# WHITAKER'S ALMANACK 1995

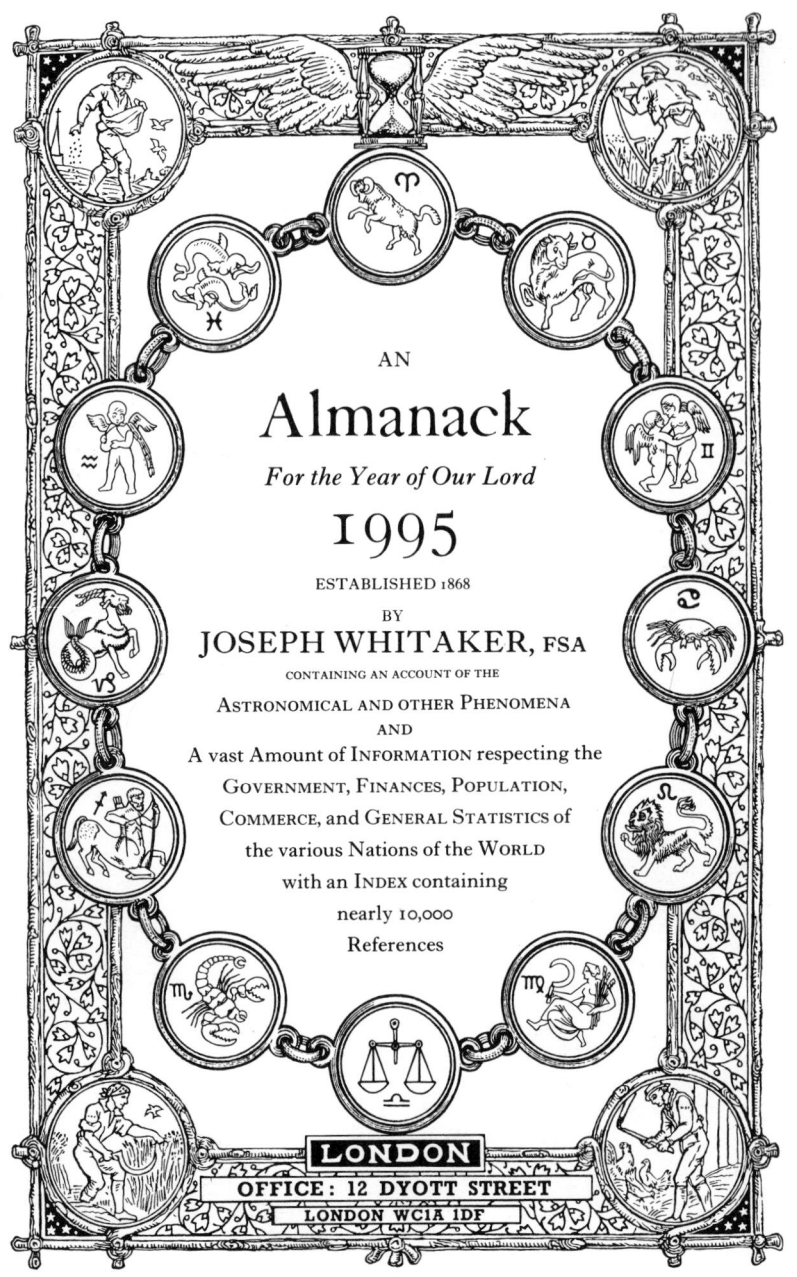

AN

# Almanack

*For the Year of Our Lord*

# 1995

ESTABLISHED 1868

BY

## JOSEPH WHITAKER, FSA

CONTAINING AN ACCOUNT OF THE

ASTRONOMICAL AND OTHER PHENOMENA

AND

A vast Amount of INFORMATION respecting the

GOVERNMENT, FINANCES, POPULATION,

COMMERCE, and GENERAL STATISTICS of

the various Nations of the WORLD

with an INDEX containing

nearly 10,000

References

## LONDON

OFFICE: 12 DYOTT STREET

LONDON WC1A 1DF

*The traditional design of the title page for Whitaker's Almanack which has appeared in each edition since 1868*

# Whitaker's Almanack

## 1995

J. WHITAKER & SONS LTD

12 DYOTT STREET · LONDON WCIA IDF

J. Whitaker and Sons Ltd
12 Dyott Street, London wc1a 1df

Whitaker's Almanack published annually since 1868
© 127th edition J. Whitaker and Sons Ltd 1994

Standard edition (1280 pages)
Cloth covers
0 85021 245 6

Leather binding
0 85021 246 4

Designed by Douglas Martin
Jacket design by Carroll Associates
Typeset by Clowes Computer Composition
Printed and bound in Great Britain by
Clays Ltd, part of St Ives plc, Bungay, Suffolk

# Contents

CONTENTS CONTINUED

# Preface

TO THE 127TH ANNUAL VOLUME 1995

Whitaker's Almanack's new format is now as well-established as its content, which we constantly seek to improve. We hope to benefit from the comments of our readers in this respect and a brief questionnaire is included in this edition.

A number of new and revised items are included in the 127th edition. The structure of the armed forces is undergoing a fundamental change at present, and the cuts and restructuring which are planned are explained in a new introduction to the Defence section.

A major engineering feat was accomplished this year with the opening of the Channel Tunnel and this is described in an article in the Transport section. Additional information has also been added to this section regarding the moves towards rail privatization, and the plans for the privatization of the coal industry are covered in the Energy section.

The sections covering historic monuments and historic houses have been amalgamated to form a single section and the information has been extensively revised, as has the section on Museums and Galleries. The results of voting in the United Kingdom in the European Parliament elections in June 1994 are included, and the article on the European Union has been revised now that the Maastricht Treaty has come into effect. This edition also carries the results of the 1994 Winter Olympic Games and Commonwealth Games.

Many organizations and individuals provide information for each edition; we appreciate the time and trouble they take and are most grateful to them for their assistance.

12 DYOTT STREET                       HILARY MARSDEN
LONDON WC1A 1DF                  *Editor*
TEL 0171-836 8911

OCTOBER 1994

# The Year 1995

## CHRONOLOGICAL CYCLES AND ERAS

| | |
|---|---|
| Dominical Letter | A |
| Epact | 29 |
| Golden Number (Lunar Cycle) | I |
| Julian Period | 6708 |
| Roman Indiction | 3 |
| Solar Cycle | 16 |

| | *Beginning* |
|---|---|
| Japanese year Heisei 7 | 1 January |
| Chinese year of the Pig | 31 January |
| Regnal year 44 | 6 February |
| Indian (Saka) year 1917 | 22 March |
| Hindu new year | 1 April |
| Sikh new year | 14 April |
| Muslim year AH 1416 | 31 May |
| Jewish year AM 5756 | 25 September |
| Roman year 2748 AUC | |

## RELIGIOUS CALENDARS

| | |
|---|---|
| Epiphany | 6 January |
| Birthday of Guru Gobind Singh Ji | 8 January |
| Makara Sankranti | 14 January |
| Ramadan, first day | 1 February |
| Vasant Panchami (Sarasvati-puja) | 4 February |
| Mahashivaratri | 27 February |
| Ash Wednesday | 1 March |
| Holi | 16 March |
| Ramanavami | 9 April |
| Good Friday | 14 April |
| Baisakhi Mela | 14 April |
| Passover, first day | 15 April |
| Easter Day (Western churches) | 16 April |
| Easter Day (Greek Orthodox) | 23 April |
| Idu-l-adha | c. 10 May |
| Rogation Sunday | 21 May |
| Ascension Day | 25 May |
| Martyrdom of Guru Arjan Dev Ji | 2 June |
| Pentecost (Whit Sunday) | 4 June |
| Feast of Weeks, first day | 4 June |
| Trinity Sunday | 11 June |
| Corpus Christi | 15 June |
| Raksha-bandhan | 10 August |
| Janmashtami | 17 August |
| Ganesh Chaturthi, first day | 29 August |
| Ganesh festival, last day | 8 September |
| Navaratri festival, first day | 25 September |
| Durga-puja | 1 October |
| Sarasvati-puja | 2 October |
| Dasara | 3 October |
| Yom Kippur (Day of Atonement) | 4 October |
| Feast of Tabernacles, first day | 9 October |
| Diwali (Hindu), first day | 21 October |
| Diwali (Hindu), last day | 25 October |
| Birthday of Guru Nanak Dev Ji | 7 November |
| Martyrdom of Guru Teg Bahadur Ji | 26 November |
| First Sunday in Advent | 3 December |
| Chanucah, first day | 18 December |
| Christmas Day | 25 December |
| Birthday of Guru Gobind Singh Ji | 28 December |

## CIVIL CALENDAR

| | |
|---|---|
| Accession of Queen Elizabeth II | 6 February |
| Duke of York's birthday | 19 February |
| St David's Day | 1 March |
| Prince Edward's birthday | 10 March |
| Commonwealth Day | 13 March |
| St Patrick's Day | 17 March |
| Birthday of Queen Elizabeth II | 21 April |
| St George's Day | 23 April |
| Coronation of Queen Elizabeth II | 2 June |
| Duke of Edinburgh's birthday | 10 June |
| The Queen's Official Birthday | 17 June |
| Princess of Wales' birthday | 1 July |
| Queen Elizabeth the Queen Mother's birthday | 4 August |
| Princess Royal's birthday | 15 August |
| Princess Margaret's birthday | 21 August |
| Lord Mayor's Day | 11 November |
| Remembrance Sunday | 12 November |
| Prince of Wales' birthday | 14 November |
| Wedding Day of Queen Elizabeth II | 20 November |
| St Andrew's Day | 30 November |

## LEGAL CALENDAR

### LAW TERMS

| | |
|---|---|
| Hilary Term | 11 January to 12 April |
| Easter Term | 25 April to 26 May |
| Trinity Term | 6 June to 31 July |
| Michaelmas Term | 2 October to 21 December |

### QUARTER DAYS

*England, Wales and Northern Ireland*

| | |
|---|---|
| Lady | 25 March |
| Midsummer | 24 June |
| Michaelmas | 29 September |
| Christmas | 25 December |

### TERM DAYS

*Scotland*

| | |
|---|---|
| Candlemas | 28 February |
| Whitsunday | 28 May |
| Lammas | 28 August |
| Martinmas | 28 November |
| Removal Terms | 28 May, 28 November |

# 1995

## JANUARY

| | | | | | |
|---|---|---|---|---|---|
| Sunday | 1 | 8 | 15 | 22 | 29 |
| Monday | 2 | 9 | 16 | 23 | 30 |
| Tuesday | 3 | 10 | 17 | 24 | 31 |
| Wednesday | 4 | 11 | 18 | 25 | |
| Thursday | 5 | 12 | 19 | 26 | |
| Friday | 6 | 13 | 20 | 27 | |
| Saturday | 7 | 14 | 21 | 28 | |

## FEBRUARY

| | | | | |
|---|---|---|---|---|
| Sunday | 5 | 12 | 19 | 26 |
| Monday | 6 | 13 | 20 | 27 |
| Tuesday | 7 | 14 | 21 | 28 |
| Wednesday | 1 | 8 | 15 | 22 |
| Thursday | 2 | 9 | 16 | 23 |
| Friday | 3 | 10 | 17 | 24 |
| Saturday | 4 | 11 | 18 | 25 |

## MARCH

| | | | | | |
|---|---|---|---|---|---|
| Sunday | | 5 | 12 | 19 | 26 |
| Monday | | 6 | 13 | 20 | 27 |
| Tuesday | | 7 | 14 | 21 | 28 |
| Wednesday | 1 | 8 | 15 | 22 | 29 |
| Thursday | 2 | 9 | 16 | 23 | 30 |
| Friday | 3 | 10 | 17 | 24 | 31 |
| Saturday | 4 | 11 | 18 | 25 | |

## APRIL

| | | | | | |
|---|---|---|---|---|---|
| Sunday | | 2 | 9 | 16 | 23 | 30 |
| Monday | | 3 | 10 | 17 | 24 |
| Tuesday | | 4 | 11 | 18 | 25 |
| Wednesday | | 5 | 12 | 19 | 26 |
| Thursday | | 6 | 13 | 20 | 27 |
| Friday | | 7 | 14 | 21 | 28 |
| Saturday | 1 | 8 | 15 | 22 | 29 |

## MAY

| | | | | |
|---|---|---|---|---|
| Sunday | | 7 | 14 | 21 | 28 |
| Monday | 1 | 8 | 15 | 22 | 29 |
| Tuesday | 2 | 9 | 16 | 23 | 30 |
| Wednesday | 3 | 10 | 17 | 24 | 31 |
| Thursday | 4 | 11 | 18 | 25 |
| Friday | 5 | 12 | 19 | 26 |
| Saturday | 6 | 13 | 20 | 27 |

## JUNE

| | | | | |
|---|---|---|---|---|
| Sunday | | 4 | 11 | 18 | 25 |
| Monday | | 5 | 12 | 19 | 26 |
| Tuesday | | 6 | 13 | 20 | 27 |
| Wednesday | | 7 | 14 | 21 | 28 |
| Thursday | 1 | 8 | 15 | 22 | 29 |
| Friday | 2 | 9 | 16 | 23 | 30 |
| Saturday | 3 | 10 | 17 | 24 |

## JULY

| | | | | | |
|---|---|---|---|---|---|
| Sunday | | 2 | 9 | 16 | 23 | 30 |
| Monday | | 3 | 10 | 17 | 24 | 31 |
| Tuesday | | 4 | 11 | 18 | 25 |
| Wednesday | | 5 | 12 | 19 | 26 |
| Thursday | | 6 | 13 | 20 | 27 |
| Friday | | 7 | 14 | 21 | 28 |
| Saturday | 1 | 8 | 15 | 22 | 29 |

## AUGUST

| | | | | |
|---|---|---|---|---|
| Sunday | | 6 | 13 | 20 | 27 |
| Monday | | 7 | 14 | 21 | 28 |
| Tuesday | 1 | 8 | 15 | 22 | 29 |
| Wednesday | 2 | 9 | 16 | 23 | 30 |
| Thursday | 3 | 10 | 17 | 24 | 31 |
| Friday | 4 | 11 | 18 | 25 |
| Saturday | 5 | 12 | 19 | 26 |

## SEPTEMBER

| | | | | |
|---|---|---|---|---|
| Sunday | | 3 | 10 | 17 | 24 |
| Monday | | 4 | 11 | 18 | 25 |
| Tuesday | | 5 | 12 | 19 | 26 |
| Wednesday | | 6 | 13 | 20 | 27 |
| Thursday | | 7 | 14 | 21 | 28 |
| Friday | 1 | 8 | 15 | 22 | 29 |
| Saturday | 2 | 9 | 16 | 23 | 30 |

## OCTOBER

| | | | | | |
|---|---|---|---|---|---|
| Sunday | 1 | 8 | 15 | 22 | 29 |
| Monday | 2 | 9 | 16 | 23 | 30 |
| Tuesday | 3 | 10 | 17 | 24 | 31 |
| Wednesday | 4 | 11 | 18 | 25 | |
| Thursday | 5 | 12 | 19 | 26 | |
| Friday | 6 | 13 | 20 | 27 | |
| Saturday | 7 | 14 | 21 | 28 | |

## NOVEMBER

| | | | | |
|---|---|---|---|---|
| Sunday | | 5 | 12 | 19 | 26 |
| Monday | | 6 | 13 | 20 | 27 |
| Tuesday | | 7 | 14 | 21 | 28 |
| Wednesday | 1 | 8 | 15 | 22 | 29 |
| Thursday | 2 | 9 | 16 | 23 | 30 |
| Friday | 3 | 10 | 17 | 24 |
| Saturday | 4 | 11 | 18 | 25 |

## DECEMBER

| | | | | | |
|---|---|---|---|---|---|
| Sunday | | 3 | 10 | 17 | 24 | 31 |
| Monday | | 4 | 11 | 18 | 25 |
| Tuesday | | 5 | 12 | 19 | 26 |
| Wednesday | | 6 | 13 | 20 | 27 |
| Thursday | | 7 | 14 | 21 | 28 |
| Friday | 1 | 8 | 15 | 22 | 29 |
| Saturday | 2 | 9 | 16 | 23 | 30 |

## PUBLIC HOLIDAYS

| | England and Wales | Scotland | Northern Ireland |
|---|---|---|---|
| New Year | 2 January | 2, 3 January | 2 January |
| St Patrick's Day | — | — | 17 March |
| *Good Friday | 14 April | 14 April | 14 April |
| Easter Monday | 17 April | — | 17 April |
| May Day | 8 May | 29 May | 8 May |
| VE Day | — | 8 May | — |
| Spring | 29 May | 1 May | 29 May |
| Battle of Boyne | — | — | 12 July |
| Summer | 28 August | 7 August | 28 August |
| *Christmas | 25, 26 December | 25, 26 December | 25, 26 December |

The May Day holiday in England, Wales and Northern Ireland has been transferred to 8 May in 1995 to mark the 50th anniversary of VE Day. Scotland has an additional holiday on 8 May.

# 1996

## JANUARY

| | | | | | |
|---|---|---|---|---|---|
| Sunday | | 7 | 14 | 21 | 28 |
| Monday | 1 | 8 | 15 | 22 | 29 |
| Tuesday | 2 | 9 | 16 | 23 | 30 |
| Wednesday | 3 | 10 | 17 | 24 | 31 |
| Thursday | 4 | 11 | 18 | 25 | |
| Friday | 5 | 12 | 19 | 26 | |
| Saturday | 6 | 13 | 20 | 27 | |

## FEBRUARY

| | | | | | |
|---|---|---|---|---|---|
| Sunday | | 4 | 11 | 18 | 25 |
| Monday | | 5 | 12 | 19 | 26 |
| Tuesday | | 6 | 13 | 20 | 27 |
| Wednesday | | 7 | 14 | 21 | 28 |
| Thursday | 1 | 8 | 15 | 22 | 29 |
| Friday | 2 | 9 | 16 | 23 | |
| Saturday | 3 | 10 | 17 | 24 | |

## MARCH

| | | | | | |
|---|---|---|---|---|---|
| Sunday | | 3 | 10 | 17 | 24 | 31 |
| Monday | | 4 | 11 | 18 | 25 | |
| Tuesday | | 5 | 12 | 19 | 26 | |
| Wednesday | | 6 | 13 | 20 | 27 | |
| Thursday | | 7 | 14 | 21 | 28 | |
| Friday | 1 | 8 | 15 | 22 | 29 | |
| Saturday | 2 | 9 | 16 | 23 | 30 | |

## APRIL

| | | | | | |
|---|---|---|---|---|---|
| Sunday | | 7 | 14 | 21 | 28 |
| Monday | 1 | 8 | 15 | 22 | 29 |
| Tuesday | 2 | 9 | 16 | 23 | 30 |
| Wednesday | 3 | 10 | 17 | 24 | |
| Thursday | 4 | 11 | 18 | 25 | |
| Friday | 5 | 12 | 19 | 26 | |
| Saturday | 6 | 13 | 20 | 27 | |

## MAY

| | | | | | |
|---|---|---|---|---|---|
| Sunday | | 5 | 12 | 19 | 26 |
| Monday | | 6 | 13 | 20 | 27 |
| Tuesday | | 7 | 14 | 21 | 28 |
| Wednesday | 1 | 8 | 15 | 22 | 29 |
| Thursday | 2 | 9 | 16 | 23 | 30 |
| Friday | 3 | 10 | 17 | 24 | 31 |
| Saturday | 4 | 11 | 18 | 25 | |

## JUNE

| | | | | | |
|---|---|---|---|---|---|
| Sunday | | 2 | 9 | 16 | 23 | 30 |
| Monday | | 3 | 10 | 17 | 24 | |
| Tuesday | | 4 | 11 | 18 | 25 | |
| Wednesday | | 5 | 12 | 19 | 26 | |
| Thursday | | 6 | 13 | 20 | 27 | |
| Friday | | 7 | 14 | 21 | 28 | |
| Saturday | 1 | 8 | 15 | 22 | 29 | |

## JULY

| | | | | | |
|---|---|---|---|---|---|
| Sunday | | 7 | 14 | 21 | 28 |
| Monday | 1 | 8 | 15 | 22 | 29 |
| Tuesday | 2 | 9 | 16 | 23 | 30 |
| Wednesday | 3 | 10 | 17 | 24 | 31 |
| Thursday | 4 | 11 | 18 | 25 | |
| Friday | 5 | 12 | 19 | 26 | |
| Saturday | 6 | 13 | 20 | 27 | |

## AUGUST

| | | | | | |
|---|---|---|---|---|---|
| Sunday | | 4 | 11 | 18 | 25 |
| Monday | | 5 | 12 | 19 | 26 |
| Tuesday | | 6 | 13 | 20 | 27 |
| Wednesday | | 7 | 14 | 21 | 28 |
| Thursday | 1 | 8 | 15 | 22 | 29 |
| Friday | 2 | 9 | 16 | 23 | 30 |
| Saturday | 3 | 10 | 17 | 24 | 31 |

## SEPTEMBER

| | | | | | |
|---|---|---|---|---|---|
| Sunday | | 1 | 8 | 15 | 22 | 29 |
| Monday | | 2 | 9 | 16 | 23 | 30 |
| Tuesday | | 3 | 10 | 17 | 24 | |
| Wednesday | | 4 | 11 | 18 | 25 | |
| Thursday | | 5 | 12 | 19 | 26 | |
| Friday | | 6 | 13 | 20 | 27 | |
| Saturday | | 7 | 14 | 21 | 28 | |

## OCTOBER

| | | | | | |
|---|---|---|---|---|---|
| Sunday | | 6 | 13 | 20 | 27 |
| Monday | | 7 | 14 | 21 | 28 |
| Tuesday | 1 | 8 | 15 | 22 | 29 |
| Wednesday | 2 | 9 | 16 | 23 | 30 |
| Thursday | 3 | 10 | 17 | 24 | 31 |
| Friday | 4 | 11 | 18 | 25 | |
| Saturday | 5 | 12 | 19 | 26 | |

## NOVEMBER

| | | | | | |
|---|---|---|---|---|---|
| Sunday | | 3 | 10 | 17 | 24 |
| Monday | | 4 | 11 | 18 | 25 |
| Tuesday | | 5 | 12 | 19 | 26 |
| Wednesday | | 6 | 13 | 20 | 27 |
| Thursday | | 7 | 14 | 21 | 28 |
| Friday | 1 | 8 | 15 | 22 | 29 |
| Saturday | 2 | 9 | 16 | 23 | 30 |

## DECEMBER

| | | | | | |
|---|---|---|---|---|---|
| Sunday | | 1 | 8 | 15 | 22 | 29 |
| Monday | | 2 | 9 | 16 | 23 | 30 |
| Tuesday | | 3 | 10 | 17 | 24 | 31 |
| Wednesday | | 4 | 11 | 18 | 25 | |
| Thursday | | 5 | 12 | 19 | 26 | |
| Friday | | 6 | 13 | 20 | 27 | |
| Saturday | | 7 | 14 | 21 | 28 | |

## PUBLIC HOLIDAYS

| | England and Wales | Scotland | Northern Ireland |
|---|---|---|---|
| New Year | 1 January | 1, 2 January | 1 January |
| St Patrick's Day | — | — | 18 March |
| *Good Friday | 5 April | 5 April | 5 April |
| Easter Monday | 8 April | — | 8 April |
| May Day | 6 May | 27 May | 6 May |
| Spring | 27 May | 6 May | 27 May |
| Battle of Boyne | — | — | 12 July |
| Summer | 26 August | 5 August | 26 August |
| *Christmas | 25, 26 December | 25, 26 December | 25, 26 December |

* In England, Wales, and Northern Ireland, Christmas Day and Good Friday are common law holidays.
In the Channel Islands, Liberation Day (9 May) is a bank and public holiday.

## FORTHCOMING EVENTS 1995

This is the UN International Year of Tolerance, the EC Year of the Young Driver, and the Arts Council Year for Literature, based in Swansea
The European City of Culture is Luxembourg
* Provisional dates

| | |
|---|---|
| 5–15 January | London International Boat Show Earls Court, London |
| 6–19 March | Cruft's Dog Show National Exhibition Centre, Birmingham |
| 16 March–9 April | Ideal Home Exhibition Earls Court, London |
| 19–21 March | London International Book Fair Olympia, London |
| 25–30 April | International Antiques Fair National Exhibition Centre, Birmingham |
| *28 April–30 September | Chichester Festival Theatre season |
| 28 April–7 October | Pitlochry Festival Theatre season Tayside |
| 29 April–20 May | Mayfest 1995 Glasgow |
| *6–20 May | Sheffield Chamber Music Festival |
| 10–14 May | Royal Windsor Horse Show Home Park, Windsor |
| 19 May–4 June | Bath International Festival |
| 22 May–27 August | Glyndebourne Festival Opera season Lewes, East Sussex |
| 23–26 May | Chelsea Flower Show Royal Hospital, Chelsea |
| 26 May–4 June | Hay-on-Wye Festival of Literature, Hereford |
| *4 June–13 August | Royal Academy Summer Exhibition Piccadilly, London |
| 9–25 June | Aldeburgh Festival of Music and Arts, Suffolk |
| 17 June | Trooping the Colour Horse Guards Parade, London |
| 1–16 July | Cheltenham International Festival of Music |
| 3–6 July | The Royal Show Stoneleigh Park, Kenilworth, Warks. |
| 5–9 July | Hampton Court Palace Flower Show East Molesey, Surrey |
| 7–16 July | York Early Music Festival |
| *12–30 July | Buxton Festival Derbyshire |
| *13–22 July | Welsh Proms 1995 St David's Hall, Cardiff |
| 18–29 July | Royal Tournament Earls Court, London |
| 21 July–16 September | Promenade Concerts season Royal Albert Hall, London |
| 4–26 August | Edinburgh Military Tattoo Edinburgh Castle |
| 5–12 August | Royal National Eisteddfod of Wales Abergele, Colwyn Bay |
| 10 August | Battle of Flowers Jersey |
| 12–13 August | Wisley Flower Show RHS Garden, Wisley |
| 13 August–2 September | Edinburgh International Festival |
| 19–26 August | Three Choirs Festival Gloucester |
| 27–28 August | Notting Hill Carnival Notting Hill, London |
| 1 September–5 November | Blackpool Illuminations |
| 2 September | Braemar Royal Highland Gathering Aberdeenshire |
| 11–15 September | TUC Annual Congress Brighton |
| *16–24 September | Southampton International Boat Show Western Esplanade, Southampton |
| 17–21 September | Liberal Democrat Conference Glasgow |
| 2–6 October | Labour Party Conference Brighton |
| 10–13 October | Conservative Party Conference Blackpool |
| *2–19 November | London International Film Festival |
| 5 November | London to Brighton Veteran Car Run |
| 5–7 November | CBI Annual Conference Bournemouth |
| 11 November | Lord Mayor's Procession and Show City of London |
| *16–26 November | Huddersfield Contemporary Music Festival |

## SPORTS EVENTS

| | |
|---|---|
| 21 January | Rugby Union: France v. Wales Parc des Princes, Paris Ireland v. England Lansdowne Road, Dublin |
| 4 February | Rugby Union: England v. France Twickenham, London Scotland v. Ireland Murrayfield, Edinburgh |
| 18 February | Rugby Union: Wales v. England Cardiff Arms Park France v. Scotland Parc des Princes, Paris |
| 4 March | Rugby Union: Ireland v. France Lansdowne Road, Dublin Scotland v. Wales Murrayfield, Edinburgh |
| 7–12 March | World Figure Skating Championships, National Exhibition Centre, Birmingham |
| 18 March | Rugby Union: England v. Scotland Twickenham, London Wales v. Ireland Cardiff Arms Park |
| 1 April | University Boat Race Putney to Mortlake, London |
| 2 April | Athletics: London Marathon |
| *14–30 April | Snooker: World Professional Championship Crucible Theatre, Sheffield |
| 29 April | Rugby League: Challenge Cup Final Wembly Stadium, London |

| | |
|---|---|
| 4–7 May | Badminton Horse Trials |
| | Badminton, Avon |
| 6 May | Rugby Union: Pilkington Cup final |
| | Twickenham, London |
| 14 May | Football: Welsh FA Cup final |
| | Cardiff Arms Park |
| 20 May | Football: FA Cup final |
| | Wembley Stadium, London |
| 24 May | Cricket: One-day International |
| | England v. West Indies |
| | Trent Bridge, Nottingham |
| 26 May | Cricket: One-day International |
| | England v. West Indies |
| | The Oval, London |
| 27 May | Football: Scottish FA Cup final |
| | Hampden Park, Glasgow |
| 28 May | Cricket: One-day International |
| | England v. West Indies |
| | Lord's, London |
| 5–10 June | Golf: British Amateur Championship |
| | Royal Liverpool and Wallasey |
| 8–12 June | Cricket: 1st Test match |
| | England v. West Indies |
| | Headingley, Leeds |
| 22–26 June | Cricket: 2nd Test Match |
| | England v. West Indies |
| | Lord's, London |
| *26 June–9 July | Lawn Tennis Championships |
| | Wimbledon, London |
| 28 June–2 July | Henley Royal Regatta |
| | Henley-on-Thames |
| 6–10 July | Cricket: 3rd Test Match |
| | England v. West Indies |
| | Edgbaston, Birmingham |
| *8–22 July | Shooting: NRA Imperial Meetings |
| | Bisley Camp, Woking, Surrey |
| *9 July | British Formula 1 Grand Prix |
| | Silverstone, Northants |
| 15 July | Cricket: Benson & Hedges Cup final |
| | Lord's, London |
| 20–23 July | Golf: Open Championship |
| | St Andrews, Fife |
| 27–31 July | Cricket: 4th Test Match |
| | England v. West Indies |
| | Old Trafford, Manchester |
| 27 July–10 August | Yachting: Admirals Cup |
| | Cowes, Isle of Wight |
| 29 July–5 August | Yachting: Cowes Week |
| | Isle of Wight |
| 5 August | Yachting: Fastnet Race |
| | Cowes/Plymouth |
| 10–14 August | Cricket: 5th Test Match |
| | England v. West Indies |
| | Trent Bridge, Nottingham |
| 24–28 August | Cricket: 6th Test Match |
| | England v. West Indies |
| | The Oval, London |
| 2 September | Cricket: NatWest Trophy final |
| | Lord's, London |
| 9–10 September | Golf: Walker Cup |
| | Royal Porthcawl, Mid Glamorgan |
| 22–24 September | Golf: Ryder Cup |
| | Oak Hill, Rochester, NY State, USA |
| 26 October– | Horse of the Year Show |
| 1 November | Wembley Arena, London |

HORSE-RACING

| | |
|---|---|
| 16 March | Cheltenham Gold Cup |
| 25 March | Lincoln Handicap |
| | Doncaster |
| 8 April | Grand National |
| | Aintree |
| 6 May | Two Thousand Guineas |
| | Newmarket |
| 7 May | One Thousand Guineas |
| | Newmarket |
| 9 June | Coronation Cup |
| | Epsom |
| 9 June | The Oaks |
| | Epsom |
| 10 June | The Derby |
| | Epsom |
| 20–23 June | Royal Ascot |
| 22 July | King George VI and Queen |
| | Elizabeth Diamond Stakes |
| | Ascot |
| 9 September | St Leger |
| | Doncaster |
| 30 September | Cambridgeshire Handicap |
| | Newmarket |
| 14 October | Cesarewitch |
| | Newmarket |

The horse-racing fixtures are the copyright of The Jockey Club

## CENTENARIES OF 1995

| | |
|---|---|
| 1695 | |
| 21 November | Henry Purcell, composer, died |
| | |
| 1795 | |
| 3 January | Josiah Wedgwood, potter, died |
| 19 May | James Boswell, biographer of Dr Johnson, died |
| 13 June | Thomas Arnold, headmaster of Rugby, born |
| 31 October | John Keats, poet, born |
| 4 December | Thomas Carlyle, essayist and historian, born |
| | |
| 1895 | |
| 1 January | J. Edgar Hoover, American head of the FBI for nearly fifty years, born |
| 24 January | Lord Randolph Churchill, politician, died |
| 1 February | John Ford, American film director, born |
| 10 March | Charles Frederick Worth, costumier, died |
| 25 April | Sir Stanley Rous, founder member of the Football Association, born |
| 29 April | Sir Malcolm Sargent, conductor, born |
| 6 May | Rudolph Valentino, film actor, born |
| 15 May | Joseph Whitaker, publisher, founder and first editor of *Whitaker's Almanack*, died |
| 24 June | Jack Dempsey, American boxer, born |

| | |
|---|---|
| 10 July | Carl Orff, German composer, born |
| 12 July | Oscar Hammerstein, American librettist, born |
| | Kirsten Flagstad, Norwegian opera singer, born |
| 26 July | Robert Graves, poet and novelist, born |
| 5 August | Friedrich Engels, German socialist, died |
| 29 August | Founding of Northern Rugby Football Union (known since 1922 as the Rugby Football League) at the George Hotel, Huddersfield |
| 28 September | Louis Pasteur, French chemist, died |
| 4 October | Buster Keaton, American film comedian, born |
| 8 October | Juan Peron, Argentine soldier and politician, born |
| 15 October | First British Motor Show, at Tunbridge Wells |
| 25 October | Sir Charles Halle, pianist and conductor, died |
| 16 November | Paul Hindemith, German composer, born |
| 27 November | Alexandre Dumas (younger), French novelist, playwright and essayist, died |
| 14 December | King George VI born |
| | Paul Éluard, French poet, born |
| 29 December | Jameson Raid in Transvaal, South Africa |
| 30 December | L. P. Hartley, novelist, born |

## CENTENARIES OF 1996

| | |
|---|---|
| 496 BC | |
| * | Sophocles, Athenian tragedian, born |
| | |
| 1096 | |
| * | First crusade to free the Holy Land begins |
| | |
| 1496 | |
| * | Santo Domingo (now capital of the Dominican Republic) founded, the first European town in the Americas |
| | |
| 1596 | |
| 13 January | Jan van Goyen, Dutch artist, born |
| 28 January | Sir Francis Drake, navigator, died |
| 31 March | René Descartes, French philosopher, born |
| | |
| 1796 | |
| 14 May | Edward Jenner carries out first vaccination against smallpox |
| 25 June (OS)/ 6 July (NS) | Nicholas I, Tsar of Russia 1801–55, born |
| 21 July | Robert Burns, poet, died |
| 10 November | Catherine II (the Great) of Russia died |

| | |
|---|---|
| 1896 | |
| 5 January | Frederic, Lord Leighton, artist and President of the Royal Academy, died |
| 1 March | Battle of Adowa: Abyssinia defeated Italy |
| 22 March | Thomas Hughes, novelist, died |
| 6 April | Modern Olympic Games revived at Athens |
| 3 May | Dodie Smith, author, born |
| 4 May | *Daily Mail* first published |
| 7 May | Kitty Godfree, lawn tennis and badminton player, born |
| 19 May | Clara Schumann, German musician, died |
| 19 June | The Duchess of Windsor (Mrs Wallis Simpson) born |
| 1 July | Harriet Beecher-Stowe, American anti-slavery novelist, died |
| 19 July | A. J. Cronin, novelist, born |
| 9 August | Jean Piaget, Swiss psychologist, born |
| 24 September | F. Scott Fitzgerald, American novelist, born |
| 3 October | William Morris, designer, poet and socialist, died |
| 1 November | Edmund Blunden, poet and scholar, born |
| 14 November | First London to Brighton 'Emancipation' car rally |
| 16 November | Sir Oswald Mosley, politician and fascist, born |
| 10 December | Alfred Nobel, Swedish chemist, died |

* exact date not known

# Astronomy

The following pages give astronomical data for each month of the year 1995. There are four pages of data for each month. All data are given for oh Greenwich Mean Time (GMT), i.e. at the midnight at the beginning of the day named. This applies also to data for the months when British Summer Time is in operation (for dates, *see* below).

The astronomical data are given in a form suitable for observation with the naked eye or with a small telescope. These data do not attempt to replace the *Astronomical Almanac* for professional astronomers.

A fuller explanation of how to use the astronomical data is given on pages 71–3.

## CALENDAR FOR EACH MONTH

The calendar for each month shows dates of religious, civil and legal significance for the year 1995.

The days in bold type are the principal holy days and the festivals and greater holy days of the Church of England as set out in the calendar of the Alternative Service Book 1980, and the calendar of Sundays set out in the Book of Common Prayer. Observance of certain festivals and greater holy days is transferred if the day falls on a principal holy day. The calendar shows the date on which holy days and festivals are to be observed in 1995.

The days in small capitals are dates of significance in the calendars of non-Anglican denominations and non-Christian religions.

The days in italic type are dates of civil and legal significance. The royal anniversaries shown in italic type are the days on which the Union flag is to be flown.

The rest of the calendar comprises days of general interest and the dates of birth or death of well-known people.

Fuller explanations of the various calendars can be found under Time Measurement and Calendars (pages 81–9).

The Zodiacal signs through which the Sun is passing during each month are illustrated. The date of transition from one sign to the next, to the nearest hour, is given under Astronomical Phenomena.

### JULIAN DATE

The Julian date on 1995 January 0.0 is 2449717.5. To find the Julian date for any other date in 1995 (at oh GMT), add the day-of-the-year number on the extreme right of the calendar for each month to the Julian date for January 0.0.

*Southern hemisphere*

| | |
|---|---|
| Autumnal equinox | March 21d 02h GMT |
| Winter solstice | June 21d 21h GMT |
| Vernal equinox | September 23d 12h GMT |
| Summer solstice | December 22d 08h GMT |

The longest day of the year, measured from sunrise to sunset, is at the summer solstice. For the remainder of this century the longest day in the United Kingdom will fall each year on 21 June. *See also* page 81.

The shortest day of the year is at the winter solstice. For the remainder of this century the shortest day in the United Kingdom will fall on 21 December in 1996, 1997, 2000, and on 22 December in 1995, 1998, 1999. *See also* page 81.

The equinox is the point at which day and night are of equal length all over the world. *See also* page 81.

In popular parlance, the seasons in the northern hemisphere comprise the following months:

| | |
|---|---|
| *Spring* | March April May |
| *Summer* | June July August |
| *Autumn* | September October November |
| *Winter* | December January February |

### BRITISH SUMMER TIME

British Summer Time is the legal time for general purposes during the period in which it is in operation. During this period, clocks are kept one hour ahead of Greenwich Mean Time. The hour of changeover is 01h Greenwich Mean Time. The duration of Summer Time in 1995 (subject to confirmation) is:

March 26 01h GMT to October 22 01h GMT

## SEASONS

The seasons are defined astronomically as follows:

| | |
|---|---|
| *Spring* | from the vernal equinox to the summer solstice |
| *Summer* | from the summer solstice to the autumnal equinox |
| *Autumn* | from the autumnal equinox to the winter solstice |
| *Winter* | from the winter solstice to the vernal equinox |

The seasons in 1995 are:

*Northern hemisphere*

| | |
|---|---|
| Vernal equinox | March 21d 02h GMT |
| Summer solstice | June 21d 21h GMT |
| Autumnal equinox | September 23d 12h GMT |
| Winter solstice | December 22d 08h GMT |

# January 1995

FIRST MONTH, 31 DAYS. *Janus*, god of the portal, facing two ways, past and future

| | | | |
|---|---|---|---|
| 1 | Sunday | **1st S. after Christmas.** Paul Revere b. 1735 | *week 1 day* 1 |
| 2 | Monday | **The Naming of Jesus.** *Bank Holiday in the UK* | 2 |
| 3 | Tuesday | *Bank Holiday in Scotland.* Josiah Wedgwood d. 1795 | 3 |
| 4 | Wednesday | Sir Isaac Pitman b. 1813. Albert Camus d. 1960 | 4 |
| 5 | Thursday | Sir Ernest Shackleton d. 1922 | 5 |
| 6 | Friday | **The Epiphany.** Richard II b. 1367 | 6 |
| 7 | Saturday | Calais regained by French 1558 | 7 |
| 8 | Sunday | **1st S. after Epiphany.** Galileo d. 1642 | *week 2 day* 8 |
| 9 | Monday | First section of London Underground opened 1863 | 9 |
| 10 | Tuesday | Archbishop William Laud exec. 1645 | 10 |
| 11 | Wednesday | *Hilary Law Sittings begin.* Alan Paton b. 1903 | 11 |
| 12 | Thursday | Hermann Goering b. 1893. Nevil Shute d. 1960 | 12 |
| 13 | Friday | James Joyce d. 1941 | 13 |
| 14 | Saturday | Lewis Carroll d. 1898. Humphrey Bogart d. 1957 | 14 |
| 15 | Sunday | **2nd S. after Epiphany.** Fanny Kemble d. 1893 | *week 3 day* 15 |
| 16 | Monday | Battle of Coruña 1809. Léo Delibes d. 1891 | 16 |
| 17 | Tuesday | Benjamin Franklin b. 1706. T. H. White d. 1964 | 17 |
| 18 | Wednesday | Versailles peace conference opened 1919. Hugh Gaitskell d. 1963 | 18 |
| 19 | Thursday | William Congreve d. 1729. James Watt b. 1736 | 19 |
| 20 | Friday | George Burns b. 1896. John Ruskin d. 1900 | 20 |
| 21 | Saturday | Concorde entered service 1976 | 21 |
| 22 | Sunday | **3rd S. after Epiphany.** Capture of Tobruk 1941 | *week 4 day* 22 |
| 23 | Monday | Stendhal b. 1783. Battle of Tripoli 1943 | 23 |
| 24 | Tuesday | Sir Winston Churchill d. 1965 | 24 |
| 25 | Wednesday | Conversion of St Paul. Virginia Woolf b. 1882 | 25 |
| 26 | Thursday | Gen. Douglas MacArthur b. 1880. Gen. Charles Gordon d. 1885 | 26 |
| 27 | Friday | J. Logie Baird first demonstrated television 1926 | 27 |
| 28 | Saturday | Henry VII b. 1457. Henry VIII d. 1547 | 28 |
| 29 | Sunday | **4th S. after Epiphany.** George III d. 1820 | *week 5 day* 29 |
| 30 | Monday | Franklin D. Roosevelt b. 1882 | 30 |
| 31 | Tuesday | *Chinese Year of the Pig.* Guy Fawkes exec. 1606 | 31 |

ASTRONOMICAL PHENOMENA

| d | h | |
|---|---|---|
| 2 | 06 | Mercury in conjunction with Moon. Mercury 7° S. |
| 2 | 21 | Mars at stationary point |
| 4 | 11 | Earth at perihelion (147 million km) |
| 5 | 13 | Saturn in conjunction with Moon. Saturn 6° S. |
| 13 | 12 | Venus at greatest elongation W.47° |
| 13 | 17 | Neptune in conjunction |
| 14 | 22 | Jupiter in conjunction with Venus. Jupiter 3° S. |
| 17 | 00 | Uranus in conjunction |
| 19 | 08 | Mercury at greatest elongation E.19° |
| 19 | 13 | Mars in conjunction with Moon. Mars 8° N. |
| 20 | 13 | Sun's longitude 300° ♒ |
| 26 | 01 | Mercury at stationary point |
| 26 | 17 | Jupiter in conjunction with Moon. Jupiter 2° S. |
| 27 | 12 | Venus in conjunction with Moon. Venus 0°.2 S. |
| 31 | 12 | Mercury in conjunction with Moon. Mercury 2° S. |

CONSTELLATIONS

The following constellations are near the meridian at

| | d | h | | d | h |
|---|---|---|---|---|---|
| December | 1 | 24 | January | 16 | 21 |
| December | 16 | 23 | February | 1 | 20 |
| January | 1 | 22 | February | 15 | 19 |

Draco (below the Pole), Ursa Minor (below the Pole), Camelopardus, Perseus, Auriga, Taurus, Orion, Eridanus and Lepus

MINIMA OF ALGOL

| d | h | d | h | d | h |
|---|---|---|---|---|---|
| 1 | 08.2 | 12 | 19.4 | 24 | 06.7 |
| 4 | 05.0 | 15 | 16.3 | 27 | 03.6 |
| 7 | 01.8 | 18 | 13.1 | 30 | 00.4 |
| 9 | 22.6 | 21 | 09.9 | | |

THE MOON

| Phases, Apsides and Node | d | h | m |
|---|---|---|---|
| ● New Moon | 1 | 10 | 56 |
| ☽ First Quarter | 8 | 15 | 46 |
| ○ Full Moon | 16 | 20 | 26 |
| ☾ Last Quarter | 24 | 04 | 58 |
| ● New Moon | 30 | 22 | 48 |
| Apogee (405,237 km) | 11 | 21 | 56 |
| Perigee (365,863 km) | 27 | 23 | 17 |

Mean longitude of ascending node on January 1, 222°

## THE SUN

s.d. 16′.3

| Day | Right Ascension | Dec. − | Equation of time | Rise 52° | Rise 56° | Transit | Set 52° | Set 56° | Sidereal time | Transit of First Point of Aries |
|---|---|---|---|---|---|---|---|---|---|---|
| | h m s | ° ′ | m s | h m | h m | h m | h m | h m | h m s | h m s |
| 1 | 18 43 54 | 23 03 | − 3 11 | 8 08 | 8 31 | 12 03 | 15 59 | 15 36 | 6 40 43 | 17 16 27 |
| 2 | 18 48 19 | 22 58 | − 3 40 | 8 08 | 8 31 | 12 04 | 16 00 | 15 37 | 6 44 39 | 17 12 31 |
| 3 | 18 52 44 | 22 53 | − 4 08 | 8 08 | 8 31 | 12 04 | 16 01 | 15 38 | 6 48 36 | 17 08 35 |
| 4 | 18 57 08 | 22 47 | − 4 36 | 8 08 | 8 30 | 12 05 | 16 02 | 15 40 | 6 52 33 | 17 04 39 |
| 5 | 19 01 32 | 22 41 | − 5 03 | 8 07 | 8 30 | 12 05 | 16 03 | 15 41 | 6 56 29 | 17 00 43 |
| 6 | 19 05 56 | 22 34 | − 5 30 | 8 07 | 8 29 | 12 06 | 16 05 | 15 42 | 7 00 26 | 16 56 47 |
| 7 | 19 10 19 | 22 27 | − 5 57 | 8 07 | 8 29 | 12 06 | 16 06 | 15 44 | 7 04 22 | 16 52 51 |
| 8 | 19 14 41 | 22 20 | − 6 23 | 8 06 | 8 28 | 12 07 | 16 07 | 15 45 | 7 08 19 | 16 48 55 |
| 9 | 19 19 03 | 22 12 | − 6 48 | 8 06 | 8 27 | 12 07 | 16 09 | 15 47 | 7 12 15 | 16 45 00 |
| 10 | 19 23 25 | 22 03 | − 7 13 | 8 05 | 8 27 | 12 07 | 16 10 | 15 49 | 7 16 12 | 16 41 04 |
| 11 | 19 27 46 | 21 54 | − 7 37 | 8 05 | 8 26 | 12 08 | 16 11 | 15 50 | 7 20 08 | 16 37 08 |
| 12 | 19 32 06 | 21 45 | − 8 01 | 8 04 | 8 25 | 12 08 | 16 13 | 15 52 | 7 24 05 | 16 33 12 |
| 13 | 19 36 26 | 21 35 | − 8 24 | 8 03 | 8 24 | 12 09 | 16 14 | 15 54 | 7 28 02 | 16 29 16 |
| 14 | 19 40 45 | 21 25 | − 8 47 | 8 02 | 8 23 | 12 09 | 16 16 | 15 55 | 7 31 58 | 16 25 20 |
| 15 | 19 45 03 | 21 15 | − 9 09 | 8 02 | 8 22 | 12 09 | 16 17 | 15 57 | 7 35 55 | 16 21 24 |
| 16 | 19 49 21 | 21 04 | − 9 30 | 8 01 | 8 21 | 12 10 | 16 19 | 15 59 | 7 39 51 | 16 17 28 |
| 17 | 19 53 38 | 20 52 | − 9 51 | 8 00 | 8 19 | 12 10 | 16 21 | 16 01 | 7 43 48 | 16 13 32 |
| 18 | 19 57 55 | 20 41 | −10 10 | 7 59 | 8 18 | 12 10 | 16 22 | 16 03 | 7 47 44 | 16 09 36 |
| 19 | 20 02 10 | 20 28 | −10 30 | 7 58 | 8 17 | 12 11 | 16 24 | 16 05 | 7 51 41 | 16 05 40 |
| 20 | 20 06 25 | 20 16 | −10 48 | 7 57 | 8 16 | 12 11 | 16 26 | 16 07 | 7 55 37 | 16 01 45 |
| 21 | 20 10 40 | 20 03 | −11 06 | 7 56 | 8 14 | 12 11 | 16 27 | 16 09 | 7 59 34 | 15 57 49 |
| 22 | 20 14 53 | 19 50 | −11 23 | 7 54 | 8 13 | 12 12 | 16 29 | 16 11 | 8 03 31 | 15 53 53 |
| 23 | 20 19 06 | 19 36 | −11 39 | 7 53 | 8 11 | 12 12 | 16 31 | 16 13 | 8 07 27 | 15 49 57 |
| 24 | 20 23 18 | 19 22 | −11 54 | 7 52 | 8 10 | 12 12 | 16 33 | 16 15 | 8 11 24 | 15 46 01 |
| 25 | 20 27 29 | 19 08 | −12 09 | 7 51 | 8 08 | 12 12 | 16 34 | 16 17 | 8 15 20 | 15 42 05 |
| 26 | 20 31 40 | 18 53 | −12 23 | 7 49 | 8 06 | 12 12 | 16 36 | 16 19 | 8 19 17 | 15 38 09 |
| 27 | 20 35 49 | 18 38 | −12 36 | 7 48 | 8 05 | 12 13 | 16 38 | 16 21 | 8 23 13 | 15 34 13 |
| 28 | 20 39 58 | 18 22 | −12 48 | 7 47 | 8 03 | 12 13 | 16 40 | 16 23 | 8 27 10 | 15 30 17 |
| 29 | 20 44 06 | 18 07 | −13 00 | 7 45 | 8 01 | 12 13 | 16 42 | 16 26 | 8 31 06 | 15 26 21 |
| 30 | 20 48 14 | 17 51 | −13 11 | 7 44 | 8 00 | 12 13 | 16 43 | 16 28 | 8 35 03 | 15 22 25 |
| 31 | 20 52 20 | 17 34 | −13 21 | 7 42 | 7 58 | 12 13 | 16 45 | 16 30 | 8 39 00 | 15 18 30 |

DURATION OF TWILIGHT (in minutes)

| Latitude | 52° | 56° | 52° | 56° | 52° | 56° | 52° | 56° |
|---|---|---|---|---|---|---|---|---|
| | 1 January | | 11 January | | 21 January | | 31 January | |
| Civil | 41 | 47 | 40 | 45 | 38 | 43 | 37 | 41 |
| Nautical | 84 | 96 | 82 | 93 | 80 | 90 | 78 | 87 |
| Astronomical | 125 | 141 | 123 | 138 | 120 | 134 | 117 | 130 |

THE NIGHT SKY

Mercury is unsuitably placed for observation for the first ten days of the month but thereafter emerges from the evening twilight to be visible low in the south-western sky at the end of evening civil twilight, until about the 27th. During its period of visibility its magnitude fades from − 0.8 to + 0.9.

Venus is a magnificent object, magnitude − 4.4, dominating the south-eastern sky for several hours before sunrise, despite its low altitude above the horizon. The old crescent Moon will be seen near the planet on the mornings of the 27th and 28th. Venus passes 3° N. of Jupiter on the 14th.

Mars, although technically a morning object, is becoming visible in the eastern sky in the evenings and by the end of the month may be detected low in the eastern sky by the end of astronomical twilight. Mars is moving slowly retrograde in Leo, passing several degrees north of Regulus towards the end of January. During the month its magnitude brightens from − 0.4 to − 1.0. The slightly reddish colour of the planet is an aid to identification.

Jupiter, magnitude − 1.8, is a brilliant morning object, low in the south-east sky before dawn. Jupiter moves from Scorpius into Ophiuchus during the month, passing 5° N. of Antares on the 23rd. On the mornings of the 26th and 27th the old Moon, four to three days before New, will be seen near the planet.

Saturn, magnitude + 1.0, is visible as an evening object in the south-west, in Aquarius.

## THE MOON

| Day | RA h m | Dec. ° | Hor. par. | Semi- diam. ′ | Sun's co- long. ° | PA of Bright Limb ° | Phase % | Age d | Rise 52° h m | Rise 56° h m | Transit h m | Set 52° h m | Set 56° h m |
|---|---|---|---|---|---|---|---|---|---|---|---|---|---|
| 1 | 18 16 | −19.5 | 60.7 | 16.5 | 262 | 120 | 0 | 29.0 | 7 40 | 7 59 | 12 05 | 16 34 | 16 16 |
| 2 | 19 18 | −17.6 | 60.2 | 16.4 | 274 | 231 | 1 | 0.5 | 8 24 | 8 40 | 13 04 | 17 51 | 17 36 |
| 3 | 20 17 | −14.6 | 59.6 | 16.2 | 286 | 244 | 4 | 1.5 | 9 00 | 9 12 | 14 00 | 19 09 | 18 58 |
| 4 | 21 13 | −10.8 | 58.7 | 16.0 | 298 | 245 | 9 | 2.5 | 9 29 | 9 37 | 14 51 | 20 25 | 20 18 |
| 5 | 22 06 | − 6.5 | 57.8 | 15.8 | 310 | 245 | 16 | 3.5 | 9 54 | 9 58 | 15 40 | 21 38 | 21 35 |
| 6 | 22 56 | − 2.1 | 56.9 | 15.5 | 322 | 245 | 25 | 4.5 | 10 17 | 10 17 | 16 27 | 22 48 | 22 50 |
| 7 | 23 45 | + 2.3 | 56.1 | 15.3 | 335 | 245 | 34 | 5.5 | 10 39 | 10 36 | 17 11 | 23 56 | — |
| 8 | 0 32 | + 6.4 | 55.4 | 15.1 | 347 | 246 | 44 | 6.5 | 11 01 | 10 54 | 17 56 | — | 0 01 |
| 9 | 1 19 | +10.2 | 54.8 | 14.9 | 359 | 248 | 53 | 7.5 | 11 25 | 11 15 | 18 40 | 1 02 | 1 11 |
| 10 | 2 06 | +13.6 | 54.4 | 14.8 | 11 | 250 | 63 | 8.5 | 11 52 | 11 38 | 19 25 | 2 06 | 2 19 |
| 11 | 2 54 | +16.3 | 54.2 | 14.8 | 23 | 253 | 72 | 9.5 | 12 22 | 12 06 | 20 11 | 3 08 | 3 24 |
| 12 | 3 42 | +18.3 | 54.1 | 14.7 | 35 | 256 | 80 | 10.5 | 12 58 | 12 40 | 20 58 | 4 08 | 4 26 |
| 13 | 4 32 | +19.6 | 54.2 | 14.8 | 48 | 259 | 87 | 11.5 | 13 41 | 13 21 | 21 47 | 5 03 | 5 22 |
| 14 | 5 23 | +20.0 | 54.4 | 14.8 | 60 | 261 | 92 | 12.5 | 14 31 | 14 11 | 22 36 | 5 53 | 6 13 |
| 15 | 6 14 | +19.5 | 54.7 | 14.9 | 72 | 261 | 97 | 13.5 | 15 27 | 15 09 | 23 25 | 6 36 | 6 55 |
| 16 | 7 06 | +18.0 | 55.1 | 15.0 | 84 | 252 | 99 | 14.5 | 16 30 | 16 14 | — | 7 14 | 7 31 |
| 17 | 7 57 | +15.8 | 55.5 | 15.1 | 96 | 172 | 100 | 15.5 | 17 36 | 17 24 | 0 13 | 7 47 | 8 00 |
| 18 | 8 47 | +12.7 | 56.0 | 15.3 | 108 | 126 | 98 | 16.5 | 18 45 | 18 36 | 1 02 | 8 15 | 8 25 |
| 19 | 9 37 | + 9.0 | 56.4 | 15.4 | 120 | 119 | 95 | 17.5 | 19 56 | 19 51 | 1 49 | 8 41 | 8 47 |
| 20 | 10 27 | + 4.8 | 56.9 | 15.5 | 132 | 117 | 90 | 18.5 | 21 08 | 21 08 | 2 37 | 9 04 | 9 07 |
| 21 | 11 17 | + 0.4 | 57.4 | 15.6 | 145 | 116 | 82 | 19.5 | 22 22 | 22 25 | 3 24 | 9 28 | 9 26 |
| 22 | 12 08 | − 4.2 | 57.9 | 15.8 | 157 | 115 | 74 | 20.5 | 23 37 | 23 44 | 4 13 | 9 52 | 9 47 |
| 23 | 13 00 | − 8.6 | 58.4 | 15.9 | 169 | 113 | 63 | 21.5 | — | — | 5 03 | 10 18 | 10 09 |
| 24 | 13 54 | −12.6 | 58.8 | 16.0 | 181 | 111 | 52 | 22.5 | 0 52 | 1 04 | 5 55 | 10 49 | 10 36 |
| 25 | 14 50 | −15.9 | 59.3 | 16.1 | 193 | 107 | 41 | 23.5 | 2 08 | 2 24 | 6 50 | 11 26 | 11 09 |
| 26 | 15 49 | −18.4 | 59.6 | 16.2 | 205 | 103 | 30 | 24.5 | 3 21 | 3 40 | 7 48 | 12 11 | 11 52 |
| 27 | 16 49 | −19.7 | 59.8 | 16.3 | 218 | 99 | 20 | 25.5 | 4 28 | 4 48 | 8 47 | 13 06 | 12 46 |
| 28 | 17 51 | −19.7 | 59.9 | 16.3 | 230 | 95 | 12 | 26.5 | 5 27 | 5 46 | 9 48 | 14 12 | 13 52 |
| 29 | 18 52 | −18.4 | 59.8 | 16.3 | 242 | 94 | 5 | 27.5 | 6 15 | 6 32 | 10 47 | 15 24 | 15 08 |
| 30 | 19 52 | −16.0 | 59.5 | 16.2 | 254 | 100 | 1 | 28.5 | 6 55 | 7 08 | 11 43 | 16 41 | 16 28 |
| 31 | 20 49 | −12.6 | 59.0 | 16.1 | 266 | 172 | 0 | 0.1 | 7 27 | 7 37 | 12 37 | 17 58 | 17 49 |

## MERCURY

| Day | RA h m | Dec. ° | Diam. ″ | Phase % | Transit h m | 5° high 52° h m | 5° high 56° h m |
|---|---|---|---|---|---|---|---|
| 1 | 19 30 | −24.0 | 5 | 95 | 12 51 | 15 47 | 15 08 |
| 3 | 19 44 | −23.5 | 5 | 94 | 12 57 | 15 58 | 15 22 |
| 5 | 19 58 | −22.8 | 5 | 92 | 13 03 | 16 10 | 15 36 |
| 7 | 20 11 | −22.1 | 5 | 89 | 13 08 | 16 22 | 15 50 |
| 9 | 20 24 | −21.2 | 6 | 86 | 13 13 | 16 34 | 16 05 |
| 11 | 20 37 | −20.3 | 6 | 82 | 13 18 | 16 46 | 16 19 |
| 13 | 20 49 | −19.3 | 6 | 78 | 13 22 | 16 58 | 16 33 |
| 15 | 21 00 | −18.3 | 6 | 72 | 13 25 | 17 09 | 16 45 |
| 17 | 21 10 | −17.2 | 6 | 66 | 13 27 | 17 18 | 16 57 |
| 19 | 21 19 | −16.1 | 7 | 58 | 13 27 | 17 25 | 17 06 |
| 21 | 21 26 | −15.1 | 7 | 49 | 13 26 | 17 30 | 17 12 |
| 23 | 21 31 | −14.1 | 8 | 40 | 13 22 | 17 32 | 17 15 |
| 25 | 21 33 | −13.3 | 8 | 30 | 13 15 | 17 29 | 17 13 |
| 27 | 21 32 | −12.8 | 9 | 21 | 13 06 | 17 23 | 17 07 |
| 29 | 21 28 | −12.4 | 9 | 13 | 12 54 | 17 11 | 16 56 |
| 31 | 21 22 | −12.4 | 10 | 6 | 12 39 | 16 56 | 16 41 |

## VENUS

| Day | RA h m | Dec. ° | Diam. ″ | Phase % | Transit h m | 5° high 52° h m | 5° high 56° h m |
|---|---|---|---|---|---|---|---|
| 1 | 15 30 | −15.2 | 29 | 43 | 8 49 | 4 48 | 5 07 |
| 6 | 15 49 | −16.3 | 27 | 46 | 8 48 | 4 54 | 5 15 |
| 11 | 16 09 | −17.3 | 26 | 49 | 8 49 | 5 01 | 5 24 |
| 16 | 16 30 | −18.3 | 24 | 52 | 8 50 | 5 09 | 5 33 |
| 21 | 16 51 | −19.1 | 23 | 54 | 8 52 | 5 18 | 5 43 |
| 26 | 17 14 | −19.9 | 22 | 56 | 8 55 | 5 26 | 5 53 |
| 31 | 17 37 | −20.4 | 21 | 58 | 8 58 | 5 34 | 6 02 |

## MARS

| Day | RA h m | Dec. ° | Diam. ″ | Phase % | Transit h m | 5° high 52° h m | 5° high 56° h m |
|---|---|---|---|---|---|---|---|
| 1 | 10 24 | +13.8 | 11 | 94 | 3 42 | 21 01 | 20 53 |
| 6 | 10 24 | +14.0 | 12 | 95 | 3 23 | 20 40 | 20 32 |
| 11 | 10 23 | +14.3 | 12 | 96 | 3 02 | 20 17 | 20 09 |
| 16 | 10 20 | +14.7 | 12 | 97 | 2 40 | 19 52 | 19 43 |
| 21 | 10 16 | +15.2 | 13 | 98 | 2 16 | 19 26 | 19 16 |
| 26 | 10 11 | +15.8 | 13 | 99 | 1 52 | 18 58 | 18 48 |
| 31 | 10 05 | +16.5 | 14 | 99 | 1 26 | 18 28 | 18 17 |

## SUNRISE AND SUNSET

| | London | | Bristol | | Birmingham | | Manchester | | Newcastle | | Glasgow | | Belfast | |
|---|---|---|---|---|---|---|---|---|---|---|---|---|---|---|
| | 0°05′ 51°30′ | | 2°35′ 51°28′ | | 1°55′ 52°28′ | | 2°15′ 53°28′ | | 1°37′ 54°59′ | | 4°14′ 55°52′ | | 5°56′ 54°35′ | |
| | h m | h m | h m | h m | h m | h m | h m | h m | h m | h m | h m | h m | h m | h m |
| 1 | 8 06 | 16 02 | 8 16 | 16 12 | 8 18 | 16 04 | 8 25 | 16 00 | 8 31 | 15 49 | 8 47 | 15 54 | 8 46 | 16 08 |
| 2 | 8 06 | 16 03 | 8 16 | 16 13 | 8 18 | 16 05 | 8 25 | 16 01 | 8 31 | 15 50 | 8 47 | 15 55 | 8 46 | 16 09 |
| 3 | 8 06 | 16 04 | 8 16 | 16 14 | 8 18 | 16 06 | 8 25 | 16 02 | 8 31 | 15 51 | 8 47 | 15 56 | 8 46 | 16 11 |
| 4 | 8 06 | 16 05 | 8 15 | 16 15 | 8 18 | 16 07 | 8 24 | 16 04 | 8 31 | 15 52 | 8 46 | 15 57 | 8 45 | 16 12 |
| 5 | 8 05 | 16 06 | 8 15 | 16 16 | 8 17 | 16 09 | 8 24 | 16 05 | 8 30 | 15 54 | 8 46 | 15 59 | 8 45 | 16 13 |
| 6 | 8 05 | 16 07 | 8 15 | 16 18 | 8 17 | 16 10 | 8 24 | 16 06 | 8 30 | 15 55 | 8 45 | 16 00 | 8 45 | 16 15 |
| 7 | 8 05 | 16 09 | 8 14 | 16 19 | 8 ˙17 | 16 11 | 8 23 | 16 07 | 8 29 | 15 56 | 8 45 | 16 02 | 8 44 | 16 16 |
| 8 | 8 04 | 16 10 | 8 14 | 16 20 | 8 16 | 16 13 | 8 23 | 16 09 | 8 29 | 15 58 | 8 44 | 16 03 | 8 43 | 16 18 |
| 9 | 8 04 | 16 11 | 8 14 | 16 21 | 8 16 | 16 14 | 8 22 | 16 10 | 8 28 | 15 59 | 8 44 | 16 05 | 8 43 | 16 19 |
| 10 | 8 03 | 16 13 | 8 13 | 16 23 | 8 15 | 16 15 | 8 21 | 16 12 | 8 27 | 16 01 | 8 43 | 16 06 | 8 42 | 16 21 |
| 11 | 8 03 | 16 14 | 8 12 | 16 24 | 8 14 | 16 17 | 8 21 | 16 13 | 8 26 | 16 03 | 8 42 | 16 08 | 8 41 | 16 22 |
| 12 | 8 02 | 16 16 | 8 12 | 16 26 | 8 14 | 16 18 | 8 20 | 16 15 | 8 26 | 16 04 | 8 41 | 16 10 | 8 41 | 16 24 |
| 13 | 8 01 | 16 17 | 8 11 | 16 27 | 8 13 | 16 20 | 8 19 | 16 16 | 8 25 | 16 06 | 8 40 | 16 11 | 8 40 | 16 25 |
| 14 | 8 00 | 16 18 | 8 10 | 16 29 | 8 12 | 16 21 | 8 18 | 16 18 | 8 24 | 16 08 | 8 39 | 16 13 | 8 39 | 16 27 |
| 15 | 8 00 | 16 20 | 8 10 | 16 30 | 8 11 | 16 23 | 8 17 | 16 20 | 8 23 | 16 09 | 8 38 | 16 15 | 8 38 | 16 29 |
| 16 | 7 59 | 16 22 | 8 09 | 16 32 | 8 10 | 16 25 | 8 16 | 16 21 | 8 22 | 16 11 | 8 37 | 16 17 | 8 37 | 16 31 |
| 17 | 7 58 | 16 23 | 8 08 | 16 33 | 8 10 | 16 26 | 8 15 | 16 23 | 8 20 | 16 13 | 8 36 | 16 19 | 8 36 | 16 32 |
| 18 | 7 57 | 16 25 | 8 07 | 16 35 | 8 09 | 16 28 | 8 14 | 16 25 | 8 19 | 16 15 | 8 34 | 16 21 | 8 35 | 16 34 |
| 19 | 7 56 | 16 26 | 8 06 | 16 37 | 8 07 | 16 30 | 8 13 | 16 27 | 8 18 | 16 17 | 8 33 | 16 23 | 8 33 | 16 36 |
| 20 | 7 55 | 16 28 | 8 05 | 16 38 | 8 06 | 16 31 | 8 12 | 16 28 | 8 17 | 16 19 | 8 32 | 16 25 | 8 32 | 16 38 |
| 21 | 7 54 | 16 30 | 8 04 | 16 40 | 8 05 | 16 33 | 8 11 | 16 30 | 8 15 | 16 20 | 8 30 | 16 27 | 8 31 | 16 40 |
| 22 | 7 53 | 16 31 | 8 03 | 16 42 | 8 04 | 16 35 | 8 10 | 16 32 | 8 14 | 16 22 | 8 29 | 16 29 | 8 29 | 16 42 |
| 23 | 7 52 | 16 33 | 8 02 | 16 43 | 8 03 | 16 37 | 8 08 | 16 34 | 8 13 | 16 24 | 8 27 | 16 31 | 8 28 | 16 44 |
| 24 | 7 50 | 16 35 | 8 00 | 16 45 | 8 02 | 16 38 | 8 07 | 16 36 | 8 11 | 16 26 | 8 26 | 16 33 | 8 27 | 16 45 |
| 25 | 7 49 | 16 37 | 7 59 | 16 47 | 8 00 | 16 40 | 8 06 | 16 37 | 8 10 | 16 28 | 8 24 | 16 35 | 8 25 | 16 47 |
| 26 | 7 48 | 16 38 | 7 58 | 16 48 | 7 59 | 16 42 | 8 04 | 16 39 | 8 08 | 16 30 | 8 23 | 16 37 | 8 24 | 16 49 |
| 27 | 7 47 | 16 40 | 7 56 | 16 50 | 7 58 | 16 44 | 8 03 | 16 41 | 8 07 | 16 32 | 8 21 | 16 39 | 8 22 | 16 51 |
| 28 | 7 45 | 16 42 | 7 55 | 16 52 | 7 56 | 16 46 | 8 01 | 16 43 | 8 05 | 16 34 | 8 19 | 16 41 | 8 21 | 16 53 |
| 29 | 7 44 | 16 44 | 7 54 | 16 54 | 7 55 | 16 48 | 8 00 | 16 45 | 8 03 | 16 36 | 8 18 | 16 43 | 8 19 | 16 55 |
| 30 | 7 42 | 16 45 | 7 52 | 16 56 | 7 53 | 16 49 | 7 58 | 16 47 | 8 02 | 16 38 | 8 16 | 16 45 | 8 17 | 16 57 |
| 31 | 7 41 | 16 47 | 7 51 | 16 57 | 7 52 | 16 51 | 7 57 | 16 49 | 8 00 | 16 41 | 8 14 | 16 47 | 8 16 | 16 59 |

## JUPITER

| Day | RA | Dec. | Transit | 5° high | |
|---|---|---|---|---|---|
| | | | | 52° | 56° |
| | h  m | °     ′ | h  m | h  m | h  m |
| 1 | 16 11.7 | −20 20 | 9 30 | 6 05 | 6 33 |
| 11 | 16 19.9 | −20 40 | 8 59 | 5 37 | 6 05 |
| 21 | 16 27.6 | −20 58 | 8 27 | 5 07 | 5 37 |
| 31 | 16 34.7 | −21 13 | 7 55 | 4 37 | 5 07 |

Diameters – equatorial 33″ polar 31″

## SATURN

| Day | RA | Dec. | Transit | 5° high | |
|---|---|---|---|---|---|
| | | | | 52° | 56° |
| | h  m | °     ′ | h  m | h  m | h  m |
| 1 | 22 41.3 | −10 14 | 15 58 | 20 30 | 20 17 |
| 11 | 22 44.7 | − 9 53 | 15 22 | 19 56 | 19 43 |
| 21 | 22 48.4 | − 9 30 | 14 47 | 19 22 | 19 10 |
| 31 | 22 52.4 | − 9 05 | 14 11 | 18 49 | 18 38 |

Diameters – equatorial 16″ polar 14″
Rings – major axis 36″ minor axis 4″

## URANUS

| Day | RA | Dec. | Transit | 10° high | |
|---|---|---|---|---|---|
| | | | | 52° | 56° |
| | h  m | °     ′ | h  m | h  m | h  m |
| 1 | 19 50.1 | −21 32 | 13 07 | 10 43 | 11 35 |
| 11 | 19 52.6 | −21 25 | 12 31 | 10 05 | 10 56 |
| 21 | 19 55.1 | −21 19 | 11 54 | 9 27 | 10 17 |
| 31 | 19 57.6 | −21 12 | 11 17 | 8 49 | 9 38 |

Diameter 4″

## NEPTUNE

| Day | RA | Dec. | Transit | 10° high | |
|---|---|---|---|---|---|
| | | | | 52° | 56° |
| | h  m | °     ′ | h  m | h  m | h  m |
| 1 | 19 37.1 | −21 00 | 12 54 | 10 25 | 11 12 |
| 11 | 19 38.7 | −20 57 | 12 17 | 9 46 | 10 33 |
| 21 | 19 40.3 | −20 53 | 11 39 | 9 08 | 9 55 |
| 31 | 19 41.9 | −20 49 | 11 01 | 8 30 | 9 16 |

Diameter 2″

# February 1995

SECOND MONTH, 28 DAYS. *Februa*, Roman festival of Purification

| | | | |
|---|---|---|---|
| 1 | *Wednesday* | RAMADAN begins. John Ford b. 1895 | *week 5 day* 32 |
| 2 | *Thursday* | **Presentation of Christ.** German surrender at Stalingrad 1943 | 33 |
| 3 | *Friday* | Gertrude Stein b. 1874. Woodrow Wilson d. 1924 | 34 |
| 4 | *Saturday* | Yalta Conference opened 1945 | 35 |
| 5 | *Sunday* | **5th S. after Epiphany.** Sir Robert Peel b. 1788 | *week 6 day* 36 |
| 6 | *Monday* | *Queen's Accession 1952.* Ronald Reagan b. 1911 | 37 |
| 7 | *Tuesday* | Sinclair Lewis b. 1885. Adolphe Sax d. 1894 | 38 |
| 8 | *Wednesday* | Jules Verne b. 1828. Sir Victor Gollancz d. 1967 | 39 |
| 9 | *Thursday* | Edward Carson b. 1854. Brendan Behan b. 1923 | 40 |
| 10 | *Friday* | Military conscription introduced in Britain 1916 | 41 |
| 11 | *Saturday* | William H. Fox-Talbot b. 1800 | 42 |
| 12 | *Sunday* | **9th S. before Easter/Septuagesima** | *week 7 day* 43 |
| 13 | *Monday* | Accession of William III and Mary II 1689 | 44 |
| 14 | *Tuesday* | St Valentine's Day. Kevin Keegan b. 1951 | 45 |
| 15 | *Wednesday* | Surrender of Singapore 1942 | 46 |
| 16 | *Thursday* | Sir Geraint Evans b. 1922. Lord Hore-Belisha d. 1957 | 47 |
| 17 | *Friday* | Molière d. 1673. Sir Edward German b. 1862 | 48 |
| 18 | *Saturday* | Martin Luther d. 1546. Robert Oppenheimer d. 1967 | 49 |
| 19 | *Sunday* | **8th S. before Easter/Sexagesima.** *Duke of York b. 1960* | *week 8 day* 50 |
| 20 | *Monday* | Sidney Poitier b. 1927. Mikhail Sholokhov d. 1984 | 51 |
| 21 | *Tuesday* | Gp Capt Douglas Bader b. 1910. Battle of Verdun 1915 | 52 |
| 22 | *Wednesday* | Sydney Smith d. 1845. Sir John Mills b. 1908 | 53 |
| 23 | *Thursday* | Handel b. 1685. Elgar d. 1934 | 54 |
| 24 | *Friday* | William C. Russell b. 1844. Joseph Rowntree d. 1925 | 55 |
| 25 | *Saturday* | Enrico Caruso b. 1873. Anthony Burgess b. 1917 | 56 |
| 26 | *Sunday* | **7th S. before Easter/Quinquagesima** | *week 9 day* 57 |
| 27 | *Monday* | Labour Party founded 1900 | 58 |
| 28 | *Tuesday* | Shrove Tuesday. Charles Blondin b. 1824 | 59 |

ASTRONOMICAL PHENOMENA

| d | h | |
|---|---|---|
| 2 | 04 | Saturn in conjunction with Moon. Saturn 6° S. |
| 3 | 23 | Mercury in inferior conjunction |
| 12 | 03 | Mars at opposition |
| 15 | 04 | Mars in conjunction with Moon. Mars 9° N. |
| 16 | 05 | Mercury at stationary point |
| 19 | 03 | Sun's longitude 330° ⌭ |
| 23 | 06 | Jupiter in conjunction with Moon. Jupiter 2° S. |
| 26 | 04 | Venus in conjunction with Moon. Venus 4° S. |
| 27 | 09 | Mercury in conjunction with Moon. Mercury 5° S. |

CONSTELLATIONS

The following constellations are near the meridian at

| | d | h | | d | h |
|---|---|---|---|---|---|
| January | 1 | 24 | February | 15 | 21 |
| January | 16 | 23 | March | 1 | 20 |
| February | 1 | 22 | March | 16 | 19 |

Draco (below the Pole), Camelopardus, Auriga, Taurus, Gemini, Orion, Canis Minor, Monoceros, Lepus, Canis Major and Puppis

MINIMA OF ALGOL

| d | h | d | h | d | h |
|---|---|---|---|---|---|
| 1 | 21.2 | 13 | 08.5 | 21 | 23.0 |
| 4 | 18.0 | 16 | 05.3 | 24 | 19.8 |
| 7 | 14.8 | 19 | 02.1 | 27 | 16.6 |
| 10 | 11.7 | | | | |

THE MOON

| Phases, Apsides and Node | | d | h | m |
|---|---|---|---|---|
| ☽ First Quarter | | 7 | 12 | 54 |
| ○ Full Moon | | 15 | 12 | 15 |
| ☾ Last Quarter | | 22 | 13 | 04 |
| Apogee (404,458 km) | | 8 | 17 | 59 |
| Perigee (370,144 km) | | 23 | 02 | 06 |

Mean longitude of ascending node on February 1, 220°

| THE SUN | | | | | | | | | | s.d. 16′.2 | |
|---|---|---|---|---|---|---|---|---|---|---|---|

| Day | Right Ascension | Dec. − | Equation of time | Rise 52° | Rise 56° | Transit | Set 52° | Set 56° | Sidereal time | Transit of First Point of Aries |
|---|---|---|---|---|---|---|---|---|---|---|
| | h  m  s | °  ′ | m  s | h  m | h  m | h  m | h  m | h  m | h  m  s | h  m  s |
| 1 | 20 56 26 | 17 17 | −13 30 | 7 41 | 7 56 | 12 14 | 16 47 | 16 32 | 8 42 56 | 15 14 34 |
| 2 | 21 00 31 | 17 00 | −13 38 | 7 39 | 7 54 | 12 14 | 16 49 | 16 34 | 8 46 53 | 15 10 38 |
| 3 | 21 04 35 | 16 43 | −13 46 | 7 38 | 7 52 | 12 14 | 16 51 | 16 36 | 8 50 49 | 15 06 42 |
| 4 | 21 08 38 | 16 25 | −13 52 | 7 36 | 7 50 | 12 14 | 16 53 | 16 39 | 8 54 46 | 15 02 46 |
| 5 | 21 12 41 | 16 08 | −13 58 | 7 34 | 7 48 | 12 14 | 16 54 | 16 41 | 8 58 42 | 14 58 50 |
| 6 | 21 16 42 | 15 49 | −14 03 | 7 33 | 7 46 | 12 14 | 16 56 | 16 43 | 9 02 39 | 14 54 54 |
| 7 | 21 20 43 | 15 31 | −14 07 | 7 31 | 7 44 | 12 14 | 16 58 | 16 45 | 9 06 35 | 14 50 58 |
| 8 | 21 24 43 | 15 12 | −14 11 | 7 29 | 7 42 | 12 14 | 17 00 | 16 47 | 9 10 32 | 14 47 02 |
| 9 | 21 28 42 | 14 53 | −14 13 | 7 27 | 7 40 | 12 14 | 17 02 | 16 50 | 9 14 29 | 14 43 06 |
| 10 | 21 32 40 | 14 34 | −14 15 | 7 25 | 7 38 | 12 14 | 17 04 | 16 52 | 9 18 25 | 14 39 10 |
| 11 | 21 36 38 | 14 15 | −14 16 | 7 24 | 7 35 | 12 14 | 17 06 | 16 54 | 9 22 22 | 14 35 15 |
| 12 | 21 40 35 | 13 55 | −14 16 | 7 22 | 7 33 | 12 14 | 17 07 | 16 56 | 9 26 18 | 14 31 19 |
| 13 | 21 44 30 | 13 35 | −14 16 | 7 20 | 7 31 | 12 14 | 17 09 | 16 58 | 9 30 15 | 14 27 23 |
| 14 | 21 48 26 | 13 15 | −14 14 | 7 18 | 7 29 | 12 14 | 17 11 | 17 01 | 9 34 11 | 14 23 27 |
| 15 | 21 52 20 | 12 55 | −14 12 | 7 16 | 7 26 | 12 14 | 17 13 | 17 03 | 9 38 08 | 14 19 31 |
| 16 | 21 56 14 | 12 34 | −14 09 | 7 14 | 7 24 | 12 14 | 17 15 | 17 05 | 9 42 04 | 14 15 35 |
| 17 | 22 00 07 | 12 13 | −14 06 | 7 12 | 7 22 | 12 14 | 17 17 | 17 07 | 9 46 01 | 14 11 39 |
| 18 | 22 03 59 | 11 52 | −14 02 | 7 10 | 7 20 | 12 14 | 17 19 | 17 09 | 9 49 58 | 14 07 43 |
| 19 | 22 07 51 | 11 31 | −13 57 | 7 08 | 7 17 | 12 14 | 17 20 | 17 12 | 9 53 54 | 14 03 47 |
| 20 | 22 11 42 | 11 10 | −13 51 | 7 06 | 7 15 | 12 14 | 17 22 | 17 14 | 9 57 51 | 13 59 51 |
| 21 | 22 15 32 | 10 48 | −13 45 | 7 04 | 7 12 | 12 14 | 17 24 | 17 16 | 10 01 47 | 13 55 55 |
| 22 | 22 19 21 | 10 27 | −13 38 | 7 02 | 7 10 | 12 14 | 17 26 | 17 18 | 10 05 44 | 13 52 00 |
| 23 | 22 23 11 | 10 05 | −13 30 | 7 00 | 7 08 | 12 13 | 17 28 | 17 20 | 10 09 40 | 13 48 04 |
| 24 | 22 26 59 | 9 43 | −13 22 | 6 58 | 7 05 | 12 13 | 17 30 | 17 22 | 10 13 37 | 13 44 08 |
| 25 | 22 30 47 | 9 21 | −13 13 | 6 56 | 7 03 | 12 13 | 17 32 | 17 25 | 10 17 33 | 13 40 12 |
| 26 | 22 34 34 | 8 58 | −13 04 | 6 54 | 7 00 | 12 13 | 17 33 | 17 27 | 10 21 30 | 13 36 16 |
| 27 | 22 38 21 | 8 36 | −12 54 | 6 51 | 6 58 | 12 13 | 17 35 | 17 29 | 10 25 27 | 13 32 20 |
| 28 | 22 42 07 | 8 13 | −12 44 | 6 49 | 6 55 | 12 13 | 17 37 | 17 31 | 10 29 23 | 13 28 24 |

DURATION OF TWILIGHT (in minutes)

| Latitude | 52° | 56° | 52° | 56° | 52° | 56° | 52° | 56° |
|---|---|---|---|---|---|---|---|---|
| | 1 February | | 11 February | | 21 February | | 28 February | |
| Civil | 37 | 41 | 35 | 39 | 34 | 38 | 34 | 38 |
| Nautical | 77 | 86 | 75 | 83 | 74 | 81 | 73 | 81 |
| Astronomical | 117 | 130 | 114 | 126 | 113 | 125 | 112 | 124 |

THE NIGHT SKY

Mercury passes through inferior conjunction on the 3rd and remains too close to the Sun for observation throughout the month.

Venus continues to be visible as a magnificent object, magnitude −4.2, low in the south-eastern sky before dawn. On the morning of the 26th the old crescent Moon, three days before New, will be seen passing about 3° north of Venus, creating a favourable opportunity for locating the planet soon after the Sun has risen, although both objects are then low in the south-south-east, Venus being about 4° below and to the right of the Moon.

Mars, magnitude −1.2, reaches opposition on the 12th and is therefore visible throughout the hours of darkness. Mars is a few degrees north of Regulus at the beginning of the month but its retrograde motion takes it to the western edge of the constellation of Leo by the end of February.

Jupiter continues to be visible as a brilliant morning object, magnitude −2.0, low in the south-east sky for several hours before dawn. On the morning of the 23rd the Moon, just past Last Quarter, passes 2° N. of Jupiter.

Saturn, magnitude +1.0, is still visible for a short time, low in the west-south-west sky in the early evening, but by the middle of the month it is lost in the gathering twilight.

Zodiacal Light. The evening cone may be observed in the western sky after the end of twilight from the 16th onwards. This faint phenomenon is only visible in good conditions, in the absence of both moonlight and artificial lighting.

## THE MOON

| Day | RA h m | Dec. ° | Hor. par. | Semi-diam. | Sun's co-long. ° | PA of Bright Limb ° | Phase % | Age d | Rise 52° h m | Rise 56° h m | Transit h m | Set 52° h m | Set 56° h m |
|---|---|---|---|---|---|---|---|---|---|---|---|---|---|
| 1 | 21 44 | − 8.5 | 58.4 | 15.9 | 278 | 232 | 2 | 1.1 | 7 55 | 8 01 | 13 28 | 19 13 | 19 09 |
| 2 | 22 36 | − 4.1 | 57.6 | 15.7 | 291 | 239 | 5 | 2.1 | 8 19 | 8 21 | 14 17 | 20 26 | 20 26 |
| 3 | 23 26 | + 0.3 | 56.8 | 15.5 | 303 | 242 | 11 | 3.1 | 8 42 | 8 41 | 15 03 | 21 37 | 21 40 |
| 4 | 0 15 | + 4.7 | 56.1 | 15.3 | 315 | 244 | 18 | 4.1 | 9 05 | 9 00 | 15 49 | 22 45 | 22 52 |
| 5 | 1 02 | + 8.7 | 55.4 | 15.1 | 327 | 246 | 27 | 5.1 | 9 29 | 9 20 | 16 34 | 23 51 | — |
| 6 | 1 50 | +12.2 | 54.9 | 15.0 | 339 | 249 | 36 | 6.1 | 9 55 | 9 43 | 17 19 | — | 0 02 |
| 7 | 2 38 | +15.2 | 54.5 | 14.8 | 352 | 252 | 45 | 7.1 | 10 24 | 10 09 | 18 05 | 0 55 | 1 09 |
| 8 | 3 27 | +17.5 | 54.3 | 14.8 | 4 | 256 | 54 | 8.1 | 10 57 | 10 40 | 18 52 | 1 55 | 2 12 |
| 9 | 4 16 | +19.0 | 54.2 | 14.8 | 16 | 259 | 64 | 9.1 | 11 37 | 11 18 | 19 40 | 2 52 | 3 11 |
| 10 | 5 06 | +19.7 | 54.3 | 14.8 | 28 | 263 | 72 | 10.1 | 12 23 | 12 04 | 20 28 | 3 44 | 4 04 |
| 11 | 5 57 | +19.6 | 54.6 | 14.9 | 40 | 267 | 80 | 11.1 | 13 17 | 12 58 | 21 17 | 4 30 | 4 50 |
| 12 | 6 48 | +18.5 | 55.0 | 15.0 | 52 | 270 | 88 | 12.1 | 14 16 | 14 00 | 22 06 | 5 11 | 5 28 |
| 13 | 7 40 | +16.5 | 55.5 | 15.1 | 64 | 271 | 93 | 13.1 | 15 21 | 15 07 | 22 55 | 5 46 | 6 01 |
| 14 | 8 31 | +13.8 | 56.1 | 15.3 | 77 | 269 | 97 | 14.1 | 16 30 | 16 20 | 23 43 | 6 16 | 6 28 |
| 15 | 9 22 | +10.3 | 56.7 | 15.4 | 89 | 250 | 100 | 15.1 | 17 41 | 17 35 | — | 6 44 | 6 51 |
| 16 | 10 13 | + 6.2 | 57.3 | 15.6 | 101 | 148 | 100 | 16.1 | 18 55 | 18 52 | 0 32 | 7 09 | 7 13 |
| 17 | 11 04 | + 1.7 | 57.8 | 15.7 | 113 | 124 | 97 | 17.1 | 20 09 | 20 11 | 1 20 | 7 33 | 7 33 |
| 18 | 11 55 | − 2.8 | 58.2 | 15.9 | 125 | 119 | 93 | 18.1 | 21 25 | 21 31 | 2 09 | 7 58 | 7 54 |
| 19 | 12 48 | − 7.3 | 58.6 | 16.0 | 137 | 115 | 86 | 19.1 | 22 41 | 22 52 | 3 00 | 8 24 | 8 16 |
| 20 | 13 42 | −11.5 | 58.9 | 16.0 | 149 | 112 | 77 | 20.1 | 23 57 | — | 3 52 | 8 54 | 8 42 |
| 21 | 14 38 | −15.0 | 59.1 | 16.1 | 162 | 108 | 67 | 21.1 | — | 0 11 | 4 46 | 9 29 | 9 13 |
| 22 | 15 35 | −17.7 | 59.2 | 16.1 | 174 | 103 | 56 | 22.1 | 1 10 | 1 28 | 5 43 | 10 10 | 9 52 |
| 23 | 16 35 | −19.3 | 59.2 | 16.1 | 186 | 99 | 45 | 23.1 | 2 18 | 2 38 | 6 40 | 11 01 | 10 41 |
| 24 | 17 35 | −19.6 | 59.2 | 16.1 | 198 | 94 | 34 | 24.1 | 3 18 | 3 38 | 7 39 | 12 01 | 11 41 |
| 25 | 18 34 | −18.8 | 59.1 | 16.1 | 210 | 89 | 24 | 25.1 | 4 09 | 4 27 | 8 37 | 13 09 | 12 51 |
| 26 | 19 33 | −16.8 | 58.9 | 16.0 | 222 | 86 | 15 | 26.1 | 4 51 | 5 06 | 9 33 | 14 21 | 14 07 |
| 27 | 20 29 | −13.8 | 58.6 | 16.0 | 235 | 84 | 8 | 27.1 | 5 25 | 5 37 | 10 26 | 15 36 | 15 26 |
| 28 | 21 24 | −10.1 | 58.1 | 15.8 | 247 | 86 | 3 | 28.1 | 5 55 | 6 02 | 11 18 | 16 51 | 16 44 |

## MERCURY

| Day | RA h m | Dec. ° | Diam. ″ | Phase % | Transit h m | 5° high 52° h m | 5° high 56° h m |
|---|---|---|---|---|---|---|---|
| 1 | 21 18 | −12.5 | 10 | 4 | 12 31 | 16 47 | 16 32 |
| 3 | 21 09 | −12.8 | 10 | 1 | 12 14 | 16 28 | 16 12 |
| 5 | 20 59 | −13.3 | 10 | 1 | 11 56 | 7 45 | 8 01 |
| 7 | 20 50 | −13.9 | 10 | 4 | 11 39 | 7 32 | 7 49 |
| 9 | 20 42 | −14.6 | 10 | 8 | 11 24 | 7 20 | 7 38 |
| 11 | 20 36 | −15.2 | 10 | 13 | 11 10 | 7 11 | 7 30 |
| 13 | 20 32 | −15.8 | 10 | 19 | 10 59 | 7 03 | 7 23 |
| 15 | 20 30 | −16.3 | 9 | 25 | 10 50 | 6 57 | 7 17 |
| 17 | 20 30 | −16.7 | 9 | 31 | 10 42 | 6 52 | 7 13 |
| 19 | 20 32 | −17.0 | 9 | 36 | 10 37 | 6 48 | 7 10 |
| 21 | 20 36 | −17.3 | 8 | 41 | 10 33 | 6 46 | 7 08 |
| 23 | 20 41 | −17.4 | 8 | 46 | 10 30 | 6 44 | 7 06 |
| 25 | 20 47 | −17.4 | 8 | 50 | 10 29 | 6 42 | 7 04 |
| 27 | 20 54 | −17.3 | 7 | 54 | 10 28 | 6 41 | 7 03 |
| 29 | 21 02 | −17.1 | 7 | 57 | 10 29 | 6 39 | 7 01 |
| 31 | 21 10 | −16.8 | 7 | 60 | 10 29 | 6 38 | 6 59 |

## VENUS

| Day | RA h m | Dec. ° | Diam. ″ | Phase % | Transit h m | 5° high 52° h m | 5° high 56° h m |
|---|---|---|---|---|---|---|---|
| 1 | 17 42 | −20.5 | 21 | 59 | 8 59 | 5 36 | 6 04 |
| 6 | 18 06 | −20.9 | 20 | 61 | 9 03 | 5 42 | 6 12 |
| 11 | 18 30 | −21.0 | 19 | 63 | 9 08 | 5 48 | 6 17 |
| 16 | 18 54 | −20.9 | 18 | 65 | 9 13 | 5 52 | 6 21 |
| 21 | 19 19 | −20.6 | 17 | 67 | 9 18 | 5 54 | 6 23 |
| 26 | 19 44 | −20.0 | 17 | 69 | 9 23 | 5 55 | 6 22 |
| 31 | 20 08 | −19.2 | 16 | 70 | 9 27 | 5 53 | 6 19 |

## MARS

| Day | RA h m | Dec. ° | Diam. ″ | Phase % | Transit h m | 5° high 52° h m | 5° high 56° h m |
|---|---|---|---|---|---|---|---|
| 1 | 10 04 | +16.6 | 14 | 99 | 1 21 | 8 14 | 8 25 |
| 6 | 9 57 | +17.3 | 14 | 100 | 0 54 | 7 51 | 8 02 |
| 11 | 9 49 | +18.0 | 14 | 100 | 0 27 | 7 27 | 7 39 |
| 16 | 9 41 | +18.7 | 14 | 100 | 23 54 | 7 03 | 7 16 |
| 21 | 9 33 | +19.2 | 14 | 100 | 23 26 | 6 39 | 6 53 |
| 26 | 9 26 | +19.7 | 13 | 99 | 23 00 | 6 15 | 6 29 |
| 31 | 9 20 | +20.0 | 13 | 98 | 22 34 | 5 51 | 6 05 |

## SUNRISE AND SUNSET

| | London | | Bristol | | Birmingham | | Manchester | | Newcastle | | Glasgow | | Belfast | |
|---|---|---|---|---|---|---|---|---|---|---|---|---|---|---|
| | 0°05′ | 51°30′ | 2°35′ | 51°28′ | 1°55′ | 52°28′ | 2°15′ | 53°28′ | 1°37′ | 54°59′ | 4°14′ | 55°52′ | 5°56′ | 54°35′ |
| | h m | h m | h m | h m | h m | h m | h m | h m | h m | h m | h m | h m | h m | h m |
| 1 | 7 39 | 16 49 | 7 49 | 16 59 | 7 50 | 16 53 | 7 55 | 16 51 | 7 58 | 16 43 | 8 12 | 16 50 | 8 14 | 17 01 |
| 2 | 7 38 | 16 51 | 7 48 | 17 01 | 7 48 | 16 55 | 7 53 | 16 53 | 7 56 | 16 45 | 8 10 | 16 52 | 8 12 | 17 04 |
| 3 | 7 36 | 16 53 | 7 46 | 17 03 | 7 47 | 16 57 | 7 52 | 16 55 | 7 54 | 16 47 | 8 08 | 16 54 | 8 10 | 17 06 |
| 4 | 7 35 | 16 54 | 7 45 | 17 05 | 7 45 | 16 59 | 7 50 | 16 57 | 7 53 | 16 49 | 8 06 | 16 56 | 8 08 | 17 08 |
| 5 | 7 33 | 16 56 | 7 43 | 17 06 | 7 43 | 17 01 | 7 48 | 16 59 | 7 51 | 16 51 | 8 04 | 16 58 | 8 07 | 17 10 |
| 6 | 7 31 | 16 58 | 7 41 | 17 08 | 7 42 | 17 03 | 7 46 | 17 01 | 7 49 | 16 53 | 8 02 | 17 00 | 8 05 | 17 12 |
| 7 | 7 30 | 17 00 | 7 40 | 17 10 | 7 40 | 17 04 | 7 44 | 17 03 | 7 47 | 16 55 | 8 00 | 17 03 | 8 03 | 17 14 |
| 8 | 7 28 | 17 02 | 7 38 | 17 12 | 7 38 | 17 06 | 7 42 | 17 05 | 7 45 | 16 57 | 7 58 | 17 05 | 8 01 | 17 16 |
| 9 | 7 26 | 17 04 | 7 36 | 17 14 | 7 36 | 17 08 | 7 41 | 17 07 | 7 43 | 16 59 | 7 56 | 17 07 | 7 59 | 17 18 |
| 10 | 7 24 | 17 05 | 7 34 | 17 16 | 7 34 | 17 10 | 7 39 | 17 09 | 7 41 | 17 02 | 7 54 | 17 09 | 7 57 | 17 20 |
| 11 | 7 23 | 17 07 | 7 33 | 17 17 | 7 33 | 17 12 | 7 37 | 17 11 | 7 39 | 17 04 | 7 52 | 17 11 | 7 55 | 17 22 |
| 12 | 7 21 | 17 09 | 7 31 | 17 19 | 7 31 | 17 14 | 7 35 | 17 13 | 7 37 | 17 06 | 7 50 | 17 14 | 7 53 | 17 24 |
| 13 | 7 19 | 17 11 | 7 29 | 17 21 | 7 29 | 17 16 | 7 33 | 17 15 | 7 34 | 17 08 | 7 47 | 17 16 | 7 50 | 17 26 |
| 14 | 7 17 | 17 13 | 7 27 | 17 23 | 7 27 | 17 18 | 7 31 | 17 17 | 7 32 | 17 10 | 7 45 | 17 18 | 7 48 | 17 28 |
| 15 | 7 15 | 17 15 | 7 25 | 17 25 | 7 25 | 17 20 | 7 29 | 17 19 | 7 30 | 17 12 | 7 43 | 17 20 | 7 46 | 17 30 |
| 16 | 7 13 | 17 16 | 7 23 | 17 26 | 7 23 | 17 22 | 7 27 | 17 21 | 7 28 | 17 14 | 7 41 | 17 22 | 7 44 | 17 32 |
| 17 | 7 11 | 17 18 | 7 21 | 17 28 | 7 21 | 17 23 | 7 24 | 17 22 | 7 26 | 17 16 | 7 38 | 17 24 | 7 42 | 17 35 |
| 18 | 7 09 | 17 20 | 7 19 | 17 30 | 7 19 | 17 25 | 7 22 | 17 24 | 7 23 | 17 18 | 7 36 | 17 27 | 7 40 | 17 37 |
| 19 | 7 07 | 17 22 | 7 17 | 17 32 | 7 17 | 17 27 | 7 20 | 17 26 | 7 21 | 17 20 | 7 34 | 17 29 | 7 37 | 17 39 |
| 20 | 7 05 | 17 24 | 7 15 | 17 34 | 7 15 | 17 29 | 7 18 | 17 28 | 7 19 | 17 23 | 7 31 | 17 31 | 7 35 | 17 41 |
| 21 | 7 03 | 17 25 | 7 13 | 17 36 | 7 13 | 17 31 | 7 16 | 17 30 | 7 17 | 17 25 | 7 29 | 17 33 | 7 33 | 17 43 |
| 22 | 7 01 | 17 27 | 7 11 | 17 37 | 7 10 | 17 33 | 7 14 | 17 32 | 7 14 | 17 27 | 7 27 | 17 35 | 7 31 | 17 45 |
| 23 | 6 59 | 17 29 | 7 09 | 17 39 | 7 08 | 17 35 | 7 12 | 17 34 | 7 12 | 17 29 | 7 24 | 17 37 | 7 28 | 17 47 |
| 24 | 6 57 | 17 31 | 7 07 | 17 41 | 7 06 | 17 37 | 7 09 | 17 36 | 7 10 | 17 31 | 7 22 | 17 40 | 7 26 | 17 49 |
| 25 | 6 55 | 17 33 | 7 05 | 17 43 | 7 04 | 17 38 | 7 07 | 17 38 | 7 07 | 17 33 | 7 19 | 17 42 | 7 24 | 17 51 |
| 26 | 6 53 | 17 34 | 7 03 | 17 44 | 7 02 | 17 40 | 7 05 | 17 40 | 7 05 | 17 35 | 7 17 | 17 44 | 7 21 | 17 53 |
| 27 | 6 51 | 17 36 | 7 01 | 17 46 | 7 00 | 17 42 | 7 03 | 17 42 | 7 03 | 17 37 | 7 14 | 17 46 | 7 19 | 17 55 |
| 28 | 6 49 | 17 38 | 6 59 | 17 48 | 6 58 | 17 44 | 7 00 | 17 44 | 7 00 | 17 39 | 7 12 | 17 48 | 7 17 | 17 57 |

## JUPITER

| Day | RA | Dec. | Transit | 5° high | |
|---|---|---|---|---|---|
| | | | | 52° | 56° |
| | h m | ° ′ | h m | h m | h m |
| 1 | 16 35.3 | −21 14 | 7 51 | 4 34 | 5 04 |
| 11 | 16 41.6 | −21 26 | 7 18 | 4 02 | 4 33 |
| 21 | 16 46.9 | −21 35 | 6 44 | 3 29 | 4 00 |
| 31 | 16 51.2 | −21 42 | 6 09 | 2 55 | 3 27 |

Diameters – equatorial 35″ polar 33″

## SATURN

| Day | RA | Dec. | Transit | 5° high | |
|---|---|---|---|---|---|
| | | | | 52° | 56° |
| | h m | ° ′ | h m | h m | h m |
| 1 | 22 52.8 | − 9 03 | 14 08 | 18 46 | 18 35 |
| 11 | 22 57.1 | − 8 36 | 13 33 | 18 14 | 18 03 |
| 21 | 23 01.6 | − 8 08 | 12 58 | 17 41 | 17 31 |
| 31 | 23 06.1 | − 7 40 | 12 23 | 17 09 | 16 59 |

Diameters – equatorial 16″ polar 14″
Rings – major axis 36″ minor axis 3″

## URANUS

| Day | RA | Dec. | Transit | 10° high | |
|---|---|---|---|---|---|
| | | | | 52° | 56° |
| | h m | ° ′ | h m | h m | h m |
| 1 | 19 57.8 | −21 11 | 11 13 | 8 46 | 9 34 |
| 11 | 20 00.2 | −21 05 | 10 36 | 8 07 | 8 55 |
| 21 | 20 02.4 | −20 59 | 9 59 | 7 29 | 8 16 |
| 31 | 20 04.5 | −20 53 | 9 22 | 6 51 | 7 38 |

Diameter 4″

## NEPTUNE

| Day | RA | Dec. | Transit | 10° high | |
|---|---|---|---|---|---|
| | | | | 52° | 56° |
| | h m | ° ′ | h m | h m | h m |
| 1 | 19 42.0 | −20 49 | 10 57 | 8 26 | 9 12 |
| 11 | 19 43.5 | −20 45 | 10 20 | 7 47 | 8 33 |
| 21 | 19 44.9 | −20 42 | 9 42 | 7 09 | 7 54 |
| 31 | 19 46.2 | −20 39 | 9 04 | 6 30 | 7 15 |

Diameter 2″

# March 1995

THIRD MONTH, 31 DAYS. *Mars*, Roman god of battle

| | | | |
|---|---|---|---|
| 1 | Wednesday | **Ash Wednesday.** St David's Day. | *week* 9 *day* 60 |
| 2 | Thursday | Cardinal Archbishop Hume of Westminster b. 1923 | 61 |
| 3 | Friday | Abolition of serfdom in Russia 1861 | 62 |
| 4 | Saturday | RNLI founded in 1824. Kenny Dalglish b. 1951 | 63 |
| 5 | Sunday | **1st S. in Lent.** Josef Stalin d. 1953 | *week* 10 *day* 64 |
| 6 | Monday | Michaelangelo b. 1474. Ivor Novello d. 1951 | 65 |
| 7 | Tuesday | Sir John Frederick Herschel b. 1792 | 66 |
| 8 | Wednesday | Otto Hahn b. 1879. Count von Zeppelin d. 1917 | 67 |
| 9 | Thursday | William Cobbett b. 1763. Ernest Bevin b. 1881 | 68 |
| 10 | Friday | *Prince Edward b. 1964.* Jan Masaryk d. 1948 | 69 |
| 11 | Saturday | Outbreak of Russian Revolution 1917 (NS) | 70 |
| 12 | Sunday | **2nd S. in Lent.** Thomas Arne b. 1710 | *week* 11 *day* 71 |
| 13 | Monday | Commonwealth Day. Uranus discovered 1781 | 72 |
| 14 | Tuesday | Carl Philipp Emanuel Bach b. 1714 | 73 |
| 15 | Wednesday | Aristotle Onassis d. 1975 | 74 |
| 16 | Thursday | Sir Austen Chamberlain d. 1937. William Beveridge d. 1963 | 75 |
| 17 | Friday | St Patrick's Day. *Bank Holiday in Northern Ireland* | 76 |
| 18 | Saturday | **St Joseph of Nazareth.** Neville Chamberlain b. 1869 | 77 |
| 19 | Sunday | **3rd S. in Lent.** A. J. Balfour d. 1930 | *week* 12 *day* 78 |
| 20 | Monday | Henrik Ibsen b. 1828. Brendan Behan d. 1964 | 79 |
| 21 | Tuesday | Archbishop Thomas Cranmer exec. 1556 | 80 |
| 22 | Wednesday | Jean-Baptiste Lully d. 1687 | 81 |
| 23 | Thursday | Princess Eugenie of York b. 1990 | 82 |
| 24 | Friday | Orde Wingate d. 1944. Viscount Montgomery of Alamein d. 1976 | 83 |
| 25 | Saturday | **The Annunciation.** Treaty of Rome 1957 | 84 |
| 26 | Sunday | **4th S. in Lent.** Mothering Sunday | *week* 13 *day* 85 |
| 27 | Monday | Wilhelm von Röntgen b. 1845. John Bright d. 1889 | 86 |
| 28 | Tuesday | Raphael b. 1483. Gen. Dwight Eisenhower d. 1969 | 87 |
| 29 | Wednesday | Sir Edwin Lutyens b. 1869. John Major b. 1943. | 88 |
| 30 | Thursday | Anna Sewell b. 1820. Beau Brummell d. 1840 | 89 |
| 31 | Friday | Andrew Marvell b. 1621. Charlotte Brontë d. 1855 | 90 |

ASTRONOMICAL PHENOMENA

| d | h | |
|---|---|---|
| 1 | 11 | Mercury at greatest elongation W.27° |
| 1 | 19 | Saturn in conjunction with Moon. Saturn 5° S. |
| 4 | 03 | Pluto at stationary point |
| 6 | 02 | Saturn in conjunction |
| 13 | 23 | Mars in conjunction with Moon. Mars 9° N. |
| 21 | 02 | Sun's longitude 0°♈ |
| 22 | 15 | Jupiter in conjunction with Moon. Jupiter 2° S. |
| 24 | 17 | Mars at stationary point. |
| 26 | 04 | Saturn in conjunction with Mercury. Saturn 0°.5 N. |
| 28 | 00 | Venus in conjunction with Moon. Venus 5° S. |
| 29 | 09 | Saturn in conjunction with Moon. Saturn 5° S. |
| 29 | 20 | Mercury in conjunction with Moon. Mercury 5° S. |

CONSTELLATIONS

The following are near the meridian at

| | d | h | | d | h |
|---|---|---|---|---|---|
| February | 1 | 24 | March | 16 | 21 |
| February | 15 | 23 | April | 1 | 20 |
| March | 1 | 22 | April | 15 | 19 |

Cepheus (below the Pole), Camelopardus, Lynx, Gemini, Cancer, Leo, Canis Minor, Hydra, Monoceros, Canis Major and Puppis

MINIMA OF ALGOL

| d | h | d | h | d | h |
|---|---|---|---|---|---|
| 2 | 13.4 | 14 | 00.7 | 25 | 12.0 |
| 5 | 10.2 | 16 | 21.5 | 28 | 08.8 |
| 8 | 07.1 | 19 | 18.3 | 31 | 05.6 |
| 11 | 03.9 | 22 | 15.2 | | |

THE MOON

| Phases, Apsides and Node | d | h | m |
|---|---|---|---|
| ● New Moon | 1 | 11 | 48 |
| ☽ First Quarter | 9 | 10 | 14 |
| ○ Full Moon | 17 | 01 | 26 |
| ☾ Last Quarter | 23 | 20 | 10 |
| ● New Moon | 31 | 02 | 09 |
| Apogee (404,346 km) | 8 | 15 | 00 |
| Perigee (366,946 km) | 20 | 13 | 20 |

Mean longitude of ascending node on March 1, 219°

## THE SUN

s.d. 16'.1

| Day | Right Ascension | Dec. | Equation of time | Rise 52° | Rise 56° | Transit | Set 52° | Set 56° | Sidereal time | Transit of First Point of Aries |
|---|---|---|---|---|---|---|---|---|---|---|
| | h m s | ° ' | m s | h m | h m | h m | h m | h m | h m s | h m s |
| 1 | 22 45 53 | −7 51 | −12 33 | 6 47 | 6 53 | 12 12 | 17 39 | 17 33 | 10 33 20 | 13 24 28 |
| 2 | 22 49 38 | −7 28 | −12 22 | 6 45 | 6 50 | 12 12 | 17 41 | 17 35 | 10 37 16 | 13 20 32 |
| 3 | 22 53 22 | −7 05 | −12 10 | 6 43 | 6 48 | 12 12 | 17 42 | 17 37 | 10 41 13 | 13 16 36 |
| 4 | 22 57 06 | −6 42 | −11 57 | 6 40 | 6 45 | 12 12 | 17 44 | 17 39 | 10 45 09 | 13 12 41 |
| 5 | 23 00 50 | −6 19 | −11 44 | 6 38 | 6 43 | 12 12 | 17 46 | 17 42 | 10 49 06 | 13 08 45 |
| 6 | 23 04 33 | −5 56 | −11 31 | 6 36 | 6 40 | 12 11 | 17 48 | 17 44 | 10 53 02 | 13 04 49 |
| 7 | 23 08 16 | −5 33 | −11 17 | 6 34 | 6 38 | 12 11 | 17 50 | 17 46 | 10 56 59 | 13 00 53 |
| 8 | 23 11 58 | −5 09 | −11 03 | 6 31 | 6 35 | 12 11 | 17 51 | 17 48 | 11 00 55 | 12 56 57 |
| 9 | 23 15 40 | −4 46 | −10 48 | 6 29 | 6 32 | 12 11 | 17 53 | 17 50 | 11 04 52 | 12 53 01 |
| 10 | 23 19 22 | −4 22 | −10 33 | 6 27 | 6 30 | 12 10 | 17 55 | 17 52 | 11 08 49 | 12 49 05 |
| 11 | 23 23 03 | −3 59 | −10 18 | 6 25 | 6 27 | 12 10 | 17 57 | 17 54 | 11 12 45 | 12 45 09 |
| 12 | 23 26 44 | −3 35 | −10 02 | 6 22 | 6 25 | 12 10 | 17 58 | 17 56 | 11 16 42 | 12 41 13 |
| 13 | 23 30 24 | −3 12 | − 9 46 | 6 20 | 6 22 | 12 10 | 18 00 | 17 58 | 11 20 38 | 12 37 17 |
| 14 | 23 34 05 | −2 48 | − 9 30 | 6 18 | 6 19 | 12 09 | 18 02 | 18 00 | 11 24 35 | 12 33 21 |
| 15 | 23 37 44 | −2 24 | − 9 13 | 6 16 | 6 17 | 12 09 | 18 04 | 18 02 | 11 28 31 | 12 29 26 |
| 16 | 23 41 24 | −2 01 | − 8 56 | 6 13 | 6 14 | 12 09 | 18 05 | 18 04 | 11 32 28 | 12 25 30 |
| 17 | 23 45 04 | −1 37 | − 8 39 | 6 11 | 6 12 | 12 09 | 18 07 | 18 07 | 11 36 24 | 12 21 34 |
| 18 | 23 48 43 | −1 13 | − 8 22 | 6 09 | 6 09 | 12 08 | 18 09 | 18 09 | 11 40 21 | 12 17 38 |
| 19 | 23 52 22 | −0 50 | − 8 04 | 6 06 | 6 06 | 12 08 | 18 11 | 18 11 | 11 44 18 | 12 13 42 |
| 20 | 23 56 01 | −0 26 | − 7 47 | 6 04 | 6 04 | 12 08 | 18 12 | 18 13 | 11 48 14 | 12 09 46 |
| 21 | 23 59 39 | −0 02 | − 7 29 | 6 02 | 6 01 | 12 07 | 18 14 | 18 15 | 11 52 11 | 12 05 50 |
| 22 | 0 03 18 | +0 21 | − 7 11 | 5 59 | 5 58 | 12 07 | 18 16 | 18 17 | 11 56 07 | 12 01 54 |
| 23 | 0 06 57 | +0 45 | − 6 53 | 5 57 | 5 56 | 12 07 | 18 17 | 18 19 | 12 00 04 | 11 57 58 |
| 24 | 0 10 35 | +1 09 | − 6 35 | 5 55 | 5 53 | 12 06 | 18 19 | 18 21 | 12 04 00 | 11 54 02 |
| 25 | 0 14 14 | +1 32 | − 6 17 | 5 52 | 5 51 | 12 06 | 18 21 | 18 23 | 12 07 57 | 11 50 06 |
| 26 | 0 17 52 | +1 56 | − 5 59 | 5 50 | 5 48 | 12 06 | 18 23 | 18 25 | 12 11 53 | 11 46 11 |
| 27 | 0 21 30 | +2 20 | − 5 40 | 5 48 | 5 45 | 12 06 | 18 24 | 18 27 | 12 15 50 | 11 42 15 |
| 28 | 0 25 09 | +2 43 | − 5 22 | 5 45 | 5 43 | 12 05 | 18 26 | 18 29 | 12 19 47 | 11 38 19 |
| 29 | 0 28 47 | +3 07 | − 5 04 | 5 43 | 5 40 | 12 05 | 18 28 | 18 31 | 12 23 43 | 11 34 23 |
| 30 | 0 32 26 | +3 30 | − 4 46 | 5 41 | 5 37 | 12 05 | 18 29 | 18 33 | 12 27 40 | 11 30 27 |
| 31 | 0 36 04 | +3 53 | − 4 28 | 5 39 | 5 35 | 12 04 | 18 31 | 18 35 | 12 31 36 | 11 26 31 |

### DURATION OF TWILIGHT (in minutes)

| Latitude | 52° | 56° | 52° | 56° | 52° | 56° | 52° | 56° |
|---|---|---|---|---|---|---|---|---|
| | 1 March | | 11 March | | 21 March | | 31 March | |
| Civil | 34 | 38 | 34 | 37 | 34 | 37 | 34 | 38 |
| Nautical | 73 | 81 | 73 | 80 | 74 | 82 | 76 | 84 |
| Astronomical | 112 | 124 | 113 | 125 | 116 | 129 | 120 | 136 |

### THE NIGHT SKY

*Mercury* is too close to the Sun for observation throughout March.

*Venus*, magnitude −4.0, is a brilliant object in the mornings, low in the south-eastern sky, but by the end of the month it is only visible for a very short time before dawn. On the morning of the 28th the old crescent Moon, three days before New, passes about 5° north of the planet.

*Mars*, not long past opposition, is visible for most of the night and is already high in the eastern sky when dusk falls. By the end of the month its brightness has fallen by a whole magnitude compared with that at opposition. Its retrograde motion has now taken it back into Cancer, reaching its second stationary point on the 24th. On the morning of the 15th the gibbous Moon passes 9° S. of the planet.

*Jupiter*, magnitude −2.2, is visible as a brilliant morning object low in the south-east sky for several hours before dawn. Jupiter is in the constellation of Ophiuchus. On the mornings of the 22nd and 23rd the old Moon will be seen near the planet.

*Saturn* passes through conjunction on the 6th and therefore remains too close to the Sun for observation in March.

*Zodiacal Light.* The evening cone may be observed stretching up from the western horizon, along the ecliptic, after the end of twilight, from the 18th onwards.

THE MOON

| Day | RA | Dec. | Hor. par. | Semi-diam. | Sun's co-long. | PA of Bright Limb | Phase | Age | Rise 52° | Rise 56° | Transit | Set 52° | Set 56° |
|---|---|---|---|---|---|---|---|---|---|---|---|---|---|
| | h m | ° | ′ | ′ | ° | ° | % | d | h m | h m | h m | h m | h m |
| 1 | 22 16 | − 5.9 | 57.6 | 15.7 | 259 | 105 | 0 | 29.1 | 6 20 | 6 24 | 12 07 | 18 04 | 18 02 |
| 2 | 23 07 | − 1.5 | 57.0 | 15.5 | 271 | 215 | 0 | 0.5 | 6 44 | 6 45 | 12 54 | 19 16 | 19 17 |
| 3 | 23 56 | + 2.9 | 56.4 | 15.4 | 283 | 237 | 3 | 1.5 | 7 08 | 7 04 | 13 40 | 20 25 | 20 31 |
| 4 | 0 45 | + 7.0 | 55.8 | 15.2 | 296 | 243 | 7 | 2.5 | 7 31 | 7 24 | 14 26 | 21 33 | 21 42 |
| 5 | 1 33 | +10.8 | 55.3 | 15.1 | 308 | 247 | 13 | 3.5 | 7 57 | 7 46 | 15 12 | 22 39 | 22 51 |
| 6 | 2 21 | +14.0 | 54.8 | 14.9 | 320 | 251 | 20 | 4.5 | 8 25 | 8 11 | 15 58 | 23 41 | 23 57 |
| 7 | 3 10 | +16.5 | 54.5 | 14.8 | 332 | 255 | 28 | 5.5 | 8 57 | 8 40 | 16 45 | — | — |
| 8 | 3 59 | +18.3 | 54.3 | 14.8 | 344 | 259 | 37 | 6.5 | 9 34 | 9 16 | 17 32 | 0 40 | 0 58 |
| 9 | 4 49 | +19.3 | 54.2 | 14.8 | 357 | 263 | 46 | 7.5 | 10 17 | 9 58 | 18 20 | 1 34 | 1 53 |
| 10 | 5 40 | +19.5 | 54.4 | 14.8 | 9 | 268 | 56 | 8.5 | 11 07 | 10 48 | 19 08 | 2 22 | 2 42 |
| 11 | 6 30 | +18.8 | 54.7 | 14.9 | 21 | 272 | 65 | 9.5 | 12 03 | 11 45 | 19 56 | 3 05 | 3 23 |
| 12 | 7 21 | +17.2 | 55.2 | 15.0 | 33 | 275 | 74 | 10.5 | 13 05 | 12 50 | 20 45 | 3 42 | 3 58 |
| 13 | 8 12 | +14.7 | 55.8 | 15.2 | 45 | 278 | 82 | 11.5 | 14 11 | 13 59 | 21 33 | 4 14 | 4 27 |
| 14 | 9 02 | +11.6 | 56.5 | 15.4 | 57 | 280 | 89 | 12.5 | 15 21 | 15 13 | 22 22 | 4 43 | 4 52 |
| 15 | 9 53 | + 7.7 | 57.3 | 15.6 | 70 | 280 | 95 | 13.5 | 16 34 | 16 30 | 23 11 | 5 09 | 5 15 |
| 16 | 10 45 | + 3.4 | 58.0 | 15.8 | 82 | 275 | 98 | 14.5 | 17 49 | 17 49 | — | 5 34 | 5 36 |
| 17 | 11 37 | − 1.2 | 58.7 | 16.0 | 94 | 216 | 100 | 15.5 | 19 06 | 19 10 | 0 00 | 6 00 | 5 58 |
| 18 | 12 30 | − 5.8 | 59.2 | 16.1 | 106 | 124 | 99 | 16.5 | 20 24 | 20 33 | 0 52 | 6 26 | 6 20 |
| 19 | 13 25 | −10.2 | 59.5 | 16.2 | 118 | 114 | 95 | 17.5 | 21 42 | 21 55 | 1 45 | 6 56 | 6 46 |
| 20 | 14 22 | −14.0 | 59.7 | 16.3 | 130 | 109 | 89 | 18.5 | 22 59 | 23 15 | 2 40 | 7 30 | 7 16 |
| 21 | 15 21 | −16.9 | 59.7 | 16.3 | 143 | 104 | 81 | 19.5 | — | — | 3 37 | 8 10 | 7 53 |
| 22 | 16 21 | −18.8 | 59.6 | 16.2 | 155 | 98 | 71 | 20.5 | 0 10 | 0 29 | 4 36 | 8 59 | 8 40 |
| 23 | 17 21 | −19.5 | 59.3 | 16.2 | 167 | 93 | 60 | 21.5 | 1 13 | 1 32 | 5 34 | 9 56 | 9 37 |
| 24 | 18 21 | −18.9 | 59.0 | 16.1 | 179 | 88 | 48 | 22.5 | 2 06 | 2 25 | 6 32 | 11 01 | 10 43 |
| 25 | 19 19 | −17.2 | 58.6 | 16.0 | 191 | 84 | 37 | 23.5 | 2 50 | 3 06 | 7 28 | 12 11 | 11 56 |
| 26 | 20 15 | −14.5 | 58.2 | 15.9 | 203 | 80 | 27 | 24.5 | 3 26 | 3 39 | 8 21 | 13 24 | 13 12 |
| 27 | 21 09 | −11.0 | 57.7 | 15.7 | 216 | 77 | 18 | 25.5 | 3 57 | 4 06 | 9 12 | 14 37 | 14 29 |
| 28 | 22 01 | − 7.1 | 57.3 | 15.6 | 228 | 76 | 10 | 26.5 | 4 23 | 4 28 | 10 01 | 15 49 | 15 45 |
| 29 | 22 51 | − 2.8 | 56.8 | 15.5 | 240 | 77 | 5 | 27.5 | 4 47 | 4 49 | 10 48 | 17 00 | 17 00 |
| 30 | 23 40 | + 1.5 | 56.3 | 15.3 | 252 | 81 | 1 | 28.5 | 5 10 | 5 09 | 11 34 | 18 09 | 18 13 |
| 31 | 0 28 | + 5.7 | 55.8 | 15.2 | 264 | 133 | 0 | 29.5 | 5 34 | 5 28 | 12 20 | 19 17 | 19 25 |

MERCURY

| Day | RA | Dec. | Diam. | Phase | Transit | 5° high 52° | 5° high 56° |
|---|---|---|---|---|---|---|---|
| | h m | ° | ″ | % | h m | h m | h m |
| 1 | 21 02 | −17.1 | 7 | 57 | 10 29 | 6 39 | 7 01 |
| 3 | 21 10 | −16.8 | 7 | 60 | 10 29 | 6 38 | 6 59 |
| 5 | 21 20 | −16.4 | 7 | 63 | 10 31 | 6 37 | 6 58 |
| 7 | 21 29 | −16.0 | 7 | 66 | 10 33 | 6 36 | 6 55 |
| 9 | 21 39 | −15.4 | 6 | 68 | 10 35 | 6 34 | 6 53 |
| 11 | 21 50 | −14.8 | 6 | 71 | 10 38 | 6 32 | 6 51 |
| 13 | 22 01 | −14.0 | 6 | 73 | 10 41 | 6 31 | 6 48 |
| 15 | 22 12 | −13.2 | 6 | 75 | 10 44 | 6 29 | 6 45 |
| 17 | 22 23 | −12.3 | 6 | 77 | 10 47 | 6 27 | 6 41 |
| 19 | 22 34 | −11.3 | 6 | 79 | 10 51 | 6 24 | 6 38 |
| 21 | 22 46 | −10.2 | 5 | 81 | 10 55 | 6 22 | 6 34 |
| 23 | 22 58 | − 9.1 | 5 | 83 | 10 59 | 6 19 | 6 31 |
| 25 | 23 10 | − 7.8 | 5 | 85 | 11 03 | 6 16 | 6 27 |
| 27 | 23 23 | − 6.5 | 5 | 86 | 11 08 | 6 14 | 6 23 |
| 29 | 23 35 | − 5.1 | 5 | 88 | 11 13 | 6 11 | 6 18 |
| 31 | 23 48 | − 3.7 | 5 | 90 | 11 18 | 6 08 | 6 14 |

VENUS

| Day | RA | Dec. | Diam. | Phase | Transit | 5° high 52° | 5° high 56° |
|---|---|---|---|---|---|---|---|
| | h m | ° | ″ | % | h m | h m | h m |
| 1 | 19 58 | −19.6 | 16 | 70 | 9 25 | 5 54 | 6 20 |
| 6 | 20 23 | −18.7 | 16 | 71 | 9 30 | 5 52 | 6 16 |
| 11 | 20 47 | −17.5 | 15 | 73 | 9 35 | 5 48 | 6 11 |
| 16 | 21 12 | −16.1 | 15 | 75 | 9 39 | 5 44 | 6 04 |
| 21 | 21 35 | −14.6 | 14 | 76 | 9 44 | 5 37 | 5 55 |
| 26 | 21 59 | −12.9 | 14 | 78 | 9 47 | 5 30 | 5 46 |
| 31 | 22 22 | −11.0 | 14 | 79 | 9 51 | 5 23 | 5 36 |

MARS

| Day | RA | Dec. | Diam. | Phase | Transit | 5° high 52° | 5° high 56° |
|---|---|---|---|---|---|---|---|
| 1 | 9 22 | +19.9 | 13 | 99 | 22 44 | 6 01 | 6 15 |
| 6 | 9 17 | +20.1 | 13 | 98 | 22 19 | 5 37 | 5 51 |
| 11 | 9 12 | +20.3 | 12 | 97 | 21 55 | 5 14 | 5 28 |
| 16 | 9 09 | +20.3 | 12 | 96 | 21 33 | 4 51 | 5 06 |
| 21 | 9 07 | +20.2 | 11 | 95 | 21 11 | 4 29 | 4 44 |
| 26 | 9 07 | +20.1 | 11 | 94 | 20 51 | 4 08 | 4 22 |
| 31 | 9 07 | +19.8 | 11 | 93 | 20 33 | 3 48 | 4 02 |

## SUNRISE AND SUNSET

| | London | | Bristol | | Birmingham | | Manchester | | Newcastle | | Glasgow | | Belfast | |
|---|---|---|---|---|---|---|---|---|---|---|---|---|---|---|
| | 0°05′ | 51°30′ | 2°35′ | 51°28′ | 1°55′ | 52°28′ | 2°15′ | 53°28′ | 1°37′ | 54°59′ | 4°14′ | 55°52′ | 5°56′ | 54°35′ |
| | h m | h m | h m | h m | h m | h m | h m | h m | h m | h m | h m | h m | h m | h m |
| 1 | 6 47 | 17 40 | 6 57 | 17 50 | 6 55 | 17 46 | 6 58 | 17 46 | 6 58 | 17 41 | 7 10 | 17 50 | 7 14 | 17 59 |
| 2 | 6 45 | 17 42 | 6 54 | 17 52 | 6 53 | 17 48 | 6 56 | 17 48 | 6 55 | 17 43 | 7 07 | 17 52 | 7 12 | 18 01 |
| 3 | 6 42 | 17 43 | 6 52 | 17 53 | 6 51 | 17 50 | 6 53 | 17 50 | 6 53 | 17 45 | 7 05 | 17 54 | 7 10 | 18 03 |
| 4 | 6 40 | 17 45 | 6 50 | 17 55 | 6 49 | 17 51 | 6 51 | 17 52 | 6 50 | 17 47 | 7 02 | 17 57 | 7 07 | 18 05 |
| 5 | 6 38 | 17 47 | 6 48 | 17 57 | 6 46 | 17 53 | 6 49 | 17 53 | 6 48 | 17 49 | 6 59 | 17 59 | 7 05 | 18 07 |
| 6 | 6 36 | 17 49 | 6 46 | 17 59 | 6 44 | 17 55 | 6 46 | 17 55 | 6 45 | 17 51 | 6 57 | 18 01 | 7 02 | 18 09 |
| 7 | 6 34 | 17 50 | 6 44 | 18 00 | 6 42 | 17 57 | 6 44 | 17 57 | 6 43 | 17 53 | 6 54 | 18 03 | 7 00 | 18 11 |
| 8 | 6 31 | 17 52 | 6 41 | 18 02 | 6 40 | 17 59 | 6 42 | 17 59 | 6 41 | 17 55 | 6 52 | 18 05 | 6 57 | 18 13 |
| 9 | 6 29 | 17 54 | 6 39 | 18 04 | 6 37 | 18 00 | 6 39 | 18 01 | 6 38 | 17 57 | 6 49 | 18 07 | 6 55 | 18 15 |
| 10 | 6 27 | 17 55 | 6 37 | 18 06 | 6 35 | 18 02 | 6 37 | 18 03 | 6 36 | 17 59 | 6 47 | 18 09 | 6 52 | 18 17 |
| 11 | 6 25 | 17 57 | 6 35 | 18 07 | 6 33 | 18 04 | 6 35 | 18 05 | 6 33 | 18 01 | 6 44 | 18 11 | 6 50 | 18 19 |
| 12 | 6 22 | 17 59 | 6 32 | 18 09 | 6 30 | 18 06 | 6 32 | 18 07 | 6 31 | 18 03 | 6 42 | 18 13 | 6 48 | 18 21 |
| 13 | 6 20 | 18 01 | 6 30 | 18 11 | 6 28 | 18 08 | 6 30 | 18 09 | 6 28 | 18 05 | 6 39 | 18 15 | 6 45 | 18 23 |
| 14 | 6 18 | 18 02 | 6 28 | 18 12 | 6 26 | 18 09 | 6 27 | 18 10 | 6 25 | 18 07 | 6 36 | 18 17 | 6 43 | 18 25 |
| 15 | 6 16 | 18 04 | 6 26 | 18 14 | 6 23 | 18 11 | 6 25 | 18 12 | 6 23 | 18 09 | 6 34 | 18 19 | 6 40 | 18 27 |
| 16 | 6 13 | 18 06 | 6 23 | 18 16 | 6 21 | 18 13 | 6 23 | 18 14 | 6 20 | 18 11 | 6 31 | 18 21 | 6 38 | 18 29 |
| 17 | 6 11 | 18 07 | 6 21 | 18 17 | 6 19 | 18 15 | 6 20 | 18 16 | 6 18 | 18 13 | 6 28 | 18 24 | 6 35 | 18 31 |
| 18 | 6 09 | 18 09 | 6 19 | 18 19 | 6 16 | 18 16 | 6 18 | 18 18 | 6 15 | 18 15 | 6 26 | 18 26 | 6 33 | 18 32 |
| 19 | 6 07 | 18 11 | 6 17 | 18 21 | 6 14 | 18 18 | 6 15 | 18 20 | 6 13 | 18 17 | 6 23 | 18 28 | 6 30 | 18 34 |
| 20 | 6 04 | 18 13 | 6 14 | 18 23 | 6 12 | 18 20 | 6 13 | 18 21 | 6 10 | 18 19 | 6 21 | 18 30 | 6 28 | 18 36 |
| 21 | 6 02 | 18 14 | 6 12 | 18 24 | 6 09 | 18 22 | 6 10 | 18 23 | 6 08 | 18 21 | 6 18 | 18 32 | 6 25 | 18 38 |
| 22 | 6 00 | 18 16 | 6 10 | 18 26 | 6 07 | 18 24 | 6 08 | 18 25 | 6 05 | 18 23 | 6 15 | 18 34 | 6 22 | 18 40 |
| 23 | 5 58 | 18 18 | 6 08 | 18 28 | 6 05 | 18 25 | 6 06 | 18 27 | 6 03 | 18 25 | 6 13 | 18 36 | 6 20 | 18 42 |
| 24 | 5 55 | 18 19 | 6 05 | 18 29 | 6 02 | 18 27 | 6 03 | 18 29 | 6 00 | 18 27 | 6 10 | 18 38 | 6 17 | 18 44 |
| 25 | 5 53 | 18 21 | 6 03 | 18 31 | 6 00 | 18 29 | 6 01 | 18 31 | 5 57 | 18 29 | 6 07 | 18 40 | 6 15 | 18 46 |
| 26 | 5 51 | 18 23 | 6 01 | 18 33 | 5 57 | 18 31 | 5 58 | 18 32 | 5 55 | 18 31 | 6 05 | 18 42 | 6 12 | 18 48 |
| 27 | 5 48 | 18 24 | 5 58 | 18 34 | 5 55 | 18 32 | 5 56 | 18 34 | 5 52 | 18 33 | 6 02 | 18 44 | 6 10 | 18 50 |
| 28 | 5 46 | 18 26 | 5 56 | 18 36 | 5 53 | 18 34 | 5 53 | 18 36 | 5 50 | 18 35 | 6 00 | 18 46 | 6 07 | 18 52 |
| 29 | 5 44 | 18 28 | 5 54 | 18 38 | 5 50 | 18 36 | 5 51 | 18 38 | 5 47 | 18 37 | 5 57 | 18 48 | 6 05 | 18 54 |
| 30 | 5 42 | 18 29 | 5 52 | 18 39 | 5 48 | 18 38 | 5 49 | 18 40 | 5 45 | 18 39 | 5 54 | 18 50 | 6 02 | 18 56 |
| 31 | 5 39 | 18 31 | 5 49 | 18 41 | 5 46 | 18 39 | 5 46 | 18 42 | 5 42 | 18 41 | 5 52 | 18 52 | 6 00 | 18 57 |

## JUPITER

| Day | RA | Dec. | Transit | 5° high | |
|---|---|---|---|---|---|
| | | | | 52° | 56° |
| | h m | ° ′ | h m | h m | h m |
| 1 | 16 50.4 | −21 41 | 6 16 | 3 02 | 3 33 |
| 11 | 16 53.8 | −21 46 | 5 40 | 2 27 | 2 58 |
| 21 | 16 56.0 | −21 48 | 5 03 | 1 50 | 2 22 |
| 31 | 16 56.9 | −21 49 | 4 25 | 1 12 | 1 43 |

Diameters – equatorial 39″ polar 36″

## SATURN

| Day | RA | Dec. | Transit | 5° high | |
|---|---|---|---|---|---|
| | | | | 52° | 56° |
| | h m | ° ′ | h m | h m | h m |
| 1 | 23 05.2 | − 7 46 | 12 30 | 7 45 | 7 55 |
| 11 | 23 09.8 | − 7 18 | 11 55 | 7 07 | 7 17 |
| 21 | 23 14.3 | − 6 50 | 11 21 | 6 30 | 6 39 |
| 31 | 23 18.8 | − 6 23 | 10 46 | 5 53 | 6 02 |

Diameters – equatorial 16″ polar 14″
Rings – major axis 35″ minor axis 2″

## URANUS

| Day | RA | Dec. | Transit | 10° high | |
|---|---|---|---|---|---|
| | | | | 52° | 56° |
| | h m | ° ′ | h m | h m | h m |
| 1 | 20 04.1 | −20 54 | 9 29 | 6 59 | 7 45 |
| 11 | 20 06.0 | −20 48 | 8 52 | 6 20 | 7 06 |
| 21 | 20 07.7 | −20 44 | 8 14 | 5 42 | 6 28 |
| 31 | 20 09.0 | −20 40 | 7 36 | 5 03 | 5 49 |

Diameter 4″

## NEPTUNE

| Day | RA | Dec. | Transit | 10° high | |
|---|---|---|---|---|---|
| | | | | 52° | 56° |
| | h m | ° ′ | h m | h m | h m |
| 1 | 19 45.9 | −20 39 | 9 11 | 6 38 | 7 23 |
| 11 | 19 47.1 | −20 36 | 8 33 | 5 59 | 6 44 |
| 21 | 19 48.0 | −20 34 | 7 55 | 5 21 | 6 05 |
| 31 | 19 48.8 | −20 32 | 7 16 | 4 42 | 5 26 |

Diameter 2″

# April 1995

FOURTH MONTH, 30 DAYS. *Aperire*, to open; Earth opens to receive seed

| | | | |
|---|---|---|---|
| 1 | *Saturday* | HINDU NEW YEAR. Royal Air Force formed 1918 | *week* 13 *day* 91 |
| 2 | *Sunday* | **5th S. in Lent.** Emile Zola b. 1840 | *week* 14 *day* 92 |
| 3 | *Monday* | Henry IV b. 1367. Kurt Weill d. 1950 | 93 |
| 4 | *Tuesday* | North Atlantic Treaty signed 1949 | 94 |
| 5 | *Wednesday* | Gen. Douglas MacArthur d. 1964. Sir Arthur ('Bomber') Harris d. 1984 | 95 |
| 6 | *Thursday* | Richard II d. 1199. Albrecht Dürer d. 1528 | 96 |
| 7 | *Friday* | William Wordsworth b. 1770. William Godwin d. 1836 | 97 |
| 8 | *Saturday* | Pablo Picasso d. 1973. Gen. Omar Bradley d. 1981 | 98 |
| 9 | *Sunday* | **Palm Sunday.** Edward IV d. 1483 | *week* 15 *day* 99 |
| 10 | *Monday* | William Hazlitt b. 1778. Evelyn Waugh d. 1966 | 100 |
| 11 | *Tuesday* | Treaty of Utrecht 1713. Dan Maskell b. 1908 | 101 |
| 12 | *Wednesday* | *Hilary Law Sittings end.* Franklin D. Roosevelt d. 1945 | 102 |
| 13 | *Thursday* | **Maundy Thursday.** John Braine b. 1922 | 103 |
| 14 | *Friday* | **Good Friday.** *Public Holiday in the UK* | 104 |
| 15 | *Saturday* | **Easter Eve.** PASSOVER begins | 105 |
| 16 | *Sunday* | **Easter Day** (Western churches) | *week* 16 *day* 106 |
| 17 | *Monday* | Bank Holiday in England, Wales and Northern Ireland | 107 |
| 18 | *Tuesday* | San Francisco earthquake 1906 | 108 |
| 19 | *Wednesday* | Charles Darwin d. 1882. Pierre Curie d. 1906 | 109 |
| 20 | *Thursday* | Adolf Hitler b. 1889. Joan Miró b. 1893 | 110 |
| 21 | *Friday* | *Queen Elizabeth II b. 1926.* Henry VII d. 1509 | 111 |
| 22 | *Saturday* | Robert Oppenheimer b. 1904 | 112 |
| 23 | *Sunday* | **1st S. after Easter.** EASTER DAY (Greek Orthodox) | *week* 17 *day* 113 |
| 24 | *Monday* | Edmund Cartwright b. 1743. Sir Stafford Cripps b. 1889 | 114 |
| 25 | *Tuesday* | **St Mark.** *Easter Law Sittings begin* | 115 |
| 26 | *Wednesday* | Alfred Krupp b. 1812. Rudolf Hess b. 1894 | 116 |
| 27 | *Thursday* | Ralph Waldo Emerson d. 1882 | 117 |
| 28 | *Friday* | Edward IV b. 1442. Benito Mussolini killed 1945 | 118 |
| 29 | *Saturday* | Sir Malcolm Sargent b. 1895 | 119 |
| 30 | *Sunday* | **2nd S. after Easter.** Adolf Hitler d. 1945 | *week* 18 *day* 120 |

ASTRONOMICAL PHENOMENA

| d | h | |
|---|---|---|
| 1 | 12 | Jupiter at stationary point |
| 10 | 09 | Mars in conjunction with Moon. Mars 8° N. |
| 13 | 12 | Saturn in conjunction with Venus. Saturn 0°.5 S. |
| 14 | 13 | Mercury in superior conjunction |
| 15 | 12 | Partial eclipse of Moon (*see* page 66) |
| 18 | 21 | Jupiter in conjunction with Moon. Jupiter 3° S. |
| 20 | 13 | Sun's longitude 30° ♉ |
| 25 | 20 | Saturn in conjunction with Moon. Saturn 5° S. |
| 27 | 01 | Venus in conjunction with Moon. Venus 4° S. |
| 27 | 22 | Neptune at stationary point |
| 29 | 18 | Annular eclipse of Sun (*see* page 66) |

CONSTELLATIONS

The following constellations are near the meridian at

| | d | h |
|---|---|---|
| March | 1 | 24 |
| March | 16 | 23 |
| April | 1 | 22 |
| April | 15 | 21 |
| May | 1 | 20 |
| May | 16 | 19 |

Cepheus (below the Pole), Cassiopeia (below the Pole), Ursa Major, Leo Minor, Leo, Sextans, Hydra and Crater

MINIMA OF ALGOL

| d | h | d | h | d | h |
|---|---|---|---|---|---|
| 3 | 02.4 | 14 | 13.7 | 23 | 04.2 |
| 5 | 23.3 | 17 | 10.5 | 26 | 01.0 |
| 8 | 20.1 | 20 | 07.4 | 28 | 21.8 |
| 11 | 16.9 | | | | |

THE MOON

| Phases, Apsides and Node | d | h | m |
|---|---|---|---|
| ☽ First Quarter | 8 | 05 | 35 |
| ○ Full Moon | 15 | 12 | 08 |
| ☾ Last Quarter | 22 | 03 | 18 |
| ● New Moon | 29 | 17 | 36 |
| Apogee (405,009 km) | 5 | 10 | 13 |
| Perigee (361,686 km) | 17 | 08 | 25 |

Mean longitude of ascending node on April 1, 217°

THE SUN                                                          s.d. 16′.0

| Day | Right Ascension | Dec. + | Equation of time | Rise 52° | Rise 56° | Transit | Set 52° | Set 56° | Sidereal time | Transit of First Point of Aries |
|---|---|---|---|---|---|---|---|---|---|---|
| | h  m  s | °  ′ | m  s | h  m | h  m | h  m | h  m | h  m | h  m  s | h  m  s |
| 1 | 0 39 43 | 4 17 | −4 10 | 5 36 | 5 32 | 12 04 | 18 33 | 18 37 | 12 35 33 | 11 22 35 |
| 2 | 0 43 22 | 4 40 | −3 52 | 5 34 | 5 29 | 12 04 | 18 35 | 18 39 | 12 39 29 | 11 18 39 |
| 3 | 0 47 01 | 5 03 | −3 35 | 5 32 | 5 27 | 12 03 | 18 36 | 18 41 | 12 43 26 | 11 14 43 |
| 4 | 0 50 40 | 5 26 | −3 17 | 5 29 | 5 24 | 12 03 | 18 38 | 18 43 | 12 47 22 | 11 10 47 |
| 5 | 0 54 19 | 5 49 | −3 00 | 5 27 | 5 22 | 12 03 | 18 40 | 18 45 | 12 51 19 | 11 06 52 |
| 6 | 0 57 58 | 6 11 | −2 42 | 5 25 | 5 19 | 12 03 | 18 41 | 18 47 | 12 55 15 | 11 02 56 |
| 7 | 1 01 37 | 6 34 | −2 25 | 5 22 | 5 16 | 12 02 | 18 43 | 18 49 | 12 59 12 | 10 59 00 |
| 8 | 1 05 17 | 6 57 | −2 08 | 5 20 | 5 14 | 12 02 | 18 45 | 18 51 | 13 03 09 | 10 55 04 |
| 9 | 1 08 57 | 7 19 | −1 52 | 5 18 | 5 11 | 12 02 | 18 47 | 18 54 | 13 07 05 | 10 51 08 |
| 10 | 1 12 37 | 7 42 | −1 35 | 5 16 | 5 09 | 12 01 | 18 48 | 18 56 | 13 11 02 | 10 47 12 |
| 11 | 1 16 17 | 8 04 | −1 19 | 5 13 | 5 06 | 12 01 | 18 50 | 18 58 | 13 14 58 | 10 43 16 |
| 12 | 1 19 58 | 8 26 | −1 03 | 5 11 | 5 04 | 12 01 | 18 52 | 19 00 | 13 18 55 | 10 39 20 |
| 13 | 1 23 39 | 8 48 | −0 47 | 5 09 | 5 01 | 12 01 | 18 53 | 19 02 | 13 22 51 | 10 35 24 |
| 14 | 1 27 20 | 9 10 | −0 32 | 5 07 | 4 58 | 12 00 | 18 55 | 19 04 | 13 26 48 | 10 31 28 |
| 15 | 1 31 01 | 9 31 | −0 17 | 5 05 | 4 56 | 12 00 | 18 57 | 19 06 | 13 30 44 | 10 27 32 |
| 16 | 1 34 43 | 9 53 | −0 02 | 5 02 | 4 53 | 12 00 | 18 59 | 19 08 | 13 34 41 | 10 23 37 |
| 17 | 1 38 25 | 10 14 | +0 12 | 5 00 | 4 51 | 12 00 | 19 00 | 19 10 | 13 38 38 | 10 19 41 |
| 18 | 1 42 08 | 10 35 | +0 26 | 4 58 | 4 48 | 11 59 | 19 02 | 19 12 | 13 42 34 | 10 15 45 |
| 19 | 1 45 51 | 10 56 | +0 40 | 4 56 | 4 46 | 11 59 | 19 04 | 19 14 | 13 46 31 | 10 11 49 |
| 20 | 1 49 34 | 11 17 | +0 53 | 4 54 | 4 43 | 11 59 | 19 05 | 19 16 | 13 50 27 | 10 07 53 |
| 21 | 1 53 18 | 11 37 | +1 06 | 4 52 | 4 41 | 11 59 | 19 07 | 19 18 | 13 54 24 | 10 03 57 |
| 22 | 1 57 02 | 11 58 | +1 18 | 4 50 | 4 39 | 11 59 | 19 09 | 19 20 | 13 58 20 | 10 00 01 |
| 23 | 2 00 47 | 12 18 | +1 30 | 4 47 | 4 36 | 11 58 | 19 10 | 19 22 | 14 02 17 | 9 56 05 |
| 24 | 2 04 32 | 12 38 | +1 42 | 4 45 | 4 34 | 11 58 | 19 12 | 19 24 | 14 06 13 | 9 52 09 |
| 25 | 2 08 17 | 12 58 | +1 53 | 4 43 | 4 31 | 11 58 | 19 14 | 19 26 | 14 10 10 | 9 48 13 |
| 26 | 2 12 04 | 13 17 | +2 03 | 4 41 | 4 29 | 11 58 | 19 16 | 19 28 | 14 14 07 | 9 44 17 |
| 27 | 2 15 50 | 13 37 | +2 13 | 4 39 | 4 27 | 11 58 | 19 17 | 19 30 | 14 18 03 | 9 40 22 |
| 28 | 2 19 37 | 13 56 | +2 22 | 4 37 | 4 24 | 11 58 | 19 19 | 19 32 | 14 22 00 | 9 36 26 |
| 29 | 2 23 25 | 14 15 | +2 31 | 4 35 | 4 22 | 11 57 | 19 21 | 19 34 | 14 25 56 | 9 32 30 |
| 30 | 2 27 13 | 14 34 | +2 40 | 4 33 | 4 20 | 11 57 | 19 22 | 19 36 | 14 29 53 | 9 28 34 |

DURATION OF TWILIGHT (in minutes)

| Latitude | 52° | 56° | 52° | 56° | 52° | 56° | 52° | 56° |
|---|---|---|---|---|---|---|---|---|
| | 1 April | | 11 April | | 21 April | | 30 April | |
| Civil | 34 | 38 | 35 | 40 | 37 | 42 | 39 | 44 |
| Nautical | 76 | 85 | 79 | 90 | 84 | 96 | 89 | 105 |
| Astronomical | 121 | 137 | 128 | 148 | 138 | 167 | 152 | 200 |

THE NIGHT SKY

Mercury passes through superior conjunction on the 14th and remains too close to the Sun for observation until late in the month. By the 26th Mercury becomes visible low in the west-north-west sky at the end of evening civil twilight, magnitude −1.0.

Venus continues to be visible as a very bright object in the mornings, magnitude −3.9. However, it can only be seen at a very low altitude above the east-south-east horizon for a very short time before dawn. The old crescent Moon, only two and a half days before New, passes about 3° N. of Venus on the morning of the 27th.

Mars, magnitude +0.2, continues to be visible as an evening object, moving eastwards from Cancer into Leo during the month.

Jupiter attains its first stationary point on the 1st, in Ophiuchus, and continues to be visible as a morning object, low in the south-east sky. By the end of the month it should be clearly visible before midnight. Its magnitude is −2.4.

Saturn is too close to the Sun for observation.

Eclipses. A partial eclipse of the Moon occurs on the 15th. An annular eclipse of the sun occurs on the 29th. (See page 66 for details).

## THE MOON

| Day | RA | Dec. | Hor. par. | Semi- diam. | Sun's co- long. | PA of Bright Limb | Phase | Age | Rise 52° | Rise 56° | Transit | Set 52° | Set 56° |
|---|---|---|---|---|---|---|---|---|---|---|---|---|---|
| | h m | ° | ' | ' | ° | ° | % | d | h m | h m | h m | h m | h m |
| 1 | 1 17 | + 9.5 | 55.3 | 15.1 | 277 | 241 | 1 | 0.9 | 5 59 | 5 50 | 13 05 | 20 24 | 20 35 |
| 2 | 2 05 | +12.9 | 54.9 | 15.0 | 289 | 250 | 4 | 1.9 | 6 26 | 6 13 | 13 51 | 21 28 | 21 42 |
| 3 | 2 54 | +15.6 | 54.5 | 14.9 | 301 | 255 | 8 | 2.9 | 6 56 | 6 41 | 14 38 | 22 28 | 22 45 |
| 4 | 3 43 | +17.7 | 54.3 | 14.8 | 313 | 259 | 14 | 3.9 | 7 31 | 7 14 | 15 25 | 23 24 | 23 43 |
| 5 | 4 33 | +19.0 | 54.2 | 14.8 | 326 | 264 | 21 | 4.9 | 8 12 | 7 53 | 16 13 | — | — |
| 6 | 5 23 | +19.4 | 54.2 | 14.8 | 338 | 268 | 29 | 5.9 | 8 59 | 8 40 | 17 01 | 0 15 | 0 34 |
| 7 | 6 13 | +19.0 | 54.3 | 14.8 | 350 | 272 | 38 | 6.9 | 9 52 | 9 34 | 17 48 | 0 59 | 1 18 |
| 8 | 7 03 | +17.7 | 54.7 | 14.9 | 2 | 276 | 48 | 7.9 | 10 51 | 10 35 | 18 36 | 1 38 | 1 55 |
| 9 | 7 53 | +15.6 | 55.2 | 15.0 | 14 | 280 | 58 | 8.9 | 11 54 | 11 41 | 19 23 | 2 12 | 2 26 |
| 10 | 8 43 | +12.7 | 55.9 | 15.2 | 27 | 283 | 67 | 9.9 | 13 01 | 12 51 | 20 11 | 2 42 | 2 52 |
| 11 | 9 33 | + 9.2 | 56.6 | 15.4 | 39 | 286 | 76 | 10.9 | 14 11 | 14 05 | 20 59 | 3 08 | 3 16 |
| 12 | 10 23 | + 5.2 | 57.5 | 15.7 | 51 | 287 | 85 | 11.9 | 15 24 | 15 22 | 21 48 | 3 34 | 3 37 |
| 13 | 11 15 | + 0.7 | 58.4 | 15.9 | 63 | 287 | 92 | 12.9 | 16 40 | 16 42 | 22 38 | 3 59 | 3 59 |
| 14 | 12 08 | − 3.9 | 59.2 | 16.1 | 75 | 286 | 97 | 13.9 | 17 58 | 18 04 | 23 31 | 4 25 | 4 21 |
| 15 | 13 03 | − 8.4 | 59.9 | 16.3 | 87 | 279 | 100 | 14.9 | 19 18 | 19 29 | — | 4 53 | 4 45 |
| 16 | 14 00 | −12.6 | 60.4 | 16.5 | 100 | 113 | 100 | 15.9 | 20 38 | 20 53 | 0 26 | 5 26 | 5 14 |
| 17 | 15 00 | −15.9 | 60.6 | 16.5 | 112 | 104 | 97 | 16.9 | 21 54 | 22 12 | 1 25 | 6 05 | 5 49 |
| 18 | 16 01 | −18.2 | 60.6 | 16.5 | 124 | 98 | 91 | 17.9 | 23 03 | 23 22 | 2 25 | 6 52 | 6 33 |
| 19 | 17 04 | −19.3 | 60.3 | 16.4 | 136 | 92 | 83 | 18.9 | — | — | 3 25 | 7 48 | 7 28 |
| 20 | 18 05 | −19.1 | 59.8 | 16.3 | 148 | 87 | 74 | 19.9 | 0 01 | 0 20 | 4 25 | 8 52 | 8 34 |
| 21 | 19 05 | −17.6 | 59.2 | 16.1 | 160 | 82 | 63 | 20.9 | 0 49 | 1 06 | 5 23 | 10 02 | 9 46 |
| 22 | 20 03 | −15.1 | 58.6 | 16.0 | 173 | 78 | 52 | 21.9 | 1 28 | 1 42 | 6 18 | 11 15 | 11 02 |
| 23 | 20 57 | −11.8 | 57.9 | 15.8 | 185 | 75 | 41 | 22.9 | 2 00 | 2 10 | 7 09 | 12 28 | 12 19 |
| 24 | 21 49 | − 7.9 | 57.3 | 15.6 | 197 | 73 | 30 | 23.9 | 2 28 | 2 34 | 7 58 | 13 40 | 13 35 |
| 25 | 22 39 | − 3.8 | 56.7 | 15.4 | 209 | 71 | 21 | 24.9 | 2 52 | 2 55 | 8 45 | 14 50 | 14 49 |
| 26 | 23 28 | + 0.4 | 56.1 | 15.3 | 221 | 71 | 13 | 25.9 | 3 15 | 3 14 | 9 31 | 15 59 | 16 01 |
| 27 | 0 16 | + 4.6 | 55.6 | 15.2 | 234 | 71 | 7 | 26.9 | 3 38 | 3 34 | 10 16 | 17 06 | 17 13 |
| 28 | 1 03 | + 8.5 | 55.2 | 15.0 | 246 | 72 | 3 | 27.9 | 4 02 | 3 54 | 11 01 | 18 12 | 18 22 |
| 29 | 1 51 | +12.0 | 54.8 | 14.9 | 258 | 73 | 1 | 28.9 | 4 28 | 4 17 | 11 47 | 19 17 | 19 30 |
| 30 | 2 40 | +14.9 | 54.5 | 14.8 | 270 | 264 | 0 | 0.3 | 4 57 | 4 43 | 12 33 | 20 19 | 20 35 |

## MERCURY

| Day | RA | Dec. | Diam. | Phase | Transit | 5° high 52° | 5° high 56° |
|---|---|---|---|---|---|---|---|
| | h m | ° | " | % | h m | h m | h m |
| 1 | 23 55 | − 2.9 | 5 | 91 | 11 20 | 6 07 | 6 12 |
| 3 | 0 08 | − 1.4 | 5 | 93 | 11 26 | 6 04 | 6 08 |
| 5 | 0 21 | + 0.3 | 5 | 95 | 11 32 | 6 01 | 6 04 |
| 7 | 0 35 | + 1.9 | 5 | 96 | 11 38 | 5 58 | 6 00 |
| 9 | 0 49 | + 3.7 | 5 | 98 | 11 44 | 5 56 | 5 56 |
| 11 | 1 04 | + 5.5 | 5 | 99 | 11 51 | 5 53 | 5 52 |
| 13 | 1 19 | + 7.3 | 5 | 100 | 11 58 | 5 51 | 5 48 |
| 15 | 1 34 | + 9.1 | 5 | 100 | 12 05 | 18 24 | 18 29 |
| 17 | 1 49 | +10.9 | 5 | 99 | 12 13 | 18 41 | 18 48 |
| 19 | 2 05 | +12.7 | 5 | 98 | 12 21 | 18 59 | 19 07 |
| 21 | 2 21 | +14.5 | 5 | 96 | 12 29 | 19 16 | 19 26 |
| 23 | 2 37 | +16.1 | 5 | 92 | 12 37 | 19 33 | 19 44 |
| 25 | 2 53 | +17.7 | 6 | 87 | 12 45 | 19 50 | 20 02 |
| 27 | 3 08 | +19.1 | 6 | 82 | 12 52 | 20 05 | 20 19 |
| 29 | 3 23 | +20.4 | 6 | 76 | 12 59 | 20 19 | 20 34 |
| 31 | 3 38 | +21.5 | 6 | 70 | 13 06 | 20 32 | 20 48 |

## VENUS

| Day | RA | Dec. | Diam. | Phase | Transit | 5° high 52° | 5° high 56° |
|---|---|---|---|---|---|---|---|
| | h m | ° | " | % | h m | h m | h m |
| 1 | 22 27 | −10.6 | 14 | 79 | 9 52 | 5 21 | 5 34 |
| 6 | 22 50 | − 8.6 | 13 | 81 | 9 55 | 5 13 | 5 23 |
| 11 | 23 12 | − 6.4 | 13 | 82 | 9 58 | 5 04 | 5 13 |
| 16 | 23 35 | − 4.2 | 13 | 83 | 10 00 | 4 54 | 5 01 |
| 21 | 23 57 | − 1.9 | 12 | 84 | 10 03 | 4 45 | 4 50 |
| 26 | 0 19 | + 0.4 | 12 | 85 | 10 06 | 4 36 | 4 39 |
| 31 | 0 42 | + 2.7 | 12 | 87 | 10 08 | 4 26 | 4 27 |

## MARS

| Day | RA | Dec. | Diam. | Phase | Transit | 5° high 52° | 5° high 56° |
|---|---|---|---|---|---|---|---|
| 1 | 9 08 | +19.8 | 10 | 93 | 20 29 | 3 44 | 3 58 |
| 6 | 9 10 | +19.4 | 10 | 92 | 20 12 | 3 24 | 3 38 |
| 11 | 9 13 | +19.0 | 10 | 92 | 19 55 | 3 05 | 3 18 |
| 16 | 9 17 | +18.5 | 9 | 91 | 19 40 | 2 47 | 2 59 |
| 21 | 9 21 | +18.0 | 9 | 91 | 19 25 | 2 29 | 2 41 |
| 26 | 9 27 | +17.4 | 8 | 90 | 19 11 | 2 11 | 2 23 |
| 31 | 9 33 | +16 8 | 8 | 90 | 18 57 | 1 54 | 2 05 |

## SUNRISE AND SUNSET

| | London | | Bristol | | Birmingham | | Manchester | | Newcastle | | Glasgow | | Belfast | |
|---|---|---|---|---|---|---|---|---|---|---|---|---|---|---|
| | 0°05′ | 51°30′ | 2°35′ | 51°28′ | 1°55′ | 52°28′ | 2°15′ | 53°28′ | 1°37′ | 54°59′ | 4°14′ | 55°52′ | 5°56′ | 54°35′ |
| | h m | h m | h m | h m | h m | h m | h m | h m | h m | h m | h m | h m | h m | h m |
| 1 | 5 37 | 18 33 | 5 47 | 18 43 | 5 43 | 18 41 | 5 44 | 18 43 | 5 40 | 18 43 | 5 49 | 18 54 | 5 57 | 18 59 |
| 2 | 5 35 | 18 34 | 5 45 | 18 44 | 5 41 | 18 43 | 5 41 | 18 45 | 5 37 | 18 44 | 5 47 | 18 56 | 5 55 | 19 01 |
| 3 | 5 32 | 18 36 | 5 42 | 18 46 | 5 39 | 18 45 | 5 39 | 18 47 | 5 35 | 18 46 | 5 44 | 18 58 | 5 52 | 19 03 |
| 4 | 5 30 | 18 38 | 5 40 | 18 48 | 5 36 | 18 46 | 5 37 | 18 49 | 5 32 | 18 48 | 5 41 | 19 00 | 5 50 | 19 05 |
| 5 | 5 28 | 18 39 | 5 38 | 18 49 | 5 34 | 18 48 | 5 34 | 18 51 | 5 30 | 18 50 | 5 39 | 19 02 | 5 47 | 19 07 |
| 6 | 5 26 | 18 41 | 5 36 | 18 51 | 5 32 | 18 50 | 5 32 | 18 53 | 5 27 | 18 52 | 5 36 | 19 04 | 5 45 | 19 09 |
| 7 | 5 24 | 18 43 | 5 34 | 18 53 | 5 29 | 18 52 | 5 29 | 18 54 | 5 25 | 18 54 | 5 34 | 19 06 | 5 42 | 19 11 |
| 8 | 5 21 | 18 44 | 5 31 | 18 54 | 5 27 | 18 53 | 5 27 | 18 56 | 5 22 | 18 56 | 5 31 | 19 08 | 5 40 | 19 13 |
| 9 | 5 19 | 18 46 | 5 29 | 18 56 | 5 25 | 18 55 | 5 25 | 18 58 | 5 20 | 18 58 | 5 28 | 19 10 | 5 37 | 19 15 |
| 10 | 5 17 | 18 48 | 5 27 | 18 58 | 5 23 | 18 57 | 5 22 | 19 00 | 5 17 | 19 00 | 5 26 | 19 12 | 5 35 | 19 17 |
| 11 | 5 15 | 18 49 | 5 25 | 18 59 | 5 20 | 18 58 | 5 20 | 19 02 | 5 15 | 19 02 | 5 23 | 19 14 | 5 33 | 19 18 |
| 12 | 5 12 | 18 51 | 5 22 | 19 01 | 5 18 | 19 00 | 5 18 | 19 03 | 5 12 | 19 04 | 5 21 | 19 16 | 5 30 | 19 20 |
| 13 | 5 10 | 18 53 | 5 20 | 19 03 | 5 16 | 19 02 | 5 15 | 19 05 | 5 10 | 19 06 | 5 18 | 19 18 | 5 28 | 19 22 |
| 14 | 5 08 | 18 55 | 5 18 | 19 04 | 5 14 | 19 04 | 5 13 | 19 07 | 5 07 | 19 08 | 5 16 | 19 20 | 5 25 | 19 24 |
| 15 | 5 06 | 18 56 | 5 16 | 19 06 | 5 11 | 19 05 | 5 11 | 19 09 | 5 05 | 19 10 | 5 13 | 19 22 | 5 23 | 19 26 |
| 16 | 5 04 | 18 58 | 5 14 | 19 08 | 5 09 | 19 07 | 5 08 | 19 11 | 5 02 | 19 12 | 5 11 | 19 24 | 5 21 | 19 28 |
| 17 | 5 02 | 19 00 | 5 12 | 19 09 | 5 07 | 19 09 | 5 06 | 19 13 | 5 00 | 19 14 | 5 08 | 19 26 | 5 18 | 19 30 |
| 18 | 4 59 | 19 01 | 5 10 | 19 11 | 5 05 | 19 11 | 5 04 | 19 14 | 4 57 | 19 16 | 5 06 | 19 28 | 5 16 | 19 32 |
| 19 | 4 57 | 19 03 | 5 07 | 19 13 | 5 03 | 19 12 | 5 01 | 19 16 | 4 55 | 19 18 | 5 03 | 19 30 | 5 13 | 19 34 |
| 20 | 4 55 | 19 05 | 5 05 | 19 14 | 5 00 | 19 14 | 4 59 | 19 18 | 4 53 | 19 19 | 5 01 | 19 32 | 5 11 | 19 36 |
| 21 | 4 53 | 19 06 | 5 03 | 19 16 | 4 58 | 19 16 | 4 57 | 19 20 | 4 50 | 19 21 | 4 58 | 19 35 | 5 09 | 19 38 |
| 22 | 4 51 | 19 08 | 5 01 | 19 18 | 4 56 | 19 18 | 4 55 | 19 22 | 4 48 | 19 23 | 4 56 | 19 37 | 5 06 | 19 40 |
| 23 | 4 49 | 19 10 | 4 59 | 19 19 | 4 54 | 19 19 | 4 53 | 19 23 | 4 46 | 19 25 | 4 53 | 19 39 | 5 04 | 19 41 |
| 24 | 4 47 | 19 11 | 4 57 | 19 21 | 4 52 | 19 21 | 4 50 | 19 25 | 4 43 | 19 27 | 4 51 | 19 41 | 5 02 | 19 43 |
| 25 | 4 45 | 19 13 | 4 55 | 19 23 | 4 50 | 19 23 | 4 48 | 19 27 | 4 41 | 19 29 | 4 49 | 19 43 | 5 00 | 19 45 |
| 26 | 4 43 | 19 14 | 4 53 | 19 24 | 4 48 | 19 25 | 4 46 | 19 29 | 4 39 | 19 31 | 4 46 | 19 45 | 4 57 | 19 47 |
| 27 | 4 41 | 19 16 | 4 51 | 19 26 | 4 46 | 19 26 | 4 44 | 19 31 | 4 37 | 19 33 | 4 44 | 19 47 | 4 55 | 19 49 |
| 28 | 4 39 | 19 18 | 4 49 | 19 28 | 4 44 | 19 28 | 4 42 | 19 32 | 4 34 | 19 35 | 4 42 | 19 49 | 4 53 | 19 51 |
| 29 | 4 37 | 19 19 | 4 47 | 19 29 | 4 42 | 19 30 | 4 40 | 19 34 | 4 32 | 19 37 | 4 39 | 19 51 | 4 51 | 19 53 |
| 30 | 4 35 | 19 21 | 4 45 | 19 31 | 4 40 | 19 31 | 4 38 | 19 36 | 4 30 | 19 39 | 4 37 | 19 53 | 4 49 | 19 55 |

## JUPITER

| Day | RA | Dec. | Transit | 5° high | |
|---|---|---|---|---|---|
| | | | | 52° | 56° |
| | h m | ° ′ | h m | h m | h m |
| 1 | 16 56.9 | −21 49 | 4 21 | 1 08 | 1 39 |
| 11 | 16 56.3 | −21 48 | 3 41 | 0 28 | 0 59 |
| 21 | 16 54.4 | −21 45 | 3 00 | 23 42 | 0 18 |
| 31 | 16 51.3 | −21 40 | 2 17 | 22 59 | 23 30 |

Diameters – equatorial 42″ polar 40″

## SATURN

| Day | RA | Dec. | Transit | 5° high | |
|---|---|---|---|---|---|
| | | | | 52° | 56° |
| | h m | ° ′ | h m | h m | h m |
| 1 | 23 19.2 | − 6 20 | 10 42 | 5 49 | 5 58 |
| 11 | 23 23.5 | − 5 55 | 10 07 | 5 12 | 5 20 |
| 21 | 23 27.5 | − 5 31 | 9 32 | 4 34 | 4 42 |
| 31 | 23 31.2 | − 5 09 | 8 56 | 3 56 | 4 04 |

Diameters – equatorial 16″ polar 14″
Rings – major axis 36″ minor axis 1″

## URANUS

| Day | RA | Dec. | Transit | 10° high | |
|---|---|---|---|---|---|
| | | | | 52° | 56° |
| | h m | ° ′ | h m | h m | h m |
| 1 | 20 09.1 | −20 40 | 7 32 | 4 59 | 5 45 |
| 11 | 20 10.1 | −20 37 | 6 54 | 4 21 | 5 06 |
| 21 | 20 10.8 | −20 35 | 6 15 | 3 42 | 4 26 |
| 31 | 20 11.2 | −20 34 | 5 36 | 3 03 | 3 47 |

Diameter 4″

## NEPTUNE

| Day | RA | Dec. | Transit | 10° high | |
|---|---|---|---|---|---|
| | | | | 52° | 56° |
| | h m | ° ′ | h m | h m | h m |
| 1 | 19 48.8 | −20 32 | 7 12 | 4 38 | 5 22 |
| 11 | 19 49.3 | −20 30 | 6 33 | 3 59 | 4 43 |
| 21 | 19 49.6 | −20 29 | 5 54 | 3 19 | 4 04 |
| 31 | 19 49.6 | −20 29 | 5 15 | 2 40 | 3 24 |

Diameter 2″

# May 1995

FIFTH MONTH, 31 DAYS. *Maia*, goddess of growth and increase

| | | | |
|---|---|---|---|
| 1 | *Monday* | **SS Philip and James.** *Bank Holiday in Scotland* | *week* 18 *day* 121 |
| 2 | *Tuesday* | Leonardo da Vinci d. 1519. Surrender of Berlin 1945 | 122 |
| 3 | *Wednesday* | Thomas Hood d. 1845. Henry Cooper b. 1934 | 123 |
| 4 | *Thursday* | Joseph Whitaker b. 1820. Marshal Josip Tito d. 1980 | 124 |
| 5 | *Friday* | Karl Marx b. 1818. Field Marshal Earl Wavell b. 1883 | 125 |
| 6 | *Saturday* | Orson Welles b. 1915. Marlene Dietrich d. 1992 | 126 |
| 7 | *Sunday* | **3rd S. after Easter.** Germany surrenders 1945 | *week* 19 *day* 127 |
| 8 | *Monday* | *Bank Holiday in the UK.* VE Day | 128 |
| 9 | *Tuesday* | Channel Islands liberated 1945 | 129 |
| 10 | *Wednesday* | Fred Astaire b. 1899. Neville Chamberlain resigned 1940 | 130 |
| 11 | *Thursday* | William Pitt (the Elder) d. 1778 | 131 |
| 12 | *Friday* | Gabriel Fauré b. 1845. John Smith d. 1994 | 132 |
| 13 | *Saturday* | 2nd Marquess of Rockingham b. 1730 | 133 |
| 14 | *Sunday* | **4th S. after Easter.** Gabriel Fahrenheit b. 1686 | *week* 20 *day* 134 |
| 15 | *Monday* | **St Matthias.** Joseph Whitaker d. 1895 | 135 |
| 16 | *Tuesday* | Film Academy Awards first presented 1929 | 136 |
| 17 | *Wednesday* | Relief of Mafeking 1900 | 137 |
| 18 | *Thursday* | Pope John Paul II b. 1920. Monte Cassino captured 1944 | 138 |
| 19 | *Friday* | James Boswell d. 1795. T. E. Lawrence d. 1935 | 139 |
| 20 | *Saturday* | Dame Barbara Hepworth d. 1975 | 140 |
| 21 | *Sunday* | **5th S. after Easter.** Alexander Pope b. 1688 | *week* 21 *day* 141 |
| 22 | *Monday* | Sir Arthur Conan Doyle b. 1859 | 142 |
| 23 | *Tuesday* | Heinrich Himmler d. 1945. Coalition Ministry dissolved 1945 | 143 |
| 24 | *Wednesday* | Queen Victoria b. 1819. Field Marshal Earl Wavell d. 1950 | 144 |
| 25 | *Thursday* | **Ascension Day.** Miles Davis b. 1926 | 145 |
| 26 | *Friday* | *Easter Law Sittings end.* Edict of Worms 1521 | 146 |
| 27 | *Saturday* | Dunkirk evacuation begun 1940. *Bismarck* sunk 1941 | 147 |
| 28 | *Sunday* | **S. after Ascension Day.** Roy Plomley d. 1985 | *week* 22 *day* 148 |
| 29 | *Monday* | *Bank Holiday in the UK.* Charles II b. 1630 | 149 |
| 30 | *Tuesday* | Joan of Arc exec. 1431 | 150 |
| 31 | *Wednesday* | MUSLIM NEW YEAR (1416). Denholm Elliott b. 1922 | 151 |

ASTRONOMICAL PHENOMENA

| d | h | |
|---|---|---|
| 1 | 07 | Mercury in conjunction with Moon. Mercury 4° N. |
| 5 | 08 | Uranus at stationary point |
| 8 | 09 | Mars in conjunction with Moon. Mars 7° N. |
| 12 | 02 | Mercury at greatest elongation E.22° |
| 16 | 03 | Jupiter in conjunction with Moon. Jupiter 2° S. |
| 20 | 17 | Pluto at opposition |
| 21 | 13 | Sun's longitude 60° II |
| 23 | 06 | Saturn in conjunction with Moon. Saturn 5° S. |
| 24 | 09 | Mercury at stationary point |
| 27 | 07 | Venus in conjunction with Moon. Venus 0°.8 S. |
| 30 | 05 | Mercury in conjunction with Moon. Mercury 3° N. |

CONSTELLATIONS

The following constellations are near the meridian at

| | d | h | | d | h |
|---|---|---|---|---|---|
| April | 1 | 24 | May | 16 | 21 |
| April | 15 | 23 | June | 1 | 20 |
| May | 1 | 22 | June | 15 | 19 |

Cepheus (below the Pole), Cassiopeia (below the Pole), Ursa Minor, Ursa Major, Canes Venatici, Coma Berenices, Bootes, Leo, Virgo, Crater, Corvus and Hydra

MINIMA OF ALGOL

Algol is inconveniently situated for observation during May.

THE MOON

| Phases, Apsides and Node | d | h | m |
|---|---|---|---|
| ☽ First Quarter | 7 | 21 | 44 |
| ○ Full Moon | 14 | 20 | 48 |
| ☾ Last Quarter | 21 | 11 | 36 |
| ● New Moon | 29 | 09 | 27 |
| Apogee (405,950 km) | 3 | 00 | 58 |
| Perigee (358,033 km) | 15 | 15 | 23 |
| Apogee (406,523 km) | 30 | 08 | 02 |

Mean longitude of ascending node on May 1, 215°

THE SUN                                                                  s.d. 15′.8

| Day | Right Ascension | Dec. + | Equation of time | Rise 52° | Rise 56° | Transit | Set 52° | Set 56° | Sidereal time | Transit of First Point of Aries |
|-----|-----------------|--------|------------------|----------|----------|---------|---------|---------|---------------|---------------------------------|
|     | h  m  s         | °  ′   | m  s             | h  m     | h  m     | h  m    | h  m    | h  m    | h  m  s       | h  m  s                         |
| 1   | 2 31 02         | 14 52  | +2 47            | 4 31     | 4 17     | 11 57   | 19 24   | 19 38   | 14 33 49      | 9 24 38                         |
| 2   | 2 34 51         | 15 10  | +2 55            | 4 30     | 4 15     | 11 57   | 19 26   | 19 40   | 14 37 46      | 9 20 42                         |
| 3   | 2 38 41         | 15 28  | +3 02            | 4 28     | 4 13     | 11 57   | 19 27   | 19 42   | 14 41 42      | 9 16 46                         |
| 4   | 2 42 31         | 15 46  | +3 08            | 4 26     | 4 11     | 11 57   | 19 29   | 19 44   | 14 45 39      | 9 12 50                         |
| 5   | 2 46 22         | 16 03  | +3 14            | 4 24     | 4 08     | 11 57   | 19 31   | 19 46   | 14 49 36      | 9 08 54                         |
| 6   | 2 50 13         | 16 20  | +3 19            | 4 22     | 4 06     | 11 57   | 19 32   | 19 48   | 14 53 32      | 9 04 58                         |
| 7   | 2 54 05         | 16 37  | +3 23            | 4 20     | 4 04     | 11 57   | 19 34   | 19 50   | 14 57 29      | 9 01 02                         |
| 8   | 2 57 58         | 16 54  | +3 27            | 4 19     | 4 02     | 11 57   | 19 36   | 19 52   | 15 01 25      | 8 57 07                         |
| 9   | 3 01 51         | 17 10  | +3 31            | 4 17     | 4 00     | 11 56   | 19 37   | 19 54   | 15 05 22      | 8 53 11                         |
| 10  | 3 05 44         | 17 26  | +3 34            | 4 15     | 3 58     | 11 56   | 19 39   | 19 56   | 15 09 18      | 8 49 15                         |
| 11  | 3 09 38         | 17 42  | +3 36            | 4 13     | 3 56     | 11 56   | 19 40   | 19 58   | 15 13 15      | 8 45 19                         |
| 12  | 3 13 33         | 17 58  | +3 38            | 4 12     | 3 54     | 11 56   | 19 42   | 20 00   | 15 17 11      | 8 41 23                         |
| 13  | 3 17 28         | 18 13  | +3 40            | 4 10     | 3 52     | 11 56   | 19 44   | 20 02   | 15 21 08      | 8 37 27                         |
| 14  | 3 21 24         | 18 28  | +3 40            | 4 09     | 3 50     | 11 56   | 19 45   | 20 04   | 15 25 05      | 8 33 31                         |
| 15  | 3 25 20         | 18 42  | +3 41            | 4 07     | 3 48     | 11 56   | 19 47   | 20 06   | 15 29 01      | 8 29 35                         |
| 16  | 3 29 17         | 18 56  | +3 40            | 4 05     | 3 46     | 11 56   | 19 48   | 20 08   | 15 32 58      | 8 25 39                         |
| 17  | 3 33 15         | 19 10  | +3 39            | 4 04     | 3 45     | 11 56   | 19 50   | 20 09   | 15 36 54      | 8 21 43                         |
| 18  | 3 37 13         | 19 24  | +3 38            | 4 03     | 3 43     | 11 56   | 19 51   | 20 11   | 15 40 51      | 8 17 47                         |
| 19  | 3 41 12         | 19 37  | +3 36            | 4 01     | 3 41     | 11 56   | 19 53   | 20 13   | 15 44 47      | 8 13 52                         |
| 20  | 3 45 11         | 19 50  | +3 33            | 4 00     | 3 39     | 11 56   | 19 54   | 20 15   | 15 48 44      | 8 09 56                         |
| 21  | 3 49 11         | 20 02  | +3 30            | 3 58     | 3 38     | 11 57   | 19 56   | 20 17   | 15 52 40      | 8 06 00                         |
| 22  | 3 53 11         | 20 15  | +3 26            | 3 57     | 3 36     | 11 57   | 19 57   | 20 18   | 15 56 37      | 8 02 04                         |
| 23  | 3 57 12         | 20 27  | +3 22            | 3 56     | 3 34     | 11 57   | 19 58   | 20 20   | 16 00 34      | 7 58 08                         |
| 24  | 4 01 13         | 20 38  | +3 17            | 3 55     | 3 33     | 11 57   | 20 00   | 20 22   | 16 04 30      | 7 54 12                         |
| 25  | 4 05 15         | 20 49  | +3 11            | 3 53     | 3 31     | 11 57   | 20 01   | 20 23   | 16 08 27      | 7 50 16                         |
| 26  | 4 09 18         | 21 00  | +3 06            | 3 52     | 3 30     | 11 57   | 20 02   | 20 25   | 16 12 23      | 7 46 20                         |
| 27  | 4 13 21         | 21 11  | +2 59            | 3 51     | 3 29     | 11 57   | 20 04   | 20 26   | 16 16 20      | 7 42 24                         |
| 28  | 4 17 24         | 21 21  | +2 52            | 3 50     | 3 27     | 11 57   | 20 05   | 20 28   | 16 20 16      | 7 38 28                         |
| 29  | 4 21 28         | 21 30  | +2 45            | 3 49     | 3 26     | 11 57   | 20 06   | 20 30   | 16 24 13      | 7 34 32                         |
| 30  | 4 25 32         | 21 40  | +2 37            | 3 48     | 3 25     | 11 57   | 20 07   | 20 31   | 16 28 09      | 7 30 37                         |
| 31  | 4 29 37         | 21 49  | +2 29            | 3 47     | 3 24     | 11 58   | 20 09   | 20 32   | 16 32 06      | 7 26 41                         |

DURATION OF TWILIGHT (in minutes)

| Latitude | 52° | 56° | 52° | 56° | 52° | 56° | 52° | 56° |
|----------|-----|-----|-----|-----|-----|-----|-----|-----|
|          | 1 May | | 11 May | | 21 May | | 31 May | |
| Civil    | 39  | 45  | 41  | 49  | 44  | 53  | 46  | 57  |
| Nautical | 90  | 106 | 97  | 121 | 106 | 143 | 116 | TAN |
| Astronomical | 154 | 209 | 179 | TAN | TAN | TAN | TAN | TAN |

THE NIGHT SKY

Mercury, except for the last week of the month, is visible low above the west-north-west horizon at the end of evening civil twilight. During this period of visibility its magnitude fades from −0.8 to +2.2. On the evening of the 1st the thin crescent Moon, only two days old, will be seen about 7° to the left of Mercury. This evening apparition is the most suitable one of the year for observers in northern temperate latitudes.

Venus, magnitude −3.9, is a bright object, visible at a very low altitude above the eastern horizon for a very short time before dawn. Conditions for detecting the planet are quite critical and observers in northern parts of the British Isles are unlikely to see it at all.

Mars is an evening object in the constellation of Leo, passing 1° N. of Regulus on the 24th. Its magnitude is then +0.8, so that it is two magnitudes fainter than when at opposition.

Jupiter, magnitude −2.5, is approaching opposition and thus visible for the greater part of the night. Jupiter is retrograding in Ophiuchus. On the morning of the 16th the Moon, almost Full, passes 2° N. of the planet.

Saturn, magnitude +1.3, gradually becomes visible as a morning object during the month, low above the east-south-east horizon before the morning twilight inhibits observation. Observers may be surprised to see it without its rings (see the notes for September on p. 49).

## THE MOON

| Day | RA | Dec. | Hor. par. | Semi-diam. | Sun's co-long. | PA of Bright Limb | Phase | Age | Rise 52° | Rise 56° | Transit | Set 52° | Set 56° |
|---|---|---|---|---|---|---|---|---|---|---|---|---|---|
| | h m | ° | ′ | ′ | ° | ° | % | d | h m | h m | h m | h m | h m |
| 1 | 3 29 | +17.2 | 54.2 | 14.8 | 283 | 263 | 2 | 1.3 | 5 30 | 5 14 | 13 20 | 21 16 | 21 35 |
| 2 | 4 18 | +18.7 | 54.1 | 14.7 | 295 | 266 | 5 | 2.3 | 6 09 | 5 51 | 14 08 | 22 09 | 22 28 |
| 3 | 5 08 | +19.3 | 54.0 | 14.7 | 307 | 270 | 10 | 3.3 | 6 54 | 6 34 | 14 55 | 22 56 | 23 15 |
| 4 | 5 58 | +19.2 | 54.1 | 14.7 | 319 | 274 | 16 | 4.3 | 7 44 | 7 26 | 15 43 | 23 37 | 23 54 |
| 5 | 6 48 | +18.1 | 54.3 | 14.8 | 332 | 278 | 23 | 5.3 | 8 40 | 8 23 | 16 30 | — | — |
| 6 | 7 38 | +16.3 | 54.6 | 14.9 | 344 | 282 | 32 | 6.3 | 9 41 | 9 26 | 17 17 | 0 12 | 0 27 |
| 7 | 8 27 | +13.7 | 55.1 | 15.0 | 356 | 285 | 41 | 7.3 | 10 45 | 10 34 | 18 03 | 0 42 | 0 54 |
| 8 | 9 15 | +10.5 | 55.8 | 15.2 | 8 | 287 | 51 | 8.3 | 11 52 | 11 44 | 18 49 | 1 09 | 1 18 |
| 9 | 10 04 | + 6.7 | 56.6 | 15.4 | 20 | 289 | 61 | 9.3 | 13 02 | 12 58 | 19 36 | 1 35 | 1 40 |
| 10 | 10 54 | + 2.5 | 57.5 | 15.7 | 33 | 291 | 71 | 10.3 | 14 14 | 14 14 | 20 25 | 1 59 | 2 01 |
| 11 | 11 45 | - 2.0 | 58.4 | 15.9 | 45 | 291 | 80 | 11.3 | 15 30 | 15 34 | 21 16 | 2 23 | 2 21 |
| 12 | 12 38 | - 6.5 | 59.3 | 16.2 | 57 | 290 | 89 | 12.3 | 16 48 | 16 57 | 22 09 | 2 50 | 2 44 |
| 13 | 13 34 | -10.8 | 60.2 | 16.4 | 69 | 290 | 95 | 13.3 | 18 08 | 18 21 | 23 06 | 3 20 | 3 10 |
| 14 | 14 33 | -14.6 | 60.8 | 16.6 | 81 | 290 | 99 | 14.3 | 19 28 | 19 45 | — | 3 55 | 3 41 |
| 15 | 15 35 | -17.4 | 61.2 | 16.7 | 94 | 60 | 100 | 15.3 | 20 43 | 21 02 | 0 06 | 4 39 | 4 21 |
| 16 | 16 38 | -19.0 | 61.2 | 16.7 | 106 | 88 | 98 | 16.3 | 21 48 | 22 08 | 1 08 | 5 32 | 5 13 |
| 17 | 17 43 | -19.3 | 61.0 | 16.6 | 118 | 85 | 93 | 17.3 | 22 43 | 23 01 | 2 11 | 6 35 | 6 16 |
| 18 | 18 45 | -18.2 | 60.4 | 16.5 | 130 | 81 | 86 | 18.3 | 23 27 | 23 42 | 3 12 | 7 46 | 7 28 |
| 19 | 19 46 | -16.0 | 59.7 | 16.3 | 142 | 77 | 77 | 19.3 | — | — | 4 10 | 9 01 | 8 46 |
| 20 | 20 43 | -12.8 | 58.9 | 16.0 | 154 | 73 | 66 | 20.3 | 0 02 | 0 14 | 5 05 | 10 16 | 10 06 |
| 21 | 21 36 | - 9.0 | 58.0 | 15.8 | 167 | 71 | 55 | 21.3 | 0 32 | 0 40 | 5 56 | 11 29 | 11 23 |
| 22 | 22 28 | - 4.8 | 57.2 | 15.6 | 179 | 69 | 45 | 22.3 | 0 58 | 1 02 | 6 44 | 12 41 | 12 39 |
| 23 | 23 17 | - 0.6 | 56.4 | 15.4 | 191 | 68 | 34 | 23.3 | 1 21 | 1 21 | 7 30 | 13 50 | 13 52 |
| 24 | 0 05 | + 3.6 | 55.8 | 15.2 | 203 | 68 | 25 | 24.3 | 1 44 | 1 41 | 8 15 | 14 58 | 15 03 |
| 25 | 0 52 | + 7.6 | 55.2 | 15.0 | 216 | 69 | 17 | 25.3 | 2 07 | 2 00 | 9 00 | 16 04 | 16 13 |
| 26 | 1 39 | +11.1 | 54.8 | 14.9 | 228 | 70 | 10 | 26.3 | 2 32 | 2 22 | 9 45 | 17 09 | 17 21 |
| 27 | 2 27 | +14.2 | 54.4 | 14.8 | 240 | 71 | 5 | 27.3 | 3 00 | 2 46 | 10 31 | 18 11 | 18 26 |
| 28 | 3 16 | +16.7 | 54.2 | 14.8 | 252 | 70 | 2 | 28.3 | 3 31 | 3 15 | 11 17 | 19 10 | 19 28 |
| 29 | 4 05 | +18.4 | 54.0 | 14.7 | 265 | 50 | 0 | 29.3 | 4 08 | 3 50 | 12 04 | 20 05 | 20 24 |
| 30 | 4 55 | +19.3 | 53.9 | 14.7 | 277 | 290 | 0 | 0.6 | 4 50 | 4 31 | 12 52 | 20 54 | 21 13 |
| 31 | 5 45 | +19.3 | 54.0 | 14.7 | 289 | 281 | 2 | 1.6 | 5 39 | 5 20 | 13 40 | 21 37 | 21 55 |

## MERCURY

| Day | RA | Dec. | Diam. | Phase | Transit | 5° high 52° | 5° high 56° |
|---|---|---|---|---|---|---|---|
| | h m | ° | ″ | % | h m | h m | h m |
| 1 | 3 38 | +21.5 | 6 | 70 | 13 06 | 20 32 | 20 48 |
| 3 | 3 52 | +22.5 | 6 | 64 | 13 11 | 20 43 | 21 00 |
| 5 | 4 05 | +23.2 | 7 | 57 | 13 16 | 20 52 | 21 10 |
| 7 | 4 17 | +23.8 | 7 | 51 | 13 20 | 20 59 | 21 18 |
| 9 | 4 27 | +24.3 | 7 | 45 | 13 23 | 21 04 | 21 24 |
| 11 | 4 37 | +24.6 | 8 | 40 | 13 24 | 21 07 | 21 27 |
| 13 | 4 46 | +24.8 | 8 | 35 | 13 25 | 21 08 | 21 28 |
| 15 | 4 53 | +24.8 | 9 | 30 | 13 24 | 21 07 | 21 27 |
| 17 | 4 59 | +24.8 | 9 | 25 | 13 21 | 21 03 | 21 24 |
| 19 | 5 04 | +24.6 | 10 | 21 | 13 18 | 20 58 | 21 19 |
| 21 | 5 07 | +24.3 | 10 | 17 | 13 13 | 20 51 | 21 10 |
| 23 | 5 09 | +23.9 | 10 | 13 | 13 06 | 20 41 | 21 00 |
| 25 | 5 09 | +23.5 | 11 | 10 | 12 58 | 20 30 | 20 48 |
| 27 | 5 07 | +22.9 | 11 | 7 | 12 49 | 20 17 | 20 35 |
| 29 | 5 06 | +22.3 | 12 | 4 | 12 39 | 20 03 | 20 20 |
| 31 | 5 03 | +21.7 | 12 | 2 | 12 28 | 19 48 | 20 04 |

## VENUS

| Day | RA | Dec. | Diam. | Phase | Transit | 5° high 52° | 5° high 56° |
|---|---|---|---|---|---|---|---|
| | h m | ° | ″ | % | h m | h m | h m |
| 1 | 0 42 | + 2.7 | 12 | 87 | 10 08 | 4 26 | 4 27 |
| 6 | 1 04 | + 5.0 | 12 | 88 | 10 11 | 4 17 | 4 16 |
| 11 | 1 27 | + 7.3 | 11 | 89 | 10 14 | 4 08 | 4 06 |
| 16 | 1 50 | + 9.5 | 11 | 90 | 10 17 | 4 00 | 3 56 |
| 21 | 2 13 | +11.6 | 11 | 91 | 10 20 | 3 52 | 3 46 |
| 26 | 2 36 | +13.7 | 11 | 92 | 10 24 | 3 45 | 3 37 |
| 31 | 3 00 | +15.6 | 11 | 93 | 10 28 | 3 39 | 3 29 |

## MARS

| Day | RA | Dec. | Diam. | Phase | Transit | 5° high 52° | 5° high 56° |
|---|---|---|---|---|---|---|---|
| 1 | 9 33 | +16.8 | 8 | 90 | 18 57 | 1 54 | 2 05 |
| 6 | 9 40 | +16.1 | 8 | 90 | 18 44 | 1 37 | 1 47 |
| 11 | 9 47 | +15.3 | 8 | 90 | 18 32 | 1 21 | 1 30 |
| 16 | 9 55 | +14.5 | 7 | 90 | 18 20 | 1 04 | 1 13 |
| 21 | 10 03 | +13.7 | 7 | 89 | 18 08 | 0 48 | 0 56 |
| 26 | 10 11 | +12.8 | 7 | 89 | 17 57 | 0 32 | 0 39 |
| 31 | 10 20 | +11.9 | 7 | 89 | 17 46 | 0 16 | 0 23 |

## SUNRISE AND SUNSET

| | London | | Bristol | | Birmingham | | Manchester | | Newcastle | | Glasgow | | Belfast | |
|---|---|---|---|---|---|---|---|---|---|---|---|---|---|---|
| | 0°05' | 51°30' | 2°35' | 51°28' | 1°55' | 52°28' | 2°15' | 53°28' | 1°37' | 54°59' | 4°14' | 55°52' | 5°56' | 54°35' |
| | h m | h m | h m | h m | h m | h m | h m | h m | h m | h m | h m | h m | h m | h m |
| 1 | 4 33 | 19 23 | 4 43 | 19 33 | 4 38 | 19 33 | 4 36 | 19 38 | 4 28 | 19 41 | 4 35 | 19 55 | 4 46 | 19 57 |
| 2 | 4 31 | 19 24 | 4 42 | 19 34 | 4 36 | 19 35 | 4 34 | 19 40 | 4 26 | 19 43 | 4 33 | 19 57 | 4 44 | 19 59 |
| 3 | 4 30 | 19 26 | 4 40 | 19 36 | 4 34 | 19 37 | 4 32 | 19 41 | 4 23 | 19 45 | 4 30 | 19 59 | 4 42 | 20 00 |
| 4 | 4 28 | 19 28 | 4 38 | 19 38 | 4 32 | 19 38 | 4 30 | 19 43 | 4 21 | 19 47 | 4 28 | 20 01 | 4 40 | 20 02 |
| 5 | 4 26 | 19 29 | 4 36 | 19 39 | 4 30 | 19 40 | 4 28 | 19 45 | 4 19 | 19 48 | 4 26 | 20 03 | 4 38 | 20 04 |
| 6 | 4 24 | 19 31 | 4 34 | 19 41 | 4 28 | 19 42 | 4 26 | 19 47 | 4 17 | 19 50 | 4 24 | 20 05 | 4 36 | 20 06 |
| 7 | 4 22 | 19 32 | 4 32 | 19 42 | 4 26 | 19 43 | 4 24 | 19 49 | 4 15 | 19 52 | 4 22 | 20 07 | 4 34 | 20 08 |
| 8 | 4 21 | 19 34 | 4 31 | 19 44 | 4 24 | 19 45 | 4 22 | 19 50 | 4 13 | 19 54 | 4 20 | 20 09 | 4 32 | 20 10 |
| 9 | 4 19 | 19 36 | 4 29 | 19 46 | 4 23 | 19 47 | 4 20 | 19 52 | 4 11 | 19 56 | 4 18 | 20 11 | 4 30 | 20 12 |
| 10 | 4 17 | 19 37 | 4 27 | 19 47 | 4 21 | 19 48 | 4 18 | 19 54 | 4 09 | 19 58 | 4 16 | 20 12 | 4 28 | 20 13 |
| 11 | 4 16 | 19 39 | 4 26 | 19 49 | 4 19 | 19 50 | 4 16 | 19 55 | 4 07 | 20 00 | 4 13 | 20 14 | 4 26 | 20 15 |
| 12 | 4 14 | 19 40 | 4 24 | 19 50 | 4 18 | 19 52 | 4 15 | 19 57 | 4 05 | 20 02 | 4 12 | 20 16 | 4 24 | 20 17 |
| 13 | 4 12 | 19 42 | 4 23 | 19 52 | 4 16 | 19 53 | 4 13 | 19 59 | 4 03 | 20 03 | 4 10 | 20 18 | 4 23 | 20 19 |
| 14 | 4 11 | 19 43 | 4 21 | 19 53 | 4 14 | 19 55 | 4 11 | 20 00 | 4 02 | 20 05 | 4 08 | 20 20 | 4 21 | 20 20 |
| 15 | 4 09 | 19 45 | 4 19 | 19 55 | 4 13 | 19 56 | 4 10 | 20 02 | 4 00 | 20 07 | 4 06 | 20 22 | 4 19 | 20 22 |
| 16 | 4 08 | 19 46 | 4 18 | 19 56 | 4 11 | 19 58 | 4 08 | 20 04 | 3 58 | 20 09 | 4 04 | 20 24 | 4 17 | 20 24 |
| 17 | 4 06 | 19 48 | 4 17 | 19 58 | 4 10 | 19 59 | 4 06 | 20 05 | 3 56 | 20 10 | 4 02 | 20 26 | 4 16 | 20 26 |
| 18 | 4 05 | 19 49 | 4 15 | 19·59 | 4 08 | 20 01 | 4 05 | 20 07 | 3 55 | 20 12 | 4 00 | 20 27 | 4 14 | 20 27 |
| 19 | 4 04 | 19 51 | 4 14 | 20 01 | 4 07 | 20 02 | 4 03 | 20 09 | 3 53 | 20 14 | 3 59 | 20 29 | 4 12 | 20 29 |
| 20 | 4 02 | 19 52 | 4 12 | 20 02 | 4 05 | 20 04 | 4 02 | 20 10 | 3 51 | 20 16 | 3 57 | 20 31 | 4 11 | 20 31 |
| 21 | 4 01 | 19 54 | 4 11 | 20 04 | 4 04 | 20 05 | 4 00 | 20 12 | 3 50 | 20 17 | 3 55 | 20 33 | 4 09 | 20 32 |
| 22 | 4 00 | 19 55 | 4 10 | 20 05 | 4 03 | 20 07 | 3 59 | 20 13 | 3 48 | 20 19 | 3 54 | 20 34 | 4 08 | 20 34 |
| 23 | 3 58 | 19 56 | 4 09 | 20 06 | 4 01 | 20 08 | 3 58 | 20 15 | 3 47 | 20 20 | 3 52 | 20 36 | 4 06 | 20 35 |
| 24 | 3 57 | 19 58 | 4 07 | 20 08 | 4 00 | 20 10 | 3 56 | 20 16 | 3 45 | 20 22 | 3 51 | 20 38 | 4 05 | 20 37 |
| 25 | 3 56 | 19 59 | 4 06 | 20 09 | 3 59 | 20 11 | 3 55 | 20 18 | 3 44 | 20 24 | 3 49 | 20 39 | 4 04 | 20 39 |
| 26 | 3 55 | 20 00 | 4 05 | 20 10 | 3 58 | 20 12 | 3 54 | 20 19 | 3 43 | 20 25 | 3 48 | 20 41 | 4 02 | 20 40 |
| 27 | 3 54 | 20 02 | 4 04 | 20 11 | 3 57 | 20 14 | 3 53 | 20 20 | 3 41 | 20 27 | 3 46 | 20 43 | 4 01 | 20 41 |
| 28 | 3 53 | 20 03 | 4 03 | 20 13 | 3 55 | 20 15 | 3 51 | 20 22 | 3 40 | 20 28 | 3 45 | 20 44 | 4 00 | 20 43 |
| 29 | 3 52 | 20 04 | 4 02 | 20 14 | 3 54 | 20 16 | 3 50 | 20 23 | 3 39 | 20 29 | 3 44 | 20 46 | 3 59 | 20 44 |
| 30 | 3 51 | 20 05 | 4 01 | 20 15 | 3 53 | 20 18 | 3 49 | 20 24 | 3 38 | 20 31 | 3 43 | 20 47 | 3 58 | 20 46 |
| 31 | 3 50 | 20 06 | 4 00 | 20 16 | 3 52 | 20 19 | 3 48 | 20 26 | 3 37 | 20 32 | 3 41 | 20 48 | 3 56 | 20 47 |

## JUPITER

| Day | RA | Dec. | Transit | 5° high | |
|---|---|---|---|---|---|
| | | | | 52° | 56° |
| | h m | ° ' | h m | h m | h m |
| 1 | 16 51.3 | −21 40 | 2 17 | 22 59 | 23 30 |
| 11 | 16 47.2 | −21 33 | 1 34 | 22 14 | 22 45 |
| 21 | 16 42.3 | −21 24 | 0 49 | 21 29 | 21 59 |
| 31 | 16 36.9 | −21 15 | 0 05 | 20 43 | 21 13 |

Diameters – equatorial 45″ polar 42″

## SATURN

| Day | RA | Dec. | Transit | 5° high | |
|---|---|---|---|---|---|
| | | | | 52° | 56° |
| | h m | ° ' | h m | h m | h m |
| 1 | 23 31.2 | − 5 09 | 8 56 | 3 56 | 4 04 |
| 11 | 23 34.5 | − 4 49 | 8 20 | 3 19 | 3 26 |
| 21 | 23 37.4 | − 4 33 | 7 44 | 2 41 | 2 48 |
| 31 | 23 39.9 | − 4 20 | 7 07 | 2 03 | 2 10 |

Diameters – equatorial 16″ polar 15″
Rings – major axis 37″ minor axis 0″

## URANUS

| Day | RA | Dec. | Transit | 10° high | |
|---|---|---|---|---|---|
| | | | | 52° | 56° |
| | h m | ° ' | h m | h m | h m |
| 1 | 20 11.2 | −20 34 | 5 36 | 3 03 | 3 47 |
| 11 | 20 11.1 | −20 35 | 4 57 | 2 23 | 3 08 |
| 21 | 20 10.8 | −20 36 | 4 17 | 1 44 | 2 29 |
| 31 | 20 10.1 | −20 39 | 3 37 | 1 04 | 1 49 |

Diameter 4″

## NEPTUNE

| Day | RA | Dec. | Transit | 10° high | |
|---|---|---|---|---|---|
| | | | | 52° | 56° |
| | h m | ° ' | h m | h m | h m |
| 1 | 19 49.6 | −20 29 | 5 15 | 2 40 | 3 24 |
| 11 | 19 49.5 | −20 30 | 4 35 | 2 01 | 2 45 |
| 21 | 19 49.1 | −20 31 | 3 56 | 1 21 | 2 06 |
| 31 | 19 48.5 | −20 32 | 3 16 | 0 42 | 1 26 |

Diameter 2″

# June 1995

SIXTH MONTH, 30 DAYS. *Junius*, Roman *gens* (family)

| | | | |
|---|---|---|---|
| 1 | *Thursday* | Battle of the Glorious First of June 1794 | *week 22 day 152* |
| 2 | *Friday* | *Coronation Day 1953.* Start of Gordon riots 1780 | 153 |
| 3 | *Saturday* | Sydney Smith b. 1771. George V b. 1865 | 154 |
| 4 | *Sunday* | **Pentecost/Whit Sunday.** FEAST OF WEEKS begins | *week 23 day 155* |
| 5 | *Monday* | UN World Environment Day | 156 |
| 6 | *Tuesday* | *Trinity Law Sittings begin.* D-Day 1944 | 157 |
| 7 | *Wednesday* | E. M. Forster d. 1970. Henry Miller d. 1980 | 158 |
| 8 | *Thursday* | John Smeaton b. 1724. George Sand d. 1876 | 159 |
| 9 | *Friday* | Lord Beaverbrook d. 1964 | 160 |
| 10 | *Saturday* | *Duke of Edinburgh b. 1921.* Andre Ampère d. 1836 | 161 |
| 11 | *Sunday* | **Trinity Sunday.** George I d. 1727 | *week 24 day 162* |
| 12 | *Monday* | **St Barnabas.** Anthony Eden b. 1897. Anne Frank b. 1929 | 163 |
| 13 | *Tuesday* | Alexander the Great d. 323 BC | 164 |
| 14 | *Wednesday* | Argentinians surrender in the Falklands 1982 | 165 |
| 15 | *Thursday* | CORPUS CHRISTI. Edward the Black Prince b. 1330 | 166 |
| 16 | *Friday* | Margaret Bondfield d. 1953. Field Marshal Earl Alexander of Tunis d. 1969 | 167 |
| 17 | *Saturday* | *Queen's Official Birthday.* Field Marshal Viscount Alanbrooke d. 1963 | 168 |
| 18 | *Sunday* | **2nd S. after Pentecost/1st S. after Trinity** | *week 25 day 169* |
| 19 | *Monday* | Metropolitan Police founded 1829 | 170 |
| 20 | *Tuesday* | Black Hole of Calcutta 1756 | 171 |
| 21 | *Wednesday* | Prince William of Wales b. 1982 | 172 |
| 22 | *Thursday* | Alexander Rose Day. Germany invaded USSR 1941 | 173 |
| 23 | *Friday* | Stanley met Livingstone 1871 | 174 |
| 24 | *Saturday* | **St John the Baptist.** Battle of Bannockburn 1314 | 175 |
| 25 | *Sunday* | **3rd S. after Pentecost/2nd S. after Trinity** | *week 26 day 176* |
| 26 | *Monday* | UN Charter signed at San Francisco 1945 | 177 |
| 27 | *Tuesday* | Sir Alfred Ayer d. 1989 | 178 |
| 28 | *Wednesday* | Berlin airlift began 1948 | 179 |
| 29 | *Thursday* | **St Peter.** Ignace Jan Paderewski d. 1941 | 180 |
| 30 | *Friday* | Elizabeth Barrett Browning d. 1861 | 181 |

ASTRONOMICAL PHENOMENA

| d | h | |
|---|---|---|
| 1 | 11 | Jupiter at opposition |
| 5 | 06 | Mercury in inferior conjunction |
| 5 | 16 | Mars in conjunction with Moon. Mars 5° N. |
| 12 | 08 | Jupiter in conjunction with Moon. Jupiter 2° S. |
| 17 | 07 | Mercury at stationary point |
| 18 | 19 | Venus in conjunction with Mercury. Venus 4° N. |
| 19 | 15 | Saturn in conjunction with Moon. Saturn 5° S. |
| 21 | | Sun's longitude 90° ♋ |
| 26 | 02 | Mercury in conjunction with Moon. Mercury 0°.6 S. |
| 26 | 16 | Venus in conjunction with Moon. Venus 3° N. |
| 29 | 16 | Mercury at greatest elongation W.22° |

CONSTELLATIONS

The following constellations are near the meridian at

| | d | h | | d | h |
|---|---|---|---|---|---|
| May | 1 | 24 | June | 15 | 21 |
| May | 16 | 23 | July | 1 | 20 |
| June | 1 | 22 | July | 16 | 19 |

Cassiopeia (below the Pole), Ursa Minor, Draco, Ursa Major, Canes Venatici, Bootes, Corona, Serpens, Virgo and Libra

MINIMA OF ALGOL

Algol is inconveniently situated for observation during June.

THE MOON

| Phases, Apsides and Node | d | h | m |
|---|---|---|---|
| ☽ First Quarter | 6 | 10 | 26 |
| ○ Full Moon | 13 | 04 | 03 |
| ☾ Last Quarter | 19 | 22 | 01 |
| ● New Moon | 28 | 00 | 50 |
| Perigee (357,010 km) | 13 | 01 | 13 |
| Apogee (406,429 km) | 26 | 11 | 03 |

Mean longitude of ascending node on June 1, 214°

## THE SUN

s.d. 15′.8

| Day | Right Ascension | Dec. + | Equation of time | Rise 52° | Rise 56° | Transit | Set 52° | Set 56° | Sidereal time | Transit of First Point of Aries |
|---|---|---|---|---|---|---|---|---|---|---|
| | h m s | ° ′ | m s | h m | h m | h m | h m | h m | h m s | h m s |
| 1 | 4 33 43 | 21 57 | +2 20 | 3 46 | 3 23 | 11 58 | 20 10 | 20 34 | 16 36 03 | 7 22 45 |
| 2 | 4 37 48 | 22 06 | +2 11 | 3 46 | 3 21 | 11 58 | 20 11 | 20 35 | 16 39 59 | 7 18 49 |
| 3 | 4 41 54 | 22 13 | +2 01 | 3 45 | 3 21 | 11 58 | 20 12 | 20 36 | 16 43 56 | 7 14 53 |
| 4 | 4 46 01 | 22 21 | +1 52 | 3 44 | 3 20 | 11 58 | 20 13 | 20 38 | 16 47 52 | 7 10 57 |
| 5 | 4 50 07 | 22 28 | +1 41 | 3 43 | 3 19 | 11 58 | 20 14 | 20 39 | 16 51 49 | 7 07 01 |
| 6 | 4 54 14 | 22 35 | +1 31 | 3 43 | 3 18 | 11 59 | 20 15 | 20 40 | 16 55 45 | 7 03 05 |
| 7 | 4 58 22 | 22 41 | +1 20 | 3 42 | 3 17 | 11 59 | 20 16 | 20 41 | 16 59 42 | 6 59 09 |
| 8 | 5 02 29 | 22 47 | +1 09 | 3 42 | 3 16 | 11 59 | 20 17 | 20 42 | 17 03 38 | 6 55 13 |
| 9 | 5 06 37 | 22 52 | +0 58 | 3 41 | 3 16 | 11 59 | 20 17 | 20 43 | 17 07 35 | 6 51 17 |
| 10 | 5 10 45 | 22 57 | +0 46 | 3 41 | 3 15 | 11 59 | 20 18 | 20 44 | 17 11 32 | 6 47 22 |
| 11 | 5 14 54 | 23 02 | +0 34 | 3 40 | 3 15 | 12 00 | 20 19 | 20 45 | 17 15 28 | 6 43 26 |
| 12 | 5 19 02 | 23 06 | +0 22 | 3 40 | 3 14 | 12 00 | 20 20 | 20 46 | 17 19 25 | 6 39 30 |
| 13 | 5 23 11 | 23 10 | +0 10 | 3 40 | 3 14 | 12 00 | 20 20 | 20 47 | 17 23 21 | 6 35 34 |
| 14 | 5 27 20 | 23 14 | −0 02 | 3 40 | 3 13 | 12 00 | 20 21 | 20 47 | 17 27 18 | 6 31 38 |
| 15 | 5 31 29 | 23 17 | −0 15 | 3 39 | 3 13 | 12 00 | 20 21 | 20 48 | 17 31 14 | 6 27 42 |
| 16 | 5 35 38 | 23 19 | −0 27 | 3 39 | 3 13 | 12 01 | 20 22 | 20 48 | 17 35 11 | 6 23 46 |
| 17 | 5 39 48 | 23 21 | −0 40 | 3 39 | 3 13 | 12 01 | 20 22 | 20 49 | 17 39 07 | 6 19 50 |
| 18 | 5 43 57 | 23 23 | −0 53 | 3 39 | 3 13 | 12 01 | 20 23 | 20 49 | 17 43 04 | 6 15 54 |
| 19 | 5 48 07 | 23 25 | −1 06 | 3 39 | 3 13 | 12 01 | 20 23 | 20 50 | 17 47 01 | 6 11 58 |
| 20 | 5 52 16 | 23 26 | −1 19 | 3 39 | 3 13 | 12 01 | 20 23 | 20 50 | 17 50 57 | 6 08 02 |
| 21 | 5 56 26 | 23 26 | −1 32 | 3 40 | 3 13 | 12 02 | 20 24 | 20 50 | 17 54 54 | 6 04 07 |
| 22 | 6 00 35 | 23 26 | −1 45 | 3 40 | 3 13 | 12 02 | 20 24 | 20 51 | 17 58 50 | 6 00 11 |
| 23 | 6 04 45 | 23 26 | −1 58 | 3 40 | 3 13 | 12 02 | 20 24 | 20 51 | 18 02 47 | 5 56 15 |
| 24 | 6 08 55 | 23 25 | −2 11 | 3 40 | 3 14 | 12 02 | 20 24 | 20 51 | 18 06 43 | 5 52 19 |
| 25 | 6 13 04 | 23 24 | −2 24 | 3 41 | 3 14 | 12 03 | 20 24 | 20 51 | 18 10 40 | 5 48 23 |
| 26 | 6 17 14 | 23 23 | −2 37 | 3 41 | 3 15 | 12 03 | 20 24 | 20 51 | 18 14 36 | 5 44 27 |
| 27 | 6 21 23 | 23 21 | −2 50 | 3 42 | 3 15 | 12 03 | 20 24 | 20 50 | 18 18 33 | 5 40 31 |
| 28 | 6 25 32 | 23 18 | −3 02 | 3 42 | 3 16 | 12 03 | 20 24 | 20 50 | 18 22 30 | 5 36 35 |
| 29 | 6 29 41 | 23 16 | −3 15 | 3 43 | 3 16 | 12 03 | 20 24 | 20 50 | 18 26 26 | 5 32 39 |
| 30 | 6 33 50 | 23 13 | −3 27 | 3 43 | 3 17 | 12 04 | 20 24 | 20 50 | 18 30 23 | 5 28 43 |

DURATION OF TWILIGHT (in minutes)

| Latitude | 52° | 56° | 52° | 56° | 52° | 56° | 52° | 56° |
|---|---|---|---|---|---|---|---|---|
| | 1 June | | 11 June | | 21 June | | 30 June | |
| Civil | 47 | 58 | 48 | 61 | 49 | 63 | 49 | 62 |
| Nautical | 117 | TAN | 125 | TAN | 128 | TAN | 125 | TAN |
| Astronomical | TAN | TAN | TAN | TAN | TAN | TAN | TAN | TAN |

### THE NIGHT SKY

*Mercury* passes through inferior conjunction on the 5th and remains too close to the Sun for observation throughout the month.

*Venus* continues to be a bright object though only visible with great difficulty for a few minutes before dawn, very low above the east-north-east horizon. Its magnitude is −3.9.

*Mars*, magnitude +1.1, continues to be visible as an evening object in Leo, in the western sky.

*Jupiter* reaches opposition on the 1st and is therefore visible throughout the hours of darkness. Jupiter is retrograding in Ophiuchus but moves back into Scorpius at the very end of the month. Its magnitude is −2.6. The Full Moon will be seen approaching Jupiter on the morning of the 12th, passing 2° N. of it after sunrise. The Moon's apparent diameter will be larger than its average value since perigee occurs less than 24 hours later.

*Saturn* is a morning object in the south-east sky, magnitude +1.2. It is in Aquarius. By the end of the month it is visible low in the east-south-east at midnight.

*Twilight*. Reference to the section above shows that astronomical twilight lasts all night for a period of around the summer solstice (i.e. in June and July), even in southern England. Under these conditions the sky never gets completely dark since the Sun is always less than 18° below the horizon.

## THE MOON

| Day | RA | Dec. | Hor. par. | Semi-diam. | Sun's co-long. | PA of Bright Limb | Phase | Age | Rise 52° | Rise 56° | Transit | Set 52° | Set 56° |
|---|---|---|---|---|---|---|---|---|---|---|---|---|---|
| | h m | ° | ' | ' | ° | ° | % | d | h m | h m | h m | h m | h m |
| 1 | 6 35 | +18.5 | 54.1 | 14.7 | 301 | 282 | 6 | 2.6 | 6 33 | 6 15 | 14 27 | 22 14 | 22 30 |
| 2 | 7 25 | +16.9 | 54.3 | 14.8 | 314 | 284 | 12 | 3.6 | 7 32 | 7 17 | 15 13 | 22 45 | 22 59 |
| 3 | 8 14 | +14.6 | 54.6 | 14.9 | 326 | 287 | 18 | 4.6 | 8 34 | 8 22 | 15 59 | 23 13 | 23 24 |
| 4 | 9 02 | +11.6 | 55.1 | 15.0 | 338 | 289 | 26 | 5.6 | 9 39 | 9 30 | 16 45 | 23 39 | 23 45 |
| 5 | 9 50 | + 8.0 | 55.7 | 15.2 | 350 | 291 | 36 | 6.6 | 10 47 | 10 41 | 17 31 | — | — |
| 6 | 10 38 | + 4.0 | 56.4 | 15.4 | 2 | 292 | 46 | 7.6 | 11 56 | 11 55 | 18 17 | 0 02 | 0 06 |
| 7 | 11 28 | − 0.3 | 57.3 | 15.6 | 15 | 293 | 56 | 8.6 | 13 08 | 13 10 | 19 05 | 0 26 | 0 26 |
| 8 | 12 18 | − 4.7 | 58.2 | 15.9 | 27 | 293 | 67 | 9.6 | 14 23 | 14 29 | 19 55 | 0 50 | 0 46 |
| 9 | 13 11 | − 9.0 | 59.1 | 16.1 | 39 | 291 | 77 | 10.6 | 15 40 | 15 51 | 20 49 | 1 17 | 1 09 |
| 10 | 14 08 | −13.0 | 60.0 | 16.4 | 51 | 290 | 86 | 11.6 | 16 59 | 17 13 | 21 46 | 1 49 | 1 37 |
| 11 | 15 07 | −16.2 | 60.7 | 16.5 | 63 | 288 | 93 | 12.6 | 18 16 | 18 34 | 22 47 | 2 27 | 2 11 |
| 12 | 16 09 | −18.5 | 61.2 | 16.7 | 76 | 289 | 98 | 13.6 | 19 27 | 19 47 | 23 50 | 3 14 | 2 56 |
| 13 | 17 14 | −19.4 | 61.4 | 16.7 | 88 | 330 | 100 | 14.6 | 20 29 | 20 48 | — | 4 13 | 3 53 |
| 14 | 18 18 | −18.9 | 61.3 | 16.7 | 100 | 68 | 99 | 15.6 | 21 20 | 21 36 | 0 53 | 5 21 | 5 02 |
| 15 | 19 22 | −17.1 | 60.8 | 16.6 | 112 | 72 | 95 | 16.6 | 22 00 | 22 14 | 1 55 | 6 36 | 6 20 |
| 16 | 20 22 | −14.2 | 60.1 | 16.4 | 124 | 71 | 88 | 17.6 | 22 33 | 22 43 | 2 53 | 7 54 | 7 42 |
| 17 | 21 19 | −10.5 | 59.2 | 16.1 | 137 | 69 | 80 | 18.6 | 23 01 | 23 07 | 3 48 | 9 12 | 9 04 |
| 18 | 22 12 | − 6.3 | 58.3 | 15.9 | 149 | 67 | 70 | 19.6 | 23 26 | 23 28 | 4 38 | 10 26 | 10 23 |
| 19 | 23 03 | − 1.9 | 57.3 | 15.6 | 161 | 67 | 60 | 20.6 | 23 50 | 23 48 | 5 27 | 11 38 | 11 39 |
| 20 | 23 52 | + 2.4 | 56.5 | 15.4 | 173 | 67 | 49 | 21.6 | — | — | 6 13 | 12 48 | 12 52 |
| 21 | 0 40 | + 6.5 | 55.7 | 15.2 | 185 | 67 | 39 | 22.6 | 0 13 | 0 08 | 6 58 | 13 55 | 14 03 |
| 22 | 1 28 | +10.2 | 55.1 | 15.0 | 198 | 69 | 30 | 23.6 | 0 37 | 0 29 | 7 43 | 15 01 | 15 12 |
| 23 | 2 16 | +13.4 | 54.6 | 14.9 | 210 | 71 | 21 | 24.6 | 1 04 | 0 52 | 8 29 | 16 04 | 16 18 |
| 24 | 3 04 | +16.0 | 54.3 | 14.8 | 222 | 73 | 14 | 25.6 | 1 34 | 1 19 | 9 15 | 17 04 | 17 21 |
| 25 | 3 53 | +18.0 | 54.1 | 14.7 | 234 | 75 | 8 | 26.6 | 2 08 | 1 51 | 10 02 | 18 00 | 18 19 |
| 26 | 4 43 | +19.1 | 54.0 | 14.7 | 247 | 75 | 4 | 27.6 | 2 49 | 2 30 | 10 49 | 18 51 | 19 10 |
| 27 | 5 33 | +19.4 | 54.0 | 14.7 | 259 | 69 | 1 | 28.6 | 3 35 | 3 16 | 11 37 | 19 36 | 19 55 |
| 28 | 6 23 | +18.9 | 54.1 | 14.7 | 271 | 7 | 0 | 29.6 | 4 27 | 4 09 | 12 24 | 20 16 | 20 32 |
| 29 | 7 13 | +17.5 | 54.2 | 14.8 | 283 | 301 | 1 | 1.0 | 5 25 | 5 09 | 13 11 | 20 49 | 21 04 |
| 30 | 8 02 | +15.3 | 54.5 | 14.9 | 296 | 294 | 4 | 2.0 | 6 26 | 6 13 | 13 58 | 21 19 | 21 30 |

## MERCURY

| Day | RA | Dec. | Diam. | Phase | Transit | 5° high 52° | 5° high 56° |
|---|---|---|---|---|---|---|---|
| | h m | ° | " | % | h m | h m | h m |
| 1 | 5 01 | +21.3 | 12 | 2 | 12 22 | 19 40 | 19 56 |
| 3 | 4 57 | +20.6 | 12 | 1 | 12 10 | 19 24 | 19 39 |
| 5 | 4 53 | +20.0 | 12 | 0 | 11 58 | 4 47 | 4 33 |
| 7 | 4 48 | +19.4 | 12 | 1 | 11 46 | 4 38 | 4 25 |
| 9 | 4 44 | +18.8 | 12 | 2 | 11 34 | 4 29 | 4 16 |
| 11 | 4 41 | +18.3 | 12 | 3 | 11 23 | 4 21 | 4 08 |
| 13 | 4 38 | +18.0 | 12 | 5 | 11 12 | 4 12 | 4 00 |
| 15 | 4 36 | +17.7 | 11 | 8 | 11 03 | 4 04 | 3 52 |
| 17 | 4 35 | +17.6 | 11 | 11 | 10 54 | 3 56 | 3 44 |
| 19 | 4 36 | +17.6 | 10 | 14 | 10 47 | 3 48 | 3 37 |
| 21 | 4 37 | +17.8 | 10 | 18 | 10 41 | 3 41 | 3 30 |
| 23 | 4 40 | +18.0 | 9 | 22 | 10 37 | 3 35 | 3 23 |
| 25 | 4 45 | +18.4 | 9 | 26 | 10 33 | 3 30 | 3 17 |
| 27 | 4 50 | +18.8 | 9 | 30 | 10 31 | 3 25 | 3 12 |
| 29 | 4 57 | +19.3 | 8 | 35 | 10 30 | 3 21 | 3 07 |
| 31 | 5 05 | +19.8 | 8 | 40 | 10 30 | 3 18 | 3 04 |

## VENUS

| Day | RA | Dec. | Diam. | Phase | Transit | 5° high 52° | 5° high 56° |
|---|---|---|---|---|---|---|---|
| | h m | ° | " | % | h m | h m | h m |
| 1 | 3 05 | +15.9 | 11 | 93 | 10 29 | 3 38 | 3 28 |
| 6 | 3 29 | +17.7 | 11 | 94 | 10 34 | 3 33 | 3 21 |
| 11 | 3 54 | +19.2 | 10 | 94 | 10 39 | 3 30 | 3 16 |
| 16 | 4 19 | +20.5 | 10 | 95 | 10 44 | 3 27 | 3 12 |
| 21 | 4 45 | +21.6 | 10 | 96 | 10 51 | 3 27 | 3 11 |
| 26 | 5 11 | +22.5 | 10 | 96 | 10 57 | 3 28 | 3 11 |
| 31 | 5 37 | +23.0 | 10 | 97 | 11 04 | 3 31 | 3 13 |

## MARS

| Day | RA | Dec. | Diam. | Phase | Transit | 5° high 52° | 5° high 56° |
|---|---|---|---|---|---|---|---|
| 1 | 10 21 | +11.7 | 7 | 89 | 17 44 | 0 13 | 0 19 |
| 6 | 10 30 | +10.7 | 6 | 90 | 17 33 | 23 54 | 0 03 |
| 11 | 10 40 | + 9.7 | 6 | 90 | 17 23 | 23 38 | 23 43 |
| 16 | 10 49 | + 8.6 | 6 | 90 | 17 12 | 23 23 | 23 26 |
| 21 | 10 59 | + 7.6 | 6 | 90 | 17 02 | 23 07 | 23 10 |
| 26 | 11 08 | + 6.4 | 6 | 90 | 16 52 | 22 51 | 22 53 |
| 31 | 11 18 | + 5.3 | 6 | 90 | 16 43 | 22 36 | 22 37 |

## SUNRISE AND SUNSET

| | London | | Bristol | | Birmingham | | Manchester | | Newcastle | | Glasgow | | Belfast | |
|---|---|---|---|---|---|---|---|---|---|---|---|---|---|---|
| | 0°05′ | 51°30′ | 2°35′ | 51°28′ | 1°55′ | 52°28′ | 2°15′ | 53°28′ | 1°37′ | 54°59′ | 4°14′ | 55°52′ | 5°56′ | 54°35′ |
| | h m | h m | h m | h m | h m | h m | h m | h m | h m | h m | h m | h m | h m | h m |
| 1 | 3 49 | 20 07 | 3 59 | 20 17 | 3 52 | 20 20 | 3 47 | 20 27 | 3 36 | 20 34 | 3 40 | 20 50 | 3 55 | 20 48 |
| 2 | 3 48 | 20 09 | 3 59 | 20 18 | 3 51 | 20 21 | 3 46 | 20 28 | 3 35 | 20 35 | 3 39 | 20 51 | 3 54 | 20 50 |
| 3 | 3 48 | 20 10 | 3 58 | 20 19 | 3 50 | 20 22 | 3 46 | 20 29 | 3 34 | 20 36 | 3 38 | 20 52 | 3 54 | 20 51 |
| 4 | 3 47 | 20 11 | 3 57 | 20 20 | 3 49 | 20 23 | 3 45 | 20 30 | 3 33 | 20 37 | 3 37 | 20 54 | 3 53 | 20 52 |
| 5 | 3 46 | 20 12 | 3 57 | 20 21 | 3 49 | 20 24 | 3 44 | 20 31 | 3 32 | 20 38 | 3 37 | 20 55 | 3 52 | 20 53 |
| 6 | 3 46 | 20 13 | 3 56 | 20 22 | 3 48 | 20 25 | 3 43 | 20 32 | 3 31 | 20 39 | 3 36 | 20 56 | 3 51 | 20 54 |
| 7 | 3 45 | 20 13 | 3 55 | 20 23 | 3 47 | 20 26 | 3 43 | 20 33 | 3 31 | 20 40 | 3 35 | 20 57 | 3 50 | 20 55 |
| 8 | 3 45 | 20 14 | 3 55 | 20 24 | 3 47 | 20 27 | 3 42 | 20 34 | 3 30 | 20 41 | 3 34 | 20 58 | 3 50 | 20 56 |
| 9 | 3 44 | 20 15 | 3 54 | 20 25 | 3 .46 | 20 28 | 3 42 | 20 35 | 3 29 | 20 42 | 3 34 | 20 59 | 3 49 | 20 57 |
| 10 | 3 44 | 20 16 | 3 54 | 20 26 | 3 46 | 20 29 | 3 41 | 20 36 | 3 29 | 20 43 | 3 33 | 21 00 | 3 49 | 20 58 |
| 11 | 3 44 | 20 17 | 3 54 | 20 26 | 3 45 | 20 29 | 3 41 | 20 37 | 3 28 | 20 44 | 3 32 | 21 01 | 3 48 | 20 59 |
| 12 | 3 43 | 20 17 | 3 53 | 20 27 | 3 45 | 20 30 | 3 40 | 20 37 | 3 28 | 20 45 | 3 32 | 21 02 | 3 48 | 20 59 |
| 13 | 3 43 | 20 18 | 3 53 | 20 28 | 3 45 | 20 31 | 3 40 | 20 38 | 3 28 | 20 46 | 3 32 | 21 02 | 3 48 | 21 00 |
| 14 | 3 43 | 20 18 | 3 53 | 20 28 | 3 45 | 20 31 | 3 40 | 20 39 | 3 27 | 20 46 | 3 31 | 21 03 | 3 47 | 21 01 |
| 15 | 3 43 | 20 19 | 3 53 | 20 29 | 3 44 | 20 32 | 3 40 | 20 39 | 3 27 | 20 47 | 3 31 | 21 04 | 3 47 | 21 01 |
| 16 | 3 43 | 20 19 | 3 53 | 20 29 | 3 44 | 20 32 | 3 40 | 20 40 | 3 27 | 20 47 | 3 31 | 21 04 | 3 47 | 21 02 |
| 17 | 3 42 | 20 20 | 3 53 | 20 30 | 3 44 | 20 33 | 3 39 | 20 40 | 3 27 | 20 48 | 3 31 | 21 05 | 3 47 | 21 02 |
| 18 | 3 42 | 20 20 | 3 53 | 20 30 | 3 44 | 20 33 | 3 39 | 20 41 | 3 27 | 20 48 | 3 31 | 21 05 | 3 47 | 21 03 |
| 19 | 3 43 | 20 21 | 3 53 | 20 30 | 3 44 | 20 34 | 3 39 | 20 41 | 3 27 | 20 49 | 3 31 | 21 06 | 3 47 | 21 03 |
| 20 | 3 43 | 20 21 | 3 53 | 20 31 | 3 44 | 20 34 | 3 40 | 20 41 | 3 27 | 20 49 | 3 31 | 21 06 | 3 47 | 21 03 |
| 21 | 3 43 | 20 21 | 3 53 | 20 31 | 3 45 | 20 34 | 3 40 | 20 42 | 3 27 | 20 49 | 3 31 | 21 06 | 3 47 | 21 04 |
| 22 | 3 43 | 20 21 | 3 53 | 20 31 | 3 45 | 20 34 | 3 40 | 20 42 | 3 27 | 20 49 | 3 31 | 21 06 | 3 47 | 21 04 |
| 23 | 3 43 | 20 22 | 3 53 | 20 31 | 3 45 | 20 34 | 3 40 | 20 42 | 3 27 | 20 50 | 3 31 | 21 07 | 3 48 | 21 04 |
| 24 | 3 44 | 20 22 | 3 54 | 20 31 | 3 45 | 20 35 | 3 41 | 20 42 | 3 28 | 20 50 | 3 32 | 21 07 | 3 48 | 21 04 |
| 25 | 3 44 | 20 22 | 3 54 | 20 31 | 3 46 | 20 35 | 3 41 | 20 42 | 3 28 | 20 50 | 3 32 | 21 07 | 3 48 | 21 04 |
| 26 | 3 44 | 20 22 | 3 55 | 20 31 | 3 46 | 20 35 | 3 41 | 20 42 | 3 29 | 20 50 | 3 33 | 21 06 | 3 49 | 21 04 |
| 27 | 3 45 | 20 22 | 3 55 | 20 31 | 3 47 | 20 34 | 3 42 | 20 42 | 3 29 | 20 49 | 3 33 | 21 06 | 3 49 | 21 04 |
| 28 | 3 45 | 20 21 | 3 55 | 20 31 | 3 47 | 20 34 | 3 42 | 20 42 | 3 30 | 20 49 | 3 34 | 21 06 | 3 50 | 21 04 |
| 29 | 3 46 | 20 21 | 3 56 | 20 31 | 3 48 | 20 34 | 3 43 | 20 41 | 3 30 | 20 49 | 3 34 | 21 06 | 3 50 | 21 04 |
| 30 | 3 46 | 20 21 | 3 57 | 20 31 | 3 48 | 20 34 | 3 44 | 20 41 | 3 31 | 20 49 | 3 35 | 21 06 | 3 51 | 21 03 |

## JUPITER

| Day | RA | Dec. | Transit | 5° high | |
|---|---|---|---|---|---|
| | | | | 52° | 56° |
| | h m | ° ′ | h m | h m | h m |
| 1 | 16 36.4 | −21 14 | 0 00 | 3 18 | 2 48 |
| 11 | 16 31.0 | −21 04 | 23 11 | 2 34 | 2 05 |
| 21 | 16 26.0 | −20 55 | 22 27 | 1 51 | 1 22 |
| 31 | 16 21.7 | −20 47 | 21 43 | 1 09 | 0 40 |

Diameters – equatorial 45″ polar 43″

## SATURN

| Day | RA | Dec. | Transit | 5° high | |
|---|---|---|---|---|---|
| | | | | 52° | 56° |
| | h m | ° ′ | h m | h m | h m |
| 1 | 23 40.1 | − 4 18 | 7 03 | 1 59 | 2 06 |
| 11 | 23 42.0 | − 4 09 | 6 26 | 1 21 | 1 28 |
| 21 | 23 43.3 | − 4 03 | 5 47 | 0 42 | 0 49 |
| 31 | 23 44.0 | − 4 02 | 5 09 | 0 03 | 0 10 |

Diameters – equatorial 17″ polar 16″
Rings – major axis 39″ minor axis 0″

## URANUS

| Day | RA | Dec. | Transit | 10° high | |
|---|---|---|---|---|---|
| | | | | 52° | 56° |
| | h m | ° ′ | h m | h m | h m |
| 1 | 20 10.0 | −20 39 | 3 33 | 1 00 | 1 46 |
| 11 | 20 09.0 | −20 42 | 2 53 | 0 21 | 1 06 |
| 21 | 20 07.8 | −20 46 | 2 13 | 23 37 | 0 27 |
| 31 | 20 06.3 | −20 51 | 1 32 | 22 57 | 23 43 |

Diameter 4″

## NEPTUNE

| Day | RA | Dec. | Transit | 10° high | |
|---|---|---|---|---|---|
| | | | | 52° | 56° |
| | h m | ° ′ | h m | h m | h m |
| 1 | 19 48.4 | −20 32 | 3 12 | 0 38 | 1 22 |
| 11 | 19 47.6 | −20 34 | 2 32 | 23 54 | 0 43 |
| 21 | 19 46.7 | −20 37 | 1 51 | 23 14 | 0 03 |
| 31 | 19 45.6 | −20 39 | 1 11 | 22 34 | 23 19 |

Diameter 2″

# July 1995

SEVENTH MONTH, 31 DAYS. *Julius* Caesar, formerly *Quintilis*, fifth month of Roman pre-Julian calendar

| | | | |
|---|---|---|---|
| 1 | *Saturday* | *Princess of Wales b. 1961.* Amy Johnson b. 1903 | *week 26 day* 182 |
| 2 | *Sunday* | **4th S. after Pentecost/3rd S. after Trinity** | *week 27 day* 183 |
| 3 | *Monday* | **St Thomas.** Robert Adam b. 1728 | 184 |
| 4 | *Tuesday* | Independence Day, USA. William Byrd d. 1623 | 185 |
| 5 | *Wednesday* | Tynwald Day. National Health Service started 1948 | 186 |
| 6 | *Thursday* | Henry II d. 1189. Aneurin Bevan d. 1960 | 187 |
| 7 | *Friday* | Edward I d. 1307. Sir Allen Lane d. 1970 | 188 |
| 8 | *Saturday* | Edmund Burke d. 1797. Vivien Leigh d. 1967 | 189 |
| 9 | *Sunday* | **5th S. after Pentecost/4th S. after Trinity** | *week 28 day* 190 |
| 10 | *Monday* | Capt. Federick Marryat b. 1792 | 191 |
| 11 | *Tuesday* | Paul Nash d. 1946. Laurence Olivier d. 1989 | 192 |
| 12 | *Wednesday* | *Bank Holiday in Northern Ireland* | 193 |
| 13 | *Thursday* | Titus Oates d. 1705. Kenneth More d. 1982 | 194 |
| 14 | *Friday* | Fête Nationale, France. Paul Kruger d. 1904 | 195 |
| 15 | *Saturday* | St Swithin's Day. Gen. John Pershing d. 1948 | 196 |
| 16 | *Sunday* | **6th S. after Pentecost/5th S. after Trinity** | *week 29 day* 197 |
| 17 | *Monday* | Isaac Watts b. 1674. Earl Grey d. 1845 | 198 |
| 18 | *Tuesday* | Gilbert White b. 1720. Jean Watteau d. 1721 | 199 |
| 19 | *Wednesday* | *Mary Rose* sank 1545. A. J. Cronin b. 1896 | 200 |
| 20 | *Thursday* | Andrew Lang d. 1912. Calouste Gulbenkian d. 1955 | 201 |
| 21 | *Friday* | Salvator Rosa b. 1615. Dame Ellen Terry d. 1928 | 202 |
| 22 | *Saturday* | **St Mary Magdalen.** Battle of Atlanta 1864 | 203 |
| 23 | *Sunday* | **7th S. after Pentecost/6th S. after Trinity** | *week 30 day* 204 |
| 24 | *Monday* | Simón Bolivár b. 1783. Capt. Matthew Webb d. 1883 | 205 |
| 25 | *Tuesday* | **St James.** First cross-channel flight 1909 | 206 |
| 26 | *Wednesday* | Francesco Cilea b. 1866. Robert Graves b. 1895 | 207 |
| 27 | *Thursday* | Sir Anton Dolin b. 1904. Korean War ended 1953 | 208 |
| 28 | *Friday* | Cyrano de Bergerac d. 1655 | 209 |
| 29 | *Saturday* | Benito Mussolini b. 1883. Luis Buñuel d. 1983 | 210 |
| 30 | *Sunday* | **8th S. after Pentecost/7th S. after Trinity** | *week 31 day* 211 |
| 31 | *Monday* | *Trinity Law Sittings end.* Leonard Cheshire d. 1992 | 212 |

ASTRONOMICAL PHENOMENA

| d | h | |
|---|---|---|
| 4 | 02 | Mars in conjunction with Moon. Mars 4° N. |
| 4 | 02 | Earth at aphelion (152 million km) |
| 6 | 08 | Saturn at stationary point |
| 9 | 14 | Jupiter in conjunction with Moon. Jupiter 2° S. |
| 17 | 00 | Saturn in conjunction with Moon. Saturn 5° S. |
| 17 | 05 | Neptune at opposition. |
| 20 | 15 | Venus in conjunction with Mercury. Venus 0°.4 S. |
| 21 | 18 | Uranus at opposition |
| 23 | 07 | Sun's longitude 120° ♌ |
| 27 | 01 | Venus in conjunction with Moon. Venus 6° N. |
| 27 | 14 | Mercury in conjunction with Moon. Mercury 6° N. |
| 28 | 02 | Mercury in superior conjunction |

CONSTELLATIONS

The following constellations are near the meridian at

| | d | h | | d | h |
|---|---|---|---|---|---|
| June | 1 | 24 | July | 16 | 21 |
| June | 15 | 23 | August | 1 | 20 |
| July | 1 | 22 | August | 16 | 19 |

Ursa Minor, Draco, Corona, Hercules, Lyra, Serpens, Ophiuchus, Libra, Scorpius and Sagittarius

MINIMA OF ALGOL

| d | h | d | h | d | h |
|---|---|---|---|---|---|
| 3 | 20.5 | 15 | 07.8 | 26 | 19.0 |
| 6 | 17.4 | 18 | 04.6 | 29 | 15.8 |
| 9 | 14.2 | 21 | 01.4 | | |
| 12 | 11.0 | 23 | 22.2 | | |

THE MOON

| Phases, Apsides and Node | d | h | m |
|---|---|---|---|
| ☽ First Quarter | 05 | 20 | 02 |
| ○ Full Moon | 12 | 10 | 49 |
| ☾ Last Quarter | 19 | 11 | 10 |
| ● New Moon | 27 | 15 | 13 |
| Perigee (358,783 km) | 11 | 10 | 07 |
| Apogee (405,690 km) | 23 | 20 | 23 |

Mean longitude of ascending node on July 1, 212°

THE SUN                                                                                                s.d. 15'.8

| Day | Right Ascension | Dec. + | Equation of time | Rise 52° | Rise 56° | Transit | Set 52° | Set 56° | Sidereal time | Transit of First Point of Aries |
|---|---|---|---|---|---|---|---|---|---|---|
| | h m s | ° ' | m s | h m | h m | h m | h m | h m | h m s | h m s |
| 1 | 6 37 58 | 23 09 | − 3 39 | 3 44 | 3 18 | 12 04 | 20 23 | 20 49 | 18 34 19 | 5 24 47 |
| 2 | 6 42 06 | 23 05 | − 3 51 | 3 45 | 3 19 | 12 04 | 20 23 | 20 49 | 18 38 16 | 5 20 51 |
| 3 | 6 46 14 | 23 01 | − 4 02 | 3 45 | 3 20 | 12 04 | 20 22 | 20 48 | 18 42 12 | 5 16 56 |
| 4 | 6 50 22 | 22 56 | − 4 13 | 3 46 | 3 21 | 12 04 | 20 22 | 20 48 | 18 46 09 | 5 13 00 |
| 5 | 6 54 30 | 22 51 | − 4 24 | 3 47 | 3 22 | 12 04 | 20 22 | 20 47 | 18 50 05 | 5 09 04 |
| 6 | 6 58 37 | 22 45 | − 4 35 | 3 48 | 3 23 | 12 05 | 20 21 | 20 46 | 18 54 02 | 5 05 08 |
| 7 | 7 02 43 | 22 39 | − 4 45 | 3 49 | 3 24 | 12 05 | 20 20 | 20 45 | 18 57 59 | 5 01 12 |
| 8 | 7 06 49 | 22 33 | − 4 54 | 3 50 | 3 25 | 12 05 | 20 20 | 20 44 | 19 01 55 | 4 57 16 |
| 9 | 7 10 55 | 22 26 | − 5 04 | 3 51 | 3 26 | 12 05 | 20 19 | 20 44 | 19 05 52 | 4 53 20 |
| 10 | 7 15 01 | 22 19 | − 5 13 | 3 52 | 3 27 | 12 05 | 20 18 | 20 43 | 19 09 48 | 4 49 24 |
| 11 | 7 19 06 | 22 12 | − 5 21 | 3 53 | 3 28 | 12 05 | 20 18 | 20 42 | 19 13 45 | 4 45 28 |
| 12 | 7 23 10 | 22 04 | − 5 29 | 3 54 | 3 30 | 12 06 | 20 17 | 20 40 | 19 17 41 | 4 41 32 |
| 13 | 7 27 15 | 21 55 | − 5 37 | 3 55 | 3 31 | 12 06 | 20 16 | 20 39 | 19 21 38 | 4 37 36 |
| 14 | 7 31 18 | 21 47 | − 5 44 | 3 56 | 3 33 | 12 06 | 20 15 | 20 38 | 19 25 34 | 4 33 41 |
| 15 | 7 35 21 | 21 38 | − 5 50 | 3 57 | 3 34 | 12 06 | 20 14 | 20 37 | 19 29 31 | 4 29 45 |
| 16 | 7 39 24 | 21 28 | − 5 57 | 3 58 | 3 35 | 12 06 | 20 13 | 20 36 | 19 33 28 | 4 25 49 |
| 17 | 7 43 26 | 21 19 | − 6 02 | 4 00 | 3 37 | 12 06 | 20 12 | 20 34 | 19 37 24 | 4 21 53 |
| 18 | 7 47 28 | 21 09 | − 6 07 | 4 01 | 3 39 | 12 06 | 20 11 | 20 33 | 19 41 21 | 4 17 57 |
| 19 | 7 51 29 | 20 58 | − 6 12 | 4 02 | 3 40 | 12 06 | 20 09 | 20 31 | 19 45 17 | 4 14 01 |
| 20 | 7 55 30 | 20 47 | − 6 16 | 4 04 | 3 42 | 12 06 | 20 08 | 20 30 | 19 49 14 | 4 10 05 |
| 21 | 7 59 30 | 20 36 | − 6 20 | 4 05 | 3 43 | 12 06 | 20 07 | 20 28 | 19 53 10 | 4 06 09 |
| 22 | 8 03 30 | 20 25 | − 6 23 | 4 06 | 3 45 | 12 06 | 20 06 | 20 27 | 19 57 07 | 4 02 13 |
| 23 | 8 07 29 | 20 13 | − 6 25 | 4 08 | 3 47 | 12 06 | 20 04 | 20 25 | 20 01 03 | 3 58 17 |
| 24 | 8 11 27 | 20 01 | − 6 27 | 4 09 | 3 48 | 12 06 | 20 03 | 20 23 | 20 05 00 | 3 54 21 |
| 25 | 8 15 25 | 19 48 | − 6 29 | 4 10 | 3 50 | 12 06 | 20 02 | 20 22 | 20 08 57 | 3 50 26 |
| 26 | 8 19 22 | 19 35 | − 6 29 | 4 12 | 3 52 | 12 06 | 20 00 | 20 20 | 20 12 53 | 3 46 30 |
| 27 | 8 23 19 | 19 22 | − 6 30 | 4 13 | 3 54 | 12 06 | 19 59 | 20 18 | 20 16 50 | 3 42 34 |
| 28 | 8 27 15 | 19 08 | − 6 29 | 4 15 | 3 55 | 12 06 | 19 57 | 20 16 | 20 20 46 | 3 38 38 |
| 29 | 8 31 11 | 18 55 | − 6 28 | 4 16 | 3 57 | 12 06 | 19 56 | 20 14 | 20 24 43 | 3 34 42 |
| 30 | 8 35 06 | 18 40 | − 6 27 | 4 18 | 3 59 | 12 06 | 19 54 | 20 12 | 20 28 39 | 3 30 46 |
| 31 | 8 39 00 | 18 26 | − 6 24 | 4 19 | 4 01 | 12 06 | 19 52 | 20 10 | 20 32 36 | 3 26 50 |

DURATION OF TWILIGHT (in minutes)

| Latitude | 52° | 56° | 52° | 56° | 52° | 56° | 52° | 56° |
|---|---|---|---|---|---|---|---|---|
| | 1 July | | 11 July | | 21 July | | 31 July | |
| Civil | 48 | 61 | 46 | 58 | 44 | 53 | 41 | 49 |
| Nautical | 124 | TAN | 116 | TAN | 107 | 144 | 98 | 122 |
| Astronomical | TAN | TAN | TAN | TAN | TAN | TAN | 180 | TAN |

THE NIGHT SKY

Mercury passes through superior conjunction on the 28th and is too close to the Sun for observation throughout the month.

Venus, magnitude − 3.9, although a bright object, can only be observed with difficulty low in the east-north-east sky just before sunrise. It is unlikely to be detected after the middle of the month as it gets closer to the Sun.

Mars is coming towards the end of its period of visibility, the period available for observation decreasing noticeably during the month. Mars, magnitude + 1.3, is low in the western sky during evening nautical twilight. By the end of July it is lost in the long twilight.

Jupiter, magnitude − 2.4, is a brilliant evening object in the southern skies, though never at any great altitude since it is 21° south of the equator. By the end of the month it is no longer visible after midnight. The gibbous Moon will be seen moving away from the planet on the evening of the 9th.

Saturn, magnitude + 1.0, continues to be visible as a morning object in the south-east sky, in Aquarius.

Uranus is at opposition on the 21st, in Sagittarius. Uranus is barely visible to the naked eye since its magnitude is + 5.6, but it is readily located with only small optical aid.

Neptune is at opposition on the 17th, in Sagittarius. It is not visible to the naked eye since its magnitude is + 7.9.

## THE MOON

| Day | RA | Dec. | Hor. par. | Semi-diam. | Sun's co-long. | PA of Bright Limb | Phase | Age | Rise 52° | Rise 56° | Transit | Set 52° | Set 56° |
|---|---|---|---|---|---|---|---|---|---|---|---|---|---|
| | h m | ° | ' | ' | ° | ° | % | d | h m | h m | h m | h m | h m |
| 1 | 8 51 | +12.5 | 54.9 | 14.9 | 308 | 293 | 8 | 3.0 | 7 31 | 7 21 | 14 44 | 21 45 | 21 53 |
| 2 | 9 39 | + 9.1 | 55.3 | 15.1 | 320 | 294 | 14 | 4.0 | 8 37 | 8 30 | 15 29 | 22 09 | 22 13 |
| 3 | 10 27 | + 5.2 | 55.8 | 15.2 | 332 | 294 | 22 | 5.0 | 9 45 | 9 42 | 16 14 | 22 32 | 22 33 |
| 4 | 11 15 | + 1.1 | 56.5 | 15.4 | 345 | 294 | 31 | 6.0 | 10 55 | 10 55 | 17 01 | 22 55 | 22 53 |
| 5 | 12 04 | − 3.2 | 57.2 | 15.6 | 357 | 294 | 41 | 7.0 | 12 06 | 12 11 | 17 49 | 23 20 | 23 14 |
| 6 | 12 55 | − 7.5 | 58.0 | 15.8 | 9 | 293 | 52 | 8.0 | 13 20 | 13 29 | 18 39 | 23 49 | 23 39 |
| 7 | 13 48 | −11.5 | 58.8 | 16.0 | 21 | 291 | 63 | 9.0 | 14 35 | 14 48 | 19 33 | — | — |
| 8 | 14 45 | −14.9 | 59.6 | 16.2 | 34 | 288 | 73 | 10.0 | 15 51 | 16 08 | 20 30 | 0 22 | 0 08 |
| 9 | 15 44 | −17.6 | 60.3 | 16.4 | 46 | 285 | 83 | 11.0 | 17 04 | 17 23 | 21 30 | 1 03 | 0 46 |
| 10 | 16 46 | −19.1 | 60.8 | 16.6 | 58 | 282 | 91 | 12.0 | 18 10 | 18 30 | 22 33 | 1 54 | 1 35 |
| 11 | 17 50 | −19.3 | 61.1 | 16.6 | 70 | 282 | 97 | 13.0 | 19 06 | 19 25 | 23 35 | 2 56 | 2 37 |
| 12 | 18 54 | −18.1 | 61.1 | 16.6 | 82 | 301 | 100 | 14.0 | 19 53 | 20 08 | — | 4 08 | 3 50 |
| 13 | 19 56 | −15.7 | 60.7 | 16.5 | 95 | 46 | 99 | 15.0 | 20 30 | 20 42 | 0 36 | 5 26 | 5 11 |
| 14 | 20 55 | −12.2 | 60.1 | 16.4 | 107 | 62 | 96 | 16.0 | 21 02 | 21 09 | 1 33 | 6 45 | 6 35 |
| 15 | 21 52 | − 8.2 | 59.3 | 16.2 | 119 | 64 | 91 | 17.0 | 21 29 | 21 33 | 2 27 | 8 03 | 7 57 |
| 16 | 22 45 | − 3.7 | 58.4 | 15.9 | 131 | 64 | 83 | 18.0 | 21 54 | 21 54 | 3 18 | 9 19 | 9 17 |
| 17 | 23 36 | + 0.7 | 57.5 | 15.7 | 143 | 65 | 74 | 19.0 | 22 18 | 22 14 | 4 07 | 10 32 | 10 34 |
| 18 | 0 26 | + 5.0 | 56.6 | 15.4 | 155 | 66 | 65 | 20.0 | 22 42 | 22 35 | 4 54 | 11 42 | 11 48 |
| 19 | 1 14 | + 8.9 | 55.8 | 15.2 | 168 | 68 | 55 | 21.0 | 23 08 | 22 57 | 5 40 | 12 49 | 12 58 |
| 20 | 2 03 | +12.4 | 55.1 | 15.0 | 180 | 70 | 45 | 22.0 | 23 37 | 23 23 | 6 26 | 13 54 | 14 06 |
| 21 | 2 51 | +15.2 | 54.6 | 14.9 | 192 | 73 | 35 | 23.0 | — | 23 53 | 7 12 | 14 55 | 15 11 |
| 22 | 3 40 | +17.4 | 54.3 | 14.8 | 204 | 76 | 27 | 24.0 | 0 10 | — | 7 58 | 15 53 | 16 11 |
| 23 | 4 30 | +18.7 | 54.1 | 14.7 | 217 | 79 | 19 | 25.0 | 0 48 | 0 29 | 8 45 | 16 46 | 17 05 |
| 24 | 5 20 | +19.3 | 54.0 | 14.7 | 229 | 82 | 12 | 26.0 | 1 32 | 1 13 | 9 33 | 17 34 | 17 53 |
| 25 | 6 10 | +19.0 | 54.1 | 14.7 | 241 | 83 | 7 | 27.0 | 2 22 | 2 03 | 10 21 | 18 15 | 18 33 |
| 26 | 7 00 | +17.9 | 54.3 | 14.8 | 253 | 82 | 3 | 28.0 | 3 18 | 3 01 | 11 08 | 18 51 | 19 07 |
| 27 | 7 50 | +16.0 | 54.6 | 14.9 | 266 | 66 | 1 | 29.0 | 4 18 | 4 04 | 11 55 | 19 23 | 19 35 |
| 28 | 8 39 | +13.3 | 54.9 | 15.0 | 278 | 335 | 0 | 0.4 | 5 22 | 5 11 | 12 42 | 19 50 | 19 59 |
| 29 | 9 28 | +10.0 | 55.3 | 15.1 | 290 | 305 | 2 | 1.4 | 6 28 | 6 20 | 13 28 | 20 15 | 20 21 |
| 30 | 10 16 | + 6.3 | 55.8 | 15.2 | 302 | 299 | 6 | 2.4 | 7 36 | 7 32 | 14 13 | 20 39 | 20 41 |
| 31 | 11 04 | + 2.2 | 56.3 | 15.3 | 315 | 297 | 11 | 3.4 | 8 45 | 8 45 | 15 00 | 21 02 | 21 01 |

## MERCURY

| Day | RA | Dec. | Diam. | Phase | Transit | 5° high 52° | 5° high 56° |
|---|---|---|---|---|---|---|---|
| | h m | ° | " | % | h m | h m | h m |
| 1 | 5 05 | +19.8 | 8 | 40 | 10 30 | 3 18 | 3 04 |
| 3 | 5 14 | +20.4 | 7 | 45 | 10 32 | 3 16 | 3 01 |
| 5 | 5 24 | +20.9 | 7 | 50 | 10 35 | 3 15 | 3 00 |
| 7 | 5 36 | +21.5 | 7 | 56 | 10 39 | 3 15 | 2 59 |
| 9 | 5 48 | +22.0 | 6 | 62 | 10 44 | 3 17 | 3 00 |
| 11 | 6 02 | +22.5 | 6 | 68 | 10 50 | 3 20 | 3 03 |
| 13 | 6 17 | +22.8 | 6 | 74 | 10 57 | 3 25 | 3 08 |
| 15 | 6 33 | +23.1 | 6 | 80 | 11 06 | 3 32 | 3 14 |
| 17 | 6 50 | +23.2 | 6 | 85 | 11 15 | 3 40 | 3 22 |
| 19 | 7 07 | +23.1 | 5 | 90 | 11 24 | 3 50 | 3 32 |
| 21 | 7 25 | +22.9 | 5 | 94 | 11 35 | 4 02 | 3 44 |
| 23 | 7 44 | +22.5 | 5 | 97 | 11 45 | 4 15 | 3 58 |
| 25 | 8 02 | +21.9 | 5 | 99 | 11 55 | 4 29 | 4 12 |
| 27 | 8 20 | +21.2 | 5 | 100 | 12 05 | 19 25 | 19 41 |
| 29 | 8 37 | +20.3 | 5 | 100 | 12 15 | 19 29 | 19 43 |
| 31 | 8 54 | +19.3 | 5 | 99 | 12 24 | 19 32 | 19 45 |

## VENUS

| Day | RA | Dec. | Diam. | Phase | Transit | 5° high 52° | 5° high 56° |
|---|---|---|---|---|---|---|---|
| | h m | ° | " | % | h m | h m | h m |
| 1 | 5 37 | +23.0 | 10 | 97 | 11 04 | 3 31 | 3 13 |
| 6 | 6 04 | +23.3 | 10 | 98 | 11 10 | 3 36 | 3 18 |
| 11 | 6 31 | +23.4 | 10 | 98 | 11 17 | 3 43 | 3 25 |
| 16 | 6 57 | +23.1 | 10 | 99 | 11 24 | 3 52 | 3 34 |
| 21 | 7 24 | +22.6 | 10 | 99 | 11 31 | 4 02 | 3 45 |
| 26 | 7 50 | +21.7 | 10 | 99 | 11 38 | 4 14 | 3 58 |
| 31 | 8 16 | +20.6 | 10 | 100 | 11 44 | 4 27 | 4 12 |

## MARS

| Day | RA | Dec. | Diam. | Phase | Transit | 5° high 52° | 5° high 56° |
|---|---|---|---|---|---|---|---|
| 1 | 11 18 | + 5.3 | 6 | 90 | 16 43 | 22 36 | 22 37 |
| 6 | 11 29 | + 4.1 | 6 | 91 | 16 33 | 22 20 | 22 20 |
| 11 | 11 39 | + 2.9 | 5 | 91 | 16 24 | 22 05 | 22 04 |
| 16 | 11 49 | + 1.7 | 5 | 91 | 16 15 | 21 49 | 21 47 |
| 21 | 12 00 | + 0.5 | 5 | 91 | 16 06 | 21 34 | 21 31 |
| 26 | 12 11 | − 0.8 | 5 | 92 | 15 57 | 21 19 | 21 14 |
| 31 | 12 22 | − 2.0 | 5 | 92 | 15 48 | 21 03 | 20 58 |

## SUNRISE AND SUNSET

| | London | | Bristol | | Birmingham | | Manchester | | Newcastle | | Glasgow | | Belfast | |
|---|---|---|---|---|---|---|---|---|---|---|---|---|---|---|
| | 0°05′ | 51°30′ | 2°35′ | 51°28′ | 1°55′ | 52°28′ | 2°15′ | 53°28′ | 1°37′ | 54°59′ | 4°14′ | 55°52′ | 5°56′ | 54°35′ |
| | h m | h m | h m | h m | h m | h m | h m | h m | h m | h m | h m | h m | h m | h m |
| 1 | 3 47 | 20 21 | 3 57 | 20 31 | 3 49 | 20 34 | 3 44 | 20 41 | 3 32 | 20 48 | 3 36 | 21 05 | 3 52 | 21 03 |
| 2 | 3 48 | 20 20 | 3 58 | 20 30 | 3 50 | 20 33 | 3 45 | 20 41 | 3 32 | 20 48 | 3 37 | 21 05 | 3 52 | 21 02 |
| 3 | 3 48 | 20 20 | 3 59 | 20 30 | 3 50 | 20 33 | 3 46 | 20 40 | 3 33 | 20 47 | 3 38 | 21 04 | 3 53 | 21 02 |
| 4 | 3 49 | 20 20 | 3 59 | 20 29 | 3 51 | 20 32 | 3 47 | 20 40 | 3 34 | 20 47 | 3 38 | 21 03 | 3 54 | 21 01 |
| 5 | 3 50 | 20 19 | 4 00 | 20 29 | 3 52 | 20 32 | 3 47 | 20 39 | 3 35 | 20 46 | 3 39 | 21 03 | 3 55 | 21 01 |
| 6 | 3 51 | 20 19 | 4 01 | 20 28 | 3 53 | 20 31 | 3 48 | 20 38 | 3 36 | 20 45 | 3 40 | 21 02 | 3 56 | 21 00 |
| 7 | 3 52 | 20 18 | 4 02 | 20 28 | 3 54 | 20 31 | 3 49 | 20 38 | 3 37 | 20 45 | 3 42 | 21 01 | 3 57 | 20 59 |
| 8 | 3 53 | 20 17 | 4 03 | 20 27 | 3 55 | 20 30 | 3 50 | 20 37 | 3 38 | 20 44 | 3 43 | 21 00 | 3 58 | 20 59 |
| 9 | 3 54 | 20 17 | 4 04 | 20 27 | 3 56 | 20 29 | 3 51 | 20 36 | 3 39 | 20 43 | 3 44 | 21 00 | 3 59 | 20 58 |
| 10 | 3 55 | 20 16 | 4 05 | 20 26 | 3 57 | 20 28 | 3 52 | 20 35 | 3 41 | 20 42 | 3 45 | 20 59 | 4 00 | 20 57 |
| 11 | 3 56 | 20 15 | 4 06 | 20 25 | 3 58 | 20 28 | 3 54 | 20 35 | 3 42 | 20 41 | 3 46 | 20 58 | 4 02 | 20 56 |
| 12 | 3 57 | 20 14 | 4 07 | 20 24 | 3 59 | 20 27 | 3 55 | 20 34 | 3 43 | 20 40 | 3 48 | 20 56 | 4 03 | 20 55 |
| 13 | 3 58 | 20 14 | 4 08 | 20 23 | 4 00 | 20 26 | 3 56 | 20 33 | 3 44 | 20 39 | 3 49 | 20 55 | 4 04 | 20 54 |
| 14 | 3 59 | 20 13 | 4 09 | 20 22 | 4 01 | 20 25 | 3 57 | 20 32 | 3 46 | 20 38 | 3 50 | 20 54 | 4 05 | 20 53 |
| 15 | 4 00 | 20 12 | 4 10 | 20 21 | 4 02 | 20 24 | 3 58 | 20 31 | 3 47 | 20 37 | 3 52 | 20 53 | 4 07 | 20 52 |
| 16 | 4 01 | 20 11 | 4 11 | 20 20 | 4 04 | 20 23 | 4 00 | 20 29 | 3 48 | 20 36 | 3 53 | 20 52 | 4 08 | 20 50 |
| 17 | 4 02 | 20 10 | 4 13 | 20 19 | 4 05 | 20 22 | 4 01 | 20 28 | 3 50 | 20 34 | 3 55 | 20 50 | 4 09 | 20 49 |
| 18 | 4 04 | 20 09 | 4 14 | 20 18 | 4 06 | 20 21 | 4 02 | 20 27 | 3 51 | 20 33 | 3 56 | 20 49 | 4 11 | 20 48 |
| 19 | 4 05 | 20 07 | 4 15 | 20 17 | 4 08 | 20 19 | 4 04 | 20 26 | 3 53 | 20 32 | 3 58 | 20 47 | 4 12 | 20 47 |
| 20 | 4 06 | 20 06 | 4 16 | 20 16 | 4 09 | 20 18 | 4 05 | 20 24 | 3 54 | 20 30 | 4 00 | 20 46 | 4 14 | 20 45 |
| 21 | 4 08 | 20 05 | 4 18 | 20 15 | 4 10 | 20 17 | 4 07 | 20 23 | 3 56 | 20 29 | 4 01 | 20 44 | 4 15 | 20 44 |
| 22 | 4 09 | 20 04 | 4 19 | 20 14 | 4 12 | 20 16 | 4 08 | 20 22 | 3 57 | 20 27 | 4 03 | 20 43 | 4 17 | 20 42 |
| 23 | 4 10 | 20 02 | 4 20 | 20 12 | 4 13 | 20 14 | 4 10 | 20 20 | 3 59 | 20 26 | 4 04 | 20 41 | 4 18 | 20 41 |
| 24 | 4 12 | 20 01 | 4 22 | 20 11 | 4 15 | 20 13 | 4 11 | 20 19 | 4 01 | 20 24 | 4 06 | 20 39 | 4 20 | 20 39 |
| 25 | 4 13 | 20 00 | 4 23 | 20 10 | 4 16 | 20 11 | 4 13 | 20 17 | 4 02 | 20 22 | 4 08 | 20 38 | 4 22 | 20 38 |
| 26 | 4 14 | 19 58 | 4 25 | 20 08 | 4 17 | 20 10 | 4 14 | 20 16 | 4 04 | 20 21 | 4 10 | 20 36 | 4 23 | 20 36 |
| 27 | 4 16 | 19 57 | 4 26 | 20 07 | 4 19 | 20 08 | 4 16 | 20 14 | 4 06 | 20 19 | 4 11 | 20 34 | 4 25 | 20 34 |
| 28 | 4 17 | 19 55 | 4 27 | 20 05 | 4 20 | 20 07 | 4 17 | 20 13 | 4 07 | 20 17 | 4 13 | 20 32 | 4 27 | 20 33 |
| 29 | 4 19 | 19 54 | 4 29 | 20 04 | 4 22 | 20 05 | 4 19 | 20 11 | 4 09 | 20 16 | 4 15 | 20 31 | 4 28 | 20 31 |
| 30 | 4 20 | 19 52 | 4 30 | 20 02 | 4 24 | 20 04 | 4 20 | 20 09 | 4 11 | 20 14 | 4 17 | 20 29 | 4 30 | 20 29 |
| 31 | 4 22 | 19 51 | 4 32 | 20 01 | 4 25 | 20 02 | 4 22 | 20 08 | 4 13 | 20 12 | 4 19 | 20 27 | 4 32 | 20 27 |

## JUPITER

| Day | RA | Dec. | Transit | 5° high | |
|---|---|---|---|---|---|
| | | | | 52° | 56° |
| | h  m | °    ′ | h  m | h  m | h  m |
| 1 | 16 21.7 | −20 47 | 21 43 | 1 09 | 0 40 |
| 11 | 16 18.3 | −20 41 | 21 01 | 0 27 | 23 54 |
| 21 | 16 16.0 | −20 37 | 20 19 | 23 42 | 23 13 |
| 31 | 16 15.0 | −20 37 | 19 39 | 23 02 | 22 33 |

Diameters – equatorial 43″ polar 40″

## SATURN

| Day | RA | Dec. | Transit | 5° high | |
|---|---|---|---|---|---|
| | | | | 52° | 56° |
| | h  m | °    ′ | h  m | h  m | h  m |
| 1 | 23 44.0 | − 4 02 | 5 09 | 0 03 | 0 10 |
| 11 | 23 44.1 | − 4 04 | 4 30 | 23 20 | 23 27 |
| 21 | 23 43.6 | − 4 10 | 3 50 | 22 41 | 22 48 |
| 31 | 23 42.5 | − 4 20 | 3 09 | 22 02 | 22 09 |

Diameters – equatorial 18″ polar 16″
Rings – major axis 41″ minor axis 0″

## URANUS

| Day | RA | Dec. | Transit | 10° high | |
|---|---|---|---|---|---|
| | | | | 52° | 56° |
| | h  m | °    ′ | h  m | h  m | h  m |
| 1 | 20 06.3 | −20 51 | 1 32 | 22 57 | 23 43 |
| 11 | 20 04.7 | −20 56 | 0 51 | 22 17 | 23 04 |
| 21 | 20 03.1 | −21 01 | 0 10 | 21 36 | 22 24 |
| 31 | 20 01.4 | −21 06 | 23 25 | 20 56 | 21 44 |

Diameter 4″

## NEPTUNE

| Day | RA | Dec. | Transit | 10° high | |
|---|---|---|---|---|---|
| | | | | 52° | 56° |
| | h  m | °    ′ | h  m | h  m | h  m |
| 1 | 19 45.6 | −20 39 | 1 11 | 3 44 | 2 59 |
| 11 | 19 44.5 | −20 42 | 0 31 | 3 03 | 2 18 |
| 21 | 19 43.4 | −20 45 | 23 46 | 2 22 | 1 37 |
| 31 | 19 42.3 | −20 48 | 23 06 | 1 41 | 0 55 |

Diameter 2″

# August 1995

EIGHTH MONTH, 31 DAYS. Julius Caesar *Augustus*, formerly *Sextilis*, sixth month of Roman pre-Julian calendar

| | | | |
|---|---|---|---|
| 1 | Tuesday | Swiss Confederation founded 1291 | *week* 31 *day* 213 |
| 2 | Wednesday | James Baldwin b. 1924. Pietro Mascagni d. 1945 | 214 |
| 3 | Thursday | Stanley Baldwin b. 1867. Joseph Conrad d. 1924 | 215 |
| 4 | Friday | *Queen Elizabeth the Queen Mother b. 1900* | 216 |
| 5 | Saturday | Lord North d. 1792. Neil Armstrong b. 1930 | 217 |
| 6 | Sunday | **The Transfiguration. 9th S. after Pentecost/8th S. after Trinity** | *week* 32 *day* 218 |
| 7 | Monday | *Bank Holiday in Scotland.* Oliver Hardy d. 1957 | 219 |
| 8 | Tuesday | Princess Beatrice of York *b.* 1988 | 220 |
| 9 | Wednesday | Atomic bomb dropped on Nagasaki 1945 | 221 |
| 10 | Thursday | Sir Charles Napier b. 1782. Herbert Hoover b. 1874 | 222 |
| 11 | Friday | First Royal Ascot horse-race meeting 1711 | 223 |
| 12 | Saturday | Glorious Twelfth. Robert Southey b. 1774 | 224 |
| 13 | Sunday | **10th S. after Pentecost/9th S. after Trinity** | *week* 33 *day* 225 |
| 14 | Monday | John Galsworthy b. 1867. Japan surrenders 1945 | 226 |
| 15 | Tuesday | *Princess Royal b. 1950.* VJ Day | 227 |
| 16 | Wednesday | Andrew Marvell d. 1678. Ted Hughes b. 1930 | 228 |
| 17 | Thursday | Blondin crosses Niagara Falls on a tightrope 1859 | 229 |
| 18 | Friday | Godfrey Evans b. 1920. George Frederick Stout d. 1944 | 230 |
| 19 | Saturday | John Flamsteed b. 1646. President Bill Clinton b. 1946 | 231 |
| 20 | Sunday | **11th S. after Pentecost/10th S. after Trinity** | *week* 34 *day* 232 |
| 21 | Monday | *Princess Margaret b. 1930.* Leon Trotsky assass. 1940 | 233 |
| 22 | Tuesday | Claude Debussy b. 1862. Viscount Nuffield d. 1963 | 234 |
| 23 | Wednesday | Constant Lambert b. 1905. Rudolf Valentino d. 1926 | 235 |
| 24 | Thursday | **St Bartholomew.** Sir Max Beerbohm b. 1872 | 236 |
| 25 | Friday | Ivan the Terrible b. 1530. Liberation of Paris 1944 | 237 |
| 26 | Saturday | John Buchan b. 1875. Christopher Isherwood b. 1904 | 238 |
| 27 | Sunday | **12th S. after Pentecost/11th S. after Trinity** | *week* 35 *day* 239 |
| 28 | Monday | *Bank Holiday in England, Wales and Northern Ireland* | 240 |
| 29 | Tuesday | Northern Rugby Football Union founded 1895 | 241 |
| 30 | Wednesday | Maria Montessori b. 1870. Raymond Massey b. 1896 | 242 |
| 31 | Thursday | John Bunyan d. 1688. Harley Granville Barker d. 1946 | 243 |

ASTRONOMICAL PHENOMENA

| d | h | |
|---|---|---|
| 1 | 14 | Mars in conjunction with Moon. Mars 2° N. |
| 2 | 17 | Jupiter at stationary point |
| 5 | 21 | Jupiter in conjunction with Moon. Jupiter 2° S. |
| 8 | 13 | Pluto at stationary point |
| 13 | 07 | Saturn in conjunction with Moon. Saturn 5° S. |
| 21 | 00 | Venus in superior conjunction |
| 23 | 15 | Sun's longitude 150° ♍ |
| 26 | 07 | Venus in conjunction with Moon. Venus 5° N. |
| 28 | 05 | Mercury in conjunction with Moon. Mercury 2° N. |
| 30 | 03 | Mars in conjunction with Moon. Mars 0°.1 N. |

CONSTELLATIONS

The following constellations are near the meridian at

| | d | h | | d | h |
|---|---|---|---|---|---|
| July | 1 | 24 | August | 16 | 21 |
| July | 16 | 23 | September | 1 | 20 |
| August | 1 | 22 | September | 15 | 19 |

Draco, Hercules, Lyra, Cygnus, Sagitta, Ophiuchus, Serpens, Aquila and Sagittarius

MINIMA OF ALGOL

| d | h | d | h | d | h |
|---|---|---|---|---|---|
| 1 | 12.6 | 12 | 23.9 | 24 | 11.1 |
| 4 | 09.5 | 15 | 20.7 | 27 | 07.9 |
| 7 | 06.3 | 18 | 17.5 | 30 | 04.7 |
| 10 | 03.1 | 21 | 14.3 | | |

THE MOON

| Phases, Apsides and Node | d | h | m |
|---|---|---|---|
| ☽ First Quarter | 4 | 03 | 16 |
| ○ Full Moon | 10 | 18 | 16 |
| ☾ Last Quarter | 18 | 03 | 04 |
| ● New Moon | 26 | 04 | 31 |
| Perigee (362,881 km) | 8 | 13 | 59 |
| Apogee (404,727 km) | 20 | 11 | 45 |

Mean longitude of ascending node on August 1, 211°

THE SUN                                                                                      s.d. 15′.8

| Day | Right Ascension | Dec. + | Equation of time | Rise 52° | Rise 56° | Transit | Set 52° | Set 56° | Sidereal time | Transit of First Point of Aries |
|---|---|---|---|---|---|---|---|---|---|---|
| | h  m  s | °  ′ | m  s | h  m | h  m | h  m | h  m | h  m | h  m  s | h  m  s |
| 1  | 8 42 54 | 18 11 | − 6 21 | 4 21 | 4 03 | 12 06 | 19 51 | 20 09 | 20 36 32 | 3 22 54 |
| 2  | 8 46 47 | 17 56 | − 6 18 | 4 22 | 4 05 | 12 06 | 19 49 | 20 07 | 20 40 29 | 3 18 58 |
| 3  | 8 50 39 | 17 41 | − 6 14 | 4 24 | 4 07 | 12 06 | 19 47 | 20 04 | 20 44 26 | 3 15 02 |
| 4  | 8 54 31 | 17 25 | − 6 09 | 4 25 | 4 08 | 12 06 | 19 46 | 20 02 | 20 48 22 | 3 11 06 |
| 5  | 8 58 23 | 17 09 | − 6 04 | 4 27 | 4 10 | 12 06 | 19 44 | 20 00 | 20 52 19 | 3 07 11 |
| 6  | 9 02 13 | 16 53 | − 5 58 | 4 29 | 4 12 | 12 06 | 19 42 | 19 58 | 20 56 15 | 3 03 15 |
| 7  | 9 06 03 | 16 37 | − 5 51 | 4 30 | 4 14 | 12 06 | 19 40 | 19 56 | 21 00 12 | 2 59 19 |
| 8  | 9 09 52 | 16 20 | − 5 44 | 4 32 | 4 16 | 12 06 | 19 38 | 19 54 | 21 04 08 | 2 55 23 |
| 9  | 9 13 41 | 16 03 | − 5 36 | 4 33 | 4 18 | 12 06 | 19 37 | 19 52 | 21 08 05 | 2 51 27 |
| 10 | 9 17 29 | 15 46 | − 5 28 | 4 35 | 4 20 | 12 05 | 19 35 | 19 49 | 21 12 01 | 2 47 31 |
| 11 | 9 21 17 | 15 28 | − 5 19 | 4 37 | 4 22 | 12 05 | 19 33 | 19 47 | 21 15 58 | 2 43 35 |
| 12 | 9 25 04 | 15 11 | − 5 09 | 4 38 | 4 24 | 12 05 | 19 31 | 19 45 | 21 19 55 | 2 39 39 |
| 13 | 9 28 50 | 14 53 | − 4 59 | 4 40 | 4 26 | 12 05 | 19 29 | 19 43 | 21 23 51 | 2 35 43 |
| 14 | 9 32 36 | 14 34 | − 4 49 | 4 41 | 4 28 | 12 05 | 19 27 | 19 40 | 21 27 48 | 2 31 47 |
| 15 | 9 36 22 | 14 16 | − 4 38 | 4 43 | 4 30 | 12 05 | 19 25 | 19 38 | 21 31 44 | 2 27 51 |
| 16 | 9 40 07 | 13 57 | − 4 26 | 4 45 | 4 32 | 12 04 | 19 23 | 19 36 | 21 35 41 | 2 23 56 |
| 17 | 9 43 51 | 13 38 | − 4 14 | 4 46 | 4 34 | 12 04 | 19 21 | 19 33 | 21 39 37 | 2 20 00 |
| 18 | 9 47 35 | 13 19 | − 4 01 | 4 48 | 4 36 | 12 04 | 19 19 | 19 31 | 21 43 34 | 2 16 04 |
| 19 | 9 51 18 | 13 00 | − 3 48 | 4 50 | 4 38 | 12 04 | 19 17 | 19 28 | 21 47 30 | 2 12 08 |
| 20 | 9 55 01 | 12 40 | − 3 34 | 4 51 | 4 40 | 12 03 | 19 15 | 19 26 | 21 51 27 | 2 08 12 |
| 21 | 9 58 43 | 12 21 | − 3 20 | 4 53 | 4 42 | 12 03 | 19 12 | 19 24 | 21 55 24 | 2 04 16 |
| 22 | 10 02 25 | 12 01 | − 3 05 | 4 54 | 4 43 | 12 03 | 19 10 | 19 21 | 21 59 20 | 2 00 20 |
| 23 | 10 06 07 | 11 41 | − 2 50 | 4 56 | 4 45 | 12 03 | 19 08 | 19 19 | 22 03 17 | 1 56 24 |
| 24 | 10 09 48 | 11 20 | − 2 35 | 4 58 | 4 47 | 12 02 | 19 06 | 19 16 | 22 07 13 | 1 52 28 |
| 25 | 10 13 29 | 11 00 | − 2 19 | 4 59 | 4 49 | 12 02 | 19 04 | 19 14 | 22 11 10 | 1 48 32 |
| 26 | 10 17 09 | 10 39 | − 2 02 | 5 01 | 4 51 | 12 02 | 19 02 | 19 11 | 22 15 06 | 1 44 36 |
| 27 | 10 20 49 | 10 18 | − 1 46 | 5 03 | 4 53 | 12 02 | 19 00 | 19 09 | 22 19 03 | 1 40 41 |
| 28 | 10 24 28 | 9 57 | − 1 29 | 5 04 | 4 55 | 12 01 | 18 57 | 19 06 | 22 22 59 | 1 36 45 |
| 29 | 10 28 07 | 9 36 | − 1 11 | 5 06 | 4 57 | 12 01 | 18 55 | 19 04 | 22 26 56 | 1 32 49 |
| 30 | 10 31 46 | 9 15 | − 0 53 | 5 07 | 4 59 | 12 01 | 18 53 | 19 01 | 22 30 53 | 1 28 53 |
| 31 | 10 35 24 | 8 53 | − 0 35 | 5 09 | 5 01 | 12 00 | 18 51 | 18 58 | 22 34 49 | 1 24 57 |

DURATION OF TWILIGHT (in minutes)

| Latitude | 52° | 56° | 52° | 56° | 52° | 56° | 52° | 56° |
|---|---|---|---|---|---|---|---|---|
| | 1 August | | 11 August | | 21 August | | 31 August | |
| Civil | 41 | 48 | 39 | 45 | 37 | 42 | 35 | 40 |
| Nautical | 97 | 120 | 89 | 106 | 83 | 96 | 79 | 89 |
| Astronomical | 177 | TAN | 153 | 205 | 138 | 166 | 127 | 147 |

THE NIGHT SKY

Mercury is unsuitably placed for observation throughout the month.

Venus is too close to the Sun for observation, superior conjunction occurring on the 20th.

Mars is unsuitably placed for observation and will remain so for the rest of the year.

Jupiter continues to be visible as a brilliant object, magnitude − 2.2, low in the southern skies in the evenings. On the 2nd it reaches its second stationary point and resumes its direct motion. Jupiter is in Scorpius. On the evening of the 5th the gibbous Moon passes 2° N. of the planet. The four Galilean satellites are readily observable with a small telescope, or even a good pair of binoculars, provided they are held rigidly. Times of eclipses and shadow transits of these satellites are given on page 70.

Saturn, although technically a morning object, is now visible in the late evening in the south-east sky. Its magnitude is + 0.9.

Meteors. The maximum of the famous Perseid meteor shower occurs on the night of the 12th to 13th. The almost Full Moon will provide a considerable hindrance to observation.

## THE MOON

| Day | RA | Dec. | Hor. par. | Semi-diam. | Sun's co-long. | PA of Bright Limb | Phase | Age | Rise 52° | Rise 56° | Transit | Set 52° | Set 56° |
|---|---|---|---|---|---|---|---|---|---|---|---|---|---|
| | h m | ° | ' | ' | ° | ° | % | d | h m | h m | h m | h m | h m |
| 1 | 11 53 | − 2.1 | 56.8 | 15.5 | 327 | 296 | 19 | 4.4 | 9 56 | 9 59 | 15 47 | 21 27 | 21 22 |
| 2 | 12 43 | − 6.3 | 57.4 | 15.6 | 339 | 294 | 28 | 5.4 | 11 08 | 11 15 | 16 36 | 21 53 | 21 45 |
| 3 | 13 35 | −10.3 | 58.0 | 15.8 | 351 | 291 | 38 | 6.4 | 12 21 | 12 32 | 17 27 | 22 24 | 22 12 |
| 4 | 14 29 | −13.8 | 58.6 | 16.0 | 4 | 288 | 49 | 7.4 | 13 35 | 13 50 | 18 21 | 23 01 | 22 45 |
| 5 | 15 26 | −16.7 | 59.2 | 16.1 | 16 | 285 | 60 | 8.4 | 14 47 | 15 04 | 19 18 | 23 46 | 23 28 |
| 6 | 16 25 | −18.5 | 59.7 | 16.3 | 28 | 281 | 71 | 9.4 | 15 54 | 16 13 | 20 18 | — | — |
| 7 | 17 27 | −19.2 | 60.1 | 16.4 | 40 | 276 | 81 | 10.4 | 16 53 | 17 12 | 21 18 | 0 41 | 0 22 |
| 8 | 18 29 | −18.6 | 60.4 | 16.5 | 52 | 273 | 89 | 11.4 | 17 43 | 18 00 | 22 18 | 1 46 | 1 28 |
| 9 | 19 30 | −16.8 | 60.4 | 16.5 | 65 | 272 | 95 | 12.4 | 18 24 | 18 38 | 23 17 | 2 59 | 2 43 |
| 10 | 20 30 | −13.8 | 60.2 | 16.4 | 77 | 281 | 99 | 13.4 | 18 59 | 19 09 | — | 4 17 | 4 05 |
| 11 | 21 28 | −10.0 | 59.7 | 16.3 | 89 | 16 | 100 | 14.4 | 19 29 | 19 34 | 0 12 | 5 36 | 5 28 |
| 12 | 22 23 | − 5.7 | 59.1 | 16.1 | 101 | 55 | 98 | 15.4 | 19 55 | 19 57 | 1 06 | 6 54 | 6 50 |
| 13 | 23 16 | − 1.2 | 58.3 | 15.9 | 113 | 61 | 93 | 16.4 | 20 20 | 20 18 | 1 56 | 8 09 | 8 09 |
| 14 | 0 07 | + 3.2 | 57.4 | 15.6 | 125 | 64 | 87 | 17.4 | 20 45 | 20 39 | 2 45 | 9 22 | 9 26 |
| 15 | 0 57 | + 7.3 | 56.6 | 15.4 | 138 | 67 | 79 | 18.4 | 21 11 | 21 02 | 3 32 | 10 32 | 10 40 |
| 16 | 1 47 | +11.0 | 55.8 | 15.2 | 150 | 69 | 70 | 19.4 | 21 39 | 21 27 | 4 19 | 11 39 | 11 50 |
| 17 | 2 36 | +14.1 | 55.2 | 15.0 | 162 | 72 | 61 | 20.4 | 22 11 | 21 56 | 5 06 | 12 43 | 12 57 |
| 18 | 3 25 | +16.5 | 54.7 | 14.9 | 174 | 76 | 51 | 21.4 | 22 47 | 22 29 | 5 53 | 13 43 | 14 00 |
| 19 | 4 15 | +18.2 | 54.4 | 14.8 | 186 | 79 | 42 | 22.4 | 23 28 | 23 10 | 6 40 | 14 38 | 14 57 |
| 20 | 5 05 | +19.0 | 54.2 | 14.8 | 199 | 83 | 33 | 23.4 | — | 23 57 | 7 28 | 15 28 | 15 47 |
| 21 | 5 55 | +19.0 | 54.2 | 14.8 | 211 | 87 | 24 | 24.4 | 0 16 | — | 8 15 | 16 12 | 16 30 |
| 22 | 6 45 | +18.2 | 54.3 | 14.8 | 223 | 90 | 17 | 25.4 | 1 10 | 0 52 | 9 03 | 16 50 | 17 06 |
| 23 | 7 35 | +16.5 | 54.6 | 14.9 | 235 | 92 | 10 | 26.4 | 2 08 | 1 53 | 9 50 | 17 23 | 17 37 |
| 24 | 8 24 | +14.1 | 55.0 | 15.0 | 248 | 93 | 5 | 27.4 | 3 11 | 2 58 | 10 37 | 17 53 | 18 03 |
| 25 | 9 14 | +11.0 | 55.5 | 15.1 | 260 | 89 | 2 | 28.4 | 4 17 | 4 08 | 11 24 | 18 19 | 18 26 |
| 26 | 10 03 | + 7.4 | 56.0 | 15.2 | 272 | 48 | 0 | 29.4 | 5 25 | 5 19 | 12 10 | 18 44 | 18 47 |
| 27 | 10 52 | + 3.4 | 56.5 | 15.4 | 284 | 313 | 1 | 0.8 | 6 34 | 6 32 | 12 57 | 19 08 | 19 08 |
| 28 | 11 41 | − 0.9 | 57.0 | 15.5 | 297 | 300 | 4 | 1.8 | 7 45 | 7 47 | 13 45 | 19 33 | 19 29 |
| 29 | 12 32 | − 5.2 | 57.5 | 15.7 | 309 | 296 | 9 | 2.8 | 8 58 | 9 04 | 14 33 | 19 59 | 19 52 |
| 30 | 13 23 | − 9.2 | 57.9 | 15.8 | 321 | 292 | 16 | 3.8 | 10 11 | 10 21 | 15 24 | 20 29 | 20 18 |
| 31 | 14 17 | −12.9 | 58.4 | 15.9 | 333 | 289 | 24 | 4.8 | 11 25 | 11 38 | 16 17 | 21 03 | 20 49 |

## MERCURY

| Day | RA | Dec. | Diam. | Phase | Transit | 5° high 52° | 56° |
|---|---|---|---|---|---|---|---|
| | h m | ° | " | % | h m | h m | h m |
| 1 | 9 03 | +18.7 | 5 | 99 | 12 28 | 19 33 | 19 45 |
| 3 | 9 19 | +17.5 | 5 | 97 | 12 36 | 19 34 | 19 45 |
| 5 | 9 34 | +16.2 | 5 | 96 | 12 44 | 19 34 | 19 44 |
| 7 | 9 49 | +14.9 | 5 | 94 | 12 51 | 19 34 | 19 42 |
| 9 | 10 03 | +13.5 | 5 | 92 | 12 57 | 19 32 | 19 40 |
| 11 | 10 17 | +12.1 | 5 | 90 | 13 03 | 19 30 | 19 36 |
| 13 | 10 30 | +10.7 | 5 | 88 | 13 08 | 19 28 | 19 33 |
| 15 | 10 43 | + 9.2 | 5 | 86 | 13 12 | 19 25 | 19 28 |
| 17 | 10 55 | + 7.8 | 5 | 84 | 13 16 | 19 21 | 19 24 |
| 19 | 11 06 | + 6.3 | 5 | 81 | 13 20 | 19 17 | 19 18 |
| 21 | 11 18 | + 4.8 | 6 | 79 | 13 23 | 19 13 | 19 13 |
| 23 | 11 28 | + 3.4 | 6 | 77 | 13 26 | 19 08 | 19 07 |
| 25 | 11 39 | + 2.0 | 6 | 75 | 13 28 | 19 03 | 19 01 |
| 27 | 11 49 | + 0.6 | 6 | 73 | 13 30 | 18 58 | 18 55 |
| 29 | 11 58 | − 0.7 | 6 | 71 | 13 32 | 18 53 | 18 48 |
| 31 | 12 07 | − 2.1 | 6 | 69 | 13 33 | 18 47 | 18 42 |

## VENUS

| Day | RA | Dec. | Diam. | Phase | Transit | 5° high 52° | 56° |
|---|---|---|---|---|---|---|---|
| | h m | ° | " | % | h m | h m | h m |
| 1 | 8 21 | +20.4 | 10 | 100 | 11 45 | 19 00 | 19 15 |
| 6 | 8 47 | +19.0 | 10 | 100 | 11 51 | 18 58 | 19 11 |
| 11 | 9 12 | +17.4 | 10 | 100 | 11 56 | 18 54 | 19 05 |
| 16 | 9 36 | +15.6 | 10 | 100 | 12 01 | 18 48 | 18 58 |
| 21 | 10 01 | +13.6 | 10 | 100 | 12 06 | 18 42 | 18 50 |
| 26 | 10 24 | +11.4 | 10 | 100 | 12 10 | 18 34 | 18 40 |
| 31 | 10 48 | + 9.2 | 10 | 100 | 12 13 | 18 26 | 18 30 |

## MARS

| Day | RA | Dec. | Diam. | Phase | Transit | 5° high 52° | 56° |
|---|---|---|---|---|---|---|---|
| 1 | 12 24 | − 2.3 | 5 | 92 | 15 46 | 21 00 | 20 55 |
| 6 | 12 35 | − 3.5 | 5 | 92 | 15 38 | 20 45 | 20 38 |
| 11 | 12 46 | − 4.8 | 5 | 93 | 15 29 | 20 30 | 20 22 |
| 16 | 12 58 | − 6.1 | 5 | 93 | 15 21 | 20 15 | 20 06 |
| 21 | 13 09 | − 7.4 | 5 | 93 | 15 13 | 20 00 | 19 50 |
| 26 | 13 21 | − 8.6 | 5 | 93 | 15 05 | 19 45 | 19 34 |
| 31 | 13 33 | − 9.9 | 5 | 94 | 14 58 | 19 30 | 19 18 |

## SUNRISE AND SUNSET

| | London | | Bristol | | Birmingham | | Manchester | | Newcastle | | Glasgow | | Belfast | |
|---|---|---|---|---|---|---|---|---|---|---|---|---|---|---|
| | 0°05′ | 51°30′ | 2°35′ | 51°28′ | 1°55′ | 52°28′ | 2°15′ | 53°28′ | 1°37′ | 54°59′ | 4°14′ | 55°52′ | 5°56′ | 54°35′ |
| | h m | h m | h m | h m | h m | h m | h m | h m | h m | h m | h m | h m | h m | h m |
| 1 | 4 23 | 19 49 | 4 33 | 19 59 | 4 27 | 20 00 | 4 24 | 20 06 | 4 14 | 20 10 | 4 20 | 20 25 | 4 33 | 20 25 |
| 2 | 4 25 | 19 48 | 4 35 | 19 57 | 4 28 | 19 59 | 4 25 | 20 04 | 4 16 | 20 08 | 4 22 | 20 23 | 4 35 | 20 24 |
| 3 | 4 26 | 19 46 | 4 36 | 19 56 | 4 30 | 19 57 | 4 27 | 20 02 | 4 18 | 20 06 | 4 24 | 20 21 | 4 37 | 20 22 |
| 4 | 4 28 | 19 44 | 4 38 | 19 54 | 4 31 | 19 55 | 4 29 | 20 00 | 4 20 | 20 04 | 4 26 | 20 19 | 4 39 | 20 20 |
| 5 | 4 29 | 19 42 | 4 39 | 19 52 | 4 33 | 19 53 | 4 30 | 19 58 | 4 21 | 20 02 | 4 28 | 20 17 | 4 41 | 20 18 |
| 6 | 4 31 | 19 41 | 4 41 | 19 51 | 4 35 | 19 51 | 4 32 | 19 57 | 4 23 | 20 00 | 4 30 | 20 15 | 4 42 | 20 16 |
| 7 | 4 32 | 19 39 | 4 42 | 19 49 | 4 36 | 19 50 | 4 34 | 19 55 | 4 25 | 19 58 | 4 32 | 20 12 | 4 44 | 20 14 |
| 8 | 4 34 | 19 37 | 4 44 | 19 47 | 4 38 | 19 48 | 4 35 | 19 53 | 4 27 | 19 56 | 4 34 | 20 10 | 4 46 | 20 12 |
| 9 | 4 35 | 19 35 | 4 46 | 19 45 | 4 39 | 19 46 | 4 37 | 19 51 | 4 29 | 19 54 | 4 36 | 20 08 | 4 48 | 20 10 |
| 10 | 4 37 | 19 33 | 4 47 | 19 43 | 4 41 | 19 44 | 4 39 | 19 49 | 4 31 | 19 52 | 4 37 | 20 06 | 4 49 | 20 08 |
| 11 | 4 39 | 19 32 | 4 49 | 19 41 | 4 43 | 19 42 | 4 41 | 19 47 | 4 32 | 19 50 | 4 39 | 20 04 | 4 51 | 20 05 |
| 12 | 4 40 | 19 30 | 4 50 | 19 40 | 4 44 | 19 40 | 4 42 | 19 45 | 4 34 | 19 47 | 4 41 | 20 01 | 4 53 | 20 03 |
| 13 | 4 42 | 19 28 | 4 52 | 19 38 | 4 46 | 19 38 | 4 44 | 19 43 | 4 36 | 19 45 | 4 43 | 19 59 | 4 55 | 20 01 |
| 14 | 4 43 | 19 26 | 4 53 | 19 36 | 4 48 | 19 36 | 4 46 | 19 40 | 4 38 | 19 43 | 4 45 | 19 57 | 4 57 | 19 59 |
| 15 | 4 45 | 19 24 | 4 55 | 19 34 | 4 49 | 19 34 | 4 48 | 19 38 | 4 40 | 19 41 | 4 47 | 19 54 | 4 59 | 19 57 |
| 16 | 4 46 | 19 22 | 4 57 | 19 32 | 4 51 | 19 32 | 4 49 | 19 36 | 4 42 | 19 39 | 4 49 | 19 52 | 5 00 | 19 54 |
| 17 | 4 48 | 19 20 | 4 58 | 19 30 | 4 53 | 19 30 | 4 51 | 19 34 | 4 44 | 19 36 | 4 51 | 19 50 | 5 02 | 19 52 |
| 18 | 4 50 | 19 18 | 5 00 | 19 28 | 4 54 | 19 28 | 4 53 | 19 32 | 4 45 | 19 34 | 4 53 | 19 47 | 5 04 | 19 50 |
| 19 | 4 51 | 19 16 | 5 01 | 19 26 | 4 56 | 19 26 | 4 54 | 19 30 | 4 47 | 19 32 | 4 55 | 19 45 | 5 06 | 19 48 |
| 20 | 4 53 | 19 14 | 5 03 | 19 24 | 4 58 | 19 23 | 4 56 | 19 27 | 4 49 | 19 29 | 4 57 | 19 42 | 5 08 | 19 45 |
| 21 | 4 54 | 19 12 | 5 04 | 19 22 | 4 59 | 19 21 | 4 58 | 19 25 | 4 51 | 19 27 | 4 59 | 19 40 | 5 10 | 19 43 |
| 22 | 4 56 | 19 10 | 5 06 | 19 19 | 5 01 | 19 19 | 5 00 | 19 23 | 4 53 | 19 25 | 5 01 | 19 38 | 5 11 | 19 41 |
| 23 | 4 58 | 19 07 | 5 08 | 19 17 | 5 03 | 19 17 | 5 01 | 19 21 | 4 55 | 19 22 | 5 03 | 19 35 | 5 13 | 19 38 |
| 24 | 4 59 | 19 05 | 5 09 | 19 15 | 5 04 | 19 15 | 5 03 | 19 19 | 4 57 | 19 20 | 5 05 | 19 33 | 5 15 | 19 36 |
| 25 | 5 01 | 19 03 | 5 11 | 19 13 | 5 06 | 19 13 | 5 05 | 19 16 | 4 59 | 19 17 | 5 07 | 19 30 | 5 17 | 19 34 |
| 26 | 5 02 | 19 01 | 5 12 | 19 11 | 5 08 | 19 10 | 5 07 | 19 14 | 5 00 | 19 15 | 5 09 | 19 28 | 5 19 | 19 31 |
| 27 | 5 04 | 18 59 | 5 14 | 19 09 | 5 09 | 19 08 | 5 08 | 19 12 | 5 02 | 19 13 | 5 11 | 19 25 | 5 21 | 19 29 |
| 28 | 5 06 | 18 57 | 5 16 | 19 07 | 5 11 | 19 06 | 5 10 | 19 09 | 5 04 | 19 10 | 5 13 | 19 23 | 5 22 | 19 26 |
| 29 | 5 07 | 18 54 | 5 17 | 19 04 | 5 13 | 19 04 | 5 12 | 19 07 | 5 06 | 19 08 | 5 14 | 19 20 | 5 24 | 19 24 |
| 30 | 5 09 | 18 52 | 5 19 | 19 02 | 5 14 | 19 01 | 5 14 | 19 05 | 5 08 | 19 05 | 5 16 | 19 18 | 5 26 | 19 22 |
| 31 | 5 10 | 18 50 | 5 20 | 19 00 | 5 16 | 18 59 | 5 15 | 19 02 | 5 10 | 19 03 | 5 18 | 19 15 | 5 28 | 19 19 |

## JUPITER

| Day | RA | Dec. | Transit | 5° high | |
|---|---|---|---|---|---|
| | | | | 52° | 56° |
| | h m | ° ′ | h m | h m | h m |
| 1 | 16 15.0 | −20 37 | 19 35 | 22 58 | 22 29 |
| 11 | 16 15.4 | −20 40 | 18 56 | 22 18 | 21 50 |
| 21 | 16 17.0 | −20 47 | 18 19 | 21 40 | 21 11 |
| 31 | 16 19.9 | −20 56 | 17 42 | 21 02 | 20 33 |

Diameters – equatorial 39″ polar 37″

## SATURN

| Day | RA | Dec. | Transit | 5° high | |
|---|---|---|---|---|---|
| | | | | 52° | 56° |
| | h m | ° ′ | h m | h m | h m |
| 1 | 23 42.3 | − 4 21 | 3 05 | 21 58 | 22 05 |
| 11 | 23 40.6 | − 4 34 | 2 24 | 21 18 | 21 25 |
| 21 | 23 38.5 | − 4 50 | 1 43 | 20 38 | 20 45 |
| 31 | 23 35.9 | − 5 08 | 1 01 | 19 57 | 20 05 |

Diameters – equatorial 19″ polar 17″
Rings – major axis 43″ minor axis 0″

## URANUS

| Day | RA | Dec. | Transit | 10° high | |
|---|---|---|---|---|---|
| | | | | 52° | 56° |
| | h m | ° ′ | h m | h m | h m |
| 1 | 20 01.2 | −21 06 | 23 21 | 1 16 | 1 05 |
| 11 | 19 59.6 | −21 11 | 22 40 | 1 12 | 0 23 |
| 21 | 19 58.2 | −21 15 | 21 59 | 0 30 | 23 37 |
| 31 | 19 56.9 | −21 18 | 21 19 | 23 45 | 22 55 |

Diameter 4″

## NEPTUNE

| Day | RA | Dec. | Transit | 10° high | |
|---|---|---|---|---|---|
| | | | | 52° | 56° |
| | h m | ° ′ | h m | h m | h m |
| 1 | 19 42.2 | −20 48 | 23 02 | 1 37 | 0 51 |
| 11 | 19 41.1 | −20 51 | 22 21 | 0 57 | 0 10 |
| 21 | 19 40.1 | −20 54 | 21 41 | 0 16 | 23 25 |
| 31 | 19 39.3 | −20 56 | 21 01 | 23 31 | 22 44 |

Diameter 2″

# September 1995

NINTH MONTH, 30 DAYS. *Septem* (seven), seventh month of Roman pre-Julian calendar

| | | | |
|---|---|---|---|
| 1 | *Friday* | Germany invaded Poland 1939 | *week 35 day* 244 |
| 2 | *Saturday* | Fire of London 1666. Battle of Omdurman 1898 | 245 |
| 3 | *Sunday* | **13th S. after Pentecost/12th S. after Trinity** | *week 36 day* 246 |
| 4 | *Monday* | Third French Republic proclaimed 1870 | 247 |
| 5 | *Tuesday* | Gp Capt Sir Douglas Bader d. 1982 | 248 |
| 6 | *Wednesday* | James II d. 1701. Elie Halévy b. 1870 | 249 |
| 7 | *Thursday* | Elizabeth I b. 1533. Leonard Cheshire b. 1917 | 250 |
| 8 | *Friday* | **Blessed Virgin Mary.** Peter Sellers b. 1925 | 251 |
| 9 | *Saturday* | Salerno landings 1943. Soap rationing ends 1950 | 252 |
| 10 | *Sunday* | **14th S. after Pentecost/13th S. after Trinity** | *week 37 day* 253 |
| 11 | *Monday* | Field Marshal Jan Smuts d. 1950 | 254 |
| 12 | *Tuesday* | H. H. Asquith b. 1852. Jesse Owens b. 1913 | 255 |
| 13 | *Wednesday* | Gen. John Pershing b. 1860. John Smith b. 1938 | 256 |
| 14 | *Thursday* | James Fenimore Cooper d. 1851 | 257 |
| 15 | *Friday* | Prince Henry of Wales b. 1984. Battle of Britain day | 258 |
| 16 | *Saturday* | John Gay b. 1685. Maria Callas d. 1977 | 259 |
| 17 | *Sunday* | **15th S. after Pentecost/14th S. after Trinity** | *week 38 day* 260 |
| 18 | *Monday* | Samuel Johnson b. 1709. Greta Garbo b. 1905 | 261 |
| 19 | *Tuesday* | George Cadbury b. 1839. Emil Zátopek b. 1922 | 262 |
| 20 | *Wednesday* | Jacob Grimm d. 1863. Kenneth More b. 1914 | 263 |
| 21 | *Thursday* | **St Matthew.** Britain abandons Gold Standard 1931 | 264 |
| 22 | *Friday* | Michael Faraday b. 1791. Irving Berlin d. 1989 | 265 |
| 23 | *Saturday* | Aldo Moro b. 1916. Pablo Neruda d. 1973 | 266 |
| 24 | *Sunday* | **16th S. after Pentecost/15th S. after Trinity** | *week 39 day* 267 |
| 25 | *Monday* | JEWISH NEW YEAR (5756). Shostakovich b. 1906 | 268 |
| 26 | *Tuesday* | Sir Barnes Wallis b. 1887. Béla Bartok d. 1945 | 269 |
| 27 | *Wednesday* | Society of Jesus afforded Papal recognition 1540 | 270 |
| 28 | *Thursday* | Louis Pasteur d. 1895. W. H. Auden d. 1973 | 271 |
| 29 | *Friday* | **St Michael and all Angels.** Lord Clive b. 1725 | 272 |
| 30 | *Saturday* | Deborah Kerr b. 1921. Truman Capote b. 1924 | 273 |

ASTRONOMICAL PHENOMENA

| d | h | |
|---|---|---|
| 2 | 05 | Jupiter in conjunction with Moon. Jupiter 3° S. |
| 9 | 04 | Mercury at greatest elongation E. 27° |
| 9 | 14 | Saturn in conjunction with Moon. Saturn 5° S. |
| 14 | 15 | Saturn at opposition |
| 22 | 09 | Mercury at stationary point |
| 23 | 12 | Sun's longitude 180° ♎ |
| 25 | 11 | Venus in conjunction with Moon. Venus 2° N. |
| 26 | 01 | Mercury in conjunction with Moon. Mercury 3° S. |
| 27 | 19 | Mars in conjunction with Moon. Mars 2° S. |
| 29 | 16 | Jupiter in conjunction with Moon. Jupiter 3° S. |
| 29 | 20 | Venus in conjunction with Mercury. Venus 4° N. |

CONSTELLATIONS

The following constellations are near the meridian at

| | d | h | | d | h |
|---|---|---|---|---|---|
| August | 1 | 24 | September | 15 | 21 |
| August | 16 | 23 | October | 1 | 20 |
| September | 1 | 22 | October | 16 | 19 |

Draco, Cepheus, Lyra, Cygnus, Vulpecula, Sagitta, Delphinus, Equuleus, Aquila, Aquarius and Capricornus

MINIMA OF ALGOL

| d | h | d | h | d | h |
|---|---|---|---|---|---|
| 2 | 01.6 | 13 | 12.8 | 25 | 00.0 |
| 4 | 22.4 | 16 | 09.6 | 27 | 20.8 |
| 7 | 19.2 | 19 | 06.4 | 30 | 17.7 |
| 10 | 16.0 | 22 | 03.2 | | |

THE MOON

| Phases, Apsides and Node | d | h | m |
|---|---|---|---|
| ☽ First Quarter | 2 | 09 | 03 |
| ○ Full Moon | 9 | 03 | 37 |
| ☾ Last Quarter | 16 | 21 | 09 |
| ● New Moon | 24 | 16 | 55 |
| Perigee (367,942 km) | 5 | 01 | 23 |
| Apogee (404,222 km) | 17 | 06 | 13 |
| Perigee (369,539 km) | 30 | 03 | 28 |

Mean longitude of ascending node on September 1, 209°

THE SUN                                                                    s.d. 15′.9

| Day | Right Ascension | Dec. | Equation of time | Rise 52° | Rise 56° | Transit | Set 52° | Set 56° | Sidereal time | Transit of First Point of Aries |
|---|---|---|---|---|---|---|---|---|---|---|
| | h m s | ° ′ | m s | h m | h m | h m | h m | h m | h m s | h m s |
| 1 | 10 39 02 | +8 32 | −0 16 | 5 11 | 5 03 | 12 00 | 18 48 | 18 56 | 22 38 46 | 1 21 01 |
| 2 | 10 42 40 | +8 10 | +0 02 | 5 12 | 5 05 | 12 00 | 18 46 | 18 53 | 22 42 42 | 1 17 05 |
| 3 | 10 46 17 | +7 48 | +0 22 | 5 14 | 5 07 | 11 59 | 18 44 | 18 51 | 22 46 39 | 1 13 09 |
| 4 | 10 49 54 | +7 26 | +0 41 | 5 16 | 5 09 | 11 59 | 18 42 | 18 48 | 22 50 35 | 1 09 13 |
| 5 | 10 53 31 | +7 04 | +1 01 | 5 17 | 5 11 | 11 59 | 18 39 | 18 45 | 22 54 32 | 1 05 17 |
| 6 | 10 57 07 | +6 42 | +1 21 | 5 19 | 5 13 | 11 58 | 18 37 | 18 43 | 22 58 28 | 1 01 22 |
| 7 | 11 00 44 | +6 20 | +1 41 | 5 21 | 5 15 | 11 58 | 18 35 | 18 40 | 23 02 25 | 0 57 26 |
| 8 | 11 04 20 | +5 57 | +2 02 | 5 22 | 5 17 | 11 58 | 18 32 | 18 38 | 23 06 22 | 0 53 30 |
| 9 | 11 07 56 | +5 35 | +2 22 | 5 24 | 5 19 | 11 57 | 18 30 | 18 35 | 23 10 18 | 0 49 34 |
| 10 | 11 11 31 | +5 12 | +2 43 | 5 25 | 5 21 | 11 57 | 18 28 | 18 32 | 23 14 15 | 0 45 38 |
| 11 | 11 15 07 | +4 49 | +3 04 | 5 27 | 5 23 | 11 57 | 18 25 | 18 30 | 23 18 11 | 0 41 42 |
| 12 | 11 18 42 | +4 27 | +3 25 | 5 29 | 5 25 | 11 56 | 18 23 | 18 27 | 23 22 08 | 0 37 46 |
| 13 | 11 22 18 | +4 04 | +3 47 | 5 30 | 5 26 | 11 56 | 18 21 | 18 24 | 23 26 04 | 0 33 50 |
| 14 | 11 25 53 | +3 41 | +4 08 | 5 32 | 5 28 | 11 56 | 18 18 | 18 22 | 23 30 01 | 0 29 54 |
| 15 | 11 29 28 | +3 18 | +4 29 | 5 34 | 5 30 | 11 55 | 18 16 | 18 19 | 23 33 57 | 0 25 58 |
| 16 | 11 33 03 | +2 55 | +4 51 | 5 35 | 5 32 | 11 55 | 18 14 | 18 16 | 23 37 54 | 0 22 02 |
| 17 | 11 36 38 | +2 32 | +5 12 | 5 37 | 5 34 | 11 55 | 18 11 | 18 14 | 23 41 50 | 0 18 07 |
| 18 | 11 40 14 | +2 08 | +5 33 | 5 38 | 5 36 | 11 54 | 18 09 | 18 11 | 23 45 47 | 0 14 11 |
| 19 | 11 43 49 | +1 45 | +5 55 | 5 40 | 5 38 | 11 54 | 18 07 | 18 08 | 23 49 44 | 0 10 15 |
| 20 | 11 47 24 | +1 22 | +6 16 | 5 42 | 5 40 | 11 54 | 18 04 | 18 06 | 23 53 40 | 0 06 19 |
| 21 | 11 50 59 | +0 59 | +6 37 | 5 43 | 5 42 | 11 53 | 18 02 | 18 03 | 23 57 37 | { 0 02 23 / 23 58 27 |
| 22 | 11 54 35 | +0 35 | +6 59 | 5 45 | 5 44 | 11 53 | 18 00 | 18 00 | 0 01 33 | 23 54 31 |
| 23 | 11 58 10 | +0 12 | +7 20 | 5 47 | 5 46 | 11 52 | 17 57 | 17 58 | 0 05 30 | 23 50 35 |
| 24 | 12 01 46 | −0 11 | +7 41 | 5 48 | 5 48 | 11 52 | 17 55 | 17 55 | 0 09 26 | 23 46 39 |
| 25 | 12 05 21 | −0 35 | +8 01 | 5 50 | 5 50 | 11 52 | 17 53 | 17 53 | 0 13 23 | 23 42 43 |
| 26 | 12 08 57 | −0 58 | +8 22 | 5 52 | 5 52 | 11 51 | 17 50 | 17 50 | 0 17 19 | 23 38 47 |
| 27 | 12 12 33 | −1 22 | +8 43 | 5 53 | 5 54 | 11 51 | 17 48 | 17 47 | 0 21 16 | 23 34 52 |
| 28 | 12 16 10 | −1 45 | +9 03 | 5 55 | 5 56 | 11 51 | 17 46 | 17 45 | 0 25 13 | 23 30 56 |
| 29 | 12 19 46 | −2 08 | +9 23 | 5 57 | 5 58 | 11 50 | 17 43 | 17 42 | 0 29 09 | 23 27 00 |
| 30 | 12 23 23 | −2 32 | +9 43 | 5 58 | 6 00 | 11 50 | 17 41 | 17 39 | 0 33 06 | 23 23 04 |

DURATION OF TWILIGHT (in minutes)

| Latitude | 52° | 56° | 52° | 56° | 52° | 56° | 52° | 56° |
|---|---|---|---|---|---|---|---|---|
| | 1 September | | 11 September | | 21 September | | 30 September | |
| Civil | 35 | 39 | 34 | 38 | 34 | 37 | 34 | 37 |
| Nautical | 79 | 89 | 76 | 84 | 74 | 82 | 73 | 80 |
| Astronomical | 127 | 146 | 120 | 135 | 115 | 129 | 113 | 126 |

THE NIGHT SKY

Mercury is too close to the Sun for observation throughout September, even though it is at greatest eastern elongation on the 9th.

Venus is unsuitably placed for observation.

Mars is too close to the Sun for observation.

Jupiter, magnitude −2.1, is still a brilliant object, low in the south-west sky in the early part of the evenings. Jupiter is in the constellation of Ophiuchus. Jupiter is near the Moon on the evenings of the 2nd and 3rd and again on the evening of the 29th.

Saturn, magnitude +0.7, is at opposition on the 14th and therefore visible throughout the hours of darkness. The rings of Saturn usually present a beautiful spectacle to the observer, even with only a small telescope, though in 1995 they are difficult to detect since the Earth passes through the ring

plane this year. It does so on two occasions – on May 22nd and August 11th, while the Sun passes through the plane on November 19th.

Zodiacal Light. The morning cone may be seen stretching up from the eastern horizon along the ecliptic before the beginning of morning twilight, from the 1st to the 7th, and again after the 22nd.

## THE MOON

| Day | RA | Dec. | Hor. par. | Semi- diam. | Sun's co- long. | PA of Bright Limb | Phase | Age | Rise 52° | Rise 56° | Transit | Set 52° | Set 56° |
|---|---|---|---|---|---|---|---|---|---|---|---|---|---|
| | h m | ° | ′ | ′ | ° | ° | % | d | h m | h m | h m | h m | h m |
| 1 | 15 13 | −15.9 | 58.7 | 16.0 | 346 | 285 | 35 | 5.8 | 12 36 | 12 53 | 17 13 | 21 45 | 21 28 |
| 2 | 16 11 | −18.0 | 59.1 | 16.1 | 358 | 280 | 46 | 6.8 | 13 43 | 14 02 | 18 10 | 22 35 | 22 16 |
| 3 | 17 10 | −18.9 | 59.3 | 16.2 | 10 | 275 | 57 | 7.8 | 14 44 | 15 03 | 19 09 | 23 35 | 23 16 |
| 4 | 18 11 | −18.8 | 59.5 | 16.2 | 22 | 271 | 68 | 8.8 | 15 36 | 15 54 | 20 07 | — | — |
| 5 | 19 11 | −17.4 | 59.6 | 16.2 | 34 | 267 | 79 | 9.8 | 16 20 | 16 34 | 21 04 | 0 43 | 0 26 |
| 6 | 20 10 | −14.9 | 59.5 | 16.2 | 47 | 263 | 87 | 10.8 | 16 56 | 17 07 | 22 00 | 1 56 | 1 43 |
| 7 | 21 07 | −11.5 | 59.3 | 16.2 | 59 | 262 | 94 | 11.8 | 17 27 | 17 35 | 22 53 | 3 13 | 3 03 |
| 8 | 22 02 | − 7.4 | 58.9 | 16.1 | 71 | 265 | 98 | 12.8 | 17 55 | 17 59 | 23 44 | 4 30 | 4 24 |
| 9 | 22 55 | − 3.1 | 58.4 | 15.9 | 83 | 309 | 100 | 13.8 | 18 21 | 18 21 | — | 5 45 | 5 44 |
| 10 | 23 47 | + 1.4 | 57.8 | 15.7 | 95 | 53 | 99 | 14.8 | 18 46 | 18 42 | 0 34 | 6 59 | 7 02 |
| 11 | 0 38 | + 5.7 | 57.1 | 15.6 | 107 | 64 | 96 | 15.8 | 19 12 | 19 05 | 1 23 | 8 11 | 8 17 |
| 12 | 1 28 | + 9.5 | 56.4 | 15.4 | 120 | 68 | 91 | 16.8 | 19 40 | 19 29 | 2 10 | 9 21 | 9 30 |
| 13 | 2 18 | +12.9 | 55.7 | 15.2 | 132 | 72 | 84 | 17.8 | 20 10 | 19 56 | 2 58 | 10 27 | 10 40 |
| 14 | 3 08 | +15.6 | 55.1 | 15.0 | 144 | 75 | 76 | 18.8 | 20 45 | 20 29 | 3 46 | 11 29 | 11 45 |
| 15 | 3 58 | +17.5 | 54.7 | 14.9 | 156 | 79 | 68 | 19.8 | 21 25 | 21 07 | 4 33 | 12 27 | 12 45 |
| 16 | 4 48 | +18.6 | 54.4 | 14.8 | 168 | 84 | 58 | 20.8 | 22 10 | 21 51 | 5 21 | 13 19 | 13 38 |
| 17 | 5 39 | +18.9 | 54.2 | 14.8 | 181 | 88 | 49 | 21.8 | 23 01 | 22 43 | 6 09 | 14 06 | 14 24 |
| 18 | 6 29 | +18.4 | 54.3 | 14.8 | 193 | 92 | 40 | 22.8 | 23 57 | 23 41 | 6 56 | 14 46 | 15 03 |
| 19 | 7 18 | +17.0 | 54.5 | 14.9 | 205 | 95 | 31 | 23.8 | — | — | 7 43 | 15 21 | 15 36 |
| 20 | 8 08 | +14.9 | 54.9 | 14.9 | 217 | 99 | 22 | 24.8 | 0 57 | 0 44 | 8 30 | 15 52 | 16 04 |
| 21 | 8 57 | +12.1 | 55.4 | 15.1 | 229 | 101 | 14 | 25.8 | 2 02 | 1 51 | 9 16 | 16 20 | 16 28 |
| 22 | 9 46 | + 8.6 | 55.9 | 15.2 | 242 | 102 | 8 | 26.8 | 3 09 | 3 01 | 10 03 | 16 46 | 16 51 |
| 23 | 10 35 | + 4.7 | 56.6 | 15.4 | 254 | 102 | 3 | 27.8 | 4 18 | 4 15 | 10 50 | 17 10 | 17 12 |
| 24 | 11 25 | + 0.5 | 57.2 | 15.6 | 266 | 94 | 1 | 28.8 | 5 29 | 5 30 | 11 38 | 17 35 | 17 33 |
| 25 | 12 16 | − 3.8 | 57.8 | 15.8 | 278 | 321 | 0 | 0.3 | 6 43 | 6 47 | 12 28 | 18 02 | 17 56 |
| 26 | 13 08 | − 8.0 | 58.4 | 15.9 | 291 | 295 | 2 | 1.3 | 7 57 | 8 06 | 13 19 | 18 31 | 18 21 |
| 27 | 14 03 | −11.9 | 58.8 | 16.0 | 303 | 289 | 6 | 2.3 | 9 12 | 9 25 | 14 12 | 19 05 | 18 51 |
| 28 | 14 59 | −15.1 | 59.1 | 16.1 | 315 | 284 | 13 | 3.3 | 10 26 | 10 42 | 15 08 | 19 45 | 19 28 |
| 29 | 15 57 | −17.4 | 59.3 | 16.1 | 327 | 280 | 22 | 4.3 | 11 36 | 11 54 | 16 06 | 20 33 | 20 15 |
| 30 | 16 57 | −18.7 | 59.3 | 16.2 | 339 | 275 | 32 | 5.3 | 12 38 | 12 57 | 17 04 | 21 30 | 21 11 |

## MERCURY

| Day | RA | Dec. | Diam. | Phase | Transit | 5° high 52° | 5° high 56° |
|---|---|---|---|---|---|---|---|
| | h m | ° | ″ | % | h m | h m | h m |
| 1 | 12 12 | − 2.7 | 6 | 67 | 13 33 | 18 44 | 18 38 |
| 3 | 12 20 | − 3.9 | 6 | 65 | 13 34 | 18 38 | 18 31 |
| 5 | 12 28 | − 5.1 | 7 | 62 | 13 34 | 18 32 | 18 24 |
| 7 | 12 36 | − 6.3 | 7 | 59 | 13 33 | 18 25 | 18 16 |
| 9 | 12 43 | − 7.3 | 7 | 56 | 13 32 | 18 18 | 18 08 |
| 11 | 12 49 | − 8.3 | 7 | 53 | 13 31 | 18 11 | 18 00 |
| 13 | 12 55 | − 9.2 | 8 | 49 | 13 28 | 18 04 | 17 52 |
| 15 | 13 00 | − 9.9 | 8 | 45 | 13 25 | 17 57 | 17 44 |
| 17 | 13 04 | −10.6 | 8 | 41 | 13 21 | 17 49 | 17 36 |
| 19 | 13 07 | −11.1 | 8 | 36 | 13 15 | 17 41 | 17 27 |
| 21 | 13 08 | −11.4 | 9 | 31 | 13 09 | 17 33 | 17 19 |
| 23 | 13 09 | −11.5 | 9 | 26 | 13 01 | 17 25 | 17 11 |
| 25 | 13 07 | −11.3 | 9 | 20 | 12 51 | 17 16 | 17 02 |
| 27 | 13 04 | −10.9 | 10 | 15 | 12 40 | 17 08 | 16 55 |
| 29 | 12 59 | −10.2 | 10 | 10 | 12 27 | 16 59 | 16 47 |
| 31 | 12 53 | − 9.2 | 10 | 5 | 12 13 | 16 51 | 16 40 |

## VENUS

| Day | RA | Dec. | Diam. | Phase | Transit | 5° high 52° | 5° high 56° |
|---|---|---|---|---|---|---|---|
| | h m | ° | ″ | % | h m | h m | h m |
| 1 | 10 52 | + 8.7 | 10 | 100 | 12 14 | 18 25 | 18 28 |
| 6 | 11 16 | + 6.3 | 10 | 100 | 12 17 | 18 15 | 18 17 |
| 11 | 11 38 | + 3.8 | 10 | 100 | 12 21 | 18 06 | 18 05 |
| 16 | 12 01 | + 1.3 | 10 | 99 | 12 24 | 17 56 | 17 53 |
| 21 | 12 24 | − 1.2 | 10 | 99 | 12 27 | 17 46 | 17 41 |
| 26 | 12 47 | − 3.8 | 10 | 99 | 12 30 | 17 35 | 17 29 |
| 31 | 13 09 | − 6.3 | 10 | 98 | 12 33 | 17 25 | 17 16 |

## MARS

| Day | RA | Dec. | Diam. | Phase | Transit | 5° high 52° | 5° high 56° |
|---|---|---|---|---|---|---|---|
| 1 | 13 36 | −10.1 | 5 | 94 | 14 56 | 19 27 | 19 14 |
| 6 | 13 48 | −11.4 | 5 | 94 | 14 49 | 19 13 | 18 58 |
| 11 | 14 01 | −12.6 | 5 | 94 | 14 42 | 18 58 | 18 43 |
| 16 | 14 14 | −13.7 | 4 | 95 | 14 35 | 18 44 | 18 27 |
| 21 | 14 27 | −14.9 | 4 | 95 | 14 28 | 18 30 | 18 12 |
| 26 | 14 40 | −16.0 | 4 | 95 | 14 22 | 18 17 | 17 57 |
| 31 | 14 54 | −17.1 | 4 | 95 | 14 16 | 18 04 | 17 42 |

## SUNRISE AND SUNSET

| | London | | Bristol | | Birmingham | | Manchester | | Newcastle | | Glasgow | | Belfast | |
|---|---|---|---|---|---|---|---|---|---|---|---|---|---|---|
| | 0°05′ | 51°30′ | 2°35′ | 51°28′ | 1°55′ | 52°28′ | 2°15′ | 53°28′ | 1°37′ | 54°59′ | 4°14′ | 55°52′ | 5°56′ | 54°35′ |
| | h m | h m | h m | h m | h m | h m | h m | h m | h m | h m | h m | h m | h m | h m |
| 1 | 5 12 | 18 48 | 5 22 | 18 58 | 5 18 | 18 57 | 5 17 | 19 00 | 5 12 | 19 00 | 5 20 | 19 12 | 5 30 | 19 17 |
| 2 | 5 14 | 18 46 | 5 24 | 18 56 | 5 19 | 18 55 | 5 19 | 18 58 | 5 14 | 18 58 | 5 22 | 19 10 | 5 32 | 19 14 |
| 3 | 5 15 | 18 43 | 5 25 | 18 53 | 5 21 | 18 52 | 5 21 | 18 55 | 5 15 | 18 55 | 5 24 | 19 07 | 5 33 | 19 12 |
| 4 | 5 17 | 18 41 | 5 27 | 18 51 | 5 23 | 18 50 | 5 22 | 18 53 | 5 17 | 18 53 | 5 26 | 19 05 | 5 35 | 19 09 |
| 5 | 5 18 | 18 39 | 5 28 | 18 49 | 5 24 | 18 48 | 5 24 | 18 50 | 5 19 | 18 50 | 5 28 | 19 02 | 5 37 | 19 07 |
| 6 | 5 20 | 18 37 | 5 30 | 18 47 | 5 26 | 18 45 | 5 26 | 18 48 | 5 21 | 18 48 | 5 30 | 19 00 | 5 39 | 19 04 |
| 7 | 5 21 | 18 34 | 5 32 | 18 44 | 5 28 | 18 43 | 5 28 | 18 46 | 5 23 | 18 45 | 5 32 | 18 57 | 5 41 | 19 02 |
| 8 | 5 23 | 18 32 | 5 33 | 18 42 | 5 29 | 18 41 | 5 29 | 18 43 | 5 25 | 18 43 | 5 34 | 18 54 | 5 43 | 18 59 |
| 9 | 5 25 | 18 30 | 5 35 | 18 40 | 5 31 | 18 38 | 5 31 | 18 41 | 5 27 | 18 40 | 5 36 | 18 52 | 5 44 | 18 57 |
| 10 | 5 26 | 18 28 | 5 36 | 18 37 | 5 33 | 18 36 | 5 33 | 18 38 | 5 28 | 18 38 | 5 38 | 18 49 | 5 46 | 18 54 |
| 11 | 5 28 | 18 25 | 5 38 | 18 35 | 5 34 | 18 34 | 5 35 | 18 36 | 5 30 | 18 35 | 5 40 | 18 46 | 5 48 | 18 52 |
| 12 | 5 29 | 18 23 | 5 39 | 18 33 | 5 36 | 18 31 | 5 36 | 18 33 | 5 32 | 18 32 | 5 42 | 18 44 | 5 50 | 18 49 |
| 13 | 5 31 | 18 21 | 5 41 | 18 31 | 5 38 | 18 29 | 5 38 | 18 31 | 5 34 | 18 30 | 5 44 | 18 41 | 5 52 | 18 47 |
| 14 | 5 33 | 18 18 | 5 43 | 18 28 | 5 39 | 18 26 | 5 40 | 18 29 | 5 36 | 18 27 | 5 46 | 18 39 | 5 54 | 18 44 |
| 15 | 5 34 | 18 16 | 5 44 | 18 26 | 5 41 | 18 24 | 5 41 | 18 26 | 5 38 | 18 25 | 5 47 | 18 36 | 5 55 | 18 42 |
| 16 | 5 36 | 18 14 | 5 46 | 18 24 | 5 43 | 18 22 | 5 43 | 18 24 | 5 40 | 18 22 | 5 49 | 18 33 | 5 57 | 18 39 |
| 17 | 5 37 | 18 11 | 5 47 | 18 21 | 5 44 | 18 19 | 5 45 | 18 21 | 5 41 | 18 20 | 5 51 | 18 31 | 5 59 | 18 37 |
| 18 | 5 39 | 18 09 | 5 49 | 18 19 | 5 46 | 18 17 | 5 47 | 18 19 | 5 43 | 18 17 | 5 53 | 18 28 | 6 01 | 18 34 |
| 19 | 5 41 | 18 07 | 5 51 | 18 17 | 5 48 | 18 15 | 5 48 | 18 16 | 5 45 | 18 14 | 5 55 | 18 25 | 6 03 | 18 31 |
| 20 | 5 42 | 18 05 | 5 52 | 18 15 | 5 49 | 18 12 | 5 50 | 18 14 | 5 47 | 18 12 | 5 57 | 18 23 | 6 04 | 18 29 |
| 21 | 5 44 | 18 02 | 5 54 | 18 12 | 5 51 | 18 10 | 5 52 | 18 11 | 5 49 | 18 09 | 5 59 | 18 20 | 6 06 | 18 26 |
| 22 | 5 45 | 18 00 | 5 55 | 18 10 | 5 53 | 18 07 | 5 54 | 18 09 | 5 51 | 18 07 | 6 01 | 18 17 | 6 08 | 18 24 |
| 23 | 5 47 | 17 58 | 5 57 | 18 08 | 5 54 | 18 05 | 5 55 | 18 06 | 5 53 | 18 04 | 6 03 | 18 15 | 6 10 | 18 21 |
| 24 | 5 49 | 17 55 | 5 59 | 18 05 | 5 56 | 18 03 | 5 57 | 18 04 | 5 55 | 18 02 | 6 05 | 18 12 | 6 12 | 18 19 |
| 25 | 5 50 | 17 53 | 6 00 | 18 03 | 5 58 | 18 00 | 5 59 | 18 02 | 5 56 | 17 59 | 6 07 | 18 09 | 6 14 | 18 16 |
| 26 | 5 52 | 17 51 | 6 02 | 18 01 | 5 59 | 17 58 | 6 01 | 17 59 | 5 58 | 17 56 | 6 09 | 18 07 | 6 16 | 18 14 |
| 27 | 5 54 | 17 48 | 6 04 | 17 58 | 6 01 | 17 56 | 6 02 | 17 57 | 6 00 | 17 54 | 6 11 | 18 04 | 6 17 | 18 11 |
| 28 | 5 55 | 17 46 | 6 05 | 17 56 | 6 03 | 17 53 | 6 04 | 17 54 | 6 02 | 17 51 | 6 13 | 18 02 | 6 19 | 18 09 |
| 29 | 5 57 | 17 44 | 6 07 | 17 54 | 6 04 | 17 51 | 6 06 | 17 52 | 6 04 | 17 49 | 6 15 | 17 59 | 6 21 | 18 06 |
| 30 | 5 58 | 17 42 | 6 08 | 17 52 | 6 06 | 17 49 | 6 08 | 17 49 | 6 06 | 17 46 | 6 17 | 17 56 | 6 23 | 18 04 |

## JUPITER

| Day | RA | Dec. | Transit | 5° high | |
|---|---|---|---|---|---|
| | | | | 52° | 56° |
| | h m | ° ′ | h m | h m | h m |
| 1 | 16 20.3 | −20 57 | 17 39 | 20 59 | 20 29 |
| 11 | 16 24.4 | −21 08 | 17 04 | 20 22 | 19 52 |
| 21 | 16 29.6 | −21 21 | 16 30 | 19 46 | 19 16 |
| 31 | 16 35.7 | −21 36 | 15 56 | 19 11 | 18 40 |

Diameters – equatorial 36″ polar 34″

## SATURN

| Day | RA | Dec. | Transit | 5° high | |
|---|---|---|---|---|---|
| | | | | 52° | 56° |
| | h m | ° ′ | h m | h m | h m |
| 1 | 23 35.7 | − 5 10 | 0 57 | 5 56 | 5 48 |
| 11 | 23 32.9 | − 5 29 | 0 15 | 5 12 | 5 04 |
| 21 | 23 30.1 | − 5 47 | 23 28 | 4 29 | 4 20 |
| 31 | 23 27.3 | − 6 05 | 22 46 | 3 45 | 3 36 |

Diameters – equatorial 19″ polar 17″
Rings – major axis 44″ minor axis 1″

## URANUS

| Day | RA | Dec. | Transit | 10° high | |
|---|---|---|---|---|---|
| | | | | 52° | 56° |
| | h m | ° ′ | h m | h m | h m |
| 1 | 19 56.8 | −21 19 | 21 14 | 23 41 | 22 51 |
| 11 | 19 55.8 | −21 21 | 20 34 | 23 00 | 22 10 |
| 21 | 19 55.1 | −21 23 | 19 54 | 22 20 | 21 30 |
| 31 | 19 54.7 | −21 24 | 19 15 | 21 40 | 20 50 |

Diameter 4″

## NEPTUNE

| Day | RA | Dec. | Transit | 10° high | |
|---|---|---|---|---|---|
| | | | | 52° | 56° |
| | h m | ° ′ | h m | h m | h m |
| 1 | 19 39.3 | −20 56 | 20 57 | 23 27 | 22 40 |
| 11 | 19 38.6 | −20 58 | 20 17 | 22 47 | 22 00 |
| 21 | 19 38.2 | −20 59 | 19 37 | 22 07 | 21 20 |
| 31 | 19 38.0 | −21 00 | 18 58 | 21 27 | 20 40 |

Diameter 2″

 # October 1995

TENTH MONTH, 31 DAYS. *Octo* (eight), eighth month of Roman pre-Julian calendar

| | | | |
|---|---|---|---|
| 1 | *Sunday* | **17th S. after Pentecost/16th S. after Trinity** | *week* 40 *day* 274 |
| 2 | *Monday* | *Michaelmas Law Sittings begin.* Gen. von Hindenberg b. 1847 | 275 |
| 3 | *Tuesday* | Francis of Assisi d. 1226. Germany reunified 1990 | 276 |
| 4 | *Wednesday* | YOM KIPPUR. Rembrandt d. 1669 | 277 |
| 5 | *Thursday* | Oxfam founded 1942. Tea rationing ended 1952 | 278 |
| 6 | *Friday* | Le Corbusier b. 1887. Thor Heyerdahl b. 1914 | 279 |
| 7 | *Saturday* | Sir Hubert Parry d. 1918. Mario Lanza d. 1959 | 280 |
| 8 | *Sunday* | **18th S. after Pentecost/17th S. after Trinity** | *week* 41 *day* 281 |
| 9 | *Monday* | FEAST OF TABERNACLES begins. Alfred Dreyfus b. 1859 | 282 |
| 10 | *Tuesday* | Henry Cavendish b. 1731. Orson Welles d. 1985 | 283 |
| 11 | *Wednesday* | Huldreich Zwingli killed 1531 | 284 |
| 12 | *Thursday* | Ramsay MacDonald b. 1866. Edith Cavell exec. 1915 | 285 |
| 13 | *Friday* | Sir Henry Irving d. 1905. Sidney Webb d. 1947 | 286 |
| 14 | *Saturday* | Gen. Dwight Eisenhower b. 1890. Rommel d. 1944 | 287 |
| 15 | *Sunday* | **19th S. after Pentecost/18th S. after Trinity** | *week* 42 *day* 288 |
| 16 | *Monday* | Houses of Parliament destroyed by fire 1834 | 289 |
| 17 | *Tuesday* | Airborne invasion of Arnhem 1944 | 290 |
| 18 | *Wednesday* | **St Luke.** Beau Nash b. 1674. Manny Shinwell b. 1884 | 291 |
| 19 | *Thursday* | Proclamation of People's Republic of China 1949 | 292 |
| 20 | *Friday* | Dame Anna Neagle b. 1904. Bud Flanagan d. 1968 | 293 |
| 21 | *Saturday* | DIWALI (Hindu) begins. Lord Nelson d. 1805 | 294 |
| 22 | *Sunday* | **20th S. after Pentecost/19th S. after Trinity** | *week* 43 *day* 295 |
| 23 | *Monday* | Battle of El Alamein began 1942 | 296 |
| 24 | *Tuesday* | Peace of Westphalia 1648. Tito Gobbi b. 1915 | 297 |
| 25 | *Wednesday* | Geoffrey Chaucer d. 1400. George II d. 1760 | 298 |
| 26 | *Thursday* | Founding of the Royal Marines 1664 | 299 |
| 27 | *Friday* | Oliver Tambo b. 1917. Charles Hawtrey d. 1988 | 300 |
| 28 | *Saturday* | **SS Simon and Jude.** Capt. James Cook b. 1728 | 301 |
| 29 | *Sunday* | **9th S. before Christmas/20th S. after Trinity** | *week* 44 *day* 302 |
| 30 | *Monday* | Angelica Kauffmann b. 1741. Sir Barnes Wallace d. 1979 | 303 |
| 31 | *Tuesday* | Hallowmass Eve. Indira Ghandi assass. 1984 | 304 |

ASTRONOMICAL PHENOMENA

| d | h | |
|---|---|---|
| 5 | 01 | Mercury in inferior conjunction |
| 5 | 04 | Neptune at stationary point |
| 6 | 13 | Uranus at stationary point |
| 6 | 18 | Saturn in conjunction with Moon. Saturn 5°S. |
| 14 | 01 | Mercury at stationary point |
| 20 | 14 | Mercury at greatest elongation W. 18° |
| 22 | 20 | Mercury in conjunction with Moon. Mercury 3° N. |
| 23 | 22 | Sun's longitude 210° ♏ |
| 24 | 05 | Total eclipse of Sun (*see* page 66) |
| 25 | 12 | Venus in conjunction with Moon. Venus 2° S. |
| 26 | 13 | Mars in conjunction with Moon. Mars 4° S. |
| 27 | 07 | Jupiter in conjunction with Moon. Jupiter 4° S. |

CONSTELLATIONS

The following constellations are near the meridian at

| | d | h | | d | h |
|---|---|---|---|---|---|
| September | 1 | 24 | October | 16 | 21 |
| September | 15 | 23 | November | 1ᵈ | 20 |
| October | 1 | 22 | November | 15 | 19 |

Ursa Major (below the Pole), Cepheus, Cassiopeia, Cygnus, Lacerta, Andromeda, Pegasus, Capricornus, Aquarius and Piscis Austrinus

MINIMA OF ALGOL

| d | h | d | h | d | h |
|---|---|---|---|---|---|
| 3 | 14.5 | 15 | 01.7 | 23 | 16.1 |
| 6 | 11.3 | 17 | 22.5 | 26 | 13.0 |
| 9 | 08.1 | 20 | 19.3 | 29 | 09.8 |
| 12 | 04.9 | | | | |

THE MOON

| Phases, Apsides and Node | d | h | m |
|---|---|---|---|
| ☽ First Quarter | 1 | 14 | 36 |
| ○ Full Moon | 8 | 15 | 52 |
| ☾ Last Quarter | 16 | 16 | 26 |
| ● New Moon | 24 | 04 | 36 |
| ○ First Quarter | 30 | 21 | 17 |
| Apogee (404,564 km) | 15 | 02 | 02 |
| Perigee (364,812 km) | 26 | 20 | 53 |

Mean longitude of ascending node on October 1, 207°

THE SUN                                                              s.d. 16′.1

| Day | Right Ascension | Dec. − | Equation of time | Rise 52° | Rise 56° | Transit | Set 52° | Set 56° | Sidereal time | Transit of First Point of Aries |
|---|---|---|---|---|---|---|---|---|---|---|
| | h  m  s | °  ′ | m  s | h  m | h  m | h  m | h  m | h  m | h  m  s | h  m  s |
| 1 | 12 26 59 | 2 55 | +10 03 | 6 00 | 6 02 | 11 50 | 17 39 | 17 37 | 0 37 02 | 23 19 08 |
| 2 | 12 30 37 | 3 18 | +10 22 | 6 02 | 6 04 | 11 49 | 17 36 | 17 34 | 0 40 59 | 23 15 12 |
| 3 | 12 34 14 | 3 41 | +10 41 | 6 03 | 6 06 | 11 49 | 17 34 | 17 31 | 0 44 55 | 23 11 16 |
| 4 | 12 37 52 | 4 05 | +11 00 | 6 05 | 6 08 | 11 49 | 17 32 | 17 29 | 0 48 52 | 23 07 20 |
| 5 | 12 41 30 | 4 28 | +11 19 | 6 07 | 6 10 | 11 49 | 17 30 | 17 26 | 0 52 48 | 23 03 24 |
| 6 | 12 45 08 | 4 51 | +11 37 | 6 08 | 6 12 | 11 48 | 17 27 | 17 24 | 0 56 45 | 22 59 28 |
| 7 | 12 48 47 | 5 14 | +11 55 | 6 10 | 6 14 | 11 48 | 17 25 | 17 21 | 1 00 42 | 22 55 33 |
| 8 | 12 52 26 | 5 37 | +12 12 | 6 12 | 6 16 | 11 48 | 17 23 | 17 18 | 1 04 38 | 22 51 37 |
| 9 | 12 56 05 | 6 00 | +12 29 | 6 13 | 6 18 | 11 47 | 17 20 | 17 16 | 1 08 35 | 22 47 41 |
| 10 | 12 59 45 | 6 23 | +12 46 | 6 15 | 6 20 | 11 47 | 17 18 | 17 13 | 1 12 31 | 22 43 45 |
| 11 | 13 03 26 | 6 45 | +13 02 | 6 17 | 6 22 | 11 47 | 17 16 | 17 11 | 1 16 28 | 22 39 49 |
| 12 | 13 07 07 | 7 08 | +13 18 | 6 19 | 6 24 | 11 47 | 17 14 | 17 08 | 1 20 24 | 22 35 53 |
| 13 | 13 10 48 | 7 31 | +13 33 | 6 20 | 6 26 | 11 46 | 17 12 | 17 06 | 1 24 21 | 22 31 57 |
| 14 | 13 14 30 | 7 53 | +13 47 | 6 22 | 6 28 | 11 46 | 17 09 | 17 03 | 1 28 17 | 22 28 01 |
| 15 | 13 18 12 | 8 15 | +14 01 | 6 24 | 6 30 | 11 46 | 17 07 | 17 01 | 1 32 14 | 22 24 05 |
| 16 | 13 21 56 | 8 38 | +14 15 | 6 25 | 6 32 | 11 46 | 17 05 | 16 58 | 1 36 10 | 22 20 09 |
| 17 | 13 25 39 | 9 00 | +14 28 | 6 27 | 6 34 | 11 45 | 17 03 | 16 56 | 1 40 07 | 22 16 13 |
| 18 | 13 29 23 | 9 22 | +14 40 | 6 29 | 6 36 | 11 45 | 17 01 | 16 53 | 1 44 04 | 22 12 18 |
| 19 | 13 33 08 | 9 43 | +14 52 | 6 31 | 6 38 | 11 45 | 16 59 | 16 51 | 1 48 00 | 22 08 22 |
| 20 | 13 36 54 | 10 05 | +15 03 | 6 32 | 6 40 | 11 45 | 16 56 | 16 48 | 1 51 57 | 22 04 26 |
| 21 | 13 40 40 | 10 27 | +15 14 | 6 34 | 6 43 | 11 45 | 16 54 | 16 46 | 1 55 53 | 22 00 30 |
| 22 | 13 44 26 | 10 48 | +15 23 | 6 36 | 6 45 | 11 45 | 16 52 | 16 44 | 1 59 50 | 21 56 34 |
| 23 | 13 48 14 | 11 09 | +15 32 | 6 38 | 6 47 | 11 44 | 16 50 | 16 41 | 2 03 46 | 21 52 38 |
| 24 | 13 52 02 | 11 30 | +15 41 | 6 40 | 6 49 | 11 44 | 16 48 | 16 39 | 2 07 43 | 21 48 42 |
| 25 | 13 55 51 | 11 51 | +15 49 | 6 41 | 6 51 | 11 44 | 16 46 | 16 36 | 2 11 39 | 21 44 46 |
| 26 | 13 59 40 | 12 12 | +15 56 | 6 43 | 6 53 | 11 44 | 16 44 | 16 34 | 2 15 36 | 21 40 50 |
| 27 | 14 03 31 | 12 33 | +16 02 | 6 45 | 6 55 | 11 44 | 16 42 | 16 32 | 2 19 33 | 21 36 54 |
| 28 | 14 07 22 | 12 53 | +16 08 | 6 47 | 6 57 | 11 44 | 16 40 | 16 29 | 2 23 29 | 21 32 58 |
| 29 | 14 11 13 | 13 13 | +16 12 | 6 48 | 6 59 | 11 44 | 16 38 | 16 27 | 2 27 26 | 21 29 03 |
| 30 | 14 15 06 | 13 33 | +16 17 | 6 50 | 7 02 | 11 44 | 16 36 | 16 25 | 2 31 22 | 21 25 07 |
| 31 | 14 18 59 | 13 53 | +16 20 | 6 52 | 7 04 | 11 44 | 16 34 | 16 23 | 2 35 19 | 21 21 11 |

DURATION OF TWILIGHT (in minutes)

| Latitude | 52° | 56° | 52° | 56° | 52° | 56° | 52° | 56° |
|---|---|---|---|---|---|---|---|---|
| | 1 October | | 11 October | | 21 October | | 31 October | |
| Civil | 34 | 37 | 34 | 37 | 34 | 38 | 36 | 40 |
| Nautical | 73 | 80 | 73 | 80 | 74 | 81 | 75 | 83 |
| Astronomical | 113 | 125 | 112 | 124 | 113 | 124 | 114 | 126 |

THE NIGHT SKY

*Mercury* passes through inferior conjunction on the 5th and is too close to the Sun for observation for the first ten days of the month. Thereafter it is visible as a morning object, low in the east-south-east sky, around the beginning of morning civil twilight. During this time its magnitude brightens from +2.0 to −0.9. On the morning of the 22nd the thin crescent Moon, only two days before New, will be seen about 8° to the right of Mercury. This morning apparition is the most suitable one of the year for observers in the British Isles.

*Venus* is unsuitably placed for observation.

*Mars* is too close to the Sun for observation.

*Jupiter* continues to be visible as a brilliant evening object, magnitude −1.9. It is visible low in the south-west sky during the early part of the evening but by the end of the month it will only be visible for about an hour after sunset.

*Saturn* is an evening object, magnitude +0.8, visible in the southern skies. Saturn is in the constellation of Aquarius.

*Eclipse.* A total eclipse of the Sun occurs on the 24th. (See page 66 for details.)

## THE MOON

| Day | RA | Dec. | Hor. par. | Semi-diam. | Sun's co-long. | PA of Bright Limb | Phase | Age | Rise 52° | Rise 56° | Transit | Set 52° | Set 56° |
|---|---|---|---|---|---|---|---|---|---|---|---|---|---|
|  | h m | ° | ' | ' | ° | ° | % | d | h m | h m | h m | h m | h m |
| 1 | 17 57 | −18.8 | 59.3 | 16.2 | 352 | 270 | 43 | 6.3 | 13 33 | 13 51 | 18 02 | 22 34 | 22 17 |
| 2 | 18 56 | −17.7 | 59.2 | 16.1 | 4 | 265 | 55 | 7.3 | 14 18 | 14 34 | 18 58 | 23 45 | 23 30 |
| 3 | 19 55 | −15.5 | 59.0 | 16.1 | 16 | 261 | 66 | 8.3 | 14 56 | 15 08 | 19 53 | — | — |
| 4 | 20 51 | −12.4 | 58.7 | 16.0 | 28 | 257 | 76 | 9.3 | 15 28 | 15 37 | 20 46 | 0 59 | 0 47 |
| 5 | 21 45 | − 8.6 | 58.4 | 15.9 | 40 | 255 | 85 | 10.3 | 15 56 | 16 01 | 21 36 | 2 13 | 2 06 |
| 6 | 22 38 | − 4.5 | 58.0 | 15.8 | 53 | 254 | 92 | 11.3 | 16 22 | 16 24 | 22 26 | 3 28 | 3 24 |
| 7 | 23 29 | − 0.1 | 57.6 | 15.7 | 65 | 255 | 97 | 12.3 | 16 47 | 16 45 | 23 14 | 4 41 | 4 41 |
| 8 | 0 20 | + 4.2 | 57.0 | 15.5 | 77 | 259 | 99 | 13.3 | 17 13 | 17 07 | — | 5 52 | 5 57 |
| 9 | 1 10 | + 8.2 | 56.5 | 15.4 | 89 | 58 | 100 | 14.3 | 17 40 | 17 30 | 0 02 | 7 02 | 7 11 |
| 10 | 2 00 | +11.7 | 55.9 | 15.2 | 101 | 72 | 98 | 15.3 | 18 09 | 17 57 | 0 49 | 8 10 | 8 22 |
| 11 | 2 50 | +14.6 | 55.4 | 15.1 | 113 | 76 | 94 | 16.3 | 18 42 | 18 27 | 1 37 | 9 15 | 9 29 |
| 12 | 3 41 | +16.8 | 54.9 | 15.0 | 125 | 80 | 89 | 17.3 | 19 20 | 19 03 | 2 25 | 10 15 | 10 32 |
| 13 | 4 31 | +18.3 | 54.5 | 14.9 | 138 | 84 | 82 | 18.3 | 20 03 | 19 45 | 3 13 | 11 10 | 11 28 |
| 14 | 5 22 | +18.8 | 54.3 | 14.8 | 150 | 89 | 74 | 19.3 | 20 52 | 20 34 | 4 01 | 11 59 | 12 18 |
| 15 | 6 12 | +18.6 | 54.2 | 14.8 | 162 | 93 | 66 | 20.3 | 21 46 | 21 29 | 4 49 | 12 42 | 12 59 |
| 16 | 7 01 | +17.5 | 54.3 | 14.8 | 174 | 97 | 57 | 21.3 | 22 44 | 22 29 | 5 36 | 13 19 | 13 34 |
| 17 | 7 50 | +15.6 | 54.5 | 14.9 | 186 | 100 | 47 | 22.3 | 23 46 | 23 34 | 6 22 | 13 51 | 14 04 |
| 18 | 8 39 | +13.1 | 54.9 | 15.0 | 199 | 103 | 38 | 23.3 | — | — | 7 08 | 14 20 | 14 29 |
| 19 | 9 27 | + 9.9 | 55.5 | 15.1 | 211 | 106 | 28 | 24.3 | 0 50 | 0 42 | 7 54 | 14 46 | 14 52 |
| 20 | 10 16 | + 6.2 | 56.2 | 15.3 | 223 | 108 | 20 | 25.3 | 1 58 | 1 53 | 8 40 | 15 11 | 15 14 |
| 21 | 11 05 | + 2.2 | 57.0 | 15.5 | 235 | 109 | 12 | 26.3 | 3 08 | 3 06 | 9 27 | 15 35 | 15 35 |
| 22 | 11 56 | − 2.1 | 57.8 | 15.7 | 247 | 109 | 6 | 27.3 | 4 20 | 4 23 | 10 16 | 16 01 | 15 57 |
| 23 | 12 48 | − 6.4 | 58.6 | 16.0 | 260 | 109 | 2 | 28.3 | 5 35 | 5 42 | 11 07 | 16 29 | 16 21 |
| 24 | 13 42 | −10.5 | 59.2 | 16.1 | 272 | 113 | 0 | 29.3 | 6 52 | 7 02 | 12 01 | 17 02 | 16 50 |
| 25 | 14 40 | −14.1 | 59.7 | 16.3 | 284 | 280 | 1 | 0.8 | 8 08 | 8 23 | 12 58 | 17 40 | 17 25 |
| 26 | 15 39 | −16.8 | 60.0 | 16.4 | 296 | 277 | 4 | 1.8 | 9 22 | 9 40 | 13 56 | 18 27 | 18 09 |
| 27 | 16 40 | −18.4 | 60.1 | 16.4 | 308 | 273 | 11 | 2.8 | 10 30 | 10 49 | 14 56 | 19 22 | 19 03 |
| 28 | 17 41 | −18.8 | 60.0 | 16.3 | 321 | 268 | 19 | 3.8 | 11 29 | 11 47 | 15 56 | 20 26 | 20 08 |
| 29 | 18 42 | −18.0 | 59.7 | 16.3 | 333 | 263 | 29 | 4.8 | 12 17 | 12 34 | 16 54 | 21 36 | 21 20 |
| 30 | 19 42 | −16.0 | 59.3 | 16.2 | 345 | 259 | 40 | 5.8 | 12 58 | 13 11 | 17 50 | 22 49 | 22 37 |
| 31 | 20 38 | −13.1 | 58.8 | 16.0 | 357 | 255 | 51 | 6.8 | 13 31 | 13 41 | 18 43 | — | 23 55 |

## MERCURY

| Day | RA | Dec. | Diam. | Phase | Transit | 5° high 52° | 5° high 56° |
|---|---|---|---|---|---|---|---|
|  | h m | ° | " | % | h m | h m | h m |
| 1 | 12 53 | − 9.2 | 10 | 5 | 12 13 | 16 51 | 16 40 |
| 3 | 12 46 | − 8.0 | 10 | 2 | 11 57 | 7 13 | 7 23 |
| 5 | 12 38 | − 6.5 | 10 | 0 | 11 42 | 6 50 | 6 58 |
| 7 | 12 31 | − 5.1 | 10 | 1 | 11 27 | 6 27 | 6 34 |
| 9 | 12 25 | − 3.7 | 10 | 5 | 11 14 | 6 06 | 6 12 |
| 11 | 12 21 | − 2.5 | 9 | 11 | 11 02 | 5 48 | 5 54 |
| 13 | 12 19 | − 1.7 | 9 | 19 | 10 53 | 5 35 | 5 40 |
| 15 | 12 20 | − 1.2 | 8 | 28 | 10 47 | 5 26 | 5 30 |
| 17 | 12 23 | − 1.1 | 8 | 38 | 10 43 | 5 21 | 5 25 |
| 19 | 12 29 | − 1.3 | 7 | 48 | 10 41 | 5 20 | 5 25 |
| 21 | 12 36 | − 1.8 | 7 | 57 | 10 40 | 5 23 | 5 28 |
| 23 | 12 45 | − 2.6 | 6 | 65 | 10 41 | 5 28 | 5 33 |
| 25 | 12 54 | − 3.6 | 6 | 72 | 10 43 | 5 35 | 5 41 |
| 27 | 13 05 | − 4.7 | 6 | 78 | 10 46 | 5 44 | 5 51 |
| 29 | 13 16 | − 5.9 | 6 | 83 | 10 50 | 5 54 | 6 02 |
| 31 | 13 28 | − 7.1 | 5 | 87 | 10 53 | 6 04 | 6 14 |

## VENUS

| Day | RA | Dec. | Diam. | Phase | Transit | 5° high 52° | 5° high 56° |
|---|---|---|---|---|---|---|---|
|  | h m | ° | " | % | h m | h m | h m |
| 1 | 13 09 | − 6.3 | 10 | 98 | 12 33 | 17 25 | 17 16 |
| 6 | 13 32 | − 8.8 | 10 | 98 | 12 36 | 17 15 | 17 03 |
| 11 | 13 56 | −11.1 | 10 | 97 | 12 40 | 17 05 | 16 50 |
| 16 | 14 20 | −13.4 | 10 | 97 | 12 44 | 16 55 | 16 38 |
| 21 | 14 44 | −15.6 | 10 | 96 | 12 48 | 16 46 | 16 26 |
| 26 | 15 08 | −17.5 | 10 | 96 | 12 53 | 16 37 | 16 15 |
| 31 | 15 33 | −19.3 | 10 | 95 | 12 59 | 16 30 | 16 04 |

## MARS

| Day | RA | Dec. | Diam. | Phase | Transit | 5° high 52° | 5° high 56° |
|---|---|---|---|---|---|---|---|
| 1 | 14 54 | −17.1 | 4 | 95 | 14 16 | 18 04 | 17 42 |
| 6 | 15 08 | −18.1 | 4 | 96 | 14 10 | 17 51 | 17 27 |
| 11 | 15 22 | −19.1 | 4 | 96 | 14 05 | 17 38 | 17 13 |
| 16 | 15 36 | −20.0 | 4 | 96 | 14 00 | 17 26 | 16 59 |
| 21 | 15 51 | −20.8 | 4 | 97 | 13 55 | 17 15 | 16 46 |
| 26 | 16 06 | −21.6 | 4 | 97 | 13 50 | 17 04 | 16 33 |
| 31 | 16 21 | −22.3 | 4 | 97 | 13 46 | 16 54 | 16 21 |

## SUNRISE AND SUNSET

| | London | | Bristol | | Birmingham | | Manchester | | Newcastle | | Glasgow | | Belfast | |
|---|---|---|---|---|---|---|---|---|---|---|---|---|---|---|
| | 0°05′ | 51°30′ | 2°35′ | 51°28′ | 1°55′ | 52°28′ | 2°15′ | 53°28′ | 1°37′ | 54°59′ | 4°14′ | 55°52′ | 5°56′ | 54°35′ |
| | h m | h m | h m | h m | h m | h m | h m | h m | h m | h m | h m | h m | h m | h m |
| 1 | 6 00 | 17 39 | 6 10 | 17 49 | 6 08 | 17 46 | 6 10 | 17 47 | 6 08 | 17 44 | 6 19 | 17 54 | 6 25 | 18 01 |
| 2 | 6 02 | 17 37 | 6 12 | 17 47 | 6 09 | 17 44 | 6 11 | 17 45 | 6 10 | 17 41 | 6 21 | 17 51 | 6 27 | 17 59 |
| 3 | 6 03 | 17 35 | 6 13 | 17 45 | 6 11 | 17 41 | 6 13 | 17 42 | 6 12 | 17 39 | 6 23 | 17 48 | 6 29 | 17 56 |
| 4 | 6 05 | 17 32 | 6 15 | 17 42 | 6 13 | 17 39 | 6 15 | 17 40 | 6 13 | 17 36 | 6 25 | 17 46 | 6 30 | 17 54 |
| 5 | 6 07 | 17 30 | 6 17 | 17 40 | 6 15 | 17 37 | 6 17 | 17 37 | 6 15 | 17 34 | 6 27 | 17 43 | 6 32 | 17 51 |
| 6 | 6 08 | 17 28 | 6 18 | 17 38 | 6 16 | 17 35 | 6 18 | 17 35 | 6 17 | 17 31 | 6 29 | 17 41 | 6 34 | 17 49 |
| 7 | 6 10 | 17 26 | 6 20 | 17 36 | 6 18 | 17 32 | 6 20 | 17 33 | 6 19 | 17 29 | 6 31 | 17 38 | 6 36 | 17 46 |
| 8 | 6 12 | 17 24 | 6 22 | 17 34 | 6 20 | 17 30 | 6 22 | 17 30 | 6 21 | 17 26 | 6 33 | 17 36 | 6 38 | 17 44 |
| 9 | 6 13 | 17 21 | 6 23 | 17 31 | 6 22 | 17 28 | 6 24 | 17 28 | 6 23 | 17 24 | 6 35 | 17 33 | 6 40 | 17 41 |
| 10 | 6 15 | 17 19 | 6 25 | 17 29 | 6 23 | 17 25 | 6 26 | 17 26 | 6 25 | 17 21 | 6 37 | 17 30 | 6 42 | 17 39 |
| 11 | 6 17 | 17 17 | 6 27 | 17 27 | 6 25 | 17 23 | 6 28 | 17 23 | 6 27 | 17 19 | 6 39 | 17 28 | 6 44 | 17 36 |
| 12 | 6 18 | 17 15 | 6 28 | 17 25 | 6 27 | 17 21 | 6 29 | 17 21 | 6 29 | 17 16 | 6 41 | 17 25 | 6 46 | 17 34 |
| 13 | 6 20 | 17 13 | 6 30 | 17 23 | 6 29 | 17 19 | 6 31 | 17 19 | 6 31 | 17 14 | 6 43 | 17 23 | 6 48 | 17 32 |
| 14 | 6 22 | 17 10 | 6 32 | 17 20 | 6 30 | 17 16 | 6 33 | 17 16 | 6 33 | 17 11 | 6 45 | 17 20 | 6 50 | 17 29 |
| 15 | 6 23 | 17 08 | 6 33 | 17 18 | 6 32 | 17 14 | 6 35 | 17 14 | 6 35 | 17 09 | 6 47 | 17 18 | 6 51 | 17 27 |
| 16 | 6 25 | 17 06 | 6 35 | 17 16 | 6 34 | 17 12 | 6 37 | 17 12 | 6 37 | 17 06 | 6 49 | 17 15 | 6 53 | 17 24 |
| 17 | 6 27 | 17 04 | 6 37 | 17 14 | 6 36 | 17 10 | 6 39 | 17 09 | 6 39 | 17 04 | 6 51 | 17 13 | 6 55 | 17 22 |
| 18 | 6 28 | 17 02 | 6 38 | 17 12 | 6 37 | 17 08 | 6 40 | 17 07 | 6 41 | 17 02 | 6 53 | 17 10 | 6 57 | 17 20 |
| 19 | 6 30 | 17 00 | 6 40 | 17 10 | 6 39 | 17 05 | 6 42 | 17 05 | 6 43 | 16 59 | 6 55 | 17 08 | 6 59 | 17 17 |
| 20 | 6 32 | 16 58 | 6 42 | 17 08 | 6 41 | 17 03 | 6 44 | 17 03 | 6 45 | 16 57 | 6 57 | 17 06 | 7 01 | 17 15 |
| 21 | 6 34 | 16 56 | 6 44 | 17 06 | 6 43 | 17 01 | 6 46 | 17 00 | 6 47 | 16 55 | 6 59 | 17 03 | 7 03 | 17 13 |
| 22 | 6 35 | 16 54 | 6 45 | 17 04 | 6 45 | 16 59 | 6 48 | 16 58 | 6 49 | 16 52 | 7 01 | 17 01 | 7 05 | 17 11 |
| 23 | 6 37 | 16 52 | 6 47 | 17 02 | 6 46 | 16 57 | 6 50 | 16 56 | 6 51 | 16 50 | 7 03 | 16 58 | 7 07 | 17 08 |
| 24 | 6 39 | 16 50 | 6 49 | 17 00 | 6 48 | 16 55 | 6 52 | 16 54 | 6 53 | 16 48 | 7 05 | 16 56 | 7 09 | 17 06 |
| 25 | 6 41 | 16 48 | 6 51 | 16 58 | 6 50 | 16 53 | 6 54 | 16 52 | 6 55 | 16 46 | 7 08 | 16 54 | 7 11 | 17 04 |
| 26 | 6 42 | 16 46 | 6 52 | 16 56 | 6 52 | 16 51 | 6 56 | 16 50 | 6 57 | 16 43 | 7 10 | 16 51 | 7 13 | 17 02 |
| 27 | 6 44 | 16 44 | 6 54 | 16 54 | 6 54 | 16 49 | 6 57 | 16 48 | 6 59 | 16 41 | 7 12 | 16 49 | 7 15 | 16 59 |
| 28 | 6 46 | 16 42 | 6 56 | 16 52 | 6 55 | 16 47 | 6 59 | 16 46 | 7 01 | 16 39 | 7 14 | 16 47 | 7 17 | 16 57 |
| 29 | 6 48 | 16 40 | 6 57 | 16 50 | 6 57 | 16 45 | 7 01 | 16 43 | 7 03 | 16 37 | 7 16 | 16 45 | 7 19 | 16 55 |
| 30 | 6 49 | 16 38 | 6 59 | 16 48 | 6 59 | 16 43 | 7 03 | 16 41 | 7 05 | 16 35 | 7 18 | 16 42 | 7 21 | 16 53 |
| 31 | 6 51 | 16 36 | 7 01 | 16 46 | 7 01 | 16 41 | 7 05 | 16 39 | 7 07 | 16 32 | 7 20 | 16 40 | 7 23 | 16 51 |

## JUPITER

| Day | RA | Dec. | | Transit | 5° high | |
|---|---|---|---|---|---|---|
| | | | | | 52° | 56° |
| | h m | ° | ′ | h m | h m | h m |
| 1 | 16 35.7 | −21 | 36 | 15 56 | 19 11 | 18 40 |
| 11 | 16 42.6 | −21 | 51 | 15 24 | 18 37 | 18 05 |
| 21 | 16 50.3 | −22 | 06 | 14 52 | 18 03 | 17 30 |
| 31 | 16 58.6 | −22 | 20 | 14 21 | 17 30 | 16 57 |

Diameters – equatorial 34″ polar 32″

## SATURN

| Day | RA | Dec. | | Transit | 5° high | |
|---|---|---|---|---|---|---|
| | | | | | 52° | 56° |
| | h m | ° | ′ | h m | h m | h m |
| 1 | 23 27.3 | − 6 | 05 | 22 46 | 3 45 | 3 36 |
| 11 | 23 24.8 | − 6 | 20 | 22 05 | 3 02 | 2 53 |
| 21 | 23 22.7 | − 6 | 33 | 21 23 | 2 19 | 2 10 |
| 31 | 23 21.0 | − 6 | 42 | 20 42 | 1 37 | 1 28 |

Diameters – equatorial 19″ polar 17″
Rings – major axis 43″ minor axis 2″

## URANUS

| Day | RA | Dec. | | Transit | 10° high | |
|---|---|---|---|---|---|---|
| | | | | | 52° | 56° |
| | h m | ° | ′ | h m | h m | h m |
| 1 | 19 54.7 | −21 | 24 | 19 15 | 21 40 | 20 50 |
| 11 | 19 54.7 | −21 | 23 | 18 35 | 21 01 | 20 11 |
| 21 | 19 55.0 | −21 | 22 | 17 56 | 20 22 | 19 32 |
| 31 | 19 55.7 | −21 | 20 | 17 18 | 19 44 | 18 54 |

Diameter 4″

## NEPTUNE

| Day | RA | Dec. | | Transit | 10° high | |
|---|---|---|---|---|---|---|
| | | | | | 52° | 56° |
| | h m | ° | ′ | h m | h m | h m |
| 1 | 19 38.0 | −21 | 00 | 18 58 | 21 27 | 20 40 |
| 11 | 19 38.0 | −21 | 00 | 18 19 | 20 48 | 20 01 |
| 21 | 19 38.3 | −21 | 00 | 17 40 | 20 09 | 19 22 |
| 31 | 19 38.8 | −20 | 59 | 17 01 | 19 31 | 18 43 |

Diameter 2″

# November 1995

ELEVENTH MONTH, 30 DAYS. *Novem* (nine), ninth month of Roman pre-Julian calendar

| | | | |
|---|---|---|---|
| 1 | *Wednesday* | **All Saints.** Benvenuto Cellini b. 1500 | *week* 44 *day* 305 |
| 2 | *Thursday* | All Souls. George Bernard Shaw d. 1950 | 306 |
| 3 | *Friday* | Vincenzo Bellini b. 1801 | 307 |
| 4 | *Saturday* | William III b. 1650. Wilfred Owen d. 1918 | 308 |
| 5 | *Sunday* | **8th S. before Christmas/21st S. after Trinity** | *week* 45 *day* 309 |
| 6 | *Monday* | Sousa b. 1854. Ignace Jan Paderewski b. 1860 | 310 |
| 7 | *Tuesday* | Marie Curie b. 1867. Gene Tunney d. 1978 | 311 |
| 8 | *Wednesday* | Milton d. 1674. Munich Putsch 1923 | 312 |
| 9 | *Thursday* | Neville Chamberlain d. 1940. Gen. Charles de Gaulle d. 1970 | 313 |
| 10 | *Friday* | Martin Luther b. 1483. Leonid Brezhnev d. 1982 | 314 |
| 11 | *Saturday* | Armistice Day 1918. Jerome Kern d. 1945 | 315 |
| 12 | *Sunday* | **7th S. before Christmas/22nd S. after Trinity** | *week* 46 *day* 316 |
| 13 | *Monday* | Edward III b. 1312. Archbishop Carey b. 1935 | 317 |
| 14 | *Tuesday* | *Prince of Wales b. 1948.* Jawaharlal Nehru b. 1889 | 318 |
| 15 | *Wednesday* | William Pitt (the Elder) b. 1708. Aneurin Bevan b. 1897 | 319 |
| 16 | *Thursday* | Suez Canal opened 1869. Sir Oswald Mosley b. 1896 | 320 |
| 17 | *Friday* | Field Marshal Viscount Montgomery of Alamein b. 1887 | 321 |
| 18 | *Saturday* | Carl von Weber b. 1786. Niels Bohr d. 1962 | 322 |
| 19 | *Sunday* | **6th S. before Christmas/23rd S. after Trinity** | *week* 47 *day* 323 |
| 20 | *Monday* | *Queen's Wedding Day 1947.* Queen Alexandra d. 1925 | 324 |
| 21 | *Tuesday* | Henry Purcell d. 1695. André Gide b. 1869 | 325 |
| 22 | *Wednesday* | General Charles de Gaulle b. 1890. Mae West d. 1981 | 326 |
| 23 | *Thursday* | Perkin Warbeck d. 1499. Manuel de Falla b. 1876 | 327 |
| 24 | *Friday* | Toulouse Lautrec b. 1864. Georges Clemenceau d. 1929 | 328 |
| 25 | *Saturday* | Andrew Carnegie b. 1835. Dame Myra Hess d. 1965 | 329 |
| 26 | *Sunday* | **5th S. before Christmas/24th S. after Trinity** | *week* 48 *day* 330 |
| 27 | *Monday* | Alexandre Dumas (the younger) d. 1895 | 331 |
| 28 | *Tuesday* | William Blake b. 1757. Enid Blyton d. 1968 | 332 |
| 29 | *Wednesday* | Gaetano Donizetti b. 1798. C. S. Lewis b. 1898 | 333 |
| 30 | *Thursday* | **St Andrew.** Sir Winston Churchill b. 1874 | 334 |

ASTRONOMICAL PHENOMENA

| d | h | |
|---|---|---|
| 2 | 22 | Saturn in conjunction with Moon. Saturn 5° S. |
| 16 | 04 | Jupiter in conjunction with Mars. Jupiter 1° N. |
| 19 | 10 | Jupiter in conjunction with Venus. Jupiter 1° N. |
| 21 | 20 | Saturn at stationary point |
| 22 | 15 | Mercury in conjunction with Moon. Mercury 3° S. |
| 22 | 19 | Sun's longitude 240° ♐ |
| 22 | 21 | Mars in conjunction with Venus. Mars 0°.2 N. |
| 23 | 05 | Mercury in superior conjunction |
| 23 | 07 | Pluto in conjunction |
| 24 | 01 | Jupiter in conjunction with Moon. Jupiter 4° S. |
| 24 | 08 | Mars in conjunction with Moon. Mars 5° S. |
| 24 | 10 | Venus in conjunction with Moon. Venus 6° S. |
| 30 | 03 | Saturn in conjunction with Moon. Saturn 5° S. |

CONSTELLATIONS

The following constellations are near the meridian at

| | d | h | | d | h |
|---|---|---|---|---|---|
| October | 1 | 24 | November | 15 | 21 |
| October | 16 | 23 | December | 1 | 20 |
| November | 1 | 22 | December | 16 | 19 |

Ursa Major (below the Pole), Cepheus, Cassiopeia, Andromeda, Pegasus, Pisces, Aquarius and Cetus

MINIMA OF ALGOL

| d | h | d | h | d | h |
|---|---|---|---|---|---|
| 1 | 06.6 | 12 | 17.8 | 24 | 05.1 |
| 4 | 03.4 | 15 | 14.7 | 27 | 01.9 |
| 7 | 00.2 | 18 | 11.5 | 29 | 22.7 |
| 9 | 21.0 | 21 | 08.3 | | |

THE MOON

| Phases, Apsides and Node | d | h | m |
|---|---|---|---|
| ○ Full Moon | 7 | 07 | 21 |
| ☾ Last Quarter | 15 | 11 | 40 |
| ● New Moon | 22 | 15 | 43 |
| ☽ First Quarter | 29 | 06 | 28 |
| Apogee (405,500 km) | 11 | 20 | 55 |
| Perigee (359,681 km) | 23 | 22 | 54 |

Mean longitude of ascending node on November 1, 206°

THE SUN                                                                                    s.d. 16'.2

| Day | Right Ascension | Dec. − | Equation of time | Rise 52° | Rise 56° | Transit | Set 52° | Set 56° | Sidereal time | Transit of First Point of Aries |
|---|---|---|---|---|---|---|---|---|---|---|
| | h m s | ° ′ | m s | h m | h m | h m | h m | h m | h m s | h m s |
| 1 | 14 22 53 | 14 12 | +16 23 | 6 54 | 7 06 | 11 44 | 16 33 | 16 21 | 2 39 15 | 21 17 15 |
| 2 | 14 26 47 | 14 31 | +16 24 | 6 56 | 7 08 | 11 44 | 16 31 | 16 18 | 2 43 12 | 21 13 19 |
| 3 | 14 30 43 | 14 50 | +16 25 | 6 57 | 7 10 | 11 44 | 16 29 | 16 16 | 2 47 08 | 21 09 23 |
| 4 | 14 34 39 | 15 09 | +16 26 | 6 59 | 7 12 | 11 44 | 16 27 | 16 14 | 2 51 05 | 21 05 27 |
| 5 | 14 38 36 | 15 28 | +16 25 | 7 01 | 7 14 | 11 44 | 16 25 | 16 12 | 2 55 02 | 21 01 31 |
| 6 | 14 42 34 | 15 46 | +16 24 | 7 03 | 7 16 | 11 44 | 16 24 | 16 10 | 2 58 58 | 20 57 35 |
| 7 | 14 46 33 | 16 04 | +16 22 | 7 05 | 7 19 | 11 44 | 16 22 | 16 08 | 3 02 55 | 20 53 39 |
| 8 | 14 50 33 | 16 22 | +16 19 | 7 06 | 7 21 | 11 44 | 16 20 | 16 06 | 3 06 51 | 20 49 43 |
| 9 | 14 54 33 | 16 39 | +16 15 | 7 08 | 7 23 | 11 44 | 16 19 | 16 04 | 3 10 48 | 20 45 48 |
| 10 | 14 58 34 | 16 57 | +16 10 | 7 10 | 7 25 | 11 44 | 16 17 | 16 02 | 3 14 44 | 20 41 52 |
| 11 | 15 02 36 | 17 13 | +16 04 | 7 12 | 7 27 | 11 44 | 16 15 | 16 00 | 3 18 41 | 20 37 56 |
| 12 | 15 06 39 | 17 30 | +15 58 | 7 14 | 7 29 | 11 44 | 16 14 | 15 58 | 3 22 37 | 20 34 00 |
| 13 | 15 10 43 | 17 46 | +15 51 | 7 15 | 7 31 | 11 44 | 16 12 | 15 57 | 3 26 34 | 20 30 04 |
| 14 | 15 14 48 | 18 02 | +15 43 | 7 17 | 7 33 | 11 44 | 16 11 | 15 55 | 3 30 31 | 20 26 08 |
| 15 | 15 18 54 | 18 18 | +15 34 | 7 19 | 7 35 | 11 45 | 16 10 | 15 53 | 3 34 27 | 20 22 12 |
| 16 | 15 23 00 | 18 33 | +15 24 | 7 21 | 7 37 | 11 45 | 16 08 | 15 51 | 3 38 24 | 20 18 16 |
| 17 | 15 27 07 | 18 49 | +15 13 | 7 22 | 7 40 | 11 45 | 16 07 | 15 50 | 3 42 20 | 20 14 20 |
| 18 | 15 31 15 | 19 03 | +15 01 | 7 24 | 7 42 | 11 45 | 16 05 | 15 48 | 3 46 17 | 20 10 24 |
| 19 | 15 35 24 | 19 18 | +14 49 | 7 26 | 7 44 | 11 45 | 16 04 | 15 46 | 3 50 13 | 20 06 28 |
| 20 | 15 39 34 | 19 32 | +14 36 | 7 28 | 7 46 | 11 46 | 16 03 | 15 45 | 3 54 10 | 20 02 33 |
| 21 | 15 43 45 | 19 45 | +14 21 | 7 29 | 7 48 | 11 46 | 16 02 | 15 43 | 3 58 06 | 19 58 37 |
| 22 | 15 47 56 | 19 59 | +14 07 | 7 31 | 7 50 | 11 46 | 16 01 | 15 42 | 4 02 03 | 19 54 41 |
| 23 | 15 52 09 | 20 12 | +13 51 | 7 33 | 7 51 | 11 46 | 16 00 | 15 41 | 4 06 00 | 19 50 45 |
| 24 | 15 56 22 | 20 24 | +13 34 | 7 34 | 7 53 | 11 47 | 15 59 | 15 39 | 4 09 56 | 19 46 49 |
| 25 | 16 00 36 | 20 36 | +13 17 | 7 36 | 7 55 | 11 47 | 15 58 | 15 38 | 4 13 53 | 19 42 53 |
| 26 | 16 04 50 | 20 48 | +12 59 | 7 37 | 7 57 | 11 47 | 15 57 | 15 37 | 4 17 49 | 19 38 57 |
| 27 | 16 09 06 | 21 00 | +12 40 | 7 39 | 7 59 | 11 47 | 15 56 | 15 36 | 4 21 46 | 19 35 01 |
| 28 | 16 13 22 | 21 11 | +12 20 | 7 40 | 8 01 | 11 48 | 15 55 | 15 34 | 4 25 42 | 19 31 05 |
| 29 | 16 17 39 | 21 21 | +12 00 | 7 42 | 8 03 | 11 48 | 15 54 | 15 33 | 4 29 39 | 19 27 09 |
| 30 | 16 21 56 | 21 32 | +11 39 | 7 43 | 8 04 | 11 49 | 15 53 | 15 32 | 4 33 35 | 19 23 13 |

DURATION OF TWILIGHT (in minutes)

| Latitude | 52° | 56° | 52° | 56° | 52° | 56° | 52° | 56° |
|---|---|---|---|---|---|---|---|---|
| | 1 November | | 11 November | | 21 November | | 30 November | |
| Civil | 36 | 40 | 37 | 41 | 38 | 43 | 39 | 45 |
| Nautical | 75 | 84 | 78 | 87 | 80 | 90 | 82 | 93 |
| Astronomical | 115 | 127 | 117 | 130 | 120 | 134 | 123 | 137 |

THE NIGHT SKY

*Mercury* is a difficult morning object for only the first two or three days of November, when it may be glimpsed low above the east-south-east horizon, around the beginning of morning civil twilight. Its magnitude is − 0.9. Afterwards Mercury is too close to the Sun for observation as it passes through superior conjunction on the 23rd.

*Venus* is too close to the Sun for observation during the first week of the month but afterwards emerges slowly from twilight and is visible as a bright evening object, low in the south-western sky just after sunset. Its magnitude is − 3.9. The thin crescent Moon is near the planet on the evenings of the 24th and 25th.

*Mars* is unsuitably placed for observation.

*Jupiter*, magnitude − 1.8, is still visible low in the south-west sky for a while after sunset during the first part of the month, gradually becoming more difficult to observe. By the end of November it is only 5° high at sunset. Jupiter is near Venus around the 18th to the 20th. In the early evenings of the 23rd and 24th Jupiter will be near the thin crescent Moon; this will be a difficult observation to make, particularly on the 23rd as the Moon is then only one day old.

*Saturn*, magnitude + 0.9, is an evening object in the southern skies but by the end of the month it is lost to view before midnight.

# 58  Astronomy

## THE MOON

| Day | RA | Dec. | Hor. par. | Semi- diam. | Sun's co- long. | PA of Bright Limb | Phase | Age | Rise 52° | Rise 56° | Transit | Set 52° | Set 56° |
|---|---|---|---|---|---|---|---|---|---|---|---|---|---|
| | h  m | ° | ′ | ′ | ° | ° | % | d | h  m | h  m | h  m | h  m | h  m |
| 1 | 21 33 | − 9.5 | 58.3 | 15.9 | 9 | 253 | 62 | 7.8 | 14 00 | 14 06 | 19 33 | 0 03 | — |
| 2 | 22 25 | − 5.5 | 57.8 | 15.7 | 21 | 251 | 73 | 8.8 | 14 26 | 14 29 | 20 22 | 1 16 | 1 12 |
| 3 | 23 16 | − 1.3 | 57.3 | 15.6 | 34 | 250 | 82 | 9.8 | 14 51 | 14 50 | 21 09 | 2 29 | 2 28 |
| 4 | 0 06 | + 3.0 | 56.7 | 15.5 | 46 | 249 | 89 | 10.8 | 15 16 | 15 11 | 21 56 | 3 39 | 3 42 |
| 5 | 0 55 | + 7.0 | 56.3 | 15.3 | 58 | 249 | 95 | 11.8 | 15 41 | 15 33 | 22 43 | 4 49 | 4 56 |
| 6 | 1 45 | +10.7 | 55.8 | 15.2 | 70 | 249 | 98 | 12.8 | 16 09 | 15 58 | 23 31 | 5 57 | 6 07 |
| 7 | 2 34 | +13.8 | 55.3 | 15.1 | 82 | 232 | 100 | 13.8 | 16 41 | 16 27 | — | 7 02 | 7 16 |
| 8 | 3 25 | +16.2 | 54.9 | 15.0 | 94 | 92 | 99 | 14.8 | 17 17 | 17 00 | 0 18 | 8 04 | 8 20 |
| 9 | 4 15 | +17.9 | 54.6 | 14.9 | 107 | 89 | 97 | 15.8 | 17 58 | 17 39 | 1 06 | 9 02 | 9 19 |
| 10 | 5 06 | +18.8 | 54.3 | 14.8 | 119 | 92 | 93 | 16.8 | 18 44 | 18 26 | 1 55 | 9 53 | 10 12 |
| 11 | 5 56 | +18.8 | 54.1 | 14.7 | 131 | 95 | 88 | 17.8 | 19 36 | 19 18 | 2 42 | 10 38 | 10 56 |
| 12 | 6 46 | +18.0 | 54.1 | 14.7 | 143 | 98 | 81 | 18.8 | 20 32 | 20 17 | 3 30 | 11 18 | 11 34 |
| 13 | 7 35 | +16.4 | 54.2 | 14.8 | 155 | 102 | 73 | 19.8 | 21 32 | 21 19 | 4 16 | 11 51 | 12 05 |
| 14 | 8 23 | +14.1 | 54.4 | 14.8 | 167 | 105 | 64 | 20.8 | 22 35 | 22 25 | 5 02 | 12 21 | 12 32 |
| 15 | 9 11 | +11.1 | 54.8 | 14.9 | 179 | 108 | 55 | 21.8 | 23 40 | 23 33 | 5 47 | 12 47 | 12 55 |
| 16 | 9 58 | + 7.7 | 55.4 | 15.1 | 192 | 110 | 45 | 22.8 | — | — | 6 32 | 13 12 | 13 17 |
| 17 | 10 46 | + 3.9 | 56.2 | 15.3 | 204 | 111 | 35 | 23.8 | 0 47 | 0 44 | 7 17 | 13 36 | 13 37 |
| 18 | 11 35 | − 0.3 | 57.0 | 15.5 | 216 | 112 | 26 | 24.8 | 1 56 | 1 57 | 8 04 | 14 00 | 13 58 |
| 19 | 12 25 | − 4.6 | 57.9 | 15.8 | 228 | 112 | 17 | 25.8 | 3 09 | 3 13 | 8 53 | 14 27 | 14 21 |
| 20 | 13 18 | − 8.7 | 58.9 | 16.0 | 240 | 111 | 9 | 26.8 | 4 24 | 4 32 | 9 45 | 14 56 | 14 47 |
| 21 | 14 14 | −12.6 | 59.7 | 16.3 | 253 | 111 | 4 | 27.8 | 5 41 | 5 53 | 10 40 | 15 32 | 15 18 |
| 22 | 15 13 | −15.7 | 60.4 | 16.5 | 265 | 118 | 1 | 28.8 | 6 58 | 7 14 | 11 39 | 16 14 | 15 58 |
| 23 | 16 15 | −17.9 | 60.8 | 16.6 | 277 | 246 | 0 | 0.3 | 8 11 | 8 29 | 12 40 | 17 07 | 16 48 |
| 24 | 17 18 | −18.9 | 61.0 | 16.6 | 289 | 262 | 3 | 1.3 | 9 16 | 9 35 | 13 42 | 18 09 | 17 50 |
| 25 | 18 22 | −18.5 | 60.8 | 16.6 | 301 | 260 | 8 | 2.3 | 10 12 | 10 29 | 14 44 | 19 20 | 19 03 |
| 26 | 19 24 | −16.8 | 60.4 | 16.5 | 314 | 257 | 16 | 3.3 | 10 57 | 11 12 | 15 42 | 20 35 | 20 21 |
| 27 | 20 23 | −14.1 | 59.8 | 16.3 | 326 | 254 | 26 | 4.3 | 11 34 | 11 45 | 16 38 | 21 51 | 21 41 |
| 28 | 21 20 | −10.6 | 59.1 | 16.1 | 338 | 251 | 36 | 5.3 | 12 05 | 12 12 | 17 30 | 23 06 | 23 00 |
| 29 | 22 13 | − 6.6 | 58.3 | 15.9 | 350 | 249 | 47 | 6.3 | 12 32 | 12 36 | 18 20 | — | — |
| 30 | 23 05 | − 2.3 | 57.5 | 15.7 | 2 | 248 | 58 | 7.3 | 12 57 | 12 57 | 19 08 | 0 19 | 0 17 |

## MERCURY

| Day | RA | Dec. | Diam. | Phase | Transit | 5° high 52° | 5° high 56° |
|---|---|---|---|---|---|---|---|
| | h  m | ° | ″ | % | h  m | h  m | h  m |
| 1 | 13 34 | − 7.8 | 5 | 89 | 10 55 | 6 10 | 6 21 |
| 3 | 13 46 | − 9.1 | 5 | 91 | 10 59 | 6 22 | 6 33 |
| 5 | 13 58 | −10.4 | 5 | 94 | 11 04 | 6 33 | 6 47 |
| 7 | 14 10 | −11.7 | 5 | 95 | 11 08 | 6 46 | 7 00 |
| 9 | 14 22 | −13.0 | 5 | 97 | 11 13 | 6 58 | 7 14 |
| 11 | 14 35 | −14.2 | 5 | 98 | 11 17 | 7 10 | 7 28 |
| 13 | 14 47 | −15.4 | 5 | 99 | 11 22 | 7 23 | 7 42 |
| 15 | 15 00 | −16.6 | 5 | 99 | 11 27 | 7 35 | 7 56 |
| 17 | 15 13 | −17.7 | 5 | 100 | 11 31 | 7 47 | 8 11 |
| 19 | 15 25 | −18.7 | 5 | 100 | 11 36 | 8 00 | 8 25 |
| 21 | 15 38 | −19.7 | 5 | 100 | 11 41 | 8 12 | 8 39 |
| 23 | 15 51 | −20.6 | 5 | 100 | 11 47 | 8 24 | 8 53 |
| 25 | 16 04 | −21.5 | 5 | 100 | 11 52 | 8 36 | 9 07 |
| 27 | 16 17 | −22.2 | 5 | 100 | 11 57 | 8 48 | 9 21 |
| 29 | 16 31 | −22.9 | 5 | 100 | 12 02 | 15 05 | 14 29 |
| 31 | 16 44 | −23.6 | 5 | 99 | 12 08 | 15 05 | 14 27 |

## VENUS

| Day | RA | Dec. | Diam. | Phase | Transit | 5° high 52° | 5° high 56° |
|---|---|---|---|---|---|---|---|
| | h  m | ° | ″ | % | h  m | h  m | h  m |
| 1 | 15 39 | −19.7 | 10 | 95 | 13 00 | 16 29 | 16 02 |
| 6 | 16 04 | −21.2 | 11 | 94 | 13 06 | 16 23 | 15 53 |
| 11 | 16 31 | −22.5 | 11 | 94 | 13 13 | 16 19 | 15 45 |
| 16 | 16 57 | −23.5 | 11 | 93 | 13 20 | 16 18 | 15 41 |
| 21 | 17 24 | −24.2 | 11 | 92 | 13 27 | 16 19 | 15 39 |
| 26 | 17 51 | −24.6 | 11 | 91 | 13 35 | 16 23 | 15 41 |
| 31 | 18 19 | −24.7 | 11 | 90 | 13 42 | 16 30 | 15 48 |

## MARS

| Day | RA | Dec. | Diam. | Phase | Transit | 5° high 52° | 5° high 56° |
|---|---|---|---|---|---|---|---|
| 1 | 16 25 | −22.4 | 4 | 97 | 13 45 | 16 53 | 16 19 |
| 6 | 16 40 | −23.0 | 4 | 97 | 13 41 | 16 44 | 16 08 |
| 11 | 16 56 | −23.5 | 4 | 98 | 13 37 | 16 35 | 15 59 |
| 16 | 17 12 | −23.8 | 4 | 98 | 13 33 | 16 28 | 15 50 |
| 21 | 17 28 | −24.1 | 4 | 98 | 13 30 | 16 22 | 15 43 |
| 26 | 17 45 | −24.3 | 4 | 98 | 13 27 | 16 18 | 15 37 |
| 31 | 18 01 | −24.4 | 4 | 98 | 13 24 | 16 14 | 15 34 |

## SUNRISE AND SUNSET

| | London | | Bristol | | Birmingham | | Manchester | | Newcastle | | Glasgow | | Belfast | |
|---|---|---|---|---|---|---|---|---|---|---|---|---|---|---|
| | 0°05′ 51°30′ | | 2°35′ 51°28′ | | 1°55′ 52°28′ | | 2°15′ 53°28′ | | 1°37′ 54°59′ | | 4°14′ 55°52′ | | 5°56′ 54°35′ | |
| | h m | h m | h m | h m | h m | h m | h m | h m | h m | h m | h m | h m | h m | h m |
| 1 | 6 53 | 16 34 | 7 03 | 16 44 | 7 03 | 16 39 | 7 07 | 16 37 | 7 09 | 16 30 | 7 22 | 16 38 | 7 25 | 16 49 |
| 2 | 6 55 | 16 32 | 7 05 | 16 43 | 7 05 | 16 37 | 7 09 | 16 36 | 7 11 | 16 28 | 7 24 | 16 36 | 7 27 | 16 47 |
| 3 | 6 56 | 16 31 | 7 06 | 16 41 | 7 06 | 16 35 | 7 11 | 16 34 | 7 13 | 16 26 | 7 27 | 16 34 | 7 29 | 16 45 |
| 4 | 6 58 | 16 29 | 7 08 | 16 39 | 7 08 | 16 33 | 7 13 | 16 32 | 7 15 | 16 24 | 7 29 | 16 32 | 7 31 | 16 43 |
| 5 | 7 00 | 16 27 | 7 10 | 16 37 | 7 10 | 16 32 | 7 15 | 16 30 | 7 17 | 16 22 | 7 31 | 16 29 | 7 33 | 16 41 |
| 6 | 7 02 | 16 26 | 7 12 | 16 36 | 7 12 | 16 30 | 7 17 | 16 28 | 7 19 | 16 20 | 7 33 | 16 27 | 7 35 | 16 39 |
| 7 | 7 03 | 16 24 | 7 13 | 16 34 | 7 14 | 16 28 | 7 18 | 16 26 | 7 21 | 16 18 | 7 35 | 16 25 | 7 37 | 16 37 |
| 8 | 7 05 | 16 22 | 7 15 | 16 32 | 7 16 | 16 26 | 7 20 | 16 24 | 7 23 | 16 16 | 7 37 | 16 23 | 7 39 | 16 35 |
| 9 | 7 07 | 16 21 | 7 17 | 16 31 | 7 17 | 16 25 | 7 22 | 16 23 | 7 25 | 16 15 | 7 39 | 16 21 | 7 41 | 16 33 |
| 10 | 7 09 | 16 19 | 7 19 | 16 29 | 7 19 | 16 23 | 7 24 | 16 21 | 7 27 | 16 13 | 7 41 | 16 20 | 7 43 | 16 31 |
| 11 | 7 10 | 16 18 | 7 20 | 16 28 | 7 21 | 16 22 | 7 26 | 16 19 | 7 29 | 16 11 | 7 43 | 16 18 | 7 45 | 16 30 |
| 12 | 7 12 | 16 16 | 7 22 | 16 26 | 7 23 | 16 20 | 7 28 | 16 18 | 7 31 | 16 09 | 7 46 | 16 16 | 7 47 | 16 28 |
| 13 | 7 14 | 16 15 | 7 24 | 16 25 | 7 25 | 16 18 | 7 30 | 16 16 | 7 33 | 16 07 | 7 48 | 16 14 | 7 49 | 16 26 |
| 14 | 7 16 | 16 13 | 7 26 | 16 23 | 7 27 | 16 17 | 7 32 | 16 14 | 7 35 | 16 06 | 7 50 | 16 12 | 7 51 | 16 25 |
| 15 | 7 17 | 16 12 | 7 27 | 16 22 | 7 28 | 16 15 | 7 34 | 16 13 | 7 37 | 16 04 | 7 52 | 16 11 | 7 53 | 16 23 |
| 16 | 7 19 | 16 10 | 7 29 | 16 20 | 7 30 | 16 14 | 7 35 | 16 11 | 7 39 | 16 02 | 7 54 | 16 09 | 7 55 | 16 21 |
| 17 | 7 21 | 16 09 | 7 31 | 16 19 | 7 32 | 16 13 | 7 37 | 16 10 | 7 41 | 16 01 | 7 56 | 16 07 | 7 57 | 16 20 |
| 18 | 7 22 | 16 08 | 7 32 | 16 18 | 7 34 | 16 11 | 7 39 | 16 09 | 7 43 | 15 59 | 7 58 | 16 06 | 7 59 | 16 18 |
| 19 | 7 24 | 16 07 | 7 34 | 16 17 | 7 35 | 16 10 | 7 41 | 16 07 | 7 45 | 15 58 | 8 00 | 16 04 | 8 01 | 16 17 |
| 20 | 7 26 | 16 05 | 7 36 | 16 15 | 7 37 | 16 09 | 7 43 | 16 06 | 7 47 | 15 56 | 8 02 | 16 02 | 8 02 | 16 16 |
| 21 | 7 28 | 16 04 | 7 37 | 16 14 | 7 39 | 16 08 | 7 44 | 16 05 | 7 49 | 15 55 | 8 04 | 16 01 | 8 04 | 16 14 |
| 22 | 7 29 | 16 03 | 7 39 | 16 13 | 7 40 | 16 06 | 7 46 | 16 03 | 7 51 | 15 54 | 8 06 | 16 00 | 8 06 | 16 13 |
| 23 | 7 31 | 16 02 | 7 41 | 16 12 | 7 42 | 16 05 | 7 48 | 16 02 | 7 53 | 15 52 | 8 08 | 15 58 | 8 08 | 16 12 |
| 24 | 7 32 | 16 01 | 7 42 | 16 11 | 7 44 | 16 04 | 7 50 | 16 01 | 7 54 | 15 51 | 8 10 | 15 57 | 8 10 | 16 10 |
| 25 | 7 34 | 16 00 | 7 44 | 16 10 | 7 45 | 16 03 | 7 51 | 16 00 | 7 56 | 15 50 | 8 11 | 15 56 | 8 12 | 16 09 |
| 26 | 7 35 | 15 59 | 7 45 | 16 09 | 7 47 | 16 02 | 7 53 | 15 59 | 7 58 | 15 49 | 8 13 | 15 54 | 8 13 | 16 08 |
| 27 | 7 37 | 15 58 | 7 47 | 16 08 | 7 49 | 16 01 | 7 55 | 15 58 | 8 00 | 15 48 | 8 15 | 15 53 | 8 15 | 16 07 |
| 28 | 7 39 | 15 57 | 7 48 | 16 08 | 7 50 | 16 00 | 7 56 | 15 57 | 8 02 | 15 47 | 8 17 | 15 52 | 8 17 | 16 06 |
| 29 | 7 40 | 15 57 | 7 50 | 16 07 | 7 52 | 16 00 | 7 58 | 15 56 | 8 03 | 15 46 | 8 19 | 15 51 | 8 18 | 16 05 |
| 30 | 7 41 | 15 56 | 7 51 | 16 06 | 7 53 | 15 59 | 7 59 | 15 55 | 8 05 | 15 45 | 8 20 | 15 50 | 8 20 | 16 04 |

## JUPITER

| Day | RA | Dec. | Transit | 5° high | |
|---|---|---|---|---|---|
| | | | | 52° | 56° |
| | h m | ° ′ | h m | h m | h m |
| 1 | 16 59.4 | −22 21 | 14 18 | 17 27 | 16 53 |
| 11 | 17 08.3 | −22 34 | 13 48 | 16 54 | 16 30 |
| 21 | 17 17.6 | −22 46 | 13 18 | 16 23 | 15 48 |
| 31 | 17 27.1 | −22 56 | 12 48 | 15 51 | 15 17 |

Diameters – equatorial 32″ polar 30″

## SATURN

| Day | RA | Dec. | Transit | 5° high | |
|---|---|---|---|---|---|
| | | | | 52° | 56° |
| | h m | ° ′ | h m | h m | h m |
| 1 | 23 20.9 | − 6 43 | 20 38 | 1 33 | 1 24 |
| 11 | 23 19.8 | − 6 48 | 19 58 | 0 52 | 0 43 |
| 21 | 23 19.4 | − 6 48 | 19 18 | 0 13 | 0 03 |
| 31 | 23 19.6 | − 6 45 | 18 39 | 23 30 | 23 21 |

Diameters – equatorial 18″ polar 16″
Rings – major axis 41″ minor axis 2″

## URANUS

| Day | RA | Dec. | Transit | 10° high | |
|---|---|---|---|---|---|
| | | | | 52° | 56° |
| | h m | ° ′ | h m | h m | h m |
| 1 | 19 55.8 | −21 20 | 17 14 | 19 40 | 18 50 |
| 11 | 19 56.9 | −21 17 | 16 36 | 19 02 | 18 13 |
| 21 | 19 58.3 | −21 13 | 15 58 | 18 25 | 17 36 |
| 31 | 19 59.9 | −21 08 | 15 20 | 17 48 | 17 00 |

Diameter 4″

## NEPTUNE

| Day | RA | Dec. | Transit | 10° high | |
|---|---|---|---|---|---|
| | | | | 52° | 56° |
| | h m | ° ′ | h m | h m | h m |
| 1 | 19 38.8 | −20 59 | 16 57 | 19 27 | 18 39 |
| 11 | 19 39.6 | −20 57 | 16 18 | 18 48 | 18 01 |
| 21 | 19 40.5 | −20 55 | 15 40 | 18 10 | 17 24 |
| 31 | 19 41.7 | −20 53 | 15 02 | 17 33 | 16 46 |

Diameter 2″

# December 1995

TWELFTH MONTH, 31 DAYS. *Decem* (ten), tenth month of Roman pre-Julian calendar

| | | | |
|---|---|---|---|
| 1 | *Friday* | Henry I d. 1135. David Ben-Gurion d. 1973 | *week* 48 *day* 335 |
| 2 | *Saturday* | Hernan Cortes d. 1547. Marquis de Sade d. 1814 | 336 |
| | | | |
| 3 | *Sunday* | **1st S. in Advent.** Sir Oswald Mosley d. 1980 | *week* 49 *day* 337 |
| 4 | *Monday* | First publication of the *Observer* 1791 | 338 |
| 5 | *Tuesday* | Repeal of Prohibition, USA 1933 | 339 |
| 6 | *Wednesday* | Joseph Conrad b. 1857. Sir Osbert Sitwell b. 1892 | 340 |
| 7 | *Thursday* | Pearl Harbor attacked 1941. Robert Graves d. 1985 | 341 |
| 8 | *Friday* | Thomas de Quincey d. 1859. James Thurber b. 1894 | 342 |
| 9 | *Saturday* | Sir Anthony van Dyck d. 1641. George Grossmith b. 1847 | 343 |
| | | | |
| 10 | *Sunday* | **2nd S. in Advent.** Paolo Uccello d. 1475 | *week* 50 *day* 344 |
| 11 | *Monday* | First motor show opened, Paris 1894 | 345 |
| 12 | *Tuesday* | Hovercraft patented 1955. John Osborne b. 1929 | 346 |
| 13 | *Wednesday* | Heinrich Heine b. 1797. Battle of the River Plate 1939 | 347 |
| 14 | *Thursday* | Stanley Baldwin d. 1947. Field Marshal Viscount Slim d. 1970 | 348 |
| 15 | *Friday* | John Paul Getty b. 1892. Charles Laughton d. 1962 | 349 |
| 16 | *Saturday* | Sir Noël Coward b. 1899. Glen Miller d. 1944 | 350 |
| | | | |
| 17 | *Sunday* | **3rd S. in Advent.** Domenico Cimarosa b. 1749 | *week* 51 *day* 351 |
| 18 | *Monday* | CHANUCAH begins. Dame Celia Johnson b. 1908 | 352 |
| 19 | *Tuesday* | Emily Brontë d. 1848. Sir Ralph Richardson b. 1902 | 353 |
| 20 | *Wednesday* | Gen. Ludendorff d. 1937. John Steinbeck d. 1968 | 354 |
| 21 | *Thursday* | *Michaelmas Law Sittings end.* Gen. George Patton d. 1945 | 355 |
| 22 | *Friday* | Giacomo Puccini b. 1858. George Eliot d. 1880 | 356 |
| 23 | *Saturday* | Richard Arkwright b. 1732. Thomas Malthus d. 1834 | 357 |
| | | | |
| 24 | *Sunday* | **4th S. in Advent.** Christmas Eve. | *week* 52 *day* 358 |
| 25 | *Monday* | **Christmas Day.** *Public Holiday in the UK* | 359 |
| 26 | *Tuesday* | **St Stephen.** *Bank Holiday in the UK* | 360 |
| 27 | *Wednesday* | **St John the Evangelist.** Rob Roy d. 1734 | 361 |
| 28 | *Thursday* | **Holy Innocents.** Brian Redhead b. 1929 | 362 |
| 29 | *Friday* | Thomas à Becket killed 1170 | 363 |
| 30 | *Saturday* | Robert Boyle d. 1691. Amelia Bloomer d. 1894 | 364 |
| | | | |
| 31 | *Sunday* | **1st S. after Christmas.** Léon Gambetta d. 1882 | *week* 53 *day* 365 |

ASTRONOMICAL PHENOMENA

| d | h | |
|---|---|---|
| 8 | 08 | Jupiter in conjunction with Mercury. Jupiter 2° N. |
| 18 | 22 | Jupiter in conjunction |
| 21 | 22 | Jupiter in conjunction with Moon. Jupiter 4° S. |
| 22 | 08 | Sun's longitude 270° ♑ |
| 23 | 06 | Mercury in conjunction with Moon. Mercury 7° S. |
| 23 | 06 | Mars in conjunction with Moon. Mars 6° S. |
| 23 | 14 | Mars in conjunction with Mercury. Mars 1° N. |
| 24 | 07 | Venus in conjunction with Moon. Venus 7° S. |
| 27 | 12 | Saturn in conjunction with Moon. Saturn 5° S. |

CONSTELLATIONS

The following constellations are near the meridian at

| | d | h | | d | h |
|---|---|---|---|---|---|
| November | 1 | 24 | December | 16 | 21 |
| November | 15 | 23 | January | 1 | 20 |
| December | 1 | 22 | January | 16 | 19 |

Ursa Major (below the Pole), Ursa Minor (below the Pole), Cassiopeia, Andromeda, Perseus, Triangulum, Aries, Taurus, Cetus and Eridanus

MINIMA OF ALGOL

| d | h | d | h | d | h |
|---|---|---|---|---|---|
| 2 | 19.6 | 14 | 06.8 | 25 | 18.1 |
| 5 | 16.4 | 17 | 03.6 | 28 | 14.9 |
| 8 | 13.2 | 20 | 00.5 | 31 | 11.7 |
| 11 | 10.0 | 22 | 21.3 | | |

THE MOON

| Phases, Apsides and Node | d | h | m |
|---|---|---|---|
| ○ Full Moon | 7 | 01 | 27 |
| ☾ Last Quarter | 15 | 05 | 31 |
| ● New Moon | 22 | 02 | 22 |
| ☽ First Quarter | 28 | 19 | 06 |
| Apogee (406,307 km) | 9 | 10 | 00 |
| Perigee (356,801 km) | 22 | 09 | 59 |

Mean longitude of ascending node on December 1, 204°

## THE SUN

s.d. 16′.3

| Day | Right Ascension | Dec. — | Equation of time | Rise 52° | Rise 56° | Transit | Set 52° | Set 56° | Sidereal time | Transit of First Point of Aries |
|---|---|---|---|---|---|---|---|---|---|---|
| | h m s | ° ′ | m s | h m | h m | h m | h m | h m | h m s | h m s |
| 1 | 16 26 14 | 21 41 | +11 18 | 7 45 | 8 06 | 11 49 | 15 53 | 15 31 | 4 37 32 | 19 19 18 |
| 2 | 16 30 33 | 21 51 | +10 56 | 7 46 | 8 08 | 11 49 | 15 52 | 15 31 | 4 41 29 | 19 15 22 |
| 3 | 16 34 52 | 22 00 | +10 33 | 7 48 | 8 09 | 11 50 | 15 51 | 15 30 | 4 45 25 | 19 11 26 |
| 4 | 16 39 12 | 22 08 | +10 09 | 7 49 | 8 11 | 11 50 | 15 51 | 15 29 | 4 49 22 | 19 07 30 |
| 5 | 16 43 33 | 22 16 | + 9 45 | 7 50 | 8 12 | 11 50 | 15 50 | 15 28 | 4 53 18 | 19 03 34 |
| 6 | 16 47 54 | 22 24 | + 9 21 | 7 52 | 8 14 | 11 51 | 15 50 | 15 28 | 4 57 15 | 18 59 38 |
| 7 | 16 52 16 | 22 31 | + 8 56 | 7 53 | 8 15 | 11 51 | 15 49 | 15 27 | 5 01 11 | 18 55 42 |
| 8 | 16 56 38 | 22 38 | + 8 30 | 7 54 | 8 17 | 11 52 | 15 49 | 15 27 | 5 05 08 | 18 51 46 |
| 9 | 17 01 01 | 22 45 | + 8 04 | 7 55 | 8 18 | 11 52 | 15 49 | 15 26 | 5 09 04 | 18 47 50 |
| 10 | 17 05 24 | 22 51 | + 7 37 | 7 56 | 8 19 | 11 53 | 15 49 | 15 26 | 5 13 01 | 18 43 54 |
| 11 | 17 09 47 | 22 56 | + 7 10 | 7 57 | 8 20 | 11 53 | 15 48 | 15 25 | 5 16 58 | 18 39 58 |
| 12 | 17 14 11 | 23 01 | + 6 43 | 7 58 | 8 22 | 11 53 | 15 48 | 15 25 | 5 20 54 | 18 36 03 |
| 13 | 17 18 36 | 23 06 | + 6 15 | 7 59 | 8 23 | 11 54 | 15 48 | 15 25 | 5 24 51 | 18 32 07 |
| 14 | 17 23 00 | 23 10 | + 5 47 | 8 00 | 8 24 | 11 54 | 15 48 | 15 25 | 5 28 47 | 18 28 11 |
| 15 | 17 27 26 | 23 14 | + 5 18 | 8 01 | 8 25 | 11 55 | 15 48 | 15 25 | 5 32 44 | 18 24 15 |
| 16 | 17 31 51 | 23 17 | + 4 49 | 8 02 | 8 26 | 11 55 | 15 49 | 15 25 | 5 36 40 | 18 20 19 |
| 17 | 17 36 17 | 23 20 | + 4 20 | 8 03 | 8 27 | 11 56 | 15 49 | 15 25 | 5 40 37 | 18 16 23 |
| 18 | 17 40 43 | 23 22 | + 3 51 | 8 04 | 8 27 | 11 56 | 15 49 | 15 25 | 5 44 33 | 18 12 27 |
| 19 | 17 45 09 | 23 24 | + 3 21 | 8 04 | 8 28 | 11 57 | 15 49 | 15 26 | 5 48 30 | 18 08 31 |
| 20 | 17 49 35 | 23 25 | + 2 52 | 8 05 | 8 29 | 11 57 | 15 50 | 15 26 | 5 52 27 | 18 04 35 |
| 21 | 17 54 01 | 23 26 | + 2 22 | 8 06 | 8 29 | 11 58 | 15 50 | 15 26 | 5 56 23 | 18 00 39 |
| 22 | 17 58 28 | 23 26 | + 1 52 | 8 06 | 8 30 | 11 58 | 15 51 | 15 27 | 6 00 20 | 17 56 43 |
| 23 | 18 02 54 | 23 26 | + 1 22 | 8 07 | 8 30 | 11 59 | 15 51 | 15 27 | 6 04 16 | 17 52 48 |
| 24 | 18 07 21 | 23 26 | + 0 52 | 8 07 | 8 31 | 11 59 | 15 52 | 15 28 | 6 08 13 | 17 48 52 |
| 25 | 18 11 47 | 23 25 | + 0 22 | 8 07 | 8 31 | 12 00 | 15 52 | 15 29 | 6 12 09 | 17 44 56 |
| 26 | 18 16 14 | 23 23 | − 0 08 | 8 08 | 8 31 | 12 00 | 15 53 | 15 29 | 6 16 06 | 17 41 00 |
| 27 | 18 20 40 | 23 21 | − 0 38 | 8 08 | 8 32 | 12 01 | 15 54 | 15 30 | 6 20 02 | 17 37 04 |
| 28 | 18 25 06 | 23 19 | − 1 07 | 8 08 | 8 32 | 12 01 | 15 55 | 15 31 | 6 23 59 | 17 33 08 |
| 29 | 18 29 32 | 23 16 | − 1 37 | 8 08 | 8 32 | 12 02 | 15 56 | 15 32 | 6 27 56 | 17 29 12 |
| 30 | 18 33 58 | 23 12 | − 2 06 | 8 08 | 8 32 | 12 02 | 15 57 | 15 33 | 6 31 52 | 17 25 16 |
| 31 | 18 38 24 | 23 09 | − 2 35 | 8 08 | 8 32 | 12 03 | 15 58 | 15 34 | 6 35 49 | 17 21 20 |

DURATION OF TWILIGHT (in minutes)

| Latitude | 52° | 56° | 52° | 56° | 52° | 56° | 52° | 56° |
|---|---|---|---|---|---|---|---|---|
| | 1 December | | 11 December | | 21 December | | 31 December | |
| Civil | 40 | 45 | 41 | 47 | 41 | 47 | 41 | 47 |
| Nautical | 82 | 93 | 84 | 96 | 85 | 97 | 84 | 96 |
| Astronomical | 123 | 138 | 125 | 141 | 126 | 142 | 125 | 141 |

THE NIGHT SKY

*Mercury* remains too close to the Sun for observation throughout the month.

*Venus*, magnitude −3.9, is a bright early evening object, being gradually visible for longer and longer after sunset as the month progresses. It will still only be seen at a very low altitude above the south-western horizon. On the evening of the 24th the thin crescent Moon, less than three days old, will be seen about 9° above Venus.

*Mars* is unsuitably placed for observation.

*Jupiter* passes through conjunction on the 18th and therefore remains too close to the Sun for observation throughout December.

*Saturn* continues to be visible as an evening object in the south and south-west skies, magnitude +1.1. Saturn is in Aquarius.

*Meteors.* The maximum of the well-known Geminid meteor shower occurs on the morning of the 14th. The gibbous Moon will be a considerable hindrance to observation as it rises well before midnight on the 13th.

## THE MOON

| Day | RA (h m) | Dec. (°) | Hor. par. (') | Semi-diam. (') | Sun's co-long. (°) | PA of Bright Limb (°) | Phase (%) | Age (d) | Rise 52° (h m) | Rise 56° (h m) | Transit (h m) | Set 52° (h m) | Set 56° (h m) |
|---|---|---|---|---|---|---|---|---|---|---|---|---|---|
| 1 | 23 55 | + 1.9 | 56.8 | 15.5 | 14 | 247 | 68 | 8.3 | 13 21 | 13 18 | 19 55 | 1 30 | 1 32 |
| 2 | 0 44 | + 6.0 | 56.2 | 15.3 | 27 | 248 | 77 | 9.3 | 13 46 | 13 39 | 20 41 | 2 40 | 2 45 |
| 3 | 1 32 | + 9.7 | 55.7 | 15.2 | 39 | 249 | 85 | 10.3 | 14 13 | 14 03 | 21 27 | 3 47 | 3 56 |
| 4 | 2 21 | +13.0 | 55.2 | 15.0 | 51 | 250 | 91 | 11.3 | 14 42 | 14 29 | 22 14 | 4 53 | 5 05 |
| 5 | 3 11 | +15.6 | 54.8 | 14.9 | 63 | 250 | 96 | 12.3 | 15 16 | 15 00 | 23 02 | 5 55 | 6 11 |
| 6 | 4 01 | +17.5 | 54.5 | 14.8 | 75 | 244 | 99 | 13.3 | 15 55 | 15 37 | 23 50 | 6 54 | 7 12 |
| 7 | 4 51 | +18.7 | 54.2 | 14.8 | 87 | 183 | 100 | 14.3 | 16 39 | 16 20 | — | 7 48 | 8 07 |
| 8 | 5 42 | +18.9 | 54.1 | 14.7 | 99 | 111 | 99 | 15.3 | 17 29 | 17 11 | 0 38 | 8 36 | 8 54 |
| 9 | 6 32 | +18.4 | 54.0 | 14.7 | 111 | 106 | 96 | 16.3 | 18 24 | 18 07 | 1 25 | 9 18 | 9 35 |
| 10 | 7 21 | +17.0 | 54.0 | 14.7 | 124 | 106 | 92 | 17.3 | 19 22 | 19 08 | 2 12 | 9 53 | 10 08 |
| 11 | 8 09 | +14.9 | 54.1 | 14.7 | 136 | 108 | 87 | 18.3 | 20 23 | 20 12 | 2 58 | 10 24 | 10 37 |
| 12 | 8 57 | +12.2 | 54.4 | 14.8 | 148 | 110 | 80 | 19.3 | 21 27 | 21 18 | 3 43 | 10 52 | 11 01 |
| 13 | 9 44 | + 9.0 | 54.7 | 14.9 | 160 | 111 | 71 | 20.3 | 22 32 | 22 27 | 4 27 | 11 16 | 11 22 |
| 14 | 10 31 | + 5.3 | 55.3 | 15.1 | 172 | 113 | 62 | 21.3 | 23 38 | 23 37 | 5 11 | 11 40 | 11 42 |
| 15 | 11 18 | + 1.3 | 56.0 | 15.3 | 184 | 113 | 52 | 22.3 | — | — | 5 56 | 12 03 | 12 02 |
| 16 | 12 06 | − 2.8 | 56.8 | 15.5 | 197 | 113 | 42 | 23.3 | 0 47 | 0 50 | 6 43 | 12 27 | 12 23 |
| 17 | 12 57 | − 6.9 | 57.7 | 15.7 | 209 | 112 | 32 | 24.3 | 1 58 | 2 05 | 7 31 | 12 54 | 12 46 |
| 18 | 13 50 | −10.8 | 58.7 | 16.0 | 221 | 111 | 22 | 25.3 | 3 13 | 3 23 | 8 23 | 13 25 | 13 14 |
| 19 | 14 46 | −14.3 | 59.7 | 16.3 | 233 | 109 | 14 | 26.3 | 4 28 | 4 42 | 9 19 | 14 02 | 13 47 |
| 20 | 15 46 | −17.0 | 60.5 | 16.5 | 245 | 108 | 7 | 27.3 | 5 43 | 6 00 | 10 18 | 14 49 | 14 31 |
| 21 | 16 48 | −18.6 | 61.1 | 16.7 | 257 | 110 | 2 | 28.3 | 6 54 | 7 13 | 11 20 | 15 46 | 15 27 |
| 22 | 17 53 | −18.9 | 61.4 | 16.7 | 270 | 163 | 0 | 29.3 | 7 56 | 8 15 | 12 23 | 16 54 | 16 35 |
| 23 | 18 57 | −17.8 | 61.4 | 16.7 | 282 | 244 | 1 | 0.9 | 8 48 | 9 05 | 13 26 | 18 09 | 17 53 |
| 24 | 20 00 | −15.5 | 61.0 | 16.6 | 294 | 249 | 6 | 1.9 | 9 31 | 9 44 | 14 25 | 19 28 | 19 16 |
| 25 | 20 59 | −12.1 | 60.4 | 16.5 | 306 | 248 | 12 | 2.9 | 10 06 | 10 15 | 15 21 | 20 47 | 20 39 |
| 26 | 21 56 | − 8.1 | 59.6 | 16.2 | 318 | 247 | 21 | 3.9 | 10 36 | 10 41 | 16 14 | 22 04 | 22 00 |
| 27 | 22 50 | − 3.8 | 58.6 | 16.0 | 331 | 246 | 31 | 4.9 | 11 02 | 11 04 | 17 04 | 23 18 | 23 18 |
| 28 | 23 42 | + 0.6 | 57.7 | 15.7 | 343 | 246 | 42 | 5.9 | 11 27 | 11 25 | 17 52 | — | — |
| 29 | 0 32 | + 4.8 | 56.8 | 15.5 | 355 | 247 | 52 | 6.9 | 11 52 | 11 47 | 18 39 | 0 29 | 0 33 |
| 30 | 1 21 | + 8.7 | 56.1 | 15.3 | 7 | 248 | 62 | 7.9 | 12 18 | 12 09 | 19 26 | 1 38 | 1 46 |
| 31 | 2 10 | +12.1 | 55.4 | 15.1 | 19 | 250 | 72 | 8.9 | 12 46 | 12 34 | 20 12 | 2 44 | 2 56 |

## MERCURY

| Day | RA (h m) | Dec. (°) | Diam. (") | Phase (%) | Transit (h m) | 5° high 52° (h m) | 5° high 56° (h m) |
|---|---|---|---|---|---|---|---|
| 1 | 16 44 | −23.6 | 5 | 99 | 12 08 | 15 05 | 14 27 |
| 3 | 16 58 | −24.1 | 5 | 99 | 12 14 | 15 06 | 14 26 |
| 5 | 17 11 | −24.6 | 5 | 98 | 12 19 | 15 07 | 14 25 |
| 7 | 17 25 | −24.9 | 5 | 98 | 12 25 | 15 10 | 14 26 |
| 9 | 17 38 | −25.2 | 5 | 97 | 12 31 | 15 13 | 14 28 |
| 11 | 17 52 | −25.4 | 5 | 96 | 12 37 | 15 17 | 14 31 |
| 13 | 18 06 | −25.5 | 5 | 95 | 12 43 | 15 22 | 14 36 |
| 15 | 18 20 | −25.5 | 5 | 94 | 12 49 | 15 28 | 14 42 |
| 17 | 18 34 | −25.4 | 5 | 92 | 12 55 | 15 36 | 14 50 |
| 19 | 18 47 | −25.2 | 5 | 91 | 13 00 | 15 44 | 14 59 |
| 21 | 19 01 | −25.0 | 5 | 88 | 13 06 | 15 52 | 15 10 |
| 23 | 19 14 | −24.6 | 5 | 86 | 13 11 | 16 02 | 15 21 |
| 25 | 19 27 | −24.1 | 6 | 83 | 13 16 | 16 11 | 15 33 |
| 27 | 19 39 | −23.5 | 6 | 79 | 13 20 | 16 21 | 15 45 |
| 29 | 19 51 | −22.8 | 6 | 74 | 13 24 | 16 31 | 15 57 |
| 31 | 20 01 | −22.1 | 6 | 69 | 13 26 | 16 40 | 16 08 |

## VENUS

| Day | RA (h m) | Dec. (°) | Diam. (") | Phase (%) | Transit (h m) | 5° high 52° (h m) | 5° high 56° (h m) |
|---|---|---|---|---|---|---|---|
| 1 | 18 19 | −24.7 | 11 | 90 | 13 42 | 16 30 | 15 48 |
| 6 | 18 46 | −24.5 | 12 | 89 | 13 50 | 16 40 | 15 59 |
| 11 | 19 13 | −24.0 | 12 | 88 | 13 57 | 16 52 | 16 14 |
| 16 | 19 40 | −23.2 | 12 | 87 | 14 04 | 17 07 | 16 32 |
| 21 | 20 06 | −22.1 | 12 | 86 | 14 11 | 17 23 | 16 51 |
| 26 | 20 32 | −20.7 | 12 | 85 | 14 17 | 17 41 | 17 12 |
| 31 | 20 58 | −19.1 | 13 | 84 | 14 22 | 17 59 | 17 34 |

## MARS

| Day | RA (h m) | Dec. (°) | Diam. (") | Phase (%) | Transit (h m) | 5° high 52° (h m) | 5° high 56° (h m) |
|---|---|---|---|---|---|---|---|
| 1 | 18 01 | −24.4 | 4 | 98 | 13 24 | 16 14 | 15 34 |
| 6 | 18 18 | −24.4 | 4 | 99 | 13 21 | 16 11 | 15 31 |
| 11 | 18 35 | −24.2 | 4 | 99 | 13 18 | 16 10 | 15 31 |
| 16 | 18 52 | −23.9 | 4 | 99 | 13 15 | 16 10 | 15 31 |
| 21 | 19 08 | −23.6 | 4 | 99 | 13 12 | 16 10 | 15 33 |
| 26 | 19 25 | −23.1 | 4 | 99 | 13 09 | 16 12 | 15 37 |
| 31 | 19 42 | −22.5 | 4 | 99 | 13 06 | 16 14 | 15 41 |

## SUNRISE AND SUNSET

| | London | | Bristol | | Birmingham | | Manchester | | Newcastle | | Glasgow | | Belfast | |
|---|---|---|---|---|---|---|---|---|---|---|---|---|---|---|
| | 0°05′ | 51°30′ | 2°35′ | 51°28′ | 1°55′ | 52°28′ | 2°15′ | 53°28′ | 1°37′ | 54°59′ | 4°14′ | 55°52′ | 5°56′ | 54°35′ |
| | h m | h m | h m | h m | h m | h m | h m | h m | h m | h m | h m | h m | h m | h m |
| 1 | 7 43 | 15 55 | 7 53 | 16 05 | 7 55 | 15 58 | 8 01 | 15 54 | 8 07 | 15 44 | 8 22 | 15 49 | 8 22 | 1ᴏ 03 |
| 2 | 7 44 | 15 55 | 7 54 | 16 05 | 7 56 | 15 57 | 8 03 | 15 54 | 8 08 | 15 43 | 8 24 | 15 48 | 8 23 | 16 02 |
| 3 | 7 46 | 15 54 | 7 55 | 16 04 | 7 58 | 15 57 | 8 04 | 15 53 | 8 10 | 15 42 | 8 25 | 15 47 | 8 25 | 16 02 |
| 4 | 7 47 | 15 53 | 7 57 | 16 04 | 7 59 | 15 56 | 8 05 | 15 52 | 8 11 | 15 41 | 8 27 | 15 47 | 8 26 | 16 01 |
| 5 | 7 48 | 15 53 | 7 58 | 16 03 | 8 00 | 15 56 | 8 07 | 15 52 | 8 13 | 15 41 | 8 28 | 15 46 | 8 28 | 16 00 |
| 6 | 7 50 | 15 53 | 7 59 | 16 03 | 8 02 | 15 55 | 8 08 | 15 51 | 8 14 | 15 40 | 8 30 | 15 45 | 8 29 | 16 00 |
| 7 | 7 51 | 15 52 | 8 01 | 16 02 | 8 03 | 15 55 | 8 09 | 15 51 | 8 15 | 15 40 | 8 31 | 15 45 | 8 30 | 15 59 |
| 8 | 7 52 | 15 52 | 8 02 | 16 02 | 8 04 | 15 54 | 8 11 | 15 50 | 8 17 | 15 39 | 8 33 | 15 44 | 8 32 | 15 59 |
| 9 | 7 53 | 15 52 | 8 03 | 16 02 | 8 05 | 15 54 | 8 12 | 15 50 | 8 18 | 15 39 | 8 34 | 15 44 | 8 33 | 15 59 |
| 10 | 7 54 | 15 51 | 8 04 | 16 02 | 8 06 | 15 54 | 8 13 | 15 50 | 8 19 | 15 39 | 8 35 | 15 44 | 8 34 | 15 58 |
| 11 | 7 55 | 15 51 | 8 05 | 16 01 | 8 07 | 15 54 | 8 14 | 15 50 | 8 20 | 15 38 | 8 37 | 15 43 | 8 35 | 15 58 |
| 12 | 7 56 | 15 51 | 8 06 | 16 01 | 8 09 | 15 54 | 8 15 | 15 50 | 8 22 | 15 38 | 8 38 | 15 43 | 8 36 | 15 58 |
| 13 | 7 57 | 15 51 | 8 07 | 16 01 | 8 10 | 15 54 | 8 16 | 15 49 | 8 23 | 15 38 | 8 39 | 15 43 | 8 38 | 15 58 |
| 14 | 7 58 | 15 51 | 8 08 | 16 01 | 8 10 | 15 54 | 8 17 | 15 49 | 8 24 | 15 38 | 8 40 | 15 43 | 8 39 | 15 58 |
| 15 | 7 59 | 15 51 | 8 09 | 16 02 | 8 11 | 15 54 | 8 18 | 15 50 | 8 25 | 15 38 | 8 41 | 15 43 | 8 39 | 15 58 |
| 16 | 8 00 | 15 52 | 8 10 | 16 02 | 8 12 | 15 54 | 8 19 | 15 50 | 8 26 | 15 38 | 8 42 | 15 43 | 8 40 | 15 58 |
| 17 | 8 01 | 15 52 | 8 11 | 16 02 | 8 13 | 15 54 | 8 20 | 15 50 | 8 26 | 15 38 | 8 43 | 15 43 | 8 41 | 15 58 |
| 18 | 8 01 | 15 52 | 8 11 | 16 02 | 8 14 | 15 54 | 8 21 | 15 50 | 8 27 | 15 38 | 8 43 | 15 43 | 8 42 | 15 58 |
| 19 | 8 02 | 15 52 | 8 12 | 16 02 | 8 14 | 15 55 | 8 21 | 15 50 | 8 28 | 15 39 | 8 44 | 15 43 | 8 43 | 15 58 |
| 20 | 8 03 | 15 53 | 8 13 | 16 03 | 8 15 | 15 55 | 8 22 | 15 51 | 8 29 | 15 39 | 8 45 | 15 44 | 8 43 | 15 59 |
| 21 | 8 03 | 15 53 | 8 13 | 16 03 | 8 16 | 15 55 | 8 23 | 15 51 | 8 29 | 15 40 | 8 45 | 15 44 | 8 44 | 15 59 |
| 22 | 8 04 | 15 54 | 8 14 | 16 04 | 8 16 | 15 56 | 8 23 | 15 52 | 8 30 | 15 40 | 8 46 | 15 45 | 8 44 | 16 00 |
| 23 | 8 04 | 15 54 | 8 14 | 16 04 | 8 17 | 15 56 | 8 24 | 15 52 | 8 30 | 15 41 | 8 46 | 15 45 | 8 45 | 16 00 |
| 24 | 8 05 | 15 55 | 8 15 | 16 05 | 8 17 | 15 57 | 8 24 | 15 53 | 8 31 | 15 41 | 8 47 | 15 46 | 8 45 | 16 01 |
| 25 | 8 05 | 15 55 | 8 15 | 16 06 | 8 17 | 15 58 | 8 24 | 15 53 | 8 31 | 15 42 | 8 47 | 15 47 | 8 46 | 16 02 |
| 26 | 8 05 | 15 56 | 8 15 | 16 06 | 8 18 | 15 58 | 8 25 | 15 54 | 8 31 | 15 43 | 8 47 | 15 47 | 8 46 | 16 02 |
| 27 | 8 06 | 15 57 | 8 15 | 16 07 | 8 18 | 15 59 | 8 25 | 15 55 | 8 31 | 15 43 | 8 48 | 15 48 | 8 46 | 16 03 |
| 28 | 8 06 | 15 58 | 8 16 | 16 08 | 8 18 | 16 00 | 8 25 | 15 56 | 8 32 | 15 44 | 8 48 | 15 49 | 8 46 | 16 04 |
| 29 | 8 06 | 15 59 | 8 16 | 16 09 | 8 18 | 16 01 | 8 25 | 15 57 | 8 32 | 15 45 | 8 48 | 15 50 | 8 46 | 16 05 |
| 30 | 8 06 | 15 59 | 8 16 | 16 10 | 8 18 | 16 02 | 8 25 | 15 58 | 8 32 | 15 46 | 8 48 | 15 51 | 8 46 | 16 06 |
| 31 | 8 06 | 16 00 | 8 16 | 16 11 | 8 18 | 16 03 | 8 25 | 15 59 | 8 32 | 15 47 | 8 48 | 15 52 | 8 46 | 16 07 |

## JUPITER

| Day | RA | Dec. | Transit | 5° high | |
|---|---|---|---|---|---|
| | | | | 52° | 56° |
| | h m | ° ′ | h m | h m | h m |
| 1 | 17 27.1 | −22 56 | 12 48 | 9 45 | 10 20 |
| 11 | 17 36.9 | −23 03 | 12 19 | 9 16 | 9 52 |
| 21 | 17 46.8 | −23 08 | 11 49 | 8 47 | 9 23 |
| 31 | 17 56.7 | −23 11 | 11 20 | 8 18 | 8 54 |

Diameters – equatorial 31″ polar 30″

## SATURN

| Day | RA | Dec. | Transit | 5° high | |
|---|---|---|---|---|---|
| | | | | 52° | 56° |
| | h m | ° ′ | h m | h m | h m |
| 1 | 23 19.6 | − 6 45 | 18 39 | 23 30 | 23 21 |
| 11 | 23 20.5 | − 6 37 | 18 01 | 22 52 | 22 43 |
| 21 | 23 22.0 | − 6 26 | 17 23 | 22 16 | 22 07 |
| 31 | 23 24.1 | − 6 10 | 16 46 | 21 40 | 21 31 |

Diameters – equatorial 17″ polar 15″
Rings – major axis 39″ minor axis 2″

## URANUS

| Day | RA | Dec. | Transit | 10° high | |
|---|---|---|---|---|---|
| | | | | 52° | 56° |
| | h m | ° ′ | h m | h m | h m |
| 1 | 19 59.9 | −21 08 | 15 20 | 17 48 | 17 00 |
| 11 | 20 01.8 | −21 02 | 14 43 | 17 12 | 16 24 |
| 21 | 20 04.0 | −20 56 | 14 05 | 16 36 | 15 49 |
| 31 | 20 06.3 | −20 49 | 13 28 | 16 00 | 15 14 |

Diameter 4″

## NEPTUNE

| Day | RA | Dec. | Transit | 10° high | |
|---|---|---|---|---|---|
| | | | | 52° | 56° |
| | h m | ° ′ | h m | h m | h m |
| 1 | 19 41.7 | −20 53 | 15 02 | 17 33 | 16 46 |
| 11 | 19 42.9 | −20 50 | 14 24 | 16 55 | 16 09 |
| 21 | 19 44.4 | −20 46 | 13 46 | 16 18 | 15 32 |
| 31 | 19 45.9 | −20 43 | 13 08 | 15 41 | 14 55 |

Diameter 2″

# 64   Astronomy

## RISING AND SETTING TIMES

### TABLE 1. SEMI-DIURNAL ARCS (HOUR ANGLES AT RISING/SETTING)

| Dec. | 0° h m | 10° h m | 20° h m | 30° h m | 40° h m | 45° h m | 50° h m | 52° h m | 54° h m | 56° h m | 58° h m | 60° h m | Dec. |
|---|---|---|---|---|---|---|---|---|---|---|---|---|---|
| 0° | 6 00 | 6 00 | 6 00 | 6 00 | 6 00 | 6 00 | 6 00 | 6 00 | 6 00 | 6 00 | 6 00 | 6 00 | 0° |
| 1° | 6 00 | 6 01 | 6 01 | 6 02 | 6 03 | 6 04 | 6 05 | 6 05 | 6 06 | 6 06 | 6 06 | 6 07 | 1° |
| 2° | 6 00 | 6 01 | 6 03 | 6 05 | 6 07 | 6 08 | 6 10 | 6 10 | 6 11 | 6 12 | 6 13 | 6 14 | 2° |
| 3° | 6 00 | 6 02 | 6 04 | 6 07 | 6 10 | 6 12 | 6 14 | 6 15 | 6 17 | 6 18 | 6 19 | 6 21 | 3° |
| 4° | 6 00 | 6 03 | 6 06 | 6 09 | 6 13 | 6 16 | 6 19 | 6 21 | 6 22 | 6 24 | 6 26 | 6 28 | 4° |
| 5° | 6 00 | 6 04 | 6 07 | 6 12 | 6 17 | 6 20 | 6 24 | 6 26 | 6 28 | 6 30 | 6 32 | 6 35 | 5° |
| 6° | 6 00 | 6 04 | 6 09 | 6 14 | 6 20 | 6 24 | 6 29 | 6 31 | 6 33 | 6 36 | 6 39 | 6 42 | 6° |
| 7° | 6 00 | 6 05 | 6 10 | 6 16 | 6 24 | 6 28 | 6 34 | 6 36 | 6 39 | 6 42 | 6 45 | 6 49 | 7° |
| 8° | 6 00 | 6 06 | 6 12 | 6 19 | 6 27 | 6 32 | 6 39 | 6 41 | 6 45 | 6 48 | 6 52 | 6 56 | 8° |
| 9° | 6 00 | 6 06 | 6 13 | 6 21 | 6 31 | 6 36 | 6 44 | 6 47 | 6 50 | 6 54 | 6 59 | 7 04 | 9° |
| 10° | 6 00 | 6 07 | 6 15 | 6 23 | 6 34 | 6 41 | 6 49 | 6 52 | 6 56 | 7 01 | 7 06 | 7 11 | 10° |
| 11° | 6 00 | 6 08 | 6 16 | 6 26 | 6 38 | 6 45 | 6 54 | 6 58 | 7 02 | 7 07 | 7 12 | 7 19 | 11° |
| 12° | 6 00 | 6 09 | 6 18 | 6 28 | 6 41 | 6 49 | 6 59 | 7 03 | 7 08 | 7 13 | 7 20 | 7 26 | 12° |
| 13° | 6 00 | 6 09 | 6 19 | 6 31 | 6 45 | 6 53 | 7 04 | 7 09 | 7 14 | 7 20 | 7 27 | 7 34 | 13° |
| 14° | 6 00 | 6 10 | 6 21 | 6 33 | 6 48 | 6 58 | 7 09 | 7 14 | 7 20 | 7 27 | 7 34 | 7 42 | 14° |
| 15° | 6 00 | 6 11 | 6 22 | 6 36 | 6 52 | 7 02 | 7 14 | 7 20 | 7 27 | 7 34 | 7 42 | 7 51 | 15° |
| 16° | 6 00 | 6 12 | 6 24 | 6 38 | 6 56 | 7 07 | 7 20 | 7 26 | 7 33 | 7 41 | 7 49 | 7 59 | 16° |
| 17° | 6 00 | 6 12 | 6 26 | 6 41 | 6 59 | 7 11 | 7 25 | 7 32 | 7 40 | 7 48 | 7 57 | 8 08 | 17° |
| 18° | 6 00 | 6 13 | 6 27 | 6 43 | 7 03 | 7 16 | 7 31 | 7 38 | 7 46 | 7 55 | 8 05 | 8 17 | 18° |
| 19° | 6 00 | 6 14 | 6 29 | 6 46 | 7 07 | 7 21 | 7 37 | 7 45 | 7 53 | 8 03 | 8 14 | 8 26 | 19° |
| 20° | 6 00 | 6 15 | 6 30 | 6 49 | 7 11 | 7 25 | 7 43 | 7 51 | 8 00 | 8 11 | 8 22 | 8 36 | 20° |
| 21° | 6 00 | 6 16 | 6 32 | 6 51 | 7 15 | 7 30 | 7 49 | 7 58 | 8 08 | 8 19 | 8 32 | 8 47 | 21° |
| 22° | 6 00 | 6 16 | 6 34 | 6 54 | 7 19 | 7 35 | 7 55 | 8 05 | 8 15 | 8 27 | 8 41 | 8 58 | 22° |
| 23° | 6 00 | 6 17 | 6 36 | 6 57 | 7 23 | 7 40 | 8 02 | 8 12 | 8 23 | 8 36 | 8 51 | 9 09 | 23° |
| 24° | 6 00 | 6 18 | 6 37 | 7 00 | 7 28 | 7 46 | 8 08 | 8 19 | 8 31 | 8 45 | 9 02 | 9 22 | 24° |
| 25° | 6 00 | 6 19 | 6 39 | 7 02 | 7 32 | 7 51 | 8 15 | 8 27 | 8 40 | 8 55 | 9 13 | 9 35 | 25° |
| 26° | 6 00 | 6 20 | 6 41 | 7 05 | 7 37 | 7 57 | 8 22 | 8 35 | 8 49 | 9 05 | 9 25 | 9 51 | 26° |
| 27° | 6 00 | 6 21 | 6 43 | 7 08 | 7 41 | 8 03 | 8 30 | 8 43 | 8 58 | 9 16 | 9 39 | 10 08 | 27° |
| 28° | 6 00 | 6 22 | 6 45 | 7 12 | 7 46 | 8 08 | 8 37 | 8 52 | 9 08 | 9 28 | 9 53 | 10 28 | 28° |
| 29° | 6 00 | 6 22 | 6 47 | 7 15 | 7 51 | 8 15 | 8 45 | 9 01 | 9 19 | 9 41 | 10 10 | 10 55 | 29° |
| 30° | 6 00 | 6 23 | 6 49 | 7 18 | 7 56 | 8 21 | 8 54 | 9 11 | 9 30 | 9 55 | 10 30 | 12 00 | 30° |
| 35° | 6 00 | 6 28 | 6 59 | 7 35 | 8 24 | 8 58 | 9 46 | 10 15 | 10 58 | 12 00 | 12 00 | 12 00 | 35° |
| 40° | 6 00 | 6 34 | 7 11 | 7 56 | 8 59 | 9 48 | 12 00 | 12 00 | 12 00 | 12 00 | 12 00 | 12 00 | 40° |
| 45° | 6 00 | 6 41 | 7 25 | 8 21 | 9 48 | 12 00 | 12 00 | 12 00 | 12 00 | 12 00 | 12 00 | 12 00 | 45° |
| 50° | 6 00 | 6 49 | 7 43 | 8 54 | 12 00 | 12 00 | 12 00 | 12 00 | 12 00 | 12 00 | 12 00 | 12 00 | 50° |
| 55° | 6 00 | 6 58 | 8 05 | 9 42 | 12 00 | 12 00 | 12 00 | 12 00 | 12 00 | 12 00 | 12 00 | 12 00 | 55° |
| 60° | 6 00 | 7 11 | 8 36 | 12 00 | 12 00 | 12 00 | 12 00 | 12 00 | 12 00 | 12 00 | 12 00 | 12 00 | 60° |
| 65° | 6 00 | 7 29 | 9 25 | 12 00 | 12 00 | 12 00 | 12 00 | 12 00 | 12 00 | 12 00 | 12 00 | 12 00 | 65° |
| 70° | 6 00 | 7 56 | 12 00 | 12 00 | 12 00 | 12 00 | 12 00 | 12 00 | 12 00 | 12 00 | 12 00 | 12 00 | 70° |
| 75° | 6 00 | 8 45 | 12 00 | 12 00 | 12 00 | 12 00 | 12 00 | 12 00 | 12 00 | 12 00 | 12 00 | 12 00 | 75° |
| 80° | 6 00 | 12 00 | 12 00 | 12 00 | 12 00 | 12 00 | 12 00 | 12 00 | 12 00 | 12 00 | 12 00 | 12 00 | 80° |

### TABLE 2. CORRECTION FOR REFRACTION AND SEMI-DIAMETER

| | m | m | m | m | m | m | m | m | m | m | m | m | |
|---|---|---|---|---|---|---|---|---|---|---|---|---|---|
| 0° | 3 | 3 | 4 | 4 | 4 | 5 | 5 | 5 | 6 | 6 | 6 | 7 | 0° |
| 10° | 3 | 3 | 4 | 4 | 4 | 5 | 5 | 6 | 6 | 6 | 7 | 7 | 10° |
| 20° | 4 | 4 | 4 | 4 | 5 | 5 | 6 | 7 | 7 | 8 | 8 | 9 | 20° |
| 25° | 4 | 4 | 4 | 4 | 5 | 6 | 7 | 8 | 8 | 9 | 11 | 13 | 25° |
| 30° | 4 | 4 | 4 | 5 | 6 | 7 | 8 | 9 | 11 | 14 | 21 | — | 30° |

NB: Regarding Table 1. If latitude and declination are of the same sign, take out the respondent directly. If they are of opposite signs, subtract the respondent from 12h.
*Examples*:

| Lat. | Dec. | Semi-diurnal arc |
|---|---|---|
| +52° | +20° | 7h 51m |
| +52° | −20° | 4h 09m |

## SUNRISE AND SUNSET

The local mean time of sunrise or sunset may be found by obtaining the hour angle from Table 1 and applying it to the time of transit. The hour angle is negative for sunrise and positive for sunset. A small correction to the hour angle, which always has the effect of increasing it numerically, is necessary to allow for the Sun's semi-diameter (16') and for refraction (34'); it is obtained from Table 2. The resulting local mean time may be converted into the standard time of the country by taking the difference between the longitude of the standard meridian of the country and that of the place, adding it to the local mean time if the place is west of the standard meridian, and subtracting it if the place is east.

*Example* – Required the New Zealand Mean Time (12h fast on GMT) of sunset on May 23 at Auckland, latitude 36° 50′ S. (or minus), longitude 11h 39m E. Taking the declination as $+20°.6$ (page 33), we find

|  | h | m |
|---|---|---|
| Tabular entry for 30° Lat. and Dec. 20°, opposite signs | + 5 | 11 |
| Proportional part for 6° 50′ of Lat. | − | 15 |
| Proportional part for 0°.6 of Dec. | − | 2 |
| Correction (Table 2) | + | 4 |
| Hour angle | 4 | 58 |
| Sun transits (page 33) | 11 | 57 |
| Longitudinal correction | + | 21 |
| New Zealand Mean Time | 17 | 16 |

## MOONRISE AND MOONSET

It is possible to calculate the times of moonrise and moonset using Table 1, though the method is more complicated because the apparent motion of the Moon is much more rapid and also more variable than that of the Sun.

The parallax of the Moon, about 57′, is near to the sum of the semi-diameter and refraction but has the opposite effect on these times. It is thus convenient to neglect all three quantities in the method outlined below.

TABLE 3. LONGITUDE CORRECTION

| X | 40m | 45m | 50m | 55m | 60m | 65m | 70m |
|---|---|---|---|---|---|---|---|
| A |  |  |  |  |  |  |  |
| h | m | m | m | m | m | m | m |
| 1 | 2 | 2 | 2 | 2 | 3 | 3 | 3 |
| 2 | 3 | 4 | 4 | 5 | 5 | 5 | 6 |
| 3 | 5 | 6 | 6 | 7 | 8 | 8 | 9 |
| 4 | 7 | 8 | 8 | 9 | 10 | 11 | 12 |
| 5 | 8 | 9 | 10 | 11 | 13 | 14 | 15 |
| 6 | 10 | 11 | 13 | 14 | 15 | 16 | 18 |
| 7 | 12 | 13 | 15 | 16 | 18 | 19 | 20 |
| 8 | 13 | 15 | 17 | 18 | 20 | 22 | 23 |
| 9 | 15 | 17 | 19 | 21 | 23 | 24 | 26 |
| 10 | 17 | 19 | 21 | 23 | 25 | 27 | 29 |
| 11 | 18 | 21 | 23 | 25 | 28 | 30 | 32 |
| 12 | 20 | 23 | 25 | 28 | 30 | 33 | 35 |
| 13 | 22 | 24 | 27 | 30 | 33 | 35 | 38 |
| 14 | 23 | 26 | 29 | 32 | 35 | 38 | 41 |
| 15 | 25 | 28 | 31 | 34 | 38 | 41 | 44 |
| 16 | 27 | 30 | 33 | 37 | 40 | 43 | 47 |
| 17 | 28 | 32 | 35 | 39 | 43 | 46 | 50 |
| 18 | 30 | 34 | 38 | 41 | 45 | 49 | 53 |
| 19 | 32 | 36 | 40 | 44 | 48 | 51 | 55 |
| 20 | 33 | 38 | 42 | 46 | 50 | 54 | 58 |
| 21 | 35 | 39 | 44 | 48 | 53 | 57 | 61 |
| 22 | 37 | 41 | 46 | 50 | 55 | 60 | 64 |
| 23 | 38 | 43 | 48 | 53 | 58 | 62 | 67 |
| 24 | 40 | 45 | 50 | 55 | 60 | 65 | 70 |

*Notation*

$\varphi$ = latitude of observer
$\lambda$ = longitude of observer (measured positively towards the west)
$T_{-1}$ = time of transit of Moon on previous day
$T_0$ = time of transit of Moon on day in question
$T_1$ = time of transit of Moon on following day
$\delta_0$ = approximate declination of Moon
$\delta_R$ = declination of Moon at moonrise
$\delta_S$ = declination of Moon at moonset
$h_0$ = approximate hour angle of Moon
$h_R$ = hour angle of Moon at moonrise
$h_S$ = hour angle of Moon at moonset
$t_R$ = time of moonrise
$t_S$ = time of moonset

*Method*

1. With arguments $\varphi$, $\delta_0$ enter Table 1 on page 64 to determine $h_0$ where $h_0$ is negative for moonrise and positive for moonset.

2. Form approximate times from
$t_R = T_0 + \lambda + h_0$
$t_S = T_0 + \lambda + h_0$

3. Determine $\delta_R$, $\delta_S$ for times $t_R$, $t_S$ respectively.

4. Re-enter Table 1 on page 64 with
    (a) arguments $\varphi$, $\delta_R$ to determine $h_R$
    (b) arguments $\varphi$, $\delta_S$ to determine $h_S$

5. Form $t_R = T_0 + \lambda + h_R + AX$
$t_S = T_0 + \lambda + h_S + AX$

where $A = (\lambda + h)$

and   $X = (T_0 - T_{-1})$   if $(\lambda + h)$   is negative
         $X = (T_1 - T_0)$   if $(\lambda + h)$   is positive

AX is the respondent in Table 3.

*Example* – To find the times of moonrise and moonset at Vancouver ($\varphi = +49°$, $\lambda = +8h\,12m$) on 1995 January 29. The starting data (page 18) are

$T_{-1} = 9h\,48m$
$T_0 = 10h\,47m$
$T_1 = 11h\,43m$
$\delta = -18°$

1. $h_0 = 4h\,32m$
2. Approximate values
    $t_R = 29d\,10h\,47m + 8h\,12m + (-4h\,32m)$
        $= 29d\,14h\,27m$
    $t_S = 29d\,10h\,47m + 8h\,12m + (+4h\,32m)$
        $= 29d\,23h\,31m$
3. $\delta_R = -17°.0$
    $\delta_S = -16°.0$
4. $h_R = -4h\,38m$
    $h_S = +4h\,43m$
5. $t_R = 29d\,10h\,47m + 8h\,12m + (-4h\,38m) + 8m$
        $= 29d\,14h\,29m$
    $t_S = 29d\,10h\,47m + 8h\,12m + (+4h\,43m) + 31m$
        $= 30d\,00h\,13m$

To get the LMT of the phenomenon the longitude is subtracted from the GMT thus:
Moonrise = 29d 14h 29m − 8h 12m = 29d 06h 17m
Moonset = 30d 00h 13m − 8h 12m = 29d 16h 01m

## ECLIPSES AND OCCULTATIONS 1995

ECLIPSES

There will be three eclipses during 1995, two of the Sun and one of the Moon. (Penumbral eclipses are not mentioned in this section as they are too difficult to observe.)

1. A partial eclipse of the Moon on April 15 is visible from the western part of North and Central America, the Pacific Ocean, Antarctica, Australasia, the Indian Ocean, and eastern and central Asia. The eclipse begins at 11h 41m and ends at 12h 55m. At maximum eclipse 12 per cent of the Moon is obscured (a small portion of the north limb).

2. An annular eclipse of the Sun on April 29 is visible as a partial eclipse from the eastern part of the central and southern United States, Central and South America, southern Mexico, Florida, and the West Indies, the Atlantic Ocean, and the extreme west of North Africa. The eclipse begins at 14h 33m and ends at 20h 32m. The track of the annular phase crosses South America from the Peru-Ecuador border through northern Brazil. The annular phase begins at 15h 40m and ends at 19h 25m: the maximum duration is 6m 37s.

3. A total eclipse of the Sun on October 24 is visible as a partial eclipse from extreme East Africa, Arabia, most of Asia (except the north-east), part of the Indian Ocean, Australasia (except southern Australia and New Zealand), and the western Pacific Ocean. The eclipse begins at 1h 52m and ends at 7h 13m. The path of totality starts in Iran, crosses Afghanistan, Pakistan, India, Myanmar (Burma), Thailand, Cambodia, south Vietnam, and north Borneo, and ends in the western Pacific Ocean. The total phase begins at 2h 52m and ends at 6h 13m: the maximum duration is 2m 10s.

LUNAR OCCULTATIONS

Observations of the times of occultations are made by both amateur and professional astronomers. Such observations are later analysed to yield accurate positions of the Moon; this is one method of determining the difference between ephemeris time and universal time.

Many of the observations made by amateurs are obtained with the use of a stop-watch which is compared with a time-signal immediately after the observation. Thus an accuracy of about one-fifth of a second is obtainable, though the observer's personal equation may amount to one-third or one-half of a second.

The list on page 67 includes most of the occultations visible under favourable conditions in the British Isles. No occultation is included unless the star is at least 10° above the horizon and the Sun sufficiently far below the horizon to permit the star to be seen with the naked eye or with a small telescope. The altitude limit is reduced from 10° to 2° for stars and planets brighter than magnitude 2.0 and such occultations are also predicted in daylight.

The column Phase shows (i) whether a disappearance (D) or reappearance (R) is to be observed; and (ii) whether it is at the dark limb (D) or bright limb (B). The column headed 'El. of Moon' gives the elongation of the Moon from the Sun, in degrees. The elongation increases from 0° at New Moon to 180° at Full Moon and on to 360° (or 0°) at New Moon again. Times and position angles (*P*), reckoned from the north point in the direction north, east, south, west, are given for Greenwich (lat. 51° 30', long. 0°) and Edinburgh (lat. 56° 00', long. 3° 12' west).

The coefficients *a* and *b* are the variations in the GMT for each degree of longitude (positive to the west) and latitude (positive to the north) respectively; they enable approximate times (to within about 1m generally) to be found for any point in the British Isles. If the point of observation is *Δλ* degrees west and *Δφ* degrees north, the approximate time is found by adding $a.\Delta\lambda + b.\Delta\phi$ to the given GMT.

*Example:* the reappearance of ZC1925 (Spica) on March 18 at Liverpool, found from both Greenwich and Edinburgh.

|  | Greenwich | Edinburgh |
|---|---|---|
|  | ° | ° |
| Longitude | 0.0 | +3.2 |
| Long. of Liverpool | +3.0 | +3.0 |
| *Δλ* | +3.0 | −0.2 |
| Latitude | +51.5 | +56.0 |
| Lat. of Liverpool | +53.4 | +53.4 |
| *Δφ* | +1.9 | −2.6 |
|  | h    m | h    m |
| GMT | 23   42.5 | 23   46.3 |
| *a.Δλ* | − 6.0 | + 0.3 |
| *b.Δφ* | + 4.6 | − 4.7 |
|  | 23   41.1 | 23   41.9 |

If the occultation is given for one station but not the other, the reason for the suppression is given by the following code:
N = star not occulted
A = star's altitude less than 10° (2° for bright stars and planets)
S = Sun not sufficiently below the horizon
G = occultation is of very short duration
In some cases the coefficients *a* and *b* are not given; this is because the occultation is so short that prediction for other places by means of these coefficients would not be reliable.

LUNAR OCCULTATIONS 1995

| Date | | ZC No. | Mag. | Phase | El. of Moon | GREENWICH | | | | EDINBURGH | | | |
|---|---|---|---|---|---|---|---|---|---|---|---|---|---|
| | | | | | | UT | a | b | P | UT | a | b | P |
| | | | | | ° | h m | m | m | ° | h m | m | m | ° |
| January | 8 | 162 | 6.9 | D.D. | 91 | N | | | | 16 51.7 | −2.1 | −0.7 | 124 |
| | 10 | 403 | 5.8 | D.D. | 113 | 18 37.5 | −1.5 | 1.2 | 67 | 18 40.1 | −1.1 | 1.7 | 53 |
| | 10 | 413 | 6.8 | D.D. | 114 | 21 0.8 | −1.5 | −0.4 | 78 | 20 55.9 | −1.3 | 0.2 | 64 |
| | 12 | 639 | 6.0 | D.D. | 134 | 16 41.8 | −0.6 | 1.7 | 84 | 16 48.5 | −0.4 | 2.0 | 72 |
| | 12 | 654 | 6.0 | D.D. | 135 | 19 31.2 | −1.3 | 1.8 | 62 | 19 36.8 | −1.0 | 2.4 | 46 |
| | 12 | 668 | 3.6 | D.D. | 136 | 22 2.0 | −1.6 | 1.1 | 53 | 22 4.2 | −1.4 | 2.2 | 35 |
| | 15 | 947 | 5.2 | D.D. | 159 | 0 22.2 | G | | 33 | N | | | |
| | 26 | 2302 | 2.9 | D.B. | 297 | 5 32.5 | −1.0 | 0.7 | 106 | 5 33.0 | −0.9 | 0.9 | 101 |
| | 26 | 2302 | 2.9 | R.D. | 297 | 6 43.5 | −1.4 | 0.4 | 277 | 6 41.5 | −1.1 | 0.5 | 280 |
| February | 8 | 617 | 6.6 | D.D. | 105 | 21 25.9 | −1.3 | −0.9 | 81 | 21 18.9 | −1.2 | −0.4 | 69 |
| March | 6 | 450 | 6.6 | D.D. | 63 | 21 57.7 | −0.3 | −0.5 | 49 | 21 55.1 | −0.5 | −0.1 | 37 |
| | 7 | 577 | 6.0 | D.D. | 74 | N | | | | 21 37.0 | G | | 161 |
| | 8 | 718 | 6.1 | D.D. | 85 | 23 2.9 | −0.3 | −1.4 | 81 | 22 55.8 | −0.4 | −1.3 | 73 |
| | 9 | 726 | 6.8 | D.D. | 85 | A | | | | 0 7.2 | 0.0 | −1.3 | 74 |
| | 11 | 1091 | 6.7 | D.D. | 116 | 18 42.7 | −1.5 | −0.1 | 110 | S | | | |
| | 11 | 1106 | 3.7 | D.D. | 118 | 22 53.5 | −0.7 | −2.2 | 126 | 22 41.8 | −0.8 | −1.9 | 118 |
| | 13 | 1237 | 6.4 | D.D. | 130 | 0 39.4 | −0.7 | −1.6 | 94 | 0 30.1 | −0.8 | −1.5 | 89 |
| | 13 | 1332 | 5.7 | D.D. | 139 | 19 52.3 | −1.7 | 2.0 | 67 | 19 59.0 | G | | 48 |
| | 18 | 1925 | 1.2 | D.B. | 205 | 23 6.5 | 0.0 | −1.7 | 171 | 23 1.2 | −0.2 | −0.6 | 159 |
| | 18 | 1925 | 1.2 | R.D. | 205 | 23 42.5 | −2.0 | 2.4 | 235 | 23 46.3 | −1.4 | 1.8 | 246 |
| April | 4 | 663 | 6.9 | D.D. | 54 | 21 39.1 | 0.0 | −1.6 | 93 | 21 32.0 | −0.1 | −1.5 | 86 |
| | 6 | 934 | 6.4 | D.D. | 76 | 23 33.7 | 0.4 | −2.0 | 129 | 23 25.4 | 0.2 | −2.1 | 123 |
| | 8 | 1073 | 6.0 | D.D. | 88 | A | | | | 0 24.2 | G | | 164 |
| | 10 | 1397 | 5.5 | D.D. | 121 | 21 45.7 | −2.3 | 0.7 | 56 | 21 43.6 | G | | 43 |
| | 12 | 1528 | 6.6 | D.D. | 135 | 1 50.9 | −0.3 | −1.9 | 122 | 1 41.3 | −0.4 | −1.9 | 119 |
| | 12 | 1623 | 5.4 | D.D. | 146 | 23 24.8 | −1.2 | −1.2 | 114 | 23 16.0 | −1.1 | −1.0 | 110 |
| May | 4 | 1029 | 5.1 | D.D. | 57 | 21 41.0 | −0.1 | −1.4 | 79 | 21 34.2 | −0.3 | −1.4 | 74 |
| | 5 | 1145 | 6.7 | D.D. | 68 | 22 29.3 | 0.1 | −1.9 | 118 | 22 20.8 | 0.0 | −1.9 | 114 |
| | 5 | 1147 | 5.1 | D.D. | 68 | 22 33.1 | −0.2 | −1.2 | 71 | 22 26.6 | −0.3 | −1.3 | 67 |
| | 10 | 1688 | 6.3 | D.D. | 126 | 20 48.9 | G | | 180 | S | | | |
| | 12 | 1925 | 1.2 | D.D. | 151 | 19 23.3 | G | | 181 | 19 16.1 | −0.1 | −0.9 | 165 |
| | 12 | 1925 | 1.2 | R.B. | 152 | 19 48.0 | G | | 225 | 19 54.7 | −1.5 | 2.2 | 239 |
| | 27 | Venus | −3.9 | D.B. | 336 | 5 35.3 | −0.6 | 1.6 | 100 | 5 41.6 | −0.4 | 1.9 | 91 |
| | 27 | Venus | −3.9 | R.D. | 337 | 6 40.9 | −0.4 | 2.7 | 223 | 6 51.0 | −0.5 | 2.4 | 234 |
| June | 1 | 1106 | 3.7 | D.D. | 38 | 21 13.3 | 0.1 | −1.2 | 71 | S | | | |
| | 12 | 2322 | 4.3 | D.D. | 164 | 0 55.0 | −1.2 | −0.9 | 89 | 0 47.8 | −1.1 | −0.7 | 84 |
| | 14 | 2826 | 4.0 | R.D. | 206 | 23 41.8 | −1.1 | 0.0 | 318 | 23 38.6 | G | | 327 |
| July | 9 | 2401 | 5.6 | D.D. | 144 | 21 53.8 | −1.5 | 0.0 | 80 | 21 49.6 | −1.3 | 0.1 | 75 |
| August | 19 | 648 | 3.9 | R.D. | 281 | 2 58.4 | −0.1 | 3.6 | 205 | 3 11.5 | −0.3 | 2.7 | 222 |
| October | 5 | 3185 | 5.3 | D.D. | 134 | 0 32.0 | −0.1 | 1.1 | 17 | N | | | |
| | 5 | 3187 | 6.2 | D.D. | 135 | 0 48.0 | −0.7 | −1.4 | 88 | 0 40.6 | −0.6 | −1.0 | 73 |
| | 14 | 832 | 4.7 | R.D. | 243 | 5 21.5 | G | | 351 | N | | | |
| November | 9 | 648 | 3.9 | R.D. | 202 | 5 3.5 | −0.8 | −1.1 | 258 | 4 55.2 | −0.8 | −1.4 | 268 |
| | 9 | 653 | 4.8 | R.D. | 202 | 5 35.1 | −0.8 | −0.3 | 231 | 5 29.8 | −0.7 | −0.8 | 243 |
| December | 9 | 1106 | 3.7 | R.D. | 211 | 21 56.0 | −0.6 | 1.7 | 265 | 22 1.0 | −0.6 | 1.4 | 279 |
| | 11 | 1341 | 4.3 | D.D. | 234 | 23 40.4 | G | | 353 | N | | | |
| | 27 | 3467 | 6.5 | D.D. | 78 | 19 25.3 | −1.6 | −2.1 | 111 | 19 13.9 | −1.3 | −1.1 | 94 |
| | 28 | 53 | 6.9 | D.D. | 91 | 21 39.9 | −0.7 | −0.7 | 64 | 21 35.6 | −0.7 | −0.2 | 49 |
| | 29 | 180 | 5.6 | D.D. | 102 | 20 15.6 | −1.4 | −0.1 | 69 | 20 12.4 | −1.1 | 0.4 | 54 |
| | 29 | 181 | 6.5 | D.D. | 102 | 20 16.6 | −1.4 | −0.1 | 69 | 20 13.4 | −1.1 | 0.4 | 54 |
| | 30 | 301 | 6.8 | D.D. | 114 | 20 4.8 | −1.7 | −0.2 | 86 | 20 0.5 | −1.3 | 0.4 | 72 |

## MEAN PLACES OF STARS 1995.5

| Name | Mag. | RA (h m) | Dec. (° ′) | Spectrum |
|---|---|---|---|---|
| α And *Alpheratz* | 2.1 | 0 08.2 | +29 04 | A0p |
| β Cassiopeiae *Caph* | 2.3 | 0 08.9 | +59 07 | F5 |
| γ Pegasi *Algenib* | 2.8 | 0 13.0 | +15 10 | B2 |
| β Hydri | 2.9 | 0 25.6 | −77 17 | G0 |
| α Phoenicis | 2.4 | 0 26.1 | −42 20 | K0 |
| α Cassiopeiae *Schedar* | 2.2 | 0 40.3 | +56 31 | K0 |
| β Ceti *Diphda** | 2.0 | 0 43.4 | −18 01 | K0 |
| γ Cassiopeiae* | Var. | 0 56.4 | +60 42 | B0p |
| β Andromedae *Mirach* | 2.1 | 1 09.5 | +35 36 | M0 |
| δ Cassiopeiae | 2.7 | 1 25.5 | +60 13 | A5 |
| α Eridani *Achernar* | 0.5 | 1 37.5 | −57 16 | B5 |
| β Arietis *Sheratan* | 2.6 | 1 54.4 | +20 47 | A5 |
| γ Andromedae *Almak* | 2.3 | 2 03.6 | +42 19 | K0 |
| α Arietis *Hamal* | 2.0 | 2 06.9 | +23 26 | K2 |
| α Ursae Minoris *Polaris* | 2.0 | 2 26.9 | +89 15 | F8 |
| β Persei *Algol** | Var. | 3 07.9 | +40 56 | B8 |
| α Persei *Mirfak* | 1.8 | 3 24.0 | +49 51 | F5 |
| η Tauri *Alcyone* | 2.9 | 3 47.2 | +24 05 | B5p |
| α Tauri *Aldebaran* | 0.9 | 4 35.7 | +16 30 | K5 |
| β Orionis *Rigel* | 0.1 | 5 14.3 | − 8 12 | B8p |
| α Aurigae *Capella* | 0.1 | 5 16.4 | +46 00 | G0 |
| γ Orionis *Bellatrix* | 1.6 | 5 24.9 | + 6 21 | B2 |
| β Tauri *Elnath* | 1.7 | 5 26.0 | +28 36 | B8 |
| δ Orionis | 2.2 | 5 31.8 | − 0 18 | B0 |
| α Leporis | 2.6 | 5 32.5 | −17 50 | F0 |
| ε Orionis | 1.7 | 5 36.0 | − 1 12 | B0 |
| ζ Orionis | 1.8 | 5 40.5 | − 1 57 | B0 |
| κ Orionis | 2.1 | 5 47.5 | − 9 40 | B0 |
| α Orionis *Betelgeuse** | Var. | 5 54.9 | + 7 24 | M0 |
| β Aurigae *Menkalinan* | 1.9 | 5 59.2 | +44 57 | A0p |
| β CMa *Mirzam* | 2.0 | 6 22.5 | −17 57 | B1 |
| α Carinae *Canopus* | −0.7 | 6 23.9 | −52 42 | F0 |
| γ Geminorum *Alhena* | 1.9 | 6 37.5 | +16 24 | A0 |
| α Canis Majoris *Sirius* | −1.5 | 6 44.9 | −16 43 | A0 |
| ε Canis Majoris | 1.5 | 6 58.4 | −28 58 | B1 |
| δ Canis Majoris | 1.9 | 7 08.2 | −26 23 | F8p |
| α Geminorum *Castor* | 1.6 | 7 34.3 | +31 54 | A0 |
| α CMi *Procyon* | 0.4 | 7 39.1 | + 5 14 | F5 |
| β Geminorum *Pollux* | 1.1 | 7 45.0 | +28 02 | K0 |
| ζ Puppis | 2.3 | 8 03.4 | −39 59 | Od |
| γ Velorum | 1.8 | 8 09.4 | −47 19 | Oap |
| ε Carinae | 1.9 | 8 22.4 | −59 30 | K0 |
| δ Velorum | 2.0 | 8 44.6 | −54 42 | A0 |
| λ Velorum *Suhail* | 2.2 | 9 07.8 | −43 25 | K5 |
| β Carinae | 1.7 | 9 13.2 | −69 42 | A0 |
| ι Carinae | 2.2 | 9 17.0 | −59 15 | F0 |
| κ Velorum | 2.6 | 9 22.0 | −54 59 | B3 |
| α Hydrae *Alphard* | 2.0 | 9 27.4 | − 8 38 | K2 |
| α Leonis *Regulus* | 1.3 | 10 08.1 | +11 59 | B8 |
| γ Leonis *Algeiba* | 1.9 | 10 19.7 | +19 52 | K0 |
| β Ursae Majoris *Merak* | 2.4 | 11 01.6 | +56 24 | A0 |
| α Ursae Majoris *Dubhe* | 1.8 | 11 03.5 | +61 47 | K0 |
| δ Leonis | 2.6 | 11 13.9 | +20 33 | A3 |
| β Leonis *Denebola* | 2.1 | 11 48.8 | +14 36 | A2 |
| γ Ursae Majoris *Phecda* | 2.4 | 11 53.6 | +53 43 | A0 |
| γ Corvi | 2.6 | 12 15.6 | −17 31 | B8 |
| α Crucis | 1.0 | 12 26.3 | −63 04 | B1 |
| γ Crucis | 1.6 | 12 30.9 | −57 05 | M3 |
| γ Centauri | 2.2 | 12 41.3 | −48 56 | A0 |
| γ Virginis | 2.7 | 12 41.4 | − 1 25 | F0 |
| β Crucis | 1.3 | 12 47.5 | −59 40 | B1 |
| ε Ursae Majoris *Alioth* | 1.8 | 12 53.8 | +55 59 | A0p |
| α Canum Venaticorum | 2.9 | 12 55.8 | +38 21 | A0p |
| ζ Ursae Majoris *Mizar* | 2.1 | 13 23.7 | +54 57 | A2p |
| α Virginis *Spica* | 1.0 | 13 25.0 | −11 08 | B2 |
| ε Centauri | 2.6 | 13 39.6 | −53 27 | B1 |
| η Ursae Majoris *Alkaid* | 1.9 | 13 47.4 | +49 20 | B3 |
| β Centauri *Hadar* | 0.6 | 14 03.5 | −60 21 | B1 |
| θ Centauri | 2.1 | 14 06.4 | −36 21 | K0 |
| α Bootis *Arcturus* | 0.0 | 14 15.4 | +19 12 | K0 |
| α Centauri *Rigil Kent* | 0.1 | 14 39.3 | −60 49 | G0 |
| ε Bootis | 2.4 | 14 44.8 | +27 06 | K0 |
| β UMi *Kochab* | 2.1 | 14 50.7 | +74 10 | K5 |
| γ Ursae Minoris | 3.1 | 15 20.7 | +71 51 | A2 |
| α CrB *Alphecca* | 2.2 | 15 34.5 | +26 44 | A0 |
| β Trianguli Australis | 3.0 | 15 54.7 | −63 25 | F0 |
| δ Scorpii | 2.3 | 16 00.1 | −22 37 | B0 |
| β Scorpii | 2.6 | 16 05.2 | −19 48 | B1 |
| α Scorpii *Antares* | 1.0 | 16 29.1 | −26 25 | M0 |
| α Trianguli Australis | 1.9 | 16 48.2 | −69 01 | K2 |
| ε Scorpii | 2.3 | 16 49.9 | −34 17 | K0 |
| α Herculis† | Var. | 17 14.4 | +14 24 | M3 |
| λ Scorpii | 1.6 | 17 33.3 | −37 06 | B2 |
| α Ophiuchi *Rasalhague* | 2.1 | 17 34.7 | +12 34 | A5 |
| θ Scorpii | 1.9 | 17 37.0 | −43 00 | F0 |
| κ Scorpii | 2.4 | 17 42.2 | −39 02 | B2 |
| γ Draconis | 2.2 | 17 56.5 | +51 29 | K5 |
| ε Sgr *Kaus Australis* | 1.9 | 18 23.9 | −34 23 | A0 |
| α Lyrae *Vega* | 0.0 | 18 36.8 | +38 47 | A0 |
| σ Sagittarii | 2.0 | 18 55.0 | −26 18 | B3 |
| β Cygni *Albireo* | 3.1 | 19 30.5 | +27 57 | K0 |
| α Aquilae *Altair* | 0.8 | 19 50.6 | + 8 51 | A5 |
| α Capricorni | 3.8 | 20 17.8 | −12 34 | G5 |
| γ Cygni | 2.2 | 20 22.1 | +40 15 | F8p |
| α Pavonis | 1.9 | 20 25.3 | −56 45 | B3 |
| α Cygni *Deneb* | 1.3 | 20 41.3 | +45 16 | A2p |
| α Cephei *Alderamin* | 2.4 | 21 18.5 | +62 34 | A5 |
| ε Pegasi | 2.4 | 21 44.0 | + 9 51 | K0 |
| δ Capricorni | 2.9 | 21 46.8 | −16 09 | A5 |
| α Gruis | 1.7 | 22 08.0 | −46 59 | B5 |
| δ Cephei† | 3.7 | 22 29.0 | +58 24 | † |
| β Gruis | 2.1 | 22 42.4 | −46 55 | M3 |
| α PsA *Fomalhaut* | 1.2 | 22 57.4 | −29 39 | A3 |
| β Pegasi *Scheat* | 2.4 | 23 03.6 | +28 04 | M0 |
| α Pegasi *Markab* | 2.5 | 23 04.5 | +15 11 | A0 |

*γ Cassiopeiae, 1994 mag. 2.5. β Persei, mag. 2.1 to 3.4.
α Orionis, mag. 0.1 to 1.2.
†α Herculis, mag. 3.1 to 3.9. δ Cephei, mag. 3.7 to 4.4,
Spectrum F5 to G0.

The positions of heavenly bodies on the celestial sphere are defined by two co-ordinates, right ascension and declination, which are analogous to longitude and latitude on the surface of the Earth. If we imagine the plane of the terrestrial equator extended indefinitely, it will cut the celestial sphere in a great circle known as the celestial equator. Similarly the plane of the Earth's orbit, when extended, cuts in the great circle called the ecliptic. The two intersections of these circles are known as the First Point of Aries and the First Point of Libra. If from any star a perpendicular be drawn to the celestial equator, the length of this perpendicular is the star's declination. The arc, measured eastwards along the equator from the First Point of Aries to the foot of this perpendicular, is the right ascension. An alternative definition of right ascension is that it is the angle at the celestial pole (where the Earth's axis, if prolonged, would meet the sphere) between the great circles to the First Point of Aries and to the star.

The plane of the Earth's equator has a slow movement, so that our reference system for right ascension and declination is not fixed. The consequent alteration in these quantities from year to year is called precession. In right ascension it is an increase of about 3s a year for equatorial stars, and larger or smaller changes in either direction for stars near the poles, depending on the right ascension of the star. In declination it varies between +20″ and −20″ according to the right ascension of the star.

A star or other body crosses the meridian when the sidereal time is equal to its right ascension. The altitude is then a maximum, and may be deduced by remembering that the altitude of the elevated pole is numerically equal to the latitude, while that of the equator at its intersection with the meridian is equal to the co-latitude, or complement of the latitude.

Thus in London (lat. 51° 30′) the meridian altitude of Sirius is found as follows:

|  | ° ′ |
|---|---|
| Altitude of equator | 38 30 |
| Declination south | 16 43 |
| Difference | 21 47 |

The altitude of Capella (Dec. +46° 00′) at lower transit is:

|  | ° ′ |
|---|---|
| Altitude of pole | 51 30 |
| Polar distance of star | 44 00 |
| Difference | 7 30 |

The brightness of a heavenly body is denoted by its magnitude. Omitting the exceptionally bright stars Sirius and Canopus, the twenty brightest stars are of the first magnitude, while the faintest stars visible to the naked eye are of the sixth magnitude. The magnitude scale is a precise one, as a difference of five magnitudes represents a ratio of 100 to 1 in brightness. Typical second magnitude stars are Polaris and the stars in the belt of Orion. The scale is most easily fixed in memory by comparing the stars with Norton's *Star Atlas* (*see* page 71). The stars Sirius and Canopus and the planets Venus and Jupiter are so bright that their magnitudes are expressed by negative numbers. A small telescope will show stars down to the ninth or tenth magnitude, while stars fainter than the twentieth magnitude may be photographed by long exposures with the largest telescopes.

## MEAN AND SIDEREAL TIME

| Acceleration | | | | Retardation | | | |
|---|---|---|---|---|---|---|---|
| h | m s | m s | s | h | m s | m s | s |
| 1 | 0 10 | 0 00 | 0 | 1 | 0 10 | 0 00 | 0 |
| 2 | 0 20 | 3 02 | 1 | 2 | 0 20 | 3 03 | 1 |
| 3 | 0 30 | 9 07 | 2 | 3 | 0 29 | 9 09 | 2 |
| 4 | 0 39 | 15 13 | 3 | 4 | 0 39 | 15 15 | 3 |
| 5 | 0 49 | 21 18 | 4 | 5 | 0 49 | 21 21 | 4 |
| 6 | 0 59 | 27 23 | 5 | 6 | 0 59 | 27 28 | 5 |
| 7 | 1 09 | 33 28 | 6 | 7 | 1 09 | 33 34 | 6 |
| 8 | 1 19 | 39 34 | 7 | 8 | 1 19 | 39 40 | 7 |
| 9 | 1 29 | 45 39 | 8 | 9 | 1 28 | 45 46 | 8 |
| 10 | 1 39 | 51 44 | 9 | 10 | 1 38 | 51 53 | 9 |
| 11 | 1 48 | 57 49 | 10 | 11 | 1 48 | 57 59 | 10 |
| 12 | 1 58 | 60 00 | | 12 | 1 58 | 60 00 | |
| 13 | 2 08 | | | 13 | 2 08 | | |
| 14 | 2 18 | | | 14 | 2 18 | | |
| 15 | 2 28 | | | 15 | 2 27 | | |
| 16 | 2 38 | | | 16 | 2 37 | | |
| 17 | 2 48 | | | 17 | 2 47 | | |
| 18 | 2 57 | | | 18 | 2 57 | | |
| 19 | 3 07 | | | 19 | 3 07 | | |
| 20 | 3 17 | | | 20 | 3 17 | | |
| 21 | 3 27 | | | 21 | 3 26 | | |
| 22 | 3 37 | | | 22 | 3 36 | | |
| 23 | 3 47 | | | 23 | 3 46 | | |
| 24 | 3 57 | | | 24 | 3 56 | | |

The length of a sidereal day in mean time is 23h 56m 04s.09. Hence 1h MT = 1h + 9s.86 ST and 1h ST = 1h − 9s.83 MT.

To convert an interval of mean time to the corresponding interval of sidereal time, enter the acceleration table with the given mean time (taking the hours and the minutes and seconds separately) and add the acceleration obtained to the given mean time. To convert an interval of sidereal time to the corresponding interval of mean time, take out the retardation for the given sidereal time and subtract.

The columns for the minutes and seconds of the argument are in the form known as critical tables. To use these tables, find in the appropriate left-hand column the two entries between which the given number of minutes and seconds lies; the quantity in the right-hand column between these two entries is the required acceleration or retardation. Thus the acceleration for 11m 26s (which lies between the entries 9m 07s and 15m 13s) is 2s. If the given number of minutes and seconds is a tabular entry, the required acceleration or retardation is the entry in the right-hand column above the given tabular entry, e.g. the retardation for 45m 46s is 7s.

*Example* – Convert 14h 27m 35s from ST to MT

|  | h | m | s |
|---|---|---|---|
| Given ST | 14 | 27 | 35 |
| Retardation for 14h | | 2 | 18 |
| Retardation for 27m 35s | | | 5 |
| Corresponding MT | 14 | 25 | 12 |

For further explanation, *see* pages 73–4.

## ECLIPSES AND SHADOW TRANSITS OF JUPITER'S SATELLITES 1995

| GMT | Sat. | Phen. |
|---|---|---|
| *d h m* | | |
| JANUARY | | |
| 4 07 46 | II | Sh.E. |
| 14 06 52 | III | Sh.E. |
| 14 07 48 | I | Sh.I. |
| 22 07 01 | I | Ec.D. |
| 23 06 20 | I | Sh.E. |
| 27 07 13 | II | Ec.D. |
| 30 06 04 | I | Sh.I. |
| FEBRUARY | | |
| 5 04 52 | II | Sh.I. |
| 5 07 18 | II | Sh.E. |
| 7 05 16 | I | Ec.D. |
| 8 06 47 | III | Ec.D. |
| 14 07 09 | I | Ec.D. |
| 15 04 19 | I | Sh.I. |
| 15 06 29 | I | Sh.E. |
| 21 04 17 | II | Ec.D. |
| 21 06 46 | II | Ec.R. |
| 22 06 13 | I | Sh.I. |
| 26 04 35 | III | Sh.I. |
| 26 06 41 | III | Sh.E. |
| MARCH | | |
| 2 04 14 | II | Sh.E. |
| 2 05 23 | I | Ec.D. |
| 3 04 44 | I | Sh.E. |
| 9 04 21 | II | Sh.I. |
| 10 04 28 | I | Sh.I. |
| 16 04 43 | III | Ec.R. |
| 18 03 37 | I | Ec.D. |
| 18 03 50 | II | Ec.R. |
| 19 03 00 | I | Sh.E. |
| 25 03 56 | II | Ec.D. |
| 25 05 30 | I | Ec.D. |
| 26 02 43 | I | Sh.I. |
| 26 04 54 | I | Sh.E. |
| APRIL | | |
| 2 04 37 | I | Sh.I. |
| 3 01 51 | I | Ec.D. |
| 3 02 32 | III | Sh.E. |
| 3 03 43 | II | Sh.E. |
| 10 03 44 | I | Ec.D. |
| 10 03 48 | II | Sh.I. |
| 10 04 22 | III | Sh.I. |
| 11 00 59 | I | Sh.I. |
| 11 03 09 | I | Sh.E. |
| 18 02 52 | I | Sh.I. |
| 19 01 02 | II | Ec.D. |
| 21 00 32 | III | Ec.R. |
| 25 04 46 | I | Sh.I. |
| 26 01 59 | I | Ec.D. |
| 26 03 38 | II | Ec.D. |
| 27 01 25 | I | Sh.E. |
| 28 00 39 | II | Sh.E. |
| 28 02 18 | III | Ec.D. |
| 28 04 30 | III | Ec.R. |
| MAY | | |
| 3 03 52 | I | Ec.D. |
| 4 01 08 | I | Sh.I. |
| 4 03 19 | I | Sh.E. |
| 5 00 42 | II | Sh.I. |
| 5 03 12 | II | Sh.E. |
| 11 03 02 | I | Sh.I. |
| 12 00 14 | I | Ec.D. |
| 12 03 16 | II | Sh.I. |
| 12 23 42 | I | Sh.E. |
| 16 00 11 | III | Sh.I. |
| 16 02 24 | III | Sh.E. |
| 19 02 07 | I | Ec.D. |
| 19 23 25 | I | Sh.I. |
| 20 01 36 | I | Sh.E. |
| 21 00 44 | II | Ec.D. |
| 27 01 19 | I | Sh.I. |
| 27 03 30 | I | Sh.E. |
| 27 22 29 | I | Ec.D. |
| 28 03 20 | II | Ec.D. |
| 28 21 59 | I | Sh.E. |
| 29 21 40 | II | Sh.I. |
| 30 00 11 | II | Sh.E. |
| JUNE | | |
| 3 00 23 | III | Ec.R. |
| 4 02 34 | I | Ec.R. |
| 4 21 42 | I | Sh.I. |
| 4 23 54 | I | Sh.E. |
| 5 21 03 | I | Ec.R. |
| 6 00 14 | II | Sh.I. |
| 6 02 45 | II | Sh.E. |
| 7 21 48 | II | Ec.R. |
| 11 23 37 | I | Sh.I. |
| 12 01 48 | I | Sh.E. |
| 12 22 57 | I | Ec.R. |
| 15 00 25 | II | Ec.R. |
| 19 01 31 | I | Sh.I. |
| 20 00 51 | I | Ec.R. |
| 20 22 11 | I | Sh.E. |
| 20 22 20 | III | Sh.E. |
| 23 21 12 | II | Sh.E. |
| 27 21 54 | I | Sh.I. |
| 28 00 02 | III | Sh.I. |
| 28 00 06 | I | Sh.E. |
| 28 21 14 | I | Ec.R. |
| 30 21 15 | II | Sh.I. |
| 30 23 47 | II | Sh.E. |
| JULY | | |
| 4 23 49 | I | Sh.I. |
| 5 23 09 | I | Ec.R. |
| 7 23 50 | II | Sh.I. |
| 9 21 32 | II | Ec.R. |
| 13 22 24 | I | Sh.E. |
| 15 21 58 | III | Ec.D. |
| 20 22 08 | I | Sh.I. |
| 21 21 27 | I | Ec.R. |
| 25 20 53 | II | Sh.E. |
| 29 20 42 | I | Sh.E. |
| AUGUST | | |
| 1 20 55 | II | Sh.I. |
| 2 22 18 | III | Sh.E. |
| 5 20 26 | I | Sh.I |
| 5 22 37 | I | Sh.E. |
| 10 21 16 | II | Ec.R. |
| 13 21 41 | I | Ec.R. |
| 20 20 19 | III | Ec.R. |
| 21 20 56 | I | Sh.E. |
| 26 20 29 | II | Sh.E. |
| 28 20 40 | I | Sh.I. |
| 29 20 01 | I | Ec.R. |
| SEPTEMBER | | |
| 2 20 40 | II | Sh.I. |
| 6 19 14 | I | Sh.E. |
| 13 18 59 | I | Sh.I. |
| 14 19 53 | III | Sh.I. |
| OCTOBER | | |
| 6 18 01 | II | Ec.R. |
| 7 18 35 | I | Ec.R. |

Jupiter's satellites transit across the disk from east to west, and pass behind the disk from west to east. The shadows that they cast also transit across the disk. With the exception at times of Satellite IV, the satellites also pass through the shadow of the planet, i.e. they are eclipsed. Just before opposition the satellite disappears in the shadow to the west of the planet and reappears from occultation on the east limb. Immediately after opposition the satellite is occulted at the west limb and reappears from eclipse to the east of the planet. At times approximately two to four months before and after opposition, both phases of eclipses of Satellite III may be seen. When Satellite IV is eclipsed, both phases may be seen.

The times given refer to the centre of the satellite. As the satellite is of considerable size, the immersion and emersion phases are not instantaneous. Even when the satellite enters or leaves the shadow along a radius of the shadow, the phase can last for several minutes. With Satellite IV, grazing phenomena can occur so that the light from the satellite may fade and brighten again without a complete eclipse taking place.

The list of phenomena gives most of the eclipses and shadow transits visible in the British Isles under favourable conditions.

| | | | |
|---|---|---|---|
| Ec. | = Eclipse | R. | = Reappearance |
| Sh. | = Shadow transit | I. | = Ingress |
| D. | = Disappearance | E. | = Egress |

## EXPLANATION OF ASTRONOMICAL DATA

Positions of the heavenly bodies are given only to the degree of accuracy required by amateur astronomers for setting telescopes, or for plotting on celestial globes or star atlases. Where intermediate positions are required, linear interpolation may be employed.

Definitions of the terms used cannot be given here. They must be sought in astronomical literature and textbooks. Probably the best source for the amateur is Norton's *Star Atlas and Reference Handbook* (Longman, 18th edition, 1989; £19.99), which contains an introduction to observational astronomy, and a series of star maps for showing stars visible to the naked eye. Certain more extended ephemerides are available in the British Astronomical Association Handbook, an annual popular among amateur astronomers (Secretary: Burlington House, Piccadilly, London WIV 9AG).

A special feature has been made of the times when the various heavenly bodies are visible in the British Isles. Since two columns, calculated for latitudes 52° and 56°, are devoted to risings and settings, the range 50° to 58° can be covered by interpolation and extrapolation. The times given in these columns are Greenwich Mean Times for the meridian of Greenwich. An observer west of this meridian must add his/her longitude (in time) and vice versa.

In accordance with the usual convention in astronomy, + and − indicate respectively north and south latitudes or declinations.

All data are, unless otherwise stated, for 0h Greenwich Mean Time (GMT), i.e. at the midnight at the beginning of the day named. Allowance must be made for British Summer Time during the period that this is in operation (*see* pages 15 and 75).

### PAGE ONE OF EACH MONTH

The calendar for each month is explained on page 15.

Under the heading Astronomical Phenomena will be found particulars of the more important conjunctions of the Sun, Moon and planets with each other, and also the dates of other astronomical phenomena of special interest.

The Constellations listed each month are those that are near the meridian at the beginning of the month at 22h local mean time. Allowance must be made for British Summer Time if necessary. The fact that any star crosses the meridian 4m earlier each night or 2h earlier each month may be used, in conjunction with the lists given each month, to find what constellations are favourably placed at any moment. The table preceding the list of constellations may be extended indefinitely at the rate just quoted.

Times of Minima of Algol are approximate times of the middle of the period of diminished light.

The principal phases of the Moon are the GMTs when the difference between the longitude of the Moon and that of the Sun is 0°, 90°, 180° or 270°. The times of perigee and apogee are those when the Moon is nearest to, and farthest from, the Earth, respectively. The nodes or points of intersection of the Moon's orbit and the ecliptic make a complete retrograde circuit of the ecliptic in about 19 years. From a knowledge of the longitude of the ascending node and the inclination, whose value does not vary much from 5°, the path of the Moon among the stars may be plotted on a celestial globe or star atlas.

### PAGE TWO OF EACH MONTH

The Sun's semi-diameter, in arc, is given once a month.

The right ascension and declination (Dec.) is that of the true Sun. The right ascension of the mean Sun is obtained by applying the equation of time, with the sign given, to the right ascension of the true Sun, or, more easily, by applying 12h to the column Sidereal Time. The direction in which the equation of time has to be applied in different problems is a frequent source of confusion and error. Apparent Solar Time is equal to the Mean Solar Time plus the Equation of Time. For example at noon on August 8 the Equation of Time is − 5m 40s and thus at 12h Mean Time on that day the Apparent Time is 12h − 5m 40s = 11h 54m 20s.

The Greenwich Sidereal Time at 0h and the Transit of the First Point of Aries (which is really the mean time when the sidereal time is 0h) are used for converting mean time to sidereal time and vice versa.

The GMT of transit of the Sun at Greenwich may also be taken as the local mean time (LMT) of transit in any longitude. It is independent of latitude. The GMT of transit in any longitude is obtained by adding the longitude to the time given if west, and vice versa.

### LIGHTING-UP TIME

The legal importance of sunrise and sunset is that the Road Vehicles Lighting Regulations 1989 (SI 1989 No. 1796) make the use of front and rear position lamps on vehicles compulsory during the period between sunset and sunrise. Headlamps on vehicles are required to be used during the hours of darkness on unlit roads or whenever visibility is seriously reduced. The hours of darkness are defined in these regulations as the period between half an hour after sunset and half an hour before sunrise.

In all laws and regulations 'sunset' refers to the local sunset, i.e. the time at which the Sun sets at the place in question. This common-sense interpretation has been upheld by legal tribunals. Thus the necessity for providing for different latitudes and longitudes, as already described, is evident.

### SUNRISE AND SUNSET

The times of sunrise and sunset are those when the Sun's upper limb, as affected by refraction, is on the true horizon of an observer at sea-level. Assuming the mean refraction to be 34′, and the Sun's semi-diameter to be 16′, the time given is that when the true zenith distance of the Sun's centre is 90° + 34′ + 16′ or 90° 50′, or, in other words, when the depression of the Sun's centre below the true horizon is 50′. The upper limb is then 34′ below the true horizon, but is brought there by refraction. It is true, of course, that an observer on a ship might see the Sun for a minute or so longer, because of the dip of the horizon, while another viewing the sunset over hills or mountains would record an earlier time. Nevertheless, the moment when the true zenith distance of the Sun's centre is 90° 50′ is a precise time dependent only on the latitude and longitude of the place, and independent of its altitude above sea-level, the contour of its horizon, the vagaries of refraction or the small seasonal change in the Sun's semi-diameter; this moment is suitable in every way as a definition of sunset (or sunrise) for all statutory purposes. (For further information, *see* footnote.)

---

SUNRISE, SUNSET AND MOONRISE, MOONSET

The tables have been constructed for the meridian of Greenwich, and for latitudes 52° and 56°. They give Greenwich Mean Time (GMT) throughout the year. To obtain the GMT of the phenomenon as seen from any other latitude and longitude in the British Isles, first interpolate or extrapolate for latitude by the usual rules of proportion. To the time thus found, the longitude (expressed in time) is to be added if west (as it usually is in Great Britain) or subtracted if east. If the longitude is expressed in degrees and minutes of arc, it must be converted to time at the rate of 1° = 4m and 15′ = 1m.

A method of calculating rise and set times for other places in the world is given on pages 64 and 65

## TWILIGHT

Light reaches us before sunrise and continues to reach us for some time after sunset. The interval between darkness and sunrise or sunset and darkness is called twilight. Astronomically speaking, twilight is considered to begin or end when the Sun's centre is 18° below the horizon, as no light from the Sun can then reach the observer. As thus defined, twilight may last several hours; in high latitudes at the summer solstice the depression of 18° is not reached, and twilight lasts from sunset to sunrise.

The need for some sub-division of twilight is met by dividing the gathering darkness into four stages.

(1) *Sunrise or Sunset*, defined as above.
(2) *Civil twilight*, which begins or ends when the Sun's centre is 6° below the horizon. This marks the time when operations requiring daylight may commence or must cease. In England it varies from about 30 to 60 minutes after sunset and the same interval before sunrise.
(3) *Nautical twilight*, which begins or ends when the Sun's centre is 12° below the horizon. This marks the time when it is, to all intents and purposes, completely dark.
(4) *Astronomical twilight*, which begins or ends when the Sun's centre is 18° below the horizon. This marks theoretical perfect darkness. It is of little practical importance, especially if nautical twilight is tabulated.

To assist observers the durations of civil, nautical and astronomical twilights are given at intervals of ten days. The beginning of a particular twilight is found by subtracting the duration from the time of sunrise, while the end is found by adding the duration to the time of sunset. Thus the beginning of astronomical twilight in latitude 52°, on the Greenwich meridian, on March 11 is found as 06h 25m − 113m = 04h 32m and similarly the end of civil twilight as 17h 57m + 34m = 18h 31m.

The letters TAN (twilight all night) are printed when twilight lasts all night.

Under the heading The Night Sky will be found notes describing the position and visibility of the planets and other phenomena.

## PAGE THREE OF EACH MONTH

The Moon moves so rapidly among the stars that its position is given only to the degree of accuracy that permits linear interpolation. The right ascension (RA) and declination (Dec.) are geocentric, i.e. for an imaginary observer at the centre of the Earth. To an observer on the surface of the Earth the position is always different, as the altitude is always less on account of parallax, which may reach 1°.

The lunar terminator is the line separating the bright from the dark part of the Moon's disk. Apart from irregularities of the lunar surface, the terminator is elliptical, because it is a circle seen in projection. It becomes the full circle forming the limb, or edge, of the Moon at New and Full Moon. The selenographic longitude of the terminator is measured from the mean centre of the visible disk, which may differ from the visible centre by as much as 8°, because of libration.

Instead of the longitude of the terminator the Sun's selenographic co-longitude (Sun's co-long.) is tabulated. It is numerically equal to the selenographic longitude of the morning terminator, measured eastwards from the mean centre of the disk. Thus its value is approximately 270° at New Moon, 360° at First Quarter, 90° at Full Moon and 180° at Last Quarter.

The Position Angle (PA) of the Bright Limb is the position angle of the midpoint of the illuminated limb, measured eastwards from the north point on the disk. The column Phase shows the percentage of the area of the Moon's disk

illuminated; this is also the illuminated percentage of the diameter at right angles to the line of cusps. The terminator is a semi-ellipse whose major axis is the line of cusps, and whose semi-minor axis is determined by the tabulated percentage; from New Moon to Full Moon the east limb is dark, and vice versa.

The times given as moonrise and moonset are those when the upper limb of the Moon is on the horizon of an observer at sea-level. The Sun's horizontal parallax (Hor. par.) is about 9″, and is negligible when considering sunrise and sunset, but that of the Moon averages about 57′. Hence the computed time represents the moment when the true zenith distance of the Moon is 90° 50′ (as for the Sun) minus the horizontal parallax. The time required for the Sun or Moon to rise or set is about four minutes (except in high latitudes). *See also* page 65 and footnote on page 71.

The GMT of transit of the Moon over the meridian of Greenwich is given; these times are independent of latitude but must be corrected for longitude. For places in the British Isles it suffices to add the longitude if west, and vice versa. For more remote places a further correction is necessary because of the rapid movement of the Moon relative to the stars. The entire correction is conveniently determined by first finding the west longitude $\lambda$ of the place. If the place is in west longitude, $\lambda$ is the ordinary west longitude; if the place is in east longitude $\lambda$ is the complement to 24h (or 360°) of the longitude and will be greater than 12h (or 180°). The correction then consists of two positive portions, namely $\lambda$ and the fraction $\lambda/24$ (or $\lambda°/360$) multiplied by the difference between consecutive transits. Thus for Sydney, New South Wales, the longitude is 10h 05m east, so $\lambda$=13h 55m and the fraction $\lambda/24$ is 0.58. The transit on the local date 1995 January 23 is found as follows:

|  |  | d | h | m |
|---|---|---|---|---|
| GMT of transit at Greenwich | Jan. | 22 | 04 | 13 |
| $\lambda$ | | | 13 | 55 |
| $0.58 \times (5h\ 03m - 4h\ 13m)$ | | | | 29 |
| GMT of transit at Sydney | | 22 | 18 | 37 |
| Corr. to NSW Standard Time | | | 10 | 00 |
| Local standard time of transit | | 23 | 04 | 37 |

As is evident, for any given place the quantities $\lambda$ and the correction to local standard time may be combined permanently, being here 23h 55m.

Positions of Mercury are given for every second day, and those of Venus and Mars for every fifth day; they may be interpolated linearly. The diameter (Diam.) is given in seconds of arc. The phase is the illuminated percentage of the disk. In the case of the inner planets this approaches 100 at superior conjunction and 0 at inferior conjunction. When the phase is less than 50 the planet is crescent-shaped or horned; for greater phases it is gibbous. In the case of the exterior planet Mars, the phase approaches 100 at conjunction and opposition, and is a minimum at the quadratures.

Since the planets cannot be seen when on the horizon, the actual times of rising and setting are not given; instead, the time when the planet has an apparent altitude of 5° has been tabulated. If the time of transit is between 00h and 12h the time refers to an altitude of 5° above the eastern horizon; if between 12h and 24h, to the western horizon. The phenomenon tabulated is the one that occurs between sunset and sunrise. The times given may be interpolated for latitude and corrected for longitude as in the case of the Sun and Moon.

The GMT at which the planet transits the Greenwich meridian is also given. The times of transit are to be corrected to local meridians in the usual way, as already described.

## PAGE FOUR OF EACH MONTH

The GMTs of sunrise and sunset for seven towns, whose adopted positions in longitude (W.) and latitude (N.) are given immediately below the name, may be used not only for these phenomena, but also for lighting-up times, which, under the Road Vehicles Lighting Regulations 1989, are from sunset to sunrise throughout the year. (*See* page 71 for a fuller explanation.)

The particulars for the four outer planets resemble those for the planets on Page Three of each month, except that, under Uranus and Neptune, times when the planet is 10° high instead of 5° high are given; this is because of the inferior brightness of these planets. The diameters given for the rings of Saturn are those of the major axis (in the plane of the planet's equator) and the minor axis respectively. The former has a small seasonal change due to the slightly varying distance of the Earth from Saturn, but the latter varies from zero when the Earth passes through the ring plane every 15 years to its maximum opening half-way between these periods. The rings were open at their widest extent in 1988.

## TIME

From the earliest ages, the natural division of time into recurring periods of day and night has provided the practical time-scale for the everyday activities of the human race. Indeed, if any alternative means of time measurement is adopted, it must be capable of adjustment so as to remain in general agreement with the natural time-scale defined by the diurnal rotation of the Earth on its axis. Ideally the rotation should be measured against a fixed frame of reference; in practice it must be measured against the background provided by the celestial bodies. If the Sun is chosen as the reference point, we obtain Apparent Solar Time, which is the time indicated by a sundial. It is not a uniform time but is subject to variations which amount to as much as a quarter of an hour in each direction. Such wide variations cannot be tolerated in a practical time-scale, and this has led to the concept of Mean Solar Time in which all the days are exactly the same length and equal to the average length of the Apparent Solar Day.

The positions of the stars in the sky are specified in relation to a fictitious reference point in the sky known as the First Point of Aries (or the Vernal Equinox). It is therefore convenient to adopt this same reference point when considering the rotation of the Earth against the background of the stars. The time-scale so obtained is known as Apparent Sidereal Time.

### GREENWICH MEAN TIME

The daily rotation of the Earth on its axis causes the Sun and the other heavenly bodies to appear to cross the sky from east to west. It is convenient to represent this relative motion as if the Sun really performed a daily circuit around a fixed Earth. Noon in Apparent Solar Time may then be defined as the time at which the Sun transits across the observer's meridian. In Mean Solar Time, noon is similarly defined by the meridian transit of a fictitious Mean Sun moving uniformly in the sky with the same average speed as the true Sun. Mean Solar Time observed on the meridian of the transit circle telescope of the Old Royal Observatory at Greenwich is called Greenwich Mean Time (GMT). The mean solar day is divided into 24 hours and, for astronomical and other scientific purposes, these are numbered 0 to 23, commencing at midnight. Civil time is usually reckoned in two periods of 12 hours, designated a.m. (*ante meridiem*, i.e. before noon) and p.m. (*post meridiem*, i.e. after noon).

### UNIVERSAL TIME

Before 1925 January 1, GMT was reckoned in 24 hours commencing at noon; since that date it has been reckoned from midnight. In view of the risk of confusion in the use of the designation GMT before and after 1925, the International Astronomical Union recommended in 1928 that astronomers should employ the term Universal Time (UT) or Weltzeit (WZ) to denote GMT measured from Greenwich Mean Midnight.

In precision work it is necessary to take account of small variations in Universal Time. These arise from small irregularities in the rotation of the Earth. Observed astronomical time is designated UT0. Observed time corrected for the effects of the motion of the poles (giving rise to a 'wandering' in longitude) is designated UT1. There is also a seasonal fluctuation in the rate of rotation of the Earth arising from meteorological causes, often called the annual fluctuation. UT1 corrected for this effect is designated UT2 and provides a time-scale free from short-period fluctuations. It is still subject to small secular and irregular changes.

### APPARENT SOLAR TIME

As has been mentioned above, the time shown by a sundial is called Apparent Solar Time. It differs from Mean Solar Time by an amount known as the Equation of Time, which is the total effect of two causes which make the length of the apparent solar day non-uniform. One cause of variation is that the orbit of the Earth is not a circle, but an ellipse, having the Sun at one focus. As a consequence, the angular speed of the Earth in its orbit is not constant; it is greatest at the beginning of January when the Earth is nearest the Sun.

The other cause is due to the obliquity of the ecliptic; the plane of the equator (which is at right angles to the axis of rotation of the Earth) does not coincide with the ecliptic (the plane defined by the apparent annual motion of the Sun around the celestial sphere) but is inclined to it at an angle of 23° 26′. As a result, the apparent solar day is shorter than average at the equinoxes and longer at the solstices. From the combined effects of the components due to obliquity and eccentricity, the equation of time reaches its maximum values in February ($-14$ minutes) and early November ($+16$ minutes). It has a zero value on four dates during the year, and it is only on these dates (approximately April 15, June 14, September 1, and December 25) that a sundial shows Mean Solar Time.

### SIDEREAL TIME

A sidereal day is the duration of a complete rotation of the Earth with reference to the First Point of Aries. The term sidereal (or 'star') time is perhaps a little misleading since the time-scale so defined is not exactly the same as that which would be defined by successive transits of a selected star, as there is a small progressive motion between the stars and the First Point of Aries due to the precession of the Earth's axis. This makes the length of the sidereal day shorter than the true period of rotation by 0.008 seconds. Superimposed on this steady precessional motion are small oscillations called nutation, giving rise to fluctuations in apparent sidereal time amounting to as much as 1.2 seconds. It is therefore customary to employ Mean Sidereal Time, from which these fluctuations have been removed. The conversion of GMT to Greenwich sidereal time (GST) may be performed by adding the value of the GST at 0h on the day in question (Page Two of each month) to the GMT converted to sidereal time using the table on page 69.

*Example* – To find the GST at August 8d 02h 41m 11s GMT

|  | h | m | s |
|---|---|---|---|
| GST at 0h | 21 | 04 | 08 |
| GMT | 2 | 41 | 11 |
| Acceleration for 2h |  |  | 20 |
| Acceleration for 41m 11s |  |  | 7 |
| Sum = GST = | 23 | 45 | 46 |

If the observer is not on the Greenwich meridian then his/her longitude, measured positively westwards from Greenwich, must be subtracted from the GST to obtain Local Sidereal Time (LST). Thus, in the above example, an observer 5h east of Greenwich, or 19h west, would find the LST as 4h 45m 46s.

EPHEMERIS TIME

In the study of the motions of the Sun, Moon and planets, observations taken over an extended period are used in the preparation of tables giving the apparent position of the body each day. A table of this sort is known as an ephemeris, and may be used in the comparison of current observations with tabulated positions. A detailed examination of the observations made over the past 300 years shows that the Sun, Moon and planets appear to depart from their predicted positions by amounts proportional to their mean motions. The only satisfactory explanation is that the time-scale to which the observations were referred was not as uniform as had been supposed. Since the time-scale was based on the rotation of the Earth, it follows that this rotation is subject to irregularities. The fact that the discrepancies between the observed and ephemeris positions were proportional to the mean motions of the bodies made it possible to secure agreement by substituting a revised time-scale and recomputing the ephemeris positions. The time-scale which brings the ephemeris into agreement with the observations is known as Ephemeris Time (ET).

The second of ET is defined in terms of the annual motion of the Earth in its orbit around the Sun (1/31556925.9747 of the tropical year for 1900 January 0d 12h ET). The precise determination of ET from astronomical observations is a lengthy process, as the accuracy with which a single observation of the Sun can be made is far less than that obtainable in, for instance, a comparison between clocks. It is therefore necessary to average the observations over an extended period. Largely on account of its faster motion, the position of the Moon may be observed with greater accuracy, and a close approximation to Ephemeris Time may be obtained by comparing observations of the Moon with its ephemeris position. Even in this case, however, the requisite standard of accuracy can only be achieved by averaging over a number of years.

In 1976 the International Astronomical Union adopted a new dynamical time-scale for general use whose scale unit is the SI second (see under Atomic Time). ET is now of little more than historical interest.

TERRESTRIAL DYNAMICAL TIME

The uniform time system used in computing the ephemerides of the solar system is Terrestrial Dynamical Time (TDT), which has replaced ET for this purpose. Except for the most rigorous astronomical calculations, it may be assumed to be the same as ET. During 1995 the estimated difference TDT − UT is 60 seconds.

ATOMIC TIME

The fundamental standards of time and frequency must be defined in terms of a periodic motion adequately uniform, enduring and measurable. Progress has made it possible to use natural standards, such as atomic or molecular oscillations. Continuous oscillations are generated in an electrical circuit, the frequency of which is then compared or brought into coincidence with the frequency characteristic of the absorption or emission by the atoms or molecules when they change between two selected energy levels. The National Physical Laboratory (NPL) routinely uses clocks of high stability produced by locking a quartz oscillator to the frequency defined by a caesium atomic beam.

International Atomic Time (TAI), established through international collaboration, is formed by combining the readings of many caesium clocks and was set close to the astronomically-based Universal Time (UT) near the beginning of 1958. It was formally recognized in 1971 and since 1988 January 1 has been maintained by the International Bureau of Weights and Measures (BIPM). The second markers are generated according to the International System (SI) definition adopted in 1967 at the 13th General Conference of Weights and Measures: 'The second is the duration of 9 192 631 770 periods of the radiation corresponding to the transition between the two hyperfine levels of the ground state of the caesium-133 atom.'

Civil time in almost all countries is now based on Co-ordinated Universal Time (UTC), which was adopted for scientific purposes on 1972 January 1. UTC differs from TAI by an integer number of seconds (determined from studies of the rate of rotation of the Earth) and was designed to make both atomic time and UT accessible with accuracies appropriate for most users. The UTC time scale is adjusted by the insertion (or, in principle, omission) of leap seconds in order to keep it within ± 0.9 s of UT. These leap seconds are introduced, when necessary, at the same instant throughout the world, either at the end of December or at the end of June. So, for example, the nineteenth leap second occurred at 0h GMT on 1994 July 1. All leap seconds so far have been positive, with 61 seconds in the final minute of the UTC month. The time 23h 59m 60s UTC is followed one second later by 0h 0m 00s of the first day of the following month. Notices concerning the insertion of leap seconds are issued by the International Earth Rotation Service (IERS) at the Observatoire de Paris.

RADIO TIME-SIGNALS

UTC is made generally available through time-signals and standard frequency broadcasts such as MSF in the UK, CHU in Canada and WWV and WWVH in the USA. These are based on national time-scales that are maintained in close agreement with UTC and provide traceability to the national time-scale and to UTC. The markers of seconds in the UTC scale coincide with those of TAI.

To disseminate the national time-scale in the UK, special signals are broadcast on behalf of the National Physical Laboratory from the BT (British Telecom) radio station at Rugby. The signals are controlled from a caesium beam atomic frequency standard and consist of a standard frequency carrier of 60 kHz (MSF) which is switched off, after being on for at least half a second, to mark every second. In part of the first second of each minute the carrier is switched on and off at 100 bits/second to signal a binary coded decimal (BCD) message giving UTC time of day and calendar information. In the other seconds the carrier is always off for at least one tenth of a second at the start and then it carries an on-off code giving similar information for British clock time together with information identifying the start of the next minute. Changes to and from summer time are made following Government announcements. Leap seconds are inserted as announced by the IERS and information provided by the BIPM on the difference between UTC and UT is also signalled. Other broadcast signals in the

UK include the BBC six pips signal, the BT Timeline ('speaking clock'), the NPL Truetime service for computers and a coded time-signal on the BBC 198 kHz transmitters, which is used for timing in the electricity supply industry. From 1972 January 1 the six pips on the BBC have consisted of five short pips from second 55 to second 59 (six pips in the case of a leap second) followed by one lengthened pip, the start of which indicates the exact minute. From 1990 February 5 these signals have been controlled by the BBC with second markers referenced to the satellite-based US navigation system GPS (Global Positioning System) and time and day referenced to the MSF transmitter. Formerly these were generated by the Royal Greenwich Observatory. The BT Timeline is compared daily with the National Physical Laboratory caesium beam atomic frequency standard at the Rugby radio station. The NPL Truetime service is directly connected to the national time scale.

Accurate timing may also be obtained from the signals of international navigation systems such as the ground-based Loran-C or Omega, or the satellite-based GPS of the USA or Russian GLONASS systems.

STANDARD TIME

In the year 1880 it was enacted by statute that the word 'time', when it occurred in any legal document relating to Great Britain, was to be interpreted, unless otherwise specifically stated, as the mean time of the Greenwich meridian. Summer time is the legal time during the period in which its use is ordained.

Since the year 1883 the system of standard time by zones has been gradually accepted, and now throughout the world a standard time which differs from that of Greenwich by an integral number of hours, either fast or slow, is used. The large territories of the United States and Canada are divided into zones approximately 7.5° on either side of central meridians. (For time zones of countries of the world, see Index.)

Variations from the standard time of some countries occur during part of the year; they are decided annually and are usually referred to as Summer Time or Daylight Saving Time.

At the 180th meridian the time can be either 12 hours fast on Greenwich Mean Time or 12 hours slow, and a change of date occurs. The internationally-recognized date or calendar line is a modification of the 180th meridian, drawn so as to include islands of any one group on the same side of the line, or for political reasons. The line is indicated by joining up the following co-ordinates:

| Lat. | Long. | Lat. | Long. |
|------|-------|------|-------|
| 60° S. | 180° | 48° N. | 180° |
| 51° S. | 180° | 53° N. | 170° E. |
| 45° S. | 172.5° W. | 65.5° N. | 169° W. |
| 15° S. | 172.5° W. | 75° N. | 180° |
| 5° S. | 180° | | |

BRITISH SUMMER TIME

In 1916 an Act ordained that during a defined period of that year the legal time for general purposes in Great Britain should be one hour in advance of Greenwich Mean Time. The Summer Time Acts 1922 to 1925 defined the period during which Summer Time was to be in force, stabilizing practice until the Second World War.

During the war the duration of Summer Time was extended and in the years 1941–5 and in 1947 Double Summer Time (two hours in advance of Greenwich Mean Time) was in force. After the war, Summer Time was extended each year in 1948–52 and 1961–4 by Order in Council.

Between 1968 October 27 and 1971 October 31 clocks were kept one hour ahead of Greenwich Mean Time throughout the year. This was known as British Standard Time.

The most recent legislation is the Summer Time Act 1972, which enacted that 'the period of summer time for the purposes of this Act is the period beginning at two o'clock, Greenwich mean time, in the morning of the day after the third Saturday in March or, if that day is Easter Day, the day after the second Saturday in March, and ending at two o'clock, Greenwich mean time, in the morning of the day after the fourth Saturday in October.'

The duration of Summer Time can be varied by Order in Council and in recent years alterations have been made to bring the operation of Summer Time in Britain closer to similar provisions in other countries of the European Union; for instance, since 1981 the hour of changeover has been 01h Greenwich Mean Time.

The duration of Summer Time in 1995 will be March 26 to October 22 (subject to confirmation).

MEAN REFRACTION

| Alt. | Ref. | Alt. | Ref. | Alt. | Ref. |
|------|------|------|------|------|------|
| ° ′ | ′ | ° ′ | ′ | ° ′ | ′ |
| 1 20 | 21 | 3 12 | 13 | 7 54 | 6 |
| 1 30 | 20 | 3 34 | 12 | 9 27 | 5 |
| 1 41 | 19 | 4 00 | 11 | 11 39 | 4 |
| 1 52 | 18 | 4 30 | 10 | 15 00 | 3 |
| 2 05 | 17 | 5 06 | 9 | 20 42 | 2 |
| 2 19 | 16 | 5 50 | 8 | 32 20 | 1 |
| 2 35 | 15 | 6 44 | 7 | 62 17 | 0 |
| 2 52 | 14 | 7 54 | | 90 00 | |
| 3 12 | | | | | |

The refraction table is in the form of a critical table (see page 69)

ASTRONOMICAL CONSTANTS

| | |
|---|---|
| Solar Parallax | 8″.794 |
| Astronomical unit | 149597870 km |
| Precession for the year 1995 | 50″.289 |
| Precession in Right Ascension | 3s.075 |
| Precession in Declination | 20″.044 |
| Constant of Nutation | 9″.202 |
| Constant of Aberration | 20″.496 |
| Mean Obliquity of Ecliptic (1995) | 23° 26′ 24″ |
| Moon's Equatorial Hor. Parallax | 57′ 02″.70 |
| Velocity of light in vacuo per second | 299792.5 km |
| Solar motion per second | 20.0 km |
| Equatorial radius of the Earth | 6378.140 km |
| Polar radius of the Earth | 6356.755 km |
| North Galactic Pole (IAU standard) | |
| | RA 12h 49m (1950.0). Dec. 27°.4 N. |
| Solar Apex | RA 18h 06m Dec. + 30° |

Length of Year (in mean solar days)

| | |
|---|---|
| Tropical | 365.24220 |
| Sidereal | 365.25636 |
| Anomalistic (perihelion to perihelion) | 365.25964 |
| Eclipse | 346.6200 |

Length of Month (mean values)

| | d | h | m | s |
|---|---|---|---|---|
| New Moon to New | 29 | 12 | 44 | 02.9 |
| Sidereal | 27 | 07 | 43 | 11.5 |
| Anomalistic (perigee to perigee) | 27 | 13 | 18 | 33.2 |

## ELEMENTS OF THE SOLAR SYSTEM

| Orb | Mean distance from Sun (Earth = 1) | km 10⁶ | Sidereal period | Synodic period | Incl. of orbit to ecliptic | Diameter | Mass (Earth = 1) | Period of rotation on axis |
|---|---|---|---|---|---|---|---|---|
| | | | days | days | ° ′ | km | | days |
| Sun | — | — | — | — | — | 1,392,530 | 332,946 | 25–35* |
| Mercury | 0.39 | 58 | 88.0 | 116 | 7 00 | 4,879 | 0.0553 | 58.646 |
| Venus | 0.72 | 108 | 224.7 | 584 | 3 24 | 12,104 | 0.8150 | 243.017r |
| Earth | 1.00 | 150 | 365.3 | — | — | 12,756e | 1.0000 | 0.997 |
| Mars | 1.52 | 228 | 687.0 | 780 | 1 51 | 6,794e | 0.1074 | 1.026 |
| Jupiter | 5.20 | 778 | 4,332.6 | 399 | 1 18 | 142,984e / 133,708p | 317.89 | 0.410e |
| Saturn | 9.54 | 1427 | 10,759.2 | 378 | 2 29 | 120,536e / 108,728p | 95.18 | 0.426e |
| Uranus | 19.18 | 2870 | 30,684.6 | 370 | 0 46 | 51,118e | 14.54 | 0.718r |
| Neptune | 30.06 | 4497 | 60,191.0 | 367 | 1 46 | 49,528e | 17.15 | 0.671 |
| Pluto | 39.80 | 5954 | 91,708.2 | 367 | 17 09 | 2,302 | 0.002 | 6.387 |

*e* equatorial, *p* polar, *r* retrograde, * depending on latitude

## THE SATELLITES

| Name | Star mag. | Mean distance from primary | Sidereal period of revolution | Name | Star mag. | Mean distance from primary | Sidereal period of revolution |
|---|---|---|---|---|---|---|---|
| EARTH | | km | d | SATURN | | km | d |
| I Moon | — | 384,400 | 27.322 | VII Hyperion | 14 | 1,481,000 | 21.277 |
| | | | | VIII Iapetus | 11 | 3,561,300 | 79.330 |
| MARS | | | | IX Phoebe | 16 | 12,952,000 | 550.5r |
| I Phobos | 12 | 9,380 | 0.319 | URANUS | | | |
| II Deimos | 13 | 23,460 | 1.262 | VI Cordelia | — | 49,770 | 0.335 |
| | | | | VII Ophelia | — | 53,790 | 0.376 |
| JUPITER | | | | VIII Bianca | — | 59,170 | 0.435 |
| XVI Metis | 17 | 127,960 | 0.295 | IX Cressida | — | 61,780 | 0.464 |
| XV Adrastea | 19 | 128,980 | 0.298 | X Desdemona | — | 62,660 | 0.474 |
| V Amalthea | 14 | 181,300 | 0.498 | XI Juliet | — | 64,350 | 0.493 |
| XIV Thebe | 16 | 221,900 | 0.675 | XII Portia | — | 66,090 | 0.513 |
| I Io | 5 | 421,600 | 1.769 | XIII Rosalind | — | 69,940 | 0.558 |
| II Europa | 5 | 670,900 | 3.551 | XIV Belinda | — | 75,260 | 0.624 |
| III Ganymede | 5 | 1,070,000 | 7.155 | XV Puck | — | 86,010 | 0.762 |
| IV Callisto | 6 | 1,880,000 | 16.689 | V Miranda | 17 | 129,390 | 1.413 |
| XIII Leda | 20 | 11,094,000 | 239 | I Ariel | 14 | 191,020 | 2.520 |
| VI Himalia | 15 | 11,480,000 | 251 | II Umbriel | 15 | 266,300 | 4.144 |
| X Lysithea | 18 | 11,720,000 | 259 | III Titania | 14 | 435,910 | 8.706 |
| VII Elara | 17 | 11,737,000 | 260 | IV Oberon | 14 | 583,520 | 13.463 |
| XII Ananke | 19 | 21,200,000 | 631r | | | | |
| XI Carme | 18 | 22,600,000 | 692r | NEPTUNE | | | |
| VIII Pasiphae | 17 | 23,500,000 | 735r | III Naiad | 25 | 48,230 | 0.294 |
| IX Sinope | 18 | 23,700,000 | 758r | IV Thalassa | 24 | 50,070 | 0.311 |
| | | | | V Despina | 23 | 52,530 | 0.335 |
| SATURN | | | | VI Galatea | 22 | 61,950 | 0.429 |
| XVIII Pan | — | 133,600 | 0.575 | VII Larissa | 22 | 73,550 | 0.555 |
| XV Atlas | 18 | 137,640 | 0.602 | VIII Proteus | 20 | 117,650 | 1.122 |
| XVI Prometheus | 16 | 139,350 | 0.613 | I Triton | 13 | 354,760 | 5.877 |
| XVII Pandora | 16 | 141,700 | 0.629 | II Nereid | 19 | 5,513,400 | 360.136 |
| XI Epimetheus | 15 | 151,420 | 0.694 | | | | |
| X Janus | 14 | 151,470 | 0.695 | PLUTO | | | |
| I Mimas | 13 | 185,520 | 0.942 | I Charon | 17 | 19,700 | 6.387 |
| II Enceladus | 12 | 238,020 | 1.370 | | | | |
| III Tethys | 10 | 294,660 | 1.888 | | | | |
| XIII Telesto | 19 | 294,660 | 1.888 | | | | |
| XIV Calypso | 19 | 294,660 | 1.888 | | | | |
| IV Dione | 10 | 377,400 | 2.737 | | | | |
| XII Helene | 18 | 377,400 | 2.737 | | | | |
| V Rhea | 10 | 527,040 | 4.518 | | | | |
| VI Titan | 8 | 1,221,850 | 15.945 | | | | |

# THE EARTH

The shape of the Earth is that of an oblate spheroid or solid of revolution whose meridian sections are ellipses not differing much from circles, whilst the sections at right angles are circles. The length of the equatorial axis is about 12,756 kilometres, and that of the polar axis is 12,714 kilometres. The mean density of the Earth is 5.5 times that of water, although that of the surface layer is less. The Earth and Moon revolve about their common centre of gravity in a lunar month; this centre in turn revolves round the Sun in a plane known as the ecliptic, that passes through the Sun's centre. The Earth's equator is inclined to this plane at an angle of 23.4°. This tilt is the cause of the seasons. In mid-latitudes, and when the Sun is high above the Equator, not only does the high noon altitude make the days longer, but the Sun's rays fall more directly on the Earth's surface; these effects combine to produce summer. In equatorial regions the noon altitude is large throughout the year, and there is little variation in the length of the day. In higher latitudes the noon altitude is lower, and the days in summer are appreciably longer than those in winter.

The average velocity of the Earth in its orbit is 30 kilometres a second. It makes a complete rotation on its axis in about 23h 56m of mean time, which is the sidereal day. Because of its annual revolution round the Sun, the rotation with respect to the Sun, or the solar day, is more than this by about four minutes (*see* page 73). The extremity of the axis of rotation, or the North Pole of the Earth, is not rigidly fixed, but wanders over an area roughly 20 metres in diameter.

# TERRESTRIAL MAGNETISM

A magnetic compass points along the horizontal component of a magnetic line of force. These directions converge on the 'magnetic dip-poles', the places where a freely suspended magnetized needle would become vertical. Not only do these poles move with time, but their exact locations are ill-defined, particularly so in the case of the north dip-pole where the lines of force on the north side of it, instead of converging radially, tend to bunch into a channel. Although it is therefore unrealistic to attempt to specify the locations of the dip-poles exactly, the present approximate adopted positions are 79°.1 N., 105°.4 W. and 64°.7 S., 138°.7 E. The two magnetic dip-poles are thus not antipodal, the line joining them passing the centre of the Earth at a distance of about 1,250 kilometres. The distances of the magnetic dip-poles from the north and south geographical poles are about 1,200 and 2,800 kilometres respectively.

There is also a 'magnetic equator', at all points of which the vertical component of the Earth's magnetic field is zero and a magnetized needle remains horizontal. This line runs between 2° and 10° north of the geographical equator in Asia and Africa, turns sharply south off the West African coast, and crosses South America through Brazil, Bolivia and Peru; it recrosses the geographical equator in mid-Pacific.

Reference has already been made to secular changes in the Earth's field. The following table indicates the changes in magnetic declination (or variation of the compass). Similar, though much smaller, changes have occurred in 'dip' or magnetic inclination. Secular changes differ throughout the world. Although the London observations strongly suggest a cycle with a period of several hundred years, an exact repetition is unlikely.

| London | | Greenwich | |
|---|---|---|---|
| 1580 | 11° 15′ E. | 1850 | 22° 24′ W. |
| 1622 | 5° 56′ E. | 1900 | 16° 29′ W. |
| 1665 | 1° 22′ W. | 1925 | 13° 10′ W. |
| 1730 | 13° 00′ W. | 1950 | 9° 07′ W. |
| 1773 | 21° 09′ W. | 1975 | 6° 39′ W. |

In order that up-to-date information on the variation of the compass may be available, many governments publish magnetic charts on which there are lines (isogonic lines) passing through all places at which specified values of declination will be found at the date of the chart.

In the British Isles, isogonic lines now run approximately north-east to south-west. Though there are considerable local deviations due to geological causes, a rough value of magnetic declination may be obtained by assuming that at 50° N. on the meridian of Greenwich, the value in 1995 is 3° 30′ west and allowing an increase of 12′ for each degree of latitude northwards and one of 30′ for each degree of longitude westwards. For example, at 53° N., 5° W., declination will be about 3° 30′ + 36′ + 150′, i.e. 6° 36′ west. The average annual change at the present time is about 6′ decrease.

The number of magnetic observatories is about 200, irregularly distributed over the globe. There are three in Great Britain, run by the British Geological Survey: at Hartland, North Devon; at Eskdalemuir, Dumfriesshire; and at Lerwick, Shetland Islands. The following are some recent annual mean values of the magnetic elements for Hartland.

| Year | Declination West | | Dip or inclination | | Horizontal force | Vertical force |
|---|---|---|---|---|---|---|
| | ° | ′ | ° | ′ | gauss | gauss |
| 1955 | 10 | 30 | 66 | 49 | 0.1859 | 0.4340 |
| 1960 | 9 | 59 | 66 | 44 | 0.1871 | 0.4350 |
| 1965 | 9 | 30 | 66 | 34 | 0.1887 | 0.4354 |
| 1970 | 9 | 06 | 66 | 26 | 0.1903 | 0.4364 |
| 1975 | 8 | 32 | 66 | 17 | 0.1921 | 0.4373 |
| 1980 | 7 | 44 | 66 | 10 | 0.1933 | 0.4377 |
| 1985 | 6 | 56 | 66 | 08 | 0.1938 | 0.4380 |
| 1990 | 6 | 15 | 66 | 10 | 0.1939 | 0.4388 |
| 1993 | 5 | 51 | 66 | 08 | 0.1943 | 0.4393 |

The normal world-wide terrestrial magnetic field corresponds approximately to that of a very strong small bar magnet near the centre of the Earth, but with appreciable smooth spatial departures. The origin and slow secular change of the normal field are not fully understood but are generally ascribed to electric currents associated with fluid motions in the Earth's core. Superimposed on the normal field are local and regional anomalies whose magnitudes may in places approach that of the normal field; these are due to the influence of mineral deposits in the Earth's crust. A small proportion of the field is of external origin, mostly associated with electric currents in the ionosphere. The configuration of the external field and the ionization of the atmosphere depend on the incident particle and radiation flux from the Sun. There are, therefore, short-term and non-periodic as well as diurnal, 27-day, seasonal and 11-year periodic changes in the magnetic field, dependent upon the position of the Sun and the degree of solar activity.

## MAGNETIC STORMS

Occasionally, sometimes with great suddenness, the Earth's magnetic field is subject for several hours to marked disturbance. During a very large storm in March 1989 the declination at Lerwick changed by almost 8° in less than an hour. In many instances, such disturbances are accompanied by widespread displays of aurorae, marked changes in the incidence of cosmic rays, an increase in the reception of 'noise' from the Sun at radio frequencies, and rapid changes in the ionosphere and induced electric currents within the Earth which adversely affect radio and telegraphic communications. The disturbances are caused by changes in the stream of ionized particles which emanates from the Sun and through which the Earth is continuously passing. Some of these changes are associated with visible eruptions on the Sun, usually in the region of sun-spots. There is a marked tendency for disturbances to recur after intervals of about 27 days, the apparent period of rotation of the Sun on its axis, which is consistent with the sources being located on particular areas of the Sun.

## ARTIFICIAL SATELLITES

To consider the orbit of an artificial satellite, it is best to imagine that one is looking at the Earth from a distant point in space. The Earth would then be seen to be rotating about its axis inside the orbit described by the rapidly revolving satellite. The inclination of a satellite orbit to the Earth's equator (which generally remains almost constant throughout the satellite's lifetime) gives at once the maximum range of latitudes over which the satellite passes. Thus a satellite whose orbit has an inclination of 53° will pass overhead all latitudes between 53° S. and 53° N., but would never be seen in the zenith of any place nearer the poles than these latitudes. If we consider a particular place on the earth, whose latitude is less than the inclination of the satellite's orbit, then the Earth's rotation carries this place first under the northbound part of the orbit and then under the southbound portion of the orbit, these two occurrences being always less than 12 hours apart for satellites moving in direct orbits (i.e. to the east). (For satellites in retrograde orbits, the words 'northbound' and 'southbound' should be interchanged in the preceding statement.) As the value of the latitude of the observer increases and approaches the value of the inclination of the orbit, so this interval gets shorter until (when the latitude is equal to the inclination) only one overhead passage occurs each day.

### OBSERVATION OF SATELLITES

The regression of the orbit around the Earth causes alternate periods of visibility and invisibility, though this is of little concern to the radio or radar observer. To the visual observer the following cycle of events normally occurs (though the cycle may start in any position): invisibility, morning observations before dawn, invisibility, evening observations after dusk, invisibility, morning observations before dawn, and so on. With reasonably high satellites and for observers in high latitudes around the summer solstice, the evening observations follow the morning observations without inter-

ruption as sunlight passing over the polar regions can still illuminate satellites which are passing over temperate latitudes at local midnight. At the moment all satellites rely on sunlight to make them visible, though a satellite with a flashing light has been suggested for a future launching. The observer must be in darkness or twilight in order to make any useful observations and the durations of twilight and the sunrise, sunset times given on Page Two of each month will be a useful guide.

Some of the satellites are visible to the naked eye and much interest has been aroused by the spectacle of a bright satellite disappearing into the Earth's shadow. The event is even more fascinating telescopically as the disappearance occurs gradually as the satellite traverses the Earth's penumbral shadow, and during the last few seconds before the eclipse is complete the satellite may change colour (in suitable atmospheric conditions) from yellow to red. This is because the last rays of sunlight are refracted through the denser layers of our atmosphere before striking the satellite.

Some satellites rotate about one or more axes so that a periodic variation in brightness is observed. This was particularly noticeable in several of the Soviet satellites.

Satellite research has provided some interesting results. Among them may be mentioned a revised value of the Earth's oblateness, 1/298.2, and the discovery of the Van Allen radiation belts.

### LAUNCHINGS

Apart from their names, e.g. Cosmos 6 Rocket, the satellites are also classified according to their date of launch. Thus 1961 α refers to the first satellite launching of 1961. A number following the Greek letter indicated the relative brightness of the satellites put in orbit. From the beginning of 1963 the Greek letters were replaced by numbers and the numbers by roman letters e.g. 1963–01A. For all satellites successfully injected into orbit the table gives the designation and names of the main objects (in the order A, B, C . . . etc.), the launch date and some initial orbital data. These are the inclination to the equator ($i$), the nodal period of revolution ($P$), the eccentricity ($e$), and the perigee height.

Although most of the satellites launched are injected into orbits less than 1,000 km high there are an increasing number of satellites in geostationary orbits, i.e. where the orbital inclination is zero, the eccentricity close to zero, and the period of revolution is 1436.1 minutes. Thus the satellite is permanently situated over the equator at one selected longitude at a mean height of 35,786 km. Already this geostationary band is crowded; for example, the television satellite Astra 1A (1988–109B) has been placed only 0°.2 away from the communication satellite Arabsat 1A (1985–15A).

## ARTIFICIAL SATELLITE LAUNCHES 1993–4

| Desig-nation | Satellite | Launch date | $i$ | $P$ | $e$ | Perigee height |
|---|---|---|---|---|---|---|
| 1993– | | | ° | m | | km |
| 26 | Alexis | April 25 | | | | |
| 27 | STS 55 | April 26 | 28.5 | 90.4 | 0.001 | 298 |
| 28 | Cosmos 2243 | April 27 | 70.3 | 88.8 | 0.004 | 191 |
| 29 | Cosmos 2244 | April 28 | 65.0 | 92.8 | 0.001 | 404 |
| 30 | Cosmos 2245 | May 11 | 82.6 | 114.0 | 0.002 | 1397 |
| 31 | Astra 1C | May 12 | 0.0 | 1435.4 | 0.004 | 35621 |
| 32 | ? | May 13 | 34.9 | 356.4 | 0.606 | 190 |
| 33 | Resurs F-2 | May 21 | 82.6 | 88.9 | 0.006 | 181 |

| Desig-nation | Satellite | Launch date | $i$ | $P$ | $e$ | Perigee height |
|---|---|---|---|---|---|---|
| | | | ° | m | | km |
| **1993–** | | | | | | |
| 34 | Progress M-18 | May 23 | 51.6 | 88.7 | 0.004 | 187 |
| 35 | Molniya 1–86 | May 26 | 62.9 | 736.7 | 0.749 | 401 |
| 36 | Cosmos 2251 | June 16 | 74.0 | 100.8 | 0.002 | 782 |
| 37 | STS 57 | June 21 | 28.5 | 93.0 | 0.005 | 395 |
| 38 | Cosmos 2252 | June 24 | 82.6 | 114.8 | 0.005 | 1410 |
| 39 | Galaxy 4 | June 25 | 6.9 | 632.7 | 0.730 | 213 |
| 40 | Resurs F-18 | June 25 | 82.6 | 89.2 | 0.002 | 223 |
| 41 | Radcal | June 25 | 89.5 | 101.5 | 0.008 | 768 |
| 42 | ? | June 26 | 34.8 | 356.5 | 0.606 | 184 |
| 43 | Soyuz TM-17 | July 1 | 51.6 | 90.1 | 0.011 | 209 |
| 44 | Cosmos 2258 | July 7 | 65.0 | 92.8 | 0.001 | 404 |
| 45 | Cosmos 2259 | July 14 | 67.1 | 89.9 | 0.013 | 179 |
| 46 | ? | July | | | | |
| 47 | Resurs F-19 | July 22 | 82.3 | 89.9 | 0.004 | 242 |
| 48 | Hispasat 2B | July 22 | 6.9 | 630.5 | 0.729 | 213 |
| 49 | Molniya 3–45 | August 4 | 62.9 | 698.7 | 0.741 | 388 |
| 50 | NOAA 13 | August 9 | 98.9 | 102.1 | 0.001 | 852 |
| 51 | Cosmos 2261 | August 10 | 62.9 | 710.8 | 0.737 | 571 |
| 52 | Progress M-19 | August 10 | 51.8 | 88.5 | 0.003 | 178 |
| 53 | Resurs F-19 | August 24 | 82.6 | 88.7 | 0.005 | 179 |
| 54 | USA 95 | August 30 | 34.9 | 355.5 | 0.605 | 192 |
| 55 | Meteor 2–21 Temisat | August 31 | 82.5 | 103.9 | 0.003 | 919 |
| 56 | USA 96 | September 3 | 27.0 | 273.7 | 0.527 | 225 |
| 57 | Cosmos 2262 | September 7 | 64.9 | 89.2 | 0.009 | 173 |
| 58 | STS 51 ACTS ORFEUS-SPA | September 12 | 28.5 | 90.3 | 0.001 | 293 |
| 59 | Cosmos 2263 | September 16 | 71.0 | 102.0 | 0.001 | 841 |
| 60 | Cosmos 2264 | September 17 | 65.0 | 92.9 | 0.002 | 402 |
| 61 | Spot-3 Stella Kitsat | September 26 | 98.7 | 101.3 | 0.000 | 817 |
| 62 | Raduga 30 | September 30 | 1.5 | 1426.1 | 0.008 | 35274 |
| 63 | Landsat 6 | October 5 | 98.5 | 100.6 | 0.000 | 784 |
| 64 | Progress M-20 | October 11 | 51.8 | 88.6 | 0.003 | 187 |
| 65 | STS 58 | October 18 | 39.0 | 90.1 | 0.001 | 280 |
| 66 | Intelsat VII F1 | October 22 | 7.0 | 630.0 | 0.731 | 172 |
| 67 | Cosmos 2265 | October 26 | 82.9 | 103.8 | 0.088 | 292 |
| 68 | USA 96 | October 26 | 55.1 | 711.7 | 0.004 | 19909 |
| 69 | Gorizont 28 | October 28 | 1.5 | 1435.5 | 0.000 | 35758 |
| 70 | Cosmos 2266 | November 2 | 83.0 | 104.8 | 0.005 | 951 |
| 71 | Cosmos 2267 | November 5 | 70.4 | 88.9 | 0.005 | 188 |
| 72 | Gorizont 29 | November 18 | 1.5 | 1399.4 | 0.001 | 35043 |
| 73 | Sodaridad 1 Meteosat 6 | November 18 | 6.9 | 631.6 | 0.730 | 212 |
| 74 | USA 97 | November 28 | 26.5 | 625.0 | 0.729 | 184 |
| 75 | STS 61 | December 2 | 28.5 | 96.3 | 0.001 | 583 |
| 76 | USA 98 | December 8 | 23.3 | 646.7 | 0.712 | 762 |
| 77 | TELSTAR 401 | December 16 | 0.1 | 1436.0 | 0.000 | 35784 |
| 78 | ? | December ? | 0.1 | 1436.2 | 0.000 | 35771 |
| 79 | Molniya 1–87 | December 22 | 62.8 | 704.4 | 0.740 | 440 |
| **1994–** | | | | | | |
| 01 | Soyuz TM-18 | January 8 | 51.7 | 88.7 | 0.001 | 203 |
| 02 | GALS 1 | January 20 | 0.3 | 1447.2 | 0.003 | 35882 |
| 03 | Meteor 3 Tubsat | January 25 | 82.6 | 109.4 | 0.001 | 1187 |
| 04 | DSPE | January 25 | 67.0 | 90.1 | 0.003 | 255 |
| 05 | Progress M-21 | January 28 | 51.6 | 92.2 | 0.000 | 384 |
| 06 | STS-60 | February 3 | 57.0 | 91.6 | 0.001 | 347 |
| 07 | OREX, VEP | February 3 | 30.5 | 93.5 | 0.001 | 446 |

| Designation | Satellite | Launch date | $i$ | $P$ | $e$ | Perigee height |
|---|---|---|---|---|---|---|
| 1994– | | | ° | m | | km |
| 08 | Raduga 1–3 | February 5 | 1.5 | 1435.7 | 0.000 | 35767 |
| 09 | USA 99 | February 7 | | | | |
| 10 | SJ 4 | February 8 | 28.5 | 637.4 | 0.732 | 206 |
| 11 | Cosmos 2268–2273 | February 12 | 82.6 | 114.3 | 0.001 | 1413 |
| 12 | Raduga 31 | February 18 | 1.5 | 1471.7 | 0.001 | 36454 |
| 13 | Galaxy 1R | February 19 | 25.6 | 712.6 | 0.650 | 2861 |
| 14 | KORONAS 1 | March 2 | 82.5 | 94.8 | 0.003 | 489 |
| 15 | STS 62 | March 9 | 39.0 | 90.4 | 0.001 | 295 |
| 16 | USA 100 | March 10 | 54.9 | 714.5 | 0.006 | 19928 |
| 17 | USA 101 | March 13 | 0.0 | 714.5 | 0.000 | 19928 |
| 18 | Cosmos 2274 | March 17 | 67.1 | 89.8 | 0.013 | 179 |
| 19 | Progress M 21 | March 22 | 51.6 | 92.3 | 0.002 | 381 |
| 20 | STS 59 | April 9 | 57.0 | 88.3 | 0.000 | 189 |
| 21 | Cosmos 2275–2277 | April 11 | 64.8 | 676.6 | 0.001 | 19120 |
| 22 | GOES 8 | April 13 | 27.1 | 767.1 | 0.766 | 133 |
| 23 | Cosmos 2278 | April 23 | 71.0 | 102.0 | 0.000 | 849 |
| 24 | Cosmos 2279 | April 26 | 82.9 | 104.8 | 0.003 | 958 |
| 25 | Cosmos 2280 | April 28 | 70.4 | 89.9 | 0.005 | 240 |

# Astronomers Royal

Instituted in 1675, the title of Astronomer Royal was given to the director of the Greenwich Observatory until 1975. Currently it is an honorary title for an outstanding astronomer, who receives a stipend of approximately £100 a year.

John Flamsteed (1646–1719), appointed 1675
Edmund Halley (1656–1742), appointed 1720
James Bradley (1693–1762), appointed 1742
Nathaniel Bliss (1700–64), appointed 1762
Nevil Maskelyne (1732–1811), appointed 1765
John Pond (1767–1836), appointed 1811
Sir George Airy (1801–92), appointed 1835
Sir William Christie (1845–1922), appointed 1881
Sir Frank Dyson (1868–1939), appointed 1910
Sir Harold Jones (1890–1960), appointed 1933
Sir Richard Woolley (1906–86), appointed 1955
Sir Martin Ryle (1918–84), appointed 1972
Sir Francis Graham-Smith (1923–), appointed 1982
Arnold Wolfendale (1927–), appointed 1991
Sir Martin Rees (1942–), appointed 1995

# Time Measurement and Calendars

## MEASUREMENTS OF TIME

Measurements of time are based on the time taken by the earth to rotate on its axis (day); by the moon to revolve round the earth (month); and by the earth to revolve round the sun (year). From these, which are not commensurable, certain average or mean intervals have been adopted for ordinary use.

### THE DAY

The day begins at midnight and is divided into 24 hours of 60 minutes, each of 60 seconds. The hours are counted from midnight up to 12 noon (when the sun crosses the meridian), and these hours are designated a.m. (*ante meridiem*); and again from noon up to 12 midnight, which hours are designated p.m. (*post meridiem*), except when the 24-hour reckoning is employed. The 24-hour reckoning ignores a.m. and p.m., and the hours are numbered 0 to 23 from midnight.

Colloquially the 24 hours are divided into day and night, day being the time while the sun is above the horizon (including the four stages of twilight defined on page 72). Day is subdivided further into morning, the early part of daytime, ending at noon; afternoon, from noon to about 6 p.m.; and evening, which may be said to extend from 6 p.m. until midnight. Night, the dark period between day and day, begins at the close of astronomical twilight (*see* page 72) and extends beyond midnight to sunrise the next day.

The names of the days are derived from Old English translations or adaptations of the Roman titles.

| | | |
|---|---|---|
| *Sunday* | Sun | Sol |
| *Monday* | Moon | Luna |
| *Tuesday* | Tiw/Tyr (god of war) | Mars |
| *Wednesday* | Woden/Odin | Mercury |
| *Thursday* | Thor | Jupiter |
| *Friday* | Frigga/Freyja | |
| | (goddess of love) | Venus |
| *Saturday* | Saeternes | Saturn |

### THE WEEK

The week is a period of seven days.

### THE MONTH

The month in the ordinary calendar is approximately the twelfth part of a year, but the lengths of the different months vary from 28 (or 29) days to 31.

### THE YEAR

The equinoctial or tropical year is the time that the earth takes to revolve round the sun from equinox to equinox, i.e. 365.24219 mean solar days, or 365 days 5 hours 48 minutes and 45 seconds.

The calendar year usually consists of 365 days, but a year containing 366 days is called bissextile (*see* Roman Calendar) or leap year, one day being added to the month of February, so that a date 'leaps over' a day of the week.

A year is a leap year if the date of the year is divisible by four without remainder, unless it is the last year of the century. The last year of a century is a leap year only if its number is divisible by 400 without remainder, e.g. the years 1800 and 1900 had only 365 days but the year 2000 will have 366 days.

### THE SOLSTICE

A solstice is the point in the tropical year at which the sun attains its greatest distance, north or south, from the Equator. In the northern hemisphere the furthest point north of the Equator marks the summer solstice and the furthest point south the winter solstice.

The date of the solstice varies according to locality. For example, if the summer solstice falls on 21 June late in the day by Greenwich time, that day will be the longest of the year at Greenwich though it may be by only a second, but it will fall on 22 June, local date, in Japan, and so 22 June will be the longest day there. The date of the solstice is also affected by the length of the tropical year, which is 365 days 6 hours less about 11 minutes 15 seconds. If a solstice happens late on 21 June in one year, it will be nearly six hours later in the next (unless the next year is a leap year), i.e. early on 22 June, and that will be the longest day.

This delay of the solstice does not continue because the extra day in leap year brings it back a day in the calendar. However, because of the 11 minutes 15 seconds mentioned above, the additional day in leap year brings the solstice back too far by 45 minutes, and the time of the solstice in the calendar is earlier, in a four-year pattern, as the century progresses. The last year of a century is in most cases not a leap year, and the omission of the extra day puts the date of the solstice later by about six hours too much. Compensation for this is made by the fourth centennial year being a leap year. The solstice has become earlier in date throughout this century and, because the year 2000 is a leap year, the solstice will get earlier still throughout the 21st century.

Similar considerations apply to the day of the winter solstice, the shortest day of the year. The difference due to locality also prevails in the same sense as for the longest day.

At Greenwich the sun sets at its earliest by the clock about ten days before the shortest day. The daily change in the time of sunset is due in the first place to the sun's movement southwards at this time of the year, which diminishes the interval between the sun's transit and its setting. However, the daily decrease of the Equation of Time causes the time of apparent noon to be continuously later day by day. This in a measure counteracts the first effect. The rates of the change of these two quantities are not equal, nor are they uniform, but are such that their combination causes the date of earliest sunset to be 12 or 13 December at Greenwich. In more southerly latitudes the effect of the movement of the sun is less, and the change in the time of sunset depends on that of the Equation of Time to a greater degree, and the date of earliest sunset is earlier than it is at Greenwich. For example, on the Equator it is about 1 November.

### THE EQUINOX

The equinox is the point at which the sun crosses the Equator and day and night are of equal length all over the world. This occurs in March and September.

### DOG DAYS

The days about the heliacal rising of the Dog Star, noted from ancient times as the hottest period of the year in the northern hemisphere, are called the Dog Days. Their incidence has been variously calculated as depending on the Greater or Lesser Dog Star (Sirius or Procyon) and their duration has been reckoned as from 30 to 54 days. A generally accepted period is from 3 July to 15 August.

## CHRISTIAN CALENDAR

In the Christian chronological system the years are distinguished by cardinal numbers before or after the birth of Christ, the period being denoted by the letters BC (Before Christ) or, more rarely, AC (*Ante Christum*), and AD (*Anno Domini* – In the Year of Our Lord). The correlative dates of the epoch are the fourth year of the 194th Olympiad, the 753rd year from the foundation of Rome, AM 3761 (Jewish chronology), and the 4714th year of the Julian period.

The system was introduced into Italy in the sixth century. Though first used in France in the seventh century, it was not universally established there until about the eighth century. It has been said that the system was introduced into England by St Augustine (AD 596), but it was probably not generally used until some centuries later. It was ordered to be used by the Bishops at the Council of Chelsea (AD 816). The actual date of the birth of Christ is somewhat uncertain.

### THE JULIAN CALENDAR

In the Julian calendar all the centennial years were leap years, and for this reason towards the close of the sixteenth century there was a difference of ten days between the tropical and calendar years; the equinox fell on 11 March of the calendar, whereas at the time of the Council of Nicaea (AD 325), it had fallen on 21 March. In 1582 Pope Gregory ordained that 5 October should be called 15 October and that of the end-century years only the fourth should be a leap year (*see* page 81).

### THE GREGORIAN CALENDAR

The Gregorian calendar was adopted by Italy, France, Spain and Portugal in 1582, by Prussia, the Roman Catholic German states, Switzerland, Holland and Flanders on 1 January 1583, by Poland in 1586, Hungary in 1587, the Protestant German and Netherland states and Denmark in 1700, and by Great Britain and Dominions (including the North American colonies) in 1752, by the omission of eleven days (3 September being reckoned as 14 September). Sweden omitted the leap day in 1700 but observed leap days in 1704 and 1708, and reverted to the Julian calendar by having two leap days in 1712; the Gregorian calendar was adopted in 1753 by the omission of eleven days (18 February being reckoned as 1 March). Japan adopted the calendar in 1872, China in 1912, Bulgaria in 1915, Turkey and Soviet Russia in 1918, Yugoslavia and Romania in 1919, and Greece in February 1923.

In the same year that the change was made in England from the Julian to the Gregorian calendar, the beginning of the new year was also changed from 25 March to 1 January (*see* page 86).

### THE ORTHODOX CHURCHES

Some Orthodox Churches still use the Julian reckoning, but the majority of Greek Orthodox Churches and the Romanian Orthodox Church have adopted a modified 'New Calendar', observing the Gregorian calendar for fixed feasts and the Julian for movable feasts.

The Orthodox Church year begins on 1 September. There are four fast periods, and in addition to Pascha (Easter), twelve great feasts, as well as numerous commemorations of the saints of the Old and New Testaments throughout the year.

### THE DOMINICAL LETTER

The Dominical Letter is one of the letters A–G which are used to denote the Sundays in successive years. If the first day of the year is a Sunday the letter is A; if the second, B; the third, C; and so on. Leap year requires two letters, the first for 1 January to 29 February, the second for 1 March to 31 December (*see* page 84).

### EPIPHANY

The feast of the Epiphany, commemorating the manifestation of Christ, later became associated with the offering of gifts by the Magi. The day was of exceptional importance from the time of the Council of Nicaea (AD 325), as the primate of Alexandria was charged at every Epiphany feast with the announcement in a letter to the churches of the date of the forthcoming Easter. The day was of considerable importance in Britain as it influenced dates, ecclesiastical and lay, e.g. Plough Monday, when work was resumed in the fields, fell on the Monday in the first full week after Epiphany.

### LENT

The Teutonic word *Lent*, which denotes the fast preceding Easter, originally meant no more than the spring season; but from Anglo-Saxon times at least it has been used as the equivalent of the more significant Latin term Quadragesima, meaning the 'forty days' or, more literally, the fortieth day. Ash Wednesday is the first day of Lent, which ends at midnight before Easter Day.

### PALM SUNDAY

Palm Sunday, the Sunday before Easter and the beginning of Holy Week, commemorates the triumphal entry of Christ into Jerusalem and is celebrated in Britain (when palm is not available) by branches of willow gathered for use in the decoration of churches on that day.

### MAUNDY THURSDAY

Maundy Thursday is the day before Good Friday, the name itself being a corruption of *dies mandati* (day of the mandate) when Christ washed the feet of the disciples and gave them the mandate to love one another.

### EASTER DAY

Easter Day is the first Sunday after the full moon which happens on, or next after, the 21st day of March; if the full moon happens on a Sunday, Easter Day is the Sunday after.

This definition is contained in an Act of Parliament (24 Geo. II c. 23) and explanation is given in the preamble to the Act that the day of full moon depends on certain tables that have been prepared. These are the tables whose essential points are given in the early pages of the Book of Common Prayer. The moon referred to is not the real moon of the heavens, but a hypothetical moon on whose 'full' the date of Easter depends, and the lunations of this 'calendar' moon consist of twenty-nine and thirty days alternately, with certain necessary modifications to make the date of its full agree as nearly as possible with that of the real moon, which is known as the Paschal Full Moon. As at present ordained, Easter falls on one of 35 days (22 March to 25 April).

### A FIXED EASTER

On 15 June 1928 the House of Commons agreed to a motion for the third reading of a bill proposing that Easter Day shall, in the calendar year next but one after the commencement of the Act and in all subsequent years, be the first Sunday after the second Saturday in April. Easter would thus fall between 9 and 15 April (inclusive), that is, on the second or third Sunday in April. A clause in the Bill provided that before it shall come into operation, regard shall be had to any opinion expressed officially by the various Christian churches. Efforts by the World Council of Churches to secure a unanimous choice of date for Easter by its member churches have so far been unsuccessful.

## ROGATION DAYS

Rogation Days are the Monday, Tuesday and Wednesday preceding Ascension Day and in the fifth century were ordered by the Church to be observed as public fasts with solemn processions and supplications. The processions were discontinued as religious observances at the Reformation, but survive in the ceremony known as 'Beating the Parish Bounds'. Rogation Sunday is the Sunday before Ascension Day.

## EMBER DAYS

The Ember Days at the four seasons are the Wednesday, Friday and Saturday (a) before the third Sunday in Advent, (b) before the second Sunday in Lent, and (c) before the Sundays nearest to the festivals of St Peter and of St Michael and All Angels.

## TRINITY SUNDAY

Trinity Sunday is eight weeks after Easter Day, on the Sunday following Pentecost (Whit Sunday). Subsequent Sundays are reckoned in the Book of Common Prayer calendar of the Church of England as 'after Trinity'.

Thomas Becket (1118–70) was consecrated Archbishop of Canterbury on the Sunday after Whit Sunday and his first act was to ordain that the day of his consecration should be held as a new festival in honour of the Holy Trinity. The observance thus originated spread from Canterbury throughout the whole of Christendom.

---

## MOVABLE FEASTS TO THE YEAR 2027

| Year | Ash Wednesday | Easter | Ascension | Pentecost (Whit Sunday) | Sundays after Pentecost | Advent Sunday |
|------|---------------|--------|-----------|-------------------------|-------------------------|---------------|
| 1995 | 1 March | 16 April | 25 May | 4 June | 20 | 3 December |
| 1996 | 21 February | 7 April | 16 May | 26 May | 21 | 1 December |
| 1997 | 12 February | 30 March | 8 May | 18 May | 22 | 30 November |
| 1998 | 25 February | 12 April | 21 May | 31 May | 20 | 29 November |
| 1999 | 17 February | 4 April | 13 May | 23 May | 21 | 28 November |
| 2000 | 8 March | 23 April | 1 June | 11 June | 19 | 3 December |
| 2001 | 28 February | 15 April | 24 May | 3 June | 20 | 2 December |
| 2002 | 13 February | 31 March | 9 May | 19 May | 22 | 1 December |
| 2003 | 5 March | 20 April | 29 May | 8 June | 19 | 30 November |
| 2004 | 25 February | 11 April | 20 May | 30 May | 20 | 28 November |
| 2005 | 9 February | 27 March | 5 May | 15 May | 22 | 27 November |
| 2006 | 1 March | 16 April | 25 May | 4 June | 20 | 3 December |
| 2007 | 21 February | 8 April | 17 May | 27 May | 21 | 2 December |
| 2008 | 6 February | 23 March | 1 May | 11 May | 23 | 30 November |
| 2009 | 25 February | 12 April | 21 May | 31 May | 20 | 29 November |
| 2010 | 17 February | 4 April | 13 May | 23 May | 21 | 28 November |
| 2011 | 9 March | 24 April | 2 June | 12 June | 18 | 27 November |
| 2012 | 22 February | 8 April | 17 May | 27 May | 21 | 2 December |
| 2013 | 13 February | 31 March | 9 May | 19 May | 22 | 1 December |
| 2014 | 5 March | 20 April | 29 May | 8 June | 19 | 30 November |
| 2015 | 18 February | 5 April | 14 May | 24 May | 21 | 29 November |
| 2016 | 10 February | 27 March | 5 May | 15 May | 22 | 27 November |
| 2017 | 1 March | 16 April | 25 May | 4 June | 20 | 3 December |
| 2018 | 14 February | 1 April | 10 May | 20 May | 22 | 2 December |
| 2019 | 6 March | 21 April | 30 May | 9 June | 19 | 1 December |
| 2020 | 26 February | 12 April | 21 May | 31 May | 20 | 29 November |
| 2021 | 17 February | 4 April | 13 May | 23 May | 21 | 28 November |
| 2022 | 2 March | 17 April | 26 May | 5 June | 19 | 27 November |
| 2023 | 22 February | 9 April | 18 May | 28 May | 21 | 3 December |
| 2024 | 14 February | 31 March | 9 May | 19 May | 22 | 1 December |
| 2025 | 5 March | 20 April | 29 May | 8 June | 19 | 30 November |
| 2026 | 18 February | 5 April | 14 May | 24 May | 21 | 29 November |
| 2027 | 10 February | 28 March | 6 May | 16 May | 22 | 28 November |

## NOTES

*Ash Wednesday* (first day in Lent) can fall at earliest on 4 February and at latest on 10 March

*Mothering Sunday* (fourth Sunday in Lent) can fall at earliest on 1 March and at latest on 4 April

*Easter Day* can fall at earliest on 22 March and at latest on 25 April

*Ascension Day* is forty days after Easter Day and can fall at earliest on 30 April and at latest on 3 June

*Pentecost (Whit Sunday)* is seven weeks after Easter and can fall at earliest on 10 May and at latest on 13 June

*Trinity Sunday* is the Sunday after Whit Sunday

*Corpus Christi* falls on the Thursday after Trinity Sunday

*Sundays after Pentecost* – there are not less than 18 and not more than 23

*Advent Sunday* is the Sunday nearest to 30 November

EASTER DAYS AND DOMINICAL LETTERS 1500 to 2030

| | | 1500–1599 | 1600–1699 | 1700–1799 | 1800–1899 | 1900–1999 | 2000–2030 |
|---|---|---|---|---|---|---|---|
| *March* | | | | | | | |
| d | 22 | 1573 | 1668 | 1761 | 1818 | | |
| e | 23 | 1505/16 | 1600 | 1788 | 1845/56 | 1913 | 2008 |
| f | 24 | | 1611/95 | 1706/99 | | 1940 | |
| g | 25 | 1543/54 | 1627/38/49 | 1722/33/44 | 1883/94 | 1951 | |
| A | 26 | 1559/70/81/92 | 1654/65/76 | 1749/58/69/80 | 1815/26/37 | 1967/78/89 | |
| b | 27 | 1502/13/24/97 | 1608/87/92 | 1785/96 | 1842/53/64 | 1910/21/32 | 2005/16 |
| c | 28 | 1529/35/40 | 1619/24/30 | 1703/14/25 | 1869/75/80 | 1937/48 | 2027 |
| d | 29 | 1551/62 | 1635/46/57 | 1719/30/41/52 | 1807/12/91 | 1959/64/70 | |
| e | 30 | 1567/78/89 | 1651/62/73/84 | 1746/55/66/77 | 1823/34 | 1902/75/86/97 | |
| f | 31 | 1510/21/32/83/94 | 1605/16/78/89 | 1700/71/82/93 | 1839/50/61/72 | 1907/18/29/91 | 2002/13/24 |
| *April* | | | | | | | |
| g | 1 | 1526/37/48 | 1621/32 | 1711/16 | 1804/66/77/88 | 1923/34/45/56 | 2018/29 |
| A | 2 | 1553/64 | 1643/48 | 1727/38/52(NS) | 1809/20/93/99 | 1961/72 | |
| b | 3 | 1575/80/86 | 1659/70/81 | 1743/63/68/74 | 1825/31/36 | 1904/83/88/94 | |
| c | 4 | 1507/18/91 | 1602/13/75/86/97 | 1708/79/90 | 1847/58 | 1915/20/26/99 | 2010/21 |
| d | 5 | 1523/34/45/56 | 1607/18/29/40 | 1702/13/24/95 | 1801/63/74/85/96 | 1931/42/53 | 2015/26 |
| e | 6 | 1539/50/61/72 | 1634/45/56 | 1729/35/40/60 | 1806/17/28/90 | 1947/58/69/80 | |
| f | 7 | 1504/77/88 | 1667/72 | 1751/65/76 | 1822/33/44 | 1901/12/85/96 | |
| g | 8 | 1509/15/20/99 | 1604/10/83/94 | 1705/87/92/98 | 1849/55/60 | 1917/28 | 2007/12 |
| A | 9 | 1531/42 | 1615/26/37/99 | 1710/21/32 | 1871/82 | 1939/44/50 | 2023 |
| b | 10 | 1547/58/69 | 1631/42/53/64 | 1726/37/48/57 | 1803/14/87/98 | 1955/66/77 | |
| c | 11 | 1501/12/63/74/85/96 | 1658/69/80 | 1762/73/84 | 1819/30/41/52 | 1909/71/82/93 | 2004 |
| d | 12 | 1506/17/28 | 1601/12/91/96 | 1789 | 1846/57/68 | 1903/14/25/36/98 | 2009/20 |
| e | 13 | 1533/44 | 1623/28 | 1707/18 | 1800/73/79/84 | 1941/52 | |
| f | 14 | 1555/60/66 | 1639/50/61 | 1723/34/45/54 | 1805/11/16/95 | 1963/68/74 | |
| g | 15 | 1571/82/93 | 1655/66/77/88 | 1750/59/70/81 | 1827/38 | 1900/06/79/90 | 2001 |
| A | 16 | 1503/14/25/36/87/98 | 1609/20/82/93 | 1704/75/86/97 | 1843/54/65/76 | 1911/22/33/95 | 2006/17/28 |
| b | 17 | 1530/41/52 | 1625/36 | 1715/20 | 1808/70/81/92 | 1927/38/49/60 | 2022 |
| c | 18 | 1557/68 | 1647/52 | 1731/42/56 | 1802/13/24/97 | 1954/65/76 | |
| d | 19 | 1500/79/84/90 | 1663/74/85 | 1747/67/72/78 | 1829/35/40 | 1908/81/87/92 | |
| e | 20 | 1511/22/95 | 1606/17/79/90 | 1701/12/83/94 | 1851/62 | 1919/24/30 | 2003/14/25 |
| f | 21 | 1527/38/49 | 1622/33/44 | 1717/28 | 1867/78/89 | 1935/46/57 | 2019/30 |
| g | 22 | 1565/76 | 1660 | 1739/53/64 | 1810/21/32 | 1962/73/84 | |
| A | 23 | 1508 | 1671 | | 1848 | 1905/16 | 2000 |
| b | 24 | 1519 | 1603/14/98 | 1709/91 | 1859 | | 2011 |
| c | 25 | 1546 | 1641 | 1736 | 1886 | 1943 | |

# HINDU CALENDAR

The Hindu calendar is a lunar calendar of twelve months, each containing 29 days, 12 hours. Each month is divided into a light fortnight (Shukla or Shuddha) and a dark fortnight (Krishna or Vadya) based on the waxing and waning of the moon. In most parts of India the month starts with the light fortnight, i.e. the day after the new moon, although in some regions it begins with the dark fortnight, i.e. the day after the full moon.

The new year begins in the month of Chaitra (March/April) and ends in the month of Phalgun (March). The twelve months, Chaitra, Vaishakh, Jyeshtha, Ashadh, Shravan, Bhadrapad, Ashvin, Kartik, Margashirsh, Paush, Magh and Phalgun, have Sanskrit names derived from twelve asterisms (constellations). There are regional variations to the names of the months but the Sanskrit names are understood throughout India.

Whenever the difference between the Hindu year of 360 lunar days (354 days 8 hours solar time) and the 365 days 6 hours of the solar year reaches the length of one Hindu lunar month (29 days 12 hours), a 'leap' month is added to the Hindu calendar.

The leap month may be added at any point in the Hindu year. The name given to the month varies according to when it occurs but is taken from the month immediately following it. Leap months occur in 1996–7 (Ashadh) and 1999–2000 (Jyeshtha).

The days of the week are called Raviwar (Sunday), Somawar (Monday), Mangalwar (Tuesday), Budhawar (Wednesday), Guruwar (Thursday), Shukrawar (Friday) and Shaniwar (Saturday). The names are derived from the Sanskrit names of the Sun, the Moon and five planets, Mars, Mercury, Jupiter, Venus and Saturn.

Most fasts and festivals are based on the lunar calendar but a few are determined by the apparent movement of the Sun, e.g. Sankranti, which is celebrated on 14/15 January to mark the start of the Sun's apparent journey northwards and a change of season.

Festivals celebrated throughout India are Chaitra (the New Year), Raksha-bandhan (the renewal of the kinship bond between brothers and sisters), Navaratri (a nine-night festival dedicated to the goddess Parvati), Dasara (the victory of Rama over the demon army), Diwali (a festival of lights), Makara Sankranti, Shivaratri (dedicated to Shiva), and Holi (a spring festival).

Regional festivals are Durga-puja (dedicated to the goddess Durga (Parvati)), Sarasvati-puja (dedicated to the goddess

Sarasvati), Ganesh Chaturthi (worship of Ganesh on the fourth day (Chaturthi) of the light half of Bhadrapad), Ramanavami (the birth festival of the god Rama) and Janmashtami (the birth festival of the god Krishna).

The main festivals celebrated in Britain are Navaratri, Dasara, Durga-puja, Diwali, Holi, Sarasvati-puja, Ganesh Chaturthi, Raksha-bandhan, Ramanavami and Janmashtami.

The dates of the main festivals in 1995 are given on page 9.

## JEWISH CALENDAR

The story of the Flood in the Book of Genesis relates that the Flood began on the 17th day of the second month, that after the end of 150 days the waters were abated, and that on the 17th day of the seventh month the Ark rested on Mount Ararat. This indicates the use of a calendar of some kind and that the writers recognized thirty days as the length of a lunation. However, after the diaspora, Jewish communities were left in considerable doubt as to the times of fasts and festivals. This led to the formation of the Jewish calendar as used today. It is said that this was done in AD 358 by Rabbi Hillel II, a descendant of Gamaliel, though some assert that it did not happen until much later.

The calendar is luni-solar, and is based on the lengths of the lunation and of the tropical year as found by Hipparchus (c.120 BC), which differ little from those adopted at the present day. The year AM 5755 (1994–5) is the 17th year of the 303rd Metonic (Minor or Lunar) cycle of 19 years and the 15th year of the 206th Solar (or Major) cycle of 28 years since the Era of the Creation. Jews hold that the Creation occurred at the time of the autumnal equinox in the year known in the Christian calendar as 3760 BC (954 of the Julian period). The epoch or starting point of Jewish chronology corresponds to 7 October 3761 BC. At the beginning of each solar cycle, the Tekufah of Nisan (the vernal equinox) returns to the same day and to the same hour.

The hour is divided into 1080 minims, and the month between one new moon and the next is reckoned as 29 days, 12 hours, 793 minims. The normal calendar year, called a Common Regular year, consists of 12 months of 30 days and 29 days alternately. Since twelve months such as these comprise only 354 days, in order that each of them shall not diverge greatly from an average place in the solar year, a thirteenth month is occasionally added after the fifth month of the civil year (which commences on the first day of the month Tishri), or as the penultimate month of the ecclesiastical year (which commences on the first day of month Nisan). The years when this happens are called Embolismic or leap years.

Of the 19 years that form a Metonic cycle, seven are leap years; they occur at places in the cycle indicated by the numbers 3, 6, 8, 11, 14, 17 and 19, these places being chosen so that the accumulated excesses of the solar years should be as small as possible.

A Jewish year is of one of the following six types:

| | |
|---|---|
| Minimal Common | 353 days |
| Regular Common | 354 days |
| Full Common | 355 days |
| Minimal Leap | 383 days |
| Regular Leap | 384 days |
| Full Leap | 385 days. |

The Regular year has alternate months of 30 and 29 days. In a Full year, whether common or leap, Marcheshvan, the second month of the civil year, has 30 days instead of 29; in

Minimal years Kislev, the third month, has 29 instead of 30. The additional month in leap years is called Adar I and precedes the month called Adar in Common years. Adar II is called Ve-Adar in leap years, and the usual Adar festivals are kept in Ve-Adar. Adar I and Adar II always have 30 days, but neither this, nor the other variations mentioned, is allowed to change the number of days in the other months which still follow the alternation of the normal twelve.

These are the main features of the Jewish calendar, which must be considered permanent because as a Jewish law it cannot be altered except by a great Sanhedrin.

The Jewish day begins between sunset and nightfall. The time used is that of the meridian of Jerusalem, which is 2h 21m in advance of Greenwich Mean Time. Rules for the beginning of sabbaths and festivals were laid down for the latitude of London in the eighteenth century and hours for nightfall are now fixed annually by the Chief Rabbi.

JEWISH CALENDAR 5755–6

AM 5755 (755) is a Regular Leap year of 13 months, 55 sabbaths and 384 days. AM 5756 (756) is a Full Common year of 12 months, 51 sabbaths and 355 days.

| Jewish Month | AM 5755 | AM 5756 |
|---|---|---|
| *Tishri* 1 | 6 September 1994 | 25 September 1995 |
| *Marcheshvan* 1 | 6 October | 25 October |
| *Kislev* 1 | 4 November | 24 November |
| *Tebet* 1 | 4 December | 24 December |
| *Shebat* 1 | 2 January 1995 | 22 January 1996 |
| *\*Adar* 1 | 1 February | |
| *†Adar* II | 3 March | 21 February |
| *Nisan* 1 | 1 April | 21 March |
| *Iyar* 1 | 1 May | 20 April |
| *Sivan* 1 | 30 May | 19 May |
| *Tammuz* 1 | 29 June | 18 June |
| *Ab* 1 | 28 July | 17 July |
| *Elul* 1 | 27 August | 16 August |

\*Known as Adar Rishon in leap years
†Known as Ve-Adar in leap years

JEWISH FASTS AND FESTIVALS
For dates of principal festivals in 1995, *see* page 9

| | |
|---|---|
| *Tishri* 1–2 | Rosh Hashanah (New Year) |
| *Tishri* 3 | \*Fast of Gedaliah |
| *Tishri* 10 | Yom Kippur (Day of Atonement) |
| *Tishri* 15–21 | Succoth (Feast of Tabernacles) |
| *Tishri* 21 | Hoshana Rabba |
| *Tishri* 22 | Shemini Atseret (Solemn Assembly) |
| *Tishri* 23 | Simchat Torah (Rejoicing of the Law) |
| *Kislev* 25 | Chanucah (Dedication of the Temple) begins |
| *Tebet* 10 | Fast of Tebet |
| *†Adar* 13 | §Fast of Esther |
| *†Adar* 14 | Purim |
| *†Adar* 15 | Shushan Purim |
| *Nisan* 15–22 | Pesach (Passover) |
| *Sivan* 6–7 | Shavuot (Feast of Weeks) |
| *Tammuz* 17 | \*Fast of Tammuz |
| *Ab* 9 | \*Fast of Ab |

\*If these dates fall on the sabbath the fast is kept on the following day
†Ve-Adar in leap years
§This fast is observed on Adar 11 (or Ve-Adar 11 in leap years) if Adar 13 falls on a sabbath

## THE MUSLIM CALENDAR

The Muslim era is dated from the *Hijrah*, or flight of the Prophet Muhammad from Mecca to Medina, the corresponding date of which in the Julian calendar is 16 July AD 622. Hijrah years (AH) are used principally in Iran, Turkey, Egypt, Malaysia, various Arab states and certain parts of India. The dating system was adopted about AD 639, commencing with the first day of the month Muharram. Muharram precedes the month in which the Hijrah took place and was recognized as the beginning of the year because it followed the month of pilgrimage.

The calendar is a lunar calendar and consists of twelve months containing an alternate sequence of 30 and 29 days, with the intercalation of one day at the end of the twelfth month at stated intervals in each cycle of 30 years. The object of the intercalation is to reconcile the date of the first day of the month with the date of the actual new moon.

Some adherents still take the date of the evening of the first physical sighting of the crescent of the New Moon as that of the first of the month.   For this reason, the beginning of a new month and the date of religious festivals can vary by a few days from the published calendars.

In each cycle of 30 years, 19 years are common and contain 354 days, and 11 years are intercalary (leap years) of 355 days, the latter being called *kabishah*. The mean length of the Hijrah years is 354 days 8 hours 48 minutes and the period of mean lunation is 29 days 12 hours 44 minutes.

To ascertain if a year is common or kabishah, divide it by 30: the quotient gives the number of completed cycles and the remainder shows the place of the year in the current cycle. If the remainder is 2, 5, 7, 10, 13, 16, 18, 21, 24, 26 or 29, the year is kabishah and consists of 355 days.

MUSLIM CALENDAR 1415–16

Hijrah year 1415 AH (remainder 5) is a kabishah year; 1416 AH (remainder 6) is a common year.

| Month (length) | 1415 AH | 1416 AH |
| --- | --- | --- |
| *Muharram* (30) | 10 June 1994 | 31 May 1995 |
| *Safar* (29) | 10 July | 30 June |
| *Rabi' I* (30) | 8 August | 29 July |
| *Rabi' II* (29) | 7 September | 28 August |
| *Jumada I* (30) | 7 October | 26 September |
| *Jumada II* (29) | 5 November | 26 October |
| *Rajab* (30) | 4 December | 24 November |
| *Shaabân* (29) | 3 January 1995 | 24 December |
| *Ramadân* (30) | 1 February | 22 January 1996 |
| *Shawwâl* (29) | 3 March | 21 February |
| *Dhû'l-Qa'da* (30) | 1 April | 21 March |
| *Dhû'l-Hijjah* (29 or 30) | 1 May | 20 April |

MUSLIM FESTIVALS

Ramadan is a month of fasting for all Muslims because it is the month in which the revelation of the *Qur'an* (Koran) began.   During Ramadan Muslims abstain from food, drink and sexual pleasure from dawn until after sunset throughout the month.

The two major festivals are *Idu-l-fitr* and *Idu-l-adha*. Idu-l-fitr marks the end of the Ramadan fast and is celebrated on the day after the sighting of the new moon of the following month.   Idu-l-adha, the festival of sacrifice (also known as the great festival), celebrates the submission of the Prophet Ibrahim (Abraham) to Allah.   Idu-l-adha falls on the tenth day of Dhul-Hijjah, coinciding with the day when those on *hajj* (pilgrimage to Mecca) sacrifice animals.

Other days accorded special recognition are:

| | |
| --- | --- |
| *Muharram* 1 | New Year's Day |
| *Muharram* 10 | Ashura (the day Prophet Nuh left the Ark and Prophet Musa was saved from Pharaoh (Sunni), the death of the Prophet's grandson Husain (Shi'ite)) |
| *Rabi'u-l-Awwal (Rabi' I)* 12 | Mawlidu-n-Nabiyy (birthday of the Prophet Muhammad) |
| *Rajab* 27 | Laylatu-l-Isra wa l-Miraj (Night of the Journey and Ascension) |
| *Ramadân* Odd-numbered nights in the last 10 of the month | Laylatu-l-Qadr (Night of Power) |
| *Dhû'l-Hijjah* 10 | Idu-l-adha (Festival of Sacrifice) |

## THE SIKH CALENDAR

The Sikh calendar is a lunar calendar of 365 days divided into 12 months. The length of the months varies between 29 and 32 days.

There are no prescribed feast days and no fasting periods.   The main celebrations are Baisakhi Mela (the new year and the anniversary of the founding of the Khalsa), Diwali Mela (festival of light), Hola Mohalla Mela (a spring festival held in the Punjab), and the Gurpurbs (anniversaries associated with the ten Gurus).

The dates of the major celebrations in 1995 are given on page 9.

## CIVIL AND LEGAL CALENDAR

THE HISTORICAL YEAR

Before the year 1752, two calendar systems were in use in England. The civil or legal year began on 25 March, while the historical year began on 1 January. Thus the civil or legal date 24 March 1658, was the same day as the historical date 24 March 1659; and a date in that portion of the year is written as 24 March 165⁸⁄₉, the lower figure showing the historical year.

THE NEW YEAR

In England in the seventh century, and as late as the 13th, the year was reckoned from Christmas Day, but in the 12th century the Anglican Church began the year with the feast of the Annunciation of the Blessed Virgin (Lady Day) on 25 March and this practice was adopted generally in the 14th century. The civil or legal year in the British Dominions (exclusive of Scotland) began with 'Lady Day' until 1751. But in and since 1752 the civil year has begun with 1 January. Certain dividends are still paid by the Bank of England on dates based on Old Style. New Year's Day in Scotland was changed from 25 March to 1 January in 1600.

On the continent of Europe, 1 January was adopted as the first day of the year by Venice in 1522, German states in 1544, Spain, Portugal, and the Roman Catholic Netherlands in 1556, Prussia, Denmark and Sweden in 1559, France in 1564, Lorraine in 1579, the Protestant Netherlands in 1583, Russia in 1725, and Tuscany in 1751.

## REGNAL YEARS

The regnal years are the years of a sovereign's reign, and each begins on the anniversary of his or her accession, e.g. regnal year 44 of the present Queen begins on 6 February 1995.

The system was used for dating Acts of Parliament until 1962. The Summer Time Act 1925, for example, is quoted as 15 and 16 Geo. V c. 64, because it became law in the parliamentary session which extended over part of both of these regnal years. Acts of a parliamentary session during which a sovereign died were usually given two year numbers, the regnal year of the deceased sovereign and the regnal year of his or her successor. Acts passed in 1952 were dated 16 Geo. VI and 1 Elizabeth II. Since 1962, Acts of Parliament have been dated by the calendar year.

## QUARTER AND TERM DAYS

Holy days and saints days were the usual means in early times for setting the dates of future and recurrent appointments. The quarter days in England and Wales are the feast of the Nativity (25 December), the feast of the Annunciation (25 March), the feast of St John the Baptist (24 June) and the feast of St Michael and All Angels (29 September).

The term days in Scotland are Candlemas (the feast of the Purification), Whitsunday, Lammas (Loaf Mass), and Martinmas (St Martin's Day). These fell on 2 February, 15 May, 1 August and 11 November respectively. However, by the Term and Quarter Days (Scotland) Act 1990, the dates of the term days were changed to 28 February (Candlemas), 28 May (Whitsunday), 28 August (Lammas) and 28 November (Martinmas).

## RED-LETTER DAYS

Red-letter days were originally the holy days and saints days indicated in early ecclesiastical calendars by letters printed in red ink. The days to be distinguished in this way were approved at the Council of Nicaea in AD 325.

These days still have a legal significance, as judges of the Queen's Bench Division wear scarlet robes on red-letter days falling during the law sittings. The days designated as red-letter days for this purpose are:

*Holy and saints days*
Conversion of St Paul, the Purification, Ash Wednesday, the Annunciation, the Ascension, the feasts of St Mark, SS Philip and James, St Matthias, St Barnabas, St John the Baptist, St Peter, St Thomas, St James, St Luke, SS Simon and Jude, All Saints, St Andrew.

*Civil calendar*
The anniversary of The Queen's accession, The Queen's birthday, and The Queen's coronation, The Queen's official birthday, the birthday of the Duke of Edinburgh, the birthday of Queen Elizabeth the Queen Mother, the birthday of the Prince of Wales, St David's Day and Lord Mayor's Day.

## PUBLIC HOLIDAYS

Public holidays are divided into two categories, common law, and statutory. Common law holidays are holidays 'by habit and custom'; in England, Wales and Northern Ireland these are Good Friday and Christmas Day.

Statutory public holidays, known as bank holidays, were first established by the Bank Holidays Act 1871. They were, literally, days on which the banks (and other public institutions) were closed and financial obligations due on that day were payable the following day. The legislation currently governing public holidays in the United Kingdom is the Banking and Financial Dealings Act 1971. It stipulates which days are to be public holidays in England, Wales, Scotland and Northern Ireland.

Certain holidays (indicated by * below) are granted annually by royal proclamation, either throughout the United Kingdom or in any place in the United Kingdom. The public holidays are:

*England and Wales*
*New Year's Day
Easter Monday
*The first Monday in May
The last Monday in May
The last Monday in August
26 December, if it is not a Sunday
27 December when 25 or 26 December is a Sunday

*Scotland*
New Year's Day, or if it is a Sunday, 2 January
2 January, or if it is a Sunday, 3 January
Good Friday
The first Monday in May
*The last Monday in May
The first Monday in August
Christmas Day, or if it is a Sunday, 26 December
*Boxing Day – if Christmas Day falls on a Sunday, 26 December is given in lieu and an alternative day is given for Boxing Day

*Northern Ireland*
*New Year's Day
17 March, or if it is a Sunday, 18 March
Easter Monday
*The first Monday in May
The last Monday in May
*12 July, or if it is a Sunday, 13 July
The last Monday in August
26 December, if it is not a Sunday
27 December if 25 or 26 December is a Sunday

For dates of public holidays in 1995 and 1996, *see* pages 10–11.

# CHRONOLOGICAL CYCLES AND ERAS

## SOLAR (OR MAJOR) CYCLE
The solar cycle is a period of twenty-eight years, in any corresponding year of which the days of the week recur on the same day of the month.

## METONIC (LUNAR, OR MINOR) CYCLE
In 432 BC, Meton, an Athenian astronomer, found that 235 lunations are very nearly, though not exactly, equal in duration to 19 solar years, and, hence, after 19 years the phases of the Moon recur on the same days of the month (nearly). The dates of full moon in a cycle of 19 years were inscribed in figures of gold on public monuments in Athens, and the number showing the position of a year in the cycle is called the golden number of that year.

## JULIAN PERIOD
The Julian period was proposed by Joseph Scaliger in 1582. The period is 7980 Julian years, and its first year coincides with the year 4713 BC. The figure of 7980 is the product of the number of years in the solar cycle, the Metonic cycle and the cycle of the Roman indiction ($28 \times 19 \times 15$).

## ROMAN INDICTION
The Roman indiction is a period of fifteen years, instituted for fiscal purposes about AD 300.

EPACT

The epact is the age of the calendar Moon, diminished by one day, on 1 January, in the ecclesiastical lunar calendar.

CHINESE CALENDAR

A lunar calendar was the sole calendar in use in China until 1911, when the government adopted the new (Gregorian) calendar for official and most business activities. The Chinese tend to follow both calendars, the lunar calendar playing an important part in personal life, e.g. birth celebrations, festivals, marriages; and in rural villages the lunar calendar dictates the cycle of activities, denoting the change of weather and farming activities.

The lunar calendar is used in Hong Kong, Singapore, Malaysia, Tibet and elsewhere in south-east Asia. The calendar has a cycle of 60 years. The new year begins at the first new moon after the sun enters the sign of Aquarius, i.e. the new year falls between 21 January and 19 February in the Gregorian calendar.

Each year in the Chinese calendar is associated with one of 12 animals: the rat, the ox, the tiger, the rabbit, the dragon, the snake, the horse, the goat or sheep, the monkey, the chicken or rooster, the dog, and the pig.

The date of the Chinese new year and the astrological sign for the years 1995–2000 are:

| 1995 | 31 January | Pig |
| 1996 | 19 February | Rat |
| 1997 | 7 February | Ox |
| 1998 | 28 January | Tiger |
| 1999 | 16 February | Rabbit |
| 2000 | 5 February | Dragon |

COPTIC CALENDAR

In the Coptic calendar, which is used by part of the population of Egypt and Ethiopia, the year is made up of 12 months of 30 days each, followed, in general, by five complementary days. Every fourth year is an intercalary or leap year and in these years there are six complementary days. The intercalary year of the Coptic calendar immediately precedes the leap year of the Julian calendar. The era is that of Diocletian or the Martyrs, the origin of which is fixed at 29 August AD 284 (Julian date).

INDIAN ERAS

In addition to the Muslim reckoning there are six eras used in India. The principal astronomical system was the Kaliyuga era, which appears to have been adopted in the fourth century AD. It began on 18 February 3102 BC. The chronological system of northern India, known as the Vikrama Samvat era, prevalent in western India, began on 23 February 57 BC. The year AD 1995 is, therefore, the year 2052 of the Vikrama era.

The Saka era of southern India dating from 3 March AD 78, was declared the uniform national calendar of the Republic of India with effect from 22 March 1957, to be used concurrently with the Gregorian calendar. As revised, year of the new Saka era begins at the spring equinox, with five successive months of 31 days and seven of 30 days in ordinary years, and six months of each length in leap years. The year AD 1995 is 1917 of the revised Saka era.

The Saptarshi era dates from the moment when the Saptarshi, or saints, were translated and became the stars of the Great Bear in 3076 BC. The Buddhists reckoned from the death of the Buddha in 543 BC (the actual date being 487 BC); and the epoch of the Jains was the death of Vardhamana, the founder of their faith, in 527 BC.

JAPANESE CALENDAR

The Japanese calendar is essentially the same as the Gregorian calendar, the years, months and weeks being of the same length and beginning on the same days as those of the Gregorian calendar. The numeration of the years is different, for Japanese chronology is based on a system of epochs or periods, each of which begins at the accession of an Emperor or other important occurrence. The method is not unlike the former British system of regnal years, but differs from it in that each year of a period closes on 31 December. The Japanese chronology begins about AD 650 and the three latest epochs are defined by the reigns of Emperors, whose actual names are not necessarily used:

*Epoch*

Taishō 1 August 1912 to 25 December 1926
Shōwa 26 December 1926 to 7 January 1989
Heisei 8 January 1989

Hence the year Heisei 7 begins on 1 January 1995.

The months are not named. They are known as First Month, Second Month, etc., First Month being equivalent to January. The days of the week are Nichiyōbi (Sun-day), Getsuyōbi (Moon-day), Kayōbi (Fire-day), Suiyōbi (Water-day), Mokuyōbi (Wood-day), Kinyōbi (Metal-day), Doyōbi (Earth-day).

THE MASONIC YEAR

Two dates are quoted in warrants, dispensations, etc., issued by the United Grand Lodge of England, those for the current year being expressed as *Anno Domini* 1995 – *Anno Lucis* 5995. This *Anno Lucis* (year of light) is based on the Book of Genesis 1:3, the 4000 year difference being derived, in modified form, from *Ussher's Notation*, published in 1654, which places the Creation of the World in 4004 BC.

OLYMPIADS

Ancient Greek chronology was reckoned in Olympiads, cycles of four years corresponding with the periodic Olympic Games held on the plain of Olympia in Elis once every four years, the intervening years being the first, second, etc., of the Olympiad which received the name of the victor at the Games. The first recorded Olympiad is that of Choroebus, 776 BC.

ZOROASTRIAN CALENDAR

Zoroastrians, followers of the Iranian prophet Zarathushtra (known to the Greeks as Zoroaster) are mostly to be found in Iran and in India, where they are known as Parsees.

The Zoroastrian era dates from the coronation of the last Zoroastrian Sasanian king in AD 631. The Zoroastrian calendar is divided into twelve months, each comprising 30 days, followed by five holy days of the Gathas at the end of each year to make the year consist of 365 days.

In order to synchronize the calendar with the solar year of 365 days, an extra month was intercalated once every 120 years. However, this intercalation ceased in the 12th century and the New Year, which had fallen in the spring, slipped back until it now falls in August. Because intercalation ceased at different times in Iran and India, there was one month's difference between the calendar followed in Iran (Kadmi calendar) and by the Parsees (Shenshai calendar).

In 1906 a group of Zoroastrians decided to bring the calendar back in line with the seasons again and restore the New Year to 21 March each year (Fasli calendar).

The Shenshai calendar (New Year in August) is mainly used by Parsees. The Fasli calendar (New Year, 21 March) is mainly used by Zoroastrians living in Iran, in the Indian subcontinent, or away from Iran.

## THE ROMAN CALENDAR

Roman historians adopted as an epoch the foundation of Rome, which is believed to have happened in the year 753 BC. The ordinal number of the years in Roman reckoning is followed by the letters AUC (*ab urbe condita*), so that the year 1995 is 2748 AUC (MMDCCXLVIII). The calendar that we know has developed from one established by Romulus, who is said to have used a year of 304 days divided into ten months, beginning with March. To this Numa added January and February, making the year consist of 12 months of 30 and 29 days alternately, with an additional day so that the total was 355. It is also said that Numa ordered an intercalary month of 22 or 23 days in alternate years, making 90 days in eight years, to be inserted after 23 February.

However, there is some doubt as to the origination and the details of the intercalation in the Roman calendar. It is certain that some scheme of this kind was inaugurated and not fully carried out, for in the year 46 BC Julius Caesar, who was then Pontifex Maximus, found that the calendar had been allowed to fall into some confusion. He therefore sought the help of the Egyptian astronomer Sosigenes, which led to the construction and adoption (45 BC) of the Julian calendar, and, by a slight alteration, to the Gregorian calendar now in use. The year 46 BC was made to consist of 445 days and is called the Year of Confusion.

In the Roman (Julian) calendar the days of the month were counted backwards from three fixed points, or days, and an intervening day was said to be so many days before the next coming point, the first and last being counted. These three points were the Kalends, the Nones, and the Ides. Their positions in the months and the method of counting from them will be seen in the table below. The year containing 366 days was called *bissextillis annus*, as it had a doubled sixth day (*bissextus dies*) before the March Kalends on 24 February – *ante diem sextum Kalendas Martias*, or a.d. VI Kal. Mart.

| Present days of the month | March, May, July, October have thirty-one days | January, August, December have thirty-one days | April, June, September, November have thirty days | February has twenty-eight days, and in leap year twenty-nine |
|---|---|---|---|---|
| 1 | Kalendis | Kalendis | Kalendis | Kalendis |
| 2 | VI ⎫ | IV ⎱ ante | IV ⎱ ante | IV ⎱ ante |
| 3 | V ⎬ ante | III ⎰ Nonas | III ⎰ Nonas | III ⎰ Nonas |
| 4 | IV ⎰ Nonas | pridie Nonas | pridie Nonas | pridie Nonas |
| 5 | III ⎭ | Nonis | Nonis | Nonis |
| 6 | pridie Nonas | VIII ⎫ | VIII ⎫ | VIII ⎫ |
| 7 | Nonis | VII ⎪ | VII ⎪ | VII ⎪ |
| 8 | VIII ⎫ | VI ⎬ ante | VI ⎬ ante | VI ⎬ ante |
| 9 | VII ⎪ | V ⎰ Idus | V ⎰ Idus | V ⎰ Idus |
| 10 | VI ⎬ ante | IV ⎪ | IV ⎪ | IV ⎪ |
| 11 | V ⎰ Idus | III ⎭ | III ⎭ | III ⎭ |
| 12 | IV ⎪ | pridie Idus | pridie Idus | pridie Idus |
| 13 | III ⎭ | Idibus | Idibus | Idibus |
| 14 | pridie Idus | XIX ⎫ | XVIII ⎫ | XVI |
| 15 | Idibus | XVIII | XVII | XV |
| 16 | XVII ⎫ | XVII | XVI | XIV |
| 17 | XVI | XVI | XV | XIII |
| 18 | XV | XV | XIV | XII |
| 19 | XIV | XIV | XIII | XI |
| 20 | XIII | XIII | XII | X ⎱ ante Kalendas |
| 21 | XII | XII ⎱ ante Kalendas | XI ⎱ ante Kalendas | IX ⎰ Martias |
| 22 | XI ⎱ ante Kalendas | XI ⎬ (of the month | X ⎬ (of the month | VIII |
| 23 | X ⎬ (of the month | X ⎰ following) | IX ⎰ following) | VII |
| 24 | IX ⎰ following) | IX | VIII | *VI |
| 25 | VIII | VIII | VII | V |
| 26 | VII | VII | VI | IV |
| 27 | VI | VI | V | III ⎭ |
| 28 | V | V | IV ⎭ | pridie Kalendas Martias |
| 29 | IV ⎭ | IV ⎭ | III | Martias |
| 30 | III | III | pridie Kalendas |  |
| 31 | pridie Kalendas (Aprilis, Iunias, Sextilis, Novembris) | pridie Kalendas (Februarias, Septembris, Ianuarias) | (Maias, Quinctilis, Octobris, Decembris) | * (repeated in leap year) |

# Calendar for Any Year 1770–2030

To select the correct calendar for any year between 1770 and 2030, consult the index below
* leap year

| Year | | Year | | Year | | Year | | Year | | Year | | Year | | Year | |
|---|---|---|---|---|---|---|---|---|---|---|---|---|---|---|---|
| 1770 | C | 1803 | M | 1836 | L* | 1869 | K | 1902 | G | 1935 | E | 1968 | D* | 2001 | C |
| 1771 | E | 1804 | B* | 1837 | A | 1870 | M | 1903 | I | 1936 | H* | 1969 | G | 2002 | E |
| 1772 | H* | 1805 | E | 1838 | C | 1871 | A | 1904 | L* | 1937 | K | 1970 | I | 2003 | G |
| 1773 | K | 1806 | G | 1839 | E | 1872 | D* | 1905 | A | 1938 | M | 1971 | K | 2004 | J* |
| 1774 | M | 1807 | I | 1840 | H* | 1873 | G | 1906 | C | 1939 | A | 1972 | N* | 2005 | M |
| 1775 | A | 1808 | L* | 1841 | K | 1874 | I | 1907 | E | 1940 | D* | 1973 | C | 2006 | A |
| 1776 | D* | 1809 | A | 1842 | M | 1875 | K | 1908 | H* | 1941 | G | 1974 | E | 2007 | C |
| 1777 | G | 1810 | C | 1843 | A | 1876 | N* | 1909 | K | 1942 | I | 1975 | G | 2008 | F* |
| 1778 | I | 1811 | E | 1844 | D* | 1877 | C | 1910 | M | 1943 | K | 1976 | J* | 2009 | I |
| 1779 | K | 1812 | H* | 1845 | G | 1878 | E | 1911 | A | 1944 | N* | 1977 | M | 2010 | K |
| 1780 | N* | 1813 | K | 1846 | I | 1879 | G | 1912 | D* | 1945 | C | 1978 | A | 2011 | M |
| 1781 | C | 1814 | M | 1847 | K | 1880 | J* | 1913 | G | 1946 | E | 1979 | C | 2012 | B* |
| 1782 | E | 1815 | A | 1848 | N* | 1881 | M | 1914 | I | 1947 | G | 1980 | F* | 2013 | E |
| 1783 | G | 1816 | D* | 1849 | C | 1882 | A | 1915 | K | 1948 | J* | 1981 | I | 2014 | G |
| 1784 | J* | 1817 | G | 1850 | E | 1883 | C | 1916 | N* | 1949 | M | 1982 | K | 2015 | I |
| 1785 | M | 1818 | I | 1851 | G | 1884 | F* | 1917 | C | 1950 | A | 1983 | M | 2016 | L* |
| 1786 | A | 1819 | K | 1852 | J* | 1885 | I | 1918 | E | 1951 | C | 1984 | B* | 2017 | A |
| 1787 | C | 1820 | N* | 1853 | M | 1886 | K | 1919 | G | 1952 | F* | 1985 | E | 2018 | C |
| 1788 | F* | 1821 | C | 1854 | A | 1887 | M | 1920 | J* | 1953 | I | 1986 | G | 2019 | E |
| 1789 | I | 1822 | E | 1855 | C | 1888 | B* | 1921 | M | 1954 | K | 1987 | I | 2020 | H* |
| 1790 | K | 1823 | G | 1856 | F* | 1889 | E | 1922 | A | 1955 | M | 1988 | L* | 2021 | K |
| 1791 | M | 1824 | J* | 1857 | I | 1890 | G | 1923 | C | 1956 | B* | 1989 | A | 2022 | M |
| 1792 | B* | 1825 | M | 1858 | K | 1891 | I | 1924 | F* | 1957 | E | 1990 | C | 2023 | A |
| 1793 | E | 1826 | A | 1859 | M | 1892 | L* | 1925 | I | 1958 | G | 1991 | E | 2024 | D* |
| 1794 | G | 1827 | C | 1860 | B* | 1893 | A | 1926 | K | 1959 | I | 1992 | H* | 2025 | G |
| 1795 | I | 1828 | F* | 1861 | E | 1894 | C | 1927 | M | 1960 | L* | 1993 | K | 2026 | I |
| 1796 | L* | 1829 | I | 1862 | G | 1895 | E | 1928 | B* | 1961 | A | 1994 | M | 2027 | K |
| 1797 | A | 1830 | K | 1863 | I | 1896 | H* | 1929 | E | 1962 | C | 1995 | A | 2028 | N* |
| 1798 | C | 1831 | M | 1864 | L* | 1897 | K | 1930 | G | 1963 | E | 1996 | D* | 2029 | C |
| 1799 | E | 1832 | B* | 1865 | A | 1898 | M | 1931 | I | 1964 | H* | 1997 | G | 2030 | E |
| 1800 | G | 1833 | E | 1866 | C | 1899 | A | 1932 | L* | 1965 | K | 1998 | I | | |
| 1801 | I | 1834 | G | 1867 | E | 1900 | C | 1933 | A | 1966 | M | 1999 | K | | |
| 1802 | K | 1835 | I | 1868 | H* | 1901 | E | 1934 | C | 1967 | A | 2000 | N* | | |

## A

| | January | February | March |
|---|---|---|---|
| Sun. | 1 8 15 22 29 | 5 12 19 26 | 5 12 19 26 |
| Mon. | 2 9 16 23 30 | 6 13 20 27 | 6 13 20 27 |
| Tue. | 3 10 17 24 31 | 7 14 21 28 | 7 14 21 28 |
| Wed. | 4 11 18 25 | 1 8 15 22 | 1 8 15 22 29 |
| Thur. | 5 12 19 26 | 2 9 16 23 | 2 9 16 23 30 |
| Fri. | 6 13 20 27 | 3 10 17 24 | 3 10 17 24 31 |
| Sat. | 7 14 21 28 | 4 11 18 25 | 4 11 18 25 |

| | April | May | June |
|---|---|---|---|
| Sun. | 2 9 16 23 30 | 7 14 21 28 | 4 11 18 25 |
| Mon. | 3 10 17 24 | 1 8 15 22 29 | 5 12 19 26 |
| Tue. | 4 11 18 25 | 2 9 16 23 30 | 6 13 20 27 |
| Wed. | 5 12 19 26 | 3 10 17 24 31 | 7 14 21 28 |
| Thur. | 6 13 20 27 | 4 11 18 25 | 1 8 15 22 29 |
| Fri. | 7 14 21 28 | 5 12 19 26 | 2 9 16 23 30 |
| Sat. | 1 8 15 22 29 | 6 13 20 27 | 3 10 17 24 |

| | July | August | September |
|---|---|---|---|
| Sun. | 2 9 16 23 30 | 6 13 20 27 | 3 10 17 24 |
| Mon. | 3 10 17 24 31 | 7 14 21 28 | 4 11 18 25 |
| Tue. | 4 11 18 25 | 1 8 15 22 29 | 5 12 19 26 |
| Wed. | 5 12 19 26 | 2 9 16 23 30 | 6 13 20 27 |
| Thur. | 6 13 20 27 | 3 10 17 24 31 | 7 14 21 28 |
| Fri. | 7 14 21 28 | 4 11 18 25 | 1 8 15 22 29 |
| Sat. | 1 8 15 22 29 | 5 12 19 26 | 2 9 16 23 30 |

| | October | November | December |
|---|---|---|---|
| Sun. | 1 8 15 22 29 | 5 12 19 26 | 3 10 17 24 31 |
| Mon. | 2 9 16 23 30 | 6 13 20 27 | 4 11 18 25 |
| Tue. | 3 10 17 24 31 | 7 14 21 28 | 5 12 19 26 |
| Wed. | 4 11 18 25 | 1 8 15 22 29 | 6 13 20 27 |
| Thur. | 5 12 19 26 | 2 9 16 23 30 | 7 14 21 28 |
| Fri. | 6 13 20 27 | 3 10 17 24 | 1 8 15 22 29 |
| Sat. | 7 14 21 28 | 4 11 18 25 | 2 9 16 23 30 |

EASTER DAYS

| March 26 | 1815, 1826, 1837, 1967, 1978, 1989 |
|---|---|
| April 2 | 1809, 1893, 1899, 1961 |
| April 9 | 1871, 1882, 1939, 1950, 2023 |
| April 16 | 1775, 1786, 1797, 1843, 1854, 1865, 1911, 1922, 1933, 1995, 2006, 2017 |
| April 23 | 1905 |

## B (LEAP YEAR)

| | January | February | March |
|---|---|---|---|
| Sun. | 1 8 15 22 29 | 5 12 19 26 | 4 11 18 25 |
| Mon. | 2 9 16 23 30 | 6 13 20 27 | 5 12 19 26 |
| Tue. | 3 10 17 24 31 | 7 14 21 28 | 6 13 20 27 |
| Wed. | 4 11 18 25 | 1 8 15 22 29 | 7 14 21 28 |
| Thur. | 5 12 19 26 | 2 9 16 23 | 1 8 15 22 29 |
| Fri. | 6 13 20 27 | 3 10 17 24 | 2 9 16 23 30 |
| Sat. | 7 14 21 28 | 4 11 18 25 | 3 10 17 24 31 |

| | April | May | June |
|---|---|---|---|
| Sun. | 1 8 15 22 29 | 6 13 20 27 | 3 10 17 24 |
| Mon. | 2 9 16 23 30 | 7 14 21 28 | 4 11 18 25 |
| Tue. | 3 10 17 24 | 1 8 15 22 29 | 5 12 19 26 |
| Wed. | 4 11 18 25 | 2 9 16 23 30 | 6 13 20 27 |
| Thur. | 5 12 19 26 | 3 10 17 24 31 | 7 14 21 28 |
| Fri. | 6 13 20 27 | 4 11 18 25 | 1 8 15 22 29 |
| Sat. | 7 14 21 28 | 5 12 19 26 | 2 9 16 23 30 |

| | July | August | September |
|---|---|---|---|
| Sun. | 1 8 15 22 29 | 5 12 19 26 | 2 9 16 23 30 |
| Mon. | 2 9 16 23 30 | 6 13 20 27 | 3 10 17 24 |
| Tue. | 3 10 17 24 31 | 7 14 21 28 | 4 11 18 25 |
| Wed. | 4 11 18 25 | 1 8 15 22 29 | 5 12 19 26 |
| Thur. | 5 12 19 26 | 2 9 16 23 30 | 6 13 20 27 |
| Fri. | 6 13 20 27 | 3 10 17 24 31 | 7 14 21 28 |
| Sat. | 7 14 21 28 | 4 11 18 25 | 1 8 15 22 29 |

| | October | November | December |
|---|---|---|---|
| Sun. | 7 14 21 28 | 4 11 18 25 | 2 9 16 23 30 |
| Mon. | 1 8 15 22 29 | 5 12 19 26 | 3 10 17 24 31 |
| Tue. | 2 9 16 23 30 | 6 13 20 27 | 4 11 18 25 |
| Wed. | 3 10 17 24 31 | 7 14 21 28 | 5 12 19 26 |
| Thur. | 4 11 18 25 | 1 8 15 22 29 | 6 13 20 27 |
| Fri. | 5 12 19 26 | 2 9 16 23 30 | 7 14 21 28 |
| Sat. | 6 13 20 27 | 3 10 17 24 | 1 8 15 22 29 |

EASTER DAYS

| April 1 | 1804, 1888, 1956 |
|---|---|
| April 8 | 1792, 1860, 1928, 2012 |
| April 22 | 1832, 1984 |

## C

| | *January* | *February* | *March* |
|---|---|---|---|
| Sun. | 7 14 21 28 | 4 11 18 25 | 4 11 18 25 |
| Mon. | 1 8 15 22 29 | 5 12 19 26 | 5 12 19 26 |
| Tue. | 2 9 16 23 30 | 6 13 20 27 | 6 13 20 27 |
| Wed. | 3 10 17 24 31 | 7 14 21 28 | 7 14 21 28 |
| Thur. | 4 11 18 25 | 1 8 15 22 | 1 8 15 22 29 |
| Fri. | 5 12 19 26 | 2 9 16 23 | 2 9 16 23 30 |
| Sat. | 6 13 20 27 | 3 10 17 24 | 3 10 17 24 31 |

| | *April* | *May* | *June* |
|---|---|---|---|
| Sun. | 1 8 15 22 29 | 6 13 20 27 | 3 10 17 24 |
| Mon. | 2 9 16 23 30 | 7 14 21 28 | 4 11 18 25 |
| Tue. | 3 10 17 24 | 1 8 15 22 29 | 5 12 19 26 |
| Wed. | 4 11 18 25 | 2 9 16 23 30 | 6 13 20 27 |
| Thur. | 5 12 19 26 | 3 10 17 24 31 | 7 14 21 28 |
| Fri. | 6 13 20 27 | 4 11 18 25 | 1 8 15 22 29 |
| Sat. | 7 14 21 28 | 5 12 19 26 | 2 9 16 23 30 |

| | *July* | *August* | *September* |
|---|---|---|---|
| Sun. | 1 8 15 22 29 | 5 12 19 26 | 2 9 16 23 30 |
| Mon. | 2 9 16 23 30 | 6 13 20 27 | 3 10 17 24 |
| Tue. | 3 10 17 24 31 | 7 14 21 28 | 4 11 18 25 |
| Wed. | 4 11 18 25 | 1 8 15 22 29 | 5 12 19 26 |
| Thur. | 5 12 19 26 | 2 9 16 23 30 | 6 13 20 27 |
| Fri. | 6 13 20 27 | 3 10 17 24 31 | 7 14 21 28 |
| Sat. | 7 14 21 28 | 4 11 18 25 | 1 8 15 22 29 |

| | *October* | *November* | *December* |
|---|---|---|---|
| Sun. | 7 14 21 28 | 4 11 18 25 | 2 9 16 23 30 |
| Mon. | 1 8 15 22 29 | 5 12 19 26 | 3 10 17 24 31 |
| Tue. | 2 9 16 23 30 | 6 13 20 27 | 4 11 18 25 |
| Wed. | 3 10 17 24 31 | 7 14 21 28 | 5 12 19 26 |
| Thur. | 4 11 18 25 | 1 8 15 22 29 | 6 13 20 27 |
| Fri. | 5 12 19 26 | 2 9 16 23 30 | 7 14 21 28 |
| Sat. | 6 13 20 27 | 3 10 17 24 | 1 8 15 22 29 |

EASTER DAYS

| | |
|---|---|
| March 25 | 1883, 1894, 1951 |
| April 1 | 1866, 1877, 1923, 1934, 1945, 2018, 2029 |
| April 8 | 1787, 1798, 1849, 1855, 1917, 2007 |
| April 15 | 1770, 1781, 1827, 1838, 1900, 1906, 1979, 1990, 2001 |
| April 22 | 1810, 1821, 1962, 1973 |

## E

| | *January* | *February* | *March* |
|---|---|---|---|
| Sun. | 6 13 20 27 | 3 10 17 24 | 3 10 17 24 31 |
| Mon. | 7 14 21 28 | 4 11 18 25 | 4 11 18 25 |
| Tue. | 1 8 15 22 29 | 5 12 19 26 | 5 12 19 26 |
| Wed. | 2 9 16 23 30 | 6 13 20 27 | 6 13 20 27 |
| Thur. | 3 10 17 24 31 | 7 14 21 28 | 7 14 21 28 |
| Fri. | 4 11 18 25 | 1 8 15 22 | 1 8 15 22 29 |
| Sat. | 5 12 19 26 | 2 9 16 23 | 2 9 16 23 30 |

| | *April* | *May* | *June* |
|---|---|---|---|
| Sun. | 7 14 21 28 | 5 12 19 26 | 2 9 16 23 30 |
| Mon. | 1 8 15 22 29 | 6 13 20 27 | 3 10 17 24 |
| Tue. | 2 9 16 23 30 | 7 14 21 28 | 4 11 18 25 |
| Wed. | 3 10 17 24 | 1 8 15 22 29 | 5 12 19 26 |
| Thur. | 4 11 18 25 | 2 9 16 23 30 | 6 13 20 27 |
| Fri. | 5 12 19 26 | 3 10 17 24 31 | 7 14 21 28 |
| Sat. | 6 13 20 27 | 4 11 18 25 | 1 8 15 22 29 |

| | *July* | *August* | *September* |
|---|---|---|---|
| Sun. | 7 14 21 28 | 4 11 18 25 | 1 8 15 22 29 |
| Mon. | 1 8 15 22 29 | 5 12 19 26 | 2 9 16 23 30 |
| Tue. | 2 9 16 23 30 | 6 13 20 27 | 3 10 17 24 |
| Wed. | 3 10 17 24 31 | 7 14 21 28 | 4 11 18 25 |
| Thur. | 4 11 18 25 | 1 8 15 22 29 | 5 12 19 26 |
| Fri. | 5 12 19 26 | 2 9 16 23 30 | 6 13 20 27 |
| Sat. | 6 13 20 27 | 3 10 17 24 31 | 7 14 21 28 |

| | *October* | *November* | *December* |
|---|---|---|---|
| Sun. | 6 13 20 27 | 3 10 17 24 | 1 8 15 22 29 |
| Mon. | 7 14 21 28 | 4 11 18 25 | 2 9 16 23 30 |
| Tue. | 1 8 15 22 29 | 5 12 19 26 | 3 10 17 24 31 |
| Wed. | 2 9 16 23 30 | 6 13 20 27 | 4 11 18 25 |
| Thur. | 3 10 17 24 31 | 7 14 21 28 | 5 12 19 26 |
| Fri. | 4 11 18 25 | 1 8 15 22 29 | 6 13 20 27 |
| Sat. | 5 12 19 26 | 2 9 16 23 30 | 7 14 21 28 |

EASTER DAYS

| | |
|---|---|
| March 24 | 1799 |
| March 31 | 1771, 1782, 1793, 1839, 1850, 1861, 1907 |
| | 1918, 1929, 1991, 2002, 2013 |
| April 7 | 1822, 1833, 1901, 1985 |
| April 14 | 1805, 1811, 1895, 1963, 1974 |
| April 21 | 1867, 1878, 1889, 1935, 1946, 1957, 2019, 2030 |

## D (LEAP YEAR)

| | *January* | *February* | *March* |
|---|---|---|---|
| Sun. | 7 14 21 28 | 4 11 18 25 | 3 10 17 24 31 |
| Mon. | 1 8 15 22 29 | 5 12 19 26 | 4 11 18 25 |
| Tue. | 2 9 16 23 30 | 6 13 20 27 | 5 12 19 26 |
| Wed. | 3 10 17 24 31 | 7 14 21 28 | 6 13 20 27 |
| Thur. | 4 11 18 25 | 1 8 15 22 29 | 7 14 21 28 |
| Fri. | 5 12 19 26 | 2 9 16 23 | 1 8 15 22 29 |
| Sat. | 6 13 20 27 | 3 10 17 24 | 2 9 16 23 30 |

| | *April* | *May* | *June* |
|---|---|---|---|
| Sun. | 7 14 21 28 | 5 12 19 26 | 2 9 16 23 30 |
| Mon. | 1 8 15 22 29 | 6 13 20 27 | 3 10 17 24 |
| Tue. | 2 9 16 23 30 | 7 14 21 28 | 4 11 18 25 |
| Wed. | 3 10 17 24 | 1 8 15 22 29 | 5 12 19 26 |
| Thur. | 4 11 18 25 | 2 9 16 23 30 | 6 13 20 27 |
| Fri. | 5 12 19 26 | 3 10 17 24 31 | 7 14 21 28 |
| Sat. | 6 13 20 27 | 4 11 18 25 | 1 8 15 22 29 |

| | *July* | *August* | *September* |
|---|---|---|---|
| Sun. | 7 14 21 28 | 4 11 18 25 | 1 8 15 22 29 |
| Mon. | 1 8 15 22 29 | 5 12 19 26 | 2 9 16 23 30 |
| Tue. | 2 9 16 23 30 | 6 13 20 27 | 3 10 17 24 |
| Wed. | 3 10 17 24 31 | 7 14 21 28 | 4 11 18 25 |
| Thur. | 4 11 18 25 | 1 8 15 22 29 | 5 12 19 26 |
| Fri. | 5 12 19 26 | 2 9 16 23 30 | 6 13 20 27 |
| Sat. | 6 13 20 27 | 3 10 17 24 31 | 7 14 21 28 |

| | *October* | *November* | *December* |
|---|---|---|---|
| Sun. | 6 13 20 27 | 3 10 17 24 | 1 8 15 22 29 |
| Mon. | 7 14 21 28 | 4 11 18 25 | 2 9 16 23 30 |
| Tue. | 1 8 15 22 29 | 5 12 19 26 | 3 10 17 24 31 |
| Wed. | 2 9 16 23 30 | 6 13 20 27 | 4 11 18 25 |
| Thur. | 3 10 17 24 31 | 7 14 21 28 | 5 12 19 26 |
| Fri. | 4 11 18 25 | 1 8 15 22 29 | 6 13 20 27 |
| Sat. | 5 12 19 26 | 2 9 16 23 30 | 7 14 21 28 |

EASTER DAYS

| | |
|---|---|
| March 24 | 1940 |
| March 31 | 1872, 2024 |
| April 7 | 1776, 1844, 1912, 1996 |
| April 14 | 1816, 1968 |

## F (LEAP YEAR)

| | *January* | *February* | *March* |
|---|---|---|---|
| Sun. | 6 13 20 27 | 3 10 17 24 | 2 9 16 23 30 |
| Mon. | 7 14 21 28 | 4 11 18 25 | 3 10 17 24 31 |
| Tue. | 1 8 15 22 29 | 5 12 19 26 | 4 11 18 25 |
| Wed. | 2 9 16 23 30 | 6 13 20 27 | 5 12 19 26 |
| Thur. | 3 10 17 24 31 | 7 14 21 28 | 6 13 20 27 |
| Fri. | 4 11 18 25 | 1 8 15 22 29 | 7 14 21 28 |
| Sat. | 5 12 19 26 | 2 9 16 23 | 1 8 15 22 29 |

| | *April* | *May* | *June* |
|---|---|---|---|
| Sun. | 6 13 20 27 | 4 11 18 25 | 1 8 15 22 29 |
| Mon. | 7 14 21 28 | 5 12 19 26 | 2 9 16 23 30 |
| Tue. | 1 8 15 22 29 | 6 13 20 27 | 3 10 17 24 |
| Wed. | 2 9 16 23 30 | 7 14 21 28 | 4 11 18 25 |
| Thur. | 3 10 17 24 | 1 8 15 22 29 | 5 12 19 26 |
| Fri. | 4 11 18 25 | 2 9 16 23 30 | 6 13 20 27 |
| Sat. | 5 12 19 26 | 3 10 17 24 31 | 7 14 21 28 |

| | *July* | *August* | *September* |
|---|---|---|---|
| Sun. | 6 13 20 27 | 3 10 17 24 31 | 7 14 21 28 |
| Mon. | 7 14 21 28 | 4 11 18 25 | 1 8 15 22 29 |
| Tue. | 1 8 15 22 29 | 5 12 19 26 | 2 9 16 23 30 |
| Wed. | 2 9 16 23 30 | 6 13 20 27 | 3 10 17 24 |
| Thur. | 3 10 17 24 31 | 7 14 21 28 | 4 11 18 25 |
| Fri. | 4 11 18 25 | 1 8 15 22 29 | 5 12 19 26 |
| Sat. | 5 12 19 26 | 2 9 16 23 30 | 6 13 20 27 |

| | *October* | *November* | *December* |
|---|---|---|---|
| Sun. | 5 12 19 26 | 2 9 16 23 30 | 7 14 21 28 |
| Mon. | 6 13 20 27 | 3 10 17 24 | 1 8 15 22 29 |
| Tue. | 7 14 21 28 | 4 11 18 25 | 2 9 16 23 30 |
| Wed. | 1 8 15 22 29 | 5 12 19 26 | 3 10 17 24 31 |
| Thur. | 2 9 16 23 30 | 6 13 20 27 | 4 11 18 25 |
| Fri. | 3 10 17 24 31 | 7 14 21 28 | 5 12 19 26 |
| Sat. | 4 11 18 25 | 1 8 15 22 29 | 6 13 20 27 |

EASTER DAYS

| | |
|---|---|
| March 23 | 1788, 1856, 2008 |
| April 6 | 1828, 1980 |
| April 13 | 1884, 1952 |
| April 20 | 1924 |

## G

|  | January | February | March |
|---|---|---|---|
| Sun. | 5 12 19 26 | 2 9 16 23 | 2 9 16 23 30 |
| Mon. | 6 13 20 27 | 3 10 17 24 | 3 10 17 24 31 |
| Tue. | 7 14 21 28 | 4 11 18 25 | 4 11 18 25 |
| Wed. | 1 8 15 22 29 | 5 12 19 26 | 5 12 19 26 |
| Thur. | 2 9 16 23 30 | 6 13 20 27 | 6 13 20 27 |
| Fri. | 3 10 17 24 31 | 7 14 21 28 | 7 14 21 28 |
| Sat. | 4 11 18 25 | 1 8 15 22 | 1 8 15 22 29 |

|  | April | May | June |
|---|---|---|---|
| Sun. | 6 13 20 27 | 4 11 18 25 | 1 8 15 22 29 |
| Mon. | 7 14 21 28 | 5 12 19 26 | 2 9 16 23 30 |
| Tue. | 1 8 15 22 29 | 6 13 20 27 | 3 10 17 24 |
| Wed. | 2 9 16 23 30 | 7 14 21 28 | 4 11 18 25 |
| Thur. | 3 10 17 24 | 1 8 15 22 29 | 5 12 19 26 |
| Fri. | 4 11 18 25 | 2 9 16 23 30 | 6 13 20 27 |
| Sat. | 5 12 19 26 | 3 10 17 24 31 | 7 14 21 28 |

|  | July | August | September |
|---|---|---|---|
| Sun. | 6 13 20 27 | 3 10 17 24 31 | 7 14 21 28 |
| Mon. | 7 14 21 28 | 4 11 18 25 | 1 8 15 22 29 |
| Tue. | 1 8 15 22 29 | 5 12 19 26 | 2 9 16 23 30 |
| Wed. | 2 9 16 23 30 | 6 13 20 27 | 3 10 17 24 |
| Thur. | 3 10 17 24 31 | 7 14 21 28 | 4 11 18 25 |
| Fri. | 4 11 18 25 | 1 8 15 22 29 | 5 12 19 26 |
| Sat. | 5 12 19 26 | 2 9 16 23 30 | 6 13 20 27 |

|  | October | November | December |
|---|---|---|---|
| Sun. | 5 12 19 26 | 2 9 16 23 30 | 7 14 21 28 |
| Mon. | 6 13 20 27 | 3 10 17 24 | 1 8 15 22 29 |
| Tue. | 7 14 21 28 | 4 11 18 25 | 2 9 16 23 30 |
| Wed. | 1 8 15 22 29 | 5 12 19 26 | 3 10 17 24 31 |
| Thur. | 2 9 16 23 30 | 6 13 20 27 | 4 11 18 25 |
| Fri. | 3 10 17 24 31 | 7 14 21 28 | 5 12 19 26 |
| Sat. | 4 11 18 25 | 1 8 15 22 29 | 6 13 20 27 |

EASTER DAYS

| March 23 | 1845, 1913 |
|---|---|
| March 30 | 1777, 1823, 1834, 1902, 1975, 1986, 1997 |
| April 6 | 1806, 1817, 1890, 1947, 1958, 1969 |
| April 13 | 1800, 1873, 1879, 1941 |
| April 20 | 1783, 1794, 1851, 1862, 1919, 1930, 2003, 2014, 2025 |

## I

|  | January | February | March |
|---|---|---|---|
| Sun. | 4 11 18 25 | 1 8 15 22 | 1 8 15 22 29 |
| Mon. | 5 12 19 26 | 2 9 16 23 | 2 9 16 23 30 |
| Tue. | 6 13 20 27 | 3 10 17 24 | 3 10 17 24 31 |
| Wed. | 7 14 21 28 | 4 11 18 25 | 4 11 18 25 |
| Thur. | 1 8 15 22 29 | 5 12 19 26 | 5 12 19 26 |
| Fri. | 2 9 16 23 30 | 6 13 20 27 | 6 13 20 27 |
| Sat. | 3 10 17 24 31 | 7 14 21 28 | 7 14 21 28 |

|  | April | May | June |
|---|---|---|---|
| Sun. | 5 12 19 26 | 3 10 17 24 31 | 7 14 21 28 |
| Mon. | 6 13 20 27 | 4 11 18 25 | 1 8 15 22 29 |
| Tue. | 7 14 21 28 | 5 12 19 26 | 2 9 16 23 30 |
| Wed. | 1 8 15 22 29 | 6 13 20 27 | 3 10 17 24 |
| Thur. | 2 9 16 23 30 | 7 14 21 28 | 4 11 18 25 |
| Fri. | 3 10 17 24 | 1 8 15 22 29 | 5 12 19 26 |
| Sat. | 4 11 18 25 | 2 9 16 23 30 | 6 13 20 27 |

|  | July | August | September |
|---|---|---|---|
| Sun. | 5 12 19 26 | 2 9 16 23 30 | 6 13 20 27 |
| Mon. | 6 13 20 27 | 3 10 17 24 31 | 7 14 21 28 |
| Tue. | 7 14 21 28 | 4 11 18 25 | 1 8 15 22 29 |
| Wed. | 1 8 15 22 29 | 5 12 19 26 | 2 9 16 23 30 |
| Thur. | 2 9 16 23 30 | 6 13 20 27 | 3 10 17 24 |
| Fri. | 3 10 17 24 31 | 7 14 21 28 | 4 11 18 25 |
| Sat. | 4 11 18 25 | 1 8 15 22 29 | 5 12 19 26 |

|  | October | November | December |
|---|---|---|---|
| Sun. | 4 11 18 25 | 1 8 15 22 29 | 6 13 20 27 |
| Mon. | 5 12 19 26 | 2 9 16 23 30 | 7 14 21 28 |
| Tue. | 6 13 20 27 | 3 10 17 24 | 1 8 15 22 29 |
| Wed. | 7 14 21 28 | 4 11 18 25 | 2 9 16 23 30 |
| Thur. | 1 8 15 22 29 | 5 12 19 26 | 3 10 17 24 31 |
| Fri. | 2 9 16 23 30 | 6 13 20 27 | 4 11 18 25 |
| Sat. | 3 10 17 24 31 | 7 14 21 28 | 5 12 19 26 |

EASTER DAYS

| March 22 | 1818 |
|---|---|
| March 29 | 1807, 1891, 1959, 1970 |
| April 5 | 1795, 1801, 1863, 1874, 1885, 1931, 1942, 1953, 2015, 2026 |
| April 12 | 1789, 1846, 1857, 1903, 1914, 1925, 1998, 2009 |
| April 19 | 1778, 1829, 1835, 1981, 1987 |

## H (LEAP YEAR)

|  | January | February | March |
|---|---|---|---|
| Sun. | 5 12 19 26 | 2 9 16 23 | 1 8 15 22 29 |
| Mon. | 6 13 20 27 | 3 10 17 24 | 2 9 16 23 30 |
| Tue. | 7 14 21 28 | 4 11 18 25 | 3 10 17 24 31 |
| Wed. | 1 8 15 22 29 | 5 12 19 26 | 4 11 18 25 |
| Thur. | 2 9 16 23 30 | 6 13 20 27 | 5 12 19 26 |
| Fri. | 3 10 17 24 31 | 7 14 21 28 | 6 13 20 27 |
| Sat. | 4 11 18 25 | 1 8 15 22 29 | 7 14 21 28 |

|  | April | May | June |
|---|---|---|---|
| Sun. | 5 12 19 26 | 3 10 17 24 31 | 7 14 21 28 |
| Mon. | 6 13 20 27 | 4 11 18 25 | 1 8 15 22 29 |
| Tue. | 7 14 21 28 | 5 12 19 26 | 2 9 16 23 30 |
| Wed. | 1 8 15 22 29 | 6 13 20 27 | 3 10 17 24 |
| Thur. | 2 9 16 23 30 | 7 14 21 28 | 4 11 18 25 |
| Fri. | 3 10 17 24 | 1 8 15 22 29 | 5 12 19 26 |
| Sat. | 4 11 18 25 | 2 9 16 23 30 | 6 13 20 27 |

|  | July | August | September |
|---|---|---|---|
| Sun. | 5 12 19 26 | 2 9 16 23 30 | 6 13 20 27 |
| Mon. | 6 13 20 27 | 3 10 17 24 31 | 7 14 21 28 |
| Tue. | 7 14 21 28 | 4 11 18 25 | 1 8 15 22 29 |
| Wed. | 1 8 15 22 29 | 5 12 19 26 | 2 9 16 23 30 |
| Thur. | 2 9 16 23 30 | 6 13 20 27 | 3 10 17 24 |
| Fri. | 3 10 17 24 31 | 7 14 21 28 | 4 11 18 25 |
| Sat. | 4 11 18 25 | 1 8 15 22 29 | 5 12 19 26 |

|  | October | November | December |
|---|---|---|---|
| Sun. | 4 11 18 25 | 1 8 15 22 29 | 6 13 20 27 |
| Mon. | 5 12 19 26 | 2 9 16 23 30 | 7 14 21 28 |
| Tue. | 6 13 20 27 | 3 10 17 24 | 1 8 15 22 29 |
| Wed. | 7 14 21 28 | 4 11 18 25 | 2 9 16 23 30 |
| Thur. | 1 8 15 22 29 | 5 12 19 26 | 3 10 17 24 31 |
| Fri. | 2 9 16 23 30 | 6 13 20 27 | 4 11 18 25 |
| Sat. | 3 10 17 24 31 | 7 14 21 28 | 5 12 19 26 |

EASTER DAYS

| March 29 | 1812, 1964 |
|---|---|
| April 5 | 1896 |
| April 12 | 1868, 1936, 2020 |
| April 19 | 1772, 1840, 1908, 1992 |

## J (LEAP YEAR)

|  | January | February | March |
|---|---|---|---|
| Sun. | 4 11 18 25 | 1 8 15 22 29 | 7 14 21 28 |
| Mon. | 5 12 19 26 | 2 9 16 23 | 1 8 15 22 29 |
| Tue. | 6 13 20 27 | 3 10 17 24 | 2 9 16 23 30 |
| Wed. | 7 14 21 28 | 4 11 18 25 | 3 10 17 24 31 |
| Thur. | 1 8 15 22 29 | 5 12 19 26 | 4 11 18 25 |
| Fri. | 2 9 16 23 30 | 6 13 20 27 | 5 12 19 26 |
| Sat. | 3 10 17 24 31 | 7 14 21 28 | 6 13 20 27 |

|  | April | May | June |
|---|---|---|---|
| Sun. | 4 11 18 25 | 2 9 16 23 30 | 6 13 20 27 |
| Mon. | 5 12 19 26 | 3 10 17 24 31 | 7 14 21 28 |
| Tue. | 6 13 20 27 | 4 11 18 25 | 1 8 15 22 29 |
| Wed. | 7 14 21 28 | 5 12 19 26 | 2 9 16 23 30 |
| Thur. | 1 8 15 22 29 | 6 13 20 27 | 3 10 17 24 |
| Fri. | 2 9 16 23 30 | 7 14 21 28 | 4 11 18 25 |
| Sat. | 3 10 17 24 | 1 8 15 22 29 | 5 12 19 26 |

|  | July | August | September |
|---|---|---|---|
| Sun. | 4 11 18 25 | 1 8 15 22 29 | 5 12 19 26 |
| Mon. | 5 12 19 26 | 2 9 16 23 30 | 6 13 20 27 |
| Tue. | 6 13 20 27 | 3 10 17 24 31 | 7 14 21 28 |
| Wed. | 7 14 21 28 | 4 11 18 25 | 1 8 15 22 29 |
| Thur. | 1 8 15 22 29 | 5 12 19 26 | 2 9 16 23 30 |
| Fri. | 2 9 16 23 30 | 6 13 20 27 | 3 10 17 24 |
| Sat. | 3 10 17 24 31 | 7 14 21 28 | 4 11 18 25 |

|  | October | November | December |
|---|---|---|---|
| Sun. | 3 10 17 24 31 | 7 14 21 28 | 5 12 19 26 |
| Mon. | 4 11 18 25 | 1 8 15 22 29 | 6 13 20 27 |
| Tue. | 5 12 19 26 | 2 9 16 23 30 | 7 14 21 28 |
| Wed. | 6 13 20 27 | 3 10 17 24 | 1 8 15 22 29 |
| Thur. | 7 14 21 28 | 4 11 18 25 | 2 9 16 23 30 |
| Fri. | 1 8 15 22 29 | 5 12 19 26 | 3 10 17 24 31 |
| Sat. | 2 9 16 23 30 | 6 13 20 27 | 4 11 18 25 |

EASTER DAYS

| March 28 | 1880, 1948 |
|---|---|
| April 4 | 1920 |
| April 11 | 1784, 1852, 2004 |
| April 18 | 1824, 1976 |

## K

|  | January | February | March |
|---|---|---|---|
| Sun. | 3 10 17 24 31 | 7 14 21 28 | 7 14 21 28 |
| Mon. | 4 11 18 25 | 1 8 15 22 | 1 8 15 22 29 |
| Tue. | 5 12 19 26 | 2 9 16 23 | 2 9 16 23 30 |
| Wed. | 6 13 20 27 | 3 10 17 24 | 3 10 17 24 31 |
| Thur. | 7 14 21 28 | 4 11 18 25 | 4 11 18 25 |
| Fri. | 1 8 15 22 29 | 5 12 19 26 | 5 12 19 26 |
| Sat. | 2 9 16 23 30 | 6 13 20 27 | 6 13 20 27 |

|  | April | May | June |
|---|---|---|---|
| Sun. | 4 11 18 25 | 2 9 16 23 30 | 6 13 20 27 |
| Mon. | 5 12 19 26 | 3 10 17 24 31 | 7 14 21 28 |
| Tue. | 6 13 20 27 | 4 11 18 25 | 1 8 15 22 29 |
| Wed. | 7 14 21 28 | 5 12 19 26 | 2 9 16 23 30 |
| Thur. | 1 8 15 22 29 | 6 13 20 27 | 3 10 17 24 |
| Fri. | 2 9 16 23 30 | 7 14 21 28 | 4 11 18 25 |
| Sat. | 3 10 17 24 | 1 8 15 22 29 | 5 12 19 26 |

|  | July | August | September |
|---|---|---|---|
| Sun. | 4 11 18 25 | 1 8 15 22 29 | 5 12 19 26 |
| Mon. | 5 12 19 26 | 2 9 16 23 30 | 6 13 20 27 |
| Tue. | 6 13 20 27 | 3 10 17 24 31 | 7 14 21 28 |
| Wed. | 7 14 21 28 | 4 11 18 25 | 1 8 15 22 29 |
| Thur. | 1 8 15 22 29 | 5 12 19 26 | 2 9 16 23 30 |
| Fri. | 2 9 16 23 30 | 6 13 20 27 | 3 10 17 24 |
| Sat. | 3 10 17 24 31 | 7 14 21 28 | 4 11 18 25 |

|  | October | November | December |
|---|---|---|---|
| Sun. | 3 10 17 24 31 | 7 14 21 28 | 5 12 19 26 |
| Mon. | 4 11 18 25 | 1 8 15 22 29 | 6 13 20 27 |
| Tue. | 5 12 19 26 | 2 9 16 23 30 | 7 14 21 28 |
| Wed. | 6 13 20 27 | 3 10 17 24 | 1 8 15 22 29 |
| Thur. | 7 14 21 28 | 4 11 18 25 | 2 9 16 23 30 |
| Fri. | 1 8 15 22 29 | 5 12 19 26 | 3 10 17 24 31 |
| Sat. | 2 9 16 23 30 | 6 13 20 27 | 4 11 18 25 |

EASTER DAYS

| | |
|---|---|
| March 28 | 1869, 1875, 1937, 2027 |
| April 4 | 1779, 1790, 1847, 1858, 1915, 1926, 1999, 2010, 2021 |
| April 11 | 1773, 1819, 1830, 1841, 1909, 1971, 1982, 1993 |
| April 18 | 1802, 1813, 1897, 1954, 1965 |
| April 25 | 1886, 1943 |

## M

|  | January | February | March |
|---|---|---|---|
| Sun. | 2 9 16 23 30 | 6 13 20 27 | 6 13 20 27 |
| Mon. | 3 10 17 24 31 | 7 14 21 28 | 7 14 21 28 |
| Tue. | 4 11 18 25 | 1 8 15 22 | 1 8 15 22 29 |
| Wed. | 5 12 19 26 | 2 9 16 23 | 2 9 16 23 30 |
| Thur. | 6 13 20 27 | 3 10 17 24 | 3 10 17 24 31 |
| Fri. | 7 14 21 28 | 4 11 18 25 | 4 11 18 25 |
| Sat. | 1 8 15 22 29 | 5 12 19 26 | 5 12 19 26 |

|  | April | May | June |
|---|---|---|---|
| Sun. | 3 10 17 24 | 1 8 15 22 29 | 5 12 19 26 |
| Mon. | 4 11 18 25 | 2 9 16 23 30 | 6 13 20 27 |
| Tue. | 5 12 19 26 | 3 10 17 24 31 | 7 14 21 28 |
| Wed. | 6 13 20 27 | 4 11 18 25 | 1 8 15 22 29 |
| Thur. | 7 14 21 28 | 5 12 19 26 | 2 9 16 23 30 |
| Fri. | 1 8 15 22 29 | 6 13 20 27 | 3 10 17 24 |
| Sat. | 2 9 16 23 30 | 7 14 21 28 | 4 11 18 25 |

|  | July | August | September |
|---|---|---|---|
| Sun. | 3 10 17 24 31 | 7 14 21 28 | 4 11 18 25 |
| Mon. | 4 11 18 25 | 1 8 15 22 29 | 5 12 19 26 |
| Tue. | 5 12 19 26 | 2 9 16 23 30 | 6 13 20 27 |
| Wed. | 6 13 20 27 | 3 10 17 24 31 | 7 14 21 28 |
| Thur. | 7 14 21 28 | 4 11 18 25 | 1 8 15 22 29 |
| Fri. | 1 8 15 22 29 | 5 12 19 26 | 2 9 16 23 30 |
| Sat. | 2 9 16 23 30 | 6 13 20 27 | 3 10 17 24 |

|  | October | November | December |
|---|---|---|---|
| Sun. | 2 9 16 23 30 | 6 13 20 27 | 4 11 18 25 |
| Mon. | 3 10 17 24 31 | 7 14 21 28 | 5 12 19 26 |
| Tue. | 4 11 18 25 | 1 8 15 22 29 | 6 13 20 27 |
| Wed. | 5 12 19 26 | 2 9 16 23 30 | 7 14 21 28 |
| Thur. | 6 13 20 27 | 3 10 17 24 | 1 8 15 22 29 |
| Fri. | 7 14 21 28 | 4 11 18 25 | 2 9 16 23 30 |
| Sat. | 1 8 15 22 29 | 5 12 19 26 | 3 10 17 24 31 |

EASTER DAYS

| | |
|---|---|
| March 27 | 1785, 1842, 1853, 1910, 1921, 2005 |
| April 3 | 1774, 1825, 1831, 1983, 1994 |
| April 10 | 1803, 1814, 1887, 1898, 1955, 1966, 1977 |
| April 17 | 1870, 1881, 1927, 1938, 1949, 2022 |
| April 24 | 1791, 1859, 2011 |

## L (LEAP YEAR)

|  | January | February | March |
|---|---|---|---|
| Sun. | 3 10 17 24 31 | 7 14 21 28 | 6 13 20 27 |
| Mon. | 4 11 18 25 | 1 8 15 22 29 | 7 14 21 28 |
| Tue. | 5 12 19 26 | 2 9 16 23 | 1 8 15 22 29 |
| Wed. | 6 13 20 27 | 3 10 17 24 | 2 9 16 23 30 |
| Thur. | 7 14 21 28 | 4 11 18 25 | 3 10 17 24 31 |
| Fri. | 1 8 15 22 29 | 5 12 19 26 | 4 11 18 25 |
| Sat. | 2 9 16 23 30 | 6 13 20 27 | 5 12 19 26 |

|  | April | May | June |
|---|---|---|---|
| Sun. | 3 10 17 24 | 1 8 15 22 29 | 5 12 19 26 |
| Mon. | 4 11 18 25 | 2 9 16 23 30 | 6 13 20 27 |
| Tue. | 5 12 19 26 | 3 10 17 24 31 | 7 14 21 28 |
| Wed. | 6 13 20 27 | 4 11 18 25 | 1 8 15 22 29 |
| Thur. | 7 14 21 28 | 5 12 19 26 | 2 9 16 23 30 |
| Fri. | 1 8 15 22 29 | 6 13 20 27 | 3 10 17 24 |
| Sat. | 2 9 16 23 30 | 7 14 21 28 | 4 11 18 25 |

|  | July | August | September |
|---|---|---|---|
| Sun. | 3 10 17 24 31 | 7 14 21 28 | 4 11 18 25 |
| Mon. | 4 11 18 25 | 1 8 15 22 29 | 5 12 19 26 |
| Tue. | 5 12 19 26 | 2 9 16 23 30 | 6 13 20 27 |
| Wed. | 6 13 20 27 | 3 10 17 24 31 | 7 14 21 28 |
| Thur. | 7 14 21 28 | 4 11 18 25 | 1 8 15 22 29 |
| Fri. | 1 8 15 22 29 | 5 12 19 26 | 2 9 16 23 30 |
| Sat. | 2 9 16 23 30 | 6 13 20 27 | 3 10 17 24 |

|  | October | November | December |
|---|---|---|---|
| Sun. | 2 9 16 23 30 | 6 13 20 27 | 4 11 18 25 |
| Mon. | 3 10 17 24 31 | 7 14 21 28 | 5 12 19 26 |
| Tue. | 4 11 18 25 | 1 8 15 22 29 | 6 13 20 27 |
| Wed. | 5 12 19 26 | 2 9 16 23 30 | 7 14 21 28 |
| Thur. | 6 13 20 27 | 3 10 17 24 | 1 8 15 22 29 |
| Fri. | 7 14 21 28 | 4 11 18 25 | 2 9 16 23 30 |
| Sat. | 1 8 15 22 29 | 5 12 19 26 | 3 10 17 24 31 |

EASTER DAYS

| | |
|---|---|
| March 27 | 1796, 1864, 1932, 2016 |
| April 3 | 1836, 1904, 1988 |
| April 17 | 1808, 1892, 1960 |

## N (LEAP YEAR)

|  | January | February | March |
|---|---|---|---|
| Sun. | 2 9 16 23 30 | 6 13 20 27 | 5 12 19 26 |
| Mon. | 3 10 17 24 31 | 7 14 21 28 | 6 13 20 27 |
| Tue. | 4 11 18 25 | 1 8 15 22 29 | 7 14 21 28 |
| Wed. | 5 12 19 26 | 2 9 16 23 | 1 8 15 22 29 |
| Thur. | 6 13 20 27 | 3 10 17 24 | 2 9 16 23 30 |
| Fri. | 7 14 21 28 | 4 11 18 25 | 3 10 17 24 31 |
| Sat. | 1 8 15 22 29 | 5 12 19 26 | 4 11 18 25 |

|  | April | May | June |
|---|---|---|---|
| Sun. | 2 9 16 23 30 | 7 14 21 28 | 4 11 18 25 |
| Mon. | 3 10 17 24 | 1 8 15 22 29 | 5 12 19 26 |
| Tue. | 4 11 18 25 | 2 9 16 23 30 | 6 13 20 27 |
| Wed. | 5 12 19 26 | 3 10 17 24 31 | 7 14 21 28 |
| Thur. | 6 13 20 27 | 4 11 18 25 | 1 8 15 22 29 |
| Fri. | 7 14 21 28 | 5 12 19 26 | 2 9 16 23 30 |
| Sat. | 1 8 15 22 29 | 6 13 20 27 | 3 10 17 24 |

|  | July | August | September |
|---|---|---|---|
| Sun. | 2 9 16 23 30 | 6 13 20 27 | 3 10 17 24 |
| Mon. | 3 10 17 24 31 | 7 14 21 28 | 4 11 18 25 |
| Tue. | 4 11 18 25 | 1 8 15 22 29 | 5 12 19 26 |
| Wed. | 5 12 19 26 | 2 9 16 23 30 | 6 13 20 27 |
| Thur. | 6 13 20 27 | 3 10 17 24 31 | 7 14 21 28 |
| Fri. | 7 14 21 28 | 4 11 18 25 | 1 8 15 22 29 |
| Sat. | 1 8 15 22 29 | 5 12 19 26 | 2 9 16 23 30 |

|  | October | November | December |
|---|---|---|---|
| Sun. | 1 8 15 22 29 | 5 12 19 26 | 3 10 17 24 31 |
| Mon. | 2 9 16 23 30 | 6 13 20 27 | 4 11 18 25 |
| Tue. | 3 10 17 24 31 | 7 14 21 28 | 5 12 19 26 |
| Wed. | 4 11 18 25 | 1 8 15 22 29 | 6 13 20 27 |
| Thur. | 5 12 19 26 | 2 9 16 23 30 | 7 14 21 28 |
| Fri. | 6 13 20 27 | 3 10 17 24 | 1 8 15 22 29 |
| Sat. | 7 14 21 28 | 4 11 18 25 | 2 9 16 23 30 |

EASTER DAYS

| | |
|---|---|
| March 26 | 1780 |
| April 2 | 1820, 1972 |
| April 9 | 1944 |
| April 16 | 1876, 2028 |
| April 23 | 1848, 1916, 2000 |

## GEOLOGICAL TIME

The earth is thought to have come into existence approximately 4,600 million years ago, but for nearly half this time, the Archean era, it was uninhabited. Life is generally believed to have emerged in the succeeding Proterozoic era. The Archean and the Proterozoic eras are often together referred to as the Precambrian.

Although primitive forms of life, e.g. algae and bacteria, existed during the Proterozoic era, it is not until the strata of Palaeozoic rocks is reached that abundant fossilized remains appear, initially of small shellfish, followed by plants, primitive fishes and, in the Devonian period (*c*.400 million BC), land-living plants and amphibia.

Since the Precambrian, there have been three great geological eras:

PALAEOZOIC ('ancient life')
*c*.570–*c*.250 million BC

*Cambrian* - Mainly sandstones, slate and shales; limestones in Scotland. Shelled fossils and invertebrates, e.g. trilobites and brachiopods appear
*Ordovician* - Mainly shales and mudstones, e.g. in north Wales; limestones in Scotland
*Silurian* - Shales, mudstones and some limestones, found mostly in Wales and southern Scotland
*Devonian* - Old red sandstone, shale, limestone and slate, e.g. in south Wales and the West Country. 'The age of fishes' - proliferation of fish fossils. First traces of land-living life
*Carboniferous* - Coal-bearing rocks, millstone grit, limestone and shale
*Permian* - Marls, sandstones and clays, named after the area of Russia where these strata are widespread. First large-scale appearance of reptile fossils

There were two great phases of mountain building in the Palaeozoic era: the Caledonian, characterized in Britain by NE–SW lines of hills and valleys; and the later Hercyian, widespread in west Germany and adjacent areas, and in Britain exemplified in E.–W. lines of hills and valleys.

The end of the Palaeozoic era was marked by the extensive glaciations of the Permian period in the southern continents and the decline of amphibians. It was succeeded by an era of warm conditions.

MESOZOIC ('middle forms of life')
*c*.250–*c*.65 million BC

*Triassic* - Mostly sandstone, e.g. in the West Midlands
*Jurassic* - Mainly limestones and clays, typically displayed in the Jura mountains, and in England in a NE–SW belt from Lincolnshire and the Wash to the Severn and the Dorset coast
*Cretaceous* - Mainly chalk, clay and sands, e.g. in Kent and Sussex

Giant reptiles were dominant during the Mesozoic era, but it was at this time that marsupial mammals first appeared, as well as *Archaeopteryx lithographica*, the earliest known species of bird. Coniferous trees and flowering plants also developed during the era and, with the birds and the mammals, were the main species to survive into the Caenozoic (or Cenozoic) era. The giant reptiles became extinct.

CAENOZOIC ('recent life')
from *c*.65 million BC

*Eocene* - The emergence of new forms of life, i.e. existing species

*Oligocene* - Fossils of a few still existing species
*Miocene* - Fossil remains show a balance of existing and extinct species
*Pliocene* - Fossil remains show a majority of still existing species
*Pleistocene* - The majority of remains are those of still existing species
*Holocene* - The present, post-glacial period. Existing species only, except for a few exterminated by man

In the last 25 million years, from the Miocene through the Pliocene periods, the Alpine-Himalayan and the circum-Pacific phases of mountain building reached their climax. During the Pleistocene period ice sheets repeatedly locked up masses of water as land ice; its weight depressed the land, but the locking-up of the water lowered the sea-level by 100–200 metres. The glaciations and interglacials of the Ice Age are extremely difficult to date and classify, but recent scientific opinion considers the Pleistocene period to have begun approximately 1.7 million years ago. The last glacial retreat, merging into the Holocene period, was 10,000 years ago.

## HUMAN DEVELOPMENT

Any consideration of the history of mankind must start with the fact that all members of the human race belong to one species of animal, i.e. *Homo sapiens*, the definition of a species being in biological terms that all its members can interbreed. As a species of mammal it is possible to group man with other similar types, known as the primates. Amongst these is found a sub-group, the apes, which includes, in addition to man, the chimpanzees, gorillas, orang-utans and gibbons. All lack a tail, have shoulder blades at the back, and a Y-shaped chewing pattern on the surface of their molars, as well as showing the more general primate characteristics of four incisors, a thumb which is able to touch the fingers of the same hand, and finger and toe nails instead of claws. All factors available to scientific study suggest that human beings have chimpanzees and gorillas as their nearest relatives in the animal world. However, there remains the possibility that there once lived creatures, now extinct, which were closer to modern man than the chimpanzees and gorillas, and which shared with modern man the characteristics of having flat faces (i.e. the absence of a pronounced muzzle), being bipedal, and possessing large brains.

There are two broad groups of extinct apes recognized by specialists. First the ramapithecines, the remains of which, mainly jaw fragments, have been found in east Africa, Asia, and Turkey. They lived about 14 to 8 million years ago, and from the evidence of their teeth it seems they chewed more in the manner of modern man than the other presently living apes. The second group, the australopithecines, have left much more numerous remains amongst which sub-groups may be detected, although the geographic spread is limited to south and east Africa. Living between 5 and 1.5 million years ago, they were closer relatives of modern man to the extent that they walked upright, did not have an extensive muzzle, and had similar types of pre-molars. The first australopithecine remains were recognized at Taung in South Africa in 1924, and subsequent discoveries include those at the famous site of Olduvai Gorge in Tanzania. Perhaps the most impressive discovery was made at Hadar in Ethiopia in 1974 when about half a skeleton, known as 'Lucy', was found.

Also in east Africa, between 2 million and 1.5 million years ago, lived a hominid group which not only walked upright, had a flat face, and a large brain case, but also made simple pebble and flake stone tools. On present evidence these habilines seem to have been the first people to make tools, however crude. This facility is related to the larger brain size and human beings are the only animals to make implements to be used in other processes. These early pebble tool users, because of their distinctive characteristics, have been grouped as a separate sub-species, now extinct, of the genus *Homo*, and are known as *Homo habilis*.

The use of fire, again a human characteristic, is associated with another group of extinct hominids whose remains, about a million years old, are found in south and east Africa, China, Indonesia, north Africa and Europe. No doubt the mastery of the techniques of making fire helped the colonization of the colder northern areas and in this respect the site of Vertesszollos in Hungary is of particular importance. *Homo erectus* is the name given to this group of fossils and it now includes a number of famous individual discoveries from earlier decades, for example, Solo Man, Heidelberg Man, and especially Peking Man who lived at the cave site at Choukoutien which has yielded evidence of fire and burnt bone.

The well-known group, Neanderthal Man, or *Homo sapiens neandertalensis*, is an extinct form of modern man who lived between about 100,000 and 40,000 years ago, thus spanning the last Ice Age. Indeed, its ability to adapt to the cold climate on the edge of the ice sheets is one of its characteristic features, the remains being found only in Europe, Asia and the Middle East. Complete neanderthal skeletons were found during excavations at Tabun in Israel, together with evidence of tool-making and the use of fire. Distinguished by very large brains, it seems that neanderthal man was the first to develop recognizable social customs, especially deliberate burial rites. Why the neanderthalers became extinct is not clear, but it may be connected with the climatic changes at the end of the Ice Ages, which would have seriously affected their food supplies; possibly they became too specialized for their own good.

The Swanscombe skull is the only known human fossil remains found in England. Some specialists see Swanscombe Man (or, more probably, woman) as a neanderthaler. Others group these remains together with the Steinheim skull from Germany, seeing both as a separate sub-species. Unfortunately there is too little evidence as yet on which to form a final judgement.

Modern Man, *Homo sapiens sapiens*, the surviving subspecies of *Homo sapiens*, had evolved to our present physical condition and had colonized much of the world by about 30,000 years ago. There are many previously distinguished individual specimens, for example Cromagnon Man, which may now be grouped together as *Homo sapiens sapiens*. It was modern man who spread to the American continent by crossing the landbridge between Siberia and Alaska and thence moved south through North America and into South America. Equally it is modern man who over the last 30,000 years has been responsible for the major developments in technology, art and civilization generally.

One of the problems for those studying fossil man is the lack in many cases of sufficient quantities of fossil bone for analysis. It is important that theories should be tested against evidence, and not the evidence made to fit the theory. The celebrated Piltdown hoax is perhaps the best-known example of 'fossils' being forged to fit what was seen in some quarters as the correct theory of man's evolution.

## CULTURAL DEVELOPMENT

The Eurocentric bias of early archaeologists meant that the search for a starting point for the development and transmission of cultural ideas, especially by migration, trade and warfare, concentrated unduly on Europe and the Near East. The Three Age system, whereby pre-history was divided into a Stone Age, a Bronze Age, and an Iron Age, was devised by Christian Thomsen, curator of the National Museum of Denmark in the early nineteenth century, to facilitate the classification of the museum's collections. The descriptive adjectives referred to the materials from which the implements and weapons were made, and came to be regarded as the dominant features of the societies to which they related. The refinement of the Three Age system once dominated archaeological thought and still remains a generally accepted concept in the popular mind. However, it is now seen by archaeologists as an inadequate model for human development.

Common sense alone suggests that there were no complete breaks between one so-called Age and another, any more than contemporaries would have regarded as a complete break between medieval and modern English history. Nor can the Three Age system be applied universally. In some areas it is necessary to insert a Copper Age, while in Africa south of the Sahara there would seem to be no Bronze Age at all; in Australia, Old Stone Age societies survived, while in South America, New Stone Age communities existed into modern times. The civilizations in other parts of the world clearly invalidate a Eurocentric theory of human development.

The concept of the 'Neolithic revolution', associated with the domestication of plants and animals, was a development of particular importance in the human cultural pattern. It reflected change from the primitive hunter/gatherer economies to a more settled agricultural way of life and therefore, so the argument goes, made possible the development of urban civilization. However, it can no longer be argued that this 'revolution' took place only in one area from which all development stemmed. Though it appears that the cultivation of wheat and barley was first undertaken, together with the domestication of cattle and goats/sheep in the Fertile Crescent, there is evidence that rice was first deliberately planted and pigs domesticated in south-east Asia, maize first cultivated in Central America, and llamas first domesticated in South America. It has been recognized increasingly in recent years that cultural changes can take place independently of each other in different parts of the world at different rates and different times. There is no need for a general diffusionist theory.

Although scholars will continue to study the particular societies which interest them, it may be possible to obtain a reliable chronological framework, in absolute terms of years, against which the cultural development of any particular area may be set. The development and refinement of radio-carbon dating and other scientific methods of producing absolute chronologies is enabling the cross-referencing of societies to be undertaken. As the techniques of dating become more rigorous in application and the number of scientifically obtained dates increases, the attainment of an absolute chronology for prehistoric societies throughout the world comes closer to being achieved.

# Tidal Tables

## CONSTANTS

The constant tidal difference may be used in conjunction with the time of high water at a standard port shown in the predictions data (pages 98–109) to find the time of high water at any of the ports or places listed below.

EXAMPLE

Required time of high water at Stranraer at 2 *January* 1995
Appropriate time of high water at *Greenock*

| | |
|---|---|
| *Morning tide* 2 *January* | 0035 hrs |
| Tidal difference | − 0020 hrs |
| High water at *Stranraer* | 0015 hrs |

The columns headed 'Springs' and 'Neaps' show the height, in metres, of the tide above datum for mean high water springs and mean high water neaps respectively.

\* data very approximate
† data for first high water springs only
H. Harbour

| Port | Diff. | | Springs | Neaps |
|---|---|---|---|---|
| | | h   m | m | m |
| Aberdeen | *Leith* | −1 19 | 4.3 | 3.4 |
| Aberdovey | *Liverpool* | −3 01 | 5.0 | 3.5 |
| Aberystwyth | *Liverpool* | −3 31 | 5.0 | 3.5 |
| Aldeburgh | *London* | −3 05 | 2.8 | 2.7 |
| Alloa | *Leith* | +0 49 | 5.6 | 4.2 |
| Amlwch | *Liverpool* | −0 35 | 7.2 | 5.7 |
| Anstruther Easter | *Leith* | −0 22 | 5.5 | 4.4 |
| Antwerp (Prosperpolder) | *London* | +0 50 | 5.8 | 4.8 |
| Appledore | *Avonmouth* | −1 16 | 7.5 | 5.2 |
| Arbroath | *Leith* | −0 33 | 5.0 | 4.1 |
| Ardrossan | *Greenock* | −0 15 | 3.2 | 2.6 |
| *Arundel | *London* | −2 04 | 3.2 | 2.1 |
| Avonmouth | *Avonmouth* | 0 00 | 13.2 | 9.8 |
| Ayr | *Greenock* | −0 25 | 3.0 | 2.5 |
| Baie de Lampaul | *London* | +2 30 | 7.4 | 5.8 |
| Ballycotton | *Avonmouth* | −1 47 | 4.2 | 3.2 |
| Banff | *Leith* | −2 44 | 3.5 | 2.8 |
| Bantry | *Liverpool* | +5 55 | 3.3 | 2.4 |
| Bardsey Island | *Liverpool* | −3 20 | 4.4 | 3.2 |
| Barmouth | *Liverpool* | −2 58 | 5.0 | 3.5 |
| Barnstaple | *Avonmouth* | −1 01 | 4.1 | 1.4 |
| Barrow (Docks) | *Liverpool* | 0 00 | 9.3 | 7.1 |
| Barry | *Avonmouth* | −0 22 | 11.4 | 8.5 |
| Belfast | *London* | −2 47 | 3.5 | 3.0 |
| Berwick | *Leith* | −0 03 | 4.7 | 3.8 |
| Bideford | *Avonmouth* | −1 16 | 5.9 | 3.6 |
| Blackpool | *Liverpool* | −0 10 | 8.9 | 7.0 |
| Blacktoft | *Hull* | +0 31 | 5.7 | 4.0 |
| Blakeney | *Hull* | +0 46 | 3.4 | 2.0 |
| Blyth | *Leith* | +0 51 | 5.0 | 3.9 |
| Boscastle | *Avonmouth* | −1 21 | 7.3 | 5.6 |
| Boulogne | *London* | −2 44 | 8.9 | 7.2 |
| Bovisand Pier | *London* | +3 55 | 5.3 | 4.3 |
| Bowling | *Greenock* | +0 15 | 4.0 | 3.3 |
| Braye (Alderney) | *London* | +5 33 | 6.2 | 4.7 |
| Brest | *London* | +2 28 | 7.5 | 5.9 |
| Bridgwater | *Avonmouth* | −0 22 | 4.6 | 1.7 |
| Bridlington | *Leith* | +2 04 | 6.1 | 4.7 |
| Bridport (W. Bay) | *London* | +4 37 | 4.1 | 3.0 |
| Brighton | *London* | −2 51 | 6.6 | 5.0 |
| Buckie | *Leith* | −2 56 | 4.1 | 3.2 |
| Bude | *Avonmouth* | −1 34 | 7.7 | 5.8 |
| Bull Sand Fort | *Hull* | −0 44 | 6.9 | 5.5 |
| Burntisland | *Leith* | 0 00 | 5.6 | 4.5 |
| Calais | *London* | −2 04 | 7.2 | 5.9 |
| Campbeltown | *Greenock* | +0 07 | 2.9 | 2.5 |
| Cape Cornwall | *Avonmouth* | −2 31 | 6.0 | 4.3 |
| Cardiff | *Avonmouth* | −0 15 | 12.2 | 9.2 |
| Cardigan Port | *Liverpool* | −3 38 | 4.7 | 3.4 |
| Carmarthen | *Avonmouth* | −0 49 | 2.6 | 0.4 |
| Cayeux | *London* | −2 55 | 10.2 | 7.9 |
| Chatham | *London* | −1 08 | 6.1 | 4.8 |
| Chepstow | *Avonmouth* | +0 20 | no data | |
| Cherbourg | *London* | −6 00 | 6.4 | 5.0 |
| Chester | *Liverpool* | +1 05 | 4.0 | 2.0 |
| Chichester H. (Entrance) | *London* | −2 40 | 4.9 | 4.0 |
| †Christchurch H. | *London* | −5 08 | 1.8 | 1.4 |
| Cobh | *Liverpool* | −5 55 | 4.2 | 3.2 |
| Coulport | *Greenock* | −0 05 | 3.4 | 2.8 |
| Coverack | *Avonmouth* | −2 02 | 5.3 | 4.2 |
| Cowes | *London* | −2 38 | 4.2 | 3.5 |
| Cromarty | *Leith* | −2 56 | 4.3 | 3.4 |
| Cromer | *Hull* | +0 15 | 5.2 | 4.1 |
| Dartmouth | *London* | +4 25 | 4.9 | 3.8 |
| Deal | *London* | −2 37 | 6.1 | 5.0 |
| Dieppe | *London* | −3 03 | 9.3 | 7.3 |
| Dingle H. | *Liverpool* | +5 34 | 4.1 | 2.8 |
| Donegal H. | *Liverpool* | −5 24 | 3.9 | 3.0 |
| Douglas (IOM) | *Liverpool* | −0 04 | 6.9 | 5.4 |
| Dover | *London* | −2 52 | 6.7 | 5.3 |
| Duclair | *London* | −1 48 | 7.5 | 6.3 |
| Duddon Bar | *Liverpool* | +0 03 | 8.5 | 6.6 |
| Dunbar | *Leith* | −0 07 | 5.2 | 4.2 |
| Dundalk (Sldr's Pt) | *Liverpool* | +0 21 | 5.1 | 4.2 |
| Dundee | *Leith* | +0 11 | 5.4 | 4.3 |
| Dungeness | *London* | −3 04 | 7.7 | 5.9 |
| Dunkirk | *London* | −1 54 | 6.0 | 4.9 |
| Eastbourne | *London* | −2 51 | 7.4 | 5.5 |
| East Loch Tarbert | *Greenock* | −0 05 | 3.4 | 2.8 |
| Exmouth Dock | *London* | +4 55 | 4.0 | 2.8 |
| Eyemouth | *Leith* | −0 20 | 4.7 | 3.7 |
| Falmouth | *London* | +3 35 | 5.3 | 4.2 |
| Ferryside | *Avonmouth* | −0 59 | 6.7 | 4.5 |
| Filey Bay | *Leith* | +1 51 | 5.8 | 4.9 |
| Fishguard | *Liverpool* | −4 01 | 4.8 | 3.4 |
| Folkestone | *London* | −3 04 | 7.1 | 5.7 |
| Formby | *Liverpool* | −0 12 | 9.0 | 7.3 |
| Fowey | *London* | +3 53 | 5.4 | 4.3 |
| Fraserburgh | *Leith* | −2 29 | 3.7 | 2.9 |
| †Freshwater | *London* | −4 48 | 2.6 | 2.3 |
| Galway | *Liverpool* | −6 08 | 5.1 | 3.9 |
| Glasgow | *Greenock* | +0 26 | 4.7 | 4.0 |
| Goole | *Hull* | +1 00 | 5.7 | 3.7 |
| Gorleston-on-Sea | *London* | −5 00 | 2.4 | 2.0 |
| Granton | *Leith* | 0 00 | 5.6 | 4.5 |
| Granville | *London* | +4 32 | 13.0 | 9.8 |
| Grimsby | *Hull* | −0 27 | 7.0 | 5.6 |
| Hartlepool | *Leith* | +0 57 | 5.4 | 4.2 |
| Harwich | *London* | −2 06 | 4.0 | 3.4 |
| Hastings | *London* | −2 57 | 7.5 | 5.8 |
| Haverfordwest | *Liverpool* | −4 51 | 2.2 | 0.3 |

| Port | Diff. | | Springs | Neaps |
|------|---|---|---|---|
| | h | m | m | m |
| Hestan Islet | Liverpool | +0 25 | 8.3 | 6.3 |
| Holyhead | Liverpool | −0 50 | 5.6 | 4.4 |
| Hook of Holland | London | −0 01 | 2.1 | 1.7 |
| †Hurst Point | London | −3 53 | 2.7 | 2.3 |
| Ijmuiden | London | +1 03 | 2.1 | 1.7 |
| Ilfracombe | Avonmouth | −1 12 | 9.2 | 6.9 |
| Inveraray | Greenock | +0 11 | 3.3 | 2.9 |
| Invergordon | Leith | −2 48 | 4.4 | 3.5 |
| Ipswich | London | −1 46 | 4.2 | 3.4 |
| Itchenor | London | −2 38 | 4.8 | 3.8 |
| Kinsale | Liverpool | −6 07 | 4.0 | 3.2 |
| Kirkcudbright | Liverpool | +0 15 | 7.5 | 5.9 |
| Kirkwall | Leith | −4 15 | 3.0 | 2.4 |
| Knights Town | Liverpool | +5 32 | 3.6 | 2.8 |
| Lamlash | Greenock | −0 26 | 3.2 | 2.6 |
| Le Havre | London | −3 55 | 7.9 | 6.6 |
| Lerwick | Leith | −3 48 | 2.2 | 1.6 |
| Limerick Dock | Liverpool | −4 27 | 6.1 | 4.6 |
| Littlehampton (Entrance) | London | −2 39 | 5.9 | 4.5 |
| Lizard Point | Avonmouth | −2 17 | 5.3 | 4.2 |
| Llanddwyn Island | Liverpool | −1 55 | 4.9 | 3.9 |
| Llanelli | Avonmouth | −0 57 | 7.8 | 5.8 |
| Loch Moidart | Greenock | +5 58 | 4.8 | 3.5 |
| Londonderry | London | −5 37 | 2.7 | 2.1 |
| Looe | London | +3 55 | 5.4 | 4.2 |
| Lossiemouth | Leith | −3 01 | 4.1 | 3.2 |
| Lowestoft | London | −4 25 | 2.4 | 2.1 |
| Lulworth Cove | London | +4 59 | 2.2 | 1.5 |
| Lundy Island | Avonmouth | −1 24 | 8.0 | 5.9 |
| Lyme Regis | London | +4 55 | 4.3 | 3.1 |
| †Lymington | London | −3 48 | 3.0 | 2.6 |
| Margate | London | −1 53 | 4.8 | 3.9 |
| Maryport | Liverpool | +0 24 | 8.6 | 6.6 |
| Menai Bridge | Liverpool | −0 30 | 7.3 | 5.8 |
| Mevagissey | London | +3 53 | 5.4 | 4.3 |
| Middlesbrough | Leith | +1 08 | 5.6 | 4.5 |
| Milford Haven | Liverpool | −5 06 | 7.0 | 5.2 |
| Minehead | Avonmouth | −0 40 | 10.6 | 7.9 |
| Montrose | Leith | −0 19 | 4.8 | 3.9 |
| Morecambe | Liverpool | +0 07 | 9.5 | 7.4 |
| Mostyn Quay | Liverpool | −0 17 | 8.5 | 6.7 |
| Newburgh | Leith | +0 48 | 4.1 | 3.0 |
| Newcastle upon Tyne | Leith | +0 53 | 5.3 | 4.1 |
| Newhaven | London | −2 46 | 6.7 | 5.1 |
| Newlyn | Avonmouth | −2 25 | 5.6 | 4.4 |
| Newport (Gwent) | Avonmouth | −0 15 | 12.1 | 8.8 |
| Newquay | Avonmouth | −1 59 | 7.0 | 5.3 |
| New Quay, Cardigan Bay | Liverpool | −3 31 | 4.9 | 3.4 |
| North Shields | Leith | +0 50 | 5.0 | 3.9 |
| North Sunderland | Leith | +0 04 | 4.8 | 3.7 |
| Oban | Greenock | +5 43 | 4.0 | 2.9 |
| Old Lynn Road | Hull | +0 07 | 7.3 | 5.8 |
| Orford Ness | London | −2 50 | 2.8 | 2.7 |
| Ostend | London | −1 32 | 5.1 | 4.2 |
| Padstow | Avonmouth | −1 46 | 7.3 | 5.6 |
| Peel (IOM) | Liverpool | −0 02 | 5.3 | 4.2 |
| Peterhead | Leith | −1 59 | 3.8 | 3.1 |
| Plymouth | London | +4 05 | 5.5 | 4.4 |
| †Poole H. (Entrance) | London | −5 18 | 2.0 | 1.6 |
| Porlock Bay | Avonmouth | −0 50 | 10.2 | 7.6 |
| Porthcawl | Avonmouth | −0 54 | 9.9 | 7.5 |
| Portmadoc | Liverpool | −2 46 | 5.1 | 3.4 |
| Portland | London | +5 09 | 2.1 | 1.4 |
| Portpatrick | Liverpool | +0 22 | 3.8 | 3.0 |
| Portsmouth | London | −2 38 | 4.7 | 3.8 |
| Port Talbot | Avonmouth | −0 54 | 9.6 | 7.3 |
| Preston | Liverpool | +0 10 | 5.3 | 3.3 |
| Pwllheli | Liverpool | −3 08 | 5.0 | 3.4 |
| Ramsey (IOM) | Liverpool | +0 10 | 7.6 | 5.9 |
| Ramsgate | London | −2 32 | 5.2 | 4.1 |
| *Rosslare H. | Liverpool | −5 24 | 1.9 | 1.4 |
| Rosyth | Leith | +0 09 | 5.8 | 4.7 |
| Ryde | London | −2 38 | 4.5 | 3.7 |
| St Helier | London | +4 48 | 11.0 | 8.1 |
| St Ives | Avonmouth | −1 56 | 6.6 | 4.9 |
| St Malo | London | +4 27 | 12.2 | 9.2 |
| St Peter Port | London | +4 54 | 9.3 | 7.0 |
| Salcombe | London | +4 10 | 5.3 | 4.1 |
| Saltash | London | +4 10 | 5.6 | 4.5 |
| Scarborough | Leith | +1 33 | 5.7 | 4.6 |
| Scheveningen | London | +1 02 | 2.2 | 1.8 |
| Scrabster | Leith | −6 06 | 5.0 | 4.0 |
| Seaham | Leith | +0 54 | 5.2 | 4.1 |
| Selsey Bill | London | −2 43 | 5.3 | 4.4 |
| Sennen Cove | Avonmouth | −2 31 | 6.1 | 4.8 |
| Sharpness Dock | Avonmouth | +0 42 | 9.3 | 5.6 |
| Sheerness | London | −1 19 | 5.8 | 4.7 |
| Shoreham | London | −2 44 | 6.3 | 4.9 |
| Silloth | Liverpool | +0 35 | 9.2 | 7.1 |
| Southampton (1st high water) | London | −2 54 | 4.5 | 3.7 |
| Southend | London | −1 23 | 5.8 | 4.7 |
| Southwold | London | −3 50 | 2.4 | 2.1 |
| Stirling | Leith | +1 15 | 2.9 | 1.6 |
| Stonehaven | Leith | −1 09 | 4.5 | 3.6 |
| Stornoway | Liverpool | −4 16 | 4.8 | 3.7 |
| Stranraer | Greenock | −0 20 | 3.0 | 2.4 |
| Stromness | Leith | −5 26 | 3.6 | 2.7 |
| Sunderland | Leith | +0 49 | 5.2 | 4.2 |
| †Swanage | London | −5 28 | 2.0 | 1.6 |
| Swansea | Avonmouth | −0 51 | 9.5 | 7.2 |
| Tarn Point | Liverpool | +0 05 | 8.3 | 6.4 |
| Tay River (Bar) | Leith | −0 19 | 5.2 | 4.2 |
| Tees River (Entrance) | Leith | +1 09 | 5.5 | 4.3 |
| Teignmouth (Approaches) | London | +4 37 | 4.8 | 3.6 |
| Tenby | Avonmouth | −1 06 | 8.4 | 6.3 |
| Tilbury | London | −0 49 | 6.4 | 5.4 |
| Tobermory | Liverpool | −5 11 | 4.4 | 3.3 |
| Torquay | London | +4 40 | 4.9 | 3.7 |
| †Totland Bay | London | −4 08 | 2.7 | 2.3 |
| Troon | Greenock | −0 25 | 3.2 | 2.6 |
| Truro | London | +3 43 | 3.5 | 2.4 |
| Walton-on-Naze | London | −2 10 | 4.2 | 3.4 |
| Waterford | Liverpool | −4 58 | 4.6 | 3.5 |
| Weston-s.-Mare | Avonmouth | −0 25 | 12.0 | 8.8 |
| *Wexford H. | Liverpool | −5 04 | 1.7 | 1.4 |
| Whitby | Leith | +1 23 | 5.6 | 4.3 |
| Whitehaven | Liverpool | +0 10 | 8.0 | 6.3 |
| Wick | Leith | −3 26 | 3.5 | 2.8 |
| Wisbech Cut | Hull | +0 03 | 7.0 | 5.1 |
| Woolwich | London | −0 20 | 7.0 | 5.9 |
| Workington | Liverpool | +0 21 | 8.1 | 6.3 |
| Worthing | London | −2 39 | 6.2 | 4.7 |
| †Yarmouth (IOW) | London | −3 43 | 3.1 | 2.5 |
| Youghal | Liverpool | −5 50 | 4.0 | 3.1 |

The tidal predictions for London Bridge, Avonmouth, Liverpool, Hull, Greenock, Leith and Dun Laoghaire on pages 98–109 have been computed by the Hydrographer of the Navy, Crown copyright reserved.

## JANUARY 1995   *High water*   GMT

| | | LONDON BRIDGE *Datum of predictions 3.20 m below* | | | | AVONMOUTH *Datum of predictions 6.50 m below* | | | | LIVERPOOL *Datum of predictions 4.93 m below* | | | | HULL (*Albert Dock*) *Datum of predictions 3.90 m below* | | | |
|---|---|---|---|---|---|---|---|---|---|---|---|---|---|---|---|---|---|
| | | hr | ht m | hr | ht m | hr | ht m | hr | ht m | hr | ht m | hr | ht m | hr | ht m | hr | ht m |
| 1 | Sunday | 00 59 | 7.0 | 13 22 | 7.2 | 06 42 | 13.5 | 19 09 | 13.5 | 10 43 | 9.7 | 23 09 | 9.6 | 05 46 | 7.4 | 18 04 | 7.6 |
| 2 | Monday | 01 48 | 7.1 | 14 13 | 7.3 | 07 32 | 13.9 | 19 58 | 13.8 | 11 32 | 9.9 | 23 58 | 9.6 | 06 36 | 7.6 | 18 48 | 7.8 |
| 3 | Tuesday | 02 35 | 7.2 | 15 03 | 7.4 | 08 19 | 14.0 | 20 45 | 13.8 | ——— | — | 12 20 | 10.0 | 07 22 | 7.6 | 19 30 | 7.9 |
| 4 | Wednesday | 03 21 | 7.2 | 15 51 | 7.4 | 09 05 | 13.9 | 21 19 | 13.5 | 00 46 | 9.5 | 13 06 | 9.9 | 08 06 | 7.5 | 20 12 | 7.9 |
| 5 | Thursday | 04 05 | 7.2 | 16 37 | 7.4 | 09 48 | 13.5 | 22 09 | 13.0 | 01 32 | 9.3 | 13 51 | 9.6 | 08 49 | 7.3 | 20 54 | 7.8 |
| 6 | Friday | 04 46 | 7.1 | 17 20 | 7.2 | 10 27 | 12.9 | 22 44 | 12.4 | 02 15 | 9.0 | 14 33 | 9.3 | 09 32 | 7.0 | 21 37 | 7.5 |
| 7 | Saturday | 05 24 | 6.9 | 18 00 | 6.9 | 11 01 | 12.2 | 23 16 | 11.7 | 02 56 | 8.6 | 15 15 | 8.9 | 10 15 | 6.6 | 22 20 | 7.1 |
| 8 | Sunday | 06 01 | 6.7 | 18 41 | 6.6 | 11 36 | 11.5 | 23 52 | 11.1 | 03 38 | 8.2 | 15 59 | 8.4 | 10 59 | 6.2 | 23 06 | 6.7 |
| 9 | Monday | 06 44 | 6.3 | 19 29 | 6.2 | ——— | — | 12 20 | 10.9 | 04 27 | 7.7 | 16 51 | 7.8 | 11 52 | 5.9 | ——— | — |
| 10 | Tuesday | 07 43 | 6.0 | 20 33 | 5.9 | 00 42 | 10.5 | 13 24 | 10.3 | 05 29 | 7.3 | 17 58 | 7.5 | 00 06 | 6.2 | 13 02 | 5.7 |
| 11 | Wednesday | 09 11 | 5.8 | 21 49 | 5.9 | 01 54 | 10.2 | 14 43 | 10.2 | 06 47 | 7.3 | 19 17 | 7.4 | 01 23 | 6.0 | 14 14 | 5.8 |
| 12 | Thursday | 10 27 | 5.8 | 22 53 | 5.9 | 03 17 | 10.3 | 15 57 | 10.5 | 07 59 | 7.5 | 20 24 | 7.7 | 02 36 | 5.9 | 15 20 | 6.0 |
| 13 | Friday | 11 26 | 6.0 | 23 47 | 6.1 | 04 28 | 10.9 | 17 00 | 11.1 | 08 54 | 8.0 | 21 17 | 8.1 | 03 43 | 6.1 | 16 17 | 6.3 |
| 14 | Saturday | ——— | — | 12 16 | 6.1 | 05 24 | 11.5 | 17 51 | 11.6 | 09 40 | 8.4 | 22 01 | 8.4 | 04 39 | 6.3 | 17 01 | 6.6 |
| 15 | Sunday | 00 33 | 6.3 | 12 59 | 6.3 | 06 09 | 12.1 | 18 33 | 12.0 | 10 21 | 8.7 | 22 41 | 8.7 | 05 23 | 6.6 | 17 38 | 6.9 |
| 16 | Monday | 01 14 | 6.4 | 13 38 | 6.5 | 06 49 | 12.4 | 19 10 | 12.2 | 10 59 | 9.0 | 23 18 | 8.9 | 05 59 | 6.8 | 18 11 | 7.1 |
| 17 | Tuesday | 01 52 | 6.6 | 14 16 | 6.7 | 07 25 | 12.6 | 19 46 | 12.4 | 11 34 | 9.1 | 23 53 | 9.0 | 06 34 | 7.0 | 18 44 | 7.3 |
| 18 | Wednesday | 02 30 | 6.8 | 14 56 | 6.9 | 08 00 | 12.8 | 20 23 | 12.7 | ——— | — | 12 09 | 9.2 | 07 09 | 7.2 | 19 19 | 7.5 |
| 19 | Thursday | 03 09 | 6.9 | 15 37 | 7.0 | 08 36 | 13.0 | 20 59 | 12.8 | 00 28 | 9.0 | 12 45 | 9.3 | 07 44 | 7.3 | 19 54 | 7.5 |
| 20 | Friday | 03 48 | 6.9 | 16 18 | 7.0 | 09 13 | 13.1 | 21 36 | 12.9 | 01 05 | 9.1 | 13 21 | 9.3 | 08 21 | 7.3 | 20 30 | 7.5 |
| 21 | Saturday | 04 24 | 6.8 | 16 57 | 6.9 | 09 50 | 13.0 | 22 13 | 12.6 | 01 42 | 9.0 | 14 00 | 9.3 | 08 58 | 7.2 | 21 07 | 7.4 |
| 22 | Sunday | 04 59 | 6.7 | 17 36 | 6.7 | 10 29 | 12.6 | 22 51 | 12.1 | 02 21 | 8.9 | 14 41 | 9.1 | 09 37 | 7.1 | 21 48 | 7.2 |
| 23 | Monday | 05 37 | 6.6 | 18 18 | 6.5 | 11 09 | 12.0 | 23 32 | 11.5 | 03 04 | 8.7 | 15 27 | 8.8 | 10 21 | 6.8 | 22 34 | 7.0 |
| 24 | Tuesday | 06 20 | 6.5 | 19 05 | 6.3 | 11 56 | 11.3 | ——— | — | 03 56 | 8.3 | 16 23 | 8.4 | 11 11 | 6.5 | 23 30 | 6.7 |
| 25 | Wednesday | 07 15 | 6.2 | 20 06 | 6.0 | 00 23 | 10.9 | 12 58 | 10.8 | 05 01 | 7.9 | 17 31 | 8.1 | ——— | — | 12 17 | 6.3 |
| 26 | Thursday | 08 30 | 6.0 | 21 25 | 6.0 | 01 38 | 10.5 | 14 30 | 10.6 | 06 18 | 7.8 | 18 49 | 8.0 | 00 46 | 6.4 | 13 45 | 6.2 |
| 27 | Friday | 09 59 | 6.0 | 22 43 | 6.2 | 03 11 | 10.7 | 15 51 | 11.1 | 07 37 | 8.1 | 20 07 | 8.2 | 02 19 | 6.4 | 15 03 | 6.5 |
| 28 | Saturday | 11 16 | 6.3 | 23 49 | 6.5 | 04 28 | 11.4 | 17 04 | 11.8 | 08 45 | 8.6 | 21 14 | 8.7 | 03 39 | 6.6 | 16 09 | 6.8 |
| 29 | Sunday | ——— | — | 12 18 | 6.7 | 05 37 | 12.4 | 18 07 | 12.7 | 09 42 | 9.2 | 22 10 | 9.2 | 04 46 | 7.0 | 17 05 | 7.2 |
| 30 | Monday | 00 45 | 6.8 | 13 13 | 7.0 | 06 33 | 13.2 | 18 59 | 13.3 | 10 33 | 9.6 | 22 59 | 9.5 | 05 41 | 7.2 | 17 52 | 7.5 |
| 31 | Tuesday | 01 34 | 7.0 | 14 02 | 7.3 | 07 21 | 13.8 | 19 45 | 13.7 | 11 19 | 9.9 | 23 45 | 9.6 | 06 27 | 7.4 | 18 33 | 7.8 |

## FEBRUARY 1995   *High water*   GMT

| | | LONDON BRIDGE | | | | AVONMOUTH | | | | LIVERPOOL | | | | HULL (*Albert Dock*) | | | |
|---|---|---|---|---|---|---|---|---|---|---|---|---|---|---|---|---|---|
| 1 | Wednesday | 02 20 | 7.2 | 14 48 | 7.4 | 08 05 | 14.1 | 20 27 | 13.8 | ——— | — | 12 04 | 10.0 | 07 08 | 7.5 | 19 13 | 8.0 |
| 2 | Thursday | 03 03 | 7.2 | 15 33 | 7.4 | 08 46 | 14.1 | 21 07 | 13.8 | 00 28 | 9.6 | 12 46 | 9.9 | 07 47 | 7.5 | 19 52 | 8.0 |
| 3 | Friday | 03 44 | 7.3 | 16 14 | 7.4 | 09 25 | 13.9 | 21 43 | 13.5 | 01 08 | 9.4 | 13 26 | 9.7 | 08 25 | 7.4 | 20 31 | 7.9 |
| 4 | Saturday | 04 22 | 7.2 | 16 52 | 7.2 | 09 59 | 13.4 | 22 14 | 12.9 | 01 45 | 9.2 | 14 03 | 9.4 | 09 02 | 7.2 | 21 09 | 7.7 |
| 5 | Sunday | 04 56 | 7.1 | 17 26 | 7.0 | 10 29 | 12.7 | 22 42 | 12.3 | 02 21 | 8.9 | 14 40 | 9.0 | 09 38 | 6.9 | 21 47 | 7.2 |
| 6 | Monday | 05 30 | 6.8 | 18 00 | 6.7 | 10 59 | 11.9 | 23 12 | 11.6 | 02 57 | 8.5 | 15 18 | 8.6 | 10 13 | 6.5 | 22 25 | 6.8 |
| 7 | Tuesday | 06 06 | 6.5 | 18 37 | 6.3 | 11 34 | 11.1 | 23 51 | 10.8 | 03 37 | 8.0 | 16 01 | 8.0 | 10 51 | 6.1 | 23 10 | 6.2 |
| 8 | Wednesday | 06 49 | 6.0 | 19 23 | 5.9 | ——— | — | 12 21 | 10.4 | 04 26 | 7.6 | 16 55 | 7.5 | 11 35 | 5.8 | ——— | — |
| 9 | Thursday | 07 45 | 5.6 | 20 22 | 5.6 | 00 45 | 10.0 | 13 34 | 9.6 | 05 33 | 7.2 | 18 10 | 7.1 | 00 18 | 5.8 | 13 07 | 5.6 |
| 10 | Friday | 09 09 | 5.3 | 21 49 | 5.5 | 02 14 | 9.7 | 15 08 | 9.7 | 07 06 | 7.2 | 19 45 | 7.3 | 01 48 | 5.6 | 14 27 | 5.7 |
| 11 | Saturday | 10 47 | 5.5 | 23 06 | 5.7 | 03 44 | 10.1 | 16 26 | 10.4 | 08 23 | 7.6 | 20 51 | 7.7 | 03 05 | 5.7 | 15 37 | 6.0 |
| 12 | Sunday | 11 46 | 5.8 | ——— | — | 04 53 | 11.0 | 17 24 | 11.2 | 09 16 | 8.1 | 21 39 | 8.2 | 04 10 | 6.0 | 16 30 | 6.4 |
| 13 | Monday | 00 01 | 6.0 | 12 33 | 6.2 | 05 44 | 11.8 | 18 09 | 11.9 | 09 59 | 8.6 | 22 20 | 8.6 | 04 58 | 6.4 | 17 12 | 6.8 |
| 14 | Tuesday | 00 48 | 6.4 | 13 15 | 6.5 | 06 26 | 12.4 | 18 48 | 12.4 | 10 38 | 9.0 | 22 58 | 9.0 | 05 37 | 6.8 | 17 48 | 7.1 |
| 15 | Wednesday | 01 30 | 6.6 | 13 55 | 6.8 | 07 04 | 12.8 | 19 26 | 12.8 | 11 14 | 9.2 | 23 33 | 9.2 | 06 12 | 7.1 | 18 23 | 7.4 |
| 16 | Thursday | 02 11 | 6.9 | 14 36 | 7.0 | 07 40 | 13.1 | 20 03 | 13.1 | 11 49 | 9.4 | ——— | — | 06 47 | 7.3 | 18 58 | 7.7 |
| 17 | Friday | 02 51 | 7.0 | 15 18 | 7.1 | 08 17 | 13.5 | 20 40 | 13.4 | 00 09 | 9.3 | 12 26 | 9.6 | 07 23 | 7.5 | 19 34 | 7.8 |
| 18 | Saturday | 03 31 | 7.1 | 15 59 | 7.1 | 08 55 | 13.7 | 21 17 | 13.5 | 00 46 | 9.4 | 13 03 | 9.7 | 07 59 | 7.6 | 20 10 | 7.8 |
| 19 | Sunday | 04 08 | 7.0 | 16 39 | 7.0 | 09 34 | 13.6 | 21 55 | 13.2 | 01 23 | 9.5 | 13 42 | 9.6 | 08 36 | 7.5 | 20 48 | 7.7 |
| 20 | Monday | 04 44 | 6.9 | 17 18 | 6.8 | 10 12 | 13.1 | 22 32 | 12.7 | 02 01 | 9.3 | 14 22 | 9.4 | 09 15 | 7.3 | 21 29 | 7.5 |
| 21 | Tuesday | 05 21 | 6.8 | 17 55 | 6.5 | 10 52 | 12.3 | 23 12 | 11.8 | 02 43 | 9.0 | 15 07 | 9.0 | 09 57 | 7.0 | 22 15 | 7.1 |
| 22 | Wednesday | 06 02 | 6.5 | 18 38 | 6.2 | 11 35 | 11.5 | ——— | — | 03 31 | 8.5 | 16 01 | 8.4 | 10 46 | 6.7 | 23 11 | 6.7 |
| 23 | Thursday | 06 51 | 6.2 | 19 32 | 5.9 | 00 00 | 11.0 | 12 35 | 10.6 | 04 34 | 8.0 | 17 10 | 7.8 | 11 48 | 6.3 | ——— | — |
| 24 | Friday | 08 03 | 5.8 | 20 55 | 5.7 | 01 12 | 10.3 | 14 09 | 10.2 | 05 57 | 7.6 | 18 38 | 7.6 | 00 28 | 6.3 | 13 19 | 6.1 |
| 25 | Saturday | 09 46 | 5.8 | 22 24 | 5.9 | 02 51 | 10.3 | 15 35 | 10.6 | 07 25 | 7.8 | 20 03 | 7.9 | 02 12 | 6.2 | 14 46 | 6.3 |
| 26 | Sunday | 11 06 | 6.2 | 23 38 | 6.3 | 04 14 | 11.1 | 16 54 | 11.5 | 08 36 | 8.4 | 21 08 | 8.5 | 03 35 | 6.5 | 15 55 | 6.7 |
| 27 | Monday | ——— | — | 12 08 | 6.7 | 05 27 | 12.2 | 17 57 | 12.5 | 09 32 | 9.0 | 22 00 | 9.0 | 04 41 | 6.8 | 16 50 | 7.1 |
| 28 | Tuesday | 00 30 | 6.7 | 13 01 | 7.1 | 06 21 | 13.1 | 18 45 | 13.2 | 10 20 | 9.5 | 22 45 | 9.4 | 05 32 | 7.1 | 17 36 | 7.4 |

## JANUARY 1995  *continued*

| | | GREENOCK | | | LEITH | | | | DUN LAOGHAIRE | | | | NOTES: |
|---|---|---|---|---|---|---|---|---|---|---|---|---|---|
| | | *Datum of predictions 1.62 m below | | | *Datum of predictions 2.90 m below | | | | †Datum of predictions 0.20 m above | | | | *Difference of height in metres from Ordnance datum (Newlyn) |
| | | hr | ht m | hr | ht m | hr | ht | hr | ht | hr | ht | | †Difference of height in metres from Ordnance datum (Dublin) |
| | | hr | m | hr | m | hr | m | hr | m | hr | m | hr | m | |
| 1 | Sunday | —— | — | 12 13 | 3.7 | 01 49 | 5.7 | 14 14 | 5.8 | 10 59 | 4.3 | 23 31 | 4.2 | hr hour |
| 2 | Monday | 00 35 | 3.5 | 12 59 | 3.8 | 02 42 | 5.8 | 15 02 | 5.9 | 11 44 | 4.4 | —— | — | m metres |
| 3 | Tuesday | 01 26 | 3.5 | 13 44 | 3.9 | 03 31 | 5.8 | 15 48 | 5.9 | 00 18 | 4.1 | 12 31 | 4.4 | |
| 4 | Wednesday | 02 13 | 3.5 | 14 26 | 4.0 | 04 19 | 5.7 | 16 34 | 5.8 | 01 06 | 4.1 | 13 16 | 4.3 | |
| 5 | Thursday | 02 56 | 3.5 | 15 07 | 3.9 | 05 07 | 5.5 | 17 21 | 5.6 | 01 53 | 4.0 | 14 03 | 4.2 | |
| 6 | Friday | 03 37 | 3.5 | 15 48 | 3.9 | 05 56 | 5.3 | 18 10 | 5.4 | 02 42 | 3.8 | 14 53 | 4.1 | |
| 7 | Saturday | 04 18 | 3.4 | 16 30 | 3.7 | 06 45 | 5.0 | 19 00 | 5.1 | 03 35 | 3.7 | 15 46 | 3.9 | |
| 8 | Sunday | 05 00 | 3.3 | 17 13 | 3.5 | 07 36 | 4.8 | 19 53 | 4.8 | 04 31 | 3.5 | 16 43 | 3.7 | |
| 9 | Monday | 05 45 | 3.2 | 18 01 | 3.3 | 08 29 | 4.6 | 20 51 | 4.6 | 05 32 | 3.4 | 17 46 | 3.6 | |
| 10 | Tuesday | 06 34 | 3.1 | 18 55 | 3.1 | 09 27 | 4.4 | 21 53 | 4.5 | 06 35 | 3.4 | 18 52 | 3.4 | |
| 11 | Wednesday | 07 31 | 3.0 | 20 06 | 2.9 | 10 28 | 4.4 | 22 55 | 4.5 | 07 35 | 3.4 | 19 54 | 3.4 | |
| 12 | Thursday | 08 50 | 3.0 | 21 54 | 2.9 | 11 26 | 4.6 | 23 52 | 4.6 | 08 31 | 3.5 | 20 51 | 3.4 | |
| 13 | Friday | 10 10 | 3.1 | 22 54 | 3.0 | —— | — | 12 20 | 4.7 | 09 22 | 3.7 | 21 41 | 3.5 | |
| 14 | Saturday | 11 02 | 3.3 | 23 40 | 3.0 | 00 43 | 4.7 | 13 08 | 5.0 | 10 05 | 3.8 | 22 24 | 3.6 | |
| 15 | Sunday | 11 43 | 3.4 | —— | — | 01 29 | 4.9 | 13 49 | 5.2 | 10 43 | 3.9 | 23 00 | 3.7 | |
| 16 | Monday | 00 20 | 3.1 | 12 19 | 3.5 | 02 09 | 5.1 | 14 27 | 5.3 | 11 17 | 4.0 | 23 32 | 3.8 | |
| 17 | Tuesday | 00 57 | 3.1 | 12 51 | 3.5 | 02 46 | 5.2 | 15 03 | 5.4 | 11 46 | 4.0 | —— | — | |
| 18 | Wednesday | 01 29 | 3.1 | 13 24 | 3.6 | 03 23 | 5.3 | 15 39 | 5.5 | 00 03 | 3.8 | 12 18 | 4.1 | |
| 19 | Thursday | 02 01 | 3.1 | 13 59 | 3.6 | 04 01 | 5.3 | 16 16 | 5.5 | 00 38 | 3.9 | 12 56 | 4.1 | |
| 20 | Friday | 02 35 | 3.2 | 14 36 | 3.7 | 04 40 | 5.3 | 16 55 | 5.4 | 01 17 | 3.9 | 13 36 | 4.1 | |
| 21 | Saturday | 03 11 | 3.2 | 15 14 | 3.7 | 05 22 | 5.3 | 17 36 | 5.3 | 01 59 | 3.9 | 14 20 | 4.1 | |
| 22 | Sunday | 03 49 | 3.2 | 15 52 | 3.6 | 06 06 | 5.2 | 18 21 | 5.2 | 02 46 | 3.9 | 15 07 | 4.0 | |
| 23 | Monday | 04 29 | 3.1 | 16 33 | 3.5 | 06 52 | 5.0 | 19 10 | 5.1 | 03 37 | 3.8 | 15 59 | 3.9 | |
| 24 | Tuesday | 05 13 | 3.1 | 17 20 | 3.3 | 07 42 | 4.9 | 20 04 | 4.9 | 04 32 | 3.7 | 16 57 | 3.8 | |
| 25 | Wednesday | 06 06 | 3.0 | 18 15 | 3.2 | 08 39 | 4.7 | 21 08 | 4.8 | 05 36 | 3.6 | 18 05 | 3.7 | |
| 26 | Thursday | 07 17 | 2.9 | 19 28 | 3.0 | 09 44 | 4.7 | 22 20 | 4.7 | 06 50 | 3.6 | 19 24 | 3.6 | |
| 27 | Friday | 09 01 | 3.0 | 21 21 | 3.0 | 10 56 | 4.8 | 23 35 | 4.9 | 08 03 | 3.7 | 20 38 | 3.7 | |
| 28 | Saturday | 10 18 | 3.2 | 22 38 | 3.1 | —— | — | 12 06 | 5.0 | 09 07 | 3.9 | 21 43 | 3.8 | |
| 29 | Sunday | 11 13 | 3.4 | 23 36 | 3.3 | 00 43 | 5.1 | 13 08 | 5.3 | 10 03 | 4.0 | 22 38 | 3.9 | |
| 30 | Monday | —— | — | 12 02 | 3.6 | 01 42 | 5.4 | 14 03 | 5.6 | 10 52 | 4.2 | 23 25 | 4.0 | |
| 31 | Tuesday | 00 28 | 3.4 | 12 48 | 3.8 | 02 33 | 5.6 | 14 51 | 5.8 | 11 35 | 4.3 | —— | — | |

## FEBRUARY 1995  *continued*

| | | GREENOCK | | | | LEITH | | | | DUN LAOGHAIRE | | | |
|---|---|---|---|---|---|---|---|---|---|---|---|---|---|
| 1 | Wednesday | 01 16 | 3.4 | 13 31 | 3.9 | 03 19 | 5.7 | 15 34 | 5.8 | 00 07 | 4.0 | 12 16 | 4.3 |
| 2 | Thursday | 01 58 | 3.5 | 14 11 | 3.9 | 04 01 | 5.6 | 16 15 | 5.8 | 00 47 | 4.0 | 12 56 | 4.3 |
| 3 | Friday | 02 36 | 3.5 | 14 49 | 3.9 | 04 43 | 5.5 | 16 56 | 5.6 | 01 25 | 3.9 | 13 36 | 4.2 |
| 4 | Saturday | 03 12 | 3.5 | 15 26 | 3.8 | 05 24 | 5.3 | 17 36 | 5.4 | 02 04 | 3.8 | 14 18 | 4.0 |
| 5 | Sunday | 03 47 | 3.5 | 16 02 | 3.7 | 06 06 | 5.1 | 18 18 | 5.1 | 02 48 | 3.7 | 15 04 | 3.9 |
| 6 | Monday | 04 24 | 3.4 | 16 40 | 3.5 | 06 49 | 4.8 | 19 01 | 4.8 | 03 35 | 3.5 | 15 53 | 3.7 |
| 7 | Tuesday | 05 04 | 3.3 | 17 22 | 3.2 | 07 33 | 4.6 | 19 52 | 4.5 | 04 30 | 3.4 | 16 51 | 3.4 |
| 8 | Wednesday | 05 49 | 3.2 | 18 09 | 3.0 | 08 26 | 4.4 | 20 59 | 4.3 | 05 36 | 3.3 | 18 02 | 3.3 |
| 9 | Thursday | 06 40 | 3.0 | 19 05 | 2.8 | 09 35 | 4.2 | 22 15 | 4.2 | 06 48 | 3.3 | 19 15 | 3.2 |
| 10 | Friday | 07 42 | 2.9 | 20 28 | 2.7 | 10 46 | 4.3 | 23 21 | 4.3 | 07 51 | 3.3 | 20 18 | 3.2 |
| 11 | Saturday | 09 16 | 2.9 | 22 30 | 2.8 | 11 47 | 4.5 | —— | — | 08 48 | 3.5 | 21 14 | 3.4 |
| 12 | Sunday | 10 32 | 3.1 | 23 19 | 2.9 | 00 17 | 4.5 | 12 40 | 4.7 | 09 37 | 3.6 | 22 00 | 3.5 |
| 13 | Monday | 11 17 | 3.3 | 23 59 | 3.0 | 01 05 | 4.8 | 13 24 | 5.0 | 10 18 | 3.8 | 22 37 | 3.6 |
| 14 | Tuesday | 11 53 | 3.4 | —— | — | 01 46 | 5.0 | 14 04 | 5.2 | 10 52 | 3.9 | 23 09 | 3.8 |
| 15 | Wednesday | 00 36 | 3.1 | 12 28 | 3.4 | 02 24 | 5.2 | 14 42 | 5.4 | 11 22 | 4.0 | 23 38 | 3.9 |
| 16 | Thursday | 01 09 | 3.1 | 13 02 | 3.5 | 03 01 | 5.4 | 15 18 | 5.5 | 11 53 | 4.1 | —— | — |
| 17 | Friday | 01 41 | 3.2 | 13 39 | 3.6 | 03 38 | 5.5 | 15 55 | 5.6 | 00 10 | 4.0 | 12 30 | 4.2 |
| 18 | Saturday | 02 14 | 3.2 | 14 17 | 3.7 | 04 17 | 5.5 | 16 34 | 5.6 | 00 49 | 4.0 | 13 11 | 4.2 |
| 19 | Sunday | 02 48 | 3.3 | 14 56 | 3.7 | 04 58 | 5.4 | 17 16 | 5.5 | 01 31 | 4.0 | 13 55 | 4.1 |
| 20 | Monday | 03 24 | 3.3 | 15 34 | 3.6 | 05 42 | 5.3 | 18 01 | 5.4 | 02 16 | 4.0 | 14 43 | 4.1 |
| 21 | Tuesday | 04 02 | 3.2 | 16 15 | 3.5 | 06 29 | 5.1 | 18 50 | 5.1 | 03 06 | 3.9 | 15 36 | 3.9 |
| 22 | Wednesday | 04 43 | 3.1 | 17 00 | 3.3 | 07 19 | 4.9 | 19 45 | 4.9 | 04 02 | 3.7 | 16 36 | 3.7 |
| 23 | Thursday | 05 33 | 3.0 | 17 53 | 3.1 | 08 16 | 4.7 | 20 49 | 4.6 | 05 07 | 3.6 | 17 49 | 3.5 |
| 24 | Friday | 06 38 | 2.9 | 19 04 | 2.8 | 09 22 | 4.5 | 22 06 | 4.6 | 06 27 | 3.5 | 19 17 | 3.5 |
| 25 | Saturday | 08 41 | 2.9 | 21 19 | 2.8 | 10 38 | 4.6 | 23 28 | 4.7 | 07 48 | 3.6 | 20 34 | 3.6 |
| 26 | Sunday | 10 04 | 3.1 | 22 35 | 3.0 | 11 53 | 4.8 | —— | — | 08 57 | 3.7 | 21 40 | 3.7 |
| 27 | Monday | 11 00 | 3.4 | 23 29 | 3.2 | 00 40 | 5.0 | 12 58 | 5.1 | 09 56 | 3.9 | 22 33 | 3.8 |
| 28 | Tuesday | 11 48 | 3.6 | —— | — | 01 37 | 5.2 | 13 52 | 5.4 | 10 45 | 4.1 | 23 18 | 3.9 |

## MARCH 1995   *High water*   GMT

London Bridge — *Datum of predictions 3.20 m below*
Avonmouth — *Datum of predictions 6.50 m below*
Liverpool — *Datum of predictions 4.93 m below*
Hull (*Albert Dock*) — *Datum of predictions 3.90 m below*

| Day | | London Bridge | | | | Avonmouth | | | | Liverpool | | | | Hull (Albert Dock) | | |
|---|---|---|---|---|---|---|---|---|---|---|---|---|---|---|---|---|
| | | hr | ht m | hr | ht m | hr | ht m | hr | ht m | hr | ht m | hr | ht m | hr | ht m | hr |
| 1 | Wednesday | 01 19 | 7.0 | 13 48 | 7.3 | 07 05 | 13.6 | 19 26 | 13.6 | 11 03 | 9.8 | 23 27 | 9.5 | 06 13 | 7.3 | 18 15 | 7.7 |
| 2 | Thursday | 02 03 | 7.2 | 14 31 | 7.4 | 07 45 | 13.9 | 20 05 | 13.8 | 11 44 | 9.8 | — | — | 06 49 | 7.4 | 18 52 | 7.9 |
| 3 | Friday | 02 44 | 7.2 | 15 11 | 7.3 | 08 23 | 14.0 | 20 41 | 13.8 | 00 05 | 9.5 | 12 22 | 9.8 | 07 24 | 7.4 | 19 29 | 7.9 |
| 4 | Saturday | 03 22 | 7.2 | 15 48 | 7.3 | 08 58 | 13.9 | 21 14 | 13.6 | 00 41 | 9.4 | 12 58 | 9.6 | 07 58 | 7.4 | 20 06 | 7.8 |
| 5 | Sunday | 03 57 | 7.2 | 16 21 | 7.1 | 09 30 | 13.5 | 21 43 | 13.2 | 01 14 | 9.2 | 13 33 | 9.3 | 08 31 | 7.3 | 20 42 | 7.6 |
| 6 | Monday | 04 29 | 7.1 | 16 52 | 7.0 | 09 58 | 12.8 | 22 10 | 12.5 | 01 48 | 9.0 | 14 08 | 9.0 | 09 03 | 7.0 | 21 17 | 7.2 |
| 7 | Tuesday | 05 02 | 6.8 | 17 24 | 6.7 | 10 26 | 12.0 | 22 37 | 11.7 | 02 22 | 8.7 | 14 44 | 8.6 | 09 34 | 6.7 | 21 52 | 6.7 |
| 8 | Wednesday | 05 36 | 6.5 | 18 00 | 6.4 | 10 56 | 11.1 | 23 08 | 10.9 | 03 00 | 8.3 | 15 25 | 8.1 | 10 07 | 6.3 | 22 30 | 6.2 |
| 9 | Thursday | 06 15 | 6.1 | 18 41 | 6.0 | 11 31 | 10.2 | 23 47 | 10.1 | 03 44 | 7.8 | 16 14 | 7.5 | 10 46 | 6.0 | 23 20 | 5.8 |
| 10 | Friday | 07 02 | 5.7 | 19 31 | 5.7 | — | — | 12 21 | 9.5 | 04 41 | 7.3 | 17 18 | 7.1 | 11 45 | 5.6 | — | — |
| 11 | Saturday | 08 03 | 5.3 | 20 37 | 5.5 | 00 48 | 9.5 | 14 07 | 9.2 | 05 59 | 7.1 | 18 48 | 7.0 | 00 05 | 5.5 | 13 36 | 5.5 |
| 12 | Sunday | 09 30 | 5.3 | 22 08 | 5.5 | 02 54 | 9.6 | 15 45 | 9.9 | 07 36 | 7.3 | 20 14 | 7.4 | 02 24 | 5.6 | 14 51 | 5.8 |
| 13 | Monday | 11 05 | 5.6 | 23 22 | 5.9 | 04 13 | 10.5 | 16 49 | 10.9 | 08 41 | 7.9 | 21 08 | 8.0 | 03 32 | 5.9 | 15 51 | 6.2 |
| 14 | Tuesday | — | — | 12 00 | 6.1 | 05 10 | 11.5 | 17 38 | 11.9 | 09 27 | 8.4 | 21 51 | 8.6 | 04 25 | 6.3 | 16 38 | 6.7 |
| 15 | Wednesday | 00 16 | 6.3 | 12 47 | 6.5 | 05 57 | 12.3 | 18 21 | 12.6 | 10 08 | 8.9 | 22 29 | 9.0 | 05 07 | 6.8 | 17 18 | 7.1 |
| 16 | Thursday | 01 02 | 6.7 | 13 30 | 6.9 | 06 37 | 12.9 | 19 00 | 13.1 | 10 45 | 9.3 | 23 07 | 9.3 | 05 44 | 7.2 | 17 56 | 7.5 |
| 17 | Friday | 01 45 | 6.9 | 14 12 | 7.1 | 07 16 | 13.4 | 19 39 | 13.5 | 11 23 | 9.6 | 23 44 | 9.6 | 06 22 | 7.5 | 18 33 | 7.7 |
| 18 | Saturday | 02 27 | 7.1 | 14 55 | 7.3 | 07 55 | 13.8 | 20 18 | 13.8 | — | — | 12 02 | 9.8 | 06 59 | 7.7 | 19 11 | 7.9 |
| 19 | Sunday | 03 09 | 7.2 | 15 38 | 7.2 | 08 35 | 14.0 | 20 57 | 13.8 | 00 23 | 9.7 | 12 43 | 9.8 | 07 36 | 7.8 | 19 50 | 7.9 |
| 20 | Monday | 03 50 | 7.2 | 16 18 | 7.1 | 09 16 | 13.8 | 21 36 | 13.5 | 01 02 | 9.7 | 13 24 | 9.8 | 08 14 | 7.7 | 20 30 | 7.8 |
| 21 | Tuesday | 04 30 | 7.1 | 16 57 | 6.8 | 09 57 | 13.3 | 22 16 | 12.9 | 01 43 | 9.6 | 14 07 | 9.5 | 08 54 | 7.5 | 21 14 | 7.5 |
| 22 | Wednesday | 05 09 | 6.9 | 17 35 | 6.5 | 10 38 | 12.5 | 22 57 | 12.0 | 02 26 | 9.2 | 14 54 | 8.9 | 09 38 | 7.1 | 22 03 | 7.1 |
| 23 | Thursday | 05 51 | 6.5 | 18 16 | 6.2 | 11 23 | 11.4 | 23 45 | 11.0 | 03 15 | 8.6 | 15 48 | 8.3 | 10 27 | 6.7 | 23 01 | 6.6 |
| 24 | Friday | 06 40 | 6.1 | 19 06 | 5.8 | — | — | 12 22 | 10.5 | 04 17 | 8.0 | 17 00 | 7.6 | 11 29 | 6.3 | — | — |
| 25 | Saturday | 07 54 | 5.8 | 20 34 | 5.6 | 00 59 | 10.3 | 13 54 | 10.1 | 05 43 | 7.6 | 18 31 | 7.4 | 00 26 | 6.2 | 12 58 | 6.1 |
| 26 | Sunday | 09 35 | 5.9 | 22 04 | 5.9 | 02 35 | 10.3 | 15 19 | 10.5 | 07 10 | 7.8 | 19 52 | 7.8 | 02 07 | 6.1 | 14 26 | 6.3 |
| 27 | Monday | 10 49 | 6.4 | 23 11 | 6.4 | 03 55 | 11.0 | 16 35 | 11.4 | 08 19 | 8.3 | 20 53 | 8.3 | 03 25 | 6.4 | 15 35 | 6.6 |
| 28 | Tuesday | 11 50 | 6.9 | — | — | 05 06 | 12.0 | 17 35 | 12.3 | 09 14 | 8.8 | 21 42 | 8.8 | 04 27 | 6.7 | 16 30 | 7.0 |
| 29 | Wednesday | 00 09 | 6.8 | 12 43 | 7.2 | 05 59 | 12.8 | 18 22 | 13.0 | 10 00 | 9.2 | 22 25 | 9.1 | 05 15 | 7.0 | 17 15 | 7.3 |
| 30 | Thursday | 00 59 | 7.1 | 13 29 | 7.4 | 06 42 | 13.3 | 19 01 | 13.3 | 10 42 | 9.5 | 23 03 | 9.3 | 05 53 | 7.1 | 17 53 | 7.5 |
| 31 | Friday | 01 43 | 7.1 | 14 10 | 7.3 | 07 20 | 13.5 | 19 37 | 13.5 | 11 21 | 9.5 | 23 39 | 9.3 | 06 26 | 7.2 | 18 30 | 7.6 |

## APRIL 1995   *High water*   GMT

| Day | | London Bridge | | | | Avonmouth | | | | Liverpool | | | | Hull (Albert Dock) | | |
|---|---|---|---|---|---|---|---|---|---|---|---|---|---|---|---|---|
| 1 | Saturday | 02 22 | 7.1 | 14 47 | 7.2 | 07 55 | 13.6 | 20 11 | 13.6 | 11 57 | 9.5 | — | — | 06 58 | 7.3 | 19 06 | 7.6 |
| 2 | Sunday | 02 58 | 7.1 | 15 20 | 7.1 | 08 29 | 13.5 | 20 43 | 13.5 | 00 12 | 9.2 | 12 32 | 9.3 | 07 30 | 7.3 | 19 42 | 7.6 |
| 3 | Monday | 03 32 | 7.0 | 15 50 | 7.0 | 09 00 | 13.2 | 21 13 | 13.1 | 00 45 | 9.1 | 13 05 | 9.1 | 08 01 | 7.2 | 20 16 | 7.3 |
| 4 | Tuesday | 04 04 | 6.9 | 16 21 | 6.9 | 09 30 | 12.7 | 21 41 | 12.5 | 01 18 | 9.0 | 13 40 | 8.9 | 08 31 | 7.0 | 20 50 | 7.0 |
| 5 | Wednesday | 04 37 | 6.7 | 16 54 | 6.7 | 09 58 | 12.0 | 22 08 | 11.8 | 01 53 | 8.7 | 14 16 | 8.5 | 09 02 | 6.8 | 21 25 | 6.6 |
| 6 | Thursday | 05 12 | 6.5 | 17 29 | 6.4 | 10 26 | 11.1 | 22 35 | 11.0 | 02 30 | 8.4 | 14 56 | 8.1 | 09 34 | 6.5 | 22 02 | 6.2 |
| 7 | Friday | 05 50 | 6.2 | 18 09 | 6.1 | 10 57 | 10.4 | 23 11 | 10.3 | 03 11 | 8.0 | 15 42 | 7.6 | 10 11 | 6.1 | 22 48 | 5.8 |
| 8 | Saturday | 06 34 | 5.9 | 18 55 | 5.9 | 11 41 | 9.7 | — | — | 04 03 | 7.5 | 16 41 | 7.2 | 11 00 | 5.8 | 23 59 | 5.5 |
| 9 | Sunday | 07 29 | 5.6 | 19 54 | 5.6 | 00 03 | 9.8 | 12 46 | 9.3 | 05 10 | 7.2 | 17 54 | 7.0 | — | — | 12 29 | 5.5 |
| 10 | Monday | 08 38 | 5.5 | 21 09 | 5.7 | 01 18 | 9.6 | 14 46 | 9.6 | 06 31 | 7.2 | 19 18 | 7.3 | 01 45 | 5.6 | 14 06 | 5.7 |
| 11 | Tuesday | 10 04 | 5.8 | 22 31 | 5.9 | 03 21 | 10.2 | 16 04 | 10.6 | 07 47 | 7.6 | 20 22 | 7.8 | 02 49 | 5.9 | 15 08 | 6.1 |
| 12 | Wednesday | 11 18 | 6.2 | 23 35 | 6.3 | 04 27 | 11.2 | 17 00 | 11.7 | 08 43 | 8.2 | 21 11 | 8.4 | 03 45 | 6.3 | 15 59 | 6.5 |
| 13 | Thursday | — | — | 12 12 | 6.7 | 05 20 | 12.2 | 17 48 | 12.6 | 09 29 | 8.8 | 21 54 | 9.0 | 04 32 | 6.8 | 16 44 | 7.0 |
| 14 | Friday | 00 27 | 6.7 | 13 00 | 7.0 | 06 06 | 13.0 | 18 31 | 13.3 | 10 12 | 9.2 | 22 36 | 9.4 | 05 14 | 7.2 | 17 27 | 7.4 |
| 15 | Saturday | 01 15 | 7.0 | 13 45 | 7.2 | 06 49 | 13.5 | 19 13 | 13.7 | 10 55 | 9.6 | 23 17 | 9.7 | 05 54 | 7.5 | 18 08 | 7.7 |
| 16 | Sunday | 02 00 | 7.2 | 14 30 | 7.3 | 07 32 | 13.9 | 19 55 | 14.0 | 11 38 | 9.8 | 23 59 | 9.8 | 06 34 | 7.7 | 18 50 | 7.9 |
| 17 | Monday | 02 46 | 7.3 | 15 14 | 7.3 | 08 16 | 14.0 | 20 37 | 14.0 | — | — | 12 23 | 9.9 | 07 14 | 7.8 | 19 32 | 7.9 |
| 18 | Tuesday | 03 31 | 7.4 | 15 58 | 7.1 | 09 00 | 13.9 | 21 20 | 13.6 | 00 43 | 9.8 | 13 09 | 9.7 | 07 55 | 7.7 | 20 17 | 7.7 |
| 19 | Wednesday | 04 17 | 7.2 | 16 40 | 6.9 | 09 44 | 13.3 | 22 04 | 13.0 | 01 28 | 9.6 | 13 55 | 9.4 | 08 37 | 7.5 | 21 04 | 7.4 |
| 20 | Thursday | 05 01 | 7.0 | 17 21 | 6.6 | 10 29 | 12.5 | 22 48 | 12.1 | 02 15 | 9.3 | 14 45 | 8.9 | 09 23 | 7.2 | 21 56 | 7.0 |
| 21 | Friday | 05 47 | 6.7 | 18 03 | 6.2 | 11 17 | 11.5 | 23 39 | 11.2 | 03 06 | 8.8 | 15 41 | 8.3 | 10 14 | 6.9 | 22 57 | 6.5 |
| 22 | Saturday | 06 38 | 6.3 | 18 54 | 6.0 | — | — | 12 15 | 10.7 | 04 08 | 8.2 | 16 50 | 7.7 | 11 14 | 6.5 | — | — |
| 23 | Sunday | 07 51 | 6.0 | 20 18 | 5.8 | 00 49 | 10.6 | 13 35 | 10.3 | 05 26 | 7.8 | 18 12 | 7.5 | 00 25 | 6.2 | 12 36 | 6.3 |
| 24 | Monday | 09 16 | 6.2 | 21 39 | 6.1 | 02 14 | 10.6 | 14 53 | 10.6 | 06 45 | 7.8 | 19 26 | 7.7 | 01 52 | 6.1 | 14 00 | 6.3 |
| 25 | Tuesday | 10 24 | 6.6 | 22 43 | 6.5 | 03 27 | 11.1 | 16 03 | 11.2 | 07 53 | 8.1 | 20 26 | 8.1 | 03 03 | 6.3 | 15 08 | 6.6 |
| 26 | Wednesday | 11 23 | 7.0 | 23 41 | 6.9 | 04 34 | 11.8 | 17 03 | 11.9 | 08 48 | 8.5 | 21 16 | 8.5 | 04 03 | 6.6 | 16 04 | 6.8 |
| 27 | Thursday | — | — | 12 16 | 7.3 | 05 28 | 12.4 | 17 52 | 12.5 | 09 36 | 8.9 | 21 59 | 8.8 | 04 50 | 6.8 | 16 50 | 7.0 |
| 28 | Friday | 00 33 | 7.0 | 13 04 | 7.3 | 06 13 | 12.7 | 18 32 | 12.8 | 10 18 | 9.1 | 22 37 | 9.0 | 05 28 | 6.9 | 17 31 | 7.2 |
| 29 | Saturday | 01 19 | 7.0 | 13 45 | 7.2 | 06 52 | 12.9 | 19 08 | 13.0 | 10 57 | 9.1 | 23 12 | 9.0 | 06 01 | 7.0 | 18 08 | 7.3 |
| 30 | Sunday | 01 59 | 6.9 | 14 21 | 7.0 | 07 27 | 13.0 | 19 42 | 13.1 | 11 33 | 9.1 | 23 45 | 9.0 | 06 33 | 7.1 | 18 45 | 7.3 |

## MARCH 1995 *continued*

| | | GREENOCK | | | LEITH | | | | DUN LAOGHAIRE | | | |
|---|---|---|---|---|---|---|---|---|---|---|---|---|
| | | *Datum of predictions 1.62 m below | | | *Datum of predictions 2.90 m below | | | | †Datum of predictions 0.20 m above | | | |
| | | hr | m | hr | m | hr | m | hr | m | hr | m | hr | m |
| 1 | Wednesday | 00 16 | 3.3 | 12 33 | 3.7 | 02 24 | 5.4 | 14 37 | 5.6 | 11 25 | 4.1 | 23 55 | 3.9 |
| 2 | Thursday | 00 59 | 3.3 | 13 14 | 3.7 | 03 03 | 5.5 | 15 17 | 5.7 | —— | — | 12 01 | 4.2 |
| 3 | Friday | 01 37 | 3.4 | 13 53 | 3.7 | 03 39 | 5.5 | 15 53 | 5.6 | 00 26 | 3.9 | 12 34 | 4.1 |
| 4 | Saturday | 02 10 | 3.4 | 14 28 | 3.7 | 04 14 | 5.4 | 16 29 | 5.5 | 00 55 | 3.8 | 13 09 | 4.0 |
| 5 | Sunday | 02 42 | 3.5 | 15 01 | 3.6 | 04 49 | 5.3 | 17 03 | 5.4 | 01 29 | 3.8 | 13 48 | 3.9 |
| 6 | Monday | 03 15 | 3.5 | 15 35 | 3.5 | 05 24 | 5.1 | 17 39 | 5.1 | 02 07 | 3.7 | 14 29 | 3.8 |
| 7 | Tuesday | 03 50 | 3.4 | 16 11 | 3.4 | 06 00 | 4.9 | 18 17 | 4.8 | 02 48 | 3.6 | 15 13 | 3.6 |
| 8 | Wednesday | 04 27 | 3.3 | 16 50 | 3.1 | 06 40 | 4.6 | 19 01 | 4.6 | 03 34 | 3.5 | 16 04 | 3.4 |
| 9 | Thursday | 05 09 | 3.1 | 17 35 | 2.9 | 07 26 | 4.4 | 19 53 | 4.3 | 04 30 | 3.3 | 17 09 | 3.2 |
| 10 | Friday | 05 59 | 3.0 | 18 31 | 2.7 | 08 22 | 4.2 | 21 17 | 4.1 | 05 50 | 3.2 | 18 33 | 3.1 |
| 11 | Saturday | 06 58 | 2.8 | 19 41 | 2.6 | 09 53 | 4.1 | 22 44 | 4.1 | 07 10 | 3.2 | 19 43 | 3.1 |
| 12 | Sunday | 08 11 | 2.8 | 21 48 | 2.6 | 11 09 | 4.3 | 23 45 | 4.4 | 08 13 | 3.3 | 20 43 | 3.3 |
| 13 | Monday | 09 41 | 2.9 | 22 47 | 2.8 | —— | — | 12 05 | 4.5 | 09 05 | 3.5 | 21 30 | 3.4 |
| 14 | Tuesday | 10 38 | 3.1 | 23 29 | 3.0 | 00 34 | 4.7 | 12 53 | 4.9 | 09 47 | 3.7 | 22 09 | 3.6 |
| 15 | Wednesday | 11 19 | 3.2 | —— | — | 01 17 | 5.0 | 13 35 | 5.2 | 10 23 | 3.8 | 22 40 | 3.8 |
| 16 | Thursday | 00 06 | 3.0 | 11 58 | 3.3 | 01 56 | 5.3 | 14 15 | 5.4 | 10 55 | 4.0 | 23 10 | 3.9 |
| 17 | Friday | 00 41 | 3.1 | 12 37 | 3.4 | 02 34 | 5.5 | 14 54 | 5.6 | 11 27 | 4.1 | 23 43 | 4.0 |
| 18 | Saturday | 01 15 | 3.2 | 13 18 | 3.5 | 03 13 | 5.6 | 15 33 | 5.7 | —— | — | 12 05 | 4.2 |
| 19 | Sunday | 01 50 | 3.3 | 13 58 | 3.6 | 03 53 | 5.7 | 16 13 | 5.8 | 00 21 | 4.1 | 12 48 | 4.2 |
| 20 | Monday | 02 25 | 3.3 | 14 39 | 3.6 | 04 34 | 5.6 | 16 57 | 5.7 | 01 05 | 4.1 | 13 34 | 4.2 |
| 21 | Tuesday | 03 01 | 3.4 | 15 19 | 3.6 | 05 19 | 5.4 | 17 44 | 5.5 | 01 51 | 4.0 | 14 24 | 4.0 |
| 22 | Wednesday | 03 40 | 3.3 | 16 01 | 3.4 | 06 07 | 5.2 | 18 35 | 5.2 | 02 43 | 3.9 | 15 20 | 3.9 |
| 23 | Thursday | 04 22 | 3.2 | 16 47 | 3.2 | 07 00 | 4.9 | 19 33 | 4.9 | 03 40 | 3.8 | 16 25 | 3.6 |
| 24 | Friday | 05 12 | 3.0 | 17 43 | 2.9 | 07 58 | 4.7 | 20 39 | 4.6 | 04 48 | 3.6 | 17 46 | 3.5 |
| 25 | Saturday | 06 20 | 2.8 | 19 09 | 2.7 | 09 08 | 4.5 | 21 59 | 4.5 | 06 12 | 3.5 | 19 11 | 3.4 |
| 26 | Sunday | 08 23 | 2.8 | 21 14 | 2.8 | 10 25 | 4.6 | 23 22 | 4.7 | 07 33 | 3.6 | 20 26 | 3.5 |
| 27 | Monday | 09 45 | 3.1 | 22 22 | 2.9 | 11 39 | 4.8 | —— | — | 08 43 | 3.7 | 21 28 | 3.6 |
| 28 | Tuesday | 10 41 | 3.3 | 23 12 | 3.1 | 00 30 | 4.9 | 12 42 | 5.0 | 09 42 | 3.9 | 22 21 | 3.8 |
| 29 | Wednesday | 11 28 | 3.4 | 23 56 | 3.2 | 01 24 | 5.2 | 13 34 | 5.3 | 10 31 | 4.0 | 23 03 | 3.8 |
| 30 | Thursday | —— | — | 12 12 | 3.5 | 02 07 | 5.3 | 14 18 | 5.4 | 11 12 | 4.0 | 23 37 | 3.8 |
| 31 | Friday | 00 35 | 3.2 | 12 53 | 3.5 | 02 43 | 5.4 | 14 56 | 5.5 | 11 44 | 4.0 | —— | — |

NOTES:
*Difference of height in metres from Ordnance datum (Newlyn)
†Difference of height in metres from Ordnance datum (Dublin)
hr hour
m metres

## APRIL 1995 *continued*

| | | GREENOCK | | | LEITH | | | | DUN LAOGHAIRE | | | |
|---|---|---|---|---|---|---|---|---|---|---|---|---|
| | | hr | m | hr | m | hr | m | hr | m | hr | m | hr | m |
| 1 | Saturday | 01 10 | 3.3 | 13 30 | 3.4 | 03 15 | 5.4 | 15 30 | 5.5 | 00 02 | 3.8 | 12 13 | 4.0 |
| 2 | Sunday | 01 42 | 3.3 | 14 04 | 3.4 | 03 45 | 5.3 | 16 03 | 5.4 | 00 29 | 3.8 | 12 46 | 3.9 |
| 3 | Monday | 02 13 | 3.4 | 14 37 | 3.4 | 04 15 | 5.2 | 16 35 | 5.3 | 01 00 | 3.8 | 13 22 | 3.8 |
| 4 | Tuesday | 02 45 | 3.4 | 15 10 | 3.3 | 04 47 | 5.1 | 17 10 | 5.1 | 01 35 | 3.7 | 14 01 | 3.7 |
| 5 | Wednesday | 03 19 | 3.4 | 15 45 | 3.2 | 05 24 | 4.9 | 17 48 | 4.9 | 02 14 | 3.7 | 14 44 | 3.6 |
| 6 | Thursday | 03 54 | 3.3 | 16 24 | 3.0 | 06 04 | 4.8 | 18 31 | 4.6 | 02 57 | 3.5 | 15 32 | 3.4 |
| 7 | Friday | 04 34 | 3.1 | 17 09 | 2.8 | 06 50 | 4.5 | 19 19 | 4.4 | 03 47 | 3.4 | 16 28 | 3.2 |
| 8 | Saturday | 05 21 | 2.9 | 18 05 | 2.6 | 07 40 | 4.3 | 20 16 | 4.2 | 04 48 | 3.2 | 17 41 | 3.1 |
| 9 | Sunday | 06 20 | 2.8 | 19 12 | 2.6 | 08 43 | 4.2 | 21 44 | 4.2 | 06 12 | 3.1 | 19 01 | 3.1 |
| 10 | Monday | 07 28 | 2.7 | 20 32 | 2.6 | 10 14 | 4.2 | 23 01 | 4.3 | 07 27 | 3.2 | 20 03 | 3.2 |
| 11 | Tuesday | 08 42 | 2.8 | 21 57 | 2.7 | 11 22 | 4.5 | 23 56 | 4.7 | 08 24 | 3.4 | 20 53 | 3.4 |
| 12 | Wednesday | 09 49 | 3.0 | 22 48 | 2.9 | —— | — | 12 14 | 4.8 | 09 09 | 3.6 | 21 32 | 3.6 |
| 13 | Thursday | 10 40 | 3.1 | 23 30 | 3.0 | 00 42 | 5.0 | 13 00 | 5.1 | 09 48 | 3.8 | 22 08 | 3.8 |
| 14 | Friday | 11 25 | 3.3 | —— | — | 01 25 | 5.3 | 13 44 | 5.5 | 10 26 | 4.0 | 22 42 | 4.0 |
| 15 | Saturday | 00 09 | 3.1 | 12 10 | 3.4 | 02 06 | 5.6 | 14 27 | 5.7 | 11 04 | 4.1 | 23 19 | 4.1 |
| 16 | Sunday | 00 48 | 3.2 | 12 55 | 3.4 | 02 48 | 5.7 | 15 11 | 5.9 | 11 44 | 4.2 | 23 58 | 4.2 |
| 17 | Monday | 01 26 | 3.3 | 13 40 | 3.5 | 03 30 | 5.8 | 15 55 | 5.9 | —— | — | 12 31 | 4.2 |
| 18 | Tuesday | 02 05 | 3.4 | 14 24 | 3.5 | 04 13 | 5.7 | 16 41 | 5.8 | 00 44 | 4.2 | 13 20 | 4.1 |
| 19 | Wednesday | 02 44 | 3.4 | 15 08 | 3.5 | 05 00 | 5.6 | 17 30 | 5.6 | 01 33 | 4.1 | 14 13 | 4.0 |
| 20 | Thursday | 03 24 | 3.4 | 15 53 | 3.3 | 05 50 | 5.3 | 18 24 | 5.3 | 02 27 | 4.0 | 15 14 | 3.8 |
| 21 | Friday | 04 08 | 3.3 | 16 44 | 3.1 | 06 45 | 5.0 | 19 24 | 4.9 | 03 27 | 3.9 | 16 22 | 3.6 |
| 22 | Saturday | 05 00 | 3.1 | 17 47 | 2.9 | 07 46 | 4.8 | 20 31 | 4.7 | 04 38 | 3.7 | 17 39 | 3.5 |
| 23 | Sunday | 06 11 | 2.9 | 19 13 | 2.7 | 08 56 | 4.6 | 21 47 | 4.6 | 05 57 | 3.6 | 18 55 | 3.5 |
| 24 | Monday | 07 55 | 2.9 | 20 49 | 2.8 | 10 09 | 4.7 | 23 01 | 4.7 | 07 13 | 3.6 | 20 05 | 3.5 |
| 25 | Tuesday | 09 18 | 3.0 | 21 55 | 2.9 | 11 16 | 4.8 | —— | — | 08 21 | 3.7 | 21 07 | 3.6 |
| 26 | Wednesday | 10 15 | 3.2 | 22 45 | 3.0 | 00 05 | 4.9 | 12 15 | 5.0 | 09 20 | 3.8 | 21 58 | 3.7 |
| 27 | Thursday | 11 03 | 3.3 | 23 28 | 3.1 | 00 59 | 5.0 | 13 07 | 5.1 | 10 10 | 3.9 | 22 40 | 3.8 |
| 28 | Friday | 11 48 | 3.3 | —— | — | 01 42 | 5.2 | 13 53 | 5.2 | 10 51 | 3.9 | 23 14 | 3.8 |
| 29 | Saturday | 00 07 | 3.1 | 12 29 | 3.2 | 02 19 | 5.2 | 14 32 | 5.3 | 11 25 | 3.8 | 23 39 | 3.8 |
| 30 | Sunday | 00 42 | 3.2 | 13 07 | 3.2 | 02 50 | 5.3 | 15 07 | 5.3 | 11 53 | 3.8 | —— | — |

## MAY 1995   *High water*   GMT

| | | LONDON BRIDGE *Datum of predictions 3.20 m below* | | | | AVONMOUTH *Datum of predictions 6.50 m below* | | | | LIVERPOOL *Datum of predictions 4.93 m below* | | | | HULL (*Albert Dock*) *Datum of predictions 3.90 m below* | | | |
|---|---|---|---|---|---|---|---|---|---|---|---|---|---|---|---|---|---|
| | | hr | ht m | hr | ht m | hr | ht m | hr | ht m | hr | ht m | hr | ht m | hr | ht m | hr | ht m |
| 1 | Monday | 02 36 | 6.8 | 14 52 | 6.9 | 08 01 | 12.9 | 20 15 | 13.0 | ---- | -- | 12 07 | 9.0 | 07 04 | 7.2 | 19 20 | 7.2 |
| 2 | Tuesday | 03 09 | 6.8 | 15 22 | 6.8 | 08 34 | 12.8 | 20 46 | 12.8 | 00 18 | 9.0 | 12 41 | 8.9 | 07 35 | 7.1 | 19 55 | 7.0 |
| 3 | Wednesday | 03 42 | 6.7 | 15 53 | 6.7 | 09 06 | 12.4 | 21 17 | 12.3 | 00 52 | 8.8 | 13 16 | 8.7 | 08 05 | 7.0 | 20 29 | 6.8 |
| 4 | Thursday | 04 16 | 6.6 | 16 28 | 6.6 | 09 36 | 11.9 | 21 45 | 11.8 | 01 27 | 8.7 | 13 52 | 8.5 | 08 36 | 6.8 | 21 04 | 6.6 |
| 5 | Friday | 04 52 | 6.5 | 17 04 | 6.5 | 10 06 | 11.3 | 22 15 | 11.2 | 02 04 | 8.4 | 14 32 | 8.2 | 09 10 | 6.6 | 21 42 | 6.3 |
| 6 | Saturday | 05 30 | 6.3 | 17 43 | 6.3 | 10 39 | 10.7 | 22 51 | 10.7 | 02 45 | 8.1 | 15 16 | 7.8 | 09 48 | 6.3 | 22 26 | 6.0 |
| 7 | Sunday | 06 13 | 6.1 | 18 27 | 6.1 | 11 20 | 10.2 | 23 39 | 10.3 | 03 33 | 7.8 | 16 08 | 7.5 | 10 34 | 6.0 | 23 23 | 5.8 |
| 8 | Monday | 07 04 | 6.0 | 19 21 | 5.9 | ---- | -- | 12 14 | 9.9 | 04 32 | 7.5 | 17 12 | 7.3 | 11 37 | 5.8 | ---- | -- |
| 9 | Tuesday | 08 07 | 5.9 | 20 30 | 5.9 | 00 40 | 10.1 | 13 26 | 9.9 | 05 40 | 7.5 | 18 23 | 7.4 | 00 50 | 5.7 | 13 11 | 5.8 |
| 10 | Wednesday | 09 19 | 6.1 | 21 44 | 6.1 | 02 04 | 10.3 | 15 04 | 10.5 | 06 49 | 7.7 | 19 30 | 7.8 | 02 04 | 6.0 | 14 23 | 6.1 |
| 11 | Thursday | 10 33 | 6.4 | 22 53 | 6.4 | 03 35 | 11.1 | 16 15 | 11.4 | 07 52 | 8.2 | 20 27 | 8.4 | 03 03 | 6.3 | 15 19 | 6.5 |
| 12 | Friday | 11 36 | 6.7 | 23 52 | 6.8 | 04 39 | 12.0 | 17 12 | 12.4 | 08 48 | 8.7 | 21 17 | 8.9 | 03 55 | 6.7 | 16 10 | 6.9 |
| 13 | Saturday | ---- | -- | 12 30 | 7.1 | 05 34 | 12.8 | 18 02 | 13.2 | 09 39 | 9.2 | 22 05 | 9.4 | 04 43 | 7.1 | 16 59 | 7.3 |
| 14 | Sunday | 00 44 | 7.0 | 13 19 | 7.2 | 06 23 | 13.4 | 18 48 | 13.7 | 10 28 | 9.5 | 22 51 | 9.7 | 05 29 | 7.4 | 17 46 | 7.5 |
| 15 | Monday | 01 35 | 7.3 | 14 06 | 7.3 | 07 11 | 13.8 | 19 35 | 14.0 | 11 17 | 9.7 | 23 38 | 9.8 | 06 12 | 7.6 | 18 33 | 7.7 |
| 16 | Tuesday | 02 24 | 7.4 | 14 52 | 7.3 | 07 59 | 13.9 | 20 21 | 14.0 | ---- | -- | 12 06 | 9.8 | 06 56 | 7.7 | 19 20 | 7.8 |
| 17 | Wednesday | 03 14 | 7.4 | 15 39 | 7.2 | 08 47 | 13.8 | 21 08 | 13.7 | 00 25 | 9.8 | 12 56 | 9.7 | 07 39 | 7.7 | 20 08 | 7.6 |
| 18 | Thursday | 04 03 | 7.3 | 16 25 | 7.0 | 09 35 | 13.4 | 21 55 | 13.1 | 01 15 | 9.7 | 13 45 | 9.4 | 08 24 | 7.6 | 20 57 | 7.4 |
| 19 | Friday | 04 52 | 7.2 | 17 09 | 6.7 | 10 22 | 12.7 | 22 42 | 12.4 | 02 05 | 9.4 | 14 37 | 9.0 | 09 11 | 7.4 | 21 50 | 7.0 |
| 20 | Saturday | 05 41 | 6.9 | 17 53 | 6.5 | 11 09 | 11.9 | 23 31 | 11.6 | 02 57 | 9.0 | 15 31 | 8.6 | 10 01 | 7.1 | 22 50 | 6.6 |
| 21 | Sunday | 06 32 | 6.6 | 18 44 | 6.3 | ---- | -- | 12 01 | 11.1 | 03 55 | 8.5 | 16 31 | 8.0 | 10 57 | 6.8 | ---- | -- |
| 22 | Monday | 07 35 | 6.4 | 19 54 | 6.2 | 00 30 | 11.0 | 13 05 | 10.7 | 05 00 | 8.1 | 17 41 | 7.7 | 00 06 | 6.3 | 12 07 | 6.5 |
| 23 | Tuesday | 08 46 | 6.4 | 21 07 | 6.3 | 01 43 | 10.8 | 14 16 | 10.6 | 06 11 | 7.9 | 18 50 | 7.7 | 01 22 | 6.1 | 13 24 | 6.4 |
| 24 | Wednesday | 09 52 | 6.7 | 22 12 | 6.6 | 02 51 | 11.0 | 15 22 | 10.9 | 07 18 | 7.9 | 19 52 | 7.8 | 02 29 | 6.2 | 14 33 | 6.5 |
| 25 | Thursday | 10 52 | 6.9 | 23 11 | 6.8 | 03 54 | 11.3 | 16 24 | 11.4 | 08 17 | 8.2 | 20 45 | 8.1 | 03 28 | 6.3 | 15 32 | 6.6 |
| 26 | Friday | 11 46 | 7.1 | ---- | -- | 04 52 | 11.7 | 17 17 | 11.9 | 09 08 | 8.4 | 21 31 | 8.4 | 04 18 | 6.5 | 16 24 | 6.7 |
| 27 | Saturday | 00 05 | 6.9 | 12 36 | 7.0 | 05 41 | 12.1 | 18 02 | 12.3 | 09 53 | 8.6 | 22 11 | 8.7 | 05 00 | 6.7 | 17 09 | 6.8 |
| 28 | Sunday | 00 53 | 6.8 | 13 19 | 6.9 | 06 23 | 12.3 | 18 41 | 12.5 | 10 34 | 8.7 | 22 47 | 8.8 | 05 37 | 6.8 | 17 50 | 6.9 |
| 29 | Monday | 01 36 | 6.7 | 13 56 | 6.8 | 07 02 | 12.4 | 19 17 | 12.6 | 11 11 | 8.8 | 23 22 | 8.8 | 06 11 | 6.9 | 18 27 | 6.9 |
| 30 | Tuesday | 02 13 | 6.6 | 14 27 | 6.7 | 07 37 | 12.4 | 19 51 | 12.6 | 11 46 | 8.8 | 23 56 | 8.8 | 06 42 | 7.0 | 19 02 | 6.9 |
| 31 | Wednesday | 02 48 | 6.6 | 14 58 | 6.7 | 08 11 | 12.3 | 20 25 | 12.5 | ---- | -- | 12 21 | 8.7 | 07 13 | 7.0 | 19 37 | 6.9 |

## JUNE 1995   *High water*   GMT

| | | LONDON BRIDGE | | | | AVONMOUTH | | | | LIVERPOOL | | | | HULL (*Albert Dock*) | | | |
|---|---|---|---|---|---|---|---|---|---|---|---|---|---|---|---|---|---|
| 1 | Thursday | 03 22 | 6.6 | 15 31 | 6.7 | 08 45 | 12.1 | 20 57 | 12.3 | 00 31 | 8.8 | 12 56 | 8.6 | 07 44 | 7.0 | 20 11 | 6.8 |
| 2 | Friday | 03 58 | 6.6 | 16 07 | 6.6 | 09 19 | 11.9 | 21 29 | 12.0 | 01 07 | 8.7 | 13 33 | 8.5 | 08 17 | 6.9 | 20 47 | 6.7 |
| 3 | Saturday | 04 35 | 6.6 | 16 45 | 6.5 | 09 52 | 11.6 | 22 02 | 11.6 | 01 43 | 8.5 | 14 11 | 8.3 | 08 53 | 6.7 | 21 25 | 6.5 |
| 4 | Sunday | 05 14 | 6.5 | 17 23 | 6.4 | 10 27 | 11.2 | 22 39 | 11.2 | 02 22 | 8.4 | 14 52 | 8.1 | 09 31 | 6.6 | 22 07 | 6.3 |
| 5 | Monday | 05 56 | 6.4 | 18 05 | 6.3 | 11 06 | 10.8 | 23 22 | 10.9 | 03 06 | 8.1 | 15 39 | 7.9 | 10 14 | 6.3 | 22 55 | 6.1 |
| 6 | Tuesday | 06 43 | 6.3 | 18 54 | 6.2 | 11 52 | 10.5 | ---- | -- | 03 58 | 7.9 | 16 34 | 7.7 | 11 06 | 6.2 | 23 55 | 6.0 |
| 7 | Wednesday | 07 40 | 6.3 | 19 56 | 6.2 | 00 14 | 10.7 | 12 50 | 10.4 | 04 59 | 7.8 | 17 38 | 7.7 | ---- | -- | 12 11 | 6.1 |
| 8 | Thursday | 08 46 | 6.3 | 21 07 | 6.3 | 01 20 | 10.6 | 14 06 | 10.5 | 06 04 | 7.9 | 18 44 | 7.9 | 01 12 | 6.1 | 13 32 | 6.2 |
| 9 | Friday | 09 57 | 6.4 | 22 17 | 6.5 | 02 45 | 11.0 | 15 30 | 11.2 | 07 09 | 8.2 | 19 48 | 8.3 | 02 21 | 6.3 | 14 40 | 6.4 |
| 10 | Saturday | 11 04 | 6.7 | 23 23 | 6.7 | 04 01 | 11.7 | 16 37 | 12.0 | 08 12 | 8.6 | 20 45 | 8.8 | 03 20 | 6.6 | 15 40 | 6.8 |
| 11 | Sunday | ---- | -- | 12 02 | 6.9 | 05 04 | 12.5 | 17 35 | 12.9 | 09 11 | 9.0 | 21 39 | 9.3 | 04 15 | 6.9 | 16 37 | 7.1 |
| 12 | Monday | 00 19 | 7.0 | 12 55 | 7.1 | 06 00 | 13.1 | 18 28 | 13.5 | 10 06 | 9.3 | 22 30 | 9.6 | 05 07 | 7.2 | 17 31 | 7.4 |
| 13 | Tuesday | 01 14 | 7.2 | 13 45 | 7.2 | 06 54 | 13.5 | 19 19 | 13.8 | 11 00 | 9.6 | 23 20 | 9.8 | 05 55 | 7.5 | 18 22 | 7.6 |
| 14 | Wednesday | 02 06 | 7.3 | 14 33 | 7.2 | 07 45 | 13.7 | 20 08 | 13.9 | 11 52 | 9.7 | ---- | -- | 06 41 | 7.7 | 19 11 | 7.6 |
| 15 | Thursday | 02 58 | 7.4 | 15 21 | 7.2 | 08 35 | 13.7 | 20 57 | 13.8 | 00 11 | 9.9 | 12 43 | 9.7 | 07 26 | 7.8 | 19 59 | 7.6 |
| 16 | Friday | 03 49 | 7.4 | 16 08 | 7.1 | 09 24 | 13.5 | 21 45 | 13.5 | 01 01 | 9.8 | 13 33 | 9.5 | 08 11 | 7.7 | 20 48 | 7.4 |
| 17 | Saturday | 04 39 | 7.4 | 16 54 | 7.0 | 10 11 | 13.0 | 22 31 | 12.9 | 01 51 | 9.6 | 14 23 | 9.2 | 08 56 | 7.6 | 21 37 | 7.1 |
| 18 | Sunday | 05 26 | 7.2 | 17 38 | 6.8 | 10 55 | 12.4 | 23 15 | 12.2 | 02 41 | 9.3 | 15 11 | 8.8 | 09 44 | 7.4 | 22 30 | 6.9 |
| 19 | Monday | 06 14 | 7.0 | 18 23 | 6.7 | 11 38 | 11.7 | ---- | -- | 03 31 | 8.9 | 16 02 | 8.4 | 10 34 | 7.1 | 23 31 | 6.4 |
| 20 | Tuesday | 07 06 | 6.7 | 19 18 | 6.5 | 00 01 | 11.5 | 12 25 | 11.1 | 04 26 | 8.4 | 16 59 | 7.9 | 11 32 | 6.7 | ---- | -- |
| 21 | Wednesday | 08 08 | 6.5 | 20 27 | 6.3 | 00 57 | 11.0 | 13 24 | 10.7 | 05 28 | 8.0 | 18 04 | 7.6 | 00 38 | 6.1 | 12 41 | 6.4 |
| 22 | Thursday | 09 15 | 6.5 | 21 37 | 6.4 | 02 03 | 10.8 | 14 32 | 10.6 | 06 36 | 7.7 | 19 10 | 7.6 | 01 43 | 6.0 | 13 51 | 6.3 |
| 23 | Friday | 10 17 | 6.5 | 22 39 | 6.5 | 03 08 | 10.8 | 15 38 | 10.8 | 07 41 | 7.7 | 20 11 | 7.8 | 02 44 | 6.1 | 14 56 | 6.3 |
| 24 | Saturday | 11 14 | 6.6 | 23 36 | 6.5 | 04 11 | 11.0 | 16 39 | 11.2 | 08 39 | 7.9 | 21 02 | 8.1 | 03 41 | 6.2 | 15 56 | 6.3 |
| 25 | Sunday | ---- | -- | 12 06 | 6.7 | 05 09 | 11.4 | 17 32 | 11.7 | 09 28 | 8.2 | 21 46 | 8.4 | 04 31 | 6.4 | 16 48 | 6.5 |
| 26 | Monday | 00 27 | 6.6 | 12 52 | 6.6 | 05 57 | 11.8 | 18 17 | 12.1 | 10 12 | 8.4 | 22 26 | 8.7 | 05 14 | 6.6 | 17 33 | 6.6 |
| 27 | Tuesday | 01 12 | 6.5 | 13 31 | 6.6 | 06 39 | 12.0 | 18 56 | 12.3 | 10 52 | 8.6 | 23 03 | 8.8 | 05 51 | 6.8 | 18 12 | 6.7 |
| 28 | Wednesday | 01 51 | 6.5 | 14 05 | 6.6 | 07 17 | 12.0 | 19 32 | 12.4 | 11 29 | 8.7 | 23 38 | 8.9 | 06 23 | 6.9 | 18 46 | 6.8 |
| 29 | Thursday | 02 27 | 6.5 | 14 39 | 6.6 | 07 52 | 12.1 | 20 06 | 12.4 | ---- | -- | 12 04 | 8.7 | 06 55 | 7.0 | 19 20 | 6.9 |
| 30 | Friday | 03 03 | 6.6 | 15 14 | 6.7 | 08 27 | 12.1 | 20 41 | 12.4 | 00 13 | 8.9 | 12 39 | 8.7 | 07 27 | 7.1 | 19 54 | 6.9 |

## MAY 1995 *continued*

| | | GREENOCK | | | | LEITH | | | | DUN LAOGHAIRE | | | |
|---|---|---|---|---|---|---|---|---|---|---|---|---|---|
| | | *Datum of predictions 1.62 m below | | | | *Datum of predictions 2.90 m below | | | | †Datum of predictions 0.20 m above | | | |
| | | | ht | | ht | | ht | | ht | | ht | | ht |
| | | hr | m | hr | m | hr | m | hr | m | hr | m | hr | m |
| 1 | Monday | 01 15 | 3.2 | 13 41 | 3.1 | 03 19 | 5.2 | 15 40 | 5.2 | 00 04 | 3.8 | 12 26 | 3.8 |
| 2 | Tuesday | 01 47 | 3.3 | 14 14 | 3.1 | 03 48 | 5.2 | 16 13 | 5.2 | 00 36 | 3.8 | 13 00 | 3.7 |
| 3 | Wednesday | 02 19 | 3.4 | 14 47 | 3.1 | 04 21 | 5.2 | 16 48 | 5.1 | 01 10 | 3.8 | 13 38 | 3.7 |
| 4 | Thursday | 02 52 | 3.4 | 15 23 | 3.0 | 04 58 | 5.0 | 17 27 | 4.9 | 01 48 | 3.7 | 14 19 | 3.6 |
| 5 | Friday | 03 27 | 3.3 | 16 03 | 2.9 | 05 39 | 4.9 | 18 09 | 4.8 | 02 31 | 3.6 | 15 05 | 3.4 |
| 6 | Saturday | 04 05 | 3.2 | 16 48 | 2.8 | 06 24 | 4.7 | 18 55 | 4.6 | 03 18 | 3.5 | 15 56 | 3.3 |
| 7 | Sunday | 04 48 | 3.0 | 17 42 | 2.7 | 07 13 | 4.5 | 19 46 | 4.5 | 04 12 | 3.4 | 16 56 | 3.2 |
| 8 | Monday | 05 42 | 2.9 | 18 43 | 2.6 | 08 07 | 4.4 | 20 47 | 4.4 | 05 15 | 3.3 | 18 03 | 3.2 |
| 9 | Tuesday | 06 47 | 2.8 | 19 49 | 2.6 | 09 12 | 4.4 | 22 01 | 4.4 | 06 25 | 3.3 | 19 11 | 3.3 |
| 10 | Wednesday | 07 57 | 2.8 | 20 59 | 2.7 | 10 26 | 4.5 | 23 08 | 4.7 | 07 29 | 3.4 | 20 05 | 3.5 |
| 11 | Thursday | 09 04 | 2.9 | 22 03 | 2.8 | 11 28 | 4.8 | —— | — | 08 25 | 3.6 | 20 52 | 3.7 |
| 12 | Friday | 10 04 | 3.1 | 22 54 | 3.0 | 00 03 | 5.0 | 12 23 | 5.1 | 09 13 | 3.8 | 21 35 | 3.9 |
| 13 | Saturday | 10 56 | 3.2 | 23 39 | 3.1 | 00 52 | 5.3 | 13 13 | 5.5 | 09 58 | 4.0 | 22 17 | 4.0 |
| 14 | Sunday | 11 45 | 3.3 | —— | — | 01 39 | 5.6 | 14 02 | 5.7 | 10 43 | 4.1 | 22 58 | 4.2 |
| 15 | Monday | 00 23 | 3.2 | 12 35 | 3.4 | 02 25 | 5.8 | 14 51 | 5.9 | 11 28 | 4.2 | 23 41 | 4.2 |
| 16 | Tuesday | 01 07 | 3.4 | 13 24 | 3.4 | 03 11 | 5.8 | 15 39 | 5.9 | —— | — | 12 17 | 4.2 |
| 17 | Wednesday | 01 49 | 3.5 | 14 13 | 3.4 | 03 57 | 5.8 | 16 28 | 5.8 | 00 29 | 4.3 | 13 10 | 4.1 |
| 18 | Thursday | 02 31 | 3.5 | 15 01 | 3.4 | 04 45 | 5.7 | 17 19 | 5.6 | 01 19 | 4.2 | 14 05 | 4.0 |
| 19 | Friday | 03 14 | 3.5 | 15 51 | 3.3 | 05 37 | 5.5 | 18 15 | 5.4 | 02 14 | 4.1 | 15 06 | 3.9 |
| 20 | Saturday | 04 00 | 3.4 | 16 44 | 3.1 | 06 33 | 5.2 | 19 14 | 5.1 | 03 15 | 4.0 | 16 11 | 3.7 |
| 21 | Sunday | 04 52 | 3.3 | 17 43 | 3.0 | 07 34 | 5.0 | 20 17 | 4.8 | 04 22 | 3.9 | 17 20 | 3.6 |
| 22 | Monday | 05 56 | 3.1 | 18 50 | 2.9 | 08 39 | 4.8 | 21 23 | 4.7 | 05 34 | 3.8 | 18 29 | 3.5 |
| 23 | Tuesday | 07 16 | 3.0 | 20 03 | 2.8 | 09 43 | 4.8 | 22 28 | 4.7 | 06 45 | 3.7 | 19 35 | 3.5 |
| 24 | Wednesday | 08 39 | 3.0 | 21 14 | 2.9 | 10 45 | 4.8 | 23 29 | 4.9 | 07 50 | 3.7 | 20 34 | 3.6 |
| 25 | Thursday | 09 44 | 3.0 | 22 10 | 2.9 | 11 42 | 4.9 | —— | — | 08 49 | 3.7 | 21 27 | 3.7 |
| 26 | Friday | 10 36 | 3.1 | 22 57 | 3.0 | 00 24 | 4.9 | 12 36 | 5.0 | 09 41 | 3.7 | 22 11 | 3.7 |
| 27 | Saturday | 11 23 | 3.0 | 23 38 | 3.1 | 01 12 | 5.0 | 13 24 | 5.0 | 10 25 | 3.7 | 22 46 | 3.8 |
| 28 | Sunday | —— | — | 12 05 | 3.0 | 01 52 | 5.1 | 14 07 | 5.1 | 11 01 | 3.7 | 23 15 | 3.8 |
| 29 | Monday | 00 16 | 3.1 | 12 45 | 3.0 | 02 27 | 5.2 | 14 45 | 5.1 | 11 32 | 3.7 | 23 43 | 3.8 |
| 30 | Tuesday | 00 51 | 3.2 | 13 21 | 3.0 | 02 58 | 5.2 | 15 20 | 5.1 | —— | — | 12 04 | 3.7 |
| 31 | Wednesday | 01 24 | 3.3 | 13 55 | 2.9 | 03 29 | 5.2 | 15 54 | 5.1 | 00 14 | 3.8 | 12 40 | 3.7 |

NOTES:
*Difference of height in metres from Ordnance datum (Newlyn)
†Difference of height in metres from Ordnance datum (Dublin)
hr hour
m metres

## JUNE 1995 *continued*

| | | GREENOCK | | | | LEITH | | | | DUN LAOGHAIRE | | | |
|---|---|---|---|---|---|---|---|---|---|---|---|---|---|
| 1 | Thursday | 01 56 | 3.3 | 14 29 | 2.9 | 04 03 | 5.2 | 16 30 | 5.1 | 00 48 | 3.8 | 13 16 | 3.7 |
| 2 | Friday | 02 29 | 3.3 | 15 05 | 2.9 | 04 40 | 5.1 | 17 09 | 5.0 | 01 26 | 3.8 | 13 56 | 3.6 |
| 3 | Saturday | 03 04 | 3.3 | 15 44 | 2.9 | 05 21 | 5.0 | 17 51 | 4.9 | 02 07 | 3.8 | 14 40 | 3.6 |
| 4 | Sunday | 03 41 | 3.3 | 16 28 | 2.8 | 06 04 | 4.9 | 18 35 | 4.8 | 02 53 | 3.7 | 15 28 | 3.5 |
| 5 | Monday | 04 21 | 3.1 | 17 16 | 2.8 | 06 51 | 4.8 | 19 22 | 4.7 | 03 43 | 3.6 | 16 19 | 3.4 |
| 6 | Tuesday | 05 08 | 3.0 | 18 10 | 2.7 | 07 40 | 4.7 | 20 14 | 4.6 | 04 37 | 3.5 | 17 16 | 3.4 |
| 7 | Wednesday | 06 05 | 2.9 | 19 09 | 2.7 | 08 35 | 4.6 | 21 13 | 4.6 | 05 36 | 3.5 | 18 17 | 3.4 |
| 8 | Thursday | 07 12 | 2.9 | 20 12 | 2.7 | 09 38 | 4.7 | 22 20 | 4.7 | 06 41 | 3.5 | 19 20 | 3.5 |
| 9 | Friday | 08 23 | 2.9 | 21 21 | 2.8 | 10 44 | 4.9 | 23 24 | 4.9 | 07 43 | 3.7 | 20 16 | 3.7 |
| 10 | Saturday | 09 31 | 3.0 | 22 23 | 2.9 | 11 47 | 5.1 | —— | — | 08 41 | 3.8 | 21 07 | 3.9 |
| 11 | Sunday | 10 31 | 3.2 | 23 16 | 3.1 | 00 21 | 5.2 | 12 46 | 5.4 | 09 35 | 4.0 | 21 56 | 4.0 |
| 12 | Monday | 11 25 | 3.3 | —— | — | 01 15 | 5.5 | 13 42 | 5.7 | 10 27 | 4.1 | 22 42 | 4.2 |
| 13 | Tuesday | 00 05 | 3.3 | 12 19 | 3.3 | 02 06 | 5.7 | 14 35 | 5.8 | 11 17 | 4.2 | 23 28 | 4.3 |
| 14 | Wednesday | 00 52 | 3.4 | 13 13 | 3.4 | 02 55 | 5.8 | 15 26 | 5.9 | —— | — | 12 06 | 4.2 |
| 15 | Thursday | 01 37 | 3.6 | 14 05 | 3.4 | 03 43 | 5.9 | 16 16 | 5.9 | 00 15 | 4.3 | 12 59 | 4.1 |
| 16 | Friday | 02 22 | 3.6 | 14 56 | 3.4 | 04 32 | 5.8 | 17 07 | 5.7 | 01 06 | 4.3 | 13 52 | 4.0 |
| 17 | Saturday | 03 06 | 3.7 | 15 44 | 3.3 | 05 23 | 5.6 | 18 01 | 5.5 | 01 59 | 4.2 | 14 49 | 3.9 |
| 18 | Sunday | 03 50 | 3.6 | 16 33 | 3.2 | 06 18 | 5.4 | 18 56 | 5.2 | 02 56 | 4.1 | 15 48 | 3.7 |
| 19 | Monday | 04 38 | 3.5 | 17 22 | 3.1 | 07 15 | 5.2 | 19 52 | 5.0 | 03 57 | 4.0 | 16 49 | 3.6 |
| 20 | Tuesday | 05 30 | 3.3 | 18 13 | 3.0 | 08 12 | 5.0 | 20 50 | 4.8 | 05 03 | 3.8 | 17 52 | 3.5 |
| 21 | Wednesday | 06 30 | 3.1 | 19 08 | 2.9 | 09 11 | 4.8 | 21 49 | 4.6 | 06 08 | 3.7 | 18 55 | 3.5 |
| 22 | Thursday | 07 42 | 3.0 | 20 10 | 2.9 | 10 10 | 4.7 | 22 49 | 4.6 | 07 13 | 3.6 | 19 54 | 3.5 |
| 23 | Friday | 09 04 | 2.9 | 21 23 | 2.9 | 11 08 | 4.7 | 23 46 | 4.7 | 08 13 | 3.6 | 20 48 | 3.6 |
| 24 | Saturday | 10 09 | 2.9 | 22 23 | 3.0 | —— | — | 12 04 | 4.8 | 09 08 | 3.6 | 21 36 | 3.7 |
| 25 | Sunday | 11 01 | 2.9 | 23 12 | 3.1 | 00 38 | 4.8 | 12 56 | 4.8 | 09 55 | 3.6 | 22 16 | 3.7 |
| 26 | Monday | 11 46 | 2.9 | 23 54 | 3.1 | 01 24 | 5.0 | 13 42 | 4.9 | 10 35 | 3.6 | 22 51 | 3.8 |
| 27 | Tuesday | —— | — | 12 28 | 2.9 | 02 04 | 5.1 | 14 23 | 5.0 | 11 11 | 3.7 | 23 23 | 3.9 |
| 28 | Wednesday | 00 31 | 3.2 | 13 06 | 2.9 | 02 39 | 5.2 | 15 00 | 5.1 | 11 44 | 3.7 | 23 53 | 3.9 |
| 29 | Thursday | 01 05 | 3.3 | 13 41 | 2.9 | 03 12 | 5.3 | 15 36 | 5.2 | —— | — | 12 16 | 3.7 |
| 30 | Friday | 01 37 | 3.3 | 14 14 | 2.9 | 03 47 | 5.3 | 16 12 | 5.2 | 00 26 | 3.9 | 12 52 | 3.7 |

## JULY 1995   *High water*   GMT

| | LONDON BRIDGE *Datum of predictions 3.20 m below* | | | | AVONMOUTH *Datum of predictions 6.50 m below* | | | | LIVERPOOL *Datum of predictions 4.93 m below* | | | | HULL (*Albert Dock*) *Datum of predictions 3.90 m below* | | | |
|---|---|---|---|---|---|---|---|---|---|---|---|---|---|---|---|---|
| | hr | ht m | hr | ht m | hr | ht m | hr | ht m | hr | ht m | hr | ht m | hr | ht m | hr | ht m |
| 1 Saturday | 03 41 | 6.7 | 15 52 | 6.7 | 09 03 | 12.1 | 21 15 | 12.4 | 00 48 | 8.8 | 13 15 | 8.6 | 08 01 | 7.1 | 20 29 | 6.9 |
| 2 Sunday | 04 20 | 6.8 | 16 29 | 6.7 | 09 38 | 12.1 | 21 49 | 12.2 | 01 23 | 8.8 | 13 50 | 8.6 | 08 36 | 7.0 | 21 06 | 6.8 |
| 3 Monday | 04 59 | 6.7 | 17 05 | 6.6 | 10 13 | 11.8 | 22 25 | 11.9 | 02 01 | 8.7 | 14 29 | 8.5 | 09 13 | 6.9 | 21 45 | 6.7 |
| 4 Tuesday | 05 38 | 6.7 | 17 44 | 6.5 | 10 50 | 11.5 | 23 05 | 11.5 | 02 41 | 8.6 | 15 11 | 8.3 | 09 53 | 6.7 | 22 28 | 6.5 |
| 5 Wednesday | 06 22 | 6.5 | 18 28 | 6.4 | 11 31 | 11.1 | 23 51 | 11.1 | 03 28 | 8.4 | 16 00 | 8.1 | 10 39 | 6.5 | 23 18 | 6.3 |
| 6 Thursday | 07 12 | 6.4 | 19 24 | 6.3 | — | — | 12 21 | 10.8 | 04 23 | 8.2 | 17 00 | 7.9 | 11 33 | 6.4 | — | — |
| 7 Friday | 08 13 | 6.2 | 20 32 | 6.2 | 00 48 | 10.8 | 13 27 | 10.6 | 05 27 | 8.1 | 18 07 | 8.0 | 00 20 | 6.2 | 12 43 | 6.3 |
| 8 Saturday | 09 24 | 6.2 | 21 46 | 6.3 | 02 07 | 10.8 | 14 53 | 10.9 | 06 35 | 8.1 | 19 16 | 8.2 | 01 40 | 6.3 | 14 05 | 6.4 |
| 9 Sunday | 10 35 | 6.4 | 22 57 | 6.5 | 03 31 | 11.3 | 16 09 | 11.6 | 07 45 | 8.4 | 20 21 | 8.7 | 02 51 | 6.5 | 15 18 | 6.6 |
| 10 Monday | 11 39 | 6.7 | — | — | 04 41 | 12.0 | 17 15 | 12.4 | 08 51 | 8.7 | 21 20 | 9.1 | 03 54 | 6.8 | 16 23 | 6.9 |
| 11 Tuesday | 00 01 | 6.8 | 12 36 | 6.9 | 05 45 | 12.7 | 18 14 | 13.2 | 09 51 | 9.1 | 22 15 | 9.6 | 04 51 | 7.1 | 17 22 | 7.2 |
| 12 Wednesday | 00 58 | 7.1 | 13 27 | 7.1 | 06 41 | 13.3 | 19 07 | 13.7 | 10 47 | 9.4 | 23 06 | 9.9 | 05 41 | 7.4 | 18 14 | 7.4 |
| 13 Thursday | 01 51 | 7.3 | 14 16 | 7.2 | 07 34 | 13.6 | 19 57 | 14.0 | 11 39 | 9.6 | 23 56 | 10.0 | 06 27 | 7.7 | 19 02 | 7.6 |
| 14 Friday | 02 42 | 7.4 | 15 03 | 7.3 | 08 23 | 13.7 | 20 44 | 14.1 | — | — | 12 28 | 9.7 | 07 11 | 7.9 | 19 47 | 7.6 |
| 15 Saturday | 03 32 | 7.5 | 15 49 | 7.3 | 09 09 | 13.7 | 21 29 | 13.9 | 00 44 | 10.0 | 13 16 | 9.6 | 07 54 | 7.9 | 20 31 | 7.5 |
| 16 Sunday | 04 20 | 7.5 | 16 33 | 7.3 | 09 53 | 13.4 | 22 12 | 13.4 | 01 32 | 9.8 | 14 01 | 9.4 | 08 37 | 7.9 | 21 16 | 7.2 |
| 17 Monday | 05 04 | 7.4 | 17 14 | 7.1 | 10 33 | 12.8 | 22 50 | 12.7 | 02 17 | 9.5 | 14 44 | 9.0 | 09 21 | 7.6 | 22 01 | 6.9 |
| 18 Tuesday | 05 47 | 7.1 | 17 54 | 6.9 | 11 08 | 12.1 | 23 25 | 11.9 | 03 01 | 9.1 | 15 26 | 8.6 | 10 06 | 7.3 | 22 48 | 6.5 |
| 19 Wednesday | 06 29 | 6.8 | 18 35 | 6.6 | 11 42 | 11.4 | — | — | 03 45 | 8.6 | 16 11 | 8.1 | 10 55 | 6.8 | 23 42 | 6.2 |
| 20 Thursday | 07 16 | 6.4 | 19 29 | 6.3 | 00 04 | 11.1 | 12 25 | 10.8 | 04 36 | 8.0 | 17 05 | 7.6 | 11 54 | 6.4 | — | — |
| 21 Friday | 08 18 | 6.1 | 20 46 | 6.0 | 00 57 | 10.5 | 13 27 | 10.3 | 05 40 | 7.5 | 18 16 | 7.4 | 00 46 | 5.9 | 13 06 | 6.0 |
| 22 Saturday | 09 33 | 6.0 | 22 03 | 6.0 | 02 12 | 10.2 | 14 46 | 10.3 | 06 57 | 7.4 | 19 31 | 7.5 | 01 53 | 5.9 | 14 18 | 5.9 |
| 23 Sunday | 10 38 | 6.1 | 23 07 | 6.1 | 03 29 | 10.3 | 16 00 | 10.7 | 08 07 | 7.5 | 20 33 | 7.8 | 02 59 | 6.0 | 15 28 | 6.0 |
| 24 Monday | 11 35 | 6.2 | — | — | 04 38 | 10.8 | 17 03 | 11.3 | 09 03 | 7.9 | 21 23 | 8.3 | 04 00 | 6.2 | 16 28 | 6.2 |
| 25 Tuesday | 00 01 | 6.2 | 12 24 | 6.3 | 05 34 | 11.4 | 17 54 | 11.9 | 09 51 | 8.3 | 22 06 | 8.6 | 04 50 | 6.5 | 17 16 | 6.4 |
| 26 Wednesday | 00 48 | 6.3 | 13 06 | 6.5 | 06 18 | 11.8 | 18 35 | 12.2 | 10 32 | 8.5 | 22 44 | 8.9 | 05 30 | 6.7 | 17 55 | 6.6 |
| 27 Thursday | 01 29 | 6.4 | 13 43 | 6.6 | 06 57 | 12.0 | 19 12 | 12.4 | 11 10 | 8.7 | 23 20 | 9.0 | 06 03 | 7.0 | 18 28 | 6.8 |
| 28 Friday | 02 06 | 6.6 | 14 20 | 6.7 | 07 33 | 12.2 | 19 47 | 12.6 | 11 46 | 8.8 | 23 54 | 9.1 | 06 35 | 7.1 | 19 00 | 7.0 |
| 29 Saturday | 02 43 | 6.8 | 14 57 | 6.8 | 08 08 | 12.3 | 20 22 | 12.7 | — | — | 12 20 | 8.9 | 07 07 | 7.3 | 19 33 | 7.2 |
| 30 Sunday | 03 22 | 6.9 | 15 35 | 6.9 | 08 44 | 12.5 | 20 57 | 12.9 | 00 28 | 9.1 | 12 54 | 8.9 | 07 41 | 7.3 | 20 08 | 7.2 |
| 31 Monday | 04 02 | 7.0 | 16 12 | 6.8 | 09 19 | 12.6 | 21 32 | 12.8 | 01 02 | 9.1 | 13 28 | 8.9 | 08 17 | 7.3 | 20 44 | 7.1 |

## AUGUST 1995   *High water*   GMT

| | LONDON BRIDGE | | | | AVONMOUTH | | | | LIVERPOOL | | | | HULL (*Albert Dock*) | | | |
|---|---|---|---|---|---|---|---|---|---|---|---|---|---|---|---|---|
| 1 Tuesday | 04 40 | 6.9 | 16 47 | 6.8 | 09 55 | 12.5 | 22 08 | 12.5 | 01 38 | 9.1 | 14 04 | 8.8 | 08 53 | 7.2 | 21 21 | 7.0 |
| 2 Wednesday | 05 18 | 6.8 | 17 23 | 6.6 | 10 31 | 12.1 | 22 46 | 12.0 | 02 17 | 9.0 | 14 44 | 8.7 | 09 31 | 7.0 | 22 01 | 6.8 |
| 3 Thursday | 05 58 | 6.6 | 18 03 | 6.5 | 11 10 | 11.5 | 23 28 | 11.4 | 03 00 | 8.8 | 15 30 | 8.4 | 10 14 | 6.8 | 22 47 | 6.6 |
| 4 Friday | 06 42 | 6.3 | 18 53 | 6.3 | 11 55 | 11.0 | — | — | 03 52 | 8.4 | 16 26 | 8.1 | 11 04 | 6.6 | 23 43 | 6.3 |
| 5 Saturday | 07 37 | 6.1 | 19 58 | 6.1 | 00 20 | 10.8 | 12 57 | 10.5 | 04 57 | 8.1 | 17 37 | 7.9 | — | — | 12 10 | 6.3 |
| 6 Sunday | 08 49 | 5.9 | 21 19 | 6.0 | 01 39 | 10.5 | 14 28 | 10.5 | 06 11 | 7.9 | 18 54 | 8.0 | 01 02 | 6.2 | 13 43 | 6.2 |
| 7 Monday | 10 10 | 6.0 | 22 39 | 6.2 | 03 11 | 10.8 | 15 50 | 11.2 | 07 30 | 8.1 | 20 06 | 8.5 | 02 28 | 6.3 | 15 07 | 6.4 |
| 8 Tuesday | 11 20 | 6.4 | 23 48 | 6.6 | 04 27 | 11.5 | 17 02 | 12.1 | 08 42 | 8.5 | 21 09 | 9.0 | 03 38 | 6.6 | 16 18 | 6.8 |
| 9 Wednesday | — | — | 12 20 | 6.8 | 05 35 | 12.4 | 18 04 | 13.1 | 09 42 | 9.0 | 22 03 | 9.6 | 04 37 | 7.0 | 17 17 | 7.1 |
| 10 Thursday | 00 46 | 7.0 | 13 12 | 7.0 | 06 32 | 13.1 | 18 56 | 13.7 | 10 35 | 9.4 | 22 52 | 9.9 | 05 28 | 7.4 | 18 06 | 7.4 |
| 11 Friday | 01 38 | 7.3 | 13 59 | 7.2 | 07 21 | 13.6 | 19 43 | 14.1 | 11 24 | 9.6 | 23 39 | 10.1 | 06 11 | 7.7 | 18 49 | 7.5 |
| 12 Saturday | 02 26 | 7.4 | 14 43 | 7.3 | 08 06 | 13.8 | 20 26 | 14.2 | — | — | 12 09 | 9.7 | 06 53 | 7.9 | 19 29 | 7.6 |
| 13 Sunday | 03 12 | 7.5 | 15 26 | 7.4 | 08 49 | 13.8 | 21 08 | 14.1 | 00 23 | 10.0 | 12 53 | 9.6 | 07 33 | 8.0 | 20 09 | 7.5 |
| 14 Monday | 03 56 | 7.5 | 16 07 | 7.4 | 09 29 | 13.6 | 21 46 | 13.6 | 01 06 | 9.8 | 13 33 | 9.4 | 08 14 | 8.0 | 20 48 | 7.3 |
| 15 Tuesday | 04 37 | 7.4 | 16 45 | 7.3 | 10 04 | 13.1 | 22 20 | 12.9 | 01 47 | 9.5 | 14 11 | 9.1 | 08 55 | 7.7 | 21 27 | 7.0 |
| 16 Wednesday | 05 14 | 7.2 | 17 21 | 7.0 | 10 35 | 12.4 | 22 49 | 12.0 | 02 26 | 9.1 | 14 47 | 8.7 | 09 36 | 7.3 | 22 06 | 6.7 |
| 17 Thursday | 05 49 | 6.8 | 17 57 | 6.7 | 11 03 | 11.6 | 23 20 | 11.1 | 03 05 | 8.6 | 15 26 | 8.2 | 10 18 | 6.8 | 22 47 | 6.3 |
| 18 Friday | 06 24 | 6.5 | 18 38 | 6.2 | 11 39 | 10.8 | — | — | 03 48 | 8.0 | 16 12 | 7.7 | 11 06 | 6.2 | 23 38 | 5.9 |
| 19 Saturday | 07 07 | 6.0 | 19 32 | 5.8 | 00 03 | 10.3 | 12 31 | 10.1 | 04 41 | 7.5 | 17 12 | 7.3 | — | — | 12 14 | 5.8 |
| 20 Sunday | 08 07 | 5.7 | 21 00 | 5.5 | 01 10 | 9.7 | 13 53 | 9.7 | 05 58 | 7.1 | 18 41 | 7.2 | 00 54 | 5.7 | 13 37 | 5.5 |
| 21 Monday | 09 46 | 5.6 | 22 32 | 5.6 | 02 47 | 9.6 | 15 23 | 10.1 | 07 33 | 7.2 | 20 01 | 7.6 | 02 11 | 5.7 | 14 55 | 5.6 |
| 22 Tuesday | 10 57 | 5.8 | 23 32 | 5.9 | 04 07 | 10.3 | 16 33 | 10.9 | 08 37 | 7.7 | 20 57 | 8.1 | 03 23 | 6.0 | 16 04 | 5.9 |
| 23 Wednesday | 11 51 | 6.1 | — | — | 05 07 | 11.1 | 17 27 | 11.7 | 09 26 | 8.1 | 21 42 | 8.6 | 04 20 | 6.3 | 16 53 | 6.3 |
| 24 Thursday | 00 20 | 6.2 | 12 37 | 6.4 | 05 53 | 11.8 | 18 10 | 12.3 | 10 08 | 8.5 | 22 21 | 8.9 | 05 03 | 6.7 | 17 31 | 6.6 |
| 25 Friday | 01 02 | 6.5 | 13 18 | 6.6 | 06 33 | 12.2 | 18 49 | 12.7 | 10 46 | 8.8 | 22 57 | 9.2 | 05 38 | 7.0 | 18 04 | 6.9 |
| 26 Saturday | 01 41 | 6.7 | 13 56 | 6.8 | 07 10 | 12.5 | 19 25 | 12.9 | 11 21 | 9.0 | 23 30 | 9.3 | 06 10 | 7.3 | 18 35 | 7.2 |
| 27 Sunday | 02 20 | 7.0 | 14 35 | 7.0 | 07 45 | 12.7 | 20 00 | 13.1 | 11 55 | 9.1 | — | — | 06 43 | 7.5 | 19 09 | 7.4 |
| 28 Monday | 02 59 | 7.1 | 15 14 | 7.1 | 08 21 | 13.0 | 20 36 | 13.3 | 00 03 | 9.4 | 12 29 | 9.2 | 07 18 | 7.6 | 19 44 | 7.5 |
| 29 Tuesday | 03 40 | 7.2 | 15 52 | 7.0 | 08 57 | 13.1 | 21 12 | 13.3 | 00 39 | 9.4 | 13 04 | 9.2 | 07 54 | 7.6 | 20 19 | 7.4 |
| 30 Wednedsay | 04 19 | 7.1 | 16 28 | 6.9 | 09 34 | 12.9 | 21 50 | 12.9 | 01 15 | 9.4 | 13 41 | 9.1 | 08 30 | 7.4 | 20 56 | 7.2 |
| 31 Thursday | 04 56 | 6.9 | 17 04 | 6.7 | 10 11 | 12.5 | 22 28 | 12.3 | 01 54 | 9.2 | 14 20 | 9.0 | 09 09 | 7.2 | 21 36 | 7.0 |

## JULY 1995  *continued*

| | GREENOCK | | | | LEITH | | | | DUN LAOGHAIRE | | | |
|---|---|---|---|---|---|---|---|---|---|---|---|---|
| | *Datum of predictions 1.62 m below | | | | *Datum of predictions 2.90 m below | | | | †Datum of predictions 0.20 m above | | | |
| | hr | ht m | hr | ht m | hr | ht m | hr | ht m | hr | ht m | hr | ht m |
| 1 Saturday | 02 09 | 3.4 | 14 48 | 2.9 | 04 23 | 5.2 | 16 50 | 5.1 | 01 02 | 3.9 | 13 30 | 3.7 |
| 2 Sunday | 02 43 | 3.4 | 15 24 | 3.0 | 05 02 | 5.2 | 17 31 | 5.1 | 01 42 | 3.9 | 14 11 | 3.7 |
| 3 Monday | 03 20 | 3.4 | 16 04 | 2.9 | 05 44 | 5.1 | 18 14 | 5.0 | 02 26 | 3.9 | 14 57 | 3.7 |
| 4 Tuesday | 03 58 | 3.3 | 16 47 | 2.9 | 06 28 | 5.0 | 18 58 | 4.9 | 03 13 | 3.8 | 15 45 | 3.6 |
| 5 Wednesday | 04 40 | 3.2 | 17 34 | 2.9 | 07 15 | 4.9 | 19 46 | 4.8 | 04 03 | 3.8 | 16 38 | 3.6 |
| 6 Thursday | 05 28 | 3.1 | 18 27 | 2.8 | 08 05 | 4.8 | 20 39 | 4.7 | 04 59 | 3.7 | 17 37 | 3.5 |
| 7 Friday | 06 27 | 3.0 | 19 28 | 2.8 | 09 03 | 4.8 | 21 41 | 4.7 | 06 02 | 3.6 | 18 42 | 3.6 |
| 8 Saturday | 07 41 | 2.9 | 20 42 | 2.8 | 10 10 | 4.8 | 22 49 | 4.8 | 07 11 | 3.7 | 19 46 | 3.7 |
| 9 Sunday | 09 02 | 3.0 | 21 58 | 2.9 | 11 19 | 5.0 | 23 55 | 5.1 | 08 19 | 3.8 | 20 46 | 3.8 |
| 10 Monday | 10 14 | 3.1 | 22 59 | 3.2 | ---- | — | 12 25 | 5.3 | 09 21 | 3.9 | 21 40 | 4.0 |
| 11 Tuesday | 11 14 | 3.2 | 23 51 | 3.4 | 00 55 | 5.3 | 13 26 | 5.5 | 10 17 | 4.0 | 22 30 | 4.2 |
| 12 Wednesday | ---- | — | 12 10 | 3.3 | 01 51 | 5.6 | 14 22 | 5.8 | 11 07 | 4.1 | 23 17 | 4.3 |
| 13 Thursday | 00 39 | 3.5 | 13 05 | 3.3 | 02 42 | 5.8 | 15 14 | 5.9 | 11 55 | 4.1 | ---- | — |
| 14 Friday | 01 26 | 3.7 | 13 56 | 3.4 | 03 30 | 5.9 | 16 02 | 5.9 | 00 02 | 4.4 | 12 44 | 4.1 |
| 15 Saturday | 02 11 | 3.8 | 14 44 | 3.4 | 04 17 | 5.9 | 16 51 | 5.8 | 00 49 | 4.3 | 13 32 | 4.0 |
| 16 Sunday | 02 53 | 3.8 | 15 27 | 3.4 | 05 05 | 5.8 | 17 40 | 5.6 | 01 37 | 4.3 | 14 21 | 3.9 |
| 17 Monday | 03 34 | 3.7 | 16 09 | 3.4 | 05 55 | 5.6 | 18 30 | 5.3 | 02 28 | 4.1 | 15 12 | 3.7 |
| 18 Tuesday | 04 16 | 3.6 | 16 50 | 3.3 | 06 46 | 5.3 | 19 19 | 5.0 | 03 20 | 4.0 | 16 06 | 3.6 |
| 19 Wednesday | 04 59 | 3.4 | 17 32 | 3.2 | 07 38 | 5.0 | 20 11 | 4.8 | 04 19 | 3.8 | 17 05 | 3.5 |
| 20 Thursday | 05 46 | 3.2 | 18 18 | 3.1 | 08 34 | 4.8 | 21 07 | 4.6 | 05 24 | 3.6 | 18 07 | 3.4 |
| 21 Friday | 06 39 | 2.9 | 19 09 | 2.9 | 09 33 | 4.6 | 22 07 | 4.5 | 06 31 | 3.5 | 19 10 | 3.4 |
| 22 Saturday | 07 51 | 2.8 | 20 14 | 2.9 | 10 35 | 4.5 | 23 08 | 4.5 | 07 35 | 3.4 | 20 08 | 3.5 |
| 23 Sunday | 09 41 | 2.8 | 21 45 | 2.9 | 11 35 | 4.5 | ---- | — | 08 34 | 3.4 | 21 01 | 3.6 |
| 24 Monday | 10 42 | 2.9 | 22 46 | 3.0 | 00 05 | 4.7 | 12 30 | 4.7 | 09 27 | 3.5 | 21 47 | 3.7 |
| 25 Tuesday | 11 29 | 2.9 | 23 32 | 3.2 | 00 56 | 4.9 | 13 19 | 4.8 | 10 11 | 3.6 | 22 26 | 3.8 |
| 26 Wednesday | ---- | — | 12 11 | 3.0 | 01 40 | 5.1 | 14 01 | 5.0 | 10 49 | 3.7 | 23 01 | 3.9 |
| 27 Thursday | 00 11 | 3.2 | 12 50 | 3.0 | 02 18 | 5.2 | 14 38 | 5.2 | 11 23 | 3.7 | 23 31 | 4.0 |
| 28 Friday | 00 45 | 3.3 | 13 25 | 3.0 | 02 53 | 5.3 | 15 14 | 5.3 | 11 53 | 3.8 | ---- | — |
| 29 Saturday | 01 16 | 3.4 | 13 56 | 3.0 | 03 27 | 5.4 | 15 50 | 5.3 | 00 01 | 4.0 | 12 26 | 3.8 |
| 30 Sunday | 01 48 | 3.4 | 14 27 | 3.0 | 04 03 | 5.4 | 16 27 | 5.3 | 00 36 | 4.0 | 13 02 | 3.8 |
| 31 Monday | 02 22 | 3.5 | 15 01 | 3.1 | 04 40 | 5.4 | 17 07 | 5.3 | 01 15 | 4.0 | 13 42 | 3.8 |

NOTES:

*Difference of height in metres from Ordnance datum (Newlyn)

†Difference of height in metres from Ordnance datum (Dublin)

hr hour

m metres

## AUGUST 1995  *continued*

| | GREENOCK | | | | LEITH | | | | DUN LAOGHAIRE | | | |
|---|---|---|---|---|---|---|---|---|---|---|---|---|
| 1 Tuesday | 02 59 | 3.5 | 15 37 | 3.1 | 05 20 | 5.3 | 17 49 | 5.2 | 01 57 | 4.0 | 14 26 | 3.8 |
| 2 Wednesday | 03 36 | 3.5 | 16 15 | 3.1 | 06 03 | 5.2 | 18 33 | 5.1 | 02 43 | 4.0 | 15 13 | 3.8 |
| 3 Thursday | 04 15 | 3.4 | 16 57 | 3.0 | 06 49 | 5.1 | 19 19 | 5.0 | 03 33 | 3.9 | 16 05 | 3.7 |
| 4 Friday | 04 59 | 3.2 | 17 46 | 2.9 | 07 39 | 5.0 | 20 11 | 4.8 | 04 29 | 3.8 | 17 03 | 3.6 |
| 5 Saturday | 05 52 | 3.0 | 18 46 | 2.9 | 08 37 | 4.8 | 21 11 | 4.7 | 05 33 | 3.6 | 18 10 | 3.6 |
| 6 Sunday | 07 02 | 2.9 | 20 09 | 2.8 | 09 45 | 4.8 | 22 22 | 4.7 | 06 51 | 3.6 | 19 25 | 3.6 |
| 7 Monday | 08 43 | 2.9 | 21 41 | 3.0 | 11 01 | 4.9 | 23 34 | 4.9 | 08 07 | 3.7 | 20 31 | 3.8 |
| 8 Tuesday | 10 08 | 3.0 | 22 46 | 3.2 | ---- | — | 12 13 | 5.1 | 09 13 | 3.8 | 21 29 | 4.0 |
| 9 Wednesday | 11 11 | 3.2 | 23 38 | 3.4 | 00 40 | 5.2 | 13 17 | 5.4 | 10 10 | 3.9 | 22 21 | 4.2 |
| 10 Thursday | ---- | — | 12 04 | 3.3 | 01 38 | 5.6 | 14 12 | 5.7 | 11 00 | 4.0 | 23 06 | 4.3 |
| 11 Friday | 00 27 | 3.6 | 12 55 | 3.4 | 02 29 | 5.8 | 15 00 | 5.8 | 11 44 | 4.1 | 23 47 | 4.3 |
| 12 Saturday | 01 13 | 3.7 | 13 42 | 3.4 | 03 15 | 5.9 | 15 45 | 5.8 | ---- | — | 12 26 | 4.0 |
| 13 Sunday | 01 55 | 3.8 | 14 23 | 3.5 | 03 58 | 5.9 | 16 28 | 5.8 | 00 28 | 4.3 | 13 07 | 4.0 |
| 14 Monday | 02 35 | 3.8 | 15 01 | 3.6 | 04 41 | 5.8 | 17 12 | 5.6 | 01 10 | 4.2 | 13 48 | 3.9 |
| 15 Tuesday | 03 12 | 3.8 | 15 37 | 3.5 | 05 25 | 5.6 | 17 55 | 5.3 | 01 54 | 4.1 | 14 32 | 3.8 |
| 16 Wednesday | 03 49 | 3.6 | 16 13 | 3.4 | 06 10 | 5.3 | 18 40 | 5.0 | 02 41 | 3.9 | 15 18 | 3.6 |
| 17 Thursday | 04 27 | 3.5 | 16 52 | 3.3 | 06 57 | 5.0 | 19 27 | 4.8 | 03 33 | 3.7 | 16 11 | 3.5 |
| 18 Friday | 05 08 | 3.2 | 17 35 | 3.2 | 07 49 | 4.7 | 20 20 | 4.5 | 04 33 | 3.5 | 17 15 | 3.4 |
| 19 Saturday | 05 55 | 3.0 | 18 24 | 3.1 | 08 51 | 4.4 | 21 23 | 4.4 | 05 45 | 3.3 | 18 23 | 3.3 |
| 20 Sunday | 06 53 | 2.7 | 19 20 | 2.9 | 10 00 | 4.3 | 22 31 | 4.4 | 06 58 | 3.3 | 19 29 | 3.4 |
| 21 Monday | 08 34 | 2.6 | 20 41 | 2.9 | 11 05 | 4.4 | 23 33 | 4.5 | 08 03 | 3.3 | 20 28 | 3.5 |
| 22 Tuesday | 10 22 | 2.8 | 22 14 | 3.0 | ---- | — | 12 03 | 4.6 | 09 00 | 3.4 | 21 19 | 3.7 |
| 23 Wednesday | 11 08 | 3.0 | 23 05 | 3.2 | 00 26 | 4.8 | 12 53 | 4.8 | 09 47 | 3.5 | 22 01 | 3.8 |
| 24 Thursday | 11 49 | 3.1 | 23 44 | 3.3 | 01 12 | 5.0 | 13 35 | 5.0 | 10 26 | 3.7 | 22 36 | 3.9 |
| 25 Friday | ---- | — | 12 26 | 3.1 | 01 51 | 5.2 | 14 12 | 5.2 | 10 59 | 3.8 | 23 07 | 4.0 |
| 26 Saturday | 00 18 | 3.3 | 13 01 | 3.1 | 02 27 | 5.4 | 14 48 | 5.4 | 11 27 | 3.8 | 23 35 | 4.1 |
| 27 Sunday | 00 50 | 3.4 | 13 31 | 3.1 | 03 02 | 5.5 | 15 24 | 5.5 | 11 57 | 3.9 | ---- | — |
| 28 Monday | 01 24 | 3.5 | 14 01 | 3.2 | 03 38 | 5.6 | 16 01 | 5.5 | 00 08 | 4.1 | 12 33 | 4.0 |
| 29 Tuesday | 02 00 | 3.5 | 14 34 | 3.2 | 04 16 | 5.6 | 16 40 | 5.5 | 00 47 | 4.2 | 13 13 | 4.0 |
| 30 Wednesday | 02 37 | 3.6 | 15 08 | 3.3 | 04 55 | 5.5 | 17 22 | 5.4 | 01 29 | 4.1 | 13 56 | 4.0 |
| 31 Thursday | 03 15 | 3.5 | 15 45 | 3.3 | 05 39 | 5.4 | 18 06 | 5.3 | 02 15 | 4.1 | 14 44 | 3.9 |

## SEPTEMBER 1995 *High water* GMT

| | | LONDON BRIDGE *Datum of predictions 3.20 m below* | | | | AVONMOUTH *Datum of predictions 6.50 m below* | | | | LIVERPOOL *Datum of predictions 4.93 m below* | | | | HULL (*Albert Dock*) *Datum of predictions 3.90 m below* | | | |
|---|---|---|---|---|---|---|---|---|---|---|---|---|---|---|---|---|---|
| | | hr | ht m | hr | ht m | hr | ht m | hr | ht m | hr | ht m | hr | ht m | hr | ht m | hr | ht m |
| 1 | Friday | 05 33 | 6.6 | 17 43 | 6.5 | 10 50 | 11.8 | 23 09 | 11.5 | 02 38 | 8.9 | 15 05 | 8.6 | 09 52 | 7.0 | 22 21 | 6.7 |
| 2 | Saturday | 06 14 | 6.3 | 18 29 | 6.2 | 11 34 | 11.0 | — | — | 03 30 | 8.4 | 16 01 | 8.2 | 10 44 | 6.6 | 23 16 | 6.4 |
| 3 | Sunday | 07 02 | 5.9 | 19 30 | 5.9 | 00 00 | 10.7 | 12 37 | 10.4 | 04 36 | 7.9 | 17 15 | 7.8 | 11 51 | 6.2 | — | — |
| 4 | Monday | 08 13 | 5.7 | 20 58 | 5.7 | 01 24 | 10.1 | 14 14 | 10.3 | 05 58 | 7.6 | 18 40 | 7.8 | 00 35 | 6.1 | 13 36 | 6.1 |
| 5 | Tuesday | 09 48 | 5.8 | 22 27 | 6.1 | 02 59 | 10.4 | 15 37 | 11.0 | 07 25 | 7.8 | 19 57 | 8.3 | 02 11 | 6.2 | 15 03 | 6.3 |
| 6 | Wednesday | 11 02 | 6.2 | 23 37 | 6.6 | 04 18 | 11.3 | 16 52 | 12.0 | 08 36 | 8.4 | 20 59 | 9.0 | 03 23 | 6.6 | 16 12 | 6.8 |
| 7 | Thursday | — | — | 12 03 | 6.7 | 05 26 | 12.3 | 17 53 | 13.1 | 09 32 | 9.0 | 21 50 | 9.5 | 04 23 | 7.0 | 17 08 | 7.1 |
| 8 | Friday | 00 33 | 7.1 | 12 54 | 7.1 | 06 19 | 13.1 | 18 41 | 13.7 | 10 20 | 9.4 | 22 36 | 9.8 | 05 11 | 7.4 | 17 53 | 7.4 |
| 9 | Saturday | 01 23 | 7.4 | 13 40 | 7.3 | 07 04 | 13.6 | 19 24 | 14.1 | 11 05 | 9.6 | 23 19 | 10.0 | 05 53 | 7.7 | 18 31 | 7.5 |
| 10 | Sunday | 02 08 | 7.5 | 14 22 | 7.4 | 07 45 | 13.8 | 20 04 | 14.1 | 11 46 | 9.6 | 23 59 | 9.9 | 06 32 | 7.9 | 19 07 | 7.5 |
| 11 | Monday | 02 50 | 7.5 | 15 02 | 7.4 | 08 23 | 13.8 | 20 42 | 14.0 | — | — | 12 24 | 9.5 | 07 11 | 8.0 | 19 42 | 7.5 |
| 12 | Tuesday | 03 30 | 7.5 | 15 40 | 7.4 | 09 00 | 13.6 | 21 17 | 13.6 | 00 38 | 9.7 | 13 01 | 9.3 | 07 50 | 7.9 | 20 18 | 7.4 |
| 13 | Wednesday | 04 06 | 7.4 | 16 17 | 7.2 | 09 33 | 13.2 | 21 48 | 12.9 | 01 15 | 9.4 | 13 36 | 9.0 | 08 29 | 7.6 | 20 53 | 7.1 |
| 14 | Thursday | 04 39 | 7.1 | 16 51 | 7.0 | 10 01 | 12.5 | 22 15 | 12.1 | 01 51 | 9.0 | 14 11 | 8.7 | 09 07 | 7.2 | 21 27 | 6.8 |
| 15 | Friday | 05 10 | 6.9 | 17 25 | 6.6 | 10 28 | 11.7 | 22 44 | 11.1 | 02 28 | 8.6 | 14 48 | 8.3 | 09 44 | 6.7 | 22 01 | 6.4 |
| 16 | Saturday | 05 44 | 6.5 | 18 03 | 6.2 | 10 59 | 10.8 | 23 19 | 10.2 | 03 09 | 8.0 | 15 31 | 7.9 | 10 24 | 6.1 | 22 40 | 6.0 |
| 17 | Sunday | 06 22 | 6.1 | 18 47 | 5.8 | 11 39 | 10.0 | — | — | 03 59 | 7.5 | 16 25 | 7.4 | 11 17 | 5.6 | 23 39 | 5.6 |
| 18 | Monday | 07 10 | 5.7 | 19 47 | 5.4 | 00 09 | 9.4 | 12 46 | 9.4 | 05 04 | 7.1 | 17 39 | 7.2 | — | — | 12 50 | 5.4 |
| 19 | Tuesday | 08 16 | 5.4 | 21 22 | 5.3 | 01 54 | 9.1 | 14 45 | 9.5 | 06 43 | 7.0 | 19 17 | 7.4 | 01 20 | 5.5 | 14 14 | 5.4 |
| 20 | Wednesday | 10 01 | 5.5 | 22 50 | 5.7 | 03 32 | 9.7 | 15 59 | 10.5 | 08 03 | 7.4 | 20 23 | 7.9 | 02 37 | 5.8 | 15 26 | 5.8 |
| 21 | Thursday | 11 10 | 5.9 | 23 44 | 6.1 | 04 34 | 10.8 | 16 55 | 11.5 | 08 55 | 8.0 | 21 10 | 8.4 | 03 40 | 6.2 | 16 19 | 6.2 |
| 22 | Friday | — | — | 12 01 | 6.3 | 05 23 | 11.7 | 17 41 | 12.3 | 09 37 | 8.5 | 21 49 | 8.9 | 04 27 | 6.6 | 16 58 | 6.7 |
| 23 | Saturday | 00 30 | 6.5 | 12 46 | 6.7 | 06 04 | 12.4 | 18 21 | 12.8 | 10 15 | 8.9 | 22 25 | 9.2 | 05 05 | 7.0 | 17 33 | 7.0 |
| 24 | Sunday | 01 12 | 6.9 | 13 27 | 6.9 | 06 42 | 12.8 | 18 58 | 13.2 | 10 50 | 9.1 | 23 01 | 9.4 | 05 41 | 7.3 | 18 07 | 7.3 |
| 25 | Monday | 01 52 | 7.1 | 14 07 | 7.1 | 07 19 | 13.2 | 19 35 | 13.5 | 11 26 | 9.3 | 23 37 | 9.6 | 06 17 | 7.6 | 18 42 | 7.6 |
| 26 | Tuesday | 02 33 | 7.3 | 14 48 | 7.2 | 07 56 | 13.4 | 20 13 | 13.7 | — | — | 12 02 | 9.4 | 06 54 | 7.7 | 19 18 | 7.6 |
| 27 | Wednesday | 03 15 | 7.3 | 15 29 | 7.2 | 08 34 | 13.5 | 20 52 | 13.6 | 00 14 | 9.6 | 12 40 | 9.5 | 07 31 | 7.7 | 19 55 | 7.6 |
| 28 | Thursday | 03 55 | 7.2 | 16 09 | 7.1 | 09 13 | 13.3 | 21 32 | 13.2 | 00 55 | 9.6 | 13 19 | 9.4 | 08 10 | 7.6 | 20 33 | 7.4 |
| 29 | Friday | 04 34 | 6.9 | 16 49 | 6.8 | 09 53 | 12.8 | 22 13 | 12.5 | 01 37 | 9.3 | 14 01 | 9.1 | 08 51 | 7.4 | 21 14 | 7.2 |
| 30 | Saturday | 05 12 | 6.6 | 17 30 | 6.5 | 10 34 | 12.0 | 22 57 | 11.5 | 02 23 | 8.9 | 14 48 | 8.7 | 09 37 | 7.0 | 22 00 | 6.8 |

## OCTOBER 1995 *High water* GMT

| | | LONDON BRIDGE | | | | AVONMOUTH | | | | LIVERPOOL | | | | HULL (*Albert Dock*) | | | |
|---|---|---|---|---|---|---|---|---|---|---|---|---|---|---|---|---|---|
| | | hr | ht m | hr | ht m | hr | ht m | hr | ht m | hr | ht m | hr | ht m | hr | ht m | hr | ht m |
| 1 | Sunday | 05 50 | 6.2 | 18 16 | 6.2 | 11 21 | 11.1 | 23 50 | 10.6 | 03 17 | 8.4 | 15 46 | 8.2 | 10 31 | 6.6 | 22 56 | 6.4 |
| 2 | Monday | 06 35 | 5.9 | 19 16 | 5.9 | — | — | 12 27 | 10.4 | 04 25 | 7.8 | 17 01 | 7.8 | 11 42 | 6.2 | — | — |
| 3 | Tuesday | 07 43 | 5.7 | 20 47 | 5.8 | 01 15 | 10.0 | 14 04 | 10.3 | 05 52 | 7.5 | 18 28 | 7.8 | 00 13 | 6.2 | 13 33 | 6.1 |
| 4 | Wednesday | 09 27 | 5.8 | 22 12 | 6.2 | 02 47 | 10.3 | 15 24 | 11.0 | 07 17 | 7.8 | 19 43 | 8.3 | 01 52 | 6.2 | 14 54 | 6.3 |
| 5 | Thursday | 10 40 | 6.3 | 23 18 | 6.8 | 04 02 | 11.2 | 16 34 | 12.0 | 08 23 | 8.3 | 20 43 | 8.8 | 03 05 | 6.6 | 16 00 | 6.7 |
| 6 | Friday | 11 40 | 6.8 | — | — | 05 07 | 12.2 | 17 33 | 12.9 | 09 15 | 8.9 | 21 32 | 9.3 | 04 03 | 7.0 | 16 52 | 7.1 |
| 7 | Saturday | 00 13 | 7.2 | 12 32 | 7.2 | 05 58 | 13.0 | 18 20 | 13.5 | 10 01 | 9.2 | 22 16 | 9.6 | 04 52 | 7.4 | 17 34 | 7.3 |
| 8 | Sunday | 01 03 | 7.5 | 13 18 | 7.3 | 06 41 | 13.4 | 19 00 | 13.8 | 10 42 | 9.4 | 22 57 | 9.7 | 05 33 | 7.6 | 18 09 | 7.4 |
| 9 | Monday | 01 46 | 7.5 | 14 00 | 7.3 | 07 19 | 13.6 | 19 38 | 13.8 | 11 20 | 9.4 | 23 35 | 9.6 | 06 11 | 7.7 | 18 42 | 7.4 |
| 10 | Tuesday | 02 26 | 7.4 | 14 38 | 7.3 | 07 55 | 13.6 | 20 14 | 13.7 | 11 56 | 9.3 | — | — | 06 49 | 7.7 | 19 16 | 7.4 |
| 11 | Wednesday | 03 02 | 7.3 | 15 15 | 7.2 | 08 30 | 13.5 | 20 48 | 13.4 | 00 10 | 9.4 | 12 30 | 9.1 | 07 27 | 7.6 | 19 49 | 7.3 |
| 12 | Thursday | 03 35 | 7.2 | 15 50 | 7.1 | 09 02 | 13.1 | 21 19 | 12.8 | 00 46 | 9.1 | 13 04 | 8.9 | 08 04 | 7.4 | 20 21 | 7.1 |
| 13 | Friday | 04 06 | 7.0 | 16 24 | 6.8 | 09 31 | 12.5 | 21 47 | 12.0 | 01 21 | 8.8 | 13 39 | 8.7 | 08 40 | 7.0 | 20 52 | 6.8 |
| 14 | Saturday | 04 37 | 6.8 | 16 59 | 6.6 | 09 59 | 11.7 | 22 15 | 11.0 | 01 58 | 8.5 | 14 16 | 8.4 | 09 15 | 6.6 | 21 24 | 6.5 |
| 15 | Sunday | 05 11 | 6.5 | 17 36 | 6.2 | 10 27 | 10.9 | 22 46 | 10.4 | 02 38 | 8.1 | 14 58 | 8.0 | 09 52 | 6.2 | 21 59 | 6.2 |
| 16 | Monday | 05 48 | 6.2 | 18 18 | 5.9 | 11 01 | 10.2 | 23 26 | 9.6 | 03 25 | 7.6 | 15 47 | 7.6 | 10 36 | 5.7 | 22 46 | 5.8 |
| 17 | Tuesday | 06 31 | 5.9 | 19 09 | 5.6 | 11 50 | 9.6 | — | — | 04 23 | 7.2 | 16 50 | 7.3 | 11 45 | 5.4 | — | — |
| 18 | Wednesday | 07 26 | 5.6 | 20 15 | 5.5 | 00 28 | 9.1 | 13 18 | 9.3 | 05 39 | 7.0 | 18 09 | 7.3 | 00 08 | 5.5 | 13 26 | 5.4 |
| 19 | Thursday | 08 44 | 5.6 | 21 40 | 5.7 | 02 41 | 9.3 | 15 15 | 10.0 | 07 08 | 7.3 | 19 27 | 7.6 | 01 48 | 5.7 | 14 36 | 5.7 |
| 20 | Friday | 10 14 | 5.9 | 22 55 | 6.1 | 03 52 | 10.3 | 16 15 | 11.1 | 08 10 | 7.8 | 20 23 | 8.2 | 02 53 | 6.0 | 15 33 | 6.2 |
| 21 | Saturday | 11 17 | 6.3 | 23 50 | 6.6 | 04 45 | 11.4 | 17 05 | 12.0 | 08 56 | 8.3 | 21 08 | 8.7 | 03 45 | 6.5 | 16 18 | 6.6 |
| 22 | Sunday | — | — | 12 08 | 6.7 | 05 31 | 12.3 | 17 49 | 12.8 | 09 37 | 8.8 | 21 49 | 9.1 | 04 29 | 6.9 | 16 58 | 7.0 |
| 23 | Monday | 00 38 | 6.9 | 12 54 | 7.0 | 06 12 | 13.0 | 18 30 | 13.3 | 10 16 | 9.2 | 22 29 | 9.5 | 05 10 | 7.3 | 17 37 | 7.4 |
| 24 | Tuesday | 01 22 | 7.2 | 13 38 | 7.2 | 06 52 | 13.5 | 19 11 | 13.7 | 10 56 | 9.5 | 23 10 | 9.7 | 05 50 | 7.6 | 18 15 | 7.6 |
| 25 | Wednesday | 02 06 | 7.3 | 14 22 | 7.3 | 07 32 | 13.7 | 19 52 | 13.9 | 11 36 | 9.7 | 23 53 | 9.8 | 06 30 | 7.7 | 18 54 | 7.7 |
| 26 | Thursday | 02 49 | 7.3 | 15 07 | 7.2 | 08 13 | 13.8 | 20 35 | 13.8 | — | — | 12 18 | 9.7 | 07 12 | 7.8 | 19 33 | 7.7 |
| 27 | Friday | 03 33 | 7.2 | 15 53 | 7.2 | 08 56 | 13.6 | 21 19 | 13.4 | 00 38 | 9.7 | 13 02 | 9.6 | 07 54 | 7.7 | 20 14 | 7.6 |
| 28 | Saturday | 04 15 | 7.0 | 16 37 | 7.0 | 09 40 | 13.0 | 22 04 | 12.7 | 01 25 | 9.4 | 13 49 | 9.3 | 08 39 | 7.5 | 20 58 | 7.3 |
| 29 | Sunday | 04 56 | 6.6 | 17 22 | 6.6 | 10 25 | 12.2 | 22 51 | 11.6 | 02 14 | 9.0 | 14 39 | 8.9 | 09 28 | 7.1 | 21 45 | 7.0 |
| 30 | Monday | 05 35 | 6.3 | 18 10 | 6.4 | 11 16 | 11.4 | 23 46 | 10.9 | 03 10 | 8.4 | 15 37 | 8.5 | 10 23 | 6.6 | 22 41 | 6.6 |
| 31 | Tuesday | 06 19 | 6.0 | 19 10 | 6.1 | — | — | 12 20 | 10.7 | 04 17 | 7.9 | 16 48 | 8.1 | 11 36 | 6.2 | 23 52 | 6.4 |

## SEPTEMBER 1995  *continued*

| | | GREENOCK | | | LEITH | | | | DUN LAOGHAIRE | | | | NOTES: |
|---|---|---|---|---|---|---|---|---|---|---|---|---|---|
| | | *Datum of predictions 1.62 m below | | | *Datum of predictions 2.90 m below | | | | †Datum of predictions 0.20 m above | | | | *Difference of height in metres from Ordnance datum (Newlyn) |
| | | hr | m ht | hr | m ht | hr | m ht | hr | m ht | hr | m ht | †Difference of height in metres from Ordnance datum (Dublin) |
| 1 | Friday | 03 54 | 3.5 | 16 25 | 3.2 | 06 26 | 5.2 | 18 54 | 5.1 | 03 06 | 3.9 | 15 37 | 3.8 |
| 2 | Saturday | 04 36 | 3.3 | 17 12 | 3.1 | 07 18 | 5.0 | 19 47 | 4.8 | 04 04 | 3.8 | 16 36 | 3.7 |
| 3 | Sunday | 05 27 | 3.1 | 18 12 | 2.9 | 08 18 | 4.8 | 20 49 | 4.7 | 05 15 | 3.6 | 17 48 | 3.6 |
| 4 | Monday | 06 38 | 2.9 | 19 46 | 2.9 | 09 29 | 4.7 | 22 04 | 4.7 | 06 42 | 3.5 | 19 10 | 3.6 |
| 5 | Tuesday | 08 41 | 2.8 | 21 29 | 3.1 | 10 53 | 4.8 | 23 21 | 4.9 | 08 02 | 3.6 | 20 21 | 3.8 |
| 6 | Wednesday | 10 08 | 3.0 | 22 32 | 3.3 | —— | — | 12 09 | 5.1 | 09 09 | 3.7 | 21 21 | 4.0 |
| 7 | Thursday | 11 04 | 3.2 | 23 23 | 3.5 | 00 28 | 5.2 | 13 11 | 5.4 | 10 05 | 3.9 | 22 12 | 4.1 |
| 8 | Friday | 11 53 | 3.4 | —— | — | 01 25 | 5.5 | 14 01 | 5.6 | 10 52 | 4.0 | 22 55 | 4.2 |
| 9 | Saturday | 00 10 | 3.7 | 12 38 | 3.4 | 02 13 | 5.7 | 14 44 | 5.7 | 11 32 | 4.0 | 23 31 | 4.3 |
| 10 | Sunday | 00 55 | 3.7 | 13 19 | 3.5 | 02 55 | 5.9 | 15 23 | 5.8 | —— | — | 12 07 | 4.0 |
| 11 | Monday | 01 35 | 3.8 | 13 56 | 3.5 | 03 35 | 5.8 | 16 01 | 5.7 | 00 06 | 4.2 | 12 41 | 3.9 |
| 12 | Tuesday | 02 12 | 3.7 | 14 29 | 3.5 | 04 13 | 5.7 | 16 38 | 5.5 | 00 45 | 4.2 | 13 16 | 3.9 |
| 13 | Wednesday | 02 47 | 3.7 | 15 03 | 3.6 | 04 51 | 5.5 | 17 16 | 5.3 | 01 24 | 4.0 | 13 54 | 3.8 |
| 14 | Thursday | 03 21 | 3.6 | 15 38 | 3.5 | 05 29 | 5.3 | 17 54 | 5.1 | 02 07 | 3.9 | 14 37 | 3.7 |
| 15 | Friday | 03 56 | 3.4 | 16 15 | 3.5 | 06 09 | 5.0 | 18 33 | 4.8 | 02 54 | 3.7 | 15 24 | 3.6 |
| 16 | Saturday | 04 35 | 3.2 | 16 57 | 3.3 | 06 54 | 4.7 | 19 18 | 4.6 | 03 48 | 3.5 | 16 21 | 3.4 |
| 17 | Sunday | 05 20 | 3.0 | 17 45 | 3.1 | 07 50 | 4.4 | 20 19 | 4.3 | 04 58 | 3.3 | 17 35 | 3.3 |
| 18 | Monday | 06 17 | 2.8 | 18 41 | 3.0 | 09 13 | 4.2 | 21 46 | 4.3 | 06 19 | 3.2 | 18 51 | 3.3 |
| 19 | Tuesday | 07 30 | 2.7 | 19 49 | 2.9 | 10 30 | 4.3 | 22 56 | 4.4 | 07 30 | 3.2 | 19 54 | 3.4 |
| 20 | Wednesday | 09 47 | 2.8 | 21 20 | 3.0 | 11 31 | 4.5 | 23 52 | 4.7 | 08 30 | 3.4 | 20 48 | 3.6 |
| 21 | Thursday | 10 38 | 3.0 | 22 25 | 3.2 | —— | — | 12 21 | 4.8 | 09 20 | 3.5 | 21 31 | 3.8 |
| 22 | Friday | 11 18 | 3.1 | 23 07 | 3.3 | 00 38 | 5.0 | 13 04 | 5.1 | 09 59 | 3.7 | 22 08 | 3.9 |
| 23 | Saturday | 11 55 | 3.2 | 23 44 | 3.4 | 01 19 | 5.2 | 13 42 | 5.3 | 10 31 | 3.8 | 22 38 | 4.0 |
| 24 | Sunday | —— | — | 12 28 | 3.2 | 01 57 | 5.5 | 14 19 | 5.5 | 11 00 | 4.0 | 23 09 | 4.2 |
| 25 | Monday | 00 20 | 3.4 | 13 00 | 3.3 | 02 34 | 5.7 | 14 56 | 5.7 | 11 30 | 4.0 | 23 42 | 4.2 |
| 26 | Tuesday | 00 58 | 3.5 | 13 32 | 3.3 | 03 12 | 5.8 | 15 34 | 5.7 | —— | — | 12 05 | 4.1 |
| 27 | Wednesday | 01 38 | 3.6 | 14 07 | 3.4 | 03 51 | 5.8 | 16 14 | 5.7 | 00 20 | 4.2 | 12 46 | 4.1 |
| 28 | Thursday | 02 17 | 3.6 | 14 43 | 3.5 | 04 33 | 5.7 | 16 56 | 5.6 | 01 05 | 4.2 | 13 30 | 4.1 |
| 29 | Friday | 02 57 | 3.6 | 15 20 | 3.4 | 05 18 | 5.6 | 17 42 | 5.4 | 01 54 | 4.1 | 14 19 | 4.0 |
| 30 | Saturday | 03 37 | 3.5 | 16 01 | 3.4 | 06 07 | 5.4 | 18 32 | 5.1 | 02 49 | 3.9 | 15 14 | 3.9 |

NOTES:
*Difference of height in metres from Ordnance datum (Newlyn)
†Difference of height in metres from Ordnance datum (Dublin)
hr  hour
m  metres

## OCTOBER 1995  *continued*

| | | GREENOCK | | | LEITH | | | | DUN LAOGHAIRE | | | |
|---|---|---|---|---|---|---|---|---|---|---|---|---|
| | | hr | m ht | hr | m ht | hr | m ht | hr | m ht | hr | m ht |
| 1 | Sunday | 04 21 | 3.3 | 16 48 | 3.2 | 07 02 | 5.1 | 19 28 | 4.9 | 03 51 | 3.7 | 16 17 | 3.8 |
| 2 | Monday | 05 14 | 3.0 | 17 50 | 3.1 | 08 05 | 4.8 | 20 34 | 4.7 | 05 09 | 3.6 | 17 33 | 3.7 |
| 3 | Tuesday | 06 35 | 2.8 | 19 32 | 3.0 | 09 21 | 4.7 | 21 52 | 4.7 | 06 36 | 3.5 | 18 55 | 3.7 |
| 4 | Wednesday | 08 40 | 2.9 | 21 11 | 3.1 | 10 47 | 4.8 | 23 09 | 4.9 | 07 53 | 3.6 | 20 07 | 3.8 |
| 5 | Thursday | 09 56 | 3.1 | 22 13 | 3.4 | 11 59 | 5.1 | —— | — | 08 59 | 3.8 | 21 08 | 4.0 |
| 6 | Friday | 10 49 | 3.3 | 23 04 | 3.6 | 00 13 | 5.2 | 12 57 | 5.3 | 09 53 | 3.9 | 22 00 | 4.1 |
| 7 | Saturday | 11 34 | 3.4 | 23 49 | 3.7 | 01 07 | 5.5 | 13 44 | 5.5 | 10 39 | 4.0 | 22 43 | 4.2 |
| 8 | Sunday | —— | — | 12 15 | 3.5 | 01 53 | 5.6 | 14 23 | 5.6 | 11 18 | 4.0 | 23 18 | 4.2 |
| 9 | Monday | 00 32 | 3.7 | 12 52 | 3.5 | 02 33 | 5.7 | 14 59 | 5.6 | 11 49 | 4.0 | 23 49 | 4.1 |
| 10 | Tuesday | 01 12 | 3.6 | 13 25 | 3.5 | 03 10 | 5.7 | 15 32 | 5.6 | —— | — | 12 16 | 4.0 |
| 11 | Wednesday | 01 48 | 3.6 | 13 58 | 3.6 | 03 45 | 5.6 | 16 04 | 5.5 | 00 22 | 4.1 | 12 49 | 3.9 |
| 12 | Thursday | 02 21 | 3.5 | 14 31 | 3.6 | 04 19 | 5.4 | 16 36 | 5.3 | 01 00 | 4.0 | 13 25 | 3.9 |
| 13 | Friday | 02 54 | 3.5 | 15 06 | 3.6 | 04 53 | 5.3 | 17 10 | 5.1 | 01 41 | 3.8 | 14 05 | 3.8 |
| 14 | Saturday | 03 29 | 3.4 | 15 42 | 3.6 | 05 31 | 5.0 | 17 48 | 4.9 | 02 26 | 3.7 | 14 49 | 3.7 |
| 15 | Sunday | 04 07 | 3.2 | 16 21 | 3.4 | 06 13 | 4.8 | 18 32 | 4.7 | 03 15 | 3.5 | 15 39 | 3.5 |
| 16 | Monday | 04 52 | 3.0 | 17 07 | 3.2 | 07 01 | 4.5 | 19 22 | 4.5 | 04 15 | 3.3 | 16 42 | 3.4 |
| 17 | Tuesday | 05 47 | 2.8 | 18 03 | 3.1 | 08 00 | 4.3 | 20 27 | 4.4 | 05 34 | 3.2 | 18 00 | 3.3 |
| 18 | Wednesday | 06 55 | 2.7 | 19 07 | 3.0 | 09 31 | 4.3 | 22 04 | 4.4 | 06 51 | 3.2 | 19 12 | 3.4 |
| 19 | Thursday | 08 23 | 2.8 | 20 18 | 3.0 | 10 46 | 4.5 | 23 08 | 4.6 | 07 53 | 3.3 | 20 08 | 3.5 |
| 20 | Friday | 09 51 | 2.9 | 21 29 | 3.1 | 11 40 | 4.7 | 23 59 | 4.9 | 08 44 | 3.5 | 20 55 | 3.7 |
| 21 | Saturday | 10 38 | 3.1 | 22 23 | 3.3 | —— | — | 12 26 | 5.1 | 09 26 | 3.7 | 21 33 | 3.9 |
| 22 | Sunday | 11 17 | 3.2 | 23 08 | 3.4 | 00 43 | 5.2 | 13 08 | 5.4 | 10 00 | 3.9 | 22 09 | 4.0 |
| 23 | Monday | 11 53 | 3.3 | 23 50 | 3.5 | 01 25 | 5.5 | 13 48 | 5.6 | 10 31 | 4.0 | 22 43 | 4.2 |
| 24 | Tuesday | —— | — | 12 29 | 3.4 | 02 06 | 5.8 | 14 29 | 5.8 | 11 05 | 4.2 | 23 21 | 4.3 |
| 25 | Wednesday | 00 33 | 3.6 | 13 06 | 3.5 | 02 47 | 5.9 | 15 09 | 5.9 | 11 41 | 4.2 | —— | — |
| 26 | Thursday | 01 16 | 3.6 | 13 43 | 3.6 | 03 29 | 6.0 | 15 51 | 5.9 | 00 02 | 4.3 | 12 23 | 4.3 |
| 27 | Friday | 02 00 | 3.6 | 14 22 | 3.6 | 04 14 | 5.9 | 16 35 | 5.7 | 00 49 | 4.2 | 13 11 | 4.2 |
| 28 | Saturday | 02 42 | 3.6 | 15 02 | 3.6 | 05 01 | 5.7 | 17 22 | 5.5 | 01 40 | 4.1 | 14 02 | 4.2 |
| 29 | Sunday | 03 26 | 3.5 | 15 45 | 3.6 | 05 53 | 5.4 | 18 15 | 5.3 | 02 39 | 3.9 | 14 59 | 4.0 |
| 30 | Monday | 04 13 | 3.3 | 16 34 | 3.4 | 06 50 | 5.1 | 19 13 | 5.0 | 03 46 | 3.8 | 16 04 | 3.9 |
| 31 | Tuesday | 05 12 | 3.1 | 17 37 | 3.2 | 07 55 | 4.9 | 20 21 | 4.8 | 05 03 | 3.6 | 17 19 | 3.8 |

## NOVEMBER 1995   *High water*   GMT

| | | LONDON BRIDGE<br>*Datum of predictions<br>3.20 m below | | | | AVONMOUTH<br>*Datum of predictions<br>6.50 m below | | | | LIVERPOOL<br>*Datum of predictions<br>4.93 m below | | | | HULL (*Albert Dock*)<br>*Datum of predictions<br>3.90 m below | | | |
|---|---|---|---|---|---|---|---|---|---|---|---|---|---|---|---|---|---|
| | | hr | ht m | hr | ht m | hr | ht m | hr | ht m | hr | ht m | hr | ht m | hr | ht m | hr | ht m |
| 1 | Wednesday | 07 27 | 5.8 | 20 31 | 6.1 | 01 01 | 10.3 | 13 47 | 10.6 | 05 38 | 7.6 | 18 07 | 8.0 | — | — | 13 17 | 6.1 |
| 2 | Thursday | 09 03 | 6.0 | 21 47 | 6.4 | 02 25 | 10.5 | 15 00 | 11.1 | 06 56 | 7.8 | 19 19 | 8.2 | 01 24 | 6.3 | 14 32 | 6.3 |
| 3 | Friday | 10 13 | 6.4 | 22 51 | 6.9 | 03 35 | 11.1 | 16 06 | 11.8 | 08 00 | 8.2 | 20 19 | 8.6 | 02 38 | 6.6 | 15 36 | 6.6 |
| 4 | Saturday | 11 13 | 6.9 | 23 47 | 7.2 | 04 38 | 11.9 | 17 04 | 12.5 | 08 53 | 8.6 | 21 10 | 8.9 | 03 38 | 6.9 | 16 28 | 6.9 |
| 5 | Sunday | — | — | 12 07 | 7.2 | 05 30 | 12.5 | 17 53 | 12.9 | 09 38 | 8.9 | 21 55 | 9.2 | 04 28 | 7.2 | 17 10 | 7.1 |
| 6 | Monday | 00 38 | 7.4 | 12 55 | 7.3 | 06 14 | 13.0 | 18 34 | 13.2 | 10 19 | 9.1 | 22 35 | 9.3 | 05 12 | 7.3 | 17 46 | 7.2 |
| 7 | Tuesday | 01 23 | 7.4 | 13 38 | 7.2 | 06 52 | 13.2 | 19 12 | 13.2 | 10 56 | 9.2 | 23 12 | 9.2 | 05 52 | 7.4 | 18 19 | 7.3 |
| 8 | Wednesday | 02 02 | 7.2 | 14 17 | 7.1 | 07 28 | 13.3 | 19 49 | 13.2 | 11 30 | 9.1 | 23 46 | 9.1 | 06 30 | 7.4 | 18 52 | 7.3 |
| 9 | Thursday | 02 36 | 7.0 | 14 53 | 7.0 | 08 03 | 13.2 | 20 23 | 13.0 | — | — | 12 03 | 9.0 | 07 07 | 7.3 | 19 23 | 7.2 |
| 10 | Friday | 03 07 | 6.9 | 15 28 | 6.8 | 08 36 | 12.9 | 20 55 | 12.6 | 00 20 | 8.9 | 12 38 | 8.9 | 07 43 | 7.1 | 19 54 | 7.1 |
| 11 | Saturday | 03 37 | 6.8 | 16 02 | 6.7 | 09 07 | 12.4 | 21 26 | 12.1 | 00 56 | 8.7 | 13 13 | 8.8 | 08 17 | 6.9 | 20 24 | 6.9 |
| 12 | Sunday | 04 09 | 6.7 | 16 37 | 6.5 | 09 37 | 11.9 | 21 56 | 11.4 | 01 33 | 8.5 | 13 50 | 8.5 | 08 51 | 6.6 | 20 56 | 6.7 |
| 13 | Monday | 04 44 | 6.5 | 17 14 | 6.3 | 10 06 | 11.2 | 22 27 | 10.8 | 02 12 | 8.2 | 14 30 | 8.3 | 09 27 | 6.3 | 21 32 | 6.4 |
| 14 | Tuesday | 05 21 | 6.3 | 17 55 | 6.2 | 10 39 | 10.6 | 23 03 | 10.2 | 02 56 | 7.8 | 15 16 | 7.9 | 10 08 | 6.0 | 22 14 | 6.1 |
| 15 | Wednesday | 06 01 | 6.1 | 18 42 | 6.0 | 11 21 | 10.1 | 23 51 | 9.7 | 03 48 | 7.5 | 16 10 | 7.6 | 11 00 | 5.8 | 23 10 | 5.9 |
| 16 | Thursday | 06 50 | 5.9 | 19 38 | 5.9 | — | — | 12 18 | 9.8 | 04 50 | 7.2 | 17 14 | 7.5 | — | — | 12 17 | 5.6 |
| 17 | Friday | 07 55 | 5.9 | 20 46 | 6.0 | 00 57 | 9.5 | 13 40 | 9.9 | 06 02 | 7.3 | 18 22 | 7.7 | 00 39 | 5.7 | 13 42 | 5.8 |
| 18 | Saturday | 09 14 | 6.0 | 22 01 | 6.2 | 02 47 | 10.0 | 15 21 | 11.6 | 07 12 | 7.7 | 19 26 | 8.1 | 02 01 | 6.0 | 14 44 | 6.1 |
| 19 | Sunday | 10 28 | 6.3 | 23 08 | 6.6 | 03 57 | 10.9 | 16 21 | 11.6 | 08 09 | 8.2 | 20 22 | 8.5 | 03 00 | 6.3 | 15 36 | 6.5 |
| 20 | Monday | 11 28 | 6.7 | — | — | 04 52 | 12.0 | 17 14 | 12.5 | 08 58 | 8.7 | 21 13 | 9.0 | 03 52 | 6.7 | 16 24 | 7.0 |
| 21 | Tuesday | 00 04 | 6.9 | 12 22 | 7.0 | 05 41 | 12.9 | 18 02 | 13.2 | 09 44 | 9.2 | 22 01 | 9.4 | 04 40 | 7.1 | 17 09 | 7.3 |
| 22 | Wednesday | 00 54 | 7.2 | 13 11 | 7.2 | 06 26 | 13.5 | 18 49 | 13.7 | 10 29 | 9.6 | 22 48 | 9.7 | 05 26 | 7.4 | 17 52 | 7.6 |
| 23 | Thursday | 01 40 | 7.3 | 13 59 | 7.4 | 07 11 | 13.9 | 19 35 | 13.9 | 11 14 | 9.8 | 23 36 | 9.8 | 06 12 | 7.7 | 18 34 | 7.7 |
| 24 | Friday | 02 27 | 7.3 | 14 48 | 7.4 | 07 57 | 14.0 | 20 22 | 13.9 | — | — | 12 01 | 9.9 | 06 57 | 7.8 | 19 17 | 7.8 |
| 25 | Saturday | 03 13 | 7.2 | 15 38 | 7.4 | 08 44 | 13.8 | 21 10 | 13.6 | 00 25 | 9.7 | 12 50 | 9.8 | 07 43 | 7.7 | 20 00 | 7.8 |
| 26 | Sunday | 03 59 | 7.0 | 16 27 | 7.2 | 09 31 | 13.4 | 21 57 | 13.0 | 01 15 | 9.5 | 13 39 | 9.6 | 08 30 | 7.6 | 20 44 | 7.6 |
| 27 | Monday | 04 43 | 6.8 | 17 14 | 7.0 | 10 19 | 12.8 | 22 45 | 12.3 | 02 07 | 9.2 | 14 30 | 9.3 | 09 20 | 7.2 | 21 32 | 7.4 |
| 28 | Tuesday | 05 25 | 6.6 | 18 03 | 6.7 | 11 08 | 12.0 | 23 35 | 11.5 | 03 01 | 8.7 | 15 25 | 8.9 | 10 14 | 6.8 | 22 24 | 7.0 |
| 29 | Wednesday | 06 10 | 6.4 | 18 57 | 6.5 | — | — | 12 05 | 11.4 | 04 01 | 8.2 | 16 26 | 8.5 | 11 20 | 6.4 | 23 26 | 6.7 |
| 30 | Thursday | 07 09 | 6.2 | 20 05 | 6.4 | 00 35 | 10.9 | 13 17 | 11.0 | 05 09 | 7.9 | 17 35 | 8.1 | — | — | 12 46 | 6.2 |

## DECEMBER 1995   *High water*   GMT

| | | LONDON BRIDGE | | | | AVONMOUTH | | | | LIVERPOOL | | | | HULL (*Albert Dock*) | | | |
|---|---|---|---|---|---|---|---|---|---|---|---|---|---|---|---|---|---|
| 1 | Friday | 08 31 | 6.2 | 21 16 | 6.5 | 01 49 | 10.7 | 14 27 | 11.1 | 06 22 | 7.8 | 18 45 | 8.1 | 00 46 | 6.5 | 13 58 | 6.2 |
| 2 | Saturday | 09 43 | 6.5 | 22 20 | 6.8 | 02 57 | 10.9 | 15 30 | 11.4 | 07 29 | 7.9 | 19 50 | 8.2 | 02 02 | 6.5 | 15 01 | 6.4 |
| 3 | Sunday | 10 45 | 6.8 | 23 18 | 7.0 | 04 00 | 11.3 | 16 30 | 11.8 | 08 25 | 8.2 | 20 45 | 8.5 | 03 06 | 6.6 | 15 57 | 6.6 |
| 4 | Monday | 11 41 | 7.0 | — | — | 04 58 | 11.9 | 17 24 | 12.2 | 09 14 | 8.5 | 21 33 | 8.7 | 04 02 | 6.8 | 16 43 | 6.8 |
| 5 | Tuesday | 00 11 | 7.1 | 12 32 | 7.1 | 05 46 | 12.3 | 18 09 | 12.5 | 09 57 | 8.8 | 22 15 | 8.8 | 04 51 | 6.9 | 17 23 | 6.9 |
| 6 | Wednesday | 00 58 | 7.1 | 13 17 | 7.0 | 06 28 | 12.7 | 18 50 | 12.7 | 10 35 | 8.9 | 22 52 | 8.9 | 05 35 | 7.0 | 17 59 | 7.1 |
| 7 | Thursday | 01 39 | 6.9 | 13 58 | 6.8 | 07 06 | 12.8 | 19 28 | 12.7 | 11 10 | 9.0 | 23 28 | 8.9 | 06 14 | 7.0 | 18 32 | 7.1 |
| 8 | Friday | 02 14 | 6.8 | 14 34 | 6.7 | 07 42 | 12.8 | 20 03 | 12.6 | 11 40 | 9.0 | — | — | 06 51 | 7.0 | 19 03 | 7.2 |
| 9 | Saturday | 02 44 | 6.7 | 15 08 | 6.7 | 08 16 | 12.7 | 20 36 | 12.4 | 00 02 | 8.8 | 12 19 | 8.9 | 07 25 | 7.0 | 19 33 | 7.2 |
| 10 | Sunday | 03 14 | 6.7 | 15 43 | 6.6 | 08 48 | 12.5 | 21 09 | 12.2 | 00 37 | 8.7 | 12 54 | 8.9 | 07 58 | 6.9 | 20 04 | 7.1 |
| 11 | Monday | 03 47 | 6.7 | 16 18 | 6.6 | 09 21 | 12.2 | 21 41 | 11.8 | 01 15 | 8.6 | 13 30 | 8.7 | 08 31 | 6.8 | 20 37 | 7.0 |
| 12 | Tuesday | 04 23 | 6.6 | 16 56 | 6.5 | 09 52 | 11.8 | 22 13 | 11.4 | 01 51 | 8.4 | 14 08 | 8.6 | 09 07 | 6.6 | 21 12 | 6.8 |
| 13 | Wednesday | 05 00 | 6.5 | 17 35 | 6.5 | 10 24 | 11.3 | 22 47 | 10.9 | 02 30 | 8.2 | 14 48 | 8.4 | 09 45 | 6.4 | 21 52 | 6.6 |
| 14 | Thursday | 05 38 | 6.4 | 18 19 | 6.4 | 11 02 | 10.9 | 23 27 | 10.5 | 03 15 | 7.9 | 15 35 | 8.1 | 10 29 | 6.2 | 22 38 | 6.3 |
| 15 | Friday | 06 22 | 6.3 | 19 09 | 6.3 | 11 48 | 10.5 | — | — | 04 08 | 7.7 | 16 30 | 7.9 | 11 21 | 6.0 | 23 34 | 6.1 |
| 16 | Saturday | 07 18 | 6.1 | 20 08 | 6.2 | 00 18 | 10.2 | 12 46 | 10.3 | 05 10 | 7.5 | 17 33 | 7.9 | — | — | 12 30 | 6.0 |
| 17 | Sunday | 08 28 | 6.1 | 21 17 | 6.3 | 01 23 | 10.1 | 14 05 | 10.5 | 06 18 | 7.7 | 18 38 | 8.1 | 00 51 | 6.1 | 13 51 | 6.1 |
| 18 | Monday | 09 43 | 6.2 | 22 28 | 6.5 | 02 56 | 10.6 | 15 34 | 11.2 | 07 23 | 8.0 | 19 41 | 8.4 | 02 12 | 6.3 | 14 55 | 6.4 |
| 19 | Tuesday | 10 53 | 6.5 | 23 32 | 6.7 | 04 11 | 11.5 | 16 39 | 12.1 | 08 23 | 8.6 | 20 42 | 8.8 | 03 15 | 6.6 | 15 52 | 6.8 |
| 20 | Wednesday | 11 54 | 6.8 | — | — | 05 11 | 12.5 | 17 38 | 12.9 | 09 17 | 9.1 | 21 38 | 9.3 | 04 13 | 6.9 | 16 45 | 7.1 |
| 21 | Thursday | 00 28 | 7.0 | 12 49 | 7.1 | 06 05 | 13.3 | 18 30 | 13.5 | 10 08 | 9.5 | 22 31 | 9.6 | 05 08 | 7.3 | 17 33 | 7.4 |
| 22 | Friday | 01 19 | 7.1 | 13 40 | 7.3 | 06 55 | 13.8 | 19 21 | 13.8 | 10 58 | 9.8 | 23 23 | 9.8 | 05 58 | 7.5 | 18 19 | 7.7 |
| 23 | Saturday | 02 07 | 7.2 | 14 32 | 7.4 | 07 45 | 14.1 | 20 11 | 14.0 | 11 48 | 10.0 | — | — | 06 47 | 7.7 | 19 03 | 7.9 |
| 24 | Sunday | 02 55 | 7.2 | 15 23 | 7.5 | 08 34 | 14.1 | 21 00 | 13.9 | 00 14 | 9.8 | 12 38 | 10.1 | 07 34 | 7.8 | 19 46 | 8.0 |
| 25 | Monday | 03 42 | 7.2 | 16 13 | 7.4 | 09 22 | 13.9 | 21 47 | 13.6 | 01 04 | 9.7 | 13 27 | 10.0 | 08 20 | 7.7 | 20 30 | 8.0 |
| 26 | Tuesday | 04 28 | 7.1 | 17 01 | 7.3 | 10 09 | 13.5 | 22 32 | 13.0 | 01 55 | 9.5 | 14 16 | 9.7 | 09 07 | 7.4 | 21 16 | 7.8 |
| 27 | Wednesday | 05 11 | 6.9 | 17 47 | 7.1 | 10 54 | 12.8 | 23 16 | 12.2 | 02 44 | 9.1 | 15 05 | 9.3 | 09 56 | 7.1 | 22 04 | 7.4 |
| 28 | Thursday | 05 54 | 6.8 | 18 35 | 6.8 | 11 40 | 12.1 | — | — | 03 34 | 8.6 | 15 56 | 8.8 | 10 51 | 6.6 | 22 57 | 7.0 |
| 29 | Friday | 06 41 | 6.6 | 19 30 | 6.6 | 00 01 | 11.5 | 12 33 | 11.4 | 04 30 | 8.1 | 16 54 | 8.3 | 11 58 | 6.3 | — | — |
| 30 | Saturday | 07 46 | 6.4 | 20 38 | 6.4 | 00 55 | 10.9 | 13 39 | 10.9 | 05 36 | 7.7 | 18 02 | 7.9 | 00 02 | 6.7 | 13 11 | 6.1 |
| 31 | Sunday | 09 06 | 6.3 | 21 45 | 6.4 | 02 06 | 10.6 | 14 47 | 10.8 | 06 48 | 7.6 | 19 13 | 7.8 | 01 18 | 6.4 | 14 17 | 6.1 |

## NOVEMBER 1995  *continued*

| | | GREENOCK | | | | LEITH | | | | DUN LAOGHAIRE | | | | NOTES: |
|---|---|---|---|---|---|---|---|---|---|---|---|---|---|---|
| | | *Datum of predictions 1.62 m below | | | | *Datum of predictions 2.90 m below | | | | †Datum of predictions 0.20 m above | | | | *Difference of height in metres from Ordnance datum (Newlyn) |
| | | hr | ht m | hr | ht m | hr | ht m | hr | ht m | hr | ht m | hr | ht m | †Difference of height in metres from Ordnance datum (Dublin) |
| 1 | Wednesday | 06 35 | 2.9 | 19 09 | 3.1 | 09 10 | 4.8 | 21 37 | 4.8 | 06 21 | 3.6 | 18 36 | 3.8 | hr  hour |
| 2 | Thursday | 08 16 | 3.0 | 20 42 | 3.2 | 10 27 | 4.8 | 22 48 | 5.0 | 07 34 | 3.7 | 19 45 | 3.9 | m  metres |
| 3 | Friday | 09 31 | 3.1 | 21 47 | 3.4 | 11 35 | 5.0 | 23 49 | 5.2 | 08 38 | 3.8 | 20 47 | 3.9 | |
| 4 | Saturday | 10 24 | 3.3 | 22 40 | 3.5 | —— | — | 12 31 | 5.2 | 09 32 | 3.9 | 21 41 | 4.0 | |
| 5 | Sunday | 11 08 | 3.4 | 23 26 | 3.5 | 00 42 | 5.3 | 13 19 | 5.4 | 10 19 | 4.0 | 22 26 | 4.1 | |
| 6 | Monday | 11 47 | 3.5 | —— | — | 01 29 | 5.4 | 13 59 | 5.5 | 10 58 | 4.0 | 23 04 | 4.0 | |
| 7 | Tuesday | 00 09 | 3.5 | 12 24 | 3.5 | 02 09 | 5.5 | 14 34 | 5.5 | 11 30 | 4.0 | 23 34 | 4.0 | |
| 8 | Wednesday | 00 49 | 3.5 | 12 58 | 3.6 | 02 46 | 5.5 | 15 05 | 5.5 | 11 57 | 4.0 | —— | — | |
| 9 | Thursday | 01 25 | 3.4 | 13 31 | 3.6 | 03 20 | 5.4 | 15 35 | 5.4 | 00 05 | 4.0 | 12 28 | 4.0 | |
| 10 | Friday | 01 58 | 3.4 | 14 04 | 3.7 | 03 53 | 5.3 | 16 06 | 5.4 | 00 42 | 3.9 | 13 02 | 4.0 | |
| 11 | Saturday | 02 32 | 3.3 | 14 38 | 3.7 | 04 28 | 5.2 | 16 40 | 5.2 | 01 20 | 3.8 | 13 40 | 3.9 | |
| 12 | Sunday | 03 07 | 3.3 | 15 14 | 3.6 | 05 06 | 5.1 | 17 19 | 5.1 | 02 01 | 3.7 | 14 21 | 3.8 | |
| 13 | Monday | 03 45 | 3.2 | 15 51 | 3.5 | 05 48 | 4.9 | 18 02 | 4.9 | 02 47 | 3.6 | 15 07 | 3.7 | |
| 14 | Tuesday | 04 28 | 3.1 | 16 33 | 3.4 | 06 34 | 4.7 | 18 50 | 4.7 | 03 40 | 3.4 | 15 58 | 3.6 | |
| 15 | Wednesday | 05 19 | 2.9 | 17 23 | 3.2 | 07 24 | 4.6 | 19 43 | 4.6 | 04 41 | 3.3 | 16 59 | 3.4 | |
| 16 | Thursday | 06 21 | 2.8 | 18 23 | 3.1 | 08 22 | 4.5 | 20 48 | 4.5 | 05 53 | 3.3 | 18 07 | 3.4 | |
| 17 | Friday | 07 28 | 2.8 | 19 28 | 3.1 | 09 37 | 4.5 | 22 06 | 4.6 | 07 02 | 3.3 | 19 13 | 3.5 | |
| 18 | Saturday | 08 42 | 2.9 | 20 36 | 3.1 | 10 48 | 4.7 | 23 11 | 4.8 | 07 58 | 3.5 | 20 07 | 3.6 | |
| 19 | Sunday | 09 48 | 3.1 | 21 40 | 3.2 | 11 43 | 5.0 | —— | — | 08 44 | 3.7 | 20 55 | 3.8 | |
| 20 | Monday | 10 38 | 3.2 | 22 34 | 3.4 | 00 03 | 5.1 | 12 33 | 5.3 | 09 25 | 3.9 | 21 38 | 4.0 | |
| 21 | Tuesday | 11 21 | 3.4 | 23 23 | 3.5 | 00 52 | 5.5 | 13 19 | 5.6 | 10 03 | 4.1 | 22 21 | 4.2 | |
| 22 | Wednesday | —— | — | 12 03 | 3.5 | 01 39 | 5.7 | 14 04 | 5.8 | 10 42 | 4.2 | 23 04 | 4.3 | |
| 23 | Thursday | 00 11 | 3.6 | 12 44 | 3.6 | 02 25 | 5.9 | 14 48 | 5.9 | 11 24 | 4.3 | 23 49 | 4.3 | |
| 24 | Friday | 00 59 | 3.6 | 13 26 | 3.7 | 03 12 | 6.0 | 15 32 | 6.0 | —— | — | 12 07 | 4.4 | |
| 25 | Saturday | 01 46 | 3.6 | 14 08 | 3.8 | 03 59 | 6.0 | 16 18 | 5.9 | 00 39 | 4.2 | 12 56 | 4.4 | |
| 26 | Sunday | 02 33 | 3.6 | 14 51 | 3.8 | 04 48 | 5.8 | 17 07 | 5.7 | 01 32 | 4.1 | 13 49 | 4.3 | |
| 27 | Monday | 03 20 | 3.5 | 15 35 | 3.7 | 05 41 | 5.5 | 18 00 | 5.4 | 02 31 | 4.0 | 14 46 | 4.2 | |
| 28 | Tuesday | 04 10 | 3.4 | 16 24 | 3.6 | 06 39 | 5.3 | 18 59 | 5.2 | 03 36 | 3.9 | 15 49 | 4.1 | |
| 29 | Wednesday | 05 07 | 3.2 | 17 22 | 3.4 | 07 41 | 5.0 | 20 04 | 5.0 | 04 45 | 3.7 | 16 58 | 3.9 | |
| 30 | Thursday | 06 13 | 3.1 | 18 34 | 3.3 | 08 47 | 4.8 | 21 12 | 4.9 | 05 56 | 3.7 | 18 08 | 3.9 | |

## DECEMBER 1995  *continued*

| | | GREENOCK | | | | LEITH | | | | DUN LAOGHAIRE | | | |
|---|---|---|---|---|---|---|---|---|---|---|---|---|---|
| | | hr | m | hr | m | hr | m | hr | m | hr | m | hr | m |
| 1 | Friday | 07 29 | 3.1 | 19 59 | 3.2 | 09 55 | 4.8 | 22 18 | 4.9 | 07 05 | 3.7 | 19 17 | 3.8 |
| 2 | Saturday | 08 48 | 3.1 | 21 14 | 3.3 | 11 00 | 4.9 | 23 18 | 5.0 | 08 09 | 3.7 | 20 20 | 3.8 |
| 3 | Sunday | 09 49 | 3.2 | 22 13 | 3.3 | 11 57 | 5.0 | —— | — | 09 05 | 3.8 | 21 17 | 3.9 |
| 4 | Monday | 10 38 | 3.3 | 23 03 | 3.4 | 00 13 | 5.1 | 12 49 | 5.1 | 09 54 | 3.9 | 22 06 | 3.9 |
| 5 | Tuesday | 11 21 | 3.4 | 23 48 | 3.3 | 01 03 | 5.2 | 13 33 | 5.2 | 10 35 | 4.0 | 22 46 | 3.9 |
| 6 | Wednesday | 11 59 | 3.5 | —— | — | 01 46 | 5.2 | 14 11 | 5.3 | 11 10 | 4.0 | 23 20 | 3.9 |
| 7 | Thursday | 00 30 | 3.3 | 12 36 | 3.6 | 02 25 | 5.3 | 14 44 | 5.4 | 11 39 | 4.0 | 23 50 | 3.8 |
| 8 | Friday | 01 07 | 3.3 | 13 10 | 3.6 | 03 00 | 5.3 | 15 15 | 5.4 | —— | — | 12 09 | 4.0 |
| 9 | Saturday | 01 41 | 3.2 | 13 43 | 3.7 | 03 34 | 5.2 | 15 46 | 5.4 | 00 23 | 3.8 | 12 43 | 4.0 |
| 10 | Sunday | 02 14 | 3.2 | 14 16 | 3.7 | 04 09 | 5.2 | 16 21 | 5.3 | 01 00 | 3.8 | 13 17 | 4.0 |
| 11 | Monday | 02 48 | 3.2 | 14 50 | 3.7 | 04 47 | 5.1 | 16 59 | 5.2 | 01 38 | 3.7 | 13 56 | 3.9 |
| 12 | Tuesday | 03 25 | 3.2 | 15 26 | 3.6 | 05 27 | 5.0 | 17 40 | 5.1 | 02 19 | 3.7 | 14 38 | 3.8 |
| 13 | Wednesday | 04 05 | 3.1 | 16 05 | 3.5 | 06 11 | 4.9 | 18 25 | 4.9 | 03 06 | 3.6 | 15 24 | 3.7 |
| 14 | Thursday | 04 50 | 3.0 | 16 48 | 3.4 | 06 57 | 4.8 | 19 13 | 4.8 | 03 57 | 3.5 | 16 14 | 3.6 |
| 15 | Friday | 05 42 | 3.0 | 17 37 | 3.2 | 07 47 | 4.7 | 20 06 | 4.7 | 04 54 | 3.4 | 17 10 | 3.6 |
| 16 | Saturday | 06 40 | 2.9 | 18 36 | 3.1 | 08 43 | 4.6 | 21 07 | 4.7 | 05 56 | 3.4 | 18 11 | 3.5 |
| 17 | Sunday | 07 45 | 2.9 | 19 44 | 3.1 | 09 48 | 4.7 | 22 16 | 4.8 | 07 01 | 3.5 | 19 16 | 3.6 |
| 18 | Monday | 08 55 | 3.0 | 20 57 | 3.2 | 10 56 | 4.9 | 23 22 | 5.0 | 07 59 | 3.6 | 20 17 | 3.7 |
| 19 | Tuesday | 10 01 | 3.1 | 22 03 | 3.3 | 11 57 | 5.1 | —— | — | 08 51 | 3.8 | 21 12 | 3.9 |
| 20 | Wednesday | 10 54 | 3.3 | 23 01 | 3.4 | 00 21 | 5.3 | 12 52 | 5.4 | 09 39 | 4.1 | 22 03 | 4.1 |
| 21 | Thursday | 11 42 | 3.5 | 23 54 | 3.5 | 01 16 | 5.6 | 13 42 | 5.7 | 10 25 | 4.2 | 22 52 | 4.2 |
| 22 | Friday | —— | — | 12 27 | 3.7 | 02 07 | 5.8 | 14 31 | 5.9 | 11 10 | 4.4 | 23 39 | 4.3 |
| 23 | Saturday | 00 46 | 3.5 | 13 13 | 3.8 | 02 57 | 6.0 | 15 17 | 6.0 | 11 55 | 4.5 | —— | — |
| 24 | Sunday | 01 37 | 3.6 | 13 57 | 3.9 | 03 46 | 6.0 | 16 04 | 6.0 | 00 29 | 4.2 | 12 44 | 4.5 |
| 25 | Monday | 02 26 | 3.6 | 14 41 | 3.9 | 04 35 | 5.8 | 16 52 | 5.8 | 01 21 | 4.2 | 13 34 | 4.4 |
| 26 | Tuesday | 03 13 | 3.6 | 15 26 | 3.9 | 05 27 | 5.6 | 17 45 | 5.6 | 02 15 | 4.1 | 14 29 | 4.3 |
| 27 | Wednesday | 04 00 | 3.5 | 16 11 | 3.8 | 06 22 | 5.4 | 18 41 | 5.4 | 03 13 | 3.9 | 15 27 | 4.2 |
| 28 | Thursday | 04 48 | 3.4 | 17 00 | 3.6 | 07 18 | 5.1 | 19 39 | 5.1 | 04 15 | 3.8 | 16 29 | 4.0 |
| 29 | Friday | 05 38 | 3.3 | 17 54 | 3.4 | 08 17 | 4.9 | 20 39 | 4.9 | 05 21 | 3.7 | 17 34 | 3.8 |
| 30 | Saturday | 06 33 | 3.2 | 18 58 | 3.2 | 09 17 | 4.7 | 21 42 | 4.8 | 06 26 | 3.6 | 18 41 | 3.7 |
| 31 | Sunday | 07 38 | 3.1 | 20 24 | 3.1 | 10 19 | 4.7 | 22 44 | 4.7 | 07 30 | 3.6 | 19 45 | 3.7 |

# World Geographical Statistics

## THE EARTH

The shape of the Earth is that of an oblate spheroid or solid of revolution whose meridian sections are ellipses, whilst the sections at right angles are circles.

DIMENSIONS

Equatorial diameter = 12,756.28 km (7,926.38 miles)
Polar diameter = 12,713.50 km (7,899.80 miles)
Equatorial circumference = 40,075.01 km (24,901.45 miles)
Polar circumference = 40,008.00 km (24,859.82 miles)

The equatorial circumference is divided into 360 degrees of longitude, which is measured in degrees, minutes and seconds east or west of the Greenwich meridian (0°) to 180° (the meridian 180° E. coinciding with 180° W.). This was internationally ratified in 1884.

Distance north and south of the Equator is measured in degrees, minutes and seconds of latitude. The Equator is 0°, the North Pole is 90° N. and the South Pole is 90° S. The Tropics lie at 23° 26′ N. (Tropic of Cancer) and 23° 26′ S. (Tropic of Capricorn). The Arctic Circle lies at 66° 34′ N. and the Antarctic Circle at 66° 34′ S. (NB The Tropics and the Arctic and Antarctic circles are of variable latitude due to the mean obliquity of the Ecliptic; the values given are for 1995.5.)

AREA, ETC.

The surface area of the Earth is 510,069,120 km² (196,938,800 miles²), of which the water area is 70.92 per cent and the land area is 29.08 per cent.

The velocity of a given point of the Earth's surface at the Equator exceeds 1,000 miles an hour (24,901.45 miles in 24 hours, viz 1,037.56 mph); the Earth's velocity in its orbit round the Sun averages 66,629 mph (584,081.400 miles in 365.256363 days). The Earth is distant from the Sun 92,955,900 miles, on average.
*Source*: Royal Greenwich Observatory

## OCEAN AREAS

| | *Area* km² | miles² |
|---|---|---|
| Pacific | 166,240,000 | 64,186,300 |
| Atlantic | 86,550,000 | 33,420,000 |
| Indian | 73,427,000 | 28,350,500 |
| Arctic | 13,223,700 | 5,105,700 |

GREATEST OCEAN DEPTHS

| *Greatest depth location* | *Depth* metres | feet |
|---|---|---|
| Mariana Trench (Pacific) | 10,924 | 35,840 |
| Puerto Rico Trench (Atlantic) | 8,605 | 28,232 |
| Java Trench (Indian) | 7,125 | 23,376 |
| Eurasian Basin (Arctic) | 5,450 | 17,880 |

## SEA AREAS

| | *Area* km² | miles² |
|---|---|---|
| South China | 2,974,600 | 1,148,500 |
| Caribbean | 2,515,900 | 971,400 |
| Mediterranean | 2,509,900 | 969,100 |
| Bering | 2,226,100 | 873,000 |
| Gulf of Mexico | 1,507,600 | 582,100 |
| Okhotsk | 1,392,000 | 537,500 |
| Japan | 1,015,000 | 391,100 |
| Hudson Bay | 730,100 | 281,900 |
| East China | 664,600 | 256,600 |
| Andaman | 564,880 | 218,100 |
| Black Sea | 507,900 | 196,100 |
| Red Sea | 453,000 | 174,900 |
| North Sea | 427,100 | 164,900 |
| Baltic Sea | 382,000 | 147,500 |
| Yellow Sea | 294,000 | 113,500 |
| Persian Gulf | 230,000 | 88,800 |

GREATEST SEA DEPTHS

| | *Maximum depth* metres | feet |
|---|---|---|
| Caribbean | 8,605 | 28,232 |
| East China | 7,507 | 24,629 |
| South China | 7,258 | 23,812 |
| Mediterranean | 5,150 | 16,896 |
| Andaman | 4,267 | 14,000 |
| Bering | 3,936 | 12,913 |
| Gulf of Mexico | 3,504 | 11,496 |
| Okhotsk | 3,365 | 11,040 |
| Japan | 3,053 | 10,016 |
| Red Sea | 2,266 | 7,434 |
| Black Sea | 2,212 | 7,257 |
| North Sea | 439 | 1,440 |
| Hudson Bay | 111 | 364 |
| Baltic Sea | 90 | 295 |
| Yellow Sea | 73 | 240 |
| Persian Gulf | 73 | 240 |

## THE CONTINENTS

There are six geographic continents, though America is often divided politically into North and Central America, and South America.

AFRICA is surrounded by sea except for the narrow isthmus of Suez in the north-east, through which is cut the Suez Canal. The Equator passes through the middle of the continent. Its extreme longitudes are 17° 20′ W. at Cape Verde, Senegal, and 51° 24′ E. at Ras Hafun, Somalia. The extreme latitudes are 37° 20′ N. at Cape Blanc, Tunisia, and 34° 50′ S. at Cape Agulhas, South Africa, about 4,400 miles apart.

NORTH AMERICA, including Mexico, is surrounded by ocean except in the south, where the isthmian states of CENTRAL AMERICA link North America with South America.

Its extreme longitudes are 168° 5' W. at Cape Prince of Wales, Alaska, and 55° 40' W. at Cape Charles, Newfoundland. The extreme continental latitudes are Point Barrow, Alaska (71°22' N.) and 14°22' N. at Ocós in the south of Mexico. The West Indies, about 65,000 square miles in area, extend from about 27° N. to 10° N. latitude.

SOUTH AMERICA lies mostly in the southern hemisphere; the Equator passes through the north of the continent. It is surrounded by ocean except where it is joined to Central America in the north by the narrow isthmus through which is cut the Panama Canal. Its extreme longitudes are 34° 47' W. at Cape Branco in Brazil and 81° 20' W. at Punta Pariña, Peru. The extreme latitudes are 12° 25' N. at Punta Gallinas, Colombia, and 55° 59' S. at Cape Horn, Chile.

ANTARCTICA lies almost entirely within the Antarctic Circle (66° 34' S.) and is the largest of the world's glaciated areas. The continent has an area of about 5.5 million square miles, 99 per cent of which is permanently ice-covered. The ice amounts to some 7.2 million cubic miles and represents more than 90 per cent of the world's fresh water. The environment is too hostile for unsupported human habitation. *See also* Countries of the World.

ASIA is the largest continent and occupies almost a third of the world's land surface. The extreme longitudes are about 26° E. on the west coast of Asia Minor and 169° 40' W. at Mys Dežneva (East Cape), Russia, a distance of about 6,000 miles. Its extreme northern latitude is 77° 45' N. at Cape Čeljuskin, Russia, and it extends over 5,000 miles south to about 1° 15' N. of the Equator. The islands of Japan, the Philippines and Indonesia ring the continent to the east and south-east.

AUSTRALIA is the smallest of the continents and lies in the southern hemisphere. It is entirely surrounded by ocean. Its extreme longitudes are 113° 9' E. at Steep Point and 153° 38' E. at Cape Byron. The extreme latitudes are 10° 40' S. at Cape York and 39° S. at South East Point.

EUROPE, including European Russia, is the smallest continent in the northern hemisphere. Its extreme latitudes are 71° 11' N. at North Cape in Norway, and 36° 23' N. at Cape Matapan in southern Greece, a distance of about 2,400 miles. Its breadth from Cape da Roca in Portugal (9° 30' W.) in the west to the Urals in the east is about 3,300 miles. The division between Europe and Asia is generally regarded as being the Ural Mountains and, in the south, the valley of the Manych, which stretches from the Caspian Sea to the mouth of the Don.

| | *Area* km² | miles² |
|---|---|---|
| Asia | 43,998,000 | 16,988,000 |
| *America | 41,918,000 | 16,185,000 |
| Africa | 29,800,000 | 11,506,000 |
| Antarctica | c.13,600,000 | c.5,500,000 |
| †Europe | 9,699,000 | 3,745,000 |
| Australia | 7,618,493 | 2,941,526 |

*North and Central America has an area of 24,255,000 km²
  (9,365,000 miles²)
†Includes 5,571,000 km² (2,151,000 miles²) of former USSR territory
  west of the Ural Mountains

## GLACIATED AREAS

It is estimated that 15,600,000 km² (6,020,000 miles²) or 10.51 per cent of the world's land surface is permanently covered with ice.

| | *Area* km² | miles² |
|---|---|---|
| South Polar regions | 13,597,000 | 5,250,000 |
| North Polar regions (incl. Greenland or Kalaallit Nunaat) | 1,965,000 | 758,500 |
| Alaska-Canada | 58,800 | 22,700 |
| Asia | 37,800 | 14,600 |
| South America | 11,900 | 4,600 |
| Europe | 10,700 | 4,128 |
| New Zealand | 984 | 380 |
| Africa | 238 | 92 |

## PENINSULAS

| | *Area* km² | miles² |
|---|---|---|
| Arabian | 3,250,000 | 1,250,000 |
| Southern Indian | 2,072,000 | 800,000 |
| Alaskan | 1,500,000 | 580,000 |
| Labradorian | 1,300,000 | 500,000 |
| Scandinavian | 800,300 | 309,000 |
| Iberian | 584,000 | 225,500 |

## LARGEST ISLANDS

| *Island (and Ocean)* | *Area* km² | miles² |
|---|---|---|
| Greenland (Arctic) | 2,175,500 | 840,000 |
| New Guinea (Pacific) | 792,500 | 306,000 |
| Borneo (Pacific) | 725,450 | 280,100 |
| Madagascar (Indian) | 587,040 | 226,658 |
| Baffin Island (Arctic) | 476,200 | 183,810 |
| Sumatra (Indian) | 427,350 | 165,000 |
| Honshu (Pacific) | 227,413 | 87,805 |
| *Great Britain (Atlantic) | 218,040 | 84,186 |
| Ellesmere Island (Arctic) | 212,745 | 82,119 |
| Victoria Island (Arctic) | 212,250 | 81,930 |
| Sulawesi (Celebes) (Indian) | 178,700 | 69,000 |
| South Island, NZ (Pacific) | 151,010 | 58,305 |
| Java (Indian) | 126,650 | 48,900 |
| Cuba (Atlantic) | 114,525 | 44,218 |
| North Island, NZ (Pacific) | 114,050 | 44,035 |
| Newfoundland (Atlantic) | 108,855 | 42,030 |
| Luzon (Pacific) | 105,880 | 40,880 |
| Iceland (Atlantic) | 103,000 | 39,770 |
| Mindanao (Pacific) | 95,247 | 36,775 |
| Ireland (Atlantic) | 82,462 | 31,839 |

*Mainland only

## LARGEST DESERTS

| | Area (approx.) km² | miles² |
|---|---|---|
| The Sahara (N. Africa) | 9,000,000 | 3,500,000 |
| Australian Desert | 1,550,000 | 600,000 |
| Arabian Desert | 1,300,000 | 500,000 |
| *The Gobi (Mongolia/China) | 1,300,000 | 500,000 |
| Kalahari Desert (Botswana/ Namibia/S. Africa) | 583,000 | 225,000 |
| Sonoran Desert (USA/Mexico) | 310,000 | 120,000 |
| Namib Desert (Namibia) | 310,000 | 120,000 |
| †Kara Kum (Turkmenistan) | 310,000 | 120,000 |
| Thar Desert (India/Pakistan) | 260,000 | 100,000 |
| Somali Desert (Somalia) | 260,000 | 100,000 |
| †Kyzyl Kum (Kazakhstan/ Uzbekistan) | 260,000 | 100,000 |
| Atacama Desert (Chile) | 180,000 | 70,000 |
| Dasht-e Lut (Iran) | 52,000 | 20,000 |
| Mojave Desert (USA) | 35,000 | 13,500 |
| Desierto de Sechura (Peru) | 26,000 | 10,000 |

*Including the Takla Makan – 320,000 km² (125,000 miles²)
†Together known as the Turkestan Desert

## DEEPEST DEPRESSIONS

| | Maximum depth below sea level metres | feet |
|---|---|---|
| Dead Sea (Jordan/Israel) | 395 | 1,296 |
| Turfan Depression (Sinkiang, China) | 153 | 505 |
| Qattara Depression (Egypt) | 132 | 436 |
| Mangyshlak peninsula (Kazakhstan) | 131 | 433 |
| Danakil Depression (Ethiopia) | 116 | 383 |
| Death Valley (California, USA) | 86 | 282 |
| Salton Sink (California, USA) | 71 | 235 |
| W. of Ustyurt plateau (Kazakhstan) | 70 | 230 |
| Prikaspiyskaya Nizmennost' (Russia/ Kazakhstan) | 67 | 220 |
| Lake Sarykamysh (Uzbekistan/ Turkmenistan) | 45 | 148 |
| El Faiyûm (Egypt) | 44 | 147 |
| Valdies peninsula, Lago Enriquillo (Dominican Republic) | 40 | 131 |

The world's largest exposed depression is the Prikaspiyskaya Nizmennost' covering the hinterland of the northern third of the Caspian Sea, which is itself 28 m (92 ft) below sea level

Western Antarctica and Central Greenland largely comprise crypto-depressions under ice burdens. The Antarctic Wilkes subglacial basin has a bedrock 2,341 m (7,680 ft) below sea-level. In Greenland (lat. 73° N., long. 39° W.) the bedrock is 365 m (1,197 ft) below sea-level

## LONGEST MOUNTAIN RANGES

| Range (location) | Length km | miles |
|---|---|---|
| Cordillera de Los Andes (W. South America) | 7,200 | 4,500 |
| Rocky Mountains (W. North America) | 4,800 | 3,000 |
| Himalaya-Karakoram-Hindu Kush (S. Central Asia) | 3,800 | 2,400 |
| Great Dividing Range (E. Australia) | 3,600 | 2,250 |
| Trans-Antarctic Mts (Antarctica) | 3,500 | 2,200 |
| Atlantic Coast Range (E. Brazil) | 3,000 | 1,900 |
| West Sumatran-Javan Range (Indonesia) | 2,900 | 1,800 |
| Aleutian Range (Alaska and NW Pacific) | 2,650 | 1,650 |
| Tien Shan (S. Central Asia) | 2,250 | 1,400 |
| Central New Guinea Range (Irian Jaya/ Papua New Guinea) | 2,000 | 1,250 |

## HIGHEST MOUNTAINS

The world's 8,000-metre mountains (with six subsidiary peaks) are all in the Himalaya-Karakoram-Hindu Kush range.

| Mountain | Height metres | feet |
|---|---|---|
| Mt Everest* | 8,848 | 29,028 |
| K2 | 8,607 | 28,238 |
| Kangchenjunga | 8,597 | 28,208 |
| Lhotse | 8,511 | 27,923 |
| Makalu I | 8,481 | 27,824 |
| Lhotse Shar | 8,383 | 27,504 |
| Dhaulagiri I | 8,167 | 26,795 |
| Manaslu I (Kutang I) | 8,156 | 26,760 |
| Cho Oyu | 8,153 | 26,750 |
| Nanga Parbat (Diamir) | 8,125 | 26,660 |
| Annapurna I | 8,091 | 26,546 |
| Gasherbrum I (Hidden Peak) | 8,068 | 26,470 |
| Broad Peak I | 8,046 | 26,400 |
| Shisha Pangma (Gosainthan) | 8,046 | 26,398 |
| Gasherbrum II | 8,034 | 26,360 |
| Annapurna East | 8,010 | 26,280 |
| Makalu South-East | 8,010 | 26,280 |
| Broad Peak Central | 8,000 | 26,246 |

*Named after Sir George Everest (1790–1866), Surveyor-General of India 1830–43, in 1863. He pronounced his name Eve-rest

The culminating summits in the other major mountain ranges are:

| Mountain (range or country) | Height metres | feet |
|---|---|---|
| Pik Pobeda (Tien Shan) | 7,439 | 24,406 |
| Cerro Aconcagua (Cordillera de Los Andes) | 6,960 | 22,834 |
| Mt McKinley, S. Peak (Alaska Range) | 6,194 | 20,320 |
| Kilimanjaro (Tanzania) | 5,894 | 19,340 |
| Hkakabo Razi (Myanmar) | 5,881 | 19,296 |
| Citlaltépetl (Orizaba) (Sierra Madre Oriental, Mexico) | 5,699 | 18,700 |

| Mountain (range or country) | Height metres | feet |
|---|---|---|
| El'brus, *W. Peak* (Caucasus) | 5,663 | 18,481 |
| Vinson Massif (E. Antarctica) | 4,897 | 16,067 |
| Puncak Jaya (Central New Guinea Range) | 4,884 | 16,023 |
| Mt Blanc (Alps) | 4,807 | 15,771 |
| Klyuchevskaya Sopka (Kamchatka peninsula, Russia) | 4,750 | 15,584 |
| Ras Dashan (Ethiopian Highlands) | 4,620 | 15,158 |
| Zard Küh (Zagros Mts, Iran) | 4,547 | 14,921 |
| Mt Kirkpatrick (Trans Antarctic) | 4,529 | 14,860 |
| Mt Belukha (Altai Mts, Russia/ Kazakhstan) | 4,505 | 14,783 |
| Mt Elbert (Rocky Mountains) | 4,400 | 14,433 |
| Mt Rainier (Cascade Range, N. America) | 4,392 | 14,410 |
| Nevado de Colima (Sierra Madre Occidental, Mexico) | 4,268 | 14,003 |
| Jebel Toubkal (Atlas Mts, N. Africa) | 4,165 | 13,665 |
| Kinabalu (Crocker Range, Borneo) | 4,101 | 13,455 |
| Kerinci (West Sumatran-Javan Range, Indonesia) | 3,800 | 12,467 |
| Jabal an Nabī Shu'ayb (N. Tihāmat, Yemen) | 3,760 | 12,336 |
| Teotepec (Sierra Madre del Sur, Mexico) | 3,703 | 12,149 |
| Thaban Ntlenyana (Drakensberg, South Africa) | 3,482 | 11,425 |
| Pico de Bandeira (Atlantic Coast Range) | 2,890 | 9,482 |
| Shishaldin (Aleutian Range) | 2,861 | 9,387 |
| Kosciusko (Great Dividing Range) | 2,228 | 7,310 |

## HIGHEST VOLCANOES

| Volcano (last major eruption) and location | Height metres | feet |
|---|---|---|
| Guallatiri (1993), Andes, Chile | 6,060 | 19,882 |
| Lascar (1991), Andes, Chile | 5,990 | 19,652 |
| Cotopaxi (1975), Andes, Ecuador | 5,897 | 19,347 |
| Tupungatito (1986), Andes, Chile | 5,640 | 18,504 |
| Nevado del Ruiz, Colombia (1985, 1992) | 5,400 | 17,716 |
| Sangay (1988), Andes, Ecuador | 5,230 | 17,159 |
| Guagua Pichincha (1988), Andes, Ecuador | 4,784 | 15,696 |
| Purace (1977), Colombia | 4,756 | 15,601 |
| Klyuchevskaya Sopka (1991), Kamchatka peninsula, Russia | 4,750 | 15,584 |
| Nevado de Colima (1991), Mexico | 4,268 | 14,003 |
| Galeras (1991), Colombia | 4,266 | 13,996 |
| Mauna Loa (1987), Hawaii Is. | 4,170 | 13,680 |
| Cameroon (1982), Cameroon | 4,070 | 13,354 |
| Acatenango (1972), Guatemala | 3,960 | 12,992 |
| Fuego (1991), Guatemala | 3,835 | 12,582 |
| Kerinci (1987), Sumatra, Indonesia | 3,800 | 12,467 |
| Erebus (1991), Ross Island, Antarctica | 3,794 | 12,450 |
| Tacana (1988), Guatemala | 3,780 | 12,400 |
| Santiaguito (1902, 1991), Guatemala | 3,768 | 12,362 |
| Rindjani (1966), Lombok, Indonesia | 3,726 | 12,224 |
| Semeru (1991), Java, Indonesia | 3,675 | 12,060 |
| Nyirgongo (1977), Zaïre | 3,475 | 11,400 |

| Volcano (last major eruption) and location | Height metres | feet |
|---|---|---|
| Koryakskaya (1957), Kamchatka, Russia | 3,456 | 11,339 |
| Irazú (1992), Costa Rica | 3,432 | 11,260 |
| Slamet (1988), Java, Indonesia | 3,428 | 11,247 |
| Spurr (1953), Alaska, USA | 3,374 | 11,069 |
| Mt Etna (1169, 1669, 1993), Sicily, Italy | 3,369 | 11,053 |
| Raung, Java, Indonesia (1991) | 3,322 | 10,932 |
| Shiveluch (1964), Kamchatka, Russia | 3,283 | 10,771 |
| Turrialba (1992), Costa Rica | 3,246 | 10,650 |
| Agung (1964), Bali, Indonesia | 3,142 | 10,308 |
| Llaima (1990), Chile | 3,128 | 10,239 |
| Redoubt (1991), Alaska, USA | 3,108 | 10,197 |
| Tjareme (1938), Java, Indonesia | 3,078 | 10,098 |
| On-Taka (1991), Japan | 3,063 | 10,049 |
| Nyamuragira (1991), Zaïre | 3,056 | 10,028 |
| Iliamna (1978), Alaska, USA | 3,052 | 10,016 |

OTHER NOTABLE VOLCANOES

| | Height metres | feet |
|---|---|---|
| Tambora (1815), Sumbawa, Indonesia | 2,850 | 9,353 |
| Mt St Helens (1980, 1986, 1991), Washington State, USA | 2,530 | 8,300 |
| Pinatubo (1991), Philippines | 1,758 | 5,770 |
| Hekla (1981, 1991), Iceland | 1,491 | 4,892 |
| Mt Pelée (1902), Martinique | 1,397 | 4,583 |
| Mt Unzen (1792, 1991), Kyushu, Japan | 1,360 | 4,462 |
| Vesuvius (AD 79, 1944), Italy | 1,280 | 4,198 |
| Kilauea (1993), Hawaii, USA | 1,242 | 4,077 |
| Stromboli (1993), Lipari Is., Italy | 926 | 3,038 |
| Krakatau (1883), Sunda Strait, Indonesia | 804 | 2,640 |
| Santorini (Thíra) (1628 BC), Aegean Sea, Greece | 566 | 1,857 |
| Vulcano (Monte Aria), Lipari Is., Italy | 499 | 1,637 |
| Tristan da Cunha (1961), South Atlantic | 243 | 800 |
| Surtsey (1963–7), off Iceland | 173 | 568 |

## LARGEST LAKES

The areas of some of these lakes are subject to seasonal variation.

| | Area km² | miles² | Length km | miles |
|---|---|---|---|---|
| Caspian Sea – Iran/ Azerbaijan/Russia/ Turkmenistan/ Kazakhstan | 371,000 | 143,000 | 1,171 | 728 |
| *Michigan – Huron, USA/Canada | 117,610 | 45,300 | 1,010 | 627 |
| Superior – Canada/USA | 82,413 | 31,820 | 563 | 350 |
| Victoria – Uganda/ Tanzania/Kenya | 69,500 | 26,828 | 362 | 225 |
| Aral Sea – Kazakhstan/ Uzbekistan | 40,400 | 15,600 | 331 | 235 |

| | Area km² | miles² | Length km | miles |
|---|---|---|---|---|
| Tanganyika – Zaïre/ Tanzania/Zambia/ Burundi | 32,900 | 12,700 | 675 | 420 |
| †Baykal (*Baikal*) – Russia | 31,500 | 12,162 | 635 | 395 |
| Great Bear – Canada | 31,328 | 12,096 | 309 | 192 |
| Malawi – Tanzania/ Malawi/Mozambique | 28,880 | 11,150 | 580 | 360 |
| Great Slave – Canada | 28,570 | 11,031 | 480 | 298 |
| Erie – Canada/USA | 25,670 | 9,910 | 388 | 241 |
| Winnipeg – Canada | 24,390 | 9,417 | 428 | 266 |
| Ontario – Canada/USA | 19,550 | 7,550 | 310 | 193 |
| Balkhash – Kazakhstan | 18,427 | 7,115 | 605 | 376 |
| Ladozhskoye (*Ladoga*) – Russia | 17,700 | 6,835 | 200 | 124 |

UNITED KINGDOM (BY COUNTRY)

| | | | | |
|---|---|---|---|---|
| Lough Neagh – Northern Ireland | 381.73 | 147.39 | 28.90 | 18.00 |
| Loch Lomond – Scotland | 71.12 | 27.46 | 36.44 | 22.64 |
| Windermere – England | 14.74 | 5.69 | 16.90 | 10.50 |
| Lake Vyrnwy – Wales (artificial) | 4.53 | 1.75 | 7.56 | 4.70 |
| Llyn Tegid (*Bala*) – Wales (natural) | 4.38 | 1.69 | 5.80 | 3.65 |

*Lakes Michigan and Huron are regarded as lobes of the same lake. The Michigan lobe has an area of 57,750 km² (22,300 miles²) and the Huron lobe an area of 59,570 km² (23,000 miles²)
†World's deepest lake (1,940 m/6,365 ft)

---

LONGEST RIVERS

| River (source and outflow) | Length km | miles |
|---|---|---|
| Nile (*Bahr-el-Nil*) (R. Luvironza, Burundi – E. Mediterranean Sea) | 6,670 | 4,145 |
| Amazon (*Amazonas*) (Lago Villafro, Peru – S. Atlantic Ocean) | 6,448 | 4,007 |
| Mississippi-Missouri (R. Red Rock, Montana – Gulf of Mexico) | 5,970 | 3,710 |
| Yenisey-Angara (W. Mongolia – Kara Sea) | 5,540 | 3,442 |
| Yangtze-Kiang (*Chang Jiang*) (Kunlun Mts, W. China – Yellow Sea) | 5,530 | 3,436 |
| Ob'-Irtysh (W. Mongolia – Kara Sea) | 5,410 | 3,362 |
| Huang He (*Yellow River*) (Bayan Har Shan range, central China – Yellow Sea) | 4,830 | 3,000 |
| Zaïre (*Congo*) (R. Lualaba, Zaïre-Zambia – S. Atlantic Ocean) | 4,700 | 2,920 |
| Amur-Argun (R. Argun, Khingan Mts, N. China – Sea of Okhotsk) | 4,670 | 2,903 |
| Lena-Kirenga (R. Kirenga, W. of Lake Baykal – Arctic Ocean) | 4,345 | 2,700 |
| Mackenzie-Peace (Tatlatui Lake, British Columbia – Beaufort Sea) | 4,240 | 2,635 |
| Mekong (Lants'ang, Tibet – South China Sea) | 4,184 | 2,600 |
| Niger (Loma Mts, Guinea – Gulf of Guinea, E. Atlantic Ocean) | 4,184 | 2,600 |
| Rió de la Plata-Paraná (R. Paranáiba, central Brazil – S. Atlantic Ocean) | 4,000 | 2,485 |

---

| River (source and outflow) | Length km | miles |
|---|---|---|
| Murray-Darling (SE Queensland – Lake Alexandrina, S. Australia) | 3,750 | 2,330 |
| Volga (Valdai plateau – Caspian Sea) | 3,690 | 2,293 |
| Zambezi (NW Zambia – S. Indian Ocean) | 3,540 | 2,200 |

OTHER NOTABLE RIVERS

| | | |
|---|---|---|
| St Lawrence (Minnesota, USA – Gulf of St Lawrence) | 3,130 | 1,945 |
| Ganges-Brahmaputra (R. Matsang, SW Tibet – Bay of Bengal) | 2,900 | 1,800 |
| Indus (R. Sengge, SW Tibet – N. Arabian Sea) | 2,880 | 1,790 |
| Danube (*Donau*) (Black Forest, SW Germany – Black Sea) | 2,850 | 1,770 |
| Tigris-Euphrates (R. Murat, E. Turkey – Persian Gulf) | 2,740 | 1,700 |
| Irrawaddy (R. Mali Hka, N. Burma – Andaman Sea) | 2,090 | 1,300 |
| Don (SE of Novomoskovsk – Sea of Azov) | 1,969 | 1,224 |

BRITISH ISLES

| | | |
|---|---|---|
| Shannon (Co. Cavan, Rep. of Ireland – Atlantic Ocean) | 386 | 240 |
| Severn (Powys, Wales – Bristol Channel) | 354 | 220 |
| Thames (Gloucestershire, England – North Sea) | 346 | 215 |
| Tay (Perthshire, Scotland – North Sea) | 188 | 117 |
| Clyde (Lanarkshire, Scotland – Firth of Clyde) | 158 | 98½ |
| Tweed (Peeblesshire, Scotland – North Sea) | 155 | 96½ |
| Bann (Upper and Lower) (Co. Down, N. Ireland – Atlantic Ocean) | 122 | 76 |

---

GREATEST WATERFALLS – BY HEIGHT

| Waterfall (river and location) | Total drop metres | feet | Greatest single leap metres | feet |
|---|---|---|---|---|
| Angel (Carrao, Venezuela) | 979 | 3,212 | 807 | 2,648 |
| Tugela (Tugela, S. Africa) | 947 | 3,110 | 410 | 1,350 |
| Utigård (Jostedal Glacier, Norway) | 800 | 2,625 | 600 | 1,970 |
| Mongefossen (Monge, Norway) | 774 | 2,540 | — | — |
| Yosemite (Yosemite Creek, USA) | 739 | 2,425 | 435 | 1,430 |
| Østre Mardøla Foss (Mardals, Norway) | 656 | 2,154 | 296 | 974 |
| Tyssestrengane (Tysso, Norway) | 646 | 2,120 | 289 | 948 |
| Cuquenán (Arabópó, Venezuela) | 610 | 2,000 | — | — |
| Sutherland (Arthur, NZ) | 580 | 1,904 | 248 | 815 |
| *Kjellfossen (Naeröfjord, Norway) | 561 | 1,841 | 149 | 490 |

*Volume often so low the fall atomizes into a 'bridal veil'

| Waterfall (river and location) | Total drop | | Greatest single leap | |
|---|---|---|---|---|
| | metres | feet | metres | feet |

BRITISH ISLES (BY COUNTRY)

| | | | | |
|---|---|---|---|---|
| Eas a' Chuàl Aluinn (Glas Bheinn, Sutherland, Scotland) | 200 | 658 | | |
| Powerscourt Falls (Dargle, Co. Wicklow, Rep. of Ireland) | 106 | 350 | | |
| Pistyll-y-Llyn (Powys/ Dyfed border, Wales) | c.73 | 230– 240 | | (cascades) |
| Pistyll Rhyadr (Clwyd/ Powys border, Wales) | 71.5 | 235 | | (single leap) |
| Caldron Snout (R. Tees, Cumbria/Durham, England) | 60 | 200 | | (cascades) |

## GREATEST WATERFALLS – BY VOLUME

| Waterfall (river and location) | Mean annual flow | |
|---|---|---|
| | m³/sec | galls/sec |
| Boyoma (R. Lualaba, Zaïre) | c.17,000 | c.3,750,000 |
| Khône (Mekong, Laos) | 11,500 | 2,530,000 |
| Niagara (Horseshoe) (R. Niagara/Lake Erie–Lake Ontario) | 3,000 | 670,000 |
| Paulo Afonso (R. São Francisco, Brazil) | 2,800 | 625,000 |
| Urubupunga (Alto Parañá, Brazil) | 2,800 | 625,000 |
| Cataratas del Iguazú (R. Iguaçu, Brazil/ Argentina) | 1,725 | 380,000 |
| Patos-Maribando (Rio Grande, Brazil) | 1,500 | 330,000 |
| Victoria (Mosi-oa-tunya) (R. Zambezi, Zambia/ Zimbabwe) | 1,000 | 220,000 |
| Churchill (R. Churchill, Canada) | 975 | 215,000 |
| Kaieteur (R. Potaro, Guyana) | 660 | 145,000 |

## TALLEST DAMS

| | metres | feet |
|---|---|---|
| Rogun, Tajikistan | 335 | 1,098 |
| Nurek, Russia | 300 | 984 |
| Grand Dixance, Switzerland | 285 | 935 |
| *Longtan, China | 285 | 935 |
| Inguri, Russia | 272 | 892 |
| Chicoasén, Mexico | 261 | 856 |
| *Tehri, India | 261 | 856 |

*under construction

The world's most massive embankment dam is the Tarbela in Pakistan, containing 148.5 million cubic metres/194.2 million cubic yards of material. The Syncrude Tailings dam in Canada will have a volume of 540 million cubic metres/ 706 million cubic yards

## TALLEST INHABITED BUILDINGS

| Building and city | Height | |
|---|---|---|
| | metres | feet |
| Sears Tower, Chicago[1] | 443 | 1,454 |
| World Trade Center, New York[2] | 417 | 1,368 |
| Empire State Building, New York[3] | 381 | 1,250 |
| Amoco Building, Chicago | 346 | 1,136 |
| John Hancock Center, Chicago | 343 | 1,127 |
| Nation's Bank Tower, Atlanta | 320 | 1,050 |
| Chrysler Building, New York | 319 | 1,046 |
| Bank of China, Hong Kong[4] | 315 | 1,033 |
| First Interstate World Center, Los Angeles | 310 | 1,017 |
| Vegas World Tower | 308 | 1,012 |
| Central Plaza, Hong Kong[5] | 306.5 | 1,005 |
| Texas Commerce Tower, Houston | 305 | 1,001 |
| State University, Moscow[6] | 302 | 994 |

[1] With TV antennae 475.18 m/1,559 ft
[2] With TV antennae, 521.2 m/1,710 ft; second tower, 415 m/1,362 ft
[3] With TV tower (added 1950–1), 430.9 m/1,414 ft
[4] With steel mast, 367.4 m/1,205 ft
[5] With steel mast, 374 m/1,227 ft
[6] Including spire

## TALLEST STRUCTURES

| Structure and location | Height | |
|---|---|---|
| | metres | feet |
| *Warszawa Radio Mast, Konstantynow, Poland | 646 | 2,120 |
| KTHI-TV Mast, Fargo, North Dakota | 629 | 2,063 |
| CN Tower, Metro Centre, Toronto, Canada | 555 | 1,822 |

*Collapsed during renovation, August 1991

## LONGEST BRIDGES – BY SPAN

| Bridge and location | Length | |
|---|---|---|
| | metres | feet |

SUSPENSION SPANS

| | | |
|---|---|---|
| Humber Estuary, Humberside, England | 1,410 | 4,626 |
| Verrazano Narrows, Brooklyn–Staten I, USA | 1,298 | 4,260 |
| Golden Gate, San Francisco Bay, USA | 1,280 | 4,200 |
| Mackinac Straits, Michigan, USA | 1,158 | 3,800 |
| Bosporus, Istanbul, Turkey | 1,074 | 3,524 |
| George Washington, Hudson River, New York City, USA | 1,067 | 3,500 |
| Ponte 25 Abril (Tagus), Lisbon, Portugal | 1,013 | 3,323 |
| Firth of Forth (road), nr Edinburgh, Scotland | 1,006 | 3,300 |
| Severn River, Severn Estuary, England | 988 | 3,240 |

The Akashi-Kaikyo road bridge (1988–98) will have a main span of 1,990 m/6,528 ft

| Bridge and location | Length | |
|---|---|---|
| | metres | feet |

CANTILEVER SPANS

Pont de Québec (rail-road), St

| Lawrence, Canada | 548.6 | 1,800 |
| Ravenswood, W. Virginia, USA | 525.1 | 1,723 |
| Firth of Forth (rail), nr Edinburgh, Scotland | 521.2 | 1,710 |
| Minato, Osaka, Japan | 510.0 | 1,673 |
| Commodore Barry, Chester, Pennsylvania, USA | 494.3 | 1,622 |
| Greater New Orleans, Louisiana, USA | 480.0 | 1,575 |
| Howrah (rail-road), Calcutta, India | 457.2 | 1,500 |

STEEL ARCH SPANS

| New River Gorge, Fayetteville, W. Virginia, USA | 518.2 | 1,700 |
| Bayonne (Kill van Kull), Bayonne, NJ– Staten I, USA | 503.5 | 1,652 |
| Sydney Harbour, Sydney, Australia | 502.9 | 1,650 |

The 'floating' bridging at Evergreen, Seattle, Washington State, USA, is 3,839 m/12,596 ft long
The longest stretch of bridgings of any kind are those between Mandeville and Jefferson, Louisiana, USA; the Lake Pontchartrain Causeway II 38.422 km/23.87 miles and Causeway I 38.352 km/23.83 miles

## LONGEST VEHICULAR TUNNELS

| Tunnel and location | Length | |
|---|---|---|
| | km | miles |
| *Seikan (rail), Tsugaru Channel, Japan | 53.90 | 33.49 |
| *Channel Tunnel, Cheriton, Kent– Sangatte, Calais | 49.94 | 31.03 |
| Moscow metro, Belyaevo–Medved Kovo, Moscow, Russia | 30.70 | 19.07 |
| Northern line tube, East Finchley– Morden, London | 27.84 | 17.30 |
| Oshimizu, Honshū, Japan | 22.17 | 13.78 |
| Simplon II (rail), Brigue, Switzerland– Iselle, Italy | 19.82 | 12.31 |
| Simplon I (rail), Brigue, Switzerland– Iselle, Italy | 19.80 | 12.30 |
| Shin-Kanmon (rail), Kanmon Strait, Japan | 18.68 | 11.61 |
| Great Appennine (rail), Vernio, Italy | 18.49 | 11.49 |
| St Gotthard (road), Göschenen– Airolo, Switzerland | 16.32 | 10.14 |
| Rokko (rail), Ōsaka–Kōbe, Japan | 16.09 | 10.00 |

*Sub-aqueous

The longest non-vehicular tunnelling in the world is the Delaware Aqueduct in New York State, USA, constructed in 1937–44 to a length of 168.9 km/105 miles

BRITISH RAIL TUNNELS

| | miles | yards |
|---|---|---|
| Severn, Bristol – Newport | 4 | 484 |
| Totley, Manchester – Sheffield | 3 | 950 |
| Standedge, Manchester – Huddersfield | 3 | 66 |
| Sodbury, Swindon – Bristol | 2 | 924 |
| Disley, Stockport – Sheffield | 2 | 346 |

| | miles | yards |
|---|---|---|
| Ffestiniog, Llandudno – Blaenau Ffestiniog | 2 | 338 |
| Bramhope, Leeds – Harrogate | 2 | 241 |
| Cowburn, Manchester – Sheffield | 2 | 182 |

## LONGEST SHIP CANALS

| Canal (opening date) | Length | | Min. depth | |
|---|---|---|---|---|
| | km | miles | metres | feet |
| White Sea-Baltic (formerly Stalin) (1933) Canalized river; canal 51.5 km/32 miles | 227 | 141.00 | 5.0 | 16.5 |
| *Suez (1869) Links Red and Mediterranean Seas | 162 | 100.60 | 12.9 | 42.3 |
| V. I. Lenin Volga-Don (1952) Links Black and Caspian Seas | 100 | 62.20 | n/a | n/a |
| Kiel (or North Sea) (1895) Links North and Baltic Seas | 98 | 60.90 | 13.7 | 45.0 |
| *Houston (1940) Links inland city with sea | 91 | 56.70 | 10.4 | 34.0 |
| Alphonse XIII (1926) Gives Seville access to sea | 85 | 53.00 | 7.6 | 25.0 |
| Panama (1914) Links Pacific Ocean and Caribbean Sea; lake chain, 78.9 km/49 miles dug | 82 | 50.71 | 12.5 | 41.0 |
| Manchester Ship (1894) Links city with Irish Channel | 64 | 39.70 | 8.5 | 28.0 |
| Welland (1931) Circumvents Niagara Falls and Rapids | 45 | 28.00 | 8.8 | 29.0 |
| Brussels (Rupel Sea) (1922) Renders Brussels an inland port | 32 | 19.80 | 6.4 | 21.0 |

*Has no locks

The first section of China's Grand Canal, running 1,780 km/1,107 miles from Beijing to Hangchou, was opened AD 610 but in undredged parts is today only 1.8 m/6 ft deep
The longest boat canal in the world is the Volga-Baltic canal from Astrakhan to St Petersburg with 2,300 route km/1,850 miles

# Distances from London by Air

The list of the distances in statute miles from London, Heathrow, to various cities (airport) abroad has been supplied by the publishers of *IATA/ Serco-IAL Ltd Air Distances Manual*, Southall, Middx.

| To | Miles |
|---|---|
| Abidjan | 3,197 |
| Abu Dhabi | 3,425 |
| Addis Ababa | 3,675 |
| Adelaide | 10,111 |
| Aden | 3,670 |
| Algiers | 1,035 |
| Amman (Queen Alia) | 2,287 |
| Amsterdam | 230 |
| Ankara | 1,770 |
| Athens | 1,500 |
| Atlanta | 4,198 |
| Auckland | 11,404 |
| Baghdad | 2,551 |
| Bahrain | 3,163 |
| Baku | 2,485 |
| Bangkok | 5,928 |
| Barbados | 4,193 |
| Barcelona | 712 |
| Basle | 447 |
| Beijing/Peking | 5,063 |
| Beirut | 2,161 |
| Belfast (Aldergrove) | 325 |
| Belgrade | 1,056 |
| Berlin (Tegel) | 588 |
| Bermuda | 3,428 |
| Berne | 476 |
| Bogota | 5,262 |
| Bombay | 4,478 |
| Boston | 3,255 |
| Brasilia | 5,452 |
| Bratislava | 817 |
| Brisbane | 10,273 |
| Brussels | 217 |
| Bucharest (Otopeni) | 1,307 |
| Budapest | 923 |
| Buenos Aires | 6,915 |
| Cairo | 2,194 |
| Calcutta | 4,958 |
| Calgary | 4,357 |
| Canberra | 10,563 |
| Cape Town | 6,011 |
| Caracas | 4,639 |
| Casablanca | 1,300 |
| Chicago (O'Hare) | 3,941 |
| Cologne | 331 |
| Colombo | 5,411 |
| Copenhagen | 608 |
| Dakar | 2,706 |
| Dallas (Fort Worth) | 4,736 |
| Dallas (Lovefield) | 4,732 |
| Damascus | 2,223 |
| Dar-es-Salaam | 4,662 |
| Darwin | 8,613 |
| Delhi | 4,180 |

| To | Miles |
|---|---|
| Denver | 4,655 |
| Detroit | 3,754 |
| Dhahran | 3,143 |
| Dhaka | 4,976 |
| Doha | 3,253 |
| Dubai | 3,414 |
| Dublin | 279 |
| Durban | 5,937 |
| Düsseldorf | 310 |
| Entebbe | 4,033 |
| Frankfurt | 406 |
| Freetown | 3,046 |
| Geneva | 468 |
| Gibraltar | 1,084 |
| Gothenburg (Landvetter) | 664 |
| Hamburg | 463 |
| Harare | 5,156 |
| Havana | 4,647 |
| Helsinki (Vantaa) | 1,148 |
| Hobart | 10,826 |
| Ho Chi Minh City | 6,345 |
| Hong Kong | 5,990 |
| Honolulu | 7,220 |
| Houston (Intercontinental) | 4,821 |
| Houston (William P. Hobby) | 4,837 |
| Islamabad | 3,767 |
| Istanbul | 1,560 |
| Jakarta | 7,295 |
| Jeddah | 2,947 |
| Johannesburg | 5,634 |
| Kabul | 3,558 |
| Karachi | 3,935 |
| Kathmandu | 4,570 |
| Khartoum | 3,071 |
| Kiev (Borispol) | 1,357 |
| Kiev (Julyany) | 1,337 |
| Kingston, Jamaica | 4,668 |
| Kuala Lumpur | 6,557 |
| Kuwait | 2,903 |
| Lagos | 3,107 |
| Larnaca | 2,036 |
| Lima | 6,303 |
| Lisbon | 972 |
| Lomé | 3,129 |
| Los Angeles | 5,439 |
| Madras | 5,113 |
| Madrid | 773 |
| Malta | 1,305 |
| Manila | 6,685 |
| Marseille | 614 |
| Mauritius | 6,075 |
| Melbourne (Essendon) | 10,504 |
| Melbourne (Tullamarine) | 10,499 |
| Mexico City | 5,529 |
| Miami | 4,414 |
| Milan (Linate) | 609 |
| Minsk | 1,176 |
| Montego Bay | 4,687 |
| Montevideo | 6,841 |
| Montreal (Mirabel) | 3,241 |
| Moscow (Sheremetievo) | 1,557 |

| To | Miles |
|---|---|
| Munich (Franz Josef Strauss) | 584 |
| Muscat | 3,621 |
| Nairobi | 4,248 |
| Naples | 1,011 |
| Nassau | 4,333 |
| New York (J. F. Kennedy) | 3,440 |
| Nice | 645 |
| Oporto | 806 |
| Oslo (Fornebu) | 722 |
| Ottawa | 3,321 |
| Palma, Majorca | 836 |
| Paris (Charles de Gaulle) | 215 |
| Paris (Le Bourget) | 215 |
| Paris (Orly) | 227 |
| Perth, Australia | 9,008 |
| Port of Spain | 4,404 |
| Prague | 649 |
| Pretoria | 5,602 |
| Reykjavik | 1,167 |
| Rhodes | 1,743 |
| Rio de Janeiro | 5,745 |
| Riyadh | 3,067 |
| Rome (Fiumicino) | 895 |
| St John's, Newfoundland | 2,308 |
| St Petersburg | 1,314 |
| Salzburg | 651 |
| San Francisco | 5,351 |
| Sao Paulo | 5,892 |
| Sarajevo | 1,017 |
| Seoul | 5,507 |
| Shanghai | 5,725 |
| Shannon | 369 |
| Singapore | 6,756 |
| Sofia | 1,266 |
| Stockholm (Arlanda) | 908 |
| Suva | 10,119 |
| Sydney | 10,568 |
| Tangier | 1,120 |
| Tehran | 2,741 |
| Tel Aviv | 2,227 |
| Tokyo (Narita) | 5,956 |
| Toronto | 3,544 |
| Tripoli | 1,468 |
| Tunis | 1,137 |
| Turin (Caselle) | 570 |
| Ulan Bator | 4,340 |
| Valencia | 826 |
| Vancouver | 4,707 |
| Venice (Tessera) | 715 |
| Vienna (Schwechat) | 790 |
| Vladivostok | 5,298 |
| Warsaw | 912 |
| Washington | 3,665 |
| Wellington | 11,692 |
| Yangon/Rangoon | 5,582 |
| Yokohama (Aomori) | 5,647 |
| Zagreb | 848 |
| Zürich | 490 |

# The United Kingdom

The United Kingdom comprises Great Britain (England, Wales and Scotland) and Northern Ireland. The Isle of Man and the Channel Islands are Crown dependencies with their own legislative systems, and not a part of the United Kingdom.

## AREA AS AT 31 MARCH 1981

| | Land miles² | km² | *Inland water miles² | km² | Total miles² | km² |
|---|---|---|---|---|---|---|
| United Kingdom | 93,006 | 240,883 | 1,242 | 3,218 | 94,248 | 244,101 |
| England | 50,058 | 129,652 | 293 | 758 | 50,351 | 130,410 |
| Wales | 7,965 | 20,628 | 50 | 130 | 8,015 | 20,758 |
| Scotland | 29,767 | 77,097 | 653 | 1,692 | 30,420 | 78,789 |
| †Northern Ireland | 5,215 | 13,506 | 246 | 638 | 5,461 | 14,144 |
| Isle of Man | 221 | 572 | — | — | 221 | 572 |
| Channel Islands | 75 | 194 | — | — | 75 | 194 |

*Excluding tidal water
†Excluding certain tidal waters that are parts of statutory areas in Northern Ireland

## POPULATION

The first official census of population in England, Wales and Scotland was taken in 1801 and a census has been taken every ten years since, except in 1941 when there was no census because of war. The last official census in the United Kingdom was taken on 21 April 1991 and the next is due in April 2001.

The first official census of population in Ireland was taken in 1841. However, all figures given below refer only to the area which is now Northern Ireland. Figures for Northern Ireland in 1921 and 1931 are estimates based on the censuses taken in 1926 and 1937 respectively.

Estimates of the population of England before 1801, calculated from the number of baptisms, burials and marriages, are:

| | | | |
|---|---|---|---|
| 1570 | 4,160,221 | 1670 | 5,773,646 |
| 1600 | 4,811,718 | 1700 | 6,045,008 |
| 1630 | 5,600,517 | 1750 | 6,517,035 |

| | United Kingdom | | | England and Wales | | | Scotland | | | Northern Ireland | | |
|---|---|---|---|---|---|---|---|---|---|---|---|---|
| *Thousands* | Total | Male | Female | Total | Male | Female | Total | Male | Female | Total | Male | Female |
| CENSUS RESULTS 1801–1991 | | | | | | | | | | | | |
| 1801 | — | — | — | 8,893 | 4,255 | 4,638 | 1,608 | 739 | 869 | — | — | — |
| 1811 | 13,368 | 6,368 | 7,000 | 10,165 | 4,874 | 5,291 | 1,806 | 826 | 980 | — | — | — |
| 1821 | 15,472 | 7,498 | 7,974 | 12,000 | 5,850 | 6,150 | 2,092 | 983 | 1,109 | — | — | — |
| 1831 | 17,835 | 8,647 | 9,188 | 13,897 | 6,771 | 7,126 | 2,364 | 1,114 | 1,250 | — | — | — |
| 1841 | 20,183 | 9,819 | 10,364 | 15,914 | 7,778 | 8,137 | 2,620 | 1,242 | 1,378 | 1,649 | 800 | 849 |
| 1851 | 22,259 | 10,855 | 11,404 | 17,928 | 8,781 | 9,146 | 2,889 | 1,376 | 1,513 | 1,443 | 698 | 745 |
| 1861 | 24,525 | 11,894 | 12,631 | 20,066 | 9,776 | 10,290 | 3,062 | 1,450 | 1,612 | 1,396 | 668 | 728 |
| 1871 | 27,431 | 13,309 | 14,122 | 22,712 | 11,059 | 11,653 | 3,360 | 1,603 | 1,757 | 1,359 | 647 | 712 |
| 1881 | 31,015 | 15,060 | 15,955 | 25,974 | 12,640 | 13,335 | 3,736 | 1,799 | 1,936 | 1,305 | 621 | 684 |
| 1891 | 34,264 | 16,593 | 17,671 | 29,003 | 14,060 | 14,942 | 4,026 | 1,943 | 2,083 | 1,236 | 590 | 646 |
| 1901 | 38,237 | 18,492 | 19,745 | 32,528 | 15,729 | 16,799 | 4,472 | 2,174 | 2,298 | 1,237 | 590 | 647 |
| 1911 | 42,082 | 20,357 | 21,725 | 36,070 | 17,446 | 18,625 | 4,761 | 2,309 | 2,452 | 1,251 | 603 | 648 |
| 1921 | 44,027 | 21,033 | 22,994 | 37,887 | 18,075 | 19,811 | 4,882 | 2,348 | 2,535 | 1,258 | 610 | 648 |
| 1931 | 46,038 | 22,060 | 23,978 | 39,952 | 19,133 | 20,819 | 4,843 | 2,326 | 2,517 | 1,243 | 601 | 642 |
| 1951 | 50,225 | 24,118 | 26,107 | 43,758 | 21,016 | 22,742 | 5,096 | 2,434 | 2,662 | 1,371 | 668 | 703 |
| 1961 | 52,709 | 25,481 | 27,228 | 46,105 | 22,304 | 23,801 | 5,179 | 2,483 | 2,697 | 1,425 | 694 | 731 |
| 1971 | 55,515 | 26,952 | 28,562 | 48,750 | 23,683 | 25,067 | 5,229 | 2,515 | 2,714 | 1,536 | 755 | 781 |
| 1981 | 55,848 | 27,104 | 28,742 | 49,155 | 23,873 | 25,281 | 5,131 | 2,466 | 2,664 | *1,533 | 750 | 783 |
| 1991 | 56,467 | 27,344 | 29,123 | 49,890 | 24,182 | 25,707 | 4,999 | 2,392 | 2,606 | 1,578 | 769 | 809 |
| †RESIDENT POPULATION: PROJECTIONS (MID-YEAR) | | | | | | | | | | | | |
| 2001 | 59,719 | 29,335 | 30,383 | 52,885 | 26,003 | 26,882 | 5,148 | 2,504 | 2,643 | 1,686 | 828 | 859 |
| 2011 | 61,110 | 30,158 | 30,952 | 54,299 | 26,820 | 27,479 | 5,078 | 2,483 | 2,595 | 1,733 | 855 | 878 |
| 2021 | 61,980 | 30,657 | 31,324 | 55,129 | 27,289 | 27,841 | 5,049 | 2,477 | 2,573 | 1,802 | 891 | 910 |
| 2031 | 62,096 | 30,680 | 31,417 | 55,240 | 27,308 | 27,933 | 4,995 | 2,451 | 2,544 | 1,861 | 921 | 940 |

*figures include 44,500 non-enumerated persons
† projections are 1991 based

*Source:* HMSO – *Annual Abstract 1994*; OPCS – Census reports

ISLANDS: Census Results 1901–91

| | Isle of Man | | | Jersey | | | *Guernsey | | |
|---|---|---|---|---|---|---|---|---|---|
| | Total | Male | Female | Total | Male | Female | Total | Male | Female |
| 1901 | 54,752 | 25,496 | 29,256 | 52,576 | 23,940 | 28,636 | 40,446 | 19,652 | 20,794 |
| 1911 | 52,016 | 23,937 | 28,079 | 51,898 | 24,014 | 27,884 | 41,858 | 20,661 | 21,197 |
| 1921 | 60,284 | 27,329 | 32,955 | 49,701 | 22,438 | 27,263 | 38,315 | 18,246 | 20,069 |
| 1931 | 49,308 | 22,443 | 26,865 | 50,462 | 23,424 | 27,038 | 40,643 | 19,659 | 20,984 |
| 1951 | 55,123 | 25,749 | 29,464 | 57,296 | 27,282 | 30,014 | 43,652 | 21,221 | 22,431 |
| 1961 | 48,151 | 22,060 | 26,091 | 57,200 | 27,200 | 30,000 | 45,068 | 21,671 | 23,397 |
| 1971 | 56,289 | 26,461 | 29,828 | 72,532 | 35,423 | 37,109 | 51,458 | 24,792 | 26,666 |
| 1981 | 64,679 | 30,901 | 33,778 | 77,000 | 37,000 | 40,000 | 53,313 | 25,701 | 27,612 |
| 1991 | 69,788 | 33,693 | 36,095 | 84,082 | 40,862 | 43,220 | 58,867 | 28,297 | 30,570 |

* Population of Guernsey, Herm, Jethou and Lithou. Figures for 1901–71 record all persons present on census night; census figures for 1981 and 1991 record all persons resident in the islands on census night

Source: 1991 Census

## RESIDENT POPULATION

### Mid-Year Estimate

| | 1982 | 1992 |
|---|---|---|
| United Kingdom | 56,306,000 | 57,998,000 |
| England | 46,794,000 | 48,378,000 |
| Wales | 2,807,000 | 2,899,000 |
| Scotland | 5,167,000 | 5,111,000 |
| Northern Ireland | 1,538,000 | 1,610,000p |

Source: HMSO – Annual Abstract of Statistics 1994

### By Age and Sex 1992

| Males | Under 16 | 65 and Over |
|---|---|---|
| United Kingdom | 6,083,000 | 3,665,000 |
| England | 5,039,000 | 3,082,000 |
| Wales | 306,000 | 201,000 |
| Scotland | 525,000 | 301,000 |
| Northern Ireland | 212,000p | 81,000p |

| Females | Under 16 | 60 and Over |
|---|---|---|
| United Kingdom | 5,764,000 | 6,956,000 |
| England | 4,772,000 | 5,807,000 |
| Wales | 290,000 | 377,000 |
| Scotland | 500,000 | 611,000 |
| Northern Ireland | 202,000p | 160,000p |

p provisional
Source: HMSO – Population Trends 76

### By Ethnic Group (1991 Census (Great Britain))

| Ethnic group | Estimated population | Percentage |
|---|---|---|
| Caribbean | 500,000 | 16.6 |
| African | 212,000 | 7 |
| Other black | 178,000 | 5.9 |
| Indian | 840,000 | 27.9 |
| Pakistani | 477,000 | 15.8 |
| Bangladeshi | 163,000 | 5.4 |
| Chinese | 157,000 | 5.2 |
| Other Asian | 198,000 | 6.6 |
| Other | 290,000 | 9.6 |
| Total ethnic minority groups | 3,015,000 | 100 |
| White | 51,874,000 | — |
| All ethnic groups | 54,889,000 | — |

Source: HMSO – Population Trends 72

### Average Density

| | Persons per hectare | |
|---|---|---|
| | 1981 | 1991 |
| England | 3.55 | 3.61 |
| Wales | 1.34 | 1.36 |
| Scotland | 0.66 | 0.65 |
| Northern Ireland | 1.12 | 1.11 |

Sources: OPCS – Census reports

## IMMIGRATION 1992

Acceptances for settlement in the UK by nationality

| Region | Number of persons |
|---|---|
| Europe: total | 4,630 |
| European Community | 930 |
| Other Western Europe | 2,510 |
| Eastern Europe | 1,180 |
| Americas: total | 7,260 |
| USA | 3,850 |
| Canada | 790 |
| Africa: total | 8,980 |
| Asia: total | 25,260 |
| Indian sub-continent | 15,070 |
| Middle East | 2,570 |
| Australasia: total | 2,340 |
| Other | 2,610 |
| Stateless | 1,490 |
| Total | 52,570 |
| Foreign | 21,760 |
| Commonwealth | 30,840 |
| Old Commonwealth | 3,120 |
| New Commonwealth | 27,710 |

Source: HMSO – Annual Abstract of Statistics 1994

## LIVE BIRTHS AND BIRTH RATES 1992

| | Live births | Birth rate* |
|---|---|---|
| United Kingdom | 781,000 | 13.5 |
| England and Wales | 690,000 | 13.4 |
| Scotland | 66,000 | 12.9 |
| Northern Ireland | 26,000 | 15.9 |

*Live births per 1,000 population
Source: HMSO – Annual Abstract of Statistics 1994

## LEGAL ABORTIONS 1992 (ENGLAND AND WALES)

| Age group | Number p |
|---|---|
| Under 16 | 3,000 |
| 16–19 | 27,600 |
| 20–34 | 111,400 |
| 35–44 | 18,100 |
| 45 and over | 450 |
| Age not stated | 10 |
| Total | 160,500 |

p provisional
Source: HMSO – *Population Trends 76*

## BIRTHS OUTSIDE MARRIAGE (UK)

| Age group | 1981 | 1992 |
|---|---|---|
| Under 20 | 30,000 | 46,000 |
| 20–24 | 33,000 | 86,000 |
| 25–29 | 16,000 | 62,000 |
| Over 30 | 13,000 | 46,000 |
| Total | 91,000 | 241,000 |

Source: HMSO – *Annual Abstract of Statistics 1994*

## MARRIAGE AND DIVORCE 1991

| | Marriages | Divorces* |
|---|---|---|
| United Kingdom | 349,739 | — |
| England and Wales | 306,756 | 158,745 |
| Scotland | 33,762 | 12,399 |
| Northern Ireland | 9,221 | 2,597 |

*Decrees absolute granted; in Northern Ireland, divorce petitions filed
Source: HMSO – *Annual Abstract of Statistics 1994*

## DEATHS AND DEATH RATES 1992

| Males | Deaths | Death rate* |
|---|---|---|
| United Kingdom | 308,535p | 10.9p |
| England and Wales | 271,732 | — |
| Scotland | 29,334 | — |
| Northern Ireland | 7,469p | — |
| Females | | |
| United Kingdom | 325,703p | 11.0p |
| England and Wales | 286,581 | — |
| Scotland | 31,603 | — |
| Northern Ireland | 7,519p | — |

* Deaths per 1,000 population
p provisional
Source: HMSO – *Annual Abstract of Statistics 1994*

## INFANT MORTALITY 1992

Deaths of infants under 1 year of age per 1,000 live births

| | Number p |
|---|---|
| United Kingdom | 6.6 |
| England and Wales | 6.6 |
| Scotland | 6.8 |
| Northern Ireland | 6.0 |

p provisional
Source: HMSO – *Annual Abstract of Statistics 1994*

## EXPECTATION OF LIFE   LIFE TABLES 1989–91 (INTERIM FIGURES)

| | England and Wales | | Scotland | | Northern Ireland | |
|---|---|---|---|---|---|---|
| Age | Male | Female | Male | Female | Male | Female |
| 0 | 73.2 | 78.7 | 71.1 | 76.7 | 71.8 | 77.6 |
| 5 | 69.0 | 74.3 | 66.8 | 72.3 | 67.5 | 73.3 |
| 10 | 64.0 | 69.4 | 61.9 | 67.4 | 62.6 | 68.3 |
| 15 | 59.1 | 64.4 | 57.0 | 62.4 | 57.6 | 63.4 |
| 20 | 54.3 | 59.5 | 52.2 | 57.5 | 52.9 | 58.4 |
| 25 | 49.5 | 54.6 | 47.5 | 52.6 | 48.2 | 53.5 |
| 30 | 44.7 | 49.7 | 42.7 | 47.7 | 43.4 | 48.6 |
| 35 | 40.0 | 44.8 | 38.0 | 42.9 | 38.7 | 43.8 |
| 40 | 35.2 | 40.0 | 33.3 | 38.1 | 33.9 | 38.9 |
| 45 | 30.5 | 35.2 | 28.7 | 33.4 | 29.3 | 34.2 |
| 50 | 26.0 | 30.6 | 24.3 | 28.8 | 24.8 | 29.6 |
| 55 | 21.7 | 26.1 | 20.1 | 24.4 | 20.6 | 25.2 |
| 60 | 17.7 | 21.8 | 16.4 | 20.4 | 16.7 | 20.9 |
| 65 | 14.2 | 17.9 | 13.0 | 16.6 | 13.3 | 17.1 |
| 70 | 11.1 | 14.3 | 10.2 | 13.2 | 10.4 | 13.5 |
| 75 | 8.5 | 11.0 | 7.9 | 10.2 | 7.9 | 10.3 |
| 80 | 6.4 | 8.2 | 5.9 | 7.6 | 5.9 | 7.6 |
| 85 | 4.9 | 5.9 | 4.4 | 5.5 | 4.3 | 5.3 |

Source: HMSO – *Annual Abstract of Statistics 1994*

## DEATHS ANALYSED BY CAUSE 1992

| | England & Wales | Scotland | N. Ireland |
|---|---|---|---|
| TOTAL DEATHS | 555,358 | 60,937 | 14,988 |
| DEATHS FROM NATURAL CAUSES | 538,677 | 58,402 | 14,407 |
| Infections and parasitic diseases | 2,633 | 270 | 41 |
| Intestinal infectious diseases | 240 | 18 | — |
| Tuberculosis of respiratory system | 309 | 40 | 8 |
| Other tuberculosis, including late effects | 263 | 23 | 5 |
| Whooping cough | 1 | — | — |
| Meningococcal infection | 162 | 9 | 7 |
| Measles | 2 | — | — |
| Malaria | 9 | — | — |
| Syphilis | 22 | 4 | — |
| Neoplasms | 145,963 | 15,312 | 3,621 |
| Malignant neoplasm of stomach | 8,285 | 828 | 213 |
| Malignant neoplasm of trachea, bronchus and lung | 33,662 | 4,308 | 771 |
| Malignant neoplasm of breast | 13,755 | 1,256 | 308 |
| Malignant neoplasm of uterus | 3,037 | 421 | 64 |
| Leukaemia | 3,616 | 284 | 66 |
| Benign and unspecified neoplasms | 1,368 | 138 | 38 |
| Endocrine, nutritional and metabolic diseases and immunity disorders | 10,605 | 742 | 60 |
| Diabetes mellitus | 8,067 | 504 | 23 |
| Nutritional deficiencies | 104 | 17 | — |
| Other metabolic and immunity disorders | 1,747 | 193 | 26 |
| Diseases of blood and blood-forming organs | 2,417 | 183 | 18 |
| Anaemias | 1,056 | 84 | 11 |
| Mental disorders | 12,950 | 1,133 | 52 |
| Diseases of nervous system and sense organs | 11,577 | 877 | 181 |
| Meningitis | 208 | 27 | 7 |
| Diseases of the circulatory system | 254,683 | 28,776 | 7,112 |
| Rheumatic heart disease | 2,136 | 186 | 62 |
| Hypertensive disease | 3,144 | 323 | 69 |
| Ischaemic heart disease | 145,904 | 16,536 | 4,313 |
| Diseases of pulmonary circulation and other forms of heart disease | 18,352 | 2,291 | 633 |
| Cerebrovascular disease | 66,291 | 7,861 | 1,691 |
| Diseases of the respiratory system | 60,388 | 6,999 | 2,423 |
| Influenza | 262 | 58 | 6 |
| Pneumonia | 26,257 | 3,729 | 1,547 |
| Bronchitis, emphysema | 6,070 | 388 | 143 |
| Asthma | 1,791 | 115 | 53 |
| Diseases of the digestive system | 18,742 | 2,122 | 405 |
| Ulcer of stomach and duodenum | 4,296 | 387 | 97 |
| Appendicitis | 130 | 10 | — |
| Hernia of abdominal cavity and other intestinal obstruction | 2,025 | 197 | 51 |
| Chronic liver disease and cirrhosis | 3,056 | 446 | 69 |
| Diseases of the genito-urinary system | 5,306 | 888 | 238 |
| Nephritis, nephrotic syndrome and nephrosis | 2,072 | 574 | 168 |
| Hyperplasia of prostate | 343 | 20 | 6 |
| Complications of pregnancy, childbirth, etc. | 45 | 7 | — |
| Abortion | 6 | — | — |
| Diseases of the skin and subcutaneous tissue | 907 | 82 | 27 |
| Diseases of the musculo-skeletal system | 5,376 | 306 | 43 |
| Congenital anomalies | 1,565 | 209 | 77 |
| Certain conditions originating in the perinatal period | 242 | 216 | 63 |
| Birth trauma, hypoxia, birth asphyxia and other respiratory conditions | 67 | 107 | 26 |
| Signs, symptoms and ill-defined conditions | 5,278 | 280 | 46 |
| Sudden infant death syndrome | 456 | 64 | 11 |
| DEATHS FROM INJURY AND POISONING | 16,681 | 2,535 | 581 |
| All accidents | 12,729 | 1,580 | 376 |
| Motor vehicle accidents | 4,114 | 468 | 165 |
| Suicide and self-inflicted injury | 3,952 | 569 | 107 |
| All other external causes | 2,294 | 386 | 98 |

*Sources:* HMSO - *Annual Abstract of Statistics 1994*; General Register Office for Scotland; General Register Office (Northern Ireland)

# The National Flag

The national flag of the United Kingdom is the Union Flag, generally known as the Union Jack. (The name 'Union Jack' derives from the use of the Union Flag on the jack-staff of naval vessels.)

The Union Flag is a combination of the cross of St George, patron saint of England, the cross of St Andrew, patron saint of Scotland, and a cross similar to that of St Patrick, patron saint of Ireland.

*Cross of St George:* cross Gules in a field Argent (red cross on a white ground).

*Cross of St Andrew:* saltire Argent in a field Azure (white diagonal cross on a blue ground).

*Cross of St Patrick:* saltire Gules in a field Argent (red diagonal cross on a white ground).

The Union Flag was first introduced in 1606 after the union of the kingdoms of England and Scotland under one sovereign. The cross of St Patrick was added in 1801 after the union of Great Britain and Ireland.

---

## DAYS FOR FLYING FLAGS

---

The correct orientation of the Union Flag when flying is with the broader diagonal band of white uppermost in the hoist (i.e. near the pole) and the narrower diagonal band of white uppermost in the fly (i.e. furthest from the pole).

It is the practice to fly the Union Flag daily on some Customs Houses. In all other cases, flags are flown on government buildings by command of The Queen.

Days for hoisting the Union Flag are notified to the Department of National Heritage by The Queen's command and communicated by the department to the other government departments. On the days appointed, the Union Flag is flown on all government buildings in London and elsewhere in the United Kingdom from 8 a.m. to sunset.

| | |
|---|---|
| The Queen's Accession | 6 February |
| Birthday of The Duke of York | 19 February |
| *St David's Day (in Wales only) | 1 March |
| Birthday of The Prince Edward | 10 March |
| Commonwealth Day (1995) | 13 March |
| Birthday of The Queen | 21 April |
| *St George's Day (in England only) | 23 April |
| Coronation Day | 2 June |
| Birthday of The Duke of Edinburgh | 10 June |
| The Queen's Official Birthday (1995) | 17 June |
| Birthday of The Princess of Wales | 1 July |
| Birthday of Queen Elizabeth the Queen Mother | 4 August |
| Birthday of The Princess Royal | 15 August |
| Birthday of The Princess Margaret | 21 August |
| Remembrance Sunday (1995) | 12 November |
| Birthday of The Prince of Wales | 14 November |
| The Queen's Wedding Day | 20 November |
| *St Andrew's Day (in Scotland only) | 30 November |

†The occasion of the opening of Parliament by The Queen

†The occasion of the prorogation of Parliament by The Queen

*Where a building has two or more flagstaffs, the appropriate national flag may be flown in addition to the Union Flag, but not in a superior position

†Flags are flown whether or not The Queen performs the ceremony in person. Flags are flown only in the Greater London area

## FLAGS AT HALF-MAST

Flags are flown at half-mast on the following occasions:

(a) From the announcement of the death up to the funeral of the Sovereign, except on Proclamation Day, when flags are hoisted right up from 11 a.m. to sunset

(b) The funerals of members of the Royal Family, subject to special commands from The Queen in each case

(c) The funerals of foreign rulers, subject to special commands from The Queen in each case

(d) The funerals of Prime Ministers and ex-Prime Ministers of the United Kingdom, subject to special commands from The Queen in each case

(e) Other occasions by special command of The Queen

On occasions when days for flying flags coincide with days for flying flags at half-mast, the following rules are observed. Flags are flown:

(a) although a member of the Royal Family, or a near relative of the Royal Family, may be lying dead, unless special commands be received from The Queen to the contrary

(b) although it may be the day of the funeral of a foreign ruler

If the body of a very distinguished subject is lying at a government office, the flag may fly at half-mast on that office until the body has left (provided it is a day on which the flag would fly) and then the flag is to be hoisted right up. On all other government buildings the flag will fly as usual.

## THE ROYAL STANDARD

The Royal Standard is hoisted only when The Queen is actually present in the building, and never when Her Majesty is passing in procession.

# The Royal Family

ELIZABETH II, by the Grace of God, of the United Kingdom of Great Britain and Northern Ireland and of her other Realms and Territories Queen, Head of the Commonwealth, Defender of the Faith

Her Majesty Elizabeth Alexandra Mary of Windsor, elder daughter of King George VI and of HM Queen Elizabeth the Queen Mother
*Born* 21 April 1926, at 17 Bruton Street, London W1
*Ascended the throne* 6 February 1952
*Crowned* 2 June 1953, at Westminster Abbey
*Married* 20 November 1947, in Westminster Abbey, HRH The Duke of Edinburgh
*Official residences:* Buckingham Palace, London SW1; Windsor Castle, Berks; Palace of Holyroodhouse, Edinburgh
*Private residences:* Sandringham, Norfolk; Balmoral Castle, Aberdeenshire
*Office:* Buckingham Palace, London SW1A 1AA. Tel: 0171-930 4832

## HUSBAND OF HM THE QUEEN

HRH THE PRINCE PHILIP, DUKE OF EDINBURGH, KG, KT, OM, GBE, AC, QSO, PC, Ranger of Windsor Park
*Born* 10 June 1921, son of Prince and Princess Andrew of Greece and Denmark (*see* page 135), naturalized a British subject 1947, created Duke of Edinburgh, Earl of Merioneth and Baron Greenwich 1947

## CHILDREN OF HM THE QUEEN

HRH THE PRINCE OF WALES (Prince Charles Philip Arthur George), KG, KT, GCB and Great Master of the Order of the Bath, AK, QSO, PC, ADC(P)
*Born* 14 November 1948, created Prince of Wales and Earl of Chester 1958, succeeded as Duke of Cornwall, Duke of Rothesay, Earl of Carrick and Baron Renfrew, Lord of the Isles and Prince and Great Steward of Scotland 1952
*Married* 29 July 1981 Lady Diana Frances Spencer, now HRH The Princess of Wales (*born* 1 July 1961, youngest daughter of the 8th Earl Spencer and the Hon. Mrs Shand Kydd), *separated* 1992
*Issue:*
(1)   HRH Prince William of Wales (Prince William Arthur Philip Louis), *born* 21 June 1982
(2)   HRH Prince Henry of Wales (Prince Henry Charles Albert David), *born* 15 September 1984
*Residences of the Prince of Wales:* St James's Palace, London SW1; Highgrove, Doughton, Tetbury, Glos.
*Residence of the Princess of Wales:* Kensington Palace, London W8 4PU
*Office:* St James's Palace, London SW1A 1BS. Tel: 0171-930 4832

HRH THE PRINCESS ROYAL (Princess Anne Elizabeth Alice Louise), KG, GCVO

*Born* 15 August 1950, declared The Princess Royal 1987
*Married* (1) 14 November 1973 Captain Mark Anthony Peter Phillips, CVO (*born* 22 September 1948); marriage dissolved 1992; (2) 12 December 1992 Commander Timothy James Hamilton Laurence, MVO (*born* 1 March 1955)
*Issue:*
(1)   Peter Mark Andrew Phillips, *born* 15 November 1977
(2)   Zara Anne Elizabeth Phillips, *born* 15 May 1981
*Residence:* Gatcombe Park, Minchinhampton, Glos.
*Office:* Buckingham Palace, London SW1A 1AA. Tel: 0171-930 4832

HRH THE DUKE OF YORK (Prince Andrew Albert Christian Edward), CVO, ADC(P)
*Born* 19 February 1960, created Duke of York, Earl of Inverness and Baron Killyleagh 1986
*Married* 23 July 1986 Sarah Margaret Ferguson, now HRH The Duchess of York (*born* 15 October 1959, younger daughter of Major Ronald Ferguson and Mrs Hector Barrantes), *separated* 1992
*Issue:*
(1)   HRH Princess Beatrice of York (Princess Beatrice Elizabeth Mary), *born* 8 August 1988
(2)   HRH Princess Eugenie of York (Princess Eugenie Victoria Helena), *born* 23 March 1990
*Residences:* Buckingham Palace, London SW1; Sunninghill Park, Ascot, Berks.
*Office:* Buckingham Palace, London SW1 1AA. Tel: 0171-930 4832

HRH THE PRINCE EDWARD (Prince Edward Antony Richard Louis), CVO
*Born* 10 March 1964
*Residence and Office:* Buckingham Palace, London SW1A 1AA. Tel: 0171-930 4832

## SISTER OF HM THE QUEEN

HRH THE PRINCESS MARGARET, COUNTESS OF SNOWDON (Princess Margaret Rose), CI, GCVO, Royal Victorian Chain, Dame Grand Cross of the Order of St John of Jerusalem
*Born* 21 August 1930, younger daughter of King George VI and HM Queen Elizabeth the Queen Mother
*Married* 6 May 1960 Antony Charles Robert Armstrong-Jones, GCVO (*born* 7 March 1930, created Earl of Snowdon 1961, Constable of Caernarvon Castle); marriage dissolved 1978
*Issue:*
(1)   David Albert Charles, Viscount Linley, *born* 3 November 1961, *married* 8 October 1993 the Hon. Serena Stanhope
(2)   Lady Sarah Chatto (Sarah Frances Elizabeth), *born* 1 May 1964, *married* 14 July 1994 Daniel Chatto
*Residence and Office:* Kensington Palace, London W8 4PU. Tel: 0171-930 3141

## MOTHER OF HM THE QUEEN

HM QUEEN ELIZABETH THE QUEEN MOTHER (Elizabeth Angela Marguerite), Lady of the Garter, Lady of

the Thistle, CI, GMVO, GBE, Dame Grand Cross of the Order of St John, Royal Victorian Chain, Lord Warden and Admiral of the Cinque Ports and Constable of Dover Castle
*Born* 4 August 1900, youngest daughter of the 14th Earl of Strathmore and Kinghorne
*Married* 26 April 1923 (as Lady Elizabeth Bowes-Lyon) Prince Albert, Duke of York, afterwards King George VI (*see* page 134)
*Residences:* Clarence House, St James's Palace, London SW1; Royal Lodge, Windsor Great Park, Berks; Castle of Mey, Caithness
*Office:* Clarence House, St James's Palace, London SW1A 1BA. Tel: 0171-930 3141

---

AUNT OF HM THE QUEEN

---

HRH PRINCESS ALICE, DUCHESS OF GLOUCESTER (Alice Christabel), GCB, CI, GCVO, GBE, Grand Cordon of Al Kamal
*Born* 25 December 1901, third daughter of the 7th Duke of Buccleuch and Queensberry
*Married* 6 November 1935 (as Lady Alice Montagu-Douglas-Scott) Prince Henry, Duke of Gloucester, third son of King George V (*see* page 134)

---

COUSINS OF HM THE QUEEN

---

HRH THE DUKE OF GLOUCESTER (Prince Richard Alexander Walter George), GCVO, Grand Prior of the Order of St John of Jerusalem
*Born* 26 August 1944
*Married* 8 July 1972 Birgitte Eva van Deurs, now HRH The Duchess of Gloucester, GCVO (*born* 20 June 1946, daughter of Asger Henriksen and Vivian van Deurs)
*Issue:*
(1)    Earl of Ulster (Alexander Patrick Gregers Richard), *born* 24 October 1974
(2)    Lady Davina Windsor (Davina Elizabeth Alice Benedikte), *born* 19 November 1977
(3)    Lady Rose Windsor (Rose Victoria Birgitte Louise), *born* 1 March 1980
*Residences:* Kensington Palace, London W8 4PU; Barnwell Manor, Peterborough, Northants. PE8 5PJ
*Office:* Kensington Palace, London W8 4PU. Tel: 0171-937 6374

HRH THE DUKE OF KENT (Prince Edward George Nicholas Paul Patrick), KG, GCMG, GCVO, ADC(P)
*Born* 9 October 1935
*Married* 8 June 1961 Katharine Lucy Mary Worsley, now HRH The Duchess of Kent, GCVO (*born* 22 February 1933, daughter of Sir William Worsley, Bt.)
*Issue:*
(1)    Earl of St Andrews (George Philip Nicholas), *born* 26 June 1962, *married* 9 January 1988 Sylvana Tomaselli, and has issue, Edward Edmund Maximilian George, Baron Downpatrick, *born* 2 December 1988; Lady Marina Charlotte Alexandra Katharine Windsor, *born* 30 September 1992
(2)    Lady Helen Taylor (Helen Marina Lucy), *born* 28 April 1964, *married* 18 July 1992 Timothy Taylor, and has issue, Columbus George Donald Taylor, *born* 6 August 1994
(3)    Lord Nicholas Windsor (Nicholas Charles Edward Jonathan), *born* 25 July 1970

*Residences:* York House, St James's Palace, London SW1 1BQ; Crocker End House, Nettlebed, Oxon.
*Office:* York House, St James's Palace, London SW1A 1BQ. Tel: 0171-930 4872

HRH PRINCESS ALEXANDRA, THE HON. LADY OGILVY (Princess Alexandra Helen Elizabeth Olga Christabel), GCVO
*Born* 25 December 1936
*Married* 24 April 1963 The Hon. Sir Angus Ogilvy, KCVO (*born* 14 September 1928, second son of 12th Earl of Airlie)
*Issue:*
(1)    James Robert Bruce Ogilvy, *born* 29 February 1964, *married* 30 July 1988 Julia Rawlinson
(2)    Marina Victoria Alexandra, Mrs Mowatt, *born* 31 July 1966, *married* 2 February 1990 Paul Mowatt, and has issue, Zenouska May Mowatt, *born* 26 May 1990; Christian Alexander Mowatt, *born* 4 June 1993
*Residence:* Thatched House Lodge, Richmond Park, Surrey
*Office:* 22 Friary Court, St James's Palace, London SW1A 1BJ. Tel: 0171-930 1860

HRH PRINCE MICHAEL OF KENT (Prince Michael George Charles Franklin), KCVO
*Born* 4 July 1942
*Married* 30 June 1978 Baroness Marie-Christine Agnes Hedwig Ida von Reibnitz, now HRH Princess Michael of Kent (*born* 15 January 1945, daughter of Baron Gunther von Reibnitz)
*Issue:*
(1)    Lord Frederick Windsor (Frederick Michael George David Louis), *born* 6 April 1979
(2)    Lady Gabriella Windsor (Gabriella Marina Alexandra Ophelia), *born* 23 April 1981
*Residences:* Kensington Palace, London W8 4PU; Nether Lypiatt Manor, Stroud, Glos.
*Office:* Kensington Palace, London W8 4PU. Tel: 0171-938 3519

---

ORDER OF SUCCESSION

---

1    HRH The Prince of Wales
2    HRH Prince William of Wales
3    HRH Prince Henry of Wales
4    HRH The Duke of York
5    HRH Princess Beatrice of York
6    HRH Princess Eugenie of York
7    HRH The Prince Edward
8    HRH The Princess Royal
9    Peter Phillips
10    Zara Phillips
11    HRH The Princess Margaret, Countess of Snowdon
12    Viscount Linley
13    Lady Sarah Chatto
14    HRH The Duke of Gloucester
15    Earl of Ulster
16    Lady Davina Windsor
17    Lady Rose Windsor
18    HRH The Duke of Kent
19    Baron Downpatrick
20    Lady Marina Charlotte Windsor
21    Lord Nicholas Windsor
22    Lady Helen Taylor
23    Columbus Taylor
24    Lord Frederick Windsor
25    Lady Gabriella Windsor
26    HRH Princess Alexandra, the Hon. Lady Ogilvy
27    James Ogilvy
28    Marina, Mrs Paul Mowatt

# Royal Households

## THE QUEEN'S HOUSEHOLD

*Lord Chamberlain*, The Earl of Airlie, KT, GCVO, PC
*Lord Steward*, The Viscount Ridley, KG, GCVO, TD
*Master of the Horse*, The Lord Somerleyton, KCVO
*Treasurer of the Household*, G. Knight, MP
*Comptroller of the Household*, D. Lightbown, MP
*Vice-Chamberlain*, S. Chapman, MP

*Gold Stick*, Maj.-Gen. Lord Michael Fitzalan-Howard,
  GCVO, CB, CBE, MC; Gen. Sir Desmond Fitzpatrick, GCB,
  DSO, MBE, MC
*Vice-Adm. of the United Kingdom*, Adm. Sir James Eberle,
  GCB
*Rear-Adm. of the United Kingdom*, Adm. Sir Nicholas Hunt,
  GCB, LVO
*First and Principal Naval Aide-de-Camp*, Adm. Sir
  Benjamin Bathurst, GCB
*Flag Aide-de-Camp*, Adm. Sir Michael Layard, KCB, CBE
*Aides-de-Camp-General*, Gen. Sir Charles Guthrie, GCB, LVO,
  OBE; Gen. Sir John Waters, KCB, CBE; Gen. Sir John
  Wilsey, KCB, CBE
*Air Aides-de-Camp*, Air Chief Marshal Sir Michael Graydon,
  GCB, CBE; Air Chief Marshal Sir Andrew Wilson, KCB, AFC

*Mistress of the Robes*, The Duchess of Grafton, GCVO
*Ladies of the Bedchamber*, The Countess of Airlie, CVO; The
  Lady Farnham
*Extra Lady of the Bedchamber*, The Marchioness of
  Abergavenny, DCVO
*Women of the Bedchamber*, Hon. Mary Morrison, DCVO;
  Lady Susan Hussey, DCVO; Lady Dugdale, DCVO; The
  Lady Elton
*Extra Women of the Bedchamber*, The Hon. Mrs Van der
  Woude, CVO; Mrs John Woodroffe, CVO; Mrs Michael
  Wall, DCVO; Lady Abel Smith, DCVO; Mrs Robert de Pass
*Equerries*, Lt.-Col. Sir Guy Acland, Bt., MVO; Maj. J. Patrick;
  Capt. E. Macfarlane (temp.)
*Extra Equerries*, Vice-Adm. Sir Peter Ashmore, KCB, KCVO,
  DSC; Lt.-Col. The Lord Charteris of Amisfield, GCB, GCVO,
  OBE, QSO, PC; Maj.-Gen. Sir Simon Cooper, KCVO; Air
  Cdre the Hon. T. Elworthy, CBE; The Rt Hon. Sir Robert
  Fellowes, KCB, KCVO; Sir Edward Ford, KCB, KCVO, ERD;
  Rear-Adm. Sir John Garnier, KCVO, CBE; Rear-Adm. Sir
  Paul Greening, GCVO; Brig. Sir Geoffrey Hardy-Roberts,
  KCVO, CB, CBE; The Rt. Hon. Sir William Heseltine, GCB,
  GCVO, AC, QSO; Lt.-Col. Sir John Johnston, GCVO, MC; Lt.-
  Col. A. Mather, OBE; Sir Peter Miles, KCVO; Lt.-Col. Sir
  John Miller, GCVO, DSO, MC; Air Cdre Sir Dennis Mitchell,
  KBE, CVO, DFC, AFC; The Lord Moore of Wolvercote, GCB,
  GCVO, CMG, QSO; Lt.-Gen. Sir John Richards, KCB, KCVO;
  Lt.-Col. W. H. M. Ross, CVO, OBE; Air Vice-Marshal Sir
  John Severne, KCVO, OBE, AFC; Lt.-Col. Sir Blair Stewart-
  Wilson, KCVO; Gp Capt P. Townsend, CVO, DSO, DFC;
  Rear-Adm. Sir Richard Trowbridge, KCVO; Lt.-Col.
  G. West, CVO; Air Cdre Sir Archie Winskill, KCVO, CBE,
  DFC, AE; Rear-Adm. R. Woodard

## THE PRIVATE SECRETARY'S OFFICE
Buckingham Palace, London SW1A 1AA

*Private Secretary to The Queen*, The Rt Hon. Sir Robert
  Fellowes, KCB, KCVO

*Deputy Private Secretary*, Sir Kenneth Scott, KCVO, CMG
*Assistant Private Secretary*, R. B. Janvrin, CVO
*Press Secretary*, C. V. Anson, LVO
*Deputy Press Secretary*, G. Crawford
*Assistant Press Secretary*, Miss P. Russell-Smith
*Chief Clerk*, Mrs G. S. Coulson, MVO
*Secretary to the Private Secretary*, Mrs J. Bean, LVO
*Clerks*, Miss A. Freeman; Mrs A. Galletley, MVO; Miss H.
  Spiller, MVO; Miss H. Staveley; Mrs E. Walsh Waring;
  Miss P. Brown; Miss M. Edwards; Mrs N. Miller; Mrs P.
  Penfold
*Press Office*, Mrs G. Middleburgh; Mrs R. Murdo-Smith,
  LVO; Miss C. Sillars
*Lady-in-Waiting's Office*, Mrs D. Phillips; Mrs J. Vince

THE QUEEN'S ARCHIVES
Round Tower, Windsor Castle, Berks

*Keeper of The Queen's Archives*, The Rt Hon. Sir Robert
  Fellowes, KCB, KCVO
*Assistant Keeper*, O. Everett, CVO
*Registrar*, Lady de Bellaigue, MVO
*Assistant Registrar*, Miss P. Clark
*Curator of the Photographic Collection*, Miss F. Dimond, LVO

## THE PRIVY PURSE AND TREASURER'S OFFICE
Buckingham Palace, London SW1A 1AA

*Keeper of the Privy Purse and Treasurer to The Queen*, Maj.
  Sir Shane Blewitt, KCVO
*Deputy Keeper of the Privy Purse and Deputy Treasurer*,
  J. Parsons, LVO
*Chief Accountant and Paymaster*, D. Walker, LVO
*Personnel Officer*, Miss P. Lloyd
*Assistant Chief Accountant and Paymaster*, Miss R. Ward
*Taxation Accountant*, Miss P. Norman
*Assistant Personnel Officer*, Mrs C. Jones
*Clerks*, Mrs C. Auton, MVO; I. Biss; Mrs N. Broad; J. Curr;
  Miss N. Mooney; Miss C. Robinson; Miss G. Wickham,
  MVO; Miss P. Green
*Land Agent, Sandringham*, J. Major, FRICS
*Resident Factor, Balmoral*, M. Leslie, LVO, FRICS

FINANCE AND PROPERTY SERVICES

*Director of Finance and Property Services*, M. Peat, CVO
*Deputy Director, Property Services*, J. Tiltman
*Superintending Architect*, S. Dhargalkar, LVO
*Senior Architect*, G. Sharpe
*Property Administrator*, Miss M. Green
*Property Accountant*, M. Bourke
*Fire Precautions and Health and Safety Manager*,
  G. Griffiths, MVO
*Fire Safety Officer*, C. Nixon
*Maintenance Manager, Buckingham Palace*, R. Brown
*Maintenance Manager, St James's and Kensington Palaces*,
  R. Mole.
*Assistant Maintenance Managers*, M. Harmer, MVO; A. Ryan
*Assistant Property Administrator*, Mrs H. Dunlop
*Management Auditor*, I. McGregor
*Assistant Management Auditor*, Mrs D. Mowbray
*Information Systems Manager*, I. Hardy
*Clerks*, Mrs. J. Hillyer; Mrs C. Sharma; Mrs J. Thomas; Miss
  R. Wickenden

WINDSOR CASTLE
*Maintenance Manager*, E. Norton
*Deputy Maintenance Manager*, P. Godwin
*Administrative Assistant*, Mrs C. Crook

ROYAL ALMONRY
*High Almoner*, The Rt. Revd the Lord Bishop of St Albans
*Hereditary Grand Almoner*, The Marquess of Exeter
*Sub-Almoner*, Revd W. Booth
*Secretary*, P. Wright, CVO
*Assistant Secretary*, C. Williams, RVM

## THE LORD CHAMBERLAIN'S OFFICE
Buckingham Palace, London SW1A 1AA

*Comptroller*, Lt.-Col. W. H. M. Ross, CVO, OBE
*Assistant Comptroller*, Lt.-Col. A. Mather, OBE
*Secretary*, P. D. Hartley, LVO
*Assistant Secretary*, J. Spencer, MVO
*State Invitations Assistant*, J. Hope
*Clerks*, Miss L. Dove; Mrs S. Scott; Mrs A. Samuelson; Miss E. Grant
*Permanent Lords-in-Waiting*, Lt.-Col. The Lord Charteris of Amisfield, GCB, GCVO, OBE, QSO, PC; The Lord Moore of Wolvercote, GCB, GCVO, CMG, QSO
*Lords-in-Waiting*, The Viscount Boyne; The Lord Camoys; The Viscount Long, CBE; The Lord Lucas of Crudwell; The Lord Inglewood
*Baronesses-in-Waiting*, The Baroness Trumpington; The Baroness Miller of Hendon
*Gentlemen Ushers*, C. Greig, CVO, CBE; Gp Capt J. Slessor; Maj. N. Chamberlayne-Macdonald, LVO, OBE; Capt. M. Barrow, DSO, RN; Capt. M. Fulford-Dobson, RN; Lt.-Gen. Sir Richard Vickers, KCB, LVO, OBE; Air Vice-Marshal B. Newton, CB, OBE; Col. M. Havergal, OBE; Rear Adm. C. H. D. Cooke-Priest, CB
*Extra Gentlemen Ushers*, Maj. T. Harvey, CVO, DSO, ERD; Maj.-Gen. Sir Cyril Colquhoun, KCVO, CB, OBE; Lt.-Col. Sir John Hugo, KCVO, OBE; Vice-Adm. Sir Ronald Brockman, KCB, CSI, CIE, CVO, CBE; Air Marshal Sir Maurice Heath, KBE, CB, CVO; Sir James Scholtens, KCVO; Sir Patrick O'Dea, KCVO; Adm. Sir David Williams, GCB; H. Davis, CVO, CM; Maj.-Gen. R. Reid, CVO, MC, CD; Lt.-Cdr. J. Holdsworth, CVO, OBE, RN; Col. G. Leigh, CVO, CBE; Lt.-Cdr. Sir Russell Wood, KCVO, VRD; Maj.-Gen. Sir Desmond Rice, KCVO, CBE; Lt.-Col. Sir Julian Paget, Bt., CVO; S. W. F. Martin, CVO; J. Haslam, CVO; Prof. Sir Norman Blacklock, KCVO, OBE, FRCS; Air Marshal Sir Roy Austen-Smith, KBE, CB, CVO, DFC; Vice-Adm. Sir David Loram, KCB, LVO
*Gentleman Usher to the Sword of State*, Gen. Sir Edward Burgess, KCB, OBE
*Gentleman Usher of the Black Rod*, Adm. Sir Richard Thomas, KCB, OBE
*Serjeants-at-Arms*, D. Walker, LVO; Maj. B. Eastwood, LVO, MBE; P. Hartley, LVO

*Marshal of the Diplomatic Corps*, Vice-Adm. Sir James Weatherall, KBE
*Vice-Marshal*, A. St J. H. Figgis, CMG

*Constable and Governor of Windsor Castle*, Gen. Sir Patrick Palmer, KBE
*Keeper of the Jewel House, Tower of London*, Maj.-Gen. G. Field, CB, OBE
*Master of The Queen's Music*, Malcolm Williamson, CBE, AO
*Poet Laureate*, Ted Hughes, OBE
*Bargemaster*, R. Crouch
*Swan Warden*, Prof. C. Perrins, LVO
*Swan Marker*, D. Barber

*Superintendent of the State Apartments, St James's Palace*, B. Andrews, BEM

## ECCLESIASTICAL HOUSEHOLD
THE COLLEGE OF CHAPLAINS

*Clerk of the Closet*, Rt. Revd Bishop of Chelmsford
*Deputy Clerk of the Closet*, Revd W. Booth
*Chaplains to The Queen*, Revd A. H. H. Harbottle, LVO; Ven. D. N. Griffiths, RD; Revd Canon J. V. Bean; Revd K. Huxley; Ven. P. Ashford; Revd Canon D. C. Gray, TD; Revd Canon E. James; Revd Canon J. Hester; Revd S. Pedley; Revd D. Tonge; Revd Canon M. A. Moxon; Revd Canon G. Murphy, LVO; Revd Canon R. H. C Lewis; Revd D. J. Burgess; Revd E. R. Ayerst; Revd R. S. Clarke; Revd Canon C. J. Hill; Revd Canon K. Pound; Revd J. Haslam; Revd Canon G. Hall; Revd Canon A. C. Hill; Revd J. C. Priestley; Revd Canon J. O. Colling; Revd Canon G. Jones; Revd Canon D. G. Palmer; Revd Canon D. H. Wheaton; Revd Canon P. Boulton; Revd Canon R. A. Bowden; Revd Canon E. Buchanan; Revd J. Robson; Revd Canon J. Stanley; Revd Canon I. Hardaker; Revd Canon L. F. Webber
*Extra Chaplains*, Revd Canon J. S. D. Mansel, KCVO, FSA; Preb. S. A. Williams, CVO; Ven. E. J. G. Ward, LVO; Revd J. R. W. Stott; Revd Canon A. D. Caesar, CVO

CHAPELS ROYAL
*Dean of the Chapels Royal*, The Bishop of London
*Sub-Dean of Chapels Royal*, Revd W. Booth
*Priests in Ordinary*, Revd G. Watkins; Revd H. Mead; Revd S. E. Young
*Organist, Choirmaster and Composer*, R. J. Popplewell, MVO, FRCO, FRCM
*Domestic Chaplain, Buckingham Palace*, Revd W. Booth
*Domestic Chaplain, Windsor Castle*, The Dean of Windsor
*Domestic Chaplain, Sandringham*, Revd Canon G. R. Hall
*Chaplain, Royal Chapel, Windsor Great Park*, Revd Canon M. Moxon
*Chaplain, Hampton Court Palace*, Revd Canon M. Moore
*Chaplain, Tower of London*, Revd Canon J. G. M. W. Murphy, LVO
*Organist and Choirmaster, Hampton Court Palace*, Prof G. Reynolds, LVO

## MEDICAL HOUSEHOLD

*Head of the Medical Household and Physician to The Queen*, R. Thompson, DM, FRCP
*Physician*, R. W. Davey, MB, BS
*Serjeant Surgeon*, B. T. Jackson, MS, FRCS
*Surgeon Oculist*, P. Holmes Sellors, LVO, BM, B.ch., FRCS
*Surgeon Gynaecologist*, M. E. Setchell, FRCS, FRCOG
*Surgeon Dentist*, N. A. Sturridge, CVO, LDS, BDS, DDS
*Orthopaedic Surgeon*, R. H. Vickers, MA, BM, B.Ch., FRCS
*Physician to the Household*, J. Cunningham, DM, FRCP
*Surgeon to the Household*, A. A. M. Lewis, MB, FRCS
*Surgeon Oculist to the Household*, T. J. ffytche, MB, FRCS
*Apothecary to The Queen and to the Household*, N. R. Southward, LVO, MB, B.chir.
*Apothecary to the Household at Windsor*, J. H. D. Briscoe, MB, B.chir., D.obst.
*Apothecary to the Household at Sandringham*, I. K. Campbell, MB, BS, FRCGP
*Coroner of The Queen's Household*, J. Burton, CBE, MB, BS

## CENTRAL CHANCERY OF THE ORDERS OF KNIGHTHOOD
St James's Palace, London SW1A 1BS

*Secretary,* Lt.-Col. A. Mather, OBE
*Assistant Secretary,* Miss R. Wells, MVO
*Clerks,* J. Bagwell Purefoy; Mrs T. Isaac; J. McGurk, MVO;
D. Pogson; Mrs F. Doyle; Mrs P. Curtis; P. van der Borgh

THE HONOURABLE CORPS OF GENTLEMEN-AT-ARMS
St James's Palace, London SW1A 1BS

*Captain,* The Lord Strathclyde
*Lieutenant,* Col. T. A. Hall, OBE
*Standard Bearer,* Maj. Sir Fergus Matheson of Matheson, Bt.
*Clerk of the Cheque and Adjutant,* Lt.-Col. R. Mayfield, DSO
*Harbinger,* Maj. Sir Philip Duncombe, Bt.

*Gentlemen of the Corps*
*Colonels,* Sir Piers Bengough, KCVO, OBE; Hon. N. Crossley, TD; T. Wilson; D. Fanshawe, OBE; J. Baker; R. ffrench Blake; Sir William Mahon, Bt.; Sir Brian Barttelot, Bt., OBE; M. J. C. Robertson, MC
*Lieutenant-Colonels,* B. Lockhart; Hon. P. H. Lewis; R. Macfarlane; Hon. G. B. Norrie; J. H. Fisher, OBE; R. Ker, MC; P. Chamberlin
*Majors,* J. A. J. Nunn; I. B. Ramsden, MBE; M. J. Drummond-Brady; A. Arkwright; G. M. B. Colenso-Jones; T. Gooch, MBE; J. B. B. Cockcroft; C. J. H. Gurney; P. D. Johnson; R. M. O. Webster
*Captain,* The Lord Monteagle of Brandon

THE QUEEN'S BODY GUARD OF THE YEOMEN OF THE GUARD
St James's Palace, London SW1A 1BS

*Captain,* The Earl of Arran
*Lieutenant,* Col. G. W. Tufnell
*Clerk of the Cheque and Adjutant,* Col. S. Longsdon
*Ensign,* Maj. C. Marriott
*Exons,* Maj. C. Enderby; Maj. M. T. N. H. Wills

## MASTER OF THE HOUSEHOLD'S DEPARTMENT

BOARD OF GREEN CLOTH
Buckingham Palace, London SW1A 1AA

*Master of the Household,* Maj.-Gen. Sir Simon Cooper, KCVO
*Deputy Master of the Household,* Lt.-Col. Sir Guy Acland, Bt., MVO
*Assistants to the Master of the Household,* M. T. Parker, MVO; P. Jackson
*Chief Clerk,* M. C. W. N. Jephson, MVO
*Chief Housekeeper,* Miss H. Colebrook, MVO
*Deputy to Assistant F,* M. Bovaird
*Senior Clerk G,* S. Stacey
*Clerks,* Miss S. Derry, LVO; Miss S. Fergus, MVO; Miss E. Henderson; Miss C. Joyce; Miss I. Spurway; A. Scovie; G. Brock
*Flower Arranger,* Mrs P. Pentney, MVO
*Palace Steward,* A. Jarred, MVO, RVM
*Royal Chef,* L. Mann, RVM
*Superintendent, Windsor Castle,* Maj. B. Eastwood, LVO, MBE
*Superintendent, The Palace of Holyroodhouse,* Lt.-Col. D. Anderson, OBE

## ROYAL MEWS DEPARTMENT
Buckingham Palace, London SW1W 0QH

*Crown Equerry,* Lt.-Col. S. Gilbart-Denham, CVO

*Veterinary Surgeon,* P. Scott Dunn, LVO, MRCVS
*Superintendent Royal Mews, Buckingham Palace,* Maj. A. Smith, MBE
*Comptroller of Stores,* Maj. L. Marsham, MVO
*Chief Clerk,* P. Almond, MVO
*Deputy Chief Clerk,* A. Marshall
*Assistant Chief Clerk,* Mrs J. Clark

## THE ROYAL COLLECTION TRUST
St James's Palace, London SW1A 1BS

*Director of Royal Collection and Surveyor of The Queen's Works of Art,* Sir Geoffrey de Bellaigue, KCVO, FBA, FSA
*Surveyor of The Queen's Pictures,* C. Lloyd
*Surveyor Emeritus of The Queen's Pictures,* Sir Oliver Millar, GCVO, FBA, FSA
*Librarian, The Royal Library, Windsor Castle,* O. Everett, CVO
*Deputy Surveyor of The Queen's Works of Art,* H. Roberts, FSA
*Librarian Emeritus,* Sir Robin Mackworth-Young, GCVO, FSA
*Director of Media Affairs,* R. Arbiter
*Curator of the Print Room,* The Hon. Mrs Roberts, MVO
*Administrator and Assistant to The Surveyors,* D. Rankin-Hunt, MVO, TD
*Assistant to The Surveyor of The Queen's Pictures,* C. Noble, MVO
*Secretary to the Director and Loans Officer (Works of Art),* Miss C. Paybody
*Exhibitions Assistant (Pictures),* Hon. C. Neville
*Senior Picture Restorer,* Miss V. Pemberton-Pigott, MVO
*Chief Restorer, Old Master Drawings,* A. Donnithorne
*Senior Furniture Restorer,* E. Fancourt, RVM
*Armourer,* J. Jackson, RVM
*Chief Binder,* R. Day, MVO, RVM
*Deputy Curator of the Print Room,* Mrs H. Ryan, MVO
*Assistant Curator (Exhibitions),* Miss T.-M. Morton
*Bibliographer,* Miss B. Wright, MVO
*Superintendent Royal Collection Hampton Court Palace,* J. Cowell, MVO
*Computer Systems Manager,* S. Patterson
*Financial Controller,* Mrs G. Johnson
*Accountant,* Miss M. O'Connell

## ROYAL COLLECTION ENTERPRISES LTD

*Managing Director,* M. E. K. Hewlett
*Personal Assistant to the Managing Director,* Mrs C. Murphy, MVO
*Financial Director,* Mrs G. Johnson
*Deputy Financial Director,* Miss J. Williams
*Retail Manager,* S. R. Spencer
*Merchandiser,* Miss R. Anderson
*Visitor Manager, Buckingham Palace,* Mrs S. Bowen
*Assistant Visitor Manager, Buckingham Palace,* Miss A. Kelly
*Administrator Public Enterprises, Windsor Castle,* Mrs A. Laing
*Assistant Administrator Public Enterprises, Windsor Castle,* Mrs H. Tarrant
*Head of Photographic Services,* Miss G. Campling
*Merchandise Consultant,* Mrs K. Munro

## ASCOT OFFICE
St James's Palace, London SW1A 1BS
Tel 0171-930 9882

*Her Majesty's Representative at Ascot,* Col. Sir Piers Bengough, KCVO, OBE
*Secretary,* Miss L. Thompson-Royds, MVO

## THE QUEEN'S HOUSEHOLD IN SCOTLAND

*Hereditary Lord High Constable*, The Earl of Erroll
*Hereditary Master of the Household*, The Duke of Argyll
*Lord Lyon King of Arms*, Sir Malcolm Innes of Edingight, KCVO, WS
*Hereditary Bearer of the Royal Banner of Scotland*, The Earl of Dundee
*Hereditary Bearer of the Scottish National Flag*, The Earl of Lauderdale
*Hereditary Keepers:*
  *Palace of Holyroodhouse*, The Duke of Hamilton and Brandon
  *Falkland Palace*, N. Crichton-Stuart
  *Stirling Castle*, The Earl of Mar and Kellie
  *Dunstaffnage Castle*, The Duke of Argyll
  *Dunconnel Castle*, Sir Fitzroy Maclean, Bt., KT, CBE
*Hereditary Carver*, Maj. Sir Ralph Anstruther, Bt., GCVO, MC
*Keeper of Dumbarton Castle*, Brig. A. S. Pearson, CB, DSO, OBE, MC, TD
*Governor of Edinburgh Castle*, Maj.-Gen. M. Scott, CBE, DSO
*Historiographer*, Prof. T. C. Smout, FBA, FRSE, FSA Scot.
*Botanist*, Prof. D. Henderson, CBE, FRSE
*Painter and Limner*, D. A. Donaldson, RSA, RP
*Sculptor in Ordinary*, Prof. Sir Eduardo Paolozzi, CBE, RA
*Astronomer*, vacant
*Heralds and Pursuivants, see page 286*

### ECCLESIASTICAL HOUSEHOLD
*Dean of the Chapel Royal*, Very Revd W. J. Morris, DD, LL.D
*Dean of the Order of the Thistle*, Very Revd G. I. Macmillan
*Chaplains in Ordinary*, Very Revd W. J. Morris, DD, LL.D.; Revd J. McLeod; Very Revd G. I. Macmillan; Revd M. D. Craig; Revd W. B. R. Macmillan, LL.D, DD.; Revd J. L. Weatherhead; Revd A. S. Todd, DD; Revd C. Robertson; Revd J. A. Simpson; Revd N. W. Drummond
*Extra Chaplains*, Very Revd R. W. V. Selby Wright, CVO, TD, DD, FRSE, FSA Scot.; Very Revd W. R. Sanderson, DD; Revd T. J. T. Nicol, MVO, MBE, MC, TD; Very Revd Prof. J. McIntyre, CVO, DD, FRSE; Revd C. Forrester-Paton; Revd H. W. M. Cant; Very Revd R. A. S. Barbour, KCVO, MC, DD; Revd K. MacVicar, MBE, DFC, TD; Very Revd W. B. Johnston, DD; Revd A. J. C. Macfarlane; Revd M. I. Levison
*Domestic Chaplain, Balmoral*, Revd J. A. K. Angus, LVO, TD

### MEDICAL HOUSEHOLD
*Physicians in Scotland*, P. Brunt, MD, FRCP; A. L. Muir, MD, FRCP
*Surgeons in Scotland*, J. Engeset, ch.M., FRCS; D. C. Carter MD, FRCS
*Apothecary to the Household at Balmoral*, D. J. A. Glass, MB, ch.B.
*Apothecary to the Household at the Palace of Holyroodhouse*, Dr J. Cormack, MD, FRCPE, FRCGP

## THE QUEEN'S BODY GUARD FOR SCOTLAND

### ROYAL COMPANY OF ARCHERS
Archers' Hall, Buccleuch Street, Edinburgh EH8 9LR

*Captain-General and Gold Stick for Scotland*, Col. the Lord Clydesmuir, KT, CB, MBE, TD
*Captains*, Maj. the Lord Home of the Hirsel, KT; The Duke of Buccleuch and Queensberry, KT, VRD; Maj. Sir Hew Hamilton-Dalrymple, Bt., KCVO; Maj. the Earl of Wemyss and March, KT
*Lieutenants*, The Earl of Airlie, KT, GCVO; Capt. Sir Iain Tennant, KT; Capt. N. E. F. Dalrymple-Hamilton, CVO, MBE, DSC, RN; The Marquess of Lothian, KCVO
*Ensigns*, Cdre Sir John Clerk of Penicuik, Bt., CBE, VRD; The Earl of Elgin and Kincardine, KT; Col. G. R. Simpson, DSO, LVO, TD; Maj. Sir David Butter, KCVO, MC
*Brigadiers*, The Earl of Minto, OBE; Maj.-Gen. Sir John Swinton, KCVO, OBE; Gen. Sir Michael Gow, GCB; The Hon. Lord Elliott, MC; Maj. the Hon. Sir Lachlan Maclean, Bt.; The Rt. Hon. Lord Younger of Prestwick, KCVO, TD; Capt. G. Burnet, LVO; The Duke of Montrose; Lt.-Gen. Sir Norman Arthur, KCB; The Hon. Sir William Macpherson of Cluny, TD; The Lord Nickson, KBE; Maj. the Lord Glenarthur; Earl of Dalkeith
*Adjutant*, Maj. the Hon. Sir Lachlan Maclean, Bt.
*Surgeon*, Dr P. A. P. Mackenzie, TD
*Chaplain*, Very Revd W. J. Morris, DD
*President of the Council and Silver Stick for Scotland*, Maj. Sir Hew Hamilton-Dalrymple, Bt., KCVO
*Vice-President*, Capt. Sir Iain Tennant, KT
*Secretary*, Capt. J. D. B. Younger
*Treasurer*, J. Martin Haldane

## HOUSEHOLD OF THE PRINCE PHILIP, DUKE OF EDINBURGH

*Treasurer*, Sir Brian McGrath, KCVO
*Private Secretary*, Brig. M. G. Hunt-Davis, CBE
*Equerry*, Maj. A. C. Richards
*Extra Equerries*, J. B. V. Orr, CVO; Sir Richard Davies, KCVO, CBE; Lord Buxton of Alsa; Brig. C. Robertson, CVO
*Temporary Equerries*, Capt. E. Bearcroft; Capt. J. Walker; Maj. J. Cosby
*Chief Clerk and Accountant*, G. D. Partington

## HOUSEHOLD OF QUEEN ELIZABETH THE QUEEN MOTHER

*Lord Chamberlain*, The Earl of Crawford and Balcarres, PC
*Private Secretary, Comptroller and Equerry*, Capt. Sir Alastair Aird, KCVO
*Assistant Private Secretary and Equerry*, Maj. R. Seymour, CVO
*Treasurer and Equerry*, Maj. Sir Ralph Anstruther, Bt., GCVO, MC
*Equerry*, Maj. C. Burgess (*temp.*)
*Extra Equerries*, Maj. Sir John Griffin, KCVO; The Lord Sinclair, CVO; Maj. W. Richardson, LVO; Maj. D. McMicking, LVO; Capt. A. Windham, LVO
*Apothecary to the Household*, Dr N. Southward, LVO, MB, B.chir.
*Surgeon-Apothecary to the Household (Royal Lodge, Windsor)*, Dr J. Briscoe, D.obst.
*Mistress of the Robes*, vacant
*Ladies of the Bedchamber*, The Lady Grimthorpe, CVO; The Countess of Scarbrough
*Women of the Bedchamber*, Dame Frances Campbell-Preston, DCVO; Lady Angela Oswald, LVO; The Hon. Mrs Rhodes; Mrs Michael Gordon-Lennox
*Extra Women of the Bedchamber*, Lady Jean Rankin, DCVO; Miss Jane Walker-Okeover; Lady Margaret Colville, CVO; Lady Elizabeth Basset, DCVO
*Clerk Comptroller*, M. Blanch, CVO

*Clerk Accountant*, J. P. Kyle, LVO
*Information Officer*, Mrs R. Murphy, LVO
*Clerks*, Miss F. Fletcher, LVO; Mrs W. Stevens

---

## HOUSEHOLD OF THE PRINCE AND PRINCESS OF WALES

---

*Private Secretary and Treasurer to the Prince of Wales*, Cdr.
  R. J. Aylard, CVO, RN
*Private Secretary to the Princess of Wales*, P. Jephson
*Deputy Private Secretary to The Prince of Wales*, S. Lamport.
*Assistant Private Secretaries to The Prince of Wales*, M.
  Butler; Dr M. Williams
*Press Secretary to the Prince of Wales*, A. Percival
*Assistant Press Secretary to the Prince of Wales*, Miss
  A. Henney
*Press Secretary to the Princess of Wales*, G. Crawford
*Equerry to the Prince of Wales*, Maj. P. J. Tabor
*Extra Equerries to the Prince of Wales*, The Hon. Edward
  Adeane, CVO; Maj.-Gen. Sir Christopher Airy, KCVO, CBE;
  Sqn. Ldr. Sir David Checketts, KCVO; Sir David Landale,
  KCVO; Sir John Riddle, Bt., CVO; G. J. Ward, CBE; Col.
  J. Q. Winter, LVO
*Ladies-in-Waiting*, Miss Anne Beckwith-Smith, LVO;
  Viscountess Campden; Mrs Max Pike; Miss Alexandra
  Loyd; Mrs James Lonsdale
*Extra Lady-in-Waiting*, Lady Sarah McCorquodale
*Secretary to the Duchy of Cornwall and Keeper of the Records*,
  J. N. C. James, CBE

---

## HOUSEHOLD OF THE DUKE AND DUCHESS OF YORK

---

*Private Secretary, Treasurer and Extra Equerry to the Duke
  and Duchess of York*, Capt. N. Blair, RN
*Comptroller and Assistant Private Secretary to the Duke and
  Duchess of York*, Mrs Jonathan Mathias
*Equerry to The Duke of York*, Capt. D. H. Thompson

---

## HOUSEHOLD OF THE PRINCE EDWARD

---

*Private Secretary*, Lt.-Col. S. G. O'Dwyer
*Assistant Private Secretary*, Mrs R. Warburton, MVO
*Clerk*, Miss L. Buggé

---

## HOUSEHOLD OF THE PRINCESS ROYAL

---

*Private Secretary*, Lt.-Col. P. Gibbs, LVO
*Assistant Private Secretary*, The Hon. Mrs Louloudis
*Ladies-in-Waiting*, Lady Carew Pole, LVO; Mrs Andrew
  Feilden, LVO; The Hon. Mrs Legge-Bourke, LVO; Mrs
  William Nunneley; Mrs Timothy Holderness-Roddam;
  Mrs Charles Ritchie; Mrs David Bowes Lyon
*Extra Ladies-in-Waiting*, Miss Victoria Legge-Bourke, LVO;
  Mrs Malcolm Innes, LVO; The Countess of Lichfield

---

## HOUSEHOLD OF THE PRINCESS MARGARET, COUNTESS OF SNOWDON

---

*Private Secretary and Comptroller*, The Lord Napier and
  Ettrick, KCVO

*Lady-in-Waiting*, The Hon. Mrs Whitehead, LVO
*Extra Ladies-in-Waiting*, Lady Elizabeth Cavendish, LVO;
  Lady Aird, LVO; Mrs Robin Benson, LVO, OBE; Lady Juliet
  Townsend, LVO; Mrs Jane Stevens, LVO; The Hon. Mrs
  Wills, LVO; The Lady Glenconner, LVO; The Countess
  Alexander of Tunis, LVO; Mrs Charles Vyvyan

---

## HOUSEHOLD OF THE DUKE AND DUCHESS OF GLOUCESTER

---

*Private Secretary, Comptroller and Equerry*, Maj.
  N. M. L. Barne
*Assistant Private Secretary to the Duchess of Gloucester*, Miss
  Suzanne Marland
*Extra Equerry*, Lt.-Col. Sir Simon Bland, KCVO
*Ladies-in-Waiting*, Mrs Michael Wigley, CVO; Mrs Euan
  McCorquodale, LVO; Mrs Howard Page
*Extra Ladies-in-Waiting*, Miss Jennifer Thomson; The Lady
  Camoys

---

## HOUSEHOLD OF PRINCESS ALICE, DUCHESS OF GLOUCESTER

---

*Private Secretary, Comptroller and Equerry*, Maj.
  N. M. L. Barne
*Extra Equerry*, Lt.-Col. Sir Simon Bland, KCVO
*Ladies-in-Waiting*, Dame Jean Maxwell-Scott, DCVO; Mrs
  Michael Harvey
*Extra Ladies-in-Waiting*, Miss Diana Harrison; The Hon.
  Jane Walsh, LVO; Miss Jane Egerton-Warburton, LVO

---

## HOUSEHOLD OF THE DUKE AND DUCHESS OF KENT

---

*Private Secretary*, N. Adamson, OBE
*Extra Equerries*, Lt.-Cdr. Sir Richard Buckley, KCVO; N.
  Adamson, OBE
*Temporary Equerry*, Capt. A. Tetley
*Ladies-in-Waiting*, Mrs Fiona Henderson, CVO; Mrs Colin
  Marsh, LVO; Mrs Julian Tomkins; Mrs Peter Troughton;
  Fiona, Lady Astor of Hever; Mrs Richard Beckett

---

## HOUSEHOLD OF PRINCE AND PRINCESS MICHAEL OF KENT

---

*Personal Secretary*, Miss E. Moore-Searson
*Equerry*, J. Kennedy
*Ladies-in-Waiting*, The Hon. Mrs Sanders; Miss Anne
  Frost; Mrs J. Fellowes

---

## HOUSEHOLD OF PRINCESS ALEXANDRA, THE HON. LADY OGILVY

---

*Comptroller and Private Secretary*, Rear-Adm. Sir John
  Garnier, KCVO, CBE
*Extra Equerry*, Maj. Sir Peter Clarke, KCVO
*Lady-in-Waiting*, Lady Mary Mumford, CVO
*Extra Ladies-in-Waiting*, Mrs Peter Afia; Lady Mary
  Colman; Lady Nicholas Gordon Lennox; The Hon. Lady
  Rowley; Dame Mona Mitchell, DCVO

# Royal Finances

## FUNDING

### THE CIVIL LIST

The Civil List dates back to the late 17th century. It was originally used by the Sovereign to pay the salaries of judges, ambassadors and other government offices as well as the expenses of the royal household. In 1760 on the accession of George III it was decided that the Civil List would be provided by Parliament in return for the King surrendering the hereditary revenues of the Crown. At that time Parliament undertook to pay the salaries of judges, ambassadors, etc. In 1831 Parliament agreed also to meet the costs of the royal palaces. Each sovereign has agreed to continue this arrangement.

The Civil List paid to The Queen is charged on the Consolidated Fund. Until 1972, the amount of money allocated annually under the Civil List was set for the duration of a reign. The system was then altered to a fixed annual payment for ten years but from 1975 high inflation made an annual review necessary. The system of payments reverted to the practice of a fixed annual payment for ten years from 1 January 1991.

The Civil List Acts provide for other members of the royal family to receive parliamentary annuities from government funds to meet the expenses of carrying out their official duties. Since 1975 The Queen has reimbursed the Treasury for the annuities paid to the Duke of Gloucester, the Duke of Kent and Princess Alexandra. Since April 1993 The Queen has reimbursed all the annuities except those paid to Queen Elizabeth the Queen Mother and the Duke of Edinburgh.

The Prince of Wales does not receive a parliamentary annuity. He derives his income from the revenues of the Duchy of Cornwall and these monies meet the official and private expenses of the Prince of Wales and his family.

The annual payments for the years 1991–2000 are:

| | |
|---|---:|
| The Queen | £7,900,000 |
| Queen Elizabeth the Queen Mother | 643,000 |
| The Duke of Edinburgh | 359,000 |
| *The Duke of York | 249,000 |
| *The Prince Edward | 96,000 |
| *The Princess Royal | 228,000 |
| *The Princess Margaret, Countess of Snowdon | 219,000 |
| *Princess Alice, Duchess of Gloucester | 87,000 |
| *The Duke of Gloucester | 175,000 |
| *The Duke of Kent | 236,000 |
| *Princess Alexandra | 225,000 |
| | 10,237,000 |
| *Refunded to the Treasury | 1,515,000 |
| Total | 8,722,000 |

### GRANT-IN-AID

Grant-in-aid is voted annually by Parliament to pay for the upkeep of the occupied royal palaces which are used as royal residences or for official or ceremonial purposes.

### THE PRIVY PURSE

The funds received by the Privy Purse pay for official expenses incurred by The Queen as head of state and for some of The Queen's private expenditure. The revenues of the Duchy of Lancaster are the principal source of income for the Privy Purse. The revenues of the Duchy were retained by George III in 1760 when the hereditary revenues were surrendered in exchange for the Civil List.

### PERSONAL INCOME

The Queen's personal income derives mostly from investments, and is used to meet private expenditure.

### DEPARTMENTAL VOTES

Other items of expenditure connected with the official duties of the royal family which fall on votes of government departments include:

Ministry of Defence – The Royal Yacht; The Queen's Flight
Foreign and Commonwealth Office – Marshal of the Diplomatic Corps; overseas visits at the request of government departments
Department of National Heritage – Royal palaces
Department of Transport – The Royal Train
HM Treasury – Central Chancery of the Orders of Knighthood

## TAXATION

The Sovereign is not legally liable to pay income tax, capital gains tax or inheritance tax. After income tax was reintroduced in 1842 some income tax was paid voluntarily by the Sovereign but over a long period these payments were phased out. In November 1992 the Prime Minister announced that The Queen had offered to pay tax on a voluntary basis from 6 April 1993, and that the Prince of Wales also wished to pay tax on a voluntary basis on his income from the Duchy of Cornwall. (He was already taxed in all other respects.)

The provisions for The Queen and the Prince of Wales to pay tax were set out in a Memorandum of Understanding on Royal Taxation presented to Parliament on 11 February 1993. The main provisions are that The Queen will pay income tax and capital gains tax in respect of her private income and assets, and on the proportion of the income and capital gains of the Privy Purse used for private purposes. Inheritance tax will be paid on The Queen's assets, except for those which pass to the next Sovereign, whether automatically or by gift or bequest. The Prince of Wales will pay income tax on income from the Duchy of Cornwall used for private purposes.

The Prince of Wales has confirmed that he intends to pay tax on the same basis following his accession to the throne.

Other members of the royal family are subject to tax as for any taxpayer.

# Military Ranks and Titles

---

### THE QUEEN

---

*Lord High Admiral of the United Kingdom*

*Colonel-in-Chief*
The Life Guards; The Blues and Royals (Royal Horse Guards and 1st Dragoons); The Royal Scots Dragoon Guards (Carabiniers and Greys); The Queen's Royal Lancers; Royal Tank Regiment; Corps of Royal Engineers; Grenadier Guards; Coldstream Guards; Scots Guards; Irish Guards; Welsh Guards; The Royal Welch Fusiliers; The Queen's Lancashire Regiment; The Argyll and Sutherland Highlanders (Princess Louise's); The Royal Green Jackets; Adjutant-General's Corps; The Governor-General's Horse Guards (of Canada); The King's Own Calgary Regiment; Canadian Forces Military Engineers Branch; Royal 22e Regiment (of Canada); Governor-General's Foot Guards (of Canada); The Canadian Grenadier Guards; Le Regiment de la Chaudiere (of Canada); 2nd Bn Royal New Brunswick Regiment (North Shore); The 48th Highlanders of Canada; The Argyll and Sutherland Highlanders of Canada (Princess Louise's); The Calgary Highlanders; Royal Australian Engineers; Royal Australian Infantry Corps; Royal Australian Army Ordnance Corps; Royal Australian Army Nursing Corps; The Corps of Royal New Zealand Engineers; Royal New Zealand Infantry Regiment; Royal New Zealand Army Ordnance Corps; Royal Malta Artillery; The Malawi Rifles

*Affiliated Colonel-in-Chief*
The Queen's Gurkha Engineers

*Captain-General*
Royal Regiment of Artillery; The Honourable Artillery Company; Combined Cadet Force; Royal Regiment of Canadian Artillery; Royal Regiment of Australian Artillery; Royal Regiment of New Zealand Artillery; Royal New Zealand Armoured Corps

*Hon. Colonel*
The Royal Mercian and Lancastrian Yeomanry

*Patron*
Royal Army Chaplains' Department

*Air Commodore-in-Chief*
Royal Auxiliary Air Force; Royal Air Force Regiment; Royal Observer Corps; Air Reserve (of Canada); Royal Australian Air Force Reserve

*Commandant-in-Chief*
Royal Air Force College, Cranwell

*Hon. Air Commodore*
RAF Marham

---

### HM QUEEN ELIZABETH THE QUEEN MOTHER

---

*Colonel-in-Chief*
1st The Queen's Dragoon Guards; The Queen's Royal Hussars (Queen's Own and Royal Irish); 9th/12th Royal Lancers (Prince of Wales's); The King's Regiment; The Royal Anglian Regiment; The Light Infantry; The Black Watch (Royal Highland Regiment); Royal Army Medical Corps; The Black Watch (Royal Highland Regiment) of Canada; The Toronto Scottish Regiment; Canadian Forces Medical Services; Royal Australian Army Medical Corps; Royal New Zealand Army Medical Corps

*Hon. Colonel*
The Royal Yeomanry; The London Scottish; Inns of Court and City Yeomanry

*Commandant-in-Chief*
Women in the Royal Navy; Women, Royal Air Force; RAF Central Flying School

---

### HRH THE PRINCE PHILIP, DUKE OF EDINBURGH

---

*Admiral of the Fleet*
*Field Marshal*
*Marshal of the Royal Air Force*

*Admiral of the Fleet, Royal Australian Navy*
*Field Marshal, Australian Military Forces*
*Marshal of the Royal Australian Air Force*

*Admiral of the Fleet, Royal New Zealand Navy*
*Field Marshal, New Zealand Army*
*Marshal of the Royal New Zealand Air Force*

*Captain-General, Royal Marines*

*Admiral*
Royal Canadian Sea Cadets

*Colonel-in-Chief*
The Royal Gloucestershire, Berkshire and Wiltshire Regiment; The Highlanders (Seaforth, Gordons and Camerons); Corps of Royal Electrical and Mechanical Engineers; Intelligence Corps; Army Cadet Force; The Royal Canadian Regiment; The Royal Hamilton Light Infantry (Wentworth Regiment) (of Canada); The Cameron Highlanders of Ottawa; The Queen's Own Cameron Highlanders of Canada; The Seaforth Highlanders of Canada; The Royal Canadian Army Cadets; The Royal Australian Corps of Electrical and Mechanical Engineers; The Australian Cadet Corps; The Royal New Zealand Corps of Electrical and Mechanical Engineers

*Deputy Colonel-in-Chief*
The Queen's Royal Hussars (Queen's Own and Royal Irish)

*Colonel*
Grenadier Guards

*Hon. Colonel*
City of Edinburgh Universities Officers' Training Corps; The Trinidad and Tobago Regiment

*Air Commodore-in-Chief*
Air Training Corps; Royal Canadian Air Cadets

*Hon. Air Commodore*
RAF Kinloss

## HRH THE PRINCE OF WALES

*Captain*, Royal Navy
*Group Captain*, Royal Air Force

*Colonel-in-Chief*
The Royal Dragoon Guards; The Cheshire Regiment; The Royal Regiment of Wales (24th/41st Foot); The Parachute Regiment; The Royal Gurkha Rifles; Army Air Corps; The Royal Canadian Dragoons; Lord Strathcona's Horse (Royal Canadians); Royal Regiment of Canada; Royal Winnipeg Rifles; Royal Australian Armoured Corps; 2nd Bn The Royal Pacific Islands Regiment

*Deputy Colonel-in-Chief*
The Highlanders (Seaforth, Gordons and Camerons)

*Colonel*
Welsh Guards

*Air Commodore-in-Chief*
Royal New Zealand Air Force

*Hon. Air Commodore*
RAF Valley

## HRH THE PRINCESS OF WALES

*Colonel-in-Chief*
The Light Dragoons; The Princess of Wales's Royal Regiment (Queen's and Royal Hampshires); The Princess of Wales's Own Regiment (of Canada); The West Nova Scotia Regiment (of Canada); The Royal Australian Survey Corps

*Hon. Air Commodore*
RAF Wittering

## HRH THE DUKE OF YORK

*Lieutenant-Commander*, Royal Navy

*Admiral*
Sea Cadet Corps

*Colonel-in-Chief*
The Staffordshire Regiment (The Prince of Wales's); The Royal Irish Regiment (27th (Inniskilling), 83rd, 87th and The Ulster Defence Regiment); Canadian Airborne Regiment

## HRH THE PRINCESS ROYAL

*Rear Admiral and Chief Commandant*
Women in the Royal Navy

*Colonel-in-Chief*
The King's Royal Hussars; Royal Corps of Signals; The Royal Scots (The Royal Regiment); The Worcestershire and Sherwood Foresters Regiment (29th/45th Foot); The Royal Logistic Corps; 8th Canadian Hussars (Princess Louise's); Canadian Forces Communications and Electronics Branch; The Grey and Simcoe Foresters; The Royal Regina Rifle Regiment; Royal Newfoundland

Regiment; Royal Australian Corps of Signals; Royal New Zealand Corps of Signals; Royal New Zealand Nursing Corps

*Affiliated Colonel-in-Chief*
The Queen's Gurkha Signals; The Queen's Own Gurkha Transport Regiment

*Hon. Colonel*
University of London Officers' Training Corps

*Hon. Air Commodore*
RAF Lyneham

*Commandant-in-Chief*
Women's Transport Service (FANY)

## HRH THE PRINCESS MARGARET, COUNTESS OF SNOWDON

*Colonel-in-Chief*
The Royal Highland Fusiliers (Princess Margaret's Own Glasgow and Ayrshire Regiment); Queen Alexandra's Royal Army Nursing Corps; The Highland Fusiliers of Canada; The Princess Louise Fusiliers; The Bermuda Regiment

*Deputy Colonel-in-Chief*
The Royal Anglian Regiment

*Hon. Air Commodore*
RAF Coningsby

## HRH PRINCESS ALICE, DUCHESS OF GLOUCESTER

*Air Chief Marshal*

*Colonel-in-Chief*
The King's Own Scottish Borderers; Royal Australian Corps of Transport; Royal New Zealand Corps of Transport

*Deputy Colonel-in-Chief*
The King's Royal Hussars; The Royal Anglian Regiment

*Air Chief Commandant*
Women, Royal Air Force

## HRH THE DUKE OF GLOUCESTER

*Deputy Colonel-in-Chief*
The Royal Gloucestershire, Berkshire and Wiltshire Regiment; The Royal Logistic Corps

*Hon. Colonel*
Royal Monmouthshire Royal Engineers (Militia)

*Hon. Air Commodore*
RAF Odiham

## HRH THE DUCHESS OF GLOUCESTER

*Colonel-in-Chief*
Royal Australian Army Educational Corps; Royal New Zealand Army Educational Corps

*Deputy Colonel-in-Chief*
  Adjutant-General's Corps

---

## HRH THE DUKE OF KENT

*Field Marshal*
*Hon. Air Vice-Marshal*

*Colonel-in-Chief*
  The Royal Regiment of Fusiliers; The Devonshire and
  Dorset Regiment; The Lorne Scots Regiment (Peel,
  Dufferin and Hamilton Regiment)

*Deputy Colonel-in-Chief*
  The Royal Scots Dragoon Guards (Carabiniers and
  Greys)

*Colonel*
  Scots Guards

*Hon. Air Commodore*
  RAF Leuchars

---

## HRH THE DUCHESS OF KENT

*Hon. Major-General*

*Colonel-in-Chief*
  The Prince of Wales's Own Regiment of Yorkshire

*Deputy Colonel-in-Chief*
  The Royal Dragoon Guards; Adjutant-General's Corps;
  The Royal Logistic Corps

---

## HRH PRINCE MICHAEL OF KENT

Major (retd), The Royal Hussars (Prince of Wales's Own)

*Hon. Commodore*
  Royal Naval Reserve

---

## HRH PRINCESS ALEXANDRA, THE HON. LADY OGILVY

*Patron*
  Queen Alexandra's Royal Naval Nursing Service

*Colonel-in-Chief*
  The King's Own Royal Border Regiment; The Queen's
  Own Rifles of Canada; The Canadian Scottish Regiment
  (Princess Mary's)

*Deputy Colonel-in-Chief*
  The Queen's Royal Lancers; The Light Infantry

*Deputy Hon. Colonel*
  The Royal Yeomanry

*Patron and Air Chief Commandant*
  Princess Mary's Royal Air Force Nursing Service

# The Royal Arms

ENGLAND

*1st and 4th quarters* (representing England) – Gules, three
  lions passant guardant in pale Or
*2nd quarter* (representing Scotland) – Or, a lion rampant
  within a double tressure flory counterflory Gules
*3rd quarter* (representing Ireland) – Azure, a harp Or,
  stringed Argent
The whole shield is encircled with the Garter

SCOTLAND

The Royal Arms shown with the Lion of Scotland in the 1st
and 4th quarters, and the Lions of England in the 2nd
quarter
  The whole shield is encircled with the Thistle

SUPPORTERS (ENGLAND)

*Dexter* (right) – a lion rampant guardant Or, imperially
  crowned (shown in Scotland on the sinister)
*Sinister* (left) – a unicorn Argent, armed, crined, and
  unguled Or, gorged with a coronet composed of crosses
  patées and fleurs-de-lis, a chain affixed, passing between
  the forelegs, and reflexed over the back (shown in
  Scotland on the dexter and imperially crowned)

CRESTS

*England* – the Royal Crown Proper thereon a lion statant
  guardant Or imperially crowned also Proper
*Scotland* – upon an imperial crown Proper a lion sejant
  affrontée Gules imperially crowned Or, holding in the
  dexter paw a sword and in the sinister a sceptre erect, also
  Proper
*Ireland* – a tower triple-towered of the First, from the portal
  a hart springing Argent, attired and hooved Or

BADGES

*England* – the red and white rose united, slipped and leaved
  proper
*Scotland* – a thistle, slipped and leaved proper
*Ireland* – a shamrock leaf slipped Vert; also a harp Or,
  stringed Argent
*United Kingdom* – the rose of England, the thistle of
  Scotland, and the shamrock of Ireland engrafted on the
  same stem proper, and an escutcheon charged as the
  Union Flag (all ensigned with the Royal Crown)
*Wales* – upon a mount Vert a dragon passant, wings
  elevated Gules

# The House of Windsor

King George V assumed by royal proclamation (17 June 1917) for his House and family, as well as for all descendants in the male line of Queen Victoria who are subjects of these realms, the name of Windsor.

KING GEORGE V (George Frederick Ernest Albert), second son of King Edward VII, *born* 3 June 1865; *married* 6 July 1893 HSH Princess Victoria Mary Augusta Louise Olga Pauline Claudine Agnes of Teck (Queen Mary, *born* 26 May 1867; *died* 24 March 1953); *succeeded* to the throne 6 May 1910; *died* 20 January 1936. *Issue:*

1. HRH PRINCE EDWARD Albert Christian George Andrew Patrick David, *born* 23 June 1894, *succeeded* to the throne as King Edward VIII, 20 January 1936; *abdicated* 11 December 1936; created *Duke of Windsor*, 1936; *married* 3 June 1937, Mrs Wallis Warfield (Her Grace The Duchess of Windsor, *born* 19 June 1896; *died* 24 April 1986), *died* 28 May 1972

2. HRH PRINCE ALBERT Frederick Arthur George, *born* 14 December 1895, *created* Duke of York 1920; *married* 26 April 1923, Lady Elizabeth Bowes-Lyon, youngest daughter of the 14th Earl of Strathmore and Kinghorne (HM Queen Elizabeth the Queen Mother, *see* page 123–4), *succeeded* to the throne as King George VI, 11 December 1936; *died* 6 Feburary 1952, having had issue (*see* page 123)

3. HRH PRINCESS (Victoria Alexandra Alice) MARY (*Princess Royal*), *born* 25 April 1897, *married* 28 February 1922, Viscount Lascelles, later the 6th Earl of Harewood (1882–1947), *died* 28 March 1965. *Issue:*
   (1) George Henry Hubert Lascelles, 7th Earl of Harewood, KBE, *born* 7 February 1923; *married* (1) 29 September 1949, Maria (Marion) Stein (marriage dissolved 1967); *issue*, (*a*) David Henry George, Viscount Lascelles, *born* 21 October 1950; (*b*) James

Edward, *born* 5 October 1953; (*c*) (Robert) Jeremy Hugh, *born* 14 February 1955; (2) 31 July 1967, Mrs Patricia Tuckwell; *issue*, (*d*) Mark Hubert, *born* 5 July 1964
   (2) Gerald David Lascelles, *born* 21 August 1924, *married* (1) 15 July 1952, Miss Angela Dowding (marriage dissolved 1978); *issue*, (*a*) Henry Ulick, *born* 19 May 1953; (2) 17 November 1978, Mrs Elizabeth Colvin; *issue*, (*b*) Martin David, *born* 9 February 1962

4. HRH PRINCE HENRY William Frederick Albert, *born* 31 March 1900, *created* Duke of Gloucester, Earl of Ulster and Baron Culloden 1928, *married* 6 November 1935, Lady Alice Christabel Montagu-Douglas-Scott, daughter of the 7th Duke of Buccleuch (HRH Princess Alice, Duchess of Gloucester, *see* page 124); *died* 10 June 1974. *Issue:*
   (1) HRH Prince William Henry Andrew Frederick, *born* 18 December 1941; *accidentally killed* 28 August 1972
   (2) HRH Prince Richard Alexander Walter George (HRH The Duke of Gloucester), *see* page 124

5. HRH PRINCE GEORGE Edward Alexander Edmund, *born* 20 December 1902, *created* Duke of Kent, Earl of St Andrews and Baron Downpatrick 1934, *married* 29 November 1934, HRH Princess Marina of Greece and Denmark (*born* 30 November OS, 1906; *died* 27 August 1968); *killed on active service*, 25 August 1942. *Issue:*
   (1) HRH Prince Edward George Nicholas Paul Patrick (HRH The Duke of Kent), *see* page 124
   (2) HRH Princess Alexandra Helen Elizabeth Olga Christabel (HRH Princess Alexandra, the Hon. Lady Ogilvy), *see* page 124
   (3) HRH Prince Michael George Charles Franklin (HRH Prince Michael of Kent), *see* page 124

6. HRH PRINCE JOHN Charles Francis, *born* 12 July 1905; *died* 18 January 1919

# Descendants of Queen Victoria

QUEEN VICTORIA (Alexandrina Victoria), *born* 24 May 1819; *succeeded* to the throne 20 June 1837; *married* 10 February 1840 (Francis) Albert Augustus Charles Emmanuel, Duke of Saxony, Prince of Saxe-Coburg and Gotha (HRH Albert, Prince Consort, *born* 26 August 1819, *died* 14 December 1861); *died* 22 January 1901. *Issue:*

1. HRH PRINCESS VICTORIA Adelaide Mary Louisa (Princess Royal) (1840–1901), *m.* 1858, Frederic (1831–88), Emperor of Germany March–June 1888. *Issue:*
   (1) HIM Wilhelm II (1859–1941), Emperor of Germany 1888–1918, *m.* (1) 1881 Princess Augusta Victoria of Schleswig-Holstein-Sonderburg-Augustenburg (1858–1921); (2) 1922 Princess Hermine of Reuss (1887–1947). *Issue:*
      (*a*) Prince Wilhelm (1882–1951), *Crown Prince* 1888–1918, *m.* 1905 Duchess Cecilie of Mecklenburg-Schwerin; *issue:* Prince Wilhelm (1906–40); Prince Ludwig Ferdinand (b. 1907), *m.* 1938 Grand Duchess Kira (*see* page 135); Prince Hubertus (1909–50); Prince Friedrich Georg (1911–66); Princess Alexandrine Irene (1915–80); Princess Cecilie (1917–75)
      (*b*) Prince Eitel-Friedrich (1883–1942), *m.* 1906 Duchess Sophie of Oldenburg (marriage dissolved 1926)
      (*c*) Prince Adalbert (1884–1948), *m.* 1914 Duchess Adelheid of Saxe-Meiningen; *issue:* Princess Victoria Marina (1917–81); Prince Wilhelm Victor (1919–89)
      (*d*) Prince August Wilhelm (1887–1949), *m.* 1908 Princess Alexandra of Schleswig-Holstein-Sonderburg-Glücksburg (marriage dissolved 1920); *issue:* Prince Alexander (1912–85)
      (*e*) Prince Oskar (1888–1958), *m.* 1914 Countess von Ruppin; *issue:* Prince Oskar (1915–39); Prince Burchard (1917–88); Princess Herzeleide (1918–89); Prince Wilhelm (b. 1922)

(*f*) Prince Joachim (1890–1920), *m.* 1916 Princess Marie of Anhalt; *issue:* Prince Karl (1916–75)
      (*g*) Princess Viktoria Luise (1892–1980), *m.* 1913 Ernst, Duke of Brunswick 1913–18 (1887–1953); *issue:* Prince Ernst (1914–87); Prince Georg (b. 1915), *m.* 1946 Princess Sophie of Greece (*see* page 135) and has issue (two sons, one daughter); Princess Frederika (1917–81), *m.* 1938 Paul I, King of the Hellenes (*see* page 135); Prince Christian (1919–81); Prince Welf Heinrich (b. 1923)
   (2) Princess Charlotte (1860–1919), *m.* 1878 Bernhard, Duke of Saxe-Meiningen 1914 (1851–1914). *Issue:*
      Princess Feodora (1879–1945), *m.* 1898 Prince Heinrich XXX of Reuss
   (3) Prince Heinrich (1862–1929), *m.* 1888 Princess Irene of Hesse (*see* page 135). *Issue:*
      (*a*) Prince Waldemar (1889–1945), *m.* Princess Calixsta of Lippe
      (*b*) Prince Sigismund (1896–1978), *m.* Princess Charlotte of Saxe-Altenburg; *issue:* Princess Barbe (b. 1920); Prince Alfred (b. 1924)
      (*c*) Prince Heinrich (1900–4)
   (4) Prince Sigismund (1864–6)
   (5) Princess Victoria (1866–1929), *m.* (1) 1890, Prince Adolf of Schaumburg-Lippe (1859–1916); (2) 1927 Alexander Zubkov
   (6) Prince Joachim Waldemar (1868–79)
   (7) Princess Sophie (1870–1932), *m.* 1889 Constantine I (1868–1923), King of the Hellenes 1913–17, 1920–3. *Issue:*
      (*a*) George II (1890–1947), King of the Hellenes 1923–4 and 1935–47, *m.* 1921 Princess Elisabeth of Roumania (marriage dissolved 1935) (*see* page 135)
      (*b*) Alexander I (1893–1920), King of the Hellenes 1917–20, *m.*

1919 Aspasia Manos; *issue:* Princess Alexandra (1921–93), *m.* 1944 King Petar II of Yugoslavia (*see* below)
(c)  Princess Helena (1896–1982), *m.* 1921 King Carol of Roumania (*see* below), (marriage dissolved 1928)
(d)  Paul I (1901–64), King of the Hellenes 1947–64, *m.* 1938 Princess Frederika of Brunswick (*see* page 134); *issue:* King Constantine II (*b.* 1940), *m.* 1964 Princess Anne-Marie of Denmark (*see* page 136), and has issue (three sons, two daughters); Princess Sophie (*b.* 1938), *m.* 1962 Juan Carlos I of Spain (*see* page 136); Princess Irene (*b.* 1942)
(e)  Princess Irene (1904–74), *m.* 1939 4th Duke of Aosta; *issue:* Prince Amedeo (*b.* 1943)
(f)  Princess Katherine (Lady Katherine Brandram) (*b.* 1913), *m.* 1947 Major R. C. A. Brandram, MC, TD; *issue:* R. Paul G. A. Brandram (*b.* 1948)
(8)  Princess Margarethe (1872–1954), *m.* 1893 Prince Friedrich Karl of Hesse (1868–1940). *Issue:*
(a)  Prince Friedrich Wilhelm (1893–1916)
(b)  Prince Maximilian (1894–1914)
(c)  Prince Philipp (1896–1980), *m.* 1925 Princess Mafalda of Italy; *issue:* Prince Moritz (*b.* 1926); Prince Heinrich (*b.* 1927); Prince Otto (*b.* 1937); Princess Elisabeth (*b.* 1940)
(d)  Prince Wolfgang (*b.* 1896), *m.* (1) 1924 Princess Marie Alexandra of Baden; (2) 1948 Ottilie Möller
(e)  Prince Richard (1901–69)
(f)  Prince Christoph (1901–43), *m.* 1930 Princess Sophie of Greece (*see* below) and has issue (two sons, three daughters)

2.  HRH PRINCE ALBERT EDWARD (HM KING EDWARD VII), *b.* 9 November 1841, *m.* 1863 HRH Princess Alexandra of Denmark (1844–1925), *succeeded* to the throne 22 January 1901, *d.* 6 May 1910. *Issue:*
(1)  Albert Victor, Duke of Clarence and Avondale (1864–92)
(2)  George (HM KING GEORGE V) (*see* page 134)
(3)  Louise (1867–1931) Princess Royal 1905–31, *m.* 1889 1st Duke of Fife (1849–1912). *Issue:*
(a)  Princess Alexandra, Duchess of Fife (1891–1959), *m.* 1913 Prince Arthur of Connaught (*see* page 136)
(b)  Princess Maud (1893–1945), *m.* 1923 11th Earl of Southesk (1893–1992); *issue:* The Duke of Fife (*b.* 1929)
(4)  Victoria (1868–1935)
(5)  Maud (1869–1938), *m.* 1896 Prince Charles of Denmark (1872–1957), later King Haakon VII of Norway 1905–57. *Issue:*
(a)  Olav V, King of Norway 1957–91 (1903–91), *m.* 1929 Princess Märtha of Sweden (1901–54); *issue:* Princess Ragnhild (*b.* 1930); Princess Astrid (*b.* 1932); Harald V, King of Norway (*b.* 1937)
(6)  Alexander (6–7 April 1871)

3.  HRH PRINCESS ALICE Maud Mary (1843–78), *m.* 1862 Prince Louis (1837–92), Grand Duke of Hesse 1877–92. *Issue:*
(1)  Victoria (1863–1950), *m.* 1884 *Admiral of the Fleet* Prince Louis of Battenberg (1854–1921), *cr.* 1st Marquess of Milford Haven 1917. *Issue:*
(a)  Alice (1885–1969), *m.* 1903 Prince Andrew of Greece (1882–1944); *issue:* Princess Margarita (1905–81) *m.* 1931 Prince Gottfried of Hohenlohe-Langenburg (*see* below); Princess Theodora (1906–69), *m.* Prince Berthold of Baden (1906–63) and has issue (2 sons, one daughter); Princess Cecilie (1911–37), *m.* George, Grand Duke of Hesse (*see* below); Princess Sophie (*b.* 1914), *m.* (1) 1930 Prince Christoph of Hesse (*see* above); (2) 1946 Prince Georg of Hanover (*see* page 134); Prince Philip, Duke of Edinburgh (*b.* 1921) (*see* page 123)
(b)  Louise (1889–1965), *m.* 1923 Gustaf VI Adolf (1882–1973), King of Sweden 1950–73
(c)  George, 2nd Marquess of Milford Haven (1892–1938), *m.* 1916 Countess Nadejda, daughter of Grand Duke Michael of Russia; *issue:* Lady Tatiana (1917–88); David Michael, 3rd Marquess (1919–70)
(d)  Louis, 1st Earl Mountbatten of Burma (1900–79), *m.* 1922 Edwina Ashley, daughter of Lord Mount Temple; *issue:* Patricia, Countess Mountbatten of Burma (*b.* 1924), Pamela (*b.* 1929)
(2)  Elizabeth (1864–1918), *m.* 1884 Grand Duke Sergius of Russia (1857–1905)
(3)  Irene (1866–1953), *m.* 1888 Prince Heinrich of Prussia (*see* page 134)
(4)  Ernst Ludwig (1868–1937), Grand Duke of Hesse 1892–1918, *m.* (1) 1894 Princess Victoria Melita of Saxe-Coburg (*see* below), (marriage dissolved 1901); (2) 1905 Princess Eleonore of Solms-Hohensolmslich. *Issue:*
(a)  Princess Elizabeth (1895–1903)

(b)  George, Grand Duke of Hesse (1906–37), *m.* Princess Cecilie of Greece (*see* above), and had issue, 2 sons, accidentally killed with parents 1937
(c)  Ludwig, Grand Duke of Hesse (1908–68), *m.* 1937 Margaret, daughter of 1st Lord Geddes
(5)  Frederick William (1870–3)
(6)  Alix (Tsaritsa of Russia) (1872–1918), *m.* 1894 Nicholas II (1868–1918) Tsar of All the Russias 1894–1917, assassinated 16 July 1918. *Issue:*
(a)  Grand Duchess Olga (1895–1918)
(b)  Grand Duchess Tatiana (1897–1918)
(c)  Grand Duchess Marie (1899–1918)
(d)  Grand Duchess Anastasia (1901–18)
(e)  Alexis, Tsarevich of Russia (1904–18)
(7)  Marie (1874–8)

4.  HRH PRINCE ALFRED Ernest Albert, Duke of Edinburgh, *Admiral of the Fleet* (1844–1900), *m.* 1874 Grand Duchess Marie Alexandrovna of Russia (1853–1920); succeeded as Duke of Saxe-Coburg and Gotha 22 August 1893. *Issue:*
(1)  Alfred (Prince of Saxe-Coburg) (1874–99)
(2)  Marie (1875–1938), *m.* 1893 Ferdinand (1865–1927), King of Roumania 1914–27. *Issue:*
(a)  Carol II (1893–1953), King of Roumania 1930–40, *m.* (2) 1921 Princess Helena of Greece (*see* above), (marriage dissolved 1928); *issue:* Michael (*b.* 1921), King of Roumania 1927–30, 1940–7, *m.* 1948 Princess Anne of Bourbon-Parma, and has issue (five daughters)
(b)  Elisabeth (1894–1956), *m.* 1921 George II, King of the Hellenes (*see* page 134)
(c)  Marie (1900–61), *m.* 1922 Alexander (1888–1934), King of Yugoslavia 1921–34; *issue:* Petar II (1923–70), King of Yugoslavia 1934–45, *m.* 1944 Princess Alexandra of Greece (*see* above) and has issue (one son); Prince Tomislav (*b.* 1928), *m.* (1) 1957 Princess Margarita of Baden (daughter of Princess Theodora of Greece and Prince Berthold of Baden, *see* above); (2) 1982 Linda Bonney; and has issue (three sons, one daughter); Prince Andrej (1929–90), *m.* (1) Princess Christina of Hesse (daughter of Prince Christoph of Hesse and Princess Sophie of Greece, *see* above); (2) 1963 Princess Kira-Melita of Leiningen (*see* below); and has issue (three sons, one daughter)
(d)  Prince Nicolas (1903–78)
(e)  Princess Ileana (1909–91), *m.* (1) 1931 Archduke Anton of Austria; (2) 1954 Dr Stefan Issarescu; *issue:* Archduke Stefan (*b.* 1932); Archduchess Maria Ileana (1933–59); Archduchess Alexandra (*b.* 1935); Archduke Dominic (*b.* 1937); Archduchess Maria Magdalena (*b.* 1939); Archduchess Elisabeth (*b.* 1942)
(f)  Prince Mircea (1913–16)
(3)  Victoria Melita (1876–1936), *m.* (1) 1894 Grand Duke Ernst Hesse (*see* above) (marriage dissolved 1901); (2) 1905 the Grand Duke Kirill of Russia (1876–1938). *Issue:*
(a)  Marie Kirillovna (1907–51), *m.* 1925 Prince Friedrich Karl of Leiningen; *issue:* Prince Emich (*b.* 1926); Prince Karl (*b.* 1928); Princess Kira-Melita (*b.* 1930), *m.* Prince Andrej of Yugoslavia (*see* above); Princess Margarita (*b.* 1932); Princess Mechtilde (*b.* 1936); Prince Friedrich (*b.* 1938)
(b)  Kira Kirillovna (1909–67), *m.* 1938 Prince Ludwig of Prussia (*see* page 134); *issue:* Prince Friedrich Wilhelm (*b.* 1939); Prince Michael (*b.* 1940); Princess Marie (*b.* 1942); Princess Kira (*b.* 1943); Prince Louis Ferdinand (1944–77); Prince Christian (*b.* 1946); Princess Xenia (*b.* 1949)
(c)  Vladimir Kirillovich (1917–92), *m.* 1948 Princess Leonida Bagration-Mukhransky; *issue:* Grand Duchess Maria (*b.* 1953), *m.* and has issue
(4)  Alexandra (1878–1942), *m.* 1896 Ernst, Prince of Hohenlohe Langenburg. *Issue:*
(a)  Gottfried (1897–1960), *m.* 1931 Princess Margarita of Greece (*see* above); *issue:* Prince Kraft (*b.* 1935), Princess Beatrix (*b.* 1936), Prince George (*b.* 1938), Prince Ruprecht and Prince Albrecht (*b.* 1944)
(b)  Maria (1899–1967), *m.* 1916 Prince Frederick of Schleswig-Holstein-Sonderburg-Glücksburg; *issue:* Prince Peter (1922–80); Princess Marie (*b.* 1927)
(c)  Princess Alexandra (1901–63)
(d)  Princess Irma (1902–86)
(5)  Princess Beatrice (1884–1966), *m.* 1909 Alfonso of Orleans, Infante of Spain. *Issue:*
(a)  Prince Alvaro (*b.* 1910), *m.* 1937 Carla Parodi-Delfino; *issue:* Princess Gerarda (*b.* 1939); Prince Alonso (1941–75); Princess Beatriz (*b.* 1943); Prince Alvaro (*b.* 1947)

(b)  Prince Alonso (1912–36)
(c)  Prince Ataulfo (1913–74)

5.  HRH Princess Helena Augusta Victoria (1846–1923), m. 1866 Prince Christian of Schleswig-Holstein-Sonderburg-Augustenburg (1831–1917). *Issue:*
(1)  Prince Christian Victor (1867–1900)
(2)  Prince Albert (1869–1931), Duke of Schleswig-Holstein 1921–31
(3)  Princess Helena (1870–1948)
(4)  Princess Marie Louise (1872–1956), m. 1891 Prince Aribert of Anhalt (marriage dissolved 1900)
(5)  Prince Harold (12–20 May 1876)

6.  HRH Princess Louise Caroline Alberta (1848–1939), m. 1871 the Marquess of Lorne, afterwards 9th Duke of Argyll (1845–1914); without issue

7.  HRH Prince Arthur William Patrick Albert, Duke of Connaught, *Field Marshal* (1850–1942), m. 1879 Princess Louisa of Prussia (1860–1917). *Issue:*
(1)  Margaret (1882–1920), m. 1905 Crown Prince Gustaf Adolf (1882–1973), afterwards King of Sweden 1950–73. *Issue:*
(a)  Gustaf Adolf, Duke of Västerbotten (1906–47), m. 1932 Princess Sibylla of Saxe-Coburg-Gotha (*see below*); *issue:* Princess Margaretha (b. 1934); Princess Birgitta (b. 1937); Princess Désirée (b. 1938); Princess Christina (b. 1943); Carl XVI Gustaf, King of Sweden (b. 1946)
(b)  Count Sigvard Bernadotte (b. 1907); m.; *issue:* Count Michael (b. 1944)
(c)  Princess Ingrid (Queen Mother of Denmark) (b. 1910), m. 1935 Frederick IX (1899–72), King of Denmark 1947–72; *issue:* Margrethe II, Queen of Denmark (b. 1940); Princess Benedikte (b. 1944); Princess Anne-Marie (b. 1946), m. 1964 Constantine II of Greece (*see page 135*)
(d)  Prince Bertil, Duke of Halland (b. 1912), m. 1976 Mrs Lilian Craig
(e)  Count Carl Bernadotte (b. 1916), m. (1) 1946 Mrs Kerstin Johnson; (2) 1988 Countess Gunnila Busler
(2)  Arthur (1883–1938), m. 1913 HH the Duchess of Fife (*see page 135*). *Issue:*
Alastair Arthur, Duke of Connaught (1914–43)
(3)  (Victoria) Patricia (1886–1974), m. 1919 Adm. Hon. Sir Alexander Ramsay. *Issue:*

Alexander Ramsay of Mar (b. 1919), m. 1956 Hon. Flora Fraser (Lady Saltoun)

8.  HRH Prince Leopold George Duncan Albert, Duke of Albany (1853–84), m. 1882 Princess Helena of Waldeck (1861–1922). *Issue:*
(1)  Alice (1883–1981), m. 1904 Prince Alexander of Teck (1874–1957), cr. 1st Earl of Athlone 1917. *Issue:*
(a)  Lady May (1906–94), m. 1931 Sir Henry Abel-Smith, KCMG, KCVO, DSO; *issue:* Anne (b. 1932); Richard (b. 1933); Elizabeth (b. 1936)
(b)  Rupert, Viscount Trematon (1907–28)
(c)  Prince Maurice (March–September 1910)
(2)  Charles Edward (1884–1954), Duke of Albany 1884 until title suspended 1917, Duke of Saxe-Coburg-Gotha 1900–18, m. 1905 Princess Victoria Adelheid of Schleswig-Holstein-Sonderburg-Glücksburg. *Issue:*
(a)  Prince Johann Leopold (1906–72), and has issue, including Ernest-Leopold (b. 1935) in whom is vested the right to petition for restoration of the Dukedom of Albany
(b)  Princess Sibylla (1908–72) m. 1932 Prince Gustav Adolf of Sweden (*see above*)
(c)  Prince Dietmar Hubert (1909–43)
(d)  Prince Caroline (1912–83), and has issue
(e)  Prince Friedrich Josias (b. 1918), and has issue

9.  HRH Princess Beatrice Mary Victoria Feodore (1857–1944), m. 1885 Prince Henry of Battenberg (1858–96). *Issue:*
(1)  Alexander, 1st Marquess of Carisbrooke (1886–1960), m. 1917 Lady Irene Denison. *Issue:*
Lady Iris Mountbatten (1920–82)
(2)  Victoria Eugénie (1887–1969), m. 1906 Alfonso XIII (1886–1941) King of Spain 1886–1931. *Issue:*
(a)  Prince Alfonso (1907–38)
(b)  Prince Jaime (1908–75)
(c)  Princess Beatrice (b. 1909)
(d)  Princess Maria (b. 1911)
(e)  Prince Juan (1913–93) Count of Barcelona, and has *issue:* Princess Maria (b. 1936); Juan Carlos I, King of Spain (b. 1938), m. 1962 Princess Sophie of Greece (*see page 135*) and has issue (1 son, 2 daughters); Princess Margarita (b. 1939)
(f)  Prince Gonzalo (1914–34)
(3)  Major Lord Leopold Mountbatten (1889–1922)
(4)  Maurice (1891–1914), died of wounds received in action

# English Kings and Queens  927 TO 1603

## HOUSES OF CERDIC AND DENMARK

| Reign | |
|---|---|
| 927–939 | Æthelstan |
| | Second son of Edward the Elder, by Ecgwynn, and grandson of Alfred |
| | Acceded to Wessex and Mercia c.924, established direct rule over Northumbria 927, effectively creating the Kingdom of England |
| | *Reigned* 15 years |
| 939–946 | Edmund I |
| | *Born* 921, fourth son of Edward the Elder, by Eadgifu |
| | *Married* (1) Ælfgifu (2) Æthelflæd |
| | *Killed* aged 25, *reigned* 6 years |
| 946–955 | Eadred |
| | Fifth son of Edward the Elder, by Eadgifu |
| | *Reigned* 9 years |
| 955–959 | Eadwig |
| | *Born* before 943, son of Edmund and Ælfgifu |
| | *Married* Ælfgifu |
| | *Reigned* 3 years |
| 959–975 | Edgar I |
| | *Born* 943, son of Edmund and Ælfgifu |
| | *Married* (1) Æthelflæd (2) Wulfthryth (3) Ælfthryth |
| | *Died* aged 32, *reigned* 15 years |
| 975–978 | Edward I (the Martyr) |
| | *Born* c.962, son of Edgar and Æthelflæd |
| | *Assassinated* aged c.16, *reigned* 2 years |
| 978–1016 | Æthelred (the Unready) |
| | *Born* c.968/969, son of Edgar and Ælfthryth |
| | *Married* (1) Ælfgifu (2) Emma, daughter of Richard I, count of Normandy |
| | 1013–14 dispossessed of kingdom by Swegn Forkbeard (king of Denmark 987–1014) |
| | *Died* aged c.47, *reigned* 38 years |
| 1016 | Edmund II (Ironside) |
| | *Born* before 993, son of Æthelred and Ælfgifu |
| | *Married* Ealdgyth |
| | *Died* aged over 23, *reigned* 7 months (April–November) |
| 1016–1035 | Cnut (Canute) |
| | *Born* c.995, son of Swegn Forkbeard, king of Denmark, and Gunhild |
| | *Married* (1) Ælfgifu (2) Emma, widow of Æthelred the Unready |
| | Gained submission of West Saxons 1015, Northumbrians 1016, Mercia 1016, king of all England after Edmund's death |
| | King of Denmark 1019–35, king of Norway 1028–35 |
| | *Died* aged c.40, *reigned* 19 years |

**1035–1040**  HAROLD I (Harefoot)
Born c.1016/17, son of Cnut and Ælfgifu
Married Ælfgifu
1035 recognized as regent for himself and his brother
Harthacnut; 1037 recognized as king
Died aged c.23, reigned 4 years

**1040–1042**  HARTHACNUT
Born c.1018, son of Cnut and Emma
Titular king of Denmark from 1028
Acknowledged king of England 1035–7 with Harold I
as regent; effective king after Harold's death
Died aged c.24, reigned 2 years

**1042–1066**  EDWARD II (the Confessor)
Born between 1002 and 1005, son of Æthelred the
Unready and Emma
Married Eadgyth, daughter of Godwine, earl of Wessex
Died aged over 60, reigned 23 years

**1066**  HAROLD II (Godwinesson)
Born c.1020, son of Godwine, earl of Wessex, and
Gytha
Married (1) Eadgyth (2) Ealdgyth
Killed in battle aged c.46, reigned 10 months (January–
October)

## THE HOUSE OF NORMANDY

**1066–1087**  WILLIAM I (the Conqueror)
Born 1027/8, son of Robert I, duke of Normandy;
obtained the Crown by conquest
Married Matilda, daughter of Baldwin, count of
Flanders
Died aged c.60, reigned 20 years

**1087–1100**  WILLIAM II (Rufus)
Born between 1056 and 1060, third son of William I;
succeeded his father in England only
Killed aged c.40, reigned 12 years

**1100–1135**  HENRY I (Beauclerk)
Born 1068, fourth son of William I
Married (1) Edith or Matilda, daughter of Malcolm III
of Scotland (2) Adela, daughter of Godfrey, count of
Louvain
Died aged 67, reigned 35 years

**1135–1154**  STEPHEN
Born not later than 1100, third son of Adela, daughter
of William I, and Stephen, count of Blois
Married Matilda, daughter of Eustace, count of
Boulogne
1141 (February–November) held captive by adherents
of Matilda, daughter of Henry I, who contested the
crown until 1153
Died aged over 53, reigned 18 years

## THE HOUSE OF ANJOU (PLANTAGENETS)

**1154–1189**  HENRY II (Curtmantle)
Born 1133, son of Matilda, daughter of Henry I, and
Geoffrey, count of Anjou
Married Eleanor, daughter of William, duke of
Aquitaine, and divorced queen of Louis VII of France
Died aged 56, reigned 34 years

**1189–1199**  RICHARD I (Coeur de Lion)
Born 1157, third son of Henry II
Married Berengaria, daughter of Sancho VI, king of
Navarre
Died aged 42, reigned 9 years

**1199–1216**  JOHN (Lackland)
Born 1167, fifth son of Henry II
Married (1) Isabella or Avisa, daughter of William, earl
of Gloucester (divorced) (2) Isabella, daughter of
Aymer, count of Angoulême
Died aged 48, reigned 17 years

**1216–1272**  HENRY III
Born 1207, son of John and Isabella of Angoulême

Married Eleanor, daughter of Raymond, count of
Provence
Died aged 65, reigned 56 years

**1272–1307**  EDWARD I (Longshanks)
Born 1239, eldest son of Henry III
Married (1) Eleanor, daughter of Ferdinand III, king
of Castile (2) Margaret, daughter of Philip III of
France
Died aged 68, reigned 34 years

**1307–1327**  EDWARD II
Born 1284, eldest surviving son of Edward I and
Eleanor
Married Isabella, daughter of Philip IV of France
Deposed January 1327, killed September 1327 aged 43,
reigned 19 years

**1327–1377**  EDWARD III
Born 1312, eldest son of Edward II
Married Philippa, daughter of William, count of
Hainault
Died aged 64, reigned 50 years

**1377–1399**  RICHARD II
Born 1367, son of Edward (the Black Prince), eldest
son of Edward III
Married (1) Anne, daughter of Emperor Charles IV
(2) Isabelle, daughter of Charles VI of France
Deposed September 1399, killed February 1400 aged
33, reigned 22 years

## THE HOUSE OF LANCASTER

**1399–1413**  HENRY IV
Born 1366, son of John of Gaunt, fourth son of Edward
III, and Blanche, daughter of Henry, duke of
Lancaster
Married (1) Mary, daughter of Humphrey, earl of
Hereford (2) Joan, daughter of Charles, king of
Navarre, and widow of John, duke of Brittany
Died aged 47, reigned 13 years

**1413–1422**  HENRY V
Born 1387, eldest surviving son of Henry IV and Mary
Married Catherine, daughter of Charles VI of France
Died aged 34, reigned 9 years

**1422–1471**  HENRY VI
Born 1421, son of Henry V
Married Margaret, daughter of René, duke of Anjou
and count of Provence
Deposed March 1461, restored October 1470
Deposed April 1471, killed May 1471 aged 49, reigned
39 years

## THE HOUSE OF YORK

**1461–1483**  EDWARD IV
Born 1442, eldest son of Richard of York, who was the
grandson of Edmund, fifth son of Edward III, and the
son of Anne, great-granddaughter of Lionel, third son
of Edward III
Married Elizabeth Woodville, daughter of Richard,
Lord Rivers, and widow of Sir John Grey
Acceded March 1461, deposed October 1470, restored
April 1471
Died aged 40, reigned 21 years

**1483**  EDWARD V
Born 1470, eldest son of Edward IV
Deposed June 1483, died probably July–September
1483, aged 12, reigned 2 months (April–June)

**1483–1485**  RICHARD III
Born 1452, fourth son of Richard of York and brother
of Edward IV
Married Anne Neville, daughter of Richard, earl of
Warwick, and widow of Edward, Prince of Wales, son
of Henry VI
Killed in battle aged 32, reigned 2 years

## THE HOUSE OF TUDOR

**1485–1509  HENRY VII**
*Born* 1457, son of Margaret Beaufort, great-granddaughter of John of Gaunt, fourth son of Edward III, and Edmund Tudor, earl of Richmond
*Married* Elizabeth, daughter of Edward IV
*Died* aged 52, *reigned* 23 years

**1509–1547  HENRY VIII**
*Born* 1491, second son of Henry VII
*Married* (1) Catherine, daughter of Ferdinand II, king of Aragon, and widow of his elder brother Arthur (divorced) (2) Anne, daughter of Sir Thomas Boleyn (executed) (3) Jane, daughter of Sir John Seymour (died in childbirth) (4) Anne, daughter of John, duke of Cleves (divorced) (5) Catherine Howard, niece of the Duke of Norfolk (executed) (6) Catherine, daughter of Sir Thomas Parr and widow of Lord Latimer
*Died* aged 55, *reigned* 37 years

**1547–1553  EDWARD VI**
*Born* 1537, son of Henry VIII and Jane Seymour
*Died* aged 15, *reigned* 6 years

**1553  JANE**
*Born* 1537, daughter of Frances, daughter of Mary Tudor, the younger sister of Henry VIII, and Henry Grey, duke of Suffolk
*Married* Lord Guildford Dudley, son of the Duke of Northumberland
*Deposed* July 1553, *executed* February 1554 aged 16, *reigned* 14 days

**1553–1558  MARY I**
*Born* 1516, daughter of Henry VIII and Catherine of Aragon
*Married* Philip II of Spain
*Died* aged 42, *reigned* 5 years

**1558–1603  ELIZABETH I**
*Born* 1533, daughter of Henry VIII and Anne Boleyn
*Died* aged 69, *reigned* 44 years

# British Kings and Queens  SINCE 1603

## THE HOUSE OF STUART

**1603–1625  JAMES I (VI OF SCOTLAND)**
*Born* 1566, son of Mary, queen of Scots and granddaughter of Margaret Tudor, elder daughter of Henry VII, and Henry Stewart, Lord Darnley
*Married* Anne, daughter of Frederick II of Denmark
*Died* aged 58, *reigned* 22 years
(*see also* page 140)

**1625–1649  CHARLES I**
*Born* 1600, second son of James I
*Married* Henrietta Maria, daughter of Henry IV of France
*Executed* 1649 aged 48, *reigned* 23 years

COMMONWEALTH DECLARED 19 May 1649
1649–53 Government by a council of state
1653–8 Oliver Cromwell, *Lord Protector*
1658–9 Richard Cromwell, *Lord Protector*

**1660–1685  CHARLES II**
*Born* 1630, eldest son of Charles I
*Married* Catherine, daughter of John IV of Portugal
*Died* aged 54, *reigned* 24 years

**1685–1688  JAMES II (VII OF SCOTLAND)**
*Born* 1633, second son of Charles I
*Married* (1) Lady Anne Hyde, daughter of Edward, earl of Clarendon (2) Mary, daughter of Alphonso, duke of Modena
Reign ended with flight from kingdom December 1688
*Died* 1701 aged 67, *reigned* 3 years

INTERREGNUM 11 December 1688 to 12 February 1689

**1689–1702  WILLIAM III**
*Born* 1650, son of William II, prince of Orange, and Mary Stuart, daughter of Charles I
*Married* Mary, elder daughter of James II
*Died* aged 51, *reigned* 13 years

*and*
**1689–1694  MARY II**
*Born* 1662, elder daughter of James II and Anne
*Died* aged 32, *reigned* 5 years

**1702–1714  ANNE**
*Born* 1665, younger daughter of James II and Anne
*Married* Prince George of Denmark, son of Frederick III of Denmark
*Died* aged 49, *reigned* 12 years

## THE HOUSE OF HANOVER

**1714–1727  GEORGE I (Elector of Hanover)**
*Born* 1660, son of Sophia (daughter of Frederick, elector palatine, and Elizabeth Stuart, daughter of James I) and Ernest Augustus, elector of Hanover
*Married* Sophia Dorothea, daughter of George William, duke of Lüneburg-Celle
*Died* aged 67, *reigned* 12 years

**1727–1760  GEORGE II**
*Born* 1683, son of George I
*Married* Caroline, daughter of John Frederick, margrave of Brandenburg-Anspach
*Died* aged 76, *reigned* 33 years

**1760–1820  GEORGE III**
*Born* 1738, son of Frederick, eldest son of George II
*Married* Charlotte, daughter of Charles Louis, duke of Mecklenburg-Strelitz
*Died* aged 81, *reigned* 59 years

REGENCY 1811–20
Prince of Wales regent owing to the insanity of George III

**1820–1830  GEORGE IV**
*Born* 1762, eldest son of George III
*Married* Caroline, daughter of Charles, duke of Brunswick-Wolfenbüttel
*Died* aged 67, *reigned* 10 years

**1830–1837  WILLIAM IV**
*Born* 1765, third son of George III
*Married* Adelaide, daughter of George, duke of Saxe-Meiningen
*Died* aged 71, *reigned* 7 years

**1837–1901  VICTORIA**
*Born* 1819, daughter of Edward, fourth son of George III
*Married* Prince Albert of Saxe-Coburg and Gotha
*Died* aged 81, *reigned* 63 years

## THE HOUSE OF SAXE-COBURG AND GOTHA

1901–1910    EDWARD VII
Born 1841, eldest son of Victoria and Albert
Married Alexandra, daughter of Christian IX of
Denmark
Died aged 68, reigned 9 years

## THE HOUSE OF WINDSOR

1910–1936    GEORGE V
Born 1865, second son of Edward VII
Married Victoria Mary, daughter of Francis, duke of
Teck
Died aged 70, reigned 25 years

1936    EDWARD VIII
Born 1894, eldest son of George V
Married (1937) Mrs Wallis Warfield
Abdicated 1936, died 1972 aged 77, reigned 10 months
(20 January to 11 December)

1936–1952    GEORGE VI
Born 1895, second son of George V
Married Lady Elizabeth Bowes-Lyon, daughter of 14th
Earl of Strathmore and Kinghorne (see also pages
123–4)
Died aged 56, reigned 15 years

1952–    ELIZABETH II
Born 1926, elder daughter of George VI
Married Philip, son of Prince Andrew of Greece (see
also page 123)
WHOM GOD PRESERVE

# Kings and Queens of Scots  1016 TO 1603

Reign
1016–1034    MALCOLM II
Born c.954, son of Kenneth II
Acceded to Alba 1005, secured Lothian c.1016,
obtained Strathclyde for his grandson Duncan c.1016,
thus forming the Kingdom of Scotland
Died aged c.80, reigned 18 years

1034–1040    DUNCAN I
Son of Bethoc, daughter of Malcolm II, and Crinan
Married a cousin of Siward, earl of Northumbria
Reigned 5 years

1040–1057    MACBETH
Born c.1005, son of a daughter of Malcolm II and
Finlaec, mormaer of Moray
Married Gruoch, granddaughter of Kenneth III
Killed aged c.52, reigned 17 years

1057–1058    LULACH
Born c.1032, son of Gillacomgan, mormaer of Moray,
and Gruoch (and stepson of Macbeth)
Died aged c.26, reigned 7 months (August–March)

1058–1093    MALCOLM III (Canmore)
Born c.1031, elder son of Duncan I
Married (1) Ingibiorg (2) Margaret (St Margaret),
granddaughter of Edmund II of England
Killed in battle aged c.62, reigned 35 years

1093–1097    DONALD III BÁN
Born c.1033, second son of Duncan I
Deposed May 1094, restored November 1094, deposed
October 1097, reigned 3 years

1094    DUNCAN II
Born c.1060, elder son of Malcolm III and Ingibiorg
Married Octreda of Dunbar
Killed aged c.34, reigned 6 months (May–November)

1097–1107    EDGAR
Born c.1074, second son of Malcolm III and Margaret
Died aged c.32, reigned 9 years

1107–1124    ALEXANDER I (The Fierce)
Born c.1077, fifth son of Malcolm III and Margaret
Married Sybilla, illegitimate daughter of Henry I of
England
Died aged c.47, reigned 17 years

1124–1153    DAVID I (The Saint)
Born c.1085, sixth son of Malcolm III and Margaret
Married Matilda, daughter of Waltheof, earl of
Huntingdon
Died aged c.68, reigned 29 years

1153–1165    MALCOLM IV (The Maiden)
Born c.1141, son of Henry, earl of Huntingdon, second
son of David I
Died aged c.24, reigned 12 years

1165–1214    WILLIAM I (The Lion)
Born c.1142, brother of Malcolm IV
Married Ermengarde, daughter of Richard, viscount of
Beaumont
Died aged c.72, reigned 49 years

1214–1249    ALEXANDER II
Born 1198, son of William I
Married (1) Joan, daughter of John, king of England
(2) Marie, daughter of Ingelram de Coucy
Died aged 50, reigned 34 years

1249–1286    ALEXANDER III
Born 1241, son of Alexander II and Marie
Married (1) Margaret, daughter of Henry III of
England (2) Yolande, daughter of the Count of Dreux
Killed accidentally aged 44, reigned 36 years

1286–1290    MARGARET (The Maid of Norway)
Born 1283, daughter of Margaret (daughter of
Alexander III) and Eric II of Norway
Died aged 7, reigned 4 years

FIRST INTERREGNUM 1290–2
Throne disputed by 13 competitors. Crown awarded to
John Balliol by adjudication of Edward I of England

## THE HOUSE OF BALLIOL

1292–1296    JOHN (Balliol)
Born c.1250, son of Dervorguilla, great-great-
granddaughter of David I, and John de Balliol
Married Isabella, daughter of John, earl of Surrey
Abdicated 1296, died 1313 aged c.63, reigned 3 years

SECOND INTERREGNUM 1296–1306
Edward I of England declared John Balliol to have
forfeited the throne for contumacy in 1296 and took
the government of Scotland into his own hands

## THE HOUSE OF BRUCE

1306–1329　ROBERT I (Bruce)
*Born* 1274, son of Robert Bruce and Marjorie, countess of Carrick, and great-grandson of the second daughter of David, earl of Huntingdon, brother of William I
*Married* (1) Isabella, daughter of Donald, earl of Mar (2) Elizabeth, daughter of Richard, earl of Ulster
*Died* aged 54, *reigned* 23 years

1329–1371　DAVID II
*Born* 1324, son of Robert I and Elizabeth
*Married* (1) Joanna, daughter of Edward II of England (2) Margaret Drummond, widow of Sir John Logie (divorced)
*Died* aged 46, *reigned* 41 years

1332 Edward Balliol, son of John Balliol, crowned King of Scots September, expelled December
1333–6 Edward Balliol restored as King of Scots

## THE HOUSE OF STEWART

1371–1390　ROBERT II (Stewart)
*Born* 1316, son of Marjorie, daughter of Robert I, and Walter, High Steward of Scotland
*Married* (1) Elizabeth, daughter of Sir Robert Mure of Rowallan (2) Euphemia, daughter of Hugh, earl of Ross
*Died* aged 74, *reigned* 19 years

1390–1406　ROBERT III
*Born* c.1337, son of Robert II and Elizabeth
*Married* Annabella, daughter of Sir John Drummond of Stobhall
*Died* aged c.69, *reigned* 16 years

1406–1437　JAMES I
*Born* 1394, son of Robert III
*Married* Joan Beaufort, daughter of John, earl of Somerset
*Assassinated* aged 42, *reigned* 30 years

1437–1460　JAMES II
*Born* 1430, son of James I
*Married* Mary, daughter of Arnold, duke of Gueldres
*Killed* accidentally aged 29, *reigned* 23 years

1460–1488　JAMES III
*Born* 1452, son of James II
*Married* Margaret, daughter of Christian I of Denmark
*Assassinated* aged 36, *reigned* 27 years

1488–1513　JAMES IV
*Born* 1473, son of James III
*Married* Margaret Tudor, daughter of Henry VII of England
*Killed* in battle aged 40, *reigned* 25 years

1513–1542　JAMES V
*Born* 1512, son of James IV
*Married* (1) Madeleine, daughter of Francis I of France (2) Mary of Lorraine, daughter of the Duc de Guise
*Died* aged 30, *reigned* 29 years

1542–1567　MARY
*Born* 1542, daughter of James V and Mary
*Married* (1) the Dauphin, afterwards Francis II of France (2) Henry Stewart, Lord Darnley (3) James Hepburn, earl of Bothwell
*Abdicated* 1567, prisoner in England from 1568, *executed* 1587, *reigned* 24 years

1567–1625　JAMES VI (and I of England)
*Born* 1566, son of Mary, queen of Scots, and Henry, Lord Darnley
Acceded 1567 to the Scottish throne, *reigned* 58 years
Succeeded 1603 to the English throne, so joining the English and Scottish crowns in one person. The two kingdoms remained distinct until 1707 when the parliaments of the kingdoms became conjoined
For British Kings and Queens since 1603, *see* pages 138–9

# Welsh Sovereigns and Princes

Wales was ruled by sovereign princes from the earliest times until the death of Llywelyn in 1282. The first English Prince of Wales was the son of Edward I, who was born in Caernarvon town on 25 April 1284. According to a discredited legend, he was presented to the Welsh chieftains as their prince, in fulfilment of a promise that they should have a prince who 'could not speak a word of English' and should be native born. This son, who afterwards became Edward II, was created 'Prince of Wales and Earl of Chester' at the Lincoln Parliament on 7 February 1301.

The title Prince of Wales is borne after individual conferment and is not inherited at birth, though some Princes have been declared and styled Prince of Wales but never formally so created (s.). The title was conferred on Prince Charles by The Queen on 26 July 1958. He was invested at Caernarvon on 1 July 1969.

INDEPENDENT PRINCES AD 844 TO 1282

| | |
|---|---|
| 844–878 | Rhodri the Great |
| 878–916 | Anarawd, son of Rhodri |
| 916–950 | Hywel Dda, the Good |
| 950–979 | Iago ab Idwal (or Ieuaf) |
| 979–985 | Hywel ab Ieuaf, the Bad |
| 985–986 | Cadwallon, his brother |
| 986–999 | Maredudd ab Owain ap Hywel Dda |
| 999–1008 | Cynan ap Hywel ab Ieuaf |
| 1018–1023 | Llywelyn ap Seisyll |
| 1023–1039 | Iago ab Idwal ap Meurig |
| 1039–1063 | Gruffydd ap Llywelyn ap Seisyll |
| 1063–1075 | Bleddyn ap Cynfyn |
| 1075–1081 | Trahaern ap Caradog |
| 1081–1137 | Gruffydd ap Cynan ab Iago |
| 1137–1170 | Owain Gwynedd |
| 1170–1194 | Dafydd ab Owain Gwynedd |
| 1194–1240 | Llywelyn Fawr, the Great |
| 1240–1246 | Dafydd ap Llywelyn |
| 1246–1282 | Llywelyn ap Gruffydd ap Llywelyn |

ENGLISH PRINCES SINCE 1301

| | |
|---|---|
| 1301 | Edward (Edward II) |
| 1343 | Edward the Black Prince, s. of Edward III |
| 1376 | Richard (Richard II), s. of the Black Prince |
| 1399 | Henry of Monmouth (Henry V) |
| 1454 | Edward of Westminster, son of Henry VI |
| 1471 | Edward of Westminster (Edward V) |
| 1483 | Edward, son of Richard III (d. 1484) |
| 1489 | Arthur Tudor, son of Henry VII |
| 1504 | Henry Tudor (Henry VIII) |
| 1610 | Henry Stuart, son of James I (d. 1612) |
| 1616 | Charles Stuart (Charles I) |
| c.1638 (s.) | Charles (Charles II) |
| 1688 (s.) | James Francis Edward (The Old Pretender) (d. 1766) |
| 1714 | George Augustus (George II) |
| 1729 | Frederick Lewis, s. of George II (d. 1751) |
| 1751 | George William Frederick (George III) |
| 1762 | George Augustus Frederick (George IV) |
| 1841 | Albert Edward (Edward VII) |
| 1901 | George (George V) |
| 1910 | Edward (Edward VIII) |
| 1958 | Charles Philip Arthur George |

# The Peerage

## and Members of the House of Lords

The rules which govern the creation and succession of peerages are extremely complicated. There are, technically, five separate peerages, the Peerage of England, of Scotland, of Ireland, of Great Britain, and of the United Kingdom. The Peerage of Great Britain dates from 1707 when an Act of Union combined the two kingdoms of England and Scotland and separate peerages were discontinued. The Peerage of the United Kingdom dates from 1801 when Great Britain and Ireland were combined under an Act of Union. Some Scottish peers have received additional peerages of Great Britain or of the United Kingdom since 1707, and some Irish peers additional peerages of the United Kingdom since 1801.

The Peerage of Ireland was not entirely discontinued from 1801 but holders of Irish peerages, whether pre-dating or created subsequent to the Union of 1801, are not entitled to sit in the House of Lords if they have no additional English, Scottish, Great Britain or United Kingdom peerage. However, they are eligible for election to the House of Commons and to vote in parliamentary elections, which other peers are not. An Irish peer holding a peerage of a lower grade which enables him to sit in the House of Lords is introduced there by the title which enables him to sit, though for all other purposes he is known by his higher title.

In the Peerage of Scotland there is no rank of Baron; the equivalent rank is Lord of Parliament, abbreviated to 'Lord' (the female equivalent is 'Lady'). All peers of England, Scotland, Great Britain or the United Kingdom who are 21 years or over, and of British, Irish or Commonwealth nationality are entitled to sit in the House of Lords.

No fees for dignities have been payable since 1937. The House of Lords surrendered the ancient right of peers to be tried for treason or felony by their peers in 1948.

### Hereditary Women Peers

Most hereditary peerages pass on death to the nearest male heir, but there are exceptions, and several are held by women (*see* pages 149 and 161).

A woman peer in her own right retains her title after marriage, and if her husband's rank is the superior she is designated by the two titles jointly, the inferior one second. Her hereditary claim still holds good in spite of any marriage whether higher or lower. No rank held by a woman can confer any title or even precedence upon her husband but the rank of a hereditary woman peer in her own right is inherited by her eldest son (or in some cases daughter).

Since the Peerage Act 1963, hereditary women peers in their own right have been entitled to sit in the House of Lords, subject to the same qualifications as men.

### Life Peers

Since 1876 non-hereditary or life peerages have been conferred on certain eminent judges to enable the judicial functions of the House of Lords to be carried out. These Lords are known as Lords of Appeal or law lords and, to date, such appointments have all been male.

Since 1958 life peerages have been conferred upon distinguished men and women from all walks of life, giving them seats in the House of Lords in the degree of Baron or Baroness. They are addressed in the same way as hereditary Lords and Barons, and their children have similar courtesy titles.

### Disclaimer of Peerages

The Peerage Act 1963 enables peers to disclaim their peerages for life. Peers alive in 1963 could disclaim within twelve months after the passing of the Act (31 July 1963); a person subsequently succeeding to a peerage may disclaim within twelve months (one month if an MP) after the date of succession, or of reaching 21, if later. The disclaimer is irrevocable but does not affect the descent of the peerage after the disclaimant's death, and children of a disclaimed peer may, if they wish, retain their precedence and any courtesy titles and styles borne as children of a peer. The disclaimer permits the disclaimant to sit in the House of Commons if elected as an MP.

The following peerages are currently disclaimed:

Earldoms: Durham (1970); Home (1963); Sandwich (1964)

Viscountcies: Hailsham (1963); Stansgate (1963)

Baronies: Altrincham (1963); Archibald (1975); Merthyr (1977); Reith (1972); Sanderson of Ayot (1971); Silkin (1972)

Peers Who Are Minors (i.e. under 21 years of age)

Earls: Craven (*b.* 1989)

Barons: Gretton (*b.* 1975)

### Contractions and Symbols

s. Scottish title
i. Irish title
* The peer holds also an Imperial title, specified after the name by Engl., Brit. or UK
° there is no 'of' in the title
*b.* born
*s.* succeeded
*m.* married
*w.* widower or widow
*M.* minor
† heir not ascertained at time of going to press

# Hereditary Peers

## ROYAL DUKES

*Style,* His Royal Highness The Duke of __
*Style of address ( formal)* May it please your Royal Highness; (*informal*) Sir

| *Created* | *Title, order of succession, name, etc.* | *Heir* |
|---|---|---|
| 1947 | *Edinburgh* (1st), The Prince Philip, Duke of Edinburgh, (*see* page 123) | The Prince of Wales |
| 1337 | *Cornwall,* Charles, Prince of Wales, *s.* 1952 (*see* page 123) | ‡ |
| 1398 | *Rothesay,* Charles, Prince of Wales, *s.* 1952 (*see* page 123) | ‡ |
| 1986 | *York* (1st), The Prince Andrew, Duke of York (*see p.* 123) | None |
| 1928 | *Gloucester* (2nd), Prince Richard, Duke of Gloucester, *s.* 1974 (*see* page 124) | Earl of Ulster (*see* page 124) |
| 1934 | *Kent* (2nd), Prince Edward, Duke of Kent, *s.* 1942 (*see* page 124) | Earl of St Andrews (*see* page 124) |

‡ The title is not hereditary but is held by the Sovereign's eldest son from the moment of his birth or the Sovereign's accession

## DUKES

*Coronet,* Eight strawberry leaves
*Style,* His Grace the Duke of __
*Wife's style,* Her Grace the Duchess of __
*Eldest son's style,* Takes his father's second title as a courtesy title
*Younger sons' style,* 'Lord' before forename and family name
*Daughters' style,* 'Lady' before forename and family name
For forms of address, *see* page 217

| *Created* | *Title, order of succession, name, etc.* | *Heir* |
|---|---|---|
| 1868 I.* | *Abercorn* (5th), James Hamilton (6th *Brit. Marq.,* 1790, and 14th *Scott. Earl,* 1606, both *Abercorn*), *b.* 1934, *s.* 1979, *m.* | Marquess of Hamilton, *b.* 1969. |
| 1701 S.* | *Argyll* (12th), Ian Campbell (5th *UK Duke Argyll,* 1892), *b.* 1937, *s.* 1973, *m.* | Marquess of Lorne, *b.* 1968. |
| 1703 S. | *Atholl* (10th), George Iain Murray, *b.* 1931, *s.* 1957. | John *M.,* *b.* 1929. |
| 1682 | *Beaufort* (11th), David Robert Somerset, *b.* 1928, *s.* 1984, *m.* | Marquess of Worcester, *b.* 1952. |
| 1694 | *Bedford* (13th), John Robert Russell, *b.* 1917, *s.* 1953, *m.* | Marquess of Tavistock, *b.* 1940. |
| 1663 S.* | *Buccleuch* (9th) & *Queensberry* (11th) (1684), Walter Francis John Montagu Douglas Scott, KT, VRD (8th *Engl. Earl, Doncaster,* 1662), *b.* 1923, *s.* 1973, *m.* | Earl of Dalkeith, *b.* 1954. |
| 1694 | *Devonshire* (11th), Andrew Robert Buxton Cavendish, MC, PC, *b.* 1920, *s.* 1950, *m.* | Marquess of Hartington, *b.* 1944. |
| 1900 | *Fife* (3rd), James George Alexander Bannerman Carnegie (12th *Scott. Earl, Southesk,* 1633, *s.* 1992), *b.* 1929, *s.* 1959. (*see* page 135). | Earl of Southesk, *b.* 1961. |
| 1675 | *Grafton* (11th), Hugh Denis Charles FitzRoy, KG, *b.* 1919, *s.* 1970, *m.* | Earl of Euston, *b.* 1947. |
| 1643 S.* | *Hamilton* (15th) & *Brandon* (12th) (*Brit.* 1711), Angus Alan Douglas Douglas-Hamilton (*Premier Peer of Scotland*), *b.* 1938, *s.* 1973, *m.* | Marquess of Douglas and Clydesdale, *b.* 1978. |
| 1766 I.* | *Leinster* (8th), Gerald FitzGerald (*Premier Duke and Marquess of Ireland*; 8th *Brit. Visct., Leinster,* 1747), *b.* 1914, *s.* 1976, *m.* | Marquess of Kildare, *b.* 1948. |
| 1719 | *Manchester* (12th), Angus Charles Drogo Montagu, *b.* 1938, *s.* 1985, *m.* | Viscount Mandeville, *b.* 1962. |
| 1702 | *Marlborough* (11th), John George Vanderbilt Henry Spencer-Churchill, *b.* 1926, *s.* 1972, *m.* | Marquess of Blandford, *b.* 1955. |
| 1707 S.* | *Montrose* (8th), James Graham (6th *Brit. Earl, Graham,* 1722), *b.* 1935, *s.* 1992, *m.* | Marquess of Graham, *b.* 1973. |
| 1483 | *Norfolk* (17th), Miles Francis Stapleton Fitzalan-Howard, KG, GCVO, CB, CBE, MC (*Premier Duke*; 12th *Eng. Baron Beaumont,* 1309, *s.* 1971; 4th *UK Baron Howard of Glossop,* 1869, *s.* 1972), *b.* 1915, *s.* 1975, *m. Earl Marshal.* | Earl of Arundel and Surrey, *b.* 1956. |
| 1766 | *Northumberland* (11th), Henry Alan Walter Richard Percy, *b.* 1953, *s.* 1988. | Lord Ralph G. A. *P., b.* 1956. |
| 1675 | *Richmond* (10th) & *Gordon* (5th) (*UK* 1876), Charles Henry Gordon Lennox (10th *Scott. Duke, Lennox,* 1675), *b.* 1929, *s.* 1989, *m.* | Earl of March and Kinrara, *b.* 1955. |

| Created | Title, order of succession, name, etc. | Heir |
|---------|----------------------------------------|------|
| 1707 S.* | *Roxburghe* (10th), Guy David Innes-Ker (5th *UK Earl, Innes,* 1837), *b.* 1954, *s.* 1974, *m.* (*Premier Baronet of Scotland*). | Marquess of Bowmont and Cessford, *b.* 1981. |
| 1703 | *Rutland* (10th), Charles John Robert Manners, CBE, *b.* 1919, *s.* 1940, *m.* | Marquess of Granby, *b.* 1959. |
| 1684 | *St Albans* (14th), Murray de Vere Beauclerk, *b.* 1939, *s.* 1988, *m.* | Earl of Burford, *b.* 1965. |
| 1547 | *Somerset* (19th), John Michael Edward Seymour, *b.* 1952, *s.* 1984, *m.* | Lord Seymour, *b.* 1982. |
| 1833 | *Sutherland* (6th), John Sutherland Egerton, TD (5th *UK Earl, Ellesmere,* 1846, *s.* 1944), *b.* 1915, *s.* 1963, *m.* | Francis R. E., *b.* 1940. |
| 1814 | *Wellington* (8th), Arthur Valerian Wellesley, KG, LVO, OBE, MC (9th *Irish Earl, Mornington,* 1760), *b.* 1915, *s.* 1972, *m.* | Marquess of Douro, *b.* 1945. |
| 1874 | *Westminster* (6th), Gerald Cavendish Grosvenor, *b.* 1951, *s.* 1979, *m.* | Earl Grosvenor, *b.* 1991. |

## MARQUESSES

*Coronet,* Four strawberry leaves alternating with four silver balls
*Style,* The Most Hon. the Marquess (of) __. In Scotland the spelling 'Marquis' is preferred for pre-Union creations
*Wife's style,* The Most Hon. the Marchioness (of) __
*Eldest son's style,* Takes his father's second title as a courtesy title
*Younger sons' style,* 'Lord' before forename and family name
*Daughters' style,* 'Lady' before forename and family name
For forms of address, *see* page 217

| Created | Title, order of succession, name, etc. | Heir |
|---------|----------------------------------------|------|
| 1916 | *Aberdeen and Temair* (6th), Alastair Ninian John Gordon (12th *Scott. Earl, Aberdeen,* 1682), *b.* 1920, *s.* 1984, *m.* | Earl of Haddo, *b.* 1955. |
| 1876 | *Abergavenny* (5th), John Henry Guy Nevill, KG, OBE, *b.* 1914, *s.* 1954, *m.* | Christopher G. C. N., *b.* 1955. |
| 1821 | *Ailesbury* (8th), Michael Sidney Cedric Brudenell-Bruce, *b.* 1926, *s.* 1974 | Earl of Cardigan, *b.* 1952. |
| 1831 | *Ailsa* (8th), Archibald Angus Charles Kennedy (20th *Scott. Earl, Cassillis,* 1509), *b.* 1956, *s.* 1994 | Lord David Kennedy, *b.* 1958. |
| 1815 | *Anglesey* (7th), George Charles Henry Victor Paget, *b.* 1922, *s.* 1947, *m.* | Earl of Uxbridge, *b.* 1950. |
| 1789 | *Bath* (7th), Alexander George Thynn, *b.* 1932, *s.* 1992, *m.* | Viscount Weymouth, *b.* 1974. |
| 1826 | *Bristol* (7th), (Frederick William) John Augustus Hervey, *b.* 1954, *s.* 1985. | Lord F. W. C. Nicholas W. H., *b.* 1961. |
| 1796 | *Bute* (7th), John Colum Crichton-Stuart (12th *Scott. Earl, Dumfries,* 1633), *b.* 1958, *s.* 1993, *m.* | Earl of Dumfries, *b.* 1989. |
| 1812 | °*Camden* (6th), David George Edward Henry Pratt, *b.* 1930, *s.* 1983. | Earl of Brecknock, *b.* 1965. |
| 1815 | *Cholmondeley* (7th), David George Philip Cholmondeley (11th *Irish Viscount, Cholmondeley,* 1661), *b.* 1960, *s.* 1990. *Lord Great Chamberlain.* | Charles G. C., *b.* 1959. |
| 1816 I.* | °*Conyngham* (7th), Frederick William Henry Francis Conyngham (7th *UK Baron, Minster,* 1821), *b.* 1924, *s.* 1974, *m.* | Earl of Mount Charles, *b.* 1951. |
| 1791 I.* | *Donegall* (7th), Dermot Richard Claud Chichester, LVO (7th *Brit. Baron, Fisherwick,* 1790, 6th *Brit. Baron, Templemore,* 1831, *s.* 1953), *b.* 1916, *s.* 1975, *m.* | Earl of Belfast, *b.* 1952. |
| 1789 I.* | *Downshire* (8th), (Arthur) Robin Ian Hill (8th *Brit. Earl, Hillsborough,* 1772), *b.* 1929, *s.* 1989, *m.* | Earl of Hillsborough, *b.* 1959. |
| 1801 I.* | *Ely* (8th) Charles John Tottenham (8th *UK Baron, Loftus,* 1801), *b.* 1913, *s.* 1969, *m.* | Viscount Loftus, *b.* 1943. |
| 1801 | *Exeter* (8th), (William) Michael Anthony Cecil, *b.* 1935, *s.* 1988, *m.* | Lord Burghley, *b.* 1970. |
| 1800 I.* | *Headfort* (6th), Thomas Geoffrey Charles Michael Taylour (4th *UK Baron, Kenlis,* 1831), *b.* 1932, *s.* 1960, *m.* | Earl of Bective, *b.* 1959. |
| 1793 | *Hertford* (8th), Hugh Edward Conway Seymour (9th *Irish Baron, Conway,* 1712), *b.* 1930, *s.* 1940, *m.* | Earl of Yarmouth, *b.* 1958. |
| 1599 S.* | *Huntly* (13th), Granville Charles Gomer Gordon (*Premier Marquess of Scotland*) (5th *UK Baron, Meldrum,* 1815), *b.* 1944, *s.* 1987, *m.* | Earl of Aboyne, *b.* 1973. |
| 1784 | *Lansdowne* (8th), George John Charles Mercer Nairne Petty-Fitzmaurice, PC (8th *Irish Earl, Kerry,* 1723), *b.* 1912, *s.* 1944, *w.* | Earl of Shelburne, *b.* 1941. |
| 1902 | *Linlithgow* (4th), Adrian John Charles Hope (10th *Scott. Earl, Hopetoun* 1703), *b.* 1946, *s.* 1987, *m.* | Earl of Hopetoun, *b.* 1969. |
| 1816 I.* | *Londonderry* (9th), Alexander Charles Robert Vane-Tempest-Stewart (6th *UK Earl, Vane,* 1823), *b.* 1937, *s.* 1955, *m.* | Viscount Castlereagh, *b.* 1972. |
| 1701 S.* | *Lothian* (12th), Peter Francis Walter Kerr, KCVO (6th *UK Baron, Kerr,* 1821), *b.* 1922, *s.* 1940, *m.* | Earl of Ancram, MP, *b.* 1945. |

| Created | Title, order of succession, name, etc. | Heir |
|---|---|---|
| 1917 | *Milford Haven* (4th), George Ivar Louis Mountbatten, *b*. 1961, *s*. 1970, *m*. | Earl of Medina, *b*. 1991. |
| 1838 | *Normanby* (5th), Constantine Edmund Walter Phipps, (9th *Irish Baron, Mulgrave,* 1767), *b*. 1954, *s*. 1994, *m*. | Lord Justin, C.P., *b*. 1958. |
| 1812 | *Northampton* (7th), Spencer Douglas David Compton, *b*. 1946, *s*. 1978, *m*. | Earl Compton, *b*. 1973. |
| 1825 I.* | *Ormonde* (7th), James Hubert Theobald Charles Butler, MBE (7th *UK Baron, Ormonde,* 1821), *b*. 1899, *s*. 1971, *w*. | None to Marquessate. To Earldoms of Ormonde and Ossory, Viscount Mountgarret, *b*. 1936 (*see* p. 151). |
| 1682 S. | *Queensberry* (12th), David Harrington Angus Douglas, *b*. 1929, *s*. 1954. | Viscount Drumlanrig, *b*. 1967. |
| 1926 | *Reading* (4th), Simon Charles Henry Rufus Isaacs, *b*. 1942, *s*. 1980, *m*. | Viscount Erleigh, *b*. 1986. |
| 1789 | *Salisbury* (6th), Robert Edward Peter Cecil, *b*. 1916, *s*. 1972, *m*. | Viscount Cranborne, PC, *b*. 1946 (*see also* Baron Cecil, page 154). |
| 1800 I.* | *Sligo* (11th), Jeremy Ulick Browne (11th *UK Baron, Monteagle,* 1806), *b*. 1939, *s*. 1991, *m*. | Sebastian U. B., *b*. 1964. |
| 1787 | °*Townshend* (7th), George John Patrick Dominic Townshend, *b*. 1916, *s*. 1921, *w*. | Viscount Raynham, *b*. 1945. |
| 1694 S.* | *Tweeddale* (13th), Edward Douglas John Hay (4th *UK Baron, Tweeddale,* 1881), *b*. 1947, *s*. 1979. | Lord Charles D. M. H., *b*. 1947. |
| 1789 I.* | *Waterford* (8th), John Hubert de la Poer Beresford (8th *Brit. Baron, Tyrone,* 1786), *b*. 1933, *s*. 1934, *m*. | Earl of Tyrone, *b*. 1958. |
| 1551 | *Winchester* (18th), Nigel George Paulet (*Premier Marquess of England*), *b*. 1941, *s*. 1968, *m*. | Earl of Wiltshire, *b*. 1969. |
| 1892 | *Zetland* (4th), Lawrence Mark Dundas (6th *UK Earl of Zetland,* 1838, 7th *Brit. Baron Dundas,* 1794), *b*. 1937, *s*. 1989, *m*. | Earl of Ronaldshay, *b*. 1965. |

---

## EARLS

---

*Coronet,* Eight silver balls on stalks alternating with eight gold strawberry leaves
*Style,* The Right Hon. the Earl (of) __
*Wife's style,* The Right Hon. the Countess (of) __
*Eldest son's style,* Takes his father's second title as a courtesy title
*Younger sons' style,* 'The Hon.' before forename and family name
*Daughters' style,* 'Lady' before forename and family name
For forms of address, *see* page 217

| Created | Title, order of succession, name, etc. | Heir |
|---|---|---|
| 1639 S. | *Airlie* (13th), David George Coke Patrick Ogilvy, KT, GCVO, PC, *b*. 1926, *s*. 1968, *m. Lord Chamberlain.* | Lord Ogilvy, *b*. 1958. |
| 1696 | *Albemarle* (10th), Rufus Arnold Alexis Keppel, *b*. 1965, *s*. 1979. | Crispian W. J. K., *b*. 1948. |
| 1952 | °*Alexander of Tunis* (2nd), Shane William Desmond Alexander, *b*. 1935, *s*. 1969, *m*. | Hon. Brian J. A., *b*. 1939. |
| 1662 S. | *Annandale and Hartfell* (11th), Patrick Andrew Wentworth Hope Johnstone, *b*. 1941, *claim established* 1985, *m*. | Lord Johnstone, *b*. 1971. |
| 1789 I. | °*Annesley* (10th), Patrick Annesley, *b*. 1924, *s*. 1979, *m*. | Hon. Philip H. A., *b*. 1927. |
| 1785 I. | *Antrim* (9th), Alexander Randal Mark McDonnell, *b*. 1935, *s*. 1977, *m*. (*Viscount Dunluce.*) | Hon. Randal A. St J. M., *b*. 1967. |
| 1762 I.* | *Arran* (9th), Arthur Desmond Colquhoun Gore (5th *UK Baron Sudley,* 1884), *b*. 1938, *s*. 1983, *m*. | Paul A. G., CMG, CVO, *b*. 1921. |
| 1955 | °*Attlee* (3rd), John Richard Attlee, *b*. 1956, *s*. 1991, *m*. | None. |
| 1714 | *Aylesford* (11th), Charles Ian Finch-Knightley, *b*. 1918, *s*. 1958, *w*. | Lord Guernsey, *b*. 1947. |
| 1937 | °*Baldwin of Bewdley* (4th), Edward Alfred Alexander Baldwin, *b*. 1938, *s*. 1976, *m*. | Viscount Corvedale, *b*. 1973. |
| 1922 | *Balfour* (4th), Gerald Arthur James Balfour, *b*. 1925, *s*. 1968, *m*. | Eustace A. G. B., *b*. 1921. |
| 1772 | °*Bathurst* (8th), Henry Allen John Bathurst, *b*. 1927, *s*. 1943, *m*. | Lord Apsley, *b*. 1961. |
| 1919 | °*Beatty* (3rd), David Beatty, *b*. 1946, *s*. 1972, *m*. | Viscount Borodale, *b*. 1973. |
| 1797 I. | *Belmore* (8th), John Armar Lowry-Corry, *b*. 1951, *s*. 1960, *m*. | Viscount Corry, *b*. 1985. |
| 1739 I. | *Bessborough* (11th), Arthur Mountifort Longfield Ponsonby (8th *UK Baron, Duncannon,* 1834), *b*. 1912, *s*. 1993, *m*. | Hon. Myles F. L. P., *b*. 1941. |
| 1815 | *Bradford* (7th), Richard Thomas Orlando Bridgeman, *b*. 1947, *s*. 1981, *m*. | Viscount Newport, *b*. 1980. |
| 1677 S. | *Breadalbane and Holland* (10th), John Romer Boreland Campbell, *b*. 1919, *s*. 1959. | None. |
| 1469 S.* | *Buchan* (17th), Malcolm Harry Erskine, (8th *UK Baron Erskine* 1806), *b*. 1930, *s*. 1984, *m*. | Lord Cardross, *b*. 1960. |

| Created | Title, order of succession, name, etc. | Heir |
|---|---|---|
| 1746 | Buckinghamshire (10th), (George) Miles Hobart-Hampden, b. 1944, s. 1983, m. | Sir John Hobart, Bt., b. 1945. |
| 1800 | °Cadogan (7th), William Gerald Charles Cadogan, MC, b. 1914, s. 1933, m. | Viscount Chelsea, b. 1937. |
| 1878 | °Cairns (6th), Simon Dallas Cairns, CBE, b. 1939, s. 1989, m. | Viscount Garmoyle, b. 1965. |
| 1455 S. | Caithness (20th), Malcolm Ian Sinclair, PC, b. 1948, s. 1965, w. | Lord Berriedale, b. 1981. |
| 1800 I. | Caledon (7th), Nicholas James Alexander, b. 1955, s. 1980, m. | Viscount Alexander, b. 1990. |
| 1661 | Carlisle (12th), Charles James Ruthven Howard, MC (12th Scott. Baron, Ruthven of Freeland, 1651, s. 1982), b. 1923, s. 1963, m. | Viscount Morpeth, b. 1949. |
| 1793 | Carnarvon (7th), Henry George Reginald Molyneux Herbert, KCVO, KBE, b. 1924, s. 1987, m. | Lord Porchester, b. 1956. |
| 1748 I.* | Carrick (10th), David James Theobald Somerset Butler (4th UK Baron, Butler, 1912), b. 1953, s. 1992, m. | Viscount Ikerrin, b. 1975. |
| 1800 I. | °Castle Stewart (8th), Arthur Patrick Avondale Stuart, b. 1928, s. 1961, m. | Viscount Stuart, b. 1953. |
| 1814 | °Cathcart (6th), Alan Cathcart, CB, DSO, MC (15th Scott. Baron, Cathcart, 1447), b. 1919, s. 1927, m. | Lord Greenock, b. 1952. |
| 1647 I. | Cavan. The 12th Earl died in 1988. Heir had not established his claim to the title at the time of going to press. | Roger C. Lambart, b. 1944. |
| 1827 | °Cawdor (7th), Colin Robert Vaughan Campbell, b. 1962, s. 1993. | Hon. Frederick W. C., b. 1965. |
| 1801 | Chichester (9th), John Nicholas Pelham, b. 1944, s. 1944, m. | Richard A. H. P., b. 1952. |
| 1803 I.* | Clancarty (8th), William Francis Brinsley Le Poer Trench (7th UK Visct. Clancarty, 1823), b. 1911, s. 1975, m. | Nicholas P. R. Le P. T., b. 1952. |
| 1776 I.* | Clanwilliam (7th), John Herbert Meade (5th UK Baron Clanwilliam, 1828), b. 1919, s. 1989, m. | Lord Gillford, b. 1960. |
| 1776 | Clarendon (7th), George Frederick Laurence Hyde Villiers, b. 1933, s. 1955, m. | Lord Hyde, b. 1976. |
| 1620 I.* | Cork (13th) & Orrery (13th)(I. 1660), Patrick Reginald Boyle (9th Brit. Baron, Boyle of Marston, 1711), b. 1910, s. 1967, m. | Hon. John W. B., DSC, b. 1916. |
| 1850 | Cottenham (8th), Kenelm Charles Everard Digby Pepys, b. 1948, s. 1968, m. | Viscount Crowhurst, b. 1983. |
| 1762 I.* | Courtown (9th), James Patrick Montagu Burgoyne Winthrop Stopford (8th Brit. Baron, Saltersford, 1796), b. 1954, s. 1975, m. | Viscount Stopford, b. 1988. |
| 1697 | Coventry (11th), George William Coventry, b. 1934, s. 1940, m. | Viscount Deerhurst, b. 1957. |
| 1857 | °Cowley (7th), Garret Graham Wellesley, b. 1934, s. 1975, m. | Viscount Dangan, b. 1965. |
| 1892 | Cranbrook (5th), Gathorne Gathorne-Hardy, b. 1933, s. 1978, m. | Lord Medway, b. 1968. |
| 1801 | Craven (9th), Benjamin Robert Joseph Craven, b. 1989, s. 1990, M. | Rupert J. E. C., b. 1926. |
| 1398 S.* | Crawford (29th) & Balcarres (12th) (S. 1651), Robert Alexander Lindsay, PC (Premier Earl on Union Roll, 5th UK Baron, Wigan, 1826, and Baron Balniel (life peerage), 1974, b. 1927, s. 1975, m. | Lord Balniel, b. 1958. |
| 1861 | Cromartie (5th), John Ruaridh Blunt Grant Mackenzie, b. 1948, s. 1989, m. | Viscount Tarbat, b. 1987. |
| 1901 | Cromer (4th), Evelyn Rowland Esmond Baring, b. 1946, s. 1991, m. | Viscount Errington, b 1994. |
| 1633 S.* | Dalhousie (16th), Simon Ramsay, KT, GCVO, GBE, MC (4th UK Baron, Ramsay, 1875), b. 1914, s. 1950, m. | Lord Ramsay, b. 1948. |
| 1725 I.* | Darnley (11th), Adam Ivo Stuart Bligh (20th Engl. Baron, Clifton of Leighton Bromswold, 1608), b. 1941, s. 1980, m. | Lord Clifton, b. 1968. |
| 1711 | Dartmouth (9th), Gerald Humphry Legge, b. 1924, s. 1962, m. | Viscount Lewisham, b. 1949. |
| 1761 | °De La Warr (11th), William Herbrand Sackville, b. 1948, s. 1988, m. | Lord Buckhurst, b. 1979. |
| 1622 | Denbigh (11th) & Desmond (10th) (I. 1622), William Rudolph Michael Feilding, b. 1943, s. 1966, m. | Viscount Feilding, b. 1970. |
| 1485 | Derby (18th), Edward John Stanley, MC, b. 1918, s. 1948, w. | Edward R. W. S., b. 1962. |
| 1553 | Devon (17th), Charles Christopher Courtenay, b. 1916, s. 1935, m. | Lord Courtenay, b. 1942. |
| 1800 I.* | Donoughmore (8th), Richard Michael John Hely-Hutchinson (8th UK Visct., Hutchinson, 1821), b. 1927, s. 1981, m. | Viscount Suirdale, b. 1952. |
| 1661 I.* | Drogheda (12th), Henry Dermot Ponsonby Moore (3rd UK Baron, Moore, 1954), b. 1937, s. 1989, m. | Viscount Moore, b. 1983. |
| 1837 | Ducie (7th), David Leslie Moreton, b. 1951, s. 1991, m. | Lord Moreton, b. 1981. |
| 1860 | Dudley (4th), William Humble David Ward, b. 1920, s. 1969, m. | Viscount Ednam, b. 1947. |
| 1660 S.* | Dundee (12th), Alexander Henry Scrymgeour (2nd UK Baron, Glassary, 1954), b. 1949, s. 1983, m. | Lord Scrymgeour, b. 1982. |
| 1669 S. | Dundonald (15th), Iain Alexander Douglas Blair Cochrane, b. 1961, s. 1986, m. | Lord Cochrane, b. 1991. |
| 1686 S. | Dunmore (11th), Kenneth Randolph Murray, b. 1913, s. 1981, w. | Viscount Fincastle, b. 1946. |
| 1822 I. | Dunraven and Mount-Earl (7th), Thady Windham Thomas Wyndham-Quin, b. 1939, s. 1965, m. | None. |
| 1833 | Durham. Disclaimed for life 1970. (Antony Claud Frederick Lambton, b. 1922, s. 1970, m.) | Hon. Edward R. L. (Baron Durham), b. 1961. |

| Created | Title, order of succession, name, etc. | Heir |
|---|---|---|
| 1837 | *Effingham* (6th), Mowbray Henry Gordon Howard (16th *Engl. Baron, Howard of Effingham*, 1554), *b*. 1905, *s*. 1946, *m*. | Cdr. David P. M. A. *H.*, *b*. 1939. |
| 1507 s.* | *Eglinton* (18th) & *Winton* (9th) (1600), Archibald George Montgomerie (6th *UK Earl, Winton*, 1859), *b*. 1939, *s*. 1966, *m*. | Lord Montgomerie, *b*. 1966. |
| 1733 I.* | *Egmont* (11th), Frederick George Moore Perceval (9th *Brit. Baron, Lovel & Holland*, 1762), *b*. 1914, *s*. 1932, *m*. | Viscount Perceval, *b*. 1934. |
| 1821 | *Eldon* (5th), John Joseph Nicholas Scott, *b*. 1937, *s*. 1976, *m*. | Viscount Encombe, *b*. 1962. |
| 1633 s.* | *Elgin* (11th), & *Kincardine* (15th) (s. 1647), Andrew Douglas Alexander Thomas Bruce (4th *UK Baron, Elgin*, 1849), KT, *b*. 1924, *s*. 1968, *m*. | Lord Bruce, *b*. 1961. |
| 1789 I.* | *Enniskillen* (7th), Andrew John Galbraith Cole (5th *UK Baron, Grinstead*, 1815) *b*. 1942, *s*. 1989, *m*. | Arthur G. *C.*, *b*. 1920. |
| 1789 I.* | *Erne* (6th), Henry George Victor John Crichton (3rd *UK Baron, Fermanagh*, 1876), *b*. 1937, *s*. 1940, *m*. | Viscount Crichton, *b*. 1971. |
| 1452 s. | *Erroll* (24th), Merlin Sereld Victor Gilbert Hay, *b*. 1948, *s*. 1978, *m*. *Hereditary Lord High Constable and Knight Marischal of Scotland*. | Lord Hay, *b*. 1984. |
| 1661 | *Essex* (10th), Robert Edward de Vere Capell, *b*. 1920, *s*. 1981, *m*. | Viscount Malden, *b*. 1944. |
| 1711 | °*Ferrers* (13th), Robert Washington Shirley, PC, *b*. 1929, *s*. 1954, *m*. | Viscount Tamworth, *b*. 1952. |
| 1789 | °*Fortescue* (8th), Charles Hugh Richard Fortescue, *b*. 1951, *s*. 1993, *m*. | Hon. Martin D. *F.*, *b*. 1924. |
| 1841 | *Gainsborough* (5th), Anthony Gerard Edward Noel, *b*. 1923, *s*. 1927, *m*. | Viscount Campden, *b*. 1950. |
| 1623 s.* | *Galloway* (13th), Randolph Keith Reginald Stewart (6th *Brit. Baron, Stewart of Garlies*, 1796), *b*. 1928, *s*. 1978, *m*. | Andrew C. *S.*, *b*. 1949. |
| 1703 s.* | *Glasgow* (10th), Patrick Robin Archibald Boyle (4th *UK Baron, Fairlie*, 1897), *b*. 1939, *s*. 1984, *m*. | Viscount of Kelburn, *b*. 1978. |
| 1806 I.* | *Gosford* (7th), Charles David Nicholas Alexander John Sparrow Acheson (5th *UK Baron, Worlingham*, 1835), *b*. 1942, *s*. 1966, *m*. | Hon. Patrick B. V. M. *A.*, *b*. 1915. |
| 1945 | *Gowrie* (2nd), Alexander Patric Greysteil Hore-Ruthven, PC (3rd *UK Baron, Ruthven of Gowrie*, 1919), *b*. 1939, *s*. 1955, *m*. | Viscount Ruthven of Canberra, *b*. 1964. |
| 1684 I.* | *Granard* (10th), Peter Arthur Edward Hastings Forbes, (5th *UK Baron, Granard*, 1806), *b*. 1957, *s*. 1992, *m*. | Viscount Forbes, *b*. 1981. |
| 1833 | °*Granville* (5th), Granville James Leveson-Gower, MC, *b*. 1918, *s*. 1953, *m*. | Lord Leveson, *b*. 1959. |
| 1806 | °*Grey* (6th), Richard Fleming George Charles Grey, *b*. 1939, *s*. 1963, *m*. | Philip K. *G.*, *b*. 1940. |
| 1752 | *Guilford* (9th), Edward Francis North, *b*. 1933, *s*. 1949, *w*. | Lord North, *b*. 1971. |
| 1619 s. | *Haddington* (13th), John George Baillie-Hamilton, *b*. 1941, *s*. 1986, *m*. | Lord Binning, *b*. 1985. |
| 1919 | °*Haig* (2nd), George Alexander Eugene Douglas Haig, OBE, *b*. 1918, *s*. 1928, *m*. | Viscount Dawick, *b*. 1961. |
| 1944 | *Halifax* (3rd), Charles Edward Peter Neil Wood (5th *UK Viscount, Halifax*, 1866), *b*. 1944, *s*. 1980, *m*. | Lord Irwin, *b*. 1977. |
| 1898 | *Halsbury* (3rd), John Anthony Hardinge Giffard, FRS, FEng., *b*. 1908, *s*. 1943, *w*. | Adam E. *G.*, *b*. 1934. |
| 1754 | *Hardwicke* (10th), Joseph Philip Sebastian Yorke, *b*. 1971, *s*. 1974. | Richard C. J. *Y.*, *b*. 1916. |
| 1812 | *Harewood* (7th), George Henry Hubert Lascelles, KBE, *b*. 1923, *s*. 1947, *m*. (*see also page* 134.) | Viscount Lascelles, *b*. 1950. |
| 1742 | *Harrington* (11th), William Henry Leicester Stanhope (8th *Brit. Viscount, Stanhope of Mahon*, 1717), *b*. 1922, *s*. 1929, *m*. | Viscount Petersham, *b*. 1945. |
| 1809 | *Harrowby* (7th), Dudley Danvers Granville Coutts Ryder, TD, *b*. 1922, *s*. 1987, *m*. | Viscount Sandon, *b*. 1951. |
| 1605 s. | *Home*. Disclaimed for life 1963. (*see* Lord Home of the Hirsel, page 164.) | Hon. David A. C. *D.-H.*, CBE, *b*. 1943. |
| 1821 | °*Howe* (7th), Frederick Richard Penn Curzon, *b*. 1951, *s*. 1984, *m*. | Charles M. P. *C.*, *b*. 1967. |
| 1529 | *Huntingdon* (16th), William Edward Robin Hood Hastings Bass, *b*. 1948, *s*. 1990, *m*. | Hon. Simon A. R. H. *H. B.*, *b*. 1950. |
| 1885 | *Iddesleigh* (4th), Stafford Henry Northcote, *b*. 1932, *s*. 1970, *m*. | Viscount St Cyres, *b*. 1957. |
| 1756 | *Ilchester* (9th), Maurice Vivian de Touffreville Fox-Strangways, *b*. 1920, *s*. 1970, *m*. | Hon. Raymond G. *F.-S.*, *b*. 1921. |
| 1929 | *Inchcape* (4th), (Kenneth) Peter (Lyle) Mackay, *b*. 1943, *s*. 1994, *m*. | Viscount Glenapp, *b*. 1979. |
| 1919 | *Iveagh* (4th), Arthur Edward Rory Guinness, *b*. 1969, *s*. 1992. | Hon. Rory M. B. *G.*, *b*. 1974. |
| 1925 | °*Jellicoe* (2nd), George Patrick John Rushworth Jellicoe, KBE, DSO, MC, PC, FRS, *b*. 1918, *s*. 1935, *m*. | Viscount Brocas, *b*. 1950. |
| 1697 | *Jersey* (9th), George Francis Child Villiers (12th *Irish Visct., Grandison*, 1620), *b*. 1910, *s*. 1923, *m*. | Viscount Villiers, *b*. 1948. |
| 1822 I. | *Kilmorey* (6th), Richard Francis Needham, PC, MP, *b*. 1942, *s*. 1977, *m*. | Viscount Newry and Morne, *b*. 1966. |
| 1866 | *Kimberley* (4th), John Wodehouse, *b*. 1924, *s*. 1941, *m*. | Lord Wodehouse, *b*. 1951. |
| 1768 I. | *Kingston* (11th), Barclay Robert Edwin King-Tenison, *b*. 1943, *s*. 1948, *m*. | Viscount Kingsborough, *b*. 1969. |
| 1633 s.* | *Kinnoull* (15th), Arthur William George Patrick Hay (9th *Brit. Baron, Hay of Pedwardine*, 1711), *b*. 1935, *s*. 1938, *m*. | Viscount Dupplin, *b*. 1962. |
| 1677 s.* | *Kintore* (13th), Michael Canning William John Keith (3rd *UK Viscount, Stonehaven*, 1938), *b*. 1939, *s*. 1989, *m*. | Lord Inverurie, *b*. 1976. |

| Created | Title, order of succession, name, etc. | Heir |
|---|---|---|
| 1914 | °*Kitchener of Khartoum* (3rd), Henry Herbert Kitchener, TD, *b.* 1919, *s.* 1937. | None. |
| 1756 I. | *Lanesborough* (9th), Denis Anthony Brian Butler, TD, *b.* 1918, *s.* 1950. | Maj. Henry A. B. C. B., *b.* 1909. |
| 1624 S. | *Lauderdale* (17th), Patrick Francis Maitland, *b.* 1911, *s.* 1968, *m.* | Viscount Maitland, *b.* 1937. |
| 1837 | *Leicester* (7th), Edward Douglas Coke, *b.* 1936, *s.* 1994, *m.* | Viscount Coke, *b.* 1965. |
| 1641 S. | *Leven* (14th) & *Melville* (13th) (s. 1690), Alexander Robert Leslie Melville, *b.* 1924, *s.* 1947, *m.* | Lord Balgonie, *b.* 1954. |
| 1831 | *Lichfield* (5th), Thomas Patrick John Anson, *b.* 1939, *s.* 1960. | Viscount Anson, *b.* 1978. |
| 1803 I.* | *Limerick* (6th), Patrick Edmund Pery, KBE (6th *UK Baron, Foxford,* 1815), *b.* 1930, *s.* 1967, *m.* | Viscount Glentworth, *b.* 1963. |
| 1572 | *Lincoln* (18th), Edward Horace Fiennes-Clinton, *b.* 1913, *s.* 1988, *m.* | Hon. Edward G. *F.-C., b.* 1943. |
| 1633 S. | *Lindsay* (16th), James Randolph Lindesay-Bethune, *b.* 1955, *s.* 1989, *m.* | Viscount Garnock, *b.* 1990. |
| 1626 | *Lindsey* (14th) *and Abingdon* (9th) (1682), Richard Henry Rupert Bertie, *b.* 1931, *s.* 1963, *m.* | Lord Norreys, *b.* 1958. |
| 1776 I. | *Lisburne* (8th), John David Malet Vaughan, *b.* 1918, *s.* 1965, *m.* | Viscount Vaughan, *b.* 1945. |
| 1822 I.* | *Listowel* (5th), William Francis Hare, GCMG, PC, (3rd *UK Baron, Hare,* 1869), *b.* 1906, *s.* 1931, *m.* | Viscount Ennismore, *b.* 1964. |
| 1905 | *Liverpool* (5th), Edward Peter Bertram Savile Foljambe, *b.* 1944, *s.* 1969, *m.* | Viscount Hawkesbury, *b.* 1972. |
| 1945 | °*Lloyd George of Dwyfor* (3rd), Owen Lloyd George, *b.* 1924, *s.* 1968, *m.* | Viscount Gwynedd, *b.* 1951. |
| 1785 I.* | *Longford* (7th), Francis Aungier Pakenham, KG, PC (6th *UK Baron, Silchester,* 1821; 1st *UK Baron, Pakenham,* 1945), *b.* 1905, *s.* 1961, *m.* | Thomas F. D. *P., b.* 1933. |
| 1807 | *Lonsdale* (7th), James Hugh William Lowther, *b.* 1922, *s.* 1953, *m.* | Viscount Lowther, *b.* 1949. |
| 1838 | *Lovelace* (5th), Peter Axel William Locke King (12th *Brit. Baron, King,* 1725), *b.* 1951, *s.* 1964, *m.* | None. |
| 1795 I.* | *Lucan* (7th), Richard John Bingham (3rd *UK Baron, Bingham,* 1934), *b.* 1934, *s.* 1964, *m.* | Lord Bingham, *b.* 1967. |
| 1880 | *Lytton* (5th), John Peter Michael Scawen Lytton (18th *Engl. Baron, Wentworth,* 1529), *b.* 1950, *s.* 1985, *m.* | Viscount Knebworth, *b.* 1989. |
| 1721 | *Macclesfield* (9th), Richard Timothy George Mansfield Parker, *b.* 1943, *s.* 1992, *m.* | Hon. J. David G. *P., b.* 1945. |
| 1800 | *Malmesbury* (6th), William James Harris, TD, *b.* 1907, *s.* 1950, *m.* | Viscount FitzHarris, *b.* 1946. |
| 1776 & 1792 | *Mansfield and Mansfield* (8th), William David Mungo James Murray (14th *Scott. Visct., Stormont,* 1621), *b.* 1930, *s.* 1971, *m.* | Viscount Stormont, *b.* 1956. |
| 1565 S. | *Mar* (14th) & *Kellie* (16th) (s. 1616), James Thorne Erskine, *b.* 1949, *s.* 1994, *m.* | Hon. Alexander D. *E., b.* 1952. |
| 1785 I. | *Mayo* (10th), Terence Patrick Bourke, *b.* 1929, *s.* 1962 | Lord Naas, *b.* 1953. |
| 1627 I.* | *Meath* (14th), Anthony Windham Normand Brabazon (5th *UK Baron, Chaworth,* 1831), *b.* 1910, *s.* 1949, *m.* | Lord Ardee, *b.* 1941. |
| 1766 I. | *Mexborough* (8th), John Christopher George Savile, *b.* 1931, *s.* 1980, *m.* | Viscount Pollington, *b.* 1959. |
| 1813 | *Minto* (6th), Gilbert Edward George Lariston Elliot-Murray-Kynynmound, OBE, *b.* 1928, *s.* 1975, *m.* | Viscount Melgund, *b.* 1953. |
| 1562 S.* | *Moray* (20th) Douglas John Moray Stuart (12th *Brit. Baron, Stuart* of *Castle Stuart,* 1796), *b.* 1928, *s.* 1974, *m.* | Lord Doune, *b.* 1966. |
| 1815 | *Morley* (6th), John St Aubyn Parker, *b.* 1923, *s.* 1962, *m.* | Viscount Boringdon, *b.* 1956. |
| 1458 S. | *Morton* (22nd), John Charles Sholto Douglas, *b.* 1927, *s.* 1976, *m.* | Lord Aberdour, *b.* 1952. |
| 1789 | *Mount Edgcumbe* (8th), Robert Charles Edgcumbe, *b.* 1939, *s.* 1982. | Piers V. *E., b.* 1946. |
| 1831 | *Munster* (7th), Anthony Charles FitzClarence, *b.* 1926, *s.* 1983, *m.* | None. |
| 1805 | °*Nelson* (9th), Peter John Horatio Nelson, *b.* 1941, *s.* 1981, *m.* | Viscount Merton, *b.* 1971. |
| 1660 S. | *Newburgh* (12th), Don Filippo Giambattista Camillo Francesco Aldo Maria Rospigliosi, *b.* 1942, *s.* 1986, *m.* | Princess Donna Benedetta F. M. *R., b.* 1974. |
| 1827 I. | *Norbury* (6th), Noel Terence Graham-Toler, *b.* 1939, *s.* 1955, *m.* | Viscount Glandine, *b.* 1967. |
| 1806 I.* | *Normanton* (6th), Shaun James Christian Welbore Ellis Agar (9th *Brit. Baron, Mendip,* 1794, 4th *UK Baron, Somerton,* 1873), *b.* 1945, *s.* 1967, *m.* | Viscount Somerton, *b.* 1982. |
| 1647 S. | *Northesk* (14th), David John MacRae Carnegie, *b.* 1954, *s.* 1994, *m.* | Lord Rosehill, *b.* 1980. |
| 1801 | *Onslow* (7th), Michael William Coplestone Dillon Onslow, *b.* 1938, *s.* 1971, *m.* | Viscount Cranley, *b.* 1967. |
| 1696 S. | *Orkney* (8th), Cecil O'Bryen Fitz-Maurice, *b.* 1919, *s.* 1951, *m.* | O. Peter *St John, b.* 1938. |
| 1925 | *Oxford and Asquith* (2nd), Julian Edward George Asquith, KCMG, *b.* 1916, *s.* 1928, *m.* | Viscount Asquith, OBE, *b.* 1952. |
| 1929 | °*Peel* (3rd), William James Robert Peel (4th *UK Viscount Peel,* 1895), *b.* 1947, *s.* 1969, *m.* | Viscount Clanfield, *b.* 1976. |
| 1551 | *Pembroke* (17th) & *Montgomery* (14th) (1605), Henry George Charles Alexander Herbert, *b.* 1939, *s.* 1969. | Lord Herbert, *b.* 1978. |
| 1605 S. | *Perth* (17th), John David Drummond, PC, *b.* 1907, *s.* 1951, *m.* | Viscount Strathallan, *b.* 1935. |

| Created | Title, order of succession, name, etc. | Heir |
|---|---|---|
| 1905 | *Plymouth* (3rd), Other Robert Ivor Windsor-Clive (15th *Engl. Baron, Windsor*, 1529), *b.* 1923, *s.* 1943, *m.* | Viscount Windsor, *b.* 1951. |
| 1785 I. | *Portarlington* (7th), George Lionel Yuill Seymour Dawson-Damer, *b.* 1938, *s.* 1959, *m.* | Viscount Carlow, *b.* 1965. |
| 1689 | *Portland* (11th), Count Henry Noel Bentinck, *b.* 1919, *s.* 1990, *m.* | Viscount Woodstock, *b.* 1953. |
| 1743 | *Portsmouth* (10th), Quentin Gerard Carew Wallop, *b.* 1954, *s.* 1984, *m.* | Viscount Lymington, *b.* 1981. |
| 1804 | *Powis* (8th), John George Herbert (9th *Irish Baron, Clive*, 1762), *b.* 1952, *s.* 1993, *m.* | Viscount Clive, *b.* 1979. |
| 1765 | *Radnor* (8th), Jacob Pleydell-Bouverie, *b.* 1927, *s.* 1968, *m.* | Viscount Folkestone, *b.* 1955. |
| 1831 I.* | *Ranfurly* (7th), Gerald Françoys Needham Knox (8th *UK Baron, Ranfurly*, 1826), *b.* 1929, *s.* 1988, *m.* | Edward J. K., *b.* 1957. |
| 1771 I. | *Roden* (10th), Robert John Jocelyn, *b.* 1938, *s.* 1993, *m.* | Hon. Thomas A. J., *b.* 1941. |
| 1801 | *Romney* (7th), Michael Henry Marsham, *b.* 1910, *s.* 1975, *m.* | Julian C. M., *b.* 1948. |
| 1703 S.* | *Rosebery* (7th), Neil Archibald Primrose (3rd *UK Earl, Midlothian*, 1911), *b.* 1929, *s.* 1974, *m.* | Lord Dalmeny, *b.* 1967. |
| 1806 I. | *Rosse* (7th), William Brendan Parsons, *b.* 1936, *s.* 1979, *m.* | Lord Oxmantown, *b.* 1969. |
| 1801 | *Rosslyn* (7th), Peter St Clair-Erskine, *b.* 1958, *s.* 1977, *m.* | Lord Loughborough, *b.* 1986. |
| 1457 S. | *Rothes* (21st), Ian Lionel Malcolm Leslie, *b.* 1932, *s.* 1975, *m.* | Lord Leslie, *b.* 1958. |
| 1861 | °*Russell* (5th), Conrad Sebastian Robert Russell, FBA, *b.* 1937, *s.* 1987, *m.* | Viscount Amberley, *b.* 1968. |
| 1915 | °*St Aldwyn* (3rd), Michael Henry Hicks Beach, *b.* 1950, *s.* 1992, *m.* | Hon. David S. H. B., *b.* 1955. |
| 1815 | *St Germans* (10th), Peregrine Nicholas Eliot, *b.* 1941, *s.* 1988. | Lord Eliot, *b.* 1966. |
| 1660 | *Sandwich*. Disclaimed for life 1964. ((*Alexander*) *Victor* (*Edward Paulet*) *Montagu*, *b.* 1906, *s.* 1962.) | John E. H. M., *b.* 1943. |
| 1690 | *Scarbrough* (12th), Richard Aldred Lumley (13th *Irish Visct., Lumley*, 1628), *b.* 1932, *s.* 1969, *m.* | Viscount Lumley, *b.* 1973. |
| 1701 S. | *Seafield* (13th), Ian Derek Francis Ogilvie-Grant, *b.* 1939, *s.* 1969, *m.* | Viscount Reidhaven, *b.* 1963. |
| 1882 | *Selborne* (4th), John Roundell Palmer, KBE, FRS, *b.* 1940, *s.* 1971, *m.* | Viscount Wolmer, *b.* 1971. |
| 1646 S. | *Selkirk* (10th), (George) Nigel Douglas-Hamilton, KT, GCMG, GBE, AFC, AE, PC, QC, *b.* 1906, *s.* 1940, *m.* | The Master of Selkirk, *b.* 1939. |
| 1672 | *Shaftesbury* (10th), Anthony Ashley-Cooper, *b.* 1938, *s.* 1961, *m.* | Lord Ashley, *b.* 1977. |
| 1756 I.* | *Shannon* (9th), Richard Bentinck Boyle (8th *Brit. Baron Carleton*, 1786), *b.* 1924, *s.* 1963. | Viscount Boyle, *b.* 1960. |
| 1442 | *Shrewsbury* & *Waterford* (22nd) (I. 1446), Charles Henry John Benedict Crofton Chetwynd Chetwynd-Talbot (*Premier Earl of England and Ireland; 7th Earl Talbot*, 1784), *b.* 1952, *s.* 1980, *m.* | Viscount Ingestre, *b.* 1978. |
| 1961 | *Snowdon* (1st), Antony Charles Robert Armstrong-Jones, GCVO, *b.* 1930, *m.* (*see also* page 123). | Viscount Linley, *b.* 1961 (*see also* page 123). |
| 1880 | °*Sondes* (5th), Henry George Herbert Milles-Lade, *b.* 1940, *s.* 1970, *m.* | None. |
| 1765 | °*Spencer* (9th), Charles Edward Maurice Spencer, *b.* 1964, *s.* 1992, *m.* | Viscount Althorp, *b.* 1994. |
| 1703 S.* | *Stair* (13th), John Aymer Dalrymple, KCVO, MBE (6th *UK Baron, Oxenfoord*, 1841), *b.* 1906, *s.* 1961, *m.* | Viscount Dalrymple, *b.* 1961. |
| 1984 | *Stockton* (2nd), Alexander Daniel Alan Macmillan, *b.* 1943, *s.* 1986. | Viscount Macmillan of Ovenden, *b.* 1974. |
| 1821 | *Stradbroke* (6th), Robert Keith Rous, *b.* 1937, *s.* 1983, *m.* | Viscount Dunwich, *b.* 1961. |
| 1847 | *Strafford* (8th), Thomas Edmund Byng, *b.* 1936, *s.* 1984, *m.* | Viscount Enfield, *b.* 1964. |
| 1606 S.* | *Strathmore* & *Kinghorne* (18th), Michael Fergus Bowes Lyon (16th *Scottish Earl, Strathmore*, 1677, & 18th *Kinghorne*, 1606; 5th *UK Earl, Strathmore* & *Kinghorne*, 1937), *b.* 1957, *s.* 1987, *m.* | Lord Glamis, *b.* 1986. |
| 1603 | *Suffolk* (21st) & *Berkshire* (14th) (1626), Michael John James George Robert Howard, *b.* 1935, *s.* 1941, *m.* | Viscount Andover, *b.* 1974. |
| 1955 | *Swinton* (2nd), David Yarburgh Cunliffe-Lister, *b.* 1937, *s.* 1972, *m.* | Hon. Nicholas J. C.-L., *b.* 1939. |
| 1714 | *Tankerville* (10th), Peter Grey Bennet, *b.* 1956, *s.* 1980. | Revd the Hon. George A. G. B., *b.* 1925. |
| 1822 | °*Temple of Stowe* (8th), (Walter) Grenville Algernon Temple-Gore-Langton, *b.* 1924, *s.* 1988, *m.* | Lord Langton, *b.* 1955. |
| 1815 | *Verulam* (7th), John Duncan Grimston (11th *Irish Visct., Grimston*, 1719; 16th *Scott. Baron, Forrester of Corstorphine*, 1633), *b.* 1951, *s.* 1973, *m.* | Viscount Grimston, *b.* 1978. |
| 1729 | °*Waldegrave* (12th), Geoffrey Noel Waldegrave, KG, GCVO, TD, *b.* 1905, *s.* 1936, *m.* | Viscount Chewton, *b.* 1940. |
| 1759 | *Warwick* (8th) & °*Brooke* (8th) (*Brit.* 1746), David Robin Francis Guy Greville, *b.* 1934, *s.* 1984. | Lord Brooke, *b.* 1957. |
| 1633 S.* | *Wemyss* (12th) & *March* (8th) (S. 1697), Francis David Charteris, KT (5th *UK Baron, Wemyss*, 1821), *b.* 1912, *s.* 1937, *w.* | Lord Neidpath, *b.* 1948. |
| 1621 I. | *Westmeath* (13th), William Anthony Nugent, *b.* 1928, *s.* 1971, *m.* | Hon. Sean C. W. N., *b.* 1965. |
| 1624 | *Westmorland* (16th), Anthony David Francis Henry Fane, *b.* 1951, *s.* 1993, *m.* | Hon. Harry St C. F., *b.* 1953. |

| Created | Title, order of succession, name, etc. | Heir |
|---------|----------------------------------------|------|
| 1876 | *Wharncliffe* (5th), Richard Alan Montagu Stuart Wortley, *b.* 1953, *s.* 1987, *m.* | Viscount Carlton, *b.* 1980. |
| 1801 | *Wilton* (7th), Seymour William Arthur John Egerton, *b.* 1921, *s.* 1927, *m.* | Baron Ebury, *b.* 1934 (*see* page 155). |
| 1628 | *Winchilsea* (16th) & *Nottingham* (11th) (1681), Christopher Denys Stormont Finch Hatton, *b.* 1936, *s.* 1950, *m.* | Viscount Maidstone, *b.* 1967. |
| 1766 I. | °*Winterton* (8th), (Donald) David Turnour, *b.* 1943, *s.* 1991, *m.* | Robert C. *T.*, *b.* 1950. |
| 1956 | *Woolton* (3rd), Simon Frederick Marquis, *b.* 1958, *s.* 1969, *m.* | None. |
| 1837 | *Yarborough* (8th), Charles John Pelham, *b.* 1963, *s.* 1991, *m.* | Lord Worsley, *b.* 1990. |

## COUNTESSES IN THEIR OWN RIGHT

*Style,* The Right Hon. the Countess (of) —
*Husband,* Untitled
*Children's style,* As for children of an Earl
For forms of address, *see* page 217

| Created | Title, order of succession, name, etc. | Heir |
|---------|----------------------------------------|------|
| 1643 S. | *Dysart* (11th in line), Rosamund Agnes Greaves, *b.* 1914, *s.* 1975. | Lady Katherine *Grant of Rothiemurchus, b.* 1918. |
| 1633 S. | *Loudoun* (13th in line), Barbara Huddleston Abney-Hastings, *b.* 1919, *s.* 1960, *m.* | Lord Mauchline, *b.* 1942. |
| c.1115 S. | *Mar* (31st in line), Margaret of Mar (*Premier Earldom of Scotland*), *b.* 1940, *s.* 1975, *m.* | Mistress of Mar, *b.* 1963. |
| 1947 | °*Mountbatten of Burma* (2nd in line), Patricia Edwina Victoria Knatchbull, CBE, *b.* 1924, *s.* 1979, *m.* | Lord Romsey, *b.* 1947 (*see also* page 153). |
| c.1235 S. | *Sutherland* (24th in line), Elizabeth Millicent Sutherland, *b.* 1921, *s.* 1963, *m.* | Lord Strathnaver, *b.* 1947. |

## VISCOUNTS

*Coronet,* Sixteen silver balls
*Style,* The Right Hon. the Viscount —
*Wife's style,* The Right Hon. the Viscountess —
*Children's style,* 'The Hon.' before forename and family name
In Scotland, the heir apparent to a Viscount may be styled 'The Master of — (title of peer)'
For forms of address, *see* page 217

| Created | Title, order of succession, name, etc. | Heir |
|---------|----------------------------------------|------|
| 1945 | *Addison* (4th), William Matthew Wand Addison, *b.* 1945, *s.* 1992, *m.* | Hon. Paul W. *A.*, *b.* 1973. |
| 1946 | *Alanbrooke* (3rd), Alan Victor Harold Brooke, *b.* 1932, *s.* 1972. | None. |
| 1919 | *Allenby* (3rd), Lt.-Col. Michael Jaffray Hynman Allenby, *b.* 1931, *s.* 1984, *m.* | Hon. Henry J. H. *A.*, *b.* 1968. |
| 1911 | *Allendale* (3rd), Wentworth Hubert Charles Beaumont, *b.* 1922, *s.* 1956. | Hon. Wentworth P. I. *B.*, *b.* 1948. |
| 1642 S. | *of Arbuthnott* (16th), John Campbell Arbuthnott, CBE, DSC, FRSE, *b.* 1924, *s.* 1966, *m.* | Master of Arbuthnott, *b.* 1950. |
| 1751 I. | *Ashbrook* (10th), Desmond Llowarch Edward Flower, KCVO, MBE, *b.* 1905, *s.* 1936, *m.* | Hon. Michael L. W. *F.*, *b.* 1935. |
| 1917 | *Astor* (4th), William Waldorf Astor, *b.* 1951, *s.* 1966, *m.* | Hon. William W. *A.*, *b.* 1979. |
| 1781 I. | *Bangor* (8th), William Maxwell David Ward, *b.* 1948, *s.* 1993, *m.* | Hon. E. Nicholas *W.*, *b.* 1953. |
| 1925 | *Bearsted* (4th), Peter Montefiore Samuel, MC, TD, *b.* 1911, *s.* 1986, *m.* | Hon. Nicholas A. *S.*, *b.* 1950. |
| 1963 | *Blakenham* (2nd), Michael John Hare, *b.* 1938, *s.* 1982, *m.* | Hon. Caspar J. *H.*, *b.* 1972. |
| 1935 | *Bledisloe* (3rd), Christopher Hiley Ludlow Bathurst, QC, *b.* 1934, *s.* 1979. | Hon. Rupert E. L. *B.*, *b.* 1964. |
| 1712 | *Bolingbroke* (7th) & *St John* (8th) (1716), Kenneth Oliver Musgrave St John, *b.* 1927, *s.* 1974. | Hon. Henry F. *St J.*, *b.* 1957. |
| 1960 | *Boyd of Merton* (2nd), Simon Donald Rupert Neville Lennox-Boyd, *b.* 1939, *s.* 1983, *m.* | Hon. Benjamin A. *L.-B.*, *b.* 1964. |

| Created | Title, order of succession, name, etc. | Heir |
|---|---|---|
| 1717 I.* | *Boyne* (10th), Gustavus Michael George Hamilton-Russell (4th *UK Baron, Brancepeth,* 1866), *b.* 1931, *s.* 1942, *m.* | Hon. Gustavus M. S. *H.-R.*, *b.* 1965. |
| 1929 | *Brentford* (4th), Crispin William Joynson-Hicks, *b.* 1933, *s.* 1983, *m.* | Hon. Paul W. *J.-H., b.* 1971. |
| 1929 | *Bridgeman* (3rd), Robin John Orlando Bridgeman, *b.* 1930, *s.* 1982, *m.* | Hon. William O. C. *B., b.* 1968. |
| 1868 | *Bridport* (4th), Alexander Nelson Hood (7th *Duke of Brontë in Sicily,* 1799, *and* 6th *Irish Baron Bridport,* 1794), *b.* 1948, *s.* 1969, *m.* | Hon. Peregrine A. N. *H., b.* 1974. |
| 1952 | *Brookeborough* (3rd), Alan Henry Brooke, *b.* 1952, *s.* 1987, *m.* | Hon. Christopher A. *B., b.* 1954. |
| 1933 | *Buckmaster* (3rd), Martin Stanley Buckmaster, OBE, *b.* 1921, *s.* 1974. | Hon. Colin J. *B., b.* 1923. |
| 1939 | *Caldecote* (2nd), Robert Andrew Inskip, KBE, DSC, FEng., *b.* 1917, *s.* 1947, *m.* | Hon. Piers J. H. *I., b.* 1947. |
| 1941 | *Camrose* (2nd), (John) Seymour Berry, TD, *b.* 1909, *s.* 1954, *m.* | Baron Hartwell, MBE, TD, *b.* 1911 (*see* page 164). |
| 1954 | *Chandos* (3rd), Thomas Orlando Lyttelton, *b.* 1953, *s.* 1980, *m.* | Hon. Oliver A. *L., b.* 1986. |
| 1665 I. | *Charlemont* (14th), John Day Caulfeild (18th *Irish Baron, Caulfeild of Charlemont,* 1620), *b.* 1934, *s.* 1985, *m.* | Hon. John D. *C., b.* 1966. |
| 1921 | *Chelmsford* (3rd), Frederic Jan Thesiger, *b.* 1931, *s.* 1970, *m.* | Hon. Frederic C. P. *T., b.* 1962. |
| 1717 I. | *Chetwynd* (10th), Adam Richard John Casson Chetwynd, *b.* 1935, *s.* 1965, *m.* | Hon. Adam D. *C., b.* 1969. |
| 1911 | *Chilston* (4th), Alastair George Akers-Douglas, *b.* 1946, *s.* 1982, *m.* | Hon. Oliver I. *A.-D., b.* 1973. |
| 1902 | *Churchill* (3rd), Victor George Spencer (5th *UK Baron Churchill,* 1815), *b.* 1934, *s.* 1973. | None to Viscountcy. To Barony, Richard H. R. *S., b.* 1926. |
| 1718 | *Cobham* (11th), John William Leonard Lyttelton (8th *Irish Baron, Westcote,* 1776), *b.* 1943, *s.* 1977, *m.* | Hon. Christopher C. *L., b.* 1947. |
| 1902 | *Colville of Culross* (4th), John Mark Alexander Colville, QC (13th *Scott. Baron, Colville of Culross,* 1604), *b.* 1933, *s.* 1945, *m.* | Master of Colville, *b.* 1959. |
| 1826 | *Combermere* (5th), Michael Wellington Stapleton-Cotton, *b.* 1929, *s.* 1969, *m.* | Hon. Thomas R. W. *S.-C., b.* 1969. |
| 1917 | *Cowdray* (3rd), Weetman John Churchill Pearson, TD (3rd *UK Baron, Cowdray,* 1910), *b.* 1910, *s.* 1933, *m.* | Hon. Michael O. W. *P., b.* 1944. |
| 1927 | *Craigavon* (3rd), Janric Fraser Craig, *b.* 1944, *s.* 1974. | None. |
| 1886 | *Cross* (3rd), Assheton Henry Cross, *b.* 1920, *s.* 1932. | None. |
| 1943 | *Daventry* (3rd), Francis Humphrey Maurice FitzRoy Newdegate, *b.* 1921, *s.* 1986, *m.* | Hon. James E. *F. N., b.* 1960. |
| 1937 | *Davidson* (2nd), John Andrew Davidson, *b.* 1928, *s.* 1970, *m.* | Hon. Malcolm W. M. *D., b.* 1934. |
| 1956 | *De L'Isle* (2nd), Philip John Algernon Sidney, MBE, (7th *Baron De L'Isle and Dudley,* 1835), *b.* 1945, *s.* 1991, *m.* | Hon. Philip W. E. *S., b.* 1985. |
| 1776 I. | *De Vesci* (7th), Thomas Eustace Vesey (8th *Irish Baron, Knapton,* 1750), *b.* 1955, *s.* 1983, *m.* | Hon. Oliver I. *V., b.* 1991. |
| 1917 | *Devonport* (3rd), Terence Kearley, *b.* 1944, *s.* 1973. | Chester D. H. *K., b.* 1932. |
| 1964 | *Dilhorne* (2nd), John Mervyn Manningham-Buller, *b.* 1932, *s.* 1980, *m.* | Hon. James E. *M.-B., b.* 1956. |
| 1622 I. | *Dillon* (22nd), Henry Benedict Charles Dillon, *b.* 1973, *s.* 1982. | Hon. Richard A. L. *D., b.* 1948. |
| 1785 I. | *Doneraile* (10th), Richard Allen St Leger, *b.* 1946, *s.* 1983, *m.* | Hon. Nathaniel W. R. St J. *St L., b.* 1971. |
| 1680 I.* | *Downe* (11th), John Christian George Dawnay (4th *UK Baron, Dawnay,* 1897), *b.* 1935, *s.* 1965, *m.* | Hon. Richard H. *D., b.* 1967. |
| 1959 | *Dunrossil* (2nd), John William Morrison, CMG, *b.* 1926, *s.* 1961, *m.* | Hon. Andrew W. R. *M., b.* 1953. |
| 1964 | *Eccles* (1st), David McAdam Eccles, CH, KCVO, PC, *b.* 1904, *m.* | Hon. John D. *E.,* CBE, *b.* 1931. |
| 1897 | *Esher* (4th), Lionel Gordon Baliol Brett, CBE, *b.* 1913. *s.* 1963, *m.* | Hon. Christopher L. B. *B., b.* 1936. |
| 1816 | *Exmouth* (10th), Paul Edward Pellew, *b.* 1940, *s.* 1970, *m.* | Hon. Edward F. *P., b.* 1978. |
| 1620 S. | *Falkland* (15th), Lucius Edward William Plantagenet Cary (*Premier Scottish Viscount on the Roll*), *b.* 1935, *s.* 1984, *m.* | Master of Falkland, *b.* 1963. |
| 1720 | *Falmouth* (9th), George Hugh Boscawen (26th *Eng. Baron, Le Despencer,* 1264), *b.* 1919, *s.* 1962, *m.* | Hon. Evelyn A. H. *B., b.* 1955. |
| 1918 | *Furness* (2nd), William Anthony Furness, *b.* 1929, *s.* 1940. | None. |
| 1720 I.* | *Gage* (8th), (Henry) Nicolas Gage, (7th *Brit. Baron, Gage,* 1790), *b.* 1934, *s.* 1993, *m.* | Hon. Henry W. *G., b.* 1975. |
| 1727 I. | *Galway* (12th), George Rupert Monckton-Arundell, *b.* 1922, *s.* 1980, *m.* | Hon. J. Philip *M., b.* 1952. |
| 1478 I.* | *Gormanston* (17th), Jenico Nicholas Dudley Preston (*Premier Viscount of Ireland*; 5th *UK Baron, Gormanston,* 1868), *b.* 1939, *s.* 1940, *w.* | Hon. Jenico F. T. *P., b.* 1974. |
| 1816 I. | *Gort* (8th), Colin Leopold Prendergast Vereker, *b.* 1916, *s.* 1975, *m.* | Hon. Foley R. S. P. *V., b.* 1951. |
| 1900 | *Goschen* (4th), Giles John Harry Goschen, *b.* 1965, *s.* 1977, *m.* | None. |
| 1849 | *Gough* (5th), Shane Hugh Maryon Gough, *b.* 1941, *s.* 1951. | None. |
| 1937 | *Greenwood* (2nd), David Henry Hamar Greenwood, *b.* 1914, *s.* 1948. | Hon. Michael G. H. *G., b.* 1923. |
| 1929 | *Hailsham.* Disclaimed for life 1963. (*see* Lord Hailsham of St Marylebone, page 164.) | Rt. Hon. Douglas M. *Hogg,* QC, MP, *b.* 1945. |
| 1891 | *Hambleden* (4th), William Herbert Smith, *b.* 1930, *s.* 1948, *m.* | Hon. William H. B. *S., b.* 1955. |
| 1884 | *Hampden* (6th), Anthony David Brand, *b.* 1937, *s.* 1975, *m.* | Hon. Francis A. *B., b.* 1970. |

| Created | Title, order of succession, name, etc. | Heir |
|---|---|---|
| 1936 | Hanworth (2nd), David Bertram Pollock, b. 1916, s. 1936, m. | Hon. David S. G. P., b. 1946. |
| 1791 I. | Harberton (10th), Thomas de Vautort Pomeroy, b. 1910, s. 1980, m. | Hon. Robert W. P., b. 1916. |
| 1846 | Hardinge (6th), Charles Henry Nicholas Hardinge, b. 1956, s. 1984, m. | Hon. Andrew H. H., b. 1960. |
| 1791 I. | Hawarden (9th), (Robert) Connan Wyndham Leslie Maude, b. 1961, s. 1991. | Hon. Thomas P. C. M., b. 1964. |
| 1960 | Head (2nd), Richard Antony Head, b. 1937, s. 1983, m. | Hon. Henry J. H., b. 1980. |
| 1550 | Hereford (18th), Robert Milo Leicester Devereux (Premier Viscount of England), b. 1932, s. 1952. | Hon. Charles R. de B. D., b. 1975. |
| 1842 | Hill (8th), Antony Rowland Clegg-Hill, b. 1931, s. 1974, m. | Peter D. R. C. C.-H., b. 1945. |
| 1796 | Hood (7th), Alexander Lambert Hood (7th Irish Baron, Hood, 1782), b. 1914, s. 1981, m. | Hon. Henry L. A. H., b. 1958. |
| 1956 | Ingleby (2nd), Martin Raymond Peake, b. 1926, s. 1966, m. | None. |
| 1945 | Kemsley (2nd), (Geoffrey) Lionel Berry, b. 1909, s. 1968, m. | Richard G. B., b. 1951. |
| 1911 | Knollys (3rd), David Francis Dudley Knollys, b. 1931, s. 1966, m. | Hon. Patrick N. M. K., b. 1962. |
| 1895 | Knutsford (6th), Michael Holland-Hibbert, b. 1926, s. 1986, m. | Hon. Henry T. H.-H., b. 1959. |
| 1945 | Lambert (3rd), Michael John Lambert, b. 1912, s. 1989, m. | None. |
| 1954 | Leathers (2nd), Frederick Alan Leathers, b. 1908, s. 1965, m. | Hon. Christopher G. L., b. 1941. |
| 1922 | Leverhulme (3rd), Philip William Bryce Lever, KG, TD, b. 1915, s. 1949, w. | None. |
| 1781 I. | Lifford (9th), (Edward) James Wingfield Hewitt, b. 1949, s. 1987, m. | Hon. James T. W. H., b. 1979. |
| 1921 | Long (4th), Richard Gerard Long, CBE, b. 1929, s. 1967, m. | Hon. James R. L., b. 1960. |
| 1957 | Mackintosh of Halifax (3rd), (John) Clive Mackintosh, b. 1958, s. 1980, m. | Hon. Thomas H. G. M., b. 1985. |
| 1955 | Malvern (3rd), Ashley Kevin Godfrey Huggins, b. 1949, s. 1978. | Hon. M. James H., b. 1928. |
| 1945 | Marchwood (3rd), David George Staveley Penny, b. 1936, s. 1979, m. | Hon. Peter G. W. P., b. 1965. |
| 1942 | Margesson (2nd), Francis Vere Hampden Margesson, b. 1922, s. 1965, m. | Capt. Hon. Richard F. D. M., b. 1960. |
| 1660 I.* | Massereene (14th) & Ferrard (7th) (1797), John David Clotworthy Whyte-Melville Foster Skeffington (7th UK Baron, Oriel, 1821), b. 1940, s. 1992, m. | Hon. Charles J. C. W.-M. F. S., b. 1973. |
| 1802 | Melville (9th), Robert David Ross Dundas, b. 1937, s. 1971, m. | Hon. Robert H. K. D., b. 1984. |
| 1916 | Mersey (4th), Richard Maurice Clive Bigham, b. 1934, s. 1979, m. | Hon. Edward J. H. B., b. 1966. |
| 1717 I.* | Midleton (12th), Alan Henry Brodrick (9th Brit. Baron, Brodrick of Peper Harow, 1796), b. 1949, s. 1988, m. | Hon. Ashley R. B., b. 1980. |
| 1962 | Mills (3rd), Christopher Philip Roger Mills, b. 1956, s. 1988, m. | None. |
| 1716 I. | Molesworth (11th), Richard Gosset Molesworth, b. 1907, s. 1961, w. | Hon. Robert B. K. M., b. 1959. |
| 1801 I.* | Monck (7th), Charles Stanley Monck (4th UK Baron, Monck, 1866), b. 1953, s. 1982 (does not use title). | Hon. George S. M., b. 1957. |
| 1957 | Monckton of Brenchley (2nd), Maj.-Gen. Gilbert Walter Riversdale Monckton, CB, OBE, MC, b. 1915, s. 1965, m. | Hon Christopher W. M., b. 1952. |
| 1946 | Montgomery of Alamein (2nd), David Bernard Montgomery, CBE, b. 1928, s. 1976, m. | Hon. Henry D. M., b. 1954. |
| 1550 I.* | Mountgarret (17th), Richard Henry Piers Butler (4th UK Baron, Mountgarret, 1911), b. 1936, s. 1966, m. | Hon. Piers J. R. B., b. 1961. |
| 1952 | Norwich (2nd), John Julius Cooper, CVO, b. 1929, s. 1954, m. | Hon. Jason C. D. B. C., b. 1959. |
| 1651 S. | of Oxfuird (13th), George Hubbard Makgill, b. 1934, s. 1986, m. | Master of Oxfuird, b. 1969. |
| 1873 | Portman, (9th), Edward Henry Berkeley Portman, b. 1934, s. 1967, m. | Hon. Christopher E. B. P., b. 1958. |
| 1743 I.* | Powerscourt (10th), Mervyn Niall Wingfield (4th UK Baron, Powerscourt, 1885), b. 1935, s. 1973, m. | Hon. Mervyn A. W., b. 1963. |
| 1900 | Ridley (4th), Matthew White Ridley, KG, GCVO, TD, b. 1925, s. 1964, m. Lord Steward. | Hon. Matthew W. R., b. 1958. |
| 1960 | Rochdale (2nd), St John Durival Kemp, b. 1938, s. 1993, m. | Hon. Jonathan H. D. K., b. 1961. |
| 1919 | Rothermere (3rd), Vere Harold Esmond Harmsworth, b. 1925, s. 1978, m. | Hon. H. Jonathan E. V. H., b. 1967. |
| 1937 | Runciman of Doxford (3rd), Walter Garrison Runciman (Garry), CBE, FBA (4th UK Baron, Runciman, 1933), b. 1934, s. 1989, m. | Hon. David W. R., b. 1967. |
| 1918 | St Davids (3rd), Colwyn Jestyn John Philipps (20th Engl. Baron Strange of Knokin, 1299, 8th Engl. Baron Hungerford, 1426, and De Moleyns, 1445), b. 1939, s. 1991, m. | Hon. Rhodri C. P., b. 1966. |
| 1801 | St Vincent (7th), Ronald George James Jervis, b. 1905, s. 1940, m. | Hon. Edward R. J. J., b. 1951. |
| 1937 | Samuel (3rd), David Herbert Samuel, PH.D., b. 1922, s. 1978, m. | Hon. Dan J. S., b. 1925. |
| 1911 | Scarsdale (3rd), Francis John Nathaniel Curzon (7th Brit. Baron, Scarsdale, 1761), b. 1924, s. 1977, m. | Hon. Peter G. N. C., b. 1949. |
| 1905 | Selby (4th), Michael Guy John Gully, b. 1942, s. 1959, m. | Hon. Edward T. W. G., b. 1967. |
| 1805 | Sidmouth (7th), John Tonge Anthony Pellew Addington, b. 1914, s. 1976, m. | Hon. Jeremy F. A., b. 1947. |
| 1940 | Simon (3rd), Jan David Simon, b. 1940, s. 1993, m. | None. |
| 1960 | Slim (2nd), John Douglas Slim, OBE, b. 1927, s. 1970, m. | Hon. Mark W. R. S., b. 1960. |
| 1954 | Soulbury (2nd), James Herwald Ramsbotham, b. 1915, s. 1971, w. | Hon. Sir Peter E. R., GCMG, GCVO, b. 1919. |
| 1776 I. | Southwell (7th), Pyers Anthony Joseph Southwell, b. 1930, s. 1960, m. | Hon. Richard A. P. S., b. 1956. |

| Created | Title, order of succession, name, etc. | Heir |
|---------|---------------------------------------|------|
| 1942 | *Stansgate*. Disclaimed for life 1963. (*Rt. Hon. Anthony Neil Wedgwood Benn*, MP, *b.* 1925, *s.* 1960, *m.*) | Stephen M. W. *B.*, *b.* 1951. |
| 1959 | *Stuart of Findhorn* (2nd), David Randolph Moray Stuart, *b.* 1924, *s.* 1971, *m.* | Hon. J. Dominic *S.*, *b.* 1948. |
| 1957 | *Tenby* (3rd), William Lloyd George, *b.* 1927, *s.* 1983, *m.* | Hon. Timothy H. G. *L. G.*, *b.* 1962. |
| 1952 | *Thurso* (2nd), Robin Macdonald Sinclair, *b.* 1922, *s.* 1970, *m.* | Hon. John A. *S.*, *b.* 1953. |
| 1983 | *Tonypandy* (1st), (Thomas) George Thomas, PC, *b.* 1909. | None. |
| 1721 | *Torrington* (11th), Timothy Howard St George Byng, *b.* 1943, *s.* 1961, *m.* | John L. *B.*, MC, *b.* 1919. |
| 1936 | *Trenchard* (3rd), Hugh Trenchard, *b.* 1951, *s.* 1987, *m.* | Hon. Alexander T. *T.*, *b.* 1978. |
| 1921 | *Ullswater* (2nd), Nicholas James Christopher Lowther, PC, *b.* 1942, *s.* 1949, *m.* | Hon. Benjamin J. *L.*, *b.* 1975. |
| 1621 I. | *Valentia* (15th), Richard John Dighton Annesley, *b.* 1929, *s.* 1983, *m.* | Hon. Francis W. D. *A.*, *b.* 1959. |
| 1964 | *Watkinson* (1st), Harold Arthur Watkinson, CH, PC, *b.* 1910, *m.* | None. |
| 1952 | *Waverley* (3rd), John Desmond Forbes Anderson, *b.* 1949, *s.* 1990. | None. |
| 1938 | *Weir* (3rd), William Kenneth James Weir, *b.* 1933, *s.* 1975, *m.* | Hon. James W. H. *W.*, *b.* 1965. |
| 1983 | *Whitelaw* (1st), William Stephen Ian Whitelaw, KT, CH, MC, PC, *b.* 1918, *m.* | None. |
| 1918 | *Wimborne* (4th), Ivor Mervyn Vigors Guest (5th *UK Baron, Wimborne*, 1880), *b.* 1968, *s.* 1993. | Hon. Julian J. *G.*, *b.* 1945. |
| 1923 | *Younger of Leckie* (3rd), Edward George Younger, OBE, TD, *b.* 1906, *s.* 1946, *w.* | Baron Younger of Prestwick, KCVO, TD, PC, *b.* 1931 (*see* page 166). |

## BARONS/LORDS

*Coronet*, Six silver balls
*Style*, The Right Hon. the Lord __ . In the Peerage of Scotland there is no rank of Baron; the equivalent rank is Lord of Parliament (*see* page 141) and Scottish peers should always be styled 'Lord', never 'Baron'
*Wife's style*, The Right Hon. the Lady __
*Children's style*, 'The Hon.' before forename and family name
In Scotland, the heir apparent to a Lord may be styled 'The Master of __ (title of peer)'
For forms of address, *see* page 217

| Created | Title, order of succession, name, etc. | Heir |
|---------|---------------------------------------|------|
| 1911 | *Aberconway* (3rd), Charles Melville McLaren, *b.* 1913, *s.* 1953, *m.* | Hon. H. Charles *M.*, *b.* 1948. |
| 1873 | *Aberdare* (4th), Morys George Lyndhurst Bruce, KBE, PC, *b.* 1919, *s.* 1957, *m.* | Hon. Alastair J. L. *B.*, *b.* 1947. |
| 1835 | *Abinger* (8th), James Richard Scarlett, *b.* 1914, *s.* 1943, *m.* | Hon. James H. *S.*, *b.* 1959. |
| 1869 | *Acton* (4th), Richard Gerald Lyon-Dalberg-Acton, *b.* 1941, *s.* 1989, *m.* | Hon. John C. F. H. *L.-D.-A.*, *b.* 1966. |
| 1887 | *Addington* (6th), Dominic Bryce Hubbard, *b.* 1963, *s.* 1982. | Hon. Michael W. L. *H.*, *b.* 1965. |
| 1955 | *Adrian* (2nd), Richard Hume Adrian, FRCP, FRS, *b.* 1927, *s.* 1977, *m.* | None. |
| 1907 | *Airedale* (4th), Oliver James Vandeleur Kitson, *b.* 1915, *s.* 1958. | None. |
| 1896 | *Aldenham* (6th), and *Hunsdon of Hunsdon* (4th) (1923), Vicary Tyser Gibbs, *b.* 1948, *s.* 1986, *m.* | Hon. Humphrey W. F. *G.*, *b.* 1989. |
| 1962 | *Aldington* (1st), Toby Austin Richard William Low, KCMG, CBE, DSO, TD, PC, *b.* 1914, *m.* | Hon Charles H. S. *L.*, *b.* 1948. |
| 1945 | *Altrincham*. Disclaimed for life 1963. (*John Edward Poynder Grigg*, *b.* 1924, *s.* 1955, *m.*) | Hon. Anthony U. D. D. *G.*, *b.* 1934. |
| 1929 | *Alvingham* (2nd), Maj.-Gen. Robert Guy Eardley Yerburgh, CBE, *b.* 1926, *s.* 1955, *m.* | Capt. Hon. Robert R. G. *Y.*, *b.* 1956. |
| 1892 | *Amherst of Hackney* (4th), William Hugh Amherst Cecil, *b.* 1940, *s.* 1980, *m.* | Hon. H. William A. *C.*, *b.* 1968. |
| 1881 | *Ampthill* (4th), Geoffrey Denis Erskine Russell, CBE, *b.* 1921, *s.* 1973. | Hon. David W. E. *R.*, *b.* 1947. |
| 1947 | *Amwell* (3rd), Keith Norman Montague, *b.* 1943, *s.* 1990, *m.* | Hon. Ian K. *M.*, *b.* 1973. |
| 1863 | *Annaly* (6th), Luke Richard White, *b.* 1954, *s.* 1990, *m.* | Hon. Luke H. *W.*, *b.* 1990. |
| 1949 | *Archibald*. Disclaimed for life 1975. (*George Christopher Archibald*, *b.* 1926, *s.* 1975, *m.*) | None. |
| 1885 | *Ashbourne* (4th), Edward Barry Greynville Gibson, *b.* 1933, *s.* 1983, *m.* | Hon. Edward C. d'O. *G.*, *b.* 1967. |
| 1835 | *Ashburton* (7th), John Francis Harcourt Baring, KG, KCVO, *b.* 1928, *s.* 1991, *m.* | Hon. Mark F. R. *B.*, *b.* 1958. |
| 1892 | *Ashcombe* (4th), Henry Edward Cubitt, *b.* 1924, *s.* 1962, *m.* | Mark E. *C.*, *b.* 1964. |
| 1911 | *Ashton of Hyde* (3rd), Thomas John Ashton, TD, *b.* 1926, *s.* 1983, *m.* | Hon. Thomas H. *A.*, *b.* 1958. |
| 1800 I. | *Ashtown* (7th), Nigel Clive Crosby Trench, KCMG, *b.* 1916, *s.* 1990, *w.* | Hon. Roderick N. G. *T.*, *b.* 1944. |

| Created | Title, order of succession, name, etc. | Heir |
|---|---|---|
| 1956 | *Astor of Hever* (3rd), John Jacob Astor, *b.* 1946, *s.* 1984, *m.* | Hon. Charles G. J. *A.*, *b.* 1990. |
| 1789 I.* | *Auckland* (9th), Ian George Eden (9th *Brit. Baron, Auckland*, 1793), *b.* 1926, *s.* 1957, *m.* | Hon. Robert I. B. *E.*, *b.* 1962. |
| 1313 | *Audley* (25th), Richard Michael Thomas Souter, *b.* 1914, *s.* 1973, *m.* | Three co-heiresses. |
| 1900 | *Avebury* (4th), Eric Reginald Lubbock, *b.* 1928, *s.* 1971, *m.* | Hon. Lyulph A. J. *L.*, *b.* 1954. |
| 1718 I. | *Aylmer* (13th), Michael Anthony Aylmer, *b.* 1923, *s.* 1982, *m.* | Hon. A. Julian *A.*, *b.* 1951. |
| 1929 | *Baden-Powell* (3rd), Robert Crause Baden-Powell, *b.* 1936, *s.* 1962, *m.* | Hon. David M. *B.-P.*, *b.* 1940. |
| 1780 | *Bagot* (9th), Heneage Charles Bagot, *b.* 1914, *s.* 1979, *m.* | Hon. C. H. Shaun *B.*, *b.* 1944. |
| 1953 | *Baillieu* (3rd), James William Latham Baillieu, *b.* 1950, *s.* 1973, *m.* | Hon. Robert L. *B.*, *b.* 1979. |
| 1607 S. | *Balfour of Burleigh* (8th), Robert Bruce, FRSE, *b.* 1927, *s.* 1967, *m.* | Hon. Victoria *B.*, *b.* 1973. |
| 1945 | *Balfour of Inchrye* (2nd), Ian Balfour, *b.* 1924, *s.* 1988, *m.* | None. |
| 1924 | *Banbury of Southam* (3rd), Charles William Banbury, *b.* 1953, *s.* 1981, *m.* | None. |
| 1698 | *Barnard* (11th), Harry John Neville Vane, TD, *b.* 1923, *s.* 1964. | Hon. Henry F. C. *V.*, *b.* 1959. |
| 1887 | *Basing* (5th), Neil Lutley Sclater-Booth, *b.* 1939, *s.* 1983, *m.* | Hon. Stuart W. *S.-B.*, *b.* 1969. |
| 1917 | *Beaverbrook* (3rd), Maxwell William Humphrey Aitken, *b.* 1951, *s.* 1985, *m.* | Hon. Maxwell F. *A*, *b.* 1977. |
| 1647 S. | *Belhaven and Stenton* (13th), Robert Anthony Carmichael Hamilton, *b.* 1927, *s.* 1961, *m.* | Master of Belhaven, *b.* 1953. |
| 1848 I. | *Bellew* (7th), James Bryan Bellew, *b.* 1920, *s.* 1981, *m.* | Hon. Bryan E. *B.*, *b.* 1943. |
| 1856 | *Belper* (4th), (Alexander) Ronald George Strutt, *b.* 1912, *s.* 1956. | Hon. Richard H. *S.*, *b.* 1941. |
| 1938 | *Belstead* (2nd), John Julian Ganzoni, PC, *b.* 1932, *s.* 1958. | None. |
| 1421 | *Berkeley* (18th), Anthony Fitzhardinge Gueterbock, OBE, *b.* 1939, *s.* 1992, *m.* | Hon. Thomas F. *G.*, *b.* 1969. |
| 1922 | *Bethell* (4th), Nicholas William Bethell, MEP, *b.* 1938, *s.* 1967, *m.* | Hon. James N. *B.*, *b.* 1967. |
| 1938 | *Bicester* (3rd), Angus Edward Vivian Smith, *b.* 1932, *s.* 1968. | Hugh C. V. *S.*, *b.* 1934. |
| 1903 | *Biddulph* (5th), (Anthony) Nicholas Colin Maitland Biddulph, *b.* 1959, *s.* 1988, *m.* | Hon. William I. R. *M. B.*, *b.* 1963. |
| 1938 | *Birdwood* (3rd), Mark William Ogilvie Birdwood, *b.* 1938, *s.* 1962, *m.* | None. |
| 1958 | *Birkett* (2nd), Michael Birkett, *b.* 1929, *s.* 1962, *m.* | Hon. Thomas *B.*, *b.* 1982. |
| 1907 | *Blyth* (4th), Anthony Audley Rupert Blyth, *b.* 1931, *s.* 1977, *m.* | Hon. Riley A. J. *B.*, *b.* 1955. |
| 1797 | *Bolton* (7th), Richard William Algar Orde-Powlett, *b.* 1929, *s.* 1963, *m.* | Hon. Harry A. N. *O.-P.*, *b.* 1954. |
| 1452 S. | *Borthwick* (23rd), John Henry Stuart Borthwick, TD, *b.* 1905, *claim succeeded* 1986, *w.* | Master of Borthwick, *b.* 1940. |
| 1922 | *Borwick* (4th), James Hugh Myles Borwick, MC, *b.* 1917, *s.* 1961, *m.* | Hon. George S. *B.*, *b.* 1922. |
| 1761 | *Boston* (10th), Timothy George Frank Boteler Irby, *b.* 1939, *s.* 1978, *m.* | Hon. George W. E. B. *I.*, *b.* 1971. |
| 1942 | *Brabazon of Tara* (3rd), Ivon Anthony Moore-Brabazon, *b.* 1946, *s.* 1974, *m.* | Hon. Benjamin R. *M.-B.*, *b.* 1983. |
| 1880 | *Brabourne* (7th), John Ulick Knatchbull, CBE, *b.* 1924, *s.* 1943, *m.* | Lord Romsey, *b.* 1947 (*see* page 149). |
| 1925 | *Bradbury* (3rd), John Bradbury, *b.* 1940, *s.* 1994, *m.* | Hon. John *B.*, *b.* 1973. |
| 1962 | *Brain* (2nd), Christopher Langdon Brain, *b.* 1926, *s.* 1966, *m.* | Hon. Michael C. *B.*, DM, FRCP, *b.* 1928. |
| 1938 | *Brassey of Apethorpe* (3rd), David Henry Brassey, OBE, *b.* 1932, *s.* 1967, *m.* | Hon. Edward *B.*, *b.* 1964. |
| 1788 | *Braybrooke* (10th), Robin Henry Charles Neville, *b.* 1932, *s.* 1990, *m.* | George *N.*, *b.* 1943. |
| 1957 | *Bridges* (2nd), Thomas Edward Bridges, GCMG, *b.* 1927, *s.* 1969, *m.* | Hon. Mark T. *B.*, *b.* 1954. |
| 1945 | *Broadbridge* (3rd), Peter Hewett Broadbridge, *b.* 1938, *s.* 1972, *m.* | Martin H. *B.*, *b.* 1929. |
| 1933 | *Brocket* (3rd), Charles Ronald George Nall-Cain, *b.* 1952, *s.* 1967, *m.* | Hon. Alexander C. C. *N.-C.*, *b.* 1984. |
| 1860 | *Brougham and Vaux* (5th), Michael John Brougham, *b.* 1938, *s.* 1967. | Hon. Charles W. *B.*, *b.* 1971. |
| 1945 | *Broughshane* (2nd), Patrick Owen Alexander Davison, *b.* 1903, *s.* 1953, *m.* | Hon. W. Kensington *D.*, DSO, DFC, *b.* 1914. |
| 1776 | *Brownlow* (7th), Edward John Peregrine Cust, *b.* 1936, *s.* 1978, *m.* | Hon. Peregrine E. Q. *C.*, *b.* 1974. |
| 1942 | *Bruntisfield* (2nd), John Robert Warrender, OBE, MC, TD, *b.* 1921, *s.* 1993, *m.* | Hon. Michael J. V. *W.*, *b.* 1949. |
| 1950 | *Burden* (2nd), Philip William Burden, *b.* 1916, *s.* 1970, *m.* | Hon. Andrew P. *B.*, *b.* 1959. |
| 1529 | *Burgh* (7th), Alexander Peter Willoughby Leith, *b.* 1935, *s.* 1959, *m.* | Hon. A. Gregory D. *L.*, *b.* 1958. |
| 1903 | *Burnham* (6th), Hugh John Frederick Lawson, *b.* 1931, *s.* 1993, *m.* | Hon. Harry F. A. *L.*, *b.* 1968. |
| 1897 | *Burton* (3rd), Michael Evan Victor Baillie, *b.* 1924, *s.* 1962, *m.* | Hon. Evan M. R. *B.*, *b.* 1949. |
| 1643 | *Byron* (13th), Robert James Byron, *b.* 1950, *s.* 1989, *m.* | Hon. Charles R. G. *B.*, *b.* 1990. |
| 1937 | *Cadman* (3rd), John Anthony Cadman, *b.* 1938, *s.* 1966, *m.* | Hon. Nicholas A. J. *C.*, *b.* 1977. |
| 1796 | *Calthorpe* (10th), Peter Waldo Somerset Gough-Calthorpe, *b.* 1927, *s.* 1945, *m.* | None. |
| 1945 | *Calverley* (3rd), Charles Rodney Muff, *b.* 1946, *s.* 1971, *m.* | Hon. Jonathan E. *M.*, *b.* 1975. |
| 1383 | *Camoys* (7th), (Ralph) Thomas Campion George Sherman Stonor, *b.* 1940, *s.* 1976, *m.* | Hon. R. William R. T. *S.*, *b.* 1974. |
| 1715 I. | *Carbery* (11th), Peter Ralfe Harrington Evans-Freke, *b.* 1920, *s.* 1970, *m.* | Hon. Michael P. *E.-F.*, *b.* 1942. |
| 1834 I.* | *Carew* (7th), Patrick Thomas Conolly-Carew (7th *UK Baron, Carew*, 1838), *b.* 1938, *s.* 1994, *m.* | Hon. William P. *C.-C.*, *b.* 1973. |
| 1916 | *Carnock* (4th), David Henry Arthur Nicolson, *b.* 1920, *s.* 1982. | Nigel *N.*, MBE, *b.* 1917. |

| Created | Title, order of succession, name, etc. | Heir |
|---|---|---|
| 1796 I.* | *Carrington* (6th), Peter Alexander Rupert Carington, KG, GCMG, CH, MC, PC (6th *Brit.* Baron, *Carrington*, 1797), *b.* 1919, *s.* 1938, *m.* | Hon. Rupert F. J. *C.*, *b.* 1948. |
| 1812 I. | *Castlemaine* (8th), Roland Thomas John Handcock, MBE, *b.* 1943, *s.* 1973, *m.* | Hon. Ronan M. E. *H* ., *b.* 1989. |
| 1936 | *Catto* (2nd), Stephen Gordon Catto, *b.* 1923, *s.* 1959, *m.* | Hon. Innes G. *C.*, *b.* 1950. |
| 1918 | *Cawley* (3rd), Frederick Lee Cawley, *b.* 1913, *s.* 1954, *m.* | Hon. John F. *C.*, *b.* 1946. |
| 1603 | *Cecil*, a subsidiary title of the Marquess of Salisbury. His heir Viscount Cranborne, PC, was given a Writ in Acceleration in this title to enable him to sit in the House of Lords whilst his father is still alive (*see also* page 144). | |
| 1937 | *Chatfield* (2nd), Ernle David Lewis Chatfield, *b.* 1917, *s.* 1967, *m.* | None. |
| 1858 | *Chesham* (6th), Nicholas Charles Cavendish, *b.* 1941, *s.* 1989, *m.* | Hon. Charles G. C. *C.*, *b.* 1974. |
| 1945 | *Chetwode* (2nd), Philip Chetwode, *b.* 1937, *s.* 1950, *m.* | Hon. Roger *C.*, *b.* 1968. |
| 1945 | *Chorley* (2nd), Roger Richard Edward Chorley, *b.* 1930, *s.* 1978, *m.* | Hon. Nicholas R. D. *C.*, *b.* 1966. |
| 1858 | *Churston* (5th), John Francis Yarde-Buller, *b.* 1934, *s.* 1991, *m.* | Hon. Benjamin F. A. *Y.-B.*, *b.* 1974. |
| 1946 | *Citrine* (2nd), Norman Arthur Citrine, *b.* 1914, *s.* 1983, *w.* | Hon. Ronald E. *C.*, *b.* 1919. |
| 1800 I. | *Clanmorris* (8th), Simon John Ward Bingham, *b.* 1937, *s.* 1988, *m.* | Robert D. de B. *B.*, *b.* 1942. |
| 1672 | *Clifford of Chudleigh* (14th), Thomas Hugh Clifford, *b.* 1948, *s.* 1988, *m.* | Hon. Alexander T. H. *C.*, *b.* 1985. |
| 1299 | *Clinton* (22nd), Gerard Nevile Mark Fane Trefusis, *b.* 1934, *title called out of abeyance* 1965, *m.* | Hon. Charles P. R. F. *T.*, *b.* 1962. |
| 1955 | *Clitheroe* (2nd), Ralph John Assheton, *b.* 1929, *s.* 1984, *m.* | Hon. Ralph *C. A.*, *b.* 1962. |
| 1919 | *Clwyd* (3rd), (John) Anthony Roberts, *b.* 1935, *s.* 1987, *m.* | Hon. J. Murray *R.*, *b.* 1971. |
| 1948 | *Clydesmuir* (2nd), Ronald John Bilsland Colville, KT, CB, MBE, TD, *b.* 1917, *s.* 1954, *m.* | Hon. David R. *C.*, *b.* 1949. |
| 1960 | *Cobbold* (2nd), David Antony Fromanteel Lytton Cobbold, *b.* 1937, *s.* 1987, *m.* | Hon. Henry F. *L. C.*, *b.* 1962. |
| 1919 | *Cochrane of Cults* (4th), (Ralph Henry) Vere Cochrane, *b.* 1926, *s.* 1990, *m.* | Hon. Thomas H. V. *C.*, *b.* 1957. |
| 1954 | *Coleraine* (2nd), (James) Martin (Bonar) Law, *b.* 1931, *s.* 1980, *w.* | Hon. James P. B. *L.*, *b.* 1975. |
| 1873 | *Coleridge* (5th), William Duke Coleridge, *b.* 1937, *s.* 1984, *m.* | Hon. James D. *C.*, *b.* 1967. |
| 1946 | *Colgrain* (3rd), David Colin Campbell, *b.* 1920, *s.* 1973, *m.* | Hon. Alastair C. L. *C.*, *b.* 1951. |
| 1917 | *Colwyn* (3rd), (Ian) Anthony Hamilton-Smith, CBE, *b.* 1942, *s.* 1966, *m.* | Hon. Craig P. *H.-S.*, *b.* 1968. |
| 1956 | *Colyton* (1st), Henry Lennox d'Aubigné Hopkinson, CMG, PC, *b.* 1902, *m.* | Alisdair J. M. *H.*, *b.* 1958. |
| 1841 | *Congleton* (8th), Christopher Patrick Parnell, *b.* 1930, *s.* 1967, *m.* | Hon. John P. C. *P.*, *b.* 1959. |
| 1927 | *Cornwallis* (3rd), Fiennes Neil Wykeham Cornwallis, OBE, *b.* 1921, *s.* 1982, *m.* | Hon. F. W. Jeremy *C.*, *b.* 1946. |
| 1874 | *Cottesloe* (5th), Cdr. John Tapling Fremantle, *b.* 1927, *s.* 1994, *m.* | Hon. Thomas F. H. *F.*, *b.* 1966. |
| 1929 | *Craigmyle* (3rd), Thomas Donald Mackay Shaw, *b.* 1923, *s.* 1944, *m.* | Hon. Thomas C. *S.*, *b.* 1960. |
| 1899 | *Cranworth* (3rd), Philip Bertram Gurdon, *b.* 1940, *s.* 1964, *m.* | Hon. Sacha W. R. *G.*, *b.* 1970. |
| 1959 | *Crathorne* (2nd), Charles James Dugdale, *b.* 1939, *s.* 1977, *m.* | Hon. Thomas A. J. *D.*, *b.* 1977. |
| 1892 | *Crawshaw* (4th), William Michael Clifton Brooks, *b.* 1933, *s.* 1946. | Hon. David G. *B.*, *b.* 1934. |
| 1940 | *Croft* (2nd), Michael Henry Glendower Page Croft, *b.* 1916, *s.* 1947, *w.* | Hon. Bernard W. H. P. *C.*, *b.* 1949. |
| 1797 I. | *Crofton* (7th), Guy Patrick Gilbert Crofton, *b.* 1951, *s.* 1989, *m.* | Hon. E. Harry P. *C.*, *b.* 1988. |
| 1375 | *Cromwell* (7th), Godfrey John Bewicke-Copley, *b.* 1960, *s.* 1982, *m.* | Hon. Thomas D. *B.-C.*, *b.* 1964. |
| 1947 | *Crook* (2nd), Douglas Edwin Crook, *b.* 1926, *s* 1989, *m.* | Hon. Robert D. E. *C.*, *b.* 1955. |
| 1920 | *Cullen of Ashbourne* (2nd), Charles Borlase Marsham Cokayne, MBE, *b.* 1912, *s.* 1932, *m.* | Hon. Edmund W. M. *C.*, *b.* 1916. |
| 1914 | *Cunliffe* (3rd), Roger Cunliffe, *b.* 1932, *s.* 1963, *m.* | Hon. Henry *C.*, *b.* 1962. |
| 1927 | *Daresbury* (3rd), Edward Gilbert Greenall, *b.* 1928, *s.* 1990, *m.* | Hon. Peter G. *G.*, *b.* 1953. |
| 1924 | *Darling* (2nd), Robert Charles Henry Darling, *b.* 1919, *s.* 1936, *m.* | Hon. R. Julian H. *D.*, *b.* 1944. |
| 1946 | *Darwen* (3rd), Roger Michael Davies, *b.* 1938, *s.* 1988, *m.* | Hon. Paul *D.*, *b.* 1962. |
| 1932 | *Davies* (3rd), David Davies, *b.* 1940, *s.* 1944, *m.* | Hon. David D. *D.*, *b.* 1975. |
| 1812 I. | *Decies* (7th), Marcus Hugh Tristram de la Poer Beresford, *b.* 1948, *s.* 1992, *m.* | Hon. Robert M. D. *de la P. B.*, *b.* 1988. |
| 1299 | *de Clifford* (27th), John Edward Southwell Russell, *b.* 1928, *s.* 1982, *m.* | Hon. William S. *R.*, *b.* 1930. |
| 1851 | *De Freyne* (7th), Francis Arthur John French, *b.* 1927, *s.* 1935, *m.* | Hon. Fulke C. A. J. *F.*, *b.* 1957. |
| 1821 | *Delamere* (5th), Hugh George Cholmondeley, *b.* 1934, *s.* 1979, *m.* | Hon. Thomas P. G. *C.*, *b.* 1968. |
| 1838 | *de Mauley* (6th), Gerald John Ponsonby, *b.* 1921, *s.* 1962, *m.* | Col. Hon. Thomas M. *P.*, TD, *b.* 1930. |
| 1937 | *Denham* (2nd), Bertram Stanley Mitford Bowyer, KBE, PC, *b.* 1927, *s.* 1948, *m.* | Hon. Richard G. G. *B.*, *b.* 1959. |
| 1834 | *Denman* (5th), Charles Spencer Denman, CBE, MC, TD, *b.* 1916, *s.* 1971, *w.* | Hon. Richard T. S. *D.*, *b.* 1946. |
| 1885 | *Deramore* (6th), Richard Arthur de Yarburgh-Bateson, *b.* 1911, *s.* 1964, *m.* | None. |
| 1887 | *De Ramsey* (4th), John Ailwyn Fellowes, *b.* 1942, *s.* 1993, *m.* | Hon. Freddie J. *F.*, *b.* 1978. |
| 1264 | *de Ros* (28th), Peter Trevor Maxwell, *b.* 1958, *s.* 1983, *m.* (*Premier Baron of England*). | Hon. Finbar J. *M.*, *b.* 1988. |
| 1881 | *Derwent* (5th), Robin Evelyn Leo Vanden-Bempde-Johnstone, LVO, *b.* 1930, *s.* 1986, *m.* | Hon. Francis P. H. *V.-B.-J.*, *b.* 1965. |

| Created | Title, order of succession, name, etc. | Heir |
|---|---|---|
| 1831 | *de Saumarez* (7th), Eric Douglas Saumarez, *b.* 1956, *s.* 1991, *m.* | Hon. Victor T. *S.*, *b.* 1956. |
| 1910 | *de Villiers* (3rd), Arthur Percy de Villiers, *b.* 1911, *s.* 1934. | Hon. Alexander C. *de V.*, *b.* 1940. |
| 1930 | *Dickinson* (2nd), Richard Clavering Hyett Dickinson, *b.* 1926, *s.* 1943, *m.* | Hon. Martin H. *D.*, *b.* 1961. |
| 1620 I.* | *Digby* (12th), Edward Henry Kenelm Digby (6th *Brit. Baron, Digby*, 1765), *b.* 1924, *s.* 1964, *m.* | Hon. Henry N. K. *D.*, *b.* 1954. |
| 1615 | *Dormer* (16th), Joseph Spencer Philip Dormer, *b.* 1914, *s.* 1975. | Geoffrey H. *D.*, *b.* 1920. |
| 1943 | *Dowding* (3rd), Piers Hugh Tremenheere Dowding, *b.* 1948, *s.* 1992. | Hon. Mark D. J. *D.*, *b.* 1949. |
| 1800 I. | *Dufferin and Clandeboye*. The 10th Baron died in 1991. Heir had not established his claim to the title at the time of going to press. | Sir John Blackwood, Bt., *b.* 1944. |
| 1929 | *Dulverton* (3rd), (Gilbert) Michael Hamilton Wills, *b.* 1944, *s.* 1992, *m.* | Hon. Robert A. H. *W.*, *b.* 1983. |
| 1800 I. | *Dunalley* (7th), Henry Francis Cornelius Prittie, *b.* 1948, *s.* 1992, *m.* | Hon. Joel H. *P.*, *b.* 1981. |
| 1324 I. | *Dunboyne* (28th), Patrick Theobald Tower Butler, VRD, *b.* 1917, *s.* 1945, *m.* | Hon. John F. *B.*, *b.* 1951. |
| 1802 | *Dunleath* (5th), Michael Henry Mulholland, *b.* 1915, *s.* 1993, *w.* | Hon. Brian H. *M.*, *b.* 1950. |
| 1439 I. | *Dunsany* (19th), Randal Arthur Henry Plunkett, *b.* 1906, *s.* 1957, *m.* | Hon. Edward J. C. *P.*, *b.* 1939. |
| 1780 | *Dynevor* (9th), Richard Charles Uryan Rhys, *b.* 1935, *s.* 1962. | Hon. Hugo G. U. *R.*, *b.* 1966. |
| 1857 | *Ebury* (6th), Francis Egerton Grosvenor, *b.* 1934, *s.* 1957, *m.* | Hon. Julian F. M. *G.*, *b.* 1959. |
| 1963 | *Egremont* (2nd), & *Leconfield* (7th) (1859), John Max Henry Scawen Wyndham, *b.* 1948, *s.* 1972, *m.* | Hon. George R. V. *W.*, *b.* 1983. |
| 1643 | *Elibank* (14th), Alan D'Ardis Erskine-Murray, *b.* 1923, *s.* 1973, *m.* | Master of Elibank, *b.* 1964. |
| 1802 | *Ellenborough* (8th), Richard Edward Cecil Law, *b.* 1926, *s.* 1945, *m.* | Maj. Hon. Rupert E. H. *L.*, *b.* 1955. |
| 1509 S.* | *Elphinstone* (18th), James Alexander Elphinstone (4th *UK Baron Elphinstone*, 1885), *b.* 1953, *s.* 1975, *m.* | Master of Elphinstone, *b.* 1980. |
| 1934 | *Elton* (2nd), Rodney Elton, TD, *b.* 1930, *s.* 1973, *m.* | Hon. Edward P. *E.*, *b.* 1966. |
| 1964 | *Erroll of Hale* (1st), Frederick James Erroll, TD, PC, *b.* 1914, *m.* | None. |
| 1964 | *Erskine of Rerrick* (2nd), Iain Maxwell Erskine, *b.* 1926, *s.* 1980. | None. |
| 1627 S. | *Fairfax of Cameron* (14th), Nicholas John Albert Fairfax, *b.* 1956, *s.* 1964, *m.* | Hon. Edward N. T. *F.*, *b.* 1984. |
| 1961 | *Fairhaven* (3rd), Ailwyn Henry George Broughton, *b.* 1936, *s.* 1973, *m.* | Capt. James H. A. *B.*, *b.* 1963. |
| 1916 | *Faringdon* (3rd), Charles Michael Henderson, *b.* 1937, *s.* 1977, *m.* | Hon. James H. *H.*, *b.* 1961. |
| 1756 I. | *Farnham* (12th), Barry Owen Somerset Maxwell, *b.* 1931, *s.* 1957, *m.* | Hon. Simon K. *M.*, *b.* 1933. |
| 1856 I. | *Fermoy* (6th), Patrick Maurice Burke Roche, *b.* 1967, *s.* 1984. | Hon. E. Hugh B. *R.*, *b.* 1972. |
| 1826 | *Feversham* (6th), Charles Antony Peter Duncombe, *b.* 1945, *s.* 1963, *m.* | Hon. Jasper O. S. *D.*, *b.* 1968. |
| 1798 I. | *ffrench* (8th), Robuck John Peter Charles Mario ffrench, *b.* 1956, *s.* 1986, *m.* | Hon. John C. M. J. F. *ff.*, *b.* 1928. |
| 1909 | *Fisher* (3rd), John Vavasseur Fisher, DSC, *b.* 1921, *s.* 1955, *m.* | Hon. Patrick V. *F.*, *b.* 1953. |
| 1295 | *Fitzwalter* (21st), (Fitzwalter) Brook Plumptre, *b.* 1914, *title called out of abeyance*, 1953, *m.* | Hon. Julian B. *P.*, *b.* 1952. |
| 1776 | *Foley* (8th), Adrian Gerald Foley, *b.* 1923, *s.* 1927, *m.* | Hon. Thomas H. *F.,* *b.* 1961. |
| 1445 S. | *Forbes* (22nd), Nigel Ivan Forbes, KBE (*Premier Lord of Scotland*), *b.* 1918, *s.* 1953, *m.* | Master of Forbes, *b.* 1946. |
| 1821 | *Forester* (8th), (George Cecil) Brooke Weld-Forester, *b.* 1938, *s.* 1977, *m.* | Hon. C. R. George *W.-F.*, *b.* 1975. |
| 1922 | *Forres* (4th), Alastair Stephen Grant Williamson, *b.* 1946, *s.* 1978, *m.* | Hon. George A. M. *W.*, *b.* 1972. |
| 1917 | *Forteviot* (4th), John James Evelyn Dewar, *b.* 1938, *s.* 1993, *m.* | Hon. Alexander J. E. *D.*, *b.* 1971. |
| 1951 | *Freyberg* (3rd), Valerian Bernard Freyberg, *b.* 1970, *s.* 1993. | None. |
| 1917 | *Gainford* (3rd), Joseph Edward Pease, *b.* 1921, *s.* 1971, *m.* | Hon. George *P.*, *b.* 1926. |
| 1818 I. | *Garvagh* (5th), (Alexander Leopold Ivor) George Canning, *b.* 1920, *s.* 1956, *m.* | Hon. Spencer G. S. de R. *C.*, *b.* 1953. |
| 1942 | *Geddes* (3rd), Euan Michael Ross Geddes, *b.* 1937, *s.* 1975, *m.* | Hon. James G. N. *G.*, *b.* 1969. |
| 1876 | *Gerard* (5th), Anthony Robert Hugo Gerard, *b.* 1949, *s.* 1992, *m.* | Hon. Rupert B. C. *G.*, *b.* 1981. |
| 1824 | *Gifford* (6th), Anthony Maurice Gifford, QC, *b.* 1940, *s.* 1961, *m.* | Hon. Thomas A. *G.*, *b.* 1967. |
| 1917 | *Gisborough* (3rd), Thomas Richard John Long Chaloner, *b.* 1927, *s.* 1951, *m.* | Hon. T. Peregrine L. *C.*, *b.* 1961. |
| 1960 | *Gladwyn* (1st), (Hubert Miles) Gladwyn Jebb, GCMG, GCVO, CB, *b.* 1900, *w.* | Hon. Miles A. G. *J.*, *b.* 1930. |
| 1899 | *Glanusk* (4th), David Russell Bailey, *b.* 1917, *s.* 1948, *m.* | Hon. Christopher R. *B.*, *b.* 1942. |
| 1918 | *Glenarthur* (4th), Simon Mark Arthur, *b.* 1944, *s.* 1976, *m.* | Hon. Edward A. *A.*, *b.* 1973. |
| 1911 | *Glenconner* (3rd), Colin Christopher Paget Tennant, *b.* 1926, *s.* 1983, *m.* | Hon. Charles E. P. *T.*, *b.* 1957. |
| 1964 | *Glendevon* (1st), John Adrian Hope, ERD, PC, *b.* 1912, *m.* | Hon. Julian J. S. *H.*, *b.* 1950. |
| 1922 | *Glendyne* (3rd), Robert Nivison, *b.* 1926, *s.* 1967, *m.* | Hon. John *N.*, *b.* 1960. |
| 1939 | *Glentoran* (2nd), Daniel Stewart Thomas Bingham Dixon, KBE, PC (NI), *b.* 1912, *s.* 1950, *w.* | Hon. Thomas R. V. *D.*, CBE, *b.* 1935. |
| 1909 | *Gorell* (4th), Timothy John Radcliffe Barnes, *b.* 1927, *s.* 1963, *m.* | Hon. Ronald A. H. *B.*, *b.* 1931. |
| 1953 | *Grantchester* (2nd), Kenneth Bent Suenson-Taylor, CBE, QC, *b.* 1921, *s.* 1976, *m.* | Hon. Christopher J. *S-. T.*, *b.* 1951. |
| 1782 | *Grantley* (7th), John Richard Brinsley Norton, MC, *b.* 1923, *s.* 1954, *m.* | Hon. Richard W. B. *N.*, *b.* 1956. |
| 1794 I. | *Graves* (9th), Evelyn Paget Graves, *b.* 1926, *s.* 1994, *m.* | Hon. Timothy E. *G.*, *b.* 1960. |

| Created | Title, order of succession, name, etc. | Heir |
|---|---|---|
| 1445 S. | *Gray* (22nd), Angus Diarmid Ian Campbell-Gray, *b.* 1931, *s.* 1946, *m.* | Master of Gray, *b.* 1964. |
| 1950 | *Greenhill* (3rd), Malcolm Greenhill, *b.* 1924, *s.* 1989. | None. |
| 1927 | *Greenway* (4th), Ambrose Charles Drexel Greenway, *b.* 1941, *s.* 1975, *m.* | Hon. Mervyn S. K. *G.*, *b.* 1942. |
| 1902 | *Grenfell* (3rd), Julian Pascoe Francis St Leger Grenfell, *b.* 1935, *s.* 1976, *m.* | Francis P. J. *G.*, *b.* 1938. |
| 1944 | *Gretton* (4th), John Lysander Gretton, *b.* 1975, *s.* 1989, *M.* | None. |
| 1397 | *Grey of Codnor* (5th), Charles Legh Shuldham Cornwall-Legh, CBE, AE, *b.* 1903, *title called out of abeyance* 1989, *w.* | Hon. Richard H. *C.-L.*, *b.* 1936. |
| 1955 | *Gridley* (2nd), Arnold Hudson Gridley, *b.* 1906, *s.* 1965, *m.* | Hon. Richard D. A. *G.*, *b.* 1956. |
| 1964 | *Grimston of Westbury* (2nd), Robert Walter Sigismund Grimston, *b.* 1925, *s.* 1979, *m.* | Hon. Robert J. S. *G.*, *b.* 1951. |
| 1886 | *Grimthorpe* (4th), Christopher John Beckett, OBE, *b.* 1915, *s.* 1963, *m.* | Hon. Edward J. *B.*, *b.* 1954. |
| 1945 | *Hacking* (3rd), Douglas David Hacking, *b.* 1938, *s.* 1971, *m.* | Hon. Douglas F. *H.*, *b.* 1968. |
| 1950 | *Haden-Guest* (4th), Peter Haden Haden-Guest, *b.* 1913, *s.* 1987, *m.* | Hon. Christopher *H.-G.*, *b.* 1948. |
| 1886 | *Hamilton of Dalzell* (4th), James Leslie Hamilton, *b.* 1938, *s.* 1990, *m.* | Hon. Gavin G. *H.*, *b.* 1968. |
| 1874 | *Hampton* (6th), Richard Humphrey Russell Pakington, *b.* 1925, *s.* 1974, *m.* | Hon. John H. A. *P.*, *b.* 1964. |
| 1939 | *Hankey* (2nd), Robert Maurice Alers Hankey, KCMG, KCVO, *b.* 1905, *s.* 1963, *m.* | Hon. Donald R. A. *H.*, *b.* 1938. |
| 1958 | *Harding of Petherton* (2nd), John Charles Harding, *b.* 1928, *s.* 1989, *m.* | Hon. William A. J. *H.*, *b.* 1969. |
| 1910 | *Hardinge of Penshurst* (3rd), George Edward Charles Hardinge, *b.* 1921, *s.* 1960, *m.* | Hon. Julian A. *H.*, *b.* 1945. |
| 1876 | *Harlech* (6th), Francis David Ormsby-Gore, *b.* 1954, *s.* 1985, *m.* | Hon. Jasset D. C. *O.-G.*, *b.* 1986. |
| 1939 | *Harmsworth* (3rd), Thomas Harold Raymond Harmsworth, *b.* 1939, *s.* 1990, *m.* | Hon. Dominic M. E. *H.*, *b.* 1973. |
| 1815 | *Harris* (6th), George Robert John Harris, *b.* 1920, *s.* 1984. | Derek M. *H.*, *b.* 1916. |
| 1954 | *Harvey of Tasburgh* (2nd), Peter Charles Oliver Harvey, *b.* 1921, *s.* 1968, *m.* | Charles J. G. *H.*, *b.* 1951. |
| 1295 | *Hastings* (22nd), Edward Delaval Henry Astley, *b.* 1912, *s.* 1956, *m.* | Hon. Delaval T. H. *A.*, *b.* 1960. |
| 1835 | *Hatherton* (8th), Edward Charles Littleton, *b.* 1950, *s.* 1985, *m.* | Hon. Thomas E. *L.*, *b.* 1977. |
| 1776 | *Hawke* (11th), Edward George Hawke, TD, *b.* 1950, *s.* 1992, *m.* | None. |
| 1927 | *Hayter* (3rd), George Charles Hayter Chubb, KCVO, CBE, *b.* 1911, *s.* 1967, *m.* | Hon. G. William M. *C.*, *b.* 1943. |
| 1945 | *Hazlerigg* (2nd), Arthur Grey Hazlerigg, MC, TD, *b.* 1910, *s.* 1949, *w.* | Hon. Arthur G. *H.*, *b.* 1951. |
| 1797 I. | *Headley* (7th), Charles Rowland Allanson-Winn, *b.* 1902, *s.* 1969, *w.* | Hon. Owain G. *A.-W.*, *b.* 1906. |
| 1943 | *Hemingford* (3rd), (Dennis) Nicholas Herbert, *b.* 1934, *s.* 1982, *m.* | Hon. Christopher D. C. *H.*, *b.* 1973. |
| 1906 | *Hemphill* (5th), Peter Patrick Fitzroy Martyn Martyn-Hemphill, *b.* 1928, *s.* 1957, *m.* | Hon. Charles A. M. *M.-H.*, *b.* 1954. |
| 1799 I.* | *Henley* (8th), Oliver Michael Robert Eden (6th *UK Baron, Northington*, 1885), *b.* 1953, *s.* 1977, *m.* | Hon. John W. O. *E.*, *b.* 1988. |
| 1800 I.* | *Henniker* (8th), John Patrick Edward Chandos Henniker-Major, KCMG, CVO, MC (4th *UK Baron, Hartismere*, 1866), *b.* 1916, *s.* 1980, *m.* | Hon. Mark I. P. C. *H.-M.*, *b.* 1947. |
| 1886 | *Herschell* (3rd), Rognvald Richard Farrer Herschell, *b.* 1923, *s.* 1929, *m.* | None. |
| 1935 | *Hesketh* (3rd), Thomas Alexander Fermor-Hesketh, PC, *b.* 1950, *s.* 1955, *m.* | Hon. Frederick H. *F.-H.*, *b.* 1988. |
| 1828 | *Heytesbury* (6th), Francis William Holmes à Court, *b.* 1931, *s.* 1971, *m.* | Hon. James W. *H. à C.*, *b.* 1967. |
| 1886 | *Hindlip* (6th), Charles Henry Allsopp, *b.* 1940, *s.* 1993, *m.* | Hon. Henry W. *A.*, *b.* 1973. |
| 1950 | *Hives* (2nd), John Warwick Hives, CBE, *b.* 1913, *s.* 1965, *m.* | Matthew P. *H.*, *b.* 1971. |
| 1912 | *Hollenden* (3rd), Gordon Hope Hope-Morley, *b.* 1914, *s.* 1977, *m.* | Hon. Ian H.-*M.*, *b.* 1946. |
| 1897 | *HolmPatrick* (4th), Hans James David Hamilton, *b.* 1955, *s.* 1991, *m.* | Hon. Ion H. J. *H.*, *b.* 1956. |
| 1933 | *Horder* (2nd), Thomas Mervyn Horder, *b.* 1910, *s.* 1955. | None. |
| 1797 I. | *Hotham* (8th), Henry Durand Hotham, *b.* 1940, *s.* 1967, *m.* | Hon. William B. *H.*, *b.* 1972. |
| 1881 | *Hothfield* (6th), Anthony Charles Sackville Tufton, *b.* 1939, *s.* 1991, *m.* | Hon. William S. *T.*, *b.* 1977. |
| 1597 | *Howard de Walden* (9th), John Osmael Scott-Ellis, TD (5th *UK Baron, Seaford*, 1826), *b.* 1912, *s.* 1946, *m.* | To Barony of Howard de Walden, four co-heiresses. To Barony of Seaford, Colin H. F. *Ellis*, *b.* 1946. |
| 1930 | *Howard of Penrith* (2nd), Francis Philip Howard, *b.* 1905, *s.* 1939, *m.* | Hon. Philip E. *H.*, *b.* 1945. |
| 1960 | *Howick of Glendale* (2nd), Charles Evelyn Baring, *b.* 1937, *s.* 1973, *m.* | Hon. David E. C. *B.*, *b.* 1975. |
| 1796 I. | *Huntingfield* (7th), Joshua Charles Vanneck, *b.* 1954, *s.* 1994, *m.* | Hon. Gerard C. A. *V.*, *b.* 1985. |
| 1866 | *Hylton* (5th), Raymond Hervey Jolliffe, *b.* 1932, *s.* 1967, *m.* | Hon. William H. M. *J.*, *b.* 1967. |
| 1933 | *Iliffe* (2nd), Edward Langton Iliffe, *b.* 1908, *s.* 1960, *m.* | Robert P. R. *I.*, *b.* 1944. |
| 1543 I. | *Inchiquin* (18th), Conor Myles John O'Brien, *b.* 1943, *s.* 1982, *m.* | Murrough R. *O'B.*, *b.* 1910. |
| 1962 | *Inchyra* (2nd), Robert Charles Reneke Hoyer Millar, *b.* 1935, *s.* 1989, *m.* | Hon. C. James C. H. *M.*, *b.* 1962. |
| 1964 | *Inglewood* (2nd), (William) Richard Fletcher-Vane, MEP, *b.* 1951, *s.* 1989, *m.* | Hon. Henry W. F. *F.-V.*, *b.* 1990. |
| 1919 | *Inverforth* (4th), Andrew Peter Weir, *b.* 1966, *s.* 1982. | Hon. John V. *W.*, *b.* 1935. |
| 1941 | *Ironside* (2nd), Edmund Oslac Ironside, *b.* 1924, *s.* 1959, *m.* | Hon. Charles E. G. *I.*, *b.* 1956. |

| Created | Title, order of succession, name, etc. | Heir |
|---|---|---|
| 1952 | *Jeffreys* (3rd), Christopher Henry Mark Jeffreys, *b.* 1957, *s.* 1986, *m.* | Hon. Arthur M. H. *J.*, *b.* 1989. |
| 1906 | *Joicey* (5th), James Michael Joicey, *b.* 1953, *s.* 1993, *m.* | Hon. William J. *J.*, *b.* 1990. |
| 1937 | *Kenilworth* (4th), (John) Randle Siddeley, *b.* 1954, *s.* 1981, *m.* | Hon. William R. J. *S.*, *b.* 1992. |
| 1935 | *Kennet* (2nd), Wayland Hilton Young, *b.* 1923, *s.* 1960, *m.* | Hon. W. A. Thoby *Y.*, *b.* 1957. |
| 1776 I.* | *Kensington* (8th), Hugh Ivor Edwardes (5th *UK Baron, Kensington*, 1886), *b.* 1933, *s.* 1981, *m.* | Hon. W. Owen A. *E.*, *b.* 1964. |
| 1951 | *Kenswood* (2nd), John Michael Howard Whitfield, *b.* 1930, *s.* 1963, *m.* | Hon. Michael C. *W.*, *b.* 1955. |
| 1788 | *Kenyon* (6th), Lloyd Tyrell-Kenyon, *b.* 1947, *s.* 1993, *m.* | Hon. Lloyd N. *T.-K.*, *b.* 1972. |
| 1947 | *Kershaw* (4th), Edward John Kershaw, *b.* 1936, *s.* 1962, *m.* | Hon. John C. E. *K.*, *b.* 1971. |
| 1943 | *Keyes* (2nd), Roger George Bowlby Keyes, *b.* 1919, *s.* 1945, *m.* | Hon. Charles W. P. *K.*, *b.* 1951. |
| 1909 | *Kilbracken* (3rd), John Raymond Godley, DSC, *b.* 1920, *s.* 1950. | Hon. Christopher J. *G.*, *b.* 1945. |
| 1900 | *Killanin* (3rd), Michael Morris, MBE, TD, *b.* 1914, *s.* 1927, *m.* | Hon. G. Redmond F. *M.*, *b.* 1947. |
| 1943 | *Killearn* (2nd), Graham Curtis Lampson, *b.* 1919, *s.* 1964, *m.* | Hon. Victor M. G. A. *L.*, *b.* 1941. |
| 1789 I. | *Kilmaine* (7th), John David Henry Browne, *b.* 1948, *s.* 1978, *m.* | Hon. John F. S. *B.*, *b.* 1983. |
| 1831 | *Kilmarnock* (7th), Alastair Ivor Gilbert Boyd, *b.* 1927, *s.* 1975, *m.* | Hon. Robin J. *B.*, *b.* 1941. |
| 1941 | *Kindersley* (3rd), Robert Hugh Molesworth Kindersley, *b.* 1929, *s.* 1976, *m.* | Hon. Rupert J. M. *K.*, *b.* 1955. |
| 1223 I. | *Kingsale* (35th), John de Courcy (*Premier Baron of Ireland*), *b.* 1941, *s.* 1969. | Nevinson R. *de C.*, *b.* 1920. |
| 1682 S.* | *Kinnaird* (13th), Graham Charles Kinnaird (5th *UK Baron, Kinnaird*, 1860), *b.* 1912, *s.* 1972, *m.* | None. |
| 1902 | *Kinross* (5th), Christopher Patrick Balfour, *b.* 1949, *s.* 1985, *m.* | Hon. Alan I. *B.*, *b.* 1978. |
| 1951 | *Kirkwood* (3rd), David Harvie Kirkwood, PH.D., *b.* 1931, *s.* 1970, *m.* | Hon. James S. *K.*, *b.* 1937. |
| 1800 I. | *Langford* (9th), Col. Geoffrey Alexander Rowley-Conwy, OBE, *b.* 1912, *s.* 1953, *m.* | Hon. Owain G. *R.-C.*, *b.* 1958. |
| 1942 | *Latham* (2nd), Dominic Charles Latham, *b.* 1954, *s.* 1970. | Anthony M. *L.*, *b.* 1954. |
| 1431 | *Latymer* (8th), Hugo Nevill Money-Coutts, *b.* 1926, *s.* 1987, *m.* | Hon. Crispin J. A. N. *M.-C.*, *b.* 1955. |
| 1869 | *Lawrence* (5th), David John Downer Lawrence, *b.* 1937, *s.* 1968. | None. |
| 1947 | *Layton* (3rd), Geoffrey Michael Layton, *b.* 1947, *s.* 1989, *m.* | Hon. David *L.*, MBE, *b.* 1914. |
| 1839 | *Leigh* (5th), John Piers Leigh, *b.* 1935, *s.* 1979, *m.* | Hon. Christopher D. P. *L.*, *b.* 1960. |
| 1962 | *Leighton of St Mellons* (2nd), (John) Leighton Seager, *b.* 1922, *s.* 1963, *m.* | Hon. Robert W. H. L. *S.*, *b.* 1955. |
| 1797 | *Lilford* (7th), George Vernon Powys, *b.* 1931, *s.* 1949, *m.* | Hon. Mark V. *P.*, *b.* 1975. |
| 1945 | *Lindsay of Birker* (3rd), James Francis Lindsay, *b.* 1945, *s.* 1994, *m.* | Hon. Thomas M. *L.*, *b.* 1915. |
| 1758 I. | *Lisle* (7th), John Nicholas Horace Lysaght, *b.* 1903, *s.* 1919, *m.* | Patrick J. *L.*, *b.* 1931. |
| 1850 | *Londesborough* (9th), Richard John Denison, *b.* 1959, *s.* 1968, *m.* | Hon. James F. *D.*, *b.* 1990. |
| 1541 I. | *Louth* (16th), Otway Michael James Oliver Plunkett, *b.* 1929, *s.* 1950, *m.* | Hon. Jonathan O. *P.*, *b.* 1952. |
| 1458 S.* | *Lovat* (15th), Simon Christopher Joseph Fraser, DSO, MC, TD (4th *UK Baron, Lovat*, 1837), *b.* 1911, *s.* 1933, *m.* | Master of Lovat *b.* 1977. |
| 1946 | *Lucas of Chilworth* (2nd), Michael William George Lucas, *b.* 1926, *s.* 1967, *m.* | Hon. Simon W. *L.*, *b.* 1957. |
| 1663 | *Lucas* (11th) & *Dingwall* (8th) (*Scottish Lordship* 1609), Ralph Matthew Palmer, *b.* 1951, *s.* 1991, *m.* | Hon. Lewis E. *P.*, *b.* 1987 |
| 1929 | *Luke* (2nd), Ian St John Lawson-Johnston, KCVO, TD, *b.* 1905, *s.* 1943, *m.* | Hon. Arthur C. St J. *L.-J.*, *b.* 1933. |
| 1914 | *Lyell* (3rd), Charles Lyell, *b.* 1939, *s.* 1943. | None. |
| 1859 | *Lyveden* (6th), Ronald Cecil Vernon, *b.* 1915, *s.* 1973, *m.* | Hon. Jack L. *V.*, *b.* 1938. |
| 1959 | *MacAndrew* (3rd), Christopher Anthony Colin MacAndrew, *b.* 1945, *s.* 1989, *m.* | Hon. Oliver C. J. *M.*, *b.* 1983. |
| 1776 I. | *Macdonald* (8th), Godfrey James Macdonald of Macdonald, *b.* 1947, *s.* 1970, *m.* | Hon. Godfrey E. H. T. *M.*, *b.* 1982. |
| 1949 | *Macdonald of Gwaenysgor* (2nd), Gordon Ramsay Macdonald, *b.* 1915, *s.* 1966, *m.* | None. |
| 1937 | *McGowan* (3rd), Harry Duncan Cory McGowan, *b.* 1938, *s.* 1966, *m.* | Hon. Harry J. C. *M.*, *b.* 1971. |
| 1922 | *Maclay* (3rd), Joseph Paton Maclay, *b.* 1942, *s.* 1969, *m.* | Hon. Joseph P. *M.*, *b.* 1977. |
| 1955 | *McNair* (3rd), Duncan James McNair, *b.* 1947, *s.* 1989, *m.* | Hon. Thomas J. *M.*, *b.* 1990. |
| 1951 | *Macpherson of Drumochter* (2nd), (James) Gordon Macpherson, *b.* 1924, *s.* 1965, *m.* | Hon. James A. *M.*, *b.* 1979. |
| 1937 | *Mancroft* (3rd), Benjamin Lloyd Stormont Mancroft, *b.* 1957, *s.* 1987, *m.* | None. |
| 1807 | *Manners* (5th), John Robert Cecil Manners, *b.* 1923, *s.* 1972, *m.* | Hon. John H. R. *M.*, *b.* 1956. |
| 1922 | *Manton* (3rd), Joseph Rupert Eric Robert Watson, *b.* 1924, *s.* 1968, *m.* | Maj. Hon. Miles R. M. *W.*, *b.* 1958. |
| 1908 | *Marchamley* (4th), William Francis Whiteley, *b.* 1968, *s.* 1994. | † |
| 1964 | *Margadale* (1st), John Granville Morrison, TD, *b.* 1906, *w.* | Hon. James I. *M.*, TD, *b.* 1930. |
| 1961 | *Marks of Broughton* (2nd), Michael Marks, *b.* 1920, *s.* 1964. | Hon. Simon R. *M.*, *b.* 1950. |
| 1964 | *Martonmere* (2nd), John Stephen Robinson, *b.* 1963, *s.* 1989. | David A. *R.*, *b.* 1965. |
| 1776 I. | *Massy* (9th), Hugh Hamon John Somerset Massy, *b.* 1921, *s.* 1958, *m.* | Hon. David H. S. *M.*, *b.* 1947. |
| 1935 | *May* (3rd), Michael St John May, *b.* 1931, *s.* 1950, *m.* | Hon. Jasper B. St J. *M.*, *b.* 1965. |
| 1928 | *Melchett* (4th), Peter Robert Henry Mond, *b.* 1948, *s.* 1973. | None. |
| 1925 | *Merrivale* (3rd), Jack Henry Edmond Duke, *b.* 1917, *s.* 1951, *m.* | Hon. Derek J. P. *D.*, *b.* 1948. |

| Created | Title, order of succession, name, etc. | Heir |
|---|---|---|
| 1911 | *Merthyr*. Disclaimed for life 1977. (*Trevor Oswin Lewis, Bt.*, CBE, *b.* 1935, *s.* 1977, *m.*) | David T. *L.*, *b.* 1977. |
| 1919 | *Meston* (3rd), James Meston, *b.* 1950, *s.* 1984, *m.* | Hon. Thomas J. D. *M.*, *b.* 1977. |
| 1838 | *Methuen* (7th), Robert Alexander Holt Methuen, *b.* 1931, *s.* 1994, *m.* | Christopher P. M. C. *Methuen-Campbell*, *b.* 1928. |
| 1711 | *Middleton* (12th), (Digby) Michael Godfrey John Willoughby, MC, *b.* 1921, *s.* 1970, *m.* | Hon. Michael C. J. *W.*, *b.* 1948. |
| 1939 | *Milford* (3rd), Hugo John Laurence Philipps, *b.* 1929, *s.* 1993, *m.* | Hon. Guy W. *P.*, *b.* 1961. |
| 1933 | *Milne* (2nd), George Douglass Milne, TD, *b.* 1909, *s.* 1948, *m.* | Hon. George A. *M.*, *b.* 1941. |
| 1951 | *Milner of Leeds* (2nd), Arthur James Michael Milner, AE, *b.* 1923, *s.* 1967, *m.* | Hon. Richard J. *M.*, *b.* 1959. |
| 1947 | *Milverton* (2nd), Revd Fraser Arthur Richard Richards, *b.* 1930, *s.* 1978, *m.* | Hon. Michael H. *R.*, *b.* 1936. |
| 1873 | *Moncreiff* (5th), Harry Robert Wellwood Moncreiff, *b.* 1915, *s.* 1942, *w.* | Hon. Rhoderick H. W. *M.*, *b.* 1954. |
| 1884 | *Monk Bretton* (3rd), John Charles Dodson, *b.* 1924, *s.* 1933, *m.* | Hon. Christopher M. *D.*, *b.* 1958. |
| 1885 | *Monkswell* (5th), Gerard Collier, *b.* 1947, *s.* 1984, *m.* | Hon. James A. *C.*, *b.* 1977. |
| 1728 | *Monson* (11th), John Monson, *b.* 1932, *s.* 1958, *m.* | Hon. Nicholas J. *M.*, *b.* 1955. |
| 1885 | *Montagu of Beaulieu* (3rd), Edward John Barrington Douglas-Scott-Montagu, *b.* 1926, *s.* 1929, *m.* | Hon. Ralph *D.-S.-M.*, *b.* 1961. |
| 1839 | *Monteagle of Brandon* (6th), Gerald Spring Rice, *b.* 1926, *s.* 1946, *m.* | Hon. Charles J. S. *R.*, *b.* 1953. |
| 1943 | *Moran* (2nd), (Richard) John (McMoran) Wilson, KCMG, *b.* 1924, *s.* 1977, *m.* | Hon. James M. *W.*, *b.* 1952. |
| 1918 | *Morris* (3rd), Michael David Morris, *b.* 1937, *s.* 1975, *m.* | Hon. Thomas A. S. *M.*, *b.* 1982. |
| 1950 | *Morris of Kenwood* (2nd), Philip Geoffrey Morris, *b.* 1928, *s.* 1954, *m.* | Hon. Jonathan D. *M.*, *b.* 1968. |
| 1945 | *Morrison* (2nd), Dennis Morrison, *b.* 1914, *s.* 1953. | None. |
| 1831 | *Mostyn* (5th), Roger Edward Lloyd Lloyd-Mostyn, MC, *b.* 1920, *s.* 1965, *m.* | Hon. Llewellyn R. L. *L.-M.*, *b.* 1948. |
| 1933 | *Mottistone* (4th), David Peter Seely, CBE, *b.* 1920, *s.* 1966, *m.* | Hon. Peter J. P. *S.*, *b.* 1949. |
| 1945 | *Mountevans* (3rd), Edward Patrick Broke Evans, *b.* 1943, *s.* 1974, *m.* | Hon. Jeffrey de C. R. *E.*, *b.* 1948. |
| 1283 | *Mowbray* (26th), *Segrave* (27th) (1283), & *Stourton* (23rd) (1448), Charles Edward Stourton, CBE, *b.* 1923, *s.* 1965, *m.* | Hon. Edward W. S. *S.*, *b.* 1953. |
| 1932 | *Moyne* (3rd), Jonathan Bryan Guinness, *b.* 1930, *s.* 1992, *m.* | Hon. Jasper J. R. *G.*, *b.* 1954. |
| 1929 | *Moynihan*. Barony dormant since the 3rd Baron died in November 1991. His trustees recognized Daniel Antony Patrick Berkeley Moynihan, (*b.* January 1991) as the financial heir of the 3rd Baron but the succession to the title is not settled. | |
| 1781 I. | *Muskerry* (9th), Robert Fitzmaurice Deane, *b.* 1948, *s.* 1988, *m.* | Hon. Jonathan F. *D.*, *b.* 1986. |
| 1627 S. | *Napier* (14th) & *Ettrick* (5th) (*UK* 1872), Francis Nigel Napier, KCVO, *b.* 1930, *s.* 1954, *m.* | Master of Napier, *b.* 1962. |
| 1868 | *Napier of Magdala* (6th), Robert Alan Napier, *b.* 1940, *s.* 1987, *m.* | Hon. James R. *N.*, *b.* 1966. |
| 1940 | *Nathan* (2nd), Roger Carol Michael Nathan, *b.* 1922, *s.* 1963, *m.* | Hon. Rupert H. B. *N.*, *b.* 1957. |
| 1960 | *Nelson of Stafford* (2nd), Henry George Nelson, FEng., *b.* 1917, *s.* 1962, *m.* | Hon. Henry R. G. *N.*, *b.* 1943. |
| 1959 | *Netherthorpe* (3rd), James Frederick Turner, *b.* 1964, *s.* 1982, *m.* | Hon. Andrew J. E. *T.*, *b.* 1993. |
| 1946 | *Newall* (2nd), Francis Storer Eaton Newall, *b.* 1930, *s.* 1963, *m.* | Hon. Richard H. E. *N.*, *b.* 1961. |
| 1776 I. | *Newborough* (7th), Robert Charles Michael Vaughan Wynn, DSC, *b.* 1917, *s.* 1965, *m.* | Hon. Robert V. *W.*, *b.* 1949. |
| 1892 | *Newton* (5th), Richard Thomas Legh, *b.* 1950, *s.* 1992, *m.* | Hon. Piers R. *L.*, *b.* 1979. |
| 1930 | *Noel-Buxton* (3rd), Martin Connal Noel-Buxton, *b.* 1940, *s.* 1980, *m.* | Hon. Charles C. *N.-B.*, *b.* 1975. |
| 1957 | *Norrie* (2nd), (George) Willoughby Moke Norrie, *b.* 1936, *s.* 1977, *m.* | Hon. Mark W. J. *N.*, *b.* 1972. |
| 1884 | *Northbourne* (5th), Christopher George Walter James, *b.* 1926, *s.* 1982, *m.* | Hon. Charles W. H. *J.*, *b.* 1960. |
| 1866 | *Northbrook* (6th), Francis Thomas Baring, *b.* 1954, *s.* 1990, *m.* | None. |
| 1878 | *Norton* (8th), James Nigel Arden Adderley, *b.* 1947, *s.* 1993, *m.* | Hon. Edward J. A. *A.*, *b.* 1982. |
| 1906 | *Nunburnholme* (4th), Ben Charles Wilson, *b.* 1928, *s.* 1974. | Hon. Charles T. *W.*, *b.* 1935. |
|  | *Oaksey, see Trevethin and Oaksey* | |
| 1950 | *Ogmore* (2nd), Gwilym Rees Rees-Williams, *b.* 1931, *s.* 1976, *m.* | Hon. Morgan R.-*W.*, *b.* 1937. |
| 1870 | *O'Hagan* (4th), Charles Towneley Strachey, *b.* 1945, *s.* 1961. | Hon. Richard T. *S.*, *b.* 1950. |
| 1868 | *O'Neill* (4th), Raymond Arthur Clanaboy O'Neill, TD, *b.* 1933, *s.* 1944, *m.* | Hon. Shane S. C. *O'N.*, *b.* 1965. |
| 1836 I.* | *Oranmore and Browne* (4th), Dominick Geoffrey Edward Browne (2nd *UK Baron Mereworth*, 1926), *b.* 1901, *s.* 1927, *m.* | Hon. Dominick G. T. *B.*, *b.* 1929. |
| 1933 | *Palmer* (4th), Adrian Bailie Nottage Palmer, *b.* 1951, *s.* 1990, *m.* | Hon. Hugo B. R. *P.*, *b.* 1980. |
| 1914 | *Parmoor* (4th), (Frederick Alfred) Milo Cripps, *b.* 1929, *s.* 1977. | M. Anthony L. *C.*, CBE, DSO, TD, QC, *b.* 1913. |
| 1937 | *Pender* (3rd), John Willoughby Denison-Pender, *b.* 1933, *s.* 1965, *m.* | Hon. Henry J. R. *D.-P.*, *b.* 1968. |
| 1866 | *Penrhyn* (6th), Malcolm Frank Douglas-Pennant, DSO, MBE, *b.* 1908, *s.* 1967, *m.* | Hon. Nigel *D.-P.*, *b.* 1909. |
| 1603 | *Petre* (18th), John Patrick Lionel Petre, *b.* 1942, *s.* 1989, *m.* | Hon. Dominic W. *P.*, *b.* 1966. |
| 1918 | *Phillimore* (5th), Francis Stephen Phillimore, *b.* 1944, *s.* 1994, *m.* | Hon. Tristan A. S. *P.*, *b.* 1977. |

| Created | Title, order of succession, name, etc. | Heir |
|---|---|---|
| 1945 | *Piercy* (3rd), James William Piercy, *b.* 1946, *s.* 1981. | Hon. Mark E. P. *P.*, *b.* 1953. |
| 1827 | *Plunket* (8th), Robin Rathmore Plunket, *b.* 1925, *s.* 1975, *m.* | Hon. Shaun A. F. S. *P.*, *b.* 1931. |
| 1831 | *Poltimore* (7th), Mark Coplestone Bampfylde, *b.* 1957, *s.* 1978, *m.* | Hon. Henry A. W. *B.*, *b.* 1985. |
| 1690 s. | *Polwarth* (10th), Henry Alexander Hepburne-Scott, TD, *b.* 1916, *s.* 1944, *m.* | Master of Polwarth, *b.* 1947. |
| 1930 | *Ponsonby of Shulbrede* (4th), Frederick Matthew Thomas Ponsonby, *b.* 1958, *s.* 1990. | None. |
| 1958 | *Poole* (2nd), David Charles Poole, *b.* 1945, *s.* 1993, *m.* | Hon. Oliver J. *P.*, *b.* 1972. |
| 1852 | *Raglan* (5th), FitzRoy John Somerset, *b.* 1927, *s.* 1964. | Hon. Geoffrey *S.*, *b.* 1932. |
| 1932 | *Rankeillour* (4th), Peter St Thomas More Henry Hope, *b.* 1935, *s.* 1967. | Michael R. *H.*, *b.* 1940. |
| 1953 | *Rathcavan* (2nd), Phelim Robert Hugh O'Neill, PC (NI), *b.* 1909, *s.* 1982, *m.* | Hon. Hugh D. T. *O'N.*, *b.* 1939. |
| 1916 | *Rathcreedan* (3rd), Christopher John Norton, *b.* 1949, *s.* 1990, *m.* | Hon. Adam G. *N.*, *b.* 1952. |
| 1868 I. | *Rathdonnell* (5th), Thomas Benjamin McClintock–Bunbury, *b.* 1938, *s.* 1959, *m.* | Hon. William L. *M.-B.*, *b.* 1966. |
| 1911 | *Ravensdale* (3rd), Nicholas Mosley, MC, *b.* 1923, *s.* 1966, *m.* | Hon. Shaun N. *M.*, *b.* 1949. |
| 1821 | *Ravensworth* (8th), Arthur Waller Liddell, *b.* 1924, *s.* 1950, *m.* | Hon. Thomas A. H. *L.*, *b.* 1954. |
| 1821 | *Rayleigh* (6th), John Gerald Strutt, *b.* 1960, *s.* 1988, *m.* | Hon. John F. *S.*, *b.* 1993. |
| 1937 | *Rea* (3rd), John Nicolas Rea, MD, *b.* 1928, *s.* 1981, *m.* | Hon. Matthew J. *R.*, *b.* 1956. |
| 1628 s. | *Reay* (14th), Hugh William Mackay, *b.* 1937, *s.* 1963, *m.* | Master of Reay, *b.* 1965. |
| 1902 | *Redesdale* (6th), Rupert Bertram Mitford, *b.* 1967, *s.* 1991. | None. |
| 1940 | *Reith.* Disclaimed for life 1972. (*Christopher John Reith*, *b.* 1928, *s.* 1971, *m.*) | Hon. James H. J. *R.*, *b.* 1971. |
| 1928 | *Remnant* (3rd), James Wogan Remnant, CVO, b. 1930, *s.* 1967, *m.* | Hon. Philip J. *R.*, *b.* 1954. |
| 1806 I. | *Rendlesham* (8th), Charles Anthony Hugh Thellusson, *b.* 1915, *s.* 1943, *w.* | Hon. Charles W. B. *T.*, *b.* 1954. |
| 1933 | *Rennell* (3rd), (John Adrian) Tremayne Rodd, *b.* 1935, *s.* 1978, *m.* | Hon. James R. D. T. *R.*, *b.* 1978. |
| 1964 | *Renwick* (2nd), Harry Andrew Renwick, *b.* 1935, *s.* 1973, *m.* | Hon. Robert J. *R.*, *b.* 1966. |
| 1885 | *Revelstoke* (5th), John Baring, *b.* 1934, *s.* 1994. | Hon. James C. *B.*, *b.* 1938. |
| 1905 | *Ritchie of Dundee* (5th), (Harold) Malcolm Ritchie, *b.* 1919, *s.* 1978, *m.* | Hon. C. Rupert R. *R.*, *b.* 1958. |
| 1935 | *Riverdale* (2nd), Robert Arthur Balfour, *b.* 1901, *s.* 1957, *w.* | Hon. Mark R. *B.*, *b.* 1927. |
| 1961 | *Robertson of Oakridge* (2nd), William Ronald Robertson, *b.* 1930, *s.* 1974, *m.* | Hon. William B. E. *R.*, *b.* 1975. |
| 1938 | *Roborough* (3rd), Henry Massey Lopes, *b.* 1940, *s.* 1992, *m.* | Hon. Massey J. H. *L.*, *b.* 1969. |
| 1931 | *Rochester* (2nd), Foster Charles Lowry Lamb, *b.* 1916, *s.* 1955, *m.* | Hon. David C. *L.*, *b.* 1944. |
| 1934 | *Rockley* (3rd), James Hugh Cecil, *b.* 1934, *s.* 1976, *m.* | Hon. Anthony R. *C.*, *b.* 1961. |
| 1782 | *Rodney* (10th), George Brydges Rodney, *b.* 1953, *s.* 1992. | Nicholas S. H. *R.*, *b.* 1947. |
| 1651 s.* | *Rollo* (13th), Eric John Stapylton Rollo (4th *UK Baron, Dunning*, 1869), *b.* 1915, *s.* 1947, *m.* | Master of Rollo, *b.* 1943. |
| 1959 | *Rootes* (3rd), Nicholas Geoffrey Rootes, *b.* 1951, *s.* 1992, *m.* | William B. *R.*, *b.* 1944. |
| 1796 I.* | *Rossmore* (7th), William Warner Westenra (6th *UK Baron, Rossmore*, 1838), *b.* 1931, *s.* 1958, *m.* | Hon. Benedict W. *W.*, *b.* 1983. |
| 1939 | *Rotherwick* (2nd), (Herbert) Robin Cayzer, *b.* 1912, *s.* 1958, *w.* | Hon. H. Robin *C.*, *b.* 1954. |
| 1885 | *Rothschild* (4th), (Nathaniel Charles) Jacob Rothschild, *b.* 1936, *s.* 1990, *m.* | Hon. Nathaniel P. V. J. *R.*, *b.* 1971. |
| 1911 | *Rowallan* (4th), John Polson Cameron Corbett, *b.* 1947, *s.* 1993, *m.* | Hon. Jason W. P. C. *C.*, *b.* 1972. |
| 1947 | *Rugby* (3rd), Robert Charles Maffey, *b.* 1951, *s.* 1990, *m.* | Hon. Timothy J. H. *M.*, *b.* 1975. |
| 1919 | *Russell of Liverpool* (3rd), Simon Gordon Jared Russell, *b.* 1952, *s.* 1981, *m.* | Hon. Edward C. S. *R.*, *b.* 1985. |
| 1876 | *Sackville* (6th), Lionel Bertrand Sackville-West, *b.* 1913, *s.* 1965, *m.* | Hugh R. I. *S.-W.*, MC, *b.* 1919. |
| 1964 | *St Helens* (2nd), Richard Francis Hughes-Young, *b.* 1945, *s.* 1980, *m.* | Hon. Henry T. *H.-Y.*, *b.* 1986. |
| 1559 | *St John of Bletso* (21st), Anthony Tudor St John, *b.* 1957, *s.* 1978. | Edmund O. *St J.*, WS, *b.* 1927. |
| 1887 | *St Levan* (4th), John Francis Arthur St Aubyn, DSC, *b.* 1919, *s.* 1978, *m.* | Hon. O. Piers *St A.*, MC, *b.* 1920. |
| 1885 | *St Oswald* (5th), Derek Edward Anthony Winn, *b.* 1919, *s.* 1984, *m.* | Hon. Charles R. A. *W.*, *b.* 1959. |
| 1960 | *Sanderson of Ayot.* Disclaimed for life 1971. (*Alan Lindsay Sanderson*, *b.* 1931, *s.* 1971, *m.*) | Hon. Michael *S.*, *b.* 1959. |
| 1945 | *Sandford* (2nd), Revd John Cyril Edmondson, DSC, *b.* 1920, *s.* 1959, *m.* | Hon. James J. M. *E.*, *b.* 1949. |
| 1871 | *Sandhurst* (5th), (John Edward) Terence Mansfield, DFC, *b.* 1920, *s.* 1964, *m.* | Hon. Guy R. J. *M.*, *b.* 1949. |
| 1802 | *Sandys* (7th), Richard Michael Oliver Hill, *b.* 1931, *s.* 1961, *m.* | None. |
| 1888 | *Savile* (3rd), George Halifax Lumley-Savile, *b.* 1919, *s.* 1931. | Hon. Henry L. T. *L.-S.*, *b.* 1923. |
| 1447 | *Saye and Sele* (21st), Nathaniel Thomas Allen Fiennes, *b.* 1920, *s.* 1968, *m.* | Hon. Richard I. *F.*, *b.* 1959. |
| 1932 | *Selsdon* (3rd), Malcolm McEacharn Mitchell-Thomson, *b.* 1937, *s.* 1963, *m.* | Hon. Callum M. M. *M.-T.*, *b.* 1969. |
| 1916 | *Shaughnessy* (3rd), William Graham Shaughnessy, *b.* 1922, *s.* 1938, *m.* | Hon. Michael J. *S.*, *b.* 1946. |
| 1946 | *Shepherd* (2nd), Malcolm Newton Shepherd, PC, *b.* 1918, *s.* 1954, *m.* | Hon. Graeme G. *S.*, *b.* 1949. |
| 1964 | *Sherfield* (1st), Roger Mellor Makins, GCB, GCMG, FRS, *b.* 1904, *w.* | Hon. Christopher J. *M.*, *b.* 1942. |
| 1902 | *Shuttleworth* (5th), Charles Geoffrey Nicholas Kay-Shuttleworth, *b.* 1948, *s.* 1975, *m.* | Hon. Thomas E. *K.-S.*, *b.* 1976. |

| Created | Title, order of succession, name, etc. | Heir |
|---|---|---|
| 1950 | *Silkin.* Disclaimed for life 1972. (*Arthur Silkin, b.* 1916, *s.* 1972, *m.*) | Hon. Christopher L. *S., b.* 1947. |
| 1963 | *Silsoe* (2nd), David Malcolm Trustram Eve, QC, *b.* 1930, *s.* 1976, *m.* | Hon. Simon R. T. *E., b.* 1966. |
| 1947 | *Simon of Wythenshawe* (2nd), Roger Simon, *b.* 1913, *s.* 1960, *m.* | Hon. Matthew *S., b.* 1955. |
| 1449 S. | *Sinclair* (17th), Charles Murray Kennedy St Clair, CVO, *b.* 1914, *s.* 1957, *m.* | Master of Sinclair, *b.* 1968. |
| 1957 | *Sinclair of Cleeve* (3rd), John Lawrence Robert Sinclair, *b.* 1953, *s.* 1985. | None. |
| 1919 | *Sinha* (4th), Susanta Prasanna Sinha, *b.* 1953, *s.* 1989, *m.* | Hon. A. K. *S., b.* 1930. |
| 1828 | *Skelmersdale* (7th), Roger Bootle-Wilbraham, *b.* 1945, *s.* 1973, *m.* | Hon. Andrew *B.-W., b.* 1977. |
| 1916 | *Somerleyton* (3rd), Savile William Francis Crossley, KCVO, *b.* 1928, *s.* 1959, *m. Master of the Horse.* | Hon. Hugh F. S. *C., b.* 1971. |
| 1784 | *Somers* (8th), John Patrick Somers Cocks, *b.* 1907, *s.* 1953, *w.* | Philip S. S. *C., b.* 1948. |
| 1780 | *Southampton* (6th), Charles James FitzRoy, *b.* 1928, *s.* 1989, *m.* | Hon. Edward C. *F., b.* 1955. |
| 1959 | *Spens* (3rd), Patrick Michael Rex Spens, *b.* 1942, *s.* 1984, *m.* | Hon. Patrick N. G. *S., b.* 1968. |
| 1640 | *Stafford* (15th), Francis Melfort William Fitzherbert, *b.* 1954, *s.* 1986, *m.* | Hon. Benjamin J. B. *F., b.* 1983. |
| 1938 | *Stamp* (4th), Trevor Charles Bosworth Stamp, MD, FRCP, *b.* 1935, *s.* 1987, *m.* | Hon. Nicholas C. T. *S., b.* 1978. |
| 1839 | *Stanley of Alderley* (8th) & *Sheffield* (8th) (1738 I.), Thomas Henry Oliver Stanley (7th *UK Baron Eddisbury,* 1848), *b.* 1927, *s.* 1971, *m.* | Hon. Richard O. *S., b.* 1956. |
| 1318 | *Strabolgi* (11th), David Montague de Burgh Kenworthy, *b.* 1914, *s.* 1953, *m.* | Andrew D. W. *K., b.* 1967. |
| 1954 | *Strang* (2nd), Colin Strang, *b.* 1922, *s.* 1978, *m.* | None. |
| 1955 | *Strathalmond* (3rd), William Roberton Fraser, *b.* 1947, *s.* 1976, *m.* | Hon. William G. *F., b.* 1976. |
| 1936 | *Strathcarron* (2nd), David William Anthony Blyth Macpherson, *b.* 1924, *s.* 1937, *m.* | Hon. Ian D. P. *M., b.* 1949. |
| 1955 | *Strathclyde* (2nd), Thomas Galloway Dunlop du Roy de Blicquy Galbraith, *b.* 1960, *s.* 1985, *m.* | Hon. Charles W. du R. de B. *G., b.* 1962. |
| 1900 | *Strathcona and Mount Royal* (4th), Donald Euan Palmer Howard, *b.* 1923, *s.* 1959, *m.* | Hon. D. Alexander S. *H., b.* 1961. |
| 1836 | *Stratheden* (6th) & *Campbell* (6th) (1841), Donald Campbell, *b.* 1934, *s.* 1987, *m.* | Hon. David A. *C., b.* 1963. |
| 1884 | *Strathspey* (6th), James Patrick Trevor Grant of Grant, *b.* 1943, *s.* 1992, *m.* | Hon. Michael P. F. *G., b.* 1953. |
| 1838 | *Sudeley* (7th), Merlin Charles Sainthill Hanbury-Tracy, *b.* 1939, *s.* 1941. | D. Andrew J. *H-T., b.* 1928. |
| 1786 | *Suffield* (11th), Anthony Philip Harbord-Hamond, MC, *b.* 1922, *s.* 1951, *m.* | Hon. Charles A. A. *H.-H., b.* 1953. |
| 1893 | *Swansea* (4th), John Hussey Hamilton Vivian, *b.* 1925, *s.* 1934, *m.* | Hon. Richard A. H. *V., b.* 1957. |
| 1907 | *Swaythling* (4th), David Charles Samuel Montagu, *b.* 1928, *s.* 1990, *m.* | Hon. Charles E. S. *M., b.* 1954. |
| 1919 | *Swinfen* (3rd), Roger Mynors Swinfen Eady, *b.* 1938, *s.* 1977, *m.* | Hon. Charles R. P. S. *E., b.* 1971. |
| 1935 | *Sysonby* (3rd), John Frederick Ponsonby, *b.* 1945, *s.* 1956. | None. |
| 1831 I. | *Talbot of Malahide* (10th), Reginald John Richard Arundell, *b.* 1931, *s.* 1987, *m.* | Hon. Richard J. T. *A., b.* 1957. |
| 1946 | *Tedder* (3rd), Robin John Tedder, *b.* 1955, *s.* 1994, *m.* | Hon. Benjamin J. *T., b.* 1985. |
| 1884 | *Tennyson* (5th), Cdr. Mark Aubrey Tennyson, DSC, *b.* 1920, *s.* 1991, *m.* | Lt.-Cdr. James A. *T.,* DSC, *b.* 1913. |
| 1918 | *Terrington* (4th), (James Allen) David Woodhouse, *b.* 1915, *s.* 1961, *m.* | Hon. C. Montague *W.,* DSO, OBE, *b.* 1917. |
| 1940 | *Teviot* (2nd), Charles John Kerr, *b.* 1934, *s.* 1968, *m.* | Hon. Charles R. *K., b.* 1971. |
| 1616 | *Teynham* (20th), John Christopher Ingham Roper-Curzon, *b.* 1928, *s.* 1972, *m.* | Hon. David J. H. I. *R.-C., b.* 1965. |
| 1964 | *Thomson of Fleet* (2nd), Kenneth Roy Thomson, *b.* 1923, *s.* 1976, *m.* | Hon. David K. R. *T., b.* 1957. |
| 1792 | *Thurlow* (8th), Francis Edward Hovell-Thurlow-Cumming-Bruce, KCMG, *b.* 1912, *s.* 1971, *w.* | Hon. Roualeyn R. *H.-T.-C.-B., b.* 1952. |
| 1876 | *Tollemache* (5th), Timothy John Edward Tollemache, *b.* 1939, *s.* 1975, *m.* | Hon. Edward J. H. *T., b.* 1976. |
| 1564 S. | *Torphichen* (15th), James Andrew Douglas Sandilands, *b.* 1946, *s.* 1975, *m.* | Douglas R. A. *S., b.* 1926. |
| 1947 | *Trefgarne* (2nd), David Garro Trefgarne, PC, *b.* 1941, *s.* 1960, *m.* | Hon. George G. *T., b.* 1970. |
| 1921 | *Trevethin* (4th), *and Oaksey* (2nd) (1947), John Geoffrey Tristram Lawrence, OBE, *b.* 1929, *s.* 1971, *m.* | Hon. Patrick J. T. *L., b.* 1960. |
| 1880 | *Trevor* (4th), Charles Edwin Hill-Trevor, *b.* 1928, *s.* 1950, *m.* | Hon. Marke C. *H.-T., b.* 1970. |
| 1461 I. | *Trimlestown* (20th), Anthony Edward Barnewall, *b.* 1928, *s.* 1990, *m.* | Hon. Raymond C. *B., b.* 1930. |
| 1940 | *Tryon* (3rd), Anthony George Merrik Tryon, *b.* 1940, *s.* 1976, *m.* | Hon. Charles G. B. *T., b.* 1976. |
| 1935 | *Tweedsmuir* (2nd), John Norman Stuart Buchan, CBE, FRSE, *b.* 1911, *s.* 1940, *m.* | Hon. William de l'A. *B., b.* 1916. |
| 1523 | *Vaux of Harrowden* (10th), John Hugh Philip Gilbey, *b.* 1915, *s.* 1977, *m.* | Hon. Anthony W. *G., b.* 1940. |
| 1800 I. | *Ventry* (8th), Andrew Wesley Daubeny de Moleyns, *b.* 1943, *s.* 1987, *m.* | Hon. Francis W. D. *de M., b.* 1965. |
| 1762 | *Vernon* (10th), John Lawrance Vernon, *b.* 1923, *s.* 1963, *m.* | Col. William R. D. *Vernon-Harcourt,* OBE, *b.* 1909. |
| 1922 | *Vestey* (3rd), Samuel George Armstrong Vestey, *b.* 1941, *s.* 1954, *m.* | Hon. William G. *V., b.* 1983. |
| 1841 | *Vivian* (6th), Nicholas Crespigny Laurence Vivian, *b.* 1935, *s.* 1991, *m.* | Hon. Charles H. C. *V., b.* 1966. |

| Created | Title, order of succession, name, etc. | Heir |
|---|---|---|
| 1934 | *Wakehurst* (3rd), (John) Christopher Loder, *b.* 1925, *s.* 1970, *m.* | Hon. Timothy W. *L.*, *b.* 1958. |
| 1723 | *Walpole* (10th), Robert Horatio Walpole (*8th Brit. Baron Walpole of Wolterton*, 1756), *b.* 1938, *s.* 1989, *m.* | Hon. Jonathan R. H. *W.*, *b.* 1967. |
| 1780 | *Walsingham* (9th), John de Grey, MC, *b.* 1925, *s.* 1965, *m.* | Hon. Robert *de G.*, *b.* 1969. |
| 1936 | *Wardington* (2nd), Christopher Henry Beaumont Pease, *b.* 1924, *s.* 1950, *m.* | Hon. William S. *P.*, *b.* 1925. |
| 1792 I. | *Waterpark* (7th), Frederick Caryll Philip Cavendish, *b.* 1926, *s.* 1948, *m.* | Hon. Roderick A. *C.*, *b.* 1959. |
| 1942 | *Wedgwood* (4th), Piers Anthony Weymouth Wedgwood, *b.* 1954, *s.* 1970, *m.* | John *W.*, CBE, MD, FRCP, *b.* 1919. |
| 1861 | *Westbury* (5th), David Alan Bethell, CBE, MC, *b.* 1922, *s.* 1961, *m.* | Hon. Richard N. *B.*, MBE, *b.* 1950. |
| 1944 | *Westwood* (3rd), (William) Gavin Westwood, *b.* 1944, *s.* 1991, *m.* | Hon. W. Fergus *W.*, *b.* 1972. |
| 1935 | *Wigram* (2nd), (George) Neville (Clive) Wigram, MC, *b.* 1915, *s.* 1960, *w.* | Maj. Hon. Andrew F. C. *W.*, MVO, *b.* 1949. |
| 1491 | *Willoughby de Broke* (21st), Leopold David Verney, *b.* 1938, *s.* 1986, *m.* | Hon. Rupert G. *V.*, *b.* 1966. |
| 1946 | *Wilson* (2nd), Patrick Maitland Wilson, *b.* 1915, *s.* 1964, *w.* | None. |
| 1937 | *Windlesham* (3rd), David James George Hennessy, CVO, PC, *b.* 1932, *s.* 1962, *w.* | Hon. James R. *H.*, *b.* 1968. |
| 1951 | *Wise* (2nd), John Clayton Wise, *b.* 1923, *s.* 1968, *m.* | Hon. Christopher J. C. *W.*, PH.D., *b.* 1949. |
| 1869 | *Wolverton* (7th), Christopher Richard Glyn, *b.* 1938, *s.* 1988. | Hon. Andrew J. *G.*, *b.* 1943. |
| 1928 | *Wraxall* (2nd), George Richard Lawley Gibbs, *b.* 1928, *s.* 1931. | Hon. Sir Eustace H. B. *G.*, KCVO, CMG, *b.* 1929. |
| 1915 | *Wrenbury* (3rd), Revd John Burton Buckley, *b.* 1927, *s.* 1940, *m.* | Hon. William E. *B.*, *b.* 1966. |
| 1838 | *Wrottesley* (6th), Clifton Hugh Lancelot de Verdon Wrottesley, *b.* 1968, *s.* 1977. | Hon. Stephen J. *W.*, *b.* 1955. |
| 1919 | *Wyfold* (3rd), Hermon Robert Fleming Hermon-Hodge, ERD, *b.* 1915, *s.* 1942. | None. |
| 1829 | *Wynford* (8th), Robert Samuel Best, MBE, *b.* 1917, *s.* 1943, *m.* | Hon. John P. R. *B.*, *b.* 1950. |
| 1308 | *Zouche* (18th), James Assheton Frankland, *b.* 1943, *s.* 1965, *m.* | Hon. William T. A. *F.*, *b.* 1984. |

## BARONESSES/LADIES IN THEIR OWN RIGHT

*Style*, The Right Hon. the Lady __, *or* The Right Hon. the Baroness __, according to her preference. Either style may be used, except in the case of Scottish titles (indicated by s.), which are not baronies (*see* page 141) and whose holders are always addressed as Lady

*Husband*, Untitled
*Children's style*, As for children of a Baron
For forms of address, *see* page 217.

| Created | Title, order of succession, name, etc. | Heir |
|---|---|---|
| 1455 | *Berners*, in abeyance between two co-heiresses, daughters of the late Baroness Berners who died in 1992. | |
| 1529 | *Braye* (8th in line), Mary Penelope Aubrey–Fletcher, *b.* 1941, *s.* 1985, *m.* | Two co-heiresses. |
| 1321 | *Dacre* (27th in line), Rachel Leila Douglas-Home, *b.* 1929, *title called out of abeyance*, 1970, *w.* | Hon. James T. A. *D.-H.*, *b.* 1952. |
| 1332 | *Darcy de Knayth* (18th in line), Davina Marcia Ingrams, *b.* 1938, *s.* 1943, *w.* | Hon. Caspar D. *I.*, *b.* 1962. |
| 1439 | *Dudley* (14th in line), Barbara Amy Felicity Hamilton, *b.* 1907, *s.* 1972, *m.* | Hon. Jim A. H. *Wallace*, *b.* 1930. |
| 1490 S. | *Herries of Terregles* (14th in line), Anne Elizabeth Fitzalan-Howard, *b.* 1938, *s.* 1975, *m.* | Lady Mary *Mumford*, CVO, *b.* 1940. |
| 1602 S. | *Kinloss* (12th in line), Beatrice Mary Grenville Freeman-Grenville, *b.* 1922, *s.* 1944, *m.* | Master of Kinloss, *b.* 1953. |
| 1681 S. | *Nairne* (12th in line), Katherine Evelyn Constance Bigham (*Katherine, Viscountess Mersey*), *b.* 1912, *s.* 1944, *w.* | The Viscount Mersey, *b.* 1934 (*see* page 151). |
| 1445 S. | *Saltoun* (20th in line), Flora Marjory Fraser, *b.* 1930, *s.* 1979, *m.* | Hon. Katharine I. M. I. *F.*, *b.* 1957. |
| 1489 S. | *Sempill* (20th in line), Ann Moira Sempill, *b.* 1920, *s.* 1965, *w.* | Master of Sempill, *b.* 1949. |
| 1628 | *Strange* (16th in line), (Jean) Cherry Drummond of Megginch, *b.* 1928, *title called out of abeyance*, 1986, *m.* | Hon. Adam H. *D. of M.*, *b.* 1953. |
| 1544/5 | *Wharton* (11th in line), Myrtle Olive Felix Robertson, *b.* 1934, *title called out of abeyance*, 1990, *m.* | Hon. Myles C. D. *R.*, *b.* 1964. |
| 1313 | *Willoughby de Eresby* (27th in line), (Nancy) Jane Marie Heathcote-Drummond-Willoughby, *b.* 1934, *s.* 1983. | Two co-heiresses. |

# Life Peers

Between 1 September 1993 and 31 August 1994, the conferment of 16 life peerages was announced, one under the Appellate Jurisdiction Act 1876 and 15 under the Life Peerages Act 1958:

LAW LORDS (27 July 1994): *The Rt. Hon. Sir Donald Nicholls

NEW YEAR'S HONOURS (30 December 1993): Sir David Nickson, KBE; Sir Patrick Wright, GCMG

QUEEN'S BIRTHDAY HONOURS (10 June 1994): Prof. Sir David Phillips, KBE, FRS; Sir Randolph Quirk, CBE; *Sir Allen Sheppard

WORKING PEERS (20 August 1994): *The Rt. Hon. Sir Peter Blaker, KCMG; *Alfred Dubs; *Mrs Josephine Farrington; *Derek Gladwin, CBE; *Charles Hambro; *the Rt. Hon. Sir Christopher Prout, TD, QC; *Miss Patricia Rawlings; *Sir Michael Shaw; *Mrs Susan Thomas, OBE; *Graham Tope, CBE

*No title gazetted at time of going to press

## CREATED UNDER THE APPELLATE JURISDICTION ACT 1876 (AS AMENDED)

### BARONS

*Created*

1986  *Ackner*, Desmond James Conrad Ackner, PC, b. 1920, m.

1981  *Brandon of Oakbrook*, Henry Vivian Brandon, MC, PC, b. 1920, m.

1980  *Bridge of Harwich*, Nigel Cyprian Bridge, PC, b. 1917, m.

1982  *Brightman*, John Anson Brightman, PC, b. 1911, m.

1991  *Browne-Wilkinson*, Nicolas Christopher Henry Browne-Wilkinson, PC, b. 1930, m. Lord of Appeal in Ordinary.

1957  *Denning*, Alfred Thompson Denning, PC, b. 1899, w.

1986  *Goff of Chieveley*, Robert Lionel Archibald Goff, PC, b. 1926, m. Lord of Appeal in Ordinary.

1985  *Griffiths*, (William) Hugh Griffiths, MC, PC, b. 1923, m.

1988  *Jauncey of Tullichettle*, Charles Eliot Jauncey, PC, b. 1925, m. Lord of Appeal in Ordinary.

1977  *Keith of Kinkel*, Henry Shanks Keith, PC, b. 1922, m. Lord of Appeal in Ordinary.

1979  *Lane*, Geoffrey Dawson Lane, AFC, b. 1918, m.

1993  *Lloyd of Berwick*, Anthony John Leslie Lloyd, PC, b. 1929, m. Lord of Appeal in Ordinary.

1992  *Mustill*, Michael John Mustill, PC, b. 1931, m. Lord of Appeal in Ordinary.

1994  *Nolan*, Michael Patrick Nolan, PC, b. 1928, m. Lord of Appeal in Ordinary.

1986  *Oliver of Aylmerton*, Peter Raymond Oliver, PC, b. 1921, m.

1980  *Roskill*, Eustace Wentworth Roskill, PC, b. 1911, m.

1977  *Scarman*, Leslie George Scarman, OBE, PC, b. 1911, m.

1992  *Slynn of Hadley*, Gordon Slynn, PC, b. 1930, m. Lord of Appeal in Ordinary.

1982  *Templeman*, Sydney William Templeman, MBE, PC, b. 1920, w.

*Created*

1964  *Wilberforce*, Richard Orme Wilberforce, CMG, OBE, PC, b. 1907, m.

1992  *Woolf*, Harry Kenneth Woolf, PC, b. 1933, m. Lord of Appeal in Ordinary.

## CREATED UNDER THE LIFE PEERAGES ACT 1958

### BARONS

*Created*

1988  *Alexander of Weedon*, Robert Scott Alexander, QC, b. 1936, m.

1976  *Allen of Abbeydale*, Philip Allen, GCB, b. 1912, m.

1961  *Alport*, Cuthbert James McCall Alport, TD, PC, b. 1912, w.

1992  *Amery of Lustleigh*, Julian Amery, PC, b. 1919, w.

1965  *Annan*, Noël Gilroy Annan, OBE, b. 1916, m.

1992  *Archer of Sandwell*, Peter Kingsley Archer, PC, QC, b. 1926, m.

1992  *Archer of Weston-super-Mare*, Jeffrey Howard Archer, b. 1940, m.

1988  *Armstrong of Ilminster*, Robert Temple Armstrong, GCB, CVO, b. 1927, m.

1992  *Ashley of Stoke*, Jack Ashley, CH, PC, b. 1922, m.

1993  *Attenborough*, Richard Samuel Attenborough, CBE, b. 1923, m.

1982  *Bancroft*, Ian Powell Bancroft, GCB, b. 1922, m.

1974  *Banks*, Desmond Anderson Harvie Banks, CBE, b. 1918, m.

1974  *Barber*, Anthony Perrinott Lysberg Barber, TD, PC, b. 1920, m.

1992  *Barber of Tewkesbury*, Derek Coates Barber, b. 1918, m.

1983  *Barnett*, Joel Barnett, PC, b. 1923, m.

1982  *Bauer*, Prof. Peter Thomas Bauer, D.SC., FBA, b. 1915.

1967  *Beaumont of Whitley*, Revd Timothy Wentworth Beaumont, b. 1928, m.

1979  *Bellwin*, Irwin Norman Bellow, b. 1923, m.

1981  *Beloff*, Max Beloff, FBA, b. 1913, m.

1981  *Benson*, Henry Alexander Benson, GBE, b. 1909, m.

1971  *Blake*, Robert Norman William Blake, FBA, b. 1916, m.

1978  *Blease*, William John Blease, b. 1914, m.

1980  *Boardman*, Thomas Gray Boardman, MC, TD, b. 1919, m.

1986  *Bonham-Carter*, Mark Raymond Bonham Carter, b. 1922, m.

1976  *Boston of Faversham*, Terence George Boston, QC, b. 1930, m.

1984  *Bottomley*, Arthur George Bottomley, OBE, PC, b. 1907, m.

1972  *Boyd-Carpenter*, John Archibald Boyd-Carpenter, PC, b. 1908, m.

1992  *Braine of Wheatley*, Bernard Richard Braine, PC, b. 1914, w.

1987  *Bramall*, Edwin Noel Westby Bramall, KG, GCB, OBE, MC, *Field Marshal*, b. 1923, m.

1976  *Briggs*, Asa Briggs, FBA, b. 1921, m.

*Created*

1976  Brimelow, Thomas Brimelow, GCMG, OBE, b. 1915, w.

1975  Brookes, Raymond Percival Brookes, b. 1909, m.

1979  Brooks of Tremorfa, John Edward Brooks, b. 1927, m.

1974  Bruce of Donington, Donald William Trevor Bruce, b. 1912, m.

1976  Bullock, Alan Louis Charles Bullock, FBA, b. 1914, m.

1988  Butterfield, (William) John (Hughes) Butterfield, OBE, DM, FRCP, b. 1920, m.

1985  Butterworth, John Blackstock Butterworth, CBE, b. 1918, m.

1978  Buxton of Alsa, Aubrey Leland Oakes Buxton, MC, b. 1918, m.

1987  Callaghan of Cardiff, (Leonard) James Callaghan, KG, PC, b. 1912, m.

1984  Cameron of Lochbroom, Kenneth John Cameron, PC, b. 1931, m.

1981  Campbell of Alloway, Alan Robertson Campbell, QC, b. 1917, m.

1974  Campbell of Croy, Gordon Thomas Calthrop Campbell, MC, PC, b. 1921, m.

1966  Campbell of Eskan, John (Jock) Middleton Campbell, b. 1912, w.

1987  Carlisle of Bucklow, Mark Carlisle, QC, PC, b. 1929, m.

1983  Carmichael of Kelvingrove, Neil George Carmichael, b. 1921.

1975  Carr of Hadley, (Leonard) Robert Carr, PC, b. 1916, m.

1987  Carter, Denis Victor Carter, b. 1932, m.

1977  Carver, (Richard) Michael (Power) Carver, GCB, CBE, DSO, MC, Field Marshal, b. 1915, m.

1990  Cavendish of Furness, (Richard) Hugh Cavendish, b. 1941, m.

1982  Cayzer, (William) Nicholas Cayzer, b. 1910, m.

1964  Chalfont, (Alun) Arthur Gwynne Jones, OBE, MC, PC, b. 1919, m.

1985  Chapple, Francis (Frank) Joseph Chapple, b. 1921, w.

1978  Charteris of Amisfield, Martin Michael Charles Charteris, GCB, GCVO, OBE, PC, Royal Victorian Chain, b. 1913, m.

1963  Chelmer, Eric Cyril Boyd Edwards, MC, TD, b. 1914, m.

1987  Chilver, (Amos) Henry Chilver, FRS, FEng., b. 1926, m.

1977  Chitnis, Pratap Chidamber Chitnis, b. 1936, m.

1992  Clark of Kempston, William Gibson Haig Clark, PC, b. 1917, m.

1979  Cledwyn of Penrhos, Cledwyn Hughes, CH, PC, b. 1916, m.

1990  Clinton-Davis, Stanley Clinton Clinton-Davis, b. 1928, m.

1978  Cockfield, (Francis) Arthur Cockfield, PC, b. 1916, w.

1987  Cocks of Hartcliffe, Michael Francis Lovell Cocks, PC, b. 1929, m.

1980  Coggan, Rt. Revd (Frederick) Donald Coggan, PC, Royal Victorian Chain, b. 1909, m.

1964  Collison, Harold Francis Collison, CBE, b. 1909, m.

1987  Colnbrook, Humphrey Edward Gregory Atkins, KCMG, PC, b. 1922, m.

1981  Constantine of Stanmore, Theodore Constantine, CBE, AE, b. 1910, w.

1992  Cooke of Islandreagh, Victor Alexander Cooke, OBE, b. 1920, m.

*Created*

1991  Craig of Radley, David Brownrigg Craig, GCB, OBE, Marshal of the Royal Air Force, b. 1929, m.

1987  Crickhowell, (Roger) Nicholas Edwards, PC, b. 1934, m.

1978  Croham, Douglas Albert Vivian Allen, GCB, b. 1917, w.

1974  Cudlipp, Hugh Cudlipp, OBE, b. 1913, m.

1979  Dacre of Glanton, Hugh Redwald Trevor-Roper, b. 1914, m.

1993  Dahrendorf, Ralf Dahrendorf, KBE, PH.D., D. PHIL., FBA, b. 1929, m.

1986  Dainton, Frederick Sydney Dainton, PH.D., SC.D., FRS, b. 1914, m.

1983  Dean of Beswick, Joseph Jabez Dean, b. 1922.

1993  Dean of Harptree, (Arthur) Paul Dean, PC, b. 1924, m.

1986  Deedes, William Francis Deedes, MC, PC, b. 1913, m.

1991  Desai, Prof. Meghnad Jagdishchandra Desai, PH.D., b. 1940, m.

1970  Diamond, John Diamond, PC, b. 1907, m.

1993  Dixon-Smith, Robert William Dixon-Smith, b. 1934, m.

1967  Donaldson of Kingsbridge, John George Stuart Donaldson, OBE, b. 1907, w.

1988  Donaldson of Lymington, John Francis Donaldson, PC, b. 1920, m.

1985  Donoughue, Bernard Donoughue, D.PHIL., b. 1934.

1987  Dormand of Easington, John Donkin Dormand, b. 1919, m.

1992  Eatwell, John Leonard Eatwell, b. 1945, m.

1983  Eden of Winton, John Benedict Eden, PC, b. 1925, m.

1992  Elis-Thomas, Dafydd Elis Elis-Thomas, b. 1946, m.

1985  Elliott of Morpeth, Robert William Elliott, b. 1920, m.

1981  Elystan-Morgan, Dafydd Elystan Elystan-Morgan, b. 1932, m.

1980  Emslie, George Carlyle Emslie, MBE, PC, FRSE, b. 1919, m.

1983  Ennals, David Hedley Ennals, PC, b. 1922, m.

1992  Ewing of Kirkford, Harry Ewing, b. 1931, m.

1983  Ezra, Derek Ezra, MBE, b. 1919, m.

1983  Fanshawe of Richmond, Anthony Henry Fanshawe Royle, KCMG, b. 1927, m.

1992  Finsberg, Geoffrey Finsberg, MBE, b. 1926, m.

1983  Fitt, Gerard Fitt, b. 1926, m.

1979  Flowers, Brian Hilton Flowers, FRS, b. 1924, m.

1967  Foot, John Mackintosh Foot, b. 1909, m.

1982  Forte, Charles Forte, b. 1908, m.

1989  Fraser of Carmyllie, Peter Lovat Fraser, PC, QC, b. 1945, m.

1974  Fraser of Kilmorack, (Richard) Michael Fraser, CBE, b. 1915, m.

1982  Gallacher, John Gallacher, b. 1920, m.

1992  Geraint, Geraint Wyn Howells, b. 1925, m.

1975  Gibson, (Richard) Patrick (Tallentyre) Gibson, b. 1916, m.

1979  Gibson-Watt, (James) David Gibson-Watt, MC, PC, b. 1918, m.

1992  Gilmour of Craigmillar, Ian Hedworth John Little Gilmour, PC, b. 1926, m.

1977  Glenamara, Edward Watson Short, CH, PC, b. 1912, m.

1965  Goodman, Arnold Abraham Goodman, CH, b. 1913.

1987  Goold, James Duncan Goold, b. 1934, w.

1976  Grade, Lew Grade, b. 1906, m.

1983  Graham of Edmonton, (Thomas) Edward Graham, b. 1925, m.

*Created*

1986  *Moore of Wolvercote*, Philip Brian Cecil Moore, GCB, GCVO, CMG, PC, *b.* 1921, *m.*

1990  *Morris of Castle Morris*, Brian Robert Morris, D.Phil., *b.* 1930, *m.*

1985  *Morton of Shuna*, Hugh Drennan Baird Morton, *b.* 1930, *m.*

1971  *Moyola*, James Dawson Chichester-Clark, PC (NI), *b.* 1923, *m.*

1984  *Mulley*, Frederick William Mulley, PC, *b.* 1918, *m.*

1985  *Murray of Epping Forest*, Lionel Murray, OBE, PC, *b.* 1922, *m.*

1979  *Murton of Lindisfarne*, (Henry) Oscar Murton, OBE, TD, PC, *b.* 1914, *m.*

1994  *Nickson*, David Wigley Nickson, KBE, FRSE, *b.* 1929, *m.*

1975  *Northfield*, (William) Donald Chapman, *b.* 1923.

1973  *O'Brien of Lothbury*, Leslie Kenneth O'Brien, GBE, PC, *b.* 1908, *m.*

1976  *Oram*, Albert Edward Oram, *b.* 1913, *m.*

1971  *Orr-Ewing*, (Charles) Ian Orr-Ewing, OBE, *b.* 1912, *m.*

1992  *Owen*, David Anthony Llewellyn Owen, CH, PC, *b.* 1938, *m.*

1991  *Palumbo*, Peter Garth Palumbo, *b.* 1935, *m.*

1992  *Parkinson*, Cecil Edward Parkinson, PC, *b.* 1931, *m.*

1975  *Parry*, Gordon Samuel David Parry, *b.* 1925, *m.*

1990  *Pearson of Rannoch*, Malcolm Everard MacLaren Pearson, *b.* 1942, *m.*

1979  *Perry of Walton*, Walter Laing Macdonald Perry, OBE, FRS, FRSE, *b.* 1921, *m.*

1987  *Peston*, Maurice Harry Peston, *b.* 1931, *m.*

1983  *Peyton of Yeovil*, John Wynne William Peyton, PC, *b.* 1919, *m.*

1994  *Phillips of Ellesmere*, Prof. David Chilton Phillips, KBE, FRS, *b.* 1924, *m.*

1975  *Pitt of Hampstead*, David Thomas Pitt, *b.* 1913, *m.*

1992  *Plant of Highfield*, Prof. Raymond Plant, PH.D., *b.* 1945, *m.*

1959  *Plowden*, Edwin Noel Plowden, GBE, KCB, *b.* 1907, *m.*

1987  *Plumb*, (Charles) Henry Plumb, MEP, *b.* 1925, *m.*

1981  *Plummer of St Marylebone*, (Arthur) Desmond (Herne) Plummer, TD, *b.* 1914, *m.*

1990  *Porter of Luddenham*, George Porter, OM, FRS, *b.* 1920, *m.*

1992  *Prentice*, Reginald Ernest Prentice, PC, *b.* 1923, *m.*

1987  *Prior*, James Michael Leathes Prior, PC, *b.* 1927, *m.*

1975  *Pritchard*, Derek Wilbraham Pritchard, *b.* 1910, *m.*

1982  *Prys-Davies*, Gwilym Prys Prys-Davies, *b.* 1923, *m.*

1987  *Pym*, Francis Leslie Pym, MC, PC, *b.* 1922, *m.*

1982  *Quinton*, Anthony Meredith Quinton, FBA, *b.* 1925, *m.*

1994  *Quirk*, Prof. (Charles) Randolph Quirk, CBE, FBA, *b.* 1920, *m.*

1978  *Rawlinson of Ewell*, Peter Anthony Grayson Rawlinson, PC, QC, *b.* 1919, *m.*

1976  *Rayne*, Max Rayne, *b.* 1918, *m.*

1983  *Rayner*, Derek George Rayner, *b.* 1926.

1987  *Rees*, Peter Wynford Innes Rees, PC, QC, *b.* 1926, *m.*

1988  *Rees-Mogg*, William Rees-Mogg, *b.* 1928, *m.*

1970  *Reigate*, John Kenyon Vaughan-Morgan, PC, *b.* 1905, *m.*

1991  *Renfrew of Kaimsthorn*, (Andrew) Colin Renfrew, FBA, *b.* 1937, *m.*

1979  *Renton*, David Lockhart-Mure Renton, KBE, TD, PC, QC, *b.* 1908, *w.*

1990  *Richard*, Ivor Seward Richard, PC, QC, *b.* 1932, *m.*

*Created*

1979  *Richardson*, John Samuel Richardson, LVO, MD, FRCP, *b.* 1910, *w.*

1983  *Richardson of Duntisbourne*, Gordon William Humphreys Richardson, KG, MBE, TD, PC, *b.* 1915, *m.*

1987  *Rippon of Hexham*, (Aubrey) Geoffrey (Frederick) Rippon, PC, QC, *b.* 1924, *m.*

1992  *Rix*, Brian Norman Roger Rix, CBE, *b.* 1924, *m.*

1961  *Robens of Woldingham*, Alfred Robens, PC, *b.* 1910, *m.*

1992  *Rodger of Earlsferry*, Alan Ferguson Rodger, PC, QC, FBA, *b.* 1944, *Lord Advocate.*

1992  *Rodgers of Quarry Bank*, William Thomas Rodgers, PC, *b.* 1928, *m.*

1977  *Roll of Ipsden*, Eric Roll, KCMG, CB, *b.* 1907, *m.*

1991  *Runcie*, Rt Revd Robert Alexander Kennedy Runcie, MC, PC, Royal Victoria Chain, *b.* 1921, *m.*

1975  *Ryder of Eaton Hastings*, Sydney Thomas Franklin (Don) Ryder, *b.* 1916, *m.*

1962  *Sainsbury*, Alan John Sainsbury, *b.* 1902, *w.*

1989  *Sainsbury of Preston Candover*, John Davan Sainsbury, KG, *b.* 1927, *m.*

1987  *St John of Fawsley*, Norman Antony Francis St John-Stevas, PC, *b.* 1929.

1985  *Sanderson of Bowden*, Charles Russell Sanderson, *b.* 1933, *m.*

1979  *Scanlon*, Hugh Parr Scanlon, *b.* 1913, *m.*

1976  *Schon*, Frank Schon, *b.* 1912, *w.*

1978  *Sefton of Garston*, William Henry Sefton, *b.* 1915, *m.*

1958  *Shackleton*, Edward Arthur Alexander Shackleton, KG, OBE, PC, FRS, *b.* 1911, *m.*

1959  *Shawcross*, Hartley William Shawcross, GBE, PC, QC, *b.* 1902, *w.*

1980  *Sieff of Brimpton*, Marcus Joseph Sieff, OBE, *b.* 1913, *m.*

1971  *Simon of Glaisdale*, Jocelyn Edward Salis Simon, PC, *b.* 1911, *m.*

1991  *Skidelsky*, Robert Jacob Alexander Skidelsky, D.Phil., *b.* 1939, *m.*

1978  *Smith*, Rodney Smith, KBE, FRCS, *b.* 1914, *m.*

1965  *Soper*, Revd Donald Oliver Soper, PH.D., *b.* 1903, *m.*

1990  *Soulsby of Swaffham Prior*, Ernest Jackson Lawson Soulsby, PH.D., *b.* 1926, *m.*

1983  *Stallard*, Albert William Stallard, *b.* 1921, *m.*

1991  *Sterling of Plaistow*, Jeffrey Maurice Sterling, CBE, *b.* 1934, *m.*

1987  *Stevens of Ludgate*, David Robert Stevens, *b.* 1936, *m.*

1992  *Stewartby*, (Bernard Harold) Ian (Halley) Stewart, RD, PC, FBA, FRSE, *b.* 1935, *m.*

1981  *Stodart of Leaston*, James Anthony Stodart, PC, *b.* 1916, *m.*

1983  *Stoddart of Swindon*, David Leonard Stoddart, *b.* 1926, *m.*

1969  *Stokes*, Donald Gresham Stokes, TD, FEng., *b.* 1914, *m.*

1971  *Tanlaw*, Simon Brooke Mackay, *b.* 1934, *m.*

1978  *Taylor of Blackburn*, Thomas Taylor, CBE, *b.* 1929, *m.*

1992  *Taylor of Gosforth*, Peter Murray Taylor, PC, *b.* 1930, *m., Lord Chief Justice of England.*

1968  *Taylor of Gryfe*, Thomas Johnston Taylor, FRSE, *b.* 1912, *m.*

1982  *Taylor of Hadfield*, Francis Taylor, *b.* 1905, *m.*

1992  *Tebbit*, Norman Beresford Tebbit, CH, PC, *b.* 1931, *m.*

1987  *Thomas of Gwydir*, Peter John Mitchell Thomas, PC, QC, *b.* 1920, *w.*

## BARONESSES

| | |
|---|---|
| *Created* | |
| 1991 | *Seccombe,* Joan Anna Dalziel Seccombe, DBE, *b.* 1930, *m.* |
| 1971 | *Seear,* (Beatrice) Nancy Seear, PC, *b.* 1913. |
| 1967 | *Serota,* Beatrice Serota, DBE, *b.* 1919, *m.* |
| 1973 | *Sharples,* Pamela Sharples, *b.* 1923, *m.* |
| 1974 | *Stedman,* Phyllis Stedman, OBE, *b.* 1916, *w.* |
| 1992 | *Thatcher,* Margaret Hilda Thatcher, OM, PC, FRS, *b.* 1925, *m.* |

| | |
|---|---|
| *Created* | |
| 1980 | *Trumpington,* Jean Alys Barker, PC, *b.* 1922, *w.* |
| 1985 | *Turner of Camden,* Muriel Winifred Turner, *b.* 1927, *m.* |
| 1985 | *Warnock,* Helen Mary Warnock, DBE, *b.* 1924, *m.* |
| 1970 | *White,* Eirene Lloyd White, *b.* 1909, *w.* |
| 1993 | *Williams of Crosby,* Shirley Vivien Teresa Brittain Williams, PC, *b.* 1930, *m.* |
| 1971 | *Young,* Janet Mary Young, PC, *b.* 1926, *m.* |

# Lords Spiritual

The Lords Spiritual are the Archbishops of Canterbury and York and 24 diocesan bishops of the Church of England. The Bishops of London, Durham and Winchester always have seats in the House of Lords; the other 21 seats are filled by the remaining diocesan bishops in order of seniority. The Bishop of Sodor and Man and the Bishop of Gibraltar are not eligible to sit in the House of Lords.

## ARCHBISHOPS

*Style,* The Most Revd and Right Hon. the Lord Archbishop of __

*Addressed as* Archbishop, *or* Your Grace

*Introduced to House of Lords*
1991 *Canterbury* (103rd), George Leonard Carey, PC, PH.D., *b.* 1935, *m. Consecrated Bishop of Bath and Wells* 1987, *trans.* 1991.
1973 *York* (95th), John Stapylton Habgood, PC, PH.D., *b.* 1927, *m. Consecrated Bishop of Durham* 1973, *trans.* 1983.

## BISHOPS

*Style,* The Right Revd the Lord Bishop of __
*Addressed as* My Lord
*elected* = date of election as diocesan bishop

*Introduced to House of Lords*
1990 *London* (131st), David Michael Hope, PC, D.Phil., *b.* 1940, *cons.* 1985, *elected* 1985, *trans.* 1991.
1994 *Durham* (93rd), (Anthony) Michael (Arnold) Turnbull, *b.* 1935, *m.,* *cons.* 1988, *elected* 1994.
1982 *Winchester* (95th), Colin Clement Walter James, *b.* 1926, *m.,* *cons.* 1973, *elected* 1977, *trans.* 1985.
1979 *Chichester* (102nd), Eric Waldram Kemp, DD, *b.* 1915, *m.,* *cons.* 1974, *elected* 1974.
1980 *Liverpool* (6th), David Stuart Sheppard, *b.* 1929, *m.,* *cons.* 1969, *elected* 1975.
1984 *Ripon* (11th), David Nigel de Lorentz Young, *b.* 1931, *m.,* *cons.* 1977, *elected* 1977.
1985 *Chelmsford* (7th), John Waine, *b.* 1930, *m.,* *cons.* 1975, *elected* 1978, *trans.* 1986.
1985 *Sheffield* (5th), David Ramsay Lunn, *b.* 1930, *cons.* 1980, *elected* 1980.
1985 *St Albans* (8th), John Bernard Taylor, *b.* 1929, *m.,* *cons.* 1980, *elected* 1980.

1985 *Newcastle* (10th), Andrew Alexander Kenny Graham, *b.* 1929, *cons.* 1977, *elected* 1981.
1987 *Worcester* (111th), Philip Harold Ernest Goodrich, *b.* 1929, *m.,* *cons.* 1973, *elected* 1982.
1987 *Chester* (39th), Michael Alfred Baughen, *b.* 1930, *m.,* *cons.* 1982, *elected* 1982.
1988 *Guildford* (7th), Michael Edgar Adie, *b.* 1929, *m.,* *cons.* 1983, *elected* 1983.
1988 *Southwark* (7th), Robert Kerr Williamson, *b.* 1932, *m.,* *cons.* 1984, *elected* 1984, *trans.* 1991.
1989 *Lichfield* (97th), Keith Norman Sutton, *b.* 1934, *m.,* *cons.* 1978, *elected* 1984.
1989 *Peterborough* (36th), William John Westwood, *b.* 1925, *m.,* *cons.* 1975, *elected* 1984.
1989 *Portsmouth* (7th), Timothy John Bavin, *b.* 1935, *cons.* 1974, *elected* 1985.
1989 *Exeter* (69th), (Geoffrey) Hewlett Thompson, *b.* 1929, *m.,* *cons.* 1974, *elected* 1985.
1990 *Bristol* (54th), Barry Rogerson, *b.* 1936, *m.,* *cons.* 1979, *elected* 1985.
1991 *Coventry* (7th), Simon Barrington-Ward, *b.* 1930, *m.,* *cons.* 1985, *elected* 1985.
1991 *Norwich* (70th), Peter John Nott, *b.* 1933, *m.,* *cons.* 1977, *elected* 1985.
1991 *St Edmundsbury and Ipswich* (8th), John Dennis, *b.* 1931, *m.,* *cons.* 1979, *elected* 1986.
1993 *Lincoln* (70th), Robert Maynard Hardy, *b.* 1936, *m.,* *cons.* 1980, *elected* 1986.
1993 *Oxford* (41st), Richard Douglas Harries, *b.* 1936, *m.,* *cons.* 1987, *elected* 1987.

*Bishops awaiting seats, in order of seniority*
*Birmingham* (7th), Mark Santer, *b.* 1936, *w.,* *cons.* 1981, *elected* 1987.
*Derby* (5th), Peter Spencer Dawes, *b.* 1928, *m.,* *cons.* 1988, *elected* 1988.
*Southwell* (9th), Patrick Burnet Harris, *b.* 1934, *m.,* *cons.* 1973, *elected* 1988.
*Rochester* (105th), (Anthony) Michael (Arnold) Turnbull, *b.* 1935, *m.,* *cons.* 1988, *elected* 1988.
*Blackburn* (7th), Alan David Chesters, *b.* 1937, *m.,* *cons.* 1989, *elected* 1989.
*Carlisle* (65th), Ian Harland, *b.* 1932, *m.,* *cons.* 1985, *elected* 1989.
*Truro* (13th), Michael Thomas Ball, *b.* 1932, *cons.* 1980, *elected* 1990.
*Ely* (67th), Stephen Whitefield Sykes, *b.* 1939, *m.,* *cons.* 1990, *elected* 1990.
*Hereford* (103rd), John Keith Oliver, *b.* 1935, *m.,* *cons.* 1990, *elected* 1990.

*Leicester* (5th), Thomas Frederick Butler, *b.* 1940, *m.*, *cons.* 1985, *elected* 1991.

*Bath and Wells* (77th), James Lawton Thompson, *b.* 1936, *m.*, *cons.* 1978, *elected* 1991.

*Wakefield* (11th), Nigel Simeon McCulloch, *b.* 1942, *m.*, *cons.* 1986, *elected* 1992.

*Bradford* (8th), David James Smith, *b.* 1935, *m.*, *cons.* 1987, *elected* 1992.

*Manchester* (10th), Christopher John Mayfield, *b.* 1935, *m.*, *cons.* 1985, *elected* 1993.

*Salisbury* (77th), David Staffurth Stancliffe, *b.* 1942, *m.*, *cons.* 1993, *elected* 1993.

*Gloucester* (39th), David Edward Bentley, *b.* 1935, *m.*, *cons.* 1986, *elected* 1993.

# The Order of St John

THE MOST VENERABLE ORDER OF THE HOSPITAL OF ST JOHN OF JERUSALEM (1888)

| | |
|---|---|
| GCStJ | Bailiff/Dame Grand Cross |
| KStJ | Knight of Justice/Grace |
| DStJ | Dame of Justice/Grace |
| ChStJ | Chaplain |
| CStJ | Commander |
| OStJ, | Officer |
| SBStJ | Serving Brother |
| SSStJ | Serving Sister |
| EsqStJ | Esquire |

*Mottoes,* Pro Fide *and* Pro Utilitate Hominum

The Order of St John, founded in the early 12th century in Jerusalem, was a religious order with a particular duty to care for the sick. In Britain the Order was dissolved by Henry VIII in 1540 but the British branch was revived in the early 19th century. The branch was not accepted by the Grand Magistracy of the Order in Rome but its search for a role in the tradition of the Hospitallers led to the founding of the St John Ambulance Association in 1877 and later the St John Ambulance Brigade; in 1882 the St John Ophthalmic Hospital was founded in Jerusalem. A royal charter was granted in 1888 establishing the British Order of St John as a British Order of Chivalry with the Sovereign as its head.

Admission to the Order is conferred in recognition of service, usually in St John Ambulance. Membership does not confer any rank, style, title or precedence on a recipient.

SOVEREIGN HEAD OF THE ORDER
HM The Queen

GRAND PRIOR
HRH The Duke of Gloucester, GCVO
*Lord Prior,* The Lord Vestey
*Prelate,* The Rt. Revd M. A. Mann, KCVO
*Chancellor,* Prof. A. R. Mellows, TD
*Bailiff of Egle,* The Lord Remnant
*Headquarters,* St John's Gate, Clerkenwell, London ECIM 4DA

## COURTESY TITLES

From this list it will be seen that, for example, the Marquess of Blandford is heir to the Dukedom of Marlborough, and Viscount Amberley to the Earldom of Russell. Titles of second heirs are also given, and the courtesy title of the father of a second heir is indicated by *; e.g. Earl of Burlington, eldest son of *Marquess of Hartington For forms of address, *see* page 217.

MARQUESSES

*Blandford – *Marlborough, D.*
Bowmont and Cessford – *Roxburghe, D.*
Douglas and Clydesdale – *Hamilton, D.*
*Douro – *Wellington, D.*
Graham – *Montrose, D.*
Granby – *Rutland, D.*
Hamilton – *Abercorn, D.*
*Hartington – *Devonshire, D.*
*Kildare – *Leinster, D.*
Lorne – *Argyll, D.*
*Tavistock – *Bedford, D.*
*Worcester – *Beaufort, D.*

EARLS

Aboyne – *Huntly, M.*
Altamont – *Sligo, M.*
Ancram – *Lothian, M.*
Arundel and Surrey – *Norfolk, D.*
*Bective – *Headfort, M.*
*Belfast – *Donegall, M.*
Brecknock – *Camden, M.*
Burford – *St Albans, D.*
Burlington – **Hartington, M.*
*Cardigan – *Ailesbury, M.*
Compton – *Northampton, M.*
*Dalkeith – *Buccleuch, D.*
Dumfries – *Bute, M.*
*Euston – *Grafton, D.*
Glamorgan – **Worcester, M.*
Grosvenor – *Westminster, D.*
*Haddo – *Aberdeen and Temair, M.*
Hillsborough – *Downshire, M.*
Hopetoun – *Linlithgow, M.*
March and Kinrara – *Richmond, D.*
*Mount Charles – *Conyngham, M.*
Mornington – **Douro, M.*
Offaly – **Kildare, M.*
Ronaldshay – *Zetland, M.*
*St Andrews – *Kent, D.*
*Shelburne – *Lansdowne, M.*
*Southesk – *Fife, D.*
Sunderland – **Blandford, M.*

*Tyrone – *Waterford, M.*
Ulster – *Gloucester, D.*
*Uxbridge – *Anglesey, M.*
Wiltshire – *Winchester, M.*
Yarmouth – *Hertford, M.*

VISCOUNTS

Althorp – *Spencer, E.*
Amberley – *Russell, E.*
Andover – *Suffolk and Berkshire, E.*
Anson – *Lichfield, E.*
Asquith – *Oxford & Asquith, E.*
Boringdon – *Morley, E.*
Borodale – *Beatty, E.*
Boyle – *Shannon, E.*
Brocas – *Jellicoe, E.*
Calne and Calstone – **Shelburne, E.*
Campden – *Gainsborough, E.*
Carlow – *Portarlington, E.*
Carlton – *Wharncliffe, E.*
Castlereagh – *Londonderry, M.*
Chelsea – *Cadogan, E.*
Chewton – *Waldegrave, E.*
Chichester – **Belfast, E.*
Clanfield – *Peel, E.*
Clive – *Powis, E.*
Coke – *Leicester, E.*
Corry – *Belmore, E.*
Corvedale – *Baldwin of Bewdley, E.*
Cranborne – *Salisbury, M.*
Cranley – *Onslow, E.*
Crichton – *Erne, E.*
Crowhurst – *Cottenham, E.*
Dalrymple – *Stair, E.*
Dangan – *Cowley, E.*
Dawick – *Haig, E.*
Deerhurst – *Coventry, E.*
Drumlanrig – *Queensberry, M.*
Dunwich – *Stradbroke, E.*
Dupplin – *Kinnoull, E.*
Ebrington – *Fortescue, E.*
Ednam – *Dudley, E.*
Emlyn – *Cawdor, E.*
Encombe – *Eldon, E.*
Ennismore – *Listowel, E.*
Enfield – *Strafford, E.*
Erleigh – *Reading, M.*
Errington – *Cromer, E.*
Feilding – *Denbigh, E.*
Fincastle – *Dunmore, E.*

FitzHarris – *Malmesbury, E.*
Folkestone – *Radnor, E.*
Forbes – *Granard, E.*
Garmoyle – *Cairns, E.*
Garnock – *Lindsay, E.*
Glandine – *Norbury, E.*
Glenapp – *Inchcape, E.*
Glentworth – *Limerick, E.*
Grimstone – *Verulam, E.*
Gwynedd – *Lloyd George of Dwyfor, E.*
Hawkesbury – *Liverpool, E.*
Ikerrin – *Carrick, E.*
Ingestre – *Shrewsbury, E.*
Ipswich – **Euston, E.*
Kelburn – *Glasgow, E.*
Kingsborough – *Kingston, E.*
Knebworth – *Lytton, E.*
Lascelles – *Harewood, E.*
Lewisham – *Dartmouth, E.*
Linley – *Snowdon, E.*
Loftus – *Ely, M.*
Lowther – *Lonsdale, E.*
Lumley – *Scarbrough, E.*
Lymington – *Portsmouth, E.*
Macmillan of Ovenden – *Stockton, E.*
Maidstone – *Winchilsea and Nottingham, E.*
Maitland – *Lauderdale, E.*
Malden – *Essex, E.*
Mandeville – *Manchester, D.*
Medina – *Milford Haven, M.*
Melgund – *Minto, E.*
Merton – *Nelson, E.*
Moore – *Drogheda, E.*
Morpeth – *Carlisle, E.*
Newport – *Bradford, E.*
Newry and Mourne – *Kilmorey, E.*
Parker – *Macclesfield, E.*
Perceval – *Egmont, E.*
Petersham – *Harrington, E.*
Pollington – *Mexborough, E.*
Raynham – *Townshend, M.*
Reidhaven – *Seafield, E.*
Ruthven of Canberra – *Gowrie, E.*
St Cyres – *Iddesleigh, E.*
Sandon – *Harrowby, E.*
Savernake – **Cardigan, E.*
Slane – **Mount Charles, E.*
Somerton – *Normanton, E.*
Stopford – *Courtown, E.*

Stormont – *Mansfield, E.*
Strathallan – *Perth, E.*
Stuart – *Castle Stewart, E.*
Suirdale – *Donoughmore, E.*
Tamworth – *Ferrers, E.*
Tarbat – *Cromartie, E.*
Vaughan – *Lisburne, E.*
Villiers – *Jersey, E.*
Weymouth – *Bath, M.*
Windsor – *Plymouth, E.*
Wolmer – *Selborne, E.*
Woodstock – *Portland, E.*

BARONS (LORD—)

Aberdour – *Morton, E.*
Apsley – *Bathurst, E.*
Ardee – *Meath, E.*
Ashley – *Shaftesbury, E.*
Balgonie – *Leven & Melville, E.*
Balniel – *Crawford and Balcarres, E.*
Berriedale – *Caithness, E.*
Bingham – *Lucan, E.*
Binning – *Haddington, E.*
Brooke – *Warwick, E.*
Bruce – *Elgin, E.*
Buckhurst – *De La Warr, E.*
Burghley – *Exeter, M.*
Cardross – *Buchan, E.*
Carnegie – **Southesk, E.*
Clifton – *Darnley, E.*
Cochrane – *Dundonald, E.*
Courtenay – *Devon, E.*
Dalmeny – *Rosebery, E.*
Doune – *Moray, E.*
Downpatrick – **St Andrews, E.*
Eliot – *St Germans, E.*
Eskdail – **Dalkeith, E.*
Formartine – **Haddo, E.*
Gillford – *Clanwilliam, E.*
Glamis – *Strathmore, E.*
Greenock – *Cathcart, E.*
Guernsey – *Aylesford, E.*
Hay – *Erroll, E.*
Herbert – *Pembroke, E.*
Howland – **Tavistock, M.*
Hyde – *Clarendon, E.*
Inverurie – *Kintore, E.*
Irwin – *Halifax, E.*
Johnstone – *Annandale and Hartfell, E.*
Kenlis – **Bective, E.*
Langton – *Temple of Stowe, E.*
La Poer – **Tyrone, E.*
Leslie – *Rothes, E.*
Leveson – *Granville, E.*

Loughborough – *Rosslyn, E.*
Maltravers – *\*Arundel and Surrey, E.*
Mauchline – *Loudoun, C.*
Medway – *Cranbrook, E.*
Montgomerie – *Eglinton and Winton, E.*
Moreton – *Ducie, E.*
Naas – *Mayo, E.*
Neidpath – *Wemyss & March, E.*
Norreys – *Lindsey & Abingdon, E.*
North – *Guilford, E.*
Ogilvy – *Airlie, E.*
Oxmantown – *Rosse, E.*
Paget de Beaudesert – *\*Uxbridge, E.*
Porchester – *Carnarvon, E.*
Ramsay – *Dalhousie, E.*
Romsey – *Mountbatten of Burma, C.*
Rosehill – *Northesk, E.*
Scrymgeour – *Dundee, E.*
Seymour – *Somerset, D.*
Strathnaver – *Sutherland, C.*
Wodehouse – *Kimberley, E.*
Worsley – *Yarborough, E.*

## PEERS' SURNAMES WHICH DIFFER FROM THEIR TITLES

The following symbols indicate the rank of the peer holding each title:
*C.* Countess
*D.* Duke
*E.* Earl
*M.* Marquess
*V.* Viscount
\* Life Peer
Where no designation is given, the title is that of an hereditary Baron or Baroness
Abney-Hastings – *Loudoun, C.*
Acheson – *Gosford, E.*
Adderley – *Norton*
Addington – *Sidmouth, V.*
Agar – *Normanton, E.*
Aitken – *Beaverbrook*
Akers-Douglas – *Chilston, V.*
Alexander – *A. of Tunis, E.*
Alexander – *A. of Weedon\**
Alexander – *Caledon, E.*
Allen – *A. of Abbeydale\**
Allen – *Croham\**
Allanson-Winn – *Headley*
Allsopp – *Hindlip*
Amery – *A. of Lustleigh\**
Anderson – *Waverley, V.*
Annesley – *Valentia, V.*
Anson – *Lichfield, E.*
Archer – *A. of Sandwell\**
Archer – *A. of Weston-super-Mare\**
Armstrong – *A. of Ilminster\**
Armstrong-Jones – *Snowdon, E.*
Arthur – *Glenarthur*
Arundell – *Talbot of Malahide*
Ashley – *A. of Stoke\**
Ashley-Cooper – *Shaftesbury, E.*
Ashton – *A. of Hyde*
Asquith – *Oxford & Asquith, E.*
Assheton – *Clitheroe*
Astley – *Hastings*
Astor – *A. of Hever*
Atkins – *Colnbrook\**
Aubrey-Fletcher – *Braye*
Bailey – *Glanusk*

Baillie – *Burton*
Baillie Hamilton – *Haddington, E.*
Baldwin – *B. of Bewdley, E.*
Balfour – *B. of Inchrye*
Balfour – *Kinross*
Balfour – *Riverdale*
Bampfylde – *Poltimore*
Banbury – *B. of Southam*
Barber – *B. of Tewkesbury\**
Baring – *Ashburton*
Baring – *Cromer, E.*
Baring – *Howick of Glendale*
Baring – *Northbrook*
Baring – *Revelstoke*
Barker – *Trumpington\**
Barnes – *Gorell*
Barnewall – *Trimlestown*
Bathurst – *Bledisloe, V.*
Beauclerk – *St Albans, D.*
Beaumont – *Allendale, V.*
Beaumont – *B. of Whitley\**
Beckett – *Grimthorpe*
Bellow – *Bellwin\**
Benn – *Stansgate, V.*
Bennet – *Tankerville, E.*
Bentinck – *Portland, E.*
Beresford – *Decies*
Beresford – *Waterford, M.*
Berry – *Camrose, V.*
Berry – *Hartwell\**
Berry – *Kemsley, V.*
Bertie – *Lindsey, E.*
Best – *Wynford*
Bethell – *Westbury*
Bewicke-Copley – *Cromwell*
Bigham – *Mersey, V.*
Bigham – *Nairne*
Bingham – *Clanmorris*
Bingham – *Lucan, E.*
Blackwood – *Dufferin & Clandeboye*
Bligh – *Darnley, E.*
Bootle-Wilbraham – *Skelmersdale*
Boscawen – *Falmouth, V.*
Boston – *B. of Faversham\**
Bourke – *Mayo, E.*
Bowes Lyon – *Strathmore, E.*
Bowyer – *Denham*
Boyd – *Kilmarnock*
Boyle – *Cork & Orrery, E.*

Boyle – *Glasgow, E.*
Boyle – *Shannon, E.*
Brabazon – *Meath, E.*
Braine – *B. of Wheatley\**
Brand – *Hampden, V.*
Brandon – *B. of Oakbrook\**
Brassey – *B. of Apethorpe*
Brett – *Esher, V.*
Bridge – *B. of Harwich\**
Bridgeman – *Bradford, E.*
Brodrick – *Midleton, V.*
Brooke – *Alanbrooke, V.*
Brooke – *Brookeborough, V.*
Brooke – *B. of Ystradfellte\**
Brooks – *B. of Tremorfa\**
Brooks – *Crawshaw*
Brougham – *Brougham and Vaux*
Broughton – *Fairhaven*
Browne – *Kilmaine*
Browne – *Oranmore and Browne*
Browne – *Sligo, M.*
Bruce – *Aberdare*
Bruce – *Balfour of Burleigh*
Bruce – *B. of Donington\**
Bruce – *Elgin and Kincardine, E.*
Brudenell-Bruce – *Ailesbury, M.*
Buchan – *Tweedsmuir*
Buckley – *Wrenbury*
Butler – *Carrick, E.*
Butler – *Dunboyne*
Butler – *Lanesborough, E.*
Butler – *Mountgarret, V.*
Butler – *Ormonde, M.*
Buxton – *B. of Alsa\**
Byng – *Strafford, E.*
Byng – *Torrington, V.*
Callaghan – *C. of Cardiff\**
Cameron – *C. of Lochbroom\**
Campbell – *Argyll, D.*
Campbell – *Breadalbane and Holland, E.*
Campbell – *C. of Alloway\**
Campbell – *C. of Croy\**
Campbell – *C. of Eskan\**
Campbell – *Cawdor, E.*
Campbell – *Colgrain*
Campbell – *Stratheden and Campbell*
Campbell-Gray – *Gray*
Canning – *Garvagh*

Capell – *Essex, E.*
Carington – *Carrington*
Carlisle – *C. of Bucklow\**
Carmichael – *C. of Kelvingrove\**
Carnegie – *Fife, D.*
Carnegie – *Northesk, E.*
Carr – *C. of Hadley\**
Cary – *Falkland, V.*
Castle – *C. of Blackburn\**
Caulfeild – *Charlemont, V.*
Cavendish – *C. of Furness\**
Cavendish – *Chesham*
Cavendish – *Devonshire, D.*
Cavendish – *Waterpark*
Cayzer – *Rotherwick*
Cecil – *Amherst of Hackney*
Cecil – *Exeter, M.*
Cecil – *Rockley*
Cecil – *Salisbury, M.*
Chalker – *C. of Wallasey\**
Chaloner – *Gisborough*
Chapman – *Northfield\**
Charteris – *C. of Amisfield\**
Charteris – *Wemyss and March, E.*
Cheshire – *Ryder of Warsaw\**
Chetwynd-Talbot – *Shrewsbury, E.*
Chichester – *Donegall, M.*
Chichester-Clark – *Moyola\**
Child Villiers – *Jersey, E.*
Cholmondeley – *Delamere*
Chubb – *Hayter*
Clark – *C. of Kempston\**
Clegg-Hill – *Hill, V.*
Clifford – *C. of Chudleigh*
Cochrane – *C. of Cults*
Cochrane – *Dundonald, E.*
Cocks – *C. of Hartcliffe\**
Cocks – *Somers*
Cokayne – *Cullen of Ashbourne*
Coke – *Leicester, E.*
Cole – *Enniskillen, E.*
Collier – *Monkswell*
Colville – *Clydesmuir*
Colville – *C. of Culross, V.*
Compton – *Northampton, M.*
Conolly-Carew – *Carew*
Constantine – *C. of Stanmore\**
Cooke – *C. of Islandreagh\**

Penny – *Marchwood, V.*
Pepys – *Cottenham, E.*
Perceval – *Egmont, E.*
Percy – *Northumberland, D.*
Perry – *P. of Southwark**
Perry – *P. of Walton**
Pery – *Limerick, E.*
Peyton – *P. of Yeovil **
Philipps – *Milford*
Philipps – *St Davids, V.*
Phillips – *P. of Ellesmere**
Phipps – *Normanby, M.*
Pitt – *P. of Hampstead**
Plant – *P. of Highfield**
Platt – *P. of Writtle**
Pleydell-Bouverie – *Radnor, E.*
Plummer – *P. of St Marylebone**
Plumptre – *Fitzwalter*
Plunkett – *Dunsany*
Plunkett – *Louth*
Pollock – *Hanworth, V.*
Pomeroy – *Harberton, V.*
Ponsonby – *Bessborough, E.*
Ponsonby – *de Mauley*
Ponsonby – *P. of Shulbrede*
Ponsonby – *Sysonby*
Porter – *P. of Luddenham**
Powys – *Lilford*
Pratt – *Camden, M.*
Preston – *Gormanston, V.*
Primrose – *Rosebery, E.*
Prittie – *Dunalley*
Ramsay – *Dalhousie, E.*
Ramsbotham – *Soulbury, V.*
Rawlinson – *R. of Ewell**
Rees-Williams – *Ogmore*
Renfrew – *R. of Kaimsthorn**
Rhys – *Dynevor*
Richards – *Milverton*
Richardson – *R. of Duntisbourne**
Rippon – *R. of Hexham**
Ritchie – *R. of Dundee*
Robens – *R. of Woldingham**
Roberts – *Clwyd*
Robertson – *R. of Oakridge*
Robertson – *Wharton*
Robinson – *Martonmere*
Robson – *R. of Kiddington**
Roche – *Fermoy*
Rodd – *Rennell*
Rodger – *R. of Earlsferry**
Rodgers – *R. of Quarry Bank**
Roll – *R. of Ipsden**
Roper-Curzon – *Teynham*
Rospigliosi – *Newburgh, E.*
Rous – *Stradbroke, E.*
Rowley-Conwy – *Langford*
Royle – *Fanshawe of Richmond**
Runciman – *R. of Doxford, V.*
Russell – *Ampthill*

Russell – *Bedford, D.*
Russell – *de Clifford*
Russell – *R. of Liverpool*
Ryder – *Harrowby, E.*
Ryder – *R. of Eaton Hastings**
Ryder – *R. of Warsaw**
Sackville – *De La Warr, E.*
Sackville-West – *Sackville*
Sainsbury – *S. of Preston Candover**
St Aubyn – *St Levan*
St Clair – *Sinclair*
St Clair-Erskine – *Rosslyn, E.*
St John – *Bolingbroke and St John, V.*
St John – *St John of Blesto*
St John-Stevas – *St John of Fawsley**
St Leger – *Doneraile, V.*
Samuel – *Bearsted, V.*
Sanderson – *S. of Ayot*
Sanderson – *S. of Bowden**
Sandilands – *Torphichen*
Saumarez – *De Saumarez*
Savile – *Mexborough, E.*
Scarlett – *Abinger*
Schreiber – *Marlesford**
Sclater-Booth – *Basing*
Scott – *Eldon, E.*
Scott-Ellis – *Howard de Walden*
Scrymgeour – *Dundee, E.*
Seager – *Leighton of St Mellons*
Seely – *Mottistone*
Sefton – *S. of Garston**
Seymour – *Hertford, M.*
Seymour – *Somerset, D.*
Shaw – *Craigmyle*
Shirley – *Ferrers, E.*
Short – *Glenamara**
Siddeley – *Kenilworth*
Sidney – *De L'Isle, V.*
Sieff – *S. of Brimpton**
Simon – *S. of Glaisdale**
Simon – *S. of Wythenshawe*
Sinclair – *Caithness, E.*
Sinclair – *S. of Cleeve*
Sinclair – *Thurso, V.*
Skeffington – *Massereene, V.*
Slynn – *S. of Hadley**
Smith – *Bicester*
Smith – *Hambleden, V.*
Smith – *Kirkhill**
Somerset – *Beaufort, D.*
Somerset – *Raglan*
Souter – *Audley*
Spencer – *Churchill, V.*
Spencer-Churchill – *Marlborough, D.*
Spring Rice – *Monteagle of Brandon*
Stanhope – *Harrington, E.*
Stanley – *Derby, E.*
Stanley – *Stanley of Alderley & Sheffield*

Stapleton-Cotton – *Combermere, V.*
Sterling – *S. of Plaistow**
Stevens – *S. of Ludgate**
Stewart – *Galloway, E.*
Stewart – *Stewartby**
Stodart – *S. of Leaston**
Stoddart – *S. of Swindon**
Stonor – *Camoys*
Stopford – *Courtown, E.*
Stourton – *Mowbray*
Strachey – *O'Hagan*
Strutt – *Belper*
Strutt – *Rayleigh*
Stuart – *Castle Stewart, E.*
Stuart – *Moray, E.*
Stuart – *S. of Findhorn, V.*
Suenson-Taylor – *Grantchester*
Taylor – *Ingrow**
Taylor – *T. of Blackburn**
Taylor – *T. of Gosforth**
Taylor – *T. of Gryfe**
Taylor – *T. of Hadfield**
Taylour – *Headfort, M.*
Temple-Gore-Langton – *Temple of Stowe, E.*
Tennant – *Glenconner*
Thellusson – *Rendlesham*
Thesiger – *Chelmsford, V.*
Thomas – *T. of Gwydir**
Thomas – *T. of Swynnerton**
Thomas – *Tonypandy, V.*
Thomson – *T. of Fleet*
Thomson – *T. of Monifieth**
Thynn – *Bath, M.*
Thynne – *Bath, M.*
Tottenham – *Ely, M.*
Trefusis – *Clinton*
Trench – *Ashtown*
Trevor-Roper – *Dacre of Glanton**
Tufton – *Hothfield*
Turner – *Netherthorpe*
Turner – *T. of Camden**
Turnour – *Winterton, E.*
Tyrell-Kenyon – *Kenyon*
Vanden-Bempde-Johnstone – *Derwent*
Vane – *Barnard*
Vane – *Inglewood*
Vane-Tempest-Stewart – *Londonderry, M.*
Vanneck – *Huntingfield*
Vaughan – *Lisburne, E.*
Vaughan-Morgan – *Reigate**
Vereker – *Gort, V.*
Verney – *Willoughby de Broke*
Vernon – *Lyveden*
Vesey – *De Vesci, V.*
Villiers – *Clarendon, E.*
Vivian – *Swansea*
Wade – *W. of Chorlton**
Walker – *W. of Worcester**
Wallace – *W. of Campsie**
Wallace – *W. of Coslany**

Wallop – *Portsmouth, E.*
Walton – *W. of Detchant**
Ward – *Bangor, V.*
Ward – *Dudley, E.*
Warrender – *Bruntisfield*
Watson – *Manton*
Wedderburn – *W. of Charlton**
Weir – *Inverforth*
Weld-Forester – *Forester*
Wellesley – *Cowley, E.*
Wellesley – *Wellington, D.*
Westenra – *Rossmore*
White – *Annaly*
White – *James of Holland Park**
White – *W. of Hull**
Whiteley – *Marchamley*
Whitfield – *Kenswood*
Williams – *Berners*
Williams – *W. of Crosby**
Williams – *W. of Elvel**
Williams – *W. of Mostyn**
Williamson – *Forres*
Willoughby – *Middleton*
Wills – *Dulverton*
Wilson – *Moran*
Wilson – *Nunburnholme*
Wilson – *W. of Langside**
Wilson – *W. of Rievaulx**
Wilson – *W. of Tillyorn**
Windsor – *Gloucester, D.*
Windsor – *Kent, D.*
Windsor-Clive – *Plymouth, E.*
Wingfield – *Powerscourt, V.*
Winn – *St Oswald*
Wodehouse – *Kimberley, E.*
Wolfson – *W. of Sunningdale**
Wood – *Halifax, E.*
Wood – *Holderness**
Woodhouse – *Terrington*
Wright – *W. of Richmond**
Wyatt – *W. of Weeford**
Wyndham – *Egremont & Leconfield*
Wyndham-Quin – *Dunraven, E.*
Wynn – *Newborough*
Yarde-Buller – *Churston*
Yerburgh – *Alvingham*
Yorke – *Hardwicke, E.*
Young – *Kennet*
Young – *Y. of Dartington**
Young – *Y. of Graffham**
Younger – *Y. of Leckie, V.*
Younger – *Y. of Prestwick**

# Orders of Chivalry

## THE MOST NOBLE ORDER OF THE GARTER (1348)

**KG**

*Ribbon*, Blue
*Motto*, Honi soit qui mal y pense
(*Shame on him who thinks evil of it*)
The number of Knights Companions
is limited to 24

SOVEREIGN OF THE ORDER
The Queen

LADIES OF THE ORDER
HM Queen Elizabeth the Queen
Mother, 1936
HRH The Princess Royal, 1994

ROYAL KNIGHTS
HRH The Duke of Edinburgh, 1947
HRH The Prince of Wales, 1958
HRH The Duke of Kent, 1985

EXTRA KNIGHTS COMPANIONS
AND LADIES
HRH Princess Juliana of the
Netherlands, 1958
HRH The Grand Duke of
Luxembourg, 1972
HM The Queen of Denmark, 1979
HM The King of Sweden, 1983
HM The King of Spain, 1988
HM The Queen of the Netherlands,
1989

KNIGHTS AND LADY COMPANIONS
Sir Cennydd Traherne, 1970
The Earl Waldegrave, 1971
The Earl of Longford, 1971
The Lord Shackleton, 1974
The Marquess of Abergavenny, 1974
The Lord Wilson of Rievaulx, 1976
The Duke of Grafton, 1976
The Lord Hunt, 1979
The Duke of Norfolk, 1983
The Lord Lewin, 1983
The Lord Richardson of
Duntisbourne, 1983
The Lord Carrington, 1985
The Lord Callaghan of Cardiff, 1987
The Viscount Leverhulme, 1988
The Lord Hailsham of St Marylebone,
1988
Lavinia, Duchess of Norfolk, 1990
The Duke of Wellington, 1990
Field Marshal Lord Bramall, 1990
Sir Edward Heath, 1992
The Viscount Ridley, 1992

The Lord Sainsbury of Preston
Candover, 1992
The Lord Ashburton, 1994
The Lord Kingsdown, 1994
Sir Ninian Stephen, 1994

*Prelate*, The Bishop of Winchester
*Chancellor*, The Marquess of
Abergavenny, KG, OBE
*Register*, The Dean of Windsor
*Garter King of Arms*, Sir Conrad Swan,
KCVO, PH.D., FSA
*Gentleman Usher of the Black Rod*,
Adm. Sir Richard Thomas, KCB,
OBE
*Secretary*, D. H. B. Chesshyre, LVO

## THE MOST ANCIENT AND MOST NOBLE ORDER OF THE THISTLE (REVIVED 1687)

**KT**

*Ribbon*, Green
*Motto*, Nemo me impune lacessit (*No
one provokes me with impunity*)
The number of Knights is limited to
16

SOVEREIGN OF THE ORDER
The Queen

LADY OF THE THISTLE
HM Queen Elizabeth the Queen
Mother, 1937

ROYAL KNIGHTS
HRH The Duke of Edinburgh, 1952
HRH The Prince of Wales, Duke of
Rothesay, 1977

KNIGHTS
The Lord Home of the Hirsel, 1962
The Earl of Wemyss and March, 1966
The Earl of Dalhousie, 1971
The Lord Clydesmuir, 1972
Sir Donald Cameron of Lochiel, 1973
The Earl of Selkirk, 1976
The Lord McFadzean, 1976
The Hon. Lord Cameron, 1978
The Duke of Buccleuch and
Queensberry, 1978
The Earl of Elgin and Kincardine,
1981
The Lord Thomson of Monifieth, 1981
The Lord MacLehose of Beoch, 1983
The Earl of Airlie, 1985
Capt. Sir Iain Tennant, 1986

The Viscount Whitelaw, 1990
Sir Fitzroy Maclean of Dunconnel,
1993

*Chancellor*, The Duke of Buccleuch
and Queensberry, KT, VRD
*Dean*, The Very Revd G. I. Macmillan
*Secretary and Lord Lyon King of Arms*,
Sir Malcolm Innes of Edingight,
KCVO, WS
*Usher of the Green Rod*, Rear-Adm.
D.A. Dunbar-Nasmith, CB, DSC

## THE MOST HONOURABLE ORDER OF THE BATH (1725)

GCB *Military*        GCB *Civil*

GCB   Knight (or Dame) Grand
      Cross
KCB   Knight Commander
DCB   Dame Commander
CB    Companion

*Ribbon*, Crimson
*Motto*, Tria juncta in uno (*Three joined
in one*)
Remodelled 1815, and enlarged many
times since. The Order is divided into
civil and military divisions. Women
became eligible for the Order from 1
January 1971

THE SOVEREIGN

GREAT MASTER AND FIRST OR
PRINCIPAL KNIGHT GRAND CROSS
HRH The Prince of Wales, KG, KT,
GCB

*Dean of the Order*, The Dean of
Westminster
*Bath King of Arms*, Air Chief Marshal
Sir David Evans, GCB, CBE
*Registrar and Secretary*, Rear-Adm. D.
E. Macey, CB
*Genealogist*, Sir Conrad Swan, KCVO,
PH.D., FSA
*Gentleman Usher of the Scarlet Rod*, Air
Vice-Marshal Sir Richard Peirse,
KCVO, CB
*Deputy Secretary*, The Secretary of the
Central Chancery of the Orders of
Knighthood
*Chancery*, Central Chancery of the
Orders of Knighthood, St James's
Palace, London SW1A 1BH

## THE ORDER OF MERIT
(1902)

OM *Military*    OM *Civil*

**OM**

*Ribbon*, Blue and crimson

This Order is designed as a special distinction for eminent men and women without conferring a knighthood upon them. The Order is limited in numbers to 24, with the addition of foreign honorary members. Membership is of two kinds, military and civil, the badge of the former having crossed swords, and the latter oak leaves

THE SOVEREIGN

HRH THE DUKE OF EDINBURGH, 1968
Dame Veronica Wedgwood, 1969
Sir Isaiah Berlin, 1971
Sir George Edwards, 1971
Sir Alan Hodgkin, 1973
The Lord Todd, 1977
Revd Prof. Owen Chadwick, KBE, 1983
Sir Andrew Huxley, 1983
Sir Michael Tippett, 1983
Frederick Sanger, 1986
Air Cdre Sir Frank Whittle, 1986
The Lord Menuhin, 1987
Prof. Sir Ernst Gombrich, 1988
Dr Max Perutz, 1988
Dame Cicely Saunders, 1989
The Lord Porter of Luddenham, 1989
The Baroness Thatcher, 1990
Dame Joan Sutherland, 1991
Prof. Francis Crick, 1991
Dame Ninette de Valois, 1992
Sir Michael Atiyah, 1992
Lucien Freud, 1993
The Lord Jenkins of Hillhead, 1993
*Honorary Member,* Mother Teresa, 1983

*Secretary and Registrar,* Sir Edward Ford, KCB, KCVO, ERD
*Chancery,* Central Chancery of the Orders of Knighthood, St James's Palace, London SW1A 1BH

## THE MOST EXALTED ORDER OF THE STAR OF INDIA (1861)

GCSI    Knight Grand Commander
KCSI    Knight Commander
CSI    Companion

*Ribbon,* Light blue, with white edges
*Motto,* Heaven's Light our Guide

THE SOVEREIGN
*Registrar,* The Secretary of the Central Chancery of the Orders of Knighthood
No conferments have been made since 1947

## THE MOST DISTINGUISHED ORDER OF ST MICHAEL AND ST GEORGE (1818)

GCMG    KCMG

GCMG    Knight (or Dame) Grand Cross
KCMG    Knight Commander
DCMG    Dame Commander
CMG    Companion

*Ribbon,* Saxon blue, with scarlet centre
*Motto,* Auspicium melioris aevi (*Token of a better age*)

THE SOVEREIGN
GRAND MASTER
HRH The Duke of Kent, KG, GCMG, GCVO, ADC
*Prelate,* The Rt. Revd the Bishop of Coventry
*Chancellor,* Sir Anthony Acland, GCMG, GCVO
*Secretary,* Sir John Coles, KCMG
*Registrar,* Sir John Graham, Bt., GCMG
*King of Arms,* Sir Oliver Wright, GCMG, GCVO, DSC
*Gentleman Usher of the Blue Rod,* Sir John Margetson, KCMG
*Dean,* The Dean of St Paul's
*Deputy Secretary,* The Secretary of the Central Chancery of the Orders of Knighthood
*Chancery,* Central Chancery of the Orders of Knighthood, St James's Palace, London SW1A 1BH

## THE MOST EMINENT ORDER OF THE INDIAN EMPIRE (1868)

GCIE    Knight Grand Commander
KCIE    Knight Commander
CIE    Companion

*Ribbon,* Imperial purple
*Motto,* Imperatricis auspiciis (*Under the auspices of the Empress*)

THE SOVEREIGN
*Registrar,* The Secretary of the Central Chancery of the Orders of Knighthood

No conferments have been made since 1947

## THE IMPERIAL ORDER OF THE CROWN OF INDIA (1877)
FOR LADIES

CI

*Badge,* the royal cipher in jewels within an oval, surmounted by an heraldic crown and attached to a bow of light blue watered ribbon, edged white
The honour does not confer any rank or title upon the recipient
No conferments have been made since 1947

HM The Queen, 1947
HM Queen Elizabeth the Queen Mother, 1931
HRH The Princess Margaret, Countess of Snowdon, 1947
HRH Princess Alice, Duchess of Gloucester, 1937
HH The Maharani of Travancore, 1929

## THE ROYAL VICTORIAN ORDER (1896)

GCVO    KCVO

GCVO    Knight or Dame Grand Cross
KCVO    Knight Commander
DCVO    Dame Commander
CVO    Commander
LVO    Lieutenant
MVO    Member

*Ribbon,* Blue, with red and white edges
*Motto,* Victoria

THE SOVEREIGN
GRAND MASTER
HM Queen Elizabeth the Queen Mother
*Chancellor,* The Lord Chamberlain
*Secretary,* The Keeper of the Privy Purse
*Registrar,* The Secretary of the Central Chancery of the Orders of Knighthood
*Chaplain,* The Revd J. Robson
*Hon. Genealogist,* D. H. B. Chesshyre, LVO

## THE MOST EXCELLENT ORDER OF THE BRITISH EMPIRE (1917)

GBE                KBE

The Order was divided into military and civil divisions in December 1918

GBE   Knight or Dame Grand Cross
KBE   Knight Commander
DBE   Dame Commander
CBE   Commander
OBE   Officer
MBE   Member

*Ribbon*, Rose pink edged with pearl grey with vertical pearl stripe in centre (military division); without vertical pearl stripe (civil division)
*Motto*, For God and the Empire

THE SOVEREIGN

GRAND MASTER
HRH The Prince Philip, Duke of Edinburgh, KG, KT, OM, GBE, PC, FRS
*Prelate*, The Bishop of London
*King of Arms*, Adm. Sir Anthony Morton, GBE, KCB
*Registrar*, The Secretary of the Central Chancery of the Orders of Knighthood
*Secretary*, Sir Robin Butler, GCB, CVO
*Dean*, The Dean of St Paul's
*Gentleman Usher of the Purple Rod*, Sir Robin Gillett, Bt., GBE, RD
*Chancery*, Central Chancery of the Orders of Knighthood, St James's Palace, London SW1A 1BH

## ORDER OF THE COMPANIONS OF HONOUR (1917)

CH

*Ribbon*, Carmine, with gold edges
This Order consists of one class only and carries with it no title. The number of awards is limited to 65 (excluding honorary members)

Anthony, Rt. Hon. John, 1981
Ashley of Stoke, The Lord, 1975
Astor, Hon. David, 1993
Baker, Dame Janet, 1993
Baker, Rt. Hon. Kenneth, 1992
Brenner, Sydney, 1986
Brooke, Rt. Hon. Peter, 1992

Carrington, The Lord, 1983
Casson, Sir Hugh, 1984
Cledwyn of Penrhos, The Lord, 1976
de Valois, Dame Ninette, 1981
Eccles, The Viscount, 1984
Fraser, Rt. Hon. Malcolm, 1977
Freud, Lucian, 1983
Gielgud, Sir John, 1977
Glenamara, The Lord, 1976
Goodman, The Lord, 1972
Gorton, Rt. Hon. Sir John, 1971
Guinness, Sir Alec, 1994
Hailsham of St Marylebone, The Lord, 1974
Hawking, Prof. Stephen, 1989
Healey, The Lord, 1979
Houghton of Sowerby, The Lord, 1967
Jones, James, 1977
Jones, Prof. Reginald, 1994
Joseph, The Lord, 1986
King, Rt. Hon. Tom, 1992
Lange, Rt. Hon. David, 1989
Needham, Joseph, 1992
Owen, The Lord, 1994
Pasmore, Victor, 1980
Perutz, Prof. Max, 1975
Powell, Anthony, 1987
Powell, Sir Philip, 1984
Pritchett, Sir Victor, 1992
Runciman, Hon. Sir Steven, 1984
Rylands, George, 1987
Sanger, Frederick, 1981
Sisson, Charles, 1993
Smith, Sir John, 1993
Somare, Rt. Hon. Sir Michael, 1978
Talboys, Rt. Hon. Sir Brian, 1981
Tebbit, The Lord, 1987
Tippett, Sir Michael, 1979
Trudeau, Rt. Hon. Pierre, 1984
Watkinson, The Viscount, 1962
Whitelaw, The Viscount, 1974
Widdowson, Dr Elsie, 1993
*Honorary Members*, Lee Kuan Yew, 1970; Dr Joseph Luns, 1971

*Secretary and Registrar*, The Secretary of the Central Chancery of the Orders of Knighthood

## THE DISTINGUISHED SERVICE ORDER (1886)

DSO

*Ribbon*, Red, with blue edges

Bestowed in recognition of especial services in action of commissioned officers in the Navy, Army and Royal Air Force and (since 1942) Mercantile Marine. The members are Companions only. A Bar may be awarded for any additional act of service

## THE IMPERIAL SERVICE ORDER (1902)

ISO

*Ribbon*, Crimson, with blue centre
Appointment as Companion of this Order is open to members of the Civil Services whose eligibility is determined by the grade they hold. The Order consists of The Sovereign and Companions to a number not exceeding 1,900, of whom 1,300 may belong to the Home Civil Services and 600 to Overseas Civil Services. The Prime Minister announced in March 1993 that no further recommendations for appointments to the Order will be made.

*Secretary*, Sir Robin Butler, GCB, CVO
*Registrar*, The Secretary of the Central Chancery of the Orders of Knighthood, St James's Palace, London SW1A 1BH

## THE ROYAL VICTORIAN CHAIN (1902)

It confers no precedence on its holders

HM THE QUEEN
HM Queen Elizabeth the Queen Mother, 1937
HRH Princess Juliana of the Netherlands, 1950
HM The King of Thailand, 1960
HIH The Crown Prince of Ethiopia, 1965
HM The King of Jordan, 1966
HM King Zahir Shah of Afghanistan, 1971
HM The Queen of Denmark, 1974
HM The King of Nepal, 1975
HM The King of Sweden, 1975
The Lord Coggan, 1980
HM The Queen of the Netherlands, 1982
Gen. Antonio Eanes, 1985
HM The King of Spain, 1986
HM The King of Saudi Arabia, 1987
HRH The Princess Margaret, Countess of Snowdon, 1990
The Lord Runcie, 1991
The Lord Charteris of Amisfield, 1992
HE François Mitterrand, 1992
HE Richard von Weizsäcker, 1992
HM The King of Norway, 1994

# Baronetage and Knightage

## BARONETS

*Style,* 'Sir' before forename and surname, followed by 'Bt.'
*Wife's style,* 'Lady' followed by surname
For forms of address, *see* page 217

There are five different creations of Baronetcies: Baronets of England (creations dating from 1611); Baronets of Ireland (creations dating from 1619); Baronets of Scotland or Nova Scotia (creations dating from 1625); Baronets of Great Britain (creations after the Act of Union 1707 which combined the kingdoms of England and Scotland); and Baronets of the United Kingdom (creations after the union of Great Britain and Ireland in 1801).

*Badge of Ulster*          *Badge of Baronets of Nova Scotia*

*Badge of Baronets of the United Kingdom*

The patent of creation limits the destination of a baronetcy, usually to male descendants of the first baronet, although special remainders allow the baronetcy to pass, if the male issue of sons fail, to the male issue of daughters of the first baronet. In the case of baronetcies of Scotland or Nova Scotia, a special remainder of 'heirs male and of tailzie' allows the baronetcy to descend to heirs general, including women. There are four existing Scottish baronets with such a remainder, one of whom, the holder of the Dunbar of Hempriggs creation, is a Baronetess.

The Official Roll of Baronets is kept at the Home Office by the Registrar of the Baronetage. Anyone who considers that he is entitled to be entered on the Roll may petition the Crown through the Home Secretary. Every person succeeding to a baronetcy must exhibit proofs of succession to the Home Secretary. A person whose name is not entered on the Official Roll will not be addressed or mentioned by the title of baronet in any official document, nor will he be accorded precedence as a baronet.

BARONETCIES EXTINCT SINCE THE LAST EDITION
Astley (*cr.* 1821), Beit (*cr.* 1924), Christison (*cr.* 1871), Hope (*cr.* 1932), Hulton (*cr.* 1905), Neville (*cr.* 1927), Nugent (*cr.* 1960) by the death of Lord Nugent of Guildford

*Registrar of the Baronetage,* R. M. Morris
*Assistant Registrar,* Mrs F. G. Bright
*Office,* Home Office, Queen Anne's Gate, London SW1H 9AT. Tel: 0171-273 3498

## KNIGHTS

*Style,* 'Sir' before forename and surname, followed by appropriate post-nominal initials if a Knight Grand Cross, Knight Grand Commander or Knight Commander

*Wife's style,* 'Lady' followed by surname
For forms of address, *see* page 217
The prefix 'Sir' is not used by knights who are clerics of the Church of England, who do not receive the accolade. Their wives are entitled to precedence as the wife of a knight but not to the style of 'Lady'.

### ORDERS OF KNIGHTHOOD

Knight Grand Cross, Knight Grand Commander, and Knight Commander are the higher classes of the Orders of Chivalry (*see* pages 174–6). Honorary knighthoods of these Orders may be conferred on men who are citizens of countries of which The Queen is not head of state. As a rule, the prefix 'Sir' is not used by honorary knights.

### KNIGHTS BACHELOR

The Knights Bachelor do not constitute a Royal Order, but comprise the surviving representation of the ancient State Orders of Knighthood. The Register of Knights Bachelor, instituted by James I in the 17th century, lapsed, and in 1908 a voluntary association under the title of The Society of Knights (now The Imperial Society of Knights Bachelor by royal command) was formed with the primary objects of continuing the various registers dating from 1257 and obtaining the uniform registration of every created Knight Bachelor. In 1926 a design for a badge to be worn by Knights Bachelor was approved and adopted; in 1974 a neck badge and miniature were added.

*Knight Principal,* Col. Sir Colin Cole, KCB, KCVO, TD
*Chairman of Council,* Sir David Napley
*Prelate,* Rt. Revd and Rt. Hon. The Bishop of London
*Hon. Registrar,* Sir Kenneth Newman, GBE, QPM
*Hon. Treasurer,* The Lord Lane of Horsell
*Clerk to the Council,* R. M. Esden
*Office,* 21 Old Buildings, Lincoln's Inn, London WC2A 3UJ

## LIST OF BARONETS AND KNIGHTS
*Revised to 31 August 1994*

Peers are not included in this list

†   Not registered on the Official Roll of the Baronetage at the time of going to press
( )   The date of creation of the baronetcy is given in parenthesis
I   Baronet of Ireland
NS   Baronet of Nova Scotia
S   Baronet of Scotland

If a baronet or knight has a double barrelled or hyphenated surname, he is listed under the final element of the name
*A full entry in italic type* indicates that the recipient of a knighthood died during the year in which the honour was conferred. The name is included for purposes of record

Abal, Sir Tei, Kt., CBE
Abbott, Sir Albert Francis, Kt., CBE
Abbott, *Vice-Adm.* Sir Peter Charles, KCB
Abdy, Sir Valentine Robert Duff, Bt. (1850)
Abel, Sir Seselo (Cecil) Charles Geoffrey, Kt., OBE
Abeles, Sir (Emil Herbert) Peter, Kt.
Abell, Sir Anthony Foster, KCMG
Abercromby, Sir Ian George, Bt. (s. 1636)
Abraham, Sir Edward Penley, Kt., CBE, FRS
Acheson, *Prof.* Sir (Ernest) Donald, KBE
Ackers, Sir James George, Kt.
Ackroyd, Sir John Robert Whyte, Bt. (1956)
Acland, Sir Antony Arthur, GCMG, GCVO
Acland, *Lt.-Col.* Sir (Christopher) Guy (Dyke), Bt., MVO (1890)
Acland, Sir John Dyke, Bt. (1644)
Acland, *Maj.-Gen.* Sir John Hugh Bevil, KCB, CBE
Adam, Sir Christopher Eric Forbes, Bt. (1917)
Adams, Sir Philip George Doyne, KCMG
Adams, Sir William James, KCMG
Adamson, Sir (William Owen) Campbell, Kt.
Adrien, *Hon.* Sir Maurice Latour-, Kt.
Adye, Sir John Anthony, KCMG
Agnew, Sir Crispin Hamlyn, Bt. (s. 1629)
†Agnew, Sir John Keith, Bt. (1895)
Agnew, Sir (William) Godfrey, KCVO, CB
Aiken, *Air Chief Marshal* Sir John Alexander Carlisle, KCB
Ainsworth, Sir (Thomas) David, Bt. (1916)
Aird, *Capt.* Sir Alastair Sturgis, KCVO
Aird, Sir (George) John, Bt. (1901)
Airey, Sir Lawrence, KCB
Airy, *Maj.-Gen.* Sir Christopher John, KCVO, CVO
Aitchison, Sir Charles Walter de Lancey, Bt. (1938)
Aitken, Sir Robert Stevenson, Kt., MD, D.Phil.
Akehurst, *Gen.* Sir John Bryan, KCB, CBE
Albert, Sir Alexis François, Kt., CMG, VRD
Albu, Sir George, Bt. (1912)
Alcock, *Air Chief Marshal* Sir (Robert James) Michael, KBE, CB
Aldous, *Hon.* Sir William, Kt.
Alexander, Sir Charles Gundry, Bt. (1945)
Alexander, Sir Claud Hagart-, Bt. (1886)
Alexander, Sir Douglas, Bt. (1921)
Alexander, Sir (John) Lindsay, Kt.
Alexander, *Prof.* Sir Kenneth John Wilson, Kt.

Alexander, Sir Michael O'Donal Bjarne, GCMG
Alexander, Sir Norman Stanley, Kt., CBE
†Alexander, Sir Patrick Desmond William Cable-, Bt. (1809)
Allan, Sir Anthony James Allan Havelock-, Bt. (1858)
Allard, Sir Gordon Laidlaw, Kt.
Allen, *Rear-Adm.* Sir David, KCVO, CBE
Allen, *Prof.* Sir Geoffrey, Kt., Ph.D., FRS
Allen, *Hon.* Sir Peter Austin Philip Jermyn, Kt.
Allen, Sir Richard Hugh Sedley, KCMG
Allen, Sir William Guilford, Kt.
Allen, Sir (William) Kenneth (Gwynne), Kt.
Alleyne, Sir George Allanmoore Ogarren, Kt.
Alleyne, *Revd* Sir John Olpherts Campbell, Bt. (1769)
Alliance, Sir David, Kt., CBE
Allinson, Sir (Walter) Leonard, KCVO, CMG
Alliott, *Hon.* Sir John Downes, Kt.
Alment, Sir (Edward) Anthony John, Kt.
Althaus, Sir Nigel Frederick, Kt.
Ambo, *Rt. Revd* George, KBE
Amet, *Hon.* Sir Arnold Karibone, Kt.
Amies, Sir (Edwin) Hardy, KCVO
Amis, Sir Kingsley William, Kt., CBE
Amory, Sir Ian Heathcoat, Bt. (1874)
Anderson, *Prof.* Sir (James) Norman (Dalrymple), Kt., OBE, QC, FBA
Anderson, *Maj.-Gen.* Sir John Evelyn, KBE
Anderson, Sir John Muir, Kt., CMG
Anderson, *Hon.* Sir Kevin Victor, Kt.
Anderson, *Vice-Adm.* Sir Neil Dudley, KBE, CB
Anderson, *Prof.* Sir (William) Ferguson, Kt., OBE
Anderton, Sir (Cyril) James, Kt., CBE, QPM
Andrew, Sir Robert John, KCB
Andrews, Sir Derek Henry, KCB, CBE
Andrews, *Hon.* Sir Dormer George, Kt.
Angus, Sir Michael Richardson, Kt.
Annesley, Sir Hugh Norman, Kt., QPM
Ansell, *Col.* Sir Michael Picton, Kt., CBE, DSO
Anson, *Vice-Adm.* Sir Edward Rosebery, KCB
Anson, Sir John, KCB
Anson, *Rear-Adm.* Sir Peter, Bt., CB (1831)
Anstey, *Brig.* Sir John, Kt., CBE, TD
Anstruther, *Maj.* Sir Ralph Hugo, Bt. GCVO, MC (s. 1694)
Antico, Sir Tristan Venus, Kt.
Antrobus, Sir Philip Coutts, Bt. (1815)
Appleyard, Sir Leonard Vincent, KCMG
Appleyard, Sir Raymond Kenelm, KBE

Arbuthnot, Sir Keith Robert Charles, Bt. (1823)
Arbuthnot, Sir William Reierson, Bt. (1964)
Archdale, *Capt.* Sir Edward Folmer, Bt., DSC, RN (1928)
Archer, *Gen.* Sir (Arthur) John, KCB, OBE
Arculus, Sir Ronald, KCMG, KCVO
Armitage, *Air Chief Marshal* Sir Michael John, KCB, CBE
Armstrong, Sir Andrew Clarence Francis, Bt., CMG (1841)
Armytage, Sir John Martin, Bt. (1738)
Arnold, *Rt. Hon.* Sir John Lewis, Kt.
Arnold, Sir Malcolm Henry, Kt., CBE
Arnold, Sir Thomas Richard, Kt., MP
Arnott, Sir Alexander John Maxwell, Bt. (1896)
Arnott, *Prof.* Sir (William) Melville, Kt., TD, MD
Arrindell, Sir Clement Athelston, GCMG, GCVO, QC
Arthur, *Lt.-Gen.* Sir (John) Norman Stewart, KCB
Arthur, Sir Stephen John, Bt. (1841)
Ash, *Prof.* Sir Eric Albert, Kt., CBE, FRS, FEng.
Ashburnham, Sir Denny Reginald, Bt. (1661)
Ashe, Sir Derick Rosslyn, KCMG
Ashley, Sir Bernard Albert, Kt.
Ashmore, *Admiral of the Fleet* Sir Edward Beckwith, GCB, DSC
Ashmore, *Vice-Adm.* Sir Peter William Beckwith, KCB, KCVO, DSC
Ashworth, Sir Herbert, Kt.
Aske, *Revd* Sir Conan, Bt. (1922)
Askew, Sir Bryan, Kt.
Asscher, *Prof.* Sir (Adolf) William, Kt., MD, FRCP
Aston, Sir Harold George, Kt., CBE
Aston, *Hon.* Sir William John, KCMG
Astor, *Hon.* Sir John Jacob, Kt., MBE
Astwood, *Hon.* Sir James Rufus, KBE
Astwood, *Lt.-Col.* Sir Jeffrey Carlton, Kt., CBE, ED
Atcherley, Sir Harold Winter, Kt.
Atiyah, Sir Michael Francis, Kt., OM, Ph.D., FRS
Atkinson, *Air Marshal* Sir David William, KBE
Atkinson, Sir Frederick John, KCB
Atkinson, Sir John Alexander, KCB, DFC
Atkinson, Sir Robert, Kt., DSC, FEng.
Attenborough, Sir David Frederick, Kt., CVO, CBE, FRS
Atwell, Sir John William, Kt., CBE, FRSE, FEng.
Atwill, Sir (Milton) John (Napier), Kt.
Audland, Sir Christopher John, KCMG
Audley, Sir George Bernard, Kt.
Auld, *Hon.* Sir Robin Ernest, Kt.
Austin, Sir Michael Trescawen, Bt. (1894)
Austin, *Vice-Adm.* Sir Peter Murray, KCB

Austin, *Air Marshal* Sir Roger Mark, KCB, AFC

†Aykroyd, Sir James Alexander Frederic, Bt. (1929)

Aykroyd, Sir William Miles, Bt., MC (1920)

Aylmer, Sir Richard John, Bt. (I. 1622)

Bacha, Sir Bhinod, Kt., CMG

Backhouse, Sir Jonathan Roger, Bt. (1901)

Bacon, Sir Nicholas Hickman Ponsonby, Bt. *Premier Baronet of England* (1611 and 1627)

Bacon, Sir Sidney Charles, Kt., CB, FEng.

Baddeley, Sir John Wolsey Beresford, Bt. (1922)

Baddiley, *Prof.* Sir James, Kt., PH.D., D.SC., FRS, FRSE

Badenoch, Sir John, Kt., DM, FRCP

Badger, Sir Geoffrey Malcolm, Kt.

Bagge, Sir (John) Jeremy Picton, Bt. (1867)

Bagnall, *Field Marshal* Sir Nigel Thomas, GCB, CVO, MC

Bailey, Sir Alan Marshall, KCB

Bailey, Sir Brian Harry, Kt., OBE

Bailey, Sir Derrick Thomas Louis, Bt., DFC (1919)

Bailey, *Prof.* Sir Harold Walter, Kt., D.Phil., FBA

Bailey, Sir John Bilsland, KCB

Bailey, Sir Richard John, Kt., CBE

Bailey, Sir Stanley Ernest, Kt., CBE, QPM

Baillie, Sir Gawaine George Hope, Bt. (1823)

Baines, *Prof.* Sir George Grenfell-, Kt., OBE

Baird, Sir David Charles, Bt. (1809)

Baird, *Lt.-Gen.* Sir James Parlane, KBE, MD

Baird, Sir James Richard Gardiner, Bt., MC (S. 1695)

Baird, *Vice-Adm.* Sir Thomas Henry Eustace, KCB

Bairsto, *Air Marshal* Sir Peter Edward, KBE, CB

Baker, Sir Robert George Humphrey Sherston-, Bt. (1796)

Baker, *Hon.* Sir (Thomas) Scott (Gillespie), Kt.

Balchin, Sir Robert George Alexander, Kt.

Balcombe, *Rt. Hon.* Sir (Alfred) John, Kt.

Balderstone, Sir James Schofield, Kt.

Baldwin, Sir Peter Robert, KCB

Balfour, *Gen.* Sir (Robert George) Victor FitzGeorge-, KCB, CBE, DSO, MC

Ball, *Air Marshal* Sir Alfred Henry Wynne, KCB, DSO, DFC

Ball, Sir Charles Irwin, Bt. (1911)

Ball, Sir Christopher John Elinger, Kt.

Ball, *Prof.* Sir Robert James, Kt., PH.D.

Balmer, Sir Joseph Reginald, Kt.

Bamford, Sir Anthony Paul, Kt.

Banham, Sir John Michael Middlecott, Kt.

Bannerman, Sir David Gordon, Bt., OBE (S. 1682)

Bannister, Sir Roger Gilbert, Kt., CBE, DM, FRCP

Barber, Sir William Francis, Bt., TD (1960)

Barbour, *Very Revd* Sir Robert Alexander Stewart, KCVO, MC

Barclay, Sir Colville Herbert Sanford, Bt. (S. 1668)

Barclay, Sir Peter Maurice, Kt., CBE

Barclay, Sir Roderick Edward, GCVO, KCMG

Barder, Sir Brian Leon, KCMG

Barker, Sir Alwyn Bowman, Kt., CMG

Barker, Sir Colin, Kt.

Barker, Sir Harry Heaton, Kt., KBE

Barker, *Hon.* Sir (Richard) Ian, Kt.

Barlow, Sir Christopher Hilaro, Bt. (1803)

Barlow, Sir (George) William, Kt., FEng.

Barlow, Sir John Kemp, Bt. (1907)

Barlow, Sir Thomas Erasmus, Bt., DSC (1902)

Barnard, Sir (Arthur) Thomas, Kt., CB, OBE

Barnard, *Capt.* Sir George Edward, Kt.

Barnard, Sir Joseph Brian, Kt.

Barnes, Sir James George, Kt., MBE

Barnes, Sir Kenneth, KCB

Barnett, Sir Oliver Charles, Kt., CBE, QC

Barnewall, Sir Reginald Robert, Bt. (I. 1623)

Baron, Sir Thomas, Kt., CBE

Barraclough, *Air Chief Marshal* Sir John, KCB, CBE, DFC, AFC

Barraclough, Sir Kenneth James Priestley, Kt., CBE, TD

Barran, Sir David Haven, Kt.

Barran, Sir John Napoleon Ruthven, Bt. (1895)

Barratt, Sir Lawrence Arthur, Kt.

Barratt, Sir Richard Stanley, Kt., CBE, QPM

Barrett, *Lt.-Gen.* Sir David William Scott-, KBE, MC

Barrett, *Lt.-Col.* Sir Dennis Charles Titchener, Kt., TD

Barrett, Sir Stephen Jeremy, KCMG

Barrington, Sir Alexander (Fitzwilliam Croker), Bt. (1831)

Barrington, Sir Nicholas John, KCMG, CVO

Barron, Sir Donald James, Kt.

Barrow, *Capt.* Sir Richard John Uniacke, Bt. (1835)

Barrowclough, Sir Anthony Richard, Kt., QC

Barry, Sir (Lawrence) Edward (Anthony Tress), Bt. (1899)

Barry, Sir (Philip) Stuart Milner-, KCVO, CB, OBE

Bartlett, Sir John Hardington, Bt. (1913)

Barton, *Prof.* Sir Derek Harold Richard, Kt., FRS, FRSE

Barttelot, *Col.* Sir Brian Walter de Stopham, Bt., OBE (1875)

Barwick, *Rt. Hon.* Sir Garfield Edward John, GCMG

Batchelor, Sir Ivor Ralph Campbell, Kt., CBE

Bate, Sir David Lindsay, KBE

Bate, Sir (Walter) Edwin, Kt., OBE

Bateman, Sir Cecil Joseph, KBE

Bateman, Sir Geoffrey Hirst, Kt., FRCS

Bateman, Sir Ralph Melton, KBE

Bates, Sir Geoffrey Voltelin, Bt., MC (1880)

Bates, Sir (John) Dawson, Bt., MC (1937)

Batho, Sir Peter Ghislain, Bt. (1928)

Bathurst, *Adm.* Sir (David) Benjamin, GCB

Bathurst, Sir Frederick Peter Methuen Hervey-, Bt. (1818)

Bathurst, Sir Maurice Edward, Kt., CMG, CBE, QC

Batten, Sir John Charles, KCVO

Battersby, *Prof.* Sir Alan Rushton, Kt., FRS

Battishill, Sir Anthony Michael William, KCB

Batty, Sir William Bradshaw, Kt., TD

Baxendell, Sir Peter Brian, Kt., CBE, FEng.

Bayliss, *Prof.* Sir Noel Stanley, Kt., CBE

Bayliss, Sir Richard Ian Samuel, KCVO, MD, FRCP

Bayly, *Vice-Adm.* Sir Patrick Uniacke, KBE, CB, DSC

Bayne, Sir Nicholas Peter, KCMG

Baynes, Sir John Christopher Malcolm, Bt. (1801)

Bazley, Sir Thomas Stafford, Bt. (1869)

Beach, *Gen.* Sir (William Gerald) Hugh, GBE, KCB, MC

Beale, *Lt.-Gen.* Sir Peter John, KBE, FRCP

Beament, Sir James William Longman, Kt., SC.D., FRS

Beattie, *Hon.* Sir Alexander Craig, Kt.

Beattie, *Hon.* Sir David Stuart, GCMG, GCVO

Beauchamp, Sir Christopher Radstock Proctor-, Bt. (1745)

Beaumont, *Capt.* the Hon. Sir (Edward) Nicholas (Canning), KCVO

Beaumont, Sir George (Howland Francis), Bt. (1661)

Beaumont, Sir Richard Ashton, KCMG, OBE

Beavis, *Air Chief Marshal* Sir Michael Gordon, KCB, CBE, AFC

Becher, Sir William Fane Wrixon, Bt., MC (1831)

Beck, Sir Edgar Charles, Kt., CBE, FEng.

Beck, Sir Edgar Philip, Kt.

Beckett, *Capt.* Sir (Martyn) Gervase, Bt., MC (1921)

Beckett, Sir Terence Norman, KBE, FEng.

Bedingfeld, *Capt.* Sir Edmund George Felix Paston-, Bt. (1661)

Beecham, Sir Jeremy Hugh, Kt.

Beecham, Sir John Stratford Roland, Bt. (1914)

Beeley, Sir Harold, KCMG, CBE

Beetham, *Marshal of the Royal Air Force* Sir Michael James, GCB, CBE, DFC, AFC

Beevor, Sir Thomas Agnew, Bt. (1784)

Begg, Sir Neil Colquhoun, KBE

Begg, *Admiral of the Fleet* Sir Varyl Cargill, GCB, DSO, DSC

Beith, Sir John Greville Stanley, KCMG

Belch, Sir Alexander Ross, Kt., CBE, FRSE

Beldam, *Rt. Hon.* Sir (Alexander) Roy (Asplan), Kt.

Belich, Sir James, Kt.

Bell, Sir Brian Ernest, KBE

Bell, Sir Gawain Westray, KCMG, CBE

Bell, Sir (George) Raymond, KCMG, CB

Bell, Sir John Lowthian, Bt. (1885)

Bell, *Hon.* Sir Rodger, Kt.

Bell, Sir Timothy John Leigh, Kt.

Bell, Sir (William) Ewart, KCB

Bell, Sir William Hollin Dayrell Morrison-, Bt. (1905)

Bellew, Sir Henry Charles Gratton-, Bt. (1838)

Bellinger, Sir Robert Ian, GBE

Bellingham, Sir Noel Peter Roger, Bt. (1796)

Bengough, *Col.* Sir Piers, KCVO, OBE

Benn, Sir (James) Jonathan, Bt. (1914)

Bennett, Sir Charles Moihi Te Arawaka, Kt., DSO

Bennett, *Air Vice-Marshal* Sir Erik Peter, KBE, CB

Bennett, *Rt. Hon.* Sir Frederic Mackarness, Kt.

Bennett, Sir Hubert, Kt.

Bennett, Sir John Mokonuiarangi, Kt.

Bennett, *Gen.* Sir Phillip Harvey, KBE, DSO

Bennett, Sir Reginald Frederick Brittain, Kt., VRD

Bennett, Sir Ronald Wilfrid Murdoch, Bt. (1929)

Benson, Sir Christopher John, Kt.

Benson, Sir (William) Jeffrey, Kt.

Bentley, Sir William, KCMG

Benyon, Sir William Richard, Kt.

Beresford, Sir (Alexander) Paul, Kt., MP

Berger, *Vice-Adm.* Sir Peter Egerton Capel, KCB, MVO, DSC

Berghuser, *Hon.* Sir Eric, Kt., MBE

Berlin, Sir Isaiah, Kt., OM, CBE

Berman, Sir Franklin Delow, KCMG

Bernard, Sir Dallas Edmund, Bt. (1954)

Berney, Sir Julian Reedham Stuart, Bt. (1620)

Berrill, Sir Kenneth Ernest, GBE, KCB

Berriman, Sir David, Kt.

Berry, *Prof.* Sir Colin Leonard, Kt., FRCPath.

Berthon, *Vice-Adm.* Sir Stephen Ferrier, KCB

Berthoud, Sir Martin Seymour, KCVO, CMG

Best, Sir Richard Radford, KCVO, CBE

Bethune, Sir Alexander Maitland Sharp, Bt. (s. 1683)

Bethune, *Hon.* Sir (Walter) Angus, Kt.

Bevan, Sir Martyn Evan Evans, Bt. (1958)

Bevan, Sir Timothy Hugh, Kt.

Beveridge, Sir Gordon Smith Grieve, Kt., FRSE, F.Eng., FRSA

Beverley, *Lt.-Gen.* Sir Henry York La Roche, KCB, OBE, RM

Beynon, *Prof.* Sir (William John) Granville, Kt., CBE, ph.D., D.SC., FRS

Bibby, Sir Derek James, Bt., MC (1959)

Bickersteth, *Rt. Revd* John Monier, KCVO

Biddulph, Sir Ian D'Olier, Bt. (1664)

Bide, Sir Austin Ernest, Kt.

Bidwell, Sir Hugh Charles Philip, GBE

Biggam, Sir Robin Adair, Kt.

Biggs, *Vice-Adm.* Sir Geoffrey William Roger, KCB

Biggs, Sir Norman Paris, Kt.

Bilas, Sir Angmai Simon, Kt., OBE

Billière, *Gen.* Sir Peter Edgar de la Cour de la, KCB, KBE, DSO, MC

Bing, Sir Rudolf Franz Josef, KBE

Bingham, *Hon.* Sir Eardley Max, Kt., QC

Bingham, *Rt. Hon.* Sir Thomas Henry, Kt.

Birch, Sir John Allan, KCVO, CMG

Birch, Sir Roger, Kt., CBE, QPM

Bird, Sir Richard Geoffrey Chapman, Bt. (1922)

Birkin, Sir John Christian William, Bt. (1905)

Birkin, Sir (John) Derek, Kt., TD

Birkmyre, Sir Archibald, Bt. (1921)

Birley, Sir Derek Sydney, Kt.

Birrell, Sir James Drake, Kt.

Birtwistle, Sir Harrison, Kt.

Bishop, Sir Frederick Arthur, Kt., CB, CVO

Bishop, Sir George Sidney, Kt., CB, OBE

Bishop, Sir Michael David, Kt., CBE

Bisson, *Rt Hon.* Sir Gordon Ellis, Kt.

Black, *Prof.* Sir Douglas Andrew Kilgour, Kt., MD, FRCP

Black, Sir James Whyte, Kt., FRCP, FRS

Black, *Adm.* Sir (John) Jeremy, GCB, DSO, MBE

Black, Sir Robert Brown, GCMG, OBE

Black, Sir Robert David, Bt. (1922)

Blackburne, *Hon.* Sir William Anthony, Kt.

Blacker, *Gen.* Sir (Anthony Stephen) Jeremy, KCB, CBE

Blacker, *Gen.* Sir Cecil Hugh, GCB, OBE, MC

†Blackett, *Maj.* Sir Francis Hugh, Bt. (1673)

Blacklock, *Surgeon Capt. Prof.* Sir Norman James, KCVO, OBE

Blackman, Sir Frank Milton, KCVO, OBE

Blackwell, Sir Basil Davenport, Kt., FEng.

Blackwood, Sir John Francis, Bt. (1814)

Blair, Sir Alastair Campbell, KCVO, TD, WS

Blair, *Lt.-Gen.* Sir Chandos, KCVO, OBE, MC

Blair, Sir Edward Thomas Hunter, Bt. (1786)

Blake, Sir Alfred Lapthorn, KCVO, MC

Blake, Sir Francis Michael, Bt. (1907)

Blake, Sir (Thomas) Richard (Valentine), Bt. (I. 1622)

Blaker, Sir John, Bt. (1919)

Blaker, *Rt. Hon.* Sir Peter Allan Renshaw, KCMG

Blakiston, Sir Ferguson Arthur James, Bt. (1763)

Bland, Sir (Francis) Christopher (Buchan), Kt.

Bland, Sir Henry Armand, Kt., CBE

Bland, *Lt.-Col.* Sir Simon Claud Michael, KCVO

Blelloch, Sir John Nial Henderson, KCB

Blennerhassett, Sir (Marmaduke) Adrian Francis William, Bt. (1809)

Blewitt, *Maj.* Sir Shane Gabriel Basil, KCVO

Blofield, *Hon.* Sir John Christopher Calthorpe, Kt.

Blois, Sir Charles Nicholas Gervase, Bt. (1686)

Blomefield, Sir Thomas Charles Peregrine, Bt. (1807)

Bloomfield, Sir Kenneth Percy, KCB

Blosse, *Capt.* Sir Richard Hely Lynch-, Bt. (1622)

Blount, Sir Walter Edward Alpin, Bt., DSC (1642)

Blunden, Sir George, Kt.

†Blunden, Sir Philip Overington, Bt. (I. 1766)

Blunt, Sir David Richard Reginald Harvey, Bt. (1720)

Blyth, Sir James, Kt.

Boardman, *Prof.* Sir John, Kt., FSA, FBA

Boardman, Sir Kenneth Ormrod, Kt.

Bodilly, *Hon.* Sir Jocelyn, Kt., VRD

Bodmer, Sir Walter Fred, Kt., ph.D., FRS

Body, Sir Richard Bernard Frank Stewart, Kt., MP

Boevey, Sir Thomas Michael Blake Crawley-, Bt. (1784)

Bogarde, Sir Dirk (Derek Niven van den Bogaerde), Kt.

Boileau, Sir Guy (Francis), Bt. (1838)

Boles, Sir Jeremy John Fortescue, Bt. (1922)

Boles, Sir John Dennis, Kt., MBE

Bolland, Sir Edwin, KCMG

Bollers, *Hon.* Sir Harold Brodie Smith, Kt.

Bolton, Sir Frederic Bernard, Kt., MC

Bona, Sir Kina, KBE

Bonallack, Sir Richard Frank, Kt., CBE

Bond, Sir Kenneth Raymond Boyden, Kt.

Bondi, *Prof.* Sir Hermann, KCB, FRS

Bonham, *Maj.* Sir Antony Lionel Thomas, Bt. (1852)

Bonsall, Sir Arthur Wilfred, KCMG, CBE

Bonsor, Sir Nicholas Cosmo, Bt., MP (1925)

Boolell, Sir Satcam, Kt.

Boon, Sir Peter Coleman, Kt.

Boord, Sir Nicolas John Charles, Bt. (1896)

Boorman, *Lt.-Gen.* Sir Derek, KCB

Booth, Sir Angus Josslyn Gore-, Bt. (I. 1760)

Booth, Sir Christopher Charles, Kt., MD, FRCP

Booth, Sir Douglas Allen, Bt. (1916)

Booth, Sir Gordon, KCMG, CVO

Booth, Sir Michael Addison John Wheeler-, KCB

Booth, Sir Robert Camm, Kt., CBE, TD

Boothby, Sir Brooke Charles, Bt. (1660)

Boreel, Sir Francis David, Bt. (1645)

Boreham, *Hon.* Sir Leslie Kenneth Edward, Kt.

Bornu, The Waziri of, KCMG, CBE

Borrie, Sir Gordon Johnson, Kt., QC

Borthwick, Sir John Thomas, Bt. MBE (1908)

Bossom, *Hon.* Sir Clive, Bt. (1953)

Boswall, Sir (Thomas) Alford Houstoun-, Bt. (1836)

Boswell, *Lt.-Gen.* Sir Alexander Crawford Simpson, KCB, CBE

Bosworth, Sir Neville Bruce Alfred, Kt., CBE

Bottomley, Sir James Reginald Alfred, KCMG

Boughey, Sir John George Fletcher, Bt. (1798)

Boulton, Sir Clifford John, GCB

Boulton, Sir (Harold Hugh) Christian, Bt. (1905)

Boulton, Sir William Whytehead, Bt., CBE, TD (1944)

Bourn, Sir John Bryant, KCB

Bourne, Sir (John) Wilfrid, KCB

Bovell, *Hon.* Sir (William) Stewart, Kt.

Bowater, Sir Euan David Vansittart, Bt. (1939)

Bowater, Sir (John) Vansittart, Bt. (1914)

Bowden, Sir Andrew, Kt., MBE, MP

Bowden, Sir Frank, Bt. (1915)

Bowen, Sir Geoffrey Fraser, Kt.

Bowen, Sir Mark Edward Mortimer, Bt. (1921)

Bowen, *Hon.* Sir Nigel Hubert, KBE

†Bowlby, Sir Richard Peregrine Longstaff, Bt. (1923)

Bowman, Sir Jeffery Haverstock, Kt.

†Bowman, Sir Paul Humphrey Armytage, Bt. (1884)

Bowmar, Sir Charles Erskine, Kt.

Bowness, Sir Alan, Kt., CBE

Bowness, Sir Peter Spencer, Kt., CBE

Boxer, *Air Vice-Marshal* Sir Alan Hunter Cachemaille, KCVO, CB, DSO, DFC

Boyce, Sir Robert Charles Leslie, Bt. (1952)

Boyd, Sir Alexander Walter, Bt. (1916)

Boyd, Sir John Dixon Iklé, KCMG

Boyd, Sir (John) Francis, Kt.

Boyd, The Hon. Sir Mark Alexander Lennox-, Kt., MP

Boyd, *Prof.* Sir Robert Lewis Fullarton, Kt., CBE, D.SC., FRS

Boyes, Sir Brian Gerald Barratt-, KBE

Boyle, Sir Stephen Gurney, Bt. (1904)

Boyne, Sir Henry Brian, Kt., CBE

Boynton, Sir John Keyworth, Kt., MC

Boyson, *Rt. Hon.* Sir Rhodes, Kt., MP

Brabham, Sir John Arthur, Kt., OBE

Bradbeer, Sir John Derek Richardson, Kt., OBE, TD

Bradbury, *Surgeon Vice-Adm.* Sir Eric Blackburn, KBE, CB

Bradford, Sir Edward Alexander Slade, Bt. (1902)

Bradley, Sir Burton Gyrth Burton-, Kt., OBE

Bradman, Sir Donald George, Kt.

Bradshaw, Sir Kenneth Anthony, KCB

Bradshaw, *Lt.-Gen.* Sir Richard Phillip, KBE

Brain, Sir (Henry) Norman, KBE, CMG

Braithwaite, Sir (Joseph) Franklin Madders, Kt.

Braithwaite, Sir Rodric Quentin, GCMG

Bramall, Sir (Ernest) Ashley, Kt.

Bramley, *Prof.* Sir Paul Anthony, Kt.

Branch, Sir William Allan Patrick, Kt.

Brancker, Sir (John Eustace) Theodore, Kt., QC

Branigan, Sir Patrick Francis, Kt., QC

Bray, Sir Theodor Charles, Kt., CBE

Brennan, *Hon.* Sir (Francis) Gerard, KBE

Brett, Sir Charles Edward Bainbridge, Kt., CBE

Brickwood, Sir Basil Greame, Bt. (1927)

Bridges, *Hon.* Sir Phillip Rodney, Kt., CMG

Brierley, Sir Ronald Alfred, Kt.

Bright, Sir Graham Frank James, Kt., MP

Bright, Sir Keith, Kt.

Brinckman, Sir Theodore George Roderick, Bt. (1831)

Brisco, Sir Donald Gilfrid, Bt. (1782)

†Briscoe, Sir Edward Home, Bt. (1910)

Brise, Sir John Archibald Ruggles-, Bt., CB, OBE, TD (1935)

Bristow, *Hon.* Sir Peter Henry Rowley, Kt.

Brittan, *Rt. Hon.* Sir Leon, Kt., QC

Brittan, Sir Samuel, Kt.

Britton, Sir Edward Louis, Kt., CBE

Broackes, Sir Nigel, Kt.

†Broadbent, Sir Andrew George, Bt. (1893)

Broadhurst, *Air Chief Marshal* Sir Harry, GCB, KBE, DSO, DFC, AFC

Brocklebank, Sir Aubrey Thomas, Bt. (1885)

Brockman, *Vice-Adm.* Sir Ronald Vernon, KCB, CSI, CIE, CVO, CBE

Brodie, Sir Benjamin David Ross, Bt. (1834)

Brogan, *Lt.-Gen.* Sir Mervyn Francis, KBE, CB

Bromhead, Sir John Desmond Gonville, Bt. (1806)

Bromley, Sir Rupert Charles, Bt. (1757)

Bromley, Sir Thomas Eardley, KCMG

Brook, Sir Robin, Kt., CMG, OBE

†Brooke, Sir Alistair Weston, Bt. (1919)

Brooke, Sir Francis George Windham, Bt. (1903)

Brooke, *Hon.* Sir Henry, Kt.

Brooke, Sir Richard Neville, Bt. (1662)

Brookes, Sir Wilfred Deakin, Kt., CBE, DSO

Brooksbank, Sir (Edward) Nicholas, Bt. (1919)

Broom, *Air Marshal* Sir Ivor Gordon, KCB, CBE, DSO, DFC, AFC

Broomfield, Sir Nigel Hugh Robert Allen, KCMG

Broughton, *Air Marshal* Sir Charles, KBE, CB

†Broughton, Sir David Delves, Bt. (1661)

Broun, Sir Lionel John Law, Bt. (s. 1686)

Brown, Sir Allen Stanley, Kt., CBE

Brown, Sir (Arthur James) Stephen, KBE

Brown, *Adm.* Sir Brian Thomas, KCB, CBE

Brown, *Lt.-Col.* Sir Charles Frederick Richmond, Bt. (1863)

Brown, Sir (Cyril) Maxwell Palmer, KCB, CMG

Brown, *Vice-Adm.* Sir David Worthington, KCB

Brown, Sir Derrick Holden-, Kt.

Brown, Sir Douglas Denison, Kt.

Brown, *Hon.* Sir Douglas Dunlop, Kt.

Brown, *Prof.* Sir (Ernest) Henry Phelps, Kt., MBE, FBA

Brown, Sir (Frederick Herbert) Stanley, Kt., CBE, FEng.

Brown, *Prof.* Sir (George) Malcolm, Kt., FRS

Brown, Sir George Noel, Kt.

Brown, Sir John Douglas Keith, Kt.

Brown, Sir John Gilbert Newton, Kt., CBE

Brown, Sir Mervyn, KCMG, OBE

Brown, *Hon.* Sir Ralph Kilner, Kt., OBE, TD

Brown, Sir Robert Crichton-, KCMG, CBE, TD

Brown, *Rt. Hon.* Sir Simon Denis, Kt.

Brown, *Rt. Hon.* Sir Stephen, Kt.

Brown, Sir Thomas, Kt.

Brown, Sir William Brian Piggott-, Bt. (1903)

Browne, *Rt. Hon.* Sir Patrick Reginald Evelyn, Kt., OBE, TD

Brownrigg, Sir Nicholas (Gawen), Bt. (1816)

Browse, *Prof.* Sir Norman Leslie, Kt., MD, FRCS

Bruce, Sir (Francis) Michael Ian, Bt. (s. 1628)

Bruce, Sir Hervey James Hugh, Bt. (1804)

Bruce, *Rt. Hon.* Sir (James) Roualeyn Hovell-Thurlow-Cumming-, Kt.

Brunner, Sir John Henry Kilian, Bt. (1895)

Brunton, Sir (Edward Francis) Lauder, Bt. (1908)

Brunton, Sir Gordon Charles, Kt.

Bryan, Sir Arthur, Kt.

Bryan, Sir Paul Elmore Oliver, Kt., DSO, MC

Bryce, *Hon.* Sir (William) Gordon, Kt., CBE

Bryson, *Adm.* Sir Lindsay Sutherland, KCB, FEng.

Buchan, Sir John, Kt., CMG

Buchanan, Sir Andrew George, Bt. (1878)

Buchanan, Sir Charles Alexander James Leith-, Bt. (1775)

Buchanan, *Prof.* Sir Colin Douglas, Kt., CBE

Buchanan, *Vice-Adm.* Sir Peter William, KBE

Buchanan, Sir Robert Wilson (Robin), Kt.

Buchanan, Sir (Ranald) Dennis, Kt., MBE

Buck, Sir (Philip) Antony (Fyson), Kt., QC

Buckley, *Rt. Hon.* Sir Denys Burton, Kt., MBE

Buckley, Sir John William, Kt.

Buckley, *Lt.-Cdr.* Sir (Peter) Richard, KCVO

Buckley, *Hon.* Sir Roger John, Kt.

Bulkeley, Sir Richard Thomas Williams-, Bt. (1661)

Bull, Sir Simeon George, Bt. (1922)

Bull, Sir Walter Edward Avenon, KCVO

Bullard, Sir Julian Leonard, GCMG

Bullus, Sir Eric Edward, Kt.

Bulmer, Sir William Peter, Kt.

Bultin, Sir Bato, Kt., MBE

Bunbury, Sir Michael William, Bt. (1681)

Bunbury, Sir (Richard David) Michael Richardson-, Bt. (I. 1787)

Bunch, Sir Austin Wyeth, Kt., CBE

Bunting, Sir (Edward) John, KBE

Bunyard, Sir Robert Sidney, Kt., CBE, QPM

Burbidge, Sir Herbert Dudley, Bt. (1916)

Burbury, *Hon.* Sir Stanley Charles, KCMG, KCVO, KBE

Burdett, Sir Savile Aylmer, Bt. (1665)

Burgen, Sir Arnold Stanley Vincent, Kt., FRS

Burgess, *Gen.* Sir Edward Arthur, KCB, OBE

Burgess, Sir (Joseph) Stuart, Kt., CBE, Ph.D., FRSC

Burgh, Sir John Charles, KCMG, CB

Burke, Sir James Stanley Gilbert, Bt. (I. 1797)

Burke, Sir (Thomas) Kerry, Kt.

Burley, Sir Victor George, Kt., CBE

Burman, Sir (John) Charles, Kt.

Burnet, Sir James William Alexander (Sir Alastair Burnet), Kt.

Burnett, *Air Chief Marshal* Sir Brian Kenyon, GCB, DFC, AFC

Burnett, Sir David Humphery, Bt., MBE, TD (1913)

Burnett, Sir John Harrison, Kt.

Burnett, Sir Walter John, Kt.

Burney, Sir Cecil Denniston, Bt. (1921)

Burns, Sir Terence, Kt.

Burns, *Maj.-Gen.* Sir (Walter Arthur) George, GCVO, CB, DSO, OBE, MC

Burrell, Sir John Raymond, Bt. (1774)

Burrenchobay, Sir Dayendranath, KBE, CMG, CVO

Burrows, Sir Bernard Alexander Brocas, GCMG

Burston, Sir Samuel Gerald Wood, Kt., OBE

Burt, *Hon.* Sir Francis Theodore Page, KCMG

Burton, Sir Carlisle Archibald, Kt., OBE

Burton, Sir George Vernon Kennedy, Kt., CBE

Burton, Sir Michael St Edmund, KCVO, CMG

Bush, *Adm.* Sir John Fitzroy Duyland, GCB, DSC

Butler, *Rt. Hon.* Sir Adam Courtauld, Kt.

Butler, Sir Clifford Charles, Kt., Ph.D., FRS

Butler, Sir (Frederick) (Edward) Robin, GCB, CVO

Butler, Sir Michael Dacres, GCMG

Butler, Sir (Reginald) Michael (Thomas), Bt. (1922)

Butler, *Hon.* Sir Richard Clive, Kt.

†Butler, Sir Richard Pierce, Bt. (1628)

Butt, Sir (Alfred) Kenneth Dudley, Bt. (1929)

Butter, *Maj.* Sir David Henry, KCVO, MC

Butterworth, Sir (George) Neville, Kt.

Buxton, *Hon.* Sir Richard Joseph, Kt.

Buxton, Sir Thomas Fowell Victor, Bt. (1840)

Buzzard, Sir Anthony Farquhar, Bt. (1929)

Byatt, Sir Hugh Campbell, KCVO, CMG

Byers, Sir Maurice Hearne, Kt., CBE, QC

Byford, Sir Lawrence, Kt., CBE, QPM

Byrne, Sir Clarence Askew, Kt., OBE, DSC

Cable, Sir James Eric, KCVO, CMG

Cadbury, Sir (George) Adrian (Hayhurst), Kt.

Cadell, *Vice-Adm.* Sir John Frederick, KBE

Cadogan, *Prof.* Sir John Ivan George, Kt., CBE, FRS, FRSE

Cahn, Sir Albert Jonas, Bt. (1934)

Cain, Sir Edward Thomas, Kt., CBE

Cain, Sir Henry Edney Conrad, Kt.

Caine, Sir Michael Harris, Kt.

Caines, Sir John, KCB

Cairncross, Sir Alexander Kirkland, KCMG

Calcutt, Sir David Charles, Kt., QC

Calderwood, Sir Robert, Kt.

Caldwell, *Surgeon Vice-Adm.* Sir (Eric) Dick, KBE, CB

Callaghan, Sir Allan Robert, Kt., CMG

Callaghan, Sir Bede Bertrand, Kt., CBE

Callard, Sir Eric John, Kt., FEng.

Callaway, *Prof.* Sir Frank Adams, Kt., CMG, OBE

Calley, Sir Henry Algernon, Kt., DSO, DFC

Callinan, Sir Bernard James, Kt., CBE, DSO, MC

Calne, *Prof.* Sir Roy Yorke, Kt., FRS

Calthorpe, Sir Euan Hamilton Anstruther-Gough-, Bt. (1929)

Cameron of Lochiel, Sir Donald Hamish, KT, CVO, TD

Cameron, Sir (Eustace) John, Kt., CBE

Cameron, *Hon.* Sir John, KT, DSC, QC (Lord Cameron)

Cameron, Sir John Watson, Kt., OBE

Campbell, Sir Alan Hugh, GCMG

Campbell, Sir Colin Moffat, Bt., MC (s. 1668)

Campbell, *Prof.* Sir Colin Murray, Kt.

Campbell, *Prof.* Sir Donald, Kt., CBE, FRCS, FRCPGlas.

Campbell, Sir Ian Tofts, Kt., CBE, VRD

Campbell, Sir Ilay Mark, Bt. (1808)

†Campbell, Sir Lachlan Philip Kemeys, Bt. (1815)

Campbell, Sir Matthew, KBE, CB, FRSE

Campbell, Sir Niall Alexander Hamilton, Bt. (1831)

Campbell, Sir Robin Auchinbreck, Bt. (s. 1628)

Campbell, Sir Thomas Cockburn-, Bt. (1821)

Campbell, *Hon.* Sir Walter Benjamin, Kt.

Campbell, *Hon.* Sir William Anthony, Kt.

Campion, Sir Harry, Kt., CB, CBE

†Carden, Sir Christopher Robert, Bt. (1887)

Carden, Sir John Craven, Bt. (I. 1787)

Carew, Sir Rivers Verain, Bt. (1661)

Carey, Sir Peter Willoughby, GCB

Carlill, *Vice-Adm.* Sir Stephen Hope, KBE, CB, DSO

Carlisle, Sir James Beethoven, GCMG

Carlisle, Sir John Michael, Kt.

Carlisle, Sir Kenneth Melville, Kt., MP

Carmichael, Sir David Peter William Gibson-Craig-, Bt. (s. 1702 and 1831)

Carmichael, Sir John, KBE

Carnac, *Revd Canon* Sir (Thomas) Nicholas Rivett-, Bt. (1836)

Carnegie, *Lt.-Gen.* Sir Robin Macdonald, KCB, OBE

Carnegie, Sir Roderick Howard, Kt.

Carnwath, Sir Andrew Hunter, KCVO

Caro, Sir Anthony Alfred, Kt., CBE

Carpenter, *Very Revd* Edward Frederick, KCVO

Carpenter, *Lt.-Gen.* the Hon. Sir Thomas Patrick John Boyd-, KBE

Carr, Sir (Albert) Raymond (Maillard), Kt.

Carr, *Air Marshal* Sir John Darcy Baker-, KBE, CB, AFC

Carrick, *Hon.* Sir John Leslie, KCMG

Carsberg, *Prof.* Sir Bryan Victor, Kt.

Carswell, *Rt. Hon.* Sir Robert Douglas, Kt.

Carter, Sir Charles Frederick, Kt., FBA

Carter, Sir Derrick Hunton, Kt., TD

Carter, Sir John, Kt., QC

Carter, Sir John Alexander, Kt.

Carter, Sir Philip David, Kt., CBE

Carter, Sir Richard Henry Alwyn, Kt.

Carter, Sir William Oscar, Kt.

Cartland, Sir George Barrington, Kt., CMG

Cartledge, Sir Bryan George, KCMG

Cary, Sir Roger Hugh, Bt. (1955)

Casey, *Rt. Hon.* Sir Maurice Eugene, Kt.

Cash, Sir Gerald Christopher, GCMG, GCVO, OBE

Cass, Sir Geoffrey Arthur, Kt.

Cass, Sir John Patrick, Kt., OBE

Cassel, Sir Harold Felix, Bt., TD, QC (1920)

Cassels, *Field Marshal* Sir (Archibald) James Halkett, GCB, KBE, DSO

Cassels, Sir John Seton, Kt., CB

Cassels, *Adm.* Sir Simon Alastair Cassillis, KCB, CBE

Cassidi, *Adm.* Sir (Arthur) Desmond, GCB

Casson, Sir Hugh Maxwell, CH, KCVO, PPRA, FRIBA

Cater, Sir Jack, KBE

Cater, Sir John Robert, Kt.

Catford, Sir (John) Robin, KCVO, CBE

Catherwood, Sir (Henry) Frederick (Ross), Kt., MEP

Catling, Sir Richard Charles, Kt., CMG, OBE

Cato, *Hon.* Sir Arnott Samuel, KCMG

Caughey, Sir Thomas Harcourt Clarke, KBE

Caulfield, *Hon.* Sir Bernard, Kt.

Cave, Sir Charles Edward Coleridge, Bt. (1896)

Cave, Sir (Charles) Philip Haddon-, KBE, CMG

Cave, Sir Robert Cave-Browne-, Bt. (1641)

Cawley, Sir Charles Mills, Kt., CBE, Ph.D.

Cayley, Sir Digby William David, Bt. (1661)

Cayzer, Sir James Arthur, Bt. (1904)

Cazalet, *Hon.* Sir Edward Stephen, Kt.

Cazalet, Sir Peter Grenville, Kt.

Cecil, *Rear-Adm.* Sir (Oswald) Nigel Amherst, KBE, CB

Chacksfield, *Air Vice-Marshal* Sir Bernard Albert, KBE, CB

Chadwick, *Revd Prof.* Henry, KBE

Chadwick, *Hon.* Sir John Murray, Kt., ED

Chadwick, Sir Joshua Kenneth Burton, Bt. (1935)

Chadwick, *Revd Prof.* (William) Owen, OM, KBE, FBA

Chan, *Rt. Hon.* Sir Julius, GCMG, KBE

Chance, Sir (George) Jeremy ffolliott, Bt. (1900)

Chandler, Sir Colin Michael, Kt.

Chandler, Sir Geoffrey, Kt., CBE

Chaney, *Hon.* Sir Frederick Charles, KBE, AFC

Chaplin, Sir Malcolm Hilbery, Kt., CBE

Chapman, Sir David Robert Macgowan, Bt. (1958)

Chapman, Sir George Alan, Kt.

Chapple, *Field Marshal* Sir John Lyon, GCB, CBE

Charles, Sir Joseph Quentin, Kt.

Charlton, Sir Robert (Bobby), Kt., CBE

Charnley, Sir (William) John, Kt., CB, FEng.

Chatfield, Sir John Freeman, Kt., CBE

Chaytor, Sir George Reginald, Bt. (1831)

Checketts, *Sqn. Ldr.* Sir David John, KCVO

Checkland, Sir Michael, Kt.

Cheetham, Sir Nicolas John Alexander, KCMG

Chessells, Sir Arthur David (Tim), Kt.

Chesterman, Sir (Dudley) Ross, Kt., Ph.D.

Chesterton, Sir Oliver Sidney, Kt., MC

Chetwood, Sir Clifford Jack, Kt.

Chetwynd, Sir Arthur Ralph Talbot, Bt. (1795)

Cheung, Sir Oswald Victor, Kt., CBE

Cheyne, Sir Joseph Lister Watson, Bt., OBE (1908)

Chichester, Sir (Edward) John, Bt. (1641)

Chilcot, Sir John Anthony, KCB

Child, Sir (Coles John) Jeremy, Bt. (1919)

Chilton, *Brig.* Sir Frederick Oliver, Kt., CBE, DSO

Chilwell, *Hon.* Sir Muir Fitzherbert, Kt.

Chinn, Sir Trevor Edwin, Kt., CVO

Chipperfield, Sir Geoffrey Howes, KCB

Chitty, Sir Thomas Willes, Bt. (1924)

Cholmeley, Sir Montague John, Bt. (1806)

Christie, Sir George William Langham, Kt.

Christie, *Hon.* Sir Vernon Howard Colville, Kt.

Christie, Sir William, Kt., MBE

Christopherson, Sir Derman Guy, Kt., OBE, D.Phil., FRS, FEng.

Chung, Sir Sze-yuen, GBE, FEng.

Clapham, Sir Michael John Sinclair, KBE

Clark, Sir Colin Douglas, Bt. (1917)

Clark, Sir Francis Drake, Bt. (1886)

Clark, Sir John Allen, Kt.

Clark, *Prof.* Sir John Grahame Douglas, Kt., CBE

Clark, Sir John Stewart-, Bt., MEP (1918)

Clark, Sir Robert Anthony, Kt., DSC

Clark, Sir Robin Chichester-, Kt.

Clark, Sir Terence Joseph, KBE, CMG, CVO

Clark, Sir Thomas Edwin, Kt.

Clarke, *Hon.* Sir Anthony Peter, Kt.

Clarke, Sir (Charles Mansfield) Tobias, Bt. (1831)

Clarke, *Prof.* Sir Cyril Astley, KBE, MD, SC.D., FRS, FRCP

Clarke, Sir Ellis Emmanuel Innocent, GCMG

Clarke, Sir Jonathan Dennis, Kt.

Clarke, *Maj.* Sir Peter Cecil, KCVO

Clarke, Sir Robert Cyril, Kt.

Clarke, Sir Rupert William John, Bt., MBE (1882)

Clay, Sir Richard Henry, Bt. (1841)

Clayton, Sir David Robert, Bt., (1732)

Clayton, Sir Robert James, Kt., CBE, FEng.

Cleaver, Sir Anthony Brian, Kt.

Cleminson, Sir James Arnold Stacey, KBE, MC

Clerk, Sir John Dutton, Bt., CBE, VRD (s. 1679)

Clerke, Sir John Edward Longueville, Bt. (1660)

Clifford, Sir Roger Joseph, Bt. (1887)

Clothier, Sir Cecil Montacute, KCB, QC

Clucas, Sir Kenneth Henry, KCB

Clutterbuck, *Vice-Adm.* Sir David Granville, KBE, CB

Coates, Sir Ernest William, Kt., CMG

Coates, Sir Frederick Gregory Lindsay, Bt. (1921)

Coats, Sir Alastair Francis Stuart, Bt. (1905)

Coats, Sir William David, Kt.

Cobban, Sir James Macdonald, Kt., CBE, TD

Cochrane, Sir (Henry) Marc (Sursock), Bt. (1903)

Cockburn, Sir John Elliot, Bt. (s. 1671)

Cockcroft, Sir Wilfred Halliday, Kt., D.Phil.

Cockerell, Sir Christopher Sydney, Kt., CBE, FRS

Cockram, Sir John, Kt.

Cockshaw, Sir Alan, Kt., FEng.

Codrington, Sir Simon Francis Bethell, Bt. (1876)

Codrington, Sir William Alexander, Bt. (1721)

Coghill, Sir Egerton James Nevill Tobias, Bt. (1778)

Cohen, Sir Edward, Kt.

Cohen, Sir Ivor Harold, Kt., CBE, TD

Cohen, Sir Stephen Harry Waley-, Bt. (1961)

Coldstream, Sir George Phillips, KCB, KCVO, QC

Cole, Sir (Alexander) Colin, KCB, KCVO, TD

Cole, Sir David Lee, KCMG, MC

Cole, Sir (Robert) William, Kt.

Coles, Sir (Arthur) John, KCMG

Colfox, Sir (William) John, Bt. (1939)

Collett, Sir Christopher, GBE

Collett, Sir Ian Seymour, Bt. (1934)

Collins, Sir Arthur James Robert, KCVO

Collins, Sir John Alexander, Kt.

Cullyear, Sir John Gowen, Kt., FEng.

Colman, *Hon.* Sir Anthony David, Kt.

Colman, Sir Michael Jeremiah, Bt. (1907)

Colquhoun, *Maj.-Gen.* Sir Cyril Harry, KCVO, CB, OBE

Colquhoun of Luss, Sir Ivar Iain, Bt. (1786)

Colt, Sir Edward William Dutton Bt. (1694)

Colthurst, Sir Richard La Touche, Bt. (1744)

Compston, *Vice-Adm.* Sir Peter Maxwell, KCB

Comyn, *Hon.* Sir James, Kt.

Conant, Sir John Ernest Michael, Bt. (1954)

Condon, Sir Paul Leslie, Kt., QPM

Connell, *Hon.* Sir Michael Bryan, Kt.

Conran, Sir Terence Orby, Kt.

Cons, *Hon.* Sir Derek, Kt.

Constable, Sir Robert Frederick Strickland-, Bt. (1641)

Cook, *Prof.* Sir Alan Hugh, Kt.

Cook, Sir Christopher Wymondham Rayner Herbert, Bt. (1886)

Cooke, Sir Charles Fletcher-, Kt., QC

Cooke, *Lt.-Col.* Sir David William Perceval, Bt. (1661)

Cooke, Sir Howard Felix Hanlan, ON, GCMG, GCVO, CD

Cooke, *Rt. Hon.* Sir Robin Brunskill, KBE

Cooksey, Sir David James Scott, Kt.

Cooley, Sir Alan Sydenham, Kt., CBE

Coop, Sir Maurice Fletcher, Kt.

Cooper, *Rt. Hon.* Sir Frank, GCB, CMG

Cooper, Sir (Frederick Howard) Michael Craig-, Kt., CBE, TD

Cooper, *Gen.* Sir George Leslie Conroy, GCB, MC

Cooper, Sir Louis Jacques Blom-, Kt., QC

Cooper, Sir Patrick Graham Astley, Bt. (1821)

Cooper, Sir Richard Powell, Bt. (1905)

Cooper, *Maj.-Gen.* Sir Simon Christie, KCVO

Cooper, Sir William Daniel Charles, Bt. (1863)

Coote, Sir Christopher John, Bt., *Premier Baronet of Ireland* (I. 1621)

Copas, *Most Revd* Virgil, KBE, DD

Cope, *Rt. Hon.* Sir John Ambrose, Kt., MP

Copisarow, Sir Alcon Charles, Kt.

Corbet, Sir John Vincent, Bt., MBE (1808)

Corbett, *Maj.-Gen.* Sir Robert John Swan, KCVO, CB

Corby, Sir (Frederick) Brian, Kt.

Corfield, *Rt. Hon.* Sir Frederick Vernon, Kt., QC

Corfield, Sir Kenneth George, Kt., FEng.

Corley, Sir Kenneth Sholl Ferrand, Kt.

Cormack, Sir Magnus Cameron, KBE

Corness, Sir Colin Ross, Kt.

Cornford, Sir (Edward) Clifford, KCB, FEng.

Cornforth, Sir John Warcup, Kt., CBE, D.Phil., FRS

Corry, Sir William James, Bt. (1885)

Cortazzi, Sir (Henry Arthur) Hugh, GCMG

Cory, Sir (Clinton Charles) Donald, Bt. (1919)

Cossons, Sir Neil, Kt., OBE

Costar, Sir Norman Edgar, KCMG

Cotter, *Lt.-Col.* Sir Delaval James Alfred, Bt., DSO (I. 1763)

Cotterell, Sir John Henry Geers, Bt. (1805)

Cotton, Sir John Richard, KCMG, OBE

Cotton, *Hon.* Sir Robert Carrington, KCMG

Cottrell, Sir Alan Howard, Kt., Ph.D., FRS, FEng.

Cotts, Sir (Robert) Crichton Mitchell, Bt. (1921)

Coulson, Sir John Eltringham, KCMG

Couper, Sir (Robert) Nicholas (Oliver), Bt. (1841)

Court, *Hon.* Sir Charles Walter Michael, KCMG, OBE

Coutts, Sir David Burdett Money-, KCVO

Couzens, Sir Kenneth Edward, KCB

Covacevich, Sir (Anthony) Thomas, Kt., DFC

Coward, *Vice-Adm.* Sir John Francis, KCB, DSO

Cowdrey, Sir (Michael) Colin, Kt., CBE

Cowen, *Rt. Hon. Prof.* Sir Zelman, GCMG, GCVO, QC

Cowie, Sir Thomas (Tom), Kt., OBE

Cowperthwaite, Sir John James, KBE, CMG

Cox, Sir Alan George, Kt., CBE

Cox, *Prof.* Sir David Roxbee, Kt., FRS

Cox, Sir (Ernest) Gordon, KBE, TD, D.SC., FRS

Cox, Sir Geoffrey Sandford, Kt., CBE

Cox, Sir (George) Trenchard, Kt., CBE, FSA

Cox, *Vice-Adm.* Sir John Michael Holland, KCB

Cox, Sir Mencea Ethereal, Kt.

Cradock, *Rt. Hon.* Sir Percy, GCMG

Craig, Sir (Albert) James (Macqueen), GCMG

Crane, Sir James William Donald, Kt., CBE

Craufurd, Sir Robert James, Bt. (1781)

Craven, *Air Marshal* Sir Robert Edward, KBE, CB, DFC

Crawford, *Prof.* Sir Frederick William, Kt., FEng.

Crawford, *Hon.* Sir George Hunter, Kt.

Crawford, Sir (Robert) Stewart, GCMG, CVO

Crawford, *Vice-Adm.* Sir William Godfrey, KBE, CB, DSC

Crawshay, *Col.* Sir William Robert, Kt., DSO, ERD, TD

Creagh, *Maj.-Gen.* Sir (Kilner) Rupert Brazier-, KBE, CB, DSO

Cresswell, *Hon.* Sir Peter John, Kt.

Crichton, Sir Andrew James Maitland-Makgill-, Kt.

Crill, Sir Peter Leslie, Kt., CBE

Cripps, Sir Cyril Humphrey, Kt.

Crisp, Sir (John) Peter, Bt. (1913)

Critchett, Sir Ian (George Lorraine), Bt. (1908)

Croft, Sir Owen Glendower, Bt. (1671)

Croft, Sir Thomas Stephen Hutton, Bt. (1818)

†Crofton, Sir Hugh Denis, Bt. (1801)

Crofton, *Prof.* Sir John Wenman, Kt.

Crofton, Sir Malby Sturges, Bt. (1838)

Croker, Sir Walter Russell, KBE

Crookenden, *Lt.-Gen.* Sir Napier, KCB, DSO, OBE

Cross, *Air Chief Marshal* Sir Kenneth Brian Boyd, KCB, CBE, DSO, DFC

Crossland, *Prof.* Sir Bernard, Kt., CBE, FEng.

Crossland, Sir Leonard, Kt.

Crossley, Sir Nicholas John, Bt. (1909)

Crouch, Sir David Lance, Kt.

Cruthers, Sir James Winter, Kt.

Cubbon, Sir Brian Crossland, GCB

Cubitt, Sir Hugh Guy, Kt., CBE

Cuckney, Sir John Graham, Kt.

Cullen, Sir (Edward) John, Kt., F.Eng.

Cumming, Sir William Gordon Gordon-, Bt. (1804)

Cuningham, Sir John Christopher Foggo Montgomery-, Bt. (NS 1672)

†Cuninghame, Sir William Henry Fairlie-, Bt. (S. 1630)

Cunliffe, Sir David Ellis, Bt. (1759)

Cunningham, Sir Charles Craik, GCB, KBE, CVO

Cunningham, *Lt.-Gen.* Sir Hugh Patrick, KBE

Cunynghame, Sir Andrew David Francis, Bt. (S. 1702)

Curle, Sir John Noel Ormiston, KCVO, CMG

Curran, Sir Samuel Crowe, Kt., D.SC., Ph.D., FRS, FRSE, FEng.

†Currie, Sir Donald Scott, Bt. (1847)

Currie, Sir Neil Smith, Kt., CBE

Curtis, Sir Barry John, Kt.

Curtis, Sir (Edward) Leo, Kt.

Curtis, *Hon.* Sir Richard Herbert, Kt.

Curtis, Sir William Peter, Bt. (1802)

Curtiss, *Air Marshal* Sir John Bagot, KCB, KBE

Curwen, Sir Christopher Keith, KCMG

Cuthbertson, Sir Harold Alexander, Kt.

Cutler, Sir (Arthur) Roden, VC, KCMG, KCVO, CBE

Cutler, Sir Charles Benjamin, KBE, ED

Cutler, Sir Horace Walter, Kt., OBE

Dacie, *Prof.* Sir John Vivian, Kt., MD, FRS

Dalais, Sir Adrien Pierre, Kt.

Dale, Sir William Leonard, KCMG

Dalrymple, *Maj.* Sir Hew Fleetwood Hamilton-, Bt., KCVO (S. 1697)

Dalton, Sir Alan Nugent Goring, Kt., CBE

Dalton, *Vice-Adm.* Sir Geoffrey Thomas James Oliver, KCB

Daly, *Lt.-Gen.* Sir Thomas Joseph, KBE, CB, DSO

Dalyell, Sir Tam, Bt., MP (NS 1685)

Daniel, Sir Goronwy Hopkin, KCVO, CB, D.Phil.

Daniel, Sir John Sagar, Kt., D.SC.

Daniell, Sir Peter Averell, Kt., TD

Danks, Sir Alan John, KBE

Darby, Sir Peter Howard, Kt., CBE, QFSM

Darell, Sir Jeffrey Lionel, Bt., MC (1795)

Dargie, Sir William Alexander, Kt., CBE

Dark, Sir Anthony Michael Beaumont-, Kt.

Darling, Sir Clifford, GCVO

Darling, Sir James Ralph, Kt., CMG, OBE

Darling, *Gen.* Sir Kenneth Thomas, GBE, KCB, DSO

Darlington, *Rear-Adm.* Sir Charles Roy, KBE

Darvall, Sir (Charles) Roger, Kt., CBE

Dashwood, Sir Francis John Vernon Hereward, Bt., *Premier Baronet of Great Britain* (1707)

Dashwood, Sir Richard James, Bt. (1684)

Daunt, Sir Timothy Lewis Achilles, KCMG

David, Sir Jean Marc, Kt., CBE, QC

Davidson, Sir Robert James, Kt., FEng.

Davie, Sir Antony Francis Ferguson-, Bt. (1847)

Davies, *Air Marshal* Sir Alan Cyril, KCB, CBE

Davies, *Hon.* Sir (Alfred William) Michael, Kt.

Davies, Sir Alun Talfan, Kt., QC

Davies, *Prof.* Sir David Evan Naughton, Kt., CBE, FRS, FEng.

Davies, Sir David Henry, Kt.

Davies, *Hon.* Sir (David Herbert) Mervyn, Kt., MC, TD

Davies, *Vice-Adm.* Sir Lancelot Richard Bell, KBE

Davies, Sir Oswald, Kt., CBE

Davies, Sir Peter Maxwell, Kt., CBE

Davies, Sir Richard Harries, KCVO, CBE

Davies, Sir Victor Caddy, Kt., OBE

Davis, Sir Charles Sigmund, Kt., CB

Davis, Sir Colin Rex, Kt., CBE

Davis, *Hon.* Sir (Dermot) Renn, Kt., OBE

Davis, Sir (Ernest) Howard, Kt., CMG, OBE

Davis, Sir John Gilbert, Bt. (1946)

Davis, Sir Maurice Herbert, Kt., OBE

Davis, Sir Rupert Charles Hart-, Kt.

Davis, *Hon.* Sir Thomas Robert Alexander Harries, KBE

Davison, *Rt. Hon.* Sir Ronald Keith, GBE, CMG

Dawbarn, Sir Simon Yelverton, KCVO, CMG

Dawson, Sir Anthony Michael, KCVO, MD, FRCP

Dawson, *Hon.* Sir Daryl Michael, KBE, CB

Dawson, Sir Hugh Michael Trevor, Bt. (1920)

Dawtry, Sir Alan (Graham), Kt., CBE, TD

Day, Sir Derek Malcolm, KCMG

Day, Sir (Judson) Graham, Kt.

Day, Sir Michael John, Kt., OBE

Day, Sir Robin, Kt.

Deakin, Sir (Frederick) William (Dampier), Kt., DSO

Dean, Sir Patrick Henry, GCMG

Deane, *Hon.* Sir William Patrick, KBE

Dearing, Sir Ronald Ernest, Kt., CB

de Bellaigue, Sir Geoffrey, KCVO

Debenham, Sir Gilbert Ridley, Bt. (1931)

de Deney, Sir Geoffrey Ivor, KCVO

Deer, Sir (Arthur) Frederick, Kt., CMG

de Hoghton, Sir (Richard) Bernard (Cuthbert), Bt. (1611)

De la Bère, Sir Cameron, Bt. (1953)

de la Mare, Sir Arthur James, KCMG, KCVO

Delamere, Sir Monita Eru, KBE

de la Rue, Sir Andrew George Ilay, Bt. (1898)

Dellow, Sir John Albert, Kt., CBE

Delve, Sir Frederick William, Kt., CBE

de Montmorency, Sir Arnold Geoffroy, Bt. (I. 1631)

Denholm, Sir John Ferguson (Ian), Kt., CBE

Denman, Sir (George) Roy, KCB, CMG

Denny, Sir Alistair Maurice Archibald, Bt. (1913)

Denny, Sir Anthony Coningham de Waltham, Bt. (I. 1782)

Dent, Sir John, Kt., CBE, FEng.

Dent, Sir Robin John, KCVO

Denton, *Prof.* Sir Eric James, Kt., CBE, FRS

Derbyshire, Sir Andrew George, Kt.

Derham, Sir Peter John, Kt.

de Trafford, Sir Dermot Humphrey, Bt. (1841)

Deverell, Sir Colville Montgomery, GBE, KCMG, CVO

Devesi, Sir Baddeley, GCMG, GCVO

De Ville, Sir Harold Godfrey Oscar, Kt., CBE

Devitt, Sir Thomas Gordon, Bt. (1916)

de Waal, Sir (Constant Henrik) Henry, KCB, QC

Dewey, Sir Anthony Hugh, Bt. (1917)

Dewhurst, *Prof.* Sir (Christopher) John, Kt.

d'Eyncourt, Sir Mark Gervais Tennyson-, Bt. (1930)

Dhenin, *Air Marshal* Sir Geoffrey Howard, KBE, AFC, GM, MD

Dhrangadhra, HH the Maharaja Raj Saheb of, KCIE

Dibela, *Hon.* Sir Kingsford, GCMG

Dick, Sir John Alexander, Kt., MC, QC

Dickenson, Sir Aubrey Fiennes Trotman-, Kt.

Dickinson, Sir Harold Herbert, Kt.

Dickinson, Sir Samuel Benson, Kt.

Dilbertson, Sir Geoffrey, Kt., CBE

Dilke, Sir John Fisher Wentworth, Bt. (1862)
Dillon, *Rt. Hon.* Sir (George) Brian (Hugh), Kt.
Dillon, Sir John Vincent, Kt., CMG
Dillon, Sir Max, Kt.
Diver, *Hon.* Sir Leslie Charles, Kt.
Dixon, Sir Jonathan Mark, Bt. (1919)
Djanogly, Sir Harry Ari Simon, Kt., CBE
Dobbs, *Capt.* Sir Richard Arthur Frederick, KCVO
Dobson, *Vice-Adm.* Sir David Stuart, KBE
Dobson, Sir Denis William, KCB, OBE, QC
Dobson, *Gen.* Sir Patrick John Howard-, GCB
Dodds, Sir Ralph Jordan, Bt. (1964)
Dodson, Sir Derek Sherborne Lindsell, KCMG, MC
Dodsworth, Sir John Christopher Smith-, Bt. (1784)
Doll, *Prof.* Sir (William) Richard (Shaboe), Kt., OBE, FRS, DM, MD, D.SC.
Dollery, Sir Colin Terence, Kt.
Donald, Sir Alan Ewen, KCMG
Donald, *Air Marshal* Sir John George, KBE
Donne, *Hon.* Sir Gaven John, KBE
Donne, Sir John Christopher, Kt.
Dookun, Sir Dewoonarain, Kt.
Dorey, Sir Graham Martyn, Kt.
Dorman, *Lt.-Col.* Sir Charles Geoffrey, Bt., MC (1923)
Dougherty, *Maj.-Gen.* Sir Ivan Noel, Kt., CBE, DSO, ED
Doughty, Sir William Roland, Kt.
Douglas, Sir (Edward) Sholto, Kt.
Douglas, Sir Robert McCallum, Kt., OBE
Douglas, *Hon.* Sir Roger Owen, Kt.
Douglas, *Rt. Hon.* Sir William Randolph, KCMG
Dover, *Prof.* Sir Kenneth James, Kt., D.Litt., FBA, FRSE
Down, Sir Alastair Frederick, Kt., OBE, MC, TD
Downes, Sir Edward Thomas, Kt., CBE
Downey, Sir Gordon Stanley, KCB
Downs, Sir Diarmuid, Kt., CBE, FEng.
Downward, Sir William Atkinson, Kt.
Dowson, Sir Philip Manning, Kt., CBE, ARA
Doyle, Sir Reginald Derek Henry, Kt., CBE
D'Oyly, Sir Nigel Hadley Miller, Bt. (1663)
Drake, Sir (Arthur) Eric (Courtney), Kt., CBE
Drake, *Hon.* Sir (Frederick) Maurice, Kt., DFC
Dreyer, *Adm.* Sir Desmond Parry, GCB, CBE, DSC
Drinkwater, Sir John Muir, Kt., QC
Driver, Sir Antony Victor, Kt.
Driver, Sir Eric William, Kt.

Drury, Sir (Victor William) Michael, Kt., OBE
Dryden, Sir John Stephen Gyles, Bt. (1733 and 1795)
du Cann, *Rt. Hon.* Sir Edward Dillon Lott, KBE
Duckmanton, Sir Talbot Sydney, Kt., CBE
Duckworth, *Maj.* Sir Richard Dyce, Bt. (1909)
du Cros, Sir Claude Philip Arthur Mallet, Bt. (1916)
Duff, *Rt. Hon.* Sir (Arthur) Antony, GCMG, CVO, DSO, DSC
Duffell, *Lt.-Gen.* Sir Peter Royson, KCB, CBE, MC
Duffus, *Hon.* Sir William Algernon Holwell, Kt.
Duffy, Sir (Albert) (Edward) Patrick, Kt., Ph.D.
Dugdale, Sir John Robert Stratford, KCVO
Dugdale, Sir William Stratford, Bt., MC (1936)
Dunbar, Sir Archibald Ranulph, Bt. (s. 1700)
Dunbar, Sir David Hope-, Bt. (s. 1664)
Dunbar, Sir Drummond Cospatrick Ninian, Bt., MC (s. 1698)
Dunbar, Sir James Michael, Bt. (s. 1694)
Dunbar of Hempriggs, Dame Maureen Daisy Helen (Lady Dunbar of Hempriggs), Btss. (s. 1706)
Duncan, Sir James Blair, Kt.
Duncombe, Sir Philip Digby Pauncefort-, Bt. (1859)
Dundas, Sir Hugh Spencer Lisle, Kt., CBE, DSO, DFC
Dunham, Sir Kingsley Charles, Kt., Ph.D., FRS, FRSE, FEng.
Dunlop, Sir Thomas, Bt. (1916)
Dunlop, Sir William Norman Gough, Kt.
Dunn, *Air Marshal* Sir Eric Clive, KBE, CB, BEM
Dunn, *Lt.-Col.* Sir (Francis) Vivian, KCVO, OBE
Dunn, *Air Marshal* Sir Patrick Hunter, KBE, CB, DFC
Dunn, *Rt. Hon.* Sir Robin Horace Walford, Kt., MC
Dunnett, Sir (Ludovic) James, GCB, CMG
Dunning, Sir Simon William Patrick, Bt. (1930)
Dunphie, *Maj.-Gen.* Sir Charles Anderson Lane, Kt., CB, CBE, DSO
Dunstan, *Lt.-Gen.* Sir Donald Beaumont, KBE, CB
†Duntze, Sir Daniel Evans, Bt. (1774)
Dupre, Sir Tumun, Kt., MBE
Dupree, Sir Peter, Bt. (1921)
Durand, Sir Edward Alan Christopher David Percy, Bt. (1892)
Durant, Sir (Robert) Anthony (Bevis), Kt., MP

Durham, Sir Kenneth, Kt.
Durie, Sir Alexander Charles, Kt., CBE
Durkin, *Air Marshal* Sir Herbert, KBE, CB
Durrant, Sir William Henry Estridge, Bt. (1784)
Duthie, *Prof.* Sir Herbert Livingston, Kt.
Duthie, Sir Robert Grieve (Robin), Kt., CBE
Duval, Sir (Charles) Gaetan, Kt.
Duxbury, *Air Marshal* Sir (John) Barry, KCB, CBE
Dyer, *Prof.* Sir (Henry) Peter (Francis) Swinnerton-, Bt., KBE, FRS (1678)
Dyke, Sir David William Hart, Bt. (1677)
Dyson, *Hon.* Sir John Anthony, Kt.
Earle, Sir (Hardman) George (Algernon), Bt. (1869)
East, Sir (Lewis) Ronald, Kt., CBE
Easton, Sir Robert William Simpson, Kt., CBE
Eastwood, Sir John Bealby, Kt.
Eaton, *Adm.* Sir Kenneth John, GBE, KCB
Eberle, *Adm.* Sir James Henry Fuller, GCB
Ebrahim, Sir (Mahomed) Currimbhoy, Bt. (1910)
Eburne, Sir Sidney Alfred William, Kt., MC
Eccles, Sir John Carew, Kt., D.Phil., FRS
Echlin, Sir Norman David Fenton, Bt. (I. 1721)
Eckersley, Sir Donald Payze, Kt., OBE
†Edge, Sir William, Bt. (1937)
Edmonstone, Sir Archibald Bruce Charles, Bt. (1774)
Edwardes, Sir Michael Owen, Kt.
Edwards, Sir Christopher John Churchill, Bt. (1866)
Edwards, Sir George Robert, Kt., OM, CBE, FRS, FEng.
Edwards, Sir (John) Clive (Leighton), Bt. (1921)
Edwards, Sir Llewellyn Roy, Kt.
Edwards, *Prof.* Sir Samuel Frederick, Kt., FRS
Egan, Sir John Leopold, Kt.
Egerton, Sir John Alfred Roy, Kt.
Egerton, Sir (Philip) John (Caledon) Grey-, Bt. (1617)
Egerton, Sir Seymour John Louis, GCVO
Egerton, Sir Stephen Loftus, KCMG
Eggleston, *Hon.* Sir Richard Moulton, Kt.
Eichelbaum, *Rt. Hon.* Sir Thomas, GBE
Eliott of Stobs, Sir Charles Joseph Alexander, Bt. (s. 1666)
Ellerton, Sir Geoffrey James, Kt., CMG, MBE
Elliot, Sir Gerald Henry, Kt.
Elliott, Sir Clive Christopher Hugh, Bt. (1917)

Elliott, *Prof.* Sir John Huxtable, Kt.,
  FBA
Elliott, Sir Randal Forbes, KBE
Elliott, *Γ ¬f.* Sir Roger James, Kt., FRS
Elliott, Sir Ronald Stuart, Kt.
Ellis, Sir John Rogers, Kt., MBE, MD,
  FRCP
Ellis, Sir Ronald, Kt., FEng.
Ellison, *Col.* Sir Ralph Harry Carr-,
  Kt., TD
Elphinstone, Sir John, Bt. (s. 1701)
Elphinstone, Sir (Maurice) Douglas
  (Warburton), Bt., TD (1816)
Elton, Sir Arnold, Kt., CBE
Elton, Sir Charles Abraham Grierson,
  Bt. (1717)
Elton, *Prof.* Sir Geoffrey Rudolph,
  Kt., FBA
Elwes, Sir Jeremy Vernon, Kt., CBE
Elwood, Sir Brian George Conway,
  Kt., CBE
Elworthy, Sir Peter Herbert, Kt.
Elyan, Sir (Isadore) Victor, Kt.
Emery, *Rt. Hon.* Sir Peter Frank
  Hannibal, Kt., MP
Empson, *Adm.* Sir (Leslie) Derek,
  GBE, KCB
Emson, *Air Marshal* Sir Reginald
  Herbert, KBE, CB, AFC
Engineer, Sir Noshirwan Phirozshah,
  Kt.
Engle, Sir George Lawrence Jose, KCB,
  QC
English, Sir Cyril Rupert, Kt.
English, Sir David, Kt.
English, Sir Terence Alexander
  Hawthorne, KBE, FRCS
Epstein, *Prof.* Sir (Michael) Anthony,
  Kt., CBE, FRS
Ereaut, Sir (Herbert) Frank Cobbold,
  Kt.
Errington, *Col.* Sir Geoffrey
  Frederick, Bt. (1963)
Errington, Sir Lancelot, KCB
Erskine, Sir (Thomas) David, Bt.
  (1821)
Esmonde, Sir Thomas Francis
  Grattan, Bt. (I. 1629)
Espie, Sir Frank Fletcher, Kt., OBE
Esplen, Sir John Graham, Bt. (1921)
Eustace, Sir Joseph Lambert, GCMG,
  GCVO
Evans, Sir Anthony Adney, Bt. (1920)
Evans, *Rt. Hon.* Sir Anthony Howell
  Meurig, Kt., RD
Evans, *Air Chief Marshal* Sir David
  George, GCB, CBE
Evans, *Air Chief Marshal* Sir David
  Parry-, GCB, CBE
Evans, *Hon.* Sir Haydn Tudor, Kt.
Evans, Sir Richard Mark, KCMG, KCVO
Evans, Sir Robert, Kt., CBE, F.Eng.
Evans, Sir (Robert) Charles, Kt.
Evans, Sir (William) Vincent (John),
  GCMG, MBE, QC
†Evans-Tipping, Sir David Gwynne,
  Bt. (1913)
Eveleigh, *Rt. Hon.* Sir Edward Walter,
  Kt., ERD

Everard, *Maj.-Gen.* Sir Christopher
  Earle Welby-, KBE, CB
Everard, Sir Robin Charles, Bt. (1911)
Everson, Sir Frederick Charles, KCMG
Every, Sir Henry John Michael, Bt.
  (1641)
Ewans, Sir Martin Kenneth, KCMG
Ewart, Sir (William) Ivan (Cecil), Bt.,
  DSC (1887)
Ewbank, *Hon.* Sir Anthony Bruce, Kt.
Ewin, Sir (David) Ernest Thomas
  Floyd, Kt., OBE, MVO
Ewing, *Vice-Adm.* Sir (Robert)
  Alastair, KBE, CB, DSC
Ewing, Sir Ronald Archibald Orr-, Bt.
  (1886)
Eyre, Sir Graham Newman, Kt., QC
Eyre, *Maj.-Gen.* Sir James Ainsworth
  Campden Gabriel, KCVO, CBE
Eyre, Sir Reginald Edwin, Kt.
Faber, Sir Richard Stanley, KCVO, CMG
Fadahunsi, Sir Joseph Odeleye, KCMG
Fagge, Sir John William Frederick,
  Bt. (1660)
Fairbairn, *Hon.* Sir David Eric, KBE,
  DFC
Fairbairn, Sir (James) Brooke, Bt.
  (1869)
Fairbairn, Sir Nicholas Hardwick, Kt.,
  QC, MP
Fairclough, Sir John Whitaker, Kt.,
  FEng.
Fairgrieve, Sir (Thomas) Russell, Kt.,
  CBE, TD
Fairhall, *Hon.* Sir Allen, KBE
Fairweather, Sir Patrick Stanislaus,
  KCMG
Falconer, *Hon.* Sir Douglas William,
  Kt., MBE
Falk, Sir Roger Salis, Kt., OBE
Falkiner, Sir Edmond Charles, Bt.
  (I. 1778)
Fall, Sir Brian James Proetel, KCMG
Falle, Sir Samuel, KCMG, KCVO, DSC
Fareed, Sir Djamil Sheik, Kt.
Farmer, Sir (Lovedin) George
  Thomas, Kt.
Farndale, *Gen.* Sir Martin Baker, KCB
Farquhar, Sir Michael Fitzroy Henry,
  Bt. (1796)
Farquharson, *Rt. Hon.* Sir Donald
  Henry, Kt.
Farquharson, Sir James Robbie, KBE
Farr, Sir John Arnold, Kt.
Farrer, Sir Charles Matthew, KCVO
Farrington, Sir Henry Francis Colden,
  Bt. (1818)
Fat, Sir (Maxime) Edouard (Lim Man)
  Lim, Kt.
Faulkner, Sir (James) Dennis
  (Compton), Kt., CBE, VRD
Fawcus, Sir (Robert) Peter, KBE, CMG
Fawkes, Sir Randol Francis, Kt.
Fay, Sir (Humphrey) Michael Gerard,
  Kt.
Fayrer, Sir John Lang Macpherson,
  Bt. (1896)
Fearn, Sir (Patrick) Robin, KCMG

Feilden, Sir Bernard Melchior, Kt.,
  CBE
Feilden, Sir Henry Wemyss, Bt.,
  (1846)
Feldman, Sir Basil Samuel, Kt.
Fell, Sir Anthony, Kt.
Fellowes, *Rt. Hon.* Sir Robert, KCB,
  KCVO
Fenn, Sir Nicholas Maxted, KCMG
Fennell, *Hon.* Sir (John) Desmond
  Augustine, Kt., OBE
Fennessy, Sir Edward, Kt., CBE
†Ferguson, Sir Ian Edward Johnson-,
  Bt. (1906)
Fergusson of Kilkerran, Sir Charles,
  Bt. (s. 1703)
Fergusson, Sir Ewan Alastair John,
  GCMG, GCVO
Fergusson, Sir James Herbert
  Hamilton Colyer-, Bt. (1866)
Feroze, Sir Rustam Moolan, Kt., FRCS
Ferris, *Hon.* Sir Francis Mursell, Kt.,
  TD
ffolkes, Sir Robert Francis Alexander,
  Bt, OBE (1774)
Field, Sir Malcolm David, Kt.
Fielding, Sir Colin Cunningham, Kt.,
  CB
Fielding, Sir Leslie, KCMG
Fiennes, Sir John Saye Wingfield
  Twisleton-Wykeham-, KCB, QC
Fiennes, Sir Maurice Alberic
  Twisleton-Wykeham-, Kt.
Fiennes, Sir Ranulph Twisleton-
  Wykeham-, Bt., OBE (1916)
Figg, Sir Leonard Clifford William,
  KCMG
Figgess, Sir John George, KBE, CMG
Figures, Sir Colin Frederick, KCMG,
  OBE
Fingland, Sir Stanley James Gunn,
  KCMG
Finlay, Sir David Ronald James Bell,
  Bt. (1964)
Finley, Sir Peter Hamilton, Kt., OBE,
  DFC
Firth, *Prof.* Sir Raymond William,
  Kt., Ph.D., FBA
Fish, Sir Hugh, Kt., CBE
Fisher, Sir George Read, Kt., CMG
Fisher, *Hon.* Sir Henry Arthur Pears,
  Kt.
Fisher, Sir Nigel Thomas Loveridge,
  Kt., MC
Fison, Sir (Richard) Guy, Bt., DSC
  (1905)
†Fitzgerald, *Revd* (Sir) Daniel Patrick,
  Bt. (1903)
FitzGerald, Sir George Peter Maurice,
  Bt., MC (*The Knight of Kerry*) (1880)
FitzHerbert, Sir Richard Ranulph, Bt.
  (1784)
Fitzpatrick, *Gen.* Sir (Geoffrey
  Richard) Desmond, GCB, DSO, MBE,
  MC
Fitzpatrick, *Air Marshal* Sir John
  Bernard, KBE, CB
Flanagan, Sir James Bernard, Kt., CBE

Flavelle, Sir (Joseph) David Ellsworth, Bt. (1917)

Fleming, *Instructor Rear-Adm.* Sir John, KBE, DSC

Fletcher, Sir Henry Egerton Aubrey-, Bt. (1782)

Fletcher, Sir James Muir Cameron, Kt.

Fletcher, Sir Leslie, Kt., DSC

Fletcher, *Air Chief Marshal* Sir Peter Carteret, KCB, OBE, DFC, AFC

Floissac, *Hon.* Sir Vincent Frederick, Kt., CMG, OBE, QC

Floyd, Sir Giles Henry Charles, Bt. (1816)

Foley, *Lt.-Gen.* Sir John Paul, KCB, OBE, MC

Foley, Sir (Thomas John) Noel, Kt., CBE

Follett, *Prof.* Sir Brian Keith, Kt., FRS

Foot, Sir Geoffrey James, Kt.

Foots, Sir James William, Kt.

Forbes, *Hon.* Sir Alastair Granville, Kt.

Forbes, *Maj.* Sir Hamish Stewart, Bt., MBE, MC (1823)

Forbes of Craigievar, Sir John Alexander Cumnock, Bt. (s. 1630)

Forbes, *Vice-Adm.* Sir John Morrison, KCB

Forbes, *Hon.* Sir Thayne John, Kt.

†Forbes of Pitsligo, Sir William Daniel Stuart-, Bt. (s. 1626)

Ford, Sir Andrew Russell, Bt. (1929)

Ford, Sir David Robert, KBE, LVO, OBE

Ford, *Maj.* Sir Edward William Spencer, KCB, KCVO

Ford, *Air Marshal* Sir Geoffrey Harold, KBE, CB, FEng.

Ford, *Prof.* Sir Hugh, Kt., FRS, FEng.

Ford, Sir James Anson St Clair-, Bt. (1793)

Ford, Sir John Archibald, KCMG, MC

Ford, Sir Richard Brinsley, Kt., CBE

Ford, *Gen.* Sir Robert Cyril, GCB, CBE

Foreman, Sir Philip Frank, Kt., CBE, FEng.

Forman, Sir John Denis, Kt., OBE

Forrest, *Prof.* Sir (Andrew) Patrick (McEwen), Kt.

Forrest, *Rear-Adm.* Sir Ronald Stephen, KCVO

Forster, Sir Archibald William, Kt., FEng.

Forster, Sir Oliver Grantham, KCMG, MVO

Forwood, Sir Dudley Richard, Bt. (1895)

Foster, *Prof.* Sir Christopher David, Kt.

Foster, Sir John Gregory, Bt. (1930)

Foster, Sir Norman Robert, Kt.

Foster, Sir Robert Sidney, GCMG, KCVO

Foulis, Sir Ian Primrose Liston-, Bt. (s. 1634)

Foulkes, Sir Nigel Gordon, Kt.

Fowden, Sir Leslie, Kt., FRS

Fowke, Sir David Frederick Gustavus, Bt. (1814)

Fowler, Sir (Edward) Michael Coulson, Kt.

Fowler, *Rt. Hon.* Sir (Peter) Norman, Kt., MP

Fox, Sir (Henry) Murray, GBE

Fox, Sir (John) Marcus, Kt., MBE, MP

Fox, *Rt. Hon.* Sir Michael John, Kt.

Fox, Sir Paul Leonard, Kt., CBE

France, Sir Arnold William, GCB

France, Sir Christopher Walter, GCB

Francis, Sir Horace William Alexander, Kt., CBE, FEng.

Frank, Sir Douglas George Horace, Kt., QC

Frank, Sir (Frederick) Charles, Kt., OBE, FRS

Frank, Sir Robert Andrew, Bt. (1920)

Frankel, Sir Otto Herzberg, Kt., D.SC., FRS

Franklin, Sir Eric Alexander, Kt., CBE

Franklin, Sir Michael David Milroy, KCB, CMG

Franks, Sir Arthur Temple, KCMG

Fraser, Sir Angus McKay, KCB, TD

Fraser, Sir Charles Annand, KCVO

Fraser, *Gen.* Sir David William, GCB, OBE

Fraser, *Air Marshal Revd* Sir (Henry) Paterson, KBE, CB, AFC

Fraser, Sir Ian, Kt., DSO, OBE

Fraser, Sir Ian James, Kt., CBE, MC

Fraser, Sir (James) Campbell, Kt.

Fraser, *Prof.* Sir James David, Bt. (1943)

Fraser, Sir William Kerr, GCB

Frederick, Sir Charles Boscawen, Bt. (1723)

Freeland, Sir John Redvers, KCMG

Freeman, Sir James Robin, Bt. (1945)

Freeman, Sir Ralph, Kt., CVO, CBE, FEng.

Freer, *Air Chief Marshal* Sir Robert William George, GBE, KCB

Freeth, *Hon.* Sir Gordon, KBE

French, *Hon.* Sir Christopher James Saunders, Kt.

Frere, *Vice-Adm.* Sir Richard Tobias, KCB

Fretwell, Sir (Major) John (Emsley), GCMG

Freud, Sir Clement Raphael, Kt.

Froggatt, Sir Leslie Trevor, Kt.

Froggatt, Sir Peter, Kt.

Frossard, Sir Charles Keith, KBE

Frost, Sir David Paradine, Kt., OBE

Frost, *Hon.* Sir (Thomas) Sydney, Kt.

Fry, Sir Peter Derek, Kt., MP

Fry, *Hon.* Sir William Gordon, Kt.

Fryberg, Sir Abraham, Kt., MBE

Fuchs, Sir Vivian Ernest, Kt., ph.D.

Fuller, *Hon.* Sir John Bryan Munro, Kt.

Fuller, Sir John William Fleetwood, Bt. (1910)

Fung, *Hon.* Sir Kenneth Ping-Fan, Kt., CBE

Furness, Sir Stephen Roberts, Bt. (1913)

Gadsden, Sir Peter Drury Haggerston, GBE, FEng.

Gage, *Hon.* Sir William Marcus, Kt.

Gairy, *Rt. Hon.* Sir Eric Matthew, Kt.

Gaius, *Rt. Revd* Saimon, KBE

Gallwey, Sir Philip Frankland Payne-, Bt. (1812)

Gamble, Sir David Hugh Norman, Bt. (1897)

Garden, *Air Marshal* Sir Timothy, KCB

Gardiner, Sir George Arthur, Kt., MP

Gardner, Sir Douglas Bruce Bruce-, Bt. (1945)

Gardner, Sir Edward Lucas, Kt., QC

Garland, *Hon.* Sir Patrick Neville, Kt.

Garland, *Hon.* Sir Ransley Victor, KBE

Garlick, Sir John, KCB

Garner, Sir Anthony Stuart, Kt.

Garnier, *Rear-Adm.* Sir John, KCVO, CBE, LVO

Garrett, *Hon.* Sir Raymond William, Kt., AFC

Garrick, Sir Ronald, Kt., CBE, F.Eng.

Garrioch, Sir (William) Henry, Kt.

Garrod, *Lt.-Gen.* Sir (John) Martin Carruthers, KCB, OBE

†Garthwaite, Sir (William) Mark (Charles), Bt. (1919)

Gaskell, Sir Richard Kennedy Harvey, Kt.

Gatehouse, *Hon.* Sir Robert Alexander, Kt.

Geddes, Sir (Anthony) Reay (Mackay), KBE

George, Sir Arthur Thomas, Kt.

Gerken, *Vice-Adm.* Sir Robert William Frank, KCB, CBE

Gery, Sir Robert Lucian Wade-, KCMG, KCVO

Gethin, Sir Richard Joseph St Lawrence, Bt. (I. 1665)

Ghurburrun, Sir Rabindrah, Kt.

Gibb, Sir Francis Ross (Frank), Kt., CBE, FEng.

Gibbings, Sir Peter Walter, Kt.

Gibbon, *Gen.* Sir John Houghton, GCB, OBE

Gibbons, Sir (John) David, KBE

Gibbons, Sir William Edward Doran, Bt. (1752)

Gibbs, *Hon.* Sir Eustace Hubert Beilby, KCVO, CMG

Gibbs, *Rt. Hon.* Sir Harry Talbot, GCMG, KBE

Gibbs, Sir Roger Geoffrey, Kt.

Gibbs, *Field Marshal* Sir Roland Christopher, GCB, CBE, DSO, MC

Gibson, Sir Alexander Drummond, Kt., CBE

†Gibson, *Revd* Sir Christopher Herbert, Bt. (1931)

Gibson, *Revd* Sir David, Bt. (1926)

Gibson, *Vice-Adm.* Sir Donald Cameron Ernest Forbes, KCB, DSC

Gibson, *Rt. Hon.* Sir Peter Leslie, Kt.

Gibson, *Rt. Hon.* Sir Ralph Brian, Kt.

Giddings, *Air Marshal* Sir (Kenneth Charles) Michael, KCB, OBE, DFC, AFC

Gielgud, Sir (Arthur) John, Kt., CH
Giffard, Sir (Charles) Sydney (Rycroft), KCMG
Gilbert, *Air Chief Marshal* Sir Joseph Alfred, KCB, CBE
†Gilbey, Sir Walter Gavin, Bt. (1893)
Giles, *Rear-Adm.* Sir Morgan Charles Morgan-, Kt., DSO, OBE, GM
Gill, Sir Anthony Keith, Kt., F.Eng.
Gillett, Sir Robin Danvers Penrose, Bt., GBE, RD (1959)
Gillmore, Sir David Howe, GCMG
Gilmour, *Col.* Sir Allan Macdonald, KCVO, OBE, MC
Gilmour, Sir John Edward, Bt., DSO, TD (1897)
Gina, Sir Lloyd Maepeza, KBE
Gingell, *Air Chief Marshal* Sir John, GBE, KCB, KCVO
Girolami, Sir Paul, Kt.
Gladstone, Sir (Erskine) William, Bt. (1846)
Glasspole, Sir Florizel Augustus, GCMG, GCVO
Glen, Sir Alexander Richard, KBE, DSC
Glenn, Sir (Joseph Robert) Archibald, Kt., OBE
Glidewell, *Rt. Hon.* Sir Iain Derek Laing, Kt.
Glock, Sir William Frederick, Kt., CBE
Glover, *Gen.* Sir James Malcolm, KCB, MBE
Glover, Sir Victor Joseph Patrick, Kt.
Glyn, Sir Alan, Kt., ERD
Glyn, Sir Anthony Geoffrey Leo Simon, Bt. (1927)
Glyn, Sir Richard Lindsay, Bt. (1759 and 1800)
Goad, Sir (Edward) Colin (Viner), KCMG
Godber, Sir George Edward, GCB, DM
Goff, Sir Robert (William) Davis-, Bt. (1905)
Gohel, Sir Jayvantsinhji Kayaji, Kt., CBE
Gold, Sir Arthur Abraham, Kt., CBE
Gold, Sir Joseph, Kt.
Goldberg, *Prof.* Sir Abraham, Kt., MD, DSC, FRCP
Golding, Sir John Simon Rawson, Kt., OBE
Goldman, Sir Samuel, KCB
Goldsmith, Sir James Michael, Kt.
Gombrich, *Prof.* Sir Ernst Hans Josef, Kt., OM, CBE, Ph.D., FBA, FSA
Gooch, Sir (Richard) John Sherlock, Bt. (1746)
Gooch, Sir Trevor Sherlock (Sir Peter), Bt. (1866)
Goodall, Sir (Arthur) David Saunders, GCMG
Goodenough, Sir Richard Edmund, Bt. (1943)
Goodhart, Sir Philip Carter, Kt.
Goodhart, Sir Robert Anthony Gordon, Bt. (1911)
Goodhart, Sir William Howard, Kt., QC
Goodhew, Sir Victor Henry, Kt.

Goodison, Sir Alan Clowes, KCMG
Goodison, Sir Nicholas Proctor, Kt.
Goodson, Sir Mark Weston Lassam, Bt. (1922)
Goodwin, Sir Matthew Dean, Kt., CBE
Goody, *Most Revd* Launcelot John, KBE
Goold, Sir George Leonard, Bt. (1801)
Gordon, Sir Alexander John, Kt., CBE
Gordon, Sir Andrew Cosmo Lewis Duff-, Bt. (1813)
Gordon, Sir Charles Addison Somerville Snowden, KCB
Gordon, Sir Keith Lyndell, Kt., CMG
Gordon, Sir (Lionel) Eldred (Peter) Smith-, Bt. (1838)
Gordon, Sir Robert James, Bt. (s. 1706)
Gordon, Sir Sidney Samuel, Kt., CBE
Gordon Lennox, Lord Nicholas Charles, KCMG, KCVO
Gore, Sir Richard Ralph St George, Bt. (I. 1622)
Goring, Sir William Burton Nigel, Bt. (1627)
Gorst, Sir John Michael, Kt., MP
Gorton, *Rt. Hon.* Sir John Grey, GCMG, CH
Goschen, Sir Edward Christian, Bt., DSO (1916)
Gosling, Sir (Frederick) Donald, Kt.
Goswell, Sir Brian Lawrence, Kt.
Goulding, Sir (Ernest) Irvine, Kt.
Goulding, Sir (William) Lingard Walter, Bt. (1904)
Gourlay, *Gen.* Sir (Basil) Ian (Spencer), KCB, OBE, MC, RM
Gourlay, Sir Simon Alexander, Kt.
Govan, Sir Lawrence Herbert, Kt.
Gow, *Gen.* Sir (James) Michael, GCB
Gow, Sir Leonard Maxwell Harper, Kt., MBE
Gowans, Sir James Learmonth, Kt., CBE, FRCP, FRS
Gowans, *Hon.* Sir (Urban) Gregory, Kt.
Graaff, Sir de Villiers, Bt., MBE (1911)
Grabham, Sir Anthony Henry, Kt.
Graham, Sir Alexander Michael, GBE
Graham, Sir Charles Spencer Richard, Bt. (1783)
Graham, Sir James Bellingham, Bt. (1662)
Graham, Sir James Thompson, Kt., CMG
Graham, Sir John Alexander Noble, Bt., GCMG (1906)
Graham, Sir John Moodie, Bt. (1964)
Graham, Sir Norman William, Kt., CB
Graham, Sir Peter, KCB, QC
Graham, Sir Peter Alfred, Kt., OBE
Graham, *Lt.-Gen.* Sir Peter Walter, KCB, CBE
†Graham, Sir Ralph Stuart, Bt. (1629)
Graham, *Hon.* Sir Samuel Horatio, Kt., CMG, OBE
Grandy, *Marshal of the Royal Air Force* Sir John, GCB, GCVO, KBE, DSO
Grant, Sir Archibald, Bt. (s. 1705)

Grant, Sir Clifford, Kt.
Grant, Sir (John) Anthony, Kt., MP
Grant, Sir (Matthew) Alistair, Kt.
Grant, Sir Patrick Alexander Benedict, Bt. (s. 1688)
Gray, Sir John Archibald Browne, Kt., SC.D., FRS
Gray, *Vice-Adm.* Sir John Michael Dudgeon, KBE, CB
Gray, *Lt.-Gen.* Sir Michael Stuart, KCB, OBE
Gray, Sir Robert McDowall (Robin), Kt.
Gray, Sir William Hume, Bt. (1917)
Gray, Sir William Stevenson, Kt.
Graydon, *Air Chief Marshal* Sir Michael James, GCB, CBE
Grayson, Sir Jeremy Brian Vincent Harrington, Bt. (1922)
Green, Sir Allan David, KCB, QC
Green, Sir (Edward) Stephen (Lycett), Bt., CBE (1886)
Green, *Hon.* Sir Guy Stephen Montague, KBE
Green, Sir Kenneth, Kt.
Green, Sir Owen Whitley, Kt.
Green, Sir Peter James Frederick, Kt.
Greenaway, Sir Derek Burdick, Bt., CBE (1933)
Greenborough, Sir John, KBE
Greenbury, Sir Richard, Kt.
Greene, Sir (John) Brian Massy-, Kt.
Greengross, Sir Alan David, Kt.
Greening, *Rear-Adm.* Sir Paul Woollven, GCVO
Greenwell, Sir Edward Bernard, Bt. (1906)
Gregson, Sir Peter Lewis, KCB
Grenside, Sir John Peter, Kt., CBE
Grey, Sir Anthony Dysart, Bt. (1814)
Grey, Sir Roger de, KCVO, PPRA
Grierson, Sir Michael John Bewes, Bt. (s. 1685)
Grierson, Sir Ronald Hugh, Kt.
Grieve, *Prof.* Sir Robert, Kt.
Griffin, *Adm.* Sir Anthony Templer Frederick Griffith, GCB
Griffin, *Maj.* Sir (Arthur) John (Stewart), KCVO
Griffin, Sir (Charles) David, Kt., CBE
Griffiths, Sir Eldon Wylie, Kt.
Griffiths, Sir John Norton-, Bt. (1922)
Grimwade, Sir Andrew Sheppard, Kt., CBE
Grindrod, *Most Revd* John Basil Rowland, KBE
Grinstead, Sir Stanley Gordon, Kt.
Grose, *Vice-Adm.* Sir Alan, KBE
Grotrian, Sir Philip Christian Brent, Bt. (1934)
Grove, Sir Charles Gerald, Bt. (1874)
Grove, Sir Edmund Frank, KCVO
Grugeon, Sir John Drury, Kt.
Grylls, Sir (William) Michael (John), Kt., MP
Guinness, Sir Alec, Kt., CH, CBE
Guinness, Sir Howard Christian Sheldon, Kt., VRD

Guinness, Sir Kenelm Ernest Lee, Bt. (1867)

Guise, Sir John Grant, Bt. (1783)

Gujadhur, Sir Radhamohun, Kt., CMG

Gull, Sir Rupert William Cameron, Bt. (1872)

Gumbs, Sir Emile Rudolph, Kt.

Gunn, *Prof.* Sir John Currie, Kt., CBE

Gunn, Sir William Archer, KBE, CMG

†Gunning, Sir Charles Theodore, Bt. (1778)

Gunston, Sir John Wellesley, Bt. (1938)

Guthrie, *Gen.* Sir Charles Ronald Llewelyn, GCB, LVO, OBE

Guthrie, Sir Malcolm Connop, Bt., (1936)

Guy, *Gen.* Sir Roland Kelvin, GCB, CBE, DSO

Habakkuk, Sir John Hrothgar, Kt., FBA

Hackett, *Gen.* Sir John Winthrop, GCB, CBE, DSO, MC

Hadlee, Sir Richard John, Kt., MBE

Hadley, Sir Leonard Albert, Kt.

Hague, *Prof.* Sir Douglas Chalmers, Kt., CBE

Halberg, Sir Murray Gordon, Kt., MBE

Hale, *Prof.* Sir John Rigby, Kt.

Hall, Sir Arnold Alexander, Kt., FRS, FEng.

Hall, *Air Marshal* Sir Donald Percy, KCB, CBE, AFC

Hall, Sir Douglas Basil, Bt., KCMG (s. 1687)

Hall, Sir Ernest, Kt., OBE

Hall, Sir (Frederick) John (Frank), Bt. (1923)

Hall, Sir John, Kt.

Hall, Sir John Bernard, Bt. (1919)

Hall, Sir Peter Edward, KBE, CMG

Hall, Sir Peter Reginald Frederick, Kt., CBE

Hall, Sir Robert de Zouche, KCMG

Hall, *Brig.* Sir William Henry, KBE, DSO, ED

Halliday, *Vice-Adm.* Sir Roy William, KBE, DSC

Hallinan, Sir (Adrian) Lincoln, Kt.

Halpern, Sir Ralph Mark, Kt.

Halsey, *Revd* Sir John Walter Brooke, Bt. (1920)

Halstead, Sir Ronald, Kt., CBE

Ham, Sir David Kenneth Rowe-, GBE

Hambling, Sir (Herbert) Hugh, Bt. (1924)

Hamburger, Sir Sidney Cyril, Kt., CBE

Hamer, *Hon.* Sir Rupert James, KCMG, ED

Hamill, Sir Patrick, Kt., QPM

Hamilton, *Rt. Hon.* Sir Archibald Gavin, Kt., MP

Hamilton, Sir Edward Sydney, Bt. (1776 and 1819)

Hamilton, Sir James Arnot, KCB, MBE, FEng.

Hamilton, *Adm.* Sir John Graham, GBE, CB

Hamilton, Sir Malcolm William Bruce Stirling-, Bt. (s. 1673)

Hamilton, Sir Michael Aubrey, Kt.

Hamilton, Sir (Robert Charles) Richard Caradoc, Bt. (s. 1646)

Hammett, *Hon.* Sir Clifford James, Kt.

Hammick, Sir Stephen George, Bt. (1834)

Hampshire, Sir Stuart Newton, Kt., FBA

Hanbury, Sir John Capel, Kt., CBE

Hancock, Sir David John Stowell, KCB

Hancock, *Air Marshal* Sir Valston Eldridge, KBE, CB, DFC

Hand, *Most Revd* Geoffrey David, KBE

Handley, Sir David John Davenport-, Kt., OBE

Hanham, Sir Michael William, Bt., DFC (1667)

Hanley, Sir Michael Bowen, KCB

Hanmer, Sir John Wyndham Edward, Bt. (1774)

Hannam, Sir John Gordon, Kt., MP

Hannay, Sir David Hugh Alexander, KCMG

Hanson, Sir Anthony Leslie Oswald, Bt. (1887)

Hanson, Sir (Charles) John, Bt. (1918)

Happold, *Prof.* Sir Edmund, Kt, FEng.

Hardcastle, Sir Alan John, Kt.

Harders, Sir Clarence Waldemar, Kt., OBE

Hardie, Sir Charles Edgar Mathewes, Kt., CBE

Hardie, Sir Douglas Fleming, Kt., CBE

Harding, Sir Christopher George Francis, Kt.

Harding, Sir George William, KCMG, CVO

Harding, *Marshal of the Royal Air Force* Sir Peter Robin, GCB

Harding, Sir Roy Pollard, Kt., CBE

Hardinge, Sir Robert Arnold, Bt. (1801)

Hardman, Sir Henry, KCB

Hardy, Sir David William, Kt.

Hardy, Sir James Gilbert, Kt., OBE

Hardy, Sir Rupert John, Bt. (1876)

Hare, Sir Philip Leigh, Bt. (1818)

Harford, Sir (John) Timothy, Bt. (1934)

Hargroves, *Brig.* Sir Robert Louis, Kt., CBE

Harington, *Gen.* Sir Charles Henry Pepys, GCB, CBE, DSO, MC

Harington, Sir Nicholas John, Bt. (1611)

Harland, *Air Marshal* Sir Reginald Edward Wynyard, KBE, CB

Harman, *Gen.* Sir Jack Wentworth, GCB, OBE, MC

Harman, *Hon.* Sir Jeremiah LeRoy, Kt.

Harmer, Sir Frederic Evelyn, Kt., CMG

Harmsworth, Sir Hildebrand Harold, Bt. (1922)

Harpham, Sir William, KBE, CMG

Harris, *Prof.* Sir Alan James, Kt., CBE, FEng.

Harris, Sir Anthony Kyrle Travers, Bt. (1953)

Harris, *Prof.* Sir Charles Herbert Stuart-, Kt., CBE, MD

Harris, *Prof.* Sir Henry, Kt., FRCP, FRCPath., FRS

Harris, *Lt.-Gen.* Sir Ian Cecil, KBE, CB, DSO

Harris, Sir Jack Wolfred Ashford, Bt. (1932)

Harris, *Air Marshal* Sir John Hulme, KCB, CBE

Harris, Sir Philip Charles, Kt.

Harris, Sir Ronald Montague Joseph, KCVO, CB

Harris, Sir William Gordon, KBE, CB, FEng.

Harrison, *Prof.* Sir Donald Frederick Norris, Kt., FRCS

Harrison, Sir Ernest Thomas, Kt., OBE

Harrison, Sir Francis Alexander Lyle, Kt., MBE, QC

Harrison, *Surgeon Vice-Adm.* Sir John Albert Bews, KBE

Harrison, *Hon.* Sir (John) Richard, Kt., ED

Harrison, *Hon.* Sir Michael Guy Vicat, Kt.

Harrison, Sir Michael James Harwood, Bt. (1961)

Harrison, *Prof.* Sir Richard John, Kt., FRS

Harrison, Sir (Robert) Colin, Bt. (1922)

Harrop, Sir Peter John, KCB

Hartley, *Air Marshal* Sir Christopher Harold, KCB, CBE, DFC, AFC

Hartley, Sir Frank, Kt., CBE, Ph.D.

Hartopp, Sir John Edmund Cradock-, Bt. (1796)

†Hartwell, Sir (Francis) Anthony Charles Peter, Bt. (1805)

Harvey, Sir Charles Richard Musgrave, Bt. (1933)

Haskard, Sir Cosmo Dugal Patrick Thomas, KCMG, MBE

Haslam, *Hon.* Sir Alec Leslie, Kt.

Haslam, *Rear-Adm.* Sir David William, KBE, CB

Hassan, Sir Joshua Abraham, GBE, KCMG, LVO, QC

Hassett, *Gen.* Sir Francis George, KBE, CB, DSO, MVO

Hastings, Sir Stephen Lewis Edmonstone, Kt., MC

Hatty, *Hon.* Sir Cyril James, Kt.

Haughton, Sir James, Kt., CBE, QPM

Havelock, Sir Wilfrid Bowen, Kt.

Hawkins, Sir Arthur Ernest, Kt.

†Hawkins, Sir Howard Caesar, Bt. (1778)

Hawkins, Sir Paul Lancelot, Kt., TD

Hawley, Sir Donald Frederick, KCMG, MBE

†Hawley, Sir Henry Nicholas, Bt. (1795)

Haworth, Sir Philip, Bt. (1911)

Hawthorne, *Prof.* Sir William Rede, Kt., CBE, SC.D., FRS, FEng.

Hay, Sir David Osborne, Kt., CBE, DSO

Hay, Sir David Russell, Kt., CBE, FRCP, MD

Hay, Sir Hamish Grenfell, Kt.

Hay, Sir James Brian Dalrymple-, Bt. (1798)

†Hay, Sir John Erroll Audley, Bt. (S. 1663)

†Hay, Sir Ronald Frederick Hamilton, Bt. (S. 1703)

Haydon, Sir Walter Robert, KCMG

Hayes, Sir Brian David, GCB

Hayes, Sir Claude James, KCMG

Hayes, *Vice-Adm.* Sir John Osier Chattock, KCB, OBE

Hayr, *Air Marshal* Sir Kenneth William, KCB, KBE, AFC

Hayter, Sir William Goodenough, KCMG

Hayward, Sir Anthony William Byrd, Kt.

Hayward, Sir Jack Arnold, Kt., OBE

Haywood, Sir Harold, KCVO, OBE

Head, Sir Francis David Somerville, Bt. (1838)

Healey, Sir Charles Edward Chadwyck-, Bt. (1919)

Heap, Sir Desmond, Kt.

Heath, *Rt. Hon.* Sir Edward Richard George, KG, MBE, MP

Heath, Sir Mark Evelyn, KCVO, CMG

Heath, *Air Marshal* Sir Maurice Lionel, KBE, CB, CVO

Heathcote, *Brig.* Sir Gilbert Simon, Bt., CBE (1733)

Heathcote, Sir Michael Perryman, Bt. (1733)

Heatley, Sir Peter, Kt., CBE

Heaton, Sir Yvo Robert Henniker-, Bt. (1912)

Heiser, Sir Terence Michael, GCB

Hele, Sir Ivor Thomas Henry, Kt., CBE

Hellaby, Sir (Frederick Reed) Alan, Kt.

Henderson, Sir Denys Hartley, Kt.

Henderson, Sir (John) Nicholas, GCMG, KCVO

Henderson, Sir William MacGregor, Kt., D.SC., FRS

Henley, Sir Douglas Owen, KCB

Henley, *Rear-Adm.* Sir Joseph Charles Cameron, KCVO, CB

Hennessy, Sir James Patrick Ivan, KBE, CMG

Hennessy, Sir John Wyndham Pope-, Kt., CBE, FBA, FSA

†Henniker, Sir Adrian Chandos, Bt. (1813)

Henry, Sir Denis Aynsley, Kt., OBE, QC

Henry, *Rt. Hon.* Denis Robert Maurice, Kt.

Henry, *Hon.* Sir Geoffrey Arama, KBE

Henry, Sir James Holmes, Bt., CMG, MC, TD, QC (1923)

Henry, *Hon.* Sir Trevor Ernest, Kt.

Hepburn, Sir John Alastair Trant Kidd Buchan-, Bt. (1815)

Herbecq, Sir John Edward, KCB

Herbert, *Adm.* Sir Peter Geoffrey Marshall, KCB, OBE

Hermon, Sir John Charles, Kt., OBE, QPM

Heron, Sir Conrad Frederick, KCB, OBE

Herries, Sir Michael Alexander Robert Young-, Kt., OBE, MC

Hervey, Sir Roger Blaise Ramsay, KCVO, CMG

Heseltine, *Rt. Hon.* Sir William Frederick Payne, GCB, GCVO

Hetherington, Sir Arthur Ford, Kt., DSC, FEng.

Hetherington, Sir Thomas Chalmers, KCB, CBE, TD, QC

Heward, *Air Chief Marshal* Sir Anthony Wilkinson, KCB, OBE, DFC, AFC

Hewetson, Sir Christopher Raynor, Kt., TD

Hewett, Sir Peter John Smithson, Bt., MM (1813)

Hewitt, Sir (Cyrus) Lenox (Simson), Kt., OBE

Hewitt, Sir Nicholas Charles Joseph, Bt. (1921)

†Heygate, Sir Richard John Gage, Bt. (1831)

Heyman, Sir Horace William, Kt.

Heywood, Sir Peter, Bt. (1838)

Hezlet, *Vice-Adm.* Sir Arthur Richard, KBE, CB, DSO, DSC

Hibbert, Sir Jack, KCB

Hibbert, Sir Reginald Alfred, GCMG

Hickey, Sir Justin, Kt.

Hickman, Sir (Richard) Glenn, Bt. (1903)

Hidden, *Hon.* Sir Anthony Brian, Kt.

Hielscher, Sir Leo Arthur, Kt.

Higgins, Sir Christopher Thomas, Kt.

Higgins, *Hon.* Sir Malachy Joseph, Kt.

Higgins, *Rt. Hon.* Sir Terence Langley, KBE, MP

Higginson, Sir Gordon Robert, Kt., Ph.D., FEng.

Higgs, Sir (John) Michael (Clifford), Kt.

Highgate, Sir James Brown, Kt., CBE

Hildyard, Sir David Henry Thoroton, KCMG, DFC

Hill, Sir Alexander Rodger Erskine-, Bt. (1945)

Hill, Sir Arthur Alfred, Kt., CBE

Hill, Sir Brian John, Kt.

Hill, Sir James Frederick, Bt. (1917)

Hill, Sir John McGregor, Kt., Ph.D., FEng.

Hill, Sir John Maxwell, Kt., CBE, DFC

†Hill, Sir John Rowley, Bt. (I. 1779)

Hill, *Vice-Adm.* Sir Robert Charles Finch, KBE, FEng.

Hillary, Sir Edmund, KBE

Hillhouse, Sir (Robert) Russell, KCB

Hills, Sir Graham John, Kt.

Hilton, *Col.* Sir Peter, KCVO, MC

Hine, *Air Chief Marshal* Sir Patrick Bardon, GCB, GBE

Hines, Sir Colin Joseph, Kt., OBE

Hinsley, *Prof.* Sir Francis Harry, Kt., OBE, FBA

Hirsch, *Prof.* Sir Peter Bernhard, Kt., Ph.D., FRS

Hirst, *Rt. Hon.* Sir David Cozens-Hardy, Kt.

Hirst, Sir Michael William, Kt.

Hoare, Sir Peter Richard David, Bt. (1786)

Hoare, Sir Timothy Edward Charles, Bt. (I. 1784)

Hobart, Sir John Vere, Bt. (1914)

Hobday, Sir Gordon Ivan, Kt.

Hobhouse, Sir Charles John Spinney, Bt. (1812)

Hobhouse, *Rt. Hon.* Sir John Stewart, Kt.

Hockaday, Sir Arthur Patrick, KCB, CMG

Hockley, *Gen.* Sir Anthony Heritage Farrar-, GBE, KCB, DSO, MC

Hodge, Sir John Rowland, Bt., MBE (1921)

Hodge, Sir Julian Stephen Alfred, Kt.

Hodges, *Air Chief Marshal* Sir Lewis MacDonald, KCB, CBE, DSO, DFC

Hodgkin, *Prof.* Sir Alan Lloyd, OM, KBE, FRS, SC.D.

Hodgkin, Sir Gordon Howard Eliot, Kt., CBE

Hodgkinson, *Air Chief Marshal* Sir (William) Derek, KCB, CBE, DFC, AFC

Hodgson, Sir Maurice Arthur Eric, Kt., FEng.

Hodgson, *Hon.* Sir (Walter) Derek (Thornley), Kt.

Hodson, Sir Michael Robin Adderley, Bt. (I. 1789)

Hoffenberg, *Prof.* Sir Raymond, KBE

Hoffman, *Rt. Hon.* Sir Leonard Hubert, Kt.

Hogg, *Maj.* Sir Arthur Ramsay, Bt., MBE (1846)

Hogg, Sir Christopher Anthony, Kt.

Hogg, Sir Edward William Lindsay-, Bt. (1905)

Hogg, *Vice-Adm.* Sir Ian Leslie Trower, KCB, DSC

Hogg, Sir John Nicholson, Kt., TD

Holcroft, Sir Peter George Culcheth, Bt. (1921)

Holden, Sir David Charles Beresford, KBE, CB, ERD

Holden, Sir Edward, Bt. (1893)

Holden, Sir John David, Bt. (1919)

Holder, Sir John Henry, Bt. (1898)

Holder, *Air Marshal* Sir Paul Davie, KBE, CB, DSO, DFC, Ph.D.

Holderness, Sir Richard William, Bt. (1920)

Holdgate, Sir Martin Wyatt, Kt., CB, Ph.D.

Holdsworth, Sir (George) Trevor, Kt.

Holland, *Hon.* Sir Christopher John, Kt.

Holland, Sir Clifton Vaughan, Kt.

Holland, Sir Geoffrey, KCB
Holland, Sir Guy (Hope), Bt. (1917)
Holland, Sir Kenneth Lawrence, Kt.,
CBE, QFSM
Holland, Sir Philip Welsby, Kt.
Holliday, *Prof.* Sir Frederick George
Thomas, Kt., CBE, FRSE
Hollings, *Hon.* Sir (Alfred) Kenneth,
Kt., MC
Hollis, *Hon.* Sir Anthony Barnard, Kt.
Holloway, *Hon.* Sir Barry Blyth, KBE
Holm, Sir Carl Henry, Kt., OBE
Holmes, *Prof.* Sir Frank Wakefield,
Kt.
Holmes, Sir Maurice Andrew, Kt.
Holmes, Sir Peter Fenwick, Kt., MC
Holroyd, *Air Marshal* Sir Frank
Martyn, KBE, CB, FEng.
Holt, *Prof.* Sir James Clarke, Kt.
Home, Sir William Dundas, Bt. (s.
1671)
Honeycombe, *Prof.* Sir Robert
William Kerr, Kt., FRS, FEng.
Honywood, Sir Filmer Courtenay
William, Bt. (1660)
Hood, Sir Alexander William Fuller-
Acland-, Bt. (1806)
Hood, Sir Harold Joseph, Bt., TD
(1922)
Hookway, Sir Harry Thurston, Kt.
Hoole, Sir Arthur Hugh, Kt.
Hope, Sir (Charles) Peter, KCMG, TD
Hope, Sir John Carl Alexander, Bt. (s.
1628)
Hopkin, Sir David Armand, Kt.
Hopkin, Sir (William Aylsham)
Bryan, Kt., CBE
Hopkins, Sir Anthony Philip, Kt., CBE
Hopkins, Sir James Sidney Rawdon
Scott-, Kt., MEP
Hopwood, Prof. Sir David Alan, Kt.,
FRS
Hordern, Sir Michael Murray, Kt.,
CBE
Hordern, *Rt. Hon.* Sir Peter
Maudslay, Kt., MP
Horlick, *Vice-Adm.* Sir Edwin John,
KBE, FEng.
Horlick, Sir John James Macdonald,
Bt. (1914)
Hornby, Sir Derek Peter, Kt.
Hornby, Sir Simon Michael, Kt.
Horne, Sir Alan Gray Antony, Bt.
(1929)
Horsfall, Sir John Musgrave, Bt., MC,
TD (1909)
Horsley, *Air Marshal* Sir (Beresford)
Peter (Torrington), KCB, CBE, MVO,
AFC
Hort, Sir James Fenton, Bt. (1767)
Hoskyns, Sir Benedict Leigh, Bt.
(1676)
Hoskyns, Sir John Austin Hungerford
Leigh, Kt.
Hotung, Sir Joseph Edward, Kt.
Houghton, Sir John Theodore, Kt.,
CBE, FRS

†Houldsworth, Sir Richard Thomas
Reginald, Bt. (1887)
Hounsfield, Sir Godfrey Newbold,
Kt., CBE
House, *Lt.-Gen.* Sir David George,
GCB, KCVO, CBE, MC
Houssemayne du Boulay, Sir Roger
William, KCVO, CMG
Howard, Sir (Hamilton) Edward de
Coucey, Bt., GBE (1955)
Howard, *Prof.* Sir Michael Eliot, Kt.,
CBE, MC
Howard, *Maj.-Gen.* Lord Michael
Fitzalan-, GCVO, CB, CBE, MC
Howell, Sir Ralph Frederic, Kt., MP
Howells, Sir Eric Waldo Benjamin,
Kt., CBE
Howard, Sir Walter Stewart, Kt., MBE
Howie, Sir James William, Kt., MD
Howlett, *Gen.* Sir Geoffrey Hugh
Whitby, KBE, MC
Hoyle, *Prof.* Sir Fred, Kt., FRS
Hoyos, *Hon.* Sir Fabriciano
Alexander, Kt.
Huckle, Sir (Henry) George, Kt., OBE
Huddie, Sir David Patrick, Kt., FEng.
Hudleston, *Air Chief Marshal* Sir
Edmund Cuthbert, GCB, CBE
Hudson, Sir Havelock Henry Trevor,
Kt.
Hudson, *Lt.-Gen.* Sir Peter, KCB, CBE
Huggins, *Hon.* Sir Alan Armstrong,
Kt.
Hugh-Jones, Sir Wynn Normington,
Kt., MVO
Hughes, Sir David Collingwood, Bt.
(1773)
Hughes, *Prof.* Sir Edward Stuart
Reginald, Kt., CBE
Hughes, Sir Jack William, Kt.
Hughes, *Air Marshal* Sir (Sidney
Weetman) Rochford, KCB, CBE, AFC
Hughes, Sir Trevor Denby Lloyd-, Kt.
Hughes, Sir Trevor Poulton, KCB
Hugo, *Lt.-Col.* Sir John Mandeville,
KCVO, OBE
Hull, *Prof.* Sir David, Kt.
Hulse, Sir (Hamilton) Westrow, Bt.
(1739)
Hume, Sir Alan Blyth, Kt., CB
Humphreys, Sir Olliver William, Kt.,
CBE
Humphreys, Sir (Raymond Evelyn)
Myles, Kt.
Hunn, Sir Jack Kent, Kt., CMG
Hunt, Sir David Wathen Stather,
KCMG, OBE
Hunt, Sir John Leonard, Kt., MP
Hunt, *Adm.* Sir Nicholas John
Streynsham, GCB, LVO
Hunt, Sir Rex Masterman, Kt., CMG
Hunt, Sir Robert Frederick, Kt., CBE,
FEng.
Hunter, *Hon.* Sir Alexander Albert,
KBE
Hunter, Sir Alistair John, KCMG
Hunter, Sir Ian Bruce Hope, Kt., MBE
Hurrell, Sir Anthony Gerald, KCVO,
CMG

Hutchinson, *Hon.* Sir Ross, Kt., DFC
Hutchison, *Lt.-Cdr.* Sir (George) Ian
Clark, Kt., RN
Hutchison, *Hon.* Sir Michael, Kt.
Hutchison, Sir Peter, Bt., CBE (1939)
Hutchison, Sir Peter Craft, Bt. (1956)
Hutton, *Rt. Hon.* Sir (James) Brian
Edward, Kt.
Huxley, *Prof.* Sir Andrew Fielding,
Kt., OM, FRS
Huxtable, *Gen.* Sir Charles Richard,
KCB, CBE
Hyatali, *Hon.* Sir Isaac Emanuel, Kt.
Hyslop, Sir Robert John (Robin)
Maxwell-, Kt.
Ibbs, Sir (John) Robin, KBE
Ihaka, *Ven.* Sir Kingi Matutaera, Kt.,
MBE
Imbert, Sir Peter Michael, Kt., QPM
Imray, Sir Colin Henry, KBE, CMG
Inge, *Field Marshal* Sir Peter
Anthony, GCB
Ingham, Sir Bernard, Kt.
Ingilby, Sir Thomas Colvin William,
Bt. (1866)
Inglis, Sir Brian Scott, Kt.
Inglis of Glencorse, Sir Roderick John,
Bt. (s. 1703)
Ingram, Sir James Herbert Charles,
Bt. (1893)
Ingram, Sir John Henderson, Kt., CBE
Inkin, Sir Geoffrey David, Kt., OBE
†Innes, Sir David Charles Kenneth
Gordon, Bt. (NS 1686)
Innes of Edingight, Sir Malcolm
Rognvald, KCVO
Innes, Sir Peter Alexander Berowald,
Bt. (s. 1628)
Inniss, *Hon.* Sir Clifford de Lisle, Kt.
Irish, Sir Ronald Arthur, Kt., OBE
Irvine, Sir Donald Hamilton, Kt., CBE,
MD, FRCGP
Irvine, *Dr* Sir Robin Orlando
Hamilton, Kt.
Irving, Sir Charles Graham, Kt.
Isaacs, Sir Kendal George Lamon,
KCMG, CBE, QC
Isham, Sir Ian Vere Gyles, Bt. (1627)
Jack, *Hon.* Sir Alieu Sulayman, Kt.
Jack, Sir David, Kt., CBE, FRS, FRSE
Jack, Sir David Emmanuel, GCMG, MBE
Jackson, *Air Chief Marshal* Sir
Brendan James, GCB
Jackson, Sir (John) Edward, KCMG
Jackson, *Hon.* Sir Lawrence Walter,
KCMG
Jackson, Sir Michael Roland, Bt.
(1902)
Jackson, Sir Nicholas Fane St George,
Bt. (1913)
Jackson, Sir Robert, Bt. (1815)
Jackson, *Gen.* Sir William Godfrey
Fothergill, GBE, KCB, MC
Jackson, Sir William Thomas, Bt.
(1869)
Jacob, Sir Isaac Hai, Kt., QC
Jacob, *Hon.* Sir Robert Raphael
Hayim (Robin), Kt.
Jacobi, Sir Derek George, Kt., CBE

Jacobi, *Dr* Sir James Edward, Kt., OBE
Jacobs, Sir David Anthony, Kt.
Jacobs, *Hon.* Sir Kenneth Sydney, KBE
Jacobs, Sir Piers, KBE
Jacobs, Sir Wilfred Ebenezer, GCMG, GCVO, OBE, QC
Jacomb, Sir Martin Wakefield, Kt.
Jaffray, Sir William Otho, Bt. (1892)
James, Sir Cynlais Morgan, KCMG
James, Sir Gerard Bowes Kingston, Bt. (1823)
James, Sir Robert Vidal Rhodes, Kt.
James, Sir Stanislaus Anthony, GCMG, OBE
Jamieson, *Air Marshal* Sir David Ewan, KBE, CB
Jansen, Sir Ross Malcolm, KBE
Jardine, Sir Andrew Colin Douglas, Bt. (1916)
Jardine, *Maj.* Sir (Andrew) Rupert (John) Buchanan-, Bt., MC (1885)
Jardine of Applegirth, Sir Alexander Maule, Bt. (s. 1672)
Jarratt, Sir Alexander Anthony, Kt., CB
Jarrett, Sir Clifford George, KBE, CB
Jawara, *Hon.* Sir Dawda Kairaba, Kt.
Jay, Sir Antony Rupert, Kt., CVO
Jeewoolall, Sir Ramesh, Kt.
Jefferson, Sir George Rowland, Kt., CBE, FEng.
Jefferson, Sir Mervyn Stewart Dunnington-, Bt. (1958)
Jeffreys, *Prof.* Sir Alec John, Kt., FRS
Jeffries, *Hon.* Sir John Francis, Kt.
Jehangir, Sir Hirji, Bt. (1908)
Jejeebhoy, Sir Rustom, Bt. (1857)
Jellicoe, Sir Geoffrey Alan, Kt., CBE, FRIBA
Jenkins, Sir Brian Garton, GBE
Jenkins, Sir Michael Romilly Heald, KCMG
Jenkins, Sir Owain Trevor, Kt.
Jenkinson, Sir John Banks, Bt. (1661)
†Jenks, Sir Maurice Arthur Brian, Bt. (1932)
Jennings, Sir Raymond Winter, Kt., QC
Jennings, *Prof.* Sir Robert Yewdall, Kt., QC
Jephcott, Sir (John) Anthony, Bt. (1962)
Jessel, Sir Charles John, Bt. (1883)
Jewkes, Sir Gordon Wesley, KCMG
Joel, *Hon.* Sir Asher Alexander, KBE
John, Sir Rupert Godfrey, Kt.
Johns, *Air Chief Marshal* Sir Richard Edward, KBE, CBE, LVO
†Johnson, Sir Allen Antony Wynn, Bt. (1818)
Johnson, *Rt. Hon.* Sir David Powell Croom-, Kt., DSC, VRD
Johnson, *Gen.* Sir Garry Dene, KCB, OBE, MC
Johnson, Sir John Rodney, KCMG
Johnson, Sir Peter Colpoys Paley, Bt. (1755)
Johnson, *Hon.* Sir Robert Lionel, Kt.

Johnson, Sir Ronald Ernest Charles, Kt., CB
Johnson, Sir Vassel Godfrey, Kt., CBE
Johnston, Sir Alexander, GCB, KBE
Johnston, Sir (David) Russell, Kt., MP
Johnston, Sir John Baines, GCMG, KCVO
Johnston, *Lt.-Col.* Sir John Frederic Dame, GCVO, MC
Johnston, *Lt.-Gen.* Sir Maurice Robert, KCB, OBE
Johnston, Sir Thomas Alexander, Bt. (s. 1626)
Johnstone, Sir Frederic Allan George, Bt. (s. 1700)
Johnstone, Sir (John) Raymond, Kt., CBE
Jolliffe, Sir Anthony Stuart, GBE
Jones, *Gen.* Sir (Charles) Edward Webb, KCB, CBE
Jones, Sir Christopher Lawrence-, Bt. (1831)
Jones, Sir David Akers-, KBE, CMG
Jones, *Air Marshal* Sir Edward Gordon, KCB, CBE, DSO, DFC
Jones, Sir (Edward) Martin Furnival, Kt., CBE
Jones, Sir Ewart Ray Herbert, Kt., D.SC., Ph.D., FRS
Jones, Sir Francis Avery, Kt., CBE, FRCP
Jones, Sir Gordon Pearce, Kt.
Jones, Sir Harry Ernest, Kt., CBE
Jones, Sir James Duncan, KCB
Jones, Sir (John) Derek Alun-, Kt.
Jones, Sir John Henry Harvey-, Kt., MBE
Jones, Sir (John) Kenneth (Trevor), Kt., CBE, QC
Jones, Sir John Lewis, KCB, CMG
Jones, Sir John Prichard-, Bt. (1910)
Jones, Sir Keith Stephen, Kt.
Jones, *Hon.* Sir Kenneth George Illtyd, Kt.
Jones, *Air Marshal* Sir Laurence Alfred, KCB, CB, AFC
Jones, Sir (Owen) Trevor, Kt.
Jones, Sir (Peter) Hugh (Jefford) Lloyd-, Kt.
Jones, Sir Richard Anthony Lloyd, KCB
Jones, Sir Robert Edward, Kt.
Jones, Sir Simon Warley Frederick Benton, Bt. (1919)
Jones, Sir (Thomas) Philip, Kt., CB
Jones, Sir (William) Emrys, Kt.
Jones, *Hon.* Sir William Lloyd Mars-, Kt., MBE
Joughin, Sir Michael, Kt., CBE
Jowitt, *Hon.* Sir Edwin Frank, Kt.
Judge, *Hon.* Sir Igor, Kt.
Jugnauth, *Rt. Hon.* Sir Anerood, KCMG, QC
Jungius, *Vice-Adm.* Sir James George, KBE
Junor, Sir John Donald Brown, Kt.
Jupp, *Hon.* Sir Kenneth Graham, Kt., MC
Kaberry, *Hon.* Sir Christopher Donald, Bt. (1960)

Kadoorie, Sir Horace, CBE
Kalo, Sir Kwamala, Kt., MBE
Kan Yuet-Keung, Sir, GBE
Kapi, *Hon.* Sir Mari, Kt., CBE
Kaputin, Sir John Rumet, KBE, CMG
Katsina, The Emir of, KBE, CMG
Katz, Sir Bernard, Kt., FRS
Kavali, Sir Thomas, Kt., OBE
Kawharu, *Prof.* Sir Ian Hugh, Kt.
Kay, *Prof.* Sir Andrew Watt, Kt.
Kay, *Hon.* Sir John William, Kt.
Kaye, Sir David Alexander Gordon, Bt. (1923)
Kaye, Sir Emmanuel, Kt., CBE
Kaye, Sir John Phillip Lister Lister-, Bt. (1812)
Keane, Sir Richard Michael, Bt. (1801)
Keatinge, Sir Edgar Mayne, Kt., CBE
Keeble, Sir (Herbert Ben) Curtis, GCMG
Keith, *Prof.* Sir James, KBE
Kellett, Sir Stanley Charles, Bt. (1801)
Kelly, *Rt. Hon.* Sir (John William) Basil, Kt.
Kelly, Sir William Theodore, Kt., OBE
Kemball, *Air Marshal* Sir (Richard) John, KCB, CBE
Kemp, Sir (Edward) Peter, KCB
Kendrew, Sir John Cowdery, Kt., CBE, SC.D., FRS
Kenilorea, *Rt. Hon.* Sir Peter, KBE
Kennard, *Lt.-Col.* Sir George Arnold Ford, Bt. (1891)
Kennaway, Sir John Lawrence, Bt. (1791)
Kennedy, Sir Clyde David Allen, Kt.
Kennedy, Sir Francis, KCMG, CBE
Kennedy, *Hon.* Sir Ian Alexander, Kt.
Kennedy, Sir Ludovic Henry Coverley, Kt.
†Kennedy, Sir Michael Edward, Bt., (1836)
Kennedy, *Rt. Hon.* Sir Paul Joseph Morrow, Kt.
Kennedy, *Air Chief Marshal* Sir Thomas Lawrie, GCB, AFC
Kennedy-Good, Sir John, KBE
Kenny, Sir Anthony John Patrick, Kt., D.Phil., D.Litt., FBA
Kenny, *Gen.* Sir Brian Leslie Graham, GCB, CBE
Kent, *Rt. Hon.* Sir Harold Simcox, GCB, QC
Kenyon, Sir George Henry, Kt.
Kermode, Sir (John) Frank, Kt., FBA
Kermode, Sir Ronald Graham Quale, KBE
Kerr, *Hon.* Sir Brian Francis, Kt.
Kerr, *Adm.* Sir John Beverley, GCB
Kerr, Sir John Olav, KCMG
Kerr, *Rt. Hon.* Sir Michael Robert Emanuel, Kt.
Kerruish, Sir (Henry) Charles, Kt., OBE
Kerry, Sir Michael James, KCB, QC
Kershaw, Sir (John) Anthony, Kt., MC
Keswick, Sir John Chippendale Lindley, Kt.
Kidd, Sir Robert Hill, KBE, CB
Kidu, *Hon.* Sir Buri (William), Kt.

Kikau, *Ratu* Sir Jone Latianara, KBE

Kilfedder, Sir James Alexander, Kt., MP

Killen, *Hon.* Denis James, KCMG

Killick, Sir John Edward, GCMG

Kilpatrick, *Prof.* Sir Robert, Kt., CBE

Kimber, Sir Charles Dixon, Bt. (1904)

Kinahan, Sir Robert George Caldwell, Kt., ERD

King, Sir Albert, Kt., OBE

King, *Gen.* Sir Frank Douglas, GCB, MBE

King, Sir John Christopher, Bt. (1888)

King, *Vice-Adm.* Sir Norman Ross Dutton, KBE

King, Sir Richard Brian Meredith, KCB, MC

King, Sir Wayne Alexander, Bt. (1815)

Kingman, *Prof.* Sir John Frank Charles, Kt., FRS

Kingsland, Sir Richard, Kt., CBE, DFC

Kingsley, Sir Patrick Graham Toler, KCVO

Kinloch, Sir David, Bt. (s. 1686)

†Kinloch, Sir David Oliphant, Bt. (1873)

Kipalan, Sir Albert, Kt.

Kirby, *Hon.* Sir Richard Clarence, Kt.

Kirkpatrick, Sir Ivone Elliott, Bt. (s. 1685)

Kirkwood, *Hon.* Sir Andrew Tristram Hammett, Kt.

Kirwan, Sir (Archibald) Laurence Patrick, KCMG, TD

Kitcatt, Sir Peter Julian, Kt., CB

Kitson, *Gen.* Sir Frank Edward, GBE, KCB, MC

Kitson, Sir Timothy Peter Geoffrey, Kt.

†Kleinwort, Sir Richard Drake, Bt. (1909)

Klug, Sir Aaron, Kt.

Knight, Sir Allan Walton, Kt., CMG

Knight, Sir Arthur William, Kt.

Knight, Sir Harold Murray, KBE, DSC

Knight, *Air Chief Marshal* Sir Michael William Patrick, KCB, AFC

Knill, Sir John Kenelm Stuart, Bt. (1893)

Knill, *Prof.* Sir John Lawrence, Kt., FEng.

Knott, Sir John Laurence, Kt., CBE

Knowles, Sir Charles Francis, Bt. (1765)

Knowles, Sir Leonard Joseph, Kt., CBE

Knowles, Sir Richard Marchant, Kt.

Knox, Sir Bryce Muir, KCVO, MC, TD

Knox, Sir David Laidlaw, Kt., MP

Knox, *Hon.* Sir John Leonard, Kt.

Knox, *Hon.* Sir William Edward, Kt.

Koraea, Sir Thomas, Kt.

Kornberg, *Prof.* Sir Hans Leo, Kt., D.SC., SC.D., Ph.D., FRS

Korowi, Sir Wiwa, GCMG

Krusin, Sir Stanley Marks, Kt., CB

Kulukundis, Sir Elias George (Eddie), Kt., OBE

Kurongku, *Most. Revd* Peter, KBE

Labouchere, Sir George Peter, GBE, KCMG

Lacon, Sir Edmund Vere, Bt. (1818)

Lacy, Sir Hugh Maurice Pierce, Bt. (1921)

Lacy, Sir John Trend, Kt., CBE

Lagesen, *Air Marshal* Sir Philip Jacobus, KCB, DFC, AFC

Laidlaw, Sir Christophor Charles Fraser, Kt.

Laing, Sir (John) Maurice, Kt.

Laing, Sir (William) Kirby, Kt., FEng.

Lake, Sir (Atwell) Graham, Bt. (1711)

Laker, Sir Frederick Alfred, Kt.

Lakin, Sir Michael, Bt. (1909)

Laking, Sir George Robert, KCMG

Lamb, Sir Albert (Larry), Kt.

Lamb, Sir Albert Thomas, KBE, CMG, DFC

Lambert, Sir Anthony Edward, KCMG

Lambert, Sir John Henry, KCVO, CMG

†Lambert, Sir Peter John Biddulph, Bt. (1711)

Lampl, Sir Frank William, Kt.

Landale, Sir David William Neil, KCVO

Landau, Sir Dennis Marcus, Kt.

Lane, Sir David William Stennis Stuart, Kt.

Lang, *Lt.-Gen.* Sir Derek Boileau, KCB, DSO, MC

Langham, Sir James Michael, Bt. (1660)

Langley, *Maj.-Gen.* Sir Henry Desmond Allen, KCVO, MBE

Langrishe, Sir Hercules Ralph Hume, Bt. (I. 1777)

Lankester, Sir Timothy Patrick, KCB

Lapsley, *Air Marshal* Sir John Hugh, KBE, CB, DFC, AFC

Lapun, *Hon.* Sir Paul, Kt.

Larcom, Sir (Charles) Christopher Royde, Bt. (1868)

Large, Sir Peter, Kt., CBE

Larmour, Sir Edward Noel, KCMG

Lasdun, Sir Denys Louis, Kt., CBE, FRIBA

Latey, *Rt. Hon.* Sir John Brinsmead, Kt., MBE

Latham, *Hon.* Sir David Nicholas Ramsey, Kt.

Latham, Sir Michael Anthony, Kt.

Latham, Sir Richard Thomas Paul, Bt. (1919)

Latimer, Sir (Courtenay) Robert, Kt., CBE

Latimer, Sir Graham Stanley, KBE

Laucke, *Hon.* Sir Condor Louis, KCMG

Lauder, Sir Piers Robert Dick-, Bt. (s. 1690)

Laughton, Sir Anthony Seymour, Kt.

Laurantus, Sir Nicholas, Kt., MBE

Laurence, Sir Peter Harold, KCMG, MC

Laurie, Sir Robert Bayley Emilius, Bt. (1834)

Lauti, *Rt. Hon.* Sir Toaripi, GCMG

Lavan, *Hon.* Sir John Martin, Kt.

Law, *Adm.* Sir Horace Rochfort, GCB, OBE, DSC

Lawes, Sir (John) Michael Bennet, Bt. (1882)

Lawler, Sir Peter James, Kt., OBE

Lawrence, Sir David Roland Walter, Bt. (1906)

Lawrence, Sir Guy Kempton, Kt., DSO, OBE, DFC

Lawrence, Sir Ivan John, Kt., QC, MP

Lawrence, Sir John Patrick Grosvenor, Kt., CBE

Lawrence, Sir John Waldemar, Bt., OBE (1858)

Lawrence, Sir William Fettiplace, Bt. (1867)

Laws, *Hon.* Sir John Grant McKenzie, Kt.

Lawson, Sir Christopher Donald, Kt.

Lawson, *Col.* Sir John Charles Arthur Digby, Bt., DSO, MC (1900)

Lawson, Sir John Philip Howard-, Bt. (1841)

Lawson, *Hon.* Sir Neil, Kt.

Lawson, *Gen.* Sir Richard George, KCB, DSO, OBE

Lawton, *Prof.* Sir Frank Ewart, Kt.

Lawton, *Rt. Hon.* Sir Frederick Horace, Kt.

Layard, *Adm.* Sir Michael Henry Gordon, KCB, CBE

Layden, Sir John (Jack), Kt.

Layfield, Sir Frank Henry Burland Willoughby, Kt., QC

Lazarus, Sir Peter Esmond, KCB

Lea, *Vice-Adm.* Sir John Stuart Crosbie, KBE

Lea, Sir Thomas William, Bt. (1892)

Leach, *Admiral of the Fleet* Sir Henry Conyers, GCB

Leach, Sir Ronald George, GBE

Leahy, Sir Daniel Joseph, Kt.

Leahy, Sir John Henry Gladstone, KCMG

Learmont, *Gen.* Sir John Hartley, KCB, CBE

Leask, *Lt.-Gen.* Sir Henry Lowther Ewart Clark, KCB, DSO, OBE

Leather, Sir Edwin Hartley Cameron, KCMG, KCVO

Leaver, Sir Christopher, GBE

Le Bailly, *Vice-Adm.* Sir Louis Edward Stewart Holland, KBE, CB

Le Cheminant, *Air Chief Marshal* Sir Peter de Lacey, GBE, KCB, DFC

Lechmere, Sir Berwick Hungerford, Bt. (1818)

Ledger, Sir Frank, (Joseph Francis), Kt.

Ledwidge, Sir (William) Bernard (John), KCMG

Lee, Sir Arthur James, KBE, MC

Lee, *Air Chief Marshal* Sir David John Pryer, GBE

Lee, *Brig.* Sir Leonard Henry, Kt., CBE

Lee, Sir Quo-wei, Kt., CBE

Lee, *Col.* Sir William Allison, Kt., OBE, TD

Leeds, Sir Christopher Anthony, Bt. (1812)

Lees, Sir David Bryan, Kt.

Lees, Sir Thomas Edward, Bt. (1897)

Lees, Sir Thomas Harcourt Ivor, Bt. (1804)

Lees, Sir (William) Antony Clare, Bt. (1937)

Leese, Sir John Henry Vernon, Bt. (1908)

Le Fanu, *Maj.* Sir (George) Victor (Sheridan), KCVO

le Fleming, Sir Quintin John, Bt. (1705)

Legard, Sir Charles Thomas, Bt. (1660)

Legg, Sir Thomas Stuart, KCB, QC

Leggatt, *Rt. Hon.* Sir Andrew Peter, Kt.

Leggatt, Sir Hugh Frank John, Kt.

Leggett, Sir Clarence Arthur Campbell, Kt., MBE

Leigh, Sir Geoffrey Norman, Kt.

Leigh, Sir Richard Henry, Bt. (1918)

Leighton, Sir Michael John Bryan, Bt. (1693)

Leitch, Sir George, KCB, OBE

Leith, Sir Andrew George Forbes-, Bt. (1923)

Le Marchant, Sir Francis Arthur, Bt. (1841)

Le Masurier, Sir Robert Hugh, Kt., DSC

Lemon, Sir (Richard) Dawnay, Kt., CBE

Leng, *Gen.* Sir Peter John Hall, KCB, MBE, MC

Lennard, *Revd* Sir Hugh Dacre Barrett-, Bt. (1801)

Leon, Sir John Ronald, Bt. (1911)

Leonard, *Rt. Revd and Rt. Hon.* Graham Douglas, KCVO

Leonard, *Hon.* Sir (Hamilton) John, Kt.

Lepping, Sir George Geria Dennis, GCMG, MBE

Le Quesne, Sir (Charles) Martin, KCMG

Le Quesne, Sir (John) Godfray, Kt., QC

Leslie, Sir Colin Alan Bettridge, Kt.

Leslie, Sir John Norman Ide, Bt. (1876)

†Leslie, Sir (Percy) Theodore, Bt. (s. 1625)

Leslie, Sir Peter Evelyn, Kt.

Lethbridge, Sir Thomas Periam Hector Noel, Bt. (1804)

Leupena, Sir Tupua, GCMG, MBE

Levene, Sir Peter Keith, KBE

Lever, Sir (Tresham) Christopher Arthur Lindsay, Bt. (1911)

Levey, Sir Michael Vincent, Kt., MVO

Levine, Sir Montague Bernard, Kt.

Levinge, Sir Richard George Robin, Bt. (I. 1704)

Levy, Sir Ewart Maurice, Bt. (1913)

Lewando, Sir Jan Alfred, Kt., CBE

Lewinton, Sir Christopher, Kt.

Lewis, Sir Kenneth, Kt.

†Lewthwaite, *Brig.* Sir Rainald Gilfrid, Bt., CVO, OBE, MC (1927)

Ley, Sir Francis Douglas, Bt., MBE, TD (1905)

Leyland, Sir Philip Vyvyan Naylor-, Bt. (1895)

Lickiss, Sir Michael Gillam, Kt.

Lickley, Sir Robert Lang, Kt., CBE, FEng.

Lidbury, Sir John Towersey, Kt.

Lidderdale, Sir David William Shuckburgh, KCB

Liggins, *Prof.* Sir Graham Collingwood, Kt., CBE, FRS

Lighthill, Sir (Michael) James, Kt., FRS

Lightman, *Hon.* Sir Gavin Anthony, Kt.

Lighton, Sir Thomas Hamilton, Bt. (I. 1791)

Lim, Sir Han-Hoe, Kt., CBE

Linacre, Sir (John) Gordon (Seymour), Kt., CBE, AFC, DFM

Lindley, Sir Arnold Lewis George, Kt., FEng.

Lindop, Sir Norman, Kt.

Lindsay, Sir James Harvey Kincaid Stewart, Kt.

Lindsay, *Hon.* Sir John Edmund Frederic, Kt.

Lindsay, Sir Ronald Alexander, Bt., (1962)

Lintott, Sir Henry John Bevis, KCMG

Lipworth, Sir (Maurice) Sydney, Kt.

Lithgow, Sir William James, Bt. (1925)

Little, *Most Revd* Thomas Francis, KBE

Littler, Sir (James) Geoffrey, KCB

Livesay, *Adm.* Sir Michael Howard, KCB

Llewellyn, Sir Henry Morton, Bt., CBE (1922)

Llewellyn, *Lt.-Col.* Sir Michael Rowland Godfrey, Bt. (1959)

Llewelyn, Sir John Michael Dillwyn-Venables-, Bt. (1890)

Lloyd, Sir Ian Stewart, Kt.

Lloyd, Sir (John) Peter (Daniel), Kt.

Lloyd, Sir Nicholas Markley, Kt.

Lloyd, Sir Richard Ernest Butler, Bt. (1960)

Loader, Sir Leslie Thomas, Kt., CBE

Loane, *Most Revd* Marcus Lawrence, KBE

Lobo, Sir Rogerio Hyndman, Kt., CBE

Lock, *Cdr.* Sir (John) Duncan, Kt.

Lockhart, Sir Simon John Edward Francis Sinclair-, Bt. (s. 1636)

Loder, Sir Giles Rolls, Bt. (1887)

Lodge, Sir Thomas, Kt.

Logan, Sir Donald Arthur, KCMG

Logan, Sir Raymond Douglas, Kt.

Lokoloko, Sir Tore, GCMG, GCVO, OBE

Lombe, *Hon.* Sir Edward Christopher Evans-, Kt.

Longden, Sir Gilbert James Morley, Kt., MBE

Longmore, *Hon.* Sir Andrew Centlivres, Kt.

Loram, *Vice-Adm.* Sir David Anning, KCB, MVO

Lorimer, Sir (Thomas) Desmond, Kt.

Lovell, Sir (Alfred Charles) Bernard, Kt., OBE, FRS

Lovelock, Sir Douglas Arthur, KCB

Loveridge, Sir John Henry, Kt., CBE

Loveridge, Sir John Warren, Kt.

Lovill, Sir John Roger, Kt., CBE

Low, Sir Alan Roberts, Kt.

Low, Sir James Richard Morrison-, Bt. (1908)

Lowe, *Air Chief Marshal* Sir Douglas Charles, GCB, DFC, AFC

Lowe, Sir Thomas William Gordon, Bt. (1918)

Lowry, Sir John Patrick, Kt., CBE

Lowson, Sir Ian Patrick, Bt. (1951)

Lowther, *Maj.* Sir Charles Douglas, Bt. (1824)

Loyd, Sir Francis Alfred, KCMG, OBE

Loyd, Sir Julian St John, KCVO

Lu, Sir Tseng Chi, Kt.

Lucas, Sir Cyril Edward, Kt., CMG, FRS

Lucas, Sir Thomas Edward, Bt. (1887)

Luce, *Rt Hon.* Sir Richard Napier, Kt.

Luckhoo, Sir Lionel Alfred, KCMG, CBE, QC

Lucy, Sir Edmund John William Hugh Cameron-Ramsay-Fairfax-, Bt. (1836)

Luddington, Sir Donald Collin Cumyn, KBE, CMG, CVO

Lumsden, Sir David James, Kt.

Lus, *Hon.* Sir Pita, Kt., OBE

Lush, *Hon.* Sir George Hermann, Kt.

Lushington, Sir John Richard Castleman, Bt. (1791)

Luttrell, *Col.* Sir Geoffrey Walter Fownes, KCVO, MC

Lyell, *Rt. Hon.* Sir Nicholas Walter, Kt., QC, MP

Lygo, *Adm.* Sir Raymond Derek, KCB

Lyle, Sir Gavin Archibald, Bt. (1929)

Lyons, Sir Edward Houghton, Kt.

Lyons, Sir James Reginald, Kt.

Lyons, Sir John, Kt.

McAdam, Sir Ian William James, Kt., OBE

Macadam, Sir Peter, Kt.

McAlpine, Sir William Hepburn, Bt. (1918)

†Macara, Sir Hugh Kenneth, Bt. (1911)

Macartney, Sir John Barrington, Bt. (I. 1799)

McAvoy, Sir (Francis) Joseph, Kt., CBE

McCaffrey, Sir Thomas Daniel, Kt.

McCall, Sir (Charles) Patrick Home, Kt., MBE, TD

McCallum, Sir Donald Murdo, Kt., CBE, FEng.

McCamley, Sir Graham Edward, Kt., MBE

McCarthy, *Rt. Hon.* Sir Thaddeus Pearcey, KBE

McClellan, *Col.* Sir Herbert Gerard Thomas, Kt., CBE, TD

McClintock, Sir Eric Paul, Kt.

McColl, Sir Colin Hugh Verel, KCMG

McCollum, *Hon.* Sir William, Kt.

McConnell, Sir Robert Shean, Bt. (1900)

McCorkell, *Col.* Sir Michael William, KCVO, OBE, TD

McCowan, *Rt. Hon.* Sir Anthony James Denys, Kt.

McCowan, Sir Hew Cargill, Bt. (1934)

McCrea, *Prof.* Sir William Hunter, Kt., FRS

McCrindle, Sir Robert Arthur, Kt.

McCullough, *Hon.* Sir (Iain) Charles (Robert), Kt.

McCusker, Sir James Alexander, Kt.

MacDermott, *Rt. Hon.* Sir John Clarke, Kt.

McDermott, Sir (Lawrence) Emmet, KBE

MacDonald, *Gen.* Sir Arthur Leslie, KBE, CB

McDonald, *Air Marshal* Sir Arthur William Baynes, KCB, AFC

McDonald, Sir Duncan, Kt., CBE, FEng.

Macdonald of Sleat, Sir Ian Godfrey Bosville, Bt. (s. 1625)

Macdonald, Sir Kenneth Carmichael, KCB

Macdonald, *Vice-Adm.* Sir Roderick Douglas, KBE

McDonald, Sir Tom, Kt., OBE

McDonald, *Hon.* Sir William John Farquhar, Kt.

MacDougall, Sir (George) Donald (Alastair), Kt., CBE, FBA

McDowell, Sir Eric Wallalce, Kt., CBE

McDowell, Sir Henry McLorinan, KBE

Mace, *Lt.-Gen.* Sir John Airth, KBE, CB

McEwen, Sir John Roderick Hugh, Bt. (1953)

McFarland, Sir John Talbot, Bt. (1914)

Macfarlane, Sir (David) Neil, Kt.

Macfarlane, Sir George Gray, Kt., CB, FEng.

McFarlane, Sir Ian, Kt.

McGeoch, *Vice-Adm.* Sir Ian Lachlan Mackay, KCB, DSO, DSC

McGrath, Sir Brian Henry, KCVO

Macgregor, Sir Edwin Robert, Bt. (1828)

MacGregor of MacGregor, Sir Gregor, Bt. (1795)

McGregor, Sir Ian Alexander, Kt., CBE, FRS

MacGregor, Sir Ian Kinloch, Kt.

McGrigor, *Capt.* Sir Charles Edward, Bt. (1831)

McIntosh, *Vice-Adm.* Sir Ian Stewart, KBE, CB, DSO, DSC

McIntosh, Sir Ronald Robert Duncan, KCB

McIntyre, Sir Donald Conroy, Kt., CBE

McIntyre, Sir Meredith Alister, Kt.

McKaig, *Adm.* Sir (John) Rae, KCB, CBE

Mackay, Sir (George Patrick) Gordon, Kt., CBE

McKay, Sir John Andrew, Kt., CBE

Mackechnie, Sir Alistair John, Kt.

McKee, *Maj.* Sir (William) Cecil, Kt., ERD

McKellen, Sir Ian Murray, Kt., CBE

McKenzie, Sir Alexander, KBE

Mackenzie, Sir Alexander Alwyne Henry Charles Brinton Muir-, Bt. (1805)

Mackenzie, *Vice-Adm.* Sir Hugh Stirling, KCB, DSO, DSC

†Mackenzie, Sir (James William) Guy, Bt. (1890)

Mackenzie, *Lt.-Gen.* Sir Jeremy John George, KCB, OBE

†Mackenzie, Sir Peter Douglas, Bt. (s. 1673)

†Mackenzie, Sir Roderick McQuhae, Bt. (s. 1703)

McKenzie, Sir Roy Allan, KBE

Mackeson, Sir Rupert Henry, Bt. (1954)

Mackie, Sir Maitland, Kt., CBE

MacKinlay, Sir Bruce, Kt., CBE

McKinnon, Sir James, Kt.

McKinnon, *Hon.* Sir Stuart Neil, Kt.

Macklin, Sir Bruce Roy, Kt., OBE

Mackworth, *Cdr.* Sir David Arthur Geoffrey, Bt. (1776)

McLaren, Sir Robin John Taylor, KCMG

MacLaurin, Sir Ian Charter, Kt.

Maclean, Sir Donald Og Grant, Kt.

Maclean of Dunconnell, Sir Fitzroy Hew, Bt., KT, CBE (1957)

McLean, Sir Francis Charles, Kt., CBE

MacLean, *Vice-Adm.* Sir Hector Charles Donald, KBE, CB, DSC

Maclean, Sir Lachlan Hector Charles, Bt. (NS 1631)

Maclean, Sir Robert Alexander, KBE

McLennan, Sir Ian Munro, KCMG, KBE

McLeod, Sir Charles Henry, Bt. (1925)

McLeod, Sir Ian George, Kt.

†MacLeod, *Hon.* Sir John Maxwell Norman, Bt. (1924)

Macleod, Sir (Nathaniel William) Hamish, KBE

McLintock, Sir Michael William, Bt. (1934)

Maclure, Sir John Robert Spencer, Bt. (1898)

McMahon, Sir Brian Patrick, Bt. (1817)

McMahon, Sir Christopher William, Kt.

Macmillan, Sir (Alexander McGregor) Graham, Kt.

MacMillan, *Lt.-Gen.* Sir John Richard Alexander, KCB, CBE

McMullin, *Rt. Hon.* Sir Duncan Wallace, Kt.

Macnab, *Brig.* Sir Geoffrey Alex Colin, KCMG, CB

Macnaghten, Sir Patrick Alexander, Bt. (1836)

McNamara, *Air Chief Marshal* Sir Neville Patrick, KBE

Macnaughton, *Prof.* Sir Malcolm Campbell, Kt.

McNee, Sir David Blackstock, Kt., QPM

McNeice, Sir (Thomas) Percy (Fergus), Kt., CMG, OBE

MacPhail, Sir Bruce Dugald, Kt.

MacPherson, Sir Keith Duncan, Kt.

Macpherson, Sir Ronald Thomas Steward (Tommy), CBE, MC, TD

Macpherson of Cluny, *Hon.* Sir William Alan, Kt., TD

McQuarrie, Sir Albert, Kt.

MacRae, Sir (Alastair) Christopher (Donald Summerhayes), KCMG

Macrae, *Col.* Sir Robert Andrew Scarth, KCVO, MBE

Macready, Sir Nevil John Wilfrid, Bt. (1923)

Mactaggart, Sir John Auld, Bt. (1938)

Macwhinnie, Sir Gordon Menzies, Kt., CBE

McWilliams, Sir Francis, GBE, FEng.

Madden, *Adm.* Sir Charles Edward, Bt., GCB (1919)

Maddocks, Sir Kenneth Phipson, KCMG, KCVO

Madel, Sir (William) David, Kt., MP

Madigan, Sir Russel Tullie, Kt., OBE

Magnus, Sir Laurence Henry Philip, Bt. (1917)

Maguire, *Air Marshal* Sir Harold John, KCB, DSO, OBE

Mahon, Sir (John) Denis, Kt., CBE

Mahon, Sir William Walter, Bt. (1819)

Maiden, Sir Colin James, Kt., D.Phil.

Main, Sir Peter Tester, Kt., ERD

Maini, Sir Amar Nath, Kt., CBE

Maino, Sir Charles, KBE

Mais, *Hon.* Sir (Robert) Hugh, Kt.

†Maitland, Sir Charles Alexander, Bt. (1818)

Maitland, Sir Donald James Dundas, GCMG, OBE

Makins, Sir Paul Vivian, Bt. (1903)

Malcolm, Sir David Peter Michael, Bt. (s. 1665)

Malet, Sir Harry Douglas St Lo, Bt. (1791)

Mallaby, Sir Christopher Leslie George, GCVO, KCMG

Mallinson, Sir William John, Bt. (1935)

Malone, *Hon.* Sir Denis Eustace Gilbert, Kt.

Mamo, Sir Anthony Joseph, Kt., OBE

Mance, *Hon.* Sir Jonathan Hugh, Kt.

Manchester, Sir William Maxwell, KBE

Mander, Sir Charles Marcus, Bt. (1911)

Manduell, Sir John, Kt., CBE

Mann, *Rt. Hon.* Sir Michael, Kt.

Mann, *Rt. Revd* Michael Ashley, KCVO

Mann, Sir Rupert Edward, Bt. (1905)

Mansel, *Revd Canon* James Seymour Denis, KCVO

Mansel, Sir Philip, Bt. (1622)

Mansfield, *Vice-Adm.* Sir (Edward) Gerard (Napier), KBE, CVO

Mansfield, *Prof.* Sir Peter, Kt., FRS

Mansfield, Sir Philip (Robert Aked), KCMG

Mantell, *Hon.* Sir Charles Barrie Knight, Kt.

Manton, Sir Edwin Alfred Grenville, Kt.

Manzie, Sir (Andrew) Gordon, KCB

Mara, *Rt. Hon.* Ratu Sir Kamisese Kapaiwai Tuimacilai, GCMG, KBE

Margetson, Sir John William Denys, KCMG

Marjoribanks, Sir James Alexander Milne, KCMG

Mark, Sir Robert, GBE

Markham, Sir Charles John, Bt. (1911)

Marking, Sir Henry Ernest, KCVO, CBE, MC

Marling, Sir Charles William Somerset, Bt. (1882)

Marr, Sir Leslie Lynn, Bt. (1919)

Marriner, Sir Neville, Kt., CBE

Marriott, Sir Hugh Cavendish Smith-, Bt. (1774)

Marsden, Sir Nigel John Denton, Bt. (1924)

Marshall, Sir Arthur Gregory George, Kt., OBE

Marshall, Sir Colin Marsh, Kt.

Marshall, Sir Denis Alfred, Kt.

Marshall, *Prof.* Sir (Oshley) Roy, Kt., CBE

Marshall, Sir Peter Harold Reginald, KCMG

Marshall, Sir Robert Braithwaite, KCB, MBE

Marshall, Sir (Robert) Michael, Kt., MP

Martell, *Vice-Adm.* Sir Hugh Colenso, KBE, CB

Martin, *Vice-Adm.* Sir John Edward Ludgate, KCB, DSC

Martin, *Prof.* Sir (John) Leslie, Kt., Ph.D.

Martin, *Prof.* Sir Laurence Woodward, Kt.

Martin, Sir (Robert) Bruce, Kt., QC

Marychurch, Sir Peter Harvey, KCMG

Masefield, Sir Peter Gordon, Kt.

Mason, *Hon.* Sir Anthony Frank, KBE

Mason, Sir (Basil) John, Kt., CB, D.SC., FRS

Mason, *Prof.* Sir David Kean, Kt., CBE

Mason, Sir Frederick Cecil, KCVO, CMG

Mason, Sir Gordon Charles, Kt., OBE

Mason, Sir John Charles Moir, KCMG

Mason, Sir John Peter, Kt., CBE

Mason, *Prof.* Sir Ronald, KCB, FRS

Matane, Sir Paulias Nguna, Kt., CMG, OBE

Mather, Sir (David) Carol (Macdonell), Kt., MC

Mather, Sir William Loris, Kt., CVO, OBE, MC, TD

Mathers, Sir Robert William, Kt.

Matheson, Sir (James Adam) Louis, KBE, CMG, FEng.

Matheson of Matheson, Sir Fergus John, Bt. (1882)

Matthews, Sir Peter Alec, Kt.

Matthews, Sir Peter Jack, Kt., CVO, OBE, QPM

Matthews, Sir Stanley, Kt., CBE

Maud, The Hon. Sir Humphrey John Hamilton, KCMG

†Maxwell, Sir Michael Eustace George, Bt. (s. 1681)

Maxwell, Sir Nigel Mellor Heron-, Bt. (s. 1683)

May, *Hon.* Sir Anthony Tristram Kenneth, Kt.

May, *Rt. Hon.* Sir John Douglas, Kt.

May, Sir Kenneth Spencer, Kt., CBE

Mayhew, *Rt. Hon.* Sir Patrick Barnabas Burke, Kt., QC, MP

Maynard, *Hon.* Sir Clement Travelyan, Kt.

Maynard, *Air Chief Marshal* Sir Nigel Martin, KCB, CBE, DFC, AFC

Medlycott, Sir Mervyn Tregonwell, Bt. (1808)

Megarry, *Rt. Hon.* Sir Robert Edgar, Kt., FBA

Megaw, *Rt. Hon.* Sir John, Kt., CBE, TD

Meinertzhagen, Sir Peter, Kt., CMG

Melhuish, Sir Michael Ramsay, KBE, CMG

Mellon, Sir James, KCMG

Melville, Sir Harry Work, KCB, Ph.D., D.SC., FRS

Melville, Sir Leslie Galfreid, KBE

Melville, Sir Ronald Henry, KCB

Mensforth, Sir Eric, Kt., CBE, F.Eng.

Menter, Sir James Woodham, Kt., Ph.D., SC.D., FRS

Menteth, Sir James Wallace Stuart-, Bt. (1838)

Menzies, Sir Peter Thomson, Kt.

Messervy, Sir (Roney) Godfrey (Collumbell), Kt.

Meyer, Sir Anthony John Charles, Bt. (1910)

Meyjes, Sir Richard Anthony, Kt.

Meyrick, Sir David John Charlton, Bt. (1880)

Meyrick, Sir George Christopher Cadafael Tapps-Gervis-, Bt. (1791)

Miakwe, *Hon.* Sir Akepa, KBE

Michael, Sir Peter Colin, Kt., CBE

Middleton, Sir George Humphrey, KCMG

Middleton, Sir Lawrence Monck, Bt. (1662)

Middleton, Sir Peter Edward, GCB

Miers, Sir (Henry) David Alastair Capel, KBE, CMG

Milbank, Sir Anthony Frederick, Bt. (1882)

Milburn, Sir Anthony Rupert, Bt. (1905)

Miles, Sir Peter Tremayne, KCVO

Miles, Sir William Napier Maurice, Bt. (1859)

Millais, Sir Geoffrey Richard Everett, Bt. (1885)

Millar, Sir Oliver Nicholas, GCVO, FBA

Millar, Sir Ronald Graeme, Kt.

Millard, Sir Guy Elwin, KCMG, CVO

Miller, Sir Donald John, Kt., FRSE, FEng.

Miller, Sir Douglas Sinclair, KCVO, CBE

Miller, Sir Hilary Duppa (Hal), Kt.

Miller, Sir (Ian) Douglas, Kt.

Miller, Sir John Holmes, Bt. (1705)

Miller, *Lt.-Col.* Sir John Mansel, GCVO, DSO, MC

Miller, Sir (Oswald) Bernard, Kt.

Miller, Sir Peter North, Kt.

Miller, Sir Ronald Andrew Baird, Kt., CBE

Miller, Sir Stephen James Hamilton, KCVO, MD, FRCS

Miller of Glenlee, Sir Stephen William Macdonald, Bt. (1788)

Millett, *Rt. Hon.* Sir Peter Julian, Kt.

Millichip, Sir Frederick Albert (Bert), Kt.

Milling, *Air Marshal* Sir Denis Crowley-, KCB, CBE, DSO, DFC

Mills, *Vice-Adm.* Sir Charles Piercy, KCB, CBE, DSC

Mills, Sir Frank, KCVO, CMG

Mills, Sir John Lewis Ernest Watts, Kt., CBE

Mills, Sir Peter Frederick Leighton, Bt. (1921)

Milman, *Lt.-Col.* Sir Derek, Bt. (1800)

Milne, Sir John Drummond, Kt.

Milner, Sir (George Edward) Mordaunt, Bt. (1717)

Milnes Coates, Sir Anthony Robert, Bt. (1911)

Mitchell, *Air Cdre* Sir (Arthur) Dennis, KBE, CVO, DFC, AFC

Mitchell, Sir David Bower, Kt., MP

Mitchell, Sir Derek Jack, KCB, CVO

Mitchell, *Prof.* Sir (Edgar) William John, Kt., CBE, FRS

Mitchell, *Hon.* Sir Stephen George, Kt.

Moate, Sir Roger Denis, Kt., MP

Mobbs, Sir (Gerald) Nigel, Kt.

Moberly, Sir John Campbell, KBE, CMG

Moberly, Sir Patrick Hamilton, KCMG

Moffat, *Lt.-Gen.* Sir (William) Cameron, KBE

Mogg, *Gen.* Sir (Herbert) John, GCB, CBE, DSO

Moir, Sir Ernest Ian Royds, Bt. (1916)

Moller, *Hon.* Sir Lester Francis, Kt.

†Molony, Sir Thomas Desmond, Bt. (1925)

Monck, Sir Nicholas Jeremy, KCB

Monro, Sir Hector Seymour Peter, Kt., MP

Montgomery, Sir (Basil Henry) David, Bt. (1801)

Montgomery, Sir (William) Fergus, Kt., MP

Mookerjee, Sir Birendra Nath, Kt.

Moollan, Sir Abdool Hamid Adam, Kt.

Moollan, *Hon.* Sir Cassam (Ismael), Kt.

Moon, Sir Peter Wilfred Giles Graham-, Bt. (1855)

†Moon, Sir Roger, Bt. (1887)

Moore, Sir Francis Thomas, Kt.

Moore, Sir Henry Roderick, Kt., CBE

Moore, Sir John Cochrane, Kt.

Moore, *Maj.-Gen.* Sir (John) Jeremy, KCB, OBE, MC

Moore, Sir John Michael, KCVO, CB, DSC

Moore, *Prof.* Sir Norman Winfrid, Bt. (1919)

Moore, Sir Patrick William Eisdell, Kt., OBE

Moore, Sir William Roger Clotworthy, Bt., TD (1932)

Mootham, Sir Orby Howell, Kt.

Morauta, Sir Mekere, Kt.

Mordaunt, Sir Richard Nigel Charles, Bt. (1611)

Moreton, Sir John Oscar, KCMG, KCVO, MC

Morgan, *Maj.-Gen.* Sir David John Hughes-, Bt., CB, CBE (1925)

Morgan, Sir Ernest Dunstan, KBE

Morgan, Sir John Albert Leigh, KCMG

Morison, *Hon.* Sir Thomas Richard Atkin, Kt.

Morland, *Hon.* Sir Michael, Kt.

Morland, Sir Robert Kenelm, Kt.

Morpeth, Sir Douglas Spottiswoode, Kt., TD

Morris, *Air Marshal* Sir Arnold Alec, KBE, CB, FEng.

Morris, Sir (James) Richard (Samuel), Kt., CBE, FEng.

Morris, Sir Keith Elliot Hedley, KBE, CMG

Morris, Sir Robert Byng, Bt. (1806)

Morrison, *Hon.* Sir Charles Andrew, Kt.

Morrison, Sir Howard Leslie, Kt., OBE

Morrison, *Rt. Hon.* Sir Peter Hugh, Kt.

Morritt, *Hon.* Sir (Robert) Andrew, Kt., CVO

Morrow, Sir Ian Thomas, Kt.

Morse, Sir Christopher Jeremy, KCMG

Morton, *Adm.* Sir Anthony Storrs, GBE, KCB

Morton, Sir (Robert) Alastair (Newton), Kt.

Moseley, Sir George Walker, KCB

Moser, *Prof.* Sir Claus Adolf, KCB, CBE, FBA

†Moss, Sir David John Edwards-, Bt. (1868)

Mostyn, *Gen.* Sir (Joseph) David Frederick, KCB, GBE

†Mostyn, Sir William Basil John, Bt. (1670)

Mott, Sir John Harmer, Bt. (1930)

Mott, Sir Nevill Francis, Kt., FRS

†Mount, Sir (William Robert) Ferdinand, Bt. (1921)

Mountain, Sir Denis Mortimer, Bt. (1922)

Mowbray, Sir John, Kt.

Mowbray, Sir John Robert, Bt. (1880)

Moynihan, Sir Noel Henry, Kt.

Muir, Sir Laurence Macdonald, Kt.

†Muir, Sir Richard James Kay, Bt. (1892)

Muirhead, Sir David Francis, KCMG, CVO

Mulcahy, Sir Geoffrey John, Kt.

Mullens, *Lt.-Gen.* Sir Anthony Richard Guy, KCB, OBE

Mummery, *Hon.* Sir John Frank, Kt.

Munn, Sir James, Kt., OBE

Munro, Sir Alan Gordon, KCMG

Munro, Sir Alasdair Thomas Ian, Bt. (1825)

Munro, Sir Ian Talbot, Bt. (s. 1634)

Munro, *Hon.* Sir Robert Lindsay, Kt., CBE

Munro, Sir Sydney Douglas Gun-, GCMG, MBE

Murley, Sir Reginald Sydney, KBE, TD, FRCS

Murphy, Sir Leslie Frederick, Kt.

Murray, *Rt. Hon.* Sir Donald Bruce, Kt.

Murray, Sir Donald Frederick, KCVO, CMG

Murray, Sir James, KCMG

Murray, Sir John Antony Jerningham, Kt., CBE

Murray, *Prof.* Sir Kenneth, Kt., FRCPath., FRS, FRSE

Murray, Sir Nigel Andrew Digby, Bt. (s. 1628)

Murray, Sir Patrick Ian Keith, Bt. (s. 1673)

†Murray, Sir Rowland William Patrick, Bt. (s. 1630)

Mursell, Sir Peter, Kt., MBE

Musgrave, Sir Christopher Patrick Charles, Bt. (1611)

Musgrave, Sir Richard James, Bt. (I. 1782)

Musson, *Gen.* Sir Geoffrey Randolph Dixon, GCB, CBE, DSO

Myers, Sir Kenneth Ben, Kt., MBE

Myers, Sir Philip Alan, Kt., OBE, QPM

Myers, *Prof.* Sir Rupert Horace, KBE

Mynors, Sir Richard Baskerville, Bt. (1964)

Nabarro, Sir John David Nunes, Kt., MD, FRCP

Naipaul, Sir Vidiadhar Surajprasad, Kt.

Nairn, Sir Michael, Bt. (1904)

Nairn, Sir Robert Arnold Spencer-, Bt. (1933)

Nairne, *Rt. Hon.* Sir Patrick Dalmahoy, GCB, MC

Naish, Sir (Charles) David, Kt.

Nalder, *Hon.* Sir Crawford David, Kt.

Nall, Sir Michael Joseph, Bt., RN (1954)

†Napier, Sir Charles Joseph, Bt. (1867)

Napier, Sir John Archibald Lennox, Bt. (s. 1627)

Napier, Sir Oliver John, Kt.

Napley, Sir David, Kt.

Neal, Sir Eric James, Kt., CVO

Neal, Sir Leonard Francis, Kt., CBE

Neale, Sir Alan Derrett, KCB, MBE

Neale, Sir Gerrard Anthony, Kt.

Neave, Sir Paul Arundell, Bt. (1795)

Nedd, *Hon.* Sir Robert Archibald, Kt.

Neill, *Rt. Hon.* Sir Brian Thomas, Kt.

Neill, Sir Francis Patrick, Kt., QC

Neill, *Rt. Hon.* Sir Ivan, Kt., PC(NI)

†Nelson, Sir Jamie Charles Vernon Hope, Bt. (1912)

Nelson, *Air Marshal* Sir (Sidney) Richard (Carlyle), KCB, OBE, MD

Nepean, *Lt.-Col.* Sir Evan Yorke, Bt. (1802)

Ness, *Air Marshal* Sir Charles Ernest, KCB, CBE

Neubert, Sir Michael John, Kt., MP

Nevile, *Capt.* Sir Henry Nicholas, KCVO

Neville, Sir Roger Albert Gartside, Kt., VRD

New, *Maj.-Gen.* Sir Laurence Anthony Wallis, Kt., CB, CBE

Newall, Sir Paul Henry, Kt., TD

Newington, Sir Michael John, KCMG

Newman, Sir Francis Hugh Cecil, Bt. (1912)

Newman, Sir Geoffrey Robert, Bt. (1836)

Newman, Sir Jack, Kt., CBE

Newman, Sir Kenneth Leslie, GBE, QPM

Newman, *Vice-Adm.* Sir Roy Thomas, KCB

Newman, *Col.* Sir Stuart Richard, Kt., CBE, TD

Newns, Sir (Alfred) Foley (Francis Polden), KCMG, CVO

Newsam, Sir Peter Anthony, Kt.

Newton, Sir (Charles) Wilfred, Kt., CBE

Newton, Sir (Harry) Michael (Rex), Bt. (1900)

Newton, Sir Kenneth Garnar, Bt., OBE, TD (1924)

Newton, Sir (Leslie) Gordon, Kt.

Ngata, Sir Henare Kohere, KBE

Niall, Sir Horace Lionel Richard, Kt., CBE

Nichol, Sir Duncan Kirkbride, Kt., CBE

Nicholas, Sir David, Kt., CBE

Nicholas, Sir Herbert Richard, Kt., OBE

Nicholas, Sir John William, KCVO, CMG

Nicholls, *Rt. Hon.* Sir Donald James, Kt.

Nicholls, *Air Marshal* Sir John Moreton, KCB, CBE, DFC, AFC

Nicholson, Sir Bryan Hubert, Kt.

†Nicholson, Sir Charles Christian, Bt. (1912)

Nicholson, *Hon.* Sir David Eric, Kt.

Nicholson, *Hon.* Sir Michael, Kt.

Nicholson, Sir Paul Douglas, Kt.

Nicholson, Sir Robin Buchanan, Kt., Ph.D., FRS, FEng.

Nicoll, Sir William, KCMG

Nicolson, Sir David Lancaster, Kt, FEng.

Nield, Sir Basil Edward, Kt., CBE, QC

Nield, Sir William Alan, GCMG, KCB

Nightingale, Sir Charles Manners Gamaliel, Bt. (1628)

Nightingale, Sir John Cyprian, Kt., CBE, BEM, QPM

Nimmo, *Hon.* Sir John Angus, Kt., CBE

Nixon, Sir Edwin Ronald, Kt., CBE

Nixon, *Revd* Sir Kenneth Michael John Basil, Bt. (1906)

Noad, Sir Kenneth Beeson, Kt., MD

Noble, Sir David Brunel, Bt. (1902)

Noble, Sir Iain Andrew, Bt., OBE (1923)

Noble, Sir (Thomas Alexander) Fraser, Kt., MBE

Nombri, Sir Joseph Karl, Kt., ISO, BEM

Norman, Sir Arthur Gordon, KBE, DFC

Norman, Sir Mark Annesley, Bt. (1915)

Norman, Sir Robert Henry, Kt., OBE

Norman, Sir Robert Wentworth, Kt.

Normanton, Sir Tom, Kt., TD

Norris, *Air Chief Marshal* Sir Christopher Neil Foxley-, GCB, DSO, OBE

Norris, Sir Eric George, KCMG

North, Sir Thomas Lindsay, Kt.

North, Sir (William) Jonathan (Frederick), Bt. (1920)

Norton, *Vice-Adm. Hon.* Sir Nicholas John Hill-, KCB

Norwood, Sir Walter Neville, Kt.

Nossal, Sir Gustav Joseph Victor, Kt., CBE

Nott, *Rt. Hon.* Sir John William Frederic, KCB

Nourse, *Rt. Hon.* Sir Martin Charles, Kt.

Nugent, Sir John Edwin Lavallin, Bt. (I. 1795)

Nugent, *Maj.* Sir Peter Walter James, Bt. (1831)

Nugent, Sir Robin George Colborne, Bt. (1806)

Nursaw, Sir James, KCB, QC

Nuttall, Sir Nicholas Keith Lillington, Bt. (1922)

Nutting, *Rt. Hon.* Sir (Harold) Anthony, Bt. (1903)

Oakeley, Sir John Digby Atholl, Bt. (1790)

Oakes, Sir Christopher, Bt. (1939)

Oakshott, Hon. Sir Anthony Hendrie, Bt. (1959)

Oates, Sir Thomas, Kt., CMG, OBE

Oatley, Sir Charles William, Kt., OBE, FRS, FEng.

Obolensky, *Prof.* Sir Dimitri, Kt.

O'Brien, Sir Frederick William Fitzgerald, Kt.

O'Brien, Sir Richard, Kt., DSO, MC

O'Brien, Sir Timothy John, Bt. (1849)

O'Brien, *Adm.* Sir William Donough, KCB, DSC

O'Connell, Sir Maurice James Donagh MacCarthy, Bt. (1869)

O'Connor, *Rt. Hon.* Sir Patrick McCarthy, Kt.

O'Dea, Sir Patrick Jerad, KCVO

Odell, Sir Stanley John, Kt.

Ogden, Sir (Edward) Michael, Kt., QC

Ogilvie, Sir Alec Drummond, Kt.

Ogilvy, Hon. Sir Angus James Bruce, KCVO

Ogilvy, Sir Francis Gilbert Arthur, Bt. (s. 1626)

Ognall, *Hon.* Sir Harry Henry, Kt.

Ohlson, Sir Brian Eric Christopher, Bt. (1920)

Okeover, *Capt.* Sir Peter Ralph Leopold Walker-, Bt. (1886)

Olewale, *Hon.* Sir Niwia Ebia, Kt.

Oliphant, Sir Mark (Marcus Laurence Elwin), KBE, FRS

Oliver, Sir (Frederick) Ernest, Kt., CBE, TD

O'Loghlen, Sir Colman Michael, Bt. (1838)

Olver, Sir Stephen John Linley, KBE, CMG

O'Neil, *Hon.* Sir Desmond Henry, Kt.

Ongley, *Hon.* Sir Joseph Augustine, Kt.

Onslow, *Rt. Hon.* Sir Cranley Gordon Douglas, KCMG, MP

Onslow, Sir John Roger Wilmot, Bt. (1797)

Oppenheim, Sir Alexander, Kt., OBE, D.SC., FRSE

Oppenheim, Sir Duncan Morris, Kt.

Oppenheimer, Sir Michael Bernard Grenville, Bt. (1921)

Oppenheimer, Sir Philip Jack, Kt.

Opperman, *Hon.* Sir Hubert Ferdinand, Kt., OBE

Orde, Sir John Alexander Campbell-, Bt. (1790)

O'Regan, *Hon.* Sir John Barry, Kt.

O'Regan, *Dr* Sir Stephen Gerard (Tipene), Kt.

Orlebar, Sir Michael Keith Orlebar Simpson-, KCMG

Ormond, Sir John Davies Wilder, Kt., BEM

Orr, Sir David Alexander, Kt., MC

Orr, Sir John Henry, Kt., OBE, QPM

Osborn, Sir John Holbrook, Kt.

Osborn, Sir Richard Henry Danvers, Bt. (1662)

Osborne, Sir Peter George, Bt. (I. 1629)

Osifelo, Sir Frederick Aubarua, Kt., MBE

Osman, Sir (Abdool) Raman Mahomed, GCMG, CBE

Osmond, Sir Douglas, Kt., CBE

Osmond, Sir (Stanley) Paul, Kt., CB

Oswald, *Admiral of the Fleet* Sir (John) Julian Robertson, GCB

Otton, Sir Geoffrey John, KCB

Otton, *Hon.* Sir Philip Howard, Kt.

Oulton, Sir Antony Derek Maxwell, GCB, QC

Outram, Sir Alan James, Bt. (1858)

Overall, Sir John Wallace, Kt., CBE, MC

Owen, Sir Geoffrey, Kt.

Owen, Sir Hugh Bernard Pilkington, Bt. (1813)

Owen, Sir Hugo Dudley Cunliffe-, Bt. (1920)

Owen, *Hon.* Sir John Arthur Dalziel, Kt.

Owo, The Olowo of, Kt.

Oxburgh, *Prof.* Sir Ernest Ronald, KBE, Ph.D., FRS

Oxford, Sir Kenneth Gordon, Kt., CBE, QPM

Packard, *Lt.-Gen.* Sir (Charles) Douglas, KBE, CB, DSO

Padmore, Sir Thomas, GCB

Page, Sir (Arthur) John, Kt.

Page, Sir Frederick William, Kt., CBE, FEng.

Page, Sir John Joseph Joffre, Kt., OBE

Paget, Sir Richard Herbert, Bt. (1886)

Pain, *Lt.-Gen.* Sir (Horace) Rollo (Squarey), KCB, MC

Pain, *Hon.* Sir Peter Richard, Kt.

Palin, *Air Chief Marshal* Sir Roger Hewlett, KCB, OBE

Palliser, *Rt. Hon.* Sir (Arthur) Michael, GCMG

Palmer, Sir Derek James, Kt.

Palmer, Sir (Charles) Mark, Bt. (1886)

Palmer, *Gen.* Sir (Charles) Patrick (Ralph), KBE

Palmer, Sir Geoffrey Christopher John, Bt. (1660)

Palmer, *Rt. Hon.* Sir Geoffrey Winston Russell, KCMG

Palmer, Sir John Chance, Kt.

Palmer, Sir John Edward Somerset, Bt. (1791)

Palmer, *Maj.-Gen.* Sir (Joseph) Michael, KCVO

Palmer, Sir Reginald Oswald, GCMG, MBE

Pantlin, Sir Dick Hurst, Kt., CBE

Paolozzi, Sir Eduardo Luigi, Kt., CBE, RA

Parbo, Sir Arvi Hillar, Kt.

Parish, Sir David Elmer Woodbine, Kt., CBE

Park, *Hon.* Sir Hugh Eames, Kt.

Parker, Sir (Arthur) Douglas Dodds-, Kt.

Parker, Sir Eric Wilson, Kt.

Parker, *Hon.* Sir Jonathan Frederic, Kt.

Parker, Sir Peter, KBE, LVO

Parker, Sir Richard (William) Hyde, Bt. (1681)

Parker, *Rt. Hon.* Sir Roger Jocelyn, Kt.

Parker, *Vice-Adm.* Sir (Wilfred) John, KBE, CB, DSC

Parker, Sir William Peter Brian, Bt. (1844)

Parkes, Sir Edward Walter, Kt., FEng.

Parkinson, Sir Nicholas Fancourt, Kt.

Parsons, Sir Anthony Derrick, GCMG, MVO, MC

Parsons, Sir (John) Michael, Kt.

Parsons, Sir Richard Edmund (Clement Fownes), KCMG

Partridge, Sir Michael John Anthony, KCB

Pascoe, *Gen.* Sir Robert Alan, KCB, MBE

Pasley, Sir John Malcolm Sabine, Bt. (1794)

Paterson, Sir Dennis Craig, Kt.

Paterson, Sir George Mutlow, Kt., OBE, QC

Paterson, Sir John Valentine Jardine, Kt.

Patnick, Sir (Cyril) Irvine, Kt., OBE, MP

Paton, Sir (Thomas) Angus (Lyall), Kt., CMG, FRS, FEng.

Pattie, *Rt. Hon.* Sir Geoffrey Edwin, Kt., MP

Pattinson, *Hon.* Sir Baden, KBE

Pattinson, Sir (William) Derek, Kt.

Paul, Sir John Warburton, GCMG, OBE, MC

Paul, *Air Marshal* Sir Ronald Ian Stuart-, KBE

Payne, Sir Norman John, Kt., CBE, FEng.

Peach, Sir Leonard Harry, Kt.

Peacock, *Prof.* Sir Alan Turner, Kt., DSC

Pearce, Sir Austin William, Kt., CBE, Ph.D., FEng.

Pearce, Sir (Daniel Norton) Idris, Kt., CBE, TD

Pearce, Sir Eric Herbert, Kt., OBE

Pearman, *Hon.* Sir James Eugene, Kt., CBE

Pearse, Sir Brian Gerald, Kt.

Pearson, Sir Francis Nicholas Fraser, Bt. (1964)

Pearson, *Gen.* Sir Thomas Cecil Hook, KCB, CBE, DSO

Peart, *Prof.* Sir William Stanley, Kt., MD, FRS

Pease, Sir (Alfred) Vincent, Bt. (1882)

Pease, Sir Richard Thorn, Bt. (1920)

Peat, Sir Gerrard Charles, KCVO

Peat, Sir Henry, KCVO, DFC

Peck, Sir Edward Heywood, GCMG

Peck, Sir John Howard, KCMG

Pedder, *Vice-Adm.* Sir Arthur Reid, KBE, CB

Pedder, *Air Marshal* Sir Ian Maurice, KCB, OBE, DFC

Peek, Sir Francis Henry Grenville, Bt. (1874)

Peek, *Vice-Adm.* Sir Richard Innes, KBE, CB, DSC

Peel, Sir John Harold, KCVO

Peel, Sir (William) John, Kt.

Peierls, Sir Rudolf Ernst, Kt., CBE, D.SC., D.Phil., FRS

Peirse, Sir Henry Grant de la Poer Beresford-, Bt. (1814)

Peirse, *Air Vice-Marshal* Sir Richard Charles Fairfax, KCVO, CB

Pelgen, Sir Harry Friedrich, Kt., MBE

†Pelly, Sir Richard John, Bt. (1840)

Pemberton, Sir Francis Wingate William, Kt., CBE

Penrose, *Prof.* Sir Roger, Kt., FRS

Percival, *Rt. Hon.* Sir (Walter) Ian, Kt., QC

Pereira, Sir (Herbert) Charles, Kt., D.SC., FRS

Perkins, *Surgeon Vice-Adm.* Sir Derek Duncombe Steele-, KCB, KCVO

Perring, Sir Ralph Edgar, Bt. (1963)

Perris, Sir David (Arthur), Kt., MBE

Perry, Sir David Howard, KCB

Perry, Sir (David) Norman, Kt., MBE

Perry, Sir Michael Sydney, Kt., CBE

Pestell, Sir John Richard, KCVO

Peterkin, Sir Neville, Kt.

Peters, *Prof.* Sir David Keith, Kt., FRCP

Petersen, Sir Jeffrey Charles, KCMG

Petersen, Sir Johannes Bjelke-, KCMG

Peterson, Sir Christopher Matthew, Kt., CBE, TD

Petit, Sir Dinshaw Manockjee, Bt. (1890)

Peto, Sir Henry George Morton, Bt. (1855)

Peto, Sir Michael Henry Basil, Bt. (1927)

Petrie, Sir Peter Charles, Bt., CMG (1918)

Pettigrew, Sir Russell Hilton, Kt.

Pettit, Sir Daniel Eric Arthur, Kt.

Philips, *Prof.* Sir Cyril Henry, Kt.

Phillips, Sir Fred Albert, Kt., CVO

Phillips, Sir Henry Ellis Isidore, Kt., CMG, MBE

Phillips, Sir Horace, KCMG

Phillips, *Hon.* Sir Nicholas Addison, Kt.

Phillips, Sir Peter John, Kt., OBE

Phillips, Sir Robin Francis, Bt. (1912)

Pickering, Sir Edward Davies, Kt.

Pickthorn, Sir Charles William Richards, Bt. (1959)

Pidgeon, Sir John Allan Stewart, Kt.

Piers, Sir Charles Robert Fitzmaurice, Bt. (I. 1661)

Pigot, Sir George Hugh, Bt. (1764)

Pigott, Sir Berkeley Henry Sebastian, Bt. (1808)

Pike, Sir Michael Edmund, KCVO, CMG

Pike, Sir Philip Ernest Housden, Kt., QC

Pilditch, Sir Richard Edward, Bt. (1929)

Pile, Sir Frederick Devereux, Bt., MC (1900)

Pile, Sir William Dennis, GCB, MBE

Pilkington, Sir Antony Richard, Kt.

Pilkington, Sir Lionel Alexander Bethune, (Sir Alastair), Kt., FRS

Pilkington, Sir Thomas Henry Milborne-Swinnerton-, Bt. (s. 1635)

Pill, *Hon.* Sir Malcolm Thomas, Kt.

Pillar, *Adm.* Sir William Thomas, GBE, KCB

Pindling, *Rt. Hon.* Sir Lynden Oscar, KCMG

Pinker, Sir George Douglas, KCVO

Pinsent, Sir Christopher Roy, Bt. (1938)

Pippard, *Prof.* Sir (Alfred) Brian, Kt., FRS

Pirie, *Gp Capt* Sir Gordon Hamish, Kt., CVO, CBE

Pitblado, Sir David Bruce, KCB, CVO

Pitcher, Sir Desmond Henry, Kt.

Pitman, Sir Brian Ivor, Kt.

Pitoi, Sir Sere, Kt., CBE

Pitt, Sir Harry Raymond, Kt., Ph.D., FRS

Pitts, Sir Cyril Alfred, Kt.

Pixley, Sir Neville Drake, Kt., MBE, VRD

Plastow, Sir David Arnold Stuart, Kt.

†Platt, Sir (Frank) Lindsey, Bt. (1958)

Platt, *Prof.* Hon. Sir Peter, Bt. (1959)

Playfair, Sir Edward Wilder, KCB

Pliatzky, Sir Leo, KCB

Plowman, *Hon.* Sir John Robin, Kt., CBE

Plumb, *Prof.* Sir John Harold, Kt.

Pohai, Sir Timothy, Kt., MBE

Pole, Sir (John) Richard (Walter Reginald) Carew, Bt. (1628)

Pole, Sir Peter Van Notten, Bt. (1791)

Pollen, Sir John Michael Hungerford, Bt. (1795)

Pollock, Sir George Frederick, Bt. (1866)

Pollock, Sir Giles Hampden Montagu-, Bt. (1872)

Pollock, *Admiral of the Fleet* Sir Michael Patrick, GCB, MVO, DSC

Ponsonby, Sir Ashley Charles Gibbs, Bt., KCVO, MC (1956)

Pontin, Sir Frederick William, Kt.

Poore, Sir Herbert Edward, Bt. (1795)

Pope, *Vice-Adm.* Sir (John) Ernle, KCB

Pope, Sir Joseph Albert, Kt., D.SC., Ph.D.

Popper, *Prof.* Sir Karl Raimund, Kt., CH, Ph.D., FRS

Popplewell, *Hon.* Sir Oliver Bury, Kt.

†Porritt, Sir Jonathon Espie, Bt. (1963)

Portal, Sir Jonathan Francis, Bt. (1901)

Porter, Sir John Simon Horsbrugh-, Bt. (1902)

Porter, Sir Leslie, Kt.

Porter, *Air Marshal* Sir (Melvin) Kenneth (Drowley), KCB, CBE

Porter, *Rt. Hon.* Sir Robert Wilson, Kt., PC(NI), QC

Posnett, Sir Richard Neil, KBE, CMG

Potter, *Hon.* Sir Mark Howard, Kt.

Potter, *Maj.-Gen.* Sir (Wilfrid) John, KBE, CB

Potter, Sir (William) Ian, Kt.

Potts, *Hon.* Sir Francis Humphrey, Kt.

Pound, Sir John David, Bt. (1905)

Pountain, Sir Eric John, Kt.

Powell, Sir (Arnold Joseph) Philip, Kt., CH, OBE, RA, FRIBA

Powell, Sir Charles David, KCMG

Powell, Sir Nicholas Folliott Douglas, Bt. (1897)

Powell, Sir Richard Royle, GCB, KBE, CMG

Power, Sir Alastair John Cecil, Bt. (1924)

Powles, Sir Guy Richardson, KBE, CMG, ED

Poynton, Sir (Arthur) Hilton, GCMG

Prendergast, Sir (Walter) Kieran, KCVO, CMG

Prentice, *Hon.* Sir William Thomas, Kt., MBE

Prescott, Sir Mark, Bt. (1938)

Preston, Sir Kenneth Huson, Kt.

Preston, Sir Peter Sansome, KCB

Preston, Sir Ronald Douglas Hildebrand, Bt. (1815)

Prevost, Sir Christopher Gerald, Bt. (1805)

Price, Sir Charles Keith Napier Rugge-, Bt. (1804)

Price, Sir David Ernest Campbell, Kt.

Price, Sir Francis Caradoc Rose, Bt. (1815)

Price, Sir Frank Leslie, Kt.

Price, Sir (James) Robert, KBE

Price, Sir Leslie Victor, Kt., OBE

Price, Sir Norman Charles, KCB

Price, Sir Robert John Green-, Bt. (1874)

Prickett, *Air Chief Marshal* Sir Thomas Other, KCB, DSO, DFC

Prideaux, Sir Humphrey Povah Treverbian, Kt., OBE

†Primrose, Sir John Ure, Bt. (1903)

Pringle, *Air Marshal* Sir Charles Norman Seton, KBE, FEng.

Pringle, *Hon.* Sir John Kenneth, Kt.

Pringle, *Lt.-Gen.* Sir Steuart (Robert), Bt., KCB, RM (s. 1683)

Pritchard, Sir Neil, KCMG

Pritchett, Sir Victor Sawdon, Kt., CH, CBE

Proby, Sir Peter, Bt. (1952)

Proud, Sir John Seymour, Kt.

Prout, *Rt. Hon.* Sir Christopher James, Kt., TD, QC, MEP

Pryke, Sir David Dudley, Bt. (1926)

Pugh, Sir Idwal Vaughan, KCB

Pugsley, *Prof.* Sir Alfred Grenvile, Kt., OBE, D.SC., FRS, FEng.

Pullen, Sir William Reginald James, KCVO

Pullinger, Sir (Francis) Alan, Kt., CBE

Pumphrey, Sir (John) Laurence, KCMG

Purchas, *Rt. Hon.* Sir Francis Brooks, Kt.

Purves, Sir William, Kt., CBE, DSO

Purvis, *Vice-Adm.* Sir Neville, KCB

Quicke, Sir John Godolphin, Kt., CBE

Quigley, Sir (William) George (Henry), Kt., CB, ph.D.

Quilliam, *Hon.* Sir (James) Peter, Kt.

Quilter, Sir Anthony Raymond Leopold Cuthbert, Bt. (1897)

Quinlan, Sir Michael Edward, GCB

Quinton, Sir James Grand, Kt.

Rabukawaqa, Sir Josua Rasilau, KBE, MVO

Radcliffe, Sir Sebastian Everard, Bt. (1813)

Radford, Sir Ronald Walter, KCB, MBE

Radzinowicz, *Prof.* Sir Leon, Kt., LL D

Rae, *Hon.* Sir Wallace Alexander Ramsay, Kt.

Raeburn, Sir Michael Edward Norman, Bt. (1923)

Raeburn, *Maj.-Gen.* Sir (William) Digby (Manifold), KCVO, CB, DSO, MBE

Raffray, Sir Piat Joseph Raymond Andre, Kt.

Raikes, *Vice-Adm.* Sir Iwan Geoffrey, KCB, CBE, DSC

Raison, *Rt. Hon.* Sir Timothy Hugh Francis, Kt.

Ralli, Sir Godfrey Victor, Bt., TD (1912)

Ramdanee, Sir Mookteswar Baboolall Kailash, Kt.

Ramphal, Sir Shridath Surendranath, GCMG

Ramphul, Sir Baalkhristna, Kt.

Ramphul, Sir Indurduth, Kt.

Ramsay, Sir Alexander William Burnett, Bt. (1806)

Ramsay, Sir Allan John (Hepple), KBE, CMG

Ramsay, Sir Thomas Meek, Kt., CMG

Ramsbotham, *Gen.* Sir David John, GCB, CBE

Ramsbotham, *Hon.* Sir Peter Edward, GCMG, GCVO

Ramsden, Sir John Charles Josslyn, Bt. (1689)

Ramsey, Sir Alfred Ernest, Kt.

Randle, *Prof.* Sir Philip John, Kt.

Ranger, Sir Douglas, Kt., FRCS

Rank, Sir Benjamin Keith, Kt., CMG

Rankin, Sir Alick Michael, Kt., CBE

Rankin, Sir Ian Niall, Bt. (1898)

Rasch, *Maj.* Sir Richard Guy Carne, Bt. (1903)

Rashleigh, Sir Richard Harry, Bt. (1831)

Ratford, Sir David John Edward, KCMG, CVO

Rattee, *Hon.* Sir Donald Keith, Kt.

Rattle, Sir Simon Dennis, Kt., CBE

Rault, Sir Louis Joseph Maurice, Kt.

Rawlins, *Surgeon Vice-Adm.* Sir John Stuart Pepys, KBE

Rawlinson, Sir Anthony Henry John, Bt. (1891)

Read, *Air Marshal* Sir Charles Frederick, KBE, CB, DFC, AFC

Read, *Gen.* Sir (John) Antony (Jervis), GCB, CBE, DSO, MC

Read, Sir John Emms, Kt.

Reade, Sir Clyde Nixon, Bt. (1661)

Reay, *Lt.-Gen.* Sir (Hubert) Alan John, KBE

Redgrave, *Maj.-Gen.* Sir Roy Michael Frederick, KBE, MC

Redmayne, Sir Nicholas, Bt. (1964)

Redmond, Sir James, Kt., FEng.

Redwood, Sir Peter Boverton, Bt. (1911)

Reece, Sir Charles Hugh, Kt.

Reece, Sir James Gordon, Kt.

Reed, *Hon.* Sir Nigel Vernon, Kt., CBE

Rees, Sir (Charles William) Stanley, Kt., TD

Rees, Sir David Allan, Kt., ph.D., D.SC., FRS

Rees, *Prof.* Sir Martin John, Kt., FRS

Reeve, Sir Anthony, KCMG

Reeves, *Most Revd* Paul Alfred, GCMG, GCVO

Reffell, *Adm.* Sir Derek Roy, KCB

Refshauge, *Maj-Gen.* Sir William Dudley, Kt., CBE

Reid, Sir Alexander James, Bt. (1897)

Reid, Sir (Harold) Martin (Smith), KBE, CMG

Reid, Sir Hugh, Bt. (1922)

Reid, Sir Norman Robert, Kt.

Reid, Sir Robert Paul, Kt.

Reiher, Sir Frederick Bernard Carl, KBE, CMG

Reilly, Sir (D'Arcy) Patrick, GCMG, OBE

Reilly, *Lt.-Gen.* Sir Jeremy Calcott, KCB, DSO

Renals, Sir Stanley, Bt. (1895)

Rendell, Sir William, Kt.

Rennie, Sir John Shaw, GCMG, OBE

Renouf, Sir Clement William Bailey, Kt.

Renouf, Sir Francis Henry, Kt.

Renshaw, Sir (Charles) Maurice Bine, Bt. (1903)

Renwick, Sir Richard Eustace, Bt. (1921)

Renwick, Sir Robin William, KCMG

Reporter, Sir Shapoor Ardeshirji, KBE

Reynolds, Sir David James, Bt. (1923)

Reynolds, Sir Peter William John, Kt., CBE

Rhodes, Sir Basil Edward, Kt., CBE, TD

Rhodes, Sir John Christopher Douglas, Bt. (1919)

Rhodes, Sir Peregrine Alexander, KCMG

Rice, *Maj.-Gen.* Sir Desmond Hind Garrett, KCVO, CBE

Rice, Sir Timothy Miles Bindon, Kt.

Richards, Sir (Francis) Brooks, KCMG, DSC

Richards, *Lt.-Gen.* Sir John Charles Chisholm, KCB, KCVO, RM

Richards, Sir Rex Edward, Kt., D.SC., FRS

Richardson, Sir Anthony Lewis, Bt. (1924)

Richardson, *Rt. Hon.* Sir Ivor Lloyd Morgan, Kt.

Richardson, Sir (John) Eric, Kt., CBE

Richardson, Sir Michael John de Rougemont, Kt.

Richardson, *Lt.-Gen.* Sir Robert Francis, KCB, CVO, CBE

Richardson, Sir Simon Alaisdair Stewart-, Bt. (s. 1630)

Riches, Sir Derek Martin Hurry, KCMG

Riches, *Gen.* Sir Ian Hurry, KCB, DSO

Richmond, Sir Alan James, Kt.

Richmond, *Rt. Hon.* Sir Clifford Parris, KBE

Richmond, Sir John Frederick, Bt. (1929)

Richmond, *Prof.* Sir Mark Henry, Kt., FRS

Rickett, Sir Denis Hubert Fletcher, KCMG, CB

Rickett, Sir Raymond Mildmay Wilson, Kt., CBE, Ph.D.

Ricketts, Sir Robert Cornwallis Gerald St Leger, Bt. (1828)

Riddell, Sir John Charles Buchanan, Bt., CVO (s. 1628)

Ridley, Sir Adam (Nicholas), Kt.

Ridsdale, Sir Julian Errington, Kt., CBE

Rigby, *Lt.-Col.* Sir (Hugh) John (Macbeth), Bt. (1929)

Riley, Sir Ralph, Kt., FRS

Ring, Sir Lindsay Roberts, GBE

Ringadoo, *Hon.* Sir Veerasamy, GCMG

Ripley, Sir Hugh, Bt. (1880)

Risk, Sir Thomas Neilson, Kt.

Rix, *Hon.* Sir Bernard Anthony, Kt.

Rix, Sir John, Kt., MBE, FEng.

Roberts, Sir Bryan Clieve, KCMG, QC

Roberts, *Hon.* Sir Denys Tudor Emil, KBE, QC

Roberts, Sir (Edward Fergus) Sidney, Kt., CBE

Roberts, Sir Frank Kenyon, GCMG, GCVO

Roberts, Sir Geoffrey Newland, Kt., CBE, AFC

Roberts, *Brig.* Sir Geoffrey Paul Hardy-, KCVO, CB, CBE

Roberts, Sir Gilbert Howland Rookehurst, Bt. (1809)

Roberts, Sir Gordon James, Kt., CBE

Roberts, *Rt. Hon.* Sir (Ieuan) Wyn Pritchard, Kt., MP

Roberts, Sir Samuel, Bt. (1919)

Roberts, Sir Stephen James Leake, Kt.

Roberts, Sir William James Denby, Bt. (1909)

Robertson, Sir John Fraser, KCMG, CBE

Robertson, Sir Lewis, Kt., CBE, FRSE

Robertson, *Prof.* Sir Rutherford Ness, Kt., CMG

Robins, Sir Ralph Harry, Kt., FEng.

Robinson, Sir Albert Edward Phineas, Kt.

†Robinson, Sir Christopher Philipse, Bt. (1854)

Robinson, Sir John James Michael Laud, Bt. (1660)

Robinson, *Rt. Hon.* Sir Kenneth, Kt.

Robinson, Sir Niall Bryan Lynch-, Bt., DSC (1920)

Robinson, Sir Wilfred Henry Frederick, Bt. (1908)

Robotham, *Hon.* Sir Lascelles Lister, Kt.

Robson, *Prof.* Sir James Gordon, Kt., CBE

Roch, *Rt. Hon.* Sir John Ormond, Kt.

Roche, Sir David O'Grady, Bt. (1838)

Rodgers, Sir (John Fairlie) Tobias, Bt. (1964)

Rodrigues, Sir Alberto Maria, Kt., CBE, ED

Roe, *Air Chief Marshal* Sir Rex David, GCB, AFC

Rogers, Sir Frank Jarvis, Kt.

Rogers, *Air Chief Marshal* Sir John Robson, KCB, CBE

Rogers, Sir Richard George, Kt., RA

Roll, *Revd* Sir James William Cecil, Bt. (1921)

Rooke, Sir Denis Eric, Kt., CBE, FRS, FEng.

Roper, *Hon.* Sir Clinton Marcus, Kt.

Ropner, Sir John Bruce Woollacott, Bt. (1952)

Ropner, Sir Robert Douglas, Bt. (1904)

Roscoe, Sir Robert Bell, KBE

Rose, *Rt. Hon.* Sir Christopher Dudley Roger, Kt.

Rose, Sir Clive Martin, GCMG

Rose, Sir David Lancaster, Bt. (1874)

Rose, *Lt.-Gen.* Sir (Hugh) Michael, KCB, CBE

Rose, Sir Julian Day, Bt. (1872 and 1909)

Rosier, *Air Chief Marshal* Sir Frederick Ernest, GCB, CBE, DSO

Ross, Sir Archibald David Manisty, KCMG

Ross, Sir (James) Keith, Bt., RD, FRCS (1960)

Ross, *Lt.-Gen.* Sir Robert Jeremy, KCB, OBE

Rosser, Sir Melvyn Wynne, Kt.

Rossi, Sir Hugh Alexis Louis, Kt.

Roth, *Prof.* Sir Martin, Kt., MD, FRCP

Rothnie, Sir Alan Keir, KCVO, CMG

Rothschild, Sir Evelyn Robert Adrian de, Kt.

Rougier, *Hon.* Sir Richard George, Kt.

Rous, Sir Anthony Gerald Roderick, KCMG, OBE

Rous, *Lt.-Gen.* the Hon. Sir William Edward, KCB, OBE

Row, *Hon.* Sir John Alfred, Kt.

Rowe, Sir Jeremy, Kt., CBE

Rowell, Sir John Joseph, Kt., CBE

Rowland, *Air Marshal* Sir James Anthony, KBE, DFC, AFC

Rowlands, *Air Marshal* Sir John Samuel, GC, KBE

Rowley, Sir Charles Robert, Bt. (1836)

Rowley, Sir Joshua Francis, Bt. (1786)

Rowling, *Rt. Hon.* Sir Wallace Edward, KCMG

Roxburgh, *Vice-Adm.* Sir John Charles Young, KCB, CBE, DSO, DSC

Royden, Sir Christopher John, Bt. (1905)

Rumbold, Sir Henry John Sebastian, Bt. (1779)

Rumbold, Sir Jack Seddon, Kt.

Runchorelal, Sir (Udayan) Chinubhai Madhowlal, Bt. (1913)

Runciman, *Hon.* Sir James Cochran Stevenson (Sir Steven Runciman), Kt., CH

Rusby, *Vice-Adm.* Sir Cameron, KCB, MVO

Russell, Sir Archibald Edward, Kt., CBE, FRS, FEng.

Russell, Sir Charles Ian, Bt. (1916)

Russell, *Hon.* Sir David Sturrock West-, Kt.

Russell, Sir George, Kt., CBE

Russell, Sir George Michael, Bt. (1812)

Russell, Sir (Robert) Mark, KCMG

Russell, Sir Spencer Thomas, Kt.

Russell, *Rt. Hon.* Sir (Thomas) Patrick, Kt.

Rutter, Sir Frank William Eden, KBE

Rutter, *Prof.* Sir Michael Llewellyn, Kt., CBE, MD, FRS

Ryan, Sir Derek Gerald, Bt. (1919)

Rycroft, Sir Richard Newton, Bt. (1784)

Ryrie, Sir William Sinclair, KCB

Sachs, *Hon.* Sir Michael Alexander Geddes, Kt.

Sainsbury, Sir Robert James, Kt.

St Aubyn, Sir (John) Arscott Molesworth-, Bt. (1689)

St George, Sir George Bligh, Bt. (l. 1766)

St Johnston, Sir Kerry, Kt.

Sainty, Sir John Christopher, KCB

Sakzewski, Sir Albert, Kt.

Salt, Sir Patrick MacDonnell, Bt. (1869)

Salt, Sir (Thomas) Michael John, Bt. (1899)

Sampson, Sir Colin, Kt., CBE, QPM

Samuel, Sir Jon Michael Glen, Bt. (1898)

Samuelson, Sir (Bernard) Michael (Francis), Bt. (1884)

Sandberg, Sir Michael Graham Ruddock, Kt., CBE

Sanders, Sir John Reynolds Mayhew-, Kt.

Sanders, Sir Robert Tait, KBE, CMG

Sanderson, Sir Frank Linton, Bt. (1920)

Sandilands, Sir Francis Edwin Prescott, Kt., CBE

Sarei, Sir Alexis Holyweek, Kt., CBE

Sarell, Sir Roderick Francis Gisbert, KCMG, KCVO

Sargant, Sir (Henry) Edmund, Kt.

Saunders, *Hon.* Sir John Anthony Holt, Kt., CBE, DSO, MC

Saunders, Sir Peter, Kt.

Sauzier, Sir (André) Guy, Kt., CBE, ED

Savage, Sir Ernest Walter, Kt.

Savile, Sir James Wilson Vincent, Kt., OBE

Saville, *Rt. Hon.* Sir Mark Oliver, Kt.

Say, *Rt. Revd* Richard David, KCVO

Schiemann, *Hon.* Sir Konrad Hermann Theodor, Kt.

Schneider, *Rt. Hon.* Sir Lancelot Raymond Adams-, KCMG

Scholey, Sir David Gerald, Kt., CBE

Scholey, Sir Robert, Kt., CBE, FEng.

Scholtens, Sir James Henry, KCVO

Schubert, Sir Sydney, Kt.

Schuster, Sir (Felix) James Moncrieff, Bt., OBE (1906)

Scipio, Sir Hudson Rupert, Kt.

Scoon, Sir Paul, GCMG, GCVO, OBE

Scopes, Sir Leonard Arthur, KCVO, CMG, OBE

Scott, Sir Anthony Percy, Bt. (1913)

Scott, Sir (Charles) Peter, KBE, CMG

Scott, Sir David Aubrey, GCMG

Scott, Sir Dominic James Maxwell-, Bt. (1642)

Scott, Sir Ian Dixon, KCMG, KCVO, CIE

Scott, Sir James Jervoise, Bt. (1962)

Scott, Sir Kenneth Bertram Adam, KCVO, CMG

Scott, Sir Michael, KCVO, CMG

Scott, Sir Oliver Christopher Anderson, Bt. (1909)

Scott, *Prof.* Sir Philip John, KBE

Scott, *Rt. Hon.* Sir Richard Rashleigh Folliott, Kt.

Scott, Sir Robert David Hillyer, Kt.

Scott, Sir Walter John, Bt. (1907)

Scott, *Rear-Adm.* Sir (William) David (Stewart), KBE, CB

Scowen, Sir Eric Frank, Kt., MD, D.SC., LL D., FRCP, FRCS

Scrivenor, Sir Thomas Vaisey, Kt., CMG

Seale, Sir John Henry, Bt. (1838)

Seaman, Sir Keith Douglas, KCVO, OBE

†Sebright, Sir Peter Giles Vivian, Bt. (1626)

Seccombe, Sir (William) Vernon Stephen, Kt.

Secombe, Sir Harry Donald, Kt., CBE

Seconde, Sir Reginald Louis, KCMG, CVO

Sedley, *Hon.* Sir Stephen John, Kt.

Seely, Sir Nigel Edward, Bt. (1896)

Seeto, Sir Ling James, Kt., MBE

Seeyave, Sir Rene Sow Choung, Kt., CBE

Seligman, Sir Peter Wendel, Kt., CBE

Senior, Sir Edward Walters, Kt., CMG

Sergeant, Sir Patrick, Kt.

Series, Sir (Joseph Michel) Emile, Kt., CBE

Serpell, Sir David Radford, KCB, CMG, OBE

Seton, Sir Iain Bruce, Bt. (S. 1663)

†Seton, Sir James Christall, Bt. (S. 1683)

Severne, *Air Vice-Marshal* Sir John de Milt, KCVO, OBE, AFC

Sewell, Sir (John) Allan, Kt., ISO

Seymour, *Cdr.* Sir Michael Culme-, Bt., RN (1809)

Shakerley, Sir Geoffrey Adam, Bt. (1838)

Shakespeare, Sir William Geoffrey, Bt. (1942)

Shapland, Sir William Arthur, Kt.

Sharp, Sir Adrian, Bt. (1922)

Sharp, Sir George, Kt., OBE

Sharp, Sir Kenneth Johnston, Kt., TD

Sharp, Sir Milton Reginald, Bt. (1920)

Sharp, Sir Richard Lyall, KCVO, CB

Sharpe, *Hon.* Sir John Henry, Kt., CBE

Shattock, Sir Gordon, Kt.

Shaw, Sir Brian Piers, Kt.

Shaw, Sir (Charles) Barry, Kt., CB, QC

Shaw, Sir (George) Neville Bowan-, Kt.

Shaw, Sir (John) Giles (Dunkerley), Kt., MP

Shaw, Sir John Michael Robert Best-, Bt. (1665)

Shaw, Sir Michael Norman, Kt.

Shaw, Sir Neil McGowan, Kt.

Shaw, Sir Robert, Bt. (1821)

Shaw, Sir Roy, Kt.

Shaw, Sir Run Run, Kt., CBE

Sheehy, Sir Patrick, Kt.

Sheen, *Hon.* Sir Barry Cross, Kt.

Sheffield, Sir Reginald Adrian Berkeley, Bt. (1755)

Shehadie, Sir Nicholas Michael, Kt., OBE

Sheil, *Hon.* Sir John, Kt.

Sheldon, *Hon.* Sir (John) Gervase (Kensington), Kt.

Shelley, Sir John Richard, Bt. (1611)

Shelton, Sir William Jeremy Masefield, Kt.

Shepheard, Sir Peter Faulkner, Kt., CBE

Shepherd, Sir Peter Malcolm, Kt., CBE

Sheppard, Sir Allen John George, Kt.

Shepperd, Sir Alfred Joseph, Kt.

Sherlock, Sir Philip Manderson, KBE

Sherman, Sir Alfred, Kt.

Sherman, Sir Louis, Kt., OBE

Shields, Sir Neil Stanley, Kt., MC

Shields, *Prof.* Sir Robert, Kt., MD

Shiffner, Sir Henry David, Bt. (1818)

Shillington, Sir (Robert Edward) Graham, Kt., CBE

Shock, Sir Maurice, Kt.

Short, *Brig.* Sir Noel Edward Vivian, Kt., MBE, MC

Shuckburgh, Sir (Charles Arthur) Evelyn, GCMG, CB

Shuckburgh, Sir Rupert Charles Gerald, Bt. (1660)

Siaguru, Sir Anthony Michael, KBE

Sich, Sir Rupert Leigh, Kt., CB

Siddall, Sir Norman, Kt., CBE, FEng.

Sidey, *Air Marshal* Sir Ernest Shaw, KBE, CB, MD

Sie, Sir Banja Tejan-, GCMG

Simeon, Sir John Edmund Barrington, Bt. (1815)

Simmons, *Air Marshal* Sir Michael George, KCB, AFC

Simmons, Sir Stanley Clifford, Kt., FRCS, FRCOG

Simonet, Sir Louis Marcel Pierre, Kt., CBE

Simpson, *Hon.* Sir Alfred Henry, Kt.

Simpson, Sir Joseph Trevor, KBE

Simpson, Sir William James, Kt.

Sinclair, Sir Clive Marles, Kt.

Sinclair, Sir George Evelyn, Kt., CMG, OBE

Sinclair, Sir Ian McTaggart, KCMG, QC

Sinclair, *Air Vice-Marshal* Sir Laurence Frank, GC, KCB, CBE, DSO

Sinclair, Sir Patrick Robert Richard, Bt. (S. 1704)

Sinclair, Sir Ronald Ormiston, KBE

Singer, *Prof.* Sir Hans Wolfgang, Kt.

Singer, *Hon.* Sir Jan Peter, Kt.

Singh, *Hon.* Sir Vijay Raghubir, Kt.

Singhania, Sir Padampat, Kt.

Sinnamon, Sir Hercules, Kt., OBE

Sitwell, Sir (Sacheverell) Reresby, Bt. (1808)

Skeet, Sir Trevor Herbert Harry, Kt., MP

Skeggs, Sir Clifford George, Kt.

Skingsley, *Air Chief Marshal* Sir Anthony Gerald, GBE, KCB

Skinner, Sir (Thomas) Keith (Hewitt), Bt. (1912)

Skipwith, Sir Patrick Alexander d'Estoteville, Bt. (1622)

Skyrme, Sir (William) Thomas (Charles), KCVO, CB, CBE, TD

Slack, Sir William Willatt, KCVO, FRCS

Slade, Sir Benjamin Julian Alfred, Bt. (1831)

Slade, *Rt. Hon.* Sir Christopher John, Kt.

Slaney, *Prof.* Sir Geoffrey, KBE

Slater, *Adm.* Sir John (Jock) Cunningham Kirkwood, GCB, LVO

Sleight, Sir Richard, Bt. (1920)

Slimmings, Sir William Kenneth MacLeod, Kt., CBE

Sloan, Sir Andrew Kirkpatrick, Kt., QPM

Sloman, Sir Albert Edward, Kt., CBE

Smallwood, *Air Chief Marshal* Sir Denis Graham, GBE, KCB, DSO, DFC

Smart, *Prof.* Sir George Algernon, Kt., MD, FRCP

Smart, Sir Jack, Kt., CBE

Smedley, Sir Harold, KCMG, MBE

Smiley, *Lt.-Col.* Sir John Philip, Bt. (1903)

Smith, Sir Alan, Kt., CBE, DFC

Smith, Sir Alexander Mair, Kt., PH.D.

Smith, Sir Andrew Colin Hugh-, Kt.

Smith, Sir Charles Bracewell-, Bt. (1947)

Smith, Sir Christopher Sydney Winwood, Bt. (1809)

Smith, *Prof.* Sir Colin Stansfield, Kt., CBE

Smith, Sir Cyril, Kt., MBE

Smith, *Prof.* Sir David Cecil, Kt., FRS

Smith, *Air Chief Marshal* Sir David Harcourt-, GBE, KCB, DFC

Smith, Sir David Iser, KCVO

Smith, Sir Douglas Boucher, KCB

Smith, Sir Dudley (Gordon), Kt., MP

Smith, *Maj.-Gen.* Sir (Francis) Brian Wyldbore-, Kt., CB, DSO, OBE

Smith, *Prof.* Sir Francis Graham-, Kt., FRS

Smith, Sir (Frank) Ewart, Kt., FEng.

Smith, Sir Geoffrey Johnson, Kt., MP

Smith, Sir Howard Frank Trayton, GCMG

Smith, Sir John Alfred, Kt., QPM

Smith, *Prof.* Sir John Cyril, Kt., CBE, QC, FBA
Smith, Sir John Hamilton-Spencer-, Bt. (1804)
Smith, Sir John Jonah Walker-, Bt. (1960)
Smith, Sir John Kenneth Newson-, Bt. (1944)
Smith, Sir John Lindsay Eric, Kt., CH, CBE
Smith, Sir John Wilson, Kt., CBE
Smith, Sir Joseph William Grenville, Kt., MD, FRCP
Smith, Sir Leslie Edward George, Kt.
Smith, *Rt. Hon.* Sir Murray Stuart-, Kt.
Smith, Sir Raymond Horace, KBE
Smith, Sir Richard Rathbone Vassar-, Bt., TD (1917)
Smith, Sir Robert Courtney, Kt., CBE
Smith, Sir Robert Hill, Bt. (1945)
Smith, *Prof.* Sir Roland, Kt.
Smith, *Air Marshal* Sir Roy David Austen-, KBE, CB, CVO, DFC
Smith, Sir (Thomas) Gilbert, Bt. (1897)
Smith, *Adm.* Sir Victor Alfred Trumper, KBE, CB, DSC
Smith, Sir William Reardon Reardon-, Bt. (1920)
Smith, Sir (William) Richard Prince-, Bt. (1911)
Smithers, *Prof.* Sir David Waldron, Kt., MD
Smithers, Sir Peter Henry Berry Otway, Kt., VRD, D.Phil.
Smithers, *Hon.* Sir Reginald Allfree, Kt.
Smyth, Sir Thomas Weyland Bowyer-, Bt. (1661)
Smyth, Sir Timothy John, Bt. (1955)
Snelling, Sir Arthur Wendell, KCMG, KCVO
Soame, Sir Charles John Buckworth-Herne-, Bt. (1697)
Sobers, Sir Garfield St Auburn, Kt.
Solomon, Sir David Arnold, Kt., MBE
Solomon, Sir Harry, Kt.
Solti, Sir Georg, KBE
Somare, *Rt. Hon.* Sir Michael Thomas, GCMG, CH
Somers, *Rt. Hon.* Sir Edward Jonathan, Kt.
Somerset, Sir Henry Beaufort, Kt., CBE
Somerville, *Brig.* Sir John Nicholas, Kt., CBE
Somerville, Sir Quentin Charles Somerville Agnew-, Bt. (1957)
Sopwith, Sir Charles Ronald, Kt.
Soutar, *Air Marshal* Sir Charles John Williamson, KBE
South, Sir Arthur, Kt.
Southby, Sir John Richard Bilbe, Bt. (1937)
Southern, Sir Richard William, Kt., FBA
Southern, Sir Robert, Kt., CBE
Southey, Sir Robert John, Kt., CMG

Southgate, Sir Colin Grieve, Kt.
Southward, Sir Leonard Bingley, Kt., OBE
Southward, Sir Ralph, KCVO, FRCP
Southwood, *Prof.* Sir (Thomas) Richard (Edmund), Kt., FRS
Southworth, Sir Frederick, Kt., QC
Souyave, *Hon.* Sir (Louis) Georges, Kt.
Sowrey, *Air Marshal* Sir Frederick Beresford, KCB, CBE, AFC
Soysa, Sir Warusahennedige Abraham Bastian, Kt., CBE
Sparkes, Sir Robert Lyndley, Kt.
Sparrow, Sir John, Kt.
Spearman, Sir Alexander Young Richard Mainwaring, Bt. (1840)
Spedding, *Prof.* Sir Colin Raymond William, Kt., CBE
Speed, Sir (Herbert) Keith, Kt., RD, MP
Speed, Sir Robert William Arney, Kt., CB, QC
Speelman, Sir Cornelis Jacob, Bt. (1686)
Speight, *Hon.* Sir Graham Davies, Kt.
Speir, Sir Rupert Malise, Kt.
Spencer, Sir Derek Harold, Kt., QC, MP
Spender, *Prof.* Sir Stephen Harold, Kt., CBE
Spicer, Sir James Wilton, Kt., MP
†Spicer, Sir Nicholas Adrian Albert, Bt., MB (1906)
Spiers, Sir Donald Maurice, Kt., CB, TD
Spooner, Sir James Douglas, Kt.
Spotswood, *Marshal of the Royal Air Force* Sir Denis Frank, GCB, CBE, DSO, DFC
Spratt, *Col.* Sir Greville Douglas, GBE, TD
Spreckley, Sir (John) Nicholas (Teague), KCVO, CMG
Spring, Sir Dryden Thomas, Kt.
Spry, *Hon.* Sir John Farley, Kt.
Stabb, *Hon.* Sir William Walter, Kt., QC
Stainton, Sir (John) Ross, Kt., CBE
Stakis, Sir Reo Argiros, Kt.
Stallard, Sir Peter Hyla Gawne, KCMG, CVO, MBE
Stamer, Sir (Lovelace) Anthony, Bt. (1809)
Stanbridge, *Air Vice-Marshal* Sir Brian Gerald Tivy, KCVO, CBE, AFC
Stanier, *Brig.* Sir Alexander Beville Gibbons, Bt., DSO, MC (1917)
Stanier, *Field Marshal* Sir John Wilfred, GCB, MBE
Stanley, *Rt. Hon.* Sir John Paul, Kt., MP
†Staples, Sir Thomas, Bt. (I. 1628)
Stapleton, Sir (Henry) Alfred, Bt. (1679)
Stark, Sir Andrew Alexander Steel, KCMG, CVO
Starke, *Hon.* Sir John Erskine, Kt.
Starkey, Sir John Philip, Bt. (1935)

Starrit, Sir James, KCVO
Statham, Sir Norman, KCMG, CVO
Staughton, *Rt. Hon.* Sir Christopher Stephen Thomas Jonathan Thayer, Kt.
Staveley, Sir John Malfroy, KBE, MC
Staveley, *Admiral of the Fleet* Sir William Doveton Minet, GCB
Stear, *Air Chief Marshal* Sir Michael James Douglas, KCB, CBE
Steel, Sir David Edward Charles, Kt., DSO, MC, TD
Steel, *Rt. Hon.* Sir David Martin Scott, KBE, MP
Steel, *Maj.* Sir (Fiennes) Michael Strang, Bt. (1938)
Steel, Sir James, Kt., CBE
Steele, Sir (Philip John) Rupert, Kt.
Steere, Sir Ernest Henry Lee-, KBE
Stenhouse, Sir Nicol, Kt.
Stening, *Col.* Sir George Grafton Lees, Kt., ED
Stephen, *Rt. Hon.* Sir Ninian Martin, KG, GCMG, GCVO, KBE
Stephenson, Sir Henry Upton, Bt. (1936)
Stephenson, *Rt. Hon.* Sir John Frederick Eustace, Kt.
Sternberg, Sir Sigmund, Kt.
Stevens, Sir Laurence Houghton, Kt., CBE
Stevenson, *Vice-Adm.* Sir (Hugh) David, KBE
Stevenson, Sir Simpson, Kt.
Stewart, Sir Alan, KBE
Stewart, Sir Alan d'Arcy, Bt. (I. 1623)
Stewart, Sir David James Henderson-, Bt. (1957)
†Stewart, Sir David John Christopher, Bt. (1803)
Stewart, Sir Edward Jackson, Kt.
Stewart, *Prof.* Sir Frederick Henry, Kt., Ph.D., FRS, FRSE
Stewart, Sir Houston Mark Shaw-, Bt., MC, TD (S. 1667)
Stewart, Sir James Douglas, Kt.
Stewart, Sir (John) Simon (Watson), Bt. (1920)
Stewart, Sir Michael Norman Francis, KCMG, OBE
Stewart, Sir Robertson Huntly, Kt., CBE
Stewart, Sir Robin Alastair, Bt. (1960)
Stewart, Sir Ronald Compton, Bt. (1937)
Stewart, *Prof.* Sir William Duncan Paterson, Kt., FRS, FRSE
Steyn, *Rt. Hon.* Sir Johan Van Zyl, Kt.
Stibbon, *Gen.* Sir John James, KCB, OBE
Stirling, Sir Alexander John Dickson, KBE, CMG
Stirling, Sir Angus Duncan Aeneas, Kt.
Stockdale, Sir Arthur Noel, Kt.
Stockdale, Sir Thomas Minshull, Bt. (1960)
Stocker, *Rt. Hon.* Sir John Dexter, Kt., MC, TD

Stoddart, *Wg Cdr.* Sir Kenneth Maxwell, KCVO, AE

Stoker, *Prof.* Sir Michael George Parke, Kt., CBE, FRCP, FRS, FRSE

Stokes, Sir John Heydon Romaine, Kt.

Stone, Sir Alexander, Kt., OBE

Stones, Sir William Frederick, Kt., OBE

Stonhouse, Sir Philip Allan, Bt. (1628)

Stonor, *Air Marshal* Sir Thomas Henry, KCB

Storey, *Hon.* Sir Richard, Bt. (1960)

Stormonth Darling, Sir James Carlisle, Kt., CBE, MC, TD

Stott, Sir Adrian George Ellingham, Bt. (1920)

Stow, Sir Christopher Philipson-, Bt., DFC (1907)

Stow, Sir John Montague, GCMG, KCVO

Stowe, Sir Kenneth Ronald, GCB, CVO

Stracey, Sir John Simon, Bt. (1818)

Strachey, Sir Charles, Bt. (1801)

Straker, Sir Michael Ian Bowstead, Kt., CBE

Strawson, *Prof.* Sir Peter Frederick, Kt., FBA

Street, *Hon.* Sir Laurence Whistler, KCMG

Streeton, Sir Terence George, KBE, CMG

Stringer, Sir Donald Edgar, Kt., CBE

Strong, Sir Roy Colin, Kt., ph.D., FSA

Stronge, Sir James Anselan Maxwell, Bt. (1803)

Stroud, *Prof.* Sir (Charles) Eric, Kt., FRCP

Strutt, Sir Nigel Edward, Kt., TD

Stuart, Sir James Keith, Kt.

Stuart, Sir Kenneth Lamonte, Kt.

†Stuart, Sir Phillip Luttrell, Bt. (1660)

Stubblefield, Sir (Cyril) James, Kt., D.SC., FRS

Stubbs, Sir James Wilfrid, KCVO, TD

Stubbs, Sir William Hamilton, Kt., Ph.D.

Stucley, *Lt.* Sir Hugh George Coplestone Bampfylde, Bt. (1859)

Studd, Sir Edward Fairfax, Bt. (1929)

Studd, Sir Peter Malden, GBE, KCVO

Studholme, Sir Henry William, Bt. (1956)

Style, *Lt.-Cdr.* Sir Godfrey William, Kt., CBE, DSC, RN

†Style, Sir William Frederick, Bt. (1627)

Suffield, Sir (Henry John) Lester, Kt.

Sugden, Sir Arthur, Kt.

Sullivan, Sir Desmond John, Kt.

Sullivan, Sir Richard Arthur, Bt. (1804)

Summerfield, *Hon.* Sir John Crampton, Kt., CBE

Summers, Sir Felix Roland Brattan, Bt. (1952)

Sunderland, *Prof.* Sir Sydney, Kt., CMG

Sutherland, *Prof.* Sir James Runciman, Kt., FBA

Sutherland, Sir John Brewer, Bt. (1921)

Sutherland, Sir Maurice, Kt.

Sutherland, Sir William George MacKenzie, Kt.

Suttie, Sir (George) Philip Grant-, Bt. (S. 1702)

Sutton, Sir Frederick Walter, Kt., OBE

Sutton, *Air Marshal* Sir John Matthias Dobson, KCB

Sutton, Sir Richard Lexington, Bt. (1772)

Swaffield, Sir James Chesebrough, Kt., CBE, RD

Swallow, Sir William, Kt.

Swan, Sir Conrad Marshall John Fisher, KCVO, ph.D.

Swan, Sir John William David, KBE

Swann, Sir Michael Christopher, Bt., TD (1906)

Swanwick, Sir Graham Russell, Kt., MBE

Swartz, *Hon.* Sir Reginald William Colin, KBE, ED

Sweetnam, Sir (David) Rodney, KCVO, CBE, FRCS

Swinburn, *Lt.-Gen.* Sir Richard Hull, KCB

Swinson, Sir John Henry Alan, Kt., OBE

Swinton, *Maj.-Gen.* Sir John, KCVO, OBE

Swire, Sir Adrian Christopher, Kt.

Swire, Sir John Anthony, Kt., CBE

Swiss, Sir Rodney Geoffrey, Kt., OBE

Swynnerton, Sir Roger John Massy, Kt., CMG, OBE, MC

Sykes, Sir Francis John Badcock, Bt. (1781)

Sykes, Sir John Charles Anthony le Gallais, Bt. (1921)

Sykes, *Prof.* Sir (Malcolm) Keith, Kt.

Sykes, Sir Richard, Kt.

Sykes, Sir Tatton Christopher Mark, Bt. (1783)

Symington, *Prof.* Sir Thomas, Kt., MD, FRSE

Symons, *Vice-Adm.* Sir Patrick Jeremy, KBE

Synge, Sir Robert Carson, Bt. (1801)

Tait, *Adm.* Sir (Allan) Gordon, KCB, DSC

Tait, Sir James Sharp, Kt., D.SC., LL D., Ph.D.

Tait, Sir Peter, KBE

Talbot, *Vice-Adm.* Sir (Arthur Allison) FitzRoy, KBE, CB, DSO

Talbot, *Hon.* Sir Hilary Gwynne, Kt.

Talboys, *Rt. Hon.* Sir Brian Edward, CH, KCB

Tancred, Sir Henry Lawson-, Bt. (1662)

Tangaroa, *Hon.* Sir Tangoroa, Kt., MBE

Tange, Sir Arthur Harold, Kt., CBE

Tapsell, Sir Peter Hannay Bailey, Kt., MP

†Tate, Sir (Henry) Saxon, Bt. (1898)

Taukala, Sir David Dawea, Kt., MBE

Tavaiqia, *Ratu* Sir Josaia, KBE

Tavare, Sir John, Kt., CBE

Taylor, *Lt.-Gen.* Sir Allan Macnab, KBE, MC

Taylor, Sir (Arthur) Godfrey, Kt.

Taylor, Sir Cyril Julian Hebden, Kt.

Taylor, Sir Edward Macmillan (Teddy), Kt., MP

Taylor, Sir James, Kt., MBE, D.SC

Taylor, Sir John Lang, KCMG

Taylor, Sir Nicholas Richard Stuart, Bt. (1917)

Taylor, *Prof.* Sir William, Kt., CBE

Teagle, *Vice-Adm.* Sir Somerford Francis, KBE

Tebbit, Sir Donald Claude, GCMG

Te Heuheu, Sir Hepi Hoani, KBE

Telford, Sir Robert, Kt., CBE, FEng.

Temple, Sir Ernest Sanderson, Kt., MBE, QC

Temple, Sir John Meredith, Kt.

Temple, Sir Rawden John Afamado, Kt., CBE, QC

Temple, *Maj.* Sir Richard Anthony Purbeck, Bt., MC (1876)

Templeton, Sir John Marks, Kt.

Tennant, *Capt.* Sir Iain Mark, KT

Tennant, Sir Anthony John, Kt.

Tennant, Sir Peter Frank Dalrymple, Kt., CMG, OBE

Teo, Sir Fiatau Penitala, GCMG, GCVO, ISO, MBE

Terry, Sir George Walter Roberts, Kt., CBE, QPM

Terry, Sir John Elliott, Kt.

Terry, Sir Michael Edward Stanley Imbert-, Bt. (1917)

Terry, *Air Chief Marshal* Sir Peter David George, GCB, AFC

Tetley, Sir Herbert, KBE, CB

Tett, Sir Hugh Charles, Kt.

Thatcher, Sir Denis, Bt., MBE, TD (1990)

Thomas, Sir Derek Morison David, KCMG

Thomas, Sir Frederick William, Kt.

Thomas, Sir (Godfrey) Michael (David), Bt. (1694)

Thomas, Sir Jeremy Cashel, KCMG

Thomas, Sir (John) Alan, Kt.

Thomas, Sir John Maldwyn, Kt.

Thomas, *Prof.* Sir John Meurig, Kt., FRS

Thomas, Sir Keith Vivian, Kt.

Thomas, Sir Robert Evan, Kt.

Thomas, *Hon.* Sir Swinton Barclay, Kt.

Thomas, Sir William James Cooper, Bt., TD (1919)

Thomas, Sir (William) Michael (Marsh), Bt. (1918)

Thomas, *Adm.* Sir (William) Richard Scott, KCB, OBE

Thompson, Sir Christopher Peile, Bt. (1890)

Thompson, Sir Donald, Kt., MP

Thompson, Sir Gilbert Williamson, Kt., OBE

Thompson, *Surgeon Vice-Adm.* Sir Godfrey James Milton-, KBE

Thompson, *Vice-Adm.* Sir Hugh Leslie Owen, KBE, FEng.

Thompson, Sir (Humphrey) Simon Meysey-, Bt. (1874)

Thompson, *Hon.* Sir John, Kt.

Thompson, *Prof.* Sir Michael Warwick, Kt., D.SC

Thompson, Sir Paul Anthony, Bt. (1963)

Thompson, Sir Peter Anthony, Kt.

Thompson, Sir Richard Hilton Marler, Bt. (1963)

Thompson, Sir (Thomas) Lionel Tennyson, Bt. (1806)

Thomson, Sir Adam, Kt., CBE

Thomson, *Air Chief Marshal Sir (Charles) John*, GCB, CBE, AFC

Thomson, Sir Evan Rees Whitaker, Kt.

Thomson, Sir (Frederick Douglas) David, Bt. (1929)

Thomson, Sir John, KBE, TD

Thomson, Sir John Adam, GCMG

Thomson, Sir John (Ian) Sutherland, KBE, CMG

Thomson, Sir Mark Wilfrid Home, Bt. (1925)

Thomson, Sir Thomas James, Kt., CBE, FRCP

Thorn, Sir John Samuel, Kt., OBE

Thorne, *Maj.-Gen.* Sir David Calthrop, KBE

Thorne, Sir Neil Gordon, Kt., OBE, TD

Thorne, Sir Peter Francis, KCVO, CBE

Thornton, Sir (George) Malcolm, Kt., MP

Thornton, *Lt.-Gen.* Sir Leonard Whitmore, KCB, CBE

Thornton, Sir Peter Eustace, KCB

Thorold, Sir Anthony Henry, Bt., OBE, DSC (1642)

Thorpe, *Hon.* Sir Mathew Alexander, Kt.

Thouron, Sir John Rupert Hunt, KBE

†Throckmorton, Sir Anthony John Benedict, Bt. (1642)

Thwaites, Sir Bryan, Kt., Ph.D.

Thwin, Sir U, Kt.

Tibbits, *Capt.* Sir David Stanley, Kt., DSC

Tickell, Sir Crispin Charles Cervantes, GCMG, KCVO

Tidbury, Sir Charles Henderson, Kt.

Tikaram, Sir Moti, KBE

Tims, Sir Michael David, KCVO

Tindle, Sir Ray Stanley, Kt., CBE

Tippet, *Vice-Adm.* Sir Anthony Sanders, KCB

Tippett, Sir Michael Kemp, Kt., OM, CH, CBE

Tirvengadum, Sir Harry Krishnan, Kt.

Titman, Sir John Edward Powis, KCVO

Tod, *Air Marshal* Sir John Hunter Hunter-, KBE, CB

Todd, Sir Ian Pelham, KBE, FRCS

Todd, *Hon.* Sir (Reginald Stephen) Garfield, Kt.

Tollemache, Sir Lyonel Humphry John, Bt. (1793)

Tololo, Sir Alkan, KBE

Tomkins, Sir Alfred George, Kt., CBE

Tomkins, Sir Edward Emile, GCMG, CVO

Tomkys, Sir (William) Roger, KCMG

Tomlinson, *Prof.* Sir Bernard Evans, Kt., CBE

Tomlinson, Sir (Frank) Stanley, KCMG

Tooley, Sir John, Kt.

Tooth, Sir (Hugh) John Lucas-, Bt. (1920)

ToRobert, Sir Henry Thomas, KBE

Tory, Sir Geofroy William, KCMG

Touche, Sir Anthony George, Bt. (1920)

Touche, Sir Rodney Gordon, Bt. (1962)

Tovey, Sir Brian John Maynard, KCMG

ToVue, Sir Ronald, Kt., OBE

Towneley, Sir Simon Peter Edmund Cosmo William, KCVO

Townsend, *Rear-Adm.* Sir Leslie William, KCVO, CBE

Townsing, Sir Kenneth Joseph, Kt., CMG

Traherne, Sir Cennydd George, KG, TD

Traill, Sir Alan Towers, GBE

Trant, *Gen.* Sir Richard Brooking, KCB

Travers, Sir Thomas à'Beckett, Kt.

Treacher, *Adm.* Sir John Devereux, KCB

Trehane, Sir (Walter) Richard, Kt.

Trelawny, Sir John Barry Salusbury-, Bt. (1628)

Trench, Sir Nigel Clive Cosby, KCMG

Trench, Sir Peter Edward, Kt., CBE, TD

Trescowthick, Sir Donald Henry, KBE

Trethowan, *Prof.* Sir William Henry, Kt., CBE, FRCP

Trevelyan, Sir George Lowthian, Bt. (1874)

Trevelyan, Sir Norman Irving, Bt. (1662)

Trewby, *Vice-Adm.* Sir (George Francis) Allan, KCB, FEng.

Trippier, Sir David Austin, Kt., RD

Tritton, Sir Anthony John Ernest, Bt. (1905)

†Trollope, Sir Anthony Simon, Bt. (1642)

Trotter, Sir Ronald Ramsay, Kt.

Troubridge, Sir Thomas Richard, Bt. (1799)

Troup, *Vice-Adm.* Sir (John) Anthony (Rose), KCB, DSC

Trowbridge, *Rear-Adm.* Sir Richard John, KCVO

Truscott, Sir George James Irving, Bt. (1909)

Tuck, Sir Bruce Adolph Reginald, Bt. (1910)

Tucker, *Hon.* Sir Richard Howard, Kt.

Tuckey, *Hon.* Sir Simon Lane, Kt.

Tudor, *Hon.* Sir James Cameron, KCMG

Tuita, Sir Mariano Kelesimalefo, Kt., OBE

Tuite, Sir Christopher Hugh, Bt., Ph.D. (1622)

Tuivaga, Sir Timoci Uluiburotu, Kt.

Tuke, Sir Anthony Favill, Kt.

Tupper, Sir Charles Hibbert, Bt. (1888)

Turbott, Sir Ian Graham, Kt., CMG, CVO

Turing, Sir John Dermot, Bt. (s. 1638)

Turnberg, *Prof.* Sir Leslie Arnold, Kt., MD, FRCP

Turnbull, Sir Richard Gordon, GCMG

Turner, Sir Colin William Carstairs, Kt., CBE, DFC

Turner, *Hon.* Sir Michael John, Kt.

Tuti, *Revd* Dudley, KBE

Tuzo, *Gen.* Sir Harry Craufurd, GCB, OBE, MC

Tweedie, *Prof.* Sir David Philip, Kt.

Tyree, Sir (Alfred) William, Kt., OBE

Tyrwhitt, Sir Reginald Thomas Newman, Bt. (1919)

Udoma, *Hon.* Sir (Egbert) Udo, Kt.

Unsworth, *Hon.* Sir Edgar Ignatius Godfrey, Kt., CMG

Unwin, Sir (James) Brian, KCB

Ure, Sir John Burns, KCMG, LVO

Urquhart, Sir Brian Edward, KCMG, MBE

Urwick, Sir Alan Bedford, KCVO, CMG

Usher, Sir Leonard Gray, KBE

Usher, Sir Robert Edward, Bt. (1899)

Ustinov, Sir Peter Alexander, Kt., CBE

Utting, Sir William Benjamin, Kt., CB

Vallance, Sir Iain David Thomas, Kt.

Vallat, Sir Francis Aimé, GBE, KCMG, QC

Vallings, *Vice-Adm.* Sir George Montague Francis, KCB

Vanderfelt, Sir Robin Victor, KBE

van der Post, Sir Laurens Jan, Kt., CBE

Vane, Sir John Robert, Kt., D.phil., D.SC., FRS

Vanneck, *Air Cdre* Hon. Sir Peter Beckford Rutgers, GBE, CB, AFC

van Straubenzee, Sir William Radcliffe, Kt., MBE

Vasquez, Sir Alfred Joseph, Kt., CBE, QC

Vaughan, Sir Gerard Folliott, Kt., MP, FRCP

Vavasour, *Cdr.* Sir Geoffrey William, Bt., DSC, RN (1828)

Veale, Sir Alan John Ralph, Kt., FEng.

Verco, Sir Walter John George, KCVO

†Verney, Sir John Sebastian, Bt. (1946)

Verney, *Hon.* Sir Lawrence John, Kt., TD

Verney, Sir Ralph Bruce, Bt., KBE (1818)

Vernon, Sir James, Kt., CBE

Vernon, Sir Nigel John Douglas, Bt. (1914)

Vesey, Sir (Nathaniel) Henry (Peniston), Kt., CBE

Vestey, Sir (John) Derek, Bt. (1921)

Vial, Sir Kenneth Harold, Kt., CBE

Vick, Sir (Francis) Arthur, Kt., OBE, Ph.D.

Vickers, *Lt.-Gen.* Sir Richard Maurice Hilton, KCB, MVO, OBE

Victoria, Sir (Joseph Aloysius) Donatus, Kt., CBE

Frederick, GBE, KCB, DSO

Vincent, Sir William Percy Maxwell, Bt. (1936)

Vinelott, *Hon.* Sir John Evelyn, Kt.

Vines, Sir William Joshua, Kt., CMG

Vyvyan, Sir John Stanley, Bt. (1645)

Waddell, Sir Alexander Nicol Anton, KCMG, DSC

Waddell, Sir James Henderson, Kt., CB

Wade, *Prof.* Sir Henry William Rawson, Kt., QC, FBA

Wade, *Air Chief Marshal* Sir Ruthven Lowry, KCB, DFC

Wagner, Sir Anthony Richard, KCB, KCVO

Waite, *Rt. Hon.* Sir John Douglas, Kt.

Wake, Sir Hereward, Bt., MC (1621)

Wakefield, Sir (Edward) Humphry (Tyrell), Bt. (1962)

Wakefield, Sir Norman Edward, Kt.

Wakefield, Sir Peter George Arthur, KBE, CMG

Wakeford, *Air Marshal* Sir Richard Gordon, KCB, OBE, MVO, AFC

Wakeley, Sir John Cecil Nicholson, Bt., FRCS (1952)

†Wakeman, Sir Edward Offley Bertram, Bt. (1828)

Walker, *Revd* Alan Edgar, Kt., OBE

Walker, *Gen.* Sir Antony Kenneth Frederick, KCB

Walker, Sir Baldwin Patrick, Bt. (1856)

Walker, Sir (Charles) Michael, GCMG

Walker, Sir Colin John Shedlock, Kt., OBE

Walker, Sir David Alan, Kt.

Walker, Sir Gervas George, Kt.

Walker, *Rt. Hon.* Sir Harold, Kt., MP

Walker, Sir Harold Berners, KCMG

Walker, *Maj.* Sir Hugh Ronald, Bt. (1906)

Walker, Sir James Graham, Kt., MBE

Walker, Sir James Heron, Bt. (1868)

Walker, *Air Marshal* Sir John Robert, KCB, CBE, AFC

Walker, Sir Michael Leolin Forestier-, Bt. (1835)

Walker, Sir Patrick Jeremy, KCB

Walker, *Gen.* Sir Walter Colyear, KCB, CBE, DSO

Wall, *Hon.* Sir Nicholas Peter Rathbone, Kt.

Wall, Sir Patrick Henry Bligh, Kt., MC, VRD

Wall, Sir Robert William, Kt., OBE

Wallace, Sir Ian James, Kt., CBE

Waller, *Hon.* Sir (George) Mark, Kt.

Waller, *Rt. Hon.* Sir George Stanley, Kt., OBE

Waller, Sir (John) Keith, Kt., CBE

Waller, Sir John Stainer, Bt. (1815)

Waller, Sir Robert William, Bt. (I. 1780)

Walley, Sir John, KBE, CB

Wallis, Sir Peter Gordon, KCVO

Wallis, Sir Timothy William, Kt.

Walsh, Sir Alan, Kt., D.SC., FRS

Walsh, *Prof.* Sir John Patrick, KBE

†Walsham, Sir Timothy John, Bt. (1831)

Walter, Sir Harold Edward, Kt.

Walters, *Prof.* Sir Alan Arthur, Kt.

Walters, Sir Dennis Murray, Kt., MBE

Walters, Sir Frederick Donald, Kt.

Walters, Sir Peter Ingram, Kt.

Walters, Sir Roger Talbot, KBE, FRIBA

Walton, Sir John Robert, Kt.

Wan, Sir Wamp, Kt., MBE

Wanstall, *Hon.* Sir Charles Gray, Kt.

Ward, *Hon.* Sir Alan Hylton, Kt.

Ward, Sir Arthur Hugh, KBE

Ward, Sir Joseph James Laffey, Bt. (1911)

Ward, *Maj.-Gen.* Sir Philip John Newling, KCVO, CBE

Ward, Sir Timothy James, Kt.

Wardale, Sir Geoffrey Charles, KCB

Wardlaw, Sir Henry (John), Bt. (s. 1631)

Wardle, Sir Thomas Edward Jewell, Kt.

Waring, Sir (Alfred) Holburt, Bt. (1935)

Warmington, *Lt.-Cdr.* Sir Marshall George Clitheroe, Bt., RN (1908)

Warner, Sir (Edward Courtenay) Henry, Bt. (1910)

Warner, Sir Edward Redston, KCMG, OBE

Warner, Sir Frederick Archibald, GCVO, KCMG

Warner, *Prof.* Sir Frederick Edward, Kt., FRS, FEng.

Warner, *Hon.* Sir Jean-Pierre Frank Eugene, Kt.

Warnock, Sir Geoffrey James, Kt.

Warren, Sir Brian Charles Pennefather, Bt. (1784)

Warren, Sir Frederick Miles, KBE

Warren, Sir (Harold) Brian (Seymour), Kt.

Warren, Sir Kenneth Robin, Kt.

Wass, Sir Douglas William Gretton, GCB

Waterhouse, *Hon.* Sir Ronald Gough, Kt.

Waterlow, Sir Christopher Rupert, Bt. (1873)

Waterlow, Sir (James) Gerard, Bt. (1930)

Waters, *Gen.* Sir (Charles) John, KCB, CBE

Wates, Sir Christopher Stephen, Kt.

Watkins, *Rt. Hon.* Sir Tasker, VC, GBE

Watson, Sir Bruce Dunstan, Kt.

Watson, Sir Duncan Amos, Kt., CBE

Watson, Sir (James) Andrew, Bt. (1866)

Watson, Sir John Forbes Inglefield-, Bt. (1895)

Watson, Sir Michael Milne-, Bt., CBE (1937)

Watson, Sir (Noel) Duncan, KCMG

Watson, *Vice-Adm.* Sir Philip Alexander, KBE, MVO

Watt, *Surgeon Vice-Adm.* Sir James, KBE, FRCS

Watt, Sir James Harvie-, Bt. (1945)

Watts, Sir Arthur Desmond, KCMG

Watts, *Lt.-Gen.* Sir John Peter Barry Condliffe, KBE, CB, MC

Wauchope, Sir Roger (Hamilton) Don-, Bt. (s. 1667)

Way, Sir Richard George Kitchener, KCB, CBE

Weatherall, *Prof.* Sir David John, Kt., FRS

Weatherall, *Vice-Adm.* Sir James Lamb, KCVO

Weatherstone, Sir Dennis, KBE

Weaver, Sir Tobias Rushton, Kt., CB

Webb, Sir Thomas Langley, Kt.

Webber, Sir Andrew Lloyd, Kt.

Webster, *Very Revd* Alan Brunskill, KCVO

Webster, *Vice-Adm.* Sir John Morrison, KCB

Webster, *Hon.* Sir Peter Edlin, Kt.

Wedderburn, Sir Andrew John Alexander Ogilvy-, Bt. (1803)

Wedgwood, Sir (Hugo) Martin, Bt. (1942)

Weinberg, Sir Mark Aubrey, Kt.

Weir, Sir Michael Scott, KCMG

Weir, Sir Roderick Bignell, Kt.

Welby, Sir (Richard) Bruno Gregory, Bt. (1801)

Welch, Sir John Reader, Bt. (1957)

Weldon, Sir Anthony William, Bt. (I. 1723)

Wellings, Sir Jack Alfred, Kt., CBE

Wells, Sir Charles Maltby, Bt., TD (1944)

Wells, Sir John Julius, Kt.

Westbrook, Sir Neil Gowanloch, Kt., CBE

Westerman, Sir (Wilfred) Alan, Kt., CBE

Weston, Sir Michael Charles Swift, KCMG, CVO

Weston, Sir (Philip) John, KCMG

Wheeler, Sir Frederick Henry, Kt., CBE

Wheeler, Sir Harry Anthony, Kt., OBE

Wheeler, *Air Chief Marshal* Sir (Henry) Neil (George), GCB, CBE, DSO, DFC, AFC

Wheeler, *Rt. Hon.* Sir John Daniel, Kt., MP

Wheeler, Sir John Hieron, Bt. (1920)

Wheeler, *Hon.* Sir Kenneth Henry, Kt.

Wheeler, *Lt.-Gen.* Sir Roger Neil, KCB, CBE

Wheler, Sir Edward Woodford, Bt. (1660)

Whishaw, Sir Charles Percival Law, Kt.

Whitaker, *Maj.* Sir James Herbert Ingham, Bt. (1936)
White, Sir Christopher Robert Meadows, Bt. (1937)
White, *Hon.* Sir Christopher Stuart Stuart-, Kt.
White, Sir David Harry, Kt.
White, Sir Frederick William George, KBE, Ph.D., FRS
White, Sir George Stanley James, Bt. (1904)
White, *Wg Cdr.* Sir Henry Arthur Dalrymple-, Bt., DFC (1926)
White, *Adm.* Sir Hugo Moresby, KCB, CBE
White, *Hon.* Sir John Charles, Kt., MBE
White, Sir John Woolmer, Bt. (1922)
White, Sir Lynton Stuart, Kt., MBE, TD
White, *Adm.* Sir Peter, GBE
White, Sir Thomas Astley Woollaston, Bt. (1802)
Whitehead, Sir John Stainton, GCMG, CVO
Whitehead, Sir Rowland John Rathbone, Bt. (1889)
Whiteley, Sir Hugo Baldwin Huntington-, Bt. (1918)
Whiteley, *Gen.* Sir Peter John Frederick, GCB, OBE, RM
Whitfield, Sir William, Kt., CBE
Whitford, *Hon.* Sir John Norman Keates, Kt.
Whitley, *Air Marshal* Sir John René, KBE, CB, DSO, AFC
Whitmore, Sir Clive Anthony, GCB, CVO
Whitmore, Sir John Henry Douglas, Bt. (1954)
Whitteridge, Sir Gordon Coligny, KCMG, OBE
Whittle, *Air Cdre* Sir Frank, OM, KBE, CB, FRS, FEng.
Whittome, Sir (Leslie) Alan, Kt.
Wickerson, Sir John Michael, Kt.
Wicks, Sir James Albert, Kt.
Wicks, Sir Nigel Leonard, KCB, CVO, CBE
Wigan, Sir Alan Lewis, Bt. (1898)
Wiggin, Sir Alfred William (Jerry), Kt., TD, MP
†Wiggin, Sir Charles Rupert John, Bt. (1892)
Wigram, *Revd Canon* Sir Clifford Woolmore, Bt. (1805)
Wilbraham, Sir Richard Baker, Bt. (1776)
Wilford, Sir (Kenneth) Michael, GCMG, CBE
Wilkes, *Gen.* Sir Michael John, KCB, CBE
Wilkins, Sir Graham John, Kt.
Wilkinson, Sir (David) Graham (Brook) Bt. (1941)
Wilkinson, *Prof.* Sir Denys Haigh, Kt., FRS
Wilkinson, *Prof.* Sir Geoffrey, Kt., FRS
Wilkinson, Sir Peter Allix, KCMG, DSO, OBE
Wilkinson, Sir Philip William, Kt.

Wilkinson, Sir William Henry Nairn, Kt.
Willatt, Sir (Robert) Hugh, Kt.
Willcocks, Sir David Valentine, Kt., CBE, MC
Williams, Sir Alastair Edgcumbe James Dudley-, Bt. (1964)
Williams, Sir Alwyn, Kt., Ph.D., FRS
Williams, Sir Arthur Dennis Pitt, Kt.
Williams, Sir (Arthur) Gareth Ludovic Emrys Rhys, Bt. (1918)
Williams, *Prof.* Sir Bruce Rodda, KBE
Williams, *Adm.* Sir David, GCB
Williams, *Prof.* Sir David Glyndwr Tudor, Kt.
Williams, Sir David Innes, Kt.
Williams, *Hon.* Sir Denys Ambrose, KCMG
Williams, Sir Donald Mark, Bt. (1866)
Williams, Sir Edgar Trevor, Kt., CB, CBE, DSO
Williams, *Prof.* Sir (Edward) Dillwyn, Kt., FRCP
Williams, *Hon.* Sir Edward Stratten, KCMG, KBE
Williams, Sir Francis John Watkin, Bt., QC (1798)
Williams, Sir Henry Sydney, Kt., OBE
Williams, Sir John Robert, KCMG
Williams, Sir Leonard, KBE, CB
Williams, Sir Osmond, Bt., MC (1909)
Williams, Sir Peter Watkin, Kt.
Williams, *Prof.* Sir Robert Evan Owen, Kt., MD, FRCP
Williams, Sir (Robert) Philip Nathaniel, Bt. (1915)
Williams, Sir Robin Philip, Bt. (1953)
Williams, Sir (William) Maxwell (Harries), Kt.
Williamson, *Marshal of the Royal Air Force* Sir Keith Alec, GCB, AFC
Williamson, Sir (Nicholas Frederick) Hedworth, Bt. (1642)
Willink, Sir Charles William, Bt. (1957)
Willis, *Hon.* Sir Eric Archibald, KBE, CMG
Willis, *Vice-Adm.* Sir (Guido) James, KBE
Willis, *Air Marshal* Sir John Frederick, KCB, CBE
Willison, *Lt.-Gen.* Sir David John, KCB, OBE, MC
Willison, Sir John Alexander, Kt., OBE
Wills, Sir David Seton, Bt. (1904)
Wills, Sir (Hugh) David Hamilton, Kt., CBE, TD
Wills, Sir John Vernon, Bt., TD (1923)
Wilmot, Sir Henry Robert, Bt. (1759)
Wilmot, *Cdr.* Sir John Assheton Eardley-, Bt., MVO, DSC, RN (1821)
Wilsey, *Gen.* Sir John Finlay Willasey, KCB, CBE
Wilson, Sir Alan Herries, Kt., FRS
Wilson, *Lt.-Gen.* Sir (Alexander) James, KBE, MC
Wilson, Sir Anthony, Kt.
Wilson, *Vice-Adm.* Sir Barry Nigel, KCB

Wilson, *Lt.-Col.* Sir Blair Aubyn Stewart-, KCVO
Wilson, Sir Charles Haynes, Kt.
Wilson, Sir David, Bt. (1920)
Wilson, Sir David Mackenzie, Kt.
Wilson, Sir Geoffrey Masterman, KCB, CMG
Wilson, Sir James William Douglas, Bt. (1906)
Wilson, Sir John Foster, Kt., CBE
Wilson, Sir John Gardiner, Kt., CBE
Wilson, *Brig.* Sir Mathew John Anthony, Bt., OBE, MC (1874)
Wilson, *Hon.* Sir Nicholas Allan Roy, Kt.
Wilson, Sir Patrick Michael Ernest David McNair-, Kt., MP
Wilson, Sir Reginald Holmes, Kt.
Wilson, Sir Robert, Kt., CBE
Wilson, Sir Robert Donald, Kt.
Wilson, *Rt. Revd* Roger Plumpton, KCVO, DD
Wilson, Sir Roland, KBE
Wilson, *Air Chief Marshal* Sir (Ronald) Andrew (Fellowes), KCB, AFC
Wilson, *Hon.* Sir Ronald Darling, KBE, CMG
Wilton, Sir (Arthur) John, KCMG, KCVO, MC
Wiltshire, Sir Frederick Munro, Kt., CBE
Windeyer, Sir Brian Wellingham, Kt.
Wingate, *Capt.* Sir Miles Buckley, KCVO
Winnington, Sir Francis Salwey William, Bt. (1755)
Winskill, *Air Cdre* Sir Archibald Little, KCVO, CBE, DFC
Winterbottom, Sir Walter, Kt., CBE
Wiseman, Sir John William, Bt. (1628)
Wolfson, Sir Brian Gordon, Kt.
Wolseley, Sir Charles Garnet Richard Mark, Bt. (1628)
†Wolseley, Sir James Douglas, Bt. (I. 1745)
Wolstenholme, Sir Gordon Ethelbert Ward, Kt., OBE
Wombwell, Sir George Philip Frederick, Bt. (1778)
Womersley, Sir Peter John Walter, Bt. (1945)
Woo, Sir Leo Joseph, Kt.
Wood, Sir Alan Marshall Muir, Kt., FRS, FEng.
Wood, Sir Anthony John Page, Bt. (1837)
Wood, Sir David Basil Hill-, Bt. (1921)
Wood, Sir Frederick Ambrose Stuart, Kt.
Wood, Sir Henry Peart, Kt., CBE
Wood, Sir Ian Clark, Kt., CBE
Wood, *Prof.* Sir John Crossley, Kt., CBE
Wood, *Hon.* Sir John Kember, Kt., MC
Wood, Sir Martin Francis, Kt., OBE
Wood, Sir Russell Dillon, KCVO, VRD
Wood, Sir William Alan, KCVO, CB
Woodcock, Sir John, Kt., CBE, QPM

Woodfield, Sir Philip John, KCB, CBE

Woodhead, *Vice-Adm.* Sir (Anthony) Peter, KCB

Woodhouse, *Rt. Hon.* Sir (Arthur) Owen, KBE, DSC

Wooding, Sir Norman Samuel, Kt., CBE

Woodroffe, *Most Revd* George Cuthbert Manning, KBE

Woodroofe, Sir Ernest George, Kt., PH.D.

Woodruff, *Prof.* Sir Michael Francis Addison, Kt., D.SC., FRS, FRCS

Woods, Sir Colin Philip Joseph, KCVO, CBE

Woods, *Rt. Revd* Robert Wilmer, KCMG, KCVO

Woodward, *Hon.* Sir (Albert) Edward, Kt., OBE

Woodward, *Adm.* Sir John Forster, GBE, KCB

Woolf, Sir John, Kt.

Woollaston, Sir (Mountford) Tosswill, Kt.

Wordie, Sir John Stewart, Kt., CBE, VRD

Worsley, *Gen.* Sir Richard Edward, GCB, OBE

Worsley, Sir (William) Marcus (John), Bt. (1838)

Worsthorne, Sir Peregrine Gerard, Kt.

Wraight, Sir John Richard, KBE, CMG

Wratten, *Air Chief Marshal* Sir William John, KBE, CB, AFC

Wraxall, Sir Charles Frederick Lascelles, Bt. (1813)

Wrey, Sir George Richard Bourchier, Bt. (1628)

Wrigglesworth, Sir Ian William, Kt.

Wright, Sir Allan Frederick, KBE

Wright, Sir Denis Arthur Hepworth, GCMG

Wright, Sir Edward Maitland, Kt., D.Phil., LL D., D.SC., FRSE

Wright, *Hon.* Sir (John) Michael, Kt.

Wright, Sir (John) Oliver, GCMG, GCVO, DSC

Wright, Sir Paul Hervé Giraud, KCMG, OBE

Wright, Sir Peter Robert, Kt., CBE

Wright, Sir Richard Michael Cory-, Bt. (1903)

Wrightson, Sir Charles Mark Garmondsway, Bt. (1900)

Wykeham, *Air Marshal* Sir Peter Guy, KCB, DSO, OBE, DFC, AFC

Wynn, Sir David Watkin Williams-, Bt. (1688)

Yacoub, *Prof.* Sir Magdi Habib, Kt., FRCS

Yang, *Hon.* Ti Liang, Kt.

Yapp, Sir Stanley Graham, Kt.

Yardley, Sir David Charles Miller, Kt., LL.D.

Yarranton, Sir Peter George, Kt.

Yarrow, Sir Eric Grant, Bt., MBE (1916)

Yeend, Sir Geoffrey John, Kt., CBE

Yellowlees, Sir Henry, KCB

Yocklunn, Sir John (Soong Chung), KCVO

Yoo Foo, Sir (François) Henri, Kt.

Youens, Sir Peter William, Kt., CMG, OBE

Young, Sir Brian Walter Mark, Kt.

Young, Sir Colville Norbert, GCMG, MBE

Young, *Lt.-Gen.* Sir David Tod, KBE, CB, DFC

Young, *Rt. Hon.* Sir George Samuel Knatchbull, Bt., MP (1813)

Young, *Hon.* Sir Harold William, KCMG

Young, Sir John Kenyon Roe, Bt. (1821)

Young, *Hon.* Sir John McIntosh, KCMG

Young, Sir Leslie Clarence, Kt., CBE

Young, Sir Norman Smith, Kt.

Young, Sir Richard Dilworth, Kt.

Young, Sir Robert Christopher Mackworth-, GCVO

Young, Sir Roger William, Kt.

Young, Sir Stephen Stewart Templeton, Bt. (1945)

Young, Sir William Neil, Bt. (1769)

Younger, *Maj.-Gen.* Sir John William, Bt., CBE (1911)

Zeeman, *Prof.* Sir (Erik) Christopher, Kt., FRS

Zeidler, Sir David Ronald, Kt., CBE

Zoleveke, Sir Gideon Pitabose, KBE

Zunz, Sir Gerhard Jacob (Jack), Kt., FEng.

Zurenuo, *Rt. Revd* Zurewe Kamong, Kt., OBE

---

# The Military Knights of Windsor

The Military Knights of Windsor take part in all ceremonies of the Noble Order of the Garter and attend Sunday morning service in St George's Chapel, Windsor Castle, as representatives of the Knights of the Garter. The Knights receive a small stipend in addition to their army pensions and quarters in Windsor Castle.

The Knights of Windsor were originally founded in 1348 after the wars in France to assist English knights, who, having been prisoners in the hands of the French, had become impoverished by the payments of heavy ransoms. When Edward III founded the Order of the Garter later the same year, he incorporated the Knights of Windsor and the College of St George into its foundation and raised the number of Knights to 26 to correspond with the number of the Knights of the Garter. Known later as the Alms Knights or Poor Knights of Windsor, their establishment was reduced under the will of King Henry VIII to 13 and Statutes were drawn up by Queen Elizabeth I.

In 1833 King William IV changed their designation to The Military Knights and granted them their present uniform which consists of a scarlet tail-coat with white cross sword-belt, crimson sash and cocked hat with plume. The badges are the Shield of St George and the Star of the Order of the Garter.

*Governor*, Maj.-Gen. Peter Downward, CB, DSO, DFC

*Military Knights*, Brig. A. L. Atkinson, OBE; Brig. J. F. Lindner, OBE, MC; Maj. W. L. Thompson, MVO, MBE, DCM; Maj. L. W. Dickerson; Maj. J. C. Cowley, DCM; Lt.-Col. N. L. West; Maj. G. R. Mitchell; MBE, BEM; Lt.-Col. R. L. C. Tamplin; Maj. P. H. Bolton, MBE; Lt.-Col. H. R. Rogers, MBE; Brig. T. W. Hackworth, OBE; Maj. R. J. Moore

*Supernumerary*, Brig. A. C. Tyler, CBE, MC

# Dames Grand Cross and Dames Commanders

*Style*, 'Dame' before forename and surname, followed by appropriate post-nominal initials. Where such an award is made to a lady already in enjoyment of a higher title, the appropriate initials follow her name
*Husband*, Untitled
For forms of address, *see* page 217

Dame Grand Cross and Dame Commander are the higher classes for women of the Order of the Bath, the Order of St Michael and St George, the Royal Victorian Order, and the Order of the British Empire. Dames Grand Cross rank after the wives of Baronets and before the wives of Knights Grand Cross. Dames Commanders rank after the wives of Knights Grand Cross and before the wives of Knights Commanders

Honorary Dame Commanders may be conferred on women who are citizens of countries of which The Queen is not head of state

LIST OF DAMES  *Revised to 31 August 1994*

Women peers in their own right and life peers are not included in this list
If a dame has a double barrelled or hyphenated surname, she is listed under the final element of the name

HM Queen Elizabeth the Queen Mother, KG, KT, CI, GMVO
HRH The Princess Royal, GCVO
HRH The Princess Margaret, Countess of Snowdon, CI, GCVO
HRH The Duchess of Gloucester, GCVO
HRH Princess Alice, Duchess of Gloucester, GCB, CI, GCVO, GBE
HRH The Duchess of Kent, GCVO
HRH Princess Alexandra of Kent, GCVO
Abaijah, Dame Josephine, DBE
Abel Smith, Lady, DCVO
Abergavenny, The Marchioness of, DCVO
Albemarle, The Countess of, DBE
Anderson, *Brig.* Hon. Dame Mary Mackenzie (Mrs Pihl), DBE
Anglesey, The Marchioness of, DBE
Anstee, Dame Margaret Joan, DCMG
Arden, *Hon.* Dame Mary Howarth (Mrs Mance), DBE
Baker, Dame Janet Abbott (Mrs Shelley), CH, DBE
Ballin, Dame Reubina Ann, DBE
Barnes, Dame (Alice) Josephine (Mary Taylor), DBE, FRCP, FRCS
Barrow, Dame Jocelyn Anita (Mrs Downer), DBE
Barrow, Dame (Ruth) Nita, GCMG
Basset, Lady Elizabeth, DCVO
Beaurepaire, Dame Beryl Edith, DBE
Bergquist, *Prof.* Dame Patricia Rose, DBE
Berry, Dame Alice Miriam, DBE
Blaize, Dame Venetia Ursula, DBE
Blaxland, Dame Helen Frances, DBE
Booth, *Hon.* Dame Margaret Myfanwy Wood, DBE
Bottomley, Dame Bessie Ellen, DBE
Bowman, Dame (Mary) Elaine Kellett-, DBE, MP
Boyd, Dame Vivienne Myra, DBE

Bracewell, *Hon.* Dame Joyanne Winifred (Mrs Copeland), DBE
Brain, Dame Margaret Anne (Mrs Wheeler), DBE
Brazill, Dame Josephine (Sister Mary Philippa), DBE
Breen, Dame Marie Freda, DBE
Bridges, Dame Mary Patricia, DBE
Brown, Dame Beryl Paston, DBE
Brown, Dame Gillian Gerda, DCVO, CMG
Browne, Lady Moyra Blanche Madeleine, DBE
Bryans, Dame Anne Margaret, DBE
Bryce, Dame Isabel Graham, DBE
Burnside, Dame Edith, DBE
Buttfield, Dame Nancy Eileen, DBE
Byford, Dame Hazel, DBE
Bynoe, Dame Hilda Louisa, DBE
Cartland, Dame Barbara Hamilton, DBE
Cartwright, Dame Mary Lucy, DBE, SC.D., D.Phil., FRS
Cartwright, Dame Silvia Rose, DBE
Casey, Dame Stella Katherine, DBE
Cayford, Dame Florence Evelyn, DBE
Charles, Dame (Mary) Eugenia, DBE
Chesterton, Dame Elizabeth Ursula, DBE
Clay, Dame Marie Mildred, DBE
Clayton, Dame Barbara Evelyn (Mrs Klyne), DBE
Cleland, Dame Rachel, DBE
Clode, Dame (Emma) Frances (Heather), DBE
Coles, Dame Mabel Irene, DBE
Cookson, Dame Catherine Ann, DBE
Corsar, The Hon. Dame Mary Drummond, DBE, RRC
Coulshed, Dame (Mary) Frances, DBE, TD
Cozens, *Brig.* Dame (Florence) Barbara, DBE, RRC
Crowe, Dame Sylvia, DBE
Daws, Dame Joyce Margaretta, DBE
Dell, Dame Miriam Patricia, DBE
Dench, Dame Judith Olivia (Mrs Williams), DBE
de Valois, Dame Ninette, OM, CH, DBE

Digby, Lady, DBE
Donaldson, Dame (Dorothy) Mary (Lady Donaldson of Lymington), GBE
Doyle, *Air Comdt.* Dame Jean Lena Annette Conan (Lady Bromet), DBE
Drake, *Brig.* Dame Jean Elizabeth Rivett-, DBE
Dugdale, Lady (Kathryn Edith Helen), DCVO
Durack, Dame Mary (Mrs H. C. Miller), DBE
Ebsworth, *Hon.* Dame Ann Marian, DBE
Emerton, Dame Audrey Caroline, DBE
Evison, Dame Helen June Patricia, DBE
Fenner, Dame Peggy Edith, DBE, MP
Fitton, Dame Doris Alice (Mrs Mason), DBE
Fookes, Dame Janet Evelyn, DBE, MP
Fraser, Dame Dorothy Rita, DBE
Friend, Dame Phyllis Muriel, DBE
Frost, Dame Phyllis Irene, DBE
Fry, Dame Margaret Louise, DBE
Gallagher, Dame Monica Josephine, DBE
Gardiner, Dame Helen Louisa, DBE, MVO
Gibbs, Dame Molly Peel, DBE
Giles, *Air Comdt.* Dame Pauline (Mrs Parsons), DBE, RRC
Golding, Dame (Cecilie) Monica, DBE
Goodman, Dame Barbara, DBE
Gordon, Dame Minita Elmira, GCMG, GCVO
Gow, Dame Jane Elizabeth (Mrs Whiteley), DBE
Grafton, The Duchess of, GCVO
Green, Dame Mary Georgina, DBE
Grey, Dame Beryl Elizabeth (Mrs Svenson), DBE
Guilfoyle, Dame Margaret Georgina Constance, DBE
Guthardt, *Revd Dr* Dame Phyllis Myra, DBE
Haig, Dame Mary Alison Glen-, DBE
Hale, *Hon.* Dame Brenda Marjorie (Mrs Farrand), DBE

Hall, Dame Catherine Mary, DBE
Hammond, Dame Joan Hood, DBE
Harris, Dame (Muriel) Diana Reader-, DBE
*Hartman, Dame (Gladys) Marea*, DBE
Heilbron, *Hon.* Dame Rose, DBE
Henderson, Dame Louise Etiennette Sidonie, DBE
Henrison, Dame Anne Elizabeth Rosina, DBE
Herbison, Dame Jean Marjory, DBE, CMG
Hercus, *Hon.* Dame (Margaret) Ann, DCMG
Hetet, Dame Rangimarie, DBE
Hill, Dame Elizabeth Mary, DBE
Hill, *Air Cdre* Dame Felicity Barbara, DBE
Hiller, Dame Wendy (Mrs Gow), DBE
Hird, Dame Thora (Mrs Scott), DBE
Horsman, Dame Dorothea Jean, DBE
Howard, Dame Rosemary Christian, DBE
Hunter, Dame Pamela, DBE
Hurley, *Prof.* Dame Rosalinde (Mrs Gortvai), DBE
Hussey, Lady Susan Katharine, DCVO
Isaacs, Dame Albertha Madeline, DBE
James, Dame Naomi Christine (Mrs Haythorne), DBE
Jenkins, Dame (Mary) Jennifer (Lady Jenkins of Hillhead), DBE
Jessel, Dame Penelope, DBE
Jones, Dame Gwyneth (Mrs Haberfeld-Jones), DBE
Kekedo, Dame Mary, DBE, BEM
Kelleher, Dame Joan, DBE
Kettlewell, *Comdt.* Dame Marion Mildred, DBE
Kilroy, Dame Alix Hester Marie (Lady Meynell), DBE
Kirby, Dame Georgina Kamiria, DBE
Kirk, Dame (Lucy) Ruth, DBE
Knight, Dame (Joan Christabel) Jill, DBE, MP
Kramer, *Prof.* Dame Leonie Judith, DBE
Lamb, Dame Dawn Ruth, DBE
Lancaster, Dame Jean, DBE
Lewis, Dame Edna Leofrida (Lady Lewis), DBE
Lister, Dame Unity Viola, DBE
Litchfield, Dame Ruby Beatrice, DBE
Lloyd, *Prof.* Dame June Kathleen, DBE, FRCP
Lowrey, *Air Comdt.* Dame Alice, DBE, RRC
Lympany, Dame Moura, DBE
Lynn, Dame Vera (Mrs Lewis), DBE
Mackinnon, Dame (Una) Patricia, DBE
Macknight, Dame Ella Annie Noble, DBE, MD
McLaren, Dame Anne Laura, DBE, FRCOG, FRS
Macmillan of Ovenden, Katharine, Viscountess, DBE
Maconchy, Dame Elizabeth Violet (Mrs Le Fanu), DBE
Major, Dame Malvina Lorraine (Mrs Fleming), DBE
Mann, Dame Ida Caroline, DBE, D.SC., FRCS

Markova, Dame Alicia, DBE
Martin, Rosamund Mary Holland-, Lady, DBE
*Mayo, Dame Eileen Rosemary (Mrs Gainsborough)*, DBE
Menzies, Dame Pattie Maie, GBE
Metge, *Dr* Dame (Alice) Joan, DBE
Miller, Dame Mabel Flora Hobart, DBE
Miller, Dame Mary Elizabeth Hedley-, DCVO, CB
Mitchell, Dame Mona, DCVO
Mitchell, *Hon.* Dame Roma Flinders, DBE
Mitchell, Dame Wendy, DBE
Morrison, *Hon.* Dame Mary Anne, DCVO
Mueller, Dame Anne Elisabeth, DCB
Muldoon, Dame Thea Dale, Lady, DBE, QSO
Munro, Dame Alison, DBE
Murdoch, Dame Elisabeth Joy, DBE
Murdoch, Dame (Jean) Iris (Mrs Bayley), DBE
Murray, Dame (Alice) Rosemary, DBE, D.Phil.
Ollerenshaw, Dame Kathleen Mary, DBE, D.Phil.
Oxenbury, Dame Shirley Anne, DBE
Park, Dame Merle Florence (Mrs Bloch), DBE
Paterson, Dame Betty Fraser Ross, DBE
Penhaligon, Dame Annette (Mrs Egerton), DBE
Plowden, The Lady, DBE
Poole, Dame Avril Anne Barker, DBE
Porter, Dame Shirley (Lady Porter), DBE
Prendergast, Dame Simone Ruth, DBE
Prentice, Dame Winifred Eva, DBE
Preston, Dame Frances Olivia Campbell-, DCVO
Price, Dame Margaret Berenice, DBE
Purves, Dame Daphne Helen, DBE
Pyke, Lady, DBE
Quinn, Dame Sheila Margaret Imelda, DBE
Railton, Dame Ruth (Mrs King), DBE
Rankin, Lady Jean Margaret Florence, DCVO
Raven, Dame Kathleen Annie (Mrs Ingram), DBE
Restieaux, *Dr* Dame Norma Jean, DBE
Riddelsdell, Dame Mildred, DCB, CBE
Ridley, Dame (Mildred) Betty, DBE
Ridsdale, Dame Victoire Evelyn Patricia (Lady Ridsdale), DBE
Rie, Dame Lucie, DBE
Rigg, Dame Diana, DBE
Robertson, *Comdt.* Dame Nancy Margaret, DBE
Roe, Dame Raigh Edith, DBE
Rue, Dame (Elsie) Rosemary, DBE
Rumbold, *Rt. Hon.* Dame Angela Claire Rosemary, DBE, MP
Salas, Dame Margaret Laurence, DBE
Saunders, Dame Cicely Mary Strode, OM, DBE, FRCP
Schwarzkopf, Dame Elisabeth Friederike Marie Olga Legge-, DBE
Scott, Dame Catherine Campbell, DBE

Scott, Dame Jean Mary Monica Maxwell-, DCVO
Scott, Dame Margaret, (Dame Catherine Margaret Mary Denton), DBE
Shenfield, Dame Barbara Estelle, DBE
Sherlock, *Prof.* Dame Sheila Patricia Violet, DBE, MD, FRCP
Sloss, *Rt. Hon.* Dame (Ann) Elizabeth (Oldfield) Butler-, DBE
Smieton, Dame Mary Guillan, DBE
Smith, *Hon.* Dame Janet Hilary (Mrs Mathieson), DBE
Smith, Dame Margaret Natalie (Maggie) (Mrs Cross), DBE
Smith, Dame Margot, DBE
Snagge, Dame Nancy Marion, DBE
Soames, Mary, Lady, DBE
Spark, Dame Muriel Sarah, DBE
Steel, *Hon.* Dame (Anne) Heather (Mrs Beattie), DBE
Stephens, *Air Comdt.* Dame Anne, DBE
Stewart, Dame Muriel Acadia, DBE
Sutherland, Dame Joan (Mrs Bonynge), OM, DBE
Szaszy, Dame Miraka Petricevich, DBE
Taylor, Dame Jean Elizabeth, DCVO
Te Atairangikaahu, Te Arikinui, Dame, DBE
Te Kanawa, Dame Kiri Janette (Mrs Park), DBE
Tilney, Dame Guinevere (Lady Tilney), DBE
Tinson, Dame Sue, DBE
Tizard, Dame Catherine Anne, GCMG, DBE
Tokiel, Dame Rosa, DBE
Tyrwhitt, *Brig.* Dame Mary Joan Caroline, DBE, TD
Uatioa, Dame Mere, DBE
Uvarov, Dame Olga, DBE
Varley, Dame Joan Fleetwood, DBE
Wagner, Dame Gillian Mary Millicent (Lady Wagner), DBE
Wall, (Alice) Anne, (Mrs Michael Wall), DCVO
Wallace, Dame (Georgina Catriona Pamela) Augusta, DBE
Warburton, Dame Anne Marion, DCVO, CMG
Warwick, Dame Margaret Elizabeth Harvey Turner-, DBE, FRCP, FRCPEd.
Waterhouse, Dame Rachel Elizabeth, DBE, ph.D.
Wedega, Dame Alice, DBE
Wedgwood, Dame (Cicely) Veronica, OM, DBE
Weston, Dame Margaret Kate, DBE
Williamson, Dame (Elsie) Marjorie, DBE, ph.D.
Winstone, Dame Dorothy Gertrude, DBE, CMG
Yonge, Dame (Ida) Felicity (Ann), DBE

# Chiefs of Clans and Names in Scotland

Only chiefs of whole Names or Clans are included, except certain special instances (marked *) who, though not chiefs of a whole name, were or are for some reason (e.g. the Macdonald forfeiture) independent. Under decision (*Campbell-Gray*, 1950) that a bearer of a 'double or triple-barrelled' surname cannot be held chief of a part of such, several others cannot be included in the list at present.

THE ROYAL HOUSE: HM The Queen

AGNEW: Sir Crispin Agnew of Lochnaw, Bt., 6 Palmerston Road, Edinburgh EH9 1TN

ANSTRUTHER: Sir Ralph Anstruther of that Ilk, Bt., KCVO, MC, Balcaskie, Pittenweem, Fife

ARBUTHNOTT: The Viscount of Arbuthnott, CBE, DSC, Arbuthnott House, Laurencekirk, Kincardineshire AB30 1PA

BARCLAY: Peter C. Barclay of that Ilk, 28A Gordon Place, London W8 4JE

BORTHWICK: The Lord Borthwick, TD, Crookston, Heriot, Midlothian EH38 5YS

BOYD: The Lord Kilmarnock, 194 Regent's Park Road, London NW1 8XP

BOYLE: The Earl of Glasgow, Kelburn, Fairlie, Ayrshire KA29 OBE

BRODIE: Ninian Brodie of Brodie, Brodie Castle, Forres, Morayshire IV36 OTE

BRUCE: The Earl of Elgin and Kincardine, KT, Broomhall, Dunfermline, Fife KY11 3DU

BUCHAN: David S. Buchan of Auchmacoy, Auchmacoy House, Ellon, Aberdeenshire

BURNETT: J. C. A. Burnett of Leys, Crathes Castle, Banchory, Kincardineshire

CAMERON: Sir Donald Cameron of Lochiel, KT, CVO, TD, Achnacarry, Spean Bridge, Inverness-shire

CAMPBELL: The Duke of Argyll, Inveraray, Argyll PA32 8XF

CARMICHAEL: Richard J. Carmichael of Carmichael, Carmichael, Thankerton, Biggar, Lanarkshire

CARNEGIE: The Duke of Fife, Elsick House, Stonehaven, Kincardineshire AB3 2NT

CATHCART: Maj.-Gen. The Earl Cathcart, CB, DSO, MC, Moor Hatches, West Amesbury, Salisbury, Wilts. SP4 7BH

CHARTERIS: The Earl of Wemyss and March, KT, Gosford House, Longniddry, East Lothian EH32 OPX

CLAN CHATTAN: M. K. Mackintosh of Clan Chattan, Maxwell Park, Gwelo, Zimbabwe

CHISHOLM: Alastair Chisholm of Chisholm (*The Chisholm*), Silver Willows, Beck Row, Bury St Edmunds

COCHRANE: The Earl of Dundonald, Lochnell Castle, Ledaig, Argyllshire

COLQUHOUN: Sir Ivar Colquhoun of Luss, Bt., Camstraddan, Luss, Dunbartonshire G83 8NX

CRANSTOUN: David A. S. Cranstoun of that Ilk, Corehouse, Lanark

CRICHTON: vacant

DARROCH: Capt. Duncan Darroch of Gourock, The Red House, Branksome Park Road, Camberley, Surrey

DEWAR: Kenneth M. J. Dewar of that Ilk and Vogrie, The Dower House, Grayshott, Nr. Hindhead, Surrey

DRUMMOND: The Earl of Perth, PC, Stobhall, Perth PH2 6DR

DUNBAR: Sir James Dunbar of Mochrum, Bt., Bld 848 C.2, 66877 Flugplatz, Ramstein, Germany

DUNDAS: David D. Dundas of Dundas, 8 Derna Road, Kenwyn 7700, South Africa

DURIE: Raymond V. D. Durie of Durie, Court House, Pewsey, Wilts.

ELIOTT: Mrs Margaret Eliott of Redheugh, Redheugh, Newcastleton, Roxburghshire

ERSKINE: The Earl of Mar and Kellie, Erskine House, Kirk Wynd, Clackmannan FK10 4JF

FARQUHARSON: Capt. A. A. C. Farquharson of Invercauld, MC, Invercauld, Braemar, Aberdeenshire AB35 5TT

FERGUSSON: Sir Charles Fergusson of Kilkerran, Bt., Kilkerran, Maybole, Ayrshire

FORBES: The Lord Forbes, KBE, Balforbes, Alford, Aberdeenshire AB33 8DR

FORSYTH: Alistair Forsyth of that Ilk, Ethie Castle, by Arbroath, Angus DD11 5SP

FRASER: The Lady Saltoun, Cairnbulg Castle, Fraserburgh, Aberdeenshire AB43 5TN

*FRASER (OF LOVAT): The Lord Lovat, DSO, MC, TD, Balblair House, Beauly, Inverness-shire IV4 7AZ

GAYRE: Lt.-Col. Robert Gayre of Gayre and Nigg, Minard Castle, Minard, Inverary, Argyll PA32 8YB

GORDON: The Marquess of Huntly, Aboyne Castle, Aberdeenshire

GRAHAM: The Duke of Montrose, Buchanan Auld House, Drymen, Stirlingshire

GRANT: The Lord Strathspey, The House of Lords, London SW1A OPW

GRIERSON: Sir Michael Grierson of Lag, Bt., 40C Palace Road, London SW2 3NJ

HAIG: The Earl Haig, OBE, Bemersyde, Melrose, Roxburghshire

HALDANE: Martin Haldane of Gleneagles, Gleneagles, Auchterarder, Perthshire

HANNAY: Ramsey W. R. Hannay of Kirkdale and of that Ilk, Cardoness House, Gatehouse-of-Fleet, Kirkcudbrightshire

HAY: The Earl of Erroll, Wolverton Farm, Wolverton, Basingstoke, Hants. RG26 5SX

HENDERSON: John W. P. Henderson of Fordell, 7 Owen Street, Toowoomba, Queensland, Australia

HUNTER: Neil A. Hunter of Hunterston, Tour d'Escas, Carretera d'Escas, La Massana, Andorra

IRVINE OF DRUM: David C. Irvine of Drum, 20 Enville Road, Bowden, Altrincham, Cheshire WA14 2PQ

JARDINE: Sir Alexander Jardine of Applegirth, Bt., Ash House, Thwaites, Millom, Cumbria LA18 5HY

JOHNSTONE: The Earl of Annandale and Hartfell, Raehills, Lockerbie, Dumfriesshire

KEITH: The Earl of Kintore, The Stables, Keith Hall, Inverurie, Aberdeenshire AB51 OLD

KENNEDY: The Marquess of Ailsa, Cassillis House, Maybole, Ayrshire

KERR: The Marquess of Lothian, KCVO, Ferniehurst Castle, Jedburgh, Roxburghshire TN8 6NX

KINCAID: Mrs Heather V. Kincaid of Kincaid, 4 Watling Street, Leintwardine, Craven Arms, Shropshire

LAMONT: Peter N. Lamont of that Ilk, St Patrick's College, Manly, NSW 2095, Australia

LEASK: Madam Leask of Leask, 1 Vincent Road, Sheringham, Norfolk

LENNOX: Edward J. H. Lennox of that Ilk, Pools Farm, Downton on the Rock, Ludlow, Shropshire

LESLIE: The Earl of Rothes, Tanglewood, West Tytherley, Salisbury, Wilts. SP5 1LX

LINDSAY: The Earl of Crawford and Balcarres, PC, Balcarres, Colinsburgh, Fife

LOCKHART: Angus H. Lockhart of the Lee, Newholme, Dunsyre, Lanark

LUMSDEN: Gillem Lumsden of that Ilk and Blanerne, Kinderslegh, Bois Avenue, Chesham Bois, Amersham, Bucks

MACALESTER: William St J. S. McAlester of Loup and Kennox, 2 Avon Road East, Christchurch, Dorset

McBAIN: J. H. McBain of McBain, 7025, North Finger Rock Place, Tucson, Arizona, USA

MALCOLM (MACCALLUM): Robin N. L. Malcolm of Poltalloch, Duntrune Castle, Lochgilphead, Argyll

MACDONALD: The Lord Macdonald (*The Macdonald of Macdonald*), Kinloch Lodge, Sleat, Isle of Skye

*MACDONALD OF CLANRANALD: Ranald A. Macdonald of Clanranald, Wester Lix Cottage, Killin, Perthshire FK21 8RD

*MACDONALD OF SLEAT (CLAN HUSTEAIN): Sir Ian Bosville Macdonald of Sleat, Bt., Thorpe Hall, Rudston, Driffield, N. Humberside YO25 OJE

*MACDONELL OF GLENGARRY: Air Cdre Aeneas R. MacDonell of Glengarry, CB, DFC, Elonbank, Castle Street, Fortrose, Ross-shire IV10 8TH

MACDOUGALL: vacant

MACDOWALL: Fergus D. H. Macdowall of Garthland, 16 Tower Road, Nepean, Ontario, Canada

MACGREGOR: Sir Gregor MacGregor of MacGregor, Bt., Bannatyne, Newtyle, Blairgowrie, Perthshire PH12 8TR

MACINTYRE: James W. MacIntyre of Glenoe, 15301 Pine Orchard Drive, Apartment 3H, Silver Spring, Maryland, USA

MACKAY: The Lord Reay, House of Lords, London SW1

MACKENZIE: The Earl of Cromartie, Castle Leod, Strathpeffer, Ross-shire IV14 9AA

MACKINNON: Madam Anne Mackinnon of Mackinnon, 16 Purleigh Road, Bridgwater, Somerset

MACKINTOSH: Lt.-Cdr. L. R. D. Mackintosh of Mackintosh, OBE (*The Mackintosh of Mackintosh*), Moy Hall, Inverness IV13 7YQ

MACLACHLAN: Madam Marjorie MacLachlan of MacLachlan, Castle Lachlan, Argyll

MACLAREN: Donald MacLaren of MacLaren and Achleskine, Achleskine, Kirkton, Balquidder, Lochearnhead

MACLEAN: The Hon. Sir Lachlan Maclean of Duart, Bt., Arngask House, Glenfarg, Perthshire PH2 9QA

MACLENNAN: vacant

MACLEOD: John MacLeod of MacLeod, Dunvegan Castle, Isle of Skye

MACMILLAN: George MacMillan of MacMillan, Finlaystone, Langbank, Renfrewshire

MACNAB: J. C. Macnab of Macnab (*The Macnab*), Leuchars Castle Farmhouse, Leuchars, Fife KY16 OEY

MACNAGHTEN: Sir Patrick Macnaghten of Macnaghten and Dundarave, Bt., Dundarave, Bushmills, Co. Antrim

MACNEACAIL: Iain Macneacail of Macneacail and Scorrybreac, 12 Fox Street, Ballina, NSW, Australia

MACNEIL OF BARRA: Ian R. Macneil of Barra (*The Macneil of Barra*), Kisimul Castle, Barra

MACPHERSON: The Hon. Sir William Macpherson of Cluny, TD, Newtown Castle, Blairgowrie, Perthshire

MACTHOMAS: Andrew P. C. MacThomas of Finegand, c/o The Clan MacThomas Society, 19 Warriston Avenue, Edinburgh

MAITLAND: The Earl of Lauderdale, 12 St Vincent Street, Edinburgh

MAKGILL: The Viscount of Oxfuird, Hill House, St Mary Bourne, Andover, Hants. SP11 6BG

MAR: The Countess of Mar, St Michael's Farm, Great Witley, Worcs. WR6 6JB

MARJORIBANKS: Andrew Marjoribanks of that Ilk

MATHESON: Maj. Sir Fergus Matheson of Matheson, Bt., Old Rectory, Hedenham, Bungay, Suffolk NR35 2LD

MENZIES: David R. Menzies of Menzies, 20 Nardina Crescent, Dalkeith, Western Australia

MOFFAT: Madam Moffat of that Ilk, St Jasual, Bullocks Farm Lane, Wheeler End Common, High Wycombe, Bucks.

MONCREIFFE: vacant

MONTGOMERIE: The Earl of Eglinton and Winton, The Dutch House, West Green, Hartley Wintney, Hants.

MORRISON: Dr Iain M. Morrison of Ruchdi, Magnolia Cottage, The Street, Walberton, Sussex

MUNRO: Patrick G. Munro of Foulis, TD, Foulis Castle, Evanton, Ross-shire IV16 9UX

MURRAY: The Duke of Atholl, Blair Castle, Blair Atholl, Perthshire

NICOLSON: The Lord Carnock, 90 Whitehall Court, London SW1A 2EL

OGILVY: The Earl of Airlie, KT, GCVO, PC, Cortachy Castle, Kirriemuir, Angus

RAMSAY: The Earl of Dalhousie, KT, GCVO, GBE, MC, Brechin Castle, Brechin, Angus DD7 6SH

RATTRAY: James S. Rattray of Rattray, Craighall, Rattray, Perthshire

ROBERTSON: Alexander G. H. Robertson of Struan (*Struan-Robertson*), The Breach Farm, Goudhurst Road, Cranbrook, Kent

ROLLO: The Lord Rollo, Pitcairns, Dunning, Perthshire PH2 9BX

ROSE: Miss Elizabeth Rose of Kilravock, Kilravock Castle, Croy, Inverness

ROSS: David C. Ross of that Ilk, The Old Schoolhouse, Fettercairn, Kincardineshire

RUTHVEN: The Earl of Gowrie, PC, Castlemartin, Kilcullen, Co. Kildare, Republic of Ireland

SCOTT: The Duke of Buccleuch and Queensberry, KT, VRD, Bowhill, Selkirk

SCRYMGEOUR: The Earl of Dundee, Birkhill, Cupar, Fife

SEMPILL: The Lady Sempill, East Lodge, Druminnor, Rhynie, Aberdeenshire AB5 4LT

SHAW: John Shaw of Tordarroch, Newhall, Balblair, By Conon Bridge, Ross-shire

SINCLAIR: The Earl of Caithness, Churchill, Chipping Norton, Oxford OX7 5UX

STIRLING: Fraser J. Stirling of Cader, 17 Park Row, Farnham, Surrey

SUTHERLAND: The Countess of Sutherland, House of Tongue, Brora, Sutherland

SWINTON: John Swinton of that Ilk, 123 Superior Avenue SW, Calgary, Alberta, Canada

URQUHART: Kenneth T. Urquhart of Urquhart, 507 Jefferson Park Avenue, Jefferson, New Orleans, Louisiana 70121, USA

WALLACE: Ian F. Wallace of that Ilk, 5 Lennox Street, Edinburgh EH4 1QB

WEDDERBURN OF THAT ILK: The Master of Dundee, Birkhill, Cupar, Fife

WEMYSS: David Wemyss of that Ilk, Invermay, Forteviot, Perthshire

# Decorations and Medals

ROYAL NAVAL AUXILIARY SICK BERTH RESERVE LONG SERVICE AND GOOD CONDUCT MEDAL
ROYAL FLEET RESERVE LONG SERVICE AND GOOD CONDUCT MEDAL
ROYAL NAVAL WIRELESS AUXILIARY RESERVE LONG SERVICE AND GOOD CONDUCT MEDAL
AIR EFFICIENCY AWARD (AE), 1942
ULSTER DEFENCE REGIMENT MEDAL
The QUEEN'S MEDAL. For champion shots in the RN, RM, RNZN, Army, RAF
CADET FORCES MEDAL, 1950
COASTGUARD AUXILIARY SERVICE LONG SERVICE MEDAL (formerly Coast Life Saving Corps Long Service Medal)
SPECIAL CONSTABULARY LONG SERVICE MEDAL
ROYAL OBSERVER CORPS MEDAL
CIVIL DEFENCE LONG SERVICE MEDAL
RHODESIA MEDAL
ROYAL ULSTER CONSTABULARY SERVICE MEDAL
SERVICE MEDAL OF THE ORDER OF ST JOHN
BADGE OF THE ORDER OF THE LEAGUE OF MERCY
VOLUNTARY MEDICAL SERVICE MEDAL, 1932
WOMEN'S VOLUNTARY SERVICE MEDAL
COLONIAL SPECIAL CONSTABULARY MEDAL

*Foreign Orders, Decorations and Medals* (in order of date)

## THE VICTORIA CROSS (1856)
FOR CONSPICUOUS BRAVERY

VC

*Ribbon*, Crimson, for all Services (until 1918 it was blue for Royal Navy)

Instituted on 29 January 1856, the Victoria Cross was awarded retrospectively to 1854, the first being held by Lt. C. D. Lucas, RN, for bravery in the Baltic Sea on 21 June 1854 (gazetted 24 February 1857). The first 62 Crosses were presented by Queen Victoria in Hyde Park, London, on 26 June 1857.

The Victoria Cross is worn before all other decorations, on the left breast, and consists of a cross-pattée of bronze, one and a half inches in diameter, with the Royal Crown surmounted by a lion in the centre, and beneath there is the inscription *For Valour*. Holders of the VC receive a tax-free annuity of £100, irrespective of need or other conditions. In 1911, the right to receive the Cross was extended to Indian soldiers, and in 1920 to Matrons, Sisters and Nurses, and the staff of the Nursing Services and other services pertaining to hospitals and nursing, and to civilians of either sex regularly or temporarily under the orders, direction or supervision of the Naval, Military, or Air Forces of the Crown.

SURVIVING RECIPIENTS OF THE VICTORIA CROSS
*as at 31 August 1994*

Agansing Rai, *Havildar*, MM (Gurkha Rifles)
1944 *World War*
Ali Haidar, *Jemadar* (Frontier Force Rifles)
1945 *World War*
Annand, *Capt.* R. W. (Durham Light Infantry)
1940 *World War*

Bhan Bhagta Gurung, *Capt.* (2nd Gurkha Rifles)
1945 *World War*
Bhandari Ram, *Capt.* (Baluch R.)
1944 *World War*
Chapman, *Sgt.* E. T., BEM (Monmouthshire R.)
1945 *World War*
Cruickshank, *Flt. Lt.* J. A. (RAFVR)
1944 *World War*
Cutler, Sir Roden, AK, KCMG, KCVO, CBE (Australia)
1941 *World War*
Ervine-Andrews, *Lt.-Col.* H. M. (E. Lancs. R.)
1940 *World War*
Fraser, *Lt.-Cdr.* I. E., DSC (RNR)
1945 *World War*
Gaje Ghale, *Subedar* (Gurkha Rifles)
1943 *World War*
Ganju Lama, *Jemadar*, MM (Gurkha Rifles)
1944 *World War*
Gardner, *Capt.* P. J., MC (RTR)
1941 *World War*
Gian Singh, *Jemadar* (Punjab R.)
1945 *World War*
Gould, *Lt.* T. W. (RN)
1942 *World War*
Hinton, *Sgt.* J. D. (NZMF)
1941 *World War*
Jamieson, *Maj.* D. A., CVO (R. Norfolk R.)
1944 *World War*
Kenna, *Pte.* E. (Australian M. F.)
1945 *World War*
Kenneally, *C-Q-M-S* J. P. (Irish Guards)
1943 *World War*
Lachiman Gurung, *Rifleman* (Gurkha Rifles)
1945 *World War*
Learoyd, *Wg Cdr.* R. A. B. (RAF)
1940 *World War*
Merritt, *Lt.-Col.* C. C. I., CD (S. Saskatchewan R.)
1942 *World War*
Norton, *Capt.* G. R., MM (SAMF)
1944 *World War*
Payne, *WO* K. (Australian Army)
1969 *Vietnam*
Place, *Rear-Adm.* B. C. G., CB, CVO, DSC (RN)
1943 *World War*
Porteous, *Col.* P. A. (RA)
1942 *World War*
Rambahadur Limbu, *Lt.*, MVO (Gurkha Rifles)
1965 *Sarawak*
Reid, *Flt. Lt.* W. (RAFVR)
1943 *World War*
Smith, *Sgt.* E. A., CD (Seaforth Highlanders of Canada)
1944 *World War*
Smythe, *Capt.* Q. G. M. (SAMF)
1942 *World War*
Speakman-Pitt, *Sgt.* W. (Black Watch)
1951 *Korea*
Tulbahadur Pun, *WOI* (Gurkha Rifles)
1944 *World War*
Umrao Singh, *Sub-Major* (IA)
1944 *World War*
Upham, *Capt.* C. H. (and Bar, 1942), (NZMF)
1941 *World War*
Watkins, *Maj. Rt. Hon.* Sir Tasker, GBE (Welch R.)
1944 *World War*
Wilson, *Lt.-Col.* E. C. T. (E. Surrey R.)
1940 *World War*

## THE GEORGE CROSS (1940)
FOR GALLANTRY

GC

*Ribbon*, Dark blue, threaded through a bar adorned with laurel leaves

Instituted 24 September 1940 (with amendments, 3 November 1942).
The George Cross is worn before all other decorations (except the VC) on the left breast (when worn by a woman it may be worn on the left shoulder from a ribbon of the same width and colour fashioned into a bow). It consists of a plain silver cross with four equal limbs, the cross having in the centre a circular medallion bearing a design showing St George and the Dragon. The inscription *For Gallantry* appears round the medallion and in the angle of each limb of the cross is the Royal cypher 'G VI' forming a circle concentric with the medallion. The reverse is plain and bears the name of the recipient and the date of the award. The cross is suspended by a ring from a bar adorned with laurel leaves on dark blue ribbon one and a half inches wide.
    The cross is intended primarily for civilians; awards to the fighting services are confined to actions for which purely military honours are not normally granted. It is awarded only for acts of the greatest heroism or of the most conspicuous courage in circumstances of extreme danger. From 1 April 1965, holders of the Cross have received a tax-free annuity of £100.
    The royal warrant which ordained that the grant of the Empire Gallantry Medal should cease authorized holders of that medal to return it to the Central Chancery of the Orders of Knighthood and to receive in exchange the George Cross. A similar provision applied to posthumous awards of the Empire Gallantry Medal made after the outbreak of war in 1939. In October 1971 all surviving holders of the Albert Medal and the Edward Medal exchanged those decorations for the George Cross.

SURVIVING RECIPIENTS OF THE GEORGE CROSS
*as at 31 August 1994*

If the recipient originally received the Empire Gallantry Medal (EGM), the Albert Medal (AM) or the Edward Medal (EM), this is indicated by the initials in parenthesis.

Archer, *Col.* B. S. T., GC, OBE, ERD, 1941
Atkinson, T., GC (EGM), 1939
Baker, J. T., GC (EM), 1929
Bamford, J., GC, 1952
Baxter, W. F., GC (EM), 1942
Beaton, J., GC, CVO, 1974
Biggs, *Maj.* K. A., GC, 1946
Bridge, *Cdr.* J., GC, GM, 1944
Butson, *Col.* A. R. C., GC, CD, MD (AM), 1948
Bywater, R. A. S., GC, GM, 1944
Durrani, *Lt.-Col.* M. K., GC, 1946
Easton, J. M. C., GC, 1941
Errington, H., GC, 1941
Fairfax, F. W., GC, 1953
Farrow, K., GC (AM), 1948
Flintoff, H. H., GC (EM), 1944
Gledhill, A. J., GC, 1967

Goad, W., GC (AM), 1943
Gregson, J. S., GC (AM), 1943
Hallowes, Mrs O. M. C., GC, MBE, Légion d'Honneur, 1946
Hawkins, E., GC, 1943
Hodge, *Capt.* A. M., GC, VRD (EGM), 1940
Johnson, *WO1 (SSM)* B., GC, 1990
Kinne, D. G., GC, 1954
Lowe, A. R., GC (AM), 1949
Lynch, J., GC, BEM (AM), 1948
McAloney, *Gp. Capt.* W. S., GC, OBE (AM), 1938
McClymont, J. M., GC (EGM), 1940
Malta, GC, 1942
Manwaring, T. G., GC (EM), 1949
May, P. R. S., GC (AM), 1947
Miller, *Lt.-Cdr.* J. B. P., GC, 1941
Moore, R. V., GC, 1940
Moss, B., GC, 1940
Naughton, F., GC (EGM), 1937
Nix, F. E., GC (EM), 1944
Patton, The Hon. John, GC, CBE, 1940
Pearson, Miss J. D. M., GC (EGM), 1940
Pratt, M. K., GC, 1978
Purves, Mrs M., GC (AM), 1949
Raweng, Awang anak, GC, 1951
Riley, G., GC (AM), 1944
Rimmer, R., GC (EGM), 1931
Rowlands, *Air Marshal* Sir John, GC, KBE, 1943
Sinclair, *Air Vice-Marshal* Sir Laurence, GC, KCB, CBE, DSO, 1941
Stevens, H. W., GC, 1958
Stronach, *Capt.* G. P., GC, 1943
Styles, *Lt.-Col.* S. G., GC, 1972
Sylvester, W. G., GC (EGM), 1940
Taylor, *Lt.-Cdr.* W. H., GC, MBE, 1941
Walker, C., GC, 1972
Walker, C. H., GC (AM), 1942
Walton, E. W. K., GC (AM), 1948
Western, D., GC (AM), 1948
Wilcox, C., GC (EM), 1949
Wiltshire, S. N., GC (EGM), 1930
Yates, P. W., GC (EM), 1932

# Forms of address

It is only possible to cover here the forms of address for peers, baronets and knights, their wife and children, and Privy Counsellors. Greater detail should be sought in one of the publications devoted to the subject.

Both formal and social forms of address are given where usage differs; nowadays, the social form is generally preferred to the formal, which increasingly is used only for official documents and on very formal occasions.

F__ represents forename
S__ represents surname

BARON - *Envelope (formal)*, The Right Hon. Lord __ ; *(social)*, The Lord __ . *Letter (formal)*, My Lord; *(social)*, Dear Lord __ . *Spoken*, Lord __ .

BARON'S WIFE - *Envelope (formal)*, The Right Hon. Lady __ ; *(social)*, The Lady __ . *Letter (formal)*, My Lady; *(social)*, Dear Lady __ . *Spoken*, Lady __ .

BARON'S CHILDREN - *Envelope (formal)*, The Hon. F__S__. *Letter*, Dear Mr/Miss/Mrs S__. *Spoken*, Mr/Miss/Mrs [F__] S__.

BARONESS IN OWN RIGHT - *Envelope*, may be addressed in same way as a Baron's wife or, if she prefers *(formal)*, The Right Hon. the Baroness __ ; *(social)*, The Baroness __ . Otherwise as for a Baron's wife.

BARONET - *Envelope*, Sir F__S__, Bt. *Letter (formal)*, Dear Sir; *(social)*, Dear Sir F__. *Spoken*, Sir F__.

BARONET'S WIFE - *Envelope*, Lady S__. *Letter (formal)*, Dear Madam; *(social)*, Dear Lady S__. *Spoken*, Lady S__.

COUNTESS IN OWN RIGHT – As for an Earl's wife.

COURTESY TITLES – The heir apparent to a Duke, Marquess or Earl uses the highest of his father's other titles as a courtesy title. (For list, *see* pages 169–70.) The holder of a courtesy title is not styled The Most Hon. or The Right Hon., and in correspondence 'The' is omitted before the title. The heir apparent to a Scottish title may use the title 'Master' (*see* below).

DAME - *Envelope*, Dame F__S__, followed by appropriate post-nominal letters. *Letter (formal)*, Dear Madam; *(social)*, Dear Dame F__. *Spoken*, Dame F__ .

DUKE - *Envelope (formal)*, His Grace the Duke of __ ; *(social)*, The Duke of __ . *Letter (formal)*, My Lord Duke; *(social)*, Dear Duke. *Spoken (formal)*, Your Grace; *(social)*, Duke.

DUKE'S WIFE - *Envelope (formal)*, Her Grace the Duchess of __ ; *(social)*, The Duchess of __ . *Letter (formal)*, Dear Madam; *(social)*, Dear Duchess. *Spoken*, Duchess.

DUKE'S ELDEST SON – *see* Courtesy titles.

DUKE'S YOUNGER SONS – *Envelope*, Lord F__S__. *Letter (formal)*, My Lord; *(social)*, Dear Lord F__. *Spoken (formal)*, My Lord; *(social)*, Lord F__.

DUKE'S DAUGHTER - *Envelope*, Lady F__S__. *Letter (formal)*, Dear Madam; *(social)*, Dear Lady F__. *Spoken*, Lady F__.

EARL – *Envelope (formal)*, The Right Hon. the Earl (of) __; *(social)*, The Earl (of) __ . *Letter (formal)*, My Lord; *(social)*, Dear Lord __ . *Spoken (formal)*, My Lord; *(social)*, Lord __ .

EARL'S WIFE - *Envelope (formal)*, The Right Hon. the Countess (of) __ ; *(social)*, The Countess (of) __ . *Letter (formal)*, Madam; *(social)*, Dear Lady __ . *Spoken (formal)*, Madam; *(social)*, Lady __ .

EARL'S CHILDREN – *Eldest son, see* Courtesy titles. *Younger sons*, The Hon. F__S__ (for forms of address, *see* Baron's children). *Daughters*, Lady F__S__ (for forms of address, *see* Duke's daughter).

KNIGHT (BACHELOR) – *Envelope*, Sir F__S__. *Letter (formal)*, Dear Sir; *(social)*, Dear Sir F__. *Spoken*, Sir F__.

KNIGHT (ORDERS OF CHIVALRY) – *Envelope*, Sir F__S__, followed by appropriate post-nominal letters. Otherwise as for Knight Bachelor.

KNIGHT'S WIFE – As for Baronet's wife.

MARQUESS – *Envelope (formal)*, The Most Hon. the Marquess of __ ; *(social)*, The Marquess of __ . *Letter (formal)*, My Lord; *(social)*, Dear Lord __ . *Spoken (formal)*, My Lord; *(social)*, Lord __ .

MARQUESS'S WIFE – *Envelope (formal)*, The Most Hon. the Marchioness of __ ; *(social)*, The Marchioness of __ . *Letter (formal)*, Madam; *(social)*, Dear Lady __ . *Spoken*, Lady __ .

MARQUESS'S CHILDREN – *Eldest son, see* Courtesy titles. *Younger sons*, Lord F__S__ (for forms of address, *see* Duke's younger sons). *Daughters*, Lady F__S__ (for forms of address, *see* Duke's daughter).

MASTER – The title is used by the heir apparent to a Scottish peerage, though usually the heir apparent to a Duke, Marquess or Earl uses his courtesy title rather than 'Master'. *Envelope*, The Master of __ . *Letter (formal)*, Dear Sir; *(social)*, Dear Master of __ . *Spoken (formal)*, Master, or Sir; *(social)*, Master, or Mr S__.

MASTER'S WIFE – Addressed as for the wife of the appropriate peerage style, otherwise as Mrs S__.

PRIVY COUNSELLOR – *Envelope*, The Right (or Rt.) Hon. F__S__. *Letter*, Dear Mr/Miss/Mrs S__. *Spoken*, Mr/Miss/Mrs S__. It is incorrect to use the letters PC after the name, unless the Privy Counsellor is a peer below the rank of Marquess and so is styled The Right Hon. because of his rank. In this case the post-nominal letters may be used in conjunction with the prefix The Right Hon.

VISCOUNT – *Envelope (formal)*, The Right Hon. the Viscount __ ; *(social)*, The Viscount __ . *Letter (formal)*, My Lord; *(social)*, Dear Lord __ . *Spoken*, Lord __ .

VISCOUNT'S WIFE – *Envelope (formal)*, The Right Hon. the Viscountess __ ; *(social)*, The Viscountess __ . *Letter (formal)*, Madam; *(social)*, Dear Lady __ . *Spoken*, Lady __ .

VISCOUNT'S CHILDREN – As for Baron's children.

# The Privy Council

The Sovereign in Council, or Privy Council, was the chief source of executive power until the system of Cabinet government developed in the 18th century. Now the Privy Council's main functions are to advise the Sovereign and to exercise its own statutory responsibilities independent of the Sovereign in Council (*see also* page 221).

Membership of the Privy Council is automatic upon appointment to certain government and judicial positions in the United Kingdom, e.g. Cabinet ministers must be Privy Counsellors and are sworn in on first assuming office. Membership is also accorded by The Queen to eminent people in the United Kingdom and independent countries of the Commonwealth of which Her Majesty is Queen, on the recommendation of the British Prime Minister. Membership of the Council is retained for life, except for very occasional removals.

The administrative functions of the Privy Council are carried out by the Privy Council Office (*see* page 344) under the direction of the Lord President of the Council, who is always a member of the Cabinet.

*Lord President of the Council*, The Rt. Hon. Antony Newton, OBE, MP
*Clerk of the Council*, N. H. Nicholls, CBE

---

MEMBERS *as at 31 August 1994*

---

HRH The Duke of Edinburgh, 1951
HRH The Prince of Wales, 1977

Aberdare, Lord, 1974
Ackner, Lord, 1980
Adams-Schneider, Sir Lancelot, 1980
Airlie, Earl of, 1984
Aitken, Jonathan, 1994
Aldington, Lord, 1954
Alebua, Ezekiel, 1988
Alison, Michael, 1981
Alport, Lord, 1960
Amery of Lustleigh, Lord, 1960
Anthony, Douglas, 1971
Archer of Sandwell, Lord, 1977
Armstrong, Ernest, 1979
Arnold, Sir John, 1979
Ashdown, Paddy, 1989
Ashley of Stoke, Lord, 1979
Avonside, Lord, 1962
Azikiwe, Nnamdi, 1960
Baker, Kenneth, 1984
Balcombe, Sir John, 1985

Barber, Lord, 1963
Barnett, Lord, 1975
Barwick, Sir Garfield, 1964
Beckett, Margaret, 1993
Beith, Alan, 1992
Beldam, Sir Roy, 1989
Belstead, Lord, 1983
Benn, Anthony, 1964
Bennett, Sir Frederic, 1985
Bevins, John, 1959
Biffen, John, 1979
Bingham, Sir Thomas, 1986
Birch, William, 1992
Bird, Vere, 1982
Bisson, Sir Gordon, 1987
Blair, Anthony, 1994
Blaker, Sir Peter, 1983
Blatch, Baroness, 1993
Bolger, James, 1991
Booth, Albert, 1976
Boothroyd, Betty, 1992
Boscawen, Hon. Robert, 1992
Bottomley, Lord, 1952
Bottomley, Virginia, 1992
Boyd-Carpenter, Lord, 1954
Boys, Michael, 1989
Boyson, Sir Rhodes, 1987
Braine, Lord, 1985
Brandon of Oakbrook, Lord, 1978
Brathwaite, Nicholas, 1991
Bridge of Harwich, Lord, 1975
Brightman, Lord, 1979
Brittan, Sir Leon, 1981
Brooke, Peter, 1988
Brown, Sir Simon, 1992
Brown, Sir Stephen, 1983
Browne, Sir Patrick, 1974
Browne-Wilkinson, Lord, 1983
Buckley, Sir Denys, 1970
Butler, Sir Adam, 1984
Butler-Sloss, Dame Elizabeth, 1988
Caithness, Earl of, 1990
Callaghan of Cardiff, Lord, 1964
Cameron of Lochbroom, Lord, 1984
Campbell of Croy, Lord, 1970
Canterbury, The Archbishop of, 1991
Carlisle of Bucklow, Lord, 1979
Carr of Hadley, Lord, 1963
Carrington, Lord, 1959
Carswell, Sir Robert, 1994
Casey, Sir Maurice, 1986
Castle of Blackburn, Baroness, 1964
Cato, Robert, 1981
Chalfont, Lord, 1964
Chalker of Wallasey, Baroness, 1987
Chan, Sir Julius, 1981
Channon, Paul, 1980
Charteris of Amisfield, Lord, 1972
Chataway, Christopher, 1970
Clark, Alan, 1991
Clark, Helen, 1990
Clark of Kempston, Lord, 1990
Clarke, Kenneth, 1984
Cledwyn of Penrhos, Lord, 1966

Cockfield, Lord, 1982
Cocks of Hartcliffe, Lord, 1976
Coggan, Lord, 1961
Colman, Fraser, 1986
Colnbrook, Lord, 1973
Colyton, Lord, 1952
Compton, John, 1983
Concannon, John, 1978
Cooke, Sir Robin, 1977
Cooper, Sir Frank, 1983
Cope, Sir John, 1988
Corfield, Sir Frederick, 1970
Cowen, Sir Zelman, 1981
Cradock, Sir Percy, 1993
Cranborne, Viscount, 1994
Crawford and Balcarres, Earl of, 1972
Crickhowell, Lord, 1979
Croom-Johnson, Sir David, 1984
Cumming-Bruce, Sir Roualeyn, 1977
Cunningham, Jack, 1993
Davies, Denzil, 1978
Davison, Sir Ronald, 1978
Dean of Harptree, Lord, 1991
Deedes, Lord, 1962
Dell, Edmund, 1970
Denham, Lord, 1981
Denning, Lord, 1948
Devonshire, Duke of, 1964
Diamond, Lord, 1965
Dillon, Sir Brian, 1982
Donaldson of Lymington, Lord, 1979
Dorrell, Stephen, 1994
Douglas, Sir William, 1977
du Cann, Sir Edward, 1964
Duff, Sir Antony, 1980
Dunn, Sir Robin, 1980
Eccles, Viscount, 1951
Eden of Winton, Lord, 1972
Eichelbaum, Sir Thomas, 1989
Emery, Sir Peter, 1993
Emslie, Lord, 1972
Ennals, Lord, 1970
Erroll of Hale, Lord, 1960
Esquivel, Manuel, 1986
Evans, Sir Anthony, 1992
Eveleigh, Sir Edward, 1977
Farquharson, Sir Donald, 1989
Fellowes, Sir Robert, 1990
Ferrers, Earl, 1982
Floissac, Sir Vincent, 1992
Foot, Michael, 1974
Foster, Derek, 1993
Fowler, Sir Norman, 1979
Fox, Sir Michael, 1981
Fraser, Malcolm, 1976
Fraser of Carmyllie, Lord, 1989
Freeman, John, 1966
Freeman, Roger, 1993
Freeson, Reginald, 1976
Gairy, Sir Eric, 1977
Garel-Jones, Tristan, 1992
Gault, Thomas, 1992
Georges, Telford, 1986
Gibbs, Sir Harry, 1972

Runcie, Lord, 1980
Russell, Sir Patrick, 1987
Ryder, Richard, 1990
Sainsbury, Hon. Timothy, 1992
St John of Fawsley, Lord, 1979
Sandiford, Erskine, 1989
Saville, Sir Mark, 1994
Scarman, Lord, 1973
Scott, Nicholas, 1989
Scott, Sir Richard, 1991
Seaga, Edward, 1981
Seear, Baroness, 1985
Selkirk, Earl of, 1955
Shackleton, Lord, 1966
Shawcross, Lord, 1946
Shearer, Hugh, 1969
Sheldon, Robert, 1977
Shephard, Gillian, 1992
Shepherd, Lord, 1965
Shore, Peter, 1967
Simmonds, Kennedy, 1984
Simon of Glaisdale, Lord, 1961
Sinclair, Ian, 1977
Slade, Sir Christopher, 1982
Slynn of Hadley, Lord, 1992
Somare, Sir Michael, 1977
Somers, Sir Edward, 1981
Stanley, Sir John, 1984

Staughton, Sir Christopher, 1988
Steel, Sir David, 1977
Stephen, Sir Ninian, 1979
Stephenson, Sir John, 1971
Stewartby, Lord, 1989
Steyn, Sir Johan, 1992
Stocker, Sir John, 1986
Stodart of Leaston, Lord, 1974
Stott, Lord, 1964
Stuart-Smith, Sir Murray, 1988
Talboys, Sir Brian, 1977
Taylor of Gosforth, Lord, 1988
Tebbit, Lord, 1981
Templeman, Lord, 1978
Thatcher, Baroness, 1970
Thomas of Gwydir, Lord, 1964
Thomson, David, 1981
Thomson of Monifieth, Lord, 1966
Thorpe, Jeremy, 1967
Tizard, Robert, 1986
Tonypandy, Viscount, 1968
Trefgarne, Lord, 1989
Trumpington, Baroness, 1992
Ullswater, Viscount, 1994
Varley, Lord, 1974
Waddington, Lord, 1987
Waite, Sir John, 1993
Wakeham, Lord, 1983

Waldegrave, William, 1990
Walker, Sir Harold, 1979
Walker of Worcester, Lord, 1970
Waller, Sir George, 1976
Watkins, Sir Tasker, 1980
Watkinson, Viscount, 1955
Weatherill, Lord, 1980
Wheeler, Sir John, 1993
Whitelaw, Viscount, 1967
Wilberforce, Lord, 1964
Williams, Alan, 1977
Williams of Crosby, Baroness, 1974
Wilson of Langside, Lord, 1967
Wilson of Rievaulx, Lord, 1947
Windlesham, Lord, 1973
Wingti, Paias, 1987
Withers, Reginald, 1977
Woodhouse, Sir Owen, 1974
Woolf, Lord, 1986
Wylie, Hon. Lord, 1970
York, The Archbishop of, 1983
Young, Baroness, 1981
Young, Sir George, 1993
Young of Graffham, Lord, 1984
Younger of Prestwick, Lord, 1979
Zacca, Edward, 1992

# The Privy Council of Northern Ireland

The Privy Council of Northern Ireland had responsibilities in Northern Ireland similar to those of the Privy Council in Great Britain until the Northern Ireland Act 1974 instituted direct rule and a United Kingdom Cabinet minister became responsible for the functions previously exercised by the Northern Ireland government.

Membership of the Privy Council of Northern Ireland is retained for life. The postnominal initials PC(NI) are used to differentiate its members from those of the Privy Council.

MEMBERS *as at 31 August 1994*

Bailie, Robin, 1971
Bleakley, David, 1971
Bradford, Roy, 1969
Craig, William, 1963
Dobson, John, 1969
Glentoran, The Lord, 1953
Kelly, Sir Basil, 1969
Kirk, Herbert, 1962
Long, William, 1966
Lowry, The Lord, 1971
McConnell, Robert, 1964

McIvor, Basil, 1971
Morgan, William, 1961
Moyola, The Lord, 1966
Neill, Sir Ivan, 1950
Porter, Sir Robert, 1969
Rathcavan, The Lord, 1969
Simpson, Robert, 1969
Taylor, John, MP, 1970
West, Henry, 1960

# Parliament

The United Kingdom constitution is not contained in any single document but has evolved in the course of time, formed partly by statute, partly by common law and partly by convention. A constitutional monarchy, the United Kingdom is governed by Ministers of the Crown in the name of the Sovereign, who is head both of the state and of the government.

The organs of government are the legislature (Parliament), the executive and the judiciary. The executive consists of HM Government (Cabinet and other Ministers) (*see* pages 231–2), government departments (*see* pages 281–369), local authorities (*see* Local Government), and public corporations operating nationalized industries or social or cultural services (*see* pages 281–369). The judiciary (*see* Law Courts and Offices) pronounces on the law, both written and unwritten, interprets statutes and is responsible for the enforcement of the law; the judiciary is independent of both the legislature and the executive.

## THE MONARCHY

The Sovereign personifies the state and is, in law, an integral part of the legislature, head of the executive, head of the judiciary, the commander-in-chief of all armed forces of the Crown and the 'Supreme Governor' of the Church of England. The seat of the monarchy is in the United Kingdom. In the Channel Islands and the Isle of Man, which are Crown dependencies, the Sovereign is represented by a Lieutenant-Governor. In the member states of the Commonwealth of which the Sovereign is head of state, her representative is a Governor-General; in United Kingdom dependencies the Sovereign is usually represented by a Governor, who is responsible to the British Government.

Although the powers of the monarchy are now very limited, restricted mainly to the advisory and ceremonial, there are important acts of government which require the participation of the Sovereign. These include summoning, proroguing and dissolving Parliament, giving royal assent to bills passed by Parliament, appointing important office-holders, e.g. government ministers, judges, bishops, and governors, conferring peerages, knighthoods and other honours, and granting pardon to a person wrongly convicted of a crime. An important function is appointing a Prime Minister, by convention the leader of the political party which enjoys, or can secure, a majority of votes in the House of Commons. In international affairs the Sovereign as head of state has the power to declare war and make peace, to recognize foreign states and governments, to conclude treaties and to annex or cede territory. However, as the Sovereign entrusts executive power to Ministers of the Crown and acts on the advice of her Ministers, which she cannot ignore, in practice royal prerogative powers are exercised by Ministers, who are responsible to Parliament.

Ministerial responsibility does not diminish the Sovereign's importance to the smooth working of government. She holds meetings of the Privy Council, gives audiences to her Ministers and other officials at home and overseas, receives accounts of Cabinet decisions, reads dispatches and signs state papers; she must be informed and consulted on every aspect of national life; and she must show complete impartiality.

## COUNSELLORS OF STATE

In the event of the Sovereign's absence abroad, it is necessary to appoint Counsellors of State under letters patent to carry out the chief functions of the Monarch, including the holding of Privy Councils and giving royal assent to acts passed by Parliament. The normal procedure is to appoint as Counsellors three or four members of the royal family among those remaining in the United Kingdom.

In the event of the Sovereign on accession being under the age of eighteen years, or at any time unavailable or incapacitated by infirmity of mind or body for the performance of the royal functions, provision is made for a regency.

## THE PRIVY COUNCIL

The Sovereign in Council, or Privy Council, was the chief source of executive power until the system of Cabinet government developed. Now its main function is to advise the Sovereign to approve Orders in Council and to advise on the issue of royal proclamations. The Council's own statutory responsibilities (independent of the powers of the Sovereign in Council) include powers of supervision over the registering bodies for the medical and allied professions. A full Council is summoned only on the death of the Sovereign or when the Sovereign announces his or her intention to marry. (For full list of Counsellors, *see* pages 218–20)

There are a number of advisory Privy Council committees, whose meetings the Sovereign does not attend. Some are prerogative committees, such as those dealing with legislative matters submitted by the legislatures of the Channel Islands and the Isle of Man or with applications for charters of incorporation; and some are provided for by statute, e.g. those for the universities of Oxford and Cambridge and the Scottish universities.

The Judicial Committee of the Privy Council is the final court of appeal from courts of the United Kingdom dependencies, courts of independent Commonwealth countries which have retained the right of appeal, courts of the Channel Islands and the Isle of Man, some professional and disciplinary committees, and church sources. The Committee is composed of Privy Counsellors who hold, or have held, high judicial office, although usually only three or five hear each case.

Administrative work is carried out by the Privy Council Office under the direction of the Lord President of the Council, a Cabinet Minister.

## PARLIAMENT

Parliament is the supreme law-making authority and can legislate for the United Kingdom as a whole or for any parts of it separately (the Channel Islands and the Isle of Man are Crown dependencies and not part of the United Kingdom). The main functions of Parliament are to pass laws, to provide (by voting taxation) the means of carrying on the work of government and to scrutinize government policy and administration, particularly proposals for expenditure. International treaties and agreements are by custom presented to Parliament before ratification.

Parliament emerged during the late thirteenth and early fourteenth centuries. The officers of the King's household and the King's judges were the nucleus of early Parliaments, joined by such ecclesiastical and lay magnates as the King might summon to form a prototype 'House of Lords', and occasionally by the knights of the shires, burgesses and proctors of the lower clergy. By the end of Edward III's reign a 'House of Commons' was beginning to appear; the first known Speaker was elected in 1377.

Parliamentary procedure is based on custom and precedent, partly formulated in the Standing Orders of both Houses (see Standing Orders, page 227), and each House has the right to control its own internal proceedings and to commit for contempt. The system of debate in the two Houses is similar; when a motion has been moved, the Speaker proposes the question as the subject of a debate. Members speak from wherever they have been sitting. Questions are decided by a vote on a simple majority. Draft legislation is introduced, in either House, as a bill. Bills can be introduced by a Government Minister or a private Member, but in practice the majority of bills which become law are introduced by the Government. To become law, a bill must be passed by each House (for parliamentary stages, see Bill, page 225) and then sent to the Sovereign for the royal assent, after which it becomes an Act of Parliament.

Proceedings of both Houses are public, except on extremely rare occasions. The minutes (called Votes and Proceedings in the Commons, and Minutes of Proceedings in the Lords) and the speeches (The Official Report of Parliamentary Debates, *Hansard*) are published daily. Proceedings are also recorded for transmission on radio and television and stored in the Parliamentary Recording Unit before transfer to the National Sound Archive. Television cameras have been allowed into the House of Lords since January 1985, and into the House of Commons since November 1989; committee meetings may also be televised.

By the Parliament Act of 1911, the maximum duration of a Parliament is five years (if not previously dissolved), the term being reckoned from the date given on the writs for the new Parliament. The maximum life has been prolonged by legislation in such rare circumstances as the two world wars (31 January 1911 to 25 November 1918; 26 November 1935 to 15 June 1945). Dissolution and writs for a general election are ordered by the Sovereign on the advice of the Prime Minister. The life of a Parliament is divided into sessions, usually of one year in length, beginning and ending most often in October or November.

## THE HOUSE OF LORDS
London SW1A 0PW
Tel 0171-219 3000

The House of Lords consists of the Lords Spiritual and Temporal. The Lords Spiritual are the Archbishops of Canterbury and York, the Bishops of London, Durham and Winchester, and the 21 senior diocesan bishops of the Church of England. The Lords Temporal consist of all hereditary peers of England, Scotland, Great Britain and the United Kingdom who have not disclaimed their peerages, life peers created under the Life Peerages Act 1958, and those Lords of Appeal in Ordinary created life peers under the Appellate Jurisdiction Act 1876, as amended (law lords). Disclaimants of an hereditary peerage lose their right to sit in the House of Lords but gain the right to vote at parliamentary elections and to offer themselves for election to the House of Commons (see also page 141). Those peers disqualified from sitting in the House include:

– aliens, i.e. any peer who is not a British citizen, a Commonwealth citizen (under the British Nationality Act 1981) or a citizen of the Republic of Ireland
– peers under the age of 21
– undischarged bankrupts or, in Scotland, those whose estate is sequestered
– peers convicted of treason

Peers who do not wish to attend sittings of the House of Lords may apply for leave of absence for the duration of a Parliament.

Until the beginning of this century the House of Lords had considerable power, being able to veto any bill submitted to it by the House of Commons, but those powers were greatly reduced by the Parliament Act of 1911 and subsequently by the Parliament Act of 1949 (see Parliament Acts 1911 and 1949, page 226).

Combined with its legislative role, the House of Lords has judicial powers as the ultimate Court of Appeal for courts in Great Britain and Northern Ireland, except for criminal cases in Scotland. These powers are exercised by the Lord Chancellor and the law lords.

Members of the House of Lords are unpaid. However, they are entitled to reimbursement of travelling expenses on parliamentary business within the UK and certain other expenses incurred for the purpose of attendance at sittings of the House, within a maximum for each day of £70.00 for overnight subsistence, £31.50 for day subsistence and incidental travel, and £30.50 for secretarial costs, postage and certain additional expenses.

COMPOSITION *as at 11 July 1994*

Archbishops and Bishops, 26
Peers by succession, 758 (17 women)
Hereditary Peers of first creation (including the Prince of Wales), 15
Life Peers under the Appellate Jurisdiction Act 1876, 21
Life Peers under the Life Peerages Act 1958, 374 (60 women)
Total 1,194
Of whom:
    Peers without Writs of Summons, 86 (2 minors)
    Peers on leave of absence from the House, 78

STATE OF PARTIES *as at 11 July 1994*

About half of the members of the House of Lords take the whip of one of the political parties. The other members sit on the cross-benches or as independents.

Conservative, 473
Labour, 114
Liberal Democrats, 54
Cross-bench, 283
Other (including Bishops), 270

## OFFICERS

The House is presided over by the Lord Chancellor, who is *ex officio* Speaker of the House. A panel of deputy Speakers is appointed by Royal Commission. The first deputy Speaker is the Chairman of Committees, appointed at the beginning of each session, a salaried officer of the House who takes the chair in committee of the whole House and in some select committees. He is assisted by a panel of deputy chairmen, headed by the salaried Principal Deputy Chairman of Committees, who is also chairman of the European Communities Committee of the House.

The permanent officers include the Clerk of the Parliaments, who is in charge of the administrative staff collectively known as the Parliament Office; the Gentleman Usher of the Black Rod, who is also Serjeant-at-Arms in attendance upon the Lord Chancellor and is responsible for security and for accommodation and services in the House of Lords; and the Yeoman Usher who is Deputy Serjeant-at-Arms and assists Black Rod in his duties.

*Speaker* (£16,825), The Rt. Hon. the Lord Mackay of Clashfern
*Private Secretary*, M. E. Ormerod
*Chairman of Committees* (£47,555), The Lord Ampthill, CBE
*Principal Deputy Chairman of Committees* (£43,576), The Lord Boston of Faversham, QC
*Clerk of the Parliaments* (£95,051), Sir Michael Wheeler-Booth, KCB
*Clerk Assistant and Prinicipal Finance Officer* (£65,990–£79,396), J. M. Davies
*Reading Clerk and Clerk of Public Bills* (£56,131–£66,283), P. D. G. Hayter, LVO
*Counsel to Chairman of Committees* (£56,131–£66,283), D. Rippengal, CB, QC; Sir James Nursaw, KCB, QC: Mrs E. Denza, CMG
*Assistant Counsel* (£39,365–£57,612), N. J. Adamson, CB, QC
*Principal Clerks* (£47,897–£66,283), J. A. Vallance White (*Judicial Office and Fourth Clerk at the Table*); M. G. Pownall (*Committees*); B. P. Keith (*Private Bills*); D. R. Beamish (*Clerk of the Journals*)
*Chief Clerks* (£39,365–£57,612), C. A. J. Mitchell; R. H. Walters, D.Phil.; Dr F. P. Tudor
*Senior Clerks* (£27,106–£41,003), E. C. Ollard; Mrs M. E. Ollard (*seconded as Secretary to the Leader of the House and Chief Whip*); A. Makower; E. J. J. Wells; T. V. Mohan; S. P. Burton; J. L. Goddard
*Clerks* (£14,416–£25,039), Mrs M. B. Bloor; D. J. Batt; Dr C. A. Mylne
*Clerk of the Records* (£39,365–£57,612), D. J. Johnson, FSA
*Deputy Clerk of the Records* (£30,680–£49,697), S. K. Ellison
*Establishment Officer* R. H. Walters, D.Phil.
*Deputy Establishment Officer* (£27,106–£41,003), G. Embleton
*Accountant* (£27,106–£49,697), C. Preece
*Assistant Accountant* (£21,789–£26,556), Miss J. M. Lansdown
*Computer Executive* (£27,106–£41,003), Ms S. C. White
*Internal Auditor* (£27,106–£41,003), C. H. Rogers
*Staff Adviser* (£27,106–£41,003), D. A. W. Dunn, ISO
*Judicial Taxing Clerk* (£21,789–£26,556), C. G. Osborne
*Librarian* (£39,365–£57,612), D. L. Jones
*Deputy Librarian* (£30,680–£49,697), P. G. Davis, Ph.D.
*Senior Library Clerk* (£27,106–£41,003), Miss I. L. Victory, Ph.D.
*Examiners of Petitions for Private Bills*, B. P. Keith; R. J. Willoughby
*Gentleman Usher of the Black Rod and Serjeant-at-Arms* (£56,131–£66,283), Adm. Sir Richard Thomas, KCB, OBE
*Yeoman Usher of the Black Rod and Deputy Serjeant-at-Arms* (£27,106–£41,003), Air Vice-Marshal D. R. Hawkins, CB, MBE
*Administration Officer* (£27,106–£41,003), Brig. A. J. M. Clark
*Staff Superintendent*, Maj. F. P. Horsfall, MBE
*Shorthand Writer* (fees), Mrs P. J. Woolger
*Editor, Official Report (Hansard)*, (£37,110–£54,262), Mrs M. E. Villiers
*Deputy Editor, Official Report* (£27,790–£44,905), G. R. Goodbarne

## THE HOUSE OF COMMONS
London SW1A 0AA
Tel 0171-219 3000

The members of the House of Commons are elected by universal adult suffrage. For electoral purposes, the United Kingdom is divided into constituencies, each of which returns one member to the House of Commons, the member being the candidate who obtains the largest number of votes cast in the constituency. To ensure equitable representation the four Boundary Commissions keep constituency boundaries under review and recommend any redistribution of seats which may seem necessary because of population movements, etc. The number of seats was raised to 640 in 1945, then reduced to 625 in 1948, and subsequently rose to 630 in 1955, 635 in 1970, 650 in 1983 and 651 in 1992. Of the present 651 seats, there are 524 for England, 38 for Wales, 72 for Scotland and 17 for Northern Ireland.

### ELECTIONS

Elections are by secret ballot, each elector casting one vote; voting is not compulsory. When a seat becomes vacant between general elections, a by-election is held.

British subjects and citizens of the Irish Republic can stand for election as Members of Parliament (MPs) provided they are 21 or over and not subject to disqualification. Those disqualified from sitting in the House include:

– undischarged bankrupts
– people sentenced to more than one year's imprisonment
– clergy of the Church of England, Church of Scotland, Church of Ireland and Roman Catholic Church
– members of the House of Lords
– holders of certain offices listed in the House of Commons Disqualification Act 1975, e.g. members of the judiciary, Civil Service, regular armed forces, police forces, some local government officers and some members of public corporations and government commissions

For entitlement to vote in parliamentary elections, *see* Legal Notes section.

A candidate does not require any party backing but his or her nomination for election must be supported by the signatures of ten people registered in the constituency. A candidate must also deposit with the returning officer £500, which is forfeit if the candidate does not receive more than 5 per cent of the votes cast. All election expenses at a general election, except the candidate's personal expenses, are subject to a statutory limit of £4,330, plus 3.7 pence for each elector in a borough constituency or 4.9 pence for each elector in a county constituency.

See pages 233–40 for an alphabetical list of MPs, pages 243–73 for the results of the last General Election, and page 241 for the results of recent by-elections.

STATE OF PARTIES *as at 31 July 1994*
Conservative, 333 (19 women)
Labour, 270 (38 women)
Liberal Democrats, 23 (3 women)
Plaid Cymru, 4
Scottish Nationalist, 3 (1 woman)
Democratic Unionist, 3
Social Democratic and Labour, 4
Ulster Popular Unionist, 1
Ulster Unionist, 9
The Speaker, 1
Total, 651 (62 women)

### BUSINESS

The week's business of the House is outlined each Thursday by the Leader of the House, after consultation between the

Chief Government Whip and the Chief Opposition Whip. A quarter to a third of the time will be taken up by the Government's legislative programme, and the rest by other business, e.g. question time. As a rule, bills likely to raise political controversy are introduced in the Commons before going on to the Lords, and the Commons claims exclusive control in respect of national taxation and expenditure. Bills such as the Finance Bill, which imposes taxation, and the Consolidated Fund Bills, which authorize expenditure, must begin in the Commons. A bill of which the financial provisions are subsidiary may begin in the Lords; and the Commons may waive its rights in regard to Lords' amendments affecting finance.

The Commons has a public register of MPs' financial and certain other interests. Members must also disclose any relevant financial interest or benefit in a matter before the House when taking part in a debate, in certain other proceedings of the House, or in consultations with other MPs, with Ministers or civil servants.

MEMBERS' PAY AND ALLOWANCES

Since 1911 members of the House of Commons have received salary payments; facilities for free travel were introduced in 1924. Members are entitled to claim income tax relief on expenses incurred in the course of their parliamentary duties. Salary rates since 1911 are as follows:

| | | | |
|---|---|---|---|
| 1911 | £400 p.a. | 1980 June | £11,750 p.a. |
| 1931 | 360 | 1981 June | 13,950 |
| 1934 | 380 | 1982 June | 14,510 |
| 1935 | 400 | 1983 June | 15,308 |
| 1937 | 600 | 1984 Jan | 16,106 |
| 1946 | 1,000 | 1985 Jan | 16,904 |
| 1954 | 1,250 | 1986 Jan | 17,702 |
| 1957 | 1,750 | 1987 Jan | 18,500 |
| 1964 | 3,250 | 1988 Jan | 22,548 |
| 1972 Jan | 4,500 | 1989 Jan | 24,107 |
| 1975 June | 5,750 | 1990 Jan | 26,701 |
| 1976 June | 6,062 | 1991 Jan | 28,970 |
| 1977 July | 6,270 | 1992 Jan | 30,854 |
| 1978 June | 6,897 | 1994 Jan | 31,687 |
| 1979 June | 9,450 | | |

In October 1969 MPs were granted an allowance for secretarial and research expenses. In 1987 this became known as the Office Costs Allowance. From April 1993 the allowance is £40,380 a year.

Since January 1972 MPs can claim reimbursement for the additional cost of staying overnight away from their main residence while on parliamentary business. This is currently £10,958 a year and since 1984 has been non-taxable.

From April 1980 provision was made enabling each MP in receipt of Office Costs Allowance to contribute sums to an approved pension scheme for the provision of a pension, or other benefits, for or in respect of persons whose salary is met by him/her from the Office Costs Allowance.

The cost of travel allowances for 1993–4 was stated in June 1994 to be £8,594,519.

MEMBERS' PENSIONS

Pension arrangements for MPs were first introduced in 1964. The arrangements currently provide a pension of one-fiftieth of salary for each year of pensionable service with a maximum of two-thirds of salary at age 65. Pension is payable normally at age 65, for men and women, or on later retirement. Pensions may be paid earlier, e.g. on ill-health retirement. The widow/widower of a former MP receives a pension of five-eighths of the late MP's pension. Pensions are index-linked. Members currently contribute 6 per cent of salary to

the pension fund; there is an Exchequer contribution, currently slightly more than the amount contributed by MPs.

The House of Commons Members' Fund provides for annual or lump sum grants to ex-MPs, their widows or widowers, and children whose incomes are below certain limits. Alternatively, payments of £2,070 a year to ex-MPs with at least ten years' service and who left the House of Commons before October 1964, and £1,294 a year to their widows or widowers are made as of right. Members contribute £24 a year and the Exchequer £215,000 a year to the fund. The net assets of the fund as at 30 September 1993 amounted to £2,568,066.

OFFICERS AND OFFICIALS

The House of Commons is presided over by the Speaker, who has considerable powers to maintain order in the House. A deputy, the Chairman of Ways and Means, and two Deputy Chairmen may preside over sittings of the House of Commons; they are elected by the House, and, like the Speaker, neither speak nor vote other than in their official capacity.

The staff of the House are employed by a Commission chaired by the Speaker. The heads of House of Commons departments are permanent officers of the House, not MPs. The Clerk of the House is the principal adviser to the Speaker on the privileges and procedures of the House, the conduct of the business of the House, and committees. The Serjeant-at-Arms is responsible for security, ceremonial, and for accommodation in the Commons part of the Palace of Westminster.

*Speaker* (£64,749), The Rt. Hon. Betty Boothroyd, MP for West Bromwich West
*Chairman of Ways and Means* (£52,790), The Rt. Hon. Michael Morris, MP for Northampton South
*First Deputy Chairman of Ways and Means* (£49,285), Geoffrey Lofthouse, MP for Pontefract and Castleford
*Second Deputy Chairman of Ways and Means* (£49,285), Dame Janet Fookes, DBE, MP for Plymouth Drake

OFFICES OF THE SPEAKER AND CHAIRMAN OF WAYS AND MEANS

*Speaker's Secretary* (£39,365–£57,612), N. Bevan, CB
*Chaplain to the Speaker*, The Revd Canon D. Gray, TD
*Secretary to the Chairman of Ways and Means*, 27,106–£41,003), Ms P. A. Helme

DEPARTMENT OF THE CLERK OF THE HOUSE

*Clerk of the House of Commons* (£95,051), D. W. Limon, CB
*Clerk Assistant* (£65,990–£79,396), W. R. McKay
*Clerk of Committees* (£65,990–£79,396), J. F. Sweetman, CB, TD
*Principal Clerks* (£47,897–£64,283)
   *Table Office*, C. B. Winnifrith
   *Public Bills*, R. B. Sands
   *Select Committees*, D. G. Millar
   *Overseas Office*, G. Cubie
   *Journals*, A. J. Hastings
   *Private Bills*, R. J. Willoughby
   *Standing Committees*, M. R. Jack, PH.D.
   *Domestic Committees*, R. W. G. Wilson
   *Financial Committees*, W. A. Proctor
   *Second Clerk of Select Committees*, Ms H. E. Irwin
*Deputy Principal Clerks* (£39,365–£57,612),
   S. A. L. Panton; Mrs J. Sharpe; Ms A. Milner-Barry;
   F. A. Cranmer; R. J. Rogers; C. R. M. Ward, PH.D.;
   D. W. N. Doig; D. L. Natzler; E. P. Silk; A. R. Kennon;
   L. C. Laurence Smyth; S. J. Patrick; D. J. Gerhold;

C. J. Poyser; D. F. Harrison; S. J. Priestley;
A. H. Doherty; P. A. Evans; R. I. S. Phillips; R. G. James
*Senior Clerks* (£27,106–£41,003), Ms P. A. Helme;
D. R Lloyd; R. A. Lambert; B. M. Hutton; J. S. Benger,
D.Phil.; Ms E. C. Samson; N. P. Walker; M. D. Hamlyn;
P. C. Seaward, D.Phil.; C. G. Lee; C. D. Stanton;
A. Y. A. Azad; C. A. Shaw (*acting*); D. Steel (*acting*);
P. Bolton (*acting*); Mrs E. A. J. Attridge (*acting*)
*Clerks of Domestic Committees* (£27,106–£41,003),
K. J. Brown; P. G. Moon
*Examiners of Petitions for Private Bills*, R. J. Willoughby;
B. P. Keith
*Registrar of Members' Interests*, R. J. Willoughby
*Taxing Officer*, R. J. Willoughby

**Vote Office**

*Deliverer of the Vote* (£39,365–£57,612), H. C. Foster
*Deputy Deliverers of the Vote* (£27,106–£41,003),
J. F. Collins (*Distribution*); F. W. Hallett (*Production*)

**Speaker's Counsel**

*Speaker's Counsel* (£54,131–£64,283), J. S. Mason, CB
*Speaker's Counsel (European legislation)* (£54,131–£64,283),
T. J. G. Pratt, CB
*Speaker's Assistant Counsel* (£39,365–£57,612), A. Akbar

**DEPARTMENT OF THE SERJEANT-AT-ARMS**

*Serjeant-at-Arms* (£54,131–£64,283) Sir Alan Urwick, KCVO,
CMG
*Deputy Serjeant-at-Arms* (£47,897–£57,612),
P. N. W. Jennings
*Assistant Serjeant-at-Arms* (£30,680–£49,697),
M. J. A. Cummins
*Deputy Assistant Serjeants-at-Arms* (£27,106–£41,003),
P. A. J. Wright; J. M. Robertson

**PARLIAMENTARY WORKS DIRECTORATE**

*Director of Works* (£51,566–£57,612), H. P. Webber
*Deputy Director of Works* (£30,680–£49,697), B. C. Sewell
*Principal Works Officers* (£27,106–£41,003), A. Makepeace;
B. R. Hall; R. Bentley; C. Hillier; M. Moone; G. Goode;
J. F. Moore; M. J. Thompson; M. Trott
*Senior Professional and Technical Officers* (£23,933–
£29,774), J. Stone; S. Howard; B. O'Boyle; C. Brown;
C. Cowell; J. Eaton; T. Fox; T. Jardine

**DEPARTMENT OF THE LIBRARY**

*Librarian* (£54,131–£64,283), Miss J. B. Tanfield
*Deputy Librarian* (£47,897–£57,612), Miss P. J. Baines
*Assistant Librarians* (£39,365–£57,612), S. Z. Young;
K. G. Cuninghame
*Deputy Assistant Librarians* (£30,680–£49,697),
Mrs J. M. Wainwright; C. C. Pond, PH.D.;
Mrs C. B. Andrews; R. C. Clements; Mrs J. M. Lourie;
R. J. Ware, D.Phil.; C. R. Barclay; Mrs J. M. Fiddick; Mrs
C. M. Gillie; R. J. Twigger; Mrs G. L. Allen
*Senior Library Clerks* (£27,106–£41,003), Ms F. Poole;
T. N. Edmonds; R. J. Cracknell; Miss O. M. Gay;
Miss E. M. McInnes; B. K. Winetrobe; Miss M. Baber;
Ms A. Walker; Mrs H. V. Holden; Miss J. Seaton;
Mrs P. L. Carling; A. J. L. Crompton; Miss V. A. Miller;
Ms H. M. Jeffs; M. P. Hillyard; S. A. Wise (*acting*); Ms J.
Roll

**DEPARTMENT OF FINANCE AND ADMINISTRATION**

*Director of Finance and Administration* (£54,131–£64,283),
J. Rodda
*Accountant* (£47,897–£57,612), A. R. Marskell
*Deputy Accountant* (£39,365–£57,612), M. Fletcher

*Assistant Accountants* (£27,106–£41,003), Mrs G.
Crowther; Mrs D. Hill (*temp.*)
*Head of Establishments Office* (£47,897–£57,612),
B. A. Wilson
*Head of Finance Office* (£39,365–£57,612), M. J. Barram
*Accountancy Development* (£27,106–£41,003), R. H. A.
Russell
*Management Accountant* (£27,106–£41,003),
Ms S. J. Peterson
*Financial Accountant* (£21,789–£26,556), Mrs N. Norman
*Deputy Head of Establishments Office* (£30,680–£49,697),
J. A. Robb
*Computer Officer* (£39,365–£57,612), R. S. Morgan
*Network Planning Officer* (£27,106–£41,003), J. Fishenden
*Internal Auditor* (£27,106–£41,003), A. A. Cameron
*Staff Inspector* (£27,106–£41,003), R. C. Collins

**DEPARTMENT OF THE OFFICIAL REPORT**

*Editor* (£47,897–£57,612), I. D. Church
*Deputy Editor* (£39,365–£57,612), P. Walker
*Principal Assistant Editors* (£30,680–£46,166), J. Gourley;
W. G. Garland; Miss H. Hales; R. V. Hadlow
*Assistant Editors* (£30,680–£46,166), Miss V. Grainger;
Miss V. A. A. Clarke; Miss G. L. Sutherland;
S. Hutchinson; Miss C. Fogarty; Miss V. A. Widgery; Ms
K. Stewart

**REFRESHMENT DEPARTMENT**

*Director of Catering Services* (£39,365–£57,612),
Mrs S. J. Harrison
*Catering Accountant* (£27,106–£41,003), D. R. W. Wood
*Operations Manager* (£27,106–£41,003), N. M. Hutson

---

## PARLIAMENTARY INFORMATION

---

The following is a short glossary of aspects of the work of
Parliament. Unless otherwise stated, references are to House
of Commons procedures.

ADJOURNMENT DEBATE – Usually a half-hour debate
introduced by a back-bencher at the end of business for the
day. The subjects raised are often local or personal issues.

BILL – Proposed legislation is termed a bill. The stages of
a public bill (for private bills, *see* page 227) in the House of
Commons are as follows:
*First Reading:* There is no debate at this stage, which
nowadays merely constitutes an order to have the bill printed
*Second Reading:* The debate on the principles of the bill
*Committee Stage:* The detailed examination of a bill, clause
by clause. In most cases this takes place in a standing
committee, or the whole House may act as a committee. A
special standing committee may take evidence before
embarking on detailed scrutiny of the bill. Very rarely, a bill
may be examined by a select committee (*see* page 227)
*Report Stage:* Detailed review of a bill as amended in
committee
*Third Reading:* Final debate on a bill
Public bills go through the same stages in the House of
Lords, except that in almost all cases the committee stage is
taken in committee of the whole House.
    A bill may start in either House, and has to pass through
both Houses to become law. Both Houses have to agree the
same text of a bill, so that the amendments made by the
second House are then considered in the originating House,
and if not agreed, sent back or themselves amended, until
agreement is reached.

CHILTERN HUNDREDS – A legal fiction, a nominal office of profit under the Crown, the acceptance of which requires an MP to vacate his seat. The Manor of Northstead is similar. These are the only means by which an MP may resign.

CLOSURE AND GUILLOTINE – To prevent deliberate waste of time of either House, a motion may be made that the question be now put. In the House of Commons, if the Speaker decides that the rights of a minority are not being prejudiced and 100 members support the closure motion in a division, if carried, the original motion is put to the House without further debate.

The guillotine represents a more rigorous and systematic application of the closure. Under this system, a bill proceeds in accordance with a rigid timetable and discussion is limited to the time allotted to each group of clauses. The closure is hardly ever used in the Lords, and there is no procedure for a guillotine. The completion of business in the Lords is ensured by agreement from all sides of the House.

CONSOLIDATED FUND BILL – A bill to authorize issue of money to maintain Government services. The bill is dealt with without debate, but afterwards members may raise topics of public or local importance.

DELEGATED LEGISLATION – Many statutes empower Ministers to make delegated legislation, with little or no reference back to Parliament, usually by means of Statutory Instruments. These fall into four broad categories:
*Affirmative Instruments*, which are subject to approval by resolutions of both Houses before they can come into or remain in force
*Negative Instruments*, which are subject to annulment by resolution of either House
*General Instruments*, which include those not required to be laid before Parliament and those which are required to be so laid but are not subject to approval or annulment
*Special Procedure Orders*, against which parties outside Parliament may lodge petitions

DISSOLUTION – Parliament comes to an end either by dissolution by the Sovereign, on the advice of the Prime Minister, or on the expiration of the term of five years for which the House of Commons was elected. Dissolution is normally effected by a royal proclamation.

EARLY DAY MOTION – A motion put on the notice paper by an MP without in general the real prospect of its being debated. Such motions are expressions of back-bench opinion.

EMERGENCY DEBATE – In the Commons a method of obtaining prompt discussion of a matter of urgency is by moving the adjournment under Standing Order No. 20 for the purpose of discussing a specific and important matter that should have urgent consideration. A member may ask leave to make this motion by giving written notice to the Speaker, usually before 12 noon, and if the Speaker considers the matter of sufficient importance and the House agrees, it is discussed usually at 7 p.m. on the following day.

FATHER OF THE HOUSE – The Member whose continuous service in the House of Commons is the longest. The present Father of the House is the Rt. Hon. Sir Edward Heath, KG, MBE, MP, elected first in 1950.

GENERAL SYNOD MEASURE – A measure passed by the national assembly of the Church of England under the Church of England Assembly (Powers) Act 1919. These measures are considered by the Joint Ecclesiastical Committee, who make a report. They are then considered by both Houses and, if approved, sent for the royal assent.

HANSARD – The official report of debates in both Houses (and in standing committees) published by HMSO, normally on the day after the sitting concerned.

HOURS OF MEETING – The House of Commons meets Monday to Thursday at 2.30 p.m., and on Friday at 9.30 a.m. Changes to these hours are under consideration. The House of Lords normally meets at 2.30 p.m. Monday to Wednesday and at 3 p.m. on Thursday. In the latter part of the session, the House of Lords sometimes sits on Fridays at 11 a.m.

HYBRIDITY – A public bill which is considered to affect specific private or local interests, as distinct from all such interests of a single category, is called a hybrid bill and is subject to a special form of scrutiny to enable people affected to object. In the House of Lords, affirmative instruments (*see* Delegated Legislation above) may also be treated as hybrid.

LEADER OF THE OPPOSITION – In 1937 the office of Leader of the Opposition was recognized and a salary was assigned to the post. Since January 1994 the salary has been £61,349 (including parliamentary salary of £23,854). The present Leader of the Opposition is the Rt. Hon. Tony Blair, MP.

THE LORD CHANCELLOR – The Lord High Chancellor of Great Britain is (*ex officio*) the Speaker of the House of Lords. Unlike the Speaker of the House of Commons, he is a member of the Government, takes part in debates and votes in divisions. He has none of the powers to maintain order that the Speaker in the Commons has, these powers being exercised in the Lords by the House as a whole. The Lord Chancellor sits in the Lords on one of the Woolsacks, couches covered with red cloth and stuffed with wool. If he wishes to address the House in any way except formally as Speaker, he leaves the Woolsack.

NAMING – When a member has been named by the Speaker for a breach of order, i.e. contrary to the practice of the House, called by surname and not addressed as the 'Hon. Member for . . . (her/his constituency)', the Leader of the House moves that the offender 'be suspended from the service of the House' for (in the case of a first offence) a period of five sitting days. Should the member offend again, the period of suspension is increased.

OPPOSITION DAY – A day on which the topic for debate is chosen by the Opposition. There are twenty such days in a normal session. On seventeen days, subjects are chosen by the Leader of the Opposition; on the remaining three days by the leader of the next largest opposition party.

PARLIAMENT ACTS 1911 AND 1949 – Under these Acts, bills may become law without the consent of the Lords.

Since at least the eighteenth century the Commons has had the privilege of having bills concerned with supply (i.e. taxation and money matters) passed without amendment by the Lords, though until 1911 the Lords retained the right to reject such bills outright.

By the Parliament Act 1911, a bill which has been endorsed by the Speaker of the House of Commons as a money bill, and has been passed by the Commons and sent up to the Lords at least one month before the end of a session, can become law without the consent of the Lords if it is not passed by them without amendment within a month.

Under the Parliament Acts 1911 and 1949, if the Lords reject any other public bill (except one to prolong the life of a Parliament) which has been passed by the Commons in two successive sessions, then that bill shall (unless the Commons direct to the contrary) become law without the consent of the Lords. The Lords have power, therefore, to delay a public bill for thirteen months from its first second reading in the House of Commons.

PRIME MINISTER'S QUESTIONS – The Prime Minister answers questions from 3.15 to 3.30 p.m. on Tuesdays and Thursdays. Nowadays the 'open question' predominates. Members tend to ask the Prime Minister what are his or her official engagements for the day; a supplementary question on virtually any topic can then be put.

PRIVATE BILL – A bill promoted by a body or an individual to give powers additional to, or in conflict with, the general law, and to which a special procedure applies to enable people affected to object.

PRIVATE MEMBERS' BILL – A public bill promoted by a Member who is not a member of the Government.

PRIVATE NOTICE QUESTION – A question adjudged of urgent importance on submission to the Speaker (in the Lords, the Leader of the House), answered at the end of oral questions, usually at 3.30 p.m.

PRIVILEGE – The following are covered by the privilege of Parliament:
(i) freedom from interference in going to, attending at, and going from, Parliament
(ii) freedom of speech in parliamentary proceedings
(iii) the printing and publishing of anything relating to the proceedings of the two Houses is subject to privilege
(iv) each House is the guardian of its dignity and may punish any insult to the House as a whole

PROROGATION – The bringing to an end, by the Sovereign on the advice of the Government, of a session of Parliament. Public bills which have not completed all their stages lapse on prorogation.

QUEEN'S SPEECH – The speech delivered by The Queen at the State Opening of Parliament, in which the Government's programme for the session is set forth. The speech is drafted by civil servants and approved by the Cabinet.

QUESTION TIME – Oral questions are answered by Ministers in the Commons from 2.30 to 3.30 p.m. every day except Friday. They are also taken at the start of the Lords sittings, with a daily limit of four oral questions.

ROYAL ASSENT – The royal assent is signified by letters patent to such bills and measures as have passed both Houses of Parliament (or bills which have been passed under the Parliament Acts 1911 and 1949). The Sovereign has not given royal assent in person since 1854. On occasion, for instance in the prorogation of Parliament, royal assent may be pronounced to the two Houses by Lords Commissioners. More usually royal assent is notified to each House sitting separately in accordance with the Royal Assent Act 1967. The old French formulae for royal assent are then endorsed on the acts by the Clerk of the Parliaments.
The power to withhold assent resides with the Sovereign but has not been exercised in the United Kingdom since 1707, in the reign of Queen Anne.

SELECT COMMITTEES – Consisting usually of ten to 15 members of all parties, select committees are a means used by both Houses in order to investigate certain matters.
Most select committees in the House of Commons are now tied to departments; each committee investigates subjects within a government department's remit. There are other House of Commons select committees dealing with public accounts (i.e. the spending by the Government of money voted by Parliament) and European legislation, and also domestic committees dealing, for example, with privilege and procedure. Major select committees usually take evidence in public; their evidence and reports are published by HMSO.
The principal select committee in the House of Lords is that on the European Communities, which has, at present,

six sub-committees dealing with all areas of Community policy. The House of Lords also has a select committee on science and technology, which appoints sub-committees to deal with specific subjects. In addition, ad hoc select committees have been set up from time to time to investigate specific subjects, e.g. overseas trade, murder and life imprisonment. There are also some joint committees of the two Houses, e.g. the Joint Committee on Statutory Instruments.

DEPARTMENTAL COMMITTEES
*Agriculture* – Chair, Sir Jerry Wiggin, MP; Clerk, Mr Walker
*Defence* – Chair, Sir Nicholas Bonsor, MP; Clerks, Mr Natzler, Mr Hennessy
*Education* – Chair, Sir Malcolm Thornton, MP; Clerk, Mr Hamlyn
*Employment* – Chair, Hon. Greville Janner, MP; Clerk, Mr Phillips
*Environment* – Chair, Robert Jones, MP; Clerks, Mr Priestley, Miss Adams
*Foreign Affairs* – Chair, Rt. Hon. David Howell, MP; Clerks, Ms Irwin, Mr Reid
*Health* – Chair, Marion Roe, MP; Clerks, Mr James, Mr Healey
*Home Affairs* – Chair, Sir Ivan Lawrence, MP; Clerks, Mr Poyser; Mr Devine
*National Heritage* – Chair, Rt. Hon. Gerald Kaufman, MP; Clerk, Mrs Sharpe
*Northern Ireland* – Chair, Sir James Kilfedder, MP, Clerk, Mr Millar
*Science and Technology* – Chair, Sir Giles Shaw, MP; Clerk, Mr Stanton
*Scottish Affairs* – Chair, William McKelvey, MP; Clerk, Mr Doherty
*Social Security* – Chair, Frank Field, MP; Clerk, Mr Lloyd
*Trade and Industry* – Chair, Richard Caborn, MP; Clerks, Mr Gerhold, Ms Gardner
*Transport* – Chair, Rt. Hon. Paul Channon, MP; Clerk, Mr Doig
*Treasury and Civil Service* – Chair, John Watts, MP; Clerks, Mr Proctor, Mr Lee
*Welsh Affairs* – Chair, Gareth Wardell, MP; Clerk, Mr Hutton

NON-DEPARTMENTAL COMMITTEES
*European Legislation* – Chair, James Hood, MP; Clerk, Mr Rogers
*Members' Interests* – Chair, Sir Geoffrey Johnson Smith, MP; Clerk, Mr Sands
*Parliamentary Commissioner* – Chair, James Pawsey, MP; Clerk, Mr Azad
*Procedure* – Chair, Rt. Hon. Sir Peter Emery, MP; Clerks, Mr Kennon, Mr Hensher
*Public Accounts* – Chair, Rt. Hon. Robert Sheldon, MP; Clerk, Dr Benger

The Privileges committee had still to be reconstituted at the time of going to press.

THE SPEAKER – The Speaker of the House of Commons is the spokesman and president of the Chamber. He or she is elected by the House at the beginning of each Parliament or when the previous Speaker retires or dies. The Speaker neither speaks in debates nor votes in divisions except when the voting is equal.

STANDING ORDERS – Rules which have from time to time been agreed by each House of Parliament to regulate the conduct of its business. These orders may be amended or repealed, and are from time to time suspended or dispensed with.

STATE OPENING – This marks the start of each new session of Parliament. Parliament is normally opened, in the presence of both Houses, by The Queen in person, who makes the speech from the throne which outlines the Government's policies for the coming session (see Queen's Speech). In the absence of The Queen, Parliament is opened by Royal Commission, and The Queen's Speech is read by one of the Lords Commissioners specially appointed by letters patent for the occasion.

STRANGERS – Anyone who is not a Member or Officer of the House is a stranger. Visitors are generally admitted to debates of both Houses but may be excluded if the House so decides. In practice this happens only in time of war.

TEN MINUTE RULE – A colloquial term for Standing Order No. 19, under which back-benchers have an opportunity on Tuesdays and Wednesdays to state for about ten minutes why a bill on a certain subject should be introduced. Time is also available for a short opposing speech.

VACANT SEATS – When a vacancy occurs in the House of Commons during a session of Parliament, the writ for the by-election is moved by a Whip of the party to which the member whose seat has been vacated belonged. If the House is in recess, the Speaker can issue a warrant for a writ, should two members certify to him that a seat is vacant.

WHIPS – In order to secure the attendance of Members of a particular party in Parliament on all occasions, and particularly on the occasion of an important vote, Whips (originally known as 'Whippers-in') are appointed. The written appeal or circular letter issued by them is also known as a 'whip', its urgency being denoted by the number of times it is underlined. Failure to respond to a three-line whip, headed 'Most important', is tantamount in the Commons to secession (at any rate temporarily) from the party. Whips are officially recognized by Parliament and are provided with office accommodation in both Houses. In both Houses, Government and some Opposition Whips receive salaries from public funds.

PUBLIC INFORMATION SERVICES
HOUSE OF COMMONS – Public Information Office, House of Commons, London SW1A 0AA. Tel: 0171-219 4272
HOUSE OF LORDS – The Journal and Information Office, House of Lords, London SW1A 0PW. Tel: 0171-219 3107

## GOVERNMENT OFFICE

The Government is the body of Ministers responsible for the administration of national affairs, determining policy and introducing into Parliament any legislation necessary to give effect to government policy. The majority of Ministers are members of the House of Commons but members of the House of Lords or of neither House may also hold ministerial responsibility. The Lord Chancellor is always a member of the House of Lords. The Prime Minister is, by current convention, always a member of the House of Commons.

### THE PRIME MINISTER
The office of Prime Minister, which had been in existence for nearly 200 years, was officially recognized in 1905 and its holder was granted a place in the table of precedence. The Prime Minister, by tradition also First Lord of the Treasury

and Minister for the Civil Service, is appointed by the Sovereign and is usually the leader of the party which enjoys, or can secure, a majority in the House of Commons. Other Ministers are appointed by the Sovereign on the recommendation of the Prime Minister, who also allocates functions amongst Ministers and has the power to obtain their resignation or dismissal individually.

The Prime Minister informs the Sovereign of state and political matters, advises on the dissolution of Parliament, and makes recommendations for important Crown appointments, the award of honours, etc.

As the chairman of Cabinet meetings and leader of a political party, the Prime Minister is responsible for translating party policy into government activity. As leader of the Government, the Prime Minister is responsible to Parliament and to the electorate for the policies and their implementation.

The Prime Minister also represents the nation in international affairs, e.g. summit conferences.

### THE CABINET
The Cabinet developed during the eighteenth century as an inner committee of the Privy Council, which was the chief source of executive power until that time. The Cabinet is composed of about twenty Ministers chosen by the Prime Minister, usually the heads of government departments (generally known as Secretaries of State unless they have a special title, e.g. Chancellor of the Exchequer), the leaders of the two Houses of Parliament, and the holders of various traditional offices.

The Cabinet's functions are the final determination of policy, control of government and co-ordination of government departments. The exercise of its functions is dependent upon enjoying majority support in the House of Commons. Cabinet meetings are held in private, taking place once or twice a week during parliamentary sittings and less often during a recess. Proceedings are confidential, the members being bound by their oath as Privy Counsellors not to disclose information about the proceedings.

The convention of collective responsibility means that the Cabinet acts unanimously even when Cabinet Ministers do not all agree on a subject. The policies of departmental Ministers must be consistent with the policies of the Government as a whole, and once the Government's policy has been decided, each Minister is expected to support it or resign.

The convention of ministerial responsibility holds a Minister, as the political head of his or her department, accountable to Parliament for the department's work. Departmental Ministers usually decide all matters within their responsibility, although on matters of political importance they normally consult their colleagues collectively. A decision by a departmental Minister is binding on the Government as a whole.

## POLITICAL PARTIES

Before the reign of William and Mary the principal officers of state were chosen by and were responsible to the Sovereign alone and not to Parliament or the nation at large. Such officers acted sometimes in concert with one another but more often independently, and the fall of one did not, of necessity, involve that of others, although all were liable to be dismissed at any moment.

In 1693 the Earl of Sunderland recommended to William III the advisability of selecting a ministry from the political party which enjoyed a majority in the House of Commons and the first united ministry was drawn in 1696 from the Whigs, to which party the King owed his throne. This group became known as the Junto and was regarded with suspicion as a novelty in the political life of the nation, being a small section meeting in secret apart from the main body of Ministers. It may be regarded as the forerunner of the Cabinet and in course of time it led to the establishment of the principle of joint responsibility of Ministers, so that internal disagreement caused a change of personnel or resignation of the whole body of Ministers.

The accession of George I, who was unfamiliar with the English language, led to a disinclination on the part of the Sovereign to preside at meetings of his Ministers and caused the appearance of a Prime Minister, a position first acquired by Robert Walpole in 1721 and retained without interruption for 20 years and 326 days.

DEVELOPMENT OF PARTIES

In 1828 the old party of the Whigs became known as Liberals, a name originally given to it by its opponents to imply laxity of principles, but gradually accepted by the party to indicate its claim to be pioneers and champions of political reform and progressive legislation. In 1861 a Liberal Registration Association was founded and Liberal Associations became widespread. In 1877 a National Liberal Federation was formed, with headquarters in London. The Liberal Party was in power for long periods during the second half of the nineteenth century and for several years during the first quarter of the twentieth century, but after a split in the party the numbers elected were small from 1931. In March 1988, a majority of the Liberals agreed on a merger with the Social Democratic Party under the title Social and Liberal Democrats; since October 1989 they have been known as the Liberal Democrats. A minority continued separately as the Liberal Party.

Soon after the change from Whig to Liberal the Tory Party became known as Conservative, a name traditionally believed to have been invented by John Wilson Croker in 1830 and to have been generally adopted about the time of the passing of the Reform Act of 1832 to indicate that the preservation of national institutions was the leading principle of the party. After the Home Rule crisis of 1886 the dissentient Liberals entered into a compact with the Conservatives, under which the latter undertook not to contest their seats, but a separate Liberal Unionist organization was maintained until 1912, when it was united with the Conservatives.

Labour candidates for Parliament made their first appearance at the general election of 1892, when there were 27 standing as Labour or Liberal-Labour. In 1900 the Labour Representation Committee was set up in order to establish a distinct Labour group in Parliament, with its own whips, its own policy, and a readiness to co-operate with any party which might be engaged in promoting legislation in the direct interest of labour. In 1906 the LRC became known as the Labour Party.

The Council for Social Democracy was announced by four former Labour Cabinet Ministers on 25 January 1981. Subsequently a number of sitting Labour Members of Parliament, together with one Conservative, joined the new group, and on 26 March 1981 the Social Democratic Party was launched. Later that year the SDP and the Liberal Party formed an electoral alliance. In 1988 a majority of the SDP agreed on a merger with the Liberal Party (*see* above) but a minority continued as a separate party under the SDP title. In June 1990 it was decided to wind up the party organization

and its three sitting MPs were known as independent social democrats. None were returned at the 1992 general election.

GOVERNMENT AND OPPOSITION

The government of the day is formed by the party which wins the largest number of seats in the House of Commons at a general election, or which has the support of a majority of members in the House of Commons. By tradition, the leader of the majority party is asked by the Sovereign to form a government, while the largest minority party becomes the official Opposition with its own leader and 'Shadow Cabinet'. Leaders of the Government and Opposition sit on the front benches of the Commons with their supporters (the back-benchers) sitting behind them.

When a party is in opposition and its leadership becomes vacant, it makes its free choice among the various personalities available; but if the party is in office, the Sovereign's choice may anticipate, and in a certain sense forestall, the decision of the party.

FINANCIAL SUPPORT

Financial support to Opposition parties was introduced in 1975 and is commonly known as Short Money, after Edward Short, the Leader of the House at that time, who introduced the scheme. For 1994–5 financial assistance is:

| | |
|---|---|
| Labour | £1,439,802.97 |
| Liberal Democrats | 297,841.08 |
| Plaid Cymru | 20,731.00 |
| SNP | 34,609.89 |
| SDLP | 21,766.56 |
| Democratic Unionists | 15,010.61 |
| Ulster Unionsts | 43,616.23 |

PARTIES

The parties included here are those with MPs sitting in the House of Commons in the present Parliament. Addresses of other political parties may be found in the Societies and Institutions section.

CONSERVATIVE AND UNIONIST PARTY
Central Office, 32 Smith Square, London SW1P 3HH
Tel 0171-222 9000
*Chairman*, The Rt. Hon. Jeremy Hanley, MP
*Deputy Chairman*, The Rt. Hon. Dame Angela Rumbold, DBE, MP; M. Dobbs; J. Maples
*Hon. Treasurer*, C. Hambro

SCOTTISH CONSERVATIVE AND UNIONIST CENTRAL OFFICE
Suite 1/1, 14 Links Place, Leith, Edinburgh EH6 7EZ
Tel 0131-555 2900
*Chairman*, Sir Michael Hirst
*Vice-Chairmen*, Miss A. Goldie; J. Carlaw; R. Robertson, MP
*Hon. Treasurer*, W. Y. Hughes, CBE
*Director of the Party in Scotland*, R. Pratt

LABOUR PARTY
150 Walworth Road, London SE17 1JT
Tel 0171-701 1234
*Parliamentary Party Leader*, The Rt. Hon. Tony Blair, MP
*Deputy Party Leader*, The Rt. Hon. John Prescott, MP
*Leader in the Lords*, The Lord Richard, PC, QC
*Chair*, David Blunkett, MP
*Vice-Chair*, G. Colling
*Treasurer*, T. Burlison
*General Secretary*, L. Whitty

SHADOW CABINET *as at end July 1994*
*Leader of the Opposition*, The Rt. Hon. Tony Blair, MP
*Deputy Leader*, The Rt. Hon. John Prescott, MP

*Treasury and Economic Affairs*, Gordon Brown, MP
*Foreign and Commonwealth Affairs*, Jack Cunningham, MP
*Home Affairs*, vacant
*Trade and Industry*, Robin Cook, MP
*Health*, David Blunkett, MP
*Employment*, The Rt. Hon. John Prescott, MP
*Transport and London*, Frank Dobson, MP
*Defence*, David Clark, MP
*Local Government*, Jack Straw, MP
*Environmental Protection*, Chris Smith, MP
*Social Security*, Donald Dewar, MP
*Education*, Ann Taylor, MP
*National Heritage*, Marjorie Mowlam, MP
*Scotland*, George Robertson, MP
*Wales*, Ron Davies, MP
*Citizen's Charter*, Michael Meacher, MP
*Development and Co-operation*, Tom Clarke, MP
*Children and the Family*, Joan Lestor, MP
Other spokesmen:
*Women*, Clare Short, MP
*Chief Secretary to the Treasury*, Harriet Harman, MP
*Agriculture*, Gavin Strang, MP
*Northern Ireland*, Kevin McNamara, MP
*Chair of the Parliamentary Labour Party*, Douglas Hoyle, MP

LABOUR CHIEF WHIPS
*House of Lords*, The Lord Graham of Edmonton
*House of Commons*, The Rt. Hon. Derek Foster, MP

LIBERAL DEMOCRATS
4 Cowley Street, London SW1P 3NB
Tel 0171-222 7999
*President*, Charles Kennedy, MP (until September 1994*)
*Hon. Treasurer*, T. Razzall
*General Secretary*, G. Elson
*Parliamentary Party Leader*, The Rt. Hon. Paddy
    Ashdown, MP
*Leader in the Lords*, The Rt. Hon. the Lord Jenkins of
    Hillhead

LIBERAL DEMOCRAT SPOKESMEN *as at 1 August 1994*
*Deputy Leader and Home Affairs*, Alan Beith, MP
*Treasury*, Malcolm Bruce, MP
*Foreign Affairs, Defence and Sport*, Menzies Campbell, MP
*Foreign Affairs and Overseas Development*, Sir David Steel,
    MP
*Health and Welfare, and Wales*, Alex Carlile, MP
*National Heritage and Constitutional Affairs*, Robert
    Maclennan, MP
*Community and Urban Affairs, Church of England*, Simon
    Hughes, MP
*Environment, Campaigns and Citizen's Charter*, Matthew
    Taylor, MP
*Europe*, Charles Kennedy, MP
*East-West Relations*, Sir Russell Johnston, MP
*Agriculture and Rural Affairs*, Paul Tyler, MP
*Local Government and Housing*, David Rendel, MP
*Scotland and Fishing*, Jim Wallace, MP
*Scotland*, Ray Mitchie, MP
*Northern Ireland*, Lord Holme of Cheltenham
*Social Security*, Archy Kirkwood, MP
*Health and Community Care*, Liz Lynne, MP
*Education and Training*, Don Foster, MP
*Family and Women's Issues*, Diana Maddock, MP
*Some spokesmanships were expected to change after the
election of a new president in September 1994

LIBERAL DEMOCRAT WHIPS
*House of Lords*, The Lord Tordoff
*House of Commons*, Archy Kirkwood, MP (*Chief Whip*);
    Simon Hughes, MP (*Deputy Whip*)

WELSH LIBERAL DEMOCRATS
57 St Mary Street, Cardiff CF1 1FE
Tel 01222-382210
*Party President*, M. Thomas, OBE, QC
*Party Leader*, Alex Carlile, QC, MP
*Chairman*, N. Phillips, OBE
*Treasurer*, B. Lopez
*Secretary*, Ms K. Lloyd

SCOTTISH LIBERAL DEMOCRATS
4 Clifton Terrace, Edinburgh EH12 5DR
Tel 0131-337 2314
*Party President*, R. Thomson
*Party Leader*, Jim Wallace, MP
*Chair*, Ms M. MacLaren
*Vice-Chairs*, M. Ford; A. Reid
*Hon. Treasurer*, N. Stephen
*Administrator*, Ms R. Grant

PLAID CYMRU
51 Cathedral Road, Cardiff CF1 9HD
Tel 01222-231944
*Party President*, Dafydd Wigley, MP
*Chairman*, J. Dixon
*Hon. Treasurer*, C. Bryant
*Chief Executive/General Secretary*, K. Davies

SCOTTISH NATIONAL PARTY
6 North Charlotte Street, Edinburgh EH2 4JH
Tel 0131-226 3661
*Parliamentary Party Leader*, Margaret Ewing, MP
*Chief Whip*, Andrew Welsh, MP
*National Convener*, Alex Salmond, MP
*Senior Vice-Convener*, Dr A. Macartney
*National Treasurer*, T. Chalmers
*National Secretary*, A. Morgan

## NORTHERN IRELAND

SOCIAL DEMOCRATIC AND LABOUR PARTY
Cranmore House, 611 Lisburn Road, Belfast BT9 7GT
Tel 01232-668100
*Parliamentary Party Leader*, John Hume, MP, MEP
*Deputy Leader*, Seamus Mallon, MP
*Chief Whip*, Eddie McGrady, MP
*Chairman*, M. Durkan
*Vice-Chairs*, J. Stephenson; Ms G. Leonard
*Hon. Treasurer*, Ms D. Field
*Party Administrator*, Mrs G. Cosgrove

ULSTER DEMOCRATIC UNIONIST PARTY
91 Dundela Avenue, Belfast BT4 3BU
Tel 01232-471155
*Parliamentary Party Leader*, I. Paisley, MP, MEP
*Deputy Leader*, Peter Robinson, MP
*Chairman*, W. J. McClure
*Deputy Chairman*, S. Gibson
*Hon. Treasurer*, D. F. Herron
*General Secretary*, N. Dodds

ULSTER UNIONIST COUNCIL
3 Glengall Street, Belfast BT12 5AE
Tel 01232-324601
*Party Leader*, The Rt. Hon. James Molyneaux, MP
*Chief Whip*, William Ross, MP
*President*, J. Cunningham
*Chairman*, J. Nicholson, MEP
*Vice-Chairman*, A. J. Wilson
*Hon. Treasurer*, J. Allen
*Party Secretary*, J. Wilson

# The Government

## THE CABINET AS AT 31 JULY 1994

*Prime Minister, First Lord of the Treasury and Minister for the Civil Service*
The Rt. Hon. John Major, MP, since November 1990
*Lord High Chancellor*
The Lord Mackay of Clashfern, PC, since October 1987
*Secretary of State for Foreign and Commonwealth Affairs*
The Rt. Hon. Douglas Hurd, CBE, MP, since October 1989
*Chancellor of the Exchequer*
The Rt. Hon. Kenneth Clarke, QC, MP, since May 1993
*Secretary of State for the Home Department*
The Rt. Hon. Michael Howard, QC, MP, since May 1993
*President of the Board of Trade and Secretary of State for Trade and Industry*
The Rt. Hon. Michael Heseltine, MP, since April 1992
*Secretary of State for Defence*
The Rt. Hon. Malcolm Rifkind, QC, MP, since April 1992
*Lord President of the Council and Leader of the House of Commons*
The Rt. Hon. Antony Newton, OBE, MP, since April 1992
*Secretary of State for the Environment*
The Rt. Hon. John Gummer, MP, since May 1993
*Chancellor of the Duchy of Lancaster and Minister of Public Service and Science*
The Rt. Hon. David Hunt, MBE, MP, since July 1994
*Secretary of State for Social Security*
The Rt. Hon. Peter Lilley, MP, since April 1992
*Minister of Agriculture, Fisheries and Food*
The Rt. Hon. William Waldegrave, MP, since July 1994
*Secretary of State for Scotland*
The Rt. Hon. Ian Lang, MP, since November 1990
*Secretary of State for Northern Ireland*
The Rt. Hon. Sir Patrick Mayhew, QC, MP, since April 1992
*Secretary of State for Health*
The Rt. Hon. Virginia Bottomley, MP, since April 1992
*Secretary of State for Education*
The Rt. Hon. Gillian Shephard, MP, since July 1994
*Secretary of State for Employment*
The Rt. Hon. Michael Portillo, MP, since July 1994
*Secretary of State for Wales*
The Rt. Hon. John Redwood, MP, since May 1993
*Secretary of State for Transport*
The Rt. Hon. Brian Mawhinney, MP, since July 1994
*Secretary of State for National Heritage*
The Rt. Hon. Stephen Dorrell, MP, since July 1994
*Lord Privy Seal and Leader of the House of Lords*
Viscount Cranborne, PC, since July 1994
*Chief Secretary to the Treasury*
The Rt. Hon. Jonathan Aitken, MP, since July 1994
*Minister Without Portfolio (Party chairman)*
The Rt. Hon. Jeremy Hanley, MP, since July 1994

## LAW OFFICERS

*Attorney-General*
The Rt. Hon. Sir Nicholas Lyell, QC, MP, since April 1992
*Lord Advocate*
The Lord Rodger of Earlsferry, PC, QC, since April 1992

*Solicitor-General*
Sir Derek Spencer, QC, MP, since April 1992
*Solicitor-General for Scotland*
Thomas Dawson, QC, since April 1992

## MINISTERS OF STATE

*Agriculture, Fisheries and Food*
Michael Jack, MP
*Defence*
The Rt. Hon. Roger Freeman, MP (*Defence Procurement*)
The Hon. Nicholas Soames, MP (*Armed Forces*)
*Education*
Eric Forth, MP
*Employment*
Ann Widdecombe, MP
*Environment*
David Curry, MP (*Minister for Local Government*)
Robert Atkins, MP (*Minister for Environment and Countryside*)
The Viscount Ullswater, PC (*Minister for Construction and Planning*)
*Foreign and Commonwealth Affairs*
The Baroness Chalker of Wallasey, PC (*Minister for Overseas Development*)
The Rt. Hon. Douglas Hogg, QC, MP; The Rt. Hon. Alastair Goodlad, MP
David Davis, MP (*Minister for Europe*)
*Health*
Gerald Malone, MP (*Minister for Health*)
*Home Office*
David Maclean, MP; The Baroness Blatch; Michael Forsyth, MP
*Northern Ireland Office*
The Rt. Hon. Sir John Wheeler, MP; Michael Ancram, MP
*Scottish Office*
The Lord Fraser of Carmyllie, PC, QC
*Social Security*
William Hague, MP (*Minister for Social Security and Disabled People*)
The Lord Mackay of Ardbrecknish
*Trade and Industry*
Richard Needham, MP (*Minister for Trade*)
Timothy Eggar, MP (*Minister for Energy and Industry*)
The Earl Ferrers, PC (*Consumer Affairs and Small Firms*)
*Transport*
John Watts, MP
*Treasury*
The Rt. Hon. Sir George Young, MP (*Financial Secretary*)
David Heathcoat-Amory, MP (*Paymaster-General*)
Anthony Nelson, MP (*Economic Secretary*)

## UNDER-SECRETARIES OF STATE

*Agriculture, Fisheries and Food*
The Earl Howe; Angela Browning, MP
*Office of the Minister for the Civil Service*
Robert Hughes, MP
*Defence*
The Lord Henley

*Education*
  Timothy Boswell, MP; Robin Squire, MP
*Employment*
  James Plaice, MP; Phillip Oppenheim, MP
*Environment*
  Sir Paul Beresford, MP; Robert Jones, MP
*Foreign and Commonwealth Affairs*
  Anthony Baldry, MP
*Health*
  The Baroness Cumberlege, CBE; The Hon. Thomas
  Sackville, MP; John Bowis, OBE, MP
*Home Office*
  Nicholas Baker, MP
*Lord Chancellor's Department*
  John Taylor, MP
*National Heritage*
  Iain Sproat, MP; The Viscount Astor
*Northern Ireland*
  Timothy Smith, MP; The Baroness Denton of Wakefield,
  CBE
*Scottish Office*
  Lord James Douglas-Hamilton, MP; Allan Stewart, MP;
  Sir Hector Monro, MP
*Social Security*
  Alistair Burt, MP; James Arbuthnot, MP; Roger Evans, MP
*Trade and Industry*
  Neil Hamilton, MP (*Corporate Affairs*)
  Charles Wardle, MP (*Industry and Energy*)
  Ian Taylor, MP (*Trade and Technology*)
*Transport*
  Steven Norris, MP; The Viscount Goschen
*Treasury*
  The Lords Commissioners, *see* Government Whips
*Welsh Office*
  Gwilym Jones, MP; Roderick Richards, MP

*Lord Commissioners*
  Timothy Wood, MP; Timothy Kirkhope, MP; Andrew
  Mackay, MP; Andrew Mitchell, MP; Derek Conway, MP
*Assistant Whips*
  Bowen Wells, MP; Simon Burns, MP; David Willetts, MP;
  Michael Bates, MP; Liam Fox, MP

## GOVERNMENT WHIPS

### HOUSE OF LORDS

*Captain of the Honourable Corps of Gentlemen-at-Arms
  (Chief Whip)*
  The Lord Strathclyde
*Captain of The Queen's Bodyguard of the Yeomen of the
  Guard (Deputy Chief Whip)*
  The Earl of Arran
*Lords-in-Waiting*
  The Viscount Long, CBE; The Lord Lucas of Crudwell;
  The Lord Inglewood
*Baronesses-in-Waiting*
  The Baroness Trumpington, PC; The Baroness Miller of
  Hendon

### HOUSE OF COMMONS

*Parliamentary Secretary to the Treasury (Chief Whip)*
  The Rt. Hon. Richard Ryder, OBE, MP
*Treasurer of HM Household (Deputy Chief Whip)*
  Gregory Knight, MP
*Comptroller of HM Household*
  David Lightbown, MP
*Vice-Chamberlain of HM Household*
  Sydney Chapman, MP

MEMBERS OF PARLIAMENT AS AT 31 JULY 1994

For abbreviations, *see* page 243
* Denotes membership of the last Parliament

*Abbott, Ms Diane J. (*b.* 1953) *Lab., Hackney North and Stoke Newington,* maj. 10,727

*Adams, Mrs Irene (*b.* 1948) *Lab., Paisley North,* maj. 9,329

Ainger, Nicholas R. (*b.* 1949) *Lab., Pembroke,* maj. 755

Ainsworth, Peter M. (*b.* 1956) *C., Surrey East,* maj. 17,656

Ainsworth, Robert W. (*b.* 1952) *Lab., Coventry North East,* maj. 11,676

*Aitken, Jonathan W. P. (*b.* 1942) *C., Thanet South,* maj. 11,513

*Alexander, Richard T. (*b.* 1934) *C., Newark,* maj. 8,229

*Alison, Rt. Hon. Michael J. H. (*b.* 1926) *C., Selby,* maj. 9,508

*Allason, Rupert W. S. (*b.* 1951) *C., Torbay,* maj. 5,787

*Allen, Graham W. (*b.* 1953) *Lab., Nottingham North,* maj. 10,743

*Alton, David P. (*b.* 1951) *LD, Liverpool, Mossley Hill,* maj. 2,606

*Amess, David A. A. (*b.* 1952) *C., Basildon,* maj. 1,480

Ancram, Michael A. F. J. K. (Earl of Ancram) (*b.* 1945) *C., Devizes,* maj. 19,712

*Anderson, Donald (*b.* 1939) *Lab., Swansea East,* maj. 23,482

Anderson, Mrs Janet (*b.* 1949) *Lab., Rossendale and Darwen,* maj. 120

*Arbuthnot, James N. (*b.* 1952) *C., Wanstead and Woodford,* maj. 16,885

*Armstrong, Miss Hilary J. (*b.* 1945) *Lab., Durham North West,* maj. 13,987

*Arnold, Jacques A. (*b.* 1947) *C., Gravesham,* maj. 5,493

*Arnold, Sir Thomas (*b.* 1947) *C., Hazel Grove,* maj. 929

*Ashby, David G. (*b.* 1940) *C., Leicestershire North West,* maj. 979

*Ashdown, Rt. Hon. J. J. D. (Paddy) (*b.* 1941) *LD, Yeovil,* maj. 8,833

*Ashton, Joseph W. (*b.* 1933) *Lab., Bassetlaw,* maj. 9,997

*Aspinwall, Jack H. (*b.* 1933) *C., Wansdyke,* maj. 13,341

*Atkins, Robert J. (*b.* 1946) *C., South Ribble,* maj. 5,973

*Atkinson, David A. (*b.* 1940) *C., Bournemouth East,* maj. 14,823

Atkinson, Peter (*b.* 1943) *C., Hexham,* maj. 13,438

Austin-Walker, John E. (*b.* 1944) *Lab., Woolwich,* maj. 2,225

*Baker, Rt. Hon. Kenneth W., CH (*b.* 1934) *C., Mole Valley,* maj. 15,950

*Baker, Nicholas B. (*b.* 1938) *C., Dorset North,* maj. 10,080

*Baldry, Antony B. (*b.* 1950) *C., Banbury,* maj. 16,720

Banks, Matthew (*b.* 1961) *C., Southport,* maj. 3,063

*Banks, Robert G., MBE (*b.* 1937) *C., Harrogate,* maj. 12,589

*Banks, Tony L. (*b.* 1943) *Lab., Newham North West,* maj. 9,171

*Barnes, Harold (*b.* 1936) *Lab., Derbyshire North East,* maj. 6,270

*Barron, Kevin J. (*b.* 1946) *Lab., Rother Valley,* maj. 17,222

Bates, Michael W. (*b.* 1961) *C., Langbaurgh,* maj. 1,564

*Batiste, Spencer L. (*b.* 1945) *C., Elmet,* maj. 3,261

*Battle, John D. (*b.* 1951) *Lab., Leeds West,* maj. 13,828

Bayley, Hugh (*b.* 1952) *Lab., York,* maj. 6,342

*Beckett, Rt. Hon. Margaret M. (*b.* 1953) *Lab., Derby South,* maj. 6,936

*Beggs, Roy (*b.* 1936) *UUP, Antrim East,* maj. 7,422

*Beith, Rt. Hon. Alan J. (*b.* 1943) *LD, Berwick-upon-Tweed,* maj. 5,043

*Bell, Stuart (*b.* 1938) *Lab., Middlesbrough,* maj. 15,784

*Bellingham, Henry C. (*b.* 1955) *C., Norfolk North West,* maj. 11,564

*Bendall, Vivian W. H. (*b.* 1938) *C., Ilford North,* maj. 9,071

*Benn, Rt. Hon. Anthony N. W. (*b.* 1925) *Lab., Chesterfield,* maj. 6,414

*Bennett, Andrew F. (*b.* 1939) *Lab., Denton and Reddish,* maj. 12,084

*Benton, Joseph E. (*b.* 1933) *Lab., Bootle,* maj. 29,442

Beresford, Sir Paul (*b.* 1946) *C., Croydon Central,* maj. 9,650

*Bermingham, Gerald E. (*b.* 1940) *Lab., St Helens South,* maj. 18,209

Berry, Roger L., D.Phil (*b.* 1948) *Lab., Kingswood,* maj. 2,370

Betts, Clive J. C. (*b.* 1950) *Lab., Sheffield, Attercliffe,* maj. 15,480

*Biffen, Rt. Hon. John W. (*b.* 1930) *C., Shropshire North,* maj. 16,211

*Blackburn, John G., PH.D. (*b.* 1933) *C., Dudley West,* maj. 5,789

*Blair, Rt. Hon. Anthony C. L. (*b.* 1953) *Lab., Sedgefield,* maj. 14,859

*Blunkett, David (*b.* 1947) *Lab., Sheffield, Brightside,* maj. 22,681

*Boateng, Paul Y. (*b.* 1951) *Lab., Brent South,* maj. 9,705

*Body, Sir Richard (*b.* 1927) *C., Holland with Boston,* maj. 13,831

*Bonsor, Sir Nicholas, Bt. (*b.* 1942) *C., Upminster,* maj. 13,821

Booth, Hartley, Ph.D. (*b.* 1946) *C., Finchley,* maj. 6,388

*Boothroyd, Rt. Hon. Betty (*b.* 1929) *The Speaker, West Bromwich West,* maj. 7,830

*Boswell, Timothy E. (*b.* 1942) *C., Daventry,* maj. 20,274

*Bottomley, Peter J. (*b.* 1944) *C., Eltham,* maj. 1,666

*Bottomley, Rt. Hon. Virginia H. B. M. (*b.* 1948) *C., Surrey South West,* maj. 14,975

*Bowden, Sir Andrew, MBE (*b.* 1930) *C., Brighton, Kemptown,* maj. 3,056

*Bowis, John C., OBE (*b.* 1945) *C., Battersea,* maj. 4,840

*Boyes, Roland (*b.* 1937) *Lab., Houghton and Washington,* maj. 20,808

*Boyson, Rt. Hon. Sir Rhodes (*b.* 1925) *C., Brent North,* maj. 10,131

*Bradley, Keith J. C. (*b.* 1950) *Lab., Manchester, Withington,* maj. 9,735

Brandreth, Gyles D. (*b.* 1948) *C., City of Chester,* maj. 1,101

*Bray, Jeremy W., ph.D. (*b.* 1930) *Lab., Motherwell South,* maj. 14,013

*Brazier, Julian W. H. (*b.* 1953) *C., Canterbury,* maj. 10,805

*Bright, Graham F. J. (*b.* 1942) *C., Luton South,* maj. 799

*Brooke, Rt. Hon. Peter L., CH (*b.* 1934) *C., City of London and Westminster South,* maj. 13,369

*Brown, J. Gordon, PH.D. (*b.* 1951) *Lab., Dunfermline East,* maj. 17,444

*Brown, Michael R. (*b.* 1951) *C., Brigg and Cleethorpes,* maj. 9,269

*Brown, Nicholas H. (*b.* 1950) *Lab., Newcastle upon Tyne East,* maj. 13,877

Browning, Mrs Angela F. (*b.* 1946) *C., Tiverton,* maj. 11,089

*Bruce, Ian C. (*b.* 1947) *C., Dorset South,* maj. 13,508

*Bruce, Malcolm G. (*b.* 1944) *LD, Gordon,* maj. 274

*Budgen, Nicholas W. (*b.* 1937) *C., Wolverhampton South West,* maj. 4,966

Burden, Richard (*b.* 1954) *Lab., Birmingham, Northfield,* maj. 630

*Burns, Simon H. M. (*b.* 1952) *C., Chelmsford,* maj. 18,260

*Burt, Alistair J. H. (*b.* 1955) *C., Bury North,* maj. 4,764

*Butcher, John P. (*b.* 1946) *C., Coventry South West,* maj. 1,436

Butler, Peter (*b.* 1951) *C., Milton Keynes North East,* maj. 14,176

*Butterfill, John V. (*b.* 1941) *C., Bournemouth West,* maj. 12,703

Byers, Stephen J. (*b.* 1953) *Lab., Wallsend,* maj. 19,470

*Caborn, Richard G. (*b.* 1943) *Lab., Sheffield Central,* maj. 17,294

*Callaghan, James (*b.* 1927) *Lab., Heywood and Middleton,* maj. 8,074

Campbell, Mrs Anne (*b.* 1940) *Lab., Cambridge,* maj. 580

*Campbell, Ronald (*b.* 1943) *Lab., Blyth Valley,* maj. 8,044

*Campbell, W. Menzies, CBE, QC (*b.* 1941) *LD, Fife North East,* maj. 3,308

*Campbell-Savours, Dale N. (*b.* 1943) *Lab., Workington,* maj. 10,449

*Canavan, Dennis A. (*b.* 1942) *Lab., Falkirk West,* maj. 9,812

Cann, James (*b.* 1946) *Lab., Ipswich,* maj. 265

*Carlile, Alexander C., QC (*b.* 1948) *LD, Montgomery,* maj. 5,209

*Carlisle, John R. (*b.* 1942) *C., Luton North,* maj. 13,094

*Carlisle, Sir Kenneth (*b.* 1941) *C., Lincoln,* maj. 2,049

*Carrington, Matthew H. M. (*b.* 1947) *C., Fulham,* maj. 6,579

*Carttiss, Michael R. H. (*b.* 1938) *C., Great Yarmouth,* maj. 5,309

*Cash, William N. P. (*b.* 1940) *C., Stafford,* maj. 10,900

*Channon, Rt. Hon. H. Paul G. (*b.* 1935) *C., Southend West,* maj. 11,902

*Chapman, Sydney B. (*b.* 1935) *C., Chipping Barnet,* maj. 13,951

Chidgey, David W. G. (*b.* 1942) *LD, Eastleigh,* maj. 9,239

Chisholm, Malcolm (*b.* 1949) *Lab., Edinburgh, Leith,* maj. 4,985

Church, Ms Judith A. (*b.* 1953), *Lab., Dagenham,* maj. 13,344

*Churchill, Winston S. (*b.* 1940) *C., Davyhulme,* maj. 4,426

Clapham, Michael (*b.* 1943) *Lab., Barnsley West and Penistone,* maj. 14,504

Clappison, W. James (*b.* 1956) *C., Hertsmere,* maj. 18,735

*Clark, David G., PH.D. (*b.* 1939) *Lab., South Shields,* maj. 13,477

*Clark, Dr Michael (*b.* 1935) *C., Rochford,* maj. 26,036

Clarke, Eric L. (*b.* 1933) *Lab., Midlothian,* maj. 10,334

*Clarke, Rt. Hon. Kenneth H., QC (*b.* 1940) *C., Rushcliffe,* maj. 19,766

*Clarke, Thomas, CBE (*b.* 1941) *Lab., Monklands West,* maj. 17,065

*Clelland, David G. (*b.* 1943) *Lab., Tyne Bridge,* maj. 15,210

Clifton-Brown, Geoffrey R. (*b.* 1953) *C., Cirencester and Tewkesbury,* maj. 16,058

*Clwyd, Ms Ann (*b.* 1937) *Lab., Cynon Valley,* maj. 21,364

Coe, Sebastian N., OBE (*b.* 1956) *C., Falmouth and Camborne,* maj. 3,267

Coffey, Ms M. Ann (*b.* 1946) *Lab., Stockport,* maj. 1,422

*Cohen, Harry (*b.* 1949) *Lab., Leyton,* maj. 11,484

*Colvin, Michael K. B. (*b.* 1932) *C., Romsey and Waterside,* maj. 15,304

Congdon, David L. (*b.* 1949) *C., Croydon North East,* maj. 7,473

Connarty, Michael (*b.* 1949) *Lab., Falkirk East,* maj. 7,969

*Conway, Derek L. (*b.* 1953) *C., Shrewsbury and Atcham,* maj. 10,965

*Cook, Francis (*b.* 1935) *Lab., Stockton North,* maj. 10,474

*Cook, R. F. (Robin) (*b.* 1946) *Lab., Livingston,* maj. 8,105

*Coombs, Anthony M. V. (*b.* 1952) *C., Wyre Forest,* maj. 10,341

*Coombs, Simon C. (*b.* 1947) *C., Swindon,* maj. 2,826

*Cope, Rt. Hon. Sir John (*b.* 1937) *C., Northavon,* maj. 11,861

*Corbett, Robin (*b.* 1933) *Lab., Birmingham, Erdington,* maj. 4,735

*Corbyn, Jeremy B. (*b.* 1949) *Lab., Islington North,* maj. 12,784

*Cormack, Patrick T. (*b.* 1939) *C., Staffordshire South,* maj. 22,633

Corston, Ms Jean (*b.* 1942) *Lab., Bristol East,* maj. 2,692

*Couchman, James R. (*b.* 1942) *C., Gillingham,* maj. 16,638

*Cousins, James M. (*b.* 1944) *Lab., Newcastle upon Tyne Central,* maj. 5,288

*Cox, Thomas M. (*b.* 1930) *Lab., Tooting,* maj. 4,107

*Cran, James D. (*b.* 1944) *C., Beverley,* maj. 16,517

*Critchley, Julian M. G. (*b.* 1930) *C., Aldershot,* maj. 19,188

*Cummings, John S. (*b.* 1943) *Lab., Easington,* maj. 26,390

*Cunliffe, Lawrence F. (*b.* 1929) *Lab., Leigh,* maj. 18,827

Cunningham, James (*b.* 1941) *Lab., Coventry South East,* maj. 1,311

*Cunningham, Rt. Hon. Dr John A. (Jack) (*b.* 1939) *Lab., Copeland,* maj. 2,439

*Currie, Mrs Edwina (*b.* 1946) *C., Derbyshire South,* maj. 4,658

*Curry, David M. (*b.* 1944) *C., Skipton and Ripon,* maj. 19,330

Dafis, Cynog G. (*b.* 1938) *PC, Ceredigion and Pembroke North,* maj. 3,193

*Dalyell, Tam (Sir Thomas Dalyell of the Binns, Bt.) (*b.* 1932) *Lab., Linlithgow,* maj. 7,026

*Darling, Alistair M. (*b.* 1953) *Lab., Edinburgh Central,* maj. 2,126

Davidson, Ian (*b.* 1950) *Lab., Glasgow, Govan,* maj. 4,125

Davies, Bryan (*b.* 1939) *Lab., Oldham Central and Royton,* maj. 8,606

*Davies, Rt. Hon. D. J. Denzil (*b.* 1938) *Lab., Llanelli,* maj. 19,270

*Davies, J. Quentin (*b.* 1944) *C., Stamford and Spalding,* maj. 22,869

*Davies, Ronald (*b.* 1946) *Lab., Caerphilly,* maj. 22,672

*Davis, David M. (*b.* 1948) *C., Boothferry,* maj. 17,535

*Davis, Terence A. G. (*b.* 1938) *Lab., Birmingham, Hodge Hill,* maj. 7,068

*Day, Stephen R. (*b.* 1948) *C., Cheadle,* maj. 15,778

Denham, John V. (*b.* 1953) *Lab., Southampton, Itchen,* maj. 551

Deva, Niranjan J. A. (*b.* 1948) *C., Brentford and Isleworth,* maj. 2,086

*Devlin, Timothy R. (*b.* 1959) *C., Stockton South,* maj. 3,369

*Dewar, Donald C. (*b.* 1937) *Lab., Glasgow, Garscadden,* maj. 13,340

*Dickens, Geoffrey K. (*b.* 1931) *C., Littleborough and Saddleworth,* maj. 4,494

*Dicks, Terence P. (*b.* 1937) *C., Hayes and Harlington,* maj. 53

*Dixon, Donald (*b.* 1929) *Lab., Jarrow,* maj. 17,907

*Dobson, Frank G. (*b.* 1940) *Lab., Holborn and St Pancras,* maj. 10,824

Donohoe, Brian H. (*b.* 1948) *Lab., Cunninghame South,* maj. 10,680

*Dorrell, Stephen J. (*b.* 1952) *C., Loughborough,* maj. 10,883

*Douglas-Hamilton, Lord James (*b.* 1942) *C., Edinburgh West,* maj. 879

*Dover, Densmore (*b.* 1938) *C., Chorley,* maj. 4,246

Dowd, James P. (*b.* 1951) *Lab., Lewisham West,* maj. 1,809

Duncan, Alan J. C. (*b.* 1957) *C., Rutland and Melton,* maj. 25,535

Duncan-Smith, G. Iain (*b.* 1954) *C., Chingford*, maj. 14,938

*Dunn, Robert J. (*b.* 1946) *C., Dartford*, maj. 10,314

*Dunnachie, James F. (*b.* 1930) *Lab., Glasgow, Pollok*, maj. 7,883

*Dunwoody, Hon. Mrs Gwyneth P. (*b.* 1930) *Lab., Crewe and Nantwich*, maj. 2,695

*Durant, Sir Anthony (*b.* 1928) *C., Reading West*, maj. 13,298

*Dykes, Hugh J. (*b.* 1939) *C., Harrow East*, maj. 11,098

Eagle, Ms Angela (*b.* 1961) *Lab., Wallasey*, maj. 3,809

*Eastham, Kenneth (*b.* 1927) *Lab., Manchester, Blackley*, maj. 12,389

*Eggar, Timothy J. C. (*b.* 1951) *C., Enfield North*, maj. 9,430

Elletson, Harold D. H. (*b.* 1960) *C., Blackpool North*, maj. 3,040

*Emery, Rt. Hon. Sir Peter (*b.* 1926) *C., Honiton*, maj. 16,511

*Enright, Derek A. (*b.* 1935) *Lab., Hemsworth*, maj. 22,075

Etherington, William (*b.* 1941) *Lab., Sunderland North*, maj. 17,004

*Evans, David J. (*b.* 1935) *C., Welwyn Hatfield*, maj. 8,465

*Evans, John (*b.* 1930) *Lab., St Helens North*, maj. 16,244

Evans, Jonathan P. (*b.* 1950) *C., Brecon and Radnor*, maj. 130

Evans, Nigel M. (*b.* 1957) *C., Ribble Valley*, maj. 6,542

Evans, Roger (*b.* 1947) *C., Monmouth*, maj. 3,204

*Evennett, David A. (*b.* 1939) *C., Erith and Crayford*, maj. 2,339

*Ewing, Mrs Margaret A. (*b.* 1945) *SNP, Moray*, maj. 2,844

Faber, David J. C. (*b.* 1961) *C., Westbury*, maj. 12,606

Fabricant, Michael L. D. (*b.* 1950) *C., Staffordshire Mid*, maj. 6,236

*Fairbairn, Sir Nicholas, QC (*b.* 1933) *C., Perth and Kinross*, maj. 2,094

*Fatchett, Derek J. (*b.* 1945) *Lab., Leeds Central*, maj. 15,020

*Faulds, Andrew M. W. (*b.* 1923) *Lab., Warley East*, maj. 7,794

*Fenner, Dame Peggy, DBE (*b.* 1922) *C., Medway*, maj. 8,786

*Field, Barry J. A., TD (*b.* 1946) *C., Isle of Wight*, maj. 1,827

*Field, Frank (*b.* 1942) *Lab., Birkenhead*, maj. 17,613

*Fishburn, J. Dudley (*b.* 1946) *C., Kensington*, maj. 3,548

*Fisher, Mark (*b.* 1944) *Lab., Stoke-on-Trent Central*, maj. 13,420

*Flynn, Paul P. (*b.* 1935) *Lab., Newport West*, maj. 7,779

*Fookes, Dame Janet, DBE (*b.* 1936) *C., Plymouth, Drake*, maj. 2,013

*Forman, F. Nigel (*b.* 1943) *C., Carshalton and Wallington*, maj. 9,943

*Forsyth, Michael B. (*b.* 1954) *C., Stirling*, maj. 703

*Forsythe, Clifford (*b.* 1929) *UUP, Antrim South*, maj. 24,559

*Forth, Eric (*b.* 1944) *C., Worcestershire Mid*, maj. 9,870

*Foster, Rt. Hon. Derek (*b.* 1937) *Lab., Bishop Auckland*, maj. 10,087

Foster, Donald M. E. (*b.* 1937) *LD, Bath*, maj. 3,768

*Foulkes, George (*b.* 1942) *Lab., Carrick, Cumnock and Doon Valley*, maj. 16,626

*Fowler, Rt. Hon. Sir Norman (*b.* 1938) *C., Sutton Coldfield*, maj. 26,036

Fox, Dr Liam (*b.* 1961) *C., Woodspring*, maj. 17,509

*Fox, Sir Marcus, MBE (*b.* 1927) *C., Shipley*, maj. 12,382

*Fraser, John D. (*b.* 1934) *Lab., Norwood*, maj. 7,216

*Freeman, Rt. Hon. Roger N. (*b.* 1942) *C., Kettering*, maj. 11,154

*French, Douglas C. (*b.* 1944) *C., Gloucester*, maj. 6,058

*Fry, Sir Peter (*b.* 1931) *C., Wellingborough*, maj. 11,816

*Fyfe, Mrs Maria (*b.* 1938) *Lab., Glasgow, Maryhill*, maj. 13,419

*Galbraith, Samuel L. (*b.* 1945) *Lab., Strathkelvin and Bearsden*, maj. 3,162

*Gale, Roger J. (*b.* 1943) *C., Thanet North*, maj. 18,210

Gallie, Philip (*b.* 1939) *C., Ayr*, maj. 85

*Galloway, George (*b.* 1954) *Lab., Glasgow, Hillhead*, maj. 4,826

Gapes, Michael J. (*b.* 1952) *Lab., Ilford South*, maj. 402

*Gardiner, Sir George (*b.* 1935) *C., Reigate*, maj. 17,664

*Garel-Jones, Rt. Hon. (W. A. T.) Tristan (*b.* 1941) *C., Watford*, maj. 9,590

Garnier, Edward (*b.* 1952) *C., Harborough*, maj. 13,543

*Garrett, John L. (*b.* 1931) *Lab., Norwich South*, maj. 6,181

*George, Bruce T. (*b.* 1942) *Lab., Walsall South*, maj. 3,178

Gerrard, Neil F. (*b.* 1942) *Lab., Walthamstow*, maj. 3,022

*Gilbert, Rt. Hon. Dr John W. (*b.* 1927) *Lab., Dudley East*, maj. 9,200

*Gill, Christopher J. F., RD (*b.* 1936) *C., Ludlow*, maj. 14,152

Gillan, Ms Cheryl E. K. (*b.* 1952) *C., Chesham and Amersham*, maj. 22,220

*Godman, Norman A., PH.D. (*b.* 1938) *Lab., Greenock and Port Glasgow*, maj. 14,979

Godsiff, Roger D. (*b.* 1946) *Lab., Birmingham, Small Heath*, maj. 13,989

*Golding, Mrs Llinos (*b.* 1933) *Lab., Newcastle under Lyme*, maj. 9,839

*Goodlad, Rt. Hon. Alistair R. (*b.* 1943) *C., Eddisbury*, maj. 12,697

*Goodson-Wickes, Dr Charles (*b.* 1945) *C., Wimbledon*, maj. 14,761

*Gordon, Mrs Mildred (*b.* 1923) *Lab., Bow and Poplar*, maj. 8,404

*Gorman, Mrs Teresa E. (*b.* 1931) *C., Billericay*, maj. 22,494

*Gorst, Sir John (*b.* 1928) *C., Hendon North*, maj. 7,122

*Graham, Thomas (*b.* 1944) *Lab., Renfrew West and Inverclyde*, maj. 1,744

*Grant, Sir Anthony (*b.* 1925) *C., Cambridgeshire South West*, maj. 19,637

*Grant, Bernard A. M. (*b.* 1944) *Lab., Tottenham*, maj. 11,968

*Greenway, Harry (*b.* 1934) *C., Ealing North*, maj. 5,966

*Greenway, John R. (*b.* 1946) *C., Ryedale*, maj. 18,439

*Griffiths, Nigel (*b.* 1955) *Lab., Edinburgh South*, maj. 4,176

*Griffiths, Peter H. S. (*b.* 1928) *C., Portsmouth North*, maj. 13,881

*Griffiths, Winston J. (*b.* 1943) *Lab., Bridgend*, maj. 7,326

*Grocott, Bruce J. (*b.* 1940) *Lab., The Wrekin*, maj. 6,648

*Grylls, Sir Michael (*b.* 1934) *C., Surrey North West*, maj. 28,394

*Gummer, Rt. Hon. John S. (*b.* 1939) *C., Suffolk Coastal*, maj. 19,285

Gunnell, W. John (*b.* 1933) *Lab., Leeds South and Morley*, maj. 7,372

*Hague, William J. (*b.* 1961) *C., Richmond (Yorks)* maj. 23,504

*Hain, Peter G. (*b.* 1950) *Lab., Neath*, maj. 23,975

Hall, Michael T. (*b.* 1952) *Lab., Warrington South*, maj. 191

*Hamilton, Rt. Hon. Sir Archibald (*b.* 1941) *C., Epsom and Ewell*, maj. 20,021

*Hamilton, M. Neil (*b.* 1949) *C., Tatton*, maj. 15,860

*Hampson, Dr Keith (*b.* 1943) *C., Leeds North West*, maj. 7,671

*Hanley, Jeremy J. (*b.* 1945) *C., Richmond and Barnes*, maj. 3,869

*Hannam, Sir John (*b.* 1929) *C., Exeter*, maj. 4,045

Hanson, David G. (*b.* 1957) *Lab., Delyn*, maj. 2,039

*Hardy, Peter (*b.* 1931) *Lab., Wentworth*, maj. 22,449

*Hargreaves, Andrew R. (*b.* 1955) *C., Birmingham, Hall Green*, maj. 3,665

*Harman, Ms Harriet (*b.* 1950) *Lab., Peckham*, maj. 12,005

*Harris, David A. (*b.* 1937) *C., St Ives*, maj. 1,645

Harvey, Nicholas B. (*b.* 1961) *LD, Devon North*, maj. 794

*Haselhurst, Alan G. B. (*b.* 1937) *C., Saffron Walden*, maj. 17,424

*Hattersley, Rt. Hon. Roy S. G. (*b.* 1932) *Lab., Birmingham, Sparkbrook,* maj. 13,572

Hawkins, Nicholas J. (*b.* 1957) *C., Blackpool South,* maj. 1,667

Hawksley, P. Warren (*b.* 1943) *C., Halesowen and Stourbridge,* maj. 9,582

*Hayes, Jeremy J. J. (*b.* 1953) *C., Harlow,* maj. 2,940

Heald, Oliver (*b.* 1954) *C., Hertfordshire North,* maj. 16,531

*Heath, Rt. Hon. Sir Edward, KG, MBE (*b.* 1916) *C., Old Bexley and Sidcup,* maj. 15,699

*Heathcoat-Amory, David P. (*b.* 1949) *C., Wells,* maj. 6,649

*Henderson, Douglas J. (*b.* 1949) *Lab., Newcastle upon Tyne North,* maj. 8,946

Hendron, Dr Joseph G. (*b.* 1932) *SDLP, Belfast West,* maj. 589

Hendry, Charles (*b.* 1959) *C., High Peak,* maj. 4,819

Heppell, John B. (*b.* 1948) *Lab., Nottingham East,* maj. 7,680

*Heseltine, Rt. Hon. Michael R. D. (*b.* 1933) *C., Henley,* maj. 18,392

*Hicks, Robert (*b.* 1938) *C., Cornwall South East,* maj. 7,704

*Higgins, Rt. Hon. Sir Terence, KBE (*b.* 1928) *C., Worthing,* maj. 16,533

*Hill, S. James A. (*b.* 1926) *C., Southampton, Test,* maj. 585

Hill, T. Keith (*b.* 1943) *Lab., Streatham,* maj. 2,317

*Hinchliffe, David M. (*b.* 1948) *Lab., Wakefield,* maj. 6,590

Hodge, Ms Margaret E. (*b.* 1944) *Lab., Barking,* maj. 11,414

*Hoey, Ms Catharine (Kate) L. (*b.* 1946) *Lab., Vauxhall,* maj. 10,488

*Hogg, Rt. Hon. Douglas M., QC (*b.* 1945) *C., Grantham,* maj. 19,588

*Hogg, Norman (*b.* 1938) *Lab., Cumbernauld and Kilsyth,* maj. 9,215

*Home Robertson, John D. (*b.* 1948) *Lab., East Lothian,* maj. 10,036

*Hood, James (*b.* 1948) *Lab., Clydesdale,* maj. 10,187

Hoon, Geoffrey W. (*b.* 1953) *Lab., Ashfield,* maj. 12,987

Horam, John R. (*b.* 1939) *C., Orpington,* maj. 12,935

*Hordern, Rt. Hon. Sir Peter (*b.* 1929) *C., Horsham,* maj. 25,072

*Howard, Rt. Hon. Michael, QC (*b.* 1941) *C., Folkestone and Hythe,* maj. 8,910

*Howarth, Alan T., CBE (*b.* 1944) *C., Stratford-upon-Avon,* maj. 22,892

*Howarth, George E. (*b.* 1949) *Lab., Knowsley North,* maj. 22,403

*Howell, Rt. Hon. David A. R. (*b.* 1936) *C., Guildford,* maj. 13,404

*Howell, Sir Ralph (*b.* 1923) *C., Norfolk North,* maj. 12,545

*Howells, Kim S., PH.D. (*b.* 1946) *Lab., Pontypridd,* maj. 19,797

*Hoyle, E. Douglas H. (*b.* 1930) *Lab., Warrington North,* maj. 12,622

Hughes, Kevin M. (*b.* 1952) *Lab., Doncaster North,* maj. 19,813

*Hughes, Robert (*b.* 1932) *Lab., Aberdeen North,* maj. 9,237

*Hughes, Robert G. (*b.* 1951) *C., Harrow West,* maj. 17,897

*Hughes, Royston J. (*b.* 1925) *Lab., Newport East,* maj. 9,899

*Hughes, Simon H. W. (*b.* 1951) *LD, Southwark and Bermondsey,* maj. 9,845

*Hume, John (*b.* 1937) *SDLP, Foyle,* maj. 13,005

*Hunt, Rt. Hon. David J. F., MBE (*b.* 1942) *C., Wirral West,* maj. 11,064

*Hunt, Sir John (*b.* 1929) *C., Ravensbourne,* maj. 19,714

*Hunter, Andrew R. F. (*b.* 1943) *C., Basingstoke,* maj. 21,198

*Hurd, Rt. Hon. Douglas R., CBE (*b.* 1930) *C., Witney,* maj. 22,568

Hutton, John M. P. (*b.* 1955) *Lab., Barrow and Furness,* maj. 3,578

*Illsley, Eric E. (*b.* 1955) *Lab., Barnsley Central,* maj. 19,361

*Ingram, Adam P. (*b.* 1947) *Lab., East Kilbride,* maj. 11,992

*Jack, J. Michael (*b.* 1946) *C., Fylde,* maj. 20,991

Jackson, Ms Glenda, CBE (*b.* 1936) *Lab., Hampstead and Highgate,* maj. 1,440

Jackson, Mrs Helen (*b.* 1939) *Lab., Sheffield, Hillsborough,* maj. 7,068

*Jackson, Robert V. (*b.* 1946) *C., Wantage,* maj. 16,473

Jamieson, David C. (*b.* 1947) *Lab., Plymouth, Devonport,* maj. 7,412

*Janner, Hon. Greville E., QC (*b.* 1928) *Lab., Leicester West,* maj. 3,978

Jenkin, Hon. Bernard (*b.* 1959) *C., Colchester North,* maj. 16,492

*Jessel, Toby F. H. (*b.* 1934) *C., Twickenham,* maj. 5,711

*Johnson Smith, Sir Geoffrey (*b.* 1924) *C., Wealden,* maj. 20,931

*Johnston, Sir Russell (*b.* 1932) *LD, Inverness, Nairn and Lochaber,* maj. 458

*Jones, Gwilym H. (*b.* 1947) *C., Cardiff North,* maj. 2,969

*Jones, Ieuan W. (*b.* 1949) *PC, Ynys Môn,* maj. 1,106

Jones, Jon O. (*b.* 1954) *Lab., Cardiff Central,* maj. 3,465

Jones, Ms Lynne M., PH.D. (*b.* 1951) *Lab., Birmingham, Selly Oak,* maj. 2,060

*Jones, Martyn D. (*b.* 1947) *Lab., Clwyd South West,* maj. 4,941

Jones, Nigel D. (*b.* 1948) *LD, Cheltenham,* maj. 1,668

*Jones, Robert B. (*b.* 1950) *C., Hertfordshire West,* maj. 13,940

*Jones, S. Barry (*b.* 1938) *Lab., Alyn and Deeside,* maj. 7,851

*Jopling, Rt. Hon. T. Michael (*b.* 1930) *C., Westmorland and Lonsdale,* maj. 16,436

Jowell, Ms Tessa (*b.* 1947) *Lab., Dulwich,* maj. 2,056

*Kaufman, Rt. Hon. Gerald B. (*b.* 1930) *Lab., Manchester, Gorton,* maj. 16,279

Keen, Alan (*b.* 1937) *Lab., Feltham and Heston,* maj. 1,995

*Kellett-Bowman, Dame Elaine, DBE (*b.* 1924) *C., Lancaster,* maj. 2,953

*Kennedy, Charles P. (*b.* 1959) *LD, Ross, Cromarty and Skye,* maj. 7,630

Kennedy, Mrs Jane (*b.* 1958) *Lab., Liverpool, Broadgreen,* maj. 7,027

*Key, S. Robert (*b.* 1945) *C., Salisbury,* maj. 8,973

Khabra, Piara C. (*b.* 1924) *Lab., Ealing, Southall,* maj. 6,866

*Kilfedder, Sir James (*b.* 1928) *UPUP, Down North,* maj. 4,934

*Kilfoyle, Peter (*b.* 1946) *Lab., Liverpool, Walton,* maj. 28,299

*King, Rt. Hon. Thomas J., CH (*b.* 1933) *C., Bridgwater,* maj. 9,716

*Kinnock, Rt. Hon. Neil G. (*b.* 1942) *Lab., Islwyn,* maj. 24,728

*Kirkhope, Timothy J. R. (*b.* 1945) *C., Leeds North East,* maj. 4,244

*Kirkwood, Archibald J. (*b.* 1946) *LD, Roxburgh and Berwickshire,* maj. 4,257

*Knapman, Roger M. (*b.* 1944) *C., Stroud,* maj. 13,405

Knight, Mrs Angela A. (*b.* 1950) *C., Erewash,* maj. 5,703

*Knight, Gregory (*b.* 1949) *C., Derby North,* maj. 4,453

*Knight, Dame Jill, DBE (*b.* 1923) *C., Birmingham, Edgbaston,* maj. 4,307

*Knox, Sir David (*b.* 1933) *C., Staffordshire Moorlands,* maj. 7,410

Kynoch, George A. B. (*b.* 1946) *C., Kincardine and Deeside,* maj. 4,495

Lait, Ms Jacqui (*b.* 1947) *C., Hastings and Rye,* maj. 6,634

*Lamont, Rt. Hon. Norman S. H. (*b.* 1942) *C., Kingston upon Thames,* maj. 10,153

*Lang, Rt. Hon. Ian B. (b. 1940) C., Galloway and Upper Nithsdale, maj. 2,468

*Lawrence, Sir Ivan, QC (b. 1936) C., Burton, maj. 5,996

Legg, Barry (b. 1949) C., Milton Keynes South West, maj. 4,687

*Leigh, Edward J. E. (b. 1950) C., Gainsborough and Horncastle, maj. 16,245

*Lennox-Boyd, Hon. Mark A. (b. 1943) C., Morecambe and Lunesdale, maj. 11,509

*Lester, James T. (b. 1932) C., Broxtowe, maj. 9,891

*Lestor, Miss Joan (b. 1931) Lab., Eccles, maj. 13,226

*Lewis, Terence (b. 1935) Lab., Worsley, maj. 10,012

Liddell, Mrs Helen (b. 1950) Lab., Monklands East, maj. 1,640

Lidington, David R., PH.D. (b. 1956) C., Aylesbury, maj. 18,860

*Lightbown, David L. (b. 1932) C., Staffordshire South East, maj. 7,192

*Lilley, Rt. Hon. Peter B. (b. 1943) C., St Albans, maj. 16,404

*Litherland, Robert K. (b. 1930) Lab., Manchester Central, maj. 18,037

*Livingstone, Ken (b. 1945) Lab., Brent East, maj. 5,971

*Lloyd, Anthony J. (b. 1950) Lab., Stretford, maj. 11,137

*Lloyd, Rt. Hon. Peter R. C. (b. 1937) C., Fareham, maj. 24,141

Llwyd, Elfyn (b. 1951) PC, Meirionnydd Nant Conwy, maj. 4,613

*Lofthouse, Geoffrey (b. 1925) Lab., Pontefract and Castleford, maj. 23,495

*Lord, Michael N. (b. 1938) C., Suffolk Central, maj. 16,031

*Loyden, Edward (b. 1923) Lab., Liverpool, Garston, maj. 12,279

Luff, Peter J. (b. 1955) C., Worcester, maj. 6,152

*Lyell, Rt. Hon. Sir Nicholas, QC (b. 1938) C., Bedfordshire Mid, maj. 25,138

Lynne, Ms Elizabeth (b. 1948) LD, Rochdale, maj. 1,839

*McAllion, John (b. 1948) Lab., Dundee East, maj. 4,564

*McAvoy, Thomas M. (b. 1943) Lab., Glasgow, Rutherglen, maj. 15,270

*McCartney, Ian (b. 1951) Lab., Makerfield, maj. 18,118

*McCrea, Revd Dr R. T. William (b. 1948) DUP, Ulster Mid, maj. 6,187

*MacDonald, Calum A. (b. 1956) Lab., Western Isles, maj. 1,703

*McFall, John (b. 1944) Lab., Dumbarton, maj. 6,129

*McGrady, Edward K. (b. 1935) SDLP, Down South, maj. 6,342

*MacGregor, Rt. Hon. John R. R., OBE (b. 1937) C., Norfolk South, maj. 17,565

*Mackay, Andrew J. (b. 1949) C., Berkshire East, maj. 28,680

*McKelvey, William (b. 1934) Lab., Kilmarnock and Loudoun, maj. 6,979

MacKinlay, Andrew S. (b. 1949) Lab., Thurrock, maj. 1,172

*Maclean, David J. (b. 1953) C., Penrith and the Border, maj. 18,449

*McLeish, Henry B. (b. 1948) Lab., Fife Central, maj. 10,578

*Maclennan, Robert A. R. (b. 1936) LD, Caithness and Sutherland, maj. 5,365

*McLoughlin, Patrick A. (b. 1957) C., Derbyshire West, maj. 18,769

*McMaster, Gordon J. (b. 1960) Lab., Paisley South, maj. 9,549

*McNair-Wilson, Sir Patrick (b. 1929) C., New Forest, maj. 20,405

*McNamara, J. Kevin (b. 1934) Lab., Hull North, maj. 15,384

MacShane, Denis (b. 1948) Lab., Rotherham, maj. 6,954

*McWilliam, John D. (b. 1941) Lab., Blaydon, maj. 13,343

*Madden, Maxwell F. (b. 1941) Lab., Bradford West, maj. 9,502

Maddock, Mrs Diana (b. 1945) LD, Christchurch, maj. 16,427

*Madel, Sir David (b. 1938) C., Bedfordshire South West, maj. 21,273

*Maginnis, Kenneth (b. 1938) UUP, Fermanagh and South Tyrone, maj. 14,113

*Mahon, Ms Alice (b. 1937) Lab., Halifax, maj. 478

Maitland, Lady Olga (b. 1944) C., Sutton and Cheam, maj. 10,756

*Major, Rt. Hon. John (b. 1943) C., Huntingdon, maj. 36,230

*Mallon, Seamus (b. 1936) SDLP, Newry and Armagh, maj. 7,091

Malone, P. Gerald (b. 1950) C., Winchester, maj. 8,121

Mandelson, Peter B. (b. 1953) Lab., Hartlepool, maj. 8,782

*Mans, Keith D. R. (b. 1946) C., Wyre, maj. 11,664

*Marek, John, PH.D. (b. 1940) Lab., Wrexham, maj. 6,716

*Marland, Paul (b. 1940) C., Gloucestershire West, maj. 4,958

*Marlow, Antony R. (b. 1940) C., Northampton North, maj. 3,908

*Marshall, David (b. 1941) Lab., Glasgow, Shettleston, maj. 14,834

*Marshall, James (b. 1941) Lab., Leicester South, maj. 9,440

*Marshall, John L. (b. 1940) C., Hendon South, maj. 12,047

*Marshall, Sir Michael (b. 1930) C., Arundel, maj. 19,863

*Martin, David J. P. (b. 1945) C., Portsmouth South, maj. 242

*Martin, Michael J. (b. 1945) Lab., Glasgow, Springburn, maj. 14,506

*Martlew, Eric A. (b. 1949) Lab., Carlisle, maj. 3,108

*Mates, Michael J. (b. 1934) C., Hampshire East, maj. 29,165

*Mawhinney, Rt. Hon. Brian S., PH.D. (b. 1940) C., Peterborough, maj. 5,376

*Maxton, John A. (b. 1936) Lab., Glasgow, Cathcart, maj. 8,001

*Mayhew, Rt. Hon. Sir Patrick, QC (b. 1929) C., Tunbridge Wells, maj. 17,132

*Meacher, Michael H. (b. 1939) Lab., Oldham West, maj. 8,333

*Meale, J. Alan (b. 1949) Lab., Mansfield, maj. 11,724

*Mellor, Rt. Hon. David J., QC (b. 1949) C., Putney, maj. 7,526

Merchant, Piers R. G. (b. 1951) C., Beckenham, maj. 15,285

*Michael, Alun E. (b. 1943) Lab., Cardiff South and Penarth, maj. 10,425

*Michie, Mrs J. Ray (b. 1934) LD, Argyll and Bute, maj. 2,622

*Michie, William (b. 1935) Lab., Sheffield, Heeley, maj. 14,954

Milburn, Alan (b. 1958) Lab., Darlington, maj. 2,798

Miller, Andrew (b. 1949) Lab., Ellesmere Port and Neston, maj. 1,989

*Mills, Iain C. (b. 1940) C., Meriden, maj. 14,699

*Mitchell, Andrew J. B. (b. 1956) C., Gedling, maj. 10,637

*Mitchell, Austin V. (b. 1934) Lab., Great Grimsby, maj. 7,504

*Mitchell, Sir David (b. 1928) C., Hampshire North West, maj. 17,848

*Moate, Sir Roger (b. 1938) C., Faversham, maj. 16,351

*Molyneaux, Rt. Hon. James H. (b. 1920) UUP, Lagan Valley, maj. 23,565

*Monro, Sir Hector, AE (b. 1922) C., Dumfries, maj. 6,415

*Montgomery, Sir Fergus (b. 1927) C., Altrincham and Sale, maj. 16,791

*Moonie, Dr Lewis G. (b. 1947) Lab., Kirkcaldy, maj. 9,126

*Morgan, H. Rhodri (b. 1939) Lab., Cardiff West, maj. 9,291

*Morley, Elliot A. (b. 1952) Lab., Glanford and Scunthorpe, maj. 8,412

*Morris, Rt. Hon. Alfred, AO (b. 1928) Lab., Manchester, Wythenshawe, maj. 11,996

Morris, Ms Estelle (b. 1952) Lab., Birmingham, Yardley, maj. 162

*Morris, Rt. Hon. John, QC (*b.* 1931) *Lab., Aberavon,* maj. 21,310

*Morris, Rt. Hon. Michael W. L. (*b.* 1936) *C., Northampton South,* maj. 16,973

*Moss, Malcolm D. (*b.* 1943) *C., Cambridgeshire North East,* maj. 15,093

*Mowlam, Dr Marjorie (*b.* 1949) *Lab., Redcar,* maj. 11,577

Mudie, George (*b.* 1945) *Lab., Leeds East,* maj. 12,697

*Mullin, Christopher J. (*b.* 1947) *Lab., Sunderland South,* maj. 14,501

*Murphy, Paul P. (*b.* 1948) *Lab., Torfaen,* maj. 20,754

*Needham, Rt. Hon. Richard F. (The Earl of Kilmorey) (*b.* 1942) *C., Wiltshire North,* maj. 16,388

*Nelson, R. Anthony (*b.* 1948) *C., Chichester,* maj. 20,887

*Neubert, Sir Michael (*b.* 1933) *C., Romford,* maj. 11,420

*Newton, Rt. Hon. Antony H., OBE (*b.* 1937) *C., Braintree,* maj. 17,494

*Nicholls, Patrick C. M. (*b.* 1948) *C., Teignbridge,* maj. 8,856

*Nicholson, David J. (*b.* 1944) *C., Taunton,* maj. 3,336

*Nicholson, Miss Emma H. (*b.* 1941) *C., Devon West and Torridge,* maj. 3,614

*Norris, Steven J. (*b.* 1945) *C., Epping Forest,* maj. 20,188

*Oakes, Rt. Hon. Gordon J. (*b.* 1931) *Lab., Halton,* maj. 18,204

O'Brien, Michael (*b.* 1954) *Lab., Warwickshire North,* maj. 1,454

*O'Brien, William (*b.* 1929) *Lab., Normanton,* maj. 8,950

*O'Hara, Edward (*b.* 1937) *Lab., Knowsley South,* maj. 22,011

Olner, William J. (*b.* 1942) *Lab., Nuneaton,* maj. 1,631

*O'Neill, Martin J. (*b.* 1945) *Lab., Clackmannan,* maj. 8,503

*Onslow, Rt. Hon. Sir Cranley, KCMG (*b.* 1926) *C., Woking,* maj. 19,842

*Oppenheim, Hon. Phillip A. C. L. (*b.* 1956) *C., Amber Valley,* maj. 712

*Orme, Rt. Hon. Stanley (*b.* 1923) *Lab., Salford East,* maj. 11,235

Ottaway, Richard G. J. (*b.* 1945) *C., Croydon South,* maj. 20,425

*Page, Richard L. (*b.* 1941) *C., Hertfordshire South West,* maj. 20,107

*Paice, James E. T. (*b.* 1949) *C., Cambridgeshire South East,* maj. 23,810

*Paisley, Revd Ian R. K. (*b.* 1926) *DUP, Antrim North,* maj. 14,936

*Parry, Robert (*b.* 1933) *Lab., Liverpool, Riverside,* maj. 17,437

*Patchett, Terry (*b.* 1940) *Lab., Barnsley East,* maj. 24,777

*Patnick, C. Irvine, OBE (*b.* 1929) *C., Sheffield, Hallam,* maj. 6,741

*Patten, Rt. Hon. John H. C. (*b.* 1945) *C., Oxford West and Abingdon,* maj. 3,539

*Pattie, Rt. Hon. Sir Geoffrey (*b.* 1936) *C., Chertsey and Walton,* maj. 22,819

*Pawsey, James F. (*b.* 1933) *C., Rugby and Kenilworth,* maj. 13,247

*Peacock, Mrs Elizabeth J. (*b.* 1937) *C., Batley and Spen,* maj. 1,408

*Pendry, Thomas (*b.* 1934) *Lab., Stalybridge and Hyde,* maj. 8,831

Pickles, Eric J. (*b.* 1952) *C., Brentwood and Ongar,* maj. 15,145

Pickthall, Colin (*b.* 1944) *Lab., Lancashire West,* maj. 2,077

*Pike, Peter L. (*b.* 1937) *Lab., Burnley,* maj. 11,491

Pope, Gregory J. (*b.* 1960) *Lab., Hyndburn,* maj. 1,960

*Porter, David J. (*b.* 1948) *C., Waveney,* maj. 6,702

*Porter, G. B. (Barry) (*b.* 1939) *C., Wirral South,* maj. 8,183

*Portillo, Rt. Hon. Michael D. X. (*b.* 1953) *C., Enfield, Southgate,* maj. 15,563

*Powell, Raymond (*b.* 1928) *Lab., Ogmore,* maj. 23,827

*Powell, William R. (*b.* 1948) *C., Corby,* maj. 342

Prentice, Mrs Bridget (*b.* 1952) *Lab., Lewisham East,* maj. 1,095

Prentice, Gordon (*b.* 1951) *Lab., Pendle,* maj. 2,113

*Prescott, Rt. Hon. John L. (*b.* 1938) *Lab., Hull East,* maj. 18,719

*Primarolo, Ms Dawn (*b.* 1954) *Lab., Bristol South,* maj. 8,919

Purchase, Kenneth (*b.* 1939) *Lab., Wolverhampton North East,* maj. 3,939

*Quin, Miss Joyce G. (*b.* 1944) *Lab., Gateshead East,* maj. 18,530

*Radice, Giles H. (*b.* 1936) *Lab., Durham North,* maj. 19,637

*Randall, Stuart J. (*b.* 1938) *Lab., Hull West,* maj. 10,585

*Rathbone, J. R. (Tim) (*b.* 1933) *C., Lewes,* maj. 12,175

Raynsford, W. R. N. (Nick) (*b.* 1945) *Lab., Greenwich,* maj. 1,357

*Redmond, Martin (*b.* 1937) *Lab., Don Valley,* maj. 13,534

*Redwood, Rt. Hon. John A. (*b.* 1951) *C., Wokingham,* maj. 25,709

*Reid, Dr John (*b.* 1947) *Lab., Motherwell North,* maj. 18,910

Rendel, David D. (*b.* 1949) *LD, Newbury,* maj. 22,055

*Renton, Rt. Hon. R. Timothy (*b.* 1932) *C., Sussex Mid,* maj. 20,528

Richards, Roderick (*b.* 1947) *C., Clwyd North West,* maj. 6,050

*Riddick, Graham E. G. (*b.* 1955) *C., Colne Valley,* maj. 7,225

*Rifkind, Rt. Hon. Malcolm L., QC (*b.* 1946) *C., Edinburgh, Pentlands,* maj. 4,290

Robathan, Andrew R. G. (*b.* 1951) *C., Blaby,* maj. 25,347

*Roberts, Rt. Hon. Sir Wyn (*b.* 1930) *C., Conwy,* maj. 995

*Robertson, George I. M. (*b.* 1946) *Lab., Hamilton,* maj. 16,603

Robertson, Raymond S. (*b.* 1959) *C., Aberdeen South,* maj. 1,517

*Robinson, Geoffrey (*b.* 1938) *Lab., Coventry North West,* maj. 6,432

Robinson, Mark N. F. (*b.* 1946) *C., Somerton and Frome,* maj. 4,341

*Robinson, Peter D. (*b.* 1948) *DUP, Belfast East,* maj. 7,787

Roche, Mrs Barbara M. R. (*b.* 1954) *Lab., Hornsey and Wood Green,* maj. 5,177

*Roe, Mrs Marion A. (*b.* 1936) *C., Broxbourne,* maj. 23,970

*Rogers, Allan R. (*b.* 1932) *Lab., Rhondda,* maj. 28,816

*Rooker, Jeffrey W. (*b.* 1941) *Lab., Birmingham, Perry Barr,* maj. 8,590

*Rooney, Terence H. (*b.* 1950) *Lab., Bradford North,* maj. 7,664

*Ross, Ernest (*b.* 1942) *Lab., Dundee West,* maj. 10,604

*Ross, William (*b.* 1936) *UUP, Londonderry East,* maj. 18,527

*Rowe, Andrew (*b.* 1935) *C., Kent Mid,* maj. 19,649

*Rowlands, Edward (*b.* 1940) *Lab., Merthyr Tydfil and Rhymney,* maj. 26,713

*Ruddock, Mrs Joan M. (*b.* 1943) *Lab., Lewisham, Deptford,* maj. 12,238

*Rumbold, Rt. Hon. Dame Angela, DBE (*b.* 1932) *C., Mitcham and Morden,* maj. 1,734

*Ryder, Rt. Hon. Richard A., OBE (*b.* 1949) *C., Norfolk Mid,* maj. 18,948

*Sackville, Hon. Thomas G. (*b.* 1950) *C., Bolton West,* maj. 1,079

*Sainsbury, Rt. Hon. Timothy A. D. (*b.* 1932) *C., Hove,* maj. 12,268

*Salmond, Alexander E. A. (*b.* 1954) *SNP, Banff and Buchan,* maj. 4,108

*Scott, Rt. Hon. Nicholas P., MBE (*b.* 1933) *C., Chelsea,* maj. 12,789

*Sedgemore, Brian C. J. (*b.* 1937) *Lab., Hackney South and Shoreditch,* maj. 9,016

*Shaw, David L. (*b.* 1950) *C., Dover,* maj. 833

*Shaw, Sir Giles (*b.* 1931) *C., Pudsey,* maj. 8,972

*Sheerman, Barry J. (*b.* 1940) *Lab., Huddersfield,* maj. 7,258

*Sheldon, Rt. Hon. Robert E. (*b.* 1923) *Lab., Ashton-under-Lyne,* maj. 10,935

*Shephard, Rt. Hon. Gillian P. (*b.* 1940) *C., Norfolk South West,* maj. 16,931

*Shepherd, Colin (*b.* 1938) *C., Hereford,* maj. 3,413

*Shepherd, Richard C. S. (*b.* 1942) *C., Aldridge-Brownhills,* maj. 11,024

*Shersby, J. Michael (*b.* 1933) *C., Uxbridge,* maj. 13,179

*Shore, Rt. Hon. Peter D. (*b.* 1924) *Lab., Bethnal Green and Stepney,* maj. 12,230

*Short, Ms Clare (*b.* 1946) *Lab., Birmingham, Ladywood,* maj. 15,283

Simpson, Alan (*b.* 1948) *Lab., Nottingham South,* maj. 3,181

*Sims, Roger E. (*b.* 1930) *C., Chislehurst,* maj. 15,276

*Skeet, Sir Trevor (*b.* 1918) *C., Bedfordshire North,* maj. 11,618

*Skinner, Dennis E. (*b.* 1932) *Lab., Bolsover,* maj. 20,660

*Smith, Andrew D. (*b.* 1951) *Lab., Oxford East,* maj. 7,538

*Smith, Christopher R., Ph.D. (*b.* 1951) *Lab., Islington South and Finsbury,* maj. 10,652

*Smith, Sir Dudley (*b.* 1926) *C., Warwick and Leamington,* maj. 8,935

Smith, Llewellyn T. (*b.* 1944) *Lab., Blaenau Gwent,* maj. 30,067

*Smith, Timothy J. (*b.* 1947) *C., Beaconsfield,* maj. 23,597

*Smyth, Revd W. Martin (*b.* 1931) *UUP, Belfast South,* maj. 10,070

*Snape, Peter C. (*b.* 1942) *Lab., West Bromwich East,* maj. 2,813

*Soames, Hon. A. Nicholas W. (*b.* 1948) *C., Crawley,* maj. 7,765

*Soley, Clive S. (*b.* 1939) *Lab., Hammersmith,* maj. 4,754

*Spearing, Nigel J. (*b.* 1930) *Lab., Newham South,* maj. 2,502

*Speed, Sir Keith, RD (*b.* 1934) *C., Ashford,* maj. 17,359

Spellar, John F. (*b.* 1947) *Lab., Warley West,* maj. 5,472

Spencer, Sir Derek, QC (*b.* 1936) *C., Brighton, Pavilion,* maj. 3,675

*Spicer, Sir James (*b.* 1925) *C., Dorset West,* maj. 8,010

*Spicer, W. Michael H. (*b.* 1943) *C., Worcestershire South,* maj. 16,151

Spink, Dr Robert M. (*b.* 1948) *C., Castle Point,* maj. 16,830

Spring, Richard J. G. (*b.* 1946) *C., Bury St Edmunds,* maj. 18,787

Sproat, Iain M. (*b.* 1938) *C., Harwich,* maj. 17,159

Squire, Ms Rachel (*b.* 1954) *Lab., Dunfermline West,* maj. 7,484

*Squire, Robin C. (*b.* 1944) *C., Hornchurch,* maj. 9,165

*Stanley, Rt. Hon. Sir John (*b.* 1942) *C., Tonbridge and Malling,* maj. 21,558

*Steel, Rt. Hon. Sir David, KBE (*b.* 1938) *LD, Tweeddale, Ettrick and Lauderdale,* maj. 2,520

*Steen, Anthony D. (*b.* 1939) *C., South Hams,* maj. 13,711

*Steinberg, Gerald N. (*b.* 1945) *Lab., City of Durham,* maj. 15,058

Stephen, B. Michael L. (*b.* 1942) *C., Shoreham,* maj. 14,286

*Stern, Michael C. (*b.* 1942) *C., Bristol North West,* maj. 45

Stevenson, George W. (*b.* 1938) *Lab., Stoke-on-Trent South,* maj. 6,909

*Stewart, J. Allan (*b.* 1942) *C., Eastwood,* maj. 11,688

*Stott, Roger, CBE (*b.* 1943) *Lab., Wigan,* maj. 21,842

*Strang, Gavin S., Ph.D. (*b.* 1943) *Lab., Edinburgh East,* maj. 7,211

*Straw, J. W. (Jack) (*b.* 1946) *Lab., Blackburn,* maj. 6,027

Streeter, Gary (*b.* 1955) *C., Plymouth, Sutton,* maj. 11,950

*Sumberg, David A. G. (*b.* 1941) *C., Bury South,* maj. 788

Sutcliffe, Gerard (*b.* 1953) *Lab., Bradford South,* maj. 9,664

Sweeney, Walter E. (*b.* 1949) *C., Vale of Glamorgan,* maj. 19

Sykes, John D. (*b.* 1956) *C., Scarborough,* maj. 11,734

*Tapsell, Sir Peter (*b.* 1930) *C., Lindsey East,* maj. 11,846

*Taylor, Sir Edward (Teddy) (*b.* 1937) *C., Southend East,* maj. 13,111

*Taylor, Ian C., MBE (*b.* 1945) *C., Esher,* maj. 20,371

*Taylor, Rt. Hon. John D. (*b.* 1937) *UUP, Strangford,* maj. 8,911

*Taylor, John M. (*b.* 1941) *C., Solihull,* maj. 25,146

*Taylor, Matthew O. J. (*b.* 1963) *LD, Truro,* maj. 7,570

*Taylor, Mrs W. Ann (*b.* 1947) *Lab., Dewsbury,* maj. 634

*Temple-Morris, Peter (*b.* 1938) *C., Leominster,* maj. 16,680

Thomason, K. Roy, OBE (*b.* 1944) *C., Bromsgrove,* maj. 13,702

*Thompson, Sir Donald (*b.* 1931) *C., Calder Valley,* maj. 4,878

*Thompson, H. Patrick (*b.* 1935) *C., Norwich North,* maj. 266

*Thompson, John (*b.* 1928) *Lab., Wansbeck,* maj. 18,174

*Thornton, Sir Malcolm (*b.* 1939) *C., Crosby,* maj. 14,806

*Thurnham, Peter G. (*b.* 1938) *C., Bolton North East,* maj. 185

Timms, Stephen C. (*b.* 1955) *Lab., Newham North East,* maj. 11,818

Tipping, S. Paddy (*b.* 1949) *Lab., Sherwood,* maj. 2,910

*Townend, John E. (*b.* 1934) *C., Bridlington,* maj. 16,358

*Townsend, Cyril D. (*b.* 1937) *C., Bexleyheath,* maj. 14,086

*Tracey, Richard P. (*b.* 1943) *C., Surbiton,* maj. 9,639

*Tredinnick, David A. S. (*b.* 1950) *C., Bosworth,* maj. 19,094

Trend, Hon. Michael St J. (*b.* 1952) *C., Windsor and Maidenhead,* maj. 12,928

*Trimble, W. David (*b.* 1944) *UUP, Upper Bann,* maj. 16,163

*Trotter, Neville G. (*b.* 1932) *C., Tynemouth,* maj. 597

*Turner, Dennis (*b.* 1942) *Lab., Wolverhampton South East,* maj. 10,240

*Twinn, Dr Ian D. (*b.* 1950) *C., Edmonton,* maj. 593

Tyler, Paul A., CBE (*b.* 1941) *LD, Cornwall North,* maj. 1,921

*Vaughan, Sir Gerard (*b.* 1923) *C., Reading East,* maj. 14,555

*Vaz, N. Keith A. S. (*b.* 1956) *Lab., Leicester East,* maj. 11,316

*Viggers, Peter J. (*b.* 1938) *C., Gosport,* maj. 16,318

*Waldegrave, Rt. Hon. William A. (*b.* 1946) *C., Bristol West,* maj. 6,071

*Walden, George G. H., CMG (*b.* 1939) *C., Buckingham,* maj. 19,791

*Walker, A. Cecil (*b.* 1924) *UUP, Belfast North,* maj. 9,625

*Walker, Rt. Hon. Sir Harold (*b.* 1927) *Lab., Doncaster Central,* maj. 10,682

*Walker, William C. (*b.* 1929) *C., Tayside North,* maj. 3,995

*Wallace, James R. (*b.* 1954) *LD, Orkney and Shetland,* maj. 5,033

*Waller, Gary P. A. (*b.* 1945) *C., Keighley,* maj. 3,596

*Walley, Ms Joan L. (*b.* 1949) *Lab., Stoke-on-Trent North,* maj. 14,777

*Ward, John D., CBE (*b.* 1925) *C., Poole,* maj. 12,831

*Wardell, Gareth L. (*b.* 1944) *Lab., Gower,* maj. 7,018

*Wardle, Charles F. (*b.* 1939) *C., Bexhill and Battle,* maj. 16,307

*Wareing, Robert N. (*b.* 1930) *Lab., Liverpool, West Derby,* maj. 20,425

Waterson, Nigel C. (*b.* 1950) *C., Eastbourne,* maj. 5,481

*Watson, Michael G. (*b.* 1949) *Lab., Glasgow Central,* maj. 11,019

*Watts, John A. (*b.* 1947) *C., Slough,* maj. 514

*Wells, Bowen (*b.* 1935) *C., Hertford and Stortford,* maj. 20,210

*Welsh, Andrew P. (*b.* 1944) *SNP, Angus East,* maj. 954

*Wheeler, Rt. Hon. Sir John (*b.* 1940) *C., Westminster North,* maj. 3,733

*Whitney, Raymond W., OBE (*b.* 1930) *C., Wycombe,* maj. 17,076

Whittingdale, John F. L., OBE (*b.* 1959) *C., Colchester South and Maldon,* maj. 21,821

Wicks, Malcolm H. (*b.* 1947) *Lab., Croydon North West,* maj. 1,526

*Widdecombe, Miss Ann N. (*b.* 1947) *C., Maidstone,* maj. 16,286

*Wiggin, Sir Jerry, TD (*b.* 1937) *C., Weston-super-Mare,* maj. 5,342

*Wigley, Dafydd (*b.* 1943) *PC, Caernarfon,* maj. 14,476

*Wilkinson, John A. D. (*b.* 1940) *C., Ruislip-Northwood,* maj. 19,791

Willetts, David L. (*b.* 1956) *C., Havant,* maj. 17,584

*Williams, Rt. Hon. Alan J. (*b.* 1930) *Lab., Swansea West,* maj. 9,478

*Williams, Dr Alan W. (*b.* 1945) *Lab., Carmarthen,* maj. 2,922

*Wilshire, David (*b.* 1943) *C., Spelthorne,* maj. 19,843

*Wilson, Brian D. H. (*b.* 1948) *Lab., Cunninghame North,* maj. 2,939

*Winnick, David J. (*b.* 1933) *Lab., Walsall North,* maj. 3,824

*Winterton, Mrs J. Ann (*b.* 1941) *C., Congleton,* maj. 11,120

*Winterton, Nicholas R. (*b.* 1938) *C., Macclesfield,* maj. 22,767

*Wise, Mrs Audrey (*b.* 1935) *Lab., Preston,* maj. 12,175

*Wolfson, G. Mark (*b.* 1934) *C., Sevenoaks,* maj. 19,154

*Wood, Timothy J. R. (*b.* 1940) *C., Stevenage,* maj. 4,888

*Worthington, Anthony (*b.* 1941) *Lab., Clydebank and Milngavie,* maj. 12,430

*Wray, James (*b.* 1938) *Lab., Glasgow, Provan,* maj. 10,703

Wright, Anthony W., D.Phil. (*b.* 1948) *Lab., Cannock and Burntwood,* maj. 1,506

*Yeo, Timothy S. K. (*b.* 1945) *C., Suffolk South,* maj. 17,289

*Young, David W. (*b.* 1930) *Lab., Bolton South East,* maj. 12,691

*Young, Rt. Hon. Sir George, Bt. (*b.* 1941) *C., Ealing, Acton,* maj. 7,007

## MEMBERS WITH SMALL MAJORITIES

The following MPs were returned in April 1992 with majorities of fewer than 1,000 votes

*Denotes membership of last Parliament

| | *Maj.* | | *Maj.* |
|---|---|---|---|
| Walter Sweeney, *C., Vale of Glamorgan* | 19 | Anne Campbell, *Lab., Cambridge* | 580 |
| *Michael Stern, *C., Bristol North West* | 45 | *James Hill, *C., Southampton Test* | 585 |
| *Terry Dicks, *C., Hayes and Harlington* | 53 | Dr Joe Hendron, *SDLP, Belfast West* | 589 |
| Phil Gallie, *C., Ayr* | 85 | *Dr Ian Twinn, *C., Edmonton* | 593 |
| Janet Anderson, *Lab., Rossendale and Darwen* | 120 | Neville Trotter, *C., Tynemouth* | 597 |
| Jonathan Evans, *C., Brecon and Radnor* | 130 | Richard Burden, *Lab., Birmingham Northfield* | 630 |
| Estelle Morris, *Lab., Birmingham Yardley* | 162 | *Ann Taylor, *Lab., Dewsbury* | 634 |
| *Peter Thurnham, *C., Bolton North East* | 185 | *Michael Forsyth, *C., Stirling* | 703 |
| Mike Hall, *Lab., Warrington South* | 191 | *Phillip Oppenheim, *C., Amber Valley* | 712 |
| *David Martin, *C., Portsmouth South* | 242 | Nick Ainger, *Lab., Pembroke* | 755 |
| Jamie Cann, *Lab., Ipswich* | 265 | *David Sumberg, *C., Bury South* | 788 |
| *Patrick Thompson, *C., Norwich North* | 266 | Nick Harvey, *LD, Devon North* | 794 |
| *Malcolm Bruce, *LD, Gordon* | 274 | *Graham Bright, *C., Luton South* | 799 |
| *William Powell, *C., Corby* | 342 | *David Shaw, *C., Dover* | 833 |
| Mike Gapes, *Lab., Ilford South* | 402 | *Lord James Douglas-Hamilton, *C., Edinburgh West* | 879 |
| *Sir Russell Johnston, *LD, Inverness, Nairn and Lochaber* | 458 | *Sir Tom Arnold, *C., Hazel Grove* | 929 |
| *Alice Mahon, *Lab., Halifax* | 478 | *Andrew Welsh, *SNP, Angus East* | 954 |
| *John Watts, *C., Slough* | 514 | *David Ashby, *C., Leicestershire North West* | 979 |
| John Denham, *Lab., Southampton Itchen* | 551 | *Sir Wyn Roberts, *C., Conwy* | 995 |

BY-ELECTIONS SINCE THE 1992 GENERAL ELECTION

|  |  |
|---|---:|
| | *Maj.* |
| NEWBURY | |
| (6 May 1993) | |
| *E*.81,081   *T*.71.25% | |
| D. Rendel, *LD* | 37,590 |
| J. Davidson, *C.* | 15,535 |
| S. Billcliffe, *Lab.* | 1,151 |
| A. Sked, *Anti-Maastricht Anti Fed.* | 601 |
| A. Bannon, *Conservative Candidate* | 561 |
| S. Martin, *Commoners Party Movement* | 435 |
| 'Lord' Sutch, *Loony* | 432 |
| J. Wallis, *Green* | 341 |
| R. Marlar, *Referendum* | 338 |
| J. Browne, *Conservative Rebel* | 267 |
| Ms L. St Clair, *Corrective* | 170 |
| W. Board, *Maastricht Referendum for Britain* | 84 |
| M. Grenville, *NLP* | 60 |
| J. Day. *People and Pensioners* | 49 |
| C. Palmer, *21st Century* | 40 |
| M. Grbin, *Defence of Children's Humanity Bosnia* | 33 |
| A. Page, *SDP* | 33 |
| Ms A. Murphy, *Comm. GB* | 32 |
| M. Stone, *Give Royal Billions to Schools* | 21 |
| *LD majority* | 22,055 |
| CHRISTCHURCH | |
| (29 July 1993) | |
| *E*.71,868   *T*.74.2% | |
| Mrs D. Maddock, *LD* | 33,164 |
| R. Hayward, *C.* | 16,737 |
| N. Lickley, *Lab.* | 1,453 |
| A. Sked, *Anti-Maastricht Anti Fed.* | 878 |
| 'Lord' Sutch, *Monster Raving Loony Rock-Roll* | 404 |
| A. Bannon, *Conservative Candidate* | 357 |
| P. Newman, *Sack Graham Taylor* | 80 |
| Ms T. B. Jackson, *Buy Daily Sport* | 67 |
| P. Hollyman, *Save NHS* | 60 |
| J. Crockard, *Highlander IV Wednesday Promotion Night* | 48 |
| M. Griffiths, *NLP* | 45 |
| M. Belcher, *Ian for King* | 23 |
| K. Fitzhugh, *Alfred Chicken* | 18 |
| J. Walley, *Rainbow Alliance Coalition* | 16 |
| *LD majority* | 16,427 |
| ROTHERHAM | |
| (5 May 1994) | |
| *E*.60,937   *T*.44.14% | |
| D. MacShane, *Lab.* | 14,912 |
| D. Wildgoose, *LD* | 7,958 |
| N. Gibb, *C.* | 2,649 |
| 'Lord' D. Sutch, *Loony* | 1,114 |
| K. Laycock, *NLP* | 173 |
| *Lab. majority* | 6,954 |
| BARKING | |
| (9 June 1994) | |
| *E*.50,454   *T*.38.6% | |
| Ms M. Hodge, *Lab.* | 13,704 |
| G. White, *LD* | 2,290 |
| Ms T. May, *C.* | 1,976 |

|  |  |
|---|---:|
| | *Maj.* |
| G. Needs, *NF* | 551 |
| G. Batten, *UK Independence* | 406 |
| Ms H. Butensky, *NLP* | 90 |
| *Lab. majority* | 11,414 |
| BRADFORD SOUTH | |
| (9 June 1994) | |
| *E*.69,914   *T*.44.0% | |
| G. Sutcliffe, *Lab.* | 17,014 |
| Ms H. Wright, *LD* | 7,350 |
| R. Farley, *C.* | 5,475 |
| 'Lord' D. Sutch, *Loony* | 727 |
| K. Laycock, *NLP* | 187 |
| *Lab. majority* | 9,664 |
| DAGENHAM | |
| (9 June 1994) | |
| *E*.59,645   *T*.37.2% | |
| Ms J. Church, *Lab.* | 15,474 |
| J. Fairrie, *C.* | 2,130 |
| P. Dunphy, *LD* | 1,804 |
| J. Tyndall, *BNP* | 1,511 |
| P. Compobassi, *UK Independence* | 457 |
| M. Leighton, *NLP* | 116 |
| *Lab. majority* | 13,344 |
| EASTLEIGH | |
| (9 June 1994) | |
| *E*.91,736   *T*.58.9% | |
| D. Chidgey, *LD* | 24,473 |
| Ms M. Birks, *Lab.* | 15,234 |
| S. Reid, *C.* | 13,675 |
| N. Farage, *UK Independence* | 952 |
| 'Lord' D. Sutch, *Loony* | 783 |
| P. Warburton, *NLP* | 145 |
| *LD majority* | 9,239 |
| NEWHAM NORTH EAST | |
| (9 June 1994) | |
| *E*.59,555   *T*.34.5% | |
| S. Timms, *Lab.* | 14,668 |
| P. Hammond, *C.* | 2,850 |
| A. Kellaway, *LD* | 821 |
| A. Scholefield, *UK Independence* | 509 |
| J. Homeless, *House Homeless People* | 342 |
| R. Archer, *NLP* | 228 |
| Ms V. Garman, *Buy the Daily Sport* | 155 |
| *Lab. majority* | 11,818 |
| MONKLANDS EAST | |
| (30 June 1994) | |
| *E*.48,391   *T*.70.17% | |
| Mrs H. Liddell, *Lab.* | 16,960 |
| Ms K. Ullrich, *SNP* | 15,320 |
| S. Gallagher, *LD* | 878 |
| Ms S. Bell, *C.* | 799 |
| A. Bremner, *Network Against Criminal Justice Bill* | 69 |
| D. Paterson, *NLP* | 58 |
| *Lab. majority* | 1,640 |

# Parliamentary statistics

## PRINCIPAL PARTIES IN PARLIAMENT SINCE 1970

|  | 1970 | 1974 Feb. | 1974 Oct. | 1979 | 1983 | 1987 | 1992 |
|---|---|---|---|---|---|---|---|
| Conservative | 330* | 296 | 276 | 339 | 397 | 375 | 336 |
| Labour | 287 | 301 | 319 | 268 | 209 | 229 | 270 |
| Liberal/LD | 6 | 14 | 13 | 11 | 17 | 17 | 20 |
| Social Democrat | — | 1 | — | — | 6 | 5 | — |
| Independent | 5† | 1 | 1 | 2 | — | — | — |
| Plaid Cymru | — | 2 | 3 | 2 | 2 | 3 | 4 |
| Scottish Nationalist | 1 | 7 | 11 | 2 | 2 | 3 | 3 |
| Democratic Unionist | — | — | — | 3 | 3 | 3 | 3 |
| SDLP | — | 1 | 1 | 1 | 1 | 3 | 4 |
| Sinn Fein | — | — | — | — | 1 | 1 | — |
| Ulster Popular Unionist | — | — | — | — | 1 | 1 | 1 |
| Ulster Unionist‡ | * | 11 | 10 | 6 | 10 | 9 | 9 |
| The Speaker | 1 | 1 | 1 | 1 | 1 | 1 | 1 |
| Total | 630 | 635 | 635 | 635 | 650 | 650 | 651 |

\* Including 8 Ulster Unionists
† Comprising: Independent Labour 1, Independent Unity 1, Protestant Unity 1, Republican Labour 1, Unity 1
‡ Comprises:
   1974 (February) United Ulster Unionist Council 11
   1974 (October) United Ulster Unionist 10
   1979 Ulster Unionist 5, United Ulster Unionist 1
   1983 Official Unionist 10

## PARLIAMENTS SINCE 1970

| Assembled | Dissolved | Duration | | |
|---|---|---|---|---|
|  |  | yr | m. | d. |
| 29 June 1970 | 8 February 1974 | 3 | 7 | 10 |
| 6 March 1974 | 20 September 1974 | 0 | 6 | 14 |
| 22 October 1974 | 7 April 1979 | 4 | 5 | 16 |
| 9 May 1979 | 13 May 1983 | 4 | 0 | 4 |
| 15 June 1983 | 18 May 1987 | 3 | 11 | 3 |
| 17 June 1987 | 16 March 1992 | 4 | 8 | 28 |
| 27 April 1992 |  |  |  |  |

## MAJORITIES IN THE HOUSE OF COMMONS SINCE 1970

| Year | Party | Maj. |
|---|---|---|
| 1970 | Conservative | 31 |
| 1974 Feb. | No majority |  |
| 1974 Oct. | Labour | 5 |
| 1979 | Conservative | 43 |
| 1983 | Conservative | 144 |
| 1987 | Conservative | 102 |
| 1992 | Conservative | 21 |

## VOTES CAST AT GENERAL ELECTIONS 1987 AND 1992*

### GENERAL ELECTION 1987

| | |
|---|---|
| Conservative | 13,760,525 |
| Labour | 10,029,944 |
| Liberal/SDP Alliance | 7,341,152 |
| Scottish Nationalist | 416,873 |
| Plaid Cymru | 123,589 |
| †Green | 89,753 |
| Others | 37,576 |

### GENERAL ELECTION 1992

| | |
|---|---|
| Conservative | 14,048,283 |
| Labour | 11,559,735 |
| Liberal Democrats | 5,999,384 |
| Scottish Nationalist | 629,552 |
| Plaid Cymru | 154,439 |
| Others | 436,207 |

*Excluding Northern Ireland seats
†Excluding Ecology candidate in Northern Ireland

## PARLIAMENTARY CONSTITUENCIES AS AT 9 APRIL 1992

The results of voting in each parliamentary division at the general election of 9 April 1992 are given below. The majority in the 1987 general election, and any subsequent by-elections, is given below the 1992 result.

*Symbols*

| | |
|---|---|
| E. | Total number of electors in the constituency at the 1992 general election |
| T. | Turnout of electors at the 1992 general election |
| * | Member of the last Parliament |

*Abbreviations*

| | |
|---|---|
| All. | Alliance Party (NI) |
| C. | Conservative |
| DUP | Democratic Unionist Party |
| Green | Green Party |
| Ind. | Independent |
| Lab. | Labour |
| L./All. | Liberal Alliance |
| LD | Liberal Democrat |
| Lib. | Liberal |
| PC | Plaid Cymru |
| SD | Social Democrat |
| SDLP | Social Democratic and Labour Party |
| SDP | Social Democrat Party |
| SF | Sinn Fein |
| SNP | Scottish National Party |
| UPUP | Ulster Popular Unionist Party |
| UUP | Ulster Unionist Party |
| ADS | After Dinner Speaker |
| AFE | Anti-Federal Europe |
| Alt. | Alternative |
| Anti Fed. | Anti Federalist League |
| Anti H. | Anti-Heseltine Independent |
| APAKBI | Anti-Paddy Ashdown Keep Britain Independent |
| AS | Anglo Saxon |
| Bastion | Bastion Party |
| BNP | British National Party |
| Brewer | Jolly Small Brewers Party |
| Brit. Ind. | British Independence Party |
| CD | Christian Democrat |
| Century | 21st Century Party |
| Choice | People's Choice |
| CL | Communist League |
| Comm. GB | Communist Party of Great Britain |
| CRA | Chauvinist Raving Alliance |
| CSP | Common Sense Party |
| C. Thatch. | Conservative Thatcherite |
| DLC | Democrat Liberal Conservative |
| DOS | Doctor of Stockwell |
| EFRA | Epping Forest Residents Association |
| ERIP | Equal Representation in Parliament |
| EUVJJ | End Unemployment Vote Justice for the Jobless |
| FDP | Fancy Dress Party |
| Fellowship | Fellowship Party |
| FP | Feudal Party |
| FTA | Fair Trials Abroad |
| FTM | Forward to Mars Party |
| Fun | Funstermentalist |
| Gremloids | Gremloids |
| Hardcore | The Altern-8-ive (Hardcore) Party |
| Homeland | Independent British Homeland Defence |
| Hove C. | Official Conservative Hove Party |
| IFM | Irish Freedom Movement |
| ILP | Independent Labour Party |
| Ind. U. | Independent Unionist |
| Int. Comm. | International Communist Party |
| Islamic | Islamic Party |
| ISS | Illegal Sunday Shopping |
| JBR | Justice from British Rail |
| Loony | Official Monster Raving Loony Party |
| Loony G. | Loony Green |
| LP | Lodestar Party |
| LTU | Labour and Trade Union |
| MBI | Morecambe Bay Independent |
| NA | Noise Abatement |
| Nat. | Nationalist |
| NF | National Front |
| NLP | Natural Law Party |
| Pensioners | Pensioners' Party |
| PP | People's Party |
| PPP | Peoples' Peace Party |
| PR | Proportional Representation |
| Prog. Soc. | Independent Progressive Socialist |
| Prot. Ref. | Protestant Reformation |
| QFL | Quality for Life Party |
| RAVA | Rainbow Ark Voters Association |
| RCC | Revolutionary Christian Communist |
| Real Bean | Real Bean |
| Rev. Comm. | Revolutionary Communist |
| Rizz | Rizz Party – Rainbow |
| Scallywagg | Scallywagg |
| SML | Scottish Militant Labour |
| SOADDA | Struck Off and Die Doctor's Alliance |
| Soc. | Socialist |
| Soc. Lab. | Socialist Labour |
| True Lab. | True Labour |
| UTCHAP | Up The Creek Have A Party |
| WAR | Workers Against Racism |
| Wessex | Save Wessex |
| Whiplash | Whiplash Corrective |
| WP | Workers' Party |
| WRP | Workers' Revolutionary Party |
| WUWC | Wake Up Wokingham Campaign |
| YSOR | Young Socialist – Occupy Ravenscraig |

## ENGLAND

**ALDERSHOT (Hants)**
E.81,754  T.78.71%

| | |
|---|---|
| *J. Critchley, C. | 36,974 |
| A. Collett, LD | 17,786 |
| J. Anthony Smith, Lab. | 8,552 |
| D. Robinson, Lib. | 1,038 |
| C. majority | 19,188 |

(June 1987, C. maj. 17,784)

**ALDRIDGE-BROWNHILLS (W. Midlands)**
E.63,404  T.82.55%

| | |
|---|---|
| *R. Shepherd, C. | 28,431 |
| N. Fawcett, Lab. | 17,407 |
| S. Reynolds, LD | 6,503 |
| C. majority | 11,024 |

(June 1987, C. maj. 12,396)

**ALTRINCHAM AND SALE (Greater Manchester)**
E.65,897  T.80.66%

| | |
|---|---|
| *Sir F. Montgomery, C. | 29,066 |
| Ms M. Atherton, Lab. | 12,275 |
| J. Mulholland, LD | 11,601 |

| | |
|---|---|
| J. Renwick, NLP | 212 |
| C. majority | 16,791 |

(June 1987, C. maj. 14,228)

**AMBER VALLEY (Derbys)**
E.70,155  T.84.69%

| | |
|---|---|
| *Hon. P. Oppenheim, C. | 27,418 |
| J. Cooper, Lab. | 26,706 |
| G. Brocklebank, LD | 5,294 |
| C. majority | 712 |

(June 1987, C. maj. 9,500)

**ARUNDEL (W. Sussex)**
E.79,241  T.77.06%

| | |
|---|---|
| *Sir M. Marshall, C. | 35,405 |
| Dr J. Walsh, LD | 15,542 |
| R. Nash, Lab. | 8,321 |
| Mrs D. Renson, Lib. | 1,103 |
| R. Corbin, Green | 693 |
| C. majority | 19,863 |

(June 1987, C. maj. 18,880)

**ASHFIELD (Notts)**
E.75,075  T.77.70%

| | |
|---|---|
| G. Hoon, Lab. | 32,018 |
| L. Robertson, C. | 19,031 |
| J. Turton, LD | 7,291 |
| Lab. majority | 12,987 |

(June 1987, Lab. maj. 4,400)

**ASHFORD (Kent)**
E.71,767  T.79.20%

| | |
|---|---|
| *K. Speed, C. | 31,031 |
| Ms C. Headley, LD | 13,672 |
| Ms D. Cameron, Lab. | 11,365 |
| Dr A. Porter, Green | 773 |
| C. majority | 17,359 |

(June 1987, C. maj. 15,488)

**ASHTON-UNDER-LYNE (Greater Manchester)**
E.58,701  T.73.87%

| | |
|---|---|
| *Rt. Hon. R. Sheldon, Lab. | 24,550 |
| J. Pinniger, C. | 13,615 |
| C. Turner, LD | 4,005 |
| C. Hall, Lib. | 907 |

J. Brannigan, *NLP* 289
*Lab. majority* 10,935
(June 1987, Lab. maj. 9,286)

AYLESBURY (Bucks)
E.79,208   T.80.29%
D. Lidington, *C.* 36,500
Ms S. Bowles, *LD* 17,640
R. Priest, *Lab.* 8,517
N. Foster, *Green* 702
B. D'Arcy, *NLP* 239
*C. majority* 18,860
(June 1987, C. maj. 16,558)

BANBURY (Oxon)
E.71,840   T.81.51%
*A. Baldry, *C.* 32,215
Ms A. Billingham, *Lab.* 15,495
G. Fisher, *LD* 10,602
Dr R. Ticiiati, *NLP* 250
*C. majority* 16,720
(June 1987, C. maj. 17,330)

BARKING (Greater London)
E.50,454   T.69.99%
*Ms J. Richardson, *Lab.* 18,224
J. Kennedy, *C.* 11,956
S. Churchman, *LD* 5,133
*Lab. majority* 6,268
(June 1987, Lab. maj. 3,409)
*See also page 241*

BARNSLEY CENTRAL (S. Yorks)
E.55,373   T.70.53%
*E. Illsley, *Lab.* 27,048
D. Senior, *C.* 7,687
S. Cowton, *LD* 4,321
*Lab. majority* 19,361
(June 1987, Lab. maj. 19,051)

BARNSLEY EAST (S. Yorks)
E.54,051   T.72.73%
*T. Patchett, *Lab.* 30,346
J. Procter, *C.* 5,569
Ms S. Anginotti, *LD* 3,399
*Lab. majority* 24,777
(June 1987, Lab. maj. 23,511)

BARNSLEY WEST AND
PENISTONE (S. Yorks)
E.63,374   T.75.75%
M. Clapham, *Lab.* 27,965
G. Sawyer, *C.* 13,461
I. Nicolson, *LD* 5,610
D. Jones, *Green* 970
*Lab. majority* 14,504
(June 1987, Lab. maj. 14,191)

BARROW AND FURNESS (Cumbria)
E.67,764   T.82.11%
J. Hutton, *Lab.* 26,568
*C. Franks, *C.* 22,990
C. Crane, *LD* 6,089
*Lab. majority* 3,578
(June 1987, C. maj. 3,928)

BASILDON (Essex)
E.67,585   T.79.61%
*D. Amess, *C.* 24,159
J. Potter, *Lab.* 22,679
G. Williams, *LD* 6,967
*C. majority* 1,480
(June 1987, C. maj. 2,649)

BASINGSTOKE (Hants)
E.82,952   T.82.79%
*A. Hunter, *C.* 37,521
D. Bull, *Lab.* 16,323
C. Curtis, *LD* 14,119
Ms V. Oldaker, *Green* 714
*C. majority* 21,198
(June 1987, C. maj. 17,893)

BASSETLAW (Notts)
E.58,583   T.92.97%
*J. Ashton, *Lab.* 29,061
Mrs C. Spelman, *C.* 19,064
M. Reynolds, *LD* 6,340
*Lab. majority* 9,997
(June 1987, Lab. maj. 5,613)

BATH (Avon)
E.63,689   T.82.54%
D. Foster, *LD* 25,718
*Rt. Hon. C. Patten, *C.* 21,950
Ms P. Richards, *Lab.* 4,102
D. McCanlis, *Green* 433
Ms M. Barker, *Lib.* 172
Dr A. Sked, *Anti Fed.* 117
J. Rumming, *Ind.* 79
*LD majority* 3,768
(June 1987, C. maj. 1,412)

BATLEY AND SPEN (W. Yorks)
E.76,417   T.79.63%
*Mrs E. Peacock, *C.* 27,629
Mrs E. Durkin, *Lab.* 26,221
G. Beever, *LD* 6,380
C. Lord, *Green* 628
*C. majority* 1,408
(June 1987, C. maj. 1,362)

BATTERSEA (Greater London)
E.68,218   T.76.63%
*J. Bowis, *C.* 26,390
A. Dubs, *Lab.* 21,550
R. O'Brien, *LD* 3,659
I. Wingrove, *Green* 584
W. Stevens, *NLP* 98
*C. majority* 4,840
(June 1987, C. maj. 857)

BEACONSFIELD (Bucks)
E.64,268   T.82.27%
*T. Smith, *C.* 33,817
Ms A. Purse, *LD* 10,220
G. Smith, *Lab.* 7,163
W. Foulds, *Ind. C.* 1,317
A. Foss, *NLP* 196
Ms J. Martin, *ERIP* 166
*C. majority* 23,597
(June 1987, C. maj. 21,339)

BECKENHAM (Greater London)
E.59,440   T.77.86%
P. Merchant, *C.* 26,323
K. Ritchie, *Lab.* 11,038
Ms M. Williams, *LD* 8,038
G. Williams, *Lib.* 643
P. Shaw, *NLP* 243
*C. majority* 15,285
(June 1987, C. maj. 13,464)

BEDFORDSHIRE MID
E.81,864   T.84.45%
*Rt. Hon. Sir N. Lyell, *C.* 40,230
R. Clayton, *Lab.* 15,092

N. Hills, *LD* 11,957
P. Cottier, *Lib.* 1,582
M. Lorys, *NLP* 279
*C. majority* 25,138
(June 1987, C. maj. 22,851)

BEDFORDSHIRE NORTH
E.73,789   T.80.03%
*Sir T. Skeet, *C.* 29,920
P. Hall, *Lab.* 18,302
M. Smithson, *LD* 10,014
Ms L. Smith, *Green* 643
B. Bench, *NLP* 178
*C. majority* 11,618
(June 1987, C. maj. 16,505)

BEDFORDSHIRE SOUTH WEST
E.79,662   T.82.39%
*W. D. Madel, *C.* 37,498
B. Elliott, *Lab.* 16,225
M. Freeman, *LD* 10,988
P. Rollings, *Green* 689
D. Gilmour, *NLP* 239
*C. majority* 21,273
(June 1987, C. maj. 22,305)

BERKSHIRE EAST
E.90,365   T.81.41%
*A. Mackay, *C.* 43,898
Ms L. Murray, *LD* 15,218
K. Dibble, *Lab.* 14,458
*C. majority* 28,680
(June 1987, C. maj. 22,626)

BERWICK-UPON-TWEED
(Northumberland)
E.54,919   T.79.12%
*A. Beith, *LD* 19,283
Dr A. Henfrey, *C.* 14,240
Dr G. Adam, *Lab.* 9,933
*LD majority* 5,043
(June 1987, L./All. maj. 13,945)

BETHNAL GREEN AND STEPNEY
(Greater London)
E.55,675   T.65.45%
*Rt. Hon. P. Shore, *Lab.* 20,350
J. Shaw, *LD* 8,120
Miss J. Emmerson, *C.* 6,507
R. Edmonds, *BNP* 1,310
S. Kelsey, *Comm. GB* 156
*Lab. majority* 12,230
(June 1987, Lab. maj. 5,284)

BEVERLEY (Humberside)
E.81,198   T.79.69%
*J. Cran, *C.* 34,503
A. Collinge, *LD* 17,986
C. Challen, *Lab.* 12,026
D. Hetherington, *NLP* 199
*C. majority* 16,517
(June 1987, C. maj. 12,595)

BEXHILL AND BATTLE (E. Sussex)
E.65,850   T.78.99%
*C. Wardle, *C.* 31,330
Ms S. Prochak, *LD* 15,023
F. Taylor, *Lab.* 4,883
J. Prus, *Green* 594
Mrs M. Smith, *CSP* 190
*C. majority* 16,307
(June 1987, C. maj. 20,519)

BEXLEYHEATH (Greater London)
E.57,684   T.82.17%
| *C. Townsend, C. | 25,606 |
| J. Browning, Lab. | 11,520 |
| Ms W. Chaplin, LD | 10,107 |
| R. Cundy, Ind. | 170 |
| C. majority | 14,086 |
(June 1987, C. maj. 11,687)

BILLERICAY (Essex)
E.80,388   T.82.34%
| *Mrs T. Gorman, C. | 37,406 |
| F. Bellard, LD | 14,912 |
| Ms A. Miller, Lab. | 13,880 |
| C. majority | 22,494 |
(June 1987, C. maj. 18,016)

BIRKENHEAD (Merseyside)
E.62,682   T.72.96%
| *F. Field, Lab. | 29,098 |
| R. Hughes, C. | 11,485 |
| P. Williams, LD | 4,417 |
| Ms T. Fox, Green | 543 |
| Ms B. Griffiths, NLP | 190 |
| Lab. majority | 17,613 |
(June 1987, Lab. maj. 15,372)

BIRMINGHAM EDGBASTON
(W. Midlands)
E.53,041   T.71.29%
| *Dame J. Knight, C. | 18,529 |
| J. Wilton, Lab. | 14,222 |
| I. Robertson-Steel, LD | 4,419 |
| P. Simpson, Green | 643 |
| C. majority | 4,307 |
(June 1987, C. maj. 8,581)

BIRMINGHAM ERDINGTON
(W. Midlands)
E.52,398   T.70.15%
| *R. Corbett, Lab. | 18,549 |
| S. Hope, C. | 13,814 |
| Dr J. Campbell, LD | 4,398 |
| Lab. majority | 4,735 |
(June 1987, Lab. maj. 2,467)

BIRMINGHAM HALL GREEN
(W. Midlands)
E.60,091   T.78.17%
| *A. Hargreaves, C. | 21,649 |
| Ms J. Slowey, Lab. | 17,984 |
| D. McGrath, LD | 7,342 |
| C. majority | 3,665 |
(June 1987, C. maj. 7,621)

BIRMINGHAM HODGE HILL
(W. Midlands)
E.57,651   T.70.82%
| *T. Davis, Lab. | 21,895 |
| Miss E. Gibson, C. | 14,827 |
| S. Hagan, LD | 3,740 |
| E. Whicker, NF | 370 |
| Lab. majority | 7,068 |
(June 1987, Lab. maj. 4,789)

BIRMINGHAM LADYWOOD
(W. Midlands)
E.56,970   T.65.92%
| *Ms C. Short, Lab. | 24,887 |
| Mrs B. Ashford, C. | 9,604 |
| B. Worth, LD | 3,068 |
| Lab. majority | 15,283 |
(June 1987, Lab. maj. 10,028)

BIRMINGHAM NORTHFIELD
(W. Midlands)
E.70,533   T.76.08%
| R. Burden, Lab. | 24,433 |
| *R. King, C. | 23,803 |
| D. Cropp, LD | 5,431 |
| Lab. majority | 630 |
(June 1987, C. maj. 3,135)

BIRMINGHAM PERRY BARR
(W. Midlands)
E.72,161   T.71.62%
| *J. Rooker, Lab. | 27,507 |
| G. Green, C. | 18,917 |
| T. Philpott, LD | 5,261 |
| Lab. majority | 8,590 |
(June 1987, Lab. maj. 6,933)

BIRMINGHAM SELLY OAK
(W. Midlands)
E.72,150   T.76.61%
| Ms L. Jones, Lab. | 25,430 |
| *A. Beaumont-Dark, C. | 23,370 |
| D. Osborne, LD | 5,679 |
| P. Slatter, Green | 535 |
| C. Barwood, NLP | 178 |
| K. Malik, Rev Comm | 84 |
| Lab. majority | 2,060 |
(June 1987, C. maj. 2,584)

BIRMINGHAM SMALL HEATH (W.
Midlands)
E.55,213   T.62.95%
| R. Godsiff, Lab. | 22,675 |
| A. Qayyum Chaudhary, C. | 8,686 |
| H. Thomas, LD | 2,575 |
| Ms H. Clawley, Green | 824 |
| Lab. majority | 13,989 |
(June 1987, Lab. maj. 15,521)

BIRMINGHAM SPARKBROOK
(W. Midlands)
E.51,677   T.66.80%
| *Rt. Hon. R. Hattersley, Lab. | 22,116 |
| M. Khamisa, C. | 8,544 |
| D. Parry, LD | 3,028 |
| C. Alldrick, Green | 833 |
| Lab. majority | 13,572 |
(June 1987, Lab. maj. 11,859)

BIRMINGHAM YARDLEY
(W. Midlands)
E.54,749   T.77.98%
| Ms E. Morris, Lab. | 14,884 |
| *A. D. G. Bevan, C. | 14,722 |
| J. Hemming, LD | 12,899 |
| Miss P. Read, NF | 192 |
| Lab. majority | 162 |
(June 1987, C. maj. 2,522)

BISHOP AUCKLAND (Durham)
E.72,572   T.76.52%
| *D. Foster, Lab. | 27,763 |
| D. Williamson, C. | 17,676 |
| W. Wade, LD | 10,099 |
| Lab. majority | 10,087 |
(June 1987, Lab. maj. 7,035)

BLABY (Leics)
E.81,790   T.83.39%
| A. Robathan, C. | 39,498 |
| Ms E. Ranson, Lab. | 14,151 |

| Ms M. Lewin, LD | 13,780 |
| J. Peacock, BNP | 521 |
| Ms S. Lincoln, NLP | 260 |
| C. majority | 25,347 |
(June 1987, C. maj. 22,176)

BLACKBURN (Lancs)
E.73,251   T.75.05%
| *J. Straw, Lab. | 26,633 |
| R. Coates, C. | 20,606 |
| D. Mann, LD | 6,332 |
| R. Field, Green | 878 |
| Mrs M. Carmichael-Grimshaw, LP | 334 |
| W. Ayliffe, NLP | 195 |
| Lab. majority | 6,027 |
(June 1987, Lab. maj. 5,497)

BLACKPOOL NORTH (Lancs)
E.58,087   T.77.55%
| H. Elletson, C. | 21,501 |
| E. Kirton, Lab. | 18,461 |
| A. Lahiff, LD | 4,786 |
| Sir G. Francis, Loony | 178 |
| H. Walker, NLP | 125 |
| C. majority | 3,040 |
(June 1987, C. maj. 7,321)

BLACKPOOL SOUTH (Lancs)
E.56,801   T.77.35%
| N. Hawkins, C. | 19,880 |
| G. Marsden, Lab. | 18,213 |
| R. Wynne, LD | 5,675 |
| D. Henning, NLP | 173 |
| C. majority | 1,667 |
(June 1987, C. maj. 6,744)

BLAYDON (Tyne & Wear)
E.66,044   T.77.69%
| *J. McWilliam, Lab. | 27,028 |
| P. Pescod, C. | 13,685 |
| P. Nunn, LD | 10,602 |
| Lab. majority | 13,343 |
(June 1987, Lab. maj. 12,488)

BLYTH VALLEY (Northumberland)
E.60,913   T.80.77%
| *R. Campbell, Lab. | 24,542 |
| P. Tracey, LD | 16,498 |
| M. Revell, C. | 7,691 |
| S. Tyley, Green | 470 |
| Lab. majority | 8,044 |
(June 1987, Lab. maj. 853)

BOLSOVER (Derbys)
E.66,693   T.78.94%
| *D. Skinner, Lab. | 33,973 |
| T. James, C. | 13,313 |
| Ms S. Barber, LD | 5,363 |
| Lab. majority | 20,660 |
(June 1987, Lab. maj. 14,120)

BOLTON NORTH EAST (Greater
Manchester)
E.58,659   T.82.26%
| *P. Thurnham, C. | 21,644 |
| D. Crausby, Lab. | 21,459 |
| B. Dunning, LD | 4,971 |
| P. Tong, NLP | 181 |
| C. majority | 185 |
(June 1987, C. maj. 813)

BOLTON SOUTH EAST (Greater Manchester)
E.65,600  T.75.53%

| | |
|---|---|
| *D. Young, *Lab.* | 26,906 |
| N. Wood-Dow, *C.* | 14,215 |
| D. Lee, *LD* | 5,243 |
| W. Hardman, *Ind. Lab.* | 2,894 |
| L. Walch, *NLP* | 290 |
| *Lab. majority* | 12,691 |

(June 1987, Lab. maj. 11,381)

BOLTON WEST (Greater Manchester)
E.71,344  T.83.53%

| | |
|---|---|
| *Hon. T. Sackville, *C.* | 26,452 |
| C. Morris, *Lab.* | 25,373 |
| Ms B. Ronson, *LD* | 7,529 |
| Ms J. Phillips, *NLP* | 240 |
| *C. majority* | 1,079 |

(June 1987, C. maj. 4,593)

BOOTHFERRY (Humberside)
E.80,747  T.79.73%

| | |
|---|---|
| *D. Davis, *C.* | 35,266 |
| Ms L. Coubrough, *Lab.* | 17,731 |
| J. Goss, *LD* | 11,388 |
| *C. majority* | 17,535 |

(June 1987, C. maj. 18,970)

BOOTLE (Merseyside)
E.69,308  T.72.46%

| | |
|---|---|
| *J. Benton, *Lab.* | 37,464 |
| C. Varley, *C.* | 8,022 |
| J. Cunningham, *LD* | 3,301 |
| Ms M. Hall, *Lib.* | 1,174 |
| T. Haynes, *NLP* | 264 |
| *Lab. majority* | 29,442 |

(June 1987, Lab. maj. 24,477)
(May 1990, Lab. maj. 23,517)
(November 1990, Lab. maj. 19,465)

BOSWORTH (Leics)
E.80,234  T.84.13%

| | |
|---|---|
| *D. Tredinnick, *C.* | 36,618 |
| D. Everitt, *Lab.* | 17,524 |
| G. Drozdz, *LD* | 12,643 |
| B. Fewster, *Green* | 716 |
| *C. majority* | 19,094 |

(June 1987, C. maj. 17,016)

BOURNEMOUTH EAST (Dorset)
E.75,089  T.72.82%

| | |
|---|---|
| *D. Atkinson, *C.* | 30,820 |
| N. Russell, *LD* | 15,997 |
| P. Brushett, *Lab.* | 7,541 |
| Ms S. Holmes, *NLP* | 329 |
| *C. majority* | 14,823 |

(June 1987, C. maj. 14,683)

BOURNEMOUTH WEST (Dorset)
E.74,738  T.75.72%

| | |
|---|---|
| *J. Butterfill, *C.* | 29,820 |
| Ms J. Dover, *LD* | 17,178 |
| B. Grower, *Lab.* | 9,423 |
| A. Springham, *NLP* | 232 |
| *C. majority* | 12,642 |

(June 1987, C. maj. 12,651)

BOW AND POPLAR (Greater London)
E.56,685  T.65.84%

| | |
|---|---|
| *Mrs M. Gordon, *Lab.* | 18,487 |
| P. Hughes, *LD* | 10,083 |
| S. Pearce, *C.* | 6,876 |

| | |
|---|---|
| J. Tyndall, *BNP* | 1,107 |
| S. Petter, *Green* | 612 |
| W. Hite, *NLP* | 158 |
| *Lab. majority* | 8,404 |

(June 1987, Lab. maj. 4,631)

BRADFORD NORTH (W. Yorks)
E.66,719  T.73.38%

| | |
|---|---|
| *T. Rooney, *Lab.* | 23,420 |
| M. Riaz, *C.* | 15,756 |
| D. Ward, *LD* | 9,133 |
| W. Beckett, *Loony* | 350 |
| M. Nasr, *Islamic* | 304 |
| *Lab. majority* | 7,664 |

(June 1987, Lab. maj. 1,663)
(November 1990, Lab. maj. 9,514)

BRADFORD SOUTH (W. Yorks)
E.69,914  T.75.61%

| | |
|---|---|
| *G. R. Cryer, *Lab.* | 25,185 |
| A. Popat, *C.* | 20,283 |
| B. Boulton, *LD* | 7,243 |
| M. Naseem, *Islamic* | 156 |
| *Lab. majority* | 4,902 |

(June 1987, Lab. maj. 309)
*See also page 241*

BRADFORD WEST (W. Yorks)
E.70,016  T.69.90%

| | |
|---|---|
| *M. Madden, *Lab.* | 26,046 |
| Dr A. Ashworth, *C.* | 16,544 |
| Dr. A. Griffiths, *LD* | 5,150 |
| P. Braham, *Green* | 735 |
| D. Pidcock, *Islamic* | 471 |
| *Lab. majority* | 9,502 |

(June 1987, Lab. maj. 7,551)

BRAINTREE (Essex)
E.78,880  T.83.41%

| | |
|---|---|
| *Rt. Hon. A. Newton, *C.* | 34,415 |
| I. Willmore, *Lab.* | 16,921 |
| Ms D. Wallis, *LD* | 13,603 |
| J. Abbott, *Green* | 855 |
| *C. majority* | 17,494 |

(June 1987, C. maj. 16,857)

BRENT EAST (Greater London)
E.53,319  T.68.82%

| | |
|---|---|
| *K. Livingstone, *Lab.* | 19,387 |
| D. Green, *C.* | 13,416 |
| M. Cummins, *LD* | 3,249 |
| Ms T. Dean, *Green* | 548 |
| Ms A. Murphy, *Comm. GB* | 96 |
| *Lab. majority* | 5,971 |

(June 1987, Lab. maj. 1,653)

BRENT NORTH (Greater London)
E.58,917  T.70.57%

| | |
|---|---|
| *Rt. Hon. Sir R. Boyson, *C.* | 23,445 |
| J. Moher, *Lab.* | 13,314 |
| P. Lorber, *LD* | 4,149 |
| T. Vipul, *Ind.* | 356 |
| T. Davids, *NLP* | 318 |
| *C. majority* | 10,131 |

(June 1987, C. maj. 15,720)

BRENT SOUTH (Greater London)
E.56,034  T.64.10%

| | |
|---|---|
| *P. Boateng, *Lab.* | 20,662 |
| R. Blackman, *C.* | 10,957 |
| M. Harskin, *LD* | 3,658 |
| D. Johnson, *Green* | 479 |

| | |
|---|---|
| C. Jani, *NLP* | 166 |
| *Lab. majority* | 9,705 |

(June 1987, Lab. maj. 7,931)

BRENTFORD AND ISLEWORTH (Greater London)
E.70,880  T.76.22%

| | |
|---|---|
| N. Deva, *C.* | 24,752 |
| Ms A. Keen, *Lab.* | 22,666 |
| Ms J. Salmon, *LD* | 5,683 |
| J. Bradley, *Green* | 927 |
| *C. majority* | 2,086 |

(June 1987, C. maj. 7,953)

BRENTWOOD AND ONGAR (Greater London)
E.65,830  T.84.70%

| | |
|---|---|
| E. Pickles, *C.* | 32,145 |
| Ms E. Bottomley, *LD* | 17,000 |
| F. Keohane, *Lab.* | 6,080 |
| Ms C. Bartley, *Green* | 535 |
| *C. majority* | 15,145 |

(June 1987, C. maj. 18,921)

BRIDGWATER (Somerset)
E.71,567  T.79.51%

| | |
|---|---|
| *Rt. Hon. T. King, *C.* | 26,610 |
| W. Revans, *LD* | 16,894 |
| P. James, *Lab.* | 12,365 |
| G. Dummett, *Green* | 746 |
| A. Body, *Ind.* | 183 |
| Ms G. Sanson, *NLP* | 112 |
| *C. majority* | 9,716 |

(June 1987, C. maj. 11,195)

BRIDLINGTON (Humberside)
E.84,829  T.77.93%

| | |
|---|---|
| *J. Townend, *C.* | 33,604 |
| J. Leeman, *LD* | 17,246 |
| S. Hatfield, *Lab.* | 15,263 |
| *C. majority* | 16,358 |

(June 1987, C. maj. 17,321)

BRIGG AND CLEETHORPES (Humberside)
E.82,377  T.77.98%

| | |
|---|---|
| *M. Brown, *C.* | 31,673 |
| I. Cawsey, *Lab.* | 22,404 |
| Ms M. Cockbill, *LD* | 9,374 |
| N. Jacques, *Green* | 790 |
| *C. majority* | 9,269 |

(June 1987, C. maj. 12,250)

BRIGHTON KEMPTOWN (E. Sussex)
E.57,646  T.76.14%

| | |
|---|---|
| *A. Bowden, *C.* | 21,129 |
| Ms G. Haynes, *Lab.* | 18,073 |
| P. Scott, *LD* | 4,461 |
| Ms E. Overall, *NLP* | 230 |
| *C. majority* | 3,056 |

(June 1987, C. maj. 9,260)

BRIGHTON PAVILION (E. Sussex)
E.57,616  T.76.81%

| | |
|---|---|
| D. Spencer, *C.* | 20,630 |
| D. Lepper, *Lab.* | 16,955 |
| T. Pearce, *LD* | 5,606 |
| I. Brodie, *Green* | 963 |
| Ms E. Turner, *NLP* | 103 |
| *C. majority* | 3,675 |

(June 1987, C. maj. 9,142)

**Bristol East (Avon)**
E.62,577   T.80.40%

| | |
|---|---|
| Ms J. Corston, *Lab.* | 22,418 |
| *J. Sayeed, *C.* | 19,726 |
| J. Kiely, *LD* | 7,903 |
| I. Anderson, *NF* | 270 |
| *Lab. majority* | 2,692 |

(June 1987, C. maj. 4,123)

**Bristol North West (Avon)**
E.72,726   T.82.35%

| | |
|---|---|
| *M. Stern, *C.* | 25,354 |
| D. Naysmith, *Lab.* | 25,309 |
| J. Taylor, *LD* | 8,498 |
| H. Long, *SD* | 729 |
| *C. majority* | 45 |

(June 1987, C. maj. 6,952)

**Bristol South (Avon)**
E.64,309   T.78.04%

| | |
|---|---|
| *Ms D. Primarolo, *Lab.* | 25,164 |
| J. Bercow, *C.* | 16,245 |
| P. Crossley, *LD* | 7,892 |
| J. Boxall, *Green* | 756 |
| N. Phillips, *NLP* | 136 |
| *Lab. majority* | 8,919 |

(June 1987, Lab. maj. 1,404)

**Bristol West (Avon)**
E.70,579   T.74.37%

| | |
|---|---|
| *Rt. Hon. W. Waldegrave, *C.* | 22,169 |
| C. Boney, *LD* | 16,098 |
| H. Bashforth, *Lab.* | 12,992 |
| A. Sawday, *Green* | 906 |
| D. Cross, *NLP* | 104 |
| B. Brent, *Rev. Comm.* | 92 |
| P. Hammond, *SOADDA* | 87 |
| T. Hedges, *Anti Fed.* | 42 |
| *C. majority* | 6,071 |

(June 1987, C. maj. 7,703)

**Bromsgrove (H & W)**
E.71,111   T.82.49%

| | |
|---|---|
| K. R. Thomason, *C.* | 31,709 |
| Ms C. Mole, *Lab.* | 18,007 |
| Ms A. Cassin, *LD* | 8,090 |
| J. Churchman, *Green* | 856 |
| *C. majority* | 13,702 |

(June 1987, C. maj. 16,685)

**Broxbourne (Herts)**
E.72,116   T.79.95%

| | |
|---|---|
| *Mrs M. Roe, *C.* | 36,094 |
| M. Hudson, *Lab.* | 12,124 |
| Mrs J. Davies, *LD* | 9,244 |
| G. Woolhouse, *NLP* | 198 |
| *C. majority* | 23,970 |

(June 1987, C. maj. 22,995)

**Broxtowe (Notts)**
E.73,123   T.83.40%

| | |
|---|---|
| *J. Lester, *C.* | 31,096 |
| J. Walker, *Lab.* | 21,205 |
| J. Ross, *LD* | 8,395 |
| D. Lukehurst, *NLP* | 293 |
| *C. majority* | 9,891 |

(June 1987, C. maj. 16,651)

**Buckingham**
E.56,063   T.84.21%

| | |
|---|---|
| *G. Walden, *C.* | 29,496 |
| T. Jones, *LD* | 9,705 |

| | |
|---|---|
| K. White, *Lab.* | 7,662 |
| L. Sheaff, *NLP* | 353 |
| *C. majority* | 19,791 |

(June 1987, C. maj. 18,526)

**Burnley (Lancs)**
E.68,952   T.74.38%

| | |
|---|---|
| *P. Pike, *Lab.* | 27,184 |
| Mrs B. Binge, *C.* | 15,693 |
| G. Birtwistle, *LD* | 8,414 |
| *Lab. majority* | 11,491 |

(June 1987, Lab. maj. 7,557)

**Burton (Staffs)**
E.75,292   T.82.43%

| | |
|---|---|
| *I. Lawrence, *C.* | 30,845 |
| Ms P. Muddyman, *Lab.* | 24,849 |
| R. Renold, *LD* | 6,375 |
| *C. majority* | 5,996 |

(June 1987, C. maj. 9,830)

**Bury North (Greater Manchester)**
E.69,529   T.84.77%

| | |
|---|---|
| *A. Burt, *C.* | 29,266 |
| J. Dobbin, *Lab.* | 24,502 |
| C. McGrath, *LD* | 5,010 |
| M. Sullivan, *NLP* | 163 |
| *C. majority* | 4,764 |

(June 1987, C. maj. 6,929)

**Bury South (Greater Manchester)**
E.65,793   T.82.10%

| | |
|---|---|
| *D. Sumberg, *C.* | 24,873 |
| Ms H. Blears, *Lab.* | 24,085 |
| A. Cruden, *LD* | 4,832 |
| Mrs N. Sullivan, *NLP* | 228 |
| *C. majority* | 788 |

(June 1987, C. maj. 2,679)

**Bury St Edmunds (Suffolk)**
E.79,967   T.78.38%

| | |
|---|---|
| R. Spring, *C.* | 33,554 |
| T. Sheppard, *Lab.* | 14,767 |
| J. Williams, *LD* | 13,814 |
| Ms J. Lillis, *NLP* | 550 |
| *C. majority* | 18,787 |

(June 1987, C. maj. 21,458)

**Calder Valley (W. Yorks)**
E.74,417   T.82.09%

| | |
|---|---|
| *Sir D. Thompson, *C.* | 27,753 |
| D. Chaytor, *Lab.* | 22,875 |
| S. Pearson, *LD* | 9,842 |
| Ms V. Smith, *Green* | 622 |
| *C. majority* | 4,878 |

(June 1987, C. maj. 6,045)

**Cambridge**
E.69,022   T.73.18%

| | |
|---|---|
| Mrs A. Campbell, *Lab.* | 20,039 |
| M. Bishop, *C.* | 19,459 |
| D. Howarth, *LD* | 10,037 |
| T. Cooper, *Green* | 720 |
| D. Brettell-Winnington, *Loony* | 175 |
| R. Chalmers, *NLP* | 83 |
| *Lab. majority* | 580 |

(June 1987, C. maj. 5,060)

**Cambridgeshire North East**
E.79,935   T.79.38%

| | |
|---|---|
| *M. Moss, *C.* | 34,288 |
| M. Leeke, *LD* | 19,195 |
| R. Harris, *Lab.* | 8,746 |
| C. Ash, *Lib.* | 998 |
| Mrs M. Chalmers, *NLP* | 227 |
| *C. majority* | 15,093 |

(June 1987, C. maj. 1,428)

**Cambridgeshire South East**
E.78,600   T.80.57%

| | |
|---|---|
| *J. Paice, *C.* | 36,693 |
| R. Wotherspoon, *LD* | 12,883 |
| M. Jones, *Lab.* | 12,688 |
| J. Marsh, *Green* | 836 |
| Ms B. Langridge, *NLP* | 231 |
| *C. majority* | 23,810 |

(June 1987, C. maj. 17,502)

**Cambridgeshire South West**
E.84,418   T.81.10%

| | |
|---|---|
| *Sir A. Grant, *C.* | 38,902 |
| Ms S. Sutton, *LD* | 19,265 |
| K. Price, *Lab.* | 9,378 |
| Ms L. Whitebread, *Green* | 699 |
| F. Chalmers, *NLP* | 225 |
| *C. majority* | 19,637 |

(June 1987, C. maj. 18,251)

**Cannock and Burntwood (Staffs)**
E.72,600   T.84.21%

| | |
|---|---|
| A. Wright, *Lab.* | 28,139 |
| *G. Howarth, *C.* | 26,633 |
| P. Treasaden, *LD* | 5,899 |
| M. Hartshorne, *Loony* | 469 |
| *Lab. majority* | 1,506 |

(June 1987, C. maj. 2,689)

**Canterbury (Kent)**
E.75,181   T.78.12%

| | |
|---|---|
| *J. Brazier, *C.* | 29,827 |
| M. Vye, *LD* | 19,022 |
| M. Whitemore, *Lab.* | 8,936 |
| Ms W. Arnall, *Green* | 747 |
| Ms S. Curphey, *NLP* | 203 |
| *C. majority* | 10,805 |

(June 1987, C. maj. 14,891)

**Carlisle (Cumbria)**
E.55,140   T.79.39%

| | |
|---|---|
| *E. Martlew, *Lab.* | 20,479 |
| C. Condie, *C.* | 17,371 |
| R. Aldersey, *LD* | 5,740 |
| Ms N. Robinson, *NLP* | 190 |
| *Lab. majority* | 3,108 |

(June 1987, Lab. maj. 916)

**Carshalton and Wallington (Surrey)**
E.65,179   T.80.94%

| | |
|---|---|
| *F. N. Forman, *C.* | 26,243 |
| T. Brake, *LD* | 16,300 |
| Ms M. Moran, *Lab.* | 9,333 |
| R. Steel, *Green* | 614 |
| D. Bamford, *Loony G.* | 266 |
| *C. majority* | 9,943 |

(June 1987, C. maj. 14,409)

CASTLE POINT (Essex)
*E.*66,229  *T.*80.50%
Dr R. Spink, *C.* — 29,629
D. Flack, *Lab.* — 12,799
A. Petchey, *LD* — 10,208
Ms I. Willis, *Green* — 683
*C. majority* — 16,830
(June 1987, C. maj. 19,248)

CHEADLE (Greater Manchester)
*E.*66,131  *T.*84.43%
*S. Day, *C.* — 32,504
Ms P. Calton, *LD* — 16,726
Ms S. Broadhurst, *Lab.* — 6,442
Ms P. Whittle, *NLP* — 168
*C. majority* — 15,778
(June 1987, C. maj. 10,631)

CHELMSFORD (Essex)
*E.*83,441  *T.*84.61%
*S. Burns, *C.* — 39,043
H. Nicholson, *LD* — 20,783
Dr R. Chad, *Lab.* — 10,010
Ms E. Burgess, *Green* — 769
*C. majority* — 18,260
(June 1987, C. maj. 7,761)

CHELSEA (Greater London)
*E.*42,371  *T.*63.31%
*Rt. Hon. N. Scott, *C.* — 17,471
Ms R. Horton, *Lab.* — 4,682
Ms S. Broidy, *LD* — 4,101
Ms N. Kortvelyessy, *Green* — 485
D. Armstrong, *Anti Fed.* — 88
*C. majority* — 12,789
(June 1987, C. maj. 13,319)

CHELTENHAM (Glos)
*E.*79,808  *T.*80.32%
N. Jones, *LD* — 30,351
J. Taylor, *C.* — 28,683
Ms P. Tatlow, *Lab.* — 4,077
M. Rendall, *AFE* — 665
H. Brighouse, *NLP* — 169
M. Bruce-Smith, *Ind.* — 162
*LD majority* — 1,668
(June 1987, C. maj. 4,896)

CHERTSEY AND WALTON (Surrey)
*E.*70,465  *T.*80.52%
*Rt. Hon. Sir G. Pattie, *C.* — 34,163
A. Kremer, *LD* — 11,344
Ms I. Hamilton, *Lab.* — 10,791
Ms S. Bennell, *NLP* — 444
*C. majority* — 22,819
(June 1987, C. maj. 17,469)

CHESHAM AND AMERSHAM (Bucks)
*E.*69,895  *T.*81.93%
Ms C. Gillan, *C.* — 36,273
A. Ketteringham, *LD* — 14,053
Ms C. Atherton, *Lab.* — 5,931
Ms C. Strickland, *Green* — 753
T. Griffith-Jones, *NLP* — 255
*C. majority* — 22,220
(June 1987, C. maj. 19,440)

CHESTER, CITY OF
*E.*63,370  *T.*83.84%
G. Brandreth, *C.* — 23,411
D. Robinson, *Lab.* — 22,310
G. Smith, *LD* — 6,867

T. Barker, *Green* — 448
S. Cross, *NLP* — 98
*C. majority* — 1,101
(June 1987, C. maj. 4,855)

CHESTERFIELD (Derbys)
*E.*71,783  *T.*77.98%
*A. Benn, *Lab.* — 26,461
A. Rogers, *LD* — 20,047
P. Lewis, *C.* — 9,473
*Lab. majority* — 6,414
(June 1987, Lab. maj. 8,577)

CHICHESTER (W. Sussex)
*E.*82,124  *T.*77.77%
*R. A. Nelson, *C.* — 37,906
P. Gardiner, *LD* — 17,019
Ms D. Andrewes, *Lab.* — 7,192
E. Paine, *Green* — 876
Ms J. Weights, *Lib.* — 643
Ms J. Jackson, *NLP* — 238
*C. majority* — 20,887
(June 1987, C. maj. 20,177)

CHINGFORD (Greater London)
*E.*55,401  *T.*78.41%
G. I. Duncan-Smith, *C.* — 25,730
P. Dawe, *Lab.* — 10,792
S. Banks, *LD* — 5,705
D. Green, *Lib.* — 602
J. Baguley, *Green* — 575
Revd C. John, *Ind.* — 41
*C. majority* — 14,938
(June 1987, C. maj. 17,955)

CHIPPING BARNET (Greater London)
*E.*57,153  *T.*78.57%
*S. Chapman, *C.* — 25,589
A. Williams, *Lab.* — 11,638
D. Smith, *LD* — 7,247
Ms D. Derksen, *NLP* — 222
C. Johnson, *Fun.* — 213
*C. majority* — 13,951
(June 1987, C. maj. 14,871)

CHISLEHURST (Greater London)
*E.*53,782  *T.*78.89%
*R. Sims, *C.* — 24,761
I. Wingfield, *Lab.* — 9,485
W. Hawthorne, *LD* — 6,683
I. Richmond, *Lib.* — 849
Dr F. Speed, *Green* — 652
*C. majority* — 15,276
(June 1987, C. maj. 14,507)

CHORLEY (Lancs)
*E.*78,531  *T.*82.81%
*D. Dover, *C.* — 30,715
R. McManus, *Lab.* — 26,469
Ms J. Ross-Mills, *LD* — 7,452
P. Leadbetter, *NLP* — 402
*C. majority* — 4,246
(June 1987, C. maj. 8,057)

CHRISTCHURCH (Dorset)
*E.*71,438  *T.*80.70%
*R. Adley, *C.* — 36,627
Revd D. Bussey, *LD* — 13,612
A. Lloyd, *Lab.* — 6,997
J. Barratt, *NLP* — 243

A. Wareham, *CRA* — 175
*C. majority* — 23,015
(June 1987, C. maj. 22,374)
*See also* page 241

CIRENCESTER AND TEWKESBURY (Glos)
*E.*88,299  *T.*82.05%
G. Clifton-Brown, *C.* — 40,258
E. Weston, *LD* — 24,200
T. Page, *Lab.* — 7,262
R. Clayton, *NLP* — 449
P. Trice-Rolph, *Ind.* — 287
*C. majority* — 16,058
(June 1987, C. maj. 12,662)

CITY OF LONDON AND WESTMINSTER SOUTH
*E.*55,021  *T.*63.08%
*Rt. Hon. P. Brooke, *C.* — 20,938
C. Smith, *Lab.* — 7,569
Ms J. Smithard, *LD* — 5,392
G. Herbert, *Green* — 458
P. Stockton, *Loony* — 147
A. Farrell, *IFM* — 107
R. Johnson, *NLP* — 101
*C. majority* — 13,369
(June 1987, C. maj. 12,034)

COLCHESTER NORTH (Essex)
*E.*86,479  *T.*79.11%
Hon. B. Jenkin, *C.* — 35,213
Dr J. Raven, *LD* — 18,721
D. Lee, *Lab.* — 13,870
M. Tariq Shabbeer, *Green* — 372
M. Mears, *NLP* — 238
*C. majority* — 16,492
(June 1987, C. maj. 13,623)

COLCHESTER SOUTH AND MALDON (Essex)
*E.*86,410  *T.*79.22%
J. Whittingdale, *C.* — 37,548
I. Thorn, *LD* — 15,727
C. Pearson, *Lab.* — 14,158
M. Patterson, *Green* — 1,028
*C. majority* — 21,821
(June 1987, C. maj. 15,483)

COLNE VALLEY (W. Yorks)
*E.*72,043  *T.*81.97%
*G. Riddick, *C.* — 24,804
J. Harman, *Lab.* — 17,579
N. Priestley, *LD* — 15,953
R. Stewart, *Green* — 443
Mrs M. Staniforth, *Loony* — 160
J. Hasty, *Ind.* — 73
J. Tattersall, *NLP* — 44
*C. majority* — 7,225
(June 1987, C. maj. 1,677)

CONGLETON (Cheshire)
*E.*70,477  *T.*84.47%
*Mrs J. A. Winterton, *C.* — 29,163
I. Brodie-Browne, *LD* — 18,043
M. Finnegan, *Lab.* — 11,927
P. Brown, *NLP* — 399
*C. majority* — 11,120
(June 1987, C. maj. 7,969)

COPELAND (Cumbria)
E.54,911   T.83.54%

| | |
|---|---|
| *Dr J. Cunningham, *Lab.* | 22,328 |
| P. Davies, *C.* | 19,889 |
| R. Putnam, *LD* | 3,508 |
| J. Sinton, *NLP* | 148 |
| *Lab. majority* | 2,439 |

(June 1987, Lab. maj. 1,894)

CORBY (Northants)
E.68,333   T.82.88%

| | |
|---|---|
| *W. Powell, *C.* | 25,203 |
| A. Feather, *Lab.* | 24,861 |
| M. Roffe, *LD* | 5,792 |
| Ms J. Wood, *Lib.* | 784 |
| *C. majority* | 342 |

(June 1987, C. maj. 1,805)

CORNWALL NORTH
E.76,844   T.81.51%

| | |
|---|---|
| P. Tyler, *LD* | 29,696 |
| *Sir G. Neale, *C.* | 27,775 |
| F. Jordan, *Lab.* | 4,103 |
| P. Andrews, *Lib.* | 678 |
| G. Rowe, *Ind.* | 276 |
| Mrs H. Treadwell, *NLP* | 112 |
| *LD majority* | 1,921 |

(June 1987, C. maj. 5,682)

CORNWALL SOUTH EAST
E.73,027   T.82.14%

| | |
|---|---|
| *R. Hicks, *C.* | 30,565 |
| R. Teverson, *LD* | 22,861 |
| Mrs L. Gilroy, *Lab.* | 5,536 |
| Miss M. Cook, *Lib.* | 644 |
| A. Quick, *Anti Fed.* | 227 |
| Miss R. Allen, *NLP* | 155 |
| *C. majority* | 7,704 |

(June 1987, C. maj. 6,607)

COVENTRY NORTH EAST
(W. Midlands)
E.64,787   T.73.20%

| | |
|---|---|
| R. Ainsworth, *Lab.* | 24,896 |
| K. Perrin, *C.* | 13,220 |
| V. McKee, *LD* | 5,306 |
| *J. Hughes, *Ind. Lab.* | 4,008 |
| *Lab. majority* | 11,676 |

(June 1987, Lab. maj. 11,867)

COVENTRY NORTH WEST
(W. Midlands)
E.50,670   T.77.63%

| | |
|---|---|
| *G. Robinson, *Lab.* | 20,349 |
| Mrs A. Hill, *C.* | 13,917 |
| Ms A. Simpson, *LD* | 5,070 |
| *Lab. majority* | 6,432 |

(June 1987, Lab. maj. 5,663)

COVENTRY SOUTH EAST
(W. Midlands)
E.48,796   T.74.87%

| | |
|---|---|
| J. Cunningham, *Lab.* | 11,902 |
| Mrs M. Hyams, *C.* | 10,591 |
| *D. Nellist, *Ind. Lab.* | 10,551 |
| A. Armstrong, *LD* | 3,318 |
| N. Tompkinson, *NF* | 173 |
| *Lab. majority* | 1,311 |

(June 1987, Lab. maj. 6,653)

COVENTRY SOUTH WEST
(W. Midlands)
E.63,474   T.80.14%

| | |
|---|---|
| *J. Butcher, *C.* | 23,225 |
| R. Slater, *Lab.* | 21,789 |
| G. Sewards, *LD* | 4,666 |
| R. Wheway, *Lib.* | 989 |
| D. Morris, *NLP* | 204 |
| *C. majority* | 1,436 |

(June 1987, C. maj. 3,210)

CRAWLEY (W. Sussex)
E.78,277   T.79.16%

| | |
|---|---|
| *Hon. A. N. Soames, *C.* | 30,204 |
| Ms L. Moffatt, *Lab.* | 22,439 |
| G. Seekings, *LD* | 8,558 |
| M. Wilson, *Green* | 766 |
| *C. majority* | 7,765 |

(June 1987, C. maj. 12,138)

CREWE AND NANTWICH (Cheshire)
E.74,993   T.81.87%

| | |
|---|---|
| *Hon. Mrs G. Dunwoody, *Lab.* | 28,065 |
| B. Silvester, *C.* | 25,370 |
| G. Griffiths, *LD* | 7,315 |
| Ms N. Wilkinson, *Green* | 651 |
| *Lab. majority* | 2,695 |

(June 1987, Lab. maj. 1,092)

CROSBY (Merseyside)
E.82,537   T.82.45%

| | |
|---|---|
| *M. Thornton, *C.* | 32,267 |
| Ms M. Eagle, *Lab.* | 17,461 |
| Ms F. Clucas, *LD* | 16,562 |
| J. Marks, *Lib.* | 1,052 |
| S. Brady, *Green* | 559 |
| N. Paterson, *NLP* | 152 |
| *C. majority* | 14,806 |

(June 1987, C. maj. 6,853)

CROYDON CENTRAL (Greater
London)
E.55,798   T.71.73%

| | |
|---|---|
| Sir P. Beresford, *C.* | 22,168 |
| G. Davies, *Lab.* | 12,518 |
| Ms D. Richardson, *LD* | 5,342 |
| *C. majority* | 9,650 |

(June 1987, C. maj. 12,617)

CROYDON NORTH EAST (Greater
London)
E.64,405   T.72.01%

| | |
|---|---|
| D. Congdon, *C.* | 23,835 |
| Ms M. Walker, *Lab.* | 16,362 |
| J. Fraser, *LD* | 6,186 |
| *C. majority* | 7,473 |

(June 1987, C. maj. 12,519)

CROYDON NORTH WEST (Greater
London)
E.57,241   T.70.76%

| | |
|---|---|
| M. Wicks, *Lab.* | 19,152 |
| *H. Malins, *C.* | 17,626 |
| Ms L. Hawkins, *LD* | 3,728 |
| *Lab. majority* | 1,526 |

(June 1987, C. maj. 3,988)

CROYDON SOUTH (Greater London)
E.64,768   T.77.57%

| | |
|---|---|
| R. Ottaway, *C.* | 31,993 |
| P. Billenness, *LD* | 11,568 |
| Miss H. Salmon, *Lab.* | 6,444 |
| M. Samuel, *Choice* | 239 |
| *C. majority* | 20,425 |

(June 1987, C. maj. 19,063)

DAGENHAM (Greater London)
E.59,645   T.70.65%

| | |
|---|---|
| *B. Gould, *Lab.* | 22,027 |
| D. Rossiter, *C.* | 15,294 |
| C. Marquand, *LD* | 4,824 |
| *Lab. majority* | 6,733 |

(June 1987, Lab. maj. 2,469)
*See also* page 241

DARLINGTON (Durham)
E.66,094   T.83.60%

| | |
|---|---|
| A. Milburn, *Lab.* | 26,556 |
| *M. Fallon, *C.* | 23,758 |
| P. Bergg, *LD* | 4,586 |
| Dr D. Clarke, *BNP* | 355 |
| *Lab. majority* | 2,798 |

(June 1987, C. maj. 2,661)

DARTFORD (Kent)
E.72,366   T.83.14%

| | |
|---|---|
| *B. Dunn, *C.* | 31,194 |
| Dr H. Stoate, *Lab.* | 20,880 |
| Dr P. Bryden, *LD* | 7,584 |
| A. Munro, *FDP* | 262 |
| Ms A. Holland, *NLP* | 247 |
| *C. majority* | 10,314 |

(June 1987, C. maj. 14,929)

DAVENTRY (Northants)
E.71,824   T.82.75%

| | |
|---|---|
| *T. Boswell, *C.* | 34,734 |
| Ms L. Koumi, *Lab.* | 14,460 |
| A. Rounthwaite, *LD* | 9,820 |
| R. France, *NLP* | 422 |
| *C. majority* | 20,274 |

(June 1987, C. maj. 19,690)

DAVYHULME (Greater Manchester)
E.61,679   T.81.82%

| | |
|---|---|
| *W. Churchill, *C.* | 24,216 |
| B. Brotherton, *Lab.* | 19,790 |
| Ms J. Pearcey, *LD* | 5,797 |
| T. Brotheridge, *NLP* | 665 |
| *C. majority* | 4,426 |

(June 1987, C. maj. 8,199)

DENTON AND REDDISH (Greater
Manchester)
E.68,463   T.76.77%

| | |
|---|---|
| *A. Bennett, *Lab.* | 29,021 |
| J. Horswell, *C.* | 16,937 |
| Dr F. Ridley, *LD* | 4,953 |
| M. Powell, *Lib.* | 1,296 |
| J. Fuller, *NLP* | 354 |
| *Lab. majority* | 12,084 |

(June 1987, Lab. maj. 8,250)

DERBY NORTH
E.73,176   T.80.65%

| | |
|---|---|
| *G. Knight, *C.* | 28,574 |
| R. Laxton, *Lab.* | 24,121 |
| R. Charlesworth, *LD* | 5,638 |
| E. Wall, *Green* | 383 |
| P. Hart, *NF* | 245 |
| N. Onley, *NLP* | 58 |
| *C. majority* | 4,453 |

(June 1987, C. maj. 6,280)

DERBY SOUTH
E.66,328  T.75.52%

| | |
|---|---:|
| *Mrs M. Beckett, *Lab.* | 25,917 |
| N. Brown, *C.* | 18,981 |
| S. Hartropp, *LD* | 5,198 |
| *Lab. majority* | 6,936 |
| (June 1987, Lab. maj. 1,516) | |

DERBYSHIRE NORTH EAST
E.70,707  T.83.61%

| | |
|---|---:|
| *H. Barnes, *Lab.* | 28,860 |
| J. Hayes, *C.* | 22,590 |
| D. Stone, *LD* | 7,675 |
| *Lab. majority* | 6,270 |
| (June 1987, Lab. maj. 3,720) | |

DERBYSHIRE SOUTH
E.82,342  T.85.49%

| | |
|---|---:|
| *Mrs E. Currie, *C.* | 34,266 |
| M. Todd, *Lab.* | 29,608 |
| Ms D. Brass, *LD* | 6,236 |
| T. Mercer, *NLP* | 291 |
| *C. majority* | 4,658 |
| (June 1987, C. maj. 10,311) | |

DERBYSHIRE WEST
E.71,201  T.84.99%

| | |
|---|---:|
| *P. McLoughlin, *C.* | 32,879 |
| R. Fearn, *LD* | 14,110 |
| S. Clamp, *Lab.* | 13,528 |
| *C. majority* | 18,769 |
| (June 1987, C. maj. 10,527) | |

DEVIZES (Wilts)
E.89,745  T.81.67%

| | |
|---|---:|
| M. Ancram, *C.* | 39,090 |
| Ms J. Mactaggart, *LD* | 19,378 |
| Ms R. Berry, *Lab.* | 13,060 |
| S. Coles, *Lib.* | 962 |
| D. Ripley, *Green* | 808 |
| *C. majority* | 19,712 |
| (June 1987, C. maj. 17,830) | |

DEVON NORTH
E.68,998  T.84.36%

| | |
|---|---:|
| N. Harvey, *LD* | 27,414 |
| *A. Speller, *C.* | 26,620 |
| P. Donner, *Lab.* | 3,410 |
| Ms C. Simmons, *Green* | 658 |
| G. Treadwell, *NLP* | 107 |
| *LD majority* | 794 |
| (June 1987, C. maj. 4,469) | |

DEVON WEST AND TORRIDGE
E.76,933  T.81.46%

| | |
|---|---:|
| *Miss E. Nicholson, *C.* | 29,627 |
| D. McBride, *LD* | 26,013 |
| D. Brenton, *Lab.* | 5,997 |
| Dr F. Williamson, *Green* | 898 |
| D. Collins, *NLP* | 141 |
| *C. majority* | 3,614 |
| (June 1987, C. maj. 6,468) | |

DEWSBURY (W. Yorks)
E.72,839  T.80.18%

| | |
|---|---:|
| *Mrs W. A. Taylor, *Lab.* | 25,596 |
| J. Whitfield, *C.* | 24,962 |
| R. Meadowcroft, *LD* | 6,570 |
| Lady J. Birdwood, *BNP* | 660 |
| N. Denby, *Green* | 471 |
| Mrs J. Marsden, *NLP* | 146 |
| *Lab. majority* | 634 |
| (June 1987, Lab. maj. 445) | |

DONCASTER CENTRAL (S. Yorks)
E.68,890  T.74.24%

| | |
|---|---:|
| *Rt. Hon. H. Walker, *Lab.* | 27,795 |
| W. Glossop, *C.* | 17,113 |
| C. Hampson, *LD* | 6,057 |
| M. Driver, *WRP* | 184 |
| *Lab. majority* | 10,682 |
| (June 1987, Lab. maj. 8,196) | |

DONCASTER NORTH (S. Yorks)
E.74,732  T.73.92%

| | |
|---|---:|
| K. Hughes, *Lab.* | 34,135 |
| R. Light, *C.* | 14,322 |
| S. Whiting, *LD* | 6,787 |
| *Lab. majority* | 19,813 |
| (June 1987, Lab. maj. 19,938) | |

DON VALLEY (S. Yorks)
E.76,327  T.76.25%

| | |
|---|---:|
| *M. Redmond, *Lab.* | 32,008 |
| N. Paget-Brown, *C.* | 18,474 |
| M. Jevons, *LD* | 6,920 |
| S. Platt, *Green* | 803 |
| *Lab. majority* | 13,534 |
| (June 1987, Lab. maj. 11,467) | |

DORSET NORTH
E.76,718  T.81.79%

| | |
|---|---:|
| *N. Baker, *C.* | 34,234 |
| Ms L. Siegle, *LD* | 24,154 |
| J. Fitzmaurice, *Lab.* | 4,360 |
| *C. majority* | 10,080 |
| (June 1987, C. maj. 11,907) | |

DORSET SOUTH
E.75,788  T.76.91%

| | |
|---|---:|
| *I. Bruce, *C.* | 29,319 |
| B. Ellis, *LD* | 15,811 |
| Dr A. Chedzoy, *Lab.* | 12,298 |
| Mrs J. Nager, *Ind.* | 673 |
| M. Griffiths, *NLP* | 191 |
| *C. majority* | 13,508 |
| (June 1987, C. maj. 15,067) | |

DORSET WEST
E.67,256  T.81.18%

| | |
|---|---:|
| *Sir J. Spicer, *C.* | 27,766 |
| R. Legg, *LD* | 19,756 |
| J. Mann, *Lab.* | 7,082 |
| *C. majority* | 8,010 |
| (June 1987, C. maj. 12,364) | |

DOVER (Kent)
E.68,962  T.83.50%

| | |
|---|---:|
| *D. Shaw, *C.* | 25,395 |
| G. Prosser, *Lab.* | 24,562 |
| M. Sole, *LD* | 6,212 |
| A. Sullivan, *Green* | 637 |
| P. Sherred, *Ind.* | 407 |
| B. Philp, *Ind. C.* | 250 |
| C. Percy, *NLP* | 127 |
| *C. majority* | 833 |
| (June 1987, C. maj. 6,541) | |

DUDLEY EAST (W. Midlands)
E.75,355  T.74.96%

| | |
|---|---:|
| *Dr J. Gilbert, *Lab.* | 29,806 |
| J. Holland, *C.* | 20,606 |
| I. Jenkins, *LD* | 5,400 |
| G. Cartwright, *NF* | 675 |
| *Lab. majority* | 9,200 |
| (June 1987, Lab. maj. 3,473) | |

DUDLEY WEST (W. Midlands)
E.86,632  T.82.08%

| | |
|---|---:|
| *J. Blackburn, *C.* | 34,729 |
| K. Lomax, *Lab.* | 28,940 |
| G. Lewis, *LD* | 7,446 |
| *C. majority* | 5,789 |
| (June 1987, C. maj. 10,244) | |

DULWICH (Greater London)
E.55,141  T.67.91%

| | |
|---|---:|
| Ms T. Jowell, *Lab.* | 17,714 |
| *G. Bowden, *C.* | 15,658 |
| Dr A. Goldie, *LD* | 4,078 |
| *Lab. majority* | 2,056 |
| (June 1987, C. maj. 180) | |

DURHAM, CITY OF
E.68,165  T.74.61%

| | |
|---|---:|
| *G. Steinberg, *Lab.* | 27,095 |
| M. Woodroofe, *C.* | 12,037 |
| N. Martin, *LD* | 10,915 |
| Ms S. J. Banks, *Green* | 812 |
| *Lab. majority* | 15,058 |
| (June 1987, Lab. maj. 6,125) | |

DURHAM NORTH
E.73,694  T.76.08%

| | |
|---|---:|
| *G. Radice, *Lab.* | 33,567 |
| Ms E. Sibley, *C.* | 13,930 |
| P. Appleby, *LD* | 8,572 |
| *Lab. majority* | 19,637 |
| (June 1987, Lab. maj. 18,433) | |

DURHAM NORTH WEST
E.61,139  T. 75.58%

| | |
|---|---:|
| *Miss H. Armstrong, Lab. | 26,734 |
| Mrs T. May, *C.* | 12,747 |
| T. Farron, LD | 6,728 |
| *Lab. majority* | 13,987 |
| (June 1987, Lab. maj. 10,162) | |

EALING ACTON (Greater London)
E.58,687  T.76.03%

| | |
|---|---:|
| *Sir G. Young, *C.* | 22,579 |
| Ms Y. Johnson, *Lab.* | 15,572 |
| L. Rowe, *LD* | 5,487 |
| Ms A. Seibe, *Green* | 554 |
| T. Pitt-Aikens, *Ind. C.* | 432 |
| *C. majority* | 7,007 |
| (June 1987, C. maj. 12,233) | |

EALING NORTH (Greater London)
E.63,528  T.78.84%

| | |
|---|---:|
| *H. Greenway, *C.* | 24,898 |
| M. Stears, *Lab.* | 18,932 |
| P. Hankinson, *LD* | 5,247 |
| D. Earl, *Green* | 554 |
| C. Hill, *NF* | 277 |
| R. Davis, *CD* | 180 |
| *C. majority* | 5,966 |
| (June 1987, C. maj. 15,153) | |

EALING SOUTHALL (Greater London)
E.65,574  T.75.49%

| | |
|---|---:|
| P. Khabra, *Lab.* | 23,476 |
| P. Treleaven, *C.* | 16,610 |
| *S. Bidwell, *True Lab.* | 4,665 |
| Ms P. Nandhra, *LD* | 3,790 |
| N. Goodwin, *Green* | 964 |
| *Lab. majority* | 6,866 |
| (June 1987, Lab. maj. 7,977) | |

EASINGTON (Durham)
E.65,061   T.72.46%
| | |
|---|---|
| *J. Cummings, *Lab.* | 34,269 |
| W. Perry, *C.* | 7,879 |
| P. Freitag, *LD* | 5,001 |
| *Lab. majority* | 26,390 |
(June 1987, Lab. maj. 24,639)

EASTBOURNE (E. Sussex)
E.76,103   T.80.97%
| | |
|---|---|
| N. Waterson, *C.* | 31,792 |
| *D. Bellotti, *LD* | 26,311 |
| I. Gibbons, *Lab.* | 2,834 |
| D. Aherne, *Green* | 391 |
| Ms T. Williamson, *Lib.* | 296 |
| *C. majority* | 5,481 |
(June 1987, C. maj 16,923)
(October 1990, LD maj. 4,550)

EASTLEIGH (Hants)
E.91,736   T.82.91%
| | |
|---|---|
| S. Milligan, *C.* | 38,998 |
| D. Chidgey, *LD* | 21,296 |
| Ms J. Sugrue, *Lab.* | 15,768 |
| *C. majority* | 17,702 |
(June 1987, C. maj. 13,355)
*See also page 241*

ECCLES (Greater Manchester)
E.64,910   T.74.12%
| | |
|---|---|
| *Miss J. Lestor, *Lab.* | 27,357 |
| G. Ling, *C.* | 14,131 |
| G. Reid, *LD* | 5,835 |
| R. Duriez, *Green* | 521 |
| Miss J. Garner, *NLP* | 270 |
| *Lab. majority* | 13,226 |
(June 1987, Lab. maj. 9,699)

EDDISBURY (Cheshire)
E.75,089   T.82.55%
| | |
|---|---|
| *A. Goodlad, *C.* | 31,625 |
| Ms N. Edwards, *Lab.* | 18,928 |
| D. Lyon, *LD* | 10,543 |
| A. Basden, *Green* | 783 |
| N. Pollard, *NLP* | 107 |
| *C. majority* | 12,697 |
(June 1987, C. maj. 15,835)

EDMONTON (Greater London)
E.63,052   T.75.66%
| | |
|---|---|
| *Dr I. Twinn, *C.* | 22,076 |
| A. Love, *Lab.* | 21,483 |
| E. Jones, *LD* | 3,940 |
| Ms E. Solley, *NLP* | 207 |
| *C. majority* | 593 |
(June 1987, C. maj. 7,286)

ELLESMERE PORT AND NESTON
(Cheshire)
E.71,572   T.84.12%
| | |
|---|---|
| A. Miller, *Lab.* | 27,782 |
| A. Pearce, *C.* | 25,793 |
| Ms E. Jewkes, *LD* | 5,944 |
| Dr M. Money, *Green* | 589 |
| Dr A. Rae, *NLP* | 105 |
| *Lab. majority* | 1,989 |
(June 1987, C. maj. 1,853)

ELMET (W. Yorks)
E.70,558   T.82.53%
| | |
|---|---|
| *S. Batiste, *C.* | 27,677 |
| C. Burgon, *Lab.* | 24,416 |

| | |
|---|---|
| Mrs A. Beck, *LD* | 6,144 |
| *C. majority* | 3,261 |
(June 1987, C. maj. 5,356)

ELTHAM (Greater London)
E.51,989   T.78.72%
| | |
|---|---|
| *P. Bottomley, *C.* | 18,813 |
| C. Efford, *Lab.* | 17,147 |
| C. McGinty, *LD* | 4,804 |
| A. Graham, *Ind. C.* | 165 |
| *C. majority* | 1,666 |
(June 1987, C. maj. 6,460)

ENFIELD NORTH (Greater London)
E.67,421   T.77.91%
| | |
|---|---|
| *T. Eggar, *C.* | 27,789 |
| M. Upham, *Lab.* | 18,359 |
| Ms S. Tustin, *LD* | 5,817 |
| J. Markham, *NLP* | 565 |
| *C. majority* | 9,430 |
(June 1987, C. maj. 14,015)

ENFIELD SOUTHGATE (Greater
London)
E.64,311   T.76.28%
| | |
|---|---|
| *M. Portillo, *C.* | 28,422 |
| Ms K. Livney, *Lab.* | 12,859 |
| K. Keane, *LD* | 7,080 |
| Ms M. Hollands, *Green* | 696 |
| *C. majority* | 15,563 |
(June 1987, C. maj. 18,345)

EPPING FOREST (Essex)
E.67,585   T.80.55%
| | |
|---|---|
| *S. Norris, *C.* | 32,407 |
| S. Murray, *Lab.* | 12,219 |
| Mrs B. Austen, *LD* | 9,265 |
| A. O'Brien, *EFRA* | 552 |
| *C. majority* | 20,188 |
(June 1987, C. maj. 21,513)
(December 1988, C. maj. 4,504)

EPSOM AND EWELL (Surrey)
E.68,138   T.80.14%
| | |
|---|---|
| *Rt. Hon. A. Hamilton, *C.* | 32,861 |
| M. Emerson, *LD* | 12,840 |
| R. Warren, *Lab.* | 8,577 |
| G. Hatchard, *NLP* | 334 |
| *C. majority* | 20,021 |
(June 1987, C. maj. 20,761)

EREWASH (Derbys)
E.75,627   T.83.78%
| | |
|---|---|
| Mrs A. Knight, *C.* | 29,907 |
| S. Stafford, *Lab.* | 24,204 |
| P. Tuck, *LD* | 8,606 |
| L. Johnson, *BNP* | 645 |
| *C. majority* | 5,703 |
(June 1987, C. maj. 9,754)

ERITH AND CRAYFORD (Kent)
E.59,213   T.79.66%
| | |
|---|---|
| *D. Evennett, *C.* | 21,926 |
| N. Beard, *Lab.* | 19,587 |
| Ms F. Jamieson, *LD* | 5,657 |
| *C. majority* | 2,339 |
(June 1987, C. maj. 6,994)

ESHER (Surrey)
E.58,840   T.80.80%
| | |
|---|---|
| *I. Taylor, *C.* | 31,115 |
| J. Richling, *LD* | 10,744 |
| Ms J. Reay, *Lab.* | 5,685 |

| | |
|---|---|
| *C. majority* | 20,371 |
(June 1987, C. maj. 19,068)

EXETER (Devon)
E.76,723   T.82.21%
| | |
|---|---|
| *Sir J. Hannam, *C.* | 26,543 |
| J. Lloyd, *Lab.* | 22,498 |
| G. Oakes, *LD* | 12,059 |
| Ms A. Micklem, *Lib.* | 1,119 |
| T. Brenan, *Green* | 764 |
| M. Turnbull, *NLP* | 98 |
| *C. majority* | 4,045 |
(June 1987, C. maj. 7,656)

FALMOUTH AND CAMBORNE
(Cornwall)
E.70,702   T.81.10%
| | |
|---|---|
| S. Coe, *C.* | 21,150 |
| Ms T. Jones, *LD* | 17,883 |
| J. Cosgrove, *Lab.* | 16,732 |
| P. Holmes, *Lib.* | 730 |
| K. Saunders, *Green* | 466 |
| F. Zapp, *Loony* | 327 |
| A. Pringle, *NLP* | 56 |
| *C. majority* | 3,267 |
(June 1987, C. maj. 5,039)

FAREHAM (Hants)
E.81,124   T.81.85%
| | |
|---|---|
| *P. Lloyd, *C.* | 40,482 |
| J. Thompson, *LD* | 16,341 |
| Ms E. Weston, *Lab.* | 8,766 |
| M. Brimecome, *Green* | 818 |
| *C. majority* | 24,141 |
(June 1987, C. maj. 18,795)

FAVERSHAM (Kent)
E.81,977   T.79.71%
| | |
|---|---|
| *R. Moate, *C.* | 32,755 |
| Ms H. Brinton, *Lab.* | 16,404 |
| R. Truelove, *LD* | 15,896 |
| R. Bradshaw, *NLP* | 294 |
| *C. majority* | 16,351 |
(June 1987, C. maj. 13,978)

FELTHAM AND HESTON (Greater
London)
E.81,221   T.73.90%
| | |
|---|---|
| A. Keen, *Lab.* | 27,660 |
| *P. Ground, *C.* | 25,665 |
| M. Hoban, *LD* | 6,700 |
| *Lab. majority* | 1,995 |
(June 1987, C. maj. 5,430)

FINCHLEY (Greater London)
E.52,907   T.77.64%
| | |
|---|---|
| H. Booth, *C.* | 21,039 |
| Ms A. Marjoram, *Lab.* | 14,651 |
| Ms H. Leighter, *LD* | 4,568 |
| A. Gunstock, *Green* | 564 |
| Ms S. Johnson, *Loony* | 130 |
| J. Macrae, *NLP* | 129 |
| *C. majority* | 6,388 |
(June 1987, C. maj. 8,913)

FOLKESTONE AND HYTHE (Kent)
E.65,856   T.79.61%
| | |
|---|---|
| *Rt. Hon. M. Howard, *C.* | 27,437 |
| Mrs L. Cufley, *LD* | 18,527 |
| P. Doherty, *Lab.* | 6,347 |
| A. Hobbs, *NLP* | 123 |
| *C. majority* | 8,910 |
(June 1987, C. maj. 9,126)

FULHAM (Greater London)
E.52,740   T.76.16%
| | |
|---|---|
| *M. Carrington, *C.* | 21,438 |
| N. Moore, *Lab.* | 14,859 |
| P. Crystal, *LD* | 3,339 |
| Ms E. Streeter, *Green* | 443 |
| J. Darby, *NLP* | 91 |
| *C. majority* | 6,579 |

(June 1987, C. maj. 6,322)

FYLDE (Lancs)
E.63,573   T.78.50%
| | |
|---|---|
| *M. Jack, *C.* | 30,639 |
| N. Cryer, *LD* | 9,648 |
| Ms C. Hughes, *Lab.* | 9,382 |
| P. Leadbetter, *NLP* | 239 |
| *C. majority* | 20,991 |

(June 1987, C. maj. 17,772)

GAINSBOROUGH AND HORNCASTLE (Lincs)
E.72,038   T.80.87%
| | |
|---|---|
| *E. Leigh, *C.* | 31,444 |
| N. Taylor, *LD* | 15,199 |
| Ms F. Jones, *Lab.* | 11,619 |
| *C. majority* | 16,245 |

(June 1987, C. maj. 9,723)

GATESHEAD EAST (Tyne & Wear)
E.64,355   T.73.63%
| | |
|---|---|
| *Miss J. Quin, *Lab.* | 30,100 |
| M. Callanan, *C.* | 11,570 |
| R. Beadle, *LD* | 5,720 |
| *Lab. majority* | 18,530 |

(June 1987, Lab. maj. 17,228)

GEDLING (Notts)
E.68,953   T.82.34%
| | |
|---|---|
| *A. J. B. Mitchell, *C.* | 30,191 |
| V. Coaker, *Lab.* | 19,554 |
| D. George, *LD* | 6,863 |
| Ms A. Miszeweka, *NLP* | 168 |
| *C. majority* | 10,637 |

(June 1987, C. maj. 16,539)

GILLINGHAM (Kent)
E.71,851   T.80.32%
| | |
|---|---|
| *J. Couchman, *C.* | 30,201 |
| P. Clark, *Lab.* | 13,563 |
| M. Wallbank, *LD* | 13,509 |
| C. MacKinlay, *Ind.* | 248 |
| D. Jolicoeur, *NLP* | 190 |
| *C. majority* | 16,638 |

(June 1987, C. maj. 12,549)

GLANFORD AND SCUNTHORPE (Humberside)
E.73,479   T.78.91%
| | |
|---|---|
| *E. Morley, *Lab.* | 30,623 |
| Dr A. Saywood, *C.* | 22,211 |
| W. Paxton, *LD* | 4,172 |
| C. Nottingham, *SD* | 982 |
| *Lab. majority* | 8,412 |

(June 1987, Lab. maj. 512)

GLOUCESTER
E.80,578   T.80.24%
| | |
|---|---|
| *D. French, *C.* | 29,870 |
| K. Stephens, *Lab.* | 23,812 |
| J. Sewell, *LD* | 10,978 |
| *C. majority* | 6,058 |

(June 1987, C. maj. 12,035)

GLOUCESTERSHIRE WEST
E.80,007   T.83.89%
| | |
|---|---|
| *P. Marland, *C.* | 29,232 |
| Ms D. Organ, *Lab.* | 24,274 |
| L. Boait, *LD* | 13,366 |
| A. Reeve, *Brit. Ind.* | 172 |
| C. Palmer, *Century* | 75 |
| *C. majority* | 4,958 |

(June 1987, C. maj. 11,679)

GOSPORT (Hants)
E.69,638   T.76.79%
| | |
|---|---|
| *P. Viggers, *C.* | 31,094 |
| M. Russell, *LD* | 14,776 |
| Ms M. Angus, *Lab.* | 7,275 |
| P. Ettie, *Pensioners* | 332 |
| *C. majority* | 16,318 |

(June 1987, C. maj. 13,723)

GRANTHAM (Lincs)
E.83,463   T.79.29%
| | |
|---|---|
| *Hon. D. Hogg, *C.* | 37,194 |
| S. Taggart, *Lab.* | 17,606 |
| J. Heppell, *LD* | 9,882 |
| J. Hiley, *Lib.* | 1,500 |
| *C. majority* | 19,588 |

(June 1987, C. maj. 21,303)

GRAVESHAM (Kent)
E.70,740   T.83.48%
| | |
|---|---|
| *J. Arnold, *C.* | 29,322 |
| G. Green, *Lab.* | 23,829 |
| D. Deedman, *LD* | 5,269 |
| A. Bunstone, *Ind.* | 273 |
| R. Khilkoff-Boulding, *ILP* | 187 |
| B. Buxton, *Soc.* | 174 |
| *C. majority* | 5,493 |

(June 1987, C. maj. 8,792)

GREAT GRIMSBY (Humberside)
E.67,427   T.75.28%
| | |
|---|---|
| *A. V. Mitchell, *Lab.* | 25,895 |
| P. Jackson, *C.* | 18,391 |
| Ms P. Frankish, *LD* | 6,475 |
| *Lab. majority* | 7,504 |

(June 1987, Lab. maj. 8,784)

GREAT YARMOUTH (Norfolk)
E.68,263   T.77.94%
| | |
|---|---|
| *M. Carttiss, *C.* | 25,505 |
| Ms B. Baughan, *Lab.* | 20,196 |
| M. Scott, *LD* | 7,225 |
| Ms P. Larkin, *NLP* | 284 |
| *C. majority* | 5,309 |

(June 1987, C. maj. 10,083)

GREENWICH (Greater London)
E.47,789   T.74.63%
| | |
|---|---|
| W. R. N. Raynsford, *Lab.* | 14,630 |
| *Mrs R. Barnes, *SD* | 13,273 |
| Mrs A. McNair, *C.* | 6,960 |
| R. McCracken, *Green* | 483 |
| R. Mallone, *Fellowship* | 147 |
| M. Hardee, *UTCHAP* | 103 |
| J. Small, *NLP* | 70 |
| *Lab. majority* | 1,357 |

(June 1987, SDP/All. maj. 2,141)

GUILDFORD (Surrey)
E.77,265   T.78.48%
| | |
|---|---|
| *Rt. Hon. D. Howell, *C.* | 33,516 |
| Mrs M. Sharp, *LD* | 20,112 |
| H. Mann, *Lab.* | 6,781 |
| A. Law, *NLP* | 234 |
| *C. majority* | 13,404 |

(June 1987, C. maj. 12,607)

HACKNEY NORTH AND STOKE NEWINGTON (Greater London)
E.54,655   T.63.53%
| | |
|---|---|
| *Ms D. Abbott, *Lab.* | 20,083 |
| C. Manson, *C.* | 9,356 |
| K. Fitchett, *LD* | 3,996 |
| Ms H. Hunt, *Green* | 1,111 |
| J. Windsor, *NLP* | 178 |
| *Lab. majority* | 10,727 |

(June 1987, Lab. maj. 7,678)

HACKNEY SOUTH AND SHOREDITCH (Greater London)
E.57,935   T.63.82%
| | |
|---|---|
| *B. Sedgemore, *Lab.* | 19,730 |
| A. Turner, *C.* | 10,714 |
| G. Wintle, *LD* | 5,533 |
| L. Lucas, *Green* | 772 |
| Ms G. Norman, *NLP* | 226 |
| *Lab. majority* | 9,016 |

(June 1987, Lab. maj. 7,522)

HALESOWEN AND STOURBRIDGE (W. Midlands)
E.77,644   T.82.28%
| | |
|---|---|
| P. W. Hawksley, *C.* | 32,312 |
| A. Hankon, *Lab.* | 22,730 |
| V. Sharma, *LD* | 7,941 |
| T. Weller, *Green* | 908 |
| *C. majority* | 9,582 |

(June 1987, C. maj. 13,808)

HALIFAX (W. Yorks)
E.73,401   T.78.69%
| | |
|---|---|
| *Ms A. Mahon, *Lab.* | 25,115 |
| T. Martin, *C.* | 24,637 |
| I. Howell, *LD* | 7,364 |
| R. Pearson, *Nat.* | 649 |
| *Lab. majority* | 478 |

(June 1987, Lab. maj. 1,212)

HALTON (Cheshire)
E.74,906   T.78.34%
| | |
|---|---|
| *Rt. Hon. G. Oakes, *Lab.* | 35,025 |
| G. Mercer, *C.* | 16,821 |
| D. Reaper, *LD* | 6,104 |
| S. Herley, *Loony* | 398 |
| N. Collins, *NLP* | 338 |
| *Lab. majority* | 18,204 |

(June 1987, Lab. maj. 14,578)

HAMMERSMITH (Greater London)
E.47,229   T.71.90%
| | |
|---|---|
| *C. Soley, *Lab.* | 17,329 |
| A. Hennessy, *C.* | 12,575 |
| J. Bates, *LD* | 3,380 |
| R. Crosskey, *Green* | 546 |
| K. Turner, *NLP* | 89 |
| Ms H. Szamuely, *Anti Fed.* | 41 |
| *Lab. majority* | 4,754 |

(June 1987, Lab. maj. 2,415)

HAMPSHIRE EAST
E.92,139   T.80.35%
| | |
|---|---|
| *M. Mates, *C.* | 47,541 |
| Ms S. Baring, *LD* | 18,376 |

J. Phillips, *Lab.* 6,840
I. Foster, *Green* 1,113
S. Hale, *RCC* 165
*C. majority* 29,165
(June 1987, C. maj. 23,786)

HAMPSHIRE NORTH WEST
*E.*73,101 *T.*80.75%
*Sir D. Mitchell, *C.* 34,310
M. Simpson, *LD* 16,462
M. Stockwell, *Lab.* 7,433
Ms D. Ashley, *Green* 825
*C. majority* 17,848
(June 1987, C. maj. 13,437)

HAMPSTEAD AND HIGHGATE
(Greater London)
*E.*58,203 *T.*73.04%
Ms G. Jackson, *Lab.* 19,193
O. Letwin, *C.* 17,753
D. Wrede, *LD* 4,765
S. Games, *Green* 594
Dr R. Prosser, *NLP* 86
Ms A. Hall, *RAVA* 44
C. Scallywag Wilson, *Scallywag* 44
Captain Rizz, *Rizz* 33
*Lab. majority* 1,440
(June 1987, C. maj. 2,221)

HARBOROUGH (Leics)
*E.*76,514 *T.*82.11%
E. Garnier, *C.* 34,280
M. Cox, *LD* 20,737
Ms C. Mackay, *Lab.* 7,483
A. Irwin, *NLP* 328
*C. majority* 13,543
(June 1987, C. maj. 18,810)

HARLOW (Essex)
*E.*68,615 *T.*82.56%
*J. Hayes, *C.* 26,608
W. Rammell, *Lab.* 23,668
Ms L. Spenceley, *LD* 6,375
*C. majority* 2,940
(June 1987, C. maj. 5,877)

HARROGATE (N. Yorks)
*E.*76,250 *T.*77.98%
*R. Banks, *C.* 32,023
T. Hurren, *LD* 19,434
A. Wright, *Lab.* 7,230
A. Warneken, *Green* 780
*C. majority* 12,589
(June 1987, C. maj. 11,902)

HARROW EAST (Greater London)
*E.*74,733 *T.*77.83%
*H. Dykes, *C.* 30,752
A. McNulty, *Lab.* 19,654
Ms V. Chamberlain, *LD* 6,360
P. Burrows, *Lib.* 1,142
Mrs S. Hamza, *NLP* 212
J. Lester, *Anti Fed.* 49
*C. majority* 11,098
(June 1987, C. maj. 18,273)

HARROW WEST (Greater London)
*E.*69,616 *T.*78.69%
*R. G. Hughes, *C.* 30,240
C. Moraes, *Lab.* 12,343
C. Noyce, *LD* 11,050
G. Aitman, *Lib.* 845

Mrs J. Argyle, *NLP* 306
*C. majority* 17,897
(June 1987, C. maj. 15,444)

HARTLEPOOL (Cleveland)
*E.*67,968 *T.*76.07%
P. Mandelson, *Lab.* 26,816
G. Robb, *C.* 18,034
I. Cameron, *LD* 6,860
*Lab. majority* 8,782
(June 1987, Lab. maj. 7,289)

HARWICH (Essex)
*E.*80,260 *T.*77.70%
I. Sproat, *C.* 32,369
Mrs P. Bevan, *LD* 15,210
R. Knight, *Lab.* 14,511
Mrs E. McGrath, *NLP* 279
*C. majority* 17,159
(June 1987, C. maj. 12,082)

HASTINGS AND RYE (E. Sussex)
*E.*71,838 *T.*74.86%
Ms J. Lait, *C.* 25,573
M. Palmer, *LD* 18,939
R. Stevens, *Lab.* 8,458
Ms S. Phillips, *Green* 640
T. Howell, *Loony* 168
*C. majority* 6,634
(June 1987, C. maj. 7,347)

HAVANT (Hants)
*E.*74,217 *T.*79.01%
D. Willetts, *C.* 32,233
S. van Hagen, *LD* 14,649
G. Morris, *Lab.* 10,968
T. Mitchell, *Green* 793
*C. majority* 17,584
(June 1987, C. maj. 16,510)

HAYES AND HARLINGTON (Greater London)
*E.*54,449 *T.*79.70%
*T. Dicks, *C.* 19,489
J. McDonnell, *Lab.* 19,436
T. Little, *LD* 4,472
*C. majority* 53
(June 1987, C. maj. 5,965)

HAZEL GROVE (Greater Manchester)
*E.*64,302 *T.*84.94%
*Sir T. Arnold, *C.* 24,479
A. Stunell, *LD* 23,550
C. McAllister, *Lab.* 6,390
M. Penn, *NLP* 204
*C. majority* 929
(June 1987, C. maj. 1,840)

HEMSWORTH (W. Yorks)
*E.*55,679 *T.*75.91%
*D. Enright, *Lab.* 29,942
G. Harrison, *C.* 7,867
Ms V. Megson, *LD* 4,459
*Lab. majority* 22,075
(June 1987, Lab. maj. 20,700)
(November 1991, Lab. maj. 11,087)

HENDON NORTH (Greater London)
*E.*51,513 *T.*75.08%
*J. Gorst, *C.* 20,569
D. Hill, *Lab.* 13,447
P. Kemp, *LD* 4,136
Ms P. Duncan, *Green* 430
Ms P. Orr, *NLP* 95
*C. majority* 7,122
(June 1987, C. maj. 10,932)

HENDON SOUTH (Greater London)
*E.*48,401 *T.*72.38%
*J. Marshall, *C.* 20,593
Ms L. Lloyd, *Lab.* 8,546
J. Cohen, *LD* 5,609
J. Leslie, *NLP* 289
*C. majority* 12,047
(June 1987, C. maj. 11,124)

HENLEY (Oxon)
*E.*64,702 *T.*79.84%
*Rt. Hon. M. Heseltine, *C.* 30,835
D. Turner, *LD* 12,443
I. Russell-Swinnerton, *Lab.* 7,676
A. Plane, *Anti H.* 431
Ms S. Banerji, *NLP* 274
*C. majority* 18,392
(June 1987, C. maj. 17,082)

HEREFORD
*E.*69,676 *T.*81.29%
*C. Shepherd, *C.* 26,727
G. Jones, *LD* 23,314
Ms J. Kelly, *Lab.* 6,005
C. Mattingly, *Green* 596
*C. majority* 3,413
(June 1987, C. maj. 1,413)

HERTFORD AND STORTFORD
*E.*76,654 *T.*81.05%
*B. Wells, *C.* 35,716
C. White, *LD* 15,506
A. Bovaird, *Lab.* 10,125
J. Goth, *Green* 780
*C. majority* 20,210
(June 1987, C. maj. 17,140)

HERTFORDSHIRE NORTH
*E.*80,066 *T.*84.44%
O. Heald, *C.* 33,679
R. Liddle, *LD* 17,148
Ms S. Bissett Johnson, *Lab.* 16,449
B. Irving, *NLP* 339
*C. majority* 16,531
(June 1987, C. maj. 11,442)

HERTFORDSHIRE SOUTH WEST
*E.*70,836 *T.*83.76%
*R. Page, *C.* 33,825
Ms A. Shaw, *LD* 13,718
A. Gale, *Lab.* 11,512
C. Adamson, *NLP* 281
*C. majority* 20,107
(June 1987, C. maj. 15,784)

HERTFORDSHIRE WEST
*E.*78,573 *T.*82.36%
*R. Jones, *C.* 33,340
Mrs E. McNally, *Lab.* 19,400
M. Trevett, *LD* 10,464
J. Hannaway, *Green* 674

J. McAuley, *NF* — 665
G. Harvey, *NLP* — 175
*C. majority* — 13,940
(June 1987, C. maj. 14,924)

HERTSMERE (Herts)
*E.*69,951   *T.*80.89%
W. J. Clappison, *C.* — 32,133
Dr D. Souter, *Lab.* — 13,398
Mrs Z. Gifford, *LD* — 10,681
Ms D. Harding, *NLP* — 373
*C. majority* — 18,735
(June 1987, C. maj. 18,106)

HEXHAM (Northumberland)
*E.*57,812   *T.*82.37%
P. Atkinson, *C.* — 24,967
I. Swithenbank, *Lab.* — 11,529
J. Wallace, *LD* — 10,344
J. Hartshorne, *Green* — 781
*C. majority* — 13,438
(June 1987, C. maj. 8,066)

HEYWOOD AND MIDDLETON
(Greater Manchester)
*E.*57,176   *T.*74.92%
*J. Callaghan, *Lab.* — 22,380
E. Ollerenshaw, *C.* — 14,306
Dr M. Taylor, *LD* — 5,262
P. Burke, *Lib.* — 757
Ms A. Scott, *NLP* — 134
*Lab. majority* — 8,074
(June 1987, Lab. maj. 6,848)

HIGH PEAK (Derbys)
*E.*70,793   *T.*84.62%
C. Hendry, *C.* — 27,538
T. Levitt, *Lab.* — 22,719
S. Molloy, *LD* — 8,861
R. Floyd, *Green* — 794
*C. majority* — 4,819
(June 1987, C. maj. 9,516)

HOLBORN AND ST PANCRAS
(Greater London)
*E.*64,480   *T.*62.99%
*F. Dobson, *Lab.* — 22,243
A. McHallam, *C.* — 11,419
Ms J. Horne-Roberts, *LD* — 5,476
P. Wolf-Light, *Green* — 959
M. Hersey, *NLP* — 212
R. Headicar, *Soc.* — 175
N. Lewis, *WAR* — 133
*Lab. majority* — 10,824
(June 1987, Lab. maj. 8,853)

HOLLAND WITH BOSTON (Lincs)
*E.*67,900   *T.*77.93%
*Sir R. Body, *C.* — 29,159
J. Hough, *Lab.* — 15,328
N. Ley, *LD* — 8,434
*C. majority* — 13,831
(June 1987, C. maj. 17,595)

HONITON (Devon)
*E.*79,223   *T.*80.74%
*Sir P. Emery, *C.* — 33,533
Ms J. Sharratt, *LD* — 17,022
R. Davison, *Lab.* — 8,142
D. Owen, *Ind. C.* — 2,175
S. Hughes, *Loony G.* — 1,442
G. Halliwell, *Lib.* — 1,005

A. Tootill, *Green* — 650
*C. majority* — 16,511
(June 1987, C. maj. 16,562)

HORNCHURCH (Greater London)
*E.*60,522   *T.*79.78%
*R. Squire, *C.* — 25,817
Ms L. Cooper, *Lab.* — 16,652
B. Oddy, *LD* — 5,366
T. Matthews, *SD* — 453
*C. majority* — 9,165
(June 1987, C. maj. 10,694)

HORNSEY AND WOOD GREEN
(Greater London)
*E.*73,491   *T.*75.85%
Mrs B. Roche, *Lab.* — 27,020
A. Boff, *C.* — 21,843
P. Dunphy, *LD* — 5,547
Ms L. Crosbie, *Green* — 1,051
P. Davies, *NLP* — 197
W. Massey, *Rev. Comm.* — 89
*Lab. majority* — 5,177
(June 1987, C. maj. 1,779)

HORSHAM (W. Sussex)
*E.*84,158   *T.*81.27%
*Sir P. Hordern, *C.* — 42,210
Ms J. Stainton, *LD* — 17,138
S. Uwins, *Lab.* — 6,745
Ms J. Elliott, *Lib.* — 1,281
T. King, *Green* — 692
J. Duggan, *PPP* — 332
*C. majority* — 25,072
(June 1987, C. maj. 23,907)

HOUGHTON AND WASHINGTON
(Tyne & Wear)
*E.*79,325   *T.*70.60%
*R. Boyes, *Lab.* — 34,733
A. Tyrie, *C.* — 13,925
O. Dumpleton, *LD* — 7,346
*Lab. majority* — 20,808
(June 1987, Lab. maj. 20,193)

HOVE (E. Sussex)
*E.*67,450   *T.*74.26%
*Hon. T. Sainsbury, *C.* — 24,525
D. Turner, *Lab.* — 12,257
A. Jones, *LD* — 9,709
N. Furness, *Hove C.* — 2,658
G. Sinclair, *Green* — 814
J. Morilly, *NLP* — 126
*C. majority* — 12,268
(June 1987, C. maj. 18,218)

HUDDERSFIELD (W. Yorks)
*E.*67,604   *T.*72.32%
*B. Sheerman, *Lab.* — 23,832
Ms J. Kenyon, *C.* — 16,574
Ms A. Denham, *LD* — 7,777
N. Harvey, *Green* — 576
M. Cran, *NLP* — 135
*Lab. majority* — 7,258
(June 1987, Lab. maj. 7,278)

HULL EAST
*E.*69,036   *T.*69.29%
*J. Prescott, *Lab.* — 30,092
J. Fareham, *C.* — 11,373
J. Wastling, *LD* — 6,050
C. Kinzell, *NLP* — 323

*Lab. majority* — 18,719
(June 1987, Lab. maj. 14,689)

HULL NORTH
*E.*71,363   *T.*66.71%
*J. K. McNamara, *Lab.* — 26,619
B. Coleman, *C.* — 11,235
A. Meadowcroft, *LD* — 9,504
G. Richardson, *NLP* — 253
*Lab. majority* — 15,384
(June 1987, Lab. maj. 12,169)

HULL WEST
*E.*56,111   *T.*65.70%
*S. Randall, *Lab.* — 21,139
D. Stewart, *C.* — 10,554
R. Tress, *LD* — 4,867
B. Franklin, *NLP* — 308
*Lab. majority* — 10,585
(June 1987, Lab. maj. 8,130)

HUNTINGDON (Cambs)
*E.*92,913   *T.*79.16%
*Rt. Hon. J. Major, *C.* — 48,662
H. Seckleman, *Lab.* — 12,432
A. Duff, *LD* — 9,386
P. Wiggin, *Lib.* — 1,045
Miss D. Birkhead, *Green* — 846
Lord D. Sutch, *Loony* — 728
M. Flanagan, *C. Thatch.* — 231
Lord Buckethead, *Gremloids* — 107
C. Cockell, *FTM* — 91
D. Shepheard, *NLP* — 26
*C. majority* — 36,230
(June 1987, C. maj. 27,044)

HYNDBURN (Lancs)
*E.*58,539   *T.*83.97%
G. Pope, *Lab.* — 23,042
*K. Hargreaves, *C.* — 21,082
Ms Y. Stars, *LD* — 4,886
S. Whittle, *NLP* — 150
*Lab. majority* — 1,960
(June 1987, C. maj. 2,220)

ILFORD NORTH (Greater London)
*E.*58,670   *T.*77.98%
*V. Bendall, *C.* — 24,698
Ms L. Hilton, *Lab.* — 15,627
R. Scott, *LD* — 5,430
*C. majority* — 9,071
(June 1987, C. maj. 12,090)

ILFORD SOUTH (Greater London)
*E.*55,741   *T.*76.83%
M. Gapes, *Lab.* — 19,418
*N. Thorne, *C.* — 19,016
G. Hogarth, *LD* — 4,126
N. Bramachari, *NLP* — 269
*Lab. majority* — 402
(June 1987, C. maj. 4,572)

IPSWICH (Suffolk)
*E.*67,261   *T.*80.32%
J. Cann, *Lab.* — 23,680
*M. Irvine, *C.* — 23,415
J. White, *LD* — 6,159
Ms J. Scott, *Green* — 591
E. Kaplan, *NLP* — 181
*Lab. majority* — 265
(June 1987, C. maj. 874)

ISLE OF WIGHT
E.99,838   T.79.76%

| | |
|---|---|
| *B. Field, *C.* | 38,163 |
| Dr P. Brand, *LD* | 36,336 |
| K. Pearson, *Lab.* | 4,784 |
| C. Daly, *NLP* | 350 |
| *C. majority* | 1,827 |

(June 1987, C. maj. 6,442)

ISLINGTON NORTH (Greater London)
E.56,270   T.67.26%

| | |
|---|---|
| *J. Corbyn, *Lab.* | 21,742 |
| Mrs L. Champagnie, *C.* | 8,958 |
| Ms S. Ludford, *LD* | 5,732 |
| C. Ashby, *Green* | 1,420 |
| *Lab. majority* | 12,784 |

(June 1987, Lab. maj. 9,657)

ISLINGTON SOUTH AND FINSBURY (Greater London)
E.55,541   T.72.52%

| | |
|---|---|
| *C. Smith, *Lab.* | 20,586 |
| M. Jones, *C.* | 9,934 |
| C. Pryce, *LD* | 9,387 |
| Ms R. Hersey, *JBR* | 149 |
| Ms M. Avino, *Loony* | 142 |
| M. Spinks, *NLP* | 83 |
| *Lab. majority* | 10,652 |

(June 1987, Lab. maj. 805)

JARROW (Tyne & Wear)
E.62,611   T.74.44%

| | |
|---|---|
| *D. Dixon, *Lab.* | 28,956 |
| T. Ward, *C.* | 11,049 |
| K. Orrell, *LD* | 6,608 |
| *Lab. majority* | 17,907 |

(June 1987, Lab. maj. 18,795)

KEIGHLEY (W. Yorks)
E.66,358   T.82.58%

| | |
|---|---|
| *G. Waller, *C.* | 25,983 |
| T. Flanagan, *Lab.* | 22,387 |
| I. Simpson, *LD* | 5,793 |
| M. Crowson, *Green* | 642 |
| *C. majority* | 3,596 |

(June 1987, C. maj. 5,606)

KENSINGTON (Greater London)
E.42,129   T.73.29%

| | |
|---|---|
| *J. D. Fishburn, *C.* | 15,540 |
| Ms A. Holmes, *Lab.* | 11,992 |
| C. Shirley, *LD* | 2,770 |
| Ms A. Burlingham-Johnson, *Green* | 415 |
| A. Hardy, *NLP* | 90 |
| Ms A. Bulloch, *Anti Fed.* | 71 |
| *C. majority* | 3,548 |

(June 1987, C. maj. 4,447)
(July 1988, C. maj. 815)

KENT MID
E.74,459   T.79.66%

| | |
|---|---|
| *A. Rowe, *C.* | 33,633 |
| T. Robson, *Lab.* | 13,984 |
| G. Colley, *LD* | 11,476 |
| G. Valente, *NLP* | 224 |
| *C. majority* | 19,649 |

(June 1987, C. maj. 14,768)

KETTERING (Northants)
E.67,853   T.82.58%

| | |
|---|---|
| *R. Freeman, *C.* | 29,115 |
| P. Hope, *Lab.* | 17,961 |
| R. Denton-White, *LD* | 8,962 |
| *C. majority* | 11,154 |

(June 1987, C. maj. 11,327)

KINGSTON UPON THAMES (Greater London)
E.51,077   T.78.41%

| | |
|---|---|
| *Rt. Hon. N. Lamont, *C.* | 20,675 |
| D. Osbourne, *LD* | 10,522 |
| R. Markless, *Lab.* | 7,748 |
| A. Amer, *Lib.* | 771 |
| D. Beaupre, *Loony* | 212 |
| G. Woollcoombe, *NLP* | 81 |
| A. Scholefield, *Anti Fed.* | 42 |
| *C. majority* | 10,153 |

(June 1987, C. maj. 11,186)

KINGSWOOD (Avon)
E.71,727   T.83.85%

| | |
|---|---|
| R. Berry, *Lab.* | 26,774 |
| *R. Hayward, *C.* | 24,404 |
| Ms J. Pinkerton, *LD* | 8,960 |
| *Lab. majority* | 2,370 |

(June 1987, C. maj. 4,393)

KNOWSLEY NORTH (Merseyside)
E.48,761   T.72.81%

| | |
|---|---|
| *G. Howarth, *Lab.* | 27,517 |
| S. Mabey, *C.* | 5,114 |
| J. Murray, *LD* | 1,515 |
| Mrs K. Lappin, *Lib.* | 1,180 |
| V. Ruben, *NLP* | 179 |
| *Lab. majority* | 22,403 |

(June 1987, Lab. maj. 21,098)

KNOWSLEY SOUTH (Merseyside)
E.62,260   T.74.77%

| | |
|---|---|
| *E. O'Hara, *Lab.* | 31,933 |
| L. Byrom, *C.* | 9,922 |
| I. Smith, *LD* | 4,480 |
| M. Raiano, *NLP* | 217 |
| *Lab. majority* | 22,011 |

(June 1987, Lab. maj. 20,846)
(September 1990, Lab. maj. 11,367)

LANCASHIRE WEST
E.77,462   T.82.55%

| | |
|---|---|
| C. Pickthall, *Lab.* | 30,128 |
| *K. Hind, *C.* | 28,051 |
| P. Reilly, *LD* | 4,884 |
| P. Pawley, *Green* | 546 |
| B. Morris, *NLP* | 336 |
| *Lab. majority* | 2,077 |

(June 1987, C. maj. 1,353)

LANCASTER (Lancs)
E.58,714   T.78.78%

| | |
|---|---|
| *Dame E. Kellett-Bowman, *C.* | 21,084 |
| Ms R. Henig, *Lab.* | 18,131 |
| J. Humberstone, *LD* | 6,524 |
| Ms G. Dowding, *Green* | 433 |
| R. Barcis, *NLP* | 83 |
| *C. majority* | 2,953 |

(June 1987, C. maj. 6,453)

LANGBAURGH (Cleveland)
E.79,566   T.83.05%

| | |
|---|---|
| M. Bates, *C.* | 30,018 |
| *A. Kumar, *Lab.* | 28,454 |

| | |
|---|---|
| P. Allen, *LD* | 7,615 |
| *C. majority* | 1,564 |

(June 1987, C. maj. 2,088)
(November 1991, C. maj. 1,975)

LEEDS CENTRAL (W. Yorks)
E.62,058   T.61.29%

| | |
|---|---|
| *D. Fatchett, *Lab.* | 23,673 |
| Mrs T. Holdroyd, *C.* | 8,653 |
| D. Pratt, *LD* | 5,713 |
| *Lab. majority* | 15,020 |

(June 1987, Lab. maj. 11,505)

LEEDS EAST (W. Yorks)
E.61,695   T.70.02%

| | |
|---|---|
| G. Mudie, *Lab.* | 24,929 |
| N. Carmichael, *C.* | 12,232 |
| P. Wrigley, *LD* | 6,040 |
| *Lab. majority* | 12,697 |

(June 1987, Lab. maj. 9,526)

LEEDS NORTH EAST (W. Yorks)
E.64,372   T.76.89%

| | |
|---|---|
| *T. Kirkhope, *C.* | 22,462 |
| F. Hamilton, *Lab.* | 18,218 |
| C. Walmsley, *LD* | 8,274 |
| J. Noble, *Green* | 546 |
| *C. majority* | 4,244 |

(June 1987, C. maj. 8,419)

LEEDS NORTH WEST (W. Yorks)
E.69,406   T.72.84%

| | |
|---|---|
| *Dr K. Hampson, *C.* | 21,750 |
| Ms B. Pearce, *LD* | 14,079 |
| Ms S. Egan, *Lab.* | 13,782 |
| D. Webb, *Green* | 519 |
| N. Nowosielski, *Lib.* | 427 |
| *C. majority* | 7,671 |

(June 1987, C. maj. 5,201)

LEEDS SOUTH AND MORLEY (W. Yorks)
E.63,107   T.72.58%

| | |
|---|---|
| W. J. Gunnell, *Lab.* | 23,896 |
| R. Booth, *C.* | 16,524 |
| Ms J. Walmsley, *LD* | 5,062 |
| R. Thurston, *NLP* | 327 |
| *Lab. majority* | 7,372 |

(June 1987, Lab. maj. 6,711)

LEEDS WEST (W. Yorks)
E.67,084   T.71.14%

| | |
|---|---|
| *J. Battle, *Lab.* | 26,310 |
| P. Bartlett, *C.* | 12,482 |
| G. Howard, *LD* | 4,252 |
| M. Meadowcroft, *Lib.* | 3,980 |
| Ms A. Mander, *Green* | 569 |
| R. Tenny, *NF* | 132 |
| *Lab. majority* | 13,828 |

(June 1987, Lab. maj. 4,692)

LEICESTER EAST
E.63,434   T.78.40%

| | |
|---|---|
| *N. K. A. S. Vaz, *Lab.* | 28,123 |
| J. Stevens, *C.* | 16,807 |
| Ms S. Mitchell, *LD* | 4,043 |
| M. Frankland, *Green* | 453 |
| D. Taylor, *Homeland* | 308 |
| *Lab. majority* | 11,316 |

(June 1987, Lab. maj. 1,924)

LEICESTER SOUTH
E.71,120 T.75.09%
| | |
|---|---|
| *J. Marshall, *Lab.* | 27,934 |
| Dr M. Dutt, *C.* | 18,494 |
| Ms A. Crumbie, *LD* | 6,271 |
| J. McWhirter, *Green* | 554 |
| Ms P. Saunders, *NLP* | 154 |
| *Lab. majority* | 9,440 |

(June 1987, Lab. maj. 1,877)

LEICESTER WEST
E.65,510 T.73.66%
| | |
|---|---|
| *Hon. G. Janner, *Lab.* | 22,574 |
| J. Guthrie, *C.* | 18,596 |
| G. Walker, *LD* | 6,402 |
| Ms C. Wintram, *Green* | 517 |
| Ms J. Rosta, *NLP* | 171 |
| *Lab. majority* | 3,978 |

(June 1987, Lab. maj. 1,201)

LEICESTERSHIRE NORTH WEST
E.72,414 T.86.11%
| | |
|---|---|
| *D. Ashby, *C.* | 28,379 |
| D. Taylor, *Lab.* | 27,400 |
| J. Beckett, *LD* | 6,353 |
| J. Fawcett, *NLP* | 229 |
| *C. majority* | 979 |

(June 1987, C. maj. 7,828)

LEIGH (Greater Manchester)
E.70,064 T.75.02%
| | |
|---|---|
| *L. Cunliffe, *Lab.* | 32,225 |
| J. Egerton, *C.* | 13,398 |
| R. Bleakley, *LD* | 6,621 |
| A. Tayler, *NLP* | 320 |
| *Lab. majority* | 18,827 |

(June 1987, Lab. maj. 16,606)

LEOMINSTER (H & W)
E.70,873 T.81.69%
| | |
|---|---|
| *P. Temple-Morris, *C.* | 32,783 |
| D. Short, *LD* | 16,103 |
| C. Chappell, *Lab.* | 6,874 |
| Ms F. Norman, *Green* | 1,503 |
| Capt. E. Carlise, *Anti Fed.* | 640 |
| *C. majority* | 16,680 |

(June 1987, C. maj. 14,075)

LEWES (E. Sussex)
E.73,918 T.81.81%
| | |
|---|---|
| *J. R. Rathbone, *C.* | 33,042 |
| N. Baker, *LD* | 20,867 |
| Ms A. Chapman, *Lab.* | 5,758 |
| A. Beaumont, *Green* | 719 |
| N. Clinch, *NLP* | 87 |
| *C. majority* | 12,175 |

(June 1987, C. maj. 13,620)

LEWISHAM DEPTFORD (Greater London)
E.57,014 T.65.05%
| | |
|---|---|
| *Mrs J. Ruddock, *Lab.* | 22,574 |
| Miss T. O'Neill, *C.* | 10,336 |
| Ms J. Brightwell, *LD* | 4,181 |
| *Lab. majority* | 12,238 |

(June 1987, Lab. maj. 6,771)

LEWISHAM EAST (Greater London)
E.57,674 T.74.78%
| | |
|---|---|
| Mrs B. Prentice, *Lab.* | 19,576 |
| *Hon. C. Moynihan, *C.* | 18,481 |

| | |
|---|---|
| J. Hawkins, *LD* | 4,877 |
| Ms G. Mansour, *NLP* | 196 |
| *Lab. majority* | 1,095 |

(June 1987, C. maj. 4,814)

LEWISHAM WEST (Greater London)
E.59,317 T.73.11%
| | |
|---|---|
| J. Dowd, *Lab.* | 20,378 |
| *J. Maples, *C.* | 18,569 |
| Ms E. Neale, *LD* | 4,295 |
| P. Coulam, *Anti Fed.* | 125 |
| *Lab. majority* | 1,809 |

(June 1987, C. maj. 3,772)

LEYTON (Greater London)
E.57,271 T.67.38%
| | |
|---|---|
| *H. Cohen, *Lab.* | 20,334 |
| Miss C. Smith, *C.* | 8,850 |
| J. Fryer, *LD* | 8,180 |
| L. de Pinna, *Lib.* | 561 |
| K. Pervez, *Green* | 412 |
| R. Archer, *NLP* | 256 |
| *Lab. majority* | 11,484 |

(June 1987, Lab. maj. 4,641)

LINCOLN
E.78,905 T.79.15%
| | |
|---|---|
| *K. Carlisle, *C.* | 28,792 |
| N. Butler, *Lab.* | 26,743 |
| D. Harding-Price, *LD* | 6,316 |
| Ms S. Wiggin, *Lib.* | 603 |
| *C. majority* | 2,049 |

(June 1987, C. maj. 7,483)

LINDSEY EAST (Lincs)
E.80,026 T.78.07%
| | |
|---|---|
| *Sir P. Tapsell, *C.* | 31,916 |
| J. Dodsworth, *LD* | 20,070 |
| D. Shepherd, *Lab.* | 9,477 |
| Ms R. Robinson, *Green* | 1,018 |
| *C. majority* | 11,846 |

(June 1987, C. maj. 8,616)

LITTLEBOROUGH AND
SADDLEWORTH (Greater
Manchester)
E.65,576 T.81.61%
| | |
|---|---|
| *G. Dickens, *C.* | 23,682 |
| C. Davies, *LD* | 19,188 |
| A. Brett, *Lab.* | 10,649 |
| *C. majority* | 4,494 |

(June 1987, C. maj. 6,202)

LIVERPOOL BROADGREEN
E.60,080 T.69.59%
| | |
|---|---|
| Mrs J. Kennedy, *Lab.* | 18,062 |
| Ms R. Cooper, *LD* | 11,035 |
| *T. Fields, *Soc. Lab.* | 5,952 |
| Mrs H. Roche, *C.* | 5,405 |
| S. Radford, *Lib.* | 1,211 |
| Mrs A. Brennan, *NLP* | 149 |
| *Lab. majority* | 7,027 |

(June 1987, Lab. maj. 6,047)

LIVERPOOL GARSTON
E.57,538 T.70.60%
| | |
|---|---|
| *E. Loyden, *Lab.* | 23,212 |
| J. Backhouse, *C.* | 10,933 |
| W. Roberts, *LD* | 5,398 |
| A. Conrad, *Lib.* | 894 |
| P. Chandler, *NLP* | 187 |
| *Lab. majority* | 12,279 |

(June 1987, Lab. maj. 13,777)

LIVERPOOL MOSSLEY HILL
E.60,409 T.68.52%
| | |
|---|---|
| *D. Alton, *LD* | 19,809 |
| N. Bann, *Lab.* | 17,203 |
| S. Syder, *C.* | 4,269 |
| B. Rigby, *NLP* | 114 |
| *LD majority* | 2,606 |

(June 1987, L./All. maj. 2,226)

LIVERPOOL RIVERSIDE
E.49,595 T.54.57%
| | |
|---|---|
| *R. Parry, *Lab.* | 20,550 |
| Dr A. Zsigmond, *C.* | 3,113 |
| M. Akbar Ali, *LD* | 2,498 |
| L. Brown, *Green* | 738 |
| J. Collins, *NLP* | 169 |
| *Lab. majority* | 17,437 |

(June 1987, Lab. maj. 20,689)

LIVERPOOL WALTON
E.70,102 T.67.40%
| | |
|---|---|
| *P. Kilfoyle, *Lab.* | 34,214 |
| B. Greenwood, *C.* | 5,915 |
| J. Lang, *LD* | 5,672 |
| T. Newall, *Lib.* | 963 |
| D. Carson, *Prot. Ref.* | 393 |
| Ms D. Raiano, *NLP* | 98 |
| *Lab. majority* | 28,299 |

(June 1987, Lab. maj. 23,253)
(July 1991, Lab. maj. 6,860)

LIVERPOOL WEST DERBY
E.56,718 T.69.84%
| | |
|---|---|
| *R. Wareing, *Lab.* | 27,014 |
| S. Fitzsimmons, *C.* | 6,589 |
| Ms G. Bundred, *LD* | 4,838 |
| D. Curtis, *Lib.* | 1,021 |
| C. Higgins, *NLP* | 154 |
| *Lab. majority* | 20,425 |

(June 1987, Lab. maj. 20,496)

LOUGHBOROUGH (Leics)
E.75,450 T.78.52%
| | |
|---|---|
| *S. Dorrell, *C.* | 30,064 |
| A. Reed, *Lab.* | 19,181 |
| A. Stott, *LD* | 8,953 |
| I. Sinclair, *Green* | 817 |
| P. Reynolds, *NLP* | 233 |
| *C. majority* | 10,883 |

(June 1987, C. maj. 17,648)

LUDLOW (Salop)
E.68,935 T.80.87%
| | |
|---|---|
| *C. Gill, *C.* | 28,719 |
| D. Phillips, *LD* | 14,567 |
| Ms B. Mason, *Lab.* | 11,709 |
| N. Appleton-Fox, *Green* | 758 |
| *C. majority* | 14,152 |

(June 1987, C. maj. 11,699)

LUTON NORTH (Beds)
E.76,857 T.81.91%
| | |
|---|---|
| *J. Carlisle, *C.* | 33,777 |
| A. McWalter, *Lab.* | 20,683 |
| Ms J. Jackson, *LD* | 7,570 |
| R. Jones, *Green* | 633 |
| K. Buscombe, *NLP* | 292 |
| *C. majority* | 13,094 |

(June 1987, C. maj. 15,573)

LUTON SOUTH (Beds)
E.73,016   T.79.10%
| | |
|---|---|
|*G. Bright, C.|25,900|
|W. McKenzie, Lab.|25,101|
|D. Rogers, LD|6,020|
|Ms L. Bliss, Green|550|
|D. Cooke, NLP|191|
|C. majority|799|
(June 1987, C. maj. 5,115)

MACCLESFIELD (Cheshire)
E.76,548   T.82.29%
| | |
|---|---|
|*N. Winterton, C.|36,447|
|Mrs M. Longworth, Lab.|13,680|
|Dr P. Beatty, LD|12,600|
|Mrs C. Penn, NLP|268|
|C. majority|22,767|
(June 1987, C. maj. 19,092)

MAIDSTONE (Kent)
E.72,834   T.80.08%
| | |
|---|---|
|*Miss A. Widdecombe, C.|31,611|
|Ms P. Yates, LD|15,325|
|Ms A. Logan, Lab.|10,517|
|Ms P. Kemp, Green|707|
|F. Ingram, NLP|172|
|C. majority|16,286|
(June 1987, C. maj. 10,364)

MAKERFIELD (Greater Manchester)
E.71,425   T.76.09%
| | |
|---|---|
|*I. McCartney, Lab.|32,832|
|Mrs D. Dickson, C.|14,714|
|S. Jeffers, LD|5,097|
|Ms S. Cairns, Lib.|1,309|
|C. Davies, NLP|397|
|Lab. majority|18,118|
(June 1987, Lab. maj. 15,558)

MANCHESTER BLACKLEY
E.55,234   T.69.31%
| | |
|---|---|
|*K. Eastham, Lab.|23,031|
|W. Hobhouse, C.|10,642|
|S. Wheale, LD|4,324|
|M. Kennedy, NLP|288|
|Lab. majority|12,389|
(June 1987, Lab. maj. 10,122)

MANCHESTER CENTRAL
E.56,446   T.56.90%
| | |
|---|---|
|*R. Litherland, Lab.|23,336|
|P. Davies, C.|5,299|
|M. Clayton, LD|3,151|
|A. Buchanan, CL|167|
|Ms V. Mitchell, NLP|167|
|Lab. majority|18,037|
(June 1987, Lab. maj. 19,867)

MANCHESTER GORTON
E.62,410   T.60.84%
| | |
|---|---|
|*Rt. Hon. G. Kaufman, Lab.|23,671|
|J. Bullock, C.|7,392|
|P. Harris, LD|5,327|
|T. Henderson, Lib.|767|
|M. Daw, Green|595|
|Ms P. Lawrence, Rev. Comm.|108|
|P. Mitchell, NLP|84|
|Ms C. Smith, Int. Comm.|30|
|Lab. majority|16,279|
(June 1987, Lab. maj. 14,065)

MANCHESTER WITHINGTON
E.63,838   T.71.27%
| | |
|---|---|
|*K. Bradley, Lab.|23,962|
|E. Farthing, C.|14,227|
|G. Hennell, LD|6,457|
|B. Candeland, Green|725|
|C. Menhinick, NLP|128|
|Lab. majority|9,735|
(June 1987, Lab. maj. 3,391)

MANCHESTER WYTHENSHAWE
E.53,548   T.69.68%
| | |
|---|---|
|*Rt. Hon. A. Morris, Lab.|22,591|
|K. McKenna, C.|10,595|
|S. Fenn, LD|3,633|
|G. Otten, Green|362|
|Ms E. Martin, NLP|133|
|Lab. majority|11,996|
(June 1987, Lab. maj. 11,855)

MANSFIELD (Notts)
E.66,964   T.82.23%
| | |
|---|---|
|*J. A. Meale, Lab.|29,932|
|G. Mond, C.|18,208|
|S. Thompstone, LD|6,925|
|Lab. majority|11,724|
(June 1987, Lab. maj. 56)

MEDWAY (Kent)
E.61,736   T.80.22%
| | |
|---|---|
|*Dame P. Fenner, C.|25,924|
|R. Marshall-Andrews, Lab.|17,138|
|C. Trice, LD|4,751|
|M. Austin, Lib.|1,480|
|P. Kember, NLP|234|
|C. majority|8,786|
(June 1987, C. maj. 9,929)

MERIDEN (W. Midlands)
E.76,994   T.78.85%
| | |
|---|---|
|*I. Mills, C.|33,462|
|N. Stephens, Lab.|18,763|
|Ms J. Morris, LD|8,489|
|C. majority|14,699|
(June 1987, C. maj. 16,820)

MIDDLESBROUGH (Cleveland)
E.58,844   T.69.85%
| | |
|---|---|
|*S. Bell, Lab.|26,343|
|P. Rayner, C.|10,559|
|Ms R. Jordan, LD|4,201|
|Lab. majority|15,784|
(June 1987, Lab. maj. 14,958)

MILTON KEYNES NORTH EAST
(Bucks)
E.62,748   T.80.95%
| | |
|---|---|
|P. Butler, C.|26,212|
|Ms M. Cosin, Lab.|12,036|
|P. Gaskell, LD|11,693|
|A. Francis, Green|529|
|Mrs M. Kavanagh-Dowsett, Ind. C.|249|
|M. Simson, NLP|79|
|C. majority|14,176|
(New constituency)

MILTON KEYNES SOUTH WEST
(Bucks)
E.66,422   T.77%
| | |
|---|---|
|B. Legg, C.|23,840|
|K. Wilson, Lab.|19,153|

| | |
|---|---|
|C. Pym, LD|7,429|
|Dr C. Field, Green|525|
|H. Kelly, NLP|202|
|C. majority|4,687|
(New constituency)

MITCHAM AND MORDEN (Greater London)
E.63,723   T.80.32%
| | |
|---|---|
|*Rt. Hon. A. Rumbold, C.|23,789|
|Ms S. McDonagh, Lab.|22,055|
|J. Field, LD|4,687|
|T. Walsh, Green|655|
|C. majority|1,734|
(June 1987, C. maj. 6,183)

MOLE VALLEY (Surrey)
E.66,949   T.81.97%
| | |
|---|---|
|*Rt. Hon. K. Baker, C.|32,549|
|M. Watson, LD|16,599|
|Dr T. Walsh, Lab.|5,291|
|Ms J. Thomas, NLP|442|
|C. majority|15,950|
(June 1987, C. maj. 16,076)

MORECAMBE AND LUNESDALE (Lancs)
E.56,426   T.78.35%
| | |
|---|---|
|*Hon. M. Lennox-Boyd, C.|22,507|
|Ms J. Yates, Lab.|10,998|
|A. Saville, LD|9,584|
|M. Turner, MBI|916|
|R. Marriott, NLP|205|
|C. majority|11,509|
(June 1987, C. maj. 11,785)

NEWARK (Notts)
E.68,801   T.82.17%
| | |
|---|---|
|*R. Alexander, C.|28,494|
|D. Barton, Lab.|20,265|
|P. Harris, LD|7,342|
|Ms P. Wood, Green|435|
|C. majority|8,229|
(June 1987, C. maj. 13,543)

NEWBURY (Berks)
E.80,252   T.82.75%
| | |
|---|---|
|Mrs J. Chaplin, C.|37,135|
|D. Rendel, LD|24,778|
|R. Hall, Lab.|3,962|
|J. Wallis, Green|539|
|C. majority|12,357|
(June 1987, C. maj. 16,658)
See also page 241

NEWCASTLE UNDER LYME (Staffs)
E.66,595   T.80.34%
| | |
|---|---|
|*Mrs L. Golding, Lab.|25,652|
|A. Brierley, C.|15,813|
|A. Thomas, LD|11,727|
|R. Lines, NLP|314|
|Lab. majority|9,839|
(June 1987, Lab. maj. 5,132)

NEWCASTLE UPON TYNE CENTRAL
E.59,973   T.71.32%
| | |
|---|---|
|*J. Cousins, Lab.|21,123|
|M. Summersby, C.|15,835|
|L. Opik, LD|5,816|
|Lab. majority|5,288|
(June 1987, Lab. maj. 2,483)

NEWCASTLE UPON TYNE EAST
E.57,165   T.70.73%

| | |
|---|---|
| *N. Brown, *Lab.* | 24,342 |
| J. Lucas, *C.* | 10,465 |
| A. Thompson, *LD* | 4,883 |
| G. Edwards, *Green* | 744 |
| *Lab. majority* | 13,877 |

(June 1987, Lab. maj. 12,500)

NEWCASTLE UPON TYNE NORTH
E.66,187   T.76.80%

| | |
|---|---|
| *D. Henderson, *Lab.* | 25,121 |
| I. Gordon, *C.* | 16,175 |
| P. Maughan, *LD* | 9,542 |
| *Lab. majority* | 8,946 |

(June 1987, Lab. maj. 5,243)

NEW FOREST (Hants)
E.75,413   T.80.76%

| | |
|---|---|
| *Sir P. McNair-Wilson, *C.* | 37,986 |
| Ms J. Vernon-Jackson, *LD* | 17,581 |
| M. Shutler, *Lab.* | 4,989 |
| Ms F. Carter, *NLP* | 350 |
| *C. majority* | 20,405 |

(June 1987, C. maj. 21,732)

NEWHAM NORTH EAST (Greater London)
E.59,555   T.60.34%

| | |
|---|---|
| *R. Leighton, *Lab.* | 20,952 |
| J. Galbraith, *C.* | 10,966 |
| J. Aves, *LD* | 4,020 |
| *Lab. majority* | 9,986 |

(June 1987, Lab. maj. 8,236)
*See also* page 241

NEWHAM NORTH WEST (Greater London)
E.46,471   T.56.02%

| | |
|---|---|
| *T. Banks, *Lab.* | 15,911 |
| M. Prisk, *C.* | 6,740 |
| A. Sawdon, *LD* | 2,445 |
| Ms A. Standford, *Green* | 587 |
| T. Jug, *Loony G.* | 252 |
| D. O'Sullivan, *Int. Comm.* | 100 |
| *Lab. majority* | 9,171 |

(June 1987, Lab. maj. 8,496)

NEWHAM SOUTH (Greater London)
E.51,143   T.60.19%

| | |
|---|---|
| *N. Spearing, *Lab.* | 14,358 |
| Ms J. Foster, *C.* | 11,856 |
| A. Kellaway, *LD* | 4,572 |
| *Lab. majority* | 2,502 |

(June 1987, Lab. maj. 2,766)

NORFOLK MID
E.80,336   T.81.64%

| | |
|---|---|
| *Rt. Hon. R. Ryder, *C.* | 35,620 |
| M. Castle, *Lab.* | 16,672 |
| J. Gleed, *LD* | 13,072 |
| Ms C. Waite, *NLP* | 226 |
| *C. majority* | 18,948 |

(June 1987, C. maj. 18,008)

NORFOLK NORTH
E.73,780   T.80.84%

| | |
|---|---|
| *R. Howell, *C.* | 28,810 |
| N. Lamb, *LD* | 16,265 |
| M. Cullingham, *Lab.* | 13,850 |
| Ms A. Zelter, *Green* | 559 |

Ms S. Jackson, *NLP*   167
*C. majority*   12,545
(June 1987, C. maj. 15,310)

NORFOLK NORTH WEST
E.77,438   T.80.67%

| | |
|---|---|
| *H. Bellingham, *C.* | 32,554 |
| Dr G. Turner, *Lab.* | 20,990 |
| A. Waterman, *LD* | 8,599 |
| S. Pink, *NLP* | 330 |
| *C. majority* | 11,564 |

(June 1987, C. maj. 10,825)

NORFOLK SOUTH
E.81,647   T.83.99%

| | |
|---|---|
| *Rt. Hon. J. MacGregor, *C.* | 36,081 |
| C. Brocklebank-Fowler, *LD* | 18,516 |
| C. Needle, *Lab.* | 12,422 |
| Ms S. Ross-Wagenknecht, *Green* | 702 |
| N. Clark, *NLP* | 320 |
| R. Peacock, *Ind.* | 304 |
| R. Watkins, *Ind. C.* | 232 |
| *C. majority* | 17,565 |

(June 1987, C. maj. 12,418)

NORFOLK SOUTH WEST
E.77,652   T.79.30%

| | |
|---|---|
| *Mrs G. Shephard, *C.* | 33,637 |
| Ms M. Page, *Lab.* | 16,706 |
| J. Marsh, *LD* | 11,237 |
| *C. majority* | 16,931 |

(June 1987, C. maj. 20,436)

NORMANTON (W. Yorks)
E.65,562   T.76.35%

| | |
|---|---|
| *W. O'Brien, *Lab.* | 25,936 |
| R. Sturdy, *C.* | 16,986 |
| M. Galdas, *LD* | 7,137 |
| *Lab. majority* | 8,950 |

(June 1987, Lab. maj. 7,287)

NORTHAMPTON NORTH
E.69,139   T.78.52%

| | |
|---|---|
| *A. Marlow, *C.* | 24,865 |
| Ms J. Thomas, *Lab.* | 20,957 |
| R. Church, *LD* | 8,236 |
| B. Spivack, *NLP* | 232 |
| *C. majority* | 3,908 |

(June 1987, C. maj. 9,256)

NORTHAMPTON SOUTH
E.83,477   T.79.90%

| | |
|---|---|
| *M. Morris, *C.* | 36,882 |
| J. Dickie, *Lab.* | 19,909 |
| G. Mabbutt, *LD* | 9,912 |
| *C. majority* | 16,973 |

(June 1987, C. maj. 17,803)

NORTHAVON (Avon)
E.83,496   T.84.16%

| | |
|---|---|
| *Rt. Hon. Sir J. Cope, *C.* | 35,338 |
| Ms H. Larkins, *LD* | 23,477 |
| Ms J. Norris, *Lab.* | 10,290 |
| Ms J. Greene, *Green* | 789 |
| P. Marx, *Lib.* | 380 |
| *C. majority* | 11,861 |

(June 1987, C. maj. 14,270)

NORWICH NORTH (Norfolk)
E.63,308   T.81.82%

| | |
|---|---|
| *H. P. Thompson, *C.* | 22,419 |
| I. Gibson, *Lab.* | 22,153 |
| D. Harrison, *LD* | 6,706 |

L. Betts, *Green*   433
R. Arnold, *NLP*   93
*C. majority*   266
(June 1987, C. maj. 7,776)

NORWICH SOUTH (Norfolk)
E.63,603   T.80.60%

| | |
|---|---|
| *J. Garrett, *Lab.* | 24,965 |
| D. Baxter, *C.* | 18,784 |
| C. Thomas, *LD* | 6,609 |
| A. Holmes, *Green* | 803 |
| B. Parsons, *NLP* | 104 |
| *Lab. majority* | 6,181 |

(June 1987, Lab. maj. 336)

NORWOOD (Greater London)
E.52,496   T.65.87%

| | |
|---|---|
| *J. Fraser, *Lab.* | 18,391 |
| J. Samways, *C.* | 11,175 |
| Ms S. Lawman, *LD* | 4,087 |
| S. Collins, *Green* | 790 |
| M. Leighton, *NLP* | 138 |
| *Lab. majority* | 7,216 |

(June 1987, Lab. maj. 4,723)

NOTTINGHAM EAST
E.67,939   T.70.08%

| | |
|---|---|
| J. Heppell, *Lab.* | 25,026 |
| *M. Knowles, *C.* | 17,346 |
| T. Ball, *LD* | 3,695 |
| A. Jones, *Green* | 667 |
| C. Roylance, *Lib.* | 598 |
| J. Ashforth, *NLP* | 283 |
| *Lab. majority* | 7,680 |

(June 1987, C. maj. 456)

NOTTINGHAM NORTH
E.69,494   T.74.98%

| | |
|---|---|
| *G. Allen, *Lab.* | 29,052 |
| I. Bridge, *C.* | 18,309 |
| A. Skelton, *LD* | 4,477 |
| A. Cadman, *NLP* | 274 |
| *Lab. majority* | 10,743 |

(June 1987, Lab. maj. 1,665)

NOTTINGHAM SOUTH
E.72,796   T.74.22%

| | |
|---|---|
| A. Simpson, *Lab.* | 25,771 |
| *M. Brandon-Bravo, *C.* | 22,590 |
| G. D. Long, *LD* | 5,408 |
| Ms J. Christou, *NLP* | 263 |
| *Lab. majority* | 3,181 |

(June 1987, C. maj. 2,234)

NUNEATON (Warwicks)
E.70,906   T.83.70%

| | |
|---|---|
| W. Olner, *Lab.* | 27,157 |
| *L. Stevens, *C.* | 25,526 |
| Ms R. Merritt, *LD* | 6,671 |
| *Lab. majority* | 1,631 |

(June 1987, C. maj. 5,655)

OLD BEXLEY AND SIDCUP (Greater London)
E.49,449   T.81.94%

| | |
|---|---|
| *Rt. Hon. E. Heath, *C.* | 24,450 |
| Ms D. Brierly, *Lab.* | 8,751 |
| D. Nicolle, *LD* | 6,438 |
| B. Rose, *Alt. C.* | 733 |
| R. Stephens, *NLP* | 148 |
| *C. majority* | 15,699 |

(June 1987, C. maj. 16,274)

OLDHAM CENTRAL AND ROYTON
(Greater Manchester)
*E*.61,333  *T*.74.20%

| | |
|---|---|
| B. Davies, *Lab.* | 23,246 |
| Mrs T. Morris, *C.* | 14,640 |
| Ms A. Dunn, *LD* | 7,224 |
| I. Dalling, *NLP* | 403 |
| *Lab. majority* | 8,606 |

(June 1987, Lab. maj. 6,279)

OLDHAM WEST (Greater
Manchester)
*E*.54,063  *T*.75.65%

| | |
|---|---|
| *M. Meacher, *Lab.* | 21,580 |
| J. Gillen, *C.* | 13,247 |
| J. Smith, *LD* | 5,525 |
| Ms S. Dalling, *NLP* | 551 |
| *Lab. majority* | 8,333 |

(June 1987, Lab. maj. 5,967)

ORPINGTON (Greater London)
*E*.57,318  *T*.83.67%

| | |
|---|---|
| J. Horam, *C.* | 27,421 |
| C. Maines, *LD* | 14,486 |
| S. Cowan, *Lab.* | 5,512 |
| R. Almond, *Lib.* | 539 |
| *C. majority* | 12,935 |

(June 1987, C. maj. 12,732)

OXFORD EAST
*E*.63,075  *T*.74.59%

| | |
|---|---|
| *A. Smith, *Lab.* | 23,702 |
| Dr M. Mayall, *C.* | 16,164 |
| M. Horwood, *LD* | 6,105 |
| Mrs C. Lucas, *Green* | 933 |
| Miss A. Wilson, *NLP* | 101 |
| K. Thompson, *Rev. Comm.* | 48 |
| *Lab. majority* | 7,538 |

(June 1987, Lab. maj. 1,288)

OXFORD WEST AND ABINGDON
*E*.72,328  *T*.76.68%

| | |
|---|---|
| *Rt. Hon. J. Patten, *C.* | 25,163 |
| Sir W. Goodhart, *LD* | 21,624 |
| B. Kent, *Lab.* | 7,652 |
| M. Woodin, *Green* | 660 |
| R. Jenking, *Lib.* | 194 |
| Miss S. Nelson, *Anti Fed.* | 98 |
| G. Wells, *NLP* | 75 |
| *C. majority* | 3,539 |

(June 1987, C. maj. 4,878)

PECKHAM (Greater London)
*E*.58,269  *T*.53.87%

| | |
|---|---|
| *Ms H. Harman, *Lab.* | 19,391 |
| C. Frazer, *C.* | 7,386 |
| Mrs R. Colley, *LD* | 4,331 |
| G. Dacres, *WRP* | 146 |
| V. Emmanuel, *Whiplash* | 140 |
| *Lab. majority* | 12,005 |

(June 1987, Lab. maj. 9,489)

PENDLE (Lancs)
*E*.64,063  *T*.82.91%

| | |
|---|---|
| G. Prentice, *Lab.* | 23,497 |
| *J. Lee, *C.* | 21,384 |
| A. Davies, *LD* | 7,976 |
| Mrs V. Thorne, *Anti Fed.* | 263 |
| *Lab. majority* | 2,113 |

(June 1987, Lab. maj. 2,639)

PENRITH AND THE BORDER
(Cumbria)
*E*.73,769  *T*.79.67%

| | |
|---|---|
| *D. Maclean, *C.* | 33,808 |
| G. Walker, *LD* | 15,359 |
| J. Metcalfe, *Lab.* | 8,871 |
| R. Gibson, *Green* | 610 |
| I. Docker, *NLP* | 129 |
| *C. majority* | 18,449 |

(June 1987, C. maj. 17,366)

PETERBOROUGH (Cambs)
*E*.87,638  *T*.75.12%

| | |
|---|---|
| *B. Mawhinney, *C.* | 31,827 |
| Ms J. Owens, *Lab.* | 26,451 |
| Ms A. Taylor, *LD* | 5,208 |
| E. Murat, *Lib.* | 1,557 |
| R. Heaton, *BNP* | 311 |
| P. Beasley, *PP* | 271 |
| C. Brettell, *NLP* | 215 |
| *C. majority* | 5,376 |

(June 1987, C. maj. 9,784)

PLYMOUTH DEVONPORT (Devon)
*E*.65,799  *T*.77.83%

| | |
|---|---|
| D. Jamieson, *Lab.* | 24,953 |
| K. Simpson, *C.* | 17,541 |
| M. Mactaggart, *LD* | 6,315 |
| H. Luscombe, *SD* | 2,152 |
| F. Lyons, *NLP* | 255 |
| *Lab. majority* | 7,412 |

(June 1987, SDP/All. maj. 6,470)

PLYMOUTH DRAKE (Devon)
*E*.51,667  *T*.75.56%

| | |
|---|---|
| *Dame J. Fookes, *C.* | 17,075 |
| P. Telford, *Lab.* | 15,062 |
| Ms V. Cox, *LD* | 5,893 |
| D. Stanbury, *SD* | 476 |
| Ms A. Harrison, *Green* | 441 |
| T. Pringle, *NLP* | 95 |
| *C. majority* | 2,013 |

(June 1987, C. maj. 3,125)

PLYMOUTH SUTTON (Devon)
*E*.67,430  *T*.81.17%

| | |
|---|---|
| G. Streeter, *C.* | 27,070 |
| A. Pawley, *Lab.* | 15,120 |
| J. Brett-Freeman, *LD* | 12,291 |
| J. Bowler, *NLP* | 256 |
| *C. majority* | 11,950 |

(June 1987, C. maj. 4,013)

PONTEFRACT AND CASTLEFORD
(W. Yorks)
*E*.64,648  *T*.74.25%

| | |
|---|---|
| *G. Lofthouse, *Lab.* | 33,546 |
| A. Rockall, *C.* | 10,051 |
| D. Ryan, *LD* | 4,410 |
| *Lab. majority* | 23,495 |

(June 1987, Lab. maj. 21,626)

POOLE (Dorset)
*E*.79,221  *T*.79.39%

| | |
|---|---|
| *J. Ward, *C.* | 33,445 |
| B. Clements, *LD* | 20,614 |
| H. White, *Lab.* | 6,912 |
| M. Steen, *Ind. C.* | 1,620 |
| A. Bailey, *NLP* | 303 |
| *C. majority* | 12,831 |

(June 1987, C. maj. 14,808)

PORTSMOUTH NORTH (Hants)
*E*.79,592  *T*.77.05%

| | |
|---|---|
| *P. Griffiths, *C.* | 32,240 |
| A. Burnett, *Lab.* | 18,359 |
| A. Bentley, *LD* | 10,101 |
| Ms H. Palmer, *Green* | 628 |
| *C. majority* | 13,881 |

(June 1987, C. maj. 18,401)

PORTSMOUTH SOUTH (Hants)
*E*.77,645  *T*.69.09%

| | |
|---|---|
| *D. Martin, *C.* | 22,798 |
| M. Hancock, *LD* | 22,556 |
| S. Rapson, *Lab.* | 7,857 |
| A. Zivkovic, *Green* | 349 |
| W. Trend, *NLP* | 91 |
| *C. majority* | 242 |

(June 1987, C. maj. 205)

PRESTON (Lancs)
*E*.64,158  *T*.71.74%

| | |
|---|---|
| *Mrs A. Wise, *Lab.* | 24,983 |
| S. O'Toole, *C.* | 12,808 |
| W. Chadwick, *LD* | 7,897 |
| Ms J. Ayliffe, *NLP* | 341 |
| *Lab. majority* | 12,175 |

(June 1987, Lab. maj. 10,645)

PUDSEY (W. Yorks)
*E*.70,847  *T*.80.14%

| | |
|---|---|
| *Sir G. Shaw, *C.* | 25,067 |
| A. Giles, *Lab.* | 16,095 |
| D. Shutt, *LD* | 15,153 |
| Ms J. Wynne, *Green* | 466 |
| *C. majority* | 8,972 |

(June 1987, C. maj. 6,436)

PUTNEY (Greater London)
*E*.61,914  *T*.77.91%

| | |
|---|---|
| *Rt. Hon. D. Mellor, *C.* | 25,188 |
| Ms J. Chegwidden, *Lab.* | 17,662 |
| J. Martyn, *LD* | 4,636 |
| K. Hagenbach, *Green* | 618 |
| P. Levy, *NLP* | 139 |
| *C. majority* | 7,526 |

(June 1987, C. maj. 6,907)

RAVENSBOURNE (Greater London)
*E*.57,259  *T*.81.24%

| | |
|---|---|
| *Sir J. Hunt, *C.* | 29,506 |
| P. Booth, *LD* | 9,792 |
| E. Dyer, *Lab.* | 6,182 |
| I. Mouland, *Green* | 617 |
| P. White, *Lib.* | 318 |
| J. Shepheard, *NLP* | 105 |
| *C. majority* | 19,714 |

(June 1987, C. maj. 16,919)

READING EAST (Berks)
*E*.72,151  *T*.75.02%

| | |
|---|---|
| *Sir G. Vaughan, *C.* | 29,148 |
| Ms G. Parker, *Lab.* | 14,593 |
| D. Thair, *LD* | 9,528 |
| Ms A. McCubbin, *Green* | 861 |
| *C. majority* | 14,555 |

(June 1987, C. maj. 16,217)

READING WEST (Berks)
*E*.67,937  *T*.77.98%

| | |
|---|---|
| *Sir A. Durant, *C.* | 28,048 |
| P. Ruhemann, *Lab.* | 14,750 |
| K. Lock, *LD* | 9,572 |

P. Unsworth, *Green* — 613
C. majority — 13,298
(June 1987, C. maj. 16,753)

REDCAR (Cleveland)
E.62,494   T.77.73%
*Dr M. Mowlam, *Lab.* — 27,184
R. Goodwill, *C.* — 15,607
C. Abbott, *LD* — 5,789
*Lab. majority* — 11,577
(June 1987, Lab. maj. 7,735)

REIGATE (Surrey)
E.71,853   T.78.54%
*Sir G. Gardiner, *C.* — 32,220
B. Newsome, *LD* — 14,556
Ms H. Young, *Lab.* — 9,150
M. Dilcliff, *SD* — 513
C. majority — 17,664
(June 1987, C. maj. 18,173)

RIBBLE VALLEY (Lancs)
E.64,996   T.85.73%
N. Evans, *C.* — 29,178
*M. Carr, *LD* — 22,636
R. Pickup, *Lab.* — 3,649
D. Beesley, *Loony G.* — 152
Ms N. Holmes, *NLP* — 112
C. majority — 6,542
(June 1987, C. maj. 19,528)
(March 1991, LD maj. 4,641)

RICHMOND AND BARNES (Greater
London)
E.53,081   T.85.01%
*J. Hanley, *C.* — 22,894
Dr J. Tonge, *LD* — 19,025
D. Touhig, *Lab.* — 2,632
Ms J. Maciejowska, *Green* — 376
C. Cunningham, *NLP* — 89
R. Meacock, *QFL* — 62
Ms A. Ellis-Jones, *Anti Fed.* — 47
C. majority — 3,869
(June 1987, C. maj. 1,766)

RICHMOND (N. Yorks)
E.82,879   T.78.41%
*W. Hague, *C.* — 40,202
G. Irwin, *LD* — 16,698
R. Cranston, *Lab.* — 7,523
M. Barr, *Ind.* — 570
C. majority — 23,504
(June 1987, C. maj. 19,576)
(Feb 1989, C. maj. 2,634)

ROCHDALE (Greater Manchester)
E.69,522   T.76.47%
Ms E. Lynne, *LD* — 22,776
D. Williams, *Lab.* — 20,937
D. Goldie-Scott, *C.* — 8,626
K. Henderson, *BNP* — 620
V. Lucker, *NLP* — 211
*LD majority* — 1,839
(June 1987, L./All. maj. 2,779)

ROCHFORD (Essex)
E.76,869   T.82.99%
*Dr M. Clark, *C.* — 38,967
N. Harris, *LD* — 12,931
D. Quinn, *Lab.* — 10,537
Ms L. Farmer, *Lib.* — 1,362
C. majority — 26,036
(June 1987, C. maj. 19,694)

ROMFORD (Greater London)
E.54,001   T.78%
*Sir M. Neubert, *C.* — 23,834
Ms E. Gordon, *Lab.* — 12,414
Ms P. Atherton, *LD* — 5,329
F. Gibson, *Green* — 546
C. majority — 11,420
(June 1987, C. maj. 13,471)

ROMSEY AND WATERSIDE (Hants)
E.82,628   T.83.15%
*M. Colvin, *C.* — 37,375
G. Dawson, *LD* — 22,071
Mrs A. Mawle, *Lab.* — 8,688
J. Spottiswood, *Green* — 577
C. majority — 15,304
(June 1987, C. maj. 15,272)

ROSSENDALE AND DARWEN (Lancs)
E.76,909   T.83.06%
Mrs J. Anderson, *Lab.* — 28,028
*D. Trippier, *C.* — 27,908
K. Connor, *LD* — 7,226
J. Gaffney, *Green* — 596
P. Gorrod, *NLP* — 125
*Lab. majority* — 120
(June 1987, C. maj. 4,982)

ROTHERHAM (S. Yorks)
E.60,937   T.71.68%
J. Boyce, *Lab.* — 27,933
S. Yorke, *C.* — 10,372
D. Wildgoose, *LD* — 5,375
*Lab. majority* — 17,561
(June 1987, Lab. maj. 16,012)
*See also* page 241

ROTHER VALLEY (S. Yorks)
E.68,303   T.74.98%
*K. Barron, *Lab.* — 30,977
T. Horton, *C.* — 13,755
K. Smith, *LD* — 6,483
*Lab. majority* — 17,222
(June 1987, Lab. maj. 15,790)

RUGBY AND KENILWORTH
(Warwicks)
E.77,766   T.83.72%
*J. Pawsey, *C.* — 34,110
J. Airey, *Lab.* — 20,863
J. Roodhouse, *LD* — 9,934
S. Withers, *NLP* — 202
C. majority — 13,247
(June 1987, C. maj. 16,264)

RUISLIP-NORTHWOOD (Greater
London)
E.54,151   T.81.91%
*J. Wilkinson, *C.* — 28,097
Ms R. Brooks, *Lab.* — 8,306
H. Davies, *LD* — 7,739
M. Sheehan, *NLP* — 214
C. majority — 19,791
(June 1987, C. maj. 16,971)

RUSHCLIFFE (Notts)
E.76,253   T.83.04%
*Rt. Hon. K. Clarke, *C.* — 34,448
A. Chewings, *Lab.* — 14,682
Dr A. Wood, *LD* — 12,660
S. Anthony, *Green* — 775

M. Maelor-Jones, *Ind. C.* — 611
D. Richards, *NLP* — 150
C. majority — 19,766
(June 1987, C. maj. 20,839)

RUTLAND AND MELTON (Leics)
E.80,976   T.80.82%
A. Duncan, *C.* — 38,603
Ms J. Taylor, *Lab.* — 13,068
R. Lustig, *LD* — 12,682
J. Berreen, *Green* — 861
R. Grey, *NLP* — 237
C. majority — 25,535
(June 1987, C. maj. 23,022)

RYEDALE (N. Yorks)
E.87,048   T.81.73%
*J. Greenway, *C.* — 39,888
Mrs E. Shields, *LD* — 21,449
J. Healey, *Lab.* — 9,812
C. majority — 18,439
(June 1987, C. maj. 9,740)

SAFFRON WALDEN (Essex)
E.74,878   T.83.21%
*A. Haselhurst, *C.* — 35,272
M. Hayes, *LD* — 17,848
J. Kotz, *Lab.* — 8,933
M. Miller, *NLP* — 260
C. majority — 17,424
(June 1987, C. maj. 16,602)

ST ALBANS (Herts)
E.74,188   T.83.47%
*Rt. Hon. P. Lilley, *C.* — 32,709
Ms M. Howes, *LD* — 16,305
K. Pollard, *Lab.* — 12,016
C. Simmons, *Green* — 734
D. Lucas, *NLP* — 161
C. majority — 16,404
(June 1987, C. maj. 10,881)

ST HELENS NORTH (Merseyside)
E.71,261   T.77.35%
*J. Evans, *Lab.* — 31,930
B. Anderson, *C.* — 15,686
J. Beirne, *LD* — 7,224
Ms A. Lynch, *NLP* — 287
*Lab. majority* — 16,244
(June 1987, Lab. maj. 14,260)

ST HELENS SOUTH (Merseyside)
E.67,507   T.73.77%
*G. Bermingham, *Lab.* — 30,391
Mrs P. Buzzard, *C.* — 12,182
B. Spencer, *LD* — 6,933
Dr H. Jump, *NLP* — 295
*Lab. majority* — 18,209
(June 1987, Lab. maj. 13,801)

ST IVES (Cornwall)
E.71,152   T.80.29%
*D. Harris, *C.* — 24,528
A. George, *LD* — 22,883
S. Warran, *Lab.* — 9,144
Dr G. Stephens, *Lib.* — 577
C. majority — 1,645
(June 1987, C. maj. 7,555)

SALFORD EAST (Greater Manchester)
E.52,616   T.64.36%

| | |
|---|---|
| *Rt. Hon. S. Orme, *Lab.* | 20,327 |
| D. Berens, *C.* | 9,092 |
| N. Owen, *LD* | 3,836 |
| M. Stanley, *Green* | 463 |
| C. Craig, *NLP* | 150 |
| *Lab. majority* | 11,235 |

(June 1987, Lab. maj. 12,056)

SALISBURY (Wilts)
E.75,916   T.79.89%

| | |
|---|---|
| *S. R. Key, *C.* | 31,546 |
| P. Sample, *LD* | 22,573 |
| S. Fear, *Lab.* | 5,483 |
| Dr S. Elcock, *Green* | 609 |
| S. Fletcher, *Ind.* | 233 |
| T. Abbott, *Wessex* | 117 |
| Ms A. Martell, *NLP* | 93 |
| *C. majority* | 8,973 |

(June 1987, C. maj. 11,443)

SCARBOROUGH (N. Yorks)
E.76,364   T.77.18%

| | |
|---|---|
| J. Sykes, *C.* | 29,334 |
| D. Billing, *Lab.* | 17,600 |
| B. Davenport, *LD* | 11,133 |
| Dr D. Richardson, *Green* | 876 |
| *C. majority* | 11,734 |

(June 1987, C. maj. 13,626)

SEDGEFIELD (Durham)
E.61,024   T.77.06%

| | |
|---|---|
| *A. Blair, *Lab.* | 28,453 |
| N. Jopling, *C.* | 13,594 |
| G. Huntington, *LD* | 4,982 |
| *Lab. majority* | 14,859 |

(June 1987, Lab. maj. 13,058)

SELBY (N. Yorks)
E.77,178   T.80.16%

| | |
|---|---|
| *Rt. Hon. M. Alison, *C.* | 31,067 |
| J. Grogan, *Lab.* | 21,559 |
| E. Batty, *LD* | 9,244 |
| *C. majority* | 9,508 |

(June 1987, C. maj. 13,779)

SEVENOAKS (Kent)
E.71,050   T.81.35%

| | |
|---|---|
| *G. M. Wolfson, *C.* | 33,245 |
| R. Walshe, *LD* | 14,091 |
| Ms J. Evans, *Lab.* | 9,470 |
| Ms M. Lawrence, *Green* | 786 |
| P. Wakeling, *NLP* | 210 |
| *C. majority* | 19,154 |

(June 1987, C. maj. 17,345)

SHEFFIELD ATTERCLIFFE (S. Yorks)
E.69,177   T.71.81%

| | |
|---|---|
| C. Betts, *Lab.* | 28,563 |
| G. Millward, *C.* | 13,083 |
| Ms H. Woolley, *LD* | 7,283 |
| G. Ferguson, *Green* | 751 |
| *Lab. majority* | 15,480 |

(June 1987, Lab. maj. 17,191)

SHEFFIELD BRIGHTSIDE (S. Yorks)
E.63,810   T.66.26%

| | |
|---|---|
| *D. Blunkett, *Lab.* | 29,771 |
| T. Loughton, *C.* | 7,090 |

| | |
|---|---|
| R. Franklin, *LD* | 5,273 |
| D. Hyland, *Int. Comm.* | 150 |
| *Lab. majority* | 22,681 |

(June 1987, Lab. maj. 24,191)

SHEFFIELD CENTRAL (S. Yorks)
E.59,059   T.56.12%

| | |
|---|---|
| *R. Caborn, *Lab.* | 22,764 |
| V. Davies, *C.* | 5,470 |
| A. Sangar, *LD* | 3,856 |
| G. Wroe, *Green* | 750 |
| M. Clarke, *EUVJJ* | 212 |
| Ms J. O'Brien, *CL* | 92 |
| *Lab. majority* | 17,294 |

(June 1987, Lab. maj. 19,342)

SHEFFIELD HALLAM (S. Yorks)
E.76,584   T.70.83%

| | |
|---|---|
| *C. I. Patnick, *C.* | 24,693 |
| Dr P. Gold, *LD* | 17,952 |
| Ms V. Hardstaff, *Lab.* | 10,930 |
| M. Baker, *Green* | 473 |
| R. Hurford, *NLP* | 101 |
| Ms T. Clifford, *Rev. Comm.* | 99 |
| *C. majority* | 6,741 |

(June 1987, C. maj. 7,637)

SHEFFIELD HEELEY (S. Yorks)
E.70,953   T.70.89%

| | |
|---|---|
| *W. Michie, *Lab.* | 28,005 |
| D. Beck, *C.* | 13,051 |
| P. Moore, *LD* | 9,247 |
| *Lab. majority* | 14,954 |

(June 1987, Lab. maj. 14,440)

SHEFFIELD HILLSBOROUGH
(S. Yorks)
E.77,343   T.77.19%

| | |
|---|---|
| Mrs H. Jackson, *Lab.* | 27,568 |
| D. Chadwick, *LD* | 20,500 |
| S. Cordle, *C.* | 11,640 |
| *Lab. majority* | 7,068 |

(June 1987, Lab. maj. 3,286)

SHERWOOD (Notts)
E.73,354   T.85.48%

| | |
|---|---|
| S. P. Tipping, *Lab.* | 29,788 |
| *A. Stewart, *C.* | 26,878 |
| J. Howard, *LD* | 6,039 |
| *Lab. majority* | 2,910 |

(June 1987, C. maj. 4,495)

SHIPLEY (W. Yorks)
E.68,816   T.82.12%

| | |
|---|---|
| *Sir M. Fox, *C.* | 28,463 |
| Ms A. Lockwood, *Lab.* | 16,081 |
| J. Cole, *LD* | 11,288 |
| C. Harris, *Green* | 680 |
| *C. majority* | 12,382 |

(June 1987, C. maj. 12,630)

SHOREHAM (W. Sussex)
E.71,252   T.81.17%

| | |
|---|---|
| B. M. L. Stephen, *C.* | 32,670 |
| M. King, *LD* | 18,384 |
| P. Godwin, *Lab.* | 6,123 |
| W. Weights, *Lib.* | 459 |
| J. Dreben, *NLP* | 200 |
| *C. majority* | 14,286 |

(June 1987, C. maj. 17,070)

SHREWSBURY AND ATCHAM (Salop)
E.70,620   T.82.45%

| | |
|---|---|
| *D. Conway, *C.* | 26,681 |
| K. Hemsley, *LD* | 15,716 |
| Ms E. Owen, *Lab.* | 15,157 |
| G. Hardy, *Green* | 677 |
| *C. majority* | 10,965 |

(June 1987, C. maj. 9,064)

SHROPSHIRE NORTH
E.82,675   T.77.68%

| | |
|---|---|
| *Rt. Hon. J. Biffen, *C.* | 32,443 |
| J. Stevens, *LD* | 16,232 |
| R. Hawkins, *Lab.* | 15,550 |
| *C. majority* | 16,211 |

(June 1987, C. maj. 14,415)

SKIPTON AND RIPON (N. Yorks)
E.75,628   T.81.34%

| | |
|---|---|
| *D. Curry, *C.* | 35,937 |
| R. Hall, *LD* | 16,607 |
| Ms K. Allott, *Lab.* | 8,978 |
| *C. majority* | 19,330 |

(June 1987, C. maj. 17,174)

SLOUGH (Berks)
E.73,889   T.78.24%

| | |
|---|---|
| *J. Watts, *C.* | 25,793 |
| E. Lopez, *Lab.* | 25,279 |
| P. Mapp, *LD* | 4,041 |
| J. Clark, *Lib.* | 1,426 |
| D. Alford, *Ind. Lab.* | 699 |
| A. Carmichael, *NF* | 290 |
| M. Creese, *NLP* | 153 |
| Ms E. Smith, *ERIP* | 134 |
| *C. majority* | 514 |

(June 1987, C. maj. 4,090)

SOLIHULL (W. Midlands)
E.77,303   T.81.61%

| | |
|---|---|
| *J. Taylor, *C.* | 38,385 |
| M. Southcombe, *LD* | 13,239 |
| Ms N. Kutapan, *Lab.* | 10,544 |
| C. Hards, *Green* | 925 |
| *C. majority* | 25,146 |

(June 1987, C. maj. 21,786)

SOMERTON AND FROME (Somerset)
E.71,354   T.82.75%

| | |
|---|---|
| M. Robinson, *C.* | 28,052 |
| D. Heath, *LD* | 23,711 |
| R. Ashford, *Lab.* | 6,154 |
| Ms L. Graham, *Green* | 742 |
| Ms J. Pollock, *Lib.* | 388 |
| *C. majority* | 4,341 |

(June 1987, C. maj. 9,538)

SOUTHAMPTON ITCHEN (Hants)
E.72,104   T.76.93%

| | |
|---|---|
| J. Denham, *Lab.* | 24,402 |
| *C. Chope, *C.* | 23,851 |
| J. Hodgson, *LD* | 7,221 |
| *Lab. majority* | 551 |

(June 1987, C. maj. 6,716)

SOUTHAMPTON TEST (Hants)
E.72,932   T.77.40%

| | |
|---|---|
| *S. J. A. Hill, *C.* | 24,504 |
| A. Whitehead, *Lab.* | 23,919 |
| Ms D. Maddock, *LD* | 7,391 |

J. Michaelis, *Green* 535
D. Plummer, *NLP* 101
*C. majority* 585
(June 1987, C. maj. 6,954)

SOUTHEND EAST (Essex)
E.56,708 T.73.80%
*Sir E. Taylor, *C.* 24,591
G. Bramley, *Lab.* 11,480
Ms J. Horne, *LD* 5,107
B. Lynch, *Lib.* 673
*C. majority* 13,111
(June 1987, C. maj. 13,847)

SOUTHEND WEST (Essex)
E.64,198 T.77.80%
*Rt. Hon. P. Channon, *C.* 27,319
Ms N. Stimson, *LD* 15,417
G. Viney, *Lab.* 6,139
A. Farmer, *Lib.* 495
C. Keene, *Green* 451
P. Warburton, *NLP* 127
*C. majority* 11,902
(June 1987, C. maj. 8,400)

SOUTH HAMS (Devon)
E.83,061 T.81.09%
*A. Steen, *C.* 35,951
V. Evans, *LD* 22,240
Ms E. Cohen, *Lab.* 8,091
C. Titmuss, *Green* 846
Mrs L. Summerville, *NLP* 227
*C. majority* 13,711
(June 1987, C. maj. 13,146)

SOUTHPORT (Merseyside)
E.71,443 T.77.60%
M. Banks, *C.* 26,081
*R. Fearn, *LD* 23,018
J. King, *Lab.* 5,637
J. Walker, *Green* 545
G. Clements, *NLP* 159
*C. majority* 3,063
(June 1987, L./All. maj. 1,849)

SOUTH RIBBLE (Lancs)
E.78,173 T.82.99%
*R. Atkins, *C.* 30,828
Dr G. Smith, *Lab.* 24,855
S. Jones, *LD* 8,928
Dr R. Decter, *NLP* 269
*C. majority* 5,973
(June 1987, C. maj. 8,430)

SOUTH SHIELDS (Tyne & Wear)
E.59,392 T.70.07%
*D. Clark, *Lab.* 24,876
J. Howard, *C.* 11,399
A. Preece, *LD* 5,344
*Lab. majority* 13,477
(June 1987, Lab. maj. 13,851)

SOUTHWARK AND BERMONDSEY
(Greater London)
E.60,251 T.62.62%
*S. Hughes, *LD* 21,459
R. Balfe, *Lab.* 11,614
A. Raca, *C.* 3,794
S. Tyler, *BNP* 530
T. Blackham, *NF* 168
Dr G. Barnett, *NLP* 113
J. Grogan, *CL* 56

*LD majority* 9,845
June 1987, L./All. maj. 2,779

SPELTHORNE (Surrey)
E.69,343 T.80.36%
*D. Wilshire, *C.* 32,627
Ms A. Leedham, *Lab.* 12,784
R. Roberts, *LD* 9,202
Ms J. Wassell, *Green* 580
D. Rea, *Loony* 338
D. Ellis, *NLP* 195
*C. majority* 19,843
(June 1987, C. maj. 20,050)

STAFFORD
E.74,663 T.82.91%
*W. Cash, *C.* 30,876
D. Kidney, *Lab.* 19,976
Mrs J. Calder, *LD* 10,702
C. Peat, *Hardcore* 178
P. Lines, *NLP* 176
*C. majority* 10,900
(June 1987, C. maj. 13,707)

STAFFORDSHIRE MID
E.73,414 T.85.66%
M. Fabricant, *C.* 31,227
*Mrs S. Heal, *Lab.* 24,991
B. Stamp, *LD* 6,432
Ms D. Grice, *NLP* 239
*C. majority* 6,236
(June 1987, C. maj. 14,654)
(March 1990, Lab. maj. 9,449)

STAFFORDSHIRE MOORLANDS
E.75,036 T.83.66%
*D. Knox, *C.* 29,240
J. Siddelley, *Lab.* 21,830
Ms C. Jebb, *LD* 9,326
M. Howson, *Anti Fed.* 2,121
P. Davies, *NLP* 261
*C. majority* 7,410
(June 1987, C. maj. 14,427)

STAFFORDSHIRE SOUTH
E.82,758 T.81.54%
*P. Cormack, *C.* 40,266
B. Wylie, *Lab.* 17,633
I. Sadler, *LD* 9,584
*C. majority* 22,633
(June 1987, C. maj. 25,268)

STAFFORDSHIRE SOUTH EAST
E.70,199 T.82.05%
*D. Lightbown, *C.* 29,180
B. Jenkins, *Lab.* 21,988
Dr G. Penlington, *LD* 5,540
Miss J. Taylor, *SD* 895
*C. majority* 7,192
(June 1987, C. maj. 10,885)

STALYBRIDGE AND HYDE (Greater
Manchester)
E.68,189 T.73.46%
*T. Pendry, *Lab.* 26,207
S. Mort, *C.* 17,376
I. Kirk, *LD* 4,740
R. Powell, *Lib.* 1,199
D. Poyzer, *Loony* 337
E. Blomfield, *NLP* 238
*Lab. majority* 8,831
(June 1987, Lab. maj. 5,663)

STAMFORD AND SPALDING (Lincs)
E.75,153 T.81.16%
*J. Q. Davies, *C.* 35,965
C. Burke, *Lab.* 13,096
B. Lee, *LD* 11,939
*C. majority* 22,869
(June 1987, C. maj. 14,007)

STEVENAGE (Herts)
E.70,233 T.83.03%
*T. Wood, *C.* 26,652
Ms J. Church, *Lab.* 21,764
A. Reilly, *LD* 9,668
A. Calcraft, *NLP* 233
*C. majority* 4,888
(June 1987, C. maj. 5,340)

STOCKPORT (Greater Manchester)
E.58,095 T.82.27%
Ms M. A. Coffey, *Lab.* 21,096
*A. Favell, *C.* 19,674
Ms A. Corris, *LD* 6,539
Ms J. Filmore, *Green* 436
D. Saunders, *NLP* 50
*Lab. majority* 1,422
(June 1987, C. maj. 2,853)

STOCKTON NORTH (Cleveland)
E.69,451 T.76.83%
*F. Cook, *Lab.* 27,918
S. Brocklebank-Fowler, *C.* 17,444
Ms S. Fletcher, *LD* 7,454
K. McGarvey, *Ind. Lab.* 550
*Lab. majority* 10,474
(June 1987, Lab. maj. 8,801)

STOCKTON SOUTH (Cleveland)
E.75,959 T.82.77%
*T. Devlin, *C.* 28,418
J. Scott, *Lab.* 25,049
Ms K. Kirkham, *LD* 9,410
*C. majority* 3,369
(June 1987, C. maj. 774)

STOKE-ON-TRENT CENTRAL (Staffs)
E.65,527 T.68.12%
*M. Fisher, *Lab.* 25,897
N. Gibb, *C.* 12,477
M. Dent, *LD* 6,073
N. Pullen, *NLP* 196
*Lab. majority* 13,420
(June 1987, Lab. maj. 9,770)

STOKE-ON-TRENT NORTH (Staffs)
E.73,141 T.73.42%
*Ms J. Walley, *Lab.* 30,464
L. Harris, *C.* 15,687
J. Redfern, *LD* 7,167
A. Morrison, *NLP* 387
*Lab. majority* 14,777
(June 1987, Lab. maj. 8,513)

STOKE-ON-TRENT SOUTH (Staffs)
E.71,316 T.74.33%
G. Stevenson, *Lab.* 26,380
R. Ibbs, *C.* 19,471
F. Jones, *LD* 6,870
Mrs E. Lines, *NLP* 291
*Lab. majority* 6,909
(June 1987, Lab. maj. 5,053)

STRATFORD-UPON-AVON
(Warwicks)
E.82,824   T.82.07%

| | |
|---|---|
| *A. Howarth, *C.* | 40,251 |
| N. Fogg, *LD* | 17,359 |
| Ms S. Brookes, *Lab.* | 8,932 |
| R. Roughan, *Green* | 729 |
| A. Saunders, *Ind. C.* | 573 |
| M. Twite, *NLP* | 130 |
| *C. majority* | 22,892 |
| (June 1987, C. maj. 21,165) | |

STREATHAM (Greater London)
E.56,825   T.69.03%

| | |
|---|---|
| K. Hill, *Lab.* | 18,925 |
| *Sir W. Shelton, *C.* | 16,608 |
| J. Pindar, *LD* | 2,858 |
| R. Baker, *Green* | 443 |
| A. Hankin, *Islamic* | 154 |
| Mrs C. Payne, *ADS* | 145 |
| J. Parsons, *NLP* | 97 |
| *Lab. majority* | 2,317 |
| (June 1987, C. maj. 2,407) | |

STRETFORD (Greater Manchester)
E.54,467   T.68.76%

| | |
|---|---|
| *A. Lloyd, *Lab.* | 22,300 |
| C. Rae, *C.* | 11,163 |
| F. Beswick, *LD* | 3,722 |
| A. Boyton, *NLP* | 268 |
| *Lab. majority* | 11,137 |
| (June 1987, Lab. maj. 9,402) | |

STROUD (Glos)
E.82,553   T.84.49%

| | |
|---|---|
| *R. Knapman, *C.* | 32,201 |
| D. Drew, *Lab.* | 18,796 |
| M. Robinson, *LD* | 16,751 |
| Ms S. Atkinson, *Green* | 2,005 |
| *C. majority* | 13,405 |
| (June 1987, C. maj. 12,375) | |

SUFFOLK CENTRAL
E.82,735   T.80.26%

| | |
|---|---|
| *M. Lord, *C.* | 32,917 |
| Ms L. Henniker-Major, *LD* | 16,886 |
| J. Harris, *Lab.* | 15,615 |
| J. Matthissen, *Green* | 800 |
| Ms J. Wilmot, *NLP* | 190 |
| *C. majority* | 16,031 |
| (June 1987, C. maj. 16,290) | |

SUFFOLK COASTAL
E.79,333   T.81.62%

| | |
|---|---|
| *Rt. Hon. J. Gummer, *C.* | 34,680 |
| P. Monk, *LD* | 15,395 |
| T. Hodgson, *Lab.* | 13,508 |
| A. Slade, *Green* | 943 |
| Ms F. Kaplan, *NLP* | 232 |
| *C. majority* | 19,285 |
| (June 1987, C. maj. 15,280) | |

SUFFOLK SOUTH
E.84,833   T.81.73%

| | |
|---|---|
| *T. Yeo, *C.* | 34,793 |
| Ms K. Pollard, *LD* | 17,504 |
| S. Hesford, *Lab.* | 16,623 |
| T. Aisbitt, *NLP* | 420 |
| *C. majority* | 17,289 |
| (June 1987, C. maj. 16,243) | |

SUNDERLAND NORTH (Tyne &
Wear)
E.72,874   T.68.86%

| | |
|---|---|
| W. Etherington, *Lab.* | 30,481 |
| Miss J. Barnes, *C.* | 13,477 |
| V. Halom, *LD* | 5,389 |
| Ms W. Lundgren, *Lib.* | 841 |
| *Lab. majority* | 17,004 |
| (June 1987, Lab. maj. 14,672) | |

SUNDERLAND SOUTH (Tyne &
Wear)
E.72,607   T.69.87%

| | |
|---|---|
| *C. Mullin, *Lab.* | 29,399 |
| G. Howe, *C.* | 14,898 |
| J. Lennox, *LD* | 5,844 |
| T. Scouler, *Green* | 596 |
| *Lab. majority* | 14,501 |
| (June 1987, Lab. maj. 12,613) | |

SURBITON (Greater London)
E.42,421   T.82.44%

| | |
|---|---|
| *R. Tracey, *C.* | 19,033 |
| Ms B. Janke, *LD* | 9,394 |
| R. Hutchinson, *Lab.* | 6,384 |
| W. Parker, *NLP* | 161 |
| *C. majority* | 9,639 |
| (June 1987, C. maj. 9,741) | |

SURREY EAST
E.57,878   T.82.53%

| | |
|---|---|
| P. Ainsworth, *C.* | 29,767 |
| R. Tomlin, *LD* | 12,111 |
| Mrs G. Roles, *Lab.* | 5,075 |
| I. Kilpatrick, *Green* | 819 |
| *C. majority* | 17,656 |
| (June 1987, C. maj. 18,126) | |

SURREY NORTH WEST
E.83,648   T.78.27%

| | |
|---|---|
| *Sir M. Grylls, *C.* | 41,772 |
| Mrs C. Clark, *LD* | 13,378 |
| M. Hayhurst, *Lab.* | 8,886 |
| Ms Y. Hockey, *Green* | 1,441 |
| *C. majority* | 28,394 |
| (June 1987, C. maj. 23,575) | |

SURREY SOUTH WEST
E.72,288   T.82.77%

| | |
|---|---|
| *Mrs V. Bottomley, *C.* | 35,008 |
| N. Sherlock, *LD* | 20,033 |
| P. Kelly, *Lab.* | 3,840 |
| N. Bedrock, *Green* | 710 |
| K. Campbell, *NLP* | 147 |
| D. Newman, *AS* | 98 |
| *C. majority* | 14,975 |
| (June 1987, C. maj. 14,343) | |

SUSSEX MID
E.80,827   T.82.85%

| | |
|---|---|
| *Rt. Hon. T. Renton, *C.* | 39,524 |
| Ms M. Collins, *LD* | 18,996 |
| Ms L. Gregory, *Lab.* | 6,951 |
| H. Stevens, *Green* | 772 |
| P. Berry, *Loony* | 392 |
| P. Hodkin, *PR* | 246 |
| Dr A. Hankey, *NLP* | 89 |
| *C. majority* | 20,528 |
| (June 1987, C. maj. 18,292) | |

SUTTON AND CHEAM (Greater
London)
E.60,949   T.82.39%

| | |
|---|---|
| Lady O. Maitland, *C.* | 27,710 |
| P. Burstow, *LD* | 16,954 |
| G. Martin, *Lab.* | 4,980 |
| J. Duffy, *Green* | 444 |
| Ms A. Hatchard, *NLP* | 133 |
| *C. majority* | 10,756 |
| (June 1987, C. maj. 15,718) | |

SUTTON COLDFIELD (W. Midlands)
E.71,410   T.79.51%

| | |
|---|---|
| *Rt. Hon. Sir N. Fowler, *C.* | 37,001 |
| J. Whorwood, *LD* | 10,965 |
| Ms J. Bott-Obi, *Lab.* | 8,490 |
| H. Meads, *NLP* | 324 |
| *C. majority* | 26,036 |
| (June 1987, C. maj. 21,183) | |

SWINDON (Wilts)
E.90,067   T.81.46%

| | |
|---|---|
| *S. Coombs, *C.* | 31,749 |
| J. D'Avila, *Lab.* | 28,923 |
| S. Cordon, *LD* | 11,737 |
| W. Hughes, *Green* | 647 |
| R. Gillard, *Loony G.* | 236 |
| V. Farrar, *Ind.* | 78 |
| *C. majority* | 2,826 |
| (June 1987, C. maj. 4,857) | |

TATTON (Cheshire)
E.71,085   T.80.83%

| | |
|---|---|
| *M. N. Hamilton, *C.* | 31,658 |
| J. Kelly, *Lab.* | 15,798 |
| Ms C. Hancox, *LD* | 9,597 |
| M. Gibson, *FP* | 410 |
| *C. majority* | 15,860 |
| (June 1987, C. maj. 17,094) | |

TAUNTON (Somerset)
E.78,036   T.82.32%

| | |
|---|---|
| *D. Nicholson, *C.* | 29,576 |
| Ms J. Ballard, *LD* | 26,240 |
| Ms J. Hole, *Lab.* | 8,151 |
| P. Leavey, *NLP* | 279 |
| *C. majority* | 3,336 |
| (June 1987, C. maj. 10,380) | |

TEIGNBRIDGE (Devon)
E.74,892   T.83.43%

| | |
|---|---|
| *P. Nicholls, *C.* | 31,272 |
| R. Younger-Ross, *LD* | 22,416 |
| R. Kennedy, *Lab.* | 8,128 |
| A. Hope, *Loony* | 437 |
| N. Hayes, *NLP* | 234 |
| *C. majority* | 8,856 |
| (June 1987, C. maj. 10,425) | |

THANET NORTH (Kent)
E.70,978   T.76.02%

| | |
|---|---|
| *R. Gale, *C.* | 30,867 |
| A. Bretman, *Lab.* | 12,657 |
| Ms J. Phillips, *LD* | 9,563 |
| Ms H. Dawe, *Green* | 873 |
| *C. majority* | 18,210 |
| (June 1987, C. maj. 17,480) | |

THANET SOUTH (Kent)
E.62,441   T.78.17%

| | |
|---|---|
| *J. Aitken, *C.* | 25,253 |
| M. James, *Lab.* | 13,740 |

W. Pitt, *LD* 8,948
Ms S. Peckham, *Green* 871
*C. majority* 11,513
(June 1987, C. maj. 13,683)

THURROCK (Essex)
*E.*69,171   *T.*78.15%
A. MacKinlay, *Lab.* 24,791
*T. Janman, *C.* 23,619
A. Banton, *LD* 5,145
C. Rogers, *Pensioners* 391
P. Compobassi, *Anti Fed.* 117
*Lab. majority* 1,172
(June 1987, C. maj. 690)

TIVERTON (Devon)
*E.*71,024   *T.*82.98%
Mrs A. Browning, *C.* 30,376
D. Cox, *LD* 19,287
Ms S. Gibb, *Lab.* 5,950
D. Morrish, *Lib.* 2,225
P. Foggitt, *Green* 1,007
B. Rhodes, *NLP* 96
*C. majority* 11,089
(June 1987, C. maj. 9,212)

TONBRIDGE AND MALLING (Kent)
*E.*77,292   *T.*82.66%
*Rt. Hon. Sir J. Stanley, *C.* 36,542
P. Roberts, *LD* 14,984
Ms M. O'Neill, *Lab.* 11,533
J. Tidy, *Green* 612
Mrs J. Hovarth, *NLP* 221
*C. majority* 21,558
(June 1987, C. maj. 16,429)

TOOTING (Greater London)
*E.*68,306   *T.*74.79%
*T. Cox, *Lab.* 24,601
M. Winters, *C.* 20,494
B. Bunce, *LD* 3,776
Ms C. Martin, *Lib.* 1,340
P. Owens, *Green* 694
F. Anklesalria, *NLP* 119
M. Whitelaw, *CD* 64
*Lab. majority* 4,107
(June 1987, Lab. maj. 1,441)

TORBAY (Devon)
*E.*71,171   *T.*80.63%
*R. Allason, *C.* 28,624
A. Sanders, *LD* 22,837
P. Truscott, *Lab.* 5,503
R. Jones, *NF* 268
Ms A. Thomas, *NLP* 157
*C. majority* 5,787
(June 1987, C. maj. 8,820)

TOTTENHAM (Greater London)
*E.*68,319   *T.*65.60%
*B. Grant, *Lab.* 25,309
A. Charalambous, *C.* 13,341
A. L'Estrange, *LD* 5,120
P. Budge, *Green* 903
Ms M. Obomanu, *NLP* 150
*Lab. majority* 11,968
(June 1987, Lab. maj. 4,141)

TRURO (Cornwall)
*E.*75,101   *T.*82.35%
*M. Taylor, *LD* 31,230
N. St Aubyn, *C.* 23,660

J. Geach, *Lab.* 6,078
L. Keating, *Green* 569
C. Tankard, *Lib.* 208
Ms M. Hartley, *NLP* 108
*LD majority* 7,570
(June 1987, L./All. maj. 4,753)

TUNBRIDGE WELLS (Kent)
*E.*76,808   *T.*78.11%
*Rt. Hon. Sir P. Mayhew, *C.* 34,162
A. Clayton, *LD* 17,030
E. Goodman, *Lab.* 8,300
E. Fenna, *NLP* 267
R. Edey, *ISS* 236
*C. majority* 17,132
(June 1987, C. maj. 16,122)

TWICKENHAM (Greater London)
*E.*63,072   *T.*84.27%
*T. Jessel, *C.* 26,804
Dr V. Cable, *LD* 21,093
M. Gold, *Lab.* 4,919
G. Gill, *NLP* 152
D. Griffith, *DLC* 103
A. Miners, *Lib.* 85
*C. majority* 5,711
(June 1987, C. maj. 7,127)

TYNE BRIDGE (Tyne & Wear)
*E.*53,079   *T.*62.64%
*D. Clelland, *Lab.* 22,328
C. Liddell-Grainger, *C.* 7,118
J. Burt, *LD* 3,804
*Lab. majority* 15,210
(June 1987, Lab. maj. 15,573)

TYNEMOUTH (Tyne & Wear)
*E.*74,955   *T.*80.39%
*N. Trotter, *C.* 27,731
P. Cosgrove, *Lab.* 27,134
P. Selby, *LD* 4,855
A. Buchanan-Smith, *Green* 543
*C. majority* 597
(June 1987, C. maj. 2,583)

UPMINSTER (Greater London)
*E.*64,138   *T.*80.46%
*Sir N. Bonsor, *C.* 28,791
T. Ward, *Lab.* 14,970
T. Hurlstone, *LD* 7,848
*C. majority* 13,821
(June 1987, C. maj. 16,857)

UXBRIDGE (Greater London)
*E.*61,744   *T.*78.87%
*J. M. Shersby, *C.* 27,487
R. Evans, *Lab.* 14,308
S. Carey, *LD* 5,900
I. Flindall, *Green* 538
M. O'Rourke, *BNP* 350
A. Deans, *NLP* 120
*C. majority* 13,179
(June 1987, C. maj. 15,970)

VAUXHALL (Greater London)
*E.*62,473   *T.*62.35%
*Ms C. Hoey, *Lab.* 21,328
B. Gentry, *C.* 10,840
M. Tuffrey, *LD* 5,678
Ms P. Shepherd, *Green* 803
A. Khan, *DOS* 156
Ms S. Hill, *Rev. Comm.* 152

*Lab. majority* 10,488
(June 1987, Lab. maj. 9,019)
(June 1989, Lab. maj. 9,766)

WAKEFIELD (W. Yorks)
*E.*69,794   *T.*76.27%
*D. Hinchliffe, *Lab.* 26,964
D. Fanthorpe, *C.* 20,374
T. Wright, *LD* 5,900
*Lab. majority* 6,590
(June 1987, Lab. maj. 2,789)

WALLASEY (Merseyside)
*E.*65,676   *T.*82.50%
Ms A. Eagle, *Lab.* 26,531
*Rt. Hon. L. Chalker, *C.* 22,722
N. Thomas, *LD* 4,177
Ms S. Davis, *Green* 650
G. Gay, *NLP* 105
*Lab. majority* 3,809
(June 1987, C. maj. 279)

WALLSEND (Tyne & Wear)
*E.*77,941   *T.*74.12%
S. Byers, *Lab.* 33,439
Miss M. Gibbon, *C.* 13,969
M. Huscroft, *LD* 10,369
*Lab. majority* 19,470
(June 1987, Lab. maj. 19,384)

WALSALL NORTH (W. Midlands)
*E.*69,604   *T.*74.98%
*D. Winnick, *Lab.* 24,387
R. Syms, *C.* 20,563
A. Powis, *LD* 6,629
K. Reynolds, *NF* 614
*Lab. majority* 3,824
(June 1987, Lab. maj. 1,790)

WALSALL SOUTH (W. Midlands)
*E.*65,642   *T.*76.26%
*B. George, *Lab.* 24,133
L. Jones, *C.* 20,955
G. Williams, *LD* 4,132
R. Clarke, *Green* 673
J. Oldbury, *NLP* 167
*Lab. majority* 3,178
(June 1987, Lab. maj. 1,116)

WALTHAMSTOW (Greater London)
*E.*49,140   *T.*72.35%
N. Gerrard, *Lab.* 16,251
*H. Summerson, *C.* 13,229
P. Leighton, *LD* 5,142
Ms J. Lambert, *Green* 594
V. Wilkinson, *Lib.* 241
A. Planton, *NLP* 94
*Lab. majority* 3,022
(June 1987, C. maj. 1,512)

WANSBECK (Northumberland)
*E.*63,457   *T.*79.29%
*J. Thompson, *Lab.* 30,046
G. Sanderson, *C.* 11,872
B. Priestley, *LD* 7,691
N. Best, *Green* 710
*Lab. majority* 18,174
(June 1987, Lab. maj. 16,789)

WANSDYKE (Avon)
*E.*77,156   *T.*84.33%
*J. Aspinwall, *C.* 31,389
D. Norris, *Lab.* 18,048

Ms D. Darby, *LD* — 14,834
F. Hayden, *Green* — 800
*C. majority* — 13,341
(June 1987, C. maj. 16,144)

WANSTEAD AND WOODFORD
(Greater London)
E.55,821   T.78.28%
*J. Arbuthnot, *C.* — 26,204
Ms L. Brown, *Lab.* — 9,319
G. Staight, *LD* — 7,362
F. Roads, *Green* — 637
A. Brickell, *NLP* — 178
*C. majority* — 16,885
(June 1987, C. maj. 16,412)

WANTAGE (Oxon)
E.68,328   T.82.68%
*R. Jackson, *C.* — 30,575
R. Morgan, *LD* — 14,102
V. Woodell, *Lab.* — 10,955
R. Ely, *Green* — 867
*C. majority* — 16,473
(June 1987, C. maj. 12,156)

WARLEY EAST (W. Midlands)
E.51,717   T.71.72%
*A. Faulds, *Lab.* — 19,891
G. Marshall, *C.* — 12,097
A. Harrod, *LD* — 4,547
A. Groucott, *NLP* — 561
*Lab. majority* — 7,794
(June 1987, Lab. maj. 5,585)

WARLEY WEST (W. Midlands)
E.57,164   T.73.90%
J. Spellar, *Lab.* — 21,386
Mrs S. Whitehouse, *C.* — 15,914
Ms E. Todd, *LD* — 4,945
*Lab. majority* — 5,472
(June 1987, Lab. maj. 5,393)

WARRINGTON NORTH (Cheshire)
E.78,548   T.77.38%
*E. D. H. Hoyle, *Lab.* — 33,019
C. Daniels, *C.* — 20,397
I. Greenhalgh, *LD* — 6,965
B. Davies, *NLP* — 400
*Lab. majority* — 12,622
(June 1987, Lab. maj. 8,013)

WARRINGTON SOUTH (Cheshire)
E.77,694   T.82.04%
M. Hall, *Lab.* — 27,819
*C. Butler, *C.* — 27,628
P. Walker, *LD* — 7,978
S. Benson, *NLP* — 321
*Lab. majority* — 191
(June 1987, C. maj. 3,609)

WARWICK AND LEAMINGTON
E.71,259   T.81.54%
*Sir D. Smith, *C.* — 28,093
M. Taylor, *Lab.* — 19,158
Ms S. Boad, *LD* — 9,645
Ms J. Alty, *Green* — 803
R. Newby, *Ind.* — 251
J. Brewster, *NLP* — 156
*C. majority* — 8,935
(June 1987, C. maj. 13,982)

WARWICKSHIRE NORTH
E.71,473   T.83.82%
M. O'Brien, *Lab.* — 27,599
*Hon. F. Maude, *C.* — 26,145
N. Mitchell, *LD* — 6,167
*Lab. majority* — 1,454
(June 1987, C. maj. 2,829)

WATFORD (Herts)
E.72,291   T.82.34%
*W. A. T. T. Garel-Jones, *C.* — 29,072
M. Jackson, *Lab.* — 19,482
M. Oaten, *LD* — 10,231
J. Hywel-Davies, *Green* — 566
L. Davis, *NLP* — 176
*C. majority* — 9,590
(June 1987, C. maj. 11,736)

WAVENEY (Suffolk)
E.84,181   T.81.81%
*D. Porter, *C.* — 33,174
E. Leverett, *Lab.* — 26,472
A. Rogers, *LD* — 8,925
D. Hook, *NLP* — 302
*C. majority* — 6,702
(June 1987, C. maj. 11,783)

WEALDEN (E. Sussex)
E.74,665   T.80.83%
*Sir G. Johnson Smith, *C.* — 37,263
M. Skinner, *LD* — 16,332
S. Billcliffe, *Lab.* — 5,579
I. Guy-Moore, *Green* — 1,002
Dr R. Graham, *NLP* — 182
*C. majority* — 20,931
(June 1987, C. maj. 20,110)

WELLINGBOROUGH (Northants)
E.73,875   T.81.89%
*P. Fry, *C.* — 32,302
P. Sawford, *Lab.* — 20,486
Ms J. Trevor, *LD* — 7,714
*C. majority* — 11,816
(June 1987, C. maj. 14,070)

WELLS (Somerset)
E.69,833   T.82.71%
*D. Heathcoat-Amory, *C.* — 28,620
H. Temperley, *LD* — 21,971
J. Pilgrim, *Lab.* — 6,126
M. Fenner, *Green* — 1,042
*C. majority* — 6,649
(June 1987, C. maj. 8,541)

WELWYN HATFIELD (Herts)
E.72,146   T.84.39%
*D. Evans, *C.* — 29,447
R. Little, *Lab.* — 20,982
R. Parker, *LD* — 10,196
Ms E. Lucas, *NLP* — 264
*C. majority* — 8,465
(June 1987, C. maj. 10,903)

WENTWORTH (S. Yorks)
E.64,914   T.74.03%
*P. Hardy, *Lab.* — 32,939
M. Brennan, *C.* — 10,490
Ms C. Roderick, *LD* — 4,629
*Lab. majority* — 22,449
(June 1987, Lab. maj. 20,092)

WEST BROMWICH EAST
(W. Midlands)
E.56,940   T.75.25%
*P. Snape, *Lab.* — 19,913
C. Blunt, *C.* — 17,100
M. Smith, *LD* — 5,360
J. Lord, *NF* — 477
*Lab. majority* — 2,813
(June 1987, Lab. maj. 983)

WEST BROMWICH WEST
(W. Midlands)
E.57,655   T.70.41%
*Miss B. Boothroyd, *Lab.* — 22,251
D. Swayne, *C.* — 14,421
Miss S. Broadbent, *LD* — 3,925
*Lab. majority* — 7,830
(June 1987, Lab. maj. 5,253)

WESTBURY (Wilts)
E.87,356   T.82.99%
*D. Faber, *C.* — 36,568
Ms V. Rayner, *LD* — 23,962
W. Stallard, *Lab.* — 9,642
P. Macdonald, *Lib.* — 1,440
P. French, *Green* — 888
*C. majority* — 12,606
(June 1987, C. maj. 10,097)

WESTMINSTER NORTH (Greater
London)
E.58,847   T.75.75%
*Sir J. Wheeler, *C.* — 21,828
Ms J. Edwards, *Lab.* — 18,095
J. Wigoder, *LD* — 3,341
Ms A. Burke, *Green* — 1,017
J. Hinde, *NLP* — 159
M. Kelly, *Anti Fed.* — 137
*C. majority* — 3,733
(June 1987, C. maj. 3,310)

WESTMORLAND AND LONSDALE
(Cumbria)
E.71,865   T.77.76%
*Rt. Hon. M. Jopling, *C.* — 31,798
S. Collins, *LD* — 15,362
D. Abbott, *Lab.* — 8,436
R. Johnstone, *NLP* — 287
*C. majority* — 16,436
(June 1987, C. maj. 14,920)

WESTON-SUPER-MARE (Avon)
E.78,839   T.79.75%
*A. W. Wiggin, *C.* — 30,022
B. Cotter, *LD* — 24,680
D. Murray, *Lab.* — 6,913
Dr R. Lawson, *Green* — 1,262
*C. majority* — 5,342
(June 1987, C. maj. 7,998)

WIGAN (Greater Manchester)
E.72,739   T.76.16%
*R. Stott, *Lab.* — 34,910
E. Hess, *C.* — 13,068
G. Davies, *LD* — 6,111
K. White, *Lib.* — 1,116
Ms A. Taylor, *NLP* — 197
*Lab. majority* — 21,842
(June 1987, Lab. maj. 20,462)

WILTSHIRE NORTH
E.85,851  T.81.71%

| | |
|---|---|
| *R. Needham, C. | 39,028 |
| Ms C. Napier, LD | 22,640 |
| Ms C. Reid, Lab. | 6,945 |
| Ms L. Howitt, Green | 850 |
| G. Hawkins, Lib. | 622 |
| S. Martienssen, Bastion | 66 |
| C. majority | 16,388 |

(June 1987, C. maj. 10,939)

WIMBLEDON (Greater London)
E.61,917  T.80.23%

| | |
|---|---|
| *Dr C. Goodson-Wickes, C. | 26,331 |
| K. Abrams, Lab. | 11,570 |
| Ms A. Willott, LD | 10,569 |
| V. Flood, Green | 860 |
| H. Godfrey, NLP | 181 |
| G. Hadley, Ind. | 170 |
| C. majority | 14,761 |

(June 1987, C. maj. 11,301)

WINCHESTER (Hants)
E.79,218  T.83.46%

| | |
|---|---|
| P. G. Malone, C. | 33,113 |
| A. Barron, LD | 24,992 |
| P. Jenks, Lab. | 4,917 |
| *J. Browne, Ind. C. | 3,095 |
| C. majority | 8,121 |

(June 1987, C. maj. 7,479)

WINDSOR AND MAIDENHEAD
(Berks)
E.77,327  T.81.68%

| | |
|---|---|
| Hon. M. Trend, C. | 35,075 |
| J. Hyde, LD | 22,147 |
| Ms C. Attlee, Lab. | 4,975 |
| R. Williams, Green | 510 |
| D. Askwith, Loony | 236 |
| Miss E. Bigg, Ind. | 110 |
| M. Grenville, NLP | 108 |
| C. majority | 12,928 |

(June 1987, C. maj. 17,836)

WIRRAL SOUTH (Merseyside)
E.61,116  T.82.37%

| | |
|---|---|
| *G. B. Porter, C. | 25,590 |
| Ms H. Southworth, Lab. | 17,407 |
| E. Cunniffe, LD | 6,581 |
| N. Birchenough, Green | 584 |
| G. Griffiths, NLP | 182 |
| C. majority | 8,183 |

(June 1987, C. maj. 10,963)

WIRRAL WEST (Merseyside)
E.62,453  T.81.57%

| | |
|---|---|
| *Rt. Hon. D. Hunt, C. | 26,852 |
| Ms H. Stephenson, Lab. | 15,788 |
| J. Thornton, LD | 7,420 |
| Ms G. Bowler, Green | 700 |
| N. Broome, NLP | 188 |
| C. majority | 11,064 |

(June 1987, C. maj. 12,723)

WITNEY (Oxon)
E.78,521  T.81.89%

| | |
|---|---|
| *Rt. Hon. D. Hurd, C. | 36,256 |
| J. Plaskitt, Lab. | 13,688 |
| I. Blair, LD | 13,393 |
| Ms C. Beckford, Green | 716 |
| Ms S. Catling, NLP | 134 |
| Miss M. Brown, FTA | 119 |

| | |
|---|---|
| C. majority | 22,568 |

(June 1987, C. maj. 18,464)

WOKING (Surrey)
E.80,842  T.79.20%

| | |
|---|---|
| *Rt. Hon. C. Onslow, C. | 37,744 |
| Mrs D. Buckrell, LD | 17,902 |
| J. Dalgleish, Lab. | 8,080 |
| Mrs T. Macintyre, NLP | 302 |
| C. majority | 19,842 |

(June 1987, C. maj. 16,544)

WOKINGHAM (Berks)
E.85,914  T.82.41%

| | |
|---|---|
| *J. Redwood, C. | 43,497 |
| P. Simon, LD | 17,788 |
| N. Bland, Lab. | 8,846 |
| P. Owen, Loony | 531 |
| P. Harriss, WUWC | 148 |
| C. majority | 25,709 |

(June 1987, C. maj. 20,387)

WOLVERHAMPTON NORTH EAST
(W. Midlands)
E.62,695  T.78%

| | |
|---|---|
| K. Purchase, Lab. | 24,106 |
| *Mrs M. Hicks, C. | 20,167 |
| M. Gwinnett, LD | 3,546 |
| K. Bullman, Lib. | 1,087 |
| Lab. majority | 3,939 |

(June 1987, C. maj. 204)

WOLVERHAMPTON SOUTH EAST
(W. Midlands)
E.56,158  T.72.86%

| | |
|---|---|
| *D. Turner, Lab. | 23,215 |
| P. Bradbourn, C. | 12,975 |
| R. Whitehouse, LD | 3,881 |
| Ms C. Twelvetrees, Lib. | 850 |
| Lab. majority | 10,240 |

(June 1987, Lab. maj. 6,398)

WOLVERHAMPTON SOUTH WEST
(W. Midlands)
E.67,288  T.78.28%

| | |
|---|---|
| *N. Budgen, C. | 25,969 |
| S. Murphy, Lab. | 21,003 |
| M. Wiggin, LD | 4,470 |
| C. Hallmark, Lib. | 1,237 |
| C. majority | 4,966 |

(June 1987, C. maj. 10,318)

WOODSPRING (Avon)
E.77,534  T.83.21%

| | |
|---|---|
| Dr L. Fox, C. | 35,175 |
| Ms N. Kirsen, LD | 17,666 |
| R. Stone, Lab. | 9,942 |
| N. Brown, Lib. | 836 |
| Ms R. Knifton, Green | 801 |
| B. Lee, NLP | 100 |
| C. majority | 17,509 |

(June 1987, C. maj. 17,852)

WOOLWICH (Greater London)
E.55,977  T.70.91%

| | |
|---|---|
| J. Austin-Walker, Lab. | 17,551 |
| *J. Cartwright, SD | 15,326 |
| K. Walmsley, C. | 6,598 |
| Ms S. Hayward, NLP | 220 |
| Lab. majority | 2,225 |

(June 1987, SDP/All. maj. 1,937)

WORCESTER
E.74,211  T.80.99%

| | |
|---|---|
| P. Luff, C. | 27,883 |
| R. Berry, Lab. | 21,731 |
| J. Caiger, LD | 9,561 |
| M. Foster, Green | 592 |
| M. Soden, Brewer | 343 |
| C. majority | 6,152 |

(June 1987, C. maj. 10,453)

WORCESTERSHIRE MID
E.84,269  T.81.07%

| | |
|---|---|
| *E. Forth, C. | 33,964 |
| Ms J. Smith, Lab. | 24,094 |
| D. Barwick, LD | 9,745 |
| P. Davis, NLP | 520 |
| C. majority | 9,870 |

(June 1987, C. maj. 14,911)

WORCESTERSHIRE SOUTH
E.80,423  T.79.99%

| | |
|---|---|
| *W. M. H. Spicer, C. | 34,792 |
| P. Chandler, LD | 18,641 |
| N. Knowles, Lab. | 9,727 |
| G. Woodford, Green | 1,178 |
| C. majority | 16,151 |

(June 1987, C. maj. 13,645)

WORKINGTON (Cumbria)
E.57,597  T.81.52%

| | |
|---|---|
| *D. Campbell-Savours, Lab. | 26,719 |
| S. Sexton, C. | 16,270 |
| Ms C. Neale, LD | 3,028 |
| D. Langstaff, Loony | 755 |
| Ms N. Escott, NLP | 183 |
| Lab. majority | 10,449 |

(June 1987, Lab. maj. 7,019)

WORSLEY (Greater Manchester)
E.72,244  T.77.74%

| | |
|---|---|
| *T. Lewis, Lab. | 29,418 |
| N. Cameron, C. | 19,406 |
| R. Boyd, LD | 6,490 |
| P. Connolly, Green | 677 |
| G. Phillips, NLP | 176 |
| Lab. majority | 10,012 |

(June 1987, Lab. maj. 7,337)

WORTHING (W. Sussex)
E.77,540  T.77.41%

| | |
|---|---|
| *Rt. Hon. T. Higgins, C. | 34,198 |
| Mrs S. Bucknall, LD | 17,665 |
| J. Deen, Lab. | 6,679 |
| Mrs P. Beever, Green | 806 |
| N. Goble, Lib. | 679 |
| C. majority | 16,533 |

(June 1987, C. maj. 18,501)

THE WREKIN (Salop)
E.90,892  T.77.14%

| | |
|---|---|
| *B. Grocott, Lab. | 33,865 |
| Mrs E. Holt, C. | 27,217 |
| A. West, LD | 8,032 |
| R. Saunders, Green | 1,008 |
| Lab. majority | 6,648 |

(June 1987, Lab. maj. 1,456)

WYCOMBE (Bucks)
E.72,564  T.78.01%

| | |
|---|---|
| *R. Whitney, C. | 30,081 |
| T. Andrews, LD | 13,005 |
| J. Huddart, Lab. | 12,222 |

| | |
|---|---|
| J. Laker, *Green* | 686 |
| A. Page, *SD* | 449 |
| T. Anton, *NLP* | 168 |
| *C. majority* | 17,076 |
| (June 1987, C. maj. 13,819) | |

WYRE (Lancs)
E.67,778   T.79.54%
| | |
|---|---|
| *K. Mans, *C.* | 29,449 |
| D. Borrow, *Lab.* | 17,785 |
| J. Ault, *LD* | 6,420 |
| R. Perry, *NLP* | 260 |
| *C. majority* | 11,664 |
| (June 1987, C. maj. 14,661) | |

WYRE FOREST (H & W)
E.73,550   T.82.36%
| | |
|---|---|
| *A. Coombs, *C.* | 28,983 |
| R. Maden, *Lab.* | 18,642 |
| M. Jones, *LD* | 12,958 |
| *C. majority* | 10,341 |
| (June 1987, C. maj. 7,224) | |

YEOVIL (Somerset)
E.73,057   T.81.98%
| | |
|---|---|
| *Rt. Hon. J. J. D. Ashdown, *LD* | 30,958 |
| J. Davidson, *Lab.* | 22,125 |
| Ms V. Nelson, *Lab.* | 5,765 |
| J. Risbridger, *Green* | 639 |

| | |
|---|---|
| D. Sutch, *Loony* | 338 |
| R. Simmerson, *APAKBI* | 70 |
| *LD majority* | 8,833 |
| (June 1987, L./All. maj. 5,700) | |

YORK (N. Yorks)
E.79,242   T.80.97%
| | |
|---|---|
| H. Bayley, *Lab.* | 31,525 |
| *C. Gregory, *C.* | 25,183 |
| Ms K. Anderson, *LD* | 6,811 |
| S. Kenwright, *Green* | 594 |
| Ms P. Orr, *NLP* | 54 |
| *Lab. majority* | 6,342 |
| (June 1987, C. maj. 147) | |

## WALES

ABERAVON (W. Glamorgan)
E.51,650   T.77.57%
| | |
|---|---|
| *Rt. Hon. J. Morris, *Lab.* | 26,877 |
| H. Williams, *C.* | 5,567 |
| Mrs M. Harris, *LD* | 4,999 |
| D. Saunders, *PC* | 1,919 |
| Capt. Beany, *Real Bean* | 707 |
| *Lab. majority* | 21,310 |
| (June 1987, Lab. maj. 20,609) | |

ALYN AND DEESIDE (Clwyd)
E.60,477   T.80.08%
| | |
|---|---|
| *S. B. Jones, *Lab.* | 25,206 |
| J. Riley, *C.* | 17,355 |
| R. Britton, *LD* | 4,687 |
| J. Rogers, *PC* | 551 |
| V. Button, *Green* | 433 |
| J. Cooksey, *Ind.* | 200 |
| *Lab. majority* | 7,851 |
| (June 1987, Lab. maj. 6,383) | |

BLAENAU GWENT
E.55,638   T.78.13%
| | |
|---|---|
| L. Smith, *Lab.* | 34,333 |
| D. Melding, *C.* | 4,266 |
| A. Burns, *LD* | 2,774 |
| A. Davies, *PC* | 2,099 |
| *Lab. majority* | 30,067 |
| (June 1987, Lab. maj. 27,861) | |

BRECON AND RADNOR (Powys)
E.51,509   T.85.94%
| | |
|---|---|
| J. P. Evans, *C.* | 15,977 |
| *R. Livsey, *LD* | 15,847 |
| C. Mann, *Lab.* | 11,634 |
| Ms S. Meredudd, *PC* | 418 |
| H. Richards, *Green* | 393 |
| *C. majority* | 130 |
| (June 1987, L./All. maj. 56) | |

BRIDGEND (Mid Glamorgan)
E.58,531   T.80.44%
| | |
|---|---|
| *W. Griffiths, *Lab.* | 24,143 |
| D. Unwin, *C.* | 16,817 |
| D. Mills, *LD* | 4,827 |
| A. Lloyd Jones, *PC* | 1,301 |
| *Lab. majority* | 7,326 |
| (June 1987, Lab. maj. 4,380) | |

CAERNARFON (Gwynedd)
E.46,468   T.78.15%
| | |
|---|---|
| *D. Wigley, *PC* | 21,439 |
| P. Fowler, *C.* | 6,963 |
| Ms S. Mainwaring, *Lab.* | 5,641 |

| | |
|---|---|
| R. Arwel Williams, *LD* | 2,101 |
| G. Evans, *NLP* | 173 |
| *PC majority* | 14,476 |
| (June 1987, PC maj. 12,812) | |

CAERPHILLY (Mid Glamorgan)
E.64,529   T.77.20%
| | |
|---|---|
| *R. Davies, *Lab.* | 31,713 |
| H. Philpott, *C.* | 9,041 |
| L. Whittle, *PC* | 4,821 |
| S. Wilson, *LD* | 4,247 |
| *Lab. majority* | 22,672 |
| (June 1987, Lab. maj. 19,167) | |

CARDIFF CENTRAL (S. Glamorgan)
E.57,716   T.74.35%
| | |
|---|---|
| J. O. Jones, *Lab.* | 18,014 |
| *I. Grist, *C.* | 14,549 |
| Ms J. Randerson, *LD* | 9,170 |
| H. Marshall, *PC* | 748 |
| C. von Ruhland, *Green* | 330 |
| B. Francis, *NLP* | 105 |
| *Lab. majority* | 3,465 |
| (June 1987, C. maj. 1,986) | |

CARDIFF NORTH (S. Glamorgan)
E.56,721   T.84.15%
| | |
|---|---|
| *G. H. Jones, *C.* | 21,547 |
| Ms J. Morgan, *Lab.* | 18,578 |
| Ms E. Warlow, *LD* | 6,487 |
| Ms E. Bush, *PC* | 916 |
| J. Morse, *BNP* | 121 |
| D. Palmer, *NLP* | 86 |
| *C. majority* | 2,969 |
| (June 1987, C. maj. 8,234) | |

CARDIFF SOUTH AND PENARTH (S. Glamorgan)
E.61,484   T.77.25%
| | |
|---|---|
| *A. Michael, *Lab.* | 26,383 |
| T. Hunter Jarvie, *C.* | 15,958 |
| P. Verma, *LD* | 3,707 |
| Ms B. Anglezarke, *PC* | 776 |
| L. Davey, *Green* | 676 |
| *Lab. majority* | 10,425 |
| (June 1987, Lab. maj. 4,574) | |

CARDIFF WEST (S. Glamorgan)
E.58,898   T.77.56%
| | |
|---|---|
| *H. R. Morgan, *Lab.* | 24,306 |
| M. Prior, *C.* | 15,015 |
| Ms J. Gasson, *LD* | 5,002 |
| Ms P. Bestic, *PC* | 1,177 |

| | |
|---|---|
| A. Harding, *NLP* | 184 |
| *Lab. majority* | 9,291 |
| (June 1987, Lab. maj. 4,045) | |

CARMARTHEN (Dyfed)
E.68,887   T. 82.70%
| | |
|---|---|
| *Dr A. W. Williams, *Lab.* | 20,879 |
| R. Thomas, *PC* | 17,957 |
| S. Cavenagh, *C.* | 12,782 |
| Mrs J. Hughes, *LD* | 5,353 |
| *Lab. majority* | 2,922 |
| (June 1987, Lab. maj. 4,317) | |

CEREDIGION AND PEMBROKE NORTH (Dyfed)
E.66,180   T.77.36%
| | |
|---|---|
| C. Dafis, *PC* | 16,020 |
| *G. Howells, *LD* | 12,827 |
| J. Williams, *C.* | 12,718 |
| J. Davies, *Lab.* | 9,637 |
| *PC majority* | 3,193 |
| (June 1987, L./All. maj. 4,700) | |

CLWYD NORTH WEST
E.67,351   T.78.64%
| | |
|---|---|
| R. Richards, *C.* | 24,488 |
| C. Ruane, *Lab.* | 18,438 |
| R. Ingham, *LD* | 7,999 |
| T. Neil, *PC* | 1,888 |
| Ms M. Swift, *NLP* | 158 |
| *C. majority* | 6,050 |
| (June 1987, C. maj. 11,781) | |

CLWYD SOUTH WEST
E.60,607   T.81.52%
| | |
|---|---|
| *M. Jones, *Lab.* | 21,490 |
| G. Owen, *C.* | 16,549 |
| G. Williams, *LD* | 6,027 |
| E. Lloyd Jones, *PC* | 4,835 |
| N. Worth, *Green* | 351 |
| Mrs J. Leadbetter, *NLP* | 155 |
| *Lab. majority* | 4,941 |
| (June 1987, Lab. maj. 1,028) | |

CONWY (Gwynedd)
E.53,576   T.78.85%
| | |
|---|---|
| *Rt. Hon. Sir W. Roberts, *C.* | 14,250 |
| Revd R. Roberts, *LD* | 13,255 |
| Ms E. Williams, *Lab.* | 10,883 |
| R. Davies, *PC* | 3,108 |
| O. Wainwright, *Ind. C.* | 637 |
| Ms D. Hughes, *NLP* | 114 |
| *C. majority* | 995 |
| (June 1987, C. maj. 3,024) | |

CYNON VALLEY (Mid Glamorgan)
*E*.49,695  *T*.76.46%
| | |
|---|---|
| *Ms A. Clwyd, Lab.* | 26,254 |
| A. Smith, *C.* | 4,890 |
| T. Benney, *PC* | 4,186 |
| M. Verma, *LD* | 2,667 |
| *Lab. majority* | 21,364 |
(June 1987, Lab. maj. 21,571)

DELYN (Clwyd)
*E*.66,591  *T*.83.40%
| | |
|---|---|
| D. Hanson, *Lab.* | 24,979 |
| M. Whitby, *C.* | 22,940 |
| R. Dodd, *LD* | 6,208 |
| A. Drake, *PC* | 1,414 |
| *Lab. majority* | 2,039 |
(June 1987, C. maj. 1,224)

GOWER (W. Glamorgan)
*E*.57,231  *T*.81.84%
| | |
|---|---|
| *G. Wardell, Lab.* | 23,455 |
| A. Donnelly, *C.* | 16,437 |
| C. Davies, *LD* | 4,655 |
| A. Price, *PC* | 1,658 |
| B. Kingzett, *Green* | 448 |
| G. Egan, *Loony G.* | 114 |
| M. Beresford, *NLP* | 74 |
| *Lab. majority* | 7,018 |
(June 1987, Lab. maj. 5,764)

ISLWYN (Gwent)
*E*.51,079  *T*.81.48%
| | |
|---|---|
| *Rt. Hon. N. Kinnock, Lab.* | 30,908 |
| P. Bone, *C.* | 6,180 |
| M. Symonds, *LD* | 2,352 |
| Ms H. Jones, *PC* | 1,636 |
| Lord Sutch, *Loony* | 547 |
| *Lab. majority* | 24,728 |
(June 1987, Lab. maj. 22,947)

LLANELLI (Dyfed)
*E*.65,058  *T*.77.80%
| | |
|---|---|
| *Rt. Hon. D. Davies, Lab.* | 27,802 |
| G. Down, *C.* | 8,532 |
| M. Phillips, *PC* | 7,878 |
| K. Evans, *LD* | 6,404 |
| *Lab. majority* | 19,270 |
(June 1987, Lab. maj. 20,935)

MEIRIONNYDD NANT CONWY
(Gwynedd)
*E*.32,413  *T*.81.47%
| | |
|---|---|
| E. Llwyd, *PC* | 11,608 |
| G. Lewis, *C.* | 6,995 |
| R. Williams, *Lab.* | 4,978 |
| Mrs R. Parry, *LD* | 2,358 |
| W. Pritchard, *Green* | 471 |
| *PC majority* | 4,613 |
(June 1987, PC maj. 3,026)

MERTHYR TYDFIL AND RHYMNEY
(Mid Glamorgan)
*E*.58,430  *T*.75.84%
| | |
|---|---|
| *E. Rowlands, Lab.* | 31,710 |
| R. Rowland, *LD* | 4,997 |
| M. Hughes, *C.* | 4,904 |
| A. Cox, *PC* | 2,704 |
| *Lab. majority* | 26,713 |
(June 1987, Lab. maj. 28,207)

MONMOUTH (Gwent)
*E*.59,147  *T*.86.06%
| | |
|---|---|
| R. Evans, *C.* | 24,059 |
| *H. Edwards, Lab.* | 20,855 |
| Mrs F. David, *LD* | 5,562 |
| M. Witherden, *Green/PC* | 431 |
| *C. majority* | 3,204 |
(June 1987, C. maj. 9,350)
(May 1991, Lab. maj. 2,406)

MONTGOMERY (Powys)
*E*.41,386  *T*.79.87%
| | |
|---|---|
| *A. Carlile, LD* | 16,031 |
| Mrs J. France-Hayhurst, *C.* | 10,822 |
| S. Wood, *Lab.* | 4,115 |
| H. Parsons, *PC* | 1,581 |
| P. Adams, *Green* | 508 |
| *LD majority* | 5,209 |
(June 1987, L./All. maj. 2,558)

NEATH (W. Glamorgan)
*E*.56,392  *T*.80.58%
| | |
|---|---|
| *P. Hain, Lab.* | 30,903 |
| D. Adams, *C.* | 6,928 |
| Dr D. Evans, *PC* | 5,145 |
| M. Phillips, *LD* | 2,467 |
| *Lab. majority* | 23,975 |
(June 1987, Lab. maj. 20,578)
(April 1991, Lab. maj. 9,830)

NEWPORT EAST (Gwent)
*E*.51,603  *T*.81.21%
| | |
|---|---|
| *R. J. Hughes, Lab.* | 23,050 |
| Mrs A. Emmett, *C.* | 13,151 |
| W. Oliver, *LD* | 4,991 |
| S. Ainley, *Green/PC* | 716 |
| *Lab. majority* | 9,899 |
(June 1987, Lab. maj. 7,064)

NEWPORT WEST (Gwent)
*E*.54,871  *T*.82.82%
| | |
|---|---|
| *P. Flynn, Lab.* | 24,139 |
| A. Taylor, *C.* | 16,360 |
| A. Toye, *LD* | 4,296 |
| P. Keelan, *PC* | 653 |
| *Lab. majority* | 7,779 |
(June 1987, Lab. maj. 2,708)

OGMORE (Mid Glamorgan)
*E*.52,195  *T*.80.62%
| | |
|---|---|
| *R. Powell, Lab.* | 30,186 |
| D. Edwards, *C.* | 6,359 |
| J. Warman, *LD* | 2,868 |
| Ms L. McAllister, *PC* | 2,667 |
| *Lab. majority* | 23,827 |
(June 1987, Lab. maj. 22,292)

PEMBROKE (Dyfed)
*E*.73,187  *T*.82.86%
| | |
|---|---|
| N. Ainger, *Lab.* | 26,253 |
| *N. Bennett, C.* | 25,498 |
| P. Berry, *LD* | 6,625 |
| C. Bryant, *PC* | 1,627 |
| R. Coghill, *Green* | 484 |
| M. Stoddart, *Anti Fed.* | 158 |
| *Lab. majority* | 755 |
(June 1987, C. maj. 5,700)

PONTYPRIDD (Mid Glamorgan)
*E*.61,685  *T*.79.25%
| | |
|---|---|
| *K. Howells, Lab.* | 29,722 |
| Dr P. Donnelly, *C.* | 9,925 |

| | |
|---|---|
| Dr D. Bowen, *PC* | 4,448 |
| S. Belzak, *LD* | 4,180 |
| Ms E. Jackson, *Green* | 615 |
| *Lab. majority* | 19,797 |
(June 1987, Lab. maj. 17,277)
(Feb. 1989, Lab. maj. 10,794)

RHONDDA (Mid Glamorgan)
*E*.59,955  *T*.76.61%
| | |
|---|---|
| *A. Rogers, Lab.* | 34,243 |
| G. Davies, *PC* | 5,427 |
| J. Richards, *C.* | 3,588 |
| P. Nicholls-Jones, *LD* | 2,431 |
| M. Fisher, *Comm. GB* | 245 |
| *Lab. majority* | 28,816 |
(June 1987, Lab. maj. 30,596)

SWANSEA EAST (W. Glamorgan)
*E*.59,196  *T*.75.56%
| | |
|---|---|
| *D. Anderson, Lab.* | 31,179 |
| H. Davies, *C.* | 7,697 |
| R. Barton, *LD* | 4,248 |
| Ms E. Bonner-Evans, *PC* | 1,607 |
| *Lab. majority* | 23,482 |
(June 1987, Lab. maj. 19,338)

SWANSEA WEST (W. Glamorgan)
*E*.59,785  *T*.73.34%
| | |
|---|---|
| *Rt. Hon. A. Williams, Lab.* | 23,238 |
| R. Perry, *C.* | 13,760 |
| M. Shrewsbury, *LD* | 4,620 |
| Dr D. Lloyd, *PC* | 1,668 |
| B. Oubridge, *Green* | 564 |
| *Lab. majority* | 9,478 |
(June 1987, Lab. maj. 7,062)

TORFAEN (Gwent)
*E*.61,104  *T*.77.47%
| | |
|---|---|
| *P. Murphy, Lab.* | 30,352 |
| M. Watkins, *C.* | 9,598 |
| M. Hewson, *LD* | 6,178 |
| Dr J. Cox, *Green/PC* | 1,210 |
| *Lab. majority* | 20,754 |
(June 1987, Lab. maj. 17,550)

VALE OF GLAMORGAN
(S. Glamorgan)
*E*.66,672  *T*.81.93%
| | |
|---|---|
| W. Sweeney, *C.* | 24,220 |
| *J. Smith, Lab.* | 24,201 |
| K. Davies, *LD* | 5,045 |
| D. Haswell, *PC* | 1,160 |
| *C. majority* | 19 |
(June 1987, C. maj 6,251)
(May 1989, Lab. maj. 6,028)

WREXHAM (Clwyd)
*E*.63,720  *T*.80.71%
| | |
|---|---|
| *J. Marek, Lab.* | 24,830 |
| O. Paterson, *C.* | 18,114 |
| A. Thomas, *LD* | 7,074 |
| G. Wheatley, *PC* | 1,415 |
| *Lab. majority* | 6,716 |
(June 1987, Lab. maj. 4,152)

YNYS MÔN (Gwynedd)
*E*.53,412  *T*.80.62%
| | |
|---|---|
| *I. W. Jones, PC* | 15,984 |
| G. Price Rowlands, *C.* | 14,878 |
| Dr R. Jones, *Lab.* | 10,126 |
| Ms P. Badger, *LD* | 1,891 |
| Mrs S. Parry, *NLP* | 182 |
| *PC majority* | 1,106 |
(June 1987, PC maj. 4,298)

## SCOTLAND

ABERDEEN NORTH (Grampian)
E.60,217   T.66.52%
| | |
|---|---|
| *R. Hughes, *Lab.* | 18,845 |
| J. McGugan, *SNP* | 9,608 |
| P. Cook, *C.* | 6,836 |
| Dr M. Ford, *LD* | 4,772 |
| *Lab. majority* | 9,237 |

(June 1987, Lab. maj. 16,278)

ABERDEEN SOUTH (Grampian)
E.58,881   T.69.78%
| | |
|---|---|
| R. Robertson, *C.* | 15,808 |
| *F. Doran, *Lab.* | 14,291 |
| J. Davidson, *SNP* | 6,223 |
| Ms I. Keith, *LD* | 4,767 |
| *C. majority* | 1,517 |

(June 1987, Lab. maj. 1,198)

ANGUS EAST (Tayside)
E.63,170   T.75.03%
| | |
|---|---|
| *A. Welsh, *SNP* | 19,006 |
| Dr R. Harris, *C.* | 18,052 |
| G. Taylor, *Lab.* | 5,994 |
| C. McLeod, *LD* | 3,897 |
| D. McCabe, *Green* | 449 |
| *SNP majority* | 954 |

(June 1987, SNP maj. 1,544)

ARGYLL AND BUTE (Strathclyde)
E.47,894   T.76.19%
| | |
|---|---|
| *Mrs J. R. Michie, *LD* | 12,739 |
| J. Corrie, *C.* | 10,117 |
| Prof. N. MacCormick, *SNP* | 8,689 |
| D. Browne, *Lab.* | 4,946 |
| *LD majority* | 2,622 |

(June 1987, L./All. maj. 1,394)

AYR (Strathclyde)
E.65,481   T.83.08%
| | |
|---|---|
| P. Gallie, *C.* | 22,172 |
| A. Osborne, *Lab.* | 22,087 |
| Mrs B. Mullin, *SNP* | 5,949 |
| J. Boss, *LD* | 4,067 |
| R. Scott, *NLP* | 132 |
| *C. majority* | 85 |

(June 1987, C. maj. 182)

BANFF AND BUCHAN (Grampian)
E.64,873   T.71.20%
| | |
|---|---|
| *A. Salmond, *SNP* | 21,954 |
| S. Manson, *C.* | 17,846 |
| B. Balcombe, *Lab.* | 3,803 |
| Mrs R. Kemp, *LD* | 2,588 |
| *SNP majority* | 4,108 |

(June 1987, SNP maj. 2,441)

CAITHNESS AND SUTHERLAND
(Highland)
E.30,905   T.71.93%
| | |
|---|---|
| *R. Maclennan, *LD* | 10,032 |
| G. Bruce, *C.* | 4,667 |
| K. MacGregor, *SNP* | 4,049 |
| M. Coyne, *Lab.* | 3,483 |
| *LD majority* | 5,365 |

(June 1987, SDP/All. maj. 8,494)

CARRICK, CUMNOCK AND DOON
VALLEY (Strathclyde)
E.55,330   T.76.94%
| | |
|---|---|
| *G. Foulkes, *Lab.* | 25,142 |
| J. Boswell, *C.* | 8,516 |

| | |
|---|---|
| C. Douglas, *SNP* | 6,910 |
| Ms M. Paris, *LD* | 2,005 |
| *Lab. majority* | 16,626 |

(June 1987, Lab. maj. 16,802)

CLACKMANNAN (Central)
E.48,963   T.78.34%
| | |
|---|---|
| *M. O'Neill, *Lab.* | 18,829 |
| A. Brophy, *SNP* | 10,326 |
| J. Mackie, *C.* | 6,638 |
| Ms A. Watters, *LD* | 2,567 |
| *Lab. majority* | 8,503 |

(June 1987, Lab. maj. 12,401)

CLYDEBANK AND MILNGAVIE
(Strathclyde)
E.47,337   T.77.79%
| | |
|---|---|
| *A. Worthington, *Lab.* | 19,637 |
| G. Hughes, *SNP* | 7,207 |
| W. Harvey, *C.* | 6,654 |
| A. Tough, *LD* | 3,216 |
| Ms J. Barrie, *NLP* | 112 |
| *Lab. majority* | 12,430 |

(June 1987, Lab. maj. 16,304)

CLYDESDALE (Strathclyde)
E.61,878   T.77.62%
| | |
|---|---|
| *J. Hood, *Lab.* | 21,418 |
| Ms C. Goodwin, *C.* | 11,231 |
| I. Gray, *SNP* | 11,084 |
| Ms E. Buchanan, *LD* | 3,957 |
| S. Cartwright, *BNP* | 342 |
| *Lab. majority* | 10,187 |

(June 1987, Lab. maj. 10,502)

CUMBERNAULD AND KILSYTH
(Strathclyde)
E.46,489   T.79.06%
| | |
|---|---|
| *N. Hogg, *Lab.* | 19,855 |
| T. Johnston, *SNP* | 10,640 |
| I. Mitchell, *C.* | 4,143 |
| Ms J. Haddow, *LD* | 2,118 |
| *Lab. majority* | 9,215 |

(June 1987, Lab. maj. 14,403)

CUNNINGHAME NORTH
(Strathclyde)
E.54,803   T.78.21%
| | |
|---|---|
| *B. Wilson, *Lab.* | 17,564 |
| Ms E. Clarkson, *C.* | 14,625 |
| D. Crossan, *SNP* | 7,813 |
| D. Herbison, *LD* | 2,864 |
| *Lab. majority* | 2,939 |

(June 1987, Lab. maj. 4,422)

CUNNINGHAME SOUTH (Strathclyde)
E.49,010   T.75.88%
| | |
|---|---|
| B. Donohoe, *Lab.* | 19,687 |
| R. Bell, *SNP* | 9,007 |
| S. Leslie, *C.* | 6,070 |
| B. Ashley, *LD* | 2,299 |
| W. Jackson, *NLP* | 128 |
| *Lab. majority* | 10,680 |

(June 1987, Lab. maj. 16,633)

DUMBARTON (Strathclyde)
E.57,222   T.77.11%
| | |
|---|---|
| *J. McFall, *Lab.* | 19,255 |
| T. Begg, *C.* | 13,126 |

| | |
|---|---|
| W. McKechnie, *SNP* | 8,127 |
| J. Morrison, *LD* | 3,425 |
| Ms D. Krass, *NLP* | 192 |
| *Lab. majority* | 6,129 |

(June 1987, Lab. maj. 5,222)

DUMFRIES (D & G)
E.61,145   T.79.97%
| | |
|---|---|
| *Sir H. Monro, *C.* | 21,089 |
| P. Rennie, *Lab.* | 14,674 |
| A. Morgan, *SNP* | 6,971 |
| N. Wallace, *LD* | 5,749 |
| G. McLeod, *Ind. Green* | 312 |
| T. Barlow, *NLP* | 107 |
| *C. majority* | 6,415 |

(June 1987, C. maj. 7,493)

DUNDEE EAST (Tayside)
E.58,959   T.72.10%
| | |
|---|---|
| *J. McAllion, *Lab.* | 18,761 |
| D. Coutts, *SNP* | 14,197 |
| S. Blackwood, *C.* | 7,549 |
| I. Yuill, *LD* | 1,725 |
| Ms S. Baird, *Green* | 205 |
| R. Baxter, *NLP* | 77 |
| *Lab. majority* | 4,564 |

(June 1987, Lab. maj. 1,015)

DUNDEE WEST (Tayside)
E.59,953   T.69.82%
| | |
|---|---|
| *E. Ross, *Lab.* | 20,498 |
| K. Brown, *SNP* | 9,894 |
| A. Spearman, *C.* | 7,746 |
| Ms E. Dick, *LD* | 3,132 |
| Ms E. Hood, *Green* | 432 |
| D. Arnold, *NLP* | 159 |
| *Lab. majority* | 10,604 |

(June 1987, Lab. maj. 16,526)

DUNFERMLINE EAST (Fife)
E.50,179   T.75.62%
| | |
|---|---|
| *J. G. Brown, *Lab.* | 23,692 |
| M. Tennant, *C.* | 6,248 |
| J. Lloyd, *SNP* | 5,746 |
| Ms T. Little, *LD* | 2,262 |
| *Lab. majority* | 17,444 |

(June 1987, Lab. maj. 19,589)

DUNFERMLINE WEST (Fife)
E.50,948   T.76.44%
| | |
|---|---|
| Ms R. Squire, *Lab.* | 16,374 |
| M. Scott-Hayward, *C.* | 8,890 |
| J. Smith, *SNP* | 7,563 |
| Ms E. Harris, *LD* | 6,122 |
| *Lab. majority* | 7,484 |

(June 1987, Lab. maj. 9,402)

EAST KILBRIDE (Strathclyde)
E.64,080   T.80.01%
| | |
|---|---|
| *A. Ingram, *Lab.* | 24,055 |
| Ms K. McAlorum, *SNP* | 12,063 |
| G. Lind, *C.* | 9,781 |
| Ms S. Grieve, *LD* | 5,377 |
| *Lab. majority* | 11,992 |

(June 1987, Lab. maj. 12,624)

EAST LOTHIAN
E.66,699   T.82.37%
| | |
|---|---|
| *J. Home Robertson, *Lab.* | 25,537 |
| J. Hepburne Scott, *C.* | 15,501 |

G. Thomson, *SNP*  7,776
T. McKay, *LD*  6,126
*Lab. majority*  10,036
(June 1987, Lab. maj. 10,105)

EASTWOOD (Strathclyde)
*E.*63,685  *T.*80.97%
*J. A. Stewart, *C.*  24,124
P. Grant-Hutchison, *Lab.*  12,436
Miss M. Craig, *LD*  8,493
P. Scott, *SNP*  6,372
Dr L. Fergusson, *NLP*  146
*C. majority*  11,688
(June 1987, C. maj. 6,014)

EDINBURGH CENTRAL (Lothian)
*E.*56,527  *T.*69.26%
*A. Darling, *Lab.*  15,189
P. Martin, *C.*  13,063
Ms L. Devine, *SNP*  5,539
A. Myles, *LD*  4,500
R. Harper, *Green*  630
D. Wilson, *Lib.*  235
*Lab. majority*  2,126
(June 1987, Lab. maj. 2,262)

EDINBURGH EAST (Lothian)
*E.*45,687  *T.*73.89%
*G. Strang, *Lab.*  15,446
K. Ward, *C.*  8,235
D. McKinney, *SNP*  6,225
D. Scobie, *LD*  3,432
G. Farmer, *Green*  424
*Lab. majority*  7,211
(June 1987, Lab. maj. 9,295)

EDINBURGH LEITH (Lothian)
*E.*56,520  *T.*71.30%
M. Chisholm, *Lab.*  13,790
Ms F. Hyslop, *SNP*  8,805
M. Bin Ashiq Rizvi, *C.*  8,496
Mrs H. Campbell, *LD*  4,975
*R. Brown, *Ind. Lab.*  4,142
A. Swan, *NLP*  96
*Lab. majority*  4,985
(June 1987, Lab. maj. 11,327)

EDINBURGH PENTLANDS (Lothian)
*E.*55,567  *T.*80.18%
*Rt. Hon. M. Rifkind, *C.*  18,128
M. Lazarowicz, *Lab.*  13,838
Ms K. Caskie, *SNP*  6,882
K. Smith, *LD*  5,597
D. Rae, *NLP*  111
*C. majority*  4,290
(June 1987, C. maj. 3,745)

EDINBURGH SOUTH (Lothian)
*E.*61,355  *T.*72.67%
*N. Griffiths, *Lab.*  18,485
S. Stevenson, *C.*  14,309
B. McCreadie, *LD*  5,961
R. Knox, *SNP*  5,727
G. Manclark, *NLP*  108
*Lab. majority*  4,176
(June 1987, Lab. maj. 1,859)

EDINBURGH WEST (Lothian)
*E.*58,998  *T.*82.67%
*Lord J. Douglas-Hamilton, *C.*  18,071
D. Gorrie, *LD*  17,192

Ms I. Kitson, *Lab.*  8,759
G. Sutherland, *SNP*  4,117
A. Fleming, *Lib.*  272
Ms L. Hendry, *Green*  234
D. Bruce, *BNP*  133
*C. majority*  879
(June 1987, C. maj. 1,234)

FALKIRK EAST (Central)
*E.*51,918  *T.*76.91%
M. Connarty, *Lab.*  18,423
R. Halliday, *SNP*  10,454
K. Harding, *C.*  8,279
Miss D. Storr, *LD*  2,775
*Lab. majority*  7,969
(June 1987, Lab. maj. 14,023)

FALKIRK WEST (Central)
*E.*50,126  *T.*76.77%
*D. Canavan, *Lab.*  19,162
W. Houston, *SNP*  9,350
M. Macdonald, *C.*  7,558
M. Reilly, *LD*  2,414
*Lab. majority*  9,812
(June 1987, Lab. maj. 13,552)

FIFE CENTRAL
*E.*56,152  *T.*74.33%
*H. McLeish, *Lab.*  21,036
Mrs T. Marwick, *SNP*  10,458
Ms C. Cender, *C.*  7,353
C. Harrow, *LD*  2,892
*Lab. majority*  10,578
(June 1987, Lab. maj. 15,709)

FIFE NORTH EAST
*E.*53,747  *T.*77.84%
*W. M. Campbell, *LD*  19,430
Mrs M. Scanlon, *C.*  16,122
D. Roche, *SNP*  3,589
Miss L. Clark, *Lab.*  2,319
T. Flynn, *Green*  294
D. Senior, *Lib.*  85
*LD majority*  3,308
(June 1987, L./All. maj. 1,447)

GALLOWAY AND UPPER
NITHSDALE (D & G)
*E.*54,474  *T.*81.66%
*Rt. Hon. I. Lang, *C.*  18,681
M. Brown, *SNP*  16,213
J. Dowson, *Lab.*  5,766
J. McKerchar, *LD*  3,826
*C. majority*  2,468
(June 1987, C. maj. 3,673)

GLASGOW CATHCART (Strathclyde)
*E.*44,689  *T.*75.38%
*J. Maxton, *Lab.*  16,265
J. Young, *C.*  8,264
W. Steven, *SNP*  6,107
G. Dick, *LD*  2,614
Ms K. Allan, *Green*  441
*Lab. majority*  8,001
(June 1987, Lab. maj. 11,203)

GLASGOW CENTRAL (Strathclyde)
*E.*48,107  *T.*63.05%
*M. Watson, *Lab.*  17,341
B. O'Hara, *SNP*  6,322
E. Stewart, *C.*  4,208

Dr A. Rennie, *LD*  1,921
Ms I. Brandt, *Green*  435
T. Burn, *Comm. GB*  106
*Lab. majority*  11,019
(June 1987, Lab. maj. 17,253)
(June 1989, Lab. maj. 6,462)

GLASGOW GARSCADDEN
(Strathclyde)
*E.*41,289  *T.*71.13%
*D. Dewar, *Lab.*  18,920
R. Douglas, *SNP*  5,580
J. Scott, *C.*  3,385
C. Brodie, *LD*  1,425
W. Orr, *NLP*  61
*Lab. majority*  13,340
(June 1987, Lab. maj. 18,977)

GLASGOW GOVAN (Strathclyde)
*E.*45,822  *T.*76.03%
I. Davidson, *Lab.*  17,051
*J. Sillars, *SNP*  12,926
J. Donnelly, *C.*  3,458
R. Stewart, *LD*  1,227
D. Spaven, *Green*  181
*Lab. majority*  4,125
(June 1987, Lab. maj. 19,509)
(Nov. 1988, SNP maj. 3,554)

GLASGOW HILLHEAD (Strathclyde)
*E.*57,223  *T.*68.80%
*G. Galloway, *Lab.*  15,148
C. Mason, *LD*  10,322
Ms A. Bates, *C.*  6,728
Miss S. White, *SNP*  6,484
Ms L. Collie, *Green*  558
Ms H. Gold, *Rev. Comm.*  73
D. Patterson, *NLP*  60
*Lab. majority*  4,826
(June 1987, Lab. maj. 3,251)

GLASGOW MARYHILL (Strathclyde)
*E.*48,426  *T.*65.16%
*Mrs M. Fyfe, *Lab.*  19,452
C. Williamson, *SNP*  6,033
J. Godfrey, *C.*  3,248
J. Alexander, *LD*  2,215
P. O'Brien, *Green*  530
M. Henderson, *NLP*  78
*Lab. majority*  13,419
(June 1987, Lab. maj. 19,364)

GLASGOW POLLOK (Strathclyde)
*E.*46,139  *T.*70.74%
*J. Dunnachie, *Lab.*  14,170
T. Sheridan, *SML*  6,287
R. Gray, *C.*  5,147
G. Leslie, *SNP*  5,107
D. Jago, *LD*  1,932
*Lab. majority*  7,883
(June 1987, Lab. maj. 17,983)

GLASGOW PROVAN (Strathclyde)
*E.*36,560  *T.*65.31%
*J. Wray, *Lab.*  15,885
Ms A. MacRae, *SNP*  5,182
A. Rosindell, *C.*  1,865
C. Bell, *LD*  948
*Lab. majority*  10,703
(June 1987, Lab. maj. 18,372)

GLASGOW RUTHERGLEN
(Strathclyde)
E.52,709  T.75.23%

| | |
|---|---|
| *T. McAvoy, *Lab.* | 21,962 |
| B. Cooklin, *C.* | 6,692 |
| J. Higgins, *SNP* | 6,470 |
| D. Baillie, *LD* | 4,470 |
| Ms B. Slaughter, *Int. Comm.* | 62 |
| *Lab. majority* | 15,270 |

(June 1987, Lab. maj. 13,995)

GLASGOW SHETTLESTON
(Strathclyde)
E.51,910  T.68.91%

| | |
|---|---|
| *D. Marshall, *Lab.* | 21,665 |
| Ms N. Sturgeon, *SNP* | 6,831 |
| N. Mortimer, *C.* | 5,396 |
| Ms J. Orskov, *LD* | 1,881 |
| *Lab. majority* | 14,834 |

(June 1987, Lab. maj. 18,981)

GLASGOW SPRINGBURN
(Strathclyde)
E.45,842  T.65.65%

| | |
|---|---|
| *M. Martin, *Lab.* | 20,369 |
| S. Miller, *SNP* | 5,863 |
| A. Barnett, *C.* | 2,625 |
| R. Ackland, *LD* | 1,242 |
| *Lab. majority* | 14,506 |

(June 1987, Lab. maj. 22,063)

GORDON (Grampian)
E.80,103  T.73.86%

| | |
|---|---|
| *M. Bruce, *LD* | 22,158 |
| J. Porter, *C.* | 21,884 |
| B. Adam, *SNP* | 8,445 |
| P. Morrell, *Lab.* | 6,682 |
| *LD majority* | 274 |

(June 1987, L./All. maj. 9,519)

GREENOCK AND PORT GLASGOW
(Strathclyde)
E.52,053  T.73.72%

| | |
|---|---|
| *N. Godman, *Lab.* | 22,258 |
| I. Black, *SNP* | 7,279 |
| Dr J. McCullough, *C.* | 4,479 |
| C. Lambert, *LD* | 4,359 |
| *Lab. majority* | 14,979 |

(June 1987, Lab. maj. 20,055)

HAMILTON (Strathclyde)
E.61,531  T.76.15%

| | |
|---|---|
| *G. Robertson, *Lab.* | 25,849 |
| W. Morrison, *SNP* | 9,246 |
| Ms M. Mitchell, *C.* | 8,250 |
| J. Oswald, *LD* | 3,515 |
| *Lab. majority* | 16,603 |

(June 1987, Lab. maj. 21,662)

INVERNESS NAIRN AND LOCHABER
(Highland)
E.69,468  T.73.27%

| | |
|---|---|
| *Sir R. Johnston, *LD* | 13,258 |
| D. Stewart, *Lab.* | 12,800 |
| F. Ewing, *SNP* | 12,562 |
| J. Scott, *C.* | 11,517 |
| J. Martin, *Green* | 766 |
| *LD majority* | 458 |

(June 1987, L./All maj. 5,431)

KILMARNOCK AND LOUDOUN
(Strathclyde)
E.62,002  T.79.99%

| | |
|---|---|
| *W. McKelvey, *Lab.* | 22,210 |
| A. Neil, *SNP* | 15,231 |
| R. Wilkinson, *C.* | 9,438 |
| Mrs K. Philbrick, *LD* | 2,722 |
| *Lab. majority* | 6,979 |

(June 1987, Lab. maj. 14,127)

KINCARDINE AND DEESIDE
(Grampian)
E.66,617  T.78.74%

| | |
|---|---|
| G. Kynoch, *C.* | 22,924 |
| *N. Stephen, *LD* | 18,429 |
| Dr A. Macartney, *SNP* | 5,927 |
| M. Savidge, *Lab.* | 4,795 |
| S. Campbell, *Green* | 381 |
| *C. majority* | 4,495 |

(June 1987, C. maj. 2,063)
(Nov. 1991, LD maj. 7,824)

KIRKCALDY (Fife)
E.51,762  T.75.06%

| | |
|---|---|
| *Dr L. Moonie, *Lab.* | 17,887 |
| S. Hosie, *SNP* | 8,761 |
| S. Wosley, *C.* | 8,476 |
| Ms S. Leslie, *LD* | 3,729 |
| *Lab. majority* | 9,126 |

(June 1987, Lab. maj. 11,570)

LINLITHGOW (Lothian)
E.61,082  T.78.66%

| | |
|---|---|
| *T. Dalyell, *Lab.* | 21,603 |
| K. MacAskill, *SNP* | 14,577 |
| Ms E. Forbes, *C.* | 8,424 |
| M. Falchikov, *LD* | 3,446 |
| *Lab. majority* | 7,026 |

(June 1987, Lab. maj. 10,373)

LIVINGSTON (Lothian)
E.61,092  T.74.62%

| | |
|---|---|
| *R. Cook, *Lab.* | 20,245 |
| P. Johnston, *SNP* | 12,140 |
| H. Gordon, *C.* | 8,824 |
| F. Mackintosh, *LD* | 3,911 |
| A. Ross-Smith, *Green* | 469 |
| *Lab. majority* | 8,105 |

(June 1987, Lab. maj. 11,105)

MIDLOTHIAN
E.60,255  T.77.87%

| | |
|---|---|
| E. Clarke, *Lab.* | 20,588 |
| A. Lumsden, *SNP* | 10,254 |
| J. Stoddart, *C.* | 9,443 |
| P. Sewell, *LD* | 6,164 |
| I. Morrice, *Green* | 476 |
| *Lab. majority* | 10,334 |

(June 1987, Lab. maj. 12,253)

MONKLANDS EAST (Strathclyde)
E.48,391  T.75.07%

| | |
|---|---|
| *Rt. Hon. J. Smith, *Lab.* | 22,266 |
| J. Wright, *SNP* | 6,554 |
| S. Walters, *C.* | 5,830 |
| P. Ross, *LD* | 1,679 |
| *Lab. majority* | 15,712 |

(June 1987, Lab. maj. 16,389)
*See also* page 241

MONKLANDS WEST (Strathclyde)
E.49,269  T.77.45%

| | |
|---|---|
| *T. Clarke, *Lab.* | 23,384 |
| K. Bovey, *SNP* | 6,319 |

| | |
|---|---|
| A. Lownie, *C.* | 6,074 |
| Ms S. Hamilton, *LD* | 2,382 |
| *Lab. majority* | 17,065 |

(June 1987, Lab. maj. 18,333)

MORAY (Grampian)
E.63,255  T.72.46%

| | |
|---|---|
| *Mrs M. Ewing, *SNP* | 20,299 |
| Ms R. Hossack, *C.* | 17,455 |
| C. Smith, *Lab.* | 5,448 |
| B. Sheridan, *LD* | 2,634 |
| *SNP majority* | 2,844 |

(June 1987, SNP maj. 3,685)

MOTHERWELL NORTH
(Strathclyde)
E.57,290  T.76.71%

| | |
|---|---|
| *Dr J. Reid, *Lab.* | 27,852 |
| D. Clark, *SNP* | 8,942 |
| R. Hargrave, *C.* | 5,011 |
| Miss H. Smith, *LD* | 2,145 |
| *Lab. majority* | 18,910 |

(June 1987, Lab. maj. 23,595)

MOTHERWELL SOUTH
(Strathclyde)
E.50,042  T.76.17%

| | |
|---|---|
| *J. Bray, *Lab.* | 21,771 |
| Mrs K. Ullrich, *SNP* | 7,758 |
| G. McIntosh, *C.* | 6,097 |
| A. Mackie, *LD* | 2,349 |
| D. Lettice, *YSOR* | 146 |
| *Lab. majority* | 14,013 |

(June 1987, Lab. maj. 16,930)

ORKNEY AND SHETLAND
E.31,472  T.65.53%

| | |
|---|---|
| *J. Wallace, *LD* | 9,575 |
| Dr P. McCormick, *C.* | 4,542 |
| J. Aberdein, *Lab.* | 4,093 |
| Mrs F. McKie, *SNP* | 2,301 |
| Ms C. Wharton, *NLP* | 115 |
| *LD majority* | 5,033 |

(June 1987, L./All. maj. 3,922)

PAISLEY NORTH (Strathclyde)
E.46,403  T.73.39%

| | |
|---|---|
| *Mrs I. Adams, *Lab.* | 17,269 |
| R. Mullin, *SNP* | 7,940 |
| D. Sharpe, *C.* | 5,576 |
| Miss E. McCartin, *LD* | 2,779 |
| D. Mellor, *Green* | 412 |
| N. Brennan, *NLP* | 81 |
| *Lab. majority* | 9,329 |

(June 1987, Lab. maj. 14,442)
(Nov. 1990, Lab. maj. 3,770)

PAISLEY SOUTH (Strathclyde)
E.47,889  T.75.01%

| | |
|---|---|
| *G. McMaster, *Lab.* | 18,202 |
| I. Lawson, *SNP* | 8,653 |
| Ms S. Laidlaw, *C.* | 5,703 |
| A. Reid, *LD* | 3,271 |
| S. Porter, *NLP* | 93 |
| *Lab. majority* | 9,549 |

(June 1987, Lab. maj. 15,785)
(Nov. 1990, Lab. maj. 5,030)

PERTH AND KINROSS (Tayside)
E.65,410  T.76.86%

| | |
|---|---|
| *Sir N. Fairbairn, *C.* | 20,195 |
| Ms R. Cunningham, *SNP* | 18,101 |

| | |
|---|---|
| M. Rolfe, *Lab.* | 6,267 |
| M. Black, *LD* | 5,714 |
| *C. majority* | 2,094 |
| (June 1987, C. maj. 5,676) | |

**RENFREW WEST AND INVERCLYDE**
(Strathclyde)
E.58,122  T.80.32%

| | |
|---|---|
| *T. Graham, *Lab.* | 17,085 |
| Ms A. Goldie, *C.* | 15,341 |
| C. Campbell, *SNP* | 9,444 |
| S. Nimmo, *LD* | 4,668 |
| D. Maltman, *NLP* | 149 |
| *Lab. majority* | 1,744 |
| (June 1987, Lab. maj. 4,063) | |

**ROSS, CROMARTY AND SKYE**
(Highland)
E.55,524  T.73.90%

| | |
|---|---|
| *C. Kennedy, *LD* | 17,066 |
| J. Gray, *C.* | 9,436 |
| R. Gibson, *SNP* | 7,618 |
| J. MacDonald, *Lab.* | 6,275 |
| D. Jardine, *Green* | 642 |
| *LD majority* | 7,630 |
| (June 1987, SDP/All. maj. 11,319) | |

**ROXBURGH AND BERWICKSHIRE**
(Borders)
E.43,485  T.77.71%

| | |
|---|---|
| *A. Kirkwood, *LD* | 15,852 |
| S. Finlay-Maxwell, *C.* | 11,595 |
| M. Douglas, *SNP* | 3,437 |
| S. Lambert, *Lab.* | 2,909 |
| *LD majority* | 4,257 |
| (June 1987, L./All maj. 4,008) | |

**STIRLING** (Central)
E.58,266  T.82.29%

| | |
|---|---|
| *M. Forsyth, *C.* | 19,174 |
| Ms K. Phillips, *Lab.* | 18,471 |
| G. Fisher, *SNP* | 6,558 |
| W. Robertson, *LD* | 3,337 |
| W. Thomson, *Green* | 342 |
| R. Sharp, *Loony* | 68 |
| *C. majority* | 703 |
| (June 1987, C. maj. 548) | |

**STRATHKELVIN AND BEARSDEN**
(Strathclyde)
E.61,116  T.82.33%

| | |
|---|---|
| *S. Galbraith, *Lab.* | 21,267 |
| M. Hirst, *C.* | 18,105 |
| T. Chalmers, *SNP* | 6,275 |
| Ms B. Waterfield, *LD* | 4,585 |
| D. Whitley, *NLP* | 90 |
| *Lab. majority* | 3,162 |
| (June 1987, Lab. maj. 2,452) | |

**TAYSIDE NORTH**
E.55,969  T.77.64%

| | |
|---|---|
| *W. Walker, *C.* | 20,283 |
| J. Swinney, *SNP* | 16,288 |
| S. Horner, *LD* | 3,791 |
| S. Maclennan, *Lab.* | 3,094 |
| *C. majority* | 3,995 |
| (June 1987, C. maj. 5,016) | |

**TWEEDDALE, ETTRICK AND
LAUDERDALE** (Borders)
E.39,493  T.78.04%

| | |
|---|---|
| *Rt. Hon. Sir D. Steel, *LD* | 12,296 |
| L. Beat, *C.* | 9,776 |
| Mrs C. Creech, *SNP* | 5,244 |
| A. Dunton, *Lab.* | 3,328 |
| J. Hein, *Lib.* | 177 |
| *LD majority* | 2,520 |
| (June 1987, L./All. maj. 5,942) | |

**WESTERN ISLES**
E.22,784  T.70.35%

| | |
|---|---|
| *C. MacDonald, *Lab.* | 7,664 |
| Ms F. MacFarlane, *SNP* | 5,961 |
| R. Heany, *C.* | 1,362 |
| N. Mitchison, *LD* | 552 |
| A. Price, *Ind.* | 491 |
| *Lab. majority* | 1,703 |
| (June 1987, Lab. maj. 2,340) | |

# NORTHERN IRELAND

**ANTRIM EAST**
E.62,839  T.62.46%

| | |
|---|---|
| *R. Beggs, *UUP* | 16,966 |
| N. Dodds, *DUP* | 9,544 |
| S. Neeson, *All.* | 9,132 |
| Miss M. Boal, *C.* | 3,359 |
| Ms A. Palmer, *NLP* | 250 |
| *UUP majority* | 7,422 |
| (June 1987, UUP maj. 15,360) | |

**ANTRIM NORTH**
E.69,124  T.65.82%

| | |
|---|---|
| *Revd I. Paisley, *DUP* | 23,152 |
| J. Gaston, *UUP* | 8,216 |
| S. Farren, *SDLP* | 6,512 |
| G. Williams, *All.* | 3,442 |
| R. Sowler, *C.* | 2,263 |
| J. McGarry, *SF* | 1,916 |
| *DUP majority* | 14,936 |
| (June 1987, DUP maj. 23,234) | |

**ANTRIM SOUTH**
E.68,013  T.62.10%

| | |
|---|---|
| *C. Forsythe, *UUP* | 29,956 |
| D. McClelland, *SDLP* | 5,397 |
| J. Blair, *All.* | 5,224 |
| H. Cushinan, *SF* | 1,220 |
| D. Martin, *Loony G.* | 442 |
| *UUP majority* | 24,559 |
| (June 1987, UUP maj. 19,587) | |

**BELFAST EAST**
E.52,833  T.67.74%

| | |
|---|---|
| *P. Robinson, *DUP* | 18,437 |
| Dr J. Alderdice, *All.* | 10,650 |
| D. Greene, *C.* | 3,314 |

| | |
|---|---|
| Ms D. Dunlop, *Ind. U.* | 2,256 |
| J. O'Donnell, *SF* | 679 |
| J. Bell, *WP* | 327 |
| G. Redden, *NLP* | 128 |
| *DUP majority* | 7,787 |
| (June 1987, DUP maj. 9,798) | |

**BELFAST NORTH**
E.55,062  T.65.22%

| | |
|---|---|
| *A. C. Walker, *UUP* | 17,240 |
| A. Maginness, *SDLP* | 7,615 |
| P. McManus, *SF* | 4,693 |
| T. Campbell, *All.* | 2,246 |
| Ms M. Redpath, *C.* | 2,107 |
| S. Lynch, *NA* | 1,386 |
| Ms M. Smith, *WP* | 419 |
| D. O'Leary, *NLP* | 208 |
| *UUP majority* | 9,625 |
| (June 1987, UUP maj. 8,560) | |

**BELFAST SOUTH**
E.52,032  T.64.54%

| | |
|---|---|
| *Revd W. M. Smyth, *UUP* | 16,336 |
| Dr A. McDonnell, *SDLP* | 6,266 |
| J. Montgomery, *All.* | 5,054 |
| L. Fee, *C.* | 3,356 |
| S. Hayes, *SF* | 1,123 |
| P. Hadden, *LTU* | 875 |
| P. Lynn, *WP* | 362 |
| Ms T. Mullan, *NLP* | 212 |
| *UUP majority* | 10,070 |
| (June 1987, UUP maj. 11,954) | |

**BELFAST WEST**
E.54,609  T.73.19%

| | |
|---|---|
| Dr J. Hendron, *SDLP* | 17,415 |
| *G. Adams, *SF* | 16,826 |
| F. Cobain, *UUP* | 4,766 |
| J. Lowry, *WP* | 750 |
| M. Kennedy, *NLP* | 213 |
| *SDLP majority* | 589 |
| (June 1987, SF maj. 2,221) | |

**DOWN NORTH**
E.68,662  T.65.47%

| | |
|---|---|
| *J. Kilfedder, *UPUP* | 19,305 |
| Dr L. Kennedy, *C.* | 14,371 |
| Ms A. Morrow, *All.* | 6,611 |
| D. Vitty, *DUP* | 4,414 |
| A. Wilmot, *NLP* | 255 |
| *UPUP majority* | 4,934 |
| (June 1987, UPUP maj. 3,953) | |

**DOWN SOUTH**
E.76,093  T.80.92%

| | |
|---|---|
| *E. McGrady, *SDLP* | 31,523 |
| D. Nelson, *UUP* | 25,181 |
| S. Fitzpatrick, *SF* | 1,843 |
| M. Healey, *All.* | 1,542 |
| Mrs S. McKenzie-Hill, *C.* | 1,488 |
| *SDLP majority* | 6,342 |
| (June 1987, SDLP maj. 731) | |

**FERMANAGH AND SOUTH TYRONE**
E.70,192  T.78.53%

| | |
|---|---|
| *K. Maginnis, *UUP* | 26,923 |
| T. Gallagher, *SDLP* | 12,810 |
| F. Molloy, *SF* | 12,604 |

D. Kettyles, *Prog. Soc.* 1,094
E. Bullick, *All.* 950
G. Cullen, *NA* 747
*UUP majority* 14,113
(June 1987, UUP maj. 12,823)

FOYLE
E.74,585   T.69.57%
*J. Hume, *SDLP* 26,710
G. Campbell, *DUP* 13,705
M. McGuinness, *SF* 9,149
Ms L. McIlroy, *All.* 1,390
G. McKenzie, *WP* 514
J. Burns, *NLP* 422
*SDLP majority* 13,005
(June 1987, SDLP maj. 9,860)

LAGAN VALLEY
E.72,645   T.67.39%
*Rt. Hon. J. H. Molyneaux, *UUP*
29,772
S. Close, *All.* 6,207
H. Lewsley, *SDLP* 4,626
T. Coleridge, *C.* 4,423
P. Rice, *SF* 3,346
Ms A.-M. Lowry, *WP* 582
*UUP majority* 23,565
(June 1987, UUP maj. 23,373)

LONDONDERRY EAST
E.75,559   T.69.79%
*W. Ross, *UUP* 30,370
A. Doherty, *SDLP* 11,843
Ms P. Davey-Kennedy, *SF* 5,320
P. McGowan, *All.* 3,613
A. Elder, *C.* 1,589
*UUP majority* 18,527
(June 1987, UUP maj. 20,157)

NEWRY AND ARMAGH
E.67,508   T.77.87%
*S. Mallon, *SDLP* 26,073
J. Speers, *UUP* 18,982
B. Curran, *SF* 6,547
Mrs E. Bell, *All.* 972
*SDLP majority* 7,091
(June 1987, SDLP maj. 5,325)

STRANGFORD
E.68,870   T.65.02%
*Rt. Hon. J. Taylor, *UUP* 19,517
S. Wilson, *DUP* 10,606
K. McCarthy, *All.* 7,585
S. Eyre, *C.* 6,782
D. Shaw, *NLP* 295
*UUP majority* 8,911
(June 1987, UUP maj. 20,646)

ULSTER MID
E.69,071   T.79.28%
*Revd Dr R. T. W. McCrea, *DUP*
23,181
D. Haughey, *SDLP* 16,994
B. McElduff, *SF* 10,248
J. McLoughlin, *Ind.* 1,996
Ms A. Gormley, *All.* 1,506
H. Hutchinson, *LTU* 389
T. Owens, *WP* 285
J. Anderson, *NLP* 164
*DUP majority* 6,187
(June 1987, DUP maj. 9,360)

UPPER BANN
E.67,446   T.67.43%
*W. D. Trimble, *UUP* 26,824
Mrs B. Rodgers, *SDLP* 10,661
B. Curran, *SF* 2,777
Dr W. Ramsey, *All.* 2,541
Mrs C. Jones, *C.* 1,556
T. French, *WP* 1,120
*UUP majority* 16,163
(June 1987, OUP maj. 17,361)
(May 1990, OUP maj. 13,849)

---

## COMMONWEALTH PARLIAMENTARY ASSOCIATION (1911)

The Commonwealth Parliamentary Association consists of 122 branches in the national, state, provincial or territorial parliaments in the countries of the Commonwealth. Conferences and general assemblies are held every year in different countries of the Commonwealth.

*President* (1993–4), Hon. Gilbert Parent, MP, Speaker of the House of Commons (*Canada*)
*Vice-President* (1993–4), Hon. M. H. Mohamed, MP, Speaker of the Parliament (*Sri Lanka*)
*Chairman of the Executive Committee* (1993– ), Colin Shepherd, MP (*United Kingdom*)
*Secretary-General*, A. R. Donahoe, QC, Suite 700, Westminster House, 7 Millbank, London SW1P 3JA

UNITED KINGDOM BRANCH

*Hon. Presidents*, The Lord Chancellor; Madam Speaker
*Chairman of Branch*, The Rt. Hon. John Major, MP

*Chairman of Executive Committee*, Sir Ivan Lawrence, QC, MP
*Secretary*, P. Cobb, OBE, Westminster Hall, Houses of Parliament, London, SW1A 0AA

## THE INTER-PARLIAMENTARY UNION (1889)

To facilitate personal contact between members of all Parliaments in the promotion of representative institutions, peace and international co-operation.

*Secretary-General*, P. Cornillon, Place du Petit-Saconnex, BP 99, 1211 Geneva 19, Switzerland

BRITISH GROUP
Palace of Westminster, London SW1A 0AA

*Hon. Presidents*, The Lord Chancellor; Madam Speaker
*President*, The Rt. Hon. John Major, MP
*Chairman*, J. Ward, CBE, MP
*Secretary*, D. Ramsay

# European Parliament

European Parliament elections take place at five-yearly intervals. In mainland Britain MEPs are elected in all constituencies on a first-past-the-post basis; in Northern Ireland three MEPs are elected by proportional representation. From 1979 to 1994 the number of seats held by the UK in the European Parliament was 81 (England 66, Wales 4, Scotland 8, Northern Ireland 3). At the June 1994 election the number of seats increased to 87 (England 71, Wales 5, Scotland 8, Northern Ireland 3).

As from 17 February 1994, nationals of member states of the European Union have the right to vote in elections to the European Parliament in the UK. British subjects and citizens of the Irish Republic can stand in the UK for election to the European Parliament provided they are 21 or over and not subject to disqualification.

MEPs receive a salary from the parliaments or governments of their respective member states, set at the level of the national parliamentary salary and subject to national taxation rules (for salary of British MEPs, see page 224).

## UK MEMBERS AS AT END JULY 1994

*Denotes membership of the last European Parliament

*Adam, Gordon J., PH.D. (b. 1934), Lab., Northumbria, maj. 66,158
*Balfe, Richard A. (b. 1944), Lab., London South Inner, maj. 59,220
*Barton, Roger (b. 1945), Lab., Sheffield, maj. 50,288
Billingham, Mrs Angela (b. 1939), Lab., Northamptonshire and Blaby, maj. 26,085
*Bowe, David R. (b. 1955), Lab., Cleveland and Richmond, maj. 57,568
*Cassidy, Bryan M. D. (b. 1934), C., Dorset and Devon East, maj. 2,264
Chichester, Giles (b. 1946), C., Devon and Plymouth East, maj. 700
*Coates, Kenneth S. (b. 1930), Lab., Nottinghamshire North and Chesterfield, maj. 76,260
*Collins, Kenneth D. (b. 1939), Strathclyde East, maj. 52,340
Corrie, John A. (b. 1935), C., Worcestershire and Warwickshire South, maj. 1,204
*Crampton, Peter D. (b. 1932), Lab., Humberside, maj. 40,618
*Crawley, Mrs Christine M. (b. 1950), Lab., Birmingham East, maj. 55,120
Cunningham, Tony (b. 1952), Lab., Cumbria and Lancashire North, maj. 22,988
*David, Wayne (b. 1957), Lab., South Wales Central, maj. 86,082
Donelly, Brendan (b. 1950), C., Sussex South and Crawley, maj. 1,746
*Donnelly, Alan J. (b. 1957), Lab., Tyne and Wear, maj. 88,380
*Elles, James E. M. (b. 1949), C., Buckinghamshire and Oxfordshire East, maj. 30,665
*Elliott, Michael N. (b. 1932), Lab., London West, maj. 42,275
Evans, Robert (b. 1956), Lab., London North West, maj. 17,442
*Ewing, Mrs Winifred M. (b. 1929), SNP, Highlands and Islands, maj. 54,916

*Falconer, Alexander (b. 1940), Lab., Scotland Mid and Fife, maj. 31,413
*Ford, J. Glyn (b. 1950), Lab., Greater Manchester East, maj. 55,986
*Green, Mrs Pauline (b. 1948), Lab., London North, maj. 48,348
Hallam, David (b. 1948), Lab., Herefordshire and Shropshire, maj. 1,850
Hardstaff, Mrs Veronica (b. 1941), Lab., Lincolnshire and Humberside South, maj. 13,745
*Harrison, Lyndon H. A. (b. 1947), Lab., Cheshire West and Wirral, maj. 47,176
Hendrick, Mark (b. 1958), Lab., Lancashire Central, maj. 12,191
*Hindley, Michael J. (b. 1947), Lab., Lancashire South, maj. 41,404
Howitt, Richard (b. 1961), Lab., Essex South, maj. 21,367
*Hughes, Stephen S. (b. 1952), Lab., Durham, maj. 111,638
*Hume, John, MP (b. 1937), SDLP, Northern Ireland, polled 161,992 votes
*Jackson, Mrs Caroline F., D.PHIL. (b. 1946), C., Wiltshire North and Bath, maj. 8,787
*Kellett-Bowman, Edward T. (b. 1931), C., Itchen, Test and Avon, maj. 6,903
Kerr, Hugh (b. 1944), Lab., Essex West and Hertfordshire East, maj. 3,067
Kinnock, Mrs Glenys (b. 1944), Lab., South Wales East, maj. 120,247
*Lomas, Alfred (b. 1928), Lab., London North East, maj. 57,085
Macartney, Allan (b. 1941), SNP, Scotland North East, maj. 31,227
McCarthy, Ms Arlene (b. 1960), Lab., Peak District, maj. 49,307
*McGowan, Michael (b. 1940), Lab., Leeds, maj. 53,082
*McIntosh, Ms Anne C. B. (b. 1954), C., Essex North and Suffolk South, maj. 3,633
*McMahon, Hugh R. (b. 1938), Lab., Strathclyde West, maj. 25,023
*McMillan-Scott, Edward H. C. (b. 1949), C., Yorkshire North, maj. 7,072
McNally, Eryl (b. 1942), Lab., Bedfordshire and Milton Keynes, maj. 33,209
*Martin, David W. (b. 1954), Lab., Lothians, maj 37,207
Mather, Graham C. S. (b. 1954), C., Hampshire North and Oxford, maj. 9,194
*Megahy, Thomas (b. 1929), Lab., Yorkshire South West, maj. 59,562
Miller, Bill (b. 1954), Lab., Glasgow, maj. 43,158
*Moorhouse, C. James O. (b. 1924), C., London South and Surrey East, maj. 8,739
Morgan, Ms Eluned (b. 1967), Lab., Wales Mid and West, maj. 29,234
*Morris, Revd David R. (b. 1930), Lab., South Wales West, maj. 84,970
Murphy, Simon (b. 1962), Lab., Midlands West, maj. 54,823
Needle, Clive (b. 1956), Lab., Norfolk, maj. 26,287
*Newens, A. Stanley (b. 1930), Lab., London Central, maj. 25,059
*Newman, Edward (b. 1953), Lab., Greater Manchester Central, maj. 42,445
*Nicholson, James F. (b. 1945), UUUP, Northern Ireland, polled 133,459 votes

*Oddy, Ms Christine M. (b. 1955), Lab., Coventry and Warwickshire North, maj. 43,901

*Paisley, Revd Ian R. K., MP (b. 1926), DUP, Northern Ireland, polled 163,246 votes

Perry, Roy (b. 1943), C., Wight and Hampshire South, maj. 5,101

*Plumb, The Lord (b. 1925), C., Cotswolds, maj. 4,268

*Pollack, Ms Anita J. (b. 1946), Lab., London South West, maj. 30,975

Provan, James L. C. (b. 1936), C., South Downs West, maj. 21,067

*Read, Ms I. M. (Mel) (b. 1939), Lab., Nottingham and Leicestershire North West, maj. 39,668

*Seal, Barry H., PH. D. (b. 1937), Lab., Yorkshire West, maj. 48,197

*Simpson, Brian (b. 1953), Lab., Cheshire East, maj. 39,279

Skinner, Peter (b. 1959), Lab., Kent West, maj. 16,777

*Smith, Alexander (b. 1943), Lab., Scotland South, maj. 45,155

*Spencer, Thomas N. B. (b. 1948), C., Surrey, maj. 27,018

Spiers, Shaun (b. 1962), Lab., London South East, maj. 8,022

*Stevens, John C. C. (b. 1955), C., Thames Valley, maj. 758

*Stewart, Kenneth A. (b. 1925), Lab., Merseyside West, maj. 51,811

*Stewart-Clark, Sir John, Bt. (b. 1929), C., Sussex East and Kent South, maj. 6,212

Sturdy, Robert (b. 1944), C., Cambridgeshire, maj. 3,942

Tappin, Michael (b. 1946), Lab., Staffordshire West and Congleton, maj. 40,277

Teverson, Robin (b. 1952), LD, Cornwall and Plymouth West, maj. 29,498

Thomas, David (b. 1955), Lab., Suffolk and Norfolk South West, maj. 12,535

*Titley, Gary (b. 1950), Lab., Greater Manchester West, maj. 58,635

*Tomlinson, John E. (b. 1939), Lab., Birmingham West, maj. 39,350

*Tongue, Ms Carole (b. 1955), Lab., London East, maj. 57,389

Truscott, Dr Peter (b. 1959), Lab., Hertfordshire, maj. 10,304

Waddington, Ms Susan (b. 1944), Lab., Leicester, maj. 20,284

Watson, Graham (b. 1956), LD, Somerset and Devon North, maj. 22,509

Watts, Mark (b. 1964), Lab., Kent East, maj. 635

*West, Norman, (b. 1935), Lab., Yorkshire South, maj. 88,309

*White, Ian (b. 1947), Lab., Bristol, maj. 29,955

Whitehead, Phillip (b. 1937), Lab., Staffordshire East and Derby, maj. 72,196

*Wilson, A. Joseph (b. 1937), Lab., Wales North, maj. 15,242

*Wynn, Terence (b. 1946), Lab., Merseyside East and Wigan, maj. 74,087

## UK CONSTITUENCIES AS AT 9 JUNE 1994

| Abbreviations | |
|---|---|
| Anti Fed. | UK Independence Anti-Federal |
| Anti Fed. C. | Official Anti-Federalist Conservative |
| Beanus | Eurobean from Planet Beanus |
| Boston | Boston Tea Party |
| Brit. | Britain |
| C. Non Fed. | Conservative Non-Federal Party |
| Capital P. | Restoration of Capital Punishment |
| Comm. | Communist |
| Comm. YBG | Communist Y Blaid Gomiwyddol |
| Const. NI | Constitutional Independence for N. Ireland |
| Corr. | Corrective Party |
| CPP | Christian People's Party |
| Home Rule | British Home Rule |
| Hum. | Humanist Party |
| ICP | International Communist Party |
| ICP4 | International Communist Party (4th International) |
| Ind. AES | Independent Anti-European Superstate |
| Ind. Brit. | Independent Britain in Europe |
| Ind. Out | Independent Out of Europe |
| Ind. Ulster | Independence for Ulster |
| Judo | European People's Party Judo Christian Alliance |
| Literal D. | Literal Democrat |
| Loony C | Raving Loony Commonsense |
| Loony CP | Monster Raving Loony Christian Party |

| | |
|---|---|
| Loony X | Monster Raving Loony Project X Party |
| MCCARTHY | Make Criminals Concerned About Our Response To Hostility and Yobbishness |
| MK | Mebyon Kernow |
| Nat. Ind. | National Independence Party |
| NCSA | Network Against Child Support Agency |
| Neeps | North East Ethnic Party, The Neeps |
| New Brit. | New Britain |
| Peace | Peace Coalition |
| Rainbow | Rainbow Connection – Oui-Say-Non-Party |
| Sceptic | Independent Euro Sceptic |
| Spirit | Spirit of Europe |
| Sportsman | Sportsman Anti-Common Market Bureaucracy |
| Subsid. | Subsidiarity Party |
| Third Way | Third Way Independence Party |
| UK Ind. | UK Independence Party |
| Ulster Ind. | Ulster Independence Movement |
| UUUP | United Ulster Unionist Party |
| For other abbreviations, see page 243 | |

---

## ENGLAND

### BEDFORDSHIRE AND MILTON KEYNES
E. 525,524   T. 38.74%

| | |
|---|---|
| E. McNally, Lab. | 94,837 |
| Mrs E. Currie, C. | 61,628 |
| Ms M. Howes, LD | 27,994 |

| | |
|---|---|
| A. Sked, UK Ind. | 7,485 |
| A. Francis, Green | 6,804 |
| A. Howes, New Brit. | 3,878 |
| L. Sheaff, NLP | 939 |
| Lab. majority | 33,209 |
| (Boundary change since June 1989) | |

### BIRMINGHAM EAST
E. 520,782   T. 29.77%

| | |
|---|---|
| *Mrs C. Crawley, Lab. | 90,291 |
| A. Turner, C. | 35,171 |
| Ms C. Cane, LD | 19,455 |
| P. Simpson, Green | 6,268 |
| R. Cook, Soc. | 1,969 |
| M. Brierley, NLP | 1,885 |
| Lab. majority | 55,120 |
| (June 1989, Lab. maj. 46,948) | |

### BIRMINGHAM WEST
E. 509,948   T. 28.49%

| | |
|---|---|
| *J. Tomlinson, Lab. | 77,957 |
| D. Harman, C. | 38,607 |
| N. McGeorge, LD | 14,603 |
| Dr B. Juby, Anti Fed. | 5,237 |
| M. Abbott, Green | 4,367 |
| A. Carmichael, NF | 3,727 |
| H. Meads, NLP | 789 |
| Lab. majority | 39,350 |
| (June 1989, Lab. maj. 30,860) | |

### BRISTOL
E. 503,218   T. 40.91%

| | |
|---|---|
| *I. White, Lab. | 90,790 |
| The Earl of Stockton, C. | 60,835 |
| J. Barnard, LD | 40,394 |
| J. Boxall, Green | 7,163 |

T. Whittingham, *UK Ind.* 5,798
T. Dyball, *NLP* 876
*Lab. majority* 29,955
(Boundary change since June 1989)

BUCKINGHAMSHIRE AND OXFORDSHIRE EAST
E. 487,692  T. 37.31%
*J. Elles, *C.* 77,037
D. Enright, *Lab.* 46,372
Ms S. Bowles, *LD* 42,836
L. Roach, *Green* 8,433
Ms A. Micklem, *Lib.* 5,111
Dr G. Clements, *NLP* 2,156
*C. majority* 30,665
(Boundary change since June 1989)

CAMBRIDGESHIRE
E. 495,383  T. 35.91%
R. Sturdy, *C.* 66,921
Ms M. Johnson, *Lab.* 62,979
A. Duff, *LD* 36,114
Ms M. Wright, *Green* 5,756
P. Wiggin, *Lib.* 4,051
F. Chalmers, *NLP* 2,077
*C. majority* 3,942
(Boundary change since June 1989)

CHESHIRE EAST
E. 502,726  T. 32.46%
*B. Simpson, *Lab.* 87,586
P. Slater, *C.* 48,307
P. Harris, *LD* 20,552
D. Wild, *Green* 3,671
P. Dixon, *Loony CP* 1,600
P. Leadbetter, *NLP* 1,488
*Lab. majority* 39,279
(Boundary change since June 1989)

CHESHIRE WEST AND WIRRAL
E. 538,571  T. 36.78%
*L. Harrison, *Lab.* 106,160
D. Senior, *C.* 58,984
I. Mottershaw, *LD* 20,746
D. Carson, *Home Rule* 6,167
M. Money, *Green* 5,096
A. Wilmot, *NLP* 929
*Lab. majority* 47,176
(Boundary change since June 1989)

CLEVELAND AND RICHMOND
E. 499,580  T. 35.26%
*D. Bowe, *Lab.* 103,355
R. Goodwill, *C.* 45,787
B. Moore, *LD* 21,574
G. Parr, *Green* 4,375
R. Scott, *NLP* 1,068
*Lab. majority* 57,568
(Boundary change since June 1989)

CORNWALL AND PLYMOUTH WEST
E. 484,697  T. 44.92%
R. Teverson, *LD* 91,113
*C. Beazley, *C.* 61,615
Mrs D. Kirk, *Lab.* 42,907
Mrs P. Garnier, *UK Ind.* 6,466
P. Holmes, *Lib.* 6,414
Ms K. Westbrook, *Green* 4,372
Dr L. Jenkin, *MK* 3,315
F. Lyons, *NLP* 921
M. Fitzgerald, *Subsid.* 606

*LD majority* 29,498
(Boundary change since June 1989)

COTSWOLDS
E. 497,588  T. 39.27%
*The Lord Plumb, *C.* 67,484
Ms T. Kingham, *Lab.* 63,216
J. Thomson, *LD* 44,269
M. Rendell, *New Brit.* 11,044
D. McCanlis, *Green* 8,254
H. Brighouse, *NLP* 1,151
*C. majority* 4,268
(Boundary change since June 1989)

COVENTRY AND WARWICKSHIRE NORTH
E. 523,448  T. 32.54%
*Ms C. Oddy, *Lab.* 89,500
Ms J. Crabb, *C.* 45,599
G. Sewards, *LD* 17,453
R. Meacham, *Free Trade* 9,432
P. Baptie, *Green* 4,360
R. Wheway, *Lib.* 2,885
R. France, *NLP* 1,098
*Lab. majority* 43,901
(Boundary change since June 1989)

CUMBRIA AND LANCASHIRE NORTH
E. 498,557  T. 40.78%
A. Cunningham, *Lab.* 97,599
*The Lord Inglewood, *C.* 74,611
R. Putnam, *LD* 24,233
R. Frost, *Green* 5,344
I. Docker, *NLP* 1,500
*Lab. majority* 22,988
(Boundary change since June 1989)

DEVON AND PLYMOUTH EAST
E. 524,320  T. 45.07%
G. Chichester, *C.* 74,953
A. Sanders, *LD* 74,253
Ms L. Gilroy, *Lab.* 47,596
D. Morrish, *Lib.* 14,621
P. Edwards, *Green* 11,172
R. Huggett, *Literal D.* 10,203
J. Everard, *Ind.* 2,629
A. Pringle, *NLP* 908
*C. majority* 700
(Boundary change since June 1989)

DORSET AND DEVON EAST
E. 531,842  T. 41.21%
*B. Cassidy, *C.* 81,551
P. Goldenberg, *LD* 79,287
A. Gardner, *Lab.* 34,856
M. Floyd, *UK Ind.* 10,548
Mrs K. Bradbury, *Green* 8,642
I. Mortimer, *C. Non-Fed.* 3,229
M. Griffiths, *NLP* 1,048
*C. majority* 2,264
(Boundary change since June 1989)

DURHAM
E. 532,051  T. 35.62%
*S. Hughes, *Lab.* 136,671
P. Bradbourn, *C.* 25,033
Dr N. Martin, *LD* 20,935
S. Hope, *Green* 5,670
C. Adamson, *NLP* 1,198
*Lab. majority* 111,638
(June 1989, Lab. maj. 86,848)

ESSEX NORTH AND SUFFOLK SOUTH
E. 497,098  T. 41.33%
*Ms A. McIntosh, *C.* 68,311
C. Pearson, *Lab.* 64,678
S. Mole, *LD* 52,536
S. de Chair, *Ind. AES* 12,409
J. Abbott, *Green* 6,641
N. Pullen, *NLP* 884
*C. majority* 3,633
(Boundary change since June 1989)

ESSEX SOUTH
E. 487,221  T. 33.08%
R. Howitt, *Lab.* 71,883
L. Stanbrook, *C.* 50,516
G. Williams, *LD* 26,132
B. Lynch, *Lib.* 6,780
G. Rumens, *Green* 4,691
M. Heath, *NLP* 1,177
*Lab. majority* 21,367
(Boundary change since June 1989)

ESSEX WEST AND HERTFORDSHIRE EAST
E. 504,095  T. 36.39%
H. Kerr, *Lab.* 66,379
*Ms P. Rawlings, *C.* 63,312
Ms G. James, *LD* 35,695
B. Smalley, *Brit.* 10,277
Ms F. Mawson, *Green* 5,632
P. Carter, *Sportsman* 1,127
L. Davis, *NLP* 1,026
*Lab. majority* 3,067
(Boundary change since June 1989)

GREATER MANCHESTER CENTRAL
E. 481,779  T. 29.11%
*E. Newman, *Lab.* 74,935
Mrs S. Mason, *C.* 32,490
J. Begg, *LD* 22,988
B. Candeland, *Green* 4,952
P. Burke, *Lib.* 3,862
P. Stanley, *NLP* 1,017
*Lab. majority* 42,445
(Boundary change since June 1989)

GREATER MANCHESTER EAST
E. 501,125  T. 27.17%
*G. Ford, *Lab.* 82,289
J. Pinniger, *C.* 26,303
A. Riley, *LD* 20,545
T. Clarke, *Green* 5,823
W. Stevens, *NLP* 1,183
*Lab. majority* 55,986
(Boundary change since June 1989)

GREATER MANCHESTER WEST
E. 512,618  T. 29.70%
*G. Titley, *Lab.* 94,129
D. Newns, *C.* 35,494
F. Harasiwka, *LD* 13,650
R. Jackson, *Green* 3,950
G. Harrison, *MCCARTHY* 3,693
T. Brotheridge, *NLP* 1,316
*Lab. majority* 58,635
(Boundary change since June 1989)

HAMPSHIRE NORTH AND OXFORD
E. 525,982  T. 38.31%
G. Mather, *C.* 72,209
Ms J. Hawkins, *LD* 63,015
J. Tanner, *Lab.* 48,525

D. Wilkinson, *UK Ind.* 8,377
Dr M. Woodin, *Green* 7,310
H. Godfrey, *NLP* 1,027
R. Boston, *Boston* 1,018
*C. majority* 9,194
(Boundary change since June 1989)

HEREFORDSHIRE AND SHROPSHIRE
E. 536,470  T. 38.69%
D. Hallam, *Lab.* 76,120
*Sir C. Prout, *C.* 74,270
J. Gallagher, *LD* 44,130
Ms F. Norman, *Green* 11,578
T. Mercer, *NLP* 1,480
*Lab. majority* 1,850
(Boundary change since June 1989)

HERTFORDSHIRE
E. 522,338  T. 40.11%
Dr P. Truscott, *Lab.* 81,821
P. Jenkinson, *C.* 71,517
D. Griffiths, *LD* 38,995
Ms L. Howitt, *Green* 7,741
M. Biggs, *New Brit.* 6,555
J. McAuley, *NF* 1,755
D. Lucas, *NLP* 734
J. Laine, *Century* 369
*Lab. majority* 10,304
(Boundary change since June 1989)

HUMBERSIDE
E. 519,013  T. 32.38%
*P. Crampton, *Lab.* 87,296
D. Stewart, *C.* 46,678
Ms D. Wallis, *LD* 28,818
Ms S. Mummery, *Green* 4,170
Ms A. Miszewska, *NLP* 1,100
*Lab. majority* 40,618
(Boundary change since June 1989)

ITCHEN, TEST AND AVON
E. 550,406  T. 41.83%
*E. Kellett-Bowman, *C.* 81,456
A. Barron, *LD* 74,553
E. Read, *Lab.* 52,416
N. Farage, *UK Ind.* 12,423
Ms F. Hulbert, *Green* 7,998
A. Miller-Smith, *NLP* 1,368
*C. majority* 6,903
(Boundary change since June 1989)

KENT EAST
E. 499,662  T. 40.34%
M. Watts, *Lab.* 69,641
*C. Jackson, *C.* 69,006
J. Macdonald, *LD* 44,549
C. Bullen, *UK Ind.* 9,414
S. Dawe, *Green* 7,196
C. Beckley, *NLP* 1,746
*Lab. majority* 635
(Boundary change since June 1989)

KENT WEST
E. 505,658  T. 37.33%
P. Skinner, *Lab.* 77,346
*B. Patterson, *C.* 60,569
J. Daly, *LD* 33,869
C. Mackinlay, *UK Ind.* 9,750
Ms P. Kemp, *Green* 5,651
J. Bowler, *NLP* 1,598
*Lab. majority* 16,777
(Boundary change since June 1989)

LANCASHIRE CENTRAL
E. 505,224  T. 33.23%
M. Hendrick, *Lab.* 73,420
*M. Welsh, *C.* 61,229
Ms J. Ross-Mills, *LD* 20,578
D. Hill, *Home Rule* 6,751
C. Maile, *Green* 4,169
Ms J. Ayliffe, *NLP* 1,727
*Lab. majority* 12,191
(Boundary change since June 1989)

LANCASHIRE SOUTH
E. 514,840  T. 33.14%
*M. Hindley, *Lab.* 92,598
R. Topham, *C.* 51,194
J. Ault, *LD* 17,008
J. Gaffney, *Green* 4,774
Mrs E. Rokas, *Ind.* 3,439
J. Renwick, *NLP* 1,605
*Lab. majority* 41,404
(Boundary change since June 1989)

LEEDS
E. 521,989  T. 30.03%
*M. McGowan, *Lab.* 89,160
N. Carmichael, *C.* 36,078
Ms J. Harvey, *LD* 17,575
M. Meadowcroft, *Lib.* 6,617
Ms C. Nash, *Green* 6,283
Ms S. Hayward, *NLP* 1,018
*Lab. majority* 53,082
(June 1989, Lab. maj. 42,518)

LEICESTER
E. 515,343  T. 37.63%
Ms S. Waddington, *Lab.* 87,048
A. Marshall, *C.* 66,764
M. Jones, *LD* 28,890
G. Forse, *Green* 8,941
Ms P. Saunders, *NLP* 2,283
*Lab. majority* 20,284
(Boundary change since June 1989)

LINCOLNSHIRE AND HUMBERSIDE
SOUTH
E. 539,981  T. 36.34%
Mrs V. Hardstaff, *Lab.* 83,172
*W. Newton Dunn, *C.* 69,427
K. Melton, *LD* 27,241
Ms R. Robinson, *Green* 8,563
E. Wheeler, *Lib.* 3,434
I. Selby, *NCSA* 2,973
H. Kelly, *NLP* 1,429
*Lab. majority* 13,745
(Boundary change since June 1989)

LONDON CENTRAL
E. 494,610  T. 32.57%
*S. Newens, *Lab.* 75,711
A. Elliott, *C.* 50,652
Ms S. Ludford, *LD* 20,176
Ms N. Kortvelyessy, *Green* 7,043
H. Le Fanu, *UK Ind.* 4,157
C. Slapper, *Soc.* 1,593
Ms S. Hamza, *NLP* 1,215
G. Weiss, *Rainbow* 547
*Lab. majority* 25,059
(June 1989, Lab. maj. 11,542)

LONDON EAST
E. 511,523  T. 33.38%
*Ms C. Tongue, *Lab.* 98,759

Ms V. Taylor, *C.* 41,370
K. Montgomery, *LD* 15,566
G. Batten, *UK Ind.* 5,974
J. Baguley, *Green* 4,337
O. Tillett, *Third Way* 3,484
N. Kahn, *NLP* 1,272
*Lab. majority* 57,389
(June 1989, Lab. maj. 27,385)

LONDON NORTH
E. 541,269  T. 34.00%
*Mrs P. Green, *Lab.* 102,059
M. Keegan, *C.* 53,711
I. Mann, *LD* 15,739
Ms H. Jago, *Green* 5,666
I. Booth, *UK Ind.* 5,099
G. Sabrizi, *Judo* 880
J. Hinde, *NLP* 856
*Lab. majority* 48,348
(June 1989, Lab. maj. 5,837)

LONDON NORTH EAST
E. 486,016  T. 26.60%
*A. Lomas, *Lab.* 80,256
S. Gordon, *C.* 23,171
K. Appiah, *LD* 10,242
Ms J. Lambert, *Green* 8,386
E. Murat, *Lib.* 2,573
P. Compobassi, *UK Ind.* 2,015
R. Archer, *NLP* 1,111
M. Fischer, *Comm. GB* 869
A. Hyland, *ICP4* 679
*Lab. majority* 57,085
(June 1989, Lab. maj. 47,767)

LONDON NORTH WEST
E. 481,272  T. 35.13%
R. Evans, *Lab.* 80,192
*The Lord Bethell, *C.* 62,750
Ms H. Leighter, *LD* 18,998
D. Johnson, *Green* 4,743
Ms A. Murphy, *Comm. GB* 858
Ms T. Sullivan, *NLP* 807
C. Palmer, *Century* 740
*Lab. majority* 17,442
(June 1989, C. maj. 7,400)

LONDON SOUTH AND SURREY EAST
E. 486,358  T. 34.38%
*J. Moorhouse, *C.* 64,813
Ms G. Rolles, *Lab.* 56,074
M. Reinisch, *LD* 32,059
J. Cornford, *Green* 7,046
J. Major, *Loony X* 3,339
A. Reeve, *Capital P.* 2,983
P. Levy, *NLP* 887
*C. majority* 8,739
(Boundary change since June 1989)

LONDON SOUTH EAST
E. 493,178  T. 35.38%
S. Spiers, *Lab.* 71,505
*P. Price, *C.* 63,483
J. Fryer, *LD* 25,271
I. Mouland, *Green* 6,399
R. Almond, *Lib.* 3,881
K. Lowne, *NF* 2,926
J. Small, *NLP* 1,025
*Lab. majority* 8,022
(Boundary change since June 1989)

LONDON SOUTH INNER
E. 510,609   T. 27.30%

| | |
|---|---|
| *R. Balfe, *Lab.* | 85,079 |
| A. Boff, *C.* | 25,859 |
| A. Graves, *LD* | 20,708 |
| S. Collins, *Green* | 6,570 |
| M. Leighton, *NLP* | 1,179 |
| *Lab. majority* | 59,220 |

(Boundary change since June 1989)

LONDON SOUTH WEST
E. 479,246   T. 34.35%

| | |
|---|---|
| *Ms A. Pollack, *Lab.* | 81,850 |
| Prof. P. Treleaven, *C.* | 50,875 |
| G. Blanchard, *LD* | 18,697 |
| T. Walsh, *Green* | 5,460 |
| A. Scholefield, *UK Ind.* | 4,912 |
| C. Hopewell, *Capital P.* | 1,840 |
| M. Simson, *NLP* | 625 |
| J. Quanjer, *Spirit* | 377 |
| *Lab. majority* | 30,975 |

(Boundary change since June 1989)

LONDON WEST
E. 505,791   T. 36.02%

| | |
|---|---|
| *M. Elliott, *Lab.* | 94,562 |
| R. Guy, *C.* | 52,287 |
| W. Mallinson, *LD* | 21,561 |
| J. Bradley, *Green* | 6,134 |
| G. Roberts, *UK Ind.* | 4,583 |
| W. Binding, *NF* | 1,963 |
| R. Johnson, *NLP* | 1,105 |
| *Lab. majority* | 42,275 |

(June 1989, Lab. maj. 14,808)

MERSEYSIDE EAST AND WIGAN
E. 518,196   T. 24.66%

| | |
|---|---|
| *T. Wynn, *Lab.* | 91,986 |
| C. Manson, *C.* | 17,899 |
| Ms F. Clucas, *LD* | 8,874 |
| J. Melia, *Lib.* | 4,765 |
| L. Brown, *Green* | 3,280 |
| G. Hutchard, *NLP* | 1,009 |
| *Lab. majority* | 74,087 |

(June 1989, Lab. maj. 76,867)

MERSEYSIDE WEST
E. 515,909   T. 26.18%

| | |
|---|---|
| *K. Stewart, *Lab.* | 78,819 |
| C. Varley, *C.* | 27,008 |
| D. Bamber, *LD* | 19,097 |
| S. Radford, *Lib.* | 4,714 |
| Ms L. Lever, *Green* | 4,573 |
| J. Collins, *NLP* | 852 |
| *Lab. majority* | 51,811 |

(June 1989, Lab. maj. 49,817)

MIDLANDS WEST
E. 533,742   T. 31.28%

| | |
|---|---|
| S. Murphy, *Lab.* | 99,242 |
| M. Simpson, *C.* | 44,419 |
| G. Baldauf-Good, *LD* | 12,195 |
| M. Hyde, *Lib.* | 5,050 |
| C. Mattingly, *Green* | 4,390 |
| J. Oldbury, *NLP* | 1,641 |
| *Lab. majority* | 54,823 |

(June 1989, Lab. maj. 42,364)

NORFOLK
E. 513,553   T. 44.25%

| | |
|---|---|
| C. Needle, *Lab.* | 102,711 |
| *P. Howell, *C.* | 76,424 |

| | |
|---|---|
| P. Burall, *LD* | 39,107 |
| A. Holmes, *Green* | 7,938 |
| B. Parsons, *NLP* | 1,075 |
| *Lab. majority* | 26,287 |

(Boundary change since June 1989)

NORTHAMPTONSHIRE AND BLABY
E. 524,916   T. 39.37%

| | |
|---|---|
| Mrs A. Billingham, *Lab.* | 95,317 |
| *A. Simpson, *C.* | 69,232 |
| K. Scudder, *LD* | 27,616 |
| Ms A. Bryant, *Green* | 9,121 |
| I. Whitaker, *Ind.* | 4,397 |
| B. Spivack, *NLP* | 972 |
| *Lab. majority* | 26,085 |

(Boundary change since June 1989)

NORTHUMBRIA
E. 516,680   T. 33.65%

| | |
|---|---|
| *G. Adam, *Lab.* | 103,087 |
| J. Flack, *C.* | 36,929 |
| L. Opik, *LD* | 20,195 |
| D. Lott, *UK Ind.* | 7,210 |
| J. Hartshorne, *Green* | 5,714 |
| L. Walch, *NLP* | 740 |
| *Lab. majority* | 66,158 |

(June 1989, Lab. maj. 60,040)

NOTTINGHAM AND LEICESTER-
SHIRE NORTH WEST
E. 507,915   T. 37.68%

| | |
|---|---|
| *Ms M. Read, *Lab.* | 95,344 |
| M. Brandon-Bravo, *C.* | 55,676 |
| A. Wood, *LD* | 23,836 |
| Ms S. Blount, *Green* | 7,035 |
| J. Downes, *UK Ind.* | 5,849 |
| P. Walton, *Ind. Out* | 2,710 |
| Mrs J. Christou, *NLP* | 927 |
| *Lab. majority* | 39,668 |

(Boundary change since June 1989)

NOTTINGHAMSHIRE NORTH AND
CHESTERFIELD
E. 490,330   T. 36.95%

| | |
|---|---|
| *K. Coates, *Lab.* | 114,353 |
| D. Hazell, *C.* | 38,093 |
| Ms S. Pearce, *LD* | 21,936 |
| G. Jones, *Green* | 5,159 |
| Ms S. Lincoln, *NLP* | 1,632 |
| *Lab. majority* | 76,260 |

(Boundary change since June 1989)

PEAK DISTRICT
E. 511,357   T. 39.02%

| | |
|---|---|
| Ms A. McCarthy, *Lab.* | 105,853 |
| R. Fletcher, *C.* | 56,546 |
| Ms S. Barber, *LD* | 29,979 |
| M. Shipley, *Green* | 5,598 |
| D. Collins, *NLP* | 1,533 |
| *Lab. majority* | 49,307 |

(Boundary change since June 1989)

SHEFFIELD
E. 476,530   T. 27.50%

| | |
|---|---|
| *R. Barton, *Lab.* | 76,397 |
| Ms S. Anginotti, *LD* | 26,109 |
| Ms K. Twitchen, *C.* | 22,374 |
| B. New, *Green* | 4,742 |
| M. England, *Comm.* | 834 |
| R. Hurford, *NLP* | 577 |
| *Lab. majority* | 50,288 |

(Boundary change since June 1989)

SOMERSET AND DEVON NORTH
E. 517,349   T. 47.09%

| | |
|---|---|
| G. Watson, *LD* | 106,187 |
| *Mrs M. Daly, *C.* | 83,678 |
| J. Pilgrim, *Lab.* | 34,540 |
| D. Taylor, *Green* | 10,870 |
| G. Livings, *New Brit.* | 7,165 |
| M. Lucas, *NLP* | 1,200 |
| *LD majority* | 22,509 |

(Boundary change since June 1989)

SOUTH DOWNS WEST
E. 486,793   T. 39.45%

| | |
|---|---|
| J. Provan, *C.* | 83,813 |
| Dr J. Walsh, *LD* | 62,746 |
| Ms L. Armstrong, *Lab.* | 32,344 |
| E. Paine, *Green* | 7,703 |
| W. Weights, *Lib.* | 3,630 |
| P. Kember, *NLP* | 1,794 |
| *C. majority* | 21,067 |

(Boundary change since June 1989)

STAFFORDSHIRE EAST AND DERBY
E. 519,553   T. 35.46%

| | |
|---|---|
| P. Whitehead, *Lab.* | 102,393 |
| Ms J. Evans, *C.* | 50,197 |
| Ms D. Brass, *LD* | 17,469 |
| I. Crompton, *UK Ind.* | 6,993 |
| R. Clarke, *Green* | 4,272 |
| R. Jones, *NF* | 2,098 |
| Ms D. Grice, *NLP* | 793 |
| *Lab. majority* | 72,196 |

(Boundary change since June 1989)

STAFFORDSHIRE WEST AND
CONGLETON
E. 502,395   T. 31.60%

| | |
|---|---|
| M. Tappin, *Lab.* | 84,337 |
| A. Brown, *C.* | 44,060 |
| J. Stevens, *LD* | 24,430 |
| D. Hoppe, *Green* | 4,533 |
| D. Lines, *NLP* | 1,403 |
| *Lab. majority* | 40,277 |

(Boundary change since June 1989)

SUFFOLK AND NORFOLK SOUTH
WEST
E. 477,668   T. 38.38%

| | |
|---|---|
| D. Thomas, *Lab.* | 74,304 |
| *A. Turner, *C.* | 61,769 |
| R. Atkins, *LD* | 37,975 |
| A. Slade, *Green* | 7,760 |
| E. Kaplan, *NLP* | 1,530 |
| *Lab. majority* | 12,535 |

(Boundary change since June 1989)

SURREY
E. 514,130   T. 37.51%

| | |
|---|---|
| *T. Spencer, *C.* | 83,405 |
| Mrs S. Thomas, *LD* | 56,387 |
| Ms F. Wolf, *Lab.* | 30,894 |
| Mrs S. Porter, *UK Ind.* | 7,717 |
| H. Charlton, *Green* | 7,198 |
| J. Walker, *Ind. Brit.* | 4,627 |
| Mrs J. Thomas, *NLP* | 2,638 |
| *C. majority* | 27,018 |

(Boundary change since June 1989)

SUSSEX EAST AND KENT SOUTH
E. 513,550   T. 41.90%

| | |
|---|---|
| *Sir J. Stewart-Clark, *C.* | 83,141 |
| D. Bellotti, *LD* | 76,929 |

| | |
|---|---|
| N. Palmer, *Lab.* | 35,273 |
| A. Burgess, *UK Ind.* | 9,058 |
| Ms R. Addison, *Green* | 7,439 |
| Ms T. Williamson, *Lib.* | 2,558 |
| P. Cragg, *NLP* | 765 |
| C. majority | 6,212 |
| (Boundary change since June 1989) | |

SUSSEX SOUTH AND CRAWLEY
E. 492,413   T. 37.64%

| | |
|---|---|
| B. Donelly, *C.* | 62,860 |
| Ms J. Edmond Smith, *Lab.* | 61,114 |
| J. Williams, *LD* | 41,410 |
| Ms P. Beever, *Green* | 9,348 |
| D. Horner, *Sceptic* | 7,106 |
| N. Furness, *Anti-Fed. C.* | 2,618 |
| A. Hankey, *NLP* | 901 |
| C. majority | 1,746 |
| (Boundary change since June 1989) | |

THAMES VALLEY
E. 543,685   T. 34.80%

| | |
|---|---|
| *J. Stevens, *C.* | 70,485 |
| J. Howarth, *Lab.* | 69,727 |
| N. Bathurst, *LD* | 33,187 |
| P. Unsworth, *Green* | 6,120 |
| J. Clark, *Lib.* | 5,381 |
| P. Owen, *Loony C* | 2,859 |
| M. Grenville, *NLP* | 1,453 |
| C. majority | 758 |
| (June 1989, C. maj. 26,491) | |

TYNE AND WEAR
E. 516,436   T. 28.02%

| | |
|---|---|
| *A. Donnelly, *Lab.* | 107,604 |
| I. Liddell-Grainger, *C.* | 19,224 |
| P. Maughan, *LD* | 8,706 |
| G. Edwards, *Green* | 4,375 |
| Ms W. Lundgren, *Lib.* | 4,164 |
| A. Fisken, *NLP* | 650 |
| Lab. majority | 88,380 |
| (June 1989, Lab. maj. 95,780) | |

WIGHT AND HAMPSHIRE SOUTH
E. 488,398   T. 37.16%

| | |
|---|---|
| R. Perry, *C.* | 63,306 |
| M. Hancock, *LD* | 58,205 |
| Ms S. Fry, *Lab.* | 40,442 |
| J. Browne, *Ind.* | 12,140 |
| P. Fuller, *Green* | 6,697 |
| W. Treend, *NLP* | 722 |
| C. majority | 5,101 |
| (Boundary change since June 1989) | |

WILTSHIRE NORTH AND BATH
E. 496,591   T. 41.46%

| | |
|---|---|
| *Mrs C. Jackson, *C.* | 71,872 |
| Ms J. Matthew, *LD* | 63,085 |
| Ms J. Norris, *Lab.* | 50,489 |
| P. Cullen, *Lib.* | 6,760 |
| M. Davidson, *Green* | 5,974 |
| T. Hedges, *UK Ind.* | 5,842 |
| D. Cooke, *NLP* | 1,148 |
| Dr J. Day, *CPP* | 725 |
| C. majority | 8,787 |
| (Boundary change since June 1989) | |

WORCESTERSHIRE AND WARWICK-
SHIRE SOUTH
E. 551,162   T. 37.98%

| | |
|---|---|
| J. Corrie, *C.* | 73,573 |
| Ms G. Gschaider, *Lab.* | 72,369 |

| | |
|---|---|
| P. Larner, *LD* | 44,168 |
| Ms J. Alty, *Green* | 9,273 |
| C. Hards, *Nat. Ind.* | 8,447 |
| J. Brewster, *NLP* | 1,510 |
| C. majority | 1,204 |
| (Boundary change since June 1989) | |

YORKSHIRE NORTH
E. 475,686   T. 38.70%

| | |
|---|---|
| *E. McMillan-Scott, *C.* | 70,036 |
| B. Regan, *Lab.* | 62,964 |
| M. Pitts, *LD* | 43,171 |
| Dr R. Richardson, *Green* | 7,036 |
| S. Withers, *NLP* | 891 |
| C. majority | 7,072 |
| (Boundary change since June 1989) | |

YORKSHIRE SOUTH
E. 523,401   T. 28.64%

| | |
|---|---|
| *N. West, *Lab.* | 109,004 |
| J. Howard, *C.* | 20,695 |
| Ms C. Roderick, *LD* | 11,798 |
| P. Davies, *UK Ind.* | 3,948 |
| J. Waters, *Green* | 3,775 |
| N. Broome, *NLP* | 681 |
| Lab. majority | 88,309 |
| (June 1989, Lab. maj. 91,784) | |

YORKSHIRE SOUTH WEST
E. 547,469   T. 29.03%

| | |
|---|---|
| *T. Megahy, *Lab.* | 94,025 |
| Mrs C. Adamson, *C.* | 34,463 |
| D. Ridgway, *LD* | 21,595 |
| A. Cooper, *Green* | 7,163 |
| G. Mead, *NLP* | 1,674 |
| Lab. majority | 59,562 |
| (Boundary change since June 1989) | |

YORKSHIRE WEST
E. 490,078   T. 34.61%

| | |
|---|---|
| *B. Seal, *Lab.* | 90,652 |
| R. Booth, *C.* | 42,455 |
| C. Bidwell, *LD* | 20,452 |
| R. Pearson, *New Brit.* | 8,027 |
| C. Harris, *Green* | 7,154 |
| D. Whitley, *NLP* | 894 |
| Lab. majority | 48,197 |
| (Boundary change since June 1989) | |

# WALES

SOUTH WALES CENTRAL
E. 477,182   T. 39.40%

| | |
|---|---|
| *W. David, *Lab.* | 115,396 |
| Ms L. Verity, *C.* | 29,314 |
| G. Llywelyn, *PC* | 18,857 |
| J. Dixon, *LD* | 18,471 |
| C. von Ruhland, *Green* | 4,002 |
| R. Griffiths, *Comm. YBG* | 1,073 |
| G. Duguay, *NLP* | 889 |
| Lab. majority | 86,082 |
| (Boundary change since June 1989) | |

SOUTH WALES EAST
E. 454,794   T. 43.07%

| | |
|---|---|
| Mrs A. Kinnock, *Lab.* | 144,907 |
| Mrs R. Blomfield-Smith, *C.* | 24,660 |
| C. Woolgrove, *LD* | 9,963 |
| C. Mann, *PC* | 9,550 |
| R. Coghill, *Green* | 4,509 |

| | |
|---|---|
| Ms S. Williams, *Welsh Soc.* | 1,270 |
| Dr R. Brussatis, *NLP* | 1,027 |
| Lab. majority | 120,247 |
| (Boundary change since June 1989) | |

SOUTH WALES WEST
E. 395,131   T. 39.92%

| | |
|---|---|
| *Revd D. Morris, *Lab.* | 104,263 |
| R. Buckland, *C.* | 19,293 |
| J. Bushell, *LD* | 15,499 |
| Ms C. Adams, *PC* | 12,364 |
| Ms J. Evans, *Green* | 4,114 |
| Ms H. Evans, *NLP* | 1,112 |
| Capt. Beany, *Beanus* | 1,106 |
| Lab. majority | 84,970 |
| (Boundary change since June 1989) | |

WALES MID AND WEST
E. 401,529   T. 48.00%

| | |
|---|---|
| Ms E. Morgan, *Lab.* | 78,092 |
| M. Phillips, *PC* | 48,858 |
| P. Bone, *C.* | 31,606 |
| Ms J. Hughes, *LD* | 23,719 |
| D. Rowlands, *UK Ind.* | 5,536 |
| Dr C. Busby, *Green* | 3,938 |
| T. Griffith-Jones, *NLP* | 988 |
| Lab. majority | 29,234 |
| (Boundary change since June 1989) | |

WALES NORTH
E. 475,829   T. 45.34%

| | |
|---|---|
| *J. Wilson, *Lab.* | 88,091 |
| D. Wigley, *PC* | 72,849 |
| G. Mon Hughes, *C.* | 33,450 |
| Ms R. Parry, *LD* | 14,828 |
| P. Adams, *Green* | 2,850 |
| D. Hughes, *NLP* | 2,065 |
| M. Cooksey, *Ind.* | 1,623 |
| Lab. majority | 15,242 |
| (Boundary change since June 1989) | |

---

# SCOTLAND

GLASGOW
E. 463,364   T. 34.46%

| | |
|---|---|
| W. Miller, *Lab.* | 83,953 |
| T. Chalmers, *SNP* | 40,795 |
| T. Sheridan, *SML* | 12,113 |
| R. Wilkinson, *C.* | 10,888 |
| J. Money, *LD* | 7,291 |
| P. O'Brien, *Green* | 2,252 |
| J. Fleming, *Soc.* | 1,125 |
| M. Wilkinson, *NLP* | 868 |
| C. Marsden, *ICP* | 381 |
| Lab. majority | 43,158 |
| (June 1989, Lab. maj. 59,232) | |

HIGHLANDS AND ISLANDS
E. 328,104   T. 39.09%

| | |
|---|---|
| *Mrs W. Ewing, *SNP* | 74,872 |
| M. Macmillan, *Lab.* | 19,956 |
| M. Tennant, *C.* | 15,767 |
| H. Morrison, *LD* | 12,919 |
| Dr E. Scott, *Green* | 3,140 |
| M. Carr, *UK Ind.* | 1,096 |
| Ms M. Gilmour, *NLP* | 522 |
| SNP majority | 54,916 |
| (June 1989, SNP maj. 44,695) | |

LOTHIANS
E. 520,943   T. 38.69%

| | |
|---|---|
| *D. Martin, *Lab.* | 90,531 |
| K. Brown, *SNP* | 53,324 |
| Dr P. McNally, *C.* | 33,526 |
| Ms H. Campbell, *LD* | 17,883 |
| R. Harper, *Green* | 5,149 |
| J. McGregor, *Soc.* | 637 |
| M. Siebert, *NLP* | 500 |
| *Lab. majority* | 37,207 |

(June 1989, Lab. maj. 38,826)

SCOTLAND MID AND FIFE
E. 546,060   T. 38.25%

| | |
|---|---|
| *A. Falconer, *Lab.* | 95,667 |
| R. Douglas, *SNP* | 64,254 |
| P. Page, *C.* | 28,192 |
| Ms H. Lyall, *LD* | 17,192 |
| M. Johnston, *Green* | 3,015 |
| T. Pringle, *NLP* | 532 |
| *Lab. majority* | 31,413 |

(June 1989, Lab. maj. 52,157)

SCOTLAND NORTH EAST
E. 575,748   T. 37.72%

| | |
|---|---|
| A. Macartney, *SNP* | 92,892 |
| *H. McCubbin, *Lab.* | 61,665 |
| Dr R. Harris, *C.* | 40,372 |
| S. Horner, *LD* | 18,008 |
| K. Farnsworth, *Green* | 2,569 |
| Ms M. Ward, *Comm. GB* | 689 |
| L. Mair, *Neeps* | 584 |
| D. Paterson, *NLP* | 371 |
| *SNP majority* | 31,227 |

(June 1989, Lab. maj. 2,613)

SCOTLAND SOUTH
E. 500,643   T. 40.14%

| | |
|---|---|
| *A. Smith, *Lab.* | 90,750 |
| A. Hutton, *C.* | 45,595 |
| Mrs C. Creech, *SNP* | 45,032 |
| D. Millar, *LD* | 13,363 |
| J. Hein, *Lib.* | 3,249 |
| Ms L. Hendry, *Green* | 2,429 |
| G. Gay, *NLP* | 539 |
| *Lab. majority* | 45,155 |

(June 1989, Lab. maj. 15,693)

STRATHCLYDE EAST
E. 492,618   T. 37.26%

| | |
|---|---|
| *K. Collins, *Lab.* | 106,476 |
| I. Hamilton, *SNP* | 54,136 |
| B. Cooklin, *C.* | 13,915 |
| R. Stewart, *LD* | 6,383 |
| A. Whitelaw, *Green* | 1,874 |
| D. Gilmour, *NLP* | 787 |
| *Lab. majority* | 52,340 |

(June 1989, Lab. maj. 60,317)

STRATHCLYDE WEST
E. 489,129   T. 40.05%

| | |
|---|---|
| *H. McMahon, *Lab.* | 86,957 |
| C. Campbell, *SNP* | 61,934 |
| J. Godfrey, *C.* | 28,414 |
| D. Herbison, *LD* | 14,772 |
| Ms K. Allan, *Green* | 2,886 |
| Ms S. Gilmour, *NLP* | 918 |
| *Lab. majority* | 25,023 |

(June 1989, Lab. maj. 39,591)

## NORTHERN IRELAND

Northern Ireland forms a three-member seat with a single transferable vote system

E. 1,150,304 T. 48.67%

| | |
|---|---|
| *Revd I. Paisley, *DUP* | 163,246 |
| *J. Hume, *SDLP* | 161,992 |
| *J. Nicholson, *UUUP* | 133,459 |
| Mrs M. Clark-Glass, *All.* | 23,157 |
| T. Hartley, *SF* | 21,273 |
| Ms D. McGuinness, *SF* | 17,195 |
| F. Molloy, *SF* | 16,747 |
| Revd H. Ross, *Ulster Ind.* | 7,858 |
| Miss M. Boal, *C.* | 5,583 |
| J. Lowry, *WP* | 2,543 |
| N. Cusack, *Ind. Lab.* | 2,464 |
| J. Anderson, *NLP* | 1,418 |
| Mrs J. Campion, *Peace* | 1,088 |
| D. Kerr, *Ind. Ulster* | 571 |
| Ms S. Thompson, *NLP* | 454 |
| M. Kennedy, *NLP* | 419 |
| R. Mooney, *Const. NI* | 400 |

# Government Departments and Public Offices

This section covers central government departments, executive agencies, regulatory bodies, other statutory independent organizations, and bodies which are government-financed or whose head is appointed by a government minister.

## THE CIVIL SERVICE

Changes are currently being introduced into the civil service with the aim of reducing its functions to a central core and privatizing or contracting out the rest of its work. Many semi-autonomous executive agencies have already been established under the 'Next Steps' programme. Executive agencies operate within a framework set by the responsible minister which specifies policies, objectives and available resources. They are usually headed by a chief executive, who is responsible for the day-to-day operations of the agency and who is accountable to the minister for the use of resources and for the performance of the agency. More than 60 per cent of the work of the civil service is now conducted by executive agencies.

Most of the Home Civil Service's senior grades have been absorbed into an Open pay and grading structure. Executive agencies are increasingly adopting their own pay and grading systems and will therefore not necessarily fit into this structure. The Open structure represents the following:

| Grade | Title |
|---|---|
| 1 | Permanent Secretary |
| 1A | Second Permanent Secretary |
| 2 | Deputy Secretary |
| 3 | Under-Secretary |
| 4 | Chief Scientific Officer B, Professional and Technology Directing A |
| 5 | Assistant Secretary, Deputy Chief Scientific Officer, Professional and Technology Directing B |
| 6 | Senior Principal, Senior Principal Scientific Officer, Professional and Technology Superintending Grade |
| 7 | Principal, Principal Scientific Officer, Principal Professional and Technology Officer |

## SALARIES

MINISTERIAL SALARIES *as at 1 January 1994*
Ministers who are Members of the House of Commons receive a reduced parliamentary salary (£23,854 in 1994) in addition to their ministerial salary.

| | |
|---|---|
| Prime Minister | £54,438 |
| Secretary of State | £40,895 |
| Minister of State (Lords) | £46,333 |
| Minister of State (Commons) | £28,936 |
| Parliamentary Under-Secretary (Lords) | £38,894 |
| Parliamentary Under-Secretary (Commons) | £21,961 |

*CIVIL SERVICE SALARIES 1994–5

| | |
|---|---|
| †Secretary of the Cabinet and Head of the Home Civil Service | £118,179 |
| †Permanent Secretary to the Treasury | £110,563 |
| †Head of the Diplomatic Service | £110,563 |
| †Grade 1 | £95,051 |
| †Grade 1A | £87,435 |
| †Grade 2 | £65,990–£79,396 |
| †Grade 3 | £52,704–£62,817 |

| | |
|---|---|
| Grade 4 | £45,278–£54,815 |
| Grade 5 | £36,739–£54,815 |
| Grade 6 | £28,213–£47,044 |
| Grade 7 | £24,724–£38,290 |
| Senior Executive Officer | £19,215–£24,780 |
| Higher Executive Officer | £15,363–£20,218 |
| Administration Trainee/HEO(D) | £13,144–£24,139 |
| Executive Officer | £11,208–£16,164 |
| Administrative Officer | £8,778–£11,636 |
| Administrative Assistant | £6,928–£9,826 |

*London Rates*

| | |
|---|---|
| †Grade 3 | £54,131–£64,283 |
| Grade 4 | £47,043–£56,953 |
| Grade 5 | £38,341–£56,953 |
| Grade 6 | £29,482–£48,879 |
| Grade 7 | £25,837–£40,012 |
| Senior Executive Officer | £20,013–£25,810 |
| Higher Executive Officer | £16,000–£21,059 |
| Executive Officer | £11,673–£16,835 |
| Administrative Officer | £9,393–£12,450 |
| Administrative Assistant | £7,412–£10,513 |

*Most grades no longer have an incremental scale; pay is based solely on performance and can be set at any level between the minimum and maximum of the range
†These grades do not attract the recruitment and retention allowance of up to £3,000 a year introduced in October 1994 to replace London weighting of up to £1,776 a year. The new allowance will be used to attract and retain staff in any part of the country at each department's discretion

---

## ADVISORY, CONCILIATION AND ARBITRATION SERVICE
27 Wilton Street, London SW1X 7AZ
Tel 0171-210 3613

---

The Advisory, Conciliation and Arbitration Service (ACAS) is an independent organization set up under the Employment Protection Act 1975 (the provisions now being found in the Trade Union and Labour Relations (Consolidation) Act 1992). ACAS is directed by a Council consisting of a full-time chairman and part-time employer, trade union and independent members, all appointed by the Secretary of State for Employment. The functions of the Service are to promote the improvement of industrial relations in general, to provide facilities for conciliation, mediation and arbitration as means of avoiding and resolving industrial disputes, and to provide advisory and information services on industrial relations matters to employers, employees and their representatives.

ACAS also has main offices in Birmingham, Bristol, Cardiff, Fleet, Glasgow, Leeds, Liverpool, Manchester, Newcastle upon Tyne and Nottingham.

*Chairman,* J. Hougham
*Chief Conciliation Officer (G4),* D. Evans
*Director of Resources (G5),* Ms H. Canter
*Director of Operations (G5),* F. Noonan
*Director of Strategy (G5),* P. Syson

## MINISTRY OF AGRICULTURE, FISHERIES AND FOOD
Whitehall Place, London SW1A 2HH
Tel 0171-238 6000; *enquiries* 0645-335577

The Ministry of Agriculture, Fisheries and Food is responsible for administering government policies on agriculture, horticulture and fisheries in England and policies relating to the safety and quality of food in the United Kingdom as a whole. In association with the Agriculture Departments of the Scottish, Welsh and Northern Ireland Offices and with the Intervention Board (*see* page 324), the Ministry is responsible for the negotiation and administration of the EC common agricultural and fisheries policies, for matters relating to the single European market, and for international agricultural and food trade policy. It commissions research to assist in the formulation and assessment of policy.

The Ministry administers policies on the control and eradication of animal, plant and fish diseases, and on assistance to capital investment in farm and horticultural businesses; it also has responsibilities relating to the protection and enhancement of the countryside and the marine environment as well as to flood defence and other rural issues.

The Ministry is responsible for ensuring public health standards in the manufacture, preparation and distribution of basic foods, and for planning to safeguard essential food supplies in times of emergency. It is responsible for government relations with the UK food and drink manufacturing industries and the food and drink importing, distributive and catering trades.

The Food Safety Directorate is responsible for many aspects of food safety and quality. These include pesticide safety approval, biotechnology, meat hygiene, animal health and welfare, and related public health issues.

*Minister*, The Rt. Hon. William Waldegrave, MP
*Principal Private Secretary* (*G7*), A. T. Cahn
*Private Secretary*, Ms S. Rimmington
*Minister of State*, Michael Jack, MP (*Farming and Fisheries*)
*Private Secretary*, Miss R. J. Gower
*Parliamentary Private Secretary*, Miss E. Nicholson, MP
*Parliamentary Secretary* (*Lords*), The Earl Howe
(*Countryside*)
*Private Secretary*, J. E. T. Hughes
*Parliamentary Secretary*, Angela Browning, MP (*Food*)
*Private Secretary*, Mrs E. C. Ratcliffe
*Parliamentary Clerk*, Miss A. Evans
*Permanent Secretary* (*G1*), R. J. Packer
*Private Secretary*, T. J. Render

## ESTABLISHMENT DEPARTMENT
*Director of Establishments* (*G3*), D. H. Griffiths

ESTABLISHMENTS (GENERAL) AND OFFICE SERVICES DIVISION
Victory House, 30–34 Kingsway, London WC2B 6TU
Tel 0171-405 4310

*Head of Division* (*G6*), G. P. Hobrough

WELFARE BRANCH
Victory House, 30–34 Kingsway, London WC2B 6TU
Tel 0171-405 4310

*Chief Welfare Officer* (*SEO*), D. J. Jones

PERSONNEL MANAGEMENT AND DEVELOPMENT DIVISION
Victory House, 30–34 Kingsway, London WC2B 6TU
Tel 0171-405 4310

*Head of Division* (*G5*), G. P. McLachlan

DEPARTMENTAL HEALTH AND SAFETY UNIT
*Head of Unit* (*G7*), C. R. Braburn

†RELOCATION TEAM
*Head of Team* (*G7*), E. G. Bacon

†STAFF TRAINING BRANCH
*Principal* (*G7*), Miss E. M. Berthoud

BUILDING AND ESTATE MANAGEMENT
Eastbury House, 30–34 Albert Embankment, London SE1 7TL
Tel 0171-238 6000

*Head of Division* (*G5*), J. A. S. Nickson

## INFORMATION DIVISION
*Chief Information Officer* (*G5*), S. Dugdale
*Chief Press Officer* (*G7*), M. Smith
*Principal Librarian* (*G7*), P. McShane

## FINANCE DEPARTMENT
19–29 Woburn Place, London WC1H 0LU
Tel 0171-270 8080

*Principal Finance Officer* (*G3*), A. R. Cruickshank

FINANCIAL POLICY DIVISION
*Head of Division* (*G5*), P. P. Nash

FINANCIAL MANAGEMENT DIVISION
*Head of Division* (*G5*), Ms J. Allfrey
*Deputy Head of Financial Management* (*G6*), J. M. Lowi

AUDIT, CONSULTANCY AND MANAGEMENT SERVICES DIVISION
*Director of Audit* (*G5*), D. V. Fisher
*Deputy Director of Audit* (*G6*), D. J. Littler

MARKET TESTING AND PROCUREMENT ADVICE
Victory House, 30–34 Kingsway, London WC2B 6TU
Tel 0171-405 4310

*Director* (*G5*), D. B. Rabey

RESOURCE MANAGEMENT STRATEGY UNIT
Government Buildings, Epsom Road, Guildford, Surrey GU1 2LD
Tel 01483-68121

*Head of Division* (*G5*), J. D. Garnett

## LEGAL DEPARTMENT
55 Whitehall, London SW1A 2EY
Tel 0171-238 6000

*Legal Adviser and Solicitor* (*G2*), J. R. Woolman
*Principal Assistant Solicitors* (*G3*), B. T. Atwood; D. J. Pearson

LEGAL DIVISION A1
*Assistant Solicitor* (*G5*), L. Gunatilleke

LEGAL DIVISION A2
Whitehall Place, London SW1A 2HH
Tel 0171-238 6000

*Assistant Solicitor* (*G5*), Mrs C. A. Davis

†At Nobel/Ergon House, 17 Smith Square, London SW1P 3JR. Tel: 0171-238 6000

LEGAL DIVISION A3
*Assistant Solicitor (G5)*, Ms C. A. Crisham

LEGAL DIVISION A4
*Assistant Solicitor (G5)*, Miss E. A. Stephens

LEGAL DIVISION A5
*Assistant Solicitor (G5)*, P. D. Davis

LEGAL DIVISION A6
*Assistant Solicitor (G5)*, T. J. Middleton

LEGAL DIVISION B1
Whitehall Place, London SW1A 2HH
Tel 0171-238 6000
*Assistant Solicitor (G5)*, P. R. Hall

LEGAL DIVISION B2
*Assistant Solicitor (G4)*, Ms S. B. Spence

LEGAL DIVISION B3
*Assistant Solicitor (G5)*, A. I. Corbett

LEGAL DIVISION B4
*Assistant Solicitor (G5)*, Dr M. R. Parke

INVESTIGATION UNIT
*Chief Investigation Officer*, L. R. Blake

## AGRICULTURAL COMMODITIES, TRADE AND FOOD PRODUCTION
*Deputy Secretary (G2)*, D. A. Hadley, CB

### EUROPEAN COMMUNITY
*Under-Secretary (G3)*, P. W. Murphy

EUROPEAN COMMUNITY DIVISION I
*Head of Division (G5)*, A. J. Lebrecht

EUROPEAN COMMUNITY DIVISION II
*Head of Division (G6)*, L. G. Mitchell

### ARABLE CROPS
*Under-Secretary (G3)*, C. J. Barnes

CEREALS AND SET-ASIDE DIVISION
*Head of Division (G4)*, G. M. Trevelyan

SUGAR, TOBACCO, OILSEEDS AND PROTEINS DIVISION
*Head of Division (G5)*, Mrs A. M. Blackburn

†HORTICULTURE AND POTATOES DIVISION
*Head of Division (G5)*, R. A. Saunderson

### LIVESTOCK GROUP
*Under-Secretary (G3)*, G. A. Hollis

BEEF DIVISION
*Head of Division (G5)*, T. D. Rossington

SHEEP AND BEEF QUOTA UNIT
*Head of Unit (G7)*, N. M. M. Cleary

SHEEP AND LIVESTOCK SUBSIDIES DIVISION
*Head of Division (G5)*, J. R. Cowan

PIGS, EGGS AND POULTRY DIVISION
*Head of Division (G5)*, G. W. Noble

MILK AND MILK PRODUCTS
*Head of Division (G5)*, B. J. Harding

### FOOD, DRINK AND MARKETING POLICY
*Under-Secretary (G3)*, J. W. Hepburn

MILK MARKETING AND LEGISLATION DIVISION
*Head of Division (G5)*, P. Elliott

FOOD INDUSTRY, MARKETING AND COMPETITION POLICY DIVISION
*Head of Division (G5)*, R. E. Melville

EXTERNAL RELATIONS AND TRADE PROMOTION DIVISION
*Head of Division (G5)*, D. V. Orchard

TRADE POLICY AND TROPICAL FOODS
*Head of Division (G5)*, Miss S. E. Brown

†MARKET TASK FORCE
*Head of Division (G5)*, H. B. Brown

†ALCOHOLIC DRINKS DIVISION
*Head of Division (G5)*, P. M. Boyling

## FOOD SAFETY
*Deputy Secretary (G2)*, C. W. Capstick, CB, CMG

### †FOOD SAFETY GROUP
*Under-Secretary (G3)*, B. H. B. Dickinson
*Chief Scientist (Fisheries and Food) (G3)*,
   Dr W. H. B. Denner

CHEMICAL SAFETY OF FOOD DIVISION
*Head of Division (G5)*, R. C. McKinley

CONSUMER PROTECTION DIVISION
*Head of Division (G5)*, C. A. Cockbill

MICROBIOLOGICAL SAFETY OF FOOD DIVISION
*Head of Division (G5)*, Mrs A. M. Pickering

FOOD SCIENCE DIVISION I
*Head of Division (G5)*, Dr J. C. Sherlock

FOOD SCIENCE DIVISION II
*Head of Division (G5)*, Dr J. R. Bell

### †CHIEF SCIENTIST'S GROUP (FOOD)
*Head of Division (G6)*, Dr D. G. Lindsay

### AGRICULTURAL INPUTS, PLANT PROTECTION AND EMERGENCIES
*Under-Secretary (G3)*, R. C. Lowson

EMERGENCIES AND FOOD PROTECTION
*Head of Division (G5)*, Dr J. R. Park

PLANT HEALTH DIVISION
*Head of Division (G5)*, A. J. Perrins

PLANT VARIETY, RIGHTS OFFICE AND SEEDS DIVISION
White House Lane, Huntingdon Road, Cambridge CB3 0LF
Tel 01223-277151
*Head of Division (G5)*, D. A. Boreham

†AGRICULTURAL RESOURCES POLICY DIVISION
*Head of Division (G5)*, A. R. Burne

## ANIMAL HEALTH AND VETERINARY GROUP
Government Buildings, Hook Rise South, Tolworth,
Surbiton, Surrey KT6 7NF
Tel 0181-330 4411
*Under-Secretary (G3)*, M. T. Haddon
*Chief Veterinary Officer (G3)*, K. C. Meldrum

ANIMAL HEALTH (ZOONOSES) DIVISION
*Head of Division (G5)*, R. J. G. Cawthorne

ANIMAL HEALTH (DISEASE CONTROL) DIVISION
*Head of Division (G5)*, T. E. D. Eddy

ANIMAL HEALTH (INTERNATIONAL TRADE) DIVISION
*Head of Division (G5)*, R. A. Bell

MEAT HYGIENE DIVISION
*Head of Division (G5)*, Mrs K. J. A. Brown

RESOURCE MANAGEMENT DIVISION
*Head of Division (G6)*, R. A. Gregg

ANIMAL WELFARE DIVISION
Tolworth Tower, Surbiton, Surrey KT6 7DX
Tel 0181-330 4411
*Head of Division (G5)*, C. J. Ryder

STATE VETERINARY SERVICE
Government Buildings, Hook Rise South, Tolworth,
Surbiton, Surrey KT15 3NB
Tel 0181-330 4411

*Director of Veterinary Field Services (G3)*, I. Crawford

LASSWADE VETERINARY LABORATORY
East of Scotland College of Agriculture, The Bush Estate,
Penicuik, Midlothian EH26 0SA
Tel 0131-445 5371
*Head of Laboratory (G6)*, Miss G. Mackenzie

COUNTRYSIDE, MARINE
ENVIRONMENT AND FISHERIES
*Deputy Secretary (G2)*, C. R. Cann

LAND USE, CONSERVATION AND
COUNTRYSIDE
†*Under-Secretary (G3)*, vacant

†COUNTRYSIDE DIVISION
*Head of Division (G5)*, R. C. McIvor

†LAND USE AND TENURE DIVISION
*Head of Division (G5)*, T. J. Osmond

†CONSERVATION POLICY DIVISION
*Head of Division (G5)*, J. E. Robbs

†ENVIRONMENTALLY-SENSITIVE AREAS
*Head of Division (G5)*, C. R. Bodrell

†LAND USE PLANNING UNIT
*Head of Division (G5)*, J. R. Mathias

†FISHERIES DEPARTMENT
*Fisheries Secretary (G3)*, S. Wentworth

FISHERIES DIVISION I
*Head of Division (G5)*, I. C. Redfern

FISHERIES DIVISION II
*Head of Division (G5)*, P. A. Cocking

FISHERIES DIVISION III
*Head of Division (G5)*, R. S. Thomas

FISHERIES DIVISION IV
*Head of Division (G6)*, B. S. Edwards

SEA FISHERIES INSPECTORATE
*Chief Inspector (G6)*, M. G. Jennings

FISHERIES RESEARCH
Pakefield Road, Lowestoft, Suffolk NR33 0HT
Tel 01502-562244

*Director of Fisheries Research and Development for Great
Britain (G4)*, D. J. Garrod, PH.D.

*Deputy Directors of Fisheries Research (G5)*, P. W. Greig-
Smith; J. W. Horwood

FISHERIES LABORATORY
Pakefield Road, Lowestoft, Suffolk NR33 0HT
Tel 01502-562244

FISHERIES LABORATORY
Remembrance Avenue, Burnham-on-Crouch, Essex
CM0 8HA
Tel 01621-782658

FISHERIES EXPERIMENT STATION
Benarth Road, Conwy, Gwynedd LL32 8UB
Tel 01492-593883

FISH DISEASES LABORATORY
33–33A Albany Road, Granby Industrial Estate,
Weymouth, Dorset DT4 9TU
Tel 01305-772137
*Officer-in-Charge (Principal Scientific Officer) (G6)*,
B. J. Hill, PH.D.

ENVIRONMENT POLICY
*Under-Secretary (G3)*, M. Madden

†ENVIRONMENTAL PROTECTION DIVISION
*Head of Division (G5)*, D. L. Dawson

†MARINE ENVIRONMENTAL PROTECTION DIVISION
*Head of Division (G5)*, G. F. Meekings

†SALMON WHALING AND INLAND FISHERIES
*Head of Division (G5)*, C. I. Llewelyn

FLOOD AND COASTAL DEFENCE DIVISION
Eastbury House, 30–34 Albert Embankment, London
SE1 7TL
Tel 0171-238 3000

*Head of Division (G5)*, R. A. Hathaway

ECONOMICS AND STATISTICS
*Under-Secretary (G3)*, R. E. Mordue

ECONOMICS (FARM BUSINESS) DIVISION
*Senior Economic Adviser (G5)*, J. P. Muriel

ECONOMICS (INTERNATIONAL) DIVISION
*Senior Economic Adviser (G5)*, Dr J. M. Slater

ECONOMICS (RESOURCE USE) DIVISION
*Senior Economic Adviser (G5)*, R. W. Irving

ECONOMICS AND STATISTICS (FOOD)
*Senior Economic Adviser (G4)*, Dr P. J. Lund

†STATISTICS (AGRICULTURAL COMMODITIES) DIVISION
*Chief Statistician (G5)*, D. Wallage

STATISTICS (CENSUS AND PRICES) DIVISION
Government Buildings, Epsom Road, Guildford,
Surrey GU1 2LD
Tel 01483-68121

*Chief Statistician (G5)*, P. F. Helm

†CHIEF SCIENTIFIC ADVISER
*Chief Scientific Adviser (G2)*, P. J. Bunyan, D.SC., PH.D.
*Chief Scientist (Agriculture) (G3)*, D. W. F. Shannon, PH.D.
*Assistant Chief Scientist (Agriculture) (G5)*, Dr M. Parker
*Scientific Liaison Officer (Fisheries) (G6)*, Dr J. Lock

RESEARCH POLICY CO-ORDINATION DIVISION
*Head of Division (G5)*, J. Suich

---

†At Nobel/Ergon House, 17 Smith Square, London SW1P 3JR. Tel:
0171-238 6000

REGIONAL ORGANIZATION
†*Director of Regional Administration (G3)*, D. J. Coates

AGENCIES AND CITIZEN'S CHARTER DIVISION
*Head of Divison (G5)*, D. P. Hunter

REGIONAL SERVICES DIVISION
†*Head of Division (G5)*, Miss V. A. Smith

REGIONAL SERVICE CENTRES
ANGLIA REGION, Block B, Government Buildings, Brooklands Avenue, Cambridge CB2 2DR. Tel: 01223-462727. *Regional Director (G5)*, Miss C. J. Rabagliati
EAST MIDLANDS REGION, Government Buildings, Block 7, Chalfont Drive, Nottingham NG8 3SN. Tel: 0115-929 1191. *Regional Director (G5)*, M. J. Finnigan
NORTH-EAST REGION, Government Buildings, Crosby Road, Northallerton, N. Yorks. DL6 1AD. Tel: 01609-773751. *Regional Director (G6)*, P. Watson
NORTHERN REGION, Eden Bridge House, Lowther Street, Carlisle, Cumbria CA3 8DX. Tel: 01228-23400. *Regional Director (G5)*, D. E. Jones
NORTH MERCIA REGION, Berkeley Towers, Nantwich Road, Crewe, Cheshire CW2 6PT. Tel: 01270-69211. *Regional Director (G6)*, R. Bettley-Smith
SOUTH-EAST REGION, Block A, Government Buildings, Coley Park, Reading, Berks. RG1 6DT. Tel: 01734-581222. *Regional Director (G5)*, R. Anderson
SOUTH MERCIA REGION, Block C, Government Buildings, Whittington Road, Worcester WR5 2LQ. Tel: 01905-763355. *Regional Director (G6)*, P. G. Gething
SOUTH-WEST REGION, Government Buildings, Alphington Road, Exeter EX2 8NQ. Tel: 01392-77951. *Regional Director (G6)*, M. R. W. Highman
WESSEX REGION, Block 3, Government Buildings, Burghill Road, Westbury-on-Trym, Bristol BS10 6NJ. Tel: 01272-591000. *Regional Director (G6)*, Mrs A. J. L. Ould

INFORMATION TECHNOLOGY DIRECTORATE
Government Buildings, Epsom Road, Guildford, Surrey GU1 2LD
Tel 01483-68121
*Director (G4)*, D. Selwood
*Assistant Directors (G5)*, A. G. Matthews; D. J. Dunthorne; *(G6)*, D. D. Brown; R. F. Syrett

EXECUTIVE AGENCIES

CENTRAL VETERINARY LABORATORY
Woodham Lane, New Haw, Addlestone, Surrey KT15 3NB
Tel 01932-341111
The Central Veterinary Laboratory provides scientific and technical expertise in animal and public health.
*Director and Chief Executive (G3)*, Dr T. W. A. Little
*Director of Research (G4)*, Dr J. A. Morris
*Director of Operations (G5)*, R. W. Saunders
*Director of Business (G5)*, vacant

VETERINARY MEDICINES DIRECTORATE
Woodham Lane, New Haw, Addlestone, Surrey KT15 3NB
Tel 01932-336911
The Veterinary Medicines Directorate is responsible for all aspects of licensing and control of animal medicines, including the protection of the consumer from hazardous or unacceptable residues.
*Chief Executive and Director of Veterinary Medicines (G4)*, Dr J. M. Rutter
*Director (Policy and Finance) (G5)*, C. J. Lawson
*Director (Licensing) (G5)*, Dr K. N. Woodward
*Licensing Manager, Pharmaceuticals and Feed Additives (G6)*, J. P. O'Brien

*Licensing Manager, Immunologicals and Suspected Adverse Reactions (SARS) (G6)*, Dr A. M. T. Lee

CENTRAL SCIENCE LABORATORY
London Road, Slough, Berks. SL3 7HJ
Tel 01753-534626
The Central Science Laboratory was enlarged in April 1994 by merging with the Food Science Laboratory, Norwich and the Torry Research Station, Aberdeen. The agency provides MAFF with technical support and policy advice on the protection and quality of the food supply and on related environmental issues.
*Chief Executive (G3)*, Dr P. I. Stanley
*Research Director (G5)*, Dr A. R. Hardy
*Head of Food Science Laboratory (G5)*, Dr J. Gilbert, Norwich Research Park, Colney Lane, Norwich NR4 7UQ. Tel: 01603-259350
*Director, Torry Research Station (G5)*, K. Whittle, PH.D., PO Box 31, 135 Abbey Road, Aberdeen AB9 8DG. Tel: 01224-877071

AGRICULTURAL DEVELOPMENT AND ADVISORY SERVICE (ADAS)
ADAS Headquarters, Oxford Spires Business Park, The Boulevard, Kidlington, Oxon. OX5 1NZ
Tel 01865-842742
The Agricultural Development and Advisory Service (ADAS) provides a comprehensive range of consultancy services to the land-based industries. It also carries out research, performs certain statutory functions and provides advice on policy for MAFF and the Welsh Office.
*Chief Executive (G2)*, Dr J. Walsh
*Director of Operations (G3)*, P. Needham
*Research Director (G4)*, Dr A. D. Hughes
*Marketing Director (G5)*, D. N. Hall
*Finance Director (G5)*, Dr C. Herring
*Personnel Director (G5)*, Ms S. Nason
*Director for Wales (G5)*, W. I. C. Davies
*Non-Executive Directors*, C. Bystram (*Chairman*); P. Christensen, CBE

PESTICIDES SAFETY DIRECTORATE
Mallard House, King's Pool, 3 Peasholme Green, York YO1 2PX
Tel 01904-640500
The Pesticides Safety Directorate is responsible for the evaluation and approval of pesticides and the development of policies relating to them, in order to protect consumers, users and the environment.
*Chief Executive (G4)*, G. K. Bruce
*Director (Policy) (G5)*, J. A. Bainton
*Director (Approvals) (G5)*, Dr A. D. Martin

MEAT HYGIENE SERVICE
This executive agency is to be launched in April 1995 and will be responsible for the fresh meat hygiene enforcement arrangements currently carried out by local authorities.
*Chief Executive-designate (G4)*, J. McNeill

INTERVENTION BOARD
— see page 324

COLLEGE OF ARMS OR HERALDS COLLEGE
Queen Victoria Street, London EC4V 4BT
Tel 0171-248 2762

The Sovereign's Officers of Arms (Kings, Heralds and Pursuivants of Arms) were first incorporated by Richard III.

The powers vested by the Crown in the Earl Marshal (the Duke of Norfolk) with regard to state ceremonial are largely exercised through the College. The College is also the official repository of the arms and pedigrees of English, Northern Irish and Commonwealth (except Canadian) families and their descendants, and its records include official copies of the records of Ulster King of Arms, the originals of which remain in Dublin. The 13 officers of the College specialize in genealogical and heraldic work for their respective clients.

Arms have been and still are granted by letters patent from the Kings of Arms. A right to arms can only be established by the registration in the official records of the College of Arms of a pedigree showing direct male line descent from an ancestor already appearing therein as being entitled to arms, or by making application through the College of Arms for a grant of arms.

The College of Arms is open Monday–Friday 10–4, when an Officer of Arms is in attendance to deal with enquiries by the public, though such enquiries may also be directed to any of the Officers of Arms, either personally or by letter.

*Earl Marshal*, His Grace the Duke of Norfolk, KG, GCVO, CB, CBE, MC

KINGS OF ARMS
*Garter*, Sir Conrad Swan, KCVO, Ph.D., FSA
*Clarenceux*, Sir Anthony Wagner, KCB, KCVO, FSA
*Norroy and Ulster*, J. P. B. Brooke-Little, CVO, FSA

HERALDS
*Chester (and Registrar)*, D. H. B. Chesshyre, LVO, FSA
*Windsor*, T. D. Mathew
*Lancaster*, P. L. Gwynn-Jones, LVO
*Somerset*, T. Woodcock, FSA
*Richmond*, P. L. Dickinson
*York*, H. E. Paston-Bedingfeld

*Earl Marshal's Secretary*, Sir Walter Verco, KCVO, Surrey Herald Extraordinary

PURSUIVANTS
*Rouge Dragon*, T. H. S. Duke
*Bluemantle*, R. J. B. Noel
*Portcullis*, W. G. Hunt, TD
*Rouge Croix*, vacant

## COURT OF THE LORD LYON
HM New Register House, Edinburgh EH1 3YT
Tel 0131-556 7255

The Court of the Lord Lyon is the Scottish Court of Chivalry (including the genealogical jurisdiction of the *Ri-Sennachie* of Scotland's Celtic Kings). The Lord Lyon King of Arms has jurisdiction, subject to appeal to the Court of Session and the House of Lords, in questions of heraldry and the right to bear arms. The Court also administers the Scottish Public Register of All Arms and Bearings and the Public Register of All Genealogies. Pedigrees are established by decrees of Lyon Court and by letters patent. As Royal Commissioner in Armory, the Lord Lyon grants patents of arms (which constitute the grantee and heirs noble in the Noblesse of Scotland) to 'virtuous and well-deserving' Scotsmen and to petitioners (personal or corporate) in Her Majesty's overseas realms of Scottish connection, and issues birthbrieves.
*Lord Lyon King of Arms*, Sir Malcolm Innes of Edingight, KCVO, WS, FSA Scot

HERALDS
*Albany*, J. A. Spens, RD, WS
*Rothesay*, Sir Crispin Agnew of Lochnaw, Bt.
*Ross*, C. J. Burnett, FSA Scot

PURSUIVANTS
*Kintyre*, J. C. G. George, FSA Scot
*Unicorn*, Alastair Campbell of Airds, FSA Scot
*Carrick*, Mrs C. G. W. Roads, MVO, FSA Scot

*Lyon Clerk and Keeper of Records*, Mrs C. G. W. Roads, MVO, FSA Scot
*Procurator-Fiscal*, D. F. Murby, WS
*Herald Painter*, Mrs J. Phillips
*Macer*, A. M. Clark

## ARTS COUNCILS

The Arts Council of Great Britain was established as an independent body in 1946 to be the principal channel for the Government's support of the arts. In April 1994 the Scottish and Welsh Arts Councils became autonomous and the Arts Council of Great Britain became the Arts Council of England.

## ARTS COUNCIL OF ENGLAND
14 Great Peter Street, London SW1P 3NQ
Tel 0171-333 0100

The Arts Council of England funds the major arts organizations in England and the ten Regional Arts Boards. It works closely with the Scottish Arts Council and the Arts Council of Wales. It will also be responsible for distributing funds raised by the National Lottery to the arts, crafts and film.

The Council also provides advice, information and help to artists, arts organizations and the general public. In common with the other Arts Councils, its objectives are to develop and improve the understanding and practice of the arts and to increase their accessibility to the public.

The Council distributes an annual grant from the Department of National Heritage; the grant for 1994–5 is £186 million.
*Chairman*, The Lord Gowrie
*Vice-Chairman*, Sir Richard Rogers
*Secretary-General*, Ms M. Allen

REGIONAL ARTS BOARDS
EASTERN ARTS BOARD, Cherry Hinton Hall, Cherry Hinton Road, Cambridge CB1 4DW. Tel: 01223-215355. *Chair*, Dr D. Harrison
EAST MIDLANDS ARTS BOARD, Mountfields House, Forest Road, Loughborough, Leics. LE11 3HU. Tel: 01509-218292. *Chair*, M. Hutchinson
LONDON ARTS BOARD, Elme House, 133 Long Acre, London WC2E 9AF. Tel: 0171-240 1313. *Chair*, C. Priestley
NORTHERN ARTS BOARD, 9–10 Osborne Terrace, Newcastle upon Tyne NE2 1NZ. Tel: 0191-281 6334. *Chair*, Mrs S. Robinson
NORTH-WEST ARTS BOARD, 12 Harter Street, Manchester M1 6HY. Tel: 0161-228 3062. *Chair*, Prof. B. Cox
SOUTH-EAST ARTS BOARD, 10 Mount Ephraim, Tunbridge Wells, Kent TN4 8AS. Tel: 01892-515210. *Chair*, B. Nicholson
SOUTHERN ARTS BOARD, 13 St Clement Street, Winchester SO23 9DQ. Tel: 01962-855099. *Chair*, D. Reid
SOUTH-WEST ARTS BOARD, Bradninch Place, Gandy Street, Exeter EX4 3LS. Tel: 01392-218188. *Chair*, Ms M. Guillebaud

WEST MIDLANDS ARTS BOARD, 82 Granville Street, Birmingham B1 2LH. Tel: 0121-631 3121. *Chair*, R. Southgate

YORKSHIRE AND HUMBERSIDE ARTS BOARD, 21 Bond Street, Dewsbury, W. Yorks. WF13 1AX. Tel: 01924-455555. *Chair*, Sir Ernest Hall

## SCOTTISH ARTS COUNCIL
12 Manor Place, Edinburgh EH3 7DD
Tel 0131-226 6051

The Scottish Arts Council funds arts organizations in Scotland and is funded directly by the Scottish Office. The grant for 1994–5 is £23.77 million.
*Chairman*, W. Brown

## ARTS COUNCIL OF WALES
Museum Place, Cardiff CF1 3NX
Tel 01222-394 711

The Arts Council of Wales funds arts organizations in Wales and is funded directly by the Welsh Office. The grant for 1994–5 is £13.54 million.
*Chairman*, Sir Richard Lloyd Jones, KCB

## ARTS COUNCIL OF NORTHERN IRELAND
185 Stranmillis Road, Belfast BT9 5DU
Tel 01232-381591

The Arts Council of Northern Ireland disburses government funds in support of the arts in Northern Ireland. It is funded by the Department of Education for Northern Ireland, and the grant for 1994–5 is £6.45 million.
*Chairman*, D. Deeny, QC

---

# ART GALLERIES, ETC

---

## ROYAL FINE ART COMMISSION
7 St James's Square, London SW1Y 4JU
Tel 0171-839 6537

Established in 1924, the Commission is an autonomous authority on the aesthetic implications of any project or development, primarily but not exclusively architectural, which affects the visual environment.
*Chairman*, The Lord St John of Fawsley, PC
*Commissioners*, Prof. R. D. Carter, CBE; Sir Philip Dowson, CBE, PRA; M. Girouard, ph.D.; The Duke of Grafton, KG, FSA; D. Hamilton Fraser, RA; M. J. Hopkins, CBE, RA; S. A. Lipton; R. MacCormac; Prof. M. MacKeith, ph.D.; H. T. Moggridge, OBE; Mrs J. Nutting; T. Osborne; Sir Philip Powell, CH, OBE, RA; Prof. J. R. Steer, FSA; J. Sutherland; Miss W. Taylor, CBE; Q. Terry; Sir William Whitfield, CBE; J. Winter, MBE; Dr G. Worsley
*Secretary (G6)*, S. Cantacuzino, CBE

## ROYAL FINE ART COMMISSION FOR SCOTLAND
9 Atholl Crescent, Edinburgh EH3 8HA
Tel 0131-229 1109

The Commission was established in 1927 and advises ministers and local authorities on the visual impact and quality of design of construction projects. It is an independent body and gives its opinions impartially.

*Chairman*, The Hon. Lord Prosser
*Commissioners*, Prof. G. Benson; Miss K. Borland; W. A. Cadell; Mrs K. Dalyell; Dr Deborah Howard, ph.D., FSA, FSA scot.; A. S. Matheson, FRIBA; G. Ogilvie-Laing; Prof. T. Ridley, FRSE; R. R. Steedman, RSA; Prof. R. Webster; R. Wedgwood
*Secretary*, C. Prosser

## NATIONAL GALLERY
Trafalgar Square, London WC2N 5DN
Tel 0171-839 3321

The National Gallery, which houses an outstanding permanent collection of Western painting since the 13th century, was founded in 1824, following a parliamentary grant of £60,000 for the purchase and exhibition of the Angerstein collection of pictures. The present site was first occupied in 1838; a substantial extension to the north of the building with a public entrance in Orange Street was opened in 1975, and the Sainsbury wing was opened in 1991. Total government grant-in-aid for 1994–5 is £18.18 million.

BOARD OF TRUSTEES
*Chairman*, N. H. Baring
*Trustees*, B. Gascoigne, FRSL; P. Troughton; The Countess of Airlie, CVO; Sir Derek Oulton, GCB, QC; E. Uglow; Sir Keith Thomas, FBA; The Hon. Simon Sainsbury; Lady Bingham; Sir Mark Richmond, sc.D.; FRS; A. Bennett; Mrs E. Monck

OFFICERS
*Director (G3)*, R. N. MacGregor
*Chief Curator (G5)*, Dr C. P. H. Brown
*Senior Curators (G6)*, Dr N. Penny; *(G7)*, Dr S. Foister; Dr D. Gordon; J. Leighton
*Chief Restorer (G5)*, M. H. Wyld
*Head of Exhibitions (G5)*, M. J. Wilson
*Scientific Adviser (G6)*, Dr A. Roy
*Director of Administration (G5)*, J. MacAuslan
*Head of Finance and Personnel (G5)*, T. Tarkowski
*Head of Press and Public Relations (G7)*, Miss J. Liddiard

## NATIONAL PORTRAIT GALLERY
St Martin's Place, London WC2H 0HE
Tel 0171-306 0055

A grant was made in 1856 to form a gallery of the portraits of the most eminent persons in British history. The present building was opened in 1896, an extension being opened in 1933. There are four outstations displaying portraits in appropriate settings: Montacute House, Gawthorpe Hall, Beningbrough Hall and Bodelwyddan Castle. Total government grant-in-aid for 1994–5 is £3.935 million.

BOARD OF TRUSTEES
*Chairman*, H. Keswick
*Trustees*, The Lord President of the Council (ex officio); The President of the Royal Academy of Arts (ex officio); Sir Oliver Millar, GCVO, FBA, FSA; J. Roberts, D.Phil.; The Lord Morris of Castle Morris, D.Phil.; Prof. N. Lynton; The Lord Weidenfeld; Sir Eduardo Paolozzi; J. Tusa; Sir Antony Acland, GCMG, GCVO; Mrs J. E. Benson, LVO, OBE; Mrs W. Tumim; Sir David Scholey, CBE; Mrs C. Tomalin; Baroness Willoughby de Eresby

*Director (G3)*, C. Saumarez-Smith, ph.D.

## TATE GALLERY
Millbank, London SW1P 4RG
Tel 0171-887 8000

The Tate Gallery comprises the national collections of British painting and 20th-century painting and sculpture. The

Gallery was opened in 1897, the cost of erection (£80,000) being defrayed by Sir Henry Tate, who also contributed the nucleus of the present collection. The Turner wing was opened in 1910, galleries to contain the collection of modern foreign painting in 1926, and a new sculpture hall in 1937. In 1979 a further extension was built, and the Clore Gallery, for the Turner Collection, was opened in 1987. The Tate Gallery Liverpool opened in 1988 and the Tate Gallery St Ives in June 1993. Total government grant-in-aid for 1994–5 is £17.2 million.

BOARD OF TRUSTEES
*Chairman*, D. Stevenson, CBE
*Trustees*, The Countess of Airlie, CVO; The Lord
   Attenborough, CBE; The Hon. Mrs J. de Botton; Sir
   Richard Carew Pole; M. Craig-Martin; R. Deacon;
   B. Gascoigne, FRSL; D. Gordon; C. Le Brun; Mrs
   P. Ridley; D. Verey

OFFICERS
*Director (G3)*, N. Serota
*Director of Public and Regional Services (G5)*, S. Nairne
*Keeper of the British Collection (G5)*, A. Wilton
*Keeper of the Modern Collection (G5)*, R. Morphet
*Curator, Tate Gallery Liverpool (G6)*, L. Biggs
*Curator, Tate Gallery St Ives (G6)*, M. Tooby

WALLACE COLLECTION
Hertford House, Manchester Square, London W1M 6BN
Tel 0171-935 0687

The Wallace Collection was bequeathed to the nation by the widow of Sir Richard Wallace, Bt. in 1897, and Hertford House was subsequently acquired by the Government. Total government grant-in-aid for 1994–5 is £1.958 million.
*Director*, Miss R. J. Savill
*Head of Administration*, A. W. Houldershaw

NATIONAL GALLERIES OF SCOTLAND
The Mound, Edinburgh EH2 2EL
Tel 0131-556 8921

The National Galleries of Scotland comprise the National Gallery of Scotland, the Scottish National Portrait Gallery and the Scottish National Gallery of Modern Art. There is also an outstation at Paxton House, Berwickshire, and another at Duff House, Banffshire, is due to open in 1995. Total government grant-in-aid for 1994–5 is £8.247 million.

TRUSTEES
*Chairman of the Trustees*, A. M. Grossart, CBE
*Trustees*, J. Packer, OBE; A. R. Cole-Hamilton; Mrs
   L. W. Gibbs; Lord Macfarlane of Bearsden; Dr
   T. Johnston; Prof. A. A. Tait; E. Hagman;
   Prof. E. Fernie; M. Shea

OFFICERS
*Director (G4)*, T. Clifford
*Keeper of Conservation (G6)*, J. P. Dick
*Keeper of Information (G7)*, Miss L. S. Callander
*Keeper of Education (G7)*, M. Cassin
*Registrar (G7)*, Miss A. Buddle
*Secretary (G6)*, Ms S. Edwards
*Buildings (G7)*, vacant
*Keeper, National Gallery of Scotland (G6)*, M. Clarke
*Keeper, Scottish National Portrait Gallery (G6)*,
   D. Thomson, PH.D.
   *Curator of Photography*, Miss S. F. Stevenson
*Keeper, Scottish National Gallery of Modern Art (G6)*,
   R. Calvocoressi

UNITED KINGDOM ATOMIC ENERGY
AUTHORITY (AEA TECHNOLOGY)
Harwell, Oxfordshire OX11 0RA
Tel 01235-821111

The UKAEA was established by the Atomic Energy Authority Act 1954. Since April 1986 the UKAEA has been required by the Government to operate on a commercial footing and in 1990 it adopted the trading name AEA Technology. It provides scientific and technical services, products and consultancy in nuclear and non-nuclear fields to governments, utilities and industries world-wide. The UKAEA has six research and engineering centres. Many of the technical staff and activities of the Warren Spring Laboratory merged with the environmental capabilities of AEA Technology in 1994 to create the National Environmental Technology Centre based within AEA Technology. The Government announced in February 1994 its intention to privatize the commercial activities of the AEA.
*Chairman (part-time)*, Sir Anthony Cleaver
*Deputy Chairman and Chief Executive*, Dr B. L. Eyre, CBE
*Members (part-time)*, Prof. Sir Peter Hirsch, FRS; J. Bullock;
   R. Sanderson, OBE; Mrs S. Shirley, OBE; Prof. M. Brady
*Secretary*, J. R. Bretherton
*Executive Director, Finance*, P. G. Daffern
*Managing Director, Services Division*, A. W. Hills
*Executive Director, Operations, AEA Technology*, Dr
   R. S. Nelson
*Chief Executive, UKAEA Government Division*, Dr
   D. Pooley

AUDIT COMMISSION FOR LOCAL
AUTHORITIES AND THE NATIONAL HEALTH
SERVICE IN ENGLAND AND WALES
1 Vincent Square, London SW1P 2PN
Tel 0171-828 1212

The Audit Commission was set up in 1983 with responsibility for the external audit of local authorities. This remit was extended from 1990 to include the audit of the National Health Service bodies in England and Wales. The Commission appoints the auditors, who may be from the District Audit Service or from a private firm of accountants. The Commission is also responsible for promoting value for money in the services provided by local authorities and health bodies.
   The Commission has 15–17 members appointed by the Secretary of State for the Environment in consultation with the Secretaries of State for Wales and for Health. Though appointed by the Secretary of State, the Commissioners are responsible to Parliament.
*Chairman*, Sir David Cooksey
*Deputy Chairman*, C. M. Stuart
*Controller of Audit*, A. Foster
*Chief Executive of District Audit Service*, D. Prince

COMMISSION FOR LOCAL AUTHORITY
ACCOUNTS IN SCOTLAND
18 George Street, Edinburgh EH2 2QU
Tel 0131-226 7346

The Commission was set up in 1975. It is responsible for securing the audit of the accounts of Scottish local authorities and certain joint boards and joint committees. Amongst its duties the Commission is required to deal with reports made by the Controller of Audit on items of account contrary to law; on incorrect accounting; and on losses due to misconduct, negligence and failure to carry out statutory duties. Since 1988 the Commission has had responsibility for value-for-money audits of authorities.

Members are appointed by the Secretary of State for Scotland.

*Chairman*, Prof. J. P. Percy
*Controller of Audit*, J. Broadfoot
*Secretary*, J. Ritchie

---

## THE BANK OF ENGLAND
Threadneedle Street, London EC2R 8AH
Tel 0171-601 4444

---

The Bank of England was incorporated in 1694 under royal charter. It is the banker of the Government, on whose behalf it executes monetary policy and manages the note issue and the national debt. It is also responsible for promoting the efficiency and competitiveness of financial services. As the central reserve bank of the country, the Bank keeps the accounts of British banks, who maintain with it a proportion of their cash resources, and of most overseas central banks. The Bank was reorganized in July 1994 and is now divided into two divisions, Monetary Stability and Financial Stability. (*See also* page 614).
*Governor*, E. A. J. George
*Deputy Governor*, R. L. Pennant-Rea
*Directors*, Sir David Cooksey; Sir Colin Corness; Mrs F. A. Heaton; Sir Christopher Hogg; Sir Martin Jacomb; P. H. Kent; Sir John Keswick; M. A. King; Sir David Lees; Ms S. V. Masters; Sir Christopher Morse, KCMG; I. Plenderleith; B. Quinn; Sir David Scholey, CBE, FRSA; Prof. Sir Roland Smith; Sir Colin Southgate
*Associate Director*, H. C. E. Harris
*Advisers to the Governor*, Sir Peter Petrie; P. C. Peddie; I. G. Watt
*Chief Cashier and Deputy Director, Banking and Market Services*, G. E. A. Kentfield
*Chief Registrar*, D. A. Bridger
*General Manager, Printing Works*, A. W. Jarvis
*Secretary*, J. R. E. Footman
*The Auditor*, M. J. W. Phillips

---

## BIOTECHNOLOGY AND BIOLOGICAL SCIENCES RESEARCH COUNCIL
Polaris House, North Star Avenue, Swindon, Wilts. SN2 1UH
Tel 01793-413200

---

The Biotechnology and Biological Sciences Research Council (BBSRC) was established in April 1994 and incorporates the work of the former Agricultural and Food Research Council and the Biotechnology Directorate and Biological Sciences Committee of the former Science and Engineering Research Council. It is an independent body funded by the Office of Science and Technology. Its aims are to promote and support research and postgraduate training relating to the under-standing and exploitation of biological systems; to advance knowledge and technology, and provide trained scientists and engineers to meet the needs of biotechnological-related industries; and to provide advice, disseminate knowledge, and promote public understanding in the fields of biotech-nology and the biological sciences. It liaises with the Scottish

Office Agriculture and Fisheries Department on research in the Scottish Agricultural and Biological Research Institutes. Government funding for 1994–5 is £171.8 million.
*Chairman*, Sir Alistair Grant
*Deputy Chairman and Chief Executive*, Prof. T. L. Blundell, FRS
*Members*, Prof. J. E. Baldwin, FRS; Dr P. J. Bunyan; Dr E. C. Dart; Prof. P. Dunnill, F.Eng.; Dr E. Finer; Prof. Sir Brian Follett, FRS; A. B. N. Gill; Dr K. W. Humphreys, CBE; Prof. S. D. Iversen; Prof. Rachel Leech; Dr T. Little; K. J. MacKenzie; Prof. Lady Noreen Murray, FRS; Dr B. M. Richards, CBE
*Deputy Chief Executive and Director of Administration (G3)*, B. G. Jamieson, PH.D.
*Heads of Groups (G5)*, S. H. Visscher (*Finance*); R. J. Price (*Human Resources*); Dr A. V. Harrison; (*Science and Technology 1*); Dr J. N. Wingfield (*Science and Technology 2*); Dr D. Yarrow (*Science and Technology 3*)

COMPUTING DIVISION
West Common, Harpenden, Herts. AL5 2JE
Tel 01582-762271
*Head of Division*, A. Windram

For institutes and units of the Biotechnology and Biological Sciences Research Council, *see* page 707

---

## BOUNDARY COMMISSIONS

---

The Commissions are constituted under the Parliamentary Constituencies Act 1986. The Speaker of the House of Commons is ex-officio chairman of all four commissions in the United Kingdom. Each of the four commissions is required by law to keep the parliamentary constituencies in their part of the United Kingdom under review. A review started after the 1992 General Election is due to be completed by the end of 1994; the final proposals must then receive parliamentary approval. Each of the three commissions in Great Britain is required by law to keep the European parliamentary constituencies in their part of Great Britain under review.

ENGLAND
St Catherine's House, 10 Kingsway, London WC2B 6JP
Tel 0171-242 0262
*Deputy Chairman*, The Hon. Mr Justice Knox
*Joint Secretaries*, R. McLeod; Mrs J. S. Morris

WALES
St Catherine's House, 10 Kingsway, London WC2B 6JP
Tel 0171-242 0262
*Deputy Chairman*, The Hon. Mr Justice Pill
*Joint Secretaries*, R. McLeod; Mrs J. S. Morris

SCOTLAND
St Andrew's House, Edinburgh EH1 3DG
Tel 0131-244 2196/3582
*Deputy Chairman*, The Hon. Lord Davidson
*Secretary*, D. K. C. Jeffrey

NORTHERN IRELAND
Frances House, 9–11 Brunswick Street, Belfast BT2 7GE
Tel 01232-321292
*Deputy Chairman*, The Hon. Mr Justice Pringle
*Secretary*, J. R. Fisher

## BRITISH BROADCASTING CORPORATION
Broadcasting House, London WIA IAA
Tel 0171-580 4468
Television Centre, Wood Lane, London W12 7RJ
Tel 0181-743 8000

The BBC was incorporated under royal charter as successor to the British Broadcasting Company Ltd, whose licence expired in 1926. Its present charter came into force on 1 August 1981, for 15 years. In July 1994 the Government published a White Paper on the future of the BBC (*see* page 1172). The chairman, vice-chairman and other governors are appointed by The Queen-in-Council. The BBC is financed by revenue from receiving licences for the home services and by grant-in-aid from Parliament for the World Service (radio). The total number of receiving licences in the UK at 31 March 1994 was 20,412,668, of which 889,074 were for monochrome receivers and 19,523,594 for colour receivers. Annual television licence fees are: monochrome £28; colour £84.50. For services, *see* Broadcasting section.

BOARD OF GOVERNORS *as at 1 July 1994*

*Chairman* (£62,120), M. Hussey
*Vice-Chairman* (£15,940), The Lord Cocks of Hartcliffe, PC
*National Governors* (*each* £15,940), Sir Kenneth Bloomfield, KCB (*N. Ireland*); Dr G. Jones (*Wales*); Sir Graham Hills, FRSE (*Scotland*)
*Governors* (*each* £7,970), W. B. Jordan, CBE; Miss J. Glover, D.phil.; Mrs S. Sadeque; Lord Nicholas Gordon Lennox, KCMG, KCVO; Mrs M. Spurr, OBE; Mrs J. Cohen; Sir David Scholey, CBE

BOARD OF MANAGEMENT
*Director-General*, J. Birt
*Deputy Director-General, Chairman, BBC Worldwide, and Managing Director, World Service*, R. Phillis
*Adviser to the Director-General*, D. Hatch, CBE
*Managing Directors*, W. Wyatt (*Network Television*); Ms E. Forgan (*Network Radio*); R. Neil (*Regional Broadcasting*); T. Hall (*News and Current Affairs*); R. Lynch (*Resources*); Dr J. Thomas (*BBC International TV*); N. Chapman (*BBC Publishing*)
*Directors*, C. Browne (*Corporate Affairs*); Ms M. Salmon (*Personnel*); Ms P. Hodgson (*Policy and Planning*); R. Baker-Bates (*Finance and Information Technology*); Ms J. Drabble (*Education*)
*Chief Executive, Enterprises*, vacant

OTHER SENIOR STAFF
*Controller, BBC1*, A. Yentob
*Controller, BBC2*, M. Jackson
*Deputy Managing Director, Network Radio and Controller, Radio 4*, M. Green
*Controller, Radio 1*, M. Bannister
*Controller, Radio 2*, Ms F. Line
*Controller, Radio 3*, N. Kenyon
*Controller, Radio 5 Live*, Ms J. Abramsky
*Controller, Scotland*, J. McCormick
*Controller, Wales*, G. Talfan Davies
*Controller, N. Ireland*, vacant
*Director of Broadcasting, World Service*, S. Younger
*Controller, Editorial Policy*, R. Ayre
*The Secretary*, M. Stevenson
*Legal Adviser*, G. Roscoe

## BRITISH COAL CORPORATION
Hobart House, Grosvenor Place, London SWIX 7AE
Tel 0171-201 4141

The British Coal Corporation (formerly the National Coal Board) was constituted in 1946 and took over the mines on 1 January 1947. Under the Coal Industry Act 1994 a new body, the Coal Authority (*see* page 296), was established to take over ownership of coal reserves and to issue licences to private sector mining companies as part of the privatization of British Coal. The British Coal Corporation will be wound up when the privatization process is completed.
*Chairman*, J. N. Clarke
*Deputy Chairman*, A. Wheeler, CBE
*Executive Members*, R. Proctor (*Finance Director*); K. Hunt (*Employee Relations*); A. D. J. Horsler (*Marketing Director*)
*Non-Executive Members*, Dr D. V. Atterton, CBE; D. B. Walker; J. P. Erbé; A. P. Hichens; Sir Robert Davidson, FEng.; Sir David Alliance, CBE; D. B. Vaughan
*Secretary*, M. S. Shelton

## THE BRITISH COUNCIL
10 Spring Gardens, London SWIA 2BN
Tel 0171-930 8466
Medlock Street, Manchester M15
Tel 0161-957 7000

The British Council was established in 1934 and incorporated by royal charter in 1940. It is an independent, non-political organization which promotes Britain abroad. It provides access to British ideas, talents and experience in education and training, books and periodicals, the English language, the arts, the sciences and technology.

The Council is represented in 108 countries and runs 187 offices, 116 libraries, 72 English language schools and 29 resource centres around the world.

The Council's annual turnover in 1994–5 is estimated at £437 million, including grants from the Foreign and Commonwealth Office and the Overseas Development Administration. The Council's own revenue in 1993–4 was in excess of £114 million.
*Chairman*, Sir Martin Jacomb
*Deputy Chairman*, The Lord Chorley
*Director-General*, J. Hanson, CBE

## BRITISH FILM COMMISSION
70 Baker Street, London WIM IDJ
Tel 0171-224 5000

The British Film Commission was established in 1992 and is funded by the Department of National Heritage. The Commission promotes the UK as an international production centre, encourages the use of locations, facilities, services and personnel, and provides a comprehensive computerized information service on all aspects of filming in the UK.
*Commissioner and Chairman of the Board*, S. W. Samuelson, CBE
*Chief Executive*, A. Patrick

## BRITISH FILM INSTITUTE
21 Stephen Street, London W1P 1PL
Tel 0171-255 1444

The British Film Institute was established in 1933 under royal charter. Its aims are to encourage the development of the art of film and its use as a record of contemporary life in Great Britain, and to foster the study, appreciation and use of films for television. It includes the National Film and Television Archive, the National Film Theatre and the Museum of the Moving Image, and it supports a network of 46 regional film theatres. The BFI Library contains the world's largest collection of material relating to film and television. Total government funding for 1994–5 is £17.1 million.
*Chairman,* J. Thomas
*Director,* W. Stevenson

## BRITISH PHARMACOPOEIA COMMISSION
Market Towers, 1 Nine Elms Lane, London SW8 5NQ
Tel 0171-273 0561

The British Pharmacopoeia Commission sets standards for medicinal products used in human and veterinary medicine. It is responsible for the British Pharmacopoeia (a publicly-available statement of the standard that a product must meet throughout its shelf-life), the British Pharmacopoeia (Veterinary) and the selection of British Approved Names. It also participates in the work of the European Pharmacopoeia on behalf of the United Kingdom. It has 15 members who are appointed by the Secretary of State for Health and the Minister for Agriculture, Fisheries and Food.
*Chairman,* Prof. D. Ganderton
*Vice-Chairman,* Prof. P. Turner, CBE
*Secretary (G6),* Dr R. C. Hutton

## BRITISH RAILWAYS BOARD
Euston House, 24 Eversholt Street, PO Box 100, London NW1 1DZ
Tel 0171-928 5151

The British Railways Board came into being in 1963 under the terms of the Transport Act 1962. Under the Railways Act 1993, the activities of the Board have been restructured in preparation for privatization. In the meantime, the Board continues as operator of train services in Great Britain. For details of privatization and railway operations, *see* Transport section.
*Chairman (£220,850),* Sir Bob Reid
*Vice-Chairman,* C. J. Campbell, CBE
*Finance and Planning,* J. J. Jerram
*Part-time non-executive members,* P. Allen, CBE; J. Aziz; J. Butler; K. H. M. Dixon; Sir William Francis, CBE; Miss K. T. Kantor; W. Wilson
*Chief Executive,* J. Welsby, CBE
*Secretary,* P. Trewin

## BRITISH STANDARDS INSTITUTION (BSI)
389 Chiswick High Road, London W4 4AL
Tel 0181-996 9000

The British Standards Institution is the recognized authority in the UK for the preparation and publication of national standards for industrial and consumer products. In consultation with the interests concerned, BSI prepares standards relating to nearly every sector of the nation's industry and trade. It also represents the UK at European and international standards meetings. About 80 per cent of its standards work is now internationally linked.

British Standards are issued for voluntary adoption, though in a number of cases compliance with a British Standard is required by legislation. BSI operates certification schemes under which industrial and consumer products are certified as complying with the relevant British Standard and may carry the Institution's certification trade marks, known as the 'Kitemark' and the 'Safety Mark'. It assesses and registers companies which meet the requirements of the quality management standard, BS5750. BSI runs one of the largest testing laboratories in Europe and has an advisory service for exporters, Technical Help to Exporters.

BSI is financed by voluntary subscriptions, an annual government grant, the sale of its publications, and fees for testing and certification. There are more than 27,000 subscribing members of BSI.
*Chief Executive,* Sir Neville Purvis, KCB

## BRITISH TOURIST AUTHORITY
Thames Tower, Black's Road, London W6 9EL
Tel 0181-846 9000

Established under the Development of Tourism Act 1969, the British Tourist Authority has specific responsibility for promoting tourism to Great Britain from overseas. It also has a general responsibility for the promotion and development of tourism and tourist facilities within Great Britain as a whole, and for advising the Government on tourism matters.
*Chairman (part-time),* Ms A. Biss
*Chief Executive,* A. Sell

## BRITISH WATERWAYS
Willow Grange, Church Road, Watford, Herts. WD1 3QA
Tel 01923-226422

British Waterways is the navigational authority for over 2,000 miles of canals and river navigations in England, Scotland and Wales. Some 380 miles are maintained and are being developed as commercial waterways for use by freight-carrying vessels. Another 1,200 miles, the cruising waterways, are being developed for boating, fishing and other leisure activities. The remaining 500 miles, the remainder waterways, are maintained with due regard to safety, public health and the preservation of amenities. Of this remaining mileage, nearly two-thirds is navigable or has been restored to navigation over the past twenty years.
*Chairman (part-time),* B. Henderson, CBE
*Vice-Chairman (part-time),* Sir Peter Hutchison, Bt.
*Members (all part-time),* J. Gordon; D. H. R. Yorke; M. Cairns; D. Porter; The Viscountess Cobham
*Chief Executive,* B. C. Dice
*Secretary and Solicitor,* R. J. Duffy

## BROADCASTING STANDARDS COUNCIL
7 The Sanctuary, London SW1P 3JS
Tel 0171-233 0544

The Council was set up in 1988 but received its statutory powers under the Broadcasting Act 1990. Its role is advisory, not regulatory. It monitors the portrayal of violence, sex and matters of taste and decency in all broadcast programmes and advertisements on television, radio, cable and satellite services. The Council publishes a code of practice, considers complaints and conducts research into audience attitudes. Members of the Council are appointed by the Secretary of State for National Heritage. The appointments are part-time.

The Government has announced plans to merge the BSC with the Broadcasting Complaints Commission (*see* page 1172).

*Chair* (£41,590), The Lady Howe of Aberavon
*Deputy Chairman* (£31,410), Dame Jocelyn Barrow, DBE
*Members* (*each* £12,510), Ms R. Bevan; Dr Jean Curtis-Raleigh; R. Kernohan, OBE; the Very Revd J. Lang; M. Parris; Ms S. O'Sullivan
*Director*, C. Shaw, CBE

## THE BROADS AUTHORITY
Thomas Harvey House, 18 Colegate, Norwich NR3 1BQ
Tel 01603-610734

The Broads Authority is a special statutory authority set up under the Norfolk and Suffolk Broads Act 1988, with powers and responsibilities similar to those of National Park Authorities. The functions of the Authority are to conserve and enhance the natural beauty of the Broads; to promote the enjoyment of the Broads by the public; and to protect the interests of navigation.

The Authority comprises 35 members, appointed by Norfolk County Council (4); Suffolk County Council (2); Broadland District Council (2); Great Yarmouth Borough Council (2); North Norfolk District Council (2); Norwich City Council (2); South Norfolk District Council (2); Waveney District Council (2); the Countryside Commission (2); English Nature (1); the Great Yarmouth Port Authority (2); the National Rivers Authority (Anglian Region) (1); the Secretary of State for the Environment (9); and two from amongst members of the Authority's statutory Navigation Committee who are not already members of the Authority.

*Chairman*, J. S. Peel, CBE, MC
*Chief Executive*, M. A. Clark

## THE CABINET OFFICE

The Cabinet Office comprises the Secretariat, who support Ministers collectively in the conduct of Cabinet business; and the Office of Public Service and Science (OPSS) which is responsible for the Citizen's Charter initiative, the Next Steps programme, the Office of Science and Technology, policy on open government, senior Civil Service and public appointments, and the management and organization of the Civil Service and recruitment into it. The OPSS is also responsible for CCTA (the Government Centre for Information Systems), the Civil Service College, the Recruitment and Assessment Services Agency, the Occupational Health Service, HMSO, the Central Office of Information and the Chessington Computer Centre.

The OPSS supports the Prime Minister in his capacity as Minister for the Civil Service, with responsibility for day-to-day supervision delegated to the Chancellor of the Duchy of Lancaster.

*Prime Minister and Minister for the Civil Service*,
The Rt. Hon. John Major, MP

## PRIME MINISTER'S OFFICE
10 Downing Street, London SW1A 2AA
Tel 0171-930 4433

*Principal Private Secretary to the Prime Minister* (*G3*),
A. Allan
*Private Secretaries to the Prime Minister* (*G5*), R. Lyne, CMG
(*Overseas Affairs*); Mrs M. Francis (*Economic Affairs*);
W. Chapman (*Parliamentary Affairs*); (*G7*), Ms
R. Reynolds (*Home Affairs*)
*Diary Secretary to the Prime Minister*, Ms A. Warburton
*Secretary for Appointments, and Ecclesiastical Secretary to the Lord Chancellor* (*G2*), J. Holroyd, CB
*Political Secretary*, J. Hill
*Policy Unit*, The Hon. Mrs S. Hogg; N. True, CBE; Mrs K. Ramsey; Miss L. Neville-Rolfe; Ms J. Rutter;
D. Green; D. Morris
*Chief Press Secretary* (*G2*), C. J. R. Meyer, CMG
*Deputy Chief Press Secretary* (*G5*), J. Haslam
*Assistant Private Secretaries to the Prime Minister*, Miss
A. B. Hordern; Miss J. L. Wilkinson
*Parliamentary Private Secretary*, J. Ward, MP
*Parliamentary Clerk*, R. Stone
*Secretary of the Cabinet and Head of Home Civil Service*,
Sir Robin Butler, GCB, CVO
*Private Secretary*, Miss M. J. Leech

## SECRETARIAT
70 Whitehall, London SW1A 2AS
Tel 0171-270 3000

*Deputy Secretaries* (*G2*), P. Lever, CMG; Mrs R. Lomax, CB;
G. C. Warner; B. Bender
*Under-Secretaries* (*G3*), R. Bird; D. J. Gould;
R. J. D. Carden; A. C. Galsworthy, CMG
*Grade 5*, A. Sandall; M. K. Collins; R. G. Wakeford;
Brig. J. A. J. Budd; S. G. Eldon
*Grade 6*, R. Hope

## OFFICE OF PUBLIC SERVICE AND SCIENCE (OPSS)
Horse Guards Road, London SW1P 3AL
70 Whitehall, London SW1A 2AS
Tel 0171-270 5811

*Chancellor of the Duchy of Lancaster and Minister of Public Service and Science*, The Rt. Hon. David Hunt, MBE, MP
*Principal Private Secretary*, J. Buck
*Private Secretary*, I. Dougal
*Special Adviser*, M. McManus
*Parliamentary Private Secretary*, N. Evans, MP
*Parliamentary Under-Secretary of State*, Robert Hughes, MP
*Private Secretary*, D. Williams
*Second Permanent Secretary* (*G1A*), R. C. Mottram
*Private Secretary*, K. Roberts
*Parliamentary Clerk*, Miss T. N. Terry
*Press Secretary* (*G5*), P. Rose

### CITIZEN'S CHARTER UNIT
Government Offices, Great George Street, London
SW1P 3AL
Tel 0171-270 1838

*Director* (*G2*), Miss E. C. Turton
*Deputy Directors* (*G5*), C. Ramsden; Mrs E. Hunter-Johnson

### EFFICIENCY UNIT
70 Whitehall, London SW1A 2AS
Tel 0171-260 0273

*Prime Minister's Adviser on Efficiency and Effectiveness*,
Sir Peter Levene, KBE

*Head of Unit (G3)*, J. Oughton
*Deputy Head of Unit (G5)*, Ms D. Kahn

ADVISORY UNIT ON MINISTERS' AGENCIES
*Adviser*, C. M. Brendish
*Grade 6*, D. R. Wood

MANAGEMENT DEVELOPMENT GROUP
*Under-Secretary (G3)*, H. H. Taylor
*Grade 5*, R. D. J. Wright *(Security)*; Mrs S. Britton *(Equal Opportunities)*; Miss S. C. Phippard *(Next Steps Project Team)*; C. J. Parry *(Development)*

TOP MANAGEMENT PROGRAMME
*Director of Programme (G3)*, H. H. Taylor
*Course Directors (G5)*, S. Mitha; Mrs M. Chapman

SENIOR AND PUBLIC APPOINTMENTS GROUP AND EUROPEAN STAFFING
*Under-Secretary (G3)*, B. Fox
*Grade 5*, D. Laughrin
*Grade 6*, J. K. Barron

MACHINERY OF GOVERNMENT
*Grade 3*, A. D. Whetnall

SECURITY
*Head of Division (G5)*, R. D. J. Wright

OFFICE OF THE CIVIL SERVICE COMMISSIONERS (OCSC)
Alencon Link, Basingstoke, Hants. RG21 1JB
Tel 01256-29222

*First Commissioner (G2)*, Mrs A. E. Bowtell, CB *(London)*
*Commissioner (G3)*, M. D. Geddes *(Chief Executive, RAS)*
*Commissioners (part-time)*, Ms U. Prashar; Mrs J. Rubin; A. Maddrell; K. E. C. Sorensen
*Secretary to the Commissioners and Head of the Office (G5)*, Miss E. M. Goodison

INFORMATION OFFICER MANAGEMENT UNIT
*Information Officer (G5)*, T. J. Perks

CCTA (THE GOVERNMENT CENTRE FOR INFORMATION SYSTEMS)
Riverwalk House, 157–161 Millbank, London SW1P 4RT
Tel 0171-217 3000
Gildengate House, Upper Green Lane, Norwich NR3 1DW
Tel 01603-694620
*Director (G3)*, R. Dibble
*Deputy Director (G4)*, W. Houldsworth

CEREMONIAL OFFICER
53 Parliament Street, London SW1A 2NG
Tel 0171-210 5056
*Grade 5*, A. J. Merifield, CB

OFFICE OF SCIENCE AND TECHNOLOGY
70 Whitehall, London SW1A 2AS
Tel 0171-270 3000
Grove House, 16 Orange Street, London WC2H 7ED
Tel 0171-270 6944
Sanctuary Buildings, Great Smith Street, London SW1P 3BT
Tel 0171-925 5000

*Chief Scientific Adviser and Head of Office (G1A)*, Prof. Sir William Stewart, FRS, FRSE
*Private Secretary (G7)*, Ms M. Smith
*Director-General of Research Councils*, Sir John Cadogan

BRANCH A
*Grade 3*, Miss H. Williams
*Grade 5*, I. Freeman *(Domestic science and technology issues)*; D. A. Warren *(International science and technology issues)*

BRANCH B
*Grade 3*, D. A. Wilkinson, CB; Dr D. G. Libby
*Grade 5*, A. A. Carter *(General Science Policy)*; R. P. Ritzema *(International Science)*
*Grade 6*, Dr K. Root *(Science Budget)*; Dr R. Dowdell

TECHNOLOGY FORESIGHT
*Under-Secretary (G3)*, Mrs H. Williams
*Grade 5*, I. Freeman
*Grade 6*, D. M. Schildt; J. G. Walshe

ESTABLISHMENT OFFICER'S GROUP
Government Offices, Great George Street, London SW1P 3AL
Tel 0171-270 3000

*Principal Establishment and Finance Officer (G3)*, R. W. D. Venning
*Deputy Establishment Officer (G5)*, G. S. Royston
*Senior Finance Officer (G6)*, Miss J. M. E. Buchan

HISTORICAL AND RECORDS SECTION
Hepburn House, Marsham Street, London SW1P 4HW
Tel 0171-217 6032
*Grade 5*, Miss P. M. Andrews

EXECUTIVE AGENCIES

CENTRAL OFFICE OF INFORMATION
— see page 294

CHESSINGTON COMPUTER CENTRE
Government Buildings, Leatherhead Road, Chessington, Surrey KT9 2LT
Tel 0181-391 3800
The Centre provides administrative and financial services to the public sector.
*Chief Executive (G5)*, R. N. Edwards

CIVIL SERVICE COLLEGE
Sunningdale Park, Ascot, Berks. SL5 0QE
Tel 01344-634000
11 Belgrave Road, London SW1V 1RB
Tel 0171-834 6644
The College provides training in management and professional skills for civil servants and for those working in the private sector.
*Chief Executive (G3)*, Dr S. H. F. Hickey
*Director of Studies (G5)*, D. R. Smith
*Business Executives (G5/G6)*, C. W. H. Aitken; M. N. Barnes; I. Cameron; Mrs P. A. Carvel; Ms E. Chennells; J. G. Fuller; M. Timmis; Miss J. A. Topham; Miss M. A. Wood

HMSO
— see pages 357–8

OCCUPATIONAL HEALTH SERVICE
18–20 Hill Street, Edinburgh EH2 3NB
Tel 0131-220 4177
The Occupational Health Service provides services and advice to all government departments and executive agencies, and to other public bodies, on matters relating to the health of their employees in their working environment.
*Chief Executive*, Dr E. C. McCloy
*Director of Medical Services*, Dr P. Litchfield

RECRUITMENT AND ASSESSMENT SERVICES (RAS)
Alencon Link, Basingstoke, Hants. RG21 1JB
Tel 01256-29222
24 Whitehall, London SW1A 2ED
Tel 0171-210 3000

RAS provides professional recruitment and staff development services to the Civil Service and other public sector bodies.
*Chief Executive,* M. D. Geddes
*Grade 5,* vacant
*Grade 6,* F. D. Bedford; K. N. Bastin; Mrs J. A. Lovegrove

---

CENTRAL ADJUDICATION SERVICES
Quarry House, Quarry Hill, Leeds LS2 7UB
Tel 0113-232 4000
New Court, 48 Carey Street, London WC2A 2LS
Tel 0171-412 1504

---

The Chief Adjudication Officer and Chief Child Support Officer are independent statutory authorities under the Social Security Act 1975 (as amended) and the Child Support Act 1991. They are appointed by the Secretary of State for Social Security to give advice to adjudication officers and child support officers, to keep under review the operation of the systems of adjudication, and to report annually to the Secretary of State on adjudication standards.

Adjudication officers make decisions of first instance on all claims for social security cash benefits, and child support officers make decisions of first instance on applications for child maintenance made to the Child Support Agency. Officers of the Chief Adjudication Officer also enter written observations on all appeals made to the Social Security Commissioners, and officers of the Chief Child Support Officer make written observations on appeals to the Child Support Commissioners.
*Chief Adjudication Officer and Chief Child Support Officer,*
  E. Hazlewood

---

CENTRAL OFFICE OF INFORMATION
Hercules Road, London SE1 7DU
Tel 0171-928 2345

---

The Central Office of Information (COI) is the government executive agency which provides publicity and information services to government departments, other executive agencies and public sector bodies. It provides consultancy, design, production, procurement and project management services for a wide range of publicity services in all media. Though the majority of COI's work is for government departments in the UK, it also produces a range of publicity materials for overseas consumption.

Administrative responsibility for the COI rests with the Minister of Public Service and Science, while the ministers whose departments it serves are responsible for the policy expressed in its work.
*Chief Executive and Head of the Government Information Service (G3),* G. M. Devereau
*Senior Personal Secretary,* Mrs J. Rodrigues

MANAGEMENT BOARD
*Members,* G. M. Devereau; K. Williamson; R. Windsor;
  D. A. Low; R. Smith
*Secretary,* Miss K. Gliding

DIRECTORS
*Director, Marketing and Client Services (G6),* S. Petherick
*Head, Business Development and Communications Services
  (G7),* W. Roberts
*Director, Advertising (G6),* M. Brodie
*Director, Research (G6),* M. Rigg
*Director, Direct Marketing (G7),* C. Noble

*Director, Press and Pictures (G6) (acting),* D. A. Low
*Director, Publications (G6),* J. Murray
*Director, Reference, Translations and Exhibitions (G6),*
  D. Beynon
*Director, Films, Television and Radio Division (G6),*
  M. Nisbet
*Principal Finance Officer (G5),* K. Williamson
*Director, Network Services (G6),* R. Haslam

NETWORK OFFICES
EASTERN, Three Crowns House, 72–80 Hills Road,
  Cambridge CB2 1LL. *Network Director (G7),* Mrs
  V. Burdon
LONDON AND SOUTH-EAST, Lincoln House, Westminster
  Bridge Road, London SE1 7DU. *Network Director (G6),*
  D. Smith
MIDLANDS, Five Ways Tower, Frederick Road,
  Edgbaston, Birmingham B15 1SH. *Network Director (G6),*
  O. J. B. Prince-White
NORTH-EAST, Wellbar House, Gallowgate, Newcastle
  upon Tyne NE1 4TB. *Network Director (G7),* H. Cozens
NORTH-WEST, Sunley Tower, Piccadilly Plaza,
  Manchester M1 4BD. *Network Director (G7),* Mrs E. Jones
SOUTH-WEST, The Pithay, Bristol BS1 2NF. *Network
  Director (G7),* P. Whitbread
YORKSHIRE AND HUMBERSIDE, City House, New Station
  Street, Leeds LS1 4JG. *Network Director (G7),* B. Garner

---

CENTRAL STATISTICAL OFFICE
Great George Street, London SW1P 3AQ
Tel 0171-270 6363/6364

---

The work of the Central Statistical Office (CSO) encompasses data collection from businesses; the preparation and publication of macro-economic statistics and social statistics abstracts; statistics relating to institutional sectors and financial statistics; the retail prices index and the family expenditure survey; liaison with international statistical bodies; and central management of the Government Statistical Service (GSS). The Central Statistical Office became an executive agency of the Treasury in 1991.
*Director and Head of the Government Statistical Service
  (G1A),* W. McLennan
*Private Secretary,* Miss F. Parrott
*Deputy Director (G2),* D. C. L. Wroe
*Head of Statistical Methods and Quality (G5),* T. Jones
*Head of Policy Secretariat (G5),* J. Pullinger

GSS AND GENERAL DIVISION
*Grade 3,* J. R. Calder
*Heads of Branches (G5),* D. C. K. Stirling (*GSS policy and
  management*); Miss J. Church (*Social and regional statistics
  and household expenditure*); Mrs M. Haworth (*Retail
  Prices*); R. J. Scott (*Registers and classification*); (G6),
  A. Machin (*Departmental Deregulation Unit*)

BUSINESS STATISTICS DIVISION
*Grade 3,* Dr M. P. G. Pepper
*Heads of Branches (G5),* K. Francombe (*Distribution and
  services*); C. J. Spiller (*Production*); G. D. Walker (*Central
  initiatives*); J. D. Kinder (*Product prices and sales*);
  M. R. Brand (*Companies and overseas*)

ECONOMIC ACCOUNTS DIVISION
*Grade 3,* J. E. Kidgell
*Heads of Branches (G5),* R. Lynch (*National accounts and
  economic assessment*); K. Mansell (*Output and
  expenditure*); P. Turnbull (*Balance of payments*);

G. Jenkinson (*Company and personal sectors*); Mrs P. Walker (*Public sector and financial accounts*); B. J. Buckingham (*Financial institutions*)

CENTRAL SERVICES DIVISION
*Grade 3*, Dr L. Mayhew
*Heads of Branches (G5)*, Dr J. Ludley (*Information systems*); D. R. Lewis (*Personnel and staff development*); H. W. Joiner (*Finance and office services*); (*G6*), I. G. Scott (*Press and Public Information*); P. Powell (*Marketing and Sales*)

---

CERTIFICATION OFFICE FOR TRADE UNIONS AND EMPLOYERS' ASSOCIATIONS
27 Wilton Street, London SW1X 7AZ
Tel 0171-210 3734/5

---

The Certification Office is an independent statutory authority. The Certification Officer is appointed by the Secretary of State for Employment and is responsible for receiving and scrutinizing annual returns from trade unions and employers' associations; for reimbursing certain costs of trade unions' postal ballots; for dealing with complaints concerning trade union elections; for ensuring observance of statutory requirements governing political funds and trade union mergers; and for certifying the independence of trade unions.
*Certification Officer*, E. G. Whybrew
*Assistant Certification Officer*, G. S. Osborne

SCOTLAND
58 Frederick Street, Edinburgh EH2 1LN
Tel 0131-226 3224
*Assistant Certification Officer for Scotland*, J. L. J. Craig

---

CHARITY COMMISSION
St Alban's House, 57–60 Haymarket, London SW1Y 4QX
Tel 0171-210 4477
Graeme House, Derby Square, Liverpool L2 7SB
Tel 0151-227 3191
Woodfield House, Tangier, Taunton, Somerset TA1 4BL
Tel 01823-345000

---

The Charity Commission is established under the Charities Act 1993 with the general function of promoting the effective use of charitable resources in England and Wales. The Commission gives information and advice to charity trustees to make the administration of their charity more effective; investigates misconduct and the abuse of charitable assets, and takes or recommends remedial action; and maintains a public register of charities. The Commission does not have at its disposal any funds with which to make grants to organizations or individuals.

At the end of 1993 the total number of registered charities was 170,932.
*Chief Commissioner (G3)*, R. Fries
*Commissioners (G3)*, R. M. C. Venables; (*G4*), J. Farquharson
*Commissioners (part-time) (G4)*, M. Webber; Mrs D. H. Yeo
*Heads of Legal Sections (G5)*, J. A. Dutton; G. S. Goodchild; K. M. Dibble; S. Slack
*Executive Director (G4)*, Mrs E. A. Shaw
*Director of Operations (G5)*, V. F. Mitchell
*Establishment Officer (G5)*, Mrs J. Cotton
*Information Systems Controller (G5)*, Ms G. Cruickshank

*Grade 6*, Miss D. F. Taylor; S. K. Sen; P. P. White; N. M. Mackenzie; R. E. Edwards; Miss V. A. Nuttall; I. M. Davies; D. C. Crick
*Grade 7*, R. E. Hatton; A. O. Polak; M. C. T. Seymour; K. M. Dickin; M. J. McManus; G. B. Ward; J. S. Holdsworth; M. Pearson; P. W. Somerfield; R. G. Dawes; Miss G. Fletcher; A. J. George; J. Thorne; I. Spencer; Mrs P. D. W. Holt; J. Kilby; R. Jones; Miss B. Lythgoe; R. A. V. Corden; J. M. Reid; Ms L. Matlock; Mrs S. E. Gillingham
*Official Custodian for Charities (G7)*, M. Fry

The departments responsible for charities in Scotland and Northern Ireland are:
SCOTLAND – Scottish Home and Health Department, Charities Division, New St Andrews House, Edinburgh EH1 3DE. Tel: 0131-244 2206
NORTHERN IRELAND – Department of Finance and Personnel, Charities Branch, Rosepark House, Upper Newtownards Road, Belfast BT4 3NR. Tel: 01232-484567

---

CHIEF ADJUDICATION OFFICER AND CHIEF CHILD SUPPORT OFFICER
— *see* Central Adjudication Services

---

CHILD SUPPORT AGENCY
— *see* page 357

---

CHURCH COMMISSIONERS
1 Millbank, London SW1P 3JZ
Tel 0171-222 7010

---

The Church Commissioners were established in 1948 by the amalgamation of Queen Anne's Bounty (established 1704) and the Ecclesiastical Commissioners (established 1836).

The Commissioners are responsible for the management of most of the Church of England's assets, the income from which is predominantly used to pay, house and pension the clergy. The Commissioners own nearly 148,000 acres of agricultural land, a number of residential estates in central London, and commercial property in Great Britain and the USA. They also carry out administrative duties in connection with pastoral reorganization and redundant churches, and have been designated by the General Synod as the central stipends authority of the Church of England.

The Commissioners are: the Archbishops of Canterbury and of York; the 41 diocesan bishops; five deans or provosts, ten other clergy and ten lay persons appointed by the General Synod; four lay persons nominated by The Queen; four persons nominated by the Archbishop of Canterbury; the Lord Chancellor; the Lord President of the Council; the First Lord of the Treasury; the Chancellor of the Exchequer; the Secretary of State for the Home Department; the Speaker of the House of Commons; the Lord Chief Justice; the Master of the Rolls; the Attorney-General; the Solicitor-General; the Lord Mayor and two Aldermen of the City of London; the Lord Mayor of York; and one representative from each of the Universities of Oxford and Cambridge.

INCOME AND EXPENDITURE
*for year ended 31 December 1993*

| INCOME | £ million |
|---|---|
| Investments | 78.0 |
| Property | 74.5 |
| Interest from loans, etc. | 15.0 |
| Total income | 167.5 |

| INCOME, *cont.* | £ *million* |
|---|---|
| Interest payable | (12.6) |
| Administration costs | (10.4) |
| Net income | 144.5 |

EXPENDITURE

| | |
|---|---|
| Clergy stipends | 58.0 |
| Clergy and widows' pensions | 69.4 |
| Clergy houses | 6.0 |
| Episcopal administration and payments to Chapters | 9.8 |
| Church buildings | 1.0 |
| Administration costs of other bodies | 2.2 |
| Total | 146.4 |
| Deficit for year | (1.9) |

Between 1988 and 1992, the value of the Church's assets fell by £800 million. In 1992–3 the value rose by £294 million.

CHURCH ESTATES COMMISSIONERS
*First,* Sir Michael Colman, Bt.
*Second,* The Rt. Hon. Michael Alison, MP
*Third,* Mrs M. H. Laird

OFFICERS
*Secretary,* P. Locke
*Deputy Secretary (Policy and Planning),* R. S. Hopgood
*Deputy Secretary (Finance and Investment),* C. W. Daws
*Assistant Secretaries:*
*The Accountant,* G. C. Baines
*Management Accountant,* B. J. Hardy
*Commercial Property,* M. G. S. Farrell
*Computer Manager,* J. W. Ferguson
*Secretariat,* W. R. Herbert
*Estates,* P. H. P. Shaw, LVO
*Investments Manager,* A. S. Hardy
*Pastoral, Houses and Redundant Churches,* M. D. Elengorn
*Stipends and Allocations (acting),* R. S. Hopgood
*Senior Architect,* J. A. Taylor
*Principals:*
*Head of Communications,* Miss A. E. Dickens
*Head of Personnel,* Miss J. H. Hudson
*Bishoprics Officer,* N. J. Neil-Smith
A. W. Atkins; Miss A. M. Mackie; G. Wills; J. A. W. Elloy;
C. R. Bullen; D. W. H. Lewis; J. W. Wallace; R. A. Scott;
M. S. Fenchelle

LEGAL DEPARTMENT
*Official Solicitor,* J. P. Guy
*Deputy Solicitor,* Miss S. M. S. Jones
*Solicitors,* Miss J. M. Bland; J. D. Carter; Miss J. A. Egar;
R. D. C. Murray; N. Pollock; Ms A. R. Usher

---

CIVIL AVIATION AUTHORITY
CAA House, 45–59 Kingsway, London WC2B 6TE
Tel 0171-379 7311

---

The CAA is responsible for the economic regulation of UK airlines by licensing air routes and air travel organizers and by approving fares; for the safety regulation of UK civil aviation by the certification of airlines and aircraft, and by licensing aerodromes, flight crew and aircraft engineers; and, through National Air Traffic Services, for the provision of air traffic control and telecommunications services. The Government has announced its intention of privatizing National Air Traffic Services.
*Chairman (part-time)* (£65,495), The Rt. Hon. C. Chataway
*Managing Director,* T. Murphy, CBE
*Secretary,* R. J. Britton

---

THE COAL AUTHORITY
200 Lichfield Lane, Berry Hill, Mansfield, Notts. NG18 4RG
Tel 01623–427162

---

The Coal Authority was established under the Coal Industry Act 1994. It will take over British Coal's ownership of coal reserves and be responsible for licensing coal mining operations. It will also deal with physical liabilities arising out of past mining, e.g. subsidence damage claims, abandoned mine shafts, the management and disposal of property, and the maintenance and availability of records.
*Chairman-designate,* Sir David White
*Chief Executive-designate,* N. Washington, OBE

---

COMMONWEALTH DEVELOPMENT CORPORATION
1 Bessborough Gardens, London SW1V 2JQ
Tel 0171-828 4488

---

The Commonwealth Development Corporation is charged with the task of assisting overseas countries in the development of their economies. Its main activity is providing long-term finance, as loans and risk capital, for projects. The Corporation's area of operations includes British dependent territories and, with ministerial approval, Commonwealth or other developing countries. At present, the Corporation is authorized to operate in more than 60 countries and territories. The Corporation is authorized to borrow up to £850 million.
*Chairman (part-time),* Sir Peter Leslie
*Deputy Chairman (part-time),* Sir Michael Caine
*Members (part-time),* Mrs A. Wright; Prof. M. Faber;
M. D. McWilliam; Prof. I. Carruthers; J. Zochonis; Sir William Ryrie, KCB; Ms C. Hayman
*Chief Executive,* Dr R. Reynolds

---

COMMONWEALTH SECRETARIAT
— *see* Index

---

COMMONWEALTH WAR GRAVES COMMISSION
2 Marlow Road, Maidenhead, Berks. SL6 7DX
Tel 01628-34221

---

The Commonwealth War Graves Commission (formerly Imperial War Graves Commission) was founded by royal charter in 1917. It is responsible for the commemoration of 1,694,930 members of the forces of the Commonwealth who fell in the two world wars. More than one million graves are maintained in 23,071 burial grounds throughout the world. Over three-quarters of a million men and women who have no known grave or who were cremated are commemorated by name on memorials built by the Commission.
The funds of the Commission are derived from the six participating governments, i.e. the UK, Australia, Canada, India, New Zealand and South Africa.
*President,* HRH The Duke of Kent, KG, GCMG, GCVO, ADC
*Chairman,* The Secretary of State for Defence in the UK
*Vice-Chairman,* Air Chief Marshal Sir Joseph Gilbert, KCB, CBE
*Members,* The Secretary of State for the Environment in the UK; The High Commissioners in London for Australia,

Canada, India, New Zealand and South Africa; Dame Janet Fookes, DBE, MP; Sir Nigel Mobbs; The Viscount Ridley, KG, GCVO, TD; Prof. R. J. O'Neill, AO; Mrs L. Golding, MP; Sir Harold Walker, KCMG; Gen. Sir John Akenhurst, KCB, CBE; Adm. Sir John Kerr, GCB
*Director-General and Secretary to the Commission,* D. Kennedy
*Deputy Directors-General*, T. F. Penfold (*Administration*); R. J. Dalley (*Operations*)
*Directors*, P. Noakes (*Finance*); A. Coombe (*Works*); D. C. Parker (*Horticulture*); D. R. Parker (*Personnel*); J. P. D. Gee (*Information and Secretariat*)
*Legal Adviser and Solicitor*, G. C. Reddie
*Hon. Artistic Adviser*, Prof. Sir Peter Shepheard, CBE
*Hon. Botanical Adviser*, Prof. G. T. Prance, D.Phil., FLS

IMPERIAL WAR GRAVES ENDOWMENT FUND
*Trustees*, H. U. A. Lambert (*Chairman*); Air Chief Marshal Sir Joseph Gilbert, KCB, CBE; The Lord Remnant, CVO
*Secretary to the Trustees*, P. Noakes

---

## COUNTRYSIDE COMMISSION
John Dower House, Crescent Place, Cheltenham, Glos. GL50 3RA
Tel 01242-521381

---

The Countryside Commission was set up in 1968 and is an independent agency which promotes the conservation and enhancement of landscape beauty in England. It encourages the provision and improvement of facilities in the countryside, and works to secure access for open air recreation. Since 1982 the Commission has been funded by an annual grant from the Department of the Environment. Members of the Commission are appointed by the Secretary of State for the Environment.

In January 1994 the Government announced that it was considering merging the work of the Countryside Commission and English Nature (*see* page 303).
*Chairman*, Sir John Johnson, KCMG
*Director-General (G3)*, M. Dower
*Directors (G5)*, R. Clarke (*Policy*); M. J. Kirby (*Operations*); M. Taylor (*Resources*)
*National Heritage Adviser*, P. Walshe
*Head of Corporate Planning (G7)*, N. Holliday
*Head of Land Use Branch (G7)*, R. Roberts
*Head of Recreation and Access Branch (G7)*, J. W. B. Worth
*Head of Public Affairs (G7)*, Ms P. Palmer
*Head of Finance and Establishments (G7)*, V. Ellis
*Head of National Parks and Planning Branch (G7)*, R. Lloyd
*Head of Environmental Protection Branch (G7)*, I. Mitchell
*Regional Officers (G7)*, K. Buchanan (*Newcastle*); Dr M. Carroll (*Cambridge*); Dr S. A. Bucknall (*Leeds*); E. Holdaway (*Bristol*); Dr Liz Newton (*Manchester*); D. E. Coleman (*London*); F. S. Walmsley (*Birmingham*)
*Special Initiatives*, Dr M. Rawson (*Community Forests*); S. Bell (*National Forest*); T. Allen (*Countryside Stewardship*)

---

## COUNTRYSIDE COUNCIL FOR WALES/ CYNGOR CEFN GWLAD CYMRU
Plas Penrhos, Fford Penrhos, Bangor, Gwynedd LL57 2LQ
Tel 01248-370444

---

The Countryside Council for Wales took over the functions of the Nature Conservancy Council in Wales and the

Countryside Commission in Wales in April 1991. It is the Government's statutory adviser on wildlife, countryside and maritime conservation matters in Wales, and it is the executive authority for the conservation of habitats and wildlife. It promotes the protection of the Welsh landscape and encourages opportunities for public access and enjoyment of the countryside. It provides grant aid to local authorities, voluntary organizations and individuals to pursue countryside management. It is funded by the Welsh Office and accountable to the Secretary of State for Wales, who appoints its members.
*Chairman*, E. M. W. Griffith, CBE
*Chief Executive*, Prof. I. Mercer
*Chief Scientist*, Prof. G. W. Jones
*Director, Resources*, R. J. Davies
*Director, Operations*, I. R. Bonner
*Chief Ecologist*, Dr M. E. Smith

---

## COVENT GARDEN MARKET AUTHORITY
Covent House, New Covent Garden Market, London SW8 5NX
Tel 0171-720 2211

---

The Covent Garden Market Authority is constituted under the Covent Garden Market Acts 1961 to 1977, the members being appointed by the Minister of Agriculture, Fisheries and Food. The Authority owns and operates the 56-acre New Covent Garden Markets (fruit, vegetables, flowers) which have been trading since 1974.
*Chairman (part-time)*, W. P. Bowman, OBE
*Members (part-time)*, P. J. Hunt; J. A. Harvey, CBE; R. Smith, OBE; Sir Peter Reynolds, CBE; Mrs A. M. Vinton
*General Manager*, Dr P. M. Liggins
*Secretary*, C. Farey

---

## CRIMINAL INJURIES COMPENSATION BOARD
Tay House, 300 Bath Street, Glasgow G2 4JR
Tel 0141-331 2726
Morley House, 26–30 Holborn Viaduct, London ECIA 2JQ
Tel 0171-842 6800

---

The Board was constituted in 1964 to administer the government scheme for *ex gratia* payments of compensation to victims of crimes of violence. In December 1993 the Government published a White Paper proposing changes to the compensation scheme, including the replacement of the Board by a new Criminal Injuries Compensation Authority (*see* page 1170).
*Chairman (part-time)* (£33,050), The Lord Carlisle of Bucklow, PC, QC
*Members*, J. F. A. Archer, QC; D. Barker, QC; Sir Derek Bradbeer, OBE; D. Brennan, QC; Sir David Calcutt, QC; H. Carlisle, QC; B. W. Chedlow, QC; J. Cherry, QC; M. Churchouse; His Hon. Sir Jonathan Clarke; Miss B. Cooper, QC; Miss D. Cotton, QC; J. D. Crowley, QC; His Hon. J. da Cunha; T. A. K. Drummond, QC; C. Fawcett, QC; Sir Richard Gaskell; E. Gee; K. Goddard, QC; G. M. Hamilton, QC; Sir Arthur Hoole; His Hon. J. Kingham; J. Law, QC; M. E. Lewer, QC; M. Lewis, QC; C. Lindsay, QC; Lord Macaulay of Bragar, QC; J. M. McGhie, QC; D. Mackay, QC; N. Miscampbell, QC; I. M. S. Park, CBE; T. Preston, QC; Miss S. Ritchie, QC; D. B. Robertson, QC; C. Seagroatt, QC; E. Stone, QC; D. O. Thomas, QC; P. Weitzman, QC; His Hon. Sir David

West-Russell; C. H. Whitby, QC; J. Leighton Williams, QC
*Director*, P. G. Spurgeon

---

CROFTERS COMMISSION
4–6 Castle Wynd, Inverness IV2 3EQ
Tel 01463-237231

---

The Crofters Commission is a statutory body established in 1955 which is responsible for reorganizing, developing and regulating crofting in the seven crofting (and former county) areas of Argyll, Caithness, Inverness, Orkney, Ross and Cromarty, Shetland and Sutherland. The Commission keeps under review all matters relating to crofting, advises the Secretary of State for Scotland on crofting matters and liaises with other relevant bodies. The Commission also administers the Crofting Counties Agricultural Grants (Scotland) Scheme 1988.
*Chairman*, H. A. M. Maclean
*Members (part-time)*, Fr. J. A. Macdonald; Mrs A. Rennie; A. Cameron; W. Ritchie; I. MacKinnon; Dr J. Watt
*Secretary (G6)*, M. Grantham

---

CROWN AGENTS FOR OVERSEA GOVERNMENTS AND ADMINISTRATIONS
St Nicholas House, St Nicholas Road, Sutton, Surrey SM1 1EL
Tel 0181-643 3311

---

Incorporated by Act of Parliament, the Crown Agents are commercial, financial and professional agents for over 100 governments and over 300 public authorities, international bodies and other organizations, primarily in the public sector.
*Chairman*, D. H. Probert
*Managing Director*, P. F. Berry

---

CROWN ESTATE
16 Carlton House Terrace, London SW1Y 5AH
Tel 0171-210 4377

---

The land revenues of the Crown in England and Wales have been collected on the public account since 1760, when George III surrendered them to Parliament and received a fixed annual payment or Civil List. At the time of the surrender the gross revenues amounted to about £89,000 and the net return to about £11,000.

In the year ended 31 March 1994, the gross income from the Crown Estate totalled £122.710 million. The sum of £78.9 million was paid to the Exchequer in 1993–4 as surplus revenue.

The land revenues in Ireland have been carried to the Consolidated Fund since 1820; from 1 April 1923, as regards the Republic of Ireland, they have been collected and administered by the Irish Government.

The land revenues in Scotland were transferred to the predecessors of the Crown Estate Commissioners in 1833.
*First Commissioner and Chairman (part-time)*, The Earl of Mansfield and Mansfield
*Second Commissioner and Chief Executive*, C. K. Howes, CB
*Commissioners (part-time)*, R. B. Caws, CBE, FRICS; P. Sober; J. N. C. James, CBE; A. S. Macdonald, CBE; J. H. M. Norris, CBE; The Lord De Ramsey
*Deputy Chief Executives*, D. E. Murray *(Property)*; D. E. G. Griffiths *(Finance and Administration)*

*Crown Estate Surveyor*, C. F. Hynes
*Asset Managers (Urban Estates)*, M. W. Dillon; J. S. Ellingford; B. T. O'Connoll; M. Tree
*Business Manager, Agricultural Estates*, R. J. Mulholland
*Asset Managers, Agricultural Estates*, J. Stumbke; I. Gorwyn
*Business Manager, Marine Estates*, F. G. Parrish
*Asset Managers, Marine Estates*, P. Davies; A. Murray
*Information Systems Manager*, D. Kingston-Smith
*Valuation and Investment Analysis Manager*, P. Shearmur
*Head of Valuation and Investment Analysis*, R. Spence
*Internal Audit Manager*, J. E. Ford
*Finance Manager*, J. G. Lelliott
*Corporate Services Manager*, M. E. Beckwith
*Legal Adviser*, M. L. Davies
*Deputy Legal Adviser*, H. Turnsek
*Solicitors*, J. B. Postgate; R. T. Hayward; M. Drayton; D. R. Apthorpe; Miss V. King; D. Harris
*Personnel Manager*, R. J. Blake
*Public Relations and Press Officer*, Mrs G. Coates
*Housing Office Manager*, R. Wyatt, 19 Bessborough Street, London SW1V 2JD. Tel: 0171-821 7144

SCOTLAND
10 Charlotte Square, Edinburgh EH2 4BR
Tel 0131-226 2741
*Crown Estate Receiver for Scotland*, M. J. Gravestock
*Asset Managers (Scottish Estates)*, N. Ruck-Keene; I. Pritchard; Ms S. Harvey
*Glenlivet Estate Ranger*, A. Wells

WINDSOR ESTATE
The Great Park, Windsor, Berks. SL4 2HT
Tel 01753-860222
*Surveyor and Deputy Ranger*, A. R. Wiseman, MVO
*Keeper of Gardens*, J. Bond

CROWN PROSECUTION SERVICE
— see page 379

---

BOARD OF CUSTOMS AND EXCISE
New King's Beam House, 22 Upper Ground, London SE1 9PJ
Tel 0171-620 1313

Commissioners of Customs were first appointed in 1671 and housed by the King in London. The Excise Department was formerly under the Inland Revenue Department and was amalgamated with the Customs Department in 1909.

HM Customs and Excise is responsible for collecting and administering customs and excise duties and value added tax, and advises the Chancellor of the Exchequer on any matters connected with them. The Department is also responsible for preventing and detecting the evasion of revenue laws and for enforcing a range of prohibitions and restrictions on the importation of certain classes of goods. In addition, the Department undertakes certain agency work on behalf of other departments, including the compilation of UK overseas trade statistics from customs import and export documents.

THE BOARD
*Chairman (G1)*, Mrs V. P. M. Strachan, CB
*Private Secretaries*, J. Wild; Ms E. Walker
*Deputy Chairman (G2)*, P. Jefferson Smith, CB; A. W. Russell
*Commissioners (G3)*, P. R. H. Allen; D. F. O. Battle; A. C. Sawyer; L. J. Harris; Mrs E. Woods; M. J. Eland; M. R. Brown

HEADQUARTERS STAFF
*Head of Information Systems (G4)*, A. G. H. Paynter
*Assistant Secretaries (G5)*, P. Kent; D. Gudgin; I. Walton;
  A. Killikelly; M. Peach; K. M. Romanski;
  B. E. G. Banks; D. C. Hewett; P. Trevett;
  B. G. Dawbarn; Mrs M. Smith; J. Campbell;
  V. C. Whittington; C. Arnott; D. P. Child; R. Kellaway;
  M. F. Knox, CBE; F. A. D. Rush; W. L. Parker;
  L. I. Stark; A. P. Allen; J. Meyler; T. Byrne;
  A. Aitchison; D. Layton; S. Kingaby; M. Joyce; B. Orr;
  H. Neuburger; J. Maclean; R. McAfee; M. Norgrove
*Head of Information (G7)*, Ms L. J. Sinclair

STATISTICAL OFFICE
*Controller (G5)*, A. H. Cowley

INVESTIGATION DIVISION
*Chief Investigation Officer (G5)*, R. Kellaway

VAT CONTROL DIRECTORATE
Queen's Dock, Liverpool L74 4AA
Tel 0151-703 8000
*Assistant Secretaries (G5)*, D. Chilver; C. J. Holloway;
  A. Howard; C. R. S. Talbot

*VAT Central Unit*
Alexander House, Victoria Avenue, Southend-on-Sea SS99
  IAA
Tel 01702-348944
*Controller (G5)*, J. Davidson

SOLICITOR'S OFFICE
*Solicitor (G2)*, D. E. J. Nissen
*Principal Assistant Solicitors (G3)*, G. Fotherby;
  R. D. S. Wylie
*Assistant Solicitors (G5)*, M. Michael; M. A. Cooper;
  M. C. K. Gasper; Miss A. E. Bolt; Miss S. G. Linton;
  J. A. Quin; I. D. Napper; J. W. Tate; D. M. North;
  C. Allen; Mrs S. Edwards; J. W. N. Tester

ACCOUNTANT AND COMPTROLLER-GENERAL'S OFFICE
*Accountant and Comptroller-General (G5)*, D. C. Hewitt
*Deputy Accountants-General (G6)*, G. B. Fox; B. Wood;
  D. J. Coyne

COLLECTORS OF CUSTOMS AND EXCISE (*G5*)
*England and Wales:*
*Birmingham*, R. A. Flavill
*Dover*, R. Crossley
*East Anglia*, R. C. Shepherd
*East Midlands*, M. D. Patten
*Leeds*, H. Peden
*Liverpool*, C. Roberts
*London Airports*, F. D. Tweddle
*London Central*, Mrs F. Boardman
*London North and West*, J. Galloway, OBE
*London Port*, R. L. H. Lawrence, CBE
*London South*, T. S. Archer
*Manchester*, J. C. Bernard
*Northampton*, A. R. Ball
*Northern England*, J. A. Rigby
*Southampton*, C. J. Packman
*South Wales and the Borders*, W. I. Stuttle
*South-west England*, P. B. Grange
*Thames Valley*, A. Bowen

*Scotland:*
*Edinburgh*, W. F. Coghill
*Glasgow and Clyde*, T. F. Jessop

*Northern Ireland:*
*Belfast*, T. W. Logan

## OFFICE OF THE DATA PROTECTION REGISTRAR
Wycliffe House, Water Lane, Wilmslow, Cheshire SK9 5AF
Tel 01625-535711 (*administration*); 01625-535777 (*enquiries*)

The Office of the Data Protection Registrar was created by
the Data Protection Act 1984. It is the Registrar's duty to
compile and maintain the Register of data users and
computer bureaux and to provide facilities for members of
the public to examine the Register; to promote observance
of data protection principles; to consider complaints made
by data subjects; to disseminate information about the Act;
to encourage the production of codes of practice by trade
associations and other bodies; to guide data users in
complying with data protection principles; to co-operate with
other parties to the Council of Europe Convention and act as
UK authority for the purposes of Article 13 of the Convention;
and to report annually to Parliament on the performance of
his functions.
*Registrar*, Mrs E. France

## MINISTRY OF DEFENCE
— see pages 392–5

## DESIGN COUNCIL
1 Oxendon Street, London SW1Y 4EE
Tel 0171-839 8000

The Design Council is incorporated by royal charter and
registered as a charity. It is the national authority on the role
of design in commercial, economic and social development.
It advises the Government and other bodies, but as a result
of a government review in 1993-4 the Council is in the
process of disposing of its existing services to industry; advice
to industry on design matters will be provided by a local
network, Business Links.
*Chairman*, J. Sorrell
*Chief Executive*, Mrs E. Ryle

## THE DUCHY OF CORNWALL
10 Buckingham Gate, London SW1E 6LA
Tel 0171-834 7346

The Duchy of Cornwall was created by Edward III in 1337
for the support of his eldest son, Edward, the Black Prince.
It is the oldest of the English duchies. Before elevation to a
dukedom, it was an earldom from 1227, when Richard, King
of the Romans and younger brother of Henry III, was created
Earl of Cornwall. Since 1503 the eldest surviving son of the
Sovereign has, as heir apparent, succeeded to the dukedom
by inheritance. The present Prince of Wales is the 24th Duke
of Cornwall, and the estate's primary function is still to
provide an income for the Duke of Cornwall and his family.
The estate is primarily agricultural, with 130,000 acres in 23
counties but mostly in the south-west of England. The Duchy
also has some residential property, a number of shops and
offices, and a Stock Exchange portfolio.

THE PRINCE'S COUNCIL
*Chairman*, HRH The Prince of Wales, KG, KT, GCB
*Lord Warden of the Stannaries*, The Lord Ashburton, KG,
  KCVO

*Receiver-General,* The Earl Cairns, CBE
*Attorney-General to the Prince of Wales,* R. J. A. Carnwath, QC
*Secretary and Keeper of the Records,* J. N. C. James, CBE
*Other members,* Earl of Shelburne; Cdr. R. J. Aylard, CVO, RN; J. E. Pugsley; A. M. J. Galsworthy; C. Howes, CB; W. N. Hood, CBE; The Earl Peel

OTHER OFFICERS
*Auditors,* I. Brindle; H. Hughes
*Sheriff* (1994–5), A. M. J. Galsworthy

---

THE DUCHY OF LANCASTER
Lancaster Place, Strand, London WC2E 7ED
Tel 0171-836 8277

The Duchy of Lancaster was created in 1351 by Edward III, when he erected Lancashire into a County Palatine; before elevation to a dukedom, it was an earldom from 1267. The estates and jurisdiction of the Duchy have been attached to the Crown since 1399, when the son of John of Gaunt, the then Duke of Lancaster, came to the throne as Henry IV. The Chancellor of the Duchy is responsible for the administration of its estates, the appointment of justices of the peace in Lancashire, Merseyside and Greater Manchester, and ecclesiastical patronage in the Duchy gift. The Chancellorship is also a Cabinet post.
*Chancellor of the Duchy of Lancaster,* The Rt. Hon. David Hunt, MBE, MP
*Attorney-General and Attorney and Serjeant within the County Palatine of Lancaster,* T. A. W. Lloyd, QC
*Receiver-General,* Maj. Sir Shane Blewitt, KCVO
*Clerk to the Council,* M. K. Ridley, CVO
*Chief Clerk,* Col. F. N. J. Davies

---

ECONOMIC AND SOCIAL RESEARCH COUNCIL
Polaris House, North Star Avenue, Swindon SN2 1UJ
Tel 01793-413000

The ESRC is an independent, government-funded body established by royal charter in 1965. It promotes and supports high-quality basic, strategic and applied social science research and related post-graduate training with the aim of increasing understanding of social and economic change and thereby enhancing the UK's industrial competitiveness, the effectiveness of public services and the quality of life. Government funding for 1994–5 is £58.9 million.
*Chairman (part-time),* Dr B. Smith, OBE
*Chief Executive,* Prof. R. Amann

For research centres, *see* pages 707–8.

---

DEPARTMENT FOR EDUCATION
Sanctuary Buildings, Great Smith Street, London SW1P 3BT
Tel 0171-925 5000

The Government Department of Education was, until the establishment of a separate office, a committee of the Privy Council appointed in 1839 to supervise the distribution of certain grants which had been made by Parliament since 1834. The Act of 1899 established the Board of Education, with a President and Parliamentary Secretary, and created a

Consultative Committee. The Education Act of 1944 established the Ministry of Education. In April 1964 the office of the Minister of Science was combined with the Ministry to form the Department of Education and Science. In July 1992, responsibility for science was transferred to the Office of Public Service and Science and the department was re-named the Department for Education. It has overall responsibility for education in England.
*Secretary of State for Education,* The Rt. Hon. Gillian Shephard, MP
*Private Secretary,* Miss P. Laidlaw
*Minister of State,* Eric Forth, MP
*Private Secretary,* Ms C. Maye
*Parliamentary Under-Secretaries of State,* Tim Boswell, MP; Robin Squire, MP
*Private Secretaries,* D. Walsh; Miss J. A. Yates
*Permanent Secretary (G1),* Sir Tim Lankester
*Private Secretary,* C. S. Wormald
*Deputy Secretaries (G2),* R. J. Dawe, CB, OBE; P. F. Owen, CB; J. C. Hedger
*Under-Secretaries (G3),* P. A. Shaw; C. A. Clark; D. M. Forrester; R. D. Horne; S. R. C. Jones; E. R. Morgan; M. J. Richardson; R. N. Ricks (*Legal Adviser*); N. J. Sanders; C. H. Saville; R. L. Smith; N. Summers

PERSONNEL AND ORGANIZATION BRANCH
*Grade 4,* Mrs H. Douglas
*Assistant Secretaries (G5),* L. B. Webb; Mrs I. Wilde
*Senior Principals (G6),* H. H. Barrick; G. H. N. Evans; S. Green
*Principals (G7),* R. Ward; K. R. Fitzgerald; M. L. Lyons; A. W. Wilshaw; Ms E. M. T. Casbon; W. N. Greenway; Miss J. A. Knight; C. Walker

INFORMATION SYSTEMS BRANCH
*Assistant Secretary (G5),* A. K. C. Gibson
*Senior Principals (G6),* P. D. Gott; E. Herbert; N. Rudd
*Principals (G7),* B. Lillburn; Mrs N. A. T. Malt; M. Midwood; A. P. Thompson; D. Craggs; J. Winkle; M. Young; J. Fitch; D. R. Pollard; M. Fisher

ANALYTICAL SERVICES BRANCH
*Head of Branch (G4),* D. Allnutt
*Chief Statisticians (G5),* J. W. Gardner; Miss P. Annesley; Miss S. J. Walton
*Head of Economics (G5),* D. J. Thompson
*Head of Operations Research Unit (G5),* R. B. Ladley
*Statisticians (G7),* A. J. Barnett; R. K. Jain; S. N. Kew; T. C. Knight; M. J. Davidson; N. Rudoe; Mrs H. E. Evans; S. K. Cook; Miss A. C. Kennedy; Miss A. C. Brown; M. R. Boothroyd; A. Ball
*Economics Advisers (G7),* J. Tarsh; M. Thompson
*Principals (G7),* A. P. O'Connor; D. S. Daniels

SCHOOL ORGANIZATION BRANCH
*Assistant Secretaries (G5),* B. Glickman; M. Hipkins; A. J. Shaw; P. J. Thorpe; J. W. Whitaker
*Chief Architect (G5),* G. J. Parker
*Chief Engineer (G6),* M. J. Patel
*Superintending Architect (G6),* J. J. Wilson
*Principals (G7),* M. E. Malt; Miss L. M. Clarke; N. R. Flint; Mrs C. K. Saville; Ms A. Barlow; K. L. R. English; D. F. Miller; M. Bell; I. Hughes; K. Mullany; A. Benson-Wilson; Mrs M. Farthing; M. Markus; Mrs A. Jackson; Mrs C. J. Crathorne; D. Robins; Ms M. Watts; Mrs L. Slater; A. Sevier; Ms A. Rushton
*Principal Architects (G7),* E. C. Bissell; Mrs D. Holt; Miss E. J. Lloyd-Jones, OBE; P. Lenssen; Miss B. M. T. Sanders; J. R. C. Brooke; A. C. Thompson; Miss

S. A. Legg; Miss L. Watson; R. H. Bishop;
T. J. Williamson; R. A. Butler; J. Bucknell
*Principal Quantity Surveyors (G7)*, A. A. Jones;
G. E. Wonnacott; D. F. Ashby
*SPTO Architects*, W. Beadling; A. V. Brock; Miss
F. A. Cowburn; J. A. Ibikunle; P. Kemp; Mrs
H. C. Nicholls; B. Goldsmith; J. Brooke
*SPTO Quantity Surveyor*, C. H. C. Marshall
*SPTO Engineer*, R. L. Daniels
*SPTO Designer*, Miss A. Wadsworth

PUPILS AND PARENTS BRANCH
*Assistant Secretaries (G5)*, T. B. Jeffery; Mrs P. A. Masters;
M. D. Phipps; A. J. Sargent
*Grade 6*, G. A. Holley
*Principals (G7)*, C. Dowe; Miss S. A. Clarke; S. Dance;
A. B. Thompson; R. Mace; M. Williams; Miss
L. Chapman; A. Short; Miss P. Ginger; C. Barnham;
M. Sharpe; Ms J. M. Saraga; J. Ford

SCHOOL FUNDING BRANCH
*Assistant Secretaries (G5)*, M. C. Stark; A. Clarke;
S. A. Marston
*Principals (G7)*, S. J. Bishop; J. Browning; P. G. Cohen;
A. J. Cromwell; C. Dee; P. W. Fulford-Jones;
R. A. V. Jacobs; Ms R. M. King; A. P. Smith

SCHOOL CURRICULUM BRANCH
*Assistant Secretaries (G5)*, Miss C. A. Bienkowska;
P. S. Lewis; M. F. Neale; S. R. Williams
*Principals (G7)*, Mrs J. Baker; Ms G. Beauchamp; Mrs
S. Jetha; J. A. Lawrence; T. Linden; I. C. Loveless;
S. A. Mellor; D. J. Noble; A. A. E. Partridge; Ms
R. D. Pearce; A. J. Pokorny; T. C. Tarrant;
B. A. R. Tovey; R. J. Wood

TEACHERS BRANCH
*Assistant Secretaries (G5)*, Ms S. L. Scales; A. J. Wye;
R. W. Chattaway
*Principals (G7)*, M. Barker; N. Cornwell; S. M. Hillier;
P. F. Curran; P. V. D. Swift; J. C. Sheridan

HIGHER EDUCATION BRANCH
*Assistant Secretaries (G5)*, A. Woollard; Mrs S. J. Trundle
*Principals (G7)*, A. Smyth; A. Callaghan; Miss K. J. Fleay;
Ms S. P. Gane

FURTHER EDUCATION BRANCH
*Head of FE Support Unit (G4)*, B. D. Short
*Assistant Secretaries (G5)*, S. T. Crowne; S. E. Kershaw;
Miss J. Partington
*Senior Principals (G6)*, E. F. H. Brittain; B. J. Smeaton
*Principals (G7)*, Mrs P. Bailey; J. Bushnell; P. Humfryes;
P. Long; E. Schuldt; C. Trudgett

STUDENT AFFAIRS BRANCH
*Assistant Secretaries (G5)*, J. P. Moore; J. S. Street
*Grade 6*, Miss C. E. Treen
*Principals (G7)*, D. D. Cook; Ms S. C. Garner; E. D. Foster;
Mrs P. Tansley; Miss J. Spatcher

INTERNATIONAL RELATIONS AND YOUTH BRANCH
*Assistant Secretaries (G5)*, Miss C. E. Hodkinson; Miss
M. d'Armenia
*Principals (G7)*, Miss L. Hanmer; Ms V. Berkeley;
D. Barwick; R. Troedson; A. Bidewell; T. Goldman

LEGAL BRANCH
*Legal Adviser (G3)*, R. N. Ricks
*Assistant Legal Advisers (G5)*, D. J. Aries; A. D. Preston;
F. D. W. Clarke
*Senior Principal Legal Officers (G6)*, N. P. Beach;
A. K. Fraser

*Principal Legal Officers (G7)*, Mrs A. E. Heilpern; Mrs
C. Manuel; C. J. Hales; Ms C. J. Reay; Miss
A. M. Goodfellow

INFORMATION BRANCH
*Grade 4*, J. W. Coe
*Senior Principal Information Officers (G6)*, K. B. Kerslake;
M. Paterson
*Chief Information Officer (G7)*, T. Cook
*Marketing Manager (G7)*, J. M. Brown

*Information Bureau and Library*
*Chief Librarian*, Miss M. Wilson

FINANCE BRANCH
*Assistant Secretaries (G5)*, R. Hull; P. F. Slade; R. J. Green;
N. J. Thirtle
*Senior Principal (G6)*, T. A. H. Tyler (*Assistant Accountant-
General*)
*Principals (G7)*, R. J. Gardner; P. G. Dalgleish;
J. J. Watson; S. D. James; S. M. Philpotts; Mrs S. Evans;
Miss B. Smart; Ms L. McAvoy; Mrs S. Todd;
N. Blackmore

EXECUTIVE AGENCY
TEACHERS PENSION AGENCY
Staindrop Road, Darlington, Co. Durham DL3 9EE
Tel 01325-392929
The Agency administers the teachers' superannuation
scheme in England and Wales.
*Chief Executive*, Mrs D. Metcalfe
*Directors*, K. M. Miles; P. M. Bleasdale; A. Allison;
D. G. Sanders

OFFICE FOR STANDARDS IN EDUCATION
(OFSTED)
Alexandra House, 33 Kingsway, London WC2B 6UF

A non-ministerial government department established in
September 1992 to keep the Secretary of State informed
about the standards and management of schools in England,
and to establish and monitor a new independent inspection
system for maintained schools in England.
*HM Chief Inspector (G2)*, C. Woodhead
*Director of Administration (G3)*, T. Flescher
*Director of Inspection (G3)*, Miss A. C. Millett
*Deputy Directors of Inspection (G4)*, A. J. Rose;
M. J. Tomlinson

TEAM MANAGERS
*Curriculum and Assessment (G5)*, T. Wylie
*Equal Opportunities and Access (G5)*, Mrs B. Fawcett
*External Relations (G5)*, P. Singh
*Finance (G5)*, B. Townsend
*Independent, International and Island Schools (G5)*, Miss
B. J. Lewis
*Management (G5)*, C. Payne
*Monitoring (G5)*, I. Shelton
*Personnel (G5)*, Miss J. Phillips
*Post-Compulsory Education (G5)*, D. West
*Quality Assurance and Development (G5)*, A. P. Matthews
*Registration (G5)*, J. Grewe
*Research and Analysis (G5)*, D. Soulsby
*Resource Planning (G5)*, D. W. Taylor
*Schools At Risk (G5)*, Miss E. Passmore
*Special Educational Needs (G5)*, Miss D. Chorley
*Teacher Education (G5)*, V. Green, CBE
*Territorial (G5)*, R. Brake
*Training and Assessment of Independent Inspectors (G5)*, Miss
E. Pagliacci

*Information (G6)*, J. Lawson
*Information Systems (G6)*, M. Childs
*Competition and Compliance (G7)*, C. Bramley

There are 27 Grade 5 Inspectors and 214 Grade 6 Inspectors

---

OFFICE OF ELECTRICITY REGULATION
Hagley House, Hagley Road, Birmingham B16 8QG
Tel 0121-456 2100
SCOTLAND: 48 Vincent Street, Glasgow G2 5TS
Tel 0141-248 5917

---

The Office of Electricity Regulation (OFFER) is the
regulatory body for the electricity supply industry in England,
Scotland and Wales. Its functions are to promote competition
in the generation and supply of electricity; to ensure that all
reasonable demands for electricity are satisfied; to protect
customers' interests in relation to prices; security of supply
and quality of services; and to promote the efficient use of
electricity. Headed by the Director-General of Electricity
Supply, OFFER was set up under the Electricity Act 1989
but is independent of ministerial control.
*Director-General of Electricity Supply*, Prof. S. C. Littlechild
*Deputy Director-General*, C. P. Carter
*Deputy Director-General for Scotland*, G. L. Sims
*Directors of Regulation and Business Affairs*, G. R. Horton;
   A. J. Boorman
*Director of Consumer Affairs*, vacant
*Technical Director*, Dr B. Wharmby
*Director of Public Affairs*, Miss J. D. Luke
*Director of Administration*, H. P. Jones
*Legal Adviser*, M. R. Brocklehurst
*Chief Examiner*, J. D. Cooper

---

OFFICE OF ELECTRICITY REGULATION
NORTHERN IRELAND
Brookmount Buildings, 42 Fountain Street, Belfast BT1 5EE
Tel 01232-311575

---

OFFER NI is the regulatory body for the electricity supply
industry in Northern Ireland.
*Director-General of Electricity Supply for Northern Ireland*,
   G. R. Horton
*Deputy Director-General*, C. H. Coulthard

---

EMPLOYMENT DEPARTMENT GROUP
Caxton House, Tothill Street, London SW1H 9NF
Tel 0171-273 3000

---

The Employment Department Group is responsible for
government policies aimed at producing a competitive,
efficient and flexible labour market. Its main objectives are
to help people acquire and improve their skills, to help
unemployed and other disadvantaged people into work, to
encourage industries to train their workforce, to protect
people at work and the public from industrial risks, and to
promote women's opportunities. The Secretary of State for
Employment is responsible for setting the strategic policy
framework in consultation with the Secretaries of State for
Scotland and Wales. In April 1994, responsibility for training
policy in Scotland and Wales within these strategic aims was
transferred to the Scottish and Welsh Offices respectively.

The Employment Department Group's policy interests
are carried out by the Department itself and by three other
bodies, all reporting to the Secretary of State for Employment.
These are the Health and Safety Commission (*see* page 312–
13), ACAS (*see* page 281) and the Employment Service (an
executive agency of the Department). The training, enterprise and education functions of the Department are carried
out by the Training, Enterprise and Education Directorate,
and the responsibility for planning and delivering government-funded training and enterprise programmes rests with
the network of 82 independent Training and Enterprise
Councils in England and Wales and with 22 Local Enterprise
Companies in Scotland (for addresses, see local telephone
directories).
*Secretary of State for Employment*, The Rt. Hon. Michael
   Portillo, MP
   *Principal Private Secretary (G5)*, P. Wanless
   *Private Secretaries*, S. Courage; Ms J. Curtis
   *Special Adviser*, Ms A. Broom
*Minister of State*, Ann Widdecombe, MP
   *Private Secretary*, P. Buckley
*Parliamentary Under-Secretaries of State*, James Paice, MP;
   The Hon. Phillip Oppenheim, MP
   *Private Secretaries*, S. Wood; Ms C. Pride
*Parliamentary Clerk*, Ms M. East
*Permanent Secretary (G1)*, Sir Nicholas Monck, KCB
   *Private Secretary*, A. Virgo
*Deputy Secretaries (G2)*, N. W. Stuart, CB; G. Reid, CB;
   I. Johnston
*Legal Adviser (G3)*, H. R. L. Purse
*Special Advisers*, I. Wilton; Ms C. Stratton

EMPLOYMENT DEPARTMENT
HEADQUARTERS

TRAINING, ENTERPRISE AND EDUCATION
DIRECTORATE
Moorfoot, Sheffield S1 4PQ
Tel 0114-275 3275

*Director-General (G2)*, Dr I. Johnston
*Director of Operations (G3)*, S. Loveman
*Head of Financial Control Unit (G5)*, N. Gregory
*Regional Directors, see* pages 348–9

*Youth and Education Policy Division*
*Director (G3)*, Mrs V. Bayliss
*Heads of Branches (G5)*; J. Robertson (*Schools and
   Partnerships Policy*); M. Brimmer (*Careers Information*);
   R. Wye (*Young People and Work*); T. Fellowes (*Further
   and Higher Education*); A. Davies (*Careers Service*)

*Training Infrastructure and Employers Division*
*Director (G3)*, N. Schofield
*Heads of Branches (G5)*, M. Nicholas (*Employer Investment*);
   J. Franklin (*European Training Policy, Programmes and
   Funding*); J. Fuller (*Qualifications and Industry Training
   Organizations*); G. Debling (*Development Strategy Unit*)

*Planning Division*
*Director (G4)*, Ms F. Everiss
*Heads of Branches (G5)*, H. Sharp (*Operational Policy*);
   J. West (*Resource Planning*); Ms L. Ammon (*Operational
   Monitoring*)

*Adults and Training Strategy Division*
*Director (G3)*, B. Heatley
*Head of Branches (G5/G6)*, D. Tansley (*Adult Training,
   Special Needs and Equal Opportunities*); J. Smith
   (*Individual Commitment*); T. Down (*Training Strategy and
   Secretariat*)

*Quality Assurance Division*
*Director (G3)*, P. Thomas
*Heads of Branches (G5)*, C. Williams (*Financial Analysis and Review*); J. Blizard (*Quality Assurance*); K. Franklin (*Quality Policy and Networking*)

INDUSTRIAL RELATIONS AND INTERNATIONAL DIRECTORATE
*Director (G2)*, G. Reid
*International Division (G3)*, C. Tucker
*Industrial Relations Division I (G3)*, Ms H. Leiser
*Industrial Relations Division II (G3)*, B. Niven
*Statistical Services Division (G3)*, P. Stibbard

RESOURCES AND STRATEGY DIRECTORATE
*Director (G2)*, N. W. Stuart, CB
*Finance and Resource Management Division (G3)*, L. Lewis
*Economics, Research and Evaluation Division (G3)*, Dr J. Robertson
*Strategy and Employment Policy Division (G3)*, P. Makeham
*Personnel and Development Division (G3)*, D. Normington
*Strategy Unit (G4)*, M. Emmott
*Business Services Division (G4)*, K. Jordan
*Information Branch (G5)*, B. Sutlieff

## THE EMPLOYMENT SERVICE
St Vincent House, 30 Orange Street London WC2H 7HT
Tel 0171-839 5600

An executive agency within the Department of Employment. The Employment Service is responsible for providing services and administering programmes to help unemployed people get back to work as quickly as possible and to make payments to those entitled to benefit.
*Chief Executive (G3 + )*, M. E. G. Fogden, CB
*Deputy Chief Executive (G3)*, D. Grover
*Director of Finance and Resources (G4)*, A. G. Johnson
*Director of Field Operations (G4)*, R. Phillips
*Director of Business Development (G4)*, K. White
*Director of Human Resources (G4)*, D. B. Price
*Regional Directors (G4)*, R. Foster (*London*); M. Raff, CBE (*West Midlands*); (*G5*), Mrs A. Le Sage (*East Midlands*); P. Robson (*Northern*); J. Roberts (*North-west*); K. Pascoe (*South-west*); G. Humphreys (*Yorkshire and Humberside*)
*Director for Scotland (G5)*, A. R. Brown
*Director for Wales (G5)*, E. B. Pearce

## ENGINEERING AND PHYSICAL SCIENCES RESEARCH COUNCIL
Polaris House, North Star Avenue, Swindon, Wilts. SN2 1ET
Tel 01793-444000

The Engineering and Physical Sciences Research Council was established in April 1994 from part of the former Science and Engineering Research Council. It is funded through the Office of Science and Technology. Its purposes are to develop the natural and physical sciences, including engineering; to maintain a fundamental capacity of research and scholarship; and to support relevant postgraduate education. EPSRC's role is to encourage and support all basic and strategic research and training in UK higher education institutions in the natural and physical sciences and engineering. Government funding for 1994–5 is £364 million.
*Chairman (part-time)*, Dr A. Rudge, OBE, FRS, FEng.
*Chief Executive*, Prof. R. Brook, OBE

*Members*, Prof. J. M. Ball, FRS; Prof. A. N. Broers, FRS, FEng.; Prof. Sir David Davies, FEng.; Dr W. D. Evans; Dr D. J. Giachardi; Prof. J. S. Higgins; Prof. B. F. G. Johnson, FRS; Dr A. Ledwith; S. Miller; Prof. J. O. Thomas, FRS; Prof. D. J. Wallace; D. A. Wilkinson

For Daresbury and Rutherford Appleton Laboratories (DRAL), *see* page 708.

## ENGLISH HERITAGE
— *see* Historic Buildings and Monuments Commission for England

## ENGLISH NATURE
Northminster House, Peterborough PE1 1UA
Tel 01733-340345

English Nature (the Nature Conservancy Council for England) was established in 1991 and is responsible for advising the Government on nature conservation in England. It promotes, directly and through others, the conservation of England's wildlife and natural features. It selects, establishes and manages National Nature Reserves and identifies and notifies Sites of Special Scientific Interest. It provides advice and information about nature conservation, and supports and conducts research relevant to these functions. Through the Joint Nature Conservation Committee (*see* page 338), it works with its sister organizations in Scotland and Wales on UK and international nature conservation issues.
In January 1994 the Government announced that it was considering merging the work of English Nature and the Countryside Commission (*see* page 297).
*Chairman*, The Earl of Cranbrook
*Chief Executive*, Dr D. R. Langslow
*Directors*, Dr K. L. Duff; E. T. Idle; Miss C. E. M. Wood; Ms S. Collins

## ENGLISH PARTNERSHIPS
16–18 Old Queen Street, London SW1H 9HP
Tel 0171-976 7070

English Partnerships, in statute the Urban Regeneration Agency, came into full operation on 1 April 1994, its primary aim being to secure the reclamation and reuse of vacant and derelict land throughout England, in partnership with the public, private and voluntary sectors.
*Chairman*, The Lord Walker of Worcester, MBE, PC
*Deputy Chairman*, Sir Idris Pearce, CBE
*Chief Executive*, D. Taylor

## DEPARTMENT OF THE ENVIRONMENT
2 Marsham Street, London SW1P 3EB
Tel 0171-276 3000

The Department of the Environment is responsible for planning and land use; local government; housing and construction; inner city areas; new towns; environmental protection; conservation areas and countryside affairs; energy efficiency; and property holdings.
*Secretary of State for the Environment*, The Rt. Hon. John Gummer, MP
　*Private Secretary*, A. G. Riddell
　*Special Advisers*, T. Burke; K. Adams; L. O'Connor

*Minister for Local Government,* David Curry, MP
  *Private Secretary,* P. Stamp
  *Parliamentary Private Secretary,* D. French, MP
*Minister for Construction and Planning,* The Viscount
  Ullswater
  *Private Secretary,* Mrs C. Mayes
*Minister for Environment and Countryside,* Robert Atkins, MP
  *Private Secretary,* Mrs T. Vokes
  *Special Adviser to Ministers of State,* J. Gray
*Parliamentary Under-Secretaries of State,* Robert Jones, MP;
  Sir Paul Beresford, MP
  *Private Secretaries,* Miss M. Cameron; Miss D. Butler
*Lord-in-Waiting,* The Viscount St Davids
  *Private Secretary,* Mrs P. Sambrook
*Parliamentary Clerk,* T. Teehan
*Permanent Secretary (G1),* A. Turnbull, CB, CVO
  *Private Secretary,* Mrs B. Houlden


ORGANIZATION AND ESTABLISHMENTS
Lambeth Bridge House, London SE1 7SB
Tel 0171-238 3000

*Principal Establishments and Finance Officer (G2),* D. J. Burr

PERSONNEL
*Director (G3),* J. A. Owen
*Grade 5,* J. Adams; K. G. Arnold; L. B. Hicks
*Grade 6,* M. A. L. Ross; R. E. Vidler; Miss J. A. Clark;
  J. Kingdom
*Chief Welfare Officer (G7),* Miss E. T. Haines

FINANCE CENTRAL
*Under-Secretary (G3),* W. F. S. Rickett
*Heads of Divisions (G5),* B. L. Glicksman; I. H. Nicol;
  D. L. H. Roberts; P. D. Walton

ADMINISTRATION RESOURCES
*Director (G3),* D. A. R. Peel
*Grade 5,* A. C. Allberry; I. S. Elrick; M. R. Haselip;
  J. J. O'Callaghan
*Grade 6,* M. J. Burt

INFORMATION
*Director (G4),* M. Granatt
*Grade 5,* J. Gee


CITIES AND COUNTRYSIDE GROUP
*Deputy Secretary (G2),* P. J. Fletcher

CITIES AND COUNTRYSIDE POLICY DIRECTORATE
*Director (G3),* M. B. Gahagan
*Heads of Divisions (G5),* J. Jacobs; A. Richardson; Mrs
  M. E. Winckler; R. O. Shaw

HOUSING AND URBAN MONITORING AND ANALYSIS
*Under-Secretary (G3),* Dr C. P. Evans
*Grade 5,* J. E. Turner; A. E. Holmans, CBE; Mrs
  J. Littlewood; M. Hughes; S. Aldridge

INTEGRATED REGIONAL OFFICES UNIT
*Grade 5,* vacant

WILDLIFE AND COUNTRYSIDE DIRECTORATE
*Under-Secretary (G3),* R. J. A. Sharp, CB
*Grade 5,* R. W. Bunce; R. M. Pritchard; R. Hepworth

CITIES, COUNTRYSIDE AND PRIVATE FINANCE
*Director (G3),* D. A. McDonald
*Grade 5,* J. P. Channing; J. McCarthy; G. L. Laufer


HOUSING AND CONSTRUCTION GROUP
*Deputy Secretary (G2),* Miss D. A. Nichols

SECRETARIAT
*Grade 7,* P. G. Tobia

HOUSING POLICY AND PRIVATE SECTOR
*Director (G4),* N. A. J. Kinghan
*Grade 5,* J. E. Roberts; Mrs H. Ghosh; C. L. L. Braun
*Grade 6,* Miss J. A. Clark

HOUSING RESOURCES AND MANAGEMENT
*Under-Secretary (G3),* Mrs M. McDonald
*Grade 5,* J. G. Grevatt; Dr J. F. A. Moore; J. N. Lithgow; Dr
  R. P. Thorogood
*Grade 6,* R. J. Wood

PROPERTY AND BUILDINGS
*Director (G4),* D. O. McCreadie
*Grade 5,* J. M. Leigh-Pollitt; P. F. Everall
*Grade 6,* W. J. Marsh; R. F. Window

ENERGY EFFICIENCY OFFICE
*Grade 3,* J. Hobson
*Grade 5,* R. J. Dinwiddy; Dr J. Miles; A. F. Galloway

CENTRAL MANAGEMENT AND ANALYSIS UNIT
*Chief Economist (G3),* N. J. Glass
*Economists (G6),* T. M. Davis; E. Evans


PROPERTY HOLDINGS AND CENTRAL
SUPPORT SERVICES
*Deputy Secretary (G2),* A. J. Lane, CB

PRINCIPAL FINANCE OFFICER AND AGENCY
SPONSORSHIP
*Under-Secretary (G3),* J. P. Henry
*Grade 5,* B. Redfern; M. H. Bowles
*Grade 6,* D. L. Smith

PROPERTY HOLDINGS DIRECTORATE
*Director (G3),* N. E. Borrett
*Grade 5,* R. W. P. Brice; A. R. Edwards
*Grade 6,* P. R. L. Hodson; D. M. Gillen
*Heads of Outstations (G6),* P. R. Stewart; J. C. Lewis;
  A. R. Jones; R. M. Barry; M. J. Hathaway;
  A. J. Partridge; C. G. H. Young


LOCAL GOVERNMENT AND PLANNING
*Deputy Secretary (G2),* C. J. S. Brearley, CB

LOCAL GOVERNMENT FINANCE POLICY
*Director, Local Government Finance Policy (G3),*
  P. J. Britton
*Heads of Divisions (G5),* M. H. Coulshed; R. J. Gibson;
  M. J. C. Faulkner; N. Dorling; Mrs P. Peneck; Dr
  C. Myerscough

LOCAL GOVERNMENT
*Under-Secretary (G3),* Mrs M. McDonald
*Heads of Divisions (G5),* Miss L. F. Bell; L. G. Packer;
  P. Rowsell
*Grade 6,* T. B. J. Crossley; J. R. Footit

PLANNING DIRECTORATE
*Under-Secretary (G3),* J. F. Ballard
*Heads of Divisions (G5),* D. N. Donaldson; R. Jones;
  M. J. Quinn; M. R. Ash; J. Zetter; R. C. Mabey;
  A. M. Oliver


LEGAL
*Solicitor and Legal Adviser (G2),* Mrs M. A. Morgan
*Deputy Solicitors (G3),* J. A. Catlin; Ms D. Unerman

*Assistant Solicitors (G3)*, P. J. Szell; *(G5)*, J. L. Comber;
I. D. Day; Mrs S. Headley; Mrs P. J. Conlon; Mrs
G. Hedley-Dent; D. W. Jordan; Miss D. C. S. Phillips;
N. S. Lefton; Ms A. Brett-Holt; D. J. Noble

## ENVIRONMENT PROTECTION
*Deputy Secretary (G2)*, F. A. Osborn, CB

HM INSPECTORATE OF POLLUTION
*Director and Chief Inspector (G3)*, Dr D. H. Slater
*Deputy Chief Inspector (G4)*, Dr A. Duncan
*Heads of Division (G5)*, Dr K. Speakman; L. N. Stuffins; Dr
D. J. Bryce; I. C. McBrayne

DIRECTORATE OF AIR, CLIMATE AND TOXIC
SUBSTANCES
*Under-Secretary (G3)*, Dr D. J. Fisk
*Heads of Division (G5)*, A. Davis; Dr N. J. King; R. Mills
*Grade 6*, Dr A. J. Apling; D. L. Pounder; Dr P. J. Corcoran;
Dr L. M. Smith; Dr M. Williams

CHIEF SCIENTIST
*Chief Scientist (G3)*, Dr D. J. Fisk
*Head of Division (G5)*, A. J. Apling

DIRECTORATE OF POLLUTION CONTROL AND WASTES
*Under-Secretary (G3)*, R. S. Dudding
*Heads of Division (G5)*, Mrs L. A. C. Simcock; N. Sanders;
Dr P. Hinchcliffe; J. Cleary; Dr N. Williams

ENVIRONMENTAL POLICY AND ANALYSIS
*Director (G3)*, A. G. Watson
*Heads of Division (G5)*, Mrs H. Hillier; J. S. Stevens;
J. W. M. Rogers; R. Wilson; P. F. Unwin

WATER DIRECTORATE
*Director (G3)*, N. W. Summerton
*Heads of Divisions (G5)*, A. J. C. Simcock; J. Vaughan;
M. Nelson; Mrs H. Chipping

*Drinking Water Inspectorate*
*Grade 5*, M. J. Rouse

## REGIONAL OFFICES
— *see* pages 348–9

## EXECUTIVE AGENCIES

BUILDING RESEARCH ESTABLISHMENT
Garston, Watford WD2 7JR
Tel 01923-894040
The BRE carries out research and provides advice on the
design, construction and performance of buildings, and
supports government departments in their related responsi-
bilities.
*Chief Executive (G3)*, R. G. Courtney
*Deputy Chief Executives (G4)*, N. O. Milbank; Dr
W. D. Woolley
*Directors of Groups and Stations (G5)*, B. O. Hall; Dr
N. J. Cook, Dr V. H. C. Crisp; Dr A. B. Birtles; J. Horan

THE BUYING AGENCY
Royal Liver Building, Pier Head, Liverpool L3 IPE
Tel 0151-227 4262
The Agency provides a professional purchasing service to
government departments and other public bodies.
*Chief Executive (G5)*, S. P. Sage

PLANNING INSPECTORATE
Tollgate House, Houlton Street, Bristol BS2 9DJ
Tel 0117-921 8950
The Inspectorate is responsible for casework involving
planning, housing, roads, environmental and related legisla-
tion.

*Chief Executive and Chief Inspector of Planning (G3)*,
C. Shepley
*Deputy Chief Inspector of Planning (G4)*, J. I. T. Dunlop
*Assistant Chief Planning Inspectors (G5)*, M. I. Montague-
Smith; J. Acton; R. E. Wilson; J. Greenfield; C. Jenkins;
Mrs S. Bruton; J. T. Graham; D. E. John
*Head of Administration (G5)*, P. N. Cheeseman
*Head of Finance, Management Services and Information
Systems (G5)*, M. Brasher

QUEEN ELIZABETH II CONFERENCE CENTRE
Broad Sanctuary, London SW1P 3EE
Tel 0171-798 4010
The Centre provides conference and banqueting facilities for
both private sector and government use.
*Chief Executive (G5)*, M. C. Buck

SECURITY FACILITIES EXECUTIVE
St Christopher House, Southwark Street, London SE1 OTE
Tel 0171-921 3995
The Agency provides a range of security support services,
products and systems.
*Chief Executive (G5)*, J. C. King

---

## ROYAL COMMISSION ON ENVIRONMENTAL
POLLUTION
Church House, Great Smith Street, London SW1P 3BZ
Tel 0171-276 2080

---

The Commission was set up in 1970 to advise on matters,
both national and international, concerning the pollution of
the environment; on the adequacy of research in this field;
and the future possibilities of danger to the environment.
*Chairman*, Sir John Houghton, CBE, FRS
*Members*, Sir Geoffrey Allen, FRS; Prof. H. Charnock, CBE,
FRS; Prof. Dame Barbara Clayton, DBE; Dr P. Doyle, CBE,
FRSE; H. R. Fell; P. R. A. Jacques, CBE;
Prof. J. H. Lawton, FRS; Prof. R. Macrory, FRSA;
Prof. J. G. Morris; Prof. E. M. Rothschild; The Earl of
Selborne, KBE, FRS; Prof. Z. A. Silberston, OBE
*Secretary*, D. R. Lewis

---

## EQUAL OPPORTUNITIES COMMISSION
Overseas House, Quay Street, Manchester M3 3HN
Tel 0161-833 9244

---

*Press Office*, Swan House, 53 Poland Street, London
W1V 3DF. Tel: 0171-287 3953
*Regional Offices*, Stock Exchange House, 7 Nelson Mandela
Place, Glasgow G2 1QW. Tel: 0141-248 5833; Caerwys
House, Windsor Place, Cardiff. Tel: 01222-343552

The Commission was set up by Parliament in 1975 as a result
of the passing of the Sex Discrimination Act. It works towards
the elimination of discrimination on the grounds of sex or
marital status and to promote equality of opportunity
between men and women generally.
*Chairwoman (£44,220)*, Ms K. Bahl
*Deputy Chairwoman (£29,650)*, Lady (Diana) Brittan
*Members*, Ms B. Hillon; Ms A. Watts, OBE; Ms N. Bray; Ms
A. Gibson; Mrs B. Kelly; Ms C. Wells; C. Mather;
P. Smith; Ms M. Berg
*Chief Executive*, P. Naish

EQUAL OPPORTUNITIES COMMISSION FOR NORTHERN
IRELAND
Chamber of Commerce House, 22 Great Victoria Street,
Belfast BT2 7BA
Tel 01232-242752
*Chair and Chief Executive*, Mrs J. Smyth

EXCHEQUER AND AUDIT DEPARTMENT
— see National Audit Office

ECGD (EXPORT CREDITS GUARANTEE
DEPARTMENT)
PO Box 2200, 2 Exchange Tower, Harbour Exchange
Square, London E14 9GS
Tel 0171-512 7000

ECGD (Export Credits Guarantee Department), the official
export credit insurer, is a separate government department
responsible to the President of the Board of Trade and
functions under the Export and Investment Guarantees Act
1991. This enables ECGD to facilitate UK exports by making
available export credit insurance to British firms engaged in
selling overseas and to guarantee repayment to banks in
Britain providing finance for export credit for goods sold on
credit terms of two years or more. The Act also empowers
ECGD to insure British private investment overseas against
political risks such as war, expropriation and restrictions on
remittances.
*Chief Executive*, W. B. Willott
*Group Directors (G3)*, M. V. Hawtin; J. R. Weiss;
　T. M. Jaffray
*Grade 5*, R. P. Burnett; P. J. Callaghan; D. C. Cooper;
　J. C. W. Croall; S. R. Dodgson; R. G. Elden;
　A. P. Fowell; R. Gotts; R. F. Lethbridge; V. P. Lunn
　Rockliffe; M. E. Maddox; M. D. Pentecost;
　R. A. Ranson; B. M. Sidwell, TD; J. S. Snowdon
*Grade 6*, G. Cassell; F. O. H. Coulson;
　R. O. L. Drummond; J. M. Foster; N. Harington;
　R. J. Healey; G. G. Jones; Ms S. Rice; D. I. Robbins;
　E. Walsby
*Grade 7*, Ms C. L. Anderson; J. S. Astruc; D. I. Calvert; Mrs
　A. C. Cowie; D. M. Cox; G. P. Cox; M. J. Crane;
　M. Cranwell; R. P. D. Crick; D. L. Dyke;
　A. C. Faulkner; G. C. Fisher; P. C. Gaudoin;
　N. F. George; R. Hardy; P. F. Henson; P. S. Hillman;
　P. Jackson; S. J. Johnson; K. Jones; C. King;
　N. A. Lambert; S. E. Lee; C. J. Leeds; M. M. Leonard;
　I. Mackay; R. A. J. D. Mayer; S. Merchack;
　A. J. E. Muckersie; P. L. Neal; G. A. Newhouse;
　J. K. Peacock; S. C. Pond; P. J. Radford;
　A. B. Redmayne; D. M. Riley; S. Rosenthal;
　P. J. Rossington; M. A. Sherane; K. R. Smith;
　R. S. Summers; J. Sweeney; J. A. Sweet; J. L. Swindon;
　Miss V. M. Taylor; Ms A. V. Thomas; C. M. Thorogood;
　T. West; J. M. Willis; I. Wilson; L. A. Woods;
　D. L. Wyatt; J. A. Youd

EXPORT GUARANTEES ADVISORY COUNCIL
*Chairman*, R. T. Fox, CBE
*Other Members*, Sir Robert Davidson; B. P. Dawe Mathews,
　TD; T. M. Evans, CBE; Sir Frank Lampl; G. W. Lynch;
　J. W. Melbourn, CBE; D. B. Newlands; Sir Derek
　Thomas, KCMG; The Viscount Weir

OFFICE OF FAIR TRADING
Field House, Bream's Buildings, London EC4A 1PR
Tel 0171-242 2858

The Office of Fair Trading is a non-ministerial government
department headed by the Director-General of Fair Trading.
It keeps commercial activities in the UK under review and
seeks to protect consumers against unfair trading practices.
The Director-General's consumer protection duties under
the Fair Trading Act 1973, together with his responsibilities
under the Consumer Credit Act 1974, the Estate Agents Act
1979, and Control of Misleading Advertisements Regulations
1988, are administered by the Office's Consumer Affairs
Division. The Competition Policy Division is concerned with
monopolies and mergers (under the Fair Trading Act 1973),
and the Director-General's other responsibilities for competition matters, including those under the Restrictive Trade
Practices Act 1976, the Resale Prices Act 1976, the
Competition Act 1980, the Financial Services Act 1986 and
the Broadcasting Act 1990. The Office is the UK competent
authority on the application of the European Commission's
competition rules, and also liaises with the Commission on
consumer protection initiatives.
*Director-General*, Sir Bryan Carsberg
*Deputy Director-General (G2)*, J. W. Preston, CB

CONSUMER AFFAIRS DIVISION
*Director (G3)*, J. F. Mills
*Assistant Directors (G5)*, P. Casey; D. W. Lightfoot;
　J. Chapman

COMPETITION POLICY DIVISION
*Director (G3)*, Dr M. Howe
*Assistant Directors (G5)*, A. J. White; R. Upson;
　H. L. Emden; C. J. C. Wright; E. L. Whitehorn

LEGAL DIVISION
*Director (G3)*, A. M. Inglese
*Assistant Directors (G5)*, M. A. Khan; P. T. Rostron

*Senior Economic Adviser (G5)*, D. Elliott
*Establishment and Finance Officer (G5)*, Miss C. Banks
*Chief Information Officer (G6)*, D. Hill

FOREIGN AND COMMONWEALTH
OFFICE
Downing Street, London SW1A 2AL
Tel 0171-270 3000

The Foreign and Commonwealth Office provides, mainly
through diplomatic missions, the means of communication
between the British Government and other governments and
international governmental organizations for the discussion
and negotiation of all matters falling within the field of
international relations. It is responsible for alerting the
British Government to the implications of developments
overseas; for protecting British interests overseas; for
protecting British citizens abroad; for explaining British
policies to, and cultivating friendly relations with, governments overseas; and for the discharge of British responsibilities to the dependent territories.

DIPLOMATIC SERVICE SALARIES *since 1 April 1994*
Permanent Under-Secretary and Head of the
　Diplomatic Service　　　　　　　　　　　£110,563
Senior Grade DS1　　　　　　　　　　　　　£95,148
Deputy Permanent Under-Secretary　　　　　£87,435

Senior Grade DS2  £65,990–£79,396
Senior Grade DS3  £54,131–£64,283
Diplomatic Service Grade 4 (DS4)  £38,341–£56,953

*Secretary of State*, The Rt. Hon. Douglas Hurd, CBE, MP
  *Principal Private Secretary*, R. J. Sawers
  *Private Secretaries*, R. Stagg; S. Smith
  *Special Advisers*, M. Maclay; M. Fraser
  *Parliamentary Private Secretary*, D. Martin, MP
*Minister of State (Minister for Overseas Development)*, The
  Baroness Chalker of Wallasey, PC
  *Private Secretary*, M. Lowcock
  *Parliamentary Private Secretary*, M. Robinson, MP
*Ministers of State*, The Rt. Hon. Douglas Hogg, QC, MP; The
  Rt. Hon. Alastair Goodlad, MP; David Davis, MP (*Minister
  for Europe*)
  *Private Secretaries*, N. S. Archer; G. J. Dorey; J. Benjamin
  *Parliamentary Private Secretary to Mr Goodlad*,
  G. Kynoch, MP
*Parliamentary Under-Secretary of State*, Tony Baldry, MP
  *Private Secretary*, N. Baird
*Parliamentary Relations Unit*, R. Thomson (*Head*);
  J. P. Rodgers (*Deputy Head and Parliamentary Clerk*)
*Permanent Under-Secretary of State and Head of the
  Diplomatic Service*, Sir John Coles, KCMG
  *Private Secretary*, S. G. McDonald
*Deputy Under-Secretary and Political Director*, Miss
  P. Neville-Jones, CMG
*Deputy Under-Secretaries (DS2):*
*Chief Clerk*, A. M. Wood, CMG
*Economic Director*, M. H. Jay, CMG
Sir Timothy Daunt, KCMG; D. J. Wright, CMG, LVO;
  J. R. Young, CMG
*Assistant Under-Secretaries (DS3):*
*Deputy Chief Clerk and Principal Establishment and Security
  Officer*, Mrs V. E. Sutherland, CMG
*Deputy Political Director and UK Perm. Rep. on the Council
  of WEU*, T. L. Richardson, CMG
*Director of Information Systems*, J. Ling, CMG
*Principal Finance Officer and Chief Inspector*, K. R. Tebbit
A. J. Beamish, CMG; R. B. Bone; A. M. Goodenough, CMG;
  D. C. B. Logan, CMG; C. O. Hum; A. F. Green, CMG;
  S. J. L. Wright; J. R. de Fonblanque; D. J. M. Dain;
  C. Battiscombe, CMG
*HM Vice-Marshal of the Diplomatic Corps*,
  A. St J. H. Figgis, CMG
*Legal Adviser (DS2)*, Sir Franklin Berman, KCMG, QC
*Second Legal Adviser*, D. H. Anderson, CMG
*Deputy Legal Advisers*, M. R. Eaton, CMG;
  K. J. Chamberlain, CMG
*Legal Counsellors*, A. Aust; Miss S. Brooks; Ms
  E. Wilmshurst; C. Whomersley

### HEADS OF DEPARTMENTS (DS4)

*\*Aid Policy Department*, S. Chakrabarti
*Aviation and Maritime Department*, A. M. Collins
*British Diplomatic Spouses Association*, Mrs C. Young
*Central European Department*, N. J. Thorpe
*Commonwealth Co-ordination Department*, D. Broad
*Commonwealth Foreign and Security Policy Unit*,
  A. D. R. Smith
*Conference on Security and Co-operation in Europe Unit*,
  C. A. Munro
*Consular Department*, S. F. Howarth
*Cultural Relations Department*, J. N. Elam

*Drugs and International Crime Department*,
  P. A. B. Thomson, CVO
*Eastern Adriatic Unit*, A. Charlton
*Eastern Department*, D. G. Manning, CMG
*\*Economic Advisers Department*, J. Rollo
*\*Economic Relations Department*, D. F. Richmond
*Environment Science and Energy Department*, G. H. Boyce
*Equatorial Africa Department*, D. R. MacLennan
*European Community Department (External)*,
  J. M. Macgregor
*European Community Department (Internal)*, A. J. Cary
*Far Eastern and Pacific Department*, G. Fry
*Home Estate Department*, D. Brown
*Hong Kong Department*, S. L. Cowper Coles
*Honours Unit*, D. E. Tarling
*Human Rights Policy Unit*, P. S. Astley
*Information Department*, Sir John Ramsden, Bt.
*Information Systems Division (Operations)*, S. I. Soutar
*Information Systems Division (Projects)*, K. Willis
*Internal Audit*, R. Elias
*Joint Assistance Unit (Central Europe)*, D. Coates
*Joint Assistance Unit (Eastern Europe)*, M. McCulloch
*†Joint Export Promotion Directorate*, M. G. Dougal
*Latin America Department*, L. G. Faulkner
*Library and Records Department*, R. M. Bone
*\*Management Review Staff*, S. R. H. Pease
*Medical and Welfare Unit*, Miss D. M. Symes, OBE
*Middle East Department*, N. W. Browne
*Migration and Visa Department*, D. I. Lewty
*National Audit Office*, R. Burwood
*Nationality, Treaty and Claims Department*, R. D. Hart
*Near East and North Africa Department*, W. G. Ehrman
*News Department*, R. N. Culshaw, MVO
*Non-Proliferation and Defence Department*, J. B. Donnelly
*North America Department*, M. E. Pellew, LVO
*Overseas Estate Department*, M. H. R. Bertram, CMG
*Overseas Inspectorate*, K. R. Tebbit (*Chief Inspector and
  Principal Finance Officer*)
*Overseas Police Adviser*, L. Grundy (*Senior Police Adviser*)
*Permanent Under-Secretary's Department*, I. R. Callan, CMG
*Personnel Management Department*, P. J. Torry
*Personnel Policy Department*, J. Poston
*Personnel Services Department*, R. G. Short, MVO
*Policy Planning Staff*, R. D. Wilkinson
*PROSPER*, C. J. Edgerton, OBE
*Protocol Department*, D. C. B. Beaumont (*First Assistant
  Marshal of the Diplomatic Corps*)
*Republic of Ireland Department*, G. R. Archer
*Research and Analysis Department, Director*, B. S. Eastwood
*Resource and Finance Department*, J. W. Thorp
*Royal Matters Unit*, J. E. Brook
*Security Department*, D. S. Broucher
*Security Co-ordination Department*, R. P. Flower
*Security Policy Department*, Ms A. J. K. Bailes
*Services Planning and Resources Department*, M. Hodge, MBE
*South Asian Department*, L. B. Smith
*South Atlantic and Antarctic Department*, P. M. Newton
*South-East Asian Department*, M. R. J. Guest
*Southern Africa Department*, C. T. W. Humfrey
*Southern European Department*, H. B. Warren-Gash
*Support Services Department*, M. Carr
*Technical Security Department*, J. Gould
*Training Department*, I. W. Mackley
*United Nations Department*, Miss M. G. D. Evans, CMG
*Western European Department*, M. L. H. Hope

---

*\*Joint Foreign and Commonwealth Office/Overseas Development
  Administration department

†Joint Foreign and Commonwealth Office/Department of Trade and
  Industry directorate

*West Indian and Atlantic Department,* G. M. Baker
*Whitley Council,* J. P. Girdlestone

## EXECUTIVE AGENCY
### WILTON PARK CONFERENCE CENTRE
Wiston House, Steyning, W. Sussex BN44 3DZ
Tel 01903-815020

The Centre organizes international affairs conferences and is hired out to government departments and commercial users.
*Chief Executive,* R. Langhorne

## THE SECRET INTELLIGENCE SERVICE (MI6)
PO Box 1300, London SE1 1BD

The Secret Intelligence Service produces secret intelligence in support of the Government's security, defence, foreign and economic policies. It was placed on a statutory footing by the Intelligence Services Act 1994.
*Director-General,* D. Spedding, CVO, OBE

## GOVERNMENT COMMUNICATIONS HEADQUARTERS (GCHQ)
Priors Road, Cheltenham, Glos. GL52 5AJ
Tel 01242-221491

GCHQ produces signal intelligence in support of the Government's security, defence, foreign and economic policies. It was placed on a statutory footing by the Intelligence Services Act 1994.
*Director,* Sir John Adye, KCMG

## CORPS OF QUEEN'S MESSENGERS
Foreign and Commonwealth Office, London SW1A 2AH
Tel 0171-270 2779

*Superintendent of the Corps of Queen's Messengers,*
  Maj. I. G. M. Bamber
*Queen's Messengers,* Maj. J. E. A. Andre;
  Cdr. D. H. Barraclough; Maj. A. N. D. Bols;
  Lt.-Cdr. K. E. Brown; Lt.-Col. W. P. A. Bush;
  Lt.-Col. M. B. de S. Clayton; Capt. G. Courtauld;
  Maj. P. C. H. Dening-Smitherman; Maj. P. T. Dunn;
  Sqn. Ldr. J. S. Frizzell; Capt. N. C. E. Gardner;
  Cdr. P. G. Gregson; Maj. D. A. Griffiths;
  Wg Cdr. J. O. Jewiss; Lt.-Col. P. S. Kerr-Smiley;
  Lt.-Col. J. M. C. Kimmins;
  Lt.-Col. R. C. Letchworth; G. F. Miller;
  Maj. D. R. Nevile; Maj. K. J. Rowbottom;
  Maj. M. R. Senior; Cdr. K. M. C. Simmons, AFC;
  Maj. P. M. O. Springfield; Maj. J. S. Steele;
  Col. D. W. F. Taylor

## FOREIGN COMPENSATION COMMISSION
Old Admiralty Building, London SW1A 2AF
Tel 0171-210 6158

The Commission was set up by the Foreign Compensation Act 1950 primarily to distribute, under Orders in Council, funds received from other governments in accordance with agreements to pay compensation for expropriated British property and other losses sustained by British nationals.
  The Commission also has the duty of registering claims for British-owned property in contemplation of agreements with other countries, and it has done so in seven instances since 1950.
*Chairman,* A. W. E. Wheeler, CBE
*Secretary,* A. N. Grant

## FORESTRY COMMISSION
231 Corstorphine Road, Edinburgh EH12 7AT
Tel 0131-334 0303

The Forestry Commission is the government department responsible for forestry policy in Great Britain. It reports directly to forestry ministers (i.e. the Minister of Agriculture, Fisheries and Food, the Secretary of State for Scotland and the Secretary of State for Wales), to whom it is responsible for advice on forestry policy and for the implementation of that policy in Great Britain. There is a statutorily-appointed Chairman and Board of Commissioners (four full-time and seven part-time) with prescribed duties and powers. The full-time Commissioners form the Executive Board.
  The Commission is organized to distinguish between its departmental, regulatory and management functions. A Policy and Resources Group is responsible for the parliamentary and policy aspects of the Commission's duties as a government department. As the Forestry Authority, the Commission provides advice and sets the standards for the forestry industry, administers the grant-aid schemes for private woodlands, carries out regulatory functions for plant health and felling control and undertakes forest research. As Forest Enterprise, the Commission manages its forestry estate on a multi-use basis. In discharging their functions, the Forestry Commissioners have a statutory duty to endeavour to achieve a reasonable balance between the needs of forestry and the environment.
  In 1993 the Government set up a review of the ownership and management of the Commission's forestry estate. In July 1994 the Government announced that the Forestry Commission would stay in the public sector, that Forest Enterprise would be replaced by a new trading body operating as an executive agency, and that measures would be taken to increase public access to forests and to encourage tree planting.
*Chairman (part-time)* (£35,913), Sir Raymond Johnstone, CBE
*Director-General and Deputy Chairman (G2),* T. R. Cutler
*Commissioner, Policy and Resources (G3),* D. S. Grundy
*Head of the Forestry Authority (G3),* R. T. Bradley
*Chief Executive, Forest Enterprise (G3),* D. L. Foot
*Secretary to the Commissioners (G5),* T. J. D. Rollinson

## REGISTRY OF FRIENDLY SOCIETIES
15 Great Marlborough Street, London W1V 2AX
Tel 0171-437 9992

The Registry of Friendly Societies is a government department serving three statutory bodies, the Building Societies Commission, the Friendly Societies Commission, and the Central Office of the Registry of Friendly Societies (together with the Assistant Registrar of Friendly Societies for Scotland).
  The Building Societies Commission was established by the Building Societies Act 1986. The Commission is responsible for the supervision of building societies and administers the system of regulation. It also advises the Treasury and other government departments on matters relating to building societies.
  The Friendly Societies Commission was established by the Friendly Societies Act 1992. Its responsibilities for the supervision of friendly societies parallel those of the Building Societies Commission for building societies.

The Central Office of the Registry of Friendly Societies provides a public registry for mutual organizations registered under the Building Societies Act 1986, Friendly Societies Acts 1974 and 1992, and the Industrial and Provident Societies Act 1965. It is responsible for the supervision of friendly societies and credit unions, and advises the Government on issues affecting those societies. The Chief Registrar also acts as the Industrial Assurance Commissioner.

BUILDING SOCIETIES COMMISSION
*Chairman,* Mrs R. E. J. Gilmore (G. Fitchew *from Dec. 1994*)
*Deputy Chairman,* H. G. Walsh
*Commissioners,* T. F. Mathews; *H. R. C. Walden, CBE; *F. E. Worsley; *F. G. Sunderland; *N. Fox Bassett; *Sir James Birrell
* part-time

FRIENDLY SOCIETIES COMMISSION
*Chairman,* D. W. Lee
*Commissioners,* F. da Rocha; *A. Wilson; *J. A. Geddes; *P. E. Couse; *Dr J. Dine
* part-time

CENTRAL OFFICE
*Chief Registrar,* Mrs R. E. J. Gilmore (G. Fitchew *from Dec. 1994*)
*Assistant Registrars (G4),* D. W. Lee; A. J. Perrett

THE REGISTRY
*First Commissioner and Chief Registrar (G2),* Mrs R. E. J. Gilmore (G. Fitchew *from Dec. 1994*)

BUILDING SOCIETIES COMMISSION STAFF
*Grade 3,* H. G. Walsh
*Grade 4,* T. F. Mathews
*Grade 5,* D. A. W. Stevens; J. M. Palmer; W. Champion; R. K. Gabbertas
*Grade 6,* N. F. Digance

FRIENDLY SOCIETIES COMMISSION STAFF
*Grade 4,* D. W. Lee
*Grade 6,* F. da Rocha

CENTRAL SERVICES STAFF
*Legal Adviser (G4),* A. J. Perrett
*Establishment and Finance Officer (G5),* K. Blackburn
*Legal Staff (G6),* P. G. Ashcroft; P. Kee; R. Caune; C. Stallard

REGISTRY OF FRIENDLY SOCIETIES, SCOTLAND
58 Frederick Street, Edinburgh, EH2 1NB
Tel 0131-226 3224
*Assistant Registrar (G5),* J. L. J. Craig, WS

---

GAMING BOARD FOR GREAT BRITAIN
Berkshire House, 168–173 High Holborn, London WC1V 7AA
Tel 0171-306 6200

---

The Board was established in 1968 and its functions are to ensure that those involved in organizing gaming and lotteries are fit to do so; to ensure that gaming is run fairly and in accordance with the law; and to advise the Home Secretary on developments in gaming so that the law can respond to change.
*Chairman (part-time)* (£31,450), Lady Littler
*Members (part-time) (each £12,610),* Sir Richard Barratt, CBE, QPM; Lady Trethowan; W. B. Kirkpatrick; B. Austin
*Secretary,* T. Kavanagh

OFFICE OF GAS SUPPLY
Stockley House, 130 Wilton Road, London SW1V 1LQ
Tel 0171-828 0898

---

The Office of Gas Supply (Ofgas) is a regulatory body set up under the Gas Act 1986. It is headed by the Director-General of Gas Supply, who is independent of ministerial control.
The principal function of Ofgas is to monitor British Gas's activities as a public gas supplier and, where necessary, to enforce the conditions of that company's authorization to act as a public gas supplier. Other functions are to investigate complaints on matters where enforcement powers may be exercisable; to fix and publish maximum charges for reselling gas; to publish information and advice for the benefit of tariff customers; to keep under review developments concerning the gas supply industry, including competition; and to settle the terms on which other suppliers have access to British Gas pipelines in the event of disagreement.
*Director-General,* Ms C. Spottiswoode
*Chief Economic Adviser,* Dr Eileen Marshall
*Legal Adviser,* D. R. M. Long
*Director, Public Affairs,* C. Webb
*Director, Consumer Affairs,* W. Macleod
*Director, Network Operations,* M. Higson
*Director, Administration,* R. Field

---

GOVERNMENT ACTUARY'S DEPARTMENT
22 Kingsway, London WC2B 6LE
Tel 0171-242 6828

---

The Government Actuary provides a consulting service to government departments, the public sector, and overseas governments. The actuaries advise on social security schemes and superannuation arrangements in the public sector at home and abroad, on population and other statistical studies, and on government supervision of insurance companies and friendly societies.
*Government Actuary,* C. D. Daykin, CB
*Directing Actuaries,* D. G. Ballantine; D. H. Loades; M. A. Pickford, CB
*Chief Actuaries,* E. I. Battersby; Ms W. M. Beaver; T. W. Hewitson; A. I. Johnston; J. C. A. Rathbone; D. I. Tomlinson; A. G. Young
*Actuaries,* W. D. B. Anderson; A. B. Chughtai; W. H. P. Davies; A. P. Gallop; Mrs B. J. Hall; C. A. Harris; P. H. Hinton; D. J. Hughes; V. P. Knowles; Mrs I. W. Lane; D. Lewis; M. K. Lunnon; A. J. Macnair; P. Merricks; P. Noonan; A. P. Pavelin; J. W. Peers; H. J. Prescott; D. E. Purchase; J. G. Spain; D. M. Webber

---

GOVERNMENT HOSPITALITY FUND
8 Cleveland Row, London SW1A 1DH
Tel 0171-210 3000

---

The Government Hospitality Fund was instituted in 1908 for the purpose of organizing official hospitality on a regular basis with a view to the promotion of international goodwill.
*Minister in Charge,* The Rt. Hon. Alastair Goodlad, MP
*Secretary,* Col. T. Earl

## DEPARTMENT OF HEALTH
Richmond House, 79 Whitehall, London SW1A 2NS
Tel 0171-210 3000

The Department of Health is responsible for the administration of the National Health Service in England and for the personal social services run by local authorities in England for children, the elderly, the infirm, the handicapped and other persons in need. It has functions relating to public and environmental health, food safety and nutrition. The Department is also responsible for the ambulance and emergency first aid services, under the Civil Defence Act 1948. The Department represents the UK at the World Health Organization.

The Department and the NHS Executive are to be streamlined and restructured around their three main responsibilities of public health, health care and social care from the autumn of 1994.

*Secretary of State for Health*, The Rt. Hon. Virginia Bottomley, MP
*Principal Private Secretary*, R. M. Creighton
*Private Secretaries*, J. Mogford; M. Yates
*Special Adviser*, R. Marsh
*Parliamentary Private Secretary*, K. Mans, MP
*Minister of State*, Gerald Malone, MP
*Private Secretary*, A. Taylor
*Parliamentary Under-Secretaries of State*, The Baroness Cumberlege, CBE; The Hon. Thomas Sackville, MP; John Bowis, OBE, MP
*Private Secretaries*, Miss A. Burnett; A. Hollebon; G. Larner
*Parliamentary Clerk*, Ms T. Fretten
*Permanent Secretary (G1)*, G. A. Hart, CB
*Private Secretary*, Ms R. Roughton
*Chief Medical Officer (G1A)*, Dr K. Calman
*Chief Executive, NHS Executive (G1A)*, A. Langlands
*Director of Research and Development*, Prof. M. Peckham

NATIONAL HEALTH SERVICE POLICY BOARD
*Chairman*, The Secretary of State for Health
*Members*, Sir James Ackers; Gerald Malone, MP (*Minister of State*); The Baroness Cumberlege, CBE; The Hon. T. Sackville, MP; J. Bowis, OBE, MP (*Parliamentary Under-Secretaries*); Dr K. Calman (*Chief Medical Officer*); A. Langlands (*Chief Executive, NHS Executive*); G. A. Hart, CB (*Permanent Secretary*); Prof. C. Chantler; P. Gummer; Mrs Y. Moores; Miss K. Jenkins; Ms S. Masters; Sir Timothy Chessels (*Chairman, London Implementation Group*); B. Baker; Dr S. Burgess, CBE; K. Ackroyd; Ms R. Fritchie; J. Greetham, CBE; Sir William Staveley, GCB; W. Wells; Sir Donald Wilson

## HEALTH AND SOCIAL SERVICES GROUP
*Deputy Secretary (G2)*, T. S. Heppell, CB

HEALTH ASPECTS OF THE ENVIRONMENT AND FOOD (ADMINISTRATIVE) DIVISION
*Under-Secretary (G3)*, B. Bridges
*Assistant Secretaries (G5)*, C. P. Kendall; R. Cunningham
*Senior Principal (G6)*, Mrs M. Fry

HEALTH CARE (ADMINISTRATIVE) DIVISION
*Under-Secretary (G3)*, Miss R. D. B. Pease
*Assistant Secretaries (G5)*, A. W. McCulloch; R. Tyrrell; I. Jewesbury; N. Boyd

COMMUNITY SERVICES DIVISION
*Under-Secretary (G3)*, T. R. H. Luce
*Assistant Secretaries (G5)*, J. A. Parker; R. P. S. Hughes, CBE; R. M. Orton; N. F. Duncan; D. P. Walden

HEALTH PROMOTION (ADMINISTRATIVE) DIVISION
*Under-Secretary (G3)*, G. J. F. Podger
*Assistant Secretaries (G5)*, J. F. Sharpe; Miss A. Mithani; Ms L. Lockyer; K. J. Guinness

P DIVISION
*Under-Secretary (G3)*, M. Jeremiah, CB
*Assistant Secretaries (G5)*, S. J. Furniss; J. Thompson; M. Siswick; S. Alcock; Ms K. James

MEDICAL DIVISIONS
*Deputy Chief Medical Officer (G2)*, Dr J. S. Metters, CB

HEALTH PROMOTION (MEDICAL) DIVISION
*Senior Principal Medical Officer (G3)*, Dr E. Rubery
*Principal Medical Officers (G4)*, Dr G. Lewis; Dr D. McInnes; Dr J. D. F. Bellamy; Dr H. Markowe; Dr D. Salisbury
*Senior Medical Officers (G5)*, Dr J. Leese; Dr E. Tebbs; Dr H. Williams; Dr M. Powlson; Dr F. Harvey; Dr K. Binysh; Dr V. Press; Dr M. Thorley; Dr M. Weir; Dr D. Ernaelsteen; Dr W. J. Modle; Dr I. A. Lister-Cheese; Dr S. Shepherd; Dr D. Milner; Dr R. Stanwell-Smith; H. Nicholas; Dr S. Gupta; Dr H. Bloom

HEALTH ASPECTS OF THE ENVIRONMENT AND FOOD (MEDICAL) DIVISION
*Senior Principal Medical Officer (G3)*, Dr G. Jones
*Principal Medical Officers (G4)*, Dr E. Smales; Dr G. E. Diggle; Dr R. Skinner; Dr M. Wiseman
*Senior Medical Officers (G5)*, Dr M. Waring; Dr N. Lazarus; Dr R. L. Maynard; Dr T. Marrs; Dr A. Bulman; Dr P. Clarke; Dr L. Robinson; Dr A. Wight; Dr F. Kennedy; Dr S. Lader; J. Hilton

HEALTH CARE (MEDICAL) DIVISION
*Senior Principal Medical Officer (G3)*, Dr P. J. Bourdillon
*Principal Medical Officer (G4)*, Dr R. Jenkins
*Senior Medical Officers (G5)*, Dr J. Ashwell; Dr N. Halliday; Dr N. Melia; Dr E. Hills; Dr A. Rejman; Dr E. Clissold; Dr S. Munday; Dr D. Brooksbank; Dr D. Kingdon; Dr E. Wilson; Dr G. Parry; Dr P. Doyle; Dr G. Glover; Dr A. Dawson; Dr C. Swinson; Dr E. Gadd; Dr G. Strathdee; Dr J. Reed, CB; Dr P. Exon; Dr W. Thorne; Dr N. Simpson

DENTAL DIVISION
*Chief Dental Officer*, R. B. Mouatt
*Senior Dental Officers*, C. Audrey; K. A. Eaton; I. R. Cooper

PHARMACEUTICAL DIVISION
*Chief Pharmaceutical Officer (G4)*, B. H. Hartley
*Deputy Chief Pharmaceutical Officer (G5)*, J. R. V. Merrills

NURSING DIVISION
*Chief Nursing Officer/Director of Nursing*, Mrs Y. Moores
*Deputy Director of Nursing*, Mrs A. Fawcett-Henesy
*Deputy Chief Nursing Officer*, J. Tait, OBE
*Principal Nursing Officer*, M. Hill

## SOCIAL SERVICES INSPECTORATE
*Chief Inspector (G2)*, H. Laming, CBE
*Deputy Chief Inspectors (G4)*, D. C. Brand; Miss C. M. Hey
*Assistant Chief Inspectors (HQ)*, J. Kennedy; F. Tolan; J. G. Smith; Mrs W. Rose

*Assistant Chief Inspectors (Regions)*, S. Allard;
J. K. Corcoran; J. Cypher; D. Gilroy; B. Riddell;
A. Jones; D. G. Lambert; Miss A. Taylor; Mrs P. K. Hall;
C. P. Brearley

## NHS EXECUTIVE

*Chief Executive*, A. Langlands
*Director of Corporate Affairs*, J. F. Shaw
*Director of Human Resources*, K. Jarrold
*Director of Finance and Corporate Information*, C. Reeves
*Medical Director*, Dr G. Winyard
*Chief Nursing Officer*, Mrs Y. Moores
*Director of Research and Development*, Prof. M. Peckham

## PERSONNEL DIRECTORATE
*Director of Human Resources (G2)*, K. Jarrold

PERSONNEL DIVISION
*Deputy Director (G3)*, J. M. Rogers
*Under-Secretary (G3)*, R. M. Drury
*Assistant Secretaries (G5)*, M. G. Sturges; Miss S. Norman;
M. Staniforth; J. Ashe; B. A. J. Bennett

RESEARCH AND DEVELOPMENT DIVISION
*Director of Research and Development*, Prof. M. Peckham
*Deputy Director of Research Management (G4)*, Prof. G.
Smith
*Assistant Secretaries (G5)*, Mrs J. Griffin; Mrs B. Soper; Dr
P. Greenaway; Dr C. Henshall
*Senior Medical Officers (G5)*, Dr R. Singh; Dr G. Lewis;
Dr J. Toy
*Senior Principal Research Officers (G6)*, Ms A. Kauder;
Dr C. Davies; Ms J. Ennis
*Nursing Officers (G6)*, Dr E. Meerabeau; Miss E. Scott

PERFORMANCE MANAGEMENT
DIRECTORATE (PRIMARY CARE)
*Under-Secretary (G3)*, J. H. Barnes
*Principal Medical Officer (G4)*, Dr P. Leech
*Assistant Secretaries (G5)*, Miss H. Gwynn; D. Hewlett;
B. Slater; W. McCarthy

HEALTH CARE DIRECTORATE
*Deputy Chief Medical Officer (G2)*, Dr G. Winyard

PUBLIC HEALTH DIVISION
*Principal Medical Officer (G4)*, Dr A. Lakhani
*Senior Medical Officers (G5)*, Dr G. Pollock; Dr J. Rees; Dr
M. Campbell-Stern; Dr G. Thomas; Dr J. Dodge; Dr
B. Rana

MEDICAL EDUCATION DIVISION
*Senior Principal Medical Officer (G3)*, J. R. W. Hangartner
*Senior Medical Officers (G5)*, Dr R. Cairncross; Dr
R. Wilson; Dr P. I. M. Allen; Dr G. Williams
*Assistant Secretary (G5)*, S. D. Catling
*Principals (G7)*, H. Tolland; T. G. Bennett; R. Haugh;
M. Fuller

## FINANCE AND CORPORATE INFORMATION
DIRECTORATE

FINANCIAL MANAGEMENT DIRECTORATE
*Director of Finance NHSHE (G2)*, C. Reeves

FINANCE BRANCH
*Under-Secretary (Health) (G3)*, A. B. Barton
*Assistant Secretaries (G5)*, J. M. Brownlee; J. C. Middleton;
K. S. Jacobsen; Ms G. Fletcher-Cook

*Senior Principals (G6)*, R. J. Tredgett; R. Churchill;
A. C. Symes; K. G. Gardner

FINANCE AND CORPORATE INFORMATION DIVISION A
*Deputy Director (G3)*, Mrs J. Firth
*Heads of Branch (G5)*, H. Gwynn; C. Dobson; M. A. Harris;
A. Angilley

FINANCE AND CORPORATE INFORMATION DIVISION B
*Deputy Director (G3)*, B. Marsden
*Heads of Branch (G5)*, B. J. Derry; J. Tomlinson; G. Smith;
S. Saunders; M. Gayton; *(G6)*, P. Macaulay; *(G7)*,
J. Dixon

FINANCE DIVISION D
*Under-Secretary (Social Security) (G3)*, J. Tross
*Assistant Secretaries (G5)*, S. Lord; Dr L. Mayhew; G. Foster

## DEPARTMENTAL RESOURCES AND
SERVICES GROUP
*Deputy Secretary (G2)*, J. Pilling

STATISTICS DIVISION
*Director of Statistics (G3)*, Mrs R. J. Butler
*Chief Statisticians (G5)*, Mrs J. Nash; R. K. Willmer;
G. J. O. Phillpotts

DEPARTMENTAL MANAGEMENT
*Principal Establishment Officer (G3)*, M. G. Lillywhite
*Assistant Secretaries (G5)*, Miss A. Stephenson; P. Allen;
Mrs S. Hughes; Ms P. A. Stewart

INFORMATION SYSTEMS DIRECTORATE
*Director of Information Systems (G4)*, Dr A. A. Holt
*Deputy Director (G5)*, C. M. O'Rourke
*Grade 6*, Miss S. Blackburn; P. Cobb; Mrs L. Wishart;
J. Bilsby; C. Horsey

ECONOMICS AND OPERATIONAL RESEARCH DIVISION
(HEALTH)
*Chief Economic Adviser (G3)*, C. H. Smee
*Senior Economic Advisers (G5)*, Dr S. Harding; J. W. Hurst

INFORMATION DIVISION
*Director of Information (G4)*, Miss R. Christopherson
*Deputy Directors (G6)*, C. P. Wilson (*news*); Mrs A. Rea
(*publicity*)

## SOLICITOR'S OFFICE
*Solicitor (G2)*, P. K. J. Thompson
*Principal Assistant Solicitor (G3)*, A. D. Roberts
*Proceedings Operational Director (G4)*, P. C. Nilsson

## ADVISORY COMMITTEES

COMMITTEE ON THE SAFETY OF MEDICINES
Market Towers, 1 Nine Elms Lane, London SW8 5NQ
Tel 0171-273 0451
*Chairman*, Prof. M. D. Rawlins

COMMITTEE ON DENTAL AND SURGICAL MATERIALS
Market Towers, 1 Nine Elms Lane, London SW8 5NQ
Tel 0171-273 0502
*Chairman*, Prof. D. E. Poswillo, CBE

ADVISORY COMMITTEE ON THE MICROBIOLOGICAL
SAFETY OF FOOD
Room 601A, Skipton House, 80 London Road, London
SE1 6LW
Tel 0171-972 5049
*Chairman*, Prof. H. M. Dick

CLINICAL STANDARDS ADVISORY GROUP
Room LG22, Wellington House, 133–155 Waterloo Road,
London SE1 8UG
Tel 0171-972 4926
*Chairman*, Sir Gordon Higginson

EXECUTIVE AGENCIES

NHS ESTATES
1 Trevelyan Square, Boar Lane, Leeds LS1 6AE
Tel 0113-254 7000

The agency provides advice and support in the area of
healthcare estate functions to the NHS and the healthcare
industry.
*Chief Executive (G3)*, J. C. Locke
*Estate Policy Director (G5)*, G. G. Mayers
*Director of Business Development (G5)*, A. R. Tanner
*Director of Resources (G5)*, L. J. Wardle
*Chief Engineer (G5)*, L. W. M. Arrowsmith
*Principal Nursing Adviser (G6)*, Mrs D. Vass

MEDICINES CONTROL AGENCY
Market Towers, 1 Nine Elms Lane, London SW8 5NQ
Tel 0171-273 3000

The Agency controls medicines through licensing, monitor-
ing and inspection, and enforces safety standards.
*Chief Executive*, Dr K. H. Jones
*Business Managers*, D. O. Hagger; R. K. Alder;
B. H. Hartley; Dr D. B. Jefferys; Dr S. M. Wood

MEDICAL DEVICES AGENCY
14 Russell Square, London WC1B 5EP
Tel 0171-972 2000

The Agency safeguards the performance, quality and safety
of medical devices.
*Director (G4)*, A. Kent

*European and Standards Business*
*Head of Business (G5)*, Dr D. C. Potter

*Device Technology and Safety*
*Head of Business (G5)*, Dr E. V. Hoxey

*DTS 1 Community Health, Non-Acute and Diagnostic, Imaging*
*Services*
*Group Manager (G6)*, A. D. C. Shipley

*DTS 2 Acute Care Services*
*Group Manager (G6)*, C. S. Bray

*Device Evaluation and Publications*
*Head of Business (G6)*, Dr N. A. Slark

*Manufacturers' Registration Scheme*
*Head of Business (G6)*, R. W. B. Allen

CORPORATE FINANCE
*Head of Business (G6)*, K. Cornelius

*Corporate Management*
*Head of Business (G6)*, T. F. Crawley

*Medical and Nursing Advice*
*Senior Medical Officers (G5)*, Dr S. M. Ludgate; Dr S. P. Vahl
*Nursing Officer (G6)*, Mrs P. A. Collinson

NHS PENSIONS
Hesketh House, 200–220 Broadway, Fleetwood, Lancs.
F47 8LG
Tel 01253-774506

The agency administers the NHS occupational pension
scheme.
*Chief Executive (G5)*, A. Cowan

NATIONAL HEALTH SERVICE

REGIONAL HEALTH AUTHORITIES
The chairmen and members of Regional Health Authorities
are appointed by the Secretary of State for Health.

ANGLIA AND OXFORD, Old Road, Headington, Oxford
OX3 7LF. *Chairman*, Sir Stuart Burgess, CBE, PH.D., FRSC;
*Executive Director*, Ms B. Stocking
NORTHERN AND YORKSHIRE, Benfield Road, Walker
Gate, Newcastle upon Tyne NE6 4PY. *Chairman*,
J. Greetham, CBE; *Executive Director*, Prof. L. Donaldson
NORTH THAMES, 40 Eastbourne Terrace, London
W2 3QR. *Chairman*, Sir William Staveley, GCB; *Executive*
*Director*, R. Kerr
NORTH WEST, 930–932 Birchwood Boulevard,
Millennium Park, Birchwood, Warrington WA3 7QN.
*Chairman*, Sir Donald Wilson; *Executive Director*,
R. Tinston
SOUTH AND WEST, King Square House, 26–27 King
Square, Bristol BS2 8EF. *Chairman*, Ms R. Fritchie;
*Executive Director*, I. Carruthers
SOUTH THAMES, 40 Eastbourne Terrace, London W2 3QR.
*Chairman*, W. Wells; *Executive Director*, C. Spry
TRENT, Fulwood House, Old Fulwood Road, Sheffield S10
3TH. *Chairman*, K. Ackroyd, CBE; *Executive Director*,
K. McLean
WEST MIDLANDS, Arthur Thompson House, 146 Hagley
Road, Birmingham B16 9PA. *Chairman*, B. W. Baker;
*Executive Director*, B. Edwards, CBE

SPECIAL HEALTH AUTHORITIES

HEALTH EDUCATION AUTHORITY, Hamilton House,
Mabledon Place, London WC1H 9TX. Tel: 0171-383 3833.
*Chairman (interim)*, A. Close; *Chief Executive*, Dr Spencer
Hagard
NATIONAL BLOOD AUTHORITY, Oak House, Reeds
Crescent, Watford, Herts. WD1 1QH. Tel: 01923-212121.
*Chairman*, Sir Colin Walker, OBE; *Chief Executive*,
J. Adey
NHS SUPPLIES AUTHORITY, Apex Plaza, Forbury Road,
Reading, Berks. RG1 1AX. Tel: 01734-595085. *Chairman*,
Sir Robin Buchanan; *National Director of Supplies*,
T. Hunt
SPECIAL HOSPITALS SERVICE AUTHORITY, Charles
House, Kensington High Street, London W14. Tel: 0171-
605 9700. The Special Hospitals Service is provided by
three hospitals: Rampton, Broadmoor and Ashworth.
*Chairman*, Mrs A. M. Nelson; *Chief Executive*, C. Kaye
CENTRE FOR APPLIED MICROBIOLOGY AND RESEARCH,
Porton Down, Salisbury, Wilts. SP4 0JG. Tel: 01980-
612100. *Director*, Prof. J. Melling, PH.D.

NATIONAL HEALTH SERVICE, SCOTLAND
—*see* Scottish Office entry

HEALTH AND SAFETY COMMISSION
Baynards House, 1 Chepstow Place, Westbourne Grove,
London W2 4TF
Tel 0171-243 6000

The Health and Safety Commission was created under the
Health and Safety at Work etc. Act 1974, with duties to
reform health and safety law, to propose new regulations,
and generally to promote the protection of people at work
and of the public from hazards arising from industrial and
commercial activity, including major industrial accidents and
the transportation of hazardous materials.

The Commission members are appointed by the Secretary of State for Employment, although the Commission assists a number of Secretaries of State concerned with aspects of its functions. It is made up of representatives of employers, trades unions and local authorities, and has a full-time chairman.

The Commission can appoint agents, and it works in conjunction with local authorities who enforce the Act in such premises as offices and warehouses.

*Chairman*, F. J. Davies, CBE
*Members*, P. Jacques, CBE; A. D. Tuffin, CBE; R. Symons, CBE; P. Gallagher; E. Carrick, Dame Rachel Waterhouse, DBE, Ph.D.; N. J. Pitcher; C. Chope; Dr G. M. Schofield
*Secretary*, T. A. Gates

---

## HEALTH AND SAFETY EXECUTIVE
Baynards House, I Chepstow Place, Westbourne Grove, London W2 4TF
Tel 0171-243 6000

The Health and Safety Executive is the Health and Safety Commission's major instrument. Through its inspectorates it enforces health and safety law in the majority of industrial premises, to protect people at work and the public. The Executive advises the Commission in its major task of laying down safety standards through regulations and practical guidance for many industrial processes, liaising as necessary with government departments and other institutions. The Executive is also the licensing authority for nuclear installations and the reporting officer on the severity of nuclear incidents in Britain. In carrying out its functions the Executive acts independently of the Government, guided only by the Commission as to general health and safety policy.

*Director-General (G2)*, J. D. Rimington, CB (*at G1A*)
*Deputy Directors-General (G2)*, D. C. T. Eves, CB (*HM Chief Inspector of Factories*); Miss J. H. Bacon

HM FACTORY INSPECTORATE
*Director of Field Operations (G3)*, Dr J. T. Carter

HM AGRICULTURAL INSPECTORATE
*HM Chief Agricultural Inspector (G3)*, F. D. Lindsay

HM MINES INSPECTORATE
*HM Chief Inspector of Mines (G3)*, K. Twist

NUCLEAR SAFETY DIVISION
*HM Chief Inspector of Nuclear Installations (G3)*, Dr S. A. Harbison

HM RAILWAY INSPECTORATE
*HM Chief Inspecting Officer of Railways (G3)*, S. S. J. Robertson

STRATEGY AND GENERAL DIVISION
*Director (G3)*, Dr J. McQuaid

TECHNOLOGY AND HEALTH SCIENCES DIVISION
Includes HM Explosives Inspectorate
*Director (G3)*, Dr A. F. Ellis

SAFETY POLICY DIVISION
*Director (G3)*, M. Addison

RESEARCH AND LABORATORY SERVICES DIVISION
*Director (G4)*, Dr A. F. Roberts

HEALTH POLICY DIVISION
*Director of Medical Services (G3)*, P. Graham

SOLICITOR'S OFFICE
*Solicitor (G4)*, B. J. Ecclestone

RESOURCES AND PLANNING DIVISION
Including the Accident Prevention Advisory Unit
*Director (G3)*, R. Hillier

OFFSHORE SAFETY DIVISION
*Chief Executive (G3)*, R. S. Allison

---

## HIGHLANDS AND ISLANDS ENTERPRISE
Bridge House, 20 Bridge Street, Inverness IVI IQR
Tel 01463-234171

Highlands and Islands Enterprise (HIE) was set up under the Enterprise and New Towns (Scotland) Act 1991. Its role is to design, direct and deliver enterprise development, training, environmental and social projects and services. HIE is made up of a strategic core body and ten Local Enterprise Companies (LECs) to which many of its individual functions are delegated. The LECs design and develop initiatives at local level covering a wide range of economic and community development, training and environmental improvements.
*Chairman*, F. Morrison
*Chief Executive*, I. A. Robertson

---

## HISTORIC BUILDINGS AND MONUMENTS COMMISSION FOR ENGLAND (ENGLISH HERITAGE)
23 Savile Row, London WIX IAB
Tel 0171-973 3000

Under the National Heritage Act 1983, the duties of the Commission are to secure the preservation of ancient monuments and historic buildings; to promote the preservation and enhancement of conservation areas; and to promote the public's enjoyment of, and advance their knowledge of, ancient monuments and historic buildings and their preservation. The Commission has advisory committees on historic buildings and areas, ancient monuments, cathedrals and churches, and London.
*Chairman*, J. Stevens, CVO
*Commissioners*, HRH The Duke of Gloucester;
   Miss J. A. Page, CBE (*Chief Executive*); Dr
   R. W. Brunskill; The Lord Cavendish of Furness; Ms
   B. Cherry; Sir Neil Cossons; Sir Hugh Cubitt; T. Farrell;
   Sir David Wilson; Mrs C. Lycett-Green; J. Seymour;
   R. Suddards; G. Wilson

---

## HISTORIC BUILDINGS COUNCIL FOR WALES
Brunel House, 2 Fitzalan Road, Cardiff CF2 IUY
Tel 01222-465511

The Council's function is to advise the Secretary of State for Wales through Cadw: Welsh Historic Monuments (*see* page 369), which is an executive agency within the Welsh Office.
*Chairman*, T. Lloyd, FSA
*Members*, W. Lindsay Evans; Prof. J. Eynon, OBE, FRIBA, FSA;
   The Earl Lloyd George of Dwyfor; R. Haslam;
   Dr P. Morgan; Mrs S. Furse; Dr S. Unwin
*Secretary*, R. W. Hughes

## HISTORIC BUILDINGS COUNCIL FOR SCOTLAND
Longmore House, Salisbury Place, Edinburgh EH9 1SH
Tel 0131-668 8787

The Historic Buildings Council for Scotland is the advisory body to the Secretary of State for Scotland on matters related to buildings of special architectural or historical interest and in particular to proposals for awards by him of grants for the repair of buildings of outstanding architectural or historical interest or lying within outstanding conservation areas.
*Chairman*, Sir Nicholas Fairbairn, QC, MP
*Members*, Sir Ilay Campbell, Bt.; Mrs P. Chalmers;
  M. Ellington; J. Hunter Blair; I. Hutchison, OBE;
  K. Martin; J. A. M. Mitchell, CB, CVO, MC; Miss
  G. Nayler; Revd C. Robertson; Prof. A. J. Rowan; Mrs
  F. Walker
*Secretary*, I. G. Dewar

## ROYAL COMMISSION ON THE HISTORICAL MONUMENTS OF ENGLAND
National Monuments Record Centre, Kemble Drive, Swindon SN2 2GZ
Tel 01793-414700

The Royal Commission on the Historical Monuments of England was established in 1908. It is the national body of architectural and archaeological survey and record. It manages England's public archive of heritage information, the National Monuments Record. The Commission's new headquarters opened to the public in July 1994.
*Chairman*, The Baroness Park of Monmouth, CMG, OBE
*Commissioners*, Prof. R. Bradley, FSA; D. J. Keene, Ph.D.;
  Prof. G. I. Meirion-Jones, Ph.D., FSA; Prof. A. C. Thomas,
  CBE, D.Litt., FSA; Prof. M. Biddle, FBA, FSA; Mrs
  B. K. Cherry, FSA; R. D. H. Gem, Ph.D., FSA;
  T. R. M. Longman; R. A. Yorke; Miss A. Riches, FSA; Dr
  M. Airs, FSA; Prof. M. Fulford, Ph.D., FSA; Dr M. Palmer,
  FSA; Miss A. Arrowsmith
*Secretary*, T. G. Hassall, FSA

## ROYAL COMMISSION ON THE ANCIENT AND HISTORICAL MONUMENTS OF WALES
Crown Building, Plas Crug, Aberystwyth, Dyfed SY23 1NJ
Tel 01970-624381

The Royal Commission was established in 1908 to make an inventory of the ancient and historical monuments of Wales and Monmouthshire. It is currently empowered by a royal warrant of 1992 to survey, record, publish and maintain a database of ancient and historical sites, structures and landscapes in Wales. The Commission is also responsible for the National Monuments Record of Wales, which is open daily for public reference.
*Chairman*, Prof. J. B. Smith
*Commissioners*, Prof. R. W. Brunskill, OBE, Ph.D., FSA; Prof.
  D. Ellis Evans, D.Phil., FBA; Prof. R. A. Griffiths, Ph.D.;
  D. Gruffydd Jones; R. M. Haslam, FSA; Prof.
  G. B. D. Jones, D.Phil., FSA; Mrs A. Nicol; S. B. Smith;
  Prof. G. J. Wainwright, MBE, Ph.D., FSA; E. Wiliam, Ph.D.,
  FSA
*Secretary*, P. R. White, FSA

## ROYAL COMMISSION ON THE ANCIENT AND HISTORICAL MONUMENTS OF SCOTLAND
John Sinclair House, 16 Bernard Terrace, Edinburgh EH8 9NX
Tel 0131-662 1446

The Royal Commission was established in 1908 and is appointed to provide for the survey and recording of ancient and historical monuments connected with the culture, civilization and conditions of life of the people in Scotland from the earliest times. It compiles and maintains the National Monuments Record of Scotland as the national record of the archaeological and historical environment. The National Monuments Record is open for reference Monday–Thursday 9.30–4.30, Friday 9.30–4.
*Chairman*, The Earl of Crawford and Balcarres, PC
*Commissioners*, Prof. J. M. Coles, Ph.D., FBA; Prof.
  J. D. Dunbar-Nasmith, CBE, FRIBA; Prof. Rosemary
  Cramp, CBE, FSA; Mrs P. E. Durham; Prof. T. C. Smout,
  CBE, FRSE, FBA; The Hon. Lord Cullen; Dr Deborah
  Howard, FSA; The Hon. P. D. E. M. Moncreiffe;
  R. A. Paxton
*Secretary*, R. J. Mercer, FSA

## ANCIENT MONUMENTS BOARD FOR WALES
Brunel House, 2 Fitzalan Road, Cardiff CF2 1UY
Tel 01222-500200

The Ancient Monuments Board for Wales advises the Secretary of State for Wales on his statutory functions in respect of ancient monuments.
*Chairman*, Prof. G. Williams, CBE, FBA, FSA
*Members*, R. B. Heaton, OBE, FRIBA; Prof. R. R. Davies, FBA,
  D.Phil.; Dr S. H. R. Aldhouse-Green, FSA; R. G. Keen;
  Miss F. Lynch, FSA; Prof. W. H. Manning, Ph.D., FSA;
  D. Moore, RD, FSA; Dr P. Smith, FSA; Prof. J. B. Smith
*Secretary*, S. Morris

## ANCIENT MONUMENTS BOARD FOR SCOTLAND
Longmore House, Salisbury Place, Edinburgh EH9 1SH
Tel 0131-668 8764

The Ancient Monuments Board for Scotland advises the Secretary of State for Scotland on the exercise of his functions, under the Ancient Monuments and Archaeological Areas Act 1979, of providing protection for monuments of national importance. Protection may be provided by including a monument in a statutory list of protected monuments, by acquisition, or by guardianship in which the Secretary of State assumes responsibility for maintenance.
*Chairman*, Prof. E. C. Fernie, FRSE, FSA, FSA scot.
*Members*, Prof. A. Fenton, CBE, FRSE, FSA scot.; J. Simpson,
  FSA scot.; Mrs E. V. W. Proudfoot, FSA, FSA scot.; Mrs
  K. Dalyell, FSA scot.; J. H. A. Gerrard, FRSA;
  T. R. H. Godden, CB; L. J. Masters, FSA; Dr A. Ritchie,
  FSA, FSA scot.; R. D. Kernohan, OBE; Dr J. Morgan, FSA
  scot.; Prof. C. D. Morris, FSA, FSA scot.; R. J. Mercer, FSA;
  W. D. H. Sellar, FSA scot.; Lady Jane Grosvenor;
  D. Hayes
*Secretary*, R. A. J. Dalziel
*Assessor*, D. J. Breeze, Ph.D., FRSE, FSA scot.

# HOME-GROWN CEREALS AUTHORITY
Hamlyn House, Highgate Hill, London N19 5PR
Tel 0171-263 3391

Set up under the Cereals Marketing Act 1965, the Authority consists of nine members representing UK cereal growers, nine representing dealers in, or processors of, grain and three independent members. The Authority's functions are to improve the production and marketing of UK-grown cereals through a research and development programme, to provide a market information service, to promote UK cereals in export markets and to support work at Food from Britain. The Authority also undertakes agency work for the Intervention Board in connection with the application in the UK of the Common Agricultural Policy for cereals.
*Chairman*, G. B. Nelson, CBE
*General Manager*, C. J. Ames

# HOME OFFICE
50 Queen Anne's Gate, London SW1H 9AT
Tel 0171-273 3000

The Home Office deals with those internal affairs in England and Wales which have not been assigned to other government departments. The Home Secretary is particularly concerned with the administration of justice; criminal law; the treatment of offenders, including probation and the prison service; the police; immigration and nationality; passport policy matters; community relations; certain public safety matters; and fire and civil emergencies services. The Home Secretary personally is the link between The Queen and the public, and exercises certain powers on her behalf, including that of the Royal Pardon.

Other subjects dealt with include electoral arrangements; addresses and petitions to The Queen; ceremonial and formal business connected with honours; requests for extradition of criminals; scrutiny of local authority byelaws; granting of licences for scientific procedures involving animals; cremations, burials and exhumations; firearms; dangerous drugs and poisons; general policy on laws relating to shops, liquor licensing, gaming and lotteries, charitable collections and marriage; theatre and cinema licensing; co-ordination of government action in relation to the voluntary social services; and race relations policy.

The Home Secretary is also the link between the UK government and the governments of the Channel Islands and the Isle of Man.
*Secretary of State for the Home Department*, The Rt. Hon. Michael Howard, QC, MP
*Principal Private Secretary (G5)*, Miss J. MacNaughton
*Private Secretaries*, J. P. Casey; C. C. R. Hudson; J. M. G. Toon
*Special Adviser*, P. Rock
*Ministers of State*, David Maclean, MP; Michael Forsyth, MP; The Baroness Blatch, CBE, PC
*Private Secretaries*, Ms S. Gooch; P. Buckley; Mrs V. Molloy
*Special Advisers*, D. Cameron; Ms R. Whetstone
*Parliamentary Private Secretary to Mr Maclean*, J. Arnold, MP; *to Baroness Blatch*, J. Clappison, MP
*Parliamentary Under-Secretary of State*, Nicholas Baker, MP
*Private Secretary*, Ms N. Smith
*Parliamentary Clerk*, Miss R. McCool
*Permanent Under-Secretary of State (G1)*, R. T. J. Wilson, CB
*Private Secretary*, C. Dolphin

*Chief Medical Officer (at Department of Health)*, Dr K. Calman

## LEGAL ADVISER'S BRANCH
*Legal Adviser (G2)*, M. L. Saunders, CB
*Principal Assistant Legal Advisers (G3)*, D. J. Bentley, CB; D. Seymour
*Assistant Legal Advisers*, R. J. Clayton; Mrs S. A. Evans; J. R. O'Meara; C. M. L. Osborne; S. A. Parker
*Senior Principal Legal Assistants*, H. M. Carter; Miss R. P. Davies; Mrs J. M. Jones; Mrs C. Price; Miss S. A. Weston

## ESTABLISHMENT, FINANCE, FIRE AND EMERGENCY PLANNING DEPARTMENTS
*Deputy Under-Secretary (G2)*, T. C. Platt

### ESTABLISHMENT DEPARTMENT
*Assistant Under-Secretary of State (G3)*, Miss M. A. Clayton (*Personnel, Organization and Management Services*)
*Heads of Divisions (G5)*, J. F. Acton; M. D. Boyle; B. W. Buck; B. M. Caffarey; C. R. Muid
*Senior Principals (G6)*, R. C. Case; J. G. Daly; A. W. Gillman; D. J. Grant; D. C. Houghton; D. Meakin; S. E. Wharton; R. Williams
*Principals (G7)*, K. Aylen; F. Bannister; J. A. Black; W. Black; P. Buley; A. Fishwick; J. Fleming; Mrs S. Fleming; P. Griffiths; Mrs G. C. Hackett; R. A. Hemmings; W. Heppolette; B. J. James; M. C. Jennings; D. G. Jones; R. Jones; A. J. Lewis; R. T. Lewis; Ms P. B. McFarlane; Miss F. Miller; Mrs J. Morgan; Mrs B. Moxon; J. T. Neil; H. O'Connor; Miss A. Reece; R. Ritchie; G. R. Sampher; T. Sargent; A. Silver; P. A. Stanton; M. Walsh; T. Ward; A. T. Williams; N. L. Willson

### ASSESSMENT CONSULTANCY UNIT
*Director (G5)*, Miss S. E. Paul
*Deputy Director (G6)*, G. J. Jones
*Principal Psychologist (G7)*, D. J. Murray

### PUBLIC RELATIONS BRANCH
*Director of Information Services (G4)*, A. E. Moorey
*Head of News (G6)*, J. G. Blakeway
*Head Publicity Officer (G6)*, C. Skinner
*Communications Co-ordinator (G6)*, T. C. Morris
*Chief Press Officer (G7)*, B. R. McBride

### FINANCE DEPARTMENT
*Assistant Under-Secretary of State (Principal Finance Officer) (G3)*, S. G. Norris
*Heads of Divisions (G5)*, R. W. Eagle; J. L. Haugh; J. A. Ingman; Ms C. Pelham; G. C. Robertson
*Senior Principals (G6)*, D. Birleson; K. Cole; P. G. Davies; A. K. Holman; R. McBurney
*Principals (G7)*, B. D. Bishop; D. Burge; Mrs C. Burrows; G. Cassell; Mrs R. Chadwick; K. I. Cole; Mrs M. Cooper; R. Daniels; G. J. Edwards; F. H. Eggleston; B. Elliott; Mrs D. Grainger; C. Harwood; S. Hobbs; P. A. Holloway; G. Hopkins; P. W. Jones; G. Laing; S. Limpkin; E. Lister; T. Oulton; C. Petter; Mrs P. Poyton; C. Roden; I. F. Rutherford; P. Sheehan; P. T. Smith, Mrs M. Thomas; S. Thornton; J. Ward

### FIRE AND EMERGENCY PLANNING DEPARTMENT
*Assistant Under-Secretary of State (G3)*, W. J. A. Innes
*Civil Emergencies Adviser*, Rear-Adm. D. K. Bawtree, CB
*Heads of Divisions (G5)*, M. J. Addison; Mrs V. V. R. Harris; R. J. Miles; Dr D. M. S. Peace
*Grade 6*, D. R. Dewick

*Principals (G7)*, Dr S. S. Athwal; Dr G. A. Carr-Hill;
N. M. Clowes; E. Cook; Mrs P. E. Culley;
C. I. Dickinson; R. C. Eaton; P. R. Edmundson; Dr
J. A. Harwood; A. E. Mantle; D. A. Peters;
A. N. Pickersgill; Dr G. E. Scott; R. C. Stephen; Dr
M. D. Thomas; K. Wallace

HM FIRE SERVICE INSPECTORATE
*HM Chief Inspector*, B. T. A. Collins, OBE
*HM Senior Inspectors*, A. F. Kilford; G. P. Reid, QFSM
*HM Inspectors*, D. Berry; S. D. Christian; D. Kent;
E. G. Pearn, QFSM; K. T. Phillips; D. Ritchie;
D. Spencer; G. K. Tinley; A. C. Wells, QFSM; D. Wright
*Senior Engineering Inspector*, R. M. Simpson, OBE
*Principal (G7)*, K. O'Sullivan

EMERGENCY PLANNING COLLEGE
The Hawkhills, Easingwold, Yorks. YO6 3EG
Tel 01347-21406

*Head of College (G6)*, A. R. Blackley
*Vice-Principal*, Col. H. H. Evans
*College Secretary (G7)*, S. Trimmins

CRIMINAL, RESEARCH AND STATISTICS
DEPARTMENTS
*Deputy Under-Secretary (G2)*, J. F. Halliday, CB

CRIMINAL POLICY DEPARTMENT
*Assistant Under-Secretary of State (G3)*, A. P. Wilson
*Heads of Divisions (G5)*, Miss C. Macready; J. M. Potts;
P. G. Spurgeon; Miss C. J. Stewart; R. C. Stoate;
N. Varney
*Chief Inspector, Drugs Branch (G6)*, A. McFarlane
*Senior Principal (G6)*, M. Rumble
*Principals (G7)*, R. Allen; R. Bradley; Miss C. F. Byrne;
P. Dawson; R. G. W. Dyce; D. H. Evans; Ms
L. Hellmuth; Ms J. L. Hutcheon; N. Jordon;
B. E. R. Kinney; Mrs P. Lutterloch; Miss
H. L. McKinnon; M. J. Narey; R. D. Parsons; D. Rigby;
Miss A. M. Rutherford; G. H. H. Sonnenberg;
J. R. Thew; P. Topping; P. F. Vallance; R. J. Wood

RESEARCH AND STATISTICS DEPARTMENT
*Assistant Under-Secretary of State (G3)*, C. P. Nuttall

RESEARCH AND PLANNING UNIT
*Head of Unit (G5)*, R. Tarling
*Grade 6*, Dr S. Field; J. M. Hough; P. J. Jordan; Mrs
P. Mayhew
*Principals (G7)*, D. C. Brown; J. A. Ditchfield; Dr
P. J. Ekblom; Ms M. Fitzgerald; J. H. Graham; Dr
P. Grove; Dr C. Hadderman; Mrs K. E. Howard; Mrs
M. B. Maniolas; T. Marshall; Ms P. M. Morgan; Miss
J. W. Mott; Dr G. I. U. Mair; A. D. Moxon;
F. P. E. Southgate; Dr I. P. Williamson

STATISTICS DEPARTMENT
*Chief Statisticians (G5)*, C. G. Lewis; J. L. Walker;
P. W. Ward
*Grade 6*, G. C. Barclay; Mrs C. L. Lehmann; R. Pape;
P. Sheriff; R. M. Taylor
*Grade 7*, Mrs J. Airs; Ms A. Barber; W. Burns; P. F. Collier;
L. Davidoff; Mrs P. Dowdeswell; N. Frater; Z. Frosztega;
I. Gaskell; Miss G. Goddard; K. M. Jackson; C. Kershaw;
M. Lock; D. A. Povey; Ms S. Richards; P. Sheriff; Dr
L. Smith; D. Turner; M. Uglow; Mrs M. Watson;
P. White; Mrs M. Wilkinson

CRIMINAL JUSTICE AND CONSTITUTIONAL
DEPARTMENT
*Assistant Under-Secretary of State (G3)*, R. M. Morris
*Heads of Divisions (G5)*, M. P. Cook; E. A. Grant;
P. J. Honour; Miss S. Marshall; P. R. C. Storr
*Grade 6*, R. G. Evans; Miss A. Fletcher; G. H. Marriage;
A. Norbury
*Principals (G7)*, Mrs P. Baskerville; Mrs M. K. Branwell;
S. L. Cox; Ms J. Davis; B. Fellows; Miss R. M. Fletton;
Ms S. Fox; J. Glaze; Ms M. Gorman; R. I. Henderson;
Mrs G. Hetherington; H. D. Hillier; J. Holland; Miss
E. James; B. D. Lane; Mrs S. J. McDougall; V. McLaren;
Mrs S. Mann; S. J. Pike; Miss S. E. Rae; R. P. Rhodes;
D. Rigby; Ms S. Roberts; D. Ross; Miss C. Rowe; Miss
J. B. Rumble; Mrs E. A. Sandars; Mrs N. M. Williams;
R. W. Wootton; R. Worthington
*HM Chief Inspector of Probation (G4)*, G. W. Smith, CBE
*HM Deputy Chief Inspector of Probation (G5)*, J. C. Haines
*HM Assistant Chief Inspector of Probation (G6)*,
G. W. Childs

ANIMALS (SCIENTIFIC PROCEDURE) INSPECTORATE
*Chief Inspector*, Dr R. M. Watt

POLICE DEPARTMENT
*Deputy Under-Secretary (G2)*, I. M. Burns, CB

POLICE DEPARTMENT
*Assistant Under-Secretaries of State (G3)*, C. L. Scoble; Miss
C. Sinclair; J. Warne; G. J. Wasserman
*Heads of Divisions (G5)*, Mrs P. G. W. Catto; Mrs
F. Clarkson; J. I. Chisholm; Mrs C. Crawford; J. B. Duke-
Evans; Mrs B. Fair; R. A. Harrington; D. A. Hill;
A. Holt; Miss D. Loudon; N. C. Sanderson;
P. N. Wrench
*Senior Principals (G6)*, J. Emery; R. A. Ginman;
M. Goulding; M. Hart; Dr G. K. Laycock; Mrs I. Posen;
D. Rowe; Dr G. Turnbull
*Principals (G7)*, Mrs J. Anderson; R. Atkins; R. C. Barron;
Dr B. J. Blain; Mrs J. Bonelle; J. W. Bradley;
K. Brennan; R. Brett; D. Brown; G. Brown; Ms
C. Checksfield; Mrs P. Cocks; G. T. Coulthard; Mrs
A. Davies; M. de Pulford; M. Dexter; Miss
J. D. Erwteman; A. Ford; C. J. Goldie; D. Greenaway;
Mrs B. J. Hawkyard; K. Hopley; S. Horlock;
G. R. Houghton; L. Hughes; A. N. Kent; Dr
D. K. Laing; J. Lane; W. P. Lawrie; E. Maclean;
P. Martin; N. F. Montgomery-Pott; Mrs G. I. Moody;
Mrs B. Moore; D. C. Moulton; Ms M. L. Newman;
M. Phillips; C. A. Pounds; P. W. Pugh; Mrs M. Rolfe;
D. G. Skene; I. Smith; K. W. Smalldon; Mrs
A. R. Stiling; R. Sutcliffe; Mrs F. Tayler; D. Theobald;
G. H. Thomas; Mrs A. Underhill; R. H. Watt; B. Webb;
G. A. Widdecombe; Dr J. Youell

POLICE SCIENTIFIC DEVELOPMENT BRANCH
Sandridge Laboratories, Woodcock Hill, Sandridge,
St Albans, Herts. AL4 9HQ
Tel 01727-865051
*Head of Laboratory (G6)*

Langhurst House, Langhurstwood Road, Nr. Horsham,
Sussex RH12 4WX
Tel 01403-55451

POLICE NATIONAL COMPUTER (HENDON DATA
CENTRE)
Aerodrome Road, Colindale, London NW9 5LN
Tel 0181-200 2424

*Head of Division (G6)*, J. Ladley

*Principals (G7)*, J. A. Henderson; D. McGarry; L. D. Watson

HM INSPECTORATE OF CONSTABULARY
*HM Chief Inspector of Constabulary* (£85,203), T. A. Morris, CBE, QPM
*HM Inspectors* (£77,037), G. J. Dear, QPM; D. Elliott, CBE, QPM; B. Hayes, CBE, QPM; D. J. O'Dowd, QPM; C. Smith, CVO, QPM

POLICE STAFF COLLEGE
Bramshill House, Basingstoke, Hants. RG27 0JW
Tel 0125 126-2931

*Commandant*, P. J. Ryan, QPM
*Deputy Commandant and Director of Courses*, Mrs S. Davies

THE SECURITY SERVICE (MI5)
PO Box 3255, London SWIP IAE
The Security Service is responsible for protecting national security. It took over responsibility for mainland intelligence about Irish terrorism from the anti-terrorist branch of the Metropolitan Police in 1992. Counter-terrorism activities account for 70 per cent of its work; 25 per cent involves counter-espionage and counter-proliferation activities, and the remaining 5 per cent involves the monitoring of subversive organizations. The Service is split into two sections, Operations and Administration. It was placed on a statutory footing by the Security Service Act 1989.
*Director-General*, Mrs S. Rimington

EQUAL OPPORTUNITIES, IMMIGRATION AND NATIONALITY DEPARTMENTS
*Deputy Under-Secretary (G2)*, A. J. Langdon

EQUAL OPPORTUNITIES AND GENERAL DEPARTMENT
*Assistant Under-Secretary of State (G3)*, M. E. Head, CVO
*Heads of Divisions (G5)*, N. M. Johnson, CBE; R. Kornicki; A. Harding
*Principals (G7)*, W. Brandon; Ms C. Dale; Mrs J. M. Flascher; Mrs D. D. Gonsalves; M. J. I. Hill; Mrs J. S. Morris; G. Sutton; R. A. Wright

*Voluntary Services Unit*
*Assistant Secretary (G5)*, D. J. Hardwick
*Principals (G7)*, R. G. W. Cook; Mrs K. Hall; Miss V. R. Hatcher; F. Smith

GAMING BOARD FOR GREAT BRITAIN
— see page 309.

IMMIGRATION AND NATIONALITY DEPARTMENT
Lunar House, 40 Wellesley Road, Croydon, Surrey, CR9 2BY
Tel 0181-686 0688

*Assistant Under-Secretaries of State (G3)*, W. A. Jeffrey; A. R. Rawsthorne
*Heads of Divisions (G5)*, D. A. L. Cooke; E. B. Nicholls; Mrs E. C. L. Pallett; Miss A. Smith; K. D. Sutton; R. M. Whalley; R. G. Yates
*Senior Principals (G6)*, C. J. Saunders; A. Walmsley
*Principals (G7)*, C. A. Allison; Mrs W. Artiss; Mrs M. Bishop; G. Brindle; W. F. Bryant; D. Burgess; J. Couch; A. Cunningham; W. M. Dawnie; J. Gilbert; V. Hogg; G. P. Hopkins; D. J. Hunt; N. Jordan; Mrs C. Kellas; C. J. Kelly; B. D. C. Mennell; T. L. Neale; C. Passey; Miss G. M. Romney; Ms C. Stewart; J. Sweet; G. Treadwell; D. Truscott; Mrs F. Webster; Mrs S. Wilmington; R. B. Woodland

*Immigration Service*
*Director (Ports) (G5)*, T. Farrage
*Director (Immigration Service Enforcement) (G5)*, C. B. Manchip

*Deputy Directors (G6)*, G. Boiling; V. Hogg; D. J. McDonough
*Assistant Directors (G7)*, B. R. Barrett; Miss G. M. Griffith; G. Maguire; D. Mould; P. Quibell; C. Passey; K. Richardson

EUROPEAN COMMUNITIES UNIT
*Head of Division (G5)*, M. J. Gillespie
*Grade 7*, Dr S. Hadjipavlou

HM PRISON SERVICE
Cleland House, Page Street, London SWIP 4LN
Tel 0171-217 3000

An executive agency within the Home Office.

NON-CIVIL SERVICE GRADE SALARIES 1994-5

| | |
|---|---|
| HM Chief Inspector of Prisons | £82,641 |
| Prison Service Governor 1 | £45,157 |
| Prison Service Governor 2 | £40,776 |
| Prison Service Governor 3 | £35,215 |
| Prison Service Governor 4 | £27,902–£30,285 |

THE PRISONS BOARD
*Chairman, and Chief Executive of the Prison Service (G2)*, D. C. Lewis
*Director of Personnel (G3)*, A. J. Butler
*Director of Finance (G3)*, B. Landers
*Director of Programmes (G3)*, A. J. Pearson
*Director of Custody (G3)*, Miss P. C. Drew
*Director of Services (G3)*, R. Tilt
*Director of Prison Health Care (G3)*, Dr R. Wool
*Non-Executive Members*, Mrs U. Banerjee; F. W. Bentley; G. Keeys; Sir Duncan Nichol, CBE

PRISON SERVICE
*Heads of Groups (G5)*, D. Ackland; I. Boon; R. Corrigan; Miss L. F. Gill; Mrs E. J. Grimsey; G. E. Guy; K. Heal; S. B. Hickson; R. C. Masefield; R. J. Weatherill; P. Wheatley; T. Wilson
*Senior Principals (G6)*, Mrs P. Almond; F. Archer; Mrs H. M. Bayne; P. Cook; C. F. Drewitt; J. Gunderson; B. Johnson; R. W. Lockett; B. S. Luetchford; Dr C. McDougall; Ms A. Nelson; P. Sleightholme
*Governors (1)*, K. Brewer; J. W. Dring; P. Earnshaw; M. O'Sullivan; J. Powls; I. Ward
*Principals (G7)*, C. Allars; Ms E. Barnard; A. J. Beasley; A. Brown; N. Burton; C. Clarke; J. Cooke; C. Crudge, OBE; L. Curran; J. A. Greenland; Mrs M. Haughey, MBE; N. Hencock; N. F. M. Home; M. W. Jarvis; Mrs V. Keating; T. Kelly; R. S. H. Kettle; K. Lockyer; M. P. Loughlin; Ms P. Lowe; K. MacKenzie; N. Maclean; M. McHugh; K. Marshall; D. Marston; C. R. Miller; Mrs E. Moody; D. S. Neal; N. Newcomen; I. Newton; J. S. Nottingham; J. Page; Ms P. Ransford; S. Reed; R. Rhodes; P. Rudgard; J. S. Sarjantson; D. Shene; S. Sirikanda; R. E. Smith; C. Spencer; D. J. Tallock; G. Thelmer; D. Thornton; M. Todd; E. Tullett; G. Utteridge; T. Watson; W. F. Whiteing; Ms A. Wickington; M. Williams; Ms L. Wilson; S. Wilson; A. Woolfenden; R. J. Wood; P. Wright
*Governors (2)*, D. Aram; Miss M. Carden; R. Curtis; C. Davidson; C. Lambert; Miss S. F. McCormick; C. Scott; M. Sheldrick; A. G. Smith; P. Wailen; C. Welsh; D. Wilson
*Chaplain-General and Archdeacon of the Prison Service*, Ven. D. Fleming
*Chief Education Officer (G6)*, I. G. Benson
*Chief Physical Education Officer (G6)*, M. W. Denton

WORKS SERVICES
Abell House, John Islip Street, London SWIP 4LH
Tel 0171-217 3000

*Director of Works (G4)*, R. Haines
*Grade 6*, M. Ireson; C. Lawton; S. Mahraj; R. Putland;
    B. Stickley
*Governor (2)*, L. Lavender
*Principals (G7)*, O. Astaniotis; P. J. Attwater; B. J. Bleet;
    J. K. Chamberlain; R. Chick; J. B. Dawson; R. D'Cruz;
    J. A. Doohan; P. Enticknap; J. V. Gleed; M. C. Hayes;
    G. E. Hickey; J. Howells; J. J. Hurley; D. Newton;
    C. Nicholls; S. Richards; M. Ryland; M. Sweeny;
    F. Thompson; R. J. Tricker; A. Weeks

INDUSTRIAL AND FARM SERVICES
Block A, Whitgift Centre, Wellesley Road, Croydon, Surrey
CR9 3LY
Tel 0181-686 8710

*Director (G5)*, P. R. A. Fulton
*Heads of Sections (G6)*, R. K. Fisher; A. Sweeney; J. Weller
*Governor (2)*, J. Smith
*Principals (G7)*, J. Cairns; J. Davies; R. Daw; J. W. Fallows;
    B. D. Feist; P. J. Goulder; J. A. Gillcrist; C. Handley;
    H. Law; G. A. Merrett; T. Senior; S. Tross; R. M. Young

SUPPLY AND TRANSPORT SERVICES
Crown House, 52 Elizabeth Street, Corby, Northants
Tel 01536-202101

*Director (G5)*, D. J. C. Kent
*Grade 6*, T. Frith
*Principals (G7)*, R. C. Brett; D. J. Brown; M. Fitzgerald;
    P. McCallum; D. J. Miller

AREA MANAGERS (GOVERNORS 1)
*Directorate of Custody (DOC)*
*East Anglia*, T. G. Murtagh, OBE
*Chilterns*, A. de Frisching
*Kent*, J. Hunter
*London North*, Miss A. M. Edwards
*London South*, P. J. Kitteridge
*South Coast*, A. Rayfield
*Wales and the West*, J. Wilkinson
*Wessex*, R. J. May

*Directorate of Programmes (DOP)*
*Central*, J. Blakey
*East Midland*, J. C. Mullens
*Mercia*, D. Curtis
*North-East*, A. H. Papps
*North-West*, D. I. Lockwood
*Trans-Pennine*, T. Bone
*Yorkshire*, M. Codd

PRISONS

ACKLINGTON (DOP), Morpeth, Northumberland
    NE65 9XF. *Governor*, F. P. Masserick
ALBANY (DOC), Newport, Isle of Wight PO30 5RS.
    *Governor*, D. M. Morrison
ALDINGTON (DOC), Ashford, Kent TN25 7BQ. *Governor*,
    D. A. Bratton
ASHWELL (DOP), Oakham, Leics. LE15 7LS. *Governor*,
    H. Reid
*ASKHAM GRANGE (DOP), Askham Richard, York YO2 3PT.
    *Governor*, H. E. Crew
BEDFORD (DOC), St Loyes Street, Bedford MK40 1HG.
    *Governor*, E. Willets
BELMARSH (DOC), Western Way, Thamesmead, London
    SE28 OEB. *Governor*, H. D. Jones

BIRMINGHAM (DOP), Winson Green Road, Birmingham
    B18 4AS. *Governor*, C. B. Scott
BLAKENHURST (private prison), Hewell Lane, Redditch,
    Worcs. B97 6QS. *Controller*, P. J. Hanglin
BLANTYRE HOUSE (DOC), Goudhurst, Cranbrook, Kent
    TN17 2NH. *Governor*, J. Semple
BLUNDESTON (DOC), Lowestoft, Suffolk NR32 5BG.
    *Governor*, S. Robinson
BRISTOL (DOC), Cambridge Road, Bristol BS7 8PS.
    *Governor*, R. D. Dixon
BRIXTON (DOC), PO Box 369, Jebb Avenue, London
    SW2 5XF. *Governor*, Dr A. Coyle
BROCKHILL (DOC), Redditch, Worcs. B97 6RD. *Governor*,
    K. Naisbitt
BULLINGDON (DOC), Padrick Haugh Road, Arncott,
    Bicester, Oxon. OX6 OPZ. *Governor*, J. Thomas-Ferrand
*BULLWOOD HALL (DOC), High Road, Hockley, Essex
    SS5 4TE. *Governor*, Mrs E. Butler
CAMP HILL (DOC), Newport, Isle of Wight PO30 5PB.
    *Governor*, W. A. Wood
CANTERBURY (DOC), Longport, Canterbury, Kent CT1 1PJ.
    *Governor*, J. L. Harrison
CARDIFF (DOC), Knox Road, Cardiff CF2 1UG. *Governor*,
    N. D. Clifford
CHANNINGS WOOD (DOC), Denbury, Newton Abbott,
    Devon TQ12 6DW. *Governor*, R. S. Brandon
CHELMSFORD (DOC), Springfield Road, Chelmsford,
    Essex CM2 6LQ. *Governor*, D. B. Sinclair
COLDINGLEY (DOC), Bisley, Woking, Surrey GU24 9EX.
    *Governor*, T. A. Ward
*COOKHAM WOOD (DOC), Cookham Wood, Rochester,
    Kent MEI 3LU. *Governor*, Mrs C. Ellis
DARTMOOR (DOC), Princetown, Yelverton, Devon
    PL20 6RR. *Governor*, J. Powls
DONCASTER (private prison), Off North Bridge,
    Marshgate, Doncaster DN5 8UX. *Controller*, J. Forster
DORCHESTER (DOC), North Square, Dorchester, Dorset
    DT1 1JD. *Governor*, R. Walker
DOWNVIEW (DOC), Sutton Lane, Sutton, Surrey SM2 5PD.
    *Governor*, D. M. Lancaster
*DRAKE HALL (DOP), Eccleshall, Staffs. ST21 6LQ.
    *Governor*, G. Hughes
*DURHAM (DOP), Old Elvet, Durham DH1 3HU. *Governor*,
    R. Mitchell
*EAST SUTTON PARK (DOC), Sutton Valence, Maidstone,
    Kent MEI7 3DF. *Governor*, Mrs C. J. Galbally
*ELMLEY (DOC), Church Road, Eastchurch, Sheerness,
    Kent MEI2 4DZ. *Governor*, W. J. Cooper
ERLESTOKE HOUSE (DOC), Devizes, Wilts. SN10 5TU.
    *Governor*, Ms A. J. Gomme
EVERTHORPE (DOP), Brough, North Humberside
    HU15 1RB. *Governor*, R. Smith
EXETER (DOC), New North Road, Exeter, Devon EX4 4EX.
    *Governor*, T. C. H. Newth
FEATHERSTONE (DOP), New Road, Featherstone,
    Wolverhampton WV10 7PU. *Governor*, C. Scott
FORD (DOC), Arundel, W. Sussex BNI8 OBX. *Governor*,
    D. A. Godfrey
FRANKLAND (DOP), Frankland, Brasside, Durham,
    DH1 5YD. *Governor*, P. Buxton, OBE
FULL SUTTON (DOP), Full Sutton, York YO4 1PS. *Governor*,
    J. W. Staples
GARTH (DOP), Ulnes Walton Lane, Leyland, Preston,
    Lancs. PR5 3NE. *Governor*, W. Rose-Quirie
GARTREE (DOP), Leicester Road, Market Harborough,
    Leics. LE16 7RP. *Governor*, R. J. Perry
GLOUCESTER (DOC), Barrack Square, Gloucester GL1 2JN.
    *Governor*, P. W. Winkley

GRENDON (DOC), Grendon Underwood, Aylesbury, Bucks. HP18 0TL. *Governor*, T. C. Newell

HASLAR (DOC), Dolphin Way, Gosport, Hants. PO12 2AW. *Governor*, I. Cruffet

HAVERIGG (DOP), Haverigg Camp, Millom, Cumbria LA18 4NA. *Governor*, B. Wilson

HEWELL GRANGE (DOP), Redditch, Worcs. B97 6QQ. *Governor*, D. W. Bamber

HIGH DOWN (DOC), Sutton Lane, Sutton, Surrey SM2 5PJ. *Governor*, S. Pryor

HIGHPOINT (DOC), Stradishall, Newmarket, Suffolk CB8 9YG. *Governor*, C. D. Sherwood

HINDLEY (DOP), Gibson Street, Bickershaw, Hindley, Wigan, Lancs. WN2 5TH. *Governor*, D. Roberts

HOLLESLEY BAY COLONY (DOC), Hollesley, Woodbridge, Suffolk IP12 3JS. *Governor*, M. F. Clarke

*HOLLOWAY (DOC), Parkhurst Road, London N7 0NU. *Governor*, Miss J. King

HOLME HOUSE (DOP), Holme House Road, Stockton-on-Tees, Cleveland TS18 2QU. *Governor*, A. K. Rawson

HULL (DOP), Hedon Road, Hull, N. Humberside HU9 5LS. *Governor*, R. Daly

KINGSTON (DOC), Milton Road, Portsmouth PO3 6AS. *Governor*, J. R. Dovell

KIRKHAM (DOP), Preston, Lancs. PR4 2RA. *Governor*, A. F. Jennings

KIRKLEVINGTON GRANGE (DOP), Yarm, Cleveland TS15 9PA. *Governor*, M. K. Lees

LANCASTER (DOP), The Castle, Lancaster LA1 1YL. *Governor*, D. G. McNaughton

LATCHMERE HOUSE (DOC), Church Road, Ham Common, Richmond, Surrey TW10 5HH. *Governor*, S. O'Neill

LEEDS (DOP), Armley, Leeds LS12 2TJ. *Governor*, A. J. Fitzpatrick

LEICESTER (DOP), Welford Road, Leicester LE2 7AJ. *Governor*, G. Ross

LEWES (DOC), Brighton Road, Lewes, E. Sussex BN7 1EA. *Governor*, J. F. Dixon

LEYHILL (DOC), Wotton-under-Edge, Glos. GL12 8HL. *Governor*, D. T. Williams

LINCOLN (DOP), Greetwell Road, Lincoln LN2 4BD. *Governor*, D. Shaw

LINDHOLME (DOP), Bawtry Road, Hatfield, Woodhouse, Doncaster DN7 6EE. *Governor*, P. Leonard

LITTLEHEY (DOC), Perry, Huntingdon, Cambs. PE18 0SR. *Governor*, M. L. Knight

LIVERPOOL (DOP), 68 Hornby Road, Liverpool L9 3DF. *Governor*, R. H. Jacques

LONG LARTIN (DOP), South Littleton, Evesham, Worcs. WR11 5TZ. *Governor*, P. Atherton

MAIDSTONE (DOC), County Road, Maidstone ME14 1UZ. *Governor*, H. Bagshaw

MANCHESTER (DOP), Southall Street, Manchester M60 9AH. *Governor*, R. P. Halward

MOORLAND (DOP), Hatfield Woodhouse, Doncaster DN7 6BW. *Governor*, C. R. Griffiths

MORTON HALL (DOP), Swinderby, Lincoln LN6 9PS. *Governor*, C. P. A. Bushell

THE MOUNT (DOC), Molyneaux Avenue, Bovingdon, Hemel Hempstead HP3 0NZ. *Governor*, Mrs M. Donnelly

*NEW HALL (DOP), Dial Wood, Flockton, Wakefield, W. Yorks. WF4 4AX. *Governor*, D. England

NORTH SEA CAMP (DOP), Freiston, Boston, Lincs. PE22 0QX. *Governor*, R. Reveley

NORWICH (DOP), Mousehold, Norwich NR1 4LU. *Governor*, Miss J. M. Fowler

NOTTINGHAM (DOP), Perry Road, Sherwood, Nottingham NG5 3AG. *Governor*, P. J. Bennett

OXFORD (DOC), New Road, Oxford OX1 1LZ. *Governor*, R. J. Talbot

PARKHURST (DOC), Newport, Isle of Wight PO30 5NX. *Governor*, J. R. Marriott

PENTONVILLE (DOC), Caledonian Road, London N7 8TT. *Governor*, W. J. Abbott

PRESTON (DOP), 2 Ribbleton Lane, Preston, Lancs. OR1 5AB. *Governor*, R. Doughty

RANBY (DOP), Ranby, Retford, Notts. DN22 8EU. *Governor*, T. J. Williams

*RISLEY (DOP), Warrington Road, Risley, Warrington WA3 6BP. *Governor*, F. B. O'Friel.

ROCHESTER (DOC), Rochester, Kent ME1 3QS. *Governor*, R. A. Chapman

RUDGATE (DOP), Wetherby, W. Yorks. LS23 7AZ. *Governor*, H. Jones

SEND (DOC), Ripley Road, Send, Woking, Surrey GU23 7LJ. *Governor*, A. French

SHEPTON MALLET (DOC), Cornhill, Shepton Mallet, Somerset BA4 5LU. *Governor*, P. O'Sullivan

SHREWSBURY (DOP), The Dana, Shrewsbury, Salop SY1 2HR. *Governor*, D. J. Bradley

STAFFORD (DOP), 54 Gaol Road, Stafford ST16 3AW. *Governor*, R. Feeney

STANDFORD HILL (DOC), Church Road, Eastchurch, Sheerness, Kent ME12 4AA. *Governor*, D. M. Twiner

STOCKEN (DOP), Stocken Hall Road, Stretton, Nr Oakham, Leics. LE15 7RD. *Governor*, D. Hall

STOKE HEATH (DOP), Market Drayton, Shropshire TF9 2JL. *Governor*, J. Alldridge

*STYAL (DOP), Wilmslow, Cheshire SK9 4HR. *Governor*, G. Walker

SUDBURY (DOP), Sudbury, Derbys. DE6 5HW. *Governor*, P. E. Salter

SWALESIDE (DOC), Eastchurch, Isle of Sheppey, Kent ME12 4AX. *Governor*, R. Tasker

SWANSEA (DOC), Oystermouth Road, Swansea SA1 2SR. *Governor*, J. Heyes

THORP ARCH (DOP), Wetherby, W. Yorks. LS23 7AY. *Governor*, G. Barnard

USK (DOC), 29 Maryport Street, Usk, Gwent NP5 1XP. *Governor*, N. J. Evans

THE VERNE (DOC), Portland, Dorset DT5 1EQ. *Governor*, T. M. Turner

WAKEFIELD (DOP), Love Lane, Wakefield WF2 9AG. *Governor*, R. S. Duncan

WANDSWORTH (DOC), PO Box 757, Heathfield Road, London SW18 3HS. *Governor*, C. G. Clarke

WAYLAND (DOC), Wayland, Griston, Thetford, Norfolk IP25 6RL. *Governor*, W. S. Duff

WELLINGBOROUGH (DOC), Millers Park, Doddington Road, Wellingborough, Northants. NN8 2NH. *Governor*, J. Whetton

WHATTON (DOP), Whatton, Notts. NG13 9FQ. *Governor*, M. A. Lewis

WHITEMOOR (DOC), Longhill Road, March, Cambs. PE15 0PR. *Governor*, R. B. Clark

WINCHESTER (DOC), Romsey Road, Winchester, Hants. SO22 5DF. *Governor*, M. K. Pascoe

WOODHILL (DOC), Tattenhoe Street, Milton Keynes MK4 4DA. *Governor*, Ms M. Gorman

WORMWOOD SCRUBBS (DOC), PO Box 757, Du Cane Road, London W12 0AE. *Governor*, J. F. Perris

WYMOTT (DOP), Moss Lane, Ulnes Walton, Leyland, Preston, Lancs. PR5 3LW. *Governor*, J. W. Mullen

---

*Women's establishments/establishments with units for women

## Young Offender Institutions

AYLESBURY (DOC), Bierton Road, Aylesbury, Bucks. HP20 IEH. *Governor*, M. Spur

BRINSFORD (DOP), New Road, Featherstone, Wolverhampton WV10 7PY. *Governor*, B. Payling

*BULLWOOD HALL (DOC), High Road, Hockley, Essex SS5 4TE. *Governor*, Mrs E. Butler

CASTINGTON (DOP), Morpeth, Northumberland NE65 9XF. *Governor*, C. Harder

DEERBOLT (DOP), Bowes Road Barnard Castle, Co. Durham DL12 9BG. *Governor*, W. J. Ginn

DOVER (DOC), The Citadel, Western Heights, Dover, Kent CT17 9DR. *Governor*, B. W. Sutton

*DRAKE HALL (DOP), Eccleshall, Staffs. ST21 6LQ. *Governor*, G. Hughes

*EAST SUTTON PARK (DOC), Sutton Valence, Maidstone, Kent ME17 3DF. *Governor*, Mrs C. J. Galbally

EASTWOOD PARK (DOC), Falfield, Wotton-under-Edge, Glos. GL12 8DB. *Governor*, P. C. Mortimore

FELTHAM (DOC), Bedfont Road, Feltham, Middx. TW13 4ND. *Governor*, J. Whitty

GLEN PARVA (DOP), Tigers Road, Wigston, Leics. LE8 2TN. *Governor*, C. Williams

GUYS MARSH (DOC), Shaftesbury, Dorset SP7 OAH. *Governor*, P. B. Tucker

HATFIELD (DOP), Hatfield, Doncaster DN7 6EL. *Governor*, J. W. Clark

HOLLESLEY BAY COLONY (DOC), Hollesley, Woodbridge, Suffolk IP12 3JS. *Governor*, M. F. Clarke

HUNTERCOMBE (DOC), Huntercombe Place, Nuffield, Henley-on-Thames RG9 5SB. *Governor*, Miss A. W. Hair

LANCASTER FARMS (DOP), Stone Row Head, off Quernmore Road, Lancaster LA1 3QZ. *Governor*, D. J. Waplington

*NEW HALL (DOP), Dial Wood, Flockton, Wakefield WF4 4AX. *Governor*, D. England

NORTHALLERTON (DOP), East Road, Northallerton, N. Yorks. DL6 INW. *Governor*, D. P. G. Appleton

ONLEY (DOC), Willoughby, Rugby, Warks. CV23 8AP. *Governor*, J. N. Brooke

PORTLAND (DOC), Easton, Portland, Dorset DT5 IDL. *Governor*, D. Brisco

PRESCOED (DOC), 29 Maryport Street, Usk, Gwent NP4 OTD. *Governor*, N. J. Evans

STOKE HEATH (DOP), Market Drayton, Salop TF9 2JL. *Governor*, J. Alldridge

*STYAL (DOP), Wilmslow, Cheshire, SK9 4HR. *Governor*, G. Walker

SWINFEN HALL (DOP), Lichfield, Staffs. WS14 9QS. *Governor*, A. J. Davis

THORN CROSS (DOP), Arley Road, Appleton Thorn, Warrington WA4 4RL. *Governor*, I. Windebank

WERRINGTON (DOP), Stoke-on-Trent ST9 ODX. *Governor*, B. Stanhope

WETHERBY (DOP), York Road, Wetherby, W. Yorks. LS22 5ED. *Governor*, P. J. Atkinson

## Remand Centres

BRINSFORD (DOP), New Road, Featherstone, Wolverhampton WV10 7PY. *Governor*, B. Payling

CARDIFF (DOC), Knox Road, Cardiff CF2 IUG. *Governor*, N. D. Clifford

EXETER (DOC), New North Road, Exeter, Devon EX4 4EX. *Governor*, T. C. H. Newth

FELTHAM (DOC), Bedfont Road, Feltham, Middx. TW13 4ND. *Governor*, J. Whitty

---

*Women's establishments/establishments with units for women

GLEN PARVA (DOP), Tigers Road, Wigston, Leics. LE8 2TN. *Governor*, C. Williams

LANCASTER FARMS (DOP), Stone Rowe Head, Off Quernmore Road, Lancaster LA1 3QZ. *Governor*, D. J. Waplington

LOW NEWTON (DOP), Brasside, Durham DH1 5SD. *Governor*, A. Holman

NORWICH (DOC), Mousehold, Norwich, Norfolk NR1 4LU. *Governor*, Miss J. M. Fowler

PUCKLECHURCH (DOC), Bristol BS17 3QJ. *Governor*, Ms S. J. Swift

READING (DOC), Forbury Road, Reading, Berks. RG1 3HY. *Governor*, J. K. Petherick

THE WOLDS (private remand prison), Everthorpe, Brough, N. Humberside HU15 2JZ. *Controller*, Mrs P. Midgley

## HM Inspectorate of Prisons

*HM Chief Inspector of Prisons*, His Hon. Judge Tumim
*HM Deputy Chief Inspector of Prisons (G5)*, B. V. Smith
*HM Inspectors*, C. Allen; J. Gallagher; E. Hornblow; D. A. Strong; B. J. Wells
*Principal (G7)*, S. E. Bass

## FIRE SERVICE COLLEGE
Moreton-in-Marsh, Glos. GL56 ORH
Tel 01608-650831

An executive agency within the Home Office.
*Chief Executive*, N. K. Finlayson
*Commandant*, F. David
*Dean*, Dr R. Willis-Lee
*Director of Administration (G7)*, J. A. Gundersen

## FORENSIC SCIENCE SERVICE HEADQUARTERS
Priory House, Gooch Street North, Birmingham B5 6QQ
Tel 0121-666 6606

An executive agency within the Home Office.
*Director-General (G3)*, Dr J. Thompson
*Head of Organization Development (G5)*, Dr P. D. B. Clarke
*Chief Scientist (G5)*, Dr A. W. Scaplehorn
*Head of Finance (G5)*, R. G. Rogers
*Head of Operations (G6)*, Dr D. J. Werrett
*Head of Business Development (G6)*, T. H. Howitt
*Grade 7*, A. D. Barclay; Dr R. K. Bramley; Dr D. A. Patterson; Dr J. A. Zoro

## PASSPORT AGENCY
Clive House, Petty France, London SW1H 9HD
Tel 0171-799 2728

An executive agency within the Home Office.
*Chief Executive (G5)*, J. E. Hayzelden, CBE
*Deputy Chief Executive and Director of Operations (G6)*, T. Lonsdale
*Director of Planning and Resources (G6)*, K. J. Sheehan
*Director of Systems (G6)*, R. G. Le Marechal
*Principals (G7)*, R. M. Bowley; J. Burgess; M. Copley; J. McColl; A. Raven; G. H. Ryan; J. Satterly; L. P. W. Sommer; R. D. Wilson

---

## HORSERACE TOTALISATOR BOARD
74 Upper Richmond Road, London SW15 2SU
Tel 0181-874 6411

---

The Horserace Totalisator Board was established by the Betting, Gaming and Lotteries Act 1963, as successor to the

Racecourse Betting Control Board. Its function is to operate totalisators on approved racecourses in Great Britain, and it also provides on- and off-course cash and credit offices. Under the Horserace Totalisator and Betting Levy Board Act 1972, it is further empowered to offer bets at starting price (or other bets at fixed odds) on any sporting event. The chairman and members of the Board are appointed by the Home Secretary.

*Chairman* (£95,000), The Lord Wyatt of Weeford
*Members*, B. McDonnell (*Chief Executive*); The Hon.
   J. Deedes; T. J. Phillips (*Finance*); J. F. Sanderson;
   The Hon. D. Sieff; C. Sporborg

## HOUSING CORPORATION
149 Tottenham Court Road, London WIP OBN
Tel 0171-393 2000

Established by Parliament in 1964, the Housing Corporation registers, promotes, funds and supervises housing associations. The Corporation's duties were extended under the provisions of the Housing Act 1988 to cover the payment of capital and revenue grants to housing associations, advice for tenants interested in Tenants' Choice, and the approval and revocation of potential new landlords under this policy.

There are over 2,200 registered associations in England providing more than 600,000 homes for people in need of housing. Housing associations are non-profit making bodies run by voluntary committees.

*Chairman*, Sir Brian Pearse
*Chief Executive*, A. Mayer

## HUMAN FERTILIZATION AND EMBRYOLOGY AUTHORITY
Paxton House, 30 Artillery Lane, London EI 7LS
Tel 0171-377 5077

The Authority was established under the Human Fertilization and Embryology Act 1990. Its function is to license persons carrying out any of the following activities: the creation or use of embryos outside the body in the provision of infertility treatment services; the use of donated gametes in infertility treatment; the storage of gametes or embryos; and research on human embryos. The Authority also keeps under review information about embryos and, when requested to do so, gives advice to the Secretary of State for Health.

*Chairman*, Prof. Sir Colin Campbell
*Deputy Chairman*, Lady Brittan
*Members*, Prof. R. J. Berry; Prof. I. Cooke; Prof. A. Cox; Ms
   J. Denton; Ms E. Forgan; Ms J. Harbison; Dr S. Hillier;
   Ph.D.; The Most Revd R. Holloway; Prof. M. Johnson;
   R. Jones; Ms P. Keith; Dr B. Lieberman; Ms A. Mays;
   Dr A. McLaren; Dr J. Naish; Rabbi Julia Neuberger;
   D. Shilson; Lady Tugendhat; J. Williams
*Chief Executive*, Mrs F. Goldhill

## INDEPENDENT COMMISSION FOR POLICE COMPLAINTS FOR NORTHERN IRELAND
Chamber of Commerce House, 22 Great Victoria Street,
Belfast BT2 7LP
Tel 01232-244821

The Commission has the power to hold independent investigations into serious complaints by members of the public against police officers in Northern Ireland.

*Chairman*, J. Grew
*Chief Executive*, B. McClelland

## INDEPENDENT REVIEW SERVICE FOR THE SOCIAL FUND
Millbank Tower, 21-24 Millbank, London, SWIP 4QU
Tel 0171-217 4799
4th Floor, Centre City Podium, 5 Hill Street,
Birmingham B5 4UB
Tel 0121-606 2100

The Social Fund Commissioner is appointed by the Secretary of State for Social Security. The Commissioner appoints Social Fund Inspectors, who provide an independent review of decisions made by Social Fund Officers in the Benefits Agency of the Department of Social Security.

*Social Fund Commissioner*, Mrs R. Mackworth, CBE

## INDEPENDENT TELEVISION COMMISSION
33 Foley Street, London WIP 7LB
Tel 0171-255 3000

The Independent Television Commission replaced the Independent Broadcasting Authority at the beginning of 1991 under the terms of the Broadcasting Act 1990. The Commission is responsible for licensing and regulating all commercially funded UK television services.

*Chairman* (£57,360), Sir George Russell, CBE
*Deputy Chairman*, J. Stevens
*Members*, Earl of Dalkeith; Prof. J. F. Fulton; Ms
   P. Mathias; Lady Popplewell; Prof. J. Ring; P. Sheth;
   R. Goddard; Mrs E. Wynne Jones
*Chief Executive*, D. Glencross, CBE
*Secretary*, M. Redley

## INDUSTRIAL INJURIES ADVISORY COUNCIL
6th Floor, The Adelphi, 1-11 John Adam Street, London
WC2N 6HT
Tel 0171-962 8066

The Industrial Injuries Advisory Council is a statutory body under the Social Security Act 1975 which considers and advises the Secretary of State for Social Security on regulations and other questions relating to industrial injuries benefits or their administration.

*Chairman*, Prof. J. M. Harrington, CBE
*Members*, Dr J. Asherson; Miss J. C. Brown;
   Prof. M. J. Cinnamond; Dr D. Coggon; Prof. A. Dayan;
   Dr C. P. Juniper; T. Mawer; Prof. A. J. Newman Taylor;
   R. Pickering; Dr E. Roman; Dr L. Rushton; Dr
   C. Taylor; O. Tudor; Ms M. Twomey
*Secretary*, R. Heigh

## BOARD OF INLAND REVENUE
Somerset House, London WC2R ILB
Tel 0171-438 6622

The Board of Inland Revenue was constituted under the Inland Revenue Board Act 1849, by the consolidation of the Board of Excise and the Board of Stamps and Taxes. In 1909 the administration of excise duties was transferred to the Board of Customs. The Board of Inland Revenue administers and collects direct taxes – mainly income tax, stamp duty, development land tax and petroleum revenue tax – and advises the Chancellor of the Exchequer on policy questions involving them.

The Department is organized into a series of accountable management units under the Next Steps programme and has its own pay structure. The day-to-day operations in assessing and collecting tax and in providing internal support services are carried out by 29 Executive Offices. The Department's Valuation Office is an executive agency responsible for valuing property for tax purposes, for compensation, for compulsory purchase, and (in England and Wales) for local rating purposes. In 1992–3 the Inland Revenue collected over £76.1 billion in tax.

THE BOARD
*Chairman (G1)*, Sir Anthony Battishill, KCB
  *Private Secretary*, Dr F. Khan
*Deputy Chairmen (G2)*, S. C. T. Matheson, CB; C. W. Corlett
*Principal Establishments Officer (G2)*, G. H. Bush

SUBJECT DIVISIONS
*Directors (G3)*, E. McGivern; M. F. Cayley; B. Mace;
  P. Lewis; I. R. Spence; E. J. Gribbon
*Assistant Directors*, R. H. Allen; R. E. Creed; R. N. Page,
  CBE; R. E. Haigh; D. L. Shaw; P. R. P. Stokes;
  A. J. O'Brien; B. Sadler; J. Evans; R. B. Willis;
  L. E. Jaundoo; I. Stewart; C. Stewart; Miss R. A. Dyall;
  M. T. Evans; M. D. R. Haigh; R. Warden;
  C. D. Sullivan; J. P. B. Bryce; P. W. Fawcett;
  M. J. G. Elliott; C. S. McNicol; Miss S. P. B. Walker;
  P. A. Michael; Mrs C. B. Hubbard; Mrs S. P. Ayling;
  A. J. H. Orhnial; B. T. Glassberg; Mrs J. McLaggan;
  A. C. Gray; J. D. Hinton; B. Jones; A. P. Beauchamp;
  R. S. Hurcombe; J. E. Morris; M. D. Phelps; M. Waters;
  A. H. Williams; P. H. Linford; J. F. McCormick; Mrs
  D. Hay; K. Hamer; J. F. Gilhooly; S. P. Norris;
  D. C. Howard; R. J. Gill; R. Thomas; T. N. Locke;
  P. C. Fielder; J. R. Streeter

PERSONNEL DIVISION
*Director of Personnel (G3)*, J. Gant
*Deputy Director*, R. Neilson
*Assistant Directors*, A. Pardoe; J. Eastman; A. J. Walker;
  Mrs A. Plumb; R. C. Cooke

MANPOWER AND SUPPORT SERVICES
*Director (G4)*, N. C. Munro
*Assistant Directors*, J. Gray; R. P. R. Tilley; D. E. Adam;
  T. A. Lawson; A. L. Hardaker

CHANGE MANAGEMENT DIVISION
*Head*, D. A. Smith
*Assistant Directors*, A. W. Kuczys; S. Banyard; Mrs
  O. A. Cahill; J. P. Gilbody; S. Hartlib; R. J. Cully

FINANCE DIVISION
*Principal Finance Officer (G3)*, R. R. Martin
*Assistant Directors*, J. H. Reed; J. R. Cavell; Miss M. A. Hill;
  R. F. Moore; J. Keelty

POLICY CO-ORDINATION UNIT
*Director*, P. Lewis
*Assistant Director*, R. Golding

BUSINESS OPERATIONS DIVISION
*Director of Operations (G3)*, M. A. Johns
*Deputy Director of Operations, Network*, D. W. Muir
*Deputy Director of Operations, Singletons*, J. M. L. Davenport

*Assistant Directors*, E. C. Jones; J. Leigh-Pemberton;
  R. J. Warner; S. J. McManus; Dr E. A. Harrison;
  D. N. Swift; J. T. Cawdron

QUALITY DEVELOPMENT DIVISION
*Director (G3)*, K. V. Deacon
*Assistant Directors*, J. W. Calder; E. C. Jones; A. McClure

EXECUTIVE OFFICES
ACCOUNTS OFFICE (CUMBERNAULD), Cumbernauld,
  Glasgow G70 5TR. *Controller*, A. Geddes, OBE
ACCOUNTS OFFICE (SHIPLEY), Shipley, Bradford, W.
  Yorks. BD98 8AA. *Controller*, P. Clark

CAPITAL TAXES OFFICE
Minford House, Rockley Road, London W14 0DF
Commerce Square, Nottingham NG1 1HS
*Controller*, B. D. Kent
*Deputy Controllers*, H. V. Capon; A. G. Nield; R. J. Draper
*Assistant Controllers*, D. J. Ferley; B. K. Lakhanpaul;
  T. J. Plumb; P. R. Twiddy; C. A. Oldridge; F. A. Cook;
  N. S. Tant; M. J. Francis; A. D. Tytherleigh;
  S. R. Gridley

CAPITAL TAXES OFFICE (SCOTLAND)
Mulberry House, 16 Picardy Place, Edinburgh, EH1 3NB
*Registrar*, I. Fraser
*Deputy Registrar*, W. Young

CORPORATE COMMUNICATIONS OFFICE
*Controller*, B. Hooper
*Press Secretary*, Mrs T. A. Middleton

ENFORCEMENT OFFICE
South Block, Barrington Road, Worthing, W. Sussex
BN12 4SG
*Controller*, K. Burns

FINANCIAL INTERMEDIARIES AND CLAIMS OFFICE
St John's House, Merton Road, Bootle L69 9BB
72 Maid Marian Way, Nottingham NG1 6AS
*Controller*, D. A. Hartnett

FINANCIAL INTERMEDIARIES AND CLAIMS OFFICE
(SCOTLAND)
Trinity Park House, South Trinity Road, Edinburgh
EH5 3SD
*Officer in Charge*, J. Duguid

FINANCIAL AND MANAGEMENT ACCOUNTING SYSTEMS
OFFICE
Barrington Road, Worthing, W. Sussex BN12 4XH
*Controller*, C. R. F. Jury

FINANCIAL SERVICES OFFICE
Barrington Road, Worthing, W. Sussex BN12 4XH
*Controller*, J. D. Easey

INFORMATION TECHNOLOGY OFFICE
*Director (G3)*, J. E. Yard
*Divisional Directors*, R. A. Assirati; P. W. Booth;
  D. B. Topple; R. H. Wearing

INTERNAL AUDIT OFFICE
22 Kingsway, London WC2B 6NR
*Chief Internal Auditor*, N. R. Buckley

OIL TAXATION OFFICE
Melbourne House, Aldwych, London WC2B 4LL
*Controller*, R. C. Mountain
*Assistant Controllers*, K. Cartwright; I. M. Griffin;
  D. Newlyn; D. J. Slattery; M. Wright

PENSION SCHEMES OFFICE
Lynwood Road, Thames Ditton, Surrey KT7 0DP
*Controller*, R. G. Lusk, CBE

SOLICITOR FOR INLAND REVENUE
*Solicitor (G2)*, B. E. Cleave
*Principal Assistant Solicitors (G3)*, J. D. H. Johnston;
   J. G. H. Bates; G. F. Butt
*Assistant Solicitors*, Miss M. P. E. Boland; A. J. Gunz;
   A. K. S. Shaw; A. P. Douglas; W. J. Durrans; S. Bousher;
   R. S. Waterson; R. F. Walters; Miss A. Hawkins;
   K. Brown; R. W. Thornhill; Miss A. E. Wyman;
   R. J. Alderman; A. G. Williams
*Board's Advisory Accountant*, T. C. Carne

SOLICITOR OF INLAND REVENUE (SCOTLAND)
80 Lauriston Place, Edinburgh EH3 9SL
*Solicitor*, I. K. Laing

SPECIAL COMPLIANCE OFFICE
Angel Court, 199 Borough High Street, London SEI 1HZ
*Controller*, F. J. Brannigan
*Group Leaders*, J. Mawson, D. F. Parrett; G. W. Lunn;
   R. A. Brown
*Board's Investigating Officer*, F. B. Dunbar

THE STAMP OFFICE
South-West Wing, Bush House, Strand, London WC2B 4QN
*Controller*, K. S. Hodgson

THE STAMP OFFICE (SCOTLAND)
Mulberry House, 16 Picardy Place, Edinburgh EHI 3NF
*Controller*, D. G. Hunter

STATISTICS AND ECONOMICS OFFICE
*Director (G3)*, R. Ward
*Chief Statisticians*, Dr G. A. Keenay; Dr G. J. Parker;
   R. J. Eason; E. Ko
*Information Technology*, Dr R. James
*Senior Economics Adviser*, W. M. McNie

TRAINING OFFICE
Royal Exchange House, Boar Lane, Leeds LSI 5PG
*Controller*, D. J. Timmons

REGIONAL OFFICES
INLAND REVENUE EAST, Midgate House, Peterborough
   PEI 1TD
INLAND REVENUE GREATER MANCHESTER, Apsley
   House, Wellington Road North, Stockport SK4 1EY
INLAND REVENUE LONDON, New Court, Carey Street,
   London WC2A 2JE
INLAND REVENUE NORTH, 100 Russell Street,
   Middlesbrough, Cleveland TSI 2RZ
INLAND REVENUE NORTH-WEST, The Triad, Stanley
   Road, Bootle, Merseyside L20 3PD
INLAND REVENUE SOUTH-EAST, Albion House, Chertsey
   Road, Woking GU2I 1BT
INLAND REVENUE SOUTH-WEST, Longbrook House,
   New North Road, Exeter EX4 4UA
INLAND REVENUE SOUTH YORKSHIRE, Sovereign
   House, 110 Queen Street, Sheffield SI 2DU
INLAND REVENUE WALES AND MIDLANDS, Chadwick
   House, Blenheim Court, Solihull, W. Midlands B91 2AA;
   Ty Rodfa, Ty Glas Avenue, Llanishen, Cardiff CF4 5TS
INLAND REVENUE SCOTLAND, 80 Lauriston Place,
   Edinburgh EH3 9SL
INLAND REVENUE NORTHERN IRELAND, Dorchester
   House, 52–58 Great Victoria Street, Belfast BT2 7QE
INLAND REVENUE LARGE GROUPS OFFICE, New Court,
   Carey Street, London WC2A 2JE

THE VALUATION OFFICE EXECUTIVE AGENCY
New Court, 48 Carey Street, London WC2A 2JE
Tel 0171-324 1183/1057
Meldrum House, 15 Drumsheugh Gardens, Edinburgh
EH3 7UN
Tel 0131-225 8511

*Chief Executive (G2)*, A. J. Langford
*Deputy Chief Executive (G3)*, R. J. Pawley
*Chief Valuer, Scotland*, A. MacLaren

---

INQUIRY INTO EXPORTS OF DEFENCE
EQUIPMENT AND DUAL-USE GOODS TO IRAQ
Room 2.2.5, 1 Palace Street, London SWIE 5HE
Tel 0171-238 3799; *Media:* 0171-238 3809

---

Sir Richard Scott was asked by the President of the Board of
Trade, after the collapse of the Matrix Churchill case in
November 1992, to examine the facts in relation to the export
from the United Kingdom of defence equipment and dual-
use goods to Iraq between December 1984 and 1990 and the
decisions reached on the export licence applications for such
goods and the basis for them; to report on whether the
relevant departments, agencies and responsible ministers
operated in accordance with the policies of the Government;
to examine and report on decisions taken by the prosecuting
authority and by those signing public interest immunity
certificates in R. v. Henderson and any other similar cases
that Lord Justice Scott considers relevant to the issues of the
inquiry; and to make recommendations. The final report of
the inquiry is expected to be published by the end of 1994.
From six weeks after publication, queries should be directed
to the Secretary to the Inquiry, c/o the Treasury Solicitor's
Department (*see* page 365).
*Inquiry headed by* The Rt. Hon. Sir Richard Scott, The Vice-
   Chancellor
*Secretary to the Inquiry (G5)*, C. P. J. Muttukumaru
*Counsel to the Inquiry*, Ms P. Baxendale, QC
*Assistant Secretary*, Miss H. M. Duffy
*Media Relations Officer (G6)*, D. Price

---

INTERCEPTION COMMISSIONER
c/o The Home Office, 50 Queen Anne's Gate, London
SWIH 9AT

---

The Commissioner is appointed by the Prime Minister. He
keeps under review the issue by the Home Secretary and the
Secretary of State for Scotland of warrants under the
Interception of Communications Act 1985 and safeguards
made in respect of intercepted material obtained through the
use of such warrants. He is also required to give all such
assistance as the Interception of Communications Tribunal
may require to enable it to carry out its functions, and to
submit an annual report to the Prime Minister with respect
to the carrying out of his functions. In 1993 the Home
Secretary issued 998 warrants, and the Secretary of State for
Scotland 122 warrants.
*Commissioner*, The Rt. Hon. the Lord Nolan

---

INTERCEPTION OF COMMUNICATIONS
TRIBUNAL
PO Box 44, London SEI OTX

---

The Tribunal comprises senior members of the legal
profession, who are appointed by The Queen. Under the
Interception of Communications Act 1985, the Tribunal is
required to investigate applications from any person who
believes that communications sent to or by them have been
intercepted in the course of their transmission by post or by
means of a public telecommunications system.

*President*, The Hon. Mr Justice Macpherson of Cluny
*Vice-President*, Sir Cecil Clothier, KCB, QC
*Members*, Sir David Calcutt, QC; I. Guild, CBE; P. Scott, QC

---

INTERVENTION BOARD
Fountain House, Queen's Walk, Reading RG1 7QW
Tel 01734-583626

---

The Intervention Board was established as a government department in 1972 and became operational in 1973. It became an executive agency in 1990. The Board is responsible for the implementation of European Community regulations covering the market support arrangements of the Common Agricultural Policy. Members are appointed by and are responsible to the Minister of Agriculture, Fisheries and Food and the Secretaries of State for Scotland, Wales and Northern Ireland.
*Chairman*, A. J. Ellis, CBE
*Chief Executive (G3)*, G. Stapleton

HEADS OF DIVISIONS
*External Trade Division (G5)*, G. N. Dixon
*Crops Division (G5)*, H. MacKinnon
*Livestock Products Division (G5)*, M. J. Griffiths
*Corporate Services Division (G5)*, J. W. M. Peffers
*Finance Division (G5)*, G. R. R. Jenkins
*Legal Division (G5)*, J. F. McCleary
*Chief Accountant (G6)*, R. Bryant
*External Operations (G6)*, J. P. Bradbury
*Procurement and Supply (G6)*, P. J. Offer
*Information Systems (G6)*, T. T. Simpson

---

LAND AUTHORITY FOR WALES
The Custom House, Customhouse Street, Cardiff CF1 5AP
Tel 01222-223444

---

The Authority is established under the Local Government Planning and Land Act 1980 and is responsible for identifying and acquiring land suitable for development in Wales and making it available for development by others.
*Chairman (part-time) (£31,625)*, Sir Geoffrey Inkin, OBE
*Chief Executive*, B. Ryan, FRICS

---

LAND REGISTRIES

---

HM LAND REGISTRY
Lincoln's Inn Fields, London WC2A 3PH
Tel 0171-917 8888

The registration of title to land was first introduced in England and Wales by the Land Registry Act 1862; HM Land Registry operates today under the Land Registration Acts 1925 to 1988. The object of registering title to land is to create and maintain a register of land owners whose title is guaranteed by the state and so to simplify the transfer, mortgage and other dealings with real property. Registration on sale is now compulsory throughout England and Wales. The register has been open to inspection by the public since December 1990.

HM Land Registry is an executive agency administered under the Lord Chancellor by the Chief Land Registrar. The

work is decentralized to a number of regional offices. The Chief Land Registrar is also responsible for the Land Charges Department and the Agricultural Credits Department.

HEADQUARTERS OFFICE
*Chief Land Registrar and Chief Executive (G2)*,
   J. J. Manthorpe, CB
*Solicitor to Land Registry (G3)*, C. J. West
*Director of Corporate Services (G4)*, E. G. Beardsall
*Senior Land Registrar (G5)*, Mrs J. G. Totty
*Director of Operations (G5)*, G. N. French
*Director of Information Technology (G5)*, P. J. Smith
*Director of Management Services (G6)*, P. R. Laker
*Land Registrar (G5)*, M. L. Wood
*Deputy Establishment Officer (G6)*, J. Hodder
*Controller of Operations Development (G6)*, A. W. Howarth

BIRKENHEAD DISTRICT LAND REGISTRY
Old Market House, Hamilton Street, Birkenhead L41 5FL
Tel 0151-473 1110
*District Land Registrar (G5)*, M. G. Garwood
*Area Manager (G6)*, J. Eccles

COVENTRY DISTRICT LAND REGISTRY
Leigh Court, Torrington Avenue, Coventry CV4 9XZ
Tel 01203-632442
*District Land Registrar (G5)*, S. P. Kelway
*Area Manager (G6)*, J. C. Lillistone

CROYDON DISTRICT LAND REGISTRY
Sunley House, Bedford Park, Croydon CR9 3LE
Tel 0181-781 9100
*District Land Registrar (G5)*, D. M. J. Moss
*Area Manager (G6)*, V. J. C. Shorney

DURHAM DISTRICT LAND REGISTRY
Southfield House, Southfield Way, Durham DH1 5TR
Tel 0191-301 3500
*District Land Registrar (G5)*, C. W. Martin
*Area Manager (G6)*, B. Warriner

GLOUCESTER DISTRICT LAND REGISTRY
Twyver House, Bruton Way, Gloucester GL1 1DQ
Tel 01452-511111
*District Land Registrar (G5)*, W. W. Budden
*Area Manager (G6)*, R. B. Johnson

HARROW DISTRICT LAND REGISTRY
Lyon House, Lyon Road, Harrow, Middx. HA1 2EU
Tel 0181-427 8811
*District Land Registrar (G5)*, J. V. Timothy
*Area Manager (G6)*, M. J. Wyatt

KINGSTON UPON HULL DISTRICT LAND REGISTRY
Earle House, Portland Street, Hull HU2 8JN
Tel 01482-223244
*District Land Registrar (G5)*, S. R. Coveney
*Area Manager (G6)*, E. Howard

LAND CHARGES AND AGRICULTURAL CREDITS
DEPARTMENT
Burrington Way, Plymouth PL5 3LP
Tel 01752-779831
*Superintendent of Land Charges (G7)*, J. Hughes

LEICESTER DISTRICT LAND REGISTRY
Thames Tower, 99 Burleys Way, Leicester LE1 3UB
Tel 0116-265 4000
*District Land Registrar (G6)*, Mrs J. A. Goodfellow
*Area Manager (G7)*, G. M. Johns

LYTHAM DISTRICT LAND REGISTRY

Birkenhead House, Lytham St Annes, Lancs. FY8 5AB
Tel 01253-849849
*District Land Registrar (G5)*, J. G. Cooper
*Area Manager (G6)*, B. Elliott

NOTTINGHAM DISTRICT LAND REGISTRY
Chalfont Drive, Nottingham NG8 3RN
Tel 0115-929 1166
*District Land Registrar (G5)*, P. J. Timothy
*Area Manager (G6)*, W. Whitaker

PETERBOROUGH DISTRICT LAND REGISTRY
Touthill Close, City Road, Peterborough PE1 1XN
Tel 01733-288288
*District Land Registrar (G5)*, L. M. Pope
*Area Manager (G6)*, B. J. Andrews

PLYMOUTH DISTRICT LAND REGISTRY
Plumer House, Tailyour Road, Crownhill, Plymouth
PL6 5HY
Tel 01752-701234
*District Land Registrar (G5)*, A. J. Pain
*Area Manager(G6)*, K. Robinson

PORTSMOUTH DISTRICT LAND REGISTRY
St Andrews Court, St Michael's Road, Portsmouth PO1 2JH
Tel 01705-865022
*District Land Registrar (G6)*, S. R. Sehrawat
*Area Manager (G7)*, R. J. Lewis

STEVENAGE DISTRICT LAND REGISTRY
Brickdale House, Swingate, Stevenage, Herts. SG1 1XG
Tel 01438-313003
*District Land Registrar (G5)*, C. Tate
*Area Manager (G6)*, A. D. Gould

SWANSEA DISTRICT LAND REGISTRY
Tybryn Glas, High Street, Swansea SA1 1PW
Tel 01792-458877
*District Land Registrar (G5)*, G. A. Hughes
*Area Manager (G6)*, R. T. Davis

TELFORD DISTRICT LAND REGISTRY
Parkside Court, Hall Park Way, Telford TF3 4LR
Tel 01952-290355
*District Land Registrar (G5)*, M. A. Roche
*Area Manager (G6)*, R. D. Moseley

TUNBRIDGE WELLS DISTRICT LAND REGISTRY
Curtis House, Hawkenbury, Tunbridge Wells, Kent
TN2 5AQ
Tel 01892-510015
*District Land Registrar (G5)*, G. R. Tooke
*Area Manager (G6)*, B. S. Crozier

WEYMOUTH DISTRICT LAND REGISTRY
1 Cumberland Drive, Weymouth, Dorset DT4 9TT
Tel 01305-776161
*District Land Registrar (G5)*, Mrs P. M. Reeson
*Area Manager (G6)*, J. Dodd

YORK DISTRICT LAND REGISTRY
James House, James Street, York YO1 3YZ
Tel 01904-450000
*District Land Registrar (G6)*, Mrs R. F. Lovel
*Area Manager (G7)*, P. Wright

COMPUTER SERVICES DIVISION
Burrington Way, Plymouth PL5 3LP
Tel 01752-779831
*Head of Services Division (G6)*, P. A. Maycock
*Head of Development Division (G6)*, R. J. Smith

REGISTERS OF SCOTLAND (EXECUTIVE
AGENCY)
Meadowbank House, 153 London Road, Edinburgh
EH8 7AU
Tel 0131-659 6111

The Registers of Scotland consist of: General Register of
Sasines and Land Register of Scotland; Register of Deeds in
the Books of Council and Session; Register of Protests;
Register of Judgments; Register of Service of Heirs; Register
of the Great Seal; Register of the Quarter Seal; Register of
the Prince's Seal; Register of Crown Grants; Register of
Sheriffs' Commissions; Register of the Cachet Seal; Register
of Inhibitions and Adjudications; Register of Entails; Register
of Hornings.
   The General Register of Sasines and the Land Register of
Scotland form the chief security in Scotland of the rights of
land and other heritable (or real) property.
*Keeper of the Registers of Scotland (G4)*, A. W. Ramage
*Senior Directors (G5)*, J. K. Mason; A. G. Rennie
*Senior Assistant Directors (G6)*, B. J. Corr; A. M. Falconer
*Strategy Director (G6)*, D. Leslie
*Assistant Directors (G7)*, D. G. Cant (*computers*); R. Glen
   (*personnel*); J. Knox (*Land Register*); D. McCallum (*Land
   Register*); L. J. Mitchell (*management services*);
   A. G. T. New (*Land Register*); I. M. Nicol (*finance*); Mrs
   P. M. Stewart (*training*)
*Assistant Keeper (G7)*, I. A. Davis
*Grade 7*, J. Anderson; J. F. Campbell; J. Cogle;
   J. S. McKinlay; D. Manson; J. B. Marshall; Mrs
   A. Moore; W. F. Rankin; J. Rynn; M. J. Wilczynski

---

LAW COMMISSION
Conquest House, 37–38 John Street, Theobalds Road,
London WC1N 2BQ
Tel 0171-411 1220

---

The Law Commission was set up in 1965, under the Law
Commissions Act 1965, to make proposals to the Government
for the examination of the law in England and Wales and for
its revision where it is unsuited for modern requirements,
obscure, or otherwise unsatisfactory. It recommends to the
Lord Chancellor programmes for the examination of different
branches of the law and suggests whether the examination
should be carried out by the Commission itself or by some
other body. The Commission is also responsible for the
preparation of Consolidation and Statute Law (Repeals) Bills.
*Chairman*, The Hon. Mr Justice Brooke
*Members*, C. Harpum; A. S. Burrows; Miss D. Faber;
   S. Silber, QC
*Secretary*, M. W. Sayers

---

SCOTTISH LAW COMMISSION
140 Causewayside, Edinburgh EH9 1PR
Tel 0131-668 2131

---

The Commission keeps the law in Scotland under review and
makes proposals for its development and reform.
*Chairman*, The Hon. Lord Davidson
*Commissioners (full-time)*, Dr E. M. Clive; Sheriff
   I. D. MacPhail, QC; (*part-time*) Prof. P. N. Love, CBE;
   W. Nimmo Smith, QC
*Secretary*, K. F. Barclay

## LAW OFFICERS' DEPARTMENTS

Attorney-General's Chambers, 9 Buckingham Gate,
London SW1E 6JP
Tel 0171-828 7155
Attorney-General's Chambers, Royal Courts of Justice,
Belfast BT1 3JY
Tel 01232-235111

The Law Officers of the Crown for England and Wales are
the Attorney-General and the Solicitor-General. The Attorney-General, assisted by the Solicitor-General, is the chief
legal adviser to the Government and is also ultimately
responsible for all Crown litigation. He has overall responsibility for the work of the Law Officers' Departments (the
Treasury Solicitor's Department, the Crown Prosecution
Service, the Serious Fraud Office and the Legal Secretariat
to the Law Officers). He has a specific statutory duty to
superintend the discharge of their duties by the Director of
Public Prosecutions (who is head of the Crown Prosecution
Service) and the Director of the Serious Fraud Office. The
Director of Public Prosecutions for Northern Ireland is
responsible to the Attorney-General for the performance of
his functions. The Attorney-General has additional responsibilities in relation to aspects of the civil and criminal law.

*Attorney-General* (\*£43,456), The Rt. Hon. Sir Nicholas
Lyell, QC, MP
  *Private Secretary*, S. A. Moore
*Solicitor-General* (\*£35,632), Sir Derek Spencer, QC, MP
  *Private Secretary*, S. A. Moore
*Parliamentary Private Secretary*, G. Streeter, MP
*Legal Secretary* (*G2*), Miss J. L. Wheldon, CB
*Deputy Legal Secretary* (*G4*), S. J. Wooler
\* Excluding reduced parliamentary salary of £23,854

## LEGAL AID BOARD

85 Grays Inn Road, London WC1X 8AA
Tel 0171-813 1000

The Legal Aid Board has the general function of ensuring
that advice, assistance and representation are available in
accordance with the Legal Aid Act 1988. In 1989 it took over
from the Law Society responsibility for administering legal
aid. The Board is a non-departmental government body
whose members are appointed by the Lord Chancellor.
*Chairman*, J. Pitts
*Members*, S. Orchard (*Chief Executive*); Ms V. Boakes;
  F. Collins; J. Crosby; Ms J. Dunkley; C. George; P. Jones;
  Ms K. Markus; Ms D. Payne; Ms P. Pearce; G. Pulman,
  QC; D. Sinker; A. Thomas

## SCOTTISH LEGAL AID BOARD

44 Drumsheugh Gardens, Edinburgh EH3 7SW
Tel 0131-226 7061

The Scottish Legal Aid Board was set up under the Legal
Aid (Scotland) Act 1986. It is responsible for ensuring that
advice, assistance and representation are available in
accordance with the Act. The Board is a non-departmental
government body whose members are appointed by the
Secretary of State for Scotland.
*Chairman*, Mrs C. A. M. Davis
*Members*, G. Barrie; Mrs K. Blair; Mrs P. A. M. Bolton; Mrs
  P. M. M. Bowman; Mrs S. Campbell; Mrs J. Couper;

A. Gilchrist; Prof. P. H. Grinyer; D. A. Leitch;
R. J. Livingstone; C. N. McEachran, QC; Sheriff
R. G. McEwan, QC; Mrs G. M. Peebles; A. F. Wylie, QC
*Chief Executive*, A. E. M. Douglas

## OFFICE OF THE LEGAL SERVICES OMBUDSMAN

22 Oxford Court, Oxford Street, Manchester M2 3WQ
Tel 0161-236 9532

The Legal Services Ombudsman is appointed by the Lord
Chancellor under the Courts and Legal Services Act 1990 to
oversee the handling of complaints against solicitors,
barristers and licensed conveyancers by their professional
bodies. A complainant must first complain to the relevant
professional body before raising the matter with the
Ombudsman. The Ombudsman is independent of the legal
profession and his services are free of charge.
*Legal Services Ombudsman*, M. Barnes
*Secretary*, S. Murray

OFFICE OF THE SCOTTISH LEGAL SERVICES
OMBUDSMAN
2 Greenside Lane, Edinburgh EH1 3AH
Tel 0131-556 5574
*Scottish Legal Services Ombudsman*, G. S. Watson

## LIBRARIES

## THE BRITISH LIBRARY

2 Sheraton Street, London W1V 4BH
Tel 0171-636 1544

The British Library is the UK's national library and occupies
the central position in the library and information network.
The Library aims to serve scholarship, research, industry,
commerce and all other major users of information. Its
services are based on collections which include over 18 million
volumes, 1 million discs, and 55,000 hours of tape recordings,
at 18 buildings in London and one complex in West
Yorkshire. The British Library is in the process of moving to
purpose-built accommodation at St Pancras, London NW1
(scheduled to open to the public in 1996).

The British Library was established in 1973 and brought
together the library departments of the British Museum, the
National Central Library, the National Lending Library for
Science and Technology, the British National Bibliography
Ltd and, in 1974, the Office for Scientific and Technical
Information. Subsequently the Library took responsibility
for the India Office Library and Records, the HMSO
Binderies, and the National Sound Archive.

Access to the Humanities and Social Sciences reading
rooms in Great Russell Street is limited to holders of a British
Library Reader's Pass; information about eligibility is
available from the Reader Admissions Office. The Aldwych
and Holborn reading rooms of the Science Reference and
Information Service are open to the general public without
charge or formality. The Library's exhibition galleries are
housed in the British Museum building in Great Russell
Street.

BRITISH LIBRARY BOARD
96 Euston Road, London NW1 2DB
Tel 0171-323 7262

*Chairman,* Sir Anthony Kenny, D.Phil., D.Litt., FBA
*Chief Executive and Deputy Chairman (G2),* B. Lang
*Directors-General (G4),* J. M. Smethurst; D. Russon
*Part-time Members,* The Lord Windlesham, CVO, PC;
  R. E. Utiger, CBE; T. J. Rix; Dame Anne Warburton,
  DCVO, CMG; H. Heaney; D. Peake; E. M. W. Griffith,
  CBE; The Hon. E. Adeane, CVO; Sir Matthew Farrer,
  KCVO; Mrs P. M. Lively, OBE; Prof. M. Anderson

### BRITISH LIBRARY, BOSTON SPA
Boston Spa, Wetherby, W. Yorks. LS23 7BQ
Tel 01937-546000
*Director-General (G4),* D. Russon

DOCUMENT SUPPLY CENTRE, *Director (G5),* D. Bradbury
NATIONAL BIBLIOGRAPHIC SERVICE. Tel: 01937-
  546585. *Director (G6),* S. J. Ede
*London Unit,* 2 Sheraton Street, London WIV 4BH. Tel: 0171-
  323 7077
ACQUISITIONS PROCESSING AND CATALOGUING,
  *Director (G5),* Mrs J. E. Butcher
COMPUTING AND TELECOMMUNICATIONS. Tel: 01937-
  546879. *Director (G5),* J. R. Mahoney

### BRITISH LIBRARY, LONDON
Great Russell Street, London WCIB 3DG
Tel 0171-636 1544

*Director-General (G4),* J. M. Smethurst
*St Pancras Project Director (G4),* D. Lyman
*Director of Project Services St Pancras Planning (G6),* Dr
  R. Coman

ADMINISTRATION, 2 Sheraton Street, London WIV 4BH.
  Tel: 0171-323 7132. *Director (G5),* R. Ball
PRESS AND PUBLIC RELATIONS, 96 Euston Road,
  London NWI 2DB. Tel: 0171-323 7111. *Head (G7),*
  M. Jackson
PUBLIC SERVICES. Tel: 0171-323 7626. *Director (G5),* Ms
  J. Carr
*Exhibitions and Education Service.* Tel: 0171-323 7595
*Reader Admissions.* Tel: 0171-323 7677
HUMANITIES AND SOCIAL SCIENCES. Tel: 0171-323
  7676.
*Director (G5),* A. Phillips
*West European Collections, Slavonic and East European
  Collections, English Language Collections.* Tel: 0171-323
  7676
*Information Branch, Official Publications and Social Science
  Service.* Tel: 0171-323 7676
*Information Sciences Service (BLISS),* Ridgmount Street,
  London WCIE 7AE. Tel: 0171-323 7688
*Newspaper Library,* Colindale Avenue, London NW9 5HE.
  Tel: 0171-323 7353
*National Sound Archive,* 29 Exhibition Road, London SW7
  2AS. Tel: 0171-412 7440
COLLECTIONS AND PRESERVATION. Tel: 0171-323 7676.
  *Director (G5),* Dr M. Foot
*Preservation Service (National Preservation Office).* Tel:
  0171-323 7612
SPECIAL COLLECTIONS. Tel: 0171-323 7513. *Director (G5),*
  Dr A. Prochaska
*Oriental and India Office Collections,* 197 Blackfriars Road,
  London SEI 8NG. Tel: 0171-412 7873
*Western Manuscripts.* Tel: 0171-323 7513
*Map Library.* Tel: 0171-323 7700
*Music Library.* Tel: 0171-323 7528
*Philatelic Collections.* Tel: 0171-323 7729

SCIENCE REFERENCE AND INFORMATION SERVICE,
  25 Southampton Buildings, London WC2A IAW. Tel: 0171-

323 7494; 9 Kean Street, London WC2B 4AT. Tel: 0171-
  323 7288. *Director (G5),* A. Gomersall
RESEARCH AND DEVELOPMENT DEPARTMENT,
  2 Sheraton Street, London WIV 4BH. Tel: 0171-323 7060.
  *Director (G6),* B. J. Perry

### NATIONAL LIBRARY OF SCOTLAND
George IV Bridge, Edinburgh EHI IEW
Tel 0131-226 4531

The Library, which was founded as the Advocates' Library
in 1682, became the National Library of Scotland in 1925. It
contains about six million books and pamphlets, 20,000
current periodicals, 230 newspaper titles and 100,000
manuscripts. It has an unrivalled Scottish collection.
  The Reading Room is for reference and research which
cannot conveniently be pursued elsewhere. Admission is by
ticket issued to an approved applicant. Opening hours:
Reading Room, weekdays, 9.30–8.30 (Wednesday, 10–
8.30); Saturday 9.30–1. Map Library, weekdays, 9.30–5
(Wednesday, 10–5); Saturday 9.30–1. Exhibition, weekdays,
10–5; Saturday 10–5; Sunday 2–5. Scottish Science Library,
weekdays, 9.30–5 (Wednesday, 10–8).

SALARIES

| | |
|---|---|
| Librarian | £44,390–£53,740 |
| Keeper | £27,660–£44,989 |
| Grade 7 | £24,239–£36,516 |

*Chairman of the Trustees,* The Earl of Crawford and
  Balcarres, PC
*Librarian and Secretary to the Trustees,* I. D. McGowan
*Secretary of the Library (Keeper),* M. C. Graham
*Grade 7,* A. Cameron; W. Jackson; J. E. McIntyre; Ms
  P. Scott
*Keepers of Printed Books,* A. M. Marchbank, PH.D.; Ms
  A. Matheson, PH.D.
*Grade 7,* T. A. Cherry; K. Gibson, PH.D.; Ms A. E. Harvey
  Wood; B. P. Hillyard, D.Phil.; S. Holland; W. A. Kelly;
  Ms J. McFarlane; J. M. Morris
*Keeper of Manuscripts,* I. C. Cunningham
*Grade 7,* I. G. Brown, PH.D., FSA; R. Duce; I. F. Maciver;
  S. M. Simpson; Ms J. M. Wilkes; Ms E. D. Yeo
*Director of Computer Services and Research (Keeper),*
  B. Gallivan
*Grade 7,* R. F. Guy
*Director of Scottish Science Library (Keeper),* Ms A. J. Bunch
*Grade 7,* J. Coll; Mrs E. Fallone; Ms M. Nisbet

### NATIONAL LIBRARY OF WALES/LLYFRGELL GENEDLAETHOL CYMRU
Aberystwyth, Dyfed SY23 3BU
Tel 01970-623816

The National Library of Wales was founded by Royal
Charter in 1907, and is maintained by annual grant from the
Treasury. It contains about four million printed books,
40,000 manuscripts, four million deeds and documents,
numerous maps, prints and drawings, and an audio-visual
collection. It specializes in manuscripts and books relating to
Wales and the Celtic peoples. It is the repository for pre-
1858 Welsh probate records, manorial records and tithe
documents, and certain legal records. Readers' room open
weekdays, 9.30–6 (Saturday 9.30–5); closed first week of
October. Admission by Reader's Ticket.
*Librarian,* J. L. Madden
*Heads of Departments,* M. W. Mainwaring (*Administration
  and Technical Services*); G. Jenkins (*Manuscripts and
  Records*); W. R. L. Griffiths (*Printed Books*); D. H. Owen
  (*Pictures and Maps*)

## LIGHTHOUSE AUTHORITIES

## CORPORATION OF TRINITY HOUSE
Trinity House, Tower Hill, London EC3N 4DH
Tel 0171-480 6601

Trinity House, the first general lighthouse and pilotage authority in the kingdom, was granted its first charter by Henry VIII in 1514. The Corporation is the general lighthouse authority for England, Wales and the Channel Islands and has statutory jurisdiction over aids to navigation maintained by local harbour authorities. It is also responsible for dealing with wrecks dangerous to navigation, except those occurring within port limits or wrecks of HM ships. The Corporation is also a deep-sea pilotage authority and a charitable organization.

The Trinity House Lighthouse Service is maintained out of the General Lighthouse Fund which is provided from light dues levied on ships calling at ports of the UK and the Republic of Ireland.

The affairs of the Corporation are controlled by a board of Elder Brethren, who are master mariners with long experience of command in the Royal Navy or merchant navy, together with figures from the world of commerce, and the Secretary. A separate board, which comprises Elder Brethren, senior staff and outside representatives, currently controls the Lighthouse Service. The Elder Brethren also act as nautical assessors in marine cases in the Admiralty Division of the High Court of Justice.

ELDER BRETHREN
*Master*, HRH The Duke of Edinburgh, KG, KT
*Deputy Master*, Capt. P. M. Edge
*Elder Brethren*, Capt. D. J. Orr; Capt. N. M. Turner, RD; HRH The Prince of Wales, KG, KT; HRH The Duke of York, CVO, ADC; Capt. Sir George Barnard, FRSA; Capt. R. N. Mayo, CBE; Capt. Sir David Tibbits, DSC, RN; Capt. D. A. G. Dickens; Capt. J. E. Bury; Capt. J. A. N. Bezant, DSC, RD, RNR; Capt. D. J. Cloke; The Lord Wilson of Rievaulx, KG, OBE, PC, FRS; Capt. Sir Miles Wingate, KCVO; The Rt. Hon. Sir Edward Heath, KG, MBE, MP; Capt. I. R. C. Saunders; Capt. P. F. Mason, CBE; Capt. T. Woodfield, OBE; Sir Eric Drake, CBE; The Lord Simon of Glaisdale, PC; Admiral of the Fleet the Lord Lewin, KG, GCB, LVO, DSC; Capt. D. T. Smith, RN; Cdr. Sir Robin Gillett, GBE, RD, RNR; The Lord Shackleton, KG, OBE, PC, FRS; Sir John Cuckney; The Lord Carrington, KG, GCMG, CH, MC, PC; Sir Brian Shaw; The Lord Mackay of Clashfern, PC; Sir Adrian Swire; Capt. P. H. King; The Lord Sterling of Plaistow, CBE, RNR; Cdr. M. J. Rivett-Carnac, RN; Rear-Adm. P. B. Lowe, CBE, LVO

OFFICERS
*Secretary and Director of Administration*, M. J. Faulkner
*Director of Finance*, K. W. Clark
*Director of Engineering*, D. A. S. Vennings
*General Manager Operations*, Capt. J. M. Barnes
*Personnel and General Services Manager*, Mrs B. C. Heesom
*Operations Administration Manager*, S. J. W. Dunning
*Legal and Information Manager*, D. I. Brewer
*Navigation Manager*, N. J. Cutmore
*Deputy Director of Engineering*, F. E. J. Holden
*Senior Inspector of Shipping*, J. R. Dunnett
*Manager, Corporate Department*, R. Dobb
*Information Officer*, H. L. Cooper

## COMMISSIONERS OF NORTHERN LIGHTHOUSES
84 George Street, Edinburgh EH2 3DA
Tel 0131-226 7051

The Commissioners of Northern Lighthouses are the general lighthouse authority for Scotland and the Isle of Man. The present board owes its origin to an Act of Parliament passed in 1786. At present the Commissioners operate under the Merchant Shipping Act 1894 and are 19 in number.

The Commissioners control 13 major manned lighthouses, 71 major automatic lighthouses, 111 minor lights and many lighted and unlighted buoys. They have a fleet of two motor vessels.

COMMISSIONERS
The Lord Advocate; the Solicitor-General for Scotland; the Lord Provosts of Edinburgh, Glasgow and Aberdeen; the Provost of Inverness; the Chairman of Argyll and Bute District Council; the Sheriffs-Principal of North Strathclyde, Tayside, Central and Fife, Grampian, Highlands and Islands, South Strathclyde, Dumfries and Galloway, Lothians and Borders, and Glasgow and Strathkelvin; T. Macgill; A. J. Struthers; W. F. Hay, CBE; J. Hann, CBE; Capt. D. M. Cowell; Adm. Sir Michael Livesay, KCB

OFFICERS
*Chief Executive*, Capt. J. B. Taylor, RN
*Secretary*, I. A. Dickson
*Engineer-in-Chief*, W. Paterson

## LOCAL COMMISSIONERS

## COMMISSION FOR LOCAL ADMINISTRATION IN ENGLAND
21 Queen Anne's Gate, London SW1H 9BU
Tel 0171-915 3210

Local Commissioners (local government ombudsmen) are responsible for investigating complaints from members of the public against local authorities (but not town and parish councils); police authorities; the Commission for New Towns and new town development corporations (housing functions); urban development corporations (town and country planning functions) and certain other authorities. The Commissioners are appointed by the Crown on the recommendation of the Secretary of State for the Environment.

Certain types of action are excluded from investigation, including personnel matters and commercial transactions unless they relate to the purchase or sale of land. Complaints can be sent direct to the Local Government Ombudsman or through a councillor, although the Local Government Ombudsman will not consider a complaint unless the council has had an opportunity to investigate and reply to a complainant.

A free booklet *Complaint about the Council? How to complain to the Local Government Ombudsman* is available from the Commission's office.
*Chairman of the Commission and Local Commissioner* (£90,148), E. B. C. Osmotherly, CB
*Vice-Chairman and Local Commissioner* (£65,307), Mrs P. A. Thomas
*Local Commissioner* (£72,500), vacant
*Member* (ex officio), The Parliamentary Commissioner for Administration
*Secretary* (£46,128), G. D. Adams

## COMMISSION FOR LOCAL ADMINISTRATION IN WALES
Derwen House, Court Road, Bridgend CF31 1BN
Tel 01656-661325

The Local Commissioner for Wales has similar powers to the Local Commissioners in England. The Commissioner is appointed by the Crown on the recommendation of the Secretary of State for Wales. A free leaflet *Your Local Ombudsman in Wales* is available from the Commission's office.
*Local Commissioner*, E. R. Moseley
*Secretary*, D. Bowen
*Member* (ex officio), The Parliamentary Commissioner for Administration

## COMMISSIONER FOR LOCAL ADMINISTRATION IN SCOTLAND
23 Walker Street, Edinburgh EH3 7HX
Tel 0131-225 5300

The Local Commissioner for Scotland has similar powers to the Local Commissioners in England, and is appointed by the Crown on the recommendation of the Secretary of State for Scotland.
*Local Commissioner*, F. C. Marks, OBE
*Deputy and Secretary*, Ms J. H. Renton

## LONDON REGIONAL TRANSPORT
55 Broadway, London SW1H 0BD
Tel 0171-222 5600

Subject to the financial objectives and principles approved by the Secretary of State for Transport, London Regional Transport has a general duty to provide or secure the provision of public transport services for Greater London.
*Chairman* (£120,000), P. Ford
*Member* (£80,600), A. J. Sheppeck
*Member, and Managing Director of London Underground Ltd* (£102,900), D. Tunnicliffe

## LORD ADVOCATE'S DEPARTMENT
2 Carlton Gardens, London SW1Y 5AA
Tel 0171-210 1010

The Law Officers for Scotland are the Lord Advocate and the Solicitor-General for Scotland. The Lord Advocate's Department is responsible for drafting Scottish legislation, for providing legal advice to other departments on Scottish questions and for assistance to the Law Officers for Scotland in certain of their legal duties.
*Lord Advocate* (£52,340), The Lord Rodger of Earlsferry, PC, QC
*Private Secretary*, A. G. Maxwell
*Solicitor-General for Scotland* (£45,539), Thomas C. Dawson, QC
*Private Secretary*, A. G. Maxwell
*Legal Secretary and First Scottish Parliamentary Counsel* (G2), J. C. McCluskie, QC
*Assistant Legal Secretaries and Scottish Parliamentary Counsel* (G3), G. M. Clark; G. Kowalski; P. J. Layden, TD; C. A. M. Wilson
*Assistant Legal Secretary and Depute Scottish Parliamentary Counsel* (G5), J. D. Harkness

*Assistant Legal Secretaries and Assistant Scottish Parliamentary Counsel* (G6/7), Miss M. Mackenzie; Miss L. A. Drummond; F. T. Coleman

## LORD CHANCELLOR'S DEPARTMENT
House of Lords, London SW1A 0PW
Trevelyan House, Great Peter Street, London SW1P 2BY
Tel 0171-210 8500

The Lord Chancellor is responsible for promoting general reforms in the civil law, for the procedure of the civil courts and for the administration of the Supreme Court (Court of Appeal, High Court and Crown Court) and county courts in England and Wales, and for legal aid schemes. He also has ministerial responsibility for magistrates' courts, which are administered locally. He is advised and assisted in raising performance standards in the Service by the new Magistrates' Courts' Service Inspectorate.
The Lord Chancellor is responsible for advising the Crown on the appointment of judges and certain other officers and is himself responsible for the appointment of Masters and Registrars of the High Court, Judges of the Principal Registry of the Family Division, district judges and magistrates. He is responsible for ensuring that letters patent and other formal documents are passed in the proper form under the Great Seal of the Realm, of which he is the custodian. The work in connection with this is carried out under his direction in the Office of the Clerk of the Crown in Chancery.
*Lord Chancellor* (£120,179), The Lord Mackay of Clashfern, PC
*Private Secretary*, M. Ormerod
*Parliamentary Secretary*, John Taylor, MP
*Private Secretary*, Ms S. Jones
*Permanent Secretary* (G1), Sir Thomas Legg, KCB, QC
*Private Secretary*, D. Willink

CROWN OFFICE
*Clerk of the Crown in Chancery* (G1), Sir Thomas Legg, KCB, QC
*Deputy Clerk of the Crown in Chancery* (G2), M. Huebner, CB
*Clerk of the Chamber*, C. I. P. Denyer

JUDICIAL APPOINTMENTS GROUP
Southside, 105 Victoria Street, London SW1E 6QT
Tel 0171-210 1630
*Head of Group* (G3), R. E. K. Holmes
*Grade 5*, D. E. Staff; R. A. Venne; R. V. Grobler; G. Norman; P. G. Taylor

LAW AND POLICY GROUPS
Trevelyan House, Great Peter Street, London SW1P 2BY
Tel 0171-210 8872
*Head of Group* (G2), M. Malone-Lee
*Grade 5*, P. G. Harris

LEGAL GROUP
Southside, 105 Victoria Street, London SW1E 6QJ
Tel 0171-210 3508
*Grade 3*, R. H. H. White
*Grade 5*, J. Watherston; M. Kron; J. Gibson; D. J. Gladwell

POLICY AND LEGAL SERVICES GROUP
Trevelyan House, Great Peter Street, London SW1P 2BY
Tel 0171-210 8843
*Grade 3*, C. W. Everett
*Grade 5*, S. Smith; M. Sayers; P. L. Jacob

## COURT SERVICE
Southside, 105 Victoria Street, London SW1E 6QT
Tel 0171-210 1733

The Court Service will become an executive agency of the Department in April 1995.

*Head (G2)*, M. Huebner, CB

COURT SERVICE BUSINESS GROUP
Trevelyan House, Great Peter Street, London SW1P 2BY
Tel 0171-210 8843

*Grade 3*, J. F. Brindley
*Grade 5*, P. Handcock; R. Sams; Miss J. Killick; Mrs
   M. Pigott
For Supreme Court departments and offices, *see* Law Courts and Offices section

### ESTABLISHMENT AND FINANCE GROUP
Trevelyan House, Great Peter Street, London SW1P 2BY
Tel 0171-210 8519

*Head of Group (G3)*, Mrs N. A. Oppenheimer
*Grade 5*, Ms H. Tuffs; A. Cogbill; P. White
*Grade 6*, Mrs J. Waters; K. Cregeen; A. Sloan

### MAGISTRATES' COURTS' SERVICE INSPECTORATE
Southside, 105 Victoria Street, London SW1E 6QJ
Tel 0171-210 1655

*Chief Inspector (G5)*, Mrs R. L. Melling
*Senior Inspectors (G6)*, Ms J. Eeles; D. Gear; C. Monson; Ms
   S. Steel

### LORD CHANCELLOR'S ADVISORY COMMITTEE ON STATUTE LAW
6 Spring Gardens, London SW1A 2BP
Tel 0171-389 3244

The Advisory Committee advises the Lord Chancellor on all matters relating to the revision, modernization and publication of the statute book.

*Chairman*, The Lord Chancellor
*Deputy Chairman*, Sir Thomas Legg, KCB, QC
*Members*, Sir Michael Wheeler-Booth, KCB; Sir Clifford
   Boulton, KCB; The Hon. Mr Justice Brooke; The Hon.
   Lord Davidson; C. Jenkins, CB, QC; J. C. McCluskie, QC;
   G. Hosker, CB, QC; R. Brodie, CB; R. H. H White;
   J. Gibson; Dr P. Freeman; (ex officio) First Legislative
   Counsel, Northern Ireland
*Secretary*, C. Carey

### LORD CHANCELLOR'S ECCLESIASTICAL OFFICE
10 Downing Street, London SW1A 2AA
Tel 0171-930 4433

*Secretary for Ecclesiastical Patronage*, J. H. Holroyd, CB
*Assistant Secretary for Ecclesiastical Patronage*,
   N. C. Wheeler

### LORD GREAT CHAMBERLAIN'S OFFICE
House of Lords, London SW1A 0AA
Tel 0171-219 3100

The Lord Great Chamberlain is a Great Officer of State, the office being hereditary since the grant of Henry I to the family of De Vere, Earls of Oxford. The Lord Great Chamberlain is responsible for the Royal Apartments of the Palace of Westminster, i.e. The Queen's Robing Room, the Royal Gallery and, in conjunction with the Lord Chancellor and Madam Speaker, Westminster Hall. The Lord Great Chamberlain has particular responsibility for the internal administrative arrangements within the House of Lords for State Openings of Parliament.

*Lord Great Chamberlain*, The Marquess of Cholmondeley
*Secretary to the Lord Great Chamberlain*, Adm. Sir Richard
   Thomas, KCB, OBE
*Clerk to the Lord Great Chamberlain*, Mrs S. E. Douglas

### LORD PRIVY SEAL'S OFFICE
Privy Council Office, 68 Whitehall, London SW1A 2AT
Tel 0171-270 3000

As leader of the House of Lords, the Lord Privy Seal is responsible to the Prime Minister for the organization of government business in the House. He also has a responsibility to the House itself to advise it on procedural matters and other difficulties which arise. The Lord Privy Seal has no departmental portfolio, but chairs a number of domestic and economic Cabinet committees.

*Lord Privy Seal, and Leader of the House of Lords*, Viscount
   Cranborne, PC
*Private Secretary*, Mrs J. M. Bailey
*Private Secretary (House of Lords)*, Mrs M. Ollard

### LOTTERY, OFFICE OF THE NATIONAL
— *see* page 337

### OFFICE OF MANPOWER ECONOMICS
22 Kingsway, London WC2B 6JY
Tel 0171-405 5944

The Office of Manpower Economics was set up in 1971. It is an independent non-statutory organization which is responsible for servicing independent review bodies which advise on the pay of various public service groups (*see* Review Bodies, page 349), the Pharmacists Review Panel and the Police Negotiating Board. The Office is also responsible for servicing *ad hoc* bodies of inquiry and for undertaking research into pay and associated matters as requested by the Government.
*Director*, M. J. Horsman
*Assistant Secretaries (G5)*, M. Emmott; P. J. H. Edwards;
   G. S. Charles; Mrs S. Webber

### MEDICAL RESEARCH COUNCIL
20 Park Crescent, London W1N 4AL
Tel 0171-636 5422

The Medical Research Council is the main government agency for the promotion of medical and related biological research. The council employs its own research staff and also provides grants for other institutions and for individuals who are not members of its own staff, thus complementing the research resources of the universities and hospitals. Government funding for 1994–5 is £269.2 million.
*Chairman*, Sir David Plastow
*Chief Executive*, Sir Dai Rees, D.SC., FRS
*Members*, Prof. A. M. Breckenridge, MD, FRCP, FRCPE, FRSE;
   K. C. Calman, MD, Ph.D., FRCS(Glas.), FRCP, FRSE; Sir
   Michael Carlisle; J. T. Carter, FRCP; Prof. T. M. Dexter,

D.SC., FRS; Prof. C. R. W. Edwards, MD, FRCP, FRCPE; Prof. J. Grimley Evans, MD, DM, FRCP, FFCM; R. E. Kendell, CBE, MD, FRCP, FRCPsych., FRCPE; Miss E. Nicholson, MP; Prof. J. R. Pattison, DM, FRCPath.; Prof. M. J. Peckham, FRCP, FRCP(Glas.), FRCR; Prof. Sir Michael Rutter, CBE, MD, FRCP, FRCPsych., FRS; Prof. Sir David Weatherall, MD, FRCP, FRCPath., FRS
*Administrative Secretary*, N. F. Morris

NEUROSCIENCES AND MENTAL HEALTH BOARD
*Chairman*, Prof. Sir Michael Rutter, CBE, MD, FRCP, FRCPsych., FRS

MOLECULAR AND CELLULAR MEDICINE BOARD
*Chairman*, Prof. T. M. Dexter, D.SC., FRS

PHYSIOLOGICAL MEDICINE AND INFECTIONS BOARD
*Chairman*, Prof. J. R. Pattison, DM, FRCPath.

HEALTH SERVICES AND PUBLIC HEALTH RESEARCH BOARD
*Chairman*, Prof. M. Roland, DM

HEADQUARTERS OFFICE
*Second Secretary*, D. C. Evered, MD, FRCP
*Director of Finance*, N. H. Winterton
*Director of Human Resources*, D. L. Smith, Ph.D.
*Director of Corporate Affairs*, J. M. Lee
*Director of Research Management*, D. R. Dunstan, Ph.D.
*Director of Industrial Collaboration and Licensing*, D. A. A. Owen, Ph.D.
*Research Strategy Manager*, M. B. Kemp, Ph.D.
*Research Business Manager*, D. J. McLaren, D.SC.
*Executive Board Secretaries*, M. M. Jepson, Ph.D.; A. B. Stone, D.Phil.; M. S. Davies, Ph.D.; R. D. A. Lang, D.Phil.; A. C. Peatfield, Ph.D.

For units of Medical Research Council, *see* pages 708–9

MENTAL HEALTH ACT COMMISSION
Maid Marian House, 56 Hounds Gate, Nottingham
NG1 6BG
Tel 0115-950 4040

The Mental Health Act Commission was established in 1983. Its functions are to keep under review the operation of the Mental Health Act 1983; to visit and interview patients detained under the Act; to investigate complaints falling within the Commission's remit; to operate the consent to treatment safeguards in the Mental Health Act; to publish a biennial report on its activities; to monitor the implementation of the Code of Practice; and to advise ministers. Commissioners are appointed by the Secretary of State for Health in the following categories: lay; legal; medical; nursing; psychology; social worker; and specialist.
*Chairman*, The Viscountess Runciman of Doxford, OBE
*Vice-Chairman*, vacant
*Chief Executive (G6)*, W. Bingley

MILLENNIUM COMMISSION
2 Little Smith Street, London SW1P 3DH
Tel 0171-416 8070

The Millennium Commission was established in February 1994. It is an independent body which will distribute 20 per cent of the net proceeds of the National Lottery to projects to mark the millennium.

*Chairman*, Rt. Hon. Stephen Dorrell, MP
*Members*, Prof. Heather Couper, FRAS; Earl of Dalkeith; The Hon. R. Dixon, CBE; Sir John Hall; The Rt. Hon. M. Heseltine, MP; S. Jenkins; M. Montague, CBE; Miss P. Scotland, QC
*Chief Executive*, N. Hinton, CBE

MONOPOLIES AND MERGERS COMMISSION
New Court, 48 Carey Street, London WC2A 2JT
Tel 0171-324 1407

The Commission was established in 1948 as the Monopolies and Restrictive Practices Commission and became the Monopolies and Mergers Commission under the Fair Trading Act 1973. Its role is to investigate and report on matters which are referred to it by the Secretary of State for Trade and Industry or the Director-General of Fair Trading or, in the case of privatized industries, by the appropriate regulator. Its decisions are determined by the criteria set out in the legislation covering the different types of reference. Nine main types of reference can be made. These are: monopolies; mergers; newspaper mergers; general, involving general practices in an industry; restrictive labour practices; competition, involving anti-competitive practices of individual firms; public sector audits; privatized industries; and Channel 3 (ITV) networking arrangements between holders of regional Channel 3 licences. The first five types of reference are made under the Fair Trading Act 1973, while the next two are covered by the Competition Act 1980. Since 1984 successive statutes have provided the Commission with a further role as an independent arbiter between certain privatized industries and their statutory regulators. References under the Broadcasting Act are made by the Independent Television Commission or the holders of regional Channel 3 licences.

The Commission consists of about 35 members, including a full-time chairman and three part-time deputy chairmen, all appointed by the Secretary of State for Trade and Industry. Each inquiry is conducted on behalf of the Commission by a group of four to six members who are appointed by the chairman.
*Chairman* (£95,060), G. D. W. Odgers
*Deputy Chairmen* (£46,685), H. H. Liesner, CB; P. H. Dean, CBE; D. G. Goyder
*Members* (£13,430/*£8,950 each), A. G. Armstrong; I. Barter; Mrs C. Blight; P. Brenan; J. S. Bridgeman; R. Davies; Prof. S. Eilon; J. Evans, MBE; A. Ferry, MBE; *N. H. Finney, OBE; Sir Archibald Forster; *Sir Ronald Halstead, CBE; *Ms P. A. Hodgson; D. J. Jenkins, MBE; *A. L. Kingshott; *N. F. Matthews; Prof. J. S. Metcalfe, CBE; Prof. P. Minford; J. D. Montgomery; *Dr D. J. Morris; *Prof. J. Pickering; *L. Priestley; M. R. Prosser; Dr A. Robinson; *J. K. Roe; *Dr L. M. Rouse; Mrs C. Tritton, QC; Prof. G. Whittington
*Secretary*, A. J. Nieduszynski
* reserve members

MUSEUMS

MUSEUMS AND GALLERIES COMMISSION
16 Queen Anne's Gate, London SW1H 9AA
Tel 0171-233 4200

Established in 1931 as the Standing Commission on Museums and Galleries, the Commission was re-named and took up new functions in September 1981. Its sponsor department is the Department of National Heritage. The Commission advises the Government, including the Department of Education for Northern Ireland, the Scottish Education Department and the Welsh Office, on museum affairs. There are 15 Commissioners, appointed by the Prime Minister.

The Commission's executive functions include providing the services of the Museums Security Adviser; the allocation of grants to the seven Area Museum Councils in England; funding and monitoring the work of the Museum Documentation Association; and directly administering a capital grant scheme for non-national museums, and various other grant schemes. The Commission administers the arrangements for government indemnities and the acceptance of works of art in lieu of inheritance tax, and it has responsibility for the two purchase grant funds for local museums managed on its behalf by the Victoria and Albert Museum and the Science Museum. The Commission's Conservation Unit advises on conservation and environmental standards, and operates grants schemes for conservators. A registration scheme for museums in the UK is operated by the Commission.

*Chairman*, G. Greene, CBE
*Members*, The Marchioness of Anglesey, DBE; J. Baer; The Baroness Brigstocke; The Viscountess Cobham; R. Foster; Adm. Sir John Kerr, GCB; J. Last, CBE; Prof. D. Michie; The Lord O'Neill, TD; The Lord Rees, PC, QC; R. H. Smith; A. Warhurst, CBE; Dame Margaret Weston, DBE
*Director and Secretary*, P. Longman

## THE BRITISH MUSEUM
Great Russell Street, London WC1B 3DG
Tel 0171-636 1555

The British Museum houses the national collection of antiquities, coins and paper money, medals, and prints and drawings. The ethnographical collections are displayed at the Museum of Mankind. The British Museum may be said to date from 1753, when Parliament approved the holding of a public lottery to raise funds for the purchase of the collections of Sir Hans Sloane and the Harleian manuscripts, and for their proper housing and maintenance. The building (Montagu House) was opened in 1759. The present buildings were erected between 1823 and the present day, and the original collection has increased to its present dimensions by gifts and purchases. Total government grant-in-aid for 1994–5 is £34.321 million.

BOARD OF TRUSTEES
*Appointed by the Sovereign*, HRH The Duke of Gloucester, GCVO
*Appointed by the Prime Minister*, The Lord Windlesham, CVO, PC (*Chairman*); N. Barber; Prof. Gillian Beer, FBA; Sir Matthew Farrer, KCVO; G. C. Greene, CBE; Prof. E. T. Hall, D.Phil., FSA, FBA; Sir Peter Harrop, KCB; M. Hopkins, CBE, RA, RIBA; Sir Joseph Hotung; S. Keswick; Hon. Mrs Marten, OBE; Sir John Morgan, KCMG; The Rt. Hon. Sir Timothy Raison; Prof. G. H. Treitel, DCL, FBA, QC; The Lord Weinstock
*Nominated by the Learned Societies*, Prof. Jean Thomas, CBE (*Royal Society*); A. Jones, RA (*Royal Academy*); Sir Claus Moser, KCB, CBE, FBA (*British Academy*); The Lord Renfrew of Kaimsthorn, FBA, FSA (*Society of Antiquaries*)
*Appointed by the Trustees of the British Museum*, Sir David Attenborough, CVO, CBE, FRS; Prof. Rosemary Cramp, CBE, FSA; The Lord Egremont; Prof. P. Lasko, CBE, FSA, FBA; Dr Jennifer Montague, FBA

OFFICERS
*Director* (*G2*), Dr R. G. W. Anderson, FRSC, FSA
*Deputy Director* (*G4*), Miss J. M. Rankine
*Secretary* (*G6*), G. B. Morris
*Head of Public Services* (*G6*), G. A. L. House
*Head of Press and Public Relations* (*SIO*), A. E. Hamilton
*Head of Design* (*G6*), Miss M. Hall, OBE
*Head of Education* (*G7*), J. F. Reeve
*Head of Administration* (*G5*), C. E. I. Jones
*Head of Building and Security Services* (*G6*), K. T. Stannard
*Head of Architectural and Building Services* (*G6*), C. J. Walker
*Head of Finance* (*G7*), D. E. Williams
*Head of Security* (*G7*), I. Slessor
*Head of Personnel and Office Services* (*G7*), Miss B. A. Hughes
*Keeper of Prints and Drawings* (*G5*), A. V. Griffiths
*Keeper of Coins and Medals* (*G5*), Dr A. M. Burnett
*Keeper of Egyptian Antiquities* (*G5*), W. V. Davies
*Keeper of Western Asiatic Antiquities* (*G5*), Dr J. E. Curtis
*Keeper of Greek and Roman Antiquities* (*G5*), Dr D. J. R. Williams
*Keeper of Medieval and Later Antiquities* (*G5*), N. M. Stratford
*Keeper of Prehistoric and Romano-British Antiquities* (*G5*), Dr I. H. Longworth, CBE
*Keeper of Japanese Antiquities* (*G5*), L. R. H. Smith
*Keeper of Oriental Antiquities* (*G5*), R. J. Knox
*Keeper of Ethnography* (*G5*), B. J. Mack
*Keeper of Scientific Research* (*G5*), Dr S. G. E. Bowman
*Keeper of Conservation* (*G5*), W. A. Oddy

## NATURAL HISTORY MUSEUM
Cromwell Road and Exhibition Road, London SW7 5BD
Tel 0171-938 9123

The Natural History Museum originates from the natural history departments of the British Museum, which grew extensively during the 19th century and in 1881 were moved to South Kensington. In 1963 the Natural History Museum became completely independent with its own body of trustees. The Zoological Museum, Tring, bequeathed by the second Lord Rothschild, has formed part of the Museum since 1938. The Geological Museum merged with the Natural History Museum in 1985. Total government grant-in-aid for 1994–5 is £27.556 million.

BOARD OF TRUSTEES
*Appointed by the Prime Minister:* Prof. R. May, FRS (*Chairman*); Sir Owen Green; The Baroness Blackstone, ph.D.; E. N. K. Clarkson, FRS; Mrs J. M. d'Abo; Sir Denys Henderson; Sir Crispin Tickell, GCMG, KCVO; Dame Anne McLaren, DBE, FRS
*Nominated by the Royal Society*, Prof. J. L. Harper, FRS
*Appointed by the Trustees of the Natural History Museum*, R. J. Carter; Prof. B. K. Follett, FRS; Sir Anthony Laughton, FRS

OFFICERS
*Director* (*G3*), N. R. Chalmers, ph.D.
*Associate Directors* (*Scientific Development*) (*G5*), Dr S. Blackmore; Dr P. Henderson
*Secretary* (*G5*), C. J. E. Legg
*Head of Development and Marketing Department* (*G6*), Mrs R. Laughton-Scott
*Marketing Manager* (*G6*), Ms J. Batchelor
*Science Marketing* (*G6*), vacant
*Public Relations Manager* (*G6*), Miss J. Bevan
*Keeper of Zoology* (*G5*), C. R. Curds, D.SC
*Director, Tring Zoological Museum* (*G6*), I. R. Bishop, OBE

*Keeper of Entomology (G5)*, Dr R. P. Lane
*Keeper of Botany (G5)*, S. Blackmore, PH.D.
*Keeper of Palaeontology (G5)*, L. R. M. Cocks, D.SC
*Keeper of Mineralogy (G5)*, P. Henderson, D.Phil
*Head of Finance (G6)*, J. Card
*Personnel Officer (G7)*, Mrs P. H. I. Orchard
*Head of Library Services (G6)*, R. E. R. Banks
*Head of Education and Exhibitions (G5)*, R. S. Miles, D.SC
*Head of Exhibition and Design (G7)*, R. M. Bloomfield, PH.D.

## THE SCIENCE MUSEUM
South Kensington, London SW7 2DD
Tel 0171-938 8000

The Science Museum, part of the National Museum of Science and Industry, houses the national collections of science, technology, industry and medicine. The Museum began as the science collection of the South Kensington Museum and first opened in 1857. In 1883 it acquired the collections of the Patent Museum and in 1909 the science collections were transferred to the new Science Museum, leaving the art collections with the Victoria and Albert Museum.

Some of the Museum's commercial aircraft, agricultural machinery, and road and rail transport collections are at Wroughton, Wilts. The Museum is also responsible for the National Railway Museum, York; the National Museum of Photography, Film and Television, Bradford; and the Concorde Exhibition at the Fleet Air Arm Museum, Yeovilton.

Total government grant-in-aid for 1994–5 is £20.425 million.

BOARD OF TRUSTEES
*Chairman*, Sir Austin Pearce, CBE
*Members*, HRH The Duke of Kent, KG, GCMG, GCVO, ADC;
   Dr Mary Archer; Prof. Sir Eric Ash, CBE, FRS, FEng.; The
   Lord Brabourne, CBE; The Viscount Downe;
   Miss M. S. Goldring, OBE; Mrs A. Higham; Mrs
   J. Kennedy; Dr Bridget Ogilvie; Sir Michael Quinlan,
   GCB; Sir Denis Rooke, CBE, FRS, FEng.; L. de Rothschild,
   CBE; Prof. Sir John Thomas, FRS; Sir Christopher Wates

OFFICERS
*Director*, Sir Neil Cossons, OBE, FSA, FRSA
*Assistant Director and Head of Resource Management*
   *Division (G5)*, J. J. Defries
*Head of Personnel and Training (G6)*, C. Gosling
*Head of Finance (G6)*, Ms A. Caine
*Assistant Director and Head of Collections Division (G5)*,
   Dr T. Wright
*Head of Physical Sciences and Engineering Group (G5)*,
   Dr D. A. Robinson
*Head of Life and Communications Technologies Group (G5)*,
   Dr R. F. Bud
*Head of Collections Management Group (G6)*, Ms S. Keene
*Assistant Director and Head of Public Affairs Division (G5)*,
   C. M. Pemberton
*Assistant Director and Head of Science Communication*
   *Division (G5)*, Prof. J. R. Durant
*Head of Education (G6)*, Dr R. Jackson
*Head of Programmes (G6)*, Dr G. Farmelo
*Assistant Director and Head of Project Development Division*
   *(G5)*, Mrs G. M. Thomas
*Head of Design (G6)*, T. Molloy
*Head of National Railway Museum (G5)*, A. Scott
*Head of National Museum of Photography, Film and*
   *Television (G5)*, Ms A. Nevill

## VICTORIA AND ALBERT MUSEUM
South Kensington, London SW7 2RL
Tel 0171-938 8500

The national museum of all branches of fine and applied art and design, the Victoria and Albert Museum descends directly from the Museum of Manufactures, which opened in Marlborough House in 1852 after the Great Exhibition of 1851. The Museum was moved in 1857 to become part of the collective South Kensington Museum. It was renamed the Victoria and Albert Museum in 1899. It also houses the National Art Library and Print Room (the National Art Slide Library is now housed at De Montfort University, Leicester).

The branch museum at Bethnal Green, which houses the Museum of Childhood, was opened in 1872 and the building is the most important surviving example of the type of glass and iron construction used by Paxton for the Great Exhibition. The Museum is also responsible for the Wellington Museum (Apsley House), and the Theatre Museum. Total government grant-in-aid for 1994–5 is £31.817 million.

BOARD OF TRUSTEES
*Chairman*, The Lord Armstrong of Ilminster, GCB, CVO
*Deputy Chairman*, Sir Michael Butler, GCMG
*Members*, The Lord Barnett, PC; Miss N. Campbell; Sir
   Clifford Chetwood; The Viscountess Cobham; E. Dawe;
   R. Fitch, CBE; Prof. C. Frayling, PH.D.; R. Gorlin;
   Pamela, Lady Harlech; Sir Terence Heiser, GCB; Sir
   Nevil Macready, Bt., CBE; Miss A. Plowden;
   Prof. M. Podro, PH.D., FBA; M. Saatchi; Prof. J. Steer, FSA
*Secretary to the Board of Trustees (G7)*, P. A. Wilson

OFFICERS
*Director (G3)*, Mrs E. A. L. Esteve-Coll
*Assistant Directors (G5)*, T. Stevens (*Collections*); J. W. Close
   (*Administration*)
*Head of Buildings and Estate (G5)*, J. G. Charlesworth
*Surveyor of Collections (G5)*, Mrs G. F. Miles
*Head of Conservation Department (G5)*, Dr J. Ashley-Smith
*Head of Finance and Central Services (G5)*, Miss R. M. Sykes
*Development Director*, vacant
*Head of Education (G6)*, D. Anderson
*Curator, Ceramics Collection (G6)*, Dr O. Watson
*Curator, Far Eastern Collection (G6)*, Miss R. Kerr
*Curator, Furniture and Woodwork Collection (G6)*, C. Wilk
*Curator, Indian and South-East Asian Collection (G6)*,
   Dr D. Swallow
*Curator, Metalwork Collection (G6)*, Mrs P. Glanville
*Head of Personnel (G6)*, Mrs G. Henchley
*Curator, Prints, Drawings and Paintings Collection (G6)*,
   Miss S. B. Lambert
*Head of Public Affairs (G5)*, R. Cole-Hamilton
*Head of Marketing and Public Relations (G7)*,
   Miss R. Griffith-Jones
*Head of Research (G5)*, P. Greenhalgh
*Curator, Sculpture Collection (G6)*, P. E. D. Williamson
*Curator, Textiles and Dress Collection (G6)*,
   Mrs V. D. Mendes
*Managing Director, V. & A. Enterprises Ltd*, M. Cass
*Curator and Chief Librarian, National Art Library (G5)*,
   J. F. van den Wateren
*Head of Bethnal Green Museum of Childhood (G6)*,
   A. P. Burton
*Head of Theatre Museum (G6)*, Ms M. Benton
*Curator of Wellington Museum (Apsley House) (E)*,
   J. R. S. Voak

## MUSEUM OF LONDON
London Wall, London EC2Y 5HN
Tel 0171-600 3699

The Museum of London illustrates the history of London from prehistoric times to the present day. It opened in 1976

and is based on the amalgamation of the former Guildhall Museum and London Museum. The Museum is controlled by a Board of Governors, appointed (nine each) by the Government and the Corporation of London. The Museum is funded jointly by the Department of National Heritage and the Corporation of London, each contributing £4.359 million in 1994–5.
*Chairman of Board of Governors*, P. Revell-Smith, CBE
*Director*, M. G. Hebditch, CBE, FSA

### COMMONWEALTH INSTITUTE
Kensington High Street, London W8 6NQ
Tel 0171-603 4535

The Commonwealth Institute has permanent exhibitions on all Commonwealth nations, special exhibitions, a Resource Centre and a Conference Centre. It is an independent statutory body funded by the British government with contributions from other Commonwealth governments. The Institute is controlled by a Board of Governors which includes the High Commissioners of all Commonwealth countries represented in London. It comprises the centre in London and the autonomous Scottish Institute in Edinburgh. Total government grant-in-aid for 1994–5 is £2.9 million.
*Director-General*, S. Cox
*Chief Administrative Officer*, P. Kennedy

### IMPERIAL WAR MUSEUM
Lambeth Road, London SE1 6HZ
Tel 0171-416 5000

The Museum, founded in 1917, illustrates and records all aspects of the two world wars and other military operations involving Britain and the Commonwealth since 1914. It was opened in its present home, formerly Bethlem Hospital or Bedlam, in 1936. The Museum also administers HMS *Belfast* in the Pool of London, Duxford Airfield near Cambridge and the Cabinet War Rooms in Westminster.

Total government grant-in-aid for 1994–5 is £10.995 million.

*Director-General (G4)*, A. C. N. Borg, CBE, PH.D., FSA
*Deputy Director-General (G5)*, R. W. K. Crawford
*Secretary (G6)*, J. J. Chadwick
*Personnel Officer (G7)*, P. L. Cracknell
*Finance Officer (G7)*, Mrs P. A. Whitfield
*Museum Superintendent (G6)*, D. A. Needham
*Information Systems Officer (G7)*, J. C. Barrett
*Director of Duxford Airfield (G5)*, E. O. Inman
*Director of HMS Belfast (G6)*, E. J. Wenzel

KEEPERS
*Department of Museum Services (G6)*, C. Dowling, D.PHIL
*Department of Documents (G6)*, R. W. A. Suddaby
*Department of Exhibits and Firearms (G6)*, D. J. Penn
*Department of Printed Books (G6)*, G. M. Bayliss, PH.D.
*Department of Art (G6)*, Miss A. H. Weight
*Department of Film (G6)*, R. B. N. Smither
*Department of Photographs (G6)*, Miss K. J. Carmichael
*Department of Sound Records (G6)*, Mrs M. A. Brooks
*Department of Marketing and Training (G6)*, Miss A. Godwin
*Curator of the Cabinet War Rooms (G7)*, P. Reed

### NATIONAL MARITIME MUSEUM
Greenwich, London SE10 9NF
Tel 0181-858 4422

Established by Act of Parliament in 1934, the National Maritime Museum illustrates the maritime history of Great Britain in the widest sense, underlining the importance of the sea and its influence on the nation's power, wealth, culture, technology and institutions. The Museum is in three groups of buildings in Greenwich Park – the main building, the Queen's House (built by Inigo Jones, 1616–35) and the Old Royal Observatory (including Wren's Flamsteed House). Total government grant-in-aid for 1994–5 is £10.971 million.
*Director*, R. L. Ormond

### NATIONAL ARMY MUSEUM
Royal Hospital Road, London SW3 4HT
Tel 0171-730 0717

The National Army Museum covers the history of five centuries of the British Army. It was established by royal charter in 1960. Total government grant-in-aid for 1994–5 is £3.108 million.
*Director*, I. G. Robertson
*Assistant Directors*, D. K. Smurthwaite; A. J. Guy; Maj. P. R. Bateman

### ROYAL AIR FORCE MUSEUM
Grahame Park Way, London NW9 5LL
Tel 0181-205 2266

Situated on the former airfield at Hendon, the Museum illustrates the development of aviation from before the Wright brothers to the present-day RAF. Total government grant-in-aid for 1994–5 is £2.906 million.
*Director*, Dr M. A. Fopp
*Deputy Director*, J. D. Freeborn
*Keepers*, D. C. R. Elliott; P. Elliott; D. F. Lawrence

### NATIONAL MUSEUMS AND GALLERIES ON MERSEYSIDE
William Brown Street, Liverpool L3 8EN
Tel 0151-207 0001

The Board of Trustees of the National Museums and Galleries on Merseyside was established in 1986 to take over responsibility for the museums and galleries previously administered by Merseyside County Council. The Board is responsible for the Liverpool Museum, the Merseyside Maritime Museum (incorporating HM Customs and Excise National Museum), the Museum of Liverpool Life, the Walker Art Gallery and Sudley House. It is grant-aided by the Department of National Heritage; the grant for 1994–5 is £16.411 million, including £2.9 million for the building of a conservation centre.
*Chairman of the Board of Trustees*, Sir Leslie Young, CBE
*Director*, R. Foster
*Head of Central Services*, P. Sudbury, PH.D.
*Keeper of Art Galleries*, J. Treuherz
*Keeper of Conservation*, J. France
*Keeper, Liverpool Museum*, E. Greenwood
*Keeper, Merseyside Maritime Museum and Museum of Liverpool Life*, M. Stammers

### NATIONAL MUSEUM OF WALES/ AMGUEDDFA GENEDLAETHOL CYMRU
Main Building, Cathays Park, Cardiff CF1 3NP
Tel 01222-397951

The National Museum of Wales comprises the Welsh Folk Museum (Amgueddfa Werin Cymru), the Roman Legionary Museum, Turner House Art Gallery, the Museum of the North, the Welsh Slate Museum, the Segontium Roman Fort Museum, the Museum of the Welsh Woollen Industry, the

Welsh Industrial and Maritime Museum, and the Graham Sutherland Gallery and Picton Castle Grounds. Total government grant-in-aid for 1994–5 is £13 million.
*President,* C. R. T. Edwards
*Vice-President,* M. C. T. Pritchard, CBE
*Director,* C. Ford, CBE
*Head of Administration,* T. Arnold
*Keepers,* M. G. Bassett, PH.D. (*Geology*); B. A. Thomas, PH.D. (*Botany*); P. M. Morgan (*Zoology*); H. S. Aldhouse-Green, PH.D. (*Archaeology*); M. Evans (*Art*) (*acting*)
*Curator, Welsh Folk Museum (Amgueddfa Werin Cymru),* Dr E. Williams
*Keepers,* E. Scourfield, PH.D.; J. W. Davies
*Officer in Charge, Roman Legionary Museum,* D. Zienkiewicz
*Keeper in Charge, Turner House Art Gallery (acting),* M. Evans
*Keeper, Museum of the North,* D. Roberts, PH.D.
*Keeper in Charge, Welsh Slate Museum,* D. Roberts, PH.D.
*Officer in Charge, Segontium Roman Fort Museum,* R. J. Brewer
*Keeper in Charge, Museum of the Welsh Woollen Industry,* E. Scourfield, PH.D.
*Keeper, Welsh Industrial and Maritime Museum,* S. Owen-Jones, PH.D.
*Officer in Charge, The Graham Sutherland Gallery and Picton Castle Grounds,* S. Moss

## NATIONAL MUSEUMS OF SCOTLAND
Chambers Street, Edinburgh EH1 IJF
Tel 0131-225 7534

The National Museums of Scotland comprise the Royal Museum of Scotland, the Museum of Antiquities, the Scottish United Services Museum, the Scottish Agricultural Museum, the Museum of Flight, the Biggar Gasworks Museum and Shambellie House Museum of Costume. Total government grant-in-aid for 1994–5 is £20 million.

BOARD OF TRUSTEES
*Chairman,* R. Smith, FSA scot.
*Members,* Prof. L. Bown, OBE; R. D. Cramond, CBE, FSA scot.; Countess of Dalkeith; Sir Nicholas Fairbairn, QC, MP; Sir Alistair Grant; Prof. P. H. Jones; D. H. Pringle, CBE; Dr Anna Ritchie; Prof. T. C. Smout, PH.D., FRSE; Sir John Thomson; Dr Veronica Van Heyingen

OFFICERS
*Director,* M. Jones, FSA, FSA scot., FRSA
*Depute Director (Resources) and Project Director, Museum of Scotland,* I. Hooper, FSA scot.
*Depute Director (Collections) and Keeper of History and Applied Art (G5),* Miss D. Idiens, FRSA, FSA scot.
*Keeper of Archaeology,* D. V. Clarke, PH.D., FSA, FSA scot.
*Keeper of Geology (G5),* W. D. I. Rolfe, PH.D., FRSE, FRSA
*Keeper of Natural History (G5),* M. Shaw, D.Phil.
*Keeper of Science, Technology and Working Life (G5),* D. J. Bryden, PH.D., FSA
*Head of Public Affairs (G6),* Ms M. Bryden
*Head of Museum Services (G6),* S. R. Elson, FSA scot.
*Head of Administration (G6),* A. G. Young
*Campaign Director, Museum of Scotland,* Ms S. Brock, PH.D., FRSA
*Keeper, Scottish United Services Museum,* S. C. Wood
*Curator, Scottish Agricultural Museum,* G. Sprott
*Curator, Museum of Flight,* Sqn. Ldr. R. M. Major
*Curator, Biggar Gasworks Museum,* J. Wood
*Keeper, Shambellie House Museum of Costume,* Miss D. Idiens, FRSA, FSA scot.

## NATIONAL ADVISORY COUNCIL FOR EDUCATION AND TRAINING TARGETS
Caxton House, Tothill Street, London SW1H 9NF
Tel 0171-273 5695
(*from Jan. 1995*) 7th Floor, 222 Grays Inn Road, London WC1X 8HR

The National Advisory Council for Education and Training Targets was established by the Government in March 1993. It monitors progress towards the National Targets for Education and Training and advises the Secretaries of State for Employment, Education and Wales on performance and policies which influence progress towards them.
*Chairman,* P. Davis
*Vice-Chairman,* M. Heron
*Members,* Sir Christopher Harding; D. Cadbury; Ms C. Galley; T. Cann, CBE; M. Walker; W. Jordan, CBE; The Baroness Perry; M. Rowarth, OBE; R. Perks, OBE
*Ex-officio,* M. Bett, CBE; Sir Brian Wolfson; Sir Anthony Cleaver
*Director,* M. Waring

## NATIONAL AUDIT OFFICE
157–197 Buckingham Palace Road, London SW1W 9SP
Tel 0171-798 7000

The National Audit Office came into existence under the National Audit Act 1983 to replace and continue the work of the former Exchequer and Audit Department. The Act reinforced the Office's total financial and operational independence from the Government and brought its head, the Comptroller and Auditor-General, into a closer relationship with Parliament as an officer of the House of Commons.

The National Audit Office provides independent information, advice and assurance to Parliament and the public about all aspects of the financial operations of government departments and many other bodies receiving public funds. This it does by examining and certifying the accounts of these organizations and by regularly publishing reports to Parliament on the results of its value for money investigations of the economy, efficiency and effectiveness with which public resources have been used. The National Audit Office is also the auditor by agreement of the accounts of certain international and other organizations. In addition, the Office authorizes the issue of public funds to government departments.
*Comptroller and Auditor-General,* Sir John Bourn, KCB
*Private Secretary,* J. Rickleton
*Deputy Comptroller and Auditor-General,* R. N. Le Marechal, CB
*Assistant Auditors-General,* T. Burr; J. A. Higgins; L. H. Hughes; J. Marshall; M. C. Pfleger
*Directors,* A. G. Brown; C. L. Press; C. K. Beauchamp; R. M. Bennett; B. Hogg; G. G. Jones; J. Parsons; J. M. Pearce; A. G. Roberts; R. A. Skeen; R. E. Spurgeon; A. Fiander; Ms M. Bibby; M. Daynes; Miss C. Mawhood; R. J. Eales; J. Colman; B. Payne; G. R. L. Osborne; R. Douglas; N. Sloan; D. Woodward; Ms W. Kenway-Smith; R. Frith
*Associate Directors,* J. J. Jones; A. Burchell; P. R. Duncombe; N. Gale; T. Griffiths; K. Hawkswell; Miss J. Lawler; J. S. McEwen; R. Parker; M. J. Reeves; P. G. Woodward; R. Goacher; M. Whitehouse; P. Cannon; R. Swan; M. Sinclair; T. Bristow; Ms P. Smith; Ms J. Wheeler; I. Summers

## NATIONAL CONSUMER COUNCIL
20 Grosvenor Gardens, London SW1W ODH
Tel 0171-730 3469

The National Consumer Council was set up by the Government in 1975 to give an independent voice to consumers in the UK. Its job is to advocate the consumer interest to decision-makers in business, industry, the public utilities, the professions, and central and local government. It does this through a combination of research and campaigning. It is funded by a grant-in-aid from the Department of Trade and Industry.
*Chairman,* Lady Wilcox
*Vice-Chairman,* Mrs A. Scully
*Members,* D. Arculus; Miss B. Brookes; A. Burton, OBE; Ms A. Daltrop; Prof. P. Fairest; Miss J. Francis; D. Gilchrist; J. Hughes; L. N. Hunter; Mrs D. Hutton; Prof. G. Jones; J. Mitchell; Ms M. McAnally; Lady McCollum; Mrs J. Varnam; Sir Geoffrey Allen
*Director,* R. Evans

## NATIONAL DEBT OFFICE
— *see* National Investment and Loans Office

## DEPARTMENT OF NATIONAL HERITAGE
2–4 Cockspur Street, London SW1Y 5DH
Tel 0171-270 3000

The Department of National Heritage was established in 1992 and is responsible for government policy relating to the arts, broadcasting, the press, museums and galleries, libraries, sport and recreation, heritage and tourism. It funds the Arts Councils and other arts bodies, including the National Heritage Memorial Fund. It also funds the Museums and Galleries Commission, the national museums and galleries in England, the British Library, the Sports Council, the British Tourist Authority and the English Tourist Board, and the British Film Institute. It is responsible for the issue of export licences on works of art, antiques and collector's items; the Government Art Collection; the built heritage, including the Royal Parks and Historic Royal Palaces executive agencies; and statistical services including the International Passenger Survey and broadcasting statistics. The Department is also responsible for policy and implementation of the National Lottery and the Millennium Fund.
*Secretary of State for National Heritage,* The Rt. Hon. Stephen Dorrell, MP
*Private Secretary,* J. Kingman
*Parliamentary Private Secretary,* G. Brandreth, MP
*Parliamentary Under-Secretaries of State,* Iain Sproat, MP; The Viscount Astor
*Private Secretaries,* N. Mackenzie; Mrs L. Sweet
*Lady-in-Waiting,* The Baroness Trumpington
*Parliamentary Clerk,* C. Hutson
*Permanent Secretary (G1),* G. H. Phillips, CB
*Private Secretary,* Ms C. Pillmen

LIBRARIES, GALLERIES AND MUSEUMS GROUP
*Head of Group (G3),* Miss M. O'Mara
*Head of Libraries and Information Services Division (G5),* P. Bolt
*Director, British Library St Pancras Project (G5),* J. R. W. Pardey
*Head of Museums and Galleries Division (G5),* P. Gregory

*Director, Government Art Collection (G6),* Dr Wendy Baron, OBE
*Head of Cultural Property Unit (G7),* Miss C. Morrison

ARTS, SPORTS AND LOTTERY GROUP
*Head of Group (G3),* A. Ramsay
*Head of Arts Division (G5),* N. Kroll
*Head of National Lottery Division (G5),* S. MacDonald
*Head of Millennium Commission Unit (G7),* Miss H. Wilkinson
*Head of Sport and Recreation Division (G5),* Miss A. Stewart

BROADCASTING AND MEDIA GROUP
*Head of Group (G3),* P. Wright
*Head of Broadcasting Policy Division (G5),* Ms S. Booth
*Head of Media Division (G5),* P. Edwards

HERITAGE AND TOURISM GROUP
*Head of Group (G3),* D. Chesterton
*Head of Heritage Division (G5),* A. Corner
*Head of Royal Estate Division (G5),* P. Douglas
*Head of Tourism Division (G5),* Ms J. Evans

RESOURCES AND SERVICES GROUP
*Director (G4),* N. Pittman
*Director of Finance and Corporate Planning (G5),* R. MacLachlan
*Director of Implementation and Review (G5),* Dr K. Gray
*Director of Personnel (G5),* G. Jones

INFORMATION
*Head of Information (G5),* Miss A. MacLean

### EXECUTIVE AGENCIES

HISTORIC ROYAL PALACES
The Birdwood Annexe, Hampton Court Palace, East Molesey, Surrey KT8 9AU
Tel 0181-977 7222

The Historic Royal Palaces agency manages the Tower of London, Hampton Court Palace, Kensington Palace, Kew Palace with Queen Charlotte's Cottage, and the Banqueting House, Whitehall.
*Chief Executive (G3),* D. C. Beeton.
*Director of Finance and Resources (G5),* Ms B. Darbyshire
*Surveyor of the Fabric (G5),* S. Bond.
*Director of Marketing (G6),* P. D. Hammond
*Curator, Historic Royal Palaces (G6),* Dr S. J. Thurley
*Administrator, Hampton Court Palace (G6),* D. J. C. MacDonald
*Resident Governor, HM Tower of London (G5),* Maj.-Gen. C. Tyler, CB (retd)
*Administrator, Kensington Palace (G7),* N. J. Arch

ROYAL PARKS
The Royal Parks Headquarters, Hyde Park, London W2 2UH
Tel 0171-298 2000

The agency is responsible for maintaining and developing the royal parks.
*Chief Executive (G5),* D. Welch

## NATIONAL HERITAGE MEMORIAL FUND
10 St James's Street, London SW1A 1EF
Tel 0171-930 0963

The National Heritage Memorial Fund is an independent body established in 1980 as a memorial to those who have died for the UK. The Fund is empowered by the National

Heritage Act 1980 to give financial assistance towards the cost of acquiring, maintaining or preserving land, buildings, works of art and other objects of outstanding interest which are also of importance to the national heritage. The Fund is administered by up to 15 trustees who are appointed by the Prime Minister. Its major source of funding is the Department of National Heritage, which gave a grant of £8.662 million for 1994–5.

TRUSTEES
*Chairman*, The Lord Rothschild
*Members*, Sir Richard Carew Pole, Bt.; The Lord Crathorne; W. L. Evans; Sir Nicholas Goodison; Sir Martin Jacomb; The Lord Macfarlane of Bearsden; Prof. P. J. Newbould; Mrs J. Nutting; Mrs C. Porteous; Cdr. L. M. M. Saunders Watson
*Director*, Miss G. Nayler

---

## NATIONAL INSURANCE JOINT AUTHORITY
The Adelphi, 1–11 John Adam Street, London WC2N 6HT
Tel 0171-962 8523

The Authority's function is to co-ordinate the operation of social security legislation in Great Britain and Northern Ireland, including the necessary financial adjustments between the two National Insurance Funds.
*Members*, The Secretary of State for Social Security; the Head of the Department of Health and Social Services for Northern Ireland.
*Secretary*, Ms G. E. Taylor

---

## NATIONAL INVESTMENT AND LOANS OFFICE
1 King Charles Street, London SW1A 2AP
Tel 0171-270 3861

The National Investment and Loans Office was set up in 1980 by the merger of the National Debt Office and the Public Works Loan Board. The Office provides staff and services for the National Debt Commissioners and the Public Works Loan Commissioners. The National Debt Office is responsible for the investment and management of statutory funds relating to the surplus monies of certain government bodies; the management of some residual operations relating to the national debt; and the facilitation of raising funds by central government following Article 104 of the Maastricht Treaty, in pursuance of section 211 of the Finance Act 1993. The function of the Public Works Loan Board is to make loans for capital purposes from central government funds to local authorities and to collect repayments.
*Director*, I. H. Peattie
*Establishment Officer*, A. G. Ladd

NATIONAL DEBT OFFICE
*Comptroller-General*, I. H. Peattie

PUBLIC WORKS LOAN BOARD
*Chairman*, Sir Robin Dent, KCVO
*Deputy Chairman*, Miss F. M. Cook, CBE
*Other Commissioners*, Miss V. J. Di Palma, OBE; G. Ross Russell; D. H. Adams; R. A. Chapman; A. Morton; G. G. Williams; R. G. Tettenborn, OBE; J. E. Scotford, CBE; A. Gillespie; A. D. Loehnis, CMG
*Secretary*, I. H. Peattie
*Assistant Secretary*, Miss L. M. Ashcroft

---

## OFFICE OF THE NATIONAL LOTTERY
2–4 Cockspur Street, London SW1Y 5DH
Tel 0171-211 2129

The Office of the National Lottery (OFLOT) was established as a non-ministerial government department in October 1993 under the National Lottery Act 1993. It will regulate the National Lottery operations and license games promoted as part of the Lottery.
*Director-General (G2)*, P. Davis
*Deputy Director-General (G5)*, Ms D. Kahn
*Head of Compliance Regulation (G5)*, K. Dunn

---

## NATIONAL RADIOLOGICAL PROTECTION BOARD
Chilton, Didcot, Oxon. OX11 0RQ
Tel 01235-831600

The National Radiological Protection Board is an independent statutory body created by the Radiological Protection Act 1970. It is the national point of authoritative reference on radiological protection for both ionizing and non-ionizing radiations.
*Chairman*, Sir Richard Southwood, FRS
*Director*, Prof. R. H. Clarke

---

## NATIONAL RIVERS AUTHORITY
Rivers House, Waterside Drive, Aztec West, Almondsbury, Bristol BS12 4UD
Tel 0117-962 4400
Eastbury House, 30–34 Albert Embankment, London SE1 7TL
Tel 0171-820 0101

The National Rivers Authority (NRA) is an independent body set up under the Water Act 1989, now the Water Resources Act 1991. Its responsibilities include monitoring the quality of water, controlling pollution, and the management of water resources, flood defence and fisheries. It has head offices in Bristol and London, and eight regional units mainly concerned with operational activities. The NRA has a board of 14 members, two of whom are appointed by the Minister of Agriculture, Fisheries and Food, one by the Secretary of State for Wales, and the rest by the Secretary of State for the Environment. Total government funding for 1994–5 is £107.6 million.
*Chairman*, The Lord Crickhowell, PC
*Chief Executive*, E. Gallagher
*Director, Water Management*, Dr C. Swinnerton
*Finance Director*, N. Reader
*Personnel Director*, P. Humphreys
*Director of Public Affairs*, M. Wilson
*Director, Operations*, K. Bond
*Director, Market Testing*, G. Mance
*Secretary and Director, Legal Services*, C. Martin

---

## DEPARTMENT FOR NATIONAL SAVINGS
Charles House, 375 Kensington High Street, London W14 8SD
Tel 0171-605 9300

The Department for National Savings was established as a government department in 1969. The Department is responsible for the administration of a wide range of schemes for personal savers.

*Director of Savings (G2)*, C. D. Butler
*Deputy Director (G3)*, D. Howard
*Head of Information Systems (G4)*, B. G. Rosser
*Establishment Officer (G5)*, D. S. Speedie
*Finance Officer (G5)*, M. A. Nicholls
*Controllers (G5)*, Miss A. Nash (*Marketing and Information*);
   A. S. McGill; D. H. Monaghan; E. B. Senior;
   P. N. S. Hickman Robertson
*Senior Principals (G6)*, D. W. Kellaway, OBE; W. J. Herd;
   D. Newton; T. Threlfall; P. Anderson; A. Muir;
   T. J. F. McMahon; J. W. Davison; J. C. Foreman
*Principals (G7)*, D. K. Paterson; A. J. V. Cummings;
   Dr A. Fort; W. J. Ferrier; H. Johnson; A. B. Wood;
   P. Finnie; C. E. Funk; I. Jordinson; B. Paley;
   J. Wheatley; C. McVey; R. A. Nichol; J. B. Dunphy;
   D. Wilson; P. B. Robinson; A. S. Lamond; D. Jeffrey;
   J. Bolam; R. W. Day; C. Dodsworth; R. R. Hesketh;
   R. J. McLelland; M. J. Tan; M. McDade; I. Rich;
   Miss J. S. Clark; M. C. Richards; M. Taylor;
   J. M. Anderson; W. Brough; S. F. Owen; W. Ward;
   J. A. Kean; D. M. F. Shedden; I. Campbell; W. Carroll;
   Mrs M. T. McLauchlan; W. Wilson; R. Rickaby;
   R. McAlpine; M. J. Verity; P. Swinbank
For details of schemes, *see* National Savings section

## NATURAL ENVIRONMENT RESEARCH COUNCIL
Polaris House, North Star Avenue, Swindon SN2 1EU
Tel 01793-411500

The Natural Environment Research Council was established in 1965 to encourage, plan and conduct research in the physical and biological sciences which relate to the natural environment and its resources. The Council carries out research and training through its own institutes and by grants, fellowships and post-graduate awards to universities and other institutions of higher education. Government funding for 1994–5 is £155.4 million.

*Chairman*, R. Malpas, CBE, FEng.
*Chief Executive*, Prof. J. Krebs, FRS
*Director of Science and Technology*, vacant
*Director of Technology Interaction Group*, vacant

CENTRAL SERVICES
NERC SCIENTIFIC SERVICES, Polaris House, North Star
   Avenue, Swindon, Wilts. SN2 1EU. Tel: 01793-411500.
   *Director*, B. J. Hinde, OBE

RESEARCH VESSEL SERVICES, No. 1 Dock, Barry,
   S. Glamorgan. Tel: 01446-737451. *Head*, Dr C. Fay

NERC COMPUTER SERVICE, Holbrook House, Station
   Road, Swindon, Wilts. SN1 1DE. Tel: 01793-411500.
   *Director*, H. J. Down

For research institutes and units of the Natural Environment Research Council, *see* page 709–10

## JOINT NATURE CONSERVATION COMMITTEE
Monkstone House, City Road, Peterborough PE1 1JY
Tel 01733-62626

The Committee was established under the Environmental Protection Act 1990 and began work in 1991. It advises the Government and others on UK and international nature conservation issues and disseminates knowledge on these subjects. It establishes common standards for the monitoring of nature conservation and research, and analyses the resulting information. It commissions research relevant to these roles, and provides guidance to English Nature, Scottish Natural Heritage, the Countryside Council for Wales and the Department of the Environment for Northern Ireland.

*Chairman*, The Earl of Selborne, KBE, FRS
*Chief Officer*, C. R. Walker, CB
*Director Life Sciences and Resources*, Dr M. W. Pienkowski
*Director Aquatic and Earth Sciences*, Dr M. A. Vincent

## NORTHERN IRELAND OFFICE
Whitehall, London SW1A 2AZ
Tel 0171-210 3000
Stormont Castle, Belfast BT4 3ST
Tel 01232-520700

The Northern Ireland Office was established in 1972, when the Northern Ireland (Temporary Provisions) Act transferred the legislative and executive powers of the Northern Ireland Parliament and Government to the UK Parliament and a Secretary of State.

The Northern Ireland Office is responsible primarily for security issues, law and order and prisons, and for matters relating to the political and constitutional future of the province. It also deals with international issues as they affect Northern Ireland, including the Anglo-Irish Agreement (*see* page 572). The Northern Ireland departments are responsible for the administration of social, industrial and economic policies.

The names of most civil servants are not listed for security reasons.

*Secretary of State for Northern Ireland*, The Rt. Hon. Sir
   Patrick Mayhew, QC, MP
*Special Adviser*, J. Caine
*Parliamentary Private Secretary*, M. Moss, MP
*Ministers of State*, Michael Ancram, MP; The Rt. Hon. Sir
   John Wheeler, MP
*Parliamentary Private Secretary to Michael Ancram*,
   R. Robertson, MP
*Parliamentary Under-Secretaries of State*, The Baroness
   Denton of Wakefield, CBE; Timothy Smith, MP
*Permanent Under-Secretary of State (G1)*, Sir John Chilcot,
   KCB
*Second Permanent Under-Secretary of State, Head of the
   Northern Ireland Civil Service (G1A)*, D. Fell, CB

LONDON
*Deputy Secretary (G2)*
*Under-Secretary (G3)*, (Security and International;
   Constitutional and Political; Economic and Social)
*Under-Secretary (G3)*, (Establishment and Finance)
*Grade 4*, (Information Services)

BELFAST
*Deputy Secretary (G2)*
*Under-Secretaries (G3)*, (Security); (Criminal Justice);
   (Political); (Establishment and Finance)

EXECUTIVE AGENCY
COMPENSATION AGENCY, Royston House, Upper Queen
   Street, Belfast BT1 6FD. Tel: 01232-2499444

# DEPARTMENT OF AGRICULTURE FOR NORTHERN IRELAND
Dundonald House, Upper Newtownards Road, Belfast
BT4 3SB
Tel 01232-520100

*Parliamentary Under-Secretary of State*, The Baroness
Denton of Wakefield, CBE
*Permanent Secretary (G2)*
*Under-Secretaries (G3)*, (Establishment and Finance);
(Commodities); (Lands); (Agricultural Service);
(Veterinary Service); (Chief Scientific Officer)

# DEPARTMENT OF ECONOMIC DEVELOPMENT NORTHERN IRELAND
Netherleigh, Massey Avenue, Belfast BT4 2JP
Tel 01232-529900

*Parliamentary Under-Secretary of State*, Timothy Smith, MP
*Permanent Secretary (G2)*
*Under-Secretaries (G3)*, (Resources Group); (Regulatory
Services Group); (Science and Technology Group)

INDUSTRIAL DEVELOPMENT BOARD, IDB House, 64
Chichester Street, Belfast BT1 4JX. Tel: 01232-233233

EXECUTIVE AGENCY

TRAINING AND EMPLOYMENT AGENCY (NORTHERN
IRELAND), Clarendon House, 9–21 Adelaide Street,
Belfast BT2 8DJ. Tel: 01232-239944

# DEPARTMENT OF EDUCATION FOR NORTHERN IRELAND
Rathgael House, Balloo Road, Bangor, Co. Down BT19 2PR
Tel 01247-279000

*Minister of State*, Michael Ancram, MP
*Permanent Secretary (G2)*
*Under-Secretaries (G3)*, (Educational Administration);
(Establishment and Finance); (Education and Training
Inspectorate)

# DEPARTMENT OF THE ENVIRONMENT FOR NORTHERN IRELAND
Parliament Buildings, Stormont, Belfast BT4 3SS
Tel: 01232-520600

*Parliamentary Under-Secretary of State*, Timothy Smith, MP
*Permanent Secretary (G2)*
*Under-Secretaries (G3)*, (Personnel, Finance and Legal
Services); (Planning and Urban Affairs); (Roads, Works
and Public Record Office); (Housing, Local Government
and Environment Service); (Land Registry, Transport,
Water Privatization and Fire Service)

EXECUTIVE AGENCIES

DRIVER AND VEHICLE LICENSING AGENCY
(NORTHERN IRELAND), County Hall, Castlerock Road,
Coleraine, Co. Londonderry BT51 3HS. Tel: 01265-44133
DRIVER AND VEHICLE TESTING AGENCY (NORTHERN
IRELAND), Balmoral Road, Belfast BT12 6QL. Tel: 01232-
681831
ORDNANCE SURVEY OF NORTHERN IRELAND, Colby
House, Stranmillis Court, Belfast BT9 5BJ. Tel: 01232-
661244
RATE COLLECTION AGENCY (NORTHERN IRELAND),
Oxford House, 49–55 Chichester Street, Belfast BT1 4HH.
Tel: 01232-231936
WATER EXECUTIVE, Northland House, Frederick Street,
Belfast BT1 2NS. Tel: 01232-244711

ADVISORY BODIES
HISTORIC BUILDINGS COUNCIL FOR NORTHERN
IRELAND, c/o Environment Service, Historic
Monuments and Buildings, 5–33 Hill Street, Belfast
BT1 2LA. Tel: 01232-235000
HISTORIC MONUMENTS COUNCIL FOR NORTHERN
IRELAND, c/o Environment Service, Historic
Monuments and Buildings, 5–33 Hill Street, Belfast
BT1 2LA. Tel: 01232-235000
COUNCIL FOR NATURE CONSERVATION AND THE
COUNTRYSIDE, c/o Environment Service, 5–33 Hill
Street, Belfast BT1 2LA. Tel: 01232-235000

# DEPARTMENT OF FINANCE AND PERSONNEL
Parliament Buildings, Stormont, Belfast BT4 3SW
Tel 01232-520400

*Minister of State*, The Rt. Hon. Sir John Wheeler, MP
*Permanent Secretary (G2)*
*Under-Secretaries (G3)*, (Supply Group); (Resources Control
and Professional Services Group); (Central Personnel
Group); (Government Purchasing Service)

NORTHERN IRELAND CIVIL SERVICE (NICS)
Stormont Castle, Belfast BT4 3TT
Tel 01232-520700

*Head of Civil Service (G1A)*, D. Fell, CB
*Under-Secretaries (G3)*, (Central Secretariat); (Legal
Services); (Office of the Legislative Council)

EXECUTIVE AGENCY

VALUATION AND LANDS AGENCY, Queen's Court, 56–66
Upper Queen Street, Belfast BT4 6FD. Tel: 01232-439303

# DEPARTMENT OF HEALTH AND SOCIAL SERVICES NORTHERN IRELAND
Dundonald House, Upper Newtownards Road, Belfast
BT4 3SF
Tel 01232-520500

*Parliamentary Under-Secretary of State*, The Baroness
Denton of Wakefield, CBE
*Permanent Secretary (G2)*
*Chief Medical Officer (G2A)*
*Under-Secretaries (G3)*, (Health and Personal Social Services
Management Executive); (Health and Personal Social
Services Policy); (Medical and Allied Services); (Central
Services)

EXECUTIVE AGENCIES

NORTHERN IRELAND CHILD SUPPORT AGENCY, Great
Northern Tower, 17 Great Victoria Street, Belfast
BT2 7AD. Tel: 01232-339000
NORTHERN IRELAND SOCIAL SECURITY AGENCY, Castle
Buildings, Stormont, Belfast BT4 3SJ. Tel: 01232-520520

# OCCUPATIONAL PENSIONS BOARD
PO Box 2EE, Newcastle upon Tyne NE99 2EE
Tel 0191-225 6414

The Occupational Pensions Board (OPB) is an independent
statutory body set up under the Social Security Act 1973 to
administer the contracting-out of occupational pensions from
the State Earnings Related Pension Scheme (SERPS), and to
advise the Secretary of State. Its functions have been extended
by subsequent legislation and it is now also responsible for

administering equal access, preservation and modification requirements and appropriate personal pension schemes. Following the Social Security Act 1990, the OPB was appointed as Registrar of Occupational and Personal Pension Schemes and granted powers to make grants to approved bodies in the field. The OPB now funds the operation of the Occupational Pensions Advisory Service (OPAS).

In June 1994 the Government published a White Paper including proposals to replace the OPB with a statutory regulator.

*Chairman,* P. D. Carr, CBE
*Deputy Chairman,* Miss C. H. Dawes
*Members,* R. J. Amy; Mrs R. Brown; R. Ellison; A. U. Lyburn; W. M. R. Ramsey, D.Phil.; K. R. Thomas; A. S. Herbert; M. R. Slack; H. M. Harris Hughes; Miss P. W. Triggs; A. Pickering
*Secretary to the Board and General Manager of Executive Office (G6),* A. Scaife

## OMBUDSMAN

— *see* Local Commissioners *and* Parliamentary Commissioner. For non-statutory Ombudsmen, *see* Index

## ORDNANCE SURVEY

Romsey Road, Maybush, Southampton SO16 4GU
Tel 01703-792000

The Ordnance Survey is the national mapping agency for Britain. It became an executive agency in 1990 and reports to the Secretary of State for the Environment.

The Ordnance Survey has military origins. It produces over 220,000 large scale maps of the country at three basic scales. These are 1:1,250 (50 inches to 1 mile) for urban areas; 1:2,500 (25 inches to 1 mile) for rural areas; and 1:10,000 (6 inches to 1 mile) for mountain and moorland. Ordnance Survey also produces a range of small scale maps and other products for general use.

*Director-General and Chief Executive,* Prof. D. Rhind
*Directors:*
*External Relations and Deputy Director-General,* J. Leonard, CBE
*Business Services,* I. Lock
*Consumer and Education Markets,* D. Davies
*Business and Professional Services,* P. Wesley
*Data Collection,* I. T. Logan
*Information Management,* B. W. Nanson
*OS International,* E. Gilbert

*Head of Finance,* D. James
*Head of Human Resources,* D. R. Evans

## OVERSEAS DEVELOPMENT ADMINISTRATION

94 Victoria Street, London SW1E 5JL
Tel 0171-917 7000
Abercrombie House, Eaglesham Road, East Kilbride, Glasgow G75 8EA
Tel 01355-844000

The Overseas Development Administration deals with British development assistance to overseas countries. This includes both capital aid on concessional terms and technical assistance (mainly in the form of specialist staff abroad and training facilities in the United Kingdom), whether provided directly to developing countries or through the various multilateral aid organizations, including the United Nations and its specialized agencies.

*Minister for Overseas Development,* The Baroness Chalker of Wallasey, PC
*Private Secretary (G7),* M. A. B. Lowcock
*Permanent Secretary (G1A),* J. M. M. Vereker
*Private Secretary,* Ms G. J. Lyons
*Deputy Secretary (G2),* R. M. Ainscow, CB
*Under-Secretaries (G3),* N. B. Hudson; B. R. Ireton; J. V. Kerby; R. G. Manning; A. J. Bennett; J. B. Wilmshurst; J. L. Faint; P. D. M. Freeman

ECONOMIC AND SOCIAL DIVISION
*Head of the Economic Service (G3),* J. B. Wilmshurst
*Senior Economic Advisers (G5),* J. C. H. Morris; B. P. Thomson; J. Roberts; M. Foster; P. J. Ackroyd
*Economic Advisers (G6),* P. L. Owen; *(G7),* P. D. Balacs; Dr F. C. Clift; J. G. Clarke; P. J. Dearden; P. D. Grant; N. F. Gregory; Dr G. Haley; A. B. D. Hall; E. Hawthorn; N. Highton
*Economists (G7),* J. L. Hoy; W. Kingsmill; M. Lewis; A. Moon; R. Teuten; Ms R. Turner; A. Whitworth; Ms C. Laing; E. Cassidy; Ms R. Phillipson; J. Burton; M. Surr; R. Moberly; Ms J. Alston; P. G. Hill
*Senior Small Enterprise Development Adviser (G6),* D. L. Wright
*Small Enterprise Development Adviser (G7),* J. R. Boulter
*Small Business Adviser (G7),* D. M. Spence
*Chief Statistician (G5),* R. M. Allen
*Statisticians (G6),* A. B. Williams; *(G7),* J. R. B. King; P. J. Crook; Ms J. J. Church; M. Dyble
*Principal Finance Management and Administration Adviser (G5),* K. L. Sparkhall
*Senior Finance Management and Administration Advisers (G6),* Dr R. Thomas; Dr G. Glentworth
*Finance Management and Administration Adviser (G7),* Dr M. Greaves
*Senior Finance and Management Advisers (G6),* D. W. Heffer; D. J. Wood; D. W. Baker; S. Sharples; J. G. Clarke
*Senior Police Adviser (G6),* L. Grundy
*Chief Social Development Adviser (G5),* Dr R. J. Eyben
*Senior Social Development Adviser (G6),* Dr S. Conlin
*Social Development Advisers (G7),* Ms P. Holden; M. Schultz; R. H. Kinnear; Dr Anne Coles
*Chief Health and Population Adviser (G5),* Dr D. Nabarro
*Senior Health and Population Adviser (G6),* R. N. Grose
*Forestry Adviser (G7),* D. Chaffey
*Purchasing Adviser (G7),* R. H. Marriott

INFORMATION DEPARTMENT
*Head of Information (G5),* A. Bearpark
*Principal Information Officer (G7),* R. W. Fosker

ADMINISTRATIVE STAFF
*Grade 5,* Miss A. M. Archbold; M. Bawden; S. Chakrabarti; J. H. S. Chard; Ms M. Cund; A. D. Davis; M. J. Dinham; J. R. Drummond; R. Elias; D. S. Fish; R. M. Graham-Harrison; B. W. Hammond; Mrs P. J. Hilton; Mrs S. Jay; Mrs B. M. Kelly, CBE; M. C. McCulloch; J. C. Machin; V. J. McClean; C. Myhill; M. A. Power; C. P. Raleigh; S. Ray; D. Sands-Smith; D. L. Stanton; G. M. Stegmann; D. P. Turner; Ms S. E. Unsworth; Miss M. Vowles; M. Wickstead; Mrs P. M. Wilkinson; R. J. Wilson
*Grade 6,* J. A. Anning; D. R. Curran; K. D. Grimshaw; N. Hoult; M. A. B. Lowcock; D. Richards; G. Toulmin; D. Trotter; G. A. Williams; A. K. C. Wood
*Grade 7,* G. F. H. Aicken; J. D. Aitken; G. Alexander; R. Allen; G. A. Armstrong; C. M. Athayde; C. B. Austin; N. Bailey; D. G. Bell; A. Bennett; F. Black; H. Britton;

W. A. Brownlie; P. J. Burton; R. T. Calvert;
P. H. Charters, OBE; D. J. Church; T. F. G. Connor;
R. G. Cousins; G. Duffy; M. J. Ellis; B. Foy; J. R. Gilbert;
M. A. Hammond; Ms V. M. Harris; B. Hefferon; Ms
A. C. Higginbottom; M. I. Holland; G. I. James;
W. Jardine; S. D. King; Mrs J. Laurence; D. Lawless;
G. G. Leader; J. Lingham; Ms M. C. McCowan;
I. M. McKendry; M. Mallalieu; P. S. Mason; J. Maund;
C. A. Metcalf; J. C. H. Millett; D. J. Moran;
M. L. S. Mosselmans; J. D. Moye; G. A. Mustard;
Ms J. C. Persey; V. R. Pheasant; R. J. Plumb;
Mrs J. Radice; C. N. Raynor; S. R. J. Robbins; Ms
J. Robinson; P. T. Rose; C. R. Roth;
Dr P. W. K. Rundell; Ms P. Schofield; D. A. Scott;
Mrs P. A. Scutt; Ms C. Seymour Smith; S. J. Sharpe; Ms
A. Siddall; R. J. Smith; Miss R. B. Stevenson;
M. J. Sexton; I. D. Stuart; D. J. C. Taylor;
E. C. N. Taylor; B. A. Thorpe; N. A. Tranter;
Ms S. T. Wardell; C. W. Warren; R. S. White;
J. M. Winter; M. C. Wood; Mrs G. B. Wright;
M. S. S. Wyatt; P. L. Zoller

ADVISORY AND SPECIALIST STAFF
*Chief Education Adviser (G5)*, Ms M. Harrison
*Senior Education Advisers (G6)*, M. D. Francis; Dr
    D. Pennycuick; M. E. Seath; Dr D. G. Swift
*Chief Engineering Adviser (G5)*, J. W. Hodges
*Senior Engineering Advisers (G6)*, A. G. Colley; C. I. Ellis;
    D. Gillett; B. Dolton; H. B. Jackson;
    P. W. D. H. Roberts; M. F. Sergeant
*Engineering Advisers (G7)*, R. J. Cadwallader; A. Barker;
    A. Smallwood; M. McCarthy; D. Robson; C. Hunt
*Senior Renewable Energy and Research Adviser (G6)*, vacant
*Senior Electrical and Mechanical Engineering Adviser (G6)*,
    R. P. Jones
*Senior Architectural and Physical Planning Advisers (G6)*,
    M. W. Parkes; W. M. Housego-Woolgar
*Chief Health and Population Advisers (G6)*, Dr P. Key, OBE;
    Miss I. Isard; Dr M. Kapila; Ms S. Simmonds;
    J. Lambert
*Chief Natural Resources Adviser (G3)*, A. J. Bennett
*Deputy Chief Natural Resources and Principal Agricultural
    Adviser (G5)*, J. M. Scott
*Deputy Chief Natural Resources Adviser (G5)*, Dr I. Haines
    (*Research*)
*Senior Natural Resources Advisers (G6)*, Ms L. C. Brown;
    B. E. Grimwood; J. R. F. Hansell; J. A. Harvey;
    D. J. Salmon; A. J. Tainsh; D. Trotman; M. J. Wilson;
    (*G7*), G. A. Gilman; Dr H. Potter; Dr P. Dobie;
    T. Barrett
*Animal Health Advisers (G6)*, G. G. Freeland;
    Dr A. D. Irvin; Ms L. Bell
*Senior Fisheries Advisers (G6)*, Dr J. Tarbit; R. W. Beales
*Senior Forestry Advisers (G6)*, W. J. Howard; R. Jenkin;
    P. Wood
*Senior Procurement Adviser (G6)*, R. Davidson
*Senior Technical Education Advisers (G6)*, C. Lewis;
    Dr G. R. H. Jones
*Industrial Training Advisers (G7)*, W. Wray; D. G. Marr
*Population Adviser (G7)*, C. Allison
*Agricultural Education and Training Adviser (G7)*, A. Hall

NATURAL RESOURCES INSTITUTE
Central Avenue, Chatham Maritime, Chatham, Kent
ME4 4TB
Tel 01634-880088

An executive agency within the ODA, the NRI provides
scientific and technical expertise in renewable natural
resources for the overseas aid programme.
*Director and Chief Executive (G3)*, G. A. Beattie

## OFFICE OF THE PARLIAMENTARY COMMISSIONER AND HEALTH SERVICE COMMISSIONER
Church House, Great Smith Street, London SW1P 3BW
Tel 0171-276 2130 (*Parliamentary Commissioner*); 0171-276
2035 (*Health Service Commissioner*)

The Parliamentary Commissioner for Administration (the
Ombudsman) is responsible for investigating complaints
referred to him by MPs from members of the public who
claim to have sustained injustice in consequence of maladministration by or on behalf of government departments and
certain non-departmental public bodies. Certain types of
action by government departments or bodies are excluded
from investigation. The Parliamentary Commissioner is also
responsible for investigating complaints, referred by MPs,
alleging that access to official information has been wrongly
refused under the Code of Practice on Access to Government
Information 1994 (*see* page 1171). Actions taken by other
public bodies (such as local authorities, the police, the Post
Office and nationalized industries) are outside the Commissioner's scope.

The Health Service Commissioners for England, for
Scotland and for Wales are responsible for investigating
complaints against National Health Service authorities and
trusts that are not dealt with by those authorities to the
satisfaction of the complainant. Complaints can be referred
direct by the member of the public who claims to have
sustained injustice or hardship in consequence of the failure
in a service provided by a relevant body, failure of that body
to provide a service or in consequence of any other action by
that body. Certain types of action are excluded, in particular,
action taken solely in consequence of the exercise of clinical
judgment. The three offices are presently held by the
Parliamentary Commissioner.

*Parliamentary Commissioner and Health Service
    Commissioner (G1)*, W. K. Reid, CB
*Deputy Parliamentary Commissioners (G3)*, J. E. Avery; Miss
    P. A. Edwards
*Deputy Health Service Commissioner (G3)*, R. A. Oswald
*Directors, Parliamentary Commissioner (G5)*, Mrs
    A. H. P. Bates; Mrs A. M. Boulton; Mrs S. P. Maunsell;
    J. L. Railton; A. Watson
*Directors, Health Service Commissioner (G5)*, J. C. Bateman;
    Miss D. C. Fordham; Mrs P. M. Newman; R. Keynes
*Establishment Officer (G6)*, T. G. Hull
*Principals, Parliamentary Commissioner (G7)*,
    Mrs C. Bentley; J. Colmans; Miss C. Corrigan; Mrs
    D. M. Eacher; D. J. Howard; P. L. Jones; S. J. Lillington;
    K. O'Brien; Mrs M. E. McKinney; G. D. Miller; Mrs
    J. J. Robins; Mrs S. E. Skingley; Miss C. A. Rees-Jenkins,
    OBE; Mrs A. Thyer; Mrs M. Vallance
*Principals, Health Service Commissioner (G7)*, Ms
    J. E. Andrews; T. J. Corkett; D. S. Coleman; E. J. Drake;
    S. J. Drummond; J. Canavan; B. P. Jones; G. M. Keil; Ms
    J. Luthert; Miss S. P. A. Pearson

## NORTHERN IRELAND PARLIAMENTARY COMMISSIONER FOR ADMINISTRATION AND NORTHERN IRELAND COMMISSIONER FOR COMPLAINTS
Progressive House, 33 Wellington Place, Belfast BT1 6HN
Tel 01232-233821

The Commissioner is appointed under legislation with
powers to investigate complaints by people claiming to have

sustained injustice in consequence of maladministration arising from action taken by a Northern Ireland government department, or any other public body within the Commissioner's remit. Staff are presently seconded from the Northern Ireland Civil Service.

*Commissioner*, Mrs J. McIvor, QSM
*Senior Director*, K. McWilliams
*Director*, G. R. Dawson
*Deputy Director*, S. P. Hughes

## PARLIAMENTARY COUNSEL
36 Whitehall, London SW1A 2AY
Tel 0171-210 6633

Parliamentary Counsel draft all government bills (i.e. primary legislation) except those relating exclusively to Scotland, the latter being drafted by the Lord Advocate's Department. They also advise on all aspects of parliamentary procedure in connection with such bills and draft government amendments to them as well as any motions (including financial resolutions) necessary to secure their introduction into, and passage through, Parliament.

*First Counsel* (£95,051), J. C. Jenkins, CB
*Second Counsel* (£83,366), D. W. Saunders, CB
*Counsel* (£65,990–£79,396), E. G. Caldwell, CB;
  E. G. Bowman, CB; G. B. Sellers, CB; E. R. Sutherland,
  CB; P. F. A. Knowles; S. C. Laws; R. S. Parker; Ms
  C. E. Johnston

## PAROLE BOARD FOR ENGLAND AND WALES
Abell House, John Islip Street, London SW1P 4LH
Tel 0171-217 5314

The Board was constituted under the Criminal Justice Act 1967 and continued under the Criminal Justice Act 1991. Its duty is to advise the Secretary of State for the Home Department with respect to matters referred to it by him which are connected with the early release or recall of prisoners. Its functions include giving directions concerning the release on licence of prisoners serving discretionary life sentences and of certain prisoners serving long-term determinate sentences; and making recommendations to the Secretary of State concerning the early release on licence of other prisoners, the conditions of parole and licences and the variation and cancellation of such conditions, and the recall of long-term and life prisoners while on licence.

*Chairman*, The Lord Belstead, PC
*Vice-Chairman*, The Hon. Mr Justice Swinton Thomas
*Secretary*, T. E. Russell

## PAROLE BOARD FOR SCOTLAND
Calton House, 5 Redheughs Rigg, Edinburgh EH12 9HW
Tel 0131-244 8755

The Board advises the Secretary of State for Scotland on the release of prisoners on licence, and related matters.

*Chairman*, J. M. Scott
*Vice-Chairman*, I. McNee
*Secretary*, H. P. Boyle

## PARTICLE PHYSICS AND ASTRONOMY RESEARCH COUNCIL
Polaris House, North Star Avenue, Swindon, Wilts. SN2 1SZ
Tel 01793-442000

The Particle Physics and Astronomy Research Council was established in April 1994 from part of the former Science and Engineering Research Council. It is an independent body funded by the Office of Science and Technology. The Council supports research into elementary particles and the fundamental forces of nature, planetary and solar research including space physics, and astronomy, astrophysics and cosmology. It funds university researchers, primarily through grants to postgraduate students and research fellowships. The Council is responsible for the funding of both national and international facilities, including the European Laboratory for Particle Physics and the European Space Agency. Government funding to the Council for 1994–5 is £184.9 million.

*Chairman*, Dr P. Williams, CBE
*Chief Executive*, Prof. K. Pounds, CBE, FRS
*Members*, Sir David Cooksey; Prof. S. Cowley; Dr D. Evans;
  J. de Fonblanque; Prof. J. Dowell, FRS; Prof. J. Enderby,
  FRS; Prof. I. Halliday; Dr Carole Jordan, FRS; Sir Martin
  Rees, FRS; Dr G. Robinson
For research establishments, *see* page 710

## PATENT OFFICE
Cardiff Road, Newport, Gwent NP9 1RH
Tel 01633-814000

The Patent Office is an executive agency of the Department of Trade and Industry. The duties of the Patent Office are to administer the Patent Acts, the Registered Designs Act and the Trade Marks Act, and to deal with questions relating to the Copyright, Designs and Patents Act 1988. The Search and Advisory Service carries out commercial searches through patent information. In 1993 the Office granted 8,330 patents and registered 8,301 designs and 32,934 trade and service marks.

*Comptroller-General* (G3), P. R. S. Hartnack
*Assistant Comptroller, Industrial Property and Copyright*
  *Department* (G4), A. Sugden
*Assistant Comptroller, Patents and Designs* (G4),
  R. J. Marchant
*Assistant Registrar, Trade Marks* (G4), Miss A. Brimelow
*Head of Marketing and Information* (Supt. Examiner),
  E. F. Blake
*Head of Administration and Resources* (G5), T. Cassidy
*Head of ADP Unit* (G6), G. Bennett

## PAYMASTER
The Office of HM Paymaster-General
HM Treasury, Parliament Street, London SW1P 3AG
Tel 0171-270 4349
Sutherland House, Russell Way, Crawley, W. Sussex
RH10 1UH
Tel 01293-560999

PAYMASTER, the Office of HM Paymaster-General, was formed by the consolidation in 1835 of various separate pay departments then existing. Its function is that of paying agent for government departments other than the revenue departments. Most of its payments are made through banks, to whose accounts the necessary transfers are made at the Bank of England. The payment of over 1.5 million public service pensions is an important feature of its work. The Office became an executive agency in 1993.

*Paymaster-General*, David Heathcoat-Amory, MP
*Assistant Paymaster-General/Chief Executive (G5)*, K. Sullens
*Grade 6*, M. D. West
*Grade 7*, D. R. Alexander; A. Edwards; T. R. George; R. G. Hollands; M. C. Kirk; D. Nunn; Mrs J. Parsons

## OFFICE OF THE PENSIONS OMBUDSMAN
11 Belgrave Road, London SW1V 1RB
Tel 0171-834 9144

The Pensions Ombudsman is appointed by the Secretary of State for Social Security under the Pension Schemes Act 1993 to deal with complaints against, and disputes with, occupational and personal pension schemes. He is completely independent.

*Pensions Ombudsman*, Dr J. T. Farrand

## POLICE COMPLAINTS AUTHORITY
10 Great George Street, London SW1P 3AE
Tel 0171-273 6450

The Police Complaints Authority was established under the Police and Criminal Evidence Act 1984 to introduce a further independent element into the procedure for dealing with complaints by members of the public against police officers in England and Wales. The Authority has powers to supervise the investigation of certain categories of serious complaints and certain statutory functions in relation to the disciplinary aspects of complaints. It does not as a rule deal with complaints about police operations; these are usually dealt with by the Chief Constable of the relevant force.

*Chairman*, Sir Leonard Peach
*Deputy Chairman (Investigations)*, J. Cartwright
*Deputy Chairman (Discipline)*, P. W. Moorhouse
*Members*, Mrs L. Cawsey; M. Chapman; N. Dholakia, OBE; Miss L. Haye; Ms A. Kelly; G. V. Marsh; W. McCall; Ms M. Meacher; L. Spencer; Brig. A. Vivian; Miss B. Wallis; E. Wignall; A. Williams

## INDEPENDENT COMMISSION FOR POLICE COMPLAINTS FOR NORTHERN IRELAND
— see page 321

## POLITICAL HONOURS SCRUTINY COMMITTEE
Cabinet Office, 53 Parliament Street, London SW1A 2NG
Tel 0171-210 5058

The function of the Political Honours Scrutiny Committee is set out in an Order of Council dated 31 May 1979. The Prime Minister submits certain particulars to the Committee about persons proposed to be recommended for honour for their political services. The Committee, after such enquiry as they think fit, report to the Prime Minister whether, so far as they believe, the persons whose names are submitted to them are fit and proper persons to be recommended.

*Chairman*, The Lord Pym, MC, PC

*Members*, The Lord Cledwyn of Penrhos, CH, PC; The Lord Thomson of Monifieth, KT, PC
*Secretary*, A. J. Merifield, CB

## OFFICE OF POPULATION CENSUSES AND SURVEYS
St Catherine's House, 10 Kingsway, London WC2B 6JP
Tel 0171-242 0262

The Office of Population Censuses and Surveys was created by the merger in 1970 of the General Register Office and the Government Social Survey Department. The Registrar-General controls the local registration service in England and Wales in the exercise of its registration and marriage duties. Copies of the original registrations of births, still births, marriages and deaths and a register of adopted children are kept at Smedley Hydro, Southport PR8 2HH. Central indexes are compiled annually and certified copies of entries may be obtained, on payment of certain fees, either by personal application from St Catherine's House or by post from Southport.

Since 1841 the Registrar-General has been responsible for taking the census of population. He also prepares and publishes a wide range of statistics and appropriate commentary relating to population, fertility, births, still births, marriages, deaths and cause of death and infectious diseases. The Registrar-General is also responsible for conducting surveys on a range of subjects for other government departments. He maintains, at Southport, the National Health Service Central Register.

Hours of access to Public Search Room, St Catherine's House, Monday–Friday, 8.30–4.30.

*Director and Registrar-General for England and Wales (G2)*, P. J. Wormald, CB
*Deputy Director and Director of Statistics (G3)*, E. J. Thompson
*Deputy Director and Chief Medical Statistician (G3)*, A. J. Fox, Ph.D.
*Deputy Registrar-General (G5)*, J. V. Ribbins
*Principal Finance Officer (G5)*, B. S. Smith
*Principal Establishment Officer (G6)*, N. E. Auckland
*Principal Information Officer (G7)*, Miss S. Wallace
*Heads of Division (G5)*, I. K. G. Arnold (*Information Technology*); M. F. G. Murphy (*Senior Medical Statistician*); R. Barnes (*Social Survey Division*); J. Craig (*Population Statistics*); Ms K. Dunnell (*Health Statistics*); B. H. Mahon (*Census*); N. Woods (*Marketing*)
*Heads of Division (G6)*, W. Jenkins (*NHS Central Register*); B. W. Meakings (*Data Services*)
*Grade 6*, B. S. T. Alcock; Mrs M. Bone; A. M. Clark; J. Denton, OBE; W. Jenkins; I. B. Knight; D. L. Pearce; R. McLeod; Mrs J. Martin; Ms J. Matheson
*Grade 7*, R. I. Armitage; F. L. Ashwood; R. A. P. Bailey; N. Bateson; R. J. Beacham; D. E. Birch; Mrs B. J. Botting; A. F. Bradbury; J. A. Brown; L. Bulusu; D. Capron; R. J. Carpenter; J. R. H. Charlton; J. Cloyne; C. J. Denham; T. L. F. Devis; J. M. Dixie; Mrs J. C. Dobbs; Ms P. A. Dodd; D. Elliot; Miss C. M. Ellis; Ms E. M. Goddard; Mrs J. R. Gregory; P. C. Gregory; J. Haskey; A. J. H. Hayes (*Chief Inspector of Registration*); P. J. Heady; G. Hughes; Mrs J. Humby; J. Jackson; S. P. King; I. B. Knight; B. G. Little; Miss C. S. J. Lloyd; D. Lockyer; W. F. Loomes; Miss E. M. McCrossan; Mrs I. MacDonald-Davies; Mrs M. Machin; A. J. Manners; V. A. Mason; H. I. Meltzer; I. D. Mills; A. Parr; M. Quinn; A. P. Read; S. Robinson-Grindey; C. I. Rooney; J. A. Salvetti;

C. Savage; Ms J. M. Sharp; Mrs S. M. Smyth; D. Stewart;
P. Stickland; Mrs L. M. Street; A. D. Teague;
A. W. Tester; Mrs M. J. Wagget; I. S. G. White;
A. J. White; E. W. Williams

## PORT OF LONDON AUTHORITY
Devon House, 58–60 St Katharine's Way, London EI 9LB
Tel 0171-265 2656

The Port of London Authority is a public trust constituted
under the Port of London Act 1908 and subsequent
legislation. It is the governing body for the Port of London,
covering the tidal portion of the River Thames from
Teddington to the seaward limit. The Board comprises a
chairman and up to seven but not less than four non-executive
members appointed by the Secretary of State for Transport,
and up to four but not less than one executive members
appointed by the Board.
*Chairman*, Sir Brian Shaw
*Vice-Chairman*, J. H. Kelly, CBE
*Chief Executive*, D. Jeffery
*Secretary*, G. E. Ennals

## THE POST OFFICE
148 Old Street, London ECIV 9HQ
Tel 0171-490 2888

Crown services for the carriage of government despatches
were set up in about 1516. The conveyance of public
correspondence began in 1635 and the mail service was made
a parliamentary responsibility with the setting up of a Post
Office in 1657. Telegraphs came under Post Office control in
1870 and the Post Office Telephone Service began in 1880.
The National Girobank service of the Post Office began in
1968. The Post Office ceased to be a government department
in 1969 when responsibility for the running of the postal,
telecommunications, giro and remittance services was transferred to a public authority called the Post Office. The 1981
British Telecommunications Act separated the functions of
the Post Office, making it solely responsible for postal
services and Girobank. Girobank was privatized in 1990. In
June 1993 the Government published a discussion document
on the future of the Post Office, in which the preferred option
was the privatization of 51 per cent of the Royal Mail and
Parcelforce, while keeping Post Office Counters in public
ownership but with greater commercial freedom.

The chairman, chief executive and members of the Post
Office Board are appointed by the Secretary of State for
Trade and Industry but responsibility for the running of the
Post Office as a whole rests with the Board in its corporate
capacity.

| FINANCIAL RESULTS | 1992–3 | 1993–4 |
|---|---|---|
| | £m | £m |
| Post Office Group | | |
| Turnover | 5,345 | 5,568 |
| Trading profit before tax | 283 | 306 |
| Royal Mail | | |
| Turnover | 4,048 | 4,223 |
| Trading profit before tax and | | |
| interest on long-term loans | 216 | 276 |

| Parcelforce | | |
|---|---|---|
| Turnover | 501 | 498 |
| Trading loss before tax and | | |
| interest on long-term loans | 12 | 17 |
| Post Office Counters | | |
| Turnover | 1,061 | 1,089 |
| Trading profit before tax and | | |
| interest on long-term loans | 43 | 34 |

POST OFFICE BOARD
*Chairman*, M. Heron
*Chief Executive*, W. Cockburn, CBE, TD
*Members*, P. Howarth (*Managing Director, Royal Mail*);
K. Williams (*Managing Director, Parcelforce*); R. Dykes
(*Managing Director, Post Office Counters Ltd*); R. Close
(*Managing Director, Finance*)
*Secretary*, Miss M. MacDonald, CBE
For postal services, *see* pages 521–3

## PRIME MINISTER'S OFFICE
— *see* page 292

## PRISONS OMBUDSMEN

The Prisons Ombudsmen are an independent point of appeal
for prisoners' grievances about their lives in prison, including
disciplinary issues. The Ombudsmen cannot investigate
grievances relating to issues which are the subject of litigation
or criminal proceedings, decisions taken by ministers on the
release of life sentence prisoners, or actions of individuals or
bodies outside the prison service (except boards of visitors).
The exclusion of grievances related to the clinical judgement
of prison medical staff is also being considered. The
Ombudsman for England and Wales was appointed in May
1994; the Ombudsman for Scotland (known as the Independent Complaints Adjudicator) will be appointed in autumn
1994.

ENGLAND AND WALES
St Vincent House, 30 Orange Street, London WC2H 7HH
Tel 0171-389 1527

*Prisons Ombudsman*, Sir Peter Woodhead, KCB

## PRIVY COUNCIL OFFICE
Whitehall, London SWIA 2AT
Tel 0171-270 3000

The Office is responsible for the arrangements leading to the
making of all royal proclamations and Orders in Council; for
certain formalities connected with ministerial changes; for
considering applications for the granting (or amendment) of
royal charters; for the scrutiny and approval of by-laws and
statutes of chartered bodies; and for the appointment of High
Sheriffs and many Crown and Privy Council appointments
to governing bodies.
*Lord President of the Council* (*and Leader of the House of
Commons*), The Rt. Hon. Antony Newton, OBE, MP
*Private Secretary*, G. D. S. Sandeman
*Special Adviser*, P. Moman
*Parliamentary Private Secretary*, J. Marshall, MP
*Clerk of the Council* (*G3*), N. H. Nicholls, CBE
*Deputy Clerk of the Council* (*G5*), R. P. Bulling
*Senior Clerk*, Miss M. A. McCullagh

PROCURATOR FISCAL SERVICE
— *see* pages 382

## PUBLIC HEALTH LABORATORY SERVICE
61 Colindale Avenue, London NW9 5DF
Tel 0181-200 1295

The Public Health Laboratory Service comprises 53 regional or area laboratories in England and Wales, the Central Public Health Laboratory and the Communicable Disease Surveillance Centre. The PHLS provides diagnostic microbiological services to hospitals, and has reference facilities that are available nationally. It collates information on the incidence of infection, and when necessary it institutes special inquiries into outbreaks and the epidemiology of infectious disease. It also undertakes bacteriological surveillance of the quality of food and water for local authorities and others. The PHLS is often called upon to advise central and local government and the hospital service on many aspects of infectious disease. It maintains close contact with veterinary organizations in areas of mutual interest, and collaborates with the World Health Organization and with national laboratory and epidemiological services overseas.

THE BOARD
*Chairman,* Dr M. P. W. Godfrey, CBE, FRCP
*Deputy Chairman,* A. Graham-Dixon, QC
*Members,* Prof. J. P. Arbuthnott, PH.D.; Dr W. Bogie;
D. F. R. Crofton; Prof. G. Crompton;
Prof. C. S. F. Easmon; Dr J. M. Forsythe; D. G. Garvie;
J. Godfrey; Dr H. H. John; Prof. M. D. Lilly;
D. Noble, CBE; Prof. F. W. O'Grady; Dr M. J. Painter;
Prof. J. R. Pattison; Prof. I. Phillips;
J. J. Skehel, PH.D., FRS; Prof. P. G. Smith, D.SC.;
G. H. Stewart; J. W. Tiffney

HEAD OFFICE
*Director,* Dr Diana Walford, FRCP, FRCPath.
*Deputy Director (Programmes),* Dr E. M. Cooke
*Deputy Director (Resources) and Board Secretary,*
  K. M. Saunders

CENTRAL PUBLIC HEALTH LABORATORY
Colindale Avenue, London NW9 5HT
*Director,* Dr M. C. Timbury

COMMUNICABLE DISEASES SURVEILLANCE CENTRE
Colindale, NW9 5EQ
*Director,* Dr C. L. R. Bartlett

OTHER SPECIAL LABORATORIES AND UNITS
ANAEROBE REFERENCE UNIT, Public Health Laboratory, Cardiff. *Director,* Prof. B. I. Duerden
CRYPTOSPROIDIUM REFERENCE UNIT, Public Health Laboratory, Rhyl. *Director,* D. N. Looker
GONOCOCCUS REFERENCE UNIT, Public Health Laboratory, Bristol. *Director,* A. E. Jephcott, MD
LEPTOSPIRA REFERENCE LABORATORY, Public Health Laboratory, Hereford. *Director,* I. R. Fergusson, TD
MALARIA REFERENCE LABORATORY, London School of Hygiene and Tropical Medicine, London WC1. *Directors,* Prof. D. J. Bradley, DM; D. C. Warhurst, PH.D., FRCPath.
MENINGOCOCCAL REFERENCE LABORATORY, Public Health Laboratory, Manchester. *Director,* J. Craske
MYCOBACTERIUM REFERENCE UNIT, Public Health Laboratory, Cardiff. *Director,* Prof. B. I. Duerden
TOXOPLASMA REFERENCE LABORATORIES, Public Health Laboratory, Swansea. *Director,* D. H. M. Joynson;

Public Health Laboratory, Tooting, London. *Director,* A. R. M. Coates
WATER AND ENVIRONMENTAL LABORATORY, Public Health Laboratory, Nottingham. *Director,* P. J. Wilkinson

REGIONAL LABORATORIES AND DIRECTORS
*Birmingham,* I. D. Farrell, PH.D.; *Bristol,* A. E. Jephcott; *Cambridge,* U. Desselberger, MD, FRCP(G); *Cardiff,* Prof. B. I. Duerden; *Leeds,* R. N. Peel; *Liverpool,* J. H. Pennington, MD; *Manchester,* J. Craske (*acting*); *Newcastle,* N. F. Lightfoot; *Oxford,* J. B. Selkon, TD; *Portsmouth,* P. A. Cockroft; *Sheffield,* P. Norman

AREA LABORATORIES
*Ashford,* C. Dulake, TD; *Bangor,* T. Howard; *Bath,* D. G. White; *Brighton,* A. Lewis; *Carlisle,* M. A. Knowles; *Carmarthen,* M. D. Simmons; *Chelmsford,* R. E. Tettmar, D.Path.; *Chester,* P. Hunter, MD; *Coventry,* P. R. Mortimer, MD; *Dorchester,* A. Rampling, PH.D.; *Epsom,* S. A. Chambers; *Exeter,* J. G. Cruickshank, MD; *Gloucester,* K. A. V. Cartwright; *Guildford,* Prof. R. Y. Cartwright; *Hereford,* I. R. Ferguson, TD; *Hull,* S. L. Mawer; *Ipswich,* P. H. Jones; *Leicester,* C. J. Mitchell; *Lincoln,* E. R. Youngs; LONDON: *Central Middlesex Hospital,* M. S. Shafi; *Dulwich,* A. H. C. Uttley, PH.D.; *Tooting,* Prof. A. R. M. Coates; *Whipps Cross,* B. Chattopadhyay, MD; *Luton,* Dr S. A. Rousseau; *Middlesbrough,* E. McKay-Ferguson, MD; *Norwich,* P. M. B. White; *Nottingham,* P. J. Wilkinson; *Peterborough,* R. S. Jobanputra, MD; *Plymouth,* D. A. B. Dance; *Poole,* W. L. Hooper; *Preston,* P. Morgan-Capner; *Reading,* P. Burden; *Rhyl,* D. N. Looker; *Salisbury,* S. Patrick; *Shrewsbury,* R. E. Warren; *Southampton,* J. A. Lowes; *Stoke-on-Trent,* J. Gray; *Swansea,* D. H. M. Joynson; *Taunton,* J. V. S. Pether; *Truro,* W. A. Telfer Brunton; *Watford,* M. T. Moulsdale; *Wolverhampton,* R. G. Thompson

## REGISTRAR OF PUBLIC LENDING RIGHT
Bayheath House, Prince Regent Street,
Stockton-on-Tees, TS18 1DF
Tel 01642-604699

Under the Public Lending Right system, in operation since 1983, payment is made from public funds to authors whose books are lent out from public libraries. Payment is made once a year (in February) and the amount each author receives is proportionate to the number of times (established from a sample) that each registered book has been lent out during the previous year.

The Registrar of PLR, who is appointed by the Secretary of State for National Heritage, compiles the register of authors and books. Only living authors resident in the UK or Germany are eligible to apply. (The term 'author' covers writers, illustrators, translators, and some editors/compilers.)

A payment of two pence was made in 1993-4 for each estimated loan of a registered book, up to a top limit of £6,000 for the books of any one registered author; the money for loans above this level is used to augment the remaining PLR payments.

In February 1994, the sum of £4.372 million was made available for distribution to 18,633 registered authors and assignees as the annual payment of PLR.

The PLR Advisory Committee advises the Secretary of State for National Heritage and the Registrar of Public Lending Right. Its members are appointed by the Secretary of State.

*Chairman of Advisory Committee*, P. S. Ziegler, CVO
*Registrar*, Dr J. Parker

PUBLIC RECORD OFFICE
— *see* below

PUBLIC TRUST OFFICE
Stewart House, 24 Kingsway, London WC2B 6JX
Tel 0171-269 7000

The Public Trust Office became an executive agency in 1994. The chief executive of the agency holds the statutory titles of Public Trustee and Accountant-General of the Supreme Court, and is accountable to the Lord Chancellor.

The Public Trustee is a trust corporation created to undertake the business of executorship and trusteeship; she can act as executor or administrator of the estate of a deceased person, or as trustee of a will or settlement. The Public Trustee is also responsible for the performance of all the administrative, but not the judicial, tasks required of the Court of Protection under Part VII of the Mental Health Act 1983, relating to the management and administration of the property and affairs of persons suffering from mental disorder. The Public Trustee also acts as Receiver when so directed by the Court, usually where there is no other person willing or able so to act.

The Accountant-General of the Supreme Court, through the Court Funds Office, is responsible for the investment and accounting of funds in court for persons under a disability, monies in court subject to litigation and statutory deposits.

The Court Funds Office is at 22 Kingsway, London WC2B 6LE. Tel: 0171-936 6000
*Chief Executive (Public Trustee and Accountant-General)*,
  Ms J. C. Lomas
*Assistant Public Trustee*, H. N. Mather
*Investment Manager*, H. Stevenson
*Chief Property Adviser*, A. Nightingale

MENTAL HEALTH SECTOR
*Head*, E. J. Dober
*Receivership Activity*, Miss G. Bradshaw
*Protection Activity*, Mrs H. M. Bratton

TRUSTS AND FUNDS SECTOR
*Head*, F. J. Eddy
*Court Funds Activity*, I. S. Price
*Trust Activity*, M. Munt

ESTABLISHMENTS AND FINANCE SECTOR
*Head*, E. A. Bloomfield
*Finance*, P. L. Hales
*Planning*, Mrs N. M. Hunt

PUBLIC WORKS LOAN BOARD
— *see* National Investment and Loans Office

COMMISSION FOR RACIAL EQUALITY
Elliot House, 10–12 Allington Street, London SW1E 5EH
Tel 0171-828 7022

The Commission was established in 1977, under the Race Relations Act 1976, to work towards the elimination of discrimination and promote equality of opportunity and good relations between different racial groups.
*Chairman*, H. Ouseley
*Deputy Chairs*, A. Ward; R. Sondhi

*Members*, R. Kent; Revd E. A. Brown; Dr M. C. K. Chan, MBE; T. A. Khan; A. Rose, OBE; R. Purkiss; Dr D. Neil; Ms M. Cunningham; Dr R. Chandran; Dr Z. Khan; M. Hastings
*Executive Director*, D. Sharma

THE RADIO AUTHORITY
Holbrook House, 14 Great Queen Street, London WC2B 5DG
Tel 0171-430 2724

The Radio Authority was established in 1991 under the Broadcasting Act 1990. Its function is to plan frequencies, to grant licences for the provision of independent radio services, and to regulate the output of the services in accordance with published codes dealing with standards for programming, advertising and sponsorship.

Members of the Authority are appointed by the Secretary of State for National Heritage; senior executive staff are appointed by the Authority.
*Chairman*, The Lord Chalfont OBE, MC, PC
*Deputy Chairman*, M. Moriarty, CB
*Members*, Mrs M. Corrigan; J. Grant; R. Sondhi; Miss J. Francis; M. Reupke; Lady Sheil; A. Reid
*Chief Executive*, P. Baldwin, CBE
*Deputy Chief Executive and Head of Regulation*, P. Brown
*Head of Development*, D. Vick
*Head of Finance*, N. Romain
*Head of Engineering*, M. Thomas
*Secretary to the Authority*, J. Norrington

RECORD OFFICES

ADVISORY COUNCIL ON PUBLIC RECORDS
*Secretariat:* Trevelyan House, Great Peter Street, London SW1P 2BY
Tel 0171-210 8810

Council members are appointed by the Lord Chancellor, under the Public Records Act 1958, to advise him on matters concerning public records in general and, in particular, on those aspects of the work of the Public Record Office which affect members of the public who make use of it. The Council meets quarterly and produces an annual report which is published alongside the Report of the Keeper of Public Records as a House of Commons sessional paper.
*Chairman*, The Master of the Rolls
*Members*, Prof. B. W. E. Alford; Sir John Blelloch; Dr A. Borg; Mrs L. Brindley; A. C. Carlile, QC, MP; Prof. R. Chapman; T. A. G. Davis, MP; Prof. R. B. Dobson; Miss A. Duncan; V. Gray; Mrs L. Lithgow; Prof. Shula Marks; D. Sumberg, MP; D. G. Vaisey
*Assessor*, Mrs S. Tyacke
*Secretary*, R. Wright

THE PUBLIC RECORD OFFICE
Ruskin Avenue, Kew, Richmond, Surrey TW9 4DU
Chancery Lane, London WC2A 1LR
Tel 0181-876 3444

The Public Records Office, originally established in 1838 under the Master of the Rolls, was placed under the direction of the Lord Chancellor in 1958. He appoints a Keeper of Public Records, whose duties are to co-ordinate and supervise the selection of records of government departments and the

English law courts for permanent preservation, to safeguard the records and to make them available to the public.

The Office holds records of central government dating from the *Domesday Book* (1086) to the present. Under the Public Records Act 1967 they are normally open to inspection when 30 years old, and are then available, without charge, in the reading rooms, Monday–Friday, 9.30–5. The museum at Chancery Lane is open Monday–Friday, 10–5 and the Census rooms are open Monday–Saturday, 9.30–5.

The Office became an executive agency in 1992.

*Keeper of Public Records (G3)*, Mrs S. Tyacke
*Central Management Department (G7)*, C. R. H. Cooper

PUBLIC SERVICES DIVISION
*Director (G5)*, C. D. Chalmers
*Reader Services Department (G6)*, Mrs A. Nicol
*Reprographic, Publishing and Publicity Department (G6)*, Dr E. Hallam Smith
*Preservation Services (G7)*, Dr H. Forde

ARCHIVAL SERVICES DIVISION
*Director (G5)*, Dr N. G. Cox
*Government Services Department (G6) (acting)*, Miss J. A. V. Rose
*Editorial Services Department (G6) (acting)*, Dr M. R. Foster

CORPORATE SERVICES DIVISION
*Director (G5)*, Dr D. Simpson
*IT Department (G7)*, Miss J. K. Lawlor
*Finance Department (G7)*, Ms P. Ewens
*Personnel Department (G7)*, N. J. Smedley
*New PRO Programme Manager (G6)*, Dr D. L. Thomas
*Office Services Department (G7)*, J. S. Harley

## HOUSE OF LORDS RECORD OFFICE

House of Lords, London SW1A 0PW
Tel 0171-219 3074

Since 1497, the records of Parliament have been kept within the Palace of Westminster. They are in the custody of the Clerk of the Parliaments. In 1946 a record department was established to supervise their preservation and their availability to the public. The search room of the office is open to the public Monday–Friday, 9.30–5 (Tuesday to 8, by appointment).

Some three million documents are preserved, including Acts of Parliament from 1497, journals of the House of Lords from 1510, minutes and committee proceedings from 1610, and papers laid before Parliament from 1531. Amongst the records are the Petition of Right, the Death Warrant of Charles I, the Declaration of Breda, and the Bill of Rights. The House of Lords Record Office also has charge of the journals of the House of Commons (from 1547), and other surviving records of the Commons (from 1572), including documents relating to private bill legislation from 1818. Among other documents are the records of the Lord Great Chamberlain, the political papers of certain members of the two Houses, and documents relating to Parliament acquired on behalf of the nation. A permanent exhibition was established in the Royal Gallery in 1979.

*Clerk of the Records (£39,365–£57,612)*, D. J. Johnson, FSA
*Deputy Clerk of the Records (£30,680–£49,697)*, S. K. Ellison
*Assistant Clerk of the Records (£12,871–£30,937)*, D. L. Prior

## ROYAL COMMISSION ON HISTORICAL MANUSCRIPTS

Quality House, Quality Court, Chancery Lane, London WC2A 1HP
Tel 0171-242 1198

The Commission was set up by royal warrant in 1869 to enquire and report on collections of papers of value for the study of history which were in private hands. In 1959 a new warrant enlarged these terms of reference to include all historical records, wherever situated, outside the Public Records and gave it added responsibilities as a central co-ordinating body to promote, assist and advise on their proper preservation and storage. The Commission has published over 200 volumes of reports.

It also maintains the National Register of Archives, which contains over 37,000 unpublished lists and catalogues of manuscript collections describing the holdings of local record offices, national and university libraries, specialist repositories and others in the UK and overseas. The NRA can be searched using computerised indices which are available in the Commission's search room.

The Commission also administers the Manorial and Tithe Documents Rules on behalf of the Master of the Rolls.

*Chairman*, G. E. Aylmer, FBA
*Commissioners*, The Lord Blake, FBA;
J. P. W. Ehrman, FBA, FSA; Prof. S. F. C. Milsom, FBA; P. T. Cormack, FSA, MP; D. G. Vaisey, FSA; The Lord Egremont and Leconfield; Mrs J. Thirsk, FBA; Sir Matthew Farrer, KCVO; Miss B. Harvey, FBA, FSA; Sir John Sainty, KCB, FSA; Prof. R. H. Campbell, PH.D.; Very Revd H. E. C. Stapleton, FSA; Sir Keith Thomas; Mrs C. M. Short; The Earl of Scarbrough; Mrs A. Dundas-Bekker
*Secretary*, C. J. Kitching, PH.D., FSA

## SCOTTISH RECORDS ADVISORY COUNCIL

HM General Register House, Edinburgh EH1 3YY
Tel 0131-556 6585

The Council was established under the Public Records (Scotland) Act 1937. Its members are appointed by the Secretary of State for Scotland and it may submit proposals or make representations to the Secretary of State, the Lord Justice General or the Lord President of the Court of Session on questions relating to the public records of Scotland.

*Chairman*, Prof. R. H. Campbell, OBE
*Secretary*, D. M. Abbott

## SCOTTISH RECORD OFFICE

HM General Register House, Edinburgh EH1 3YY
Tel 0131-556 6585

The history of the national archives of Scotland can be traced back to the 13th century. The Scottish Record Office keeps the administrative records of pre-Union Scotland, the registers of central and local courts of law, the public registers of property rights and legal documents, and many collections of local and church records and private archives. Certain groups of records, mainly the modern records of government departments in Scotland, the Scottish railway records, the plans collection, and private archives of an industrial or commercial nature, are preserved in the branch repository at the West Register House in Charlotte Square. The search rooms in both buildings are open Monday–Friday, 9–4.45. A permanent exhibition at the West Register House and changing exhibitions at the General Register House are open to the public on weekdays, 10–4. The National Register of Archives (Scotland), which is a branch of the Scottish Record Office, is based in the West Register House.

The Scottish Record Office became an executive agency of the Scottish Office in April 1993.
*Keeper of the Records of Scotland*, P. M. Cadell

## CORPORATION OF LONDON RECORDS OFFICE
Guildhall, London EC2P 2EJ
Tel 0171-332 1251

The Corporation of London Records Office contains the municipal archives of the City of London which are regarded as the most complete collection of ancient municipal records in existence. The collection includes charters of William the Conqueror, Henry II, and later kings and queens to 1957; ancient custumals: Liber Horn, Dunthorne, Custumarum, Ordinacionum, Memorandorum and Albus, Liber de Antiquis Legibus, and collections of Statutes; continuous series of judicial rolls and books from 1252 and Council minutes from 1275; records of the Old Bailey and Guildhall Sessions from 1603; financial records from the 16th century; the records of London Bridge from the 12th century; and numerous subsidiary series and miscellanea of historical interest. Readers' Room open Monday–Friday, 9.30–4.45.
*Keeper of the City Records*, The Town Clerk
*City Archivist*, J. R. Sewell
*Deputy City Archivist*, Mrs J. M. Bankes

## RED DEER COMMISSION
Knowsley, 82 Fairfield Road, Inverness IV3 5LH
Tel 01463-231751

The Red Deer Commission has the general functions of furthering the conservation and control of red and sika deer in Scotland and of keeping under review all matters relating to roe deer. It has the statutory duty, with powers, to prevent damage to agriculture and forestry by red and sika deer. The Commission also has the power to advise in the interest of conservation any owner of land on questions relating to the carrying of stocks of red deer, sika deer and roe deer on that land, and to carry out research into matters of scientific importance relating to deer.
*Chairman (part-time)*, P. Gordon-Duff-Pennington, OBE
*Chief Executive and Secretary*, A. Rinning
*Technical Director*, R. W. Youngson

## REGIONAL GOVERNMENT OFFICES

In April 1994 integrated government offices were set up in the English regions to bring together the existing regional offices of the Department of the Environment, the Department of Transport, the Department of Trade and Industry and the Training, Enterprise and Education Directorate of the Department of Employment. Each integrated regional office is headed by a senior regional director, who is accountable to the relevant Secretary of State. The offices are administering a new single budget for development and regeneration which combines the budgets of more than 20 previously separate programmes.

EASTERN
*Secretariat:* Heron House, 49–53 Goldington Road, Bedford MK40 3LL
Tel 01234-363161

*Senior Regional Director (G3)*, J. Turner

*Regional Directors (G5)*, C. Dunabin (*Housing*); R. A. Bird (*Planning and Transport*); J. Hall (*Trade and Industry*); Ms C. Johnson (*Employment and Training*)

EAST MIDLANDS
*Secretariat:* Cranbrook House, Cranbrook Street, Nottingham NG1 1EY
Tel 0115-935 2416

*Senior Regional Director (G3)*, M. Lanyon
*Regional Directors (G4)*, D. Morrison (*Environment and Transport*); (*G5*), M. Briggs (*Trade and Industry*); P. Launer (*Employment and Training*)

LONDON
*Secretariat:* Room P2/023, 2 Marsham Street, London SW1P 3EB
Tel 0171-276 5825

*Senior Regional Director (G2)*, R. Young
*Regional Directors (G3)*, Ms A. Heath (*Environment*); I. Yass (*Transport*); (*G5*), J. Hagestadt (*Trade and Industry*); Ms W. Harris (*Employment and Training*)

MERSEYSIDE
*Secretariat:* Room 402, Graeme House, Derby Square, Liverpool L2 7SU
Tel 0151-224 6300

*Senior Regional Director (G3)*, J. Stoker
*Regional Directors (G5)*, I. Urqhart (*Housing, Europe and Transport*); S. Dunmore (*Urban and Economic Affairs*); Ms P. Jackson (*Trade and Industry*); P. Houton (*Employment and Training*)

NORTH-EAST
*Secretariat:* Room 406, Stangate House, 2 Groat Market, Newcastle upon Tyne NE1 1YN
Tel 0191-235 7722

*Senior Regional Director (G3)*, Ms P. Denham
*Regional Directors (G5)*, Ms C. Caudle (*Environment and Transport*); R. Bell (*Regeneration*); A. Dell (*Trade and Industry*); K. Heslop (*Employment and Training*)

NORTH-WEST
*Secretariat:* 20th Floor, Sunley Tower, Piccadilly Plaza, Manchester M1 4BE
Tel 0161-838 5555

*Senior Regional Director (G3)*, Miss M. Neville-Rolfe
*Regional Directors (G3)*, J. Plowman (*Environment and Transport*); (*G4*), B. Chapman (*Trade and Industry*); (*G5*), B. Isherwood (*Regeneration*); P. Styche (*Housing and Planning*); P. Keen (*Employment and Training*)

SOUTH-EAST
*Secretariat:* Room 522, Charles House, 375 Kensington High Street, London W14 8QH
Tel 01345-125341

*Senior Regional Director (G3)*, Ms G. Ashmore
*Regional Directors (G5)*, B. Wilson (*Planning*); T. Radice (*Regeneration, Housing and Environment*); Ms A. Baker (*Transport*); E. Beston (*Trade and Industry*); D. Main (*Employment and Training*)

SOUTH-WEST
*Secretariat:* 4th Floor, The Pithay, Bristol BS1 2NQ
Tel 0117-945 6992

*Senior Regional Director (G3)*, B. Leonard
*Regional Directors (G5)*, S. McQuillin (*acting*) (*Devon and Cornwall*); P. Botham (*acting*) (*Environment and Transport*); J. Bowder (*Trade and Industry*); Ms W. Mauger (*Employment and Training*)

WEST MIDLANDS
*Secretariat:* 6th Floor, 77 Paradise Circus, Queensway, Birmingham BI 2DT
Tel 0121-212 5050

*Senior Regional Director (G3),* D. Ritchie
*Regional Directors (G4),* Dr M. Sutton *(Trade and Industry);*
(G5), Ms P. Holland *(Single Regeneration Budget);*
J. Northover *(Housing and Environment);* J. Darlington *(Planning and Transport);* H. Tollyfield *(Employment and Training)*

YORKSHIRE AND HUMBERSIDE
*Secretariat:* Room GO1, 25 Queen Street, Leeds LS1 2TW
Tel 0113-280 0600

*Senior Regional Director (G3),* J. Walker
*Regional Directors (G5),* I. Crowther *(Housing, Planning and Transport);* Ms E. Kerry *(Regeneration);* Ms S. Seymour *(Trade and Industry);* G. Dyche *(Employment and Training);* (G6), N. Best *(Strategy and Resources)*

---

## REVENUE ADJUDICATOR'S OFFICE

3rd Floor, Haymarket House, 28 Haymarket, London SW1Y 4SP
Tel 0171-930 2292

---

The Revenue Adjudicator is appointed by the Board of Inland Revenue to consider complaints about how the Inland Revenue or the Valuation Office Agency have handled someone's affairs. The Adjudicator's Office opened in July 1993.
*Revenue Adjudicator,* Ms E. Filkin
*Head of Office,* D. I. Richardson

---

## REVIEW BODIES

---

The secretariat for these bodies is provided by the Office of Manpower Economics *(see* page 330)

### ARMED FORCES PAY

The Review Body on Armed Forces Pay was appointed in 1971 to advise the Prime Minister on the pay and allowances of members of naval, military and air forces of the Crown and of any women's service administered by the Defence Council.
*Chairman,* G. M. Hourston
*Members,* C. M. Bolton; J. C. L. Cox; J. Crosby; The Baroness Dean of Thornton-le-Fylde; Air Chief Marshal Sir Roger Palin, KCB, OBE; Mrs D. Venables

### DOCTORS' AND DENTISTS' REMUNERATION

The Review Body on Doctors' and Dentists' Remuneration was set up in 1971 to advise the Prime Minister on the remuneration of doctors and dentists taking any part in the National Health Service.
*Chairman,* C. B. Gough
*Members,* D. G. Boyd; Ms T. Boyden; Miss S. Field; D. Fredjohn, MBE; Dr E. Nelson; D. Penton; Prof. G. F. Thomason, CBE

### NURSING STAFF, MIDWIVES, HEALTH VISITORS AND PROFESSIONS ALLIED TO MEDICINE

The Review Body for nursing staff, midwives, health visitors and professions allied to medicine was set up in 1983 to advise the Prime Minister on the remuneration of nursing staff, midwives and health visitors employed in the National Health Service; and also of physiotherapists, radiographers, remedial gymnasts, occupational therapists, orthoptists, chiropodists, dietitians and related grades employed in the National Health Service.
*Chairman,* M. Bett, CBE
*Members,* Mrs S. Gleig; J. Hildreth; Ms R. Lea; Miss A. Mackie, OBE; Dr Gillian Raab; Prof. G. F. Thomason, CBE; Miss D. Whittingham

### SCHOOL TEACHERS

The School Teachers' Review Body (STRB) is a statutory body, set up under the School Teachers' Pay and Conditions Act 1991. It is required to examine and report on such matters relating to the statutory conditions of employment of school teachers in England and Wales as may be referred to it by the Secretary of State for Education. The STRB's reports are submitted to the Prime Minister and the Secretary of State and the latter is required to publish them.
*Chairman,* J. Gardiner
*Members,* Mrs B. Amey; Sir Alan Cox, CBE; Mrs J. Cuthbertson; P. Halsey, CB, LVO; M. Harding; Mrs G. Rostron; Mrs A. Vinton

### SENIOR SALARIES

A Top Salaries Review Body was set up in 1971 to advise the Prime Minister on the remuneration of the higher judiciary and other judicial appointments, senior civil servants, and senior officers of the armed forces. In 1993 its name was changed to the Senior Salaries Review Body, and its remit was officially extended to cover the pay, pensions and allowances of MPs, ministers and others whose pay is determined by a Ministerial and Other Salaries Order, and the allowances of peers. It is also required to reward performance where appropriate, and to take into account equal opportunities policy.
*Chairman,* The Lord Nickson, KBE
*Members,* Prof. G. Bain; Sir Cecil Clothier, KCB, QC; Mrs R. Day; G. M. Hourston; Miss P. Mann; Mrs Y. Newbold; Sir Michael Perry, CBE; H. S. Pigott; Sir Anthony Wilson

---

## ROYAL BOTANIC GARDEN EDINBURGH

Inverleith Row, Edinburgh EH3 5LR
Tel 0131-552 7171

---

The Royal Botanic Garden (RBG) Edinburgh originated as the Physic Garden, established in 1670 beside the Palace of Holyroodhouse. Since 1986, RBG Edinburgh has been administered by a Board of Trustees established under the National Heritage (Scotland) Act 1985.

RBG Edinburgh is an international centre for scientific research on plant diversity, maintaining collections of living plants and reference resources, including a herbarium of some two million specimens of preserved plants. Other statutory functions of RBG Edinburgh include the provision of education and information on botany and horticulture, and the provision of public access to the living plant collections.

The Garden moved to its present site at Inverleith, Edinburgh in 1821. There are also three specialist gardens: Younger Botanic Garden Benmore, near Dunoon, Argyllshire; Logan Botanic Garden, near Stranraer, Wigtownshire; and Dawyck Botanic Garden, near Stobo, Peeblesshire.

Public opening hours: RBG Edinburgh, daily (except Christmas Day and New Year's Day) November–February 10–4; March–April and September–October 10–6; May–August 10–8; specialist gardens, March–October 10–6.
*Chairman of the Board of Trustees*, Prof. M. Wilkins, FRSE
*Regius Keeper*, Prof. D. S. Ingram
*Deputy Keeper*, Dr D. J. Mann

## ROYAL BOTANIC GARDENS KEW
Richmond, Surrey TW9 3AB
Tel 0181-940 1171
Wakehurst Place, Ardingly, nr. Haywards Heath, W. Sussex RH17 6TN
Tel 01444-892701

The Royal Botanic Gardens (RBG) Kew were originally laid out as a private garden for Kew House for George III's mother, HRH Princess Augusta, in 1759. They were much enlarged in the 19th century, notably by the inclusion of the grounds of the former Richmond Lodge. In 1965 the garden at Wakehurst Place was acquired; it is owned by the National Trust and managed by RBG Kew. Under the National Heritage Act 1983 a Board of Trustees was set up to administer the Gardens which in 1984 became an independent body supported by a grant-in-aid.

The functions of RBG Kew are to carry out research into plant sciences, to disseminate knowledge about plants and to provide the public with the opportunity to gain knowledge and enjoyment from the Gardens' collections. There are extensive national reference collections of living and preserved plants and a comprehensive library and archive. The main emphasis is on plant conservation and bio-diversity.

Open daily (except Christmas Day and New Year's Day) from 9.30 a.m. The closing hour varies from 4 p.m. in mid-winter to 6 p.m. on weekdays and 7.30 p.m. on Sundays and Bank Holidays in mid-summer. Admission (1994), £4.00. Concessionary schemes available. Museums open 9.30 a.m.; Glasshouses, 9.30–4.30 (winter); 9.30–5.30 (summer). No dogs except guide-dogs for the blind.

BOARD OF TRUSTEES
*Chairman*, R. A. E. Herbert
*Members*, R. P. Bauman; The Viscount Blakenham; C. D. Brickell, CBE; Prof. W. G. Chaloner, FRS; Sir Philip M. Dowson, CBE, RA; Mrs A. Lennox-Boyd; Prof. R. May, FRS; J. Pettifer; Jane Renfrew, PH.D.; The Earl of Selbourne, KBE, FRS; Mrs V. R. Wakefield
*Director*, Dr G. T. Prance, FRS

## ROYAL COMMISSION FOR THE EXHIBITION OF 1851
Sherfield Building, Imperial College of Science, Technology and Medicine, London SW7 2AZ
Tel 0171-225 6110

The Royal Commission was incorporated by supplemental charter as a permanent Commission after winding up the affairs of the Great Exhibition of 1851. Its object is to promote scientific and artistic education by means of funds derived from its Kensington estate, purchased with the surplus left over from the Great Exhibition.
*President*, HRH The Duke of Edinburgh, KG, KT, PC
*Chairman, Board of Management*, Sir Denis Rooke, CBE, FRS
*Secretary to Commissioners*, M. C. Neale, CB

## THE ROYAL MINT
Llantrisant, nr Pontyclun, Mid Glamorgan CF7 8YT
Tel 01443-222111

The prime responsibility of the Royal Mint is the provision of United Kingdom coinage, but it actively competes in world markets for a share of the available circulating coin business and, based on the last ten years, two-thirds of the 15,000 tonnes of coins produced annually is exported to more than 100 countries. The Mint also manufactures special proof and uncirculated quality coins in gold, silver and other metals; military and civil decorations and medals; commemorative and prize medals; and royal and official seals.

The Royal Mint became an executive agency responsible to the Chancellor of the Exchequer in April 1990.
*Master of the Mint*, The Chancellor of the Exchequer (ex officio)
*Deputy Master and Comptroller*, R. de L. Holmes

## ROYAL NATIONAL THEATRE BOARD
South Bank, London, SE1 9PX
Tel 0171-928 2033

The chairman and members of the Board of the Royal National Theatre are appointed by the Secretary of State for National Heritage.
*Chairman*, The Lady Soames, DBE
*Members*, The Hon. P. Benson; The Hon. Lady Cazalet; M. Codron, CBE; Lady Greenbury; Ms S. Hall; S. Lipton; Sir Derek Mitchell, KCB, CVO; D. Nandy; M. Oliver; The Rt. Hon. Sir Michael Palliser, GCMG; L. Sieff, OBE; T. Stoppard, CBE; S. Yassukovich, CBE
*Company Secretary and Head of Finance*, A. Blackstock
*Board and Committee Secretary*, M. McGregor

## RURAL DEVELOPMENT COMMISSION
141 Castle Street, Salisbury, Wilts. SP1 3TP
Tel 01722-336255

The Rural Development Commission was formed in 1988 by the merger of the Development Commission for Rural England and the Council for Small Industries in Rural Areas. Statutorily it is the Development Commission, but it is known as the Rural Development Commission as this is a better indication of its functions. It is funded by government grant-in-aid. It advises the Government on economic and social matters affecting rural areas, and its prime aim is to stimulate job creation and the provision of essential services in the countryside.
*Chairman*, The Lord Shuttleworth
*Deputy Chairman*, R. Thompson
*Chief Executive*, R. Butt
*Deputy Chief Executive*, J. Taylor

## SCOTT INQUIRY
— see page 323

## SCOTTISH COURTS ADMINISTRATION
— see page 380

## SCOTTISH ENTERPRISE
120 Bothwell Street, Glasgow G2 7JP
Tel 0141-248 2700

In 1991 Scottish Enterprise took over the economic development and environmental improvement functions of the Scottish Development Agency and the training functions of the Training Agency in lowland Scotland. Its remit is to further the development of Scotland's economy, to enhance the skills of the Scottish workforce, to promote Scotland's international competitiveness and to improve the environment. Many of its functions are contracted out to a network of local enterprise companies. Through Locate in Scotland (*see* page 353), Scottish Enterprise is also concerned with attracting firms to Scotland.
*Chairman*, Prof. D. MacKay
*Chief Executive*, C. Beveridge
*Senior Management Team*, C. Aitken; P. Brady;
R. Crawford; R. Downes; R. Griggs; J. Lord;
R. Macfarlane; A. Proctor

## SCOTTISH HOMES
Thistle House, 91 Haymarket Terrace, Edinburgh EH12 5HE
Tel 0131-313 0044

Scottish Homes, the national housing agency for Scotland, aims to improve the quality and variety of housing available in Scotland by working in partnership with the public and private sectors. The agency is a major funder of new and improved housing provided by housing associations and private developers. It is currently transferring its own 50,000 rented houses to alternative landlords. It is also involved in housing research and in piloting innovative housing solutions. Board members are appointed by the Secretary of State for Scotland.
*Chairman*, Sir James Mellon
*Chief Executive*, P. McKinlay

## SCOTTISH NATURAL HERITAGE
12 Hope Terrace, Edinburgh EH9 2AS
Tel 0131-447 4784

Scottish Natural Heritage came into existence in 1992 under the Natural Heritage (Scotland) Act 1991. It provides advice on nature conservation to all those whose activities affect wildlife, landforms and features of geological interest in Scotland, and seeks to develop and improve facilities for the enjoyment of the Scottish countryside.
*Chairman*, M. Magnusson, KBE
*Chief Executive*, R. Crofts
*Chief Scientific Adviser*, M. B. Usher
*Director of Policy*, J. Thomson
*Director of Communications*, D. Campbell
*Director of Resources*, Ms L. Montgomery

## SCOTTISH OFFICE

The Secretary of State for Scotland is responsible in Scotland for a wide range of statutory functions which in England and Wales are the responsibility of a number of departmental ministers. He also works closely with ministers in charge of Great Britain departments on topics of special significance to Scotland within their fields of responsibility. His statutory functions are administered by five main departments: the Scottish Office Agriculture and Fisheries Department, the Scottish Office Education Department, the Scottish Office Environment Department, the Scottish Office Home and Health Department, and the Scottish Office Industry Department. These departments plus Central Services are collectively known as the Scottish Office.

In addition there are a number of other Scottish departments for which the Secretary of State has some degree of responsibility; these include the Scottish Courts Administration, the General Register Office, the Scottish Record Office and the Department of the Registers of Scotland. The Secretary of State also bears ministerial responsibility for the activities in Scotland of several statutory bodies, such as the Forestry Commission, whose functions extend throughout Great Britain.

Dover House, Whitehall, London, SW1A 2AU
Tel 0171-270 3000

*Secretary of State for Scotland*, The Rt. Hon. Ian Lang, MP
   *Private Secretary (G5)*, M. B. Foulis
   *Special Advisers*, A. Young; G. Mackay
   *Parliamentary Private Secretary*, S. Coombs, MP
*Minister of State*, The Lord Fraser of Carmyllie, PC, QC
   *(Education, Health and Home Affairs, and General European Issues)*
   *Private Secretary*, Ms S. J. Morrell
*Parliamentary Under-Secretaries of State*, Lord James Douglas-Hamilton, MP; J. Allan Stewart, MP; Sir Hector Monro, MP
   *Private Secretaries*, Ms J. Macbeth; Mrs J. Serafini; D. T. Robb
   *Parliamentary Clerk*, Mrs L. J. Stirling
*Permanent Under-Secretary of State (G1)*, Sir Russell Hillhouse, KCB
   *Private Secretary*, Miss S. C. Gartside

LIAISON DIVISION
*Assistant Secretary (G5)*, E. W. Ferguson

St Andrew's House, Edinburgh EH1 3DG
Tel 0131-556 8400

MANAGEMENT GROUP SUPPORT STAFF
*Principal (G7)*, Ms M. M. A. McGinn

CENTRAL SERVICES
*Grade 2*, G. R. Wilson, CB

PERSONNEL GROUP
16 Waterloo Place Edinburgh, EH1 3DN
Tel 0131-556 8400

*Principal Establishment Officer (G3)*, C. C. MacDonald
*Assistant Secretaries (G5)*, G. D. Calder; W. R. J. McQueen
*Senior Principals (G6)*, C. D. Henderson; I. C. Henderson; W. E. Bennet

ADMINISTRATIVE SERVICES
James Craig Walk, Edinburgh EH1 3BA
Tel 0131-556 8400

*Director of Administrative Services (G4)*, R. S. B. Gordon
*Assistant Secretary (G5)*, D. Stevenson
*Head of Information Technology (G5)*, A. M. Brown
*Head of IT Services (G6)*, I. W. Goodwin
*Director of Telecommunications (G6)*, K. Henderson
*Chief Estates Officer (G6)*, R. I. K. White, FRICS

FINANCE DIVISION
New St Andrew's House, Edinburgh EH1 3TG
Tel 0131-556 8400

*Principal Finance Officer (G3)*, Miss E. A MacKay
*Assistant Secretaries (G5)*, J. S. Aldridge; Dr P. S. Collings;
D. Crawley; Ms I. M. Low; B. Naylor; D. G. N. Reid;
W. T. Tait
*Director of Financial Systems Unit (G6)*, R. Smith

SOLICITOR'S OFFICE
For the Scottish departments and certain UK services,
including HM Treasury, in Scotland

*Solicitor (G2)*, R. Brodie, CB
*Deputy Solicitor (G3)*, N. W. Boe
*Divisional Solicitors (G5)*, K. F. Barclay; R. Bland (*seconded
to Scottish Law Commission*); G. C. Duke; I. H. Harvie;
R. M. Henderson; J. L. Jamieson; H. F. Macdiarmid;
J. G. S. Maclean; N. Raven; Mrs L. A. Wallace

SCOTTISH OFFICE INFORMATION DIRECTORATE
For the Scottish departments and certain UK services

*Director (G5)*, Ms E. S. B. Drummond
*Deputy Director (G6)*, W. A. McNeill

## SCOTTISH OFFICE AGRICULTURE AND FISHERIES DEPARTMENT
Pentland House, 47 Robb's Loan, Edinburgh EH14 1TY
Tel 0131-556 8400

*Secretary (G2)*, K. J. MacKenzie
*Under-Secretary (G3)*, T. A. Cameron
*Fisheries Secretary (G3)*, G. Robson
*Assistant Secretaries (G5)*, D. R. Dickson; J. Duffy;
I. W. Gordon; R. A. Grant; A. K. MacLeod;
A. J. Matheson; K. W. Moore; A. J. Rushworth;
I. M. Whitelaw
*Chief Agricultural Officer (G4)*, W. A. Macgregor
*Deputy Chief Agricultural Officer (G5)*, J. I. Woodrow
*Assistant Chief Agricultural Officers (G6)*, D. R. J. Craven;
J. A. Hardie; J. G. Muir; A. Robb; A. J. Robertson
*Chief Agricultural Economist (G6)*, J. R. Wildgoose, D.Phil.
*Chief Meat and Livestock Inspector (G7)*, vacant
*Chief Food and Dairy Officer (G7)*, D. J. MacDonald
*Chief Surveyor (G6)*, N. Taylor, FRICS
*Scientific Adviser (G5)*, T. W. Hegarty, Ph.D.
*Senior Principal Scientific Officers (G6)*, Dr D. Jenkinson;
Mrs L. A. D. Turl

SCOTTISH AGRICULTURAL SCIENCE AGENCY
East Craigs, Edinburgh EH12 8NJ
Tel 0131-556 8400

An executive agency within the Scottish Office. The Agency
provides scientific information and advice on agricultural
and horticultural crops and the environment, and has various
statutory and regulatory functions.
*Director (G5)*, Dr R. K. M. Hay
*Deputy Director (G6)*, S. R. Cooper
*Senior Principal Scientific Officer (G6)*, A. D. Ruthven

FISHERIES RESEARCH SERVICES
Marine Laboratory, PO Box 101, Victoria Road, Torry,
Aberdeen AB9 8DB
Tel 01224-876544

*Director of Fisheries Research for Scotland (G4)*,
Prof. A. D. Hawkins, Ph.D., FRSE
*Deputy Director (G6)*, D. N. MacLennan
*Senior Principal Scientific Officers (G6)*, R. M. Cook, Ph.D.;
J. M. Davies, Ph.D.; A. L. S. Munro, Ph.D.;
P. A. M. Stewart, Ph.D.; C. S. Wardle, Ph.D

*Freshwater Fisheries Laboratory*
Faskally, Pitlochry, Perthshire PH16 5LB
Tel 01796-472060

*Senior Principal Scientific Officers (G6)*, R. G. J. Shelton,
Ph.D.; J. E. Thorpe, Ph.D.
*Inspector of Salmon and Freshwater Fisheries for Scotland
(G7)*, R. B. Williamson

*Scottish Fisheries Protection Agency*
Pentland House, 47 Robb's Loan, Edinburgh EH14 1TW
Tel 0131-556 8400

An executive agency within the Scottish Office. The Agency
enforces fisheries law and regulations in Scottish waters and
ports.
*Chief Executive (G5)*, A. K. MacLeod
*Director of Policy and Resources (G6)*, J. B. Roddin
*Director of Operations (G6)*, R. J. Walker
*Marine Superintendent*, Capt. R. M. Mill-Irving

## SCOTTISH OFFICE ENVIRONMENT DEPARTMENT
New St Andrew's House, Edinburgh EH1 3TG
Tel 0131-556 8400

*Secretary (G2)*, H. H. Mills
*Under-Secretaries (G3)*, J. S. Graham; S. F. Hampson;
A. M. Russell
*Assistant Secretaries (G5)*, M. T. Affolter; M. Batho;
J. T. Birley; D. J. Chalmers; J. A. Ewing; Dr
J. M. Francis; J. W. L. Lonie; D. F. Middleton;
J. N. Randall; E. C. Reavley; J. A. Rennie; A. M. Russell

PROFESSIONAL STAFF
*Chief Engineer (G3)*, A. C. Paton
*Deputy Chief Engineer (G5)*, T. D. Macdonald
*Assistant Chief Engineers (G6)*, P. Bolton; D. MacFarlane;
P. Wright
*Director of Building and Chief Architect (G3)*, J. E. Gibbons,
Ph.D., FSA SCOT.
*Deputy Director of Building and Deputy Chief Architect (G5)*,
C. Gray
*Deputy Director (G6)*, A. J. Wyllie
*Chief Planner (G4)*, A. Mackenzie
*Deputy Chief Planner (G5)*, D. R. Dare
*Assistant Chief Planners (G6)*, A. W. Denham; I. R. Duncan;
S. G. Fulton; T. Williamson
*HM Chief Industrial Pollution Inspector (G5)*,
I. W. W. Wright

LOCAL GOVERNMENT FINANCE GROUP
New St Andrew's House, Edinburgh EH1 3TB
Tel 0131-556 8400

*Assistant Secretaries (G5)*, A. G. Beattie; K. W. McKay

INQUIRY REPORTERS
16 Waterloo Place, Edinburgh EH1 3DN
Tel 0131-556 8400

*Chief Reporter (G3)*, Miss G. Pain
*Deputy Chief Reporter (G5)*, R. M. Hickman

HISTORIC SCOTLAND
Longmore House, Salisbury Place, Edinburgh EH9 1SH
Tel 0131-668 8600

An executive agency within the Scottish Office. The agency's
role is to protect Scotland's historic monuments, buildings
and lands, and to promote public understanding and
enjoyment of them.
*Chief Executive (G3)*, G. N. Munro
*Directors (G5)*, F. J. Lawrie; D. Macniven, TD; I. Maxwell;
*(G6)*, S. Rosie

*Chief Inspector of Ancient Monuments*, Dr D. J. Breeze
*Chief Inspector, Building Division*, J. R. Hume

## SCOTTISH OFFICE INDUSTRY DEPARTMENT

New St Andrew's House, Edinburgh EH1 3TG
Tel 0131-556 8400

*Secretary (G2)*, P. MacKay, CB
*Under-Secretaries (G3)*, J. W. Elvidge; E. J. Weeple
*Assistant Secretaries (G5)*, D. A. Brew; D. A. Campbell;
   M. J. P. Cunliffe; A. W. Fraser; I. F. Gray;
   P. Hetherington; R. N. Irvine; R. MacEwan; R. Tait;
   G. M. D. Thomson
*Senior Economic Advisers (G5)*, Dr A. Goudie; C. L. Wood

PROFESSIONAL STAFF
*Director of Roads (G3)*, J. A. L. Dawson
*Deputy Chief Engineer (Roads) (G5)*, J. A. Howison
*Deputy Chief Engineer (Bridges) (G5)*, J. Innes
*Assistant Chief Engineers (G6)*, N. B. MacKenzie;
   I. McIntosh

INDUSTRIAL EXPANSION
Alhambra House, 45 Waterloo Street, Glasgow G2 6AT
Tel 0141-248 2855

*Under-Secretary (G3)*, G. Robson
*Industrial Adviser*, Dr C. K. Benington
*Scientific Adviser*, I. McGhee
*Assistant Secretaries (G5)*, J. W. H. Irvine; J. McGhee;
   J. Meldrum

LOCATE IN SCOTLAND
120 Bothwell Street, Glasgow G2 7JP
Tel 0141-248 2700

*Director (G4)*, R. Crawford
*Senior Principal (G6)*, W. Malone
*Principal (G7)*, A. McCabe; P. A. D. Ritchie
*Director (North America)*, R. Crawford

SCOTTISH TRADE INTERNATIONAL
120 Bothwell Street, Glasgow G2 7JP
Tel 0141-248 2700

*Director*, D. Taylor

## SCOTTISH OFFICE EDUCATION DEPARTMENT

New St Andrew's House, Edinburgh EH1 3TG
Tel 0131-556 8400

*Secretary (G2)*, G. R. Wilson, CB
*Under-Secretaries (G3)*, W. A. P. Weatherston, CB;
   J. S. B. Martin
*Assistant Secretaries (G5)*, D. S. Henderson; R. D. Jackson;
   T. J. Kelly; G. McHugh; Miss M. MacLean; *Mrs
   V. MacNiven; *Mrs N. S. Munro
*Chief Statistician (G5)*, G. C. Jones

* part-time

HM INSPECTORS OF SCHOOLS
*Senior Chief Inspector (G3)*, T. N. Gallacher
*Deputy Senior Chief Inspectors (G4)*, W. T. Beveridge;
   D. A. Osler
*Chief Inspectors (G5)*, J. Boyes; G. H. C. Donaldson; Miss
   K. M. Fairweather; G. P. D. Gordon; D. E. Kelso;
   J. J. McDonald; A. S. McGlynn; M. Roebuck;
   H. M. Stalker; R. M. S. Tuck
There are 90 Grade 6 Inspectors.

STUDENT AWARDS AGENCY FOR SCOTLAND
Gyleview House, 3 Redheughs Rigg, Edinburgh EH12 9HH
Tel 0131-244 5715

An executive agency within the Scottish Office.
*Chief Executive*, K. MacRae
*Deputy Chief Executive*, J. G. Donnelly

## SCOTTISH OFFICE HOME AND HEALTH DEPARTMENT

St Andrew's House, Edinburgh EH1 3DG
Tel 0131-556 8400

*Secretary (G2)*, J. Hamill
*Under-Secretaries (G3)*, D. Belfall; N. G. Campbell;
   D. J. Essery; Mrs G. M. Stewart
*Assistant Secretaries (G5)*, Mrs M. H. Brannan; J. T. Brown;
   Mrs M. B. Gunn; C. M. A. Lugton; C. K. McIntosh;
   P. M. Russell; R. H. Scott
*Senior Principal (G6)*, N. MacLeod

NATIONAL HEALTH SERVICE IN SCOTLAND
MANAGEMENT EXECUTIVE
*Chief Executive*, G. Scaife
*Director of Strategic Management*, G. A. Anderson
*Director of Finance*, vacant
*Director of Administration*, Dr D. Steel
*Director of Information Services*, C. B. Knox
*Director of Manpower*, M. Sibbald
*Assistant Secretaries (G5)*, W. J. Farquhar; W. Moyes;
   Mrs A. Robson; G. M. D. Thomson; G. W. Tucker
*Assistant Director (G6)*, H. R. McCallum
*Senior Principal (G6)*, Miss J. McGregor

MEDICAL SERVICES
*Chief Medical Officer (G2)*, Prof. R. E. Kendell, CBE, MD
*Deputy Chief Medical Officer (G3)*, Dr A. B. Young, FRCPE
*Principal Medical Officers*, Dr J. V. Basson;
   Dr C. F. Fleming; Dr Margaret Hennigan; Dr Rosalind
   Skinner; Dr Elizabeth Sowler
*Senior Medical Officers*, R. E. G. Aitken, TD; Dr Angela
   Anderson; I. R. Bashford; P. W. Brooks; S. Capewell; Dr
   D. J. Ewing; Dr A. Findlay; Dr D. Jolliffe; Ms E. Keel;
   Dr Sheila Lawson; Dr Patricia Madden; Dr A. MacLeod;
   B. T. Potter; Dr R. Simmons; Dr O. A. Thores
*Chief Scientist*, Prof. I. A. D. Bouchier, CBE, FRCP
*Chief Dental Officer*, J. R. Wild
*Deputy Chief Dental Officer*, M. Yewe-Dyer
*Regional Dental Officers*, K. J. McKenzie; M. G. Platt; Miss
   A. J. Power; G. A. Reid
*Chief Nursing Officer*, Miss A. Jarvie
*Chief Pharmacist (G5)*, W. Scott
*Chief Research Officer*, Dr C. P. A. Levein
*Senior Principal Research Officers (G6)*, Dr
   D. M. McAllister; Dr Jacqueline Tombs

SOCIAL WORK SERVICES GROUP
43 Jeffrey Street, Edinburgh EH1 1DN
Tel 0131-556 8400

*Assistant Secretaries (G5)*, G. A. Anderson; Ms L. J. Clare;
   Mrs R. Menlowe; J. W. Sinclair
*Chief Inspector of Social Work Services*, A. Skinner
*Assistant Chief Inspectors*, Mrs H. Dempster;
   Ms M. L. Hunt; F. A. O'Leary; D. Pia; I. C. Robertson

MISCELLANEOUS APPOINTMENTS
*HM Chief Inspector of Constabulary*, J. Boyd, CBE, QPM
*HM Chief Inspector of Prisons*, A. H. Bishop, CB
*Commandant, Scottish Police College*, H. I. Watson, QPM
*HM Chief Inspector of Fire Services*, N. Morrison
*Commandant, Scottish Fire Service Training School*,
   C. F. McManus, QFSM
*Secretary, Scottish Health Service Advisory Council*,
   W. J. Farquhar

SCOTTISH OFFICE PENSIONS AGENCY
St Margaret's House, 151 London Road, Edinburgh EH8 7TG
Tel 0131-244 3217

An executive agency within the Scottish Office. The Agency is responsible for the pension arrangements of some 300,000 people, mainly NHS and teaching services employees and pensioners.
*Chief Executive*, N. MacLeod
*Directors (G7)*, G. Mowat (*Policy*); A. M. Small (*Operations*); J. Edgar (*Resources and Customer Services*)

SCOTTISH PRISON SERVICE
Calton House, 5 Redheughs Rigg, Edinburgh EH12 9HW
Tel 0131-556 8400

An executive agency within the Scottish Office.
*Chief Executive of Scottish Prison Service (G3)*, E. W. Frizzell
*Deputy Chief Executive and Director of Prisons (G5)*, A. R. Walker
*Director, Human Resources (G5)*, J. D. Gallagher
*Director, Finance and Information Services (G5)*, W. Pretswell
*Director, Strategy and Planning (G5)*, D. A. Stewart
*Deputy Director, Regime Services and Supplies (G6)*, N. Harvey
*Deputy Director, Estates and Buildings (G6)*, D. D. Sutherland
*Area Director, South and West (G5)*, J. Milne
*Area Director, North and East (G5)*, J. Pearce
*Governor, Scottish Prison Service College*, R. L. Houchin

PRISONS

ABERDEEN, Craiginches, Aberdeen AB9 2HN. *Governor*, W. A. R. Rattray
BARLINNIE, Barlinnie, Glasgow G33 2QX. *Governor*, P. Withers
BARLINNIE SPECIAL UNIT, Barlinnie, Glasgow G33 2QX. *Governor*, Ms S. Brooks
CASTLE HUNTLY YOUNG OFFENDERS INSTITUTION, Castle Huntly, Longforgan, nr Dundee DD2 5HL. *Governor*, Mrs M. Wood
CORNTON VALE, Cornton Road, Stirling FK9 5NY. *Governor*, R. H. H. Colen
DUMFRIES YOUNG OFFENDERS INSTITUTION, Terregles Street, Dumfries DG2 9AX. *Governor*, G. Taylor
DUNGAVEL, Dungavel House, Strathaven, Lanarkshire ML10 6RF. *Governor*, J. Bywalec
EDINBURGH, Saughton, Edinburgh EH1 3LN. *Governor*, J. Durno
FRIARTON, Friarton, Perth PH2 8DW. *Governor*, E. A. Gordon
GLENOCHIL PRISON AND YOUNG OFFENDERS INSTITUTION, King O'Muir Road, Tullibody, Clackmannanshire FK10 3AD. *Governor*, L. McBain
GREENOCK, Gateside, Greenock PA16 9AH. *Governor*, D. E. Gunn
INVERNESS, Porterfield, Inverness IV2 3HH. *Governor*, W. M. Weir
LONGRIGGEND REMAND INSTITUTION, Longriggend, nr Airdrie, Lanarkshire ML6 7TL. *Governor*, A. F. King
LOW MOSS, Low Moss, Bishopbriggs, Glasgow G64 2QB. *Governor*, W. Davidson
NORANSIDE, Noranside, Fern, By Forfar, Angus DD8 3QY. *Governor*, E. Brownsmith
PENNINGHAME, Penninghame, Newton Stewart DG8 6RG. *Governor*, H. Ross
PERTH, 3 Edinburgh Road, Perth PH2 8AT. *Governor*, M. Duffy

PETERHEAD, Salthouse Head, Peterhead, Aberdeenshire AB4 6YY. *Governor*, A. P. Spencer
POLMONT YOUNG OFFENDERS INSTITUTION, Brightons, Falkirk, Stirlingshire FK2 0AB. *Governor*, W. McKinlay
SHOTTS, Shotts ML7 4LF. *Governor*, G. M. Shearer, OBE
SHOTTS ALTERNATIVE UNIT, Shotts ML7 4LF. *Governor*, A. McVicar

MENTAL WELFARE COMMISSION FOR SCOTLAND
25 Drumsheugh Gardens, Edinburgh EH3 7NS
Tel 0131-225 7034

*Chairman*, Sheriff H. J. Aronson
*Commissioners*, Mrs A. Baxter; P. H. Brodie; R. G. Davis; Ms A. M. Green; Mrs M. Jeffcoat; Dr M. Livingston; Dr D. McCall-Smith; Dr M. McCreadie; J. Murray; Miss L. M. Noble; J. G. Sutherland
*Medical Commissioners*, J. A. T. Dyer; A. Jacques
*Social Work Commissioner*, C. E. McGregor
*Secretary*, R. Mitchell

COUNSEL TO THE SECRETARY OF STATE FOR SCOTLAND UNDER THE PRIVATE LEGISLATION PROCEDURE (SCOTLAND) ACT 1936
50 Frederick Street, Edinburgh EH2 1EX
Tel 0131-226 6499

*Senior Counsel*, G. S. Douglas, QC
*Junior Counsel*, N. M. P. Morrison

NATIONAL HEALTH SERVICE, SCOTLAND

HEALTH BOARDS

ARGYLL AND CLYDE, Ross House, Hawkhead Road, Paisley. *Chairman*, R. R. Reid; *General Manager*, I. C. Smith
AYRSHIRE AND ARRAN, PO Box 13, Hunters Avenue, Ayr. *Chairman*, J. W. G. Donaldson, CBE; *General Manager*, J. M. Eckford, OBE
BORDERS, Huntlyburn, Melrose, Roxburghshire. *Chairman*, D. A. C. Kilshaw; *General Manager*, D. A. Peters, OBE
DUMFRIES AND GALLOWAY, Nithbank, Dumfries. *Chairman*, J. A. M. McIntyre, OBE; *General Manager*, D. Banks
FIFE, Springfield House, Cupar. *Chairman*, R. Baker, OBE; *General Manager*, Miss P. Frost
FORTH VALLEY, 33 Spittal Street, Stirling. *Chairman*, Mrs J. D. Isbister; *General Manager*, D. Hird
GRAMPIAN, Summerfield House, Eday Road, Aberdeen. *Chairman*, C. MacLeod, CBE; *General Manager*, F. E. L. Hartnett, OBE
GREATER GLASGOW, 112 Ingram Street, Glasgow. *Chairman*, Sir Robert Calderwood; *General Manager (acting)*, T. A. Divers
HIGHLAND, Reay House, 17 Old Edinburgh Road, Inverness. *Chairman*, J. D. M. Robertson, CBE; *General Manager*, Dr G. V. Stone
LANARKSHIRE, 14 Beckford Street, Hamilton, Lanarkshire. *Chairman*, I. Livingstone, OBE; *General Manager*, Prof. F. Clark, CBE
LOTHIAN, 148 The Pleasance, Edinburgh. *Chairman*, Dr J. W. Baynham, CBE; *General Manager*, J. Lusby
ORKNEY, Balfour Hospital, New Scapa Road, Kirkwall, Orkney. *Chairman*, J. Leslie; *General Manager*, E. Jackson
SHETLAND, Brevik House, Lerwick. *Chairman*, Mrs F. Grains, OBE; *General Manager*, B. J. Atherton

TAYSIDE, PO Box 75, Vernonholme, Riverside Drive, Dundee. *Chairman*, J. C. MacFarlane, OBE; *General Manager*, Miss L. Barrie

WESTERN ISLES, 37 South Beach Street, Stornoway, Isle of Lewis. *Chairman*, A. Matheson; *General Manager*, R. Mullan

## HEALTH EDUCATION BOARD FOR SCOTLAND
Woodburn House, Canaan Lane, Edinburgh EH10 4SG
Tel 0131-447 8044

*Chairman*, E. Walker
*General Manager*, Dr A. Tannahill

## STATE HOSPITAL
Carstairs Junction, Lanark ML11 8RP
Tel 01555-840293

*Chairman*, P. Hamilton-Grierson
*General Manager*, R. Manson

## COMMON SERVICES AGENCY
Trinity Park House, South Trinity Road, Edinburgh EH5 3SE
Tel 0131-552 6255

*Chairman*, G. Scaife
*General Manager*, J. T. Donald

## GENERAL REGISTER OFFICE
New Register House, Edinburgh EH1 3YT
Tel 0131-334 0380

The General Register Office for Scotland is an executive agency of the Scottish Office. It is the office of the Registrar-General for Scotland, who has responsibility for civil registration and the taking of censuses in Scotland and has in his custody the following records: the statutory registers of births, deaths, still births, adoptions, marriages and divorces; the old parish registers (recording births, marriages, deaths, etc., before civil registration began in 1855); and records of censuses of the population in Scotland. Hours of public access: Monday–Thursday 9–4.30; Friday 9–4.
*Registrar-General (G4)*, Dr C. M. Glennie, CBE
*Deputy Registrar-General (G5)*, B. V. Philp
*Senior Principal (G6)*, D. A. Orr
*Principals (G7)*, D. B. L. Brownlee; R. C. Lawson; F. D. Garvie
*Statisticians (G7)*, J. Arrundale; G. W. L. Jackson; F. G. Thomas

## SEA FISH INDUSTRY AUTHORITY
18 Logie Mill, Logie Green Road, Edinburgh EH7 4HG
Tel 0131-558 3331

Established under the Fisheries Act 1981, the Authority is required to promote the efficiency of the sea fish industry. It carries out research relating to the industry and gives advice on related matters. It provides training, promotes the marketing, consumption and export of sea fish and sea fish products, and may provide financial assistance for the improvement of fishing vessels in respect of essential safety equipment.
*Chairman*, B. Skipper, CBE
*Chief Executive*, P. D. Chaplin
*Assistant Secretary*, D. Robertson
*Technical Director*, J. E. Tumilty
*Marketing Director*, R. M. Kennedy
*Training Director*, K. Waind

## THE SECURITY SERVICE COMMISSIONER
c/o The Home Office, 50 Queen Anne's Gate, London SW1H 9AT

The Commissioner is appointed by the Prime Minister. He keeps under review the issue of warrants by the Home Secretary under the Security Service Act 1989, and is required to help the Security Service Tribunal by investigating complaints which allege interference with property and by offering all such assistance in discharging its functions as it may require. He is also required to submit an annual report on the discharge of his functions to the Prime Minister.
*Commissioner*, The Rt. Hon. Lord Justice Stuart-Smith

## SECURITY SERVICE TRIBUNAL
PO Box 18, London SE1 0TZ

The Security Service Act 1989 established a tribunal of three to five senior members of the legal profession, independent of the Government and appointed by The Queen, to investigate complaints from any person about anything which they believe the Security Service has done to them or to their property.
*President*, The Rt. Hon. Lord Justice Simon Brown
*Vice-President*, Sheriff J. McInnes, QC
*Member*, Sir Richard Gaskell

## SERIOUS FRAUD OFFICE
Elm House, 10–16 Elm Street, London, WC1X 0BJ
Tel 0171-239 7272

The Serious Fraud Office is an autonomous department under the superintendence of the Attorney-General. Its remit is to investigate and prosecute serious and complex fraud. (Other fraud cases are currently handled by the fraud investigation unit of the Crown Prosecution Service, but the Government is proposing to establish a single body to handle all fraud cases.) The scope of its powers covers England, Wales and Northern Ireland. The staff includes lawyers, accountants and other support staff; investigating teams work closely with the police.
*Director*, G. Staple
*Deputy Director*, J. Knox

## DEPARTMENT OF SOCIAL SECURITY
Richmond House, 79 Whitehall, London, SW1A 2NS
Tel 0171-210 3000

The Department of Social Security is responsible for the payment of benefits and the collection of contributions under the National Insurance and Industrial Injuries schemes, and for the payment of child benefit, one-parent benefit, Income Support and Family Credit. It administers the Social Fund, and is responsible for assessing the means of applicants for legal aid. It is also responsible for the payment of war pensions.
*Secretary of State for Social Security*, The Rt. Hon. Peter Lilley, MP
*Private Secretary*, Ms J. Rintoul
*Special Adviser*, P. Barnes

*Parliamentary Private Secretary*, P. Merchant, MP
*Minister of State*, William Hague, MP (*Social Security and Disabled People*)
*Private Secretary*, I. Spur
*Minister of State*, The Lord Mackay of Ardbrecknish
*Private Secretary*, Ms C. Poulson
*Parliamentary Under-Secretaries of State*, Alistair Burt, MP; Roger Evans, MP; James Arbuthnot, MP
*Private Secretaries*, D. Higlett; Ms H. Nicholas
*Parliamentary Private Secretary*, I. Bruce, MP
*Permanent Secretary (G1)*, Sir Michael Partridge, KCB
*Private Secretary*, Ms H. Todd

## RESOURCE MANAGEMENT AND PLANNING GROUP
*Deputy Secretary (G2)*, B. Gilmore

CORPORATE STRATEGY AND PERSONNEL DIVISION
*Grade 3*, S. Hewitt
*Chief Statisticians (G5)*, N. Dyson; M. McDowall
*Senior Economic Advisers (G5)*, J. Ball; G. Harris
*Deputy Chief Scientific Officer (G5)*, D. Barnbrook
*Chief Research Officer (G5)*, Ms S. Duncan

*ANALYTICAL SERVICES DIVISION
*Director (G3)*, D. Stanton

FINANCE DIVISION
*Grade 3*, J. Tross

## SOCIAL SECURITY POLICY GROUP
*Deputy Secretary (G2)*, R. A. Birch

*SOCIAL SECURITY DIVISION A
*Under-Secretary (G3)*, B. Walmsley
*Assistant Secretaries (G5)*, N. Ward; K. Limm; J. Groombridge; Mrs C. Rookes; Mrs A. Lingwood

*SOCIAL SECURITY DIVISION B
*Under-Secretary (G3)*, M. Whippman
*Assistant Secretaries (G5)*, B. Calderwood; Miss G. Moor; C. B. Evans; Mrs L. Richards

*SOCIAL SECURITY DIVISION C
*Under Secretary (G3)*, Miss M. Peirson
*Assistant Secretaries (G5)*, Mrs C. Souter; Miss J. Liebling; D. Hill; Ms J. Clayton

*SOCIAL SECURITY DIVISION D
*Under-Secretary (G3)*, R. Brown
*Assistant Secretaries (G5)*, Ms N. Bastin; D. Jackson; O. C. L. Thorpe; R. H. Layton; I. Williams

*SOCIAL SECURITY DIVISION E
*Under-Secretary (G3)*, D. Brereton
*Assistant Secretaries (G5)*, S. Wilcox; D. Allsop
*Grade 6*, P. Morgan

INFORMATION DIVISION
*Head of Information (G5)*, S. Reardon
*Deputy Head of Information (G6)*, T. Grace
*Principal Information Officer (G7)*, J. Bretherton
*Chief Publicity Officer (G7)*, Ms H. Midlane

## SOLICITOR'S OFFICE
*Solicitor (G2)*, P. K. J. Thompson

SOLICITOR'S DIVISION A
New Court, 48 Carey Street, London WC2A 2LS
Tel 0171-412 1342

---

*At the Adelphi, 1–11 John Adam Street, London WC2N 6HT. Tel: 0171-962 8000

*Principal Assistant Solicitor (G3)*, Mrs G. S. Kerrigan
*Assistant Solicitors (G5)*, D. P. Dunleavy; J. M. Swainson; Mrs M. Astbury; Mrs G. Massiah; Miss A. V. Windsor; K. K. Baublys

SOLICITOR'S DIVISION B
New Court, 48 Carey Street, London WC2A 2LS
Tel 0171-412 1370

*Proceedings Operational Director (G4)*, P. C. Nilsson
*Assistant Solicitors (G5)*, S. M. Cooper; R. G. S. Aitken; R. S. Powell; C. G. Blake

SOLICITOR'S DIVISION C
New Court, 48 Carey Street, London WC2A 2LS
Tel 0171-412 1466

*Principal Assistant Solicitor (G3)*, A. D. Roberts
*Assistant Solicitors (G5)*, Miss R. Lester; P. Milledge; R. J. Dormer; J. F. McCleary; J. P. Canlin

## MAXWELL PENSIONS UNIT
7 St James's Square, London SW1Y 4JU
Tel 0171-839 3599

*Director (G5)*, R. P. Cleasby

## EXECUTIVE AGENCIES

BENEFITS AGENCY
Quarry House, Quarry Hill, Leeds LS2 7UA
Tel 0113-232 4000

The Agency administers claims for and payments of social security benefits.
*Chief Executive (G2)*, M. Bichard
  *Private Secretary (G4)*, T. Moran
*Directors (G3)*, D. Riggs (*finance*); G. Bardwell (*personnel*)
*Directors of Territories (G3)*, A. J. Laurance (*Scotland/Northern England*); (*G4*), A. Cleveland (*Southern England*); I. Stewart (*Wales/Central England*)

*Benefits Agency Medical Services*
*Director (G3)*, Dr P. Castaldi
*Principal Medical Officers*, Dr M. Aylward; Dr P. Dewis; Dr C. Hudson; Dr P. Doughty

INFORMATION TECHNOLOGY SERVICES AGENCY
4th Floor, Verulam Point, Station Way, St Albans, Herts. AL1 5HE
Tel 01727-815838

The Agency maintains and oversees policies on information technology strategy, procurement, technical standards and security.
*Chief Executive*, I. Magee
*Directors*, K. Caldwell; G. McCorkell; S. Williams; J. Thomas; U. Brennan; N. Haighton; G. Hextall; P. Graham
*Non-Executive Director*, T. Drury

CONTRIBUTIONS AGENCY
DSS Longbenton, Benton Park Road,
Newcastle upon Tyne NE98 1YX
Tel 0191-225 7665

The Agency collects and records National Insurance contributions, maintains individual records, and provides an advisory service.
*Chief Executive (G3)*, vacant
*Deputy Chief Executive (G5)*, G. Bertram
*Directors*, K. Wilson; S. Heminsley; R. Roberts, OBE; D. Gatenby; A. Cass; I. Hutton
*Non-Executive Director*, J. Wilson

RESETTLEMENT AGENCY
Euston Tower, 286 Euston Road, London, NW1 3DN
Tel 0171-388 1188

The Agency operates hostels for single homeless people, provides incentives for voluntary organizations or local authorities to purchase the hostels, and undertakes related activities.
*Chief Executive (G5)*, A. J. Ward

CHILD SUPPORT AGENCY
Millbank Tower, 21–24 Millbank, London SW1P 4QU
Tel 0171-210 3000

The Agency was set up in April 1993. It is responsible for the administration of the Child Support Act and for the assessment, collection and enforcement of maintenance payments for all new cases; by 1996 it will have re-assessed all existing cases where the parent with care is claiming benefit. It is expected to examine existing non-benefit cases in 1996–7 and be fully operational from 1997. The House of Commons Social Security select committee published the report of an inquiry into the Agency's work in December 1993; its recommendations led to measures which extended the phasing-in period for payments, increased protection to absent parents on low incomes, and reduced payments for older children. The committee is conducting a second inquiry into whether further measures should be taken to ensure that the method of assessing maintenance is simpler, more flexible and fairer. In 1993–4 the Agency took on 858,000 cases and completed 205,000 assessments. It saved £418 million in benefit payments against a target of £530 million. The target for 1994–5 is £460 million.
*Chief Executive (G4)*, Miss A. Chant

WAR PENSIONS AGENCY
Norcross, Blackpool, Lancs. FY5 3WP
Tel 01253-858858

The Agency administers the payment of war disablement pensions and provides welfare services and support to war disablement pensioners, war widows and their dependants and carers. It became an executive agency in April 1994.
*Chief Executive*, P. Mathison

*Central Advisory Committee on War Pensions*
Room 1138, The Adelphi, 1–11 John Adam Street, London WC2N 6HT
Tel 0171-962 8028
*Secretary*, S. Adams

SOCIAL SECURITY ADVISORY
COMMITTEE
New Court, Carey Street, London, WC2A 2LS
Tel 0171-412 1507

The Social Security Advisory Committee (SSAC) was established by the Social Security Act 1980 to advise the Secretary of State for Social Security and the Department of Health and Social Services for Northern Ireland on all social security matters except those relating to benefits for industrial injuries and diseases and occupational pensions. The Social Security Housing Benefit Act 1982 added housing benefit to the Committee's responsibilities.
*Chairman*, M. Bett, CBE
*Members*, Mrs J. Anelay, OBE; A. Dilnot; Revd G. H. Good, OBE; N. Hardwick; M. Hastings; Prof. A. I. Ogus; Hon. Mrs R. H. P. Price; B. Rigby; Lady Scott, CBE; Dr

A. V. Stokes, OBE; Prof. Olive Stevenson, CBE; O. Tudor; R. G. Wendt
*Secretary*, L. C. Smith

SPORTS COUNCIL
16 Upper Woburn Place, London WC1H 0QP
Tel 0171-388 1277

The Sports Council, created under royal charter, promotes the development of sport and fosters the provision of facilities for sport and recreation in Great Britain. Government funding for 1994–5 is £49.8 million. In July 1994 the Government announced proposals to replace the Sports Council with a United Kingdom Sports Council and an English Sports Council.
*Chairman*, Sir Peter Yarranton
*Directors-General (acting)*, D. Casey; D. Mason

For Sports Councils for Scotland, Wales and N. Ireland, *see* page 712.

HMSO (HER MAJESTY'S STATIONERY OFFICE)
St Crispins, Duke Street, Norwich NR3 1PD
Tel 01603-622211

HMSO (Her Majesty's Stationery Office) was established in 1786 and is the government executive agency that provides printing, binding and business supplies to government departments and publicly funded organizations. HMSO is also the Government's publisher, and has bookshops for the sale of government publications in six major cities as well as appointed agents in other cities. HMSO obtains most of its supplies and printing from commercial sources by competitive tender, apart from about 20 per cent of its printing requirement, such as Hansard and Bills and Acts of Parliament, which are produced in its own printing works. HMSO is a self-financing government trading fund and competes for its business with other commercial suppliers.
*Controller and Chief Executive*, P. I. Freeman, CB
*Executive Assistant*, Mrs J. B. Ward
*Deputy Chief Executive*, M. D. Lynn
*Director-General of Corporate Services*, P. J. Macdonald
*Director of Change*, A. J. Davies

HEADS OF DIVISIONS
*Publications*, C. N. Southgate
*Office Supplies*, A. M. Cole
*Print Procurement*, B. Ekers
*Finance and Planning*, C. J. Penn
*Information Technology*, D. C. Kerry
*Technological Innovation*, J. R. Eveson
*Engineering and Estates*, W. E. Scott
*Human Resources*, J. McDonald
*Office Equipment*, V. C. Bell
BIRMINGHAM – *Bookshop*, 258 Broad Street, Birmingham B1 2HE
BRISTOL, Distribution Park, Hawkley Drive, Woodlands Lane, Bradley Stoke, Bristol BS12 0BF. *Bookshop*, 33 Wine Street, Bristol BS1 2BH
LONDON – *Publications Centre*, 51 Nine Elms Lane, London SW8 5DR. *Bookshop*, 49 High Holborn, London WC1V 6HB
MANCHESTER, Broadway, Chadderton, Oldham, Lancs. OL9 9QH. *Bookshop*, 9–21 Princess Street, Manchester M60 8AS

SCOTLAND, South Gyle Crescent, Edinburgh EH12 9EB. *Director, Edinburgh*, G. W. Bedford. *Bookshop*, 71 Lothian Road, Edinburgh EH3 9AZ
NORTHERN IRELAND, IDB House, Chichester Street, Belfast BT1 4PS. *Director, Belfast*, M. McNeill. *Bookshop*, 16 Arthur Street, Belfast BT1 4GD

---

## STUDENT LOANS COMPANY LTD

100 Bothwell Street, Glasgow G2 7JD
Tel 0141-306 2000

---

The Company was established in 1989 to administer the student loans scheme on behalf of the Government. In 1992–3 345,000 students took out loans with a total value of more than £226.5 million.
*Chief Executive*, R. J. Harrison, CBE

---

## OFFICE OF TELECOMMUNICATIONS

50 Ludgate Hill, London EC4M 7JJ
Tel 0171-634 8700

---

The Office of Telecommunications (Oftel) is a non-ministerial government department which is responsible for supervising telecommunications activities in the UK. Its principal functions are to ensure that holders of telecommunications licences comply with their licence conditions; to maintain and promote effective competition in telecommunications; and to promote the interests of purchasers and other users of telecommunication services and apparatus in respect of prices, quality and variety.

The Director-General has powers to deal with anti-competitive practices and monopoly situations. He also has a duty to consider all reasonable complaints and representations about telecommunication apparatus and services.

*Director-General*, D. G. Cruickshank
*Deputy Director-General*, Mrs A. Walker
*Director of Competition*, Mrs A. Taylor
*Director of Consumer Affairs*, Ms C. Farnish
*Director of Licensing*, Ms S. Chambers
*Director of Licence Compliance*, Mrs P. Sellers
*Technical Director*, P. Walker
*Economic Director*, A. Bell
*Director of Information*, D. Redding

---

## TOURIST BOARDS

(For British Tourist Authority, *see* page 291)

---

The English Tourist Board, the Scottish Tourist Board, the Wales Tourist Board and the Northern Ireland Tourist Board are responsible for developing and marketing the tourist industry in their respective countries. The Boards' main objectives are to promote holidays and to encourage the provision and improvement of tourist amenities.

ENGLISH TOURIST BOARD, Thames Tower, Black's Road, London W6 9EL. Tel: 0181-846 9000. *Chief Executive*, J. East
SCOTTISH TOURIST BOARD, 23 Ravelston Terrace, Edinburgh EH4 3EU. Tel: 0131-332 2433. *Chief Executive*, D. D. Reid
WALES TOURIST BOARD, Brunel House, 2 Fitzalan Road, Cardiff CF2 1UY. Tel: 01222-499909. *Chief Executive*, P. Loveluck, CBE

NORTHERN IRELAND TOURIST BOARD, St Anne's Court, 59 North Street, Belfast BT1 1NB. Tel: 01232-231221. *Chief Executive*, I. Henderson

---

## DEPARTMENT OF TRADE AND INDUSTRY

Ashdown House, 123 Victoria Street, London SW1E 6RB
Tel 0171-215 5000
*Enterprise Initiative*: Tel 0800-500200
*Business in Europe*: Tel 01272-444888
*Innovation Enquiry Line*: Tel 0800-442001

---

The Department is responsible for:
(a) international trade policy, including the promotion of UK trade interests in the European Community, GATT, OECD, UNCTAD and other international organizations
(b) the promotion of UK exports and assistance to exporters
(c) policy in relation to industry and commerce, including policy towards small firms, regional policy and regional industrial assistance (some of this applying only to England), and policy in relation to the Post Office
(d) competition policy and consumer protection, including relations with the Office of Fair Trading, the Office of Telecommunications and the Monopolies and Mergers Commission; co-ordination of policy on deregulation
(e) the development of national policies in relation to all forms of energy and the development of new sources of energy; international aspects of energy policy. Links with British Coal, the Atomic Energy Authority, the electricity supply industry, the nuclear power construction industry, and the oil and gas industries
(f) policy on science and technology research and development; space; standards, quality and design; the Laboratory of the Government Chemist, the National Engineering Laboratory, the National Physical Laboratory and the National Weights and Measures Laboratory (all executive agencies)
(g) company legislation and the Companies House executive agency; the Insolvency Service executive agency; the regulation of insurance companies; the Radiocommunications Agency (executive agency); and the Patent Office and Accounts Services executive agencies

*President of the Board of Trade and Secretary of State for Trade and Industry*, The Rt. Hon. Michael Heseltine, MP
*Principal Private Secretary*, P. Smith
*Private Secretaries*, N. Welch; M. Hilton
*Special Advisers*, Lady Strathnever; Dr A. Kemp; A. J. Allen
*Chief Economic Adviser*, Dr W. Eltis
*Personal Adviser*, Sir Peter Levene, KBE
*Parliamentary Private Secretary*, R. Ottaway, MP
*Minister for Industry and Energy*, Timothy Eggar, MP
*Private Secretary*, M. Baldwin
*Parliamentary Private Secretary*, P. Luff, MP
*Minister for Export and Trade*, The Rt. Hon. Richard Needham, MP
*Private Secretary*, V. Marthaler
*Parliamentary Private Secretary*, A. Rowe, MP
*Minister for Consumer Affairs and Small Firms*, The Earl Ferrers, PC
*Private Secretary*, I. Gibbons
*Parliamentary Under-Secretary of State for Trade and Technology*, Ian Taylor, MP
*Private Secretary*, J. Walker
*Parliamentary Under-Secretary of State for Industry and Energy*, Charles Wardle, MP

*Private Secretary*, I. McKenzie
*Parliamentary Under-Secretary of State for Corporate Affairs*, Neil Hamilton, MP
*Private Secretary*, P. Hadley
*British Overseas Trade Board Chairman*, Sir Derek Hornby
*Private Secretary*, R. Pringle
*Parliamentary Clerk*, T. Williams
*Permanent Secretary (G1)*, Sir Peter Gregson, KCB
*Private Secretary*, C. Parker
*Deputy Secretaries (G2)*, C. W. Roberts, CB (*Trade Policy and Export Promotion*); R. Williams, CB (*Regional and Small Firms*); B. Hilton, CB (*Laboratories*); A. Hammond, CB (*The Solicitor*); C. Henderson, CB (*Energy*); R. J. Priddle, CB (*Corporate and Consumer Affairs*); A. C. Hutton (*Principal Establishment and Finance Officer*); A. Macdonald, CB (*Industry*)

## DIVISIONAL ORGANIZATION

‡AEROSPACE DIVISION
*Head of Division (G3)*, R. Foster
*Heads of Branches (G5)*, Ms R. J. Anderson; M. Ralph; S. I. Charik; Miss V. Evans

ATOMIC ENERGY
1 Palace Street, London SW1E 5HE

*Head of Division (G3)*, Dr T. E. Walker
*Heads of Branches (G5)*, Mrs H. Haddon; Dr D. Lumley; S. D. Spivey

BRITISH NATIONAL SPACE CENTRE
Bridge Place, 88–89 Eccleston Square, London SW1V 1PT
*Director-General (G3)*, D. R. Davis
*Deputy Director-General (G4)*, D. Leadbeater
*Heads of Branches (G5)*, Dr R. Jude; H. Evans; (*G6*), Dr D. Williams; J. Thomas; Dr P. Murdin

CHEMICALS AND BIOTECHNOLOGY DIVISION
*Head of Division (G3)*, Dr E. G. Finer
*Heads of Branches (G5)*, Ms G. Alliston; Dr E. A. M. Baker; N. Owen

COAL DIVISION
1 Palace Street, London SW1E 5HE
*Head of Division (G3)*, W. I. MacIntyre, CB
*Heads of Branches (G5)*, J. A. V. Collett; N. Hirst; A. Berry

COAL PRIVATIZATION UNIT
1 Palace Street, London SW1E 5HE
*Head of Division (G3)*, P. Loughead
*Grade 5*, Ms F. S. Price

COMPANIES DIVISION
10–18 Victoria Street, London SW1H 0NN
*Head of Division (G3)*, Mrs S. Brown
*Heads of Branches (G5)*, N. D. Peace; J. Healey; F. C. Jenkins; D. E. Love

COMPETITION POLICY DIVISION
*Head of Division (G3)*, A. J. Pryor
*Heads of Branches (G5)*, A. Cooper; C. C. Bridge

COMPETITIVENESS DIVISION
*Head of Division (G3)*, Dr R. Dobbie
*Heads of Branches (G5)*, M. Gibson; J. Rees

CONSUMER AFFAIRS DIVISION
10–18 Victoria Street, London SW1H 0NN
*Head of Division (G3)*, J. Dorken
*Heads of Branches (G5)*, D. Jones; P. D. Atkinson; M. Oldham; D. W. Hellings

DEREGULATION UNIT
*Director (G3)*, G. Dart
*Heads of Branches (G5)*, R. M. Watson; Miss M. N. Carter; Miss A. Willcocks

ECONOMICS AND STATISTICS DIVISION
*Chief Economic Adviser (G3)*, D. R. Coates
*Heads of Branches (G5)*, Dr D. S. Higham; S. Penneck; M. S. Bradbury

ELECTRICITY AND NUCLEAR FUELS DIVISION
1 Palace Street, London SW1E 5HE
*Head of Division (G3)*, C. C. Wilcock
*Heads of Branches (G5)*, S. F. D. Powell; J. H. T. Green; Dr P. Fenwick; Miss S. Haird; D. Hauser

‡ELECTRONICS AND ENGINEERING DIVISION
*Head of Division (G3)*, R. M. Rumbelow
*Heads of Branches (G5)*, T. J. Soane; S. C. Pride; Dr I. Eddison; J. C. Octon

ENERGY POLICY AND ANALYSIS UNIT
1 Palace Street, London SW1E 5HE
*Head of Division (G4)*, N. Hartley
*Heads of Branches (G5)*, H. Charman; D. Hodgson; S. A. Price; G. C. White; Dr R. Van Slooten

‡ENVIRONMENT AND ENERGY TECHNOLOGIES DIVISION
*Head of Division (G3)*, Dr C. Hicks
*Heads of Branches (G5)*, C. Brewer; Dr A. Eggington; A. Steele; G. Bevan

EUROPEAN COMMUNITY AND TRADE RELATIONS DIVISION
*Head of Division (G3)*, W. L. Stow
*Grade 4*, S. Fremantle
*Heads of Branches (G5)*, J. Rhodes; D. I. Richardson; M. D. C. Johnson

EXPORT CONTROL AND NON-PROLIFERATION DIVISION
Kingsgate House, 66–74 Victoria Street, London SW1E 6SW
*Head of Division (G3)*, R. J. Meadway
*Heads of Branches (G5)*, M. V. Coolican; P. H. Agrell

EXPORTS TO ASIA, AFRICA AND AUSTRALASIA DIVISION
Kingsgate House, 66–74 Victoria Street, London SW1E 6SW
*Head of Division (G3)*, M. M. Baker
*Heads of Branches (G5)*, G. Hopson; M. Cohen; I. Cliff; (*G6*), A. E. Reynolds

EXPORTS TO EUROPE AND THE AMERICAS DIVISION
*Head of Division (G3)*, N. Thornton
*Heads of Branches (G5)*, K. D. Levinson; B. Hampton; S. Lyle Smythe; K. Timmins; (*G6*), L. Rabstaff

FINANCE AND RESOURCE MANAGEMENT DIVISION
*Head of Division (G3)*, M. K. O'Shea
*Heads of Branches (G5)*, D. T. Smith; Mrs M. Bloom; J. Hobday; J. P. Clayton

INFORMATION DIVISION
*Head of Information (G4)*, Ms J. M. Caines
*Head of News (G6)*, A. Marre

*Publicity*
Bridge Place, 88–89 Eccleston Square, London SW1V 1PT
*Head of Branch (G5)*, Miss P. R. A. Freedman

‡At 151 Buckingham Palace Road, London SW1W 9SS

INSURANCE DIVISION
10–18 Victoria Street, London SW1H 0NN
*Head of Division (G3),* J. Spencer
*Heads of Branches (G5),* R. Allen; R. Hobbs; J. Alty;
    K. Long

INTERNAL AUDIT
1 Palace Street, London SW1E 5HE
*Head of Internal Audit (G5),* A. C. Elkington

INTERNATIONAL TRADE POLICY DIVISION
*Head of Division (G3),* J. Cooke
*Heads of Branches (G5),* J. Hunt; J. Startup; S. J. Bowen;
    C. B. Moir

INVESTIGATIONS DIVISION
*Head of Division (G3),* M. G. Roberts
*Grade 4,* Mrs T. J. Dunstan
*Inspector of Companies (G4),* G. Harp
*Heads of Branches (G5),* S. L. Parkinson; A. Mier; Miss
    H. Pottle; H. Bradshaw; Mrs B. Chase; A. Robertshaw

INVEST IN BRITAIN BUREAU
Kingsgate House, 66–74 Victoria Street, London SW1E 6SW
*Chief Executive (G3),* A. Fraser
*Head of Branch (G5),* J. C. S. Priston

JOINT EXPORT PROMOTION DIRECTORATE (FCO/DTI)
Kingsgate House, 66–74 Victoria Street, London SW1E 6SW
*Director-General of Export Promotion (G3),* F. R. Mingay,
    CMG
*Directors (G5),* D. Saunders; (DS4) M. Dougal

‡MANAGEMENT AND TECHNOLOGY SERVICES DIVISION
*Head of Division (G3),* Dr K. C. Shotton
*Heads of Branches (G5),* C. W. Johnston; Dr K. Poulter; Dr
    R. Hinder; Dr M. S. Draper

OIL AND GAS DIVISION
1 Palace Street, London SW1E 5HE
*Head of Division (G3),* M. J. Michell
*Heads of Branches (G5),* M. H. Atkinson; (RES2),
    J. R. V. Brooks; B. Coleman; (PS2), G. N. Marriott
*Director of Oil and Gas Royalties Office (G6),* J. F. Craven

*Gas and Oil Measurement Branch*
3 Tigers Road, Wigston, Leicester LE18 4UX
Tel 0116 278 5354
*Director (G5),* J. Plant

*Oil and Gas Office (Aberdeen)*
Atholl House, 86–88 Guild Street, Aberdeen AB9 1DR
Tel 01224-213557
*Grade 5,* A. S. Wilson

OIL AND GAS PROJECTS AND SUPPLIES OFFICE
Alhambra House, 45 Waterloo Street, Glasgow G2 6AS
Tel 0141-221 8777
1 Palace Street, London SW1E 5HE
Tel 0171-215 5000
*Chief Executive (G3),* D. Watson
*Heads of Branches (G5),* A. E. Maule; Mrs R. E. Ebbers;
    H. M. Whiteside; (G6), J. Roddie

PERSONNEL DIVISION
1 Palace Street, London SW1E 5HE
*Head of Division (G3),* Miss P. Boys
*Heads of Branches (G5),* J. Thompson; R. Rogers; A. Mantle

PROJECTS EXPORT PROMOTION DIVISION
*Head of Division (G3),* D. J. Hall
*Heads of Branches (G5),* A. G. Atkinson; D. Marsh;
    N. M. S. Armour

REGIONAL DEVELOPMENT DIVISION
Kingsgate House, 66–74 Victoria Street, London SW1E 6SW
*Head of Division (G3),* vacant
*Director, IDU (G3),* A. Dunnett
*Heads of Branches (G5),* R. H. S. Wells, CBE; K. Holt; Mrs
    M. A. Wilks; Miss D. Gane; D. A. Miner

SERVICES MANAGEMENT DIVISION
Kingsgate House, 66–74 Victoria Street, London SW1E 6SW
*Head of Division (G3),* Dr R. Heathcote
*Grade 4,* R. J. Wheeler
*Heads of Branches (G5),* E. Tomlin; R. Nicklen; Mrs
    E. Drage; B. Avery

SMALL FIRMS AND BUSINESS LINK DIVISION
St Mary's House, Level 2, Moorfoot, Sheffield S1 4PQ
Tel 0114-270 1356
Kingsgate House, 66–74 Victoria Street, London SW1E 6SW
Tel 0171-215 5000
*Head of Division (G3),* H. V. Brown
*Heads of Branches (G5),* J. M. Reid; R. M. Anderson;
    M. Garrod

SOLICITOR'S OFFICE
10–18 Victoria Street, London SW1H 0NN
*The Solicitor (G2),* A. Hammond, CB
*Grade 3,* P. H. Bovey; Miss K. Morton; J. M. Stanley;
    C. Kerse
*Assistant Solicitors (G5),* M. Bucknill; J. Burnett; Mrs
    J. Darvell; Miss P. A. E. Granados; R. D. B. Green;
    A. S. W. Hyett; D. H. M. Ingham; D. S. Mangat;
    I. K. Mathers; S. G. Milligan; R. Nicklen; Miss
    E. N. O'Flynn; R. C. Perkins; Miss G. Richmond;
    J. W. Roberts; A. M. Susman; B. Welch; A. J. Woods

‡TECHNOLOGY AND INNOVATION POLICY DIVISION
*Head of Division (G3),* Dr D. Evans
*Heads of Branches (G5),* R. T. King; I. C. Downing;
    P. E. Mason; P. L. Bunn; J. M. Barber; G. C. Riggs; Dr
    A. Keddie; C. M. Cruickshank

‡TELECOMMUNICATIONS AND POSTS DIVISION
*Head of Division (G3),* P. Salvidge
*Grade 4,* S. R. Temple
*Heads of Branches (G5),* D. D. Sibbick; P. Waller;
    N. McMillan; J. S. Neilson; D. A. Hendon; N. Worman;
    Dr D. Walker

‡TEXTILES AND RETAILING DIVISION
*Head of Division (G3),* I. M. Jones
*Heads of Branches (G5),* T. L. Roberts; C. L. Jackson

‡VEHICLES, METALS AND MINERALS DIVISION
*Head of Division (G3),* M. Stanley
*Heads of Branches (G5),* T. M. H. Shearer; H. P. Brown;
    B. F. Harding; (G6), R. Poole

BRITISH OVERSEAS TRADE BOARD
Kingsgate House, 66–74 Victoria Street, London SW1E 6SW
Tel 0171-215 5000

*President,* The President of the Board of Trade
*Chairman,* Sir Derek Hornby
*Vice-Chairman,* HRH The Duke of Kent, KG, GCMG, GCVO
*Members,* Dr D. Baldwin, CBE; G. J. Bull; Sir Colin
    Chandler; Sir Alan Cockshaw; Mrs H. M. Cropper;
    I. L. Dale, OBE; H. Davies; Mrs J. Hall; Dr A. Hayes, CB;
    D. Lanigan, CBE; R. Mingay, CMG; The Rt. Hon. Sir

‡At 151 Buckingham Palace Road, London SW1W 9SS

Michael Palliser, GCMG; D. Peake; C. W. Roberts, CB;
B. D. Taylor, CBE; B. W. Willott; D. Wright, CMG, LVO
*Secretary (G5)*, D. Saunders

## REGIONAL OFFICES
— *see* pages 348-9

## EXECUTIVE AGENCIES

ACCOUNTS SERVICES AGENCY
PO Box 100, Caerleon House, Cleppa Park, Newport,
Gwent NP1 9YG
Tel 01633-652200
The Agency is expected to be privatized by the spring of
1995.
*Director and Chief Executive (G5)*, D. M. Hoddinott

COMPANIES HOUSE
Companies House, Crown Way, Cardiff CF4 3UZ
Tel 01222-388588
Companies House incorporates companies, registers
company documents and provides company information.
*Registrar of Companies for England and Wales (G4)*,
D. Durham
London Search Room, 55-71 City Road, London EC1Y 1BB
Tel 0171-253 9393
102 George Street, Edinburgh EH2 3DJ
Tel 0131-225 5774
*Registrar for Scotland*, J. Henderson

THE INSOLVENCY SERVICE
PO Box 203, 5th Floor, 21 Bloomsbury Street, London
WC1B 3QW
Tel 0171-291 1110
The Service administers and investigates the affairs of
bankrupt individuals and companies; reports any resulting
criminal offences; disqualifies directors in corporate failures;
regulates insolvency practitioners; provides banking and
investment services for bankruptcy and liquidation funds;
and provides advice to ministers.
*Inspector-General of the Insolvency Service and Chief
Executive*, P. R. Joyce
*Deputy Inspectors-General*, D. J. Flynn; M. Osborne

LABORATORY OF THE GOVERNMENT CHEMIST
Queens Road, Teddington, Middx. TW11 OLY
Tel 0181-943 7000
The Laboratory provides chemical analysis and
measurement services to several government departments
and other bodies.
*Government Chemist (G3)*, Dr R. Worswick

NATIONAL ENGINEERING LABORATORY
East Kilbride, Glasgow G75 0QU
Tel 013552-20222
The National Engineering Laboratory is expected to be
privatized during 1995.
*Chief Executive (G3)*, W. Edgar

NATIONAL PHYSICAL LABORATORY
Queen's Road, Teddington, Middx. TW11 0LW
Tel 0181-977 3222
The Laboratory develops and disseminates national
measurement standards.
*Chief Executive and Director (G3)*, Dr P. B. Clapham

NATIONAL WEIGHTS AND MEASURES LABORATORY
Stanton Avenue, Teddington, Middx. TW11 0JZ
Tel 0181-943 7272

The Laboratory administers weights and measures
legislation.
*Chief Executive (G5)*, Dr S. Bennett

PATENT OFFICE
— *see* page 342

RADIOCOMMUNICATIONS AGENCY
Waterloo Bridge House, Waterloo Road, London SE1 8UA
Tel 0171-215 2150
The Agency is responsible for most civil radio matters other
than telecommunications broadcasting policy and the radio
equipment market.
*Chief Executive (G3)*, J. Norton
*Heads of Branches (G5)*, M. Goddard; R. Louth; A. Grilli;
D. Reed; R. M. Skiffins; B. A. Maxwell

---

## DEPARTMENT OF TRANSPORT
2 Marsham Street, London SW1P 3EB
Tel 0171-276 3000

---

The Department of Transport is responsible for land, sea
and air transport, including sponsorship of the rail and bus
industries; airports; domestic and international civil aviation;
shipping and the ports industry; navigational lights, pilotage,
HM Coastguard and marine pollution; motorways and other
trunk roads; oversight of road transport including vehicle
standards, registration and licensing, driver testing and
licensing, bus and road freight licensing, regulation of taxis
and private hire cars and road safety; and oversight of local
authorities' transport planning, including payment of Trans-
port Supplementary Grant.
   The Department is expected to relocate to Great Minster,
Horseferry Road, London SW1 in the autumn of 1995.
*Secretary of State for Transport*, The Rt. Hon. Dr Brian
Mawhinney, MP
   *Private Secretary*, Ms U. O'Brien
*Minister of State*, John Watts, MP
   *Private Secretary*, Ms S. M. Watkins
*Parliamentary Under-Secretaries*, The Viscount Goschen
   (*Roads and Traffic*); Steven Norris, MP (*Transport in
   London*)
   *Private Secretaries*, J. Nicholls; Miss S. Gray
*Parliamentary Clerk*, Miss P. Gaunt
*Permanent Under-Secretary of State (G1)*, A. P. Brown
   *Private Secretary*, D. Gurr

INFORMATION
*Head of Information (G5)*, M. J. Helm

AIR ACCIDENTS INVESTIGATION BRANCH
Royal Aerospace Establishment, Farnborough, Hants.
GU14 6TD
Tel 01252-510300
*Chief Inspector of Air Accidents (G4)*, K. P. R. Smart
*Grade 5*, R. C. McKinlay

MARINE ACCIDENTS INVESTIGATION BRANCH
5-7 Brunswick Place, Southampton SO1 2AN
Tel 01703-232424
*Chief Inspector of Marine Accidents (G5)*, Capt.
P. B. Marriott

TRANSPORT SECURITY
*Director and Co-ordinator (G4)*, H. Ditmas
*Grade 5*, Mrs A. M. Moss

LEGAL
*Head of Division (G3)*, M. C. P. Thomas

CENTRAL SERVICES

*Principal Establishment and Finance Officer (G2)*,
  D. J. Rowlands, CB

PERSONNEL
Lambeth Bridge House, London SE1 7SB
Tel 0171-238 3000

*Director of Personnel (G3)*, R. A. Allan
*Grade 5*, R. D. Bayly; D. L. McMillan
*Grade 6*, B. Meakins; E. M. Gibbons
*Chief Welfare Officer (G7)*, Miss E. T. Haines

FINANCE
*Under-Secretary (G3)*, Ms E. A. Hopkins
*Heads of Divisions (G5)*, M. N. Lambirth; S. K. Reeves
*Accounting Adviser (G4)*, A. R. Allum

EXECUTIVE AGENCIES DIRECTORATE
*Under-Secretary (G3)*, J. Phillips
*Grade 5*, J. L. Gansler; S. P. Connolly; A. C. Melville;
  P. A. A. Sanders

INTERNAL AUDIT
Ashdown House, Sedlescombe Road North, Hastings,
E. Sussex TN37 7GA
Tel 01424-458306

*Head of Branch (G5)*, M. J. Reece

CENTRAL SERVICES UNIT
Ashdown House, Sedlescombe Road North, Hastings,
E. Sussex TN37 7GA
Tel 01424-458306

*Grade 4*, M. R. Newey
*Heads of Divisions (G5)*, D. E. Bridge; G. L. Jones;
I. R. Heawood
*Grade 6*, I. Harris

ECONOMIC AND TRANSPORT POLICY
*Chief Economic Adviser (G3)*, Dr J. H. Rickard
*Grade 5*, T. E. Worsley; M. C. Mann; D. R. Instone

STATISTICS
Romney House, 43 Marsham Street, London SW1P 3PY
Tel 0171-276 8513

*Under-Secretary (G3)*, D. W. Flaxen
*Grade 5*, Miss B. J. Wood; Dr R. L. Butchart; P. J. Capell;
  R. P. Donachie

CHIEF SCIENTIST
*Chief Scientist (G4)*, Dr D. H. Metz

INFRASTRUCTURE
*Deputy Secretary (G2)*, N. L. J. Montagu, CB

RAILWAY INFRASTRUCTURE
*Under-Secretary (G3)*, C. R. Grimsey
*Heads of Divisions (G4)*, Dr J. H. Denning; (G5),
  A. Burchell; M. R. Fawcett; R. J. Griffins; Miss
  P. M. Williams; P. D. Burgess

RAILWAY PRIVATIZATION
*Under-Secretaries (G3)*, P. Wood; Mrs J. M. Williams
*Grade 4*, P. J. Coby
*Heads of Divisions (G5)*, P. H. McCarthy; B. Wadsworth;
  R. C. Bennett; R. S. Peal; M. J. Fuhr

PORTS DIVISION
*Head of Division (G5)*, P. R. Smith

AIRPORT INFRASTRUCTURE
*Under-Secretary (G3)*, H. B. Wenban-Smith
*Grade 5*, Ms A. M. Munro

ROAD INFRASTRUCTURE
*Grade 3*, H. C. S. Derwent
*Grade 5*, R. W. Linnard; M. A. Walsh; Dr
  C. M. Woodman; G. D. Rowe

OPERATIONS
*Deputy Secretary (G2)*, J. W. S. Dempster, CB

PUBLIC TRANSPORT LONDON
*Under-Secretary (G3)*, vacant
*Heads of Divisions (G5)*, A. B. Murray; E. C. Neve

URBAN AND LOCAL TRANSPORT
*Under-Secretary (G3)*, J. R. Coates, CB
*Heads of Divisions (G5)*, P. E. Pickering; M. R. Pitwood;
  A. S. D. Whybrow; Dr R. M. Kimber

ROAD AND VEHICLE SAFETY
*Under-Secretary (G3)*, Miss S. J. Lambert
*Heads of Divisions (G5)*, I. R. Jordan; Dr P. H. Martin;
  P. E. Butler
*Grade 6*, J. Winder

TRAFFIC AREA OFFICES
*Licensing Authorities and Traffic Commissioners*
EASTERN (Nottingham and Cambridge), Brig. C. M. Boyd
NORTH-EASTERN (Newcastle upon Tyne and Leeds),
  K. R. Waterworth
NORTH-WESTERN (Manchester), M. S. Albu
SCOTTISH (Edinburgh), Brig. M. W. Betts
SOUTH-EASTERN AND METROPOLITAN (Eastbourne),
  Brig. M. H. Turner
SOUTH WALES (Cardiff), J. M. C. Pugh
WESTERN (Bristol), Air Vice-Marshal R. G. Ashford, CBE
WEST MIDLANDS (Birmingham), J. M. C. Pugh

CHIEF MECHANICAL ENGINEER'S OFFICE
*Director and Chief Mechanical Engineer (G5)*,
  M. St J. Fendick

DEPARTMENTAL MEDICAL ADVISER
*Grade 4*, Dr J. F. Taylor

CIVIL AVIATION DIRECTORATE
*Under-Secretary (G3)*, H. B. Wenban-Smith
*Grade 5*, Ms A. Munro; Ms M. J. Clare

EUROPEAN DIVISION
*Head of Division (G5)*, J. S. Neve

INTERNATIONAL AVIATION DIRECTORATE
*Under-Secretary (G3)*, A. J. Goldman
*Grade 4*, D. S. Evans
*Heads of Divisions (G5)*, D. B. Cooke; R. S. Balme;
  A. T. Baker

UK DELEGATION TO THE CHANNEL TUNNEL SAFETY
AUTHORITY
Church House, Great Smith Street, London SW1P 3BL
Tel 0171-276 2014

*Grade 3*, E. Ryder, CB
*Grade 5*, A. P. Moss

SHIPPING AND FREIGHT DIRECTORATE
*Under-Secretary (G3)*, R. E. Clarke
*Heads of Divisions (G5)*, L. S. Moyle; J. F. Wall;
  R. T. Bishop; J. R. Fells
*Grade 7*, A. Crosswell

REGIONAL OFFICES
— *see* pages 348–9

# EXECUTIVE AGENCIES

## HIGHWAYS AGENCY

St Christopher House, Southwark Street, London SEI OTE
Tel 0171-928 3666

The Agency is responsible for the management and maintenance of the motorway and trunk road network and for road construction and improvement.
*Chief Executive (G2)*, L. J. Haynes
*Director, Finance Directorate (G3)*, B. J. Billington
*Director, Strategy Directorate (G4)*, P. G. Collis
*Director, Human Resources Directorate (G5)*, K. A. Wyatt
*Grade 4, Restructuring and Property Team*, N. E. Firkins
*Director, Engineering and Environmental Policy Directorate (G3)*, T. A. Rochester
*Director, Road Programme Directorate (G3)*, A. Whitfield
*Director, Motorway Widening Unit (G4)*, D. York
*Director, London Regional Office (G4)*, D. A. Holland
*Director, Network Management and Maintenance Directorate (G3)*, J. W. Fellows

*Regional Construction Programme Divisions*

*Eastern,* Bedford – *Director (G4)*, J. A. Kerman; *Grade 5,* J. P. Boud
*East Midlands,* Nottingham – *Director (G5)*, K. McKenzie
*Northern,* Newcastle upon Tyne – *Director (G5)*, D. Ward
*North-West,* Manchester – *Director (G4)*, A. J. Homer; *Grade 5,* E. A. Sherwin
*South-East,* Dorking – *Director (G4)*, B. A. Sperring; *Grade 5,* M. G. Quinn
*South-West,* Bristol – *Director (G4)*, P. E. Nutt; *Grade 5,* J. D. Gill
*West Midlands,* Birmingham – *Director (G4)*, P. E. Nutt; *Grade 5,* J. M. Bradley
*Yorkshire and Humberside,* Leeds – *Director (G4)*, A. J. Homer; *Grade 5,* R. R. Bineham

*Regional Network Management Divisions*

*Eastern – Director (G5)*, R. T. Thorndike
*East Midlands – Director (G5)*, K. McKenzie
*Northern – Director (G5)*, D. Ward
*North-West – Director (G5)*, M. M. Niven
*South-East – Director (G5)*, A. D. Rowland
*South-West – Director (G5)*, vacant
*West Midlands – Director (G5)*, W. S. C. Wadrup
*Yorkshire and Humberside – Director (G5)*, J. R. Wilkins

## VEHICLE INSPECTORATE

Berkeley House, Croydon Street, Bristol BS5 ODA
Tel 0117-954 3274

The Agency carries out annual testing and inspection of heavy goods and other vehicles and administers the MOT testing scheme.
*Chief Executive (G4)*, R. J. Oliver
*Deputy Chief Executive (G5)*, J. A. T. David
*Director of Administration (G6)*, K. Walton

## DRIVING STANDARDS AGENCY

Stanley House, Talbot Street, Nottingham NGI 5GU
Tel 0115-947 4222

The Agency's role is to carry out driving tests and approve driving instructors.
*Chief Executive (G5)*, Dr S. J. Ford

## TRANSPORT RESEARCH LABORATORY

Crowthorne, Berks. RGII 6AU
Tel 01344-773131

The Agency conducts and manages transport research and provides advice.

*Chief Executive (G3)*, H. J. Wootton
*Operations Director (G4)*, Dr R. S. Hinsley
*Grade 5,* Dr P. H. Bly; J. Porter; D. H. Goody;
D. A. Lynam; G. M. Clarke; P. B. Hunt; E. D. Gould

## DRIVER AND VEHICLE LICENSING AGENCY

Longview Road, Morriston, Swansea SA6 7JL
Tel 01792-782318

The Agency issues driving licences, registers and licenses vehicles, and collects excise duty.
*Chief Executive (G3)*, S. R. Curtis
*Heads of Divisions (G5)*, R. J. Verge; T. J. Horton
*Grade 6,* P. G. Desborough

## MARINE SAFETY AGENCY

Spring Place, 105 Commercial Road, Southampton SOI OZD
Tel 01703-329100

The Agency's role is to develop, promote and enforce high standards of marine safety and to minimize the risk of pollution of the marine environment from ships.
*Chief Executive (G4)*, R. M. Bradley
*Grade 5,* P. J. Hambling; W. A. Graham; Capt. D. Bell
*Grade 6,* R. Padgett

## COASTGUARD AGENCY

Spring Place, 105 Commercial Road, Southampton SOI OZD
Tel 01703-329100

The Agency's role is to minimize loss of life among seafarers and coastal users, and to minimize pollution from ships to sea and coastline.
*Chief Executive (G4)*, C. J. Harris
*Chief Coastguard (G5)*, Cdr D. T. Ancona, RN (retd)
*Grade 6,* D. Cockram

## VEHICLE CERTIFICATION AGENCY

1 Eastgate Office Centre, Eastgate Road, Bristol BS5 6XX
Tel 0117-951 5151

The Agency tests and certificates vehicles to UK and international standards.
*Chief Executive (G5)*, D. W. Harvey

---

# THE TREASURY

Parliament Street, London SWIP 3AG
Tel 0171-270 3000

---

The Office of the Lord High Treasurer has been continuously in commission for well over 200 years. The Lord High Commissioners of HM Treasury are the First Lord of the Treasury (who is also the Prime Minister), the Chancellor of the Exchequer and five junior Lords. This Board of Commissioners is assisted at present by the Chief Secretary, a Parliamentary Secretary who is also the government Chief Whip, a Financial Secretary, an Economic Secretary, the Paymaster-General, and the Permanent Secretary.

The Prime Minister and First Lord is not primarily concerned in the day-to-day aspects of Treasury business. The junior lords are government whips in the House of Commons. The management of the Treasury devolves upon the Chancellor of the Exchequer and, under him, the Chief Secretary, the Financial Secretary, the Economic Secretary and the Paymaster-General. All Treasury ministers are concerned in tax matters.

The Chief Secretary is responsible for the control of public expenditure; pay in the public sector, including nationalized industries but excluding the Civil Service; parliamentary pay; procurement policy; export credit; and efficiency in the public sector.

The Financial Secretary discharges the traditional responsibility of the Treasury for the largely formal procedure for the voting of funds by Parliament. He also has responsibility for other parliamentary financial business; the legislative programme; Inland Revenue duties and taxes; privatization policy; competition and deregulation policy; and Civil Service pay, management and industrial relations.

The Economic Secretary has responsibility for monetary policy; the financial system (including banks, building societies and other financial institutions); the Government Actuary's Department; the Central Statistical Office; international financial business; Economic and Monetary Union; stamp duties; the Valuation Office; the Royal Mint; the Department for National Savings; the Registry of Friendly Societies; the National Investment and Loans Office; public expenditure casework; and the Treasury Bulletin and Economic Briefing.

The Paymaster-General is responsible for Customs and Excise duties and taxes; women's issues; charities; the environment (including energy efficiency); the EC budget; general accounting issues; PAYMASTER (the office of Paymaster-General); and ministerial correspondence. PAYMASTER (*see* pages 342–3) acts as a clearing bank and provides financial information for all government departments; it has particular responsibility for public sector pensions.

A fundamental review of the running costs and organization of the Treasury was due to be completed by the autumn of 1994.

*Prime Minister and First Lord of the Treasury,*
  The Rt. Hon. John Major, MP
*Chancellor of the Exchequer* (*£40,895),
  The Rt. Hon. Kenneth Clarke, QC, MP
  *Principal Private Secretary,* N. I. MacPherson
  *Private Secretary,* I. Rogers
  *Special Advisers,* Mrs T. Keswick; D. Ruffley
*Chief Secretary to the Treasury* (*£40,895), The
  Rt. Hon. Jonathan Aitken, MP
  *Private Secretary,* P. T. Wanless
*Financial Secretary to the Treasury* (*£28,936), The Rt. Hon.
  Sir George Young, Bt., MP
  *Private Secretary,* J. O. F. Kingman
*Economic Secretary* (*£28,936), Anthony Nelson, MP
  *Private Secretary,* S. G. Meck
*Paymaster-General* (*£28,936), David Heathcoat-Amory, MP
  *Private Secretary,* M. Young
*Parliamentary Secretary to the Treasury and Government
  Chief Whip* (*£34,037), The Rt. Hon. Richard Ryder,
  OBE, MP
  *Private Secretary,* M. Maclean
*Treasurer of HM Household and Deputy Chief Whip*
  (*£28,936), Gregory Knight, MP
*Lord Commissioners of the Treasury* (*£18,620),
  T. Wood, MP; T. J. R. Kirkhope, MP; A. J. MacKay, MP;
  A. Mitchell, MP; D. Conway, MP
*Assistant Whips* (*£18,620), B. Wells, MP; M. Bates, MP;
  D. Willetts, MP; Dr L. Fox, MP; S. Burns, MP
*Parliamentary Clerk,* D. S. Martin
*Panel of Independent Forecasters to the Treasury,* W. Godley;
  G. Davies; T. Congdon; A. Britton; D. Currie;
  P. Minford
*Permanent Secretary to the Treasury* (*G1*), Sir Terence Burns
  *Private Secretary,* Miss S. M. A. James
*Second Permanent Secretaries* (*G1A*), Sir Nigel Wicks, KCB,
  CVO, CBE (*Overseas Finance*); R. P. Culpin, CB, CVO (*Public
  Expenditure*)

---

*In addition to a reduced parliamentary salary of £23,854

*Head of Government Economics Service and Chief Economic
  Adviser to the Treasury,* Prof. A. Budd
*Head of Government Accountancy Service and Chief
  Accountancy Adviser to the Treasury,* A. Likierman
*Deputy Secretaries* (*G2*), C. W. Kelly (*Public Finance*);
  vacant (*Overseas Finance*); A. J. C. Edwards, CB (*Public
  Services, and General Expenditure*); S. A. Robson (*Industry
  and Financial Institutions*); R. Mountfield, CB (*Civil
  Service Management and Pay*)

## CENTRAL DIVISIONS
PERSONNEL, FINANCE AND SUPPORT
*Director* (*G3*), P. R. C. Gray
*Assistant Secretaries* (*G5*), E. I. Cooper; Ms C. Slocock;
  D. Batt; J. J. Heywood
*Senior Principals* (*G6*), J. W. Stevens; D. J. Baker;
  D. N. Walters; P. Tickner

INFORMATION DIVISION
*Assistant Secretary* (*G5*), A. Hudson
*Deputy Head of Division* (*G6*), A. Kilpatrick

## INDUSTRY AND FINANCIAL INSTITUTIONS
INDUSTRY GROUP
*Under-Secretary* (*G3*), M. L. Williams
*Assistant Secretaries* (*G5*), C. R. Pickering; T. R. Fellgett;
  W. Guy

PUBLIC ENTERPRISES GROUP
*Under-Secretary* (*G3*), I. P. Wilson
*Assistant Secretaries* (*G5*), F. K. Jones; P. Wynn Owen;
  H. J. Bush

BANKING GROUP
*Under-Secretary* (*G3*), vacant
*Assistant Secretaries* (*G5*), C. Farthing; Ms E. Young;
  R. Ireson

SECURITIES AND INVESTMENT GROUP
*Under-Secretary* (*G3*), A. Whiting
*Grade 5,* Mrs P. C. Diggle; R. Pratt; Ms J. Simpson

EDUCATION, TRAINING AND EMPLOYMENT GROUP
*Under-Secretary* (*G3*), D. N. Sedgwick
*Assistant Secretaries* (*G5*), Ms R. Thompson; M. C. Mercer

## PUBLIC SERVICES
SOCIAL SERVICES AND TERRITORIAL GROUP
*Under-Secretary* (*G3*), Miss G. M. Noble
*Assistant Secretaries* (*G5*), J. Halligan; J. W. Grice; S. Kelly

LOCAL GOVERNMENT GROUP
*Under-Secretary* (*G3*), J. Beastall
*Assistant Secretaries* (*G5*), R. Bent; I. V. W. Taylor; Dr
  D. J. Compton

PROCUREMENT GROUP
*Director,* P. Forshaw, CBE
*Deputy Director,* M. J. Hoare

TREASURY OFFICER OF ACCOUNTS GROUP
*Under-Secretary* (*G3*), vacant
*Assistant Secretary* (*G4*), F. Martin

## GENERAL EXPENDITURE POLICY
GENERAL EXPENDITURE POLICY GROUP
*Under-Secretary* (*G3*), E. J. W. Gieve
*Assistant Secretaries* (*G5*), J. Hibberd; Mrs R. M. Dunn;
  D. Deaton

DEFENCE POLICY, MANPOWER AND MATERIEL GROUP
*Under-Secretary* (*G3*), Ms A. Perkins
*Assistant Secretaries* (*G5*), R. J. Devereux; M. E. Donnelly

OPERATIONAL RESEARCH
*Assistant Secretary (G5),* J. B. Jones

OVERSEAS FINANCE
INTERNATIONAL FINANCE GROUP
*Under-Secretary (G3),* D. L. C. Peretz
*Assistant Secretaries (G5),* D. Owen; J. S. Cunliffe; D. Roe

AID AND EXPORT FINANCE GROUP
*Under-Secretary (G3),* J. E. Mortimer
*Assistant Secretaries (G5),* S. N. Wood; M. G. Richardson

EUROPEAN COMMUNITY GROUP
*Under-Secretary (G3),* D. J. Bostock
*Assistant Secretaries (G5),* P. M. Rayner; N. J. Ilett; T. J. Sutton

GOVERNMENT ACCOUNTANCY SERVICE
MANAGEMENT UNIT AND ACCOUNTANCY ADVICE GROUP
*Grade 4,* D. Cooke
*Senior Principals (G6),* C. Butler; P. Holden

TREASURY REPRESENTATIVES IN USA
*Economic Minister and UK Representative IMF/IBRD,* H. P. Evans

CHIEF ECONOMIC ADVISER'S SECTOR

FORECASTS AND ANALYSIS GROUP
*Under-Secretary (G3),* C. J. Mowl
*Senior Economic Advisers (G5),* C. M. Kelly; S. Brooks

MEDIUM TERM AND POLICY ANALYSIS GROUP
*Under-Secretary (G3),* C. Riley
*Assistant Secretaries (G5),* D. Savage; S. W. Matthews

PUBLIC SERVICES ECONOMICS DIVISION
*Under-Secretary (G3),* M. J. Spackman
*Assistant Secretaries (G5),* R. Weeden; M. A. Parsonage; R. B. Stannard

ECONOMIC BRIEFING UNIT
*Assistant Secretary (G5),* P. L. Patterson

PUBLIC SECTOR FINANCE
*Assistant Secretary (G5),* A. W. Ritchie

PUBLIC FINANCE
FISCAL POLICY GROUP
*Under-Secretary (G3),* Mrs A. F. Case
*Assistant Secretaries (G5),* A. Sharples; R. P. Short

MONETARY GROUP
*Under-Secretary (G3),* A. O'Donnell, CB
*Assistant Secretaries (G5),* J. P. McIntyre; S. Pickford

EXCHEQUER FUNDS AND ACCOUNTS DIVISION
*Assistant Secretary (G5),* N. M. Hansford (*Treasury Accountant*)

CIVIL SERVICE MANAGEMENT AND PAY

CIVIL SERVICE PAY
*Under-Secretary (G3),* S. W. Boys-Smith
*Assistant Secretaries (G5),* Mrs S. D. Brown; R. J. Evans

PERSONNEL POLICY GROUP
*Under-Secretary (G3),* B. A. E. Taylor
*Assistant Secretaries (G5),* D. G. Pain; D. W. Rayson; J. Dixon; J. Strachan

MANAGEMENT POLICY
*Under-Secretary (G3),* R. I. G. Allen
*Assistant Secretary (G5),* M. Perfect; J. Barker; (*G6*), D. Wilson

SPECIALIST SUPPORT GROUP
*Grade 4,* C. J. A. Chivers
*Grade 5,* I. S. Thomson; S. D. Truman

THE TREASURY SOLICITOR
DEPARTMENT OF HM PROCURATOR-GENERAL AND TREASURY SOLICITOR
Queen Anne's Chambers, 28 Broadway, London SW1H 9JS
Tel 0171-210 3000

The Treasury Solicitor's Department provides legal services for many government departments. Those without their own lawyers are provided with legal advice, and both they and other departments are provided with litigation services. The Treasury Solicitor is also the Queen's Proctor, and is responsible for collecting Bona Vacantia on behalf of the Crown.
*HM Procurator-General and Treasury Solicitor (G1),* G. A. Hosker, CB, QC
*Deputy Treasury Solicitor (G2),* D. A. Hogg

TREASURY ADVISORY DIVISION
*Grade 2 (Legal),* M. A. Blythe
*Grade 5,* Mrs P. A. Dayer; M. J. Hemming; Mrs V. Collett; Miss J. V. Stokes
*Grade 6,* Miss P. F. Henderson; Ms S. C. Grundy; Ms S. Cochrane; A. Barsby; C. Barton
*Grade 7,* Mrs J. Kron; C. Marquand; Ms R. Sandby-Thomas

CENTRAL ADVISORY DIVISION
*Grade 5,* Mrs I. G. Letwin
*Grade 7,* Ms M. Garner

LITIGATION DIVISION
*Grade 3,* P. Ridd
*Grade 4,* F. L. Croft; D. Brummell
*Grade 5,* Mrs D. Babar; A. D. Lawton; A. Leithead; P. R. Messer; J. B. C. Oliver; D. F. Pascho; R. J. Phillips; A. J. Sandal; M. Sturdy; P. F. O. Whitehurst
*Grade 6,* A. P. M. Aylett; Miss J. Brooks; P. Carroll; J. M. Crane; J. N. Desai; Miss H. Fassnidge; P. D. F. Grant; J. D. Howes; Miss L. F. Nicoll; F. G. O'Connell; D. Palmer; Miss A. J. Rees; H. O. J. R. Shepheard; D. A. Stalker; A. Turek; R. J. Walter
*Grade 7,* T. C. Adcock; C. Ashford; Miss R. Barry; J. P. Betteley; L. Blake; Miss R. Brown; A. P. Chapman; Miss D. Cooper; Miss A. Coult; Ms A. Dick; J. Gladysz; S. P. Higgins; L. John-Charles; Ms J. Linney; Miss C. I. Martin; J. B. Matthews; Ms M. McNally; P. J. Moran; Miss C. R. Musaala-Mukasa; S. Nasser; A. C. Nwanodi; L. O'Dea; R. C. J. Opie; Miss D. Oram; R. M. Pierce; J. A. Ramnarine; Ms S. Ridley; M. E. Robinson; Miss C. M. Smith; D. Trinchero; G. Tuttle

QUEEN'S PROCTOR DIVISION
*Queen's Proctor,* G. A. Hosker, CB, QC
*Assistant Queen's Proctor,* Mrs D. Babar

ESTABLISHMENTS, FINANCE AND DEPARTMENTAL SERVICES DIVISION
*Principal Establishment and Finance Officer and Security Officer (G5),* A. J. E. Hollis
*Departmental Services Manager and Deputy Establishment and Security Officer (G7),* C. A. Woolley
*Personnel Officer (G7),* Ms H. Donnelly
*Finance Officer (G7),* R. B. Smith
*Head of Information Systems (G7),* G. N. Younger
*Business Support Manager (G7),* J. Hoadly

BONA VACANTIA DIVISION
*Grade 5,* Miss S. L. Sargant
*Grade 6,* M. R. M. Davis; P. F. Nockles
*Senior Legal Assistant,* S. A. Tobin
*Grade 7,* Mrs P. L. Woods; Mrs A. Evans; Ms J. C. Shotter;
   D. Reid; N. Gajjar

EUROPEAN DIVISION
*Grade 3,* J. E. G. Vaux
*Grade 5,* J. E. Collins; D. Macrae
*Grade 6,* Miss S. L. Hudson; Ms A. F. Golding
*Grade 7,* Miss B. J. Gardner; J. D. Colahan

NATIONAL HERITAGE DIVISION
*Grade 5,* P. C. Jenkins
*Grade 6,* S. T. Harker
*Grade 7,* Miss M. Brown; G. Evans

OFFICE OF PUBLIC SERVICE AND SCIENCE DIVISION
*Grade 5,* M. C. Carpenter
*Grade 6,* P. Kilgarriff
*Grade 7,* Miss S. Litchfield

MINISTRY OF DEFENCE DIVISION
Metropole Building, Northumberland Avenue, London
WC2N 5BL
Tel 0171-218 4691
*Grade 3,* D. F. W. Pickup
*Grade 5,* J. R. J. Braggins; Miss V. F. Dewhurst;
   J. N. Ashworth
*Grade 6,* P. Visagie; P. A. Sorenson; J. J. Cooper;
   M. G. Truran
*Grade 7,* Miss E. Polledri; G. Brzezina; M. Pulver; Ms
   M. Healey; Ms J. A. Murnane; Ms E. C. P. Lane;
   J. Ziegel

DEPARTMENT FOR EDUCATION DIVISION
Sanctuary Buildings, Great Smith Street, London SW1P 3BT
Tel 0171-925 5000
*Grade 3,* R. N. Ricks
*Grade 5,* D. J. Aries; F. D. W. Clarke; A. D. Preston
*Grade 6,* A. K. Fraser; N. P. Beach
*Grade 7,* C. J. Reay; C. J. Hales; Ms C. Manuel; Mrs
   A. Heilpern; Ms A. Goodfellow

DEPARTMENT OF EMPLOYMENT DIVISION
Caxton House, Tothill Street, London SW1H 9NF
Tel 0171-273 3000
*Grade 3,* H. R. L. Purse
*Grade 5,* R. J. Baker; C. House; Miss R. Jeffries;
   N. A. D. Lambert
*Grade 6,* R. H. Britten; S. J. Gibbon; J. K. Winayak;
   M. W. Smith; A. W. Stewart
*Grade 7,* R. Creasy; J. C. Youdell; M. W. Benney

DEPARTMENT OF TRANSPORT DIVISION
2 Marsham Street, London SW1P 3EB
Tel 0171-276 3000
*Grade 3,* M. C. P. Thomas
*Grade 4,* Miss J. Richardson
*Grade 5,* R. G. Bellis; P. D. Coopman; C. W. M. Ingram;
   A. G. Jones; R. Lines
*Grade 6,* G. W. M. Galliford; A. Lancaster;
   A. M. H. Prosser; S. W. Rock; N. C. Thomas;
   V. Edwards; J. Hall; G. Claydon; J. Jordan; A. L. Norris;
   H. Roberts; N. Magyar
*Senior Legal Assistants,* B. J. Hammersley; A. K. Johnston
*Grade 7,* R. C. Drabble; B. Golds; R. J. R. Jones; I. Adams;
   M. P. Gold; Ms K. H. Booth

GOVERNMENT PROPERTY LAWYERS
Riverside Chambers, Castle Street, Taunton, Somerset
TA1 4AP

Tel 01823-345200
An executive agency within the Treasury Solicitor's Department.
*Chief Executive (G3),* A. D. Osborne
*Deputy Chief Executive (G4),* P. Horner
*Group Directors (G5),* M. Benmayor; P. L. Noble;
   M. F. Rawlins; A. M. Scarfe
*Director of Lands Advisory (G6),* R. C. Paddock
*Assistant Directors of Lands Advisory (G7),* T. P. Baker;
   S. R. Bould
*Finance and Personnel Director (G7),* M. J. Robbins

COUNCIL ON TRIBUNALS
7th Floor, 22 Kingsway, London WC2B 6LE
Tel 0171-936 7045

The Council on Tribunals is an independent statutory body. It keeps under review the constitution and working of the various tribunals which have been placed under its general supervision, and considers and reports on administrative procedures relating to statutory inquiries. It is consulted by government departments on proposals for legislation affecting tribunals and inquiries, and on proposals where the need for an appeals procedure may arise. It also offers advice on draft primary legislation. Some 70 tribunals are currently under the Council's supervision.

The Scottish Committee of the Council generally considers Scottish tribunals and matters relating only to Scotland.

Members of the Council are appointed by the Lord Chancellor and the Lord Advocate. The Scottish Committee is composed partly of members of the Council designated by the Lord Advocate and partly of others appointed by him. The Parliamentary Commissioner for Administration is ex officio a member of both the Council and the Scottish Committee.

*Chairman,* The Lord Archer of Sandwell, PC, QC
*Members,* The Parliamentary Commissioner for
   Administration; Mrs A. Anderson; G. A. Anderson;
   T. N. Biggart, CBE, WS (*Chairman of the Scottish
   Committee*); M. B. Dempsey; Mrs S. Friend;
   T. R. H. Godden, CB; C. Heaps; B. Hill, CBE;
   Prof. M. J. Hill; W. N. Hyde; R. H. Jones, CVO; Dr
   C. A. Kaplan; L. F. Read, QC; Prof. M. Partington
*Secretary,* J. D. Saunders

SCOTTISH COMMITTEE
20 Walker Street, Edinburgh EH3 7HR
Tel 0131-220 1236
*Chairman,* T. N. Biggart, CBE, WS
*Members,* The Parliamentary Commissioner for
   Administration; G. A. Anderson; Mrs H. Sheerin, OBE;
   Mrs C. A. M. Davis; J. Langan; Ms M. Burns
*Secretary,* Mrs A. E. Scotland

TRIBUNALS
— *see* pages 384–7

UNRELATED LIVE TRANSPLANT
REGULATORY AUTHORITY
Department of Health, Room 520, Eileen House,
80–94 Newington Causeway, London SE1 6EF
Tel 0171-972 2739

The Unrelated Live Transplant Regulatory Authority (ULTRA) is a statutory body established in 1990. In every case where the transplant of an organ within the definition of the Human Organ Transplants Act 1989 is proposed between a living donor and a recipient who are not genetically related, the proposal must be referred to ULTRA. Applications must be made by registered medical practitioners.

The Authority comprises a chairman and ten members appointed by the Secretary of State for Health. The secretariat is provided by Department of Health officials.

*Chairman*, Prof. M. Bobrow
*Members*, Revd Prof. G. R. Dunstan; Dr P. A. Dyer; Mrs D. Eccles; Prof. M. G. McGeown; S. G. Macpherson; Dr N. P. Mallick; Prof. J. R. Salaman; Miss F. Smithers; Miss S. M. Taber; J. Wellbeloved
*Administrative Secretary*, J. R. Walden
*Medical Secretary*, Dr E. Hills

## WALES YOUTH AGENCY
Leslie Court, Lon-y-Llyn, Caerphilly, Mid Glamorgan CF8 1BQ
Tel 01222-880088

The Wales Youth Agency is a non-departmental public body funded by the Welsh Office. Its functions include the encouragement and development of the partnership between statutory and voluntary agencies relating to young people; the promotion of staff development and training; and the extension of marketing and information services in the relevant fields. The board of directors is appointed by the Secretary of State for Wales; directors do not receive a salary.

*Chairman of the Board of Directors*, G. Davies
*Vice-Chairman of the Board of Directors*, Dr H. Williamson
*Executive Director*, B. Williams

## OFFICE OF WATER SERVICES
Centre City Tower, 7 Hill Street, Birmingham B5 4UA
Tel 0121-625 1300

The Office of Water Services (Ofwat) was set up under the Water Act 1989 to support the Director-General of Water Services, who regulates the economic framework of the water industry in England and Wales. His main duties are to ensure that water and sewerage companies (*see* page 508) can carry out and finance the functions specified in the Water Act, and to protect the interests of water consumers. The Director-General has established ten regional customer service committees which investigate complaints and identify customer concerns. The Ofwat National Customer Council is a non-statutory body set up by the Director-General in 1993 to represent the views of water customers nationally.

The Director-General is independent of ministerial control and directly accountable to Parliament.

*Director-General of Water Services*, I. C. R. Byatt

## WELSH DEVELOPMENT AGENCY
Pearl House, Greyfriars Road, Cardiff CF1 3XX
Tel 01222-222666

The Welsh Development Agency was established under the Welsh Development Agency Act 1975 and came into existence in 1976. Its remit is to help further the regeneration of the economy and improve the environment in Wales. The Agency's main activities include helping to boost the growth,

profitability and competitiveness of indigenous Welsh companies; building speculative and bespoke factories and encouraging investment by the private sector in site development; grant-aiding land reclamation; and stimulating quality urban and rural regeneration and development. Through its International Division it also promotes inward investment into Wales.

*Chairman*, D. Rowe-Beddoe
*Deputy Chairman*, Dr R. Bichan
*Chief Executive*, B. Hartop

## WELSH OFFICE

The Welsh Office has responsibility in Wales for ministerial functions relating to health and personal social services; education, except for terms and conditions of service and student awards; training; the Welsh language, arts and culture; the implementation of the Citizen's Charter in Wales; local government; housing; water and sewerage; environmental protection; sport; agriculture and fisheries; forestry; land use, including town and country planning and countryside and nature conservation; new towns; non-departmental public bodies and appointments in Wales; ancient monuments and historic buildings and the Welsh Arts Council; roads; tourism; financial assistance to industry; the Strategic Development Scheme in Wales and the Programme for the Valleys; the operation of the European Regional Development Fund in Wales and other European Community matters; civil emergencies; and all financial aspects of these matters, including Welsh rate support grant.

Gwydyr House, Whitehall, London SW1A 2ER
Tel 0171-270 3000

*Secretary of State for Wales*, The Rt. Hon. John Redwood, MP
*Private Secretary*, Miss K. Jennings
*Parliamentary Private Secretary*, D. Evennett, MP
*Parliamentary Under-Secretaries*, Gwilym Jones, MP; Roderick Richards, MP
*Private Secretaries*, V. R. Watkin; M. Parkinson
*Special Adviser*, H. Williams
*Parliamentary Clerk*, A. Green
*Permanent Secretary (G1)*, M. C. Scholar, CB
*Private Secretary*, R. Shearer

Cathays Park, Cardiff CF1 3NQ
Tel 01222-825111

LEGAL GROUP
*Legal Adviser (G3)*, D. G. Lambert
*Assistant Solicitors (G5)*, P. J. Murrin; J. H. Turnbull
*Lawyers (G6)*, H. D. Evans; J. D. H. Evans; Miss A. L. Ferguson; C. P. Jones; C. G. Longville; A. J. Park; Mrs A. T. Parkes; Mrs P. Turnbull; A. J. Watkins; A. Widdrington
*Senior Legal Assistant*, D. H. J. Williams
*Lawyers (G7)*, Mrs R. Cleal; Mrs K. R. Davies; T. R. E. Heywood; Miss E. A. Hume; Ms T. L. Jones; Miss J. Lewis; C. Mayers; Ms S. Olley; M. Partridge; Miss E. Stallard; Mrs A. Titmuss; Miss C. Troddyn; Mrs R. J. Wiles

INFORMATION DIVISION
*Director of Information (G5)*, H. G. Roberts
*Chief Press Officer (G7)*, R. Lehnert
*Principal Publicity Officer (G7)*, W. J. Edwards

ESTABLISHMENT GROUP
*Principal Establishment Officer (G3)*, C. D. Stevens
*Heads of Divisions (G5)*, R. M. Abel; G. A. Thomas;
   Ms H. Angus
*Chief Statistician (G5)*, W. R. L. Alldritt
*Head of Health Intelligence Unit (G6)*, M. R. Brand
*Head of Training and Education Intelligence Unit (G6)*,
   P. J. Fullerton
*Principals (G7)*, R. J. Callen; Mrs J. Leitch; P. Lunn;
   Mrs B. Hollick; M. Stevenson; P. H. Skellon; C. Tudor;
   D. D. Baird; Mrs J. Blamire; H. C. L. Green
*Principal Research Officer (G7)*, Mrs M. A. J. Gronow
*Statisticians (G7)*, E. Swires Hennessy; J. D. James;
   H. M. Jones; R. Jones; Mrs K. M. Phillips; Mrs
   C. Fullerton; Miss D. R. Carter; P. J. Demery; Mrs
   C. M. Roberts; Mrs S. Leake; R. T. Kilpatrick
*Medical Director of Cancer Registry*, Dr M. Cotter
*NHS (G9) Secondee*, A. M. Jackson

FINANCE GROUP
*Principal Finance Officer (G3)*, R. A. Wallace
*Heads of Divisions (G5)*, D. T. Richards; L. A. Pavelin
*Senior Economic Adviser (G5)*, M. G. Phelps
*Grade 6*, M. G. Horlock
*Head of Internal Audit (G6)*, D. Howarth
*Principals (G7)*, B. R. Davies; M. H. Harper; Mrs H. Usher;
   Mrs E. A. O. Morse; Mrs S. V. Beacham
*Economic Adviser (G7)*, V. W. F. McPherson
*Principal Research Officer (G7)*, E. G. Darwin

## AGRICULTURE, ECONOMIC DEVELOPMENT AND INDUSTRY AND TRAINING
*Deputy Secretary (G2)*, J. F. Craig, CB

AGRICULTURE DEPARTMENT
*Head of Department (G3)*, L. K. Walford
*Heads of Divisions (G5)*, G. Podmore; D. R. Thomas
*Principals (G7)*, Mrs B. Harding; A. G. Huws; Ms
   A. Jackson; R. F. Patterson; C. E. Taylor; B. E. Price;
   P. N. S. Wolfenden; A. Aggett
*Divisional Executive Officers (G7)*, W. K. Griffiths
   (*Carmarthen*); E. Hughes (*Caernarfon*); J. C. Alexander
   (*Llandrindod Wells*)

ECONOMIC DEVELOPMENT GROUP
*Head of Group (G3)*, M. J. Cochlin
*Heads of Divisions (G5)*, B. J. Mitchell;
   Miss E. N. M. Davies; M. L. Evans
*Principals (G7)*, M. H. Bendon; Dr M. C. Dunn;
   Ms J. M. Gordon; A. D. Lansdown; Dr I. I. Thomas;
   R. Keveren; J. Atkins

INDUSTRY AND TRAINING DEPARTMENT
*Director (G3)*, D. W. Jones
*Industrial Director (G4)*, J. Cameron
*Heads of Divisions (G5)*, G. T. Evans; H. Brodie;
   N. E. Thomas; (*G6*), Dr R. J. Loveland
*Principals (G7)*, Dr A. Peters; C. Burdett; J. R. Evans;
   J. Love; Mrs L. Somme-Dew; K. Sleight; J. Grimes;
   G. Jones; I. Shuttleworth; C. Francis; K. Smith; Mrs
   K. Phillips; Mrs J. Gronow; R. Waller; M. J. A. Roberts;
   D. O'Brien; Mrs N. Barry; G. Madden; K. J. Orchard

## EDUCATION, HOUSING, HEALTH AND SOCIAL SERVICES, TRANSPORT, LOCAL GOVERNMENT, PLANNING AND ENVIRONMENT
*Deputy Secretary (G2)*, J. W. Lloyd, CB

EDUCATION DEPARTMENT
*Head of Department (G3)*, S. H. Martin
*Heads of Divisions (G5)°*, W. G. Davies; H. Evans;
   R. J. Davies; Dr H. F. Rawlings
*Principals (G7)°*, Mrs J. Booker; P. F. Brown; D. A. Bullen;
   Mrs L. L. Changkee; B. Dare; R. O. Evans;
   Mrs J. Hopkins; G. R. Jones; Mrs C. Peat;
   M. G. Richards; D. M. Rolph

OFFICE OF HM CHIEF INSPECTOR FOR SCHOOLS IN WALES
*Chief Inspector (G4)°*, R. L. James
*Staff Inspectors (G5)°*, S. J. Adams; J. R. N. Evans;
   T. E. Parry; G. Thomas; P. Thomas; Mrs I. Thomas;
   C. Abbott
There are 45 Grade 6 Inspectors.
*Head of Administration (G7)*, J. Roberts

HOUSING, LOCAL GOVERNMENT FINANCE AND SOCIAL SERVICES GROUP
*Head of Group (G3)*, R. W. Jarman
*Heads of Divisions (G5)*, D. Adams; M. J. Clancy;
   Mrs B. J. M. Wilson; Mrs E. A. Taylor
*Chief Inspector, Social Services Inspectorate (Wales) (G5)*,
   D. G. Evans
*Deputy Chief Inspectors*, J. F. Mooney; R. C. Woodward
*Grade 6*, A. C. Elmer; M. J. Shanahan
*Principals (G7)*, Mrs K. Cassidy; L. Conway;
   D. B. Hilbourne; D. Hobbs; J. Kilner; R. Norris; Ms
   J. Allen; W. S. Atwill; P. J. Higgins; Mrs J. Westlake;
   D. A. Powell
*Social Services Inspectors (G7)*, D, Barker; D. A. Brushett;
   G. H. Davies; Miss R. E. Evans; I. Forster;
   Mrs J. Jenkins; C. D. Vyvyan; Mrs P. White
*Principal Professional and Technology Officers (G7)*,
   G. N. Harding; W. Ross

HEALTH DEPARTMENT
*Director (G3)*, P. R. Gregory
*Heads of Divisions (G5)*, D. H. Jones; D. A. Pritchard;
   C. L. Jones; B. Wilcox; R. C. Williams; A. G. Thornton
*Principals (G7)*, Mrs J. D. Annand; M. A. C. Brooke;
   M. D. Chown; P. Davenport; R. J. Dodd; J. Morgan;
   R. A. Williams; D. W. Evans; Mrs C. Lines; D. Boyland;
   I. Heppenstall; M. F. Webb; J. Toman; E. J. McDonald;
   R. A. Jones; Ms J. Plastow; Mrs J. E. Wood;
   R. O'Sullivan; G. Thomas; C. Coombs

HEALTH PROFESSIONAL GROUP
*Chief Medical Officer (G3)*, Dr D. J. Hine

*Public Health Sub Group (HPG M1)*
*Deputy Chief Medical Officer (G4)*, Dr A. M. George
*Senior Medical Officers (G5)*, Dr J. Ludlow; Dr J. G. Avery

*Hospital Services Sub Group (HPG M2)*
*Principal Medical Officer (G4)*, Dr B. Fuge
*Senior Medical Officers (G5)*, Dr D. Salter; Dr D. W. Owen;
   Dr P. Lyne

*Community and Primary Care Services Sub Group (HPG M3)*
*Principal Medical Officer (G4)*, Dr J. K. Richmond
*Senior Medical Officers (G5)*, D. E. Davies; Dr R. Owen; Dr
   H. N. Williams
*Medical Adviser (part time)*, Dr J. Andrew
*Chief Dental Officer (G5)*, D. M. Heap
*Senior Dental Officer (G5)*, P. Langmaid
*Dental Officer (G6)*, J. D. O. Parkholm
*Chief Scientific Adviser (G5)*, Dr J. A. V. Pritchard
*Deputy Scientific Adviser (G6)*, Dr E. O. Crawley
*Chief Pharmaceutical Adviser (G5)*, Dr G. B. A. Veitch
*Deputy Pharmaceutical Adviser (G6)*, Mrs D. Kay Roberts

*Chief Environmental Health Adviser (G5)*, R. Alexander
*Deputy Environmental Health Adviser (G6)*, D. Worthington

NURSING DIVISION
*Chief Nursing Officer*, Miss M. Bull
*Deputy Chief Nursing Officer*, Mrs B. Melvin
*Nursing Officers*, Mrs S. M. Drayton; P. Johnson; Mrs
J. Sait; M. F. Tonkin

TRANSPORT, PLANNING AND ENVIRONMENT GROUP
*Head of Group (G3)*, G. C. G. Craig
*Director of Highways (G4)*, K. J. Thomas°
*Deputy Director of Highways (G5)*, J. G. Evans*
*Heads of Divisions (G5)*, A. H. H. Jones; D. I. Westlake°
*Chief Planning Adviser (G5)*, W. P. Roderick
*Superintending Engineers (G6)*, J. R. Rees*; B. H. Hawker,
OBE*
*Chief Estates Adviser (G6)*, G. K. Hoad
*Senior Principal (G6)*, P. R. Marsden
*Scientific Adviser (G6)*, Dr H. Prosser
*Principals (G7)*, P. M. Bishop; M. D. Evans; T. W. Hunter;
H. R. Payne; Mrs C. R. Jones; G. R. Jones; D. Hadfield°;
R. D. Macey; G. Quarrell; D. C. Quinlan°
*Principal Planning Officers (G7)*, L. Owen; J. V. Spear
*Principal Research Officers (G7)*, A. S. Dredge;
Ms L. J. Roberts
*Principal Estates Officer (G7)*, R. W. Wilson
*Principal Professional and Technology Officers, Highways
Directorate° (G7)*, M. J. Gilbert*; I. A. Grindulais;
A. P. Howcroft; A. L. Perry; R. H. Powell; S. C. Shouler;
J. Collins; K. J. Alexander; R. H. Hooper*; R. K. Cone;
J. Dawkins; T. Dorken; R. Shaw; M. J. A. Parker;
V. S. Pownall*

LOCAL GOVERNMENT REORGANIZATION GROUP
*Head of Group (G3)*, J. D. Shortridge
*Principals (G7)*, I. R. Miller; A. C. Wood; Mrs J. Harris

HM INSPECTORATE OF POLLUTION FOR WALES
11th Floor, Brunel House, 2 Fitzalan Road, Cardiff CF2 1TT
Tel 01222-49558

*Inspector, Hazardous Wastes (G7)*, G. Taylor
*Inspector, Radiation and Chemicals (G7) (acting)*,
Dr C. Hardman
*Inspector, Water (G7)*, A. A. Houlden

## HEALTH AUTHORITIES

CLWYD, Preswylfa, Hendy Road, Mold, Clwyd CH7 1PZ.
*Chief Executive Director*, B. F. Jones
EAST DYFED, Starling Park House, Johnstown,
Carmarthen, Dyfed SA31 3HL. *Managing Director*,
M. Ponton
GWENT, Brecon House, Mamhilad Park Estate, Pontypool,
Gwent. *Joint Chief Executive*, J. Hallett
GWYNEDD, Coed Mawr, Bangor, Gwynedd LL57 1IP.
*District General Manager*, C. H. Thomas
MID GLAMORGAN, District Headquarters, Albert Road,
Pontypridd CF37 1LA. *District General Manager*,
E. J. Thomas
PEMBROKESHIRE, Old Medical Centre, Winch Lane,
Haverfordwest, Dyfed SA61 1RN. *Chief Executive*,
M. Ponton
POWYS, Mansion House, Bronllys, Brecon, Powys LD3 0LS.
*District General Manager*, Dr D. Bevan

SOUTH GLAMORGAN, Temple of Peace and Health,
Cathays Park, Cardiff CF1 3NW. *District General Manager*,
G. L. Harrhy
WEST GLAMORGAN, The Oldway Centre, 36 Orchard
Street, Swansea SA1 5AQ. *Chief Executive Director*,
A. Beddow

## EXECUTIVE AGENCIES

AGRICULTURAL DEVELOPMENT AND ADVISORY
SERVICE (ADAS)
— *see* page 285

CADW: WELSH HISTORIC MONUMENTS
Brunel House, Fitzalan Road, Cardiff CF2 1UY
Tel 01222-465511
Cadw supports the preservation, conservation, appreciation
and enjoyment of the built heritage in Wales.
*Chief Executive*, E. A. J. Carr
*Director of Properties in Care*, J. H. Pavitt
*Director of Policy and Administration*, R. W. Hughes
*Conservation Architect (G6)*, J. D. Hogg
*Principal Inspector of Ancient Monuments and Historic
Buildings*, J. R. Avent
*Inspectors of Ancient Monuments and Historic Buildings*,
J. K. Knight; A. D. McLees; Dr S. E. Rees;
R. C. Turner; M. J. Yates

PLANNING INSPECTORATE
Cathays Park, Cardiff CF1 3NQ
Tel 01222-823892
A joint executive agency of the Department of the
Environment and the Welsh Office (*see* page 305).
*Chief Executive and Chief Planning Officer (G3)*, H. S. Crow
*Assistant Chief Planning Inspector (G5)*, D. F. Harris

---

WOMEN'S NATIONAL COMMISSION
Level 4, Caxton House, Tothill Street, London SW1H 9NF
Tel 0171-273 5486

---

The Women's National Commission is an advisory committee to the Government. Its remit is to ensure by all possible
means that the informed opinions of women are given their
due weight in the deliberations of the Government. The
Commission's 50 members are all women who are elected or
appointed by national organizations with a large and active
membership of women. The organizations include the
women's sections of the major political parties, trade unions
and religious groups, professional women's organizations
and other bodies broadly representative of women.
*Government Co-Chairman*, The Baroness Denton of
Wakefield, CBE
*Elected Co-Chairman*, Ms M. Rooney
*Joint Secretaries*, Ms J. Bailey; Ms W. Brown

---

Based at:
°Ty Glas Road, Llanishen, Cardiff CF4 5LE. Tel: 01222-761456
*Government Buildings, Dinerth Road, Rhos-on-Sea, Colwyn Bay
LL28 4UL. Tel: 01492-44261

# Law Courts and Offices

The Judicial Committee of the Privy Council is the final court of appeal from courts of the United Kingdom dependencies and courts of independent Commonwealth countries which have retained the right of appeal (Antigua and Barbuda, the Bahamas, Barbados, Belize, Brunei, Dominica, The Gambia, Jamaica, Kiribati, Mauritius, New Zealand, Singapore, St Christopher and Nevis, St Lucia, St Vincent and the Grenadines, Trinidad and Tobago, and Tuvalu). The Committee also hears appeals from courts of the Channel Islands and the Isle of Man, the disciplinary and health committees of the medical and allied professions, and some ecclesiastical appeals under the Pastoral Measure 1983.

The Judicial Committee includes the Lord Chancellor, the Lords of Appeal in Ordinary (*see* page 371) and other members of the Privy Council who hold or have held high judicial office, and certain judges from the Commonwealth. Commonwealth appeals are usually heard by a board of five judges.

PRIVY COUNCIL OFFICE (JUDICIAL COMMITTEE), Downing Street, London SW1A 2AJ. Tel: 0171-270 0483
*Registrar of the Privy Council*, D. H. O. Owen
*Chief Clerk*, K. N. Stringer

# The Judicature of England and Wales

The legal system of England and Wales is separate from those of Scotland and Northern Ireland and differs from them in law, judicial procedure and court structure, although there is a common distinction between civil law (disputes between individuals) and criminal law (acts harmful to the community).

The supreme judicial authority for England and Wales is the House of Lords, which is the ultimate Court of Appeal from all courts in Great Britain and Northern Ireland (except criminal courts in Scotland) for all cases except those concerning the interpretation and application of European Community law, including preliminary rulings requested by British courts and tribunals, which are decided by the European Court of Justice (*see* pages 761–2). As a Court of Appeal the House of Lords consists of the Lord Chancellor and the Lords of Appeal in Ordinary (law lords).

The Supreme Court of Judicature comprises the Court of Appeal, the High Court of Justice and the Crown Court. The High Court of Justice is the superior civil court and is divided into three divisions. The Chancery Division is concerned mainly with equity, bankruptcy and contentious probate business. The Queen's Bench Division deals with commercial and maritime law, serious personal injury and medical negligence cases, cases involving a breach of contract and professional negligence actions. The Family Division deals with matters relating to family law. Sittings are held at the Royal Courts of Justice in London or at 26 Crown Court centres outside the capital. High Court judges sit alone to hear cases at first instance. Appeals from lower courts are heard by two or three judges, or by single judges of the appropriate division. The Restrictive Practices Court, set up under the Restrictive Trade Practices Act 1956, and the Official Referees' Courts, which deal almost exclusively with cases concerning the construction industry, are also part of the High Court. Appeals from the High Court are heard in the Court of Appeal (Civil Division), presided over by the Master of the Rolls, and may go on to the House of Lords.

In criminal matters the decision to prosecute in the majority of cases rests with the Crown Prosecution Service, the independent prosecuting body in England and Wales (*see* page 379). At the head of the service is the Director of Public Prosecutions, who discharges her duties under the superintendence of the Attorney-General. Certain categories of offence continue to require the Attorney-General's consent for prosecution.

The Crown Court sits in about 90 centres, divided into six circuits, and is presided over by High Court judges, full-time circuit judges, and part-time recorders, sitting with a jury in all trials which are contested. It deals with trials of the more serious criminal offences, the sentencing of offenders committed for sentence by magistrates' courts (when the magistrates consider their own power of sentence inadequate), and appeals from magistrates' courts. Magistrates usually sit with a circuit judge or recorder to deal with appeals and committals for sentence. Appeals from the Crown Court, either against sentence or conviction, are made to the Court of Appeal (Criminal Division), presided over by the Lord Chief Justice. A further appeal from the Court of Appeal to the House of Lords can be brought if a point of law of general public importance is considered to be involved.

Minor criminal offences (summary offences) are dealt with in magistrates' courts, which usually consist of three unpaid lay magistrates (justices of the peace) sitting without a jury, who are advised on points of law and procedure by a legally-qualified clerk to the justices. There were 30,054 justices of the peace at 1 January 1994. In busier courts a full-time, salaried and legally-qualified stipendiary magistrate presides alone. Cases involving people under 16 are heard in youth courts, specially constituted magistrates' courts which sit apart from other courts. Preliminary proceedings in a serious case to decide whether there is evidence to justify committal for trial in the Crown Court are also held in the magistrates' courts. Appeals from magistrates' courts against sentence or conviction are made to the Crown Court. Appeals upon a point of law are made to the High Court, and may go on to the House of Lords.

Most minor civil cases are dealt with by the county courts, of which there are about 270 (details may be found in the local telephone directory). For cases involving small claims there are special arbitration facilities and simplified procedures. Where there are financial limits on county court jurisdiction, claims which exceed those limits may be tried in the county courts with the consent of the parties, or in certain circumstances on transfer from the High Court. Outside London, bankruptcy proceedings can be heard in designated county courts. Magistrates' courts can deal with certain classes of civil case and committees of magistrates license public houses, clubs and betting shops. For the implementation of the Children Act 1989, a new structure of hearing centres was set up in October 1991 for family proceedings cases, involving magistrates' courts (family proceedings courts), divorce county courts, family hearing centres and care centres. Appeals in family matters heard in the family proceedings courts go to the Family Division of the High Court; affiliation appeals and appeals from decisions of the licensing committees of magistrates go to the Crown Court. Appeals from county courts are heard in the Court of Appeal (Civil Division), and may go on to the House of Lords.

Coroners' courts investigate violent and unnatural deaths or sudden deaths where the cause is unknown. Cases may be brought before a local coroner (a senior lawyer or doctor) by doctors, the police, various public authorities or members of the public. Where a death is sudden and the cause is unknown, the coroner may order a post-mortem examination to determine the cause of death rather than hold an inquest in court.

For a summary of the Government's interim response to the recommendations of the Royal Commission on Criminal Justice, *see* page 1171.

## THE HOUSE OF LORDS
AS FINAL COURT OF APPEAL

*The Lord High Chancellor*
The Rt. Hon. the Lord Mackay of Clashfern, *born* 1927, *apptd* 1987

LORDS OF APPEAL IN ORDINARY (each £109,435)
*Style*, The Rt. Hon. Lord —

Rt. Hon. Lord Keith of Kinkel, *born* 1922, *apptd* 1977
Rt. Hon. Lord Goff of Chieveley, *born* 1926, *apptd* 1986
Rt. Hon. Lord Jauncey of Tullichettle, *born* 1925, *apptd* 1988
Rt. Hon. Lord Browne-Wilkinson, *born* 1930, *apptd* 1991
Rt. Hon. Lord Mustill, *born* 1931, *apptd* 1992
Rt. Hon. Lord Slynn of Hadley, *born* 1930, *apptd* 1992
Rt. Hon. Lord Woolf, *born* 1933, *apptd* 1992
Rt. Hon. Lord Lloyd of Berwick, *born* 1929, *apptd* 1993
Rt. Hon. Lord Nolan, *born* 1928, *apptd* 1994
Rt. Hon. Lord Nicholls, *born* 1933, *apptd* 1994

*Registrar*, The Clerk of the Parliaments (*see* page 223)

## SUPREME COURT OF JUDICATURE

## COURT OF APPEAL

*The Master of the Rolls* (£109,435), The Rt. Hon. Sir Thomas Bingham, *born* 1933, *apptd* 1992
*Secretary*, Miss V. Seymour
*Clerk*, D. G. Grimmett

LORDS JUSTICES OF APPEAL (each £104,922)
*Style*, The Rt. Hon. Lord/Lady Justice [surname]

Rt. Hon. Sir Brian Neill, *born* 1923, *apptd* 1985
Rt. Hon. Sir Martin Nourse, *born* 1932, *apptd* 1985
Rt. Hon. Sir Iain Glidewell, *born* 1924, *apptd* 1985
Rt. Hon. Sir John Balcombe, *born* 1925, *apptd* 1985
Rt. Hon. Sir Patrick Russell, *born* 1926, *apptd* 1987
Rt. Hon. Dame Elizabeth Butler-Sloss, DBE, *born* 1933, *apptd* 1988
Rt. Hon. Sir Murray Stuart-Smith, *born* 1927, *apptd* 1988
Rt. Hon. Sir Christopher Staughton, *born* 1933, *apptd* 1988
Rt. Hon. Sir Michael Mann, *born* 1930, *apptd* 1988
Rt. Hon. Sir Donald Farquharson, *born* 1928, *apptd* 1989
Rt. Hon. Sir Anthony McCowan, *born* 1928, *apptd* 1989

Rt. Hon. Sir Roy Beldam, *born* 1925, *apptd* 1989
Rt. Hon. Sir Andrew Leggatt, *born* 1930, *apptd* 1990
Rt. Hon. Sir Johan Steyn, *born* 1932, *apptd* 1992
Rt. Hon. Sir Paul Kennedy, *born* 1935, *apptd* 1992
Rt. Hon. Sir David Hirst, *born* 1925, *apptd* 1992
Rt. Hon. Sir Simon Brown, *born* 1937, *apptd* 1992
Rt. Hon. Sir Anthony Evans, *born* 1934, *apptd* 1992
Rt. Hon. Sir Christopher Rose, *born* 1937, *apptd* 1992
Rt. Hon. Sir Leonard Hoffman, *born* 1934, *apptd* 1992
Rt. Hon. Sir John Waite, *born* 1932, *apptd* 1993
Rt. Hon. Sir John Roch, *born* 1934, *apptd* 1993
Rt. Hon. Sir Peter Gibson, *born* 1934, *apptd* 1993
Rt. Hon. Sir John Hobhouse, *born* 1932, *apptd* 1993
Rt. Hon. Sir Denis Henry, *born* 1931, *apptd* 1993
Rt. Hon. Sir Mark Saville, *born* 1936, *apptd* 1994
Rt. Hon. Sir Peter Millett, *born* 1932, *apptd* 1994
Rt. Hon. Sir Swinton Thomas, *born* 1931, *apptd* 1994
Rt. Hon. Sir Andrew Morritt, CVO, *born* 1938, *apptd* 1994

*Ex officio Judges*, The Lord High Chancellor; the Lord Chief Justice of England; the Master of the Rolls; the President of the Family Division; and the Vice-Chancellor

COURT OF APPEAL (CRIMINAL DIVISION)

*Judges*, The Lord Chief Justice of England; the Master of the Rolls; Lords Justices of Appeal; and Judges of the High Court of Justice

COURTS-MARTIAL APPEAL COURT

*Judges*, The Lord Chief Justice of England; the Master of the Rolls; Lords Justices of Appeal; and Judges of the High Court of Justice

## HIGH COURT OF JUSTICE

CHANCERY DIVISION

*President*, The Lord High Chancellor
*The Vice-Chancellor* (£104,922), The Rt. Hon. Sir Richard Scott, *born* 1934, *apptd* 1994
*Clerk*, W. Northfield, BEM

JUDGES (each £95,051)
*Style*, The Hon. Mr/Mrs Justice [surname]

Hon. Sir John Vinelott, *born* 1923, *apptd* 1978
Hon. Sir Jean-Pierre Warner, *born* 1924, *apptd* 1981
Hon. Sir Jeremiah Harman, *born* 1930, *apptd* 1982
Hon. Sir John Knox, *born* 1925, *apptd* 1985
Hon. Sir William Aldous, *born* 1936, *apptd* 1988
Hon. Sir John Mummery, *born* 1938, *apptd* 1989
Hon. Sir Donald Rattee, *born* 1937, *apptd* 1989
Hon. Sir Francis Ferris, TD, *born* 1932, *apptd* 1990
Hon. Sir John Chadwick, ED, *born* 1941, *apptd* 1991
Hon. Sir Jonathan Parker, *born* 1937, *apptd* 1991
Hon. Sir John Lindsay, *born* 1935, *apptd* 1992
Hon. Dame Mary Arden, DBE, *born* 1947, *apptd* 1993
Hon. Sir Edward Evans-Lombe, *born* 1937, *apptd* 1993
Hon. Sir Robin Jacob, *born* 1941, *apptd* 1993
Hon. Sir William Blackburne, *born* 1944, *apptd* 1993
Hon. Sir Gavin Lightman, *born* 1939, *apptd* 1994
Hon. Sir Robert Walker, *born* 1938, *apptd* 1994
Hon. Sir Robert Carnwath, *born* 1945, *apptd* 1994

HIGH COURT OF JUSTICE IN BANKRUPTCY

*Judges*, The Vice-Chancellor and judges of the Chancery Division of the High Court

COMPANIES COURT

*Judges*, The Vice Chancellor and judges of the Chancery
Division of the High Court

PATENT COURT (APPELLATE SECTION)

*Judges*, The Hon. Mr Justice Aldous; The Hon. Mr Justice
Mummery; The Hon. Mr Justice Jacob

## QUEEN'S BENCH DIVISION

*The Lord Chief Justice of England* (£118,179) The Rt. Hon.
the Lord Taylor of Gosforth, *born* 1930, *apptd* 1992
*Private Secretary*, E. Adams
*Clerk*, J. Bond

JUDGES (each £95,051)
*Style*, The Hon. Mr/Mrs Justice [surname]

Hon. Sir Haydn Tudor Evans, *born* 1920, *apptd* 1974
Hon. Sir Ronald Waterhouse, *born* 1926, *apptd* 1978
Hon. Sir Maurice Drake, DFC, *born* 1923, *apptd* 1978
Hon. Sir Christopher French, *born* 1925, *apptd* 1979
Hon. Sir Charles McCullough, *born* 1931, *apptd* 1981
Hon. Sir Oliver Popplewell, *born* 1927, *apptd* 1983
Hon. Sir William Macpherson of Cluny, TD, *born* 1926,
*apptd* 1983
Hon. Sir Philip Otton, *born* 1933, *apptd* 1983
Hon. Sir Michael Hutchison, *born* 1933, *apptd* 1983
Hon. Sir Richard Tucker, *born* 1930, *apptd* 1985
Hon. Sir Robert Gatehouse, *born* 1924, *apptd* 1985
Hon. Sir Patrick Garland, *born* 1929, *apptd* 1985
Hon. Sir Michael Turner, *born* 1931, *apptd* 1985
Hon. Sir John Alliott, *born* 1932, *apptd* 1986
Hon. Sir Harry Ognall, *born* 1934, *apptd* 1986
Hon. Sir Konrad Schiemann, *born* 1937, *apptd* 1986
Hon. Sir John Owen, *born* 1925, *apptd* 1986
Hon. Sir Humphrey Potts, *born* 1931, *apptd* 1986
Hon. Sir Richard Rougier, *born* 1932, *apptd* 1986
Hon. Sir Ian Kennedy, *born* 1930, *apptd* 1986
Hon. Sir Nicholas Phillips, *born* 1938, *apptd* 1987
Hon. Sir Robin Auld, *born* 1937, *apptd* 1988
Hon. Sir Malcolm Pill, *born* 1938, *apptd* 1988
Hon. Sir Stuart McKinnon, *born* 1938, *apptd* 1988
Hon. Sir Mark Potter, *born* 1937, *apptd* 1988
Hon. Sir Henry Brooke, *born* 1936, *apptd* 1988
Hon. Sir Igor Judge, *born* 1941, *apptd* 1988
Hon. Sir Edwin Jowitt, *born* 1929, *apptd* 1988
Hon. Sir Scott Baker, *born* 1937, *apptd* 1988
Hon. Sir Michael Morland, *born* 1929, *apptd* 1989
Hon. Sir Mark Waller, *born* 1940, *apptd* 1989
Hon. Sir Roger Buckley, *born* 1939, *apptd* 1989
Hon. Sir Anthony Hidden, *born* 1936, *apptd* 1989
Hon. Sir Michael Wright, *born* 1932, *apptd* 1990
Hon. Sir Charles Mantell, *born* 1937, *apptd* 1990
Hon. Sir John Blofeld, *born* 1932, *apptd* 1990
Hon. Sir Peter Cresswell, *born* 1944, *apptd* 1991
Hon. Sir Anthony May, *born* 1940, *apptd* 1991
Hon. Sir John Laws, *born* 1945, *apptd* 1992
Hon. Dame Ann Ebsworth, DBE, *born* 1937, *apptd* 1992
Hon. Sir Simon Tuckey, *born* 1941, *apptd* 1992
Hon. Sir David Latham, *born* 1942, *apptd* 1992
Hon. Sir John Kay, *born* 1943, *apptd* 1992
Hon. Sir Christopher Holland, *born* 1937, *apptd* 1992
Hon. Sir Richard Curtis, *born* 1933, *apptd* 1992
Hon. Sir Stephen Sedley, *born* 1939, *apptd* 1992
Hon. Dame Janet Smith, DBE, *born* 1940, *apptd* 1992
Hon. Sir Anthony Colman, *born* 1938, *apptd* 1992
Hon. Sir Anthony Clarke, *born* 1943, *apptd* 1993
Hon. Sir John Dyson, *born* 1943, *apptd* 1993
Hon. Sir Thayne Forbes, *born* 1938, *apptd* 1993

Hon. Sir Michael Sachs, *born* 1932, *apptd* 1993
Hon. Sir Stephen Mitchell, *born* 1941, *apptd* 1993
Hon. Sir Rodger Bell, *born* 1939, *apptd* 1993
Hon. Sir Michael Harrison, *born* 1939, *apptd* 1993
Hon. Sir Bernard Rix, *born* 1944, *apptd* 1993
Hon. Dame Heather Steel, DBE, *born* 1940, *apptd* 1993
Hon. Sir Richard Buxton, *born* 1938, *apptd* 1993
Hon. Sir William Gage, *born* 1938, *apptd* 1993
Hon. Sir Jonathan Mance, *born* 1943, *apptd* 1993
Hon. Sir Andrew Longmore, *born* 1944, *apptd* 1993
Hon. Sir Thomas Morison, *born* 1939, *apptd* 1993

## FAMILY DIVISION

*President* (£104,922) Rt. Hon. Sir Stephen Brown, *born*
1929, *apptd* 1988
*Secretary*, Mrs S. Leung
*Clerk*, Mrs S. Bell

JUDGES (each £95,051)
*Style*, The Hon. Mr/Mrs Justice [surname]

Hon. Sir Anthony Ewbank, *born* 1925, *apptd* 1980
Hon. Sir Anthony Hollis, *born* 1927, *apptd* 1982
Hon. Sir Mathew Thorpe, *born* 1938, *apptd* 1988
Hon. Sir Edward Cazalet, *born* 1936, *apptd* 1988
Hon. Sir Alan Ward, *born* 1938, *apptd* 1988
Hon. Sir Robert Johnson, *born* 1933, *apptd* 1989
Hon. Sir Douglas Brown, *born* 1931, *apptd* 1989
Hon. Dame Joyanne Bracewell, DBE, *born* 1934, *apptd* 1990
Hon. Sir Michael Connell, *born* 1939, *apptd* 1991
Hon. Sir Peter Singer, *born* 1944, *apptd* 1993
Hon. Sir Nicholas Wall, *born* 1945, *apptd* 1993
Hon. Sir Andrew Kirkwood, *born* 1944, *apptd* 1993
Hon. Sir Nicholas Wilson, *born* 1945, *apptd* 1993
Hon. Sir Christopher Stuart-White, *born* 1933, *apptd* 1993
Hon. Dame Brenda Hale, DBE, *born* 1945, *apptd* 1994

## RESTRICTIVE PRACTICES COURT

*Judge*, The Hon. Mr Justice Warner
*Lay Members*, B. M. Currie; Sir Lewis Robertson, CBE;
R. Garrick, CBE; S. J. Ahearne; J. A. Graham;
Mrs D. H. Hatfield; S. McDowall; J. A. Scott

## OFFICIAL REFEREES' COURTS
St Dunstan's House, 133–137 Fetter Lane, London
EC4A IHD
Tel 0171–936 7429

JUDGES (each £82,641)

His Hon. Judge Lewis, QC (*Senior Official Referee*)
His Hon. Judge Bowsher, QC
His Hon. Judge Loyd, QC
His Hon. Judge Hicks, QC
His Hon. Judge Havery, QC
His Hon. Judge Lloyd, QC
His Hon. Judge Newman, QC

*Chief Clerk*, Miss B. Joy

## LORD CHANCELLOR'S DEPARTMENT
— *see* Government Departments and Public Offices

## SUPREME COURT DEPARTMENTS AND OFFICES
Royal Courts of Justice, London WC2A 2LL
Tel 0171–936 6000

ADMINISTRATOR'S OFFICE
*Administrator (G5)*, G. E. Calvett
*Deputy Administrator (G6)*, I. Hyams
*Secretary to the Family Division (G6)*, R. P. Knight

ADMIRALTY AND COMMERCIAL REGISTRY AND MARSHAL'S OFFICE
*Registrar (£58,974)*, P. Miller
*Marshal and Chief Clerk (G7)*, A. Ferrigno

BANKRUPTCY DEPARTMENT
*Chief Registrar (£69,497)*, G. L. Pimm
*Bankruptcy Registrars (£58,974)*, W. S. James;
   J. A. Simmonds; D. G. Scott; P. J. S. Rawson
*Chief Clerk (SEO)*, M. Brown

CENTRAL OFFICE OF THE SUPREME COURT
*Senior Master of the Supreme Court (QBD), and Queen's Remembrancer (£69,497)*, W. K. Topley
*Masters of the Supreme Court (QBD) (£58,974)*,
   P. B. Creightmore; D. L. Prebble; G. H. Hodgson;
   R. L. Turner; J. Trench; M. Tennant; P. Miller;
   N. O. G. Murray; I. H. Foster; G. H. Rose; P. G. A. Eyre
*Chief Clerk (Central Office) (G7)*, C. F. Jones

CHANCERY DIVISION
*Chief Clerk (G7)*, P. Emery

CHANCERY CHAMBERS
*Chief Master of the Supreme Court (£69,497)*,
   J. M. Dyson
*Masters of the Supreme Court (£58,974)*, J. S. Gowers;
   G. A. Barratt; J. I. Winegarten; J. A. Moncaster
*Chief Clerk (SEO)*, G. Robinson
*Conveyancing Counsel of the Supreme Court*, W. D. Ainger;
   H. M. Harrod; A. C. Taussig

COMPANIES COURT
*Registrar (£58,974)*, M. Buckley
*Chief Clerk (SEO)*, M. Brown

COURT OF APPEAL CIVIL DIVISION
*Registrar (£69,497)*, J. D. R. Adams
*Chief Clerk (SEO)*, Miss H. M. Goddard

COURT OF APPEAL CRIMINAL DIVISION
*Registrar (£69,497)*, M. McKenzie, QC
*Deputy Registrar (G5)*, M. N. Farmer
*Chief Clerk (G7)*, K. M. Dickerson

COURTS-MARTIAL APPEALS OFFICE
*Registrar (£69,497)*, M. McKenzie, QC
*Chief Clerk (G7)*, K. M. Dickerson

CROWN OFFICE OF THE SUPREME COURT
*Master of the Crown Office, and Queen's Coroner and Attorney (£69,497)*, M. McKenzie, QC
*Head of Crown Office (G5)*, Mrs L. Knapman
*Chief Clerk (G7)*, K. M. Dickerson

EXAMINERS OF THE COURT
Empowered to take examination of witnesses in all Divisions of the High Court

R. G. Wood; Mrs G. M. Kenne; Miss L. Driscoll;
R. M. Planterose; Miss V. E. I. Selvaratnam

RESTRICTIVE PRACTICES COURT
*Clerk of the Court*, M. Buckley
*Chief Clerk (SEO)*, M. Brown

SUPREME COURT TAXING OFFICE
*Chief Master (£69,497)*, P. T. Hurst
*Masters of the Supreme Court (£58,974)*, C. R. N. Martyn;
   M. Ellis; T. H. Seager Berry; C. C. Wright; P. A. Rogers;
   G. N. Pollard
*Chief Clerk (Administration) (G7)*, R. Cuthbert
*Chief Taxing Officer (G7)*, T. J. Ryan

COURT OF PROTECTION
Stewart House, 24 Kingsway, London WC2B 6HD
Tel 0171-269 7000
*Master (£69,497)*, Mrs A. B. Macfarlane

ELECTION PETITIONS OFFICE
Room E218, Royal Courts of Justice, Strand, London WC2A 2LL
Tel 0171-936 6131
The office accepts petitions and deals with all matters relating to the questioning of parliamentary, European Parliament and local government elections, and with applications for relief under the Representation of the People legislation.
*Prescribed Officer*, W. K. Topley
*Chief Clerk*, Miss J. L. Waine

OFFICE OF THE LORD CHANCELLOR'S VISITORS
Rochester House, 33 Greycoat Street, London SWIP 2QF
Tel 0171-210 1389
*Legal Visitor*, A. R. Tyrrell
*Medical Visitors*, A. G. Fullerton; K. Khan; D. Parr;
   J. Roberts; W. B. Spry; E. Mateu

OFFICIAL RECEIVERS' DEPARTMENT
21 Bloomsbury Street, London WCIB 3SS
Tel 0171-323 3090
*Senior Official Receiver*, M. C. A. Osborne
*Official Receivers*, M. J. Pugh; L. T. Cramp;
   J. Norris

OFFICIAL SOLICITOR'S DEPARTMENT
81 Chancery Lane, London WC2B 6HD
Tel 0171-911 7105
*Official Solicitor to the Supreme Court*, P. M. Harris
*Deputy Official Solicitor*, H. J. Baker
*Chief Clerk (G7)*, R. Lancaster

PRINCIPAL REGISTRY (FAMILY DIVISION)
Somerset House, London WC2R ILP
Tel 0171-936 6000
*Senior District Judge (£69,497)*, G. B. N. A. Angel
*District Judges (£58,974)*, T. G. Guest; J. E. Artro-Morris;
   R. B. Rowe; B. P. F. Kenworthy-Browne;
   Mrs K. T. Moorhouse; M. J. Segal; R. Conn;
   Miss I. M. Plumstead; G. J. Maple; Miss H. C. Bradley;
   K. J. White; A. R. S. Bassett-Cross; N. A. Grove;
   M. C. Berry; Miss S. M. Bowman; C. Million; P. Waller;
   Miss P. Cushing; R. Harper
*Secretary (G6)*, R. P. Knight

*District Probate Registrars*
*Birmingham and Stoke-on-Trent*, C. Marsh
*Brighton and Maidstone*, M. N. Emery
*Bristol, Exeter and Bodmin*, P. L. Speyer
*Ipswich, Norwich and Peterborough*, E. R. Alexander

*Leeds, Lincoln and Sheffield*, A. P. Dawson
*Liverpool, Lancaster and Chester*, B. J. Thomas
*Llandaff, Bangor, Carmarthen and Gloucester*, R. F. Yeldam
*Manchester and Nottingham*, M. A. Moran
*Newcastle, Carlisle, York and Middlesbrough*, P. Sanderson
*Oxford*, R. R. Da Costa
*Winchester*, A. K. Biggs

## OFFICE OF THE JUDGE ADVOCATE OF THE FLEET
The Law Courts, Barker Road, Maidstone ME16 8EQ
Tel 01622-754966

*Judge Advocate of the Fleet* (£69,497), His Hon. Judge Waley, VRD, QC

## OFFICE OF THE JUDGE ADVOCATE-GENERAL OF THE FORCES
(*Joint Service for the Army and the Royal Air Force*)
22 Kingsway, London WC2B 6LE
Tel 0171-305 7910

*Judge Advocate-General* (£82,641), His Hon. Judge J. W. Rant, QC
*Vice-Judge Advocate-General* (£69,497), E. G. Moelwyn-Hughes
*Assistant Judge Advocates-General* (£45,150–£52,100), A. P. Pitts; D. M. Berkson; M. A. Hunter; T. R. King; T. G. Pontius; J. P. Camp
*Deputy Judge Advocates* (£31,600–£44,300), Miss S. E. Woollam; R. C. C. Seymour; I. H. Pearson

## HIGH COURT AND CROWN COURT CENTRES

First-tier centres deal with both civil and criminal cases and are served by High Court and circuit judges. Second-tier centres deal with criminal cases only and are served by High Court and circuit judges. Third-tier centres deal with criminal cases only and are served only by circuit judges.

MIDLAND AND OXFORD CIRCUIT
*First-tier* – Birmingham, Lincoln, Nottingham, Oxford, Stafford, Warwick
*Second-tier* – Leicester, Northampton, Shrewsbury, Worcester
*Third-tier* – Coventry, Derby, Grimsby, Hereford, Peterborough, Stoke-on-Trent, Wolverhampton
*Circuit Administrator*, L. Oates, 2 Newton Street, Birmingham B4 7LU. Tel: 0121–627 1700
*Courts Administrators: Birmingham Group*, P. Barton; *Nottingham Group*, Mrs E. A. Folman; *Stafford Group*, A. F. Parker

NORTH-EASTERN CIRCUIT
*First-tier* – Leeds, Newcastle upon Tyne, Sheffield, Teesside
*Second-tier* – York
*Third-tier* – Bradford, Doncaster, Durham
*Circuit Administrator*, P. J. Farmer, 17th Floor, West Riding House, Albion Street, Leeds LS1 5AA. Tel: 0113–244 1841
*Courts Administrators: Leeds Group*, P. Delany, OBE; *Newcastle upon Tyne Group*, K. Budgen; *Sheffield Group*, G. Bingham

NORTHERN CIRCUIT
*First-tier* – Carlisle, Liverpool, Manchester, Preston
*Third-tier* – Barrow-in-Furness, Bolton, Burnley, Lancaster
*Circuit Administrator*, R. A. Vincent, 15 Quay Street, Manchester M60 9FD. Tel: 0161–833 1005
*Courts Administrators: Manchester Group*, Mrs A. Prior; *Liverpool Group*, D. A. Beaumont; *Preston Group*, Mrs C. A. Mayer

SOUTH-EASTERN CIRCUIT
*First-tier* – Chelmsford, Lewes, Norwich
*Second-tier* – Ipswich, London (Central Criminal Court), Luton, Maidstone, Reading, St Albans
*Third-tier* – Aylesbury, Bury St Edmunds, Cambridge, Canterbury, Chichester, Guildford, King's Lynn, London (Croydon, Harrow, Inner London Session House, Isleworth, Kingston upon Thames, Knightsbridge, Middlesex Guildhall, Snaresbrook, Southwark and Wood Green, Woolwich), Southend
*Circuit Administrator*, B. Cooke, New Cavendish House, 18 Maltravers Street, London WC2R 3EU. Tel: 0171–936 7235
*Deputy Circuit Administrator*, P. Stockton
*Courts Administrators: Chelmsford Group*, M. Littlewood; *Maidstone Group*, Mrs H. Hartwell; *Kingston Group*, J. L. Powell; *London (Civil)*, P. Risk; *London (Crime)*, G. F. Addicott

The High Court in Greater London sits at the Royal Courts of Justice.

WALES AND CHESTER CIRCUIT
*First-tier* – Caernarfon, Cardiff, Chester, Mold, Swansea
*Second-tier* – Carmarthen, Merthyr Tydfil, Newport, Welshpool
*Third-tier* – Dolgellau, Haverfordwest, Knutsford, Warrington
*Circuit Administrator*, V. Grove, Churchill House, Churchill Way, Cardiff CF1 4HH. Tel: 01222–396925
*Courts Administrators: Cardiff Group*, G. Jones; *Chester Group*, T. D. Beckett

WESTERN CIRCUIT
*First-tier* – Bristol, Exeter, Truro, Winchester
*Second-tier* – Dorchester, Gloucester, Plymouth
*Third-tier* – Barnstaple, Bournemouth, Devizes, Newport (IOW), Portsmouth, Salisbury, Southampton, Swindon, Taunton
*Circuit Administrator*, R. J. Clark, Bridge House, Sion Place, Clifton, Bristol BS8 4BN. Tel: 0117–974 3763
*Courts Administrators: Bristol Group*, A. C. Butler; *Exeter Group*, J. Ardern; *Winchester Group*, D. Ryan

## CIRCUIT JUDGES

*Senior Circuit Judges*, each £82,641
*Circuit Judges*, each £69,497
*Style*, His/Her Hon. Judge [surname]

MIDLAND AND OXFORD CIRCUIT
*Senior Presiding Judge*, Hon. Mr Justice Rougier
W. A. L. Allardice; F. A. Allen; Miss C. Alton; B. J. Appleby, QC; M. J. Astill; D. P. Bennett; R. S. A. Benson; I. J. Black, QC; R. W. A. Bray; D. W. Brunning; J. J. Cavell; F. A. Chapman; P. N. R. Clark; R. R. B. Cole; T. G. E. Corrie; P. F. Crane; *P. J. Crawford, QC (Recorder of Birmingham)*; I. T. R. Davidson, QC; P. N. de Mille; T. M. Dillon, QC; C. H. Durman; B. A. Farrer, QC; Miss E. N. Fisher;

J. E. Fletcher; A. C. Geddes; R. J. H. Gibbs, QC; V. E. Hall;
J. Hall; D. R. D. Hamilton; S. T. Hammond;
G. C. W. Harris, QC; M. K. Harrison-Hall; T. R. Heald;
C. R. Hodson; J. R. Hopkin; R. H. Hutchinson;
J. E. M. Irvine; R. P. V. Jenkins; J. G. Jones;
A. W. P. King; M. K. Lee, QC; M. H. Mander;
K. Matthewman, QC; W. D. Matthews; R. G. May;
H. R. Mayor, QC; N. Micklem; P. R. Morrell; J. I. Morris;
A. J. H. Morrison; M. D. Mott; A. J. D. Nicholl;
R. T. N. Orme; R. C. C. O'Rorke; J. F. F. Orrell;
D. S. Perrett, QC; C. J. Pitchers; R. F. D. Pollard;
F. M. Potter; D. P. Pugsley; J. R. Pyke; J. A. O. Shand;
J. R. S. Smyth; D. P. Stanley; P. J. Stretton; G. C. Styler;
H. C. Tayler, QC; A. B. Taylor; K. J. Taylor; M. B. Ward;
D. J. R. Wilcox; H. Wilson; J. W. Wilson;
K. S. W. Wilson Mellor, QC; C. G. Young

## NORTH-EASTERN CIRCUIT

*Senior Presiding Judge*, Hon. Mr Justice Waller

J. Altman; T. G. F. Atkinson; G. Baker, QC;
P. M. Baker, QC; T. W. Barber; G. N. Barr Young;
D. R. Bentley, QC; A. N. J. Briggs; D. M. A. Bryant;
J. W. M. Bullimore; B. Bush; M. C. Carr; M. L. Cartlidge;
P. J. Charlesworth; P. J. Cockroft; G. J. K. Coles, QC;
J. Crabtree; M. T. Cracknell; W. H. R. Crawford, QC;
Mrs J. Davies; E. J. Faulks; P. J. Fox, QC; A. N. Fricker, QC;
M. S. Garner; A. R. Goldsack, QC; S. P. Grenfell;
W. Hannah; G. F. R. Harkins; J. A. Henham;
D. Herrod, QC; P. M. L. Hoffman; R. Hunt;
A. E. Hutchinson, QC; N. H. Jones, QC; G. H. Kamil;
T. D. Kent-Jones, TD; C. F. Kolbert; G. M. Lightfoot;
R. P. Lowden; A. G. McCallum; A. C. Macdonald;
Miss M. B. M. MacMurray, QC; M. K. Mettyear;
A. L. Myerson, QC; D. A. Orde; Miss H. E. Paling;
*D. M. Savill, QC; R. M. Scott; A. Simpson; J. Stephenson;
*R. A. R. Stroyan, QC (*Recorder of Newcastle upon Tyne*);
Mrs L. Sutcliffe; R. C. Taylor; J. D. G. Walford; M. Walker;
P. H. C. Walker

## NORTHERN CIRCUIT

*Senior Presiding Judge*, Hon. Mr Justice Morland

M. P. Allweis; H. H. Andrew, QC; J. F. Appleton;
A. W. Bell; R. C. W. Bennett; Miss I. Bernstein;
M. S. Blackburn; R. Brown; I. B. Campbell;
F. B. Carter, QC; B. I. Caulfield; D. Clark; D. C. Clarke, QC;
G. M. Clifton; I. W. Crompton; G. P. Crowe, QC;
Ms J. M. P. Daley; *R. E. Davies, QC (*Recorder of
Manchester*); M. Dean, QC; Miss A. E. Downey;
B. R. Duckworth; S. B. Duncan; T. K. Earnshaw;
D. M. Evans, QC; S. J. D. Fawcus; P. S. Fish; J. R. B. Geake;
D. S. Gee; J. A. D. Gilliland, QC; R. G. Hamilton;
J. A. Hammond; F. D. Hart, QC; M. Hedley;
T. D. T. Hodson; F. R. B. Holloway; R. C. Holman;
Miss M. Holt; N. J. L. G. Howarth; G. W. Humphries;
C. E. F. James; P. M. Kershaw, QC (*Commercial Circuit
Judge*); H. L. Lachs; C. N. Lees; J. M. Lever, QC;
R. J. D. Livesey, QC; R. Lockett; D. Lynch; D. I. Mackay;
J. B. Macmillan; D. G. Maddison; B. C. Maddocks;
C. J. Mahon; J. A. Morgan; F. D. Owen, TD;
R. E. I. Pickering; D. A. Pirie; A. J. Proctor; J. H. Roberts;
Miss G. D. Ruaux; H. S. Singer; W. P. Smith;
Miss E. M. Steel; C. B. Tetlow; J. P. Townend;
I. J. C. Trigger; P. W. G. Urquhart; I. S. Webster;
W. R. Wickham (*Recorder of Liverpool*); B. Woodward

## SOUTH-EASTERN CIRCUIT

*Senior Presiding Judge*, Hon. Mr Justice Blofeld

J. R. S. Adams; F. J. Aglionby; J. A. Baker; J. B. Baker, QC;
M. J. D. Baker; P. V. Baker, QC; A. F. Balston;
G. S. Barham; C. J. A. Barnett, QC; W. E. Barnett, QC;
K. Bassingthwaighte; G. A. Bathurst Norman;
P. J. L. Beaumont, QC; N. E. Beddard; G. J. Binns;
J. E. Bishop; B. M. B. Black; P. C. Bowsher, QC;
A. V. Bradbury; P. N. Brandt; L. J. Bromley, QC;
A. E. Brooks; R. G. Brown; J. M. Bull, QC; G. N. Butler, QC;
*N. M. Butter, QC; H. J. Byrt, QC; C. V. Callman;
B. E. Capstick, QC; B. L. Charles, QC; A. W. Clark;
D. J. Clarkson, QC; P. C. Clegg; M. Cohen, QC;
S. H. Colgan; P. H. Collins; C. C. Colston, QC; S. S. Coltart;
Viscount Colville of Culross, QC; J. S. Colyer, QC;
C. D. Compston; T. A. C. Coningsby, QC; R. D. Connor;
M. J. Cook; R. A. Cooke; G. H. Coombe; M. R. Coombe;
A. Cooray; Dr E. Cotran; R. C. Cox; D. L. Croft, QC;
G. L. Davies; I. H. Davies, TD; W. L. M. Davies, QC;
W. N. Denison, QC (*Common Serjeant*); J. E. Devaux;
K. M. Devlin; M. N. Devonshire, TD; A. E. J. Diamond, QC;
W. H. Dunn, QC; A. H. Durrant; C. M. Edwards;
Q. T. Edwards, QC; F. P. L. Evans; J. K. Q. Evans;
S. J. Evans; J. D. Farnworth; P. Fingret; J. J. Finney;
P. Ford; J. J. Fordham; G. C. F. Forrester; J. R. B. Fox-
Andrews, QC; Ms D. A. Freedman; R. Gee; L. Gerber;
Miss A. F. Goddard, QC; S. A. Goldstein; P. W. Goldstone;
M. B. Goodman; C. G. M. Gordon; J. B. Gosschalk;
J. H. Gower, QC; M. Graham, QC; B. S. Green, QC;
P. B. Greenwood; D. J. Griffiths; G. D. Grigson;
R. B. Groves, TD, VRD; N. T. Hague, QC;
A. B. R. Hallgarten, QC; Miss G. Hallon; P. J. Halnan;
J. Hamilton; R. E. Hammerton; C. R. H. Hardy;
B. Hargrove, OBE, QC; J. P. Harris, DSC; M. F. Harris;
R. O. Havery, QC; R. G. Hawkins, QC; R. J. Haworth;
A. H. Head; J. C. Hicks; A. N. Hitching; D. Holden;
A. C. W. Hordern, QC; R. W. Howe; M. Hucker; Sir David
Hughes-Morgan, Bt., CB, CBE; J. G. Hull, QC; M. J. Hyam;
D. A. Inman; Dr P. J. E. Jackson; C. P. James;
T. J. C. Jospeh; M. Kennedy, QC; A. M. Kenny;
L. G. Krikler; L. H. C. Lait; P. St J. H. Langan, QC;
Capt. J. B. R. L. Langdon, RN; G. F. B. Laughland, QC;
R. Laurie; T. Lawrence; D. M. Levy, QC;
E. A. G. Lewis, QC; H. J. Lloyd, QC; F. R. Lockhart;
D. B. D. Lowe; R. H. Lownie; Mrs N. M. Lowry;
R. J. Lowry, QC; J. A. T. Loyd, QC; Capt. S. Lyons;
K. M. McHale; K. A. Machin, QC; M. B. McMullan;
K. C. Macrae; J. R. Main, QC; B. A. Marder, QC;
F. J. M. Marr-Johnson; L. A. Marshall; D. N. N. Martineau;
N. A. Medawar, QC; D. B. Meier; D. J. Mellor;
G. D. Mercer; A. L. Mildon, QC; D. Q. Miller; D. Morton
Jack; R. T. Moss; J. I. Murchie; T. M. E. Nash;
Mrs N. F. Negus; M. H. D. Neligan;
C. W. F. Newman, QC; Mrs M. F. Norrie;
Ms S. F. Norwood; P. W. O'Brien; M. A. Oppenheimer;
D. A. Paiba; Mrs N. Pearce; Miss V. A. Pearlman;
J. R. Peppitt, QC; F. H. L. Petre; A. J. Phelan;
N. A. J. Philpot; D. C. Pitman; J. R. Platt; P. B. Pollock;
W. D. C. Poulton; H. C. Pownall, QC;
R. J. C. V. Prendergast; J. E. Previté, QC; B. H. Pryor, QC;
J. E. Pullinger; J. W. Rant, QC; E. V. P. Reece; G. K. Rice;
M. S. Rich, QC; K. A. Richardson, QC; G. Rivlin, QC;
S. D. Robbins; J. H. P. Roberts; D. A. H. Rodwell, QC;
J. W. Rogers, QC; G. H. Rooke, TD, QC; P. C. R. Rountree;
J. H. Rucker; T. R. G. Ryland; R. B. Sanders;
Maj.-Gen. D. H. D. Selwood; J. S. Sennitt; J. L. Sessions;
J. D. Sheerin; D. R. A. Sich; A. G. Simmons;
K. T. Simpson; P. R. Simpson; M. Singh, QC;
J. K. E. Slack, TD; S. P. Sleeman; P. M. J. Slot;
F. B. Smedley, QC; C. M. Smith, QC; S. A. R. Smith;
R. J. Southan; S. B. Spence; *R. O. C. Stable, QC;

C. J. Sumner; W. F. C. Thomas; A. G. Y. Thorpe;
A. H. Tibber; C. H. Tilling; A. M. Troup; S. Tumim;
J. T. Turner; C. J. M. Tyrer; Mrs A. P. Uziell-Hamilton;
J. E. van der Werff; Sir Lawrence Verney, TD (*Recorder of London*); A. O. R. Vick, QC; T. L. Viljoen;
Miss M. S. Viner, CBE, QC; A. F. Waley, VRD, QC;
D. B. Watling, QC; V. B. Watts; *F. J. White;
S. R. Wilkinson; S. M. Willis; G. N. Worthington;
E. G. Wrintmore; K. H. Zucker, QC

WALES AND CHESTER CIRCUIT

*Senior Presiding Judge*, Hon. Mr Justice Curtis

M. R. Burr; T. R. Crowther, QC; G. H. M. Daniel;
R. D. G. David, QC; D. T. A. Davies; J. B. S. Diehl, QC;
D. E. H. Edwards; G. O. Edwards, QC; Lord Elystan-Morgan; D. R. Evans, QC; T. M. Evans, QC;
*M. Gibbon, QC; D. M. Hughes; G. J. Jones;
H. D. H. Jones; G. E. Kilfoil;
T. E. I. Lewis-Bowen; D. G. Morgan; D. G. Morris;
D. C. Morton; T. H. Moseley, QC; D. A. Phillips;
P. J. Price, QC; E. J. Prosser, QC; H. W. J. ap Robert;
H. E. P. Roberts, QC; S. M. Stephens, QC;
D. B. Williams, TD; H. V. Williams, QC

WESTERN CIRCUIT

*Senior Presiding Judge*, Hon. Mr Justice Auld

M. F. Addison; S. T. Bates, QC; P. T. S. Batterbury;
J. F. Beashel; C. L. Boothman; M. J. L. Brodrick;
J. M. J. Burford, QC; R. D. H. Bursell, QC; J. R. Chalkley;
M. G. Cotterill; G. W. A. Cottle; Ms H. Counsell;
S. C. Darwall Smith; Mrs S. P. Darwall Smith;
Mrs L. H. Davies; M. Dyer; *P. Fallon, QC; P. D. Fanner;
J. D. Foley; D. L. Griffiths; Mrs C. M. A. Hagen;
G. B. Hutton; R. E. Jack, QC; A. G. H. Jones;
D. McCarraher, VRD; T. N. Mackean;
Miss S. M. D. McKinney; I. S. McKintosh; I. G. McLean;
J. G. McNaught; T. J. Milligan; E. G. Neville;
S. K. O'Malley; S. K. Overend; R. C. Pryor, QC;
J. N. P. Rudd; R. M. Shawcross; D. A. Smith, QC;
W. E. M. Taylor; P. M. Thomas; A. A. R. Thompson, QC;
H. J. M. Tucker, QC; D. M. Webster, QC; J. H. Weeks, QC;
J. R. Whitley; J. A. J. Wigmore; K. M. Willcock, QC;
J. C. Willis; J. H. Wroath

RECORDERS (each £332 per day)

R. D. I. Adam; J. D. R. Adams; R. J. P. Aikens, QC;
J. F. Akast; D. J. Ake; R. Akenhead, QC;
I. D. G. Alexander, QC; C. D. Allan; C. A. Alldis;
W. P. Andreae-Jones, QC; P. J. Andrews, QC;
R. A. Anelay, QC; A. R. L. Ansell; M. G. Anthony;
Miss L. E. Appleby, QC; J. F. A. Archer, QC;
Lord Archer of Sandwell, PC, QC; A. J. Arlidge, QC;
E. K. Armitage, QC; P. J. B. Armstrong; G. K. Arran;
R. Ashton; P. Ashworth, QC; J. M. Aspinall; E. G. Aspley;
B. Atchley; N. J. Atkinson, QC; M. G. Austin-Smith, QC;
M. J. S. Axtell; W. S. Aylen, QC; J. F. Badenoch, QC;
A. B. Baillie; M. F. Baker, QC; N. R. J. Baker, QC;
S. W. Baker; C. G. Ball, QC; A. Barker, QC; B. J. Barker, QC;
D. Barker, QC; G. E. Barling, QC; R. O. Barlow;
D. N. Barnard; D. M. W. Barnes, QC; H. J. Barnes;
T. P. Barnes, QC; K. E. Barnett; R. A. Barratt, QC;
J. E. Barry; R. Bartfield; G. R. Bartlett, QC;
J. C. T. Barton, QC; D. C. Bate, QC; S. D. Batten, QC;
P. J. Batty; J. J. Baughan, QC; R. A. Bayliss; J. Beatson;
C. H. Beaumont; C. O. M. Bedingfield, TD, QC;
C. O. J. Behrens; R. W. Belben; The Hon. M. J. Beloff, QC;
H. P. D. Bennett, QC; J. M. Bennett; P. Bennett, QC;
H. L. Bentham; D. M. Berkson; M. Bethel, QC;

J. P. V. Bevan; J. C. Beveridge, QC; Mrs C. V. Bevington;
N. Bidder; M. G. Binning; P. V. Birkett, QC; W. J. Birtles;
P. W. Birts, QC; H. O. Blacksell, QC; J. A. Blair-Gould;
A. N. H. Blake; C. Bloom, QC; D. J. Blunt, QC;
J. G. Boal, QC; D. R. L. Bodey, QC; J. G. Boggis, QC;
G. T. K. Boney, QC; Miss J. A. M. Bonvin; D. J. Boulton;
S. N. Bourne-Arton, QC; P. H. Bowers; S. C. Boyd, QC;
J. J. Boyle; W. T. S. Braithwaite, QC; N. D. Bratza, QC;
G. B. Breen; D. J. Brennan, QC; M. L. Brent, QC;
G. J. B. G. Brice, QC; J. N. W. Bridges-Adams;
A. J. Brigden; P. J. Briggs; R. P. Brittain; J. Bromley-Davenport; S. C. Brown, QC; D. J. M. Browne, QC;
J. N. Browne; A. J. N. Brunner, QC; R. V. Bryan;
A. Bueno, QC; D. L. Bulmer; J. P. Burgess; J. K. Burke, QC;
J. P. Burke; H. W. Burnett, QC; R. H. Burns;
S. J. Burnton, QC; M. J. Burton, QC; K. Bush;
A. J. Butcher, QC; Miss J. Butler; A. N. L. Butterfield, QC;
C. W. Byers; M. D. Byrne; Mrs B. A. Calvert, QC;
D. Calvert-Smith; R. Camden Pratt, QC;
Miss S. M. C. Cameron, QC; A. N. Campbell, QC;
J. Q. Campbell; G. M. C. Carey, QC; A. C. Carlile, QC, MP;
The Lord Carlisle of Bucklow, PC, QC; H. B. H. Carlisle, QC;
M. J. Carroll; J. J. Carter-Manning, QC; R. Carus, QC;
B. E. F. Catlin; J. A. Chadwin, QC; N. M. Chambers, QC;
D. C. Champion; V. R. Chapman; J. M. Cherry, QC;
J. R. Cherryman, QC; C. F. Chruszcz, QC; C. H. Clark, QC;
C. S. C. S. Clarke, QC; P. W. Clarke; S. P. Clarke;
A. S. L. Cleary; W. Clegg, QC; M. F. Coates; W. P. Coates;
D. J. Cocks, QC; J. J. Coffey; T. A. Coghlan;
W. J. Coker, QC; J. R. Cole; N. J. Coleman;
N. B. C. Coles, QC; A. R. Collender, QC; P. N. Collier, QC;
A. D. Collins, QC; J. M. Collins; Ms M. Colton;
Mrs J. R. Comyns; G. D. Conlin; J. G. Connor; C. S. Cook;
A. E. M. Cooper; Miss B. P. Cooper, QC; P. J. Cooper, QC;
P. E. Copley; Miss S. M. Corkhill; C. J. Cornwall;
P. J. Cosgrove, QC; Miss D. R. Cotton, QC; J. S. Coward, QC;
P. R. Cowell; B. R. E. Cox, QC; P. J. Cox, DSC, QC;
D. I. Crigman, QC; M. L. S. Cripps; C. A. Critchlow;
J. F. Crocker; D. R. Crome; J. D. Crowley, QC;
E. J. R. Crowther, OBE; W. R. H. Crowther, QC;
H. M. Crush; D. M. Cryan; T. S. Culver;
Miss E. A. M. Curnow, QC; J. T. Curran; P. D. Curran;
J. W. O. Curtis, QC; M. J. Curwen; K. C. Cutler;
A. J. G. Dalziel; P. M. Darlow; G. W. Davey;
C. P. M. Davidson; A. R. M. Davies; J. T. L. Davies;
R. L. Davies, QC; A. W. Dawson; D. H. Day, QC;
J. J. Deave; J. B. Deby, QC; P. G. Dedman;
Mrs P. A. Deeley; C. F. Dehn, QC; P. A. de la Piquerie;
M. A. de Navarro, QC; W. E. Denny, CBE, QC;
R. L. Denyer, QC; S. C. Desch, QC; H. A. D. de Silva;
T. Deva Pillay; P. N. Digney; C. E. Dines;
A. D. Dinkin, QC; I. J. Dobkin; R. A. M. Doggett;
Ms B. Dohmann, QC; D. T. Donaldson, QC;
A. M. Donne, QC; A. K. Dooley; P. H. Downes; J. Dowse;
S. M. Duffield; P. R. Dunkels, QC; R. T. Dutton;
J. M. Dyson; D. Eady, QC; Miss D. B. Eaglestone;
H. W. P. Eccles, QC; Miss S. M. Edwards, QC;
D. F. Elfer, QC; G. Elias, QC; E. A. Elliott; D. R. Ellis;
J. A. Elvidge; C. Elwen; R. M. Englehart, QC;
T. M. English; G. A. Ensor; D. A. Evans, QC;
D. H. Evans, QC; G. W. R. Evans, QC; M. J. Evans;
Sir Graham Eyre, QC; T. M. Faber; W. D. Fairclough;
R. B. Farley, QC; D. J. Farrer, QC; K. J. Farrow;
P. E. Feinberg, QC; R. Fernyhough, QC; D. T. Fish;
D. P. Fisher; G. D. Flather, CBE, QC; P. E. J. Focke, QC;
R. A. Fordham, QC; A. J. Forrest; M. D. P. Fortune;
J. R. Foster, QC; Miss R. M. Foster; J. H. Fryer-Spedding, OBE; M. T. Fugard, CB; M. Gale, QC;
C. J. E. Gardner, QC; C. R. Garside, QC; J. W. Gaskell;

R. C. Gaskell; S. A. G. L. Gault; A. H. Gee, QC; D. S. Geey; W. George; J. S. Gibbons; C. A. H. Gibson; F. H. S. Gilbert, QC; N. B. D. Gilmour, QC; L. Giovene; A. T. Glass, QC; H. B. Globe, QC; H. K. Goddard, QC; H. A. Godfrey, QC; Ms L. S. Godfrey, QC; J. J. Goldberg, QC; J. B. Goldring, QC; P. H. Goldsmith, QC; L. C. Goldstone, QC; I. F. Goldsworthy, QC; A. J. J. Gompertz, QC; A. A. Gordon; J. P. Gorman, QC; J. R. W. Goss; T. J. C. Goudie, QC; C. O. G. Gould; A. A. Goymer; G. Gozem; A. S. Grabiner, QC; R. A. Grant; C. A. St J. Gray, QC; G. Gray, QC; J. M. Gray; R. M. K. Gray, QC; H. Green, QC; J. C. Greenwood; J. G. Grenfell, QC; R. D. Grey, QC; J. C. Griffiths, CMG, QC; J. P. G. Griffiths; J. D. Griggs; M. G. Grills; M. S. E. Grime, QC; Mrs H. M. Grindrod, QC; P. Grobel; M. A. W. Grundy; S. J. Gullick; A. S. Hacking, QC; M. F. Haigh; J. W. Haines; D. R. Halbert; D. J. Hale; J. P. N. Hallam; D. T. Hallchurch; Miss H. C. Hallett, QC; A. W. Hamilton, QC; G. M. Hamilton, TD, QC; P. L. Hamlin; J. Hampton; J. L. Hand, QC; Miss R. S. A. Hare; R. D. Harman, QC; G. T. Harrap; P. J. Harrington, QC; D. M. Harris, QC; R. D. Harrison; R. M. Harrison, QC; H. M. Harrod; C. P. Hart-Leverton, QC; B. Harvey; C. S. Harvey, MBE, TD; M. L. T. Harvey, QC; T. S. A. Hawkesworth, QC; J. M. Haworth; R. W. P. Hay; Prof. D. J. Hayton; R. Hayward-Smith, QC; A. J. Healey; M. J. Heath; T. B. Hegarty, QC; G. E. Heggs; R. A. Henderson, QC; R. H. Q. Henriques, QC; M. J. Henshell; P. J. M. Heppel, QC; R. C. Herman; M. S. Heslop; R. B. Hickman; B. J. Higgs, QC; E. M. Hill, QC; J. W. Hillyer; A. J. H. Hilton, QC; Ms E. J. Hindley, QC; W. T. J. Hirst; J. D. Hitchen; S. A. Hockman, QC; The Hon. Mary Hogg, QC; A. J. C. Hoggett, QC; D. A. Hollis, VRD, QC; E. J. Holman, QC; C. J. Holmes; J. F. Holt; R. M. Hone; A. T. Hoolahan, QC; A. Hooper, QC; P. J. C. R. Hooton; S. Hopkins; M. A. P. Hopmeier; K. A. D. Hornby; M. Horowitz, QC; C. P. Hotten, QC; B. F. Houlder, QC; R. Houlker, QC; The Rt. Hon. M. Howard, QC, MP; M. N. Howard, QC; C. I. Howells; M. J. Hubbard, QC; A. P. G. Hughes, QC; P. T. Hughes, QC; R. P. Hughes; T. M. Hughes, QC; J. Hugill, QC; L. D. Hull; D. P. Hunt; D. R. N. Hunt, QC; P. J. Hunt, QC; I. G. A. Hunter, QC; M. Hussain, QC; B. A. Hytner, QC; R. A. G. Inglis; A. B. Issard-Davies; D. G. A. Jackson; M. R. Jackson; R. M. Jackson; I. E. Jacob; P. J. Jacobs; N. F. B. Jarman, QC; J. M. Jarvis, QC; A. H. Jeffreys; D. A. Jeffreys, QC; J. Jeffs, QC; J. D. Jenkins, QC; D. B. Johnson, QC; D. A. F. Jones; N. G. Jones; R. A. Jones, QC; S. E. Jones, QC; T. G. Jones; W. H. Joss; H. M. Joy; P. S. L. Joyce, QC; M. D. L. Kalisher, QC; M. L. Kallipetis, QC; I. G. F. Karsten, QC; S. S. Katkhuda; M. R. Kay, QC; R. G. Kaye, QC; M. L. Keane; D. N. Keating, QC; K. R. Keen, QC; D. W. Keene, QC; B. R. Keith, QC; C. L. Kelly; C. J. B. Kemp; D. Kennett Brown; L. D. Kershen, QC; G. M. Khayat, QC; R. I. Kidwell, QC; T. R. King; T. R. A. King, QC; W. M. Kingston, QC; R. C. Klevan, QC; B. J. Knight, QC; M. S. Knott; Miss P. E. Knowles; S. E. Kramer; Miss L. J. Kushner, QC; P. E. Kyte, QC; L. P. Laity; P. M. Lakin; C. A. Lamb; D. G. Lane, QC; G. J. H. Langley, QC; B. R. Latham, QC; S. W. Lawler, QC; Sir Ivan Lawrence, QC, MP; M. H. Lawson, QC; G. S. Lawson-Rogers, QC; P. L. O. Leaver, QC; D. Lederman, QC; B. W. T. Leech; I. Leeming, QC; C. H. de V. Leigh, QC; Sir Godfrey Le Quesne, QC; H. B. G. Lett; B. H. Leveson, QC; S. Levine; A. E. Levy, QC; M. E. Lewer, QC; A. K. Lewis, QC; B. W. Lewis; M. ap G. Lewis, QC; R. S. Lewis;

C. C. D. Lindsay, QC; S. J. Linehan, QC; J. S. Lipton; B. J. E. Livesey, QC; C. G. Llewellyn-Jones, QC; S. H. Lloyd; J. Lloyd-Eley, QC; D. Lloyd Jones; C. J. Lockhart-Mummery, QC; A. J. C. Lodge, QC; D. C. Lovell-Pank, QC; G. W. Lowe; N. H. Lowe; G. W. Lowther; F. D. L. Loy; G. Lumley; Rt. Hon. Sir Nicholas Lyell, QC, MP; E. Lyons, QC; D. L. McCarthy; A. W. McCreath; A. G. McDowall; A. G. MacDuff, QC; D. D. McEvoy, QC; R. J. McGregor-Johnson; R. D. Machell, QC; J. V. Machin; B. M. McIntyre; C. C. Mackay, QC; D. L. Mackie; I. McLeod; N. R. B. Macleod, QC; N. J. C. McLusky; T. Maher; A. R. Malcolm; M. E. Mann, QC; The Hon. G. R. J. Mansfield; A. C. B. Markham-David; R. L. Marks; A. S. Marron, QC; R. G. Marshall-Andrews, QC; H. R. A. Martineau; C. G. Masterman; D. Matheson, QC; P. R. Matthews; P. B. Mauleverer, QC; R. B. Mawrey, QC; R. Maxwell, QC; Mrs P. R. May; M. Meggeson; N. F. Merriman, QC; J. T. Milford, QC; R. A. Miller; S. M. Miller, QC; J. B. M. Milmo, QC; D. C. Milne, QC; N. A. Miscampbell, QC, MP; C. R. Mitchell; D. C. Mitchell; F. I. Mitchell; N. J. Mitchell; J. E. Mitting, QC; E. G. Moelwyn-Hughes; C. R. D. Moger, QC; H. J. Montlake; R. J. Moore; M. J. Moore-Bick, QC; M. G. C. Moorhouse; H. M. Morgan; G. E. Moriarty, QC; A. P. Morris, QC; The Rt. Hon. J. Morris, QC, MP; C. Morris-Coole; T. J. Mort; A. G. Moses, QC; C. J. Moss, QC; P. C. Mott, QC; Miss M. J. S. Mowat; R. W. Moxon-Browne, QC; J. H. Muir; J. Mulcahy, QC; F. J. Muller, QC; I. P. Murphy, QC; M. J. A. Murphy, QC; N. O. G. Murray; N. J. Mylne, QC; H. G. Narayan; J. O. Neligan; R. F. Nelson, QC; D. E. Neuberger, QC; R. E. Newbold; A. R. H. Newman, QC; S. A. G. Newman, QC; G. Nice, QC; C. A. A. Nicholls, QC; C. V. Nicholls, QC; M. C. Nicholson; A. S. T. E. Nicol; B. Nolan, QC; Col. A. P. Norris, OBE; J. M. Norris; P. H. Norris; J. G. Nutting; D. P. O'Brien, QC; E. M. Ogden, QC; S. Oliver-Jones; C. P. L. Openshaw, QC; D. B. W. Ouseley, QC; G. V. Owen, QC; R. M. Owen, QC; T. W. Owen; S. R. Page; D. C. J. Paget, QC; A. O. Palmer, QC; A. W. Palmer, QC; A. D. W. Pardoe, QC; S. A. B. Parish; A. E. W. Park, QC; G. C. Parkins, QC; G. E. Parkinson; M. P. Parroy, QC; D. J. Parry; D. J. T. Parry; E. O. Parry; M. A. Parry Evans; N. S. K. Pascoe, QC; A. Patience, QC; J. G. Paulusz; Prof. D. S. Pearl; R. J. Pearse Wheatley; B. P. Pearson; D. H. Penry-Davey, QC; J. Perry, QC; M. Pert, QC; B. J. Phelvin; J. A. Phillips; W. B. Phillips; J. C. Phipps; M. A. Pickering, QC; C. J. Pitchford, QC; The Hon. B. M. D. Pitt; A. P. Pitts; Miss E. F. Platt, QC; R. Platts; J. R. Playford, QC; A. G. S. Pollock, QC; T. G. Pontius; D. A. Poole; A. R. Porten, QC; L. R. Portnoy; M. J. Pratt, QC; S. Pratt; T. W. Preston; G. A. L. Price, QC; J. A. Price, QC; N. L. Price, QC; R. N. M. Price; A. C. Pugh, QC; G. V. Pugh, QC; C. P. B. Purchas, QC; R. M. Purchas, QC; N. R. Purnell, QC; P. O. Purnell, QC; Q. C. W. Querelle; D. A. Radcliffe; D. W. Radford; Ms A. J. Rafferty, QC; T. W. H. Raggatt, QC; A. Rankin, QC; A. D. Rawley, QC; P. R. Raynor, QC; L. F. Read, QC; J. H. Reddihough; A. R. F. Redgrave, QC; J. Reeder, QC; P. Rees; C. E. Reese, QC; J. R. Reid, QC; P. C. Reid; M. P. Reynolds; P. C. Rhodes; R. E. Rhodes, QC; D. G. Rice; D. W. Richards; H. A. Richardson; N. P. Riddell; S. V. Riordan, QC; Miss J. H. Ritchie; Miss S. A. Ritchie, QC; J. A. Roberts, QC; J. D. Roberts; J. M. Roberts; J. M. G. Roberts, QC; P. E. Robertshaw; A. J. Robertson; V. Robinson, QC; D. E. H. Robson, QC; G. W. Roddick, QC; Miss D. J. Rodgers; J. M. T. Rogers, QC; K. S. Rokison, QC; W. M. Rose;

J. G. Ross; J. G. Ross Martyn; P. C. Rouch; J. J. Rowe, QC;
R. J. Royce, QC; R. J. Rubery; A. A. Rumbelow, QC;
A. P. Russell; R. R. Russell; A. Rutherford; G. C. Ryan, QC;
J. R. T. Rylance; C. N. Salmon; J. E. A. Samuels, QC;
Miss A. O. H. Sander; A. T. Sander; G. R. Sankey, QC;
J. H. B. Saunders, QC; M. P. Sayers, QC; R. J. Scholes, QC;
A. R. G. Scott-Gall; R. J. Seabrook, QC; C. Seagroatt, QC;
M. R. Selfe; W. P. L. Sellick; O. M. Sells; D. Serota, QC;
A. J. Seys-Llewellyn; A. R. F. Sharp; P. P. Shears;
S. J. Sher, QC; J. M. Shorrock, QC; S. R. Silber, QC;
P. F. Singer, QC; J. C. N. Slater, QC; E. Slinger; A. C. Smith;
A. T. Smith, QC; R. D. H. Smith, QC; R. S. Smith, QC;
Ms Z. P. Smith; S. M. Solley, QC; R. F. Solman; E. Somerset
Jones, QC; R. C. Southwell, QC, R. C. E. Southwell;
M. H. Spence, QC; Sir Derek Spencer, QC, MP;
J. Spencer, QC; M. G. Spencer, QC; S. M. Spencer, QC;
R. V. Spencer Bernard; D. P. Spens; L. Spittle; R. W. Spon-
Smith; D. W. Steel, QC; D. Steer, QC; M. T. Steiger, QC;
D. H. Stembridge, QC; Mrs L. J. Stern, QC;
A. W. Stevenson, TD; J. S. H. Stewart, QC;
R. M. Stewart, QC; W. R. Stewart Smith; G. J. C. Still;
D. A. Stockdale; D. M. A. Stokes, QC; M. G. T. Stokes, QC;
E. D. R. Stone, QC; P. L. Storr; T. M. F. Stow, QC;
D. M. A. Strachan, QC; M. Stuart-Moore, QC; F. R. C. Such;
A. B. Suckling, QC; J. M. Sullivan, QC; Ms L. E. Sullivan, QC;
D. M. Sumner; J. P. C. Sumption, QC; P. J. Susman;
R. P. Sutton, QC; J. A. Swanson; D. R. Swift; L. Swift, QC;
M. R. Swift, QC; Miss H. H. Swindells; C. J. M. Symons, QC;
J. A. Tackaberry, QC; R. K. K. Talbot; G. F. Tattersall, QC;
E. Taylor; M. J. Taylor; J. J. Teare; A. D. Temple, QC;
V. B. A. Temple, QC; M. H. Tennant; M. I. Tennant;
D. M. Thomas, OBE, QC; D. O. Thomas, QC; P. A. Thomas;
R. J. L. Thomas, QC; R. L. Thomas, QC; R. U. Thomas, QC;
P. J. Thompson; A. C. L. Thornton, QC; J. Tiley;
M. B. Tillett; J. W. Tinnion; R. N. Titheridge, QC;
R. S. W. Tonking; J. K. Toulmin, CMG, QC;
R. G. Toulson, QC; J. B. S. Townend, QC; C. M. Treacy, QC;
H. B. Trethowan; A. D. H. Trollope, QC;
M. G. Tugendhat, QC; H. W. Turcan; D. A. Turner, QC;
P. A. Twigg, QC; A. R. Tyrrell, QC; N. E. Underhill, QC;
J. G. G. Ungley; N. P. Valios, QC; A. R. Vandermeer, QC;
D. A. J. Vaughan, QC; M. J. D. Vere-Hodge, QC;
C. D. Voelcker; J. P. Wadsworth; D. St J. Wagstaff;
S. P. Waine; J. J. Wait; R. Wakefield; R. M. Wakerley, QC;
W. H. Waldron, QC; R. A. Walker, QC; R. J. Walker, QC;
T. E. Walker, QC; Sir Jonah Walker-Smith, Bt.;
S. P. Waller; B. Walsh, QC; T. M. Walsh; C. T. Walton;
J. C. Warner; J. Warren, QC; D. E. B. Waters; Sir James
Watson, Bt.; C. D. G. Waud; B. J. Waylen; A. R. Webb;
R. S. Webb, QC; M. Weisman; P. Weitzman, QC;
C. S. Welchman; C. P. C. Whelon; G. Whitburn, QC;
C. H. Whitby, QC; W. J. M. White;
D. R. B. Whitehouse, QC; P. G. Whiteman, QC;
P. J. M. Whiteman, TD; A. Whitfield, QC;
D. G. Widdicombe, QC; R. Wigglesworth; J. S. Wiggs;
A. D. F. Wilcken; K. H. P. Wilkinson; N. V. M. Wilkinson;
D. B. Williams; G. H. G. Williams; Lord Williams of
Mostyn, QC; G. Williams; J. L. Williams, QC;
M. J. Williams; W. L. Williams, QC; S. W. Williamson, QC;
A. M. Wilson, QC; C. Wilson-Smith, QC; G. W. Wingate-
Saul, QC; R. J. Winstanley; M. E. Wolff; J. S. Wolstenholme;
H. Wolton, QC; D. A. Wood, QC; D. R. Wood; N. A. Wood;
W. R. Wood; L. G. Woodley, QC; Miss S. Woodley;
J. T. Woods; W. C. Woodward, QC; D. R. Woolley, QC;
N. G. Wootton; T. H. Workman; Miss A. M. Worrall, QC;
D. Worsley; P. F. Worsley, QC; J. J. Wright;
D. E. M. Young, QC

PROVINCIAL (each £56,974)

*Cheshire*, P. K. Dodd, OBE, *apptd* 1991
*Devon*, vacant
*East and West Sussex*, P. C. Tain, *apptd* 1992
*Greater Manchester*, W. D. Fairclough, *apptd* 1982;
   Miss J. E. Hayward, *apptd* 1991; A. Berg, *apptd* 1994
*Hampshire*, T. G. Cowling, *apptd* 1989
*Humberside*, N. H. White, *apptd* 1985
*Lancashire/Merseyside*, J. Finestein, *apptd* 1992
*Leicestershire*, vacant
*Merseyside*, N. G. Wootton, *apptd* 1976; D. R. G. Tapp,
   *apptd* 1992; P. S. Ward, *apptd* 1994; P. J. Firth, *apptd*
   1994
*Middlesex*, N. A. McKittrick, *apptd* 1989; S. Somjee, *apptd*
   1991; S. N. Day, *apptd* 1991
*Mid Glamorgan*, B. R. Oliver, *apptd* 1983; J. T. Curran,
   *apptd* 1990
*Norfolk*, N. P. Heley, *apptd* 1994
*North-East London*, G. E. Cawdron, *apptd* 1993
*Nottinghamshire*, P. F. Nuttall, *apptd* 1991; M. L. R. Harris,
   *apptd* 1991
*Shropshire*, P. H. R. Browning, *apptd* 1994
*South Glamorgan*, G. R. Watkins, *apptd* 1993
*South Yorkshire*, J. A. Browne, *apptd* 1992; J. E. Barry,
   *apptd* 1985; W. D. Thomas, *apptd* 1989;
   M. A. Rosenberg, *apptd* 1993
*Staffordshire*, P. G. G. Richards, *apptd* 1991
*West Midlands*, W. M. Probert, *apptd* 1983; B. Morgan,
   *apptd* 1989; I. Gillespie, *apptd* 1991; M. F. James, *apptd*
   1991; C. M. McColl, *apptd* 1994
*West Yorkshire*, F. D. L. Loy, *apptd* 1972; Mrs P. A. Hewitt,
   *apptd* 1990; G. A. K. Hodgson, *apptd* 1993

METROPOLITAN

*Chief Metropolitan Stipendiary Magistrate and Chairman of
   Committee of Magistrates for Inner London Area*
   (*£69,924), P. G. N. Badge, *apptd* 1992 (*Bow Street*)

*Magistrates* (each £60,974)

*Bow Street*, The Chief Magistrate; R. D. Bartle, *apptd* 1972;
   J. G. Connor, *apptd* 1979; H. N. Evans, *apptd* 1994
*Camberwell Green*, C. P. M. Davidson, *apptd* 1984;
   T. H. Workman, *apptd* 1986; H. Gott, *apptd* 1992;
   Mrs E. Rees, *apptd* 1994; Miss E. Roscoe, *apptd* 1994
*Clerkenwell*, M. L. R. Romer, *apptd* 1972; C. J. Bourke,
   *apptd* 1972; B. Loosley, *apptd* 1989
*Greenwich and Woolwich*, W. A. Kennedy, *apptd* 1991;
   D. A. Cooper, *apptd* 1991; P. S. Wallis, *apptd* 1993
*Highbury Corner*, D. Barr, *apptd* 1976; Miss D. Quick, *apptd*
   1986; G. Wicks, *apptd* 1987; P. Simpson, *apptd* 1993
*Horseferry Road*, A. R. Davies, *apptd* 1985; T. Maher, *apptd*
   1983; G. Breen, *apptd* 1986; Mrs K. R. Keating, *apptd*
   1987
*Marlborough Street*, J. Q. Campbell, *apptd* 1981;
   Miss D. Wickham, *apptd* 1989
*Marylebone*, G. L. J. Noel, *apptd* 1975; D. Kennet Brown,
   *apptd* 1982; A. C. Baldwin, *apptd* 1990; T. English, *apptd*
   1986; K. Maitland-Davies, *apptd* 1984
*Old Street*, M. A. Johnstone, *apptd* 1980; C. Pratt, *apptd*
   1990
*South-Western*, S. G. Clixby, *apptd* 1981; C. D. Voelcker,
   *apptd* 1982; A. Ormerod, *apptd* 1988
*Thames*, D. M. Fingleton, *apptd* 1980; G. E. Parkinson,
   *apptd* 1982; N. Crichton, *apptd* 1987; I. Bing, *apptd* 1989

*Tower Bridge*, Mrs J. R. Comyns, *apptd* 1982; R. D. Philips, *apptd* 1989; M. Kelly, *apptd* 1992
*Wells Street*, Miss A. M. Jennings, *apptd* 1972; I. M. Baker, *apptd* 1990; Ms G. Babington-Browne, *apptd* 1991; M. J. Read, *apptd* 1993
*West London*, H. J. Cook, *apptd* 1975; D. Thomas, *apptd* 1990
*Unattached Magistrates*, A. Evans, *apptd* 1990; C. S. F. Black, *apptd* 1993; S. Dawson, *apptd* 1994

COMMITTEE OF MAGISTRATES FOR INNER LONDON AREA
65 Romney Street, London SWIP 3RD
Tel 0171-799 3332

*Principal Chief Clerk and Clerk to the Committee* (£53,023–£61,087), G. D. Painter
*Chief Clerk (Training)* (£*47,848), P. Unwin

* 1993–4 figure

## CROWN PROSECUTION SERVICE
50 Ludgate Hill, London EC4M 7EX
Tel 0171-273 8000

The Crown Prosecution Service (CPS) is responsible for the independent review and conduct of criminal proceedings instituted by police forces in England and Wales, with the exception of cases conducted by the Serious Fraud Office (*see* page 355) and certain minor offences.

The Director of Public Prosecutions is the head of the Service and discharges her statutory functions under the superintendence of the Attorney-General.

The Service comprises a headquarters office and 13 areas covering England and Wales. Each of the CPS areas is supervised by a Chief Crown Prosecutor.

For salaries, *see* page 281

*Director of Public Prosecutions (G1)*, Mrs B. Mills, QC
*Principal Establishment and Finance Officer (G3)*, D. Nooney
*Director (Casework) (G3)*, C. Newell
*Director (Operations) (G3)*, G. Duff
*Director (Policy) (G3)*, K. Ashken

CPS AREAS

CPS ANGLIA, Queen's House, 58 Victoria Street, St Albans AL1 3HZ. Tel: 01727-844753. *Chief Crown Prosecutor (G4)*, R. J. Chronnell
CPS EAST MIDLANDS, 2 King Edward Court, King Edward Street, Nottingham NG1 1EL. Tel: 0115-948 0480. *Chief Crown Prosecutor (G4)*, B. T. McArdle
CPS HUMBER, Belgrave House, 47 Bank Street, Sheffield S1 2EH. Tel: 0114-276 1601. *Chief Crown Prosecutor (G4)*, D. Adams
CPS LONDON, Portland House, Stag Place, London SW1E 5BH. Tel: 0171-828 9050. *Chief Crown Prosecutor (G3)*, G. D. Etherington
CPS MERSEY/LANCASHIRE, 7th Floor (South), Royal Liver Building, Pier Head, Liverpool L3 1HN. Tel: 0151-236 7575. *Chief Crown Prosecutor (G4)*, C. Woodcock
CPS MIDLANDS, 14th Floor, Colmore Gate, 2 Colmore Row, Birmingham B3 2QA. Tel: 0121-629 7202. *Chief Crown Prosecutor (G4)*, T. M. McGowran
CPS NORTH, Benton House, 136 Sandyford Road, Newcastle upon Tyne NE2 1QE. Tel: 0191-230 0800. *Chief Crown Prosecutor (G4)*, D. V. Dickenson
CPS NORTH-WEST, PO Box 377, 8th Floor, Sunlight House, Quay Street, Manchester M60 3LU. Tel: 0161-837 7402. *Chief Crown Prosecutor (G4)*, A. R. Taylor
CPS SEVERN/THAMES, Artillery House, Heritage Way, Droitwich, Worcester WR9 8YB. Tel: 01905-793703. *Chief Crown Prosecutor (G4)*, A. S. R. Clarke
CPS SOUTH-EAST, Stoke Mill, Woking Road, Guildford, Surrey GU1 1AQ. Tel: 01483-573255. *Chief Crown Prosecutor (G4)*, D. E. J. Dracup
CPS SOUTH-WEST, Hawkins House, Pynes Hill, Rydon Lane, Exeter EX2 5SS. Tel: 01392-422555. *Chief Crown Prosecutor (G4)*, P. Boeuf
CPS WALES, Tudor House, 16 Cathedral Road, Cardiff CF1 9LJ. Tel: 01222-783037. *Chief Crown Prosecutor (G4)*, R. A. Prickett
CPS YORKSHIRE, 6th Floor, Ryedale Building, 60 Piccadilly, York YO1 1NS. Tel: 01904-610726. *Chief Crown Prosecutor (G4)*, D. M. Sharp, CBE

# The Scottish Judicature

Scotland has a legal system separate from and differing greatly from the English legal system in enacted law, judicial procedure and the structure of courts.

In Scotland the system of public prosecution is headed by the Lord Advocate and is independent of the police, who have no say in the decision to prosecute. The Lord Advocate, discharging his functions through the Crown Office in Edinburgh, is responsible for prosecutions in the High Court, sheriff courts and district courts. Prosecutions in the High Court are prepared by the Crown Office and conducted in court by one of the law officers, by an advocate-depute, or by a solicitor advocate. In the inferior courts the decision to prosecute is made and prosecution is preferred by procurators fiscal, who are lawyers and full-time civil servants subject to the directions of the Crown Office. A permanent legally-qualified civil servant known as the Crown Agent is responsible for the running of the Crown Office and the organization of the Procurator Fiscal Service, of which he is the head.

Scotland is divided into six sheriffdoms, each with a full-time Sheriff Principal. The sheriffdoms are further divided into sheriff court districts, each of which has a legally-qualified, resident sheriff or sheriffs, who are the judges of the court.

In criminal cases sheriffs principal and sheriffs have the same powers; sitting with a jury of 15 members, they may try more serious cases on indictment, or, sitting alone, may try lesser cases under summary procedure. Minor summary offences are dealt with in district courts which are administered by the district and the islands local government authorities and presided over by lay justices of the peace (of whom there are about 4,400) and, in Glasgow only, by stipendiary magistrates. Juvenile offenders (children under 16) may be brought before an informal children's hearing comprising three local lay people. The superior criminal court is the High Court of Justiciary which is both a trial and an appeal court. Cases on indictment are tried by a High Court judge, sitting with a jury of 15, in Edinburgh and on circuit in other towns. Appeals from the lower courts against conviction or sentence are heard also by the High Court, which sits as an appeal court only in Edinburgh. There is no further appeal to the House of Lords in criminal cases.

In civil cases the jurisdiction of the sheriff court extends to most kinds of action. Appeal against decisions of the sheriff may be made to the Sheriff Principal and thence to the Court of Session, or direct to the Court of Session, which sits only in Edinburgh. The Court of Session is divided into the Inner and the Outer House. The Outer House is a court of first instance in which cases are heard by judges sitting singly, sometimes with a jury of 12. The Inner House, itself subdivided into two divisions of equal status, is mainly an appeal court. Appeals may be made to the Inner House from the Outer House as well as from the sheriff court. An appeal may be made from the Inner House to the House of Lords.

The judges of the Court of Session are the same as those of the High Court of Justiciary, the Lord President of the Court of Session also holding the office of Lord Justice General in the High Court. Senators of the College of Justice are Lords Commissioners of Justiciary as well as judges of the Court of Session. On appointment, a Senator takes a judicial title, which is retained for life. Although styled 'The Hon./Rt. Hon. Lord —', the Senator is not a peer.

The office of coroner does not exist in Scotland. The local procurator fiscal inquires privately into sudden and suspicious deaths and may report findings to the Crown Agent. In some cases a fatal accident inquiry may be held before the sheriff.

## COURT OF SESSION AND HIGH COURT OF JUSTICIARY

*The Lord President and Lord Justice General* (£109,439)
The Rt. Hon. Lord Hope (David Hope), *born* 1938, *apptd* 1989

### INNER HOUSE

*Lords of Session* (each £104,922)

FIRST DIVISION

The Lord President
Hon. Lord Allanbridge (William Stewart), *born* 1925, *apptd* 1977
Hon. Lord Cowie (William Cowie), *born* 1926, *apptd* 1977
Hon. Lord Mayfield (Ian MacDonald, MC), *born* 1921, *apptd* 1981

SECOND DIVISION

*Lord Justice Clerk* (£108,922), The Rt. Hon. Lord Ross (Donald Ross), *born* 1927, *apptd* 1985
Rt. Hon. Lord Murray (Ronald Murray), *born* 1922, *apptd* 1979
Hon. The Lord McCluskey, *born* 1929, *apptd* 1984
Hon. Lord Morison (Alastair Morison), *born* 1931, *apptd* 1985

### OUTER HOUSE

*Lords of Session* (each £95,051)

Hon. Lord Davidson (Charles Davidson) (*seconded to Scottish Law Commission*), *born* 1929, *apptd* 1983

Hon. Lord Sutherland (Ranald Sutherland), *born* 1932, *apptd* 1985
Hon. Lord Weir (David Weir), *born* 1931, *apptd* 1985
Hon. Lord Clyde (James Clyde), *born* 1932, *apptd* 1985
Hon. Lord Cullen (Douglas Cullen), *born* 1935, *apptd* 1986
Hon. Lord Prosser (William Prosser), *born* 1934, *apptd* 1986
Hon. Lord Kirkwood (Ian Kirkwood), *born* 1932, *apptd* 1987
Hon. Lord Coulsfield (John Cameron), *born* 1934, *apptd* 1987
Hon. Lord Milligan (James Milligan), *born* 1934, *apptd* 1988
Hon. The Lord Morton of Shuna, *born* 1930, *apptd* 1988
Hon. Lord Caplan (Philip Caplan), *born* 1929, *apptd* 1989
Rt. Hon. The Lord Cameron of Lochbroom, *born* 1931, *apptd* 1989
Hon. Lord Marnoch (Michael Bruce), *born* 1938, *apptd* 1990
Hon. Lord MacLean (Ranald MacLean), *born* 1938, *apptd* 1990
Hon. Lord Penrose (George Penrose), *born* 1938, *apptd* 1990
Hon. Lord Osborne (Kenneth Osborne), *born* 1937, *apptd* 1990
Hon. Lord Abernethy (John Cameron), *born* 1938, *apptd* 1992
Hon. Lord Johnston (Alan Charles Macpherson), *born* 1942, *apptd* 1994

## COURT OF SESSION AND HIGH COURT OF JUSTICIARY

Parliament House, Parliament Square, Edinburgh EH1 1RQ
Tel 0131-225 2595

*Principal Clerk of Session and Justiciary* (£36,019–£53,470), H. S. Foley
*Deputy Principal Clerk of Justiciary and Administration* (£24,239–£37,539), E. Cumming
*Deputy Principal Clerk of Session and Principal Extractor* (£24,239–£37,539), M. Weir
*Deputy Principal Clerk (Keeper of the Rolls)* (£24,239–£37,539), T. M. Thomson
*Depute Clerks of Session and Justiciary* (£19,215–£24,780), N. J. Dowie; I. Smith; T. Higgins; T. B. Cruickshank; Q. Oliver; F. Shannly; A. S. Moffat; D. J. Shand; G. Ellis; D. G. Lynn; R. Cockburn; W. Dunn; A. Finlayson; C. Armstrong; S. Hindes; P. Crow; R. McMillan; G. Prentice; C. Cockburn; S. F. Bain; S. Walker; R. Jenkins; J. O. McLean

## SCOTTISH COURTS ADMINISTRATION

26–27 Royal Terrace, Edinburgh EH7 5AH
Tel 0131-556 0755

The Scottish Courts Administration is responsible to the Secretary of State for Scotland for the organization, administration and staffing of the court offices (except the district courts) and to the Lord Advocate for certain aspects of court procedures, jurisdiction and legislation, law reform and other matters.

The Scottish Court Service will become an executive agency in April 1995.
*Director* (G3), G. Murray, CB
*Deputy Director (Court Organization and Management)* (G5), vacant
*Deputy Director (Assistant Solicitor)* (G5), P. M. Beaton
*Chief Executive-designate, Scottish Court Service Executive Agency*, M. Ewart

## SHERIFF COURT OF CHANCERY

27 Chambers Street, Edinburgh EH1 1LB
Tel 0131–225 2525

The Court deals with service of heirs and completion of title in relation to heritable property.
*Sheriff of Chancery*, C. G. B. Nicholson, QC

## HM COMMISSARY OFFICE

27 Chambers Street, Edinburgh EH1 1LB
Tel 0131–225 2525

The Office is responsible for issuing confirmation, a legal document entitling a person to execute a deceased person's will, and other related matters.
*Commissary Clerk*, I. E. Scott

## SCOTTISH LAND COURT

1 Grosvenor Crescent, Edinburgh EH12 5ER
Tel 0131–225 3595

The court deals with disputes relating to agricultural and crofting land in Scotland.
*Chairman* (£82,641), The Hon. Lord Philip (Alexander Philip), QC
*Members*, D. D. McDiarmid; D. M. MacDonald; J. Kinloch (*part-time*)
*Principal Clerk*, K. H. R. Graham

---

## SHERIFFDOMS

---

SALARIES

| | |
|---|---|
| Sheriff Principal | £82,641 |
| Sheriff | £69,497 |
| Regional Sheriff Clerk | £27,660–£53,470 |
| Sheriff Clerk | £11,208–£37,539 |

*Floating Sheriff

## GRAMPIAN, HIGHLANDS AND ISLANDS

*Sheriff Principal*, D. J. Risk
*Regional Sheriff Clerk*, J. Robertson

SHERIFFS AND SHERIFF CLERKS

*Aberdeen and Stonehaven*, D. W. Bogie; G. C. Warner; D. Kelbie; L. A. S. Jessop; *Sheriff Clerks*, D. Nicoll; I. Smith
*Peterhead and Banff*, K. A. McLernan; *Sheriff Clerk*, A. Hempseed; *Sheriff Clerk Depute*, W. H. Connon
*Elgin*, N. McPartlin; *Sheriff Clerk*, M. McBey
*Inverness, Lochmaddy, Portree, Stornoway, Dingwall, Tain, Wick and Dornoch*, W. J. Fulton; D. Booker-Milburn; J. O. A. Fraser; E. Stewart; *Sheriff Clerk*, J. Robertson
*Kirkwall and Lerwick*, G. S. MacKenzie; *Sheriff Clerks Depute*, R. Cantwell; A. C. Norris
*Fort William*, D. Noble (also *Oban and Campbeltown*); *Sheriff Clerk Depute*, D. Hood

## TAYSIDE, CENTRAL AND FIFE

*Sheriff Principal*, J. J. Maguire, QC
*Regional Sheriff Clerk*, J. S. Doig

SHERIFFS AND SHERIFF CLERKS

*Arbroath and Forfar*, K. A. Veal; G. N. R. Stein; *Sheriff Clerks*, M. Herbertson; P. Dougan

*Dundee*, R. A. Davidson; A. L. Stewart; *Sheriff Clerk*, J. S. Doig
*Perth*, J. F. Wheatley; J. C. McInnes, QC; *Sheriff Clerk*, W. Jones
*Falkirk*, A. V. Sheehan; A. J. Murphy; *Sheriff Clerk*, D. Forrester
*Stirling*, A. Pollock; R. E. G. Younger; *Sheriff Clerk*, J. Clark
*Alloa*, W. M. Reid; *Sheriff Clerk*, G. McHeard
*Cupar*, C. Smith (also *Dundee*); *Sheriff Clerk*, R. Hughes
*Dunfermline*, J. S. Forbes; C. W. Palmer; *Sheriff Clerk*, W. McCulloch
*Kirkcaldy*, W. J. Christie; Mrs L. G. Patrick; *Sheriff Clerk*, I. Hay

## LOTHIAN AND BORDERS

*Sheriff Principal*, C. G. B. Nicholson, QC
*Regional Sheriff Clerk*, I. E. Scott

SHERIFFS AND SHERIFF CLERKS

*Edinburgh*, N. E. D. Thomson; J. L. M. Mitchell; P. G. B. McNeill, PH.D., QC; Miss H. J. Aronson, QC; R. G. Craik, QC; G. I. W. Shiach; Miss I. A. Poole; R. J. D. Scott; A. M. Bell; J. M. S. Horsburgh; G. W. S. Presslie; J. A. Farrell; *A. Lothian; *F. J. Keane; *Sheriff Clerk*, I. E. Scott
*Peebles*, N. E. D. Thomson, CBE (also *Edinburgh*); *Sheriff Clerk*, I. E. Scott
*Linlithgow*, H. R. MacLean; G. R. Fleming; *Sheriff Clerk*, R. Sinclair
*Haddington*, G. W. S. Presslie (also *Edinburgh*); *Sheriff Clerk*, J. O'Donnell
*Jedburgh and Duns*, J. V. Paterson; *Sheriff Clerk*, J. W. Williamson
*Selkirk*, J. V. Paterson; *Sheriff Clerk*, L. McFarlane

## NORTH STRATHCLYDE

*Sheriff Principal*, R. C. Hay, CBE
*Regional Sheriff Clerk*, A. A. Brown

SHERIFFS AND SHERIFF CLERKS

*Oban and Campbeltown*, D. Noble (also *Fort William*); *Sheriff Clerk Deputes*, G. Whitelaw; P. G. Hay
*Dumbarton*, J. T. Fitzsimons; T. Scott; S. W. H. Fraser; *Sheriff Clerk*, N. R. Weir
*Paisley*, R. G. Smith; C. N. Stoddart; J. Spy; C. K. Higgins; A. W. Noble; *C. G. McKay; *Sheriff Clerk*, A. A. Brown
*Greenock*, J. Herald (also *Rothesay*); Sir Stephen Young; *Sheriff Clerk*, J. Tannahill
*Kilmarnock*, T. M. Croan; D. B. Smith; T. F. Russell; *Sheriff Clerk*, J. Shaw
*Dunoon*, A. Noble (also *Dumbarton*); *Sheriff Clerk Depute*, Mrs C. Carson

## GLASGOW AND STRATHKELVIN

*Sheriff Principal*, N. D. MacLeod, QC
*Regional Sheriff Clerk*, C. McLay

SHERIFFS AND SHERIFF CLERKS

*Glasgow*, A. C. Horsfall, QC (*seconded to Scottish Lands Tribunal*); A. A. Bell, QC; B. Kearney; G. H. Gordon, QC; A. C. McKay; J. C. M. Jardine; Mrs D. J. B. Robertson; B. A. Lockhart; I. G. Pirie; Mrs A. L. A. Duncan; W. G. Stevenson, QC; G. J. Evans; E. H. Galt; A. C. Henry; J. K. Mitchell; A. G. Johnston; J. P. Murphy; M. Sischy; S. A. O. Raeburn; A. B. Wilkinson; D. Convers; J. McGowan; *Sheriff Clerk*, C. McLay

## SOUTH STRATHCLYDE, DUMFRIES AND GALLOWAY

*Sheriff Principal*, G. L. Cox, QC
*Regional Sheriff Clerk*, H. Findlay, OBE

### SHERIFFS AND SHERIFF CLERKS

*Hamilton*, L. Cameron; A. C. MacPherson; W. F. Lunny;
    D. G. Russell; V. J. Canavan (also *Airdrie*); W. E. Gibson;
    H. Stirling; *C. B. Miller; *Sheriff Clerk*, P. Yelney
*Lanark*, J. D. Allan; *Sheriff Clerk*, D. Fyffe
*Ayr*, N. Gow, QC; R. G. McEwan, QC; *Sheriff Clerk*,
    G. W. Waddell
*Stranraer and Kirkcudbright*, J. R. Smith; *Sheriff Clerk*
    (*Stranraer*), W. McIntosh; *Sheriff Clerk (Kirkcudbright)*,
    B. Lindsay
*Dumfries*, K. G. Barr; M. J. Fletcher; *Sheriff Clerk*,
    P. McGonigle
*Airdrie*, J. H. Stewart; V. J. Canavan (also *Hamilton*);
    R. H. Dickson; I. C. Simpson; *Sheriff Clerk*, H. Findlay

## STIPENDIARY MAGISTRATES

### GLASGOW

R. Hamilton, *apptd* 1984; J. B. C. Nisbet, *apptd* 1984;
R. B. Christie, *apptd* 1985; Mrs J. A. M. MacLean, *apptd*
1990

## PROCURATOR FISCAL SERVICE

### CROWN OFFICE
25 Chambers Street, Edinburgh EH1 1LA
Tel 0131-226 2626

*Crown Agent* (£64,307–£75,328), J. D. Lowe
*Deputy Crown Agent* (£44,390–£53,740), N. McFadyen

### PROCURATORS FISCAL

SALARIES 1993–4
Regional Procurator Fiscal–grade 3        £52,704–£62,817

Regional Procurator Fiscal–grade 4        £44,390–£51,732
Procurator Fiscal–upper level             £36,019–£47,921
Procurator Fiscal–lower level             £25,900–£40,939

### GRAMPIAN, HIGHLANDS AND ISLANDS REGION

*Regional Procurator Fiscal*, A. D. Vannett (*Aberdeen*)
*Procurators Fiscal*, E. K. Barbour (*Stonehaven*);
    A. J. M. Colley (*Banff*); I. S. McNaughtan (*Peterhead*);
    G. K. Buchanan (*Elgin*); A. N. MacDonald (*Wick*);
    C. B. McClory (*Portree and Lochmaddy*); Mrs D. Wilson
    (*Stornoway*); H. T. Westwater (*Dornoch* and *Tain*);
    W. W. Orr (*Inverness*); D. K. Adam (*Kirkwall* and
    *Lerwick*); Mrs A. Neizer (*Fort William*); D. R. Hingston
    (*Dingwall*)

### TAYSIDE, CENTRAL AND FIFE REGION

*Regional Procurator Fiscal*, B. K. Heywood (*Dundee*)
*Procurators Fiscal*, Mrs B. Bott (*Arbroath*); J. F. McKay
    (*Forfar*); I. A. McLeod (*Perth*); G. E. Scott (*Falkirk*);
    K. Valentine (*Stirling*); I. D. Douglas (*Alloa*);
    E. B. Russell (*Cupar*); R. T. Hamilton (*Dunfermline*);
    F. R. Crowe (*Kirkcaldy*)

### LOTHIAN AND BORDERS REGION

*Regional Procurator Fiscal*, R. F. Lees (*Edinburgh*)
*Procurators Fiscal*, R. F. Lees (*Peebles*); Miss L. M. Ruxton
    (*Linlithgow*); A. J. P. Reith (*Haddington*); A. R. G. Fraser
    (*Duns* and *Jedburgh*); D. McNeill (*Selkirk*)

### NORTH STRATHCLYDE REGION

*Regional Procurator Fiscal*, J. D. Friel (*Paisley*)
*Procurators Fiscal*, I. Henderson (*Campbeltown*);
    C. C. Donnelly (*Dumbarton*); J. Macdonald (*Greenock* and
    *Rothesay*); D. L. Webster (*Dunoon*); J. G. MacGlennan
    (*Kilmarnock*); B. R. Maguire (*Oban*)

### GLASGOW AND STRATHKELVIN REGION

*Regional Procurator Fiscal*, A. C. Normand (*Glasgow*)

### SOUTH STRATHCLYDE, DUMFRIES AND GALLOWAY REGION

*Regional Procurator Fiscal*, W. G. Carmichael (*Hamilton*)
*Procurators Fiscal*, S. R. Houston (*Lanark*); N. G. O'Brien
    (*Ayr*); F. Walkinshaw (*Stranraer*); D. J. Howdle
    (*Dumfries* and *Kirkcudbright*); A. T. Wilson (*Airdrie*)

# Northern Ireland Judicature

In Northern Ireland the legal system and the structure of courts closely resemble those of England and Wales; there are, however, often differences in enacted law.

The Supreme Court of Judicature of Northern Ireland comprises the Court of Appeal, the High Court of Justice and the Crown Court. The practice and procedure of these courts is similar to that in England. The superior civil court is the High Court of Justice, from which an appeal lies to the Northern Ireland Court of Appeal; the House of Lords is the final civil appeal court.

The Crown Court, served by High Court and county court judges, deals with criminal trials on indictment. Cases are heard before a judge and, except those involving offences specified under emergency legislation, a jury. Appeals from the Crown Court against conviction or sentence are heard by the Northern Ireland Court of Appeal; the House of Lords is the final court of appeal.

The decision to prosecute in cases tried on indictment and in summary cases of a serious nature rests in Northern Ireland with the Director of Public Prosecutions, who is responsible to the Attorney-General. Minor summary offences are prosecuted by the police.

Minor criminal offences are dealt with in magistrates' courts by a full-time, legally qualified resident magistrate and, where an offender is under 17, by juvenile courts each consisting of a resident magistrate and two lay members specially qualified to deal with juveniles (at least one of whom must be a woman). In July 1994 there were 982 justices of the peace in Northern Ireland. Appeals from magistrates' courts are heard by the county court, or by the Court of Appeal on a point of law or an issue as to jurisdiction.

Magistrates' courts in Northern Ireland can deal with certain classes of civil case but most minor civil cases are dealt with in county courts. Judgments of all civil courts are enforceable through a centralized procedure administered by the Enforcement of Judgments Office.

## SUPREME COURT OF JUDICATURE
The Royal Courts of Justice, Belfast BT1 3JF
Tel 01232–235111

*Lord Chief Justice of Northern Ireland* (£109,435),
The Rt. Hon. Sir Brian Hutton, *born* 1931, *apptd* 1988
*Principal Secretary*, D. A. Lavery

LORDS JUSTICES OF APPEAL (each £104,922)
*Style*, The Rt. Hon. Lord Justice [surname]

Rt. Hon. Sir Basil Kelly, *born* 1920, *apptd* 1984
Rt. Hon. Sir John MacDermott, *born* 1927, *apptd* 1987
Rt. Hon. Sir Robert Carswell, *born* 1934, *apptd* 1993

PUISNE JUDGES (each £95,051)
*Style*, The Hon. Mr Justice [surname]

Hon. Sir Michael Nicholson, *born* 1933, *apptd* 1986
Hon. Sir William McCollum, *born* 1933, *apptd* 1987
Hon. Sir Anthony Campbell, *born* 1936, *apptd* 1988
Hon. Sir John Sheil, *born* 1938, *apptd* 1989
Hon. Sir Brian Kerr, *born* 1948, *apptd* 1993
Hon. Sir John Pringle, *born* 1929, *apptd* 1993
Hon. Sir Malachy Higgins, *born* 1944, *apptd* 1993

MASTERS OF THE SUPREME COURT (each £56,974)
*Master, Queen's Bench and Appeals and Clerk of the Crown*,
  J. W. Wilson, QC
*Master, High Court*, Mrs D. M. Kennedy
*Master, Office of Care and Protection*, F. B. Hall
*Master, Chancery Office*, R. A. Ellison

*Master, Bankruptcy and Companies Office*, J. B. C. Glass
*Master, Probate and Matrimonial Office*, R. T. Millar
*Master, Taxing Office*, J. C. Napier

## COUNTY COURTS

JUDGES (each £82,641)
*Style*, His Hon. Judge [surname]

Judge Russell, QC; Judge Curran, QC; Judge McKee, QC; Judge Gibson, QC; Judge Hart, QC; Judge Petrie, QC; Judge Smyth, QC; Judge Burgess, Judge Markey, QC; Judge McKay, QC; Judge Chambers, QC (*Chief Social Security and Child Support Commissioner*)

RECORDERS (each £82,641)
*Belfast*, Rt. Hon. Judge Sir Robert Porter, QC
*Londonderry*, Judge Martin, QC

## MAGISTRATES' COURTS

RESIDENT MAGISTRATES (each £56,974)
There are 17 resident magistrates in Northern Ireland.

## CROWN SOLICITOR'S OFFICE
PO Box 410, Royal Courts of Justice, Belfast BT1 3JY
Tel 01232–235111

*Crown Solicitor*, N. P. Roberts

## DEPARTMENT OF THE DIRECTOR OF PUBLIC PROSECUTIONS
Royal Courts of Justice, Belfast BT1 3NX
Tel 01232–235111

*Director of Public Prosecutions*, A. Fraser, CB, QC
*Deputy Director of Public Prosecutions*, D. Magill

## NORTHERN IRELAND COURT SERVICE
Windsor House, Bedford Street, Belfast BT2 7LT
Tel 01232–328594

*Director (G3)*

# Ecclesiastical Courts

Original jurisdiction is exercised by the consistory court of each diocese in England, presided over by the Chancellor of that diocese. Appellate jurisdiction is exercised by the provincial courts detailed below, by the Court for Ecclesiastical Causes Reserved, and by commissions of review (the membership of these being newly constituted for each case).

COURT OF ARCHES (PROVINCE OF CANTERBURY)
*Registry*, 16 Beaumont Street, Oxford OX1 2LZ
Tel 01865–241974

*Dean of the Arches*, The Rt. Worshipful Sir John Owen

COURT OF THE VICAR-GENERAL OF THE PROVINCE OF CANTERBURY
*Registry*, 16 Beaumont Street, Oxford OX1 2LZ
Tel 01865–241974

*Vicar-General*, The Rt. Worshipful Miss S. Cameron, QC

CHANCERY COURT OF YORK
*Registry*, 1 Peckitt Street, York YO1 1SG
Tel 01904–623487

*Auditor*, The Rt. Worshipful Sir John Owen

THE VICAR-GENERAL OF THE PROVINCE OF YORK
*Registry*, 1 Peckitt Street, York YO1 1SG
Tel 01904–623487

*Vicar-General*, His Honour the Worshipful Judge
  T. A. C. Coningsby, QC

COURT OF FACULTIES
*Registry*, 1 The Sanctuary, London SW1P 3JT
Tel 0171–222 5381

Office for the issue of special and common marriage licences, appointment of notaries public, etc. Office hours, Monday–Friday, 10–4.

*Master of the Faculties*, The Rt. Worshipful Sir John Owen

# Tribunals

## AGRICULTURAL LAND TRIBUNALS

c/o Land Use and Tenure Division, Ministry of Agriculture, Fisheries and Food, Nobel House, 17 Smith Square, London SWIP 3JR
Tel 0171–238 3000

Agricultural Land Tribunals were set up under the Agriculture Act 1947 and settle disputes and other issues between agricultural landlords and tenants. They also settle drainage disputes between neighbours.

There are seven tribunals covering England and one covering Wales. For each tribunal the Lord Chancellor appoints a chairman and one or more deputies, who must be barristers or solicitors of at least seven years standing. The Lord Chancellor also appoints lay members to three statutory panels of members: the 'landowners' panel, the 'farmers' panel and the 'drainage' panel.

Each of the eight tribunals is an independent statutory body with jurisdiction only within its own area. A separate tribunal is constituted for each case, and consists of a chairman (who may be the chairman or one of the deputy chairmen) and two lay members nominated by the chairman. The chairmen and deputy chairmen are entitled to claim a fee of £233 per day.

*Chairmen (England)*, W. D. Greenwood; K. J. Fisher; P. A. de la Piquerie; C. H. Beaumont; M. K. Lee; G. L. Newsom; His Hon. Judge Robert Taylor
*Chairman (Wales)*, W. J. Owen

## COMMONS COMMISSIONERS

Golden Cross House, Duncannon Street, London WC2N 4JF
Tel 0171–210 4584

The Commons Commissioners are responsible for deciding disputes arising under the Commons Registration Act 1965 and the Common Land (Rectification of Registers) Act 1989. They also enquire into the ownership of unclaimed common land. Commissioners are appointed by the Lord Chancellor.
*Chief Commons Commissioner (£80,428)*, M. Roth
*Commissioners*, I. L. R. Romer; D. M. Burton
*Clerk*, Miss F. A. A. Buchan

## COPYRIGHT TRIBUNAL

Room 4/6, Hazlitt House, 45 Southampton Buildings, London WC2A 1AR
Tel 0171–438 4776

The Copyright Tribunal is the successor to the Performing Right Tribunal which was established by the Copyright Act 1956 to resolve various classes of copyright dispute, principally in the field of collective licensing. Its jurisdiction was extended by the Copyright, Designs and Patents Act 1988 and the Broadcasting Act 1990.

The chairman and two deputy chairmen are appointed by the Lord Chancellor. Up to eight ordinary members are appointed by the Secretary of State for Trade and Industry.
*Chairman*, J. M. Bowers
*Secretary*, Mrs K. M. Adams

## DATA PROTECTION TRIBUNAL

c/o The Home Office, Queen Anne's Gate, London SW1H 9AT
Tel 0171–273 3386

The Data Protection Tribunal was established under the Data Protection Act 1984 to determine appeals against decisions of the Data Protection Registrar (*see* page 299). The chairman and two deputy chairmen are appointed by the Lord Chancellor and must be legally qualified. Lay members are appointed by the Home Secretary to represent the interests of data users or data subjects.

A tribunal consists of a legally-qualified chairman sitting with equal numbers of the lay members appointed to represent the interests of data users and data subjects. The chairman and members receive an *ad hoc* daily fee when the tribunal is sitting.
*Chairman*, J. A. C. Spokes, QC
*Secretary*, M. Jones

## EMPLOYMENT APPEAL TRIBUNAL

*Central Office*, Audit House, 58 Victoria Embankment, London EC4Y 0DS
Tel 0171–273 1041
*Divisional Office*, 11 Melville Crescent, Edinburgh EH3 7LU
Tel 0131–225 3963

The Employment Appeal Tribunal was established as a superior court of record under the provisions of the Employment Protection Act 1975, hearing appeals on a question of law arising from any decision of an industrial tribunal.

A tribunal consists of a legally-qualified chairman and two lay members, one from each side of industry. They are appointed by The Queen on the recommendation of the Lord Chancellor and the Secretary of State for Employment.
*President*, The Hon. Mr Justice Mummery
*Scottish Chairman*, The Hon. Lord Coulsfield
*Registrar*, Miss V. J. Selio

## IMMIGRATION APPELLATE AUTHORITIES

Thanet House, 231 Strand, London WC2R 1DA
Tel 0171–353 8060

The Immigration Appeal Adjudicators hear appeals from immigration decisions concerning the need for, and refusal of, leave to enter or remain in the UK, decisions to make deportation orders and directions to remove persons subject to immigration control from the UK. The Immigration Appeal Tribunal hears appeals direct from decisions to make deportation orders in matters concerning conduct contrary to the public good. Its principal jurisdiction is, however, the hearing of appeals from adjudicators by the party (Home Office or individual) who is aggrieved by the decision. Appeals are subject to leave being granted by the tribunal.

An adjudicator sits alone. The tribunal sits in divisions of three – normally a legally qualified member and two lay members. Members of the tribunal and adjudicators are appointed by the Lord Chancellor.

IMMIGRATION APPEAL TRIBUNAL
*President* (£69,497), G. W. Farmer
*Vice-Presidents*, Prof. D. C. Jackson; Mrs J. Chatwani

IMMIGRATION APPEAL ADJUDICATORS
*Chief Adjudicator* (£69,497), vacant
*Deputy Chief Adjudicator*, R. G. Care

---

INDEPENDENT TRIBUNAL SERVICE
City Gate House, 39–45 Finsbury Square, London EC2A IPX
Tel 0171-814 6500

---

The service is the judicial authority which exercises judicial and administrative control over the independent social security and child support appeal tribunals, medical and disability appeal tribunals and vaccine damage tribunals.
*President* (£73,497), His Hon. Judge Bassingthwaighte
*Chief Executive*, Mrs V. Willcocks

---

INDUSTRIAL TRIBUNALS

---

CENTRAL OFFICE (ENGLAND AND WALES)
19–29 Woburn Place, London WCIH OLU
Tel 0171-273 8659

Industrial Tribunals for England and Wales sit in 11 regions. The tribunals deal with matters of employment law, redundancy, dismissal, contract disputes, sexual and racial discrimination and related areas of dispute which may arise in the workplace. The tribunals are funded by the Department of Employment.

Chairmen, who may be full-time or part-time, are legally qualified. They are appointed by the Lord Chancellor. Tribunal members are nominated by the CBI and TUC, and appointed by the Secretary of State for Employment.
*President* (£82,641), His Hon. Judge T. Lawrence

CENTRAL OFFICE (SCOTLAND)
St Andrew House, 141 West Nile Street, Glasgow GI 2RU
Tel 0141-331 1601

Tribunals in Scotland have the same remit as those in England and Wales. Chairmen are appointed by the Lord President of the Court of Session and lay members by the Secretary of State for Employment.
*President* (£82,641), Mrs D. Littlejohn

---

INDUSTRIAL TRIBUNALS AND THE FAIR EMPLOYMENT TRIBUNAL (NORTHERN IRELAND)
Long Bridge House, 20–24 Waring Street, Belfast BTI 2EB
Tel 01232-327666

---

The industrial tribunal system in Northern Ireland was set up in 1965 and is similar to the system operating in the rest of the UK. The main legislation in Northern Ireland giving jurisdiction to industrial tribunals to hear complaints relating to employment matters corresponds to legislation enacted in Great Britain, except that there is no equivalent legislation to the Race Relations Act.

Since 1 January 1990 there has been a separate Fair Employment Tribunal in Northern Ireland. The Fair

Employment Tribunal hears and determines individual cases of alleged religious or political discrimination in employment. Employers can also appeal to the Fair Employment Tribunal if they consider the directions of the Fair Employment Commission to be unreasonable, inappropriate or unnecessary, and the Fair Employment Commission can make application to the Tribunal for the enforcement of undertakings or directions with which an employer has not complied.

The president, vice-president and part-time chairmen of the Fair Employment Tribunal are appointed by the Lord Chancellor. The full-time chairman and the part-time chairmen of the industrial tribunals and the panel members to both the industrial tribunals and the Fair Employment Tribunal are appointed by the Department of Economic Development Northern Ireland.
*President of the Industrial Tribunals and the Fair Employment Tribunal* (£82,641), J. Maguire
*Vice-President of the Industrial Tribunals and the Fair Employment Tribunal*, Mrs M. Perceval-Price
*Secretary*, J. Murphy

---

LANDS TRIBUNAL
48–49 Chancery Lane, London WC2A IJR
Tel 0171-936 7200

---

The Lands Tribunal is an independent judicial body constituted by the Lands Tribunal Act 1949 for the purpose of determining a wide range of questions relating to the valuation of land, rating appeals from local valuation courts and the discharge or modification of restrictive covenants. The Act also empowers the tribunal to accept the function of arbitration under references by consent. The tribunal consists of a president and a number of other members, who are appointed by the Lord Chancellor.
*President* (£73,497), His Hon. Judge Marder, QC
*Members* (£69,497), Dr T. Hoyes, FRICS; M. S. J. Hopper, FRICS
*Members (part-time)* (£316 per day), J. C. Hill, TD; His Hon. Judge Rich, QC; A. P. Musto, FRICS; P. H. Clarke, FRICS
*Registrar*, C. A. McMullan

---

LANDS TRIBUNAL FOR SCOTLAND
1 Grosvenor Crescent, Edinburgh EHI2 5ER
Tel 0131-225 7996

---

The Lands Tribunal for Scotland was constituted by the Lands Tribunal Act 1949. Its remit is the same as the tribunal for England and Wales but also covers questions relating to tenants rights. The president is appointed by the Lord President of the Court of Session.
*President* (£82,641), The Hon. Lord Philip, QC
*Members* (£69,497), Sheriff A. C. Horsfall, QC; A. R. MacLeary; J. Devine (*full-time*); R. A. Edwards, CBE, WS (*part-time*)
*Clerk*, D. Pentland

---

MENTAL HEALTH REVIEW TRIBUNALS

---

The Mental Health Review Tribunals are independent judicial bodies established under the Mental Health Act 1959 and which now operate under the Mental Health Act 1983. They are responsible for reviewing the cases of patients compulsorily detained under the Act's provisions. They have the power to discharge the patient and, in the case of unrestricted patients, to re-classify the patient, to recommend leave of absence, delayed discharge, transfer to another hospital, or that a guardianship order be made. There are eight tribunals in England, each headed by a regional chairman who is appointed by the Lord Chancellor's Department on a part-time basis. Each tribunal is made up of at least three members, and must include a lawyer, who acts as president (£221 per day), a medical member (£220.70 per day) and a lay member (£91 per day).

The Medical Health Review Tribunals' secretariat is based in five regional offices:

LIVERPOOL, 3rd Floor, Cressington House, 249 St Mary's Road, Garston, Liverpool L19 0NF. Tel: 0151-494 0095. *Clerk*, Mrs B. Foot

LONDON (NORTH), Spur 3, Block 1, Government Buildings, Honeypot Lane, Stanmore, Middx. HA7 1AY. Tel: 0171-972 3738. *Clerk*, P. Barnett

LONDON (SOUTH), Block 3, Crown Offices, Kingston Bypass Road, Surbiton, Surrey KT6 5QN. Tel: 0181-398 4166. *Clerk*, Mrs J. Innes

NOTTINGHAM, Spur A, Block 5, Government Buildings, Chalfont Drive, Western Boulevard, Nottingham NG8 3RZ. Tel: 0115-929 4222. *Clerk*, M. Chapman

WALES, 1st Floor, New Crown Buildings, Cathays Park, Cardiff CF1 3NQ. Tel: 01222-823036. *Clerk*, Mrs C. Thomas

## NATIONAL HEALTH SERVICE TRIBUNAL

The NHS Tribunal inquires into representations that the continued inclusion of a family practitioner (doctor, dentist, pharmacist or optician) on a Family Practitioner Committee's list would be prejudicial to the efficiency of the services concerned. The tribunal sits when required, about eight times a year, and usually in London.
*Chairman*, A. Whitfield, QC
*Clerk*, I. D. Keith, East Hookers, Twineham, nr Haywards Heath, W. Sussex RH17 5NN. Tel: 01444-881345

## NATIONAL HEALTH SERVICE TRIBUNAL (SCOTLAND)
Erskine House, 68 Queen Street, Edinburgh EH2 4NN
Tel 0131-226 6541

The tribunal was set up under the National Health Service (Scotland) Act 1978, and exists to consider representations that the continued inclusion of a registered medical practitioner, dental practitioner, optometrist or pharmacist on a health board's list would be prejudicial to the continuing efficiency of the service in question.

The tribunal meets when required and is composed of a chairman, one lay member, and one practitioner member drawn from a representative professional panel. The chairman is appointed by the Lord President of the Court of Session, and the lay member and the members of the professional panel are appointed by the Secretary of State for Scotland. The chairman and members receive an *ad hoc* daily fee when the tribunal is sitting.
*Chairman*, W. C. Galbraith, QC
*Lay member*, J. D. M. Robertson
*Clerk to the Tribunal*, D. G. Brash, WS

## PENSIONS APPEAL TRIBUNALS

CENTRAL OFFICE (ENGLAND AND WALES)
48–49 Chancery Lane, London WC2A 1JR
Tel 0171-936 7034

The Pensions Appeal Tribunals are responsible for hearing appeals from ex-servicemen or women and widows who have had their claims for a war pension rejected by the Secretary of State for Social Security. The Entitlement Appeal Tribunals hear appeals in cases where the Secretary of State has refused to grant a war pension. The Assessment Appeal Tribunals hear appeals against the Secretary of State's assessment of the degree of disablement caused by an accepted condition.

The tribunal members are appointed by the Lord Chancellor.
*President* (£56,974), J. R. T. Holt
*Secretary*, Mrs A. Bartram

PENSIONS APPEAL TRIBUNALS FOR SCOTLAND
20 Walker Street, Edinburgh EH3 7HS
Tel 0131-220 1404
*President*, A. C. Hamilton, QC

## OFFICE OF THE SOCIAL SECURITY AND CHILD SUPPORT COMMISSIONERS
Harp House, 83–86 Farringdon Street, London EC4A 4DH
Tel 0171-353 5145
23 Melville Street, Edinburgh EH3 7PW
Tel 0131-225 2201

The Social Security Commissioners are the final statutory authority to decide appeals relating to entitlement to social security benefits. The Child Support Commissioners are the final statutory authority to decide appeals relating to child support. Appeals may be made in relation to both matters only on a point of law. The Commissioners' jurisdiction covers England, Wales and Scotland. There are 17 commissioners; they are all qualified lawyers.
*Chief Social Security Commissioner and Chief Child Support Commissioner* (£69,497), His Hon. Judge Machin, QC
*Secretary*, S. Hill (*London*); R. Lindsay (*Edinburgh*)

## OFFICE OF THE SOCIAL SECURITY AND CHILD SUPPORT COMMISSIONERS FOR NORTHERN IRELAND
Lancashire House, 5 Linenhall Street, Belfast BT2 8AA
Tel 01232-332344

The role of Northern Ireland Social Security and Child Support Commissioners is similar to that of the Commissioners in Great Britain. There are two commissioners for Northern Ireland.
*Chief Commissioner* (£82,641), His Hon. Judge Chambers, QC
*Registrar of Appeals*, W. D. Pollock

## THE SOLICITORS' DISCIPLINARY TRIBUNAL
227–228 Strand WC2A 1BA
Tel 0171-242 0219

The Solicitors' Disciplinary Tribunal was constituted under the provisions of the Solicitors Act 1974. It is an independent

statutory body whose members are appointed by the Master of the Rolls. The tribunal considers applications made to it alleging either professional misconduct and/or a breach of the statutory rules by which solicitors are bound against an individually named solicitor, former solicitor, or registered foreign lawyer. The tribunal's jurisdiction extends to solicitor's clerks, in respect of whom they may make an order restricting that clerk's employment by solicitors.
*President*, G. B. Marsh
*Clerk*, Mrs S. C. Elson

## SPECIAL COMMISSIONERS OF INCOME TAX
15–19 Bedford Avenue, London WC1B 3AS
Tel 0171–631 4242

The Special Commissioners are an independent body appointed by the Lord Chancellor to hear complex appeals against decisions of the Board of Inland Revenue and its officials. There are three full-time and 14 part-time commissioners; all are legally qualified.
*Presiding Special Commissioner* (£82,641), His Hon. Stephen Oliver, QC
*Special Commissioners* (£56,974), T. H. K. Everett; D. A. Shirley
*Clerk*, R. P. Lester

## TRAFFIC COMMISSIONERS
c/o Western Traffic Area, The Gaunt's House, Denmark Street, Bristol BS1 5DR
Tel 0117-975 5065

The Traffic Commissioners are responsible for the licensing of operators of heavy goods and public service vehicles, and they also have responsibility for appeals relating to the licensing of operators and for disciplinary cases involving the conduct of drivers of these vehicles. There are seven Commissioners in the eight traffic areas covering Great Britain. Each Traffic Commissioner constitutes a tribunal for the purposes of the Tribunals and Inquiries Act 1971. For Traffic Area Offices and Commissioners, *see* page 362.
*Senior Traffic Commissioner*, Air Vice-Marshal R. G. Ashford, CBE

## TRANSPORT TRIBUNAL
48–49 Chancery Lane, London, WC2A 1JR
Tel 0171–936 7494

The Transport Tribunal was set up in 1947 and hears appeals against decisions made by Traffic Commissioners at public inquiries. The tribunal consists of a legally-qualified president, two legal members who may sit as chairmen, and five lay members. The president and legal members are appointed by the Lord Chancellor and the lay members are appointed by the Secretary of State for Transport.
*President (part-time)*, His Hon. Judge H. Wilson
*Legal members* (£233 per day), His Hon. Judge Brodrick (*part-time*); R. Owen, QC
*Lay members* (£186 per day), T. W. Hall; J. W. Whitworth; G. Simms; Miss E. B. Haran; P. Rogers
*Secretary*, Mrs A. Bartram

## VALUATION TRIBUNALS
c/o Warwickshire Valuation Tribunal, 2nd Floor, Walton House, 11 Parade, Leamington Spa, Warks. CV32 4DG
Tel 01926-421875

The Valuation Tribunals hear appeals concerning the council tax, non-domestic rating and land drainage rates in England and Wales. They also have residual jurisdiction to hear appeals concerning the community charge, the pre-1990 rating list, disabled rating and mixed hereditaments. There are 56 Valuation Tribunals in England, and eight in Wales. Each tribunal is a separate independent body; those in England are funded by the Department of the Environment and those in Wales by the Welsh Office. A separate tribunal is constituted for each hearing, and normally consists of a chairman and two other members. Members are appointed by the local authority/authorities, and serve on a voluntary basis. A National Committee of Valuation Tribunals considers all matters affecting Valuations Tribunals in England, and the Council of Wales, Valuation Tribunal Presidents, performs the same function in Wales.
*President, National Committee of Valuation Tribunals*, A. H. W. Kennard
*Secretary, National Committee of Valuation Tribunals*, B. P. Massen
*President, Council of Wales, Valuation Tribunal Presidents*, T. D. M. John

## VAT AND DUTIES TRIBUNALS
15–19 Bedford Avenue, London WC1B 3AS
Tel 0171–631 4242

VAT Tribunals are administered by the Lord Chancellor's Department in England and Wales, and by the Secretary of State in Scotland. They are independent and decide disputes between taxpayers and the Commissioners of Customs and Excise, who manage VAT. In England and Wales, the president and chairmen are appointed by the Lord Chancellor, and members are appointed by the Treasury. Chairmen in Scotland are appointed by the Lord President of the Court of Session.
*President* (£82,641), His Hon. Stephen Oliver, QC
*Vice-President, England and Wales* (£56,974), A. W. Simpson
*Vice-President, Scotland* (£56,974), R. A. Bennett, CBE, QC
*Vice-President, Northern Ireland* (£56,974), D. C. Morgan, QC
*Registrar*, R. P. Lester

TRIBUNAL CENTRES
EDINBURGH, 44 Palmerston Place, Edinburgh EH12 5BJ. Tel: 0131–226 3551
LONDON (including Belfast), 15–19 Bedford Avenue, London WC1B 3AS. Tel: 0171–631 4242
MANCHESTER, Warwickgate House, Warwick Road, Old Trafford, Manchester M16 0GP. Tel: 0161–872 6471

# The Police Service

There are 52 police forces in the United Kingdom, each responsible for law enforcement in its area. Most forces' area is conterminous with an English or Welsh county or Scottish region, though there are several combined forces. Law enforcement in London is carried out by the Metropolitan Police and the City of London Police; in Northern Ireland by the Royal Ulster Constabulary; and by the Isle of Man, States of Jersey, and Guernsey forces in their respective islands and bailiwicks. The National Criminal Intelligence Service was set up in April 1992.

Each police force is maintained by a police authority. The authorities of English and Welsh forces comprise committees of local councillors, magistrates and independent members; in Scotland, the regional and islands councils are the authorities. In London the authority for the Metropolitan Police is the Home Secretary, and that for the City of London Police is a committee of the Corporation of London and includes councillors and magistrates. In Northern Ireland the Secretary of State appoints the police authority.

Police authorities are financed by central and local government grants and a precept on the council tax. Subject to the approval of the Home Secretary and to regulations, they appoint the chief constable. In England and Wales they are responsible for publishing annual policing plans and annual reports, setting local objectives and a budget, and levying the precept. The responsibilities of police authorities in Scotland will be altered by the Local Government Bill replacing the two-tier local government structure with unitary authorities. The structure and responsibilities of the police authority in Northern Ireland are under review.

The Home Secretary and the Secretaries of State for Scotland and Northern Ireland are responsible for the organization, administration and operation of the police service. They make regulations covering matters such as police ranks, discipline, hours of duty, and pay and allowances. All police forces are subject to inspection by HM Inspectors of Constabulary, who report to the respective Secretary of State.

The investigation and resolution of a serious complaint against a police officer in England and Wales is subject to the scrutiny of the Police Complaints Authority. An officer who is dismissed or reduced in rank may appeal to the Police Appeal Tribunal, consisting of a legally qualified chairman, a member of the police authority, and two police representatives. In Scotland, chief constables are obliged to investigate a complaint against one of their officers; if there is a suggestion of criminal activity, the complaint is investigated by an independent public prosecutor. In Northern Ireland complaints are investigated by the Independent Commission for Police Complaints.

## BASIC RATES OF PAY *from 1 September 1994*

| | |
|---|---|
| Chief Constable | £58,002–£73,728 |
| Deputy Chief Constable | £51,090–£58,983 |
| Assistant Chief Constable | £48,657 |
| Chief Superintendent (rank abolished April 1995) | £40,071–£42,549 |
| Superintendent | £37,596–£45,012 |
| Chief Inspector | £30,081–£33,384 |
| Inspector | £27,642–£30,081 |
| Sergeant | £21,372–£24,927 |
| Constable | £13,992–£22,146 |

*Metropolitan Police*
(excluding London weighting and London allowance)

| | |
|---|---|
| Metropolitan Commissioner | £90,148 |
| Deputy Commissioner | £78,555 |
| Assistant Commissioner | £69,300 |
| Deputy Assistant Commissioner | £55,440 |
| Commander | £48,657 |
| Chief Superintendent (rank abolished April 1995) | £40,071–£42,549 |
| Superintendent | £37,596–£45,012 |
| Chief Inspector | £31,347–£34,650 |
| Inspector | £28,908–£31,347 |
| Sergeant | £21,372–£24,927 |
| Constable | £13,992–£22,146 |

### THE SPECIAL CONSTABULARY

The Special Constabulary is the part-time volunteer branch of the police force. Special Constables have full police powers within their force area and undertake regular officers' routine policing duties when required, thus freeing regulars at times of emergency for those tasks which only they can perform. There were 20,566 Special Constables in England and Wales at the end of 1993.

### THE NATIONAL CRIMINAL INTELLIGENCE SERVICE (NCIS)

The function of the National Criminal Intelligence Service (NCIS) is to gather, collate and disseminate information and intelligence on serious crime of a regional, national and international nature. It is independent of any other police organization.

*Headquarters:* PO Box 8000, Spring Gardens, Tinworth Street, London SEII 5EN. Tel: 0171-238 8000
*Strength,* 499
*Director-General,* A. H. Pacey, CBE, QPM
*Deputy Director-General (Director (Intelligence)),* J. P. Hamilton
*Director, International Division,* P. J. Byrne, MBE
*Director, UK Division,* R. Hills
*Director, Resources Division,* R. Creedon

---

## POLICE AUTHORITIES

---

*Strength:* actual strength of force as at mid June 1994
*Chair:* Chairman/Convener of the Police Authority/Police Committee

### ENGLAND

AVON AND SOMERSET CONSTABULARY, *HQ,* PO Box 37, Valley Road, Portishead, Bristol BS20 8QJ. Tel: 0117-981 8181. *Strength,* 3,023; *Chief Constable,* D. J. Shattock, QPM; *Chair,* D. Heath, CBE

BEDFORDSHIRE POLICE, *HQ,* Woburn Road, Kempston, Bedford MK43 9AX. Tel: 01234-841212. *Strength,* 1,132; *Chief Constable,* A. Dyer, QPM; *Chair,* elected at each meeting

CAMBRIDGESHIRE CONSTABULARY, *HQ,* Hinchingbrooke Park, Huntingdon, Cambs. PE18 8NP. Tel: 01480-456111. *Strength,* 1,241; *Chief Constable,* D. G. Gunn, QPM; *Chair,* H. J. Fitch

CHESHIRE CONSTABULARY, *HQ*, Castle Esplanade, Chester, CHI 2PP. Tel: 01244-350000. *Strength*, 1,893; *Chief Constable*, J. M. Jones, QPM; *Chair*, J. H. Collins, OBE

CLEVELAND CONSTABULARY, *HQ*, PO Box 70, Ladgate Lane, Middlesbrough, Cleveland TS8 9EH. Tel: 01642-326326. *Strength*, 1,431; *Chief Constable*, B. B. D. Shaw, QPM; *Chair*, I. Jeffrey

CUMBRIA CONSTABULARY, *HQ*, Carleton Hall, Penrith, Cumbria CAIO 2AU. Tel: 01768-891999. *Strength*, 1,177; *Chief Constable*, A. G. Elliott, QPM; *Chair*, R. Watson

DERBYSHIRE CONSTABULARY, *HQ*, Butterley Hall, Ripley, Derbyshire DE5 3RS. Tel: 01773-570100. *Strength*, 1,840; *Chief Constable*, J. F. Newing, QPM; *Chair*, E. H. Swain

DEVON AND CORNWALL CONSTABULARY, *HQ*, Middlemoor, Exeter EX2 7HQ. Tel: 01392-52101. *Strength*, 2,903; *Chief Constable*, J. S. Evans, QPM; *Chair*, S. J. Day

DORSET POLICE FORCE, *HQ*, Winfrith, Dorchester, Dorset DT2 8DZ. Tel: 01929-462727. *Strength*, 1,286; *Chief Constable*, B. H. Weight, QPM; *Chair*, Sir Stephen Hammick, Bt.

DURHAM CONSTABULARY, *HQ*, Aykley Heads, Durham DHI 5TT. Tel: 0191-386 4929. *Strength*, 1,374; *Chief Constable*, F. W. Taylor, QPM; *Chair*, J. Richardson

ESSEX POLICE, *HQ*, PO Box 2, Springfield, Chelmsford CM2 6DA. Tel: 01245-491491. *Strength*, 2,923; *Chief Constable*, J. H. Burrow, CBE; *Chair*, R. H. Boyd

GLOUCESTERSHIRE CONSTABULARY, *HQ*, Holland House, Lansdown Road, Cheltenham, Glos. GL51 6QH. Tel: 01242-521321. *Strength*, 1,164; *Chief Constable*, A. J. P. Butler, PH.D.; *Chair*, R. Somers

GREATER MANCHESTER POLICE, *HQ*, PO Box 22 (S. West PDO), Chester House, Boyer Street, Manchester M16 ORE. Tel: 0161-872 5050. *Strength*, 6,945; *Chief Constable*, D. Wilmot, QPM; *Chair*, S. Murphy

HAMPSHIRE CONSTABULARY, *HQ*, West Hill, Winchester, Hants. SO22 5DB. Tel: 01962-868133. *Strength*, 3,265; *Chief Constable*, J. C. Hoddinott, CBE, QPM; *Chair*, M. J. Clark

HERTFORDSHIRE CONSTABULARY, *HQ*, Stanborough Road, Welwyn Garden City, Herts. AL8 6XF. Tel: 01707-331177. *Strength*, 1,673; *Chief Constable*, P. Sharpe; *Chair*, F. Peacock

HUMBERSIDE POLICE, *HQ*, Queens Gardens, Kingston upon Hull, N. Humberside HUI 3DJ. Tel: 01482-26111. *Strength*, 2,036; *Chief Constable*, D. A. Leonard, QPM; *Chair*, I. A. Cawsey

KENT CONSTABULARY, *HQ*, Sutton Road, Maidstone, Kent ME15 9BZ. Tel: 01622-690690. *Strength*, 3,130; *Chief Constable*, J. D. Phillips, QPM; *Chair*, Sir John Grugeon

LANCASHIRE CONSTABULARY, *HQ*, PO Box 77, Hutton, Preston PR4 5SB. Tel: 01772-614444. *Strength*, 3,170; *Chief Constable*, R. B. Johnson, CBE, QPM; *Chair*, Mrs R. B. Henig

LEICESTERSHIRE CONSTABULARY, *HQ*, PO Box 999, Leicester LE99 1AZ. Tel: 0116-253 0066. *Strength*, 1,817; *Chief Constable*, K. Povey, QPM; *Chair*, R. A. Wann

LINCOLNSHIRE POLICE, *HQ*, PO Box 999, Lincoln LN5 7PH. Tel: 01522-532222. *Strength*, 1,204; *Chief Constable*, J. P. Bensley; *Chair*, B. Fippard

MERSEYSIDE POLICE, *HQ*, PO Box 59, Canning Place, Liverpool L69 1JD. Tel: 0151-709 6010. *Strength*, 4,772; *Chief Constable*, J. Sharples, QPM; *Chair*, H. N. Williams, OBE

NORFOLK CONSTABULARY, *HQ*, Martineau Lane, Norwich NRI 2DJ. Tel: 01603-768769. *Strength*, 1,432; *Chief Constable*, K. R. Williams, QPM; *Chair*, P. R. Mason

NORTHAMPTONSHIRE POLICE, *HQ*, Wootton Hall, Northampton NN4 0JQ. Tel: 01604-700700. *Strength*, 1,190; *Chief Constable*, E. Crew, QPM; *Chair*, Dr M. Dickie

NORTHUMBRIA POLICE, *HQ*, Ponteland, Newcastle upon Tyne NE20 OBL. Tel: 01661-872555. *Strength*, 3,590; *Chief Constable*, J. A. Stevens, QPM; *Chair*, G. Gill

NORTH YORKSHIRE POLICE, *HQ*, Newby Wiske Hall, Newby Wiske, Northallerton, N. Yorks. DL7 9HA. Tel: 01609-783131. *Strength*, 1,333; *Chief Constable*, D. M. Burke, QPM; *Chair*, elected at each meeting

NOTTINGHAMSHIRE CONSTABULARY, *HQ*, Sherwood Lodge, Arnold, Nottingham NG5 8PP. Tel: 0115-967 0999. *Strength*, 2,325; *Chief Constable*, D. Crompton, QPM; *Chair*, C. P. Winterton

SOUTH YORKSHIRE POLICE, *HQ*, Snig Hill, Sheffield S3 8LY. Tel: 0114-276 8522. *Strength*, 3,020; *Chief Constable*, R. Wells, QPM; *Chair*, Sir John Layden

STAFFORDSHIRE POLICE, *HQ*, Cannock Road, Stafford STI7 0QG. Tel: 01785-57717. *Strength*, 2,215; *Chief Constable*, C. H. Kelly, CBE, QPM; *Chair*, J. T. Meir

SUFFOLK CONSTABULARY, *HQ*, Martlesham Heath, Ipswich IP5 7QS. Tel: 01473-613500. *Strength*, 1,234; *Chief Constable*, A. T. Coe, QPM; *Chair*, C. C. Jones

SURREY POLICE, *HQ*, Mount Browne, Sandy Lane, Guildford, Surrey GU3 1HG. Tel: 01483-571212. *Strength*, 1,625; *Chief Constable*, D. J. Williams, QPM; *Chair*, A. C. Tisdall

SUSSEX POLICE, *HQ*, Malling House, Church Lane, Lewes, E. Sussex BN7 2DZ. Tel: 01273-475432. *Strength*, 3,009; *Chief Constable*, P. Whitehouse, QPM; *Chair*, D. Bellotti

THAMES VALLEY POLICE, *HQ*, Oxford Road, Kidlington, Oxon. OX5 2NX. Tel: 01865-846000. *Strength*, 3,883; *Chief Constable*, C. Pollard, QPM; *Chair*, D. J. Priestley

WARWICKSHIRE CONSTABULARY, *HQ*, PO Box 4, Leek Wootton, Warwick CV35 7QB. Tel: 01926-415000. *Strength*, 1,037; *Chief Constable*, P. D. Joslin, QPM; *Chair*, M. Singh

WEST MERCIA CONSTABULARY, *HQ*, PO Box 55, Hindlip Hall, Hindlip, Worcester WR3 8SP. Tel: 01905-723000. *Strength*, 2,094; *Chief Constable*, D. C. Blakey, QPM; *Chair*, P. H. Fallows, TD

WEST MIDLANDS POLICE, *HQ*, PO Box 52, Lloyd House, Colmore Circus, Queensway, Birmingham B4 6NQ. Tel: 0121-626 5000. *Strength*, 6,973; *Chief Constable*, R. Hadfield, QPM; *Chair*, Mrs M. Whitehouse

WEST YORKSHIRE POLICE, *HQ*, PO Box 9, Laburnum Road, Wakefield, W. Yorks. WF1 3QP. Tel: 01924-375222. *Strength*, 5,037; *Chief Constable*, K. Hellawell, QPM; *Chair*, T. Brennan

WILTSHIRE CONSTABULARY, *HQ*, London Road, Devizes, Wilts. SNIO 2DN. Tel: 01380-722341. *Strength*, 1,161; *Chief Constable*, W. R. Girven, QPM; *Chair*, Mrs J. M. Wood

## WALES

DYFED–POWYS POLICE, *HQ*, PO Box 99, Llangunnor, Carmarthen, Dyfed SA31 2PF. Tel: 01267-236444. *Strength*, 972; *Chief Constable*, R. White, QPM; *Chair*, T. G. Parry

GWENT CONSTABULARY, *HQ*, Croesyceiliog, Cwmbran, Gwent NP44 2XJ. Tel: 01633-838111. *Strength*, 1,010; *Chief Constable*, A. T. Burden; *Chair*, B. Sutton

NORTH WALES POLICE, *HQ*, Glan-y-Don, Colwyn Bay, Clwyd LL29 8AW. Tel: 01492-517171. *Strength*, 1,352; *Chief Constable*, M. J. Argent; *Chair*, W. E. Conway

SOUTH WALES CONSTABULARY, *HQ*, Cowbridge Road, Bridgend, Mid Glamorgan CF31 3SU. Tel: 01656-655555. *Strength*, 3,083; *Chief Constable*, W. R. Lawrence, QPM; *Chair*, R. Jones

## SCOTLAND

CENTRAL SCOTLAND POLICE, *HQ*, Randolphfield, Stirling FK8 2HD. Tel: 01786-456000. *Strength*, 657; *Chief Constable*, W. J. M. Wilson, QPM; *Convener*, J. Anderson, CBE

DUMFRIES AND GALLOWAY CONSTABULARY, *HQ*, Cornwall Mount, Dumfries DG1 1PZ. Tel: 01387-52112. *Strength*, 380; *Chief Constable*, H. R. Cameron, QPM; *Chair*, K. Cameron

FIFE CONSTABULARY, *HQ*, Wemyss Road, Dysart, Kirkcaldy, Fife KY1 2YA. Tel: 01592-652611. *Strength*, 779; *Chief Constable*, W. M. Moodie, CBE, QPM; *Chair*, R. Gough, CBE

GRAMPIAN POLICE, *HQ*, Queen Street, Aberdeen AB9 1BA. Tel: 01224-639111. *Strength*, 1,172; *Chief Constable*, I. T. Oliver, QPM, PH.D.; *Chair*, B. Topping

LOTHIAN AND BORDERS POLICE, *HQ*, Fettes Avenue, Edinburgh EH4 1RB. Tel: 0131-311 3131. *Strength*, 2,492; *Chief Constable*, Sir William Sutherland, QPM; *Chair*, R. B. Martin

NORTHERN CONSTABULARY, *HQ*, Perth Road, Inverness IV2 3SY. Tel: 01463-715555. *Strength*, 654; *Chief Constable*, H. C. MacMillan, CBE, QPM; *Chair*, vacant

STRATHCLYDE POLICE, *HQ*, 173 Pitt Street, Glasgow G2 4JS. Tel: 0141-204 2626. *Strength*, 6,954; *Chief Constable*, L. Sharp, QPM; *Chair*, J. Jennings

TAYSIDE POLICE, *HQ*, PO Box 59, West Bell Street, Dundee DD1 9JU. Tel: 01382-23200. *Strength*, 1,057; *Chief Constable*, J. W. Bowman, CBE, QPM; *Chair*, A. Shand

## NORTHERN IRELAND

ROYAL ULSTER CONSTABULARY, *HQ*, Brooklyn, Knock Road, Belfast BT5 6LE. Tel: 01232-650222. *Strength*, 8,511; *Chief Constable*, Sir Hugh Annesley, QPM; *Chair*, D. Cooke

## ISLANDS

ISLAND POLICE FORCE, *HQ*, Hospital Lane, St Peter Port, Guernsey GY1 2QN. Tel: 01481-725111. *Strength*, 141; *Chief Officer*, M. Le Moignan, QPM; *President, States Committee for Home Affairs*, M. Torode

STATES OF JERSEY POLICE, *HQ*, Rouge Bouillon, PO Box 789, St Helier, Jersey JE2 3ZA. Tel: 01534-612612. *Strength*, 232; *Chief Officer*, R. H. Le Breton; *Chair*, M. Wavell

ISLE OF MAN CONSTABULARY, *HQ*, Glencrutchery Road, Douglas, Isle of Man IM2 4RG. Tel: 01624-631212. *Strength*, 212; *Chief Constable*, R. E. N. Oake; *Minister for Home Affairs*, The Hon. A. A. Callin

---

## METROPOLITAN POLICE SERVICE
New Scotland Yard, Broadway, London SW1H 0BG
Tel 0171-230 1212

---

Establishment, 27,605

*Commissioner*, Sir Paul Condon, QPM
*Deputy Commissioner*, Sir John Smith, QPM
*Receiver*, G. L. Angel

TERRITORIAL OPERATIONS DEPARTMENT
*Assistant Commissioner*, R. A. Hunt, OBE, QPM
*Deputy Assistant Commissioner*, D. N. Meynell, OBE
*Commanders*, J. J. Allinson; D. A. Ray
*Director of Support Administration*, B. Reeves

OPERATIONAL AREAS
*Assistant Commissioners*, A. J. Speed, QPM (*Central*); B. H. Skitt, BEM, QPM (*North-West*); A. Dunn (*North-East*); W. I. R. Johnston, QPM (*South-East*); P. Manning (*South-West*)
*Deputy Assistant Commissioners*, M. B. Taylor, QPM; A. G. Fry, QPM; L. T. Roach, QPM; D. Flanders; M. J. Sullivan, QPM; T. J. Siggs, OBE
*Commanders*, T. O. Jones, MBE; L. J. Poole, QPM; D. M. T. Kendrick, QPM; J. F. Purnell, CGM; B. J. Luckhurst; T. D. Laidlaw, QPM; A. V. Comben; J. Townshend; H. N. L. Blenkin; C. R. Pearman; A. L. Rowe; P. R. Nove

SPECIALIST OPERATIONS DEPARTMENT
*Assistant Commissioner*, D. C. Veness, QPM
*Deputy Assistant Commissioner*, J. A. Hawley, QPM
*Commanders*, K. G. Churchill-Coleman, OBE, QPM; D. Buchanan; R. C. Marsh, QPM; D. M. Tucker; B. G. Moss; J. G. D. Grieve

*Metropolitan Police Laboratory*
*Director*, Dr B. Sheard
*Deputy Directors*, G. J. O. Lee; M. R. Loveland; P. D. Martin; Dr W. D. C. Wilson

PERSONNEL DEPARTMENT
*Director of Personnel*, H. Maslen
*Commanders*, B. F. Aitchison (*Training*); L. Poole, QPM (*Police Personnel Management*)

INSPECTION AND REVIEW
*Assistant Commissioner*, P. J. J. Winship, QPM
*Commander*, J. D. Gibson

COMPLAINTS INVESTIGATION BUREAU
*Commander (acting)*, B. Byrne

CENTRAL STAFF
*Commander*, M. Briggs

DIRECTORATE OF PUBLIC AFFAIRS
*Director of Public Affairs*, Ms S. Cullum

SOLICITOR'S DEPARTMENT
*Solicitor*, C. S. Porteous, CBE

DIRECTORATE OF PERFORMANCE REVIEW AND MANAGEMENT SERVICES
*Director*, Mrs S. M. Merchant

FINANCE DEPARTMENT
*Director of Finance*, J. A. Crutchlow

PROPERTY SERVICES DEPARTMENT
*Director of Property Services*, T. G. Lawrence

DEPARTMENT OF TECHNOLOGY
*Director of Technology*, N. Boothman

---

## CITY OF LONDON POLICE
26 Old Jewry, London EC2R 8DJ
Tel 0171-601 2222

---

Strength (August 1994), 936

*Commissioner* (£76,233), W. Taylor, QPM
*Assistant Commissioner* (£59,424), C. Coxall, QPM
*Commander* (£48,657), R. Friend

*Chief Superintendents*:
   *'B' Division*, J. Todd
   *'C' Division*, P. Eskriett
   *CID*, T. Dickinson
   *Company Fraud*, R. Knevett
   *Management Support*, M. Campbell
   *Operational Support*, T. Hillier

---

BRITISH TRANSPORT POLICE
15 Tavistock Place, London WC1H 9SJ
Tel 0171-388 7541

---

Strength (March 1994), 2,155
The Force provides a policing service to the British Railways
Board, Railtrack and London Underground Ltd. Police
stations are located throughout England, Wales and Scotland.
The Chief Constable reports to the British Transport Police
Committee, a statutory body set up under the Transport Act
1962. The members of the Committee are appointed by the
British Railways Board and London Underground Ltd.
*Chief Constable*, D. O'Brien, OBE, QPM
*Deputy Chief Constable*, A. Parker, QPM

---

MINISTRY OF DEFENCE POLICE
Ministry of Defence, Empress State Building,
Lillie Road, London SW6 1TR
Tel 0171-824 4444

---

Strength (June 1994), 4,882
The Ministry of Defence Police is a statutory police force
directly responsible to the Secretary of State for Defence for
the policing of all military land, stations and establishments
in the United Kingdom. It is due to become a defence agency
in 1995.
*Chief Constable*, J. Reddington, QPM
*Deputy Chief Constable*, W. E. E. Boreham, OBE
*Head of Secretariat*, J. A. Smallwood

---

ROYAL PARKS CONSTABULARY
The Old Police House, Hyde Park, London W2 2UH
Tel 0171-298 2054

---

Strength (March 1994), 185
The Royal Parks Constabulary is maintained by the Royal
Parks Agency, an executive agency of the Department of
National Heritage, and is responsible for the policing of eight
royal parks in and around London. These comprise an area
in excess of 6,300 acres. Officers of the Force are appointed
under the Parks Regulations Act 1872 as amended.
*Chief Officer*, W. Ross
*Deputy Chief Officer (acting)*, A. McLean

---

UNITED KINGDOM ATOMIC ENERGY
AUTHORITY CONSTABULARY
Building E6, Culham Laboratory, Abingdon,
Oxon. OX14 3DB
Tel 01235-463760

---

Strength (July 1994), 486
The Constabulary is responsible for policing United Kingdom
Atomic Energy Authority and British Nuclear Fuels PLC

establishments and for escorting nuclear material between
establishments. The Chief Constable is responsible, through
the Atomic Energy Authority Police Committee, to the
President of the Board of Trade.
*Chief Constable*, H. J. McMorris, QPM
*Deputy Chief Constable*, E. H. Miller

---

STAFF ASSOCIATIONS

---

ASSOCIATION OF CHIEF POLICE OFFICERS OF
   ENGLAND, WALES AND NORTHERN IRELAND, Room
   311, Wellington House, 67–73 Buckingham Gate,
   London SW1E 6BE. Tel: 0171-230 7184. Represents the
   Chief Constables, Deputy Chief Constables and Assistant
   Chief Constables of England, Wales and Northern
   Ireland, and officers of the rank of Commander and
   above in the Metropolitan and City of London Police.
   *General Secretary*, Miss M. C. E. Burton
THE POLICE SUPERINTENDENTS' ASSOCIATION OF
   ENGLAND AND WALES, 67A Reading Road,
   Pangbourne, Reading RG8 7JD. Tel: 01734-844005.
   Represents officers of the rank of Superintendent and
   Chief Superintendent. *Secretary*, Chief Supt. D. A. Clark
THE POLICE FEDERATION OF ENGLAND AND WALES,
   15–17 Langley Road, Surbiton, Surrey KT6 6LP. Tel: 0181-
   399 2224. Represents officers up to and including the
   rank of Chief Inspector. *General Secretary*, L. Williams;
   *Chairman*, F. H. J. Broughton
ASSOCIATION OF CHIEF POLICE OFFICERS IN
   SCOTLAND, Police Headquarters, Fettes Avenue,
   Edinburgh EH4 1RB. Tel: 0131-311 3051. Represents the
   Chief Constables, Deputy Chief Constables and Assistant
   Chief Constables of the Scottish police forces. *Hon.
   Secretary*, Sir William Sutherland, QPM
THE ASSOCIATION OF SCOTTISH POLICE
   SUPERINTENDENTS, Secretariat, 173 Pitt Street,
   Glasgow G2 4JS. Tel: 0141-221 5796. Represents officers
   of the rank of Superintendent and Chief Superintendent.
   *Hon. Secretary*, Chief Supt. J. Urquhart
THE SCOTTISH POLICE FEDERATION, 5 Woodside Place,
   Glasgow G3 7QF. Tel: 0141-332 5234. Represents officers
   up to and including the rank of Chief Inspector. *General
   Secretary*, D. J. Keil
THE SUPERINTENDENT ASSOCIATION OF NORTHERN
   IRELAND, Ormiston House, Hawthornden Road, Belfast
   BT4 3JW. Tel: 01232-700129. Represents Superintendents
   and Chief Superintendents in the RUC. *Hon. Secretary*,
   Chief Supt. A. Donald
THE POLICE FEDERATION FOR NORTHERN IRELAND,
   Royal Ulster Constabulary, Garnerville, Garnerville
   Road, Belfast BT4 2NX. Tel: 01232-760831. Represents
   officers up to and including the rank of Chief Inspector.
   *Secretary*, D. A. McClurg

# Defence

The armed forces of the United Kingdom comprise the Royal Navy, the Army and the Royal Air Force. The Queen is commander-in-chief of all the armed forces. The Ministry of Defence, headed by a Secretary of State, provides the support structure for the armed forces. Within the Ministry of Defence, the Defence Council has overall responsibility for running the armed forces. The Chief of Staff of each service reports through the Chief of the Defence Staff to the Secretary of State on matters relating to the running of his service. The Chief of Staff also chairs the executive committee of the appropriate service board, which manages the service in accordance with centrally-determined objectives and budgets. The military-civilian Defence Staff, headed by the Vice-Chief of the Defence Staff, is responsible for policy and strategy, operational requirements and commitments. The mainly civilian Office of Management and Budget deals with budgets, resource planning and civilian personnel management, and the Procurement Executive is responsible for purchasing equipment. The Defence Intelligence Staff and the Defence Scientific Staff also form part of the Ministry of Defence.

As a result of the 'Front Line First' defence costs study, a corporate main board will be established below ministerial level with responsibility for policy, management and finance. An MoD Head Office composed of a unified Central Staff with three small headquarters staffs supporting the individual Chiefs of Staff will replace the Office of Management and Budget, the Defence Staff and the Defence Scientific Staff. A permanent Joint Headquarters will be set up at Northwood to connect the policy and strategic functions of the MoD Head Office with the conduct of operations and to strengthen the policy/executive division. Financial planning, personnel, telecommunications and security structures will also be reorganized and the Procurement Executive will be further streamlined. A new executive agency will bring together all the major MoD non-nuclear science and technology organizations, including the Defence Research Agency, the Defence Operations Analysis Centre, the Chemical and Biological Defence Establishment and the Directorate-General of Test and Evaluation.

ARMED FORCES STRENGTHS *as at 1 April 1994*

| All Services | 254,488 |
|---|---|
| Men | 236,726 |
| Women | 17,762 |
| Royal Naval Services | 55,779 |
| Men | 51,529 |
| Women | 4,250 |
| Army | 123,028 |
| Men | 115,976 |
| Women | 7,052 |
| Royal Air Force | 75,681 |
| Men | 69,221 |
| Women | 6,460 |

## DEFENCE CUTS

DEFENCE SPENDING PLANS

| | £ million |
|---|---|
| *1993–4 | 23,450 |
| 1994–5 | 22,890 |
| 1995–6 | 22,130 |
| 1996–7 | 22,230 |

*Estimated outturn, including provision for the security and intelligence services which was transferred to a new Cabinet Office Vote from 1 April 1994

SERVICE PERSONNEL

The table below includes plans for 11,600 job reductions in the support and administrative areas of the armed forces under the July 1994 'Front Line First' defence costs study.

| | Royal Navy | Army | RAF |
|---|---|---|---|
| 1990 strength | 63,200 | 152,800 | 89,700 |
| 1991 target for 1995 | 55,000 | 116,000 | 75,000 |
| April 1994 target for 1995 | 51,000 | 120,000 | 70,000 |
| July 1994 target for 2000 | 49,100 | 117,800 | 62,500 |

MoD CIVILIAN PERSONNEL

The figures below include plans for 7,100 job reductions in civilian personnel under the July 1994 'Front Line First' defence costs study.

| | |
|---|---|
| 1990–1 level | 170,642 |
| February 1994 level | 144,010 |
| April 1994 target for 1996 | 128,700 |
| July 1994 target for 2000 | 121,600 |

There are expected to be further reductions in service and civilian personnel by 2000.

DEPLOYMENT AS AT EARLY 1994

Outside Great Britain, army units were stationed in Antarctica, Ascension Island, Belize, Brunei, Cyprus, the Falkland Islands, Germany, Gibraltar, the Gulf, Hong Kong (the Brigade of Gurkhas), and Northern Ireland. Royal Air Force units were stationed in Belize, the central Atlantic, the Channel, Cyprus, the eastern Atlantic and North Sea, the Falkland Islands, Germany, Gibraltar, the Gulf, Hong Kong, Italy, Northern Ireland, Turkey and the former Yugoslavia.

Members of the British armed forces were also deployed with the United Nations Force in Cyprus (UNFICYP), the United Nations Iraq-Kuwait Observer Mission (UNIKOM), and the United Nations Protection Force in the former Yugoslavia (UNPROFOR).

## MINISTRY OF DEFENCE
Main Building, Whitehall, London SW1A 2HB
Tel 0171-218 9000

For ministerial and civil service salaries, *see page 281*
For Services salaries, *see pages 402–4*
*Secretary of State for Defence*, The Rt. Hon. Malcolm Rifkind, QC, MP
*Special Advisers*, C. Blunt; C. Littmoden
*Parliamentary Private Secretary*, H. Bellingham, MP
*Minister of State for the Armed Forces*, The Hon. Nicholas Soames, MP
*Minister of State for Defence Procurement*, The Rt. Hon. Roger Freeman, MP
*Parliamentary Under-Secretary of State*, The Lord Henley
*Permanent Under-Secretary of State (G1)*, Sir Christopher France, GCB
*Chief of the Defence Staff*, Field Marshal Sir Peter Inge, GCB

THE DEFENCE COUNCIL

The Defence Council is responsible for running the Armed Forces. It is chaired by the Secretary of State for Defence and consists of: the Ministers of State; the Permanent Under-Secretary of State; the Chief of the Defence Staff and the Vice-Chief of the Defence Staff; the Parliamentary Under-Secretary of State; the Chief Scientific Adviser; the Chief of Defence Procurement; the Second Permanent Under-Secretary of State; the Chief of the Naval Staff; the Chief of the General Staff; and the Chief of the Air Staff.

## DEFENCE STAFF

*Vice-Chief of the Defence Staff*, Adm. Sir Jock Slater, GCB, LVO
*Defence Services Secretary*, Air Vice-Marshal P. J. Harding, CB, CBE, AFC

### DEFENCE COMMITMENTS STAFF

*Deputy CDS (Commitments)*, Vice-Adm. the Hon. Sir Nicholas Hill-Norton, KCB
*Asst Under-Secretary (Commitments) (G3)*, W. D. Reeves, CB
*Asst CDS (Overseas)*, Air Vice-Marshal N. B. Baldwin, CBE

### DEFENCE LOGISTICS STAFF

*Asst CDS (Logistics)*, Rear-Adm. F. B. Goodson, OBE
*Deputy CDS (Systems)*, Vice-Adm. M. G. Rutherford, CBE
*Asst CDS, Operational Requirements (Sea)*, Rear-Adm. J. A. Trewby
*Asst CDS, Operational Requirements (Land)*, Maj.-Gen. S. Cowan, CBE
*Asst CDS, Operational Requirements (Air)*, Air Vice-Marshal C. C. C. Coville
*Asst CDS (CIS)*, Maj.-Gen. W. J. P. Robins, OBE

### DEFENCE PROGRAMMES AND PERSONNEL STAFF

*Deputy CDS (Programmes and Personnel)*, Lt.-Gen. the Hon. Sir Thomas Boyd-Carpenter, KBE
*Asst CDS (Programmes)*, Air Vice-Marshal G. A. Robertson, CBE

### DEFENCE MEDICAL SERVICES DIRECTORATE

*Surgeon-General*, Surgeon Vice-Adm. A. L. Revell, QHS
*Director, Defence Dental Services*, Air Vice-Marshal J. Mackey, QHDS
*Director, Defence Nursing Services*, Commandant Nursing Officer Miss J. Titley

### POLICY

*Deputy Under-Secretary (Policy) (G2)*, D. B. Omand
*Asst Under-Secretary (Policy) (G3)*, G. W. Hopkinson
*Asst CDS (Policy and Nuclear)*, Rear-Adm. D. F. A. Henderson

### DEFENCE INFORMATION STAFF

*Press Secretary and Chief of Information (G4)*, Ms G. Samuel
*Deputy Press Secretary and Director of Public Relations (G5)*, A. Armstrong
*Director, Public Relations (Navy)*, Capt. C. Esplin-Jones, RN
*Director, Public Relations (Army)*, Brig. P. Trousdell
*Director, Public Relations (RAF)*, Air Cdre G. McRobbie

### DEFENCE INTELLIGENCE STAFF

*Chief of Defence Intelligence*, Lt.-Gen. Sir John Foley, KCB, OBE, MC
*Director-General, Intelligence (Assessments)*
*Director-General, Scientific and Technical Intelligence*
*Director-General, Management and Support of Intelligence*
*Director, Defence Intelligence (Secretariat) (G5)*

## NAVY DEPARTMENT

*Chief of the Naval Staff and First Sea Lord*, Adm. Sir Benjamin Bathurst, KCB

*C.-in-C. Naval Home Command and Second Sea Lord*, Adm. Sir Michael Layard, KCB, CBE, ADC
*Asst Chief of Naval Staff*, Rear-Adm. J. R. Brigstocke (*until April 1995*)
*Commandant-General Royal Marines*, Lt.-Gen. Sir Robert Ross, KCB, OBE
*Naval Secretary and Director-General, Naval Manning*, Rear-Adm. A. W. J. West, DSC
*Chief of Fleet Support*, Vice-Adm. Sir Richard Frere, KCB
*Asst Under-Secretary (Fleet Support) (G3)*, A. J. D. Pawson
*Director-General, Fleet Support (Ships) (G3)*, B. V. Babbington
*Director-General, Fleet Support (Equipment and Systems)*, Rear-Adm. J. R. Shiffner
*Director-General, Supplies and Transport (N) (G3)*, D. G. Jones
*Director-General, Fleet Support (Operations and Plans)*, Rear-Adm. J. H. Dunt
*Director-General, Aircraft (Navy)*, Rear-Adm. R. C. Moylan-Jones
*Director-General, Naval Medical Services*, Surgeon Rear-Adm. A. Craig, QHP
*Director, Dental Services (Royal Navy)*, Surgeon Cdre T. J. C. Hall, OBE, QHDS
*Director, Nursing Services (Royal Navy)*, Principal Nursing Officer Miss C. M. Taylor
*Director-General, Naval Chaplaincy Services*, Ven. M. W. Bucks, QHC
*Hydrographer of the Royal Navy and Chief Executive, Hydrographic Office*, Rear-Adm. N. R. Essenhigh

## GENERAL STAFF

*Chief of the General Staff*, Gen. Sir Charles Guthrie, GCB, LVO, OBE, ADC (*Gen.*)
*Asst Chief of the General Staff*, Maj.-Gen. M. J. D. Walker, CBE
*Director-General, Communications and Information Systems (Army) and Signals Officer in Chief (Army)*, Maj.-Gen. A. H. Boyle
*Director-General, TA*, Maj.-Gen. A. I. J. Kennedy, CBE
*Director-General, Military Survey*, Maj.-Gen. M. P. B. G. Wilson
*Director-General, Army Training*, Maj.-Gen. R. W. M. McAfee
*Inspector-General, Doctrine and Training*, Lt.-Gen. Sir Peter Duffell, KCB, CBE, MC
*Director-General, Land Warfare*, Maj.-Gen. M. A. Willcocks
*Director, Royal Armoured Corps*, Maj.-Gen. J. M. F. C. Hall, OBE
*Director, Royal Artillery*, Maj.-Gen. I. G. C. Durie, CBE
*Director, Infantry*, Maj.-Gen. R. A. Pett, MBE
*Director, Army Air Corps*, Maj.-Gen. S. W. St J. Lytle
*Engineer-in-Chief (Army)*, Maj.-Gen. G. W. Field, CB, OBE

## ARMY DEPARTMENT

*Military Secretary*, Maj.-Gen. R. J. Hayman-Joyce, CBE
*Adjutant-General*, Gen. Sir Michael Wilkes, KCB, CBE
*Director-General, HQ Directorate Adjutant-General's Corps*, Maj.-Gen. R. D. Grist, CB, OBE
*Director-General, Army Manning and Recruiting*, Maj.-Gen. J. F. Deverell, OBE
*Director, Staff and Personnel Support (Army)*, Brig. C. Geal, OBE
*Provost Marshal (Army)*, Brig. I. Cameron
*Director, Army Legal Services*, Maj.-Gen. A. P. V. Rogers, OBE
*Director, Educational and Training Services (Army)*, Brig. J. M. Macfarlane

Director, Women, Brig. J. M. Roulstone
Quartermaster-General, Lt.-Gen. the Hon. Sir William
Rous, KCB, OBE
Asst Under-Secretary (Quartermaster) (G3), Dr A. M. Fox
Director-General, Logistics Policy (Army), Maj.-Gen.
P. J. Sheppard, CBE
Director, Army Veterinary and Remount Services, Brig.
A. H. Parker-Bowles, OBE
Director-General, Logistic Support (Army), Maj.-Gen.
D. L. Burden, CBE
Director-General, Equipment Support (Army), Maj.-Gen.
P. J. G. Corp
Chief Executive, Army Base Repair Organization,
Brig. J. R. Drew
Director-General, Army Medical Services, Maj.-Gen.
F. B. Mayes, QHS
Director, Army Dental Services, Brig. C. D. Parkinson
Director, Army Nursing Services, Brig. H. S. Dixon-Nuttall,
QHNS
Chaplain-General, Revd J. Harkness, CB, CBE, QHC

## AIR FORCE DEPARTMENT

Chief of the Air Staff, Air Chief Marshal Sir Michael
Graydon, GCB, CBE, ADC
Asst Chief of Air Staff, Air Vice-Marshal P. T. Squire, DFC,
AFC
Director-General, Strategic Policy and Plans, Air Vice-
Marshal P. G. Beer, CBE, LVO
Chief Executive, National Air Traffic Services (G3),
D. J. McLauchlan
Director-General, Policy and Planning, NATS, Air Vice-
Marshal J. D. L. Feesey
Air Member for Personnel, Air Chief Marshal Sir Andrew
Wilson, KCB, AFC, ADC
Air Secretary and AOC RAF Personnel Management Centre,
Air Vice-Marshal R. P. O'Brien, OBE
Air Officer Training, vacant
Director, Legal Services (RAF) Air Vice-Marshal
G. W. Carleton
Air Officer Commanding-in-Chief and Air Member for
Logistics, Air Chief Marshal Sir Michael Alcock, KBE, CB
Air Officer Commanding Information Systems and Signals
Units, Air Vice-Marshal J. B. Main, OBE
Director-General, Support Management (RAF), Air Vice-
Marshal C. G. Terry, OBE
Director-General, Medical Services (RAF), Air Vice-Marshal
J. A. Baird, QHP
Director, Dental Services (RAF), Air Cdre D. W. Marchant
Director, Nursing Services (RAF), Gp Capt V. Hand, QHNS
Chaplain-in-Chief (RAF), Ven. B. H. Lucas, CB, QHC
Chief Executive, RAF Support Command Maintenance
Group, Air Vice-Marshal R. H. Kyle, MBE

## DEFENCE SCIENTIFIC STAFF

Chief Scientific Adviser (G1A), Prof. Sir David Davies, KBE
Deputy Chief Scientific Adviser (G2), P. D. Ewins, CB
Asst Chief Scientific Advisers (G3), Dr G. D. Coley
(Projects); G. H. B. Jordan (Capabilities); P. M. Sutcliffe
(Research); (G4) A. L. C. Quigley (Nuclear)
Chief Executive, Chemical and Biological Defence
Establishment (G3), Dr G. S. Pearson, CB
Chief Executive, Defence Operational Analysis Centre (G4),
Dr D. Leadbeater

## OFFICE OF MANAGEMENT AND BUDGET

Second Permanent Under-Secretary of State (G1A),
J. M. Stewart, CB

Deputy Under-Secretaries (G2), J. F. Howe, OBE (Civilian
Management); J. K. Ledlie, CB, OBE (Personnel and
Logistics); R. T. Jackling, CBE (Resources, Finance and
Programmes)
Asst Under-Secretaries (G3), T. J. Brack, CB (General
Finance); I. D. Fauset (Civilian Personnel Management);
D. C. R. Heyhoe (Civilian Policy Management);
C. V. Balmer (Management Strategy); Miss A. Walker
(Service Personnel); R. P. Hatfield (Director-General of
Management Audit); B. R. Hawtin (Programmes);
D. Fisher (Systems); Dr M. Harte (Director-General,
Information Technology Systems); B. W. Stanley (Director,
Works Services); T. F. W. B. Knapp (Infrastructure and
Logistics); D. F. W. Pickup (Legal Adviser)
Chief Statistical Adviser and Chief Executive of Defence
Analytical Services Agency, P. Altobell
Chief Executive, Defence Accounts Agency (G4),
M. J. Dymond
Chief Constable, Ministry of Defence Police, J. Reddington,
QPM

## PROCUREMENT EXECUTIVE

Chief of Defence Procurement (G1), Dr M. K. McIntosh

### POLICY AND ADMINISTRATION

Deputy Under-Secretary (Defence Procurement) (G2),
M. J. V. Bell
Asst Under-Secretary (Business Strategy) (G3), J. A. Gulvin
Asst Under-Secretary (Finance) (G3), Ms D. J. Seammen
President of the Ordnance Board, Rear-Adm. M. R. Thomas
Director-General, Test and Evaluation (G3), B. Miller
Director-General, Defence Contracts (G3), G. E. Roe
Principal Director, Accountancy, Estimating and Pricing
Services (G4), J. V. A. Crawford

### DEFENCE EXPORT SERVICES ORGANIZATION

Head of Defence Export Services (G2), Sir Alan Thomas, KCB
Military Deputy to Head of DES, Rear-Adm. J. F. T. G. Salt
(retd)
Director-General, Marketing (G3), N. Paren, CB
Asst Under-Secretary (Export Policy and Finance) (G3),
C. T. Sandars
Director-General, Saudi Armed Forces Project, Air Marshal
I. D. Macfadyen, CB, OBE
Director, Malaysian Project (G5), J. B. Taylor
Director, Kuwait Programme, Brig. C. R. Burson

### CONTROLLER OF THE NAVY

Controller of the Navy, Vice-Adm. R. Walmsley
Principal Director of Contracts (Navy) (G4), A. T. Phipps
Director-General, Submarines and Deputy Controller (G3),
C. V. Betts
Director-General, Surface Ships, Rear-Adm. F. P. Scourse,
MBE
Director-General, Surface Weapons (G4), S. Stagg
Director-General, Underwater Weapons (G4), D. McArthur
Chief, Strategic Systems Executive, Rear-Adm. R. O. Irwin
Director-General, Strategic Weapons Systems (G4),
Dr J. P. Catchpole

### MASTER-GENERAL OF THE ORDNANCE

Master-General of the Ordnance, Gen. Sir Jeremy Blacker,
KCB, CBE
Director-General, Policy and Special Projects,
J. G. H. Walker
Principal Director, Contracts (Ordnance) (G4), R. C. Harford
Director-General, Guided Weapons and Electronic Systems
(G3), J. D. Maines

*Director-General, Land Fighting Systems*, Maj.-Gen.
A. C. P. Stone

AIR SYSTEMS CONTROLLERATE

*Controller, Aircraft*, Air Marshal Sir Roger Austin, KCB, AFC
*Principal Director, Contracts (Air)* (*G4*), S. L. Porter
*Director-General, Aircraft 1*, (*G3*), J. A. Gordon
*Director-General, Aircraft 2*, Air Vice-Marshal
P. C. Norriss, AFC
*Director-General, Avionics Weapons and Information Systems*
(*G3*), G. N. Beaven

NUCLEAR PROGRAMMES

*Deputy Controller (Nuclear)* (*G3*), G. L. Sturgess
*Chief Executive, Atomic Weapons Establishment* (*G2*),
B. H. Richards

DEFENCE AGENCIES

ARMY BASE REPAIR ORGANIZATION, Portway, Monxton
Road, Andover, Hants. SP11 8HT. Tel: 01264-383184.
*Chief Executive*, Brig. J. R. Drew
CHEMICAL AND BIOLOGICAL DEFENCE
ESTABLISHMENT, Porton Down, Salisbury, Wilts. SP4
0JQ. Tel: 01980-612000. *Chief Executive* (*G3*), Dr
G. S. Pearson, CB
DEFENCE ACCOUNTS AGENCY, Warminster Road, Bath
BA1 5AA. Tel: 01225-884884. *Chief Executive* (*G4*),
M. J. Dymond
DEFENCE ANALYTICAL SERVICES AGENCY,
Northumberland House, Northumberland Avenue,
London WC2N 5BP. Tel: 0171-218 0872. *Chief Executive*
(*G4*), P. Altobell
DEFENCE OPERATIONAL ANALYSIS CENTRE, Broadoaks,
Parvis Road, West Byfleet, Surrey KT14 6LY. Tel: 01252-
340035. *Chief Executive* (*G4*), Dr D. Leadbetter
DEFENCE POSTAL AND COURIER SERVICE, Inglis
Barracks, Mill Hill, London NW7 1PY. Tel: 0181-818 6417.
*Director and Chief Executive*, Brig. T. M. Brown
DEFENCE RESEARCH AGENCY, Farnborough, Hants.
GU14 6TD. Tel: 01252-392000. *Chief Executive* (*G2*),
J. A. R. Chisholm
HYDROGRAPHIC OFFICE, Taunton, Somerset TA1 2DN.
Tel: 01823-337900. *Chief Executive, and Hydrographer of
the Royal Navy*, Rear-Adm. N. R. Essenhigh
METEOROLOGICAL OFFICE, London Road, Bracknell,
Berks. RG12 2SZ. Tel: 01344-420242. *Chief Executive*
(*G3*), Prof. J. C. R. Hunt, FRS
MILITARY SURVEY, Elmwood Avenue, Feltham, Middx.
TW13 7AE. Tel: 0181-818 2193. *Chief Executive*, Maj.-Gen.
M. P. B. G. Wilson
MINISTRY OF DEFENCE POLICE (*see* page 391) – to
become an agency in 1995
NAVAL AIRCRAFT REPAIR ORGANIZATION, Royal Naval
Yard, Fleetlands, Gosport, Hants. PO13 0AW. Tel: 01329-
826225. *Chief Executive*, Capt. W. S. Graham
RAF SUPPORT COMMAND MAINTENANCE GROUP,
RAF Brampton, Huntingdon, Cambs. PE18 8QL. Tel:
01480-52151. *Chief Executive*, Air Vice-Marshal
R. H. Kyle
RAF TRAINING GROUP – to be launched in late 1994

---

# The Royal Navy

LORD HIGH ADMIRAL OF THE UNITED KINGDOM
HM The Queen

ADMIRALS OF THE FLEET
HRH The Prince Philip, Duke of Edinburgh, KG, KT, OM,
GBE, AC, QSO, PC, *apptd* 1953
Sir Varyl Begg, GCB, DSO, DSC, *apptd* 1968
The Lord Hill-Norton, GCB, *apptd* 1971
Sir Michael Pollock, GCB, LVO, DSC, *apptd* 1974
Sir Edward Ashmore, GCB, DSC, *apptd* 1977
The Lord Lewin, KG, GCB, LVO, DSC, *apptd* 1979
Sir Henry Leach, GCB, *apptd* 1982
Sir William Staveley, GCB, *apptd* 1989
Sir Julian Oswald, GCB, *apptd* 1993

ADMIRALS

Bathurst, Sir Benjamin, GCB, ADC (*Chief of the Naval Staff
and First Sea Lord*)
Slater, Sir Jock, GCB, LVO (*Vice-Chief of the Defence Staff*)
White, Sir Hugo, KCB, CBE (*C.-in-C. Fleet*)
Layard, Sir Michael, KCB, CBE, ADC (*C.-in-C. Naval Home
Command and Second Sea Lord*)

VICE-ADMIRALS

Hill-Norton, The Hon. Sir Nicholas, KCB (*Deputy CDS
(Commitments)*)
Newman, Sir Roy, KCB (*Flag Officer South and Naval Base
Comd. Devonport*)
Biggs, Sir Geoffrey, KCB
Morgan, C. C. (*Flag Officer Scotland, N. England and N.
Ireland*)
Frere, Sir Richard, KCB (*Chief of Fleet Support*)
Abbott, Sir Peter, KCB (*Deputy Supreme Allied Commander
Atlantic*)
Moore, M. A. C., LVO (*Chief of Staff to Commander, Allied
Naval Forces Southern Europe*)
Boyce, M. C., OBE (*Flag Officer Surface Flotilla, until April
1995*)
Rutherford, M. G., CBE (*Deputy CDS (Systems)*)
Walmsley, R. (*Controller of the Navy*)
Revell, A. L., QHS (*Surgeon-General*)
Tod, J. J. R., CBE (*Deputy Comd. Fleet*)
Gretton, M. P. (*Supreme Allied Commander Atlantic's
Representative in Europe*)

REAR-ADMIRALS

Woodard, R. N. (*Flag Officer Royal Yachts*)
Wilkinson, N. J., CB (*Commandant, Joint Services Defence
College, Greenwich*)
Brigstocke, J. R. (*Asst Chief of Naval Staff, until April 1995*)
Shiffner, J. R. (*Director-General, Fleet Support (Equipment
and Systems)*)
Lang, J. S.
Sanders, J. T., CB, OBE (*Flag Officer Gibraltar, until December
1994*)
Moylan-Jones, R. C. (*Director-General, Aircraft (Navy)*)
Rankin, N. E., CBE (*Flag Officer Portsmouth, until April
1995*)
England, T. J. (*Chief Staff Officer (Support)/Fleet*)
Tolhurst, J. G. (*Flag Officer Sea Training*)
Garnett, I. D. G. (*Flag Officer Naval Aviation*)
Irwin, R. O. (*Chief, Strategic Systems Executive*)
Goodson, F. B., OBE (*Asst CDS (Logistics)*)
Blackham, J. J. (*Chief of Staff to C.-in-C. NAVHOME*)
Dunt, J. H. (*Director-General, Fleet Support (Operations and
Plans)*)
Lane-Nott, R. C. (*Flag Officer Submarines and Comd. Sub.
Area East Atlantic*)
Essenhigh, N. R. (*Hydrographer of the Navy and Chief
Executive, Hydrographic Office Defence Support Agency*)
Craig, A., QHP (*Director-General, Naval Medical Services*)

Haddacks, P. K. (*Asst CDS (Policy and Requirements*) *to Supreme Allied Commander Europe*)
West, A. W. J., DSC (*Naval Secretary and Director-General, Naval Manning*)
Trewby, J. A. (*Asst CDS Operational Requirements (Sea)*)
Clarke, J. P., LVO, MBE (*Flag Officer Training and Recruiting*)
Scourse, F. P., MBE (*Director-General, Surface Ships*)
Blackburn, D. A. J. (*Head of British Defence Staff Washington*)
Thomas, M. R. (*President of the Ordnance Board*)
Henderson, D. F. A. (*Asst CDS (Policy and Nuclear*))
Franklyn, P. M. (*Commander, UK Task Group*)
Perowne, J. F. (*Senior Naval Member, Royal College of Defence Studies, from Jan. 1995*)

---

## HM FLEET AS AT 1 APRIL 1994

---

### SUBMARINES

TRIDENT
*Operational:* Vanguard†, Victorious†

POLARIS
*Operational:* Renown, Repulse, Resolution

FLEET
*Operational:* Sceptre, Spartan, Splendid, Superb, Talent, Tireless, Torbay, Trenchant, Triumph, Valiant
*Refitting/standby:* Sovereign, Trafalgar, Turbulent

TYPE 2400
*Operational:* Unicorn, Unseen, Upholder, Ursula

### ANTI-SUBMARINE WARFARE (ASW) CARRIERS

*Operational:* Ark Royal, Illustrious, Invincible

### ASSAULT SHIPS

*Operational:* Fearless
*Refitting/standby:* Intrepid

### DESTROYERS

TYPE 42
*Operational:* Birmingham, Cardiff, Edinburgh, Exeter, Glasgow, Liverpool, Manchester, Newcastle, Nottingham, Southampton
*Refitting/standby:* Gloucester, York

### FRIGATES

TYPE 23
*Operational:* Argyll, Iron Duke, Lancaster, Marlborough, Monmouth, Montrose†, Norfolk, Northumberland*, Richmond*, Westminster†

TYPE 22
*Operational:* Beaver, Boxer, Brave, Brazen, Brilliant, Broadsword, Campbelltown, Chatham, Cornwall, Coventry, Cumberland, Sheffield
*Refitting/standby:* Battleaxe, London

TYPE 21
*Operational:* Active, Avenger

LEANDER CLASS
*Refitting/standby:* Andromeda

### OFFSHORE PATROL

CASTLE CLASS
*Operational:* Dumbarton Castle
*Refitting/standby:* Leeds Castle

ISLAND CLASS
*Operational:* Alderney, Anglesey, Guernsey, Lindisfarne, Orkney, Shetland

### MINEHUNTERS

HUNT CLASS
*Operational:* Atherstone, Berkeley, Bicester, Brecon, Brocklesby, Cattistock, Chiddingfold, Cottesmore, Dulverton, Hurworth, Ledbury, Middleton, Quorn

SANDOWN CLASS
*Operational:* Bridport†, Cromer†, Inverness, Sandown, Walney†

### PATROL CRAFT

BIRD CLASS
*Operational:* Cygnet, Kingfisher, Redpole

PEACOCK CLASS
*Operational:* Peacock, Plover, Starling

RIVER CLASS
*Operational:* Blackwater
*Refitting/standby:* Arun, Itchen, Orwell, Spey

TON CLASS
*Operational:* Wilton

COASTAL TRAINING CRAFT[1]
*Operational:* Archer, Biter, Blazer, Charger, Dasher, Example, Exploit, Explorer, Express, Puncher, Pursuer, Smiter

GIBRALTAR SEARCH AND RESCUE CRAFT
*Operational:* Ranger, Trumpeter

### ROYAL YACHT

*Operational:* Britannia

### ICE PATROL SHIP

*Operational:* Endurance

### SURVEY SHIPS

*Operational:* Beagle, Bulldog, Hecla, Herald, Roebuck
*Refitting/standby:* Gleaner

### SOLD/DECOMMISSIONED 1993-4

Alacrity, Amazon, Ambuscade, Arrow, Brinton, Carron, Dovey, Helford, Helmsdale, Humber, Iveston, Jersey, Kellington, Nurton, Opportune, Opossum, Oracle, Ribble, Scylla, Sheraton, Waveney

*   Under construction at 1 April 1994 and planned to enter service 1994–5
†   Engaged in trials or training at 1 April 1994
1   Coastal training craft are operated by the University Royal Naval Units

### ROYAL FLEET AUXILIARY (RFA)

The Royal Fleet Auxiliary supplies ships of the fleet with fuel, food, water, spares and ammunition while at sea. Its ships are manned by merchant seamen. In April 1994 there were 21 ships in the RFA.

## FLEET AIR ARM

The Fleet Air Arm was established in 1937 and operates aircraft (including helicopters) for the Royal Navy. In April 1994 there were 203 aircraft in the Fleet Air Arm.

## ROYAL NAVAL RESERVE (RNR)

The Royal Naval Reserve is a totally integrated part of the Royal Navy. It comprises about 3,500 men and women nationwide who volunteer to train in their spare time for a variety of sea and shore tasks which they would carry out in time of tension or war.
*Director, Naval Reserves*, Capt. T. J. Norman-Walker

## ROYAL NAVAL AUXILIARY SERVICE (RNXS)

Formed 1962; disbanded 31 March 1994

## ROYAL MARINES

The Corps of Royal Marines was formed in 1664 and is part of the Naval Service. The Royal Marines provide Britain's sea soldiers and in particular 3 Commando Brigade Royal Marines, which is trained and equipped for mountain and cold weather warfare and provides the fleet military landing force. Royal Marines also serve in HM Ships and the Special Boat Service, and provide detachments for other naval and amphibious operations. They also provide the Naval Band Service. The Corps is about 6,500 strong.
*Commandant-General, Royal Marines*, Lt.-Gen. Sir Robert Ross, KCB, OBE
*Major-Generals*, A. M. Keeling, CB, CBE (*MGRM*); J. S. Chester, OBE (*Royal College Defence Studies*)

## ROYAL MARINES RESERVE (RMR)

The Royal Marines Reserve is a force of commando-trained volunteers who train to combat-readiness in order to support the regular Royal Marines should the need arise. About 50 per cent are trained and equipped for arctic warfare and most regular Royal Marine specializations are open to the reservist. There are RMR centres in London, Glasgow, Bristol, Liverpool and Newcastle, each with a number of outlying detachments. The present strength of the RMR is about 1,100.
*Director*, Brig. R. S. Tailyour

## QUEEN ALEXANDRA'S ROYAL NAVAL NURSING SERVICE

The first nursing sisters were appointed to naval hospitals in 1884 and the Queen Alexandra's Royal Naval Nursing Service (QARNNS) gained its current title under the patronage of Queen Alexandra in 1902. Nursing ratings were introduced in 1960 and men were integrated into the Service in 1982; both men and women serve as officers and ratings. Female medical assistants were introduced in 1987. Qualified staff and learners are mainly based at the UK Royal Naval Hospitals, and continue their responsibility for the health and fitness of naval personnel. The strength is about 600.
*Patron*, HRH Princess Alexandra, the Hon. Lady Ogilvy
*Matron-in-Chief*, Principal Nursing Officer Miss C. M. Taylor

## WOMEN'S ROYAL NAVAL SERVICE

Formed 1917; temporarily disbanded between the First and Second World Wars; disbanded 1 November 1993

# The Army

THE QUEEN

FIELD MARSHALS
HRH The Prince Philip, Duke of Edinburgh, KG, KT, OM, GBE, AC, QSO, PC, *apptd* 1953
Sir James Cassels, GCB, KBE, DSO, *apptd* 1968
The Lord Carver, GCB, CBE, DSO, MC, *apptd* 1973
Sir Roland Gibbs, GCB, CBE, DSO, MC, *apptd* 1979
The Lord Bramall, KG, GCB, OBE, MC, *apptd* 1982
Sir John Stanier, GCB, MBE, *apptd* 1985
Sir Nigel Bagnall, GCB, CVO, MC, *apptd* 1988
Sir Richard Vincent, GBE, KCB, DSO (*Chairman of NATO's Military Committee*), *apptd* 1991
Sir John Chapple, GCB, CBE (*Governor and C.-in-C. Gibraltar*), *apptd* 1992
HRH The Duke of Kent, KG, GCMG, GCVO, ADC, *apptd* 1993
Sir Peter Inge, GCB (*Chief of the Defence Staff*), *apptd* 1994

GENERALS
Waters, Sir John, KCB, CBE, ADC (*D. SACEUR*)
Jones, Sir Edward, KCB, CBE, Col. Cmdt. 2 RGJ
Guthrie, Sir Charles, GCB, LVO, OBE, ADC (*Gen.*), Col. Cmdt. Int. Corps (*Chief of the General Staff*)
Johnson, Sir Garry, KCB, OBE, MC, Col. 10 GR, Col. Cmdt. The Light Division (*C.-in-C. AFNORTH*)
Wilsey, Sir John, KCB, CBE, ADC (*Gen.*), Col. Cmdt. Royal Logistic Corps (*C.-in-C. UK Land Forces*)
Wilkes, Sir Michael, KCB, CBE, Col. Cmdt. Hon. Artillery Company (TA) (*Adjutant-General*)
Blacker, Sir Jeremy, KCB, CBE, Col. Cmdt. RTR, Col. Cmdt. RAC (*Master-General of the Ordnance*)

LIEUTENANT-GENERALS
Swinburn, Sir Richard, KCB (*Deputy C.-in-C., HQ UK Land Forces*)
Mackenzie, Sir Jeremy, KCB, OBE, Col. Cmdt. AG Corps (*Cmdt. NATO Rapid Reaction Corps*)
Rous, The Hon. Sir William, KCB, OBE, Col. Coldstream Guards (*Quartermaster-General*)
Beale, Sir Peter, KBE, QHP
Duffell, Sir Peter, KCB, CBE, MC, Col. The Royal Gurkha Rifles (*Inspector-General, Doctrine and Training*)
Boyd-Carpenter, the Hon. Sir Thomas, KBE (*Deputy CDS (Programmes and Personnel)*)
Wheeler, Sir Roger, KCB, CBE (*GOC Northern Ireland*)
Rose, Sir Michael, KCB, CBE, QGM (*Comd. Bosnia-Hercegovina Command*)
Foley, Sir John, KCB, OBE, MC (*Chief of Defence Intelligence*)
Denison-Smith, A. A., MBE (*GOC S District*)

MAJOR-GENERALS
Hayman-Joyce, R. J., CBE (*Military Secretary*)
Cowan, S., CBE, Col. QGS (*Asst CDS Operational Requirements (Land)*)
Grist, R. D., CB, OBE, Col. Royal Gloucestershire, Berkshire and Wiltshire (*Director-General, HQ Directorate AG Corps*)

Thomson, D. P., CB, CBE, MC, Col. The Argyll and Sutherland Highlanders (Princess Louise's) (*Senior Army Member, Royal College of Defence Studies*)

Harley, A. G. H., CB, OBE (*Comd. British Forces Cyprus*)

Wallace, C. B. Q., OBE, Col. Cmdt. RMP (*Comdt. Staff College*)

Field, G. W., CB, OBE, Col. Cmdt. Royal Logistic Corps (*Engineer-in-Chief (Army)*)

Heath, M. S., CB, CBE, Col. Cmdt. Corps of REME (*Team Leader, Army Costs Study*)

Stone, A. C. P., CB, Col. Cmdt. Royal Regiment of Artillery (*Director-General, Land Fighting Systems*)

Meier, A. L., OBE

Smith, R. A., DSO, OBE, QGM, Col. Cmdt. Parachute Regiment, Col. Cmdt. REME Equipment Support Organization (*Asst CDS (Operations/Security)*)

Toyne-Sewell, T. P. (*Team Leader, Tri-Service Study into Services Recruiting Organizations*)

Pett, R. A., MBE, Col. Cmdt. The King's Division (*Director, Infantry*)

Boyle, A. H. (*Director-General, CIS (Army) and Signals Officer-in-Chief (Army)*)

Burton, E. F. G., OBE (*Cmdt. RMCS*)

Freer, I. L., CB, CBE, Col. Cmdt. POW Division (*GOC Wales and Western District*)

Regan, M. D., OBE (*Director-General, AG Corps*)

Courage, W. J., CB, MBE (*Chief of Joint Services Liaison Organization Bonn*)

Mayes, F. B., QHS, FRCS (*Director-General, Army Medical Services*)

Dutton, B. H., CBE (*Comd. British Forces Hong Kong*)

Grant, S. C. (*Chief of Staff HQ BAOR*)

Lytle, S. W. St J. (*Director, Army Air Corps*)

Pike, H. W. R., DSO, MBE, Col. SASC (*Cmdt. RMAS*)

Walker, M. J. D., CBE, Col. Cmdt. The Queen's Division, Col. Cmdt. AAC (*Asst Chief of General Staff*)

Sheppard, P. J., CBE (*Director-General, Logistics Policy (Army)*)

Carr-Smith, S. R. (*Chief C3 NACISA*)

Jackson, M. D., CBE (*GOC 3 (UK) Division*)

Kennedy, A. I. G., CBE (*Director-General, TA*)

Mackay-Dick, I. C., MBE (*GOC London District*)

Scott, M. I. E., CBE, DSO, Col. Cmdt. The Scottish Division (*GOC Scotland*)

Burden, D. L., CBE (*Director-General, Logistic Support (Army)*)

Craig, R. P., MD, FRCS, QHS (*Cmdt. MED. UK Land Forces*)

Cordingley, P. A. J., DSO (*GOC E District*)

Willcocks, M. A. (*Director-General, Land Warfare*)

Deverell, J. F., OBE (*Director-General, Army Manning and Recruiting*)

Pigott, A. D., CBE (*Chief of Staff HQ ACE Rapid Reaction Corps*)

Robins, W. J. P., OBE (*Asst CDS (CIS)*)

McAfee, R. W. M. (*Director-General, Army Training*)

White, M. S., CBE (*Director of Support LANDCENT*)

Cowan, G. O., CBE, Col. Cmdt. Brigade of Gurkhas (*Cmdt. Royal Army Medical College*)

Cordy-Simpson, R. A. (*GOC 1 Armd Division*)

Wilson, M. P. B. G. (*Director-General, Military Survey*)

Vyvyan, C. G. C. (*Chief of Staff HQ UK Land Forces*)

Hall, J. M. F. C., OBE (*Director, Royal Armoured Corps*)

Richards, N. W. F., OBE (*Chief Combat Support ACE Rapid Reaction Corps*)

Leask, A. de C. L., CBE (*Comd. Land Forces and DD Ops. N. Ireland*)

Durie, I. G. C., CBE (*Director, Royal Artillery*)

Corp, P. J. G. (*Director-General, Equipment Support (Army)*)

Rogers, A. P. V., OBE (*Director, Army Legal Services*)

Pack, S. J. (*Comd. British Forces Gibraltar, from Dec. 1994*)

## CONSTITUTION OF THE BRITISH ARMY

The regular forces include the following arms, branches and corps. Soldiers' record offices are shown at the end of each group; records of officers are maintained at the Ministry of Defence.

THE ARMS

HOUSEHOLD CAVALRY – The Household Cavalry Regiment (The Life Guards and The Blues and Royals). *Records*, Queen's Park, Chester

ROYAL ARMOURED CORPS – Cavalry Regiments: 1st The Queen's Dragoon Guards; The Royal Scots Dragoon Guards (Carabiniers and Greys); The Royal Dragoon Guards; The Queen's Royal Hussars (The Queen's Own and Royal Irish); 9th/12th Royal Lancers (Prince of Wales's); The King's Royal Hussars; The Light Dragoons; The Queen's Royal Lancers; Royal Tank Regiment comprising two regular regiments. *Records*, Queen's Park, Chester

ARTILLERY – Royal Regiment of Artillery. *Records*, Imphal Barracks, Fulford Road, York

ENGINEERS – Corps of Royal Engineers. *Records*, Kentigern House, Brown Street, Glasgow

SIGNALS – Royal Corps of Signals. *Records*, Kentigern House, Brown Street, Glasgow

THE INFANTRY

The Foot Guards and regiments of Infantry of the Line are grouped in divisions as follows:

GUARDS DIVISION – Grenadier, Coldstream, Scots, Irish and Welsh Guards. *Records*, Imphal Barracks, Fulford Road, York

SCOTTISH DIVISION – The Royal Scots (The Royal Regiment); The Royal Highland Fusiliers (Princess Margaret's Own Glasgow and Ayrshire Regiment); The King's Own Scottish Borderers; The Black Watch (Royal Highland Regiment); The Highlanders (Seaforth, Gordons and Camerons); The Argyll and Sutherland Highlanders (Princess Louise's). *Records*, Imphal Barracks, Fulford Road, York

QUEEN'S DIVISION – The Princess of Wales's Royal Regiment (Queen's and Royal Hampshire's); The Royal Regiment of Fusiliers; The Royal Anglian Regiment. *Records*, Higher Barracks, Exeter

KING'S DIVISION – The King's Own Royal Border Regiment; The King's Regiment; The Prince of Wales's Own Regiment of Yorkshire; The Green Howards (Alexandra, Princess of Wales's Own Yorkshire Regiment); The Queen's Lancashire Regiment; The Duke of Wellington's Regiment (West Riding). *Records*, Imphal Barracks, Fulford Road, York

PRINCE OF WALES'S DIVISION – The Devonshire and Dorset Regiment; The Cheshire Regiment; The Royal Welch Fusiliers; The Royal Regiment of Wales (24th/41st Foot); The Royal Gloucestershire, Berkshire and Wiltshire Regiment; The Worcestershire and Sherwood Foresters Regiment (29th/45th Foot); The Staffordshire Regiment (The Prince of Wales's). *Records*, Imphal Barracks, Fulford, York

LIGHT DIVISION – The Light Infantry; The Royal Green Jackets. *Records*, Higher Barracks, Exeter

BRIGADE OF GURKHAS – The Royal Gurkha Rifles; The Queen's Gurkha Engineers; Queen's Gurkha Signals; The

Queen's Own Gurkha Transport Regiment. *Records*, Record Office, Brigade of Gurkhas, Hong Kong, BFPO 1 (from Jan. 1995, Church Crookham, Hants.)
THE ROYAL IRISH REGIMENT (one general service and six home service battalions) – 27th (Inniskilling), 83rd, 87th and the Ulster Defence Regiment. *Records*, Imphal Barracks, Fulford Road, York
THE PARACHUTE REGIMENT (three regular battalions) – *Records*, Higher Barracks, Exeter
SPECIAL AIR SERVICE REGIMENT – *Records*, Higher Barracks, Exeter
ARMY AIR CORPS – *Records*, Higher Barracks, Exeter

THE SERVICES

Royal Army Chaplain's Department – *Regimental HQ* and *Depot*, Bagshot Park, Surrey
The Royal Logistic Corps – *Records*, Kentigern House, Brown Street, Glasgow; South Wigston, Leicester; Higher Barracks, Exeter
Royal Army Medical Corps, Royal Army Dental Corps and Queen Alexandra's Royal Army Nursing Corps – *Records*, Queen's Park, Chester
Adjutant-General's Corps – *Records*, Queen's Park, Chester
Corps of Royal Electrical and Mechanical Engineers Equipment Support Organization – *Records*, Glen Parva Barracks, Saffron Road, Wigston, Leicester
Small Arms School Corps – *Records*, Higher Barracks, Exeter
General Service Corps – *Records*, Imphal Barracks, Fulford Road, York
Royal Army Veterinary Corps, Intelligence Corps, Army Physical Training Corps, Officers Training Corps – *Records*, Higher Barracks, Exeter

ARMY EQUIPMENT HOLDINGS

The Army is equipped (as at 1 January 1994) with 957 tanks, 3,762 armoured combat vehicles or ACV lookalikes, 492 artillery pieces, 42 landing craft and 302 helicopters.

THE TERRITORIAL ARMY (TA)

The Territorial Army is designed to provide a highly-trained and well-equipped force which will complete the Regular Army order of battle in a time of national emergency. It is also intended to make greater use of the TA in peacetime. The structure of the TA is currently under review. Its establishment is approximately 59,000.

QUEEN ALEXANDRA'S ROYAL ARMY NURSING CORPS

The Queen Alexandra's Royal Army Nursing Corps (QARANC) was founded in 1902 as Queen Alexandra's Imperial Military Nursing Service (QAIMNS) and gained its present title in 1949. The QARANC has trained nurses for the register since 1950 and has many other nursing employments. Since 1 April 1992 men have been eligible to join the QARANC. The Corps provides service in military hospitals in the United Kingdom (including Northern Ireland), Germany, Hong Kong, Cyprus, Falkland Islands, Belize and wherever they may be needed world-wide.
*Colonel-in-Chief*, HRH The Princess Margaret, Countess of Snowdon, GCVO, CI
*Matron-in-Chief (Army) and Director, Army Nursing Services*, Brig. H. S. Dixon-Nuttall, QHNS

WOMEN'S ROYAL ARMY CORPS
Formed 1 February 1949; disbanded April 1992

# The Royal Air Force

THE QUEEN

MARSHALS OF THE ROYAL AIR FORCE
HRH The Prince Philip, Duke of Edinburgh, KG, KT, OM, GBE, AC, QSO, PC, *apptd* 1953
Sir John Grandy, GCB, GCVO, KBE, DSO, *apptd* 1971
Sir Denis Spotswood, GCB, CBE, DSO, DFC, *apptd* 1974
Sir Michael Beetham, GCB, CBE, DFC, AFC, *apptd* 1982
Sir Keith Williamson, GCB, AFC, *apptd* 1985
The Lord Craig of Radley, GCB, OBE, *apptd* 1988
Sir Peter Harding, GCB, ADC, *apptd* 1993

AIR CHIEF MARSHALS
Graydon, Sir Michael, GCB, CBE, ADC (*Chief of the Air Staff*)
Stear, Sir Michael, KCB, CBE (*Deputy C.-in-C. Allied Forces Central Europe*)
Wilson, Sir Andrew, KCB, AFC, ADC (*Air Member for Personnel*)
Alcock, Sir Michael, KBE, CB (*Air Officer Commanding-in-Chief and Air Member for Logistics*)
Johns, Sir Richard, KCB, CBE, LVO (*C.-in-C. Allied Forces North-Western Europe*)
Wratten, Sir William, KBE, CB, AFC (*AOC.-in-C. Strike Command and Comd. Allied Air Forces North-Western Europe*)

AIR MARSHALS
Walker, Sir John, KCB, CBE, AFC
Austin, Sir Roger, KCB, AFC (*Controller, Aircraft*)
Harris, Sir John, KCB, CBE (*AOC No. 18 Group*)
Willis, Sir John, KCB, CBE (*AOC.-in-C. RAF Support Command*)
Garden, Sir Timothy, KCB (*Commandant, Royal College of Defence Studies*)
Allison, J. S., CBE (*Chief of Staff and Deputy C.-in-C. Strike Command*)
Macfadyen, I. D., CB, OBE (*Director-General, Saudi Armed Forces Project*)

AIR VICE-MARSHALS
Harding, P. J., CB, CBE, AFC (*Defence Services Secretary*)
Cousins, D., CB, AFC (*Cmdt. RAF College, Cranwell*)
Dodworth, P., CB, OBE, AFC
Baird, J. A., QHP (*Director-General, Medical Services (RAF)*)
Beer, P. G., CBE, LVO (*Chief of Staff and Director-General, Strategic Policy and Plans*)
French, D. R., CB, MBE
Saunders, D. J., CBE (*Air Officer Engineering and Supply*)
Squire, P. T., DFC, AFC (*Asst Chief of the Air Staff*)
Robertson, G. A., CBE (*Asst CDS (Programmes)*)
Lucas, Ven. B. H., QHC (*Chaplain-in-Chief (RAF)*)
Brook, J. M., CB, QHS
Chapple, R., QHP (*Principal Medical Officer, RAF Support Command*)
Cheshire, J. A., CB, CBE (*UK Military Representative to NATO Military Committee, Brussels*)
Norriss, P. C., AFC (*Director-General, Aircraft 2*)

Rae, W. M., CB (*Senior Director of Staff, Royal College of Defence Studies*)
Kyle, R. H., MBE (*Chief Executive, RAF Support Command Maintenance Group*)
Mackey, J., QHDS (*Director, Defence Dental Services*)
Sherrington, T. B., OBE (*Air Officer Admin., RAF Support Command*)
Carleton, G. W. (*Director, Legal Services (RAF)*)
Coville, C. C. C. (*Asst CDS Operational Requirements (Air)*)
O'Brien, R. P., OBE (*Air Secretary and AOC RAF Personnel Management Centre*)
Bagnall, A. J. C., CB, OBE (*AOC No. 11 Group*)
May, J. A. G., CBE (*Air Staff, HQ Strike Command*)
Baldwin, N. B., CBE (*Asst CDS (Overseas)*)
Donaldson, M. P., MBE (*Cmdt. RAF Staff College, Bracknell*)
Terry, C. G., OBE (*Director-General, Support Management (RAF)*)
Main, J. B., OBE (*Air Officer Commanding Information Systems and Signals Units*)
Goddard, P. J.
Feesey, J. D. L. (*Director-General, Policy and Planning, NATS*)
Goodall, R. H., CBE, AFC (*AOC No. 2 Group*)
Day, J. R. (*AOC No. 1 Group*)
Hull, D. H., QHS (*Dean of Air Force Music*)
Henderson, D. F. A., CBE (*Operations Division, HQ Strike Command*)
Jenner, T. I.

---

## CONSTITUTION OF THE ROYAL AIR FORCE

Since April 1994, the RAF has consisted of three commands: Strike Command, Logistics Command, and Personnel and Training Command. Strike Command is the RAF's operational command for the UK and designated locations abroad (including Germany); its roles include strike/attack, air defence, control and reporting, maritime surveillance, air reconnaissance, air-to-air refuelling, offensive support, air transport, aero-medical facilities, and search and rescue. Logistics Command is responsible for all logistics, engineering support, and maintenance. Personnel and Training Command is responsible for air and ground training, hospitals, and personnel administration.

The Royal Air Force is equipped (as at 1 April 1994) with:
*Aircraft* – 256 Tornado, 7 Sentry, 56 Harrier, 53 Jaguar, 17 Canberra, 29 Nimrod, 19 VC10, 9 Tristar, 60 Hercules, 25 Hawk, 11 BAe, 2 Andover
*Helicopters* – 40 Puma, 47 Wessex, 19 Sea King, 10 Chinook, 7 Gazelle
Miscellaneous training aircraft, etc.
Rapier missiles

## ROYAL AUXILIARY AIR FORCE (RAUXAF)

Formed in 1924, the Auxiliary Air Force served with great distinction in the Second World War and in recognition of its war record King George VI conferred the prefix 'Royal' in 1947. The Royal Auxiliary Air Force supports the RAF in maritime air operations, air and ground defence of major airfields, air movements, and aero-medical evacuation. Plans have been announced for the merger of the RAUXAF and the RAFVR.
*Air Commodore-in-Chief,* HM The Queen
*Director of Personnel Management (Airmen) and Controller of Reserve Forces (RAF),* Air Cdre M. L. Jackson, OBE

## ROYAL AIR FORCE VOLUNTEER RESERVE (RAFVR)

The Royal Air Force Volunteer Reserve was created in 1936 with the object of providing training for the increased number of aircrew who were seen as necessary for the forthcoming conflict. The RAFVR was reconstituted in 1947 following war service. It provides specialist personnel who fill specific wartime intelligence support, photo interpretation and public relations appointments. A small number of RAFVR aircrew are employed to augment regular crews on Nimrod (Maritime Reconnaissance) aircraft in wartime. Plans have been announced for the merger of the RAFVR and the RAUXAF.
*Director of Personnel Management (Airmen) and Controller of Reserve Forces (RAF),* Air Cdre M. L. Jackson, OBE

---

## PRINCESS MARY'S ROYAL AIR FORCE NURSING SERVICE

---

The Princess Mary's Royal Air Force Nursing Service (PMRAFNS) is open to both male and female candidates. Commissions are offered to those who are Registered General Nurses (RGN) with a minimum of two years experience after obtaining RGN and normally with a second qualification. RGNs with no additional experience or qualification are also recruited as non-commissioned officers in the grade of Staff Nurse.
*Air Chief Commandant,* HRH Princess Alexandra, the Hon. Lady Ogilvy, GCVO
*Matron-in-Chief,* Group Captain V. M. Hand, QHNS

---

## WOMEN'S ROYAL AIR FORCE
Formed 1 April 1918; disbanded 1920
Re-formed 1949; disbanded 1 April 1994

---

## ROYAL OBSERVER CORPS
Established in 1925; stood down 31 March 1992

---

## SERVICE SALARIES

The following rates of pay have been introduced as part of the 1994 pay award for service personnel. These rates apply from 1 April 1994 to 1 January 1995, when the second stage of the pay award will be implemented and pay will rise by approximately 0.9 per cent.

The increasing integration of women in the armed services is reflected in equal pay for equal work and the X factor addition is now the same for men and women (11.5 per cent).

Annual salaries are derived from daily rates in whole pence and rounded to the nearest £.

The pay rates shown are for Army personnel. The rates apply also to personnel of equivalent rank and pay band in the other services.

### OFFICERS' SALARIES

#### MAIN SCALE

| Rank | Daily | Annual | Rank | Daily | Annual |
|---|---|---|---|---|---|
| Second Lieutenant | £35.48 | £12,950 | Special List Lieutenant-Colonel | £103.76 | £37,872 |
| Lieutenant | | | Lieutenant-Colonel | | |
| On appointment | 46.92 | 17,126 | On appointment with less than 19 years service | 105.57 | 38,533 |
| After 1 year in the rank | 48.15 | 17,575 | After 2 years in the rank or with 19 years service | 108.35 | 39,548 |
| After 2 years in the rank | 49.38 | 18,024 | After 4 years in the rank or with 21 years service | 111.13 | 40,562 |
| After 3 years in the rank | 50.61 | 18,473 | After 6 years in the rank or with 23 years service | 113.91 | 41,577 |
| After 4 years in the rank | 51.84 | 18,922 | After 8 years in the rank or with 25 years service | 116.70 | 42,596 |
| Captain | | | Colonel | | |
| On appointment | 59.71 | 21,794 | On appointment | 122.95 | 44,877 |
| After 1 year in the rank | 61.32 | 22,382 | After 2 years in the rank | 126.19 | 46,059 |
| After 2 years in the rank | 62.94 | 22,973 | After 4 years in the rank | 129.41 | 47,235 |
| After 3 years in the rank | 64.56 | 23,564 | After 6 years in the rank | 132.65 | 48,417 |
| After 4 years in the rank | 66.17 | 24,152 | After 8 years in the rank | 135.88 | 49,596 |
| After 5 years in the rank | 67.79 | 24,743 | Brigadier | 150.81 | 55,046 |
| After 6 years in the rank | 69.40 | 25,331 | Major-General | 163.82 | 59,794 |
| Major | | | Lieutenant-General | 187.31 | 68,368 |
| On appointment | 75.25 | 27,466 | General | 260.41 | 95,050 |
| After 1 year in the rank | 77.12 | 28,149 | Field Marshal | 323.78 | 118,180 |
| After 2 years in the rank | 78.99 | 28,831 | | | |
| After 3 years in the rank | 80.85 | 29,510 | | | |
| After 4 years in the rank | 82.71 | 30,189 | | | |
| After 5 years in the rank | 84.58 | 30,872 | | | |
| After 6 years in the rank | 86.44 | 31,551 | | | |
| After 7 years in the rank | 88.31 | 32,233 | | | |
| After 8 years in the rank | 90.18 | 32,916 | | | |

## SALARIES OF OFFICERS COMMISSIONED FROM THE RANKS (LIEUTENANTS AND CAPTAINS ONLY)

| YEARS OF COMMISSIONED SERVICE | YEARS OF NON-COMMISSIONED SERVICE FROM AGE 18 | | | | | |
|---|---|---|---|---|---|---|
| | Less than 12 years | | 12 years but less than 15 years | | 15 years or more | |
| | Daily | Annual | Daily | Annual | Daily | Annual |
| On appointment | £65.62 | £23,951 | £68.95 | £25,167 | £72.29 | £26,386 |
| After 1 year service | 67.29 | 24,561 | 70.63 | 25,780 | 73.38 | 26,784 |
| After 2 years service | 68.95 | 25,167 | 72.29 | 26,386 | 74.46 | 27,178 |
| After 3 years service | 70.63 | 25,780 | 73.38 | 26,784 | 75.55 | 27,576 |
| After 4 years service | 72.29 | 26,386 | 74.46 | 27,178 | 76.62 | 27,966 |
| After 5 years service | 73.38 | 26,784 | 75.55 | 27,576 | 77.71 | 28,364 |
| After 6 years service | 74.46 | 27,178 | 76.62 | 27,966 | 78.79 | 28,758 |
| After 8 years service | 75.55 | 27,576 | 77.71 | 28,364 | 79.88 | 29,156 |
| After 10 years service | 76.62 | 27,966 | 78.79 | 28,758 | 79.88 | 29,156 |
| After 12 years service | 77.71 | 28,364 | 79.88 | 29,156 | 79.88 | 29,156 |
| After 14 years service | 78.79 | 28,758 | 79.88 | 29,156 | 79.88 | 29,156 |
| After 16 years service | 79.88 | 29,156 | 79.88 | 29,156 | 79.88 | 29,156 |

The pay structure below officer level is divided into pay bands. Jobs at each rank are allocated to bands according to their score in the job evaluation system.

Scale A: committed to serve/have completed less than 6 years

Scale B: committed to serve/have completed 6 years but less than 9 years

Scale C: committed to serve/have completed more than 9 years

Daily rates of pay effective from 1 April 1994 are:

## SALARIES OF WARRANT OFFICERS AND SENIOR NCOs

| Rank | Scale A | | | | Scale B | | | | Scale C | | | |
|---|---|---|---|---|---|---|---|---|---|---|---|---|
| | Band 4 | Band 5 | Band 6 | Band 7 | Band 4 | Band 5 | Band 6 | Band 7 | Band 4 | Band 5 | Band 6 | Band 7 |
| Sergeant | £43.62 | £47.96 | £52.70 | £  — | £43.92 | £48.26 | £53.00 | £  — | £44.37 | £48.71 | £53.45 | £  — |
| Staff Sergeant | 46.13 | 50.46 | 55.22 | 60.95 | 46.43 | 50.76 | 55.52 | 61.25 | 46.88 | 51.21 | 55.97 | 61.70 |
| Warrant Officer | | | | | | | | | | | | |
| Class 2 | 49.32 | 53.67 | 59.52 | 65.38 | 49.62 | 53.97 | 59.82 | 65.68 | 50.07 | 54.42 | 60.27 | 66.13 |
| Class 1 | 52.60 | 56.93 | 62.86 | 68.70 | 52.90 | 57.23 | 63.16 | 69.00 | 53.35 | 57.68 | 63.61 | 69.45 |

## SALARIES OF ADULT PERSONNEL OF THE RANK OF CORPORAL AND BELOW

| Rank | Scale A | | | Scale B | | | Scale C | | |
|---|---|---|---|---|---|---|---|---|---|
| | Band 1 | Band 2 | Band 3 | Band 1 | Band 2 | Band 3 | Band 1 | Band 2 | Band 3 |
| Private | | | | | | | | | |
| Class 4 | £22.21 | £  — | £  — | £22.51 | £  — | £  — | £22.96 | £  — | £  — |
| Class 3 | 24.88 | 28.90 | 33.34 | 25.18 | 29.20 | 33.64 | 25.63 | 29.65 | 34.09 |
| Class 2 | 27.83 | 31.86 | 36.31 | 28.13 | 32.16 | 36.61 | 28.58 | 32.61 | 37.06 |
| Class 1 | 30.20 | 34.22 | 38.66 | 30.50 | 34.52 | 38.96 | 30.95 | 34.97 | 39.41 |
| Lance-Corporal | | | | | | | | | |
| Class 3 | 30.20 | 34.22 | 38.66 | 30.50 | 34.52 | 38.96 | 30.95 | 34.97 | 39.41 |
| Class 2 | 32.27 | 36.29 | 41.10 | 32.57 | 36.59 | 41.40 | 33.02 | 37.04 | 41.85 |
| Class 1 | 34.71 | 38.74 | 43.54 | 35.01 | 39.04 | 43.84 | 35.46 | 39.49 | 44.29 |
| Corporal | | | | | | | | | |
| Class 2 | 37.28 | 41.29 | 46.11 | 37.58 | 41.59 | 46.41 | 38.03 | 42.04 | 46.86 |
| Class 1 | 40.01 | 44.04 | 48.85 | 40.31 | 44.34 | 49.15 | 40.76 | 44.79 | 49.60 |

# Relative Rank – Armed Forces

| | Royal Navy | | Army | | Royal Air Force |
|---|---|---|---|---|---|
| 1 | Admiral of the Fleet | 1 | Field Marshal | 1 | Marshal of the RAF |
| 2 | Admiral (Adm.) | 2 | General (Gen.) | 2 | Air Chief Marshal |
| 3 | Vice-Admiral (Vice-Adm.) | 3 | Lieutenant-General (Lt.-Gen.) | 3 | Air Marshal |
| 4 | Rear-Admiral (Rear-Adm.) | 4 | Major-General (Maj.-Gen.) | 4 | Air Vice-Marshal |
| 5 | Commodore (1st & 2nd class) (Cdre) | 5 | Brigadier (Brig.) | 5 | Air Commodore (Air Cdre) |
| 6 | Captain (Capt.) | 6 | Colonel (Col.) | 6 | Group Captain (Gp Capt) |
| 7 | Commander (Cdr.) | 7 | Lieutenant-Colonel (Lt.-Col.) | 7 | Wing Commander (Wg Cdr.) |
| 8 | Lieutenant-Commander (Lt.-Cdr.) | 8 | Major (Maj.) | 8 | Squadron Leader (Sqn. Ldr.) |
| 9 | Lieutenant (Lt.) | 9 | Captain (Capt.) | 9 | Flight Lieutenant (Flt. Lt.) |
| 10 | Sub-Lieutenant (Sub-Lt.) | 10 | Lieutenant (Lt.) | 10 | Flying Officer (FO) |
| 11 | Acting Sub-Lieutenant (Acting Sub-Lt.) | 11 | Second Lieutenant (2nd Lt.) | 11 | Pilot Officer (PO) |

## SERVICE RETIRED PAY ON COMPULSORY RETIREMENT

Those who leave the services having served at least five years, but not long enough to qualify for the appropriate immediate pension, now qualify for a preserved pension and terminal grant, both of which are payable at age 60. The tax-free resettlement grants shown below are payable on release to those who qualify for a preserved pension and who have completed nine years service from age 21 (officers) or 12 years from age 18 (other ranks).

The annual rates for army personnel are given. The rates apply also to personnel of equivalent rank in the other services, including the nursing services.

### OFFICERS

Applicable to officers who give full pay service on the active list on or after 31 March 1994

| No. of years reckonable service over age 21 | Capt. and below* | Major* | Lt.-Col. | Colonel | Brigadier | Major-General | Lieutenant-General | General |
|---|---|---|---|---|---|---|---|---|
| 16 | £ 7,219 | £ 8,604 | £11,271 | £ — | £ — | £ — | £ — | £ — |
| 17 | 7,552 | 9,013 | 11,793 | — | — | — | — | — |
| 18 | 7,885 | 9,422 | 12,314 | 14,341 | — | — | — | — |
| 19 | 8,218 | 9,831 | 12,836 | 14,948 | — | — | — | — |
| 20 | 8,551 | 10,240 | 13,357 | 15,555 | — | — | — | — |
| 21 | 8,884 | 10,648 | 13,879 | 16,162 | — | — | — | — |
| 22 | 9,217 | 11,057 | 14,400 | 16,769 | 19,358 | — | — | — |
| 23 | 9,550 | 11,466 | 14,922 | 17,376 | 19,969 | — | — | — |
| 24 | 9,883 | 11,875 | 15,443 | 17,983 | 20,581 | 22,356 | — | — |
| 25 | 10,216 | 12,284 | 15,965 | 18,591 | 21,192 | 23,020 | — | — |
| 26 | 10,549 | 12,693 | 16,487 | 19,198 | 21,804 | 23,685 | — | — |
| 27 | 10,882 | 13,102 | 17,008 | 19,805 | 22,416 | 24,349 | 27,841 | — |
| 28 | 11,215 | 13,511 | 17,530 | 20,412 | 23,027 | 25,014 | 28,601 | — |
| 29 | 11,548 | 13,920 | 18,051 | 21,019 | 23,639 | 25,678 | 29,360 | — |
| 30 | 11,881 | 14,328 | 18,573 | 21,626 | 24,251 | 26,342 | 30,120 | 41,875 |
| 31 | 12,214 | 14,737 | 19,094 | 22,233 | 24,862 | 27,007 | 30,879 | 42,931 |
| 32 | 12,547 | 15,146 | 19,616 | 22,840 | 25,474 | 27,671 | 31,639 | 43,987 |
| 33 | 12,880 | 15,555 | 20,137 | 23,447 | 26,085 | 28,336 | 32,398 | 45,043 |
| 34 | 13,213 | 15,964 | 20,659 | 24,054 | 26,697 | 29,000 | 33,158 | 46,099 |

*Field Marshal* – active list retired pay at the rate of £57,317 a year

*Including Quartermaster

### WARRANT OFFICERS, NCOS AND PRIVATES

Applicable to soldiers who give full pay service on or after 21 March 1994

| Number of years reckonable service | Below Corporal | Corporal | Sergeant | Staff Sergeant | Warrant Officer Class II | Warrant Officer Class I |
|---|---|---|---|---|---|---|
| 22 | £4,191 | £5,355 | £5,884 | £ 6,687 | £ 6,924 | £ 7,651 |
| 23 | 4,337 | 5,542 | 6,089 | 6,931 | 7,169 | 7,926 |
| 24 | 4,484 | 5,729 | 6,295 | 7,165 | 7,415 | 8,201 |
| 25 | 4,630 | 5,916 | 6,500 | 7,398 | 7,660 | 8,476 |
| 26 | 4,776 | 6,103 | 6,706 | 7,632 | 7,906 | 8,751 |
| 27 | 4,922 | 6,290 | 6,911 | 7,866 | 8,151 | 9,026 |
| 28 | 5,069 | 6,477 | 7,116 | 8,100 | 8,397 | 9,301 |
| 29 | 5,215 | 6,664 | 7,322 | 8,334 | 8,642 | 9,576 |
| 30 | 5,361 | 6,850 | 7,527 | 8,567 | 8,888 | 9,852 |
| 31 | 5,507 | 7,037 | 7,733 | 8,801 | 9,133 | 10,127 |
| 32 | 5,654 | 7,224 | 7,938 | 9,035 | 9,379 | 10,402 |
| 33 | 5,800 | 7,411 | 8,143 | 9,269 | 9,624 | 10,677 |
| 34 | 5,946 | 7,598 | 8,349 | 9,503 | 9,870 | 10,952 |
| 35 | 6,092 | 7,785 | 8,554 | 9,736 | 10,115 | 11,227 |
| 36 | 6,239 | 7,972 | 8,760 | 9,970 | 10,361 | 11,502 |
| 37 | 6,385 | 8,159 | 8,965 | 10,204 | 10,606 | 11,777 |

### RESETTLEMENT GRANTS

Terminal grants are in each case three times the rate of retired pay or pension. There are special rates of retired pay for certain other ranks not shown above. Lower rates are payable in cases of voluntary retirement.

A gratuity of £2,470 is payable for officers with short service commissions for each year completed. Resettlement grants are: officers £8,491; non-commissioned ranks £5,609.

# Nobel Prizes

For prize winners for the years 1901–90, *see* earlier editions of *Whitaker's Almanack*.

The Nobel Prizes are awarded each year from the income of a trust fund established by the Swedish scientist Alfred Nobel, the inventor of dynamite, who died on 10 December 1896, leaving a fortune of £1,750,000. The prizes are awarded to those who have contributed most to the common good in the domain of:

*Physics*
  awarded by the Royal Swedish Academy of Sciences;
*Chemistry*
  awarded by the Royal Swedish Academy of Sciences;
*Physiology or Medicine*
  awarded by the Karolinska Institute;
*Literature*
  awarded by the Swedish Academy of Arts;
*Peace*
  awarded by a five-person committee elected by the Norwegian Storting;
*Economic Sciences* (instituted 1969)
  awarded by the Royal Swedish Academy of Sciences.

The first awards were made in 1901 on the fifth anniversary of Nobel's death. The prizes are awarded every year on 10 December, the anniversary of Nobel's death.

The Trust is administered by the board of directors of the Nobel Foundation, Stockholm, consisting of five members and three deputy members. The Swedish Government appoints a chairman and a deputy chairman, the remaining members being appointed by the awarding authorities.

The awards have been distributed as follows:
*Physics*
American 57, British 20, German 19 (1948–90, West German 8), French 11, Soviet 7, Dutch 6, Swedish 4, Austrian 3, Danish 3, Italian 3, Japanese 3, Chinese 2, Swiss 2, Canadian 1, Indian 1, Irish 1, Pakistani 1.
*Chemistry*
American 38, German 27 (1948–90, West German 10), British 23, French 7, Swiss 5, Swedish 4, Canadian 3, Dutch 2, Argentinian 1, Austrian 1, Belgian 1, Czech 1, Finnish 1, Hungarian 1, Italian 1, Japanese 1, Norwegian 1, Soviet 1.
*Physiology or Medicine*
American 70, British 23, German 14 (1948–90, West German 4), French 7, Swedish 7, Danish 5, Swiss 5, Austrian 4, Belgian 4, Italian 3, Australian 2, Canadian 2, Dutch 2, Hungarian 2, Russian 2, Argentinian 1, Japanese 1, Portuguese 1, South African 1, Spanish 1.
*Literature*
French 12, American 10, British 8, Swedish 7, German 6 (1948–90, West German 1), Italian 5, Spanish 5, Danish 3, Norwegian 3, Soviet 3, Chilean 2, Greek 2, Irish 2, Polish 2, Swiss 2, Australian 1, Belgian 1, Colombian 1, Czech 1, Egyptian 1, Finnish 1, Guatemalan 1, Icelandic 1, Indian 1, Israeli 1, Japanese 1, Mexican 1, Nigerian 1, South African 1, Trinidadian 1, Yugoslav 1, Stateless 1.
*Peace*
American 17, Institutions 16, British 9, French 9, Swedish 5, German 4 (1948–90, West German 1), South African 4, Belgian 3, Swiss 3, Argentinian 2, Austrian 2, Norwegian 2, Soviet 2, Burmese 1, Canadian 1, Costa Rican 1, Danish 1, Dutch 1, Egyptian 1, Guatemalan 1, Irish 1, Israeli 1, Italian 1, Japanese 1, Mexican 1, Polish 1, Tibetan 1, Vietnamese 1, Yugoslav 1.
*Economics*
American 21, British 6, Norwegian 2, Swedish 2, Dutch 1, French 1, Soviet 1.

| Prize | 1991 | 1992 | 1993 |
|---|---|---|---|
| *Physics* | Prof. P.-G. de Gennes (French) | Prof. G. Charpak (French) | Dr R. Hulse (American) Dr J. Taylor (American) |
| *Chemistry* | Prof. R. Ernst (Swiss) | Prof. R. Marcus (American) | Prof. M. Smith (Canadian) Dr K. Mullis (American) |
| *Physiology or Medicine* | E. Neher (German) B. Sakmann (German) | Dr E. Krebs (American) Dr E. Fischer (American) | Dr R. Roberts (British) Prof. P. Sharp (American) |
| *Literature* | N. Gordimer (South African) | D. Walcott (Trinidadian) | Ms T. Morrison (American) |
| *Peace* | Aung San Suu Kyi (Burmese) | Sra R. Menchú (Guatemalan) | N. Mandela (South African) Pres. F. W. de Klerk (South African) |
| *Economics* | Prof. R. Coase (British) | G. S. Becker (American) | Prof. R. Fogel (American) Prof. D. North (American) |

# The Christian Churches

## The Church of England

The Church of England is the established (i.e. state) church in England and the mother church of the Anglican Communion. It originated in the conflicts between church and state throughout the Middle Ages, culminating in the Act of Supremacy issued by Henry VIII in 1534. This repudiated papal supremacy and declared the King to be the supreme head of the Church in England. Since 1559 the English monarch has been termed the Supreme Governor of the Church of England. The Thirty-Nine Articles, a set of doctrinal statements which, together with the Book of Common Prayer of 1662 and the Ordinal, define the position of the Church of England, were adopted in their final form in 1571 and include the emphasis on personal faith and the authority of the scriptures common to the Protestant Reformation throughout Europe.

The Church of England is divided into the two provinces of Canterbury and York, each under an archbishop. The two provinces are subdivided into 44 dioceses. Decisions on matters concerning the Church of England are made by the General Synod, established in 1970. It also discusses and expresses opinion on any other matter of religious or public interest. The General Synod has 574 members in total, divided between three houses: the House of Bishops, the House of Clergy and the House of Laity. It is presided over jointly by the Archbishops of Canterbury and York and normally meets twice a year. The Synod has the power, delegated by Parliament, to frame statute law (known as a Measure) on any matter concerning the Church of England. A Measure must be laid before both Houses of Parliament, who may accept or reject it but cannot amend it. Once accepted the Measure is submitted for Royal Assent and then has the full force of law. The Synod appoints a number of committees, boards and councils which deal with, or advise on, a wide range of matters. In addition to the General Synod, there are synods of clergy and laity at diocesan level.

In 1990 the Church of England had an electoral roll membership of 1.4 million, of whom about 1.1 million regularly attended Sunday services. There are (1993 figures) two archbishops, 104 diocesan, suffragan and (stipendiary) assistant bishops, 10,080 male and 737 female full-time stipendiary clergy, and over 16,000 churches and places of worship. (The Diocese in Europe is not included in these figures.)

### THE ORDINATION OF WOMEN

On 11 November 1992, the General Synod of the Church of England voted to permit the ordination of women as priests. In the House of Bishops there were 39 votes (75 per cent) in favour of the legislation and 13 (25 per cent) against; in the House of Clergy, 176 (70.4 per cent) in favour and 74 (29.6 per cent) against; and in the House of Laity, 169 (67.3 per cent) in favour and 82 (32.7 per cent) against. The legislation was presented to the Ecclesiastical Committee of Parliament in early 1993. The Committee found the legislation expedient, and affirmative resolutions were passed in both Houses of Parliament in the autumn of 1993. The legislation received royal assent and the petition to promulge (proclaim) the canon was submitted to the Crown. The canon was promulged in the General Synod in February 1994 and the first 32 women priests were ordained on 12 March 1994 by the Bishop of Bristol, the Rt. Revd Dr Barry Rogerson, in Bristol Cathedral.

The Priests (Ordination of Women) Measure 1993 contains provisions safeguarding the position of bishops and parishes who are opposed to the priestly ministry of women. In November 1993 the General Synod agreed to the appointment of up to three 'provincial visitors' to work with those who are unable to accept the ministry of bishops ordaining women priests. The provincial visitors, who are suffragan bishops, are allowed to carry out confirmations and ordinations in parishes opposed to women priests, as long as they have the permission of the diocesan bishop. In February 1994 two provincial visitors were appointed, in the new sees of Ebbsfleet (Province of Canterbury) and Beverley (Province of York). A third see, Richborough (Province of Canterbury) was created but not filled. Diocesan bishops are also able to depute a suffragan to ordain women; authorize a suffragan to minister to clergy and parishes whose views differ from his own; or make similar arrangements with bishops in neighbouring dioceses. The General Synod also approved an Act setting out the practical arrangements to provide pastoral care for all, irrespective of their views on the ordination of women to the priesthood. Clergy who still feel compelled to leave the ministry will be entitled to generous financial assistance.

GENERAL SYNOD OF THE CHURCH OF ENGLAND, Church House, Dean's Yard, London SW1P 3NZ. Tel: 0171-222 9011. *Secretary-General*, P. Mawer
HOUSE OF BISHOPS: *Chairman*, The Archbishop of Canterbury; *Vice-Chairman*, The Archbishop of York
HOUSE OF CLERGY: *Joint Chairmen*, Revd Dr J. Sentamu; Canon J. Stanley
HOUSE OF LAITY: *Chairman*, Prof. J. D. McClean, CBE; *Vice-Chairman*, Dr Christina Baxter

### STIPENDS 1994–5

| | |
|---|---|
| Archbishop of Canterbury | £44,640 |
| Archbishop of York | £39,105 |
| Bishop of London | £36,450 |
| Bishop of Durham | £32,165 |
| Bishop of Winchester | £26,815 |
| Other diocesan bishops | £24,200 |
| Suffragan bishops | £19,895 |
| Deans and provosts | £19,895 |
| Residentiary canons | £16,270 |
| Incumbents and clergy of similar status | £13,200* |

*national average

### STIPENDIARY CLERGY *as at 31 December 1993*

| | Male | Female |
|---|---|---|
| Bath and Wells | 238 | 17 |
| Birmingham | 208 | 22 |
| Blackburn | 270 | 8 |
| Bradford | 125 | 9 |
| Bristol | 150 | 22 |
| Canterbury | 183 | 12 |
| Carlisle | 167 | 10 |
| Chelmsford | 444 | 28 |
| Chester | 300 | 12 |
| Chichester | 347 | 9 |
| Coventry | 160 | 12 |
| Derby | 204 | 14 |
| Durham | 263 | 18 |
| Ely | 154 | 12 |

| | Male | Female |
|---|---|---|
| Exeter | 286 | 8 |
| Gloucester | 182 | 17 |
| Guildford | 194 | 21 |
| Hereford | 126 | 8 |
| Leicester | 174 | 11 |
| Lichfield | 369 | 39 |
| Lincoln | 231 | 21 |
| Liverpool | 267 | 28 |
| London | 557 | 47 |
| Manchester | 334 | 21 |
| Newcastle | 171 | 9 |
| Norwich | 214 | 10 |
| Oxford | 449 | 38 |
| Peterborough | 180 | 7 |
| Portsmouth | 137 | 6 |
| Ripon | 163 | 24 |
| Rochester | 231 | 16 |
| St Albans | 298 | 31 |
| St Edmundsbury and Ipswich | 188 | 13 |
| Salisbury | 245 | 13 |
| Sheffield | 214 | 16 |
| Sodor and Man | 20 | 0 |
| Southwark | 387 | 44 |
| Southwell | 202 | 18 |
| Truro | 135 | 4 |
| Wakefield | 192 | 15 |
| Winchester | 253 | 9 |
| Worcester | 160 | 17 |
| York | 308 | 21 |
| TOTAL | 10,080 | 737 |

# Province of Canterbury

## CANTERBURY

103RD ARCHBISHOP AND PRIMATE OF ALL ENGLAND
Most Revd and Rt. Hon. George L. Carey, PH.D., *cons.* 1987,
*trans.* 1991, *apptd* 1991; Lambeth Palace, London SEI 7JU.
*Signs* George Cantuar:

BISHOPS SUFFRAGAN
*Dover*, Rt. Revd J. Richard A. Llewellin, *cons.* 1985, *apptd*
1992; Upway, St Martin's Hill, Canterbury, CTI IPR
*Maidstone*, Rt. Revd Gavin H. Reid, *cons.* 1992, *apptd* 1992;
Bishop's House, Pett Lane, Charing, Ashford TN27 ODL
*Ebbsfleet*, Rt. Revd John Richards, *cons.* 1994, *apptd* 1994
(provincial episcopal visitor); The Rectory, Church
Leigh, Stoke-on-Trent, Staffs. STIO 4PT
*Richborough*, vacant (provincial episcopal visitor)

DEAN
Very Revd John Arthur Simpson, *apptd* 1986

CANONS RESIDENTIARY
P. Brett, *apptd* 1983; Ven. M. Till, *apptd* 1986; Revd
R. H. C. Symon
*Organist*, D. Flood, FRCO, *apptd* 1988

ARCHDEACONS
*Canterbury*, Ven. M. Till, *apptd* 1986
*Maidstone*, Ven. P. Evans, *apptd* 1989

*Vicar-General of Province and Diocese*, Chancellor
S. Cameron, QC
*Commissary-General*, vacant
*Joint Registrars of the Province*, F. E. Robson, OBE; B. J. T.
Hanson

*Registrar of the Diocese*, A. O. E. Davies
*Diocesan Secretary*, D. Kemp, Diocesan House, Lady
Wootton's Green, Canterbury CTI INQ. Tel: 01227-459401

## LONDON

131ST BISHOP
Rt. Revd and Rt. Hon. David M. Hope, D.phil., *cons.* 1985,
*trans.* 1991, *apptd* 1991; 8 Barton Street, London
SWIP 3NE. *Signs* David Londin:

AREA BISHOPS
*Edmonton*, Rt. Revd Brian J. Masters, *cons.* 1982, *apptd*
1984; I Regent's Park Terrace, London NWI 7EE
*Kensington*, vacant; 19 Campden Hill Square, London
W8 7JY
*Stepney*, Rt. Revd Richard C. Chartres; 63 Coborn Road,
London E3 2DB
*Willesden*, Rt. Revd Graham G. Dow; 173 Willesden Lane,
London NW6 7YN

BISHOP SUFFRAGAN
*Fulham*, Rt. Revd C. John Klyberg, *cons.* 1985, *apptd* 1985;
4 Cambridge Place, London W8 5PB

DEAN OF ST PAUL'S
Very Revd T. Eric Evans, *apptd* 1988

CANONS RESIDENTIARY
Ven. G. Cassidy, *apptd* 1987; C. J. Hill, *apptd* 1989;
R. J. Halliburton, *apptd* 1990; M. J. Saward, *apptd* 1991
*Registrar and Receiver of St Paul's*, Brig. R. W. Acworth, CBE
*Organist*, J. Scott, FRCO, *apptd* 1990

ARCHDEACONS
*Charing Cross*, Rt. Revd C. J. Klyberg, *apptd* 1989
*Hackney*, Ven. C. Young, *apptd* 1992
*Hampstead*, vacant
*London*, Ven. G. Cassidy, *apptd* 1987
*Middlesex*, Ven. T. J. Raphael, *apptd* 1983
*Northolt*, Ven. M. Colclough, *apptd* 1992

*Chancellor*, Miss S. Cameron, QC, *apptd* 1992
*Registrar*, D. W. Faull, OBE
*Diocesan Secretary*, C. J. A. Smith, 36 Causton Street,
London SWIP 4AU. Tel: 0171-932 1100

## WINCHESTER

95TH BISHOP
Rt. Revd Colin C. W. James, *cons.* 1973, *trans.* 1977 and
1985, *apptd* 1985; Wolvesey, Winchester SO23 9ND. *Signs*
Colin Winton:

BISHOPS SUFFRAGAN
*Basingstoke*, Rt. Revd D. Geoffrey Rowell, *cons.* 1994, *apptd*
1994; Little Acorns, Boynes Wood Road, Medstead
GU34 5EA
*Southampton*, Rt. Revd John F. Perry, *cons.* 1989, *apptd*
1989; Ham House, The Crescent, Romsey SO51 7NG

DEAN
Very Revd Trevor R. Beeson, *apptd* 1987

*Dean of Jersey (A Peculiar)*, Very Revd John Seaford, *apptd*
1993

*Dean of Guernsey (A Peculiar)*, Very Revd Jeffery Fenwick, *apptd* 1989

CANONS RESIDENTIARY
A. K. Walker, *apptd* 1987; Ven. A. F. Knight, *apptd* 1991; P. B. Morgan, *apptd* 1994

*Organist*, D. Hill, FRCO, *apptd* 1988

ARCHDEACONS
*Basingstoke,* Ven. A. F. Knight, *apptd* 1990
*Winchester,* Ven. A. G. Clarkson, *apptd* 1984

*Chancellor,* C. Clark, *apptd* 1993
*Registrar and Legal Secretary,* P. M. White
*Diocesan Secretary,* R. Anderton, Church House, 9 The Close, Winchester, Hants. SO23 9LS. Tel: 01962-844644

---

## BATH AND WELLS

76TH BISHOP
Rt. Revd James L. Thompson, *cons.* 1978, *apptd* 1991; The Palace, Wells BA5 2PD. *Signs* James Bath & Wells

BISHOP SUFFRAGAN
*Taunton,* Rt. Revd J. H. Richard Lewis, *cons.* 1992, *apptd* 1992; Sherford Farm House, Sherford, Taunton TA1 3RF

DEAN
Very Revd Richard Lewis, *apptd* 1990

CANONS RESIDENTIARY
C. E. Thomas, *apptd* 1983; P. de N. Lucas, *apptd* 1988; G. O. Farran, *apptd* 1985

*Organist,* A. Crossland, FRCO, *apptd* 1970

ARCHDEACONS
*Bath,* Ven. J. E. Burgess, *apptd* 1975
*Taunton,* Ven. R. M. C. Frith, *apptd* 1992
*Wells,* Ven. R. Ackworth, *apptd* 1993

*Chancellor,* T. Briden, *apptd* 1993
*Registrar, Secretary and Chapter Clerk,* T. Berry
*Diocesan Secretary,* N. Denison, The Old Deanery, Wells, Somerset BA5 2UG. Tel: 01749-670777

---

## BIRMINGHAM

7TH BISHOP
Rt. Revd Mark Santer, *cons.* 1981, *apptd* 1987; Bishop's Croft, Harborne, Birmingham B17 0BG. *Signs* Mark Birmingham

BISHOP SUFFRAGAN
*Aston,* Rt. Revd John Austin, *cons.* 1992, *apptd* 1992; Strensham House, 8 Strensham Hill, Moseley, Birmingham B13 8AG

STIPENDIARY ASSISTANT BISHOP
Rt. Revd Michael Whinney, *cons.* 1982, *apptd* 1989

PROVOST
Very Revd Peter A. Berry, *apptd* 1986

CANONS RESIDENTIARY
Ven. C. J. G. Barton, *apptd* 1990; A. H. F. Luff, *apptd* 1992

*Organist,* M. Huxley, FRCO, *apptd* 1986

ARCHDEACONS
*Aston,* Ven. C. J. G. Barton, *apptd* 1990
*Birmingham,* Ven. J. F. Duncan, *apptd* 1985

*Coleshill,* vacant
*Chancellor,* His Honour Judge Aglionby, *apptd* 1970
*Registrar and Legal Secretary,* H. Carslake
*Diocesan Secretary,* Canon J. Pendorf, 175 Harborne Park Road, Harborne, Birmingham B17 0BH. Tel: 0121-427 5141

---

## BRISTOL

54TH BISHOP
Rt. Revd Barry Rogerson, *cons.* 1979, *apptd* 1985; Bishop's House, Clifton Hill, Bristol BS8 1BW. *Signs* Barry Bristol

BISHOP SUFFRAGAN
*Swindon,* Rt. Revd Michael Doe, *cons.* 1994, *apptd* 1994; Mark House, Field Rise, Old Town, Swindon SN1 4HP

DEAN
Very Revd Dr A. Wesley Carr, *apptd* 1987

CANONS RESIDENTIARY
A. L. J. Redfern, *apptd* 1987; J. L. Simpson, *apptd* 1989; P. F. Johnson, *apptd* 1990

*Organist,* C. Brayne, *apptd* 1990

ARCHDEACONS
*Bristol,* Ven. D. J. Banfield, *apptd* 1990
*Swindon,* Ven. M. Middleton, *apptd* 1992

*Chancellor,* Sir David Calcutt, QC, *apptd* 1971
*Registrar and Secretary,* D. Ratcliffe
*Diocesan Secretary,* Mrs L. Farrall, Diocesan Church House, 23 Great George Street, Bristol, Avon BS1 5QZ. Tel: 0117-921 4411

---

## CHELMSFORD

7TH BISHOP
Rt. Revd John Waine, *cons.* 1975, *apptd* 1986; Bishopscourt, Margaretting, Ingatestone CM4 0HD. *Signs* John Chelmsford

BISHOPS SUFFRAGAN
*Barking,* Rt. Revd Roger F. Sainsbury, *cons.* 1991, *apptd* 1991; 110 Capel Road, Forest Gate, London E7 0JS
*Bradwell,* Rt. Revd Laurence Green, *cons.* 1993, *apptd* 1993; The Vicarage, Orsett Road, Horndon-on-the-Hill, Stanford-le-Hope, Essex SS17 8NS
*Colchester,* Rt. Revd Edward Holland, *cons.* 1986, *apptd* 1995; 1 Fitzwalter Road, Lexden, Colchester CO3 3SS

PROVOST
Very Revd John H. Moses, PH.D., *apptd* 1982

CANONS RESIDENTIARY
T. Thompson, *apptd* 1988; B. P. Thompson, *apptd* 1988

*Organist,* Dr G. Elliott, PH.D., FRCO, *apptd* 1981

ARCHDEACONS
*Colchester,* Ven. E. C. F. Stroud, *apptd* 1983
*Harlow,* Ven. M. J. Fox, *apptd* 1993
*Southend,* Ven. D. Jennings, *apptd* 1992
*West Ham,* Ven. T. J. Stevens, *apptd* 1991

*Chancellor,* Miss S. M. Cameron, QC, *apptd* 1970
*Diocesan Registrar,* B. Hood
*Diocesan Secretary,* M. Walker, 53 New Street, Chelmsford, Essex CM1 1AT. Tel: 01245-266731

## CHICHESTER

102ND BISHOP
Rt. Revd Eric W. Kemp, DD, *cons.* 1974, *apptd* 1974; The Palace, Chichester PO19 1PY. *Signs* Eric Cicestr:

BISHOPS SUFFRAGAN
*Horsham*, Rt. Revd Lindsay Urwin, *cons.* 1993, *apptd* 1993; Diocesan Church House, 9 Brunswick Square, Hove, E. Sussex BN3 1EN
*Lewes*, Rt. Revd Ian P. M. Cundy, *cons.* 1992, *apptd* 1992; Beacon House, Berwick, Polegate BN26 6ST

DEAN
Very Revd John D. Treadgold, LVO, *apptd* 1989

CANONS RESIDENTIARY
R. T. Greenacre, *apptd* 1975; J. F. Hester, *apptd* 1985

*Organist*, A. J. Thurlow, FRCO, *apptd* 1980

ARCHDEACONS
*Chichester*, Ven. M. Brotherton, *apptd* 1991
*Horsham*, Ven. W. C. L. Filby, *apptd* 1983
*Lewes and Hastings*, Ven. H. Glaisyer, *apptd* 1991

*Chancellor*, His Honour Judge Q. T. Edwards, QC, *apptd* 1978
*Legal Secretary and Registrar*, C. L. Hodgetts
*Diocesan Secretary*, J. Prichard, Diocesan Church House, 9 Brunswick Square, Hove, E. Sussex BN3 1EN. Tel: 01273-329023

## COVENTRY

7TH BISHOP
Rt. Revd Simon Barrington-Ward, *cons.* 1985, *apptd* 1985; The Bishop's House, 23 Davenport Road, Coventry CV5 6PW. *Signs* Simon Coventry

BISHOP SUFFRAGAN
*Warwick*, Rt. Revd George C. Handford, *cons.* 1990, *apptd* 1990; 139 Kenilworth Road, Coventry CV4 7AF

PROVOST
Very Revd John F. Petty, *apptd* 1987

CANONS RESIDENTIARY
P. Oestreicher, *apptd* 1986; M. Sadgrove, *apptd* 1987; V. Faull, *apptd* 1994

*Organist*, A. P. Leddington Wright, *apptd* 1984

ARCHDEACONS
*Coventry*, Ven. H. I. L. Russell, *apptd* 1989
*Warwick*, Ven. M. J. J. Paget-Wilkes, *apptd* 1990

*Chancellor*, W. M. Gage, *apptd* 1980
*Registrar*, D. J. Dumbleton
*Diocesan Secretary*, J. Allen, Church House, Palmerston Road, Coventry CV5 6FJ. Tel: 01203-674328

## DERBY

5TH BISHOP
Rt. Revd Peter S. Dawes, *cons.* 1988, *apptd* 1988; The Bishop's House, 6 King Street, Duffield, Belper, Derbys. DE56 4EU. *Signs* Peter Derby

BISHOP SUFFRAGAN
*Repton*, Rt. Revd F. Henry A. Richmond, *cons.* 1986, *apptd* 1986; Repton House, Lea, Matlock DE4 5JP

PROVOST
Very Revd Benjamin H. Lewers, *apptd* 1981

CANONS RESIDENTIARY
G. A. Chesterman, *apptd* 1989; Ven. I. Gatford, *apptd* 1992; G. O. Marshall, *apptd* 1992; R. M. Parsons, *apptd* 1993
*Organist*, P. Gould, *apptd* 1982

ARCHDEACONS
*Chesterfield*, Ven. G. R. Phizackerley, *apptd* 1978
*Derby*, Ven. I. Gatford, *apptd* 1992

*Chancellor*, J. W. M. Bullimore, *apptd* 1981
*Registrar*, J. S. Battie
*Diocesan Secretary*, R. Carey, Derby Church House, Full Street, Derby DE1 3DR. Tel: 01332-382233

## ELY

67TH BISHOP
Rt. Revd Stephen W. Sykes, *cons.* 1990, *apptd* 1990; The Bishop's House, Ely CB7 4DW. *Signs* Stephen Ely

BISHOP SUFFRAGAN
*Huntingdon*, Rt. Revd William G. Roe, D.phil., *cons.* 1980, *apptd* 1980; 14 Lynn Road, Ely, Cambs. CB6 1DA

DEAN
Very Revd Michael Higgins, *apptd* 1991

CANONS RESIDENTIARY
D. J. Green, *apptd* 1980; J. Rone, *apptd* 1989
*Organist*, P. Trepte, FRCO, *apptd* 1991

ARCHDEACONS
*Ely*, Ven. J. Watson, *apptd* 1993
*Huntingdon*, Ven. R. K. Sledge, *apptd* 1978
*Wisbech*, vacant

*Chancellor*, W. Gage, QC
*Joint Registrars*, W. H. Godfrey; P. F. B. Beesley (*Legal Secretary*)
*Diocesan Secretary*, D. Phillips, Bishop Woodford House, Barton Road, Ely, Cambs. CB7 4DX. Tel: 01353-663579

## EXETER

69TH BISHOP
Rt. Revd G. Hewlett Thompson, *cons.* 1974, *apptd* 1985; The Palace, Exeter EX1 1HY. *Signs* Hewlett Exon:

BISHOPS SUFFRAGAN
*Crediton*, Rt. Revd Peter E. Coleman, *cons.* 1984, *apptd* 1984; 10 The Close, Exeter EX1 1EZ
*Plymouth*, Rt. Revd Richard S. Hawkins, *cons.* 1988, *apptd* 1988; 31 Riverside Walk, Tamerton Foliot, Plymouth PL5 4AQ

DEAN
Very Revd Richard Montague Stephens Eyre, *apptd* 1981

CANONS RESIDENTIARY
A. C. Mawson, *apptd* 1979; Ven. J. Richards, *apptd* 1981; K. C. Parry, *apptd* 1991

*Organist*, L. A. Nethsingha, FRCO, *apptd* 1973

ARCHDEACONS
*Barnstaple*, Ven. T. Lloyd, *apptd* 1989
*Exeter*, Ven. A. F. Tremlett, *apptd* 1994
*Plymouth*, Ven. R. G. Ellis, *apptd* 1982
*Totnes*, vacant

*Chancellor*, Sir David Calcutt, QC, *apptd* 1971
*Registrar*, R. K. Wheeler
*Diocesan Secretary*, Revd R. Huddleson, Diocesan House, Palace Gate, Exeter, Devon EX1 1HX. Tel: 01392-72686

## GIBRALTAR IN EUROPE

BISHOP
Rt. Revd John Hind, *cons.* 1991, *apptd* 1993; 14 Tufton Street, London SW1P 3QZ. *Signs* John Gibraltar

BISHOP SUFFRAGAN
*In Europe*, vacant

AUXILIARY BISHOPS
Rt. Revd E. M. H. Capper, OBE, *cons.* 1967, *apptd* 1973; Rt. Revd D. de Pina Cabral, *cons.* 1967, *apptd* 1976; Rt. Revd A. W. M. Weeks, CB, *cons.* 1977, *apptd* 1988; Rt. Revd E. Devenport, *apptd* 1992

*Vicar-General*, Revd W. G. Reid
*Dean, Cathedral Church of the Holy Trinity, Gibraltar*, Very Revd B. W. Horlock, OBE
*Chancellor, Pro-Cathedral of St Paul, Valletta, Malta*, Canon P. Cousins
*Chancellor, Pro-Cathedral of the Holy Trinity, Brussels, Belgium*, Canon N. Walker

ARCHDEACONS
*Aegean*, Ven. G. B. Evans
*North-West Europe*, Ven. G. G. Allen
*France*, Ven. M. Draper
*Gibraltar*, Ven. K. Robinson
*Italy*, Rt. Revd E. Devenport
*Scandinavia*, Ven. G. A. C. Brown
*Switzerland*, Ven. P. J. Hawker

*Chancellor*, Sir David Calcutt, QC
*Diocesan Registrar and Legal Secretary*, J. G. Underwood
*Diocesan Secretary*, Revd W. G. Reid, 14 Tufton Street, London SW1P 3QZ. Tel: 0171-976 8001

## GLOUCESTER

39TH BISHOP
Rt. Revd David Bentley, *cons.* 1986, *apptd* 1993; Bishopscourt, Gloucester GL1 2BQ. *Signs* David Gloucester

BISHOP SUFFRAGAN
*Tewkesbury*, Rt. Revd G. D. Jeremy Walsh, *cons.* 1986, *apptd* 1986; Green Acre, Hempsted, Gloucester GL2 6LG

DEAN
Very Revd Kenneth N. Jennings, *apptd* 1982

CANONS RESIDENTIARY
R. D. M. Grey, *apptd* 1982; R. P. Greenwood, *apptd* 1986; N. Chatfield, *apptd* 1992; N. Heavisides, *apptd* 1993

*Organist*, D. Briggs, FRCO, *apptd* 1994

ARCHDEACONS
*Cheltenham*, Ven. J. A. Lewis, *apptd* 1988
*Gloucester*, Ven. C. J. H. Wagstaff, *apptd* 1982

*Chancellor and Vicar-General*, Ms D. J. Rogers, *apptd* 1990
*Registrar*, C. G. Peak
*Diocesan Secretary*, M. Williams, Church House, College Green, Gloucester GL1 2LY. Tel: 01452-410022

## GUILDFORD

7TH BISHOP
Rt. Revd John W. Gladwin, *cons.* 1994, *apptd* 1994; Willow Grange, Woking Road, Guildford GU4 7QS. *Signs* John Guildford

BISHOP SUFFRAGAN
*Dorking*, Rt. Revd David P. Wilcox, *cons.* 1986, *apptd* 1986; 13 Pilgrims Way, Guildford GU4 8AD

DEAN
Very Revd Alexander G. Wedderspoon, *apptd* 1987

CANONS RESIDENTIARY
F. S. Telfer, *apptd* 1973; R. D. Fenwick, *apptd* 1990
*Organist*, A. Millington, FRCO, *apptd* 1982

ARCHDEACONS
*Dorking*, Ven. C.W. Herbert, *apptd* 1990
*Surrey*, Ven. J. S. Went, *apptd* 1989

*Chancellor*, His Hon. Judge Goodman
*Legal Secretary and Registrar*, P. F. B. Beesley
*Diocesan Secretary*, Mrs K. Ingate, Diocesan House, Quarry Street, Guildford GU1 3XG. Tel: 01483-571826

## HEREFORD

103RD BISHOP
Rt. Revd John Oliver, *cons.* 1990, *apptd* 1990; The Palace, Hereford HR4 9BN. *Signs* John Hereford

BISHOP SUFFRAGAN
*Ludlow*, Rt. Revd Dr John Saxbee, *cons.* 1994, *apptd* 1994; Bishop's House, Halford, Craven Arms, Shropshire SY7 9BT

DEAN
Very Revd Robert A. Willis, *apptd* 1992

CANONS RESIDENTIARY
P. Iles, *apptd* 1983; J. Tiller, *apptd* 1984; J. Butterworth, *apptd* 1994
*Organist*, Dr R. Massey, FRCO, *apptd* 1974

ARCHDEACONS
*Hereford*, Ven. L. G. Moss, *apptd* 1992
*Ludlow*, Ven. J. C. Saxbee, *apptd* 1992

*Chancellor*, J. M. Henty
*Joint Registrars*, V. T. Jordan; P. Beesley
*Diocesan Secretary*, Miss S. Green, The Palace, Hereford HR4 9BL. Tel: 01432-353863

## LEICESTER

5TH BISHOP
Rt. Revd Thomas F. Butler, PH.D., *cons.* 1985, *apptd* 1991; Bishop's Lodge, 10 Springfield Road, Leicester LE2 3BD. *Signs* Thomas Leicester

STIPENDIARY ASSISTANT BISHOP
Rt. Revd Godfrey Ashby, *cons.* 1980, *apptd* 1988

PROVOST
Very Revd Derek Hole, *apptd* 1992

CANONS RESIDENTIARY
M. T. H. Banks, *apptd* 1988; M. Wilson, *apptd* 1988

*Organist*, J. T. Gregory, *apptd* 1994

ARCHDEACONS
*Leicester*, Ven. M. Edson, *apptd* 1994
*Loughborough*, Ven. I. Stanes, *apptd* 1992

*Chancellor*, N. Seed, *apptd* 1989
*Registrars*, P. C. E. Morris; R. H. Bloor
*Diocesan Secretary*, J. Cryer, Church House, 3–5 St Martin's
   East, Leicester LEI 5FX. Tel: 0116-262 7445

## LICHFIELD

97TH BISHOP
Rt. Revd Keith N. Sutton, *cons.* 1978, *apptd* 1984; Bishop's
   House, The Close, Lichfield WS13 7LG. *Signs* Keith
   Lichfield

BISHOPS SUFFRAGAN
*Shrewsbury*, Rt. Revd David M. Hallatt, *cons.* 1994, *apptd*
   1994; Athlone House, 68 London Road, Shrewsbury SY2
   6PG
*Stafford*, Rt. Revd Michael C. Scott-Joynt, *cons.* 1987, *apptd*
   1987; Ash Garth, Broughton Crescent, Barlaston ST12
   9DD
*Wolverhampton*, Rt. Revd Michael G. Bourke, *cons.* 1993,
   *apptd* 1993; 61 Richmond Road, Wolverhampton WV3
   9JH

DEAN
Very Revd Tom Wright, *apptd* 1993

CANONS RESIDENTIARY
Ven. R. B. Ninis, *apptd* 1974; A. N. Barnard, *apptd* 1977;
   J. Howe, *apptd* 1988

*Organist*, A. Lumsden, *apptd* 1992

ARCHDEACONS
*Lichfield*, Ven. R. B. Ninis, *apptd* 1974
*Salop*, Ven. G. Frost, *apptd* 1987
*Stoke-on-Trent*, Ven. D. Ede, *apptd* 1989

*Chancellor*, His Honour Judge Shand
*Diocesan Registrar*, J. P. Thorneycroft
*Diocesan Secretary*, D. R. Taylor, St Mary's House, The
   Close, Lichfield, Staffs. WS13 7LD. Tel: 01543-414551

## LINCOLN

70TH BISHOP
Rt. Revd Robert M. Hardy, *cons.* 1980, *apptd* 1987;
   Bishop's House, Eastgate, Lincoln LN2 1QQ. *Signs* Robert
   Lincoln

BISHOPS SUFFRAGAN
*Grantham*, Rt. Revd William Ind, *cons.* 1987, *apptd* 1987;
   Fairacre, Barrowby High Road, Grantham NG31 8NP
*Grimsby*, Rt. Revd David Tustin, *cons.* 1979, *apptd* 1979;
   Bishop's House, Church Lane, Irby-upon-Humber,
   Grimsby DN37 7JR

DEAN
Very Revd Brandon D. Jackson, *apptd* 1989

CANONS RESIDENTIARY
B. R. Davis, *apptd* 1977; A. J. Stokes, *apptd* 1992; V. White,
   *apptd* 1994

*Organist*, C. S. Walsh, FRCO, *apptd* 1988

ARCHDEACONS
*Lincoln*, Ven. M. P. Brackenbury, *apptd* 1988
*Lindsey*, vacant
*Stow*, Ven. R. J. Wells, *apptd* 1989

*Chancellor*, His Honour Judge Goodman, *apptd* 1971
*Registrar and Legal Secretary*, D. M. Wellman
*Diocesan Secretary*, Capt. D. Williamson, RN, The Old
   Palace, Lincoln LN2 1PU. Tel: 01522-529241

## NORWICH

70TH BISHOP
Rt. Revd Peter J. Nott, *cons.* 1977, *apptd* 1985; Bishop's
   House, Norwich, NR3 1SB. *Signs* Peter Norvic:

BISHOPS SUFFRAGAN
*Lynn*, Rt. Revd David Conner, *cons.* 1994, *apptd* 1994; The
   Old Vicarage, Castle Acre, King's Lynn PE32 2AA
*Thetford*, Rt. Revd Hugo F. de Waal, *cons.* 1992, *apptd*
   1992; Rectory Meadow, Bramerton, Norwich NR14 7DW

DEAN
Very Revd John P. Burbridge, *apptd* 1983

CANONS RESIDENTIARY
M. F. Perham, *apptd* 1992; Ven. C. J. Offer, *apptd* 1994;
   R. J. Hammer, *apptd* 1994

*Organist*, D. Cooper, *apptd* 1994

ARCHDEACONS
*Lynn*, Ven. A. C. Foottit, *apptd* 1987
*Norfolk*, Ven. A. M. Handley, *apptd* 1993
*Norwich*, Ven. C. J. Offer, *apptd* 1994

*Chancellor*, His Honour J. H. Ellison, VRD, *apptd* 1955
*Registrar and Secretary*, J. W. F. Herring
*Diocesan Secretary*, Dr B. Martin, Diocesan House, 109
   Dereham Road, Easton, Norwich, Norfolk NR9 5ES. Tel:
   01603-880853

## OXFORD

41ST BISHOP
Rt. Revd Richard D. Harries, *cons.* 1987, *apptd* 1987;
   Diocesan Church House, North Hinksey, Oxford
   OX2 0NB. *Signs* Richard Oxon:

AREA BISHOPS
*Buckingham*, Rt. Revd Colin J. Bennetts, *cons.* 1994, *apptd*
   1994; Sheridan, Grimms Hill, Great Missenden HP16 9BD
*Dorchester*, Rt. Revd Anthony J. Russell, *cons.* 1988, *apptd*
   1988; Holmby House, Sibford Ferris, Banbury, Oxon.
   OX15 5RG
*Reading*, Rt. Revd John F. E. Bone, *cons.* 1989, *apptd* 1989;
   Greenbanks, Old Bath Road, Sonning, Reading RG4 0SY

DEAN OF CHRIST CHURCH
Very Revd John H. Drury, *apptd* 1991

CANONS RESIDENTIARY
Ven. F. V. Weston, *apptd* 1982; O. M. T. O'Donovan,
D.Phil., *apptd* 1982; J. M. Pierce, *apptd* 1987; J. S. K. Ward,
*apptd* 1991; Rt. Revd A. R. M. Gordon, *apptd* 1991; Prof.
P. Hinchcliff, *apptd* 1991

*Organist*, S. Darlington, FRCO, *apptd* 1985

ARCHDEACONS
*Berkshire*, Ven. M. A. Hill, *apptd* 1992
*Buckingham*, Ven. J. A. Morrison, *apptd* 1989
*Oxford*, Ven. F. V. Weston, *apptd* 1982

*Chancellor*, P. T. S. Boydell, QC, *apptd* 1958
*Registrar and Legal Secretary*, Dr F. E. Robson
*Secretary to the Diocesan Board of Finance*, T. Landsbert,
Diocesan Church House, North Hinksey, Oxford
OX2 ONB. Tel: 01865-244566

## PETERBOROUGH

36TH BISHOP
Rt. Revd William J. Westwood, *cons.* 1975, *apptd* 1984; The
Palace, Peterborough PEI IYA. *Signs* William Petriburg:

BISHOP SUFFRAGAN
*Brixworth*, Rt. Revd Paul E. Barber, *cons.* 1989, *apptd* 1989;
4 The Avenue, Dallington, Northampton NNI 4RZ

DEAN
Very Revd Michael Bunker, *apptd* 1992

CANONS RESIDENTIARY
T. R. Christie, *apptd* 1980; J. Higham, *apptd* 1983;
T. Willmott, *apptd* 1989

*Organist*, C. S. Gower, FRCO, *apptd* 1977

ARCHDEACONS
*Northampton*, Ven. M. R. Chapman, *apptd* 1991
*Oakham*, Ven. B. Fernyhough, *apptd* 1977

*Chancellor*, T. A. C. Coningsby, QC, *apptd* 1989
*Registrar and Legal Secretary*, R. Hemingray
*Diocesan Secretary*, P. Haines, The Palace, Peterborough,
Cambs. PEI IYB. Tel: 01733-64448

## PORTSMOUTH

7TH BISHOP
Rt. Revd Timothy J. Bavin, *cons.* 1974, *apptd* 1985;
Bishopswood, Fareham, Hants. PO14 INT. *Signs* Timothy
Portsmouth

PROVOST
Very Revd Michael Yorke, *apptd* 1994

CANONS RESIDENTIARY
C. J. Bradley, *apptd* 1990; D. T. Isaac, *apptd* 1990; Jane
Hedges, *apptd* 1993

*Organist*, A. Lucas, FRCO, *apptd* 1990

ARCHDEACONS
*Isle of Wight*, Ven. A. H. M. Turner, *apptd* 1986
*Portsmouth*, Ven. G. P. Knowles, *apptd* 1993

*Chancellor*, His Honour Judge Aglionby, *apptd* 1978
*Registrar*, Miss H. A. G. Tyler
*Diocesan Secretary*, M. Jordan, Cathedral House, St
Thomas's Street, Portsmouth, Hants. PO1 2HA. Tel:
01705-825731

## ROCHESTER

105TH BISHOP
Rt. Revd Dr Michael Nazir-Ali, *cons.* 1984, *apptd* 1994;
Bishopscourt, Rochester MEI ITS. *Signs* Michael Roffen:

BISHOP SUFFRAGAN
*Tonbridge*, Rt. Revd Brian A. Smith, *cons.* 1993, *apptd* 1993;
Bishop's Lodge, St Botolph's Road, Sevenoaks TNI3 3AG

DEAN
Very Revd Edward F. Shotter, *apptd* 1990

CANONS RESIDENTIARY
E. R. Turner, *apptd* 1981; R. J. R. Lea, *apptd* 1988;
J. Armson, *apptd* 1989; N. Warren, *apptd* 1989

*Organist*, B. Ferguson, FRCO, *apptd* 1977

ARCHDEACONS
*Bromley*, Ven. G. Norman, *apptd* 1994
*Rochester*, Ven. N. L. Warren, *apptd* 1989
*Tonbridge*, Ven. R. J. Mason, *apptd* 1977

*Chancellor*, His Honour Judge M. B. Goodman, *apptd* 1971
*Registrar*, O. R. Woodfield
*Diocesan Secretary*, P. Law, St Nicholas Church, Boley Hill,
Rochester MEI ISL. Tel: 01634-830333

## ST ALBANS

8TH BISHOP
Rt. Revd John B. Taylor, *cons.* 1980, *apptd* 1980; Abbey
Gate House, St Albans AL3 4HD. *Signs* John St Albans

BISHOPS SUFFRAGAN
*Bedford*, Rt. Revd John H. Richardson, *cons.* 1994, *apptd*
1994; 168 Kimbolton Road, Bedford MK41 8DN
*Hertford*, Rt. Revd Robin J. N. Smith, *cons.* 1990, *apptd*
1990; Hertford House, Abbey Mill Lane, St Albans AL3
4HE

DEAN
Very Revd Christopher Lewis, *apptd* 1993

CANONS RESIDENTIARY
C. Garner, *apptd* 1984; G. R. S. Ritson, *apptd* 1987;
M. Sansom, *apptd* 1988; C. R. J. Foster, *apptd* 1994

*Organist*, Dr B. Rose, *apptd* 1988

ARCHDEACONS
*Bedford*, Ven. M. L. Lesiter, *apptd* 1993
*St Albans*, Ven. P. B. Davies, *apptd* 1987

*Chancellor*, His Honour Judge Bursell, QC, *apptd* 1992
*Registrar and Legal Secretary*, D. N. Cheetham
*Diocesan Secretary*, L. Nicholls, Holywell Lodge, 41
Holywell Hill, St Albans ALI IHE. Tel: 01727-854532

## ST EDMUNDSBURY AND IPSWICH

8TH BISHOP
Rt. Revd John Dennis, *cons.* 1979, *apptd* 1986; Bishop's
House, 4 Park Road, Ipswich IPI 3ST. *Signs* John St
Edmundsbury and Ipswich

BISHOP SUFFRAGAN
*Dunwich*, Rt. Revd Jonathan S. Bailey, *cons.* 1992, *apptd*
    1992; The Old Vicarage, Stowupland, Stowmarket IP14
    4BQ

PROVOST
vacant

CANONS RESIDENTIARY
A. M. Shaw, *apptd* 1989; M. E. Mingins, *apptd* 1993
*Organist*, M. Cousins, *apptd* 1993

ARCHDEACONS
*Ipswich*, Ven. T. A. Gibson, *apptd* 1987
*Sudbury*, vacant
*Suffolk*, Ven. G. Arrand, *apptd* 1994

*Chancellor*, His Honour Sir John Blofeld, QC, *apptd* 1974
*Registrar*, J. D. Mitson
*Diocesan Secretary*, I. Dodd, 13–15 Tower Street, Ipswich
    IP1 3BG. Tel: 01473-211028

---

## SALISBURY

---

77TH BISHOP
Rt. Revd David S. Stancliffe, *cons.* 1993, *apptd* 1993; South
    Canonry, The Close, Salisbury SP1 2ER. *Signs* David
    Sarum

BISHOPS SUFFRAGAN
*Ramsbury*, Rt. Revd Peter St G. Vaughan, *cons.* 1989, *apptd*
    1989; Bishop's House, Urchfont, Devizes, Wilts. SN10 4QH
*Sherborne*, Rt. Revd John D. G. Kirkham, *cons.* 1976, *apptd*
    1976; Little Bailie, Sturminster Marshall, Wimborne BH21
    4AD

DEAN
Very Revd the Hon. Hugh G. Dickinson, *apptd* 1986

CANONS RESIDENTIARY
D. J. C. Davies, *apptd* 1985; J. R. Stewart, *apptd* 1990;
    D. M. K. Durston, *apptd* 1992

*Organist*, R. G. Seal, FRCO, *apptd* 1968

ARCHDEACONS
*Dorset*, Ven. G. E. Walton, *apptd* 1982
*Sarum*, Ven. B. J. Hopkinson, *apptd* 1986
*Sherborne*, Ven. P. C. Wheatley, *apptd* 1991
*Wilts*, Ven. B. J. Smith, *apptd* 1980

*Chancellor*, His Honour J. H. Ellison, VRD, *apptd* 1955
*Registrar and Legal Secretary*, F. M. Broadbent
*Diocesan Secretary*, Lt.-Col. C. C. G. Ross, Church House,
    Crane Street, Salisbury SP1 2QB. Tel: 01722-411922

---

## SOUTHWARK

---

8TH BISHOP
Rt. Revd Robert K. Williamson, *cons.* 1984, *trans.* 1991,
    *apptd* 1991; Bishop's House, 38 Tooting Bec Gardens,
    London SW16 1QZ. *Signs* Robert Southwark

AREA BISHOPS
*Croydon*, Rt. Revd Wilfred D. Wood, DD, *cons.* 1985, *apptd*
    1985; St Matthew's House, George Street, Croydon CRO
    1PE
*Kingston upon Thames*, Rt Revd Martin Wharton, *cons.*
    1992, *apptd* 1992; *Office*, Whitelands College, West Hill,
    London SW15 3SN

*Woolwich*, Rt. Revd A. Peter Hall, *cons.* 1984, *apptd* 1984;
    8B Hilly Fields Crescent, London SE4 1QA

PROVOST
Very Revd Colin B. Slee, *apptd* 1994

CANONS RESIDENTIARY
I. Smith-Cameron, *apptd* 1972; Dr M. Kitchen, *apptd* 1988;
    D. Painter, *apptd* 1991
*Organist*, P. Wright, FRCO, *apptd* 1989

ARCHDEACONS
*Croydon*, Ven. V. A. Davies, *apptd* 1994
*Lambeth*, Ven. C. R. B. Bird, *apptd* 1988
*Lewisham*, Ven. G. Kuhrt, *apptd* 1989
*Reigate*, Ven. P. B. Coombs, *apptd* 1988
*Southwark*, Ven. D. L. Bartles-Smith, *apptd* 1985
*Wandsworth*, Ven. D. Gerrard, *apptd* 1989

*Chancellor*, R. M. K. Gray, QC, *apptd* 1990
*Registrar*, P. Morris
*Diocesan Secretary*, M. Cawte, Trinity House, 4 Chapel
    Court, Borough High Street, London SE1 1HW. Tel: 0171-
    403 8686

---

## TRURO

---

13TH BISHOP
Rt. Revd Michael T. Ball, *cons.* 1980, *apptd* 1990; Lis
    Escop, Truro TR3 6QQ. *Signs* Michael Truro

BISHOP SUFFRAGAN
*St Germans*, Rt. Revd Graham R. James, *cons.* 1993, *apptd*
    1993; 32 Falmouth Road, Truro TRI 2HX

DEAN
Very Revd David J. Shearlock, *apptd* 1982

CANONS RESIDENTIARY
Ven. R. L. Ravenscroft, *apptd* 1988; P. R. Gay, *apptd* 1994;
    K. P. Mellor, *apptd* 1994
*Organist*, A. Nethsingha, FRCO, *apptd* 1994

ARCHDEACONS
*Cornwall*, Ven. R. L. Ravenscroft, *apptd* 1988
*Bodmin*, Ven. R. D. C. Whiteman, *apptd* 1989

*Chancellor*, P. T. S. Boydell, QC, *apptd* 1957
*Registrar and Secretary*, M. J. Follett
*Diocesan Secretary*, C. B. Gorton, Diocesan House,
    Kenwyn, Truro TRI 3DU. Tel: 01872-74351

---

## WORCESTER

---

111TH BISHOP
Rt. Revd Philip H. E. Goodrich, *cons.* 1973, *apptd* 1982;
    The Bishop's House, Hartlebury Castle, Kidderminster
    DY11 7XX. *Signs* Philip Worcester

BISHOP SUFFRAGAN
*Dudley*, Rt. Revd Dr Rupert Hoare, *cons.* 1993, *apptd* 1993;
    The Bishop's House, Brooklands, Halesowen Road,
    Cradley Heath B64 7JF

DEAN
Very Revd Robert M. C. Jeffery, *apptd* 1987

CANONS RESIDENTIARY
Ven. F. Bentley, *apptd* 1984; D. G. Thomas, *apptd* 1987;
    I. M. MacKenzie, *apptd* 1989
*Organist*, Dr D. Hunt, FRCO, *apptd* 1975

ARCHDEACONS
*Dudley*, Ven. J. Gathercole, *apptd* 1987
*Worcester*, Ven. F. Bentley, *apptd* 1984

*Chancellor*, P. T. S. Boydell, QC, *apptd* 1959
*Registrar*, M. Huskinson
*Diocesan Secretary*, J. Stanbury, The Old Palace, Deansway, Worcester WR1 2JE. Tel: 01905-20537

## ROYAL PECULIARS

### WESTMINSTER
*The Collegiate Church of St Peter*
*Dean*, Very Revd Michael Mayne, *apptd* 1986
*Sub Dean and Archdeacon*, A. E. Harvey, *apptd* 1987
*Canons of Westminster*, A. E. Harvey, *apptd* 1982; D. C. Gray, *apptd* 1987; C. D. Semper, *apptd* 1987
*Chapter Clerk and Receiver-General*, Rear-Adm. K. A. Snow, CB, *apptd* 1987
*Organist*, M. Neary, FRCO, *apptd* 1988
*Registrar*, S. J. Holmes, MVO, *apptd* 1984, 20 Dean's Yard, London SW1P 3PA

### WINDSOR
*The Queen's Free Chapel of St George within Her Castle of Windsor*
*Dean*, Very Revd Patrick R. Mitchell, FSA, *apptd* 1989
*Canons Residentiary*, J. A. White, *apptd* 1982; D. M. Stanesby, PH.D., *apptd* 1985; A. A. Coldwells, *apptd* 1987; M. A. Moxon, *apptd* 1990
*Chapter Clerk*, Lt.-Col. N. J. Newman, *apptd* 1990
*Organist*, J. Rees-Williams, FRCO, *apptd* 1991

# Province of York

## YORK

95TH ARCHBISHOP AND PRIMATE OF ENGLAND
Most Revd and Rt. Hon. John S. Habgood, PH.D., *cons.* 1973, *trans.* 1983, *apptd* 1983; Bishopthorpe, York YO2 1QE. *Signs* John Ebor:

BISHOPS SUFFRAGAN
*Hull*, Rt. Revd James S. Jones, *cons.* 1994, *apptd* 1994; Hullen House, Woodfield Lane, Hessle, Hull HU13 0ES
*Selby*, Rt. Revd Humphrey V. Taylor, *cons.* 1991, *apptd* 1991; 10 Precentor's Court, York YO1 2ES
*Whitby*, Rt. Revd Gordon Bates, *cons.* 1983, *apptd* 1983; 60 West Green, Stokesley, Middlesbrough TS9 5BD
*Beverley*, Rt. Revd John Gaisford, *cons.* 1994 *apptd* 1994 (provincial episcopal visitor); 2 Lovat Drive, Knutsford, Cheshire WA16 3NS

DEAN
Very Revd Raymond Furnell, *apptd* 1994

CANONS RESIDENTIARY
R. A. Hockley, *apptd* 1976; J. Toy, PH.D., *apptd* 1983; R. Metcalfe, *apptd* 1988

*Organist*, P. Moore, FRCO, *apptd* 1983

ARCHDEACONS
*Cleveland*, Ven. C. J. Hawthorn, *apptd* 1991
*East Riding*, Ven. H. F. Buckingham, *apptd* 1988

*York*, Ven. G. B. Austin, *apptd* 1988
*Official Principal and Auditor of the Chancery Court*, J. A. D. Owen, QC
*Chancellor of the Diocese*, His Honour Judge Coningsby, QC, *apptd* 1977
*Vicar-General of the Province and Official Principal of the Consistory Court*, His Honour Judge Coningsby, QC
*Registrar and Legal Secretary*, L. P. M. Lennox
*Diocesan Secretary*, K. W. Dodgson, Church House, Ogleforth, York YO1 2JE. Tel: 01904-611696

## DURHAM

92ND BISHOP
Rt. Revd A. Michael A. Turnbull, *cons.* 1988, *apptd* 1994; Auckland Castle, Bishop Auckland DL14 7NR. *Signs* Michael Dunelm

BISHOP SUFFRAGAN
*Jarrow*, Rt. Revd Alan Smithson, *cons.* 1990, *apptd* 1990; The Old Vicarage, Hallgarth, Pittington, Durham DH6 1AB

DEAN
Very Revd John R. Arnold, *apptd* 1989

CANONS RESIDENTIARY
M. C. Perry, *apptd* 1970; R. L. Coppin, *apptd* 1974; Ven. J. D. Hodgson, *apptd* 1983; D. W. Brown, *apptd* 1990; G. S. Pedley, *apptd* 1993

*Organist*, J. B. Lancelot, FRCO, *apptd* 1985

ARCHDEACONS
*Auckland*, Ven. G. G. Gibson, *apptd* 1993
*Durham*, Ven. J. D. Hodgson, *apptd* 1993

*Chancellor*, His Honour Judge Bursell, QC, *apptd* 1989
*Registrar and Legal Secretary*, D. M. Robertson
*Diocesan Secretary*, W. Hurworth, Auckland Castle, Bishop Auckland, Co. Durham DL14 7QJ. Tel: 01388-604515

## BLACKBURN

7TH BISHOP
Rt. Revd Alan D. Chesters, *cons.* 1989, *apptd* 1989; Bishop's House, Ribchester Road, Blackburn BB1 9EF. *Signs* Alan Blackburn

BISHOPS SUFFRAGAN
*Burnley*, Rt. Revd Martyn W. Jarrett, *cons.* 1994, *apptd* 1994; Dean House, 449 Padiham Road, Burnley BB12 6TE
*Lancaster*, Rt. Revd John Nicholls, *cons.* 1990, *apptd* 1990; Wheatfields, 7 Dallas Road, Lancaster LA1 1TN

PROVOST
Very Revd David Frayne, *apptd* 1992

CANONS RESIDENTIARY
J. M. Taylor, *apptd* 1976; M. A. Kitchener, *apptd* 1990; S. R. Hull, *apptd* 1994; K. J. Parfitt, *apptd* 1994
*Organist*, R. Sayer, *apptd* 1994

ARCHDEACONS
*Blackburn*, Ven. W. D. Robinson, *apptd* 1986
*Lancaster*, Ven. K. H. Gibbons, *apptd* 1981

*Chancellor*, J. W. M. Bullimore, *apptd* 1990
*Registrar*, T. A. Hoyle

*Diocesan Secretary*, D. Dunderdale (*until March 1995*), Diocesan Office, Cathedral Close, Blackburn BB1 5AA. Tel: 01254-54421

---

## BRADFORD

---

**8TH BISHOP**
Rt. Revd David J. Smith, *cons.* 1987, *apptd* 1992; Bishopscroft, Ashwell Road, Heaton, Bradford BD9 4AU. *Signs* David Bradford

**PROVOST**
Very Revd John S. Richardson, *apptd* 1990

**CANONS RESIDENTIARY**
K. H. Cook, *apptd* 1977; C. G. Lewis, *apptd* 1993

*Organist*, A. Horsey, FRCO, *apptd* 1986

**ARCHDEACONS**
*Bradford*, Ven. D. H. Shreeve, *apptd* 1984
*Craven*, Ven. M. L. Grundy, *apptd* 1994

*Chancellor*, D. M. Savill, QC, *apptd* 1976
*Registrar and Secretary*, J. G. H. Mackrell
*Diocesan Secretary*, M. Halliday, Cathedral Hall, Stott Hill, Bradford BD1 4ET. Tel: 01274-725958

---

## CARLISLE

---

**65TH BISHOP**
Rt. Revd Ian Harland, *cons.* 1985, *apptd* 1989; Rose Castle, Dalston, Carlisle CA5 7BZ. *Signs* Ian Carliol:

**BISHOP SUFFRAGAN**
*Penrith*, Rt. Revd Richard Garrard, *cons.* 1994, *apptd* 1994; The Rectory, Great Salkeld, Penrith CA11 9NA

**DEAN**
Very Revd Henry E. C. Stapleton, *apptd* 1988

**CANONS RESIDENTIARY**
R. A. Chapman, *apptd* 1978; R. C. Johns, *apptd* 1989; D. T. I. Jenkins, *apptd* 1991; Ven. D. C. Turnbull, *apptd* 1993

*Organist*, J. Suter, FRCO, *apptd* 1991

**ARCHDEACONS**
*Carlisle*, Ven. D. C. Turnbull, *apptd* 1993
*West Cumberland*, Ven. J. R. Packer, *apptd* 1991
*Westmorland and Furness*, Ven. L. J. Peat, *apptd* 1989

*Chancellor*, His Honour Judge Aglionby, *apptd* 1991
*Registrar and Secretary*, Mrs S. Holmes
*Diocesan Secretary*, Canon D. Jenkins, Church House, West Walls, Carlisle CA3 8UE. Tel: 01228-22573

---

## CHESTER

---

**39TH BISHOP**
Rt. Revd Michael A. Baughen, *cons.* 1982, *apptd* 1982; Bishop's House, Chester CH1 2JD. *Signs* Michael Cestr:

**BISHOPS SUFFRAGAN**
*Birkenhead*, Rt. Revd Michael L. Langrish, *cons.* 1993, *apptd* 1993; 67 Bidston Road, Oxton, Birkenhead L43 6TR

*Stockport*, Rt. Revd Geoffrey M. Turner, *cons.* 1994, *apptd* 1994; Bishop's Lodge, Back Lane, Dunham Town, Altrincham, Cheshire WA14 4SG

**DEAN**
Very Revd Stephen S. Smalley, *apptd* 1986

**CANONS RESIDENTIARY**
R. M. Rees, *apptd* 1990; O. A. Conway, *apptd* 1991; Dr T. J. Dennis, *apptd* 1994; J. W. S. Newcome, *apptd* 1994

*Organist*, R. Fisher, FRCO, *apptd* 1968

**ARCHDEACONS**
*Chester*, Ven. C. Hewetson, *apptd* 1994
*Macclesfield*, Ven. R. J. Gillings, *apptd* 1994

*Chancellor*, H. H. Lomas, *apptd* 1977
*Registrar and Legal Secretary*, A. K. McAllester
*Diocesan Secretary*, P. J. Mills, Diocesan House, Raymond Street, Chester CH1 4PN. Tel: 01244-379222

---

## LIVERPOOL

---

**6TH BISHOP**
Rt. Revd David S. Sheppard, *cons.* 1969, *apptd* 1975; Bishop's Lodge, Woolton Park, Liverpool L25 6DT. *Signs* David Liverpool

**BISHOP SUFFRAGAN**
*Warrington*, Rt. Revd Michael Henshall, *cons.* 1976, *apptd* 1976; Martinsfield, Elm Avenue, Great Crosby, Liverpool L23 2SX

**DEAN**
Very Revd Rhys D. C. Walters, OBE, *apptd* 1983

**CANONS RESIDENTIARY**
M. M. Wolfe, *apptd* 1982; D. J. Hutton, *apptd* 1983; H. Thomas, *apptd* 1988; M. C. Boyling, *apptd* 1994

*Organist*, Prof. I. Tracey, *apptd* 1980

**ARCHDEACONS**
*Liverpool*, Ven. R. L. Metcalf, *apptd* 1994
*Warrington*, Ven. C. D. S. Woodhouse, *apptd* 1981

*Chancellor*, R. G. Hamilton
*Registrar and Cathedral Chapter Clerk*, R. H. Arden
*Diocesan Secretary*, K. Cawdron, Church House, 1 Hanover Street, Liverpool L1 3DW. Tel: 0151-709 9722

---

## MANCHESTER

---

**10TH BISHOP**
Rt. Revd Christopher J. Mayfield, *cons.* 1985, *apptd* 1993; Bishopscourt, Bury New Road, Manchester M7 0LE. *Signs* Christopher Manchester

**BISHOPS SUFFRAGAN**
*Bolton*, Rt. Revd David Bonser, *cons.* 1991, *apptd* 1991; 4 Sandfield Drive, Lostock, Bolton BL6 4DU
*Hulme*, Rt. Revd Colin J. F. Scott, *cons.* 1984, *apptd* 1984; 1 Raynham Avenue, Didsbury, Manchester M20 0BW
*Middleton*, Rt. Revd Stephen Venner, *cons.* 1994, *apptd* 1994; The Hollies, Manchester Road, Rochdale OL11 3QY

**DEAN**
Very Revd Kenneth Riley, *apptd* 1993

CANONS RESIDENTIARY
Ven. R. B. Harris, *apptd* 1980; J. R. Atherton, PH.D., *apptd*
1984; B. Duncan, *apptd* 1986; A. E. Radcliffe, *apptd* 1991

*Organist*, C. Stokes, *apptd* 1992

ARCHDEACONS
*Bolton*, Ven. L. M. Davies, *apptd* 1992
*Manchester*, Ven. R. B. Harris, *apptd* 1980
*Rochdale*, Ven. J. M. M. Dalby, *apptd* 1991

*Chancellor*, G. C. H. Spafford, *apptd* 1976
*Registrar*, M. Darlington
*Diocesan Secretary*, Mrs J. Park, Diocesan Church House,
90 Deansgate, Manchester M3 2GH. Tel: 0161-833 9521

---

## NEWCASTLE

IOTH BISHOP
Rt. Revd Andrew A. K. Graham, *cons.* 1977, *apptd* 1981;
Bishop's House, 29 Moor Road South, Gosforth,
Newcastle upon Tyne NE3 IPA. *Signs* A. Newcastle

STIPENDIARY ASSISTANT BISHOP
Rt. Revd Kenneth Gill, *cons.* 1972, *apptd* 1980

PROVOST
Very Revd Nicholas G. Coulton, *apptd* 1990

CANONS RESIDENTIARY
R. Langley, *apptd* 1985; P. R. Strange, *apptd* 1986;
I. F. Bennett, *apptd* 1988; Ven. P. Elliott, *apptd* 1993

*Organist*, T. G. Hone, FRCO, *apptd* 1987

ARCHDEACONS
*Lindisfarne*, Ven. M. E. Bowering, *apptd* 1987
*Northumberland*, Ven. P. Elliott, *apptd* 1993

*Chancellor*, His Honour A. J. Blackett-Ord, CVO, *apptd* 1971
*Registrar and Secretary*, R. R. V. Nicholson
*Diocesan Secretary*, D. Hide, Church House, Grainger Park
Road, Newcastle upon Tyne NE4 8SX. Tel: 0191-226 0622

---

## RIPON

IITH BISHOP
Rt. Revd David N. de L. Young, *cons.* 1977, *apptd* 1977;
Bishop Mount, Ripon HG4 5DP. *Signs* David Ripon

BISHOP SUFFRAGAN
*Knaresborough*, Rt. Revd Malcolm J. Menin, *cons.* 1986,
*apptd* 1986; 16 Shaftesbury Avenue, Roundhay, Leeds
LS8 IDT

DEAN
Very Revd Christopher R. Campling, *apptd* 1984

CANONS RESIDENTIARY
D. G. Ford, *apptd* 1980; P. J. Marshall, *apptd* 1985;
M. R. Glanville-Smith, *apptd* 1990

*Organist*, R. Perrin, FRCO, *apptd* 1966

ARCHDEACONS
*Leeds*, Ven. J. M. Oliver, *apptd* 1992
*Richmond*, Ven. K. Good, *apptd* 1993

*Chancellor*, His Honour Judge Grenfell, *apptd* 1992
*Registrar and Legal Secretary*, J. R. Balmforth
*Diocesan Secretary*, G. M. Royal, Diocesan Office, St Mary's
Street, Leeds LS9 7DP. Tel: 0113-248 7487

---

## SHEFFIELD

5TH BISHOP
Rt. Revd David R. Lunn, *cons.* 1980, *apptd* 1980;
Bishopscroft, Snaithing Lane, Sheffield S10 3LG. *Signs*
David Sheffield

BISHOP SUFFRAGAN
*Doncaster*, Rt. Revd. Michael F. Gear, *cons.* 1993, *apptd*
1993; Bishops Lodge, Hooton Roberts, Rotherham S65
4PF

PROVOST
vacant

CANONS RESIDENTIARY
T. M. Page, *apptd* 1982; Ven. S. R. Lowe, *apptd* 1988;
C. M. Smith, *apptd* 1991; Jane E. M. Sinclair, *apptd* 1993

*Organist*, S. Lole, *apptd* 1994

ARCHDEACONS
*Doncaster*, Ven. B. L. Holdridge, *apptd* 1994
*Sheffield*, Ven. S. R. Lowe, *apptd* 1988

*Chancellor*, Prof. J. D. McClean, *apptd* 1992
*Registrar and Legal Secretary*, C. P. Rothwell
*Diocesan Secretary*, C. A. Beck, FCIS, Diocesan Church
House, 95–99 Effingham Street, Rotherham S65 IBL. Tel:
0114-283 7547

---

## SODOR AND MAN

79TH BISHOP
Rt. Revd Noel D. Jones, CB, *cons.* 1989, *apptd* 1989; The
Bishop's House, Quarterbridge Road, Douglas, Isle of
Man IM2 3RF. *Signs* Noel Sodor and Man

CANONS
B. H. Kelly, *apptd* 1980; B. H. Partington, *apptd* 1985;
J. Sheen, *apptd* 1991; F. H. Bird, *apptd* 1993

ARCHDEACON
*Isle of Man*, Ven. D. A. Willoughby, *apptd* 1982

*Vicar-General and Chancellor*, P. W. S. Farrant
*Registrar*, C. J. Callow
*Diocesan Secretary*, The Hon. C. Murphy, c/o Cooil
Voorath, The Cronk, Ballaugh, Isle of Man IM7 5AX. Tel:
01624-897880

---

## SOUTHWELL

9TH BISHOP
Rt. Revd Patrick B. Harris, *cons.* 1973, *apptd* 1988; Bishop's
Manor, Southwell NG25 OJR. *Signs* Patrick Southwell

BISHOP SUFFRAGAN
*Sherwood*, Rt. Revd Alan W. Morgan, *cons.* 1989, *apptd*
1989; Sherwood House, High Oakham Road, Mansfield
NG18 5AJ

PROVOST
Very Revd David Leaning, *apptd* 1991

CANONS RESIDENTIARY
D. P. Keene, *apptd* 1981; I. G. Collins, *apptd* 1985;
M. Austin, *apptd* 1992

*Organist*, P. Hale, *apptd* 1989

ARCHDEACONS
*Newark*, Ven. D. C. Hawtin, *apptd* 1992
*Nottingham*, Ven. T. O. Walker, *apptd* 1991

*Chancellor*, J. Shand, *apptd* 1981
*Registrar*, C. C. Hodson
*Diocesan Secretary*, B. Noake, Dunham House, Westgate,
   Southwell, Notts. NG25 0JL. Tel: 01636-814331

## WAKEFIELD

11TH BISHOP
Rt. Revd Nigel S. McCulloch, *cons.* 1986, *apptd* 1992;
   Bishop's Lodge, Woodthorpe Lane, Wakefield WF2 6JL.
   *Signs* Nigel Wakefield

BISHOP SUFFRAGAN
*Pontefract*, Rt. Revd John Finney, *cons.* 1993, *apptd* 1993;
   Pontefract House, 181A Manygates Lane, Wakefield
   WF2 7DR

PROVOST
Very Revd John E. Allen, *apptd* 1982

CANONS RESIDENTIARY
R. D. Baxter, *apptd* 1986; I. C. Knox, *apptd* 1989;
D. O'Connor, *apptd* 1992; G. Nairn-Briggs, *apptd* 1992
*Organist*, J. Bielby, FRCO, *apptd* 1972

ARCHDEACONS
*Halifax*, vacant
*Pontefract*, Ven. J. Flack, *apptd* 1992

*Chancellor*, P. Collier, QC, *apptd* 1992
*Registrar and Secretary*, L. Box
*Diocesan Secretary*, J. Clark, Church House, 1 South Parade,
   Wakefield WF1 1LP. Tel: 01924-371802

# The Anglican Communion

The Anglican Communion consists of 31 independent
provincial or national Christian Churches throughout the
world, many of which are in Commonwealth countries and
originated from missionary activity by the Church of England.
There is no single world authority linking the Communion,
but all recognize the leadership of the Archbishop of
Canterbury and have strong ecclesiastical and historical links
with the Church of England. Every ten years all the bishops
in the Communion meet at the Lambeth Conference,
convened by the Archbishop of Canterbury. The Conference
has no policy-making authority but is an important forum for
the discussion of issues of common concern. The Anglican
Consultative Council was set up in 1968 to function between
conferences and the meeting of the Primates every two years.
   There are about 70 million Anglicans and 800 archbishops
and bishops world-wide.

## THE CHURCH IN WALES

The Anglican Church was the established church in Wales
from the 16th century until 1920, when the estrangement of
the majority of Welsh people from Anglicanism resulted in
disestablishment. Since then the Church in Wales has been
an autonomous province consisting of six sees, with one of
the diocesan bishops being elected Archbishop of Wales by
an electoral college comprising elected lay and clerical
members.
   The legislative body of the Church in Wales is the
Governing Body, which has 349 members in total, divided
between the three orders of bishops, clergy and laity. It is
presided over by the Archbishop of Wales and meets twice
annually. Its decisions are binding upon all members of the
Church. There are about 104,000 members of the Church in
Wales, with six bishops, about 700 stipendiary clergy and
1,142 parishes.

THE GOVERNING BODY OF THE CHURCH IN WALES,
   39 Cathedral Road, Cardiff CF1 9XF. Tel: 01222-231638.
   *Secretary-General*, J. W. D. McIntyre

10TH ARCHBISHOP OF WALES, Most Revd Alwyn
   R. Jones (Bishop of St Asaph), *elected* 1991

THE RT. REVD BISHOPS
*Bangor* (79*th*), Rt. Revd Dr Barry C. Morgan, *b.* 1947, *cons.*
   1993, *apptd* 1992; Tŷ'r Esgob, Bangor LL57 2SS. *Signs*
   Barry Bangor. *Stipendiary clergy*, 71
*Llandaff* (101*st*), Rt. Revd Roy T. Davies, *b.* 1934, *cons.*
   1985, *apptd* 1985; Llys Esgob, The Cathedral Green,
   Llandaff, Cardiff CF5 2YE. *Signs* Roy Landav. *Stipendiary
   clergy*, 168
*Monmouth* (8*th*), Rt. Revd Rowan D. Williams, *b* 1950, *cons.*
   1992, *apptd* 1992; Bishopstow, Stow Hill, Newport NP9
   4EA. *Signs* Rowan Monmouth. *Stipendiary clergy*, 110
*St Asaph* (74*th*), Most Revd Alwyn R. Jones, *b.* 1934, *cons.*
   1982, *apptd* 1982; Esgobty, St Asaph, Clwyd LL17 0TW.
   *Signs* Alwyn Cambrensis. *Stipendiary clergy*, 112
*St David's* (125*th*), Rt. Revd J. Ivor Rees, *b.* 1926, *cons.*
   1988, *apptd* 1991; Llys Esgob, Abergwili, Dyfed SA31 2JG.
   *Signs* Ivor St Davids. *Stipendiary clergy*, 132
*Swansea and Brecon* (7*th*), Rt. Revd Dewi M. Bridges, *b.*
   1933, *cons.* 1988, *apptd* 1988; Ely Tower, Brecon, Powys
   LD3 9DE. *Signs* Dewi Swansea & Brecon. *Stipendiary
   clergy*, 100

The stipend of a diocesan bishop of the Church in Wales is
£23,610 a year from 1994

## THE EPISCOPAL CHURCH IN SCOTLAND

The Episcopal Church in Scotland was founded after the Act
of Settlement (1690) established the presbyterian nature of
the Church of Scotland. The Episcopal Church is in full
communion with the Church of England but is autonomous.
The governing authority is the General Synod, an elected
body of 160 members which meets once a year. The diocesan
bishop who convenes and presides at meetings of the General
Synod is called the Primus and is elected by his fellow
bishops.
   There are 55,929 members of the Episcopal Church in
Scotland, of whom 35,036 are communicants. There are
seven bishops, 202 clergy, and 341 churches and places of
worship.

THE GENERAL SYNOD OF THE EPISCOPAL CHURCH IN
   SCOTLAND, 21 Grosvenor Crescent, Edinburgh
   EH12 5EE. Tel: 0131-225 6357. *Secretary-General*,
   J. Simpson

PRIMUS OF THE EPISCOPAL CHURCH IN SCOTLAND,
   Most Revd Richard F. Holloway (Bishop of Edinburgh),
   *elected* 1992

THE RT. REVD BISHOPS
*Aberdeen and Orkney*, A. Bruce Cameron, *b.* 1941, *cons.*
   1992, *apptd* 1992. *Clergy* 14

*Argyll and the Isles*, Douglas M. Cameron, *b.* 1935, *cons.* 1992, *apptd* 1992. *Clergy* 10

*Brechin*, Robert T. Halliday, *b.* 1932, *cons.* 1990, *apptd* 1990. *Clergy* 15

*Edinburgh*, Richard F. Holloway, *b.* 1933, *cons.* 1986, *apptd* 1986. *Clergy* 65

*Glasgow and Galloway*, John M. Taylor, *b.* 1932, *cons.* 1991, *apptd* 1991. *Clergy* 45

*Moray, Ross and Caithness*, Gregor Macgregor, *b.* 1933, *cons.* 1994, *apptd* 1994. *Clergy* 16

*St Andrews, Dunkeld and Dunblane*, Michael G. Hare-Duke, *b.* 1925, *cons.* 1969, *apptd* 1969. *Clergy* 30

The stipend of a diocesan bishop of the Episcopal Church in Scotland was £16,956 in 1994

---

## THE CHURCH OF IRELAND

---

The Anglican Church was the established church in Ireland from the 16th century but never secured the allegiance of a majority of the Irish and was disestablished in 1871. The Church in Ireland is divided into the provinces of Armagh and Dublin, each under an archbishop. The provinces are subdivided into 12 dioceses.

The legislative body is the General Synod, which has 660 members in total, divided between the House of Bishops and the House of Representatives. The Archbishop of Armagh is elected by the House of Bishops; other episcopal elections are made by an electoral college.

There are about 375,000 members of the Church of Ireland, with two archbishops, ten bishops, about 600 clergy and about 1,000 churches and places of worship.

CENTRAL OFFICE, Church of Ireland House, Church Avenue, Rathmines, Dublin 6. Tel: 00-353-14-978422. *Assistant Secretary of the General Synod*, D. G. Meredith

### PROVINCE OF ARMAGH

ARCHBISHOP OF ARMAGH AND PRIMATE OF ALL IRELAND, Most Revd Robert H. A. Eames, PH.D., *b.* 1937, *cons.* 1975, *trans.* 1986. *Clergy* 53

THE RT. REVD BISHOPS
*Clogher*, Brian D. A. Hannon, *b.* 1936, *cons.* 1986, *apptd* 1986. *Clergy* 34

*Connor*, Samuel G. Poyntz, PH.D., *b.* 1926, *cons.* 1978, *trans.* 1987. *Clergy* 115

*Derry and Raphoe*, James Mehaffey, PH.D., *b.* 1931, *cons.* 1980, *apptd* 1980. *Clergy* 52

*Down and Dromore*, Gordon McMullan, PH.D., TH.D., *b.* 1934, *cons.* 1980, *trans.* 1986. *Clergy* 112

*Kilmore, Elphin and Ardagh*, Michael H. G. Mayes, *b.* 1941, *cons.* 1993, *apptd* 1993. *Clergy* 29

*Tuam, Killala and Achonry*, John R. W. Neill, *b.* 1945, *cons.* 1986, *apptd* 1986. *Clergy* 10

### PROVINCE OF DUBLIN

ARCHBISHOP OF DUBLIN, BISHOP OF GLENDALOUGH, AND PRIMATE OF IRELAND, Most Revd Donald A. Caird, DD, *b.* 1925, *cons.* 1970, *trans.* 1976, 1985. *Clergy* 88

THE RT. REVD BISHOPS
*Cashel and Ossory*, Noel V. Willoughby, *b.* 1926, *cons.* 1980, *apptd* 1980. *Clergy* 39

*Cork, Cloyne and Ross*, Robert A. Warke, *b.* 1930, *cons.* 1988, *apptd* 1988. *Clergy* 28

*Limerick and Killaloe*, Edward F. Darling, *b.* 1933, *cons.* 1985, *apptd* 1985. *Clergy* 22

*Meath and Kildare*, Most Revd Walton N. F. Empey, *b.* 1934, *cons.* 1981, *trans.* 1985. *Clergy* 20

---

# Anglican Communion Overseas

---

## ANGLICAN CHURCH OF AOTEAROA, NEW ZEALAND AND POLYNESIA

---

PRIMATE AND ARCHBISHOP OF AOTEAROA, NEW ZEALAND AND POLYNESIA, The Most Revd Brian N. Davis (Bishop of Wellington), *cons.* 1980, *apptd* 1986

THE RT. REVD BISHOPS
*Aotearoa*, Whakahuhui Vercoe, *cons.* 1981, *apptd* 1981
*Auckland*, Bruce Gilberd, *cons.* 1985, *apptd* 1985
*Christchurch*, David Coles, *cons.* 1990, *apptd* 1990
*Dunedin*, Penelope Jamieson, *cons.* 1990, *apptd* 1990
*Nelson*, Derek Eaton, *cons.* 1990, *apptd* 1990
*Polynesia*, Jabez Bryce, *cons.* 1975, *apptd* 1975
*Waiapu*, Murray Mills, *cons.* 1991, *apptd* 1991
*Waikato*, David Moxon, *cons.* 1993, *apptd* 1993
*Wellington*, see above

---

## ANGLICAN CHURCH OF AUSTRALIA

---

PRIMATE OF AUSTRALIA, The Most Revd Keith Rayner (Archbishop of Melbourne), *cons.* 1969, *apptd* 1991

### PROVINCE OF NEW SOUTH WALES
METROPOLITAN
*Archbishop of Sydney*, The Most Revd R. Harry Goodhew, *cons.* 1982, *apptd* 1993

THE RT. REVD BISHOPS
*Armidale*, Peter Chiswell, *cons.* 1976, *apptd* 1976
*Bathurst*, Bruce W. Wilson, *cons.* 1984, *apptd* 1989
*Canberra and Goulburn*, George V. Browning, *apptd* 1993
*Grafton*, Bruce A. Schultz, *cons.* 1985, *apptd* 1985
*Newcastle*, Roger A. Herft, *apptd* 1993
*Riverina*, Bruce Q. Clark, *apptd* 1993

### PROVINCE OF QUEENSLAND
METROPOLITAN
*Archbishop of Brisbane*, The Most Revd Peter Hollingworth, *cons.* 1985, *apptd* 1990

THE RT. REVD BISHOPS
*Carpentaria*, Anthony F. B. Hall-Matthews, *cons.* 1984
*North Queensland*, John Lewis, *cons.* 1971
*Northern Territory*, Richard F. Appleby, *apptd* 1992
*Rockhampton*, George A. Hearn, *cons.* 1981

### PROVINCE OF SOUTH AUSTRALIA
METROPOLITAN
*Archbishop of Adelaide*, The Most Revd Ian G. C. George, *cons.* 1989, *apptd* 1991

THE RT. REVD BISHOPS
*The Murray*, Graham H. Walden, *cons.* 1981, *apptd* 1989
*Willochra*, W. David H. McCall, *cons.* 1987, *apptd* 1987

### PROVINCE OF VICTORIA
METROPOLITAN
*Archbishop of Melbourne*, The Most Revd Keith Rayner, *cons.* 1969, *apptd* 1990 (*see above*)

THE RT. REVD BISHOPS
*Ballarat,* R. David Silk, *cons.* 1994, *apptd* 1994
*Bendigo,* vacant
*Gippsland,* vacant
*Wangaratta,* vacant

## PROVINCE OF WESTERN AUSTRALIA
METROPOLITAN
*Archbishop of Perth,* The Most Revd Peter F. Carnley,
PH.D., *cons.* 1981, *apptd* 1981

THE RT. REVD BISHOPS
*Bunbury,* Hamish J. U. Jamieson, *cons.* 1974, *apptd* 1984
*North-West Australia,* Anthony Nicholls, *cons.* 1992, *apptd*
1992

## EXTRA-PROVINCIAL DIOCESE
*Bishop of Tasmania,* Rt. Revd Phillip K. Newell, AO, *cons.*
1982, *apptd* 1982

---

## EPISCOPAL ANGLICAN CHURCH OF BRAZIL
*Igreja Episcopal Anglicana Do Brasil*

---

PRIMATE, The Most Revd Glauco Soares de Lima (Bishop
of South Central Brazil), *cons.* 1989, *apptd* 1994

THE RT. REVD BISHOPS
*Brasilia,* Almir dos Santos, *cons.* 1989, *apptd* 1989
*Central Brazil,* Sydney A. Ruiz, *cons.* 1985, *apptd* 1985
*Northern Brazil,* Clovis E. Rodrigues, *cons.* 1985, *apptd* 1986
*Pelotas,* Luiz O. P. Prado, *cons.* 1987, *apptd* 1989
*South Central Brazil,* see above, *apptd* 1989
*Southern Brazil,* Claudio V. S. Gastal, *cons.* 1984, *apptd* 1984
*South-Western Brazil,* Jubal P. Neves, *cons.* 1993, *apptd*
1993

---

## CHURCH OF THE PROVINCE OF BURUNDI

---

ARCHBISHOP OF PROVINCE, The Most Revd Samuel
Sindamuka (Bishop of Matana), *cons.* 1975, *apptd* 1989

THE RT. REVD BISHOPS
*Bujumbura,* Pie Ntukamazina, *cons.* 1990, *apptd* 1990
*Buye,* Samuel Ndayisenga, *apptd* 1979
*Gitega,* Jean Nduwayo, *apptd* 1985
*Matana,* see above

---

## ANGLICAN CHURCH OF CANADA

---

ARCHBISHOP AND PRIMATE, The Most Revd Michael
G. Peers, *cons.* 1977, *elected* 1986

## PROVINCE OF BRITISH COLUMBIA
METROPOLITAN
*Archbishop of Kootenay,* The Most Revd David Crawley,
*cons.* 1990, *elected* 1994

THE RT. REVD BISHOPS
*British Columbia,* Barry Jenks, *cons.* 1992, *elected* 1992
*Caledonia,* John Hannen, *cons.* 1981, *elected* 1981
*Cariboo,* James Cruickshank, *cons.* 1992, *elected* 1992
*Kootenay,* see above, *elected* 1990
*New Westminster,* Michael Ingham, *cons.* 1994, *elected* 1993
*Yukon,* Ronald Ferris, *cons.* 1981, *elected* 1981

## PROVINCE OF CANADA
METROPOLITAN
*Archbishop of Western Newfoundland,* The Most Revd
Stewart S. Payne, *cons.* 1978, *elected* 1990

THE RT. REVD BISHOPS
*Central Newfoundland,* Edward Marsh, *cons.* 1990, *elected*
1990
*Eastern Newfoundland and Labrador,* Donald Harvey, *cons.*
1993, *elected* 1992
*Fredericton,* George Lemon, *cons.* 1989, *elected* 1989
*Montreal,* Andrew Hutchison, *cons.* 1990, *elected* 1990
*Nova Scotia,* Arthur Peters, *cons.* 1982, *elected* 1982
*Quebec,* Bruce Stavert, *cons.* 1991, *elected* 1991
*Western Newfoundland,* see above

## PROVINCE OF ONTARIO
METROPOLITAN
*Archbishop of Huron,* The Most Revd Percival O'Driscoll,
*cons.* 1987, *elected* 1993

THE RT. REVD BISHOPS
*Algoma,* vacant
*Huron,* see above
*Moosonee,* Caleb Lawrence, *cons.* 1980, *elected* 1980
*Niagara,* Walter Asbil, *cons.* 1990, *elected* 1990
*Ontario,* Peter Mason, *cons.* 1992, *elected* 1992
*Ottawa,* John Baycroft, *cons.* 1985, *elected* 1993
*Toronto,* Terence Finlay, *cons.* 1986, *elected* 1990

## PROVINCE OF RUPERT'S LAND
METROPOLITAN
*Archbishop of Calgary,* The Most Revd Barry Curtis, *cons.*
1983, *elected* 1994

THE RT. REVD BISHOPS
*Arctic,* J. Christopher Williams, *cons.* 1987, *elected* 1991
*Athabasca ,* John Clarke, *cons.* 1992, *elected* 1992
*Brandon,* Malcolm Harding, *cons.* 1992, *elected* 1992
*Calgary,* see above, *elected* 1983
*Edmonton,* Kenneth Genge, *cons.* 1988, *elected* 1988
*Keewatin,* Thomas Collings, *cons.* 1991, *elected* 1991
*Qu' Appelle,* Eric Bays, *cons.* 1986, *elected* 1986
*Rupert's Land,* Patrick Lee, *cons.* 1994, *elected* 1994
*Saskatchewan,* Anthony Burton, *cons.* 1993, *elected* 1993
*Saskatoon,* Thomas Morgan, *cons.* 1985, *elected* 1993

---

## CHURCH OF THE PROVINCE OF CENTRAL
## AFRICA

---

ARCHBISHOP OF PROVINCE, The Most Revd Walter
P. K. Makhulu (Bishop of Botswana), *cons.* 1979, *apptd*
1980

THE RT. REVD BISHOPS
*Botswana,* see above
*Central Zambia,* Clement Shaba, *cons.* 1984, *apptd* 1984
*Harare,* Ralph Hatendi, *cons.* 1979, *apptd* 1981
*Lake Malawi,* Peter Nyanja, *cons.* 1978, *apptd* 1978
*The Lundi,* Jonathan Siyachitema, *cons.* 1981, *apptd* 1981
*Lusaka,* Stephen Mumba, *cons.* 1981, *apptd* 1981
*Manicaland,* Elijah Masuko, *cons.* 1981, *apptd* 1981
*Matabeleland,* Theophilus Naledi, *cons.* 1987, *apptd* 1987
*Northern Zambia,* Bernard Malango, *cons.* 1988, *apptd* 1988
*Southern Malawi,* Nathaniel Aipa, *cons.* 1987, *apptd* 1987

# CHURCH OF THE PROVINCE OF THE INDIAN OCEAN

ARCHBISHOP OF PROVINCE, The Most Revd French Chang-Him (Bishop of Seychelles), *cons.* 1979, *apptd* 1984

THE RT. REVD BISHOPS
*Antananarivo*, Remi Rabenirina, *cons.* 1984, *apptd* 1984
*Antsiranana*, Keith Benzies, OBE, *cons.* 1982, *apptd* 1982
*Mauritius*, Rex Donat, *cons.* 1984, *apptd* 1984
*Seychelles, see* above
*Toamasina*, Donald Smith, *cons.* 1990, *apptd* 1990

# THE HOLY CATHOLIC CHURCH IN JAPAN
*Nippon Sei Ko Kai*

PRIMATE, The Most Revd James T. Yashiro (Bishop of Kita Kanto), *cons.* 1985, *apptd* 1994

THE RT. REVD BISHOPS
*Chubu*, Samuel W. Hoyo, *cons.* 1987, *apptd* 1987
*Hokkaido*, Augustine H. Amagi, *cons.* 1987, *apptd* 1987
*Kita Kanto, see* above 1985
*Kobe*, John J. Furumoto, *cons.* 1992, *apptd* 1992
*Kyoto*, John T. Okano, *cons.* 1991, *apptd* 1991 (*until March 1995*)
*Kyushu*, Joseph N. Iida, *cons.* 1982, *apptd* 1982
*Okinawa*, Paul S. Nakamura, *cons.* 1972, *apptd* 1972
*Osaka*, Christopher I. Kikawada, *cons.* 1975, *apptd* 1975 (*until March 1995*)
*Tohoku*, William T. Murakami, *cons.* 1993, *apptd* 1993
*Tokyo*, John M. Takeda, *cons.* 1988, *apptd* 1988
*Yokohama*, Raphael S. Kajiwara, *cons.* 1984, *apptd* 1984

# THE EPISCOPAL CHURCH IN JERUSALEM AND THE MIDDLE EAST

PRESIDENT-BISHOP, Rt. Revd Samir Kafity, *apptd* 1986

THE RT. REVD BISHOPS
*Jerusalem*, Samir Kafity, *cons.* 1984, *apptd* 1986
*Iran*, Iraj Mottahedeh, *cons.* 1990, *apptd* 1990
*Egypt*, Ghais A. Malik, *cons.* 1984, *apptd* 1984
*Cyprus and the Gulf*, John Brown, *cons.* 1986, *apptd* 1986

# CHURCH OF THE PROVINCE OF KENYA

ARCHBISHOP OF PROVINCE, The Most Revd Dr Manasses Kuria (Bishop of Nairobi), *cons.* 1970, *apptd* 1980

THE RT. REVD BISHOPS
*Butere*, Horace Etemesi, *cons.* 1993, *apptd* 1993
*Eldoret*, Stephen Kewasis, *cons.* 1992, *apptd* 1992
*Embu*, Moses Njue, *cons.* 1990, *apptd* 1990
*Kajiado*, vacant
*Katakwa*, Eliud Okiring, *cons.* 1991, *apptd* 1991
*Kirinyaga*, David Gitari, *cons.* 1975, *apptd* 1975
*Machakos*, Benjamin Nzimbi, *cons.* 1985, *apptd* 1985
*Maseno North*, vacant
*Maseno South*, Henry Okullu, *cons.* 1974, *apptd* 1974
*Maseno West*, Joseph Wesonga, *cons.* 1991, *apptd* 1991
*Mombasa*, Julius Kalu, *cons.* 1994, *apptd* 1994
*Mount Kenya Central*, Julius G. Gachuche, *cons.* 1993, *apptd* 1993

*Mount Kenya South*, George Njuguna, *cons.* 1984, *apptd* 1984
*Mount Kenya West*, Alfred Chipman, *cons.* 1993, *apptd* 1993
*Mumias*, William C. W. Shikukule, *cons.* 1993, *apptd* 1993
*Nairobi, see* above
*Nakuru*, Stephen M. Njihia, *cons.* 1990, *apptd* 1990
*Nambale*, Josiah M. Were, *cons.* 1993, *apptd* 1993
*Southern Nyanza*, Haggai Nyang', *cons.* 1990, *apptd* 1993
*Taita/Taveta*, Samson M. Mwaluda, *cons.* 1993, *apptd* 1993

# CHURCH OF THE PROVINCE OF KOREA

ARCHBISHOP OF PROVINCE, The Most Revd Simon S. Kim (Bishop of Seoul), *apptd* 1993

THE RT. REVD BISHOPS
*Pusan*, Bundo C. H. Kim, *apptd* 1988
*Seoul, see* above
*Taejon*, Paul Hwan Yoon, *apptd* 1988

# CHURCH OF THE PROVINCE OF MELANESIA

ARCHBISHOP OF PROVINCE, The Most Revd Ellison L. Pogo (Bishop of Central Melanesia), *cons.* 1981, *apptd* 1994

THE RT. REVD BISHOPS
*Central Melanesia, see* above
*Hanuato'o*, James Mason, *cons.* 1991, *apptd* 1991
*Malaita*, Raymond Aumae, *cons.* 1990, *apptd* 1990
*Temotu*, Lazarus Munamua, *cons.* 1987, *apptd* 1987
*Vanuatu*, Michael Tavoa, *cons.* 1990, *apptd* 1990
*Ysabel*, Walter Siba, *cons.* 1990, *apptd* 1994

# CHURCH OF THE PROVINCE OF MYANMAR

ARCHBISHOP OF PROVINCE, The Most Revd Andrew Mya Han (Bishop of Yangon), *cons.* 1988, *apptd* 1988

THE RT. REVD BISHOPS
*Hpa'an*, Daniel Hoi Kyin, *cons.* 1992, *apptd* 1992
*Mandalay*, Andrew Hla Aung, *cons.* 1988, *apptd* 1988
*Myitkyina*, John Shan Lon, *cons.* 1994, *apptd* 1994
*Sittwe*, Barnabas Theaung Hawi, *cons.* 1978, *apptd* 1980
*Toungoo*, John Wilme, *cons.* 1994, *apptd* 1994
*Yangon (Rangoon), see* above

# CHURCH OF THE PROVINCE OF NIGERIA

ARCHBISHOP OF THE PROVINCE, The Most Revd Joseph Adetiloye (Bishop of Lagos), *apptd* 1991

THE RT. REVD BISHOPS
*Aba*, A. O. Iwuagwu, *apptd* 1985
*Abuja*, Peter Akinole, *apptd* 1989
*Akoko*, J. O. K. Olowokure, *apptd* 1986
*Akure*, Emmanuel Gbonigi, *apptd* 1983
*Asaba*, Roland Nwosu, *apptd* 1977

*Awka,* Maxwell Anikwenwa, *apptd* 1987
*Bauchi,* Emmanuel O. Chukwuma, *apptd* 1990
*Benin,* John George, *apptd* 1985
*Calabar,* W. G. Ekprikpo
*Egbado,* Timothy Bolaji
*Egba-Egbado,* T. I. Akintayo, *apptd* 1977
*Ekiti,* C. A. Akinbola, *apptd* 1986
*Enugu,* Gideon Otubelu, *apptd* 1969
*Ibadan,* Gideon Olajide, *apptd* 1988
*Ife,* Gabriel Oloniyo
*Ijebu,* Abraham Olowoyo, *apptd* 1990
*Ijebu Remo,* E. O. I. Ogundana, *apptd* 1984
*Ilesha,* E. A. Ademowo, *apptd* 1989
*Jos,* B. A. Kwashi
*Kaduna,* Titus Ogbonyomi, *apptd* 1975
*Kafanchan,* William Diya, *apptd* 1990
*Kano,* B. O. Omosebi, *apptd* 1990
*Katsina,* J. S. Kwasu, *apptd* 1990
*Kwara,* Herbert Haruna, *apptd* 1974
*Lagos, see above, apptd* 1985
*Maiduguri,* E. K. Mani, *apptd* 1990
*Makurdi,* Nathan Nyom
*Mbaise,* Cyril Chukwka
*Minna,* Nathaniel Yisa, *apptd* 1990
*The Niger,* Jonathan Onyemelukwe, *apptd* 1975
*Niger Delta,* Samuel Elenwo, *apptd* 1981
*Oke-Osun,* Abraham O. Awoson
*Okigwe/Orlu,* Samuel Ebo, *apptd* 1984
*Ondo,* Samuel Aderin, *apptd* 1981
*Osun,* Seth Fagbemi, *apptd* 1987
*Owerri,* Benjamin Nwankiti, *apptd* 1968
*Owo,* Peter A. Adebiyi
*Sabon Gidaora,* Albert A. Agbaje
*Sokoto,* J. A. Idowu-Fearon, *apptd* 1990
*Uyo,* Ebenezar Nglass
*Warri,* Nathaniel Enuku
*Yola,* Chris O. Efobi, *apptd* 1990

---

## ANGLICAN CHURCH OF PAPUA NEW GUINEA

ARCHBISHOP OF PROVINCE, The Most Revd Bevan
   Meredith (Bishop of New Guinea Islands), *cons.* 1967,
   *elected* 1990

THE RT. REVD BISHOPS
*Aipo Rongo,* Paul Richardson, *cons.* 1987, *elected* 1987
*Dogura,* Tevita Talanoa, *cons.* 1992, *elected* 1992
*New Guinea Islands, see above, elected* 1977
*Popondota,* vacant
*Port Moresby,* Isaac Gadebo, *cons.* 1983, *elected* 1983

---

## PHILIPPINE EPISCOPAL CHURCH

PRIME BISHOP, The Most Revd Narciso V. Ticobay, *cons.*
   1986, *apptd* 1993

THE RT. REVD BISHOPS
*Central Philippines,* Manuel C. Lumpias, *cons.* 1977, *apptd*
   1978
*North Central Philippines,* Joel A. Pachao, *cons.* 1993, *apptd*
   1993
*Northern Luzon,* Ignacio C. Soliba, *cons.* 1990, *apptd* 1990
*Northern Philippines,* Robert L. Longid, *cons.* 1983, *apptd*
   1986
*Southern Philippines,* James B. Manguramas, *cons.* 1993,
   *apptd* 1993

---

## CHURCH OF THE PROVINCE OF RWANDA

ARCHBISHOP OF THE PROVINCE, The Most Revd
   Augustin Nshamihigo (Bishop of Shyira), *apptd* 1992

THE RT. REVD BISHOPS
*Butare,* Justin Ndandali, *apptd* 1992
*Byunba,* Onesphore Rwaje
*Cyangugu,* Daniel Nduhura
*Kibungo,* Augustin Mvunabandi
*Kigali,* Adonia Sebununguri, *cons.* 1965
*Kigeme,* Norman Kayumba
*Shyira, see above, apptd* 1984
*Shyogwe,* Samuel Musubyimana

---

## CHURCH OF THE PROVINCE OF SOUTHERN AFRICA

METROPOLITAN
*Archbishop of Cape Town,* The Most Revd Desmond
   M. B. Tutu, *cons.* 1976, *trans.* 1986

THE RT. REVD BISHOPS
*Bloemfontein,* Thomas Stanage, *cons.* 1978, *trans.* 1982
*Christ the King,* Peter Lee, *cons.* 1990, *apptd* 1990
*George,* Derek Damant, *cons.* 1985, *apptd* 1985
*Grahamstown,* David Russell, *cons.* 1986, *trans.* 1987
*Johannesburg,* Duncan Buchanan, *cons.* 1986, *apptd* 1986
*Kimberley and Kuruman,* W. N. Ndungane, *cons.* 1991,
   *apptd* 1991
*Klerksdorp,* David Nkwe, *cons.* 1990, *apptd* 1990
*Lebombo,* Dinis Sengulane, *cons.* 1976, *apptd* 1976
*Lesotho,* Philip Mokuku, *cons.* 1978, *apptd* 1978
*Namibia,* James Kauluma, *cons.* 1978, *apptd* 1981
*Natal,* Michael Nuttall, *cons.* 1975, *trans.* 1982
*Niassa,* Paulino Manhique, *cons.* 1986, *apptd* 1986
*Port Elizabeth,* Eric Pike, *cons.* 1989, *trans.* 1993
*Pretoria,* Richard Kraft, *cons.* 1982, *apptd* 1982
*St Helena,* John Ruston, *cons.* 1985, *trans.* 1991
*St John's,* Jacob Dlamini, *cons.* 1980, *apptd* 1985
*St Mark the Evangelist,* Rollo Le Feuvre, *cons.* 1987, *apptd*
   1987
*South-Eastern Transvaal,* David Beetge, *cons.* 1990, *apptd*
   1990
*Swaziland,* Lawrence Zulu, *cons.* 1975, *trans.* 1993
*Umzimvubu,* Geoffrey Davies, *cons.* 1987, *apptd* 1991
*Zululand,* Peter Harker, *cons.* 1993, *apptd* 1993

*Order of Ethiopia,* Sigqibo Dwane, *cons.* 1983, *apptd* 1983

---

## ANGLICAN CHURCH OF THE SOUTHERN CONE OF AMERICA

PRESIDING BISHOP, Rt. Revd Colin Bazley (Bishop of
   Chile), *cons.* 1969

THE RT. REVD BISHOPS
*Argentina,* David Leake, *cons.* 1969, *apptd* 1990
*Chile, see above, apptd* 1977
*Northern Argentina,* Maurice Sinclair, *cons.* 1990, *apptd* 1990
*Paraguay,* John Ellison, *cons.* 1988, *apptd* 1988
*Peru,* vacant
*Uruguay,* Harold Godfrey, *cons.* 1986, *apptd* 1986

## PROVINCE OF THE EPISCOPAL CHURCH OF THE SUDAN

ARCHBISHOP OF PROVINCE, The Most Revd Benjamin W. Yugusuk (Bishop of Juba)

THE RT. REVD BISHOPS
*Bor,* Nathaniel Garang
*Juba, see* above
*Kajokeji,* Manaseh B. Dawidi
*Khartoum,* Bulus Idris Tia
*Malakal,* Kedekia Mabier
*Maridi,* Joseph Marona
*Mundri,* Eluzai Munda
*Rumbek,* Gabriel R. Jur
*Wau (acting),* Gabriel R. Jur
*Western Sudan,* Kurkeil M. Khamis
*Yambio,* Daniel Zindo, *cons.* 1984, *apptd* 1984
*Yei,* Seme L. Solomona

## CHURCH OF THE PROVINCE OF TANZANIA

ARCHBISHOP OF PROVINCE, The Most Revd John A. Ramadhani (Bishop of Zanzibar and Tanga), *cons.* 1980, *apptd* 1984

THE RT. REVD BISHOPS
*Central Tanganyika,* Godfrey Mhogolo, *cons.* 1989, *apptd* 1989
*Dar es Salaam,* Basil Sambano, *cons.* 1992, *apptd* 1992
*Kagera,* Edwin Nyamubi, *cons.* 1993, *apptd* 1993
*Mara,* vacant
*Masasi,* Christopher Sadiki, *cons.* 1992, *apptd* 1992
*Morogoro,* Dudley Mageni, *cons.* 1987, *apptd* 1987
*Mount Kilimanjaro,* Simon Makundi, *cons.* 1991, *apptd* 1991
*Mpwapwa,* Simon Chiwanga, *cons.* 1991, *apptd* 1991
*Rift Valley,* Alpha Mohamed, *cons.* 1982, *apptd* 1991
*Ruaha,* Donald Mtetemela, *cons.* 1982, *apptd* 1990
*Ruvuma,* Stanford Shauri, *cons.* 1989, *apptd* 1989
*South-West Tanganyika,* Charles Mwaigoga, *cons.* 1983, *apptd* 1983
*Tabora,* Francis Ntiruka, *cons.* 1989, *apptd* 1989
*Victoria Nyanza,* John Changae, *cons.* 1993, *apptd* 1993
*Western Tanganyika,* Gerard Mpango, *cons.* 1983, *apptd* 1983
*Zanzibar and Tanga, see* above

## CHURCH OF THE PROVINCE OF UGANDA

ARCHBISHOP OF THE PROVINCE, The Most Revd Dr Yona Okoth (Bishop of Kampala), *cons.* 1972, *apptd* 1984

THE RT. REVD BISHOPS
*Bukedi,* Nicodemus Okille, *apptd* 1984
*Bunyoro-Kitara,* Yonasani Rwakaikara
*Busoga,* Cyprian Bamwoze, *apptd* 1972
*East Ankole,* Elisha Kyamugambi, *cons.* 1992, *apptd* 1992
*Kampala, see* above
*Karamoja,* Peter Lomongin, *apptd* 1987
*Kigezi,* William Rukirande
*Lango,* Melchizedek Otim, *apptd* 1976
*Luwero,* M. Bugimbi, *cons.* 1990, *apptd* 1990
*Madi and West Nile,* Caleb Nguma, *apptd* 1991
*Mbale,* Akisoferi M. Wesonga

*Mityana,* Wilson Mutebi, *apptd* 1977
*Muhabura,* Ernest M. Shalita, *cons.* 1990, *apptd* 1990
*Mukono,* Livingstone Mpalanyi-Nkoyoyo, *apptd* 1985
*Namirembe,* Misaeri Kauma, *apptd* 1985
*Nebbi,* Henry L. Orombi, *cons.* 1993, *apptd* 1993
*North Mbale,* Peter Mudonyi, *cons.* 1992, *apptd* 1992
*North Kigezi,* Yustasi Ruhindi, *apptd* 1981
*Northern Uganda,* Gideon Oboma
*Ruwenzori,* Eustace Kamanyire, *apptd* 1981
*Soroti,* Geresom Ilukor, *apptd* 1976
*South Ruwenzori,* Zebidee Masereka
*West Ankole,* Yorumu Bamunoba, *apptd* 1977
*West Buganda,* Christopher Senyonjo, *apptd* 1974

## EPISCOPAL CHURCH IN THE USA

PRESIDING BISHOP AND PRIMATE, Most Revd Edmond Lee Browning, DD, *cons.* 1968, *apptd* 1986

RT. REVD BISHOPS
*Province I*
*Connecticut,* Clarence Coleridge, *cons.* 1981, *apptd* 1994
*Maine,* Edward C. Chalfant, *cons.* 1984, *apptd* 1986
*Massachusetts,* David E. Johnson, *cons.* 1985, *apptd* 1986
*New Hampshire,* Douglas E. Theuner, *cons.* 1986, *apptd* 1986
*Rhode Island,* George E. Hunt, *cons.* 1980, *apptd* 1980
*Vermont,* Mary A. Mcleod, *cons.* 1993, *apptd* 1993
*Western Massachusetts,* Robert S. Denig, *cons.* 1993, *apptd* 1993

*Province II*
*Albany,* David S. Ball, *cons.* 1984, *apptd* 1984
*Central New York,* David B. Joslin, *cons.* 1991, *apptd* 1992
*Europe, Convocation of American Churches in,* Jeffery Rowthorn, *cons.* 1987
*\*Haiti,* Zaché Duracin, *cons.* 1993, *apptd* 1994
*Long Island,* Orris Walker, *cons.* 1988, *apptd* 1991
*New Jersey,* Mellick Belshaw, *cons.* 1975, *apptd* 1983
*New York,* Richard Grein, *cons.* 1981, *apptd* 1989
*Newark,* John S. Spong, *cons.* 1976, *apptd* 1979
*Rochester,* William G. Burrill, *cons.* 1984, *apptd* 1984
*\*Virgin Islands,* vacant
*Western New York,* David C. Bowman, *cons.* 1986, *apptd* 1987

*Province III*
*Bethlehem,* J. Mark Dyer, *cons.* 1982, *apptd* 1983
*Central Pennsylvania,* Charlie F. McNutt, *cons.* 1980, *apptd* 1982
*Delaware,* C. Cabell Tennis, *cons.* 1986, *apptd* 1986
*Easton,* Martin G. Townsend, *cons.* 1986, *apptd* 1986
*Maryland,* Charles Longest (*Bishop-in-charge*), *cons.* 1989
*North-Western Pennsylvania,* Robert D. Rowley jun., *cons.* 1989, *apptd* 1991
*Pennsylvania,* Allen L. Bartlett, *cons.* 1986, *apptd* 1987
*Pittsburgh,* Alden M. Hathaway, *cons.* 1981, *apptd* 1983
*Southern Virginia,* Frank Vest, *cons.* 1985, *apptd* 1991
*South-Western Virginia,* A. Heath Light, *cons.* 1979, *apptd* 1979
*Virginia,* Peter J. Lee, *cons.* 1984, *apptd* 1985
*Washington,* Ronald Haines, *cons.* 1986, *apptd* 1990
*West Virginia,* John H. Smith, *cons.* 1989, *apptd* 1989

*missionary diocese

## Province IV

*Alabama,* Robert O. Miller, *cons.* 1988, *apptd* 1988
*Atlanta,* Frank K. Allan, *cons.* 1988, *apptd* 1989
*Central Florida,* John Howe, *cons.* 1989, *apptd* 1990
*Central Gulf Coast,* Charles F. Duvall, *cons.* 1981, *apptd* 1981
*East Carolina,* B. Sidney Saunders, *cons.* 1979, *apptd* 1983
*East Tennessee,* Robert G. Tharp, *cons.* 1991, *apptd* 1992
*Florida,* Stephen Jecko, *cons.* 1994, *apptd* 1994
*Georgia,* Harry W. Shipps, *cons.* 1984, *apptd* 1985
*Kentucky,* Ted Gulick, *cons.* 1964
*Lexington,* Don A. Wimberley, *cons.* 1984, *apptd* 1985
*Louisiana,* James B. Brown, *cons.* 1976, *apptd* 1976
*Mississippi,* Alfred C. Marble jun., *cons.* 1991, *apptd* 1993
*North Carolina,* Robert Johnson, *cons.* 1994, *apptd* 1994
*South Carolina,* Edward Salmon jun., *cons.* 1990, *apptd* 1990
*South-East Florida,* Calvin O. Schofield jun., *cons.* 1979,
    *apptd* 1980
*South-West Florida,* Rogers Harris, *cons.* 1989, *apptd* 1989
*Tennessee,* Bertram N. Herlong, *cons.* 1993, *apptd* 1993
*Upper South Carolina,* William A. Beckham, *cons.* 1979,
    *apptd* 1979
*West Tennessee,* Alex D. Dickson jun., *cons.* 1983, *apptd* 1983
*Western North Carolina,* Robert Johnson, *cons* 1989, *apptd*
    1990

## Province V

*Chicago,* Frank T. Griswold III, *cons.* 1985, *apptd* 1987
*Eau Claire,* William C. Wantland, *cons.* 1980, *apptd* 1980
*Fond Du Lac,* Russell Jacobus, *cons.* 1994, *apptd* 1994
*Indianapolis,* Edward W. Jones, *cons.* 1977, *apptd* 1977
*Michigan,* R. Stewart Wood, *cons.* 1990, *apptd* 1990
*Milwaukee,* Roger J. White, *cons.* 1984, *apptd* 1985
*Missouri,* Hays Rockwell, *cons.* 1991, *apptd* 1993
*Northern Indiana,* Francis C. Gray, *cons.* 1986, *apptd* 1987
*Northern Michigan,* Thomas K. Ray, *cons.* 1982, *apptd* 1982
*Ohio,* J. Clark Grew, *cons.* 1994, *apptd* 1994
*Quincy,* Edward Macburney, *cons.* 1988, *apptd* 1988
*Southern Ohio,* Herbert Thompson jun., *cons.* 1988, *apptd*
    1992
*Springfield,* Peter H. Beckwith, *cons.* 1991
*Western Michigan,* Edward L. Lee jun., *cons.* 1989, *apptd*
    1989

## Province VI

*Colorado,* William Winterrowd, *cons.* 1991, *apptd* 1991
*Iowa,* C. Christopher Epting, *cons.* 1988, *apptd* 1988
*Minnesota,* James Jelinek, *cons.* 1993, *apptd* 1993
*Montana,* Charles I. Jones, *cons.* 1986, *apptd* 1986
*Nebraska,* James E. Krotz, *cons.* 1989, *apptd* 1989
*North Dakota,* Andrew H. Fairfield, *cons.* 1990, *apptd* 1990
*South Dakota,* Creighton Robertson, *cons.* 1994, *apptd* 1994
*Wyoming,* Bob G. Jones, *cons.* 1977, *apptd* 1977

## Province VII

*Arkansas,* Larry Maze, *cons.* 1994, *apptd* 1994
*Dallas,* James Stanton, *cons.* 1993, *apptd* 1993
*Fort Worth,* Clarence C. Pope jun., *cons.* 1985, *apptd* 1986
*Kansas,* William E. Smalley, *cons.* 1989, *apptd* 1989
*North-West Texas,* Sam B. Hulsey, *cons.* 1980, *apptd* 1980
*Oklahoma,* Robert M. Moodey, *cons.* 1988, *apptd* 1989
*Rio Grande,* Terence Kelshaw, *cons.* 1989, *apptd* 1989
*Texas,* Maurice M. Benitez, *cons.* 1980, *apptd* 1980
*West Missouri,* John C. Buchanan, *cons.* 1989, *apptd* 1989
*West Texas,* John H. MacNaughton, *cons.* 1986, *apptd* 1987
*Western Kansas,* John F. Ashby, *cons.* 1981, *apptd* 1981
*Western Louisiana,* Robert Hargrove, *cons.* 1989, *apptd* 1990

## Province VIII

*Alaska,* Stephen Charleston, *cons.* 1991, *apptd* 1991
*Arizona,* Robert R. Shahan, *cons.* 1992, *apptd* 1993
*California,* William E. Swing, *cons.* 1979, *apptd* 1980
*El Camino Real,* Richard L. Skimpfky, *cons.* 1990, *apptd*
    1990
*Eastern Oregon,* Rustin R. Kimsey, *cons.* 1980, *apptd* 1980
*Hawaii,* Donald P. Hart, *cons.* 1986, *apptd* 1986
*Idaho,* John Thornton, *cons.* 1990, *apptd* 1990
*Los Angeles,* Frederick L. Borsch, *cons.* 1988, *apptd* 1988
*Navajoland Area Mission,* Steven T. Plummer, *cons.* 1989,
    *apptd* 1989
*Nevada,* Stewart C. Zabriskie, *cons.* 1986, *apptd* 1986
*Northern California,* Jerry A. Lamb, *cons.* 1991, *apptd* 1992
*Olympia,* Vincent W. Warner, *cons.* 1989, *apptd* 1990
*Oregon,* Robert L. Ladehoff, *cons.* 1985, *apptd* 1986
*San Diego,* Gethin B. Hughes, *cons.* 1992, *apptd* 1992
*San Joaquin,* John-David Schofield, *cons.* 1988, *apptd* 1989
*Spokane,* Frank Terry, *cons.* 1990, *apptd* 1991
*Taiwan,* John C. T. Chien, *cons.* 1988, *apptd* 1988
*Utah,* George E. Bates, *cons.* 1986, *apptd* 1986

## Province IX

*Central Ecuador,* Neptali L. Moreno, *cons.* 1990, *apptd* 1990
*Colombia,* Bernardo Merino-Botero, *cons.* 1979, *apptd* 1979
*Cuernavaca,* Jose G. Saucedo, *cons.* 1958, *apptd* 1989
*Dominican Republic,* Julio C. Holguin, *apptd* 1991
*Guatemala,* Armando Guerra-Soria, *cons.* 1982, *apptd* 1982
*Honduras,* Leopold Frade, *cons.* 1984, *apptd* 1984
*Mexico,* Sergio Carranza-Gomez, *cons.* 1989, *apptd* 1989
*Nicaragua,* Sturdie W. Downs, *cons.* 1985, *apptd* 1985
*Northern Mexico,* German Martinez, *cons.* 1987, *apptd* 1987
*Panama,* James H. Ottley, *cons.* 1984, *apptd* 1984
*El Salvador,* Martin Barahona, *cons.* 1992, *apptd* 1992
*South-East Mexico,* Claro H. Rames, *cons.* 1980, *apptd* 1989
*Western Mexico,* Samuel Espinoza-Venegas, *cons.* 1981,
    *apptd* 1983

## Extra-Provincial

*Costa Rica,* Cornelius J. Wilson, *cons.* 1978, *apptd* 1978
*Puerto Rico,* David Alvarez, *cons.* 1987, *apptd* 1987
*Venezuela,* Onell A. Soto, *cons.* 1987, *apptd* 1987

## CHURCH OF THE PROVINCE OF WEST AFRICA

ARCHBISHOP OF PROVINCE, The Most Revd Robert
Okine (Bishop of Koforidua), *cons.* 1981, *apptd* 1993

THE RT. REVD BISHOPS
*Accra,* Francis Thompson, *cons.* 1983, *apptd* 1983
*Bo,* Samuel Gbonda, *cons.* 1994, *apptd* 1994
*Cape Coast,* Kobina Quashie, *apptd* 1992
*Freetown,* Prince Thompson, *cons.* 1981, *apptd* 1981
*Gambia,* Solomon Johnson, *cons.* 1990, *apptd* 1990
*Guinea,* vacant
*Koforidua, see above, apptd* 1981
*Kumasi,* Edmund Yeboah, *cons.* 1985, *apptd* 1985
*Liberia,* vacant
*Sekondi,* Theophilus Annobil, *cons.* 1981, *apptd* 1981
*Sunyani/Tamale,* Joseph Dadson, *cons.* 1981, *apptd* 1981

The Anglican Church of Cameroon is a missionary area of
the Province

---

*missionary diocese

# CHURCH IN THE PROVINCE OF THE WEST INDIES

ARCHBISHOP OF PROVINCE, The Most Revd Orland Lindsay (Bishop of North-Eastern Caribbean and Aruba), cons. 1970, apptd 1986

THE RT. REVD BISHOPS
*Barbados,* Drexel Gomez, CMG, cons. 1972, apptd 1972
*Belize,* Desmond Smith, cons. 1989, apptd 1989
*Guyana,* Randolph George, cons. 1976, apptd 1980
*Jamaica,* Neville de Souza, cons. 1973, apptd 1979
*Nassau and the Bahamas,* Michael Eldon, CMG, cons. 1971, apptd 1972
*North-Eastern Caribbean and Aruba, see above*
*Trinidad and Tobago,* Clive Abdulah, cons. 1970, apptd 1970
*Windward Islands,* Philip Elder, cons. 1966

# CHURCH OF THE PROVINCE OF ZAÏRE

ARCHBISHOP OF THE PROVINCE, The Most Revd Byanka Njojo (Bishop of Boga-Zaïre), cons. 1980, apptd 1992

THE RT. REVD BISHOPS
*Boga-Zaïre, see above, apptd* 1980
*Bukavu,* Balufuga Dirokpa, cons. 1982, apptd 1982
*Kisangani,* Sylvestre Mugera, cons. 1980, apptd 1980
*Nord Kivu,* Methusela Musubaho, cons. 1992, apptd 1992
*Shaba,* Emmanuel Mbona, cons. 1980, apptd 1980

# OTHER CHURCHES AND EXTRA-PROVINCIAL DIOCESES

ANGLICAN CHURCH OF BERMUDA, The Rt. Revd William Down, apptd 1990
EPISCOPAL CHURCH OF CUBA, The Rt. Revd Emilio H. Albalate
HONG KONG AND MACAO, The Rt. Revd Peter Kwong
KUCHING, The Rt. Revd Datuk John Leong Chee Yun
SABAH, The Rt. Revd Yong Ping Chung, apptd 1991
SINGAPORE, The Rt. Revd Moses Leng Kong Tay, apptd 1982
WEST MALAYSIA, The Rt. Revd Tan Sri John Savarimuthu, apptd 1973
LUSITANIAN CHURCH (*Portuguese Episcopal Church*), The Rt. Revd Fernando da Luz Soares, apptd 1971
SPANISH REFORMED CHURCH, The Rt. Revd Arturo Sánchez Galan, apptd 1982

# The Church of Scotland

The Church of Scotland is the established (i.e. state) church of Scotland. The Church is Reformed and evangelical in doctrine, and presbyterian in constitution. In 1560 the jurisdiction of the Roman Catholic Church in Scotland was abolished and the first assembly of the Church of Scotland ratified the Confession of Faith, drawn up by a committee including John Knox. In 1592 Parliament passed an Act guaranteeing the liberties of the Church and its presbyterian government. James VI (James I of England) and later Stuart monarchs attempted to restore episcopacy, but a presbyterian church was finally restored in 1690 and secured by the Act of Settlement (1690) and the Act of Union (1707). The Free Church of Scotland was formed in 1843 in a dispute over patronage and state interference; in 1900 most of its ministers joined with the United Presbyterian Church (formed in 1847) to form the United Free Church of Scotland. In 1929 most of this body rejoined the Church of Scotland to form the united Church of Scotland.

The Church of Scotland is presbyterian in its organization, i.e. based on a hierarchy of councils of ministers and elders and, since 1990, of members of a diaconate. At local level the kirk session consists of the parish minister and ruling elders. At district level the presbyteries, of which there are 47, consist of all the ministers in the district, one ruling elder from each congregation, and those members of the diaconate who qualify for membership. The General Assembly is the supreme authority, and is presided over by a Moderator chosen annually by the Assembly. The Sovereign, if not present in person, is represented by a Lord High Commissioner who is appointed each year by the Crown.

The Church of Scotland has about 753,000 members, 1,260 ministers and 1,700 churches. There are about 100 ministers and other personnel working overseas.

*Lord High Commissioner* (1994), Lady Fraser
*Moderator of the General Assembly* (1994), The Rt. Revd J. A. Simpson
*Principal Clerk,* The Very Revd J. L. Weatherhead, DD
*Deputy Clerk,* Revd F. A. J. MacDonald
*Procurator,* A. Dunlop, QC
*Law Agent and Solicitor of the Church,* R. A. Paterson
*Parliamentary Agent,* I. McCulloch (*London*)
*General Treasurer,* W. G. P. Colledge
CHURCH OFFICE, 121 George Street, Edinburgh EH2 4YN.
Tel: 0131-225 5722

PRESBYTERIES AND CLERKS
*Edinburgh,* Revd W. P. Graham
*West Lothian,* Revd D. Shaw
*Lothian,* J. D. McCulloch
*Melrose and Peebles,* Revd C. A. Duncan
*Duns,* Revd A. C. D. Cartwright
*Jedburgh,* Revd N. R. Combe
*Annandale and Eskdale,* Revd C. B. Haston
*Dumfries and Kirkcudbright,* Revd G. M. A. Savage
*Wigtown and Stranraer,* Revd D. Dutton
*Ayr,* Revd J. Crichton
*Irvine and Kilmarnock,* Revd C. G. F. Brockie
*Ardrossan,* Revd D. Broster
*Lanark,* Revd I. D. Cunningham
*Paisley,* Revd J. P. Cubie
*Greenock,* Revd D. Mill
*Glasgow,* Revd A. Cunningham
*Hamilton,* Revd J. H. Wilson
*Dumbarton,* Revd D. P. Munro
*South Argyll,* Revd R. H. McNidder
*Dunoon,* Revd R. Samuel
*Lorn and Mull,* Revd W. Hogg
*Falkirk,* Revd D. E. McClements
*Stirling,* Revd G. A. McCutcheon
*Dunfermline,* Revd W. E. Farquhar
*Kirkcaldy,* Revd B. L. Tomlinson
*St Andrews,* Revd J. W. Patterson
*Dunkeld and Meigle,* Revd A. F. Chisholm
*Perth,* Revd D. Main
*Dundee,* Revd J. A. Roy
*Angus,* Revd R. J. Ramsay

*Aberdeen*, Revd H. C. Sefton
*Kincardine and Deeside*, Revd J. W. S. Brown
*Gordon*, Revd I. U. Thomson
*Buchan*, Revd R. Neilson
*Moray*, Revd J. T. Stuart
*Abernethy*, Revd J. A. I. MacEwan
*Inverness*, Revd R. J. V. Logan
*Lochaber*, Revd A. Ramsay
*Ross*, Revd R. M. MacKinnon
*Sutherland*, Revd J. L. Goskirk
*Caithness*, Revd M. G. Mappin
*Lochcarron/Skye*, Revd A. I. Macarthur
*Uist*, Revd A. P. J. Varwell
*Lewis*, Revd T. S. Sinclair
*Orkney (Finstown)*, Revd T. Hunt
*Shetland (Lerwick)*, Revd M. Cheyne
*England (London)*, Revd W. A. Cairns
*Europe (Portugal)*, Revd R. Hill

# The Roman Catholic Church

The Roman Catholic Church is one world-wide Christian Church acknowledging as its head the Bishop of Rome, known as the Pope (Father). The Pope is held to be the successor of St Peter and thus invested with the power which was entrusted to St Peter by Jesus Christ. A direct line of succession is therefore claimed from the earliest Christian communities. Papal authority over the doctrine and jurisdiction of the Church in western Europe developed early and was unrivalled after the split with the Eastern Orthodox Church until the Protestant Reformation in the 16th century. With the fall of the Roman Empire the Pope also became an important political leader. His temporal power is now limited to the 107 acres of the Vatican City State.

The Pope exercises spiritual authority over the Church with the advice and assistance of the Sacred College of Cardinals, the supreme council of the Church. He is also advised about the concerns of the Church locally by his ambassadors, who liaise with the Bishops' Conference in each country.

In addition to advising the Pope, those members of the Sacred College of Cardinals who are under the age of 80 also elect a successor following the death of a Pope. The assembly of the Cardinals at the Vatican for the election of a new Pope is known as the Conclave in which, in complete seclusion, the Cardinals elect by a secret ballot; a two-thirds majority is necessary before the vote can be accepted as final. When a Cardinal receives the necessary votes, the Dean of the Sacred College formally asks him if he will accept election and the name by which he wishes to be known. On his acceptance of the office the Conclave is dissolved and the First Cardinal Deacon announces the election to the assembled crowd in St Peter's Square. On the first Sunday or Holyday following the election, the new Pope assumes the pontificate at High Mass in St Peter's Square. A new pontificate is dated from the assumption of the pontificate.

The number of cardinals was fixed at 70 by Pope Sixtus V in 1586, but has been steadily increased since the pontificate of John XXIII and now stands at 143 (as at end May 1994).

The Roman Catholic Church universally and the Vatican City State are run by the Curia, which is made up of the Secretariat of State, the Sacred Council for the Public Affairs of the Church, and various congregations, secretariats and tribunals assisted by commissions and offices. The congregations are permanent commissions for conducting the affairs

of the Church and are made up of cardinals, one of whom occupies the office of prefect. Below the Secretariat of State and the congregations are the secretariats and tribunals, all of which are headed by cardinals. (The Curial cardinals are analagous to ministers in charge of government departments.)

The Vatican State has its own diplomatic service, with representatives known as nuncios. Papal nuncios with full diplomatic recognition are given precedence over all other ambassadors to the country to which they are appointed; where precedence is not recognized the Papal representative is known as a pro-nuncio. Where the representation is only to the local churches and not to the government of a country, the Papal representative is known as an apostolic delegate. The Roman Catholic Church has an estimated 890.9 million adherents world-wide.

SOVEREIGN PONTIFF

His Holiness Pope John Paul II (Karol Wojtyla), *born* Wadowice, Poland, 18 May 1920; *ordained priest* 1946; *appointed Archbishop* of Krakow 1964; *created Cardinal* 1967; *assumed pontificate* 16 October 1978

SECRETARIAT OF STATE

*Secretary of State*, HE Cardinal Angelo Sodano
*First Section (General Affairs)*, Mgr G. Re (Archbishop of Vescovio)
*Second Section (Relations with other states)*, Mgr J. L. Tauran (Archbishop of Telepte)

BISHOPS' CONFERENCE

The Roman Catholic Church in England and Wales is governed by the Bishops' Conference, membership of which includes the Diocesan Bishops, the Apostolic Exarch of the Ukrainians, the Bishop of the Forces and the Auxiliary Bishops. The Conference is headed by the President (Cardinal Basil Hume, Archbishop of Westminster) and Vice-President (the Archbishop of Liverpool). There are five departments, each with an episcopal chairman: the Department for Christian Life and Worship (the Archbishop of Southwark), the Department for Mission and Unity (the Bishop of East Anglia), the Department for Catholic Education and Formation (the Bishop of Leeds), the Department for Christian Responsibility and Citizenship (the Bishop of Middlesbrough), and the Department for International Affairs (the Bishop of Salford).

The Bishops' Standing Committee, made up of all the Archbishops and the chairman of each of the above departments, has general responsibility for continuity and policy between the plenary sessions of the Conference. It prepares the Conference agenda and implements its decisions. It is serviced by a General Secretariat. There are also agencies and consultative bodies affiliated to the Conference.

The Bishops' Conference of Scotland has as its president Archbishop Winning of Glasgow and is the permanently constituted assembly of the Bishops of Scotland. To promote its work, the Conference establishes various agencies which have an advisory function in relation to the Conference. The more important of these agencies are called Commissions and each one has a Bishop President who, with the other members of the Commissions, are appointed by the Conference.

The Irish Episcopal Conference has as its acting president Archbishop Connell of Dublin. Its membership comprises all the Archbishops and Bishops of Ireland and it appoints various Commissions to assist it in its work. There are three types of Commissions: (a) those made up of lay and clerical members chosen for their skills and experience, and staffed by full-time expert secretariats; (b) Commissions whose members are selected from existing institutions and whose services are supplied on a part-time basis; and (c) Commissions of Bishops only.

The Roman Catholic Church in Britain and Ireland has an estimated 8,992,092 members, 11 archbishops, 67 bishops, 12,698 priests, and 8,588 churches and chapels open to the public.

Bishops' Conferences secretariats:

ENGLAND AND WALES, 39 Eccleston Square, London SW1V 1PD. Tel: 0171-630 8220. *General Secretary*, The Rt. Revd Philip Carroll

SCOTLAND, Candida Casa, 8 Corsehill Road, Ayr, Scotland KA7 2ST. Tel: 01292-256750. *General Secretary*, The Rt. Revd Maurice Taylor, Bishop of Galloway

IRELAND, Iona, 67 Newry Road, Dundalk, Co. Louth. *Executive Secretary*, Revd Gerard Clifford

---

## GREAT BRITAIN

---

APOSTOLIC NUNCIO TO THE UNITED KINGDOM OF GREAT BRITAIN AND NORTHERN IRELAND
The Most Revd Luigi Barbarito, 54 Parkside, London SW19 5NE. Tel: 0181-946 1410

## ENGLAND AND WALES

THE MOST REVD ARCHBISHOPS
*Westminster*, HE Cardinal Basil Hume, *cons.* 1976
  *Auxiliaries*, Victor Guazzelli, *cons.* 1970; Vincent Nichols, *cons.* 1992; James J. O'Brien, *cons.* 1977; Patrick O'Donoghue, *cons.* 1983
  *Clergy*, 832
  *Archbishop's Residence*, Archbishop's House, Ambrosden Avenue, London SW1P 1QJ. Tel: 0171-834 4717
*Birmingham*, Maurice Couve de Murville, *cons.* 1982, *apptd* 1982
  *Auxiliaries*, Terence Brain, *cons.* 1991; Philip Pargeter, *cons.* 1989
  *Clergy*, 496
  *Diocesan Curia*, Cathedral House, St Chad's Queensway, Birmingham B4 6EX. Tel: 0121-236 5535
*Cardiff*, John A. Ward, *cons.* 1981, *apptd* 1983
  *Clergy*, 144
  *Diocesan Curia*, Archbishop's House, 41–43 Cathedral Road, Cardiff CF1 9HD. Tel: 01222-220411
*Liverpool*, Derek Worlock, *cons.* 1965, *apptd* 1976
  *Auxiliaries*, John Rawsthorne, *cons.* 1981; Vincent Malone, *cons.* 1989
  *Clergy*, 558
  *Diocesan Curia*, 152 Brownlow Hill, Liverpool L3 5RQ. Tel: 0151-709 4801
*Southwark*, Michael Bowen, *cons.* 1970, *apptd* 1977
  *Auxiliaries*, Charles Henderson, *cons.* 1972; Howard Tripp, *cons.* 1980; John Jukes, *cons.* 1980
  *Clergy*, 555
  *Diocesan Curia*, Archbishop's House, 150 St George's Road, London SE1 6HX. Tel: 0171-928 5592

THE RT. REVD BISHOPS
*Arundel and Brighton*, Cormac Murphy-O'Connor, *cons.* 1977. *Clergy*, 329. *Diocesan Curia*, Bishop's House, The Upper Drive, Hove, E. Sussex BN3 6NE. Tel: 01273-506387
*Brentwood*, Thomas McMahon, *cons.* 1980, *apptd* 1980. *Clergy*, 188. *Bishop's Office*, Cathedral House, Ingrave Road, Brentwood, Essex CM15 8AT. Tel: 01277-232266

*Clifton*, Mervyn Alexander, *cons.* 1972, *apptd* 1975. *Clergy*, 258. *Diocesan Curia*, Egerton Road, Bishopston, Bristol BS7 8HU. Tel: 0117-924 1378
*East Anglia*, Alan Clark, *cons.* 1969, *apptd* 1976. *Clergy*, 131. *Diocesan Curia*, The White House, 21 Upgate, Poringland, Norwich NR14 7SH. Tel: 01508-492202
*Hallam*, Gerald Moverley, *cons.* 1968, *apptd* 1980. *Clergy*, 103. *Bishop's Residence*, 'Quarters', Carsick Hill Way, Sheffield S10 3LT. Tel: 0114-230 9101
*Hexham and Newcastle*, Michael Ambrose Griffiths, *cons.* 1992. *Clergy*, 292. *Diocesan Curia*, Bishop's House, East Denton Hall, 800 West Road, Newcastle upon Tyne NE5 2BJ. Tel: 0191-228 0003
  *Auxiliary*, Owen Swindelhurst, *cons.* 1977
*Lancaster*, John Brewer, *cons.* 1971, *apptd* 1985. *Clergy*, 250. *Bishop's Residence*, Bishop's House, Cannon Hill, Lancaster LA1 5NG. Tel: 01524-32231
*Leeds*, David Konstant, *cons.* 1977, *apptd* 1985. *Clergy*, 249. *Diocesan Curia*, 7 St Marks Avenue, Leeds LS2 9BN. Tel: 0113-244 4788
*Menevia (Wales)*, Daniel Mullins, *cons.* 1970, *apptd* 1987. *Clergy*, 62. *Diocesan Curia*, 115 Walter Road, Swansea SA1 5RE. Tel: 01792-644017
*Middlesbrough*, John Crowley, *cons.* 1986, *apptd* 1992. *Clergy*, 197. *Diocesan Curia*, 50A The Avenue, Linthorpe, Middlesbrough, Cleveland TS5 6QT. Tel: 01642-850505
  *Auxiliary*, Thomas O'Brien, *cons.* 1981
*Northampton*, Patrick Leo McCartie, *cons.* 1977. *Clergy*, 160. *Diocesan Curia*, Bishop's House, Marriott Street, Northampton NN2 6AW. Tel: 01604-715635
*Nottingham*, James McGuinness, *cons.* 1972, *apptd* 1975. *Clergy*, 226. *Diocesan Curia*, Willson House, Derby Road, Nottingham NG1 5AW. Tel: 0115-947 2972
*Plymouth*, Christopher Budd, *cons.* 1986. *Clergy*, 160. *Diocesan Curia*, Vescourt, Hartley Road, Plymouth PL3 5LR. Tel: 01752-772950
*Portsmouth*, F. Crispian Hollis, *cons.* 1987, *apptd* 1989. *Clergy*, 273. *Bishop's Residence*, Bishop's House, Edinburgh Road, Portsmouth, Hants. PO1 3HG. Tel: 01705-820894
*Salford*, Patrick Kelly, *cons.* 1984. *Clergy*, 407. *Diocesan Curia*, Cathedral House, 250 Chapel Street, Salford M3 5LL. Tel: 0161-834 9052
*Shrewsbury*, Joseph Gray, *cons.* 1969, *apptd* 1980. *Clergy*, 220. *Diocesan Curia*, 2 Park Road South, Birkenhead, Merseyside L43 4UX. Tel: 0151-652 9855
*Wrexham (Wales)*, vacant. *Clergy*, 95. *Diocesan Curia*, Bishop's House, Sontley Road, Wrexham, Clwyd LL13 7EW. Tel: 01978-262726

## SCOTLAND

THE MOST REVD ARCHBISHOPS
*St Andrews and Edinburgh*, Keith Patrick O'Brian, *cons.* 1985
  *Auxiliary*, Kevin Rafferty, *cons.* 1990
  *Clergy*, 213
  *Diocesan Curia*, 106 Whitehouse Loan, Edinburgh EH9 1BD. Tel: 0131-452 8244
*Glasgow*, Thomas Winning, *cons.* 1971, *apptd* 1974
  *Clergy*, 338
  *Diocesan Curia*, 196 Clyde Street, Glasgow G1 4JY. Tel: 0141-226 5898

THE RT. REVD BISHOPS
*Aberdeen*, Mario Conti, *cons.* 1977. *Clergy*, 59. *Bishop's Residence*, 156 King's Gate, Aberdeen AB2 6BR. Tel: 01224-319154

*Argyll and the Isles*, Roderick Wright, *cons.* 1990. *Clergy*, 35.
   *Diocesan Curia*, St Mary's, Belford Road, Fort William,
   Inverness-shire PH33 6BT. Tel: 01397-706046
*Dunkeld*, Vincent Logan, *cons.* 1981. *Clergy*, 67. *Diocesan
   Curia*, 26 Roseangle, Dundee DD1 4LR. Tel: 01382-25453
*Galloway*, Maurice Taylor, *cons.* 1981. *Clergy*, 75. *Diocesan
   Curia*, 8 Corsehill Road, Ayr KA7 2ST. Tel: 01292-266750
*Motherwell*, Joseph Devine, *cons.* 1977, *apptd* 1983.
   *Clergy*, 190. *Diocesan Curia*, Coursington Road,
   Motherwell ML1 1PW. Tel: 01698-269114
*Paisley*, John A. Mone, *cons.* 1984, *apptd* 1988. *Clergy*, 98.
   *Diocesan Curia*, Cathedral House, 8 East Buchanan
   Street, Paisley, Renfrewshire PA1 1HS. Tel: 0141-889 3601

---

## IRELAND

---

There is one hierarchy for the whole of Ireland. Several of
the dioceses have territory partly in the Republic of Ireland
and partly in Northern Ireland.

APOSTOLIC NUNCIO TO IRELAND
   The Most Revd Emanuele Gerada (titular Archbishop of
   Nomenta), 183 Navan Road, Dublin 7. Tel: 00 353 1-
   380577

THE MOST REVD ARCHBISHOPS
*Armagh*, HE Cardinal Cahal B. Daly, *cons.* 1990
   *Auxiliary*, Gerard Clifford, *cons.* 1991
   *Clergy*, 271
   *Diocesan Curia*, Ara Coeli, Armagh BT61 7QY. Tel: 01861-
   522045
*Cashel*, Dermot Clifford, *cons.* 1986
   *Clergy*, 122
   *Archbishop's Residence*, Archbishop's House, Thurles, Co.
   Tipperary. Tel: 00 353 504-21512
*Dublin*, Desmond Connell, *cons.* 1988, *apptd* 1988
   *Auxiliaries*, Donal Murray, *cons.* 1982; Dermot
   O'Mahony, *cons.* 1975; James Moriarty, *cons.* 1992;
   Eamonn Walsh, *cons.* 1990; Desmond Williams, *cons.*
   1985
   *Clergy*, 994
   *Archbishop's Residence*, Archbishop's House,
   Drumcondra, Dublin 9. Tel: 00 353 1-8373732
*Tuam*, vacant
   *Auxiliary*, Michael Neary, *cons.* 1992
   *Clergy*, 165
   *Archbishop's Residence*, Archbishop's House, Tuam, Co.
   Galway. Tel: 00 353 93-24166

THE MOST REVD BISHOPS
*Achonry*, Thomas Flynn, *cons.* 1975. *Clergy*, 55. *Bishop's
   Residence*, Bishop's House, Ballaghadaderreen, Co.
   Roscommon. Tel: 00 353 907-60021
*Ardagh and Clonmacnois*, Colm O'Reilly, *cons.* 1983.
   *Clergy*, 108. *Diocesan Office*, Bishop's House, St
   Michael's, Longford, Co. Longford. Tel: 00 353 43-
   46432
*Clogher*, Joseph Duffy, *cons.* 1979. *Clergy*, 124. *Bishop's
   Residence*, Bishop's House, Monaghan. Tel: 00 353 47-
   81019
*Clonfert*, Joseph Kirby, *cons.* 1988. *Clergy*, 76. *Bishop's
   Residence*, St Brendan's, Coorheen, Loughrea, Co.
   Galway. Tel: 00 353 91-41560
*Cloyne*, John Magee, *cons.* 1987. *Clergy*, 155. *Diocesan
   Centre*, Cobh, Co. Cork. Tel: 00 353 21-811430
*Cork and Ross*, Michael Murphy, *cons.* 1976. *Clergy*, 360.
   *Diocesan Office*, Bishop's House, Redemption Road,
   Cork. Tel: 00 353 21-301717
   *Auxiliary*, John Buckley, *cons.* 1984

*Derry*, vacant. *Clergy*, 149. *Bishop's Residence*, Bishop's
   House, St Eugene's Cathedral, Derry BT48 9AP. Tel:
   01504-262302
   *Auxiliary*, Francis Lagan, *cons.* 1988
*Down and Connor*, Patrick J. Walsh, *cons.* 1991. *Clergy*, 324.
   *Bishop's Residence*, Lisbreen, 73 Somerton Road, Belfast,
   Co. Antrim DT15 4DE. Tel: 01232-776185
   *Auxiliaries*, Anthony Farquhar, *cons.* 1983; William
   Philbin, *cons.* 1991
*Dromore*, Francis Brooks, *cons.* 1976. *Clergy*, 71. *Bishop's
   Residence*, Bishop's House, Violet Hill, Newry, Co. Down
   BT35 6PN. Tel: 01693-62444
*Elphin*, Dominic Conway, *cons.* 1970. *Clergy*, 104. *Bishop's
   Residence*, St Mary's, Sligo. Tel: 00 353 71-62670
*Ferns*, Brendon Comiskey, *cons.* 1980. *Clergy*, 148. *Bishop's
   Office*, Bishop's House, Summerhill, Wexford. Tel:
   00 353 53-22177
*Galway and Kilmacduagh*, James McLoughlin, *cons.* 1993.
   *Diocesan Office*, The Cathedral, Galway. Tel: 00 353 91-
   63566
*Kerry*, vacant. *Clergy*, 143. *Bishop's Residence*, Bishop's
   House, Killarney, Co. Kerry. Tel: 00 353 64-31168
*Kildare and Leighlin*, Laurence Ryan, *cons.* 1984.
   *Clergy*, 225. *Bishop's Residence*, Bishop's House, Carlow.
   Tel: 00 353 503-31102
*Killala*, Thomas Finnegan, *cons.* 1970. *Clergy*, 51. *Bishop's
   Residence*, Bishop's House, Ballina, Co. Mayo. Tel:
   00 353 96-21518
*Killaloe*, vacant. *Clergy*, 186. *Bishop's Residence*,
   Westbourne, Ennis, Co. Clare. Tel: 00 353 65-28638
*Kilmore*, Francis McKiernan, *cons.* 1972. *Clergy*, 103.
   *Bishop's Residence*, Bishop's House, Cullies, Co. Cavan.
   Tel: 00 353 49-31496
*Limerick*, Jeremiah Newman, *cons.* 1974. *Clergy*, 234.
   *Diocesan Offices*, 66 O'Connell Street, Limerick. Tel:
   00 353 61-315856
*Meath*, Michael Smith, *cons.* 1984, *apptd* 1990. *Clergy*, 270.
   *Bishop's Residence*, Bishop's House, Dublin Road,
   Mullingar, Co. Westmeath. Tel: 00 353 44-48841
*Ossory*, Laurence Forristal, *cons.* 1980. *Clergy*, 125. *Bishop's
   Residence*, Sion House, Kilkenny. Tel: 00 353 56-62448
*Raphoe*, Seamus Hegarty, *cons.* 1984. *Clergy*, 102. *Bishop's
   Residence*, Ard Adhamhnáin, Letterkenny, Co. Donegal.
   Tel: 00 353 74-21208
*Waterford and Lismore*, William Lee, *cons.* 1993. *Clergy*,
   206. *Bishop's Residence*, Woodleigh, Summerville
   Avenue, Waterford. Tel: 00 353 51-71432

---

## RESIDENTIAL ARCHBISHOPRICS THROUGHOUT THE WORLD

ALBANIA
*Durrës-Tirana*, Brok K. Mirdita
*Shkodër*, Frano Illia

ALGERIA
*Algiers*, Henri Teissier

ANGOLA
*Huambo*, Francisco Viti
*Luanda*, HE Cardinal Alexandre do Nascimento
*Lubango*, Manuel Franklin da Costa

ARGENTINA
*Bahia Blanca*, Romulo Garcia
*Buenos Aires*, HE Cardinal Antonio Quarracino

*Córdoba*, HE Cardinal Raúl Francisco Primatesta
*Corrientes*, vacant
*La Plata*, Carlos Galán
*Mendoza*, Candido Genaro Rubiolo
  *Coadjutor*, Jose M. Arancibia
*Paraná*, Estanislao Esteban Karlic
*Resistencia*, Carmelo J. Giaquinta
*Rosario*, Eduardo Vicente Miras
*Salta*, Moises J. Blanchoud
*San Juan de Cuyo*, Italo Severino Di Stefano
*Santa Fe*, Edgardo Gabriel Storni
*Tucumán*, vacant

AUSTRALIA
*Adelaide*, Leonard Anthony Faulkner
*Brisbane*, John A. Bathersby
*Canberra*, Francis P. Carroll
*Hobart*, Joseph E. D'Arcy
*Melbourne*, Thomas Francis Little
*Perth*, Barry J. Hickey
*Sydney*, HE Cardinal Edward B. Clancy

AUSTRIA
*Salzburg*, Georg Eder
*Vienna*, HE Cardinal Hans Hermann Groer

BANGLADESH
*Dhaka*, Michael Rozario

BELARUS
*Minsk-Mohilev Archdiocese*, Kazimierz Swiatek

BELGIUM
*Malines-Bruxelles*, HE Cardinal Godfried Danneels

BENIN
*Cotonou*, Isidore de Souzá

BOLIVIA
*Cochabamba*, Rene Fernandez Apaza
*La Paz*, Luis Sainz Hinojosa
*Santa Cruz de la Sierra*, Julio T. Sandoval
*Sucre*, Jesus G. Pérez Rodriguez

BOSNIA HERCEGOVINA
*Vrhbosna, Sarajevo*, Vinko Puljić

BRAZIL
*Aparacida*, Geraldo Maria de Morais Penido
*Aracaju*, Luciano José Cabral Duarte
*Bélem do Pará*, Vicente Joaquim Zico
*Belo Horizonte*, Serafim Fernandes de Araújo
*Botucatu*, Antonio M. Mucciolo
*Brasilia*, HE Cardinal Jose Freire Falcao
*Campinas*, Gilberto Pereira Lopes
*Campo Grande*, Vitorio Pavanello
*Cascavel*, Armando Cirio
*Cuiaba*, Bonifacio Piccinini
*Curitiba*, Pedro Antonio Fedalto
*Diamantina*, Geraldo Majelo Reis
*Florianópolis*, Eusebio Oscar Scheid
*Fortaleza*, HE Cardinal Aloisio Lorscheider
*Goiania*, Antonio Ribeiro de Oliveira
*Juiz de Fora*, Clovis Frainer
*Londrina*, Albano Bortoletto Cavallin
*Maceió*, Edvaldo G. Amaral
*Manaus*, Luiz S. Vieira
*Mariana*, Luciano Mendes de Almeida
*Maringá*, Jaime Luis Coelho
*Natal*, Heitor de Araujo Sales
*Niteroi*, Carlos A. Navarro
*Olinda and Recife*, José Cardoso Sobrinho
*Paraiba*, José M. Pires

*Porto Alegre*, Altamiro Rossato
*Porto Velho*, José Martins da Silva
*Pouso Alegre*, João Bergese
*Ribeirão Preto*, Arnaldo Ribeiro
*São Luis do Maranhão*, Paulo Eduardo de Andrade Ponte
*São Paulo*, HE Cardinal Paulo Evaristo Arns
*São Salvador da Bahia*, HE Cardinal Lucas Moreira Neves
*São Sebastião do Rio de Janeiro*, HE Cardinal Eugenio de Araújo Sales
*Sorocaba*, José Lambert
*Teresina*, Miguel F. Camara Filho
*Uberaba*, Benedito de Ulhôa Vieira
*Vitória*, Silvestre L. Scandian

BURKINA
*Ouagadougou*, HE Cardinal Paul Zoungrana

BURUNDI
*Gitega*, Joachim Ruhuna

CAMEROON
*Bamenda*, Paul Verdzekov
*Douala*, HE Cardinal Christian W. Tumi
*Garoua*, Antoine Ntalou
*Yaoundé*, Jean Zoa

CANADA
*Edmonton*, Joseph N. MacNeil
*Gatineau-Hull*, Roger Ebacher
*Grouard-McLennon*, Henri Légaré
*Halifax*, Austin-Emile Burke
*Keewatin-Le Pas*, Peter Alfred Sutton
*Kingston*, Francis John Spence
*Moncton*, Donat Chiasson
*Montreal*, Jean-Claude Turcotte
*Ottawa*, Marcel A. Gervais
*Quebec*, Maurice Couture
*Regina*, vacant
*Rimouski*, Bertrand Blanchet
*St Boniface*, Antoine Hacault
*St Johns, Newfoundland*, James H. MacDonald
*Sherbrooke*, Jean Marie Fortier
*Toronto*, Aloysius Matthew Ambrosic
*Vancouver*, Adam J. Exner
*Winnipeg*, Leonard J. Wall; (Ukrainian Rite), Michael Bzdel

CAUCASIA
*Caucasia Apostolic Administrator*, Jean-Paul Gobel

CENTRAL AFRICAN REPUBLIC
*Bangui*, Joachim N'Dayen

CHAD
*Ndjamena*, Charles Vandame

CHILE
*Antofagasta*, Patricio Infante Alfonso
*Concepción*, Antonio M. Casamitjana
*La Serena*, Francisco J. Cox Huneeus
*Puerto Montt*, Savino B. Cazzaro Bertollo
*Santiago de Chile*, Carlos Oviedo Cavada

CHINA
*Anking, Huai-Ning*, vacant
*Canton*, Dominic Tang Yee-Ming
*Changsha*, vacant
*Chungking*, vacant
*Foochow, Min-Hou*, vacant
*Hangchow*, vacant
*Hankow*, vacant
*Kaifeng*, vacant
*Kunming*, vacant
*Kweyang*, vacant

*Lanchow*, vacant
*Mukden*, vacant
*Nanchang*, vacant
*Nanking*, vacant
*Nanning*, vacant
*Peking (Beijing)*, vacant
*Sian*, vacant
*Suiyüan*, Francis Wang Hsueh-Ming
*Taiyuan*, vacant
*Tsinan*, vacant

COLOMBIA
*Barranquilla*, Felix Maria Torres Parra
*Bogotá*, HE Cardinal Mario Revollo Bravo
*Bucaramanga*, Dario Castrillon Hoyos
*Cali*, Pedro Rubiano Sáenz
*Cartagena*, Carlos José Ruiseco Vieira
*Ibague*, Juan S. Jaramillo
*Manizales*, José de Jesús Pimiento Rodriguez
*Medellin*, Hector Rueda Hernández
*Nueva Pamplona*, Rafael Sarmiento Peralta
*Popayán*, Alberto G. Jaramillo
*Santa Fe de Antioquia*, Ignacio Gomez Afistizabal
*Tunja*, Augusto Trujillo Arango

CONGO
*Brazzaville*, Barthélémy Batantu

COSTA RICA
*San José*, Román Arrieta Villalobos

CÔTE D'IVOIRE
*Abidjan*, HE Cardinal Bernard Yago

CROATIA
*Rijeka-Senj*, Anton Tamarut
*Split-Makarska*, Ante Juric
*Zadar*, Marijan Oblak
*Zagreb*, HE Cardinal Franjo Kuharić

CUBA
*San Cristóbal de la Habana*, Jaime Lucas Ortega y Alamino
*Santiago de Cuba*, Pedro Meurice Estiu

CYPRUS
*Cyprus* (Maronite Seat at Nicosia), Boutros Gemayel

CZECH REPUBLIC
*Olomouc*, Jan Graubner
*Praha*, Miloslav Vlk

DOMINICAN REPUBLIC
*Santiago de los Caballeros*, Juan A. F. Santana
*Santo Domingo*, HE Cardinal Nicolás de Jesús López Rodriguez

ECUADOR
*Cuenca*, Alberto Luna Tobar
*Guayaquil*, Ignacio Larrea Holguin
*Quito*, Antonio J. González Zumárraga

EQUATORIAL GUINEA
*Malabo*, Idlefonso Obama Obono

ETHIOPIA
*Addis Ababa*, HE Cardinal Paul Tzadua

FRANCE
*Aix*, Bernard Panafieu
*Albi*, Roger Meindre
*Auch*, Gabriel Vanel
*Avignon*, Raymond Bouchex
*Besançon*, Lucien Daloz
*Bordeaux*, Pierre Eyt
*Bourges*, Pierre Plateau

*Cambrai*, Jacques Delaporte
*Chambéry*, Claude Feidt
*Lyon*, vacant
*Marseilles*, HE Cardinal Robert Coffy
*Paris*, HE Cardinal J. M. Lustiger
*Reims*, Jean Balland
*Rennes*, Jacques Jullien
*Rouen*, Joseph Duval
*Sens*, Gérard Defois
*Strasbourg*, Charles Amarin Brand
*Toulouse*, André Collini
*Tours*, Jean Honoré

FRENCH POLYNESIA
*Papeete*, Michel Coppenrath

GABON
*Libreville*, André Fernand Anguilé

GERMANY
*Bamberg*, Elmar Maria Kredel
*Berlin*, George M. Sterzinsky
*Cologne*, HE Cardinal Joachim Meisner
*Freiburg im Breisgau*, Oskar Saier
*Munich and Freising*, HE Cardinal Friedrich Wetter
*Paderborn*, Johannes Joachim Degenhardt

GHANA
*Accra*, Dominic K. Andoh
*Cape Coast*, Peter Kodwo A. Turkson
*Tamale*, Peter Poreiku Dery

GREECE
*Athens*, Nicholaos Foscolos
*Corfu*, Antonio Varthalitis
*Naxos*, Nicolaos Printesis
*Rhodes*, vacant (Apostolic Administrator, Nicholaos Foscolos)

GUATEMALA
*Guatemala*, Prospero Penados del Barrio

GUINEA
*Conakry*, Robert Sarah

HAITI
*Cap-Haitien*, François Gayot
*Port au Prince*, François-Wolff Ligondé

HONDURAS
*Tegucigalpa*, Oscar A. Maradiaga

HONG KONG
*Hong Kong*, HE Cardinal J. B. Wu Cheng Chung

HUNGARY
*Eger*, Istvan Seregely
*Esztergom*, HE Cardinal Laslo Paskai
*Kalocsa*, Laszlo Danko

INDIA
*Agra*, Cecil de Sa
*Bangalore*, Alphonsus Mathias
*Bhopal*, Eugene D' Souza
*Bombay*, HE Cardinal I. Pimenta
*Calcutta*, Henry Sebastian D'Souza
*Changanacherry*, Joseph Powathil
*Cuttack-Bhubaneswar*, Raphael Cheenath
*Delhi*, Alan de Lastic
*Ernakulam*, HE Cardinal Anthony Padiyara
*Goa and Daman*, Raul Nicolau Gonsalves
*Hyderabad*, Saminini Arulappa
*Madras and Mylapore*, vacant
*Madurai*, Marianus Arokiasamy
*Nagpur*, Leobard D'Souza
*Pondicherry and Cuddalore*, Michael Augustine

*Ranchi*, Telesphore P. Toppo
*Shillong-Gauhati*, Hubert D'Rosario
*Trivandrum* (Syrian Melekite Rite), Benedict Varghese
　Gregorios Thangalathil
*Verapoly*, Cornelius Elanjikal

INDONESIA
*Ende*, Donatus Djagom
*Jakarta*, Leo Soekoto
*Kupang*, Gregorius Manteiro
*Medan*, Alfred Gonti Pius Datubara
*Merauke*, Jacobus Duivenvoorde
*Pontianak*, Hieronymus Herculanus Bumbun
*Semarang*, Julius R. Darmaatmadja
*Ujung Pandang*, R. P. Francis van Roessel

IRAN
*Ahváz*, Hanna Zora
*Tehran*, Youhannan Semaan Issayi
*Urmyá*, Thomas Meram

IRAQ
*Arbil*, Stephane Babaca
*Baghdad* (Latin Rite), Paul Dahdah; (Syrian Rite), Athanase
　M. S. Matoka; (Armenian Rite), Paul Coussa
*Basra*, Yousif Thomas
*Kirkuk*, André Sana
*Mosul*, Georges Garmo

ISRAEL (*see also* Patriarchs, page 432)
*Akka* (Greek Melekite Catholic Rite), Maximos Salloum

ITALY
*Acerenza*, Michele Scandiffio
*Amalfi*, Beniamino De Palma
*Ancona*, Franco Festorazzi
*Bari*, Mariano Magrassi
*Benevento*, Serafino Sprovieri
*Bologna*, HE Cardinal Giacomo Biffi
*Brindisi*, Settimio Todisco
*Cagliari*, Otterino Pietro Alberti
*Camerino*, Piergiorgio Nesti
*Campobasso-Boiano*, Ettore Di Filippo
*Capua*, Luigi Diligenza
*Catania*, Luigi Bommarito
*Catanzaro*, Antonio Cantisani
*Chieti*, vacant
*Conza*, Mario Milano
*Cosenza*, Dino Trabalzini
*Crotone-Santa Severina*, Giuseppe Agostino
*Fermo*, Cleto Bellucci
*Ferrara*, Luigi Maverna
*Florence*, HE Cardinal Silvano Piovanelli
*Foggia*, Giuseppe Casale
*Gaeta*, Vincenzo Farano
*Genoa*, HE Cardinal Giovanni Canestri
*Gorizia and Gradisca*, Antonio Vitale Bommarco
*Lanciano*, Enzio d'Antonio
*L'Aquila*, Mario Peressin
*Lecce*, Cosmo F. Ruppi
*Lucca*, Bruno Tommasi
*Manfredonia*, Vincenzo D'Addario
*Matera*, Antonio Ciliberti
*Messina*, Ignazio Cannavó
*Milan*, HE Cardinal Carlo Maria Martini
*Modena*, Santo B. Quadri
*Monreale*, Salvatore Cassisa
*Naples*, HE Cardinal Michele Giordano
*Oristano*, Pier Luigi Tiddia
*Otranto*, Francesco Cacucci
*Palermo*, HE Cardinal Salvatore Pappalardo

*Perugia*, Ennio Antonelli
*Pescara-Penne*, Francesco Cuccarese
*Pisa*, Alessandro Plotti
*Potenza*, Ennio Appignanesi
*Ravenna*, Luigi Amaducci
*Reggio Calabria*, Vittorio L. Mondello
*Rossano-Cariati*, Andrea Cassone
*Salerno*, Gerardo Pierro
*Sassari*, Salvatore Isgrò
*Siena*, Gaetano Bonicelli
*Siracusa*, Giuseppe Costanzo
*Sorrento*, Felice Cece
*Spoleto*, Antonio Ambrosanio
*Taranto*, Luigi Papa
*Trani and Barletta*, Carmelo Cassati
*Trento*, Giovanni Sartori
*Turin*, HE Cardinal Giovanni Saldarini
*Udine*, Alfredo Battisti
*Urbino*, Donato U. Bianchi
*Vercelli*, Tarcisio Bertone

JAMAICA
*Kingston*, Samuel Emmanuel Carter

JAPAN
*Nagasaki*, Francis Xavier Shimamoto
*Osaka*, Paul Hisao Yasuda
*Tokyo*, Peter Seiichi Shirayanagi

JORDAN
*Petra and Filadelfia* (Greek Melekite Catholic Rite), George
　El-Murr

KAZAKHSTAN
*Karaganda Apostolic Administration* (Latin Rite), Apostolic
　Administrator, Mgr Jan Lenga (titular Bishop of Arba)

KENYA
*Kisumu*, Zaccharus Okoth
*Mombasa*, John Njenga
*Nairobi*, HE Cardinal Maurice Otunga
*Nyeri*, Nicodemus Kirima

KOREA
*Kwangju*, Victorinus Kong-Hi Youn
*Seoul*, HE Cardinal Stephen Sou Hwan Kim
*Taegu*, Paul Moun-Hi Ri

LATVIA
*Riga*, Jánis Pujats

LEBANON
*Antelias* (Maronite Rite), Joseph Mohsen Bechara
*Baalbek, Eliopoli* (Greek Melekite Catholic Rite), Salim
　Bustros
*Baniyas* (Greek Melekite Catholic Rite), Antoine Hayek
*Beirut* (Greek Melekite Catholic Rite), Habib Bacha;
　(Maronite Rite), Khalil Abinader
*Saïda* (Greek Melekite Catholic Rite), Georges Kwaiter
*Tripoli* (Maronite Rite), Gabriel Toubia; (Greek Melekite
　Catholic Rite), Elias Nijmé
*Tyre* (Greek Melekite Catholic Rite), Jean A. Haddad;
　(Maronite Rite), Maroun Sader
*Zahle and Furzol* (Greek Melekite Catholic Rite), Andre
　Haddad

LESOTHO
*Maseru*, Bernard Mohlalisi

LIBERIA
*Monrovia*, Michael Kpakala Francis

LITHUANIA
*Kaunas*, HE Cardinal Vincentas Sladkevicius
*Vilnius*, Audris J. Bačkis

LUXEMBOURG
*Luxembourg*, Fernand Franck

MADAGASCAR
*Antananarive*, vacant
*Antsiranana*, Albert Joseph Tsiahoana
*Fianarantsoa*, Philibert Randriambololona

MALAWI
*Blantyre*, James Chiona

MALAYSIA
*Kuala Lumpur*, Anthony S. Fernandez
*Kuching*, Peter Chung Hoan Ting

MALI
*Bamako*, Luc Auguste Sangaré

MALTA
*Malta*, Joseph Mercieca

MARTINIQUE
*Fort de France*, Maurice Marie-Sainte

MEXICO
*Acapulco*, Rafael Bello Ruiz
*Antequera*, Hector G. Martìnez
*Chihuahua*, José Fernández Arteaga
*Durango*, José M. Perez
*Guadalajara*, Juan Sandoval Iniguez
*Hermosillo*, Carlos Quintero Arce
*Jalapa*, Sergio Obeso Rivera
*Mexico City*, HE Cardinal Ernesto Corripio Ahumada
*Monterrey*, Adolfo Suarez Rivera
*Morelia*, Estanislao Alcarez Figueroa
*Puebla de los Angeles*, Rosendo Huesca Pacheco
*San Luis Potosi*, Arturo A. Szymanski Ramirez
*Tlalnepantla*, Manuel P. Gil Gonzalez
*Yucatán*, Manuel Castro Ruiz

MONACO
*Monaco*, Joseph-Marie Sardou

MOROCCO
*Rabat*, Hubert Michon
*Tangier*, Antonio J. Peteiro Freire

MOZAMBIQUE
*Beira*, Jaime P. Goncalves
*Maputo*, HE Cardinal Alexandre José Maria dos Santos
*Nampula*, Manuel Vieira Pinto

MYANMAR (BURMA)
*Mandalay*, Alphonse U. Than Aung
*Yangon (Rangoon)*, Gabriel Thohey Mahn Gaby

NAMIBIA
*Windhoek*, Bonifatius Haushiku

NETHERLANDS
*Utrecht*, HE Cardinal Adrianus J. Simonis

NEW ZEALAND
*Wellington*, HE Cardinal Thomas Stafford Williams

NICARAGUA
*Managua*, HE Cardinal Miguel Obando Bravo

NIGERIA
*Jos*, Gabriel G. Ganaka
*Kaduna*, Peter Yariyok Jatau
*Lagos*, Anthony Okogie
*Onitsha*, Stephen Nweke Ezeanya

OCEANIA
*Agaña*, Anthony Sablan Apuron
*Honiara*, Adrian Thomas Smith

*Nouméa*, Michel-Marie-Bernard Calvet
*Papeete*, Michel-Gaspard Copenrath
*Samoa, Apia and Tokelau*, HE Cardinal Pio Taofino'u
*Suva*, Petero Mataca

PAKISTAN
*Karachi*, vacant
    *Coadjutor*, Simeon Pereira

PANAMA
*Panama*, Jose Dimas C. Delgado

PAPUA NEW GUINEA
*Madang*, Benedict To Varpin
*Mount Hagen*, Michael Meier
*Port Moresby*, Peter Kurongku
*Rabaul*, Karl Hesse

PARAGUAY
*Asuncion*, Felipe Santiago B. Avalos

PERU
*Arequipa*, Fernando Vargas Ruiz de Somocurcio
*Ayacucho o Huamanga*, vacant
*Cuzco*, Alcides Mendoza Castro
*Huancayo*, vacant
*Lima*, Augusto Vargas Alzamora
*Piura*, Oscar Rolando Cantuarias Pastor
*Trujillo*, Manuel Prado Pérez-Rosas

PHILIPPINES
*Caceres*, Leonardo Legazpi
*Cagayan de Oro*, Jesus B. Tuquib
*Capiz*, Onesimo C. Gordoncillo
*Cebu*, HE Cardinal Ricardo Vidal
*Cotabato*, Philip Frances Smith
*Davao*, Antonio Mabutas
*Jaro*, Alberto J. Piamonte
*Lingayen-Dagupan*, Oscar V. Cruz
*Lipa*, Gaudencio B. Rosales
*Manila*, HE Cardinal Jaime L. Sin
*Nueva Segovia*, Orlando Quevedo
*Ozamiz*, Jesus Dosado
*Palo*, Pedro R. Dean
*San Fernando*, Paciano Aniceto
*Tuguegarao*, Diosdado A. Talamayan
*Zamboanga*, Francisco Raval Cruces

POLAND
*Bialystok*, Stanislaw Szymecki
*Czestochowa*, Stanislaw Nowak
*Gdańsk*, Tadeusz Goclowski
*Gniezno*, Henryk Muszyński
*Katowice*, Damian Zimoń
*Kraków*, HE Cardinal Franciszek Macharski
*Lodz*, Wladyslaw Ziolek
*Lublin*, Boleslaw Pylak
*Poznań*, Jerzy Stroba
*Przemyśl of the Latins*, Jozef Michalik
*Szczecin-Kamień*, Marian Przykucki
*Warmia*, Edmund Piszcz
*Warsaw*, HE Cardinal Józef Glemp
*Wroclaw*, HE Cardinal Henryk Roman Gulbinowicz

PORTUGAL
*Braga*, Eurico Dias Nogueira
*Evora*, Maurilio Jorge Quintal de Gouveia

PUERTO RICO
*San Juan*, HE Cardinal Luis Aponte Martinez

ROMANIA
*Alba Julia* (Latin Rite), Gyorgy-Miklos Jakubinyi
*Bucarești*, Ioan Robu

*Fagaras and Alba Julia* (Romanian Byzantine Rite), Lucian Muresan

RUSSIA
*Moscow Apostolic Administration* (covering European Russia), Apostolic Administrator, Archbishop Tadeusz Kondrusiewicz
*Novosibirsk Apostolic Administration* (covering Siberia), Apostolic Administrator, Mgr Joseph Werth, SJ (titular Bishop of Bulna)

RWANDA
*Kigali*, vacant

ST LUCIA
*Castries*, Kelvin E. Felix

EL SALVADOR
*San Salvador*, Arturo Rivera Damas

SENEGAL
*Dakar*, HE Cardinal Hyacinthe Thiandoum

SIERRA LEONE
*Freetown and Bo*, Joseph Ganda

SINGAPORE
*Singapore*, Gregory Yong Sooi Ngean

SLOVAK REPUBLIC
*Trnava*, Jan Sokol

SLOVENIA
*Ljubljana*, Alojzij Suštar

SOUTH AFRICA
*Bloemfontein*, Peter John Butelezi
*Cape Town*, Lawrence Patrick Henry
*Durban*, Wilfrid Fox Napier
*Pretoria*, George Francis Daniel

SPAIN
*Barcelona*, Ricardo Maria Carles Gordó
*Burgos*, Santiago Martinez Acebes
*Granada*, José Méndez Asensio
*Madrid*, HE Cardinal Angel Suquia Goicoechea
*Oviedo*, Gabino Diaz Merchán
*Pamplona*, Fernando S. Aquilar
*Santiago de Compostela*, Antonio Rouco Varela
*Sevilla*, Carlos Amigo Vallejo
*Tarragona*, Ramon Torrella Cascante
*Toledo*, HE Cardinal Marcelo González Martin
*Valencia*, Agustin Garcia-Gasco Vicente
*Valladolid*, José Delicado Baeza
*Zaragoza*, Elíaz Yanez Alvarez

SRI LANKA
*Colombo*, Nicholas Marcus Fernando

SUDAN
*Juba*, Paulino Lukudu Loro
*Khartoum*, Gabriel Zubeir Wako

SYRIA
*Alep, Beroea, Halab* (Greek Melekite Catholic Rite), Néophytes Edelby; (Syrian Rite), Raboula A. Beylouni; (Maronite Rite), Pierre Callaos; (Armenian Rite), Boutros Marayati
*Baniyas* (Greek Melekite Catholic Rite), Antoine Hayek
*Bosra, Bostra*, Boulos Nassif Borkhoche
*Damascus* (Greek Melekite Catholic Rite), S. B. Maximos V. Hakim; (Syrian Rite), Eustache J. Mounayer; (Maronite Rite), Hamid A. Mourany
*Hassaké-Nisibi*, Georges Habib Hafouri
*Homs, Emesa* (Greek Melekite Catholic Rite), Abraham Nehmé; (Syrian Catholic Rite), Basile Daoud
*Laodicea* (Greek Melekite Catholic Rite), Michel Yatim

TAIWAN
*Taipei*, Joseph Ti-Kang

TANZANIA
*Dar es Salaam*, Polycarp Pengo
*Mwanza*, Antony Mayala
*Songea*, Norbert W. Mtega
*Tabora*, Mario E. A. Mgulunde

THAILAND
*Bangkok*, HE Cardinal Michael Michai Kitbunchu
*Tharé and Nonseng*, Lawrence Khai Saen-Phon-On

TOGO
*Lomé*, Philippe F. K. Kpodzro

TRINIDAD
*Port of Spain*, Gordon Anthony Pantin

TURKEY
*Diarbekir*, Paul Karatas
*Istanbul (Constantinople)*, Jean Tcholakian
*Izmir*, Giuseppe G. Bernardini

UGANDA
*Kampala*, Emmanuel Wamala

UKRAINE
*Lvov* (Latin Rite), Marian Jaworski (Archbishop of Lvov of the Latins); (Ukrainian Rite), HE Cardinal Myroslav I. Lubachivsky (Major Archbishop of Lvov of the Ukrainians)

URUGUAY
*Montevideo*, José Gottardi Cristelli

USA
*Anchorage*, Francis Thomas Hurley
*Atlanta*, John F. Donoghue
*Baltimore*, William Henry Keeler
*Boston*, HE Cardinal Bernard F. Law
*Chicago*, HE Cardinal Joseph L. Bernardin
*Cincinnati*, Daniel E. Pilarczyk
*Denver*, James Francis Stafford
*Detroit*, Adam J. Maida
*Dubuque*, Daniel W. Kucera
*Hartford*, Daniel A. Cronin
*Indianapolis*, Daniel Mark Buechlein
*Kansas City*, James P. Keleher
*Los Angeles*, HE Cardinal Roger M. Mahony
*Louisville*, Thomas C. Kelly
*Miami*, Edward A. McCarthy
*Milwaukee*, Rembert G. Weakland
*Mobile*, Oscar H. Lipscomb
*Newark*, Theodore E. McCarrick
*New Orleans*, Francis B. Schulte
*New York*, HE Cardinal John J. O'Connor
*Oklahoma City*, Eusebius Joseph Beltran
*Omaha*, Elden Curtiss
*Philadelphia*, HE Cardinal Anthony J. Bevilacqua; (Ukrainian Rite), Stephen Sulyk
*Pittsburgh* (Byzantine Rite), vacant
*Portland (Oregon)*, William J. Levada
*St Louis (Missouri)*, Justin F. Rigali
*St Paul and Minneapolis*, John Robert Roach
*San Antonio*, Patrick F. Flores
*San Francisco*, John R. Quinn
*Santa Fe*, Administrator, Michael Sheehan
*Seattle*, Thomas J. Murphy
*Washington*, HE Cardinal James A. Hickey

VENEZUELA
*Barquisimeto*, Julio Manuel Chirivella Varela
*Caracas*, HE Cardinal José Ali Lebrún Moratinos

*Ciudad Bolivar*, Medardo Luzardo Romero
*Cumana*, Alfredo J. R. Figueroa
*Maracaibo*, Ramon O. Perez Morales
*Mérida*, Baltazar P. Cardozo
*Valencia*, Jorge Liberato Urosa Savino

VIETNAM
*Hanoi*, Paul Joseph Pham Dinh Tung
*Hue Apostolic Administrator*, Etienne N. N. Thê
*Thanh-Phô Hôchiminh*, Paul Nguyên Van Binh

WEST INDIES
*Castries*, Kelvin Edward Felix, OBE

YUGOSLAV FEDERAL REPUBLIC
*Bar*, Petar Perkolić
*Belgrade*, Franc Perko

ZAÏRE
*Bukavu*, Christophe Munzihirwa Mwene Ngabo
*Kananga*, Bakole wa Ilunga
*Kinshasa*, HE Cardinal Frederick Etsou-Nzabi-
Bamungwabi
*Kisangani*, Laurent Monsengwo Pasinya
*Lubumbashi*, Kabanga Songasonga
*Mbandaka-Bikoro*, Joseph Kumuondala Mbimba

ZAMBIA
*Kasama*, James Spaita
*Lusaka*, Adrian Mungandu

ZIMBABWE
*Harare*, Patrick Chakaipa

## PATRIARCHS IN COMMUNION WITH THE ROMAN CATHOLIC CHURCH

*Alexandria*, HB Stephanos II Ghattas (Patriarch for Catholic Copts); HB Parthenios III (Greek Orthodox Patriarch of Alexandria and All Africa)
*Antioch*, HB Ignace Antoine II Hayek (Patriarch for Syrian rite Catholics); HB Maximos V. Hakim (Patriarch for Greek Melekite rite Catholics); HB Nasrallah Pierre Sfeir (Patriarch for Maronite rite Catholics)
*Jerusalem*, HB Michel Sabbah (Patriarch for Latin rite Catholics); HB Maximos V. Hakim (Patriarch for Greek Melekite rite Catholics)
*Babilonia of the Chaldeans*, HB Raphael I Bidawid
*Cilicia of the Armenians*, HB Jean Pierre XVIII Kasparian (Patriarch for Armenian rite Catholics)
*Oriental India*, Archbishop Raul Nicolau Gonsalves
*Lisbon*, HE Cardinal Antonio Ribeiro
*Venice*, HE Cardinal Marco Ce

# Other Churches in the UK

## AFRICAN AND AFRO-CARIBBEAN CHURCHES

There are more than 160 Christian churches or groups of African or Afro-Caribbean origin in the United Kingdom. These include the Apostolic Faith Church, the Cherubim and Seraphim Church, the New Testament Church Assembly, the New Testament Church of God and the Wesleyan Holiness Church.

The Afro-West Indian United Council of Churches and the Council of African and Afro-Caribbean Churches UK (which was initiated as the Council of African and Allied Churches in 1979 to give one voice to the various Christian churches of African origin in the UK) are the media through which the member churches can work jointly to provide services they cannot easily provide individually.

There are about 70,000 adherents of African and Afro-Caribbean churches in the United Kingdom, and about 1,000 congregations. The Afro-West Indian United Council of Churches has about 30,000 individual members, 135 ministers and 65 places of worship. The Council of African and Afro-Caribbean Churches UK has about 15,000 members, 250 ministers and 75 congregations.

AFRO-WEST INDIAN UNITED COUNCIL OF CHURCHES, Overstone Hall Conference Centre, Main House, Overstone Park, Overstone, Northampton NN6 0AD. Tel: 01604-645944. *Chairman*, Revd E. Brown
COUNCIL OF AFRICAN AND AFRO-CARIBBEAN CHURCHES UK, 31 Norton House, Sidney Road, London SW9 0UJ. Tel: 0171-274 5589. *Chairman*, His Grace The Most Revd Father Olu A. Abiola

## ASSOCIATED PRESBYTERIAN CHURCHES OF SCOTLAND

The Associated Presbyterian Churches came into being in 1989 as a result of a division within the Free Presbyterian Church of Scotland. Following two controversial disciplinary cases, the culmination of deepening differences within the Church, a Deed of Separation was drawn up by several members of the Church's synod. This held that the Church, in contravention of its constitution, had denied its members freedom of judgement in matters relating to the application of the Christian faith to daily living. A presbytery was formed calling itself the Associated Presbyterian Churches (APC). The APC claims that it represents the Free Presbyterian Church of Scotland as constituted in 1893. The Associated Presbyterian Churches has about 1,000 members, 13 ministers and 20 churches.
*Clerk of the Scottish Presbytery*, D. K. Laing, 1 Golden Square, Aberdeen AB9 1HA. Tel: 01862-87541

## THE BAPTIST CHURCH

Baptists trace their origins to John Smyth, who in 1609 in Amsterdam reinstituted the baptism of conscious believers as the basis of the fellowship of a gathered church. Members of Smyth's church established the first Baptist church in England in 1612. They came to be known as 'General' Baptists and their theology was Arminian, whereas a later group of Calvinists who adopted the baptism of believers came to be known as 'Particular' Baptists. The two sections of the Baptists were united into one body, the Baptist Union of Great Britain and Ireland, in 1891. In 1988 the title was changed to the Baptist Union of Great Britain.

Baptists emphasize the complete independence of the local church, although individual churches are linked in various kinds of associations. There are international bodies (such as the Baptist World Alliance) and national bodies, but many Baptist churches belong to neither. However, in Great Britain the majority of churches and associations belong to the Baptist Union of Great Britain. There are also Baptist Unions in Wales, Scotland and Ireland which are much smaller than the Baptist Union of Great Britain, and there is some overlap of membership.

There are over 38 million Baptist church members worldwide; in the Baptist Union of Great Britain there are 160,000 members, 1,820 pastors and 2,118 churches. In the Baptist Union of Scotland there are 15,287 members, 130 pastors and 169 churches. In the Baptist Union of Wales there are 25,384 members, 117 pastors and 544 churches. In the Baptist Union of Ireland there are 8,505 members, 72 pastors and 103 churches.

*President of the Baptist Union of Great Britain* (1994–5), Revd S. J. Gaukroger

*General Secretary*, Revd D. R. Coffey, Baptist House, PO Box 44, 129 Broadway, Didcot, Oxon. OX11 8RT. Tel: 01235-512077

## THE CHURCH OF CHRIST, SCIENTIST

The Church of Christ, Scientist was founded by Mary Baker Eddy in the USA in 1879 to 'reinstate primitive Christianity and its lost element of healing'. Christian Science teaches the need for spiritual regeneration and salvation from sin, but is best known for its reliance on prayer alone in the healing of sickness. Adherents believe that such healing is a law, or Science, and is in direct line with that practised by Jesus Christ (revered, not as God, but as the Son of God) and by the early Christian Church.

The denomination consists of The First Church of Christ, Scientist, in Boston, Massachusetts, USA (The Mother Church) and its branch churches in over 60 countries world-wide. Branch churches are democratically governed by their members, while a five-member Board of Directors, based in Boston, is authorized to transact the business of The Mother Church. The Bible and Mary Baker Eddy's book, *Science and Health with Key to the Scriptures*, are used at services; there are no clergy. Those engaged in full-time healing are called practitioners, of whom there are 3,500 world-wide.

No membership figures are available, since Mary Baker Eddy felt that numbers are no measure of spiritual vitality and ruled that such statistics should not be published. There are over 2,400 branch churches world-wide, including nearly 200 in the United Kingdom.

CHRISTIAN SCIENCE COMMITTEE ON PUBLICATION, 2 Elysium Gate, 126 New Kings Road, London SW6 4LZ. Tel: 0171-371 0600. *District Manager for Great Britain and Ireland*, A. Grayson

## THE CHURCH OF JESUS CHRIST OF LATTER-DAY SAINTS

The Church (often referred to as 'the Mormons') was founded in New York State, USA, in 1830, and came to Britain in 1837. The oldest continuous branch in the world is to be found in Preston, Lancs. Mormons are Christians who claim to belong to the Restored Church of Jesus Christ. They believe that true Christianity died when the last original apostle died, but that it was given back to the world by God and Christ through Joseph Smith, the Church's founder and first president. They accept and use the Bible as scripture, but believe in continuing revelation from God and that additional scriptures, including Smith's testimony *The Book of Mormon: Another Testament of Jesus Christ*. The importance of the family is central to the Church's beliefs and practices. Church members set aside Monday evenings as Family Home Evenings when Christian family values are taught. Polygamy was formally discontinued in 1890.

The Church has no paid ministry; local congregations are headed by a leader chosen from amongst their number. The world governing body, based in Utah, USA, is the three-man

First Presidency, assisted by The Quorum of the Twelve Apostles.

There are about 9 million members world-wide, with about 165,000 adherents in Britain in over 340 congregations.

*President of the Europe North Area (including Britain)*, Elder K. Johnson

BRITISH HEADQUARTERS, Church Offices, 751 Warwick Road, Solihull, W. Midlands B91 3DQ. Tel: 0121-711 2244

## THE CONGREGATIONAL FEDERATION

The Congregational Federation was founded by members of Congregational churches in England and Wales who did not join the United Reformed Church (q.v.) in 1972. There are also churches in Scotland and Australia. The Federation exists to encourage congregations of believers to worship in free assembly, but has no authority over them and emphasizes their right to independence and self-government.

The Federation has 9,455 members, 118 ministers, 36 pastors, about 260 lay preachers and 311 churches.

*President of the Federation* (1994–5), Mrs A. Adams

*General Secretary*, G. M. Adams, The Congregational Centre, 4 Castle Gate, Nottingham NG1 7AS. Tel: 0115-941 3801

## THE FREE CHURCH OF ENGLAND

The Free Church of England is a union of two bodies in the Anglican tradition, the Free Church of England, founded in 1844 as a protest against the Oxford Movement in the established Church, and the Reformed Episcopal Church, founded in America in 1873 but which also had congregations in England. As both Churches sought to maintain the historic faith, tradition and practice of the Anglican Church since the Reformation, they decided to unite as one body in England in 1927. The historic episcopate was conferred on the English Church in 1876 through the line of the American bishops, who had pioneered an open table Communion policy towards members of other denominations.

The Free Church of England has 1,550 members, 38 ministers and 26 churches in England. It also has three house churches and three ministers in New Zealand, and one church and one minister in St Petersburg, Russia.

*General Secretary*, Revd W. J. Lawler, 45 Broughton Road, Wallasey, Merseyside L44 4DT. Tel: 0151-638 2564

## THE FREE CHURCH OF SCOTLAND

The Free Church of Scotland was formed in 1843 when over 400 ministers withdrew from the Church of Scotland as a result of interference in the internal affairs of the church by the civil authorities. In 1900, all but 26 ministers joined with others to form the United Free Church (most of which rejoined the Church of Scotland in 1929). In 1904 the remaining 26 ministers were recognized by the House of Lords as continuing the Free Church of Scotland.

The Church maintains strict adherence to the Westminster Confession of Faith (1648) and accepts the Bible as the sole rule of faith and conduct. Its General Assembly meets annually. It also has links with Reformed Churches overseas. The Free Church of Scotland has about 20,000 members, 110 ministers and 140 churches.

*General Treasurer,* I. D. Gill, The Mound, Edinburgh
EH1 2LS. Tel: 0131-226 5286

## THE FREE PRESBYTERIAN CHURCH OF SCOTLAND

The Free Presbyterian Church of Scotland was formed in 1893 by two ministers of the Free Church of Scotland who refused to accept a Declaratory Act passed by the Free Church General Assembly in 1892. The Free Presbyterian Church of Scotland is Calvinistic in doctrine and emphasizes observance of the Sabbath. It adheres strictly to the Westminster Confession of Faith of 1648.

The Church has about 3,000 members in Scotland and about 11,000 in overseas congregations. It has 22 ministers and 34 churches.

*Moderator,* Revd N. M. Ross, 10 Achany Road, Dingwall
IV15 9JB. Tel: 01349-64351

*Clerk of Synod,* Revd D. B. MacLeod, 8 Colinton Road, Edinburgh EH10 5DS. Tel: 0131-447 1920

## THE INDEPENDENT METHODIST CHURCHES

The Independent Methodist Churches seceded from the Wesleyan Methodist Church in 1805 and remained independent when the Methodist Church in Great Britain was formed in 1932. They are mainly concentrated in the industrial areas of the north of England.

The churches are Methodist in doctrine but their organization is congregational. All the churches are members of the Independent Methodist Connexion of Churches. The controlling body of the Connexion is the Annual Meeting, to which churches send delegates. The Connexional President is elected annually. Between annual meetings the affairs of the Connexion are handled by departmental committees. Ministers are appointed by the churches and trained through the Connexion. The ministry is open to both men and women and is unpaid.

There are 3,600 members, 124 ministers and 103 churches in Great Britain.

*Connexional President* (1994–5), G. J. Lomas

*General Secretary,* J. M. Day, The Old Police House, Croxton, Stafford ST21 6PE. Tel: 0163-082 671

## JEHOVAH'S WITNESSES

The movement now known as Jehovah's Witnesses grew from a Bible study group formed by Charles Taze Russell in 1872 in Pennsylvania, USA. In 1896 it adopted the name of the Watch Tower Bible and Tract Society, and in 1931 its members became known as Jehovah's Witnesses. Jehovah's (God's) Witnesses believe in the Bible as the Word of God, and consider it to be inspired and historically accurate. They take the scriptures literally, except where there are obvious indications that they are figurative or symbolic, and reject the doctrine of the Trinity. Witnesses believe that the earth will remain for ever and that all those approved of by Jehovah will have eternal life on a cleansed and beautified earth; only 144,000 will go to heaven to rule with Christ. They believe that the second coming of Christ and his thousand-year reign on earth have been imminent since 1914, and that Armaged-

don (a final battle in which evil will be defeated) will precede Christ's rule of peace. They refuse to take part in military service, and do not accept stimulants or blood transfusions. They publish a magazine, *The Watchtower.*

The 12-member world governing body is based in New York, USA. Witnesses world-wide are divided into branches, countries or areas, districts, circuits and congregations. There are overseers at each level, and two assemblies are held annually for each circuit. There is no paid ministry, but each congregation has elders assigned to look after various duties and every Witness is assigned homes to visit in their congregation.

There are about 4,800,000 Jehovah's Witnesses world-wide, with 125,000 Witnesses in the United Kingdom organized into more than 1,350 congregations.

BRITISH ISLES HEADQUARTERS, IBSA House, The Ridgeway, London NW7 1RP. Tel: 0181-906 2211

## THE LUTHERAN CHURCH

Lutheranism is based on the teachings of Martin Luther, the German leader of the Protestant Reformation. The authority of the scriptures is held to be supreme over Church tradition and creeds, and the key doctrine is that of justification by faith alone.

Lutheranism is one of the largest Protestant denominations and it is particularly strong in northern Europe and the USA. Some Lutheran churches are episcopal, while others have a synodal form of organization; unity is based on doctrine rather than structure. Most Lutheran churches are members of the Lutheran World Federation, based in Geneva.

Lutheran services in Great Britain are held in many languages to serve members of different nationalities. English-language congregations are members either of the Lutheran Church in Great Britain–United Synod, or of the Evangelical Lutheran Church of England. The United Synod and most of the various national congregations are members of the Lutheran Council of Great Britain.

There are over 70 million Lutherans world-wide; in Great Britain there are 27,000 members, 45 ministers and 100 churches.

*Chairman of the Lutheran Council of Great Britain,* Very Revd R. J. Patkai, 8 Collingham Gardens, London SW5 0HW. Tel: 0171-373 1141

## THE METHODIST CHURCH

The Methodist movement started in England in 1729 when the Revd John Wesley, an Anglican priest, and his brother Charles met with others in Oxford and resolved to conduct their lives and study by 'rule and method'. In 1739 the Wesleys began evangelistic preaching and the first Methodist chapel was founded in Bristol in the same year. In 1744 the first annual conference was held, at which the Articles of Religion were drawn up. Doctrinal emphases included repentance, faith, the assurance of salvation, social concern and the priesthood of all believers. After John Wesley's death in 1791 the Methodists withdrew from the established Church to form the Methodist Church. Methodists gradually drifted into many groups, but in 1932 the Wesleyan Methodist Church, the United Methodist Church and the Primitive Methodist Church united to form the Methodist Church in Great Britain as it now exists.

The governing body and supreme authority of the Methodist Church is the Conference, but there are also 33 district synods, consisting of all the ministers and selected lay people in each district, and circuit meetings of the ministers and lay people of each circuit.

There are over 60 million Methodists world-wide; in Great Britain (1992 figures) there are 408,107 members, 3,601 ministers, 10,414 lay preachers and 6,950 churches.

*President of the Conference in Great Britain* (1994–5), Revd Dr L. J. Griffiths
*Vice-President of the Conference* (1994–5), Sr C. Walters
*Secretary of the Conference*, Revd B. E. Beck, Methodist Church, Conference Office, 1 Central Buildings, Storeys Gate, London SW1H 9NH. Tel: 0171-222 8010

## THE METHODIST CHURCH IN IRELAND

The Methodist Church in Ireland is closely linked to British Methodism but is autonomous. It has 18,722 members, 197 ministers, 310 lay preachers and 234 churches.

*President of the Conference in Ireland* (1994–5) *and Secretary of the Conference in Ireland*, Revd E. T. I. Mawhinney, 1 Fountainville Avenue, Belfast BT9 6AN. Tel: 01232-324554

## THE ORTHODOX CHURCH

The Orthodox Church (or Eastern Orthodox Church) is a communion of self-governing Christian churches recognizing the honorary primacy of the Oecumenical Patriarch of Constantinople.

In the first millennium of the Christian era the faith was slowly formulated. Between AD 325 and 787 there were seven Oecumenical Councils at which bishops from the entire Christian world assembled to resolve various doctrinal disputes which had arisen. The estrangement between East and West began after Constantine moved the centre of the Roman Empire from Rome to Constantinople, and it gained momentum after the temporal administration was divided. Linguistic and cultural differences between Greek East and Latin West served to encourage separate ecclesiastical developments which became pronounced in the tenth and early eleventh centuries.

The administration of the church was divided between five ancient patriarchates: Rome and all the West, Constantinople (the imperial city – the 'New Rome'), Jerusalem and all Palestine, Antioch and all the East, and Alexandria and all Africa. Of these, only Rome was in the Latin West and after the Great Schism in 1054, Rome developed a structure of authority centralized on one source, the Papacy, while the Orthodox East maintained the style of localized administration.

To the older patriarchates were later added the Patriarchates of Russia, Georgia, Serbia, Bulgaria and Romania. The Orthodox Church also includes autocephalous (self-governing) national churches in Greece, Cyprus, Poland, Albania, Czechoslovakia and Sinai, and autonomous national churches in Finland and Japan. The Estonian and Latvian Orthodox Churches are in practice part of the Moscow Patriarchate. The Belorussians and Ukrainians have recently been given greater autonomy by Moscow, but some Ukrainians have broken away to establish an independent Ukrainian Patriarchate. In Macedonia the local hierarchy has declared itself independent of the Serbian Patriarchate. The Russian dioceses in the diaspora fall into four groups: those under the direct control of the Moscow Patriarchate; the Russian Orthodox Church Outside Russia, sometimes known as the Synod in Exile; the Russian Archdiocese centred at the cathedral in rue Daru, Paris, which is part of the Patriarchate in Constantinople; and the Orthodox Church in America, which was granted autocephalous status in 1970.

The position of Orthodox Christians is that the faith was fully defined during the period of the Oecumenical Councils. In doctrine it is strongly trinitarian, and stresses the mystery and importance of the sacraments. It is episcopal in government. The structure of the Orthodox Christian year differs from that of Western Churches (*see* page 82).

Orthodox Christians throughout the world are estimated to number about 150 million.

PATRIARCHS
*Archbishop of Constantinople, New Rome and Oecumenical Patriarch*, Bartholomew, *elected* 1991
*Pope and Patriarch of Alexandria and All Africa*, Parthenios III, *elected* 1987
*Patriarch of Antioch and All the East*, Ignatios IV, *elected* 1979
*Patriarch of Jerusalem and All Palestine*, Diodoros, *elected* 1981
*Patriarch of Moscow and All Russia*, Alexei II, *elected* 1990
*Archbishop of Tbilisi and Mtskheta, Catholicos-Patriarch of All Georgia*, Ilia II, *elected* 1977
*Archbishop of Pec, Metropolitan of Belgrade and Karlovci, Patriarch of Serbia*, Paul, *elected* 1990
*Archbishop of Bucharest and Patriarch of Romania*, Teoctist, *elected* 1986
*Metropolitan of Sofia and Patriarch of Bulgaria*, Maxim, *elected* 1971
*Patriarch of Kiev and All Ukraine*, no Patriarch agreed upon owing to division among the Ukrainian Orthodox

ORTHODOX CHURCHES IN THE UK

THE GREEK ORTHODOX CHURCH (PATRIARCHATE OF CONSTANTINOPLE)
The presence of Greek Orthodox Christians in Britain dates back to 1677 when Archbishop Joseph Geogirenes of Samos fled from Turkish persecution and came to London, where a church was built for him in Soho. The present Greek cathedral in Moscow Road, Bayswater, was opened for public worship in 1879 and the Diocese of Thyateira and Great Britain was established in 1922. There are now 87 parishes in Great Britain, served by eight bishops and 87 churches.

In Great Britain the Patriarchate of Constantinople is represented by Archbishop Gregorios of Thyateira and Great Britain, 5 Craven Hill, London W2 3EN. Tel: 0171-723 4787.

THE RUSSIAN ORTHODOX CHURCH (PATRIARCHATE OF MOSCOW) AND THE RUSSIAN ORTHODOX CHURCH OUTSIDE RUSSIA
The earliest records of Russian Orthodox Church activities in Britain date from the visit to England of Tsar Peter I at the beginning of the 18th century. Clergy were sent from Russia to serve the chapel established to minister to the staff of the Imperial Russian Embassy in London.

After 1917 the Church of Russia was persecuted. The Patriarch of Moscow, St Tikhon the New Martyr, anathematized both the atheistic persecutors of the Church and all who collaborated with them. Because of the civil war normal administrative contact with Russian Orthodox Christians outside the country was impossible, and he therefore authorized the establishment of a higher church administration, i.e. a synod in exile, by Russian bishops who were then outside Russia. This is the origin of the Russian Orthodox Church Outside Russia. The attitude of the Church of Russia to the former Soviet regime was always a source of contention between the two hierarchies; tensions are now lessening but remain unresolved.

In Britain the Patriarchate of Moscow is represented by Metropolitan Anthony of Sourozh, 67 Ennismore Gardens, London SW7 INH. Tel: 0171-584 0096. He is assisted by one archbishop, one bishop and about 13 priests. There are 15 parishes.

The Russian Orthodox Church Outside Russia is represented by Archbishop Mark of Richmond and Great Britain (who is also Archbishop of Berlin and Germany), 14 St Dunstan's Road, London W6 8RB. Tel: 0181-748 4232. There are eight parishes and two monasteries, served by six priests.

THE SERBIAN ORTHODOX CHURCH (PATRIARCHATE OF SERBIA)

There was a small congregation of Orthodox Christian Serbs in London before the Second World War, but most Serbian parishes in Britain have been established since 1945. There is no resident bishop as the parishes are part of the Serbian Orthodox Diocese of Western Europe, which has its centre in Germany. There are five main parishes in Britain and several smaller communities served by seven priests.

In Britain the Patriarchate of Serbia is represented by the Episcopal Vicar, the Very Revd Milun Kostic, 89 Lancaster Road, London W11 1QQ. Tel: 0171-727 8367.

OTHER NATIONALITIES

Latvian, Polish and some Belorussian Orthodox parishes in Britain are under the care of the Patriarchate of Constantinople. The Patriarchates of Antioch, Bulgaria and Romania are represented by one priest each. Both the Ukrainian Autocephalous Orthodox Church and the Belorussian Autocephalic Orthodox Church have a few parishes in Britain.

ORTHODOX CHURCH PUBLIC RELATIONS OFFICE, St George Orthodox Information Service, 64 Prebend Gardens, London W6 OXU. Tel: 0181-741 9624. *Secretary*, A. Bond

## PENTECOSTAL CHURCHES

Pentecostalism is inspired by the descent of the Holy Spirit upon the apostles at Pentecost. The movement began in Los Angeles, USA, in 1906 and is characterized by baptism with the Holy Spirit, divine healing, speaking in tongues (glossolalia), and a literal interpretation of the scriptures. The Pentecostal movement in Britain dates from 1907. Initially, groups of Pentecostalists were led by laymen and did not organize formally. However, in 1915 the Elim Foursquare Gospel Alliance (more usually called the Elim Pentecostal Church) was founded in Ireland by George Jeffreys and in 1924 about 70 independent assemblies formed a fellowship, the Assemblies of God in Great Britain and Ireland. The Apostolic Church grew out of the 1904–5 revivals in South Wales and was established in 1916, and the New Testament Church of God was established in England in 1953. In recent years many aspects of Pentecostalism have been adopted by the growing charismatic movement within the Roman Catholic Church and Protestant and Eastern Orthodox churches.

There are about 22 million Pentecostalists world-wide, with about 125,000 adult adherents in Great Britain and Ireland.

THE APOSTOLIC CHURCH, International Administration Offices, PO Box 389, 24–27 St Helens Road, Swansea, West Glamorgan SA1 1ZH. Tel: 01792-473992. *President*, Pastor P. Cawthorne; *Administrator*, Pastor M. Davies. The Apostolic Church has about 130 churches, 5,500 adherents and 83 ministers

THE ASSEMBLIES OF GOD IN GREAT BRITAIN AND IRELAND, General Offices, 106–114 Talbot Street, Nottingham NG1 5GH. Tel: 0115-947 4525. *General Superintendent*, W. Shenton; *General Administrator*, B. D. Varnam. The Assemblies of God has 630 churches, about 75,000 adherents (including children) and 663 accredited ministers

THE ELIM PENTECOSTAL CHURCH, PO Box 38, Cheltenham, Glos. GL50 3HN. Tel: 01242-519904. *General Superintendent*, Pastor I. W. Lewis; *Administrator*, Pastor B. Hunter. The Elim Pentecostal Church has about 470 churches, 50,000 adherents and 475 accredited ministers

THE NEW TESTAMENT CHURCH OF GOD, Main House, Overstone Park, Overstone, Northampton NN6 0AD. Tel: 01604-645944. *National Overseer*, Revd Dr S. E. Arnold. The New Testament Church of God has 106 organized congregations, 7,042 baptized members, about 20,000 adherents and 232 accredited ministers

## THE PRESBYTERIAN CHURCH IN IRELAND

The Presbyterian Church in Ireland is Calvinistic in doctrine and presbyterian in constitution. Presbyterianism was established in Ireland as a result of the Ulster plantation in the early 17th century, when English and Scottish Protestants settled in the north of Ireland.

There are 21 presbyteries and five regional synods under the chief court known as the General Assembly. The General Assembly meets annually and is presided over by a Moderator who is elected for one year. The ongoing work of the Church is undertaken by 18 boards under which there are a number of specialist committees.

There are about 330,000 Presbyterians in Ireland, mainly in the north, in 562 congregations and with 400 ministers.

*Moderator* (1994–5), Rt. Revd Dr D. McGaughey
*Clerk of Assembly and General Secretary*, Revd S. Hutchinson, Church House, Belfast BT1 6DW. Tel: 01232-322284

## THE PRESBYTERIAN CHURCH OF WALES

The Presbyterian Church of Wales or Calvinistic Methodist Church of Wales is Calvinistic in doctrine and presbyterian in constitution. It was formed in 1811 when Welsh Calvinists severed the relationship with the established church by ordaining their own ministers. It secured its own confession of faith in 1823 and a Constitutional Deed in 1826, and since 1864 the General Assembly has met annually, presided over by a Moderator elected for a year. The doctrine and constitutional structure of the Presbyterian Church of Wales was confirmed by Act of Parliament in 1931–2.

The Church has 55,690 members, 128 ministers and 977 churches.

*Moderator* (1994–5), Revd I. Lloyd
*General Secretary*, Revd D. H. Owen, 53 Richmond Road, Cardiff CF2 3UP. Tel: 01222-494913

## THE RELIGIOUS SOCIETY OF FRIENDS (QUAKERS)

Quakerism is a movement, not a church, which was founded in the 17th century by George Fox and others in an attempt to revive what they saw as 'primitive Christianity'. The movement was based originally in the Midlands, Yorkshire and north-west England, but there are now Quakers in 36 countries around the world. The colony of Pennsylvania, founded by William Penn, was originally Quaker.

Emphasis is placed on the experience of God in daily life rather than on sacraments or religious occasions. There is no church calendar. Worship is largely silent and there are no appointed ministers; the responsibility for conducting a meeting is shared equally among those present. Social reform and religious tolerance have always been important to Quakers, together with a commitment to non-violence in resolving disputes.

There are 213,800 Quakers world-wide, with over 19,000 in Great Britain and Ireland. There are about 460 meeting houses in Great Britain.

CENTRAL OFFICES: (GREAT BRITAIN) Friends House, Euston Road, London NW1 2BJ. Tel: 0171-387 3601; (IRELAND) Swanbrook House, Morehampton Road, Dublin 4. Tel: 00 353 1-683684

---

## THE SALVATION ARMY

---

The Salvation Army was founded by a Methodist minister, William Booth, in the east end of London in 1865, and has since become established in 95 countries world-wide. It was first known as the Christian Mission, and took its present name in 1878 when it adopted a quasi-military command structure intended to inspire and regulate its endeavours and to reflect its view that the Church was engaged in spiritual warfare. Salvationists emphasize evangelism, social work and the relief of poverty.

The world leader, known as the General, is elected by a High Council composed of the Chief of the Staff and senior ranking officers known as commissioners.

There are about 1.5 million soldiers, 16,455 active officers (full-time ordained ministers) and 14,068 corps (churches) and outposts world-wide. In Great Britain and Ireland there are 55,000 soldiers, 1,807 active officers and 992 worship centres.

*General*, P. Rader
*UK Territorial Commander*, Commissioner D. Pender
TERRITORIAL HEADQUARTERS, PO Box 249, 101 Queen Victoria Street, London EC4P 4EP. Tel: 0171-236 5222

---

## THE SEVENTH-DAY ADVENTIST CHURCH

---

The Seventh-day Adventist Church was founded in 1863 in the USA. Its members look forward to the second coming of Christ and observe the Sabbath as a day of rest, worship and ministry. The Church bases its faith and practice wholly on the Bible and has developed 27 fundamental beliefs.

The World Church is divided into 12 divisions, each made up of unions of churches. The Seventh-day Adventist Church in the British Isles is known as the British Union of Seventh-day Adventists and is a member of the Trans-European Division. In the British Isles the administrative organization of the church is arranged in three tiers: the local churches; the regional conferences for south England, north England, Wales, Scotland and Ireland, which are held every three years; and the national 'union' conference which is held every five years.

There are over 7 million Adventists and 36,032 churches in 204 countries world-wide. In the United Kingdom and

Ireland there are 18,242 members, 155 ministers and 245 churches.
*President of the British Union Conference* (1991–6), Pastor C. R. Perry
BRITISH ISLES HEADQUARTERS, Stanborough Park, Watford WD2 6JP. Tel: 01923-672251

---

## UNDEB YR ANNIBYNWYR CYMRAEG
*The Union of Welsh Independents*

---

The Union of Welsh Independents was formed in 1872 and is a voluntary association of Welsh Congregational Churches and personal members. It is entirely Welsh-speaking. Congregationalism in Wales dates back to 1639 when the first Welsh Congregational Church was opened in Gwent. Member Churches are Calvinistic in doctrine and congregationalist in organization. Each church has complete independence in the government and administration of its affairs.

The Union has about 47,000 members, 115 ministers and 605 chapels.

*President of the Union* (1994–5), Mrs M. Davies, MBE
*General Secretary*, Revd D. Morris Jones, Tŷ John Penry, 11 Heol Sant Helen, Swansea SA1 4AL. Tel: 01792-467040

---

## UNITARIAN AND FREE CHRISTIAN CHURCHES

---

Unitarianism has its historical roots in the Judaeo-Christian tradition but denies the exclusive divinity of Christ and the doctrine of the trinity. It allows the individual to embrace insights from all the world's faiths and philosophies, as there is no formal creed. It is accepted that beliefs may evolve in the light of personal experience.

Unitarian communities first became established in Poland and Transylvania in the 16th century. The first avowedly Unitarian place of worship in the British Isles opened in London in 1774. The General Assembly of Unitarian and Free Christian Churches came into existence in 1928 as the result of the amalgamation of two earlier organizations.

There are about 10,000 Unitarians in Great Britain and Ireland, and 150 Unitarian ministers. About 250 self-governing congregations and fellowship groups, including a small number overseas, are members of the General Assembly.

GENERAL ASSEMBLY OF UNITARIAN AND FREE CHRISTIAN CHURCHES, Essex Hall, 1–6 Essex Street, Strand, London WC2R 3HY. Tel: 0171-240 2384. *General Secretary*, J. J. Teagle

---

## THE UNITED REFORMED CHURCH

---

The United Reformed Church was formed by the union of most of the Congregational churches in England and Wales with the Presbyterian Church of England in 1972.

Congregationalism dates from the mid 16th century. It is Calvinistic in doctrine, and its followers form independent self-governing congregations bound under God by covenant, a principle laid down in the writings of Robert Browne (1550–1633). From the late 16th century the movement was driven underground by persecution, but the cause was defended at the Westminster Assembly in 1643 and the Savoy Declaration of 1658 laid down its principles.

Congregational churches formed county associations for mutual support and in 1832 these associations merged to form the Congregational Union of England and Wales.

The Presbyterian Church in England also dates from the mid 16th century, and was Calvinistic and evangelical in its doctrine. It was governed by a hierarchy of courts.

In the 1960s there was close co-operation locally and nationally between Congregational and Presbyterian Churches. This led to union negotiations and a Scheme of Union, supported by Act of Parliament in 1972. In 1981 a further unification took place, with the Reformed Association of Churches of Christ becoming part of the URC. In its basis the United Reformed Church reflects local church initiative and responsibility with a conciliar pattern of oversight. The General Assembly is the central body, and is made up of equal numbers of ministers and lay members.

The United Reformed Church is divided into 12 Provinces, each with a Provincial Moderator who chairs the Synod, and 75 Districts. There are 115,000 members, 799 full-time stipendiary ministers, 196 non-stipendiary ministers and 1,800 local churches.

*General Secretary*, Revd A. G. Burnham, 86 Tavistock Place, London WC1H 9RT. Tel: 0171-916 2020

## THE WESLEYAN REFORM UNION

The Wesleyan Reform Union was founded by Methodists who left or were expelled from Wesleyan Methodism in 1849 following a period of internal conflict. Its doctrine is conservative evangelical and its organization is congregational, each church having complete independence in its government and administration of its affairs. The main concentration of churches is in Yorkshire.

The Union has 2,698 members, 20 ministers, 143 lay preachers and 122 churches.

*President* (1994–5), N. Sowerby
*General Secretary*, Revd E. W. Downing, Wesleyan Reform Church House, 123 Queen Street, Sheffield S1 2DU. Tel: 0114-272 1928

# Archbishops of Canterbury since 1414

Henry Chichele (1362–1443), translated 1414
John Stafford (?–1452), translated 1443
John Kemp (c.1380–1454), translated 1452
Thomas Bourchier (c.1410–86), translated 1454
John Morton (c.1420–1500), translated 1486
Henry Deane (?–1503), translated 1501
William Warham (1450–1532), translated 1503
Thomas Cranmer (1489–1556), translated 1533
Reginald Pole (1500–58), translated 1556
Matthew Parker (1504–75), translated 1559
Edmund Grindal (c. 1519–83), translated 1576
John Whitgift (c.1530–1604), translated 1583
Richard Bancroft (1544–1610), translated 1604
George Abbot (1562–1633), translated 1611
William Laud (1573–1645), translated 1633
William Juxon (1582–1663), translated 1660
Gilbert Sheldon (1598–1677), translated 1663
William Sancroft (1617–93), translated 1678
John Tillotson (1630–94), translated 1691
Thomas Tenison (1636–1715), translated 1695
William Wake (1657–1737), translated 1716

John Potter (c. 1674–1747), translated 1737
Thomas Herring (1693–1757), translated 1747
Matthew Hutton (1693–1758), translated 1757
Thomas Secker (1693–1768), translated 1758
Hon. Frederick Cornwallis (1713–83), translated 1768
John Moore (1730–1805), translated 1783
Charles Manners-Sutton (1755–1828), translated 1805
William Howley (1766–1848), translated 1828
John Bird Sumner (1780–1862), translated 1848
Charles Longley (1794–1868), translated 1862
Archibald Campbell Tait (1811–82), translated 1868
Edward White Benson (1829–96), translated 1883
Frederick Temple (1821–1902), translated 1896
Randall Davidson (1848–1930), translated 1903
Cosmo Lang (1864–1945), translated 1928
William Temple (1881–1944), translated 1942
Geoffrey Fisher (1887–1972), translated 1945
Michael Ramsey (1904–88), translated 1961
Donald Coggan (1909–), translated 1974
Robert Runcie (1921–), translated 1980
George Carey (1935–), translated 1991

# Popes since 1800

The family name is in italics

Pius VII, *Chiaramonti*, elected 1800
Leo XII, *della Genga*, elected 1823
Pius VIII, *Castiglioni*, elected 1829
Gregory XVI, *Cappellari*, elected 1831
Pius IX, *Mastai-Ferretti*, elected 1846
Leo XIII, *Pecci*, elected 1878
Pius X, *Sarto*, elected 1903
Benedict XV, *della Chiesa*, elected 1914

Pius XI, *Ratti*, elected 1922
Pius XII, *Pacelli*, elected 1939
John XXIII, *Roncalli*, elected 1958
Paul VI, *Montini*, elected 1963
John Paul I, *Luciani*, elected 1978
John Paul II, *Wojtyla*, elected 1978

Adrian IV is the only Englishman to be elected pope. He was born Nicholas Breakspear at Langley, near St Albans, and was elected Pope in 1154 on the death of Anastasius IV. He died in 1159.

# Non-Christian Faiths

## BUDDHISM

Buddhism originated in northern India, in the teachings of Siddharta Gautama, who was born near Kapilavastu about 560 BC. After a long spiritual quest he experienced enlightenment beneath a tree at the place now known as Bodhgaya, and began missionary work.

Fundamental to Buddhism is the concept that there is no such thing as a permanent soul or self; when someone dies, consciousness is the only one of the elements of which they were composed which is lost. All the other elements regroup in a new body and carry with them the consequences of the conduct of the earlier life (known as the law of *karma*). This cycle of death and rebirth is broken only when the state of *nirvana* has been reached. Buddhism steers a middle path between belief in personal immortality and belief in death as the final end.

The Four Noble Truths of Buddhism (*dukkha*, suffering; *tanha*, a thirst or desire for continued existence which causes dukkha; *nirvana*, the final liberation from desire and ignorance; and *ariya*, the path to nirvana) are all held to be universal and to sum up the *dhamma* or true nature of life. Necessary qualities to promote spiritual development are *sila* (morality), *samadhi* (meditation) and *panna* (wisdom).

There are two main schools of Buddhism: *Theravada* Buddhism, the earliest extant school, which is more traditional, and *Mahayana* Buddhism, which began to develop about 100 years after the Buddha's death and is more liberal; it teaches that all people may attain Buddahood. Important schools which have developed within Mahayana Buddhism are *Zen* Buddhism, *Nichiren* Buddhism and Pure Land Buddhism or *Amidism*. There are also distinctive Tibetan forms of Buddhism. Buddhism began to establish itself in the West at the beginning of the 20th century.

The scripture of Theravada Buddhism is the *Pali Canon*, which dates from the first century BC. Mahayana Buddhism uses a Sanskrit version of the Pali Canon but also has many other works of scripture.

There is no set time for Buddhist worship, which may take place in a temple or in the home. Worship centres around *paritta* (chanting), acts of devotion centring on the image of the Buddha, and, where possible, offerings to a relic of the Buddha. Buddhist festivals vary according to local traditions and within Theravada and Mahayana Buddhism. For religious purposes Buddhists use solar and lunar calendars, the New Year being celebrated in April. Other festivals mark events in the life of the Buddha.

There is no supreme governing authority in Buddhism. In the United Kingdom communities representing all schools of Buddhism have developed and operate independently. The Buddhist Society was established in 1924; it runs courses and lectures, and publishes books about Buddhism. It represents no one school of Buddhism.

There are estimated to be at least 300 million Buddhists world-wide, and about 275 organizations and groups, an estimated 25,000 adherents and 15 temples or monasteries in the United Kingdom.

THE BUDDHIST SOCIETY, 58 Eccleston Square, London SW1V 1PH. Tel: 0171-834 5858. *General Secretary*, R. C. Maddox

## HINDUISM

Hinduism has no historical founder but is known to have been highly developed in India by about 1200 BC. Its adherents originally called themselves Aryans; Muslim invaders first called the Aryans 'Hindus' (derived from the word 'Sindhu', the name of the river Indus) in the eighth century.

Hinduism's evolution has been complex and it embraces many different religious beliefs, mythologies and practices. Most Hindus hold that *satya* (truthfulness), *ahimsa* (non-violence), honesty, physical labour and tolerance of other faiths are essential for good living. They believe in one supreme spirit (*Brahman*), and in the transmigration of *atman* (the soul). Most Hindus accept the doctrine of *karma* (consequences of actions), the concept of *samsara* (successive lives) and the possibility of all atmans achieving *moksha* (liberation from samsara) through *jnana* (knowledge), *yoga* (meditation), *karma* (work or action) and *bhakti* (devotion).

Most Hindus offer worship to *murtis* (images or statues) representing different aspects of Brahman, and follow their *dharma* (religious and social duty) according to the traditions of their *varna* (social class), *ashrama* (stage in life), *jati* (caste) and *kula* (family).

Hinduism's sacred texts are divided into *shruti* ('heard' or divinely inspired), including the *Vedas*; or *smriti* ('remembered' tradition), including the *Ramayana*, the *Mahabharata*, the *Puranas* (ancient myths), and the sacred law books. Most Hindus recognize the authority of the *Vedas*, the oldest holy books, and accept the philosophical teachings of the *Upanishads*, the *Vedanta Sutras* and the *Bhagavad-Gita*.

Brahman is formless, limitless and all-pervading, and is represented in worship by murtis which may be male or female and in the form of a human, animal or bird. Brahma, Vishnu and Shiva are the most important gods worshipped by Hindus; their respective consorts are Saraswati, Lakshmi and Durga or Parvati, also known as Shakti. There are held to have been ten *avatars* (incarnations) of Vishnu, of whom the most important are Rama and Krishna. Other popular gods are Ganesha, Hanuman and Subrahmanyam. All gods are seen as aspects of the supreme God, not as competing deities.

Orthodox Hindus revere all gods and goddesses equally, but there are many sects, including the Hare-Krishna movement (ISKCon), the Arya Samaj, the Swami Narayan Hindu mission and the Satya Sai-Baba movement. Worship in the sects is concentrated on one deity to the exclusion of others. In some sects a human *guru* (spiritual teacher), usually the head of the organization, is revered more than the deity, while in other sects the guru is seen as the source of spiritual guidance.

Hinduism does not have a centrally-trained and ordained priesthood. The pronouncements of the *shankaracharyas* (heads of monasteries) of Shringeri, Puri, Dwarka and Badrinath are heeded by the orthodox but may be ignored by the various sects.

The commonest form of worship is a *puja*, in which offerings of red and yellow powders, rice grains, water, flowers, food, fruit, incense and light are made to the image of a deity. Puja may be done either in a home shrine or a *mandir* (temple). Many British Hindus celebrate life-cycle rituals with Sanskrit mantras for naming a baby, the sacred thread (an initiation ceremony), marriage and cremation. For details of the Hindu calendar, main festivals etc, *see* pages 84–5.

The largest communities of Hindus in Britain are in Leicester, London, Birmingham and Bradford, and developed as a result of immigration from India, east Africa and Sri Lanka. Many Hindus now are British by birth, with English as their first language; the main ethnic languages are Gujarati, Hindi, Punjabi, Tamil, Bengali and Marathi.

There are an estimated 800 million Hindus world-wide; there are about 360,000 adherents and over 150 temples in the UK.

ARYA PRATINIDHI SABHA (UK), 69A Argyle Road, London W13 0LY
BHARATIYA VIDYA BHAVAN, Old Church Building, 4A Castletown Road, London W14 9HQ. Tel: 0171-381 3086. *Executive Director,* M. Krishnamurti
INTERNATIONAL SOCIETY FOR KRISHNA CONSCIOUSNESS (ISKCon), Bhaktivedanta Manor, Letchmore Heath, nr Watford, Herts. WD2 8EP. Tel: 01923-857244. *Director,* M. Fleming
NATIONAL COUNCIL OF HINDU TEMPLES, c/o Santan Mandir, Weymouth Street, off Catherine Street, Leicester LE1 2JE. Tel: 01772-720413. *General Secretary,* V. Aery
SWAMINARAYAN HINDU MISSION, 54–62 Meadow Garth, London NW10 8HD. Tel: 0181-965 2651
VISHWA HINDU PARISHAD (UK), 48 Wharfedale Gardens, Thornton Heath, Surrey CR7 6LB. Tel: 0181–679 7505. *General Secretary,* K. Ruparelia

## ISLAM

Islam (which means 'peace arising from submission to the will of Allah' in Arabic) is a monotheistic religion which originated in Arabia through the Prophet Muhammad, who was born in Mecca in AD 570. Islam spread to Egypt, North Africa, Spain and the borders of China in the century following the prophet's death, and is now the predominant religion in Indonesia, the Near and Middle East, North and parts of West Africa, Pakistan, Bangladesh, Malaysia and some of the republics of the former Soviet Union. There are also large Muslim communities in many other countries.

For Muslims (adherents of Islam), God (*Allah*) is one and holds absolute power. His commands were revealed to mankind through the prophets, who include Abraham, Moses and Jesus, but his message was gradually corrupted until revealed finally and in perfect form to Muhammad through the angel *Jibril* (Gabriel) over a period of 23 years. This last, incorruptible message has been recorded in the *Qur'an* (Koran), which contains 114 divisions called *surahs*, each made up of *ayahs*, and is held to be the essence of all previous scriptures. The *Ahadith* are the records of the Prophet Muhammad's deeds and sayings (the *Sunnah*) as recounted by his immediate followers. A culture and a system of law and theology gradually developed to form a distinctive Islamic civilization. Islam makes no distinction between sacred and worldly affairs and provides rules for every aspect of human life. The *Shari'a* is the sacred law of Islam based upon prescriptions derived from the Qur'an and the Sunnah of the Prophet.

The 'five pillars of Islam' are *shahada* (a declaration of faith in the oneness and supremacy of Allah); *salat* (formal prayer, to be performed five times a day facing the holy city of Mecca); *zakat* (alms-giving); *saum* (fasting during the month of Ramadan); and *hajj* (pilgrimage to Mecca); some

Muslims would add *jihad* (striving for the cause of good and resistance to evil).

Two main groups developed among Muslims. *Sunni* Muslims accept the legitimacy of Muhammad's first four *caliphs* (successors as head of the Muslim community) and of the authority of the Muslim community as a whole. About 90 per cent of Muslims are Sunni Muslims. *Shi'ites* recognize only Muhammad's son-in-law Ali as his rightful successor and the *Imams* (descendants of Ali, not to be confused with *imams* (prayer leaders or religious teachers)) as the principal legitimate religious authority. The largest group within *Shi'ism* is *Twelver Shi'ism*, which has been the official school of law and theology in Iran since the 16th century; other subsects include the *Ismailis* and the *Druze*, the latter being an offshoot of the Ismailis and differing considerably from the main body of Muslims.

There is no organized priesthood, but holy men such as *ulama, imams* and *ayatollahs* are accorded great respect. The *Sufis* are the mystics of Islam. Mosques are centres for worship and teaching and also for social and welfare activities. For details of the Muslim calendar and festivals, *see* page 86.

Islam was first known in western Europe in the eighth century AD when 800 years of Muslim rule began in Spain. Later, Islam spread to eastern Europe. More recently, Muslims came to Europe from Africa, the Middle East and Asia in the late 19th century. Both the Sunni and Shi'ah traditions are represented in Britain, but the majority of Muslims in Britain adhere to Sunni Islam.

The largest communities are in London, Liverpool, Manchester, Birmingham, Bradford, Cardiff, Edinburgh and Glasgow. There is no central organization, but the Islamic Cultural Centre, which is the London Central Mosque, and the Imams and Mosques Council are influential bodies; there are many other Muslim organizations in Britain.

There are about 1,000 million Muslims world-wide, with at least one million adherents and over 350 mosques in Britain.

ISLAMIC CULTURAL CENTRE, 146 Park Road, London NW8 7RG. Tel: 0171-724 3363. *Director,* Dr M. A. al-Ghamdi
IMAMS AND MOSQUES COUNCIL, 20–22 Creffield Road, London W5 3RP. Tel: 0181-992 6636. *Director of the Council and Principal of the Muslim College,* Dr M. A. Z. Badawi

## JUDAISM

Judaism is the oldest monotheistic faith. The primary authority of Judaism is the Hebrew Bible or *Tanakh*, which records how the descendants of Abraham were led by Moses out of their slavery in Egypt to Mount Sinai where God's law (*Torah*) was revealed to them as the chosen people. The *Talmud*, which consists of commentaries on the *Mishnah* (the first text of rabbinical Judaism), is also held to be authoritative, and may be divided into two main categories: the *halakah* (dealing with legal and ritual matters) and the *Aggadah* (dealing with theological and ethical matters not directly concerned with the regulation of conduct). The *Midrash* comprises rabbinic writings containing biblical interpretations in the spirit of the *Aggadah*. The *halakah* has become a source of division; Orthodox Jews regard Jewish law as derived from God and therefore unalterable; Reform and Liberal Jews seek to interpret it in the light of contemporary considerations; and Conservative Jews aim to maintain most of the traditional rituals but to allow changes in accordance with that tradition. Reconstructionist Judaism, a 20th-century movement, regards Judaism as a culture rather than a theological system and therefore accepts all forms of Jewish practice.

The family is the basic unit of Jewish ritual, with the synagogue playing an important role as the centre for public worship and religious study. A synagogue is led by a group of laymen who are elected to office; there are no priestly roles. The Rabbi is primarily a teacher and spiritual guide. The Sabbath is the central religious observance. For details of the Jewish calendar, fasts and festivals, *see* page 85. Most British Jews are descendants of either the *Ashkenazim* of central and eastern Europe or the *Sephardim* of Spain and Portugal.

The Chief Rabbi of the United Hebrew Congregations of the Commonwealth is appointed by a Chief Rabbinate Conference, and is the rabbinical authority of the Orthodox sector of the Ashkenazi Jewish community. His authority is not recognized by the Reform Synagogues of Great Britain (the largest progressive group), the Union of Liberal and Progressive Synagogues, the Union of Orthodox Hebrew Congregations, the Federation of Synagogues, the Sephardi community, or the Assembly of Masorti Synagogues. He is, however, generally recognized both outside the Jewish community and within it as the public religious representative of the totality of British Jewry.

The *Beth Din* (Court of Judgment) is the rabbinic court. The *Dayanim* (Assessors) adjudicate in disputes or on matters of Jewish law and tradition; they also oversee dietary law administration. The Chief Rabbi is President of the *Beth Din* of the United Synagogue.

The Board of Deputies of British Jews was established in 1760 and is the representative body of British Jewry. The basis of representation is mainly synagogal, but communal organizations are also represented. It watches over the interests of British Jewry and seeks to counter anti-Jewish discrimination.

There are over 12.5 million Jews world-wide; in Great Britain and Ireland there are an estimated 300,000 adherents and about 350 synagogues. Of these, 185 congregations and about 150 rabbis and ministers are under the jurisdiction of the Chief Rabbi. A further 99 orthodox congregations have a more independent status, and 72 congregations do not recognize the authority of the Chief Rabbi.

CHIEF RABBINATE, Adler House, Tavistock Square, London WC1H 9HN. Tel: 0171-387 1066. *Chief Rabbi*, Dr Jonathan Sacks; *Executive Director*, J. Kestenbaum
BETH DIN (COURT OF THE CHIEF RABBI), Adler House, Tavistock Square, London WC1H 0EP. Tel: 0171-387 5772. *Registrar*, J. Phillips; *Dayanim*, Rabbi C. Ehrentreu; Rabbi I. Binstock; Rabbi C. D. Kaplin; Rabbi I. D. Berger
BOARD OF DEPUTIES OF BRITISH JEWS, Woburn House, Tavistock Square, London WC1H 0EZ. Tel: 0171-387 3952. *President*, E. Tabachnik, QC; *Chief Executive*, N. A. Nagler
ASSEMBLY OF MASORTI SYNAGOGUES, 766 Finchley Road, London NW11 7TH. Tel: 0181-201 8772. *Administrator*, vacant
FEDERATION OF SYNAGOGUES, 65 Watford Way, London NW4 3AQ. Tel: 0181-202 2263. *Administrator*, G. Kushner
REFORM SYNAGOGUES OF GREAT BRITAIN, The Sternberg Centre for Judaism, Manor House, 80 East End Road, London N3 2SY. Tel: 0181-349 4731. *Chief Executive*, Rabbi T. Bayfield
SPANISH AND PORTUGUESE JEWS' CONGREGATION, 2 Ashworth Road, London W9 1JY. Tel: 0171-289 2573. *Chief Executive*, Mrs J. Velleman

UNION OF LIBERAL AND PROGRESSIVE SYNAGOGUES, The Montagu Centre, 21 Maple Street, London W1P 6DS. Tel: 0171-580 1663. *Director*, Mrs R. Rosenberg
UNION OF ORTHODOX HEBREW CONGREGATIONS, 40 Queen Elizabeth's Walk, London N16 0HH. Tel: 0181-802 6226. *Executive Director*, Rabbi A. Klein
UNITED SYNAGOGUE HEAD OFFICE, Woburn House, Tavistock Square, London WC1H 0EZ. Tel: 0171-387 4300. *Chief Executive*, J. M. Lew

## SIKHISM

The Sikh religion dates from the birth of Guru Nanak in the Punjab in 1469. The word 'guru' means teacher, but in Sikh tradition it has come to represent the divine presence of God giving inner spiritual guidance. Nanak's role as the human vessel of the divine guru was passed on to nine successors, the last of whom (Guru Gobind Singh) died in 1708. The immortal guru is now held to reside in the sacred scripture, *Guru Granth Sahib*, and so to be present in all Sikh gatherings.

Guru Nanak taught that there is one God and that different religions are like different roads leading to the same destination. He condemned religious conflict, ritualism and caste prejudices. The fifth Guru, Guru Arjan, compiled the Sikh Holy Book, a collection of hymns (*gurbani*) known as the *Adi Granth*. It includes the writings of the first five Gurus and selected writings of Hindu and Muslim saints whose views are in accord with the Guru's teachings. Guru Arjan also built the Golden Temple at Amritsar, the centre of Sikhism. The tenth Guru, Guru Gobind Singh, passed on the guruship to the sacred scripture, Guru Granth Sahib. He also founded the *Khalsa*, an order intended to fight against tyranny and injustice. Male initiates to the order added 'Singh' to their given names and women added 'Kaur'. Guru Gobind Singh also made five symbols obligatory: *kaccha* (a special undergarment), *kara* (a steel bangle), *kirpan* (a small sword), *kesh* (long unshorn hair, and consequently the wearing of a turban), and *kangha* (a comb). These practices are still compulsory for those Sikhs who are initiated into the *Khalsa* (the *Amritdharis*). Those who do not seek initiation are known as *Sahajdharis*.

There are no professional priests in Sikhism; anyone with a reasonable proficiency in the Punjabi language can conduct a service. Worship can be offered individually or communally, and in a private house or a *gurdwara* (temple). Sikhs are forbidden to eat meat prepared by ritual slaughter; they are also asked to abstain from smoking, alcohol and other intoxicants. For details of the Sikh calendar and main celebrations, *see* page 86.

Sikhs first came to Britain in the 1950s, mainly for economic and political reasons. The largest Sikh communities are in London, Bradford, Leeds, Huddersfield, Birmingham, Nottingham, Coventry and Wolverhampton. Every gurdwara manages its own affairs and there is no central body in the UK. The Sikh Missionary Society UK works for the advancement of Sikhism and provides an information service.

There are about 12.5 million Sikhs world-wide and an estimated 400,000 adherents and 170 gurdwaras in Great Britain.

SIKH MISSIONARY SOCIETY UK, 10 Featherstone Road, Southall, Middx. UB2 5AA. Tel: 0181-574 1902. *Hon. Secretary*, T. S. Manget

# Development Corporations

## NEW TOWNS

### COMMISSION FOR THE NEW TOWNS
Glen House, Stag Place, London SWIE 5AJ
Tel 0171-828 7722

The Commission was established under the New Towns Act 1959. Its remit is to hold, manage and turn to account the property of development corporations transferred to the Commission; and to dispose of property so transferred and any other property held by it, as soon as it considers it expedient to do so. In carrying out its remit the Commission must have due regard to the convenience and welfare of persons residing, working or carrying on business there and, until disposal, the maintenance and enhancement of the value of the land held and return obtained from it.

The Commission has such responsibilities in Basildon, Bracknell, Central Lancashire, Corby, Crawley, Harlow, Hatfield, Hemel Hempstead, Milton Keynes, Northampton, Peterborough, Redditch, Skelmersdale, Stevenage, Telford, Warrington and Runcorn, Washington, and Welwyn Garden City. The Commission has minimal responsibilities (principally financial and litigation) in Aycliffe and Peterlee, and Cwmbran following the wind-up of their development corporations in 1988.
*Chairman*, Sir Neil Shields, MC
*Deputy Chairman*, The Lord Finsberg, MBE
*Members*, R. B. Caws, CBE; The Lord Bellwin; Sir Brian Jenkins, GBE; M. H. Mallinson; F. C. Graves, OBE; J. Trustram Eve; Ms W. Luscombe; Lady Marsh
*Chief Executive*, N. J. Walker

#### REGIONAL OFFICES
NORTH (Central Lancashire, Skelmersdale, Warrington and Runcorn, Washington, Aycliffe and Peterlee), New Town House, Buttermarket Street, Warrington WAI 2LF. Tel: 01925-651144. *Director*, J. Leigh
CENTRAL (Milton Keynes, Corby, Northampton), Saxon Court, 502 Avebury Boulevard, Central Milton Keynes MK9 3HS. Tel: 01908-692692. *Director*, J. Napleton
WEST MIDLANDS (Redditch, Telford), Jordan House West, Hall Court, Hall Park Way, Telford TF3 4NN. Tel: 01952-293131. *Director*, C. Mackrell
SOUTH (Basildon, Bracknell, Crawley, Harlow, Hatfield, Hemel Hempstead, Peterborough, Stevenage, Welwyn Garden City), Glen House, Stag Place, London SWIE 5AJ. Tel: 0171-828 7722. *Director*, G. D. Johnston

## DEVELOPMENT CORPORATIONS

### WALES

DEVELOPMENT BOARD FOR RURAL WALES (1977), Ladywell House, Newtown, Powys SY16 IJB. Tel: 01686-626965. *Chairman*, D. Rowe-Beddoe.

### SCOTLAND

CUMBERNAULD, Strathclyde (1956), Cumbernauld House, Cumbernauld G67 3JH. *Chairman*, D. W. Mitchell, CBE. *Chief Executive*, D. Millan. Area, 7,788 acres. Population, 50,600. Estimated eventual population, 60,000
EAST KILBRIDE, Strathclyde (1947), Atholl House, East Kilbride, Glasgow G74 ILU. *Chairman*, J. A. Denholm,

CBE. *Managing Director*, J. C. Shaw. Area, 10,250 acres. Population, 70,300. Estimated eventual population, 82,500
GLENROTHES, Fife (1948), Balgonie Road, Markinch, Glenrothes KY7 6AH. *Chairman*, Prof. C. Blake, CBE. *General Manager*, J. A. F. McCombie. Area, 5,757 acres. Population, 39,700. Estimated eventual population, 44,000
IRVINE, Ayrshire (1966), Perceton House, Irvine, Ayrshire KAII 2AL. *Chairman*, M. Crichton, CBE. *Managing Director*, Brig. R. A. Rickets. Area, 16,000 acres. Population, 56,000. Estimated eventual population, 70,000
LIVINGSTON, West Lothian (1962), Sidlaw House, Almondvale North, Livingston, West Lothian EH54 6QA. *Chairman*, R. S. Watt, CBE. *Chief Executive*, J. A. Pollock. Area, 6,868 acres. Population, 43,800. Estimated eventual population, 50,000

## URBAN DEVELOPMENT CORPORATIONS

Urban development corporations were established under the Local Government, Planning and Land Act 1980. Their remit is to bring land and buildings in selected areas back into effective use by developing infrastructure, housing, employment and the environment. The corporations encourage business, especially from overseas, to invest in the area and can provide grants to assist commercial and industrial development.

### ENGLAND

BIRMINGHAM HEARTLANDS (1992), Waterlinks House, Richard Street, Birmingham, B7 4AA. Tel: 0121-333 3060. *Chairman*, Sir Reginald Eyre; *Chief Executive*, J. Beeston. Area, 1,000 hectares
BLACK COUNTRY (1987), Black Country House, Rounds Green Road, Oldbury B69 2RD. Tel: 0121-511 2000. *Chairman*, G. Carter, CBE; *Chief Executive*, D. Morgan. Area, 2,600 hectares
BRISTOL (1989), 2nd Floor, Techno House, Redcliffe Way, Bristol BSI 6NX. Tel: 0117-925 5222. *Chairman*, C. Thomas; *Chief Executive*, M. Collinge. Area, 360 hectares
CENTRAL MANCHESTER (1988), Churchgate House, 56 Oxford Street, Manchester MI 6EU. Tel: 0161-236 1166. *Chairman*, Dr J. Grigor; *Chief Executive*, J. Glester. Area, 187 hectares
LEEDS (1988), South Point, South Accommodation Road, Leeds LS10 IPP. Tel: 0113-244 6273. *Chairman*, P. Hartley; *Chief Executive*, M. Eagland. Area, 540 hectares
LONDON DOCKLANDS (1981), Thames Quay, 191 Marsh Wall, London E14 9TJ. Tel: 0171-512 3000. *Chairman*, M. Pickard; *Chief Executive*, E. Sorenson. Area, 2,226 hectares
MERSEYSIDE (1981), Royal Liver Buildings, Pier Head, Liverpool L3 IJH. Tel: 0151-236 6090. *Chairman*, Sir Desmond Pitcher; *Chief Executive*, C. Farrow. Area, 960 hectares
PLYMOUTH (1993), Royal William Yard, Plymouth PLI 3RP. Tel: 01752-256132. *Chairman*, Sir Robert Gerken; *Chief Executive*, J. Collinson. Area, 67 hectares
SHEFFIELD (1988), Don Valley House, Saville Street East, Sheffield S4 7UQ. Tel: 0114-272 0100. *Chairman*, H. Sykes; *Chief Executive*, G. Kendall. Area, 800 hectares

TEESSIDE (1987), Dunedin House, Riverside Quay, Stockton-on-Tees TS17 6BJ. Tel: 01642–677123. *Chairman,* R. Norman, OBE; *Chief Executive,* D. Hall. Area, 4,600 hectares

TRAFFORD PARK (1987), Waterside, Trafford Wharf Road, Trafford Park, Manchester M17 IEX. Tel: 0161–848 8000. *Chairman,* W. Morgan; *Chief Executive,* M. Shields. Area, 1,270 hectares

TYNE AND WEAR (1987), Scotswood House, Newcastle Business Park, Newcastle upon Tyne NE4 7YL. Tel: 0191–226 1234. *Chairman,* Sir Paul Nicholson; *Chief Executive,* A. Balls. Area, 2,400 hectares

WALES

CARDIFF BAY (1987), Baltic House, Mount Stuart Square, Cardiff CF1 6DH. Tel: 01222–585858. *Chairman,* Sir Geoffrey Inkin, OBE; *Chief Executive,* M. Boyce. Area, 1,094 hectares

NORTHERN IRELAND

LAGANSIDE (1989), Clarendon Building, 15 Clarendon Road, Belfast BT1 3BG. Tel: 01232–328507. *Chairman,* The Duke of Abercorn; *Chief Executive,* G. Mackey. Area, 122 hectares

---

# The Cinque Ports

As their name implies, the Cinque Ports were originally five in number: Hastings, New Romney, Hythe, Dover and Sandwich. They were formed during the eleventh century to defend the Channel coast and, after the Norman Conquest, were recognized as a Confederation by a charter of 1278. The 'antient towns' of Winchelsea and Rye were added at some time after the Conquest. The other members of the Confederation, known as Limbs, are Lydd, Faversham, Folkestone, Deal, Tenterden, Margate and Ramsgate.

Until 1855 the duty of the Cinque Ports was to provide ships and men for the defence of the state in return for considerable privileges, such as tax exemptions and the framing of by-laws. Of these privileges only jurisdiction in Admiralty remains.

The Barons of the Cinque Ports have the ancient privilege of attending the Coronation ceremony and are allotted special places in Westminster Abbey.

*Lord Warden of the Cinque Ports,* HM Queen Elizabeth the Queen Mother

*Judge, Court of Admiralty,* G. Darling, RD, QC

*Registrar,* I. G. Gill, LVO, 3 Waterloo Crescent, Dover, Kent CT16 1LA. Tel: 01304-225225

LORD WARDENS OF THE CINQUE PORTS *since* 1904

| | |
|---|---|
| The Marquess Curzon | 1904 |
| The Prince of Wales | 1905 |
| The Earl Brassey | 1908 |
| The Earl Beauchamp | 1913 |
| The Marquess of Reading | 1934 |
| The Marquess of Willingdon | 1936 |
| Winston Churchill | 1941 |
| Sir Robert Menzies | 1965 |
| HM Queen Elizabeth the Queen Mother | 1978 |

# Education

For addresses of national education departments, *see* Government Departments and Public Offices. For other addresses, *see* Education Directory

Responsibility for education in the United Kingdom is largely decentralized. Overall responsibility for all aspects of education in England lies with the Secretary of State for Education; in Wales with the Secretary of State for Wales; in Scotland with the Secretary of State for Scotland acting through the Scottish Office Education Department; and in Northern Ireland with the Secretary of State for Northern Ireland.

The main concerns of the education departments (the Department for Education (DFE), the Welsh Office, the Scottish Office Education Department (SOED), and the Department of Education for Northern Ireland (DENI)) are the formulation of national policies for education, and the maintenance of consistency in educational standards. They are responsible for the broad allocation of resources for education, for the rate and distribution of educational building and for the supply, training and superannuation of teachers. Hitherto, none of the education departments have run any schools or colleges directly, nor employed any teachers. However, under the provisions of the Education Reform Act 1988 and the Self-Governing Schools etc. (Scotland) Act 1989 the Welsh office and the Scottish Office Education Department fund individual schools which have opted out of local education authority control and applied for direct funding from the Secretaries of State; those in England are funded by the Funding Agency for Schools (FAS). In addition, the Department for Education, in association with sponsors from industry, funds the City Technology Colleges (CTCs), the City College for the Technology of the Arts and pays grants to the new Technology Colleges. Technology Academies are proposed on a similar basis in Scotland.

Schools in Northern Ireland providing integrated education are able to apply for grant-maintained status from the Department of Education for Northern Ireland.

## EXPENDITURE

The Department for Education, the Welsh Office, the Scottish Office and the Northern Ireland Office act within a framework of estimates approved by Parliament.

In real terms expenditure on education by central government departments was (£ million):

|  | 1993–4 estimated outturn | 1994–5 planned |
|---|---|---|
| DFE | 9,817 | 10,410 |
| Welsh Office | 424.6 | 484.7 |
| SOED | 1,192 | 1,318 |
| DENI | 1,243 | 1,291 |

In the United Kingdom in 1991–2, central government provisional expenditure on education was (£million):

| | |
|---|---|
| Schools | 17,187 |
| Further and higher education | 7,395 |
| Other education and related expenditure | 2,974 |

Most of this expenditure is incurred by local authorities, which make their own expenditure decisions according to their local situations and needs and which, until April 1993, were also responsible for funding most further education courses. The bulk of direct expenditure by the DFE, the Welsh Office and SOED is directed towards supporting higher education in universities and colleges through the Higher Education Funding Councils (HEFCs) and further education and sixth form colleges through the Further Education Funding Councils (FEFCs) in England and Wales and directly from central government in Scotland. In addition, the DFE funds grant-maintained schools through the Funding Agency for Schools (FAS) and CTCs in the schools sector.

The Welsh Office also funds grants for higher and further education, grant-maintained schools, educational services and research, and supports bilingual education and the Welsh language.

In Scotland the bulk of expenditure on education is at a local level by the regional and islands councils. In addition to those outlined above, the main elements of central government expenditure are grant-aided special schools, self-governing schools, student awards, curriculum development, special educational needs and community education.

The Department of Education for Northern Ireland finances higher education, teacher education, teacher salaries and superannuation, student awards, grant-maintained integrated schools, and voluntary grammar schools. Remaining expenditure is by education and library boards at local level.

Current net expenditure on education by local education authorities in England and Wales, regional and islands councils in Scotland, and education and library boards in Northern Ireland is as follows (£million):

|  | 1993–4 estimated outturn | 1994–5 planned |
|---|---|---|
| England | 19,843 | 17,087 |
| Wales | 1,240.1 | 1,243.9 |
| Scotland | 2,427 | 2,460 |
| Northern Ireland | 886 | 898 |

## LOCAL EDUCATION ADMINISTRATION

The education service at present is a national service in which the provision of most school education is locally administered;* its administration is still largely decentralized.

In England and Wales the education service is administered by local education authorities (LEAs), which carry the day-to-day responsibility for providing most state primary and secondary education in their areas, although the planning and supply of school places is to be shared with the Funding Agency for Schools (FAS) as the number of pupils in grant-maintained schools grows. They also share with the Further Education Funding Councils the duty to provide adult education to meet the needs of their areas.

Each local education authority was formerly required by statute to appoint an education committee, or committees, authorized to exercise on its behalf any of its functions with respect to education, except the power to borrow money. The passing of the Education Act 1993 removed this requirement and LEAs are now free to organize themselves as they think fit.

The LEAs own and maintain schools and colleges, build new ones and provide equipment. Most of the public money spent on education is disbursed by the local authorities. LEAs are financed largely from the council tax and aggregate external finance (AEF) from the Department of the Environment in England and the Welsh Office in Wales.

The powers of local education authorities as regards the control of schools have been modified in recent years. The

Education (No. 2) Act 1986 legislated for equal numbers of parents and local authority representatives as governors in most maintained schools. The process was continued by the Education Reform Act 1988, which delegated control of their budgets directly to all schools. It also provided for schools to opt out of local authority control. These grant-maintained (GM) schools are funded by the Funding Agency for Schools in England. Those in Wales are funded by the Welsh Office at present but the Schools Funding Council for Wales will take over when the number of grant-maintained schools warrants the change. The Education Act 1993 facilitated opting out and enabled primary schools to apply for grant-maintained status as a group as well as individually. It also provided for an Education Association to be set up to take over the management of failing schools where both the LEA and the governing body have not brought about the improvements identified as necessary.

The duty of providing education locally in Scotland rests with the nine regional and three islands councils. They are responsible for the construction of buildings, the employment of teachers and other staff, and the provision of equipment and materials. Management is to be devolved to all primary and secondary schools by April 1996, although the deadline has been extended to April 1998 in primary schools with headteachers who teach full-time, and to April 1997 in all special schools. The councils' responsibility for the curricula taught in schools is shared with headteachers under the guidance of the Secretary of State for Scotland and the Scottish Consultative Council on the Curriculum.

The powers of local authorities over educational institutions under their control have been reduced also in Scotland. Under the School Boards (Scotland) Act 1988, education authorities are required to establish school boards consisting of parents and teachers as well as co-opted members, responsible among other things for the appointment of staff. The Self-Governing Schools etc. (Scotland) Act 1989 provides for schools to withdraw from local authority control and become self-governing; for the institution of Technology Academies directly funded by central government; for the composition of further education college councils on which at least half the members are employers, and for the delegation of substantial functions to these new councils.

Education is administered locally in Northern Ireland by five education and library boards, whose costs are met in full by DENI. A review of educational administration is taking place but no major changes will be introduced before 1997. All grant-aided schools include elected parents and teachers on their boards of governors. Provision has been made for schools wishing to provide integrated education to have grant-maintained integrated status from the outset. All schools and colleges of further education have full responsibility for their own budgets, including staffing costs.

The Council for Catholic Maintained Schools forms an upper tier of management for Catholic schools and provides advice on matters relating to management and administration.

### The Inspectorate

Under the Education (Schools) Act 1992, the Office for Standards in Education (OFSTED), headed by HM Chief Inspector of Schools in England (HMCI), was created separately from the DFE. Its counterpart in Wales is the Office of HM Chief Inspector of Schools in Wales (OHMCI Wales). OFSTED's remit is to inspect, report on and improve standards of achievement and quality of education through regular independent inspection, public reporting and informed advice. A new system of inspection by independent registered inspectors has been set up, which provides a full inspection for all state schools every four years, starting from September 1993 for secondary schools and September 1994 for primary and special schools. OFSTED selects the teams of independent inspectors following bids for the contracts. A summary of the inspection report must be sent to parents of each pupil, followed by a copy of the governors' action plan thereon. The inspection of further and higher education in England and Wales is the responsibility of inspectors appointed to the respective funding councils. HM Inspectorate in Scotland carries out the inspection of schools and further education institutions in that country, and in addition requires schools to produce a document setting out their educational targets for the two years ahead and a report on progress over the previous two years. The inspection of higher education is the responsibility of inspectors appointed to the Higher Education Funding Council for Scotland. Inspection is carried out in Northern Ireland by the Education and Training Inspectorate of the Department of Education which also performs an advisory function to the Secretary of State for Northern Ireland. From September 1992 a five-year cycle of inspection was introduced.

There were, in 1994–5, 240 HMIs who act as special advisers to OFSTED and about 6,000 independent inspectors in England, 53 HMIs and about 385 independent inspectors in Wales, 102 in Scotland and 60 members of the Inspectorate in Northern Ireland.

## SCHOOLS AND PUPILS

Schooling is compulsory in Great Britain for all children between five and 16 years and between five and 16 years in Northern Ireland. Some provision is made for children under five and many pupils remain at school after the minimum leaving age. No fees are charged in any publicly maintained school in England, Wales and Scotland. In Northern Ireland, fees are paid by pupils in preparatory departments of grammar schools, but pupils admitted to the secondary departments of grammar schools do not pay fees.

In the United Kingdom, parents have a right to express a preference for a particular school and have a right to appeal if dissatisfied. Parental choice has been increased by the introduction of a policy known as more open enrolment whereby schools are required to admit children up to the limit of their capacity if there is a demand for places, and to publish their criteria for selection if they are over-subscribed, in which case parents have a right of appeal.

The 'Parents' Charter', available free from education departments, is a booklet which tells parents about the education system. Schools are now required to make available information about themselves, their public examination results, truancy rates, and destination of leavers. Corporal punishment is no longer legal in publicly maintained schools in the United Kingdom.

### Fall and Rise in Numbers

In primary education, and increasingly in secondary education, pupil numbers in the United Kingdom declined through the 1980s. In nursery and primary schools pupil numbers reached their lowest figure of 4.5 million in 1990. Numbers are expected to increase gradually year by year until by 2000 they reach about 5.3 million. In secondary schools pupil numbers peaked at 4.6 million in 1981. They stood at 3.5 million in 1991 and are projected to rise to 3.9 million in 2000.

ENGLAND AND WALES

There are two main categories of school in England and Wales: publicly maintained schools, which charge no fees; and independent schools, which charge fees (*see* pages 448–9). Most publicly maintained schools are maintained by local education authorities. However, as a result of the Education Reform Act 1988, there are now two other categories: grant-maintained schools, which are funded through the Funding Agency for Schools in England and by the Welsh office in Wales. These comprise primary and secondary schools which, although still providing free education, have applied to opt out of local education authority control in favour of grant-maintained status; and City Technology Colleges (*see* below). There are 31,861 schools in the maintained sector and 2,488 independent schools.

Maintained schools are of two types: (i) county schools (16,666 in 1993) which are owned by LEAs and wholly funded by them. They are non-denominational and provide primary and secondary education; and (ii) voluntary schools (7,515 in 1993) which also provide primary and secondary education. Although the buildings are in many cases provided by the voluntary bodies (mainly religious denominations), they are financially maintained by an LEA.

Voluntary schools are of three kinds: controlled (3,093), aided (4,357) and special agreement (65). In controlled schools the LEA bears all costs. In aided schools the building is usually provided by the voluntary body. The managers or governors are responsible for repairs to the school building and for improvements and alterations to it, though the Department for Education may reimburse part of approved capital expenditure, while the LEA pays for internal maintenance and other running costs. Special agreement schools are those where the LEA may, by special agreement, pay between one-half and three-quarters of the cost of building a new, or extending an existing, voluntary school, almost always a secondary school. There are no special agreement schools in Wales. In voluntary schools the majority of the managers or governors are appointed by the voluntary body and at least one by the LEA. The managers or governors control the appointment of teachers. Expenditure is normally apportioned between the authority and the voluntary body.

All publicly maintained schools have a governing body usually made up of a number of parent representatives, governors appointed by the LEA if the school is LEA maintained, the headteacher (unless he or she chooses otherwise), and serving teachers. The Education Act 1993 allows schools to appoint up to four sponsor governors from business who will be expected to provide financial and managerial assistance. Parental involvement in the running of schools has increased considerably in recent years, and parents have also been given the power to decide by ballot whether their child's school should opt out of local authority control and become grant-maintained. Governors are responsible for the overall policies of schools and their academic aims and objectives; they also control matters of school discipline and the appointment and dismissal of staff. Under the Education (Schools) Act 1992, governing bodies select inspectors for their schools, are responsible for action as a result of inspection reports and are required to make these reports and their action plans thereon available to parents. The Education Reform Act 1988 delegated control of the administration of the major part of school budgets, including staffing costs, from LEAs directly to schools under the Local Management of Schools (LMS) initiative. In April 1995 the proportion of the budget which must be delegated will rise from 85 per cent to 95 per cent. LEAs continue to retain responsibility for various services, including transport and school meals.

*Technology Colleges* – In autumn 1993, building on the technology schools initiative which ran from 1991 to 1993, the Government published a detailed prospectus for grant-maintained and voluntary-aided secondary schools wishing to become Technology Colleges specializing in the teaching of technology, mathematics and science. In addition to the normal funding arrangements, they receive business sponsorship (up to four sponsor governors may sit on governing bodies) and complementary capital grants from central government, together with annual grants to assist the delivery of an enhanced curriculum. In September 1994, 42 schools began operating as technology colleges.

*Grant-maintained (GM) schools* – All secondary and primary schools are eligible to apply for grant-maintained status, subject to a ballot of parents. GM schools are maintained directly by the Secretary of State and the Welsh office, not the LEA, and are wholly run by their own governing body. The Funding Agency for Schools (FAS) was set up in April 1994 to take over the payment of grants to grant-maintained schools in England. The Schools Funding Council for Wales will be instituted when the number of GM schools, 16 in July 1994, justifies the change in funding arrangements. In June 1994 there were 928 schools operating under grant-maintained status, 594 secondary schools, and 334 primary schools. By September 1994 there were projected to be nearly 1,000 grant-maintained schools in operation.

*City Technology Colleges (CTCs)* and *City Colleges for the Technology of the Arts (CCTAs)* are state-aided but independent of LEAs. Their aim is to widen the choice of secondary education in disadvantaged urban areas and to teach a broad curriculum with an emphasis on science, technology, business understanding and arts technologies. Capital costs are shared by government and sponsors from industry and commerce, and running costs are covered by a per capita grant from the DFE in line with comparable costs in an LEA maintained school. The first city technology college opened in September 1988 in Solihull. By September 1993 there were 15. The first CCTA, known as Britschool, opened in Croydon in September 1991.

SCOTLAND

Schools in Scotland fall into three main categories: education authority schools (3,798) (known as public schools), which are managed by the regional and islands councils and financed jointly by the councils and central government; grant-aided schools (10), conducted by voluntary managers who receive grants direct from the Scottish Office Education Department; and independent schools (121), which receive no direct grant and charge fees, but are subject to inspection and registration. An additional category is created under the provisions of the Self-Governing Schools etc. (Scotland) Act 1989, of schools opting to be managed entirely by a board of management consisting of the headmaster, parent and staff representatives and co-opted members. The change of status will require a ballot of parents and the publication of proposals by the board, and the achievement of self-government is subject to a final decision by the Secretary of State. These schools will remain in the public sector and will be funded by direct government grant set to match the resources the school would have received under education authority management. One has so far been established.

Under the School Boards (Scotland) Act 1988, education authorities are required to establish school boards to participate in the administration and management of schools. These boards consist of elected parents and staff members as well as co-opted members.

*Technology Academies (TAs)* – The Self-Governing Schools etc. (Scotland) Act 1989 provides for setting up technology academies in areas of urban deprivation. These secondary schools are intended to be so placed as to draw on a wide catchment, and to offer a broad curriculum with an emphasis on science and technology. They are to be founded and managed in partnership with industrial sponsors, with central government meeting the running costs by grant-aid thereafter. None has yet been set up.

NORTHERN IRELAND

There are three main categories of grant-aided school in Northern Ireland: controlled schools (695), which are controlled by the education and library boards with all costs paid from public funds; voluntary maintained schools (578), mainly under Roman Catholic management, which receive grants towards capital costs and running costs in whole or in part; and voluntary grammar schools (52), which may be under Roman Catholic or non-denominational management and receive grants from the Department of Education for Northern Ireland. All grant-aided schools include elected parents and teachers on their boards of governors, whose responsibilities also include financial management under the Local Management of Schools (LMS) initiative. About 85 per cent of the potential funds available to schools are now delegated to them. Legislation has been introduced under which voluntary maintained and voluntary grammar schools can apply for designation as a new category of voluntary school, which is eligible for a 100 per cent as opposed to 85 per cent grant. Such schools are managed by a board of governors on which no single interest group has a majority of nominees. There are also 18 independent schools in Northern Ireland.

The majority of children in Northern Ireland are educated in schools which in practice are segregated on religious lines. Integrated schools exist to educate Protestant and Roman Catholic children together. There are two types: grant-maintained integrated schools which are funded by DENI; and controlled integrated schools funded by the education and library boards. Procedures are also in place for balloting parents in existing segregated schools to determine whether they want instead to have integrated schools. By September 1994, 23 integrated schools had been established, six of them secondary.

THE STATE SYSTEM

NURSERY EDUCATION – Nursery education is for children from two to five years and is not compulsory. It takes place in nursery schools or nursery classes in primary schools. In 1991–2, 817,400 pupils under five years of age were receiving education in maintained nursery and primary schools, an increase of 18,000 on the previous year. Of the total, 84,700 were in nursery schools, 676,900 in primary schools, and 49,100 in non-maintained nursery schools. Expressed as a percentage of the population aged three and four years, the 817,400 represented 52.7 per cent, compared to 51.6 per cent in the previous year. Many children also attend pre-school playgroups organized by parents and voluntary bodies such as the Pre-School Playgroups Association.

PRIMARY EDUCATION – Primary education begins at five years in Great Britain and four years in Northern Ireland, and is almost always co-educational. In England, Wales and Northern Ireland the transfer to secondary school is generally made at 11 years. In Scotland, the primary school course lasts for seven years and pupils transfer to secondary courses at about the age of 12.

Primary schools consist mainly of infants' schools for children aged five to seven, junior schools for those aged seven to 11, and combined junior and infant schools for both age groups. First schools in some parts of England cater for ages five to ten as the first stage of a three-tier system: first, middle and secondary. Many primary schools provide nursery classes for children under five (*see* above).

The number of primary schools in the United Kingdom in 1991–2 was 23,958, which was 177 fewer than in 1990–1, with 4,998,500 full- and part-time pupils, of which 817,400 were under five. Between 1991 and 2000 primary school pupil numbers are projected to rise by about 9.6 per cent.

Pupil-teacher ratios in maintained primary schools were:

|                  | 1990–1 | 1991–2 |
|------------------|--------|--------|
| England          | 22.0   | 22.0   |
| Wales            | 22.3   | 22.3   |
| Scotland         | 19.5   | 19.5   |
| Northern Ireland | 22.9   | 22.6   |
| UK               | 21.8   | 21.6   |

The average size of classes 'as taught' fell to 23.8 in 1991 but rose to 25.5 in 1993.

MIDDLE SCHOOLS – Middle schools (which take children from first schools), mostly in England, cover varying age ranges between eight and 14 and usually lead on to comprehensive upper schools.

SECONDARY EDUCATION – Secondary schools are for children aged 11 to 16 and for those who choose to stay on to 18. At 16, many students prefer to move on to tertiary or sixth form colleges (*see* page 453). Most secondary schools in England, Wales and Scotland are co-educational. The largest secondary schools have over 2,000 pupils but only 21.4 per cent of the schools take over 1,000 pupils.

In England and Wales the main types of secondary schools are: comprehensive schools (85.4 per cent of pupils in England, 99.1 in Wales), whose admission arrangements are without reference to ability or aptitude; middle deemed secondary schools for children aged variously between eight and 14 years who then move on to senior comprehensive schools at 12, 13 or 14 (6.4 per cent of pupils in England); secondary modern schools (3.6 per cent of pupils in England) providing a general education with a practical bias; secondary grammar schools (3.8 per cent of pupils in England) with selective intake providing an academic course from 11 to 16–18 years; and technical schools (0.1 per cent in England), providing an integrated academic and technical education.

In January 1992 there were in England and Wales 3,009,800 pupils in maintained secondary schools, including 10.3 per cent in England and 12.8 per cent in Wales who were 16 or over. After falling by 16 per cent between 1987 and 1991, numbers are projected to rise 11.3 per cent by 2000.

Pupil-teacher ratios improved steadily from 15.7 in 1987 to 15.3 in 1990 in England and Wales, then rose to 15.9 in 1993. The average class size in England and Wales in 1993 was 21.4.

In Scotland all pupils in education authority secondary schools attend schools with a comprehensive intake. Most of these schools provide a full range of courses appropriate to all levels of ability from first to sixth year. In 1992–3 there were 303,077 pupils in education authority schools, of whom 21.7 per cent were 16 or over. Numbers are projected to increase to 328,000 in 2001. Pupil-teacher ratios worsened from 12.4 in 1991 to 12.8 in 1993. The average class size in 1993 rose to 19.4.

In most areas of Northern Ireland there is a selective system of secondary education with pupils transferring either to grammar schools or secondary schools at 11–12 years of age. Parents can choose the school they would like their children to attend and all those who apply must be admitted if they meet the criteria. If a school is over-subscribed beyond its statutory admissions number, selection is on the basis of published criteria, which, for most grammar schools, place emphasis on performance in the transfer procedure tests which are administered by the Northern Ireland Council for the Curriculum, Examinations and Assessment. When parents consider that a school has not applied its criteria fairly they have access to independent appeals tribunals. Grammar schools provide an academic type of secondary education with A-levels at the end of the seventh year, while secondary non-grammar schools follow a curriculum suited to a wider range of aptitudes and abilities.

In 1993 there were 145,500 pupils in public sector secondary schools, of whom 88,005 (60.5 per cent) attended non-grammar secondary and 57,507 (39.5 per cent) attended grammar schools. Of all pupils 15.7 per cent were 16 or over. Pupil-teacher ratios in Northern Ireland were 15.4 in 1992.

SPECIAL EDUCATION – Special education is provided for children with special educational needs, usually because they have a disability which either prevents or hinders them from making use of educational facilities of a kind generally provided for children of their age in schools within the area of the local authority concerned. Wherever possible, such children are educated in ordinary schools, taking the parents' wishes into account and schools are required to publish their policy for pupils with special educational needs. LEAs are required to identify and secure provision for the needs of children with learning difficulties, involving the parents in any decision and drawing up a formal statement of the child's special educational needs and how it intends to meet them. Parents have a right to appeal if they disagree with the statement.

Maintained special schools are run by education authorities which pay all the costs of maintenance, but by April 1994 Local Management of Schools (LMS) was extended to those able and wishing to manage their own budgets. These schools are also able to apply to become grant-maintained. Non-maintained special schools are run by voluntary bodies; they may receive some grant from central government for capital expenditure and for equipment, but their current expenditure is met primarily from the fees charged to education authorities for pupils placed in them. Some independent schools provide education wholly or mainly for children with special educational needs and are required to meet similar standards to those for maintained and non-maintained special schools. It is intended that pupils with special education needs should have access to as much of the national curriculum as possible, but there is provision for them to be exempt from it or for it to be modified to suit their capabilities. The Education Act 1993 set statutory time limits for LEAs to provide assessments and statements, gave parents greater choice of schools and extended their right of appeal by establishing the Special Educational Needs (SEN) Tribunal.

In January 1992 in the United Kingdom there was a total of 111,700 full-time pupils in special schools and 700 in hospital schools in England, Wales and Northern Ireland. Of the 111,700, 94,700 were in England, 3,600 in Wales, 8,600 in Scotland and 4,100 in Northern Ireland. Numbers have decreased since 1975–6 as education authorities in England, Wales and Northern Ireland must now ensure that children with special needs are educated as far as possible in ordinary schools with support teaching.

In Scotland, school placing is a matter of agreement between education authorities and parents. Parents have the right to say which school they want their child to attend, and a right of appeal where their wishes are not being met. Whenever possible, children with special needs are integrated into ordinary schools. However, for those who require a different environment or specialized facilities, there are special schools, both grant-aided by central government and independent, and special classes within ordinary schools.

The Self-Governing Schools etc. (Scotland) Act 1989 obliges education authorities to respond to reasonable requests for independent special schools, and provides for them to send children with special needs to schools outside Scotland if appropriate provision is not available within the country. A new centre has been opened which practises conductive education methods for children with motor impairments.

ALTERNATIVE PROVISION

There is no legal obligation on parents in the United Kingdom to educate their children at school provided that the local education authority is satisfied that the child is receiving full-time education suited to its age, abilities and aptitudes. The education authority need not be informed that a child is being educated at home unless the child is already registered at a state school. In this case the parents must arrange for the child's name to be removed from the school's register (by writing to the headteacher) before education at home can begin. Failure to de-register a child leaves the parents liable to prosecution for condoning non-attendance.

In most cases an initial visit is made by an education adviser or education welfare officer, and sometimes subsequent inspections are made, but practice varies according to the individual education authority. There is no requirement for parents educating their children at home to be in possession of a teaching qualification.

Further advice on educating children other than at school can be obtained from Education Otherwise (*see* page 461).

INDEPENDENT SCHOOLS

Independent schools receive no grants from public funds. They charge fees, and are owned and managed under special trusts, with profits being used for the benefit of the schools concerned. There is a wide variety of provision, from kindergartens to large day and boarding schools, and from experimental schools to traditional institutions. A number of independent schools have been instituted by religious and ethnic minorities.

All independent schools in the United Kingdom are open to inspection by approved inspectors (*see* page 445) and must register with the appropriate government education department. The education departments lay down certain minimum standards and can make schools remedy any unacceptable features of their building or instruction and exclude any unsuitable teacher or proprietor. Most independent schools offer a similar range of courses to state schools and enter pupils for the same public examinations. Introduction of the national curriculum and the associated education targets and assessment procedures is not obligatory in the independent sector.

The term public schools is often applied to those independent schools in membership of the Headmasters' Conference, the Governing Bodies Association or the Governing Bodies of Girls' Schools Association. Most public schools are single-sex (about half of them for girls) but there are some mixed schools and an increasing number of schools have mixed sixth forms.

Preparatory schools are so-called because they prepare children for the common entrance examination to senior independent schools. Most cater for boys from about seven to 13 years, some are for girls, and an increasing number are co-educational. The common entrance examination is set by the Common Entrance Examination Board, but marked by the independent school to which the pupil intends to go. It is taken at 13 by boys, and from 11 to 13 by girls.

In 1993 there were in England 2,247 independent schools with 560,245 full-time and part-time pupils and a pupil-teacher ratio of 10.4.

In Wales in 1992–3 there were 65 independent schools, with 11,164 pupils and a pupil-teacher ratio of 9.7.

In Scotland in 1992–3 there were 121 registered independent schools with 33,300 pupils and a pupil-teacher ratio of 10.6. Most independent schools in Scotland follow the English examination system, i.e. GCSE followed by A-levels, although some take the Scottish Education Certificate at Ordinary/Standard grade followed by Highers or Advanced Highers.

There are 18 independent schools in Northern Ireland with 963 pupils and a pupil-teacher ratio of 11.3.

## ASSISTED PLACES SCHEME

The Assisted Places Scheme enables children to attend independent secondary schools which their parents could not otherwise afford. The scheme provides help with tuition fees and other expenses, except boarding costs, on a sliding scale depending on the family's income. The take-up rate for places available at age 11 to 13 at the 303 participating schools in England and Wales is around 99 per cent, and the proportion of pupils receiving full fee remission is about 37 per cent. In the 1993–4 academic year, 34,578 places were offered in England and Wales. The 55 participating schools in Scotland admitted about 3,000 pupils on the scheme in 1993–4, which, unlike that in England and Wales, is cash-limited. The proportion of pupils receiving full fee remission was about 47 per cent.

The scheme is administered and funded in England by the Department for Education, in Wales by the Welsh Office, and in Scotland by the Scottish Office Education Department. The scheme does not operate in Northern Ireland as the independent sector admits non-fee-paying pupils. There is, however, a similar scheme known as the Talented Children's Scheme to help pupils gifted in music and dance.

Further information can be obtained from the Independent Schools Information Service (*see* page 461).

## THE CURRICULUM

### ENGLAND AND WALES

The Education Reform Act 1988 legislated for the progressive introduction of a national curriculum in primary and secondary schools between autumn 1989 and autumn 1997. During the period of compulsory schooling for children aged five to 16 the curriculum originally included mathematics, English (or Welsh in Wales) and science as core subjects and history, geography, technology, music, art, physical education and (for pupils in secondary schools) a modern foreign language as foundation subjects. The national curriculum is at present being revised to reduce the burden on schools and there are proposals to reduce the time devoted to it. Meanwhile, for 14 to 16 year-olds, history and geography are being removed as compulsory subjects, and technology and modern foreign languages have both been suspended as compulsory subjects pending review, although schools are still being encouraged to make all these subjects available. Religious education is required to be available in schools, with the curriculum devised locally, but parents have the right to remove their children if they wish. For the core subjects attainment tests have been instituted at the end of the first three key stages of education. Those for seven and 14 year-olds are already in place; those for 11 year-olds were piloted in 1994 for introduction in 1995. Teachers will also make their own assessments of their pupils' progress in English, mathematics and science to set alongside the test results. At 16 the GCSE and vocational equivalents will be the main form of assessment. Plans to use the test results at

seven and 14 in compiling publicly available comparative tables of schools have been abandoned as a result of resistance from schools and only A, AS, GCSE and GNVQ results have featured for 1994. However, it is planned that the results of tests on 11 year-olds will be published when the tests are introduced in 1995. Teachers have expressed dissatisfaction with the tests since their inception on account of excessive workload and the denial of teachers' own professional accountability. In response to their concerns the government review of the manageability of the national curriculum and testing system announced that there would be fewer and shorter tests for seven and 14 year-olds and that teachers would have discretion over making and recording assessments. In addition, it is intended to introduce external marking for tests of 11 and 14 year-olds; to fund assistance for teachers of seven year-olds administering tests and to teachers of other age groups in certain circumstances; and to end mandatory external auditing of teachers' own assessment of classroom work, retaining it only for English and mathematics testing of 11 year-olds. In 1994 about 30 per cent of 14 year-olds did the tests and a majority of primary schools tested seven year-olds. About 75 per cent of schools took part in the pilot tests for 11 year-olds.

In Wales in 1992–3 the Welsh language was in use as the main or secondary medium of instruction or taught as a second language in 93 per cent of primary schools. In secondary schools Welsh was taught as a first or second language in 92.6 per cent of schools. It constitutes a core subject of the national curriculum in Welsh-speaking schools and a foundation subject in the others, although there is provision for exemptions to be made.

In England the School Curriculum and Assessment Authority (SCAA), funded by the Department for Education, is responsible for the promotion and support of curriculum development, in addition to advising the Secretary of State on the school curriculum and school tests/examinations. In Wales its functions are performed by the Curriculum and Assessment Authority for Wales, funded by the Welsh Office.

### SCOTLAND

The content and management of the curriculum in Scotland is the responsibility of education authorities and individual headteachers. Advice and guidance is provided by the Scottish Office Education Department and the Scottish Consultative Council on the Curriculum. Scotland effectively has a national curriculum for 14 to 16 year-olds, who are required to study English, mathematics and a science subject plus five other subjects. These form the core area, supplemented by other activities forming the elective area. There is a recommended percentage of class time to be devoted to each area over the two years. Provision is made for teaching in Gaelic in Gaelic-speaking areas.

The Scottish Consultative Council on the Curriculum, which is responsible for development and advisory work on the curriculum in Scotland, has undertaken a major review of the balance of the primary curriculum, and has produced national guidelines for each of the curricular areas for the age group five to 14. There are new guidelines on assessment across the whole curriculum, and standardized national testing is being phased in for English language and mathematics at five stages for this age group which are taken when teachers think the pupils are ready. For 16–18 year-olds, there is available a modular system of vocational courses in addition to academic courses.

### NORTHERN IRELAND

Major programmes of curriculum review and development are in progress in primary and secondary schools. A curriculum common to all schools is to be introduced by 1995–6, with six broad areas of study within which nine subjects will be compulsory; religious education will be included as a compulsory part of the curriculum. The Irish language will be a compulsory subject in Irish-medium primary schools and can be chosen as the compulsory foreign language in secondary schools. Arrangements for the assessment of pupils for all compulsory subjects, broadly in line with those in England and Wales, are proposed at the ages of eight, 11, 14 and 16. Voluntary pilot assessments were carried out by June 1993 for 11 and 14 year-olds and in May 1994 for eight-year-olds and are to be repeated in 1994–5. The GCSE will be used to assess 16 year-olds. In Northern Ireland, as in England and Wales, teachers are dissatisfied with the assessment arrangements which have as a result been simplified.

The Northern Ireland Council for the Curriculum, Assessment and Examinations (NICCAE) monitors and advises the department on all matters relating to the curriculum and assessment arrangements in grant-aided schools in Northern Ireland. It conducts GCSE, A and AS level examinations, pupil assessment at key stages and administers the transfer procedure tests.

RECORDS OF ACHIEVEMENT

The National Record of Achievement sets down the range of a school-leaver's achievements and activities both inside and outside the classroom, including those not tested by examination. It is issued to all those leaving school in England and Wales. It is not compulsory in Scotland but is available to all education authorities for issue to school leavers. Under the Education (Schools) Act 1992, parents in England and Wales must receive a written yearly progress report on all aspects of their children's achievements. There is a similar commitment for Northern Ireland. In Scotland the school report card has been revised to give parents more information on their children's progress.

TECHNICAL AND VOCATIONAL EDUCATION INITIATIVE

The Technical and Vocational Education Initiative (TVEI), administered and funded by the Department of Employment in England, the Welsh Office in Wales and the Scottish Office Industry Department in Scotland, operates across the curriculum within a framework of general education. It aims to make the secondary curriculum more relevant to adult life and work. It is a national scheme with criteria which complement and are compatible with the requirements of the national curriculum in England and Wales. Participation is voluntary, and is open to all maintained schools and colleges providing for young people of all abilities aged 14 to 18. TVEI is not an examination or a qualification.

THE PUBLIC EXAMINATION SYSTEM

ENGLAND, WALES AND NORTHERN IRELAND

Until the end of 1987, secondary school pupils at the end of compulsory schooling around the age of 16, and others, took the General Certificate of Education (GCE) Ordinary-level or the Certificate of Secondary Education (CSE). From 1988 these were replaced by a single system of examinations, the General Certificate of Secondary Education (GCSE), which is usually taken after five years of secondary education. The GCSE is the main method of assessing the performance of pupils at age 16 in all national curriculum subjects required to be assessed at the end of compulsory schooling and the structure of the exam is being adapted in accordance with national curriculum requirements.

The GCSE differs from its predecessors in that there are syllabuses based on national criteria covering course objec-

tives, content and assessment methods; differentiated assessment (i.e. different papers or questions for different ranges of ability); and grade-related criteria (i.e. grades awarded on absolute rather than relative performance). The GCSE certificates are awarded on a seven-point scale, A to G. From 1994 there has been an additional 'starred' A grade (A*), to recognize the achievement of the highest attainers at GCSE. Grades A to C are the equivalent of the corresponding O-level grades A to C or CSE grade 1. Grades D, E, F and G record achievement at least as high as that represented by CSE grades 2 to 5. All GCSE syllabuses, assessments and grading procedures are monitored by the School Curriculum and Assessment Authority (see pages 449, 451) to ensure that they conform to the national criteria. GCSE examinations are offered to schools/exam centres by Examining Groups.

Of school leavers in the United Kingdom who left school without A-levels or SCE H-grades in 1991–2, 45.9 per cent had achieved one or more graded GCSE or SCE O or Standard grade results.

From September 1991, many maintained schools have offered BTEC Firsts (see page 453) and it is hoped that more schools will offer BTEC Nationals. National Vocational Qualifications in the form of General NVQs have been available to students in schools from September 1992 (see page 454).

The General Diploma will be introduced in 1995 for 16–18 year-olds achieving GCSE at grades A* to C in English, mathematics and science, plus two other GCSEs at the same grades or their vocational equivalent.

Advanced (A-level) examinations are taken by those who choose to continue their education after GCSE. A-level courses last two years and have traditionally provided the foundation for entry to higher education. A-levels are marked on a seven-point scale, from A to E, N (narrow failure) and U (unclassified), which latter grade will not be certificated. A new 'starred' grade A is proposed to recognize exceptional performance.

Advanced Supplementary level (AS-level) examinations were introduced in September 1987, as an alternative to, and to complement, A-level examinations. AS-levels are for full-time A-level students but are also open to other students. An AS-level syllabus covers not less than half the amount of ground covered by the corresponding A-level syllabus and, where possible, is related to it. An AS-level course lasts two years and requires not less than half the teaching time of the corresponding A-level course, and two AS-levels are equivalent to one A-level. AS-level courses are intended to supplement and broaden A-level studies, and examinations are held at the same time as A-levels. AS-level passes are graded A to E, with grade standards related to the A-level grades.

A mixture of A-level courses in the subjects to be specialized in and AS-levels form the standard for admission to higher education.

In the United Kingdom in 1991–2, 32 per cent of all 17 year-olds (29 per cent of boys, 34 per cent of girls) achieved one or more A-level or SCE H-grade result. This figure includes those continuing their education in maintained further education establishments including tertiary colleges, as well as school leavers.

Of school leavers alone (636,000), 25.8 per cent achieved at least one A-level or SCE H-grade (24 per cent of boys, 27.7 per cent of girls). Of those in Great Britain obtaining two or more A-levels, or three or more SCE H-grades, 19 per cent studied sciences (26 per cent of boys, 12 per cent of girls), 41 per cent studied arts/social studies (32 per cent of boys, 50 per cent of girls), and 40 per cent (42 per cent of boys, 38 per cent of girls) studied a combination of science and arts/social studies.

Most examining boards allow the option of an additional paper of greater difficulty to be taken by A-level candidates to obtain what is known as a Special-level or Scholarship-level qualification. S-level papers are available in most of the traditional academic subjects and are marked on a three-point scale.

The City and Guilds Diploma of Vocational Education superseded the Certificate of Pre-Vocational Education (CPVE) in schools and colleges in England, Wales and Northern Ireland from September 1992. It is intended for a wide ability range, including pupils who might not go on to A-levels but would like to continue their education on completion of compulsory secondary schooling.

The Diploma of Vocational Education provides recognition of achievement at three levels: foundation, intermediate and national; the two latter broadly corresponding to the GNVQ (see page 454) at levels 2 and 3. Within guidelines schools and colleges design their own courses, which stress activity-based learning, core skills of application of numbers, communication and information technology, and work experience. The Diploma of Vocational Education is mainly for those who want to find out what aptitudes they may have and to prepare themselves for work, but who are not yet committed to a particular occupation. It can be taken alongside other courses such as GCSEs, A- or AS-levels. The Diploma at foundation level continues to be available.

## CO-ORDINATION AND ADVISORY BODIES

The School Curriculum and Assessment Authority (SCAA) is funded wholly by the Department for Education and advises the Government on all school curriculum examination and assessment matters in England.

The Curriculum and Assessment Authority for Wales and the Northern Ireland Council for the Curriculum, Assessment and Examinations (NICCEA) perform the same function in Wales and Northern Ireland. The Curriculum and Assessment Authority for Wales is funded by the Welsh Office and NICCEA is funded by the Department of Education for Northern Ireland.

## SCOTLAND

The system of public examinations in Scotland is different from that elsewhere in the United Kingdom. At the end of the fourth year of secondary education, at about the age of 16, pupils take either the Ordinary grade of the Scottish Certificate of Education Examination or the Standard grade. By 1994-5, the Ordinary grade will have been replaced by Standard grade courses and examinations, which have been designed to suit every level of ability, with assessment against nationally determined standards of performance.

For most courses there are three separate examination papers at the end of the two-year Standard grade course. They are set at Credit (leading to awards at grade 1 or 2), General (leading to awards at grade 3 or 4) and Foundation (leading to awards at grade 5 or 6) levels. Grade 7 is available to those who, although they have completed the course, have shown no significant level of attainment. Normally pupils will take examinations covering two pairs of grades, either grades 1-4 or grades 3-6.

Pupils may attempt as many of a wide range of subjects as they are capable of, in either the Ordinary/Standard grades or in the Higher grade which is normally taken one year after Ordinary/Standard grades, at the age of 17 or thereabouts; the latter consist of modules with a mixture of internal and external assessment. The shorter course means that Higher grades are normally studied to a lesser depth than A-levels; on the other hand it is common for pupils to be presented for four or more Higher grades at a single diet of the examination.

The Certificate of Sixth Year Studies (CSYS) is designed to give direction and purpose to sixth-year work by encouraging pupils who have completed their main subjects at Higher grade to study a maximum of three of these subjects in depth. In the 1997-8 session CSYS will be replaced by Advanced Higher courses. For students who do not wish to progress to Advanced Higher level there will be an externally-assessed exit point at Higher level, which those progressing will by-pass. Vocationally-orientated subjects are to be included both at Higher and Advanced Higher level. Pupils may also use the sixth year to gain improved or additional Higher grades or Ordinary/Standard grades.

The examining body for the Scottish Certificate of Education and the Certificate of Sixth Year Studies is the Scottish Examination Board.

National Certificates were introduced in 1984-5 as an alternative to, and to complement, Highers and CSYS. They are awarded to pupils normally over the age of 16 who have successfully completed a programme of vocational courses based on modular study units, and the assessment system is based on national criteria. National Certificates are validated by the Scottish Vocational Education Council (see also page 453).

## THE INTERNATIONAL BACCALAUREATE

The International Baccalaureate is an internationally recognized two-year pre-university course and examination designed to facilitate the mobility of students and to promote international understanding. Candidates must offer one subject from each of six subject groups, at least three at higher level and the remainder at subsidiary level. Single subjects can be offered, for which a certificate is received. There are 29 schools and colleges in the United Kingdom which offer the International Baccalaureate diploma.

## TEACHERS

### ENGLAND AND WALES

Teachers are appointed by local education authorities, school governing bodies, or school managers. Those in publicly maintained schools must be approved as qualified. Approval was formerly given by the Department for Education but is now the function of the Teacher Training Agency, subject to criteria published by the Secretaries of State. To become a qualified teacher it is necessary to have successfully completed a course of initial teacher training, usually either a Bachelor of Education (B.Ed.) degree or the Postgraduate Certificate of Education (PGCE), but a one-year course is being considered which will qualify certain non-graduates to teach at nursery and infant level. Teacher training was hitherto largely integrated with the rest of higher education, with training places concentrated in universities and institutes or colleges of education, but it has now become largely school-based, with student teachers on secondary PGCE courses spending two-thirds of their training in the classroom. From September 1993 individual schools or consortia of schools and CTCs were invited to bid for funds from the DFE to carry out their own teacher training, including recruitment of students, subject to approval of their proposed training programme and monitoring and evaluation by OFSTED. Funds are given to schools to meet the costs of designing and delivering the courses, and students receive flat-rate bursaries. Changes have also been made to primary phase teacher training to make it more school-based and to give schools a role in course design and delivery. Under the articled teacher scheme, graduates are paid a bursary in addition to a salary to complete a school-based PGCE course over two years involving a progressively increasing teaching load. The scheme ceased in September 1993 when intake was restricted to primary phase teacher training only.

The Teacher Training Agency (TTA) began operations in September 1994, funding all types of teacher training, whether run by schools, universities or colleges, and some educational research. These provisions in England were formerly funded by the Higher Education Funding Council in respect of education institutions, and for schools by LEAs. The TTA will accredit those institutions which meet the standards set by the Secretaries of State for their courses, replacing CATE (*see* below), and will also be a central source of advice and information on teacher training. The TTA will exercise only its non-funding functions for Wales, where the institutions will be funded by the HEFCW.

With certain exceptions the profession at present has an all-graduate entry. Teachers in further education are not required to have qualified teacher status, though roughly half have a teaching qualification and most have industrial, commercial or professional experience.

The licensed teacher scheme is designed to attract into the teaching profession entrants over 24 years of age without formal teaching qualifications but with relevant training and experience. All licensees are required to have the equivalent of two years' higher education in the United Kingdom and the equivalent of grade C in GCSE maths and English. Local education authorities are involved in devising a suitable two-year training programme for any licensed teachers they may appoint to their schools; for grant-maintained schools and City Technology Colleges this will be a matter for the schools themselves. LEAs have discretion to recommend qualified teacher status after one year for a licensee with at least two years' experience as an instructor prior to becoming a licensed teacher. The TTA will in future grant licences for this programme.

The Specialist Teacher Assistant (STA) scheme was introduced in September 1994 to provide trained support to qualified teachers in the teaching of reading, writing and arithmetic to young pupils. Training will be part-time over one year and results in a Specialist Teacher Assistant Record (STAR), which would count towards entry to teacher training.

## SCOTLAND

All teachers in maintained schools must be registered with the General Teaching Council for Scotland. They are registered provisionally for a two-year probationary period which can be extended if necessary. Only graduates are accepted as entrants to the teaching profession in Scotland. As a result of a review of initial teacher training instituted in 1992 a greater proportion of training is now classroom-based. The mentor teacher scheme is designed to provide students with support from designated experienced teachers on classroom management and performance. The colleges of education provide both in-service and pre-service training for teachers and are funded by the Scottish Higher Education Funding Council.

## NORTHERN IRELAND

Teacher training in Northern Ireland is provided by the two universities and two colleges of education. The colleges are concerned with teacher education mainly for the primary school sector. They also provide B.Ed. courses for intending secondary school teachers of religious education, commercial studies, and craft, design and technology. With these exceptions, the training of teachers for secondary schools is provided in the education departments of the universities. A professional qualification is not mandatory to teach in secondary schools. The Licensed Teacher route is not accepted for qualified teacher status in Northern Ireland. A review of primary and secondary teacher training has taken

place as a result of which student teachers will spend more time in the classroom and will have the support of a mentoring arrangement with an experienced teacher. The current probationary year is to be replaced by a two-year induction period. These changes will take place over the academic years 1995–6 to 1996–7.

## ACCREDITATION OF TRAINING INSTITUTIONS

The Council for the Accreditation of Teacher Education (CATE) until September 1994 advised central government on the accreditation, content and quality of initial teacher training courses in England, Wales and Northern Ireland, monitoring and disseminating good practice. Its functions for England and Wales were then taken over by the Teacher Training Agency. For Northern Ireland a co-ordinating committee for teacher education is proposed.

In Scotland all training courses in colleges of education must be approved by the Scottish Office Education Department and a validating body.

## NEWLY-TRAINED TEACHERS

Of teachers who in 1991 had successfully completed initial training courses in the United Kingdom, 12,100 had completed a postgraduate course and 7,900 a course for non-graduates.

Because of a shortage of teachers in a number of secondary subjects, a tax-free bursary scheme for trainee teachers on one- or two-year full-time courses has been introduced. The scheme, which was administered by the DFE, transferred to the TTA in September 1994. The subjects are: physics or chemistry, or a combination of the two; mathematics; modern languages (including Welsh in Wales); technology; craft, design and technology (CDT). The bursary is £1,000 a year.

## SERVING TEACHERS

In 1991–2 there were 549,000 teachers (full-time and full-time equivalent) in public sector schools and establishments of further and higher education in the United Kingdom, excluding universities. Of these, 457,000 were in maintained schools and 87,000 in further education. There were 208,000 full-time teachers in public sector primary schools, 230,000 in public sector secondary schools and 19,000 in special schools.

## SALARIES

Qualified teachers in England and Wales, other than heads and deputy heads, are paid on an 18-point scale ranging from £11,571 to £31,323 (September 1994 figures). Entry points and placement depend on qualifications, experience, responsibilities, excellence, and recruitment and retention factors as calculated by the relevant body, i.e. in grant-maintained schools and LEA schools with delegated budgets, the governing body; otherwise the LEA. Headteachers' salaries range from £23,811 to £52,152 and deputy headteachers' salaries range from £23,055 to £37,923. Qualified teachers in Northern Ireland are paid on an 18-point scale as of April 1994 ranging from £11,571 to £31,323. Salaries for principals range from £23,811 to £52,152 and vice-principals from £23,055 to £33,923. There is a statutory superannuation scheme in maintained schools.

Teachers in Scotland are paid (April 1993 figures) on a ten-point scale from £11,562 to £19,218. The entry point depends on type of qualification, and additional allowances are payable under certain circumstances. Headteachers are paid on a scale from £24,375 to £45,150 and deputy headteachers from £24,375 to £33,783, depending on whether the school is primary or secondary and the size of school roll.

# FURTHER EDUCATION

The Education Reform Act 1988 defines further education as all provision outside schools to people aged over 16 of education up to and including A-level and its equivalent. The Further Education Funding Councils for England and Wales, the Scottish Office Education Department and the Education and Library Boards in Northern Ireland have a duty to secure provision of adequate facilities for further education in their territories.

## ENGLAND AND WALES

The Further and Higher Education Act 1992 removed all further education and sixth form colleges from local authority control as of April 1993, and provided for them to be funded directly by central government through the Further Education Funding Council for England (FEFCE) and the Further Education Funding Council for Wales (FEFCW). These councils are also responsible for the assessment of quality, in which the Councils' inspectorates play a key role. The colleges are controlled by autonomous further education corporations, including substantial representation from business, which own their own assets and employ their own staff. Their funding is determined in part by the number of students recruited.

In England and Wales further education courses are taught at a variety of institutions. These range from universities which were formerly polytechnics, colleges of higher education and colleges of further education (many of which also offer higher education courses) to tertiary colleges and sixth form colleges, which concentrate on the provision of normal sixth form school courses as well as a range of vocational courses. A number of institutions specific to a particular form of training, e.g. the Royal College of Music, are also involved.

Teaching staff in further education establishments are not necessarily required to have teaching qualifications although many do so, but they are subject to regular appraisal of teaching performance.

Much of the post-school provision outside the higher education sector is broadly vocational in purpose. It ranges from lower-level technical and commercial courses through courses for those aiming at higher-level posts in industry, commerce and administration, to professional courses. Facilities for GCSE courses, the Diploma of Vocational Education, AS-levels and A-level courses are also provided (see pages 450–1). These courses can form the foundation for progress to higher education qualifications.

The main courses and examinations in the vocational field, all of which link in with the National Vocational Qualification (NVQ) framework (see below), are offered by the following bodies, but there are also many others:

The Business and Technology Education Council (BTEC) provides programmes of study across a wide range of subject areas. The main qualifications are the BTEC First Certificate and the BTEC First Diploma; the BTEC National Certificate and the BTEC National Diploma; BTEC NVQs; and BTEC foundation, intermediate and advanced GNVQs in some vocational areas. BTBC First and National diplomas are to be phased out gradually in most areas by September 1996 as GNVQs are introduced.

City and Guilds of London Institute (C&G) is the UK's largest awarding body. It specialises in developing qualifications and assessments for work-related and general education and leisure. It awards nationally recognized certificates in over 400 subjects, many of which are NVQs. Its progressive structure of awards spans seven levels, from foundation to the highest level of professional competence.

RSA (Royal Society of Arts) Examinations Board schemes cover a wide range of vocational qualifications, including business administration, management, language schemes, information technology and teaching qualifications. Many schemes are offered at levels matching those established by the NCVQ (see below), and a policy operates of credit accumulation, so that candidates can take a single unit or complete qualifications.

There are 404 further education establishments in England and Wales and 1,956 adult education centres. In 1992–3 there were 529,812 full-time and sandwich-course students and 758,843 part-time students on further education courses.

## SCOTLAND

Further education comprises non-advanced courses up to SCE Highers grade, GCE A-level and SCOTVEC vocational courses. Under the Further and Higher Education (Scotland) Act 1992 funding of further education colleges was transferred to central government from the education authorities in April 1993; a further education funding council is proposed at a later stage. Courses are taught mainly at colleges of further education, including technical colleges, and in some schools.

Since April 1993 further education colleges have been self-governing, with boards of management which run the colleges and employ staff. The boards include the principal and staff and student representatives among their ten to 16 members, and at least half the members must have experience of commerce, industry or the practice of a profession.

The Scottish Vocational Education Council (SCOTVEC) provides qualifications for most occupations (paralleling the work of the National Council for Vocational Qualifications and the Business and Technology Education Council, City and Guilds of London Institute, the Royal Society of Arts and other bodies in England, Wales and Northern Ireland). It provides at non-advanced level the National Certificate which covers the whole range of non-advanced further education provision in Scotland. Students may study for the National Certificate on a full-time, part-time, open learning or work-based basis. The system is based on modules, and National Certificate modules can be taken in further education colleges, secondary schools and other centres, normally from the age of 16 onwards. SCOTVEC also offers modular advanced-level HNC/HND qualifications and a few post-graduate or post-experience qualifications which are available in further education colleges and higher education institutions. Scottish Vocational Qualifications (SVQs) correspond to the system of NVQs which operates in the rest of the UK. SVQs are essentially work-based but are also available in further education colleges and other centres.

The Record of Education and Training (RET) has been introduced to provide a single certificate recording SCOTVEC achievements; an updated version is provided as and when necessary.

In 1991–2 there were 35,312 full-time and sandwich-course students and 97,500 part-time students on non-advanced vocational courses of further education in the 43 further education colleges, 15 central institutions and five colleges of education then in existence.

## NORTHERN IRELAND

The Education and Library Boards are obliged to submit for approval to the Department of Education for Northern Ireland, schemes setting out the principles to be applied by the boards in planning the further education provision to be made by colleges under their management.

The colleges of further education are at present maintained by the Education and Library Boards, but financial powers and responsibilities are delegated to the boards of governors of the colleges. The boards of governors must include at least 50 per cent membership from the professions, local business or industry, or other fields of employment relevant to the activities of the college. The review of further education provision which took place during 1991–2 recommended that college and course provision should be rationalized by the amalgamation of some colleges. From September 1994 the mergers reduced the number of free-standing institutions from 24 to 17. No decisions have yet been taken regarding the central funding of colleges in Northern Ireland, either through a funding council or directly by DENI.

On reaching school-leaving age, pupils may attend colleges of further education to pursue the same type of vocational courses as are provided in colleges in England and Wales, administered by the same examining bodies.

In 1991–2 Northern Ireland had 24 institutions of further education with 309 out-centres. In 1991–2 there were 20,486 full-time students and 55,440 part-time students on non-advanced vocational courses of further education.

COURSE INFORMATION

Applications for further education courses are generally made directly to the colleges concerned. Information on further education courses in the United Kingdom and addresses of colleges can be found in the *Directory of Further Education* published annually by the Careers Research and Advisory Centre.

NATIONAL VOCATIONAL QUALIFICATIONS

The National Council for Vocational Qualifications (NCVQ) was set up by the Government in October 1986 to achieve a coherent national framework for vocational qualifications in England, Wales and Northern Ireland. The Council does not award qualifications but works with and through the established examining and awarding bodies to reform the existing vocational qualifications system and introduce simplified arrangements. SCOTVEC (*see* above) performs similar functions in Scotland, but its role includes the awarding of qualifications.

The name and style National Vocational Qualification is accorded to qualifications accredited by NCVQ. The NVQ framework is currently based on five levels incorporating qualifications up to and including the Higher National standard. From September 1992 General National Vocational Qualifications (GNVQs) were introduced into colleges and schools. They cover broad categories in the NVQ framework and are aimed at those wishing to familiarize themselves with a range of opportunities. Advanced GNVQ or the vocational A-level (formerly level 3) is designed to be equivalent to two A-levels; intermediate (formerly level 2) is equivalent to four or five good GCSEs. Foundation GNVQs (formerly level 1) became available in September 1994.

The National Record of Achievement (NRA) replaced the National Record of Vocational Achievement (NRVA) in autumn 1993 (*see* page 450).

# HIGHER EDUCATION

The term higher education is used to describe education above A-level, Higher grade and their equivalent, which is provided mainly in universities and colleges of higher education.

The Further and Higher Education Act 1992 and parallel legislation in Scotland removed the distinction between higher education provided by the universities, which were funded by the Universities Funding Council (UFC), and that provided in England and Wales by the former polytechnics and colleges of higher education, funded by the Polytechnics and Colleges Funding Council (PCFC), and in Scotland by the former central institutions and other institutions funded by central government. All are now funded by the Higher Education Funding Councils for England, Wales and Scotland. The Acts also provided for other changes to bring the non-university sector in line with the universities, including the right for all polytechnics, and other higher education institutions which satisfy the necessary criteria, to award their own taught course and research degrees and to adopt the title of university. All the polytechnics and art colleges have since adopted the title of university. The change of name does not affect the legal constitution of the institutions.

In 1991–2, there were 844,400 full-time and sandwich-course students in higher education in the United Kingdom, of whom 88,100 were from overseas. The number of part-time students in the United Kingdom, including the Open University, was 456,000. The proportion of 16- to 20-year-olds entering full-time higher education in Great Britain rose from 16.1 per cent in 1985–6 to 23.1 per cent in 1991–2. The number of mature entrants (those aged 21 and over when starting an undergraduate course and 25 and over when starting a postgraduate course) to higher education in Great Britain in 1991 (excluding those at the Open University) was 278,200, up by 107 per cent on 1980. The number of full-time students on science courses in 1991–2 was 140,100, of whom 49,600 were female.

UNIVERSITIES AND COLLEGES

The universities are self-governing institutions established by royal charter or Act of Parliament. They have academic freedom and are responsible for their own academic appointments, curricula and student admissions and award their own degrees.

Responsibility for universities in England rests with the Secretary of State for Education, and in their territories the Secretaries of State for Scotland, Wales and Northern Ireland. Advice to the Government on matters relating to the universities is provided by the Higher Education Funding Councils for England, Wales and Scotland, and by the Northern Ireland Higher Education Council. The HEFCs receive a block grant from central government which they allocate to the universities and colleges. The grant is allocated directly by central government in Northern Ireland.

There are now 86 universities in the United Kingdom, where only 47 existed prior to the Further and Higher Education Acts 1992. Of these 86, 70 are in England (including one federal university), two (one a federal institution) in Wales, 12 in Scotland and two in Northern Ireland.

The universities which pre-date the 1992 Acts each have their own system of internal government, but broad similarities exist. Most are run by two main bodies: the senate, which deals primarily with academic issues and consists of members elected from within the university; and the council, which is the supreme body and is responsible for all appointments and promotions, and bidding for and allocation of financial resources. At least half the members of the council are drawn from outside the university. Joint committees of senate and council are becoming increasingly common.

In 1992–3, at the 47 universities which were funded through the UFC (two in Northern Ireland, eight in Scotland, a single federal university in Wales, and the remainder in England), there were 435,617 full-time students (22,708 from EC countries; 45,633 from other overseas countries) and 75,506 part-time students. Women formed 45.3 per cent of the full-time total and 46.4 per cent of the part-time total.

Those universities which were formerly polytechnics and the colleges of higher education are run by higher education corporations (HECs), which are controlled by boards of governors whose members were initially appointed by the Secretaries of State but which will subsequently make their own appointments. At least half the members of each board must be drawn from industry, business, commerce and the professions.

In England and Wales, there were 441,482 students in the 33 polytechnics in 1991–2. Of these, 429,668 were on higher education courses, of whom 305,440 were full-time or sandwich-course students. In the 50 colleges of higher education in England and Wales in 1991–2, there were 151,384 students, 136,100 of these on higher education courses and of whom 99,350 were full-time or sandwich-course students.

In 1991–2 there were 357 major establishments in higher education (maintained, assisted by LEAs, in receipt of direct grant from the DFE, or voluntary) outside the PCFC sector. In England and Wales in 1991–2 they catered for 124,319 students on higher education courses funded by the PCFC, including 34,714 on full-time or sandwich courses. The higher education courses in these establishments are now funded by the HEFCs for England and Wales, and their further education courses are funded through the FEFCs.

The non-residential Open University provides courses nationally leading to degrees. Teaching is through a combination of television and radio programmes, correspondence, tutorials, short residential courses and local audio-visual centres. No qualifications are needed for entry. The Open University offers a modular programme of undergraduate courses by credit accumulation and post-experience and postgraduate courses, including a programme of higher degrees which comprises B.Phil., M.Phil. and Ph.D. through research, and MA, MBA and M.Sc. through taught courses. The Open University throughout the UK is funded by the Higher Education Funding Council for England. In 1994, about 90,000 undergraduates were registered at the Open University, of whom about 48 per cent were women and 52 per cent were men. Estimated cost (year 1994) of a six-credit degree was around £2,800.

The independent University of Buckingham provides a two-year course leading to a bachelor's degree and its tuition fees were £8,712 for 1994. It receives no capital or recurrent income from the Government but its students are eligible for mandatory awards from local education authorities. Its academic year consists of four terms of ten weeks each.

## ACADEMIC STAFF

Each university and college appoints its own academic staff on its own conditions. However, there is a common salary structure and, except for Oxford and Cambridge, a common career structure in those universities formerly funded by the UFC; and a common salary structure for the former PCFC sector. The Education Reform Act 1988 appointed the University Commissioners to secure changes to university statutes abolishing the granting of tenure, thus enabling staff to be dismissed for good cause and for redundancy.

The Education Reform Act 1988 took polytechnics and higher education colleges in England and Wales out of local education authority control, turning them into employers on their own account. The Polytechnics and Colleges Employers' Forum was set up to look after terms and conditions of employment in its sector. It has combined with the salaries and industrial relations department of the Committee of Vice Chancellors and Principals to form the Universities and

Colleges Employers Association (UCEA), a pay agency for universities and colleges.

Teaching staff in higher education require no formal teaching qualification, but teacher trainers are required to spend a certain amount of time in schools to ensure that they have sufficient recent practical experience.

In 1992–3, there were 58,666 full-time and part-time academic staff in universities funded by the UFC and 120,011 in institutions formerly in the PCFC sector in England and Wales or centrally funded in Scotland and Northern Ireland.

Salary scales for staff in the former UFC sector differ from those in the former polytechnics and colleges; it is hoped to amalgamate them over the next few years. The 1994–5 salary scales for non-clinical academic staff in universities formerly funded by the UFC are:

| | |
|---|---|
| Lecturer grade A | £13,941–£19,326 |
| Lecturer grade B | £20,133–£25,735 |
| Senior lecturer | £27,108–£30,533 |
| Professor from | £31,158 |

The salaries of clinical academic staff are kept broadly comparable to those of doctors and dentists in the National Health Service.

Salary scales for lecturers in the former polytechnics, now universities, and colleges of further and higher education in England, Wales and Northern Ireland are (September 1993):

| | |
|---|---|
| Lecturer | £11,067–£20,745 |
| Senior lecturer | £19,362–£25,584 |
| Principal lecturer | £24,198–£30,426 |
| Head of Department from £26,304 | |

The salary scales for staff in Scotland are (April 1994–5):

| | |
|---|---|
| Lecturer | £14,223–£25,527 |
| Senior lecturer | £23,412–£30,264 |
| Head of department/professor | from £31,215 |

## FINANCE

Although universities and colleges are expected to look to a much wider range of funding sources than before, and to generate additional revenue in collaboration with industry, they are still largely financed, directly or indirectly, from government resources.

In the academic year 1992–3 the total recurrent income of the 47 universities funded by the UFC was £5,406 million (£4,870 million in 1991–2). The exchequer grant was £1,621 million (£1,564 million in 1991–2), forming 30 per cent of total income (32.1 per cent in 1991–2), compared to 1976–7 when it formed 75 per cent. Income from research grants and contracts in 1992–3 was £1,106 million, an increase of 17.6 per cent on the previous year.

In the academic year 1992–3 the PCFC recurrent grant to institutions and LEAs for higher education courses was £883 million (£842 million in 1991–2).

## COURSES

In the United Kingdom all universities, including the Open University, and some colleges award their own degrees and other qualifications and can act as awarding and validating bodies for neighbouring colleges which are not yet accredited. These functions, and the accreditation of institutions to award their own degrees, were formerly effected by the Council for National Academic Awards until it ceased to operate in October 1992. The Higher Education Quality Council (HEQC), funded by institutional contributions, has been set up to advise the Secretaries of State on applications for degree-awarding powers.

Higher education courses last full-time for at least four weeks or, if part-time, involve more than 60 hours of instruction. Facilities exist for full-time and part-time study, day release, sandwich or block release. Credit accumulation and transfer (CATS) is a system of study which is now becoming widely available. It allows a student to achieve a final qualification by accumulating credits for courses of study successfully achieved, or even professional experience, over a period. Credit transfer information and values are carried on an electronic database called ECCTIS 2000, which is available in most careers offices and many schools and colleges.

Higher education courses include: first degree and postgraduate (including research); Diploma in Higher Education (Dip.HE); Higher National Diploma (HND) and Higher National Certificate (HNC); and preparation for professional examinations. The in-service training of teachers is also included, but from September 1994 was funded in England only by the TTA (see page 452), not the HEFC.

The Diploma of Higher Education (Dip.HE) is a two-year diploma usually intended to serve as a stepping-stone to a degree course or other further study. The Dip.HE is awarded by the institution itself if it is accredited; by an accredited institution of its choice if not. The BTEC Higher National Certificate (HNC) is awarded after two years part-time study. The BTEC Higher National Diploma (HND) is awarded after two years full-time, or three years sandwich-course or part-time study.

With the exception of certain Scottish universities where master is sometimes used for a first degree in arts subjects, undergraduate courses lead to the title of Bachelor, Bachelor of Arts (BA) and Bachelor of Science (B.Sc.) being the most common. For a higher degree the titles are, Master of Arts (MA), Master of Science (M.Sc.) (usually taught courses) and the research degrees of Master of Philosophy (M.Phil.) and Doctor of Philosophy (Ph.D. or, at a few universities, D.Phil.).

Most undergraduate courses at British universities and colleges of higher education run for three years, except in Scotland and at the University of Keele where they may take four years. Professional courses in subjects such as medicine, dentistry and veterinary science take longer. Details of courses on offer and of predicted entry requirements for the following year's intake are provided in *University and College Entrance: Official Guide* published annually by Universities and Colleges Admissions Service (UCAS), which includes degree, Dip.HE and HND courses at all universities (excluding the Open University) and most colleges of HE (for address, see page 463).

Postgraduate studies vary in length. Taught courses which lead to certificates, diplomas or master's degrees usually take one year full-time or two years part-time. Research degrees take from two to three years full-time and much longer if completed on a part-time basis. Details of taught courses and research degree opportunities can be found in *Graduate Studies* published annually for the Careers Research and Advisory Centre (CRAC) by Hobsons Publishing PLC (for address, see page 463).

Post-experience short courses are forming an increasing part of higher education provision, reflecting the need to update professional and technical training. Most of these courses fund themselves.

## ADMISSIONS

Apart from quotas for medical, dental and veterinary students, there are no limits set for student intakes and the individual university or college decides which students to accept. The formal entry requirements to most degree courses are two A-levels at grade E or above (or equivalent), and to HND courses one A-level (or equivalent). In practice, most offers of places require qualifications in excess of this, higher requirements usually reflecting the popularity of a course. These requirements do not, however, exclude applications from students with a variety of non-GCSE qualifications or unquantified experience and skills.

For admission to a degree, Dip.HE or HND, potential students apply through a central clearing house. All universities and most colleges providing higher education courses in the United Kingdom are members of the Universities and Colleges Admission Service (UCAS), which replaced the former Universities Central Council on Admissions (UCCA) and Polytechnics Central Admissions System (PCAS). (The only exception among universities is the Open University, which conducts its own admissions.) Applicants are supplied with an application form and a *UCAS Handbook*, available from schools, colleges and careers offices or direct from UCAS, and may apply to a maximum of eight institutions/courses on the UCAS form.

There are a number of studio-based art and design courses for which applications are made through the Art and Design Admissions Registry. Applications for undergraduate teacher training courses are made through UCAS.

For admission as a postgraduate student, universities and colleges normally require a good first degree in a subject related to the proposed course of study or research, but other experience and qualifications will be considered on merit. Most applications are made to individual institutions but there are two clearing houses of relevance. Postgraduate teacher training courses in England, Wales and Northern Ireland utilise the Graduate Teacher Training Registry (see page 463). Postgraduate teacher training courses in Scotland are at present applied to through the Teacher Education Admissions Clearing House (TEACH), which will, however, be wound up after handling the intake for session 1994-5; procedures for admission to these courses in subsequent years have yet to be decided. For social work the Social Work Admissions System operates (see page 463).

## SCOTLAND

As a result of changes brought about by the Further and Higher Education (Scotland) Act 1992, the Scottish Higher Education Funding Council (SHEFC) now funds 23 institutions of higher education, including 13 universities. The universities are broadly managed as described above and each institution of higher education is managed by an independent governing body which includes representatives of industrial, commercial, professional and educational interests. Most of the courses outside the universities have a vocational orientation and a substantial number are sandwich courses.

In 1991-2, there was a total of 151,089 students enrolled on courses of higher education outside the universities. Of these, 113,671 attended higher education institutions and 37,418 were on higher education courses in further education colleges. Of the total number, 71 per cent were on full-time or sandwich courses.

Applications to institutions of higher education in Scotland are made through UCAS, except for applications for postgraduate teacher training courses made through TEACH (see page 463) up to and including student intake for the session 1994-5. Details of initial teacher training courses can be obtained from colleges of education and those universities offering such courses, and from the Committee of Scottish Higher Education Principals (COSHEP).

## NORTHERN IRELAND

In Northern Ireland advanced courses are provided by 24 institutions of further education and by the two universities. As well as offering first and postgraduate degrees, the University of Ulster offers courses leading to the BTEC Higher National Diploma and professional qualifications. Applications to undertake courses of higher education other than degree courses are made to the institutions direct. Applications for degree courses are made through UCAS.

In 1991–2, 4,095 students were enrolled on advanced courses of higher education in the institutions of further education, 43.5 per cent of whom were women. There were 951 students on full-time or sandwich courses.

## FEES

The tuition fees for students with mandatory awards (*see* below) are paid by the grant-awarding body. Students from member states of the European Community pay fees at home student rates. Since 1980–1 students from outside the EC have paid fees that are meant to cover the cost of their education, but financial help is available under a number of schemes. Information about these schemes is available from British Council offices world-wide.

Universities and colleges are free to set their own charges and the Committee of Vice-Chancellors and Principals no longer recommends minimum fees for students from non-EC countries for those institutions formerly in the UFC sector. Undergraduate fees for the academic year 1994–5 for home and EC students are £750 for arts courses (band 1), £1,600 for laboratory or workshop based courses, mainly science (band 2), and £2,800 for clinical courses (band 3).

For postgraduate students, the maximum tuition fee that will be reimbursed through the awards system is £2,350 in 1994–5.

## GRANTS FOR STUDENTS

Students in the United Kingdom who plan to take a full-time or sandwich course of further study after leaving school may be eligible for a grant. A parental contribution is deductible on a sliding scale dependent on income. For married students this may be deducted from their spouse's income instead. However, parental contribution is not deducted from the grant to students over 25 years of age who have been self-supporting for at least three years. The main rates of mandatory grant have been frozen since 1991–2 as it is envisaged that students will increasingly support themselves by loans. Tuition fees are paid in full for all students in receipt of a grant, regardless of parental income, and they are usually paid direct to the university or college by the education authority.

Grants are paid by local education authorities in England, Wales and Northern Ireland, of which 100 per cent of the cost is reimbursed by central government, and by the Scottish Office Education Department in Scotland through the Students Award Agency. Applications are made to the authority in the area in which the student normally lives. Applications should not, however, be made earlier than January preceding the start of the course. ·

### TYPES OF GRANT

Grants are of two kinds: mandatory and discretionary. Mandatory grants are those which awarding authorities must pay to students who are attending designated courses and who can satisfy certain other conditions. Such a grant is awarded normally to enable the student to attend only one designated course and there is no general entitlement to an award for any particular number of years. Discretionary grants are those for which each awarding authority has discretion to decide its own policy.

Designated courses are those full-time or sandwich courses leading to: a degree; the Diploma of Higher Education; the BTEC Higher National Diploma; initial teacher-training courses, including those for the postgraduate certificate of education and the art teachers' certificate or diploma; a university certificate or diploma course lasting at least three years; other qualifications which are specifically designated as being comparable to first degree courses; and the

SCOTVEC Higher National Diploma. The local education authority should be consulted for advice about eligibility for a grant.

A means-tested maintenance grant, usually paid once a term, covers periods of attendance during term as well as the Christmas and Easter vacations, but not the summer vacation. It is subject to deduction on account of the student's own income and her/his parents' or spouse's income. The basic grant rates for 1994–5 are: £2,560 if living in a hall of residence or lodgings and studying within the London area (£2,495 for students from Scotland); £2,040 as above but outside the London area (£1,975 for students from Scotland); £1,615 if living at the parental home (£1,480 for students in Scotland). Additional allowances are available if, for example, the course requires a period of study abroad.

LEA and Scottish Office Education Department expenditure on student fees and maintenance in 1992–3 was £2,990 million; 750,370 mandatory awards were made.

### STUDENT LOANS

The Education (Student Loans) Act 1990 legislated for interest-free but indexed top-up loans of up to £1,375 in 1994–5 to be made available to eligible students in the United Kingdom. The government expects that at least £470 million will be taken up in loans in 1994–5.

Students apply direct to the Student Loans Company Ltd (see page 358), which will require a certificate of eligibility from their place of study. Loans are available to students on designated courses within the scope of mandatory awards and the same residency conditions apply. Repayment is normally over five to seven years, although it can be deferred if income is below about £14,000 a year.

### ACCESS FUNDS

Access funds are allocated by education departments to the appropriate funding councils in England, Wales and Scotland and administered by further and higher education institutions. In Northern Ireland they are allocated by central government to the institutions direct. They are available to students whose access to higher education might otherwise be inhibited by financial considerations or where real financial difficulties are faced. For the academic year 1994–5, provision in the United Kingdom will be £33.3 million.

### POSTGRADUATE AWARDS

Unlike funding for undergraduates, which is mandatory for most degree and equivalent level courses, grants for postgraduate study are usually discretionary. Grants are also often dependent on the class of first degree, especially for research degrees.

A number of schemes of postgraduate bursaries or studentships for residents in England and Wales are funded by the Department for Education, the six government research councils, the Ministry of Agriculture, Fisheries and Food, and the British Academy, which awards grants for study in the humanities.

In Scotland postgraduate funding is provided by the Scottish Office Education Department, the Scottish Office Agriculture and Fisheries Department, and the research councils in England and Wales.

Awards in Northern Ireland are made by the Department of Education for Northern Ireland, the Department of Agriculture for Northern Ireland, and the Medical Research Council.

In 1991–2 in the United Kingdom 27,400 awards were made. The national rates for twelve-month studentships in 1994–5 are: £5,555 in college or lodgings in London; £4,415 in college or lodgings outside London; £3,255 for those living with parents or spouse's parents. The rates for 30-week bursaries for 1994–5 are: £3,295 in college or lodgings in London; £2,600 in college or lodgings outside London; £1,965 if living with parents or spouse's parents.

## ADULT AND CONTINUING EDUCATION

The term adult education covers a broad spectrum of educational activities ranging from non-vocational courses of general interest, through the acquiring of special vocational skills needed in industry or commerce, to study for a degree at the Open University.

Until the passing of the Further and Higher Education Act 1992, local education authorities were the main providers of adult and continuing education in England and Wales and had a statutory duty to do so. The Further Education Funding Councils are now responsible for, and fund, those courses which take place in their sector and lead to academic and vocational qualifications, prepare students to undertake further or higher education courses, or confer basic skills. Advanced courses of continuing education are funded by the Higher Education Funding Councils. Courses which do not fall within the remit of the funding councils continue to be the responsibility of the LEAs. Funding in Northern Ireland is through the education and library boards and in Scotland by the Scottish Office Education Department and by the education authorities.

### PROVIDERS

Courses specifically for adults are provided by many bodies. They include, in the statutory sector: local education authorities in England and Wales; the regional and islands education authorities in Scotland and the Scottish Office Education Department; education and library boards in Northern Ireland; further education colleges; higher education colleges; universities, especially the Open University and Birkbeck College of the University of London; residential colleges; the BBC, independent television and local radio stations. There are also a number of voluntary bodies.

The local education authorities in England and Wales operate through 'area' adult education centres (1,956 in 1992), institutes or colleges, and the adult studies departments of colleges of further education. The regional and islands education authorities in Scotland fund adult education, including that provided by the universities and the Workers' Educational Association, at vocational further education colleges (48 in 1992). In addition, the Scottish Office Education Department provides grants to a number of voluntary organizations. Provision in the statutory sector in Northern Ireland is the responsibility of the universities and the education and library boards, which operate 17 further education colleges and a number of community schools.

The involvement of universities in adult education and continuing education has diversified considerably and is supported by a variety of administrative structures ranging from dedicated departments to a devolved approach. Birkbeck College in the University of London caters solely for part-time students. Those institutions and colleges formerly in the PCFC sector in England and Wales, because of their range of courses and flexible patterns of student attendance, provide opportunities in the field of adult and continuing education. The Forum for the Advancement of Continuing Education (FACE) promotes collaboration between institutions of higher education active in this area. The Open University, in partnership with the BBC, provides distance teaching leading to first degrees, and also offers post-experience and higher degree courses (*see* page 472).

Of the voluntary bodies, the biggest is the Workers' Educational Association (WEA) which operates throughout the United Kingdom, reaching about 180,000 adult students annually. The FEFCs for England and Wales, the Scottish Office Education Department, the Department of Education for Northern Ireland and local education authorities make grants towards provision.

The National Institute of Adult Continuing Education (England and Wales) (NIACE) provides information and advice to organizations and individuals on all aspects of adult continuing education. NIACE conducts research, project and development work, and is funded by the DFE, the LEAs and other funding bodies. The Welsh committee, NIACE Cymru, receives financial support from the Welsh Office, support in kind from the Welsh Joint Education Committee, and advises government, voluntary bodies and education providers on adult continuing education and training matters in Wales. In Scotland advice on adult and community education, and promotion thereof, is provided by the Scottish Community Education Council. The Northern Ireland Council for Adult Education has an advisory role. Its membership includes representatives of the education and library boards and of most organizations involved in the field, together with an assessor appointed by DENI.

Membership of the Universities Association for Continuing Education is open to any university or university college in the United Kingdom. It promotes university continuing education, facilitates the interchange of information, and supports research and development work in continuing education.

### COURSES

Although lengths vary, most courses are part-time. Long-term residential colleges grant-aided by the DFE, the Welsh Office or the Scottish Office provide full-time courses lasting one or two years. Some colleges and centres offer short-term residential courses, lasting from a few days to a few weeks, in a wide range of subjects. Local education authorities directly sponsor many of the colleges, while others are sponsored by universities or voluntary organizations. A list of courses, *Residential Short Courses*, is published by NIACE.

### GRANTS

Although full-time courses at degree level attract mandatory awards, for courses below that level all students over the age of 19 must pay a fee. However, discretionary grants may be available. Adult education bursaries for students at the long-term residential colleges of adult education are the responsibility of the colleges themselves. The awards are administered for the colleges by the Awards Officer of the Residential Colleges Committee for students resident in England and are funded by the FEFC for England in English colleges; for colleges in Wales they are funded and administered by the FEFC for Wales; for colleges in Scotland by the Scottish Office Education Department; and for colleges in Northern Ireland by the Department of Education for Northern Ireland. A booklet *Adult Education Bursaries* can be obtained from the Awards Officer, Adult Education Bursaries, c/o Ruskin College (*see* page 474).

### NUMBERS

There are no comprehensive statistics covering all aspects of adult education. However, enrolments on evening courses in the United Kingdom numbered 1,732,000 in 1991–2 (66.2 per cent women). This number included 961,000 students at adult education centres. In 1992–3, liberal adult education and professional updating short courses organized by those institutions formerly funded by the UFC were attended by 952,954 students, an increase of 9.5 per cent on 1991–2.

# Education Directory

## LOCAL EDUCATION AUTHORITIES

### ENGLAND

COUNTY COUNCILS

AVON, PO Box 57, Avon House North, St James Barton, Bristol BS99 7EB. Tel: 0117-987 4121. *Director,* G. Badman

BEDFORDSHIRE, County Hall, Cauldwell Street, Bedford MK42 9AP. Tel: 01234-363222. *Director,* D. G. Wadsworth

BERKSHIRE, Shire Hall, Shinfield Park, Reading RG2 9XE. Tel: 01734-233401. *Chief Education Officer,* S. R. Goodchild

BUCKINGHAMSHIRE, Walton Street, Aylesbury HP20 1UZ. Tel: 01296-395000. *Chief Education Officer,* S. Sharp

CAMBRIDGESHIRE, Castle Court, Shire Hall, Cambridge CB3 0AP. Tel: 01223-317667. *Director,* J. Ferguson

CHESHIRE, County Hall, Chester CHI ISF. Tel: 01244-602424. *Director,* D. Cracknell

CLEVELAND, Woodlands Road, Middlesbrough TS1 3BN. Tel: 01642-248155. *County Education Officer,* B. Worthy

CORNWALL, County Hall, Truro TRI 3BA. Tel: 01872-74282. *Secretary of Education,* J. Harris

CUMBRIA, 5 Portland Square, Carlisle CAI 1PU. Tel: 01228-23456. *Director,* Ms P. Black

DERBYSHIRE, County Offices, Matlock DE4 3AG. Tel: 01629-580000. *Chief Education Officer,* Mrs V. Hannon

DEVON, County Hall, Topsham Road, Exeter EX2 4QG. Tel: 01392-382059. *Chief Education Officer,* S. W. Jenkin

DORSET, County Hall, Colliton Park, Dorchester DTI 1XJ. Tel: 01305-251000. *Director,* R. H. Ely

DURHAM, County Hall, Durham DHI 5UJ. Tel: 0191-386 4411. *Director,* K. Mitchell

EAST SUSSEX, PO Box 4, County Hall, St Anne's Crescent, Lewes BN7 1SG. Tel: 01273-481000. *County Education Officer,* D. Mallen

ESSEX, PO Box 47, A Block, County Hall, Victoria Road South, Chelmsford CMI 1LD. Tel: 01245-492759. *County Education Officer,* R. M. Sharp

GLOUCESTERSHIRE, Shire Hall, Westgate Street, Gloucester GLI 2TP. Tel: 01452-425000. *Director,* K. D. Anderson

HAMPSHIRE, The Castle, Winchester SO23 8UJ. Tel: 01962-841841. *County Education Officer,* P. J. Coles

HEREFORD AND WORCESTER, County Hall, Spetchley Road, Worcester WR5 2NP. Tel: 01905-763763. *County Education Officer,* D. A. J. Stanley

HERTFORDSHIRE, County Hall, Hertford SG13 8DE. Tel: 01992-555701. *County Education Officer,* Mrs H. du Quesnay

HUMBERSIDE, County Hall, Cross Street, Beverley HUI7 9BA. Tel: 01482-867131. *Director,* Dr M. W. Garnett

ISLE OF WIGHT, County Hall, Newport PO30 1UD. Tel: 01983-821000. *Director,* Dr J. A. Williams

KENT, Springfield, Maidstone MEI4 2LJ. Tel: 01622-671411. *Director,* R. Pryke

LANCASHIRE, PO Box 61, County Hall, Preston PRI 8RJ. Tel: 01772-254868. *Chief Education Officer,* A. J. Collier

LEICESTERSHIRE, County Hall, Glenfield, Leicester LE3 8RF. Tel: 0116-232 3232. *Director,* vacant

LINCOLNSHIRE, County Offices, Newland, Lincoln LNI 1YL. Tel: 01522-553292. *Director,* N. J. Riches

NORFOLK, County Hall, Martineau Lane, Norwich NRI 2DH. Tel: 01603-222300. *Director,* M. H. Edwards

NORTHAMPTONSHIRE, PO Box 149, County Hall, Northampton NNI 1AU. Tel: 01604-236236. *Director,* R. Atkinson

NORTHUMBERLAND, County Hall, Morpeth NE61 2EF. Tel: 01670-533000. *Director,* C. C. Tipple

NORTH YORKSHIRE, County Hall, Racecourse Lane, Northallerton DL7 8AE. Tel: 01609-780780. *Director,* F. F. Evans

NOTTINGHAMSHIRE, County Hall, West Bridgford, Nottingham NG2 7QP. Tel: 0115-982 3823. *Director,* vacant

OXFORDSHIRE, Macclesfield House, New Road, Oxford OXI INA. Tel: 01865-815449. *Chief Education Officer,* Mrs J. Stephens

SHROPSHIRE, The Shirehall, Abbey Foregate, Shrewsbury SY2 6ND. Tel: 01743-254301. *County Education Officer,* Ms C. Adams

SOMERSET, County Hall, Taunton TAI 4DY. Tel: 01823-333451. *Chief Education Officer,* N. Henwood

STAFFORDSHIRE, Tipping Street, Stafford STI6 2DH. Tel: 01785-223121. *Chief Education Officer,* Dr P. J. Hunter

SUFFOLK, St Andrew House, County Hall, Ipswich IP4 1LJ. Tel: 01473-230000. *County Education Officer,* D. J. Peachey

SURREY, County Hall, Penrhyn Road, Kingston upon Thames KTI 2DJ. Tel: 0181-541 9501. *County Education Officer,* Ms J. H. Barrows

WARWICKSHIRE, PO Box 24, 22 Northgate Street, Warwick CV34 4SR. Tel: 01926-410410. *Director,* Ms M. Maden

WEST SUSSEX, County Hall, West Street, Chichester PO19 1RF. Tel: 01243-777100. *Director,* R. D. C. Bunker

WILTSHIRE, County Hall, Trowbridge BAI4 8JB. Tel: 01225-713000. *Director,* Dr K. Robinson

METROPOLITAN DISTRICT COUNCILS

BARNSLEY, Berneslai Close, Barnsley. Tel: 01226-770770. *Director,* M. Warrington

BIRMINGHAM, Council House, Margaret Street, B3 3BU. Tel: 0121-235 2872. *Chief Education Officer,* T. Brighouse

BOLTON, Paderborn House, Civic Centre, BLI 1JW. Tel: 01204-22311. *Chief Education Officer,* B. Hughes

BRADFORD, Flockton House, Flockton Road, BD4 7RY. Tel: 01274-751700. *Education Officer (acting),* K. Sutcliffe

BURY, Athenaeum House, Market Street, BL9 0BN. Tel: 0161-705 5652. *Chief Education Officer,* J. Beech

CALDERDALE, Northgate House, Halifax HXI 1UN. Tel: 01422-357257. *Director,* Miss J. Tonge

COVENTRY, New Council Offices, CVI 5RR. Tel: 01203-831500. *Chief Education Officer,* Ms C. Goodwin

DONCASTER, PO Box 266, The Council House, DNI 3BN. Tel: 01302-734444. *Director,* A. M. Taylor

DUDLEY, Westox House, 1 Trinity Road, DYI 1JB. Tel: 01384-452200. *Chief Education Officer,* R. K. Westerby

GATESHEAD, Civic Centre, Regent Street, NE8 1HH. Tel: 0191-477 1011. *Director,* D. Arbon

KIRKLEES, Oldgate House, 2 Oldgate, Huddersfield HDI 6QW. Tel: 01484-422133. *Chief Education Officer,* R. Vincent

KNOWSLEY, Huyton Hey Road, Huyton, Merseyside L36 5YH. Tel: 0151-443 3220. *Director of Educataion,* P. Wylie

LEEDS, Merrion House, 110 Merrion Centre, LS2 8DT. Tel: 0113-234 8080. *Chief Education Officer,* Mrs J. A. M. Strong

LIVERPOOL, 14 Sir Thomas Street, LI 6BJ. Tel: 0151-225 2799. *Director,* M. F. Cogley

MANCHESTER, Cumberland House, Crown Square, M60 3BB. Tel: 0161-234 7121. *Education Officer,* R. Jobson

NEWCASTLE UPON TYNE, Civic Centre, NEI 8PU. Tel: 0191-232 8520. *Education Officer,* N. Purser

NORTH TYNESIDE, Stephenson House, Stephenson Street, North Shields NE30 IQA. Tel: 0191-257 5544. *Education Officer,* J. C. Benneworth

OLDHAM, Old Town Hall, Middleton Road, Chadderton, OL9 6PP. Tel: 0161-911 4203. *Education Officer,* W. R. Kneen, PH.D.

ROCHDALE, PO Box 70, Municipal Offices, Smith Street, OL16 IYD. Tel: 01706-47474. *Director,* Mrs D. Cavanagh

ROTHERHAM, Norfolk House, Walker Place, Rotherham, S65 IAN. Tel: 01709-382121. *Education Officer,* B. H. Yemm

ST HELENS, Rivington Centre, Rivington Road WA10 4ND. Tel: 01744-24061. *Director,* B. M. Mainwaring

SALFORD, Chapel Street, M3 5LT. Tel: 0161-832 9751. *Chief Education Officer,* D. Johnston

SANDWELL, PO Box 41, Shaftesbury House, 402 High Street, West Bromwich B70 9LT. Tel: 0121-525 7366. *Director,* S. Gallacher

SEFTON, Town Hall, Oriel Road, Bootle, Merseyside L20 7AE. Tel: 0151-933 6003. *Education Officer,* J. A. Marsden

SHEFFIELD, PO Box 67, Leopold Street, SI IRJ. Tel: 0114-273 4420/1. *Director,* Ms A. Muller

SOLIHULL, PO Box 20, Council House, B91 3QU. Tel: 0121-704 6000. *Director,* C. J. Trinick

SOUTH TYNESIDE, Town Hall and Civic Offices, Westoe Road, South Shields NE32 IRU. Tel: 0191-427 1717. *Education Officer,* I. L. Reid

STOCKPORT, Stopford House, Piccadilly, SKI 3XE. Tel: 0161-474 3808. *Director,* M. K. J. Hunt

SUNDERLAND, PO Box 101, Civic Centre, SR2 7DN. Tel: 0191-567 6161. *Education Officer,* D. A. Bowers

TAMESIDE, Council Offices, Wellington Road, Ashton-under-Lyne OL6 6DL. Tel: 0161-342 8355. *Director,* A. M. Webster

TRAFFORD, Sale Town Hall, School Road, Sale M33 IAL. Tel: 0161-872 2101. *Director,* A. Lee

WAKEFIELD, County Hall, WFI 2QL. Tel: 01924-295500. *Education Officer,* J. McLeod

WALSALL, Civic Centre, Darwall Street, WSI IDQ. Tel: 01922-6523000. *Education Officer,* M. J. Quinn

WIGAN, Gateway House, Standishgate, WNI IAE. Tel: 01942-44991. *Education Officer (acting),* M. Roxburgh

WIRRAL, Hamilton Building, Conway Street, Birkenhead L41 4FD. Tel: 0151-666 2121. *Director,* D. Rigby

WOLVERHAMPTON, Civic Centre, St Peter's Square, WVI IRR. Tel: 01902-27811. *Director,* R. Lockwood

LONDON

*Inner London borough

BARKING AND DAGENHAM, Town Hall, Barking, Essex IGII 7LU. Tel: 0181-592 4500. *Education Officer,* A. Larbalastier

BARNET, Old Town Hall, Friern Barnet Lane, NII 3DL. Tel: 0181-368 1255. *Education Officer,* J. Bailey

BEXLEY, Hill View, Hill View Drive, Welling, Kent DAI6 5RY. Tel: 0181-303 7777. *Director,* P. McGee

BRENT, Chesterfield House, 9 Park Lane, Wembley, Middx. HA9 7RW. Tel: 0181-900 5443. *Director,* G. Benham

BROMLEY, Civic Centre, Stockwell Close, BRI 3UH. Tel: 0181-464 3333. *Director,* A. Baxter

*CAMDEN, Crowndale Centre, 218–220 Eversholt Street, NWI IBD. Tel: 0171-911 1525. *Education Officer,* P. Mitchell

*CITY OF LONDON, Education Department, Corporation of London, PO Box 270, Guildhall, EC2P 2EJ. Tel: 0171-332 1750. *City Education Officer,* D. Smith

*CITY OF WESTMINSTER, City Hall, Victoria Street, SWIE 6QP. Tel: 0171-798 2771. *Education Officer,* Mrs D. Tuck

CROYDON, Taberner House, Park Lane, CR9 ITP. Tel: 0181-686 4433. *Director,* P. Benians

EALING, Perceval House, 14–18 Uxbridge Road, W5 2HL. Tel: 0181-758 5484. *Director,* M. Herrman

ENFIELD, PO Box 56, Civic Centre, Silver Street, ENI 3XQ. Tel: 0181-366 6565. *Director,* G. Hutchinson

*GREENWICH, Riverside House, Woolwich High Street, Woolwich, SEI8 6DN. Tel: 0181-854 8888. *Director,* J. Kramer

*HACKNEY, Edith Cavell Building, Enfield Road, NI 5LZ. Tel: 0171-214 8400. *Director,* G. John

*HAMMERSMITH AND FULHAM, Cambridge House, Cambridge Grove, W6 4LE. Tel: 0181-748 3020. *Director,* Ms C. Whatford

HARINGEY, 48 Station Road, N22 4TR. Tel: 0181-975 9700. *Director,* R. L. Jones

HARROW, PO Box 22, Civic Centre, Harrow HAI 2UW. Tel: 0181-863 5611. *Director,* Mrs C. Gilbert

HAVERING, Mercury House, Mercury Gardens, Romford RMI 3DR. Tel: 01708-772222. *Director,* C. Hardy

HILLINGDON, Civic Centre, Uxbridge, Middx. UB8 IUW. Tel: 01895-250111. *Education Officer,* Mrs G. Andrews

HOUNSLOW, Civic Centre, Lampton Road, TW3 4DN. Tel: 0181-862 5301. *Director,* J. D. Trickett

*ISLINGTON, Laycock Street, NI ITH. Tel: 0171-457 5753. *Education Officer,* H. Nicolle

*KENSINGTON AND CHELSEA, Town Hall, Hornton Street, W8 7NX. Tel: 0171-937 5464. *Education Officer,* M. Stoten

KINGSTON UPON THAMES, Guildhall, KTI IEU. Tel: 0181-547 5220. *Director,* W. Dickinson

*LAMBETH, Blue Star House, 234–244 Stockwell Road, SW9 9SP. Tel: 0171-926 2248. *Chief Education Officer,* Mrs B. Burchell

*LEWISHAM, Laurence House, I Catford Road, SE6 4RU. Tel: 0181-695 6000. *Director,* L. Fullick

MERTON, Civic Centre, London Road, Morden, Surrey SM4 5DX. Tel: 0181-545 3276. *Director,* Ms L. Kant

NEWHAM, Broadway House, 322 High Street, E15 IAJ. Tel: 0181-555 5552. *Director,* I. Harrison

REDBRIDGE, Lynton House, 255–259 High Road, Ilford, IGI INN. Tel: 0181-478 3020. *Director,* D. Capper

RICHMOND UPON THAMES, Regal House, London Road, Twickenham, TWI 3QS. Tel: 0181-891 1411. *Director,* G. Alexander

*SOUTHWARK, I Bradenham Close, SE17 2BA. Tel: 0171-525 5000. *Education Officer,* G. Mott

SUTTON, The Grove, Carshalton, Surrey SM5 3AL. Tel: 0181-770 5000. *Director,* C. Blurton

*TOWER HAMLETS, Mulberry Place, 5 Clove Crescent, EI4 2BG. (The office will relocate in 1995) Tel: 0171-512 4200. *Education Officer,* Mrs A. Sofer

WALTHAM FOREST, Municipal Offices, High Road, Leyton EIO 5QJ. Tel: 0181-527 5544. *Director,* A. Lockhart

*WANDSWORTH, Town Hall, Wandsworth High Street, SW18 2PU. Tel: 0181-871 7890. *Director (acting)*, P. Robinson

## WALES

### COUNTY COUNCILS

CLWYD, Shire Hall, Mold CH7 6NB. Tel: 01352-702500. *Director*, K. McDonogh
DYFED, Pibwrlwyd, Carmarthen SA31 2NH. Tel: 01267-233333. *Director*, J. G. Ellis
GWENT, County Hall, Cwmbran NP44 2XG. Tel: 01633-838838. *Director*, J. D. Griffiths
GWYNEDD, County Offices, Caernarfon LL57 3BY. Tel: 01286-672255. *Director*, G. Jarvis
MID GLAMORGAN, County Hall, Cathays Park, Cardiff CFI 3NE. Tel: 01222-820820. *Director*, K. Davies
POWYS, County Hall, Llandrindod Wells LDI 5LG. Tel: 01597-826000. *Director*, M. R. J. Barker
SOUTH GLAMORGAN, County Hall, Atlantic Wharf, Cardiff CFI 5UW. Tel: 01222-872000. *Director*, T. P. Davies
WEST GLAMORGAN, County Hall, Swansea SAI 3SN. Tel: 01792-471111. *Director*, H. G. Roberts

## SCOTLAND

### REGIONAL AND ISLANDS COUNCILS

BORDERS, Regional Headquarters, Newtown St Boswells, Melrose TD6 OSA. Tel: 01835-823301. *Director*, I. Dutton
CENTRAL, Regional Council Offices, Viewforth, Stirling FK8 2ET. Tel: 01786-442000. *Director*, Mrs M. Allan
DUMFRIES AND GALLOWAY, 30 Edinburgh Road, Dumfries DGI IJQ. Tel: 01387-61234. *Director*, W. C. Fordyce
FIFE, Fife House, North Street, Glenrothes KY7 5LT. Tel: 01592-414141. *Director*, B. Welsh
GRAMPIAN, Woodhill House, Westburn Road, Aberdeen AB9 2LU. Tel: 01224-664600. *Director*, D. Paterson
HIGHLAND, Regional Buildings, Glenurquhart Road, Inverness IV3 5NX. Tel: 01463-702802. *Director*, A. C. Gilchrist
LOTHIAN, 40 Torphichen Street, Edinburgh EH3 8JJ. Tel: 0131-229 9166. *Director*, Ms E. Reid
ORKNEY, Council Offices, Kirkwall KW15 INY. Tel: 01856-873535. *Director*, J. Anderson
SHETLAND, Schlumberger Industrial Estate, Lerwick ZEI OPY. Tel: 01595-3535. *Director*, J. Halcrow
STRATHCLYDE, 20 India Street, Glasgow G2 4PF. Tel: 0141-249 4150. *Director*, F. Pignatelli
TAYSIDE, Tayside House, 28 Crichton Street, Dundee DDI 3RJ. Tel: 01382-23281. *Director*, A. B. Watson
WESTERN ISLES, Council Offices, Sandwick Road, Stornoway, Isle of Lewis PA87 2BW. Tel: 01851-703773. *Director*, N. R. Galbraith

## NORTHERN IRELAND

### EDUCATION AND LIBRARY BOARDS

BELFAST, Board Headquarters, 40 Academy Street, Belfast BTI 2NQ. Tel: 01232-329211. *Chief Executive*, T. G. J. Moag
NORTH EASTERN, County Hall, 182 Galgorm Road, Ballymena, Co. Antrim BT42 IHN. Tel: 01266-653333. *Chief Executive*, G. Topping
SOUTH EASTERN, 18 Windsor Avenue, Belfast BT9 6EF. Tel: 01232-381188. *Chief Executive*, T. Nolan, OBE
SOUTHERN, 3 Charlemont Place, The Mall, Armagh BT61 9AX. Tel: 01861-523811. *Chief Executive*, J. G. Kelly

WESTERN, I Hospital Road, Omagh, Co. Tyrone BT79 OAW. Tel: 01662-240240. *Chief Executive*, M. H. F. Murphy, OBE

## ISLANDS

GUERNSEY, PO Box 32, Grange Road, St Peter Port GYI 3AU. Tel: 01481-710821. *Director*, J. D. Stephenson
JERSEY, PO Box 142, St Saviour JE4 8QJ. Tel: 01534-509500. *Director*, B. Grady
ISLE OF MAN, Department of Education, Murray House, Mount Havelock, Douglas IMI 2SG. Tel: 01624-685801. *Director*, G. Baker
ISLES OF SCILLY, Town Hall, St Mary's TR21 OLW. Tel: 01720-22537. *Secretary for Education*, P. S. Hygate

---

## ADVISORY BODIES

---

### SCHOOLS

EDUCATION OTHERWISE, PO Box 120, Leamington Spa, Warks. CV32 7ER. *Helpline*, tel: 01926-886828
INTERNATIONAL BACCALAUREATE, Examinations Office, Pascal Close, St Mellons, Cardiff CF3 OYP. Tel: 01222-770770. *Director of Examinations*, C. Carthew
NATIONAL ADVISORY COUNCIL FOR EDUCATION TRAINING AND TARGETS, Room 559, Caxton House, Tothill Street, London SWIH 9NF. Tel: 0171-273 5695. *Director*, M. Waring
NATIONAL COUNCIL FOR EDUCATIONAL TECHNOLOGY, Milburn Hill Road, Science Park, Coventry CV4 7JJ. Tel: 01203-416994. *Chief Executive*, Mrs M. Bell
SPECIAL EDUCATIONAL NEEDS TRIBUNAL, Department for Education, Sanctuary Buildings, Great Smith Street, London SWIP 3BT. Tel: 0171-925 5042. *Secretary*, Ms J. Saraga

### INDEPENDENT SCHOOLS

ASSISTED PLACES COMMITTEE, 26 Queen Anne's Gate, London SWIH 9AN. Tel: 0171-222 9595. *Secretary*, Mrs M. L. Shaw
COMMON ENTRANCE BOARD, Jordan House, Christchurch Road, New Milton, Hants. BH25 6QJ. Tel: 01425-621111. *Administrator*, Mrs J. Williams
GOVERNING BODIES ASSOCIATION, Windleshaw Lodge, Withyham, Nr. Hartfield, E. Sussex TN7 4DB. Tel: 01892-770879. *Secretary*, D. G. Banwell
GOVERNING BODIES OF GIRLS' SCHOOLS ASSOCIATION, Windleshaw Lodge, Withyham, Nr. Hartfield, E. Sussex TN7 4DB. Tel: 01892-770879. *Secretary*, D. G. Banwell
INDEPENDENT SCHOOLS INFORMATION SERVICE, 56 Buckingham Gate, London SWIE 6AG. Tel: 0171-630 8793/4. *National Director*, D. J. Woodhead

### FURTHER EDUCATION

FURTHER EDUCATION UNIT, Unit 3, Citadel Place, Tinworth Street, London SEII 5EH. Tel: 0171-962 1280. *Chief Officer*, G. Stanton
NATIONAL COUNCIL FOR VOCATIONAL QUALIFICATIONS, 222 Euston Road, London NWI 2BZ. Tel: 0171-387 9898. *Chief Executive*, J. Hillier

*Regional Advisory Councils*

ASSOCIATION OF COLLEGES IN THE EASTERN REGION, Merlin Place, Milton Road, Cambridge CB4 4DP. Tel: 01223–424022. *Chief Officer*, A. Young

CENTRA (NORTH WEST EDUCATION AND TRAINING SERVICES) LTD, Walkden Road, Worsley, Manchester M28 7QA. Tel: 0161-702 8700. *Chief Executive*, R. S. Welsh

EMFEC (EAST MIDLAND FURTHER EDUCATION COUNCIL), Robins Wood House, Robins Wood Road, Aspley, Nottingham NG8 3NH. Tel: 0115-929 3291. *Chief Executive*, R. Ainscough

LASER ADVISORY COUNCIL (LONDON AND SOUTH EAST), Chenies House, 21 Bedford Square, London WC1B 3HH. Tel: 0171-637 3073. *Director*, L. South

NORTHERN COUNCIL FOR FURTHER EDUCATION, 5 Grosvenor Villas, Grosvenor Road, Newcastle upon Tyne NE2 2RU. Tel: 0191-281 3242. *Director*, J. F. Pearce

SOUTHERN REGIONAL COUNCIL FOR FURTHER EDUCATION AND TRAINING, The Mezzanine Suite, PO Box 2055, Civic Centre, Reading RG1 7ET. Tel: 01734-390592. *Chief Officer*, B. J. Knowles

SOUTH WEST ASSOCIATION FOR FURTHER EDUCATION AND TRAINING, Bishops Hull House, Bishops Hull, Taunton, Somerset TA1 5RA. Tel: 01823-335491. *Chief Executive*, F. S. Fisher

WELSH JOINT EDUCATION COMMITTEE, 245 Western Avenue, Cardiff CF5 2YX. Tel: 01222-561231. *Secretary*, C. Heycock

YORKSHIRE AND HUMBERSIDE ASSOCIATION FOR FURTHER AND HIGHER EDUCATION, Dewsbury Business and Media Centre, 13 Wellington Road East, Dewsbury, W. Yorks. WF13 1XG. Tel: 01924-450900. *Chief Executive*, Prof. N. Woodhead

### HIGHER EDUCATION

ASSOCIATION OF COMMONWEALTH UNIVERSITIES, John Foster House, 36 Gordon Square, London WC1H 0PF. Tel: 0171-387 8572. *Secretary-General*, Dr A. Christodoulou, CBE

COMMITTEE OF VICE-CHANCELLORS AND PRINCIPALS OF THE UNIVERSITIES OF THE UNITED KINGDOM, 29 Tavistock Square, London WC1H 9EZ. Tel: 0171-387 9231. *Chairman*, Dr K. Edwards; *Secretary* T. U. Burgner

HIGHER EDUCATION QUALITY COUNCIL, 344–354 Gray's Inn Road, London WC1X 8BP. Tel: 0171-837 2223. *Company Secretary*, G. L. Middleton

NORTHERN IRELAND HIGHER EDUCATION COUNCIL, c/o Department of Education for Northern Ireland, Rathgael House, Balloo Road, Bangor BT19 7PR. Tel: 01247-279333. *Chairman*, Sir Kenneth Bloomfield, KCB

### CURRICULUM COUNCILS, ETC.

CURRICULUM AND ASSESSMENT AUTHORITY FOR WALES, Castle Buildings, Womanby Street, Cardiff CF1 9SX. Tel: 01222-344946. *Chief Executive*, J. V. Williams

NORTHERN IRELAND COUNCIL FOR THE CURRICULUM, ASSESSMENT AND EXAMINATIONS, Stranmillis College, Stranmillis Road, Belfast BT9 5DY. Tel: 01232-381414. *Chief Executive*, Mrs C. Coxhead

SCHOOL CURRICULUM AND ASSESSMENT AUTHORITY, Newcombe House, 45 Notting Hill Gate, London W11 3JB. Tel: 0171-229 1234. *Chairman*, Sir Ron Dearing; *Chief Executive*, C. Woodhead

SCOTTISH CONSULTATIVE COUNCIL ON THE CURRICULUM, Gardyne Road, Broughty Ferry, Dundee DD5 1NY. Tel: 01382-455053. *Chief Executive*, C. E. Harrison

TVEI UNIT, Schools Policy Branch, Employment Department, Room E435, Moorfoot, Sheffield S1 4PQ. Tel: 0114-259 3857

## EXAMINING BODIES

### GCSE

NORTHERN EXAMINATIONS AND ASSESSMENT BOARD, Devas Street, Manchester M15 6EX. Tel: 0161-953 1180. *Chief Executive*, Mrs K. Tattersall

NORTHERN IRELAND COUNCIL FOR THE CURRICULUM, ASSESSMENT AND EXAMINATIONS, Beechill House, 42 Beechill Road, Belfast BT8 4RS. Tel: 01232-704666. *Chief Executive*, Mrs C. Coxhead

SOUTHERN EXAMINING GROUP, Stag Hill House, Guildford, Surrey GU2 5XJ. Tel: 01483-506506/01865-510085. *Joint Secretaries*, J. A. Day; J. Pailing

UNIVERSITY OF LONDON EXAMINATIONS AND ASSESSMENT COUNCIL, The Lindens, 139 Lexden Road, Colchester CO3 3RL. Tel: 01206-549595; Stewart House, 32 Russell Square, London WC1B 5DN. Tel: 0171-331 4000. *Chief Executive*, A. Smith

WELSH JOINT EDUCATION COMMITTEE, 245 Western Avenue, Cardiff CF5 2YX. Tel: 01222-561231. *Secretary*, C. Heycock

WEST MIDLANDS EXAMINATIONS BOARD, Mill Wharf, Mill Street, Birmingham B6 4BU. Tel: 0121-628 2000. *Secretary*, B. Swift

### A-LEVEL

ASSOCIATED EXAMINING BOARD, Stag Hill House, Guildford, Surrey GU2 5XJ. Tel: 01483-506506. *Secretary-General*, J. A. Day

NORTHERN EXAMINATIONS AND ASSESSMENT BOARD, Devas Street, Manchester M15 6EX. Tel: 0161-953 1180. *Chief Executive*, Mrs K. Tattersall

NORTHERN IRELAND COUNCIL FOR THE CURRICULUM, ASSESSMENT AND EXAMINATIONS, Beechill House, 42 Beechill Road, Belfast BT8 4RS. Tel: 01232-704666. *Chief Executive*, Mrs C. Coxhead

OXFORD AND CAMBRIDGE SCHOOLS EXAMINATION BOARD, Purbeck House, Purbeck Road, Cambridge CB2 2PU. Tel: 01223-411211. *Secretary-General*, H. F. King

OXFORD AND CAMBRIDGE SCHOOLS EXAMINATION BOARD, Elsfield Way, Oxford OX2 8EP. Tel: 01865-54421. *Secretary (acting)*, J. G. Lloyd

UNIVERSITY OF CAMBRIDGE LOCAL EXAMINATIONS SYNDICATE, Syndicate Buildings, 1 Hills Road, Cambridge CB1 2EU. Tel: 01223-553311. *Secretary*, M. P. Halstead

UNIVERSITY OF LONDON EXAMINATIONS AND ASSESSMENT COUNCIL, Stewart House, 32 Russell Square, London WC1B 5DN. Tel: 0171-331 4000. *Chief Executive*, A. Smith

UNIVERSITY OF OXFORD DELEGACY OF LOCAL EXAMINATIONS, Ewert House, Ewert Place, Summertown, Oxford OX2 7BZ. Tel: 01865-54291. *Secretary*, J. Pailing

WELSH JOINT EDUCATION COMMITTEE, 245 Western Avenue, Cardiff CF5 2YX. Tel: 01222-561231. *Secretary*, C. Heycock

### SCOTLAND

SCOTTISH EXAMINATION BOARD, Ironmills Road, Dalkeith, Midlothian EH22 1LE. Tel: 0131-663 6601. *Chief Executive*, H. A. Long, PH.D.

SCOTTISH VOCATIONAL EDUCATION COUNCIL, Hanover House, 24 Douglas Street, Glasgow G2 7NQ. Tel: 0141-248 7900. *Chief Executive*, T. J. McCool

## FURTHER EDUCATION

BUSINESS AND TECHNOLOGY EDUCATION COUNCIL, Central House, Upper Woburn Place, London WC1H OHH. Tel: 0171-413 8400. *Chief Executive*, Dr C. Townsend

CITY AND GUILDS OF LONDON INSTITUTE, 76 Portland Place, London WIN 4AA. Tel: 0171-278 2468. *Director-General*, Dr N. Carey

RSA EXAMINATIONS BOARD, Westwood Way, Coventry CV4 8HS. Tel: 01203-470033. *Chief Executive*, M. F. Cross

VOCATIONAL EDUCATION UNIT, 46 Britannia Street, London WCIX 9RG. Tel: 0171-278 2468. *Chairman*, P. Wates; *Division Manager*, Ms H. Aylett

## FUNDING COUNCILS

### SCHOOLS

FUNDING AGENCY FOR SCHOOLS, Albion Wharf, 25 Skeldergate, York YOI 2XL. Tel: 01904-661603. *Chairman*, Sir Christopher Benson; *Chief Executive*, M. Collier

### FURTHER EDUCATION

FURTHER EDUCATION FUNDING COUNCIL FOR ENGLAND, Cheylesmore House, Quinton Road, Coventry CVI 2WT. Tel: 01203-863000. *Chief Executive*, Sir William Stubbs

FURTHER EDUCATION FUNDING COUNCIL FOR WALES, Lambourne House, Cardiff Business Park, Llanishen, Cardiff CF4 5GL. Tel: 01222-761861. *Chief Executive*, Prof. J. A. Andrews

SCOTTISH FURTHER EDUCATION FUNDING UNIT, Scottish Office Education Department, 43 Jeffrey Street, Edinburgh EHI IDN. Tel: 0131-244 5378. *Director*, J. G. Henderson

### HIGHER EDUCATION

HIGHER EDUCATION FUNDING COUNCIL FOR ENGLAND, Northavon House, Coldharbour Lane, Bristol BS16 1QD. Tel: 01272-317317. *Chief Executive*, Prof. G. Davies, FEng.

HIGHER EDUCATION FUNDING COUNCIL FOR WALES, Lambourne House, Cardiff Business Park, Llanishen, Cardiff CF4 5GL. Tel: 01222-761861. *Chief Executive*, Prof. J. A. Andrews

SCOTTISH HIGHER EDUCATION FUNDING COUNCIL, Donaldson House, 97 Haymarket Terrace, Edinburgh EHI2 5HD. Tel: 0131-313 6500. *Chief Executive*, Prof. J. Sizer

TEACHER TRAINING AGENCY, c/o Department of Education, Sanctuary Buildings, Great Smith Street, London SWIP 3BT. *Chairman*, G. Parker

## ADMISSIONS AND COURSE INFORMATION

ART AND DESIGN ADMISSIONS REGISTRY, Penn House, 9 Broad Street, Hereford HR4 9AP. Tel: 01432-266653. *Registrar*, T. W. M. Gourdie

CAREERS RESEARCH AND ADVISORY CENTRE (CRAC), Sheraton House, Castle Park, Cambridge CB3 OAX. Tel: 01223-460277. *Director*, D. Blandford.

*Publishers*, Hobsons Publishing PLC, Bateman Street, Cambridge CB2 ILZ

COMMITTEE OF SCOTTISH HIGHER EDUCATION PRINCIPALS (COSHEP), St Andrew House, 141 West Nile Street, Glasgow GI 2RN. Tel: 0141-353 1880. *Secretary*, Dr R. L. Crawford

GRADUATE TEACHER TRAINING REGISTRY, Fulton House, Jessop Avenue, Cheltenham, Glos. GL50 3SH. Tel: 01242-225868. *Registrar*, M. Griffiths

SOCIAL WORK ADMISSIONS SYSTEM, Fulton House, Jessop Avenue, Cheltenham GL50 3SH. Tel: 01242-225977. *Admissions Officer*, M. Griffiths

TEACHER EDUCATION ADMISSIONS CLEARING HOUSE (TEACH) (Scottish postgraduate only), PO Box 165, Holyrood Road, Edinburgh EH8 8AT. *Registrar*, Miss R. C. Williamson

UNIVERSITIES AND COLLEGES ADMISSIONS SERVICE, Fulton House, Jessop Avenue, Cheltenham GL50 3SH. Tel: 01242-222444. *Chief Executives*, M. A. Higgins (*Corporate Affairs*); P. A. Oakley (*Applications*)

## UNIVERSITIES

### THE UNIVERSITY OF ABERDEEN (1495)
Regent Walk, Aberdeen AB9 IFX
Tel 01224-272000
Full-time Students (1993–4), 9,500
*Chancellor*, Sir Kenneth Alexander, FRSE (1987)
*Principal*, Prof. J. Maxwell Irvine, PH.D.
*Secretary*, N. R. D. Begg
*Rector*, I. Hamilton, QC (1994–6)

### ANGLIA POLYTECHNIC UNIVERSITY (1992)
Victoria Road South, Chelmsford, Essex CMI ILL
Tel 01245-493131
Full-time Students (1992–3), 7,863
*Chancellor*, The Lord Prior, PC
*Vice-Chancellor*, M. J. Salmon
*Head of Student Administration*, D. Davis

### ASTON UNIVERSITY (1966)
Aston Triangle, Birmingham B4 7ET
Tel 0121-359 3611
Full-time Students (1993–4), 4,252
*Chancellor*, Sir Adrian Cadbury (1979)
*Vice-Chancellor*, Prof. Sir Frederick Crawford, PH.D., D.Eng., D.SC., FEng.
*Registrar and Secretary*, R. D. A. Packham

### THE UNIVERSITY OF BATH (1966)
Claverton Down, Bath BA2 7AY
Tel 01225-826826
Full-time Students (1993–4), 5,400
*Chancellor*, Sir Denys Henderson (1993)
*Vice-Chancellor*, Prof. V. D. Vandelinde
*Registrar*, J. Bursey

### THE UNIVERSITY OF BIRMINGHAM (1900)
Edgbaston, Birmingham BI5 2TT
Tel 0121-414 3344
Full-time Students (1992–3), 13,000
*Chancellor*, Sir Alexander Jarratt, CB (1983)
*Vice-Chancellor*, Prof. Sir Michael Thompson, D.SC.
*Registrar and Secretary*, D. R. Holmes

BOURNEMOUTH UNIVERSITY (1992)
(formerly Bournemouth Polytechnic)
Poole House, Talbot Campus, Fern Barrow,
Dorset BH12 5BB
Tel 01202-524111
*Full-time Students* (1992-3), 8,000
*Chancellor*, The Baroness Cox (1992)
*Vice-Chancellor*, Dr B. R. MacManus
*Secretary and Registrar*, Miss B. Chamberlain

THE UNIVERSITY OF BRADFORD (1966)
Bradford BD7 1DP
Tel 01274-733466
*Full-time Students* (1993-4), 6,692
*Chancellor*, Sir Trevor Holdsworth (1992)
*Vice-Chancellor*, Prof. D. J. Johns, Ph.D., D.Sc. (1989)
*Registrar and Secretary*, N. Andrews

THE UNIVERSITY OF BRIGHTON (1992)
(formerly Brighton Polytechnic)
Mithras House, Lewes Road, Brighton BN2 4AT
Tel 01273-600900
*Full-time Students* (1993-4), 9,780
*Chairman of the Board*, M. J. Aldrich
*Director*, Prof. D. J. Watson
*Deputy Director*, D. E. House

THE UNIVERSITY OF BRISTOL (1909)
Senate House, Tyndall Avenue, Bristol BS8 1TH
Tel 0117-930 3030
*Full-time Students* (1993-4), 10,252
*Chancellor*, Sir Jeremy Morse, KCMG (1989)
*Vice-Chancellor*, Sir John Kingman, FRS
*Registrar*, J. H. M. Parry

BRUNEL UNIVERSITY (1966)
Uxbridge, Middx. UB8 3PH
Tel 01895-274000
*Full-time Students* (1993-4), 5,290
*Chancellor*, The Earl of Halsbury, FRS (1966)
*Vice-Chancellor*, Prof. M. J. H. Sterling
*Secretary-General and Registrar*, D. Neave

THE UNIVERSITY OF BUCKINGHAM (1983)
Founded 1976 as University College at Buckingham
Buckingham MK18 1EG
Tel 01280-814080
*Full-time Students* (1993-4), 978
*Chancellor*, The Baroness Thatcher, OM, PC, FRS (1992)
*Vice-Chancellor*, The Rt. Hon. Sir Richard Luce (1992)
*Registrar and Secretary*, M. Lavis, Ph.D.

THE UNIVERSITY OF CAMBRIDGE
University Offices, The Old Schools, Cambridge CB2 1TN
Tel 01223-337733
Number of undergraduates in residence 1994-5: *Men*,
6,083; *Women*, 4,553

UNIVERSITY OFFICERS, ETC.

*Chancellor*, HRH The Duke of Edinburgh, KG, KT, OM, GBE,
PC (1977)
*Vice-Chancellor*, Prof. Sir David Williams (*Wolfson*) (1989)
*High Steward*, The Lord Runcie, PC, DD (1991)
*Deputy High Steward*, The Lord Richardson of
Duntisbourne, PC, MBE, TD (1983)
*Commissary*, The Lord Oliver of Aylmerton, PC (*Trinity
Hall*) (1989)
*Proctors*, J. K. Thompson (*Clare*); R. B. Thorpe, Ph.D.
(*Churchill*) (1994)

*Orator*, A. J. Bowen (*Jesus*) (1993)
*Registrary*, S. G. Fleet, Ph.D. (*Downing*) (1983)
*Deputy Registrary*, N. J. B. A. Branson, Ph.D. (*Darwin*)
(1993)
*Librarian*, P. K. Fox (*Selwyn*) (1994)
*Treasurer*, Ms J. Womack (*Trinity*) (1993)
*Secretary-General of the Faculties*, D. A. Livesey,
Ph.D. (*Emmanuel*) (1992)
*Director of the Fitzwilliam Museum*, S. S. Jervis (*Corpus
Christi*) (1990)

COLLEGES AND HALLS, ETC.
with dates of foundation

CHRIST'S (1505), *Master*, Prof. Sir Hans Kornberg, Ph.D.,
D.SC., SC.D., FRS (1983)
CHURCHILL (1960), *Master*, Prof. A. N. Broers, Ph.D., FRS
(1990)
CLARE (1326), *Master*, Prof. B. A. Hepple (1993)
CLARE HALL (1966), *President*, Prof. G. P. K. Beer, Litt..D.,
FBA (1994)
CORPUS CHRISTI (1352), *Master*, Prof. E. A. Wrigley,
Ph.D. (1994)
DARWIN (1964), *Master*, Prof. G. E. R. Lloyd, Ph.D., FBA
(1989)
DOWNING (1800), *Master*, P. Mathias, CBE, Litt.D., FBA
(1987)
EMMANUEL (1584), *Master*, The Lord St John of Fawsley,
PC, Ph.D. (1991)
FITZWILLIAM (1966), *Master*, Prof. A. W. Cuthbert, Ph.D.,
FRS (1991)
GIRTON (1869), *Mistress*, Mrs J. J. d'A. Campbell, CMG
(1992)
GONVILLE AND CAIUS (1348), *Master*, Prof. P. Gray, SC.D.,
FRS (1988)
HOMERTON (1824) (for B.Ed. students), *Principal*,
Mrs K. B. Pretty, Ph.D. (1991)
HUGHES HALL (1885) (for post-graduate students),
*President*, J. T. Dingle, D.SC. (1993)
JESUS (1496), *Master*, Prof. the Lord Renfrew of
Kaimsthorn, SC.D. (1986)
KING'S (1441), *Provost*, Prof. P. P. G. Bateson, SC.D., FRS
(1987)
*LUCY CAVENDISH COLLEGE (1965) (for women research
students and mature and affiliated undergraduates),
*President*, Baroness Perry of Southwark (1994)
MAGDALENE (1542), *Master*, Prof. J. B. Gurdon, D.Phil.,
FRS (1995)
*NEW HALL (1954), *President*, Mrs V. L. Pearl, Ph.D. (1981)
*NEWNHAM (1871), *Principal*, Ms O. S. O'Neill (1992)
PEMBROKE (1347), *Master*, Sir Roger Tomkys, KCMG (1992)
PETERHOUSE (1284), *Master*, Prof. Sir John Meurig
Thomas, FRS (1993)
QUEENS' (1448), *President*, Revd J. C. Polkinghorne, SC.D.,
FRS (1989)
ROBINSON (1977), *Warden*, Prof. the Lord Lewis of
Newnham, SC.D., FRS (1977)
ST CATHARINE'S (1473), *Master*, Prof. Sir Terence English
(1993)
ST EDMUND'S (1896), *Master*, R. M. Laws, CBE, Ph.D.
(1986)
ST JOHN'S (1511), *Master*, Prof. P. Goddard, Ph.D., FRS
(1994)
SELWYN (1882), *Master*, D. Harrison, CBE, SC.D., F.Eng.
(1993)
SIDNEY SUSSEX (1596), *Master*, Prof. G. Horn, SC.D., FRS
(1992)
TRINITY (1546), *Master*, Sir Michael Atiyah, Ph.D., FRS,
FRSE (1990)

TRINITY HALL (1350), *Master*, Sir John Lyons, PH.D.
(1984)
WOLFSON (1965), *President*, G. Johnson PH.D. (1994)
*Colleges for women only

THE UNIVERSITY OF CENTRAL ENGLAND
IN BIRMINGHAM (1992)
(formerly Birmingham Polytechnic)
Perry Barr, Birmingham B42 2SU
Tel 0121-331 5000
Full-time Students (1993–4), 15,057
*Chancellor*, The Lord Mayor of Birmingham
*Vice-Chancellor*, Dr P. C. Knight
*Secretary and Registrar*, Ms M. Penlington

THE UNIVERSITY OF CENTRAL LANCASHIRE
(1992)
(formerly Lancashire Polytechnic)
Preston PRI 2HE
Tel 01772-201201
Full-time Students (1993–4), 12,200
*Rector and Chief Executive*, B. Booth
*Head of Academic Administration*, L. Munro
*Secretary*, Ms P. M. Ackroyd

THE CITY UNIVERSITY (1966)
Northampton Square, London ECIV OHB
Tel 0171-477 8000
Full-time Students (1992–3), 5,833
*Chancellor*, The Rt. Hon. the Lord Mayor of London
*Vice-Chancellor and Principal*, Prof. R. N. Franklin, D.phil.,
D.SC.
*Registrar*, A. H. Seville, PH.D.
*Secretary*, M. M. O'Hara

COVENTRY UNIVERSITY (1992)
(formerly Coventry Polytechnic)
Priory Street, Coventry CVI 5FB
Tel 01203-631313
Full-time Students (1993–4), 14,900
*Vice-Chancellor*, M. Goldstein, PH.D., D.SC.
*Registrar*, J. Gledhill, PH.D.
*Secretary*, Ms L. Arlidge

DE MONTFORT UNIVERSITY (1992)
(formerly Leicester Polytechnic)
The Gateway, Leicester LEI 9BH
Tel 0116-255 1551
Full-time Students (1993–4), 18,000
*Chancellor*, Dame Anne Mueller
*Vice-Chancellor and Chief Executive*, Prof. K. Barker, CBE
*Registrar*, E. Critchlow
*Secretary*, A. Denny

THE UNIVERSITY OF DERBY (1993)
(formerly Derbyshire College of Higher Education)
Kedleston Road, Derby DE22 IGB
Tel 01332-622222
Full-time Students (1993–4), 7,500
*Vice-Chancellor*, Prof. R. Waterhouse
*Registrar and Secretary*, Mrs J. Fry

THE UNIVERSITY OF DUNDEE (1967)
Dundee DDI 4HN
Tel 01382-23181
Full-time Students (1993–4), 6,700
*Chancellor*, Sir James Black, FRCP, FRS (1992)
*Principal and Vice-Chancellor*, Dr I. J. Graham-Bryce

*Secretary*, R. Seaton
*Rector*, S. Fry (1992–5)

THE UNIVERSITY OF DURHAM
Founded 1832; re-organized 1908, 1937 and 1963
Old Shire Hall, Durham DHI 3HP
Tel 0191-374 2000
Full-time Students (1993–4), 7,825
*Chancellor*, Sir Peter Ustinov, CBE, FRSL
*Vice-Chancellor and Warden*, Prof. E. A. V. Ebsworth, PH.D.,
D.SC., FRSE
*Registrar and Secretary*, J. C. F. Hayward

COLLEGES

COLLINGWOOD, *Principal*, G. H. Blake, PH.D.
GRADUATE SOCIETY, *Principal*, M. Richardson, PH.D.
GREY, *Master*, V. E. Watts
HATFIELD, *Master*, Prof. J. P. Barber, PH.D.
ST AIDAN'S, *Principal*, R. J. Williams
ST CHAD'S, *Principal*, The Revd Dr D. Arnold
ST CUTHBERT'S SOCIETY, *Principal*, S. G. C. Stoker
ST HILD AND ST BEDE, *Principal*, J. V. Armitage, PH.D.
ST JOHN'S, *Principal*, D. V. Day
ST MARY'S, *Principal*, Miss J. M. Kenworthy
TREVELYAN, *Principal (acting)*, G. Marshall, PH.D.
UNIVERSITY (DURHAM), *Master*, E. C. Salthouse, PH.D.
UNIVERSITY (STOCKTON), *Principal*, J. C. F. Hayward
USHAW, *President*, Rt. Revd Mgr R. Atherton, OBE
VAN MILDERT, *Principal*, Dr J. Turner

THE UNIVERSITY OF EAST ANGLIA (1963)
Norwich NR4 7TJ
Tel 01603-56161
Full-time Students (1993–4), 6,569
*Chancellor*, Sir Geoffrey Allen, FEng, FRS (1994)
*Vice-Chancellor*, Prof. D. C. Burke, CBE, PH.D.
*Registrar and Secretary*, M. G. E. Paulson-Ellis, OBE

THE UNIVERSITY OF EAST LONDON (1992)
(formerly Polytechnic of East London)
Longbridge Road, Dagenham, Essex RM8 2AS
Tel 0181-590 7722
Full-time Students (1993–4), 11,000
*Vice-Chancellor*, Prof. F. Gould
*Secretary and Registrar*, A. Ingle

THE UNIVERSITY OF EDINBURGH (1583)
Old College, South Bridge, Edinburgh EH8 9YL
Tel 0131-650 1000
Full-time Students (1993–4), 15,560
*Chancellor*, HRH The Prince Philip, Duke of Edinburgh,
KG, KT, OM, GBE, PC, FRS (1952)
*Vice-Chancellor and Principal*, Prof. S. Sutherland, FBA, FRSE
*Registrar and Secretary*, M. J. B. Lowe, PH.D.
*Rector*, Dr. M. Macleod (1994–7)

THE UNIVERSITY OF ESSEX (1964)
Wivenhoe Park, Colchester CO4 3SQ
Tel 01206-873333
Full-time Students (1993–4), 5,083
*Chancellor*, The Rt. Hon. Sir Patrick Nairne, GCB, MC (1983)
*Vice-Chancellor*, Prof. R. J. Johnston, PH.D.
*Registrar and Secretary*, A. F. Woodburn

THE UNIVERSITY OF EXETER (1955)
Northcote House, The Queen's Drive, Exeter EX4 4QJ
Tel 01392-263263
Full-time Students (1993–4), 8,266
*Chancellor*, Sir Rex Richards, D.SC., FRS (1981)

*Vice-Chancellor*, Sir Geoffrey Holland, KCB
*Academic Registrar and Secretary*, I. H. C. Powell

## GLAMORGAN UNIVERSITY (1992)
(formerly Polytechnic of Wales)
Pontypridd, Mid Glamorgan CF37 1DL
Tel 01443-480480
Full-time Students (1993–4), 9,827
*Chancellor*, The Lord Rees, PC, QC
*Vice-Chancellor*, Prof. A. L. Webb
*Academic Registrar*, J. O'Shea
*Secretary*, J. L. Bracegirdle

## THE UNIVERSITY OF GLASGOW (1451)
Glasgow G12 8QQ
Tel 0141-339 8855
Full-time Students (1993–4), 15,449
*Chancellor*, Sir Alexander Cairncross, KCMG, FBA, Ph.D., LLD
   (1972)
*Vice-Chancellor*, Sir William Fraser, GCB, LL D, FRSE
*Registrar*, J. M. Black
*Secretary*, R. Ewen, OBE, TD
*Rector*, J. Ball (1993–6)

## GLASGOW CALEDONIAN UNIVERSITY (1993)
Cowcaddens Road, Glasgow G4 0BA
Tel 0141-331 3000
Full-time Students (1993–4), 9,530
*Chancellor*, The Lord Nickson, KBE
*Vice-Chancellor*, Prof. J. S. Mason, Ph.D.
*Secretary*, B. M. Murphy

## THE UNIVERSITY OF GREENWICH (1992)
(formerly Thames Polytechnic)
Wellington Street, Woolwich, London SE18 6PF
Tel 0181-316 8000
Full-time Students (1993–4), 13,539
*Chancellor*, The Baroness Young
*Vice-Chancellor*, Dr D. Fussey
*Academic Registrar*, A. I. Mayfield
*Secretary*, J. Charles

## HERIOT-WATT UNIVERSITY (1966)
Riccarton, Edinburgh EH14 4AS
Tel 0131-449 5111
Full-time Students (1992–3), 8,894
*Chancellor*, The Lord Mackay of Clashfern, PC, QC, FRSE
   (1979)
*Principal and Vice-Chancellor*, Prof. A. G. J. MacFarlane,
   CBE, Ph.D., FRS, FRSE, FEng. (1989)
*Registrar*, D. Sturgeon
*Secretary*, P. L. Wilson

## THE UNIVERSITY OF HERTFORDSHIRE (1992)
(formerly Hatfield Polytechnic)
College Lane, Hatfield, Herts. AL10 9AB
Tel 01707-279000
Full-time Students (1993–4), 12,102
*Chancellor*, Sir Brian Corby
*Vice-Chancellor*, Prof. N. K. Buxton
*Registrar and Secretary*, P. G. Jeffreys

## THE UNIVERSITY OF HUDDERSFIELD (1992)
(formerly Polytechnic of Huddersfield)
Queensgate, Huddersfield HD1 3DH
Tel 01484-422288
Full-time Students (1993–4), 9,988
*Chancellor*, R. C. Cross, OBE

*Vice-Chancellor and Rector*, Prof. K. J. Durrands, CBE
*Secretary and Head of Administration*, D. J. Lock
*Academic Registrar*, M. E. Bond

## THE UNIVERSITY OF HULL (1954)
Cottingham Road, Hull HU6 7RX
Tel 01482-46311
Full-time Students (1993–4), 9,000
*Chancellor*, The Lord Armstrong of Ilminster, GCB, CVO
*Vice-Chancellor*, Prof. D. Dilks, FRSL
*Registrar and Secretary*, P. A. Bolton

## THE UNIVERSITY OF HUMBERSIDE (1992)
(formerly Humberside Polytechnic)
Cottingham Road, Hull HU6 7RT
Tel 01482-440550
Full-time Students (1993–4), 8,989
*Pro-Chancellor*, Dr Harry Hooper, CBE
*Vice-Chancellor*, Prof. R. King
*Registrar*, F. Marks
*Secretary*, Miss M. Harries-Jenkins

## THE UNIVERSITY OF KEELE (1962)
Keele, Newcastle under Lyme, Staffs. ST5 5BG
Tel 01782-621111
Full-time Students (1993–4), 5,188
*Chancellor*, Sir Claus Moser, KCB, CBE, FBA (1986)
*Vice-Chancellor*, Prof. B. E. Fender, CMG, Ph.D.
*Registrar*, D. Cohen, Ph.D.

## THE UNIVERSITY OF KENT AT CANTERBURY (1965)
Tanglewood, Giles Lane, Canterbury CT2 7LX
Tel 01227-764000
Full-time Students (1993–4), 6,549
*Chancellor*, R. Horton (1990)
*Vice-Chancellor*, R. Sibson, Ph.D.
*Registrar*, T. Mead, Ph.D.

## KINGSTON UNIVERSITY (1992)
(formerly Kingston Polytechnic)
Penrhyn Road, Kingston upon Thames,
Surrey KT1 2EE
Tel 0181-547 2000
Full-time Students (1993–4), 11,000
*Chancellor*, Sir Frank Lampl
*Vice-Chancellor*, R. C. Smith, CBE, Ph.D.
*Secretary*, E. Lang

## THE UNIVERSITY OF LANCASTER (1964)
Lancaster LA1 4YW
Tel 01524-65201
Full-time Students (1993–4), 7,030
*Chancellor*, HRH Princess Alexandra, the Hon. Lady
   Ogilvy, GCVO (1964)
*Vice-Chancellor*, Prof. H. J. Hanham, Ph.D.
*Secretary*, S. A. C. Lamley

## THE UNIVERSITY OF LEEDS (1904)
Leeds LS2 9JT
Tel 0113-243 1751
Full-time Students (1993–4), 17,500
*Chancellor*, HRH The Duchess of Kent, GCVO (1966)
*Vice-Chancellor*, Prof. A. G. Wilson
*Registrar*, vacant

## LEEDS METROPOLITAN UNIVERSITY (1992)
(formerly Leeds Polytechnic)
Calverley Street, Leeds LS1 3HE
Tel 0113-283 2600

Full-time Students (1993–4), 14,200
*Principal and Chief Executive*, Prof. L. Wagner
*Secretary*, M. Wilkinson

THE UNIVERSITY OF LEICESTER (1957)
University Road, Leicester LEI 7RH
Tel 0116-252 2522
Full-time Students (1993–4), 8,245
*Chancellor*, The Lord Porter of Luddenham, OM, Ph.D.,
SC.D., FRS (1985)
*Vice-Chancellor*, K. J. R. Edwards, Ph.D.
*Registrar*, K. J. Julian

THE UNIVERSITY OF LIVERPOOL (1903)
PO Box 147, Liverpool L69 3BX
Tel 0151-794 2011
Full-time Students (1993–4), 12,000
*Chancellor*, Sir Alastair Pilkington (1994)
*Vice-Chancellor*, Prof. P. N. Love, CBE
*Registrar and Secretary*, M. D. Carr

LIVERPOOL JOHN MOORES UNIVERSITY
(1992)
(formerly Liverpool Polytechnic)
Rodney House, 70 Mount Pleasant, Liverpool L3 5UX
Tel 0151-231 2121
Full-time Students (1992–3), 19,000
*Chancellor*, J. Moores, CBE
*Vice-Chancellor*, Prof. P. Toyne
*Registrar*, Ms A. Richardson
*Secretary*, P. Blackburn

THE UNIVERSITY OF LONDON (1836)
Senate House, Malet Street, London WCIE 7HU
Tel 0171-636 8000
Internal Students (1993–4), 67,567, External Students,
21,754
*Visitor*, HM The Queen in Council
*Chancellor*, HRH The Princess Royal, GCVO, FRS (1981)
*Vice-Chancellor*, Prof. A. Rutherford, CBE
*Chairman of the Council*, The Lord Rippon of Hexham, PC,
QC
*Chairman of Convocation*, Prof. Sir William Taylor, CBE
*Principal*, P. Holwell

COLLEGES OF THE UNIVERSITY

BIRKBECK COLLEGE, Malet Street, London
WCIE 7HX. *Master*, The Baroness Blackstone, Ph.D.
GOLDSMITHS COLLEGE, Lewisham Way, New Cross,
London SE14 6NW. *Warden*, Prof. K. J. Gregory, Ph.D.
IMPERIAL COLLEGE OF SCIENCE, TECHNOLOGY AND
MEDICINE (includes St Mary's Hospital Medical School),
London SW7 2AZ. *Rector*, Prof. Sir Ronald Oxburgh, KBE,
FRS
INSTITUTE OF EDUCATION, 20 Bedford Way, London
WCIH OAL. *Director*, Prof. P. Mortimore
KING'S COLLEGE LONDON (includes King's College
School of Medicine and Dentistry), Strand, London
WC2R 2LS. *Principal*, Prof. A. Lucas, Ph.D.
LONDON SCHOOL OF ECONOMICS AND POLITICAL
SCIENCE, Houghton Street, London WC2A 2AE. *Director*,
J. M. Ashworth, Ph.D., D.SC.
QUEEN MARY AND WESTFIELD COLLEGE, Mile End
Road, London EI 4NS. *Principal*, Prof. G. Zellick, Ph.D.
ROYAL HOLLOWAY, Egham Hill, Egham, Surrey TW20
OEX. *Principal*, Prof. N. Gowar
ROYAL VETERINARY COLLEGE, Royal College Street,
London NW1 OTU. *Principal and Dean*,
Prof. L. E. Lanyon, Ph.D.

SCHOOL OF ORIENTAL AND AFRICAN STUDIES,
Thornhaugh Street, London WCIH OXG. *Director*,
M. D. McWilliam
SCHOOL OF PHARMACY, 29–39 Brunswick Square,
London WCIN IAX. *Dean*, Prof. A. T. Florence, Ph.D.,
FRSE
UNIVERSITY COLLEGE LONDON (including UCL Medical
School), Gower Street, London WCIE 6BT. *Provost*,
Dr D. H. Roberts, CBE, FRS
WYE COLLEGE, Wye, Ashford, Kent TN25 5AH. *Principal*,
Prof. J. H. D. Prescott, Ph.D.
*HEYTHROP COLLEGE, Kensington Square, London
w8 5HQ. *Principal*, Revd B. A. Callaghan, SJ

*Not in receipt of HEFCE grants

MEDICAL SCHOOLS

CHARING CROSS AND WESTMINSTER MEDICAL
SCHOOL, The Reynolds Building, St Dunstan's Road,
London W6 8RP. *Dean*, Prof. R. M. Greenhalgh, FRCS
KING'S COLLEGE SCHOOL OF MEDICINE AND
DENTISTRY, Bessemer Road, London SE5 9PJ. *Dean*, I.
Gainsford
THE LONDON HOSPITAL MEDICAL COLLEGE, Turner
Street, London EI 2AD. *Dean*, Prof. Sir Colin Berry,
FRCPath
ROYAL FREE HOSPITAL SCHOOL OF MEDICINE,
Rowland Hill Street, London NW3 2PF. *Dean*,
Prof. A. J. Zuckerman, MD, FRCP
ST BARTHOLOMEW'S HOSPITAL MEDICAL COLLEGE,
West Smithfield, London ECIA 7BE. *Dean*, Prof.
L. H. Rees, MD, FRCP
ST GEORGE'S HOSPITAL MEDICAL SCHOOL, Cranmer
Terrace, London SW17 ORE. *Dean*, Prof. Sir
William Asscher, MD, FRCP, FRCPath.
ST MARY'S HOSPITAL MEDICAL COLLEGE (Faculty of
Imperial College), Norfolk Place, London W2 IPG. *Dean*,
Prof. P. Richards
UCL MEDICAL SCHOOL (Faculty of University College
London), Rayne Institute, Gower Street, London
WCIE 6BT. *Dean*, Prof. J. R. Pattison
UNITED MEDICAL AND DENTAL SCHOOLS OF GUY'S
AND ST THOMAS' HOSPITALS, Guy's, London Bridge,
London SEI 9RT; St Thomas', Lambeth Palace Road,
London SEI 7EH. *Principal*, Prof. C. Chantler

POSTGRADUATE MEDICAL INSTITUTIONS

LONDON SCHOOL OF HYGIENE AND TROPICAL
MEDICINE, Keppel Street, London WCIE 7HT. *Dean*,
Prof. R. G. Feachem, Ph.D, D.SC.(med)
ROYAL POSTGRADUATE MEDICAL SCHOOL, Du Cane
Road, London W12 ONN. *Dean*, Prof. Sir Colin
Dollery, FRCP
BRITISH POSTGRADUATE MEDICAL FEDERATION, 33
Millman Street, London WCIN 3EJ. *Director*,
Dr M. Green, DM, FRCP
Comprises:
EASTMAN DENTAL INSTITUTE, Gray's Inn Road, London
WCIX 8LD. *Dean*, Prof. G. B. Winter, D.ch.
INSTITUTE OF CANCER RESEARCH, Royal Cancer
Hospital, 17A Onslow Gardens, London
SW7 3AL. *Director*, Prof. P. B. Garland, Ph.D., FRSE
INSTITUTE OF CHILD HEALTH, 30 Guilford Street,
London WCIN IEH. *Dean*, Prof. R. J. Levinsky, MD, FRCP
INSTITUTE OF NEUROLOGY, National Hospital, Queen
Square, London WCIN 3BG. *Dean*, Prof. D. N. Landon
INSTITUTE OF OPHTHALMOLOGY, 11–43 Bath Street,
London ECIV 9EL. *Dean*, N. S. C. Rice, MD, FRCS

INSTITUTE OF PSYCHIATRY, De Crespigny Park, Denmark Hill, London SE5 8AF. *Dean,* Dr S. A. Checkley, FRCP, FRCPsych.

NATIONAL HEART AND LUNG INSTITUTE, Dovehouse Street, London SW3 6LY. *Dean,* Prof. T. Clark, MD, FRCP

SENATE INSTITUTES

BRITISH INSTITUTE IN PARIS, 9–11 Rue de Constantine, 75340, Paris. *Director,* Prof. C. L. Campos, L-ès-L., Ph.D. *London office:* Senate House, Malet Street, London WCIE 7HU

CENTRE FOR DEFENCE STUDIES, King's College London, Strand, London WC2R 2LS. *Director,* Prof. L. Freedman

COURTAULD INSTITUTE OF ART, North Block, Somerset House, Strand, London WC2R 0RN. *Director,* Prof. C. M. Kauffmann, Ph.D., FSA

INSTITUTE OF ADVANCED LEGAL STUDIES, Charles Clore House, 17 Russell Square, London WCIB 5DR. *Director,* Prof. T. C. Daintith

INSTITUTE OF CLASSICAL STUDIES, 31–34 Gordon Square, London WCIH 0PY. *Director,* Prof. R. R. K. Sorabji, FBA

INSTITUTE OF COMMONWEALTH STUDIES, 28 Russell Square, London WCIB 5DS. *Director,* Prof. J. Manor

INSTITUTE OF GERMANIC STUDIES, 29 Russell Square, London WCIB 5DP. *Hon. Director,* E. M. Batley

INSTITUTE OF HISTORICAL RESEARCH, Senate House, Malet Street, London WCIE 7HU. *Director,* Prof. P. K. O'Brien, D.phil.

INSTITUTE OF LATIN AMERICAN STUDIES, 31 Tavistock Square, London WCIH 9HA. *Director,* Prof. V. G. Bulmer-Thomas, D.Phil.

INSTITUTE OF ROMANCE STUDIES, Senate House, Malet Street, London WCIE 7HU. *Hon. Director,* Prof. A. Lavers, L-ès-L, Ph.D.

INSTITUTE OF UNITED STATES STUDIES, Senate House, Malet Street, London WCIE 7HU. *Director,* Prof. G. L. McDowell, Ph.D.

INSTITUTE OF ZOOLOGY, Royal Zoological Society, Regent's Park, London NW1 4RY. *Director,* Prof. A. P. F. Flint, Ph.D., D.SC.

SCHOOL OF SLAVONIC AND EAST EUROPEAN STUDIES, Senate House, Malet Street, London WCIE 7HU. *Director,* Prof. M. A. Branch, Ph.D.

UNIVERSITY MARINE BIOLOGICAL STATION MILLPORT, Isle of Cumbrae, Scotland KA28 0EG. *Director,* Prof. J. Davenport

WARBURG INSTITUTE, Woburn Square, London WCIH 0AB. *Director,* Prof. C. N. J. Mann, Ph.D.

ASSOCIATED INSTITUTIONS

JEWS' COLLEGE, 44A Albert Road, London NW4 2SJ. *Principal,* Rabbi Dr D. Sinclair

LONDON BUSINESS SCHOOL, Sussex Place, Regent's Park, London NW1 4SA. *Principal,* Prof. G. Bain, D.phil.

ROYAL ACADEMY OF MUSIC, Marylebone Road, London NW1 5HT. *Principal,* L. Harrell

ROYAL COLLEGE OF MUSIC, Prince Consort Road, London SW7 2BS. *Director,* M. G. Matthews, FRSA, FRCM

TRINITY COLLEGE OF MUSIC, Mandeville Place, London W1M 6AQ. *Principal,* P. Jones, CBE, FRCM

## LONDON GUILDHALL UNIVERSITY (1993)
31 Jewry Street, London EC3N 2EY
Tel 0171-320 1000
Full-time Students (1993–4), 8,597
*Principal,* HRH The Prince Philip, Duke of Edinburgh, KG, KT, OM, GBE, PC, FRS
*Provost,* Prof. R. Floud, D.phil.

*Registrar,* B. High
*Academic Secretary,* E. N. Winders

## LOUGHBOROUGH UNIVERSITY OF TECHNOLOGY (1966)
Loughborough LE11 3TU
Tel 01509-263171
Full-time Students (1993–4), 9,419
*Chancellor,* Sir Denis Rooke, CBE, FRS, FEng (1989)
*Vice-Chancellor,* Prof. D.Wallace, Ph.D., FRS, FRSE
*Registrar,* D. E. Fletcher, Ph.D.
*Academic Secretary,* N. A. McHard

## UNIVERSITY OF LUTON (1993)
(formerly Luton College of Higher Education)
Park Square, Luton LU1 3JU
Tel 01582-34111
Full-time Students (1993–4), 10,500
*Chancellor,* Sir David Plastow
*Vice-Chancellor,* Dr A. Wood
*Academic Registrar,* R. M. Driver

## THE UNIVERSITY OF MANCHESTER
(Founded 1851; re-organized 1880 and 1903)
Oxford Road, Manchester M13 9PL
Full-time Students (1993–4), c.15,000
*Chancellor,* vacant
*Vice-Chancellor,* Prof. M. B. Harris, CBE, Ph.D.
*Academic Secretary,* D. A. Richardson

## UNIVERSITY OF MANCHESTER INSTITUTE OF SCIENCE AND TECHNOLOGY (1824)
PO Box 88, Manchester M60 1QD
Tel 0161-236 3311
Full-time Students (1993–4), 6,040
*Chancellor,* Sir John Mason, CB, D.SC., FRS (1986)
*Principal,* Prof. H. C. A. Hankins, Ph.D.
*Secretary and Registrar,* E. Newcomb

## MANCHESTER METROPOLITAN UNIVERSITY (1992)
(formerly Manchester Polytechnic)
All Saints, Manchester M15 6BH
Tel 0161-247 2000
Full-time Students (1993–4), 23,020
*Chancellor,* The Duke of Westminster
*Director,* Sir Kenneth Green
*Registrar,* J. Karczewski-Slowikowski
*Secretary,* R. O. Yeo

## MIDDLESEX UNIVERSITY (1992)
(formerly Middlesex Polytechnic)
White Hart Lane, London N17 8HR
Tel 0181-362 5000
Full-time Students (1993–4), 13,795
*Chancellor,* The Baroness Platt of Writtle
*Vice-Chancellor,* Prof. D. Melville, Ph.D.
*Registrar,* G. Jones

## NAPIER UNIVERSITY (1992)
(formerly Napier Polytechnic)
219 Colinton Road, Edinburgh EH14 1DJ
Tel 0131-444 2266
Full-time Students (1993–4), 7,685
*Chancellor,* The Lord Younger of Prestwick, KCVO, TD, PC, FRSE
*Vice-Chancellor and Principal,* Prof. J. Mavor
*Secretary and Registrar,* I. J. Miller

## THE UNIVERSITY OF NEWCASTLE UPON TYNE
(Founded 1852; re-organized 1908, 1937 and 1963)
6 Kensington Terrace, Newcastle upon Tyne NE1 7RU
Tel 0191-222 6000
Full-time Students (1993–4), 11,495
*Chancellor*, The Viscount Ridley, KG, TD (1989)
*Vice-Chancellor*, J. R. G. Wright
*Registrar*, D. E. T. Nicholson

## THE UNIVERSITY OF NORTH LONDON (1992)
(formerly Polytechnic of North London)
166–220 Holloway Road, London N7 8DB
Tel 0171-607 2789
Full-time Students (1993–4), 9,130
*Vice-Chancellor and Chief Executive*, B. Roper
*Academic Registrar*, Dr M. Storey
*Secretary*, C. Wragg

## THE UNIVERSITY OF NORTHUMBRIA AT NEWCASTLE (1992)
(formerly Newcastle upon Tyne Polytechnic)
Ellison Place, Newcastle upon Tyne NE1 8ST
Tel 0191-232 6002
Full-time Students (1993–4), 11,295
*Chancellor*, The Lord Glenamara, CH, PC
*Vice-Chancellor*, Prof. L. Barden, CBE, Ph.D., D.SC.
*Registrar and Secretary*, R. A. Bott

## THE UNIVERSITY OF NOTTINGHAM (1948)
University Park, Nottingham NG7 2RD
Tel 0115-948 4848
Full-time Students (1993–4), 11,400
*Chancellor*, Sir Ron Dearing, CB (1993)
*Vice-Chancellor*, Prof. Sir Colin Campbell
*Registrar*, D. Allen

## NOTTINGHAM TRENT UNIVERSITY (1992)
Burton Street, Nottingham NG1 4BU
Tel 0115-941 8418
Full-time Students (1992–3), 13,877
*Vice-Chancellor*, Prof. R. Cowell, Ph.D.
*Academic Registrar*, A. E. Foster, OBE

## THE UNIVERSITY OF OXFORD
University Offices, Wellington Square, Oxford OX1 2JD
Tel 01865-270001
Number of students in residence 1993–4:
*Men*, 8,910; *Women*, 5,828

UNIVERSITY OFFICERS, ETC.

*Chancellor*, The Lord Jenkins of Hillhead, PC
  (*Balliol*), elected 1987
*High Steward*, The Lord Goff of Chieveley, PC (*Lincoln* and
  *New College*), elected 1990
*Vice-Chancellor*, Dr P. M. North, CBE, QC, FBA (*Jesus*),
  elected 1993
*Proctors*, Dr J. Pallot (*Christ Church*); Dr A. Avramides (*St
  Hilda's*), elected 1994
*Assessor*, J. M. Landers (*All Souls*), elected 1994
*Public Orator*, J. Griffin (*Balliol*), elected 1992
*Bodley's Librarian*, D. G. Vaisey (*Exeter*), elected 1986
*Keeper of Archives*, J. Hackney (*Wadham*), elected 1988
*Director of the Ashmolean Museum*, C. J. White (*Worcester*),
  elected 1985
*Registrar of the University*, A. J. Dorey, D.PHIL. (*Linacre*),
  elected 1979
*Surveyor to the University*, P. M. R. Hill, elected 1993
*Secretary of Faculties*, A. P. Weale (*Worcester*), elected 1984

*Secretary of the Chest*, I. G. Thompson (*Merton*), elected 1986
*Deputy Registrar* (*Administration*), P. W. Jones (*Green*),
  elected 1991

OXFORD COLLEGES AND HALLS
with dates of foundation

ALL SOULS (1438), *Warden*, Prof. J. Davis (1994)
BALLIOL (1263), *Master*, C. R. Lucas, D.PHIL. (1994)
BRASENOSE (1509), *Principal*, The Lord Windlesham, CVO,
  PC (1989)
CHRIST CHURCH (1546), *Dean*, Very Revd J. H. Drury
  (1991)
CORPUS CHRISTI (1517), *President*, Prof. Sir Keith
  Thomas, FBA (1986)
EXETER (1314), *Rector*, Prof. M. Butler (1994)
GREEN (1979), *Warden*, Sir Crispin Tickell, GCMG, KCVO
  (1990)
HERTFORD (1874), *Principal*, Prof. Sir Christopher
  Zeeman, FRS (1988)
JESUS (1571), *Principal*, Dr P. M. North, CBE, FBA (1984)
KEBLE (1868), *Warden*, A. Cameron, FBA, FSA (1994)
KELLOG COLLEGE (formerly Rewley House) (1990),
  *President*, G. P. Thomas, Ph.D. (1990)
LADY MARGARET HALL (1878), *Principal*, D. M. Stewart
  (1979)
LINACRE (1962), *Principal*, Sir Bryan Cartledge, KCMG
  (1988)
LINCOLN (1427), *Rector*, E. K. Anderson, FRSE (1994)
MAGDALEN (1458), *President*, A. D. Smith, CBE (1988)
MERTON (1264), *Warden*, Dr. J Rawson, FBA (1994)
NEW COLLEGE (1379), *Warden*, H. McGregor, QC, DCL
  (1985)
NUFFIELD (1937), *Warden*, Prof. A. Atkinson, FBA (1994)
ORIEL (1326), *Provost*, E. W. Nicholson, DD, FBA (1990)
PEMBROKE (1624), *Master*, Prof. R. Stevens, DCL (1993)
QUEEN'S (1340), *Provost*, G. Marshall (1993)
ST ANNE'S (1952) (Originally Society of Oxford Home-
  Students (1879)), *Principal*, Mrs R. L. Deech (1991)
ST ANTONY'S (1950), *Warden*, The Lord Dahrendorf, KBE,
  Ph.D., FBA (1987)
ST CATHERINE'S (1962), *Master*, The Lord Plant of
  Highfield (1994)
ST CROSS (1965), *Master*, R. C. Repp, D.PHIL. (1987)
ST EDMUND HALL (*c.* 1278), *Principal*, J. C. B. Gosling
  (1983)
*ST HILDA'S (1893), *Principal*, Miss E. Llewellyn-Smith, CB
  (1990)
ST HUGH'S (1886), *Principal*, D. Wood, QC (1991)
ST JOHN'S (1555), *President*, W. Hayes, D.PHIL. (1987)
ST PETER'S (1929), *Master*, J. P. Barron, D.PHIL. (1991)
SOMERVILLE (1879), *Principal*, Mrs C. E. Hughes, CMG
  (1989)
TRINITY (1554), *President*, Sir John Burgh, KCMG, CB (1987)
UNIVERSITY (1249), *Master*, W. J. Albery, D.PHIL., FRS
  (1989)
WADHAM (1612), *Warden*, J. S. Flemming (1993)
WOLFSON (1966), *President*, Sir David Smith, D.PHIL. (1994)
WORCESTER (1714), *Provost*, R. G. Smethurst (1991)
BLACKFRIARS (1921), *Regent*, Revd B. E. A. Davies (1994)
CAMPION HALL (1896), *Master*, Revd J. A. Munitiz (1989)
GREYFRIARS (1910), *Warden*, Revd M. W. Sheehan,
  D.PHIL. (1990)
MANCHESTER (1786), *Principal*, Revd R. Waller, Ph.D.
  (1990)
MANSFIELD (1886), *Principal*, D. J. Trevelyan, CB (1989)

* College for women only

REGENT'S PARK (1810), *Principal*, Revd P. S. Fiddes, D.phil. (1989)
ST BENET'S HALL (1897), *Master*, Revd H. Wansbrough, OSB (1991)

OXFORD BROOKES UNIVERSITY (1993)
Headington, Oxford OX3 OBP
Tel 01865-483410
Full-time Students (1993–4), 10,774
*Chancellor*, Ms H. Kennedy, QC
*Vice-Chancellor*, Dr C. Booth
*Deputy Vice-Chancellor, Corporate Services*, B. Summers

THE UNIVERSITY OF PAISLEY (1992)
(formerly Paisley College of Technology)
High Street, Paisley PA1 2BE
Tel 0141-848 3000
Full-time Students (1993–4), 6,162
*Chancellor*, Sir Robert Easton, CBE
*Vice-Chancellor and Principal*, Prof. R. W. Shaw
*Registrar*, D. Rigg
*Secretary*, J. Fraser

UNIVERSITY OF PLYMOUTH (1992)
(formerly Polytechnic SouthWest)
Drake Circus, Plymouth PL4 8AA
Tel 01752-600600
Full-time Students (1993–4), 11,997
*Vice-Chancellor*, Prof. J. Bull
*Registrar*, Dr C. J. Sparrow

UNIVERSITY OF PORTSMOUTH (1992)
(formerly Portsmouth Polytechnic)
University House, Winston Churchill Avenue, Portsmouth PO1 2UP
Tel 01705-827681
Full-time Students (1993–4), 11,307
*Chancellor*, The Lord Palumbo
*Vice-Chancellor*, N. Merritt
*Academic Registrar*, R. Moore
*Secretary*, D. Hunt

THE QUEEN'S UNIVERSITY OF BELFAST (1908)
Belfast BT7 1NN
Tel 01232-245133
Full-time Students (1993–4), 10,612
*Chancellor*, Sir David Orr
*President and Vice-Chancellor*, Sir Gordon Beveridge, Ph.D., FRSE
*Academic Secretary*, Dr G. Baird
*Administrative Secretary*, D. Wilson

THE UNIVERSITY OF READING (1926)
Whiteknights, PO Box 217, Reading RG6 2AH
Tel 01734-875123
Full-time Students (1993–4), 9,286
*Chancellor*, The Lord Carrington, KG, GCMG, CH, MC, PC (1992)
*Vice-Chancellor*, Prof. R. Williams
*Registrar*, D. C. R. Frampton

THE ROBERT GORDON UNIVERSITY (1992)
(formerly Robert Gordon Institute of Technology)
Schoolhill, Aberdeen AB9 1FR
Tel 01224-262000
Full-time Students (1993–4), 6,016
*Chancellor*, Sir Bob Reid
*Vice-Chancellor and Principal*, Dr D. A. Kennedy

*Academic Registrar*, Mrs H. Douglas
*Secretary*, D. Caldwell

THE UNIVERSITY OF ST ANDREWS (1411)
College Gate, St Andrews KY16 9AJ
Tel 01334-76161
Full-time Students (1993–4), 5,234
*Chancellor*, Sir Kenneth Dover, D.Litt., FRSE, FBA (1981)
*Vice-Chancellor and Principal*, Prof. S. Arnott, Ph.D., FRS, FRSE
*Secretary of Court*, D. J. Corner
*Rector*, D. Findlay QC (1993–6)

THE UNIVERSITY OF SALFORD (1967)
Salford M5 4WT
Tel 0161-745 5000
Full-time Students (1993–4), 6,995
*Chancellor*, vacant
*Vice-Chancellor*, Prof. T. M. Husband, Ph.D, FEng.
*Registrar*, M. D. Winton, Ph.D.

THE UNIVERSITY OF SHEFFIELD (1905)
Western Bank, Sheffield S10 2TN
Tel 0114-276 8555
Full-time Students (1993–4), 14,000
*Chancellor*, The Lord Dainton, Ph.D., SC.D., FRS (1979)
*Vice-Chancellor*, Prof. G. G. Roberts
*Registrar and Secretary*, Dr J. S. Padley

SHEFFIELD HALLAM UNIVERSITY (1992)
(formerly Sheffield Polytechnic)
Pond Street, Sheffield S1 1WB
Tel 0114-272 0911
Full-time Students (1993–4), 16,856
*Chancellor*, Sir Bryan Nicholson
*Vice-Chancellor*, J. Stoddart
*Registrar*, Ms J. Tory
*Secretary*, Ms S. Neocosmos

THE UNIVERSITY OF SOUTHAMPTON (1952)
Highfield, Southampton SO9 5NH
Tel 01703-595000
Full-time Students (1993–4), 10,080
*Chancellor*, The Earl Jellicoe, KBE, DSO, MC, PC, FRS (1984)
*Vice-Chancellor*, Prof. H. Newby, Ph.D.
*Secretary and Registrar*, J. F. D. Lauwerys
*Academic Registrar*, R. Knight

SOUTH BANK UNIVERSITY (1992)
(formerly South Bank Polytechnic)
103 Borough Road, London SE1 OAA
Tel 0171-928 8989
Full-time Students (1993–4), 15,274
*Chairman of the Board of Governors*, C. McLaren
*Vice-Chancellor*, Prof. G. Bernbaum
*Registrar*, vacant
*Secretary*, Ms L. Gander

STAFFORDSHIRE UNIVERSITY (1992)
(formerly Staffordshire Polytechnic)
College Road, Stoke-on-Trent ST4 2DE
Tel 01782-744531
Full-time Students (1993–4), 10,000
*Chancellor*, The Lord Ashley of Stoke, CH, PC
*Vice-Chancellor*, K. B. Thompson
*Academic Registrar*, Miss F. Francis
*Secretary*, K. Sproston

THE UNIVERSITY OF STIRLING (1967)
Stirling FK9 4LA
Tel 01786-73171
Full-time Students (1993–4), 5,200
*Chancellor*, The Lord Balfour of Burleigh, FRSE (1988)
*Principal and Vice-Chancellor*, Prof. A. Miller, ph.d., FRSE
*Registrar*, D. J. Farrington, D.phil.
*Secretary*, R. G. Bomont

THE UNIVERSITY OF STRATHCLYDE (1964)
16 Richmond Street, Glasgow GI IXQ
Tel 0141-552 4400
Full-time Students (1993–4), 13,239
*Chancellor*, The Lord Tombs, LL D, D.SC., FEng. (1990)
*Principal and Vice-Chancellor*, Prof. J. P. Arbuthnott
*Secretary*, P. W. A. West

THE UNIVERSITY OF SUNDERLAND (1992)
(formerly Sunderland Polytechnic)
Langham Tower, Ryhope Road, Sunderland SR2 7EE
Tel 0191-515 2000
Full-time Students (1993–4), 12,054
*Vice-Chancellor*, Ms A. Wright, ph.d.
*Academic Registrar*, S. Porteous
*Secretary*, J. D. Pacey

THE UNIVERSITY OF SURREY (1966)
Guildford, Surrey GU2 5XH
Tel 01483-300800
Full-time Students (1993–4), 5,685
*Chancellor*, HRH The Duke of Kent, KG, GCMG, GCVO
   (1977)
*Vice-Chancellor*, Prof. R. J. Dowling, ph.d., FEng.
*Secretary and Registrar*, H. W. B. Davies

THE UNIVERSITY OF SUSSEX (1961)
Falmer, Brighton BNI 9RH
Tel 01273-678416
Full-time Students (1993–4), 8,214
*Chancellor*, The Duke of Richmond and Gordon (1985)
*Vice-Chancellor*, Prof. G. Conway
*Registrar and Secretary*, G. Lockwood, D.phil.

THE UNIVERSITY OF TEESSIDE (1992)
(formerly Teesside Polytechnic)
Middlesbrough, Cleveland TSI 3BA
Tel 01642-218121
Full-time Students (1992–3), 6,995
*Chancellor*, Sir Leon Brittan
*Vice-Chancellor*, Prof. D. Fraser
*University Secretary*, J. M. McClintock

THAMES VALLEY UNIVERSITY (1992)
(formerly Polytechnic of West London)
St Mary's Road, Ealing, London W5 5RF
Tel 0181-579 5000
Full-time Students (1993–4), 11,500
*Chancellor*, P. Hamlyn, CBE
*Vice-Chancellor*, Dr M. Fitzgerald
*Academic Registrar*, Ms A. Denton
*Secretary*, Ms M. Joyce

THE UNIVERSITY OF ULSTER (1984)
(Amalgamation of New University of Ulster and Ulster
Polytechnic)
Cromore Road, Coleraine BT52 ISA
Tel 01265-44141
Full-time Students (1993–4), 11,700
*Chancellor*, Rabbi J. Neuberger

*Vice-Chancellor*, Prof. T. A. Smith
*Academic Registrar*, K. Millar, ph.d.

THE UNIVERSITY OF WALES (1893)
King Edward VII Avenue, Cathays Park, Cardiff CFI 3NS
Tel 01222-382656
*Chancellor*, HRH The Prince of Wales, KG, KT, GCB, PC
   (1976)
*Vice-Chancellor*, Prof. K. O. Morgan, D.phil., FBA
*Secretary-General*, J. D. Pritchard

COLLEGES
ST DAVID'S UNIVERSITY COLLEGE, Lampeter, Dyfed
   SA48 7ED. Tel: 01570-422351. *Principal*, Prof.
   K. Robbins, D.Litt., D.phil., FRSE (1992)
UNIVERSITY COLLEGE OF NORTH WALES, Bangor,
   Gwynedd LL57 2DG. Tel: 01248-351151. *Principal*, Prof.
   E. Sunderland, ph.d. (1984)
UNIVERSITY COLLEGE OF SWANSEA, Singleton Park,
   Swansea SA2 8PP. Tel: 01792-205678. *Principal*, Prof.
   R. H. Williams, ph.d., FRS (1994)
UNIVERSITY COLLEGE OF WALES, Old College, King
   Street, Aberystwyth, Dyfed SY23 2AX. Tel: 01970-623111.
   *Principal*, Prof. K. O. Morgan, D.phil., FBA (1979)
UNIVERSITY OF WALES COLLEGE OF CARDIFF, PO Box
   920, Cardiff CFI 3XP. Tel: 01222-874000. *Principal*, Prof.
   E. B. Smith, ph.d., D.sc. (1993)
UNIVERSITY OF WALES COLLEGE OF MEDICINE, Heath
   Park, Cardiff CF4 4XN. Tel: 01222-747747. *Provost*, Prof.
   I. R. Cameron, FRCP (1994)

THE UNIVERSITY OF WARWICK (1965)
Coventry CV4 7AL
Tel 01203-523876
Full-time Students (1993–4), 12,700
*Chancellor*, Sir Shridath Surendranath Ramphal, GCMG, QC
   (1989)
*Vice-Chancellor*, Prof. Sir Brian Follett, FRS, D.sc.
*Registrar*, M. L. Shattock, OBE
*Secretary*, A. L. Jones

THE UNIVERSITY OF WESTMINSTER (1992)
(formerly Polytechnic of Central London)
309 Regent Street, London WIR 8AL
Tel 0171-911 5000
Full-time Students (1992–3), 6,000
*Rector*, Prof. T. E. Burlin
*Deputy-Rector*, Dr G. M. Copland
*Registrar*, Ms J. Hopkinson

THE UNIVERSITY OF THE WEST OF
ENGLAND, BRISTOL (BRISTOL UWE) (1992)
(formerly Bristol Polytechnic)
Coldharbour Lane, Frenchay, Bristol BS16 1QY
Tel 01272-656261
Full-time Students (1993–4), 12,288
*Chancellor*, Dame Elizabeth Butler-Sloss, DBE
*Vice-Chancellor*, A. C. Morris
*Academic Registrar*, Ms M. J. Carter
*Secretary*, W. Evans

THE UNIVERSITY OF WOLVERHAMPTON
(1992)
(formerly Wolverhampton Polytechnic)
Wulfruna Street, Wolverhampton WVI ISB
Tel 01902-321000
Full-time Students (1993–4), 17,089
*Chancellor*, The Earl of Shrewsbury and Talbot
*Vice-Chancellor/Director*, Prof. M. J. Harrison
*Pro-Vice-Chancellor/Assistant Director*, G. R. Brooks

## THE UNIVERSITY OF YORK (1963)
Heslington, York YO1 5DD
Tel 01904-430000
Full-time Students (1993–4), 5,300
*Chancellor,* Dame Janet Baker, DBE
*Vice-Chancellor,* Prof. R. U. Cooke
*Registrar,* D. J. Foster

## CRANFIELD UNIVERSITY (1969)
Cranfield, Beds. MK43 0AL
Tel 01234-750111
Cranfield University (formerly the Cranfield Institute of Technology) grants degrees in applied science, engineering, technology and management.
Full-time Students (1993–4), 2,227
*Chancellor,* The Lord Kings Norton, PH.D., FEng. (1969)
*Vice-Chancellor,* Prof. F. R. Hartley, D.SC.
*Secretary and Registrar,* J. K. Pettifer

## THE OPEN UNIVERSITY (1969)
Walton Hall, Milton Keynes MK7 6AA
Tel 01908-274066
Students and clients (1994), *c.*200,000
Tuition by correspondence linked with special radio and television programmes, video and audio cassettes, residential schools and a locally-based tutorial and counselling service. The University awards degrees of BA, B.SC., B.Phil., MA, MBA, MBA (Technology), M.SC., M.Phil., PH.D., D.SC. and D.Litt. There are eight faculties: arts; education; health, welfare and community education; management; mathematics and computing; science; social sciences; technology; and a wide range of qualification courses and study packs.
*Chancellor,* The Rt. Hon. Betty Boothroyd
*Vice-Chancellor,* Sir John Daniel
*Secretary,* D. J. Clinch

## THE ROYAL COLLEGE OF ART (1837)
Kensington Gore, London SW7 2EU
Tel 0171-584 5020
Under royal charter (1967) the Royal College of Art grants the degrees of Doctor, Doctor of Philosophy, Master of Philosophy, Master of Arts and Master of Design.
Students (1993–4), 730 (all postgraduate)
*Provost,* The Earl of Gowrie, PC (1986)
*Rector and Vice-Provost,* Prof. A. Jones
*Registrar,* A. Selby

## COLLEGES

It is not possible to name here all the colleges offering courses of higher or further education. The list of English colleges that follows is confined to those in the Higher Education Funding Council for England sector; there are many more colleges in England providing higher education courses, some with HEFCFE funding.

The list of colleges in Wales, Scotland and Northern Ireland includes institutions providing at least one full-time course leading to a first degree granted by an accredited validating body. It does not include colleges forming part of a polytechnic or a university.

## ENGLAND

BATH COLLEGE OF HIGHER EDUCATION, Newton Park, Newton St Loe, Bath BA2 9BN. Tel: 01225-873701.
*Director and Chief Executive,* B. L. Gomes da Costa

BISHOP GROSSETESTE COLLEGE, Lincoln LN1 3DY. Tel: 01522-527347. *Principal,* Prof. L. Marsh, OBE, D.Phil.
BOLTON INSTITUTE OF HIGHER EDUCATION, Deane Road, Bolton BL3 5AB. Tel: 01204-528851. *Principal,* R. Oxtoby, PH.D.
BRETTON HALL, West Bretton, Wakefield, W. Yorks. WF4 4LG. Tel: 01924-830261. *Principal,* Prof. G.H. Bell
BUCKINGHAMSHIRE COLLEGE, Queen Alexandra Road, High Wycombe, Bucks. HP11 2JZ. Tel: 01494-522141. *Director,* P. B. Mogford
CANTERBURY CHRIST CHURCH COLLEGE, North Holmes Road, Canterbury, Kent CT1 1QU. Tel: 01227-767700. *Principal,* M. H. A. Berry, TD
THE CENTRAL SCHOOL OF SPEECH AND DRAMA, Embassy Theatre, Eton Avenue, London NW3 3HY. Tel: 0171-722 8183. *Principal,* R. S. Fowler
CHELTENHAM AND GLOUCESTER COLLEGE OF HIGHER EDUCATION, PO Box 220, The Park, Cheltenham, Glos. GL50 2QF. Tel: 01242-532700. *Director,* Miss J. O. Trotter, OBE
CHESTER COLLEGE, Cheyney Road, Chester CH1 4BJ. Tel: 01244-375444. *Principal,* Revd E. V. Binks
CHICHESTER INSTITUTE OF HIGHER EDUCATION, College Lane, Chichester, West Sussex PO19 4PE. Tel: 01243-787911. *Director,* Dr J. F. Wyatt
COLLEGE OF ST MARK AND ST JOHN, Derriford Road, Plymouth PL6 8BH. Tel: 01752-777188. *Principal,* J. E. Anderson
DARTINGTON COLLEGE OF ARTS, Totnes, Devon TQ9 6EJ. Tel: 01803-862224. *Principal,* Prof. K. Thompson
EDGE HILL COLLEGE OF HIGHER EDUCATION, St Helens Road, Ormskirk, Lancs. L39 4QP. Tel: 01695-575171. *Director,* Dr. J. Cater
FALMOUTH SCHOOL OF ART AND DESIGN, Woodlane, Falmouth, Cornwall TR11 4RA. Tel: 01326-211077. *Principal,* Prof. A. G. Livingston
HARPER ADAMS AGRICULTURAL COLLEGE, Newport, Shropshire TF10 8NB. Tel: 01952-820280. *Principal,* G. R. McConnell
HOMERTON COLLEGE, Cambridge CB2 2PH. Tel: 01223-411141. *Principal,* Mrs K. Pretty, PH.D.
INSTITUTE OF ADVANCED NURSING, Royal College of Nursing, 20 Cavendish Square, London W1M 0AB. Tel: 0171-355 1396. *Principal,* J. C. A. Wells
KENT INSTITUTE OF ART AND DESIGN, Oakwood Park, Maidstone ME16 8AG (*also* New Dover Road, Canterbury CT1 3AN; and Fort Pitt, Rochester ME1 1DZ). Tel: 01622-757286. *Director,* P. I. Williams
KING ALFRED'S COLLEGE, Winchester SO22 4NR. Tel: 01962-841515. *Principal,* Prof. J. P. Dickinson
LIVERPOOL INSTITUTE OF HIGHER EDUCATION, PO Box 6, Stand Park Road, Liverpool L16 9JD. Tel: 0151-737 3000. *Rector,* J. Burke, OBE, PH.D.
THE LONDON INSTITUTE, 65 Davies Street, London W1Y 2AA. Tel: 0171-514 6000. *Rector,* Prof. J. C. McKenzie
Comprising:
*Camberwell College of Arts,* Peckham Road, London SE5 8UF
*Central St Martins College of Art and Design,* Southampton Row, London WC1B 4AP
*Chelsea College of Art and Design,* Manresa Road, London SW3 6LS
*London College of Fashion,* 20 John Prince's Street, London W1M 9HE
*London College of Printing and Distributive Trades,* Elephant and Castle, London SE1 6SB

LOUGHBOROUGH COLLEGE OF ART AND DESIGN, Radmoor, Loughborough, Leics. LE11 3BT. Tel: 01509-261515. *Principal*, I. Pugh

LSU COLLEGE OF HIGHER EDUCATION, The Avenue, Southampton SO17 1BG. Tel: 01703-228761. *Principal*, Dr A. C. Chitnis

NENE COLLEGE, Park Campus, Boughton Green Road, Northampton NN2 7AL. Tel: 01604-735500. *Director*, S. M. Gaskell, PH.D.

NEWMAN COLLEGE, Genners Lane, Bartley Green, Birmingham B32 3NT. Tel: 0121-476 1181. *Principal*, Joan S. Cuming, PH.D.

RAVENSBOURNE COLLEGE OF DESIGN AND COMMUNICATION, Walden Road, Chislehurst, Kent BR7 5SN. Tel: 0181-468 7071. *Director*, Prof. R. Baker

ROEHAMPTON INSTITUTE, Senate House, Roehampton Lane, London SW15 5PU. Comprises Digby Stuart College, Froebel Institute College, Southlands College and Whitelands College. Tel: 0181-392 3000. *Rector*, S. C. Holt, PH.D.

ROSE BRUFORD COLLEGE, Lamorbey Park, Sidcup, Kent DA15 9DF. Tel: 0181-300 3024. *Principal*, R. Ely

ROYAL ACADEMY OF MUSIC, Marylebone Road, London NW1 5HT. Tel: 0171-873 7373. *Principal*, L. Harrell

ROYAL COLLEGE OF MUSIC, Prince Consort Road, London SW7 2BS. Tel: 0171-589 3643. *Director*, Ms J. Ritterman, PH.D.

ROYAL NORTHERN COLLEGE OF MUSIC, 124 Oxford Road, Manchester M13 9RD. Tel: 0161-273 6283. *Principal*, Sir John Manduell, CBE

S. MARTIN'S COLLEGE, Lancaster LA1 3JD. Tel: 01524-63446. *Principal*, D. Edynbry, PH.D.

SALFORD COLLEGE OF TECHNOLOGY, Frederick Road, Salford M6 6PU. Tel: 0161-736 6541. *Principal*, J. Squires

SOUTHAMPTON INSTITUTE OF HIGHER EDUCATION, East Park Terrace, Southampton SO14 0UU. Tel: 01703-319267. *Director*, D. G. Leyland

SURREY INSTITUTE OF ART AND DESIGN, Falkner Road, The Hart, Farnham, Surrey GU9 7DS. Tel: 01252-722441. *Director*, N. J. Taylor

TRINITY AND ALL SAINTS' COLLEGE, Brownberrie Lane, Horsforth, Leeds LS18 5HD. Tel: 0113-283 7100. *Principal*, Dr G. L. Turnbull

TRINITY COLLEGE OF MUSIC, 11–13 Mandeville Place, London W1M 6AQ. Tel: 0171-935 5773. *Principal*, G. Henderson

UNIVERSITY COLLEGE OF RIPON AND YORK ST JOHN, Lord Mayor's Walk, York YO3 7EX. Tel: 01904-656771. *Principal*, Prof. G. P. McGregor

UNIVERSITY COLLEGE SCARBOROUGH, THE NORTH RIDING COLLEGE, Filey Road, Scarborough, N. Yorks. YO11 3AZ. Tel: 01723-362392. *Principal*, R. A. Withers, PH.D.

WESTHILL COLLEGE, Hamilton Building, Weoley Park Road, Selly Oak, Birmingham B29 6LL. Tel: 0121-472 7245. *Principal*, Dr J. G. Priestley

WESTMINSTER COLLEGE, Oxford OX2 9AT. Tel: 01865-247644. *Principal*, Revd Dr K. B. Wilson, OBE

WINCHESTER SCHOOL OF ART, Park Avenue, Winchester, Hants. SO23 8DL. Tel: 01962-842500. *Principal*, M. Sadler-Forster

WORCESTER COLLEGE OF HIGHER EDUCATION, Henwick Grove, Worcester WR2 6AJ. Tel: 01905-748080. *Principal*, Ms D. Urwin

## WALES

CARDIFF INSTITUTE OF HIGHER EDUCATION, Western Avenue, Llandaff, Cardiff CF5 2YB. Tel: 01222-551111. *Director*, J. D. Winslow

GWENT COLLEGE OF HIGHER EDUCATION, College Crescent, Caerleon, Newport, Gwent NP6 1XJ. Tel: 01633-430088. *Principal*, Dr K. J. Overshott

INSTITUTE OF HEALTH CARE STUDIES, University Hospital of Wales, Heath Park, Cardiff CF4 4XW. Tel: 01222-744416. *Dean*, M. Booy

LLANDRILLO COLLEGE, Llandudno Road, Rhos-on-Sea, Colwyn Bay, Clwyd LL28 4HZ. Tel: 01492-546666. *Principal*, W. S. H. Evans

NORMAL COLLEGE, Bangor, Gwynedd LL57 2PX. Tel: 01248-370171. *Principal*, H. G. Roberts, PH.D.

THE NORTH-EAST WALES INSTITUTE (NEWI Plas Coch), Mold Road, Wrexham, Clwyd LL11 2AW. Tel: 01978-290666. Also NEWI Cartrefle at Cefn Road, Wrexham LL13 9NL, NEWI College of Art and Design Technology at Regent Street, Wrexham LL11 and NEWI Deeside at Kelsterton Road, Connah's Quay, Deeside CH5 4BR. *Principal*, Prof. J. O. Williams, PH.D, D.SC.

SWANSEA INSTITUTE OF HIGHER EDUCATION, Townhill Road, Swansea SA2 0UT. Tel: 01792-481000. *Principal*, G. Stockdale, PH.D.

TRINITY COLLEGE, Carmarthen, Dyfed, SA31 3EP. Tel: 01267-237971. *Principal*, D. C. Jones-Davies, OBE

WELSH AGRICULTURAL COLLEGE, Llanbadarn Fawr, Aberystwyth, Dyfed SY23 3AL. Tel: 01970-624471. *Principal*, Dr J. H. Harries

WELSH COLLEGE OF MUSIC AND DRAMA, Castle Grounds, Cathays Park, Cardiff CF1 3ER. Tel: 01222-342854. *Principal*, E. Fivet

## SCOTLAND

BELL COLLEGE OF TECHNOLOGY, Almada Street, Hamilton, Lanarkshire ML3 0JB. Tel: 01698-283100. *Principal*, J. Reid

EDINBURGH COLLEGE OF ART, Lauriston Place, Edinburgh EH3 9DF. Tel: 0131-221 6000. *Principal*, Prof. A. J. Rowan, PH.D.

GLASGOW SCHOOL OF ART, 167 Renfrew Street, Glasgow G3 6RQ. Tel: 0141-353 4500. *Director*, Prof. D. Cameron

NORTHERN COLLEGE OF EDUCATION, Hilton Place, Aberdeen AB9 1FA. Tel: 01224-283500; Gardyne Road, Dundee DD5 1NY. Tel: 01382-464000. *Principal*, D. A. Adams

QUEEN MARGARET COLLEGE, Clerwood Terrace, Edinburgh EH12 8TS. Tel: 0131-317 3000. *Principal*, Prof. D. F. Leach

ROYAL SCOTTISH ACADEMY OF MUSIC AND DRAMA, 100 Renfrew Street, Glasgow G2 3DB. Tel: 0141-332 4101. *Principal*, Dr P. Ledger, CBE, FRSE

SAC (SCOTTISH AGRICULTURAL COLLEGE), Central Office, West Mains Road, Edinburgh EH9 3JG. Tel: 0131-662 1303. Campuses at Aberdeen, Auchincruive, and Edinburgh. *Principal and Chief Executive*, Prof. P. C. Thomas

ST ANDREW'S COLLEGE OF EDUCATION, Duntocher Road, Bearsden, Glasgow G61 4QA. Tel: 0141-943 1424. *Principal*, Prof. B. J. McGettrick, OBE

SCOTTISH COLLEGE OF TEXTILES, Netherdale, Galashiels, Selkirkshire TD1 3HF. Tel: 01896-753351. *Principal*, Prof. C. E. R. Maddox, PH.D.

## NORTHERN IRELAND

DOWN COLLEGE OF FURTHER EDUCATION, Market Street, Downpatrick, Co. Down BT30 6ND. Tel: 01396-615815. *Principal*, T. P. Walsh

ST MARY'S COLLEGE, 191 Falls Road, Belfast BT12 6FE. Tel: 01232-327678. *Principal*, Revd M. O'Callaghan

STRANMILLIS COLLEGE, Stranmillis Road, Belfast BT9 5DY. Tel: 01232-381271. *Principal*, Dr J. R. McMinn

## ADULT AND CONTINUING EDUCATION

FORUM FOR THE ADVANCEMENT OF CONTINUING EDUCATION, Department of Continuing Education, Westminster College, Oxford OX2 9AT. Tel: 01865-247644. *Secretary*, Dr. P. Percy

NATIONAL INSTITUTE OF ADULT CONTINUING EDUCATION, 21 De Montfort Street, Leicester LEI 7GE. Tel: 0116-255 1451. *Director*, A. Tuckett

NIACE CYMRU, 245 Western Avenue, Cardiff CF5 2YX. Tel: 01222-571201. *Associate Director for Wales*, Ms A. Poole

NORTHERN IRELAND COUNCIL FOR ADULT EDUCATION, c/o Western Education and Library Board, 1 Hospital Road, Omagh, Co. Tyrone BT79 0AW. Tel: 01662-240240. *Chairman*, M. H. F. Murphy, OBE

THE RESIDENTIAL COLLEGES COMMITTEE, c/o Ruskin College, Oxford OX1 2HE. Tel: 01865-56360. *Awards Officer*, Mrs F. A. Bagchi

SCOTTISH COMMUNITY EDUCATION COUNCIL, Rosebery House, 9 Haymarket Terrace, Edinburgh EH12 5EZ. Tel: 0131-313 2488. *Executive Director*, C. McConnell

THE UNIVERSITIES ASSOCIATION FOR CONTINUING EDUCATION, Department of Adult Continuing Education, University of Leeds, Leeds LS2 9JT. Tel: 0113-233 3222. *Secretary*, Prof. R. Taylor

THE WORKER'S EDUCATIONAL ASSOCIATION, Temple House, 17 Victoria Park Square, London E2 9PB. Tel: 0181-983 1515. *General Secretary*, R. Lochrie

LONG-TERM RESIDENTIAL COLLEGES FOR ADULT EDUCATION

COLEG HARLECH, Harlech, Gwynedd LL46 2PU. Tel: 01766-780363. *Warden*, J. W. England

CO-OPERATIVE COLLEGE, Stanford Hall, Loughborough, Leics. LE12 5QR. Tel: 01509-852333. *Principal*, Dr R. Houlton

FIRCROFT COLLEGE, 1018 Bristol Road, Selly Oak, Birmingham B29 6LH. Tel: 0121-472 0116. *Principal*, K. Jackson

HILLCROFT COLLEGE, South Bank, Surbiton, Surrey KT6 6DF. Tel: 0181-399 2688. For women only. *Principal*, Ms E. Aird

NEWBATTLE ABBEY COLLEGE, Dalkeith, Midlothian EH22 3LL. Tel: 0131-663 1921. *Principal*, W. M. Conboy

NORTHERN COLLEGE, Wentworth Castle, Stainborough, Barnsley, S. Yorks. S75 3ET. Tel: 01226-285426. *Principal*, R. H. Fryer

PLATER COLLEGE, Pullens Lane, Oxford OX3 0DT. Tel: 01865-741676. *Principal*, M. Blades

RUSKIN COLLEGE, Walton Street, Oxford OX1 2HE. Tel: 01865-54331. *Principal*, S. Yeo, D.Phil.

## Professional Education

*Excluding postgraduate study*

The organizations listed below are those which, by providing specialist training or conducting examinations, control entry into a profession, or organizations responsible for maintaining a register of those with professional qualifications in their sector.

Many professions now have a largely graduate entry, and possession of a first degree can exempt entrants from certain of the professional examinations. Enquiries about obtaining professional qualifications should be made to the relevant professional organization(s). Details of higher education providers of first degrees may be found in *University and College Entrance: Official Guide*.

## ACCOUNTANCY

The main bodies granting membership on examination after a period of practical work are:

INSTITUTE OF CHARTERED ACCOUNTANTS IN ENGLAND AND WALES, Chartered Accountants' Hall, PO Box 433, Moorgate Place, London EC2P 2BJ. Tel: 0171-920 8100. *Secretary and Chief Executive*, A. J. Colquhoun

INSTITUTE OF CHARTERED ACCOUNTANTS OF SCOTLAND, 27 Queen Street, Edinburgh EH2 1LA. Tel: 0131-225 5673. *Chief Executive*, P. W. Johnston

CHARTERED ASSOCIATION OF CERTIFIED ACCOUNTANTS, 29 Lincoln's Inn Fields, London WC2A 3EE. Tel: 0171-242 6855. *Chief Executive*, Mrs A. L. Rose

CHARTERED INSTITUTE OF MANAGEMENT ACCOUNTANTS, 63 Portland Place, London WIN 4AB. Tel: 0171-637 2311. *Secretary*, Sir George Vallings, KCB

CHARTERED INSTITUTE OF PUBLIC FINANCE AND ACCOUNTANCY, 3 Robert Street, London WC2N 6BH. Tel: 0171-895 8823. *Secretary*, N. P. Hepworth, OBE

## ACTUARIAL SCIENCE

Two professional organizations grant qualifications after examination:

INSTITUTE OF ACTUARIES, Staple Inn Hall, High Holborn, London WC1V 7QJ. Tel: 0171-242 0106. *Secretary-General*, A. G. Tait. Enquiries to Actuarial Education Service, Napier House, 4 Worcester Street, Oxford OX1 2AW. Tel: 01865-794144

FACULTY OF ACTUARIES IN SCOTLAND, 40 Tristle Street, Edinburgh EH2 1EN. Tel: 0131-557 1575. *Secretary*, W. W. Mair

## ARCHITECTURE

The Education and Professional Development Committee of the Royal Institute of British Architects sets standards and guides the whole system of architectural education throughout the United Kingdom. The RIBA recognizes courses at 39 schools of architecture in the UK for exemption from their own examinations.

THE ROYAL INSTITUTE OF BRITISH ARCHITECTS, 66 Portland Place, London WIN 4AD. Tel: 0171-580 5533. *President*, Dr F. Duffy; *Director-General*, A. Reid, PH.D.

Schools of architecture outside the universities include:

THE ARCHITECTURAL ASSOCIATION, 34–36 Bedford Square, London WC1B 3ES. *Secretary*, E. A. Le Maistre

## BANKING

Professional organizations granting qualifications after examination are:
CHARTERED INSTITUTE OF BANKERS, 10 Lombard Street, London EC3V 9AS. Tel: 0171-623 3531. *Chief Executive*, G. Shreeve
CHARTERED INSTITUTE OF BANKERS IN SCOTLAND, 19 Rutland Square, Edinburgh EH1 2DE. Tel: 0131-229 9869. *Chief Executive*, Dr C. W. Munn

## BIOLOGY, CHEMISTRY, PHYSICS

Professional qualifications are awarded by:
INSTITUTE OF BIOLOGY, 20–22 Queensberry Place, London SW7 2DZ. Tel: 0171-581 8333. *President*, Prof. F. A. Herbert; *General Secretary*, Dr R. H. Priestley
ROYAL SOCIETY OF CHEMISTRY, Burlington House, Piccadilly, London W1V 0BN. Tel: 0171-437 8656. *President*, Prof. C. W. Rees, FRS; *Secretary-General*, Dr T. Inch
INSTITUTE OF PHYSICS, 47 Belgrave Square, London SW1X 8QX. Tel: 0171-235 6111. *Chief Executive*, Dr A. Jones

## BUILDING

Examinations are conducted by:
CHARTERED INSTITUTE OF BUILDING, Englemere, King's Ride, Ascot, Berks. SL5 8BJ. Tel: 01344-23355. *Chief Executive*, K. Banbury
INSTITUTE OF BUILDING CONTROL, 21 High Street, Ewell, Epsom, Surrey KT17 1SB. Tel: 0181-393 6860. *Director*, Ms R. Raywood
INSTITUTE OF CLERKS OF WORKS OF GREAT BRITAIN, 41 The Mall, London W5 3TJ. Tel: 0181-579 2917/8. *Secretary*, A. P. Macnamara

## BUSINESS, MANAGEMENT AND ADMINISTRATION

Professional bodies conducting training and/or examinations in business, administration, management or commerce include:
AMETS (ASSOCIATION FOR MANAGEMENT EDUCATION AND TRAINING IN SCOTLAND), c/o University of Stirling, Stirling FK9 4LA. Tel: 01786-450906. *Vice-Chairman*, M. Makower
CAM FOUNDATION (COMMUNICATIONS, ADVERTISING AND MARKETING EDUCATION FOUNDATION), Abford House, 15 Wilton Road, London SW1V 1NJ. Tel: 0171-828 7506. *Registrar*, Ms K. Hutchinson
CHARTERED INSTITUTE OF HOUSING, Octavia House, Westwood Business Park, Westwood Way, Coventry CV4 8JP. Tel: 01203-694433. *Chief Executive*, P. McGurk
CHARTERED INSTITUTE OF MARKETING, Moor Hall, Cookham, Maidenhead, Berks. SL6 9QH. Tel: 01628-524922. *Director-General*, S. Cuthbert
CHARTERED INSTITUTE OF PURCHASING AND SUPPLY, Easton House, Easton on the Hill, Stamford,

Lincs. PE9 3NZ. Tel: 01780-56777. *Director-General*, P. Thomson
CHARTERED INSTITUTE OF TRANSPORT, 80 Portland Place, London W1N 4DP. *Director-General*, R. P. Botwood
FACULTY OF SECRETARIES AND ADMINISTRATORS, Brightstowe, Catteshall Lane, Godalming, Surrey GU7 1LT. Tel: 01483-454213. *Secretary*, Mrs D. M. Rummery
INSTITUTE OF ADMINISTRATIVE MANAGEMENT, 40 Chatsworth Parade, Petts Wood, Orpington, Kent BR5 1RW. Tel: 01689-875555. *Chief Executive*, Prof. G. Robinson
INSTITUTE OF CHARTERED SECRETARIES AND ADMINISTRATORS, 16 Park Crescent, London W1N 4AH. Tel: 0171-580 4741. *Chief Executive*, M. J. Ainsworth
INSTITUTE OF CHARTERED SHIPBROKERS, 3 Gracechurch Street, London EC3V 0AT. Tel: 0171-283 1361. *Secretary*, J. H. Parker
INSTITUTE OF EXPORT, Export House, 64 Clifton Street, London EC2A 4HB. Tel: 0171-247 9812. *Director-General*, I. J. Campbell
INSTITUTE OF HEALTH SERVICES MANAGEMENT, 39 Chalton Street, London NW1 1JD. Tel: 0171-388 2626. *Director*, R. Rowden
INSTITUTION OF MANAGEMENT, Management House, Cottingham Road, Corby, Northants. NN17 1TT. Tel: 01536-204222. *Director-General*, R. Young
INSTITUTE OF PERSONNEL AND DEVELOPMENT, IPD House, Camp Road, London SW19 4UX. Tel: 0181-946 9100. *Director-General*, G. Armstrong
INSTITUTE OF PRACTITIONERS IN ADVERTISING, 44 Belgrave Square, London SW1X 8QS. Tel: 0171-235 7020. *Secretary*, J. Raad
HENLEY MANAGEMENT COLLEGE, Greenlands, Henley-on-Thames, Oxon. RG9 3AU. Tel: 01491-571454. *Principal*, Prof. R. Wild
LONDON BUSINESS SCHOOL, Sussex Place, Regent's Park, London NW1 4SA. Tel: 0171-262 5050. *Principal*, Prof. G. Bain, PH.D.
MANCHESTER BUSINESS SCHOOL, Booth Street West, Manchester M15 6PB. Tel: 0161-275 6333. *Director*, Prof. J. A. Arnold
LONDON CHAMBER OF COMMERCE AND INDUSTRY EXAMINATIONS BOARD, Marlowe House, Station Road, Sidcup, Kent DA15 7BJ. Tel: 0181-302 0261. *Chief Executive*, W. J. Swords

## DANCE

ROYAL ACADEMY OF DANCING, 36 Battersea Square, London SW11 3RA. Tel: 0171-223 0091. *Chief Executive*, D. Watchman; *Artistic Director*, J. Byrne
ROYAL BALLET SCHOOL, 155 Talgarth Road, London W14 9DE. Tel: 0181-748 6335. Also at White Lodge, Richmond Park, Surrey TW10 5HR. Tel: 0181-876 5547. *Director*, Dame Merle Park, DBE
IMPERIAL SOCIETY OF TEACHERS OF DANCING, Euston Hall, Birkenhead Street, London WC1H 8BE. Tel: 0171-837 9967. *General Secretary*, M. J. Browne

## DEFENCE

ROYAL COLLEGE OF DEFENCE STUDIES, Seaford House, 37 Belgrave Square, London SW1X 8NS. Tel: 0171-915 4800. Prepares selected senior officers and officials for responsibilities in the direction and management of defence and security. *Commandant*, Air Marshal Sir Timothy Garden, KCB

ROYAL NAVAL COLLEGES
ROYAL NAVAL COLLEGE, Greenwich, London SE10 9NN. Tel: 0181-858 2154. *Admiral President*, Rear-Adm. J. R. Brigstocke; *Dean of the College*, Prof. G. Till, PH.D.
BRITANNIA ROYAL NAVAL COLLEGE, Dartmouth, Devon TQ6 0HJ. Tel: 01803-832141. Provides general and academic officer training. *Captain*, Capt. S. Moore
ROYAL NAVAL ENGINEERING COLLEGE, Manadon, Plymouth PL5 3AQ. Provides BA, B.Eng., M.Sc. and specialist training in naval engineering. Students are selected uniformed officers of the Royal Navy, Commonwealth and foreign navies, and civilians. *Captain*, Capt. P. A. M. Thomas; *Dean*, Capt. B. M. Leavey; *Executive Officer*, Cdr. S. P. C. Westwood

MILITARY COLLEGES
STAFF COLLEGE, Camberley, Surrey GU15 4NP. Tel: 01276-412691. *Commandant*, Maj.-Gen. C. B. Q. Wallace, OBE
ROYAL MILITARY ACADEMY SANDHURST, Camberley, Surrey GU15 4PQ. Tel: 01276-63344. *Commandant*, Maj.-Gen. H. W. R. Pike, DSO, MBE
ROYAL MILITARY COLLEGE OF SCIENCE, Shrivenham, Swindon, Wilts. SN6 8LA. Tel: 01793-785435. Students from UK and overseas study from degree to postgraduate levels in management, science and technology. There is an increasing range of research and consultancy activity as the College is now a faculty of Cranfield University. *Commandant*, Maj.-Gen. E. F. B. Burton, OBE; *Principal*, Prof. A. C. Baynham, PH.D.
DIRECTORATE OF EDUCATIONAL AND TRAINING SERVICES, Director-General Adjutant General's Corp, Worthydown, Winchester, Hants SO21 2RG. Tel: 01962-887672/3. *Director*, Brig. J. M. Macfarlane

ROYAL AIR FORCE COLLEGES
ROYAL AIR FORCE STAFF COLLEGE, Bracknell, Berks. RG12 3DD. Prepares selected senior officers for high-grade command and staff appointments. Two-thirds of the students are RAF officers; the others are officers from the other UK Services and overseas air forces. *Air Officer Commanding and Commandant*, Air Vice-Marshal M. P. Donaldson
ROYAL AIR FORCE COLLEGE, Cranwell, Sleaford, Lincs. NG34 8HB. Provides initial officer training for officers of the RAF and PMRAFNS. The initial specialist training for officers of the Engineer and Supply Branches, advanced specialist training for officers of the General Duties, Engineer and Supply Branches and basic flying training for pilots of the General Duties Branch are also conducted at Cranwell. *Air Officer Commanding and Commandant*, Air Vice-Marshal D. Cousins, CB, AFC
ROYAL AIR FORCE SCHOOL OF EDUCATION AND TRAINING SUPPORT, RAF Newton, Nottingham NG13 8HL. Tel: 01949-20771. *Commanding Officer*, Gp Capt J. Rennie

## DENTISTRY

To be entitled to be registered in the Dentists Register, a person must hold the degree or diploma in dental surgery of

a university in the United Kingdom or the diploma of any of the licensing authorities (The Royal College of Surgeons of England and of Edinburgh, and the Royal College of Physicians and Surgeons of Glasgow). Nationals of an EC member state holding an appropriate European diploma, and holders of certain overseas diplomas, may also be registered. The Dentists Register is maintained by by:
THE GENERAL DENTAL COUNCIL, 37 Wimpole Street, London W1M 8DQ. Tel: 0171-486 2171. *Registrar*, N. T. Davies, MBE

## DIETETICS
*See also* FOOD AND NUTRITION SCIENCE

The professional association is the British Dietetic Association. Full membership is open to dietitians holding a recognized qualification, who may also become State Registered Dietitians through the Council for Professions Supplementary to Medicine (*see* Medicine)
THE BRITISH DIETETIC ASSOCIATION, 7th Floor, Elizabeth House, 22 Suffolk Street, Queensway, Birmingham B1 1LS. Tel: 0121-643 5483

## DRAMA

The national validating body for courses providing training in drama for the professional theatre is the National Council for Drama Training. It currently has accredited courses at the following: Academy of Live and Recorded Arts; Arts Educational Schools; Birmingham School of Speech Training & Dramatic Art; Bristol Old Vic Theatre School; Central School of Speech and Drama; Drama Centre, London; Drama Studio; Guildford School of Acting; Guildhall School of Music and Drama; London Academy of Music and Dramatic Art; Manchester Polytechnic School of Theatre; Mountview Theatre School; Queen Margaret College, Edinburgh; Rose Bruford College; Royal Academy of Dramatic Art; Royal Scottish Academy of Music and Drama; Webber Douglas Academy of Dramatic Art; Welsh College of Music and Drama.
The accreditation of a course in a school does not necessarily imply that other courses of different type or duration in the same school are also accredited
THE NATIONAL COUNCIL FOR DRAMA TRAINING, 5 Tavistock Place, London WC1H 9SN. *Secretary*, Miss E. M. McKay

## ENGINEERING

The Engineering Council supervises the engineering profession through the 41 nominated engineering institutions who are represented on its Board for Engineers' Registration. Working with and through the institutions, the Council sets the standards for the registration of individuals, and also the accreditation for academic courses in universities and colleges and the practical training in industry.
THE ENGINEERING COUNCIL, 10 Maltravers Street, London WC2R 3ER. Tel: 0171-240 7891. *Director-General*, D. Siler
The principal qualifying bodies are:
BRITISH COMPUTER SOCIETY, 1 Sanford Street, Swindon SN1 1HJ. Tel: 01793 417417. *Chief Executive*, G. Kirkpatrick

CHARTERED INSTITUTION OF BUILDING SERVICES ENGINEERS, Delta House, 222 Balham High Road, London SW12 9BS. Tel: 0181-675 5211. *Secretary*, A. V. Ramsay

INSTITUTION OF CHEMICAL ENGINEERS, The Davis Building, 165–171 Railway Terrace, Rugby, Warks. CV21 3HQ. Tel: 01788-578214. *Chief Executive*, Dr T. J. Evans

INSTITUTION OF CIVIL ENGINEERS, Great George Street, London SW1P 3AA. Tel: 0171-222 7722. *Secretary*, R. Dobson

INSTITUTION OF ELECTRICAL ENGINEERS, Savoy Place, London WC2R OBL. Tel: 0171-240 1871. *Secretary*, Dr J. C. Williams, FEng.

INSTITUTE OF ENERGY, 18 Devonshire Street, London WIN 2AU. Tel: 0171-580 7124. *Secretary*, J. E. H. Leach

INSTITUTION OF GAS ENGINEERS, 21 Portland Place, London WIN 3AF. Tel: 0171-636 6603. *Secretary*, D. J. Chapman

INSTITUTE OF MARINE ENGINEERS, The Memorial Building, 76 Mark Lane, London EC3R 7JN. Tel: 0171-481 8493. *Secretary*, J. E. Sloggett

INSTITUTE OF MATERIALS, 1 Carlton House Terrace, London SW1Y 5DB. Tel: 0171-839 4071. *Secretary*, Dr J. A. Catterall

INSTITUTE OF MEASUREMENT AND CONTROL, 87 Gower Street, London WCIE 6AA. Tel: 0171-387 4949. *Secretary*, M. J. Yates

INSTITUTION OF MECHANICAL ENGINEERS, 1 Birdcage Walk, London SW1H 9JJ. Tel: 0171-222 7899. *Director-General*, Dr R. Pike

INSTITUTION OF MINING ENGINEERS, Danum House, 6A South Parade, Doncaster DNI 2DY. Tel: 01302-320486. *Secretary*, G. J. M. Woodrow

INSTITUTION OF MINING AND METALLURGY, 44 Portland Place, London WIN 4BR. Tel: 0171-580 3802. *Secretary*, M. J. Jones

INSTITUTION OF STRUCTURAL ENGINEERS, 11 Upper Belgrave Street, London SW1X 8BH. Tel: 0171-235 4535. *Secretary*, Dr J. W. Dougill

ROYAL AERONAUTICAL SOCIETY, 4 Hamilton Place, London W1V OBQ. Tel: 0171-499 3515. *Director*, R. J. Kennett

ROYAL INSTITUTION OF NAVAL ARCHITECTS, 10 Upper Belgrave Street, London SW1X 8BQ. Tel: 0171-235 4622. *Secretary*, J. Rosewarn

---

## FOOD AND NUTRITION SCIENCE
*See also* DIETETICS

Scientific and professional bodies include:
INSTITUTE OF FOOD SCIENCE & TECHNOLOGY, 10 Cambridge Court, 210 Shepherd's Bush Road, London W6 7NL. Tel: 0171-603 6316. *Executive Secretary*, Ms H. G. Wild

NUTRITION SOCIETY, 10 Cambridge Court, 210 Shepherds Bush Road, London W6 7NJ. Tel: 0171-602 0228. *Hon. Secretary*, Dr R. F. Grimble

---

## FORESTRY AND TIMBER STUDIES

Professional organizations include:
ROYAL FORESTRY SOCIETY OF ENGLAND, WALES AND NORTHERN IRELAND, 102 High Street, Tring, Herts.,

HP23 4AF. Tel: 01442-822028. *Director*, J. E. Jackson, Ph.D.

ROYAL SCOTTISH FORESTRY SOCIETY, 62 Queen Street, Edinburgh EH2 4NA. Tel: 0131-228 8142. *Director*, M. Osborne

INSTITUTE OF CHARTERED FORESTERS, 7A St Colme Street, Edinburgh EH3 6AA. Tel: 0131-225 2705. *Secretary*, Mrs M. W. Dick

COMMONWEALTH FORESTRY ASSOCIATION, c/o Oxford Forestry Institute, South Parks Road, Oxford OX1 3RB. Tel: 01865-275072. *Chairman*, P. J. Wood

---

## FUEL AND ENERGY SCIENCE

The principal professional bodies are:
INSTITUTE OF ENERGY, 18 Devonshire Street, London WIN 2AU. Tel: 0171-580 7124. *Secretary*, J. Leach

INSTITUTION OF GAS ENGINEERS, 21 Portland Place, London WIN 3AF. Tel: 0171-636 6603. *Secretary*, D. J. Chapman

INSTITUTE OF PETROLEUM, 61 New Cavendish Street, London WIM 8AR. Tel: 0171-467 7100. *Director-General*, I. Ward

---

## HOTELKEEPING, CATERING AND INSTITUTIONAL MANAGEMENT
*See also* DIETETICS, and FOOD and NUTRITION SCIENCE

The qualifying professional body in the subjects is:
HOTEL CATERING AND INSTITUTIONAL MANAGEMENT ASSOCIATION, 191 Trinity Road, London SW17 7HN. Tel: 0181-672 4251. *Chief Executive*, J. Logie

---

## INDUSTRIAL AND VOCATIONAL TRAINING

There are 120 industry training organizations, employer-led independent organizations whose role includes setting the standards of National and Scottish Vocational Qualifications.
NATIONAL COUNCIL OF INDUSTRY TRAINING ORGANIZATIONS, 5 George Lane, Royston, Herts. SG8 9AR. Tel: 01763-247285. *Chairman*, P. Morley; *Administrator*, Mrs C. Armstrong

---

## INSURANCE

Organizations conducting examinations and awarding diplomas are:
ASSOCIATION OF AVERAGE ADJUSTERS, 200 Aldersgate Street, London ECIA 4JJ. Tel: 0171-956 0099. *Hon. Secretary*, D. W. Taylor

CHARTERED INSURANCE INSTITUTE, 20 Aldermanbury, London EC2V 7HY. Tel: 0171-606 3835. *Director-General*, Prof. D. E. Bland

CHARTERED INSTITUTE OF LOSS ADJUSTERS, Manfield House, 376 Strand, London WC2R OLR. Tel: 0171-240 1496. *Director*, A. F. Clack

## JOURNALISM

Courses for trainee newspaper journalists are available at 20 centres. One-year full-time courses are available for selected students. Particulars of all these courses are available from the National Council for the Training of Journalists. Short courses for experienced journalists are also arranged by the National Council.

For periodical journalists, there are eight centres running courses approved by the Periodicals Training Council.

THE NATIONAL COUNCIL FOR TRAINING OF JOURNALISTS, Latton Bush Centre, Southern Way, Harlow, Essex CM18 7BL. Tel: 01279-430009. *Chief Executive,* R. Selwood

THE PERIODICALS TRAINING COUNCIL, Imperial House, 15–19 Kingsway, London WC2B 6UN. Tel: 0171-836 8798. *Executive Director,* D. Longbottom, MBE

## LAW

### THE BAR

Admission to the Bar of England and Wales is controlled by the Inns of Court, admission to the Bar of Northern Ireland by the Honorable Society of the Inn of Court of Northern Ireland and admission as an Advocate of the Scottish Bar is controlled by the Faculty of Advocates. The governing body of the barristers' branch of the legal profession in England and Wales is the General Council of the Bar. The governing body in Northern Ireland is the Honorable Society of the Inn of Court of Northern Ireland, and the Faculty of Advocates is the governing body of the Scottish Bar. The education and examination of students for the Bar of England and Wales is superintended by the Council of Legal Education.

THE GENERAL COUNCIL OF THE BAR, 3 Bedford Row, London WC1R 4DB. Tel: 0171-242 0082. *Chairman,* R. Seabrook, QC; *Chief Executive,* N. Morison

*The Inns of Court*

THE INNER TEMPLE, London EC4Y 7HL. Tel: 0171-797 8175. *Treasurer,* The Rt. Hon. Lord Justice Hirst; *Sub-Treasurer,* Brig. P. Little

THE MIDDLE TEMPLE, London EC4Y 9AT. *Treasurer,* D. A. Hollis, QC; *Deputy Treasurer,* Brig. C. T. J. Wright

GRAY'S INN, 8 South Square, London WC1R 5EU. *Treasurer,* The Rt. Hon. Sir Iain Glidewell; *Under-Treasurer,* D. Machin

LINCOLN'S INN, London WC2A 3TL. Tel: 0171-405 1393. *Treasurer,* The Lord Oliver of Aylmerton, PC; *Under-Treasurer,* Capt. P. M. Carver, RN

THE COUNCIL OF LEGAL EDUCATION, Inns of Court School of Law, 39 Eagle Street, London WC1R 4AJ. Tel: 0171-404 5787. *Chairman,* The Hon. Mr Justice Phillips; *Dean, Inns of Court School of Law,* Mrs M. A. Phillips

FACULTY OF ADVOCATES, Advocates Library, Parliament House, Edinburgh EH1 1RF. Tel: 0131-226 5071. *Dean,* A. R. Hardie, QC; *Clerk,* J. R. Doherty

THE HONORABLE SOCIETY OF THE INN OF COURT OF NORTHERN IRELAND, Royal Courts of Justice, Belfast BT1 3JF. Tel: 01232-235111. *Treasurer* (1994), His Hon. Judge Markey, QC; *Under-Treasurer,* J. A. L. McLean, QC

### SOLICITORS

Qualifications for solicitor are obtainable only from one of the Law Societies, which control the education and examination of articled clerks, and the admission of solicitors.

LAW SOCIETY OF ENGLAND AND WALES, 113 Chancery Lane, London WC2A 1PL. Tel: 0171-242 1222. *President* (1994–5), R. C. Elly; *Vice-President* (1994–5), J. A. E. Young; *Secretary-General,* J. W. Hayes

THE COLLEGE OF LAW provides courses for the Law Society examinations at Braboeuf Manor, St Catherine's, Guildford, Surrey GU3 1HA; 14 Store Street, London WC1E 7DE; Christleton Hall, Chester CH3 7AB; Bishopthorpe Road, York YO2 1QA

THE SOLICITORS COMPLAINTS BUREAU, Victoria Court, 8 Dormer Place, Leamington Spa, Warks CV32 5AE. Tel: 01926-820082. The Bureau is an independent arm of the Law Society set up to handle complaints about solicitors.

LAW SOCIETY OF SCOTLAND, Law Society's Hall, 26 Drumsheugh Gardens, Edinburgh EH3 7YR. Tel: 0131-226 7411. *President* (1994–5), K. A. Ross; *Secretary,* K. W. Pritchard, OBE

LAW SOCIETY OF NORTHERN IRELAND, Law Society House, 90–106 Victoria Street, Belfast BT1 3JZ. Tel: 01232-231614. *Secretary,* M. C. Davey

## LIBRARIANSHIP AND INFORMATION SCIENCE/MANAGEMENT

The Library Association accredits degree and postgraduate courses in library and information science which are offered by 17 universities in the UK. A full list of accredited degree and postgraduate courses is available from the Education Department. The Association also maintains a professional register of Chartered Members open to graduate ordinary members of the Association.

THE LIBRARY ASSOCIATION, 7 Ridgmount Street, London WC1E 7AE. Tel: 0171-636 7543. *Chief Executive,* R. Shimmon

## MATERIALS STUDIES

The qualifying body is:

INSTITUTE OF MATERIALS, 1 Carlton House Terrace, London SW1Y 5DB. Tel: 0171-839 4071. *Secretary,* Dr J. A. Catterall

## MEDICINE

### EXAMINING BODY FOR DIPLOMAS

UNITED EXAMINING BOARD, Apothecaries Hall, Black Friars Lane, London EC4V 6EJ. Tel: 0171-236 1180. *Chairman,* P. Edmond; *Registrar,* A. M. Wallington-Smith

### COLLEGES/SOCIETIES HOLDING POSTGRADUATE MEMBERSHIP AND DIPLOMA EXAMINATIONS

ROYAL COLLEGE OF ANAESTHETISTS, 48–49 Russell Square, London WC1B 4JY. Tel: 0171-813 1900. *President,* Prof. C. Prys-Roberts; *Chief Executive,* Sir Geoffrey de Deney, KCVO

ROYAL COLLEGE OF GENERAL PRACTITIONERS, 14 Princes Gate, London SW7 1PU. Tel: 0171-581 3232. *President,* Dr L. Newman, OBE; *Hon. Secretary,* Dr W. Reith

ROYAL COLLEGE OF OBSTETRICIANS AND GYNAECOLOGISTS, 27 Sussex Place, London NW1 4RG. Tel: 0171-262 5425. *President,* Prof. G. V. P. Chamberlain, RD, FRCOG; *Secretary,* P. A. Barnett

ROYAL COLLEGE OF PATHOLOGISTS, 2 Carlton House Terrace, London SW1Y 5AF. Tel: 0171-930 5863. *President,* Prof. A. J. Bellingham, FRCP, FRCPath.; *Secretary,* K. Lockyer

ROYAL COLLEGE OF PHYSICIANS, 11 St Andrews Place, London NW1 4LE. Tel: 0171-935 1174. *President,* Prof. Sir Leslie Turnberg; *Secretary,* D. B. Lloyd

ROYAL COLLEGE OF PHYSICIANS OF EDINBURGH, 9 Queen Street, Edinburgh EH2 1JQ. Tel: 0131-225 7324. *President,* Dr A. D. Toft; *Secretary,* Dr J. StJ. Thomas

ROYAL COLLEGE OF PHYSICIANS AND SURGEONS OF GLASGOW, 234–242 St Vincent Street, Glasgow G2 5RJ. Tel: 0141-221 6072. *President,* N. McKay; *Hon. Secretary,* Dr B. Williams

ROYAL COLLEGE OF PSYCHIATRISTS, 17 Belgrave Square, London SW1X 8PG. Tel: 0171-235 2351. *President,* Dr F. Caldicott; *Secretary,* Mrs V. Cameron

ROYAL COLLEGE OF RADIOLOGISTS, 38 Portland Place, London W1N 3DG. Tel: 0171-636 4432. *President,* Dr C. H. Paine; *Secretary,* A. J. Cowles

ROYAL COLLEGE OF SURGEONS OF ENGLAND, 35–43 Lincoln's Inn Fields, London WC2A 3PN. Tel: 0171-405 3474. *President,* Prof. Sir Norman Browse, PRCS; *Secretary,* R. H. E. Duffett

ROYAL COLLEGE OF SURGEONS OF EDINBURGH, Nicolson Street, Edinburgh EH8 9DW. Tel: 0131-556 6206. *President,* Prof. Sir Robert Shields; *Secretary,* I. B. Macleod, FRCSed.

SOCIETY OF APOTHECARIES OF LONDON, Black Friars Lane, London EC4V 6EJ. Tel: 0171-236 1180. *Clerk,* Lt.-Col. R. J. Stringer

## PROFESSIONS SUPPLEMENTARY TO MEDICINE

The standard of professional education in biomedical sciences, chiropody, dietetics, occupational therapy, orthoptics, physiotherapy and radiography is the responsibility of seven professional boards, which also publish an annual register of qualified practitioners. The work of the boards is co-ordinated by the Council for Professions Supplementary to Medicine.

THE COUNCIL FOR PROFESSIONS SUPPLEMENTARY TO MEDICINE, Park House, 184 Kennington Park Road, London SE11 4BU. Tel: 0171-582 0866. *Registrar,* R. Pickis

### BIOMEDICAL SCIENCES

Qualifications from higher or further education establishments and training in medical laboratories are required for progress to the professional examinations and qualifications of the INSTITUTE OF BIOMEDICAL SCIENCE, 12 Coldbath Square, London EC1R 5HL. Tel: 0171-636 8192. *Chief Executive,* A. Potter

### CHIROPODY

Professional recognition is granted by the Society of Chiropodists and Podiatrists to students who are awarded B.Sc. degrees in Podiatry or Podiatric Medicine after attending a course of full-time training for three or four years at one of the 14 recognized schools in the UK (11 in England and Wales, two in Scotland and one in Northern Ireland). Qualifications granted and degrees recognized by the Society are approved by the Chiropodists Board for the purpose of

State Registration, which is a condition of employment within the National Health Service.

THE SOCIETY OF CHIROPODISTS AND PODIATRISTS, 53 Welbeck Street, London W1M 7HE. Tel: 0171-486 3381. *General Secretary,* J. G. C. Trouncer

*See also* DIETETICS

### OCCUPATIONAL THERAPY

Professional qualifications are awarded by the College of Occupational Therapists upon completion of one of the 31 training courses approved by the College.

THE COLLEGE OF OCCUPATIONAL THERAPISTS, 6–8 Marshalsea Road, London SE1 1HL. Tel: 0171-357 6480. *Secretary,* M. D. Hall, OBE, GM

*See also* OPHTHALMIC OPTICS

### ORTHOPTICS

Orthoptists undertake the diagnosis and treatment of all types of squint and other anomalies of binocular vision, working in close collaboration with ophthalmologists. The training and maintenance of professional standards are the responsibility of the Orthoptists Board of the Council for Professions Supplementary to Medicine. The professional body is the British Orthoptic Society. Training is at degree level.

THE BRITISH ORTHOPTIC SOCIETY, Tavistock House North, Tavistock Square, London WC1H 9HX. *Hon. Secretary,* Mrs A. Charnock

### PHYSIOTHERAPY

Full-time three- or four-year degree courses are available at 31 recognized schools in the UK. Information about courses leading to eligibility for Membership of the Chartered Society of Physiotherapy and to State Registration is available from THE CHARTERED SOCIETY OF PHYSIOTHERAPY, 14 Bedford Row, London WC1R 4ED. Tel: 0171-242 1941. *Secretary,* T. Simon

### RADIOGRAPHY AND RADIOTHERAPY

In order to practise both diagnostic and therapeutic radiography in the United Kingdom, it is necessary to have successfully completed a course of education and training recognized by the Privy Council. Such courses are offered by universities and colleges throughout the United Kingdom and lead to the award of a degree in radiography. Further information is available from the college.

THE COLLEGE OF RADIOGRAPHERS, 14 Upper Wimpole Street, London W1M 8BN. Tel: 0171-935 5726. *Deputy Chief Executive,* P. M. Smith

## COMPLEMENTARY MEDICINE

Professional courses are validated by:

INSTITUTE FOR COMPLEMENTARY MEDICINE, PO Box 194, LONDON SE16 1QZ. Tel: 0171-237 5165. *Director,* A. Baird

## MERCHANT NAVY TRAINING SCHOOLS

### OFFICERS

MARITIME OPERATIONS CENTRE, Southampton Institute of Higher Education, Newtown Road, Warsash, Southampton SO3 9ZL. Tel: 01489-576161. *Head of Centre,* Capt. G. B. Angas

## SEAFARERS

INDEFATIGABLE SCHOOL, Plas Llanfair, Llanfairpwll, Anglesey LL61 6NT. Tel: 01248-714338. *Headmaster,* Capt. P. White

NATIONAL SEA TRAINING COLLEGE, Denton, Gravesend, Kent DA12 2HR. Tel: 01474-363656. *Principal,* M. Bolton

## MUSIC

ASSOCIATED BOARD OF THE ROYAL SCHOOLS OF MUSIC, 14 Bedford Square, London WC1B 3JG. The Board conducts music examinations in centres throughout the world for the Royal Academy of Music and the Royal College of Music in London, the Royal Northern College of Music, Manchester and the Royal Scottish Academy of Music and Drama, Glasgow. *Chief Executive,* R. Morris

ROYAL ACADEMY OF MUSIC, Marylebone Road, London NW1 5HT. Tel: 0171-873 7373. *Principal,* L. Harrell

ROYAL COLLEGE OF MUSIC, Prince Consort Road, London SW7 2BS. Tel: 0171-589 3643. *Director,* Dr J. Ritterman

ROYAL NORTHERN COLLEGE OF MUSIC, 124 Oxford Road, Manchester M13 9RD. Tel: 0161-273 6283. *Principal,* Sir John Manduell, CBE

ROYAL SCOTTISH ACADEMY OF MUSIC AND DRAMA, 100 Renfrew Street, Glasgow G2 3DB. Tel: 0141-332 4101. *Principal,* Dr P. Ledger, CBE

ROYAL COLLEGE OF ORGANISTS, 7 St Andrew Street, London EC4A 3LQ. Tel: 0171-936 3606. *Clerk,* V. Waterhouse

GUILDHALL SCHOOL OF MUSIC AND DRAMA, Silk Street, London EC2Y 8DT. Tel: 0171-628 2571. *Principal,* I. Horsbrugh

LONDON COLLEGE OF MUSIC, Thames Valley University, St Mary's Road, London W5 5RF. Tel: 0181-231 2304. *General Manager,* R. D. Roberts

TRINITY COLLEGE OF MUSIC, 11–13 Mandeville Place, London W1M 6AQ. Tel: 0171-935 5773. *Principal,* G. Henderson

## NURSING

Courses leading to registration as a nurse are at least three years in length. There are also some programmes which are combined with degrees. Students study in colleges of nursing or in institutions of higher education. Courses offer a combination of theoretical and practical experience in a wide variety of settings. Depending on the type of course, students will register in adult, child, mental health or mental handicap (learning disabilities) nursing. A wide variety of specialist programmes are available after registration, for example in district nursing or occupational health nursing.

The Royal College of Nursing, within its Institute of Advanced Nursing Education, provides education at post-basic level in hospital, occupational health and community health fields. Advanced courses are held in preparation for senior posts in management and teaching; and other short and special courses.

THE ROYAL COLLEGE OF NURSING OF THE UNITED KINGDOM, 20 Cavendish Square, London W1M 0AB. Tel: 0171-409 3333. *General Secretary,* Miss C. Hancock; *Principal of the Institute of Advanced Nursing Education,* J. C. A. Wells.

UK CENTRAL COUNCIL FOR NURSING, MIDWIFERY AND HEALTH VISITING, 23 Portland Place, London W1N 3AF. Tel: 0171-637 7181. *Registrar and Chief Executive,* C. Ralph

ENGLISH NATIONAL BOARD FOR NURSING, MIDWIFERY AND HEALTH VISITING, Victory House, 170 Tottenham Court Road, London W1P 0HA. Tel: 0171-388 3131. *Chief Executive Officer,* A. P. Smith

WELSH NATIONAL BOARD FOR NURSING, MIDWIFERY AND HEALTH VISITING, Floor 13, Pearl Assurance House, Greyfriars Road, Cardiff CF1 3AG. Tel: 01222-395535. *Chief Executive Officer,* D. A. Ravey

NATIONAL BOARD FOR NURSING, MIDWIFERY AND HEALTH VISITING FOR SCOTLAND, 22 Queen Street, Edinburgh EH2 1NT. Tel: 0131-226 7371. *Chief Executive Officer,* Mrs E. C. Mitchell

NATIONAL BOARD FOR NURSING, MIDWIFERY AND HEALTH VISITING FOR NORTHERN IRELAND, RAC House, 79 Chichester Street, Belfast BT1 4JE. Tel: 01232-238152. *Chief Executive Officer,* Dr O. D'A. Slevin

## OPHTHALMIC OPTICS

Professional bodies are:

THE BRITISH COLLEGE OF OPTOMETRISTS, 10 Knaresborough Place, London SW5 0TG. Tel: 0171-373 7765. Grants qualifications as an optometrist. *General Secretary,* P. D. Leigh

THE ASSOCIATION OF BRITISH DISPENSING OPTICIANS, 6 Hurlingham Business Park, Sulivan Road, London SW6 3DU. Tel: 0171-736 0088. Grants qualifications as a dispensing optician. *Registrar,* D. G. Baker

## PHARMACY

Information may be obtained from the Secretary and Registrar of the Royal Pharmaceutical Society of Great Britain.

ROYAL PHARMACEUTICAL SOCIETY OF GREAT BRITAIN, 1 Lambeth High Street, London SE1 7JN. *Secretary and Registrar,* J. Ferguson

## PHOTOGRAPHY

The professional body is:

BRITISH INSTITUTE OF PROFESSIONAL PHOTOGRAPHY, Fox Talbot House, 2 Amwell End, Ware, Herts. SG12 9HN. Tel: 01920-464011. *Chief Executive,* A. Mair

## PRINTING

Details of training courses in printing can be obtained from the Institute of Printing and the British Printing Industries Federation. In addition to these examining and organizing bodies, examinations are held by various independent regional examining boards in further education.

BRITISH PRINTING INDUSTRIES FEDERATION, 11 Bedford Row, London WC1R 4DX. Tel: 0171-242 6904. *Director-General,* G. C. Stanley

INSTITUTE OF PRINTING, 8 Lonsdale Gardens, Tunbridge Wells, Kent TNI INU. Tel: 01892-538118. *Secretary-General*, D. Freeland

## SOCIAL WORK

The Central Council for Education and Training in Social Work promotes education and training for social work and social care throughout the UK. It approves education and training programmes, including those leading to its qualifying award, the Diploma in Social Work.
THE CENTRAL COUNCIL FOR EDUCATION AND TRAINING IN SOCIAL WORK, Derbyshire House, St Chad's Street, London WC1H 8AD. Tel: 0171-278 2455. *Chairman*, J. Greenwood; *Director*, T. Hall

## SPEECH THERAPY

The College of Speech and Language Therapists provides details of courses leading to qualification as a speech and language therapist. Other professionals may become Associates of the College. A directory of registered members is published annually.
THE COLLEGE OF SPEECH AND LANGUAGE THERAPISTS, 7 Bath Place, London EC2A 3DR. Tel: 0171-613 3855. *Director*, Mrs S. Davis

## SURVEYING

The qualifying professional bodies include:
ROYAL INSTITUTION OF CHARTERED SURVEYORS (incorporating The Institute of Quantity Surveyors), 12 Great George Street, London SW1P 3AD. Tel: 0171-334 3701. *Chief Executive*, M. Pattison
ARCHITECTS AND SURVEYORS INSTITUTE, 15 St Mary Street, Chippenham, Wilts. SN15 3JN. Tel: 01249-444505. *Chief Executive*, B. A. Hunt
ASSOCIATION OF BUILDING ENGINEERS, Jubilee House, Billing Brook Road, Weston Favell, Northampton NN3 8NW. Tel: 01604-404121. *Chief Executive*, B. D. Hughes
INSTITUTE OF REVENUES, RATING AND VALUATION, 41 Doughty Street, London WC1N 2LF. Tel: 0171-831 3505. *Director*, C. Farrington
INCORPORATED SOCIETY OF VALUERS AND AUCTIONEERS (1968), 3 Cadogan Gate, London SW1X 0AS. Tel: 0171-235 2282. *Chief Executive*, H. Whitty

## TEACHING

To become a qualified teacher it is necessary to have successfully completed a course of initial teacher training. Non-graduates usually qualify by way of a three- or four-year course leading to a Bachelor of Education (B.Ed.) honours degree, but some universities offer first degree courses (BA, B.Sc.) taken concurrently with a certificate of education. Graduates take a one-year postgraduate certificate of education (PGCE).
Details of courses in England and Wales are contained in the *Handbook of Degree and Advanced Courses* published annually by the National Association of Teachers in Further and Higher Education. Details of courses in Scotland can be obtained from the colleges of education, from COSHEP, and from TEACH (*see* page 463). Details of courses in Northern Ireland can be obtained from the Department of Education for Northern Ireland. Applications for teacher training courses in Northern Ireland are made to the institutions direct.
Teacher training is increasingly school-based and in future schools, or consortia of schools, will be able to carry out their own teacher-training, subject to approval of their training scheme. State-run school-based schemes already established include the licensed teacher scheme in England and Wales, and the mentor teacher scheme in Scotland (*see also* pages 451-2).
For applications, *see* page 456.

## TEXTILES

THE TEXTILE INSTITUTE, International Headquarters, 10 Blackfriars Street, Manchester M3 5DR. Tel: 0161-834 8457. *Chief Executive*, R. G. Denyer

## THEOLOGICAL COLLEGES

The number of students training for the ministry for the academic year 1993-4 is shown in parenthesis.

ANGLICAN

CRANMER HALL, St John's College, Durham DH1 3RJ. (80). *Warden*, Revd J. Pritchard
LINCOLN THEOLOGICAL COLLEGE, Wordsworth Street, Lincoln LN1 3BP. (65). *Warden*, Revd Canon W. M. Jacob, PH.D.
OAK HILL COLLEGE, Chase Side, London N14 4PS. (98). *Principal*, Revd Canon R. G. Bridger
COLLEGE OF THE RESURRECTION, Mirfield, W. Yorks. WF14 0BW. (28). *Principal*, Revd Dr D. J. Lane
RIDLEY HALL, Cambridge CB3 9HG. (54). *Principal*, Revd G. A. Cray
RIPON COLLEGE, Cuddesdon, Oxford OX44 9EX. (75). *Principal*, Revd Canon J. H. Garton
ST JOHN'S COLLEGE, Chilwell Lane, Bramcote, Nottingham NG9 3DS. (100). *Principal*, Revd Dr J. Goldingay
ST MICHAEL'S THEOLOGICAL COLLEGE, Llandaff, Cardiff CF5 2YJ. (38). *Warden*, Revd Canon J. H. L. Rowlands
ST STEPHEN'S HOUSE, 16 Marston Street, Oxford OX4 1JX. (55). *Principal*, Revd Canon E. R. Barnes
THEOLOGICAL INSTITUTE OF THE SCOTTISH EPISCOPAL CHURCH, 21 Inverleith Terrace, Edinburgh EH3 5NS. (30). *Principal*, Revd Canon K. Mason
TRINITY COLLEGE, Stoke Hill, Bristol BS9 1JP. (130). *Principal (acting)*, Revd M. Roberts
WESTCOTT HOUSE, Jesus Lane, Cambridge CB5 8BP. (53). *Principal*, Revd M. G. V. Roberts
WYCLIFFE HALL, 54 Banbury Road, Oxford OX2 6PW. (68). *Principal*, Revd Dr R. T. France

BAPTIST

BRISTOL BAPTIST COLLEGE, Woodland Road, Bristol BS8 1UN. (18). *Principal*, Revd Dr B. Haymes
NORTHERN BAPTIST COLLEGE, Northern Federation for Training in Ministry, Luther King House, Brighton

Grove, Rusholme, Manchester M14 5JP. (30). *Principal,*
Revd Dr R. L. Kidd
NORTH WALES BAPTIST COLLEGE, Ffordd Ffriddoedd,
Bangor, Gwynedd LL57 2EH. (2). *Principal,* Revd
J. R. Rowlands
REGENT'S PARK COLLEGE, Oxford OX1 2LB. (27).
*Principal,* Revd Dr P. S. Fiddes
THE SCOTTISH BAPTIST COLLEGE, 12 Aytoun Road,
Glasgow G41 5RN. (20). *Principal,* Revd
K. B. E. Roxburgh
SOUTH WALES BAPTIST COLLEGE, 54 Richmond Road,
Cardiff CF2 3UR. (20). *Principal,* Revd D. H. Matthews
SPURGEON'S COLLEGE, South Norwood Hill, London
SE25 6DJ. (140). *Principal,* Revd M. Quicke

CHURCH OF SCOTLAND

CHRIST'S COLLEGE, 25 High Street, Old Aberdeen
AB2 3EE. (35). *Master,* Revd Prof. A. Main, TD, PH.D.
NEW COLLEGE, Mound Place, Edinburgh EH1 2LU. (45).
*Principal,* Revd Prof. D. B. Forrester
TRINITY COLLEGE, 4 The Square, University of Glasgow,
Glasgow G12 8QQ. (61). *Principal,* Revd
Prof. G. M. Newlands

CONGREGATIONAL

COLLEGE OF THE WELSH INDEPENDENTS, 38 Pier
Street, Aberystwyth, Dyfed. *Principal,* Revd Dr
E. S. John
SCOTTISH CONGREGATIONAL COLLEGE, 20 Inverleith
Terrace, Edinburgh EH3 5NS. (10). *Principal,*
Revd Dr J. W. S. Clark

ECUMENICAL

QUEEN'S COLLEGE, Somerset Road, Edgbaston,
Birmingham B15 2QH. (75). *Principal,* Revd P. Fisher

METHODIST

EDGHILL THEOLOGICAL COLLEGE, 9 Lennoxvale, Belfast
BT9 5BY. (13). *Principal,* Revd D. Cooke, PH.D.
HARTLEY VICTORIA COLLEGE, Northern Federation for
Training in Ministry, Luther King House, Brighton
Grove, Manchester M14 5JP. (24). *Principal,* Revd
G. Slater
LINCOLN THEOLOGICAL COLLEGE, Wordsworth Street,
Lincoln LN1 3BP. (65). *Warden,* Revd Canon
W. M. Jacob, PH.D.
WESLEY COLLEGE, College Park Drive, Henbury Road,
Bristol BS10 7QD. (60). *Principal,* Dr H. McKeating
WESLEY HOUSE, Jesus Lane, Cambridge CB5 8BJ. (34).
*Principal,* Revd Dr I. H. Jones
WESLEY STUDY CENTRE, 55 The Avenue, Durham
DH1 4EB. (17). *Director,* Revd B. Luscombe, PH.D.

NON-DENOMINATIONAL

ST MARY'S COLLEGE, The University, St Andrews, Fife
KY16 9JU. (180). *Principal,* Dr R. A. Piper

PRESBYTERIAN

UNION THEOLOGICAL COLLEGE, Belfast BT7 1JT. (37).
*Principal,* Revd Prof. T. S. Reid

PRESBYTERIAN CHURCH OF WALES

UNITED THEOLOGICAL COLLEGE, Aberystwyth SY23 2LT.
(36). *Principal,* Revd Prof. E. ap Nefydd Roberts

ROMAN CATHOLIC

ALLEN HALL COLLEGE, 28 Beaufort Street, London
SW3 5AA. (50). *Principal,* Revd K. Barltrop, STL

CAMPION HOUSE COLLEGE, 112 Thornbury Road,
Isleworth, Middx. TW7 4NN. (35). *Principal,*
Revd C. C. Dykehoff, SJ
OSCOTT COLLEGE, Chester Road, Sutton Coldfield,
W. Midlands B73 5AA. (66). *Rector,* Rt. Revd
Mgr P. McKinney, STL
SCOTUS COLLEGE, 2 Chesters Road, Bearsden, Glasgow
G61 4AG. (50). *Rector,* Rt Revd Mgr M. J. Conway
ST JOHN'S SEMINARY, Wonersh, Guildford, Surrey
GU5 0QX. (40). *Rector,* Rt. Revd Mgr P. Smith
USHAW COLLEGE, Durham DH7 9RH. (92). *Principal,*
Rt. Revd Mgr R. Atherton, OBE

UNITARIAN

UNITARIAN COLLEGE, Northern Federation for Training
in Ministry, Luther King House, Brighton Grove,
Rusholme, Manchester M14 5JP. (5). *Principal,* Revd
L. Smith, PH.D.

UNITED REFORMED

BALA-BANGOR INDEPENDENT COLLEGE, Bangor
LL57 2EH. (15). *Principal,* R. T. Jones, D.Phil., DD
MANSFIELD COLLEGE, Mansfield Road, Oxford OX1 3TF.
(20). *Principal,* D. J. Trevelyan, CB
NORTHERN COLLEGE, Northern Federation for Training
in Ministry, Luther King House, Brighton Grove,
Rusholme, Manchester M14 5JP. (28). *Principal,* Revd Dr
D. R. Peel
WESTMINSTER COLLEGE, Madingley Road, Cambridge
CB3 0AA. (35). *Principal,* Revd M. H. Cressey

JEWISH

JEWS' COLLEGE, Albert Road, London NW4 2SJ. (12).
*Principal,* Rabbi Dr D. Sinclair
LEO BAECK COLLEGE, Sternberg Centre for Judaism, 80
East End Road, London N3 2SY. (18). *Principal,* Rabbi
Dr J. Magonet

---

## TOWN AND COUNTRY PLANNING

Degree and diploma courses in town planning are accredited
by the Royal Town Planning Institute.
THE ROYAL TOWN PLANNING INSTITUTE, 26 Portland
Place, London W1N 4BE. Tel: 0171-636 9107. *Secretary-
General,* D. Fryer, OBE

---

## TRANSPORT

Qualifying examinations in transport management and
logistics leading to chartered professional status are con-
ducted by the Chartered Institute of Transport.
THE CHARTERED INSTITUTE OF TRANSPORT, 80
Portland Place, London W1N 4DP. Tel: 0171-636 9952.
*Director,* A. M. J. Pomeroy

# Independent Schools

The following pages list those independent schools whose Head is a member of the Headmasters' Conference, the Society of Headmasters and Headmistresses of Independent Schools or the Girls' Schools Association

---

## THE HEADMASTERS' CONFERENCE

---

*Chairman* (1995), H. R. Wright (King Edward's School, Birmingham)
*Secretary*, V. S. Anthony, 130 Regent Road, Leicester LE1 7PG. Tel: 0116-285 4810
*Membership Secretary*, R. N. P. Griffiths, 1 Russell House, Bepton Road, Midhurst, W. Sussex GU29 9NB. Tel: 01730-815635. The annual meeting is, as a rule, held at the end of September

\* Woodard Corporation School, 1 The Sanctuary, London SW1P 3JT. Tel: 0171-222 5381
† Girls in VI form
‡ Co-educational
° 1993 figures

| Name of School | Foun-ded | No. of pupils | Annual fees £ | | Head (with date of appointment) |
|---|---|---|---|---|---|
| | | | Boarding | Day | |
| ENGLAND AND WALES | | | | | |
| Abbotsholme School, Staffs. | 1889 | 238‡ | 10,764 | 7,254 | D. J. Farrant (1984) |
| Abingdon School, Oxon. | 1256 | 750 | 9,420 | 5,010 | M. St J. Parker (1975) |
| Ackworth School, W. Yorks. | 1779 | 430‡ | 9,105 | 5,187 | D. S. Harris (1989) |
| Aldenham School, Herts. | 1597 | 365† | 11,070 | 7,470 | S. Borthwick (1994) |
| Alleyn's School, London SE22 | 1619 | 907‡ | — | 5,475 | Dr C. H. R. Niven (1992) |
| Allhallows School, Dorset | 1515 | 230‡ | 10,956 | 5,478 | P. S. Larkman, LVO (1983) |
| Ampleforth College (*RC*), Yorks. | 1802 | 562 | 11,520 | 5,940 | Revd G. F. L. Chamberlain, OSB (1993) |
| \*Ardingly College, W. Sussex | 1858 | 450‡ | 11,085 | 8,805 | J. W. Flecker (1980) |
| Arnold School, Blackpool | 1896 | 810‡ | — | 3,549 | W. T. Gillen (1993) |
| Ashville College, Harrogate | 1877 | 350‡ | 8,336 | 4,474 | M. H. Crosby (1987) |
| Bablake School, Coventry | 1560 | 850‡ | — | 3,495 | Dr S. Nuttall (1991) |
| Bancroft's School, Essex | 1727 | 725‡ | — | 5,298 | Dr P. C. D. Southern (1985) |
| Barnard Castle School, Co. Durham | 1883 | 500† | 7,959 | 4,710 | F. S. McNamara (1980) |
| Batley Grammar School, W. Yorks. | 1612 | 585† | — | 3,390 | C. S. Parker (1986) |
| Bedales School, Hants. | 1893 | 403‡ | 12,378 | 8,940 | R. E. I. Newton (1992) |
| Bedford School | 1552 | 710 | 10,635 | 6,645 | Dr I. P. Evans (1990) |
| Bedford Modern School | 1566 | 986 | 8,043 | 4,200 | P. J. Squire (1977) |
| Berkhamsted School, Herts. | 1541 | 624 | 10,410 | 6,390 | Revd K. H. Wilkinson (1989) |
| Birkenhead School, Merseyside | 1860 | 750 | — | 3,459 | S. J. Haggett (1988) |
| Bishop's Stortford College, Herts. | 1868 | 330† | 10,020 | 7,230 | S. G. G. Benson (1984) |
| \*Bloxham School, Oxon. | 1860 | 350† | 11,580 | 8,985 | D. K. Exham (1991) |
| Blundell's School, Devon | 1604 | 372† | 11,145 | 6,795 | J. Leigh (1992) |
| Bolton School | 1524 | 1,000 | — | 4,398 | A. W. Wright (1983) |
| Bootham School, York | 1823 | 324‡ | 9,450 | 6,135 | I. M. Small (1988) |
| Bradfield College, Berks. | 1850 | °580† | °11,475 | °8,606 | P. B. Smith (1985) |
| Bradford Grammar School | 1662 | 967‡ | — | 3,660 | D. A. G. Smith (1974) |
| Brentwood School, Essex | 1557 | 1,022† | 9,580 | 5,482 | J. A. B. Kelsall (1993) |
| Brighton College, E. Sussex | 1845 | 470‡ | 11,385 | 7,485 | J. D. Leach (1987) |
| Bristol Cathedral School | 1542 | 479† | — | 3,903 | K. J. Riley (1994) |
| Bristol Grammar School | 1532 | 1,020‡ | — | 3,705 | C. E. Martin (1986) |
| Bromsgrove School, Worcs. | 1553 | 615‡ | 9,510 | 5,955 | T. M. Taylor (1986) |
| Bryanston School, Dorset | 1928 | 660‡ | 12,720 | 8,481 | T. D. Wheare (1983) |
| Bury Grammar School, Lancs. | 1634 | 670 | — | 3,534 | K. Richards (1990) |
| Canford School, Dorset | 1923 | 482‡ | 11,900 | 8,925 | J. D. Lever (1992) |
| Caterham School, Surrey | 1811 | 750† | 10,698 | 5,520 | R. Davey (1995) |
| Charterhouse, Surrey | 1611 | 700† | 12,222 | 10,083 | P. Hobson (1993) |
| Cheadle Hulme School, Cheshire | 1855 | 910‡ | — | 3,894 | D. J. Wilkinson (1990) |
| Cheltenham College, Glos. | 1841 | °559† | °11,370 | °8,595 | P. D. V. Wilkes (1990) |
| Chetham's School of Music, Manchester | 1653 | 280‡ | 15,288 | 11,841 | Revd P. F. Hullah (1992) |
| Chigwell School, Essex | 1629 | 360† | 9,108 | 5,991 | A. R. M. Little (1989) |
| Christ College, Brecon | 1541 | 370† | 8,913 | 6,804 | S. W. Hockey (1982) |
| Christ's Hospital, W. Sussex | 1553 | 830‡ | varies | — | R. C. Poulton (1987) |

| Name of School | Foun-ded | No. of pupils | Annual fees £ Boarding | Day | Head (with date of appointment) |
|---|---|---|---|---|---|
| Churcher's College, Hants. | 1722 | 581‡ | 8,982 | 4,800 | G. W. Buttle (1988) |
| City of London, London EC4 | 1442 | 870 | — | 5,553 | B. G. Bass (1990) |
| City of London Freemen's School, Surrey | 1854 | 387‡ | 8,586 | 5,499 | D. C. Haywood (1987) |
| Clifton College, Bristol | 1862 | 649‡ | 11,685 | 8,190 | H. Monro (1990) |
| Colfe's School, London SE12 | 1652 | 700† | — | 4,674 | Dr D. Richardson (1990) |
| Colston's Collegiate School, Bristol | 1710 | 400‡ | 9,510 | 5,400 | S. B. Howarth (1988) |
| Cranleigh School, Surrey | 1863 | 540† | 11,970 | 8,985 | A. Hart (1984) |
| Culford School, Suffolk | 1881 | 580‡ | 9,630 | 6,300 | J. Richardson (1992) |
| Dame Allan's School, Newcastle upon Tyne | 1705 | 400† | — | 3,432 | T. A. Willcocks (*Principal*) (1988) |
| Dauntsey's School, Wilts. | 1543 | 630‡ | 10,149 | 6,249 | C. R. Evans (1985) |
| Dean Close School, Cheltenham | 1884 | 440‡ | 11,700 | 8,160 | C. J. Bacon (1979) |
| *Denstone College, Staffs. | 1873 | 300‡ | 10,272 | 7,323 | H. C. K. Carson (1990) |
| Douai School (*RC*), Berks. | 1903 | 200‡ | 10,125 | 6,525 | Revd E. Power (1993) |
| Dover College, Kent | 1871 | 262‡ | 10,950 | 5,970 | M. P. G. Wright (1991) |
| Downside School (*RC*), Somerset | 1607 | 400 | 10,836 | 6,945 | Dom. A. Bellenger (1991) |
| Dulwich College, London SE21 | 1619 | 1,383 | 11,910 | 5,955 | A. C. F. Verity (*Master*) (1986) |
| Durham School | 1414 | 343† | 11,085 | 7,209 | M. A. Lang (1982) |
| Eastbourne College, E. Sussex | 1867 | 480† | 11,292 | 8,349 | C. M. P. Bush (1993) |
| *Ellesmere College, Shropshire | 1884 | 340‡ | 9,900 | 6,800 | D. R. du Croz (1988) |
| Eltham College, London SE9 | 1842 | 580† | 11,061 | 5,241 | D. M. Green (1990) |
| Emanuel School, London SW11 | 1594 | 750 | — | 4,326 | T. Jones-Parry (1994) |
| Epsom College, Surrey | 1855 | 656† | 11,151 | 8,284 | A. H. Beadles (1993) |
| Eton College, Berks. | 1440 | 1,270 | 12,384 | — | J. E. Lewis (1994) |
| Exeter School | 1633 | 720† | 7,452 | 3,942 | N. W. Gamble (1992) |
| Felsted School, Essex | 1564 | 360‡ | 11,880 | 9,375 | S. C. Roberts (1993) |
| Forest School, London E17 | 1834 | 820† | 8,280 | 5,274 | A. Boggis (*Warden*) (1992) |
| Framlingham College, Suffolk | 1864 | 436‡ | 9,270 | 5,949 | Mrs. G. M. Randall (1994) |
| Frensham Heights, Surrey | 1925 | 300‡ | 11,250 | 7,200 | P. de Voile (1993) |
| Giggleswick School, N. Yorks. | 1512 | 310‡ | 11,100 | 7,362 | A. P. Millard (1993) |
| Gresham's School, Norfolk | 1555 | 450‡ | 10,845 | 7,605 | J. H. Arkell (1991) |
| Haberdashers' Aske's School, Herts. | 1690 | 1,100 | — | 5,334 | K. Dawson (1987) |
| Haileybury, Herts. | 1862 | 584† | 12,240 | 8,874 | D. J. Jewell (1987) |
| Hampton School, Middx. | 1557 | 915 | — | 4,650 | G. G. Able (1988) |
| Harrow School, Middx. | 1571 | 800 | 12,900 | — | N. R. Bomford (1991) |
| Hereford Cathedral School | 1384 | °586‡ | 7,650 | 4,350 | Dr H. C. Tomlinson (1988) |
| Highgate School, London N6 | 1565 | 600 | 10,725 | 6,825 | R. P. Kennedy (1989) |
| Hulme Grammar School, Oldham | 1611 | 740 | — | 3,426 | G. F. Dunkin (1987) |
| *Hurstpierpoint College, W. Sussex | 1849 | 350‡ | 10,980 | 8,760 | S. A. Watson (1986) |
| Hymers College, Hull | 1889 | 720 | — | 3,330 | J. C. Morris (1990) |
| Ipswich School, Suffolk | 1390 | 610† | 8,211 | 4,797 | I. G. Galbraith (1993) |
| John Lyon School, Middx. | 1876 | 505 | — | 5,115 | Revd T. J. Wright (1986) |
| Kelly College, Devon | 1877 | 330‡ | 10,950 | 6,750 | C. H. Hirst (1985) |
| Kent College, Canterbury | 1885 | 530‡ | 9,627 | 5,400 | R. J. Wicks (1980) |
| Kimbolton School, Cambs. | 1600 | 560‡ | 8,595 | 4,995 | R. V. Peel (1987) |
| King Edward VI School, Southampton | 1553 | 936‡ | — | 4,497 | T. R. Cookson (1990) |
| King Edward VII School, Lytham | 1908 | 520 | — | 4,260 | P. J. Wilde (1993) |
| King Edward's School, Bath | 1552 | 690† | — | 4,056 | P. J. Winter (1993) |
| King Edward's School, Birmingham | 1552 | °875 | — | °4,074 | H. R. Wright (*Chief Master*) (1991) |
| King Edward's School, Witley, Surrey | 1553 | 510‡ | 8,625 | 6,000 | R. J. Fox (1988) |
| King Henry VIII School, Coventry | 1545 | 840‡ | — | 3,495 | T. J. Vardon (1994) |
| *King's College, Taunton | 1880 | 445‡ | 10,980 | 7,380 | R. S. Funnell (1988) |
| King's College School, London SW19 | 1829 | 700 | — | 5,940 | R. M. Reeve (1980) |
| King's School, Bruton, Somerset | 1519 | 307† | 10,650 | 7,545 | R. I. Smyth (1993) |
| King's School, Canterbury | 600 | 710‡ | 12,300 | 8,490 | Revd Canon A. C. J. Phillips (1986) |
| King's School, Chester | 1541 | 520 | — | 3,894 | A. R. D. Wickson (1981) |
| King's School, Ely, Cambs. | 970 | 399‡ | 11,046 | 7,398 | R. H. Youdale (1992) |
| King's School, Macclesfield | 1502 | 1,100† | — | 3,960 | A. G. Silcock (1987) |
| King's School, Rochester, Kent | 604 | 320‡ | 10,923 | 6,225 | Dr I. R. Walker (1986) |
| King's School, Tynemouth | 1860 | 660‡ | — | 3,510 | Dr D. Younger (1993) |
| King's School, Worcester | 1541 | 777‡ | 8,793 | 5,091 | Dr J. M. Moore (1983) |

| Name of School | Foun-ded | No. of pupils | Annual fees £ | | Head (with date of appointment) |
|---|---|---|---|---|---|
| | | | Boarding | Day | |
| Kingston Grammar School, Surrey | 1561 | 600‡ | — | 5,130 | C. D. Baxter (1991) |
| Kingswood School, Bath | 1748 | 445‡ | 10,680 | 6,810 | G. M. Best (1987) |
| *Lancing College, W. Sussex | 1848 | 524† | 11,625 | 8,736 | C. J. Saunders (1993) |
| Latymer Upper School, London w6 | 1624 | 950 | — | 5,298 | C. Diggory (1991) |
| Leeds Grammar School | 1552 | 1,047 | — | 4,104 | B. W. Collins (1986) |
| Leicester Grammar School | 1981 | 585‡ | — | 3,900 | J. B. Sugden (1989) |
| Leighton Park School, Reading | 1890 | 384‡ | 10,710 | 8,037 | J. A. Chapman (1986) |
| The Leys School, Cambridge | 1875 | 400‡ | 11,400 | 8,430 | Revd J. C. A. Barrett (1990) |
| Liverpool College | 1840 | 250‡ | — | 3,918 | B. R. Martin (1992) |
| Llandovery College, Dyfed | 1848 | 245‡ | 8,886 | 5,799 | Dr C. E. Evans (*Warden*) (1988) |
| Lord Wandsworth College, Hants. | 1912 | 365† | 9,012 | 7,044 | G. de W. Waller (1993) |
| Loughborough Grammar School | 1495 | 940 | 7,884 | 4,230 | D. N. Ireland (1984) |
| Magdalen College School, Oxford | 1480 | 496 | 8,694 | 4,581 | P. M. Tinniswood (*Master*) (1991) |
| Malvern College, Worcs. | 1865 | 670‡ | 11,790 | 8,580 | R. de C. Chapman (1983) |
| Manchester Grammar School | 1515 | 1,450 | — | 3,990 | G. M. Stephen, ph.d (*High Master*) (1994) |
| Marlborough College, Wilts. | 1843 | 800‡ | 12,120 | 8,550 | E. J. H. Gould (1993) |
| Merchant Taylors' School, Liverpool | 1620 | 703 | — | 3,600 | S. J. R. Dawkins (1986) |
| Merchant Taylors' School, Middx. | 1561 | 740 | 10,500 | 6,350 | J. R. Gabitass (1991) |
| Millfield, Street, Somerset | 1935 | 1,250‡ | 12,930 | 7,920 | C. S. Martin (1990) |
| Mill Hill School, London nw7 | 1807 | 545† | 11,010 | 7,290 | E. A. M. MacAlpine (1992) |
| Monkton Combe School, Bath | 1868 | 320‡ | 11,280 | 7,830 | M. J. Cuthbertson (1990) |
| Monmouth School, Gwent | 1614 | 543 | 7,899 | 4,743 | R. D. Lane (1982) |
| Mount St Mary's College (*RC*), Sheffield | 1842 | 310‡ | 8,718 | 5,892 | P. Fisher (1991) |
| Newcastle under Lyme School | 1874 | 1,149‡ | — | 3,408 | Dr R. M. Reynolds (*Principal*) (1990) |
| Norwich School | 1250 | 600† | — | 4,284 | C. D. Brown (1984) |
| Nottingham High School | 1513 | 830 | — | 4,365 | D. T. Witcombe, ph.d. (1970) |
| Oakham School, Rutland | 1584 | 1,000‡ | 11,010 | 6,090 | G. Smallbone (1985) |
| The Oratory School (*RC*), Berks. | 1859 | 400 | 11,310 | 7,905 | S. W. Barrow (1992) |
| Oundle School, Northants. | 1556 | 826‡ | 12,021 | — | D. B. McMurray (1984) |
| Pangbourne College, Berks. | 1917 | 400† | 10,860 | 7,620 | A. B. E. Hudson (1988) |
| Perse School, Cambridge | 1615 | 476† | — | 4,215 | N. Richardson (1994) |
| Plymouth College | 1877 | 640 | 8,292 | 4,326 | A. J. Morsley (1992) |
| Pocklington School, York | 1514 | 603‡ | 8,355 | 4,566 | J. N. D. Gray (1992) |
| Portsmouth Grammar School | 1732 | 780‡ | — | 4,356 | A. C. V. Evans (1983) |
| Prior Park College (*RC*), Bath | 1830 | 460‡ | 9,696 | 5,361 | J. W. R. Goulding (1989) |
| Queen Elizabeth GS, Wakefield | 1591 | 745‡ | — | 3,945 | R. P. Mardling (1985) |
| Queen Elizabeth's GS, Blackburn | 1567 | 1,050† | — | 3,720 | P. F. Johnston (1978) |
| Queen Elizabeth's Hospital, Bristol | 1590 | 512 | 6,546 | 3,729 | Dr R. Gliddon (1985) |
| Queen's College, Taunton | 1843 | 470‡ | 8,820 | 5,760 | C. T. Bradnock (1991) |
| Radley College, Oxon. | 1847 | 620 | 11,850 | — | R. M. Morgan (*Warden*) (1991) |
| Ratcliffe College (*RC*), Leicester | 1844 | 475‡ | 8,745 | 5,832 | Revd K. A. Tomlinson (1993) |
| Reading Blue Coat School | 1646 | 540† | 8,970 | 4,920 | Revd A. Sanders (1974) |
| Reed's School, Surrey | 1813 | 330† | 9,894 | 7,479 | D. E. Prince (1983) |
| Reigate Grammar School, Surrey | 1675 | 790† | — | 4,596 | J. G. Hamlin (1982) |
| Rendcomb College, Glos. | 1920 | 230‡ | 10,413 | 8,235 | J. Tolputt (1987) |
| Repton School, Derby | 1557 | 580‡ | 11,160 | 8,400 | G. E. Jones (1987) |
| RNIB New College, Worcester | 1987 | 121‡ | 21,420 | 14,280 | Revd B. R. Manthorp (1980) |
| Rossall School, Lancs. | 1844 | 430‡ | 11,400 | 5,700 | R. D. W. Rhodes (1987) |
| Royal Grammar School, Guildford | 1552 | 832 | — | 5,481 | T. M. S. Young (1992) |
| Royal Grammar School, Newcastle upon Tyne | 1545 | 944 | — | 3,441 | J. F. X. Miller (1994) |
| Royal Grammar School, Worcester | 1291 | 780 | — | 4,200 | W. A. Jones (1993) |
| Rugby School, Warwicks. | 1567 | 675‡ | 12,270 | 7,275 | M. B. Mavor, cvo (1990) |
| Rydal School, Clwyd | 1885 | 330‡ | 9,381 | 6,864 | N. W. Thorne (1991) |
| Ryde School (with Upper Chine), Isle of Wight | 1921 | 490‡ | 8,025 | 4,020 | M. D. Featherstone (1990) |
| St Albans School, Herts. | 1570 | 630† | — | 5,164 | A. R. Grant (1993) |
| St Ambrose College, Cheshire | 1946 | 700 | — | 3,300 | G. E. Hester (1991) |
| St Anselm's College (*RC*), Birkenhead | 1933 | 620 | — | 3,111 | C. Cleugh (1993) |
| St Bede's College (*RC*), Manchester | 1876 | 988‡ | — | 3,720 | J. Byrne (1983) |

| Name of School | Foun-ded | No. of pupils | Annual fees £ | | Head (with date of appointment) |
|---|---|---|---|---|---|
| | | | Boarding | Day | |
| St Bees School, Cumbria | 1583 | 290‡ | 10,041 | 6,909 | P. A. Chamberlain (1988) |
| St Benedict's School (RC), London w5 | 1902 | 564† | — | 4,635 | Dr A. J. Dachs (1987) |
| St Dunstan's College, London se6 | 1888 | 820‡ | — | 5,064 | J. D. Moore (1993) |
| St Edmund's College (RC), Herts. | 1568 | 550‡ | 9,015 | 5,769 | D. J. J. McEwen (1984) |
| St Edmund's School, Canterbury | 1749 | 300‡ | 11,580 | 7,560 | A. N. Ridley (1994) |
| St Edward's College (RC), Liverpool | 1853 | 680‡ | — | 3,390 | J. E. Waszek (1992) |
| St Edward's School, Oxford | 1863 | 565† | 11,790 | 8,850 | D. Christie (Warden) (1988) |
| St George's College (RC), Surrey | 1869 | 497† | — | 6,255 | P. McLaughlin (1994) |
| St John's School, Surrey | 1851 | 400† | 9,900 | 6,900 | C. H. Tongue (1993) |
| St Lawrence College, Kent | 1879 | 350‡ | 10,800 | 7,200 | J. H. Binfield (1983) |
| St Mary's College (RC), Merseyside | 1919 | 570‡ | — | 3,642 | W. Hammond (1991) |
| St Paul's School, London sw13 | 1509 | 752 | 12,057 | 7,782 | R. S. Baldock (High Master) (1992) |
| St Peter's School, York | 627 | 474‡ | 10,055 | 5,985 | R. N. Pittman (1985) |
| Sedbergh School, Cumbria | 1525 | 402 | 11,325 | 7,935 | Dr R. G. Baxter (1982) |
| Sevenoaks School, Kent | 1418 | 940‡ | 11,178 | 6,804 | R. P. Barker (1981) |
| Sherborne School, Dorset | 1550 | 640 | 12,135 | 9,255 | P. H. Lapping (1988) |
| Shrewsbury School | 1552 | 695 | 11,850 | 8,355 | F. E. Maidment (1988) |
| Silcoates School, W. Yorks. | 1820 | 409‡ | — | 5,160 | A. P. Spillane (1991) |
| Solihull School, W. Midlands | 1560 | 806† | — | 3,930 | A. Lee (1983) |
| Stamford School, Lincs. | 1532 | 577 | 7,782 | 3,891 | G. J. Timm (1978) |
| Stockport Grammar School | 1487 | 1,005‡ | — | 3,636 | D. R. J. Bird (1985) |
| Stonyhurst College (RC), Lancs. | 1593 | 400† | 11,031 | 6,849 | Dr R. G. G. Mercer (1985) |
| Stowe School, Bucks. | 1923 | 540† | 12,597 | 8,652 | J. G. L. Nichols (1989) |
| Sutton Valence School, Kent | 1576 | 340‡ | 10,656 | 6,822 | N. A. Sampson (1994) |
| Taunton School | 1847 | 500‡ | 11,070 | 7,080 | B. B. Sutton (1987) |
| Tettenhall College, Staffs. | 1863 | 358‡ | 8,880 | 5,475 | Dr P. Bodkin (1994) |
| Tonbridge School, Kent | 1553 | 660 | 12,351 | 8,715 | J. M. Hammond (1990) |
| Trent College, Derbys. | 1868 | 685‡ | 10,015 | 6,125 | J. S. Lee (1988) |
| Trinity School, Surrey | 1596 | 850 | — | 4,911 | B. J. Lennon (1995) |
| Truro School | 1879 | 832‡ | 8,259 | 4,434 | G. A. G. Dodd (1993) |
| University College School, London nw3 | 1830 | 700 | — | 6,495 | G. D. Slaughter (1983) |
| Uppingham School, Leics. | 1584 | 600† | 12,150 | 7,290 | S. C. Winkley (1991) |
| Warwick School | 914 | 810 | 9,330 | 4,350 | P. J. Cheshire (1988) |
| Wellingborough School, Northants. | 1595 | 396‡ | 8,985 | 5,025 | F. R. Ullmann (1993) |
| Wellington College, Berks. | 1856 | 804† | 11,850 | 8,655 | C. J. Driver (1989) |
| Wellington School, Somerset | 1937 | 795‡ | 7,698 | 4,194 | A. J. Rogers (1990) |
| Wells Cathedral School, Somerset | 1180 | 615‡ | 8,688 | 5,103 | J. S. Baxter (1987) |
| West Buckland School, Devon | 1858 | 445‡ | 8,544 | 4,635 | M. Downward (1979) |
| Westminster School, London sw1 | 1560 | 660† | 12,390 | 8,430 | D. M. Summerscale (1986) |
| Whitgift School, Surrey | 1596 | 1,050 | — | 5,235 | C. A. Barnett, d.phil. (1991) |
| William Hulme's GS, Manchester | 1887 | 780‡ | — | 4,133 | P. A. Briggs (1987) |
| Winchester College, Hants. | 1382 | 681 | 12,786 | 9,591 | J. P. Sabben-Clare (1985) |
| Wisbech Grammar School, Cambs. | 1379 | 635‡ | — | 4,290 | R. S. Repper (1988) |
| Wolverhampton Grammar School | 1512 | 710‡ | — | 4,479 | B. St J. Trafford (1990) |
| Woodbridge School, Suffolk | 1662 | 500‡ | 8,376 | 5,097 | S. H. Cole (1994) |
| Woodhouse Grove School, Bradford | 1812 | 560‡ | 8,535 | 5,025 | D. W. Welsh (1991) |
| *Worksop College, Notts. | 1895 | 330‡ | 10,320 | 7,125 | R. A. Collard (1994) |
| Worth School (RC), W. Sussex | 1959 | 305 | 11,100 | 7,401 | Fr C. Jamison (1994) |
| Wrekin College, Shropshire | 1880 | 270‡ | 10,890 | 5,970 | P. Johnson (1991) |
| Wycliffe College, Glos. | 1882 | 300‡ | 11,310 | 7,920 | D. C. M. Prichard (1994) |
| Yarm School, Cleveland | 1978 | 470 | — | 4,584 | R. Neville Tate (1978) |
| **SCOTLAND** | | | | | |
| Daniel Stewart's and Melville College, Edinburgh | 1832 | 760 | 7,782 | 3,978 | P. J. F. Tobin (Principal) (1989) |
| Dollar Academy, Clackmannanshire | 1818 | 740‡ | 8,757 | 3,951 | J. S. Robertson (Rector) (1994) |
| Dundee High School | 1239 | 1,100‡ | — | 3,723 | R. Nimmo, obe (Rector) (1977) |
| The Edinburgh Academy | 1824 | 531† | 10,602 | 5,013 | A. J. D. Rees (Rector) (1992) |
| Fettes College, Edinburgh | 1870 | 343‡ | 11,730 | 7,875 | M. T. Thyne, frse (1988) |
| George Heriot's School, Edinburgh | 1659 | 1,317‡ | — | 3,624 | K. P. Pearson (1983) |
| George Watson's College, Edinburgh | 1741 | 1,267‡ | 7,953 | 3,987 | F. E. Gerstenberg (Principal) (1985) |

| Name of School | Foun-ded | No. of pupils | Annual fees £ | | Head (with date of appointment) |
|---|---|---|---|---|---|
| | | | Boarding | Day | |
| Glasgow Academy | 1845 | 615‡ | — | 4,080 | D. Comins (Rector) (1994) |
| Glenalmond College, Perthshire | 1841 | 255† | 11,100 | 7,395 | I. G. Templeton (Warden) (1992) |
| Gordonstoun School, Moray | 1934 | 474‡ | 11,550 | 7,452 | M. C. S.-R. Pyper (1990) |
| High School of Glasgow | 1124 | 614‡ | — | 4,059 | R. G. Easton (1983) |
| Hutchesons' Grammar School, Glasgow | 1641 | 1,151‡ | — | 3,474 | D. R. Ward (Rector) (1987) |
| Kelvinside Academy, Glasgow | 1878 | 470 | — | 4,050 | J. H. Duff (Rector) (1980) |
| Loretto School, E. Lothian | 1827 | 305‡ | 11,055 | 7,368 | Revd N. W. Drummond (1984) |
| Merchiston Castle School, Edinburgh | 1833 | 380 | 10,950 | 7,080 | D. M. Spawforth (1981) |
| Morrison's Academy, Crieff | 1860 | 643‡ | 9,900 | 3,540 | H. A. Ashmall (Rector) (1979) |
| Robert Gordon's College, Aberdeen | 1729 | 950‡ | 8,200 | 3,700 | G. A. Allan (1978) |
| Strathallan School, Perthshire | 1913 | 430‡ | 10,500 | 7,485 | A. McPhail (1993) |

NORTHERN IRELAND

| Name of School | Foun-ded | No. of pupils | Annual fees £ | | Head (with date of appointment) |
|---|---|---|---|---|---|
| Bangor Grammar School, Co. Down | 1856 | 915 | — | 400 | T. W. Patton (1979) |
| Belfast Royal Academy | 1785 | 1,350‡ | — | °185 | W. M. Sillery (1980) |
| Campbell College, Belfast | 1894 | 675 | 4,945 | 945 | Dr R. J. I. Pollock (1987) |
| Coleraine Academical Institution | 1856 | 850 | 5,675 | 2,604 | R. S. Forsythe (1984) |
| Methodist College, Belfast | 1868 | 1,769‡ | 5,433 | 140 | T. W. Mulryne (1988) |
| Portora Royal School, Enniskillen | 1618 | 430 | — | nil | R. L. Bennett (1983) |
| Royal Belfast Academical Institution | 1810 | 1,020 | — | 360 | R. M. Ridley (1990) |

CHANNEL ISLANDS AND ISLE OF MAN

| Name of School | Foun-ded | No. of pupils | Annual fees £ | | Head (with date of appointment) |
|---|---|---|---|---|---|
| Elizabeth College, Guernsey | 1563 | 570† | 5,925 | 2,355 | J. H. F. Doulton (1988) |
| King William's College, Isle of Man | 1668 | 330‡ | 10,845 | 7,725 | S. A. Westley (1989) |

EUROPE

| Name of School | Foun-ded | No. of pupils | Annual fees £ | | Head (with date of appointment) |
|---|---|---|---|---|---|
| Aiglon College, Switzerland | 1949 | 280‡ | Fr.50,220 | Fr.34,275 | R. McDonald (1994) |
| British School in the Netherlands | 1935 | 520‡ | — | Gld.18,975 | M. J. Cooper (Principal) (1990) |
| British School of Brussels | 1970 | 529‡ | — | Fr.580,000 | Ms J. M. Bray (Principal) (1993) |
| The English School, Nicosia, Cyprus | 1900 | 830‡ | — | C£1,600 | A. M. Hudspeth (1988) |
| The International School of Geneva | 1924 | 1,110‡ | Fr.41,255 | Fr.18,040 | G. Walker, OBE (Director-General) (1991) |
| The International School of Paris | 1964 | 220‡ | — | Fr.77,000 | N. M. Prentki (1988) |
| St Columba's College, Dublin | 1843 | 300‡ | Ir£5,520 | Ir£3,150 | T. E. Macey (Warden) (1988) |
| St George's English School, Rome | 1958 | 380‡ | — | L18.3m | B. Gardner (1994) |
| Sir James Henderson School, Milan | 1969 | 170† | — | L13.4m | C. T. G. Leech (1986) |

**OTHER OVERSEAS MEMBERS**

AFRICA

FALCON COLLEGE, PO Esigodini, Zimbabwe. Head, P. N. Todd

HILTON COLLEGE, Natal 3245, SA. Head, P. Marsh

MICHAELHOUSE, Balgowan, Natal 3275, SA. Head, J. H. Pluke

PETERHOUSE, Marondera, Zimbabwe. Head, Revd Dr A. J. Megahey

ST GEORGE'S COLLEGE, Harare, Zimbabwe. Head, M. F. Hackett

DIOCESAN COLLEGE, Rondebosch, SA. Head, C. Watson

ST JOHN'S COLLEGE, Johannesburg, SA. Head, W. Macfarlane

ST STITHIAN'S COLLEGE, Randburg, SA. Head, D. B. Wylde

AUSTRALIA

ANGLICAN CHURCH GRAMMAR SCHOOL, Brisbane. Head, C. V. Ellis

BRIGHTON GRAMMAR SCHOOL, Brighton, Victoria. Head, R. L. Rofe

BRISBANE BOYS' COLLEGE, Brisbane. Head, G. M. Cujes

CAMBERWELL GRAMMAR SCHOOL, Canterbury, Victoria 3101. Head, C. F. Black

CANBERRA GS, Redhill, ACT 2603. Head, T. C. Murray

CAULFIELD GRAMMAR SCHOOL, East St Kilda, Victoria. Head, S. H. Newton

CHRIST CHURCH GRAMMAR SCHOOL, Claremont 6010, W. Australia. Head, J. J. S. Madin

CHURCH OF ENGLAND GRAMMAR SCHOOL, Melbourne. Head, A. J. de V. Hill

CHURCH OF ENGLAND GRAMMAR SCHOOL, Sydney, NSW. Head, R. A. I. Grant

CRANBROOK SCHOOL, Sydney, NSW. Head, Dr B. N. Carter

GEELONG CHURCH OF ENGLAND GRAMMAR SCHOOL,
Corio. *Head*, vacant
THE GEELONG COLLEGE, Geelong, Victoria. *Head*,
A. P. Sheahan
GUILDFORD GRAMMAR SCHOOL, W. Australia. *Head*,
J. M. Moody
HAILEYBURY COLLEGE, Keysborough, Victoria 3175.
*Head*, A. H. M. Aikman
HALE SCHOOL, Wembley Downs, W. Australia. *Head*,
K. G. Tregonning
KING'S SCHOOL, Parramatta, NSW. *Head*, J. A. Wickham
KINROSS WOLAROI SCHOOL, NSW. *Head*,
A. E. S. Anderson
KNOX GS, Wahroonga 2076, NSW. *Head*, Dr I. Paterson
ST PETER'S COLLEGE, St Peter's, S. Australia. *Head*,
Dr A. J. Shinkfield
SCOTCH COLLEGE, Adelaide, S. Australia. *Head*,
W. M. Miles
SCOTCH COLLEGE, Hawthorn, Melbourne, Victoria. *Head*,
Dr F. G. Donaldson
SCOTCH COLLEGE, Swanbourne, W. Australia. *Head*,
W. R. Dickinson
SCOTS COLLEGE, Sydney, NSW. *Head*, G. A. W. Renney
THE SOUTHPORT SCHOOL, Southport, Queensland. *Head*,
B. A. Cook
SYDNEY GRAMMAR SCHOOL, NSW. *Head*,
Dr R. D. Townsend
WESLEY COLLEGE, Melbourne. *Head*, D. G. McArthur

CANADA

BRENTWOOD COLLEGE SCHOOL, Vancouver, BC. *Head*,
W. T. Ross
GLENLYON-NORFOLK SCHOOL, Victoria, BC. *Head*,
D. Brooks
HILLFIELD-STRATHALLAN COLLEGE, Hamilton, Ontario.
*Head*, M. B. Wansbrough
PICKERING COLLEGE, Newmarket, Ontario. *Head*,
S. H. Clark
ST ANDREW'S COLLEGE, Aurora, Ontario. *Head*,
R. P. Bedard
TORONTO FRENCH SCHOOL. *Head*, A. S. Troubetzkoy
TRINITY COLLEGE SCHOOL, Port Hope, Ontario. *Head*,
R. C. N. Wright
UPPER CANADA COLLEGE, Toronto. *Head*, J. D. Blakey

HONG KONG

ISLAND SCHOOL, Borrett Road. *Head*, D. J. James
KING GEORGE V SCHOOL, Kowloon. *Head*,
M. J. Behennah

INDIA

LAWRENCE SCHOOL, Sanawar. *Head*, Sumer Singh
THE SCINDIA SCHOOL, GWALIOR. *Head*, Dr S. D. Singh

NEW ZEALAND

CHRIST'S COLLEGE, Christchurch, Canterbury. *Head*,
Dr M. J. Rosser
KING'S COLLEGE, Auckland. *Head*, J. S. Taylor
ST ANDREW'S COLLEGE, Christchurch, Canterbury. *Head*,
Dr A. J. Rentoul
THE COLLEGIATE SCHOOL, Wanganui. *Head*,
T. S. McKinley
WAITAKI BOYS' HIGH SCHOOL, Oamaru. *Head*,
B. R. Gollop

PHILIPPINES

BRENT SCHOOL, Baguio City. *Head*, P. Gysin

SOUTH AMERICA

ACADEMIA BRITANICA CUSCATLECA, El Salvador. *Head*,
A. J. McGuiggan
MARKHAM COLLEGE, Lima, Peru. *Head*, W. J. Baker
ST ANDREW'S SCOTS SCHOOL, Buenos Aires, Argentina.
*Head*, K. Prior
ST GEORGE'S COLLEGE, Quilmes, Argentina. *Head*,
N. P. O. Green
ST PAULS' SCHOOL, São Paulo, Brazil. *Head*,
M. T. M. C. McCann
THE BRITISH SCHOOLS, Montevideo, Uruguay. *Head*,
J. H. Sidwell

ADDITIONAL MEMBERS

The headteachers of some maintained schools are by
invitation Additional Members of the HMC. They include
the following:

DURHAM JOHNSTONE SCHOOL, Durham. *Head*,
J. Dunford
EGGBUCKLAND COMMUNITY COLLEGE, Plymouth. *Head*,
H. Green
HABERDASHERS' ASKE'S HATCHAM BOYS' SCHOOL,
Pepys Road, London SE14. *Head*, G. J. Walker
HAYWARDS HEATH SIXTH FORM COLLEGE, W. Sussex.
*Head*, B. W. Derbyshire
THE JUDD SCHOOL, Tonbridge, Kent. *Head*,
K. A. Starling
KING EDWARD VI CAMP HILL SCHOOL FOR BOYS,
Birmingham. *Head*, R. Dancey
LISKEARD SCHOOL, Cornwall. *Head*, A. D. Wood
THE LONDON ORATORY SCHOOL, London SW6. *Head*,
J. C. McIntosh
PRESCOT SCHOOL, Merseyside. *Head*, P. A. Barlow
PRINCE HENRY'S GRAMMAR SCHOOL, Otley, W Yorks.
*Head*, M. Franklin
PRINCE WILLIAM SCHOOL, Oundle, Cambs. *Head*,
C. J. Lowe
THE ROYAL GRAMMAR SCHOOL, Lancaster. *Head*,
P. J. Mawby
ST BARTHOLOMEW'S SCHOOL, Newbury, Bucks. *Head*,
R. P. H. Mermagen
ST JOHN'S SCHOOL, Marlborough, Wilts. *Head*, J. Price
WESTMINSTER CITY SCHOOL, London SW1. *Head*,
M. Billingham

## SOCIETY OF HEADMASTERS AND HEADMISTRESSES OF INDEPENDENT SCHOOLS

The Society was founded in 1961 and, in general, represents smaller boarding schools.

*Hon. Secretary*, A. E. R. Dodds, Mantons, Park Road, Winchester, Hants. SO23 7BE. Tel: 01962-862579

Headmasters of the following schools are members of both HMC and SHMIS; details of these schools appear in the HMC list: Abbotsholme School, Ackworth School, Bedales School, Churcher's College, City of London Freemen's School, Colston's Collegiate School, King's School, Tyne-mouth, Lord Wandsworth College, Pangbourne College, Reading Blue Coat School, Reed's School, Rendcomb College, Ryde School, St George's College, Silcoates School, Tettenhall College, West Buckland School, Wisbech Grammar School, Woodbridge School, Yarm School

\* Woodard Corporation School
† Girls in VI form
‡ Co-educational

| Name of School | Founded | No. of pupils | Annual fees £ | | Head (with date of appointment) |
|---|---|---|---|---|---|
| | | | Boarding | Day | |
| Austin Friars School (*RC*), Carlisle | 1951 | 296‡ | 7,245 | 4,149 | M. G. Taylor (1994) |
| Bearwood College, Berks. | 1827 | 218 | 9,750 | 5,400 | Dr R. J. Belcher (1993) |
| Bedstone College, Shropshire | 1948 | 170‡ | 9,180 | 5,931 | M. S. Symonds (1990) |
| Bembridge School, Isle of Wight | 1919 | 300‡ | 8,910 | 4,440 | J. High (1986) |
| Bentham School, N. Yorks | 1726 | 220‡ | 8,394 | 4,194 | N. K. D. Ward (1992) |
| Bethany School, Kent | 1866 | 270‡ | 9,078 | 5,808 | W. M. Harvey (1988) |
| Birkdale School, Sheffield | 1904 | 453† | — | 4,290 | Revd M. D. A. Hepworth (1983) |
| Box Hill School, Surrey | 1959 | 278‡ | 9,672 | 5,994 | Dr R. A. S. Atwood (1987) |
| Carmel College (*Jewish*), Oxon. | 1948 | 216‡ | 13,065 | 7,305 | P. D. Skelker (1984) |
| Claremont Fan Court School, Surrey | 1932 | 378‡ | 8,580 | 5,400 | Mrs P. B. Farrar (*Principal*) (1994) |
| Clayesmore School, Dorset | 1896 | 280‡ | 10,860 | 7,605 | D. J. Beeby (1986) |
| Cokethorpe School, Oxon. | 1957 | 195‡ | 11,490 | 7,560 | D. G. Crawford (1989) |
| Duke of York's Royal Military School, Dover | 1803 | 489 | 800 | — | Col. G. H. Wilson (1992) |
| Elmhurst Ballet School, Surrey | 1903 | 255‡ | 8,736 | 6,405 | J. McNamara (1994) |
| Embley Park School, Romsey, Hants. | 1946 | 225‡ | 9,460 | 5,790 | D. F. Chapman (1987) |
| Ewell Castle School, Surrey | 1926 | 320† | — | 4,215 | R. A. Fewtrell (1983) |
| Friends' School, Essex | 1702 | 250‡ | 9,582 | 5,946 | Miss S. H. Evans (1989) |
| Fulneck School (Boys), W. Yorks. | 1753 | 225‡ | 8,400 | 4,485 | I. D. Cleland (1980) |
| \*Grenville College, Devon | 1954 | 380 | 9,480 | 4,650 | M. C. V. Cane, PH.D. (1992) |
| Halliford School, Middx. | 1956 | 276† | — | 4,260 | J. R. Crook (1984) |
| Hipperholme Grammar School, Halifax | 1648 | 370‡ | — | 3,264 | C. C. Robinson (1988) |
| Keil School, Dumbarton | 1915 | 220‡ | 8,862 | 4,944 | J. A. Cummings (1993) |
| Kingham Hill School, Oxon. | 1886 | 210‡ | 9,069 | 5,442 | M. Payne (*Warden*) (1990) |
| King's School, Gloucester | 1541 | 350‡ | 8,700 | 5,100 | P. Lacey (1992) |
| Kirkham Grammar School, Lancs. | 1549 | 520‡ | 6,651 | 3,504 | B. Stacey (1991) |
| Langley School, Norfolk | 1910 | 266‡ | 9,435 | 4,965 | S. J. W. McArthur (1989) |
| Lord Mayor Treloar College, Hants. | 1908 | 242‡ | 34,351 | 25,764 | H. Heard (1990) |
| Milton Abbey School, Dorset | 1954 | 230 | 11,055 | 7,380 | R. H. Hardy (1987) |
| Oswestry School, Shropshire | 1407 | 283‡ | 8,664 | 5,115 | J. V. Light (1992) |
| The Purcell School (music), Middx. | 1962 | 157‡ | 13,980 | 8,265 | K. J. Bain (1984) |
| Rannoch School, Perthshire | 1959 | 270‡ | 10,020 | 5,490 | M. Barratt (1982) |
| Rishworth School, W. Yorks. | 1724 | 560‡ | 8,940 | 4,620 | M. J. Elford (1993) |
| Rougemont School, Gwent | 1919 | 250‡ | — | 4,305 | G. R. Sims (1991) |
| Royal Hospital School, Ipswich | 1712 | 600‡ | 7,350 | — | M. A. B. Kirk (1983) |
| Royal Russell School, Surrey | 1853 | 450‡ | 9,600 | 5,070 | R. D. Balaam (1981) |
| Royal School, Dungannon, N. Ireland | 1614 | 691‡ | 5,505 | 85 | P. D. Hewitt (1984) |
| Royal Wolverhampton School | 1850 | 300‡ | 8,700 | 4,980 | P. Gorring (1985) |
| Ruthin School, Clwyd | 1574 | 160‡ | 10,450 | 5,985 | J. S. Rowlands (1993) |
| St Bede's School, E. Sussex | 1979 | 390‡ | 10,950 | 6,750 | R. A. Perrin (1978) |
| St David's College, Gwynedd | 1965 | 240 | 8,928 | 5,805 | W. Seymour (1991) |
| Scarborough College, N. Yorks. | 1898 | 413‡ | 9,057 | 4,911 | D. S. Hempsall, PH.D. (1985) |
| Seaford College, W. Sussex | 1884 | 312† | 9,500 | 5,750 | R. C. Hannaford (1990) |
| Shebbear College, Devon | 1841 | 240‡ | 8,880 | 4,785 | R. J. Buley (1983) |
| Shiplake College, Oxon. | 1959 | 320 | 10,200 | 7,290 | N. V. Bevan (1988) |
| Sibford School, Oxon. | 1842 | 300‡ | 9,180 | 4,800 | J. Dunston (1990) |
| Sidcot School, Avon | 1808 | 370‡ | 9,282 | 5,550 | C. J. Greenfield (1986) |
| Stafford Grammar School, Staffs. | 1982 | 285‡ | — | 3,810 | M. James (1992) |
| Stanbridge Earls School, Hants. | 1952 | 193‡ | 11,310 | 8,490 | H. Moxon (1984) |
| Warminster School, Wilts. | 1707 | 332‡ | 8,700 | 5,085 | T. D. Holgate (1990) |

## GIRLS' SCHOOLS ASSOCIATION

THE GIRLS' SCHOOLS ASSOCIATION, 130 Regent Road, Leicester LEI 7PG. Tel: 0116-254 1619
*President* (1994–5), Mrs P. Penney
*Secretary*, Ms S. Cooper

CSC Church Schools Company, 1A Doughty Street, London WC1N 2PH. Tel: 0171-404 3134
§ Girls Public Day School Trust, 26 Queen Anne's Gate, London SW1H 9AN. Tel: 0171-222 9595
\* Woodard Corporation School
† Boys in VI form
‡ Co-educational
° 1993 figures

| Name of School | Founded | No. of pupils | Annual fees £ | | Head (with date of appointment) |
|---|---|---|---|---|---|
| | | | Boarding | Day | |
| ENGLAND AND WALES | | | | | |
| Abbey School, Reading | 1887 | 720 | — | 3,960 | Miss B. C. L. Sheldon (1991) |
| Abbot's Hill, Herts. | 1912 | 163 | 9,795 | 5,775 | Mrs J. Kingsley (1979) |
| Adcote School, Shropshire | 1907 | 109 | 8,925 | 4,950 | Mrs S. B. Cecchet (1979) |
| Alice Ottley School, Worcester | 1883 | 588 | — | 4,515 | Miss C. Sibbit (1986) |
| Amberfield School, Ipswich | 1952 | 266 | — | 3,630 | Mrs L. A. Lewis (1992) |
| Ashford School, Kent | 1910 | 397 | 8,997 | 5,202 | Mrs P. Metham (1992) |
| Atherley School, Southampton (*CSC*) | 1926 | 275 | — | 4,171 | Mrs C. Madinaveitia (1995) |
| Badminton School, Bristol | 1858 | 300 | 10,725 | 5,925 | C. J. T. Gould (1981) |
| §Bath High School | 1875 | 409 | — | 3,804 | Miss M. A. Winfield (1985) |
| Battle Abbey School, E. Sussex | 1912 | 120‡ | 8,820 | 5,460 | D. J. A. Teall (1982) |
| Bedford High School | 1882 | 780 | 8,589 | 4,500 | Miss M. L. Churm (1994) |
| Bedgebury School, Kent | 1860 | 335 | 10,299 | 6,375 | Mrs M. E. A. Kaye (1987) |
| Beechwood School (*RC*), Kent | 1915 | 178 | 10,290 | 6,150 | T. Hodkinson (1994) |
| §Belvedere School, Liverpool | 1880 | 474 | — | 3,804 | Mrs C. H. Evans (1992) |
| Benenden School, Kent | 1923 | 435 | 12,150 | — | Mrs G. D. duCharme (1985) |
| Berkhamsted School, Herts. | 1888 | 352 | 10,680 | 6,390 | Miss V. E. M. Shepherd (1980) |
| §Birkenhead High School | 1901 | 709 | — | 3,804 | Mrs K. R. Irving (1986) |
| §Blackheath High School, London SE3 | 1880 | 356 | — | 4,428 | Miss R. K. Musgrave (1989) |
| Bolton School, Lancs. | 1877 | 800 | — | 4,398 | Miss E. J. Panton (1993) |
| Bradford Girls' Grammar School | 1875 | 650 | — | 3,852 | Mrs L. J. Warrington (1986) |
| §Brighton and Hove High School | 1876 | 522 | — | 3,804 | Miss R. A. Woodbridge (1989) |
| Brigidine School, Windsor | 1948 | 260 | — | 4,212 | Mrs M. B. Cairns (1986) |
| §Bromley High School, Kent | 1883 | 570 | — | 4,428 | Mrs E. J. Hancock (1989) |
| Bruton School, Somerset | 1900 | 560 | 6,540 | 3,543 | Mrs J. M. Wade (1987) |
| Burgess Hill School, W. Sussex | 1906 | 370 | 8,775 | 5,220 | Mrs R. F. Lewis (1993) |
| Bury Grammar School, Lancs. | 1884 | 814 | — | 3,534 | Miss J. M. Lawley (1987) |
| Casterton School, Cumbria | 1823 | 345 | 8,682 | 5,442 | A. F. Thomas (1990) |
| §Central Newcastle High School | 1895 | 594 | — | 3,804 | Mrs A. M. Chapman (1985) |
| Channing School, London N6 | 1885 | 320 | — | 5,445 | Mrs I. R. Raphael (1984) |
| §Charters-Ancaster School, E. Sussex | 1906 | 178 | 8,832 | 4,692 | Mrs K. Lewis (1990) |
| Cheltenham Ladies' College, Glos. | 1853 | 840 | 11,805 | 7,500 | Miss E. Castle (*Principal*) (1987) |
| City of London School for Girls, London EC2 | 1894 | 545 | — | 4,726 | Lady France, OBE (1986) |
| Clifton High School, Bristol | 1877 | 463 | 8,655 | 4,575 | Mrs J. D. Walters (1985) |
| Cobham Hall, Kent | 1962 | 175 | 12,300 | 8,250 | Mrs R. J. McCarthy (1989) |
| Colston's Girls' School, Bristol | 1891 | 500 | — | 3,402 | Mrs J. P. Franklin (1989) |
| Combe Bank School, Kent | 1868 | 230 | — | 5,190 | Miss N. Spurr (1993) |
| Commonweal Lodge School, Surrey | 1916 | 150 | — | 4,350 | Miss J. M. Brown (1982) |
| Cranford House School, Oxon. | 1931 | 80 | — | 4,350 | Mrs A. B. Gray (1992) |
| Croft House School, Dorset | 1941 | 120 | 9,360 | 6,600 | M. P. Hawkins (1993) |
| Croham Hurst School, Surrey | 1899 | 340 | — | 4,245 | Miss S. C. Budgen (1994) |
| §Croydon High School, Surrey | 1874 | 700 | — | 4,428 | Mrs P. E. Davies (1990) |
| Dame Alice Harpur School, Bedford | 1882 | 753 | — | 4,017 | Mrs R. Randle (1990) |
| Dame Allan's Girls' School, Newcastle upon Tyne | 1705 | 400† | — | 3,432 | T. A. Willcocks (*Principal*) (1988) |
| Derby High School | 1892 | 312 | — | 4,170 | Dr G. H. Goddard (1983) |
| Downe House, Berks. | 1907 | 560 | 11,835 | 8,880 | Miss S. Cameron (1989) |

| Name of School | Founded | No. of pupils | Annual fees £ | | Head (with date of appointment) |
|---|---|---|---|---|---|
| | | | Boarding | Day | |
| Dunottar School, Surrey | 1926 | 300 | — | 4,275 | Miss J. Burnell (1986) |
| Durham High School | 1884 | 425 | — | 4,170 | M. L. Walters (1992) |
| Edgbaston Church of England College | 1886 | 350 | — | 4,185 | Mrs A. Varley-Tipton (1992) |
| Edgbaston High School | 1876 | 510 | — | 4,095 | Mrs S. J. Horsman (1987) |
| Edgehill College, Devon | 1884 | 380 | 8,940 | 4,875 | Mrs E. M. Burton (1987) |
| Elmslie Girls' School, Lancs. | 1918 | 350 | — | 3,705 | Miss E. M. Smithies (1978) |
| Farlington School, W. Sussex | 1896 | 235 | 8,910 | 5,550 | Mrs P. Mawer (1992) |
| Farnborough Hill, Hants. | 1889 | 530 | — | 4,026 | Sr E. McCormack (1988) |
| Farringtons and Stratford House, Kent | 1911 | 300 | 8,631 | 4,725 | Mrs B. J. Stock (1987) |
| Felixstowe College, Suffolk | 1929 | 200 | 10,551 | 6,576 | Mrs B. Patterson (1993) |
| Fernhill Manor School, Hants. | 1890 | 120 | 7,800 | 4,965 | Revd A. J. Folks (1985) |
| Francis Holland School, London NW1 | 1878 | 365 | — | 4,950 | Mrs P. H. Parsonson (1988) |
| Francis Holland School, London SW1 | 1881 | 175 | — | 5,475 | Mrs J. A. Anderson (1982) |
| Gateways School, Leeds | 1941 | 286 | — | 3,369 | Mrs S. A. Fatkin (*acting*) |
| Godolphin School, Wilts. | 1726 | 371 | 10,266 | 6,150 | Mrs H. Fender (1990) |
| Godolphin and Latymer School, London W6 | 1905 | 700 | — | 5,385 | Miss M. Rudland (1986) |
| Greenacre School, Surrey | 1933 | 209 | — | 4,770 | Mrs P. M. Wood (1990) |
| The Grove School, Hindhead, Surrey | 1877 | 170 | 9,219 | 5,769 | C. Brooks (1984) |
| Guildford High School (*CSC*) | 1888 | 465 | — | 4,821 | Mrs S. H. Singer (1991) |
| Haberdashers' Aske's School for Girls, Herts. | 1873 | 847 | — | 3,915 | Mrs P. Penney (1991) |
| Haberdashers' Monmouth School, Gwent | 1891 | 545 | 7,896 | 4,350 | Mrs D. L. Newman (1992) |
| Harrogate Ladies' College | 1893 | 370 | 8,655 | 5,820 | Mrs J. A. Smith (1993) |
| Headington School, Oxford | 1915 | 554 | 8,607 | 4,311 | Miss E. M. Tucker (1982) |
| Heathfield School, Ascot, Berks. | 1900 | 215 | 11,925 | — | Mrs J. Benammar (1992) |
| §Heathfield School, Pinner, Middx. | 1900 | 311 | — | 4,428 | Mrs J. Merritt (1988) |
| Hethersett Old Hall School, Norwich | 1928 | 199 | 8,100 | 4,140 | Mrs V. M. Redington (1983) |
| Highclare School, W. Midlands | 1932 | 302† | — | 3,465 | Mrs C. A. Hanson (1973) |
| Hollygirt School, Nottingham | 1877 | 220 | — | 3,330 | Mrs M. R. Banks (1985) |
| Holy Child School, Birmingham | 1933 | 171 | — | 4,290 | Mrs J. Hill (1993) |
| Holy Trinity College, Bromley | 1886 | 310 | — | 3,999 | Mrs D. Bradshaw (1994) |
| Holy Trinity School, Kidderminster | 1903 | 200 | — | 3,240 | Mrs S. M. Bell (1990) |
| Howell's School, Denbigh, Clwyd | 1859 | 212 | 11,451 | 6,249 | Mrs M. Steel (1991) |
| §Howell's School, Llandaff, Cardiff | 1860 | 558 | — | 3,804 | Mrs C. J. Fitz (1991) |
| Hull High School (*CSC*) | 1890 | 242 | 6,045 | 3,795 | Mrs M. A. Benson (1994) |
| Hulme Grammar School, Oldham | 1895 | 520 | — | 3,426 | Miss M. S. Smolenski (1992) |
| §Ipswich High School | 1878 | 430 | — | 3,804 | Miss V. MacCuish (1993) |
| James Allen's Girls' School, London SE22 | 1741 | 750 | °6,732 | 5,505 | Mrs M. Gibbs (1994) |
| Kent College | 1885 | 233‡ | 10,080 | 6,030 | Miss B. Crompton (1990) |
| King Edward VI High School for Girls, Birmingham | 1883 | 545 | — | 4,020 | Miss E. W. Evans (1977) |
| King's HS for Girls, Warwick | 1879 | 550 | — | 3,888 | Mrs J. M. Anderson (1987) |
| Kingsley School, Warwicks. | 1884 | 451 | — | 4,050 | Mrs M. A. Webster (1988) |
| Lady Eleanor Holles School, Middx. | 1711 | 646 | — | 4,755 | Miss E. M. Candy (1981) |
| La Retraite Leehurst School, Wilts. | 1953 | °200 | — | °3,840 | Mrs M. Paisey (1986) |
| La Sagesse Convent High School, Newcastle upon Tyne | 1906 | 350 | — | 3,540 | Miss L. Clark (1994) |
| La Sagesse Convent School, Hants. | 1896 | 105 | — | 2,976 | Sr Thomas Cox (1977) |
| Lavant House School, W. Sussex | 1952 | 120 | 9,525 | 5,820 | Mrs Y. Graham (1990) |
| Leeds Girls' High School | 1876 | °615 | — | °3,954 | Miss P. A. Randall (1977) |
| Leicester High School | 1906 | 300 | — | 4,050 | Mrs P. A. Watson (1992) |
| Loughborough High School | 1850 | 540 | — | 3,807 | Miss J. E. L. Harvatt (1978) |
| Luckley-Oakfield School, Berks. | 1895 | 290 | 7,740 | 4,800 | R. C. Blake (1984) |
| Malvern Girls' College, Worcs. | 1893 | 475 | 11,025 | 7,350 | Dr A. Lee (1994) |
| Manchester High School | 1874 | 715 | — | 3,735 | Miss E. M. Diggory (1994) |
| Manor House School, Little Bookham, Surrey | 1927 | 200 | 7,569 | 5,184 | Mrs L. Mendes (1989) |
| Maynard School, Exeter | 1877 | 490 | — | 3,900 | Miss F. Murdin (1980) |
| Merchant Taylors' School, Liverpool | 1888 | 650 | — | 3,600 | Mrs J. Mills (1994) |
| Micklefield Wadhurst School, E. Sussex | 1910 | 200 | 9,855 | 6,270 | Miss A. M. Phillips (1994) E. Reynolds (1994) |
| Moira House School, E. Sussex | 1875 | 279 | 10,305 | 6,651 | A. R. Underwood (1975) |
| More House School, London SW1 | 1953 | 230 | — | 5,205 | Miss M. Connell (1991) |
| Moreton Hall, Shropshire | 1913 | 280 | 10,428 | 7,230 | J. Forster (1992) |
| Mount School, York | 1831 | 240 | 9,720 | 6,135 | Miss B. J. Windle (1986) |

| Name of School | Foun-ded | No. of pupils | Annual fees £ | | Head (with date of appointment) |
|---|---|---|---|---|---|
| | | | Boarding | Day | |
| Newcastle upon Tyne Church HS | 1885 | 393 | — | 3,465 | Miss P. E. Davies (1974) |
| New Hall School, Essex | 1642 | 430 | 10,110 | 6,474 | Sr Margaret Mary Horton (1986) |
| Northampton High School | 1878 | 535 | — | 3,960 | Mrs L. A. Mayne (1988) |
| North Foreland Lodge, Hants. | 1909 | 180 | 10,275 | — | Miss D. L. Matthews (1983) |
| North London Collegiate School | 1850 | 740 | — | 4,611 | Mrs J. L. Clanchy (1986) |
| Northwood College, Middx. | 1878 | 548 | — | 4,584 | Mrs J. A. Mayou (1991) |
| §Norwich High School | 1875 | 666 | — | 3,804 | Mrs V. C. Bidwell (1985) |
| §Nottingham High School | 1875 | 822 | — | 3,804 | Mrs C. Bowering (1984) |
| §Notting Hill and Ealing High School | 1873 | 555 | — | 4,428 | Mrs S. M. Whitfield (1991) |
| Ockbrook School, Derby | 1799 | 203 | 6,576 | 3,546 | Ms M. Rennie, PH.D. (1987) |
| Old Palace School, Surrey | 1887 | 600 | — | 3,717 | Miss K. L. Hilton (1974) |
| §Oxford High School | 1875 | 560 | — | 3,804 | Mrs J. Townsend (1981) |
| Palmers Green High School, London N21 | 1905 | 140 | — | 3,885 | Mrs S. Grant (1989) |
| Parsons Mead, Surrey | 1897 | 440 | 10,461 | 4,785 | Miss E. B. Plant (1990) |
| Penrhos College, Clwyd | 1880 | 220 | 8,970 | 6,150 | C. M. J. Allen (1993) |
| Perse School for Girls, Cambridge | 1881 | 540 | — | 4,275 | Mrs H. S. Smith (1989) |
| *Peterborough High School | 1939 | 193 | 7,863 | 3,915 | Mrs A. Storey (1977) |
| Pipers Corner School, Bucks. | 1930 | 360 | 8,877 | 5,304 | Dr M. M. Wilson (1986) |
| Polam Hall, Co. Durham | 1848 | 325 | 8,469 | 4,143 | Mrs H. C. Hamilton (1987) |
| §Portsmouth High School | 1882 | 539 | — | 3,804 | Mrs J. M. Dawtrey (1984) |
| Princess Helena College, Herts. | 1820 | 152 | 9,690 | 6,750 | Miss H. Davidson-Wall (1990) |
| Prior's Field, Surrey | 1902 | 220 | 9,435 | 6,270 | Mrs J. M. McCallum (1987) |
| §Putney High School, London SW15 | 1893 | 575 | — | 4,428 | Mrs E. Merchant (1991) |
| Queen Anne's School, Berks. | 1698 | 345 | 10,650 | 6,900 | Mrs D. Forbes (1993) |
| Queen Ethelburga's College, York | 1912 | 200 | 9,585 | 6,075 | Mrs G. L. Richardson (1993) |
| Queen Margaret's School, York | 1901 | 360 | 9,825 | 6,225 | Dr G. A. H. Chapman (1993) |
| Queen Mary School, Lytham, Lancs. | 1930 | 575 | — | 3,513 | Miss M. C. Ritchie (1981) |
| Queen's College, London W1 | 1848 | 370 | — | 5,565 | Lady Goodhart (1991) |
| Queen's Gate School, London SW7 | 1891 | 220 | — | 5,160 | Mrs A. M. Holyoak (Principal) (1988) |
| Queen's School, Chester | 1878 | 430 | — | 4,050 | Miss D. M. Skilbeck (1989) |
| Queenswood, Herts. | 1894 | 406 | 11,001 | 6,510 | Mrs A. M. B. Butler (1981) |
| Redland High School, Bristol | 1882 | 480 | — | 3,777 | Mrs C. Lear (1989) |
| Red Maids' School, Bristol | 1634 | 500 | 7,212 | 3,636 | Miss S. Hampton (1987) |
| Rickmansworth Masonic School, Herts. | 1788 | 520 | 7,133 | 4,941 | Mrs I. M. Andrews (1992) |
| Roedean School, Brighton | 1885 | 440 | 12,405 | — | Mrs A. R. Longley (1984) |
| Rosemead, W. Sussex | 1919 | 185 | 9,345 | 5,370 | Mrs H. Kingham (Principal) (1991) |
| Royal Naval School, Surrey | 1840 | 250 | 9,222 | 5,823 | Dr J. L. Clough (1987) |
| Royal School, Bath | 1864 | 300 | 10,680 | 6,813 | Mrs E. McKendrick (1994) |
| Runton and Sutherland School, Norfolk | 1875 | 102 | 9,300 | 5,670 | Mrs D. J. Buckenham (1993) |
| Rye St Antony School (RC), Oxford | 1930 | 330 | 7,950 | 4,875 | Miss A. M. Jones (1990) |
| St Albans High School, Herts. | 1889 | 680 | — | 4,506 | Mrs C. Y. Daly (1994) |
| St Andrew's School, Bedford | 1897 | 151 | — | 3,315 | Mrs J. E. Stephen (1991) |
| St Anne's School, Cumbria | 1863 | 240 | 8,859 | 5,874 | C. M. G. Jenkins (1993) |
| St Antony's-Leweston School (RC), Dorset | 1891 | 288 | 9,831 | 6,411 | Miss C. Denley Lloyd (1993) |
| St Catherine's School, Surrey | 1885 | 440 | 8,929 | 5,445 | Mrs C. Oulton (1994) |
| *School of St Clare, Penzance | 1889 | 95 | 7,965 | 4,206 | I. Halford (1986) |
| St David's School, Middx. | 1716 | 242† | 8,595 | 4,950 | Mrs J. G. Osborne (1985) |
| St Dunstan's Abbey, Devon | 1850 | 200 | 6,750 | 4,290 | R. A. Bye (1991) |
| St Elphin's School, Derbys. | 1844 | 178 | 9,384 | 5,466 | Mrs V. E. Fisher (1994) |
| St Felix School, Suffolk | 1897 | 260 | 9,885 | 6,345 | Mrs S. R. Campion (1991) |
| St Francis' College (RC), Herts. | 1933 | 199 | 9,210 | 4,725 | Miss M. Hegarty (1993) |
| St Gabriel's School, Berks. | 1929 | 166 | — | 4,827 | D. Cobb (1990) |
| St George's School, Ascot, Berks. | 1923 | 286 | 11,325 | 6,525 | Mrs A. M. Griggs (1989) |
| School of S. Helen and S. Katharine, Oxon. | 1903 | 520 | 7,680 | 4,155 | Mrs C. L. Hall (1993) |
| St Helen's School, Middx. | 1899 | 575 | 8,565 | 4,545 | Mrs Y.A. Burne, PH.D. (1987) |
| *S. Hilary's School, Cheshire | 1880 | 133 | — | 3,885 | Mrs J. Tracey (1985) |
| St James's and the Abbey, Worcs. | 1896 | 190 | 10,476 | 6,984 | Miss E. M. Mullenger (1986) |
| St Joseph's Convent School (RC), Berks. | 1909 | 420 | — | 3,615 | Mrs V. Brookes (1990) |
| St Joseph's School, Lincoln | 1905 | 236 | 7,665 | 3,885 | Mrs M. Bradley (1994) |
| St Leonards-Mayfield School, E. Sussex | 1850 | 525 | 9,738 | 6,490 | Sr J. Sinclair (1980) |

| Name of School | Founded | No. of pupils | Annual fees £ | | Head (with date of appointment) |
|---|---|---|---|---|---|
| | | | Boarding | Day | |
| St Margaret's School, Bushey, Herts. | 1749 | 430 | 8,040 | 5,085 | Miss M. de Villiers (1992) |
| *St Margaret's School, Exeter | 1904 | 440 | 6,240 | 3,810 | Mrs M. D'Albertanson (1993) |
| St Martin's School, Solihull, W. Midlands | 1941 | 260 | — | 4,230 | Mrs S. J. Williams (1989) |
| *School of S. Mary and S. Anne, Abbots Bromley, Staffs. | 1874 | 280 | 10,245 | 6,828 | A. Grigg (1989) |
| St Mary's Convent School, Worcester | 1934 | 400 | — | 3,315 | Miss G. Morrissey (1995) |
| St Mary's Hall, Brighton | 1836 | 250 | 8,730 | 5,784 | Mrs P. J. James (1992) |
| St Mary's School (RC), Ascot, Berks. | 1885 | 340 | 10,995 | 6,597 | Sr M. M. Orchard (1982) |
| St Mary's School, Calne, Wilts. | 1872 | 315 | 10,950 | 6,495 | Miss D. H. Burns (1985) |
| St Mary's School, Cambridge | 1898 | 590 | 6,489 | 3,622 | Miss M. Conway (1989) |
| St Mary's School, Colchester | 1908 | 245 | — | 3,504 | Mrs G. M. G. Mouser (1981) |
| St Mary's School, Gerrards Cross | 1872 | 210 | — | 4,845 | Mrs J. P. G. Smith (1984) |
| St Mary's School (RC), Shaftesbury | 1945 | 300 | 9,300 | 5,940 | Sr M. Campion Livesey (1985) |
| St Mary's School, Wantage, Oxon. | 1873 | 257 | 10,350 | — | Mrs S. Bodinham (1994) |
| St Maur's Convent School, Weybridge | 1898 | 400 | — | 4,725 | Mrs M. E. Dodds (1991) |
| St Michael's, Limpsfield, Surrey | 1850 | 109 | 10,005 | 5,850 | Ms M. J. Hustler, ph.d. (1989) |
| St Paul's Girls' School, London w6 | 1904 | 611 | — | 6,012 | Miss J. Gough (High Mistress) (1992) |
| St Swithun's School, Winchester | 1884 | 445 | 10,695 | 6,495 | Miss J. E. Jefferson (1986) |
| St Teresa's School, Dorking | 1928 | 360 | 10,335 | 4,785 | L. Allan (1987) |
| Selwyn School, Glos. | — | 170 | 8,430 | 4,800 | Miss L. M. Brown (1994) |
| §Sheffield High School | 1878 | 537 | — | 4,428 | Mrs M. A. Houston (1989) |
| Sherborne School for Girls, Dorset | 1899 | 468 | 10,800 | 7,200 | Miss J. M. Taylor (1985) |
| §Shrewsbury High School | 1885 | 423 | — | 3,804 | Miss S. Gardner (1990) |
| Sir William Perkins's School, Surrey | 1725 | 590 | — | 3,750 | Miss S. Ross (1994) |
| §South Hampstead High School, London NW3 | 1876 | 616 | — | 4,428 | Mrs J. G. Scott (1993) |
| Stamford High School, Lincs. | 1876 | 713 | 7,824 | 3,912 | Miss G. K. Bland (1978) |
| Stonar School, Wilts. | 1921 | 500 | 9,180 | 5,085 | Mrs S. Hopkinson (1985) |
| Stover School, Devon | 1932 | 203 | 7,920 | 4,158 | Mrs W. E. Lunel (1984) |
| Stratford House School, Kent | 1912 | °230 | — | °4,260 | Mrs A. A. Williamson (1974) |
| §Streatham Hill and Clapham High School, London sw2 | 1887 | 409 | — | 4,428 | Miss G. M. Ellis (1979) |
| Sunderland High School (CSC) | 1884 | 230‡ | — | 3,750 | Miss C. Rendle-Short (1993) |
| Surbiton High School (CSC), Surrey | 1884 | °510 | — | °4,428 | Miss G. Perry (1993) |
| §Sutton High School, Surrey | 1884 | 537 | — | 4,428 | Miss A. E. Cavendish (1980) |
| §Sydenham High School, London SE26 | 1887 | 481 | — | 4,428 | Mrs G. Baker (1988) |
| Talbot Heath, Dorset | 1886 | 500 | 8,268 | 4,713 | Mrs C. Dipple (1991) |
| Teesside High School, Cleveland | 1970 | 399 | — | 3,501 | Mrs J. Coles (1982) |
| Tormead School, Surrey | 1905 | 590 | — | 4,860 | Mrs H. E. M. Alleyne (1992) |
| Truro High School | 1880 | 308 | 7,695 | 4,215 | J. Graham-Brown (1992) |
| Tudor Hall School, Oxon. | 1850 | 260 | 9,795 | 6,105 | Miss N. Godfrey (1984) |
| Ursuline Convent School, Kent | 1904 | 300 | 10,158 | 5,148 | Sr M. Murphy (1977) |
| Ursuline High School, Ilford | 1903 | 400 | — | 4,122 | Miss J. Reddington (1990) |
| Wakefield Girls' High School | 1878 | 762 | — | 3,945 | Mrs P. A. Langham (1987) |
| Walthamstow Hall, Kent | 1838 | 350 | 10,275 | 5,535 | Mrs J. S. Lang (1983) |
| Wentworth Milton Mount, Dorset | 1871 | 260 | 8,385 | 5,241 | Miss S. Coe (1991) |
| Westfield School, Newcastle upon Tyne | 1962 | 212 | — | 3,942 | Mrs M. Farndale (1990) |
| West Heath, Kent | 1867 | 96 | 10,710 | 7,530 | Mrs A. Williamson (1994) |
| Westholme School, Lancs. | 1923 | 650 | — | 3,345 | Mrs L. Croston (Principal) (1988) |
| Westonbirt, Glos. | 1928 | 252 | 10,374 | 6,678 | Mrs G. Hylson-Smith (1986) |
| §Wimbledon High School, London sw19 | 1880 | 545 | — | 4,428 | Mrs E. M. Baker (1992) |
| Wispers School, Surrey | 1946 | 130 | 8,820 | 5,685 | L. H. Beltran (1979) |
| Withington Girls' School, Manchester | 1890 | 490 | — | 3,585 | Mrs M. Kenyon (1986) |
| Woldingham School, Surrey | 1842 | 500 | 10,914 | 6,609 | Ms P. Dineen, ph.d. (1985) |
| Wroxall Abbey School, Warwick | 1872 | °100 | °9,075 | °5,325 | Mrs J. M. Gowen (1993) |
| Wychwood School, Oxford | 1897 | 160 | 6,630 | 4,185 | Mrs M. L. Duffill (1981) |
| Wycombe Abbey School, Bucks. | 1896 | 485 | 11,880 | 8,910 | Mrs J. M. Goodland (1989) |

| Name of School | Foun-ded | No. of pupils | Annual fees £ | | Head (with date of appointment) |
|---|---|---|---|---|---|
| | | | Boarding | Day | |
| Wykeham House School, Fareham, Hants. | 1913 | °250 | — | °3,546 | Mrs E. M. Moore (1983) |
| York College for Girls (*CSC*) | 1908 | 175 | — | 4,884 | Mrs J. L. Clare (1982) |
| SCOTLAND | | | | | |
| Kilgraston School, Perthshire | 1930 | 270 | 9,180 | 5,100 | Mrs J. L. Austin (1993) |
| Laurel Bank School, Glasgow | 1903 | 250 | — | 4,032 | Miss L. G. Egginton (1984) |
| Mary Erskine School, Edinburgh | 1694 | 650 | 7,782 | 3,978 | P. F. J. Tobin (*Principal*) (1989) |
| Park School, Glasgow | 1880 | 250 | — | 3,780 | Mrs M. E. Myatt (1986) |
| St Denis and Cranley School, Edinburgh | 1858 | 150 | 8,940 | 4,410 | Mrs J. M. Munro (1984) |
| St George's School, Edinburgh | 1888 | 550 | 8,247 | 4,272 | Dr J. McClure (1994) |
| St Leonards School, St Andrews | 1877 | 270 | 11,421 | 6,018 | Mrs L. E. James (1988) |
| St Margaret's School, Aberdeen | 1846 | 227 | — | 3,528 | Miss L. M. Ogilvie (1989) |
| St Margaret's School, Edinburgh | 1890 | 369 | 8,010 | 3,960 | Miss A. Mitchell (1994) |
| Wellington School for Girls, Ayr | 1849 | 250 | 8,910 | 4,470 | Mrs D. A. Gardner (1988) |
| CHANNEL ISLANDS | | | | | |
| The Ladies' College, Guernsey | 1872 | 334 | — | 1,950 | Miss M. Macdonald (1993) |

# Social Welfare

## National Health Service

*and Local Authority Personal Social Services*

The National Health Service came into being on 5 July 1948 as a result of the National Health Service Act 1946, covering England and Wales, and separate legislation for Scotland and Northern Ireland. The Acts placed a duty on the relevant Secretaries of State to promote the establishment of a comprehensive health service designed to secure improvement in the mental and physical health of the people and the prevention, diagnosis and treatment of illness. The National Health Service is administered in England by the Secretary of State for Health, and in Wales, Scotland and Northern Ireland by the Secretaries of State for Wales, Scotland and Northern Ireland.

The National Health Service covers a comprehensive range of hospital, specialist, family practitioner (medical, dental, ophthalmic and pharmaceutical), artificial limb and appliance, ambulance, and community health services. Everyone normally resident in the UK is entitled to use any of these services, there are no contribution conditions and the charges made (except those for amenity beds) are reduced or waived in cases of hardship.

In addition, the Secretary of State for Health is responsible under the Local Authority Social Services Act 1970 for the provision by local authorities of social services for the elderly, the disabled, those with mental disorders and for families and children.

The NHS is financed mainly from taxation and the cost met from moneys voted by Parliament. The present level of expenditure is £39 billion per annum.

### STRUCTURE

The National Health Service and Community Care Act 1990 introduced wide-ranging reforms in management and patient care. The Act provides for more streamlined Regional and District Health Authorities and Family Health Services Authorities, and for the establishment of NHS Trusts, which operate as self-governing health care providers. One result of the Act is that health care is provided through NHS contracts, where one body (the purchaser) is responsible for obtaining the appropriate health care for its population from another body (the provider). From 1 April 1993, the Community Care Reforms introduced major changes in the way care is administered for the elderly, the mentally ill, the physically handicapped and people with learning disabilities.

From 1 April 1994 the Regional Health Authorities (RHAs) in England were reduced from 14 to eight in preparation for their abolition, subject to parliamentary consent. They are to be replaced by eight NHS Executive regional offices. They are responsible for regional planning, the allocation of resources to District Health Authorities, Family Health Services Authorities and general practitioner fundholders, and the promotion of national policies and priorities. They are directly accountable to the Secretary of State for Health and provide the link between the DHAs and FHSAs, and the NHS Management Executive. Legislation is also planned to allow DHAs and FHSAs to merge.

The 145 District Health Authorities (DHAs) are responsible for purchasing health care for the people who live within their areas, and for the operational management of health services and planning within regional and national strategic guidelines. DHAs' resources are allocated by RHAs, to which they are also accountable for their performance. As a result of the reforms, some DHAs have merged to form larger bodies, allowing them to increase their purchasing power and make better use of resources.

---

## HEALTH SERVICES

---

### FAMILY DOCTOR SERVICE

In England and Wales the Family Doctor Service (or General Medical Services) is managed by 98 Family Health Services Authorities (FHSAs) which also organize the general dental, pharmaceutical and ophthalmic services for their areas. There is a Family Health Services Authority for one or more DHAs. In England the chairman is appointed by the Secretary of State and the non-executive members by the RHA. In Wales the chairman and non-executive members are appointed by the Secretary of State. There are nine non-executive members: a general medical practitioner, a general dental practitioner, a community pharmacist, a nurse, and five lay members.

Any doctor may take part in the Family Doctor Service (provided the area in which he/she wishes to practise has not already an adequate number of doctors) and about 28,000 general practitioners in England and Wales do so. They may at the same time have private fee-paying patients. Family doctors are paid for their NHS work in accordance with a scheme of remuneration which includes a basic practice allowance, capitation fees, reimbursement of certain practice expenses and payments for out-of-hours work.

The National Health Service and Community Care Act 1990 enables general practitioner practices with at least 7,000 patients to apply for fundholding status (a number of smaller practices form units in order to achieve fundholding status). This makes the practice responsible for its own NHS budget for a specified range of goods and services. There are currently 1,673 fundholding units, comprising 2,040 practices. Fundholding practices are monitored by the FHSAs on behalf of the RHAs.

Everyone aged 16 or over can choose their doctor (parents or guardians choose for children under 16) and the doctor is also free to accept a person or not as he or she chooses. A person may change their doctor if they wish, by going to the surgery of a general practioner of their choice who is willing to accept them, and either handing in their medical card to register or filling in a form. When people are away from home they can still use the Family Doctor Service if they ask to be treated as temporary residents, and in an emergency, if a person's own doctor is not available, any doctor in the service will give treatment and advice.

Patients are treated either in the doctor's surgery or, when necessary, at home. Doctors may prescribe for their patients all drugs and medicines which are medically necessary for their treatment and also a certain number of surgical appliances (the more elaborate being provided through hospitals).

### DENTAL SERVICE

Dentists, like doctors, may take part in the NHS and also have private patients. About 16,000 of the dentists available for general practice in England provide NHS general dental services. They are responsible to the FHSAs in whose areas they provide services.

Patients are free to go to any dentist who is taking part in the NHS and willing to accept them. Dentists are paid a capitation fee for patients registered with them who are under 18 years of age. They receive payment for items of treatment for individual adult patients and, in addition, a continuing care payment for those registered with them.

Patients are asked to pay 80 per cent of the cost of NHS dental treatment. The maximum charge for a course of treatment is £275. There is no charge for arrest of bleeding, repairs to dentures, home visits by the dentist or re-opening a surgery in an emergency (in these two cases, payment will be for treatment given in the normal way). The following are exempt from dental charges/have charges remitted:

(i)    young people under 18
(ii)   full-time students under 19
(iii)  expectant mothers who were pregnant when accepted for treatment
(iv)   women who have had a child in the previous 12 months
(v)    people who receive Income Support or Family Credit and their dependants

Leaflet AB11 available from post offices and leaflet D11 available from local social security offices explain how other people on a low income can, depending on their financial circumstances, get free treatment or help with charges.

PHARMACEUTICAL SERVICE

Patients may obtain medicines, appliances and oral contraceptives prescribed under the NHS from any pharmacy whose owner has entered into arrangements with the FHSA to provide this service. Almost all pharmacy owners have done so and display notices that they dispense under the NHS; the number of these pharmacies in England and Wales at the end of 1990 was about 10,400. There are also some appliance suppliers who only provide special appliances. In country areas where access to a pharmacy may be difficult, patients may be able to obtain medicines, etc., from their doctor.

Except for contraceptives (for which there is no charge), a charge of £4.75 is payable for each item supplied unless the patient is exempt and the declaration on the back of the prescription form is completed. Exemptions cover:

(i)    children under 16
(ii)   full-time students under 19
(iii)  men aged 65 and over
(iv)   women aged 60 and over
(v)    pregnant women
(vi)   mothers who have had a baby within the last 12 months
(vii)  people suffering from certain medical conditions
(viii) people who receive Income Support or Family Credit and their dependants
(ix)   people who hold an AG2 certificate issued by the Health Benefits Unit, and their dependants
(x)    war pensioners (for their accepted disablements)

Prepayment certificates (£24.60 valid for four months, £67.70 valid for a year) may be purchased by those patients not entitled to exemption who require frequent prescriptions. Further information about the exemption and prepayment arrangements is given in leaflet P11.

GENERAL OPHTHALMIC SERVICES

General Ophthalmic Services, which are administered by Family Practitioner Committees, form part of the ophthalmic services available under the NHS. The NHS sight test is available free to:

(i)    children under 16
(ii)   full-time students under the age of 19
(iii)  people in receipt of Income Support and Family Credit, and their partners
(iv)   people prescribed complex lenses
(v)    the registered blind and partially sighted
(vi)   diagnosed diabetic and glaucoma patients
(vii)  close relatives aged 40 or over of diagnosed glaucoma patients

Those on a low income may qualify for help with the cost.

Certain groups are automatically entitled to help with the purchase of glasses under an NHS voucher scheme:

(i)    children under 16
(ii)   full-time students under 19
(iii)  people in receipt of Income Support or Family Credit, and their partners
(iv)   people wearing certain complex lenses
(v)    people whose spectacles are lost or damaged as a result of their disability, injury or illness

The value of the voucher depends on the lenses required. Vouchers may be used to help pay for the glasses or contact lenses of the patient's choice. People with a low income may claim help on form AG1. Glasses or contact lenses should not be purchased until the result of a claim is known as no refunds can be given. Booklet G11 gives further details.

Diagnosis and specialist treatment of eye conditions is available through the Hospital Eye Service as well as the provision of glasses of a special type.

Testing of sight may be carried out by any ophthalmic medical practitioner or ophthalmic optician and can cost up to £18. The optician must give the prescription, and a voucher if eligible, to the patient who can take this to any supplier of glasses of his/her choice to have dispensed. However, only registered opticians can supply glasses to children and to people registered as blind or partially sighted.

PRIMARY HEALTH CARE SERVICES

Primary health care services include the general medical, dental, ophthalmic and pharmaceutical services. They also include community services run by district health authorities, health centres and clinics, family planning outside the hospital service, and preventive activities in the community including vaccination, immunization and fluoridation.

The district nursing and health visiting services include community psychiatric nursing for mentally ill people living outside hospital, and school nursing for the health surveillance of schoolchildren of all ages. Ante- and post-natal care and chiropody are also an integral part of the primary health care service.

COMMUNITY CHILD HEALTH SERVICES

Pre-school services at GP surgeries or child health clinics provide regular surveillance of children's physical, mental and emotional health and development, and advice to parents on their children's health and welfare.

The School Health Service provides for the medical and dental examination of schoolchildren, and advises the local education authority, the school, the parents and the pupil of any health factors which may require special consideration during the pupil's school life. GPs are increasingly undertaking child health surveillance to improve the preventive health care of children.

HOSPITALS AND OTHER SERVICES

The Secretary of State for Health has a duty to provide, to such extent as he/she considers necessary to meet all reasonable requirements, hospital and other accommodation; medical, dental, nursing and ambulance services; other facilities for the care of expectant and nursing mothers and young children; facilities for the prevention of illness and the care and after-care of persons suffering from illness; and such other services as are required for the diagnosis and treatment of illness. Rehabilitation services (occupational therapy, physiotherapy and speech therapy) may also be provided for those who need it and surgical and medical appliances are supplied in appropriate cases. NHS services and equipment should be free of charge unless current legislation on prescriptions states otherwise.

Specialists and consultants who take part in the NHS can engage in private practice, including the treatment of their private patients in NHS hospitals.

*Trusts*

The National Health Service and Community Care Act 1990 enables hospitals and other providers of health care to become independent of health authority control as self-governing NHS Trusts run by boards of directors. The Trusts derive their income principally from contracts to provide health services to health authorities and fund-holding general practitioners. By April 1994 there were 419 NHS Trusts representing the majority of hospitals and community units. Applications from 14 units wishing to become Trusts in April 1995 are under consideration.

*Charges*

In a number of hospitals, accommodation is available for the treatment of private in-patients who undertake to pay the full costs of hospital accommodation and services and (usually) separate medical fees to a specialist as well. The amount of the medical fees is a matter for agreement between doctor and patient. Hospital charges for private resident patients are determined by DHAs or NHS Trusts, either on a local basis or in line with a central 'model' list.

Certain hospitals have accommodation in single rooms or small wards which, if not required for patients who need privacy for medical reasons, may be made available to patients who desire it as an amenity. These patients are still NHS patients and are treated as such.

There is no charge for drugs supplied to NHS hospital in-patients but out-patients pay £4.75 per item unless they are exempt.

With certain exceptions, hospital out-patients have to pay fixed charges for dentures, contact lenses and certain appliances. Glasses may be obtained either from the hospital or an optician and the charge will be related to the type of lens prescribed and the choice of frame.

## PERSONAL SOCIAL SERVICES

Local authorities are responsible for personal social services within their area. Each authority has a Director of Social Services and a Social Services Committee responsible for the social services functions placed upon them by the Local Authority Social Services Act 1970.

# National Insurance and Related Cash Benefits

The state insurance and assistance schemes, comprising schemes of national insurance and industrial injuries insurance, national assistance, and non-contributory old age pensions came into force from 5 July 1948. The Ministry of Social Security Act 1966 replaced national assistance and non-contributory old age pensions with a scheme of non-contributory benefits. These and subsequent measures relating to social security provision in Great Britain were consolidated by the Social Security Act 1975; the Social Security (Consequential Provisions) Act 1975; and the Industrial Injuries and Diseases (Old Cases) Act 1975. Corresponding measures were passed for Northern Ireland. The Social Security Pensions Act 1975 introduced a new State pensions scheme, which came into force on 6 April 1978, and the graduated pension scheme 1961 to 1975 has been wound up, existing rights being preserved. The Pensioners' Payments and Social Security Act 1979 provided for a £10 bonus for pensioners in 1979 and for the payment of a bonus in succeeding years at levels then to be determined. The Child Benefit Act 1975 replaced family allowances (introduced 1946) with child benefit and one parent benefit. Some of this legislation has been superseded by the provisions of the Social Security Acts 1968 to 1992.

## NATIONAL INSURANCE SCHEME

The National Insurance (NI) scheme operates under the Social Security Contributions and Benefits Act 1992 and the Social Security Administration Act 1992, and orders and regulations made thereunder. The scheme is financed by contributions payable by earners, employers and others (such as non-employed persons, paying voluntary contributions). It provides the funds required for paying benefits payable under the Social Security Acts out of the National Insurance Fund and not out of other public money, and for the making of payments towards the cost of the National Health Service. In 1991 the Redundancy Fund was absorbed into the National Insurance Fund. The yearly Treasury supplement to the National Insurance Fund was abolished in April 1989. A Treasury grant was introduced from April 1993.

### CONTRIBUTIONS

Contributions are of four classes:

CLASS 1 CONTRIBUTIONS

These are earnings-related, based on a percentage of the employee's earnings.
(a) primary Class 1 contributions are payable by employed earners and office-holders over age 16 with gross earnings at or above the lower earnings limit of £57.00 per week. Employees earning less than the lower earnings limit do not pay any contributions. For those with gross earnings at or above this level, contributions are payable on all earnings up to an upper limit of £430.00 per week. 'Gross earnings' include overtime pay, commission, bonus, etc., without deduction of any superannuation contributions. Contributions are paid at 2 per cent of earnings up to the lower earnings limit, plus contributions at a higher percentage on earnings between the lower earning limit and the employees' upper earnings limit. Employees contributing at the reduced rate continue to

pay at that rate on earnings up to and including the employees' upper earnings limit.

(b) secondary Class 1 contributions are payable by employers of employed earners, and by the appropriate authorities in the case of office-holders. In 1985 the upper earnings limit for employers' contributions was abolished and secondary contributions are payable on all the employee's earnings if they reach or exceed £57.00 per week.

Women who marry for the first time no longer have a right to elect not to pay the full contribution rate. Married women and widows who before 12 May 1977 elected not to pay contributions at the full rate retain the right to pay a reduced rate over the same earnings range, which includes a contribution to the National Health Service. They lose this right if, after 5 April 1978, there are two consecutive tax years in which they receive no earnings on which primary Class 1 contributions are payable and in which they have not been at any time self-employed earners. No primary contributions are due on earnings paid for a period on or after the employee's pension age, even when retirement is deferred.

Primary contributions are deducted from earnings by the employer and are paid, together with the employer's contributions, to the Inland Revenue along with income tax collected under the PAYE system.

CLASS 2 CONTRIBUTIONS

These are flat-rate, paid weekly by self-employed earners over age 16. Those with earnings below £3,200 a year for the tax year 1994-5 can apply for exemption from liability to pay Class 2 contributions. People who while self-employed are exempted from liability to pay contributions on the grounds of small earnings may pay either Class 2 or Class 3 contributions voluntarily. Self-employed earners (whether or not they pay Class 2 contributions) may also be liable to pay Class 4 contributions based on profits or gains within certain limits. There are special rules for those who are concurrently employed and self-employed.

Married women and widows can no longer choose not to pay Class 2 contributions. Those who elected not to pay Class 2 contributions before 12 May 1977 retain the right until there is a period of two consecutive tax years after 5 April 1978 in which they were not at any time either self-employed earners or had earnings on which primary Class 1 contributions were payable.

Class 2 contributions may be paid by direct debit through a bank or National Giro account following a quarterly bill.

CLASS 3 CONTRIBUTIONS

These are voluntary flat-rate contributions payable by persons over school-leaving age who would otherwise be unable to qualify for retirement pension and certain other benefits because they have an insufficient record of Class 1 or Class 2 contributions. Married women and widows who on or before 11 May 1977 elected not to pay Class 1 (full rate) or Class 2 contributions cannot pay Class 3 contributions while they retain this right.

Payment may be made by direct debit through a bank or National Giro account following a quarterly bill.

CLASS 4 CONTRIBUTIONS

These are payable by self-employed earners, whether or not they pay Class 2 contributions, on annual profits or gains from a trade, profession or vocation chargeable to income tax under Schedule D, where these fall between £6,490 and £22,360 a year. The maximum Class 4 contribution, payable on profits or gains of £22,360 or more, is £1,158.51.

Class 4 contributions are generally assessed and collected by the Inland Revenue along with Schedule D income tax.

Self-employed persons under 16 or who at the beginning of a tax year are over pension age even where retirement is deferred, are not liable to pay Class 4 contributions. There are special rules for people who have more than one job or who pay Class 1 contributions on earnings which are chargeable to income tax under Schedule D.

Regulations state the cases in which earners may be exempted from liability to pay contributions, and the conditions upon which contributions are credited to persons who are exempted. Leaflet NI 208 is obtainable from local social security offices.

For the period 6 April 1994 to 5 April 1995 the earnings brackets determining Class 1 contributions are:

| | Weekly earnings |
|---|---|
| 1 | £57.00– 99.99 |
| 2 | 100.00–144.99 |
| 3 | 145.00–199.99 |
| 4 | 200.00–430.00 |
| 5 | over 430.00 |

CONTRIBUTION RATES *from 6 April 1994 to 5 April 1995*

CLASS 1 CONTRIBUTIONS – NOT CONTRACTED OUT
*Employee's rates*

| Earnings bracket | Percentage of reckonable income | | | |
|---|---|---|---|---|
| | On first £57.00 | | On earnings from £57.00–£430.00 | |
| | standard | reduced | standard | reduced |
| 1 | 2 | 3.85 | 10 | 3.85 |
| 2 | 2 | 3.85 | 10 | 3.85 |
| 3 | 2 | 3.85 | 10 | 3.85 |
| 4 | 2 | 3.85 | 10 | 3.85 |
| 5 | *2 | *3.85 | *10 | *3.85 |

*To a maximum of £430.00 per week

CLASS 1 CONTRIBUTIONS – CONTRACTED OUT
(*see also* page 499)
*Employee's rates*

| Earnings bracket | On first £57.00 | | On earnings from £57.00–£430.00 | |
|---|---|---|---|---|
| | standard | reduced | standard | reduced |
| 1 | 2 | 3.85 | 8.2 | 3.85 |
| 2 | 2 | 3.85 | 8.2 | 3.85 |
| 3, 4, 5 | 2 | 3.85 | 8.2 | 3.85 |

*Employer's rates*

| Earnings bracket | On first £57.00 | On earnings from £57.00–£430.00 | On any earnings over £430.00 |
|---|---|---|---|
| 1 | 3.6 | 0.6 | 0 |
| 2 | 5.6 | 2.6 | 0 |
| 3 | 7.6 | 4.6 | 0 |
| 4 | 10.2 | 7.2 | 0 |
| 5 | 10.2 | 7.2 | 10.2 |

CLASS 2 CONTRIBUTIONS, £5.65 weekly flat rate

CLASS 3 CONTRIBUTIONS, £5.55

CLASS 4 CONTRIBUTIONS, 7.3% of profits or gains

The Social Security (Contributions) Act 1991 added a new class of contributions: 1A, payable in respect of car fuel by persons liable to pay secondary Class 1 contributions. It has effect with regard to the 1991-2 tax year and thereafter.

# THE STATE EARNINGS RELATED PENSION SCHEME (SERPS)

The Social Security Pensions Act 1975, which came into force in April 1978, aims to reduce reliance upon means-tested benefit in old age, in widowhood and in chronic ill-health by providing better pensions; to ensure that occupational pension schemes which are contracted out of part of the state scheme fulfil the conditions of a good scheme; that pensions are adequately protected against inflation; and that in both the state and occupational schemes men and women are treated equally.

Under the state earnings-related pension scheme, retirement, invalidity and widow's pensions for employees are related to the earnings on which NI contributions have been paid. For employees of either sex with a complete insurance record, the scheme provides a category A retirement pension in two parts, a basic and an additional pension. The basic pension corresponds to the old personal flat-rate national insurance pension. The additional pension is 1.25 per cent of average earnings between the lower weekly earnings limit for Class 1 contribution liability and the upper earnings limit for each year of such earnings under the scheme, and will thus build up to 25 per cent in twenty years. Retirement, widow's and invalidity pensions under the new scheme started to be paid in April 1979. Since 6 April 1979 the basic retirement pension has been augmented for employed earners by the additional pension related to earnings, but it will be twenty years before these additional pensions become payable at the full rate.

The additional pension will be calculated in a different way for individuals who reach pension age after 6 April 1999. The changes are to be phased in over ten years. From 2010 a lifetime's earnings will be included in the calculation and for years from 1988-9 onwards the accrual rate on these surplus earnings will be 20 per cent. The accrual rate on surplus earnings for the years from 1978-9 to 1987-8 will remain at 25 per cent.

Actual earnings are to be revalued in terms of the earnings level current in the last complete tax year before pension age (or death or incapacity). Both components of pensions in payment will be uprated annually in line with the movement of prices. Graduated retirement pensions in payment, and rights to such pensions earned by people who are still working, will be brought into the annual review of benefits.

Self-employed persons pay contributions towards the basic pension. Employees with earnings below the lower limit and people not in employment may contribute voluntarily for basic pension. Although no primary Class 1 contributions or Class 2 or Class 4 contributions are payable by persons who work beyond pension age (65 for men, 60 for women), the employer's liability for secondary Class 1 contributions continues if earnings are at or above the lower earnings limit. Class 4 contributions are still payable up to the end of the tax year during which pension age is reached.

Widows will get the whole of any additional pensions earned by their husbands with their widowed mother's allowances or widow's pensions; and can add to the retirement pensions earned by their own contributions any additional pensions earned by their husbands up to the maximum payable on one person's contributions. Men whose wives die when they are both over pension age can add together their own and their wives' pension rights in the same way as widows.

The scheme permits years of home responsibilities to reduce the number of qualifying years (since 1978) needed by women for retirement pension; and the 'half-test', by which a married woman who married before age 55 could not qualify for a Category A retirement pension unless she had contributed on earnings at the basic level in at least half the years between marriage and pension age, has been abolished with effect from 22 December 1984. The range of short-term social security benefits and industrial injury benefits under the Social Security Act 1975 continues with only minor changes.

## CONTRACTED-OUT AND PERSONAL PENSION SCHEMES

Members of occupational pension schemes which meet the standards laid down in the Social Security Pensions Act 1975 or the Social Security Act 1986 can be contracted-out of the earnings-related part of the state scheme relating to retirement and widows' benefits.

Until 6 April 1988 occupational pension schemes could contract out only if they promised a pension that was related to earnings (a contracted-out salary-related scheme). They must provide a pension that is not less than the guaranteed minimum pension (GMP), which is broadly equivalent to the state earnings-related pension. Since 6 April 1988 occupational pension schemes which promise a minimum level of contributions (a contracted-out money purchase scheme) have also been able to contract out. They provide a pension based on the fund built up in the scheme over the years plus the results of the way they have been invested.

Since July 1988 employees whose employers do not provide a pension scheme have been able to start their own personal pension instead of staying in the state earnings-related pension scheme. Since 6 April 1988, this choice has been open to all employees even if their employer does have a pension scheme. A personal pension, like a contracted-out money purchase scheme, provides a pension based on the fund built up in the scheme over the years plus the results of the way they have been invested.

The decision on whether or not an occupational pension scheme may become contracted-out lies with the Occupational Pension Board, an independent statutory body which has a general responsibility for supervising contracting-out. They also consider and approve personal pension schemes which can be used instead of state additional pension.

The state earnings-related pension payable to a member of a contracted-out salary-related scheme, or his widow, will be reduced by the amount of GMP payable (which in the case of a widow must be at least half of the late husband's GMP entitlement). Members of contracted-out money purchase schemes and personal pension schemes, or their widows, have no GMP entitlement as such. But the state earnings-related pension payable will be reduced by an amount equivalent to a GMP (or widow's GMP).

Since 6 April 1988 contracted-out salary-related schemes must also provide a widower's GMP which must be at least half of the late wife's GMP entitlement built up from 6 April 1988. (A scheme need not provide entitlement to a GMP for widowers of earners dying before April 1989.) Contracted-out money purchase schemes and personal pension schemes must provide half-rate widower's benefit.

In contracted-out schemes, both the employee and the employer pay the full ordinary rate of contribution on the first £57.00 (1994-5 figure) of earnings but earnings above that amount attract a lower rate of contribution from the employee, and from the employer where the employee's earnings are under £430.00; where the employee's earnings exceed this amount, the full ordinary rate of contribution is payable only by the employer and the employee has no liability for contributions on these earnings (*see also* page 498).

An employee who chooses a personal pension in place of SERPS or their employer's pension scheme must pay NI contributions at the full ordinary rate (the employer's share must also be paid at the same rate). The DSS pays the difference between the lower contracted-out rate and the full ordinary rate directly into the personal pension scheme.

## NATIONAL INSURANCE FUND

The National Insurance Fund receives all social security contributions (less only the National Health Service and Redundancy Fund and Maternity Pay Fund allocations and the National Insurance surcharge for taxation purposes) and it bears the cost of all contributory benefits provided by the Social Security Acts and the cost of administration.

Approximate receipts and payments of the National Insurance Fund for the year ended 31 March 1993, were as follows:

| *Receipts* | £'000 |
|---|---|
| Balance, 1 April 1992 | 8,333,300 |
| Contributions under the Social Security Acts (net of SSP/SMP) | 33,597,351 |
| Compensation from Consolidated Fund for SSP/SMP recoveries | 1,089,000 |
| Income from investments | 924,586 |
| Other receipts | 49,282 |
| | 43,993,519 |

| *Payments* | £'000 | £'000 |
|---|---|---|
| Unemployment benefit | 1,760,158 | |
| Sickness benefit | 364,000 | |
| Invalidity benefit | 6,209,602 | |
| Maternity allowance | 31,500 | |
| Widow's benefit | 1,010,000 | |
| Guardian's allowance and child's special allowance | 2,000 | |
| Retirement pension | 26,705,927 | |
| Pensioners' lump sum payments | 115,110 | 36,198,297 |
| Personal pensions | | 2,654,226 |
| Transfers to Northern Ireland | | 40,000 |
| Administration | | 1,332,005 |
| Other payments | | 10,523 |
| Redundancy payments | | 322,224 |
| Balance, 31 March 1993 | | 3,436,244 |
| | | 43,993,519 |

NB: There have been changes to the National Insurance Fund. Payments will no longer be paid into surcharges or the Maternity Pay Fund. However, residual payments are still being paid in respect of late paid contributions for premium years.

## BENEFITS

The benefits payable under the Social Security Acts are as follows:

CONTRIBUTORY BENEFITS
Unemployment benefit
Sickness benefit
Invalidity pension and allowance
Maternity allowance
Widow's benefit, comprising widow's payment, widowed
  mother's allowance and widow's pension
Retirement pensions, categories A and B

NON-CONTRIBUTORY BENEFITS
Child benefit
One parent benefit
Guardian's allowance
Invalid care allowance
Mobility allowance
Severe disablement allowance
Attendance allowance
Disability Living Allowance
Disability Working Allowance
Retirement pensions, categories C and D
Income Support
Family Credit
Social Fund

BENEFITS FOR INDUSTRIAL INJURIES, DISABLEMENT AND DEATH

OTHER
Statutory sick pay
Statutory maternity pay

Leaflets relating to the various benefits and payments are obtainable from local social security offices.

The Social Security Acts empower the Secretary of State to increase certain rates of benefit by order approved by both Houses of Parliament, and require him to increase certain rates by such an order if an annual review shows that they have not retained their value in relation to the general level of prices obtaining in Great Britain as measured by the Retail Price Index. The latest order providing for increases in benefit rates took effect from the week commencing 11 April 1994. It did not apply to all benefits.

## CONTRIBUTORY BENEFITS

Entitlement to contributory benefits depends on contribution conditions being satisfied either by the claimant or by some other person (depending on the kind of benefit). The class or classes of contribution which for this purpose are relevant to each benefit are:

| *Short-term benefits* | |
|---|---|
| Unemployment benefit | Class 1 |
| Sickness benefit | Class 1 or 2 |
| Maternity allowance | Class 1 or 2 |

| *Long-term benefits* | |
|---|---|
| Widow's benefits | |
| Category A retirement pension | } Class 1, 2 or 3 |
| Category B retirement pension | |
| Invalidity benefit | Class 1 or 2 |

The system of contribution conditions relates to yearly levels of earnings on which contributions have been paid. The contribution conditions for different benefits are set out in leaflets available at local social security offices.

UNEMPLOYMENT BENEFIT

Benefit is payable in a period of interruption of employment for up to 312 days a year, excluding Sundays. Spells of unemployment and sickness not separated by more than eight weeks count as one period of interruption of employment. A person who has exhausted benefit requalifies when he/she has again worked as an employed earner for at least 16 hours a week for 13 weeks. These weeks need not be consecutive but must generally fall within 26 weeks prior to the date of the claim.

There are disqualifications from receiving benefit, e.g. for a period not exceeding 26 weeks if a person has lost their employment through misconduct, or has voluntarily left employment without just cause, or has, without good cause, refused an offer of employment or training.

## SICKNESS BENEFIT

State sickness benefit currently is payable for up to 28 weeks of sickness in a period of interruption of employment. It is to be replaced in April 1995 by incapacity benefit (*see* below)

There are disqualifications from receiving sickness benefit for a period not exceeding six weeks if a person has become incapable of work through his/her own misconduct or fails without good cause to attend for or submit himself/herself to prescribed medical or other examination or treatment, or observe prescribed rules of behaviour.

Statutory sick pay (SSP) was introduced in April 1983 and replaces the employee's entitlement to state sickness benefit, which is not payable as long as any SSP liability remains. Since 6 April 1986 employers are responsible for paying SSP to their employees for up to 28 weeks of sickness in any period of incapacity for work. SSP is subject to PAYE and to NI deductions. Employees who cannot get SSP can claim state sickness benefit instead. Employers can no longer recover any SSP costs. Employers whose gross annual NI liability is £20,000 or less will be fully reimbursed once their employee has received four weeks of SSP in one spell of sickness.

## INVALIDITY BENEFIT

Normally, after 28 weeks of sickness, state sickness benefit or SSP (where applicable) is replaced by an invalidity pension. In addition, an invalidity allowance is payable if incapacity for work begins more than five years before pension age. The allowance varies according to the age at which invalidity began. If still in payment at pension age invalidity allowance is offset by entitlement to an additional earnings-related pension and/or a guaranteed minimum pension.

## INCAPACITY BENEFIT

Incapacity Benefit will replace State Sickness Benefit and Invalidity Benefit from 13 April 1995.

The new benefit will have short-term and long-term elements. Short-term benefit will consist of a lower rate payable for the first 28 weeks of sickness, equivalent to the current rate of sickness benefit, and a higher rate payable after 28 weeks, equivalent to the higher rate of SSP. Long-term benefit will be payable after 52 weeks at a rate equivalent to the current basic rate of invalidity benefit and will not be payable after pension age. The terminally ill and those entitled to the highest rate care component of disability living allowance will be able to get the long-term rate after 28 weeks rather than 52 weeks. Incapacity benefit will be taxable after 28 weeks of incapacity.

Two rates of age addition will be paid with long-term benefit based on the claimant's age when incapacity started. The higher rate will be payable where incapacity for work commenced before the age of 35; and the lower rate where incapacity commenced before the age of 45. There will be no earnings-related additional pension with incapacity benefit.

A medical test of incapacity for work will also be introduced for incapacity benefit as well as other benefits paid on the basis of incapacity for work. The medical test will apply after 28 weeks of incapacity for work and will assess ability to perform a range of work-related activities rather than the ability to perform a specific job.

## MATERNITY BENEFIT

Statutory maternity pay (SMP) is administered by employers. The state maternity allowance scheme covers women who are self-employed or otherwise do not qualify for SMP.

In general, employers pay SMP to pregnant women who have been employed by them full or part-time for at least 26 weeks, and who have earned at least the lower earnings limit for the payment of NI contributions. All women who meet these conditions receive payment of 90 per cent of earnings for six weeks, followed by a maximum of 12 weeks at £52.50. Women have some choice in deciding when to begin maternity leave but SMP is not payable for any week in which work is done. Employers are reimbursed for 92 per cent of the SMP they pay (104 per cent for those whose NI liability is under £20,000).

A woman may qualify for maternity allowance (MA) if she has been working and paying contributions at the full rate for at least 26 weeks in the 66-week period which ends one week before the baby is due. She also has an element of choice in deciding when to stop work and receive MA, which is not payable for any period she works. Women employed at the 15th week before the baby is due will receive £52.50 per week for 18 weeks, and self-employed and unemployed women will receive £44.55 for up to 18 weeks.

## WIDOW'S BENEFITS

Only the late husband's contributions of any class count for widow's benefit in any of its three forms:

*Widow's Payment* – may be received by a woman who at her husband's death is under 60, or whose husband was not entitled to a Category A retirement pension when he died

*Widowed Mother's Allowance* – payable to a widow if she is entitled or treated as entitled to child benefit, or if she is expecting her husband's baby

*Widow's Pension* – a widow may receive this pension if aged 45 or over at the time of her husband's death or when her widowed mother's allowance ends. If aged 55 or over she will receive the full widow's pension rate

Widow's benefit of any form ceases upon re-marriage or during a period in which she lives with a man as his wife.

## RETIREMENT PENSION: CATEGORIES A AND B

A Category A pension is payable for life to men or women on their own contributions if they are over pension age (65 for a man and 60 for a woman).

Where a person defers making a claim at 65 (60 for a woman) or later opts to be treated as if he/she had not made a claim, and does not draw a Category A pension, the weekly rate of pension is increased when he or she finally makes a claim or reaches the age of 70 (65 for a woman), in respect of weeks when pension is forgone during the five years after reaching minimum pension age. Details of the increase in the rate of pension due to deferred retirement are given in leaflet NP46, available at social security offices. If a married man defers his own Category A pension, his wife has to defer receiving her Category B pension based on his contribution record. During this time she earns increments to the Category B pension, provided she does not claim retirement pension or Graduated Retirement Benefit in her own right; increments are payable to her (and not her husband) when they both claim their pensions.

A Category B pension is normally payable for life to a woman on her husband's contributions when he has claimed, or is over 70, and has qualified for his own Category A pension, and she has reached 60. It is also payable on widowhood after 60 whether or not the late husband had retired and qualified for his own pension. The pension is payable at the rate of the increase for a wife while the husband is alive, and at the single person's rate on widowhood after 60. Where a woman is widowed before she reaches 60, a Category B pension is paid to her on reaching 60 at the same rate as her widow's pension if she claims. If a woman qualifies for a pension of each category she receives whichever pension is the larger.

The earnings rule, which stated that a man aged 65 to 70, or a woman aged 60 to 65 who has qualified for pension would have it reduced if he or she earned more than a certain amount, was abolished on 1 October 1989. Where an adult dependant is living with the claimant, an Adult Dependants increase (£45.45) will only be payable if the dependant's earnings do not exceed the standard rate of unemployment benefit for a single person under pensionable age (*see* below). For the purpose of the dependency rule only, earnings will include payments by way of occupational or personal pension. The earnings of a separated spouse affect the increase of retirement pension if they exceed £34.50 a week.

Unemployment, sickness or invalidity benefit is payable to men between 65 and 70, and women between 60 and 65 who have not claimed their retirement pension and who would have been entitled to a retirement pension if they had claimed at pension age. This applies in the case of sickness and invalidity benefit (incapacity benefit from 13 April 1995) if incapacity for work is the result of an industrial accident or prescribed disease. These rates of benefit for people over pension age are shown in leaflet NI 196. A retirement pension will be increased by the amount of any invalidity allowance the pensioner was getting within the period of eight weeks and one day before reaching minimum pension age but this will be offset against any additional pension or GMP. An age addition of 25p per week is payable if a retirement pensioner is aged 80 or over.

### GRADUATED RETIREMENT BENEFIT

Graduated NI contributions were first payable from April 1961 and were calculated as a percentage of earnings between certain bands. They were discontinued in April 1975. Any graduated pension which an employed person over 18 and under 70 (65 for a woman) had earned by paying graduated contributions would be paid when the contributor claims retirement pension or at 70 (65 for a woman), in addition to any retirement pension for which he or she qualifies.

Graduated retirement benefit is at the rate of 7.48p a week (April 1994) for each 'unit' of graduated contributions paid by the employee (half a unit or more counts as a whole unit). A unit of contributions is £7.50 for men and £9.00 for women of graduated contributions paid.

A wife can get a graduated pension in return for her own graduated contributions, but not for her husband's. A widow, or a widower whose wife died after 5 April 1979 when they were both over pensionable age, gets a graduated addition to his/her retirement pension equal to half of any graduated additions earned by his/her late spouse, plus any additions earned by his/her own graduated contributions. If a person defers making a claim beyond 65 (60 for a woman), entitlement may be increased by one seventh of a penny per £1 of its weekly rate for each complete week of deferred retirement, as long as the retirement is deferred for a minimum of seven weeks.

### WEEKLY RATES OF BENEFIT
*from week commencing 11 April 1994*

*Unemployment Benefit: standard rate*

| | |
|---|---|
| Person under pension age | £44.45 |
| Increase for wife/other adult dependant | 28.05 |
| *Person over pension age | 57.60 |
| Increase for wife/other adult dependant | 34.50 |

*Sickness Benefit: standard rate*

| | |
|---|---|
| Person under pension age | 43.45 |
| Increase for wife/other adult dependant | 28.05 |
| *Person over pension age | 55.25 |

| | |
|---|---|
| Increase for wife/other adult dependant | 33.10 |

*\*Invalidity Pension*

| | |
|---|---|
| Person (under or over pension age) | 57.60 |
| Increase for wife/other adult dependant | 34.50 |

*Invalidity Allowance: maximum amount payable*

| | |
|---|---|
| Higher rate | 12.15 |
| Middle rate | 7.60 |
| Lower rate | 3.80 |

*Maternity Allowance*

| | |
|---|---|
| Employed | £52.50 |
| Self-employed or unemployed | £44.55 |

*Widow's Benefits*

| | |
|---|---|
| Widow's Payment (lump sum) | 1,000.00 |
| *Widowed Mother's Allowance | 57.60 |
| *Widow's Pension | 57.60 |

*\*Retirement Pension: categories A and B*

| | |
|---|---|
| Single person | 57.60 |
| Increase for wife/other adult dependant | 34.50 |

*These benefits attract an increase for each dependent child (in addition to child benefit) of £9.80 for the first or only child and £11 for each subsequent child

## NON-CONTRIBUTORY BENEFITS

### CHILD BENEFIT

Child benefit is payable for virtually all children aged under 16, and for those aged 16 to 18 who are studying full-time up to and including A-level or equivalent standard. It is also payable for a short period if the child has left school recently and is registered for work or youth training at a careers office.

### ONE PARENT BENEFIT

This benefit may be paid to a person in receipt of child benefit who is responsible for bringing up one or more children on his/her own. It is a flat rate non-means tested, non-contributory benefit payable for the eldest child.

### GUARDIAN'S ALLOWANCE

Where the parents of a child are dead, the person who has the child in his/her family may claim a guardian's allowance in addition to child benefit. The allowance, in exceptional circumstances, is payable on the death of only one parent.

### INVALID CARE ALLOWANCE

Invalid care allowance is payable to persons of working age who are not gainfully employed because they are regularly and substantially engaged in caring for a severely disabled person who is receiving attendance allowance, the middle or highest rate of disability living allowance or constant attendance allowance with either a war or services pension, industrial disablement workman's compensation, or an allowance under the Pneumoconiosis, Byssinosis and Miscellaneous Diseases Benefit Scheme.

### SEVERE DISABLEMENT ALLOWANCE

Persons under pensionable age who have been continuously incapable of work for a period of at least 28 weeks but who do not qualify for a contributory invalidity pension may be entitled to severe disablement allowance. People who first become incapable of work after their twentieth birthday must be at least 80 per cent disabled.

### ATTENDANCE ALLOWANCE

This is payable to disabled people over 65 who need a lot of care or supervision because of physical or mental disability for a period of at least six months. People not expected to live for six months because of an illness do not have to wait six months. The allowance has two rates: the lower rate is for day or night care, and the higher rate is for day and night care.

## DISABILITY LIVING ALLOWANCE

This is payable to disabled people under 65 who have personal care and mobility needs because of an illness or disability for a period of at least three months and are likely to need care for a further six months or more. People not expected to live for six months because of an illness do not have to wait three months. The allowance has two components: the care component, which has three rates, and the mobility component, which has two rates. The rates depend on the care and mobility needs of the claimant. The mobility component is payable only to those aged five or over.

## DISABILITY WORKING ALLOWANCE

This is a tax-free, income-related benefit for people who are working 16 hours a week or more but have an illness or disability which puts them at a disadvantage in getting a job. To qualify a person must be aged 16 or over and must, at the date of the claim, have one of the 'qualifying benefits', such as disability living allowance. The amount payable depends on the size of the family and weekly income. DWA is not payable if any savings exceed £16,000.

## RETIREMENT PENSION: CATEGORIES C AND D

A Category C pension is provided, subject to a residence test, for persons who were over pensionable age on 5 July 1948, and for women whose husbands are so entitled if they are over pension age, with increases for adult and child dependants. A Category D pension is provided for others when they reach 80 if they are not already getting a retirement pension of any category or if they are getting that pension at less than these rates. An age addition of 25p per week is payable if persons entitled to retirement pension are aged 80 or over.

### WEEKLY RATES OF BENEFIT
*from week commencing 6 April 1994*

| | |
|---|---:|
| *Child Benefit (first child)* | £10.20 |
| Each subsequent child | 8.25 |
| *One Parent Benefit* | |
| First or only child of certain lone parents | 6.15 |
| *Guardian's Allowance (eldest child)* | 9.80 |
| Each subsequent child | 11.00 |
| *\*Severe Disablement Allowance* | |
| †Basic rate | £34.80 |
| Under 40 | 12.15 |
| 40–49 | 7.65 |
| 50–59 | 3.80 |
| Increase for wife/other adult dependant | 20.65 |
| *\*Invalid Care Allowance* | 34.50 |
| Increase for wife/other adult dependant | 20.65 |
| *Attendance Allowance* | |
| Higher rate | 45.70 |
| Lower rate | 30.55 |
| *Disability Living Allowance* | |
| *Care component* | |
| Higher rate | 45.70 |
| Middle rate | 30.55 |
| Lower rate | 12.15 |
| *Mobility component* | |
| Higher rate | 31.95 |
| Lower rate | 12.15 |

| | |
|---|---:|
| *Disability Working Allowance* | |
| Single person | 46.05 |
| Couple or single parent | 63.75 |
| Child aged under 11 | 11.20 |
| aged 11–15 | 18.55 |
| aged 16–17 | 23.05 |
| aged 18 | 32.20 |
| ‡*Applicable amount* (income threshold) | |
| Single person | 43.00 |
| Couple or single parent | 71.70 |
| *Retirement Pension: categories \*C and D* | |
| Single person | 34.50 |
| Increase for wife/other adult dependant | 20.65 |
| (not payable with Category D pension) | |

\* These benefits attract an increase for each dependent child (in addition to child benefit) of £9.80 for the first or only child and £11 for each subsequent child
† The age addition applies to the age when incapacity began
‡ 70 pence is deducted from the maximum DWA payable (this is obtained by adding up the appropriate allowance for each person in the family) for every pound coming in each week over the appropriate applicable amount. Where weekly income is below the applicable amount, maximum DWA is payable

## INCOME SUPPORT

Income support is a benefit for those aged 18 and over (although certain vulnerable 16- and 17-year-olds may be eligible) whose income falls below set levels. Others who may be eligible include people who are: over 60; bringing up children alone; unable to work through sickness or disability; caring for a disabled person; unemployed or working part-time. Except in special cases income support is not available to those who work for more than 16 hours per week or who have a partner who works for more than 16 hours per week.

Income support is not payable if the claimant, or claimant and partner, have capital or savings in excess of £8,000. For capital or savings in excess of £3,000 a deduction of £1 is made for every £250, or part of £250, held.

Sums payable depend on fixed allowances laid down by law for people in different circumstances. If both partners are entitled to income support, either may claim it for the couple. People receiving income support will be able to receive housing benefit, help with mortgage or home loan interest and help with health care. They may also be eligible for help with exceptional expenses from the Social Fund. Leaflet IS20 gives a detailed explanation of income support.

Special rates may apply to some people living in residential care or nursing homes. Details are available from local social security offices.

### INCOME SUPPORT PREMIUMS

Income support premiums are additional weekly payments for those with special needs. People qualifying for more than one premium will normally only receive the highest single premium for which they qualify. However, family premium, disabled child's premium, severe disability premium and carer premium are payable in addition to other premiums.

People with children qualify for a family premium if they have at least one child; a disabled child's premium if they have a child who receives attendance allowance or certain components of disability living allowance or is registered blind; or a lone parent premium if they are bringing up one or more children alone. If someone receives invalid care allowance, they qualify for the carer premium.

Long-term sick or disabled people qualify for a disability premium if they or their partner are receiving certain benefits because they are disabled or cannot work; are registered blind; or if the claimant, but not their partner, has been sending in doctor's statements for at least 28 weeks stating inability to work through sickness. If someone is living alone and they are in receipt of attendance allowance or disability living allowance, without anyone receiving invalid care allowance for looking after them, they may qualify for a severe disability premium in addition to a disability premium.

People qualify for a pensioner premium if they or their partner are aged between 60 and 74, an enhanced pensioner premium if they or their partner are aged between 75 and 79, and a higher pensioner premium if they or their partner are aged 80 or over. A higher pensioner premium is also payable to people aged between 60 and 79 who receive attendance allowance, mobility allowance, invalidity benefit or severe disablement allowance, or who are registered blind. A higher pensioner premium may be paid as well as a severe disability premium. Enhanced pensioner premium is payable to qualifying pensioners in addition to pensioner premium.

### WEEKLY RATES OF BENEFIT
*from week commencing 6 April 1994*

*Income Support*

| Single people | |
|---|---|
| aged 16–17 | £27.50 |
| aged 16–17 (certain circumstances) | 36.15 |
| aged 18–24 | 36.15 |
| aged 25 and over | 45.70 |
| aged 18 and over and a single parent | 45.70 |

| Couples* | |
|---|---|
| both under 18 | 54.55 |
| both aged 18 or over | 71.70 |

| For each child in a family | |
|---|---|
| under 11 | 15.65 |
| aged 11–15 | 23.00 |
| †aged 16–17 | 27.50 |
| †aged 18 and over | 36.15 |

*Premiums*

| | |
|---|---|
| Family Premium | 10.05 |
| Disabled Child's Premium | 19.45 |
| Lone Parent Premium | 5.10 |
| Disability Premium | |
|   Single | 19.45 |
|   Couple | 27.80 |
| Severe Disability Premium | |
|   Single | 34.30 |
|   Couple (one person qualified) | 34.30 |
|   Couple (both qualified) | 68.60 |
| Pensioner Premium | |
|   Single | 18.25 |
|   Couple | 27.55 |
| Higher Pensioner Premium | |
|   Single | 24.70 |
|   Couple | 35.30 |
| Enhanced Pensioner Premium | |
|   Single | 20.35 |
|   Couple | 30.40 |

*Where one or both partners are aged under 18, their personal allowance will depend on their situation
†If in full-time education up to A-level or equivalent standard

## FAMILY CREDIT

Family credit is a tax-free benefit for working families with children. To qualify, a family must include at least one child under 16 (under 19 if in full-time education up to A-level or equivalent standard) and the claimant, or partner if there is one, must be working for at least 16 hours per week. It does not matter which partner is working and they may be employed or self-employed. The right to family credit does not depend on NI contributions and the same rates of benefit are paid to one- and two-parent families. Family credit is not payable if the claimant, or claimant and partner, have capital or savings in excess of £8,000. The rate of benefit is affected if capital or savings in excess of £3,000 are held. The rate of benefit payable depends upon the claimant's (and partner's) net income (excluding child benefit), number of children, and children's ages. Family credit, one parent benefit, and the first £15.00 of any maintenance in payment are paid for 26 weeks and the amount payable will usually remain the same throughout this period, regardless of change of circumstances. In certain cases where there are formal childcare arrangements for children under 11, costs of up to £40 per week will be taken into account. Payment is made weekly via post offices or every four weeks directly into a bank or building society account. Family credit is claimed by post. A claim pack FC1 which includes a claim form can be obtained at a post office or social security office or call the Family Credit Helpline on 01253-500050. In two-parent families the woman should claim.

### WEEKLY RATES OF BENEFIT
*from week commencing 5 April 1994*

The maximum amount will be payable where net income is no more than £71.70 per week. Where net income exceeds that amount, the maximum credit is reduced by 70 per cent of the excess and the result is the family credit payable. The maximum rate consists of:

| | |
|---|---|
| Adult credit (for one or two parents) | £44.30 |
| plus for each child | |
| aged under 11 | 11.20 |
| aged 11–15 | 18.55 |
| aged 16–17 | 23.05 |
| aged 18 | 32.20 |

---

## CLAIMS AND QUESTIONS

---

With a few exceptions, claims and questions relating to social security benefits are decided by statutory authorities who act independently of the Department of Social Security and Department of Employment.

The first of the statutory authorities, the Adjudication Officer, determines entitlement to benefit. A client who is dissatisfied with that decision has the right of appeal to an independent social security appeal tribunal. There is a further right of appeal to a Social Security Commissioner against the tribunal's decision but leave to appeal must first be obtained. Appeals to the Commissioner must be on a point of law. Provision is also made for the determination of certain questions by the Secretary of State for Social Services.

Disablement questions are decided by adjudicating medical authorities or medical appeal tribunals. Appeal to the Commissioner against a tribunal's decision is with leave and on a point of law only.

Leaflet NI246, which is available from social security offices, explains how to appeal, and leaflet NI260 is a guide to reviews and appeals.

## THE SOCIAL FUND

The Social Fund helps people with expenses which are difficult to meet from regular income. Regulated maternity, funeral and cold weather payments are decided by Adjudication Officers and are not cash-limited. Discretionary community care grants, and budgeting and crisis loans are decided by Social Fund Officers and come out of a yearly budget which is allocated to each district (1994–5, grants £97 million; loans £255 million).

### REGULATED PAYMENTS

#### Maternity Payments

A payment of up to £100 for each baby expected, born or adopted. It is payable to people on income support, disability working allowance and family credit and is non-repayable.

#### Funeral Payments

Payable for reasonable funeral expenses incurred by people receiving income support, disability working allowance, family credit or housing benefit. It is recoverable from the estate of the deceased.

#### Cold Weather Payments

£7 for any consecutive seven days when the average temperature is 0°C or below. Paid to people on income support who are pensioners, disabled or parents with a child under the age of five. It is non-repayable.

### DISCRETIONARY PAYMENTS

#### Community Care Grants

They are intended to help people on income support to move into the community or avoid institutional care; ease exceptional pressures on families; and/or meet certain essential travelling expenses. They are usually non-repayable.

#### Budgeting Loans

These are interest-free loans to people who have been receiving income support for at least six months, for intermittent expenses that may be difficult to budget for.

#### Crisis Loans

These are interest-free loans to anyone, whether receiving benefit or not, who is without resources in an emergency, where there is no other means of preventing serious risk or damage to health or safety.

Loans are normally repaid over a period of up to 78 weeks at 15, 10 or 5 per cent of income support (less housing costs), depending on other commitments.

### SAVINGS

Savings over £500 (£1,000 for people aged 60 or over) are taken into account for maternity and funeral payments, community care grants and budgeting loans. All savings are taken into account for crisis loans.

### APPEALS AND REVIEWS

For regulated payment there is a right of appeal to an independent Social Security Appeal Tribunal and thereafter to a Social Security Commissioner. For discretionary payments there is a review system where persons can ask for a review at the local office with a further right of review to an independent Social Fund Inspector.

## INDUSTRIAL INJURIES, DISABLEMENT AND DEATH BENEFITS

The industrial injuries scheme, administered under the Social Security Contributions and Benefits Act 1992, provides a range of benefits designed to compensate for disablement resulting from an industrial accident (i.e. an accident arising out of and in the course of an employed earner's employment) or from a prescribed disease due to the nature of a person's employment. Rates of benefit are increased periodically.

### BENEFITS

Disablement benefit is normally payable 15 weeks (90 days) after the date of accident or onset of disease if the employed earner suffers from loss of physical or mental faculty such that the resulting disablement is assessed at not less than 14 per cent. The amount of disablement benefit payable varies according to the degree of disablement (in the form of a percentage) assessed by an adjudicating medical authority or medical appeal tribunal.

Disablement assessed at less than 14 per cent does not normally attract basic benefit except for certain chest diseases. A weekly pension is payable where the assessment of disablement is between 14 and 100 per cent (assessments of 14 to 19 per cent are payable at the 20 per cent rate). Payment can be made for a limited period or for life. The basic rates are applicable to adults and to juveniles entitled to an increase for a child or adult dependant; other juveniles receive lower rates.

Basic rates of pension are not related to the pensioner's loss of earning power, and are payable whether he/she is in work or not. There is provision for increases of pension if the pensioner requires constant attendance or if his/her disablement is exceptionally severe. A pensioner may draw SSP, sickness or invalidity benefit as appropriate, in addition to disablement pension, during spells of incapacity for work.

Regulations impose certain obligations on claimants and beneficiaries and on employers, including, in the case of claimants for disablement benefit, that of submitting themselves for medical examination.

### SUPPLEMENTARY ALLOWANCES

Special schemes under the Industrial Injuries and Diseases (Old Cases) Act 1975 provide supplementary allowances to those entitled to receive weekly payments of workmen's compensation for loss of earnings due to injury at work, or disease contracted during employment before 5 July 1948 when the industrial injuries scheme was introduced. Other schemes under the Act provide allowances to those who contracted slowly-developing diseases during employment before July 1948 where neither workmen's compensation nor industrial injuries benefits are payable. A lump sum death benefit of up to £300 may also be payable to a dependant of such a person. Leaflet NI196 provides details relating to these allowances.

Weekly Rates of Benefit
*from 6 April 1994*
*\*Disablement Benefit/Pension*
Degree of disablement

| | |
|---|---|
| 100 per cent | £93.20 |
| 90 | 83.88 |
| 80 | 74.56 |
| 70 | 65.24 |
| 60 | 55.92 |
| 50 | 46.60 |
| 40 | 37.28 |
| 30 | 27.96 |
| 20 | 18.64 |
| †Unemployability supplement | 57.60 |
| Addition for adult dependant (subject to earnings rule) | 34.50 |
| Reduced earnings allowance (maximum) | 37.28 |
| Constant attendance allowance (normal maximum rate) | 37.40 |
| Exceptionally severe disablement allowance | 37.40 |

\*There is a weekly benefit for those under 18 with no dependants which is set at a lower rate
†This benefit attracts an increase for each dependent child (in addition to child benefit) of £9.80 for the first child and £11 for each subsequent child

CLAIMS AND QUESTIONS

Provision is made for the determination of certain questions by the Secretary of State for Social Security, and of 'disablement questions' by a medical board (or a single doctor) or, on appeal, by a medical appeal tribunal. An appeal on a point of law against a medical appeal tribunal decision is determined by the Social Security Commissioner.

Claims for benefit and certain questions arising in connection with a claim for or award of benefit (e.g. whether the accident arose out of and in the course of the employment) are determined by an adjudication officer appointed by the Secretary of State, or a social security appeal tribunal, or in certain circumstances, on further appeal, by the Commissioners.

# War Pensions

War pensions are awarded under The Naval, Military and Air Forces, Etc. (Disablement and Death) Service Pensions Order 1983.

The War Pensions Agency, an executive agency of the Department of Social Security (DSS), awards war pensions to members of the armed forces in respect of the periods 4 August 1914 to 30 September 1921 and subsequent to 3 September 1939 (including present members of the armed forces). There is also a scheme for civilians and civil defence workers in respect of the 1939–45 war, and other schemes for groups such as merchant seamen and Polish armed forces who served under British command.

War pensions for the period 1 October 1921 to 2 September 1939 are dealt with by the Ministry of Defence, which is also responsible for the Armed Forces Pension Scheme.

PENSIONS

War disablement pension is awarded for the disabling effects of any injury, wound or disease which is attributable to, or

has been aggravated by, conditions of service in the armed forces. It cannot be paid until the serviceman or woman has left the armed forces.

Disablement is assessed by comparison of the disabled person's health with that of a normal, healthy person of the same age and sex, without taking into account the disabled person's earning capacity or occupation, and is expressed on a percentage scale up to 100 per cent. Disablement of 20 per cent and above, for which a pension is awarded, is assessed in steps of 10 per cent. Maximum assessment does not necessarily imply total incapacity. For assessment of less than 20 per cent a lump sum is usually payable. No award is made where disablement in respect of noise-induced sensori-neural hearing loss is assessed at less than 20 per cent.

The dependency allowance, formerly payable in respect of a wife or child, was abolished in April 1992 and an equivalent amount incorporated into the basic war disablement pension.

War widow's pension is awarded where death occurs as a result of service or where a war disablement pensioner was receiving constant attendance allowance at the time of his death, or would have been receiving it if he were not in hospital, in which case his widow has automatic entitlement to a war widow's pension, regardless of the cause of death. Additional allowances are payable for dependent children, in addition to child benefit.

A lower weekly rate is payable to war widows of men below the rank of Lieutenant-Colonel who are under the age of 40, without children and capable of maintaining themselves. This is increased to the standard rate at age 40.

Rank additions to both disablement gratuities and widow's pensions may be paid where the rank held was above that of private (or equivalent).

SUPPLEMENTARY ALLOWANCES

A number of supplementary allowances may be awarded to a war pensioner which are intended to meet various needs, such as mobility, unemployability, constant nursing care, which may result from disablement or death and take account of its particular effect on the pensioner or spouse.

The principal supplementary allowances are:

*Unemployability supplement* – paid to a war pensioner whose pensioned disablement is so serious as to make him unemployable. An invalidity allowance may also be payable if the incapacity for work began more than five years before normal retirement age.

*Allowance for lowered standard of occupation* – awarded to a partially disabled pensioner whose pensioned disablement permanently prevents him from following his pre-service occupation and from doing another job of equivalent financial standard. The allowance, together with the basic war disablement pension, must not exceed pension at the 100 per cent rate.

*Constant attendance allowance*– awarded if the pensioner is receiving a pension at the 80 per cent rate or more and needs a great deal of care because of the disability. It is paid at one of four rates depending on how much care is needed.

*Widow's child's allowance* – paid in addition to child benefit.

Other supplementary allowances include exceptionally severe disablement allowance, severe disablement occupational allowance, treatment allowance, mobility supplement, comforts allowance, clothing allowance, age allowance, widow's age allowance, and education allowance. There is a supplementary rent allowance available on a war widow's pension.

Decisions on supplementary allowances are made on a discretionary basis and there is no provision for a statutory right of appeal against them. However, war pensioners may discuss any aspect of their pension position with their local war pensions committee, which may be able to arrange help or make representations to the DSS.

### WAR PENSIONERS ABROAD

The DSS is responsible for the payment of war pensions, and, where necessary, meeting the cost of treatment for accepted disablement, to pensioners who reside overseas. They receive the same pension rates and annual upratings as war pensioners in this country.

### SOCIAL SECURITY BENEFITS

Most social security benefits are paid in addition to the basic war disablement pension or war widow's pension. Any retirement pension for which a war widow qualifies on her own contributions, and any graduated retirement benefit or additional earnings related pension inherited from her husband, can be paid in addition to her war widow's pension.

A war pensioner or war widow who claims income support, family credit or disability working allowance has the first £10 of pension disregarded. A similar provision operates for housing benefit and council tax benefit; but the local authority may, at its discretion, disregard any or all of the balance.

### CLAIMS AND QUESTIONS

Where a claim is made no later than seven years after the termination of service, the claimant does not have to prove that the disablement or death on which the claim is based is related to service and receives the benefit of any reasonable doubt. Where a claim is made more than seven years after the termination of service the claimant has to show that disablement or death is related to service. However, the claim succeeds if reliable evidence is produced which raises a reasonable doubt whether or not disablement or death is related to service. There is no time limit for making a claim for war pension.

Independent pensions appeal tribunals hear appeals against the decisions of the DSS on entitlement and assessment of disablement in respect of the 1939–45 war and subsequent service cases. There are no time limits within which an entitlement appeal must be made but there are time limits within which an assessment appeal should be made. However, there are now no rights of appeal in the 1914–21 war disablement cases, the great majority of which were given final assessment in the 1920s with a 12 months' right of appeal at the time. An appeal by a 1914 war widow must be made within twelve months of the date on which the rejection of the claim is notified.

### WAR PENSIONERS WELFARE SERVICE

The DSS operates a war pensioners welfare service to advise and assist war pensioners and their widows on any matters affecting their welfare. Welfare officers are attached to war pensioners' welfare offices located in the major towns, and the service is available to any war pensioner or war widow who needs it.

The current rates of all war pensions and allowances are listed in leaflet MPL154 *Rates of War Pensions and Allowances*, obtainable from war pensioners welfare offices; the Leaflets Unit, PO Box 21, Stanmore, Middx. HA7 1AY; or by phoning the War Pension Helpline on 01253-858858.

### WEEKLY RATES OF PENSIONS AND ALLOWANCES
*from week commencing 6 April 1994*

*War Disablement pension*
Degree of disablement:

| | |
|---|---|
| 100 per cent | £98.90 |
| 90 per cent | 89.01 |
| 80 per cent | 79.12 |
| 70 per cent | 69.23 |
| 60 per cent | 59.34 |
| 50 per cent | 49.45 |
| 40 per cent | 39.56 |
| 30 per cent | 29.67 |
| 20 per cent | 19.78 |

*Unemployability supplement*

| | |
|---|---|
| Personal allowance | 61.10 |
| Increase for wife/other adult dependant | 34.50 |
| Increase for first child | 9.80 |
| Increase for other children | 11.00 |

*Allowance for lowered standard of occupation*

| | |
|---|---|
| (maximum) | 37.28 |

*Widow's pension*
(widow of Private or equivalent rank)

| | |
|---|---|
| Standard rate | 74.70 |
| Increase for first child | 13.90 |
| Increase for other children | 15.10 |
| Childless widow under 40 | 17.28 |

*Widow's age allowance*

| | |
|---|---|
| aged 65–69 | 8.50 |
| aged 70–79 | 16.40 |
| aged 80 and over | 24.40 |

# The Water Industry

## ENGLAND AND WALES

In England and Wales the Secretaries of State for the Environment and for Wales and the Director-General of Water Services are responsible for the general oversight of the industry and for ensuring that the private water companies fulfil their statutory obligation to provide water supply and sewerage services.

The Minister of Agriculture, Fisheries and Food and the Secretary of State for Wales are responsible for policy relating to land drainage, flood protection, sea defences and the protection and development of fisheries.

The National Rivers Authority is responsible for water quality and the control of pollution, the management of water resources and nature conservation. The Drinking Water Inspectorate and local authorities are responsible for the quality of drinking water.

### THE WATER COMPANIES

Until the end of 1989, nine regional water authorities in England and the Welsh Water Authority in Wales were responsible for water supply and the development of water resources, sewerage and sewage disposal, pollution control, freshwater fisheries, flood protection, water recreation, and environmental conservation. The Water Act 1989 provided for the creation of a privatized water industry under public regulation, and the functions of the regional water authorities were taken over by ten water holding companies and the regulatory bodies.

Of the 99 per cent of the population of England and Wales who are connected to a public water supply, 75 per cent are supplied by the new water companies (through their principal operating subsidiaries, the water service companies). The remaining 25 per cent are supplied by statutory water companies which were already in the private sector. Most of these have now converted to public limited company (PLC) status. The ten water service companies are also responsible for sewerage and sewage disposal in England and Wales.

### Water Service Companies

ANGLIAN WATER SERVICES LTD, Compass House, Chivers Way, Histon, Cambs. CB4 4ZY
DWR CYMRU (WELSH WATER), Cambrian Way, Brecon, Powys LD3 7HP
NORTHUMBRIAN WATER LTD, Abbey Road, Pity Me, Durham DH1 5FS
NORTH WEST WATER LTD, Dawson House, Liverpool Road, Great Sankey, Warrington WA5 3LW
SEVERN TRENT WATER LTD, 2297 Coventry Road, Sheldon, Birmingham B26 3PU
SOUTHERN WATER SERVICES LTD, Southern House, Yeoman Road, Worthing, W. Sussex BN13 3NX
SOUTH WEST WATER SERVICES LTD, Peninsula House, Rydon Lane, Exeter EX2 7HR
THAMES WATER UTILITIES LTD, Nugent House, Vastern Road, Reading RG1 8DB
WESSEX WATER SERVICES LTD, Wessex House, Passage Street, Bristol BS2 0JQ
YORKSHIRE WATER SERVICES LTD, West Riding House, 67 Albion Street, Leeds LS1 5AA

### REGULATORY BODIES

The Director-General of Water Services is appointed by the Secretaries of State for the Environment and for Wales. Independent of ministers and directly accountable to Parliament, his main duties are to ensure that the water companies can carry out and finance the functions specified in the Water Act 1989 and to protect the interests of water consumers. All the water companies are subject to a system of price control which sets a limit on the average increase in their prices each year. The Office of Water Services (*see* page 367) was set up to support the director-general's activities.

An independent national body, the National Rivers Authority (*see* page 337) was established under the Water Act 1989 to take over the regulatory and river management functions of the regional water authorities. It has statutory duties and powers in relation to water resources, pollution control, flood defence, fisheries, recreation, conservation and navigation in England and Wales.

The Drinking Water Inspectorate (*see* page 305) was established under the Water Act 1989, and is responsible for assessing the quality of the drinking water supplied by the water companies and for inspecting the companies themselves. The inspectors also investigate any accidents affecting drinking water quality. The Chief Inspector presents an annual report to the Secretaries of State for the Environment and for Wales.

### METHODS OF CHARGING

In England and Wales, most householders still pay for domestic water supply and sewerage services through charges based on the assessed value of their property under the old domestic rating system. Industrial and most commercial users are charged according to consumption, which is recorded by meter.

The abolition of domestic rates means that new methods of charging the private consumer for water and sewerage services must be found. The Water Industry Act 1991 gives the water companies until 2000 to decide on and introduce a suitable method of charging. The main options under consideration are a flat-rate licence fee, property banding, and metering. Individual water companies are currently assessing the results of trials of domestic metering.

## SCOTLAND

Overall responsibility for national water policy in Scotland rests with the Secretary of State for Scotland. Most aspects of water policy are administered through the Scottish Office Environment Department, but fisheries and certain aspects of land drainage are the responsibility of the Scottish Office Agriculture and Fisheries Department.

Water supply and sewerage services are at present local authority responsibilities and are provided by the nine regional councils and the three islands councils.

The Central Scotland Water Development Board was established in 1967 with the main statutory function of developing new sources of water supply for the purpose of providing water in bulk to water authorities whose limits of supply are within the board's area, i.e. Central, Fife, Lothian, Strathclyde and Tayside Regional Councils. In November 1992 the Government published a consultation paper which set out eight options for the future structure of water and sewerage services in Scotland, ranging from privatization to retention of the services in local authority control. Following the consultation, the Secretary of State announced in July 1993 that three public water authorities would be established to own and operate current water and sewerage assets and to arrange new investment to maximize private sector involvement. The authorities will be in place by April 1996, with a new independent representative body being set up to protect consumers' interests.

Seven river purification boards and the Islands Councils of Orkney, Shetland and the Western Isles have the specific duty of promoting the cleanliness of Scotland's rivers, lochs and coastal waters and conserving water resources. They are responsible for the prevention and control of pollution within their own areas.

CENTRAL SCOTLAND WATER DEVELOPMENT BOARD, Balmore, Torrance, Glasgow G64 4AJ. *Director,* W. G. Mitchell

METHODS OF CHARGING

Domestic consumers pay a council water charge or pay by water metering; sewerage services are paid for through the council tax. Non-domestic consumers pay non-domestic water rates or metered charges, and non-domestic sewerage rates. Charges and rates are currently set by each regional and islands council.

NORTHERN IRELAND

In Northern Ireland ministerial responsibility for water services lies with the Secretary of State for Northern Ireland. The Department of the Environment for Northern Ireland, operating through the Water Executive, is responsible for policy and co-ordination with regard to supply, distribution and cleanliness of water, and the provision and maintenance of sewerage services.

The Water Executive is divided into four regions, the Eastern, Northern, Western and Southern Divisions. These are based in Belfast, Ballymena, Londonderry and Craigavon respectively.

On major issues the Department of the Environment for Northern Ireland seeks the views of the Northern Ireland Water Council, a body appointed to advise the Department on the exercise of its water and sewerage functions. The Council includes representatives from agriculture, angling, industry, commerce, tourism, trade unions and local government.

METHODS OF CHARGING

Usually householders do not pay separately for water and sewerage services; the costs of these services are allowed for in the Northern Ireland regional rate. Water consumed by industry, commerce and agriculture in excess of 100 cubic metres (22,000 gallons) per half year is charged through meters. Traders operating from industrially derated premises are required to pay for the treatment and disposal of the trade effluent which they discharge into the public sewerage system.

# HM Coastguard

Founded in 1822, originally to guard the coasts against smuggling, HM Coastguard's role today is the very different one of guarding and saving life at sea. The Service is responsible for co-ordinating all civil maritime search and rescue operations around the 10,500 mile coastline of Great Britain and Northern Ireland and 1,000 miles into the Atlantic. In addition, it co-operates with search and rescue organizations of neighbouring countries in western Europe and around the Atlantic seaboard. The Service maintains a 24-hour radar watch on the Dover Strait, providing a Channel navigation information service for all shipping in one of the busiest sea lanes in the world. It also liaises very closely with the off-shore oil and gas industry and with passenger ship companies.

Since 1978 HM Coastguard has been organized into six regions, each with a Regional Controller, operating from a Maritime Rescue Co-ordination Centre. Each region is subdivided into districts under District Controllers, operating from Maritime Rescue Sub-Centres. In all there are 21 of these centres. They are on 24-hour watch and are fitted with a comprehensive range of communications equipment. They are supported by some 357 smaller stations manned by part-time Auxiliary Coastguards under the direction of Regulars, each of which keeps its parent centre fully informed of day-to-day casualty risk, particularly on the more remote danger spots around the coast.

Between 1 January and 31 December 1993, the 450 Regular and 3,500 Auxiliary Coastguards co-ordinated 9,611 incidents requiring search and rescue facilities, resulting in assistance being given to 17,106 persons. All distress telephone and radio calls are centralized on the 21 centres, which are on the alert for people or vessels in distress, shipping hazards and oil slicks. Using modern telecommunications equipment, including satellite, they can alert and co-ordinate the most appropriate rescue facilities; RNLI lifeboats, Royal Navy, RAF or Coastguard helicopters, fixed-wing aircraft, naval vessels, ships in the vicinity, or Coastguard shore and cliff rescue teams.

For those who regularly sail in local waters or make longer passages, the Coastguard Yacht and Boat Safety Scheme provides a valuable free service. Its aim is to give the Coastguard a record of the details of craft, their equipment fit and normal operating areas. Yacht and Boat Safety Scheme cards are available from all Coastguard stations, harbourmasters' offices, and most yacht clubs and marinas as well as Coastguard Headquarters.

Members of the public who see an accident or a potentially dangerous incident on or around the coast should dial 999 and ask for the Coastguard.

On 1 April 1994 HM Coastguard and the Marine Pollution Control Unit together formed the Coastguard Agency, an executive agency of the Department of Transport.

*Coastguard Headquarters and Office of the Chief Coastguard,* Spring Place, 105 Commercial Road, Southampton SO15 1EG. Tel: 01703 – 329100.

# Energy

## THE COAL INDUSTRY

Coal has been mined in Britain for centuries and the availability of coal was crucial to the industrial revolution of the 18th and 19th centuries. Mines were in private ownership until 1947 when they were nationalized and came under the management of the National Coal Board (now the British Coal Corporation). In addition to producing coal at its own deep-mine and opencast sites, British Coal is responsible for licensing private operators of deep mines employing up to 150 workers and opencast mines.

In October 1992 British Coal announced that it would close 31 of its 50 deep mines by March 1993. Public concern led to a government review of the decision. The conclusions of the review, published in March 1993 in the White Paper *The Prospects for Coal* (for summary, *see* Whitaker's Almanack 1994), confirmed that the earlier assessment of the prospects for the industry were realistic but proposed to give temporary support to the industry to give it a better chance of a competitive future. Despite this support, the continuing decline in the demand for coal meant that by the end of 1993 only 24 deep mines remained operational, including Asfordby, Leics., and Maltby, S. Yorks., which are under development and not in full operation. British Coal has offered to the private sector pits which it does not intend to continue in production; in 1993 it advertised 28 mines for lease and licence, and by the end of 1993 was negotiating for the licence of six mines.

The main domestic customer of the coal industry is the electricity supply industry, but the latter's demand for coal has declined as it turns increasingly to alternative fuels. In the first ten months of 1993, the amount of coal consumed at power stations was 15.7 per cent less than during the corresponding period in 1992. National Power has announced that it expects to close ten of its 18 coal-fired power stations by 2000, so the long-term prospects for the coal industry are poor and further mine closures are expected.

### PRIVATIZATION

Under the Coal Industry Act 1994, a new body, the Coal Authority, was established to take over ownership of coal reserves and to issue licences to private mining companies as part of the privatization of British Coal. The Coal Authority will also deal with the physical legacy of mining, e.g. subsidence damage claims, and will be responsible for holding and making available all existing records.

The Government intends to offer the mines for sale in five businesses based in the separate regions of Scotland, Wales and the North-East and two based on the central areas of the Midlands and Yorkshire. British Coal will continue under licence from the Coal Authority until privatization is complete and will then be wound up.

**SUPPLY AND DEMAND** 1992 *million tonnes*

*Supply*

| | |
|---|---|
| Production of deep-mined coal | 65.8 |
| Production of opencast coal | 18.4 |
| Recovered slurry, fines, etc. | 0.6 |
| Imports | 20.4 |
| Change in colliery stocks | +2.2 |
| Change in stocks at opencast sites | +0.6 |
| Total supply | 102.4 |

*Home consumption*

| | |
|---|---|
| Electricity supply industry | 79.0 |
| Coke ovens | 9.0 |
| Low temperature carbonization plants | 0.6 |
| Manufactured fuel plants | 0.7 |
| Railways | — |
| Collieries | 0.1 |
| Industry (disposals to users) | 6.1 |
| Domestic (disposals to users) | 4.2 |
| Public services | 0.7 |
| Miscellaneous | 0.2 |
| Total home consumption | 100.6 |
| Overseas shipments and bunkers | 0.7 |
| Total consumption and shipments | 101.3 |
| *Change in distributed stocks | +1.2 |
| †Balance | −0.1 |

*Stock change excludes industrial and domestic stocks
†This is the balance between supply and consumption, shipments and changes in known distributed stocks
*Source:* HMSO – *Annual Abstract of Statistics 1994*

## THE GAS INDUSTRY

The gas industry in the United Kingdom was nationalized in 1949 under the Gas Act 1948, and operated as the Gas Council. The Gas Act 1972 replaced the Gas Council with the British Gas Corporation and led to greater centralization of the industry. The British Gas Corporation was privatized in 1986 as British Gas PLC and is currently the main supplier of gas in Great Britain. The Office of Gas Supply (*see* page 309) is the regulatory body for the gas industry.

In July 1993 the Monopolies and Mergers Commission found that British Gas's integrated business in Great Britain as a gas trader and the owner of the gas transportation system was against the public interest, and it recommended that the company divest itself of its gas supply business in Great Britain. In December 1993 the President of the Board of Trade announced that competition would be introduced into the domestic gas supply market in April 1996, and that British Gas should separate fully its supply and transportation operations; it would not be required to divest itself of its supply business. Competition would be limited to 5 per cent of the market in the year to April 1997, and 10 per cent in the year to April 1998, when all restrictions would be removed.

In May 1994 a consultation document, *Competition and Choice in the Gas Market* (*see* page 1172), was published jointly by the Department of Trade and Industry and the Office of Gas Supply.

FUEL INPUT AND GAS OUTPUT: GAS SALES 1992
*giga-watt hours*

*Fuel input to gas industry*

| | |
|---|---:|
| Petroleum (*million tonnes*) | — |
| *Petroleum gases | 50 |
| Natural gas | — |
| Coke oven gas | — |
| Total to gas works | 50 |
| Natural gas for direct supply | 621,143 |
| Total fuel input | 621,193 |

*Gas output and sales*
Gas output:

| | |
|---|---:|
| Town gas | 32 |
| Natural gas supplied direct | 621,143 |
| Gross total available | 621,175 |
| Own use | −2,651 |
| †Statistical difference | −24,493 |
| Total sales | 594,031 |

*Analysis of gas sales*

| | |
|---|---:|
| Power stations | 27,051 |
| Final users: | |
| Iron and steel industry | 14,198 |
| Other industries | 117,942 |
| Domestic | 330,100 |
| Public administration | 43,207 |
| Agriculture | 1,179 |
| Miscellaneous | 55,494 |

*Butane, propane, ethane and refinery tail gases
†Supply greater than recorded demand (−). Includes losses in distribution
Source: HMSO - *Annual Abstract of Statistics 1994*

## BRITISH GAS PLC

The principal business of British Gas is the purchase, transmission and sale of natural gas to domestic, industrial and commercial customers in Great Britain. British Gas has hydrocarbon exploration and production operations offshore and onshore, both in Great Britain and overseas, and it has an interest in gas-related activities world-wide.

British Gas is divided into three parts: the UK Gas Business, Exploration and Production, and Global. In December 1993 it announced that it would restructure its UK operations to separate its gas supply business from its gas transportation business. Its regional structure was abolished and replaced by five gas business units and a support services unit. The business units are: British Gas TransCo, which provides transportation and storage services to shippers; British Gas (Public Supply), which sells gas to domestic and other customers using less than 2,500 therms per year; British Gas Contract Trading, which sells gas to industrial and commercial customers using more than 2,500 therms per year; British Gas Retail, which markets gas appliances through a national chain of shops; and British Gas Service, which handles the servicing and installation of gas central heating and other equipment.

BRITISH GAS PLC, Rivermill House, 152 Grosvenor Road, London SW1V 3JL. Tel: 0171-821 1444. *Chairman*, R. V. Giordano; *Chief Executive*, C. H. Brown

### SUPPLY AND TRANSMISSION

British Gas obtains natural gas from fields on mainland Britain, in coastal waters and in the North Sea. It also imports

gas from other countries. In 1992 total production from UK continental shelf fields of gas contracted to British Gas was 61,216 million cubic metres, of which 60,927 million cubic metres was offshore production and 289 million cubic metres was onshore production.

The mainland national transmission system is operated by British Gas, with other gas suppliers entering contracts with British Gas to use the system. British Gas operates six reception terminals. The length of mains in use in 1993 was 265,000 km: 247,000 km of distribution mains and 18,000 km of transmission mains.

### SALES 1993

| Total gas sold and used: | GWh |
|---|---:|
| Residential | 340,164 |
| Commercial | 74,897 |
| Industrial | 139,829 |
| Total | 554,890 |

| Charges for domestic use from 1 Oct. 1993: | pence |
|---|---:|
| Standing charge per day | 10.1 |
| Unit charges | pence per kilowatt hour |
| Annual consumption | |
| First 146,536 KWh | 1.477 |
| 146,537–293,071 KWh | 1.409 |
| 293,072–439,607 KWh | 1.375 |
| 439,608–732,678 KWh | 1.341 |

### BRITISH GAS FINANCE
£ million

| | 1992 | 1993 |
|---|---:|---:|
| *Turnover* | | |
| UK gas supply | 8,129 | 8,055 |
| Overseas gas supply | 883 | 965 |
| Exploration and production | 995 | 1,219 |
| UK marketing activities | 786 | 763 |
| Other activities | 184 | 238 |
| Less: intra-group sales | (723) | (854) |
| Total | 10,254 | 10,386 |
| *Operating costs* include: | | |
| Raw materials and consumables | 3,664 | 3,601 |
| Gas Levy | 282 | 240 |
| Employee costs | 1,691 | 1,726 |
| Exceptional charges | 320 | 1,683 |
| Current cost depreciation | 1,196 | 1,337 |
| Total | 9,151 | 10,696 |
| Current cost operating profit (loss) | 1,109 | (351) |
| Gearing adjustment | 41 | 65 |
| Net interest payable | (311) | (357) |
| Current cost profit (loss) before tax | 846 | (613) |
| Current cost profit (loss) after tax | 475 | 536 |
| Minority shareholders' interest | (2) | 3 |
| Current cost profit (loss) attributable to British Gas shareholders | 473 | (533) |
| Dividends | (613) | (628) |
| Transfer from reserves | (140) | (1,161) |

## THE ELECTRICITY SUPPLY INDUSTRY

Under the Electricity Act 1989 twelve new public electricity supply companies were formed from the twelve area electricity boards in England and Wales. The companies were floated on the stock market in 1990. Four new companies were formed from the Central Electricity Generating Board: three new generating companies (National Power PLC, Nuclear Electric PLC and PowerGen PLC) and the

National Grid Company PLC. National Power PLC and PowerGen PLC were floated on the stock market in 1991, the Government retaining a 40 per cent holding in both companies.

In Scotland, three new companies were formed: Scottish Power PLC, Scottish Hydro-Electric PLC and Scottish Nuclear Ltd. Flotation of Scottish Power PLC and Scottish Hydro-Electric PLC on the stock market took place in 1991.

A trade and representational organization, the Electricity Association, was created by the newly formed British electricity companies; its principal subsidiaries were Electricity Association Services Ltd (for representational and professional services) and Electricity Association Technology Ltd (for distribution and utilization research, development and technology transfer). Electricity Association Technology Ltd (now renamed EA Technology Ltd) left the Electricity Association group of companies in April 1993.

The Office of Electricity Regulation (*see* page 302) is the regulatory body for the industry.

ELECTRICITY ASSOCIATION SERVICES LTD, 30 Millbank, London SW1P 4RD. Tel: 0171–344 5700. *Chief Executive*, P. E. E. Daubeney

EA TECHNOLOGY LTD, Capenhurst, Chester CH1 6ES. Tel: 0151-339 4181. *Managing Director*, Dr S. F. Exell

SUPPLY COMPANIES

THE NATIONAL GRID COMPANY PLC, National Grid House, Kirby Corner Road, Coventry CV4 8JY. Tel: 01203–537777. *Chief Executive*, D. Jones

NATIONAL POWER PLC, Windmill Hill Business Park, Whitehill Way, Swindon, Wilts. SN5 9NX. Tel: 01793–877777. *Chief Executive*, J. Baker

NUCLEAR ELECTRIC PLC, Barnett Way, Barnwood, Glos GL4 7RS. Tel: 01452–652222. *Chairman*, J. Collier

POWERGEN PLC, 53 New Broad Street, London EC2M 1JJ. Tel: 0171–638 5742. *Chief Executive*, E. Wallis

REGIONAL ELECTRICITY COMPANIES

EASTERN ELECTRICITY PLC, PO Box 40, Wherstead, Ipswich IP2 9AQ

EAST MIDLANDS ELECTRICITY PLC, PO Box 4 North PDO, 398 Coppice Road, Arnold, Nottingham NG5 7HX

LONDON ELECTRICITY PLC, Templar House, 81–87 High Holborn, London WC1V 6NU

MANWEB PLC, Sealand Road, Chester CH1 4LR

MIDLANDS ELECTRICITY PLC, Mucklow Hill, Halesowen, W. Midlands B62 8BP

NORTHERN ELECTRIC PLC, Carliol House, Newcastle upon Tyne NE99 1SE

NORWEB PLC, Talbot Road, Manchester M16 0MQ

SEEBOARD PLC, Forest Gate, Brighton Road, Crawley, W. Sussex RH11 9BH

SOUTHERN ELECTRIC PLC, Littlewick Green, Maidenhead, Berks SL6 3QB

SWALEC PLC, St Mellons, Cardiff CF3 9XW

SOUTH WESTERN ELECTRICITY PLC, 800 Park Avenue, Aztec West, Almondsbury, Avon BS12 4SE

YORKSHIRE ELECTRICITY GROUP PLC, Scarcroft, Leeds LS14 3HS

SCOTTISH COMPANIES

SCOTTISH HYDRO-ELECTRIC PLC, 16 Rothesay Terrace, Edinburgh EH3 7SE. Tel: 0131-225 1361. *Chief Executive*, R. Young

SCOTTISH NUCLEAR LTD, 3 Redwood Crescent, Peel Park, East Kilbride G74 5PR. Tel: 0135 52–66266. *Chief Executive*, Dr R. C. Jeffrey

SCOTTISH POWER PLC, 1 Atlantic Quay, Glasgow G2 8SP. Tel: 0141–248 8200. *Chief Executive*, Dr I. Preston

GENERATION, SUPPLY AND CONSUMPTION
*gigawatt-hours*

| | 1991 | 1992 |
|---|---|---|
| *Electricity generated* | | |
| All generating companies: total | 322,805 | 326,879 |
| Conventional steam stations | 245,042 | 239,805 |
| Nuclear stations | 70,543 | 78,468 |
| Gas turbines and oil engines | 355 | 363 |
| Hydro-electric stations: | | |
| Natural flow | 4,580 | 5,514 |
| Pumped storage | 1,523 | 1,703 |
| Other (mainly wind) | 762 | 1,026 |
| *Electricity used on works: total* | 20,111 | 20,526 |
| Major generating companies | 18,420 | 18,757 |
| Other generators | 1,691 | 1,769 |
| *Electricity supplied (gross)* | | |
| All generating companies: total | 302,694 | 306,352 |
| Conventional steam stations | 232,865 | 227,275 |
| Nuclear stations | 62,761 | 70,643 |
| Gas turbines and oil engines | 310 | 314 |
| Hydro-electric stations: | | |
| Natural flow | 4,561 | 5,494 |
| Pumped storage | 1,465 | 1,641 |
| Other (mainly wind) | 732 | 985 |
| *Electricity used in pumping* | | |
| Major generating companies | 2,109 | 2,261 |
| *Electricity supplied (net): total* | 300,526 | 304,091 |
| Major generating companies | 280,649 | 283,478 |
| Other generators | 19,937 | 20,613 |
| Net imports | 16,407 | 16,693 |
| Electricity available | 316,993 | 320,785 |
| Losses in transmission, etc | 26,152 | 27,618 |
| *Electricity consumption: total* | 290,841 | 293,167 |
| Fuel industries | 9,794 | 9,969 |
| Final users: total | 281,048 | 283,198 |
| Industrial sector | 99,570 | 100,902 |
| Domestic sector | 98,098 | 99,482 |
| Other sectors | 83,380 | 82,814 |

*Source:* HMSO - *Annual Abstract of Statistics 1994*

# Transport

## GOODS TRANSPORT 1992

| | |
|---|---|
| TOTAL TONNE KILOMETRES (*thousand millions*) | 208.3 |
| Road | 126.5 |
| Rail (British Rail only) | 15.3 |
| Water: coastwise oil products* | 30.1 |
| Water: other* | 25.0 |
| Pipelines (except gases) | 11.2 |
| TOTAL (*million tonnes*) | 1,923 |
| Road | 1,555 |
| Rail (British Rail only) | 125 |
| Water: coastwise oil products* | 43 |
| Water: other* | 97 |
| Pipelines (except gases) | 106 |

*'Coastwise' includes all sea traffic within the UK, Isle of Man and Channel Islands. 'Other' means other coastwise plus inland waterway traffic and one-port traffic

## PASSENGER TRANSPORT 1992p
*Thousand million passenger kilometres (estimated)*

| | |
|---|---|
| TOTAL | 611 |
| Air | 5 |
| Rail* | 38 |
| Road: Public service vehicles | 43 |
|     Cars, vans and taxis | 515 |
|     Motorcycles | 5 |
|     Pedal cycles | 5 |

p provisional
*Including London Regional Transport and Passenger Transport Executive railway systems

## SEAPORT TRAFFIC 1992†   *Million gross tonnes*

| | |
|---|---|
| FOREIGN TRAFFIC: *Imports* | |
| Bulk fuel traffic | 76.5 |
| Other bulk traffic | 42.6 |
| Container and roll-on traffic | 42.8 |
| Semi-bulk traffic | 14.9 |
| Conventional traffic | 1.2 |
| All imports | 117.9 |
| FOREIGN TRAFFIC: *Exports* | |
| Bulk fuel traffic | 88.8 |
| Other bulk traffic | 20.5 |
| Container and roll-on traffic | 34.2 |
| Semi-bulk traffic | 5.2 |
| Conventional traffic | 1.1 |
| All exports | 149.9 |
| DOMESTIC TRAFFIC | |
| Bulk fuel traffic | 98.1 |
| Other bulk traffic | 37.8 |
| Container and roll-on traffic | 9.1 |
| Semi-bulk traffic | 0.3 |
| Conventional traffic | 0.3 |
| Non-oil traffic with UK offshore installations | 5.0 |
| All domestic traffic | 150.7 |
| TOTAL FOREIGN AND DOMESTIC TRAFFIC | 478.5 |

†All data are for Great Britain

*Source of all data:* HMSO – *Annual Abstract of Statistics 1994*

## AIR PASSENGERS 1993*

| | |
|---|---|
| ALL UK AIRPORTS: TOTAL | 113,897,887 |
| LONDON AREA AIRPORTS: TOTAL | 72,879,617 |
|   Battersea Heliport | 3,215 |
|   Gatwick | 20,151,339 |
|   Heathrow | 47,899,107 |
|   London City | 244,001 |
|   Luton | 1,872,487 |
|   †Southend | 9,713 |
|   Stansted | 2,702,970 |
| OTHER UK AIRPORTS: TOTAL | 41,015,055 |
|   Aberdeen | 2,333,849 |
|   Barrow-in-Furness | 651 |
|   Belfast | 2,200,186 |
|   Belfast City | 846,307 |
|   Bembridge | 521 |
|   Benbecula | 36,063 |
|   ‡Biggin Hill | 7,152 |
|   Birmingham | 4,202,685 |
|   Blackpool | 99,831 |
|   Bournemouth | 82,869 |
|   Bristol | 1,139,602 |
|   Cambridge | 29,144 |
|   Cardiff | 800 704 |
|   Carlisle | 3,405 |
|   Coventry | 10,102 |
|   Dundee | 23,955 |
|   East Midlands | 1,392,090 |
|   Edinburgh | 2,870,618 |
|   Exeter | 177,814 |
|   Glasgow | 5,169,922 |
|   Gloucestershire | 8,876 |
|   Hawarden | 138 |
|   Humberside | 216,191 |
|   Inverness | 245,355 |
|   Islay | 18,338 |
|   Isle of Man | 507,553 |
|   Isles of Scilly–St Mary's | 99,671 |
|     –Tresco | 20,781 |
|   Kent International | 11,848 |
|   Kirkwall | 111,122 |
|   Leeds/Bradford | 719,601 |
|   Lerwick (Tingwall) | 4,433 |
|   Liverpool | 461,075 |
|   Londonderry | 31,086 |
|   Lydd | 1,515 |
|   Manchester | 13,099,080 |
|   Newcastle | 2,143,022 |
|   Norwich | 204,948 |
|   Penzance Heliport | 83,814 |
|   Plymouth | 78,527 |
|   Prestwick | 14,124 |
|   Scatsta | 13,173 |
|   Shoreham | 2,249 |
|   Southampton | 420,346 |
|   Stornoway | 88,782 |
|   Sumburgh | 450,735 |
|   Teesside | 346,272 |
|   Tiree | 5,664 |
|   Unst | 145,574 |
|   Wick | 33,692 |
| CHANNEL IS. AIRPORTS: TOTAL | 2,432,472 |
|   Alderney | 77,313 |
|   Guernsey | 760,717 |
|   Jersey | 1,594,442 |

*Total terminal transit, scheduled and charter passengers
†January to November 1993 only
‡From June 1993 only

*Source:* Civil Aviation Authority

## AERODROMES/AIRPORTS

The following aerodromes in the UK, the Isle of Man and the Channel Islands are either state owned or licensed for use by civil aircraft. A number of unlicensed aerodromes not included in this list are also available for private use by special permission. Aerodromes designated as Customs airports are printed in small capitals. Customs facilities are available at certain other aerodromes by special arrangement.

BAA    Owned by BAA PLC
H      Licensed for helicopters
HIAL   Operated by Highland and
       Islands Airports Ltd
J      Military aerodromes – civil
       availability by prior
       permission
M      Owned by municipal authority
P      Private ownership
S      Government owned and
       operated

### ENGLAND AND WALES

Aberporth, Dyfed   J
Andrewsfield, Essex
Barrow (Walney Island), Cumbria
Bembridge, IOW
Benson, Oxon   J
Beverley/Linley Hill, N. Humberside
BIGGIN HILL, Kent   P
BIRMINGHAM   P
Blackbushe, Hants
BLACKPOOL, Lancs   P
Bodmin, Cornwall
Boscombe Down, Wilts   J
Bourn, Cambridge
BOURNEMOUTH, Dorset   P
BRISTOL   P
Brize Norton, Oxford   J
Brough, N. Humberside
Caernarfon, Gwynedd
CAMBRIDGE   P
CARDIFF   P
Carlisle, Cumbria   M
Chichester (Goodwood), Sussex
Chivenor, Devon   J
Church Fenton, N. Yorks   J
Clacton, Essex
Compton Abbas, Dorset
Cosford, Wolverhampton   J
COVENTRY, W. Midlands   M
Cranfield, Beds
Cranwell, Lincs   J
Crowfield, Suffolk
Culdrose, Cornwall   J
Deenethorpe, Northants
Denham, Bucks
Derby
Dishforth, N. Yorks   J
Dunkeswell, Devon
Dunsfold, Surrey   M
Duxford, Cambs   M
Eaglescott, Devon
Earls Colne, Halstead
EAST MIDLANDS, Derbys   P
Elstree, Herts

EXETER, Devon
Fairoaks, Surrey
Farnborough, Hants   S
Fenland, Lincs
Filton, Bristol
Finningley, S. Yorks   J
Fowlmere, Cambs
Full Sutton, N. Yorks
Gloucestershire (Staverton)   P
Great Yarmouth (North Denes),
   Norfolk   H
Halfpenny Green, Staffs
Halton, Bucks   J
Haverfordwest, Dyfed   M
Hawarden, Clwyd
Hucknall, Notts
HUMBERSIDE   P
Ipswich, Suffolk
Isle of Wight/Sandown
Land's End (St Just), Cornwall
Lashenden, Headcorn, Kent
LEEDS/BRADFORD   P
Lee-on-Solent, Hants   J
Leicester
Linton-on-Ouse, Yorks   J
Little Gransden, Beds
LIVERPOOL   P
Llanbedr, Gwynedd   J
LONDON/CITY
LONDON/GATWICK   BAA
LONDON/HEATHROW   BAA
LONDON/STANSTED   BAA
London/Westland Heliport   H
LUTON, Beds   P
LYDD, Kent
Lyneham, Wilts   J
MANCHESTER   P
Manchester (Barton)
MANSTON/KENT INTERNATIONAL
   J
Marston Moor, York
Mona, Gwynedd   J
Netherthorpe, S. Yorks
NEWCASTLE UPON TYNE   P
Newton, Notts   J
Northampton (Sywell)
Northolt, Middx   J
NORWICH, Norfolk   M
Nottingham
Old Sarum, Wilts
Oxford (Kidlington)
Penzance, Cornwall   H
Perranporth, Cornwall
Peterborough (Conington)
Peterborough (Sibson)
PLYMOUTH (ROBOROUGH), Devon
Portland Naval, Dorset   JH
Redhill, Surrey
Retford/Gamston, Notts
Rochester, Kent
St Mawgan, Cornwall   J
Sandtoft, Humberside
Scilly Isles (St Mary's)   M
Seething, Norfolk
Shawbury, Shropshire   J
Sherburn-in-Elmet, N. Yorks
Shipdham, Norfolk
Shobdon, Herefordshire
SHOREHAM, W. Sussex   P
Silverstone, Northants
Sleap, Shropshire
SOUTHAMPTON/Eastleigh   P

SOUTHEND, Essex   P
Stapleford, Essex
Sturgate, Lincs
Swansea, W. Glam   M
TEESSIDE, Cleveland   P
Thruxton, Hants
Tresco, Isles of Scilly   H
Turweston, Northants
Valley, Gwynedd   J
Warton, Lancs
Wattisham, Suffolk   J
Wellesbourne Mountford, Warwick
Welshpool, Powys
Weston, Avon   H
White Waltham, Berks
Wickenby, Lincs
Woodford, Gtr Manchester
Woodvale, Merseyside   J
Wycombe Air Park (Booker), Bucks
Yeovil, Somerset
Yeovilton, Somerset   J

### SCOTLAND

ABERDEEN (DYCE)   BAA
Barra, Hebrides
Benbecula, Hebrides   HIAL
Cumbernauld, Strathclyde
Dundee   M
Eday, Orkneys   M
EDINBURGH   BAA
Fair Isle, Shetlands
Fife/Glenrothes   M
Flotta, Orkneys
GLASGOW   BAA
Inverness (Dalcross)   HIAL
Islay (Port Ellen), Hebrides   HIAL
Kirkwall, Orkneys   HIAL
Lerwick (Tingwall), Shetlands   M
Leuchars, Fife   J
Machrihanish, Kintyre   J
North Ronaldsay, Orkneys   M
Papa Westray, Orkneys   M
Perth (Scone)
PRESTWICK, Ayrshire   BAA
Sanday, Orkneys   M
Scatsta, Shetlands
Stornoway, Hebrides   HIAL
Stronsay, Orkneys   M
SUMBURGH, Shetlands   HIAL
Tiree, Hebrides   HIAL
Unst, Shetlands   M
West Freugh, Dumfries   S
Westray, Orkneys   M
Whalsay, Shetlands
Wick, Caithness   HIAL

### NORTHERN IRELAND

BELFAST (ALDERGROVE)
Belfast (City)
Enniskillen (St Angelo), Co.
   Fermanagh   P
Londonderry (Eglinton)   M
Newtownards, Co. Down

### ISLANDS

ALDERNEY, CI   S
GUERNSEY, CI   S
JERSEY, CI   S
RONALDSWAY, IOM   S

## RAILWAYS

Britain pioneered railways and a railway network was developed across Britain by private companies in the course of the 19th century. In 1948 the main railway companies were nationalized and were run by a public authority, the British Transport Commission. The Commission was replaced by the British Railways Board on 1 January 1963. On 1 April 1994 the British Railways Board ceased to be responsible for the provision of rail services in Britain but continues as operator (under the operating name British Rail) of all train services until they are sold or franchised to the private sector.

Prior to privatization, management of the railways had been organized into the business sectors of InterCity, Network SouthEast, Regional Railways, Trainload Freight and Railfreight Distribution. These businesses have ceased to exist corporately but the names will continue to be used for trading purposes in the short term. European Passenger Services Ltd was set up to manage international passenger rail services through the Channel Tunnel and ownership was transferred to the Government in May 1994.

### PRIVATIZATION

Since 1 April 1994, ownership of track and land has been vested in Railtrack, a government-owned company. Railtrack manages the track and charges for access to it and is responsible for signalling and timetabling. It does not operate train services. It owns the freehold of stations, but station management is being privatized under management contract or lease arrangements. Initially, Railtrack's infrastructure support functions are being provided by 30 British Rail service companies; these companies will be restructured and privatized. Railtrack will invest in infrastructure principally using finance raised by track charges, and will take investment decisions in consultation with rail operators. Railtrack itself will eventually be privatized.

Passenger services have been divided into 25 train-operating units, which will be run by British Rail as 'shadow' franchises before gradually being franchised to private sector operators. The private sector will also be able to run completely new services with a right of open access to the track. The Government will continue to subsidize loss-making but socially necessary rail services. The new franchising director will award franchises by competitive tendering, will monitor the performance of the franchisees, and allocate and administer government subsidy payments.

The first 'shadow' franchise, set up in October 1993, was the Victoria-Gatwick Express; five more were established in April 1994. All six will be offered for sale in 1995. A further seven franchises are to be privatized by the end of 1996, and the remaining 12 at a later date.

British Rail's passenger rolling stock has been divided between three subsidiary companies which will lease rolling stock to franchisees, open-access operators and, pending franchising, to British Rail's 25 operating units. The three companies will be privatized in 1995. Trainload Freight and the contract services business of Railfreight Distribution have been merged and split into three geographically-based companies, which will be privatized in due course. The European business of Railfreight Distribution will be privatized when the Channel Tunnel freight services have been established. The domestic and deep-sea container business of Railfreight Distribution (Freightliner) is being sold separately during 1994. Rail Express Systems, which carries Royal Mail letters for the Post Office, will be privatized as a single entity as soon as possible.

The new independent Rail Regulator will be responsible for the licensing of new railway operators, approving access agreements, promoting the use and development of the network, and protecting the interests of rail users.

BRITISH RAILWAYS BOARD, *see* page 291
RAILTRACK, 40 Bernard Street, London WC1N 1LG. Tel: 0171-928 5151. *Chairman,* R. Horton. *Chief Executive,* J. Edmonds, CBE
OFFICE OF PASSENGER RAIL FRANCHISING (OPRAF), 26 Old Queen Street, London SW1H 9HP. Tel: 0171-799 8800. *Franchising Director,* R. Salmon
OFFICE OF THE RAIL REGULATOR (ORR), 1 Waterhouse Square, Holborn Bars, 138–142 Holborn, London EC1N 2SU. Tel: 0171-282 2000. *Rail Regulator,* J. Swift

### BRITISH RAIL OPERATIONS

At 31 March 1994, British Rail had 23,452 miles of standard gauge lines and sidings in use, representing 10,275 miles of route of which 3,087 miles were electrified. Standard rail on main line has a weight of 110 lb per yard. British Rail had 1,885 locomotives (1,625 diesel-electric and 260 electric); 1,820 diesel multiple-unit vehicles, 6,570 electric multiple-unit vehicles and 2,502 locomotive-hauled vehicles.

Loaded train miles run in passenger service totalled 228.1 million. Passenger journeys made during the year totalled 713.2 million, including 341.3 million made by holders of season tickets. The average distance of each passenger journey on ordinary fare was 35.7 miles; and on season ticket, 16.4 miles. Passenger stations in use in 1994 numbered 2,493 and freight terminals 60.

There were 13,871 freight vehicles and 910 other vehicles in the non-passenger-carrying stock. Train miles run in freight service totalled 26 million.

On 31 March 1994 British Rail employed 115,546 staff (124,791 at 31 March 1993). Including subsidiaries, the group total at 31 March 1994 was 121,025 (133,060 at 31 March 1993).

### FINANCIAL RESULTS

British Rail's profit and loss account for 1993–4 showed a deficit of £108.4 million after interest and extraordinary items, compared with a deficit of £163.9 million in 1992–3. The railway operating surplus was £23 million compared with a deficit of £94.3 million for the previous year.

| | £ million |
|---|---|
| *Railways* | 1993–4 |
| Turnover (including grants) | |
| InterCity | 896.8 |
| Network SouthEast | 1,114.6 |
| Regional Railways | 817.3 |
| Trainload Freight | 432.1 |
| Railfreight Distribution | 159.5 |
| Parcels | 78.4 |
| Other | 146.8 |
| Total | 3,645.5 |
| | |
| Operating expenditure | |
| Train operation | 601.4 |
| Train provision | 156.5 |
| Operations control | 270.0 |
| Train maintenance | 555.7 |
| Terminals | 428.4 |
| Commercial services | 100.6 |
| Security | 40.2 |
| Track, signalling and telecommunications | 552.5 |
| Train catering | 42.2 |
| General expenses | 482.4 |
| Depreciation and amortisation | 266.4 |
| Deferred grant income | (191.8) |

| | |
|---|---|
| Non-rail business | 154.9 |
| Exceptional items | 163.1 |
| Total | 3,622.5 |
| | |
| Operating profit | 23.0 |
| Profit on disposal of fixed assets | 37.8 |
| Restructuring costs | (48.3) |
| Interest and similar charges | (120.9) |
| Group loss | (108.4) |

The costs of restructuring the operations of British Rail in 1992–4 prior to privatization were £102 million, of which £43.9 million was offset by government grants. A further £81 million is expected to be spent in 1994–5. In 1992–4 £372.2 million was spent on voluntary severance schemes for 17,000 employees and on rationalization costs, of which £124.7 million was offset by government grants.

ACCIDENTS ON RAILWAYS

| | 1991–2 | 1992–3 |
|---|---|---|
| *Train accidents: total* | 960 | 1,152 |
| Persons killed: total | 11 | 5 |
| Passengers | 2 | 0 |
| Railway staff | 2 | 1 |
| Others | 7 | 4 |
| Persons injured: total | 391 | 153 |
| Passengers | 307 | 66 |
| Railway staff | 65 | 74 |
| Others | 19 | 13 |
| *Other accidents through movement of railway vehicles* | | |
| Persons killed | 73 | 38 |
| Persons injured | 2,360 | 2,558 |
| *Other accidents on railway premises* | | |
| Persons killed | 10 | 7 |
| Persons injured | 6,900 | 7,524 |
| *Trespassers and suicides* | | |
| Persons killed | 242 | 244 |
| Persons injured | 92 | 89 |

THE CHANNEL TUNNEL

The earliest recorded scheme for a submarine transport connection between Britain and France was in 1802. Tunnelling has begun simultaneously on both sides of the Channel three times, in 1881, in the early 1970s, and on 1 December 1987, when construction workers began to bore the first of the three tunnels which form the current project. They 'holed through' the first tunnel (the service tunnel) on 1 December 1990. Tunnelling was completed in June 1991.

In January 1986 the contract for construction and operation of the tunnel and its services was awarded to an Anglo-French private-sector company called CTG-FM, subsequently renamed Eurotunnel. Eurotunnel's costs from establishment in 1986 to the first commercial service in 1994 were £8,750 million. The funds available to Eurotunnel amount to £10,500 million, raised through equity and loans. Eurotunnel expect to break even in 1998, and the projected costs until that time are estimated at £10,500 million.

The submarine link comprises three tunnels. There are two rail tunnels, each carrying trains in one direction, which measure 24.93 ft (7.6 m) in diameter. Between them lies a smaller service tunnel, measuring 15.75 ft (4.8 m) in diameter. The service tunnel is linked to the rail tunnels by 130 cross-passages for maintenance and safety purposes. The tunnels are 31 miles (50 km) long, 24 miles (38 km) of which is under the sea-bed at an average depth of 132 ft (40 m).

There are two cross-over caverns, the largest man-made undersea caverns in existence, where sliding doors can be moved so that trains may cross from one tunnel to the other in emergencies or during large maintenance jobs.

The rail terminals are situated at Folkestone and Calais, and the tunnels go underground at Shakespeare Cliff, Dover, and Sangatte, west of Calais. Eurotunnel has combined passport controls on both sides of the Channel so that passengers only stop once for frontier controls and continue their journey uninterrupted once through the tunnel.

SERVICES

There will be a combination of services running through the tunnels. The all-passenger service, on newly-designed Eurostar trains, will provide a London-to-Paris service (approximate journey time, 3 hours) and a London-to-Brussels service (approximate journey time, 3 hours 10 minutes). The vehicle shuttle service, Le Shuttle, will use specially-designed trains capable of holding any form of passenger vehicle except heavy goods vehicles (HGVs), which will be carried on separate trains. All passengers, apart from HGV drivers, stay with their vehicles for the duration of the journey. Le Shuttle will run between Folkestone and Calais, taking approximately 35 minutes terminal to terminal.

The tunnel was officially opened by The Queen and President Mitterrand on 6 May 1994; HGV services began on 19 May, with the tunnel fully operational for freight traffic from 13 June. Passenger services were intended to start directly after the official opening but because of delays in commissioning the new rolling-stock, passenger services were rescheduled to begin in October 1994.

RAIL LINKS

The route for the British rail link was confirmed by the Secretary of State for Transport (John MacGregor) on 24 January 1994 following a report by Union Railways, a British Rail subsidiary. Decisions on two of the controversial sections of the route at Ashford and Pepper Hill in Kent were confirmed on 28 April. The rail link will run from Folkestone to a new terminal at St Pancras station, London. It will pass through Ashford and Detling, under the North Downs and the Thames to West Thurrock where it will turn westwards through Rainham to a tunnel at Barking which will carry it through to St Pancras via Stratford. A hybrid bill concerning the route is expected to be ready for Parliament by autumn 1994.

Construction of the rail link is expected to cost £2,700 million, and be financed jointly with the private sector. A private sector company will be responsible for design, construction and ownership of the rail link, and will take over Union Railways and European Passenger Services, who will operate international services from London to the Channel tunnel. Construction is expected to be completed in 2002.

Infrastructure developments in France have been completed and high-speed trains can now run from Calais to Paris, linking the Channel tunnel with the high-speed European network. The new lines from Calais to Lille and Lille to Paris have been privately financed at a cost of 17,000 million francs. There is a new station at Lille which has been designed to cope with the increased volume of European traffic, expected to double by 1997. The construction of Lille Europe station has been financed by SNCF at a cost of 252 million francs.

# ROADS

## HIGHWAY AUTHORITIES

The powers and responsibilities of highway authorities in England and Wales are set out in the Highways Acts 1980; for Scotland there is separate legislation.

Responsibility for trunk road motorways and other trunk roads in Great Britain rests in England with the Secretary of State for Transport, in Scotland with the Secretary of State for Scotland, and in Wales with the Secretary of State for Wales. The costs of construction, improvement and maintenance are paid for by central government. The highway authority for non-trunk roads in England and Wales is, in general, the county council, metropolitan district council or London borough council in whose area the roads lie, and in Scotland the regional or islands council. In Northern Ireland the Department of the Environment (Northern Ireland) is responsible for public roads and their maintenance and construction.

## EXPENDITURE

Transport Supplementary Grant (TSG) is a block grant and was introduced in England and Wales in 1975 to replace a variety of specific grants paid towards local transport expenditure.

In England TSG is only paid towards capital spending on highways and the regulation of traffic, current expenditure having been subsumed by rate support grant (now called revenue support grant) since 1985. TSG is also paid towards capital spending on bridge assessment and strengthening; towards structural maintenance on the primary route network; and towards all principal 'A' roads. In Wales Transport Grant is paid to the Welsh county councils towards capital expenditure only, current expenditure having been subsumed by rate support grant.

Grant rates are determined by the respective Secretaries of State; at present, grant is paid at 50 per cent of expenditure accepted for grant in England and Wales.

For the financial year 1994–5 local authorities in England will receive £329.4 million in TSG. Total estimated expenditure on building and maintaining motorways and trunk roads in 1992–3 was £1.96 billion in England; estimated outturn for 1993–4 is £2.09 billion.

In the financial year 1994–5, local authorities in Wales will receive £33 million in TG. Total expenditure on roads in Wales in 1992–3 was £302 million.

Total capital expenditure on local roads was estimated to be £193 million in Scotland in 1993–4, and total expenditure on building and maintaining trunk roads was £233 million.

## ROAD LENGTHS (in miles) as at April 1993

|  | Total roads | Trunk roads (including motorways) | Motorways* |
|---|---|---|---|
| England | 173,160 | 6,502 | 1,670 |
| Wales | 20,888 | 1,058 | 77 |
| Scotland | 32,306 | 1,939 | 158 |
| N. Ireland | 15,048 | 1,443† | 70 |
| UK | 241,402 | 10,942 | 1,975 |

*There were in addition 29 miles of local authority motorway in England and 19 miles in Scotland

†'A' roads; there are no designated trunk roads in N. Ireland

## MOTORWAYS

The network in England and Wales is based on five main routes:

| M1 | London to Yorkshire |
|---|---|
| M4 | London to South Wales |
| M5 | Birmingham, Bristol, Exeter |
| M6 | Birmingham to Carlisle |
| M62 | Lancashire to North Humberside |

Other important motorways include:

| M2 | Medway towns |
|---|---|
| M3 | London to Winchester |
| M11 | London to Cambridge |
| M18 | Rotherham to Goole |
| M20 | London to Folkestone |
| M25 | London orbital route |
| M40 | London to Birmingham |
| M56 | North Cheshire |
| M180 | South Humberside |

Motorways in Scotland include:

| M8 | Edinburgh, Glasgow, Greenock |
|---|---|
| M9 | Edinburgh to Stirling |
| M73 | Maryville to Mollisburn |
| M74 | Nether Abington to Millbank |
| M80 | Stirling to Haggs/Glasgow (M8) to Stepps |
| M85 | Friarton Bridge to Perth |
| M90 | Inverkeithing to Perth |
| M876 | Dennyloanhead (M80) to Kincardine Bridge |

## DRIVING TESTS

The number of car driving tests conducted in Great Britain in 1993 was 1,511,014, of which 48.3 per cent resulted in a pass. In addition a total of 63,224 LGV/PCV (large goods vehicle/passenger carrying vehicle) tests were undertaken, of which 50.1 per cent were successful. A total of 80,687 motorcycle tests were undertaken, of which 70.2 per cent were successful.

## MOTOR VEHICLES

The number of vehicles in Great Britain with current licences in 1993 was:

| Private and light goods | 22,558,000 |
|---|---|
| Motor cycles, scooters, mopeds | 653,000 |
| Public transport vehicles | 107,000 |
| Heavy goods vehicles | 432,000 |
| Agricultural tractors | 318,000 |
| Others | 55,000 |
| Total | 25,089,000 |

This total includes 966,000 Crown vehicles and vehicles exempt from licensing.

## BUSES AND COACHES 1992–3 (Great Britain)

| Number of vehicles (31 March 1993) | 72,600 |
|---|---|
| Vehicle kilometres (millions) | 3,864 |
| Local bus passenger journeys (millions) | 4,483 |
| Passenger receipts (£ million) | 3,033 |

## ROAD ACCIDENTS 1993

| Road accidents | 228,865 |
|---|---|
| Vehicles involved: | |
|     Pedal cycles | 24,593 |
|     Motor vehicles | 386,299 |
| Total casualties | 306,020 |
|     Pedestrians | 48,098 |
|     Vehicle users | 257,922 |

| | | |
|---|---|---|
| Killed* | | 3,814 |
| Pedestrians | | 1,241 |
| Pedal cycles | | 186 |
| All two-wheeled motor vehicles | | 427 |
| Cars and taxis | | 1,760 |
| Others | | 200 |

*Died within 30 days of accident

| | Killed | Injured |
|---|---|---|
| 1965 | 7,952 | 389,986 |
| 1970 | 7,499 | 355,869 |
| 1975 | 6,366 | 318,584 |
| 1980 | 6,010 | 323,000 |
| 1985 | 5,165 | 312,359 |
| 1990 | 5,217 | 335,924 |
| 1991 | 4,568 | 306,701 |
| 1992 | 4,229 | 306,444 |
| 1993 | 3,814 | 302,206 |

## LICENCES

### VEHICLE LICENSES

Since 1974 registration and first licensing of vehicles has been through local offices (known as Vehicle Registration Offices) of the Department of Transport's Driver and Vehicle Licensing Centre in Swansea. The records of existing vehicles are held at Swansea. Local facilities for relicensing are available as follows:

(i) with a licence reminder (form V11) in person at any post office which deals with vehicle licensing, or post it to the post office shown on the form

(ii) with a vehicle licence renewal (form V10). You may normally apply in person at any licensing post office. You will need to take your vehicle registration document with you; if this is not available you must complete form V62 which is held at post offices. Postal applications can be made to the post offices shown on form V100, available at any post office. This form also provides guidance on registering and licensing vehicles.

Details of the present duties chargeable on motor vehicles are available at post offices and Vehicle Registration Offices. The Vehicles (Excise) Act 1971 provides *inter alia* that any vehicle kept on a public road but not used on roads is chargeable to excise duty as if it were in use.

### VEHICLE EXCISE DUTY RATES *since 1 December 1993*

| | 12 months £ | 6 months £ |
|---|---|---|
| *Motor Cars* | | |
| Those first constructed before 1 January 1947 | 70.00 | 38.50 |
| Others | 130.00 | 71.50 |
| *Motor Cycles* | | |
| With or without sidecar, not exceeding 150 cc | 15.00 | — |
| With or without sidecar, 150–250 cc | 35.00 | — |
| Others | 55.00 | 30.25 |
| *Tricycles (not over 450 kg)* | | |
| Not over 150 cc | 15.00 | — |
| Others | 55.00 | 30.25 |
| *Hackney Carriages* | | |
| Seating less than 9 persons | 130.00 | 71.50 |
| Seating 9–16 persons | 150.00 | 82.50 |
| Seating 17–35 persons | 200.00 | 110.00 |
| Seating 36–60 persons | 300.00 | 165.00 |
| Seating over 60 persons | 450.00 | 247.50 |

### DRIVING LICENCE FEES *since 1 February 1993*

*Full Licence*

| | |
|---|---|
| First full licence | £21.00 |
| Changing a provisional to a full licence after passing a driving test | free |
| Renewal of licence issued after 30 September 1982 | £6.00 |
| Medical renewal | free |
| Medical renewal (over 70) | £6.00 |
| Removing endorsements | £6.00 |
| New licence after a period of disqualification | £12.00 |

*Provisional Licence*

| | |
|---|---|
| First provisional licence | £21.00 |
| Renewal of provisional licence issued before 1 October 1982 | £21.00 |

| | |
|---|---|
| *Duplicate Licence* | £6.00 |
| *Exchange Licence* | £6.00 |

The minimum age for driving motor cars, light goods vehicles up to 3.5 tonnes and motor cycles is 17 (moped, 16).

### DRIVING TEST FEES (weekday rate/evening and Saturday rate)

| | |
|---|---|
| For cars | £27.50/£37.50 |
| *For motor cycles | £35/£46.50 |
| For lorries, buses | £62/£80 |
| For invalid carriages | free |

*The first part of the motor cycle test, now known as Compulsory Basic Training, is no longer conducted by the Department of Transport but by appointed motor cycle training organizations, who conduct the majority of basic training tests within the framework of their own training courses and are free to set their own fee. The fee for a certificate of completion of a Compulsory Basic Training course is £5

An extended driving test was introduced in 1992 for those convicted of dangerous driving. The fee is £55/£77.50 (car) or £70/£92 (motorcycle)

### MoT TESTING

Cars, motor cycles, motor caravans, light goods and dual-purpose vehicles more than three years old must be covered by a current MoT test certificate. Copies of the legislation governing MoT testing can be obtained from any bookshop which stocks HMSO publications. The legislation comprises the Road Traffic Act 1988 (Sections 45 and 46), the Motor Vehicles (Test) Regulations 1981, and subsequent amendments.

## PRINCIPAL MERCHANT FLEETS OF THE WORLD

| Flag | 1983 No. | Gross tonnage | 1988 No. | Gross tonnage | 1992 No. | Gross tonnage | 1993 No. | Gross tonnage |
|---|---|---|---|---|---|---|---|---|
| Panama | 5,376 | 35,196,771 | 5,283 | 45,369,271 | 5,424 | 52,485,614 | 5,564 | 57,618,623 |
| Liberia | 1,956 | 62,816,709 | 1,525 | 50,117,615 | 1,661 | 55,917,675 | 1,611 | 53,918,534 |
| Greece | 3,085 | 37,252,628 | 1,900 | 21,927,073 | 1,877 | 25,738,640 | 1,929 | 29,134,435 |
| Japan | 10,504 | 39,954,868 | 9,634 | 31,103,800 | 9,923 | 25,101,697 | 9,950 | 24,247,525 |
| Cyprus | 689 | 5,232,110 | 1,390 | 18,338,438 | 1,463 | 20,487,370 | 1,591 | 22,842,009 |
| Bahamas | 154 | 2,822,264 | 603 | 9,031,692 | 1,090 | 20,616,451 | 1,121 | 21,224,164 |
| Norway (NIS) | — | — | 260 | 7,444,014 | 839 | 20,211,536 | 785 | 19,383,417 |
| Russia | — | — | — | — | 4,909 | 16,301,753 | 5,335 | 16,813,761 |
| China | 1,233 | 9,111,125 | 1,827 | 12,891,825 | 2,346 | 13,899,468 | 2,510 | 14,944,999 |
| Malta | 170 | 1,075,264 | 364 | 2,788,809 | 931 | 11,004,869 | 1,037 | 14,163,357 |
| *United States of America | 6,185 | 17,200,606 | 6,080 | 16,140,194 | 5,830 | 14,448,245 | 5,646 | 14,086,835 |
| Singapore | 848 | 6,605,775 | 752 | 7,278,838 | 998 | 9,905,142 | 1,129 | 11,034,831 |
| Philippines | 918 | 3,174,681 | 1,476 | 9,574,226 | 1,521 | 8,470,441 | 1,469 | 8,466,171 |
| Hong Kong | 312 | 5,206,581 | 389 | 7,402,886 | 395 | 7,266,973 | 418 | 7,664,300 |
| Korea (South) | 1,779 | 7,089,899 | 1,916 | 7,407,166 | 2,116 | 7,407,194 | 2,085 | 7,047,183 |
| Italy | 1,609 | 9,232,089 | 1,621 | 7,622,529 | 1,625 | 7,512,891 | 1,548 | 7,030,237 |
| India | 693 | 6,363,633 | 785 | 6,137,582 | 871 | 6,545,970 | 886 | 6,574,733 |
| Taiwan | 530 | 3,420,623 | 607 | 4,688,979 | 645 | 6,192,796 | 651 | 6,071,191 |
| St Vincent | 47 | 81,745 | 240 | 918,954 | 840 | 4,698,481 | 961 | 5,287,171 |
| Ukraine | — | — | — | — | 1,068 | 5,221,961 | 1,124 | 5,264,478 |
| Brazil | 689 | 5,634,490 | 716 | 6,100,641 | 600 | 5,347,820 | 573 | 5,216,063 |
| Turkey | 741 | 2,845,339 | 862 | 3,244,896 | 901 | 4,135,924 | 948 | 5,043,840 |
| Germany | 2,231 | 8,127,137† | 1,728 | 5,405,606† | 1,320 | 5,360,064 | 1,234 | 4,978,566 |
| Denmark (DIS) | — | — | — | — | 458 | 4,735,837 | 467 | 4,615,542 |
| Iran | 289 | 1,933,479 | 383 | 4,716,691 | 409 | 4,571,394 | 431 | 4,443,972 |
| United Kingdom | 2,516 | 17,217,718 | 1,909 | 5,572,566 | 1,576 | 4,081,240 | 1,532 | 4,116,868 |
| Bermuda | 75 | 942,046 | 114 | 4,207,760 | 94 | 3,338,357 | 96 | 3,139,736 |
| Netherlands | 1,330 | 4,958,715 | 1,149 | 3,267,589 | 1,027 | 3,345,531 | 1,006 | 3,085,644 |
| Romania | 387 | 2,537,322 | 467 | 3,627,483 | 433 | 2,981,336 | 443 | 2,866,962 |
| Australia | 605 | 2,101,532 | 674 | 2,358,822 | 641 | 2,688,503 | 633 | 2,861,786 |
| France | 1,166 | 9,422,967 | 919 | 4,046,828 | 823 | 3,483,968 | 775 | 2,701,333 |
| Poland | 795 | 3,484,704 | 713 | 3,418,057 | 635 | 3,108,704 | 591 | 2,645,716 |
| Canada | 1,307 | 3,426,853 | 1,225 | 2,912,772 | 1,139 | 2,610,035 | 1,049 | 2,540,984 |
| Indonesia | 1,488 | 1,935,255 | 1,728 | 2,124,802 | 2,029 | 2,367,193 | 2,041 | 2,440,471 |
| Sweden | 668 | 3,467,334 | 624 | 2,060,354 | 648 | 2,884,056 | 614 | 2,438,789 |
| Kuwait | 246 | 2,818,156 | 212 | 938,795 | 197 | 2,258,190 | 207 | 2,217,911 |
| Marshall Islands | — | — | — | — | 36 | 1,675,899 | 57 | 2,197,961 |
| Malaysia | 411 | 1,626,679 | 486 | 1,578,095 | 556 | 2,047,626 | 572 | 2,165,692 |
| Norway | 2,295 | 18,524,521 | 1,826 | 2,397,631 | 1,597 | 2,018,977 | 1,514 | 2,152,258 |

NIS   Norwegian International Ship Register – offshore registry
*Excluding ships of United States Reserve Fleet
†Including the former German Democratic Republic
DIS   Danish International Register of Shipping – offshore registry

*Source:* Lloyd's Register of Shipping

## MERCHANT SHIPS COMPLETED DURING 1993

| Country of Build | No. | Gross tonnage | For Registration in | No. | Gross tonnage |
|---|---|---|---|---|---|
| Japan | 598 | 9,085,924 | Panama | 150 | 5,209,742 |
| Korea (South) | 97 | 4,466,762 | Liberia | 55 | 3,011,270 |
| Germany | 88 | 963,134 | Japan | 417 | 1,343,730 |
| Denmark | 32 | 959,842 | Norway (NIS) | 28 | 1,203,662 |
| Taiwan | 11 | 589,532 | Bahamas | 34 | 1,150,996 |
| Spain | 39 | 555,507 | Greece | 13 | 952,645 |
| *China | 42 | 475,887 | Denmark (DIS) | 26 | 768,326 |
| Italy | 29 | 468,856 | Singapore | 59 | 648,430 |
| Poland | 30 | 330,866 | Germany | 55 | 579,710 |
| Brazil | 10 | 315,376 | Hong Kong | 20 | 485,959 |
| United Kingdom | 18 | 229,474 | Cyprus | 22 | 468,140 |
| *Ukraine | 22 | 228,128 | Italy | 37 | 452,387 |
| Finland | 5 | 182,025 | Philippines | 13 | 368,412 |
| Croatia | 7 | 164,511 | China | 36 | 276,658 |
| Norway | 37 | 160,899 | Taiwan | 11 | 274,278 |
| Netherlands | 57 | 152,200 | United Kingdom | 12 | 220,841 |
| Romania | 8 | 120,245 | Netherlands | 41 | 173,810 |
| Portugal | 11 | 97,761 | Russia | 92 | 169,402 |
| *Russia | 66 | 56,861 | Norway | 18 | 161,261 |
| Singapore | 32 | 53,837 | Marshall Islands | 1 | 160,347 |
| Indonesia | 17 | 53,785 | Australia | 13 | 156,841 |
| Bulgaria | 8 | 51,350 | Malta | 7 | 154,618 |
| France | 9 | 40,800 | Brazil | 8 | 153,548 |
| Turkey | 12 | 35,483 | French Antarctic Territory | 2 | 145,471 |
| India | 19 | 30,040 | Isle of Man | 5 | 123,775 |
| Canada | 5 | 26,035 | Finland | 4 | 121,762 |
| Australia | 38 | 19,993 | Romania | 2 | 103,401 |
| Slovakia | 7 | 15,538 | Indonesia | 22 | 101,241 |
| Malaysia | 32 | 15,235 | India | 24 | 101,052 |
| Other countries | 119 | 79,052 | Other countries | 278 | 783,223 |
| **World Total** | **1,505** | **20,024,938** | **World Total** | **1,505** | **20,024,938** |

*Information incomplete
NIS   Norwegian International Ship Register – offshore registry
DIS   Danish International Register of Shipping – offshore registry

*Source:* Lloyd's Register of Shipping

# Communications

## Postal Services

In 1969 the Post Office ceased to be a government department. The responsibility for running postal services was transferred to a public authority called the Post Office, which also administered telecommunications in the United Kingdom. The British Telecommunications Act 1981 separated the postal and telecommunications functions and gave the Secretary of State for Trade and Industry powers to suspend the monopoly of the Post Office in certain areas and to issue licences to other bodies to provide an alternative service. Non-Post Office bodies are now permitted to transfer mail between document exchanges and to deliver letters, provided that a minimum fee of £1 per letter is charged. Charitable organizations are allowed to carry and deliver Christmas and New Year cards.

---

### INLAND POSTAL SERVICES AND REGULATIONS

---

#### INLAND LETTER POST RATES

| Not over | 1st class | 2nd class |
|---|---|---|
| 60 g | 25p | 19p |
| 100 g | 38p | 29p |
| 150 g | 47p | 36p |
| 200 g | 57p | 43p |
| 250 g | 67p | 52p |
| 300 g | 77p | 61p |
| 350 g | 88p | 70p |
| 400 g | £1.00 | 79p |
| 450 g | £1.13 | 89p |
| 500 g | £1.25 | 98p |
| 600 g | £1.55 | £1.20 |
| 700 g | £1.90 | £1.40 |
| 750 g | £2.05 | £1.45 (not |
| 800 g | £2.15 | admissible |
| 900 g | £2.35 | over 750 g) |
| 1,000 g | £2.50 | |
| Each extra 250 g or part thereof | 65p | |

Postcards travel at the same rates

#### UK PARCEL RATES

| Not over | | Not over | |
|---|---|---|---|
| 1 kg | £2.65 | 8 kg | £5.80 |
| 2 kg | £3.25 | 10 kg | £6.75 |
| 4 kg | £4.50 | 30 kg | £8,10 |
| 6 kg | £5.00 | | |

#### STAMPS

There is a two-tier postal delivery system in the UK with first class letters normally being delivered the following day and second class post within three days.

Postage stamps are sold in values of 1p, 2p, 4p, 5p, 6p, 10p, 19p, 20p, 25p, 29p, 30p, 35p, 36p, 38p, 41p, 50p, £1, £1.50, £2.00, £5.00, and £10.00.

Books of stamps costing 50p or £1, or single first or second class stamps, are available from electronic vending machines at some main post offices. At post office counters books are sold containing ten first class stamps (£2.50) and ten second class stamps (£1.90). Rolls of 25p and 19p stamps are also sold. Mixed value rolls are only available on special order from post offices. The sale of postage stamps has been extended to outlets other than post offices, including stationers and newsagents.

#### PREPAID STATIONERY

Aerogrammes to all destinations, 36p.
Forces Aerogrammes, free to certain destinations. Other mail charged at a concessionary rate.
Prepaid envelopes:

| Size | DL | C5 | C4 |
|---|---|---|---|
| Postage paid to | 100g | 350g | 500g |
| Special delivery | £3.30 | £3.80 | £4.20 |
| Registered plus* | £3.90 | £4.40 | £4.80 |

*Includes compensation up to £1,500

Printed postage stamps cut from envelopes, postcards, newspaper wrappers, etc., may be used as stamps in payment of postage, provided that they are not imperfect or defaced.

#### POSTAL ORDERS

Postal orders (British pattern) are issued and paid at nearly all post offices in the UK. They are also paid in the Irish Republic, and issued and/or paid in many other countries overseas.

Postal orders are printed with a counterfoil for denominations of 50p and £1, followed by £1 steps to £10, £15 and £20. Postage stamps may be affixed in the space provided to increase the value of the postal order by up to 49p.

Charges (in addition to the value of the postal order): Up to £1, 25p; £2–£4, 42p; £5–£7, 55p; £8–£10, 65p; £15, 75p; £20, 80p.

The name of the payee must be inserted on the postal order. If not presented within six months of the last day of the month of issue, orders must be sent to the local customer services manager of Post Office Counters Ltd (the address and telephone number can be found in the telephone directory), to ascertain whether the order may still be paid, although if the counterfoil has been retained postal orders not more than four years out of date may be paid when presented with the counterfoil at a post office.

#### OTHER SERVICES

*Cash on Delivery Service*

(Inland, excluding Irish Republic and HM ships). A trade charge (amount to be collected) up to £500 can, under certain conditions, be collected from addresses and remitted to the sender of a parcel containing an invoice. Invoice values of over £100 are only collectable at Post Office premises.

Charge per parcel (exclusive of postage and registration): Customers under contract, £1.70; other customers, £2.00; COD enquiry, £1.70.

*Certificate of Posting*

Issued free on request at time of posting.

*Compensation*

(Royal Mail inland only): compensation up to a maximum of £24 may be paid where it can be shown that a letter was damaged or lost in the post due to the fault of the Post Office, its employees or agents. The onus of making up properly any parcel sent by post lies with the sender. The Post Office does not accept any responsibility for loss arising from faulty packing.

Parcelforce: compensation up to £20 per parcel will be paid for loss or damage if a certificate of posting has been obtained. A Compensation Fee Certificate of Posting can also be obtained; 65p, up to £150 compensation, £1.20, up to £500 compensation.

### Newspaper Post

Copies of newspapers registered at the Post Office may be posted by the publisher or their agents in wrappers open at both ends, in unsealed envelopes approved by the Post Office, or without covers and tied by string which can be removed without cutting. Wrappers and envelopes must be prominently marked 'newspaper post' in the top left-hand corner. No writing or additional printing is permitted, other than the words 'with compliments', name and address of sender, request for return if undeliverable and a reference to a page. Items receive first class letter service.

Newspapers posted by the public, or supplements to registered newspapers dispatched apart from their ordinary publications, are transmitted under the conditions governing the first or second class letter services.

### Prohibited Articles

Prohibitions include offensive or dangerous articles, packets likely to impede Post Office sorters, and certain kinds of advertisement.

### Recorded Delivery

The recorded delivery service provides a record of posting and delivery of inland letters and ensures a signature on delivery. No compensation is available for money or jewellery sent by this service. Charge, 55p. To confirm delivery, call LocalCall 0645-272100 and quote the number on the bar-coded receipt. (Also for Registered and Special Delivery.)

### Redirection

(i) By agent of addressee – mail other than parcels, business reply and freepost items may be reposted free not later than the day after delivery (not counting Sundays and public holidays) if unopened and if original addressee's name is unobscured. Parcels may be redirected free of charge within the same time limits only if the original and substituted address are in the same local parcel delivery area (or within the London postal area). Registered packets, which must be taken to a post office, are re-registered free only up to the day after delivery.
(ii) By the Post Office – requests for redirection of mail should be made on printed forms obtainable from the Post Office and must be signed by the person to whom the letters are to be addressed. A fee is payable for each different surname on the application form.

Charges: Up to 1 calendar month, £6.00; up to 3 calendar months, £13.00; up to 12 calendar months, £30.00.

### Registered

(Inland first class letters only). All packets intended for registration must be handed to the post office and a certificate of posting obtained. The registration fee is £3.00 for compensation up to a £500 claim. Registered Plus, price £3.30, is for items worth between £500 and £2,200.

Consequential Loss Insurance provides cover up to £10,000 for items worth more than their material value:

| Compensation up to | Standard fee in addition to registered fee and postage |
|---|---|
| £1,000 | £0.45 |
| £2,500 | £0.60 |

| Compensation up to | Standard fee in addition to registered fee and postage |
|---|---|
| £5,000 | £0.85 |
| £7,500 | £1.10 |
| £10,000 | £1.35 |

Compensation in respect of currency or other forms of monetary worth is given only if money is sent by registered letter post in one of the special envelopes sold officially (see Prepaid Stationery). Compensation cannot be paid in the case of any packet containing anything not legally transmissible by post. Compensation is paid for fragile articles only if they have been adequately packed. No compensation is paid for deterioration due to delay of perishable articles or for damage to exceptionally fragile articles.

### Special Delivery

Offers next-day delivery service by 12.30 p.m. to most UK destinations, collecting a signature on delivery. Charge, £2.70 plus first class postage.

### Undelivered Mail

Undelivered mail is returned to the sender provided the return address is indicated either on the outside of the envelope or inside. If the sender's address is not available, items not containing property are destroyed. If the packet contains something of value it is retained for up to three months. Exceptionally, items in the minimum weight step on which a rebate of postage has been allowed are destroyed unopened unless there is a return address shown on the outside of the cover. In addition, undeliverable second class mail which contains newspapers, magazines or commercial advertising is destroyed.

### Unpaid Mail

All unpaid or underpaid letters are treated as second class mail. The recipient is charged the amount of underpayment plus 15p per item. Parcels over 750 g are charged at first class rates plus 15p.

## SPECIAL DELIVERY SERVICES

### Datapost

A guaranteed service for the delivery of documents and packages: (i) Datapost Sameday offers same working day collection and delivery in many areas; (ii) Datapost 10 and Datapost 12 offer next working day delivery nationwide. Datapost 10 for delivery before 10 a.m. and Datapost 12 for delivery before noon are available to certain destinations only. Items may be collected or handed in at post offices. There are also Datapost links with a number of overseas countries. Parcelforce 24 and 48 offer a similar guaranteed service to Datapost, 24 being delivered the following working day and 48 the working day after.

### Royal Mail Special Delivery

This service offers special messenger treatment, where necessary, to ensure next day delivery of first class letters and packets. The fee of £2.70 is refunded if next working day delivery is not achieved, provided that items are posted before latest recommended posting times.

### Swiftair

Express delivery of airmail letters and packets up to 2 kg anywhere in the world. Items normally arrive at least one day in advance of normal air mail. Charge (in addition to postage), £2.70.

## OVERSEAS POSTAL SERVICES AND REGULATIONS

### OVERSEAS SURFACE MAIL RATES

*Letters*

| Not over | | Not over | |
|---|---|---|---|
| 20 g | 30p | 450 g | £2.75 |
| 60 g | 50p | 500 g | £3.04 |
| 100 g | 72p | 750 g | £4.49 |
| 150 g | £1.01 | 1,000 g | £5.94 |
| 200 g | £1.30 | 1,250 g | £7.39 |
| 250 g | £1.59 | 1,500 g | £8.84 |
| 300 g | £1.88 | 1,750 g | £10.29 |
| 350 g | £2.17 | 2,000 g | £11.74 |
| 400 g | £2.46 | | |

### AIRMAIL LETTER RATES

*Europe: Letters*

| Not over | | Not over | |
|---|---|---|---|
| 20 g | 25p | 260 g | £1.74 |
| 20 g non EC | 30p | 280 g | £1.86 |
| 40 g | 42p | 300 g | £1.98 |
| 60 g | 54p | 320 g | £2.10 |
| 80 g | 66p | 340 g | £2.22 |
| 100 g | 78p | 360 g | £2.34 |
| 120 g | 90p | 380 g | £2.46 |
| 140 g | £1.02 | 400 g | £2.58 |
| 160 g | £1.14 | 420 g | £2.70 |
| 180 g | £1.26 | 440 g | £2.82 |
| 200 g | £1.38 | 460 g | £2.94 |
| 220 g | £1.50 | 480 g | £3.06 |
| 240 g | £1.62 | *500 g | £3.18 |
| * Max. 2 kg | | | |

*Outside Europe: Letters*

| | Not over 10 g | Not over 20 g | Each extra 20 g |
|---|---|---|---|
| Zone 1 | 41p | 60p | 32p |
| Zone 2 | 41p | 60p | 42p |

For airmail letter zones outside Europe, *see* pages 527–8

### OTHER SERVICES

*Advice of Delivery*

Written confirmation of delivery from the post office at the stated destination. Charge: 40p plus postage.

*Cash on Delivery*

This is an optional extra service only available when using Parcelforce International Standard or Economy service. The following fee is added to postage charges, based on the value of the item to be delivered:

| Value | Fee |
|---|---|
| Up to £200 | £5.00 |
| £200–£400 | £9.50 |
| £400–£600 | £14.50 |
| £600–£1,000 | £18.50 |
| £1,000–£1,500 | £22.50 |

For inland parcels the delivery fee is £3.00.

*Compensation*

If a certificate of posting is produced, compensation may be given for loss or damage in the UK to uninsured parcels to or from most overseas countries. No compensation will be paid for any loss or damage due to the action of the Queen's Enemies.

*Export Restrictions*

Under Department of Trade and Industry regulations the exportation of some goods by post is prohibited except under Department of Trade licence. Enquiries should be addressed to the Export Data Branch, Overseas Trade Divisions, Department of Trade and Industry, 1 Victoria Street, London SW1H 0ET. Tel: 0171-215 5000.

*International Recorded Delivery*

Provides the same service as Recorded Delivery in the UK (*see* page 522). This service is recommended for items of little or no monetary value. Compensation is available up to £25. Charge: £2.50 plus airmail postage.

*International Registered*

Packets containing valuable papers, documents or articles such as jewellery can be insured as letters, or as parcels if the country of destination does not accept dutiable goods in the letter post. For HM ships abroad and also members of the Army and RAF overseas using BFPO numbers, parcels only are insurable up to £140 at a fee of £1.20.

Charges: Compensation up to £500, £3.00 plus airmail postage; up to £1,000, £4.00 plus airmail postage.

*International Reply Coupons*

Coupons are used to prepay replies to letters. They are exchangeable abroad for stamps representing the minimum surface mail letter rate from the country concerned to the UK. Charge: 60p each.

*Poste Restante*

Solely for the convenience of travellers and for three months only in any one town. A packet may be addressed to any post office, except town sub-offices, and should have the words 'Poste Restante' or 'to be called for' in the address. Redirection from a Poste Restante is undertaken for up to three months. Letters at a seaport for an expected ship are kept for two months; otherwise letters are kept for two weeks, or for one month if originating from abroad. At the end of this period mail is treated as undeliverable, unless bearing a request for return.

*Small Packets Post*

This service permits the transmission of goods up to 2 kg to all countries, in the same mails as printed papers (NB: To Australia, Cuba, Myanmar (Burma) and Papua New Guinea there is a limit of 500 g). Packets can be sealed and can contain personal correspondence if it relates to the contents of the packet. Registration is allowed as insurance as long as the item is packed in a way which complies with appropriate insurance regulations. A customs declaration is required and the packet must be endorsed 'small packet' and marked with a return address.

Instructions for the disposal of undelivered packets must be given at the time of posting. A packet which cannot be delivered will be returned to the sender at his/her expense.

### SMALL PACKETS POST RATES

*Surface Mail: World-wide*

| Not over | | Not over | |
|---|---|---|---|
| 100 g | 48p | 450 g | £1.60 |
| 150 g | 64p | 500 g | £1.76 |
| 200 g | 80p | 750 g | £2.56 |
| 250 g | 96p | 1,000 g | £3.36 |
| 300 g | £1.12 | 1,500 g | £4.96 |
| 350 g | £1.28 | 2,000 g | £6.56 |
| 400 g | £1.44 | | |

# Public Telecommunications Services

Under the British Telecommunications Act 1981 the functions of the Post Office were divided between two separate organizations. The Post Office retained control of postal services and British Telecom (now BT) was created to provide a telecommunications service. The Act also provided for a limited relaxation of the telecommunications monopoly. This was further advanced by the Telecommunications Act 1984, which removed BT's monopoly on running the public telecommunications system. British Telecom was privatized as a public limited company in 1984.

The Telecommunications Act 1984 also established the Office of Telecommunications (Oftel) as the independent regulatory body for the telecommunications industry (*see also* Government Departments and Public Offices).

## PUBLIC TELECOMMUNICATIONS OPERATORS

Until recently there were three licensed fixed-link public telecommunications operators (PTOs) in the UK: BT, Mercury Communications Ltd, and Kingston Communications (Hull) PLC. In 1988 the Government announced its intention to license up to six other operators to provide one-way satellite communications systems; during 1989 three of these operators were granted temporary licences and the Government announced that such operators could offer services throughout Europe, rather than in the UK only, as previously indicated. In March 1991 the Government announced that it was opening up the existing duopoly of the two major fixed-link operators and would be encouraging applications for telecommunications licences. Since then there have been 12 recipients of major licences included in the 44 licences issued by the Department of Trade and Industry. There are 31 applications under consideration.

BT's obligations under its operating licence include the provision of a universal telecommunications service; a service in rural areas; and essential services, such as public call boxes and emergency services.

Mercury Communications is licensed to provide national and international public telecommunications services for residential and business customers. These services utilize the digital network created by Mercury. Mercury can also provide the following services: (i) public and private telephone services; (ii) national and international telex; (iii) international switched data services; (iv) electronic messaging (electronic mail and access to telex via a personal computer); (v) data network services; (vi) customer equipment; (vii) mobile communications services; and (viii) Mercury paging.

## PRIVATE TELEPHONE SERVICES

There are over 260 private telephone companies which offer information on a variety of subjects such as the weather, stock market analysis, horoscopes, etc., on the BT network. Other services are available on Mercury's network.

The lines and equipment are provided by BT under condition that services adhere to the codes of practice of the Independent Committee for the Supervision of Standards of Telephone Information Practice. All services are charged at 48p per minute (peak and standard rate) or 36p per minute (cheap rate).

## MOBILE TELEPHONE SYSTEMS

Cellular telephone network systems allow calls to be made to and from mobile telephones. The two companies licensed by the Department of Trade and Industry to provide competing cellular telephone systems are Cellnet, jointly owned by BT and Securicor, and Racal Vodafone Ltd, owned by the Racal Electronics Group. Cellular phones can be identified by the number prefixes 0831, 0836, 0850, 0860, or 0881 and calls to them are charged at the 'm' rate.

## CODE CHANGES IN 1995

On 16 April 1995 all UK codes will change with the addition of a 1 as their second digit. Bristol, Leeds, Leicester, Nottingham and Sheffield codes will change completely. The international code will change from 010 to 00. For further information call the BT Helpline, 0800-010101, or the Mercury Helpline, 0500-041995.

---

## INLAND TELEPHONES

An individual customer can install an extension telephone socket or apparatus in their own home without the need to buy the items from any of the licensed public telecommunications operators. However, it is necessary to possess a special style of master-socket which must be supplied by the public network operator. Although an individual need not buy or rent an apparatus from a PTO, a telephone bought from a retail outlet must be of an approved standard compatible with the public network (indicated by a green disc on the label).

BT EXCHANGE LINE RENTALS (*including VAT*)

| | Per quarter |
|---|---|
| Residential, exclusive | £23.69 |
| Light user scheme | £23.69 |
| Business, exclusive | £32.66 |

BT TELEPHONE APPARATUS RENTAL

| | |
|---|---|
| Residential | from £3.80 |
| Business | from £4.70 |
| Private payphone | from £36.50 |

EXCHANGE LINE CONNECTION AND TAKE-OVER CHARGES (*including VAT*)

| BT | |
|---|---|
| New customer | £116.33 |
| Removing customer | £0.00 |
| Take-over of existing lines: | |
| Simultaneous (same day) | £0.00 |
| Non-simultaneous | £25.00 |

| *Mercury* | |
|---|---|
| Initial and annual administration charge | £11.75 |

RATES

BT local and dialled national calls are charged in 4.2p units when made from ordinary lines and in 10p units when made from payphones. Mercury charges are calculated to the nearest 100th of a second. All charges are subject to VAT, except those from payphones which are VAT inclusive. VAT charges on ordinary lines are calculated as a percentage of the total quarterly (BT)/monthly (Mercury) bill.

The length of time per unit/charge per second depends on the time of day and the distance of the call:

| BT | Mercury | |
|---|---|---|
| Daytime | Standard | Monday to Friday 8 a.m. to 6 p.m. |
| Cheap | Economy | Monday to Friday 6 p.m. to 8 a.m.* |
| Weekend† | Weekend | Midnight Friday to midnight Sunday |

*also Christmas Day, Boxing Day and New Year's Day
†national calls only

Local rate

'a' rate – up to 35 miles (56 km)

'b1' rate – frequently used routes over 35 miles (56 km)

'b' rate – over 35 miles (56 km) (including Channel Islands and Isle of Man)

'm' rate – dialled calls to mobile phones

'p1' rate – Callstream (except for certain prefixed call charges) and information and entertainment services

## PREFIXED CALL CHARGES

0800, 0500 – free

0345, 0645 – charged at local rate

0370, 0374, 0385, 0831, 0836, 0850, 0860 and 0881 – charged at 'm' rate

0336, 0338, 0660, 0839, 0881, 0891, 0898, 08364 – charged at 'p1' rate

0956 – Mercury One-2-One mobile phone

## DIALLED CALL TIME pence per minute charges (incl. VAT)

|  | BT | Mercury |
| --- | --- | --- |
| *Local* |  |  |
| Daytime | 5.00 | * |
| Cheap | 1.67 | * |
| Weekend | n/a | * |
| *'a' rate* |  |  |
| Daytime/Standard | 8.33 | 7.29 |
| Cheap/Economy | 5.00 | 2.82 |
| Weekend | 3.33 | 2.82 |
| *'b1' rate* |  |  |
| Daytime/Standard | 10.00 | 8.23 |
| Cheap/Economy | 6.67 | 4.70 |
| Weekend | 3.33 | 2.94 |
| *'b' rate* |  |  |
| Daytime/Standard | 13.33 | 10.34 |
| Cheap/Economy | 8.33 | 6.23 |
| Weekend | 3.33 | 2.94 |
| *'m' rate* |  |  |
| Daytime | 39.67 | 32.90† |
| Cheap | 26.33 | 21.90† |
| *'p1' rate* |  |  |
| Daytime | 49.67 | varies |
| Cheap | 39.67 | varies |

*Mercury advises customers to use BT for local calls

†Calls to Mercury One-2-One mobile phones are charged at the following pence per minute rates:

| Mon.–Fri. | 0900–1300 | 15.25 |
| Mon.–Fri. | 0800–0900 1300–1800 | 11.15 |
| All other times |  | 7.15 |

## OPERATOR-CONNECTED CALLS

Operator-connected calls from ordinary lines are generally subject to a three-minute minimum charge (and thereafter by the minute) which varies with distance and time of day. Operator-connected calls from payphones are charged in three-minute periods at the payphone tariff. For calls that have to be placed through the operator because a dialled call has failed, the charge is equivalent to the dialled rate, subject normally to the three-minute minimum.

Higher charges apply to other operator-connected calls, including special services calls and those to mobile phones, the Irish Republic and the Channel Islands.

## PHONECARDS

BT phonecards to the value of £2, £5, £10 and £20 are available from post offices and other outlets for use in specially designated public telephone boxes. Each phonecard unit is equivalent to a 10p coin in a payphone.

Mercury public phones accept phonecards (£2, £4 and £10) and all major credit cards, but not cash. Charges are made per second.

Special public payphones at major railway stations and airports also accept commercial credit cards.

## INTERNATIONAL TELEPHONES

All UK customers have access to International Direct Dialling (IDD) and can dial direct to numbers on most exchanges in over 200 countries world-wide. Details about how to make calls are given in dialling code information and in the International Telephone Guide.

For countries without IDD, calls have to be made through the International Operator. All operator-connected calls are subject to a three-minute minimum charge. Thereafter the call is charged by the minute.

Countries which can be called on IDD fall into one of 13 international charge bands depending on location. Charges in each band also vary according to the time of day; cheap rate dialled calls are available to all countries at certain times, but there is no reduced rate for operator-connected calls. Details of current international telephone charges can be obtained from the International Operator.

For International Dialling Codes, *see* pages 527–8

## OTHER TELECOMMUNICATIONS SERVICES

### TELEX SERVICE

There are now 208 countries that can be reached by the BT telex service from the UK, over 200 of them by direct dialling.

For most customers, direct dialled calls to international destinations are charged in six-second units. Units cost between 4.5p and 13.5p depending upon the country called. Calls via the BT operator are charged in one-minute steps with a three-minute minimum, plus a surcharge of £1.30 a call. Operator-connected calls are charged at between 39p and £1.60 a minute depending upon the country called.

Calls made via BT's Telex Plus store and forward facility attract normal telex charges and a handling charge of 13p for inland delivered messages and 30p for international delivered messages.

### TELEMESSAGE

Telemessages can be sent by telephone or telex within the UK for 'hard copy' delivery the next working day, including Saturdays. To achieve this, a telemessage must be telephoned/telexed before 10 p.m. Monday to Saturday (7 p.m. Sundays and Bank Holidays). Dial 100 (190 in London, Birmingham and Glasgow) and ask for the Telemessage Service or see the telex directory for codes.

A telemessage costs £5 for the first 50 words and £2.75 for each subsequent group of 50 words – the name and address are free. A sender's copy costs 85p. A selection of cards is available for special occasions at 80p per card. All prices are subject to VAT.

INTERNATIONAL TELEMESSAGE

Telemessage is also available to the USA. For next working day delivery a telemessage must be filed by 10 p.m. UK time Monday to Saturday (7 p.m. Sundays and Bank Holidays). US addresses must include the ZIP code. Charges are £7.25 for the first 50 words and £3.60 for each subsequent group of 50 words. The name and address are free but all charges are subject to VAT.

## BT SERVICES

OPERATOR SERVICES – 100
  For difficulties
  For the following call services: alarm calls (booking charge £2.70); advice of duration and charge (charge £1.80); charge card calls (charge £1.50); freefone calls; international personal calls (charge £2.15–£4.30); transferred charge calls (charge £1.80); subscriber controlled transfer (All charges exclude VAT)
INTERNATIONAL OPERATOR – 155

DIRECTORY ENQUIRIES – 192
INTERNATIONAL DIRECTORY ENQUIRIES – 153
EMERGENCY SERVICES – 999
  Services include fire service; police service; ambulance service; coastguard; lifeboat; cave rescue; mountain rescue
FAULTS – 151
TELEMESSAGE – 100 (190 in London, Birmingham and Glasgow)
INTERNATIONAL TELEMESSAGE – 100 (190 in London, Birmingham and Glasgow). The service is only available to the USA
INTERNATIONAL TELEGRAMS – 100 (190 in London, Birmingham and Glasgow). The service is available world-wide
MARITIME SERVICES – 100
  Includes Ship's Telegram Service and Ship's Telephone Service
BT INMARSAT SATELLITE SERVICE – 155
ALL OTHER CALL ENQUIRIES – 191

# Forecast Services

## WEATHERCALL SERVICE

To obtain local weather forecasts by telephone or fax, dial the prefix code followed by the appropriate regional code. The prefix for telephone calls is 0891-500 4; the prefix for faxes is 0891-44 99. A helpdesk can be faxed on 0171-613 5000

| | |
|---|---|
| Greater London | 01 |
| Kent, Surrey and Sussex | 02 |
| Dorset, Hampshire and IOW | 03 |
| Devon and Cornwall | 04 |
| Wiltshire, Glos., Avon and Somerset | 05 |
| Berks., Bucks. and Oxfordshire | 06 |
| Beds., Herts. and Essex | 07 |
| Norfolk, Suffolk and Cambridgeshire | 08 |
| West, Mid and South Glamorgan and Gwent | 09 |
| Shropshire, Hereford and Worcester | 10 |
| Central Midlands | 11 |
| East Midlands | 12 |
| Lincolnshire and Humberside | 13 |
| Dyfed and Powys | 14 |
| Gwynedd and Clwyd | 15 |
| North-west England | 16 |
| West and South Yorkshire | 17 |
| North-east England | 18 |
| Cumbria and the Lake District | 19 |
| South-west Scotland | 20 |
| West Central Scotland | 21 |
| Edinburgh, South Fife, Lothian and Borders | 22 |
| East Central Scotland | 23 |
| Grampian and East Highlands | 24 |
| North-west Scotland | 25 |
| Caithness, Orkney and Shetland | 26 |
| Northern Ireland | 27 |

Calls are charged at 39p per minute cheap rate, 49p at all other times (subject to change)

## MARINECALL SERVICE

To obtain information about weather conditions up to twelve miles off the coast, dial the prefix code 0891 500, followed by the appropriate area code

| | |
|---|---|
| Scotland North | 451 |
| Scotland East | 452 |
| North-east | 453 |
| East | 454 |
| Anglia | 455 |
| Channel East | 456 |
| Mid-Channel | 457 |
| South-west | 458 |
| Bristol Channel | 459 |
| Wales | 460 |
| North-west | 461 |
| Clyde | 462 |
| Caledonia | 463 |
| Minch | 464 |
| Ulster | 465 |
| English Channel | 992 |

Calls are charged at 39p per minute cheap rate, 49p at all other times (subject to change)

# Airmail and IDD Codes

| Country | AZ | IDD from UK‡ | IDD to UK |
| --- | --- | --- | --- |

| Country | AZ | IDD from UK‡ | IDD to UK |
| --- | --- | --- | --- |
| Cambodia | 1 | 010 855 | † |
| Cameroon | 1 | 010 237 | 00 44 |
| Canada | 1 | 010 1 | 011 44 |
| Canary Islands | ec | 010 34 | 07p44 |
| Cape Verde | e | 010 238 | † |
| Cayman Islands | 1 | 010 1 809 | 0 44 |
| Central African Republic | 1 | 010 236 | † |
| Chad | 1 | 010 235 | † |
| Chile | 1 | 010 56 | 00 44 |
| China | 2 | 010 86 | 00 44 |
| Colombia | 1 | 010 57 | 90 44 |
| Comoros | 1 | 010 269 | † |
| Congo | 1 | 010 242 | 00 44 |
| Cook Islands | 2 | 010 682 | 00 44 |
| Costa Rica | 1 | 010 506 | 00 44 |
| Côte d'Ivoire | 1 | 010 225 | 00 44 |
| Croatia | e | 010 385 | 99 44 |
| Cuba | 1 | 010 53 | |
| Cyprus | e | 010 357 | 00 44 |
| Czech Republic | e | 010 42 | 00 44 |
| Denmark | ec | 010 45 | 009 44 |
| Djibouti | 1 | 010 253 | 00 44 |
| Dominica | 1 | 010 1 809 | 011 44 |
| Dominican Republic | 1 | 010 1 809 | † |
| Ecuador | 1 | 010 593 | 00 44 |
| Egypt | 1 | 010 20 | 00 44 |
| Equatorial Guinea | 1 | 010 240 | † |
| Estonia | e | 010 372 | 810 44 |
| Ethiopia | 1 | 010 251 | |
| Falkland Islands | 1 | 010 500 | 01 44 |
| Faroe Islands | e | 010 298 | 009 44 |
| Fiji | 2 | 010 679 | 05 44 |
| Finland | e | 010 358 | 990 44 |
| France | ec | 010 33 | 19p44° |
| French Guiana | 1 | 010 594 | † |
| French Polynesia | 2 | 010 689 | 00 44 |
| Gabon | 1 | 010 241 | 00 44 |
| The Gambia | 1 | 010 220 | 00 44 |
| Georgia | e | 010 7 | 810 44 |
| Germany | ec | 010 49 | 00 44 |
| Ghana | 1 | 010 233 | 00 44 |
| Gibraltar | ec | 010 350 | 00 44 |
| Greece | ec | 010 30 | 00 44 |
| Greenland | e | 010 299 | 009 44 |
| Grenada | 1 | 010 1 809 | 011 44 |
| Guadeloupe | 1 | 010 590 | 00 44 |
| Guam | 2 | 010 671 | 00 44 |
| Guatemala | 1 | 010 502 | 00 44 |
| Guinea | 1 | 010 224 | † |
| Guinea-Bissau | 1 | 010 245 | † |
| Guyana | 1 | 010 592 | 011 44 |
| Haiti | 1 | 010 509 | † |
| Honduras | 1 | 010 504 | 00 44 |
| Hong Kong | 1 | 010 852 | 001 44 |
| Hungary | e | 010 36 | 00 44 |
| Iceland | e | 010 354 | 90 44 |
| India | 1 | 010 91 | 00 44 |
| Indonesia | 1 | 010 62 | 00 44 |
| Iran | 1 | 010 98 | 00 44 |
| Iraq | 1 | 010 964 | 00 44 |
| Irish Republic | ec | 010 353 | 00 44 |
| Israel | 1 | 010 972 | 00 44 |
| Italy | ec | 010 39 | 00 44 |
| Jamaica | 1 | 010 1 809 | † |
| Japan | 2 | 010 81 | 001 44 |
| Jordan | 1 | 010 962 | 00 44* |
| Kazakhstan | e | 010 7 | 810 44 |

## AIRMAIL ZONES (AZ)

The table includes airmail letter zones for countries outside
Europe, and destinations to which European and European
Union airmail letter rates apply (*see also* page 523).
(*Source: Post Office*)

| | |
| --- | --- |
| 1 | airmail zone 1 |
| 2 | airmail zone 2 |
| e | Europe |
| ec | European Union |

## INTERNATIONAL DIRECT DIALLING (IDD)

International dialling codes are composed of four elements
which are dialled in sequence:

(i)   the international code‡
(ii)  the country code (*see below*)
(iii) the area code
(iv)  the customer's telephone number

Calls to some countries must be made via the international
operator. (*Source: BT*)

‡   From 16 April 1995 the international code will be 00.
    From August 1994 both the 010 and 00 codes may be
    available
†   Calls must be made via the international operator
p   A pause in dialling is necessary whilst waiting for a
    second tone
p*  Only in Bruges, Ostende and Veurne
°   Second tone may not always be audible
*   Varies in some areas

| Country | AZ | IDD from UK‡ | IDD to UK |
| --- | --- | --- | --- |
| Afghanistan | 1 | 010 93 | † |
| Albania | e | 010 355 | † |
| Algeria | 1 | 010 213 | 00p44 |
| Andorra | ec | 010 33 628 | 0p44 |
| Angola | 1 | 010 244 | † |
| Anguilla | 1 | 010 1 809 | 001 44 |
| Antigua and Barbuda | 1 | 010 1 809 | 011 44 |
| Argentina | 1 | 010 54 | 00 44 |
| Armenia | e | 010 7 | 810 44 |
| Aruba | 1 | 010 297 | † |
| Ascension Island | 1 | 010 247 | |
| Australia | 2 | 010 61 | 00 11 44 |
| Austria | e | 010 43 | 00 44 |
| Azerbaijan | e | 010 994 | 810 44 |
| Azores | ec | 010 351 | 00 44 |
| Bahamas | 1 | 010 1 809 | 011 44 |
| Bahrain | 1 | 010 973 | 0 44 |
| Bangladesh | 1 | 010 880 | 00 44 |
| Barbados | 1 | 010 1 809 | 011 44 |
| Belarus | e | 010 7 | 810 44 |
| Belgium | ec | 010 32 | 00p44* |
| Belize | 1 | 010 501 | † |
| Benin | 1 | 010 229 | 00p44 |
| Bermuda | 1 | 010 1 809 | 1 44 |
| Bhutan | 1 | 010 975 | 00 44 |
| Bolivia | 1 | 010 591 | 00 44 |
| Bosnia-Hercegovina | e | 010 387 | 99 44 |
| Botswana | 1 | 010 267 | 00 44 |
| Brazil | 1 | 010 55 | 00 44 |
| British Virgin Islands | 1 | 010 1 809 49 | 011 44 |
| Brunei | 1 | 010 673 | 00 44 |
| Bulgaria | e | 010 359 | 00 44 |
| Burkina Faso | 1 | 010 226 | |
| Burundi | 1 | 010 257 | 90 44 |

| Country | AZ | IDD from UK‡ | IDD to UK | Country | AZ | IDD from UK‡ | IDD to UK |
|---|---|---|---|---|---|---|---|
| Kenya | 1 | 010 254 | 00 44 | Russia | e | 010 7 | 810 44 |
| Kiribati | 2 | 010 686 | 09 44 | Rwanda | 1 | 010 250 | 00 44 |
| Korea, North | 2 | 010 850 | 010 44 | St Helena | 1 | 010 290 | 01 44 |
| Korea, South | 2 | 010 82 | 001 44 | St Kitts and Nevis | 1 | 010 1 809 | † |
| Kuwait | 1 | 010 965 | 00 44 | St Lucia | 1 | 010 1 809 | 0 44 |
| Kyrgystan | e | 010 7 | 810 44 | St Pierre and Miquelon | 1 | 010 508 | 19p44 |
| Laos | 1 | 00 856 | † | St Vincent and the | | | |
| Latvia | e | 010 371 | 810 44 | Grenadines | 1 | 010 1 809 | 00 44 |
| Lebanon | 1 | 010 961 | 00 44 | El Salvador | 1 | 010 503 | 00 44 |
| Lesotho | 1 | 010 266 | 00 44 | Samoa, American | 2 | 010 684 | 144 |
| Liberia | 1 | 010 231 | 00 44 | San Marino | ec | 010 378 | 00 44 |
| Libya | 1 | 010 218 | 00 44 | São Tomé and | | | |
| Liechtenstein | e | 010 41 75 | 00 44 | Príncipe | 1 | 010 239 | † |
| Lithuania | e | 010 370 | 810 44 | Saudi Arabia | 1 | 010 966 | 00 44 |
| Luxembourg | ec | 010 352 | 00 44 | Senegal | 1 | 010 221 | 00p44 |
| Macao | 1 | 010 853 | 00 44 | Seychelles | 1 | 010 248 | 0 44 |
| Madagascar | 1 | 010 261 | 16p44 | Sierra Leone | 1 | 010 232 | † |
| Madeira | ec | 010 351 91 | 00 44* | Singapore | 1 | 010 65 | 005 44 |
| Malawi | 1 | 010 265 | 101 44 | Slovak Republic | e | 010 42 | 00 44 |
| Malaysia | 1 | 010 60 | 00 44 | Slovenia | e | 010 386 | 99 44 |
| Maldives | 1 | 010 960 | 00 44 | Solomon Islands | 2 | 010 677 | 00 44 |
| Mali | 1 | 010 223 | 00 44 | Somalia | 1 | 010 252 | † |
| Malta | e | 010 356 | 00 44 | South Africa | 1 | 010 27 | 09 44 |
| Mariana Islands, | | | | Spain | ec | 010 34 | 07p44 |
| Northern | 2 | 010 670 | 010 44 | Sri Lanka | 1 | 010 94 | 00 44 |
| Marshall Islands | 2 | 010 692 | 012 44 | Sudan | 1 | 010 249 | † |
| Martinique | 1 | 010 596 | 19p44 | Suriname | 1 | 010 597 | 00 44 |
| Mauritania | 1 | 010 222 | 00 44 | Swaziland | 1 | 010 268 | 00 44 |
| Mauritius | 1 | 010 230 | 00 44 | Sweden | e | 010 46 | 009 44p |
| Mayotte | 1 | 010 269 | 19p44 | Switzerland | e | 010 41 | 00 44 |
| Mexico | 1 | 010 52 | 98 44 | Syria | 1 | 010 963 | 00 44 |
| Micronesia, Federated | | | | Taiwan | 2 | 010 886 | 002 44 |
| States of | 2 | 010 691 | | Tajikistan | e | 010 7 | 810 44 |
| Moldova | e | 010 373 | 810 44 | Tanzania | 1 | 010 255 | 00 44 |
| Monaco | ec | 010 33 93 | 19p44 | Thailand | 1 | 010 66 | 001 44 |
| Mongolia | 2 | 010 976 | † | Tibet | 1 | 010 86 | 00 44 |
| Montserrat | 1 | 010 1 809 | † | Togo | 1 | 010 228 | 00 44 |
| Morocco | 1 | 010 212 | 00p44 | Tonga | 2 | 010 676 | 00 44 |
| Mozambique | 1 | 010 258 | 00 44 | Trinidad and Tobago | 1 | 010 1 809 | 01 44 |
| Myanmar | 1 | 010 95 | 0 44 | Tristan da Cunha | 1 | † | |
| Namibia | 1 | 010 264 | 09 44 | Tunisia | 1 | 010 216 | 00 44 |
| Nauru | 2 | 010 674 | 00 44 | Turkey | e | 010 90 | 9p944 |
| Nepal | 1 | 010 977 | 00 44 | Turkmenistan | e | 010 7 | 810 44 |
| Netherlands | ec | 010 31 | 00 44 | Turks and Caicos | | | |
| Netherlands Antilles | 1 | 010 599 | 00 44 | Islands | 1 | 010 1 809 | 0 44 |
| New Caledonia | 2 | 010 687 | 00 44 | Tuvalu | 2 | 010 688 | † |
| New Zealand | 2 | 010 64 | 00 44 | Uganda | 1 | 010 256 | 00 44 |
| Nicaragua | 1 | 010 505 | 00 44 | Ukraine | e | 010 7 | 810 44 |
| Niger | 1 | 010 227 | 00 44 | United Arab Emirates | 1 | 010 971 | 00 44 |
| Nigeria | 1 | 010 234 | 009 44 | Uruguay | 1 | 010 598 | 00 44 |
| Niue | 2 | 010 683 | | USA | 1 | 010 1 | 011 44 |
| Norfolk Island | 2 | 010 672 | | Alaska | | 010 1 907 | 011 44 |
| Norway | e | 010 47 | 095 44 | Hawaii | | 010 1 808 | 011 44 |
| Oman | 1 | 010 968 | 00 44 | Uzbekistan | e | 010 7 | 810 44 |
| Pakistan | 1 | 010 92 | 00 44 | Vanuatu | 2 | 010 678 | 00 44 |
| Palau | 2 | 010 6809 | | Vatican City State | ec | 010 39 66982 | |
| Panama | 1 | 010 507 | 00 44 | Venezuela | 1 | 010 58 | 00 44 |
| Papua New Guinea | 2 | 010 675 | 05 44 | Vietnam | 1 | 010 84 | † |
| Paraguay | 1 | 010 595 | 002 44 | Virgin Islands (US) | 1 | 010 1 809 | 011 44 |
| | | | 003 44 | Western Samoa | 2 | 010 685 | † |
| Peru | 1 | 010 51 | 00 44 | Yemen | | | |
| Philippines | 2 | 010 63 | 00 44 | north | 1 | 010 967 | 00 44 |
| Poland | e | 010 48 | 0p044 | south | 1 | 010 965 | 00 44 |
| Portugal | ec | 010 351 | 00 44 | Yugoslav Fed. Rep. | e | 010 381 | 99 44 |
| Puerto Rico | 1 | 010 1 809 | 135 44 | Zaire | 1 | 010 243 | 00 44 |
| Qatar | 1 | 010 974 | 044 | Zambia | 1 | 010 260 | 00 44 |
| Réunion | 1 | 010 262 | 19p44 | Zimbabwe | 1 | 010 263 | 110 44 |
| Romania | e | 010 40 | 00 44 | | | | |

# Local Government

The Local Government Acts of 1972 and 1985, the Local Government (Scotland) Act 1973 and the London Government Act 1963 are the main Acts which have brought about the present structure of local government in Great Britain. This structure has been in effect in England and Wales since 1974, with alterations in 1986 with the abolition of the metropolitan counties and the Greater London Council; and in Scotland since 1975.

The structure is based on two tiers of local authorities (county or regional councils and district councils) in the non-metropolitan areas; and a single tier of metropolitan and London borough councils in the six metropolitan areas of England and in London respectively.

The structure of local government in England is currently being reviewed by the Local Government Commission. The county and district councils on the Isle of Wight are to be replaced with a single unitary authority with effect from April 1995, and the Commission has proposed similar changes for other areas of England.

Legislation passed in 1994 abolishes the two-tier structure in Wales and Scotland with effect from 1 April 1996 and replaces it with a single tier of unitary authorities.

Local authorities are empowered or required by various Acts of Parliament to carry out functions in their areas. The legislation concerned comprises public general Acts and 'local' Acts which local authorities have promoted as private bills.

## ELECTIONS

Local elections are normally held on the first Thursday in May. Generally, all British subjects or citizens of the Republic of Ireland of 18 years or over who are resident on the qualifying date in the area for which the election is being held, are entitled to vote at local government elections. A register of electors is prepared and published annually by local electoral registration officers.

A returning officer has the overall responsibility for an election. Voting takes place at polling stations, arranged by the local authority and under the supervision of a presiding officer specially appointed for the purpose. Candidates, who are subject to various statutory qualifications and disqualifications designed to ensure that they are suitable persons to hold office, must be nominated by electors for the electoral area concerned.

In England, the Local Government Commission is responsible for carrying out periodic reviews of electoral arrangements and making proposals to the Secretary of State for changes found necessary. Legislation is before Parliament to set up mechanisms to deal with these matters in Wales and Scotland.

LOCAL GOVERNMENT COMMISSION FOR ENGLAND, Dolphyn Court, 10–11 Great Turnstile, Lincoln's Inn Fields, London WC1V 7JU. Tel: 0171-430 8400

## INTERNAL ORGANIZATION

The council as a whole is the final decision-making body within any authority. Councils are free to a great extent to make their own internal organizational arrangements.

Normally, questions of policy are settled by the full council, while the administration of the various services is the responsibility of committees of councillors. Day-to-day decisions are delegated to the council's officers, who act within the policies laid down by the councillors.

## FINANCE

Local government in England, Wales and Scotland is financed from four sources: the council tax, non-domestic rates, government grants, and income from fees and charges for services. (For arrangements in Northern Ireland, see page 533.)

## COUNCIL TAX

Under the Local Government Finance Act 1992, from 1 April 1993 the council tax replaced the community charge (which had been introduced in April 1989 in Scotland and April 1990 in England and Wales in place of domestic rates).

The council tax is a local tax levied by each local council. Liability for the council tax bill usually falls on the owner-occupier or tenant of a dwelling which is their sole or main residence. Council tax bills may be reduced because of the personal circumstances of people resident in a property, and there are discounts in the case of dwellings occupied by fewer than two adults.

In England and Wales, each county council and each district council sets its own council tax rate. The district councils collect the combined council tax and the county councils claim their share from the district councils' collection funds. In Scotland each regional, island and district council sets its own rate of council tax.

The tax relates to the value of the dwelling. Each dwelling is placed in one of eight valuation bands, ranging from A to H, based on the property's estimated market value as at 1 April 1991.

The valuation bands and ranges of values in England, Wales and Scotland are:

### England

| | | | |
|---|---|---|---|
| A | Up to £40,000 | E | £88,001–£120,000 |
| B | £40,001–£52,000 | F | £120,001–£160,000 |
| C | £52,001–£68,000 | G | £160,001–£320,000 |
| D | £68,001–£88,000 | H | Over £320,000 |

### Wales

| | | | |
|---|---|---|---|
| A | Up to £30,000 | E | £66,001–£90,000 |
| B | £30,001–£39,000 | F | £90,001–£120,000 |
| C | £39,001–£51,000 | G | £120,001–£240,000 |
| D | £51,001–£66,000 | H | Over £240,000 |

### Scotland

| | | | |
|---|---|---|---|
| A | Up to £27,000 | E | £58,001–£80,000 |
| B | £27,001–£35,000 | F | £80,001–£106,000 |
| C | £35,001–£45,000 | G | £106,001–£212,000 |
| D | £45,001–£58,000 | H | Over £212,000 |

The council tax within a local area varies between the different bands according to proportions laid down by law. The charge attributable to each band as a proportion of the Band D charge set by the council is approximately:

| | | | |
|---|---|---|---|
| A | 67% | E | 122% |
| B | 78% | F | 144% |
| C | 89% | G | 167% |
| D | 100% | H | 200% |

The band D rate is given in the tables on pages 551–7 (England), 563 (London), 566 (Wales), and 570–1 (Scotland). There may be variations from the given figure within each district council area because of different parish precepts being levied.

## NON-DOMESTIC RATES

Non-domestic (business) rates have been collected since 1 April 1990 by billing authorities, i.e. district councils in England and Wales, and regional and islands councils in Scotland. In respect of England and Wales, the Local Government Finance Act 1988 provides for liability for rates to be assessed on the basis of a poundage (multiplier) tax on the rateable value of property (hereditaments). The multiplier is set by central government and rates are collected by the billing authority for the area where a property is located. Rate income collected by billing authorities is paid into a national non-domestic rating (NNDR) pool and redistributed to individual authorities on the basis of the adult population figure as prescribed by the Secretary of State. For the years 1990–1 to 1994–5 actual payment of rates in certain cases are subject to transitional arrangements, to phase in the larger increases and reductions in rates resulting from the combined effects of the 1990 revaluation and the introduction of a uniform national business rate (UBR).

Rates are levied in Scotland in accordance with the Local Government (Scotland) Act 1975. Poundages for each local authority are prescribed by the Secretary of State for Scotland. Rate income is pooled and redistributed to local authorities on a per capita basis. For the years 1990–1 to 1994–5, payment of rates is subject to transitional arrangements to phase in the effect of the 1990 revaluation.

Rateable values for the rating lists came into force on 1 April 1990. They are derived from the rental value of property as at 1 April 1988 and determined on certain statutory assumptions by valuation officers of the Valuation Office Agency. New property which is added to the list, and significant changes to existing property, necessitate amendments to the rateable value on the same basis. Rating lists remain in force until the next general revaluation. A new rating list, based on rents as at 1 April 1993, will come into force on 1 April 1995. Any transitional arrangements had yet to be announced at the time of going to press.

Certain types of property are exempt from rates, e.g. agricultural land and buildings, and places of public religious worship. Charities and other non-profit-making organizations may receive full or partial relief. Specified classes of empty property are liable to pay rates at 50 per cent in England and Wales.

## GOVERNMENT GRANTS

In addition to specific grants in support of revenue expenditure on particular services, central government pays revenue support grant to local authorities. This grant is paid to each county/regional and district council so that if each authority spends at a level sufficient to provide a standard level of service, it can set the same council tax.

## COMPLAINTS

Commissioners for Local Administration in England, Wales and Scotland (*see* pages 328–9) are responsible for investigating complaints from members of the public who claim to have suffered injustice as a consequence of maladministration in local government or in certain local bodies.

The Northern Ireland Commissioner for Complaints fulfils a similar function in Northern Ireland, investigating complaints about local authorities and certain public bodies.

## THE QUEEN'S REPRESENTATIVES

The Lord Lieutenant of a county is the permanent local representative of the Crown in that county. The appointment of Lord Lieutenants is now regulated by the Reserve Forces Act 1980. They are appointed by the Sovereign on the recommendation of the Prime Minister. The retirement age is 75. The office of Lord Lieutenant dates from 1557, and its holder was originally responsible for the maintenance of order and for local defence in the county. The duties of the post include attending on royalty during official visits to the county, performing certain duties in connection with armed forces of the Crown (and in particular the reserve forces), and making presentations of honours and awards on behalf of the Crown. In England, Wales and Northern Ireland, the Lord Lieutenant usually also holds the office of *Custos Rotulorum*. As such, he acts as head of the county's commission of the peace (which recommends the appointment of magistrates).

The office of Sheriff (from the Old English shire-reeve) of a county was created in the tenth century. The Sheriff was the special nominee of the Sovereign, and the office reached the peak of its influence under the Norman kings. The Provisions of Oxford (1258) laid down a yearly tenure of office. Since the mid-16th century the office has been purely civil, with military duties taken over by the Lord Lieutenant of the county. The Sheriff (commonly known as 'High Sheriff') attends on royalty during official visits to the county, acts as the returning officer during parliamentary elections in county constituencies, attends the opening ceremony when a High Court judge goes on circuit, executes High Court writs, and appoints under-sheriffs to act as deputies. The appointments and duties of the High Sheriffs in England and Wales are laid down by the Sheriffs Act 1887.

The serving High Sheriff submits a list of names of possible future sheriffs to a tribunal which chooses three names to put to the Sovereign. The tribunal nominates the High Sheriff annually on 12 November and the Sovereign pricks the name of the Sheriff to succeed in the following year. The term of office runs from 25 March to the following 24 March (the civil and legal year before 1752). No person may be chosen twice in three years if there is any other suitable person in the county.

## CIVIC DIGNITIES

District councils may petition for a royal charter granting borough or 'City' status to the district.

In England and Wales the chairman of a borough or county borough council may be called a mayor, and the chairman of a city council a Lord Mayor. Parish councils in England and Wales may call themselves 'town councils', in which case their chairman is the town mayor.

In Scotland the chairman of a district council may be known as a convenor; a provost is the equivalent of a mayor. The chairmen of the councils for the cities of Aberdeen, Dundee, Edinburgh and Glasgow are Lord Provosts.

## ENGLAND

(For London, *see* below)

England outside Greater London is divided into counties. Each county is divided into districts. There are 39 non-metropolitan counties; each of these is divided into non-metropolitan districts, of which there are 296. These districts have populations broadly in the range of 60,000 to 100,000; some however, have larger populations, because of the need to avoid dividing large towns, and some in mainly rural areas have smaller populations. The Local Government Commission is currently reviewing this structure.

Six metropolitan counties cover the main conurbations outside Greater London: Tyne and Wear, West Midlands, Merseyside, Greater Manchester, West Yorkshire and South

Yorkshire. They are divided into 36 metropolitan districts, most of which have a population of over 200,000.

There are also about 10,000 parishes, in 219 of the non-metropolitan and 18 of the metropolitan districts.

ELECTIONS

For districts, non-metropolitan counties, and for about 8,000 parishes, there are elected councils, consisting of directly elected councillors. The councillors elect annually one of their number as chairman.

Generally, councillors serve four years and there are no elections of district and parish councillors in county election years. In metropolitan districts, one-third of the councillors for each ward are elected each year except in the year when county elections take place elsewhere. Non-metropolitan districts can choose whether to have elections by thirds or whole council elections. In the former case, one-third of the council, as nearly as may be, is elected in each year of metropolitan district elections. If whole council elections are chosen, these are held in the year midway between county elections.

FUNCTIONS

In non-metropolitan areas, functions are divided between the districts and counties, those requiring the larger area or population for their efficient performance going to the county. The metropolitan district councils, with the larger population in their areas, already had wider functions than non-metropolitan councils, and following abolition of the metropolitan county councils were given most of their functions also. A few functions continue to be exercised over the larger area by joint bodies, made up of councillors from each district.

The allocation of functions is as follows:

*County councils:* education; strategic planning; traffic, transport and highways; police; fire service; consumer protection; refuse disposal; smallholdings; social services; libraries

*Non-metropolitan district councils:* local planning; housing; highways (maintenance of certain urban roads and off-street car parks); building regulations; environmental health; refuse collection; cemeteries and crematoria

*Metropolitan district councils:* their functions are all those listed above, except that fire, civil defence, police and passenger transport (and in some cases, refuse disposal) are exercised by joint bodies

*Concurrently by county and district councils:* recreation (parks, playing fields, swimming pools); museums; encouragement of the arts, tourism and industry

PARISH COUNCILS

Parishes with 200 or more electors must generally have parish councils, which means that over three-quarters of the parishes have councils. A parish council comprises at least five members, the number being fixed by the district council. Elections are held every four years, at the time of the election of the district councillor for the ward including the parish. All parishes have parish meetings, comprising the electors of the parish. Where there is no council, the meeting must be held at least twice a year.

Parish council functions include: allotments; encouragement of arts and crafts; community halls, recreational facilities (e.g. open spaces, swimming pools), cemeteries and crematoria; and many minor functions. They must also be given an opportunity to comment on planning applications. They may, like county and district councils, spend limited sums for the general benefit of the parish. They levy a precept on the district councils for their funds.

FINANCE

Aggregate external finance for 1994–5 was originally determined at £34,313 million. Of this, specific and special grants were estimated at £5,131 million. £18,499 million was in respect of revenue support grant and £10,685 million was support from the national non-domestic rate pool. Total standard spending by local authorities considered for grant purposes was £42,654 million.

The average council taxes, expressed in terms of Band C, two-adult properties for 1994–5, were: inner London boroughs £465; outer London boroughs £480; London £475; metropolitan districts £572; non-metropolitan districts £509. The average for England was £516.

National non-domestic rate (or uniform business rate) for 1994–5 is 42.3p. The amount estimated to be raised from central, local and Crown lists is £11.2 billion. Total rateable value held on local authority lists at 31 December 1993 was £30.3 billion. The amount to be redistributed to authorities from the pool in 1994–5 is £10.7 billion.

Under the Local Government and Housing Act 1989, local authorities have four main ways of paying for capital expenditure: borrowing and other forms of extended credit; capital grants from central government towards some types of capital expenditure; 'usable' capital receipts from the sale of land, houses and other assets; and revenue.

The amount of capital expenditure which a local authority can finance by borrowing (or other forms of credit) is effectively limited by the credit approvals issued to it by central government. Most credit approvals can be used for any local authority service; these are known as basic credit approvals. Others are for particular projects or services; these are known as supplementary credit approvals.

Generally, the 'usable' part of a local authority's capital receipts consists of 25 per cent of receipts from the sale of council houses and 50 per cent of most other receipts. The balance has to be set aside as provision for repaying debt and meeting other credit liabilities.

EXPENDITURE

Local authority budgeted net revenue expenditure for 1994–5 was (1994–5 cash prices):

| Service | £m |
| --- | --- |
| Education | 18,660 |
| School catering | 391 |
| Libraries, museums and art galleries | 737 |
| Personal social services | 6,497 |
| Police | 5,759 |
| Fire | 1,206 |
| Other Home Office services | 831 |
| Local transport | 2,362 |
| Local environmental services | 5,278 |
| Agricultural services | 40 |
| Consumer protection and trading standards | 139 |
| Employment | 168 |
| Non-housing revenue account housing | 378 |
| Housing benefits | 4,392 |
| Parish precepts | 116 |
| *New net current expenditure* | 44,955 |
| Capital charges | 2,534 |
| Capital charged to revenue | 705 |
| Other non-current expenditure | 3,265 |
| Interest receipts | −611 |
| *Gross revenue expenditure* | 52,849 |

| | |
|---|---|
| Specific and special grants outside AEF* | −8,368 |
| Other income | −50 |
| *Revenue expenditure* | 44,432 |
| Specific and special grants inside AEF* | −4,866 |
| *Net revenue expenditure* | 39,566 |

AEF = aggregate external finance
*Includes only those grants in support of budgeted revenue expenditure

## LONDON

Since the abolition of the Greater London Council in 1986, the Greater London area has not had a single local government body. The area is divided into 32 borough councils, which have a status similar to the metropolitan district councils in the rest of England, and the Corporation of the City of London.

### LONDON BOROUGH COUNCILS

The London boroughs have whole council elections every four years, in the year immediately following the county council election year. The next elections will be held in 1998.

The borough councils have responsibility for the following functions: building regulations; cemeteries and crematoria; consumer protection; education; youth employment; environmental health; electoral registration; food; drugs; housing; leisure services; libraries; local planning; local roads; museums; parking; recreation (parks, playing fields, swimming pools); refuse collection and street cleansing; social services; town planning; and traffic management.

### THE CORPORATION OF THE CITY OF LONDON

(*see also* pages 558–60)

The Corporation of the City of London is the local authority for the City of London. Its legal definition is 'The Mayor and Commonalty and Citizens of the City of London'. It is governed by the Court of Common Council, which consists of the Lord Mayor, 24 other aldermen, and 132 common councilmen. The Lord Mayor and two sheriffs are nominated annually by the City guilds (the livery companies) and elected by the Court of Aldermen. Aldermen and councilmen are elected by businesses in the 25 wards into which the City is divided; councilmen must stand for re-election annually. The Council is a legislative assembly, and there are no political parties.

The Corporation has the same functions as the London borough councils. In addition, it runs the City of London Police; is the health authority for the Port of London; has health control of animal imports throughout Greater London, including at Heathrow airport; owns and manages public open spaces throughout Greater London; runs the Central Criminal Court; and runs Billingsgate, Smithfield and Spitalfields markets.

### THE CITY GUILDS (LIVERY COMPANIES)

The livery companies of the City of London grew out of early medieval religious fraternities and began to emerge as trade and craft guilds, retaining their religious aspect, in the 12th century. From the early 14th century, only members of the trade and craft guilds could call themselves citizens of the City of London. The guilds began to be called livery companies, because of the distinctive livery worn by the most prosperous guild members on ceremonial occasions, in the late 15th century.

By the early 19th century the power of the companies within their trades had begun to wane, but those wearing the livery of a company continued to play an important role in the government of the City of London. Liverymen still have the right to nominate the Lord Mayor and sheriffs, and most members of the Court of Common Council are liverymen (*see also* page 560).

### GREATER LONDON SERVICES

After the abolition of the Greater London Council (GLC) in 1986, the London boroughs took over most of its functions. Successor bodies have also been set up for certain functions.

The London Residuary Body (LRB) was set up in 1986 to deal with residual matters of the GLC which could not easily be transferred elsewhere. The LRB completed its work in relation to the GLC in 1990, when it became responsible for residual matters relating to the Inner London Education Authority, which was abolished on 1 April 1990. The LRB has now transferred most residual Greater London matters to the London Borough of Bromley and inner London matters to the Royal Borough of Kensington and Chelsea. Its sole remaining responsibility is the disposal of County Hall.

LONDON RESIDUARY BODY, c/o Town Hall, Royal Borough of Kensington and Chelsea, Hornton Street, London W8 7NX. Tel: 0171-938 4028

## WALES

Since 1974 Wales, including the former Monmouthshire, has been divided into eight counties. Each county is divided into districts, of which there are 37. Under the Local Government (Wales) Act 1994, all county and district councils will be abolished and replaced by a single tier of 22 county and county borough councils with effect from 1 April 1996. The new authorities will be elected in May 1995. Each will inherit all the functions of the existing county and district councils, except fire services (which will be provided by three combined fire authorities) and National Parks (which will become the responsibility of three independent boards).

The new county and county borough councils are: Anglesey; Caernarfonshire and Merionethshire; Cardiff; Cardiganshire, Carmarthenshire; Denbighshire; Flintshire; Monmouthshire, Pembrokeshire; Powys; Swansea; Aberconwy and Colwyn; Blaenau Gwent; Bridgend; Caerphilly; Merthyr Tydfil; Neath and Port Talbot; Newport; Rhondda, Cynon, Taff; Torfaen; Vale of Glamorgan; Wrexham.

### COMMUNITY COUNCILS

In Wales parishes have been replaced by communities. Unlike England, where many areas are not in any parish, communities have been established for the whole of Wales, approximately 865 communities in all. Community meetings may be convened as and when desired.

Community councils exist in 735 communities and further councils may be established at the request of a community meeting. Community councils have broadly the same range of powers as English parish councils. Community councillors are elected en bloc at the same time as a district council election and for a term of four years.

### FINANCE

Aggregate external finance for 1994–5 is £2,419.2 million. This comprises revenue support grant of £1,740.1 million, specific grants of £215.1 million, and support from the national non-domestic rate pool of £464 million. Total standard spending by local authorities considered for grant purposes is £2,704.8 million.

The average council tax levied in Wales for 1994–5 is £350, comprising county councils £287 and district councils £64.

National non-domestic rates (or uniform business rate) in Wales for 1994–5 is 44.8p. The amount estimated to be raised is £464 million. Total rateable value held on local authority lists at 31 December 1993 was £1,073 million.

## SCOTLAND

Since 1975, mainland Scotland has been divided for local government purposes into nine regions within which there are 53 districts. Under the Local Government (Scotland) Bill currently before Parliament, the existing regional and district councils will be abolished on 1 April 1996 and replaced by a single tier of unitary councils. The new authorities will be elected in May 1995. Each will inherit all the functions of the existing regional and district councils, except water and sewerage (which will be provided by three public bodies whose members will be appointed by the Secretary of State for Scotland) and reporters panels (which will become a national agency).

In the three islands areas, Orkney, Shetland and the Western Isles, there are single-tier islands councils responsible for most local authority functions.

### ELECTIONS

For the regional, islands and district councils, there are councils consisting of directly elected councillors. The councillors serve for four years, elections to district councils taking place midway between regional council elections.

In 1994 the register showed 3,946,264 electors in Scotland.

### FUNCTIONS

*Regional councils:* education; social work; strategic planning; the provision of infrastructure such as roads, water and sewerage; consumer protection; flood prevention; coast protection; valuation and rating; the police and fire services; civil defence; electoral registration; public transport; registration of births, deaths and marriages
*District councils:* housing; leisure and recreation, including tourism, parks, libraries, museums and galleries; development control and building control; environmental health, including cleansing; refuse collection and disposal; food hygiene, inspection of shops, offices and factories, clean air, markets and slaughterhouses, burial and cremation; licensing, including liquor, cinemas and theatres, taxis, street traders, betting and gaming, and charitable collections; allotments; public conveniences; the administration of district courts

### COMMUNITY COUNCILS

Unlike the parish councils of England or community councils of Wales, Scottish community councils are not local authorities. Their purpose as defined in statute is to ascertain and express the views of the communities which they represent, and to take in the interests of their communities such action as appears to be expedient or practicable. Over 1,000 community councils have been established under schemes drawn up by district and islands councils in Scotland.

### FINANCE

In 1992–3 a total of £1,256.3 million was received from non-domestic rates by local authorities. The average non-domestic rate levied was 55p. Total non-domestic water rate income was £23,639,000 and the average non-domestic water rate levied was 5p. Income from the non-domestic sewerage rate was £94,052,000 and the average non-domestic sewerage rate levied was 4.7p. Total metered water income was £83,859,000 and the average metered water rate levied was 39p.

The 1992–3 community charge income received by local authorities totalled £938,981,000 and the average personal community charge levied was £297.46. The community water charge receipts were £102,899,000 and the average community water charge levied was £32.82.

Provisional figures for 1993–4 show total receipts from non-domestic rates of £1,187.22 million and £908.87 million from the council tax. The average non-domestic rate per £ levied for 1993–4 was 51.3p and the average Band D council tax payable was £559. The average Band D council water charge payable was £74.

## NORTHERN IRELAND

For the purpose of local government Northern Ireland has a system of 26 single-tier district councils.

### ELECTIONS

There are 582 members of the councils, elected for periods of four years at a time on the principle of proportional representation.

### FUNCTIONS

The district councils have three main roles. These are:
*Executive:* responsibility for a wide range of local services including building regulations; community services; consumer protection; cultural facilities; environmental health; miscellaneous licensing and registration provisions, including dog control; litter prevention; recreational and social facilities; refuse collection and disposal; street cleansing; and tourist development
*Representative:* nominating representatives to sit as members of the various statutory bodies responsible for the administration of regional services such as drainage, education, electricity, fire, health and personal social services, and libraries
*Consultative:* acting as the medium through which the views of local people are expressed on the operation in their area of other regional services, notably conservation (including water supply and sewerage services), planning, and roads, provided by those departments of central government which have an obligation, statutory or otherwise, to consult the district councils about proposals affecting their areas

### FINANCE

Local government in Northern Ireland is funded by a system of rates (a local property tax calculated by using the rateable value of a property multiplied by an amount per pound of rateable value). Rates are collected by the Department of the Environment for Northern Ireland and consist of a regional rate made by the Department of Finance and Personnel and a district rate made by individual district councils.

In 1993–4 a total of £323 million was raised in domestic rates in Northern Ireland and the total rateable value was £218.8 million. The average domestic poundage levied was 147.35p and the average non-domestic rate poundage was 221.35p.

# Political Composition of Local Councils

AS AT END MAY 1994

*Abbreviations:*

| | |
|---|---|
| C. | Conservative |
| Com. | Communist |
| Dem. | Democrat |
| Green | Green |
| Ind. | Independent |
| Lab. | Labour |
| Lib. | Liberal |
| LD | Liberal Democrat |
| MK | Mebyon Kernow |
| NP | Non-political/Non-party |
| PC | Plaid Cymru |
| RA | Ratepayers'/Residents' Associations |
| SD | Social Democrat |
| SNP | Scottish National Party |

## ENGLAND

### COUNTY COUNCILS

| | |
|---|---|
| Avon | *Lab.* 34, *C.* 25, *LD* 17 |
| Bedfordshire | *Lab.* 31, *C.* 28, *LD* 13, *Ind.* 1 |
| Berkshire | *LD* 32, *Lab.* 25, *C.* 15, *Ind.* 2, *Lib.* 1, *vacant* 1 |
| Buckinghamshire | *C.* 39, *LD* 16, *Lab.* 13, *Ind.* 3 |
| Cambridgeshire | *C.* 33, *Lab.* 21, *LD* 21, *Ind.* 1, *Lib.* 1 |
| Cheshire | *Lab.* 35, *C.* 22, *LD* 14 |
| Cleveland | *Lab.* 52, *C.* 14, *LD* 11 |
| Cornwall | *LD* 43, *Ind.* 21, *Lab.* 8, *C.* 6, *MK* 1 |
| Cumbria | *Lab.* 39, *C.* 28, *LD* 14, *Ind.* 2 |
| Derbyshire | *Lab.* 54, *C.* 21, *LD* 8, *Ind.* 1 |
| Devon | *LD* 41, *Lab.* 21, *C.* 18, *Ind.* 4, *Lib.* 1 |
| Dorset | *LD* 39, *C.* 28, *Lab.* 6, *Ind.* 4 |
| Durham | *Lab.* 56, *C.* 6, *LD* 6, *Ind.* 4 |
| East Sussex | *LD* 30, *C.* 22, *Lab.* 18 |
| Essex | *Lab.* 33, *C.* 32, *LD* 32, *Ind.* 1 |
| Gloucestershire | *LD* 30, *Lab.* 20, *C.* 12, *Others* 1 |
| Hampshire | *LD* 48, *C.* 29, *Lab.* 24, *Ind.* 1 |
| Hereford and Worcester | *C.* 25, *Lab.* 24, *LD* 22, *Ind.* 5 |
| Hertfordshire | *Lab.* 30, *C.* 26, *LD* 19, *Ind.* 2 |
| Humberside | *Lab.* 43, *C.* 22, *LD* 10 |
| Isle of Wight | *LD* 29, *C.* 9, *Ind.* 4, *Others* 1 |
| Kent | *C.* 41, *Lab.* 30, *LD* 28 |
| Lancashire | *Lab.* 54, *C.* 34, *LD* 11 |
| Leicestershire | *Lab.* 37, *C.* 31, *LD* 17 |
| Lincolnshire | *C.* 32, *Lab.* 25, *LD* 15, *Ind.* 4 |
| Norfolk | *C.* 33, *Lab.* 32, *LD* 17, *Ind.* 2 |
| Northamptonshire | *Lab.* 36, *C.* 27, *LD* 5 |
| Northumberland | *Lab.* 39, *C.* 14, *LD* 11, *Ind.* 1, *vacant* 1 |
| North Yorkshire | *LD* 35, *C.* 29, *Lab.* 22, *Ind.* 9, *Ind. Lab.* 1 |
| Nottinghamshire | *Lab.* 58, *C.* 24, *LD* 6 |
| Oxfordshire | *C.* 25, *Lab.* 24, *LD* 20, *Green* 1 |
| Shropshire | *C.* 26, *Lab.* 23, *LD* 14, *Ind.* 3 |
| Somerset | *LD* 41, *C.* 13, *Lab.* 2, *Ind.* 1 |
| Staffordshire | *Lab.* 52, *C.* 21, *LD* 5, *Ind.* 2, *RA* 1, *Ratepayer* 1 |
| Suffolk | *Lab.* 32, *C.* 25, *LD* 19, *Ind.* 4 |
| Surrey | *C.* 34, *LD* 29, *Lab.* 8, *RA* 3, *Ind.* 2 |
| Warwickshire | *Lab.* 30, *C.* 19, *LD* 10, *Ind.* 3 |
| West Sussex | *LD* 34, *C.* 26, *Lab.* 10, *Ind.* 1 |
| Wiltshire | *LD* 33, *C.* 18, *Lab.* 17 |

## METROPOLITAN DISTRICT COUNCILS

### GREATER MANCHESTER

| | |
|---|---|
| Bolton | *Lab.* 37, *C.* 15, *LD* 6, *Ind. Lab.* 1, *vacant* 1 |
| Bury | *Lab.* 24, *C.* 21, *LD* 3 |
| Manchester | *Lab.* 78, *LD* 16, *C.* 4, *Others* 1 |
| Oldham | *Lab.* 29, *LD* 23, *C.* 7, *Ind. LD* 1 |
| Rochdale | *Lab.* 23, *LD* 22, *C.* 14, *Ind.* 1 |
| Salford | *Lab.* 55, *C.* 4, *Lib.* 1 |
| Stockport | *LD* 29, *Lab.* 18, *C.* 13, *Ind.* 3 |
| Tameside | *Lab.* 48, *C.* 8, *Others* 1 |
| Trafford | *C.* 35, *Lab.* 23, *LD* 5 |
| Wigan | *Lab.* 63, *LD* 5, *C.* 2, *Ind. Lab.* 1, *vacant* 1 |

### MERSEYSIDE

| | |
|---|---|
| Knowsley | *Lab.* 61, *C.* 2, *Ind.* 2, *Ind. Lab.* 1 |
| Liverpool | *Lab.* 44, *LD* 44, *C.* 2, *Lib.* 2, *Others* 7 |
| St Helens | *Lab.* 33, *LD* 14, *C.* 5, *Others* 2 |
| Sefton | *Lab.* 26, *C.* 24, *LD* 19 |
| Wirral | *Lab.* 30, *C.* 28, *LD* 8 |

### SOUTH YORKSHIRE

| | |
|---|---|
| Barnsley | *Lab.* 62, *C.* 2, *Ind.* 2 |
| Doncaster | *Lab.* 54, *C.* 9 |
| Rotherham | *Lab.* 63, *C.* 3 |
| Sheffield | *Lab.* 56, *LD* 22, *C.* 8, *Ind. Lab.* 1 |

### TYNE AND WEAR

| | |
|---|---|
| Gateshead | *Lab.* 51, *LD* 12, *C.* 1, *Ind. Lab.* 1, *Lib.* 1 |
| Newcastle upon Tyne | *Lab.* 60, *LD* 13, *C.* 5 |
| North Tyneside | *Lab.* 36, *C.* 16, *LD* 8 |
| South Tyneside | *Lab.* 54, *LD* 5, *Others* 1 |
| Sunderland | *Lab.* 64, *C.* 7, *LD* 3, *vacant* 1 |

### WEST MIDLANDS

| | |
|---|---|
| Birmingham | *Lab.* 63, *C.* 40, *LD* 14 |
| Coventry | *Lab.* 41, *C.* 13 |
| Dudley | *Lab.* 38, *C.* 33, *LD* 1 |
| Sandwell | *Lab.* 43, *C.* 22, *Lib.* 7 |
| Solihull | *C.* 22, *Lab.* 15, *LD* 8, *Ind. RA* 5, *Ind.* 1 |
| Walsall | *Lab.* 25, *C.* 22, *LD* 9, *Ind.* 4 |
| Wolverhampton | *Lab.* 31, *C.* 26, *LD* 3 |

### WEST YORKSHIRE

| | |
|---|---|
| Bradford | *Lab.* 51, *C.* 35, *LD* 4 |
| Calderdale | *C.* 23, *Lab.* 22, *LD* 7, *Ind.* 2 |
| Kirklees | *Lab.* 35, *C.* 21, *LD* 15, *Others* 1 |
| Leeds | *Lab.* 67, *C.* 23, *LD* 8, *Ind.* 1 |
| Wakefield | *Lab.* 56, *C.* 5, *Ind. Lab.* 2 |

## NON-METROPOLITAN DISTRICT COUNCILS

\* denotes councils where one-third of councillors retire each year except in the year of county council elections

| | |
|---|---|
| *Adur | *LD* 25, *C.* 11, *RA* 2, *Lab.* 1 |
| Allerdale | *Lab.* 30, *C.* 11, *Ind.* 11, *LD* 3 |

| | |
|---|---|
| Alnwick | *LD* 16, *C.* 4, *Lab.* 2, *Ind.* 1, *Others* 6 |
| *Amber Valley | *Lab.* 24, *C.* 15, *Ind.* 2, *RA* 1, *Others* 1 |
| Arun | *C.* 35, *LD* 13, *Lab.* 6, *Ind.* 2 |
| Ashfield | *Lab.* 32, *C.* 1 |
| Ashford | *C.* 28, *LD* 12, *Lab.* 6, *Ind.* 1, *Ind. C.* 1, *Others* 1 |
| Aylesbury Vale | *C.* 27, *LD* 24, *Ind.* 6, *Lab.* 1 |
| Babergh | *C.* 16, *Ind.* 9, *Lab.* 6, *LD* 5, *Others* 6 |
| *Barrow-in-Furness | *Lab.* 24, *C.* 13, *Ind.* 1 |
| *Basildon | *C.* 21, *Lab.* 13, *LD* 8 |
| *Basingstoke and Deane | *C.* 28, *LD* 13, *Lab.* 11, *Ind.* 5 |
| *Bassetlaw | *Lab.* 30, *C.* 16, *LD* 2, *Ind.* 1, *Ind. Lab.* 1 |
| *Bath | *LD* 29, *C.* 17, *Lab.* 2 |
| Berwick-upon-Tweed | *LD* 11, *Ind.* 7, *C.* 5, *Lab.* 1, *NP* 1, *Others* 3 |
| Beverley | *C.* 31, *LD* 19, *Lab.* 2, *Ind.* 1 |
| Blaby | *C.* 30, *LD* 5, *Ind.* 3, *Lab.* 1 |
| *Blackburn | *Lab.* 36, *C.* 17, *LD* 4, *Ind.* 1, *vacant* 2 |
| Blackpool | *Lab.* 27, *C.* 10, *LD* 6, *vacant* 1 |
| Blyth Valley | *Lab.* 30, *LD* 17 |
| Bolsover | *Lab.* 35, *RA* 2 |
| Boothferry | *C.* 18, *Lab.* 12, *Ind.* 5 |
| Boston | *C.* 12, *Lab.* 8, *LD* 8, *Ind.* 6 |
| Bournemouth | *LD* 25, *C.* 21, *Lab.* 6, *Ind.* 5 |
| Bracknell Forest | *C.* 32, *Lab.* 7, *LD* 1 |
| Braintree | *C.* 24, *Lab.* 21, *LD* 6, *Ind.* 5, *RA* 4 |
| Breckland | *C.* 32, *Ind.* 11, *Lab.* 8, *LD* 2 |
| *Brentwood | *LD* 25, *C.* 12, *Ind.* 1, *Lab.* 1 |
| Bridgnorth | *C.* 12, *Ind.* 8, *NP* 7, *LD* 3, *Ind. Lab.* 2, *Lab.* 1 |
| *Brighton | *Lab.* 27, *C.* 21 |
| *Bristol | *Lab.* 40, *C.* 19, *LD* 8, *vacant* 1 |
| *Broadland | *C.* 22, *LD* 15, *Ind.* 6, *Lab.* 6 |
| Bromsgrove | *C.* 26, *Lab.* 14, *SD* 1 |
| *Broxbourne | *C.* 32, *Lab.* 5, *LD* 4, *vacant* 1 |
| Broxtowe | *C.* 26, *Lab.* 15, *LD* 6, *Ind.* 1, *vacant* 1 |
| *Burnley | *Lab.* 33, *LD* 9, *C.* 4, *Ind. Lab.* 1, *vacant* 1 |
| *Cambridge | *Lab.* 19, *LD* 16, *C.* 7 |
| *Cannock Chase | *Lab.* 31, *C.* 8, *LD* 3 |
| Canterbury | *LD* 23, *C.* 17, *Lab.* 8, *Ind.* 1 |
| Caradon | *Ind.* 21, *LD* 9, *C.* 6, *RA* 3, *Lab.* 1, *vacant* 1 |
| *Carlisle | *Lab.* 27, *C.* 20, *LD* 3, *Ind.* 1 |
| Carrick | *LD* 20, *Ind.* 11, *C.* 9, *Lab.* 4, *vacant* 1 |
| Castle Morpeth | *Ind.* 9, *Lab.* 9, *LD* 9, *C.* 7 |
| Castle Point | *C.* 36, *Lab.* 1, *vacant* 2 |
| Charnwood | *C.* 32, *Lab.* 15, *LD* 4, *Ind.* 1 |
| Chelmsford | *C.* 29, *LD* 21, *Ind.* 4, *Lab.* 2 |
| *Cheltenham | *LD* 26, *C.* 10, *Lab.* 2, *Others* 3 |
| *Cherwell | *C.* 31, *Lab.* 16, *LD* 4, *Ind.* 1 |
| *Chester | *C.* 23, *Lab.* 19, *LD* 16, *Ind.* 2 |
| Chesterfield | *Lab.* 31, *LD* 13, *C.* 3 |
| Chester-le-Street | *Lab.* 27, *Ind.* 4, *C.* 1, *LD* 1 |
| Chichester | *C.* 32, *LD* 15, *Ind.* 3 |
| Chiltern | *C.* 40, *LD* 8, *RA* 2 |
| *Chorley | *C.* 21, *Lab.* 21, *LD* 5, *Ind.* 1 |
| Christchurch | *C.* 13, *Ind.* 11, *LD* 1 |
| Cleethorpes | *Lab.* 16, *C.* 13, *LD* 12 |
| *Colchester | *LD* 34, *C.* 19, *Lab.* 6, *RA* 1 |
| *Congleton | *LD* 27, *C.* 13, *Lab.* 5 |
| Copeland | *Lab.* 28, *C.* 19, *Ind.* 2, *NP* 1, *vacant* 1 |
| Corby | *Lab.* 22, *C.* 2, *Ind.* 1, *LD* 1, *vacant* 1 |
| Cotswold | *Ind.* 15, *C.* 9, *LD* 6, *Ind. C.* 1, *Lab.* 1, *Others* 13 |
| *Craven | *LD* 14, *C.* 11, *Ind.* 6, *Lab.* 3 |
| *Crawley | *Lab.* 23, *C.* 7, *LD* 2 |
| *Crewe and Nantwich | *Lab.* 29, *C.* 25, *LD* 3 |
| Dacorum | *C.* 38, *Lab.* 15, *LD* 5 |
| Darlington | *Lab.* 30, *C.* 17, *LD* 2, *Others* 3 |
| Dartford | *C.* 25, *Lab.* 20, *RA* 2 |
| *Daventry | *C.* 18, *Lab.* 12, *Ind.* 3, *LD* 2 |
| *Derby | *Lab.* 25, *C.* 18, *LD* 1 |
| Derbyshire Dales | *C.* 25, *LD* 10, *Lab.* 4 |
| Derwentside | *Lab.* 39, *Ind.* 14, *C.* 2 |
| Dover | *C.* 27, *Lab.* 22, *LD* 6, *Ind.* 1 |
| Durham | *Lab.* 29, *LD* 14, *Ind.* 6 |
| Easington | *Lab.* 40, *Ind.* 4, *Lib.* 4, *Ind. Lab.* 1, *vacant* 2 |
| *Eastbourne | *LD* 19, *C.* 11 |
| East Cambridgeshire | *Ind.* 23, *LD* 7, *C.* 5, *Ind. C.* 1, *Lab.* 1 |
| East Devon | *C.* 41, *LD* 11, *Green* 2, *Ind.* 2, *Ind. C.* 1, *Lib.* 1, *Others* 2 |
| East Dorset | *C.* 18, *LD* 14, *RA* 2, *Others* 2 |
| East Hampshire | *LD* 21, *C.* 15, *Ind.* 6 |
| East Hertfordshire | *C.* 34, *LD* 10, *Ind.* 3, *Lab.* 2, *RA* 1 |
| *Eastleigh | *LD* 23, *C.* 18, *Lab.* 3 |
| East Lindsey | *Ind.* 44, *C.* 6, *Lab.* 4, *LD* 4, *Green* 1 |
| East Northamptonshire | *C.* 24, *Lab.* 9, *LD* 3 |
| East Staffordshire | *Lab.* 23, *Ind. C.* 12, *C.* 6, *LD* 5 |
| East Yorkshire | *C.* 18, *Ind.* 11, *LD* 6, *Lab.* 5, *SD* 3 |
| Eden | *Ind.* 33, *LD* 4 |
| *Ellesmere Port and Neston | *Lab.* 30, *C.* 11 |
| *Elmbridge | *C.* 22, *RA* 20, *LD* 10, *Lab.* 7, *Ind.* 1 |
| *Epping Forest | *C.* 27, *Lab.* 14, *RA* 10, *LD* 6, *SD* 2 |
| Epsom and Ewell | *RA* 30, *LD* 6, *Lab.* 3 |
| Erewash | *Lab.* 27, *C.* 21, *Ind.* 2, *LD* 2 |
| *Exeter | *Lab.* 16, *C.* 12, *LD* 6, *Lib.* 2 |
| *Fareham | *LD* 16, *C.* 14, *Ind. C.* 10, *Lab.* 2 |
| Fenland | *C.* 26, *Lab.* 6, *Ind.* 4, *LD* 4 |
| Forest Heath | *C.* 17, *Ind.* 4, *LD* 3, *Lab.* 1 |
| Forest of Dean | *Lab.* 25, *Ind.* 8, *LD* 7, *C.* 3, *Ind. C.* 1, *Others* 5 |
| Fylde | *C.* 22, *RA* 9, *LD* 5, *Lab.* 1, *Others* 12 |
| Gedling | *C.* 38, *Lab.* 15, *LD* 3, *Ind.* 1 |
| *Gillingham | *LD* 20, *C.* 13, *Lab.* 8, *Ind. LD* 1 |
| Glanford | *C.* 20, *Ind.* 10, *Lab.* 8, *Green* 3 |
| *Gloucester | *Lab.* 17, *C.* 11, *LD* 7 |
| *Gosport | *LD* 16, *C.* 6, *Ind.* 4, *Lab.* 4 |
| Gravesham | *Lab.* 23, *C.* 21 |
| *Great Grimsby | *Lab.* 28, *C.* 9, *LD* 5, *Ind.* 3 |
| *Great Yarmouth | *Lab.* 27, *C.* 19, *LD* 2 |
| Guildford | *C.* 20, *LD* 18, *Lab.* 6, *Ind.* 1 |
| *Halton | *Lab.* 44, *LD* 7, *C.* 2 |
| Hambleton | *C.* 24, *Ind.* 13, *LD* 5, *SD* 3, *Lab.* 2 |
| Harborough | *C.* 19, *LD* 10, *Ind.* 4, *Lab.* 4 |
| *Harlow | *Lab.* 33, *C.* 6, *LD* 3 |
| *Harrogate | *LD* 37, *C.* 19, *Ind.* 2, *Lab.* 2 |
| *Hart | *LD* 14, *C.* 13, *Ind.* 8 |

| | |
|---|---|
| *Hartlepool | *Lab.* 26, *C.* 12, *LD* 8, *Ind.* 1 |
| *Hastings | *LD* 12, *Lab.* 10, *C.* 8, *Ind.* 2 |
| *Havant | *C.* 16, *Lab.* 12, *LD* 11, *Ind.* 3 |
| *Hereford | *LD* 22, *Lab.* 4, *C.* 1 |
| *Hertsmere | *C.* 19, *Lab.* 14, *LD* 5, *Ind.* 1 |
| High Peak | *Lab.* 17, *C.* 14, *LD* 10, *Ind.* 3 |
| Hinckley and Bosworth | *C.* 21, *LD* 8, *Lab.* 4, *Ind.* 1 |
| Holderness | *Ind.* 24, *LD* 7 |
| Horsham | *C.* 27, *LD* 14, *Ind.* 2 |
| Hove | *C.* 21, *Lab.* 6, *LD* 3 |
| *Huntingdonshire | *C.* 36, *Lab.* 12, *Ind. Lab.* 4, *Ind.* 1 |
| *Hyndburn | *Lab.* 32, *C.* 13, *LD* 1, *vacant* 1 |
| *Ipswich | *Lab.* 33, *C.* 14, *LD* 1 |
| Kennet | *C.* 17, *Ind.* 14, *LD* 8, *Lab.* 1 |
| Kerrier | *LD* 16, *Ind.* 13, *Lab.* 10, *C.* 5 |
| Kettering | *Lab.* 17, *C.* 12, *SD* 8, *Ind.* 5, *Others* 2, *vacant* 1 |
| King's Lynn and West Norfolk | *C.* 38, *Lab.* 16, *LD* 5, *Ind.* 1 |
| *Kingston upon Hull | *Lab.* 53, *LD* 6, *C.* 1 |
| Kingswood | *Lab.* 25, *C.* 18, *Lib.* 5, *Ind.* 2 |
| Lancaster | *Lab.* 24, *C.* 15, *Ind.* 13, *LD* 8 |
| Langbaurgh on Tees | *Lab.* 29, *C.* 22, *LD* 7, *Ind. Lab.* 1 |
| Leicester | *Lab.* 37, *C.* 12, *LD* 7 |
| *Leominster | *Ind.* 15, *LD* 8, *C.* 6, *Ind. C.* 3, *Lab.* 2, *Green* 1, *vacant* 1 |
| Lewes | *LD* 27, *C.* 19, *Ind.* 2 |
| Lichfield | *C.* 36, *Lab.* 16, *Ind. Lab.* 3, *Ind.* 1 |
| *Lincoln | *Lab.* 30, *C.* 3 |
| Luton | *Lab.* 27, *C.* 9, *LD* 9, *Green* 1, *Ind. C.* 1, *Ind. Lab.* 1 |
| *Macclesfield | *C.* 32, *LD* 15, *Lab.* 10, *RA* 3 |
| *Maidstone | *C.* 22, *LD* 17, *Lab.* 10, *Ind.* 5, *vacant* 1 |
| Maldon | *C.* 16, *Ind.* 10, *LD* 4 |
| Malvern Hills | *Ind.* 18, *LD* 16, *C.* 14, *Green* 1, *Ind. C.* 1, *Lab.* 1 |
| Mansfield | *Lab.* 38, *C.* 5, *LD* 2, *vacant* 1 |
| Medina | *C.* 18, *LD* 12, *Lab.* 3, *Ind.* 2, *Others* 1 |
| Melton | *C.* 18, *LD* 7, *vacant* 1 |
| Mendip | *LD* 21, *C.* 12, *Ind.* 7, *Lab.* 3 |
| Mid Bedfordshire | *C.* 42, *Lab.* 4, *Lib.* 4, *Ind.* 3 |
| Mid Devon | *Ind.* 27, *LD* 8, *Lib.* 2, *Ind. SD* 1, *Lab.* 1, *vacant* 1 |
| Middlesbrough | *Lab.* 37, *C.* 9, *Lib.* 5, *Ind.* 1, *vacant* 1 |
| Mid Suffolk | *C.* 15, *LD* 11, *Lab.* 9, *Ind. C.* 5 |
| *Mid Sussex | *C.* 34, *LD* 14, *Ind.* 4, *Lab.* 2 |
| *Milton Keynes | *Lab.* 20, *C.* 14, *LD* 11, *Lab.* 3 |
| *Mole Valley | *LD* 21, *C.* 11, *Ind.* 8, *Lab.* 1 |
| Newark and Sherwood | *Lab.* 28, *C.* 18, *LD* 5, *Ind.* 3 |
| Newbury | *LD* 24, *C.* 18, *Ind.* 2, *Lab.* 1 |
| *Newcastle under Lyme | *Lab.* 33, *LD* 14, *C.* 9 |
| New Forest | *LD* 30, *C.* 22, *Ind.* 6 |
| Northampton | *Lab.* 21, *C.* 17, *LD* 5 |
| Northavon | *LD* 25, *C.* 19, *Lab.* 11, *NP* 1, *vacant* 1 |
| *North Bedfordshire | *C.* 22, *Lab.* 16, *LD* 11, *Ind.* 4 |
| North Cornwall | *Ind.* 28, *LD* 7, *Lab.* 2, *C.* 1 |
| North Devon | *LD* 30, *Ind.* 11, *C.* 3 |
| North Dorset | *Ind.* 20, *LD* 12, *vacant* 1 |
| North East Derbyshire | *Lab.* 30, *C.* 12, *Ind.* 3, *LD* 3, *Ind. C.* 1, *vacant* 4 |
| *North Hertfordshire | *C.* 25, *Lab.* 18, *LD* 5, *Ind.* 1, *RA* 1 |

| | |
|---|---|
| North Kesteven | *NP* 25, *Lab.* 6, *LD* 5, *Ind.* 2, *vacant* 1 |
| North Norfolk | *C.* 16, *NP* 12, *LD* 7, *Lab.* 6, *Ind.* 5 |
| North Shropshire | *Ind.* 31, *C.* 4, *Lab.* 4, *LD* 1 |
| North Warwickshire | *Lab.* 19, *C.* 12, *Ind.* 1, *NP* 1, *vacant* 1 |
| North West Leicestershire | *Lab.* 26, *C.* 10, *Ind. C.* 4 |
| North Wiltshire | *LD* 29, *C.* 15, *Ind.* 3, *Lab.* 3, *NP* 2 |
| *Norwich | *Lab.* 35, *LD* 11, *C.* 2 |
| Nottingham | *Lab.* 37, *C.* 17, *Green* 1 |
| *Nuneaton and Bedworth | *Lab.* 37, *C.* 8 |
| *Oadby and Wigston | *LD* 19, *C.* 7 |
| Oswestry | *Ind.* 10, *C.* 9, *Lab.* 6, *LD* 4 |
| *Oxford | *Lab.* 36, *C.* 7, *LD* 7, *Green* 1 |
| *Pendle | *Lab.* 23, *LD* 21, *C.* 7 |
| *Penwith | *C.* 10, *Lab.* 8, *LD* 8, *Ind.* 6, *MK* 1, *vacant* 1 |
| *Peterborough | *C.* 21, *Lab.* 18, *Lib.* 5, *Ind.* 2, *Ind. Lab.* 1, *LD* 1 |
| Plymouth | *Lab.* 40, *C.* 18, *Ind. Lab.* 1, *LD* 1 |
| Poole | *LD* 20, *C.* 16 |
| *Portsmouth | *C.* 14, *Lab.* 14, *LD* 7, *Ind.* 2, *vacant* 2 |
| *Preston | *Lab.* 31, *C.* 19, *LD* 7 |
| *Purbeck | *C.* 9, *LD* 8, *Ind.* 5 |
| *Reading | *Lab.* 28, *C.* 12, *LD* 5 |
| *Redditch | *Lab.* 19, *C.* 9, *LD* 1 |
| *Reigate and Banstead | *C.* 22, *LD* 12, *Lab.* 11, *RA* 3, *Ind.* 1 |
| Restormel | *LD* 30, *Ind.* 11, *C.* 2, *Lab.* 1 |
| Ribble Valley | *C.* 23, *LD* 15, *Lab.* 1 |
| Richmondshire | *Ind.* 34 |
| Rochester upon Medway | *C.* 22, *Lab.* 21, *LD* 7 |
| *Rochford | *LD* 21, *C.* 10, *Lab.* 7, *RA* 2 |
| *Rossendale | *C.* 20, *Lab.* 15, *Ind. C.* 1 |
| Rother | *C.* 18, *LD* 16, *Ind.* 8, *Lab.* 3 |
| *Rugby | *C.* 19, *Lab.* 16, *RA* 6, *LD* 4, *Ind.* 3 |
| *Runnymede | *C.* 26, *Lab.* 9, *Ind.* 6, *LD* 1 |
| Rushcliffe | *C.* 43, *LD* 6, *Lab.* 5 |
| *Rushmoor | *C.* 23, *LD* 13, *Lab.* 8, *Ind.* 1 |
| Rutland | *Ind.* 8, *C.* 7, *LD* 4, *vacant* 1 |
| Ryedale | *LD* 20, *Ind.* 14, *C.* 6, *Lab.* 2 |
| *St Albans | *LD* 29, *C.* 19, *Lab.* 9 |
| St Edmundsbury | *C.* 26, *Lab.* 11, *LD* 5, *Ind.* 2 |
| Salisbury | *C.* 32, *Ind.* 10, *LD* 10, *Lab.* 6 |
| Scarborough | *C.* 16, *Lab.* 16, *Ind.* 9, *LD* 8 |
| *Scunthorpe | *Lab.* 34, *C.* 5, *SD* 1 |
| Sedgefield | *Lab.* 32, *LD* 10, *Ind.* 4, *C.* 2, *Others* 1 |
| Sedgemoor | *C.* 26, *Lab.* 12, *LD* 7, *Ind.* 4 |
| Selby | *C.* 22, *Lab.* 13, *Ind.* 10, *LD* 3, *Ind. Lab.* 2 |
| Sevenoaks | *C.* 31, *Ind.* 11, *LD* 11 |
| Shepway | *LD* 32, *C.* 19, *Ind.* 2, *Lab.* 2, *vacant* 1 |
| *Shrewsbury and Atcham | *C.* 16, *Lab.* 15, *LD* 11, *Ind.* 6 |
| *Slough | *Lab.* 28, *Lib.* 5, *C.* 4, *Ind.* 1, *Ind. Lab.* 1 |
| *Southampton | *Lab.* 23, *LD* 14, *C.* 8 |
| *South Bedfordshire | *C.* 35, *Lab.* 10, *LD* 7, *Ind.* 1 |
| South Bucks | *C.* 30, *Ind.* 10, *LD* 1 |
| *South Cambridgeshire | *C.* 22, *Ind.* 20, *LD* 7, *Lab.* 6 |
| South Derbyshire | *Lab.* 21, *C.* 10, *Ind. C.* 2, *NP* 1 |
| *Southend-on-Sea | *C.* 18, *LD* 14, *Lab.* 7 |

| | |
|---|---|
| South Hams | *C.* 24, *Ind.* 14, *LD* 4, *Ind. C.* 1, *Others* 1 |
| *South Herefordshire | *Ind.* 26, *LD* 7, *C.* 2, *Others* 4 |
| South Holland | *Lab.* 10, *C.* 7, *Ind.* 2, *Others* 19 |
| South Kesteven | *C.* 23, *Lab.* 13, *Ind.* 11, *LD* 9, *Lib.* 1 |
| *South Lakeland | *LD* 18, *C.* 14, *Ind.* 13, *Lab.* 6, *vacant* 1 |
| South Norfolk | *C.* 22, *LD* 22, *Ind.* 3 |
| South Northamptonshire | *C.* 29, *Ind.* 9, *Lab.* 2 |
| South Oxfordshire | *C.* 28, *LD* 9, *Ind.* 5, *Lab.* 5, *RA* 3 |
| South Ribble | *C.* 33, *Lab.* 14, *LD* 6, *vacant* 1 |
| South Shropshire | *NP* 11, *C.* 5, *Ind.* 5, *LD* 5, *Ind. C.* 1, *Lab.* 1, *Others* 12 |
| South Somerset | *LD* 41, *C.* 14, *Ind.* 5 |
| South Staffordshire | *C.* 37, *Lab.* 9, *LD* 3, *Ind.* 1 |
| South Wight | *LD* 10, *C.* 7, *Ind.* 7 |
| Spelthorne | *C.* 33, *Lab.* 4, *LD* 3 |
| Stafford | *C.* 29, *Lab.* 17, *LD* 12, *Ind.* 2 |
| Staffordshire Moorlands | *RA* 24, *C.* 13, *Lab.* 9, *LD* 5, *Ind.* 3, *Others* 2 |
| *Stevenage | *Lab.* 31, *C.* 4, *LD* 4 |
| Stockton-on-Tees | *Lab.* 27, *C.* 17, *LD* 10, *Ind.* 1 |
| *Stoke-on-Trent | *Lab.* 49, *C.* 11 |
| *Stratford-upon-Avon | *C.* 26, *LD* 22, *Ind.* 5, *Lab.* 2 |
| *Stroud | *C.* 18, *Lab.* 14, *LD* 13, *Ind.* 6, *Green* 4 |
| Suffolk Coastal | *C.* 36, *Ind.* 7, *Lab.* 6, *LD* 6 |
| Surrey Heath | *C.* 29, *LD* 6, *Ind. Lab.* 1 |
| *Swale | *LD* 19, *C.* 17, *Lab.* 12, *Ind.* 1 |
| *Tamworth | *Lab.* 20, *C.* 8, *Ind.* 2 |
| *Tandridge | *C.* 22, *LD* 17, *Lab.* 3 |
| Taunton Deane | *LD* 31, *C.* 12, *Lab.* 6, *Ind.* 4 |
| Teesdale | *Ind.* 22, *Lab.* 7, *C.* 2 |
| Teignbridge | *Ind.* 22, *C.* 19, *LD* 13, *Lab.* 4 |
| Tendring | *LD* 21, *C.* 16, *Lab.* 12, *Ind.* 8, *Others* 3 |
| Test Valley | *C.* 25, *LD* 16, *Ind.* 1, *NP* 1, *vacant* 1 |
| Tewkesbury | *Ind.* 21, *C.* 7, *LD* 4, *Lab.* 3, *vacant* 1 |
| *Thamesdown | *Lab.* 33, *C.* 12, *LD* 8, *Ind.* 1 |
| Thanet | *C.* 30, *Lab.* 14, *Ind.* 8, *LD* 2 |
| *Three Rivers | *C.* 20, *LD* 20, *Lab.* 7, *Ind.* 1 |
| *Thurrock | *Lab.* 28, *C.* 7, *Ind.* 4 |
| *Tonbridge and Malling | *C.* 32, *LD* 17, *Lab.* 6 |
| *Torbay | *LD* 20, *C.* 12, *Lab.* 2, *Others* 2 |
| Torridge | *Ind.* 15, *C.* 5, *LD* 5, *Lab.* 4, *Ind. C.* 3, *Green* 1, *Others* 3 |
| *Tunbridge Wells | *C.* 24, *LD* 20, *Lab.* 3, *Ind.* 1 |
| Tynedale | *C.* 18, *Lab.* 14, *LD* 9, *Ind.* 6 |
| Uttlesford | *C.* 22, *LD* 13, *Ind.* 6, *Lab.* 1 |
| Vale of White Horse | *C.* 28, *LD* 19, *Ind.* 2, *Lab.* 2 |
| Vale Royal | *Lab.* 32, *C.* 24, *LD* 3, *Ind.* 1 |
| Wansbeck | *Lab.* 44, *Lib.* 2 |
| Wansdyke | *C.* 22, *Lab.* 20, *Ind.* 3, *LD* 2 |
| Warrington | *Lab.* 42, *LD* 9, *C.* 8, *Ind. Lab.* 1 |
| Warwick | *C.* 24, *Lab.* 10, *LD* 8, *RA* 3 |
| *Watford | *Lab.* 20, *C.* 9, *LD* 7 |
| *Waveney | *Lab.* 27, *C.* 17, *LD* 4 |
| Waverley | *C.* 27, *LD* 27, *Lab.* 2, *vacant* 1 |
| Wealden | *C.* 44, *LD* 9, *Ind.* 5 |
| Wear Valley | *LD* 20, *Lab.* 9, *Ind.* 6, *Others* 5 |
| Wellingborough | *C.* 19, *Lab.* 12, *Ind.* 2, *Ind. C.* 1 |
| *Welwyn Hatfield | *Lab.* 24, *C.* 23 |
| West Devon | *Ind.* 16, *LD* 8, *C.* 4, *Green* 1, *Lab.* 1 |

| | |
|---|---|
| West Dorset | *C.* 17, *LD* 12, *NP* 12, *Ind.* 7, *Lab.* 4, *Ind. C.* 1, *SD* 1, *vacant* 1 |
| *West Lancashire | *Lab.* 29, *C.* 26 |
| *West Lindsey | *LD* 13, *Ind.* 10, *C.* 9, *Lab.* 5 |
| *West Oxfordshire | *Ind.* 18, *C.* 13, *LD* 12, *Lab.* 6 |
| West Somerset | *Ind.* 21, *C.* 4, *Lab.* 3, *LD* 2, *Others* 2 |
| West Wiltshire | *LD* 23, *Lib.* 4, *Ind.* 2, *Lab.* 2, *Others* 10, *vacant* 2 |
| *Weymouth and Portland | *LD* 14, *Lab.* 9, *C.* 6, *Ind.* 3, *Ind. RA* 3 |
| *Winchester | *LD* 28, *C.* 17, *Lab.* 6, *Ind.* 4 |
| Windsor and Maidenhead | *C.* 26, *LD* 25, *RA* 7 |
| *Woking | *C.* 16, *LD* 13, *Lab.* 5, *Ind. C.* 1 |
| *Wokingham | *C.* 34, *LD* 20 |
| Woodspring | *C.* 34, *LD* 16, *Ind.* 4, *Lab.* 3, *Green* 1, *vacant* 1 |
| *Worcester | *Lab.* 23, *C.* 9, *LD* 4 |
| *Worthing | *LD* 19, *C.* 17 |
| Wrekin | *Lab.* 32, *C.* 9, *Ind.* 3, *LD* 2 |
| Wychavon | *C.* 32, *LD* 9, *Lab.* 6, *Ind.* 2 |
| Wycombe | *C.* 37, *LD* 11, *Lab.* 9, *Ind.* 3 |
| Wyre | *C.* 32, *Lab.* 17, *LD* 4, *Ind.* 2, *RA* 1 |
| *Wyre Forest | *Lab.* 18, *LD* 15, *C.* 8, *Ind.* 1 |
| *York | *Lab.* 33, *C.* 7, *LD* 5 |

## GREATER LONDON BOROUGHS

| | |
|---|---|
| Barking and Dagenham | *Lab.* 48, *Ind.* 3 |
| Barnet | *C.* 29, *Lab.* 25, *LD* 6 |
| Bexley | *C.* 24, *Lab.* 24, *LD* 14 |
| Brent | *C.* 33, *Lab.* 28, *LD* 5 |
| Bromley | *C.* 32, *LD* 21, *Lab.* 7 |
| Camden | *Lab.* 47, *C.* 7, *LD* 5 |
| City of Westminster | *C.* 45, *Lab.* 15 |
| Croydon | *Lab.* 40, *C.* 30 |
| Ealing | *Lab.* 48, *C.* 20. *LD* 3 |
| Enfield | *Lab.* 41, *C.* 25 |
| Greenwich | *Lab.* 47, *C.* 8, *SD* 4, *LD* 3 |
| Hackney | *Lab.* 44, *LD* 10, *C.* 6 |
| Hammersmith and Fulham | *Lab.* 34, *C.* 15, *LD* 1 |
| Haringey | *Lab.* 57, *C.* 2 |
| Harrow | *LD* 29, *C.* 17, *Lab.* 14, *Ind.* 3 |
| Havering | *Lab.* 31, *RA* 17, *C.* 11, *LD* 4 |
| Hillingdon | *Lab.* 43, *C.* 25, *Ind. Lab.* 1 |
| Hounslow | *Lab.* 49, *C.* 6, *LD* 5 |
| Islington | *Lab.* 39, *LD* 12, *C.* 1 |
| Kensington and Chelsea | *C.* 39, *Lab.* 15 |
| Kingston upon Thames | *LD* 26, *C.* 18, *Lab.* 6 |
| Lambeth | *Lab.* 24, *LD* 24, *C.* 16 |
| Lewisham | *Lab.* 63, *LD* 3, *C.* 1 |
| Merton | *Lab.* 40, *C.* 10, *Ind.* 3, *RA* 1 |
| Newham | *Lab.* 59, *LD* 1 |
| Redbridge | *Lab.* 29, *C.* 24, *LD* 9 |
| Richmond upon Thames | *LD* 43, *C.* 7, *Lab.* 2 |
| Southwark | *Lab.* 34, *LD* 27, *C.* 3 |
| Sutton | *LD* 47, *Lab.* 5, *C.* 4 |
| Tower Hamlets | *Lab.* 43, *LD* 7 |
| Waltham Forest | *Lab.* 27, *C.* 16, *LD* 14 |
| Wandsworth | *C.* 45, *Lab.* 16 |

## WALES

### COUNTY COUNCILS

| | |
|---|---|
| Clwyd | *Lab.* 33, *Ind.* 11, *C.* 7, *PC* 4, *Others* 8, *vacant* 1 |
| Dyfed | *Ind.* 31, *Lab.* 22, *LD* 8, *PC* 7, *C.* 1, *RA* 1 |
| Gwent | *Lab.* 56, *C.* 5, *LD* 1, *PC* 1 |
| Gwynedd | *Ind.* 26, *PC* 18, *Lab.* 9, *LD* 7, *Others* 2 |
| Mid Glamorgan | *Lab.* 59, *PC* 9, *Ind.* 3, *C.* 1, *vacant* 2 |
| Powys | *Ind.* 35, *Lab.* 6, *LD* 4, *Others* 1 |
| South Glamorgan | *Lab.* 40, *C.* 12, *LD* 8, *Ind.* 1, *PC* 1 |
| West Glamorgan | *Lab.* 47, *Ind.* 6, *C.* 3, *LD* 3, *PC* 1, *SD* 1 |

### DISTRICT COUNCILS

| | |
|---|---|
| Aberconwy | *Lab.* 11, *LD* 10, *C.* 9, *Ind.* 6, *NP* 4, *PC* 1 |
| Alyn and Deeside | *Lab.* 26, *C.* 6, *Ind.* 5, *Ind. C.* 2, *LD* 2, *Ind. Lab.* 1, *vacant* 1 |
| Arfon | *PC* 15, *Ind.* 13, *Lab.* 8, *LD* 2, *Others* 1 |
| Blaenau Gwent | *Lab.* 32, *RA* 5, *Ind.* 3, *PC* 2, *C.* 1, *Lib.* 1 |
| Brecknock | *Ind.* 29, *Lab.* 13, *LD* 2 |
| Cardiff | *Lab.* 39, *C.* 16, *LD* 9, *Ind.* 1 |
| Carmarthen | *Ind.* 27, *Lab.* 6, *PC* 2, *LD* 1, *RA* 1 |
| Ceredigion | *Ind.* 30, *LD* 9, *PC* 4, *Lab.* 1 |
| Colwyn | *Ind.* 11, *LD* 11, *C.* 6, *Lab.* 3, *Lib.* 1, *RA* 1, *vacant* 1 |
| Cynon Valley | *Lab.* 25, *PC* 11, *Ind.* 1, *Others* 1 |
| Delyn | *Ind.* 21, *Lab.* 14, *LD* 3, *C.* 2, *PC* 2 |
| Dinefwr | *Lab.* 15, *Ind.* 9, *PC* 5, *NP* 2, *vacant* 1 |
| Dwyfor | *Ind.* 22, *PC* 7 |
| Glyndŵr | *Ind.* 26, *Lab.* 4, *Ind. Lab.* 2, *LD* 2, *PC* 1 |
| Islwyn | *Lab.* 30, *PC* 5 |
| Llanelli | *Lab.* 20, *LD* 5, *Green* 3, *PC* 2, *Ind.* 1, *Others* 4 |
| Lliw Valley | *Lab.* 22, *Ind.* 6, *PC* 4, *C.* 1 |
| Meirionnydd | *PC* 13, *Lab.* 5, *Ind.* 1, *Others* 22 |
| Merthyr Tydfil | *Lab.* 20, *Ind.* 12, *PC* 1 |
| Monmouth | *C.* 21, *Lab.* 14, *Ind.* 3, *LD* 1, *vacant* 1 |
| Montgomeryshire | *Ind.* 37, *LD* 5, *Lab.* 2, *C.* 1, *PC* 1 |
| Neath | *Lab.* 24, *PC* 5, *LD* 2, *Ind.* 1, *Others* 1, *vacant* 1 |
| Newport | *Lab.* 43, *C.* 4 |
| Ogwr | *Lab.* 38, *C.* 8, *Ind. Lab.* 1, *LD* 1, *vacant* 1 |
| Port Talbot | *Lab.* 21, *RA* 6, *SD* 2, *Ind.* 1, *LD* 1 |
| Preseli Pembrokeshire | *Ind.* 36, *Lab.* 2, *C.* 1, *LD* 1 |
| Radnorshire | *Ind.* 25, *Lab.* 4, *LD* 2, *C.* 1, *Green* 1 |
| Rhondda | *Lab.* 23, *PC* 7, *RA* 3 |
| Rhuddlan | *Ind.* 21, *Lab.* 11 |
| Rhymney Valley | *Lab.* 27, *PC* 12, *Ind.* 4, *Ind. Lab.* 1, *RA* 1, *vacant* 1 |
| South Pembrokeshire | *NP* 27, *Lab.* 2, *PC* 1 |

| | |
|---|---|
| Swansea | *Lab.* 32, *LD* 8, *C.* 6, *Ind.* 6 |
| Taff-Ely | *Lab.* 20, *PC* 14, *Ind.* 4, *LD* 2, *C.* 1, *RA* 1, *SD* 1 |
| Torfaen | *Lab.* 36, *Ind.* 3, *LD* 3, *C.* 1, *Others* 1 |
| Vale of Glamorgan | *Lab.* 20, *C.* 19, *PC* 3, *Others* 4 |
| Wrexham Maelor | *Lab.* 29, *Ind.* 6, *LD* 5, *C.* 4, *Lib.* 1, *PC* 1 |
| Ynys Môn | *Ind.* 26, *PC* 7, *Lab.* 5, *C.* 1 |

## SCOTLAND

### REGIONAL AND ISLANDS COUNCILS

| | |
|---|---|
| Borders | *Ind.* 10, *LD* 8, *SNP* 6, *C.* 2, *NP* 1 |
| Central | *Lab.* 23, *SNP* 6, *C.* 4, *Ind.* 2 |
| Dumfries and Galloway | *Lab.* 11, *Ind.* 8, *LD* 5, *C.* 3, *SNP* 3, *Lib.* 1, *Others* 4 |
| Fife | *Lab.* 28, *LD* 12, *SNP* 4, *Com.* 1, *Ind.* 1 |
| Grampian | *LD* 18, *SNP* 17, *Lab.* 12, *C.* 8, *Ind.* 2 |
| Highland | *Ind.* 31, *Lab.* 10, *SNP* 4, *LD* 3, *C.* 2, *Lib.* 2, *Others* 2 |
| Lothian | *Lab.* 36, *C.* 5, *LD* 4, *SNP* 4 |
| Orkney | *Ind.* 28 |
| Shetland | *NP* 11, *Ind.* 5, *LD* 2, *Lab.* 1, *Ind. Lab.* 1, *Others* 6 |
| Strathclyde | *Lab.* 86, *SNP* 7, *LD* 6, *C.* 3, *Ind.* 2 |
| Tayside | *SNP* 22, *Lab.* 16, *C.* 4, *LD* 2, *Ind.* 1, *Ind. Lab.* 1 |
| Western Isles | *Ind.* 24, *Lab.* 4, *vacant* 2 |

### DISTRICT COUNCILS

| | |
|---|---|
| Aberdeen | *Lab.* 27, *LD* 13, *C.* 10, *SNP* 2 |
| Angus | *RA* 11, *C.* 7, *Ind.* 2, *LD* 1 |
| Annandale and Eskdale | *LD* 9, *Ind.* 5, *Lab.* 1, *Lib.* 1 |
| Argyll and Bute | *Ind.* 10, *C.* 4, *LD* 3, *SNP* 2, *Lab.* 1, *Others* 5, *vacant* 1 |
| Badenoch and Strathspey | *Ind.* 11 |
| Banff and Buchan | *Ind.* 10, *SNP* 7, *LD* 1 |
| Bearsden and Milngavie | *C.* 5, *LD* 4, *vacant* 1 |
| Berwickshire | *C.* 8, *Ind.* 3, *Lib.* 1 |
| Caithness | *Ind.* 16 |
| Clackmannan | *Lab.* 8, *SNP* 3, *C.* 1 |
| Clydebank | *Lab.* 7, *SNP* 3, *C.* 1, *Ind.* 1 |
| Clydesdale | *Lab.* 7, *SNP* 4, *C.* 3, *Ind.* 2 |
| Cumbernauld and Kilsyth | *Lab.* 7, *SNP* 5 |
| Cumnock and Doon Valley | *Lab.* 10 |
| Cunninghame | *Lab.* 20, *C.* 6, *SNP* 3, *Ind.* 1 |
| Dumbarton | *Lab.* 8, *C.* 5, *SNP* 2, *Ind.* 1 |
| Dundee | *Lab.* 27, *C.* 11, *SNP* 5, *Ind. C.* 1 |
| Dunfermline | *Lab.* 22, *LD* 5, *SNP* 4, *C.* 2, *Others* 1 |
| East Kilbride | *Lab.* 12, *C.* 2, *SNP* 2 |
| East Lothian | *Ind. Lab.* 9, *C.* 7, *SNP* 1 |
| Eastwood | *C.* 8, *RA* 2, *Lab.* 1, *SNP* 1 |
| Edinburgh | *Lab.* 31, *C.* 22, *LD* 7, *SNP* 2 |
| Ettrick and Lauderdale | *Ind.* 15, *SNP* 1 |
| Falkirk | *Lab.* 16, *SNP* 12, *Ind.* 5, *C.* 3 |
| Glasgow | *Lab.* 55, *C.* 4, *Ind. Lab.* 2, *SNP* 2, *LD* 1, *Others* 2 |
| Gordon | *Ind.* 9, *LD* 5, *C.* 2 |

| | |
|---|---|
| Hamilton | *Lab.* 15, *C.* 2, *Lib.* 2, *Ind. Lab.* 1 |
| Inverclyde | *Lab.* 10, *LD* 8, *C.* 1, *vacant* 1 |
| Inverness | *Ind.* 13, *Lab.* 8, *LD* 5, *Lib.* 1, *SNP* 1 |
| Kilmarnock and Loudoun | *Lab.* 8, *SNP* 7, *C.* 3 |
| Kincardine and Deeside | *C.* 5, *Ind.* 5, *LD* 1, *SNP* 1 |
| Kirkcaldy | *Lab.* 24, *SNP* 7, *Ind.* 3, *C.* 2, *LD* 2, *Others* 2 |
| Kyle and Carrick | *C.* 16, *Lab.* 9 |
| Lochaber | *Ind.* 4, *NP* 4, *Lab.* 3, *SNP* 3, *Ind. Lab.* 1 |
| Midlothian | *Lab.* 12, *C.* 2, *SNP* 1 |
| Monklands | *Lab.* 17, *SNP* 3 |
| Moray | *Ind.* 8, *SNP* 7, *Lab.* 2, *C.* 1 |
| Motherwell | *Lab.* 22, *SNP* 4, *C.* 2, *Ind.* 2 |
| Nairn | *Ind.* 8, *C.* 1, *SNP* 1 |
| Nithsdale | *Lab.* 9, *Ind.* 8, *C.* 5, *SNP* 5, *LD* 1 |
| North East Fife | *LD* 13, *C.* 4, *Ind.* 1 |
| Perth and Kinross | *C.* 16, *SNP* 5, *Ind.* 3, *Lab.* 3, *LD* 2 |
| Renfrew | *Lab.* 22, *SNP* 11, *C.* 7, *SD* 3, *Ind.* 2 |
| Ross and Cromarty | *Ind.* 18, *SD* 4 |
| Roxburgh | *Ind.* 7, *LD* 5, *C.* 2, *NP* 1, *SNP* 1 |
| Skye and Lochalsh | *Ind.* 9, *LD* 1, *SNP* 1 |
| Stewartry | *Ind.* 4, *C.* 1, *Others* 7 |
| Stirling | *C.* 10, *Lab.* 10 |
| Strathkelvin | *Lab.* 9, *C.* 6 |
| Sutherland | *Ind.* 14 |
| Tweeddale | *Ind.* 7, *Lab.* 1, *LD* 1, *SNP* 1 |
| West Lothian | *Lab.* 11, *SNP* 10, *C.* 2, *Ind.* 1 |
| Wigtown | *Ind.* 6, *NP* 5, *C.* 1, *Lab.* 1, *SNP* 1 |

# England

## POSITION AND EXTENT

The Kingdom of England lies between 55° 46′ and 49° 57′ 30″ N. latitude (from a few miles north of the mouth of the Tweed to the Lizard), and between 1° 46′ E. and 5° 43′ W. (from Lowestoft to Land's End). England is bounded on the north by the Cheviot Hills; on the south by the English Channel; on the east by the Straits of Dover (Pas de Calais) and the North Sea; and on the west by the Atlantic Ocean, Wales and the Irish Sea. It has a total area of 50,351 sq. miles (130,410 sq. km): land 50,058 sq. miles (129,652 sq. km); inland water 293 sq. miles (758 sq. km).

## POPULATION

The population at the 1991 Census was 46,382,050 (males 22,469,707; females 23,912,343). The average density of the population in 1991 was 3.6 persons per hectare.

## FLAG

The flag of England is the cross of St George, a red cross on a white field (cross gules in a field argent). The cross of St George, the patron saint of England, has been used since the 13th century.

## RELIEF

There is a marked division between the upland and lowland areas of England. In the extreme north the Cheviot Hills (highest point, The Cheviot, 2,674 ft) form a natural boundary with Scotland. Running south from the Cheviots, though divided from them by the Tyne Gap, is the Pennine range (highest point, Cross Fell, 2,930 ft), the main orological feature of the country. The Pennines culminate in the Peak District of Derbyshire (Kinder Scout, 2,088 ft). West of the Pennines are the Cumbrian mountains, which include Scafell Pike (3,210 ft), the highest peak in England, and to the east are the Yorkshire Moors, their highest point being Urra Moor (1,490 ft).

In the west, the foothills of the Welsh mountains extend into the bordering English counties of Shropshire (the Wrekin, 1,334 ft; Long Mynd, 1,694 ft) and Hereford and Worcester (the Malvern Hills – Worcestershire Beacon, 1,394 ft). Extensive areas of high land and moorland are also to be found in the south-western peninsula formed by Somerset, Devon and Cornwall: principally Exmoor (Dunkery Beacon, 1,704 ft), Dartmoor (High Willhays, 2,038 ft) and Bodmin Moor (Brown Willy, 1,377 ft). Ranges of low, undulating hills run across the south of the country, including the Cotswolds in the Midlands and south-west, the Chilterns to the north of London, and the North (Kent) and South (Sussex) Downs of the south-east coastal areas.

The lowlands of England lie in the Vale of York, East Anglia and the area around the Wash. The lowest-lying are the Cambridgeshire Fens in the valleys of the Great Ouse and the River Nene, which are below sea-level in places. Since the 17th century extensive drainage has brought much of the Fens under cultivation. The North Sea coast between the Thames and the Humber, low-lying and formed of sand and shingle for the most part, is subject to erosion and defences against further incursion have been built along many stretches.

## HYDROGRAPHY

The Severn is the longest river in Great Britain, rising in the north-eastern slopes of Plynlimon (Wales) and entering England in Shropshire with a total length of 220 miles (354 km) from its source to its outflow into the Bristol Channel, where it receives on the east the Bristol Avon, and on the west the Wye, its other tributaries being the Vyrnwy, Tern, Stour, Teme and Upper (or Warwickshire) Avon. The Severn is tidal below Gloucester, and a high bore or tidal wave sometimes reverses the flow as high as Tewkesbury (13½ miles above Gloucester). The scenery of the greater part of the river is very picturesque and beautiful, and the Severn is a noted salmon river, some of its tributaries being famous for trout. Navigation is assisted by the Gloucester and Berkeley Ship Canal (16¼ miles), which admits vessels of 350 tons to Gloucester. The Severn Tunnel was begun in 1873 and completed in 1886 at a cost of £2,000,000 and after many difficulties from flooding. It is 4 miles 628 yards in length (of which 2¼ miles are under the river). The Severn road bridge between Haysgate, Gwent, and Almondsbury, Glos., with a centre span of 3,240 ft, was opened in 1966.

The longest river wholly in England is the Thames, with a total length of 215 miles (346 km) from its source in the Cotswold hills to the Nore, and is navigable by ocean-going ships to London Bridge. The Thames is tidal to Teddington (69 miles from its mouth) and forms county boundaries almost throughout its course; on its banks are situated London, Windsor Castle, the oldest royal residence still in regular use, Eton College, the first of the public schools, and Oxford, the oldest university in the kingdom.

Of the remaining English rivers those flowing into the North Sea are the Tyne, Wear, Tees, Ouse and Trent from the Pennine Range, the Great Ouse (160 miles), which rises in Northamptonshire, and the Orwell and Stour from the hills of East Anglia. Flowing into the English Channel are the Sussex Ouse from the Weald, the Itchen from the Hampshire Hills, and the Axe, Teign, Dart, Tamar and Exe from the Devonian hills. Flowing into the Irish Sea are the Mersey, Ribble and Eden from the western slopes of the Pennines and the Derwent from the Cumbrian mountains.

The English Lakes, noteworthy for their picturesque scenery and poetic associations, lie in Cumbria, the largest being Windermere (10 miles long), Ullswater and Derwentwater.

## ISLANDS

The Isle of Wight is separated from Hampshire by the Solent. The capital, Newport, stands at the head of the estuary of the Medina, Cowes (at the mouth) being the chief port. Other centres are Ryde, Sandown, Shanklin, Ventnor, Freshwater, Yarmouth, Totland Bay, Seaview and Bembridge.

Lundy (the name means Puffin Island), 11 miles northwest of Hartland Point, Devon, is about two miles long and about half a mile broad (average), with a total area of about 1,116 acres, and a population of about 20. It became the property of the National Trust in 1969 and is now principally a bird sanctuary.

The Isles of Scilly consist of about 140 islands and skerries (total area, 6 sq. miles/10 sq. km) situated 28 miles southwest of Land's End. Only five are inhabited: St Mary's, St Agnes, Bryher, Tresco and St Martin's. The population is 1,978. The entire group has been designated a Conservation Area, a Heritage Coast, and an Area of Outstanding Natural Beauty, and has been given National Nature Reserve status by the Nature Conservancy Council because of its unique flora and fauna. Tourism and the winter/spring flower trade for the home market form the basis of the economy of the Isles. The island group is a recognized rural development area.

# EARLY HISTORY

## PREHISTORIC INHABITANTS

Archaeological evidence suggests that England has been inhabited since at least the Palaeolithic period, though the extent of the various Palaeolithic cultures was dependent upon the degree of glaciation. The succeeding Neolithic and Bronze Age cultures have left abundant remains throughout the country, the best-known of these being the henges and stone circles of Stonehenge (ten miles north of Salisbury, Wilts.) and Avebury (Wilts.), both of which are believed to have been of religious significance. In the latter part of the Bronze Age the Goidels, a people of Celtic race, and in the Iron Age other Celtic races of Brythons and Belgae, invaded the country and brought with them Celtic civilization and dialects, place names in England bearing witness to the spread of the invasion over the whole kingdom.

## THE ROMAN CONQUEST

The Roman conquest of Gaul (57–50 BC) brought Britain into close contact with Roman civilization, but although Julius Caesar raided the south of Britain in 55 BC and 54 BC, conquest was not undertaken until nearly 100 years later. In AD 43 the Emperor Claudius dispatched Aulus Plautius, with a well-equipped force of 40,000, and himself followed with reinforcements in the same year. Success was delayed by the resistance of Caratacus (Caractacus), the British leader from AD 48–51, who was finally captured and sent to Rome, and by a great revolt in AD 61 led by Boudicca (Boadicea), Queen of the Iceni; but the south of Britain was secured by AD 70, and Wales and the area north to the Tyne by about AD 80.

In AD 122, the Emperor Hadrian visited Britain and built a continuous rampart, since known as Hadrian's Wall, from Wallsend to Bowness (Tyne to Solway). The work was entrusted by the Emperor Hadrian to Aulus Platorius Nepos, legate of Britain from AD 122 to 126, and it was intended to form the northern frontier of the Roman Empire.

The Romans administered Britain as a province under a Governor, with a well-defined system of local government, each Roman municipality ruling itself and its surrounding territory, while London was the centre of the road system and the seat of the financial officials of the Province of Britain. Colchester, Lincoln, York, Gloucester and St Albans stand on the sites of five Roman municipalities, and Wroxeter, Caerleon, Chester, Lincoln and York were at various times the sites of legionary fortresses. Well-preserved Roman towns have been uncovered at (or near) Silchester (*Calleva Atrebatum*), ten miles south of Reading, Wroxeter (*Viroconium Cornoviorum*), near Shrewsbury, and St Albans (*Verulamium*) in Hertfordshire.

Four main groups of roads radiated from London, and a fifth (the Fosse) ran obliquely from Lincoln through Leicester, Cirencester and Bath to Exeter. Of the four groups radiating from London, one ran south-east to Canterbury and the coast of Kent, a second to Silchester and thence to parts of western Britain and south Wales, a third (later known as Watling Street) ran through Verulamium to Chester, with various branches, and the fourth reached Colchester, Lincoln, York and the eastern counties.

In the fourth century Britain was subject to raids along the east coast by Saxon pirates, which led to the establishment of a system of coast defence from the Wash to Southampton Water, with forts at Brancaster, Burgh Castle (Yarmouth), Walton (Felixstowe), Bradwell, Reculver, Richborough, Dover, Lympne, Pevensey and Porchester (Portsmouth). The Irish (Scoti) and Picts in the north were also becoming more aggressive; from about AD 350 incursions became more frequent and more formidable. As the Roman Empire came under attack increasingly towards the end of the fourth century, many troops were removed from Britain for service in other parts of the empire. The island was eventually cut off from Rome by the Teutonic conquest of Gaul, and with the withdrawal of the last Roman garrison early in the fifth century, the Romano-British were left to themselves.

## SAXON SETTLEMENT

According to legend, the British King Vortigern called in the Saxons to defend him against the Picts, the Saxon chieftains being Hengist and Horsa, who landed at Ebbsfleet, Kent, and established themselves in the Isle of Thanet; but the events during the one and a half centuries between the final break with Rome and the re-establishment of Christianity are unclear. However, it would appear that in the course of this period the raids turned into large-scale settlement by invaders traditionally known as Angles (England north of the Wash and East Anglia), Saxons (Essex and southern England) and Jutes (Kent and the Weald), which pushed the Romano-British into the mountainous areas of the north and west, Celtic culture outside Wales and Cornwall surviving only in topographical names. Various kingdoms were established at this time which attempted to claim overlordship of the whole country, hegemony finally being achieved by Wessex (capital, Winchester) in the ninth century. This century also saw the beginning of raids by the Vikings (Danes), which were resisted by Alfred the Great (871–899), who fixed a limit to the advance of Danish settlement by the Treaty of Wedmore (878), giving them the area north and east of Watling Street, on condition that they adopt Christianity.

In the tenth century the kings of Wessex recovered the whole of England from the Danes, but subsequent rulers were unable to resist a second wave of invaders. England paid tribute (*Danegeld*) for many years, and was invaded in 1013 by the Danes and ruled by Danish kings from 1016 until 1042, when Edward the Confessor was recalled from exile in Normandy. On Edward's death in 1066 Harold Godwinson (brother-in-law of Edward and son of Earl Godwin of Wessex) was chosen King of England. After defeating (at Stamford Bridge, Yorkshire, 25 September) an invading army under Harald Hadraada, King of Norway (aided by the outlawed Earl Tostig of Northumbria, Harold's brother), Harold was himself defeated at the Battle of Hastings on 14 October 1066, and the Norman conquest secured the throne of England for Duke William of Normandy, a cousin of Edward the Confessor.

## CHRISTIANITY

Christianity reached the Roman province of Britain from Gaul in the third century (or possibly earlier); Alban, traditionally Britain's first martyr, was put to death as a Christian during the persecution of Diocletian (22 June 303), at his native town Verulamium; and the Bishops of Londinium, Eboracum (York), and Lindum (Lincoln) attended the Council of Arles in 314. However, the Anglo-Saxon invasions submerged the Christian religion in England until the sixth century when conversion was undertaken in the north from 563 by Celtic missionaries from Ireland led by St Columba, and in the south by a mission sent from Rome in 597 which was led by St Augustine, who became the first archbishop of Canterbury. England appears to have been converted again by the end of the seventh century and followed, after the Council of Whitby in 663, the practices of the Roman Church, which brought the kingdom into the mainstream of European thought and culture.

## PRINCIPAL CITIES

### BIRMINGHAM

Birmingham (West Midlands) is Britain's second city. It is a focal point in national communications networks with a rapidly expanding International Airport. The generally accepted derivation of 'Birmingham' is the *ham* (dwelling-place) of the *ing* (family) of *Beorma*, presumed to have been a Saxon. During the Industrial Revolution the town grew into a major manufacturing centre. In 1889 Birmingham was granted City status.

Despite the decline in manufacturing, Birmingham is still a major hardware trade and motor component industry centre. As well as the National Exhibition Centre and the Aston Science Park, recent developments include the International Convention Centre and the National Indoor Arena. An Urban Development Agency was set up in 1986.

The principal buildings are the Town Hall (1832–4); the Council House (1879); Victoria Law Courts (1891); the University (1909); the 13th-century Church of St Martin-in-the-Bullring (rebuilt 1873); the Cathedral (formerly St Philip's Church) (1711) and the Roman Catholic Cathedral of St Chad (1839–41).

### BRADFORD

Bradford (West Yorkshire) lies on the southern edge of the Yorkshire Dales National Park, including within its boundaries the village of Haworth, home of the Brontë sisters, and Ilkley Moor.

Originally a Saxon township, Bradford received a market charter in 1251 but developed only slowly until the industrialization of the textile industry brought rapid growth during the 19th century. The prosperity of that period is reflected in much of the city's architecture, particularly the public buildings: City Hall (1873), Wool Exchange (1867), St George's Hall (Concert Hall, 1853), Cartwright Hall (Art Gallery, 1904) and the Technical College (1882). Other chief buildings are the Cathedral (15th century) and Bolling Hall (14th century).

Textiles still play an important part in the city's economy but industry is now more broadly based, including engineering and micro-electronics. The city has a strong financial services sector, and a growing tourism industry.

### BRISTOL

Bristol (Avon) was a Royal Borough before the Norman Conquest. The earliest form of the name is *Bricgstow*. In 1373 it received from Edward III a charter granting it county status.

The chief buildings include the 12th-century Cathedral (with later additions), with Norman chapter house and gateway, the 14th-century Church of St Mary Redcliffe, Wesley's Chapel, Broadmead, the Merchant Venturers' Almshouses, the Council House (1956), Guildhall, Exchange (erected from the designs of John Wood in 1743), Cabot Tower, the University and Clifton College. The Roman Catholic Cathedral at Clifton was opened in 1973.

The Clifton Suspension Bridge, with a span of 702 feet over the Avon, was projected by Brunel in 1836 but was not completed until 1864. Brunel's SS *Great Britain*, the first ocean-going propeller-driven ship, is now being restored in the City Docks from where she was launched in 1843. The docks themselves have been extensively restored and redeveloped.

### CAMBRIDGE

Cambridge, a settlement far older than its ancient University, lies on the River Cam or Granta. The city is a county town and regional headquarters. Its industries include electronics, flour milling, cement making, the manufacture of scientific instruments and the growing area of biotechnology. Among its open spaces are Jesus Green, Sheep's Green, Coe Fen, Parker's Piece, Christ's Pieces, the University Botanic Garden, and the Backs, or lawns and gardens through which the Cam winds behind the principal line of college buildings. East of the Cam, King's Parade, upon which stand Great St Mary's Church, Senate House and King's College Chapel with Wilkins' screen, joins Trumpington Street to form one of the most beautiful thoroughfares in Europe.

University and college buildings provide the outstanding features of Cambridge architecture but several churches (especially St Benet's, the oldest building in the City, and St Sepulchre's, the Round Church) are also notable. The modern Guildhall (1939) stands on a site of which at least part has held municipal buildings since 1224.

### CANTERBURY

Canterbury, the Metropolitan City of the Anglican Communion, has a history going back to prehistoric times. It was the Roman *Durovernum Cantiacorum* and the Saxon *Cant-wara-byrig* (stronghold of the men of Kent). Here in 597 St Augustine began the conversion of the English to Christianity, when Ethelbert, King of Kent, was baptized.

Of the Benedictine St Augustine's Abbey, burial place of the Jutish Kings of Kent (whose capital Canterbury was), only ruins remain. St Martin's Church, on the eastern outskirts of the city, is stated by Bede to have been the place of worship of Queen Bertha, the Christian wife of King Ethelbert, before the advent of St Augustine.

In 1170 the rivalry of Church and State culminated in the murder in Canterbury Cathedral, by Henry II's knights, of Archbishop Thomas Becket, whose shrine became a great centre of pilgrimage, as described by Chaucer in his *Canterbury Tales*. After the Reformation pilgrimages ceased, but the prosperity of the city was strengthened by an influx of Huguenot refugees, who introduced weaving. The Elizabethan poet and playwright Christopher Marlowe was born and reared in Canterbury, and there are also literary associations with Defoe, Dickens, Joseph Conrad and Somerset Maugham.

The Cathedral, with architecture ranging from the 11th to the 15th centuries, is world famous. Modern pilgrims are attracted particularly to the Martyrdom, the Black Prince's Tomb, the Warriors' Chapel and the many examples of medieval stained glass.

The medieval city walls are built on Roman foundations and the 14th-century West Gate is one of the finest buildings of its kind in the country.

The 1,000 seat Marlowe Theatre is the base for the Canterbury Arts Festival each autumn.

### CARLISLE

Carlisle is situated at the confluence of the River Eden and River Caldew, 309 miles north-west of London and about ten miles from the Scottish border. It was granted a charter in 1158.

The city stands at the western end of Hadrian's Wall and dates from the original Roman settlement of *Luguvalium*. Granted to Scotland in the tenth century, Carlisle is not included in the Domesday Book. William Rufus reclaimed the area in 1092 and the castle and city walls were built to guard Carlisle and the western border; the citadel is a Tudor addition to protect the south of the city. Until the Union of the Crowns in 1603, Carlisle changed hands several times and was frequently besieged. During the Civil War the city remained Royalist; in 1745 it supported the Young Pretender.

The Cathedral, originally a 12th-century Augustinian priory, was enlarged in the 13th and 14th centuries after the diocese was created in 1133. To the south is a restored Tithe Barn and nearby the 18th-century church of St Cuthbert, the third to stand on a site dating from the seventh century.

Carlisle is the major shopping, commercial and agricultural centre for the area, and industries include the manufacture of metal goods, biscuits and textiles. However, the largest employer is the services sector, notably in central and local government, retailing and transport. The city has an important communications position at the centre of a network of major roads, as an important stage on the main west coast rail services, and with its own airport at Crosby.

## CHESTER

Chester is situated on the River Dee, and was granted Borough and City status in 1974. Its recorded history dates from the first century when the Romans founded the fortress of *Deva*. The city's name is derived from the Latin *castra* (a camp or encampment). During the Middle Ages, Chester was the principal port of north-west England but declined with the silting of the Dee estuary and competition from Liverpool. The city was also an important military centre, notably during Edward I's Welsh campaigns and the Elizabethan Irish campaigns. During the Civil War, Chester supported the King and was besieged from 1643 to 1646. Chester's first charter was granted c.1175 and the city was incorporated in 1506. The office of Sheriff is the earliest created in the country (c.1120s), and in 1992 the Mayor was granted the title of Lord Mayor. He/she also enjoys the title 'Admiral of the Dee'.

The city's architectural features include the city walls (an almost complete two-mile circuit), the unique Rows (covered galleries above the street-level shops), the Victorian Gothic Town Hall (1869), the Castle (rebuilt 1788 and 1822) and numerous half-timbered buildings. The Cathedral was a Benedictine abbey until the Dissolution. Remaining monastic buildings include the chapter house, refectory and cloisters and there is a modern free-standing bell tower. The Norman church of St John the Baptist was a cathedral church in the early Middle Ages.

Chester is primarily a regional service centre and has considerable tourist appeal. In 1984 the city was awarded Development Area status, which has attracted a range of nationally-known companies to expand or locate in Chester.

## COVENTRY

Coventry (West Midlands) is an important industrial centre, producing vehicles, machine tools, agricultural machinery, man-made fibres, aerospace components and telecommunications equipment. New investment has come from the financial services, power transmission, professional services and educational sectors.

The city owes its beginning to Leofric, Earl of Mercia, and his wife Godiva who, in 1043, founded a Benedictine monastery. The guildhall of St Mary dates from the 14th century, three of the city's churches date from the 14th and 15th centuries, and 16th-century almshouses may still be seen. Coventry's first cathedral was destroyed at the Reformation, its second in the 1940 blitz (the walls and spire remain) and the new cathedral designed by Sir Basil Spence, consecrated in 1962, now draws innumerable visitors.

Coventry is the home of the University of Warwick and its Science Park, Coventry University, the rapidly-expanding Westwood Business Park, the award-winning Cable and Wireless College, and the Museum of British Road Transport.

## DERBY

Derby stands on the banks of the River Derwent, and its name dates back to 880 when the Danes settled in the locality and changed the original Saxon name of *Northworthy* to *Deoraby*.

Derby has a wide range of industries: its products include aero engines, pipework, specialized mechanical engineering equipment, textiles, chemicals, plastics and the Royal Crown Derby porcelain. The city is an established railway centre, the site of British Rail's Technical Centre with its research laboratories.

Buildings of interest include St Peter's Church and the Old Abbey Building (14th century), the Cathedral (1525), St Mary's Roman Catholic Church (1839) and the Industrial Museum, formerly the Old Silk Mill (1721). The traditional city centre is complemented by the new Eagle Centre and 'out-of-centre' retail developments. In addition to the Derby Playhouse, the Assembly Rooms are a multi-purpose venue.

The first charter granting a Mayor and Aldermen was that of Charles I in 1637. Previous charters date back to 1154. It was granted City status in 1977.

## DURHAM

The city of Durham is a district in the county of Durham and a major tourist attraction because of its prominent Norman Cathedral and Castle set high on a wooded peninsula overlooking the River Wear. The Cathedral was founded as a shrine for the body of St Cuthbert in 995. The present building dates from 1093 and among its many treasures is the tomb of the Venerable Bede (673–735). Durham's Prince Bishops had unique powers up to 1836, being lay rulers as well as religious leaders. As a palatinate Durham could have its own army, nobility, coinage and courts. The Castle was the main seat of the Prince Bishops for nearly 800 years; it is now used as a college by the University. The University, founded on the initiative of Bishop William Van Mildert, is England's third oldest. Its students live in 14 colleges spread across the city.

Among other buildings of interest is the Guildhall in the Market Place which dates originally from the 14th century. Much work has been carried out to conserve this area, forming part of the city's major contribution to the Council of Europe's Urban Renaissance Campaign. Annual events include Durham's Regatta in June (claimed to be the oldest rowing event in Britain) and the Annual Gala (formerly Durham Miners' Gala) in July.

In the past 20 years the economy of Durham has undergone a significant change with the replacement of mining as the dominant industry by 'white collar' employment. Although still a predominantly rural area, the industrial and commercial sector is growing and a wide range of manufacturing and service industries are based on industrial estates in and around the city.

## EXETER

Exeter lies on the River Exe ten miles from the sea. It was granted a Royal Charter by Henry II. The Romans founded *Isca Dumnoniorum* in the first century AD, and in the third century a stone wall (most of which remains) was built, providing protection against Saxon, and then Danish invasions. After the Conquest, the city led resistance to William in the west, until reduced by siege. The Normans built the ringwork castle of Rougemont, the gatehouse and one tower of which remain, although the rest was pulled down in 1784. The first bridge across the Exe was built in the early 13th century. The city's main port was situated downstream at Topsham until the construction in the 1560s of the first true canal in England, the re-development of which in 1700 brought seaborne trade direct to the city. Exeter was the Royalist headquarters in the west during the Civil War.

The diocese of Exeter was established by Edward the Confessor in 1050, although a minster existed near the Cathedral site from the late seventh century. A new cathedral was built in the 12th century but the present building was begun c.1275, although incorporating the Norman towers, and completed about a century later. The Guildhall dates from the 12th century and there are many other medieval buildings in the city, as well as buildings in the Georgian and Regency styles, and the Custom House (1680). Damage suffered by bombing in 1942 led to the redevelopment of the city centre.

Exeter's prosperity from medieval times was based on trade in wool and woollen cloth (commemorated by Tuckers Hall), which remained at its height until the late 18th century when export trade was hit by the French wars. Subsequently Exeter has developed as an administrative and commercial centre, notably in the distributive trades, light manufacturing industries and tourism.

## KINGSTON UPON HULL

Hull (officially Kingston upon Hull) lies in the mostly rural county of Humberside, at the junction of the River Hull with the Humber, 22 miles from the North Sea. It is one of the great seaports of the United Kingdom. It has docks covering a water area of 172 acres, equipped to handle cargoes by unit-load techniques, and is a departure point for car ferry services to continental Europe. There is a great variety of industry and service industries, as well as increasing tourism and conference business.

The city, restored after heavy air raid damage during the Second World War, has good office and administrative buildings, its municipal centre being the Guildhall, its educational centres the University of Hull and Humberside University and its religious centre the Parish Church of the Holy Trinity. The old town area is being renovated and includes a marina and shopping complex. Just west of the city is the Humber Bridge, the world's longest single span suspension bridge.

Kingston upon Hull was so named by Edward I. City status was accorded in 1897 and the office of Mayor raised to the dignity of Lord Mayor in 1914.

## LEEDS

Leeds (West Yorkshire), situated in the lower Aire Valley, is a junction for road, rail, canal and air services and an important commercial centre. Seventy-three per cent of employment is in services, notably the distributive trades, public administration, medical services and business services. The main manufacturing industries are mechanical engineering, printing and publishing, metal goods and furniture.

The principal buildings are the Civic Hall (1933), the Town Hall (1858), the Municipal Buildings and Art Gallery (1884) with the Henry Moore Gallery (1982), the Corn Exchange (1863) and the University. The Parish Church (St Peter's) was rebuilt in 1841; the 17th-century St John's Church has a fine interior with a famous English Renaissance screen; the last remaining 18th-century church in the city is Holy Trinity in Boar Lane (1727). Kirkstall Abbey (about three miles from the centre of the city), founded by Henry de Lacy in 1152, is one of the most complete examples of Cistercian houses now remaining. Temple Newsam, birthplace of Lord

Darnley, was acquired by the Council in 1922. The present house was largely rebuilt by Sir Arthur Ingram in about 1620. Adel Church, about five miles from the centre of the city, is a fine Norman structure.

Leeds was first incorporated by Charles I in 1626. The earliest forms of the name are *Loidis* or *Ledes*, the origins of which are obscure.

## LEICESTER

Leicester is situated geographically in the centre of England. It dates back to pre-Roman times and was one of the five Danish *Burghs*. In 1589 Queen Elizabeth I granted a Charter to the City and the ancient title was confirmed by letters patent in 1919. Under local government reorganization Leicester retained its designation as a City.

The principal industries of the city are hosiery, knitwear, footwear manufacturing and engineering. The growth of Leicester as a hosiery centre increased rapidly from the introduction there of the first stocking frame in 1670 and today it has some of the largest hosiery factories in the world.

The principal buildings in the city are the Town Hall, the New Walk Centre, the University of Leicester, De Montfort University, De Montfort Hall, one of the finest concert halls in the provinces seating over 2,750 people, and the Granby Halls, an indoor sports facility. The ancient Churches of St Martin (now Leicester Cathedral), St Nicholas, St Margaret, All Saints, St Mary de Castro, and buildings such as the Guildhall, the 14th-century Newarke Gate, the Castle and the Jewry Wall Roman site still exist. The Haymarket Theatre was opened in 1973 and The Shires shopping centre in 1992.

## LINCOLN

Situated 40 miles inland on the River Witham, Lincoln derives its name from a contraction of *Lindum Colonia*, the settlement founded in AD 48 by the Romans to command the crossing of Ermine Street and Fosse Way. Sections of the third-century Roman city wall can be seen, including an extant gateway (Newport Arch), and excavations have discovered traces of a sewerage system unique in Britain. The Romans also drained the surrounding fenland and created a canal system, laying the foundations of Lincoln's agricultural prosperity, and also of the city's importance in the medieval wool trade as a port and Staple town.

As one of the Five Boroughs of the Danelaw, Lincoln was an important trading centre in the ninth and tenth centuries and medieval prosperity from the wool trade lasted until the 14th century, enabling local merchants to build parish churches (of which three survive), and attracting in the 12th century a Jewish community (Jew's House and Court, Aaron's House). However, the removal of the Staple to Boston in 1369 heralded a decline from which the city only recovered fully in the 19th century when improved fen drainage made Lincoln agriculturally important, and improved canal and rail links led to industrial development, mainly in the manufacture of machinery, components and engineering products.

The castle was built shortly after the Conquest and is unusual in having two mounds; on one motte stands a Keep (Lucy's Tower) added in the 12th century. The Cathedral was begun c.1073 when the first Norman bishop moved the see of Lindsey to Lincoln, but was mostly destroyed by fire and earthquake in the 12th century. Rebuilding was begun by St Hugh and completed over a century later. The Wren library contains manuscripts including one of the four surviving originals of the Magna Carta. Other notable architectural features of the city are the 12th-century High Bridge, the oldest in Britain still to carry buildings, and the

Guildhall situated above the 15th–16th century Stonebow gateway.

## LIVERPOOL

Liverpool (Merseyside) on the right bank of the River Mersey, three miles from the Irish Sea, is the United Kingdom's foremost port for the Atlantic trade. Tunnels link Liverpool with Birkenhead and Wallasey.

There are 2,100 acres of dockland on both sides of the river and the Gladstone and Royal Seaforth Docks can accommodate the largest vessels afloat. Annual tonnage of cargo handled is approximately 27.8 million tonnes. The main imports are crude oil, grain, ores, edible oils, timber, containers and break-bulk cargo. Liverpool Free Port, Britain's largest, was opened in 1984.

Liverpool was created a free borough in 1207 and a city in 1880. From the early 18th century it expanded rapidly with the growth of industrialization and the Atlantic trade. Surviving buildings from this date include the Bluecoat Chambers (1717, formerly the Bluecoat School), the Town Hall (1754, rebuilt to the original design 1795), and buildings in Rodney Street, Canning Street and the suburbs. Notable from the 19th and 20th centuries are the Anglican Cathedral, built from the designs of Sir Giles Gilbert Scott (the foundation stone was laid in 1904, and the building was completed only in 1980), the Catholic Metropolitan Cathedral (designed by Sir Frederick Gibberd, consecrated 1967) and St George's Hall (1838–54), regarded as one of the finest modern examples of classical architecture. The recently refurbished Albert Dock (designed by Jesse Hartley) contains the Merseyside Maritime Museum and Tate Gallery, Liverpool.

In 1852 an Act was obtained for establishing a public library, museum and art gallery; as a result Liverpool had one of the first public libraries in the country. The Brown, Picton and Hornby libraries now form one of the country's major libraries. The Victoria Building of Liverpool University, the Royal Liver, Cunard and Mersey Docks & Harbour Company buildings at the Pier Head, the Municipal Buildings and the Philharmonic Hall are other examples of the City's fine buildings. Britain's first International Garden Festival was held in Liverpool in 1984.

## MANCHESTER

Manchester (the *Mamucium* of the Romans, who occupied it in AD 79) is a commercial and industrial centre with a population engaged in the engineering, chemical, clothing, food processing and textile industries and in education. Banking, insurance and a growing leisure industry are among the prime commercial activities. The city is connected with the sea by the Manchester Ship Canal, opened in 1894, 35¼ miles long, and accommodating ships up to 15,000 tons. Manchester Airport handles more than 13 million passengers yearly.

The principal buildings are the Town Hall, erected in 1877 from the designs of Alfred Waterhouse, together with a large extension of 1938; the Royal Exchange (1869, enlarged 1921); the Central Library (1934); Heaton Hall; the 17th-century Chetham Library; the Rylands Library (1900), which includes the Althorp collection; the University precinct; the 15th-century Cathedral (formerly the parish church); G-MEX and the Free Trade Hall. Manchester is the home of the Hallé Orchestra, the Royal Northern College of Music, the Royal Exchange Theatre and seven public art galleries. Metrolink, the new light rail system, opened in 1992.

The town received its first charter of incorporation in 1838 and was created a city in 1853. The title of City was retained under local government reorganization.

## NEWCASTLE UPON TYNE

Newcastle upon Tyne (Tyne and Wear), on the north bank of the River Tyne, is eight miles from the North Sea. A Cathedral and University city, it is the administrative, commercial and cultural centre for north-east England and the principal port. It is an important manufacturing centre with a wide variety of industries.

The principal buildings include the Castle Keep (12th century), Black Gate (13th century), Blackfriars (13th century), West Walls (13th century), St Nicholas's Cathedral (15th century, fine lantern tower), St Andrew's Church (12th–14th century), St John's (14th–15th century), All Saints (1786 by Stephenson), St Mary's Roman Catholic Cathedral (1844), Trinity House (17th century), Sandhill (16th-century houses), Guildhall (Georgian), Grey Street (1834–9), Central Station (1846–50), Laing Art Gallery (1904), University of Newcastle Physics Building (1962) and Medical Building (1985), Civic Centre (1963), Central Library (1969) and Eldon Square Shopping Development (1976). Open spaces include the Town Moor (927 acres) and Jesmond Dene. Nine bridges span the Tyne at Newcastle.

The City derives its name from the 'new castle' (1080) erected as a defence against the Scots. In 1400 it was made a County, and in 1882 a City.

## NORWICH

Norwich (Norfolk) grew from an early Anglo-Saxon settlement near the confluence of the Rivers Yare and Wensum, and now serves as provincial capital for the predominantly agricultural region of East Anglia. The name is thought to relate to the most northerly of a group of Anglo-Saxon villages or *wics*. The city's first known Charter was granted in 1158 by Henry II.

Norwich serves its surrounding area as a market town and commercial centre, banking and insurance being prominent among the city's businesses. From the 14th century until the Industrial Revolution, Norwich was the regional centre of the woollen industry, but now the biggest single industry is financial services and principal trades are engineering, printing, shoemaking, double glazing, and the production of chemicals, clothing, confectionery and other foodstuffs. Norwich is accessible to seagoing vessels by means of the River Yare, entered at Great Yarmouth, 20 miles to the east.

Among many historic buildings are the Cathedral (completed in the 12th century and surmounted by a 15th-century spire 315 feet in height), the keep of the Norman castle (now a museum and art gallery), the 15th-century flint-walled Guildhall (now a tourist information centre), some thirty medieval parish churches, St Andrew's and Blackfriars' Halls, the Tudor houses preserved in Elm Hill and the Georgian Assembly House. The University of East Anglia is located on a site at Earlham on the city's western boundary.

## NOTTINGHAM

Nottingham stands on the River Trent and is connected by canal with the Atlantic Ocean and the North Sea. *Snotingaham* or *Notingeham*, literally the homestead of the people of Snot, is the Anglo-Saxon name for the Celtic settlement of *Tigguocobauc*, or the house of caves. In 878, Nottingham became one of the Five Boroughs of the Danelaw following a treaty signed by Alfred the Great and the Danish King Guthrum. William the Conqueror ordered the construction of Nottingham Castle, while the town itself developed rapidly under Norman rule. Its laws and rights were later formally recognized by Henry II's Charter in 1155. The Castle became a favoured residence of King John. In 1642 King Charles I raised his personal standard at Nottingham Castle at the start of the Civil War.

Nottingham is a major sporting centre, home to Nottingham Forest FC, Notts County FC (the world's oldest Football league side), Nottingham Racecourse and the National Watersports Centre. The principal industries include textiles, pharmaceuticals, food manufacturing, engineering and telecommunications. There are two universities within the city boundaries.

Architecturally, Nottingham has a wealth of notable buildings, particularly those designed in the Victorian era by T. C. Hine and Watson Fothergill. The City Council owns the Castle, of Norman origin but restored in 1878, Wollaton Hall (1580-8), Newstead Abbey (home of Lord Byron), the Guildhall (1888) and Council House (1929). St Mary's, St Peter's and St Nicholas's Churches are of interest, as is the Roman Catholic Cathedral (Pugin, 1842-4).

Nottingham was granted City status in 1897.

## OXFORD

Oxford is a University city, an important industrial centre, and a market town. Industry played a minor part in Oxford until the motor industry was established in 1912.

It is for its architecture that Oxford is of most interest to the visitor, its oldest specimens being the reputedly Saxon tower of St Michael's church, the remains of the Norman castle and city walls, and the Norman church at Iffley. It is chiefly famous, however, for its Gothic buildings, such as the Divinity Schools, the Old Library at Merton College, William of Wykeham's New College, Magdalen College and Christ Church and many other college buildings. Later centuries are represented by the Laudian quadrangle at St John's College, the Renaissance Sheldonian Theatre by Wren, Trinity College Chapel, and All Saints Church; Hawksmoor's mock-Gothic at All Souls College, and the 18th-century Queen's College. In addition to individual buildings, High Street and Radcliffe Square, just off it, both form architectural compositions of great beauty. Most of the Colleges have gardens, those of Magdalen, New College, St John's (designed by 'Capability' Brown) and Worcester being the largest.

## PLYMOUTH

Plymouth is situated on the borders of Devon and Cornwall at the confluence of the Rivers Tamar and Plym. The city has a long maritime history; it was the home port of Sir Francis Drake and the starting point for his circumnavigation of the world, as well as the last port of call for the *Mayflower* when the Pilgrim Fathers sailed for the New World in 1620. Today Plymouth is host to many international yacht races. The Barbican harbour area has many Elizabethan buildings and on Plymouth Hoe stands Smeaton's lighthouse, the third to be built on the Eddystone Rocks 13 miles offshore.

Following extensive war damage, the city centre, comprising a large shopping centre, municipal offices, law courts and public buildings, has been rebuilt. The main employment is provided at the naval base, though many industrial firms and service industries have become established in the post-war period and the city is a growing tourism centre. In 1982 the Theatre Royal was opened. In conjunction with the Cornwall County Council, the Tamar Bridge was constructed linking the city by road with Cornwall.

## PORTSMOUTH

Portsmouth occupies Portsea Island, Hampshire, with boundaries extending to the mainland. It is a centre of industry and commerce, including many high technology and manufacturing industries. It is the British headquarters

of several major international companies. The Royal Navy base still has a substantial work force, although this has decreased in recent years. The commercial port and continental ferry port is owned and run by the City Council, and carries passengers and vehicles to France and northern Spain.

A major port since the 16th century, Portsmouth is also a thriving seaside resort catering for thousands of visitors annually. Among many historic attractions are Lord Nelson's flagship, HMS *Victory*, the Tudor warship *Mary Rose*, Britain's first 'ironclad', HMS *Warrior*, the D-Day Museum, Charles Dickens' birthplace at 393 Old Commercial Road, the Royal Naval and Royal Marine museums, Southsea Castle (built by Henry VIII), the Round Tower and Point Battery, which for hundreds of years have guarded the entrance to Portsmouth Harbour, Fort Nelson on Portsdown Hill and the Sealife Centre.

## ST ALBANS

The origins of St Albans, situated on the River Ver, stem from the Roman town of *Verulamium*. Named after the first Christian martyr in Britain, who was executed here, St Albans has developed around the Norman Abbey and Cathedral Church (consecrated 1115), built partly of materials from the old Roman city. The museums house Iron Age and Roman artefacts and the Roman Theatre, unique in Britain, has a stage as opposed to an amphitheatre. Archaeological excavations in the city centre continue also to reveal evidence of pre-Roman, Saxon and medieval occupation.

The town's significance grew to the extent that it was a signatory and venue for the drafting of the Magna Carta. It was also the scene of riots during the Peasants' Revolt, the French King John was imprisoned there after the Battle of Poitiers, and heavy fighting took place there during the Wars of the Roses.

Previously controlled by the Abbot, the town achieved a Royal Charter in 1553 and City status in 1877. The street market, first established in 1553, is still an important feature of the city, as are many hotels and inns which survive from the days when St Albans was an important coach stop. Tourist attractions include historic churches and houses, and a 15th-century clock tower.

The city now contains a wide range of firms, with special emphasis on micro-technology and electronics, particularly in the medical field. In addition, it is the home of the Royal National Rose Society, and of Rothamsted Park, the agricultural research centre.

## SHEFFIELD

Sheffield (South Yorkshire), the centre of the special steel and cutlery trades, is situated at the junction of the Sheaf, Porter, Rivelin and Loxley valleys with the River Don. Though its cutlery, silverware and plate have long been famous, Sheffield has other and now more important industries: special and alloy steels, engineering, tool-making and financial services. Research in glass, metallurgy and other fields is carried out.

The parish church of St Peter and St Paul, founded in the 12th century, became the Cathedral Church of the Diocese of Sheffield in 1914. The Roman Catholic Cathedral Church of St Marie (founded 1847) was created Cathedral for the new diocese of Hallam in 1980. Parts of the present building date from c.1435. The principal buildings are the Town Hall (1897, 1923 and 1977), the Cutlers' Hall (1832), the University (1905 and more recent extensions, including 19-storey Arts Tower), City Hall (1932), Graves Art Gallery (1934), Mappin Art Gallery and the Crucible Theatre. The restored 19th-century Lyceum theatre opened in 1990.

Sheffield was created a city in 1893 and in 1974 retained its city status.

*Master Cutler* (1994–5) *of the Company of Cutlers in Hallamshire*, C. J. Jewitt

## SOUTHAMPTON

Southampton is the leading British deep-sea port on the Channel and is situated on one of the finest natural harbours in the world. The first Charter was granted by Henry II and Southampton was created a county of itself in 1447. In 1964 it was granted city status by Royal Charter.

There were Roman and Saxon settlements on the site of the city, which has been an important port since the time of the Conquest due to its natural deep-water harbour. The oldest church is St Michael's (1070) which has a black tournai marble font and an unusually tall spire built in the 18th century as a landmark for navigators of Southampton Water. Other buildings and monuments within the city walls are the Tudor House, God's House Tower, Bargate Museum, the Tudor Merchants Hall, the Weigh-house, West Gate, King John's House, Long House, Wool House, the ruins of Holy Rood Church, St Julien's Church and the Mayflower Memorial. The medieval town walls, built for artillery, are among the most complete in Europe. Public open spaces total over 1,000 acres in extent and comprise 9 per cent of the city's area. The Common covers an area of 328 acres in the central district of the city and is mostly natural parkland. Two recent additions to work in marine technology in Southampton are a leading oceanographic research centre (part of the University) and the recently developed marine science and technology business park.

## STOKE-ON-TRENT

Stoke-on-Trent (Staffordshire), standing on the River Trent and familiarly known as The Potteries, is the main centre of employment for the population of North Staffordshire. The city is the largest clayware producer in the world (china, earthenware, sanitary goods, refractories, bricks and tiles) and also has a wide range of other manufacturing industry, including steel, chemicals, engineering and tyres. Extensive reconstruction has been carried on in recent years.

The city was formed by the federation in 1910 of the separate municipal authorities of Tunstall, Burslem, Hanley, Stoke, Fenton, and Longton, all of which are now combined in the present City of Stoke-on-Trent.

## WINCHESTER

Winchester, the ancient capital of England, is situated on the River Itchen. The city is rich in architecture of all types but the Cathedral takes pride of place. The longest Gothic cathedral in the world, it was built in 1079–93 and exhibits examples of Norman, Early English and Perpendicular styles. Winchester College, founded in 1382, is one of the most famous public schools, the original building (of 1393) remaining largely unaltered. St Cross Hospital, another great medieval foundation, lies one mile south of the city. The almshouses were founded in 1136 by Bishop Henry de Blois, and Cardinal Henry Beaufort added a new almshouse of 'Noble Poverty' in 1446. The chapel and dwellings are of great architectural interest, and visitors may still receive the 'Wayfarer's Dole' of bread and ale.

Recent excavations have done much to clarify the origins and development of Winchester. Part of the forum and several of the streets of the Roman town have been discovered; and excavations in the Cathedral Close have uncovered the entire site of the Anglo-Saxon cathedral (known as the Old Minster) and parts of the New Minster, built by Alfred's son Edward the Elder and the burial place of the Alfredian dynasty. The original burial place of St Swithun, before his remains were translated to a site in the present cathedral, was also uncovered.

Excavations in other parts of the city have thrown much light on Norman Winchester, notably on the site of the Royal Castle, adjacent to which the new Law Courts have been built, and in the grounds of Wolvesey Castle, where the great house built by Bishops Giffard and Henry de Blois in the 12th century has been uncovered. The Great Hall, built by Henry III between 1222 and 1236 survives. It houses the Arthurian Round Table.

## YORK

The city of York (North Yorkshire) is an archiepiscopal seat. Its recorded history dates from AD 71, when the Roman Ninth Legion established a base under Petilius Cerealis which later became the fortress of *Eburacum*. In Anglo-Saxon times the city was the royal and ecclesiastical centre of Northumbria, and after capture by a Viking army in AD 866 it became the capital of the Viking kingdom of Jorvik. By the 14th century the city had become a great mercantile centre, mainly owing to its control of the wool trade, and was used as the chief base against the Scots. Under the Tudors its fortunes declined, though Henry VIII made it the head-quarters of the Council of the North. Recent excavations on many sites, including Coppergate, have greatly expanded knowledge of Roman, Viking and medieval urban life.

With its development as a railway centre in the 19th century the commercial life of York expanded. The principal industries are the manufacture of chocolate, railway coaches, scientific instruments, and sugar. It is the location of several government departments.

The city is rich in examples of architecture of all periods. The earliest church was built in AD 627 and, in the 12th to 15th centuries, the present Minster was built in a succession of styles. Other examples within the city are the medieval city walls and gateways, churches and guildhalls. Domestic architecture includes the Georgian mansions of The Mount, Micklegate and Bootham. Its museums include York Castle Museum, the National Railway Museum and the Jorvik Viking Centre.

# English Counties and Shires

## LORD LIEUTENANTS AND HIGH SHERIFFS

| County/Shire | Lord Lieutenant | High Sheriff, 1994–5 |
|---|---|---|
| Avon | Sir John Wills, Bt., TD | C. Marsden-Smedley |
| Bedfordshire | S. C. Whitbread | B. E. Howard |
| Berkshire | J. R. Henderson, CVO, OBE | Maj. the Hon. J. D. A. J. Monson |
| Buckinghamshire | Cdr. the Lord Cottesloe | J. M. Wheeler |
| Cambridgeshire | J. G. P. Crowden | F. J. Grounds |
| Cheshire | W. Bromley-Davenport | R. J. McAlpine |
| Cleveland | The Lord Gisborough | G. D. Saul |
| Cornwall | The Viscount Falmouth | A. M. J. Galsworthy |
| Cumbria | J. Cropper | F. J. R. Boddy |
| Derbyshire | J. K. Bather | Mrs G. M. Hutchinson |
| Devon | Lt.-Col. the Earl of Morley | The Countess of Arran |
| Dorset | The Lord Digby | Capt. M. Fulford-Dobson, RN |
| Durham | D. J. Grant, CBE | N. D. B. Straker |
| East Sussex | Adm. Sir Lindsay Bryson, KCB | The Lady Lloyd of Berwick |
| Essex | The Lord Braybrooke | Mrs E. B. P. Ward-Thomas |
| Gloucestershire | H. W. G. Elwes | Col. R. A. Coxwell-Rogers |
| Greater London | Field Marshal the Lord Bramall, GCB, OBE, MC | A. J. Butterwick |
| Greater Manchester | Col. J. B. Timmins, OBE, TD | J. B. Zochonis |
| Hampshire | Mrs F. M. Fagan | C. A. Palmer-Tomkinson |
| Hereford and Worcester | Capt. T. R. Dunne | G. M. Clive |
| Hertfordshire | S. A. Bowes Lyon | Lady Staughton |
| Humberside | R. A. Bethell | T. W. Boyd |
| Isle of Wight | *The Lord Mottistone, CBE | M. G. Ball |
| Kent | The Lord Kingsdown, PC | Mrs R. C. Teacher |
| Lancashire | Sir Simon Towneley, KCVO | Mrs J. J. Duckworth |
| Leicestershire | T. G. M. Brooks | J. M. S. Whitehead, CBE |
| Lincolnshire | Capt. Sir Henry N. Nevile, KCVO | S. J. E. Turner |
| Merseyside | A. W. Waterworth | Mrs A. Samuels, OBE |
| Norfolk | T. J. Colman | F. Cator |
| Northamptonshire | J. L. Lowther, CBE | Mrs L. A. Perry |
| Northumberland | The Viscount Ridley, KG, TD | Mrs M. L. Skeggs |
| North Yorkshire | Sir Marcus Worsley, Bt. | R. E. Howard-Vyse |
| Nottinghamshire | Sir Andrew Buchanan, Bt. | R. B. Godwin-Austen |
| Oxfordshire | Sir Ashley Ponsonby, Bt., KCVO, MC | D. P. Mason |
| Shropshire | The Viscount Boyne | J. H. G. Lywood |
| Somerset | Col. Sir Walter Luttrell, KCVO, MC | Elizabeth, Lady Gass |
| South Yorkshire | J. H. Neill, CBE, TD | M. G. S. Frampton, TD |
| Staffordshire | J. A. Hawley, TD | Col. M. P. K. Beatty, CBE, TD |
| Suffolk | The Lord Belstead | Brig. A. B. D. Gurdon, CBE |
| Surrey | R. E. Thornton, OBE | T. F. Goad |
| Tyne and Wear | Sir Ralph Carr-Ellison, TD | R. C. Spoor, OBE |
| Warwickshire | Capt. the Viscount Daventry | H. D. Warriner |
| West Midlands | R. R. Taylor, OBE | Sir Adrian Cadbury |
| West Sussex | Maj.-Gen. Sir Philip Ward, KCVO, CBE | P. Longley |
| West Yorkshire | J. Lyles | C. W. D. Sutcliffe |
| Wiltshire | Field Marshal Sir Roland Gibbs, GCB, CBE, DSO, MC | Mrs A. R. Grange |

* Lord Lieutenant and Governor

## COUNTY COUNCILS: Area, Population, Finance

| Council | Administrative headquarters | Area (hectares) | Population 1992* | Total demand upon collection fund 1994 |
|---|---|---|---|---|
| Avon | Avon House North, St James Barton, Bristol | 134,628 | 968,400 | £173,631,767 |
| Bedfordshire | County Hall, Bedford | 123,468 | 536,500 | 360,600,000 |
| Berkshire | Shire Hall, Reading | 125,901 | 758,100 | 132,800,000 |
| Buckinghamshire | County Hall, Aylesbury | 188,279 | 645,700 | 109,691,000 |
| Cambridgeshire | Shire Hall, Cambridge | 340,181 | 677,700 | 100,089,699 |
| Cheshire | County Hall, Chester | 233,325 | 966,900 | 173,080,907 |
| Cleveland | Municipal Buildings, Middlesbrough | 59,079 | 560,000 | 87,275,804 |
| Cornwall | County Hall, Truro | 356,442† | 475,400† | 78,909,671 |
| Cumbria | The Courts, Carlisle | 682,451 | 490,200 | 85,929,000 |
| Derbyshire | County Offices, Matlock | 263,098 | 947,400 | 155,566,307 |
| Devon | County Hall, Exeter | 671,096 | 1,045,100 | 627,715,000 |
| Dorset | County Hall, Dorchester | 265,433 | 664,300 | 117,860,800 |
| Durham | County Hall, Durham | 243,369 | 607,000 | 76,415,000 |
| East Sussex | Pelham House, St Andrews Lane, Lewes | 179,530 | 720,600 | 127,780,000 |
| Essex | County Hall, Chelmsford | 367,167 | 1,555,800 | 248,074,000 |
| Gloucestershire | Shire Hall, Gloucester | 264,270 | 541,400 | 94,133,000 |
| Hampshire | The Castle, Winchester | 378,022 | 1,587,500 | 232,200,000 |
| Hereford and Worcester | County Hall, Worcester | 392,650 | 690,400 | 109,846,000 |
| Hertfordshire | County Hall, Hertford | 163,601 | 994,200 | 169,187,000 |
| Humberside | County Hall, Beverley, N. Humberside | 351,256 | 881,400 | 143,300,000 |
| Isle of Wight | County Hall, Newport, IOW | 38,063 | 125,600 | 22,333,000 |
| Kent | County Hall, Maidstone | 373,063 | 1,538,300 | 251,000,000 |
| Lancashire | County Hall, Preston | 306,957 | 1,413,600 | 238,887,000 |
| Leicestershire | County Hall, Leicester | 255,297 | 902,300 | 131,438,780 |
| Lincolnshire | County Offices, Lincoln | 591,791 | 596,800 | 90,485,063 |
| Norfolk | County Hall, Norwich | 537,482 | 763,000 | 115,898,826 |
| Northamptonshire | County Hall, Northampton | 236,721 | 590,100 | 89,956,262 |
| Northumberland | County Hall, Morpeth | 503,165 | 307,200 | 44,995,895 |
| North Yorkshire | County Hall, Northallerton | 831,236 | 723,000 | 119,000,000 |
| Nottinghamshire | County Hall, Nottingham | 216,090 | 1,025,200 | 169,128,000 |
| Oxfordshire | County Hall, Oxford | 260,798 | 587,100 | 95,112,000 |
| Shropshire | The Shirehall, Shrewsbury | 349,013 | 412,800 | 63,700,000 |
| Somerset | County Hall, Taunton | 345,233 | 472,400 | 81,000,000 |
| Staffordshire | County Buildings, Stafford | 271,616 | 1,051,900 | 145,935,076 |
| Suffolk | County Hall, Ipswich | 379,664 | 648,000 | 101,097,443 |
| Surrey | County Hall, Kingston upon Thames | 167,924 | 1,036,700 | 189,148,000 |
| Warwickshire | Shire Hall, Warwick | 198,052 | 492,000 | 88,700,000 |
| West Sussex | County Hall, Chichester | 198,935 | 712,600 | 125,200,000 |
| Wiltshire | County Hall, Trowbridge | 347,883 | 579,300 | 97,587,000 |

\* *Source: HMSO – OPCS Key Population and Vital Statistics 1992*
† Including Isles of Scilly

## THE ISLES OF SCILLY

The islands of the Scillies group are administered by the Council of the Isles of Scilly, a 21-member non-political body, which combines the powers and duties of a county council and a district council under the Local Government Act 1972 and the Isles of Scilly Orders 1978. Legislation is specifically applied to the Isles of Scilly by Special Order. The Council is responsible for education, fire services, highways, planning, social services, water, and the airport. The police service is administered by the Devon and Cornwall Police Authority, of which the Council is a member. The Isles are part of the St Ives electoral division.

*Administrative Headquarters*, Town Hall, St Mary's, Isles of Scilly TR21 0LW

*Chairman of the Council*, J. P. Greenlaw

*Clerk and Chief Executive*, P. S. Hygate

*Chief Technical Officer*, B. M. Lowen

## COUNTY COUNCILS: Officers and Chairman

| Council | Chief Executive | County Treasurer | Chairman of County Council |
|---|---|---|---|
| Avon | B. D. Smith | C. Reynell (*acting*) | Mrs M. Hudson |
| Bedfordshire | D. Cleggett | *B. Phelps | Mrs K. Burley |
| Berkshire | °G. B. Scotford, OBE | †I. Thompson | C. Clarence |
| Buckinghamshire | C. M. Garrett | *J. Beckerlegg | K. I. Ross |
| Cambridgeshire | A. G. Lister | *D. Earle | C. Bradford |
| Cheshire | M. E. Pitt | ‡‡J. E. H. Whiteoak | Ms D. McConnell |
| Cleveland | B. Stevenson | †P. Riley | E. Wood |
| Cornwall | S. F. Nicol | *R. N. Lester | P. B. Cocks, CBE |
| Cumbria | J. E. Burnet | R. F. Mather | W. Cameron |
| Derbyshire | ‡J. S. Raine | P. Swaby | J. McKay |
| Devon | R. D. Clark | J. Glasby | R. A. Westlake |
| Dorset | P. K. Harvey | A. P. Peel | Mrs P. A. Hymers |
| Durham | K. W. Smith | J. Kirkby | J. Mackintosh |
| East Sussex | °°Mrs C. Miller | J. Davies | L. Hamilton |
| Essex | K. W. S. Ashurst | K. D. Neale | T. E. Dale |
| Gloucestershire | M. Honey | **J. R. Cockroft | F. R. Thompson |
| Hampshire | A. R. Hodgson | J. E. Scotford | K. W. E. Lane |
| Hereford and Worcester | J. W. Turnbull | P. Middleborough | J. W. Wardle, MBE |
| Hertfordshire | B. Briscoe | **Mrs L. Homer | M. D. Colne |
| Humberside | J. A. Parkes | *G. T. Southern | Ms V. Wilson |
| Isle of Wight | J. S. Horsnell | J. B. W. Proctor | Mrs V. A. Anderson |
| Kent | P. R. Sabin | *P. Martin | J. Purchese |
| Lancashire | G. A. Johnson | B. G. Aldred | E. M. Fail |
| Leicestershire | J. B. Sinnott | R. Hale | T. G. Howatt |
| Lincolnshire | R. J. D. Procter | M. Spink | R. Rainsforth |
| Norfolk | B. J. Capon, CBE | R. D. Summers | L. E. Austin |
| Northamptonshire | A. J. Greenwell, CBE | *R. Paver | Mrs E. M. Dicks |
| Northumberland | °°K. Morris | *K. Morris | J. Morris |
| North Yorkshire | J. A. Ransford | ††L. Cornfield | Ms B. Graham |
|  |  | ††J. Moore |  |
| Nottinghamshire | P. Housden | R. Latham | P. Burgess |
| Oxfordshire | J. Harwood | C. Gray | Ms M Ferriman |
| Shropshire | A. Barnish | N. Pursey | G. Raxster |
| Somerset | B. M. Tanner | C. N. Bilsland | R. B. Clark |
| Staffordshire | B. A. Price | R. G. Tettenborn, OBE | J. O'Leary |
| Suffolk | P. F. Bye | P. B. Atkinson | E. M. Wiles |
| Surrey | D. J. Thomas | ‡‡P. Derrick | Mrs C. Gerard |
| Warwickshire | I. G. Caulfield | S. R. Freer | D. Forwood |
| West Sussex | B. Fieldhouse | D. P. Rigg | C. Robinson |
| Wiltshire | I. A. Browning | *D. Chalker | P. L. Jeffries |

\* Director of Finance
° County Manager
† County Finance Officer
‡ County Director
** Director of Corporate Services
°° Managing Director
†† Deputy
‡‡ Director of Resources

# Metropolitan Councils

Small capitals denote City status

| Council | Population 1992* | Band D charge 1994 | Chief Executive | Mayor (a) Lord Mayor 1994–5 |
|---|---|---|---|---|
| Greater Manchester | 2,573,500 | | | |
| Bolton | 263,800 | £650.51 | B. Collinge | T. Anderton |
| Bury | 180,600 | 568.62 | D. J. Burton | R. Fletcher |
| Manchester | 434,600 | 670.11 | A. Sandford | (a) Ms S. Smith |
| Oldham | 220,300 | 683.00 | C. Smith | F. Heap |
| Rochdale | 205,700 | 674.82 | J. F. D. Pierce | J. E. Beasley |
| Salford | 230,300 | 740.09 | J. C. Willis | V. Prior |
| Stockport | 288,900 | 689.73 | J. R. Schultz | J. P. MacCarron |
| Tameside | 221,000 | 687.60 | M. Greenwood | Ms P. L. Haslam |
| Trafford | 216,000 | 544.50 | W. A. Lewis | K. Rogers |
| Wigan | 312,500 | 593.54 | S. M. Jones | W. S. Simmons |
| | | | | |
| Merseyside | 1,445,600 | | | |
| Knowsley | 155,500 | 651.30 | D. G. Henshaw | H. Bailey |
| Liverpool | 479,000 | 799.10 | P. Bounds | (a) R. Johnston |
| St Helens | 180,900 | 651.62 | Mrs C. A. Hudson | J. Fletcher |
| Sefton | 294,900 | 651.33 | G. J. Haywood | N. Fanning |
| Wirral | 335,300 | 683.54 | A. White | S. Dunn |
| | | | | |
| South Yorkshire | 1,304,400 | | | |
| Barnsley | 224,800 | 543.09 | J. A. Edwards, OBE | Mrs J. Watts |
| Doncaster | 293,500 | 491.90 | J. D. Hale | G. Gallimore |
| Rotherham | 255,100 | 603.72 | J. Bell | Mrs S. Walker |
| Sheffield | 531,000 | 622.75 | Mrs P. Gordon | (a) I. Saunders |
| | | | | |
| Tyne and Wear | 1,134,400 | | | |
| Gateshead | 203,100 | 657.00 | L. N. Elton | Ms P. Murray |
| Newcastle upon Tyne | 281,700 | 711.17 | G. N. Cook | (a) R. C. Brown |
| North Tyneside | 195,200 | 689.67 | †C. A. Roberts | R. A. Usher |
| South Tyneside | 157,300 | 614.25 | P. J. Haigh | Mrs J. Phipps |
| Sunderland | 297,200 | 540.88 | C. Sinclair | (a) D. G. Whalen |
| | | | | |
| West Midlands | 2,630,600 | | | |
| Birmingham | 1,009,100 | 632.16 | M. T. Lyons | (a) Sir Richard Knowles |
| Coventry | 304,600 | 753.11 | I. Roxburgh | (a) H. N. Nolan |
| Dudley | 311,000 | 582.98 | A. V. Astling | J. Simpson |
| Sandwell | 294,000 | 629.28 | F. N. Summers | J. P. Padden |
| Solihull | 200,900 | 535.00 | J. Scampion | E. S. Pemberton |
| Walsall | 263,500 | 553.68 | D. C. Winchurch | K. Sears |
| Wolverhampton | 247,500 | 552.96 | N. H. Perry, Ph.D. | S. A. Ledsam |
| | | | | |
| West Yorkshire | 2,093,500 | | | |
| Bradford | 477,500 | 562.46 | R. Penn | (a) D. Mangham |
| Calderdale | 193,900 | 673.36 | M. Ellison | S. J. Pearson |
| Kirklees | 383,300 | 712.38 | R. V. Hughes | H. Sheldon |
| Leeds | 721,800 | 599.37 | J. P. Smith | (a) Mrs C. Myers |
| Wakefield | 317,100 | 543.37 | R. Mather | D. Lund |

*Source:* HMSO – OPCS Key Population and Vital Statistics 1992
† Head of Paid Service

# Non-Metropolitan Councils

SMALL CAPITALS denote CITY status
§ denotes Borough status
Source of population figures: HMSO – OPCS Key Population and Vital Statistics 1992

| Council | Population 1992 | Band D charge 1994 | Chief Executive | Chairman 1994-5 (a) Mayor (b) Lord Mayor |
|---|---|---|---|---|
| Adur, West Sussex | 58,100 | £586.19 | F. M. G. Staden | Mrs S. Bucknall |
| §Allerdale, Cumbria | 96,900 | 623.04 | *C. J. Hart | (a) Mrs C. C. McCarron-Holmes |
| Alnwick, Northumberland | 30,300 | 535.99 | L. St Ruth | I. McArthur |
| §Amber Valley, Derbyshire | 113,000 | 597.52 | °P. M. Carney | (a) R. M. Buzzard |
| Arun, West Sussex | 132,200 | 544.73 | I. Sumnall | Mrs G. Hurle-Hobbs |
| Ashfield, Nottinghamshire | 109,800 | 647.45 | S. Beedham | Mrs D. Tyler |
| §Ashford, Kent | 93,600 | 518.18 | E. H. W. Mexter | (a) A. J. Hoad |
| Aylesbury Vale, Bucks. | 150,300 | 480.23 | B. J. Quoroll | J. W. Cartwright |
| Babergh, Suffolk | 80,000 | 498.42 | D. C. Bishop | Mrs J. Law |
| §Barrow-in-Furness, Cumbria | 73,600 | 696.00 | T. O. Campbell (acting) | (a) Mrs E. Willacy |
| Basildon, Essex | 161,800 | 615.06 | J. C. Rosser | F. Tomlin |
| §Basingstoke and Deane, Hants. | 146,000 | 485.84 | Ms K. Sporle | (a) J. L. Shears |
| Bassetlaw, Notts. | 105,400 | 659.29 | M. S. Havenhand | Mrs M. Hall |
| BATH, Avon | 83,900 | 550.27 | N. C. Abbott | (a) H. Routledge |
| §Bedford | 137,300 | 435.52 | L. W. Gould | (a) D. A. Jones |
| §Berwick-upon-Tweed, Northumberland | 26,900 | 518.60 | E. O. Cawthorn | (a) A. Easton |
| §Beverley, Humberside | 113,600 | 638.65 | M. Rice | (a) Mrs D. Wright |
| Blaby, Leics. | 84,300 | 521.63 | †E. Hemsley | L. C. Bolton |
| §Blackburn, Lancs. | 138,300 | 680.43 | G. L. Davies | (a) E. M. Arnold |
| §Blackpool, Lancs. | 152,000 | 682.11 | G. E. Essex-Crosby | (a) S. R. Beilby |
| §Blyth Valley, Northumberland | 80,500 | 603.46 | D. Crawford | (a) Mrs D. Westwood |
| Bolsover, Derbyshire | 71,500 | 541.68 | J. R. Fotherby | D. E. Reynolds |
| §Boothferry, Humberside | 64,800 | 558.79 | J. W. Barber | (a) Mrs E. M. Redfern |
| §Boston, Lincs. | 54,000 | 562.14 | I. Ward | (a) C. Marshall |
| §Bournemouth, Dorset | 159,300 | 535.50 | D. Newell | (a) J. Millward |
| §Bracknell Forest, Berks. | 100,300 | 501.26 | A. J. Targett | (a) A. Ward |
| Braintree, Essex | 121,100 | 531.96 | Ms A. Ralph | M. F. Hall |
| Breckland, Norfolk | 109,900 | 502.92 | R. Garnett | T. J. Wilding |
| Brentwood, Essex | 71,000 | 520.65 | C. P. Sivell | (a) D. P. Higgins |
| Bridgnorth, Shropshire | 50,300 | 523.72 | Mrs T. M. Elliott | M. G. Pate |
| §Brighton, East Sussex | 154,600 | 564.65 | G. Jones | (a) T. Framroze |
| BRISTOL, Avon | 396,600 | 733.07 | Ms L. de Groot (acting) | (b) Mrs C. Warren |
| Broadland, Norfolk | 107,400 | 498.60 | J. H. Bryant | H. Bowyer |
| Bromsgrove, Hereford and Worcs. | 92,600 | 529.04 | R. P. Bradshaw | Miss M. Y. Butt |
| §Broxbourne, Herts. | 82,700 | 520.90 | M. J. Walker | (a) J. R. S. Morton |
| §Broxtowe, Notts. | 109,600 | 640.28 | M. Brown | (a) Mrs J. K. Moodie |
| §Burnley, Lancs. | 92,500 | 679.86 | R. Ellis | (a) L. Harrison |
| CAMBRIDGE | 111,200 | 551.86 | R. Hammond | (a) J. E. Rosenstiel |
| Cannock Chase, Staffs. | 90,400 | 589.12 | M. G. Kemp | D. Thomas |
| CANTERBURY, Kent | 130,600 | 573.89 | C. Gay | (b) W. Hornsby |
| Caradon, Cornwall | 78,000 | 561.38 | J. Neal | B. E. de St Paër-Gotch |
| CARLISLE, Cumbria | 102,700 | 644.46 | R. S. Brackley | (a) C. Paisley |
| Carrick, Cornwall | 83,800 | 564.94 | P. M. Talbot | D. C. Hancock |
| §Castle Morpeth, Northumberland | 50,100 | 641.35 | P. Wilson | (a) I. McConnell-Wood |
| §Castle Point, Essex | 86,600 | 590.94 | B. Rollinson | Mrs M. L. Grant |
| §Charnwood, Leics. | 150,100 | 548.17 | S. M. Peatfield | A. J. B. Thornton |
| §Chelmsford, Essex | 154,500 | 537.02 | R. M. C. Hartley | (a) M. J. C. Dilloway |
| §Cheltenham, Glos. | 107,400 | 584.80 | C. Nye | (a) Miss D. M. A. Griggs |
| Cherwell, Oxon. | 128,400 | 460.27 | G. J. Handley | B. V. Wood |
| CHESTER, Cheshire | 119,500 | 605.68 | P. F. Durham | (b) J. G. Smith |
| §Chesterfield, Derbyshire | 100,600 | 611.12 | D. R. Shaw | (a) R. A. Matthews |

* General Manager
° Borough Secretary
† Finance and General Manager

| Council | Population 1992 | Band D charge 1994 | Chief Executive | Chairman 1994–5 (a) Mayor (b) Lord Mayor |
|---|---|---|---|---|
| Chester-le-Street, Co. Durham | 52,900 | £537.46 | J. A. Greensmith | A. Dunn |
| Chichester, West Sussex | 102,200 | 492.24 | C. E. Evans | Capt. S. A. Stuart, CBE, RN |
| Chiltern, Bucks. | 90,300 | 509.74 | D. G. Sainsbury | A. Dibbo |
| §Chorley, Lancs. | 97,100 | 643.65 | J. W. Davies | (a) A. Gee |
| §Christchurch, Dorset | 41,700 | 524.26 | C. H. Dewsnap | (a) E. J. Coope |
| §Cleethorpes, Humberside | 70,100 | 720.61 | P. Daniel | (a) Mrs M. Solomon |
| §Colchester, Essex | 148,600 | 534.78 | J. Cobley | (a) J. A. R. Webb |
| §Congleton, Cheshire | 85,100 | 539.64 | Miss C. L. Pointer | (a) A. Mather |
| §Copeland, Cumbria | 71,800 | 625.09 | *R. G. Smith | (a) J. Henney |
| Corby, Northants. | 53,200 | 570.30 | T. Simmons | (a) T. McGivern |
| Cotswold, Glos. | 76,200 | 506.14 | N. Howells | Mrs M. F. Brown |
| Craven, North Yorkshire | 51,000 | 533.33 | †H. H. Crabtree | Mrs M. Nicholson |
| §Crawley, W. Sussex | 88,500 | 540.00 | M. D. Sander | (a) D. W. Murdoch |
| §Crewe and Nantwich, Cheshire | 107,700 | 614.79 | A. Wenham | (a) P. Birchall |
| §Dacorum, Herts. | 134,500 | 522.01 | K. Hunt | (a) Mrs J. A. Dunbavand |
| §Darlington, Co. Durham | 100,100 | 590.91 | H. R. C. Owen | (a) J. Williams |
| §Dartford, Kent | 81,900 | 525.17 | C. R. Shepherd | (a) B. Smith |
| Daventry, Northants. | 63,300 | 548.07 | R. J. Symons, RD | S. J. Osborne |
| DERBY | 227,100 | 582.50 | R. H. Cowlishaw | (a) N. S. Dhindsa |
| Derbyshire Dales | 68,400 | 614.17 | D. Wheatcroft | C. H. Birch |
| Derwentside, Co. Durham | 87,200 | 583.75 | N. F. Johnson | E. Turner |
| Dover, Kent | 106,100 | 559.49 | J. P. Moir, TD | P. T. Wilson |
| DURHAM | 87,700 | 511.59 | C. G. Firmin | (a) W. D. Cavanagh |
| Easington, Co. Durham | 99,400 | 535.17 | *P. Innes | A. Westgarth |
| §Eastbourne, East Sussex | 85,600 | 607.65 | Dr M. Blanch | R. Parsons |
| East Cambridgeshire | 61,300 | 452.16 | T. T. G. Hardy | J. E. Seaman |
| East Devon | 119,100 | 547.96 | F. J. Vallender | F. A. C. Pinney, OBE |
| East Dorset | 79,400 | 534.53 | A. Breakwell | D. J. Durley |
| East Hampshire | 104,500 | 494.32 | B. P. Roynon | Miss K. M. Dell |
| East Hertfordshire | 118,100 | 496.07 | R. J. Bailey | N. Poulton |
| §Eastleigh, Hants. | 108,100 | 475.74 | C. Tapp | (a) Mrs R. Jones |
| East Lindsey, Lincs. | 119,800 | 533.58 | ‡P. Haigh | R. B. Shields |
| East Northamptonshire | 69,100 | 552.24 | R. K. Heath | J. Chatburn |
| East Staffordshire | 98,200 | 542.75 | F. W. Saunders | F. P. Edginton |
| §East Yorkshire, Humberside | 86,700 | 621.00 | J. H. Gibson | (a) D. J. V. Evans |
| Eden, Cumbria | 46,400 | 610.97 | I. W. Bruce | E. S. C. Wooff |
| §Ellesmere Port and Neston, Cheshire | 81,200 | 629.11 | S. Ewbank | (a) W. G. Ible |
| §Elmbridge, Surrey | 114,800 | 577.72 | D. W. L. Jenkins | (a) E. Mallett |
| Epping Forest, Essex | 118,200 | 611.51 | J. Burgess | Mrs J. Davis |
| §Epsom and Ewell, Surrey | 68,600 | 520.87 | D. J. Smith | (a) D. P. Hughes |
| §Erewash, Derbyshire | 107,200 | 615.54 | vacant | (a) T. Moloney |
| EXETER, Devon | 106,500 | 562.21 | B. Frowd | (a) R. Yeo |
| §Fareham, Hants. | 100,900 | 495.45 | A. A. Davies | (a) Mrs T. A. Short |
| Fenland, Cambs. | 77,000 | 499.80 | N. R. Topliss | A. R. German |
| Forest Heath, Suffolk | 61,200 | 475.02 | S. W. Catchpole | R. Crane |
| Forest of Dean, Glos. | 75,500 | 600.30 | °R. A. Willis | B. W. Hobman |
| §Fylde, Lancs. | 72,900 | 571.96 | J. P. Johnson | (a) G. Bamber |
| §Gedling, Notts. | 111,800 | 648.27 | W. Brown | (a) E. Godfrey |
| §Gillingham, Kent | 96,200 | 533.97 | J. A. McBride | (a) Mrs S. G. Clark |
| §Glanford, Humberside | 72,600 | 668.51 | D. D. H. Cameron | (a) W. J. P. England |
| GLOUCESTER | 105,400 | 554.54 | G. Garbutt | (a) T. Workman |
| §Gosport, Hants. | 76,500 | 515.35 | M. S. Friend | (a) Mrs A. J. Whitbread |
| §Gravesham, Kent | 93,500 | 506.81 | E. V. J. Seager | (a) W. Cook |
| §Great Grimsby, Humberside | 91,500 | 690.00 | R. S. G. Bennett | (a) A. Bovier |
| §Great Yarmouth, Norfolk | 89,000 | 520.94 | R. Packham | (a) Mrs C. Batley |
| §Guildford, Surrey | 127,200 | 528.69 | D. T. Watts | (a) D. May |
| §Halton, Cheshire | 124,500 | 620.38 | M. Cuff | (a) L. Temple |
| Hambleton, North Yorkshire | 81,300 | 466.00 | C. Spencer | L. H. Groves |
| Harborough, Leics. | 69,300 | 539.14 | M. C. Wilson | R. Marriott |
| Harlow, Essex | 74,600 | 706.50 | *D. Byrne | Ms A. Garner |

\* General Manager
† Head of Paid Service
‡ Director of Central Services
° Director of Administrative Services

| Council | Population 1992 | Band D charge 1994 | Chief Executive | Chairman 1994–5 (a) Mayor (b) Lord Mayor |
|---|---|---|---|---|
| §Harrogate, North Yorkshire | 146,400 | £580.73 | P. M. Walsh | (a) R. M. O'Neill |
| Hart, Hants. | 82,300 | 489.34 | G. R. Jelbart | Mrs A. Kern |
| §Hartlepool, Cleveland | 91,900 | 723.56 | B. J. Dinsdale | (a) Mrs S. G. Hanson |
| §Hastings, East Sussex | 83,900 | 589.46 | R. A. Carrier | (a) R. Stevens |
| §Havant, Hants. | 118,700 | 541.09 | J. E. Palmer (acting) | (a) Mrs A. D. Atterbury |
| Hereford | 51,100 | 526.50 | C. E. S. Willis | (a) Mrs C. D. L. Gundy |
| §Hertsmere, Hertfordshire | 89,900 | 547.63 | †P. Copland | (a) J. W. Kentish |
| §High Peak, Derbyshire | 86,700 | 624.51 | R. P. H. Brady | (a) Mrs E. J. Inglefield |
| §Hinckley and Bosworth, Leics. | 98,000 | 487.53 | ‡I. G. Brady (acting) | (a) Mrs P. M. Willis |
| §Holderness, Humberside | 51,800 | 635.76 | A. Johnson | (a) Mrs A. M. Suggit |
| Horsham, West Sussex | 110,500 | 460.63 | M. J. Pearson | Mrs S. L. A. Walker |
| §Hove, East Sussex | 90,400 | 573.30 | J. P. Teasdale | (a) L. A. Hamilton |
| Huntingdonshire, Cambs. | 149,200 | 467.02 | T. J. Gee | G. J. Dodson |
| §Hyndburn, Lancs. | 78,900 | 688.41 | M. J. Wedgeworth | (a) R. J. Goggin |
| §Ipswich, Suffolk | 116,000 | 698.31 | J. D. Hehir | (a) I. Grimwood |
| Kennet, Wilts. | 72,300 | 493.69 | P. L. Owens | D. J. Godwin |
| Kerrier, Cornwall | 89,000 | 529.39 | G. G. Cox | Miss P. N. Aston |
| §Kettering, Northants. | 78,200 | 549.63 | P. Walker | (a) E. Bellamy-Tall |
| §King's Lynn and West Norfolk | 131,800 | 514.00 | A. E. Pask | (a) J. B. Howling |
| Kingston upon Hull, Humberside | 268,500 | 678.69 | D. Stephenson | (b) Mrs M. Bell |
| §Kingswood, Avon | 91,200 | 617.85 | A. Smith | (a) C. Peacock |
| Lancaster, Lancs. | 131,300 | 650.00 | °W. Pearson | (a) J. Yates |
| §Langbaurgh-on-Tees, Cleveland | 145,900 | 718.32 | K. Abigail | (a) S. Tombe |
| Leicester | 285,400 | 664.96 | I. Farookhi | (b) Mrs M. E. W. Bell |
| Leominster, Hereford and Worcs. | 40,000 | 530.06 | G. R. Chilton | M. O. Harrison |
| Lewes, East Sussex | 88,900 | 547.16 | J. N. Crawford | Ms A. G. E. Appleton |
| Lichfield, Staffs. | 93,900 | 515.83 | J. T. Thompson | Mrs E. J. Bayliss |
| Lincoln | 85,600 | 564.91 | A. Sparke | (a) R. Hurst |
| §Luton, Beds. | 176,200 | 555.60 | J. C. Southwell | (a) Mrs D. Stewart |
| §Macclesfield, Cheshire | 151,000 | 603.33 | B. W. Longden | (a) R. F. Short |
| §Maidstone, Kent | 138,000 | 571.36 | J. D. Makepeace | (a) F. Winckless |
| Maldon, Essex | 52,600 | 506.43 | E. A. P. Plumridge | F. Delderfield |
| Malvern Hills, Hereford and Worcs. | 88,400 | 525.78 | M. J. Jones | T. W. Hunt |
| Mansfield, Notts. | 102,000 | 677.04 | R. P. Goad | D. Hales |
| §Medina, Isle of Wight | 72,000 | 547.01 | *J. Sprake | (a) J. Effemey |
| §Melton, Leics. | 46,100 | 561.26 | **P. J. G. Herrick | (a) C. O. Chapman |
| Mendip, Somerset | 98,200 | 567.93 | G. Jeffs | W. Mackay |
| Mid Bedfordshire | 113,000 | 494.67 | C. A. Tucker | Mrs C. M. Barnes |
| Mid Devon | 64,800 | 575.17 | M. I. R. Bull | Mrs M. E. Turner |
| §Middlesbrough, Cleveland | 145,600 | 725.74 | J. R. Foster | (a) R. K. Brady |
| Mid Suffolk | 78,700 | 517.04 | H. McFarlane | R. M. Melvin |
| Mid Sussex | 123,300 | 511.74 | B. J. Grimshaw | W. E. Knighton |
| §Milton Keynes, Bucks. | 181,000 | 580.03 | M. J. Murray | (a) E. Ellis |
| Mole Valley, Surrey | 79,400 | 516.60 | A. A. Huggins | D. J. Edge |
| Newark and Sherwood, Notts. | 103,900 | 650.14 | †R. G. Dix | W. S. Greig |
| Newbury, Berks. | 139,800 | 523.65 | P. E. McMahon | A. Thorpe |
| §Newcastle under Lyme, Staffs. | 122,700 | 568.17 | D. F. Hill | (a) Mrs E. Caddy |
| New Forest, Hants. | 162,400 | 488.91 | P. A. D. Hyde | Mrs J. K. Vernon-Jackson, MBE |
| §Northampton | 186,000 | 619.11 | R. J. B. Morris | (a) A. J. Hargrave |
| Northavon, Avon | 135,700 | 622.91 | F. Maude | R. M. McGurk |
| North Cornwall | 74,900 | 547.80 | D. H. Westwell | K. F. White |
| North Devon | 85,700 | 568.56 | D. T. Cunliffe | E. J. Kingston |
| North Dorset | 54,100 | 481.83 | A. J. Bridgeman | B. R. Clarke |
| North East Derbyshire | 99,100 | 617.31 | ‡Mrs C. A. Gilbey | Mrs T. M. Lide |
| North Hertfordshire | 113,700 | 517.84 | J. S. Philp | M. Hughes |
| North Kesteven, Lincs. | 80,300 | 564.59 | S. Lamb | Mrs J. Morris |
| North Norfolk | 92,700 | 500.00 | T. V. Nolan | P. D. Blaxell |

† Managing Director
‡ Head of Paid Service
° Clerk
* General Manager
** Borough Secretary and Clerk

| Council | Population 1992 | Band D charge 1994 | Chief Executive | Chairman 1994-5 (a) Mayor (b) Lord Mayor |
|---|---|---|---|---|
| North Shropshire | 53,800 | £556.10 | D. Pearce | E. J. Dodd |
| §North Warwickshire | 61,300 | 642.26 | D. Monks | (a) L. J. Smith |
| North West Leicestershire | 82,500 | 542.35 | J. E. White | Mrs A. U. Smith |
| North Wiltshire | 115,300 | 476.51 | H. Miles | A. S. R. Jackson |
| NORWICH, Norfolk | 127,700 | 598.60 | J. R. Packer | (b) Ms B. Ferris |
| NOTTINGHAM | 282,500 | 630.56 | E. F. Cantle | (b) V. B. Gapper |
| §Nuneaton and Bedworth, Warwickshire | 118,300 | 654.21 | ‡‡J. Walton | (a) R. G. Copland |
| §Oadby and Wigston, Leics. | 53,500 | 591.26 | Mrs R. E. Hyde | (a) A. J. Morris |
| §Oswestry, Shropshire | 34,400 | 553.47 | D. A. Towers | (a) Mrs E. Harrison |
| OXFORD | 131,500 | 605.81 | R. S. Block | (b) W. W. Buckingham |
| §Pendle, Lancs. | 85,600 | 695.15 | S. Barnes | (a) L. Atkinson |
| Penwith, Cornwall | 59,900 | 489.62 | ‡F. H. Murton | Mrs S. M. Menadue |
| PETERBOROUGH, Cambs. | 156,200 | 530.09 | W. E. Samuel | (a) Mrs R. G. E. Day |
| PLYMOUTH, Devon | 257,600 | 603.11 | Mrs A. Stone | (b) W. T. Ainsworth |
| §Poole, Dorset | 136,300 | 531.20 | J. W. Brooks | (a) F. J. Winwood |
| PORTSMOUTH, Hants. | 189,500 | 497.87 | *N. Gurney | (b) Dr A. D. Burnett |
| §Preston, Lancs. | 131,500 | 691.80 | G. Driver | (a) I. W. Hall |
| Purbeck, Dorset | 43,800 | 468.51 | P. B. Croft | D. B. Humphry |
| §Reading, Berks. | 137,100 | 593.00 | Ms S. Pierce | (a) G. H. Ford |
| §Redditch, Hereford and Worcs. | 78,600 | 586.62 | †Ms S. Manzie | (a) D. Baddeley |
| §Reigate and Banstead, Surrey | 118,600 | 550.58 | M. Bacon | (a) Mrs D. H. Bowes |
| §Restormel, Cornwall | 87,900 | 569.36 | D. Brown | (a) B. J. Higman |
| §Ribble Valley, Lancs. | 51,500 | 643.92 | O. Hopkins | (a) Mrs K. Hodkinson |
| Richmondshire, N. Yorkshire | 46,500 | 531.43 | H. Tabiner | Mrs L. Miller |
| ROCHESTER UPON MEDWAY, Kent | 147,600 | 450.18 | R. I. Gregory | (a) Mrs A. D. Marsh |
| Rochford, Essex | 75,900 | 517.32 | P. W. Hughes | M. I. Handford |
| §Rossendale, Lancs. | 66,000 | 711.91 | J. S. Hartley | (a) R. A. Wilkinson |
| Rother, East Sussex | 83,500 | 524.88 | D. F. Powell | C. A. Bayliss |
| §Rugby, Warwickshire | 86,500 | 551.59 | J. S. R. Lawton | (a) A. J. Reeve |
| §Runnymede, Surrey | 74,900 | 484.71 | T. N. Williams | (a) F. J. Tourlamain |
| §Rushcliffe, Notts. | 100,300 | 609.78 | J. Saxton | (a) Mrs J. Dixon |
| §Rushmoor, Hants. | 87,700 | 510.91 | R. Upton | (a) P. R. Lillywhite |
| Rutland, Leics. | 33,400 | 555.07 | K. R. Emslie | Mrs P. R. Holloway |
| Ryedale, North Yorkshire | 92,100 | 516.30 | M. Walker | E. Thomas |
| ST ALBANS, Herts. | 126,900 | 536.96 | E. A. Hackford | (a) A. Nowell |
| §St Edmundsbury, Suffolk | 92,400 | 540.63 | G. R. N. Toft | (a) Mrs J. A. Bone |
| Salisbury, Wilts. | 108,400 | 500.66 | D. R. J. Rawlinson | K. A. Edwards |
| §Scarborough, N. Yorkshire | 109,200 | 529.47 | J. M. Trebble | (a) Mrs E. Bosomworth |
| §Scunthorpe, Humberside | 62,000 | 675.70 | I. M. Hutchinson | (a) J. Towndrow |
| Sedgefield, Co. Durham | 91,700 | 534.17 | A. J. Roberts | J. T. O'Brien |
| Sedgemoor, Somerset | 100,000 | 565.80 | A. G. Lovell | K. W. W. Dyer |
| Selby, North Yorkshire | 92,800 | 505.89 | J. C. Edwards | S.C. Tuvey |
| Sevenoaks, Kent | 109,200 | 494.98 | B. C. Cova, MBE | M. J. A. Stevens |
| Shepway, Kent | 94,600 | 570.42 | R. J. Thompson | R. A. Pascoe |
| §Shrewsbury and Atcham | 92,700 | 543.94 | D. Bradbury | (a) J. W. L. Pritchard |
| §Slough, Berks. | 102,900 | 488.79 | °C. Coppell | (a) R. Sibley |
| SOUTHAMPTON, Hants. | 208,200 | 529.45 | E. A. Urquhart | (a) E. Read |
| South Bedfordshire | 110,100 | 543.48 | T. D. Rix | J. L. Steward |
| South Buckinghamshire | 63,000 | 484.60 | C. Furness | Prof. C. A. Hogarth |
| South Cambridgeshire | 122,800 | 435.75 | J. S. Ballantyne | C. W. Tulitt |
| South Derbyshire | 73,600 | 541.17 | T. Day | P. Coxon |
| §Southend-on-Sea, Essex | 165,100 | 533.19 | °D. Moulson | (a) Miss M. R. Haine |
| South Hams, Devon | 78,500 | 530.80 | F. G. Palmer | J. W. Squire |
| South Herefordshire | 52,900 | 503.93 | A. Hughes | J. W. Edwards |
| South Holland, Lincs. | 68,700 | 558.66 | C. J. Simpkins | Mrs A. M. Newton |
| South Kesteven, Lincs. | 111,300 | 538.32 | K. R. Cann | J. Thompson |
| South Lakeland, Cumbria | 98,900 | 619.78 | A. F. Winstanley | Mrs E. M. Braithwaite |
| South Norfolk | 104,200 | 501.75 | A. G. T. Kellett | Mrs R. Tilbrook |

‡‡ Borough Manager
‡Head of Paid Service
* City Manager
† Borough Director
° Clerk

| Council | Population 1992 | Band D charge 1994 | Chief Executive | Chairman 1994–5 (a) Mayor (b) Lord Mayor |
|---|---|---|---|---|
| South Northamptonshire | 71,800 | £543.76 | K. Whitehead | Mrs J. Buxton |
| South Oxfordshire | 121,800 | 503.46 | R. Watson | Mrs J. M. Day |
| §South Ribble, Lancs. | 102,700 | 648.55 | J. B. R. Leadbetter | (a) Ms E. Webster |
| South Shropshire | 39,400 | 531.85 | G. C. Biggs | J. McCormick |
| South Somerset | 145,000 | 567.17 | M. Usher | R. Madelin |
| South Staffordshire | 106,200 | 463.73 | L. Barnfild | Mrs H. V. Harding |
| §South Wight, IOW | 53,600 | 547.49 | D. W. Jaggar | (a) Mrs A. E. Le Brecht |
| §Spelthorne, Surrey | 91,600 | 542.40 | M. B. Taylor | (a) A. Hirst |
| §Stafford | 120,600 | 537.77 | J. K. M. Krawiec | (a) K. F. Brown |
| Staffordshire Moorlands | 95,900 | 571.01 | A. W. Law | R. G. Locker |
| §Stevenage, Herts. | 75,800 | 587.98 | H. L. Miller | (a) R. J. Smith |
| §Stockton-on-Tees, Cleveland | 176,600 | 661.10 | °F. F. Theobalds | (a) K. Dobinson |
| STOKE-ON-TRENT, Staffs. | 252,900 | 603.81 | B. Smith | (b) R. Leigh |
| Stratford-upon-Avon, Warwicks. | 107,300 | 614.52 | I. B. Prosser | G. H. Freeman |
| Stroud, Glos. | 105,400 | 601.92 | R. M. Ollin | Mrs S. M. Bruce |
| Suffolk Coastal | 111,300 | 530.91 | T. K. Griffin | M. Morton |
| §Surrey Heath | 80,800 | 542.42 | N. M. Pughe | (a) F. W. Chipperfield |
| §Swale, Kent | 116,800 | 504.54 | W. Croydon, CBE | (a) L. T. Vaughan |
| §Tamworth, Staffs. | 71,100 | 536.75 | G. Morrell | (a) Mrs M. Lewis |
| Tandridge, Surrey | 77,800 | 549.09 | P. J. D. Thomas | D. R. Newland |
| §Taunton Deane, Somerset | 97,700 | 513.62 | *Mrs S. Douglas | (a) D. S. Applegate |
| Teesdale, Co. Durham | 24,400 | 550.52 | C. E. Fell | K. Coates |
| Teignbridge, Devon | 111,400 | 542.13 | P. B. Young | D. J. Miller |
| Tendring, Essex | 128,200 | 532.29 | D. Mitchell-Gears | Mrs P. Manning |
| §Test Valley, Hants. | 103,400 | 479.46 | G. Blythe | (a) R. Gardiner |
| §Tewkesbury, Glos. | 71,400 | 431.21 | **R. A. Wheeler | (a) G. F. Kent |
| §Thamesdown, Wilts. | 173,600 | 545.49 | D. M. Kent | (a) D. Glaholm |
| Thanet, Kent | 126,200 | 577.49 | D. Ralls, CBE, DFC | T. Cole |
| Three Rivers, Herts. | 81,600 | 543.21 | A. Robertson | D. Frankland |
| §Thurrock, Essex | 131,200 | 553.59 | K. Barnes | (a) B. Palmer |
| §Tonbridge and Malling, Kent | 102,100 | 523.34 | T. Thompson | (a) T. Barton |
| §Torbay, Devon | 121,600 | 552.25 | D. P. Hudson | (a) J. Nicholls |
| Torridge, Devon | 53,400 | 526.72 | R. K. Brasington | Mrs P. J. Paddon |
| §Tunbridge Wells, Kent | 101,800 | 502.81 | R. J. Stone | (a) H. R. Wright |
| Tynedale, Northumberland | 57,300 | 559.14 | A. Baty | A. Rubery |
| Uttlesford, Essex | 66,600 | 526.72 | K. Ivory | Mrs J. E. Menell |
| Vale of White Horse, Oxon. | 112,300 | 468.40 | †D. J. Heavens | K. H. Davies |
| §Vale Royal, Cheshire | 114,200 | 622.37 | W. R. T. Woods | (a) A. N. Ford |
| Wansbeck, Northumberland | 62,100 | 591.78 | A. G. White | J. Tweddle |
| Wansdyke, Avon | 80,700 | 589.83 | *P. May | J. E. Hotter |
| §Warrington, Cheshire | 183,700 | 599.82 | M. I. M. Sanders | (a) M. F. Hannon |
| Warwick | 118,500 | 590.38 | J. V. Picking | P. Byrd |
| §Watford, Herts. | 76,100 | 609.25 | D. Plank | Ms M. Green |
| Waveney, Suffolk | 108,500 | 542.67 | M. Berridge | Mrs S. M. Bostock |
| §Waverley, Surrey | 115,300 | 538.61 | G. W. Nuttall | (a) J. H. Wooton |
| Wealden, East Sussex | 133,700 | 564.51 | D. R. Holness | P. Clifford |
| Wear Valley, Co. Durham | 63,600 | 593.06 | †Mrs E. M. Ashness | Mrs J. Jobson |
| §Wellingborough, Northants. | 68,700 | 293.49 | W. B. Veal | (a) M. Waters |
| Welwyn Hatfield, Herts. | 95,100 | 545.93 | D. Riddle | S. Atkinson |
| §West Devon | 46,600 | 566.97 | J. S. Ligo | (a) Mrs B. M. Cheeseman |
| West Dorset | 87,300 | 509.15 | R. C. Rennison | Mrs J. D. Cockerill |
| West Lancashire | 109,800 | 656.39 | B. A. Knight | W. G. Roberts |
| West Lindsey, Lincs. | 77,100 | 535.84 | R. W. Nelsey | A. H. Frith |
| West Oxfordshire | 93,100 | 486.34 | N. J. B. Robson | C. R. M. Fox |
| West Somerset | 31,700 | 562.35 | C. Rockall | Mrs M. Lyons |
| West Wiltshire | 109,700 | 552.59 | D. G. Latham | J. B. Wesley |
| §Weymouth and Portland, Dorset | 62,400 | 551.49 | M. N. Ashby | (a) Mrs B. Dench |
| WINCHESTER, Hants. | 99,500 | 468.46 | D. H. Cowan | (a) R. Pearce |
| §Windsor and Maidenhead, Berks. | 135,500 | 530.96 | G. B. Blacker | (a) D. Outwin |
| §Woking, Surrey | 87,600 | 528.84 | P. Russell | (a) D. Thornton |

° Clerk
* General Manager
** Borough Secretary
† Director of Administration

| Council | Population 1992 | Band D charge 1994 | Chief Executive | Chairman 1994-5 (a) Mayor (b) Lord Mayor |
|---|---|---|---|---|
| Wokingham, Berks. | 142,500 | £542.34 | Mrs G. C. Norton | G. Parkinson |
| Woodspring, Avon | 180,500 | 624.71 | C. A. Stephens | K. W. Lacey |
| WORCESTER | 86,000 | 558.56 | ††D. Wareing | (a) D. Inight |
| §Worthing, West Sussex | 98,000 | 554.82 | M. J. Ball | (a) B. J. Lynn |
| Wrekin, Shropshire | 142,200 | 600.09 | D. G. Hutchison | M. Smith |
| Wychavon, Hereford and Worcs. | 103,900 | 531.04 | T. Du Sautoy | Mrs M. Mathews |
| Wycombe, Bucks. | 161,100 | 509.44 | R. J. Cummins | (a) R. Barber |
| §Wyre, Lancs. | 103,300 | 648.00 | M. Brown | (a) Mrs J. Hutch |
| Wyre Forest, Hereford and Worcs. | 96,900 | 539.43 | W. S. Baldwin | M. M. G. Oborski |
| YORK, North Yorkshire | 103,800 | 550.17 | J. Cairns | (b) D. Wilde |

†† Director of Community Services

# Roman Names of English Towns and Cities

| | | | |
|---|---|---|---|
| Bath | *Aquae Sulis* | Leicester | *Ratae Corieltauvorum* |
| Canterbury | *Durovernum Cantiacorum* | Lincoln | *Lindum* |
| Carlisle | *Luguvalium* | London | *Londinium* |
| Chelmsford | *Caesaromagus* | Manchester | *Mamucium* |
| Chester | *Deva* | Newcastle upon Tyne | *Pons Aelius* |
| Chichester | *Noviomagus Regnensium* | Pevensey | *Anderetium* |
| Cirencester | *Corinium Dobunnorum* | Rochester | *Durobrivae* |
| Colchester | *Camulodunum* | St Albans | *Verulamium* |
| Doncaster | *Danum* | Salisbury (Old Sarum) | *Sorviodunum* |
| Dorchester | *Durnovaria* | Silchester | *Calleva Atrebatum* |
| Dover | *Dubris* | Winchester | *Venta Belgarum* |
| Exeter | *Isca Dumnoniorum* | Wroxeter | *Viroconium Cornoviorum* |
| Gloucester | *Glevum* | York | *Eburacum* |

# London

## THE CORPORATION OF LONDON
(*see also* page 532)

The City of London is the historic centre at the heart of London known as 'the square mile' around which the vast metropolis has grown over the centuries. The City's residential population is 5,400. The civic government is carried on by the Corporation of the City of London through the Court of Common Council.

The City is the financial and business centre of London and includes the head offices of the principal banks, insurance companies and mercantile houses, in addition to buildings ranging from the historic interest of the Roman Wall and the 15th-century Guildhall, to the massive splendour of St Paul's Cathedral and the architectural beauty of Wren's spires.

The City of London was described by Tacitus in AD 62 as 'a busy emporium for trade and traders'. Under the Romans it became an important administration centre and hub of the road system. Little is known of London in Saxon times, when it formed part of the kingdom of the East Saxons. In 886 Alfred recovered London from the Danes and reconstituted it a burgh under his son-in-law. In 1066 the citizens submitted to William the Conqueror who in 1067 granted them a charter, which is still preserved, establishing them in the rights and privileges they had hitherto enjoyed.

### THE MAYORALTY

The Mayoralty was probably established about 1189, the first Mayor being Henry Fitz Ailwyn who filled the office for 23 years and was succeeded by Fitz Alan (1212–14). A new charter was granted by King John in 1215, directing the Mayor to be chosen annually, which has ever since been done, though in early times the same individual often held the office more than once. A familiar instance is that of 'Whittington, thrice Lord Mayor of London' (in reality four times, 1397, 1398, 1406, 1419); and many modern cases have occurred. The earliest instance of the phrase 'Lord Mayor' in English is in 1414. It was used more generally in the latter part of the 15th century and became invariable from 1535 onwards. At Michaelmas the liverymen in Common Hall choose two Aldermen who have served the office of Sheriff for presentation to the Court of Aldermen, and one is chosen to be Lord Mayor for the following mayoral year.

### LORD MAYOR'S DAY

The Lord Mayor of London was previously elected on the feast of St Simon and St Jude (28 October), and from the time of Edward I, at least, was presented to the King or to the Barons of the Exchequer on the following day, unless that day was a Sunday. The day of election was altered to 16 October in 1346, and after some further changes was fixed for Michaelmas Day in 1546, but the ceremonies of admittance and swearing-in of the Lord Mayor continued to take place on 28 and 29 October respectively until 1751. In 1752, at the reform of the calendar, the Lord Mayor was continued in office until 8 November, the 'New Style' equivalent of 28 October. The Lord Mayor is now presented to the Lord Chief Justice at the Royal Courts of Justice on the second Saturday in November to make the final declaration of office, having been sworn in at Guildhall on the preceding day. The procession to the Royal Courts of Justice is popularly known as the Lord Mayor's Show.

### REPRESENTATIVES

Aldermen are mentioned in the 11th century and their office is of Saxon origin. They were elected annually between 1377 and 1394, when an Act of Parliament of Richard II directed them to be chosen for life.

The Common Council, elected annually on the first Friday in December, was, at an early date, substituted for a popular assembly called the *Folkmote*. At first only two representatives were sent from each ward, but the number has since been greatly increased.

### OFFICERS

Sheriffs were Saxon officers; their predecessors were the *wic-reeves* and *portreeves* of London and Middlesex. At first they were officers of the Crown, and were named by the Barons of the Exchequer; but Henry I (in 1132) gave the citizens permission to choose their own Sheriffs, and the annual election of Sheriffs became fully operative under King John's charter of 1199. The citizens lost this privilege, as far as the election of the Sheriff of Middlesex was concerned, by the Local Government Act 1888; but the liverymen continue to choose two Sheriffs of the City of London, who are appointed on Midsummer Day and take office at Michaelmas.

The office of Chamberlain is an ancient one, the first contemporary record of which is 1237. The Town Clerk (or Common Clerk) is mentioned in 1274.

### ACTIVITIES

The work of the Corporation is assigned to a number of committees which present reports to the Court of Common Council. These Committees are: City Lands and Bridge House Estates, Policy and Resources, Finance, Planning and Transportation, Central Markets, Billingsgate and Leadenhall Markets, Spitalfields Market, Police, Port and City of London Health and Social Services, Libraries, Art Galleries and Records, Boards of Governors of Schools, Music and Drama (Guildhall School of Music and Drama), Establishment, Housing, Gresham (City side), Hampstead Heath Management, Epping Forest and Open Spaces, West Ham Park, Privileges, Barbican Residential and Barbican Centre (Barbican Arts and Conference Centre).

The City's estate, in the possession of which the Corporation of London differs from other municipalities, is managed by the City Lands and Bridge House Estates Committee, the chairmanship of which carries with it the title of Chief Commoner. *Chairman* (1994), J. Holland.

The Honourable the Irish Society (The Irish Chamber, Guildhall, London EC2P 2EJ. *Clerk*, S. Waley), which manages the Corporation's estates in Ulster, consists of a Governor and five other Aldermen, the Recorder, and 19 Common Councilmen, of whom one is elected Deputy Governor.

### THE LORD MAYOR 1993–4*
*The Rt. Hon. the Lord Mayor*, Sir Paul Newall, TD
*Secretary*, Air Vice-Marshal M. Dicken, CB

### THE SHERIFFS 1994–5
R. E. Nichols (*Alderman, Candlewick*) and J. P. Charkham; *elected*, 24 June 1994; *assumed office*, 28 September 1994

### OFFICERS
*Town Clerk*, S. Jones, apptd 1991
*Chamberlain*, B. P. Harty, apptd 1983

* The Lord Mayor for 1994–5 was elected on Michaelmas Day. See Stop-press

## THE ALDERMEN

| Name and Ward | CC | Ald. | Shff. | Lord Mayor |
|---|---|---|---|---|
| Cdr. Sir Robin Gillett, Bt., GBE, RD, *Bassishaw* | 1965 | 1969 | 1973 | 1976 |
| Sir Peter Gadsden, GBE, *Farringdon Wt.* | 1969 | 1971 | 1970 | 1979 |
| Sir Christopher Leaver, GBE, *Dowgate* | 1973 | 1974 | 1979 | 1981 |
| Sir Alan Traill, GBE, *Langbourn* | 1970 | 1975 | 1982 | 1984 |
| Sir David Rowe-Ham, GBE, *Bridge* | — | 1976 | 1984 | 1986 |
| Sir Greville Spratt, GBE, TD, *Castle Baynard* | — | 1978 | 1984 | 1987 |
| Sir Christopher Collett, GBE, *Broad Street* | 1973 | 1979 | 1985 | 1988 |
| Sir Hugh Bidwell, GBE, *Billingsgate* | — | 1979 | 1986 | 1989 |
| Sir Alexander Graham, GBE, *Queenhithe* | 1978 | 1979 | 1986 | 1990 |
| Sir Brian Jenkins, GBE, *Cordwainer* | — | 1980 | 1987 | 1991 |
| Sir Francis McWilliams, GBE, *Aldersgate* | 1978 | 1980 | 1988 | 1992 |
| Sir Paul Newall, TD, *Walbrook* | 1980 | 1981 | 1989 | 1993 |

*All the above have passed the Civic Chair*

| | | | | |
|---|---|---|---|---|
| Christopher Walford, *Farringdon Wn.* | — | 1982 | 1990 | |
| Neil Young, *Bread Street* | 1980 | 1982 | 1991 | |
| Roger Cork, *Tower* | 1978 | 1983 | 1992 | |
| Leonard Chalstrey, *Vintry* | 1981 | 1984 | 1993 | |
| Richard Nichols, *Candlewick* | 1983 | 1984 | 1994 | |
| Bryan Toye, *Lime Street* | — | 1983 | | |
| Peter Bull, *Cheap* | 1968 | 1984 | | |
| Sir Peter Levene, KBE, *Portsoken* | 1983 | 1984 | | |
| Clive Martin, OBE, TD, *Aldgate* | — | 1985 | | |
| David Howard, *Cornhill* | 1972 | 1986 | | |
| James Oliver, *Bishopsgate* | 1980 | 1987 | | |
| Gavyn Arthur, *Cripplegate* | 1988 | 1991 | | |
| Robert Finch, *Coleman Street* | — | 1992 | | |

## THE COMMON COUNCIL OF LONDON

*Deputy:* Each Common Councilman so described serves as deputy to the Alderman of her/his ward

| | |
|---|---|
| Angell, E. H. (1991) | *Cripplegate Wt.* |
| Anstee, N. J. (1987) | *Aldersgate* |
| Archibald, *Deputy* W. W. (1986) | *Cornhill* |
| Bailey, J. (1993) | *Cripplegate Wt.* |
| Ballard, K. A., MC (1969) | *Castle Baynard* |
| Balls, H. D. (1970) | *Castle Baynard* |
| Barker, *Deputy* J. A. (1981) | *Cripplegate Wt.* |
| Barnes-Yallowley, H. M. F. (1986) | *Coleman Street* |
| Beale, *Deputy* M. J. (1979) | *Lime Street* |
| Bird, J. L. (1977) | *Bridge* |
| Biroum-Smith, P. L. (1988) | *Dowgate* |
| Block, S. A. A. (1983) | *Cheap* |
| Bradshaw, D. J. (1991) | *Cripplegate Wn.* |
| Bramwell, F. M. (1983) | *Langbourn* |
| Brewer, D. W. (1992) | *Bassishaw* |
| Brewster, J. W., OBE (1994) | *Bassishaw* |
| Brighton, R. L. (1984) | *Portsoken* |
| Brooks, W. I. B. (1988) | *Billingsgate* |
| Brown, *Deputy* D. T. (1971) | *Walbrook* |
| Caspi, D. (1994) | *Bridge* |
| Cassidy, *Deputy* M. J. (1989) | *Coleman Street* |
| Catt, B. F. (1982) | *Farringdon Wn.* |
| Challis, G. H., CBE (1978) | *Langbourn* |
| Clements, *Deputy* G. E. I. (1960) | *Farringdon Wt.* |
| Cohen, Mrs C. M. (1986) | *Lime Street* |
| Cole, Lt.-Col. Sir Colin, KCB, KCVO, TD (1964) | *Castle Baynard* |
| Collinson, Miss A. H. (1991) | *Farringdon Wt.* |
| Cope, Dr J. (1963) | *Farringdon Wt.* |
| Cotgrove, D. (1991) | *Lime Street* |
| Coven, *Deputy* Mrs E. O., CBE (1972) | *Dowgate* |
| Currie, Miss S. E. M. (1985) | *Cripplegate Wt.* |
| Daily-Hunt, R. B. (1989) | *Cripplegate Wt.* |
| David, C. P. (1984) | *Aldgate* |
| Davis, C. B. (1991) | *Bread Street* |
| de Silva, D., QC (1980) | *Farringdon Wt.* |
| Dove, W. H., MBE (1993) | *Bishopsgate* |
| Dowson, G. R. (1992) | *Cripplegate Wn.* |
| Dunitz, A. A. (1984) | *Portsoken* |
| Edwards, *Deputy* R. D. K. (1978) | *Bassishaw* |
| Eskenzi, A. N. (1970) | *Farringdon Wn.* |
| Evans, Mrs J. (1975) | *Farringdon Wt.* |
| Eve, R. A. (1980) | *Cheap* |
| Everett, K. M. (1984) | *Candlewick* |
| Falk, F. A., TD (1984) | *Farringdon Wt.* |
| Farthing, R. B. C. (1981) | *Aldgate* |
| Fell, J. A. (1982) | *Queenhithe* |
| FitzGerald, *Deputy* R. C. A. (1981) | *Bread Street* |
| Floyd-Ewin, *Deputy* Sir David, LVO, OBE (1963) | *Castle Baynard* |
| Forbes, G. B. (1993) | *Bishopsgate* |
| Frankenberg, P. B. (1989) | *Cordwainer* |
| Fraser, S. J. (1993) | *Coleman Street* |
| Fraser, W. B. (1981) | *Vintry* |
| Frazer, C. M. (1993) | *Farringdon Wt.* |
| Galloway, A. D. (1981) | *Broad Street* |
| Ginsburg, S. (1990) | *Bishopsgate* |
| Gold, R. (1965) | *Castle Baynard* |
| Gowman, Miss A. (1991) | *Dowgate* |
| Graves, A. C. (1985) | *Bishopsgate* |
| Halliday, Mrs P. (1992) | *Walbrook* |
| Harding, N. H., OBE (1970) | *Farringdon Wn.* |
| Hardwick, Dr P. B. (1987) | *Aldgate* |
| Hart, *Deputy* M. G. (1970) | *Bridge* |
| Haynes, J. E. H. (1986) | *Cornhill* |
| Henderson, *Deputy* J. S., OBE (1975) | *Langbourn* |
| Henderson-Begg, M. (1977) | *Coleman Street* |
| Hill-Smith, A. G. L. (1992) | *Farringdon Wt.* |
| Holland, *Deputy* J. (1972) | *Aldgate* |
| Horlock, *Deputy* H. W. S. (1969) | *Farringdon Wn.* |
| Hughesdon, J. S. (1991) | *Broad Street* |
| Jackson, L. St J. T. (1978) | *Bread Street* |
| Jennings, I. G. (1988) | *Cripplegate Wn.* |
| Keep, Mrs B. (1987) | *Cripplegate Wn.* |
| Kellett, Mrs M. W. F. (1986) | *Tower* |
| Kemp, D. L. (1984) | *Coleman Street* |
| Knowles, S. K. (1984) | *Candlewick* |
| Langton Way, J. H. (1992) | *Cripplegate Wt.* |
| Lawson, G. C. H. (1971) | *Portsoken* |
| Littlestone, N. (1993) | *Aldersgate* |
| MacLellan, A. P. W. (1989) | *Walbrook* |
| McNeil, I. D. (1977) | *Lime Street* |
| Malins, J. H., QC (1981) | *Farringdon Wt.* |
| Martin, R. C. (1986) | *Queenhithe* |
| Martinelli, P. J. (1994) | *Bassishaw* |
| Mayhew, Miss J. (1986) | *Queenhithe* |
| Mitchell, C. R. (1971) | *Castle Baynard* |
| Mizen, *Deputy* D. H. (1979) | *Broad Street* |
| Mobsby, *Deputy* D. J. L. (1985) | *Billingsgate* |
| Morgan, *Deputy* B. L., CBE (1963) | *Bishopsgate* |
| Moss, A. D. (1989) | *Tower* |
| Nash, *Deputy* Mrs J. C. (1983) | *Aldersgate* |

Neary, J. E. (1982) — *Aldgate*
Newman, Mrs P. B. (1989) — *Aldersgate*
Northall-Laurie, P. D. (1975) — *Walbrook*
Owen, Mrs J. (1975) — *Langbourn*
Owen-Ward, J. R. (1983) — *Bridge*
Parmley, A. C. (1992) — *Vintry*
Pembroke, *Deputy* Mrs A. M. F. (1978) — *Cheap*
Ponsonby of Shulbrede, The Lady
  (1981) — *Farringdon Wt.*
Pulman, *Deputy* G. A. G. (1983) — *Tower*
Punter, C. (1993) — *Cripplegate Wn.*
Reed, *Deputy* J. L., MBE (1967) — *Farringdon Wn.*
Revell-Smith, *Deputy* P. A., CBE (1959) — *Vintry*
Rigby, P. P., CBE (1972) — *Farringdon Wn.*
Robinson, Mrs D. C. (1989) — *Bishopsgate*
Rodgers, Miss E. H. L. (1987) — *Vintry*
Roney, *Deputy* E. P. T., CBE (1974) — *Bishopsgate*
Samuel, *Deputy* Mrs I., MBE (1971) — *Portsoken*
Sargant, K. A. (1991) — *Cornhill*
Saunders, *Deputy* R. (1975) — *Candlewick*
Savory, M. B. (1980) — *Broad Street*
Scriven, R. G. (1984) — *Candlewick*
Sellon, S. A., OBE, TD (1990) — *Cordwainer*
Shalit, D. M. (1972) — *Farringdon Wn.*
Sharp, *Deputy* Mrs I. M. (1974) — *Queenhithe*
Sherlock, M. R. C. (1992) — *Dowgate*
Simpson, A. S. J. (1987) — *Aldersgate*
Simpson, Mrs S. G. (1992) — *Aldersgate*
Snyder, *Deputy* M. J. (1986) — *Cordwainer*
Spanner, J. H., TD (1984) — *Broad Street*
Stitcher, *Deputy* G. M., CBE (1966) — *Farringdon Wt.*
Stone, H. V. (1993) — *Billingsgate*
Taylor, J. A. F., TD (1991) — *Bread Street*
Trotter, J. (1993) — *Billingsgate*
Walsh, S. (1989) — *Farringdon Wt.*
White, Dr J. W. (1986) — *Cornhill*
Willoughby, P. J. (1985) — *Bishopsgate*
Wilmot, R. T. D. (1973) — *Cordwainer*
Wilson, A. B., CBE (1984) — *Cheap*
Wixley, G. R. A., TD (1964) — *Coleman Street*
Woodward, *Deputy* C. D., CBE (1971) — *Cripplegate Wn.*
Wooldridge, F. D. (1988) — *Farringdon Wn.*

# The City Guilds (Livery Companies)

The constitution of the livery companies has been unchanged for centuries. There are three ranks of membership; freemen, liverymen and assistants. A person can become a freeman by patrimony (through a parent having been a freeman); by servitude (through having served an apprenticeship to a freeman); or by redemption (by purchase).

Election to the livery is the prerogative of the company, who can elect any of its freemen as liverymen. Assistants are usually elected from the livery and form a Court of Assistants which is the governing body of the company. The Master (in some companies called the Prime Warden) is elected annually from the assistants.

As at June 1994, 22,938 liverymen of the guilds were entitled to vote at elections at Common Hall.

The order of precedence, omitting extinct companies, is given in parenthesis after the name of each company in the list below. In certain companies the election of Master or Prime Warden for the year does not take place till the autumn. In such cases the Master or Prime Warden for 1993-4 is given.

## THE TWELVE GREAT COMPANIES
*In order of civic precedence*

MERCERS (*1*). *Hall*, Ironmonger Lane, London EC2V 8HE. *Livery*, 250. *Clerk*, G. M. M. Wakeford. *Master*, D. M. Watney

GROCERS (*2*). *Hall*, Princes Street, London EC2R 8AD. *Livery*, 305. *Clerk*, C. G. Mattingley, CBE. *Master*, Viscount Glenapp

DRAPERS (*3*). *Hall*, Throgmorton Street, London EC2N 2DQ. *Livery*, 242. *Clerk*, A. L. Lang, MBE. *Master*, Capt. P. A. Bence-Trower, RN

FISHMONGERS (*4*). *Hall*, London Bridge, London EC4R 9EL. *Livery*, 371. *Clerk*, K. S. Waters. *Prime Warden*, The Lord Strathcona and Mount Royal

GOLDSMITHS (*5*). *Hall*, Foster Lane, London EC2V 6BN. *Livery*, 275. *Clerk*, R. D. Buchanan-Dunlop, CBE. *Prime Warden*, The Lord Tombs

MERCHANT TAYLORS (*6/7*). *Hall*, 30 Threadneedle Street, London EC2R 8AY. *Livery* 318. *Clerk*, Capt. D. A. Wallis, RN. *Master*, J. R. Perring

SKINNERS (*6/7*). *Hall*, 8 Dowgate Hill, London EC4R 2SP. *Livery*, 370. *Clerk*, Capt. D. H. Dyke, CBE, LVO, RN. *Master*, The Hon. Sir Richard Clive Butter

HABERDASHERS (*8*). *Hall*, Staining Lane, London EC2V 7DD. *Livery*, 320. *Clerk*, Capt. M. E. Barrow, DSO, RN. *Master*, A. D. Pilcher

SALTERS (*9*). *Hall*, 4 Fore Street, London EC2Y 5DE. *Livery*, 159. *Clerk*, Col. M. P. Barneby. *Master*, J. R. S. Homan

IRONMONGERS (*10*). *Hall*, Shaftesbury Place, Barbican, London EC2Y 8AA. *Livery*, 127. *Clerk*, J. A. Oliver. *Master*, J. M. Edwards, CBE, QC

VINTNERS (*11*). *Hall*, Upper Thames Street, London EC4V 3BJ. *Livery*, 311. *Clerk*, Brig. G. Read, CBE. *Master*, D. J. B. Rutherford, OBE

CLOTHWORKERS (*12*). *Hall*, Dunster Court, Mincing Lane, London EC3R 7AH. *Livery*, 200. *Clerk*, M. G. T. Harris. *Master*, J. S. Latham

## OTHER CITY GUILDS
*In alphabetical order*

ACTUARIES (*91*). *Livery*, 175. *Clerk*, P. D. Esslemont, 16A Cadogan Square, London SW1X 0JU. *Master*, J. J. Simon

AIR PILOTS AND AIR NAVIGATORS, GUILD OF (*81*). *Livery*, 395. *Grand Master*, HRH The Prince Philip, Duke of Edinburgh, KG, KT. *Clerk*, Gp Capt J. W. Tritton, AFC, Cobham House, 291 Gray's Inn Road, London WC1X 8QF. *Master*, Capt. C. L. Hodgkinson

APOTHECARIES, SOCIETY OF (*58*). *Hall*, Black Friars Lane, London EC4V 6EJ. *Livery*, 1,350. *Clerk*, Lt.-Col. R. J. Stringer. *Master*, J. Chalstrey

ARBITRATORS (*93*). *Livery*, 250. *Clerk*, Lt.-Col. I. R. P. Green, 2 Bolts Hill, Castle Camps, Cambs. CB1 6TL. *Master*, The Rt. Hon Sir Ian Percival, QC

ARMOURERS AND BRASIERS (*22*). *Hall*, 81 Coleman Street, London EC2R 5BJ. *Livery*, 122. *Clerk*, Cdr. T. J. K. Sloane. *Master*, Revd. P. E. de D. Warburton

BAKERS (*19*). *Hall*, Harp Lane, London EC3R 6DP. *Livery*, 415. *Clerk* (*acting*), J. W. Tompkins. *Master*, T. Beale

BARBERS (*17*). *Hall*, Monkwell Square, Wood Street, London EC2Y 5BL. *Livery*, 224. *Clerk*, Col. A. B. Harfield, CBE. *Master*, R. Simmons

BASKETMAKERS (*52*). *Livery*, 380. *Clerk*, A. Gillett, 7 Kinghorn Street, London ECIA 7HT. *Prime Warden*, Maj. G. J. Flint-Shipman.

BLACKSMITHS (*40*). *Livery*, 230. *Clerk*, R. C. Jorden, 27 Cheyne Walk, Grange Park, London N21 1DB. *Prime Warden*, B. J. M. Iles

BOWYERS (*38*). *Livery*, 111. *Clerk*, J. R. Owen-Ward, 261 Green Lanes, London N13 4XE. *Master*, J. F. G. James-Crook

BREWERS (*14*). *Hall*, Aldermanbury Square, London EC2V 7HR. *Livery*, 129. *Clerk*, C. W. Dallmeyer. *Master*, M. J. Griffiths

BRODERERS (*48*). *Livery*, 155. *Clerk*, P. J. C. Crouch, 11 Bridge Road, East Molesey, Surrey KT8 9EU. *Master*, The Lord Slynn of Hadley, PC

BUILDERS MERCHANTS (*88*). *Livery*, 215. *Clerk*, Miss S. Robinson, TD, 14 Charterhouse Square, London ECIM 6AX. *Master*, M. Pares

BUTCHERS (*24*). *Hall*, 87 Bartholomew Close, London ECIA 7EB. *Livery*, 782. *Clerk*, A. H. Emus. *Master*, H. Arnold

CARMEN (*77*). *Livery*, 430. *Clerk*, Lt.-Col. G. T. Pearce, MBE, 35–37 Ludgate Hill, London EC4M 7JN. *Master*, M. E. G. Taylor

CARPENTERS (*26*). *Hall*, 1 Throgmorton Avenue, London EC2N 2JJ. *Livery*, 150. *Clerk*, Maj.-Gen. P. T. Stevenson, OBE. *Master*, Capt. K. G. Hamon

CHARTERED ACCOUNTANTS (*86*). *Livery*, 342. *Clerk*, G. H. Kingsmill, The Grove, Hinton Parva, Swindon SN4 0DH. *Master*, F. B. Harrison, CBE

CHARTERED ARCHITECTS (*98*). *Livery*, 118. *Clerk*, L. W. Groome, OBE, 5 Claylands Place, London SW8 1NZ. *Master*, Prof. J. M. Welbank

CHARTERED SECRETARIES AND ADMINISTRATORS (*87*). *Livery*, 232. *Hon. Clerk*, W. C. Hammond, MBE, St Dunstan's House, Carey Lane, London EC2V 8AA. *Master*, Col. G. E. Cauchi, CBE

CHARTERED SURVEYORS (*85*). *Livery*, 345. *Clerk*, Mrs A. L. Jackson, 16 St Mary-at-Hill, London EC3R 8EE. *Master*, Sir Brian Hill

CLOCKMAKERS (*61*). *Livery*, 216. *Hall*, St Dunstan's House, Carey Lane, London EC2V 8AA. *Clerk*, Gp Capt P. H. Gibson, MBE. *Master*, S. J. Thornton

COACHMAKERS AND COACH-HARNESS MAKERS (*72*). *Livery*, 400. *Clerk*, Maj. W. H. Wharfe, 149 Banstead Road, Ewell, Epsom, Surrey KT17 3HL. *Master*, A. R. Maidens

CONSTRUCTORS (*99*). *Livery*, 112. *Clerk*, A. W. J. Appleton, Graves End House, Woodbury, Salterton, Exeter EX5 1PG. *Master*, P. M. R. Olley

COOKS (*35*). *Livery*, 75. *Clerk*, M. C. Thatcher, 35 Great Peter Street, London SW1P 3LR. *Master*, R. P. Horne

COOPERS (*36*). *Hall*, 13 Devonshire Square, London EC2M 4TH. *Livery*, 260. *Clerk*, J. A. Newton. *Master*, P. J. S. Allington, OBE

CORDWAINERS (*27*). *Livery* 150. *Clerk*, Lt.-Col. J. R. Blundell, RM, Eldon Chambers, 30 Fleet Street, London EC4Y 1AA. *Master*, J. D. W. Birts

CURRIERS (*29*). *Livery*, 95. *Clerk*, Gp Capt F. J. Hamilton, Kestrel Cottage, East Knoyle, Salisbury SP3 6AD. *Master*, Sir Frank Sanderson, Bt.

CUTLERS (*18*). *Hall*, Warwick Lane, London EC4M 7GR. *Livery*, 100. *Clerk*, K. S. G. Hinde, TD. *Master*, C. V. M. Latham

DISTILLERS (*69*). *Livery*, 280. *Clerk*, C. V. Hughes, 71 Lincoln's Inn Fields, London WC2A 3JF. *Master*, M. W. Druitt

DYERS (*13*). *Hall*, Dowgate Hill, London EC4R 2ST. *Livery*, 125. *Clerk*, J. R. Chambers. *Prime Warden*, D. Blackburn

ENGINEERS (*94*). *Livery*, 285. *Clerk*, Cdr. B. D. Gibson, 1 Carlton House Terrace, London SW1Y 5DB. *Master*, Rear-Adm. J. S. Grove, CB, OBE

ENVIRONMENTAL CLEANERS (*97*). *Livery*, 180. *Clerk*, S. J. Holt, Whitethorns, Rannoch Road, Crowborough, E. Sussex TN6 1RA. *Master*, A. G. Raven

FAN MAKERS (*76*). *Livery*, 200. *Clerk*, Lt.-Col. I. R. P. Green, 2 Bolts Hill, Castle Camps, Cambs. CB1 6GL. *Master*, G. D. E. Bilton

FARMERS (*80*). *Hall*, 3 Cloth Street, London ECIA 7LD. *Livery*, 300. *Clerk*, Miss M. L. Winter. *Master*, Mrs E. R. Wheatley-Hubbard, OBE

FARRIERS (*55*). *Livery*, 375. *Clerk*, H. W. H. Ellis, 37 The Uplands, Loughton, Essex IG10 1NQ. *Master*, Dr J. C. Garham

FELTMAKERS (*63*). *Livery*, 170. *Clerk*, Lt.-Col. C. J. Holroyd, Providence Cottage, Chute Cadley, Andover, Hants. SP11 9EB. *Master*, G. R. D. Farr

FLETCHERS (*39*). *Hall*, 3 Cloth Street, London ECIA 7LD. *Livery*, 105. *Clerk*, J. R. Owen-Ward. *Master*, A. Mackenzie

FOUNDERS (*33*). *Hall*, 1 Cloth Fair, London ECIA 7HT. *Livery*, 170. *Clerk*, A. J. Gillett. *Master*, Dr D. V. Atterton, CBE

FRAMEWORK KNITTERS (*64*). *Livery*, 214. *Clerk*, D. A. Tate, Parkville House, Bridge Street, Pinner, Middx. HA5 3JD. *Master*, P. C. Osborne

FRUITERERS (*45*). *Livery*, 275. *Clerk*, Cdr. M. T. H. Styles, Denmead Cottage, Chawton, Alton, Hants. GU34 1SB. *Master*, M. C. Wallis

FUELLERS (*95*). *Livery*, 85. *Clerk*, Wg Cdr. H. F. C. Squire, OBE, 4 Maycross Avenue, Morden, Surrey SM4 4DA. *Master*, W. M. Pybus

FURNITURE MAKERS (*83*). *Livery*, 260. *Clerk*, Wg Cdr. G. Acklam, MBE, 30 Harcourt Street, London W1H 2AA. *Master*, R. H. Leigh

GARDENERS (*66*). *Livery*, 248. *Clerk*, Col. N. G. S. Gray, 25 Luke Street, London EC2A 4AR. *Master*, N. A. Chalmers

GIRDLERS (*23*). *Hall*, Basinghall Avenue, London EC2V 5DD. *Livery*, 80. *Clerk*, N. Wyldbore-Smith. *Master*, J. P. Reeve

GLASS-SELLERS (*71*). *Livery*, 180. *Hon. Clerk*, B. J. Rawles, 43 Aragon Avenue, Thames Ditton, Surrey KT7 0PY. *Master*, J. S. Horne

GLAZIERS AND PAINTERS OF GLASS (*53*). *Hall*, 9 Montague Close, London SE1 9DD. *Livery*, 280. *Clerk*, P. R. Batchelor. *Master*, J. B. R. Vartan

GLOVERS (*62*). *Livery*, 270. *Clerk*, Mrs M. Hood, 71 Ifield Road, London SW10 9AU. *Master*, J. Gratwick, OBE

GOLD AND SILVER WYRE DRAWERS (*74*). *Livery*, 330. *Clerk*, J. R. Williams, 50 Cheyne Avenue, London E18 2DR. *Master*, R. F. H. Vanderpump

GUNMAKERS (*73*). *Livery*, 276. *Clerk*, F. B. Brandt, TD, The Proof House, 48–50 Commercial Road, London E1 1LP. *Master*, R. N. Young

HORNERS (*54*). *Livery*, 280. *Clerk*, S. J. Holt, Whitethorns, Rannoch Road, Crowborough, E. Sussex TN6 1RA. *Master* Dr E. M. Hunt

INFORMATION TECHNOLOGISTS (*100*). *Livery*, 251. *Clerk*, Mrs G. Davies (*acting*), Epworth House, 25 City Road, London EC1Y 1AA. *Master*, Sir Brian Jenkins, GBE

INNHOLDERS (*32*). *Hall*, College Street, London EC4R 2RH. *Livery*, 133. *Clerk*, J. R. Edwardes Jones. *Master*, H. E. Harrison

INSURERS (*92*). *Hall*, 20 Aldermanbury, London EC2V 7HY. *Livery*, 362. *Clerk*, V. D. Webb. *Master*, T. Roberts, CBE

JOINERS AND CEILERS (*41*). *Livery*, 134. *Clerk*, D. A. Tate, Parkville House, Bridge Street, Pinner, Middx. HA5 3JD. *Master*, A. M. Young

LAUNDERERS (*89*). *Hall,* 9 Montague Close, London SEI 9DD. *Livery,* 205. *Clerk,* M. Bennett. *Master,* B. St J. Mowbray

LEATHERSELLERS (*15*). *Hall,* 15 St Helen's Place, London EC3A 6DQ. *Livery,* 150. *Clerk,* Rear-Adm. P. B. Rowe, CBE, LVO. *Master,* J. R. D. Scriven

LIGHTMONGERS (*96*). *Livery,* 124. *Clerk,* S. H. Birch, 53 Leithcote Gardens, London SW16 2UX. *Master,* M. P. T. Keevill

LORINERS (*57*). *Livery,* 390. *Clerk,* J. R. Williams, 50 Cheyne Avenue, London E18 2DR. *Master,* Sir Francis McWilliams, GBE

MAKERS OF PLAYING CARDS (*75*). *Livery,* 145. *Clerk,* M. J. Smyth, 6 The Priory, Godstone, Surrey RH9 8NL. *Master,* E. B. H. Chappell

MARKETORS (*90*). *Livery,* 220. *Clerk,* N. Boakes, Europower House, Lower Road, Cookham, Maidenhead, Berks. SL6 9EH. *Master,* T. Corrigan

MASONS (*30*). *Livery,* 125. *Clerk,* T. F. Ackland, 261 Green Lanes, London N13 4XE. *Master,* S. Mason

MASTER MARINERS, HONOURABLE COMPANY OF (*78*). HQS *Wellington,* Temple Stairs, Victoria Embankment, London WC2R 2PN. *Livery,* 250. *Clerk,* J. A. V. Maddock. *Admiral,* HRH The Duke of Edinburgh, KG, KT. *Master,* Capt. T. J. Sandell

MUSICIANS (*50*). *Livery,* 315. *Clerk,* S. F. N. Waley, 2–4 Carey Street, London EC4Y 8AA. *Master,* A. P. Pool

NEEDLEMAKERS (*65*). *Livery,* 235. *Clerk,* M. G. Cook, 5 Staple Inn, London WCIV 7QH. *Master,* R. Hadley

PAINTER-STAINERS (*28*). *Hall,* 9 Little Trinity Lane, London EC4V 2AD. *Livery,* 310. *Clerk,* Wg Cdr. B. C. Pratt. *Master,* A. H. Stevenson

PATTENMAKERS (*70*). *Livery,* 200. *Clerk,* P. Merritt, 25 Wellesley Road, London W4 4BU. *Master,* R. S. Sancroft-Baker

PAVIORS (*56*). *Livery,* 250. *Clerk,* R. F. Coe, 154 Dukes Avenue, New Malden, Surrey KT3 4HR. *Master,* I. J. Dussek

PEWTERERS (*16*). *Hall,* Oat Lane, London EC2V 7DE. *Livery,* 107. *Clerk,* Maj.-Gen. J. St J. Grey, CB. *Master,* P. S. Johnson

PLAISTERERS (*46*). *Hall,* 1 London Wall, London EC4Y 5JU. *Livery,* 208. *Clerk,* H. Mott. *Master,* H. Kersey

PLUMBERS (*31*). *Livery,* 360. *Clerk,* Cdr. A. J. Roberts, OBE, 49 Queen Victoria Street, London EC4N 4SE. *Master,* J. Jones

POULTERS (*34*). *Livery,* 164. *Clerk,* A. W. Scott, 23 Orchard Drive, Chorleywood, Herts. WD3 5QN. *Master,* R. P. Juniper

SADDLERS (*25*). *Hall,* 40 Gutter Lane, London EC2V 6BR. *Livery,* 70. *Clerk,* Gp Capt W. S. B. Martin, CBE. *Master,* H. J. C. Pulley

SCIENTIFIC INSTRUMENT MAKERS (*84*). *Hall,* 9 Montague Close, London SEI 9DD. *Livery,* 227. *Clerk,* F. G. Everard. *Master,* W. J. Goldfinch

SCRIVENERS (*44*). *Livery,* 154. *Clerk,* H. J. W. Harman, Westminster Bank Chambers, 11 Bridge Road, East Molesey, Surrey KT8 9EU. *Master,* B. J. Ducker

SHIPWRIGHTS (*59*). *Livery,* 430. *Clerk,* Capt. R. F. Channon, RN, Ironmongers' Hall, Barbican, London EC2Y 8AA. *Permanent Master,* HRH The Duke of Edinburgh, KG, KT. *Prime Warden,* M. C. Robinson

SOLICITORS (*79*). *Livery,* 340. *Clerk,* Miss S. M. Robinson, TD, 14 Charterhouse Square, London ECIM 6AX. *Master,* H. M. Crush

SPECTACLE MAKERS (*60*). *Livery,* 360. *Clerk,* C. J. Eldridge, Apothecaries' Hall, Black Friars Lane, London EC4V 6EL. *Master,* D. Evershed-Martin

STATIONERS AND NEWSPAPER MAKERS (*47*). *Hall,* Ave Maria Lane, London EC4M 7DD. *Livery,* 439. *Clerk,* Capt. P. Hames, RN. *Master,* R. K. Haselden

TALLOW CHANDLERS (*21*). *Hall,* 4 Dowgate Hill, London EC4R 2SH. *Livery,* 180. *Clerk,* Brig. W. K. L. Prosser, CBE, MC. *Master,* Prof. P. G. Moore, TD

TIN PLATE WORKERS alias Wire Workers (*67*). *Livery,* 168. *Clerk,* S. J. Holt, Whitethorns, Rannoch Road, Crowborough, E. Sussex TN6 IRA. *Master,* K. W. C. Reed

TOBACCO PIPE MAKERS AND TOBACCO BLENDERS (*82*). *Livery,* 180. *Clerk,* I. J. Kimmins, Penwood, Penwood End, Hook Heath, Woking, Surrey GU22 0JU. *Master,* P. J. Redman

TURNERS (*51*). *Livery,* 155. *Clerk,* R. G. Woodwark, DSC, 33A Hill Avenue, Amersham, Bucks. HP6 5BX. *Master,* A. C. Hamilton

TYLERS AND BRICKLAYERS (*37*). *Livery,* 129. *Clerk,* F. A. G. Rider, 6 Martin Lane, Cannon Street, London EC4R 0DP. *Master,* C. G. H. Grellier

UPHOLDERS (*49*). *Livery,* 200. *Clerk,* W. R. Wallis, Charrington House, The Causeway, Bishop's Stortford CH23 2EW. *Master,* Judge R. Cole

WAX CHANDLERS (*20*). *Hall,* Gresham Street, London EC2V 7AD. *Livery,* 80. *Clerk,* T. Wood. *Master,* G. S. Planner

WEAVERS (*42*). *Livery,* 128. *Clerk,* J. G. Ouvry, Saddlers' House, Gutter Lane, London EC2V 6BR. *Upper Bailiff,* Sir Richard Baker Wilbraham, Bt.

WHEELWRIGHTS (*68*). *Livery,* 246. *Clerk,* M. R. Francis, Greenup, Milton Avenue, Gerrards Cross, Bucks. SL9 8QW. *Master,* K. A. Wells

WOOLMEN (*43*). *Livery,* 126. *Clerk,* F. Allen, Hollands, Hedsor Road, Bourne End, Bucks. SL8 5EC. *Master,* The Princess Royal

PARISH CLERKS (*No livery*). *Members,* 98. *Clerk,* B. J. N. Coombes, 1 Dean Trench Street, London SWIP 3HB. *Master,* P. A. G. Stickley

WATER CONSERVATORS (*No livery*). *Freeman,* 143. *Clerk,* R. A. Riley, 20 Aldermanbury, London EC2V 7GF. *Master,* P. A. Banks.

WATERMEN AND LIGHTERMEN (*No livery*). *Craft Owning Freemen,* 350. *Hall,* 16 St Mary-at-Hill, London EC3R 8EE. *Clerk,* Lt.-Col. C. P. Cameron, MC. *Master,* J. K. Badcock

WORLD TRADERS (*No livery*). *Freemen,* 104. *Clerk,* J. Norman, 13 Pinewood Road, Branksome Park, Poole, Dorset BHI3 6JP. *Master,* Revd Canon P. Delaney

## LONDON BOROUGH COUNCILS

| Council | Municipal offices | Population 1992 | Band D charge 1994 | Chief Executive (*Managing Director) | Mayor (a) Lord Mayor 1994-5 |
|---|---|---|---|---|---|
| Barking and Dagenham | °Dagenham, RM10 7BN | 146,200 | £513.00 | W. C. Smith | G. J. Bramley |
| Barnet | †The Burroughs, Hendon, NW4 4BG | 302,300 | 569.40 | M. M. Caller | E. Hillman |
| Bexley | ‡Bexleyheath, Kent DA6 7LB | 219,500 | 510.00 | T. Musgrave | R. Allen |
| Brent | †Forty Lane, Wembley, HA9 9EZ | 247,000 | 597.60 | C. Wood | D. Games |
| Bromley | °Bromley, BR1 3UH | 293,400 | 472.00 | N. T. Palk | M. Tickner |
| §Camden | †Euston Road, NW1 2RU | 180,800 | 659.52 | J. Smith | W. Budd |
| §CITY OF WESTMINSTER | City Hall, Victoria Street, SW1E 6QP | 188,600 | 245.00 | *W. C. Roots | (a) Mrs A. Hooper |
| Croydon | Taberner House, Park Lane, Croydon CR9 3JS | 320,700 | 527.00 | D. Wechsler | W. Garratt |
| Ealing | °Uxbridge Road, W5 2HL | 283,700 | 470.00 | Ms G. Goy | V. Sharma |
| Enfield | °Enfield, EN1 3XA | 262,600 | 580.00 | Ms M. Arnold | Ms R. Smythe |
| §Greenwich | †Wellington Street, SE18 6PW | 215,000 | 632.16 | C. Roberts | Ms V. Morse |
| §Hackney | †Mare Street, E8 1EA | 189,600 | 659.85 | J. White | N. Tallent |
| §Hammersmith and Fulham | †King Street, W6 9JU | 156,100 | 526.61 | *N. Newton | Ms J. Caruana |
| Haringey | °Wood Green, N22 4LE | 211,000 | 686.84 | G. Singh | E. Prescott |
| Harrow | °Harrow, HA1 2UH | 204,900 | 549.00 | A. G. Redmond | J. Cowan |
| Havering | †Romford, RM1 3BD | 231,300 | 495.00 | D. R. Bradley | J. Hoepelman |
| Hillingdon | °Uxbridge, UB8 1UW | 237,600 | 546.43 | C. Rippingale | E. A. J. Harris |
| Hounslow | °Lampton Road, Hounslow, TW3 4DN | 206,800 | 588.07 | R. Kerslake | G. Agarwal |
| §Islington | †Upper Street, N1 2UD | 174,800 | 647.26 | E. W. Dear | M. Boye-Anawomah |
| §Kensington and Chelsea (RB) | †Hornton Street, W8 7NX | 146,900 | 489.27 | R. A. Taylor | Ms D. Weatherhead |
| Kingston upon Thames (RB) | Guildhall, Kingston upon Thames KT1 1EU | 137,800 | 538.35 | T. Hornsby | B. Bennett |
| §Lambeth | †Brixton Hill, SW2 1RW | 258,800 | 629.84 | H. Gilby | Ms P. Watson |
| §Lewisham | †Catford, SE6 4RU | 240,000 | 559.53 | Barry Quirk (acting) | G. Garcha |
| Merton | °London Road, Morden, SM4 5DX | 172,800 | 495.32 | Ms H. Rabbats | M. Searle |
| Newham | †East Ham, E6 2RP | 223,700 | 594.00 | D. Stevenson | Ms M. Knight |
| Redbridge | †Ilford, IG1 1DD | 232,000 | 510.00 | M. J. Frater | Ms L. Perham |
| Richmond upon Thames | °York Street, Twickenham, TW1 3AA | 165,000 | 540.79 | R. L. Harbord | A. Manners |
| §Southwark | †Peckham Road, SE5 8UB | 227,400 | 569.44 | W. Coomber | D. McCarthy |
| Sutton | ‡St Nicholas Way, Sutton, SM1 1EA | 172,000 | 541.62 | Ms P. Hughes | Ms S. Siggins |
| §Tower Hamlets | 107 Commercial Street, E1 6BG | 168,500 | 553.00 | Ms S. Dean (acting) | A. Downes |
| Waltham Forest | †Forest Road, Walthamstow, E17 4JF | 218,300 | 587.07 | A. Tobias | M. Khan |
| §Wandsworth | †Wandsworth, SW18 2PU | 265,900 | 139.00 | G. K. Jones | Mrs B. Jeffery |

§   Inner London Borough
RB Royal Borough
°   Civic Centre
†   Town Hall
‡   Civic Offices
*Source of population statistics*: HMSO – *OPCS Key Population and Vital Statistics 1992*

# Wales

The 1991 figure represents a slight decline from 18.9 per cent in 1981 (1971, 20.8 per cent; 1961, 26 per cent).

## POSITION AND EXTENT

The Principality of Wales (Cymru) occupies the extreme west of the central southern portion of the island of Great Britain, with a total area of 8,015 sq. miles (20,758 sq. km): land 7,965 sq. miles (20,628 sq. km); inland water 50 sq. miles (130 sq. km). It is bounded on the north by the Irish Sea, on the south by the Bristol Channel, on the east by the English counties of Cheshire, Shropshire, Hereford and Worcester, and Gloucestershire, and on the west by St George's Channel.

Across the Menai Straits is the island of Ynys Môn (Anglesey) (276 sq. miles), communication with which is facilitated by the Menai Suspension Bridge (1,000 ft long) built by Telford in 1826, and by the tubular railway bridge (1,100 ft long) built by Stephenson in 1850. Holyhead harbour, on Holy Isle (north-west of Anglesey), provides accommodation for ferry services to Dublin (70 miles).

## POPULATION

The population at the 1991 Census was 2,811,865 (males 1,356,886; females 1,454,979). The average density of population in 1991 was 1.36 persons per hectare.

## RELIEF

Wales is a country of extensive tracts of high plateau and shorter stretches of mountain ranges deeply dissected by river valleys. Lower-lying ground is largely confined to the coastal belt and the lower parts of the valleys. The highest mountains are those of Snowdonia in the north-west (Snowdon, 3,559 ft), Berwyn (Aran Fawddwy, 2,971 ft), Cader Idris (Pen y Gadair, 2,928 ft), Dyfed (Plynlimon, 2,467 ft), and the Black Mountain, Brecon Beacons and Black Forest ranges in the south-east (Carmarthen Van, 2,630 ft, Pen y Fan, 2,906 ft, Waun Fâch, 2,660 ft).

## HYDROGRAPHY

The principal river rising in Wales is the Severn (see page 540), which flows from the slopes of Plynlimon to the English border. The Wye (130 miles) also rises in the slopes of Plynlimon. The Usk (56 miles) flows into the Bristol Channel, through Gwent. The Dee (70 miles) rises in Bala Lake and flows through the Vale of Llangollen, where an aqueduct (built by Telford in 1805) carries the Pontcysyllte branch of the Shropshire Union Canal across the valley. The estuary of the Dee is the navigable portion, 14 miles in length and about five miles in breadth, and the tide rushes in with dangerous speed over the 'Sands of Dee'. The Towy (68 miles), Teifi (50 miles), Taff (40 miles), Dovey (30 miles), Taf (25 miles) and Conway (24 miles), the last named broad and navigable, are wholly Welsh rivers.

The largest natural lake is Bala (Llyn Tegid) in Gwynedd, nearly four miles long and about one mile wide. Lake Vyrnwy is an artificial reservoir, about the size of Bala, and forms the water supply of Liverpool; Birmingham is supplied from reservoirs in the Elan and Claerwen valleys.

## WELSH LANGUAGE

According to the 1991 Census results, the percentage of persons of three years and over able to speak Welsh was:

| | | | |
|---|---|---|---|
| Clwyd | 18.2 | Powys | 20.2 |
| Dyfed | 43.7 | S. Glamorgan | 6.5 |
| Gwent | 2.4 | W. Glamorgan | 15.0 |
| Gwynedd | 61.0 | | |
| Mid Glamorgan | 8.5 | Wales | 18.7 |

### FLAG

The flag of Wales, the Red Dragon (Y Ddraig Goch), is a red dragon on a field divided white over green (per fess argent and vert a dragon passant gules). The flag was augmented in 1953 by a royal badge on a shield encircled with a riband bearing the words Ddraig Goch Ddyry Cychwyn and imperially crowned, but this augmented flag is rarely used.

## EARLY HISTORY

### CELTS AND ROMANS

The earliest inhabitants of whom there is any record appear to have been subdued or exterminated by the Goidels (a people of Celtic race) in the Bronze Age. A further invasion of Celtic Brythons and Belgae followed in the ensuing Iron Age. The Roman conquest of southern Britain and Wales was for some time successfully opposed by Caratacus (Caractacus or Caradog), chieftain of the Catuvellauni and son of Cunobelinus (Cymbeline). South-east Wales was subjugated and the legionary fortress at Caerleon-on-Usk established by about AD 75–77; the conquest of Wales was completed by Agricola about AD 78. Communications were opened up by the construction of military roads from Chester to Caerleon-on-Usk and Caerwent, and from Chester to Conwy (and thence to Carmarthen and Neath). Christianity was introduced during the Roman occupation, in the fourth century.

### ANGLO-SAXON ATTACKS

The Anglo-Saxon invaders of southern Britain drove the Celts into the mountain stronghold of Wales, and into Strathclyde (Cumberland and south-west Scotland) and Cornwall, giving them the name of Waelisc (Welsh), meaning 'foreign'. The West Saxons' victory of Deorham (AD 577) isolated Wales from Cornwall and the battle of Chester (AD 613) cut off communication with Strathclyde and northern Britain. In the eighth century the boundaries of the Welsh were further restricted by the annexations of Offa, King of Mercia, and counter-attacks were largely prevented by the construction of an artificial boundary from the Dee to the Wye (Offa's Dyke).

In the ninth century Rhodri Mawr (844–878) united the country and successfully resisted further incursions of the Saxons by land and raids of Norse and Danish pirates by sea, but at his death the three provinces of Gwynedd (north), Powys (mid) and Deheubarth (south) were divided among his three sons, Anarawd, Mervyn and Cadell. Cadell's son Hywel Dda ruled a large part of Wales and codified its laws but the provinces were not united again until the rule of Llewelyn ap Seisyllt (husband of the heiress of Gwynedd) from 1018 to 1023.

### THE NORMAN CONQUEST

After the Norman conquest of England, William I created palatine counties along the Welsh frontier, and the Norman barons began to make encroachments into Welsh territory. The Welsh princes recovered many of their losses during the civil wars of Stephen's reign and in the early 13th century Owen Gruffydd, prince of Gwynedd, was the dominant figure in Wales. Under Llywelyn ap Iorwerth (1194–1240) the Welsh united in powerful resistance to English incursions and Llywelyn's privileges and de facto independence were recognized in Magna Carta. His grandson, Llywelyn ap

Gruffydd, was the last native prince; he was killed in 1282 during hostilities between the Welsh and English, allowing Edward I of England to establish his authority over the country. On 7 February 1301, Edward of Caernarvon, son of Edward I, was created Prince of Wales, a title which has subsequently been borne by the eldest son of the sovereign.

Strong Welsh national feeling continued, expressed in the early 15th century in the rising led by Owain Glyndŵr, but the situation was altered by the accession to the English throne in 1485 of Henry VII of the Welsh House of Tudor. Wales was politically assimilated to England under the Act of Union of 1535, which extended English laws to the Principality and gave it parliamentary representation for the first time.

### EISTEDDFOD

The Welsh are a distinct nation, with a language and literature of their own, and the national bardic festival (Eisteddfod), instituted by Prince Rhys ap Griffith in 1176, is still held annually (for date, see page 12). These *Eisteddfodau* (sessions) form part of the *Gorsedd* (assembly), which is believed to date from the time of Prydian, a ruling prince in an age many centuries before the Christian era.

---

### PRINCIPAL CITIES

### CARDIFF

Cardiff (South Glamorgan), at the mouth of the Rivers Taff, Rhymney and Ely, is the capital city of Wales and a major administrative, commercial and business centre. It has many industries, including steel and cigars, and its flourishing port is within the Cardiff Bay area, subject of a major redevelopment over the next five years.

The many fine buildings include the City Hall, the National Museum of Wales, University Buildings, Law Courts, Welsh Office, County Hall, Police Headquarters, the Temple of Peace and Health, Llandaff Cathedral, the Welsh National Folk Museum at St Fagans, Cardiff Castle, the New Theatre, the Sherman Theatre and the Cardiff College of Music and Drama. More recent buildings include St David's Hall, Cardiff International Arena and World Trade Centre, and the Welsh National Ice Rink.

### SWANSEA

Swansea (*Abertawe*) is a city and a seaport of West Glamorgan. The Gower peninsula was brought within the city boundary under local government reform in 1974. The trade of the port includes coal, steel products, containerized goods and the import and export of petroleum products and petrochemicals.

The principal buildings are the Norman Castle (rebuilt *c*.1330), the Royal Institution of South Wales, founded in 1835 (including Library), the University College at Singleton, and the Guildhall, containing the Brangwyn panels. New buildings include the Industrial and Maritime Museum, the new Maritime Quarter and Marina and the leisure centre.

Swansea was chartered by the Earl of Warwick, *c*.1158–84, and further charters were granted by King John, Henry III, Edward II, Edward III and James II, Cromwell (two) and the Marcher Lord William de Breos.

# Welsh Counties

## LORD LIEUTENANTS AND HIGH SHERIFFS

| County | Lord Lieutenant | High Sheriff, 1994-5 |
| --- | --- | --- |
| Clwyd | Sir William Gladstone, Bt. | Capt. N. M. Archdale |
| Dyfed | D. C. Mansel Lewis | Dr J. G. Jenkins |
| Gwent | R. Hanbury-Tenison | S. A. J. P. Bosanquet |
| Gwynedd | R. E. Meuric Rees, CBE | R. H. Davies |
| Mid Glamorgan | M. A. McLaggan | Col. T. U. Buckthought |
| Powys | M. L. Bourdillon | Mrs S. A. G. Ballance |
| South Glamorgan | Capt. N. Lloyd-Edwards | Mrs J. Cory |
| West Glamorgan | vacant | C. R. Rees |

## COUNTY COUNCILS: AREA, POPULATION, FINANCE

| Council | Administrative headquarters | Area (hectares) | *Population 1992 | Total demand upon collection fund 1994 |
| --- | --- | --- | --- | --- |
| Clwyd | Shire Hall, Mold | 243,015 | 414,600 | £44,298,000 |
| Dyfed | County Hall, Carmarthen | 576,575 | 351,100 | 41,574,043 |
| Gwent | County Hall, Cwmbran | 137,652 | 449,300 | 36,417,000 |
| Gwynedd | County Offices, Caernarfon | 386,331 | 239,800 | 25,100,000 |
| Mid Glamorgan | County Hall, Cathays Park, Cardiff | 101,749 | 542,800 | 46,300,000 |
| Powys | County Hall, Llandrindod Wells | 507,716 | 119,200 | 12,441,000 |
| South Glamorgan | County Hall, Atlantic Wharf, Cardiff | 41,622 | 410,500 | 36,622,092 |
| West Glamorgan | County Hall, Swansea | 81,960 | 371,200 | 38,417,000 |

* *Source*: HMSO – *OPCS Key Population and Vital Statistics 1992*

COUNTY COUNCILS: Officers and Chairman

| Council | Chief Executive | County Treasurer | Chairman of County Council |
|---------|-----------------|------------------|----------------------------|
| Clwyd | E. R. Davies | A. Bell | P. Walker |
| Dyfed | W. J. Phillips | H. Morse | Dr E. Davies |
| Gwent | M. J. Perry | J. P. Walsh | W. J. Gore |
| Gwynedd | H. V. Thomas | T. D. Heald | A. Owen |
| Mid Glamorgan | D. H. Thomas, CBE | L. M. James | T. Richards |
| Powys | N. M. Pringle | †J. Wrightson | D. M. Jones |
| South Glamorgan | B. Davies | °K. Bray | A. A'Herne |
| West Glamorgan | A. G. Corless | °S. G. Dunster | F. C. Evans |

† County Finance Officer
° Director of Finance

# District Councils

SMALL CAPITALS denote CITY status
§ denotes Borough status

| Council | *Population 1992 | Band D charge 1994 | Chief Executive | Chairman 1994–5 (a) Mayor (b) Lord Mayor |
|---------|------------------|--------------------|-----------------|-------------------------------------------|
| §Aberconwy, Gwynedd | 54,100 | £344.29 | A. G. Carr | (a) A. Barrett |
| Alyn and Deeside, Clwyd | 74,500 | 360.26 | D. Salisbury | W. A. Roberts |
| §Arfon, Gwynedd | 56,100 | 352.74 | D. L. Jones | (a) B. Jones |
| §Blaenau Gwent, Gwent | 76,900 | 306.20 | R. Leadbeter, OBE | (a) K. Barnes |
| §Brecknock, Powys | 41,500 | 327.12 | R. O. Doylend | (a) Mrs I. B. Lewis |
| CARDIFF, South Glamorgan | 295,600 | 291.21 | R. L. Knight | (b) D. R. Ormonde |
| Carmarthen, Dyfed | 56,200 | 348.20 | R. R. Morgan | D. H. Merriman |
| Ceredigion, Dyfed | 67,900 | 379.37 | D. Morgan | D. L. Evans |
| §Colwyn, Clwyd | 56,400 | 360.74 | C. D. Barker | (a) Mrs R. W. Jones |
| §Cynon Valley, Mid Glamorgan | 65,600 | 346.32 | T. B. Roberts, OBE | (a) T. Dower |
| §Delyn, Clwyd | 69,700 | 346.54 | P. J. McGreevy | (a) K. Corbett |
| §Dinefwr, Dyfed | 38,700 | 373.60 | E. W. Harries | (a) J. Davies |
| Dwyfor, Gwynedd | 27,300 | 287.04 | E. M. Royles | J. R. Jones |
| Glyndŵr, Clwyd | 42,000 | 346.46 | J. H. Parry | E. E. Williams |
| §Islwyn, Gwent | 67,200 | 301.14 | B. Bird | (a) Mrs J. M. Morgan |
| §Llanelli, Dyfed | 74,600 | 377.87 | D. B. Parry-Jones | (a) S. R. Cosslett |
| §Lliw Valley, West Glamorgan | 64,200 | 358.08 | B. J. Preedy | (a) M. G. Dennis |
| Meirionnydd, Gwynedd | 32,900 | 262.86 | G. W. Hughes | H. L. Williams |
| §Merthyr Tydfil, Mid Glamorgan | 60,100 | 340.14 | R. V. Morris | (a) E. Thomas |
| §Monmouth, Gwent | 76,700 | 311.40 | G. Cummings | (a) W. J. Parker |
| Montgomeryshire, Powys | 53,700 | 323.20 | N. J. Bardsley | H. B. Williams |
| §Neath, West Glamorgan | 66,300 | 324.48 | S. Penny | (a) C. E. Henrywood |
| §Newport, Gwent | 137,200 | 319.19 | R. D. Blair | (a) E. Travers |
| §Ogwr, Mid Glamorgan | 134,200 | 341.93 | J. G. Cole | (a) R. D. Power |
| §Port Talbot, West Glamorgan | 51,100 | 376.59 | I. K. Lewis | (a) Mrs O. Jones |
| Preseli Pembrokeshire, Dyfed | 71,200 | 359.59 | I. W. R. David | P. A. Stock |
| Radnorshire, Powys | 24,000 | 326.25 | G. C. Read | P. G. Harrison |
| §Rhondda, Mid Glamorgan | 79,300 | 289.53 | G. Evans | (a) B. Rowland |
| §Rhuddlan, Clwyd | 55,000 | 358.58 | E. O. Lake | (a) P. W. Owen |
| Rhymney Valley, Mid Glamorgan | 104,000 | 338.87 | M. T. Benyon | Mrs C. Forehead |
| South Pembrokeshire, Dyfed | 42,700 | 341.70 | G. H. James | W. Rees |
| SWANSEA, West Glamorgan | 189,400 | 384.66 | A. K. B. Boatswain | (b) R. G. Davies |
| §Taff-Ely, Mid Glamorgan | 99,700 | 327.04 | D. Gethin | (a) A. J. Wells |
| §Torfaen, Gwent | 91,300 | 304.36 | M. B. Mehta | (a) M. H. Morgan |
| §Vale of Glamorgan, South Glamorgan | 114,800 | 282.99 | M. P. A. Smith | (a) R. H. Davies |
| §Wrexham Maelor, Clwyd | 117,200 | 356.40 | R. J. Dutton, CBE | (a) A. Griffiths |
| §Ynys Môn (Isle of Anglesey), Gwynedd | 69,300 | 346.40 | E. L. Gibson | (a) O. G. Jones |

* Source: HMSO – OPCS Key Population and Vital Statistics 1992

# Scotland

## POSITION AND EXTENT

The Kingdom of Scotland occupies the northern portion of the main island of Great Britain and includes the Inner and Outer Hebrides, and the Orkney, Shetland, and many other islands. It lies between 60° 51′ 30″ and 54° 38′ N. latitude and between 1° 45′ 32″ and 6° 14′ W. longitude, with England to the south, the Atlantic Ocean on the north and west, and the North Sea on the east.

The greatest length of the mainland (Cape Wrath to the Mull of Galloway) is 274 miles, and the greatest breadth (Buchan Ness to Applecross) is 154 miles. The customary measurement of the island of Great Britain is from the site of John o' Groats house, near Duncansby Head, Caithness, to Land's End, Cornwall, a total distance of 603 miles in a straight line and approximately 900 miles by road.

The total area of Scotland is 30,420 sq. miles (78,789 sq. km); land 29,767 sq. miles (77,097 sq. km), inland water 653 sq. miles (1,692 sq. km).

## POPULATION

The population at the 1991 Census was 4,998,567 (males 2,391,961; females 2,606,606). The average density of the population in 1991 was 0.65 persons per hectare.

## RELIEF

There are three natural orographic divisions of Scotland. The southern uplands have their highest points in Merrick (2,766 ft), Rhinns of Kells (2,669 ft), and Cairnsmuir of Carsphairn (2,614 ft), in the west; and the Tweedsmuir Hills in the east (Hartfell 2,651 ft, Dollar Law 2,682 ft, Broad Law 2,756 ft).

The central lowlands, formed by the valleys of the Clyde, Forth and Tay, divide the southern uplands from the northern Highlands, which extend almost from the extreme north of the mainland to the central lowlands, and are divided into a northern and a southern system by the Great Glen.

The Grampian Mountains, which entirely cover the southern Highland area, include in the west Ben Nevis (4,406 ft), the highest point in the British Isles, and in the east the Cairngorm Mountains (Cairn Gorm 4,084 ft, Braeriach 4,248 ft, Ben Macdui 4,296 ft). The north-western Highland area contains the mountains of Wester and Easter Ross (Carn Eige 3,880 ft, Sgurr na Lapaich 3,775 ft).

Created, like the central lowlands, by a major geological fault, the Great Glen (60 miles long) runs between Inverness and Fort William, and contains Loch Ness, Loch Oich and Loch Lochy. These are linked to each other and to the north-east and south-west coasts of Scotland by the Caledonian Canal, providing a navigable passage between the Moray Firth and the Inner Hebrides.

## HYDROGRAPHY

The western coast is fragmented by peninsulas and islands, and indented by fjords (sea-lochs), the longest of which is Loch Fyne (42 miles long) in Argyll. Although the east coast tends to be less fractured and lower, there are several great drowned inlets (firths), e.g. Firth of Forth, Firth of Tay, Moray Firth, as well as the Firth of Clyde in the west.

The lochs are the principal hydrographic feature. The largest in Scotland and in Britain is Loch Lomond (27 sq. miles), in the Grampian valleys; the longest and deepest is Loch Ness (24 miles long and 800 feet deep), in the Great Glen; and Loch Shin (20 miles long) and Loch Maree in the Highlands.

The longest river is the Tay (117 miles), noted for its salmon. It flows into the North Sea, with Dundee on the estuary, which is spanned by the Tay Bridge (10,289 ft) opened in 1887 and the Tay Road Bridge (7,365 ft) opened in 1966. Other noted salmon rivers are the Dee (90 miles) which flows into the North Sea at Aberdeen, and the Spey (110 miles), the swiftest flowing river in the British Isles, which flows into Moray Firth. The Tweed, which gave its name to the woollen cloth produced along its banks, marks in the lower stretches of its 96-mile course the border between Scotland and England.

The most important river commercially is the Clyde (106 miles), formed by the junction of the Daer and Portrail water, which flows through the city of Glasgow to the Firth of Clyde. During its course it passes over the picturesque Falls of Clyde, Bonnington Linn (30 ft), Corra Linn (84 ft), Dundaff Linn (10 ft) and Stonebyres Linn (80 ft), above and below Lanark. The Forth (66 miles), upon which stands Edinburgh, the capital, is spanned by the Forth (Railway) Bridge (1890), which is 5,330 feet long, and the Forth (Road) Bridge (1964), which has a total length of 6,156 feet (over water) and a single span of 3,000 feet.

The highest waterfall in Scotland, and the British Isles, is Eas a'Chùal Aluinn with a total height of 658 feet (200 m), which falls from Glas Bheinn in Sutherland. The Falls of Glomach, on a head-stream of the Elchaig in Wester Ross, have a drop of 370 feet.

## GAELIC LANGUAGE

According to the 1991 Census, 1.4 per cent of the population of Scotland, mainly in the Highlands and western coastal regions, were able to speak the Scottish form of Gaelic.

## FLAG

The flag of Scotland is known as the Saltire. It is a white diagonal cross on a blue field (saltire argent in a field azure) and represents St Andrew, the patron saint of Scotland.

## THE SCOTTISH ISLANDS

The Hebrides did not become part of the Kingdom of Scotland until 1266, when they were ceded to Alexander III by Magnus of Norway. Orkney and Shetland fell to the Scottish Crown as a pledge for the unpaid dowry of Margaret of Denmark, wife of James III, in 1468, the Danish claims to suzerainty being relinquished in 1590 when James VI married Anne of Denmark.

## ORKNEY

The Orkney Islands (total area 375½ sq. miles) lie about six miles north of the mainland, separated from it by the Pentland Firth. Of the 90 islands and islets (holms and skerries) in the group, about one-third are inhabited.

The total population at the 1981 Census was 19,040; the 1981 populations of the islands shown here include those of smaller islands forming part of the same civil parish.

| | |
|---|---|
| Mainland, 14,299 | Shapinsay, 345 |
| Eday, 154 | South Ronaldsay, 1,188 |
| Hoy and Graemsay, 80 | Stronsay, 462 |
| Papa Westray, 94 | Walls and Flotta, 761 |
| Rousay and Egilsay, 264 | Westray, 741 |
| Sanday and North Ronaldsay, 652 | |

The islands are rich in Pictish and Scandinavian remains, the most notable being the Stone Age village of Skara Brae, the burial chamber of Maeshowe, the many brochs (Pictish towers) and St Magnus Cathedral. Scapa Flow, between the Mainland and Hoy, was the war station of the British Grand Fleet from 1914 to 1919 and the scene of the scuttling of the surrendered German High Seas Fleet (21 June, 1919).

Most of the islands are low-lying and fertile, and farming (principally beef cattle) is the main industry. Flotta, to the south of Scapa Flow, is now the site of the oil terminal for the Piper, Claymore and Tartan fields in the North Sea. The capital is Kirkwall (population 6,881) on Mainland.

SHETLAND

The Shetland Islands have a total area of 551 sq. miles and a population at the 1981 Census of 27,271. They lie about 50 miles north of the Orkneys, with Fair Isle about half-way between the two groups. Out Stack, off Muckle Flugga, one mile north of Unst, is the most northerly part of the British Isles (60° 51′ 30″ N. lat.).

There are over 100 islands, of which 16 are inhabited. Populations at the 1981 census were:

| | |
|---|---|
| Mainland, 22,184 | Muckle Roe, 101 |
| Bressay, 335 | Out Skerries, 79 |
| East and West Burra | Papa Stour, 29 |
| and Trondra, 930 | Unst, 1,206 |
| Fair Isle, 69 | Whalsay, 1,026 |
| Fetlar, 102 | Yell, 1,168 |
| Foula, 39 | |

Shetland's many archaeological sites include Jarlshof, Mousa and Clickhimin, and its long connection with Scandinavia has resulted in a strong Norse influence on its place-names and dialect.

Industries include fishing, knitwear and farming. In addition to the fishing fleet there are fish processing factories, while the traditional handknitting of Fair Isle and Unst is supplemented now with machine-knitted garments. Farming is mainly crofting, with sheep being raised on the moorland and hills of the islands. Latterly the islands have become an important centre of the North Sea oil industry, with pipelines from the Brent and Ninian fields running to the terminal at Sullom Voe, the largest of its kind in Europe. Lerwick is the main centre for supply services for offshore oil exploration and development.

The capital is Lerwick (population 7,901) on Mainland.

THE HEBRIDES

Until the closing years of the 13th century the Hebrides included other Scottish islands in the Firth of Clyde, the peninsula of Kintyre (Argyllshire), the Isle of Man, and the (Irish) Isle of Rathlin. The origin of the name is stated to be the Greek *Eboudai*, latinized as *Hebudes* by Pliny, and corrupted to its present form. The Norwegian name *Sudreyjar* (Southern Islands) was latinized as *Sodorenses*, a name that survives in the Anglican bishopric of Sodor and Man.

There are over 500 islands and islets, of which about 100 are inhabited, though mountainous terrain and extensive peat bogs mean that only a fraction of the total area is under cultivation. Stone, Bronze and Iron Age settlement has left many remains, including those at Callanish on Lewis, and Norse colonization has influenced language, customs and place-names. Occupations include farming (mostly crofting and stock-raising), fishing and the manufacture of tweeds and other woollens. Tourism is also an important factor in the economy.

The Inner Hebrides lie off the west coast of Scotland and relatively close to the mainland. The largest and best-known is Skye (area 643 sq. miles; pop. 8,139; chief town, Portree), which contains the Cuillin Hills (Sgurr Alasdair 3,257 ft), the Red Hills (Beinn na Caillich 2,403 ft), Bla Bheinn (3,046 ft) and The Storr (2,358 ft). Skye is also famous as the refuge of the Young Pretender in 1746. Other islands in the Highland Region include Raasay (pop. 182), Rum, Eigg and Muck.

Islands in the Strathclyde Region include Arran (pop. 4,726) containing Goat Fell (2,868 ft); Coll and Tiree (pop.

933); Colonsay and Oronsay (pop. 137); Islay (area 235 sq. miles; pop. 3,997); Jura (area 160 sq. miles; pop. 239) with a range of hills culminating in the Paps of Jura (Beinn-an-Oir, 2,576 ft, and Beinn Chaolais, 2,477 ft); and Mull (area 367 sq. miles; pop. 2,605; chief town Tobermory) containing Ben More (3,171 ft).

The Outer Hebrides, separated from the mainland by the Minch, now form the Western Isles Islands Council area (area 1,119 sq. miles; population at the 1981 Census 31,842). The main islands are Lewis with Harris (area 770 sq. miles, pop. 23,390), whose chief town, Stornoway (pop. 13,409), is the administrative headquarters; North Uist (pop. 1,454); South Uist (pop. 2,223); Benbecula (pop. 1,988) and Barra (pop. 1,232). Other inhabited islands include Bernera (292), Berneray (134), Eriskay (219), Grimsay (206), Scalpay (461) and Vatersay (108).

---

EARLY HISTORY

PREHISTORIC INHABITANTS

The Picts, believed to be of non-Aryan origin, seem to have inhabited the whole of northern Britain and to have spread over the north of Ireland. Remains are most frequent in Caithness and Sutherland and the Orkney Islands.

Celts arrived from Belgic Gaul during the latter part of the Bronze Age and in the early Iron Age, and except in the extreme north of the mainland and in the islands, the civilization and speech of the people were definitely Celtic at the time of the Roman invasion of Britain.

THE ROMAN INVASION

In AD 79–80 Julius Agricola extended the Roman conquests in Britain by advancing into Caledonia and building a line of fortifications across the isthmus between the Forth and Clyde, but after a victory at Mons Graupius he was recalled. Hadrian's Wall, mostly complete by AD 130, marked the frontier until about AD 143 when the frontier moved north to the Forth–Clyde isthmus and was secured by the Antonine Wall. From about AD 155 the Antonine Wall was damaged by frequent attacks and by the end of the second century the northern limit of Roman Britain had receded to Hadrian's Wall.

THE SCOTS

After the withdrawal or absorption of the Roman garrison of Britain there were many years of tribal warfare between the Picts and Scots (the Gaelic tribe then dominant in Ireland), the Brythonic Waelisc (Welsh) of Strathclyde (south-west Scotland and Cumberland), and the Anglo-Saxons of Lothian. The Waelisc were isolated from their kinsmen in Wales by the victory of the West Saxons at Chester (613), and towards the close of the ninth century the Scots under Kenneth Mac Alpin became the dominant power in Caledonia. In the reign of Malcolm I (943–954) Strathclyde was brought into subjection, the English lowland kingdom (Lothian) being conquered by Malcolm II (1005–1034).

From the late 11th century until the mid 16th century there were constant wars between Scotland and England, the outstanding figures in the struggle being William Wallace, who defeated the English at Stirling Bridge (1297) and Robert Bruce, who won the battle of Bannockburn (1314). James IV and many of his nobles fell at the disastrous battle of Flodden (1513).

## THE JACOBITE REVOLTS

In 1603 James VI of Scotland succeeded Elizabeth I on the throne of England (his mother, Mary Queen of Scots, was the great-granddaughter of Henry VII), his successors reigning as sovereigns of Great Britain, although political union of the two countries did not occur until 1707. After the abdication (by flight) in 1688 of James VII and II, the crown devolved upon William III (grandson of Charles I) and Mary (elder daughter of James VII and II). In 1689 Graham of Claverhouse roused the Highlands on behalf of James VII and II, but died after a military success at Killiecrankie.

After the death of Anne (younger daughter of James VII and II), the throne devolved upon George I (great-grandson of James VI and I). In 1715, armed risings on behalf of James Stuart (the Old Pretender) led to the indecisive battle of Sheriffmuir, and the Jacobite movement died down until 1745, when Charles Stuart (the Young Pretender) defeated the Royalist troops at Prestonpans and advanced to Derby (1746). From Derby, the adherents of 'James VIII and III' (the title claimed for his father by Charles Stuart) fell back on the defensive, and the movement was finally crushed at Culloden (16 April 1746).

## PRINCIPAL CITIES

### ABERDEEN

Aberdeen, 130 miles north-east of Edinburgh, received its charter as a Royal Burgh in 1179. Scotland's third largest city, Aberdeen is the second largest Scottish fishing port and the main centre for offshore oil exploration and production. It is also an ancient university town and distinguished research centre. Other industries include engineering, food processing, textiles, paper manufacturing and chemicals.

Places of interest include King's College, St Machar's Cathedral, Brig o' Balgownie, Duthie Park and Winter Gardens, Hazlehead Park, the Kirk of St Nicholas, Mercat Cross, Marischal College and Marischal Museum, Provost Skene's House, Art Gallery, James Dun's House, Satrosphere Hands-On Discovery Centre, and Provost Ross's House (maritime museum).

### DUNDEE

Dundee, a Royal Burgh, is situated on the north bank of the Tay estuary. The city's port and dock installations are important to the offshore oil industry and the airport also provides servicing facilities. Principal industries include textiles, computers and other electronic industries, lasers, printing, tyre manufacture, food processing, carpets, engineering and clothing manufacture. Six sites have Enterprise Zone status, including the Technology Park, airport and port.

The unique City Churches – three churches under one roof, together with the 15th-century St Mary's Tower – are the most prominent architectural feature. Discovery Point, the visitor centre at Discovery Quay, relates the voyage of RRS *Discovery*, the Dundee-built ship which took Capt. Scott to the Antarctic.

### EDINBURGH

Edinburgh is the capital of and seat of government in Scotland. The city is built on a group of hills and contains in Princes Street one of the most beautiful thoroughfares in the world.

The principal buildings are the Castle, which includes St Margaret's Chapel, the oldest building in Edinburgh, and near it, the Scottish National War Memorial; the Palace of Holyroodhouse; Parliament House, the present seat of the judicature; three universities (Edinburgh, Heriot-Watt, Napier); St Giles' Cathedral (restored 1879–83); St Mary's (Scottish Episcopal) Cathedral (Sir Gilbert Scott); the General Register House (Robert Adam); the National and the Signet Libraries; the National Gallery; the Royal Scottish Academy; and the National Portrait Gallery.

### GLASGOW

Glasgow, a Royal Burgh, is the principal commercial and industrial centre in Scotland. The city occupies the north and south banks of the Clyde, formerly one of the chief commercial estuaries in the world. The principal industries include engineering, electronics, finance, chemicals and printing. The city has also developed recently as a tourism and conference centre.

The chief buildings are the 13th-century Gothic Cathedral, the University (Sir Gilbert Scott), the City Chambers, the Royal Concert Hall, St Mungo Museum of Religious Life and Art, Pollok House, the School of Art (Mackintosh), Kelvingrove Art Galleries, the Burrell Collection museum and the Mitchell Library. The city is home to the Scottish National Orchestra, Scottish Opera and Scottish Ballet.

## LORD LIEUTENANTS

| Region | Title | Name |
|---|---|---|
| Borders | Berwickshire | Maj.-Gen. Sir John Swinton, KCVO, OBE |
| | Roxburgh, Ettrick and Lauderdale | The Duke of Buccleuch and Queensberry, KT, VRD |
| | Tweeddale | Capt. J. D. B. Younger |
| Central | Clackmannan | vacant |
| | Stirling and Falkirk | Lt.-Col. J. Stirling of Garden, CBE, TD |
| Dumfries and Galloway | Dumfries | Capt. R. C. Cunningham-Jardine |
| | The Stewartry of Kirkcudbright | Sir Michael Herries, OBE, MC |
| | Wigtown | Maj. E. S. Orr Ewing |
| Fife | Fife | The Earl of Elgin and Kincardine, KT |
| Grampian | Aberdeenshire | Capt. C. A. Farquharson |
| | Banffshire | J. A. S. McPherson, CBE |
| | Kincardineshire | The Viscount of Arbuthnott, CBE, DSC, FRSE |
| | Morayshire | Air Vice-Marshal G. A. Chesworth, CB, OBE, DFC |

| Region | Title | Name |
|---|---|---|
| Highland | Caithness | The Viscount Thurso |
| | Inverness | Lt.-Cdr. L. R. D. Mackintosh of Mackintosh, OBE |
| | Nairn | The Earl of Leven and Melville |
| | Ross and Cromarty | Capt. R. W. K. Stirling of Fairburn, TD |
| | Sutherland | Maj.-Gen. D. Houston, CBE |
| Lothian | East Lothian | Sir Hew Hamilton-Dalrymple, Bt., KCVO |
| | Midlothian | Capt. G. W. Burnett, LVO |
| | West Lothian | The Earl of Morton |
| Strathclyde | Argyll and Bute | Col. A. Fletcher, OBE |
| | Ayrshire and Arran | Maj. R. Y. Henderson, TD |
| | Dumbartonshire | Brig. D. D. G. Hardie, TD |
| | Lanarkshire | H. B. Sneddon, CBE |
| | Renfrewshire | Maj. J. D. M. Crichton Maitland |
| Tayside | Angus | The Earl of Airlie, KT, GCVO, PC |
| | Perth and Kinross | Maj. Sir David Butter, KCVO, MC |
| Orkney | Orkney | Brig. M. G. Dennison |
| Shetland | Shetland | J. H. Scott |
| Western Isles | Western Isles | The Viscount Dunrossil, CMG |

The Lord Provosts of the four city districts of Aberdeen, Dundee, Edinburgh and Glasgow are Lord Lieutenants for those districts *ex officio*

# Scottish Regions and Islands

REGIONAL AND ISLANDS COUNCILS: Area, Population, Finance

| Council | Administrative headquarters | Area (hectares) | Population (latest estimate) | Band D charge 1994 | Band D water charge per household 1994 |
|---|---|---|---|---|---|
| Borders | Newtown St Boswells | 471,253 | 105,300 | £384.00 | £92.00 |
| Central | Stirling | 263,455 | 272,900 | 444.00 | 47.00 |
| Dumfries and Galloway | Dumfries | 639,561 | 147,900 | 389.00 | 84.00 |
| Fife | Glenrothes | 131,201 | 351,200 | 472.00 | 59.00 |
| Grampian | Aberdeen | 869,772 | 528,100 | 389.00 | 89.00 |
| Highland | Inverness | 2,539,759 | 206,900 | 403.92 | 88.31 |
| Lothian | Edinburgh | 171,595 | 750,600 | 490.00 | 78.00 |
| Orkney | Kirkwall | 97,581 | 19,600 | 440.00 | 123.00 |
| Shetland | Lerwick | 143,268 | 22,522 | 409.85 | 116.30 |
| Strathclyde | Glasgow | 1,350,283 | 2,286,800 | 396.00 | 80.00 |
| Tayside | Dundee | 749,165 | 395,200 | 445.00 | 69.00 |
| Western Isles | Stornoway, Lewis | 289,798 | 29,600 | 463.00 | 194.00 |

REGIONAL AND ISLAND COUNCILS: Officers and Conveners

| Council | Chief Executive | Director of Finance | Convener |
|---|---|---|---|
| Borders | K. J. Clark, CBE | P. Jeary | The Earl of Minto, OBE |
| Central | D. Sinclair | S. C. Craig | Mrs A. Wallace |
| Dumfries and Galloway | I. F. Smith | J. C. Stewart | A. Baldwick |
| Fife | Dr J. A. Markland | A. E. Taylor | R. Gough, CBE |
| Grampian | A. G. Campbell | A. McLean | Ms R. Kemp |
| Highland | R. H. Stevenson | A. M. Jamieson | D. J. McPherson, CBE |
| Lothian | T. Aitchison | D. B. Chynoweth | E. Milligan |
| Orkney | R. H. Gilbert | D. H. Robertson | H. Halcro-Johnston |
| Shetland | M. E. Green | A. Matthews | L. S. Smith |
| Strathclyde | N. McIntosh | A. Gillespie | W. Perry |
| Tayside | R. W. Black | I. B. McIver | Mrs F. E. Duncan |
| Western Isles | B. W. Stewart | R. Bennie | D. M. Mackay |

# District Councils

| Council | Administrative headquarters | Population (latest estimate) | Band D charge 1994 | Chief Executive | Chairman (a) Convener (b) Provost (c) Lord Provost |
|---|---|---|---|---|---|
| Aberdeen City (5) | Aberdeen | 213,000 | £179.00 | A. Mearns | (c) J. Wyness |
| Angus (9) | Forfar | 96,500 | 99.00 | P. B. Regan | (b) B. M. C. Milne |
| Annandale and Eskdale (3) | Annan | 37,130 | 121.00 | §W. J. Davidson | (a) D. T. R. Wilson |
| Argyll and Bute (8) | Lochgilphead | 63,350 | 184.00 | M. A. J. Gossip, CBE | G. McMillan |
| Badenoch and Strathspey (6) | Kingussie | 10,399 | 99.00 | Mrs J. M. Fraser | A. Gordon |
| Banff and Buchan (5) | Banff | 88,020 | 99.00 | R. M. Blackburn | (a) W. R. Cruickshank, OBE |
| Bearsden and Milngavie (8) | Bearsden | 41,000 | 126.00 | I. C. Laurie | (b) I. J. Miller |
| Berwickshire (1) | Duns | 19,350 | 64.80 | R. A. Christie | Capt. J. Evans |
| Caithness (6) | Wick | 26,710 | 86.00 | A. Beattie | (a) J. M. Young, OBE |
| Clackmannan (2) | Alloa | 47,643 | 170.21 | R. Allan | (a) J. Watson |
| Clydebank (8) | Clydebank | 47,500 | 180.00 | J. T. McNally | (b) J. McAllister |
| Clydesdale (8) | Lanark | 58,290 | 196.00 | P. W. Daniels | (a) Mrs E. Logan |
| Cumbernauld and Kilsyth (8) | Cumbernauld | 63,930 | 183.00 | J. Hutton | (b) C. Combe |
| Cumnock and Doon Valley (8) | Cumnock | 42,954 | 180.00 | K. W. Inch | (a) E. Ross |
| Cunninghame (8) | Irvine | 139,020 | 165.00 | B. Devine | (a) S. Dewar |
| Dumbarton (8) | Dumbarton | 77,222 | 199.00 | ‡M. J. Watters | (b) P. O'Neill |
| Dundee City (9) | Dundee | 171,520 | 221.00 | A. Stephen | (c) T. M. McDonald |
| Dunfermline (4) | Dunfermline | 129,830 | 124.00 | K. Drennan | (b) Ms M. Millar |
| East Kilbride (8) | East Kilbride | 82,777 | 175.00 | J. Jarvie | (b) S. Crawford |
| East Lothian (7) | Haddington | 85,140 | 130.00 | M. Duncan | G. M. Wanless |
| Eastwood (8) | Giffnock | 60,600 | 99.00 | M. D. Henry | (b) L. M. Rosin |
| Edinburgh City (7) | Edinburgh | 418,914 | 245.36 | W. M. Blythe | (c) Rt. Hon. N. Irons |
| Ettrick and Lauderdale (1) | Galashiels | 35,000 | 102.60 | C. M. Anderson | (b) W. Hardie |
| Falkirk (2) | Falkirk | 142,800 | 92.00 | W. Weir | (b) J. Constable |
| Glasgow City (8) | Glasgow | 681,470 | 225.00 | T. J. Monaghan | (c) Rt. Hon. J. Shields |
| Gordon (5) | Inverurie | 77,080 | 90.00 | M. C. Barron | (b) R. G. Bisset |
| Hamilton (8) | Hamilton | 105,202 | 215.00 | M. Docherty | (b) S. Casserly |
| Inverclyde (8) | Greenock | 90,103 | 167.00 | R. McPherson | (b) A. Robertson |
| Inverness (6) | Inverness | 62,245 | 111.00 | B. Wilson | (b) W. A. E. Fraser |
| Kilmarnock and Loudoun (8) | Kilmarnock | 79,861 | 145.23 | R. W. Jenner | (b) D. Coffey |
| Kincardine and Deeside (5) | Stonehaven | 54,990 | 58.50 | T. Hyder | (a) Mrs D. Ewing |
| Kirkcaldy (4) | Kirkcaldy | 148,450 | 160.00 | §D. A. Watt | (a) R. King, OBE |
| Kyle and Carrick (8) | Ayr | 112,658 | 220.00 | I. R. D. Smillie | (b) G. T. Macdonald |
| Lochaber (6) | Fort William | 19,195 | 144.00 | D. A. B. Blair | N. M. Clark |
| Midlothian (7) | Dalkeith | 79,910 | 150.00 | T. Muir | (a) D. Molloy |
| Monklands (8) | Coatbridge | 102,379 | 218.00 | M. V. P. Hart | (b) R. Gilson |
| Moray (5) | Elgin | 83,616 | 99.00 | J. P. Summers | (a) E. Aldridge |
| Motherwell (8) | Motherwell | 143,730 | 179.00 | J. Bonomy | (b) W. Wilson |
| Nairn (6) | Nairn | 10,600 | 109.00 | †A. M. Kerr | (b) J. Cattanach |
| Nithsdale (3) | Dumfries | 57,220 | 129.00 | T. Orr | (b) Mrs J. McMurdo |
| North-East Fife (4) | Cupar | 69,930 | 159.00 | D. M. Abbott | Mrs I. M. Carter |
| Perth and Kinross (9) | Perth | 129,070 | 110.00 | H. Robertson | (b) Mrs J. McCormack |
| Renfrew (8) | Paisley | 201,000 | 189.00 | *A. I. Cowe | (b) W. Orr |
| Ross and Cromarty (6) | Dingwall | 49,184 | 143.00 | R. Mair | (a) Maj. A. Cameron, MBE |
| Roxburgh (1) | Hawick | 35,350 | 99.00 | W. R. Millan | Mrs M. S. Turnbull |
| Skye and Lochalsh (6) | Portree | 11,870 | 109.00 | D. H. Noble | J. F. Munro |
| Stewartry (3) | Kirkcudbright | 23,690 | 70.00 | J. C. Howie | (a) J. Nelson, MBE, TD |
| Stirling (2) | Stirling | 81,630 | 136.00 | G. Bonner | (a) Mrs P. Greenhill |
| Strathkelvin (8) | Kirkintilloch | 85,191 | 219.00 | C. Mallon | (b) R. M. Coyle |
| Sutherland (6) | Golspie | 13,190 | 102.00 | †J. Allison | (a) Mrs A. Magee |
| Tweeddale (1) | Peebles | 15,375 | 85.00 | G. H. T. Garvie | D. Suckling |
| West Lothian (7) | Bathgate | 146,430 | 91.00 | A. M. Linkston | (a) J. McGinley |
| Wigtown (3) | Stranraer | 30,077 | 123.00 | A. Geddes | W. Service |

§ General Manager
‡ District Secretary
† Director of Administration
* Managing Director

*Regions*
(1) Borders
(2) Central
(3) Dumfries and Galloway
(4) Fife
(5) Grampian
(6) Highland
(7) Lothian
(8) Strathclyde
(9) Tayside

# Northern Ireland

Northern Ireland has a total area of 5,461 sq. miles (14,144 sq. km): land, 5,215 sq. miles (13,506 sq. km); inland water and tideways, 246 sq. miles (638 sq. km).

The population of Northern Ireland at the 1991 Census was 1,577,836 (males, 769,071; females, 808,765). The average density of population in 1991 was 1.11 persons per hectare.

In 1991 the number of persons in the various religious denominations (expressed as percentages of the total population) were: Roman Catholic, 38.4; Presbyterian, 21.4; Church of Ireland, 17.7; Methodist, 3.8; others 7.7; none, 3.7; not stated, 7.3.

---

## PRINCIPAL CITIES

---

### BELFAST

Belfast, the administrative centre of Northern Ireland, is situated at the mouth of the River Lagan at its entrance to Belfast Lough. The city grew, owing to its easy access by sea to Scottish coal and iron, to be a great industrial centre.

The principal buildings are of a relatively recent date and include the Parliament Buildings at Stormont, the City Hall, the Law Courts, the Public Library and the Museum and Art Gallery.

Belfast received its first charter of incorporation in 1613 and was created a city in 1888; the title of Lord Mayor was conferred in 1892.

### LONDONDERRY

Londonderry (originally Derry) is situated on the River Foyle, and was reputedly founded in AD 546 by St Columba. It has important associations with the City of London. The Irish Society was created by the City of London in 1610, and under its royal charter of 1613 it fortified the city and was for long closely associated with its administration. Because of this connection the city was incorporated in 1613 under the new name of Londonderry.

The city is famous for the great siege of 1688–9, when for 105 days the town held out against the forces of James II until relieved by sea. The city walls are still intact and form a circuit of almost a mile around the old city.

Interesting buildings are the Protestant Cathedral of St Columb's (1633) and the Guildhall, reconstructed in 1912 and containing a number of beautiful stained glass windows, many of which were presented by the livery companies of London.

---

## CONSTITUTION AND GOVERNMENT

---

As part of the United Kingdom, Northern Ireland is subject to the same fundamental constitutional provisions which apply to the rest of the United Kingdom. It had its own parliament and government from 1921 to 1972, but after increasing civil unrest the Northern Ireland (Temporary Provisions) Act 1972 transferred the legislative and executive powers of the Northern Ireland parliament and government to the UK Parliament and a Secretary of State. The Northern Ireland Constitution Act 1973 provided for devolution in Northern Ireland through an assembly and executive, and in

January 1974 a power-sharing executive was formed by the Northern Ireland political parties. This arrangement collapsed in May 1974 and since then Northern Ireland has been governed by direct rule under the provisions of the Northern Ireland Act 1974. This allows Parliament to approve all laws for Northern Ireland and places the Northern Ireland department under the direction and control of the Secretary of State for Northern Ireland.

Attempts have been made by successive governments to find a means of restoring a widely acceptable form of devolved government to Northern Ireland. A 78-member Assembly was elected by proportional representation in 1982. However, it was dissolved four years later after it failed to discharge its responsibilities of making proposals for the resumption of devolved government and of monitoring the work of the Northern Ireland departments.

In 1985 the governments of the United Kingdom and the Republic of Ireland signed the Anglo-Irish Agreement, establishing an intergovernmental conference in which the Irish government may put forward views and proposals on certain aspects of Northern Ireland affairs.

In 1990 further dialogue between the Government and the constitutional political parties in Northern Ireland was established as a means of exploring the extent of the common ground which existed between them at that time. A formula, known as the three-stranded approach, for political talks about the future of Northern Ireland and its relationship with the United Kingdom and the Republic of Ireland was agreed in 1991. Strand 1 of the talks between the Government and the four main local constitutional political parties began in April 1992. Strand 2, involving the government of the Republic of Ireland, took place between July and November 1992. Although round table talks ended in November 1992, the process has continued since September 1993 in the form of private bilateral discussion with three of the four main Northern Ireland parties (the DUP have declined to participate) to explore the basis upon which they can come together for further dialogue.

Bilateral discussions have also been taking place between the British and Irish governments to develop a framework to carry the talks process forward, building on the principles of the joint declaration (the Downing Street declaration) made by the Prime Minister and the Taoiseach on 15 December 1993. This outlined an agreed framework from which a peace process could start, and said that all democratically-mandated parties could be involved in the talks as long as they permanently renounced paramilitary violence. The president of Sinn Fein (Gerry Adams) later called for clarification of details of the declaration and of the Government's long-term intentions regarding Ireland. In response to specific questions from Sinn Fein the Government provided a commentary detailing its stated position on Northern Ireland. At the time of going to press, this situation had not been resolved. (*See also* Events of the Year.)

### FLAG

The official national flag of Northern Ireland is now the Union Flag. The flag formerly in use (a white, six-pointed star in the centre of a red cross on a white field, enclosing a red hand and surmounted by a crown) has not been used since the imposition of direct rule.

---

### FINANCE

---

Taxation in Northern Ireland is largely imposed and collected by the United Kingdom government. After deducting the cost of collection and of Northern Ireland's contributions to the European Community the balance, known as the Attributed Share of Taxation, is paid over to the Northern Ireland Consolidated Fund. Northern Ireland's revenue is insufficient to meet its expenditure and is supplemented by a grant-in-aid.

|  | 1993–4* | 1994–5** |
|---|---|---|
| Public income | £6,014,467,844 | £6,322,470,000 |
| Public expenditure | 5,983,267,764 | 6,322,470,000 |

* Outturn
** Estimate

## PRODUCTION

The products of the engineering, shipbuilding and aircraft industries, which employed 34,000 persons in 1991, were valued at £1,676 million. The textile industries, employing about 10,400 persons, produced products valued at approximately £448 million. The food and drink industry, employing about 22,000 persons, produced goods valued at £3,571 million.

In 1992 1,224 persons were employed in mining and quarrying operations in Northern Ireland and the minerals raised (20,055,834 tonnes) were valued at £37,245,379.

## COMMUNICATIONS

### SEAPORTS

The total tonnage handled by Northern Ireland ports in 1993 was 18 million. Regular ferry, freight and container services operate to ports in Great Britain and Europe from 18 ports, including Belfast, Coleraine, Larne, Londonderry and Warrenpoint.

### ROAD AND RAIL

The Northern Ireland Transport Holding Company is largely responsible for the supervision of the subsidiary companies, Ulsterbus and Citybus (which operate the public road passenger services) and Northern Ireland Railways. Road freight services are also provided by a large number of hauliers operating competitively under licence.

### AIR

Belfast International Airport was privatized during 1994 and is operated by MEBO (Management/Employee Buy Out). It has substantial passenger and freight handling facilities and provides scheduled and chartered services on domestic and international routes.

Scheduled services also operate from Belfast City Airport to 19 UK destinations and from Eglinton Airport to two UK destinations.

# Northern Ireland Counties

| County | Area* (sq. miles) | Lord Lieutenant | High Sheriff, 1994 |
|---|---|---|---|
| Antrim | 1,093 | The Lord O'Neill | A. D. Frazer |
| ‡Belfast City | 25 | Col. J. E. Wilson, OBE | Mrs M. M. Crooks |
| Armagh | 484 | The Earl of Caledon | J. E. Lamb |
| Down | 945 | Col. W. S. Brownlow | M. G. B. Browne |
| Fermanagh | 647 | The Earl of Erne | W. R. M. Farrell |
| †Londonderry | 798 | Col. M. W. McCorkell, OBE, TD | W. S. P. Clark |
| ‡Londonderry City | 3.4 | J. T. Eaton, CBE, TD | G. F. W. Price |
| Tyrone | 1,211 | The Duke of Abercorn | R. N. A. Lowry |

* Excluding inland waters and tideways
‡ Denotes County Borough
† Excluding the City of Londonderry

# District Councils

§ Denotes Borough Council

| Council | Population (30 June 1992) | Net Annual Value | Council Clerk | Chairman †Mayor 1994 |
|---|---|---|---|---|
| §Antrim, Co. Antrim | 44,500 | £6,775,611 | S. J. Magee | †T. E. Wallace |
| §Ards, Co. Down | 65,500 | 7,902,518 | D. J. Fallows | †J. Shields |
| Armagh, Co. Armagh | 51,700 | 5,280,789 | D. R. D. Mitchall | J. F. Nicholson |
| §Ballymena, Co. Antrim | 56,800 | 8,583,413 | M. G. Rankin | †Revd R. Coulter |
| §Ballymoney, Co. Antrim | 24,300 | 2,676,689 | J. C. Alderdice | †C. J. Cousley |

| Council | Population (30 June 1992) | Net Annual Value | Council Clerk | Chairman †Mayor 1994 |
|---|---|---|---|---|
| Banbridge, Co. Down | 33,800 | £3,999,680 | R. Gilmore | J. Walsh |
| Belfast, Co. Antrim and Co. Down | 287,500 | 54,846,109 | J. Hanna | H. Smyth (*Lord Mayor*) |
| §Carrickfergus, Co. Antrim | 33,600 | 4,617,693 | R. Boyd | †S. Crowe |
| §Castlereagh, Co. Down | 62,000 | 8,281,261 | J. White | †J. Bell |
| §Coleraine, Co. Londonderry | 51,500 | 7,778,339 | W. E. Andrews | †D. McClarty |
| Cookstown, Co. Tyrone | 34,000 | 3,167,150 | M. McGuckin | S. A. Glasgow |
| §Craigavon, Co. Armagh | 76,000 | 10,644,971 | E. A. McKinley | †B. Maguinness |
| Derry, Co. Londonderry | 97,600 | 12,290,361 | J. Keanie | †J. R. Guy |
| Down, Co. Down | 58,800 | 6,207,545 | O. O'Connor | J Cochrane |
| Dungannon, Co. Tyrone | 45,700 | 4,748,375 | W. J. Beattie | J. Canning |
| | | | | D. J. Brady |
| Fermanagh, Co. Fermanagh | 54,200 | 5,851,235 | G. Burns, MBE | G. Gallagher |
| §Larne, Co. Antrim | 29,700 | 4,017,317 | G. McKinley | †Mrs R. A. Armstrong |
| §Limavady, Co. Londonderry | 29,300 | 2,950,275 | J. K. Stevenson | †I. Grant |
| §Lisburn, Co. Antrim and Co. Down | 100,300 | 13,784,400 | M. S. Fielding | †W. H. Lewis |
| Magherafelt, Co. Londonderry | 36,400 | 3,674,442 | J. A. McLaughlin | R. A. Montgomery |
| Moyle, Co. Antrim | 14,700 | 1,545,122 | R. G. Lewis | R. A. McIlroy |
| Newry and Mourne, Co. Down and Co. Armagh | 83,700 | 8,259,684 | K. O'Neill | T. D. Kennedy |
| §Newtownabbey, Co. Antrim | 75,300 | 11,431,032 | J. Campbell | †J. Robinson |
| §North Down, Co. Down | 72,500 | 9,671,161 | A. McDowell | †Rt. Hon. R. Bradford |
| Omagh, Co. Tyrone | 45,600 | 4,494,364 | J. P. McKinney | W. Breen |
| Strabane, Co. Tyrone | 35,500 | 3,189,836 | Dr V. R. Eakin | E. Turner |

# Patron Saints

ST GEORGE
*Patron Saint of England*

St George is believed to have been born in Cappadocia, of Christian parents, in the latter part of the third century and to have served with distinction as a soldier under the Emperor Diocletian, including a visit to England on a military mission. When the persecution of Christians was ordered, St George sought a personal interview to remonstrate with the Emperor and after a profession of faith resigned his military commission. Arrest and torture followed and he was martyred at Nicomedia on 23 April 303, a day ordered to be kept in remembrance as a national festival by the Council of Oxford in 1222, although it was not until the reign of Edward III that he was made patron saint of England.

St George's connection with a dragon seems to date from the close of the sixth century and to be due to the transfer of his remains from Nicomedia to Lydda, close to the scene of the legendary exploit of Perseus in rescuing Andromeda and slaying the sea monster, credit for which became attached to the Christian martyr.

ST DAVID
*Patron Saint of Wales*

St David is believed to have been born towards the beginning and to have died towards the end of the sixth century. St David was an eloquent preacher, who founded the monastery at Menevia, now St David's. He became the patron of Wales, but there is no record of any papal canonization before 1181. His annual festival is observed on 1 March.

ST ANDREW
*Patron Saint of Scotland*

St Andrew, one of the Christian Apostles and brother of Simon Peter, was born at Bethsaida on the Sea of Galilee and lived at Capernaum. He preached the Gospel in Asia Minor and in Scythia along the shores of the Black Sea and became the patron saint of Russia. It is believed that he suffered crucifixion at Patras in Achaea, on a *crux decussata* (now known as St Andrew's Cross) and that his relics were removed from Patras to Constantinople and thence to St Andrews, probably in the eighth century, since which time he has been the patron saint of Scotland. The festival of St Andrew is held on 30 November.

ST PATRICK
*Patron Saint of Ireland*

St Patrick was born, probably in England, about 389 and was carried off to Ireland as a slave about 16 years later, escaping to Gaul at the age of 22. He was ordained deacon at Auxerre and having been consecrated Bishop in 432 was dispatched to Wicklow to reorganize the Christian communities in Ireland. He founded the see of Armagh and introduced Latin into Ireland as the language of the Church. He died *c.*461 and his festival is celebrated on 17 March.

# The Isle of Man

*Ellan Vannin*

The Isle of Man is an island situated in the Irish Sea, in latitude 54° 3′–54° 25′ N. and longitude 4° 18′–4° 47′ W., nearly equidistant from England, Scotland and Ireland. Although the early inhabitants were of Celtic origin, the Isle of Man was part of the Norwegian Kingdom of the Hebrides until 1266, when this was ceded to Scotland. Subsequently granted to the Stanleys (Earls of Derby) in the 15th century and later to the Dukes of Atholl, it was brought under the administration of the Crown in 1765. The island forms the bishopric of Sodor and Man.

The total land area is 221 sq. miles (572 sq. km). The report on the 1991 Census showed a resident population of 69,788 (males, 33,693; females, 36,095). The main language in use is English. There are no remaining native speakers of Manx Gaelic but 643 people are able to speak the language.

CAPITAL – ΨDouglas; population (1991), 22,214. ΨCastletown (3,152) is the ancient capital; the other towns are ΨPeel (3,829) and ΨRamsey (6,496)

FLAG – A red flag charged with three conjoined armoured legs in white and gold

TYNWALD DAY – 5 July.

## GOVERNMENT

The Isle of Man is a self-governing Crown dependency, having its own parliamentary, legal and administrative system. The British Government is responsible for international relations and defence. Under the UK Act of Accession, Protocol 3, the island's relationship with the European Community is limited to trade alone and does not extend to financial aid. The Lieutenant-Governor is The Queen's personal representative in the island.

The legislature, Tynwald, is the oldest parliament in the world in continuous existence. It has two branches: the Legislative Council and the House of Keys. The Council consists of the President of Tynwald, the Bishop of Sodor and Man, the Attorney-General (who does not have a vote) and eight members elected by the House of Keys. The House of Keys has 24 members, elected by universal adult suffrage. The branches sit separately to consider legislation and sit together, as Tynwald Court, for most other parliamentary purposes.

The presiding officer in Tynwald Court is the President of Tynwald, elected by the members, who also presides over sittings of the Legislative Council. The presiding officer of the House of Keys is Mr Speaker, who is elected by members of the House.

The principal members of the Manx Government are the Chief Minister and nine departmental ministers, who comprise the Council of Ministers.

*Lieutenant-Governor*, His Excellency Air Marshal Sir
 Laurence Jones, KCB, AFC
 *ADC to the Lieutenant-Governor*, M. M. Wood
*President of Tynwald*, The Hon. Sir Charles Kerruish, OBE
*Speaker, House of Keys*, The Hon. J. C. Cain
*The First Deemster and Clerk of the Rolls*, His Honour
 J. W. Corrin
*Clerk of Legislative Council*, T. A. Bawden
*Clerk of Tynwald, Secretary to the House of Keys and Counsel
 to the Speaker*, Prof. T. St J. N. Bates
*Attorney-General*, J. M. Kerruish
*Chief Minister*, The Hon. M. R. Walker, CBE
*Chief Secretary*, J. F. Kissack
*Chief Financial Officer*, J. A. Cashen

## ECONOMY

Most of the income generated in the island is earned in the services sector with financial and business services being considerably larger than the traditional industry of tourism. Manufacturing industry is also a major generator of income whilst the island's other traditional industries of agriculture and fishing now play a smaller role in the economy.

Under the terms of Protocol 3, the island has free access to EC markets for its products.

A 20-acre freeport has been developed adjacent to the main airport at Ronaldsway.

The island's unemployment rate is approximately 4 per cent and price inflation is around 3 per cent per annum.

## FINANCE

The island's Budget for 1994–5 provided for net expenditure of £200,523,000. The principal sources of government revenue are taxes on income and expenditure. Income tax is payable at a rate of 15 per cent on the first £17,000 of taxable income of resident individuals and 20 per cent on the balance, after personal allowances. The rate of income tax is 20 per cent on the whole taxable income of non-residents and companies. By agreement with the British Government, the island keeps most of its rates of indirect taxation (Value Added Tax and duties) the same as those in the United Kingdom, but this agreement may be terminated by either party. A reciprocal agreement on national insurance benefits and pensions exists between the Governments of the Isle of Man and the United Kingdom. Taxes are also charged on property (rates), but these are comparatively low.

The major government expenditure items are health, social security and education, which account for 59 per cent of the government budget. The island makes a voluntary annual contribution to the United Kingdom for defence and other external services.

Although the island has a limited relationship with the European Community, it neither contributes money to nor receives funds from the EC budget.

# The Channel Islands

The Channel Islands, situated off the north-west coast of France (at distances of from ten to 30 miles), are the only portions of the Dukedom of Normandy still belonging to the Crown, to which they have been attached since the Conquest. They were the only British territory to come under German occupation during the Second World War, following invasion on 30 June to 1 July 1940. The islands were relieved by British forces on 9 May 1945, and 9 May (Liberation Day) is now observed as a bank and public holiday.

The islands consist of Jersey (28,717 acres/11,630 ha), Guernsey (15,654 acres/6,340 ha), and the dependencies of Guernsey: Alderney (1,962 acres/795 ha), Brechou (74/30), Great Sark (1,035/419), Little Sark (239/97), Herm (320/130), Jethou (44/18) and Lihou (38/15) – a total of 48,083 acres/19,474 ha, or 75 sq. miles/194 sq. km. In 1991 the population of Jersey was 84,082; and of Guernsey, 58,867; Alderney, 2,297 and Sark, 575. The official languages are English and French but French is being supplanted by English, which is the language in daily use. In country districts of Jersey and Guernsey and throughout Sark a Norman-French *patois* is also in use, though to a declining extent.

## GOVERNMENT

The islands are Crown dependencies with their own legislative assemblies (the States in Jersey, Guernsey and Alderney, and the Court of Chief Pleas in Sark), and systems of local administration and of law, and their own courts. Acts passed by the States require the sanction of The Queen-in-Council. The British Government is responsible for defence and international relations. The Channel Islands have trading rights alone within the European Community; these rights do not include financial aid.

In both Bailiwicks the Lieutenant-Governor and Commander-in-Chief, who is appointed by the Crown, is the personal representative of The Queen and the channel of communication between the Crown (via the Privy Council) and the island's government.

The government of each Bailiwick is conducted by committees appointed by the States. Justice is administered by the Royal Courts of Jersey and Guernsey, each consisting of the Bailiff and 12 elected Jurats. The Bailiffs of Jersey and Guernsey, appointed by the Crown, are President of the States and of the Royal Courts of their respective islands.

Each Bailiwick constitutes a deanery under the jurisdiction of the Bishop of Winchester (*see* Index).

## ECONOMY

A mild climate and good soil have led to the development of intensive systems of agriculture and horticulture, which form a significant part of the economy. Equally important are invisible earnings, principally from tourism and banking and finance, the low rate of income tax (20p in the £ in Jersey and Guernsey; no tax of any kind in Sark) and the absence of super-tax and death duties making the islands a popular tax-haven.

Principal exports are agricultural produce and flowers; imports are chiefly machinery, manufactured goods, food, fuel and chemicals. Trade with the UK is regarded as internal.

British currency is legal tender in the Channel Islands but each Bailiwick issues its own coins and notes (*see* page 613). They also issue their own postage stamps; UK stamps are not valid.

## JERSEY

*Lieutenant-Governor and Commander-in-Chief of Jersey*, His Excellency Air Marshal Sir John Sutton, KCB, *apptd* 1990
  *Secretary and ADC*, Col. A. J. C. Woodrow, OBE
*Bailiff of Jersey*, Sir Peter Crill, CBE
*Deputy Bailiff*, P. M. Bailhache
*Attorney-General*, M. C. St J. Burt
*Receiver-General*, Gp Capt R. Green, OBE
*Solicitor-General*, S. C. Nicolle
*Greffier of the States*, G. H. C. Coppock
*States Treasurer*, G. M. Baird

### FINANCE

| Year to 31 Dec. | 1992 | 1993 |
| --- | --- | --- |
| Revenue | £377,235,237 | £383,865,789 |
| Revenue expenditure | 377,331,511 | 338,721,115 |
| Capital expenditure | 51,106,748 | 45,504,889 |
| Public debt | 0 | 0 |

CHIEF TOWN – ΨSt Helier, on the south coast of Jersey
FLAG – A white field charged with a red saltire cross, and the arms of Jersey in the upper centre

## GUERNSEY AND DEPENDENCIES

*Lieutenant-Governor and Commander-in-Chief of the Bailiwick of Guernsey and its Dependencies*, His Excellency Vice-Adm. Sir John Coward, KCB, DSO, *apptd* 1994
  *Secretary and ADC*, Capt. D. P. L. Hodgetts
*Bailiff of Guernsey*, Sir Graham Dorey
*Deputy Bailiff*, de V. G. Carey
*HM Procureur and Receiver-General*, A. C. K. Day, QC
*HM Comptroller*, G. R. Rowland, QC
*States Supervisor*, M. J. Brown

### FINANCE

| Year to 31 Dec. | 1992 | 1993 |
| --- | --- | --- |
| Revenue | £157,145,000 | £158,659,600 |
| Expenditure | 140,661,000 | 148,953,206 |

CHIEF TOWNS – Ψ St Peter Port, on the east coast of Guernsey; St Anne on Alderney
FLAG – White, bearing a red cross of St George, with a gold cross overall in the centre

### ALDERNEY

*President of the States*, E. W. Baron
*Clerk of the States*, D. V. Jenkins
*Clerk of the Court*, A. Johnson

### SARK

*Seigneur of Sark*, J. M. Beaumont
*The Seneschal*, L. P. de Carteret
*The Greffier*, J. P. Hamon

### OTHER DEPENDENCIES

Brechou, Lihou and Jethou are leased by the Crown. Herm is leased by the States of Guernsey.

# Conservation and Heritage

## Countryside Conservation

### NATIONAL PARKS

#### ENGLAND AND WALES

The ten National Parks of England and Wales were set up under the provisions of the National Parks and Access to the Countryside Act 1949 to conserve and protect scenic landscapes from inappropriate development and to provide access to the land for public enjoyment.

The Countryside Commission is the statutory body which has the power to designate National Parks in England, and the Countryside Council for Wales is responsible for National Parks in Wales. Designations in England are confirmed by the Secretary of State for the Environment, and those in Wales by the Secretary of State for Wales. The designation of a National Park does not affect the ownership of the land or remove the rights of the local community. Although the parks are administered through local government, the majority of the land is owned by private landowners (74 per cent) or by bodies such as the National Trust (7 per cent) and the Forestry Commission (7 per cent). The National Park Authorities own only 2.3 per cent of the land in the National Parks.

Under the Local Government Act 1972, National Park Authorities (NPAs) are the authorities responsible for park administration. They also influence land use and development, and deal with planning applications. Two-thirds of the members of each authority are appointed by the county and district councils within whose boundaries the parks lie. One-third of the members are appointed by the relevant Secretary of-State with advice from the Countryside Commission or the Countryside Council for Wales. The NPAs appoint the National Park Officer for the National Park they administer.

In the Peak District and the Lake District the NPAs are special boards: the Peak Park Joint Planning Board and the Lake District Special Planning Board. These are autonomous authorities which are financially independent, unlike the authorities in the other eight parks which are county council committees.

Central government provides 75 per cent of the funding for the parks through the National Park Supplementary Grant. The remaining 25 per cent is supplied by the local authorities concerned. Approved net expenditure for all National Parks in England and Wales in 1994-5 was £28,664,000.

The Countryside Commission has stated that other areas are regarded as being worthy of National Parks status. Two areas considered as having equivalent status are the Broads and the New Forest (*see* page 578).

The National Parks (with date designation confirmed) are:

BRECON BEACONS (1957), 1,351 sq. km/522 sq. miles – The park lies in Powys (66 per cent), Dyfed, Gwent and Mid Glamorgan. The park is centred on the Beacons, Pen y Fan, Corn Du and Cribyn, but also includes the valley of the Usk, the Black Mountains to the east and the Black Mountain to the west. There are information centres at Brecon, Craig-y-nos Country Park, Abergavenny and Llandovery, a study centre at Danywenallt and a day visitor centre near Libanus.

*Information Office*, 7 Glamorgan Street, Brecon, Powys LD3 7DP. Tel: 01874-624437. *National Park Officer*, M. Fitton

DARTMOOR (1951 and 1994), 954 sq. km/368 sq. miles – The park lies wholly in Devon. It consists of moorland and rocky granite tors, and is rich in prehistoric remains. There are information centres at Newbridge, Tavistock, Bovey Tracey, Steps Bridge, Princetown and Postbridge. *Information Office*, Parke, Haytor Road, Bovey Tracey, Devon TQ13 9JQ. Tel: 01626-832093. *National Park Officer*, N. Atkinson

EXMOOR (1954), 693 sq. km/268 sq. miles – The park lies in Somerset (71 per cent) and Devon. Exmoor is a moorland plateau inhabited by wild ponies and red deer. There are many ancient remains and burial mounds. There are information centres at Lynmouth, County Gate, Dulverton and Combe Martin. *Information Office*, Exmoor House, Dulverton, Somerset TA22 9HL. Tel: 01398-23665. *National Park Officer*, K. Bungay

LAKE DISTRICT (1951), 2,292 sq. km/885 sq. miles – The park lies wholly in Cumbria. The Lake District includes England's highest mountains (Scafell Pike, Helvellyn and Skiddaw) but it is most famous for its glaciated lakes. There are information centres at Keswick, Waterhead, Hawkshead, Seatoller, Bowness, Grasmere, Coniston, Glenridding and Pooley Bridge, an information van at Gosforth and a park centre at Brockhole, Windermere. *Information Office*, Brockhole, Windermere, Cumbria LA23 1LJ. Tel: 01539-446601. *National Park Officer*, J. Toothill

NORTHUMBERLAND (1956), 1,049 sq. km/405 sq. miles – The park lies wholly in Northumberland. It is an area of hill country stretching from Hadrian's Wall to the Scottish Border. There are information centres at Ingram, Once Brewed, Rothbury, Housesteads, Harbottle and Kielder, and an information caravan at Cawfields. *Information Office*, Eastburn, South Park, Hexham, Northumberland NE46 1BS. Tel: 01434-605555. *National Park Officer*, G. Taylor

NORTH YORK MOORS (1952), 1,436 sq. km/554 sq. miles – The park lies in North Yorkshire (96 per cent) and Cleveland. It consists of woodland and moorland, and includes the Hambleton Hills and the Cleveland Way. There are information centres at Danby, Pickering, Sutton Bank, Ravenscar, Helmsley and Hutton-le-Hole, and a day study centre at Danby. *Information Office*, The Old Vicarage, Bondgate, Helmsley, York YO6 5BP. Tel: 01439-70657. *National Park Officer*, D. Statham

PEAK DISTRICT (1951), 1,438 sq. km/555 sq. miles – The park lies in Derbyshire (64 per cent), Staffordshire, South Yorkshire, Cheshire, West Yorkshire and Greater Manchester. The Peak District includes the gritstone moors of the 'dark peak' and the limestone dales of the 'white peak'. There are information centres at Bakewell, Edale, Fairholmes and Castleton, and information points at Torside (in the Longdendale Valley) and at Hartington (former station).

*Information Office*, Aldern House, Baslow Road, Bakewell, Derbyshire DE45 1AE. Tel: 01629-814321. *National Park Officer*, C. Harrison

PEMBROKESHIRE COAST (1952), 584 sq. km/225 sq. miles – The park lies wholly in Dyfed. It consists of cliffs, moorland and Skomer Island. There are information centres at Tenby, St David's, Pembroke, Newport, Kilgetty, Haverfordwest and Broad Haven.
*Information Office*, County Offices, Haverfordwest, Dyfed SA61 1QZ. Tel: 01437-764591. *National Park Officer*, N. Wheeler

SNOWDONIA (1951), 2,142 sq. km/827 sq. miles – Snowdonia lies wholly in Gwynedd. It is an area of deep valleys and rugged mountains. There are information centres at Aberdovey, Bala, Betws y Coed, Blaenau Ffestiniog, Conwy, Harlech, Dolgellau and Llanberis.
*Information Office*, Penrhyndeudraeth, Gwynedd LL48 6LS. Tel: 01766-770274. *National Park Officer*, A. Jones

YORKSHIRE DALES (1954), 1,769 sq. km/683 sq. miles – The park lies in North Yorkshire (88 per cent) and Cumbria. The Yorkshire Dales are composed primarily of limestone overlaid in places by millstone grit. The three peaks of Ingleborough, Whernside and Pen-y-Ghent are within the park. There are information centres at Clapham, Grassington, Hawes, Aysgarth Falls, Malham and Sedbergh.
*Information Office*, Yorebridge House, Bainbridge, Leyburn, North Yorkshire DL8 3BP. Tel: 01969-50456. *National Park Officer*, R. Harvey

Two other areas considered to have equivalent status to national parks are the Broads and the New Forest. The Broads Authority, a special statutory authority, was established in 1989 to develop, conserve and manage the Norfolk and Suffolk Broads (*see also* Government Departments and Public Offices). The Government declared in 1992 its intention of giving the New Forest a status equivalent to that of a National Park by declaring it an 'area of national significance'.

THE BROADS (1989), 303 sq. km/117 sq. miles – The Broads are located between Norwich and Great Yarmouth on the flood plains of the five rivers flowing through the area to the sea. The area is one of fens, winding waterways, woodland and marsh. The forty or so broads are man-made, and are connected to the rivers by dykes, providing over 200 km of navigable waterways. There are information centres at Beccles, Hoveton, North-west Tower (Yarmouth), Ranworth and Toad Hole.
*Broads Authority*, Thomas Harvey House, 18 Colegate, Norwich NR3 1BQ. Tel: 01603-610734. *Chief Executive*, A. Clark

THE NEW FOREST, 376 sq. km/145 sq. miles – The forest has been protected since 1079 when it was declared a royal hunting forest. The area consists of forest, ancient woodland and heathland. Much of the Forest is managed by the Forestry Commission, which provides several camp-sites. The main villages are Brockenhurst, Burley and Lyndhurst, which has a visitor centre.
*The Forestry Commission*, Office of the Deputy Surveyor of the New Forest and the New Forest Committee, The Queen's House, Lyndhurst, Hants. SO43 7NH. Tel: 01703-284149

SCOTLAND AND NORTHERN IRELAND

The National Parks and Access to the Countryside Act 1949 dealt only with England and Wales and made no provision for Scotland or Northern Ireland. Although there are no national parks in these two countries, there is power to designate them in Northern Ireland under the Amenity Lands Act 1965 and the Nature Conservation and Amenity Lands Order (Northern Ireland) 1985. In 1989 the Scottish Office asked Scottish Natural Heritage to report on whether national parks should be designated in Scotland.

AREAS OF OUTSTANDING NATURAL BEAUTY

ENGLAND AND WALES

Under the National Parks and Access to the Countryside Act 1949, provision was made for the designation of Areas of Outstanding Natural Beauty (AONBs) by the Countryside Commission. The Countryside Act 1968 further defines the role of AONBs, suggesting that they should show due regard for the interests of other land users, such as agriculture and forestry groups. The Countryside Commission continues to be responsible for AONBs in England but since April 1991 the Countryside Council for Wales has been responsible for the Welsh AONBs. Designations in England are confirmed by the Secretary of State for the Environment and those in Wales by the Secretary of State for Wales.

Although less emphasis is placed upon the provision of open-air enjoyment for the public than in the national parks, AONBs are areas which are no less beautiful and require the same degree of protection to conserve and enhance the natural beauty of the countryside. This includes protecting flora and fauna, geological and other landscape features. In AONBs planning and management responsibilities are split between county and district councils (there are 17 which cross county boundaries). Finance for the AONBs is provided by grant-aid.

The forty Areas of Outstanding Natural Beauty (with date designation confirmed) are:

ANGLESEY (1967), 215 sq. km/83 sq. miles – The area extends along the entire coastline of the island, except for breaks around the urban areas and in the vicinity of Wylfa

ARNSIDE AND SILVERDALE (1972), 75 sq. km/29 sq. miles – The area embraces the upper half of Morecambe Bay, the Kent estuary, and includes extensive tidal flats in the Bay

BLACKDOWN HILLS (1991), 370 sq. km/143 sq. miles – An area of greensand ridges in Devon and Somerset extending from Cullompton in the west to Chard in the east, south of Taunton to north of Honiton

CANNOCK CHASE (1958), 68 sq. km/26 sq. miles – An area of high heathland in Staffordshire. Deer continue to roam over the Chase

CHICHESTER HARBOUR (1964), 74 sq. km/29 sq. miles – The area extends from Hayling Island to Apuldram and includes Thorney Island

CHILTERNS (1965; extended 1990), 833 sq. km/322 sq. miles – Chalk downlands running from South Oxfordshire north-eastwards to Bedfordshire, including the outlying group of hills beyond Luton

CLWYDIAN RANGE (1985), 156 sq. km/60 sq. miles – A prominent ridge extending southwards from Prestatyn on the north Wales coast. Offa's Dyke runs along the crest of the range

CORNWALL (1959; Camel estuary 1983), 958 sq. km/370 sq. miles – A number of separate areas including Bodmin Moor, most of the Land's End peninsula, the coast between St Michael's Mount and St Austell (with Falmouth omitted), the Fowey estuary; in north Cornwall most of the coast to Bedruthan Steps and between Perranporth and Godrevy Towans, and the Camel estuary

COTSWOLDS (1966; extended 1990), 2,038 sq. km/787 sq. miles – The area of limestone hills above the Vales of Gloucester and Evesham

CRANBORNE CHASE AND WEST WILTSHIRE DOWNS (1983), 983 sq. km/379 sq. miles – A mainly chalkland and greensand area covering parts of Wiltshire, Dorset, Hampshire and Somerset, including the wooded remnants of the ancient Chase

DEDHAM VALE (1970; extended 1978, 1991), 90 sq. km/35 sq. miles – The area on the Essex/Suffolk border where John Constable painted

EAST DEVON (1963), 268 sq. km/103 sq. miles – The coastline between Exmouth and Lyme Regis, with Sidmouth, Beer and Seaton omitted. Inland, Gittisham Hill, East Hill and Woodbury and Aylebeare Commons are included

NORTH DEVON (1960), 171 sq. km/66 sq. miles – Includes most of the North Devon coastline, from just north of Bude to the boundary of the Exmoor National Park

SOUTH DEVON (1960), 337 sq. km/130 sq. miles – Includes the coast between Bolt Head and Bolt Tail, Salcombe, Slapton Sands and Dartmouth, and the estuaries and valleys of the Yealm, Erme, Avon and Dart

DORSET (1959), 1,129 sq. km/436 sq. miles – The coastline between Lyme Regis and Poole, with the Isle of Portland and Weymouth omitted, stretching inland to include the Purbeck Hills and the downs of Hardy country

FOREST OF BOWLAND (1964), 802 sq. km/310 sq. miles – A moorland area mostly in Lancashire running westward from the River Ribble, with a small outlying area east of the Ribble which includes Pendle Hill

GOWER (1956), 189 sq. km/73 sq. miles – A peninsula in West Glamorgan, known for its coastline

EAST HAMPSHIRE (1962), 383 sq. km/148 sq. miles – A chalkland area stretching from the outskirts of Winchester to the Sussex border about 10 miles inland

SOUTH HAMPSHIRE COAST (1967), 77 sq. km/30 sq. miles – The coastline between Hurst Castle and Calshot Castle, extending inland up the River Beaulieu for about six miles

HIGH WEALD (1983), 1,460 sq. km/564 sq. miles – The area covers parts of East and West Sussex, Kent and Surrey. It is predominantly wooded, and includes larger heathland areas like Ashdown Forest, the remnants of the old Wealden forests

HOWARDIAN HILLS (1987), 204 sq. km/79 sq. miles – Wooded hills which rise above the Vales of York and Pickering

KENT DOWNS (1968), 878 sq. km/339 sq. miles – Running east and south-east from the Surrey border near Westerham to the coast near Dover and Folkestone, with a coastal outlier at South Foreland and a narrow strip of the old sea cliff escarpment west of Hythe overlooking Romney Marsh

LINCOLNSHIRE WOLDS (1973), 558 sq. km/215 sq. miles – The area extends in a south-easterly direction from Laceby and Caistor in the north to the region of Spilsby, about ten miles west of the coast

LLEYN (1957), 155 sq. km/60 sq. miles – The peninsula forming the westernmost part of the county of Gwynedd

MALVERN HILLS (1959), 105 sq. km/40 sq. miles – The whole range of the Malvern Hills in the county of Hereford and Worcester, just touching Gloucestershire

MENDIP HILLS (1972; extended 1989), 198 sq. km/76 sq. miles – Comprising over half of the Mendip Hills, the area stretches from Bleadon Hill to the A39 road north of Wells and includes Cheddar Gorge and Wookey Hole

NIDDERDALE (1994), 603 sq. km/233 sq. miles – The eastern fringe of the Yorkshire Pennines, containing moorland and dales such as the Skell, Washburn, and Nidderdale itself

NORFOLK COAST (1968), 451 sq. km/174 sq. miles – An almost continuous coastal strip three to five miles in depth from Hunstanton to Bacton, with a further small strip between Sea Palling and Winterton-on-Sea. The area includes part of the Sandringham estate

NORTH PENNINES (1988), 1,998 sq. km/766 sq. miles – The northern limit of the Pennine chain, covering parts of Cumbria, Co. Durham and Northumberland

NORTHUMBERLAND COAST (1958), 135 sq. km/52 sq. miles – Stretches from just south of Berwick to Amble and includes Holy Island and the Farne Islands

QUANTOCK HILLS (1957), 99 sq. km/38 sq. miles – A range of sandstone hills in Somerset

ISLES OF SCILLY (1976), 16 sq. km/6 sq. miles – About 140 islands and skerries in the Scillies group of which only five are inhabited. There are a number of Sites of Special Scientific Interest

SHROPSHIRE HILLS (1959), 804 sq. km/310 sq. miles – Most of south-west Shropshire between the Welsh border and the boundary with Hereford and Worcester, including the region around Clun, the area of the Stiperstones, the Long Mynd and Wenlock Edge, with the tongues of land running north-east to the Wrekin and south towards Ludlow

SOLWAY COAST (1964), 115 sq. km/44 sq. miles – A stretch of coastline in Cumbria from Maryport to the estuaries of the Rivers Eden and Esk (with Silloth omitted) backed by the Solway Plain

SUFFOLK COAST AND HEATHS (1970), 403 sq. km/156 sq. miles – The area includes 38 miles of coastline and parts of the Stour and Orwell estuaries, while the Rivers Deben, Alde and Blyth flow through it

SURREY HILLS (1958), 419 sq. km/162 sq. miles – An area to the east and south of Guildford, including the Hog's Back and the ridge of the North Downs

SUSSEX DOWNS (1966), 983 sq. km/379 sq. miles – The area includes the chalk escarpment of the South Downs from Beachy Head to the Hampshire border, and stretches down to the coast between Eastbourne and Seaford

NORTH WESSEX DOWNS (1972), 1,730 sq. km/668 sq. miles – An upland area in Hampshire, Wiltshire, Oxfordshire and Berkshire, bounded by the Marlborough and Lambourn Downs in the west, the Chiltern Hills in the east and Salisbury Plain in the south

ISLE OF WIGHT (1963), 189 sq. km/73 sq. miles – A number of separate areas comprising stretches of coastline, the Yar Valley, the high downland behind Ventnor and the chalk ridge which runs from Newport to Culver Cliff and Foreland

WYE VALLEY (1971), 326 sq. km/126 sq. miles – The deep, wooded river valley running through the counties of Gwent, Gloucestershire, and Hereford and Worcester

Proposals for further designations include the Tamar valley in Devon/Cornwall.

## NORTHERN IRELAND

The Department of the Environment for Northern Ireland, with advice from the Council for Nature Conservation and the Countryside, designates Areas of Outstanding Natural Beauty in Northern Ireland. At present there are nine and these cover a total area of approximately 284,948 hectares (704,121 acres).

ANTRIM COAST AND GLENS, Co. Antrim, 70,600 ha/
   174,452 acres
CAUSEWAY COAST, Co. Antrim, 4,200 ha/10,378 acres
LAGAN VALLEY, Co. Down, 2,072 ha/5,119 acres
LECALE COAST, Co. Down, 3,108 ha/7,679 acres
MOURNE, Co. Down, 57,012 ha/140,876 acres
NORTH DERRY, Co. Londonderry, 12,950 ha/31,999 acres
RING OF GULLION, Co. Armagh, 15,353 ha/37,938 acres
SPERRIN, Co. Tyrone/Co. Londonderry, 101,006 ha/
   249,585 acres
STRANGFORD LOUGH, Co. Down, 18,647 ha/46,077 acres

---

## NATIONAL SCENIC AREAS

---

No Areas of Outstanding Natural Beauty are designated in Scotland. However, National Scenic Areas have a broadly equivalent status. Scottish Natural Heritage recognizes areas of national scenic significance. At present there are 40, covering a total area of 1,001,800 hectares (2,475,448 acres).

Development within National Scenic Areas is dealt with by the local planning authority, who are required to consult Scottish Natural Heritage concerning certain categories of development. Land management uses can also be modified in the interest of scenic conservation. The Secretary of State for Scotland has limited powers of intervention should a planning authority and Scottish Natural Heritage disagree.

| | hectares | acres |
|---|---|---|
| BORDER | | |
| Eildon and Leaderfoot | 3,600 | 8,896 |
| Upper Tweeddale | 10,500 | 25,945 |
| CENTRAL | | |
| *Loch Lomond | 11,200 | 27,675 |
| *Loch Rannoch and Glen Lyon | 1,300 | 3,212 |
| The Trossachs | 4,600 | 11,367 |
| DUMFRIES AND GALLOWAY | | |
| East Stewartry Coast | 4,500 | 11,119 |
| Fleet Valley | 5,300 | 13,096 |
| Nith Estuary | 9,300 | 22,980 |
| GRAMPIAN | | |
| *The Cairngorm Mountains | 29,800 | 73,636 |
| *Deeside and Lochnagar | 32,200 | 79,566 |
| HIGHLAND | | |
| Assynt-Coigach | 90,200 | 222,884 |
| *Ben Nevis and Glen Coe | 79,600 | 196,692 |
| *The Cairngorm Mountains | 37,400 | 92,415 |
| The Cuillin Hills | 21,900 | 54,115 |
| Dornoch Firth | 7,500 | 18,532 |
| Glen Affric | 19,300 | 47,690 |
| Glen Strathfarrar | 3,800 | 9,390 |
| Kintail | 15,500 | 38,300 |
| Knoydart | 39,500 | 97,604 |
| Kyle of Tongue | 18,500 | 45,713 |
| Loch Shiel | 13,400 | 33,111 |
| Morar, Moidart and Ardna-
   murchan | 13,500 | 33,358 |
| North-west Sutherland | 20,500 | 50,655 |
| The Small Isles | 15,500 | 38,300 |
| Trotternish | 5,000 | 12,355 |
| Wester Ross | 145,300 | 359,036 |
| ORKNEY ISLANDS | | |
| Hoy and West Mainland | 14,800 | 36,571 |
| SHETLAND ISLANDS | | |
| Shetland | 11,600 | 28,664 |

| STRATHCLYDE | | |
|---|---|---|
| *Ben Nevis and Glen Coe | 17,500 | 43,242 |
| Jura | 21,800 | 53,868 |
| Knapdale | 19,800 | 48,926 |
| Kyles of Bute | 4,400 | 10,872 |
| *Loch Lomond | 16,200 | 40,030 |
| Loch na Keal, Isle of Mull | 12,700 | 31,382 |
| Lynn of Lorn | 4,800 | 11,861 |
| North Arran | 23,800 | 58,810 |
| Scarba, Lunga and the Garvel-
   lachs | 1,900 | 4,695 |
| TAYSIDE | | |
| *Ben Nevis and Glen Coe | 4,500 | 11,119 |
| *Deeside and Lochnagar | 7,800 | 19,274 |
| *Loch Rannoch and Glen Lyon | 47,100 | 116,384 |
| Loch Tummel | 9,200 | 22,733 |
| River Earn | 3,000 | 7,413 |
| River Tay | 5,600 | 13,838 |
| WESTERN ISLES | | |
| St Kilda | 900 | 2,224 |
| South Lewis, Harris and North
   Uist | 109,600 | 270,822 |
| South Uist Machair | 6,100 | 15,073 |
| TOTAL | 1,001,800 | 2,475,448 |

*National Scenic Areas in more than one region

# Nature Conservation Areas

---

## SITES OF SPECIAL SCIENTIFIC INTEREST

---

Site of Special Scientific Interest (SSSI) is a legal designation applied to land in England, Scotland or Wales which English Nature (EN), Scottish Natural Heritage (SNH), or the Countryside Council for Wales (CCW) identifies as being of special interest because of its flora, fauna, geological or physiographical features. In some cases, SSSI are managed as nature reserves.

EN, SNH and CCW must notify the designation of a SSSI to the local planning authority, every owner/occupier of the land, and the Secretary of State for the Environment (or Secretary of State for Scotland or for Wales where applicable). Forestry and agricultural departments and a number of other bodies are also informed of this designation.

Objections to the designation of a SSSI can be made and ultimately considered at a full meeting of the Council of EN or the Statutory Protection Committee of CCW. In Scotland an objection will be dealt with by the appropriate regional board or the main board of SNH, depending on the nature of the objection. Unresolved objections on scientific grounds must be referred to the Advisory Committee for SSSI.

The protection of these sites depends on the co-operation of individual landowners and occupiers. Owner/occupiers must consult EN, SNH or CCW and gain written consent before they can undertake certain listed activities on the site. Funds are available through management agreements and grants to assist owners and occupiers in conserving sites' interests. As a last resort a site can be purchased.

As at 31 March 1994 there were 6,057 SSSI in Britain, covering 1,923,155 hectares (4,751,911 acres).

|  | no. | hectares | acres |
|---|---|---|---|
| England | 3,794 | 871,066 | 2,152,404 |
| Scotland | 1,373 | 846,830 | 2,092,517 |
| Wales | 890 | 205,259 | 506,990 |

## NORTHERN IRELAND

In Northern Ireland 54 Areas of Special Scientific Interest (ASSIs) have been established by the Department of the Environment for Northern Ireland. These cover a total area of 54,408 hectares (134,388 acres).

## NATIONAL NATURE RESERVES

National Nature Reserves are defined in the National Parks and Access to the Countryside Act 1949 as land designated for the study and preservation of flora and fauna, or of geological or physiographical features.

English Nature (EN), Scottish Natural Heritage (SNH) or the Countryside Council for Wales (CCW) can designate as a National Nature Reserve land which is being managed as a nature reserve under an agreement with one of the statutory nature conservation agencies; land held and managed by EN, SNH or CCW; or land held and managed as a nature reserve by another approved body. EN, SNH or CCW can turn to the appropriate Secretary of State to impose by-laws for the protection of the reserves from undesirable development.

As at 31 March 1994 there were 270 National Nature Reserves in Britain, covering 187,579 hectares (463,495 acres).

|  | no. | hectares | acres |
|---|---|---|---|
| England | 150 | 59,327 | 146,597 |
| Scotland | 71 | 114,838 | 283,765 |
| Wales | 49 | 13,414 | 33,133 |

## NORTHERN IRELAND

National Nature Reserves are established and managed by the Department of the Environment for Northern Ireland, with advice from the Council for Nature Conservation and the Countryside. There are 45 National Nature Reserves covering 4,574 hectares (11,297 acres).

## LOCAL NATURE RESERVES

Local Nature Reserves are defined in the National Parks and Access to the Countryside Act 1949 as land designated for the study and preservation of flora and fauna, or of geological or physiographical features. The Act gives local authorities in England and Wales and district councils in Scotland the power to acquire, declare and manage local nature reserves in consultation with English Nature, Scottish Natural Heritage and the Countryside Council for Wales. Conservation trusts can also own and manage non-statutory local nature reserves.

As at 31 March 1994 there were 429 designated Local Nature Reserve areas in Britain, covering 22,994 hectares (56,814 acres).

|  | no. | hectares | acres |
|---|---|---|---|
| England | 393 | 15,748 | 38,913 |
| Scotland | 15 | 3,332 | 8,233 |
| Wales | 21 | 3,914 | 9,668 |

An additional 17.19 km of linear trails are designated as Local Nature Reserves.

## FOREST NATURE RESERVES

Forest Enterprise (part of the Forestry Commission) has created 46 Forest Nature Reserves from conservation sites within its estate. Their purpose is to protect and conserve special forms of natural habitat, flora and fauna existing in forested areas. Forest Enterprise has 400 SSSI on its estates, some of which are also Forest Nature Reserves.

Forest Nature Reserves extend in size from under 50 hectares (124 acres) to 500 hectares (1,236 acres). The largest include the Black Wood of Rannoch, by Loch Rannoch; Cannop Valley Oakwoods, Forest of Dean; Culbin Forest, near Forres; Glen Affric, near Fort Augustus; Kylerhea, Skye; Pembrey, Carmarthen Bay; Starr Forest, in Galloway Forest Park; and Wyre Forest, near Kidderminster.

## NORTHERN IRELAND

There are 36 Forest Nature Reserves in Northern Ireland, covering 1,759 hectares (4,346 acres). They are designated and administered by the Forest Service, a division of the Department of Agriculture for Northern Ireland. There are also 15 National Nature Reserves on Forest Service-owned property.

## MARINE NATURE RESERVES

The Wildlife and Countryside Act 1981 gives the Secretary of State for the Environment (and the Secretaries of State for Wales and for Scotland where appropriate) power to designate Marine Nature Reserves, and English Nature, Scottish Natural Heritage and the Countryside Council for Wales powers to select and manage these reserves.

Marine Nature Reserves provide protection for marine flora and fauna, and geological and physiographical features on land covered by tidal waters or parts of the sea in or adjacent to Great Britain. Reserves also provide opportunities for study and research.

The two statutory Marine Nature Reserves are:

LUNDY (1986), Bristol Channel
SKOMER (1990), Dyfed

Other areas proposed for designation as reserves are: the Menai Strait, Bardsey Island, and part of the Lleyn peninsula, Gwynedd.

A number of non-statutory marine reserves have been set up by conservation groups.

# Wildlife Conservation

## PROTECTED SPECIES

The Wildlife and Countryside Act 1981 gives legal protection to a wide range of wild animals and plants. Subject to parliamentary approval, the Secretary of State for the Environment may vary the animals and plants given legal protection. The most recent variation of Schedules 5 and 8 came into effect in October 1992.

### ANIMALS, ETC.

Under Section 9 and Schedule 5 of the Act it is illegal without a licence to kill, injure, take, possess or sell any of the animals mentioned below (whether alive or dead) and to disturb its place of shelter and protection or to destroy that place.

†Adder (*Vipera berus*)
§Allis shad (*alosa alosa*)
Anemone, Ivell's Sea (*Edwardsia ivelli*)
Anemone, Startlet Sea (*Nematostella vectensis*)
Apus (*Triops cancriformis*)
Bat, Horseshoe (*Rhinolophidae*, all species)
Bat, Typical (*Vespertilionidae*, all species)
Beetle (*Graphoderus zonatus*)
Beetle (*Hypebaeus flavipes*)
Beetle (*Paracymus aeneus*)
Beetle, Lesser Silver Water (*Hydrochara caraboides*)
§§Beetle, Mire Pill (*Curimopsis nigrita*)
Beetle, Rainbow Leaf (*Chrysolina cerealis*)
Beetle, Violet Click (*Limoniscus violaceus*)
Burbot (*Lota lota*)
*Butterfly, Adonis Blue (*Lysandra bellargus*)
*Butterfly, Black Hairstreak (*Strymonidia pruni*)
*Butterfly, Brown Hairstreak (*Thecla betulae*)
*Butterfly, Chalkhill Blue (*Lysandra coridon*)
*Butterfly, Chequered Skipper (*Carterocephalus palaemon*)
*Butterfly, Duke of Burgundy Fritillary (*Hamearis lucina*)
*Butterfly, Glanville Fritillary (*Melitaea cinxia*)
Butterfly, Heath Fritillary (*Mellicta athalia* (or *Melitaea athalia*))
Butterfly, High Brown Fritillary (*Argynnis adippe*)
Butterfly, Large Blue (*Maculinea arion*)
*Butterfly, Large Copper (*Lycaena dispar*)
*Butterfly, Large Heath (*Coenonympha tullia*)
*Butterfly, Large Tortoiseshell (*Nymphalis polychloros*)
*Butterfly, Lulworth Skipper (*Thymelicus acteon*)
*Butterfly, Marsh Fritillary (*Eurodryas aurinia*)
*Butterfly, Mountain Ringlet (*Erebia epiphron*)
*Butterfly, Northern Brown Argus (*Aricia artaxerxes*)
*Butterfly, Pearl-bordered Fritillary (*Boloria euphrosyne*)
*Butterfly, Purple Emperor (*Apatura iris*)
*Butterfly, Silver Spotted Skipper (*Hesperia comma*)
*Butterfly, Silver-studded Blue (*Plebejus argus*)
*Butterfly, Small Blue (*Cupido minimus*)
Butterfly, Swallowtail (*Papilio machaon*)
*Butterfly, White Letter Hairstreak (*Stymonida w-album*)

*Butterfly, Wood White (*Leptidea sinapis*)
Cat, Wild (*Felis silvestris*)
Cicada, New Forest (*Cicadetta montana*)
**Crayfish, Atlantic Stream (*Austropotamobius pallipes*)
Cricket, Field (*Gryllus campestris*)
Cricket, Mole (*Gryllotalpa gryllotalpa*)
Dolphin (*Cetacea*)
Dormouse (*Muscardinus avellanarius*)
Dragonfly, Norfolk Aeshna (*Aeshna isosceles*)
*Frog, Common (*Rana temporaria*)
Grasshopper, Wart-biter (*Decticus verrucivorus*)
Hatchet Shell, Northern (*Thyasira gouldi*)
Lagoon Snail (*Paludinella littorina*)
Lagoon Snail, De Folin's (*Caecum armoricum*)
Lagoon Worm, Tentacled (*Alkmaria romijni*)
Leech, Medicinal (*Hirudo medicinalis*)
Lizard, Sand (*Lacerta agilis*)
‡Lizard, Viviparous(*Lacerta vivipara*)
Marten, Pine (*Martes martes*)
Moth, Barberry Carpet (*Pareulype berberata*)
Moth, Black-veined (*Siona lineata* (or *Idaea lineata*))
Moth, Essex Emerald (*Thetidia smaragdaria*)
Moth, New Forest Burnet (*Zygaena viciae*)
Moth, Reddish Buff (*Acosmetia caliginosa*)
Moth, Sussex Emerald (*Thalera fimbrialis*)
Moth, Viper's Bugloss (*Hadena irregularis*)
Mussel, Freshwater Pearl (*Margaritifera margaritifera*)
Newt, Great Crested (or Warty) (*Triturus cristatus*)
*Newt, Palmate (*Triturus helveticus*)
*Newt, Smooth (*Triturus vulgaris*)
Otter, Common (*Lutra lutra*)
Porpoise (*Cetacea*)
Sandworm, Lagoon (*Armandia cirrhosa*)
Sea Fan, Pink (*Eunicella verrucosa*)
Sea-Mat, Trembling (*Victorella pavida*)
Sea Slug, Lagoon (*Tenellia adspersa*)
Shrimp, Fairy (*Chirocephalus diaphanus*)
Shrimp, Lagoon Sand (*Gammarus insensibilis*)
‡Slow-worm (*Anguis fragilis*)
Snail, Glutinous (*Myxas glutinosa*)
Snail, Sandbowl (*Catinella arenaria*)
‡Snake, Grass (*Natrix natrix* (*Natrix helvetica*))
Snake, Smooth (*Coronella austriaca*)
Spider, Fen Raft (*Dolomedes plantarius*)
Spider, Ladybird (*Eresus niger*)
Squirrel, Red (*Sciurus vulgaris*)
Sturgeon (*Acipenser sturio*)
*Toad, Common (*Bufo bufo*)
Toad, Natterjack (*Bufo calamita*)
Turtle, Marine (*Dermochelyidae* and *Cheloniidae*, all species)
Vendace (*Coregonus albula*)
Walrus (*Odobenus rosmarus*)
Whale (*Cetacea*)
Whitefish (*Coregonus lavaretus*)

### PLANTS

Under Section 13 and Schedule 8 of the Wildlife and Countryside Act 1981, it is illegal without a licence to pick, uproot, sell or destroy any of the plants mentioned below and, unless authorized, to uproot any wild plant.

Adder's tongue, Least (*Ophioglossum lusitanicum*)
Alison, Small (*Alyssum alyssoides*)
Blackwort (*Southbya nigrella*)
Broomrape, Bedstraw (*Orobanche caryophyllacea*)

---

*the offence relates to 'sale' only
**the offence relates to 'taking' and 'sale' only
†the offence relates to 'killing and injuring' only
‡the offence relates to 'killing, injuring and sale'
§the offence relates to 'killing, injuring and taking'
§§the offence relates only to damaging, destroying or obstructing access to a shelter or protection, or disturbing during occupation of such

Broomrape, Oxtongue (*Orobanche loricata*)
Broomrape, Thistle (*Orobanche reticulata*)
Cabbage, Lundy (*Rhynchosinapis wrightii*)
Calamint, Wood (*Calamintha sylvatica*)
Caloplaca, Snow (*Caloplaca nivalis*)
Catapyrenium, Tree (*Catapyrenium psoromoides*)
Catchfly, Alpine (*Lychnis alpina*)
Catillaria, Laurer's (*Catellaria laureri*)
Centaury, Slender (*Centaurium tenuiflorum*)
Cinquefoil, Rock (*Potentilla rupestris*)
Cladonia, Upright Mountain (*Cladonia stricta*)
Clary, Meadow (*Salvia pratensis*)
Club-rush, Triangular (*Scirpus triquetrus*)
Colt's-foot, Purple (*Homogyne alpina*)
Cotoneaster, Wild (*Cotoneaster integerrimus*)
Cottongrass, Slender (*Eriophorum gracile*)
Cow-wheat, Field (*Melampyrum arvense*)
Crocus, Sand (*Romulea columnae*)
Crystalwort, Lizard (*Riccia bifurca*)
Cudweed, Broad-leaved (*Filago pyramidata*)
Cudweed, Jersey (*Gnaphalium luteoalbum*)
Cudweed, Red-tipped (*Filago lutescens*)
Diapensia (*Diapensia lapponica*)
Dock, Shore (*Rumex rupestris*)
Earwort, Marsh (*Jamesoniella undulifolia*)
Eryngo, Field (*Eryngium campestre*)
Fern, Dickie's bladder (*Cystopteris dickieana*)
Fern, Killarney (*Trichomanes speciosum*)
Flapwort, Norfolk (*Leiocolea rutheana*)
Fleabane, Alpine (*Erigeron borealis*)
Fleabane, Small (*Pulicaria vulgaris*)
Frostwort, Pointed (*Gymnomitrion apiculatum*)
Galingale, Brown (*Cyperus fuscus*)
Gentian, Alpine (*Gentiana nivalis*)
Gentian, Dune (*Gentianella uliginosa*)
Gentian, Early (*Gentianella anglica*)
Gentian, Fringed (*Gentianella ciliata*)
Gentian, Spring (*Gentiana verna*)
Germander, Cut-leaved (*Teucrium botrys*)
Germander, Water (*Teucrium scordium*)
Gladiolus, Wild (*Gladiolus illyricus*)
Goosefoot, Stinking (*Chenopodium vulvaria*)
Grass-poly (*Lythrum hyssopifolia*)
Grimmia, Blunt-leaved (*Grimmia unicolor*)
Gyalecta, Elm (*Gyalecta ulmi*)
Hare's-ear, Sickle-leaved (*Bupleurum falcatum*)
Hare's-ear, Small (*Bupleurum baldense*)
Hawk's-beard, Stinking (*Crepis foetida*)
Hawkweed, Northroe (*Hieracium northroense*)
Hawkweed, Shetland (*Hieracium zetlandicum*)
Hawkweed, Weak-leaved (*Hieracium attenuatifolium*)
Heath, Blue (*Phyllodoce caerulea*)
Helleborine, Red (*Cephalanthera rubra*)
Helleborine, Young's (*Epipactis youngiana*)
Horsetail, Branched (*Equisetum ramosissimum*)
Hound's-tongue, Green (*Cynoglossum germanicum*)
Knawel, Perennial (*Scleranthus perennis*)
Knotgrass, Sea (*Polygonum maritimum*)
Lady's-slipper (*Cypripedium calceolus*)
Lecanactis, Churchyard (*Lecanactis hemisphaerica*)
Lecanora, Tarn (*Lecanora archariana*)
Lecidea, Copper (*Lecidea inops*)
Leek, Round-headed (*Allium sphaerocephalon*)
Lettuce, Least (*Lactuca saligna*)
Lichen, Arctic Kidney (*Nephroma arcticum*)
Lichen, Ciliate Strap (*Heterodermia leucomelos*)
Lichen, Coralloid Rosette (*Heterodermia propagulifera*)
Lichen, Ear-lobed Dog (*Peltigera lepidophora*)
Lichen, Forked Hair (*Bryoria furcellata*)

Lichen, Golden Hair (*Teloschistes flavicans*)
Lichen, Orange Fruited Elm (*Caloplaca luteoalba*)
Lichen, River Jelly (*Collema dichotomum*)
Lichen, Scaly Breck (*Squamarina lentigera*)
Lichen, Stary Breck (*Buellia asterella*)
Lily, Snowdon (*Lloydia serotina*)
Liverwort (*Petallophyllum ralfsi*)
Liverwort, Lindenberg's Leafy (*Adelanthus lindenbergianus*)
Marsh-mallow, Rough (*Althaea hirsuta*)
Marshwort, Creeping (*Apium repens*)
Milk-parsley, Cambridge (*Selinum carvifolia*)
Moss (*Drepanocladius vernicosus*)
Moss, Alpine Copper (*Mielichoferia mielichoferi*)
Moss, Baltic Bog (*Sphagnum balticum*)
Moss, Blue Dew (*Saelania glaucescens*)
Moss, Blunt-leaved Bristle (*Orthotrichum obtusifolium*)
Moss, Bright Green Cave (*Cyclodictyon laetevirens*)
Moss, Cordate Beard (*Barbula cordata*)
Moss, Cornish Path (*Ditrichum cornubicum*)
Moss, Derbyshire Feather (*Thamnobryum angustifolium*)
Moss, Dune Thread (*Bryum mamillatum*)
Moss, Glaucous Beard (*Barbula glauca*)
Moss, Green Shield (*Buxbaumia viridis*)
Moss, Hair Silk (*Plagiothecium piliferum*)
Moss, Knothole (*Zygodon forsteri*)
Moss, Large Yellow Feather (*Scorpidium turgescens*)
Moss, Millimetre (*Micromitrium tenerum*)
Moss, Multifruited River (*Cryphaea lamyana*)
Moss, Nowell's Limestone (*Zygodon gracilis*)
Moss, Rigid Apple (*Bartramia stricta*)
Moss, Round-leaved Feather (*Rhyncostegium rotundifolium*)
Moss, Schleicher's Thread (*Bryum schleicheri*)
Moss, Triangular Pygmy (*Acaulon triquetrum*)
Moss, Vaucher's Feather (*Hypnum vaucheri*)
Mudwort, Welsh (*Limosella australis*)
Naiad, Holly-leaved (*Najas marina*)
Naiad, Slender (*Najas flexilis*)
Orache, Stalked (*Halimione pedunculata*)
Orchid, Early Spider (*Ophrys sphegodes*)
Orchid, Fen (*Liparis loeselii*)
Orchid, Ghost (*Epipogium aphyllum*)
Orchid, Lapland Marsh (*Dactylorhiza lapponica*)
Orchid, Late Spider (*Ophrys fuciflora*)
Orchid, Lizard (*Himantoglossum hircinum*)
Orchid, Military (*Orchis militaris*)
Orchid, Monkey (*Orchis simia*)
Pannaria, Caledonia (*Pannaria ignobilis*)
Parmelia, New Forest (*Parmelia minarum*)
Parmentaria, Oil Stain (*Parmentaria chilensis*)
Pear, Plymouth (*Pyrus cordata*)
Penny-cress, Perfoliate (*Thlaspi perfoliatum*)
Pennyroyal (*Mentha pulegium*)
Pertusaria, Alpine Moss (*Pertusaria bryontha*)
Physcia, Southern Grey (*Physcia tribacioides*)
Pigmyweed (*Crassula aquatica*)
Pine, Ground (*Ajuga chamaepitys*)
Pink, Cheddar (*Dianthus gratianopolitanus*)
Pink, Childling (*Petroraghia nanteuilii*)
Plantain, Floating Water (*Luronium natans*)
Pseudocyphellaria, Ragged (*Pseudocyphellaria lacerata*)
Psora, Rusty Alpine (*Psora rubiformis*)
Ragwort, Fen (*Senecio paludosus*)
Ramping-fumitory, Martin's (*Fumaria martinii*)
Rampion, Spiked (*Phyteuma spicatum*)
Restharrow, Small (*Ononis reclinata*)
Rock-cress, Alpine (*Arabis alpina*)
Rock-cress, Bristol (*Arabis stricta*)
Rustworth, Western (*Marsupella profunda*)
Sandwort, Norwegian (*Arenaria norvegica*)

Sandwort, Teesdale (*Minuartia stricta*)
Saxifrage, Drooping (*Saxifraga cernua*)
Saxifrage, Marsh (*Saxifraga hirulus*)
Saxifrage, Tufted (*Saxifraga cespitosa*)
Solenopsora, Serpentine (*Solenopsora liparina*)
Solomon's-seal, Whorled (*Polygonatum verticillatum*)
Sow-thistle, Alpine (*Cicerbita alpina*)
Spearwort, Adder's-tongue (*Ranunculus ophioglossifolius*)
Speedwell, Fingered (*Veronica triphyllos*)
Speedwell, Spiked (*Veronica spicata*)
Star-of-Bethlehem, Early (*Gagea bohemica*)
Starfruit (*Damasonium alisma*)
Stonewort, Bearded (*Chara canescens*)
Stonewort, Foxtail (*Lamprothamnium papulosum*)
Strapwort (*Corrigiola litoralis*)
Turpswort (*Geocalyx graveolens*)
Violet, Fen (*Viola persicifolia*)
Viper's-grass (*Scorzonera humilis*)
Water-plantain, Ribbon-leaved (*Alisma gramineum*)
Wood-sedge, Starved (*Carex depauperata*)
Woodsia, Alpine (*Woodsia alpina*)
Woodsia, Oblong (*Woodsia ilvensis*)
Wormwood, Field (*Artemisia campestris*)
Woundwort, Downy (*Stachys germanica*)
Woundwort, Limestone (*Stachys alpina*)
Yellow-rattle, Greater (*Rhinanthus serotinus*)

## WILD BIRDS

The Wildlife and Countryside Act 1981 lays down a close
season for wild birds (other than game birds) from 1 February
to 31 August inclusive, each year. Exceptions to these dates
are made for:
*Capercaillie* and (except Scotland) *Woodcock* – 1 February to
30 September
*Snipe* – 1 February to 11 August
*Wild Duck* and *Wild Goose* (below high water mark) –
21 February to 31 August

Birds which may be killed or taken outside the close season
(except on Sundays and on Christmas Day in Scotland, and
on Sundays in prescribed areas of England and Wales) are
the above-named, plus coot, certain wild duck (gadwall,
goldeneye, mallard, pintail, pochard, shoveler, teal, tufted
duck, wigeon), certain wild geese (Canada, greylag, pink-
footed, white-fronted (in England and Wales only)), moorhen,
golden plover and woodcock.
   Certain wild birds may be killed or taken subject to the
conditions of a general licence at any time by authorized
persons: crow, collared dove, gull (great and lesser black-
backed or herring), jackdaw, jay, magpie, pigeon (feral or
wood), rook, sparrow (house), and starling.
   All other British birds are fully protected by law throughout
the year.

---

## CLOSE SEASONS AND TIMES

---

## GAME BIRDS

In each case the dates are inclusive:

*Black game* – 11 December to 19 August (31 August in
   Somerset, Devon and New Forest)
*\*Grouse* – 11 December to 11 August
*\*Partridge* – 2 February to 31 August
*\*Pheasant* – 2 February to 30 September
*\*Ptarmigan* – (Scotland only) 11 December to 11 August

\* It is also unlawful in England and Wales to kill this game
on a Sunday or Christmas Day

## HUNTING AND GROUND GAME

There is no statutory close time for fox-hunting or rabbit-
shooting, nor for hares. However, by an Act passed in 1892
the sale of hares or leverets in Great Britain is prohibited
from 1 March to 31 July inclusive under a penalty of £1.
The recognized date for the opening of the fox-hunting
season is 1 November, and it continues till the following
April.

## DEER

The statutory close seasons for deer (all dates inclusive) are:

|  | England and Wales | Scotland |
|---|---|---|
| Fallow deer | | |
| Male | 1 May–31 July | 1 May–31 July |
| Female | 1 Mar.–31 Oct. | 16 Feb.–20 Oct. |
| Red deer | | |
| Male | 1 May–31 July | 21 Oct.–30 June |
| Female | 1 Mar.–31 Oct. | 16 Feb.–20 Oct. |
| Roe deer | | |
| Male | 1 Nov.–31 Mar. | 21 Oct.–31 Mar. |
| Female | 1 Mar.–31 Oct. | 1 April–20 Oct. |
| Sika deer | | |
| Male | 1 May–31 July | 21 Oct.–30 June |
| Female | 1 Mar.–31 Oct. | 16 Feb.–20 Oct. |
| Red/Sika hybrids | | |
| Male | — | 21 Oct.–30 June |
| Female | — | 16 Feb.–20 Oct. |

## ANGLING

Where local by-laws neither specify nor dispense with an
annual close season, the following are statutory close times
(dates inclusive):
*Coarse fishing* – 15 March to 15 June
*Game fishing* – Trout, 1 October to end February; salmon, 1
   November to 31 January

Close seasons vary in accordance with local by-laws. It is
necessary in all cases to check with the National Rivers
Authority regional office covering the area (details can be
found in the local telephone directory).
   The NRA introduced in 1994 a two-tiered rod fishing
licence which covers different categories of fish. The previous
seven-day licence has been extended to cover eight consecutive days and a new one-day licence has been introduced.
Purchase of a national rod fishing licence is legally required
of anglers wishing to fish with rod and line in all waters
within the area of the NRA.

|  | Salmon & sea trout | Non-migratory trout and coarse fish |
|---|---|---|
| Full annual | £45.00 | £15.00 |
| Concessionary annual | 22.50 | 7.50 |
| Eight-day | 13.50 | 4.50 |
| One-day | 4.50 | 1.50 |

Concessionary licences are available for juniors (12–16 years),
for senior citizens (65 years and over), and disabled who are
in receipt of invalidity benefit or severe disability allowance.
Those in receipt of a war pension which includes unemployability supplements are also eligible.

# Historic Buildings

The following is a selection of the many historic houses, castles and monuments open to the public. The admission charges given are the standard charges for 1994–5; many properties have concessionary rates for children, etc. Opening hours vary. Many properties are closed in winter and some are also closed in the mornings. Most properties are closed on Christmas Eve, Christmas Day, Boxing Day and New Year's Day, and many are closed on Good Friday. During the winter season, most English Heritage monuments are closed on Mondays and monuments in the care of Cadw: Welsh Historic Monuments are closed on Sunday mornings. Information about a specific property should be checked by telephone.

\* Closed in winter (usually November-March)
† Closed in winter, and in mornings in summer

## ENGLAND

EH English Heritage property
NT National Trust property

\*A LA RONDE (NT), Exmouth, Devon. Tel: 01395–265514. Closed Fri. and Sat. Adm. £3.00. Unique 16–sided house built in 1796

\*ALNWICK CASTLE, Northumberland. Tel: 01665–510777. Adm. £4.00. The second-largest inhabited castle in England, with Italian Renaissance-style interior

ALTHORP, Northants. Tel: 01604–770107. Opening times and prices subject to change. House originally built in early 16th century. Fine art collection

†ANGLESEY ABBEY (NT), Cambs. Tel: 01223–811200. Closed Mon. (except Bank Holidays) and Tues. Adm. £4.75; gardens only, £3.00. House built c.1600; bought by Lord Fairhaven in early 20th century. Outstanding grounds with unique statuary

†ARUNDEL CASTLE, W. Sussex. Tel: 01903–883136. Closed Sat. Adm. charge. Castle dating from the Norman Conquest. Seat of the Dukes of Norfolk

AVEBURY (NT, managed by EH), Wilts. Adm. free. Remains of stone circles constructed 4,000 years ago surrounding the later village of Avebury. Also *Avebury Museum*. Tel: 01672–539250. Adm. £1.35

BANQUETING HOUSE, Whitehall, London SW1. Tel: 0171–839 8919. Closed Sun. and Bank Holidays. Adm. £2.90. Designed by Inigo Jones; ceiling paintings by Rubens. Site of the execution of Charles I

\*BASILDON PARK (NT), Berks. Tel: 01734–843040. Closed Mon. (except Bank Holidays) and Tues. Adm. £3.50; grounds only, £2.50. Palladian house built in 1776; unusual octagonal room

BATTLE ABBEY (EH), E. Sussex. Tel: 01424–773792. Adm. £3.00. Remains of the abbey founded by William the Conqueror on the site of the Battle of Hastings

BEAULIEU, Hants. Tel: 01590–612345. Adm. charge. House and gardens, Beaulieu Abbey and exhibition of monastic life, National Motor Museum (*see also* page 592)

BEESTON CASTLE (EH), Cheshire. Tel: 01829–260464. Adm. £2.00. Thirteenth-century inner ward with gatehouse and towers, and remains of large outer ward

†BELTON HOUSE (NT), Grantham, Lincs. Tel: 01476–66116. Closed Mon. (except Bank Holidays) and Tues. Adm. £4.30. Fine 17th-century house in landscaped park

\*BELVOIR CASTLE, nr. Grantham, Lincs. Tel: 01476–870262. Closed Mon. and Fri. except Bank Holidays. Adm. £4.00. Seat of the Dukes of Rutland; 19th-century Gothic-style castle

\*BERKELEY CASTLE, Glos. Tel: 01453–810332. Closed Mon. except Bank Holidays. Adm. £3.80. Completed 1153; site of the murder of Edward II (1327). Elizabethan terraced gardens

\*BLENHEIM PALACE, Woodstock, Oxon. Tel: 01993–811325. Adm. charge. Seat of the Dukes of Marlborough and Winston Churchill's birthplace; designed by Vanbrugh

†BLICKLING HALL (NT), Norfolk. Tel: 01263–733084. Closed Mon. (except Bank Holidays) and Thurs. Adm. £4.50; garden only, £2.50. Jacobean house with 18th-century alterations; state rooms, Long Gallery, formal gardens, temple and orangery

BODIAM CASTLE (NT), E. Sussex. Tel: 01580–830436. Closed Mon. in winter. Adm. £2.50. Well-preserved medieval moated castle

BOLSOVER CASTLE (EH), Derbys. Tel: 01246–823349. Adm. £2.10. Notable for its 17th-century buildings

BOSCOBEL HOUSE (EH), Shropshire. Tel: 01902–850244. Closed Jan. Adm. £3.15. Timber-framed 17th-century hunting lodge with later alterations

†BOUGHTON HOUSE, Northants. Tel: 01536–515731. House open Aug. only; grounds May to Sept. except Fri. State rooms by prior booking. Adm. £4.00; grounds £1.50. French-style 17th-century house

\*BOWOOD HOUSE, Wilts. Tel: 01249–812102. Adm. £4.50. An 18th-century house in Capability Brown park, with lake, temple and arboretum

\*BROADLANDS, Hants. Tel: 01794–516878. Closed Fri. (except Good Friday and in Aug.). Adm. £5.00. Palladian mansion in Capability Brown parkland. Mountbatten exhibition

BRONTË PARSONAGE, Haworth, W. Yorks. Tel: 01535–642323. Closed mid Jan.-mid Feb. Adm. £3.60. Home of the Brontë sisters; museum and memorabilia

BUCKFAST ABBEY, Devon. Tel: 01364–643301. Adm. free. Abbey church erected between 1907 and 1938

\*BUCKINGHAM PALACE, London SW1. Tel: 0171–493 3175. Open daily for eight weeks from early August each year. Adm. £8.00. The Palace was purchased by George III in 1762 and has been the Sovereign's London home since 1837. Eighteen state rooms, including the throne room; also the picture gallery

BUCKLAND ABBEY (NT), Devon. Tel: 01822–853607. Closed Thurs. In winter open only weekend afternoons, and Wed. afternoon for pre-booked parties. Adm. £4.00. A 13th-century Cistercian monastery. Home of Sir Francis Drake

\*BURGHLEY HOUSE, Stamford, Lincs. Tel: 01780–52451. Adm. £4.80. Late Elizabethan house; vast state apartments

†CALKE ABBEY (NT), Derbys. Tel: 01332–863822. Closed Thurs. and Fri. Adm. £4.50, by timed ticket. Baroque 18th-century mansion

CARISBROOKE CASTLE (EH), Isle of Wight. Tel: 01983–522107. Adm. £3.20. Norman castle; prison of Charles I 1647–8

CARLISLE CASTLE (EH), Cumbria. Tel: 01228–591922. Adm. £2.00. Medieval castle, prison of Mary Queen of Scots

*CARLYLE'S HOUSE (NT), Cheyne Row, London SW3. Tel: 0171-352 7087. Home of Thomas Carlyle

CASTLE ACRE PRIORY (EH), Norfolk. Tel: 01760-755394. Adm. £2.10. Remains include 12th-century church and prior's lodgings

*CASTLE DROGO (NT), Devon. Tel: 01647-433306. Closed Fri. Adm. £4.60; grounds only, £2.00. Granite castle designed by Lutyens

*CASTLE HOWARD, N. Yorks. Tel: 01653-684333. Adm. £6.00. Designed by Vanbrugh 1699-1726; mausoleum designed by Hawksmoor

CASTLE RISING CASTLE (EH), Norfolk. Tel: 01553-631330. Adm. £1.25. A 12th-century keep in a massive earthwork with gatehouse and bridge

†CHARTWELL (NT), Kent. Tel: 01732-866368. Closed Fri. and Mon. (except Bank Holidays). Adm. £4.20; grounds only, £2.00. Home of Sir Winston Churchill

*CHATSWORTH, Derbys. Tel: 01246-582204. Adm. charge. Tudor mansion with later additions in magnificent parkland

CHESTERS ROMAN FORT (EH), Northumberland. Tel: 01434-681379. Adm. £2.00. Fine example of a Roman cavalry fort

*CHYSAUSTER ANCIENT VILLAGE (EH), Cornwall. Tel: 01736-61889. Adm. £1.30. Romano-Cornish village, 2nd and 3rd century AD, on a probably late Iron Age site

CLIFFORD'S TOWER (EH), York. Tel: 01904-646940. Adm. £1.50. A 13th-century tower built on a mound

†CLIVEDEN (NT), Berks. Tel: 01628-605069. House open Thurs. and Sun. only, gardens daily. Adm. £3.80, £1.00 extra for house. Former home of the Astors, now a hotel set in garden and woodland

CORBRIDGE ROMAN SITE (EH), Northumberland. Tel: 01434-632349. Adm. £2.00. Excavated central area of a Roman town and successive military bases

CORFE CASTLE (NT), Dorset. Tel: 01929-481294. Nov.-Jan. open weekend afternoons only. Adm. £2.90. Ruined former royal castle dating from 11th century

†CROFT CASTLE (NT), Herefordshire. Tel: 01568-780246. Closed Mon. (except Bank Holidays) and Tues.; April and Oct. open weekends only. Adm. £3.00. Pre-Conquest border castle with Georgian-Gothic interior

DEAL CASTLE (EH), Kent. Tel: 01304-372762. Adm. £2.00. Largest and most complete of the coastal defence forts built by Henry VIII

DICKENS HOUSE, Doughty Street, London WC1. Tel: 0171-405 2127. Closed Sun. Adm. £3.00. House occupied by Dickens 1837-9; manuscripts, furniture and portraits

DR JOHNSON'S HOUSE, 17 Gough Square, London EC4. Tel: 0171-353 3745. Closed Sun. and Bank Holidays. Adm. £3.00. Home of Samuel Johnson

DOVE COTTAGE, Grasmere, Cumbria. Tel: 015394-35544. Closed Jan. and early Feb. Adm. £3.70. Wordsworth's home 1799-1808; museum and memorabilia

DOVER CASTLE (EH), Kent. Tel: 01304-201628. Adm. £5.25. Castle with Roman, Saxon and Norman features, and wartime operations rooms

DUNSTANBURGH CASTLE (EH), Northumberland. Tel: 01665-576231. Adm. £1.25. A 14th-century castle on a cliff, with a substantial gatehouse-keep

FARLEIGH HUNGERFORD CASTLE (EH), Somerset. Tel: 01225-754026. Adm. £1.25. Late 14th-century castle with two courts and chapel with tomb of Sir Thomas Hungerford

*FARNHAM CASTLE KEEP (EH), Surrey. Tel: 01252-713393. Adm. £1.80. Large 12th-century shell-keep on motte

FOUNTAINS ABBEY (NT), nr. Ripon, N. Yorks. Tel: 01765-608888. Closed Fri. Nov.-Jan. Adm. £4.00. Ruined Cistercian monastery; 18th-century landscaped gardens of Studley Royal estate

FRAMLINGHAM CASTLE (EH), Suffolk. Tel: 01728-724189. Adm. £1.80. Castle (c.1200) with high curtain walls enclosing an almshouse (1639)

FURNESS ABBEY (EH), Cumbria. Tel: 01229-823420. Adm. £2.00. Remains of church and conventual buildings founded in 1123

GLASTONBURY ABBEY, Somerset. Tel: 01458-832267. Adm. £2.00. Ruins of a 12th-century abbey rebuilt after fire. Site of an early Christian settlement

GOODRICH CASTLE (EH), Herefordshire. Tel: 01600-890538. Adm. £1.80. Remains of 13th- and 14th-century castle with 12th-century keep

GREENWICH, London SE10. *Royal Observatory*. Closed Sun. mornings. Adm. charge. Former Royal Observatory (founded 1675) where the time ball and zero meridian of longitude can be seen. *The Queen's House*. Tel: 0181-858 4422. Closed Sun. mornings. Adm. charge. Designed for Queen Anne, wife of James I, by Inigo Jones. *Painted Hall and Chapel* (Royal Naval College). Closed mornings and Thurs. Visitors are admitted to Sunday service in the chapel at 11 a.m. except during college vacations

GRIMES GRAVES (EH), Norfolk. Tel: 01842-810656. Adm. £1.25. Neolithic flint mines. One shaft can be descended

*GUILDHALL, London EC2. Tel: 0171-606 3030. Closed Sat. Adm. free. Centre of civic government of the City. Built c.1440; facade built 1788-9

*HADDON HALL, Derbys. Tel: 01629-812855. Closed Mon. (except Bank Holidays) and Sun. in July and Aug. except Bank Holiday weekend. Adm. £4.00. Well-preserved 12th-century manor house

HAILES ABBEY (EH), Glos. Tel: 01242-602398. Adm. £1.90. Ruins of a Cistercian monastery founded in 1246, with museum

*HAM HOUSE (NT), Richmond, Surrey. Tel: 0181-940 1950. Closed Thurs., also Sat. and Sun. mornings Nov.-Dec. Adm. £4.00; garden open all year except Mon., adm. free. Stuart house with fine interiors

HAMPTON COURT PALACE, East Molesey, Surrey. Tel: 0181-781 9500. Adm. £7.00. A 16th-century palace with additions by Wren. Gardens with maze; Tudor tennis court (summer only)

†HARDWICK HALL (NT), Derbys. Tel: 01246-850430. Closed Mon. (except Bank Holidays), Tues. and Fri. Adm. £5.50; garden open daily, adm. £2.00. Built 1591-7 by Bess of Hardwick; notable furnishings

*HARDY'S COTTAGE (NT), Higher Bockhampton, Dorset. Tel: 01305-262366. Interior open only by appointment. Adm. £2.50. Garden open daily except Thurs., adm. free. Birthplace of Thomas Hardy

*HAREWOOD HOUSE, W. Yorks. Tel: 0113-288 6467. Adm. charge. An 18th-century house designed by John Carr and Robert Adam; park by Capability Brown

†HATFIELD HOUSE, Herts. Tel: 01707-262823. Closed Mon. (except Bank Holidays). Adm. charge. Jacobean house built by Robert Cecil, and the family home of the Cecils. Surviving wing of royal Palace of Hatfield (1497)

HELMSLEY CASTLE (EH), N. Yorks. Tel: 01439-770442. Adm. £1.80. A 12th-century keep and curtain wall with 16th-century domestic buildings. Spectacular earthwork defences

†HEVER CASTLE, Kent. Tel: 01732-865224. Adm. charge. A 13th-century double-moated castle, childhood home of Anne Boleyn

*HOLKER HALL, Cumbria. Tel: 015395–58328. Closed Sat. Adm. charge. Former home of the Dukes of Devonshire; award-winning gardens

†HOLKHAM HALL, Norfolk. Tel: 01328–710227. Closed Fri. and Sat. Adm. £3.00. Fine Palladian mansion

HOUSESTEADS ROMAN FORT (EH), Northumberland. Tel: 01434–344363. Adm. £2.20. Excavated infantry fort on Hadrian's Wall with extra-mural civilian settlement

†HUGHENDEN MANOR (NT), High Wycombe. Tel: 01494–532580. Closed Mon. (except Bank Holidays) and Tues. Adm. £3.50. Home of Disraeli; small formal garden

JANE AUSTEN'S HOUSE, Chawton, Hants. Tel: 01420–83262. Open daily April-Oct., weekends only Jan.-Feb., Wed.-Sun. only Nov., Dec. and March. Adm. £1.50. Jane Austen's home 1809–17

KEATS HOUSE, Keats Grove, London NW3. Tel: 0171–435 2062. Closed mornings and Sat. afternoons in winter. Adm. free. Home of John Keats 1818–20

*KELMSCOTT MANOR, nr. Lechlade, Glos. Tel: 01367–252486. Open Wed. only. (Thurs. and Fri. by written application.) Adm. £5.00. Summer home of William Morris, with products of Morris and Co.

KENILWORTH CASTLE (EH), Warks. Tel: 01926–52078. Adm. £1.80. Castle showing many styles of building from 1155 to 1649

KENSINGTON PALACE, London W8. Tel: 0171–937 9561. Adm. £4.50. Closed for refurbishment from autumn 1995. Built in 1605 and enlarged by Wren; bought by William and Mary in 1689. Birthplace of Queen Victoria

KENWOOD (EH), Hampstead Lane, London NW3. Tel: 0181–348 1286. Adm. free. Adam villa housing the Iveagh bequest of paintings and furniture. Open-air concerts in summer

*KEW PALACE, Surrey. Tel: 0181–332 5189. Adm. £1.20. Built in 1631 as the Dutch House; residence of George III. Also Queen Charlotte's Cottage, weekends and Bank Holidays only. Adm. 70p. Joint ticket £1.50

†KINGSTON LACY HOUSE (NT), Dorset. Tel: 01202–883402. Closed Thurs. and Fri. Adm. £5.20; grounds only, £2.00. A 17th-century house with 18th- and 19th-century alterations; important collection of paintings

†KNEBWORTH HOUSE, Herts. Tel: 01438–812661. Adm. £4.50; grounds only, £3.00. Tudor manor house concealed by 19th-century Gothic decoration; Lutyens gardens

†KNOLE (NT), Kent. Tel: 01732–450608. Closed Mon. (except Bank Holidays) and Tues. Adm. £4.00; park free to pedestrians. House dating from the 15th century set in parkland; fine art treasures

LAMBETH PALACE, London SE1. Tel: 0171–928 8282. Visits by written application a year in advance. Official residence of the Archbishop of Canterbury. A 19th-century house with parts dating from the 12th century

*LANERCOST PRIORY (EH), Cumbria. Tel: 016977–3030. Adm. 80p. The nave of the Augustinian priory church, c.1166, is still used; remains of other claustral buildings

*LANHYDROCK (NT), Cornwall. Tel: 01208–73320. Closed Mon. (except Bank Holidays). Garden open daily including in winter. Adm. £5.00. House dating from the 17th century; 42 rooms, including servants quarters and kitchen

LEEDS CASTLE, Kent. Tel: 01622–765400. Open daily; mornings only in winter. Adm. £7.00; park only, £5.50. Castle dating from the 9th century, on two islands in a lake

LINCOLN CASTLE. Tel: 01522–511068. Adm. £2.00. Built by William the Conqueror in 1068

LINDISFARNE PRIORY (EH), Northumberland. Tel: 01289–89200. Open all year, subject to tide times. Adm. £2.00.

Bishopric of the Northumbrian kingdom destroyed by the Danes; re-established in the 11th century as a Benedictine priory, now ruined

†LITTLE MORETON HALL (NT), Cheshire. Tel: 01260–272018. Closed Mon. (except Bank Holidays) and Tues. Adm. £2.80 (weekends and Bank Holidays, £3.60). Timber-framed moated manor house with a knot garden

LONGLEAT HOUSE, Warminster. Tel: 01985–844400. Open daily; safari park closed winter. Adm. charge. Elizabethan house in Italian Renaissance style

LULLINGSTONE ROMAN VILLA (EH), Kent. Tel: 01322–863467. Adm. £2.00. Large villa occupied for much of the Roman period; fine mosaics

†LUTON HOO, Beds. Tel: 01582–22955. Open Fri.-Sun. and Bank Holiday Mon. Adm. £5.00. Houses the Wernher collection of china, glass, pictures and other objets d'art

MANSION HOUSE, London EC4. Tel: 0171–626 2500. Group visits only, by prior arrangement. The official residence of the Lord Mayor of London

MARBLE HILL HOUSE (EH), Twickenham, Middx. Tel: 0181–892 5115. Adm. free. English Palladian villa with Georgian paintings and furniture

*MICHELHAM PRIORY, E. Sussex. Tel: 01323–844224. Adm. £3.50. Tudor house built onto an Augustinian priory

MIDDLEHAM CASTLE (EH), N. Yorks. Tel: 01969–23899. Adm. £1.25. A 12th-century keep within later fortifications and domestic buildings. Childhood home of Richard III

†MONTACUTE HOUSE (NT), Somerset. Tel: 01935–823289. Closed Tues. Grounds open all year. Adm. £4.70; grounds only, £2.60. Elizabethan house built of Ham Hill stone

MOUNT GRACE PRIORY (EH), N. Yorks. Tel: 01609–883494. Adm. £2.00. Carthusian monastery, with remains of monastic buildings

NETLEY ABBEY (EH), Hants. Tel: 01703–453076. Adm. free. Remains of Cistercian abbey and ruined Tudor house

OLD SARUM (EH), Wilts. Tel: 01722–335398. Adm. £1.35. Earthworks enclosing remains of the castle and the 11th-century cathedral

ORFORD CASTLE (EH), Suffolk. Tel: 013944–50472. Adm. £1.80. Circular keep of c.1170 and remains of coastal defence castle built by Henry II

*OSBORNE HOUSE (EH), Isle of Wight. Tel: 01983–200022. Adm. £5.50. Queen Victoria's seaside residence

†OSTERLEY PARK HOUSE (NT), Isleworth, Middx. Tel: 0181–560 3918. Closed Mon. (except Bank Holidays) and Tues. Grounds open all year. Adm. £3.50; grounds free. Elizabethan mansion set in parkland

PENDENNIS CASTLE (EH), Cornwall. Tel: 01326–316594. Adm. £2.10. Well-preserved coastal defence castle built by Henry VIII

†PENSHURST PLACE, Kent. Tel: 01892–870307. Adm. £4.95; grounds only, £3.50. House with medieval Baron's Hall and 14th-century gardens

†PETWORTH (NT), W. Sussex. Tel: 01798–342207. Closed Mon. (except Bank Holidays) and Fri. Adm. £4.00. Late 17th-century house set in deer park

PEVENSEY CASTLE (EH), E. Sussex. Tel: 01323–762604. Adm. charge. Walls of a 4th-century Roman fort enclosing remains of an 11th-century castle

PEVERIL CASTLE (EH), Derbys. Tel: 01433–620613. Adm. £1.25. A 12th-century castle defended on two sides by precipitous rocks

†POLESDEN LACY (NT), Surrey. Tel: 01372–458203. Closed Mon. (except Bank Holidays) and Tues., open weekends only in March. Grounds open daily all year. Adm. £5.50;

grounds only £2.50. Regency villa remodelled in the Edwardian era. Fine paintings and furnishings

PORTCHESTER CASTLE (EH), Hants. Tel: 01705–378291. Adm. £2.00. Walls of a late Roman fort enclosing a Norman keep and an Augustinian priory church

*POWDERHAM CASTLE, Devon. Tel: 01626–890243. Closed Sat. Adm. charge. Medieval castle with 18th- and 19th-century alterations

†RABY CASTLE, Co. Durham. Tel: 01833–660202. Closed Sat. (except Bank Holiday weekends). Limited opening in May and June. Adm. £3.30; grounds only, £1.00. A 14th-century castle with walled gardens

†RAGLEY HALL, Warks. Tel: 01789–762090. Closed Mon. (except Bank Holidays) and Fri. Adm. £4.00. A 17th-century house with gardens, park and lake

RICHBOROUGH CASTLE (EH), Kent. Tel: 01304–612013. Adm. £1.80. Landing-site of the Claudian invasion in AD 43, with third-century stone walls

RICHMOND CASTLE (EH), N. Yorks. Tel: 01748–822493. Adm. £1.60. A 12th-century keep with 11th-century curtain wall and gatehouse

RIEVAULX ABBEY (EH), N. Yorks. Tel: 014396–228. Adm. £2.20. Founded c.1132. Remains of a Cistercian abbey, with fine 13th-century choir and claustral buildings

ROCHESTER CASTLE (EH), Kent. Tel: 01634–402276. Adm. £2.00. An 11th-century castle partly on the Roman city wall, with a square keep of c.1130

†ROCKINGHAM CASTLE, Northants. Tel: 01536–770240. Open Sun. and Thurs. only (and Bank Holiday Mon. and Tues., and Tues. in Aug.). Adm. £3.60; gardens only, £2.20. Built by William the Conqueror

ROYAL PAVILION, Brighton. Tel: 01273–603005. Adm. charge. Palace of George IV. Chinoiserie interiors with much of the original furniture

†RUFFORD OLD HALL (NT), Lancs. Tel: 01704–821254. Closed Thurs. and Fri. Adm. £3.00; garden only £1.60. A 15th-century hall with unique screen

ST AUGUSTINE'S ABBEY (EH), Canterbury, Kent. Tel: 01227–767345. Adm. £1.50. Remains of Benedictine monastery, with Norman church, on site of abbey founded AD 598 by St Augustine

ST MAWES CASTLE (EH), Cornwall. Tel: 01326–270526. Adm. £1.35. Coastal defence castle built by Henry VIII comprising central tower and three bastions

*ST MICHAEL'S MOUNT (NT), Cornwall. Tel: 01736–710507. Closed Sat. and Sun. No regular ferry service in winter; castle open as tide, weather and circumstances permit. Adm. £3.20. A 14th-century castle with later additions and alterations, off the coast at Marazion

*SANDRINGHAM, Norfolk. Tel: 01553–772675. Closed for three weeks in the summer, on Sun. mornings and when the Royal Family is in residence. Adm. £3.50; grounds only, £2.50. The Queen's private residence; a neo-Jacobean house built in 1870

SCARBOROUGH CASTLE (EH), N. Yorks. Tel: 01723–372451. Adm. £1.50. Remains of 12th-century keep and curtain walls

SHERBORNE CASTLE, Dorset. Tel: 01935–813182. Closed Mon. and Tues. in winter. Adm. £1.25. Early 12th-century castle owned by Sir Walter Raleigh

†SHUGBOROUGH (NT), Staffs. Tel: 01889–881388. Adm. house, servants' quarters and farm, £7.50; house only, £3.50. House set in 18th-century park with monuments, temples and pavilions in the Greek Revival style

SKIPTON CASTLE, N. Yorks. Tel: 01756–792442. Closed Sun. mornings. Adm. £2.90. D-shaped castle with six round towers and beautiful inner courtyard

†SMALLHYTHE PLACE (NT), Kent. Tel: 01580–762334. Closed Thurs.-Fri. (open Good Friday). Adm. £2.50. Half-timbered 16th-century house; home of Ellen Terry 1899–1928

†STANFORD HALL, Leics. Tel: 01788–860250. Open Sat.-Sun.; also Bank Holiday Mon. and Tues. Adm. £3.20; grounds only, £1.80. William and Mary house with unique collection of Stuart portraits. Motorcycle museum

STONEHENGE (EH), Wilts. Tel: 01980–624715. Adm. £2.85. Prehistoric monument consisting of a series of concentric stone circles surrounded by a ditch and bank

STONELEIGH ABBEY, Warks. Tel: 01926–52116. Open by appointment only; closed weekends. Early 18th-century Georgian mansion on the site of a Cistercian abbey

†STONOR PARK, Oxon. Tel: 01491–638587. Opening days vary. Adm. £3.50. Medieval house with Georgian facade. Centre of Roman Catholicism after the Reformation

†STOURHEAD (NT), Wilts. Tel: 01985–844785. Closed Thurs.-Fri. Gardens open daily all year. Adm. £4.10; gardens, £4.10. English Palladian mansion with famous gardens

*STRATFIELD SAYE HOUSE, Berks. Tel: 01256–882882. Closed Fri. Wellington Country Park, open daily. Adm. charge. House built 1630–40; home of the Dukes of Wellington since 1817

STRATFORD-UPON-AVON, Warks. *Shakespeare's Birthplace* with Shakespeare Centre; *Anne Hathaway's Cottage*, home of Shakespeare's wife; *Mary Arden's House*, home of Shakespeare's mother; *New Place*, where Shakespeare died; and *Hall's Croft*, home of Shakespeare's daughter. Tel: 01789–204016. Adm. charges. Also *Grammar School* attended by Shakespeare, *Royal Shakespeare Theatre* (burnt down 1926, rebuilt 1932) and *Swan Theatre* (opened 1986)

†SUDELEY CASTLE, Glos. Tel: 01242–602308. Adm. £4.90. Castle built in 1442; restored in the 19th century

*SYON HOUSE, Brentford, Middx. Tel: 0181–560 0881. Closed Mon. (except Bank Holidays) and Tues. Adm. charge. Built on the site of a former monastery; Adam interior

TILBURY FORT (EH), Essex. Tel: 01375–858489. Adm. £1.80. A Henry VIII coastal fort, extended by Charles II

TINTAGEL CASTLE (EH), Cornwall. Tel: 01840–770328. Adm. £2.10. A 12th-century cliff-top castle and Dark Age settlement site

TOWER OF LONDON, London EC3. Tel: 0171–709 0765. Adm. charge. Royal palace and fortress begun by William the Conqueror in 1078. Houses the Crown Jewels and the national collection of arms and armour

*TRERICE (NT), Cornwall. Tel: 01637–875404. Closed Tues. Adm. £3.60. Elizabethan manor house

TYNEMOUTH CASTLE AND PRIORY (EH), Tyne and Wear. Tel: 0191–257 1090. Adm. £1.25. Remains of a Benedictine priory, founded 1090, on Saxon monastic site. Coastal batteries (open Fri.-Mon. afternoons) with reconstructed First World War magazine

WALMER CASTLE (EH), Kent. Tel: 01304–364288. Closed Jan.-Feb. and when the Lord Warden is in residence. Adm. £3.00. One of Henry VIII's coastal defence castles, now the residence of the Lord Warden of the Cinque Ports

WALTHAM ABBEY (EH), Essex. Adm. free. Ruined abbey including the nave of the abbey church c.1120, 'Harold's Bridge' and the late 14th-century gatehouse. Traditionally the burial place of Harold II (1066)

WARKWORTH CASTLE (EH), Northumberland. Tel: 01665–711423. Adm. £1.80. A 15th-century keep amidst earlier ruins, with a 14th-century hermitage (open summer weekends only) upstream

WARWICK CASTLE. Tel: 01926–408000. Adm. £7.75. Medieval castle in Capability Brown parkland

WHITBY ABBEY (EH), N. Yorks. Tel: 01947–603568. Adm. £1.50. Remains of a 13th- and 14th-century Benedictine church on the site of a monastery founded in AD 657

*WILTON HOUSE, Wilts. Tel: 01722–743115. Adm. £5.50. House completed in 1653 on the site of a Tudor house and Saxon abbey

WINDSOR CASTLE, Berks. Tel: 01753–868286. State apartments closed when The Queen is in residence. Adm. £8.00, including the castle precincts. Official residence of The Queen and the oldest royal residence still in regular use. State apartments, Queen Mary's Dolls' House, Exhibition of The Queen's Presents and Royal Carriages. Restoration work in progress on fire-damaged state rooms (which may still be viewed). Also *St George's Chapel*. Tel: 01753–865538; *Royal Mausoleum*, Frogmore Gardens. Tel: 01753–831118 for recorded information

WOBURN ABBEY, Beds. Tel: 01525–290666. Closed Mon.-Fri. in winter. Adm. £6.50. Built on the site of a Cistercian abbey; seat of the Dukes of Bedford. Important art collection; deer park with wildlife

WROXETER ROMAN CITY (EH), Shropshire. Tel: 01743–761330. Adm. £1.80. The 2nd-century public baths and part of the forum of the Roman town of Viroconium

## WALES

c Property of Cadw: Welsh Historic Monuments
NT National Trust property

BEAUMARIS CASTLE (C), Anglesey. Tel: 01248–810361. Adm. £1.50. Fine concentrically-planned castle, still almost intact

CAERLEON ROMAN AMPHITHEATRE (C), Gwent. Tel: 01633–422518. Adm. £1.50 (including Roman Fortress Baths, *see below*). Late 1st-century arena surrounded by bank for spectators

CAERLEON ROMAN FORTRESS BATHS (C), Gwent. Tel: 01633–422518. Adm. £1.50 (including Roman Amphitheatre, *see above*), joint ticket with Legionary Museum £2.50. Rare example of a legionary bath-house

CAERNARFON CASTLE (C), Gwynedd. Tel: 01286–677617. Adm. £3.50. Important Edwardian castle built, with the town wall, between 1283 and 1330

CAERPHILLY CASTLE (C), Mid Glamorgan. Tel: 01222–883143. Adm. £2.00. Concentrically-planned castle (c.1270) notable for its scale and use of water defences

CARDIFF CASTLE, S. Glamorgan. Tel: 01222–822083. Adm. charge. Castle built on the site of a Roman fort; spectacular towers and rich interior

CASTELL COCH (C), S. Glamorgan. Tel: 01222–810101. Adm. £2.00. Rebuilt 1875–90 on medieval foundations

CHEPSTOW CASTLE (C), Gwent. Tel: 01291–624065. Adm. £2.90. Rectangular keep amid extensive fortifications

CONWY CASTLE (C), Gwynedd. Tel: 01492–592358. Adm. £2.90. Built by Edward I to guard the Conwy ferry

CRICCIETH CASTLE (C), Gwynedd. Tel: 01341–422854. Adm. £2.00. Native Welsh 13th-century castle, altered by Edward I

DENBIGH CASTLE (C), Clwyd. Tel: 01745–813979. Adm. £1.50. Remains of the castle (1282-1322), including triangular gatehouse

HARLECH CASTLE (C), Gwynedd. Tel: 01766–780552. Adm. £2.90. Well-preserved Edwardian castle, constructed 1283–9, on an outcrop above the former shore-line

PEMBROKE CASTLE, Dyfed. Tel: 01646–681510. Adm. £2.00. Castle founded in 1093, with a Great Tower 75 feet tall; birthplace of King Henry VII

†PENRHYN CASTLE (NT), Bangor. Tel: 01248–353084. Closed Tues. Adm. £4.40; garden only, £2.00. Neo-Norman castle built in the 19th century. Industrial railway museum

PORTMEIRION, Gwynedd. Tel: 01766–770228. Adm. £3.00 (April-Oct.), £1.50 (Nov.-March). Village in Italianate style

†POWIS CASTLE (NT), Powys. Tel: 01938–554336. Closed Mon. (except Bank Holidays) and Tues. (except July and Aug.). Adm. £5.80; museum and garden only, £3.80. Medieval castle with interior in variety of styles; 17th-century gardens and Clive of India museum

RAGLAN CASTLE (C), Gwent. Tel: 01291–690228. Adm. £2.00. Remains of 15th-century castle with moated hexagonal keep

ST DAVIDS BISHOP'S PALACE (C), Dyfed. Tel: 01437–720517. Adm. £1.50. Remains of residence of Bishops of St Davids dating from 1280–1350

TINTERN ABBEY (C), Gwent. Tel: 01291–689251. Adm. £2.00. Remains of 13th-century church and conventual buildings of a Cistercian monastery

TRETOWER COURT AND CASTLE (C), Powys. Tel: 01874–730279. Adm. £2.00. Medieval house with remains of castle nearby

## SCOTLAND

HS Historic Scotland property
NTS National Trust for Scotland property

ANTONINE WALL (HS), Central and Strathclyde regions. Adm. free. Built about AD 142, consists of ditch, turf rampart and road, with forts every two miles

BALMORAL CASTLE, Grampian. Tel: 013397–42334. Open May-July. Closed Sun. Adm. £2.50. Mid 19th-century Baronial-style castle built for Victoria and Albert. The Queen's private residence

BLACK HOUSE, ARNOL (HS), Lewis, Western Isles. Tel: 01851–71395. Closed Sun.; also Fri. in winter. Adm. £1.50. Traditional Lewis thatched house

*BLAIR CASTLE, Tayside. Tel: 01796–481207. Adm. £4.50. Mid 18th-century mansion with 13th-century tower; seat of the Dukes of Atholl

*BONAWE IRONWORKS (HS), Strathclyde. Tel: 01866–2432. Closed Sun. mornings. Adm. £2.00. Charcoal-fuelled ironworks

†BOWHILL, SELKIRK. Tel: 01750–20732. House open July only; grounds early May to late summer except Fri. Adm. £3.50; grounds only, £1.00. Seat of the Dukes of Buccleuch and Queensberry. Fine collection of paintings, including portrait miniatures

BROUGH OF BIRSAY (HS), Orkney. Adm. free. Remains of Norse church and village on the tidal island of Birsay

CAERLAVEROCK CASTLE (HS), nr. Dumfries. Tel: 01387–77244. Adm. £2.00. Closed Sun. mornings. Fine early classical Renaissance building

CALLANISH STANDING STONES (HS), Lewis, Western Isles. Adm. free. Standing stones in a cross-shaped setting, dating from 3000 BC

CATHERTUNS (BROWN AND WHITE) (HS), Tayside. Adm. free. Two large Iron Age hill forts

*CAWDOR CASTLE, Inverness. Tel: 01667–404615. Adm. £4.00; grounds only, £2.00. A 14th-century tower-house with 17th-century additions

CLAVA CAIRNS (HS), Highland. Adm. free. Late Neolithic or early Bronze Age cairns

*CRATHES CASTLE (NTS), Grampian. Tel: 01330–844525. Gardens and grounds open all year. Adm. £4.00; gardens and grounds only, £2.00. A 16th-century baronial castle in woodland, fields and gardens

*CULZEAN CASTLE (NTS), Strathclyde. Tel: 016556–274. Country park open all year. Adm. £5.50; country park only, £3.00. An 18th-century Adam castle with oval staircase and round drawing-room

*DRUMLANRIG CASTLE, nr. Dumfries. Tel: 01848–331682. Closed Sun. mornings and Thurs. Adm. £4.00; country park only, £2.00. Castle with baroque decorative features and notable art and furniture collections

DRYBURGH ABBEY (HS), Borders. Tel: 01835–22381. Closed Sun. mornings. Adm. £2.00. A 12th-century abbey containing tomb of Sir Walter Scott

*DUNVEGAN CASTLE, Skye. Tel: 01470–521310. Closed Sun. mornings. Adm. £4.00; gardens only, £2.40. A 13th-century castle with later additions; the home of the chiefs of the Clan MacLeod. Boat trips to a seal colony

EDINBURGH CASTLE (HS), Lothian. Tel: 0131–225 9846. Adm. £5.00; War Memorial free. Includes the Scottish National War Memorial, Scottish United Services Museum and historic apartments

EDZELL CASTLE (HS), Tayside. Tel: 01356–648631. Closed Sun. mornings; also Thurs. afternoons and Fri. in winter. Adm. £2.00. Medieval tower house incorporated in a 16th-century courtyard mansion; walled garden

*EILEAN DONAN CASTLE, Wester Ross. Tel: 0159985–202. Adm. £1.50. A 13th-century castle with Jacobite relics

ELGIN CATHEDRAL (HS), Grampian. Tel: 01343–547171. Closed Sun. mornings; also Thurs. afternoons and Fri. in winter. Adm. £1.20. A 13th-century cathedral with fine chapterhouse

*FLOORS CASTLE, Kelso. Tel: 01573–223333. Closed Fri. and Sat. (except July-Aug.). Adm. £3.40. Largest inhabited castle in Scotland; seat of the Dukes of Roxburghe

FORT GEORGE (HS), Highland. Tel: 01667–462777. Closed Sun. mornings. Adm. £2.50. An 18th-century artillery fort

*GLAMIS CASTLE, Tayside. Tel: 01307–840242. Adm. £4.20; grounds only, £2.00. Seat of the Lyon family (later Earls of Strathmore and Kinghorne) since 1372

GLASGOW CATHEDRAL (HS), Strathclyde. Tel: 0141–552 6891. Closed Sun. mornings. Adm. free. Medieval cathedral with elaborately vaulted crypt

GLENELG BROCHS (HS), Highland. Adm. free. Two broch towers with well-preserved structural features

HERMITAGE CASTLE (HS), Borders. Tel: 01387–376222. Closed Sun. mornings; also Mon.-Fri. in winter. Adm. £1.20. Ruined castle dating from the 14th century

*HOPETOUN HOUSE, nr. Edinburgh. Tel: 0131–331 2451. Adm. £3.80. House designed by Sir William Bruce, enlarged by William Adam

HUNTLY CASTLE (HS), Grampian. Tel: 01466–793191. Closed Sun. mornings; also Thurs. afternoons and Fri. in winter. Adm. £2.00. Ruin of a 16th- and 17th- century house

*INVERARY CASTLE, Argyll. Tel: 01499–2203. Closed Fri. (except July-Aug.) and Sun. morning. Woods open all year. Adm. £3.00. Gothic-style 18th-century castle; seat of the Dukes of Argyll

IONA ABBEY, Inner Hebrides. Tel: 016817–404. Adm. £2.00. Monastery founded by St Columba in AD 563, now restored

*JARLSHOF (HS), Shetland. Tel: 01950–60112. Closed Sun. mornings. Adm. £2.00. Remains of Bronze Age village

JEDBURGH ABBEY (HS), Borders. Tel: 01835–863925. Closed Sun. mornings. Adm. £2.50. Romanesque and early Gothic church founded about 1138

KELSO ABBEY (HS), Borders. Closed Sun. mornings. Adm. free. Remains of west end of great abbey church founded 1128

LINLITHGOW PALACE (HS), Lothian. Tel: 01506–842896. Closed Sun. mornings. Adm. £2.00. Ruin of royal palace in a park setting. Birthplace of Mary, Queen of Scots

MAES HOWE CHAMBERED CAIRN (HS), Orkney. Tel: 01856–76217. Closed Sun. mornings. Adm. £2.00. Prehistoric tomb

*MEIGLE SCULPTURED STONES (HS), Tayside. Adm. £1.20. Pictish stones

MELROSE ABBEY (HS), Borders. Tel: 01896–822562. Closed Sun. mornings. Adm. £2.50. Ruin of Cistercian abbey founded c.1136

MOUSA BROCH (HS), Shetland. Adm. free. Finest surviving Iron Age broch tower

NETHER LARGIE CAIRNS (HS), Argyll and Bute. Adm. free. Bronze Age and Neolithic cairns

NEW ABBEY CORNMILL (HS), nr. Dumfries. Tel: 01387–85260. Closed Sun. mornings; also Thurs. afternoons and Fri. in winter. Adm. £1.50. Water-powered oatmeal mill in working order

PALACE OF HOLYROODHOUSE, Edinburgh. Tel: 0131–556 7371. Closed Sun. in winter, and when The Queen is in residence. Adm. charge. The Queen's official Scottish residence. Main part of the palace built 1671–9

RING OF BROGAR (HS), Orkney. Adm. free. Neolithic circle of upright stones with an enclosing ditch spanned by causeways

RUTHWELL CROSS (HS), Dumfries and Galloway. Adm. free. Seventh-century Anglian cross

ST ANDREWS CASTLE AND CATHEDRAL (HS), Fife. Tel: 01334–77196 (castle); 01334–72563 (cathedral). Adm. £2.00 (castle); £1.50 (cathedral). Closed Sun. mornings. Ruins of 13th-century castle and remains of the largest cathedral in Scotland

*SCONE PALACE, Perth. Tel: 01738–52300. Closed Sun. mornings (except July and Aug.). Adm. £4.20. House built 1802–13 on the site of a medieval palace

SKARA BRAE (HS), Orkney. Tel: 01856–84815. Closed Sun. mornings. Adm. £2.50. Prehistoric village

*SMAILHOLM TOWER (HS), Borders. Closed Sun. mornings. Adm. £1.50. Well-preserved rectangular tower

STIRLING CASTLE (HS), Central. Tel: 01786–450000. Adm. £3.50. Great Hall and gatehouse of James IV, palace of James V, Chapel Royal remodelled by James VI, artillery fortifications

TANTALLON CASTLE (HS), Lothian. Tel: 01620–2727. Closed Sun. mornings; also Thurs. afternoons and Fri. in winter. Adm. £2.00. Fortification with earthwork defences and a 14th-century curtain wall with towers

*THREAVE CASTLE (HS), Dumfries and Galloway. Tel: 01831–168512. Closed Sun. mornings. Adm. £1.50, including ferry trip. Late 14th-century tower with artillery fortification. On an island, reached by boat; long walk to castle

URQUHART CASTLE (HS), Loch Ness. Tel: 01456–450551. Adm. £3.00. Remains of a large castle with a well-preserved tower on the western shore of Loch Ness

# NORTHERN IRELAND

DE Property in the care of the Northern Ireland
Department of the Environment
NT National Trust property

BALLYCOPELAND WINDMILL (DE), Millisle, Co. Down.
Tel: 01247–861413. Close Sun. mornings. Adm. £1.00.
Late 18th-century tower mill, fully restored to working
order

CARRICKFERGUS CASTLE (DE), Co. Antrim. Tel: 01960–
351273. Closed Sun. mornings. Adm. £2.50. Castle
begun in 1180 and garrisoned until 1928

*CASTLE COOLE (NT), Enniskillen. Tel: 01365–322690.
Closed Thurs., and Bank Holiday weekend mornings.
Adm. £2.40; grounds, adm. free. Eighteenth-century
mansion by James Wyatt

†CASTLE WARD (NT), Co. Down. Tel: 01396–881204.
Closed Thurs. May-Aug., and Mon.-Fri. Sept.-Oct.
Grounds open all year. Adm. £2.50; grounds, adm. free.
An 18th-century house with Classical west front and
Gothic east front; Victorian laundry

*DEVENISH ISLAND (DE), Co. Fermanagh. Closed Sun.
mornings. Adm. £2.25. Island monastery founded in the
6th century by St Molaise

†DOWNHILL CASTLE (NT), Co. Londonderry. Tel: 01238–
510721. Closed Mon.-Fri. (except Bank Holidays) in
April-June and Sept. Grounds open all year. Adm. free.
Ruins of palatial house in landscaped estate including
Mussenden Temple

DUNLUCE CASTLE (DE), Co. Antrim. Tel: 012657–31938.
Closed Sun. morning and Mon. Adm. £1.50. Ruins of
16th-century stronghold of the MacDonnells, Lords of the
Isles

†FLORENCE COURT (NT), Co. Fermanagh. Tel: 01365–
348249. Closed Tues.; also Mon.-Fri. (except Bank
Holidays) in April, May and Sept. Grounds open all year.
Adm. £2.40; grounds, £1.50. Mid 18th-century house
with rococo plasterwork

GREY ABBEY (DE), Co. Down. Tel: 01247–788585. Closed
Sun. morning and Mon.; Mon.-Fri. in winter. Adm £1.00.
Substantial remains of a Cistercian abbey founded in 1193

HILLSBOROUGH FORT (DE), Co. Down. Closed Sun.
mornings. Adm. free. Artillery fort built in 1650 and
remodelled in the 18th century

†MOUNT STEWART (NT), Co. Down. Tel: 012477–88387.
Closed Tues.; also Mon.-Fri. April and Oct. Adm. £3.30;
garden and temple only, £2.70. An 18th-century house,
childhood home of Lord Castlereagh

NENDRUM MONASTERY (DE), Mahee Island, Co. Down.
Closed Sun. mornings. Adm 75p. Founded in the fifth
century by St Machaoi; museum on site

NEWTOWNARDS PRIORY (DE), Co. Down. Opened on
request. Adm. 75p. Remains of a Dominican friary

*TULLY CASTLE (DE), Co. Fermanagh. Closed Sun.
mornings. Adm. £1.00. Fortified house and bawn built in
1613

*WHITE ISLAND (DE), Co. Fermanagh. Closed Sun.
mornings. Adm. £2.25. Tenth-century monastery and
12th-century church. Access by ferry

# Museums and Galleries

The following is a selection of the many museums and art galleries in the United Kingdom. The admission charges given are the standard charges for 1994–5, where a charge is made; many museums have concessionary rates for children, etc. Opening hours vary. Most museums are closed on Christmas Eve, Christmas Day, Boxing Day and New Year's Day; many are closed on Good Friday, and some are closed on May Day Bank Holiday. Some smaller museums close at lunchtimes. Information about a specific museum or gallery should be checked by telephone.
* Local authority museum/gallery

## ENGLAND

BARNARD CASTLE, Co. Durham – *The Bowes Museum*, Westwick Road. Tel: 01833–690606. Closed Sun. mornings. Adm. charge. European art from the late medieval period to the 19th century; music and costume galleries; English period rooms from Elizabeth I to Victoria

BATH – *American Museum in Britain*, Claverton Manor. Tel: 01225–460503. Closed in the mornings and on Mon. (except Bank Holidays); also closed in winter (except on application). Adm. charge. American decorative arts from the 17th to 19th centuries
*Museum of Costume*, Bennett Street. Tel: 01225–461111. Adm. £3.20. Fashion from the 16th century to the present day
*Roman Baths Museum*, Abbey Church Yard. Tel: 01225–461111. Adm. (including 18th-century Pump Room) £5.00. Museum adjoins the remains of a Roman baths and temple complex
*Victoria Art Gallery*, Bridge Street. Tel: 01225–461111. Closed Sun. and Bank Holidays. Adm. free. European Old Masters and British art since the 18th century, especially topographical views

BEAMISH, Co. Durham – *The North of England Open Air Museum*. Tel: 01207–231811. Closed Mon. and Fri. in winter. Adm. charge. Recreated northern town c.1900, with rebuilt and furnished local buildings, a tramway, a colliery village, a railway station, and a working farm with agricultural machinery and animals (only town and tramway in winter)

BEAULIEU, Hants. – *National Motor Museum*. Tel: 01590–612345. Adm. charge. Displays of over 250 vehicles dating from 1894 to the present day

BEVERLEY, N. Humberside – *Museum of Army Transport*, Flemingate. Tel: 01482–860445. Adm. charge. Field workshop, amphibious assault landing, railway section and aircraft

BIRMINGHAM – *Aston Hall*, Albert Road. Tel: 0121–327 0062. Closed mornings and in winter. Adm. free. Jacobean house containing paintings, furniture and tapestries from 17th to 19th centuries
*Birmingham Nature Centre*, Edgbaston. Tel: 0121–472 7775. Closed Mon.-Fri. in winter. Adm. free. Indoor and outdoor enclosures displaying British wildlife
*City Museum and Art Gallery*, Chamberlain Square. Tel: 0121–235 2834. Closed Sun. mornings. Adm. free. Includes notable collection of Pre-Raphaelites
*Museum of Science and Industry*, Newhall Street. Tel: 0121–235 1661. Closed Sun. mornings. Adm. free.

Vehicles and industrial machinery from the Industrial Revolution to the present; interactive science centre and mechanical musical instrument collection

BRADFORD – *Cartwright Hall Art Gallery*, Lister Park. Tel: 01274–493313. Closed Mon. (except Bank Holidays). Adm. free. British 19th- and 20th-century fine art
*Industrial Museum and Horses at Work*, Moorside Road. Tel: 01274–631756. Closed Mon. (except Bank Holidays). Adm. free. Engineering, textiles, transport and social history exhibits, including recreated back-to-back cottages
*National Museum of Photography, Film and Television*, Pictureville. Tel: 01274–727488. Closed Mon. Adm. free. Photography, film and television equipment and materials, including the only IMAX cinema in the UK and the only public Cinerama theatre in the world

BRIGHTON – *Brighton Museum and Art Gallery*, Church Street. Tel: 01273–603005. Closed Wed., and Sun. mornings. Adm. free. Includes Old Master paintings, the Willett collection of English pottery and porcelain, and Art Nouveau and Art Deco works

BRISTOL – *Blaise Castle House Museum*, Henbury. Tel: 0117–950 6789. Closed Mon. Adm. free. Agricultural and social history collections in an 18th-century mansion
*Bristol Industrial Museum*, Prince Street. Tel: 0117–925 1470. Closed Mon. Adm. £1.00. Industrial, maritime and transport collections
*City Museum and Art Gallery*, Queen's Road. Tel: 0117–927 3571. Adm. £2.00. Includes fine and applied art, oriental art, and Bristol ceramics and paintings

CAMBRIDGE – *Duxford Airfield*, Duxford. Tel: 01223–835000. Adm. £5.95. Displays of military and civil aircraft, tanks, guns and naval exhibits
*Fitzwilliam Museum*, Trumpington Street. Tel: 01223–332900. Closed Mon. (except Bank Holidays) and Sun. mornings. Lower galleries closed afternoons (except Sat.); upper galleries closed mornings (except Sat.). Adm. free. Antiquities, fine and applied arts, clocks, ceramics, manuscripts, furniture, sculpture, coins and medals and temporary exhibitions

CARLISLE – *Tullie House Museum and Art Gallery*, Castle Street. Tel: 01228–34781. Closed Sun. mornings. Adm. charge to Border galleries only; ground floor, Old Tullie House and Jacobean galleries, adm. free. Prehistoric archaeology, Hadrian's Wall, Viking and medieval Cumbria, and the social history of Carlisle; also British 19th- and 20th-century art and English porcelain

CHESTER – *Grosvenor Museum*, Grosvenor Street. Tel: 01244–321616. Closed Sun. mornings. Adm. free. Roman collections, natural history, art, clocks, local history and costume

CHICHESTER – *Weald and Downland Open Air Museum*, Singleton. Tel: 01243–811348. Open March-Oct. daily. Adm. £4.20. Rescued vernacular buildings from south-east England rebuilt on a downland site; includes medieval houses, agricultural and rural craft buildings and a working watermill

COLCHESTER – *Colchester Castle Museum*, Castle Park. Tel: 01206–712939. Closed Sun. mornings and winter. Adm. £2.50. Local archaeological antiquities and displays on Roman Colchester; tours of the Roman vaults, castle walls and chapel with medieval and prison displays

COVENTRY – *Herbert Art Gallery and Museum*, Jordan Well. Tel: 01203–832381. Closed Sun. mornings. Local history, archaeology and industry, natural history including a major collection of insects, and fine and decorative art

*Museum of British Road Transport*, Hales Street. Tel: 01203–832425. Adm. charge. Hundreds of motor vehicles and bicycles

CRICH, nr. Matlock, Derbys. – *National Tramway Museum*. Tel: 01773–852565. Closed in winter. Open weekends and Bank Holidays, and Mon.-Thurs. April-Sept., and some Fridays. Adm. charge. Open-air working museum with tram rides

DERBY – *Derby Museum and Art Gallery*, The Strand. Tel: 01332–255586. Closed Sun. mornings and Bank Holiday mornings. Adm. free. Includes paintings by Joseph Wright of Derby and Derby porcelain

*Industrial Museum*, off Full Street. Tel: 01332–255308. Closed Sun. mornings and Bank Holiday mornings. Adm. 30p. Rolls-Royce aero engine collection and a railway engineering gallery

DORCHESTER – *Dorset County Museum*, High West Street. Tel: 01305–262735. Closed Sun. except July and Aug. Adm. £1.95. Includes a collection of Thomas Hardy's manuscripts, books, notebooks and drawings

EXETER – *Exeter Maritime Museum*, The Haven. Tel: 01392–58075. Adm. £3.85. Collection of working boats

*Royal Albert Memorial Museum*, Queen Street. Tel: 01392–265858. Closed Sun. Adm. free. Natural history, archaeology, ethnography, and fine and decorative art including Exeter silver

HALIFAX – *Eureka! The Museum for Children*, Discovery Road. Tel: 01426–983191. Open daily. Adm. £4.50 (over age 12), £3.50 (ages 3–12), free (under age 3). Family ticket £13.50. Museum designed for children up to age 12

HULL – *Ferens Art Gallery*, Queen Victoria Square. Tel: 01482–593912. Closed Sun. mornings. Adm. free. European art, especially Dutch 17th-century paintings, British portraits from 17th to 20th centuries, and marine paintings

*Town Docks Museum*, Queen Victoria Square. Tel: 01482–593902. Closed Sun. mornings. Adm. free. Whaling, fishing and navigation exhibits

HUNTINGDON – *Cromwell Museum*, Grammar School Walk. Tel: 01480–425830. Closed Mon. and Bank Holidays (except Good Friday); also closed mornings (except Sat.) in winter. Adm. free. Portraits and memorabilia relating to Oliver Cromwell

IPSWICH – *Christchurch Mansion and Wolsey Art Gallery*, Christchurch Park. Tel: 01473–213761. Closed Sun. mornings and Mon. Adm. free. Tudor house with paintings by Gainsborough, Constable and other Suffolk artists; furniture and 18th-century ceramics. Art gallery for temporary exhibitions

KEIGHLEY, W. Yorks. – *Cliffe Castle Museum and Art Gallery*, Spring Gardens Lane. Tel: 01274–758230. Closed Mon. (except Bank Holidays). Adm. free. Natural history, geology and folk life exhibits in a Victorian mansion

LEEDS – *Abbey House Museum*, Kirkstall. Tel: 0113–275 5821. Closed Sun. mornings. Adm. charge. Toys, games, dolls, and three full-sized period streets

*City Art Gallery*, The Headrow. Tel: 0113–247 8248. Closed Sun. and Bank Holidays. Adm. free. British and European paintings including English watercolours, modern sculpture, Henry Moore gallery, print room

*City Museum*, Calverley Street. Tel: 0113–246 2632. Closed Sun. and Mon. Adm. free. Natural history, archaeology, ethnography and coin collections

LEICESTER – *Jewry Wall Museum of Archaeology*, St Nicholas Circle. Tel: 0116–247 3021. Closed Sun. mornings. Adm. free. Archaeology, Roman Jewry Wall and Baths, and mosaics

*Leicestershire Museum and Art Gallery*, New Walk. Tel: 0116–255 4100. Closed Sun. mornings. Adm. free. Includes notable collection of German Expressionist paintings

*Snibston Discovery Park*, Coalville. Tel: 01530–510851. Adm. charge. Open-air science and industry museum on site of a coal mine; country park with nature trail

LINCOLN – *Museum of Lincolnshire Life*, Burton Road. Tel: 01522–528448. Closed Sun. mornings in winter. Adm. charge. Social history and agricultural collection

*National Cycle Museum*, Union Road. Tel: 01522–545091. Adm. charge. Cycles from the early 19th century to the present

*Usher Gallery*, Lindum Road. Tel: 01522–527980. Closed Sun. mornings. Adm. charge. Watches, miniatures, porcelain, silver; collection of Peter de Wint works; Lincolnshire topography; Tennyson memorabilia

LIVERPOOL – *Lady Lever Art Gallery*, Wirral. Tel: 0151–645 3623. Closed Sun. mornings. Adm. free. Paintings, furniture and porcelain

*Liverpool Museum*, William Brown Street. Tel: 0151–207 0001. Closed Sun. mornings. Adm. free (except to the Planetarium). Includes Egyptian mummies, weapons and classical sculpture; planetarium, aquarium, vivarium and natural history centre

*Merseyside Maritime Museum*, Albert Dock. Tel: 0151–207 0001. Joint adm. charge with the Museum of Liverpool Life. Floating exhibits, working displays and craft demonstrations

*Museum of Liverpool Life*, Mann Island. Tel: 0151–207 0001. Joint adm. charge with the Merseyside Maritime Museum. The history of Liverpool

*Sudley Art Gallery*, Mossley Hill Road. Tel: 0151–724 3245. Closed Sun. mornings. Adm. free. Late 18th- and 19th-century British paintings in a former shipowner's home

*Tate Gallery Liverpool*, Albert Dock. Tel: 0151–709 3223. Closed Mon. (except Bank Holidays). Adm. free. Twentieth-century painting and sculpture

*Walker Art Gallery*, William Brown Street. Tel: 0151–207 0001. Closed Sun. mornings. Adm. free. Paintings from the 14th to 20th centuries

LONDON: GALLERIES – *Barbican Art Gallery*, Barbican Centre, EC2. Tel: 0171–638 4141. Temporary exhibitions

*Courtauld Institute Galleries*, Somerset House, Strand, WC2. Tel: 0171–873 2526. Closed Sun. mornings. Adm. £3.00. The University of London galleries

*Dulwich Picture Gallery*, College Road, SE21. Tel: 0181–693 5254. Closed Sun. mornings and Mon. Adm. £2.00. Built by Sir John Soane to house the Bourgeois collection

*Hayward Gallery*, South Bank Centre, SE1. Tel: 0171–928 3144. Adm. £5.00. Temporary exhibitions

*National Gallery*, Trafalgar Square, WC2. Tel: 0171–839 3321. Closed Sun. mornings. Adm. free. Western painting from the 13th to 20th centuries; Early Renaissance collection in the Sainsbury wing

*National Portrait Gallery*, St Martin's Place, WC2. Tel: 0171–306 0055. Closed Sun. mornings. Adm. free. Portraits of eminent people in British history; galleries of 20th-century portraits and photographs

*Percival David Foundation of Chinese Art*, Gordon Square, WC1. Tel: 0171-387 3909. Closed weekends. Adm. free. Chinese ceramics; reference library
*Photographers Gallery*, Great Newport Street, WC2. Tel: 0171-831 1772. Closed Sun. Adm. free. Temporary exhibitions
*The Queen's Gallery*, Buckingham Palace, SW1. Tel: 0171-799 2331. Closed Mon. (except Bank Holidays) and Sun. mornings. Adm. £3.00. Art from the royal collection
*Royal Academy of Arts*, Piccadilly, W1. Tel: 0171-439 7438. Adm. charge. British art since 1750 and temporary exhibitions; annual Summer Exhibition
*Serpentine Gallery*, Kensington Gardens, W2. Tel: 0171-402 6075. Adm. free. Temporary exhibitions
*Tate Gallery*, Millbank, SW1. Tel: 0171-821 1313. Closed Sun. mornings. Adm. free. British painting and 20th-century painting and sculpture
*Wallace Collection*, Manchester Square, W1. Tel: 0171-935 0687. Closed Sun. mornings. Adm. free. Paintings and drawings, French 18th-century furniture, armour, porcelain and clocks
*Whitechapel Art Gallery*, Whitechapel High Street, E1. Tel: 0171-377 0107. Closed Mon. Adm. free to most exhibitions. Temporary exhibitions
LONDON: MUSEUMS – *Bank of England Museum*, Threadneedle Street, EC2. Tel: 0171-601 5545. Closed Sun. and Bank Holidays (except in summer); also closed Sat. Adm. free. History of the Bank since 1694
*Bethnal Green Museum of Childhood*, Cambridge Heath Road, E2. Tel: 0181-980 3204. Closed Sun. mornings and Fri. Adm. free but donations invited. Toys, games and exhibits relating to the social history of childhood
*British Museum*, Great Russell Street, WC1. Tel: 0171-636 1555. Closed Sun. mornings. Adm. free. Antiquities, coins, medals, prints and drawings, European history galleries
*Cabinet War Rooms*, King Charles Street, SW1. Tel: 0171-930 6961. Adm. £3.90. Underground rooms used by Churchill and the Government during the Second World War
*Commonwealth Institute*, Kensington High Street, W8. Tel: 0171-603 4535. Closed Sun. mornings. Adm. £1.00. Exhibitions on Commonwealth nations, visual arts and crafts
*Cutty Sark*, Greenwich, SE10. Tel: 0181-858 3445. Closed in winter. Adm. £3.25. Restored and rerigged tea clipper with exhibits on board. Sir Francis Chichester's round-the-world yacht, *Gipsy Moth IV*, can also be seen (separate adm. charge 50p)
*Design Museum*, Shad Thames, SE1. Tel: 0171-407 6261. Adm. £4.50. The development of design and the mass-production of consumer objects
*Geffrye Museum*, Kingsland Road, E2. Tel: 0171-739 9893. Closed Mon., and Sun. and Bank Holiday mornings. Adm. free. English urban domestic interiors since 1600; also paintings, furniture , decorative arts and walled herb garden
*Horniman Museum and Gardens*, London Road, SE23. Tel: 0181-699 1872. Closed Sun. mornings. Adm. free. Museum of ethnography, musical instruments and natural history. Reference library (by appointment)
*Imperial War Museum*, Lambeth Road, SE1. Tel: 0171-416 5000. Reference departments closed Sat. (except by appointment) and Sun. Adm. £3.90 (free after 4.30 p.m. daily). All aspects of the two world wars and other military operations involving Britain and the Commonwealth since 1914

*Jewish Museum*, Albert Street, NW1. Tel: 0171-284 1997. Closed Fri., Sat., public and Jewish holidays. Adm. £2.50. Jewish life, history and religion
*London Transport Museum*, Covent Garden, WC2. Tel: 0171-379 6344. Adm. charge. Vehicles, photographs and graphic art relating to the history of London public transport
*MCC Museum*, Lord's, NW8. Tel: 0171-289 1611. Open match days (closed Sun. mornings); also conducted tours by appointment with Tours Manager. Adm. charge. Cricket museum
*Museum of London*, London Wall, EC2. Tel: 0171-600 3699. Closed Sun. mornings and Mon. Adm. £3.50 (free after 4.30 p.m. daily). History of London from prehistoric times to present day
*Museum of Mankind*, Burlington Gardens, W1. Tel: 0171-636 1555. Closed Sun. mornings. Adm. free. The ethnographical collections of the British Museum
*Museum of the Moving Image*, South Bank, SE1. Tel: 0171-401 2636. Adm. £5.50. History of the moving image in cinema and television
*National Army Museum*, Royal Hospital Road, SW3. Tel: 0171-730 0717. Adm. free. History of the British army; the Indian Army room at the Royal Military Academy, Sandhurst, Camberley, Surrey, may be viewed by appointment
*National Maritime Museum*, Greenwich, SE10. Tel: 0181-858 4422. Closed Sun. mornings. Reference library closed Sat. (except by appointment) and Sun. Comprises the main building, the Old Royal Observatory, the Queen's House (*see page 586*), and a Special Exhibitions Centre. Adm. charge. Maritime history of Britain
*Natural History Museum*, Cromwell Road, SW7. Tel: 0171-938 9123. Adm. £5.00. Natural history collections
*Royal Air Force Museum*, Hendon, NW9. Tel: 0181-205 2266. Adm. charge. Aviation from before the Wright brothers to the present-day RAF; historic aircraft
*Royal Mews*, Buckingham Palace, SW1. Tel: 0171-799 2331. Open Tues.-Thurs. in summer, Wed. only in winter. Adm. £3.00. Carriages, coaches, stables and horses
*Science Museum*, Exhibition Road, SW7. Tel: 0171-938 8000. Closed Sun. and Bank Holiday weekends. Adm. charge. Science, technology, industry and medicine collections
*Shakespeare Globe Exhibition*, Bankside, SE1. Tel: 0171-928 6406. Adm. £4.00. Recreation of Elizabethan theatre using 16th-century techniques
*Sherlock Holmes Museum*, Baker Street, NW1. Tel: 0171-935 8866. Adm. £5.00. Recreated rooms of the fictional detective
*Sir John Soane's Museum*, Lincoln's Inn Fields, WC2. Tel: 0171-405 2107. Closed Sun. and Mon. Adm. free. Art and antiques
*Theatre Museum*, Russell Street, WC2. Tel: 0171-836 7891. Closed Mon. Adm. £3.00. History of the performing arts
\**Tower Bridge Walkway and Museum*, SE1. Tel: 0171-378 1928. Adm. £5.00. History of the bridge and display of Victorian steam machinery; panoramic views from walkways
*Victoria and Albert Museum*, Cromwell Road, SW7. Tel: 0171-938 8500. Closed Mon. mornings. Includes National Art Library and Print Room (closed Sun. and Mon.) Adm. free but donations invited. Fine and applied art and design, including furniture, glass, textiles and dress collections

*Wellington Museum* (Apsley House), Hyde Park Corner, w1. Tel: 0171-499 5676. Closed until June 1995. Adm. charge. Wellington's home after Waterloo, known as No. 1 London; paintings, sculpture, silver and porcelain
*Wimbledon Lawn Tennis Museum*, Church Road, sw19. Tel: 0181-946 6131. Closed Sun. mornings and Mon. Adm. £2.50. Tennis trophies, fashion and memorabilia
MANCHESTER – *\*City Art Galleries*, Mosley Street and Princess Street. Tel: 0161-236 5244. Closed Sun. mornings. Adm. free. Includes Old Masters, Turner, Gainsborough, Stubbs, the Pre-Raphaelites and 20th century art
*\*Gallery of English Costume*, Rusholme. Tel: 0161-224 5217. Closed Sun. mornings and Tues. (weekend opening subject to change). Adm. free. Exhibits from the 16th to 20th centuries
*Manchester Museum*, Oxford Road. Tel: 0161-275 2634. Closed Sun. Adm. free. Botany, Egyptology, geology, zoology, entomology, ethnography and natural history collections
*Museum of Science and Industry*, Castlefield. Tel: 0161-832 1830. Adm. £3.50. On site of world's oldest passenger railway station; galleries relating to space, energy, power, transport, aviation and social history; interactive science centre
*Whitworth Art Gallery*, Oxford Road. Tel: 0161-273 4865. Closed Sun. Adm. free. Watercolours, drawings, prints, textiles, wallpapers and 20th-century British art
NEWCASTLE UPON TYNE – *\*Laing Art Gallery*, Higham Place. Tel: 0191-232 7734. Closed Sun. mornings. Adm. free. British and European art, ceramics, glass, silver, textiles and costume; local arts and crafts
*\*Newcastle Discovery* (Museum of Science and Engineering), West Blandford Square. Tel: 0191-232 6789. Closed Sun. Local history, fashion, power, and Tyneside's maritime history; hands-on science centre
NEWMARKET – *National Horseracing Museum*, High Street. Tel: 01638-667333. Closed Mon. (except Bank Holidays, July and Aug.), Sun. mornings and Jan.-March. Adm. £3.30. Paintings, trophies and exhibits relating to horseracing
NORWICH – *\*Castle Museum*. Tel: 01603-223624. Closed Sun. mornings. Adm. charge. Art (including Norwich school), archaeology, silver and glass; guided tours of battlements and dungeons
NOTTINGHAM – *\*Brewhouse Yard Museum*, Castle Boulevard. Tel: 0115-948 3504. Adm. free. Daily life from the 17th to 20th centuries
*\*Castle Museum*. Tel: 0115-948 3504. Adm. free. Paintings, archaeology, ceramics, ethnography, silver and glass; history of Nottingham
*\*Industrial Museum*, Wollaton Park. Tel: 0115-928 4602. Closed Sun. mornings, and Mon.-Wed. and Fri. in winter. Adm. free (except Sat., Sun. and Bank Holidays) Lacemaking machinery, steam engines and transport exhibits
*\*Natural History Museum*, Wollaton Park. Tel: 0115-928 1333. Closed Sun. mornings. Adm. free (except Sat., Sun. and Bank Holidays) Local natural history and wildlife dioramas
OXFORD – *Ashmolean Museum*, Beaumont Street. Tel: 01865-278000. Closed Mon. (except Bank Holidays) and Sun. mornings. Adm. free. European and Oriental fine and applied arts, archaeology, Egyptology and numismatics
*Museum of Modern Art*, Pembroke Street. Tel: 01865-722733. Closed Sun. mornings and Mon. Temporary exhibitions

*Oxford University Museum*, Parks Road. Tel: 01865-272950. Closed mornings (except for school parties) and Sun. Adm. free. Entomology, geology, mineralogy and zoology
PLYMOUTH – *\*City Museum and Art Gallery*, Drake Circus. Tel: 01752-668000. Closed Mon. (except Bank Holidays) and Sun. Adm. free. Includes temporary exhibitions
*\*The Dome*, The Hoe. Tel: 01752-600608. Adm. charge. Maritime history museum
PORTSMOUTH – *\*Charles Dickens Birthplace Museum*, Old Commercial Road. Tel: 01705-827261. Closed in winter. Adm. charge. Dickens memorabilia
*\*D-Day Museum*, Clarence Esplanade. Tel: 01705-827261. Adm. charge. Includes the Overlord Embroidery
*Naval Heritage Area*, HM Naval Base. Story of the Royal Navy using HMS *Victory* (tel: 01705-819604), HMS *Warrior* (tel: 01705-291379), and the *Mary Rose* (tel: 01705-750521). Separate adm. charge to each
*Royal Naval Museum*, HM Naval Base. Tel: 01705-733060. Adm. charge. Includes Nelson memorabilia
PRESTON – *\*Harris Museum and Art Gallery*, Market Square. Tel: 01772-257112. Closed Sun. Adm. free. British art since the 18th century, ceramics, glass, costume and local history
ST ALBANS – *\*Verulamium Museum*, St Michael's. Tel: 01727-819339. Closed Sun. mornings. Adm. £2.50. Iron Age and Roman Verulamium, including wall plasters, jewellery, mosaics and room reconstructions
ST IVES, Cornwall – *Tate Gallery St Ives*, Porthmeor Beach. Tel: 01736-796226. Closed Mon. Sept.-May except Bank Holidays. Adm. £2.50. Twentieth-century works from the St Ives collection. Includes admission to Barbara Hepworth Museum and Sculpture Garden
SHEFFIELD – *\*City Museum*, Weston Park. Tel: 0114-276 8588. Closed Mon. Adm. free. Includes cutlery, Sheffield plate, and Peak district archaeology
*\*Graves Art Gallery*, Surrey Street. Tel: 0114-273 5858. Closed Sun. mornings and Mon. Adm. free. British art from the 16th to 20th centuries. Old Masters and non-European art
*\*Kelham Island Industrial Museum*, off Alma Street. Tel: 0114-272 2106. Closed Fri. and Sat. Adm. charge. Local industrial and social history
*\*Mappin Art Gallery*, Weston Park. Tel: 0114-272 6281. Closed Sun. mornings and Mon. Adm. free. British and European art from the 18th to 20th centuries
*\*Shepherd Wheel*, off Hangingwater Road. Tel: 0114-236 7731. Closed Mon. and Tues. Adm. free. Water-powered cutlery-grinding wheel and workshops
STOKE-ON-TRENT – *\*Etruria Industrial Museum*, Shelton. Tel: 01782-287557. Closed Mon. and Tues. Adm. free. Britain's sole surviving steam-powered potter's mill
*\*City Museum and Art Gallery*, Hanley. Tel: 01782-202173. Closed Sun. mornings. Adm. free. Pottery and porcelain collections
*Gladstone Pottery Museum*, Longton. Tel: 01782-319232. Closed Sun. mornings; closed in winter. Adm. charge. A working Victorian pottery
Pottery factory tours are available by arrangement Mon.-Fri., except during factory holidays, at the following: *Royal Doulton*, Nile Street, Burslem; *Spode*, Church Street, Stoke; *Beswick*, Gold Street, Longton; *Royal Grafton China*, Marlborough Road, Longton; *Wedgwood*, Barlaston
STYAL, Cheshire – *Quarry Bank Mill*. Tel: 01625-527468. Closed Mon. in winter. Adm. charge. Water-powered cotton mill illustrating history of cotton industry; weaving demonstrations; restored Apprentice House

TRING, Herts. – *Tring Zoological Museum*, Akeman Street. Tel: 01442-824181. Closed Sun. mornings. Adm. £2.00. Display of more than 4,000 animal species

WAKEFIELD – *Yorkshire Sculpture Park*, West Bretton. Tel: 01924-830302. Adm. free. Sculpture by Moore, Hepworth and others in open air; public workshops and temporary exhibitions

WORCESTER – *City Museum and Art Gallery*, Foregate Street. Tel: 01905-25371. Closed Thurs. and Sun. Adm. free. Includes a military museum and changing art exhibitions
*Dyson Perrins Museum and Royal Worcester Porcelain Works*, Severn Street. Tel: 01905-23221. Closed Sun. Adm. £1.50. Worcester porcelain collection; factory tours on weekdays

WROUGHTON, nr. Swindon, Wilts. – *Science Museum*, Wroughton Airfield. Tel: 01793-814466. Open selected summer weekends only. Adm. charge. Air displays and some of the Science Museum's transport and agricultural collection

YEOVIL, Somerset – *Fleet Air Arm Museum*, Royal Naval Air Station, Yeovilton. Tel: 01935-840565. Adm. charge. History of naval aviation; historic aircraft, including Concorde 002
*Montacute House*, Montacute. Tel: 01935-823289. Closed mornings and on Tues.; also closed in winter. Adm. £4.80. Elizabethan and Jacobean portraits from the National Portrait Gallery

YORK – *Beningbrough Hall*, Shipton-by-Beningbrough. Tel: 01904-470666. Closed Thurs. and Fri. (except Good Friday and July-Aug.); also closed in winter. Adm. £4.50. Portraits from the National Portrait Gallery
*Castle Museum*. Tel: 01904-653611. Adm. £3.95. Reconstructed streets; costume and military collections
*City Art Gallery*, Exhibition Square. Tel: 01904-623839. Closed Sun. mornings. Adm. free. European and British painting spanning seven centuries; modern pottery
*Jorvik Viking Centre*, Coppergate. Tel: 01904-643211. Adm. £3.95. Reconstruction of Viking York
*National Railway Museum*, Leeman Road. Tel: 01904-621261. Adm. £4.20. Includes locomotives, rolling stock and carriages
*Yorkshire Museum*, Museum Gardens. Tel: 01904-629745. Closed Sun. mornings in winter. Adm. £3.00. Yorkshire life from Roman to medieval times; geology gallery

## WALES

CAERLEON, Gwent – *Roman Legionary Museum*. Tel: 01633-423134. Closed Sun. mornings. Adm. charge. Material from the site of the Roman fortress of Isca and its suburbs

CARDIFF – *National Museum of Wales*, Cathays Park. Tel: 01222-397951. Closed Sun. mornings and Mon. (except Bank Holidays). Adm. charge. Includes natural sciences, archaeology and Impressionist paintings
*Welsh Folk Museum*, St Fagans. Tel: 01222-569441. Closed Sun. in winter. Adm. charge. Open-air museum with re-erected buildings, agricultural equipment and costume
*Welsh Industrial and Maritime Museum*, Bute Street. Tel: 01222-481919. Closed Mon., and Sun. mornings. Adm. charge. Power, railways, locomotives and shipping exhibitions; miniature railway

LLANBERIS, Gwynedd – *Museum of the North*. Tel: 01286-870636. Closed Nov.-April (except by appointment). Adm. charge. Multi-media presentation of Welsh history, including the electricity supply industry
*Welsh Slate Museum*. Tel: 01286-870630. Closed in winter. Adm. charge. Original 19th-century plant and machinery in a disused slate quarry; recreated workshops and crafts demonstrations

LLANDYSUL, Dyfed – *Museum of the Welsh Woollen Industry*, Dre-fach Felindre. Tel: 01559-370929. Closed Sun., and Sat. in winter. Adm. charge. Exhibitions, a working woollen mill and craft workshops

ST ASAPH, Clwyd – *Bodelwyddan Castle*, Bodelwyddan. Tel: 01745-583539. Closed Fri. (except July-Aug.) and Mon. and Fri. in winter. Adm. charge. Portraits from the National Portrait Gallery

SWANSEA – *Glyn Vivian Art Gallery and Museum*, Alexandra Road. Tel: 01792-655006. Closed Mon. (except Bank Holidays). Adm. free. Paintings, ceramics, Swansea pottery and porcelain, clocks, glass and Welsh art
*Swansea Maritime and Industrial Museum*, Museum Square. Tel: 01792-650351. Closed Mon. (except Bank Holidays). Adm. free. Includes a working woollen mill and historic boats

## SCOTLAND

ABERDEEN – *Aberdeen Art Gallery*, Schoolhill. Tel: 01224-646333. Closed Sun. mornings. Adm. free. Art from the 18th to 20th centuries
*Aberdeen Maritime Museum*, Shiprow. Tel: 01224-585788. Closed Mon. Adm. free. Maritime history, including shipbuilding and North Sea oil

EDINBURGH – *City Art Centre*, Market Street. Tel: 0131-529 3541. Closed Sun. Adm. free. Late 19th- and 20th-century art and temporary exhibitions
*Commonwealth Institute Scotland*, Rutland Square. Tel: 0131-229 6668. Closed weekends. Adm. free. Exhibitions relating to countries of the Commonwealth
*Huntly House Museum*, Canongate. Tel: 0131-529 4143. Closed Sun. Adm. free. Local history, silver, glass and Scottish pottery
*Museum of Antiquities*, Queen Street. Tel: 0131-255 7534. Closed Sun. mornings. Adm. free. Scotland since the Stone Age
*Museum of Childhood*, High Street. Tel: 0131-529 4142. Closed Sun. Adm. free. Toys, games, clothes and exhibits relating to the social history of childhood
*Museum of Flight*, East Fortune Airfield, nr North Berwick. Tel: 01620-880308. Closed in winter. Adm. charge. Display of more than 30 aircraft
*National Gallery of Scotland*, The Mound. Tel: 0131-556 8921. Closed Sun. mornings. Adm. free. Paintings, drawings and prints from the 16th to 20th centuries, and the national collection of Scottish art
*People's Story*, Canongate. Tel: 0131-529 4057. Closed Sun. Adm. free. Edinburgh life since the 18th century
*Royal Museum of Scotland*, Chambers Street. Tel: 0131-225 7534. Closed Sun. mornings. Adm. free. Scottish and international collections from prehistoric times to the present
*Scottish Agricultural Museum*, Ingliston. Tel: 0131-225 7534. Closed in winter and on Sun., also on Sat. in May and Sept. Adm. free. History of agriculture in Scotland

*Scottish National Portrait Gallery*, Queen Street.
Tel: 0131–556 8921. Closed Sun. mornings. Adm. free.
Portraits of eminent people in Scottish history, and the
national collection of photography
*Scottish National Gallery of Modern Art*, Belford Road.
Tel: 0131–556 8921. Closed Sun. mornings. Adm. free.
Twentieth-century painting, sculpture and graphic art
*Scottish United Services Museum*, Edinburgh Castle.
Tel: 0131–225 7534. Closed Sun. mornings in winter.
Adm. free. History of the armed forces of Scotland
\*The Writer's Museum*, Lawnmarket. Tel: 0131–529 4901.
Closed Sun. Adm. free. Robert Louis Stevenson, Walter
Scott and Robert Burns exhibits
FORT WILLIAM – *West Highland Museum*, Cameron
Square. Tel: 01397–702169. Closed Sun. mornings.
Includes tartan collections and exhibits relating to 1745
uprising
GLASGOW – *Glasgow Art Gallery and Museum*,
Kelvingrove. Tel: 0141–221 9600. Adm. free. Includes
Old Masters, 19th-century French paintings and armour
collection
*Burrell Collection*, Pollokshaws Road. Tel: 0141–649 7151.
Adm. free. Nineteenth-century paintings, textiles,
furniture, ceramics, stained glass and silver
*Hunterian Art Gallery*, Hillhead Street. Tel: 0141–330
5431. Closed Sun. Adm. free. Rennie Mackintosh and
Whistler collections; also Old Masters and modern prints
*McLellan Galleries*, Sauchiehall Street. Tel: 0141–331
1854. Closed Sun. mornings. Adm. charge. Temporary
exhibitions
*Museum of Transport*, Bunhouse Road. Tel: 0141–221
9600. Adm. free. Includes a reproduction of a 1938
Glasgow street, cars since the 1930s, trams and a Glasgow
subway station
*People's Palace Museum*, Glasgow Green. Tel: 0141–554
0223. Adm. free. History of Glasgow since 1175
*Pollok House*, Pollokshaws Road. Tel: 0141–632 0274.
Adm. free. Spanish paintings, furniture, silver and
ceramics
*St Mungo Museum of Religious Life and Art*, Castle Street.
Tel: 0141–553 2557. Adm. free. Explores universal
themes through objects of all the main global religions

## NORTHERN IRELAND

BELFAST – *Ulster Museum*, Botanic Gardens. Tel: 01232–
381251. Closed weekend mornings. Adm. free. Irish
antiquities, natural and local history, fine and applied arts
HOLYWOOD, Co. Down – *Ulster Folk and Transport
Museum*, Cultra. Tel: 01232–428428. Closed Sun.
mornings, and also Sat. mornings in winter. Adm. £3.00.
Indoor galleries and reconstructed buildings in the open
air
OMAGH, Co. Tyrone – *Ulster American Folk Park*,
Castletown. Tel: 01662–243292. Closed weekends in
winter. Adm. £3.00. Open-air museum telling the story
of Ulster's emigrants to America; restored or recreated
thatched houses, log cabins and craft workshops; ship and
dockside gallery

# Sights of London

For historic buildings, museums and galleries in London, *see* pages 585–596

ALEXANDRA PALACE AND PARK, Wood Green, London N22 4AY. Tel: 0181-365 2121. The Victorian Palace was severely damaged by fire in 1980 but was restored, and reopened in 1988. Alexandra Palace now provides modern facilities for exhibitions, sports, conferences and leisure activities. There is an ice rink, open daily.

BARBICAN CENTRE, Silk Street, London EC2Y 8DS. Tel: 0171-638 4141 ext. 7537/8. Owned, funded and managed by the Corporation of London, the Barbican Centre opened in 1982 and houses the 1,166-seat Barbican Theatre, along with a 200-seat studio theatre (The Pit), and the 2,026-seat Barbican Hall. There are also three cinemas, two art galleries, a sculpture court, a lending library, trade exhibition and conference facilities.

BRIDGES. The bridges over the Thames (from east to west) are:

*The Queen Elizabeth II Bridge*, opened 1991, from Dartford to Thurrock

*Tower Bridge*, opened 1894 (*see also* page 594)

*London Bridge*, opened after rebuilding by Rennie, 1831; the new London Bridge opened 1973

*Alexandra Bridge* (railway bridge), built 1863–6

*Southwark Bridge* (Rennie), built 1814–19; rebuilt 1912–21

*Blackfriars Railway Bridge*, completed 1864

*Blackfriars Bridge*, built 1760–9; rebuilt 1860–9; widened 1907–10

*Waterloo Bridge* (Rennie), opened 1817; rebuilt 1937–42

*Hungerford Railway Bridge* (Brunel), suspension bridge built 1841–5; replaced by present railway and footbridge 1863

*Westminster Bridge* (width 84 ft), opened 1750; rebuilt 1854–62

*Lambeth Bridge*, built 1862; rebuilt 1929–32

*Vauxhall Bridge*, built 1811–16; rebuilt 1895–1906

*Grosvenor Bridge* (railway bridge), built 1859–60; rebuilt 1963–7

*Chelsea Bridge*, built 1851–8; replaced by suspension bridge 1934; widened 1937

*Albert Bridge*, opened 1873; restructured (Bazalgette) 1884; strengthened 1971–3

*Battersea Bridge* (Holland), opened 1772; rebuilt (Bazalgette) 1890

*Battersea Railway Bridge*, opened 1863

*Wandsworth Bridge*, opened 1873; rebuilt 1940

*Putney Railway Bridge*, opened 1889

*Putney Bridge*, built 1727–9; rebuilt (Bazalgette) 1882–6; starting point of Oxford and Cambridge Boat Race

*Hammersmith Bridge*, built 1824–7; rebuilt (Bazalgette) 1883–7

*Barnes Railway Bridge* (also pedestrian), built 1846–9; restructured 1893

*Chiswick Bridge*, opened 1933

*Kew Railway Bridge*, opened 1869

*Kew Bridge*, built 1758–9; rebuilt and renamed King Edward VII Bridge 1903

*Richmond Lock*; lock, weir and footbridge opened 1894

*Twickenham Bridge*, opened 1933

*Richmond Railway Bridge*, opened 1848; restructured 1906–8

*Richmond Bridge*, built 1774–7; widened 1937

*Teddington Lock*, footbridge opened 1889; marks the end of the tidal reach of the Thames

*Kingston Bridge*, built 1825–8; widened 1914

*Hampton Court Bridge*, built 1753; replaced by iron bridge 1865; present bridge built 1933

CEMETERIES. *Abney Park*, Stamford Hill, N16 (35 acres), tomb of General Booth, founder of the Salvation Army, and memorials to many Nonconformist divines. *Brompton*, Old Brompton Road, SW10 (40 acres), graves of Sir Henry Cole, Emmeline Pankhurst, John Wisden. *City of London Cemetery and Crematorium*, Aldersbrook Road, E12 (200 acres). *Golders Green Crematorium*, Hoop Lane, NW11 (12 acres), with Garden of Rest and memorials to many famous men and women. *Hampstead*, Fortune Green Road, NW6 (36 acres), graves of Kate Greenaway, Lord Lister, Marie Lloyd. *Highgate*, Swains Lane, N6 (38 acres), tombs of George Eliot, Herbert Spencer, Faraday and Marx; guided tours only, west side, £3.00. *Kensal Green*, Harrow Road, W10 (70 acres), tombs of Thackeray, Trollope, Sydney Smith, Wilkie Collins, Tom Hood, George Cruikshank, Leigh Hunt, I. K. Brunel and Charles Kemble. Churchyard of the former *Marylebone Chapel*, Marylebone High Street, W1, Charles Wesley and his son Samuel Wesley buried; chapel demolished in 1949, now Garden of Rest. *Nunhead*, Linden Grove, SE15 (26 acres), badly vandalized and closed in 1969, recently restored and opened for burials. *St Marylebone Cemetery and Crematorium*, East End Road, N2 (47 acres). *West Norwood Cemetery and Crematorium*, Norwood High Street, SE27 (42 acres), tombs of Sir Henry Bessemer, Sir Hiram Maxim, Mrs Beeton, Sir Henry Tate and Joseph Whitaker (*Whitaker's Almanack*).

CENOTAPH, Whitehall, London SW1. The word 'cenotaph' means 'empty tomb'. It is the monument erected 'To the Glorious Dead', as a memorial to all ranks of the sea, land and air forces who gave their lives in the service of the Empire during the First World War. Designed by Sir Edwin Lutyens and erected as a temporary memorial in 1919, it was replaced by a permanent structure unveiled by George V on Armistice Day 1920. An additional inscription was made after the Second World War to commemorate those who gave their lives in that conflict.

CHARTERHOUSE, Sutton's Hospital, Charterhouse Square, London EC1M 6AN. Tel: 0171-253 9503. A Carthusian monastery from 1371 to 1537, purchased in 1611 by Thomas Sutton, who endowed it as a hospital for aged men 'of gentle birth' and a school for poor scholars (removed to Godalming in 1872). Open to visitors on Wednesdays at 2.15 (April–July). Admission £2.00. *Registrar and Clerk to the Governors*, Lt.-Col. I. Macdonald.

CHELSEA PHYSIC GARDEN, 66 Royal Hospital Road, London SW3 4HS. Tel: 0171-352 5646. A garden of general botanical research, maintaining a wide range of rare and unusual plants. The garden was established in 1673 by the Society of Apothecaries. Open Wednesday and Sunday p.m. during summer months. All enquiries to the Curator.

DOWNING STREET, London SW1. Number 10 Downing Street is the official town residence of the Prime Minister, No. 11 of the Chancellor of the Exchequer and No. 12 is the office of the Government Whips. The street was named after Sir George Downing, Bt., soldier and diplomatist, who was MP for Morpeth from 1660 to 1684. *Chequers*, a Tudor mansion in the Chilterns about three miles from Princes Risborough, was presented by Lord and Lady Lee of Fareham in 1917 to serve, from 1921, as a country residence for the Prime Minister of the day.

GEORGE INN, Borough High Street, London SE1. The last galleried inn in London, built in 1677. Now run as an ordinary public house.

GREENWICH, London SE10. *The Royal Naval College* was until 1873 the Greenwich Hospital. It was built by Charles II, largely from designs by John Webb, and by Queen Anne and William III, from designs by Wren. It stands on the site of an ancient royal palace and of the more recent Palace of Placentia constructed by Humphrey, Duke of Gloucester (1391–1447), son of Henry IV. Henry VIII, Mary I and Elizabeth I were born in the royal palace (which reverted to the Crown in 1447) and Edward VI died there. *Greenwich Park* (196½ acres) was enclosed by Humphrey, Duke of Gloucester, and laid out by Charles II from the designs of Le Nôtre. On a hill in Greenwich Park is the former Royal Observatory (founded 1675). Its buildings are now managed by the National Maritime Museum (*see* page 594) and the first observatory is named Flamsteed House, after John Flamsteed (1646–1719), the first Astronomer Royal. *Cutty Sark*, the last of the famous tea clippers, has been preserved as a memorial to ships and men of a past era (*see* page 594). The yacht *Gipsy Moth IV* is preserved alongside the *Cutty Sark*.

HORSE GUARDS, Whitehall, London SW1. Archway and offices built about 1753. The mounting of the guard takes place at 11 a.m. (10 a.m. on Sundays) and the dismounted inspection at 4 p.m. Only those on the Lord Chamberlain's list may drive through the gates and archway into *Horse Guards' Parade* (230,000 sq. ft), where the Colour is 'trooped' on The Queen's official birthday.

THE HOUSES OF PARLIAMENT, Westminster, London SW1. The royal palace of Westminster, originally built by Edward the Confessor, was the normal meeting place of Parliament from about 1340. St Stephen's Chapel was used from about 1550 for the meetings of the House of Commons, which had previously been held in the Chapter House or Refectory of Westminster Abbey. The House of Lords met in an apartment of the royal palace.

The fire of 1834 destroyed much of the palace and the present Houses of Parliament were erected on the site from the designs of Sir Charles Barry and Augustus Welby Pugin between 1840 and 1867. The Chamber of the House of Commons was destroyed by bombing in 1941 and a new Chamber designed by Sir Giles Gilbert Scott was used for the first time in 1950.

*Westminster Hall* was the only part of the old palace of Westminster to survive the fire of 1834. It was built by William Rufus (1097–9) and altered by Richard II (1394–9). The hammerbeam roof of carved oak dates from 1396–8. The Hall was the scene of the trial of Charles I.

*The Victoria Tower* of the House of Lords is about 330 ft high, and when Parliament is sitting the Union flag flies by day from its flagstaff. *The Clock Tower* of the House of Commons is about 320 ft high and contains 'Big Ben', the hour bell said to be named after Sir Benjamin Hall, First Commissioner of Works when the original bell was cast in 1856. This bell, which weighed 16 tons 11 cwt, was found to be cracked in 1857. The present bell (13½ tons) is a recasting of the original and was first brought into use in 1859. The dials of the clock are 23 ft in diameter, the hands being 9 ft and 14 ft long (including balance piece). A light is displayed from the Clock Tower at night when Parliament is sitting.

For security reasons tours of the Houses of Parliament are available only to those who have made advance arrangements through an MP or peer.

Admission to the Strangers' Gallery of the House of Lords is arranged by a peer or by queue via St Stephen's Entrance. Admission to the Strangers' Gallery of the House of Commons is by Members' order (Members' orders should be sought several weeks in advance), or by queue via St Stephen's Entrance. Queues are usually shorter after 6 p.m., Monday–Thursday. Overseas visitors may write to the Public Information Office, or obtain cards of introduction from their Embassy or High Commission.

INNS OF COURT. The *Inner* and *Middle Temple*, Fleet Street/Victoria Embankment, London EC4, have occupied since the early 14th century the site of the buildings of the Order of Knights Templars. *Inner Temple Hall* is open by appointment on application to the Treasurer's Office. *Middle Temple Hall* (1562–70) is open when not in use, Monday–Friday 10–11.30 and 3–4; closed on public holidays. In Middle Temple Gardens (not open to the public) Shakespeare (Henry VI, Part I) places the incident which led to the 'Wars of the Roses' (1455–85).

*Temple Church*, London EC4, has a nave which forms one of five remaining round churches in England. Open Wednesday–Friday 10–4. Services: 8.30 and 11.15 a.m. except in August and September. *Master of the Temple*, Revd Canon J. Robinson.

*Lincoln's Inn*, Chancery Lane/Lincoln's Inn Fields, London WC2, occupies the site of the palace of a former Bishop of Chichester and of a Black Friars monastery. The Hall and Library Buildings are of 1845, although the Library is first mentioned in 1474; the old Hall (early 16th century) and the Chapel were rebuilt c.1619–23. Halls open by appointment, Chapel and Gardens, Monday–Friday 12–2.30. Chapel services Sunday 11.30 a.m. during law terms. *Lincoln's Inn Fields* (7 acres). The Square was laid out by Inigo Jones.

*Gray's Inn*, Holborn/Gray's Inn Road, London WC1. Early 14th century. Hall 1556–8. Chapel services 11.15 a.m. (during law dining terms only). Holy Communion first Sunday in every month except August–September. Gardens open Monday–Friday 12–2.30. Tel: 0171-405 8164. No other 'Inns' are active, but there are remains of *Staple Inn*, a gabled front on Holborn (opposite Gray's Inn Road). *Clement's Inn* (near St Clement Danes Church), *Clifford's Inn*, Fleet Street, and *Thavies Inn*, Holborn Circus, are all rebuilt. *Serjeants' Inn*, Fleet Street and another (demolished 1910) of the same name in Chancery Lane, were composed of Serjeants-at-Law, the last of whom died in 1922.

KEW GARDENS, Surrey – *see* index.

LLOYD'S, Lime Street, London EC3M 7HA. Society of private underwriters which evolved during the 18th century from Lloyds Coffee House. The present building was opened for business in May 1986, and houses the Lutine Bell. Underwriting is on four floors with a total area of 114,000 sq. ft. A visitors' gallery is open Monday–Friday for pre-booked groups.

LONDON PARKS, ETC.
Maintained by the Crown
*Bushy Park* (1,099 acres), Surrey. Adjoining Hampton Court, contains avenue of horse-chestnuts enclosed in a fourfold avenue of limes planted by William III. 'Chestnut Sunday' (when the trees are in full bloom with their 'candles') is usually about 1 to 15 May
*Green Park* (49 acres), London W1. Between Piccadilly and St James's Park, with Constitution Hill leading to Hyde Park Corner
*Greenwich Park* (196½ acres), London SE10
*Hampton Court Gardens* (54 acres), Surrey
*Hampton Court Green* (17 acres), Surrey
*Hampton Court Park* (622 acres), Surrey
*Hyde Park* (341 acres), London W1/W2. From Park Lane to Kensington Gardens, containing the Serpentine. Fine gateway at Hyde Park Corner, with Apsley House, the Achilles Statue, Rotten Row and the Ladies' Mile. To the north-east is the Marble Arch, originally erected by George

IV at the entrance to Buckingham Palace and re-erected in the present position in 1851

*Kensington Gardens* (275 acres), London W2/W8. From the western boundary of Hyde Park to Kensington Palace, containing the Albert Memorial

*Kew, Royal Botanic Gardens, see* Index

*Regent's Park* and *Primrose Hill* (464 acres), London NW1. From Marylebone Road to Primrose Hill surrounded by the Outer Circle and divided by the Broad Walk leading to the Zoological Gardens

*Richmond Park* (2,469 acres), Surrey

*St James's Park* (93 acres), London SW1. From Whitehall to Buckingham Palace. Ornamental lake of 12 acres. The original suspension bridge built in 1857 was replaced in 1957. The Mall leads from the Admiralty Arch to Buckingham Palace, Birdcage Walk from Storey's Gate to Buckingham Palace

Maintained by the Corporation of London

*Ashtead Common* (500 acres), Surrey

*Burnham Beeches* and *Fleet Wood* (540 acres), Bucks. Purchased by the Corporation for the benefit of the public in 1880, Fleet Wood (65 acres) being presented in 1921

*Coulsdon Common* (133 acres), Surrey

*Epping Forest* (6,000 acres), Essex. Purchased by the Corporation and opened to the public in 1882. The present Forest is 12 miles long by 1 to 2 miles wide, about one-tenth of its original area

*Farthing Downs* (121 acres), Surrey

*Hampstead Heath* (789 acres), London NW3. Including Golders Hill (36 acres) and Parliament Hill (271 acres)

*Highgate Wood* (70 acres), London

*Kenley Common* (138 acres), Surrey

*Queen's Park* (30 acres), London

*Riddlesdown* (90 acres), Surrey

*Spring Park* (51 acres), Kent

*West Ham Park* (77 acres), London

*West Wickham Common* (25 acres), Kent

*Woodredon and Warlies Park Estate* (740 acres), Waltham Abbey

Also smaller open spaces within the City of London, including *Finsbury Circus Gardens*

LONDON PLANETARIUM, Marylebone Road, London NW1 5LR. Tel: 0171-486 1121. Open daily (except Christmas Day), star show and Space Trail 12.20–4.40. Admission charge.

MADAME TUSSAUD'S, Marylebone Road, London NW1 5LR. Tel: 0171-935 6861. Waxwork exhibition. Open daily (except Christmas Day) 10–5.30. Admission charge.

MARKETS. The London markets (mostly administered by the Corporation of the City of London) provide foodstuffs for 8–9 million people. *Billingsgate* (fish), Thames Street site dating from 1875, a market site for over 1,000 years, moved to the Isle of Dogs in January 1982). *Borough*, SE1 (vegetables, fruit, flowers, etc.), established on present site 1756, privately owned and run. *Covent Garden* (vegetables, fruit, flowers, etc.), established in 1661 under a charter of Charles II, moved in 1973 to a 64-acre site at Nine Elms. *Leadenhall*, EC3 (meat, poultry, fish, etc.), built 1881, part recently demolished. *London Fruit Exchange*, Brushfield Street, built by Corporation of London 1928–9 as buildings for Spitalfields market; not connected with the market since it moved in 1991. *Petticoat Lane*, Middlesex Street, E1, a market has existed on the site for over 500 years, now a Sunday morning market selling almost anything. *Portobello Road*, W11, originally for herbs and horse-trading from 1870; became famous for antiques after the closure of the Caledonian Market in 1948; Saturdays. *Smithfield, Central Meat, Fish, Fruit, Vegetable and Poultry Markets*, built 1851–66, the site of St Bartholomew's Fair from 12th to 19th century, new hall built 1963, market refurbished 1993–4. *Spitalfields*, E1 (vegetables, fruit, etc.), established 1682, modernized 1928, moved to Leyton in May 1991.

MARLBOROUGH HOUSE, Pall Mall, London SW1A 5HX. Built by Wren for the first Duke of Marlborough and completed in 1711, the house reverted to the Crown in 1835. In 1863 it became the London house of the Prince of Wales and was the London home of Queen Mary until her death in 1953. In 1959 Marlborough House was given by The Queen as a centre for Commonwealth government conferences and it was opened as such in 1962. The Queen's Chapel, Marlborough Gate, begun in 1623 from the designs of Inigo Jones for the Infanta Maria of Spain, and completed for Queen Henrietta Maria, is open to the public for services on Sundays at 8.30 a.m. and 11.15 a.m. between Easter Day and end July (*see* St James's Palace for winter services in The Chapel Royal).

LONDON MONUMENT (commonly called The Monument), Monument Street, London EC3. Built from designs of Wren, 1671–7, to commemorate the Great Fire of London, which broke out in Pudding Lane on 2 September 1666. The fluted Doric column is 120 ft high; the moulded cylinder above the balcony supporting a flaming vase of gilt bronze is an additional 42 ft; and the column is based on a square plinth 40 ft high (with fine carvings on the west face) making a total height of 202 ft. Splendid views of London from gallery at top of column (311 steps). As total refurbishment planned for 1993 onwards, check with Town Clerk's office for access. Tel: 0171-606 3030.

MONUMENTS (sculptor's name in parenthesis). *Albert Memorial* (Durham), Kensington Gore; *Royal Air Force* (Blomfield), Victoria Embankment; *Viscount Alanbrooke,* Whitehall; *Beaconsfield,* Parliament Square; *Beatty* (Macmillan), Trafalgar Square; *Belgian Gratitude* (setting by Blomfield, statue by Rousseau), Victoria Embankment; *Boadicea* (or Boudicca), Queen of the Iceni (Thornycroft), Westminster Bridge; *Brunel* (Marochetti), Victoria Embankment; *Burghers of Calais* (Rodin), Victoria Tower Gardens, Westminster; *Burns* (Steel), Embankment Gardens; *Carlyle* (Boehm), Chelsea Embankment; *Cavalry* (Jones), Hyde Park; *Edith Cavell* (Frampton), St Martin's Place; *Cenotaph* (Lutyens), Whitehall; *Charles I* (Le Sueur), Trafalgar Square; *Charles II* (Gibbons), South Court, Chelsea Hospital; *Cleopatra's Needle* (68¼ ft high, *c.*1500 BC, erected on the Thames Embankment in 1877–8; the sphinxes are Victorian; *Clive* (Tweed), King Charles Street; *Captain Cook* (Brock), The Mall; *Crimean,* Broad Sanctuary; *Oliver Cromwell* (Thornycroft), outside Westminster Hall; *Cunningham* (Belsky), Trafalgar Square; *Gen. Charles de Gaulle* Carlton Gardens; *Lord Dowding* (Faith Winter), Strand; *Duke of Cambridge* (Jones), Whitehall; *Duke of York* (124 ft), Carlton House Terrace; *Edward VII* (Mackennal), Waterloo Place; *Elizabeth I* (1586, oldest outdoor statue in London; from Ludgate), Fleet Street; *Eros* (Shaftesbury Memorial) (Gilbert), Piccadilly Circus; *Marechal Foch* (Mallisard, copy of one in Cassel, France), Grosvenor Gardens; *Charles James Fox* (Westmacott), Bloomsbury Square; *George III* (Cotes Wyatt), Cockspur Street; *George IV* (Chantrey), riding without stirrups, Trafalgar Square; *George V* (Reid Dick), Old Palace Yard; *George VI* (Macmillan), Carlton Gardens; *Gladstone* (Thornycroft), Strand; *Guards'* (Crimea) (Bell), Waterloo Place; (Great War) (Ledward, figures, Bradshaw, cenotaph), Horse Guards' Parade; *Haig* (Hardiman), Whitehall; *Sir Arthur (Bomber) Harris* (Faith Winter), Strand; *Irving* (Brock), north side of National Portrait Gallery; *James II* (Gibbons and/or pupils), Trafalgar Square; *Jellicoe* (Wheeler),

Trafalgar Square; *Samuel Johnson* (Fitzgerald), opposite St Clement Danes; *Kitchener* (Tweed), Horse Guards' Parade; *Abraham Lincoln* (Saint-Gaudens, copy of one in Chicago), Parliament Square; *Milton* (Montford), St Giles, Cripplegate; *The Monument* (*see* above); *Mountbatten*, Foreign Office Green; *Nelson* (170 ft 2 in), Trafalgar Square, with Landseer's lions (cast from guns recovered from the wreck of the *Royal George*); *Florence Nightingale* (Walker), Waterloo Place; *Palmerston* (Woolner), Parliament Square; *Peel* (Noble), Parliament Square; *Pitt* (Chantrey), Hanover Square; *Portal* (Nemon), Embankment Gardens; *Prince Consort* (Bacon), Holborn Circus; *Queen Elizabeth Gate*, Hyde Park Corner; *Raleigh* (Macmillan), Whitehall; *Richard I (Coeur de Lion)* (Marochetti), Old Palace Yard; *Roberts* (Bates), Horse Guards' Parade; *Franklin D. Roosevelt* (Reid Dick), Grosvenor Square; *Royal Artillery* (South Africa) (Colton), The Mall; (Great War), Hyde Park Corner; *Captain Scott* (Lady Scott), Waterloo Place; *Shackleton* (Sarjeant Jagger), Kensington Gore; *Shakespeare* (Fontana, copy of one by Scheemakers in Westminster Abbey), Leicester Square; *Smuts* (Epstein), Parliament Square; *Sullivan* (Goscombe John), Victoria Embankment; *Trenchard* (Macmillan), Victoria Embankment; *Victoria Memorial*, in front of Buckingham Palace; *George Washington* (Houdon copy), Trafalgar Square; *Wellington* (Boehm), Hyde Park Corner; (Chantrey) riding without stirrups, outside Royal Exchange; *John Wesley* (Adams Acton), City Road; *William III* (Bacon), St James's Square; *Wolseley* (Goscombe John), Horse Guards' Parade.

PORT OF LONDON. The Port of London covers the tidal section of the River Thames from Teddington to the seaward limit (Tongue light vessel), a distance of 150 km. The governing body is the Port of London Authority (PLA). Eighty-eight per cent of the total port traffic is handled at privately operated riverside terminals between Fulham and Canvey Island, the rest at the enclosed dock at Tilbury, 40 km below London Bridge. Passenger vessels and cruise liners can be handled at moorings at Greenwich, Tower Bridge and Tilbury.

ROMAN REMAINS. The city wall of Roman *Londinium* was largely rebuilt during the medieval period but sections may be seen near the White Tower in the Tower of London; at Tower Hill; at Coopers' Row; at All Hallows, London Wall, its vestry being built on the remains of a semi-circular Roman bastion; at St Alphage, London Wall, showing a succession of building repairs from the Roman until the late medieval period; and at St Giles, Cripplegate. Sections of the great forum and basilica, more than 165 metres square, have been encountered during excavations in the area of Leadenhall, Gracechurch Street and Lombard Street. Traces of Roman activity along the river include a massive riverside wall built in the late Roman period, and a succession of Roman timber quays along Lower and Upper Thames Street.

Other major buildings are the Provincial Governor's Palace in Cannon Street; the amphitheatre at Guildhall; remains of a bath-building, preserved in Lower Thames Street; and the Temple of Mithras in Walbrook.

ROYAL ALBERT HALL, Kensington Gore, London SW7 2AP. Tel: 0171-589 3203. The elliptical hall, one of the largest in the world, was completed in 1871, and since 1941 has been the venue each summer for the Promenade Concerts founded in 1895 by Sir Henry Wood. Other events include pop and classical music concerts, dance, opera, sporting events, conferences and banquets.

ROYAL HOSPITAL, CHELSEA, Royal Hospital Road, London SW3 4SL. Tel: 0171-730 0161. Founded by Charles II in 1682, and built by Wren; opened in 1692 for old and disabled soldiers. Open Monday–Saturday 10–12, daily 2–

4. The extensive grounds include the former Ranelagh Gardens and are the venue for the Chelsea Flower Show each May. *Governor*, Gen. Sir Brian Kenny, GCB, CBE; *Lt.-Governor and Secretary*, Maj.-Gen. F. G. Sugden, CB, CBE.

ROYAL OPERA HOUSE, Covent Garden, London WC2E 9DD. Home of The Royal Ballet (1931) and The Royal Opera (1946). The Royal Opera House is the third theatre to be built on the site, opening 1858; the first was opened in 1732.

ST JAMES'S PALACE, Pall Mall, London SW1. Built by Henry VIII; the Gatehouse and Presence Chamber remain; later alterations were made by Wren and Kent. The Chapel Royal is open for services on Sundays at 8.30 a.m. and 11.15 a.m. between the beginning of October and Good Friday (*see* Marlborough House for summer services in The Queen's Chapel). Representatives of foreign powers are still accredited 'to the Court of St James's'. *Clarence House* (1825) in the palace precinct is the home of The Queen Mother.

ST PAUL'S CATHEDRAL, London EC4M 8AD. Built 1675–1710, cost £747,660. The cross on the dome is 365 ft above the ground level, the inner cupola 218 ft above the floor. 'Great Paul' in the south-west tower weighs nearly 17 tons. The organ by Father Smith (enlarged by Willis and rebuilt by Mander) is in a case carved by Grinling Gibbons, who also carved the choir stalls. Open for sightseeing Monday–Saturday 8.30–4.00. Admission to cathedral and crypt: £3.00, children £2.00; Galleries £2.50/£1.50. Services: Sundays, 8, 10.30, 11.30 and 3.15. Weekdays, 7.30, 8, 12.30 and 5 (Saturday Mattins 10 a.m.).

SOMERSET HOUSE, Strand and Victoria Embankment, London WC2. The river façade (600 ft. long) was built in 1776–86 from the designs of Sir William Chambers; the eastern extension, which houses part of King's College, was built by Smirke in 1829. Somerset House was the property of Lord Protector Somerset, at whose attainder in 1552 the palace passed to the Crown, and it was a royal residence until 1692.

SOUTH BANK, London SE1. The arts complex on the south bank of the River Thames includes the South Bank Centre, owned and managed by the South Bank Board, which consists of the 2,903-seat *Royal Festival Hall* (opened in 1951 for the Festival of Britain), the adjacent 1,056-seat *Queen Elizabeth Hall*, the 368-seat *Purcell Room*, and the 77-seat Voice Box. Tel: 0171-928 8800.

The *National Film Theatre* (opened 1952), administered by the British Film Institute, has three auditoria showing almost 2,000 films a year. The London Film Festival is held here every November. Tel: 0171-928 3232.

The *Royal National Theatre* opened in 1976 and stages classical, modern, new and neglected plays in its three auditoria: the 1,160-seat Olivier theatre, the 890-seat Lyttelton theatre and the Cottesloe theatre which seats up to 400. Tel: 0171-928 2252.

SOUTHWARK CATHEDRAL, London SE1 9DA. Mainly 13th century, but the nave is largely rebuilt. The tomb of John Gower (1330–1408) is between the Bunyan and Chaucer memorial windows in the north aisle; Shakespeare's effigy backed by a view of Southwark and the Globe Theatre in the south aisle; the tomb of Bishop Andrews (died 1626) is near the screen. The lady chapel was the scene of the consistory courts of the reign of Mary (Gardiner and Bonner) and is still used as a consistory court. John Harvard, after whom Harvard University is named, was baptized here in 1607, and the chapel by the north choir aisle is his memorial chapel. Open 8.30–6, admission free. Services: Sundays, 11, 3. Weekdays, 12.45, 5.30 (sung on Tuesdays and Fridays), Saturdays, 12 noon.

THAMES EMBANKMENTS. The *Victoria Embankment*, on the north side from Westminster to Blackfriars, was constructed by Sir Joseph Bazalgette (1819–91) for the Metropolitan Board of Works, 1864–70; the seats, of which the supports of some are a kneeling camel, laden with spicery, and of others a winged sphinx, were presented by the Grocers' Company and by W. H. Smith, MP, in 1874; the *Albert Embankment*, on the south side from Westminster Bridge to Vauxhall, 1866–9; the *Chelsea Embankment*, 1871–4. The total cost exceeded £2,000,000. Bazalgette also inaugurated the London main drainage system, 1858–65. A medallion (*Flumini vincula posuit*) has been placed on a pier of the Victoria Embankment to commemorate the engineer.

THAMES FLOOD BARRIER. Officially opened in May 1984, though first used in February 1983, the barrier consists of ten rising sector gates which span 570 yards from bank to bank of the Thames at Woolwich Reach. When not in use the gates lie horizontally, allowing shipping to navigate the river normally; when the barrier is closed, the gates turn through 90 degrees to stand vertically more than 50 feet above the river bed. The barrier took eight years to complete and can be raised within about 30 minutes.

THAMES TUNNELS. The *Rotherhithe Tunnel*, opened 1908, connects Commercial Road, London E14, with Lower Road, Rotherhithe; it is 1 mile 332 yards long, of which 525 yards are under the river. The first *Blackwall Tunnel* (northbound vehicles only), opened 1897, connects East India Dock Road, Poplar, with Blackwall Lane, East Greenwich. The height restriction on the northbound tunnel is 13ft 4in. A second tunnel (for southbound vehicles only) opened 1967. The lengths of the tunnels measured from East India Dock Road to the Gate House on the south side are 6,215 ft (old tunnel) and 6,152 ft. *Greenwich Tunnel* (pedestrians only), opened 1902, connects the Isle of Dogs, Poplar, with Greenwich; it is 406 yards long. The *Woolwich Tunnel* (pedestrians only), opened 1912, connects North and South Woolwich below the passenger and vehicular ferry from North Woolwich Station, London E16, to High Street, Woolwich, London SE18; it is 552 yards long.

WALTHAM CROSS, Herts. At Waltham Cross is one of the crosses (partly restored) erected by Edward I to mark a resting place of the corpse of Queen Eleanor on its way to Westminster Abbey. Ten crosses were erected, but only those at Geddington, Northampton and Waltham survive; 'Charing' Cross originally stood near the spot now occupied by the statue of Charles I at Whitehall.

WESTMINSTER ABBEY, London SW1. Built between 1050 and 1745; contains the chapel of Henry VII, chapter house and cloisters; Edward the Confessor's shrine, tombs of kings and queens and many other monuments, including the grave of 'The Unknown Warrior' and Poets' Corner. The Coronation Chair encloses the Stone of Scone, removed from Scotland by Edward I in 1296. Open on weekdays 9.20–6 (9.20–7.45 Wednesday). Admission to the Royal Chapels, Poets' Corner, Quire and Statesmen's Aisle £4.00, con. £2.00/£1.00. Last admission Monday–Friday 4 p.m., Saturday 5 p.m. Wednesday 6–8 p.m. free. Nave open on Sundays between services. Services: Sundays, 8, 10, 11.15, 3, 6.30 (generally preceded by an organ recital). Monday–Friday, 7.30, 8, 12.30, 5. Saturdays, 8, 9.20, 3.

WESTMINSTER CATHEDRAL, Ashley Place, London SW1P 1QW. Roman Catholic cathedral built 1895–1903 from the designs of J. F. Bentley. The campanile is 283 feet high. Cathedral open 6.45 a.m.–8 p.m. Masses: Sundays, 7, 8, 9, 10.30 (sung), 12, 5.30 and 7; Solemn Vespers and Benediction 3.30. Monday–Friday, 7, 8, 8.30, 9, 10.30, 12.30, 1.05 and 5.30 (sung). Morning Prayer 7.40, Vespers 5. Saturdays 7, 8, 8.30, 9, 10.30 (sung), 12.30 and 6, Morning Prayer 7.40, Vespers 5.30. Holy days of obligation, Low Masses 7, 8, 8.30, 9, 10.30, 12.30, 1.05, 5.30 (sung) and 7.

ZOOLOGICAL GARDENS (London Zoo), Regent's Park, London NW1. Tel: 0171-722 3333. Opened in 1828. Open daily (except Christmas Day) March–September 10–5.30, 10–4 in winter. Admission £6.95, con. £5.95/£4.95.

LONDON TOURISM BOARD AND CONVENTION BUREAU, Tourist Information Centre, Victoria Station Forecourt, London SW1V 1JU. Tel: 0171-730 3488

# Hallmarks

Hallmarks are the symbols stamped on gold, silver or platinum articles to indicate that they have been tested at an official Assay Office and that they conform to one of the legal standards. With certain exceptions, all gold, silver, or platinum articles are required by law to be hallmarked before they are offered for sale. Hallmarking was instituted in England in 1300 under a statute of Edward I.

## MODERN HALLMARKS

Normally a complete modern hallmark consists of four symbols – the sponsor's mark, the assay office mark, the standard mark and the date letter. Additional marks have been authorized from time to time.

### SPONSOR'S MARK

Instituted in England in 1363, the sponsor's mark was originally a device such as a bird or fleur-de-lis. Now it consists of the initial letters of the name or names of the manufacturer or firm. Where two or more sponsors have the same initials, there is a variation in the surrounding shield or style of letters.

### STANDARD MARK

The standard mark indicates that the content of the precious metal in the alloy from which the article is made, is not less than the legal standard. The legal standard is the minimum content of precious metal by weight in parts per thousand, and the standards are:

| | | |
|---|---|---|
| Gold | 916.6 | (22 carat) |
| | 750 | (18 carat) |
| | 585 | (14 carat) |
| | 375 | (9 carat) |
| Silver | 958.4 | (Britannia) |
| | 925 | (sterling) |
| Platinum | 950 | |

The metals are marked as follows, if they are manufactured in the United Kingdom:

GOLD – a crown followed by the millesimal figure for the standard, e.g. 916 for 22 carat (see table above)

SILVER – Britannia silver: a full-length figure of Britannia. Sterling silver: a lion passant (England) or a lion rampant (Scotland)

 *Britannia Silver*

 *Sterling Silver (England)*

 *Sterling Silver (Scotland)*

PLATINUM – an orb

### ASSAY OFFICE MARK

This mark identifies the particular assay office at which the article was tested and marked. The existing assay offices in Britain are:

LONDON, Goldsmiths' Hall, London EC2V 8AQ.
Tel: 0171-606 8975

BIRMINGHAM, Newhall Street, Birmingham B3 1SB.
Tel: 0121-236 6951

 *Gold and platinum*

 *Silver*

SHEFFIELD, 137 Portobello Street, Sheffield S1 4DS.
Tel: 0114-275 5111

EDINBURGH, 9 Granton Road, Edinburgh EH5 3QJ.
Tel: 0131-551 2189

Assay offices formerly existed in other towns, e.g. Chester, Exeter, Glasgow, Newcastle, Norwich and York, each having its own distinguishing mark.

### DATE LETTER

The date letter shows the year in which an article was assayed and hallmarked. Each alphabetical cycle has a distinctive style of lettering or shape of shield. The date letters were different at the various assay offices and the particular office must be established from the assay office mark before reference is made to tables of date letters.

The table on page 604 shows specimen shields and letters used by the London Assay Office on silver articles in each period from 1498. The same letters are found on gold articles but the surrounding shield may differ. Since 1 January 1975, each office has used the same style of date letter and shield for all articles.

## OTHER MARKS

### FOREIGN GOODS

Since 1842 foreign goods imported into Britain have been required to be hallmarked before sale. The marks consist of the importer's mark, a special assay office mark, the figure denoting fineness (fineness mark) and the annual date letter.

The following are the assay office marks for gold imported articles. For silver and platinum the symbols remain the same but the shields differ in shape.

 *London*

 *Birmingham*

 *Sheffield*

 *Edinburgh*

## CONVENTION HALLMARKS

Special marks at authorized assay offices of the signatory countries of the International Convention (Austria, Denmark, Finland, Ireland, Norway, Portugal, Sweden, Switzerland and the UK) are legally recognized in the United Kingdom as approved hallmarks. These consist of a sponsor's mark, a common control mark, a fineness mark (arabic numerals showing the standard in parts per thousand), and an assay office mark. There is no date letter.

The fineness marks are:

| | | |
|---|---|---|
| Gold | 750 | (18 carat) |
| | 585 | (14 carat) |
| | 375 | (9 carat) |
| Silver | 925 | (sterling) |
| Platinum | 950 | |

The common control marks are:

 Gold (18 carat)

 Silver

 Platinum

## DUTY MARKS

In 1784 an additional mark of the reigning sovereign's head was introduced to signify that the excise duty had been paid. The mark became obsolete on the abolition of the duty in 1890.

## COMMEMORATIVE MARKS

There are three other marks to commemorate special events, the Silver Jubilee of King George V and Queen Mary in 1935, the Coronation of Queen Elizabeth II in 1953, and her Silver Jubilee in 1977.

---

## LONDON (GOLDSMITHS' HALL) DATE LETTERS FROM 1498

---

| | | from | to |
|---|---|---|---|
| | Black letter, small | 1498–9 | 1517–8 |
| | Lombardic | 1518–9 | 1537–8 |
| | Roman and other capitals | 1538–9 | 1557–8 |
| | Black letter, small | 1558–9 | 1577–8 |
| | Roman letter, capitals | 1578–9 | 1597–8 |
| | Lombardic, external cusps | 1598–9 | 1617–8 |
| | Italic letter, small | 1618–9 | 1637–8 |
| | Court hand | 1638–9 | 1657–8 |

| | | from | to |
|---|---|---|---|
| | Black letter, capitals | 1658–9 | 1677–8 |
| | Black letter, small | 1678–9 | 1696–7 |
| | Court hand | 1697 | 1715–6 |
| | Roman letter, capitals | 1716–7 | 1735–6 |
| | Roman letter, small | 1736–7 | 1738–9 |
| | Roman letter, small | 1739–40 | 1755–6 |
| | Old English, capitals | 1756–7 | 1775–6 |
| | Roman letter, small | 1776–7 | 1795–6 |
| | Roman letter, capitals | 1796–7 | 1815–6 |
| | Roman letter, small | 1816–7 | 1835–6 |
| | Old English, capitals | 1836–7 | 1855–6 |
| | Old English, small | 1856–7 | 1875–6 |
| | Roman letter, capitals [A to M square shield N to Z as shown] | 1876–7 | 1895–6 |
| | Roman letter, small | 1896–7 | 1915–6 |
| | Black letter, small | 1916–7 | 1935–6 |
| | Roman letter, capitals | 1936–7 | 1955–6 |
| | Italic letter, small | 1956–7 | 1974 |
| | Italic letter, capitals | 1975 | |

# Economic Statistics

GENERAL GOVERNMENT RECEIPTS  *£ billion*

| | Outturn 1992–3 | Estimated outturn 1993–4* | Estimated outturn 1994–5* |
|---|---|---|---|
| Taxes on income, expenditure and capital | 171.4 | 176 | 196 |
| Social security receipts | 37.4 | 39 | 43 |
| Interest and dividends | 5.0 | 6 | 5 |
| Other receipts | 9.6 | 9 | 8 |
| Total general government receipts | 223.3 | 230 | 252 |
| *of which:* | | | |
| North Sea revenues | 1.3 | 1.5 | 2 |

* Rounded to the nearest £1 billion
*Source:* HM Treasury - *Financial Statement and Budget Report 1994-5*

## THE NEW CONTROL TOTAL AND GENERAL GOVERNMENT EXPENDITURE
(EXCLUDING PRIVATIZATION PROCEEDS)  *£ million*

| | Estimated outturn 1993–4 | Plans/ projections 1994–5 |
|---|---|---|
| Central government expenditure | 170,100 | 172,900 |
| Local authority expenditure | 70,200 | 71,700 |
| Financing requirements of nationalized industries | 4,690 | 3,190 |
| Reserve | — | 3,500 |
| Adjustment | −300 | |
| New control total | 244,700 | 251,300 |
| Cyclical social security | 14,000 | 15,000 |
| Central government debt interest | 19,400 | 22,500 |
| Accounting adjustments | 8,000 | 9,000 |
| General government expenditure excluding privatization proceeds | 286,100 | 297,300 |
| GGE excluding privatization proceeds as a percentage of GDP | 45% | 43.75% |

*Source:* HM Treasury - *Financial Statement and Budget Report 1994-5*

NEW CONTROL TOTAL EXPENDITURE BY DEPARTMENT  *£ million*

| | Estimated outturn 1993–4 | New plans 1994–5 |
|---|---|---|
| Defence | 23,410 | 23,490 |
| Foreign Office | 1,490 | 1,220 |
| Overseas Development | 2,280 | 2,310 |
| Agriculture, Fisheries and Food | 3,050 | 2,810 |
| Trade and Industry | 3,630 | 2,270 |
| ECGD | −40 | −90 |
| Employment | 3,620 | 3,770 |
| Transport | 6,150 | 5,850 |
| DoE – Housing | 7,720 | 7,430 |
| DoE – Environment | 2,320 | 1,980 |
| DoE – PSA | 110 | 110 |
| DoE – Local government | 29,340 | 29,920 |
| Home Office | 6,010 | 6,260 |
| Legal departments | 2,550 | 2,730 |
| Education | 9,820 | 10,490 |
| National Heritage | 990 | 980 |
| Health | 30,090 | 31,730 |
| Social Security | 67,300 | 68,800 |
| Scotland | 13,630 | 14,110 |
| Wales | 6,330 | 6,650 |
| Northern Ireland | 7,110 | 7,390 |
| Chancellor of the Exchequer's departments | 3,450 | 3,430 |
| Cabinet Office– OPSS | 1,250 | 1,320 |
| Cabinet Office – other, etc. | 480 | 500 |
| European Communities | 2,450 | 1,350 |
| Local authority self-financed expenditure | 10,400 | 11,000 |
| Reserve | — | 3,500 |
| Adjustment | −300 | |
| New control total | 244,700 | 251,300 |

*Source:* HM Treasury - *Financial Statement and Budget Report 1994-5*

EXTERNAL FINANCING REQUIREMENTS OF NATIONALIZED INDUSTRIES  *£ million*

| | Estimated outturn 1993–4 | Plans 1994–5 |
|---|---|---|
| Trade and Industry | 2,280 | 950 |
| British Coal | 1,750 | 700 |
| British Shipbuilders | −10 | 0 |
| Nuclear Electric | 730 | 480 |
| Post Office | −180 | −230 |
| Transport | 2,320 | 2,220 |
| British Rail | 1,470 | 1,220* |
| Union Railways | 40 | 40 |
| Civil Aviation Authority | 100 | 60 |
| London Transport | 720 | 900 |
| DoE – Environment | 50 | 50 |
| British Waterways Board | 50 | 50 |
| Scotland | 30 | −30 |
| Caledonian MacBrayne Ltd | 10 | 10 |
| Scottish Nuclear | −30 | −40 |
| Scottish Transport Group | 40 | — |
| Total | 4,690 | 3,190 |

* To be split between BR, Railtrack and the Office of Passenger Rail Franchising
*Source:* HM Treasury - *Financial Statement and Budget Report 1994-5*

LOCAL AUTHORITY EXPENDITURE  *£ million*

|  | Estimated outturn 1993–4 | Plans 1994–5 |
|---|---|---|
| CURRENT | | |
| *Aggregate External Finance and transitional arrangements* | | |
| England | | |
| National non-domestic rate payments | 11,560 | |
| Revenue support grant | 17,050 | |
| Specific grants | 4,660 | |
| Total | 33,270 | 34,310† |
| Scotland | | |
| National non-domestic rate payments | 1,190 | |
| Revenue support grant | 3,620 | |
| Specific grants | 400 | |
| Total | 5,210 | 5,270† |
| Wales | | |
| National non-domestic rate payments | 470 | |
| Revenue support grant | 1,670 | |
| Specific grants | 210 | |
| Total | 2,350 | 2,420† |
| TOTAL | 40,830 | 42,000 |
| Other current grants | 13,090 | 13,180 |
| TOTAL CURRENT | 53,900 | 55,200 |
| CAPITAL | | |
| Capital grants | 1,750 | 1,510 |
| Credit approvals | 4,170 | 4,050 |
| Total capital | 5,920 | 5,560 |
| TOTAL | 59,800 | 60,700 |

†Breakdown of total not available
*Source:* HM Treasury – *Financial Statement and Budget Report 1994-5*

---

PUBLIC SECTOR BORROWING REQUIREMENT

|  | Outturn 1992–3 | Budget forecast 1993–4 | Latest forecast |
|---|---|---|---|
| PSBR (£ billion) | 36.7 | 50.1 | 49.8 |
| As % of GDP | 6 | 8 | 7¾ |
| PSBR excluding privatization proceeds (£ billion) | 44.8 | 55.6 | 55.2 |
| As % of GDP | 7½ | 8¾ | 8¾ |

*Source:* HM Treasury – *Financial Statement and Budget Report 1994-5*

---

GDP BY INDUSTRY 1992 BEFORE DEPRECIATION BUT AFTER STOCK APPRECIATION
*£ million*

| | |
|---|---|
| Agriculture, hunting, forestry and fishing | 9,309 |
| Mining and quarrying, including gas and oil extraction | 9,842 |
| Manufacturing | 114,698 |
| Electricity, gas and water supply | 13,717 |
| Construction | 32,002 |
| Wholesale and retail trade; repairs; hotels and restaurants | 72,549 |
| Transport, storage and communication | 41,613 |
| Financial intermediation; real estate; renting and business activities | 121,704 |
| Public administration, national defence and compulsory social security | 36,605 |
| Education; health; social work | 52,509 |
| Other services, including sewerage and refuse disposal | 32,892 |
| *Total* | 537,440 |
| *less* adjustment for financial services | 23,058 |
| Statistical discrepancy (income adjustment) | 212 |
| *Gross domestic product* | 514,594 |

*Source:* HMSO – *Annual Abstract of Statistics 1994*

---

UNEMPLOYMENT BY STANDARD REGIONS
SEASONALLY ADJUSTED, AT MID APRIL 1994*

|  | Total | % of workforce |
|---|---|---|
| United Kingdom | 2,682,500 | 9.5 |
| England: | | |
| North | 161,000 | 11.4 |
| Yorkshire and Humberside | 228,700 | 9.7 |
| East Midlands | 171,200 | 8.9 |
| East Anglia | 75,500 | 7.3 |
| South East | 845,600 | 9.3 |
| South West | 194,900 | 8.5 |
| West Midlands | 252,100 | 9.8 |
| North West | 297,500 | 9.9 |
| Wales | 123,500 | 9.8 |
| Scotland | 233,600 | 9.4 |
| Northern Ireland | 99,000 | 13.3 |

NOTE: Percentages calculated using mid-1993 estimates of total employees in employment, unemployed, self-employed and HM Forces, and participants in work-related government training schemes
* provisional
*Source:* Department of Employment

# Trade

BALANCE OF PAYMENTS 1992  £ MILLION

CURRENT ACCOUNT
Visible trade

| | |
|---|---|
| Exports (fob) | 107,047 |
| Imports (fob) | 120,453 |
| Visible balance | − 13,406 |
| Invisibles | |
| Credits | 108,438 |
| Debits | 103,652 |
| Invisibles balance | 4,786 |
| *of which:* | |
| Services balance | 4,069 |
| Interest, profits and dividends balance | 5,777 |
| Transfers balance | − 5,060 |
| CURRENT BALANCE | − 8,620 |

*TRANSACTIONS IN EXTERNAL ASSETS AND LIABILITIES
Investment overseas by UK residents

| | |
|---|---|
| Direct | − 9,424 |
| Portfolio | − 32,818 |
| Total UK investment overseas | − 42,242 |
| Investment in the UK by overseas residents | |
| Direct | 10,343 |
| Portfolio | 21,390 |
| Total overseas investment in UK | 31,733 |
| Foreign currency lending abroad by UK banks | − 14,995 |
| Foreign currency borrowing abroad by UK banks | 21,460 |
| Net foreign currency transactions of UK banks | 6,465 |
| Sterling lending abroad by UK banks | − 10,842 |
| Sterling borrowing and deposit liabilities abroad of UK banks | 2,840 |
| Net sterling transactions of UK banks | − 8,002 |
| Deposits with and lending to banks abroad by UK non-bank private sector | − 7,871 |
| Borrowing from banks abroad by: | |
| UK non-bank private sector | 8,018 |
| Public corporations | − 506 |
| General government | 993 |
| Official reserves (additions to −, drawings on +) | 1,406 |
| Other external assets of: | |
| UK non-bank private sector and public corporations | − 9,749 |
| General government | − 682 |
| Other external liabilities of: | |
| UK non-bank private sector and public corporations | 31,319 |
| General government | − 2,562 |
| NET TRANSACTIONS IN ASSETS AND LIABILITIES | 8,319 |
| BALANCING ITEM | 301 |

* Assets: increase − /decrease +
Liabilities: increase + /decrease −
*Source:* HMSO - *Annual Abstract of Statistics 1994*

VISIBLE TRADE OF THE UK ON A BALANCE OF
PAYMENTS BASIS  *£ million*

| | Exports | Imports | Visible balance |
|---|---|---|---|
| 1983 | 60,700 | 62,237 | − 1,537 |
| 1984 | 70,265 | 75,601 | − 5,336 |
| 1985 | 77,991 | 81,336 | − 3,345 |
| 1986 | 72,627 | 82,186 | − 9,559 |
| 1987 | 79,153 | 90,735 | − 11,582 |
| 1988 | 80,346 | 101,826 | − 21,480 |
| 1989 | 92,154 | 116,837 | − 24,683 |
| 1990 | 101,718 | 120,527 | − 18,809 |
| 1991 | 103,413 | 113,697 | − 10,284 |
| 1992 | 107,047 | 120,453 | − 13,406 |

*Source:* HMSO - *Annual Abstract of Statistics 1994*

VALUE OF UK EXPORTS 1992p BY DESTINATION
*£ million*

| | |
|---|---|
| European Community | 60,702.3 |
| Other western Europe | 8,548.1 |
| North America | 13,971.2 |
| Other OECD countries | 3,873.0 |
| Oil-exporting countries | 6,013.0 |
| Eastern Europe and CIS | 1,702.7 |
| Other countries | 12,716.7 |
| Total | 108,507.5 |

p provisional
*Source:* HMSO - *Annual Abstract of Statistics 1994*

VALUE OF UK IMPORTS 1992p BY SOURCE
*£ million*

| | |
|---|---|
| European Community | 65,609.3 |
| Other western Europe | 14,509.0 |
| North America | 15,718.9 |
| Other OECD countries | 8,884.6 |
| Oil-exporting countries | 3,078.5 |
| Eastern Europe and CIS | 1,644.3 |
| Other countries | 15,637.7 |
| Total | 125,866.8 |

p provisional
*Source:* HMSO - *Annual Abstract of Statistics 1994*

VALUE OF UNITED KINGDOM IMPORTS (cif) 1992 BY SECTIONS AND DIVISIONS

| | £ million | | £ million |
|---|---|---|---|
| TOTAL UK IMPORTS | 125,866.8 | *Manufactured goods classified chiefly by material* | 20,670.4 |
| | | Leather, leather manufactures, nes, and | |
| *Food and live animals chiefly for food* | 11,401.4 | dressed furskins | 187.4 |
| Live animals chiefly for food | 211.3 | Rubber manufactures, nes | 995.9 |
| Meat and meat preparations | 2,033.0 | Cork and wood manufactures (excluding | |
| Dairy products and birds' eggs | 1,111.4 | furniture) | 847.2 |
| Fish, crustaceans and molluscs, and | | Paper, paperboard, and articles of paper | |
| preparations thereof | 996.0 | pulp, of paper or of paperboard | 3,801.3 |
| Cereals and cereal preparations | 1,004.2 | Textile yarn, fabrics, made-up articles, nes, | |
| Vegetables and fruit | 3,118.0 | and related products | 3,940.5 |
| Sugar, sugar preparations and honey | 761.8 | Non-metallic mineral manufactures, nes | 3,217.6 |
| Coffee, tea, cocoa, spices, and manufactures | | Iron and steel | 2,513.7 |
| thereof | 890.4 | Non-ferrous metals | 2,589.7 |
| Feeding-stuff for animals (not including | | Manufactures of metal, nes | 2,577.3 |
| unmilled cereals) | 716.7 | | |
| Miscellaneous edible products and | | *Machinery and transport equipment* | 47,317.0 |
| preparations | 558.7 | Power generating machinery and | |
| | | equipment | 3,611.8 |
| *Beverages and tobacco* | 2,025.5 | Machinery specialized for particular | |
| Beverages | 1,565.0 | industries | 3,206.9 |
| Tobacco and tobacco manufactures | 460.5 | Metalworking machinery | 800.5 |
| | | General industrial machinery and | |
| *Crude materials, inedible, except fuels* | 4,668.2 | equipment, nes, and machine parts, nes | 4,518.1 |
| Hides, skins and furskins, raw | 76.8 | Office machines and automatic data | |
| Oil seeds and oleaginous fruit | 228.5 | processing equipment | 8,360.9 |
| Crude rubber (including synthetic and | | Telecommunications, sound recording and | |
| reclaimed) | 228.9 | reproducing apparatus and equipment | 3,555.7 |
| Cork and wood | 1,024.6 | Electrical machinery, apparatus and | |
| Pulp and waste paper | 629.6 | appliances, nes, and electrical parts thereof | |
| Textile fibres (other than wool tops) and | | (including non-electrical counterparts, nes, | |
| their wastes (not manufactured into yarn or | | of electrical household type equipment) | 7,738.2 |
| fabric) | 480.7 | Road vehicles (including air cushion | |
| Crude fertilizers and crude minerals | | vehicles) | 12,118.5 |
| (excluding coal, petroleum and precious | | Other transport equipment | 3,406.3 |
| stones) | 264.0 | | |
| Metalliferous ores and metal scrap | 1,163.5 | *Miscellaneous manufactured articles* | 19,106.6 |
| Crude animal and vegetable materials | 571.7 | Sanitary, plumbing, heating and lighting | |
| | | fixtures and fittings, nes | 390.4 |
| *Mineral fuels, lubricants and related materials* | 7,014.1 | Furniture and parts thereof | 1,053.7 |
| Petroleum, petroleum products and related | | Travel goods, handbags and similar | |
| materials | 5,326.6 | containers | 311.6 |
| Coal, coke, gas and electric current | 1,687.5 | Articles of apparel and clothing accessories | 4,477.9 |
| | | Footwear | 1,152.5 |
| *Animal and vegetable oils, fats and waxes* | 422.7 | Professional, scientific and controlling | |
| | | instruments and apparatus, nes | 2,621.0 |
| *Total manufactured goods* | 98,712.3 | Photographic apparatus, equipment and | |
| | | supplies and optical goods, nes, watches and | |
| *Chemicals and related products* | 11,618.3 | clocks | 1,635.0 |
| Organic chemicals | 2,792.6 | Miscellaneous manufactured articles, nes | 7,464.4 |
| Inorganic chemicals | 950.2 | | |
| Dyeing, tanning and colouring materials | 687.0 | *Commodities and transactions not classified* | |
| Medicinal and pharmaceutical products | 1,663.4 | *elsewhere* | 1,622.5 |
| Essential oils and perfume materials; toilet, | | | |
| polishing and cleansing materials | 941.1 | | |
| Fertilizers, manufactured | 257.4 | | |
| Plastics in primary forms | 2,008.5 | | |
| Plastics in non-primary forms | 1,028.1 | | |
| Chemical materials | 1,289.9 | | |

nes  not elsewhere specified

*Source:* HMSO – *Annual Abstract of Statistics 1994*

## VALUE OF UNITED KINGDOM EXPORTS (fob) 1992 BY SECTIONS AND DIVISIONS

| | £ million |
|---|---|
| TOTAL UK EXPORTS | 108,507.5 |
| *Food and live animals chiefly for food* | 5,289.5 |
| Live animals chiefly for food | 339.2 |
| Meat and meat preparations | 826.7 |
| Dairy products and birds' eggs | 534.6 |
| Fish, crustaceans and molluscs, and preparations thereof | 567.8 |
| Cereals and cereal preparations | 1,203.5 |
| Vegetables and fruit | 330.6 |
| Sugar, sugar preparations and honey | 300.1 |
| Coffee, tea, cocoa, spices and manufactures thereof | 508.5 |
| Feeding-stuff for animals (not including unmilled cereals) | 337.4 |
| Miscellaneous edible products and preparations | 341.1 |
| *Beverages and tobacco* | 3,417.4 |
| Beverages | 2,447.7 |
| Tobacco and tobacco manufactures | 969.7 |
| *Crude materials, inedible, except fuels* | 1,879.3 |
| Hides, skins and furskins, raw | 130.9 |
| Oil seeds and oleaginous fruit | 36.6 |
| Crude rubber (including synthetic and reclaimed) | 209.0 |
| Cork and wood | 29.7 |
| Pulp and waste paper | 38.9 |
| Textile fibres (other than wool tops) and their wastes (not manufactured into yarn or fabric) | 487.7 |
| Crude fertilizers and crude minerals (excluding coal, petroleum and precious stones) | 366.5 |
| Metalliferous ores and metal scrap | 457.7 |
| Crude animal and vegetable materials | 122.3 |
| *Mineral fuels, lubricants and related materials* | 6,967.4 |
| Petroleum, petroleum products and related materials | 6,660.6 |
| Coal, coke, gas and electric current | 306.8 |
| *Animal and vegetable oils, fats and waxes* | 86.0 |
| *Total manufactured goods* | 88,842.8 |
| *Chemicals and related products* | 14,976.3 |
| Organic chemicals | 3,699.2 |
| Inorganic chemicals | 1,185.1 |
| Dyeing, tanning and colouring materials | 1,282.2 |
| Medicinal and pharmaceutical products | 2,993.2 |
| Essential oils and perfume materials; toilet, polishing and cleansing materials | 1,469.4 |
| Fertilizers, manufactured | 110.6 |
| Plastics in primary forms | 1,325.8 |
| Plastics in non-primary forms | 812.4 |
| Chemical materials | 2,098.5 |

nes  not elsewhere specified

| | £ million |
|---|---|
| *Manufactured goods classified chiefly by material* | 15,482.3 |
| Leather, leather manufactures, nes, and dressed furskins | 265.4 |
| Rubber manufactures, nes | 975.6 |
| Cork and wood manufactures (excluding furniture) | 129.4 |
| Paper, paperboard, and articles of paper pulp, of paper or of paperboard | 1,730.4 |
| Textile yarn, fabrics, made-up articles, nes, and related products | 2,457.4 |
| Non-metallic mineral manufactures, nes | 2,955.4 |
| Iron and steel | 3,004.4 |
| Non-ferrous metals | 1,752.7 |
| Manufactures of metal, nes | 2,211.7 |
| *Machinery and transport equipment* | 44,420.1 |
| Power generating machinery and equipment | 5,536.6 |
| Machinery specialized for particular industries | 4,048.1 |
| Metalworking machinery | 698.3 |
| General industrial machinery and equipment, nes, and machine parts, nes | 4,579.5 |
| Office machines and automatic data processing equipment | 6,616.8 |
| Telecommunications and sound recording and reproducing apparatus and equipment | 2,857.8 |
| Electrical machinery, apparatus and appliances, nes, and electrical parts thereof (including non-electrical counterparts, nes, of electrical household type equipment) | 6,354.5 |
| Road vehicles (including air cushion vehicles) | 8,893.6 |
| Other transport equipment | 4,834.9 |
| *Miscellaneous manufactured articles* | 13,964.1 |
| Sanitary, plumbing, heating and lighting fixtures and fittings, nes | 273.6 |
| Furniture and parts thereof | 620.4 |
| Travel goods, handbags and similar containers | 75.3 |
| Articles of apparel and clothing accessories | 2,084.1 |
| Footwear | 340.7 |
| Professional, scientific and controlling instruments and apparatus, nes | 3,077.2 |
| Photographic apparatus, equipment and supplies and optical goods, nes, watches and clocks | 1,379.4 |
| Miscellaneous manufactured articles, nes | 6,113.4 |
| *Commodities and transactions not classified elsewhere* | 2,025.1 |

*Source:* HMSO – *Annual Abstract of Statistics 1994*

## HOUSEHOLDS AND THEIR EXPENDITURE 1992[1]

NUMBER OF HOUSEHOLDS

| | |
|---|---|
| SUPPLYING DATA | 7,418 |
| Total number of persons | 18,174 |
| Total number of adults[2] | 13,563 |

HOUSEHOLD PERCENTAGE
DISTRIBUTION BY TENURE

| | |
|---|---|
| Rented unfurnished | 28.4% |
| Rented furnished | 3.8% |
| Rent-free | 2.0% |
| Owner-occupied | 65.8% |

AVERAGE NUMBER OF PERSONS
PER HOUSEHOLD

| | |
|---|---|
| All persons | 2.450 |
| Males | 1.182 |
| Females | 1.268 |
| Adults[2] | 1.828 |
| Persons under 65 | 1.460 |
| Persons 65 and over | 0.369 |
| Children[2] | 0.621 |
| Children under 2 | 0.071 |
| Children 2 and under 5 | 0.111 |
| Children 5 and under 18 | 0.439 |
| Persons economically active | 1.169 |
| Persons not economically active | 1.281 |
| Men 65 and over, women 60 and over | 0.399 |
| Others | 0.882 |

AVERAGE WEEKLY HOUSEHOLD EXPENDITURE ON
COMMODITIES AND SERVICES

| | Weekly average £ | As % of total |
|---|---|---|
| Housing[3] | 47.36 | 17.4 |
| Fuel, light and power | 13.02 | 4.8 |
| Food | 47.66 | 17.5 |
| Alcoholic drink | 11.06 | 4.1 |
| Tobacco | 5.38 | 2.0 |
| Clothing and footwear | 16.39 | 6.0 |
| Household goods | 21.90 | 8.1 |
| Household services | 13.40 | 4.9 |
| Personal goods and services | 10.18 | 3.7 |
| Motoring expenditure | 35.66 | 13.1 |
| Fares and other travel costs | 7.20 | 2.6 |
| Leisure goods | 13.32 | 4.9 |
| Leisure services | 27.56 | 10.1 |
| Miscellaneous | 1.75 | 0.6 |
| Total | 271.83 | 100.0 |

[1] Information derived from the Family Expenditure Survey; relates to
the UK
[2] Adults = all persons 18 and over and married persons under 18
Children = all unmarried persons under 18
[3] Excludes mortgage payments but includes imputed expenditure (i.e.
the weekly equivalent of rateable value)
*Source:* HMSO – *Annual Abstract of Statistics 1994*

## SOURCES OF HOUSEHOLD INCOME 1992*

AVERAGE WEEKLY INCOME BY SOURCE (£)

| | |
|---|---|
| Wages and salaries | 222.74 |
| Self-employment | 29.57 |
| Investments | 20.80 |
| Annuities and pensions (other than social security benefits | 19.58 |
| Social security benefits | 45.04 |
| Other sources | 5.20 |
| Total | 342.93 |

SOURCES AS A PERCENTAGE OF TOTAL HOUSEHOLD
INCOME (%)

| | |
|---|---|
| Wages and salaries | 65.0 |
| Self-employment | 8.6 |
| Investments | 6.1 |
| Annuities and pensions (other than social security benefits | 5.7 |
| Social security benefits | 13.1 |
| Other sources | 1.5 |
| Total | 100.0 |

* Information derived from the Family Expenditure Survey; relates to
the UK. Number of households supplying data, 7,418
*Source:* HMSO – *Annual Abstract of Statistics 1994*

## AVAILABILITY OF CERTAIN DURABLE GOODS 1992*
PERCENTAGE OF HOUSEHOLDS

| | |
|---|---|
| Car | 67.6 |
| One | 45.1 |
| Two | 18.7 |
| Three or more | 3.8 |
| Central heating, full or partial | 81.8 |
| Washing machine | 87.9 |
| Refrigerator or fridge/freezer | 99.2 |
| Freezer or fridge/freezer | 83.5 |
| Television | 98.3 |
| Telephone | 88.4 |
| Home computer | 19.1 |
| Video recorder | 69.3 |

* Information derived from the Family Expenditure Survey; relates to
the UK. Number of households supplying data, 7,418
*Source:* HMSO – *Annual Abstract of Statistics 1994*

# The Cost of Living

The first cost of living index to be calculated took July 1914 as 100 and was based on the pattern of expenditure of working-class families in 1904. The cost of living index was superseded in 1947 by the general index of retail prices (RPI), although the older term is still popularly applied to it.

## GENERAL INDEX OF RETAIL PRICES

The general index of retail prices measures the changes month by month in the average level of prices of goods and services purchased by most households in the United Kingdom. The spending pattern on which the index is based is revised each year, mainly using information from the Family Expenditure Survey. The expenditure of certain higher income households and of households mainly dependent on state pensions is excluded.

The index is compiled using a selection of over 600 goods and services and the prices charged for these items are collected at regular intervals in about 180 locations throughout the country. For the index, the price changes are weighted in accordance with the pattern of consumption of the average family.

## INFLATION RATE

The twelve-monthly percentage change in the 'all items' index of the RPI is usually referred to as the rate of inflation. The percentage change in prices between any two months/years can be obtained using the following formula:

$$\frac{\text{Later date RPI} - \text{Earlier date RPI}}{\text{Earlier date RPI}} \times 100$$

e.g. to find the rate of inflation for 1988, using the annual averages for 1987 and 1988:

$$\frac{106.9 - 101.9}{101.9} \times 100 = 4.9\%$$

## PURCHASING POWER OF THE POUND

Changes in the internal purchasing power of the pound may be defined as the 'inverse' of changes in the level of prices; when prices go up, the amount which can be purchased with a given sum of money goes down. To find the purchasing power of the pound in one month or year, given that it was 100p in a previous month or year, the calculation would be:

$$100p \times \frac{\text{Earlier month/year RPI}}{\text{Later month/year RPI}}$$

Thus, if the purchasing power of the pound is taken to be 100p in 1975, the comparable purchasing power in 1993 would be:

$$100p \times \frac{34.2}{140.7} = 24.31p$$

For longer term comparisons, it has been the practice to use an index which has been constructed by linking together the RPI for the period 1962 to date; an index derived from the consumers expenditure deflator for the period from 1938 to 1962; and the prewar 'Cost of Living' index for the period 1914 to 1938. This long-term index enables the internal purchasing power of the pound to be calculated for any year from 1914 onwards. It should be noted that these figures can only be approximate.

| | Long-term index of consumer goods and services (Jan. 1987 = 100) | Comparable purchasing power of £1 in 1993 | Rate of inflation (annual average) |
|---|---|---|---|
| 1914 | 2.8 | 50.25 | |
| 1915 | 3.5 | 40.20 | |
| 1920 | 7.0 | 20.10 | |
| 1925 | 5.0 | 28.14 | |
| 1930 | 4.5 | 31.27 | |
| 1935 | 4.0 | 35.18 | |
| 1938 | 4.4 | 31.98 | |
| *There are no official figures for 1939–45* | | | |
| 1946 | 7.4 | 19.01 | |
| 1950 | 9.0 | 15.63 | |
| 1955 | 11.2 | 12.56 | |
| 1960 | 12.6 | 11.17 | |
| 1965 | 14.8 | 9.51 | |
| 1970 | 18.5 | 7.61 | |
| 1975 | 34.2 | 4.11 | |
| 1980 | 66.8 | 2.11 | 18.0 |
| 1981 | 74.8 | 1.88 | 11.9 |
| 1982 | 81.2 | 1.73 | 8.6 |
| 1983 | 84.9 | 1.66 | 4.6 |
| 1984 | 89.2 | 1.58 | 5.0 |
| 1985 | 94.6 | 1.49 | 6.1 |
| 1986 | 97.8 | 1.44 | 3.4 |
| 1987 | 101.9 | 1.38 | 4.2 |
| 1988 | 106.9 | 1.32 | 4.9 |
| 1989 | 115.2 | 1.22 | 7.8 |
| 1990 | 126.1 | 1.12 | 9.5 |
| 1991 | 133.5 | 1.05 | 5.9 |
| 1992 | 138.5 | 1.02 | 3.7 |
| 1993 | 140.7 | 1.00 | 1.6 |

# Finance

## British Currency

### COIN

| | |
|---|---|
| *Gold Coins* | *Nickel-Brass Coins* |
| *One hundred pounds | Two pounds £2 |
| £100 | One pound £1 |
| *Fifty pounds £50 | |
| *Twenty-five pounds £25 | *Cupro-Nickel Coins* |
| *Ten pounds £10 | Crown £5 (since 1990) |
| Five pounds £5 | 50 pence 50p |
| Two pounds £2 | Crown 25p (pre-1990) |
| Sovereign £1 | 20 pence 20p |
| Half-Sovereign 50p | ‡10 pence 10p |
| | §5 pence 5p |
| *Silver Coins* | |
| †*Maundy Money* | *Bronze Coins* |
| Fourpence 4p | 2 pence 2p |
| Threepence 3p | 1 penny 1p |
| Twopence 2p | |
| Penny 1p | *Copper-plated Steel Coins* |
| | 2 pence 2p |
| | 1 penny 1p |

*Britannia gold bullion coins, introduced in October 1987
†Gifts of special money distributed by the Sovereign annually on Maundy Thursday to the number of aged poor men and women corresponding to the Sovereign's own age
‡New 10 pence coin introduced on 30 September 1992
§New 5 pence coin introduced on 27 June 1990

### GOLD COIN

Gold ceased to circulate during the First World War. Since then controls on buying, selling and holding gold coin have been imposed at various times but subsequently have been revoked. Under the Exchange Control (Gold Coins Exemption) Order 1979 gold coins may now be imported and exported without restriction, except gold coins which are more than fifty years old and valued at a sum in excess of £8,000; these cannot be exported without specific authorization from the Department of Trade and Industry.

On 1 April 1982 the Government introduced VAT (currently 17.5 per cent) on sales of all gold coin.

### SILVER COIN

Prior to 1920 silver coins were struck from sterling silver, an alloy of which 925 parts in 1,000 were silver. In 1920 the proportion of silver was reduced to 500 parts. From 1 January 1947 all 'silver' coins, except Maundy money, have been struck from cupro-nickel, an alloy of copper 75 parts and nickel 25 parts, except for the 20p, composed of copper 84 parts, nickel 16 parts. Maundy coins continue to be struck from sterling silver.

### BRONZE COIN

Bronze, introduced in 1860 to replace copper, is an alloy of copper 97 parts, zinc 2.5 parts and tin 0.5 part. These proportions have been subject to slight variations in the past. Bronze was replaced by copper-plated steel in September 1992.

The 'remedy' is the amount of variation from standard permitted in weight and fineness of coins when first issued from the Mint.

### LEGAL TENDER

Gold, dated 1838 onwards, if not below least current weight, is legal tender to any amount. £5 (Crown since 1990), £2 and £1 coins are legal tender to any amount; 50p, 25p (Crown pre-1990) and 20p coins are legal tender up to £10; 10p and 5p coins are legal tender up to £5, and 2p and 1p coins are legal tender for amounts up to 20p.

Farthings ceased to be legal tender on 31 December 1960, the halfpenny on 1 August 1969, the halfcrown on 1 January 1970, the threepence and penny on 31 August 1971, the sixpence on 30 June 1980, the decimal halfpenny on 31 December 1984, the old 5p on 31 December 1990, and the old 10p on 30 June 1993.

The decimal system was introduced on 15 February 1971. Since 1982 the word 'new' in 'new pence' displayed on decimal coins has been dropped.

The Channel Islands and the Isle of Man issue their own coinage, which are legal tender only in the island of issue. For denominations, *see* page 613.

| Metal | | Standard weight (g) | Standard diameter (cm) |
|---|---|---|---|
| Penny | bronze | 3.564 | 2.032 |
| Penny | copper-plated steel | 3.564 | 2.032 |
| 2 pence | bronze | 7.128 | 2.591 |
| 2 pence | copper-plated steel | 7.128 | 2.591 |
| 5p | cupro-nickel | 3.25 | 1.80 |
| 10p | cupro-nickel | 6.5 | 2.45 |
| 20p | cupro-nickel | 5.0 | 2.14 |
| 25p Crown | cupro-nickel | 28.276 | 3.861 |
| 50p | cupro-nickel | 13.5 | 3.0 |
| £1 | nickel-brass | 9.5 | 2.25 |
| £2 | nickel-brass | 15.98 | 2.84 |
| £5 Crown | cupro-nickel | 28.28 | 3.861 |

### BANKNOTES

Bank of England notes are currently issued in denominations of £5, £10, £20 and £50 for the amount of the fiduciary note issue, and are legal tender in England and Wales. Banknotes which are no longer legal tender are payable when presented at the head office of the Bank of England in London.

The old white notes for £10, £20, £50, £100, £500 and £1,000, which were issued until April 1943, ceased to be legal tender in May 1945, and the old white £5 note in March 1946.

The white £5 note issued between October 1945 and September 1956, the £5 notes issued between 1957 and 1963, (bearing a portrait of Britannia) and the first series to bear a portrait of The Queen, issued between 1963 and 1971, ceased to be legal tender in March 1961, June 1967 and September 1973 respectively.

The series of £1 notes issued during the years 1928 to 1960 and the 10s. notes of the same type issued from 1928 to 1961 (those without the royal portrait) ceased to be legal tender in May and October 1962 respectively. The £1 note first issued in March 1960 (bearing on the back a representation of Britannia) and the £10 note first issued in February 1964 (bearing a lion on the back) both bearing a portrait of The Queen on the front ceased to be legal tender in June 1979.

The £1 note first issued in 1978 ceased to be legal tender on 11 March 1988. The 10s. note was replaced by the 50p coin in October 1969, and ceased to be legal tender on 21 November 1970.

The D series of banknotes was introduced in 1970. The predominant identifying feature of each note was the portrayal on the back of a prominent figure from Britain's history, namely:

£5    The Duke of Wellington
£10   Florence Nightingale
£20   William Shakespeare
£50   Sir Christopher Wren

The £20 note was introduced in July 1970, the £5 note in November 1971, the £10 note in February 1975, the £1 note in February 1978 and the £50 note in March 1981. The D series notes ceased to be legal tender on the following dates: £1 note, 11 March 1988; £5 note, 29 November 1991; £20 note, 19 March 1993; £10 note, 20 May 1994. The £1 coin was introduced on 21 April 1983 to replace the £1 note.

A new E series of notes was introduced in June 1990 when a new £5 was issued, followed by a £20 note in June 1991, a £10 note in April 1992 and a £50 note in April 1994. This new series replaces the D series. The historical figures portrayed in this series are:

£5    George Stephenson
£10   Charles Dickens
£20   Michael Faraday
£50   Sir John Houblon

NOTE CIRCULATION

Note circulation is highest at the two peak spending periods of the year, around Christmas and during the summer holiday period. A peak of £20,345 million was reached immediately prior to Christmas 1993, a 6.7 per cent increase on the previous year.

The proportion of the total value of £1 notes in circulation at end February 1994 compared with the previous year was constant at 0.3 per cent. £5 notes increased from 6.9 per cent to 7.0 per cent. £10 notes increased from 31.5 per cent to 32.5 per cent. £20 and £50 notes increased from 36.0 per cent and 16.1 per cent to 42.2 per cent and 17.9 per cent respectively.

On 28 February 1994 the values of notes in circulation were:

| | |
|---|---|
| £1 | £57,290,370 |
| £5 | £1,135,087,910 |
| £10 | £5,245,336,140 |
| £20 | £6,817,802,100 |
| £50 | £2,883,911,450 |

OTHER BANKNOTES

SCOTLAND – Banknotes are issued by three Scottish banks. The Royal Bank of Scotland and the Bank of Scotland issue notes for £5, £10, £20 and £100. The Royal Bank of Scotland also issues £1 notes. The Clydesdale Bank issues notes for £5, £10, £20, £50, £100. Scottish notes are not legal tender in Scotland but they are an authorized currency and enjoy there a status comparable to that of the Bank of England note.

NORTHERN IRELAND – Banknotes are issued by four banks in Northern Ireland. The Northern Bank and the Ulster Bank issue notes for £5, £10, £20, £50 and £100. First Trust Bank and the Bank of Ireland issue notes for £5, £10, £20 and £100. Northern Ireland notes are not legal tender in Northern Ireland but they circulate widely and enjoy a status comparable to that of Bank of England notes.

CHANNEL ISLANDS – The States of Jersey issues its own currency notes and coinage. The note denominations are for £1, £5, £10, £20 and £50. The seven denominations of coin are: 1p, 2p, 5p, 10p, 20p, 50p and £1. The States of Guernsey issues its own currency notes and coinage. The notes are for £1, £5, £10, £20 and £50. The eight denominations of coin are 1p, 2p, 5p, 10p, 20p, 50p, £1 and £2.

THE ISLE OF MAN – The Isle of Man Government issues notes for £1, £5, £10, £20 and £50. Although these notes are only legal tender in the Isle of Man, they are accepted at face value in branches of the clearing banks in the United Kingdom. The Isle of Man issues coins for 1p, 2p, 5p, 10p, 20p, 50p, £1, £2 and £5.

Although none of the series of notes specified above is legal tender in the United Kingdom, they are generally accepted by the banks irrespective of their place of issue. At one time the banks made a commission charge for handling Scottish and Irish notes but this was abolished some years ago.

# Slang Terms for Money

(Reproduced from *Whitaker's Almanack* 1891)

In addition to the ordinary terms there are others which, although puzzling to a foreigner, are tolerably well understood in this country. In Scotland, a man who flies 'kites' may not be worth a 'bodle', and in England not worth a 'mag' – coins which no one ever saw. Such a man will toss you for a 'bob'. He, of course, would be shunned by the lady who lost a 'pony' on last year's Oaks, and by her husband who lost a 'monkey' on the Derby at Epsom a day or two previously. A gentleman who is worth a 'plum' (£100,000) need never be short of 'tin'; while the outcast who begs a few 'coppers' in order to procure a bed generally has no 'blunt'. The following words are commonly in use:

| | |
|---|---|
| A Joey = 4d. | A Pony = £25 |
| A Tanner = 6d. | A Monkey = £500 |
| A Bob = 1s. | A Kite = An accommodation Bill |
| Half a Bull = 2s. 6d. | Browns = Copper or bronze |
| A Bull = 5s. | Tin = Money generally |
| A Quid = £1 | Blunt = Silver, or money in general |

# Banking

Deposit-taking institutions may be broadly divided into two sectors: the monetary sector, which is predominantly banks and is supervised by the Bank of England; and those institutions outside the monetary sector, of which the most important are the building societies and the National Savings Bank.

The main institutions within the British banking system are the Bank of England (the central bank), the clearing banks (the major retail banks), the merchant banks, the overseas banks, and the discount houses.

The Banking Act 1987 established a single category of authorized institutions eligible to carry out banking business. Under the 1987 Act, the Bank of England exercises a regulatory role over the banking system, and ensures the efficient functioning of payment and settlement systems and efficient services. In its role as the central bank, the Bank of England also acts as banker to the Government and as a note-issuing authority. It is responsible for executing monetary policy and therefore sets the base rates.

BANK BASE RATES 1993–4

| 23 November 1993 | 5.5% |
| 8 February 1994 | 5.25% |
| 12 September 1994 | 5.75% |

## CLEARING BANKS

The clearing banks are Abbey National, Bank of Scotland, Barclays, Clydesdale, Co-operative, Coutts, Girobank, Lloyds, Midland, National Westminster, the Royal Bank of Scotland Group, the TSB and the Yorkshire Bank.

Banking hours differ throughout Great Britain. Many banks in England and Wales are experimenting with longer hours and Saturday morning opening, and hours vary from branch to branch. Current minimum opening hours are:

ENGLAND AND WALES: Monday–Friday 9.30–3.30 (City of London town clearers 9.30–3)

SCOTLAND: Monday–Wednesday, Friday, 9.15–4.45; Thursday 9.15–5.30

NORTHERN IRELAND: Open four days a week 10–3; open one day a week 9.30–5

## CLEARING SERVICES

The Association for Payment Clearing Services (APACS) manages the payment clearing systems and oversees money transmission in the UK. It is an umbrella organization for three separate companies:

BACS Ltd is the UK's automated clearing house for bulk clearing of electronic debits and credits (e.g. direct debits and salary credits).

The Cheque and Credit Clearing Company Ltd operates bulk clearing systems for inter-bank cheques and paper credit items.

CHAPS and Town Clearing Company Ltd provides same-day clearing for high value electronic funds transfers and cheques.

Membership of APACS and the operational clearing companies is open to any appropriately regulated financial institution providing payment services and meeting the relevant membership criteria. As at June 1994, APACS had 23 members, comprising the major banks and building societies.

ASSOCIATION FOR PAYMENT CLEARING SERVICES (APACS), Mercury House, Triton Court, 14 Finsbury Square, London EC2A 1BR. Tel: 0171–711 6200. *Head of Public Affairs*, R. Tyson-Davies

BACS LTD, De Havilland Road, Edgware, Middlesex HA8 5QA. *Chief Executive*, G. Younger

CHEQUE AND CREDIT CLEARING COMPANY LTD, Mercury House, Triton Court, 14 Finsbury Square, London EC2A 1BR. *Chief Inspector*, P. M. Rowe

CHAPS AND TOWN CLEARING COMPANY LTD, Mercury House, Triton Court, 14 Finsbury Square, London EC2A 1BR. *Chief Inspector*, P. M. Rowe

## BANKING SERVICES

Retail banks now offer a wide variety of financial services to companies and individuals, including current and deposit accounts, loan facilities, automated teller (cashpoint) machines, cheque guarantee cards, credit cards and debit cards.

FINANCIAL RESULTS 1993

| Bank Group | P/L before taxation £m | P/L after taxation £m | Total assets £m | Number of UK branches |
|---|---|---|---|---|
| Abbey National | 704 | 390 | 83,800 | 680 |
| *Bank of Scotland | 268.7 | 163.4 | 30,748 | 310 |
| Barclays | 664 | 382 | 166,008 | 2,400 |
| Clydesdale | 89.2 | 58.8 | 5,561.7 | 314 |
| Co-operative | 17.8 | 11.1 | 3,223 | 109 |
| Coutts & Co. | 79 | n/a | 10,549 | 18 |
| Girobank | n/a | n/a | n/a | n/a |
| Lloyds | 1,031 | 694 | 71,636 | 1,930 |
| Midland | 844 | 672 | 76,431 | 1,740 |
| National Westminster | 989 | 643 | 152,862 | 2,553 |
| The Royal Bank of Scotland Group PLC | 265.2 | 184.3 | 36,293.8 | 800 |
| †Yorkshire Bank | 131.3 | 86 | 3,966 | 270 |

*For year ended 28 February 1994
†For year ended September 1993

## AUTHORIZED INSTITUTIONS

Banking in the United Kingdom is regulated by the Banking Act 1987 as amended by the European Community's Second Banking Co-ordination Directive, which came into effect on 1 January 1993.

The Directive permits banks incorporated in one EC member state to carry on certain banking activities in another member state without the need for authorization by that state. Consequently, the Bank of England no longer authorizes banks incorporated in other EC states with branches in the UK so that they may accept deposits in the UK; the authorization of their home state supervisor is sufficient provided that certain notification requirements are met. However, UK-incorporated subsidiaries of banks incorporated in other EC states which wish to accept deposits in the UK continue to need authorization by the Bank of England.

As at 28 February 1994, a total of 518 institutions were authorized to carry out business in the UK:

| | |
|---|---|
| Authorized under the Banking Act 1987 | 389 |
| UK-incorporated | 232 |
| Incorporated outside the EEA | 157 |
| European authorized institutions | 129 |
| With UK branches entitled to accept deposits in UK | 97 |
| Other EAIs | 32 |
| TOTAL | 518 |

The following lists show the institutions authorized or entitled to accept deposits in the UK and covered by the UK's deposit protection scheme, as at 2 September 1994.

## AUTHORIZED BY THE BANK OF ENGLAND

UK-INCORPORATED
(Including partnerships formed under the law of any part of the UK)

*In administration

ABC International Bank PLC
ANZ Grindlays Bank PLC
AY Bank Ltd
Abbey National PLC
Abbey National Treasury Services PLC
Adam & Company PLC
Afghan National Credit & Finance Ltd
Airdrie Savings Bank
Alexanders Discount PLC
Alliance Trust (Finance) Ltd
Allied Bank Philippines (UK) PLC
Allied Trust Bank Ltd
Anglo-Romanian Bank Ltd
Henry Ansbacher & Co. Ltd
Arbuthnot Latham & Co. Ltd
Assemblies of God Property Trust
Associates Capital Corporation Ltd
Avco Trust PLC

Bank Leumi (UK) PLC
Bank of America International Ltd
Bank of Boston Ltd
Bank of Cyprus (London) Ltd
Bank of Montreal Europe Ltd
Bank of Scotland
Bank of Scotland Treasury Services PLC
Bank of Tokyo International Ltd
Bank of Wales PLC
Bankers Trust International PLC

Banque Nationale de Paris PLC
The Baptist Union Corporation Ltd
Barclays Bank PLC
Barclays Bank Trust Company Ltd
Barclays de Zoete Wedd Ltd
Baring Brothers & Co. Ltd
Belmont Bank Ltd
Beneficial Bank PLC
*British and Commonwealth Merchant Bank PLC
The British Bank of the Middle East
The British Linen Bank Ltd
British Railways Savings Company Ltd
Brown, Shipley & Co. Ltd

CIBC Bank PLC
CLF Municipal Bank PLC
Caledonian Bank PLC
Cater Allen Ltd
Central Hispano Bank (UK) Ltd
The Charities Aid Foundation Money Management Company Ltd
Chartered Trust PLC
Charterhouse Bank Ltd
Chase Investment Bank Ltd
Chemical Investment Bank Ltd
Citibank International PLC
City Trust Ltd
Clive Discount Company Ltd
Close Brothers Ltd
Clydesdale Bank PLC
Commercial Bank Trust PLC
Commercial Bank of London PLC
Confederation Bank Ltd
Consolidated Credits Bank Ltd
The Co-operative Bank PLC
County NatWest Ltd
Coutts & Co.
Credit Suisse Financial Products

Daiwa Europe Bank PLC
Dalbeattie Finance Co. Ltd
Dao Heng Bank (London) PLC
Davenham Trust PLC
The Dorset, Somerset & Wilts. Investment Society Ltd
Dryfield Trust PLC
Dunbar Bank PLC
Duncan Lawrie Ltd

Eccles Savings and Loans Ltd
Exeter Bank Ltd

FIBI Bank (UK) PLC
Fairmount Trust Ltd
FennoScandia Bank Ltd
Financial & General Bank PLC
James Finlay Bank Ltd
First National Bank PLC
First National Commercial Bank PLC
The First Personal Bank PLC
First Trust Bank (AIB Group Northern Ireland PLC)
Robert Fleming & Co. Ltd
Ford Credit Europe PLC
Foreign & Colonial Management Ltd
Forward Trust Ltd
Forward Trust Personal Finance Ltd
Frizzell Banking Services Ltd

Gartmore Money Management Ltd
Gerrard & National Ltd
Girobank PLC
Goldman Sachs Ltd
Granville Trust Ltd

Gresham Trust PLC
Guinness Mahon & Co. Ltd

HFC Bank PLC
HSBC Investment Banking Ltd
Habibsons Bank Ltd
Hambros Bank Ltd
Hampshire Trust PLC
The Hardware Federation Finance Co. Ltd
Harrods Bank Ltd
Harton Securities Ltd
Havana International Bank Ltd
The Heritable & General Investment Bank Ltd
Hill Samuel Bank Ltd
C. Hoare & Co.
Julian Hodge Bank Ltd
Humberclyde Finance Group Ltd
Hungarian International Bank Ltd

3i PLC
3i Group PLC
IBJ International PLC
International Mexican Bank Ltd
Iran Overseas Investment Bank Ltd
Italian International Bank PLC

Jordan International Bank PLC
Leopold Joseph & Sons Ltd

KDB Bank (UK) Ltd
KEXIM Bank (UK) Ltd
King & Shaxson Ltd
Kleinwort Benson Ltd
Kleinwort Benson Investment Management Ltd
Korea Long Term Credit Bank International Ltd

LTCB International Ltd
Lazard Brothers & Co. Ltd
Lloyds Bank PLC
Lloyds Bank (BLSA) Ltd
Lloyds Bowmaker Ltd
Lloyds Private Banking Ltd
Lombard Bank Ltd
Lombard & Ulster Ltd
Lombard North Central PLC
London Scottish Bank PLC
London Trust Bank PLC
Lordsvale Finance PLC

MBNA International Bank Ltd
McNeill Pearson Ltd
W. M. Mann & Co. (Investments) Ltd
Marks and Spencer Financial Services Ltd
Matheson Bank Ltd
Matlock Bank Ltd
Meghraj Bank Ltd
Mellon Europe Ltd
Mercury Provident PLC
Merrill Lynch International Bank Ltd
The Methodist Chapel Aid Association Ltd
Midland Bank PLC
Midland Bank Trust Company Ltd
Minories Finance Ltd
Minster Trust Ltd
Samuel Montagu & Co. Ltd
Morgan Grenfell & Co. Ltd
Moscow Narodny Bank Ltd
*Mount Banking Corporation Ltd
Mutual Trust and Savings Ltd

NIIB Group Ltd
NWS Bank PLC
National Bank of Egypt International Ltd

National Bank of Kuwait (International) PLC
The National Mortgage Bank PLC
National Westminster Bank PLC
NationsBank Europe Ltd
The Nikko Bank (UK) PLC
Noble Grossart Ltd
Nomura Bank International PLC
Northern Bank Ltd
Northern Bank Executor & Trustee Company Ltd
Nykredit Mortgage Bank PLC

Omega Trust Co. Ltd

PaineWebber International Bank Ltd
Pointon York Ltd
The Private Bank and Trust Company Ltd

Ralli Investment Company Ltd
R. Raphael & Sons PLC
Rathbone Bros. & Co. Ltd
Rea Brothers Ltd
Reliance Bank Ltd
Republic Mase Bank Ltd
Riggs AP Bank Ltd
Riyad Bank Europe Ltd
N. M. Rothschild & Sons Ltd
Royal Bank of Canada Europe Ltd
The Royal Bank of Scotland PLC
RoyScot Trust PLC

SBI European Bank Ltd
Sabanci Bank PLC
Sanwa International PLC
Saudi American Bank (UK) Ltd
Saudi International Bank (Al-Bank Al-Saudi Al-Alami Ltd)
Schroder Leasing Ltd
J. Henry Schroder Wagg & Co. Ltd
Scotiabank (UK) Ltd
Scottish Amicable Money Managers Ltd
Seccombe Marshall & Campion PLC
Secure Trust Bank PLC
Singer & Friedlander Ltd
Smith & Williamson Securities
Southsea Mortgage & Investment Co. Ltd
Standard Bank London Ltd
Standard Chartered Bank
Svenska International PLC

TSB Bank PLC
TSB Bank Scotland PLC
Tokai Bank Europe Ltd
Toronto Dominion Bank Europe Ltd
Turkish Bank (UK) Ltd
Tyndall Bank PLC

UBAF Bank Ltd
UCB Bank PLC
Ulster Bank Ltd
Union Discount Company Ltd
The United Bank of Kuwait PLC
United Dominions Trust Ltd
United Trust Bank Ltd
Unity Trust Bank PLC

Wagon Finance Ltd
S. G. Warburg & Co. Ltd
Weatherbys & Co. Ltd
Wesleyan Savings Bank Ltd
Western Trust & Savings Ltd
West Merchant Bank Ltd
Whiteaway Laidlaw Bank Ltd
*Wimbledon & South West Finance PLC
Wintrust Securities Ltd

Woodchester Credit Lyonnais PLC
Yamaichi Bank (UK) PLC
Yorkshire Bank PLC

INCORPORATED OUTSIDE THE EUROPEAN ECONOMIC AREA
(Including partnerships or other unincorporated associations formed under the law of any member state of the European Community other than the UK)

†Provisional liquidator appointed

ABSA Bank Ltd
Allied Bank of Pakistan Ltd
American Express Bank Ltd
Arab African International Bank
Arab Bank PLC
Arab Banking Corporation BSC
Arab National Bank
Asahi Bank Ltd
Ashikaga Bank Ltd
Australia & New Zealand Banking Group Ltd

BSI – Banca della Svizzera Italiana
Banca Serfin SA
Banco de la Nación Argentina
Banco do Brasil SA
Banco do Estado de São Paulo SA
Banco Mercantil de São Paulo SA
Banco Nacional de México SNC
Banco Real SA
Bancomer SA
Bangkok Bank Public Company Ltd
Bank Julius Baer & Co. Ltd
Bank Bumiputra Malaysia Berhad
PT Bank Ekspor Impor Indonesia (Persero)
Bank Handlowy w Warszawie SA
Bank Hapoalim BM
Bank Mellat
Bank Melli Iran
PT Bank Negara Indonesia (Persero)
Bank of America Illinois
Bank of America NT & SA
Bank of Baroda
The Bank of N. T. Butterfield & Son Ltd
Bank of Ceylon
Bank of China
The Bank of East Asia Ltd
The Bank of Fukuoka Ltd
Bank of India
Bank of Montreal
The Bank of New York
The Bank of Nova Scotia
Bank of Seoul
The Bank of Tokyo Ltd
Bank of Western Australia Ltd
The Bank of Yokohama Ltd
Bank Saderat Iran
Bank Sepah-Iran
Bank Tejarat
Bank von Ernst & Co. Ltd
Bankers Trust Company
Beirut Riyad Bank SAL

Canadian Imperial Bank of Commerce
Canara Bank
Chang Hwa Commercial Bank Ltd
The Chase Manhattan Bank NA
Chemical Bank
The Chiba Bank Ltd
Cho Hung Bank

The Chuo Trust & Banking Co. Ltd
Citibank NA
Commercial Bank of Korea Ltd
Commonwealth Bank of Australia
CoreStates Bank NA
Crédit Suisse
Cyprus Credit Bank Ltd
The Cyprus Popular Bank Ltd
The Dai-Ichi Kangyo Bank Ltd
The Daiwa Bank Ltd
The Development Bank of Singapore Ltd
Discount Bank and Trust Company

Emirates Bank International Ltd

First Bank of Nigeria PLC
First Commercial Bank
First Fidelity Bank NA
The First National Bank of Boston
The First National Bank of Chicago
Fleet Bank of Massachusetts, NA
French Bank of Southern Africa Ltd
The Fuji Bank Ltd

Ghana Commercial Bank
Gulf International Bank BSC

Habib Bank AG Zurich
Habib Bank Ltd
Hanil Bank
Harris Trust and Savings Bank
The Hiroshima Bank Ltd
The Hokkaido Takushoku Bank Ltd
The Hokuriku Bank Ltd
The Hongkong and Shanghai Banking Corporation Ltd

The Industrial Bank of Japan Ltd

The Joyo Bank Ltd

Korea Exchange Bank
Korea First Bank

The Long-Term Credit Bank of Japan Ltd

Macquarie Bank Ltd
Malayan Banking Berhad
Mashreq Bank PSC
Mellon Bank NA
Merchants National Bank & Trust Company of Indianapolis (National City Bank, Indiana)
The Mitsubishi Bank Ltd
The Mitsubishi Trust and Banking Corporation
The Mitsui Trust & Banking Co. Ltd
Morgan Guaranty Trust Company of New York
Multibanco Comermex SA

NBD Bank, NA
Nacional Financiera SNC
National Australia Bank Ltd
National Bank of Abu Dhabi
National Bank of Canada
The National Bank of Dubai Ltd
National Bank of Pakistan
NationsBank of North Carolina NA
Nedcor Bank Ltd
The Nippon Credit Bank Ltd
The Norinchukin Bank
The Northern Trust Company

Oversea-Chinese Banking Corporation Ltd
Overseas Trust Bank Ltd
Overseas Union Bank Ltd

Philippine National Bank

Qatar National Bank SAQ

†Rafidain Bank
Republic National Bank of New York
The Riggs National Bank of Washington DC
Riyad Bank
Royal Bank of Canada

The Sakura Bank Ltd
The Sanwa Bank Ltd
Saudi American Bank
Shanghai Commercial Bank Ltd
Shinhan Bank
The Siam Commercial Bank Public Company Ltd
Sonali Bank
State Bank of India
State Street Bank and Trust Company
The Sumitomo Bank Ltd
The Sumitomo Trust & Banking Co. Ltd
Swiss Bank Corporation
Syndicate Bank

TC Ziraat Bankasi
The Thai Farmers Bank Public Company Ltd
The Tokai Bank Ltd
The Toronto-Dominion Bank
The Toyo Trust & Banking Company Ltd
Türkiye İş Bankasi AŞ

Uco Bank
Union Bancaire Privée CBI-TDB
Union Bank of Nigeria PLC
Union Bank of Switzerland
United Bank Ltd
United Mizrahi Bank Ltd
United Overseas Bank Ltd

Westpac Banking Corporation

The Yasuda Trust & Banking Co. Ltd

Zambia National Commercial Bank Ltd
Zivnostenská Banka AS

## EUROPEAN AUTHORIZED INSTITUTIONS ENTITLED TO ESTABLISH BRANCHES IN THE UK

The following are entitled to establish branches in the UK for the purpose of accepting deposits in the UK. The country of the home state supervisory authority is in parenthesis.

ABN AMRO Bank NV (Netherlands)
AIB Capital Markets PLC (Republic of Ireland)
AIB Finance Ltd (Republic of Ireland)
ASLK-CGER Bank NV-SA (Belgium)
Allied Irish Banks PLC (Republic of Ireland)
Anglo Irish Bank Corporation PLC (Republic of Ireland)

BfG Bank AG (Germany)
Banca Cassa di Risparmio di Torino SpA (Italy)
Banca Commerciale Italiana (Italy)
Banca di Roma SpA (Italy)
Banca March SA (Spain)
Banca Nazionale dell'Agricoltura SpA (Italy)
Banca Nazionale del lavoro SpA (Italy)
Banca Popolare di Milano (Italy)
Banca Popolare di Novara (Italy)
Banco Ambrosiano Veneto SpA (Italy)
Banco Bilbao-Vizcaya (Spain)
Banco Central Hispanoamericano SA (Spain)
Banco de Sabadell (Spain)
Banco di Napoli SpA (Italy)
Banco di Sicilia SpA (Italy)

Banco Español de Crédito SA (Spain)
Banco Espirito Santo e Comercial de Lisboa (Portugal)
Banco Exterior de España SA (Spain)
Banco Nacional Ultramarino SA (Portugal)
Banco Português do Atlântico (Portugal)
Banco Santander (Spain)
Banco Totta & Açores SA (Portugal)
Bank Austria AG (Austria)
Bank Brussels Lambert (Belgium)
Bankgesellschaft Berlin AG (Germany)
The Bank of Ireland (Republic of Ireland)
Banque Arabe et Internationale d'Investissement (France)
Banque Banorabe (France)
Banque Française de l'Orient (France)
Banque Française du Commerce Extérieur (France)
Banque Indosuez (France)
Banque Internationale à Luxembourg SA (Luxembourg)
Banque Nationale de Paris (France)
Banque Paribas (France)
Bayerische Hypotheken-und Wechsel-Bank AG (Germany)
Bayerische Landesbank Girozentrale (Germany)
Bayerische Vereinsbank AG (Germany)
Belgolaise SA (Belgium)
Berliner Bank AG (Germany)
Berliner Handels-und Frankfurter Bank (Germany)
Byblos Bank Belgium SA (Belgium)

CARIPLO (Cassa di Risparmio delle Provincie Lombarde SpA) (Italy)
Caisse Nationale de Crédit Agricole (France)
Cassa di Risparmio di Verona Vicenza Belluno e Ancona SpA (Italy)
Christiania Bank og Kreditkasse (Norway)
Commerzbank AG (Germany)
Compagnie Financière de CIC et de l'Union Européenne (France)
Confederacion Española de Cajas de Ahorros (Spain)
Creditanstalt-Bankverein (Austria)
Crédit Commercial de France (France)
Crédit du Nord (France)
Crédit Lyonnais (France)
Crédit Lyonnais Bank Nederland NV (Netherlands)
Credito Italiano (Italy)

Den Danske Bank Aktieselskab (Denmark)
Den norske Bank AS (Norway)
Deutsche Bank AG (Germany)
Deutsche Genossenschaftsbank (Germany)
Dresdner Bank AG (Germany)

Ergobank SA (Greece)

First National Building Society (Republic of Ireland)

Generale Bank (Belgium)
GiroCredit Bank Aktiengesellschaft der Sparkassen (Austria)
Gota Bank (Sweden)

Hamburgische Landesbank Girozentrale (Germany)

ICS Building Society (Republic of Ireland)
Internationale Nederlanden Bank NV (Netherlands)
Ionian and Popular Bank of Greece SA (Greece)
Irish Permanent Building Society (Republic of Ireland)
Istituto Bancario San Paolo di Torino SpA (Italy)

Jyske Bank (Denmark)

Kansallis-Osake-Pankki (Finland)
Kas-Associatie NV (Netherlands)
Kredietbank NV (Belgium)

Landesbank Berlin Girozentrale (Germany)

Landesbank Hessen-Thüringen Girozentrale (Germany)

MeesPierson NV (Netherlands)
Monte dei Paschi di Siena (Italy)

National Bank of Greece SA (Greece)
Nordbanken (Sweden)
Norddeutsche Landesbank Girozentrale (Germany)

Postipankki Ltd (Finland)

Rabobank Nederland (Coöperatieve Centrale Raiffeisen-
Boerenleenbank BA) (Netherlands)

Raiffeisen Zentralbank Osterreich AG (Austria)

Skandinaviska Enskilda Banken (Sweden)
Société Générale (France)
Südwestdeutsche Landesbank Girozentrale (Germany)
Svenska Handelsbanken (Sweden)
SwedBank (Sweden)

Ulster Investment Bank Ltd (Republic of Ireland)
Unibank AS (Denmark)
Union Bank of Finland Ltd (Finland)

Westdeutsche Landesbank Girozentrale (Germany)

# The National Debt

Net central government borrowing each year represents an addition to the National Debt. At the end of March 1993 the National Debt amounted to some £248,600 million of which about £20,200 million was in currencies other than sterling. Of the £228,400 million sterling debt, £163,600 million consisted of gilt-edged stock; of this, 28 per cent had a maturity of up to five years, 45 per cent a maturity of over five years and up to 15 years, and 27 per cent a maturity of over 15 years or undated. The remaining sterling debt was made up mainly of national savings (£39,000 million), certificates of tax deposits, Treasury bills, and Ways and Means advances (very short-term internal government borrowing).

Sizeable trust funds have been established over the past fifty years for the purpose of reducing the National Debt. The National Fund was established in 1927 with an original gift of £100,653,656; it is administered by Baring Brothers & Co. Ltd. The Elsie Mackay Fund was established in 1929 with an original gift of £527,809 to run for 45–50 years. It was wound up in 1979, when it was valued at £4,902,864. The John Buchanan Fund was established in 1932 with gifts totalling £36,702 to run for 50 years. It was wound up in 1982, when it was valued at £204,138.

# The Stock Exchange

The International Stock Exchange of the United Kingdom and Republic of Ireland Ltd serves the needs of government, industry and investors by providing facilities for raising capital and a central market-place for securities trading. There are 8,547 securities listed on the London Stock Exchange, which have a value of approximately £3,226,000 million. In 1993 securities worth some £2,828,200 million changed hands. This central market-place covers government stocks (called gilts) and UK and overseas company shares (called equities and fixed interest stocks) and traditional options.

## BIG BANG

During 1986 the London Stock Exchange went through the greatest period of change in its two-hundred year history. In March 1986 it opened its doors for the first time to overseas and corporate membership of the Exchange, allowing banks, insurance companies and overseas securities houses to become members of the Exchange and to buy existing member firms. On 27 October 1986, three major reforms took place, changes which became known as 'Big Bang':

1  Abolition of scales of minimum commissions, allowing clients to negotiate freely with their brokers about the charge for their services
2  Abolition of the separation of member firms into brokers and jobbers. Under the new system, firms are broker/dealers, able to act as agents on behalf of clients; to act as principals buying and selling shares for their own account; and to become registered market makers, making continuous buying and selling prices in specific securities
3  The introduction of the Stock Exchange Automated Quotations (SEAQ) system. Market makers input their buying and selling prices into SEAQ, which displays the competing quotations on a composite page onscreen. For all but the smallest, least frequently traded UK companies, the volume of shares traded is also updated continuously throughout the day

Of all these changes, the implementation of SEAQ has had the most visible effect. Dealing in stocks and shares now takes place via the telephone in the firms' own dealing rooms, rather than face to face on the floor of the Exchange. The new systems also provide increased investor protection. All deals taking place via the Exchange's SEAQ system are recorded on a database which can be used to resolve disputes or to carry out investigations.

Members of the London Stock Exchange buy and sell shares on behalf of the public, as well as institutions such as pension funds or insurance companies. In return for transacting the deal, the broker will charge a commission, which is usually based upon the value of the transaction. The market makers, or wholesalers, in each security do not charge a commission for their services, but will quote the broker two prices, a price at which they will buy and a price at which they will sell. It is the middle of these two prices which is published in lists of Stock Exchange prices in newspapers.

## REGULATORY BODIES

On 12 November 1986 members of the Exchange agreed to merge with members of the international broking community in London, based outside the Exchange, in order to form two new bodies: the International Stock Exchange of the United Kingdom and Republic of Ireland Ltd, and the Securities and Futures Authority. These two regulatory bodies were formed under the provisions of the Financial Services Act 1986, which requires investment businesses to be authorized and regulated by a self-regulating organization (SRO) of which the Securities and Futures Authority is one. The Act also requires business to be conducted through a recognized investment exchange (RIE). The London Stock Exchange is an RIE, regulating three main markets: UK equities, international equities and gilts.

## PRIMARY MARKETS

The Exchange serves the needs of industry by providing a mechanism where companies can raise capital for development and growth through the issue of securities. For a company entering the market for the first time there are two possible Stock Exchange markets, depending upon the size, history and requirements of the company. The first is the listed market, which exists for well-established companies, which must comply with stringent criteria relating to all aspects of their operations. At present, companies coming to this market require a three-year trading record with a minimum of 25 per cent of the shares held in public hands. The Unlisted Securities Market was established in 1980 with less rigorous entry requirements designed with the smaller and newer company in mind. Companies at present are required to provide a two-year trading record and a minimum of 10 per cent of the shares must be in public hands. Owing to the lack of distinction between the two markets, the Unlisted Securities Market will be closed at the end of 1996.

Once admitted to the Exchange, all companies are obliged to keep their shareholders informed of their progress, making announcements of a price-sensitive nature through the Exchange's company announcements department.

## THE GOVERNING BOARD

The International Stock Exchange has its headquarters in London, and representative offices around the UK and the Republic of Ireland. At present there are 386 member firms.

The interests of the membership of the London Stock Exchange are reflected in the governing board, whose members are responsible for overall policy and the strategic direction of the Exchange. The board consists of representatives drawn from listed companies, investors and other major users, elected at the annual general meeting, and the Government Broker, the Chief Executive and up to five senior executives of the Stock Exchange.

LONDON STOCK EXCHANGE, Old Broad Street, London EC2N 1HP. Tel: 0171-797 1000
*Chairman,* J. Kemp-Welch
*Chief Executive,* M. Lawrence

# Mutual Societies

## FRIENDLY SOCIETIES IN BRITAIN

Friendly societies are voluntary mutual organizations, the main purposes of which are the provision of relief or maintenance during sickness, unemployment or retirement, and the provision of life assurance. Many of the older traditional societies complement their business activities by social activity and a general care for individual members in ways normally outside the scope of a purely commercial organization. There are three main categories of friendly societies: societies with separately registered branches, commonly called orders; centralized societies, which conduct business directly with members (having no separately registered branches); and collecting societies. Collecting societies conduct industrial assurance business and are subject to the requirements of the Industrial Assurance Acts in addition to the Friendly Societies Acts. Industrial assurance is life assurance for which the premiums are payable at intervals of less than two months and are received by means of collectors who make house-to-house visits for the purpose.

Long before the term 'friendly society' came into use, the seeds of voluntary mutual insurance had been sown in the ancient religious and trade guilds. Guilds had become widespread in Britain by the 14th century. By then, the purely charitable character of the original guilds had largely changed with the emergence of numerous small institutions adopting primitive mutual insurance methods of a regular flat rate contribution to insure relief when sick or in old age and a payment to the widow in the event of death. The present register of friendly societies includes several societies which have been in existence for more than 200 years, the oldest, operating in Scotland, being the Incorporation of Carters in Leith, established in 1555.

The first Act for the encouragement and protection of friendly societies in this country was not passed until 1793, but various amending Acts were passed during the next century as the result of the recommendations of successive select committees (including a Royal Commission in 1871). The rules and other documents of societies deposited with local justices passed into the custody of the Registrar of Friendly Societies following the Act of 1846. Those relating to some societies no longer on the register have been transferred to the Public Record Office for permanent preservation.

The Friendly Societies Act 1974 allows three other main classes of society to be registered: benevolent societies, working men's clubs and specially authorized societies. Benevolent societies are established for any charitable or benevolent purpose, to provide the same type of benefits as would be permissible for a friendly society, but in contrast the benefits must be for persons who are not members instead of, or in addition to, members. Working men's clubs provide social and recreational facilities for members. Specially authorized societies are registered for any purpose authorized by the Treasury as a purpose to which some or all of the provisions of the 1974 Act ought to be extended. Examples are societies for the promotion of science, literature and the fine arts, or to enable members to pursue an interest in sports and games.

The most recent legislation, the Friendly Societies Act 1992, created a new legislative framework for friendly societies, enabling them to provide a wider range of services to their members and allowing them to compete on more equal terms with other financial institutions. At the same time it provided for more flexible prudential supervision to safeguard members of societies.

The Act enables friendly societies to incorporate and establish subsidiaries to provide various financial and other services to their members and the public. The activities which subsidiaries are able to conduct as the relevant provisions have come into force under subordinate legislation include those to establish and manage unit trust schemes and Personal Equity Plans; to arrange for the provision of credit, whether as agents or providers; to carry on long-term or general insurance business; to provide insurance intermediary services; to provide fund management services for trustees of pension funds; to administer estates and execute trusts of wills; and to establish and manage sheltered housing, residential homes for the elderly, hospitals and nursing homes.

The Act established a new framework to oversee friendly societies, including a Friendly Societies Commission, whose principal functions are to regulate the activities of friendly societies, promote their financial stability and protect members' funds. All friendly societies carrying on insurance or non-insurance business require authorization by the Commission, which has a broad range of prudential powers. Friendly societies were also to be brought within the scope of the Policyholders Protection Act 1975, the statutory investor protection scheme covering insurance policyholders.

The principal statistics at the end of 1992 are given in the table below.

| | No. of societies | No. of members 000s | Benefits paid £000s | Total funds £000s |
|---|---|---|---|---|
| Orders and branches | 1,255* | 341† | 8,438† | 189,632† |
| Collecting societies | 27 | 13,148‡ | 262,214 | 3,736,281 |
| Other centralized societies | 360 | 2,913 | 317,898 | 2,931,752 |
| Benevolent societies | 78 | 323 | 4,687 | 33,232 |
| Working men's clubs | 2,345 | 1,275° | n/a | 162,793° |
| Specially authorized societies | | | | |
| Loans | 8 | 15 | n/a | 431 |
| Others | 133 | 98 | 807 | 22,316 |

\* 17 orders, 1,238 branches
† 1991 figure
° 1990 figure
‡ Assurances

## INDUSTRIAL AND PROVIDENT SOCIETIES IN BRITAIN

The familiar 'Co-op' societies are amongst the wide variety which are registered under the Industrial and Provident Societies Act 1965. This consolidating Act, which is administered by the Chief Registrar of Friendly Societies, provides for the registration of societies and lays down the broad framework within which they must operate. Internal relations of societies are governed by their registered rules.

Registration under the Act confers upon a society corporate status by its registered name with perpetual succession and a common seal, and limited liability. A society qualifies for registration if it is carrying on an industry, business or trade, and it satisfies the Registrar either (a) that it is a bona fide co-operative society, or (b) that in view of the fact that its business is being, or is intended to be, conducted for the benefit of the community, there are special reasons why it should be registered under the Act rather than as a company under the Companies Act.

The Credit Unions Act 1979 added a new class of society registerable under the 1965 Act. It also made provision for the supervision of these savings and loan bodies. Unlike other classes, where the role of the Registry is solely that of a registration authority, it is for credit unions the prudential supervisor, seeking to encourage the prudent safekeeping of investors' money.

During 1992 the number of registered societies of all classes decreased by 40 to 11,348 but the number of credit unions increased by 56 to 383. The largest group in terms of turnover was that consisting of the retail societies, which includes those trading under the 'Co-op' sign, with sales in 1992 of £5,888 million. The principal statistics at the end of 1992 are given in the table below.

| | No. of societies | No. of members 000s | Funds of members £000s | Total assets £000s |
|---|---|---|---|---|
| Retail | 173 | 7,220 | 1,273,037 | 2,854,043 |
| Wholesale and productive | 201 | 182 | 475,901 | 1,327,211 |
| Agricultural | 1,066 | 290 | 221,666 | 510,540 |
| Fishing | 94 | 7 | 6,068 | 17,936 |
| Clubs | 3,796 | 1,952* | 205,084* | 331,916* |
| General service | 1,168 | 490 | 6,949,214 | 7,965,469 |
| Housing | 4,467 | 172 | 15,769,974 | 22,631,811 |
| Credit unions | 383 | 88 | 30,769 | 32,489 |
| TOTAL | 11,348 | 10,402 | 24,931,713 | 35,671,415 |

* 1989 figures

## BUILDING SOCIETIES IN THE UK

The Building Societies Act 1986 gave building societies a completely new legal framework, the first since the initial comprehensive building society legislation in 1874. The new Act applies to societies throughout the United Kingdom.

The 1986 Act made provision for a Building Societies Commission to promote the protection of shareholders and depositors, the financial stability of societies, and to administer the system of regulation of building societies provided under the Act. The First Commissioner and Chairman of the Commission is also Chief Registrar of Friendly Societies (see Index). Much of the Act is concerned with the powers of control of the Commission and provision in relation to the management of societies, accounts, audit and so on. But the greatest impact flowed from the new powers which societies could adopt, leading to an increased range of services which they might provide. There were also some significant changes in relation to members' rights.

Under an earlier Act, raising funds to make loans was the only purpose for which a building society could exist. Under the 1986 Act that has only to be its principal purpose. The constitutional provisions include the right of members to have access to the register of members, entitlement to have

notices of meetings and to vote, and the right of members to have a resolution circulated.

In addition to traditional mortgage business, the power of societies to lend in respect of shared ownership, index-linked and equity-linked schemes is given. Societies may also lend the deposit, lend on registered land before the borrower is registered as the owner and on other equitable interests. Provision is also made for societies to make advances secured on land outside the United Kingdom. Larger societies were able, for the first time, to make unsecured loans, and to make loans on mobile homes.

Under the 1962 Act building societies could only hold land for the purposes of running their business. The 1986 Act gave building societies power to hold and develop land as a commercial asset. However, the land has to be primarily for residential purposes, or adjoining land, or for purposes incidental to the holding of residential land.

An investor protection scheme and the Investor Protection Board which administers it were established under the Act. The scheme comes into operation on the insolvency of a building society and protects the first £20,000 of a person's shares. Joint holdings are split between the holders so that, for example, a husband and wife can each have £20,000 of protected investment. The Board determines the percentage of protected investment in each case; there is a statutory maximum of 90 per cent.

On mergers, the main difference is that borrowers have a vote. For a merger to be approved at least 50 per cent of borrowers who exercise their right to vote must vote in favour, as well as 75 per cent of qualifying share investors who vote. Provision is also made for a society to convert to company status. During 1989 the Abbey National became the first, and as yet the only, building society to complete the process.

Societies were also empowered to offer for the first time the following services:
(a) Money transmission services
(b) Foreign exchange services
(c) Making or receiving of payments as agents
(d) Management, as agents, of mortgage investments
(e) Management, as agents, of land (larger societies only)
(f) Arranging for the provision of services relating to the acquisition or disposal of investments for individuals
(g) Establishment and management of personal equity plans
(h) Arranging for the provision of credit to individuals
(i) Establishment and management of unit trust schemes for the provision of pensions (through a subsidiary)
(j) Establishment and administration of pension schemes
(k) Arranging for the provision of insurance of any description
(l) Giving advice on insurance of any description
(m) Estate agency service (through a subsidiary)
(n) Surveys and valuations of land
(o) Conveyancing services

Technical problems emerged in relation to these services and in June 1988 Parliament made Orders which allowed societies to have the power to own up to 100 per cent of a life assurance company, 15 per cent of a general insurance company, 100 per cent of a stockbroking company and to offer an additional range of financial services including executorship and trusteeship, hire purchase, and leasing and safe deposit facilities. The Orders also included an increase in the limit on unsecured personal loans from £5,000 to £10,000.

The Government announced a review of the 1986 Act early in 1994. The outcome of the first stage of the review included a package of measures designed to give societies opportunities to develop and introduce extra competition into markets where they have not previously been able to operate directly. Amongst the measures is the power to own a general insurance company offering buildings, contents and mortgage payments protection insurance policies.

OMBUDSMAN SCHEME

Societies must belong to an ombudsman scheme for the investigation of complaints. Matters to be covered by the scheme include operation of share and deposit accounts, loans (but not the making of new loans), money transmission services, foreign exchange services, agency payments and receipts, and the provision of credit. Grounds for complaint include breach of the Act or contract, unfair treatment or maladministration, and where the complainant has suffered pecuniary loss or expense or inconvenience. A society must agree to be bound by decisions of the adjudicator unless it agrees to give notice to its members and the public of its

reasons for not doing so. For address of the Building Societies Ombudsman scheme, *see* Index.

BUILDING SOCIETIES 1992–3

|  | 1992 | 1993 |
|---|---|---|
| No. of societies – total | 105 | 101 |
| – authorized | 88 | 84 |
| No. of shareholders (000s) | 37,533 | 37,809 |
| No. of depositors (000s) | 5,920 | 5,486 |
| No. of borrowers (000s) | 7,141 | 7,229 |
| Share balances (£m) | 187,108 | 194,975 |
| Deposit balances (£m) | 59,910 | 64,861 |
| Mortgage balances (£m) | 213,323 | 224,168 |
| Total assets (£m) | 265,224 | 281,152 |
| Advances during year |  |  |
| No. (000s) | 1,205 | 1,011 |
| Amount (£m) | 35,698 | 33,183 |

## MORTGAGE ARREARS AND REPOSSESSIONS

The economic recession resulted in a sharp rise in mortgage arrears and repossessions, with more than 75,000 properties repossessed in 1991. That total fell by 7,000 in 1992 as a result of a greater willingness by societies to enter into arrangements with borrowers. The number continued to

decline in 1993 and there was also a reduction during the year in the number of loans where repayments were more than six months in arrears. Details of loans outstanding and properties repossessed for recent years are shown below.

|  | 1987 | 1988 | 1989 | 1990 | 1991 | 1992 | 1993 |
|---|---|---|---|---|---|---|---|
| No. of loans at end year (000s) | 8,283 | 8,564 | 9,125 | 9,415 | 9,815 | 9,922 | 10,137 |
| Properties repossessed in year |  |  |  |  |  |  |  |
| Number | 26,390 | 18,510 | 15,810 | 43,890 | 75,540 | 68,540 | 58,540 |
| % | 0.32 | 0.22 | 0.17 | 0.47 | 0.77 | 0.70 | 0.58 |

## INTEREST RATES: MORTGAGE AND SHARE

The interest rates prevailing on mortgage lending and share investment vary from society to society and in relation to the type or amount of loan or investment. General rate changes are made in response to market conditions and recent rates, with the dates of change, are given below.

The interval between the payments or compounding of interest is crucial in determining the competitiveness of particular societies' accounts. In order to make a true comparison of interest rates, the annual percentage rate or APR, which should appear in all advertisements and leaflets, must be used.

|  | May '92 | Sept. '92 | Oct. '92 | Nov. '92 | Jan. '93 | Feb. '93 | Nov. '93 | Dec. '93 | Jan. '94 |
|---|---|---|---|---|---|---|---|---|---|
| Gross average rate for all share accounts % | 8.93 | 8.41 | 7.52 | 6.59 | 6.25 | 5.84 | 5.72 | 5.32 | 5.31 |
| Predominant mortgages rate % | 10.70 | 9.95 | 9.34 | 8.55 | 8.09 | 7.99 | 7.94 | 7.72 | 7.68 |

SOCIETIES WITH TOTAL ASSETS EXCEEDING £1 MILLION AT END OF FINANCIAL YEAR 1993

| Name of Society (abbreviated*) and head office address | Share investors | Total assets £'000 |
|---|---|---|
| Alliance and Leicester, 49 Park Lane, London WIY 4EQ | 2,998,300 | 21,086,200 |
| Barnsley, Regent Street, Barnsley, South Yorks S70 2EH | 31,722 | 178,954 |
| Bath Investment, 20 Charles Street, Bath BA1 1HY | 12,750 | 49,276 |
| Beverley, 57 Market Place, Beverley, N. Humberside HU17 8AA | 5,713 | 35,438 |
| Birmingham Midshires, PO Box 81, 35–49 Lichfield Street, Wolverhampton WV1 1EL | 679,062 | 4,327,187 |
| Bradford and Bingley, Crossflatts, Bingley, West Yorks. BD16 2UA | 1,490,370 | 13,864,398 |
| Bristol and West, Broad Quay, Bristol BS99 7AX | 1,040,879 | 8,140,500 |
| Britannia, Britannia House, Cheadle Road, Leek, Staffs. ST13 5RG | 1,312,460 | 12,905,500 |
| Buckinghamshire, High Street, Chalfont St Giles, Bucks. HP8 4QB | 6,080 | 52,643 |
| Cambridge, 32 St Andrew's Street, Cambridge CB2 3AR | 48,600 | 322,514 |
| Catholic, 7 Strutton Ground, London SW1P 2HY | 3,257 | 22,628 |
| Century, 21 Albany Street, Edinburgh EH1 3QW | 1,485 | 10,697 |
| Chelsea, Thirlestaine Hall, Thirlestaine Road, Cheltenham, Glos. GL53 7AL | 208,222 | 2,210,082 |
| Cheltenham and Gloucester, Barnett Way, Gloucester GL4 7RL | 969,000 | 17,686,600 |
| Chesham, 12 Market Square, Chesham, Bucks. HP5 1ER | 12,704 | 80,247 |
| Cheshire, Castle Street, Macclesfield, Chesire SK11 6AH | 212,100 | 1,367,172 |
| Chorley and District, 49–51 St Thomas's Road, Chorley, Lancs. PR7 1JL | 9,561 | 61,146 |
| City and Metropolitan, 219 High Street, Bromley, Kent BR1 1PR | 9,158 | 93,743 |
| Clay Cross Benefit, Eyre Street, Clay Cross, Chesterfield S45 9NS | 3,200 | 15,618 |
| Coventry, PO Box 9, High Street, Coventry CV1 5QN | 474,486 | 2,966,439 |
| Cumberland, Cumberland House, Castle Street, Carlisle CA3 8RX | 134,482 | 516,280 |
| Darlington, Tubwell Row, Darlington, Co. Durham DL1 1NX | 44,108 | 267,696 |
| Derbyshire, Duffield Hall, Duffield, Derby DE56 1AG | 296,756 | 1,645,058 |
| Dudley, Dudley House, Stone Street, Dudley DY1 1NP | 18,539 | 76,217 |
| Dunfermline, 12 East Port, Dunfermline, Fife KY12 7LD | 140,780 | 811,911 |
| Earl Shilton, 22 The Hollow, Earl Shilton, Leicester LE9 7NB | 9,601 | 53,684 |
| Ecology, 18 Station Road, Cross Hills, Keighley, West Yorks BD20 7EH | 3,253 | 13,017 |
| Furness, 51–55 Duke Street, Barrow-in-Furness LA14 1RT | 64,208 | 337,118 |
| Gainsborough, 26 Lord Street, Gainsborough, Lincs. DN21 2DB | 5,325 | 27,222 |
| Greenwich, 279–283 Greenwich High Road, London SE10 8NL | 24,000 | 151,415 |
| Halifax, Trinity Road, Halifax, West Yorks HX1 2RG | 7,340,400 | 67,157,100 |
| Hanley Economic, Granville House, Festival Park, Hanley, Stoke-on-Trent, Staffs. ST1 5TB | 29,117 | 167,157 |
| Harpenden, 14 Station Road, Harpenden, Herts. AL5 4SE | 9,302 | 40,374 |
| Hinckley and Rugby, Upper Bond Street, Hinckley, Leics. LE10 1DG | 42,194 | 249,003 |
| Holmesdale, 43 Church Street, Reigate, Surrey RH2 0AE | 5,307 | 58,853 |
| Ilkeston Permanent, 24–26 South Street, Ilkeston, Derby DE7 5HQ | 4,029 | 16,325 |
| Ipswich, 44 Upper Brook Street, Ipswich IP4 1DP | 30,271 | 164,864 |
| Kent Reliance, Reliance House, Manor Road, Chatham, Kent ME4 6AF | 44,400 | 229,249 |
| Lambeth, 118–120 Westminster Bridge Road, London SE1 7XE | 53,757 | 524,074 |
| Leeds and Holbeck, 105 Albion Street, Leeds LS1 5AS | 286,574 | 2,452,929 |
| Leeds Permanent, Permanent House, 1 Lovell Park Road, Leeds LS1 1NS | 3,497,883 | 19,492,500 |
| Leek United, 50 St Edward Street, Leek, Staffs. ST13 5DH | 49,326 | 334,223 |
| Londonderry Provident, 31A Carlisle Road, Londonderry BT48 6JJ | 1,029 | 6,861 |
| Loughborough, 6 High Street, Loughborough, Leics. LE11 2QB | 13,019 | 97,777 |
| Manchester, 18–20 Bridge Street, Manchester M3 3BU | 9,533 | 86,759 |
| Mansfield, Regent House, Regent Street, Mansfield, Notts. NG18 1SS | 18,968 | 104,693 |
| Market Harborough, Welland House, The Square, Market Harborough, Leics. LE16 7PD | 30,574 | 194,022 |
| Marsden, 6–20 Russell Street, Nelson, Lancs. BB9 7NJ | 56,200 | 254,664 |
| Melton Mowbray, 39 Nottingham Street, Melton Mowbray, Leics. LE13 1NR | 30,724 | 187,228 |
| Mercantile, 75 Howard Street, North Shields, Tyne and Wear NE30 1AQ | 22,801 | 129,869 |
| Monmouthshire, John Frost Square, Newport, Gwent NP9 1PX | 24,856 | 152,209 |
| National and Provincial, Provincial House, Bradford BD1 1NL | 2,217,440 | 12,719,800 |
| National Counties, National Counties House, Church Street, Epsom, Surrey KT17 4NL | 16,017 | 362,028 |
| Nationwide, Nationwide House, Pipers Way, Swindon SN38 1NW | 6,400,331 | 35,283,758 |
| Newbury, 17–20 Bartholomew Street, Newbury, Berks. RG14 5LY | 29,271 | 218,222 |
| Newcastle, Grainger Chambers, Hood Street, Newcastle upon Tyne NE1 6JP | 146,844 | 1,186,134 |
| North of England, 50 Fawcett Street, Sunderland SR1 1SA | 229,673 | 1,509,764 |
| Northern Rock, Northern Rock House, Gosforth, Newcastle upon Tyne NE3 4PL | 946,355 | 7,279,414 |
| Norwich and Peterborough, Peterborough Business Park, Lynchwood, Peterborough PE2 6WZ | 171,296 | 1,383,896 |
| Nottingham, 5–13 Upper Parliament Street, Nottingham NG1 2BX | 134,323 | 819,233 |
| Nottingham Imperial, Imperial Building, 29 Bridgford Road, West Bridgford, Nottingham NG2 6AU | 6,630 | 37,696 |
| Penrith, 7 King Street, Penrith, Cumbria CA11 7AR | 6,305 | 46,211 |
| Portman, Portman House, Richmond Hill, Bournemouth, Dorset BH2 6EP | 534,409 | 3,055,300 |

| *Name of Society (abbreviated\*) and head office address* | *Share investors* | *Total assets £'000* |
|---|---|---|
| Principality, PO Box 89, Principality Buildings, Queen Street, Cardiff CF1 1UA | 231,019 | 1,198,474 |
| Progressive, 33–37 Wellington Place, Belfast BT1 6HH | 44,368 | 319,670 |
| Saffron Walden, Herts. and Essex, 1A Market Street, Saffron Walden, Essex CB10 1HX | 38,311 | 215,738 |
| Scarborough, Prospect House, 442/444 Scalby Road, Scarborough, North Yorks. YO12 6EE | 70,560 | 406,728 |
| Scottish, 23 Manor Place, Edinburgh EH3 7XE | 16,939 | 104,965 |
| Shepshed, Bull Ring, Shepshed, Loughborough, Leics. LE12 9QD | 7,164 | 31,191 |
| Skipton, The Bailey, Skipton, North Yorks. BD23 1DN | 215,021 | 2,908,386 |
| Stafford Railway, 4 Market Square, Stafford ST16 2JH | 8,550 | 44,940 |
| Staffordshire, Jubilee House, PO Box 66, 84 Salop Street, Wolverhampton WV3 0SA | 189,828 | 955,060 |
| Standard, 64 Church Way, North Shields, Tyne and Wear NE29 0AF | 2,674 | 14,826 |
| Stroud and Swindon, Rowcroft, Stroud, Glos. GL5 3BG | 97,603 | 523,641 |
| Swansea, 11 Cradock Street, Swansea SA1 3EW | 3,381 | 29,960 |
| Teachers, Allenview House, Hanham Road, Wimborne, Dorset BH21 1AG | 10,765 | 120,430 |
| Tipton and Coseley, 70 Owen Street, Tipton, West Midlands DY4 8HG | 16,629 | 89,855 |
| Tynemouth, 53–55 Howard Street, North Shields, Tyne and Wear NE30 1AN | 6,623 | 47,878 |
| Universal, Universal House, Kings Manor, Newcastle upon Tyne NE1 6PA | 25,500 | 184,887 |
| Vernon, 19 St Petersgate, Stockport, Cheshire SK1 1HF | 27,099 | 115,404 |
| West Bromwich, 374 High Street, West Bromwich, West Midlands B70 8LR | 294,810 | 1,344,541 |
| West Cumbria, Cumbria House, Murray Road, Workington CA14 2AD | 6,973 | 35,956 |
| Woolwich, Watling Street, Bexleyheath, Kent DA6 7RR | 3,285,000 | 25,233,600 |
| Yorkshire, Yorkshire House, Yorkshire Drive, Bradford BD5 8LJ | 708,004 | 5,346,867 |

\* 'Building Society' are the last words in every society's name

# National Savings

NATIONAL SAVINGS BANK

On 31 May 1994, there were about 15,932,626 active accounts with the sum of approximately £1,454.5 million due to depositors in ordinary accounts and about 4,769,360 active accounts with the sum of approximately £9,110.7 million due to depositors in investment accounts.

Interest is earned at 3.25 per cent per year on each ordinary account for every complete calendar month in which the balance is £500 or more, provided the account is kept open for the whole of 1994 (31 December 1993 to 1 January 1995); and at 2.9 per cent per year for other months or for accounts opened or closed during 1994. The minimum deposit is £10; maximum balance £10,000 plus interest credited. On 31 May 1994 the average amount held in ordinary accounts was approximately £91.

The investment account pays a higher rate of interest (the current rate can be found at any post office). The minimum deposit is £20; maximum balance £100,000 plus interest credited. On 31 May 1994 the average amount held in investment accounts was approximately £1,910.

PREMIUM BONDS

Premium Bonds are a government security which were first introduced on 1 November 1956. Premium Bonds enable savers to enter a regular draw for tax-free prizes, while retaining the right to get their money back. A sum equivalent to interest on each bond is put into a prize fund and distributed by weekly and monthly prize draws. (The rate of interest is 5.2 per cent a year from 1 April 1994.) The prizes are drawn by ERNIE (electronic random number indicator equipment) and are free of all UK income tax and capital gains tax.

Bonds are in units of £1, with a minimum purchase of £100; above this, purchases must be in multiples of £10, up to a maximum holding limit of £20,000 per person. Winners of £50 and £100 prize warrants will be invited to return their prize warrants to National Savings, Blackpool, if they wish to reinvest. This transaction cannot be made through the Post Office. Bonds can only be held in the name of an individual and not by organizations.

Bonds become eligible for prizes once they have been held for one clear calendar month following the month of purchase. Each £1 unit can win only one prize per draw, but it will be awarded the highest for which it is drawn. Bonds remain eligible for prizes until they are repaid. When a holder dies, bonds remain eligible for prizes up to and including the twelfth monthly draw after the month in which the holder dies.

By April 1994 bonds to the value of £6,795 million had been sold. Of these £3,108 million had been cashed, leaving £3,687 million still invested. By the April 1994 prize draw, 45 million prizes totalling £2,666 million had been distributed since the first prize draw in June 1957.

INCOME BONDS

National Savings Income Bonds were introduced in 1982. They are particularly suitable for those who want to receive regular monthly payments of interest while preserving the full cash value of their capital. The bonds are sold in multiples of £1,000. The minimum holding is £2,000 and the maximum £250,000 (sole or joint holding).

Interest is calculated on a day-to-day basis and paid monthly. Interest is taxable, but is paid without deduction of tax at source. The bonds have a guaranteed life of ten years, but may be repaid at par before maturity on giving three months' notice. If repayment of a bond is made within the first year of purchase, interest from the date of purchase to the date of repayment is earned at half rate. If the sole or sole surviving holder dies, however, no fixed period of notice is required and there is no loss of interest for repayment made within the first year.

Net investment in National Savings Income Bonds was £10,974 million at the end of April 1994.

PENSIONERS GUARANTEED INCOME BONDS

Pensioners Guaranteed Income Bonds were introduced in January 1994 and are designed for people aged 65 and over who wish to receive regular monthly payments with a rate of interest that is fixed for a five year period whilst preserving the full cash value of their investment.

The minimum limit for each purchase is £500. The maximum holding is £20,000 (£40,000 for a joint holding); within these limits Bonds can be bought for any amount in pounds and pence. The rate of interest is fixed and guaranteed for the first five years. Interest is taxable, but is paid without deduction of tax at source.

Holders can apply for repayment (or part repayment of a Bond subject to the minimum holding limits) by giving 60 days notice (if repayment is before the fifth anniversary date). No interest is earned during the notice period. If repayment is requested within two weeks of any fifth anniversary of purchase, there is no formal period of notice. On the death of a holder or sole surviving investor in a joint holding repayment will be made without notice. Interest will be paid in full up to the date of repayment.

Net investment in Pensioners Guaranteed Income Bonds was £802.4 million at the end of March 1994.

CHILDREN'S BONUS BONDS

Children's Bonus Bonds were introduced in July 1991. The latest issue, Issue F, was introduced on 17 December 1993. They can be bought for any child under 16 and will go on growing in value until he or she is 21. The bonds are sold in multiples of £25. The minimum holding is £25, the maximum holding in Issue F is £1,000 per child. This is in addition to holdings of earlier issues of the bond (excluding interest and bonuses). Bonds for children under 16 must be held by a parent or guardian.

Children's Bonus Bonds (Issue F) earn 5 per cent a year over five years. A bonus (14.92 per cent) of the purchase price is added at the fifth anniversary. This is equal to 7.35 per cent a year compound. All returns are totally exempt from UK income tax. No interest is earned on bonds cashed in before the first anniversary of purchase. Bonuses are only payable if the bond is held until the next bonus date. Bonds over five years old continue to earn interest and bonuses until the holder is 21, when they should be cashed in. If bonds are not cashed in on the holder's 21st birthday, they earn no interest after that birthday.

FIRST OPTION BONDS

FIRST (Fixed Interest Rate Savings Tax-paid) Option Bonds were introduced in July 1992. They offer guaranteed rates without the need for long-term commitment for personal savers over 16. They can be held indefinitely and will continue to grow in value at rates of interest fixed for 12 months at a time. Tax is deducted from the interest at source. The minimum purchase is £1,000 and the maximum holding is £250,000. Withdrawals can be made without penalty at any anniversary date and there is no formal notice period for repayment. No interest is earned on repayments before the first anniversary.

## CAPITAL BONDS

National Savings Capital Bonds were introduced in January 1989. The latest series, Series H, was introduced on 17 December 1993. Capital Bonds offer capital growth over five years with guaranteed returns at fixed rates. The interest is taxable each year (for those who pay income tax) but is not deducted at source. The minimum purchase is £100. There is a maximum holding limit of £250,000 from Series B onwards.

Capital Bonds will be repaid in full with all interest gained at the end of five years. No interest is earned on bonds repaid in the first year. Reinvestment or extension terms may also be available.

## YEARLY PLAN

The National Savings Yearly Plan was introduced on 2 July 1984. It offers a guaranteed tax-free return. Applicants agree to make 12 monthly payments, leading to the issue of a Yearly Plan Certificate. The maximum guaranteed rate of interest is earned if the certificate is held for a full four years. Applications may be made by any individuals aged seven or over; in the name of children under seven years; and by not more than two trustees for a sole beneficiary.

Payments must be made on the same date every month by standing order from a bank or other acceptable account. Only one payment may be made in any one month and must be in multiples of £5. Minimum monthly contribution is £20, maximum £400. Net investment in National Savings Yearly Plan was £540,169,271 at 30 April 1994.

## GILTS ON THE NATIONAL SAVINGS STOCK REGISTER

Government stock or 'gilts' are Stock Exchange securities issued by the Government. They usually have a life of between five and 20 years and most pay a guaranteed fixed rate of interest twice a year throughout this period. When they reach the end of this period they are 'redeemed' (which means repaid) at their face value.

The National Savings Stock Register (NSSR) enables investors to buy and sell gilts by post. It is now possible to have most new issues of gilts registered on the NSSR. Interest on gilts held on the NSSR, although taxable, is paid in full without deduction of tax at source.

## NATIONAL SAVINGS CERTIFICATES

### RECENT ISSUES

The amount, including accrued interest, index-linked increase or bonus remaining to the credit of investors in National Savings Certificates on 30 April 1994 was approximately £17,750.1 million. In 1993–4, approximately £3,364 million was subscribed and £2,206.1 million (excluding interest, index-linked increase or bonus) was repaid. Interest, index-linked increase, bonus or other sum payable is free of UK income tax (including investment income surcharge) and capital gains tax.

From June 1982, savings certificates of the 7th to 34th Issues will be extended on general extension rates as they reach the end of their existing extension periods. The percentage interest rate is determined by the Treasury and any change in this general extension rate will be applicable from the first of the month following its announcement. Under the system, a certificate earns interest for each complete period of three months beyond the expiry of the previous extension terms. Within each three-month period, interest is calculated separately for each month at the rate applicable from the beginning of that month. The interest

for each month is one-twelfth of the annual rate (i.e. it does not vary with the number of days in the month) and is capitalized annually on the anniversary of the date of purchase. The current rate of interest under the general extension rate is given in leaflets available at post offices.

### RETIREMENT ISSUE

2 June 1975–15 November 1980

*Maximum holding:* 120 units

*Unit cost:* £10

*Interest per unit:* the repayment value, subject to their being held a year, is related to the movement of the UK General Index of Retail Prices.* Certificates of the Retirement Issue were only on sale to men aged 65 years or over and women aged 60 years or over, but may now be transferred to anyone

### SECOND INDEX-LINKED ISSUE

17 November 1980–29 June 1985

*Maximum holding:* 1,000 units

*Unit cost:* £10

*Interest per unit:* the repayment value, subject to their being held a year, is related to the movement of the UK General Index of Retail Prices*

### THIRD INDEX-LINKED ISSUE

1 July 1985–31 July 1986

*Maximum holding:* 200 units

*Unit cost:* £25

*Interest per unit:* the repayment value, subject to their being held for one year, is related to the movement of the UK General Index of Retail Prices. In addition, there is guaranteed extra interest of 2.5 per cent for the first year; 2.75 per cent for the second year; 3.25 per cent for the third year; 4 per cent for the fourth year, and 5.25 per cent for the fifth year. This interest is worth 3.54 per cent compound over a full five years. Certificates held beyond the fifth anniversary earn index-linking plus half a per cent interest on each following anniversary**

### FOURTH INDEX-LINKED ISSUE

1 August 1986–30 June 1990

*Maximum holding:* 200 units

*Unit cost:* £25

*Interest per unit:* the repayment value, subject to their being held for one year, is related to the movement of the UK General Index of Retail Prices. In addition, there is guaranteed extra interest of 3 per cent for the first year; 3.25 per cent for the second year; 3.5 per cent for the third year; 4.5 per cent for the fourth year, and 6 per cent for the fifth year. This interest is worth 4.04 per cent compound over a full five years. Certificates held beyond the fifth anniversary earn index-linking plus half a per cent interest on each following anniversary**

### THIRTY-FOURTH ISSUE

22 July 1988–16 June 1990

*Maximum holding:* 40 units, plus facilities to hold up to a further 400 units

*Unit cost:* £25

*Value after five years:* £35.89

*Interest per unit:* after one year the repayment value increases by 6 per cent for ordinarily held 34th Issue. However, reinvestment certificates earn interest during the first year at a rate of 6 per cent a year for each three-month period. Thereafter, all 34th Issue earn 6.25 per cent after two years; 6.5 per cent after three years; 7 per cent after four years; and 7.5 per cent after five years**

### THIRTY-FIFTH ISSUE

18 June 1990–14 March 1991

*Maximum holding:* 40 units, plus special facilities to hold up to a further 400 units

*Unit cost:* £25

*Value after five years:* £39.36

*Interest per unit:* after one year the repayment value increases by 6.5 per cent for ordinarily held 35th Issue. However, reinvestment certificates earn interest during the first year at a rate of 6.5 per cent a year. Thereafter, all 35th Issue earn 7 per cent after two years; 7.75 per cent after three years; 8.5 per cent after four years; and 9.5 per cent after five years

### FIFTH INDEX-LINKED ISSUE

2 July 1990–12 November 1992

*Maximum holding:* 400 units, plus special facilities to hold up to a further 400 units

*Unit cost:* £25

*Interest per unit:* the repayment value, subject to their being held for one year, is related to the movement of the UK General Index of Retail Prices. In addition, there is guaranteed extra interest which is paid from the date of purchase for each full year the certificates are held. After the first year the return is the Retail Price Index (RPI) only. Certificates repaid before the first anniversary date earn RPI for each complete month held from the purchase date. For the second year, the RPI plus 0.5 per cent; for the third, the RPI plus 1 per cent; for the fourth, the RPI plus 2 per cent; and at the fifth anniversary, RPI plus 4.5 per cent

### SIXTH INDEX-LINKED ISSUE
7 December 1992–16 December 1993

*Maximum holding:* 400 units, plus special facilities to hold up to a further 800

*Unit cost:* £100; reinvestment certificates £25

*Interest per unit:* the repayment value, subject to their being held for one year, is related to the movement of the UK General Index of Retail Prices. In addition, there is a guaranteed extra interest of 1.5 per cent for the first year; 2 per cent for the second year; 2.75 per cent for the third year; 3.75 per cent for the fourth year; and 6.32 per cent for the fifth year. This is worth 3.25 per cent compound over the full five years. Certificates repaid before the first anniversary date earn RPI plus extra interest of 1.5 per cent a year for each complete month

### THIRTY-SIXTH ISSUE
2 April 1991–2 May 1992

*Maximum holding:* 400 units, plus special facilities to hold up to a further 400

*Unit cost:* £25

*Value after five years:* £37.59

*Interest per unit:* after one year the repayment value increases by 5.5 per cent for ordinarily held 36th Issue. However, reinvestment certificates earn interest during the first year at a rate of 5.5 per cent a year. Thereafter, all 36th Issue earn 6 per cent after two years; 6.75 per cent after three years; 7.5 per cent after four years; and 8.5 per cent after five years

### THIRTY-SEVENTH ISSUE
13 May 1992–5 August 1992

*Maximum holding:* 300 units, plus special facilities to hold up to a further 400

*Unit cost:* £25

*Value after five years:* £36.74

*Interest per unit:* after one year the repayment value increases by 5.5 per cent for ordinarily held 37th Issue. However, reinvestment certificates earn interest during the first year at a rate of 5.5 per cent a year. After one year, £1.38 is added; during the second year, 41 pence per completed three months; during the third year, 56 pence per completed three months; during the fourth year, 71 pence per completed three months; and during the fifth year, 91 pence per completed three months

### THIRTY-EIGHTH ISSUE
24 August 1992–22 September 1992

*Maximum holding:* 200 units, plus special facilities to hold up to a further 400

*Unit cost:* £25

*Value after five years:* £35.89

*Interest per unit:* after one year the repayment value increases by 5.25 per cent for ordinarily held 38th Issue. However, reinvestment certificates earn interest during the first year at a rate of 5.25 per cent a year. After one year, £1.31 is added; during the second year, 41 pence per completed three months; during the third year, 50 pence per completed three months; during the fourth year, 63 pence per completed three months; and during the fifth year, 86 pence per completed three months

### THIRTY-NINTH ISSUE
5 October 1992–12 November 1992

*Maximum holding:* 50 units, plus special facilities to hold up to a further 100

*Unit cost:* £100

*Value after five years:* £138.63

*Interest per unit:* after one year the repayment value increases by 4.6 per cent for ordinarily held 39th Issue. However, reinvestment certificates earn interest during the first year at a rate of 4.6 per cent a year. After one year, £4.60 is added; during the second year, £1.37 per completed three months; during the third year, £1.86 per

completed three months; during the fourth year, £2.32 per completed three months; and during the fifth year, £2.96 per completed three months

### FORTIETH ISSUE
7 December 1992–

*Maximum holding:* 400 units, plus special facilities to hold up to a further 800

*Unit cost:* £100; reinvestment certificates £25

*Value after five years:* £132.25

*Interest per unit:* after one year the repayment value increases by 4 per cent for ordinarily held 40th Issue. However, reinvestment certificates earn interest during the first year at a rate of 4 per cent a year. On a £100 unit after one year, £4 is added; during the second year, £1.15 per completed three months; during the third year, £1.56 per completed three months; during the fourth year, £1.54 per completed three months; and during the fifth year, £2.42 per completed three months

### SEVENTH INDEX-LINKED ISSUE
17 December 1993–

*Maximum holding:* 400 units, plus special facilities to hold up to a further 800

*Unit cost:* £100; reinvestment certificates £25

*Interest per unit:* the repayment value, subject to their being held for one year, is related to the movement of the UK General Index of Retail Prices. In addition, there is a guaranteed extra interest of 1.25 per cent for the first year; 1.75 per cent for the second year; 2.5 per cent for the third year; 3.5 per cent for the fourth year and 6.07 per cent for the fifth year. This is worth 3 per cent compound over the full five years. Certificates repaid before the first anniversary date will earn RPI plus extra interest of 1.25 per cent a year for each complete month

### FORTY-FIRST ISSUE
17 December 1993–

*Maximum holding:* 400 units, plus special facilities to hold up to a further 800

*Unit cost:* £100; reinvestment certificates £25

*Value after five years:* £130.08

*Interest per unit:* after one year the repayment value increased by 3.65 per cent for ordinarily held 41st Issue. However, reinvestment certificates if encashed before the first anniversary earn interest at 3.65 per cent for each complete period of three months. On a £100 unit after one year, £3.65 is added; during the second year, £1.05 per completed three months; during the third year, £1.45 per completed three months; during the fourth year, £1.82 per completed three months; and during the fifth year, £2.28 per completed three months

*Index-linked certificates of the Retirement and 2nd Issues were eligible for annual supplements to index-linking. Seven supplements were introduced, the final one for 1988–9. At the fifth anniversary there is a bonus of 4 per cent of the purchase price, and at the tenth anniversary there is a second bonus of 4 per cent of the capitalized value at the fifth anniversary. All supplements and bonuses are fully index-linked once earned

**As announced by the Treasury

# Insurance

The Insurance Companies Act 1982 empowers the Department of Trade and Industry to authorize corporate bodies to transact insurance in the United Kingdom provided they comply with the financial and other regulations detailed in the Act. At the end of 1993 there were 823 insurance companies with authorization to transact one or more classes of insurance business in the UK.

Under the Financial Services Act 1986, the Securities and Investments Board (SIB) is empowered to make, monitor and enforce rules about the conduct of investment business. Insurance companies offering investment contracts like life insurance, pensions, unit trusts and annuities can either obtain authorization direct from SIB or from the Life Assurance and Unit Trust Regulatory Organization (LAUTRO). Insurance companies offering other investment services may require authorization by other SROs such as the Investment Management Regulatory Organization (IMRO).

A single SRO for life insurance, pensions and related contracts has been proposed. The Personal Investment Authority (PIA) will take over the work of LAUTRO, FIMBRA, some parts of IMRO and the regulatory function of the SIB itself. Although the UK's largest life insurer has indicated that it will not join, the PIA was expected to be operational by July 1994.

## THE EUROPEAN COMMUNITY

The Single European Act 1986 set out a programme of over 300 EC directives intended to achieve the removal of barriers to a free market within the community. In November 1989 a 'single licence' system was proposed for the insurance sector. This envisages the supervisor in the insurer's home country carrying out all the financial supervision necessary. This would mean a UK insurer authorized by the Department of Trade would automatically satisfy the supervisory authority in all other EC countries.

In December 1993 the Department of Trade and Industry issued a consultation document on implementation of the Third Life and Non-Life (Framework) Directives in the UK and draft regulations were laid before Parliament in May 1994, clearing the way to the single European insurance market from 1 July 1994.

## INSURANCE PREMIUM TAX

In the November 1993 Budget the Chancellor introduced an insurance premium tax on all non-life policies. The tax will be levied at a rate of 2.5 per cent on gross premiums payable on or after 1 October 1994.

In addition to the obvious effect on premium rates, the tax also presents insurers with an administrative burden, but the imposition of the tax was not entirely unexpected as a similar tax is levied in many other European countries.

## ASSOCIATION OF BRITISH INSURERS

Ninety per cent of the world-wide business of insurance companies is transacted by the 450 members of the Association of British Insurers (51 Gresham Street, London EC2V 7HQ), a trade association which represents both life and general insurers. On general insurance (motor, household, holiday, etc.), ABI acts as a regulatory organization for insurance intermediaries who do not qualify to be registered brokers.

## INSURANCE BROKERS

The Insurance Brokers Registration Act 1977 empowers the Insurance Brokers Registration Council (15 St Helen's Place, London EC3A 6DS) as the statutory body responsible for the registration of insurance brokers. The Council is responsible for the registration and training of insurance brokers, conduct of business, and discipline, and it lays down rules relating to such matters as accounting practice, staff qualifications, advertising, etc.

It is possible to act as an insurance intermediary without being registered with the IBRC but unregistered intermediaries are forbidden to use the words 'Insurance Broker' as a title.

*IBRC Registered Brokers 1993*

| | |
|---|---|
| Registered individuals | 15,127 |
| Limited companies registered | 2,594 |
| Sole traders and partnerships | 2,091 |
| (containing 1,263 partners and directors) | |

CONTRIBUTION TO THE BALANCE OF PAYMENTS

| | 1991 | 1992 |
|---|---|---|
| Insurance | £3,570m | £4,340m |

---

## GENERAL INSURANCE

---

Results for 1993 continued the improvement begun in 1992, with insurance companies recording their first trading profit since 1989. The world-wide trading result was a profit of 5.4 per cent of premium income, compared with a loss of 2.7 per cent in 1992. This turn-around was attributed to reduced operating costs, the initial impact of premium increases imposed in 1992, loss prevention initiatives and the initial benefits of action against fraudulent claims.

In the UK, motor insurance recorded a small profit (1 per cent of premiums) which has not occurred for over ten years. Non-motor insurance also improved but still stayed in the red with a small loss of 1.9 per cent of premiums. Elsewhere in the world, general insurance losses were reduced but remained at substantial levels for both motor and non-motor business. The USA market remained particularly difficult, with an underwriting loss of 10.4 per cent of premiums.

General insurers were affected in 1993 by the explosion in Bishopsgate in the City of London, which meant that the provisions of the Reinsurance (Acts of Terrorism) Act 1993 were brought into use. This Act makes the Government the final reinsurer for claims arising from terrorist acts. In the event, despite some inaccurate first estimates of the cost of the damage from sources outside the insurance market, the Government was not required to contribute. Another significant event was the House of Lords ruling on the Cambridge Water Company v. Eastern Counties Leather PLC case in December 1993. The Court of Appeal had ruled that a company was liable in respect of pollution even when it had no reason to believe that its activities were likely to cause damage. The House of Lords overturned this ruling and introduced a 'foreseeability' test.

WORLD-WIDE GENERAL BUSINESS UNDERWRITING RESULT

| | 1992 | | | | 1993 | | | |
|---|---|---|---|---|---|---|---|---|
| | UK | USA | Other | Total | UK | USA | Other | Total |
| **Motor** | | | | | | | | |
| Premiums (£m) | 5,732 | 1,610 | 2,873 | 10,215 | 6,374 | 1,662 | 3,005 | 11,042 |
| Profit/loss (£m) | −579 | −132 | −228 | −939 | 66 | −112 | −249 | −295 |
| % of premiums | −10.1 | −8.2 | −7.9 | −9.2 | 1.0 | −6.8 | −6.3 | −2.7 |
| **Non-motor** | | | | | | | | |
| Premiums (£m) | 10,569 | 1,970 | 3,408 | 15,947 | 11,911 | 2,413 | 4,990 | 19,314 |
| Profit/loss (£m) | −1,634 | −333 | −521 | −2,488 | −222 | −313 | −383 | −917 |
| % of premiums | −15.5 | −16.9 | −15.3 | −15.6 | −1.9 | −13.0 | −7.7 | −4.7 |

NET PREMIUM INCOME BY TERRITORY 1993

| | UK £m | Other EC countries £m | USA £m | Other overseas £m | Total (world-wide) £m | Increase % |
|---|---|---|---|---|---|---|
| Motor | 6,374 | 1,256 | 1,662 | 1,750 | 11,042 | 8.1 |
| Non-motor | 11,911 | 1,443 | 2,413 | 3,547 | 19,314 | 21.1 |
| Marine, Aviation and Transport | 1,302 | 102 | 75 | 91 | 1,570 | −31.1 |
| Other three-year business | 1,305 | 153 | 122 | 782 | 2,363 | −12.5 |
| *Total general business* | 20,893 | 2,954 | 4,272 | 6,169 | 34,288 | 10.1 |
| Ordinary long-term | 44,624 | 3,010 | 2,619 | 3,721 | 53,974 | 5.6 |
| Industrial long-term | 1,343 | — | — | — | 1,343 | −2.7 |
| *Total long-term business* | 45,967 | 3,010 | 2,619 | 3,721 | 55,317 | 5.4 |

## BRITISH INSURANCE COMPANIES IN 1993

The following insurance company figures refer to members of the Association of British Insurers, and also to certain non-members.

CLAIMS STATISTICS

| | 1992 £m | 1993 £m | |
|---|---|---|---|
| **Fire claims** | | | |
| Commercial fires | 613 | 423 | (−31%) |
| Domestic fires | 237 | 224 | (−5%) |
| **Theft claims** | | | |
| Commercial theft (inc. money) | 277 | 235 | (−15%) |
| Domestic theft | 750 | 744 | (−0.8%) |

WORLD-WIDE GENERAL BUSINESS TRADING RESULT

| | 1992 £m | 1993 £m |
|---|---|---|
| Net written premiums | 31,139 | 34,288 |
| Underwriting profit/loss for one year account business | | |
| Motor | −939 | −295 |
| Non-motor | −2,488 | −917 |
| Transfer to profit and loss account for other business | | |
| Marine, Aviation, Transport | −663 | −392 |
| Other | −784 | −564 |
| Total underwriting result | −4,874 | −2,168 |
| Investment income | 4,048 | 4,035 |
| Overall trading profit | −826 | 1,867 |
| Profit as % of premium income | −2.7% | 5.4% |

## LLOYD'S OF LONDON

Lloyd's of London is an incorporated society of private underwriters who provide an international market for almost all types of insurance. Lloyd's currently earns a gross premium income of around £8,000 million for underwriters each year. Much of this business comes from outside Great Britain and makes a valuable contribution to the balance of payments.

Today, as it was three centuries ago, a policy is underwritten at Lloyd's by private individuals with unlimited liability. Now that Lloyd's members are numbered in their thousands, however, the method of underwriting is the same only in principle. Specialist underwriters accept insurance risks at Lloyd's on behalf of members (often referred to as 'names') grouped into syndicates. There are currently around 17,000 members in some 349 syndicates of varying sizes, some with over 2,000 names, each managed by an underwriting agent approved by the Council of Lloyd's.

Lloyd's membership is drawn from many sources. Industry, commerce and the professions are strongly represented, while many members work at Lloyd's either for brokerage firms or for underwriting agencies. Underwriting membership of Lloyd's is open to anyone provided they meet the stringent financial requirements of the Corporation of Lloyd's. Substantial financial assets have to be shown and a deposit lodged with the Corporation as security for underwriting liabilities. This deposit, which must be in the form of approved securities, is determined at 30 per cent of the member's annual premium income and showing nominal means.

Lloyd's is incorporated by an Act of Parliament (Lloyd's Acts 1871–1982) and is governed by a council of 18 members. Market management is handled by a Market Board of 19 members (comprising six working members of the Council, the chief executive officer, six further working members, three external members and three Corporation executives). Regulation is supervised by a Board of 16 members (comprising six nominated members of the Council, five external members of the Council, four working members and the Solicitor to the Corporation).

The Corporation is a non-profit making body chiefly financed by its members' subscriptions. It provides the premises, administrative staff and services enabling Lloyd's underwriting syndicates to conduct their business. It does not, however, assume corporate liability for the risks accepted by its members, who remain responsible to the full extent of their personal means for their underwriting affairs.

Lloyd's syndicates have no direct contact with the public. All business is transacted through insurance brokers accredited by the Corporation of Lloyd's. In addition, non-Lloyd's brokers in the United Kingdom, when guaranteed by Lloyd's brokers, are able to deal directly with Lloyd's motor syndicates, a facility which has made the Lloyd's market more accessible to the insuring public.

Lloyd's also provides the most comprehensive shipping intelligence service available in the world. The enormous volume of shipping and other information received from Lloyd's agents, shipowners, news agencies and other sources throughout the world, is collated and distributed to the media as well as to the maritime and commercial sectors in general. *Lloyd's List* is London's oldest daily newspaper and contains news of general commercial interest as well as shipping information. *Lloyd's Shipping Index*, also published daily, lists some 25,000 ocean-going vessels in alphabetical order and gives the latest known report of each.

### DEVELOPMENTS IN 1993

Lloyd's system of reporting results three years in arrears added to the market's woes in 1993 as, at a time when the insurance companies (who work on a one year account) were reporting improving underwriting results, Lloyd's was still reporting the heavy losses of 1991. These poor results added to the misery of the internal wrangles which beset the market during the year. Lloyd's names became increasingly open about the size of their losses and many joined action groups determined to seek legal redress for what they felt was negligent handling and advice by members' agents.

The chief executive officer, Peter Middleton, and chairman David Rowland have pursued the proposals in Lloyd's first-ever business plan. This has involved the cutting of costs, the introduction of corporate members and an attempt to set up a reinsurance company (NewCo) to take on the losses of the past and ensure that new investors are insulated from becoming involved in them. At the end of 1993 Lloyd's published its £900 million settlement offer to the 21,000 members in dispute with their agents for losses which could, in part, be judged to be due to misconduct or negligence. Despite the offer, the acrimony and legal action continues.

### LLOYD'S MEMBERSHIP AND CAPACITY

| | 1991 | 1992 | 1993 |
|---|---|---|---|
| Membership | 26,539 | 22,259 | 19,537 |
| Gross market capacity | £11,382m | £10,046m | £8,878m |
| Average capacity per member | £455,000 | £451,000 | £454,000 |

### LLOYD'S GLOBAL ACCOUNTS *as at 31 December 1993*

| | 1990 £000 | 1991 £000 |
|---|---|---|
| Gross premiums | 9,325,817 | 9,675,415 |
| Premiums in respect of reinsurance ceded | 4,045,318 | 3,661,510 |
| Net premiums | 5,280,499 | 6,013,905 |
| Reinsurance premiums received from closed year of account | 5,683,087 | 3,955,316 |
| Reserves brought forward in respect of run-off years of account | 3,377,056 | 7,013.948 |
| *Total premiums* | 14,340,642 | 16,983,169 |
| Gross claims | 16,722,073 | 13,340,401 |
| Reinsurance recoveries | 10,817,870 | 7,119,112 |
| Net claims | 5,904,203 | 6,221,289 |
| Reinsurance premiums paid to close the account | 3,936,440 | 4,010,233 |
| Reserves retained in respect of run-off years of account | 6,917,651 | 8,745,115 |
| *Total claims* | 16,758,294 | 18,976,637 |
| Underwriting result | (2,417,652) | (1,993,468) |
| Loss on currency exchange | (90,013) | (82,672) |
| Syndicate expenses | (696,408) | (747,581) |
| Adjustment in respect of double count | 595,831 | 533,262 |
| Net underwriting result/balance | (2,608,242) | (2,290,459) |
| Gross investment income | 590,612 | 578,519 |
| Gross investment appreciation | 155,414 | 135,724 |
| Gross investment return | 746,026 | 714,243 |
| Loss before personal expenses and tax | (1,862,216) | (1,576,216) |
| Members' personal expenses | 456,845 | 471,575 |
| Loss before tax and after double count adjustment | (2,319,061) | (2,047,791) |

### LLOYD'S RESULTS 1991

| | Marine 1990 £m | 1991 £m | Non-marine 1990 £m | 1991 £m |
|---|---|---|---|---|
| Net premiums | 1,703.4 | 1,435.6 | 2,619.1 | 3,393 |
| Pure year result | (892.9) | (452) | (20.4) | (62.3) |

| | Aviation 1990 £m | 1991 £m | Motor 1990 £m | 1991 £m |
|---|---|---|---|---|
| Net premiums | 324 | 432.2 | 753.2 | 634 |
| Pure year result | (14) | (106.6) | (10.1) | 5.9 |

## LIFE INSURANCE AND PENSIONS

Premium income continued at record levels for 1993, with UK premium income increasing by 6.2 per cent to £46 billion. Total payments to UK policyholders were also at record levels, increasing by 9.8 per cent to £30.5 billion. Examination of the figures reveals a move away from annual premium contracts (up by 13.8 per cent) to single premium business (up 29.2 per cent) reflecting the more uncertain nature of the employment market.

UK pensions also showed a rise in premium income but the 1.2 per cent rise was appreciably lower than in previous years. Here again the economic climate was the major factor.

In September 1993 the Pension Law Review Committee (the Goode Committee) published its report, which was largely welcomed by the life insurance companies who are pension providers. Discussions with the Department of Social Security on certain issues continue but it is expected that the resultant Pensions Bill will be before Parliament in the 1994–5 session.

At the end of 1993 the Securities and Investment Board published the result of the investigation into the quality of advice given on transfers out of company pension schemes into personal pensions. This found that in only 9 per cent of cases was there satisfactory documentary evidence that good advice had been given. The industry was at pains to point out that this did not mean that the advice was inappropriate for all the remaining 91 per cent but a major investigation is now under way. Estimates of the likely compensation bill range from £100 million to £1 billion.

### PREMIUM INCOME FOR WORLD-WIDE LONG-TERM INSURANCE BUSINESS

| | 1992 £m | 1993 £m |
|---|---|---|
| *Ordinary Branch* | | |
| Business written in UK | | |
| Annual premiums | | |
| Life | 10,277 | 10,517 |
| Annuities | 84 | 69 |
| Pensions | 9,104 | 9,159 |
| Single premiums | | |
| Life | 7,609 | 9,834 |
| Annuities | 904 | 872 |
| Pensions | 13,524 | 13,746 |
| Other | 400 | 427 |
| Business written overseas | | |
| Annual premiums | 4,261 | 4,832 |
| Single premiums | 4,926 | 4,518 |
| *Industrial Branch* | 1,380 | 1,343 |
| *Total* | 52,469 | 55,317 |

### PAYMENTS TO POLICYHOLDERS

| | 1992 £m | 1993 £m |
|---|---|---|
| *Ordinary Branch* | | |
| Payments to UK policyholders | 25,544 | 28,316 |
| Payments to overseas policyholders | 5,132 | 5,569 |
| *Industrial Branch* | | |
| Payments to UK policyholders | 2,214 | 2,166 |
| *Total* | 32,890 | 36,051 |

### INDIVIDUAL PENSIONS: NEW BUSINESS 1992–3

| | Annual premium policies | | Single policy premiums | | Renewed single premiums £m |
|---|---|---|---|---|---|
| | No. new policies | New premiums £m | No. new policies | New premiums £m | |
| NON-LINKED | | | | | |
| 1992 | 711,000 | 564 | 367,000 | 3,167 | n/a |
| 1993 | 488,000 | 496 | 251,000 | 2,093 | 596 |
| 1993 | | | | | |
| 1st quarter | 138,000 | 126 | 66,000 | 537 | 163 |
| 2nd quarter | 137,000 | 143 | 79,000 | 565 | 158 |
| 3rd quarter | 105,000 | 109 | 50,000 | 476 | 112 |
| 4th quarter | 109,000 | 119 | 56,000 | 516 | 163 |
| LINKED | | | | | |
| 1992 | 919,000 | 553 | 414,000 | 2,477 | n/a |
| 1993 | 795,000 | 638 | 516,000 | 2,226 | 378 |
| 1993 | | | | | |
| 1st quarter | 197,000 | 142 | 100,000 | 485 | 85 |
| 2nd quarter | 215,000 | 166 | 119,000 | 548 | 101 |
| 3rd quarter | 187,000 | 150 | 164,000 | 549 | 75 |
| 4th quarter | 196,000 | 180 | 133,000 | 645 | 117 |

INVESTMENTS OF INSURANCE COMPANIES 1993

| Investment of funds | Long-term business £m | General business £m |
|---|---|---|
| Index-linked British Government securities | 8,741 | 647 |
| British Government authority securities (excluding those in line 1) | 60,027 | 11,028 |
| Other government, provincial and municipal stocks | 30,495 | 13,567 |
| Debentures, loan stocks, preference and guaranteed stocks and shares | 40,677 | 9,671 |
| Ordinary stocks and shares | 247,391 | 17,143 |
| Mortgages | 16,792 | 1,392 |
| Real property and ground rents | 35,549 | 3,580 |
| Other invested assets | 21,290 | 8,561 |
| 'Net current assets' | 1,227 | 8,844 |
| Total net assets | 462,189 | 74,433 |
| Gross income for year on investment holdings (gross of tax and interest paid) | 22,327 | 4,247 |
| Interest payable in year | 304 | 212 |

## DIRECTORY OF INSURANCE COMPANIES

*Classes of insurance undertaken*
G    General
L    Life
M    Marine
Re   Reinsurance

*Group membership*
(CU)    Commercial Union
(ES)    Eagle Star
(GA)    General Accident
(GRE)   Guardian Royal Exchange
(NU)    Norwich Union
(R)     Royal
(SA)    Sun Alliance & London

| Nature of business | Name of company | Head Office address |
|---|---|---|
| L | Abbey Life | 80 Holdenhurst Road, Bournemouth BH8 8AL |
| GLM Re | AGF | 41 Botolph Lane, London EC3R 8DL |
| GM Re | Albion | 9–13 Fenchurch Buildings, London EC3M 5HR |
| GLM | Alliance Assurance (SA) | 1 Bartholomew Lane, London EC2N 2AB |
| L | Allied Dunbar | Allied Dunbar Centre, Swindon SN1 1EL |
| L | American Life | 2–8 Altyre Road, Croydon CR9 2LG |
| G | Ansvar | 31 St Leonards Road, Eastbourne BN21 3UR |
| GM | Atlas (GRE) | Royal Exchange, London EC3V 3LS |
| L | Australian Mutual Provident | 100 Temple Street, Bristol BS1 6EA |
| L | Axa Equity and Law | Amersham Road, High Wycombe HP13 5AL |
| G | Baptist | 1 Merchant Street, London E3 4LY |
| L | Barclays Life | 94 St Paul's Churchyard, London EC4M 8EH |
| G Re | Black Sea and Baltic | 65 Fenchurch Street, London EC3M 4EV |
| GLM | Bradford (SA) | North Park, Halifax HX1 2TU |
| L | Britannia Life | Britannia Court, 50 Bothwell Street, Glasgow G2 6HR |
| GL | Britannic | Moor Green, Moseley, Birmingham B13 8QF |
| M | British & Foreign Marine (R) | New Hall Place, Liverpool |
| Engineering | British Engine (R) | Longridge House, Manchester M60 4DT |
| GLM | British Equitable (GRE) | Royal Exchange, London EC3V 3LS |
| L | British Life Office | Reliance House, Mount Ephraim, Tunbridge Wells, Kent TN4 8BL |
| G | British Oak (GRE) | Royal Exchange, London EC3V 3LS |
| G | Builders' Accident | 31–33 Bedford Street, London, WC2E 9EL |
| L | Caledonian (GRE) | Royal Exchange, London EC3V 3LS |
| GM | Cambrian (GRE) | Royal Exchange, London EC3V 3LS |
| L | Canada Life | Canada Life House, Potters Bar, Herts EN6 5BA |
| GM | Car & General (GRE) | Royal Exchange, London EC3V 3LS |
| L | Century Life | Century House, 5 Old Bailey, London EC4M 7BA |
| GL | Cigna | PO Box 42, Greenock, Renfrewshire PA15 1AB |
| L | Citibank Life | 21–23 Perrymount Road, Haywards Heath, W. Sussex RH16 3TP |
| L | City of Glasgow Friendly | 200 Bath Street, Glasgow G2 4HJ |
| L | Clerical, Medical Group | 15 St James Square, London SW1Y 4LQ |
| L | Colonial Mutual | Colonial Mutual House, Chatham Maritime, Kent ME14 4YY |
| GLM Re | Commercial Union | St Helen's, 1 Undershaft, London EC3P 3DQ |
| L | Commercial Union Life | St Helen's, 1 Undershaft, London EC3P 3DQ |
| L | Confederation Life | Lytton Way, Stevenage, Herts SG1 2NN |
| G | Congregational and General | Currer House, Currer Street, Bradford BD1 5BA |

| Nature of business | Name of company | Head Office address |
|---|---|---|
| GLM | Co-operative | Miller Street, Manchester M60 OAL |
| GLM Re | Cornhill | 32 Cornhill, London EC3V 3LJ |
| L | Crown Financial Management | Crown House, Crown Square, Woking GU21 1XW |
| G | Direct Line Insurance | 3 Edridge Road, Croydon CR9 1AG |
| GM | Dominion | 52–54 Leadenhall Street, London EC3A 2AQ |
| GLM Re | Eagle Star | 60 St Mary Axe, London EC3A 8JQ |
| GL | Ecclesiastical | Beaufort House, Brunswick Road, Gloucester GL1 1JZ |
| GL | Economic | Economic House, 25 London Road, Sittingbourne ME10 1PE |
| Animal Ins. | Equine and Livestock | PO Box 100, Ouseburn, York YO5 9SZ |
| L | Equitable Life | 55 Basinghall Street, London EC2V 5DR |
| G | Federation General | PO Box 196, Redhill, Surrey RH1 1FG |
| L | Friends' Provident | United Kingdom House, Castle Street, Salisbury SP1 3SH |
| G | Gan Minster | Minster House, Arthur Street, London EC4R 9BJ |
| GM Re | General Accident | Pitheavlis, Perth, Scotland PH2 0NH |
| L Re | General Accident Life | 2 Rougier Street, York YO1 1HR |
| GLM Re | GRE | Royal Exchange, London EC3V 3LS |
| G | Gresham Fire & Accident | 11 Queen Victoria Street, London EC4N 4XP |
| GM | Guarantee Society (GA) | 42–47 Minories, London EC3N 1BX |
| L | Guardian Assurance (GRE) | Royal Exchange, London EC3V 3LS |
| GM | Hibernian | Haddington Road, Dublin 4 |
| L | Hill Samuel | NLA Tower, Addiscombe Road, Croydon CR9 6BP |
| GL | Ideal | Pitmaston, Birmingham B13 8NG |
| L | Irish Life | Irish Life Centre, Victoria Street, St Albans AL1 5TS |
| GF | Iron Trades | Iron Trades House, 21–24 Grosvenor Place, London SW1X 7JA |
| L | LAS Group | Britannia Court, 50 Bothwell Street, Glasgow G2 6HR |
| L | Laurentian Life | Laurentian House, Barnwood, Glos GL4 7RZ |
| GLM Re | Legal and General | Temple Court, 11 Queen Victoria Street, London EC4N 4TP |
| L | Liberty Life | Liberty House, Station Road, New Barnet EN5 1PA |
| GF | Licenses & General (GRE) | Royal Exchange, London EC3V 3LS |
| L | Lincoln National (UK) PLC | 1 Olympic Way, Wembley HA9 0NB |
| GM | Liverpool Marine & General (SA) | 1 Bartholomew Lane, London EC2N 2AB |
| L | Liverpool Victoria Friendly | Victoria House, Southampton Row, London WC1B 4DB |
| GM | Local Government Guarantee (GRE) | Royal Exchange, London EC3V 3LS |
| GM Re | Lombard General | Lombard House, 182 High Street, Tonbridge TN9 1BY |
| GM | London & Edinburgh | The Warren, Worthing, W. Sussex BN14 9QD |
| L | London & Manchester | Winslade Park, Exeter, Devon EX5 1DS |
| GM | London & Scottish (CU) | St Helen's, 1 Undershaft, London EC3 |
| L | M & G Assurance | Three Quays. Tower Hill, London EC3R 6BQ |
| L | Manulife | St George's Way, Stevenage SG1 1HP |
| M | Marine (R) | 34–36 Lime Street, London EC3 |
| M | Maritime (NU) | Surrey Street, Norwich NR1 3NS |
| L | Medical, Sickness, Annuity and Life | Pynes Hill House, Rydon Lane, Exeter EX2 5SP |
| Re | Mercantile & General | Moorfields House, Moorfields, London EC4R 9BJ |
| L | Merchant Investors (MI Group) | St Bartholomew's House, Lewins Mead, Bristol BS1 2NH |
| GF | Methodist | Brazennose House, Brazennose Street, Manchester M2 5AS |
| L | MGM Assurance | MGM House, Heene Road, Worthing BN11 2DY |
| G | Motor Union (GRE) | Royal Exchange, London EC3V 3LS |
| L | NPI | NPI House, Tunbridge Wells, Kent TN1 2UE |
| GL | Nalgo Insurance Association | 137 Euston Road, London NW1 2AU |
| G | National Guarantee & Suretyship (CU) | St Helen's, 1 Undershaft, London EC3P 3DQ |
| L | National Mutual Life | The Priory, Hitchin, Herts. SG5 2DQ |
| Engineering | National Vulcan Eng. Ins. Group (SA) | St Mary's Parsonage, Manchester M60 9AP |
| G | Navigators & General (ES) | 113 Queens Road, Brighton BN1 3XN |
| GL Re | NFU Avon | Tiddington Road, Stratford-upon-Avon CV37 7BJ |
| G | NIG Skandia | Crown House, 145 City Road, London EC1V 1LP |
| L | NM Financial Management | Enterprise House, Isambard Brunel Road, Portsmouth PO1 2AW |
| GM Re | Norwich Union Fire | PO Box 6, Surrey Street, Norwich NR1 3NS |
| L | Norwich Union Life | PO Box 6, Surrey Street, Norwich NR1 3NS |
| Re | NRG Victory Reinsurance | Castle Hill Avenue, Folkestone CT20 2TF |
| GLM Re | Pearl | The Pearl Centre, Lynchwood, Peterborough PE2 6FY |
| GL Sickness | Permanent | Pynes Hill House, Pynes Hill, Rydon Lane, Exeter EX2 5SP |
| GLM | Phoenix (SA) | 1 Bartholomew Lane, London EC2N 2AB |
| L | Property Growth | Leon House, High Street, Croydon CR9 1LU |
| L | Provident Life Association | Provident Way, Basingstoke, Hants RG21 2SZ |
| L | Provident Mutual Life | Six Hills Way, Stevenage, Herts SG1 2ST |
| F | Provincial | Stramongate, Kendal, Cumbria LA9 4BE |
| GLM Re | Prudential | 142 Holborn Bars, London EC1N 2NH |
| GL | Refuge | Refuge House, Alderley Road, Wilmslow, Cheshire SK9 1PF |
| GM | Reliance Marine (GRE) | Royal Exchange, London EC3V 3LS |

| Nature of business | Name of company | Head Office address |
|---|---|---|
| L | Reliance Mutual | Reliance House, Mount Ephraim, Tunbridge Wells, Kent TN4 8BL |
| G | Road Transport & General (GA) | Pitheavlis, Perth PH2 0NH |
| G | Royal Exchange | Royal Exchange, London EC3V 3LS |
| L | Royal Heritage Life | Royal Insurance House, Business Park, Peterborough PE2 6GG |
| L | Royal Life | PO Box 30, New Hall Place, Liverpool L69 3HS |
| L | Royal Liver Friendly | Royal Liver Building, Pier Head, Liverpool L3 1HT |
| GL | Royal London | Royal London House, Middleborough, Colchester CO1 1RA |
| L | Royal National Pension Fund for Nurses | Burdett House, 15 Buckingham Street, Strand, London WC2N 6ED |
| F | Salvation Army | 117–121 Judd Street, London WC1H 9NN |
| L | Save & Prosper | 1 Finsbury Avenue, London EC2M 2QY |
| L | Scottish Amicable | 150 St Vincent Street, Glasgow G2 5NQ |
| Engineering | Scottish Boiler (GA) | Pitheavlis, Perth, Scotland PH2 0NH |
| L | Scottish Equitable | 28 St Andrew Square, Edinburgh EH2 1YF |
| M | Scottish General (GA) | PO Box 896, 103 Westerhill Road, Bishopbriggs, Glasgow G64 2QX |
| L | Scottish Legal Life | 95 Bothwell Street, Glasgow G2 7HY |
| L | Scottish Life | 19 St Andrew Square, Edinburgh EH2 2YA |
| L | Scottish Mutual | 109 St Vincent Street, Glasgow G2 5HN |
| L | Scottish Provident Institution | 6 St Andrew Square, Edinburgh EH2 2YA |
| GLM | Scottish Union & National (NU) | Surrey Street, Norwich NR1 3NS |
| L | Scottish Widows' | 15 Dalkeith Road, Edinburgh EH16 5BU |
| GM | Sea (SA) | 1 Bartholomew Lane, London EC2N 2AB |
| L | Stalwart Assurance | Stalwart House, 142 South Street, Dorking RH4 2EV |
| L | Standard Life | 3 George Street, Edinburgh EH2 2X2 |
| GM | State Assurance (GRE) | Royal Exchange, London EC3V 3LS |
| GLM | Sun Alliance and London | 1 Bartholomew Lane, London EC2N 2AB |
| GM | Sun Insurance Office (SA) | 1 Bartholomew Lane, London EC2N 2AB |
| L | Sun Life Assurance | 107 Cheapside, London EC2N 6DU |
| L Re | Sun Life of Canada | Basing View, Basingstoke, Hants RG21 2DZ |
| L | Swiss Life | PO Box 127, Swiss Life House, 101 London Road, Sevenoaks, Kent TN13 1BG |
| L | Swiss Pioneer Life | 16 Crosby Road North, Waterloo, Liverpool L22 0NY |
| GL | Teacher's Assurance | 12 Christchurch Road, Bournemouth BH1 3LW |
| L | Tunstall & District | Station Chambers, Tunstall, Stoke-on-Trent ST6 6DU |
| M | Ulster Marine (GA) | Pitheavlis, Perth PH2 0NH |
| GM | Union Insurance Society of Canton (GRE) | Royal Exchange, London EC3V 3LS |
| GL | United Friendly | 42 Southwark Bridge Road, London SE1 9HE |
| GL Re | Wesleyan Assurance | Colmore Circus, Birmingham B4 6AR |
| L | Windsor Life | Windsor House, Telford, Salop TF3 4NB |
| GM Re | Zurich | Zurich House, Stanhope Road, Portsmouth PO1 1DU |
| L | Zurich Life | Hippodrome House, 11 Guildhall Walk, Portsmouth PO1 2RL |

# Investment Business Regulation

The growth of Britain's financial services industry in the 1970s and 1980s left the regulatory structure existing at that time inadequate to deal with the new competitive climate or to provide the necessary safeguards for the investing public. Under the Financial Services Act 1986, a new supervisory framework was set up to regulate companies conducting investment business and new criminal offences were created. The Act came into force on 29 April 1988, when it became a criminal offence to conduct investment business without authorization, unless specifically exempt from the authorization requirement.

The Securities and Investments Board (SIB) is the designated agency under the Financial Services Act 1986 for regulating the activities of investment businesses in the UK. Although not a statutory body, the SIB has statutory powers under the Act to recognize self-regulating organizations, professional bodies, investment exchanges and clearing houses, and directly to authorize firms to undertake investment business in the UK.

The SIB oversees the regulation of all investment business in the UK. It is not responsible for areas involving public issues, takeovers and mergers, and insider dealing investigation. Its area of authority overlaps with that of the Bank of England, the Department of Trade and Industry (for insurance companies) and the Building Societies Commission where their respective member bodies are carrying out investment business.

The regulatory sanctions of the SIB are as follows:

1   It may issue public or private reprimands
2   It may restrict business
3   It may suspend authorization
4   It may withdraw authorization
5   In certain cases it may take out a civil injunction
6   It may petition the courts for the winding up of companies
7   It may ban persons from the industry for life

CENTRAL REGISTER
Checkline 0171-929 3652

The SIB maintains a register (the Central Register) of all firms who are authorized to carry on investment business. The entry for each firm gives its name, address and telephone number; an SIB reference number; its authorization status; its appropriate regulatory body; and whether it can handle client money.

INVESTORS COMPENSATION SCHEME

The Investors Compensation Scheme, run by a management company as part of the overall investor protection offered by the SIB, comes into play when authorized firms become insolvent owing money to private investors. It is funded by means of a levy on all member firms, according to their size and category. The maximum compensation that the scheme can pay to an investor is £48,000.

SECURITIES AND INVESTMENTS BOARD LTD, Gavrelle House, 2–14 Bunhill Row, London EC1Y 8RA. Tel: 0171-638 1240

## SELF-REGULATING ORGANIZATIONS

The SIB recognizes self-regulating organizations (SROs), which are responsible to the SIB for ensuring financial supervision in their respective sectors of investment business. Most members of the financial services industry obtain their authorization by being members of an SRO.

The following are recognized by the SIB as being able to provide proper regulation of the investment business carried out by their members, and the necessary standard of investor protection:

*FIMBRA (Financial Intermediaries, Managers and Brokers Regulatory Organization), Hertsmere House, Hertsmere Road, London E14 4AB. Tel: 0171-538 8860
IMRO (Investment Management Regulatory Organization), Broadwalk House, Appold Street, London EC2A 2LL. Tel: 0171-628 6022
*LAUTRO (Life Assurance and Unit Trust Regulatory Organization), Centre Point, 103 New Oxford Street, London WC1A 1QH. Tel: 0171-379 0444
PIA (Personal Investment Authority), 3 Royal Exchange Buildings, London EC3V 3NL. Tel: 0171-929 0072
SFA (Securities and Futures Authority Ltd), Cottons Centre, Cottons Lane, London SE1 2QB. Tel: 0171-378 9000

IMRO also regulates the activities of friendly societies.
* The SIB recognized the PIA as the main SRO for the retail sector with effect from 18 July 1994. Recognition of FIMBRA and LAUTRO is to be withdrawn on 1 October 1994; the process of derecognition will be staged over 15 months.

## RECOGNIZED PROFESSIONAL BODIES

The SIB is empowered to recognize professional bodies (RPBs) who, as a result, can authorize their members for investment business. Such business must not form the whole or main part of the total business undertaken by the firm.

INSTITUTE OF CHARTERED ACCOUNTANTS IN ENGLAND AND WALES, Chartered Accountants Hall, PO Box 433, Moorgate Place, London EC2P 2BJ. Tel: 0171-920 8100
INSTITUTE OF CHARTERED ACCOUNTANTS OF SCOTLAND, 27 Queen Street, Edinburgh EH2 1LA. Tel: 0131-225 5673
INSTITUTE OF CHARTERED ACCOUNTANTS IN IRELAND, 11 Donegall Square South, Belfast BT1 5JE. Tel: 01232-321600
CHARTERED ASSOCIATION OF CERTIFIED ACCOUNTANTS, 29 Lincoln's Inn Fields, London WC2A 3EE. Tel: 0171-242 6855
THE LAW SOCIETY, Law Society House, 50–52 Chancery Lane, London WC2A 1SX. Tel: 0171-242 1222
LAW SOCIETY OF SCOTLAND, Law Society's Hall, 26 Drumsheugh Gardens, Edinburgh EH3 7YR. Tel: 0131-226 7411
LAW SOCIETY OF NORTHERN IRELAND, Law Society's House, 90–106 Victoria Street, Belfast BT1 3JZ. Tel: 01232-231614
INSTITUTE OF ACTUARIES, Staple Inn Hall, High Holborn, London WC1V 7QJ. Tel: 0171-242 0106
INSURANCE BROKERS REGISTRATION COUNCIL, 15 St Helen's Place, London EC3A 6DS. Tel: 0171-588 4387

## RECOGNIZED INVESTMENT EXCHANGES

Investment exchanges are exempt from needing authorization from the SIB as an investment business. However, to be a recognized investment exchange (RIE), each must fulfil the following requirements: adequate financial resources; proper conduct of business rules; a proper market in its products; procedures for recording transactions; effective monitoring and enforcement of rules; proper arrangements for the clearing and performance of contracts.

INTERNATIONAL PETROLEUM EXCHANGE (IPE), International House, 1 St Katharine's Way, London EI 9UN. Tel: 0171-481 0643

LONDON COMMODITY EXCHANGE LTD, 1 Commodity Quay, St Katharine Docks, London EI 9AX. Tel: 0171-481 2080

LONDON INTERNATIONAL FINANCIAL FUTURES AND OPTIONS EXCHANGE (LIFFE), Cannon Bridge, London EC4R 3XX. Tel: 0171-623 0444

LONDON METAL EXCHANGE LTD (LME), Plantation House, Fenchurch Street, London EC3M 3AP. Tel: 0171-626 3311

THE LONDON SECURITIES AND DERIVATIVES EXCHANGE LTD (OMLX), 107 Cannon Street, London EC4N 5AD. Tel: 0171-283 0678

The following exchanges are recognized by the Treasury as offering adequate investor protection:

INTERNATIONAL STOCK EXCHANGE OF THE UNITED KINGDOM AND THE REPUBLIC OF IRELAND (LSE), Old Broad Street, London EC2N 1HP. Tel: 0171-588 2355

CHICAGO BOARD OF TRADE (CBOT), European Office, 52–54 Gracechurch Street, London EC3V OEH. Tel: 0171-929 0021

CHICAGO MERCANTILE EXCHANGE (CME), Pinnacle House, 23–26 St Dunstan's Hill, London EC3R 8HL. Tel: 0171-623 2550

MEFF RENTA FIJA, Via Laietana, 58-08003 Barcelona, Spain. Tel: 00-34 3 412 1128

MEFF RENTA VARIABLE, Torre Picasso, Planta 26, 28020 Madrid, Spain. Tel: 00-34 1 585 0800

NATIONAL ASSOCIATION OF SECURITIES DEALERS AUTOMATED QUOTATIONS SYSTEM (NASDAQ), 43 London Wall, London EC2M 5TB. Tel: 0171-374 6969

NEW YORK MERCANTILE EXCHANGE (NYMEX), 35 Piccadilly, W1V 9PB. Tel: 0171-437 2933

SYDNEY FUTURES EXCHANGE, 30–32 Grosvenor Street, Sydney, NSW 2000, Australia. Tel: 00–612 256 0555

## RECOGNIZED CLEARING HOUSES

A recognized clearing house (RCH) must satisfy the same kind of criteria to obtain recognition as the RIEs. There is one RCH which acts as a clearing house for some of the above RIEs:

LONDON CLEARING HOUSE LTD (LCH), Roman Wall House, 1–2 Crutched Friars, London EC3N 2AN. Tel: 0171-265 2000

## DESIGNATED INVESTMENT EXCHANGES

The SIB has drawn up a list of 51 overseas exchanges (known as DIEs) who appear to have operating procedures broadly equivalent to those of the RIEs. Designation merely shows that an exchange meets certain basic criteria but carries no guarantee.

## OMBUDSMEN SCHEMES

Independent ombudsmen schemes have been set up for banks, building societies, and insurance companies. They provide an independent and impartial method of resolving disputes that arise between a company and its customer. In each ombudsman scheme there is a council which appoints and supervises the Ombudsman. The Ombudsman Council is composed of people representing public and consumer

interests and member companies. The schemes are funded in various ways: annual subscription from member companies, a levy on member companies according to the size of their assets, or a charge for each complaint handled against a particular company.

IMRO has also appointed an independent ombudsman, the Investment Ombudsman, who is responsible for resolving disputes that arise between a customer and a member company of IMRO. The Investment Ombudsman scheme is funded by IMRO but operates independently.

The Pensions Ombudsman is appointed by the Secretary of State for Social Security under the Pension Schemes Act 1993, and is responsible to Parliament. He can resolve grievances between an individual and his/her pension scheme (but not National Insurance benefits). His decisions are binding on both parties. A statutory levy on pension schemes, based on the number of members therein, contributes to the funding of the scheme.

THE OFFICE OF THE BANKING OMBUDSMAN, 70 Gray's Inn Road, London WC1X 8NB. Tel: 0171-404 9944. *Banking Ombudsman*, L. Shurman

THE OFFICE OF THE BUILDING SOCIETIES OMBUDSMAN, Grosvenor Gardens House, 35–37 Grosvenor Gardens, London SW1X 7AW. Tel: 0171-931 0044. *Building Societies Ombudsman*, B. Murphy

THE INSURANCE OMBUDSMAN BUREAU, City Gate One, 135 Park Street, London SE1 9EA. Tel: 0171-928 4488. *Insurance Ombudsman*, Dr J. T. Farrand, QC; *Deputy Ombudsman*, L. Slade

THE OFFICE OF THE INVESTMENT OMBUDSMAN, 6 Frederick's Place, London EC2R 8BT. Tel: 0171-796 3065. *Investment Ombudsman*, R. Youard

THE PENSIONS OMBUDSMAN, 11 Belgrave Road, London SW1V 1RB. Tel: 0171-834 9144. *Pensions Ombudsman*, Dr J. T. Farrand

## THE TAKEOVER PANEL

The Takeover Panel was set up in 1968 in response to concern about practices unfair to shareholders in take-over bids for public and certain private companies. Its principal objective is to ensure equality of treatment, and fair opportunity for all shareholders to consider on its merits an offer that would result in the change of control of a company. It is a non-statutory body that operates the City Code on Take-overs and Mergers.

The chairman, deputy chairmen and three lay members of the panel are appointed by the Bank of England. The remainder are representatives of the banking, insurance, investment, pension fund and accountancy professional bodies, the CBI, IMRO and the Stock Exchange.

THE TAKEOVER PANEL, PO Box 226, The Stock Exchange Building, London, EC2P 2JX. Tel: 0171-382 9026. *Chairman*, Sir David Calcutt, QC

# Taxation

## INCOME TAX

Income tax is charged on the total income of individuals for a year of assessment commencing on 6 April and ending on the following 5 April. The rates of tax and the calculation of liability will frequently differ, sometimes substantially, as between one year of assessment and another. The following information is confined to the year of assessment 1994–5, ending on 5 April 1995.

Liability to income tax is determined by establishing the taxable income for a year of assessment. The income will be reduced by an individual's personal allowance and some other reliefs. The first £3,000 of taxable income remaining is assessable to income tax at the lower rate of 20 per cent and the next £20,700 at the basic rate of 25 per cent. Should any excess remain over £23,700 (£3,000 plus £20,700) this will be taxable at the higher rate of 40 per cent.

The three rates apply to the assessment of both earned and investment income. There is little distinction between the two classes, although the receipt of earned income may produce an entitlement to some allowances not available against investment income. Special rules apply to tax on company dividends. Certain allowances and reliefs are given as a deduction from tax payable.

The tables below show the income tax payable for 1994–5 by an individual on the amount of income specified, after deducting the personal allowance and providing relief for the married couple's allowance, where appropriate. Elderly persons over the age of 74 years may pay rather less tax. Some taxpayers may be entitled to transitional allowances and other reliefs which reduce the tax payable below the amount shown by the tables.

Trustees administering settled property are chargeable to income tax at the basic rate of 25 per cent. Where the trustees retain discretionary powers or income is accumulated, there will also be liability to the additional rate of 10 per cent. Companies residing in the United Kingdom are not liable to income tax but suffer corporation tax on income, profits and gains.

The charge to income tax broadly arises on all taxable income accruing from sources in the United Kingdom. Individuals who are resident in this territory may also become liable on income arising overseas. An individual is resident in the United Kingdom if he or she normally resides here. Persons not normally residing in the United Kingdom may become resident if they visit this territory for periods which average three months or more throughout a period of years, or are present for at least 183 days in a particular year.

Income arising overseas will often incur liability to foreign taxation. If that income is also chargeable to United Kingdom income tax, excessive liability could well arise. The United Kingdom has concluded double taxation agreements with many overseas territories and these ensure that the same slice of income is not doubly taxed. In the absence of such an agreement, foreign tax suffered can usually be relieved under the domestic code when calculating liability to United Kingdom income tax.

### INDEPENDENT TAXATION

For many years the income of a married woman 'living with' her husband was treated as that of the husband for income tax purposes. This did not generally apply in the year of marriage and it remained possible for the couple to exercise the right of separate assessment or for the wife to be separately assessed as a single person on her earned income. However, the husband was usually responsible for submitting income tax returns, for discharging income tax on the combined incomes and dealing generally with taxation matters.

## SINGLE PERSONS AND MARRIED WOMEN

| Income | Persons under 65 | | Persons 65 or over* | |
|---|---|---|---|---|
| £ | Income tax £ | Average rate % | Income tax £ | Average rate % |
| 4,000 | 111 | 2.8 | — | — |
| 5,000 | 311 | 6.2 | 160 | 3.2 |
| 6,000 | 511 | 8.5 | 360 | 6.0 |
| 7,000 | 739 | 10.6 | 560 | 8.0 |
| 8,000 | 989 | 12.4 | 800 | 10.0 |
| 9,000 | 1,239 | 13.8 | 1,050 | 11.7 |
| 10,000 | 1,489 | 14.9 | 1,300 | 13.0 |
| 12,000 | 1,989 | 16.6 | 1,800 | 15.0 |
| 14,000 | 2,489 | 17.8 | 2,300 | 16.4 |
| 16,000 | 2,989 | 18.7 | 2,989 | 18.7 |
| 18,000 | 3,489 | 19.4 | 3,489 | 19.4 |
| 20,000 | 3,989 | 19.9 | 3,989 | 19.9 |
| 25,000 | 5,239 | 21.0 | 5,239 | 21.0 |
| 30,000 | 6,917 | 23.1 | 6,917 | 23.1 |
| 40,000 | 10,917 | 27.3 | 10,917 | 27.3 |
| 50,000 | 14,917 | 29.8 | 14,917 | 29.8 |
| 60,000 | 18,917 | 31.5 | 18,917 | 31.5 |
| 100,000 | 34,917 | 34.9 | 34,917 | 34.9 |

\* Persons aged 75 or over suffer less tax on income falling below £16,000 on this table

## MARRIED MEN

| Income | Couples under 65 | | Couples 65 or over† | |
|---|---|---|---|---|
| £ | Income tax £ | Average rate % | Income tax £ | Average rate % |
| 4,000 | — | — | — | — |
| 5,000 | — | — | — | — |
| 6,000 | 167 | 2.8 | — | — |
| 7,000 | 395 | 5.6 | 27 | 0.4 |
| 8,000 | 645 | 8.1 | 267 | 3.3 |
| 9,000 | 895 | 9.9 | 517 | 5.7 |
| 10,000 | 1,145 | 11.4 | 767 | 7.7 |
| 12,000 | 1,645 | 13.7 | 1,267 | 10.6 |
| 14,000 | 2,145 | 15.3 | 1,767 | 12.6 |
| 16,000 | 2,645 | 16.5 | 2,447 | 15.3 |
| 18,000 | 3,189 | 17.7 | 3,189 | 17.7 |
| 20,000 | 3,645 | 18.2 | 3,645 | 18.2 |
| 25,000 | 4,895 | 19.6 | 4,895 | 19.6 |
| 30,000 | 6,573 | 21.9 | 6,573 | 21.9 |
| 40,000 | 10,573 | 26.4 | 10,573 | 26.4 |
| 50,000 | 14,573 | 29,1 | 14,573 | 29.1 |
| 60,000 | 18,573 | 31.0 | 18,573 | 31.0 |
| 100,000 | 34,573 | 34.6 | 34,573 | 34.6 |

† Persons aged 75 or over suffer less tax on income falling below £18,000 on this table

This practice ceased to apply on 6 April 1990 with the introduction of independent taxation. A husband and wife are now independently taxed, with each entitled to a personal allowance. In most situations any unused personal allowance available to one spouse cannot be transferred to the other. A married man 'living with' his wife can obtain a married couple's allowance. In the absence of any claim, this allowance must be used by the husband but where any balance remains the surplus may be transferred to the wife. It is possible for a married woman to claim half the basic married couple's allowance as of right. In addition, the entire basic allowance may be obtained by the wife, if her husband so agrees.

Each spouse may obtain other allowances and reliefs where the underlying conditions are satisfied. Income must be accurately allocated between a husband and wife by reference to the individual beneficially entitled to that income. Where income arises from jointly-held assets, this must be apportioned equally between husband and wife. However, in those cases where the beneficial interests in jointly-held assets are not equal, a special declaration can be made to apportion income by reference to the actual interests in that income.

## INCOME TAXABLE

Income tax is assessed and collected under several Schedules. Each Schedule determines the extent of liability and establishes the amount to be included in taxable income. In some instances the actual income arising in a year of assessment will be charged to income tax for that year.

A different basis of assessment may be used for income taxable under Cases I to V of Schedule D. Throughout a period of many years income has been assessed under these Cases on a 'preceding year' basis. This involves measuring income for the year by reference to that arising in a previous year or period but there are special rules where a new source is acquired or an existing source discontinued. The 'preceding year' basis is being replaced by a 'current year' basis of assessment. This requires that business profits assessable under Case I or Case II of Schedule D will be those for the accounting period ending in the year of assessment, with special adjustments for the opening and closing years of a business. Other income assessable under Schedule D will be that which arises in the actual year of assessment.

The new 'current year' basis will apply at the outset for new sources commenced on and after 5 April 1994. Sources existing before that date will become subject to the current year basis in 1997–8, although transitional rules will apply to achieve a smooth transition from the old basis to the new.

Following the withdrawal of income tax liability for most commercial woodlands in the United Kingdom, Schedule B no longer applies. The contents of the remaining schedules are shown below.

### Schedule A

Tax is charged on annual profits arising from the ownership or occupation of land in the United Kingdom. This will include rents, ground rents and other income from land. Expenditure incurred by the landlord on maintenance, repairs, insurance and management can be subtracted from the annual profits. This Schedule does not include profits from farming, market gardening or woodlands, nor does it extend to mineral rents and royalties. Premiums arising on the grant of a lease for a period not exceeding fifty years are assessed to income tax as rent. However, the amount of the taxable premium may be reduced by 2 per cent for each complete year, after the first year, of the leasing period. Income from furnished lettings is assessable under Case VI of Schedule D, unless an option is exercised for such income to be assessed under Schedule A. Where income arises from furnished holiday lettings, additional expenditure may be included in calculating income chargeable to tax. Income from furnished holiday lettings is treated as earned income.

Receipts not exceeding £3,250 annually and received by an individual from letting property furnished in his or her own home are not chargeable to tax.

### Schedule C

This Schedule is confined to interest or dividends on government or public authority funds and certain payments made out of the public revenues of overseas countries.

### Schedule D

This Schedule is divided into six Cases, as follows:

*Cases I and II* – Profits arising from trades, professions and vocations, including farming and market gardening. Capital expenditure incurred on assets used for business purposes will often produce an entitlement to capital allowances which reduce the profits chargeable. These profits may also be reduced following the submission of claims for loss relief and other matters.

*Case III* – Interest on government stocks not taxed at source (e.g. War Loan and British Savings Bonds), interest on National Savings Bank deposits and discounts. Interest up to £70 on ordinary National Savings Bank deposits is exempt from income tax. The exemption applies to both husband and wife separately. Interest on National Savings Bank Special Investment accounts is not exempt.

*Cases IV and V* – Interest from overseas securities, rents, dividends and all other income accruing outside the United Kingdom. Assessment is based on the full amount of income arising, whether remitted to the United Kingdom or retained overseas, but individuals who are either not domiciled in the United Kingdom or who are ordinarily resident overseas may be taxed on a remittance basis. Overseas pensions are taxable but the amount arising may be reduced by 10 per cent for assessment purposes. Dividends on overseas investments are chargeable only at the lower rate of 20 per cent and the higher rate of 40 per cent.

*Case VI* – Sundry profits and annual receipts not assessed under any other Case or Schedule. These may include insurance commissions, post-cessation receipts, income from furnished lettings, and numerous other receipts specifically charged under Case VI.

### Schedule E

All emoluments from an office or employment are assessable under this Schedule. There are three Cases, as follows:

*Case I* – This applies to all emoluments of an individual resident and ordinarily resident in the United Kingdom.

*Case II* – Of application where the individual is not resident or not ordinarily resident and extends to emoluments for duties undertaken in the United Kingdom.

*Case III* – Applies in rare situations to other emoluments remitted to the United Kingdom.

Although earnings for overseas duties may be assessable under Case I where the employee is resident and ordinarily resident in the United Kingdom, a foreign earnings deduction of 100 per cent may be available, which reduces the overseas assessable earnings to nil. This deduction can be obtained where duties are performed overseas for a continuous period reaching or exceeding 365 days and is confined to earnings from the overseas activity.

A 'receipts basis' applies for determining the year of assessment in which earnings must be taxed. Where emoluments are assessable under Case I or Case II, the date of receipt will comprise the earlier of:

(a) the date of payment
(b) the date entitlement arises

In the case of company directors it is the earliest of the two dates given above with the addition of the following three which establish the time of receipt:

(c) the date emoluments are credited in the company's books

(d) where emoluments for a period are determined after the end of that period, the date of determination

(e) where emoluments for a period are determined in that period, the last day of that period

The emoluments assessable under Schedule E include all salaries, wages, director's fees and other money sums. In addition, there is a wide range of benefits which must be added to taxable emoluments. These include the provision of living accommodation on advantageous terms and advantages arising from the use of vouchers.

Further taxable benefits accrue to directors and also to employees receiving emoluments of £8,500 or more in the year of assessment. These benefits include the reimbursement of expenses, the availability of motor cars for private motoring, the provision of petrol or other fuel for private motoring, the use of vans, the provision of interest-free loans, and other benefits provided at the employer's expense. The cost of providing a limited range of child care facilities may be excluded.

In arriving at the amount to be assessed under Schedule E, all expenses incurred wholly, exclusively and necessarily in the performance of the duties may be deducted. This includes fees and subscriptions paid to certain professional bodies and learned societies. Fees paid to managers by entertainers, actors and others assessable under Schedule E may be deducted, up to a maximum of 17.5 per cent of earnings.

Compensation for loss of office and other sums received on the termination of an office or employment are assessable to tax. However, the first £30,000 may be excluded with only the balance remaining chargeable, unless the compensatory payment is linked with the retirement of the recipient.

Earnings received from an approved profit-related pay scheme are exempt from income tax.

*Schedule F*

This Schedule is concerned with company dividends and distributions. A United Kingdom resident company paying a dividend or making a distribution must account to the Inland Revenue for advance corporation tax. A shareholder residing in the United Kingdom obtains the dividend or distribution together with a tax credit equal to one-quarter of the sum received for 1994–5. The dividend or distribution is regarded as having suffered income tax, equal to the tax credit, at the lower rate of 20 per cent. Where the shareholder is not liable, or not fully liable, at that rate a repayment can be obtained. Dividends or distributions are not liable to tax at the difference between the lower rate of 20 per cent and the basic rate of 25 per cent. However, shareholders liable at the higher rate of 40 per cent will incur further liability on the grossed-up equivalent of the sum received at the rate of 40 per cent, less the tax credit of 20 per cent.

Some payments made by an unquoted trading company to redeem or purchase its own shares are not treated as distributions.

*Building society interest and bank interest*

Many payments of interest by building societies and banks are received after the deduction of income tax at the basic rate of 25 per cent. However, investors not liable to income tax at the basic rate may arrange to receive interest gross, with no tax being deducted on payment. Others who suffer income tax by deduction can obtain a repayment in whole or in part if they are not fully liable at the basic rate.

INCOME NOT TAXABLE

This includes interest on National Savings Certificates, most scholarship income, bounty payments to members of the armed services and annuities payable to the holders of certain awards. Dividend income arising from investments in personal equity plans may be exempt from tax. Income received under most maintenance agreements and court orders made after 30 June 1988 will not be liable to tax. Nor will payments made under many deeds of covenant executed after 14 March 1988 be recognized for tax purposes, unless the recipient is a charity. Interest arising on a Tax Exempt Special Savings Account (TESSA) opened with a building society or bank will be exempt from tax, if the account is maintained throughout a five-year period.

SOCIAL SECURITY BENEFITS

Many social security benefits are not liable to income tax. These include income support, family credit, maternity allowance, long-term sickness benefit, child benefit, invalidity benefit, war widow's pension, disability living allowance and numerous others. Among the limited range of benefits which are taxable is the retirement pension, widow's pension, widowed mother's allowance, and unemployment benefits. Short-term sick pay and maternity pay payable by an employer are also chargeable to tax.

It is expected that both invalidity benefit and sickness benefit will be replaced by a new incapacity benefit from 6 April 1995 and made chargeable to income tax.

PAY AS YOU EARN

The Pay As You Earn system is not an independent form of taxation but has been designed to collect income tax by deduction from most emoluments. When paying emoluments to employees, an employer is usually required to deduct income tax and account for that tax to the Inland Revenue. In many cases this deduction procedure will fully exhaust the individual's liability to income tax, unless there is other income. The date of 'receipt' used for assessment purposes (*see* above) also identifies the date of 'payment' when establishing liability for PAYE.

From May 1994 the PAYE system is also used to collect tax on certain payments made 'in kind'. This includes payment in the form of gold bullion and marketable securities, among others.

ALLOWANCES

The allowances available to individuals for 1994–5 are outlined below.

*Personal allowance*

Each individual receives a basic personal allowance of £3,445. This is increased to £4,200 for individuals over the age of 64 on 5 April 1995, and further increased to £4,370 for those over the age of 74 on the same date. The increased allowance is available for those who died during the year of assessment but who would otherwise have achieved the appropriate age not later than 5 April 1995.

The amount of the increased personal allowance for older taxpayers will be reduced by one-half of total income in excess of £14,200. This reduction in the allowance will continue until it has been reduced to the basic personal allowance of £3,445.

Apart from limited transitional matters mentioned below, any unused part of the personal allowance of one spouse cannot be transferred to the other.

The personal allowance is given as a deduction in calculating taxable income and may therefore produce relief at the rate of 20, 25 or 40 per cent, as appropriate.

*Married couple's allowance*

A married man who was 'living with' his wife at any time in the year ending on 5 April 1995 is entitled to a married couple's allowance. The basic allowance is £1,720. This may be increased to £2,665 if either the husband or the wife is 65 years or over at any time in the year ending on 5 April 1995. A further increase to £2,705 can be obtained where either party to the marriage was 75 or over on 5 April 1995. Where an individual would otherwise have reached either age by 5 April 1995, but who died earlier in the year, the increased allowance is given.

The amount of the increased married couple's allowance may be reduced where the income of the husband (excluding the income of the wife) exceeds £14,200. The reduction will comprise:

(a) one-half of the husband's total income in excess of £14,200, less

(b) the amount of any reduction made when calculating the husband's increased personal allowance

This reduction in the married couple's allowance cannot reduce that allowance below the basic amount of £1,720.

If husband and wife were married during 1994-5 the married couple's allowance of £1,720, or any increased sum, must be reduced by one-twelfth for each complete month commencing on 6 April 1994, and preceding the date of marriage.

Unlike the personal allowance, the married couple's allowance does not reduce taxable income. Relief is granted by reducing the tax payable by 20 per cent of the allowance. Should the allowance exceed taxable income, no tax will be due.

In the absence of any further action the married couple's allowance will be given to the husband. If he is unable to utilize all or any part of that allowance, due to an absence of income, the husband may transfer the unused portion to his wife. The decision whether or not to transfer remains at the discretion of the husband.

However, a wife may file an election to obtain one-half of the basic married couple's allowance as of right, leaving the husband with the balance of that allowance. Alternatively, the couple may jointly elect that the entire basic allowance should be allocated to the wife only. Except in the year of marriage, the election must be made before the commencement of the year of assessment to which it is to apply. Should either spouse be unable to utilize his or her share of the married couple's allowance the unused part may be transferred to the other spouse.

*Additional personal allowance*

An allowance of £1,720 is available to a single person who has a qualifying child resident with him or her in 1994-5. The allowance can also be obtained by a married man whose wife is totally incapacitated by physical or mental infirmity throughout the year.

A 'qualifying child' for 1994-5 must be born during the year, be under the age of 16 years at the commencement of the year, or be over the age of 16 at the commencement of the year and either receiving full-time instruction at a university, college, school or other educational establishment or undergoing training for a trade, profession or vocation throughout a minimum period of two years. It is not necessary that the child is the claimant's own, a stepchild of the claimant, an illegitimate child if the parents married after the child's birth, or an adopted child under the age of 18 at the time of adoption. Alternatively it must be shown that the child was either born during 1994-5 or under the age of 18 at the commencement of the year and maintained by the claimant at his or her own expense during the whole of the succeeding twelve-month period.

Only one additional personal allowance of £1,720 can be obtained by an individual notwithstanding the number of children involved. Where an unmarried couple are living together as husband and wife, it is not possible for both to obtain the additional personal allowance. The allowance is given by reducing tax payable at the rate of 20 per cent of £1,720.

*Widow's bereavement allowance*

For the year of assessment in which a husband dies his surviving widow may obtain a widow's bereavement allowance which is £1,720 for 1994-5. It is a requirement that the parties were 'living together' immediately before the husband's death. A similar allowance will be available in the year following death, unless the widow remarried in the year of death. No widow's bereavement allowance can be obtained for future years. Here also relief is granted by reducing tax payable at the rate of 20 per cent of £1,720.

*Blind person's allowance*

An allowance of £1,200 is available to an individual if at any time during the year ending on 5 April 1995, he or she was registered as blind on a register maintained by a local authority. If the individual is 'living with' a wife or husband, any unused part of the blind person's allowance can be transferred to the other spouse. The allowance reduces taxable income and may therefore give rise to relief at the taxpayer's highest rate of tax suffered.

*Transitional allowances*

There are three limited transitional allowances which are intended to ensure that the introduction of independent taxation on 6 April 1990 did not increase liability to income tax for subsequent years. These allowances comprise:

(a) an increased personal allowance available to a wife where the husband cannot fully use that allowance in 1994-5

(b) a special personal allowance available to a husband where his wife falls into a higher age group, namely over 64 or over 74

(c) a married couple's allowance available to a separated husband not 'living with' his wife if the separation occurred before 6 April 1990

LIFE ASSURANCE RELIEF

Life assurance deduction relief is limited to premiums paid on policies made before 14 March 1984. No relief is available for policies issued after this date. Where the terms of a policy made before 14 March 1984 are subsequently varied or extended to produce increased benefits, future premiums paid may no longer qualify for relief.

When paying premiums under a qualifying policy made before 14 March 1984, the payer will deduct and retain income tax at the rate of 12.5 per cent. The ability to retain deductions made in this manner is not affected by the payer's liability to income tax on taxable income. No restriction to the deduction procedure arises if aggregate premiums paid during a year of assessment do not exceed £1,500 (calculated before deducting tax). Should premiums exceed this amount, relief will be confined to £1,500 or one-sixth of total income, whichever is the greater. Where sums deducted exceed the maximum limit, the excess must be accounted for to the Inland Revenue.

OTHER RELIEFS

In addition to personal and blind person's allowances, which reduce taxable income, and other allowances which reduce tax payable, further reliefs may be available to an individual. These include payments of interest.

In some instances, interest paid by a business proprietor may be included when calculating profits chargeable to income tax under Case I or Case II of Schedule D. Many private individuals cannot obtain relief in this manner and must satisfy stringent requirements before relief will be forthcoming. In general terms, before interest can qualify for relief it must be paid for a qualifying purpose. Relief will not be available to the extent that interest exceeds a reasonable commercial rate and no relief is forthcoming for interest on an overdraft.

For 1994–5 relief will be available on the following payments:

(a) Interest on a loan to purchase, develop or improve an interest in land owned by the individual and used as the only or main residence of that individual. 'Land' includes large houseboats and also caravans used for residential purposes. No relief is available for interest on loans applied after 5 April 1988 for the development or improvement of land, unless the work involves the construction of a new building. Relief is available for interest paid on a loan applied to acquire a property which is the only or main residence of a dependent relative, a separated spouse or a divorced former spouse, but only where that person occupied the property before 6 April 1988. Relief may also be forthcoming for interest on a loan used to acquire some other property, perhaps to be used as the only or main residence on retirement, by an individual who is compelled to occupy property by reason of his or her work. If the loan, or aggregate of several loans, exceeds £30,000, relief is restricted to interest on that amount. Where two or more persons apply loans after 31 July 1988 to acquire interests in a single building, those persons cannot, collectively, obtain relief for interest on more than £30,000 in relation to that building. Relief is given by reducing tax payable at the rate of 20 per cent. There can be no relief at the increased rates of 25 or 40 per cent.

(b) Interest on a loan to purchase or improve an interest in land which is let or available for letting at a commercial rent. This interest is only capable of being deducted from rental income

(c) Interest on a loan made to acquire an interest in a close company or in a partnership, or to advance money to such a person

(d) Interest on a loan to a member of a partnership to acquire machinery or plant for use in the partnership business

(e) Interest on a loan to an employed person to acquire machinery or plant for the purposes of his/her employment

(f) Interest on a loan made for the purpose of contributing capital to an industrial co-operative

(g) Interest on a loan applied for investment in an employee-controlled company

(h) Interest on a loan made to elderly persons for the purchase of an annuity where the loan is secured on land. If the loan exceeds £30,000, relief is limited to interest on this amount. This relief is restricted to income tax at the basic rate of 25 per cent.

(i) Interest on a loan to personal representatives to provide funds for the payment of capital transfer tax or inheritance tax

Relief for many payments of mortgage interest is obtained through a special scheme known as MIRAS (mortgage interest relief at source). This applies to interest paid to a building society, bank, insurance company and certain other approved persons. When making payments of this nature in 1994–5 the payer will deduct and retain income tax at the rate of 20 per cent. This will provide the payer with full relief at that rate and no other relief will be necessary. Qualifying payments of interest outside the MIRAS scheme continue to produce relief by reducing tax payable at the rate of 20 per cent.

Other relief under headings (b) to (i) (but not (h)) are given by deducting interest from taxable income. This enables the taxpayer to obtain relief at his or her top rate suffered.

Many employees pay contributions to an approved occupational pension scheme. The amount of their contributions may be deducted when calculating emoluments assessable under Schedule E. Relief should also be available for any additional voluntary contributions paid.

Self-employed individuals and those receiving earnings not covered by an occupational pension scheme may contribute under personal pension scheme arrangements. These individuals may also pay premiums under retirement annuity schemes, if the arrangements were concluded before 1 July 1988. Contributions paid under both headings may obtain income tax relief by deduction from taxable income, subject to maximum limits.

Subject to a maximum of £100,000 in any one year, the cost of subscribing for shares in an unquoted company may qualify for relief under the Enterprise Investment Scheme. Many requirements must be satisfied before this relief can be obtained, but husband and wife may each take advantage of the £100,000 annual maximum. Relief is given by reducing tax payable at the rate of 20 per cent of the share subscription cost.

## THE CHANGING SYSTEM

The income tax system which applies in the United Kingdom is in the process of considerable change. Until recently nearly all allowances and reliefs available to an individual were deducted when calculating taxable income. This enabled the amount of income tax otherwise payable to be reduced at the top rate suffered by the taxpayer. Whilst some allowances and reliefs continue to reduce the tax burden in this manner, there are an increasing number which do not reduce taxable income but reduce the amount of tax. For example, the married couple's allowance, additional personal allowance, widow's bereavement allowance, relief for mortgage interest, and relief for subscriptions under the Enterprise Investment Scheme all apply to reduce the tax burden at the lower rate of 20 per cent. Therefore an individual incurring liability at 40 per cent only obtains relief at one-half this rate. Certain of these reliefs are likely to be further reduced to 15 per cent for 1995–6.

Dividend income now effectively suffers income tax at the lower rate of 20 per cent, although shareholders incurring personal liability at the higher rate of 40 per cent must suffer an additional 20 per cent by direct assessment. There is no liability at the basic rate of 25 per cent on dividends.

The long established 'preceding year' basis for calculating trading and professional profits is being abandoned and replaced by a current year basis.

In 1996–7 many taxpayers will be provided with the option of adopting self-assessment rather than supplying the Inland Revenue with details of income and awaiting assessments showing the proper amount of tax due. This self-assessment will not be confined to income tax but will extend to capital gains tax also. These changes are having, and will continue to have, a considerable impact on the taxation commitments of many individuals.

# CAPITAL GAINS TAX

An individual is chargeable to capital gains tax on chargeable gains which accrue to him or her during a year of assessment ending on 5 April. The application of the tax has been amended substantially in recent years and the following information is confined to the year of assessment 1994–5, ending on 5 April 1995.

Liability extends to individuals who are either resident or ordinarily resident for the year but special rules apply where a person permanently leaves the United Kingdom or comes to this territory for the purpose of acquiring residence. Non-residents are not liable to capital gains tax unless, exceptionally, they carry on a business in the United Kingdom through a branch or agency.

Trustees residing in the United Kingdom are chargeable to capital gains tax but chargeable gains accruing to companies are assessable to corporation tax.

Capital gains tax is chargeable on the total of chargeable gains which accrue to a person in a year of assessment, after subtracting allowable losses arising in the same year. Unused allowable losses brought forward from some earlier year may be offset against current chargeable gains but in the case of individuals this must not reduce the net chargeable gains for 1994–5 below £5,800. It is possible to utilize trading losses against chargeable gains where those losses have not been offset against income.

## RATE OF TAX

Where the net chargeable gains accruing to an individual during 1994–5 do not exceed £5,800 there will be no liability to capital gains tax. If the net gains exceed £5,800 the excess is chargeable at the taxpayer's marginal rate of income tax. This is achieved by adding to the amount of income chargeable to income tax the excess net chargeable gains. The rate attributable to this top slice will disclose the rate of capital gains tax payable, which may be at 20 per cent, 25 per cent, 40 per cent or a combination of the three. Although income tax rates are used, capital gains tax remains a separate tax.

Capital gains tax for 1994–5 normally falls due for payment on or before 1 December 1995. If the return or other information recording chargeable gains is delayed, interest may become chargeable.

## HUSBAND AND WIFE

Following the introduction of independent taxation on 6 April 1990 a husband and wife 'living together' are separately assessed to capital gains tax. Each spouse must independently calculate his or her gains and losses, with each entitled to the annual exemption of £5,800. No liability to capital gains tax arises from the transfer of assets between husband and wife 'living together'.

## DISPOSAL OF ASSETS

Before liability to capital gains tax can arise a disposal, or deemed disposal, of an asset must take place. This occurs not only where assets are sold or exchanged but applies on the making of a gift. There is also a disposal of assets where any capital sum is derived from assets, for example, where compensation is received for loss or damage to an asset.

The date on which a disposal must be treated as having taken place will determine the year of assessment into which the chargeable gain or allowable loss falls. In those cases where a disposal is made under an unconditional contract, the time of disposal will be that when the contract was entered into and not the subsequent date of conveyance or transfer. A disposal under a conditional contract or option is treated as taking place when the contract becomes unconditional or the option is exercised. Disposals by way of gift are undertaken when the gift becomes effective.

## VALUATION OF ASSETS

The amount actually received as consideration for the disposal of an asset will be the sum from which very limited outgoings must be deducted for the purpose of establishing the gain or loss. In some cases, however, the consideration passing will not accurately reflect the value of the asset and a different basis must be used. This applies, in particular, where an asset is transferred by way of gift or otherwise than by a bargain made at arm's length. Such transactions are deemed to take place for a consideration representing market value, which will determine both the disposal proceeds accruing to the transferor and the cost of acquisition to the transferee.

Market value represents the price which an asset might reasonably be expected to fetch on a sale in the open market. In the case of unquoted shares or securities, it is to be assumed that the hypothetical purchaser in the open market would have available all the information which a prudent prospective purchaser of shares or securities might reasonably require if he were proposing to purchase them from a willing vendor by private treaty and at arm's length. This is an important consideration as the amount of information deemed to be available to a hypothetical purchaser may materially affect the price 'reasonably' offered in an open market situation. The market value of unquoted shares or securities will usually be established following negotiations with the Shares Valuation Division of the Capital Taxes Office. The valuation of land and interests in land in the United Kingdom will be dealt with by the District Valuer.

Special rules apply to determine the market value of shares quoted on the Stock Exchange.

## DEDUCTION FOR OUTGOINGS

Once the actual or notional disposal proceeds have been determined, it only remains to subtract eligible outgoings for the purpose of computing the gain or loss. There is the general rule that any outgoings deducted, or which are available to be deducted, when calculating income tax liability must be ignored. Subject to this, deductions will usually be limited to:

(a) the cost of acquiring the asset, together with incidental costs wholly and exclusively incurred in connection with the acquisition

(b) expenditure incurred wholly and exclusively on the asset in enhancing its value, being expenditure reflected in the state or nature of the asset at the time of the disposal, and any other expenditure wholly and exclusively incurred in establishing, preserving or defending title to, or a right over, the asset

(c) the incidental costs of making the disposal

Where the disposal concerns a leasehold interest having less than 50 years to run, any expenditure falling under (a) and (b) must be written off throughout the duration of the lease. This recognizes that a lease is a wasting asset which, at the termination of the leasing period, will retain no value.

## ASSETS HELD ON 31 MARCH 1982

Where the disposal relates to assets held on 31 March 1982, the actual cost of acquisition will not usually enter into the calculation of gain. It is to be assumed that such assets were acquired on 31 March 1982 for a consideration representing market value on that date. The increase in value, if any, occurring before 31 March 1982 will not be assessable to capital gains tax.

INDEXATION ALLOWANCE

An indexation allowance may be available on the disposal of an asset. This allowance is based on percentage increases in the retail prices index between the month of March 1982 or, if later, the month in which expenditure is incurred, and the month of disposal. The increase is applied to the items of expenditure in (a) and (b) above to determine the amount of the indexation allowance. However, if the asset was acquired before 31 March 1982, the allowance will be based on market value at 31 March 1982.

Previously the indexation allowance could be subtracted from the gain, added to the loss or used to convert a gain into a loss. However, where the disposal has taken place after 29 November 1993 the indexation allowance may only be applied to reduce a gain. It cannot increase the amount of a loss, and where the allowance exceeds the amount of a gain it only remains necessary to reduce the gain to nil.

As a transitional measure some limited relief is available to individuals undertaking the disposal of assets between 30 November 1993 and 5 April 1995. To the extent that the indexation allowance cannot be used, due to the absence of sufficient gains, up to a maximum of £10,000 the otherwise disallowed indexation allowance can be utilized. Should any balance remain unused at 5 April 1995 that balance cannot be carried forward and any benefit will be lost.

EXEMPTIONS

There is a general exemption from liability to capital gains tax where the net gains of an individual for 1994–5 do not exceed £5,800. This general exemption applies separately to a husband and to his wife where the parties are 'living together'.

The disposal of many assets will not give rise to chargeable gains or allowable losses and these assets include:
(a) private motor cars
(b) government securities
(c) loan stock and other securities (but not shares)
(d) options and contracts relating to securities within (b) and (c)
(e) National Savings Certificates, Premium Bonds, Defence Bonds and National Development Bonds
(f) currency of any description acquired for personal expenditure outside the United Kingdom
(g) decorations awarded for valour
(h) betting wins and pools, lottery or games prizes
(i) compensation or damages for any wrong or injury suffered by an individual in his/her person or in his/her profession or vocation
(j) life assurance and deferred annuity contracts where the person making the disposal is the original beneficial owner
(k) dwelling-houses and land enjoyed with the residence which is an individual's only or main residence
(l) tangible movable property, the consideration for the disposal of which does not exceed £6,000
(m) certain tangible movable property which is a wasting asset having a life not exceeding 50 years
(n) assets transferred to charities and other bodies
(o) works of art, historic buildings and similar assets
(p) assets used to provide maintenance funds for historic buildings
(q) assets transferred to trustees for the benefit of employees

DWELLING-HOUSES

Exemption from capital gains tax will usually be available for any gain which accrues to an individual from the disposal of, or of an interest in, a dwelling-house or part of a dwelling-house which has been his/her only or main residence. The exemption extends to land which has been occupied and

enjoyed with the residence as its garden or grounds. Some restriction may be necessary where the land exceeds half a hectare.

The gain will not be chargeable to capital gains tax if the dwelling-house, or part, has been the individual's only or main residence throughout the period of ownership, or throughout the entire period except for all or any part of the last three years. A proportionate part of the gain will be exempt in other cases if the dwelling-house has been the individual's only or main residence for part only of the period of ownership. In the case of property acquired before 31 March 1982, the period of ownership is treated as commencing on this date.

Where part of the dwelling-house has been used exclusively for business purposes, that part of the gain attributable to business use will not be exempt. It will be comparatively unusual for any part to be used exclusively for such a purpose, except perhaps in the case of doctors' or dentists' surgeries.

In those cases where part of a qualifying dwelling-house has been used to provide rented residential accommodation this non-personal use may frequently be ignored when calculating exemption from capital gains tax, unless relatively substantial sums are involved.

Dwellings occupied by dependent relatives or separated or divorced former spouses, may also qualify for the exemption, but only where occupation commenced before 6 April 1988.

ROLL-OVER RELIEF – BUSINESS ASSETS

Persons carrying on business will often undertake the disposal of an asset and use the proceeds to finance the acquisition of a replacement asset. Where this situation arises a claim for roll-over relief may be available. The broad effect of such a claim is that all or part of the gain arising on the disposal of the old asset may be disregarded. The gain or part is then subtracted from the cost of acquiring the replacement asset. As this cost is reduced, any gain arising from the future disposal of the replacement asset will be correspondingly increased, unless of course a further roll-over situation then develops.

It remains a requirement that both the old and the replacement asset must be used for the purpose of the taxpayer's business. Relief will only be available if the acquisition of the replacement asset takes place within a period commencing twelve months before, and ending three years after, the disposal of the old asset, although the Board of Inland Revenue retain a discretion to extend this period where the circumstances were such that it was impossible for the taxpayer to acquire the replacement asset before the expiration of the normal time limit.

Whilst many business assets qualify for roll-over relief there are exceptions.

ROLL-OVER RELIEF – SHARES

An additional form of roll-over relief was introduced for disposals taking place after 15 March 1993 and matched with the acquisition of shares in unquoted companies. Stringent requirements had to be satisfied before relief could be obtained and few taxpayers were able to take advantage of the provisions. However, the scope of roll-over relief was widened significantly for disposals taking place after 29 November 1993. Gains arising on the disposal of virtually any asset will enable an individual, and some trustees, to contemplate the availability of roll-over relief. It is a necessary requirement that the individual or trustee making the disposal acquires shares in a qualifying unquoted trading company. Most shareholdings in trading companies will qualify, with the notable exception of those carrying on the business of farming and some forms of property development.

An unusual feature of roll-over relief on the reinvestment in shares is that, subject to upper limits, the individual or trustee can roll over any part of the chargeable gain arising on the disposal of assets. The ability to select the amount to be rolled over enables the claimant to leave undisturbed the remaining gain, which can be offset against available losses or perhaps used to absorb the annual exemption of £5,800.

## Hold-over Relief – Gifts

The gift of an asset is treated as a disposal made for a consideration equal to market value, with a corresponding acquisition by the transferee at an identical value. In the case of gifts made by individuals and a limited range of trustees to a transferee resident in the United Kingdom, a form of hold-over relief may be available. Relief is limited to the transfer of certain assets, including the following:

(a) assets used for the purposes of a trade or similar activity carried on by the transferor or his/her personal company
(b) shares or securities of a trading company which is neither quoted on a stock exchange nor dealt in on the Unlisted Securities Market
(c) shares or securities of a trading company which is quoted or listed but which is the transferor's personal company
(d) many interests in agricultural property qualifying for business property relief or agricultual property relief for inheritance tax purposes
(e) assets involved in transactions which are lifetime transfers for inheritance tax purposes, other than potentially exempt transfers

The effect of the claim is similar to that following a claim for roll-over relief on the disposal of business assets, but adjustments will be necessary where some consideration is given for the transfer, the asset has not been used for business purposes throughout the period of ownership, or not all assets of a company are used for business purposes.

## Retirement Relief

Retirement relief is available to an individual who disposes by way of sale or gift of the whole or part of a business. It does not necessarily follow that the isolated disposal of assets will represent the disposal of the whole or part of a business. The main condition for granting this relief is that throughout a period of at least one year the business has been owned either by the individual or by a trading company in which the individual retained a sufficient shareholding interest. The relief extends also to cases where an individual disposes by way of sale or gift of shares or securities of a company. It must be demonstrated that the company was a trading company, that the individual retained a sufficient shareholding interest, and that he/she was engaged as a full-time working officer or employee.

An individual who has attained the age of 55 years at the time of a disposal taking place after 29 November 1993 may obtain retirement relief up to a maximum of £625,000. The amount of this relief must be reduced if the conditions have not been satisfied throughout a one-year period. With a single exception no retirement relief can be obtained if the disposal occurs before the individual's 55th birthday. This exception arises where an individual is compelled to retire early on the grounds of ill-health. The normal retirement relief may then be obtained. Any retirement relief must be subtracted from the net gains arising on disposal, leaving the balance remaining, if any, chargeable to capital gains tax in the normal manner.

## Death

No capital gains tax is chargeable on the value of assets retained at the time of death. However, the personal representatives administering the deceased's estate are deemed to acquire those assets for a consideration representing market value on death. This ensures that any increase in value occurring before the date of death will not be chargeable to capital gains tax. If a legatee or other person acquires an asset under a will or intestacy no chargeable gain will accrue to the personal representatives, and the person taking the asset will also be treated as having acquired it at the time of death for its then market value.

# INHERITANCE TAX

Liability to inheritance tax may arise on a limited range of lifetime gifts and other dispositions and also on the value of assets retained, or deemed to be retained, at the time of death. An individual's domicile at the time of any gift or on death is an important matter. Domicile will generally be determined by applying normal rules, although special considerations may be necessary where an individual was previously domiciled in the United Kingdom but subsequently acquired a domicile of choice overseas. Where a person was domiciled in the United Kingdom at the time of a disposition or on death the location of assets is immaterial and full liability to inheritance tax arises. Individuals domiciled outside the United Kingdom are, however, chargeable to inheritance tax only on transactions affecting assets located in the United Kingdom.

The assets of husband and wife are not merged for inheritance tax purposes. Each spouse is treated as a separate individual entitled to receive the benefit of his or her exemptions, reliefs and rates of tax. Where husband and wife retain similar assets, for example shares in the same family company, special 'related property' provisions may require the merger of those assets for valuation purposes only.

## Lifetime Gifts and Dispositions

Gifts and dispositions made during lifetime fall under four broad headings, namely:
(a) dispositions which are not transfers of value
(b) exempt transfers
(c) potentially exempt transfers
(d) chargeable transfers

### Dispositions which are not transfers of value

Several lifetime transactions are not treated as transfers of value and may be entirely disregarded for inheritance tax purposes. These include transactions not intended to confer gratuitous benefit, the provision of family maintenance, the waiver of the right to receive remuneration or dividends, and the grant of agricultural tenancies for full consideration.

### Exempt transfers

Certain other transfers are treated as exempt transfers and incur no liability to inheritance tax. The main exempt transfers are listed below:

*Transfers between spouses* – Transfers between husband and wife are usually exempt. However, if the transferor is, but the transferee spouse is not, domiciled in the United Kingdom, transfers will be exempt only to the extent that the total does not exceed £55,000. Unlike the requirement used for income tax and capital gains tax purposes, it is immaterial whether husband and wife are living together.

*Annual exemption* – The first £3,000 of gifts and other dispositions made in a year ending on 5 April is exempt. If the exemption is not used, or not wholly used, in any year the balance may be carried forward to the following year only. The annual exemption will only be available for a potentially exempt transfer if that transfer subsequently becomes chargeable by reason of the donor's death.

*Small gifts* – Outright gifts of £250 or less to any person in one year ending 5 April are exempt.

*Normal expenditure* – A transfer made during lifetime and comprising normal expenditure is exempt. To obtain this exemption it must be shown that:

(a) the transfer was made as part of the normal expenditure of the transferor
(b) taking one year with another, the transfer was made out of income
(c) after allowing for all transfers of value forming part of normal expenditure the transferor was left with sufficient income to maintain his or her usual standard of living

*Gifts in consideration of marriage* – These are exempt if they satisfy certain requirements. The amount allowed will be governed by the relationship between the donor and a party to the marriage. The allowable amounts comprise:

(a) gifts by a parent, £5,000
(b) gifts by a grandparent, £2,500
(c) gifts by a party to the marriage, £2,500
(d) gifts by other persons, £1,000

*Gifts to charities* – Gifts to charities are exempt from liability.

*Gifts to political parties* – Gifts to political parties which satisfy certain requirements are generally exempt.

*Gifts for national purposes* – Gifts made to an extensive list of bodies are exempt from liability. These include, among others: the National Gallery, the British Museum, the National Trust, the National Art Collections Fund, the National Heritage Memorial Fund, the Historic Buildings and Monuments Commission for England (English Heritage), any local authority, any university or university college in the United Kingdom.

A number of other gifts made for the public benefit are also exempt.

*Potentially exempt transfers*

Lifetime gifts and dispositions which are neither to be ignored nor comprise exempt transfers incur possible liability to inheritance tax. However, relief is available for a range of potentially exempt transfers. These comprise gifts made by an individual to:

(a) a second individual
(b) trustees administering an accumulation and maintenance trust
(c) trustees administering a disabled person's trust

The accumulation and maintenance trust mentioned in (b) must achieve that on reaching a specified age, not exceeding 25 years, a beneficiary will become absolutely entitled to trust assets or obtain an interest in possession in the income of those assets.

Additions to the above list affect settled property administered by trustees where an individual, or individuals, retain an interest in possession. The transfer of assets to, the removal of assets from, or the rearrangement of interests in such property comprise potentially exempt transfers if the person transferring an interest and the person benefiting from the transfer are both individuals.

No immediate liability to inheritance tax will arise on the making of a potentially exempt transfer. Should the donor survive for a period of seven years, immunity from liability will be confirmed. However, the donor's death within the seven-year *inter vivos* period produces liability, as explained later, if the amounts involved are sufficiently substantial.

*Chargeable transfers*

Any remaining lifetime gifts or dispositions which are neither to be ignored nor represent exempt transfers or potentially exempt transfers, incur liability to inheritance tax. The range of such chargeable transfers is severely limited and is broadly confined to transfers made to or affecting discretionary trusts, transfers to non-individuals and transfers involving companies.

GIFTS WITH RESERVATION

A lifetime gift of assets made at any time after 17 March 1986 may incur additional liability to inheritance tax if the donor retains some interest in the subject matter of the gift. This may arise, for example, where a parent transfers a dwelling-house to a son or daughter and continues to occupy the property or to enjoy some benefit from that property. The retention of a benefit may be ignored where it is enjoyed in return for full consideration, perhaps a commercial rent, or where the benefit arises from changed circumstances which could not have been foreseen at the time of the original gift. The gift with reservation provisions will not usually apply to most exempt transfers.

There are three possibilities which may arise where the donor reserves or enjoys some benefit from the subject matter of a previous gift and subsequently dies, namely:

(a) if no benefit is enjoyed within a period of seven years before death there can be no further liability
(b) if the benefit ceased to be enjoyed within a period of seven years before the date of death, the original donor is deemed to have made a potentially exempt transfer representing the value of the asset at the time of cessation
(c) if the benefit is enjoyed at the time of death, the value of the asset must be included in the value of the deceased's estate on death

It must be emphasized that the existence of a benefit enjoyed at any time within a period of seven years before death will establish liability to tax on gifts with reservation, notwithstanding that the gift may have been made many years earlier, providing it was undertaken after 17 March 1986.

DEATH

Immediately before the time of death an individual is deemed to make a transfer of value. This transfer will comprise the value of assets forming part of the deceased's estate after subtracting most liabilities. Any exempt transfers may, however, be excluded. These include transfers for the benefit of a surviving spouse, a charity and a qualifying political party, together with bequests to approved bodies and for national purposes.

Death may also trigger three additional liabilities, namely:

(a) A potentially exempt transfer made within the period of seven years ending on death loses its potential status and becomes chargeable to inheritance tax
(b) The value of gifts made with reservation may incur liability if any benefit was enjoyed within a period of seven years preceding death
(c) Additional tax may become payable for chargeable lifetime transfers made within seven years before death

VALUATIONS

The valuation of assets is an important matter as this will establish the value transferred for lifetime dispositions and also the value of a person's estate at the time of death. The value of property will represent the price which might reasonably be expected from a sale in the open market. This price cannot be reduced on the grounds that, should the whole property be placed on the market simultaneously, values would be depressed.

In some cases it may be necessary to incorporate the value of 'related property'. This will include property comprised in the estate of the transferor's spouse and certain property previously transferred to charities. The purpose of the related property valuation rules is not to add the value of the property to the estate of the transferor. Related property must be merged to establish the aggregate value of the respective interests and this value is then apportioned, usually on a *pro rata* basis, to the separate interests.

The value of shares and securities quoted on the Stock Exchange will be determined by extracting figures from the daily list of official prices.

Where quoted shares and securities are sold or the quotation is suspended within a period of twelve months following the date of death, a claim may be made to substitute the proceeds or subsequent value for the value on death. This claim will only be beneficial if the gross proceeds realized are lower or the value has fallen below market value at the time of death. A similar claim may be available for interests in land sold within a period of four years following death.

## RELIEF FOR ASSETS

Special relief is made available for certain assets, notably woodlands, agricultural property and business property. The effect of this relief is summarized below.

### Woodlands

Where woodlands pass on death the value will usually be included in the deceased's estate. However, an election may be made in respect of land in the United Kingdom on which trees or underwood is growing to delete the value of those assets. Relief is confined to the value of trees or underwood and does not extend to the land on which they are growing. Liability to inheritance tax will arise if and when the trees or underwood are sold on a future occasion.

### Agricultural property

Relief is available for the agricultural value of agricultural property. Such property must be occupied and used for agricultural purposes and relief is confined to the agricultural value.

The value transferred, either on a lifetime gift or on death, must be determined. This value may then be reduced by a percentage. The percentage has changed from time to time but for events taking place after 9 March 1992 a 100 per cent deduction will be available if the transferor retained vacant possession or could have obtained that possession within a period of twelve months following the transfer. In other cases, notably including land let to tenants, a lower deduction of 50 per cent is available.

It remains a requirement that the agricultural property was either occupied by the transferor for the purposes of agriculture throughout a two-year period ending on the date of the transfer, or was owned by him/her throughout a period of seven years ending on that date and also occupied for agricultural purposes.

### Business property

Where the value transferred is attributable to relevant business property, that value may be reduced by a percentage. The reduction in value applies to:

(a) property consisting of a business or an interest in a business
(b) shares or securities of an unquoted company which provided the transferor with control
(c) unquoted shares or securities not falling within (b) which provided the transferor with more than 25 per cent of voting rights
(d) other unquoted shares or securities not falling within (c)
(e) shares or securities of a quoted company which provided the transferor with control
(f) any land, building, machinery or plant which, immediately before the transfer, was used wholly or mainly for the purposes of a business carried on by a company of which the transferor had control
(g) any land, building, machinery or plant which, immediately before the transfer, was used wholly or mainly for the purposes of a business carried on by a partnership of which the transferor was a partner
(h) any land, building, machinery or plant which, immediately before the transfer, was used wholly or mainly for the purposes of a business carried on by the transferor and was then settled property in which he retained an interest in possession

Here also the percentage deductions have changed, but for events occurring after 9 March 1992 a deduction of 100 per cent is available for assets falling within (a), (b) or (c). A reduced deduction of 50 per cent can be obtained for assets within (d) to (h).

It is a general requirement that the property must have been retained for a period of two years before the transfer or death and restrictions may be necessary if the property has not been used wholly for business purposes. The same slice of property cannot obtain both business property relief and the relief available for agricultural property.

## CALCULATION OF TAX PAYABLE

The calculation of inheritance tax payable adopts the use of a cumulative total. Each chargeable lifetime transfer is added to the total with a final addition made on death. The top slice added to the total for the current event determines the rate at which inheritance tax must be paid. However, the cumulative total will only include transfers made within a period of seven years before the current event and those undertaken outside this period must be excluded. Although inheritance tax was only introduced on 18 March 1986, the seven-year cumulative total will include chargeable lifetime gifts made before that date, subject to the seven-year limitation.

### Lifetime chargeable transfers

The value transferred by the limited range of lifetime chargeable transfers must be added to the seven-year cumulative total to calculate whether any inheritance tax is due. Should the nil rate band be exceeded, tax will be imposed on the excess at one-half of the rate shown below. However, if the donor dies within a period of seven years from the date of the chargeable lifetime transfer, additional tax may be due. This is calculated by applying tax at the full rate (in substitution for the one-half rate previously used). The amount of tax is then reduced to a percentage by applying tapering relief. This percentage is governed by the number of years from the date of the lifetime gift to the date of death and is as follows:

### Period of years before death

| | |
|---|---|
| Not more than 3 | 100% |
| More than 3 but not more than 4 | 80% |
| More than 4 but not more than 5 | 60% |
| More than 5 but not more than 6 | 40% |
| More than 6 but not more than 7 | 20% |

Should this exercise produce liability greater than that previously paid at the one-half rate on the lifetime transfer, additional tax, representing the difference, must be discharged. Where the calculation shows an amount falling below tax paid on the lifetime transfer, no additional liability can arise nor will the deficiency become repayable.

Tapering relief will, of course, only be available if the calculation discloses a liability to inheritance tax. There can be no liability to the extent that the lifetime transfer falls within the nil rate band.

*Potentially exempt transfers*

Where a potentially exempt transfer loses immunity from liability, due to the donor's death within the seven-year *inter vivos* period, the value transferred by that transfer enters into the cumulative total. Any liability to inheritance tax will be calculated by applying the full rate shown below, reduced to the percentage governed by tapering relief if the original transfer occurred more than three years before death. Here also liability can only arise to the extent, if any, that the nil rate band is exceeded.

*Death*

The final addition to the seven-year cumulative total will comprise the value of an estate on death. Inheritance tax will be calculated by applying the full rate shown below to the extent the nil rate band is exceeded. No tapering relief can be obtained.

RATES OF TAX

In earlier times there were several rates of inheritance tax which progressively increased as the value transferred grew in size. However, for events taking place after 9 March 1992, a nil rate applies to the initial slice of £150,000. Any excess is charged at the single positive rate of 40 per cent.

Only one-half of the 40 per cent rate (namely 20 per cent) will be applicable for chargeable lifetime transfers.

The above rate and rateband is likely to be amended on future occasions.

PAYMENT OF TAX

Inheritance tax usually falls due for payment six months after the end of the month in which the chargeable transaction takes place. Where a transfer, other than that made on death, occurs after 5 April and before the following 1 October, tax falls due on the following 30 April, although there are some exceptions to this general rule.

Inheritance tax attributable to the transfer of certain land, controlling shareholding interests, unquoted shares, businesses and interests in businesses, together with agricultural property, may usually be satisfied by instalments spread over ten years. Except in the case of non-agricultural land, where interest is charged on outstanding instalments, no liability to interest arises where tax is paid on the due date. In all cases, delay in the payment of tax may incur liability to interest.

SETTLED PROPERTY

Complex rules apply to establish inheritance tax liability on settled property. Where a person is beneficially entitled to an interest in possession, that person is effectively deemed to own the property in which the interest subsists. It follows that where the interest comes to an end during the beneficiary's lifetime and some other person becomes entitled to the property or interest, the beneficiary is treated as having made a transfer of value. However, this will usually comprise a potentially exempt transfer. In addition, no liability will arise where the property vests in the absolute ownership of the previous beneficiary. The death of a person entitled to an interest in possession will require the value of the underlying property to be added to the value of the deceased's estate.

In the case of other settled property where there is no interest in possession (e.g. discretionary trusts), liability to tax will arise on each ten-year anniversary of the trust. There will also be liability if property ceases to be held on discretionary trusts before the first ten-year anniversary date is reached or between anniversaries. The rate of tax suffered will be governed by several considerations, including previous dispositions made by the settlor, transactions concluded by the trustees, and the period throughout which property has been held in trust.

Accumulation and maintenance settlements which require assets to be distributed, or interests in income to be created, not later than a beneficiary's twenty-fifth birthday may be exempt from any liability to inheritance tax.

# CORPORATION TAX

Profits, gains and income accruing to companies resident in the United Kingdom incur liability to corporation tax. Non-resident companies are immune from this tax unless they carry on a trade in the United Kingdom through a permanent establishment, branch or office. Companies residing outside the United Kingdom may be liable to income tax at the basic rate on other income arising in the United Kingdom, perhaps from letting property. The following comments are confined to companies resident in the United Kingdom and have little application to those residing overseas.

Liability to corporation tax is governed by the profits, gains or income for an accounting period. This is usually the period for which financial accounts are made up, and in the case of companies preparing accounts to the same accounting date annually will comprise successive periods of twelve months.

RATE OF TAX

The amount of profits or income for an accounting period must be determined on normal taxation principles. The special rules which apply to individuals where a source of income is acquired or discontinued are ignored and consideration is confined to the actual profits or income for an accounting period.

The rate of corporation tax is fixed for a financial year ending on 31 March. Where the accounting period of a company overlaps this date and there is a change in the rate of corporation tax, profits and income must be apportioned.

In recent years the rate of corporation tax has been as follows:

*Financial year*

| | |
|---|---|
| 12 months ending 31 March 1990 | 35% |
| 31 March 1991 | 34% |
| 31 March 1992, 1993, 1994, 1995 | 33% |

SMALL COMPANIES RATE

Where the profits of a company do not exceed stated limits, corporation tax becomes payable at the following small companies rate. It is the amount of profits and not the size of the company which governs the application of this rate.

*Financial year*

| | |
|---|---|
| 12 months ending 31 March 1990, 1991, 1992, 1993, 1994, 1995 | 25% |

The level of profits which a company may derive without losing the benefit of the small companies rate is frequently changed. For the year ending on 31 March 1995 the limit is £300,000. However, if profits exceed £300,000 but fall below £1,500,000 marginal small companies rate relief applies. The broad effect of marginal relief is that the first £300,000 of profits is taxed at the small companies rate of 25 per cent. Profits falling in the margin then incur liability at the marginal rate of 35 per cent. Different upper limits and marginal rates applied for earlier years. Where the accounting period of a company overlaps 31 March, profits must be apportioned to establish the appropriate rate for each part of those profits.

The lower limit of £300,000 and the upper limit of £1,500,000 apply for a period of twelve months in duration and must be proportionately reduced for shorter periods. Some restriction in the small companies rate and the marginal rate may be necessary if there are two or more associated companies, namely companies under common control.

The small companies rate is not available for close investment-holding companies. These are mainly investment companies, other than those receiving most of their income from letting land and property.

## CAPITAL GAINS

Chargeable gains arising to a company are calculated in a manner similar to that used for individuals. However, companies cannot obtain the annual exemption of £5,800 or the special indexation allowance for loss-making disposals made before 6 April 1995. Nor are they assessed to capital gains tax. In place of this tax companies suffer liability to corporation tax on chargeable gains. Tax is suffered on the full chargeable gain, after subtracting relief for losses, if any.

## DISTRIBUTIONS

Dividends and other qualifying distributions made by a United Kingdom resident company are not satisfied after deduction of income tax. However, when making a distribution a company is required to account to the Inland Revenue for advance corporation tax. The amount of this tax is based on the distribution and changes in the rate have been introduced throughout a three-year period as follows:

| Distribution | Rate |
|---|---|
| Year ending 5 April 1993 | one third |
| Year ending 5 April 1994 | nine thirty-firsts |
| Year ending 5 April 1995 | one quarter |

Advance corporation tax accounted for in this manner in relation to distributions made in an accounting period may usually be set against a company's corporation tax liability for the same period. Some restrictions are imposed on the amount which can be offset but any surplus may be carried forward, or perhaps carried backwards, and set against corporation tax paid or due for other accounting periods.

A United Kingdom resident shareholder receiving a qualifying distribution also obtains a tax credit based on the distribution made. Over the same three-year period the tax credit will be calculated as follows:

| Distribution | Rate |
|---|---|
| Year ending 5 April 1993 | one third |
| Year ending 5 April 1994 | one quarter |
| Year ending 5 April 1995 | one quarter |

The total income of the individual therefore comprises the aggregate of the distribution and the tax credit. It will be noted that whilst the rate of advance corporation tax and amount of the tax credit are identical for the first and last of the three years, the amounts differed in 1993–4.

For 1993–4 and 1994–5 a distribution is treated as having suffered income tax at the lower rate of 20 per cent. If the individual is not liable, or not fully liable, to income tax at this rate all or part of the tax credit can be refunded by the Inland Revenue. There is no liability on distributions at the basic rate of 25 per cent. However, individuals with substantial income incur liability to income tax at the higher rate of 40 per cent on the aggregate of the distribution and the tax credit. With tax deemed to have been suffered at the lower rate of 20 per cent the additional liability will be limited to the excess over this rate, which is also 20 per cent.

## INTEREST

On making many payments of interest a company is required to deduct income tax at the basic rate and account for the tax deducted to the Inland Revenue. The gross amount of interest paid will usually comprise a charge on income to be offset against profits on which corporation tax becomes payable.

## GROUPS OF COMPANIES

Each company within a group is separately charged to corporation tax on profits, gains and income. However, where one group member realizes a loss, other than a capital loss, a claim may be made to offset the deficiency against profits of some other member of the same group.

Claims are also available to avoid the payment of advance corporation tax on distributions, or the deduction of income tax on the payment of interest, for transactions between members of a group of companies. The transfer of capital assets from one member of a group to a fellow member will incur no liability to tax on chargeable gains.

## PAY AND FILE

For accounting periods ending after 30 September 1993 a new 'pay and file' system now affects all companies. Under this system tax is payable on a self-assessment basis nine months following the end of the accounting period involved, with accounts and returns being submitted three months later. Failure to satisfy corporation tax or to submit documents within these time limits will result in a liability to discharge interest and penalties.

# VALUE ADDED TAX

Unlike income tax, capital gains tax, inheritance tax and corporation tax, which are collected and administered by the Inland Revenue, value added tax is the responsibility of Customs and Excise. Value added tax is charged on the value of the supplies made by a registered trader and extends to both the supply of goods and the supply of services.

For many years liability to account for value added tax also arose on the value of goods imported into the United Kingdom. This liability remains where goods are imported from many overseas sources. However, substantial changes were introduced with the commencement of the European 'single market' on 1 January 1993. Where goods are imported by a trader from a second trader in a member state of the European Community there is no value added tax on importation. In place of importation tax there is an acquisition tax whereby a trader who acquires goods must include the acquisition in his normal value added tax return and account for the tax due. A United Kingdom trader who exports goods to a member state will not be required to account for value added tax on the supply, if that trader observes the requirements laid down by regulations.

## REGISTRATION

All traders, including professional men and women, together with companies, making taxable supplies of a value exceeding stated limits are required to register for value added tax purposes. Taxable supplies represent the supply of goods and services potentially chargeable with value added tax. The limits which govern mandatory registration are amended annually but from 1 December 1993 an unregistered trader must register:

(a) at any time, if there are reasonable grounds for believing that the value of taxable supplies in the next 30 days will exceed £45,000

(b) at the end of any month if the value of taxable supplies in the last 12 months then ending has exceeded £45,000. Liability to register under (b) may be avoided if it can be shown that the value of supplies in the period of 12 months then beginning will not exceed £43,000. There may, however, be liability to register immediately where a business is taken over from another trader as a 'going concern'.

Where the limits governing mandatory registration have been exceeded, it is necessary for the trader to notify Customs and Excise. Failure to provide prompt notification may have unfortunate results as the person concerned will be required to account for value added tax from the proper registration date.

A trader whose taxable supplies do not reach the mandatory registration limits may apply for voluntary registration. This step may be thought advisable to recover input tax or to compete with other registered traders.

A registered trader may submit an application for de-registration if the value of taxable supplies subsequently falls. From 1 December 1993, an application for de-registration can be made if the value of taxable supplies for the year beginning on the application date is not expected to exceed £43,000.

### INPUT TAX

A registered trader will both suffer tax (input tax) when obtaining goods or services for the purposes of his business and also become liable to account for tax (output tax) on the value of goods and services which he supplies. Relief can usually be obtained for input tax suffered, either by setting that tax against output tax due or by repayment. Most items of input tax can be relieved in this manner but there are exceptions, including the prohibition of relief for the cost of business entertaining. Where a registered trader makes both exempt supplies and also taxable supplies to his customers or clients, there may be some restriction in the amount of input tax which can be recovered.

### OUTPUT TAX

When making a taxable supply of goods or services a registered trader must account for output tax, if any, on the value of the supply. Usually the price charged by the registered trader will be increased by adding value added tax but failure to make the required addition will not remove liability to account for output tax.

### EXEMPT SUPPLIES

No value added tax is chargeable on the supply of goods or services which are treated as exempt supplies. These include the provision of burial and cremation facilities, insurance, finance and education. The granting of a lease to occupy land or the sale of land will usually comprise an exempt supply, but there are numerous exceptions. In particular, the sale of new non-domestic buildings or certain buildings used by charities cannot be treated as exempt supplies.

A taxable person may elect to tax rents and other supplies of buildings and agricultural land not used for residential or charitable purposes.

Exempt supplies do not enter into the calculation of taxable supplies which governs liability to mandatory registration. Such supplies made by a registered trader may, however, limit the amount of input tax which can be relieved. It is for this reason that the election may be useful.

### RATES OF TAX

Two rates of value added tax have applied since 1 April 1991, namely:

(a) a zero, or nil, rate
(b) a standard rate of 17.5 per cent

Although no tax is due on a zero-rated supply, this does comprise a taxable supply which must be included in the calculation governing liability to register.

### ZERO-RATING

A large number of supplies are zero-rated, including, among others:

(a) the supply of many items of food and drink for human consumption. This does not include ice creams, chocolates, sweets, potato crisps and alcoholic drinks. Nor does it extend to supplies made in the course of catering or to items supplied for consumption in a restaurant or café. Whilst the supply of cold items, e.g. sandwiches, for consumption away from the supplier's premises, is zero-rated, the supply of hot food, for example fish and chips, is not
(b) animal feeding stuffs
(c) sewerage and water, unless supplied for industrial purposes
(d) books, brochures, pamphlets, leaflets, newspapers, maps and charts
(e) talking books for the blind and handicapped, and wireless sets for the blind
(f) supplies of services, other than professional services, when constructing a new domestic building or a building to be used by a charity. The supply of materials for such a building is also zero-rated, together with the sale or the grant of a long lease for these buildings. Alterations to some protected buildings are also zero-rated
(g) the transportation of persons in a vehicle, ship or aircraft designed to carry not less than twelve persons
(h) supplies of drugs, medicines and other aids for the handicapped
(i) supplies of clothing and footwear for young persons
(j) exports

Supplies of electricity, gas and coal for domestic use ceased to be zero-rated after 31 March 1994. However, supplies made immediately after this date are subject to a reduced tax rate of 8 per cent, which is expected to increase to 17.5 per cent one year later.

This list is not exhaustive but indicates the wide range of supplies which may be zero-rated.

### COLLECTION OF TAX

Registered traders submit value added tax returns for accounting periods. Each accounting period is usually three months in duration but arrangements can be made to submit returns on a monthly basis. Very large traders must account for tax on a monthly basis but this does not affect the three-monthly return. The return will show both the output tax due for supplies made by the trader in the accounting period and also the input tax for which relief is claimed. If the output tax exceeds input tax the balance must be remitted with the value added tax return. Where input tax suffered exceeds the output tax due the registered trader may claim recovery of the excess from Customs and Excise.

This basis for collecting tax explains the structure of value added tax. Where supplies are made between registered traders the supplier will account for an amount of tax which will usually be identical to the tax recovered by the person to whom the supply is made. However, where the supply is made to a person who is not a registered trader there can be no recovery of input tax and it is on this person that the final burden of value added tax eventually falls.

In those cases where goods are acquired by a United Kingdom trader from a supplier within a member state of the European Community the trader must also account for the tax due on acquisition.

An optional scheme is available for registered traders having an annual turnover of taxable supplies not exceeding £350,000. Such traders may, if they wish, render returns annually. Nine equal payments of value added tax will be paid on account, with a final balancing payment accompanying submission of the return.

## BAD DEBTS

Many retailers operate special retail schemes for calculating the amount of value added tax due. These schemes are, broadly, based on the volume of consideration received in an accounting period. Should a customer fail to pay for goods or services supplied, there will be no consideration on which value added tax falls to be calculated.

To avoid the problem of bad debts incurred by traders not operating a special retail scheme, an optional system of cash accounting is available. This scheme, confined to traders with annual taxable supplies not exceeding £350,000, enables returns to be made on a cash basis, in substitution for the normal supply basis. Traders using such a scheme will not, of course, include bad debts in the calculation of cash receipts.

Where neither the cash accounting arrangements nor the special retail scheme applies, output tax falls due on the value of the supply and liability is not affected by failure to receive consideration. However, where a debt is more than six months old and is written off in the supplier's books, relief for bad debts will be forthcoming.

## OTHER SPECIAL SCHEMES

In addition to the schemes for retailers, there are several special schemes applied to calculate the amount of value added tax due and which also limit the ability to recover input tax. These schemes apply to the supply of second-hand motor cars, motor cycles, caravans, boats, electronic organs, aircraft and firearms, together with works of art, antiques and collectors' pieces.

## FARMERS

Farmers may elect to apply a special flat rate scheme. This scheme is available to farmers who are not registered traders. Under the scheme a flat-rate addition of 4 per cent may be made on sales, with the amount of the addition being retained by the farmer. Registered traders to whom such a supply is made may treat the 4 per cent addition as recoverable input tax.

# Stamp Duties

Stamp duty is a tax on documents. There are a number of separate duties, under different heads of charge. The Finance Act 1990 included provisions abolishing all the stamp duty charges on transactions in shares from a date to be fixed by Treasury order (which has not yet been made). The Finance Act 1991 removed the stamp duty charges on documents relating to all other types of property except land and buildings, again from a date to be specified (no date yet specified). In the list of documents which follows, those which will be affected by the above provisions are indicated with an asterisk*.

AGREEMENT FOR LEASE, *see* LEASES

AGREEMENT FOR SALE OF PROPERTY

Charged with *ad valorem* duty as if an actual conveyance on sale, with certain exceptions, e.g. agreements for the sale of land, stocks and shares, goods, wares or merchandise, or a ship (*see* S. 59 (1), Stamp Act 1891). If *ad valorem* duty is paid on an agreement in accordance with this provision, the subsequent conveyance or transfer is not chargeable with any *ad valorem* duty and the Commissioners will upon application either place a denoting stamp on such conveyance or transfer or will transfer the *ad valorem* duty thereto. Further, if such an agreement is rescinded, not performed, etc., the Commissioners will return the *ad valorem* duty paid.

AGREEMENT UNDER SEAL

Subject to exemptions, 50p

ASSIGNMENT

By way of sale, *see* CONVEYANCE
By way of gift, *see* VOLUNTARY DISPOSITION

ASSURANCE, *see* INSURANCE POLICIES

*BEARER INSTRUMENT

Inland bearer instrument, i.e. share warrant, stock certificate to bearer or any other instrument to bearer by which stock can be transferred, issued by a company or body formed or established in the UK, 1.5 per cent.

Overseas bearer instrument, i.e. such an instrument issued in Great Britain by a company formed out of the UK, 1.5 per cent.

BILL OF SALE, ABSOLUTE, *see* CONVEYANCE ON SALE

CAPITAL DUTY

This was charged at 1 per cent on every £100 or fraction of £100 of the actual value of assets contributed by the members of a company provided the place of effective management of the company was in Great Britain, or its registered office was in Great Britain but the place of its effective management was outside the EC (Finance Act 1973). The tax was abolished by the Finance Act 1988 in respect of transactions entered into on or after 16 March 1988.

CONTRACT, *see* AGREEMENT

*CONTRACT OR GRANT FOR PAYMENT OF A SUPERANNUATION ANNUITY

For every £10 or fractional part of £10, 5p

CONVEYANCE OR TRANSFER ON SALE
(In the case of a Voluntary Disposition, *see* below)

Conveyance or transfer on sale of any property (except stock or marketable securities), where the conveyance or transfer contains a certificate of value certifying that the transaction does not form part of a larger transaction or a series of transactions in respect of which the aggregate amount or value of the consideration exceeds £60,000, *nil*

Exceeds £60,000 (for every £100 or fraction of £100), £1

The limit was increased from £30,000 to £60,000 for documents executed after 15 March 1993

If the conveyance or transfer on sale does not contain the appropriate statement, duty at the full rate of £1 for every £100 or fraction of £100 will be payable whatever the amount of the consideration.

However, if the consideration does not exceed £500, and the instrument does not contain a certificate of value, there are graduated duties ranging from 50p to £5.

Conveyances to charities are exempt from duty under this head provided the instrument is stamped with a denoting stamp.

CONVEYANCE OR TRANSFER OF ANY OTHER KIND

Fixed duty, 50p

However, under the Stamp Duty (Exempt Instruments) Regulations 1987, instruments which would otherwise fall under this head are exempt from stamp duty provided that the document is duly certified. The certificate must contain a sufficient description of the category into which the instrument falls, and must be signed by the transferor, his solicitor or agent: 'I/We hereby certify that this instrument falls within category . . . in the Schedule to the Stamp Duty (Exempt Instruments) Regulations 1987.'

COVENANT, for original creation and sale of any annuity, *see* CONVEYANCE

DECLARATION OF TRUST

Not being a will or settlement, 50p

DEMISE, *see* LEASES

DUPLICATE OR COUNTERPART

Same duty as original, but not to exceed, 50p

GIFT, *see* VOLUNTARY DISPOSITION

*GUARANTEE

If under seal, 50p

INSURANCE POLICIES, LIFE

Exceeding £50 and not exceeding £1,000, for every £100 or part of £100, 5p

Exceeding £1,000, for every £1,000 or any fractional part of £1,000, 50p

Made after 1 August 1966 for period not exceeding two years, 5p

The Finance Act 1989 abolished this charge for policies made after 31 December 1989.

### Leases (including Agreements for Leases)

Lease or tack for any definite term less than a year of any furnished dwelling-house or apartments where the rent for such term exceeds £500, £1

Of any lands, tenements, etc., in consideration of any rent, according to the following:

| Annual rent not exceeding | †Term not exceeding 7 yrs | 35 yrs | 100 yrs | Exceeding 100 yrs |
|---|---|---|---|---|
| £ | £ p | £ p | £ p | £ p |
| 5 | Nil | 0.10 | 0.60 | 1.20 |
| 10 | Nil | 0.20 | 1.20 | 2.40 |
| 15 | Nil | 0.30 | 1.80 | 3.60 |
| 20 | Nil | 0.40 | 2.40 | 4.80 |
| 25 | Nil | 0.50 | 3.00 | 6.00 |
| 50 | Nil | 1.00 | 6.00 | 12.00 |
| 75 | Nil | 1.50 | 9.00 | 18.00 |
| 100 | Nil | 2.00 | 12.00 | 24.00 |
| 150 | Nil | 3.00 | 18.00 | 36.00 |
| 200 | Nil | 4.00 | 24.00 | 48.00 |
| 250 | Nil | 5.00 | 30.00 | 60.00 |
| 300 | Nil | 6.00 | 36.00 | 72.00 |
| 350 | Nil | 7.00 | 42.00 | 84.00 |
| 400 | Nil | 8.00 | 48.00 | 96.00 |
| 450 | Nil | 9.00 | 54.00 | 108.00 |
| 500 | Nil | 10.00 | 60.00 | 120.00 |
| *Exceeding £500, for every £50 or fraction thereof* | 0.50 | 1.00 | 6.00 | 12.00 |

†If the term is indefinite the same duty is payable as if the term did not exceed seven years.

Where a consideration other than rent is payable, the same rule applies where the consideration does not exceed £60,000 as under conveyance or transfer on sale (except stock or marketable securities), provided that any rent payable does not exceed £600 a year and a certificate of value is included in the conveyance or transfer.

Leases to charities are exempt from duty under this head provided the instrument is stamped with a denoting stamp.

### Mortgages, exempt.

### Receipts for Salaries, Wages and Superannuation, and other like allowances, exempt.

### *Transfer of Stock and Shares by sale, 0.5 per cent

### *Unit Trust Instrument

Any trust instrument of a unit trust scheme, for every £100 or fraction of £100 of the amount or value of the property subject to the trusts created or recorded by the instrument, 25p

By the Finance Act 1989, the transfer of units in certain authorized unit trusts is no longer subject to duty.

### Voluntary Disposition, *inter vivos,* 50p

The Commissioners as a general rule allow deeds, etc., to be stamped after execution.

### Without Penalty, on Payment of Duty only

Deeds and instruments not otherwise excepted, within 30 days of first execution.

NB. Where wholly executed abroad, the period begins to run from the date of arrival in the UK.

### Penalties Enforceable on Stamping in Addition to Duty

Instruments presented after the proper time (subject to special provisions in some cases and subject to the Commissioner's power to mitigate), a penalty equal to the unpaid duty (and interest thereon if duty exceeds £10) plus £10

# Legal Notes

## IMPORTANT

The purpose of these notes is to outline some of the more common parts of the law as they may affect the average person. They are believed to be correct at the time of going to press. However, the law is constantly developing and changing, and it is always best to take expert advice. Anyone who does not have a solicitor already and is unable to find one through the recommendation of a friend, can contact the Citizens' Advice Bureau (whose address can be obtained from the telephone directory or from any post office or town hall). Each CAB has a list of solicitors in the area who deal with particular types of problem. Alternatively, assistance can be sought from The Law Society, 113 Chancery Lane, London WC2A 1PL or The Law Society of Scotland, 26 Drumsheugh Gardens, Edinburgh EH3 7YR.

The legal aid and legal advice and assistance schemes exist to make the help of the trained lawyer available to those who would not otherwise be able to afford legal advice. The best policy is to go to a solicitor without delay; timely advice will set your mind at rest but sitting on your rights can mean that you lose them.

It is not necessary for a dispute to have arisen before advice is sought from a solicitor; the legal advice and assistance scheme enables a solicitor to advise you on your rights, for instance under a tenancy agreement, the estate of a deceased person or in connection with matrimonial and consumer matters, and to write letters or take other steps on your behalf. Entitlement to take advantage of the scheme depends on your means (*see* pages 673, 674, 675) but a solicitor or Citizens' Advice Bureau will be able to advise about entitlement.

## BRITISH CITIZENSHIP

There are three types of citizenship: British Citizenship; Citizenship of the British Dependent Territories; and British Overseas Citizenship.

### Acquisition of citizenship on change of law

The British Nationality Act 1981 which came into force on 1 January 1983 made substantial changes to the law of citizenship, which before that date did not distinguish between the three types of citizenship referred to above. Almost all persons who were then both citizens of the UK and colonies and who had a right of abode in the UK became British citizens when the Act came into force. Most UK and colonies citizens who did not have a right of abode in the UK became Citizens of the British Dependent Territories. This type of citizenship was, broadly speaking, conferred on citizens of the UK and colonies by birth, naturalization or registration in dependent territories. Dependent territories include Hong Kong, Gibraltar, the Falkland Islands, and St Helena and its dependencies. Any UK and colonies citizen who, on 1 January 1983, did not acquire either British or British Dependent Territories Citizenship became a British Overseas Citizen.

### Later acquisition of British citizenship

British citizenship is acquired automatically by those born in the UK (including, for this purpose, the Channel Islands and the Isle of Man) who have a parent who is a British citizen or a parent who is settled in the UK. Certain other categories of children born in the UK also acquire this type of citizenship, i.e. foundlings, those whose parents subsequently settle in the UK, those who live in the UK for ten years from birth and those adopted in the UK.

A person born outside the UK may acquire British citizenship in the following ways:

(a) if one of his/her parents is a British citizen otherwise than by descent, e.g. parent was born in the UK

(b) if one of his/her parents is a British citizen serving the Crown overseas

(c) if the Secretary of State consents to his/her registration while he/she is a minor

(d) if he/she is a Citizen of the British Dependent Territories, a British Overseas Citizen, a British subject or a British Protected Person (these last two are residual categories of people who have not acquired one of the three types of citizenship) and has been lawfully resident in the UK for five years without any time restriction

(e) if he/she is a British Dependent Territories Citizen who is a national of the UK for the purposes of the EC (i.e. a Gibraltarian)

(f) if he/she is naturalized. Naturalization may be applied for only by adults and the Secretary of State has a discretion whether to permit it. The basic requirements are five years' residence, good character, sufficient knowledge of the English or Welsh language, and an intention to reside in the UK permanently. The requirements are somewhat less restrictive in the case of an applicant who is married to a British citizen

### Acquisition of British Dependent Territories and British Overseas Citizenship after the Act

These citizenships are intended for persons connected with certain Commonwealth countries other than the UK. In the case of dependent territories the rules are very similar to those for acquiring British citizenship, except that the connection is with the dependent territory rather than with the UK. British Overseas Citizenship may be acquired by the wife and minor children of a British Overseas Citizen in certain circumstances.

### Retention of nationality by persons born in or who are citizens of the Republic of Ireland

By the Ireland Act 1949, a person who was born before 6 December 1922 in what is now the Republic of Ireland (Eire) and was a British subject immediately before 1 January 1949, is not deemed to have ceased to be a British subject unless either he/she (a) was domiciled in the Irish Free State on 6 December 1922, (b) was on or after 10 April 1935 and before 1 January 1949 permanently resident there, or (c) had before 1 January 1949 been registered as a citizen of Eire under the laws of that country.

In addition, by the British Nationality Act 1948, any citizen of Eire who immediately before 1 January 1949 was also a British subject can retain that status by submitting at any time a claim to the Home Secretary on any of the following grounds:

(a) he/she has been in the service of the United Kingdom government

(b) he/she holds a British passport issued in the United Kingdom or in any colony, protectorate, United Kingdom mandated or trust territory

(c) he/she has associations by way of descent, residence or otherwise with any such place

(d) on complying with similar legislation in any of the 'dominions'

The British Nationality Act 1981 provides that persons who have made a claim may continue to be British subjects. Any citizen of Eire who was a British subject before 1 January 1949 and who has not yet made a claim may do so provided that:

(a) he/she is or has been in Crown service under the government of the United Kingdom

(b) he/she has associations by way of descent, residence or otherwise with the United Kingdom or any dependent territory

*Renunciation and resumption*

A person may cease to be a British citizen by renouncing his/her citizenship (with the consent of the Secretary of State in wartime). The renunciation is required to be registered with the Secretary of State and will be revoked if no new citizenship or nationality is acquired within six months. Once renounced, citizenship may be reacquired if the renunciation was necessary to retain or acquire some other citizenship or nationality. Similar rules as to renunciation and reacquisition apply in the case of British Dependent Territories Citizenships and of renunciation (but not reacquisition) in the case of British Overseas Citizenship.

*Status of aliens*

Property may be held by an alien in the same manner as by a natural-born British subject, but he/she may not hold public office, exercise the franchise or own a British ship or aircraft. The Republic of Ireland Act 1949 declares that the Republic, though not part of HM Dominions, is not a foreign country, and any reference in an Act of Parliament to foreigners, aliens, foreign countries, etc., shall be construed accordingly.

## CONSUMER LAW

### THE SUPPLY OF GOODS AND SERVICES

(1) The Sale of Goods Act 1979 provides protection to the purchaser of goods, by implying certain terms into every contract for the sale of goods. These implied terms are:

(a) A condition that the seller will pass good title to the buyer (unless the seller agrees to transfer only such title as he or his principal has) and warranties that the goods will be free from undisclosed encumbrances, and that the buyer will enjoy quiet possession of the goods

(b) Where there is a sale of goods by description, a condition that the goods will correspond with that description, and where the sale is by sample and description, a condition that the bulk of the goods shall correspond with both sample and description

(c) Where the seller sells goods in the course of a business, a condition that the goods will be of merchantable quality, unless before the contract is made, the buyer has examined the goods and ought to have noticed the defect, bearing in mind the purchaser's knowledge of the goods and the extent of the examination, or unless the seller has specifically drawn the attention of the buyer to the defect. Merchantable quality means fit for the purpose for which goods of the kind are commonly bought, taking into account any description applied to them, the price and other relevant circumstances

(d) A condition that where the seller sells goods in the course of a business, the goods are reasonably fit for any purpose made known to the seller by the buyer, unless the buyer does not rely on the seller's skill and judgment, or it would be unreasonable for him to do so

(e) Where there is a sale of goods by sample, conditions that the bulk of the goods shall correspond with the sample in quality, that the buyer will have a reasonable opportunity of comparing the bulk with the sample, and that the goods are free from any defect rendering them unmerchantable, which would not be apparent from the sample

For these purposes, the broad difference between a condition and a warranty is that the remedy for a breach of an implied condition may enable the buyer to reject the goods and recover damages if he has suffered loss, whereas the remedy for a breach of warranty will only enable the buyer to recover damages.

It is possible for a seller to exclude some of the above terms from a contract, subject to restrictions imposed by the Unfair Contract Terms Act 1977 as given below. These restrictions give more protection where the buyer 'deals as consumer'. In a contract of sale of goods, a buyer 'deals as consumer' where there is a sale by a seller in the course of a business, where the goods are of a type ordinarily bought for private use or consumption, and where the goods are sold to a person who does not buy or hold himself out as buying them in the course of a business. A buyer in a sale by auction or competitive tender never 'deals as consumer'.

The 1977 Act prohibits the exclusion of the implied terms given in (b) to (e) above, where the buyer 'deals as consumer'. In sales where the buyer does not 'deal as consumer', terms purporting to exclude these implied terms may be relied upon only to the extent that it would be reasonable to allow reliance. The Act provides guidelines for determining whether it would be reasonable to allow reliance. The implied terms in (a) above cannot be excluded whether the buyer 'deals as consumer' or not.

(2) Similar terms to those implied in contracts of sale of goods are implied into contracts of hire-purchase by the Supply of Goods (Implied Terms) Act 1973, and the 1977 Act limits the exclusion of these implied terms in a similar manner.

(3) Under the Supply of Goods and Services Act 1982, terms similar to those in the Sale of Goods Act relating to quiet possession, compliance with description, merchantable quality, fitness for purpose and correspondence with sample are implied into other types of contract under which ownership of goods passes (e.g. a contract for 'work and materials' such as a supply of new parts during the servicing of a motor car) and also into contracts for the hire of goods. In the case of contracts under which ownership of goods is to pass, there is also an implied condition as to title.

The 1977 Act limits the exclusion of these implied terms in a similar manner to the implied terms in the Sale of Goods Act.

(4) The Supply of Goods and Services Act 1982 also implies into a contract for the supply of services terms that the supplier will use reasonable care and skill, carry out the service within a reasonable time (unless the time is agreed) and make a reasonable charge (unless the charge is agreed).

(5) The Trade Descriptions Act 1968 provides that it is a criminal offence for a trader or businessman to apply a false trade description to any goods, or to supply or offer to supply any goods to which a false trade description has been applied. A trade description includes a description as to quantity, size, method, place and date of manufacture, other history, composition, other physical characteristics, fitness for purpose, behaviour or accuracy, testing or approval. It is also an

offence to give a false indication as to the price of goods. Prosecutions are brought by trading standards inspectors.

(6) The Fair Trading Act 1973 is also designed to protect the consumer. It provides for the appointment of a Director-General of Fair Trading, whose duties include keeping under review commercial activities in the UK relating to the supply of goods or services to consumers, and to collect information to discover practices that may adversely affect the economic interests of the consumer. He may refer certain consumer trade practices to the Consumer Protection Advisory Committee, or of his own initiative take proceedings against firms that are trading unfairly. He may also publish information and advice to consumers. Examples of practices which have been prohibited by virtue of references made under this Act include the use of certain void exclusion clauses in contracts for the sale of goods and hire-purchase, and advertisements by traders appearing to sell as private persons.

(7) The Consumer Protection Act 1987 makes the producer of a product liable for any damage exceeding £275 caused by a defect in that product, subject to certain defences.

(8) The Consumer Protection (Cancellation of Contracts Concluded Away from Business Premises) Regulations 1987 allow consumers a seven-day period in which to cancel most contracts for supply of goods or services exceeding £35 in cost, where these contracts have been made following an unsolicited visit to the consumer's home or workplace.

*Scotland*

The Sale of Goods Act 1979, a consolidating Act, applies with some modification to Scotland. For example, it is not necessary in Scotland to distinguish between the words condition and warranty. The remedies of the buyer in both cases are the same, i.e. the buyer can either within a reasonable time reject the goods and treat the contract as repudiated, or retain the goods and treat the failure to perform such material part as a breach which may give rise to a claim for compensation or damages. The Trade Descriptions Act 1968 applies with minor modifications to Scotland. The Supply of Goods and Services Act 1982 does not extend to Scotland.

CONSUMER CREDIT

The Consumer Credit Act 1974 provides a system for the protection of the consumer, of licensing and control of all matters relating to the provision of credit or to the supply of goods on hire or hire-purchase, administered by the Director-General of Fair Trading. A licence is required to carry on a consumer credit or consumer hire business, or to deal in credit brokerage, debt adjusting, counselling or collecting, for which group licences are available. Any 'fit' person may apply to the Director-General of Fair Trading for a licence, which is normally renewable after ten years. A licence is not necessary if such types of business are only transacted 'occasionally' or if exempt agreements only are involved.

For the Act's provisions to apply, the agreement must be 'regulated', i.e. be to individuals or partnerships only; must not be exempt, e.g. certain loans by local authorities or building societies; and the total credit must not exceed £15,000. The terms of a regulated agreement can be varied by the creditor, but only if the agreement gives him the right to do so and the debtor receives notice in the prescribed form.

To be enforceable the agreement must be properly executed, and the specified information must be given during the antecedent negotiations for the contract. These are conducted by the creditor, credit broker or supplier (these being the creditor's agents) and begin when the parties first begin discussions.

The agreement must state certain information such as the amount of credit, the annual percentage rate of interest, and the amount and timing of repayments.

An agreement is cancellable under the Act if oral representations were made in the debtor's presence during antecedent negotiations and the debtor signed the agreement other than at the creditor's (or credit-broker's or negotiator's) place of business. Time for cancellation expires five clear days after the debtor receives a second copy of the agreement. The agreement must inform the debtor of his right to cancel and how to cancel.

Where there are arrangements or connections between the creditor and supplier, the former is generally liable for any misrepresentation or breach of contract by the latter, and will thus be liable to indemnify the debtor.

If the debtor is in arrears or is otherwise in breach of the agreement, the creditor may not enforce the agreement, e.g. by repossessing goods, without serving a default notice on the debtor. This notice will give the debtor a chance to remedy the default. Even if the default is not remedied by the debtor, if the agreement is a hire-purchase or conditional sale agreement, the creditor cannot repossess the goods without an order of the court if the debtor has paid one-third of the total price of the goods.

Where the agreement requires the debtor to make grossly exorbitant payments or is contrary to the ordinary principles of fair dealing, the court can reopen it either at the debtor's request or during enforcement proceedings and (*inter alia*) alter the terms of the contract or set aside any obligations it imposes so as to do justice between the parties. Whether an agreement is such an extortionate credit bargain is decided by reference (*inter alia*) to interest rates prevailing at the date of agreement, the pressure for finance the debtor was under, etc.

If a credit reference agency was used to check the debtor's financial standing the creditor must give the agency's name to the debtor, who is entitled to see the agency's file on him/her on payment of a fee of £1.

*Scotland*

The Consumer Credit Act also extends to Scotland and goes far in assimilating the Scots law on this topic with English law. The Supply of Goods (Implied Terms) Act 1973 also applies to Scotland. Parts II and III only of the Unfair Contract Terms Act 1977 apply to Scotland.

RECEIPTS

The law on receipts in Scotland is governed by the Prescription and Limitations (Scotland) Act 1973, which for this purpose came into force on 25 July 1976. Receipts need only be kept for a period of five years and if a creditor does not make a relevant claim within that period no action can be raised.

---

# THE CROWN – PROCEEDINGS AGAINST

---

Before 1947, proceedings against the Crown were generally possible only by a procedure known as a petition of right, which placed the litigant at a considerable disadvantage. However, by the Crown Proceedings Act 1947, which came into operation on 1 January 1948, the Crown, in its public capacity, is largely placed in the same position as a subject, although some procedural disadvantages remain, e.g. the enforcement of judgments against the Crown.

## Scotland

*Scotland*

The 1947 Act as amended extends to Scotland and has the effect of bringing the practice of the two countries as closely together as the different legal systems will permit. While formerly actions against the Crown, when permissible, were confined to the Court of Session, proceedings may now be brought in the Sheriff Court.

The Act lays down that arrestment of money in the hands of the Crown or of a government department is competent in any case where arrestment in the hands of a subject would have been competent, but an exception is made in respect of National Savings Bank deposits. Section 2 (1) of the Law Reform (Miscellaneous Provisions) (Scotland) Act 1966 removes the privilege whereby the wages of Crown servants, other than serving members of the armed forces, are exempt from arrestment in execution.

---

# DEATHS

---

## REGISTRATION

REGISTRATION
(For Certificates, *see* page 664)

*England and Wales*

When a death takes place, information of it must be given in person to the local Registrar of Births and Deaths, and the register signed in his/her presence by a relative of the deceased present at the death or in attendance during the last illness; or by some other relative of the deceased; in default of any relatives by (a) a person present at the death, or the occupier of the house in which the death happened, or (b) an inmate of the house, or (c) the person arranging the disposal of the body.

The registration must be made within five days of the death, or within the same time written notice of the death must be sent to the Registrar. If the deceased was attended during his/her last illness by a registered medical practitioner, a certificate of cause of death must be sent by the doctor to the Registrar. The doctor must give to the informant of the death a written notice of the signing of the certificate, which must be delivered to the Registrar.

If the death is not registered within five days (or 14 days if written notice of the occurrence of the death is sent to him/her), the Registrar may require any one of the above-mentioned persons to attend to register at a stated time and place. Failure to comply involves a penalty. The registration of a death is free of charge. After 12 months no death can be registered without the Registrar-General's consent.

Whenever the death of a child is registered, particulars of the name and occupation of the mother are to be entered in the register.

It is essential that a certificate for disposal should be obtained from the Registrar before the funeral or cremation. No fee is chargeable for this certificate. A body must not be disposed of until either the Registrar has given a certificate to the effect that he/she has registered or received notice of the death, or until the Coroner has made a disposal order.

A person disposing of a body must within 96 hours deliver to the Registrar a notification as to the date, place, and means of the disposal of the body.

*Still births: see* page 663.

*Death at sea:* the master of a British ship must record any death on board and send particulars to the Registrar-General of Shipping.

*Death abroad:* consular officers are authorized to register deaths of British subjects occurring abroad. Certificates are obtainable at the Registrar-General's Office, London. If the deceased was of Scottish domicile, particulars are sent to the Registrar-General for Scotland.

With regard to the registration of deaths of members of the armed forces and deaths occurring on HM ships and aircraft, *see* the Registration of Births, etc. Act 1957.

*Scotland*

The Registration of Births, Deaths and Marriages (Scotland) Act 1965 supersedes provisions in former Acts.

Personal notification within eight days must be given to the Registrar of either the registration district in which the death took place, or any registration district in which the deceased was ordinarily resident immediately before his/her death. When a body is found and the place of death is not known, notification must be given to the Registrar of either the registration district in which the body was found or any other registration district appropriate by virtue of the preceding sentence. When a person dies (in or out of Scotland) in a ship, aircraft or land vehicle during a journey and the body is conveyed therein to any place in Scotland the death shall, unless the Registrar-General otherwise directs, be deemed to have occurred at that place.

The register must be signed in the presence of the Registrar by one of the following: (a) any relative of the deceased; (b) any person present at the death; (c) the deceased's executor or other legal representative; (d) the occupier, at the time of the death, of the premises where the death took place; (e) if these fail, any other person having knowledge of the particulars to be registered. Failure to comply involves a penalty.

The medical practitioner who attended the deceased during the last illness must sign a certificate of the cause of death within seven days. If there is no such medical practitioner, any medical practitioner who is able to do so may sign the certificate. At the time of registering the death the Registrar shall, without charge, give the informant a certificate of registration, and the person to whom the certificate is given must hand it to the undertaker before cremation. A body may, however, be interred before death is registered, in which case the undertaker must deliver a certificate of burial to the Registrar within three days.

## BURIAL

BURIAL

The duty of burial is placed on the deceased person's executors (if any appointed); it is also a recognized obligation of the parent of a child, and of a householder where the body lies. Funeral expenses of a reasonable amount will be repayable out of the deceased's estate in priority to any other claims. Directions as to place and mode of burial are frequently contained in the deceased's will, in some memorandum placed with private papers, or may have been communicated verbally to a relative. Consequently, steps should immediately be taken to ascertain the deceased's wishes from the above sources. If the wishes are considered objectionable, they are not necessarily enforceable; legal advice should be taken. A person may legally leave directions for the anatomical examination of his/her body. As to the place of burial, the parish churchyard is the normal burying place for parishioners or any person dying in the parish, but nowadays this will apply only in villages and smaller towns. In populous districts cemeteries and crematoria have been established, either by the local council or a private company, and burials will take place there in accordance with the regulations. For an exclusive right to a burial space in the churchyard, a faculty is required from the Ecclesiastical Court. Poor persons may be buried at the public expense by the local authority. As to the necessity for obtaining a Registrar's certificate or authority from the Coroner for disposal, *see* above.

## CREMATION

Under the Cremation Acts 1902 and 1952, regulations are made by the Home Secretary dealing fully with the cremation of a body, disposal of ashes, etc., and containing numerous safeguards.

If cremation is desired it is advisable for instructions to be left in writing to that effect. However, in Scotland, even if the deceased wished his/her body to be cremated or anatomically dissected, relatives can still veto his/her wishes.

To arrange for cremation, the executor or near relative should instruct the undertaker to that effect and obtain from him the forms required by statute.

## INTESTACY

As regards deaths on or after 15 March 1977, the position is governed by the Administration of Estates Act 1925, as amended by the Intestates' Estates Act 1952, the Family Provision Act 1966 and Orders made thereunder. If the intestate leaves a spouse and issue, the spouse takes:
(a) the 'personal chattels'
(b) £125,000 with interest at 6 per cent from death until payment
(c) a life interest in half of the rest of the estate
This life interest can be capitalized at the option of the spouse. Personal chattels are articles of household use or ornament (including motor cars), not used for business purposes. The rest of the estate goes to the issue.

If the intestate leaves a spouse and no issue, but leaves a parent or brother or sister of the whole blood or issue of such brothers and sisters the spouse takes
(a) the 'personal chattels'
(b) £200,000 with interest at 6 per cent from death until payment
(c) half of the rest of the estate absolutely
The other half of the rest of the estate goes to the parents, equally if more than one, or, if none, to the brothers and sisters of the whole blood or issue of such brothers and sisters.

If the intestate leaves a spouse, but no issue, no parents and no brothers or sisters of the whole blood or their issue, the spouse takes the whole estate absolutely.

If resident therein at the intestate's death, the surviving spouse may generally require the personal representatives to appropriate the interest of the intestate in the matrimonial home in or towards satisfaction of any absolute interest of the spouse, including the capitalized value of a life interest. In certain cases, leave of court is required. On a partial intestacy any benefit (other than personal chattels specifically bequeathed) received by the surviving spouse under the will must be brought into account against the statutory legacy of £125,000 or £200,000, as the case may be. If there is no surviving spouse, the estate is distributed among those who survive the intestate in the following order (those entitled under earlier numbers taking to the exclusion of those entitled under later numbers):
(1) children
(2) father or mother (equally, if both alive)
(3) brothers and sisters of the whole blood
(4) brothers and sisters of the half blood
(5) grandparents (equally, if more than one alive)
(6) uncles and aunts of the whole blood
(7) uncles and aunts of the half blood
(8) the Crown, Duchy of Lancaster or the Duke of Cornwall
In cases (1), (3), (4), (6) and (7), the persons entitled lose their interests unless they or their issue not only survive the intestate, but also attain eighteen or marry under that age,

their shares going to the persons (if any) within the same group who do attain eighteen or marry. Moreover, in the same cases, succession is not per capita, but *per stirpes*, i.e. by stocks or families. Thus, if the intestate leaves one child and two grandchildren, being the children of a child of the intestate who predeceased the intestate, the two grandchildren represent their deceased parent and take between them one-half of the issue's share, the remaining half going to the surviving child. Similarly, nephews and nieces represent a deceased brother, and so on.

When the deceased died partially intestate (i.e. leaving a will which disposed of only part of his/her property), the above rules apply to the intestate part.

Children must bring into account (hotchpot) any substantial advances received from the intestate during his/her lifetime before claiming any further share under the intestacy. Special hotchpot provisions apply to partial intestacy.

In respect of deaths occurring on or after 4 April 1988, Section 18 of the Family Law Reform Act 1987 provides that references to any relationship between two persons shall, unless the contrary intention appears, be construed without regard to whether or not the father and mother of either of them, or the father and mother of any person through whom the relationship is deduced, have or had been married to each other at any time.

In respect of deaths after March 1976 the provisions of the Inheritance (Provision for Family and Dependants) Act 1975 may allow other persons to claim provision out of the estate. *See* page 659.

For personal application for letters of administration, *see* page 660.

### Scotland

The Succession (Scotland) Act 1964, provides that the whole estate of any person dying intestate shall devolve without distinction between heritable and moveable property. By that Act the surviving spouse of an intestate may, as a prior right (in addition to legal rights, *see* below), claim the matrimonial home to a maximum of £110,000, or a choice of one matrimonial home if more than one (or in certain circumstances the value thereof), with its furniture and plenishings not exceeding £20,000 in value, plus the sum of £30,000 if the deceased left issue or, if no issue, the sum of £50,000. These figures have applied since 26 November 1993 and may be increased from time to time by order of the Secretary of State.

The fact that a person was born illegitimate no longer has any effect in their rights of succession as against a legitimate child, by virtue of the Law Reform (Parent and Child) (Scotland) Act 1986.

Legal rights, referred to above, are:
*Jus relicti(ae)* – the right of a surviving spouse to one half of the deceased's net moveable estate after satisfaction of prior rights if there are no surviving children, or to one-third if there are any surviving children
*Legitim* – the right of surviving children to one-half of the net moveable estate of deceased parents if no surviving spouse, or one-third of the net moveable estate of deceased parents after satisfaction of prior rights where there is a surviving spouse.
There are no legal rights in heritage.
In general, the lines of succession are:
(1) descendants
(2) collaterals
(3) ascendants and their collaterals, and so on in the ascending scale
The Crown is *ultimus haeres*
The right of representation, i.e. the right of the issue of a person who would have succeeded if he/she had survived the

intestate, is open to any line of succession where previously it was limited to apply only when there were next of kin or the issue of predeceasing next of kin. The surviving mother of an intestate now has equal rights of succession with the surviving father, where formerly these were restricted. The intestate's maternal relations, who prior to the Act had no rights of succession, are now on an equal footing with the paternal relations. Where the intestate is survived only by parents and by brothers and sisters (collaterals), half of the estate is taken by the parents and the other half by the brothers and sisters, those of the whole blood being preferred to those of the half blood. Where, however, succession opens to collaterals (which expression can include the brothers and sisters of an ancestor of the intestate) of the half blood, they shall rank equally amongst themselves, whether related to the intestate (or his/her ancestor) through their father or their mother.

## WILLS

The following notes and those on intestacy must be read subject to the provisions of the Inheritance (Provision for Family and Dependants) Act 1975, which can affect the estate of anyone dying domiciled in England and Wales after March 1976. Very broadly, a spouse, former spouse who has not remarried, a child of the deceased or one treated by the deceased as a child of his/her family, or any person maintained by him/her at his/her death may apply to the Court under the Act. If the Court thinks that the will or the law of intestacy or both do not make reasonable provision for the applicant, it may order payment out of the net estate of maintenance or a lump sum. It may also order the transfer of property or vary certain trusts, and the powers can affect property disposed of by the deceased in his/her lifetime intending to defeat the Act. It is up to the applicant to take the initiative, and the application must generally be made within six months of the grant of probate or letters of administration.

### Making a Will

Every person over the age of 18 should make a will. However small the estate, the rules of intestacy (*see* above) may not reflect a person's wishes as to his/her property. In any case a will can do more than just deal with property. It can in particular appoint executors, give directions as to the disposal of the body and appoint guardians to take care of children in the event of the parents' death. For the wealthier person an appropriately drawn will can operate to reduce the burden of inheritance tax.

It is considered desirable for a will to be properly drawn up by a solicitor. Although normally the making of a will is not one of the services which can be provided under the legal advice and assistance scheme, it can be provided for certain special categories of person such as the aged and infirm (*see* page 674).

In no circumstances should one person prepare a will for another person where the former is to take any benefit under it. This can easily lead to a suggestion of undue influence, which may cause the will to be held bad.

Assuming a lawyer is not employed, a person having resolved to make a will must remember that it is only after a person is dead, and cannot explain his/her meaning, that his/her will can be open to dispute. It is the more necessary, therefore, to express what is meant in language of the utmost clarity, avoiding the use of any word or expression that admits of another meaning than the one intended. Avoid the use of legal terms, such as heirs and issue, when the same thing may be expressed in plain language. If in writing the will a mistake is made, it is better to rewrite the whole. Before

a will is executed (*see* page 660), an alteration may be made by striking through the words with a pen, but opposite to such alteration the testator and witnesses should write their names or place their initials. Never scratch out a word with a knife or other instrument; no alteration of any kind whatever must be made after the will is executed. If the testator afterwards wishes to change the disposition of his/her estate, it is best to make a new will, revoking the old one. The use of codicils should be left to a lawyer.

A will should be written in ink and very legibly, on a single sheet of paper. Although forms of wills must vary to suit different cases, the following forms may be found useful to those who, in cases of emergency, are called upon to draw up wills, either for themselves or others. Nothing more complicated should be attempted. The forms should be studied in conjunction with the following notes:

> This is the last will and testament of me [*Thomas Smith*] of [*Vine Cottage, Silver Street, Reading, Berks.*] which I make this [*thirteenth*] day of [*February* 1995] and whereby I revoke all previous wills and testamentary dispositions.
>
> 1. I hereby appoint [*John Green of _____ and Richard Brown of _____*] to be the executor(s) of this my will.
>
> 2. I give all my property real and personal to [*my wife Mary* or *my sons Raymond and David equally* or as the case may be].
>
> Signed by the testator in the presence of us both present at the same time who, at his request, in his presence and in the presence of each other have hereunto set our names as witnesses.
>
> Thomas Smith
> *Signature of Testator;*
>
> William Jones (*signed*)
> of Green Gables, South Street, Reading, tailor.
>
> Henry Morgan (*signed*)
> of 16 North Street, Reading, butcher.

Should it be desired to give legacies and/or gifts of specific property, instead of giving the whole estate to one or more persons, the form above should be used with the substitution for clause 2 of the following clauses:

> 2. I give to _____ of _____ the sum of £_____ and to _____ of _____ the sum of £_____ and to _____ of _____ all my books [*or as the case may require*].
>
> 3. All the residue of my property real and personal I give to _____ of _____.

### Terms

Real property includes freehold land and houses, while personal property includes debts due, arrears of rents, money, leasehold property, house furniture, goods, assurance policies, stocks and shares in companies, and the like. The words 'my money', apart from the context, will normally only include actual real money. The expression 'goods and chattels' should not be used. In giving particular property, ordinary language is sufficient, e.g. my house, Vine Cottage, Silver Street, Reading, Berks. Such specific gifts fail if not owned by the testator at his/her death.

### Residuary legatees

It is well in all cases where legacies or specific gifts are made, to leave to some person or persons 'the residue of my property', although it may be thought that the whole of the property has been disposed of in legacies, etc., already mentioned in the will. It should be remembered that a will operates on property owned at the time of death.

*Execution of a will, and witnesses*

The testator should sign his/her name at the foot or end of the will, in the presence of two witnesses, who will immediately afterwards sign their names in the testator's and in each other's presence. A person who has been left any gift or share of residue in the will, or whose wife or husband has been left such a gift, should not be an attesting witness. Their attestation would be good, but they would forfeit the gift. It is better that a person named as executor should not be a witness. Husband and wife may both be witnesses, provided neither is a legatee. If a solicitor be appointed executor, it is lawful to direct that his/her ordinary fees and charges shall be paid; but in this case the solicitor (as an interested party) must not be a witness to the will.

It is desirable that the witnesses should be fully described, as they may possibly be wanted at some future time. If the testator be too ill to sign, even by a mark, another person may sign the testator's name to the will for him/her, in his/her presence and by his/her direction, and in this case it should be shown that the testator knew the contents of the document. The attestation clause should therefore be worded:

Signed by Thomas Brown, by the direction and in the presence of the testator, Thomas Smith, in the joint presence of us, who thereupon signed our names in his presence and in the presence of each other, the will having been first read over to the testator, who appeared fully to understand the same.

Where there is any suspicion that the testator is not, by reason of age or infirmity, fully in command of his/her faculties it is desirable to ask his/her doctor to act as a witness (*see* Testamentary capacity below).

A blind person may make a will in braille. If the testator is blind the will should be read aloud to him/her in the presence of the witnesses, and the fact mentioned in the attestation clause. A blind person cannot witness a will.

If by inadvertence the testator should have signed his/her will without the witnesses being present, then the attestation should be: 'The testator acknowledged his signature already made as his signature to his last will and testament, in the joint presence,' etc. Any omission in the observance of these details may invalidate the will. The stringency of the law as to signature and witnessing of a will is only relaxed in favour of soldiers, sailors and airmen in certain circumstances.

*Executors*

It is usual to appoint two executors, although one is sufficient; any number up to and including four may be appointed. The name and address of each executor should be given in full. An executor may be a legatee. Thus a child of full age or wife to whom the whole or a portion of the estate is left may be appointed sole executor, or one of two executors. The addresses of the executors are not essential, but it is desirable here as elsewhere, to avoid ambiguity or vagueness.

*Lapsed legacies*

If a legatee dies in the lifetime of the testator, the legacy generally lapses and falls into the residue. Where a residuary legatee predeceases the testator, his/her share of the residuary estate will not generally pass to the other residuary legatees, but will pass to the persons entitled on the deceased's intestacy. In all such cases it is desirable to make a new will.

An important exception to the general rule of lapse stated above is contained in the Administration of Justice Act 1982, where there is a gift to a child or remoter issue of the testator who dies before the testator leaving issue who survive the testator. In such a case the gift will pass to the issue of the deceased child.

*Testamentary capacity*

A person under the age of 18 cannot make a will (except for soldiers, sailors and airmen in exceptional circumstances).

So far as mental capacity is concerned the testator must be able to understand and appreciate the nature and effect of making a will, the property of which he/she can dispose and the claims to which he/she ought to give effect. If a person is not mentally able to make a will, provision exists (under the Mental Health Act 1983) for the Court to do this for him/her.

REVOCATION

A later will revokes an earlier will if it expressly says so, or is completely inconsistent with it. Otherwise the earlier one is revoked only in so far as it is inconsistent with the later one. A will may also be revoked by burning, tearing or otherwise destroying the will with the intention of revoking it. Such destruction must either be by the testator or by some other person in the testator's presence and at his/her direction. It is not sufficient to obliterate the will with a pen. Marriage in every case acts as the revocation of a will, except that under the Administration of Justice Act 1982, there is a provision to the effect that if it appears from a will that at the time it was made the testator was expecting to be married to a particular person and that he/she intended that the will (or a disposition in the will) should not be revoked by the marriage to that person, the will will not be revoked by marriage to that person. The Act also provides that where after a testator has made a will the testator's marriage is terminated by a decree of divorce or nullity, any gift to a spouse shall lapse and any appointment of the spouse as executor shall be omitted from the will unless the will shows a contrary intention.

PROBATE OR LETTERS OF ADMINISTRATION

Application for probate or for letters of administration may be made in person at the Personal Application Department of the Principal Registry of the Family Division, a district probate registry or sub-registry, or a probate office, by the executors or persons entitled to a grant of probate. Applicants should bring (a) the will, if any; (b) a certificate of death; (c) particulars of all property and assets left by the deceased; and (d) a list of debts and funeral expenses.

Intending applicants, before attending at a registry or probate office, should write or telephone to the nearest probate registry or sub-registry for the necessary forms. Postal or telephone applications cannot be dealt with at the local probate offices, which are part-time only.

Certain property can be disposed of on death without a grant of probate or administration, or in pursuance of a nomination made by the deceased, provided the amount involved does not exceed £5,000. (See The Administration of Estates (Small Payments) Act 1965.)

WHERE TO FIND A PROVED WILL

A will proved since 1858 must have been proved either at the Principal Registry at Somerset House, or a district registry. In the former case the original will itself is preserved at Somerset House, the copy of which probate has been granted is in the hands of the executors who proved the will, and another copy for Parliament is bound up in a folio volume of wills made by testators of that initial and date. The indices to these volumes may be examined at Somerset House and a copy of any will read. In the latter case, the original will proved in the district registry is kept there and may be seen or a copy obtained, but a copy is sent to and filed at Somerset House, where also it may be seen. A general index of grants, both probates and administrations, is prepared and printed annually in lexicographical form, and may be seen at either the Principal Registry or a district registry. This index is usually ready by about October of the following year.

## Recent deaths

A system introduced in 1975 enables a person to discover when a grant of probate or letters of administration is made which may be invaluable to a creditor of the deceased or applicant under the Inheritance (Provision for Family and Dependants) Act 1975 (*see* page 659). A standing search may be made by sending a request in the form set out below to the Record Keeper at the Principal Registry of the Family Division with a small fee. The searcher will receive particulars of any grant made in the previous 12 months or the following six months, including names and addresses of the executors or administrators and the registry in which the grant was made.

## Form of search

In the High Court of Justice
Family Division
The Principal Registry (Probate)
I/We apply for the entry of a standing search so that there shall be sent to me/us an office copy of every grant of representation in England and Wales in the estate of:
Full name of deceased:
Alternative or alias name
Full address
Exact date of death

Which either has issued not more than twelve months before the entry of this application or issues within six months hereafter
Signed _____ (full address).

## SCOTLAND

A domiciled Scotsman, unlike a domiciled Englishman, cannot in certain circumstances dispose effectively of the entirety of his estate. If he leaves a widow and children, the widow is entitled to a one-third share in the whole of the moveable estate (her *jus relictae*), and the children are entitled to another one-third share equally between them (their *legitim*). If he leaves a widow but no children, or children but no widow, the *jus relictae* or *legitim* is increased to a one-half share of the net moveable estate. The remaining portion is known as the dead's part. A surviving husband and children have comparable rights (*jus relicti* and *legitim*) in the wife's estate. The dead's part is the only portion of which the testator can freely dispose. Legacies and bequests are payable only out of the dead's part. All debts are payable out of the whole estate before any division.

Pupils, i.e. a girl up to the age of 12 or a boy up to the age of 14, cannot make wills. Formerly a minor could dispose only of moveables but since the passing of the Succession (Scotland) Act 1964, a minor has a like capacity to test on heritable property.

A will must be in writing and may be typewritten or even in pencil. A will may be either:
(a) holograph, i.e. written, dated and subscribed by the testator himself/herself, in which case no witnesses are necessary; a printed form filled up by the testator or a typewritten document is not necessarily a holograph but may become so if the testator writes, in hand, at the foot of the form or document the words 'adopted as holograph' followed by his/her signature and the date. Words written on erasure or marginal additions or interlineations in holograph writings, if proved to be in the handwriting of the maker of the deed, are valid
(b) attested, i.e. signed in presence of two witnesses. It is not necessary that these witnesses should sign in the presence

of one another, or even that they should see the testator signing so long as the testator acknowledges his/her signature to the witnesses

The Conveyancing and Feudal Reform (Scotland) Act 1970, whilst altering generally the rules for the subscription of deeds, specifically (s. 44 (2)) makes no change in the rules applying to wills, which must still be signed by the testator on every page. If the testator cannot write or is blind, the will may be authenticated by a law agent, notary public or justice of the peace and two witnesses. It is better that the will is not witnessed by a beneficiary thereunder, although this circumstance will not invalidate the attestation of the will or (as it would in England) the gift. A parish minister may act as a notary for the purpose of subscribing a will in his own parish.

Wills may be registered in the Books of the Sheriffdom in which the deceased died domiciled, or in the Books of Council and Session at HM General Register House, Edinburgh. The original deed may be inspected on payment of a small fee and a certified official copy may be obtained. A Scottish will is not revoked by the subsequent marriage of the testator. The subsequent birth of a child for whom no testamentary provision has been made may revoke a will. A will may be revoked by a subsequent will, either expressly or by implication; but in so far as the two can be read together, both wills have effect. If a subsequent will is revoked, the earlier will is revived.

### CONFIRMATION

Confirmation, the Scottish equivalent of probate, is obtained in the sheriff court of the sheriffdom in which the deceased was domiciled at the date of his/her death or, where the deceased had no fixed domicile or died abroad, in the Commissariat of Edinburgh. Executors are either 'nominate' or 'dative'. An executor nominate is one nominated by the deceased in the will or, where such person has predeceased the testator, by the residuary beneficiary. An executor dative is one appointed by the court in the case of intestacy or where the deceased had failed to name an executor in the will and there is no residuary beneficiary. In the former case the deceased's next-of-kin are all entitled to be declared executors dative. An inventory of the deceased's estate and a schedule of debts, together with an affidavit, must first be given up. In estates under £17,000 gross, confirmation is obtained under a simplified procedure at reduced fees.

### PRESUMPTION OF SURVIVORSHIP

The Succession (Scotland) Act 1964 provides, by s. 31, that where two persons die in circumstances indicating that they died simultaneously or if it is uncertain which was the survivor, the younger will be deemed to have survived the elder unless the elder person left testamentary provision in favour of the younger, whom failing in favour of a third person, the younger person having died intestate (partially or wholly); but if the persons so dying were husband and wife, neither shall be presumed to have survived the other.

## EMPLOYMENT

### WAGES AND SICK PAY

Under the Wages Act 1986, subject to certain exceptions, employers may not make deductions from an employee's wages unless authorized by statute or contract or with the employee's prior written consent. There is an upper limit of one-tenth of gross pay for deductions from retail workers' wages on account of cash or stock shortages.

Under the Social Security and Housing Benefits Act 1982 as amended, an employee absent from work because of illness or injury is entitled to receive Statutory Sick Pay (SSP) from the employer for a maximum period of 28 weeks in any period of three years. No payment is made for the first three days of any period of illness.

Under the Statutory Sick Pay Act 1994, employers no longer receive any state reimbursement of SSP (except for small employers whose contributions do not exceed £20,000 in any year). The 1994 Act also provides that women employees between the ages of 60 and 65 are now entitled to SSP.

The Equal Pay Act 1970, which extends to Scotland, prevents discrimination as regards terms and conditions of employment between men and women employed on like work in the same employment.

### PARTICULARS OF TERMS OF EMPLOYMENT

Under the Employment Protection (Consolidation) Act 1978 (as amended), an employer must give each employee working more than eight hours a week and based in Great Britain, within two months of the beginning of the employment a written statement containing the following particulars of the contract between them:

(a) the date when the employment began (when continuous employment began if previous work counts as continuous with this job)
(b) the rate of remuneration (or how it is calculated)
(c) the intervals at which wages are paid
(d) the hours of work
(e) the employee's entitlement to holidays (including public holidays) and holiday pay
(f) the title of the employee's job
(g) the place or places of work
(h) terms relating to sickness, injury and sick pay
(i) details of any pension scheme
(j) the length of notice which the employee should give and receive in order to terminate the contract, or when it is to end if it is a fixed term contract.
(k) particulars of any collective agreement which directly affects the terms of employment
(l) if the employee is required to work outside the UK for more than one month, the period of such work and the currency in which payment is made.

In addition, the written particulars must specify any disciplinary rules; and also must identify the person to whom the employee can apply if dissatisfied with any disciplinary decision or to seek redress of any grievance, and what further steps may ensue.

### TERMINATION OF EMPLOYMENT

An employee may be dismissed without notice if guilty of gross breach of contract, such as disobedience to a lawful order or dishonesty. The employee is then entitled only to wages accrued due at the date of dismissal.

In other cases, the employee is entitled to reasonable notice which, under the Employment Protection (Consolidation) Act 1978, must not be less than one week if he/she has been continuously employed for four weeks but less than two years; after two years it is two weeks' notice, increasing by one week's notice for each further full year worked up to a maximum of 12 weeks' notice after 12 years' service.

An employer who wrongfully dismisses an employee (i.e. with less than the length of notice to which he/she is entitled) is generally liable to pay wages for the period of proper notice.

An employee who has a fixed term contract has no claim against his/her employer for breach of contract (wrongful dismissal) if the contract is not renewed when it expires. If he/she is wrongfully dismissed before the contract expires, he/she is generally entitled to remuneration payable over the full period of the contract.

An employee may be entitled to a redundancy payment or to compensation for unfair dismissal if the employment has been terminated by the employer (with or without proper notice) or he/she has a fixed term contract which expires without being renewed or the employment has been terminated by the employee by reason of the employer's breach of contract.

Under the Employment Protection (Consolidation) Act 1978, an employee who satisfies the foregoing conditions and has been continuously employed for two years and who is dismissed by reason of redundancy may be entitled to a redundancy payment calculated by reference to his/her age, pay and length of service.

The Employment Protection (Consolidation) Act 1978 also enables an employee who is unfairly dismissed to complain to an industrial tribunal (generally within three months of dismissal). The onus will then be on the employer to prove that the dismissal was due to capability, conduct, redundancy, illegality or some other substantial reason justifying dismissal. The tribunal must decide whether the employer acted reasonably in dismissing the employee. If the employer fails to prove that the dismissal was due to one or more of the above five reasons, or the tribunal decides that the employer did not act reasonably in dismissing the employee, the dismissal will be unfair, in which case the tribunal can:

(a) order re-engagement or reinstatement
(b) award compensation consisting of a basic and a compensatory award

For an employee to bring himself/herself within the unfair dismissal provisions, he/she must have been continuously employed for a period of two years.

All complaints of unfair dismissal are referred to a conciliation officer or the Department of Employment and a high proportion of complaints are disposed of in this way.

### DISCRIMINATION

Discrimination on the grounds of sex or marital status is made unlawful by the Sex Discrimination Act 1975. The provisions of the Sex Discrimination Act are similar to those of the Race Relations Act 1976 which make discrimination on 'racial grounds' unlawful. 'Racial grounds' include colour, race, nationality, or ethnic or national origins. The Equal Opportunities Commission and the Commission for Racial Equality have the function of eliminating such discriminations and may provide assistance in pursuing allegations of discrimination.

# FAMILY LAW

## ADOPTION OF CHILDREN

In England and Wales the adoption of children is mainly governed by the Adoption Act 1976, as amended by the Children Act 1989. A court order is necessary to legalize the adoption, which, when completed, has the effect of making the adopted child the child of the adopter as if he or she had been born to the adopter in lawful wedlock, and the original rights and duties of the natural parents are thereby cut. The adopter has full rights as to residence, education, etc., and the child is treated as his/hers for the purpose of any devolution of property on an intestacy occurring or under any disposition made after the adoption order. The application may be made to the High Court (Family Division) or to a county court or family proceedings court.

Orders may be made in favour of married couples, single, widowed or divorced persons, but not of one party to a marriage alone unless the other spouse cannot be found, is physically or mentally incapable of making an application, or they are separated in circumstances likely to be permanent. A person aged under 21 cannot adopt.

The child's parents or guardians must consent unconditionally to the making of the order unless the court dispenses with the consent, which it may do if the parent cannot be found or is incapable of giving consent, is withholding consent unreasonably, or has neglected or ill-treated the child.

Restrictions are placed on societies which may arrange adoptions.

An adopted person aged over 18 may apply to the Registrar-General for information to enable him/her to obtain a full certificate of his/her birth, but before being supplied with the information he/she will be informed that counselling services are available to him/her. The 1989 Act provides for the creation of a new register (the Adoption Contact Register) in which details of those who have had their children adopted, and of adopted persons themselves, may be recorded.

An adopter and the adopted child are within the prohibited degrees for the purposes of marriage to one another.

All adoptions in Great Britain are registered in the Registers of Adopted Children kept by the Registrars-General in London and Edinburgh respectively. Certificates from these registers, including short certificates which contain no reference to adoptions, can be obtained on conditions similar to those relating to birth certificates (*see* below).

*Scotland*

The law is consolidated in the Adoption (Scotland) Act 1978 as amended by the Children Act 1989. The law relating to fostering is consolidated in the Foster Children (Scotland) Act 1984. A petition for adoption is presented either to the sheriff court or the Court of Session. As in England, the petitioner(s) must be 21 or over and may be a married couple or one person who, if married, is living apart permanently from his or her spouse. The consent of the child's natural parents/guardians is required unless dispensed with, or the child is already free for adoption.

The Succession (Scotland) Act 1964 gives the adopted child the same rights of succession as a child born to the adopter in wedlock but deprives him/her of any such rights in the estates of his natural parents.

## BIRTHS (REGISTRATION)

When a birth takes place, personal information of it must be given to the Registrar of Births and Deaths for the sub-district in which the birth occurred, and the register signed in his/her presence by the father or mother of the child; or, if they fail, by (a) the occupier of the house in which the birth happened; (b) a person present at the birth; or (c) the person having charge of the child. The duty of attending to the registration therefore rests firstly on the parents. The mother is responsible for the registration of the birth of an illegitimate child.

The registration is required to be made within 42 days of the birth. Failure to do this without reasonable cause involves liability to a penalty. The registration of a birth is free. In England or Wales, the informant, instead of attending before the registrar of the sub-district where the birth occurred, may make a declaration of the particulars required to be registered in the presence of any registrar. Under the National Health Service Act 1977, notice of every birth must be given by the father, or person in attendance on the mother, to the district medical officer of health by post within 36 hours of the birth. This is in addition to the registration already mentioned.

*Still birth*: a still birth must be registered, and a certificate signed by the doctor or midwife who was present at the birth or who has examined the body of the child must be produced to the registrar. The certificate must, where possible, state the cause of death and the estimated duration of the pregnancy. A still birth may only be registered within three months of the birth.

*Re-registration*: the re-registration of the birth of a person legitimated by the subsequent marriage of the parents is provided for in the Births and Deaths Registration Act 1953, as amended by the Family Law Reform Act 1987. Special provisions apply to the registration and re-registration of births of abandoned children, and the re-registration of births of illegitimate children showing the father's name; the mother must normally be party to the latter application.

*Birth at sea*: the master of a British ship must record any birth on board and send particulars to the Registrar-General of Shipping.

*Birth abroad*: consular officers are authorized to register births of British subjects occurring abroad. Certificates are obtainable in due course at the Registrar-General's Office, London.

The registration of births occurring out of the United Kingdom among members of the armed forces or occurring on board HM ships and aircraft, is provided for by the Registration of Births, Deaths and Marriages (Special Provisions) Act 1957, applicable also to Scotland.

*Scotland*

The Registration of Births, Deaths and Marriages (Scotland) Act 1965 supersedes former Acts. Personal notification within 21 days of any birth must be given to the registrar of either the registration district in which the birth took place, or any registration district in which the mother of the child was ordinarily resident at the time of the birth. In the case of a foundling child, dead or alive, when the place of birth is not known, notification must be given to the registrar of the registration district in which the child, or the body, was found, within two months from the date on which the child was found. When a child is born (in or out of Scotland) in a ship, aircraft or land vehicle during a journey and the child is conveyed therein to any place in Scotland, the birth shall, unless the Registrar-General otherwise directs, be deemed to have occurred at that place.

The register must be signed in the presence of the registrar by the father or mother of the child; or, if they fail, by (a) any relative of either parent who has knowledge of the birth; (b) the occupier of the premises in which the child was, to the knowledge of that occupier, born; (c) any person present at the birth; (d) any person having charge of the child. Failure without reasonable cause involves a penalty.

The name of the father of a child born out of wedlock may be entered in the register of births at the time of registration if jointly requested by the mother and father, and the latter's name may also be recorded at a later date on declaration by both parents. A free abbreviated certificate of birth will be issued to the informant at the time of registration.

*Still birth*: a still birth must be registered and a certificate, signed by the doctor or certified midwife present at the birth or who has examined the body of the child, must be produced.

*Re-registration*: provision is made for the re-registration of the birth of a person made legitimate by the subsequent marriage of the parents or whose birth entry is affected by any matter respecting status or paternity, or has been so made as to imply that he/she is a foundling.

## CERTIFICATES OF BIRTHS, DEATHS OR MARRIAGES

Certificates of births, deaths or marriages in England and Wales can be obtained at the Office of Population Censuses and Surveys (OPCS), St Catherine's House, 10 Kingsway, London WC2B 6JP, or from the Superintendent Registrar having the legal custody of the register containing the entry of which a certificate is required. Certificates of marriage can also be obtained from the incumbent of the church in which the marriage took place, or from the Nonconformist minister (or other authorized person) where the marriage takes place in a registered building.

A standard certificate of birth, death or marriage may be obtained from the Superintendent Registrar for a fee of £5.50 or from the registrar for a fee of £2.50. One short birth certificate is issued free of charge at registration. The fee for the issue of a short birth certificate by the Superintendent Registrar is £3.00 and by a registrar, £2.00. Certificates of birth, death or marriage for special purposes cost £2.00.

When a certificate is required, the nearest register office will be able to advise on the best way of obtaining it and any fees payable. As a rule, copies of entries in the registers may be obtained by a personal visit to OPCS at St Catherine's House, London, or by postal application (provided sufficient information is given to identify the certificate required) from Smedley Hydro, Trafalgar Road, Birkdale, Southport PR8 2HH. Copies obtained from the Superintendent Registrar cost £5.50; copies obtained from a registrar cost £2.50. For a general search in the indexes of not more than six successive hours and where the object is not stated, the fee is £15.00. No fee is payable for a search in the indexes when a particular entry in the register is specified.

Records of births, deaths and marriages registered in England and Wales since 1837 are kept at the Office of Population Censuses and Surveys, St Catherine's House, 10 Kingsway, London WC2B 6JP. The Society of Genealogists, 14 Charterhouse Buildings, Goswell Road, London ECIM 7BA, possesses many records of baptisms, marriages and deaths prior to 1837, including copies in whole or in part of about 4,000 parish registers.

### Scotland

Certificates of births, deaths or marriages registered from 1855 (when compulsory registration commenced in Scotland) can be obtained personally at the General Register Office, New Register House, Edinburgh EH1 3YT, or from the appropriate local registrar, on payment of the fee of £10 for a full extract entry of birth, death or marriage (£12 by post), and £10 for an abbreviated certificate of birth (£12 by post). An abbreviated certificate of registration of death is issued free of charge for National Insurance purposes in certain cases. A Register of Divorces (which includes decrees of declaration of nullity of marriage) is kept by the Registrar-General at the General Register Office. The fee for an extract decree is £10 (£12 by post). The fees for searches of the registers vary according to the nature of the search and/or of the application; rates are available from the General Register Office.

There are also available at the General Register Office old parish registers of the date prior to 1855, which were formerly kept under the administration of the established Church of Scotland. An extract of an entry in these registers may be obtained for a fee of £12.00 (which includes the search fee).

The Registration of Presumed Deaths (Prescription of Particulars) (Scotland) Regulations 1978 as read with Presumption of Death (Scotland) Act 1977 prescribe the particulars to be notified by the clerk of court to the Registrar-General after a decree or variation order has been granted in an action of declarator of death of a missing person.

## DIVORCE, SEPARATION AND ANCILLARY MATTERS

Matrimonial suits may be conveniently divided into two classes: those in which it is sought to annul the marriage because of some defect; and those in which, the marriage being admitted, it is sought to end the marriage or the duties arising from it. By virtue of the Matrimonial and Family Proceedings Act 1984, all matrimonial causes are commenced in one of the divorce county courts designated by the Lord Chancellor or in the Divorce Registry in London. If the suit becomes defended, it may be transferred to the High Court.

### NULLITY OF MARRIAGE

Nullity of marriage is now mainly governed as to England and Wales by the Matrimonial Causes Act 1973. A marriage is void *ab initio* if the parties were within the prohibited degrees of affinity; or were not male and female; if it was bigamous; if one of the parties was under the age of consent, i.e. 16; or, in the case of a polygamous marriage entered into outside England and Wales, if either party was at the time of the marriage domiciled in England or Wales. Where the formalities of the marriage were defective, the marriage is generally void if both parties knew of the defect (e.g. where marriage took place otherwise than in an authorized building). However, absence of the consent of parents or guardians (or of the court or other authority, in lieu thereof) in the case of minors does not invalidate the marriage.

A marriage is voidable (i.e. a decree of nullity may be obtained but until such time the marriage remains valid) on the following grounds:

(a) incapacity of either party to consummate
(b) respondent's wilful refusal to consummate
(c) that either party did not validly consent to the marriage, whether in consequence of duress, mistake, unsoundness of mind or otherwise
(d) that either party at the time of marriage was a mentally disordered person
(e) that at the time of marriage the respondent was suffering from communicable venereal disease
(f) that at the time of the marriage the respondent was pregnant by another man

In cases (e) and (f), the petitioner must have been ignorant of the grounds at the date of the marriage. In cases (c), (d), (e) and (f) proceedings must be instituted within three years of the marriage, although leave may be obtained to petition outside this period in the case of certain persons suffering from mental illness. In all cases the court shall not grant a decree where the petitioner has led the respondent to believe that he/she would not seek a decree and it would be unjust for it to be granted.

The 1973 Act provides that a decree of nullity in a voidable marriage only annuls the marriage from the date of the decree. The marriage remains valid until the decree, and any children of the marriage are legitimate. Children of a void marriage are illegitimate unless the father was domiciled in England or Wales at the child's birth (or father's death, if earlier), and at the time of conception (or marriage if later) both or either of the parents reasonably believed the marriage was valid.

A spouse's insistence upon the use of contraceptives will not constitute wilful refusal to consummate within (b) above, even though there has been no normal intercourse, but it may in certain circumstances constitute unreasonable behaviour for the purpose of divorce. Further, it has been allowed as a defence to a charge of desertion against the aggrieved party.

## JUDICIAL SEPARATION AND DIVORCE

The second class of suit includes a suit for judicial separation (which does not dissolve a marriage) and a suit for divorce (which, if successful, dissolves the marriage altogether and leaves the parties at liberty to marry again). Either spouse may petition for judicial separation. It is not necessary to prove that the marriage has broken down irretrievably and the facts listed below are grounds for judicial separation.

## DIVORCE

The sole ground on which a divorce is obtained by either husband or wife is the irretrievable breakdown of the marriage. However, the court is precluded from holding that a marriage has irretrievably broken down unless it is satisfied of one or more of the following facts:

(a) that the respondent has committed adultery since the marriage and the petitioner finds it intolerable to live with the respondent
(b) that the respondent has behaved in such a way that the petitioner cannot reasonably be expected to continue cohabitation
(c) desertion by the respondent for two years immediately before the petition
(d) five years' separation immediately before the petition (but only two years where the respondent consents to the decree). Matrimonial Causes Act 1973

The foregoing is subject to a clause prohibiting any petition for divorce (but not for judicial separation) before the lapse of one year from the date of the marriage.

Desertion may be defined as a voluntary withdrawal from cohabitation by one spouse without just cause and against the wishes of the other. Where one spouse is guilty of conduct of a serious nature which forces the other to leave, the party at fault is said to be guilty of constructive desertion.

### Encouragement of reconciliation

The 1973 Act requires the solicitor for the petitioner in certain cases to certify whether the possibility of a reconciliation has been discussed with the petitioner and whether or not the solicitor has given the petitioner the names and addresses of persons qualified to help effect a reconciliation.

A total period of less than six months during which the parties have resumed living together is to be disregarded in determining whether the prescribed period of desertion or separation has been continuous. Similar provision for effecting a reconciliation exists in relation to the other proofs of breakdown, but a petitioner cannot rely on an act of adultery by the other party if they have lived together for more than six months after discovery of that act of adultery.

### Obtaining the decree nisi

Where the suit is defended, i.e. the respondent opposes the dissolution or the fact/ground on which the petitioner seeks it, the petition will be heard by a judge in open court, the parties giving oral evidence. Where the suit is undefended, the evidence will normally take the form of a sworn written statement made by the petitioner which will be sent to the court and read over by a district judge. If the district judge is satisfied that the petitioner has proved the contents of the petition, he/she will simply fix a date for the pronouncement

of the decree nisi in open court, it being unnecessary for either party to attend. Only if the district judge is not satisfied as above will he/she order that the petition be heard formally by the judge.

### Children

After giving his/her certificate in relation to the decree nisi, the district judge must consider whether he/she should exercise any of his/her powers under the Children Act 1989. If the district judge thinks it may be necessary to exercise those powers, he/she can in exceptional circumstances delay the grant of the decree absolute.

### Decree absolute

Every decree of divorce or nullity is in the first instance a decree nisi, and the marriage subsists until the decree is made absolute, usually six weeks after decree nisi on the petitioner's application. After the decree absolute either party is free to remarry.

### Maintenance, etc

The court has wide powers to order either party to the marriage to make financial provision (e.g. periodical payments, a lump sum, the transfer of property) for the other party or, in certain circumstances, any child of the family, having regard to the party's means, the recipient's needs and all the important aspects of the case. These so-called ancillary matters often present more difficulty than the divorce itself, especially where they affect the home, and may go on long after the marriage is dissolved. There is, however, nothing to stop financial matters being negotiated by the parties through their solicitors before the divorce goes through.

The jurisdiction of the court to make child maintenance orders has been restricted by the Child Support Act 1991. Under this Act, a government agency, the Child Support Agency, has become responsible for assessing the maintenance that absent parents should pay for their natural children.

The court may, where the husband has neglected to provide reasonable maintenance for the wife or children, order the husband to make provision for the wife and, in certain circumstances, the children, even though no matrimonial suit is pending between the parties to the marriage, and while such an order is in force the court may also make orders relating to the children.

## ORDERS REGARDING CHILDREN

The Court may make orders in respect of children in connection with a suit for divorce, nullity or judicial separation (see above), or with an application to the family proceedings court (see below) whether the suit succeeds or not. In addition, if there is no other matrimonial suit involved, a parent may apply for orders under the Children Act 1989, and any person interested may apply to the High Court for the child to be made a ward of court.

In all cases the welfare of the child is the paramount consideration. The categories of child who may be covered by any particular type of proceedings differ according to the nature of those proceedings and to the nature of the particular relief sought, but it should be borne in mind that in connection with divorce, nullity and judicial separation a child which has been treated by the spouses as a child of the family may be included as a 'child of the family' as well as the children of the spouses themselves. This also applies to most maintenance cases in the family proceedings court (see below). It should be borne in mind that where there is financial need (because of continuing education or disability, for instance), maintenance may be ordered for children even beyond the age of majority.

Any dispute relating to the above matters should be placed in the hands of a solicitor without delay.

## SEPARATION BY AGREEMENT

Husband and wife may enter into an agreement to separate and live apart but the agreement, to be valid, must be followed by an immediate separation. It is most desirable to consult a solicitor in every such case, who will often advise obtaining a court order by consent.

## FAMILY PROCEEDINGS COURT

For many years the law relating to domestic proceedings in magistrates' courts (now family proceedings courts) was out of line with the divorce law which was reformed in 1969. The Domestic Proceedings and Magistrates' Courts Act 1978 took effect in early 1981 and now contains the relevant law.

A husband or wife can apply to a family proceedings court for a matrimonial order on the grounds that the other spouse: (a) has failed to pay reasonable maintenance for the applicant; (b) has failed to make a proper contribution towards the reasonable maintenance of a child of the family; (c) has deserted the applicant; or (d) has behaved in such a way that the applicant cannot reasonably be expected to live with the respondent.

If the case is proved the court can order: (a) periodical payments for the applicant; (b) periodical payments for a child of the family (except where the court's jurisdiction has been superseded by the Child Support Agency, *see* above); or (c) a lump sum (not exceeding £1,000) for the benefit of the applicant and/or for any child of the family.

In deciding what orders (if any) to make, the court must consider a number of guidelines which are similar to those governing financial orders on divorce. There are also special provisions relating to consent orders and separation by agreement. The court also has powers to make orders relating to a child of the family and these orders together with orders for child maintenance can be made even though the court makes no order for spouse maintenance. Other provisions of the Act relate to interim orders, and variation, discharge and revival of orders. An order may be enforceable even though the parties are living together, but in some cases it will cease to have effect if they continue to do so for six months. The hearing of matrimonial disputes is separate from ordinary court business, and the public are not admitted.

## DOMESTIC VIOLENCE

The Domestic Violence and Matrimonial Proceedings Act 1976, the Domestic Proceedings and Magistrates' Courts Act 1978 and the Matrimonial Homes Act 1983 have made it easier for one spouse who has been subjected to violence by the other to obtain an order to restrain further violence and if need be to have the other excluded from the home. Such orders can be obtained very quickly, and a person disobeying them is liable to be imprisoned for contempt of court. There are some differences of detail between the three Acts; in particular the 1976 Act also applies to unmarried couples. Such orders may also be obtained in the course of suits for divorce and judicial separation.

## SCOTLAND

### NULLITY OF MARRIAGE

A declaration of nullity of marriage may be obtained on the ground of any impediment, such as consanguinity and affinity, subsistence of a previous marriage, nonage of one of the parties, incapacity or insanity of one of the parties, or by the absence of genuine consent. The financial provisions on divorce contained in the Family Law (Scotland) Act 1985 also apply to an action for declaration of nullity of marriage.

## JUDICIAL SEPARATION

Under the Divorce (Scotland) Act 1976, a decree of judicial separation can be obtained by proof of the same facts necessary to obtain decree of divorce, except that for the principle of irretrievable breakdown there is substituted that of grounds justifying separation. This type of action is competent in both the Court of Session and the sheriff court.

## DIVORCE

Actions of divorce could formerly only be raised in the Court of Session, having jurisdiction to entertain such actions only if either of the parties to the marriage in question is domiciled in Scotland on the date when the action is begun, or was habitually resident in Scotland throughout the period of one year ending with that date. As from 1 May 1984, however, when the Divorce Jurisdiction, Court Fees and Legal Aid (Scotland) Act 1983 came into force, actions of divorce may also be raised in the sheriff courts provided the above conditions are complied with, and provided either party to the marriage was resident in the sheriffdom for a period of 40 days ending with the date the action was begun, or was resident in the sheriffdom for a period of not less than 40 days ending not more than 40 days before the date the action was begun.

The Scots law of divorce is governed by the Divorce (Scotland) Act 1976, which for the purposes of divorce came into force on 1 January 1977. The sole ground of divorce is irretrievable breakdown of the marriage. This can be established only in one of the following ways:

(a) The defending spouse has committed adultery since the date of the marriage. It is not necessary for the pursuing spouse to prove that the fact of adultery made it intolerable to live with the defending spouse

(b) The defending spouse has behaved in such a way that the pursuing spouse cannot reasonably be expected to cohabit with him or her. It is immaterial whether or not the conduct founded upon is active or passive

(c) The defending spouse has deserted the pursuing spouse for a continuous period of two years. There must be no question of the pursuing spouse having refused a genuine and reasonable offer to adhere. Nor is irretrievable breakdown established if cohabitation is resumed for a period of more than three months after the two-year period has expired

(d) There has been no cohabitation at any time during a continuous period of two years immediately preceding the action between the parties to the action, and the defending spouse consents to the divorce being granted

(e) There has been no cohabitation at any time during a continuous period of five years, as in (d), except that on the expiry of the five-year period, the consent of the defending spouse is not required

The facts of desertion and separation are not interrupted by the parties cohabiting for a period or periods not exceeding six months. However, such a period or periods of cohabitation would not be included in the calculation of the two-year or five-year periods.

### *Encouragement of reconciliation*

The burden of promoting a reconciliation between spouses in a divorce action in Scotland falls upon the court by virtue of the 1976 Act. Where an action of divorce has been raised, it may be postponed by the court to enable the parties to seek to effect a reconciliation, if the court feels that there may be a reasonable prospect of such reconciliation. If the parties do cohabit during such postponement, no account shall be taken of such cohabitation if the action later proceeds.

*Maintenance, etc.*

The 1976 Act also provides that either party to a marriage can apply to the court at any time prior to decree being granted for: (a) an order for interim custody of all or some of the children of the marriage under 16 years of age; (b) an order for access to all or some of the children of the marriage under 16 years of age in the custody of the other party.

The financial provisions on divorce in the 1976 Act have been superseded by the Family Law (Scotland) Act 1985, which allows either party to the marriage to apply to the court for an order for payment of a capital sum or a periodical allowance or for an incidental order. The Act sets out principles to be applied by the court, one of these being that the financial provisions awarded to a party who has been dependent for financial support on the other party should be given over a period of not more than three years.

The Act also defines the rights and obligations of aliment between parents and children, thereby excluding aliment between grandparents and grandchildren and of children to parents, and provides that a child is entitled to aliment up to the age of 18 or to 25 if in full-time further education, and for the claiming of aliment whether in connection with an action of divorce, etc., or independently.

*Procedure*

Appearance in court at a proof in an undefended divorce action has been unnecessary since April 1978. A full proof is still necessary if the action is defended in any respect. In place of court appearance, affidavits (statements sworn before a notary public) by the pursuer and any witnesses are lodged in the court together with a Minute by the solicitor craving decree.

A simplified procedure for 'do-it-yourself' divorce was introduced in January 1983 for certain divorces. Thus, if the action is based on (d) or (e) above and will not be opposed, and if there are no children under 16 and no financial claims, then the applicant can write directly to the local sheriff court or to the Court of Session, Divorce Section (SP), Parliament House, Edinburgh, for the appropriate forms to enable him or her to proceed. The fee is £55 unless the applicant receives Income Support, Family Credit or legal advice and assistance, in which case there is no fee.

CUSTODY OF CHILDREN

In actions for divorce and separation, the court has a discretion in awarding the custody of the children of the parties. The welfare of the children is the paramount consideration, and the mere fact that a spouse, by reason of his or her behaviour, brought about the breakdown of the marriage does not of itself preclude him or her from being awarded custody. The Children Act 1975, as amended, also applies to Scotland.

DOMESTIC VIOLENCE

The Matrimonial Homes (Family Protection) (Scotland) Act 1981, as amended, provides that one spouse, whether or not he or she has title to the matrimonial home, can obtain an exclusion order suspending the other spouse's occupancy rights in the matrimonial home. The court (either Court of Session or sheriff court) is empowered to make such an order if satisfied that it is necessary to protect the applicant or any child of the family from any conduct, actual or threatened or reasonably apprehended, of the other spouse which would be injurious to the physical or mental health of the applicant or child. In making the order the court may include a warrant for the summary ejection of the non-applicant spouse from the matrimonial home and for an interdict prohibiting him/her from entering it.

ILLEGITIMACY AND LEGITIMATION

The Children Act 1989 gives the mother parental responsibility for her child when not married to the father. The father can acquire parental responsibility by agreement with her (in prescribed form) or by court order.

*Prima facie* every child born of a married woman during a marriage is legitimate; and this presumption can only be rebutted by strong evidence. However, under the Family Law Reform Act 1969, any presumption of law as to the legitimacy (or illegitimacy) of any person may in civil proceedings be rebutted by evidence showing that it is more probable than not that the person is illegitimate (or legitimate) and in any proceedings where paternity is in question, blood tests may be ordered. If, however, the husband and wife are separated under an order of the court, a child conceived by the wife during such separation is presumed not to be the husband's child.

LEGITIMATION

The Legitimacy Act 1976 consolidates earlier legislation dating back to 1 January 1927. Where the parents of an illegitimate person marry, or have married, whether before or after that date, the marriage, if the father is at the date thereof domiciled in England or Wales, renders that person, if living, legitimate as from 1 January 1927, or from the date of the marriage, whichever last happens. Marriage legitimates a person even though the father or mother was married to a third person at the time when the illegitimate person was born. It is the duty of the parents to supply to the Registrar-General information for re-registration of the birth of a legitimate child.

*Declarations of legitimacy*

A person claiming that he, his parents, or any remoter ancestor has become legitimated, may petition the High Court or the county court for the necessary declaration.

*Rights and duties of legitimated persons*

A legitimated person, his/her spouse or children may take property under an intestacy occurring after the date of legitimation, or under any disposition (e.g. a will) coming into operation after such date, as if he/she had been legitimate. He/she must maintain all persons whom he/she would be bound to maintain had he/she been born legitimate, and he/she is entitled to the benefit of any Act of Parliament which confers rights on legitimate persons to recover damages or compensation. The Act specially provides that nothing therein contained is to render any person capable of succeeding to or transmitting a right to any dignity or title.

PROPERTY RIGHTS OF ILLEGITIMATE CHILDREN

By the Family Law Reform Act 1969 the rights of an illegitimate child on an intestacy were broadly equated with those of a legitimate child, and in any disposition made after 31 December 1969, any reference to children or other relatives was, unless the contrary intention appears, to be construed as including any person who is illegitimate or who is related through another person who is illegitimate. However, these provisions of the 1969 Act have been replaced by the general provision of the Family Law Reform Act 1987 (*see* page 658).

SCOTLAND

The Law Reform (Parent and Child) Scotland Act 1986 implemented the Scottish Law Commission's report on illegitimacy. The Act contains a general provision granting equal status to all persons whatever the marital status of their parents. The mother of an illegitimate child may raise an action of affiliation and aliment against the father, either in the Court of Session or, more usually, in the sheriff court. Where in any such action the court finds that the defender is the father of the child, the court shall, in awarding expenses, or aliment, have regard to the means of the parties and the whole circumstances of the case. The court may, upon application by the mother or by the father of any illegitimate child, or in any action for aliment for an illegitimate child, make such order as it may think fit regarding the custody of such child and the right of access thereto of either parent, having regard to the welfare of the child and to the conduct of the parents and to the wishes as well of the mother as of the father and may on the application of either parent recall or vary such order. The obligation of the mother and of the father of an illegitimate child to provide aliment for such child shall (without prejudice to any obligation attaching at common law) endure until the child attains the age of sixteen.

Legitimation

By Scottish law an illegitimate child is legitimated by and on the date of the subsequent marriage of its parents and there is no objection to there having been an impediment to the marriage of the parents at the time of the child's conception; see the Legitimation (Scotland) Act 1968, which came into operation on 8 June 1968, on which date thousands of existing illegitimate children were regarded as legitimated. By the Registration of Births, Deaths and Marriages (Scotland) Act 1965, a child so legitimated who has already been registered as illegitimate may be re-registered as legitimate. The consent of the father of an illegitimate child to its adoption is not required unless he has been awarded parental rights by the court.

## MARRIAGE

Marriage According to Rites of the Church of England

*Marriage by banns*

The Marriage Act 1949 prescribes audible publication according to the rubric, on three Sundays preceding the ceremony during morning service or, if there is no morning service on a Sunday on which the banns are to be published, during evening service. Where the parties reside in different parishes, the banns must be published in both. Under the Act, banns may be published and the marriage solemnized in the parish church, which is the usual place of worship of the persons to be married or either of them, although neither of such persons dwells in such parish; but this publication of banns is in addition to any other publication required by law and does not apply if the church or the residence of either party is in Wales. The Act provides specially for the case where one of the parties resides in Scotland and the other in England, the publication being then in the parish in England in which one party resides, and, according to the law and custom in Scotland, in the place where the other party resides. After the lapse of three months from the last time of publication, the banns become useless, and the parties must either obtain a licence (*see* below), or submit to the republication of banns.

*Marriage by licence*

Marriage licences are of two kinds:

*Common Licence:* a common licence, dispensing with the necessity for banns, is granted by the archbishops and bishops through their surrogates, for marriages in any church or chapel duly licensed for marriages. A common licence can be obtained in London by application at the Faculty Office

(1 The Sanctuary, London SW1 3JT) and (for marriages in London) at the Bishop of London's Diocesan Registry (1 The Sanctuary, London SW1 3JT), by one of the parties about to be married. In the country they may be obtained at the offices of the bishop's registrars, but licences obtained at the bishop's diocesan registry only enable the parties to be married in the diocese in which they are issued; those procured at the Faculty Office are available for all England and Wales. No instructions, either verbal or in writing, can be received, except from one of the parties. Affidavits are prepared from the personal instructions of one of the parties about to be married, and the licence is delivered to the party upon payment of a fee (*see* page 670). Before a licence can be granted one of the parties must make an affidavit that there is no legal impediment to the intended marriage; and also that one of such parties has had his or her usual place of abode for the space of fifteen days immediately preceding the issuing of the licence within the parish or ecclesiastical district of the church in which the marriage is to be solemnized, or that the church in which the marriage is to be solemnized is the usual place of worship of the parties or one of them. In the country there may generally be found a parochial clergyman (surrogate) before whom the affidavit may be taken, and whose office it is to deliver the licence personally to the applicant. (In some dioceses it is necessary for the surrogate to procure the licence from the bishop's registry.) The licence continues in force for three months from its date.

*Special Licence:* a special licence is granted by the Archbishop of Canterbury, in special circumstances, for marriage at any place with or without previous residence in the district, or at any time, etc.; but the reasons assigned must meet with the archbishop's approval. Application must be made to the Faculty Office. For fee, *see* page 670.

*Marriage under Superintendent Registrar's certificate*

A marriage may be performed in church on the Superintendent Registrar's certificate (*see* below) without banns, provided that the incumbent's consent is obtained. One of the parties must be resident within the ecclesiastical parish of the church in which the marriage is to take place unless the church is the usual place of worship of the parties or one of them.

Marriage under Superintendent Registrar's Certificate

The following marriages may be solemnized on the authority of a Superintendent Registrar's certificate (either with or without a licence):

(a) a marriage in a registered building, e.g. a Nonconformist church registered for the solemnization of marriages therein

(b) a marriage in a register office

(c) a marriage according to the usages of the Society of Friends (commonly called Quakers)

(d) a marriage between two persons professing the Jewish religion according to the usages of the Jews

(e) a marriage according to the rites of the Church of England (*see* above – in this case the marriage can only be without licence)

(f) a marriage of a person who is housebound or is detained at the place where he or she normally resides (*see* page 669)

Notice of the intended marriage must be given as follows:

*Marriage by certificate (without licence):* if both parties reside in the same registration district, they must both have resided there for seven days before the notice can be given. It may then be given by either party. If the parties reside in different registration districts, notice must be given by each to the Superintendent Registrar of the district in which he or she resides, and the preliminary residential qualification of seven days must be fulfilled by each before either notice can be given.

*Marriage by certificate (with licence):* one notice only is necessary, whether the parties live in the same or in different registration districts. Either party may give the notice, which must be given to the Superintendent Registrar of any registration district in which one of the parties has resided for the period of 15 days immediately preceding the giving of notice, but both parties must be resident in England or Wales on the day notice is given.

The notice (in either case) must be in the prescribed form and must contain particulars as to names, marital status, occupation, residence, length of residence, and the building in which the marriage is to take place. The notice must also contain or have added at the foot thereof a solemn declaration that there is no legal impediment to the marriage, and, in the case of minors, that the consent of the person whose consent to the marriage is required by law (*see* Minors, page 670) has been duly given, and that the residential qualifications mentioned above have been complied with. A person making a false declaration renders himself or herself liable to prosecution for perjury. The notice is entered in the marriage notice book.

### Issue of certificate

*Without licence:* the notice (or an exact copy thereof) is affixed in some conspicuous place in the Superintendent Registrar's office for 21 days next after the notice was entered in the marriage notice book. After the lapse of this period the Superintendent Registrar may, provided no impediment is shown, issue his certificate for the marriage which can then take place at any time within three months from the date of the entry of the notice.

*With licence:* the notice in this case is not affixed in the office of the Superintendent Registrar. After the lapse of one whole day (other than a Sunday, Christmas Day or Good Friday) from the date of entry of the notice, the Superintendent Registrar may, provided no impediment is shown, issue his certificate and licence for the marriage, which can then take place on any day within three months from the date of entry of the notice.

### SOLEMNIZATION OF THE MARRIAGE

#### In a registered building

The marriage must generally take place at a building within the district of residence of one of the parties, but if the usual place of worship of either is outside the district of his or her residence, it may take place in such usual place of worship. Further, if there is not within the district of residence of one of the parties a registered building within which marriages are solemnized according to the rites and ceremonies which the parties desire to adopt in solemnizing their marriage, it may take place in an appropriate registered building in the nearest district.

The presence of a Registrar of Marriages is not necessary at marriages at registered buildings which have adopted the provisions of section 43 of the Marriage Act 1949. This section provides for the appointment of an authorized person (a person, usually the minister or an official of the building, certified by the trustees or governing body as having been duly authorized for the purpose) who must be present and must register the marriage.

The marriage must be solemnized between the hours of 8 a.m. and 6 p.m., with open doors, in the presence of two or more witnesses. The parties must at some time during the ceremony make the following declaration: 'I do solemnly declare that I know not of any lawful impediment why I, A. B., may not be joined in matrimony to C. D.' Also each of the parties must say to the other: 'I call upon these persons here present to witness that I, A. B., do take thee, C. D., to be my lawful wedded wife [or husband],' or, if the marriage is solemnized in the presence of an authorized person without the presence of a registrar, each party may say in lieu thereof: 'I, A. B., do take thee, C. D., to be my wedded wife [or husband].'

#### In a register office

The marriage may be solemnized in the office of the Superintendent Registrar to whom notice of the marriage has been given. The marriage must be solemnized between the hours of 8 a.m. and 6 p.m., with open doors, in the presence of the Superintendent Registrar or a registrar of the registration district of that Superintendent Registrar, and in the presence of two witnesses. The parties must make the following declaration: 'I do solemnly declare that I know not of any lawful impediment why I, A. B., may not be joined in matrimony to C. D.,' and each party must say to the other: 'I call upon these persons here present to witness that I, A. B., do take thee, C. D., to be my lawful wedded wife [or husband].'

No religious ceremony may take place in the register office, though the parties may, on production of their marriage certificate, go through a subsequent religious ceremony in any church or persuasion of which they are members.

#### Other cases

If both parties are members of the Society of Friends (Quakers), or if, not being in membership, they have been authorized by the Society of Friends to solemnize their marriage in accordance with its usages, they may be married in a Friends' meeting-house. The marriage must be registered by the registering officer of the Society appointed to act for the district in which the meeting-house is situated. The presence of a Registrar of Marriages is not necessary.

If both parties are Jews they may marry according to their usages in a synagogue which has a certified marriage secretary, or in a private dwelling-house at any hour; the building may be situated within or without the district of residence. The marriage must be registered by the secretary of the synagogue of which the man is a member. The presence of a Registrar of Marriages is not necessary.

### MARRIAGE UNDER REGISTRAR-GENERAL'S LICENCE

The main purpose of the Marriage (Registrar-General's Licence) Act 1970, which came into force on 1 January 1971, is to enable non-Anglicans to be married in unregistered premises where one of the persons to be married is seriously ill, is not expected to recover, and cannot be moved to registered premises.

### DETAINED AND HOUSEBOUND PERSONS

The Marriage Act 1983 (which does not extend to Scotland) enables marriages of detained persons and housebound persons to be solemnized at their place of residence . The Act came into operation on 1 May 1984.

### MARRIAGE IN ENGLAND OR WALES WHEN ONE PARTY LIVES IN SCOTLAND OR NORTHERN IRELAND

Notice for a marriage by a Superintendent Registrar's certificate in a register office or registered building may be given in the usual way by the party resident in England. As regards Scotland, the party there should give notice of intention to marry to the Registrar. As regards Northern Ireland, the party there, after a residence of seven days, must give notice to the District Registrar of Marriages. Notice cannot be given for such marriages to take place by certificate with licence of the Superintendent Registrar.

Marriage of such parties may take place in a church of the Church of England after the publication of banns, or by ecclesiastical licence.

CIVIL FEES from 1 April 1994
*Marriage by Superintendent Registrar's certificate*
If both parties live in same district
In register office, £37.00
In a registered building when presence of registrar is required, £49.00
If the parties live in different districts
In register office, £55.00
In a registered building when presence of registrar is required, £67.00

*Marriage by Superintendent Registrar's licence*
In register office, £82.00
In a registered building when presence of registrar is required, £94.00

Total fees for the preliminaries to marriage by Registrar-General's licence, £15.00

*Marriage of a housebound or detained person*
For attendance of Superintendent Registrar at residence of housebound or detained person to attest notice of marriage, £32.00
For attendance of Superintendent Registrar at residence of housebound or detained person, £32.00
For attendance of registrar at residence of housebound or detained person, £31.00

In the case of a registered building, further fees may be payable to the minister or the authorities of the building.

ECCLESIASTICAL FEES from 1 April 1994
*Marriage after banns*
Parties residing in same parish, £100.00
Parties residing in different parishes, £116.00

*Marriages by common licence*
Fee for licence varies, but usually £45.00
Fee to Church authorities for ceremony, £90.00

*Marriage on the authority of the Superintendent Registrar's certificate*
Parties residing in same registration district, £108.00
Parties residing in different districts, £126.00

*Marriage by special licence*
Fee payable at Faculty Office, £90.00

*Marriage of a housebound or detained person*
For attendance of a Superintendent Registrar at residence of a housebound or detained person to attest marriage, £32.00
*For entering notice of marriage, £18.00

*Two notices are required to be given if the parties reside in different registration districts
Further fees may be payable for additional facilities at the marriage, e.g. the organist's fee
Some of the above fees may not apply to the Church in Wales

MISCELLANEOUS NOTES

*Consanguinity and affinity*
A marriage between persons within the prohibited degrees of consanguinity or affinity is void. Relaxations have, however, been made by various statutes which have now been replaced by the Marriage Act 1949 (see 1st Schedule to

the Act) and the Marriage (Enabling) Act 1960. It is now permitted to contract a marriage with:
(a) sister, aunt or niece of a former wife (whether she is living or not)
(b) former wife of brother, uncle or nephew (whether he is living or not)
No member of the clergy can be compelled to solemnize any of the foregoing marriages, but he/she may allow his church to be used for the purpose by another minister.

The Marriage (Prohibited Degrees of Relationship) Act 1986 makes further provision with regard to the marriage of persons related by affinity, e.g. after section 1 of the Act came into force, a marriage between a man and the daughter or granddaughter of his former wife will not be void by reason only of that relationship if both parties have attained 21 at the time of the marriage and the younger party has not at any time before attaining 18 been a child of the family in relation to the other party.

*Minors*
Persons under 18 years of age are generally required to obtain the consent of certain persons (Marriage Act 1949, section 3 and 2nd Schedule as amended by the Children Act 1989). Where both parents are living, both must consent. Where one is dead, the survivor, or, if there is a guardian appointed by the deceased parent, the guardian and the survivor must consent. (For the position where the parents of the child were not married to each other at the time of birth, see Schedule 12, paragraph 5 to the Children Act 1989.) No consent is required in the case of a minor's second marriage. In certain exceptional cases consent may be dispensed with, e.g. the insanity of a parent.

If consent is refused the court may, on application being made, consent to the marriage; application can be made for this purpose to the High Court, the county court, or a court of summary jurisdiction. The Act prohibits any marriage where either party is under 16 years of age.

SCOTLAND

According to the law of Scotland, marriage is a contract which is completed by the mutual consent of the parties. The Marriage (Scotland) Act 1977, which came into force on 1 January 1978, states or restates the law in convenient form. References in this section are to that Act.

IMPEDIMENTS TO MARRIAGE
These are: (a) nonage, i.e. where either party is under the age of 16; (b) forbidden degrees of relationship (Section 2) as amended by the Marriage Prohibited Degrees of Relationship Act 1986; (c) subsisting previous marriage; (d) incapacity to understand the nature of the contract; (e) both parties of the same sex; (f) non-residence, i.e. if the requirements of prior residence of one or other of the parties in Scotland have not been complied with.

The Act also states the grounds on which certain marriages may be declared void, but this is amended by the Law Reform (Miscellaneous Provisions) (Scotland) Act 1980 which prevents a marriage being rendered void solely due to the failure to comply with certain formalities, provided the particulars of that marriage are entered in a register of marriages by or at the behest of an appropriate registrar.

REGULAR AND IRREGULAR MARRIAGES

*Regular marriages*
A regular marriage is one which is celebrated by a minister of religion or authorized registrar or other celebrant specified in the Act. The parties must submit to the district registrar a

statutory notice of intention to marry, the fee for which is £10.00 each. The registrar will then enter the parties' names and particulars in the marriage notice book which must also show the intended date of the marriage. The registrar must then display the notice of intention to marry in a prominent public place until the intended date, and any person claiming an interest may lodge written objections thereto with the registrar (Section 5). The registrar, after 14 clear days of receipt of the marriage notice and on being satisfied that there are no legal impediments to the marriage, will issue to either or both parties a marriage schedule. The 14-day period may be shortened in exceptional circumstances. The marriage schedule must be produced to the celebrant of the marriage. The fee for the solemnization ceremony in a register office is £40.00. After the ceremony the marriage must be registered within three days with the Registrar-General for inclusion in the Register of Births, Deaths and Marriages. Within one month of the ceremony, the fee for an extract marriage certificate is £7; thereafter it is £10.

*Irregular marriages*

Since the Marriage (Scotland) Act 1939 the only form of irregular marriage to be recognized by law, marriage by habit and repute, remains competent under the 1977 Act. If the parties live together constantly as husband and wife and are held to be such by the general repute of the neighbourhood and among their friends and relations, then there may arise a presumption from which marriage can be inferred. Before such a marriage can be registered, however, a decree of declarator of marriage must be obtained from the Deputy Principal Clerk of the Court of Session. It is the duty of the Deputy Principal Clerk to register the decree as soon as it is granted.

# JURY SERVICE

Every parliamentary or local elector between the ages of 18 and 70 who has resided in the United Kingdom, Channel Islands or Isle of Man for at least five years since he/she attained the age of 13 will be qualified to serve on a jury unless he/she is ineligible or disqualified.

Ineligible persons include those who have at any time been judges, magistrates and certain senior court officials, those who within the previous ten years have been concerned with the law (such as barristers and solicitors and their clerks, court officers, coroners, police, prison and probation officers); priests of any religion and vowed members of religious communities; and certain sufferers from mental illness.

Disqualified persons are those who have at any time been sentenced by a court in the United Kingdom, Channel Islands or Isle of Man, to a term of imprisonment or custody for life or five years or more, or a person who in the last ten years has (a) served any part of a sentence of imprisonment, youth custody or detention; (b) been detained in a young offender institution; (c) had passed on him/her or made in respect of him/her a suspended sentence of imprisonment or order for detention; or (d) had made in respect of him/her a community service order. A person who at any time in the last five years has been placed on probation is also disqualified.

Some others are excusable as of right. These include persons over 65, members and officers of the Houses of Parliament, full-time serving members of the armed forces, registered and practising members of the medical, dental, nursing, veterinary and pharmaceutical professions, and any person who has served on a jury in the two years before he/she is summoned. In other cases the court may excuse a juror at its discretion, e.g. where the service would be a hardship to the juror, or defer the date of attendance.

If a person serves on a jury knowing himself/herself to be disqualified or ineligible, he/she is liable to be fined up to £5,000 or £500 respectively.

A juror is entitled to subsistence and travelling expenses, compensation for other expenses incurred in consequence of attendance for jury service, loss of earnings and loss of national insurance benefits, but certain maximum figures (which are revised from time to time) are laid down.

A verdict of a jury must normally be unanimous but after two hours' consideration (or such longer period as the court thinks reasonable), a majority verdict is acceptable if ten jurors agree to it (or nine if the size of the jury has been reduced to ten, e.g. by illness during the trial).

Jury trial is now very unusual in civil cases but a person charged with any but the least serious crimes is entitled to be tried by a jury. The defendant may object to any juror if he/she can show that that juror ought not to be on the jury, e.g. because he/she is ineligible or is biased against him/her.

The Coroners Act 1988 (which does not extend to Scotland) makes provision in relation to qualification to serve on coroners' juries.

*Scotland*

It is the duty of the sheriff principal of each sheriffdom, in respect of each sheriff court district in the sheriffdom, to maintain a book (the general jury book) containing the names and designations of persons within the district who are qualified and liable to serve as jurors. The book, which is compiled from information which every householder is required to provide, is kept open for the inspection by any person, upon payment of a nominal fee, at the sheriff clerk's office for the district.

Under s.1 of the Law Reform (Miscellaneous Provisions) (Scotland) Act 1980, every man or woman between the ages of 18 and 65 who is for the time being registered as a parliamentary or local government elector and who has been ordinarily resident in the United Kingdom, the Channel Islands or the Isle of Man for any period of at least five years since attaining the age of 13 years, is qualified to serve on a jury.

Ineligible persons include those who at any time within the past ten years have been judges of the supreme courts, sheriffs and certain other senior court officials, those who at any time within the past five years have been concerned with the administration of justice (such as advocates and their clerks, solicitors, court staff, police officers, prison officers, sheriff officers, procurator fiscals, and members of parole boards and children's panels), and certain sufferers from mental illness.

The same rules for disqualified persons operate in Scotland as in England.

Those excusable as of right are members and officers of the Houses of Parliament, full-time serving members of the armed forces, registered and practising members of the medical, dental, nursing, veterinary and pharmaceutical professions, ministers of religion and other persons in holy orders, and any person who has attended for jury service in the past five years.

If a person serves on a jury knowing himself/herself to be disqualified or ineligible, he/she is liable to be fined up to £5,000 or £1,000 respectively. Jurors failing to attend without good cause are liable to a maximum fine of £200.

Part II of the Juries Act 1949 (amended by regulations following thereon and by the Law Reform (Miscellaneous Provisions) (Scotland) Act 1980) applies only to Scotland and provides, *inter alia*, for the payment of travelling expenses and subsistence allowances to jurors and for loss of earnings.

The number of a jury in a civil cause in the Court of Session is 12 and in the sheriff court seven. In a criminal trial the number is 15.

## LANDLORD AND TENANT

Although basically the relationship between the parties to a lease is governed by the lease itself, the position is complicated by numerous statutory provisions. The few points dealt with may show the desirability of seeking professional assistance in these matters. Important provisions include the following:

(1) The Agricultural Holdings Act 1986, among other things, regulates the length of notice necessary to determine an agricultural tenancy, the tenant's right to remove fixtures on the land, his right to compensation for damage done by game, for improvements and for disturbance, and his right to require the consent of the Agricultural Land Tribunal to the operation of a notice to quit.

(2) The Landlord and Tenant Acts 1927 and 1954, as amended: Part II of the 1954 Act gives security of tenure to the tenant of most business premises, and in effect the tenant can only be ousted on one or more of the seven grounds set out in the Act. In some cases, where the landlord can resume possession, the tenant is entitled to compensation.

(3) The complicated mass of legislation regarding dwelling-houses is embodied in the Rent Act 1977 and the Housing Act 1988.

If a tenancy of a house is within the Rent Act, the tenant has a personal right to reside there, and may only be ousted on certain grounds. Tenancies with full Rent Act protection are known as regulated tenancies. The maximum rent recoverable under such a tenancy is the rent agreed between the landlord and tenant, unless a fair rent has been registered, in which case that is the maximum. Application for the registration of a fair rent may be made by either the landlord or tenant, to the local rent officer, and appeal against his decision lies to the rent assessment committee.

Since the Housing Act 1988 came into force on 15 January 1989, it has not generally been possible to create a new regulated tenancy, although the above protection remains for existing regulated tenancies. Tenancies granted on or after 15 January 1989 are known as assured tenancies provided they satisfy certain conditions, which are broadly the same as those for regulated tenancies under the 1977 Act. However, the rent payable by an assured tenant is either that agreed with the landlord or the open market rent fixed by the rent assessment committee.

(4) The Protection from Eviction Act 1977, as amended by the Housing Act 1988, provides that if any person with intent to cause the residential occupier of any premises to give up the occupation thereof does any act calculated to interfere with the peace or comfort of the residential occupier or members of the household, that person shall be guilty of an offence. A further provision prevents a landlord enforcing without a court order a right to possession against a tenant who is not protected by any security of tenure legislation, and there are special rules in such cases relating to agricultural employees.

(5) A notice to quit any dwelling-house must be given at least four weeks before it is to take effect, and must be in writing and in the prescribed statutory form.

(6) Part I of the Landlord and Tenant Act 1954 applies to most tenancies of houses for over 21 years at a ground rent.

Where it applies, the contractual tenancy is continued until brought to an end in the manner prescribed by the Act, and in effect the landlord can only get possession on limited grounds.

Further, under the Leasehold Reform Act 1967, tenants of houses under leases for over 21 years at a low rent are in most cases given a right to purchase the freehold or to take an extended lease for a term of fifty years, provided the tenant at the time when he/she seeks to exercise the right has been occupying the house as his/her residence for the last three years or for periods amounting to three years in the last ten years.

(7) Full Rent Act or Housing Act protection is available only if a dwelling-house is let on a tenancy. If the occupier of a dwelling-house has a mere licence to occupy, he/she does not have protection. Further, even if he/she has a tenancy, he/she will not be protected if a low rent is payable. For these reasons, many occupants of houses owned by farmers and occupied by farm workers did not enjoy full security of tenure. The Rent (Agriculture) Act 1976 contains detailed provisions conferring security of tenure on certain agricultural workers housed by their employers and on their successors on death.

(8) Under the Landlord and Tenant Act 1985 (which does not extend to Scotland), in a lease of a dwelling-house granted for a term of less than seven years, there is implied a covenant by the landlord (a) to keep in repair the structure and exterior of the house and (b) to keep in repair and proper working order the installations in the house for the supply of water, gas and electricity, for sanitation, and for space heating or heating water.

(9) The Housing Act 1985 gives security of tenure to many tenants of local authorities and certain other bodies. Further, and subject to certain conditions, such tenants may have the right to purchase their houses or to take a long lease of their flats.

(10) Tenants of flats and other dwellings are given a number of special rights by the Landlord and Tenant Act 1987, as amended by the Housing Act 1988.

### Scotland

A lease is a contract, the relationship of the parties being governed by the terms thereof. As is also the case in England, legislation has played an important part in regulating that relationship. Thus, what at common law was an agreement binding only the parties to the deed, becomes in virtue of the Leases Act 1449, a contract binding the landlord's successors, as purchasers or creditors, provided the following four conditions are observed: (a) the lease, if for more than one year, must be in writing; (b) there must be a rent; (c) there must be a term of expiry; and (d) the tenant must have entered into possession.

It would be impracticable to enter here upon a general discussion of this branch of the law. A few important provisions include:

(1) The Agricultural Holdings (Scotland) Act 1991 is a consolidating Act applicable to Scotland. It contains provisions similar to those in the English Act alluded to in the preceding section.

The Small Landholders Act 1911 provided for the setting up of the Land Court, which has jurisdiction over a large proportion of agricultural and pastoral land in Scotland.

(2) In Scotland business premises are not controlled by statute to so great an extent as in England, but the Tenancy of Shops (Scotland) Act 1949 gives a measure of security to tenants of shops. This Act enables the tenant of a shop who

is threatened with eviction to apply to the sheriff for a renewal of the tenancy. If the landlord has offered to sell the property to the tenant at an agreed price the application for a renewal of the tenancy may be dismissed. Reference should be made to Section 1 (3) of the 1949 Act for particulars of other circumstances in which the sheriff has a discretion to dismiss an application. The Act extends to premises held by the Crown or government departments, either as landlord or tenant.

(3) Many leases contain references to the term and quarter days in connection with the expiry of the lease payment dates or for rent reviews. At common law these days and dates are respectively Candlemas (2 February), Whitsunday (15 May), Lammas (1 August) and Martinmas (11 November). The Term and Quarter Days (Scotland) Act 1990 amends these dates to 28 February, 28 May, 28 August and 28 November respectively, with effect from 13 July 1991, unless, in the case of a deed executed before that date an application had been made to a sheriff for a declaration that a date other than the statutory date should apply. Where a pre-existing deed contains a reference to a specific date instead of or in addition to a day, then it is that date which shall apply.

(4) The Housing (Scotland) Act 1987 consolidates previous legislation in regard to the extensive powers and duties to local authorities in relation to housing. Included therein is the general provision regarding the rights of public sector tenants to purchase the houses which they occupy and the restrictions regarding this right in certain circumstances where the house has been designed or adapted for occupation by the elderly. This Act also makes provision for secure tenancies for public sector tenants.

(5) The Housing (Scotland) Act 1988 creates, with certain exceptions, two new forms of tenancy for tenancies created after 2 January 1989: assured tenancies, and short assured tenancies. The assured tenancy significantly reduces the concept of security of tenure and abolishes any method of regulating rent other than market forces. The short assured tenancy lasts for at least six months and if properly constituted will allow the landlord to recover possession on its expiry. Provision is made for a tenant to apply to the rent assessment committee to fix a rent based on the rent a landlord might reasonably expect for a short assured tenancy of the property.

(6) For most tenancies created before 2 January 1989, the Rent (Scotland) Act 1984 will continue to apply. It defines regulated tenancies, which may be either furnished or unfurnished, and lays down the system by which a landlord or tenant may obtain from the Rent Office registration of a fair rent. The Act gives to tenants of either furnished or unfurnished lets a substantial degree of security of tenure. There are, however, certain exceptions; they do not apply to tenancies where the interest belongs to the Crown or to a government department or to a local authority, a development corporation of a new town or a housing corporation. There must be a true tenancy for the Act to apply. It does not apply to licencees such as lodgers or persons allowed to occupy houses on a grace and favour basis or to services occupiers.

The Act regulates the short tenancy, a category of let under which, on compliance with certain conditions, the landlord can be assured of recovering possession on the expiry of the stipulated period of let. The Act defines the circumstances in which generally a landlord may apply for increased rent as a consequence of having carried out improvements to the property, and also lays down the system of phasing such rent increases. On the death of a statutory successor to a tenancy, the tenancy may pass for a second time to a member of the family or a relative who has been in residence in the house for a period of at least six months.

The Act further lays down the duties and functions of rent officers and rent assessment committees with regard to unfurnished accommodation and for rent tribunals for furnished accommodation.

The Secretary of State for Scotland is given power in the 1988 Act to repeal or amend those sections of the 1984 Act relating to the phasing of rent increases. The other major features of the 1988 Act are to establish Scottish Homes, and to permit public sector properties to be transferred to Scottish Homes or a landlord approved by Scottish Homes.

# LEGAL AID

The Legal Aid Act 1988 (as amended) is designed to make legal aid and advice more readily available for persons of small and moderate means. The main structure of the service is contained in the Act itself and the regulations made thereunder, administered by the Legal Aid Board.

## CIVIL PROCEEDINGS

Legal aid is available for proceedings (including matrimonial causes) in the House of Lords, Court of Appeal, High Court, county courts, Lands Tribunal, Employment Appeal Tribunal, Restrictive Practices Court, before the Commons Commissioners, and civil proceedings in magistrates' courts. In any event, an application for legal aid will not be approved if it appears that the applicant would gain only a trivial advantage from the proceedings. Further, proceedings wholly or partly in respect of defamation are excepted from the scheme, as are also relator actions and election petitions. Legal aid is not available for proceedings before tribunals, other than those mentioned above. It is generally not available for obtaining the decree in undefended divorce and judicial separation, although the legal advice and assistance scheme (see below) is, and legal aid is still available to deal with property, disputes over children, etc., arising in the suit.

Where a person is concerned in proceedings only in a representative, fiduciary or official capacity, his/her personal resources are not to be taken into account in considering eligibility for legal aid. In certain public law proceedings under the Children Act 1989, non-means tested legal aid is available. Apart from this, eligibility in civil proceedings depends upon an applicant's disposable income and disposable capital. The figures change frequently; particulars can be obtained from a solicitor, the Law Society or a Citizens' Advice Bureau. Disposable income is calculated by making deductions from gross income in respect of certain matters such as dependants, interest on loans, income tax, rent and other matters for which the applicant must or reasonably may provide. Disposable capital is calculated by excluding from gross capital part of the value of the house in which the applicant resides, furniture and household possessions; allowances are made in respect of dependants. Except in cases where they are living apart or have a contrary interest, any resources of a person's wife or husband or cohabitee are to be treated as that person's resources. These figures will be assessed by the Department of Social Security and will be referred to the Legal Aid Board, who will determine whether reasonable grounds exist for the grant of a civil aid certificate. Appeal from refusal of a certificate lies to an area committee. A person resident in England or Wales desiring legal aid should apply for a certificate to the appropriate area director for the area in which he or she resides; if resident elsewhere, application should be made to an area director in London. If a certificate is granted, the applicant may select his/her solicitor, and, if necessary, counsel from a panel. The costs of the assisted person's solicitor and counsel will be paid out of the legal aid fund. When, however, damages or property are recovered or preserved by the assisted person, the legal aid fund has a charge over them in respect of these costs less any contribution towards costs recovered from the unsuccessful party. In matrimonial cases, maintenance is exempt, as is the first £2,500 of any property settlement. The court may order that the costs of a successful unassisted party shall be paid out of the legal aid fund.

In an urgent case, e.g. domestic violence or to restrain the kidnapping abroad of a child, legal aid may be granted without the applicant's means being fully investigated beforehand. If on a full examination later he/she is found financially ineligible, he/she is liable to pay all the costs incurred on his/her behalf.

### LEGAL ADVICE AND ASSISTANCE

The scheme is governed by the Legal Aid Act 1988. Under the legal advice and assistance scheme a client may obtain such advice or assistance as is normally provided by a solicitor. If necessary, the advice of a barrister may be obtained but, with the exception of domestic proceedings in a family proceedings court and certain other proceedings (see below), the scheme does not extend to taking any step in any proceedings before any court or tribunal. Where legal aid is available for civil proceedings (see above) or in criminal cases (see below), the scheme covers work done in making application for such legal aid.

A person (other than one receiving advice and assistance at a police station or from a duty solicitor) is eligible for advice or assistance under the scheme provided his/her disposable capital and his/her disposable income do not exceed limits in force from time to time or if he/she is eligible for Income Support or Family Credit. In calculating disposable income, income tax and National Insurance contributions are deducted. For a married man or person with children or other dependants, further deductions will be made from both income and capital. It is intended that the financial limits shall approximate to those applying for legal aid in civil proceedings (see page 673). Except when they are separated or have conflicting interests, the means of husband and wife or cohabiting couple will be aggregated for the purpose of determining financial eligibility. Particulars may be obtained from a solicitor, the Law Society or a Citizens' Advice Bureau.

Unless the solicitor's firm holds a franchise, a solicitor cannot do more than two hours' work, or three hours' in the case of divorce (where acting for the petitioner), without leave of the area legal aid committee. The solicitor's costs are paid out of any monies recovered in respect of costs or damages from another party (although this may be waived by leave of the area committee in cases of hardship) and the balance will be paid by the legal aid fund.

The Act also extends the scheme to cover the costs of a solicitor who is present within the precincts of a family proceedings court or county court and is requested by the court to advise or represent a person who is in need of help.

In April 1980 the scheme was enlarged to cover the cost of representation in domestic proceedings in a magistrates' court. It has since been extended to cover the representation of patients before Mental Health Review Tribunals. Subject to financial eligibility limits, application is made to the area or local committee for 'approval of assistance by way of representation' which will replace legal aid for such proceedings. The two-hour limit referred to above will not apply. An applicant who is outside the financial limits but eligible for legal aid will still have to apply for a legal aid certificate as before. Free advice and assistance, and assistance by way of representation from a duty solicitor, are also

available in limited circumstances to persons appearing before a magistrates' court charged with a criminal offence.

In January 1986 the scheme was further extended to provide free advice and assistance to all suspects detained at a police station, whether arrested or merely helping police with their enquiries, and free representation for all arrested persons who are the subject of an application for a warrant of further detention under the Police and Criminal Evidence Act 1984. Such persons may instruct a solicitor of their choice or take advantage of the duty solicitor scheme which has now been extended to cover police stations.

### CRIMINAL PROCEEDINGS

The Legal Aid Act 1988 provides for legal aid in criminal proceedings. A criminal court (e.g. magistrates' court, Crown Court) has power to order legal aid to be granted where it appears desirable to do so in the interests of justice. The court shall make an order in certain cases, e.g. where a person is committed for trial on a charge of murder. However, the court may not make an order unless it appears to the court that the person's disposable income and capital are such that he/she requires assistance in meeting the costs of the particular proceedings in question. Application should be made to the appropriate court where proceedings are to take place.

An applicant shall be required to make a contribution towards the costs of his/her case if his/her disposable income and capital exceed certain prescribed limits. Persons in receipt of Income Support are automatically exempt. In order to ascertain the amount of this contribution an applicant will have to produce written evidence of his/her means. Investigation of means will be carried out by the court. Any person who falls into arrears with the payment of contribution is liable to have the order revoked.

Any practising barrister or solicitor may act for a legally aided person in criminal proceedings unless excluded by reason of misconduct. In general, where legal aid is given it will normally include representation by both counsel and solicitor. However, in connection with magistrates' courts, representation will be by solicitor alone unless the offence is a serious one.

Where any doubt arises about the grant of a legal aid order, that doubt is to be resolved in favour of the applicant. The court also has power to amend or revoke a legal aid order. Legal aid may also be granted in connection with appellate proceedings, e.g. on appeal to the Criminal Division of the Court of Appeal under the Criminal Appeal Act 1968.

## SCOTLAND

Legal aid in Scotland is governed by the Legal Aid (Scotland) Act 1986 and the regulations made thereunder. This Act established the Scottish Legal Aid Board, which has the general function of securing that legal aid and legal advice and assistance are available in accordance with the Act, and of administering the Scottish Legal Aid Fund.

### CIVIL PROCEEDINGS

Civil legal aid is available in relation to civil proceedings in the House of Lords in appeals from the Court of Session, in the Court of Session, the Lands Valuation Appeal Court, the Scottish Land Court, the sheriff court, the Lands Tribunal for Scotland, the Employment Appeals Tribunal and to the European Court of Human Rights. Civil legal aid is granted if, on application to the Board, the Board is satisfied that there is *probabilis causa litigandi* and that it is reasonable in the particular circumstances of the case that legal aid should be awarded. As in England, eligibility and any contribution required from an applicant is dependent on their disposable income and disposable capital. Information on current financial limits can be obtained from the Scottish Legal Aid Board, a solicitor, or a Citizens' Advice Bureau.

A person believing himself/herself to be eligible may instruct any solicitor of his/her own choice. If a court action is not immediately contemplated, application will be made for legal advice and assistance which operates in a similar manner to the legal advice and assistance scheme in England. If proceedings are contemplated then a formal application for civil legal aid will be made and there are special provisions for emergency applications in appropriate circumstances.

If proceedings are decided against a person in receipt of legal aid the court shall determine a reasonable sum in the circumstances as an appropriate award of expenses to be made against the applicant. The court may make an award out of the fund only if proceedings were instituted by the legally assisted person and the court is satisfied that the resisting party would suffer severe financial hardship unless the order is made, and if the court is satisfied that in all the circumstances it is just and equitable that an award be made. If monies are recovered by a legally assisted person these fall to be paid to the Scottish Legal Aid Board who will then determine the appropriate level of contribution from the sums received which should be made to the expenses of their litigation.

### CRIMINAL PROCEEDINGS

Legal aid in criminal causes is also administered under the Legal Aid (Scotland) Act 1986. The procedure for application for criminal legal aid is dependent on the circumstances of each case. In serious cases heard before a jury under solemn procedure it is for the court to decide whether to grant legal aid. Applications for legal aid must normally be made on the prescribed forms to the clerk of the court in question and an applicant is required to provide therein particulars of the merits of his/her case and his/her financial circumstances. In summary criminal causes, however, the procedure is dependent on whether the applicant is in custody; if so he/she is entitled to automatic free legal aid from the duty solicitor. If the applicant is not in custody and wishes to plead guilty, he/she is ineligible for full legal aid but may be entitled to criminal legal advice and assistance, and in some circumstances may qualify for assistance by way of representation which will enable his/her solicitor to appear and make a plea in mitigation on his/her behalf. If he/she is not in custody and wishes to plead not guilty, he/she can apply to the Scottish Legal Aid Board for criminal legal aid on the prescribed form not later than fourteen days after the first court appearance at which he/she made the plea, and legal aid shall be granted only if the Board is satisfied that the accused cannot meet the expenses of the case without undue hardship and that it is in the interest of justice as defined by the 1986 Act.

(b) making a material change in use

It is expressly provided that if one dwelling-house is converted into two or more dwelling-houses, this involves a material change in use.

The following do not constitute 'development':

(a) maintaining, improving or altering the interior of a building, provided there is no material change to the exterior, with the exception that any expansion, or works begun for the expansion, of a building below ground level constitutes development

(b) changing the use of property within the curtilage of a dwelling-house for a purpose incidental to the use of the dwelling-house as such. (It will, however, be development if building operations are carried out)

Application can be made to the local planning authority to determine whether or not an operation or change of use constitutes development.

### PLANNING PERMISSION

Application for planning permission is not always necessary, as the Secretary of State may make development orders giving general permission for a specified type of development, e.g. enlargement of a dwelling-house (including erection of a garage), so long as the cubic content of the original dwelling (external measurement) is not exceeded by more than 70 cubic metres or 15 per cent, whichever is greater, subject to a maximum of 115 cubic metres. However, in the case of a terraced house, the limitation is 50 cubic metres or 10 per cent, whichever is the greater, subject to the maximum of 115 cubic metres.

Appeal against refusal of permission lies to the Secretary of State and from his decision, in limited circumstances, to the High Court. If the result of the appeal is unsatisfactory, an applicant may in certain circumstances require the local authority to purchase the land.

### SCOTLAND

The Town and Country Planning (Scotland) Act 1972 consolidates the statute law relating to town and country planning in Scotland.

The uses of buildings are classified by the Town and Country Planning (Use Classes) (Scotland) Order 1988 (as amended). Changes in use prior to 31 December 1984 are immune from enforcement proceedings.

Development normally requires to be commenced within five years from the date of granting permission.

The 1972 Act contains provisions for an appeal to the Secretary of State against the refusal of planning permission. The decision of the Secretary of State is final.

Sections 87 and 92 of the Local Government, Planning and Land Act 1980 contain important provisions on planning applications and, unlike certain parts of this Act, extend to Scotland.

## TOWN AND COUNTRY PLANNING

The Town and Country Planning Act 1990 (consolidating earlier Acts) as amended by the Planning and Compensation Act 1991, contains far-reaching provisions affecting the liberty of an owner of land to develop and use it at will. A person has generally to get planning permission from the local planning authority before carrying out any development on the land.

Development includes:

(a) carrying out of building, engineering, mining or other operations

## VOTERS' QUALIFICATIONS

The franchise is governed by the Representation of the People Acts 1983 and 1985 (as amended by the Representation of the People Acts 1989 and 1990). Those entitled to vote as electors at a parliamentary election in any constituency are all persons resident thereon the qualifying date who, at that date and on the date of the poll, are Commonwealth citizens or citizens of the Republic of Ireland and who are not subject to any legal incapacity to vote and who on the date of the poll are at least 18 years of age. However, a person is not entitled to vote at a parliamentary election in any constituency in Northern Ireland unless he/she was resident in Northern Ireland during the whole of the period of three months ending on the qualifying date for that election. Also, no person can use his/her vote unless he/she is on the register of electors kept for the constituency. A person who is of voting age on the date of the poll at a parliamentary or local government election is entitled to vote, whether or not he/she was of voting age on the qualifying date. Accordingly, a qualified person will be entitled to be registered in a register of parliamentary electors or a register of local government electors if he/she will attain voting age within twelve months from the date on which the register is required to be published. Subject to certain conditions, the 1985 Act extends the franchise to British citizens overseas.

The register is prepared by the registration officer in each constituency in Great Britain. It is the registration officer's duty to have a house-to-house or other official inquiry made as to the persons entitled to be registered and to publish preliminary electors' lists showing the persons appearing to him/her to be entitled to be registered. Any person whose name is omitted may claim registration, and any person on the list may object to the inclusion therein of other persons' names; the registration officer determines the claims and objections.

Voters at a parliamentary or local government election must generally vote in person at the allotted polling station, except for those entitled to vote by post or at any polling station, and those for whom proxies have been appointed. Certain people can apply to be treated as absent voters at a parliamentary election and thus able to vote by post; among these are registered service voters, those unable by reason of blindness or other physical incapacity to go in person to the polling station, and those no longer at their qualifying address or unable to go in person from their qualifying address to the polling station without making a journey by air or sea.

Unless entitled to vote by post, a person registered as a service voter may vote by proxy at a parliamentary or local government election. A proxy may also be appointed by a registered elector, where the registration officer is satisfied that the applicant's circumstances on the date of the poll are likely to be such that he/she cannot reasonably be expected to vote in person at the allotted polling station. The appointment of a person to vote as proxy at parliamentary elections has effect also for the purposes of local government elections.

# The Probation Service

## ENGLAND AND WALES

The Probation Service is employed in each area (55 in total) by an independent committee of justices and it provides a professional social work agency in the courts, with responsibility for a wide range of duties which include:

(a) a pre-sentence report service for the criminal courts
(b) provision of a range of non-custodial measures involving the supervision of offenders in the community
(c) supervisory aftercare for offenders released from custody, together with social work in penal establishments and help for the families of those serving sentences
(d) an enquiry, conciliation and supervision service in the divorce and domestic courts
(e) support for and promotion of preventive and containment measures in the community designed to reduce the level of crime and domestic breakdown

It is a direct grant service funded 80 per cent from the Home Office and 20 per cent from the relevant local authority.

Its national representative bodies are:

THE CENTRAL PROBATION COUNCIL, 38 Belgrave Square, London SW1X 8NT. Tel: 0171-245 9364. *Director*, I. Miles

THE ASSOCIATION OF CHIEF OFFICERS OF PROBATION, 20–30 Lawefield Lane, Wakefield WF2 8SP. Tel: 01924–361156. *General Secretary*, Ms M. Honeyball

THE NATIONAL ASSOCIATION OF PROBATION OFFICERS, 3 Chivalry Road, London SW11 1HT. Tel: 0171-223 4887. *General Secretary*, Ms J. McKnight

## SCOTLAND

The probation service in Scotland is a statutory duty of local authorities under s. 27 of the Social Work (Scotland) Act 1968. Social workers have to supervise and provide advice, guidance and assistance to those persons living in their area who are subject to a court's supervision order. This is done by social workers as part of their normal duties and not by a separate probation staff.

# Intellectual Property

## COPYRIGHT

Copyright protects all original literary, dramatic, musical and artistic works, published editions of works, computer programs, sound recordings, films (including video) and broadcasts (including cable and satellite broadcasts). Under copyright the creators of these works can control the various ways in which their material may be exploited, the rights broadly covering copying, adapting, issuing copies to the public, performing in public, and broadcasting the material.

Copyright protection in the United Kingdom is automatic and there is no registration system. The normal term of copyright protection in literary, dramatic, musical and artistic works is the life of the author plus 50 years (increased to 70 years in the member states of the European Union from July 1995). Other forms of copyright usually last for 50 years or less.

The main international treaties protecting copyright are the Berne Convention for the Protection of Literary and Artistic Works, the Rome Convention for the Protection of Performers, Producers of Phonograms and Broadcasting Organizations, and the Universal Copyright Convention (UCC); the United Kingdom is a signatory to these conventions. Copyright material created by UK nationals or residents is protected in each country which is a member of the conventions by the national law of that country. A full list of participating countries may be obtained from the Patent Office.

### Licensing

Reproduction of copyright material without seeking permission in each instance may be permitted under licence. In the UK the Copyright Licensing Agency, formed in 1982 by the Authors' Licensing and Collecting Society and the Publishers Licensing Society, licenses the reprographic copying of literary works. The International Federation of Reproduction Rights Organizations facilitates agreements between its member licensing agencies and on behalf of its members with organizations such as the World Intellectual Property Organization, UNESCO, the European Union and the Council of Europe.

### Legal Deposit

Publishers are legally obliged to send one copy of a new publication to each of the copyright deposit libraries within one month of publication. The aim of legal deposit is to keep a complete national archive of published works as a current reference and information source. The copyright deposit libraries are the British Library, the Bodleian Library in Oxford, Cambridge University Library, the National Library of Scotland, the National Library of Wales, and Trinity College Library in Dublin.

The duties of the British Library's Legal Deposit Office are split between two locations. Books and other publications are deposited at Boston Spa, and newspapers and periodicals at the Newspaper Legal Deposit Office in London. All publications for the other four copyright libraries in the UK are dealt with by the Agent for Copyright Libraries.

## PATENTS

A patent is a document issued by the Patent Office relating to an invention and giving the proprietor monopoly rights, effective within the United Kingdom (including the Isle of Man). In return the patentee pays a fee to cover the costs of processing the patent and publicly discloses details of the invention.

To qualify for a patent an invention must be new, must exhibit an inventive step, and must be capable of industrial application. The patent is valid for a maximum of 20 years from the date on which the application was filed, subject to payment of annual fees from the end of the fourth year.

The Patent Office, established in 1852, is responsible for ensuring that all stages of an application comply with the Patents Act 1977, and that the invention meets the criteria for a patent. Patent Office Examiners check that the invention is new and innovative by searching previously published documents on the Patent Office databank, which contains details of some two million British patents, together with published international and European applications. The contents of the databank and of the Science Reference Library, which developed from the library established at the Patent Office, are available to the public.

The World Intellectual Property Organization (WIPO), a United Nations body, is responsible for administering many of the international conventions on intellectual property. The Patent Co-operation Treaty allows inventors to file a single application for patent rights in some or all of the 60 contracting states. This application is searched by an International Searching Authority and published by the International Bureau of WIPO. It may also be the subject of an (optional) international preliminary examination. Applicants must then deal directly with the patent offices in the countries where they are seeking patent rights.

The European Patent Convention, linked to the Patent Co-operation Treaty, allows inventors to obtain patent rights in all 17 contracting states by filing a single European patent application which is processed by the European Patent Office (EPO). Once granted, the patent is subject to national laws in each signatory country. To comply with security requirements, an applicant resident in the UK must file a European patent application with the UK Patent Office unless the Patent Office gives permission for it to be filed directly with the EPO. The EPO office for international patent documentation (Inpadoc) is based in Vienna and acts as an information, collection and reference centre for patent offices around the world.

## TRADE MARKS

Trade marks are a means of identification, whether a word or device or a combination of both, a logo, or the shape of goods or their packaging, which enable traders to make their goods or services readily distinguishable from those supplied by other traders. Registration prevents other traders using the same or a similar trade mark for similar products or services for which the mark is registered.

In the UK trade marks are registered at the Trade Marks Registry in the Patent Office. In order to qualify for registration a mark must be capable of distinguishing its proprietor's goods or services from those of other undertakings. It should be non-deceptive and not easily confused with a mark that has already been registered for the same or similar goods or services. The relevant current legislation is the Trade Marks Act 1994.

It is possible to obtain an international trade mark registration, effective in over 30 countries, under the Madrid Agreement. Although the UK is not a party to this agreement, following revision of UK trade marks law the UK government will be able to ratify the protocol to the Madrid Agreement. This will allow British companies to obtain international trade mark registration through a single application to WIPO in those countries party to the protocol.

EC trade mark regulation is now in force and will be administered by the Office for the Harmonization of the Single Market (trade marks and designs) in Alicante, Spain. The office, due to open in 1996, will register EC trade marks, which will be a unitary right valid throughout the European Union. The national registration of trade marks in member states will continue in parallel with the EC trade mark.

## DESIGN PROTECTION

Design protection covers the outward appearance of an article and takes two forms in the UK, registered design and design right, which are not mutually exclusive. Registered design protects the aesthetic appearance of an article, including shape, configuration, pattern or ornament, although artistic works such as sculptures are excluded, being generally protected by copyright. In order to qualify for protection, a design must be new and materially different from earlier UK published designs. The owner of the design must apply to the Designs Registry at the Patent Office. Initial registration lasts for five years and is extendible in five-yearly steps to a maximum of 25 years. The current legislation is the Registered Designs Act 1949 (as amended).

There is no international design registry currently available to UK applicants; in general, separate applications must be made in each country in which protection is sought. Proposals for an EC design regulation are being discussed. If adopted, these would result in a unitary design right valid throughout the European Union, obtainable via a single application.

Design right is an automatic right which applies to the shape or configuration of articles and does not require registration. Unlike registered design, two-dimensional designs do not qualify for protection but designs of semiconductor chips (topographies) are protected by design right. Designs must be original and non-commonplace. The term of design right is ten years from first marketing of the design and the right is effective only in the UK. The current legislation is Part 3 of the Copyright, Designs and Patents Act 1988.

## ORGANIZATIONS

AGENT FOR THE COPYRIGHT LIBRARIES, 100 Euston Street, London NW1 2HQ. Tel: 0171-380 0240. *Agent* A. T. Smail

AUTHORS' LICENSING AND COLLECTING SOCIETY, 33 Alfred Place, London WC1E 7DP. Tel: 0171-255 2034

CHARTERED INSTITUTE OF PATENT AGENTS, Staple Inn Buildings, London WC1V 7PZ. Tel: 0171-405 9450

COPYRIGHT LICENSING AGENCY LTD, 90 Tottenham Court Road, London W1P 9HE. Tel: 0171-436 5931

DESIGNS REGISTRY, The Patent Office, Cardiff Road, Newport, Gwent NP9 1RH. Tel: 01633-814000

EUROPEAN PATENT OFFICE, *Headquarters*, Erhardstrasse 27, D-8000 Munich 2, Germany

INPADOC, Schottenfeldgasse 29, Pastfach 82, A-1072, Vienna, Austria

INTERNATIONAL FEDERATION OF REPRODUCTION RIGHTS ORGANIZATIONS (IFFRO), Goethestrasse 49, D-8000 Munich 2, Germany

LEGAL DEPOSIT OFFICE, The British Library, Boston Spa, Wetherby, West Yorkshire LS23 7BY. Tel: 01937-546600

NEWSPAPER LEGAL DEPOSIT OFFICE, The British Library, 120 Colindale Avenue, London NW9 5LF. Tel: 0171-323 7353

THE PATENT OFFICE, Cardiff Road, Newport, Gwent NP9 1RH. Tel: 01633-814000

PUBLISHERS LICENSING SOCIETY, 90 Tottenham Court Road, London W1P 9HE. Tel: 0171-436 5931

SCIENCE REFERENCE LIBRARY, 25 Southampton Buildings, London WC2A 1AW. Tel: 0171-323 7494

TRADE MARKS REGISTRY, The Patent Office, Cardiff Road, Newport, Gwent NP9 1RH. Tel: 01633-814000

WORLD INTELLECTUAL PROPERTY ORGANIZATION (WIPO), 34 chemin des Colombettes, 1211 Geneva 20, Switzerland

# The Media

## Broadcasting

### FUTURE OF THE BBC

The BBC's present charter expires in 1996. In anticipation of this the Government initiated a debate about the future of public service broadcasting with a Green Paper, *The Future of the BBC*, published on 24 November 1992. The BBC published a charter review document, *Extending Choice*, on 26 November 1992 outlining the BBC's view of its future. On 27 May 1993, after a period of consultation and debate, the BBC published *Responding to the Green Paper*. A White Paper was published in July 1994 (*see page 1172*).

### TELEVISION

The British Broadcasting Corporation (*see* page 290) is responsible for public service broadcasting in the UK. Its constitution and finances are governed by royal charter and by a licence and agreement. Its role is to provide high-quality programmes with wide-ranging appeal that educate, inform and entertain.

The Independent Television Commission (*see* page 321) is the regulator and licenser for independent television companies. The ITV franchises for the 15 regional companies and for breakfast television were allocated new ten-year licences from January 1993. In January 1994 it was announced that an ITV company may own two licences, 20 per cent of a third, and 5 per cent of any subsequent licence.

A new independent national television channel was due to be established by the autumn of 1993, but the ITC decided not to award the licence to Channel Five Holdings Ltd, the only applicant. The ITC is now inviting bids again for the licence.

All channels are broadcast in colour on 625 lines UHF from a network of transmitting stations which are owned and operated by the BBC and by National Transcommunications Ltd. Transmissions are available to more than 99 per cent of the population.

### BBC TELEVISION

Television Centre, Wood Lane, London W12 7RJ
Tel 0181-743 8000

The BBC's experiments in television broadcasting started in 1929 and in 1936 the BBC began the world's first public service of high-definition television from Alexandra Palace. The BBC broadcasts two national television services, BBC 1 and BBC 2; outside England these services are designated BBC Scotland on 1, BBC Scotland on 2, BBC 1 Northern Ireland, BBC 2 Northern Ireland, BBC Wales on 1 and BBC Wales on 2.

### BBC WORLD SERVICE TELEVISION

80 Wood Lane, London W12 OTT
Tel 0181-576 2783

World Service Television (WSTV) was set up in 1991 to establish a world-wide television service and assume responsibility for the BBC's satellite television interests. Its core service is a 24-hour news and information channel which is now broadcast in Europe, Asia, Africa, Canada and Japan, and is expected to start broadcasting in the USA in 1995. An Arabic language channel for the Middle East and North Africa began in 1994. In partnership with Pearson PLC, the BBC planned to launch two pan-European satellite services, one entertainment and one news and information, by the end of 1994.

### INDEPENDENT TELEVISION

INDEPENDENT TELEVISION NETWORK CENTRE
200 Gray's Inn Road, London WC1X 8HF
Tel 0171-843 8000

The ITV Network Centre is wholly owned by the ITV companies and undertakes the commissioning and scheduling of those television programmes which are shown across the ITV network. It also provides a range of services to the ITV companies where a common approach is required.

Programmes for the network are commissioned from the ITV companies as well as from independent producers. As the Centre has no legal status as a broadcaster, commissions must then be contracted jointly with one of the ITV companies. The scheduling of all networked programmes is submitted for general approval to the network companies' heads of broadcasting, who sit on the ITV Broadcast Board.

ITV's governing body is the Council, comprising heads of the ITV companies and chaired by the elected representative of the ITV companies.
*Chief Executive*, A. Quinn
*Network Director*, M. Plantin

INDEPENDENT TELEVISION NETWORK COMPANIES
ANGLIA TELEVISION (owned by Meridian) (*eastern England*), Anglia House, Norwich NR1 3JG. Tel: 01603-615151
BORDER TELEVISION PLC (*the Borders*), Television Centre, Carlisle CA1 3NT. Tel: 01228-25101
CARLTON TELEVISION LTD (*London (weekdays)*), 101 St Martin's Lane, London WC2N 4AZ. Tel: 0171-240 4000
CENTRAL INDEPENDENT TELEVISION PLC (owned by Carlton) (*the Midlands*), Central House, Broad Street, Birmingham B1 2JP. Tel: 0121-643 9898
CHANNEL TELEVISION LTD (*Channel Islands*), The Television Centre, St Helier, Jersey JE2 3ZD. Tel: 01534-68999
GRAMPIAN TELEVISION PLC (*northern Scotland*), Queen's Cross, Aberdeen AB9 2XJ. Tel: 01224-646464
GRANADA TELEVISION LTD (*north-west England*), Granada TV Centre, Quay Street, Manchester M60 9EA. Tel: 0161-832 7211
HTV GROUP (*Wales and western England*), HTV Wales, Television Centre, Culverhouse Cross, Cardiff CF5 6XJ. Tel: 01222-590590; HTV Ltd, Television Centre, Bath Road, Bristol BS4 3HG. Tel: 0117-977 8366
LONDON WEEKEND TELEVISION (owned by Granada) (*London (weekends)*), London Television Centre, Upper Ground, London SE1 9LT. Tel: 0171-620 1620
MERIDIAN BROADCASTING LTD (*south and south-east England*), Television Centre, Southampton SO9 5HZ. Tel: 01703-222555
SCOTTISH TELEVISION PLC (*central Scotland*), Cowcaddens, Glasgow G2 3PR. Tel: 0141-332 9999
TYNE TEES TELEVISION LTD (*north-east England*), The Television Centre, City Road, Newcastle upon Tyne NE1 2AL. Tel: 0191-261 0181

ULSTER TELEVISION PLC (*Northern Ireland*), Havelock House, Ormeau Road, Belfast BT7 IEB. Tel: 01232-328122

WESTCOUNTRY TELEVISION LTD (*south-west England*), Western Wood Way, Langage Science Park, Plymouth PL7 5BG. Tel: 01752-333333

YORKSHIRE TELEVISION LTD (*Yorkshire*), The Television Centre, Leeds LS3 IJS. Tel: 0113-243 8283

### OTHER INDEPENDENT TELEVISION COMPANIES

CHANNEL FOUR TELEVISION COMPANY LTD, 124 Horseferry Road, London SW1P 2TX. Tel: 0171-396 4444. Provides a service to the UK except Wales, and is charged to cater for interests under-represented by the ITV network companies

GMTV LTD (*breakfast television*), The London Television Centre, Upper Ground, London SE1 9LT. Tel: 0171-827 7000

INDEPENDENT TELEVISION NEWS LTD, ITN House, 200 Gray's Inn Road, London WC1X 8XD. Tel: 0171-833 3000

TELETEXT UK LTD, 101 Farm Lane, London SW6 1QJ. Tel: 0171-386 5000. Provides teletext services for the ITV companies and Channel 4

WELSH FOURTH CHANNEL AUTHORITY (Sianel Pedwar Cymru), Parc Ty Glas, Llanishen, Cardiff CF4 5DU. Tel: 01222-747444. S4C schedules Welsh language programmes and relays most Channel 4 programmes

### DIRECT BROADCASTING BY SATELLITE TELEVISION

BRITISH SKY BROADCASTING LTD, 6 Centaurs Business Park, Isleworth, Middx. TW7 5QD. Tel: 0171-705 3000. Broadcasts seven channels which are wholly owned by Sky. Twelve channels are available in the multi-channel package which is broadcast, but not owned, by Sky. Five new channels were launched in October 1994.

## RADIO

The BBC provides both national and local radio services. The Radio Authority (*see* page 346) is the regulator and licenser for independent radio companies.

Three independent national radio stations have been licensed since 1991; the latest, Talk Radio UK Ltd, is to begin broadcasting in 1995. Five independent regional local radio licences have been awarded and stations will begin broadcasting on or after 1 September 1994 (*see* page 682). Since January 1991 the Authority has awarded more than 35 new local radio licences, has readvertised 68 local licences, and has a further 60 to be readvertised by the end of 1995.

### BBC RADIO

Broadcasting House, Portland Place, London W1A 1AA
Tel 0171-580 4468

BBC Radio broadcasts five national services to the UK, Isle of Man and the Channel Islands. There is also a tier of national regional services in Wales, Scotland and Northern Ireland and 38 local radio stations in England and the Channel Islands. In Wales there are two regional services based on the Welsh and English languages respectively.

### BBC NATIONAL SERVICES

RADIO 1 (Pop and rock music, information and comedy) – 24 hours a day. *Frequencies:* FM 97.6–99.8 MHz, coverage 98.6%

RADIO 2 (Popular music, entertainment, comedy and the arts) – 24 hours a day. *Frequencies:* FM 88–90.2 MHz, coverage 98.6%

RADIO 3 (Classical music, drama, documentaries, poetry, and schools programmes) – 6.30 a.m.–12.45 a.m. daily. *Frequencies:* FM 90.2–92.4 MHz, coverage 98.6%

RADIO 4 (News, documentaries, drama, entertainment, and cricket in season) – 5.55 a.m.–12.40 a.m. daily. *Frequencies:* FM in England 92.4–94.6 MHz, elsewhere 92.4–96.1 and 103.5–105 MHz, coverage 98.6%; LW 198kHz/1515m, plus eight local fillers on MW

RADIO 5 LIVE (News and sport) – 24 hours a day. *Frequencies:* 693 kHz and 909 kHz, plus one local filler

### BBC NATIONAL REGIONAL SERVICES

RADIO SCOTLAND *Frequencies:* MW 810 kHz plus two local fillers; FM 92.4–96.1 and 103.5–105 MHz, coverage 94%. Local programmes on FM as above: ABERDEEN (also MW 990 kHz); HIGHLAND; RADIO NAN GAIDHEAL (Gaelic service) ORKNEY; SHETLAND; SOLWAY (also MW 585 kHz); TWEED

RADIO ULSTER *Frequencies:* MW 1341 kHz, plus two local fillers; FM 92.4–96.1 MHz, coverage 96%. Local programmes on RADIO FOYLE *Frequencies:* MW 792 kHz; FM 93.1 MHz

RADIO WALES *Frequency:* MW 882 kHz plus two local fillers, coverage 96%. Local programmes on RADIO CLWYD *Frequency:* MW 657 kHz

RADIO CYMRU (Welsh-language) *Frequencies:* FM 92.4–96.1 and 103.5–105 MHz, coverage 96%

### BBC LOCAL RADIO STATIONS

There are 38 local stations serving England and the Channel Islands:

BBC 3 COUNTIES RADIO, PO Box 3CR, Luton, Beds. LU1 5XL. Tel: 01582-441000. *Frequencies:* MW 1161/630 kHz, 95.5/103.8FM

BERKSHIRE, Broadcasting House, 42A Portman Road, Reading, Berks. RG3 1NB. Tel: 01734-567056. *Frequencies:* 94.6/95.4/104.1/104.4 FM

BRISTOL, 3 Tyndalls Park Road, Bristol BS8 1PP. Tel: 0117-974 1111. *Frequencies:* MW 1548 kHz, 94.9/95.5/104.6 FM

CAMBRIDGESHIRE, Broadcasting House, 104 Hills Road, Cambridge CB2 1LD. Tel: 01223-315970. *Frequencies:* MW 1026 kHz, 95.7 FM

CLEVELAND, PO Box 1548, Newport Road, Middlesbrough, Cleveland TS1 5DG. Tel: 01642-225211. *Frequencies:* MW 1548 kHz, 95.0/95.8 FM

CORNWALL, Phoenix Wharf, Truro, Cornwall TR1 1UA. Tel: 01872-75421. *Frequencies:* MW 630/657 kHz, 95.2/96.0/103.9 FM

CUMBRIA, Hilltop Heights, London Road, Carlisle CA1 2NA. Tel: 01228-59244. *Frequencies:* MW 756/1458/837 kHz, 95.2/95.6/96.1/104.2 FM

CWR (COVENTRY AND WARWICKSHIRE RADIO), 25 Warwick Road, Coventry CV1 2WR. Tel: 01203-559911. *Frequencies:* 94.8/103.7 FM

DERBY, 56 St Helen's Street, Derby DE1 3HL. Tel: 01332-361111. *Frequencies:* MW 1116 kHz, 94.2/95.3/104.5 FM

DEVON, PO Box 5, Broadcasting House, Seymour Road, Plymouth PO1 1XT. Tel: 01752-260323. *Frequencies:* MW 801/990/1458/801 kHz, 103.4/96.0/95.8/94.8 FM

ESSEX, PO Box 765, 198 New London Road, Chelmsford CM2 9AB. Tel: 01245-262393. *Frequencies:* MW 765/729/1530 kHz, 103.5/95.3 FM

GLOUCESTERSHIRE, London Road, Gloucester GL1 1SW. Tel: 01452-308585. *Frequencies:* 95.0/104.7 FM

GLR (GREATER LONDON RADIO), 35A Marylebone High Street, London W1A 4LG. Tel: 0171-224 2424. *Frequencies:* MW 1458 kHz, 94.9 FM

GMR (GREATER MANCHESTER RADIO), New Broadcasting House, Oxford Road, Manchester M60 1SJ. Tel: 0161-200 2000. *Frequencies:* MW 1458 kHz, 95.1 FM

GUERNSEY, Commerce House, Les Banques, St Peter Port, Guernsey. Tel: 01481-728977. *Frequencies:* MW 1116 kHz, 93.2 FM

HEREFORD AND WORCESTER, 43 Broad Street, Hereford HR4 9HH. Tel: 01432-355252; and Hylton Road, Worcester WR2 5WW. Tel: 01905-748485. *Frequencies:* MW 738/819 kHz, 104.6/104.0/94.7 FM

HUMBERSIDE, 9 Chapel Street, Hull HU1 3NU. Tel: 01482-23232. *Frequencies:* MW 1485 kHz, 95.9 FM

JERSEY, Broadcasting House, Rouge Bouillon, St Helier, Jersey. Tel: 01534-70000. *Frequencies:* MW 1026 kHz, 88.8 FM

KENT, Sun Pier, Chatham, Kent ME4 4EZ. Tel: 01634-830505. *Frequencies:* MW 1035/774/1602 kHz, 96.7/104.2 FM

LANCASHIRE, 20–26 Darwen Street, Blackburn BB2 2EA. Tel: 01254-62411. *Frequencies:* MW 855/1557 kHz, 95.5/104.5/103.9 FM

LEEDS, Broadcasting House, Woodhouse Lane, Leeds LS2 9PN. Tel: 0113-244 2131. *Frequencies:* MW 774 kHz, 92.4/95.3 FM

LEICESTER, Epic House, Charles Street, Leicester LE1 3SH. Tel: 0116-251 6688. *Frequencies:* MW 837 kHz, 104.9 FM

LINCOLNSHIRE, Radion Buildings, Newport, Lincoln LN1 3XY. Tel: 01522-511411. *Frequencies:* MW 837 kHz, 104.9 FM

MERSEYSIDE, 55 Paradise Street, Liverpool L1 3BP. Tel: 0151-708 5500. *Frequencies:* MW 1485 kHz, 95.8 FM

NEWCASTLE, Broadcasting Centre, Barrack Road, Fenham, Newcastle upon Tyne NE99 1RN. Tel: 0191-232 4141. *Frequencies:* MW 1458 kHz, 95.4/104.4/96.0 FM

NORFOLK, Norfolk Tower, Surrey Street, Norwich NR1 3PA. Tel: 01603-617411. *Frequencies:* MW 855/873 kHz, 95.1/104.4 FM

NORTHAMPTON, Broadcasting House, Abington Street, Northampton NN1 2BE. Tel: 01604-239100. *Frequencies:* 104.2/106.3 FM

NOTTINGHAM, York House, Mansfield Road, Nottingham NG1 3JB. Tel: 0115-941 5161. *Frequencies:* MW 1584/1521 kHz, 103.8/95.5 FM

OXFORD, 269 Banbury Road, Oxford OX2 7DW. Tel: 01865-311444. *Frequency:* 95.2 FM

SHEFFIELD, Ashdell Grove, 60 Westbourne Road, Sheffield S10 2QU. Tel: 0114-268 6185. *Frequencies:* MW 1035 kHz, 94.7/104.1/88.6 FM

SHROPSHIRE, 2–4 Boscobel Drive, Shrewsbury SY1 3TT. Tel: 01743-248484. *Frequencies:* MW 1584 kHz, 95.0/96.0 FM

SOLENT, Broadcasting House, Havelock Road, Southampton SO1 0XR. Tel: 01703-631311. *Frequencies:* MW 999/1359 kHz, 96.1 FM

SOUTHERN COUNTIES, Broadcasting House, Guildford, Surrey GU2 5AP. Tel: 01483-306113; Marlborough Place, Brighton BN1 1TU. Tel: 01273-680231. *Frequencies:* MW 1485/1161/1368 kHz, 95.0/95.1/95.3/104.5/104.6/104.0 FM

STOKE, Conway House, Cheapside, Hanley, Stoke-on-Trent ST1 1JJ. Tel: 01782-208080. *Frequencies:* MW 1503 kHz, 94.6 FM

SUFFOLK, Broadcasting House, St Matthew's Street, Ipswich IP1 3EP. Tel: 01473-250000. *Frequencies:* 95.5/103.9/104.6 FM

WILTSHIRE SOUND, Broadcasting House, 56–58 Prospect Place, Swindon SN1 3RW. Tel: 01793-513626. *Frequencies:* MW 1332/1368 kHz, 103.6/103.4/103.5 FM

WM (WEST MIDLANDS), Pebble Mill Road, Birmingham B5 7SD. Tel: 0121-414 8484. *Frequencies:* MW 828/1458 kHz, 95.6 FM

YORK, 20 Bootham Row, York YO3 7BR. Tel: 01904-641351. *Frequencies:* MW 666/1260 kHz, 103.7/104.3/95.5 FM

## BBC WORLD SERVICE

Bush House, Strand, London WC2B 4PH
Tel 0171-240 3456

The BBC World Service broadcasts 880 hours of programmes a week in 39 languages including English. Eighty-four transmitters are used, 38 of them in the UK and 46 at relay stations overseas. In addition the World Service supplies more than 540 hours of programmes a week for other radio stations.

In 1994 the World Service was reorganized into six regions, each responsible for programmes in English as well as regional languages.

AFRICA AND THE MIDDLE EAST, Arabic, Hausa, Somali and Swahili; English programmes including *Network Africa* and *Focus on Africa*.

ASIA PACIFIC, Burmese, Cantonese, Indonesian, Mandarin, Thai and Vietnamese; English programmes including *Dateline East Asia*.

EUROPE, Albanian, Bulgarian, Croatian, Czech, Finnish, French, German, Greek, Hungarian, Polish, Romanian, Serbian, Slovak, Slovene and Turkish; English programmes including *Europe Today*.

FORMER SOVIET UNION AND SOUTH-WEST ASIA, Russian, Ukrainian, Pashto and Persian.

SOUTH ASIA, Bengali, Hindi, Nepali, Sinhala, Tamil and Urdu; English programmes including *South Asia Report*.

THE AMERICAS, Portuguese for Brazil, Spanish; English programmes including *Caribbean Report* and *Calling the Falklands*.

BBC ENGLISH teaches English world-wide through radio, television and a wide range of published courses

BBC MONITORING provides regional summaries and a teleprinted news service from the output of overseas radio and television stations

BBC TOPICAL TAPES produces programmes in English for radio stations in 50 countries

BBC TRANSCRIPTION sells a wide range of BBC radio programmes on CD to broadcasters in over 100 countries

BBC TRAINING runs journalism, management and skills training courses for overseas broadcasters

BBC MARSHALL PLAN OF THE MIND TRUST produces business skills radio courses for Russia and Ukraine.

BBC INTERNATIONAL BROADCASTING AND AUDIENCE RESEARCH carries out audience research and sells printed publications and data

## INDEPENDENT RADIO

INDEPENDENT NATIONAL RADIO STATIONS

CLASSIC FM, Academic House, 24–28 Oval Road, London NW1 7DQ. Tel: 0171-284 3000. 24 hours a day. *Frequencies:* 99.9–101.9 FM

VIRGIN 1215, 1 Golden Square, London WIR 4DJ. Tel: 0171-434 1215. 24 hours a day. *Frequencies:* MW 1242/1266/1215/1197 kHz

TALK RADIO UK LTD, Media Ventures International, 25A Foubert's Place, London WIV IHE. Tel: 0171-287 8000. 24 hours a day. *Frequencies:* MW 1053/1089 kHz

INDEPENDENT REGIONAL LOCAL RADIO STATIONS

CENTURY RADIO (*North-east*), PO Box 100, Gateshead NE8 2YY. Tel: 0191-477 6666

GALAXY RADIO (*Severn Estuary*), Broadcast Centre, Portland Square, Bristol BS2 8RZ. Tel: 01272-240111

HEART FM (*West Midlands*), c/o The Chrysalis Building, Bramley Road, London W10 6SP. Tel: 0171-221 2213

JFM (*North-west*), The World Trade Centre, Exchange Quay, Manchester M5 3EQ. Tel: 0161-877 1004

SCOT FM (*Central Scotland*), 1 The Shed, Albert Quay, Leith Docks, Edinburgh EH6 7DN. Tel: 0131-554 6677

INDEPENDENT LOCAL RADIO STATIONS

AIRE FM, PO Box 2000, Leeds LS3 ILR. Tel: 0113-245 2299. *Frequency:* 96.3 FM

THE BAY, PO Box 969, St George's Quay, Lancaster LA1 3LD. Tel: 01524-848747. *Frequencies:* 96.9/102.3/103.2 FM

BEACON RADIO, 267 Tettenhall Road, Wolverhampton WV6 0DQ. Tel: 01902-757211. *Frequency:* 97.2/103.1 FM

BREEZE, Radio House, Clifftown Road, Southend-on-Sea, Essex SSI ISX. Tel: 01702-333711. *Frequency:* MW 1359/1431 kHz

BRMB FM, Aston Road North, Birmingham B6 4BX. Tel: 0121-359 4481. *Frequency:* 96.4 FM

BRUNEL CLASSIC GOLD, PO Box 2000, Swindon SN4 7EX. Tel: 01793-440301; PO Box 2000, Bristol BS99 7SN. Tel: 0117-927 9911. *Frequencies:* MW 1260 kHz (Bristol); 1161 kHz (Swindon); 936 kHz (West Wilts.)

CAPITAL AND GOLD, Euston Tower, London NWI 3DR. Tel: 0171-608 6080. *Frequencies:* MW 1548 kHz, (Gold) 95.8 FM

CENTRAL FM, Stirling Enterprise Park, Kerse Road, Stirling FK7 7YJ. Tel: 01786-451188. *Frequency:* 103.1 FM

CFM, PO Box 964, Carlisle, Cumbria CA1 3NG. Tel: 01228-818964. *Frequency:* 96.4 FM

CHANNEL 103 FM, 6 Tunnell Street, St Helier, Jersey JE2 4LU. Tel: 01543-888103. *Frequency:* 103.7 FM

CHILTERN RADIO PLC, Broadcast Centre, Chiltern Road, Dunstable, Beds. LU6 1HQ. Tel: 01582-666001. *Frequencies:* MW 828 kHz, 97.6 FM(Luton), 792 kHz, 96.9 FM (Bedford)

CHOICE FM, 16–18 Trinity Gardens, London SW9 8DP. Tel: 0171-738 7969. *Frequency:* 96.9 FM

CHOICE FM, c/o 175 Hamstead Road, Handsworth Wood, Birmingham B20 2RL. Tel: 0121-553 6199. *Frequency:* 102.4 FM

CITY FM, PO Box 967, Liverpool L69 1TQ. Tel: 0151-227 5100. *Frequency:* 96.7 FM

CLYDE 1 AND 2, Clydebank Business Park, Clydebank, Glasgow G81 2RX. Tel: 0141-306 2200. *Frequencies:* MW 1152 kHz, 102.5 FM

COOL FM, PO Box 974, Belfast BT1 IRT. Tel: 01247-817181. *Frequency:* 97.4 FM

COUNTRY 1035, PO Box 1035, London SW6 3QQ. Tel: 0171-384 1175. *Frequency:* 1035 kHz

DEVONAIR RADIO, 35–37 St David's Hill, Exeter EX4 4DA. Tel: 01392-430703. *Frequencies:* MW 666 kHz, 97.0 FM (Exeter); 954 kHz, 96.4 FM (Torbay); 103 FM (East Devon)

DOWNTOWN RADIO, Newtownards, Co. Down BT23 4ES. Tel: 01247-815555. *Frequencies:* MW 1026 kHz, 96.6/96.4/102.4 FM

ELEVEN SEVENTY AM, PO Box 1170, High Wycombe, Bucks. HP13 6YT. Tel: 01494-446611. *Frequency:* MW 1170 kHz

ESSEX RADIO PLC, Radio House, Clifftown Road, Southend-on-Sea, Essex SS1 ISX. Tel: 01702-333711. *Frequencies:* 96.3 FM (Southend), 102.6 FM (Chelmsford)

FORTH FM, Forth House, Forth Street, Edinburgh EHI 3LF. Tel: 0131-556 9255. *Frequencies:* 97.3/97.6 FM

FORTUNE 1458, PO Box 1458, Quay West, Trafford Park, Manchester M17 1FL. Tel: 0161-877 1458. *Frequency:* 1458 kHz

FOX FM, Brush House, Pony Road, Cowley, Oxford OX4 2XR. Tel: 01865-748787. *Frequencies:* 102.6 FM (Oxford); 97.4 FM (Banbury)

GALAXY RADIO, 25 Portland Square, Bristol BS2 8RZ. Tel: 0117-924 0111. *Frequencies:* 97.2 FM; 101 FM (Seven Estuary)

GEM-AM, 29–31 Castle Gate, Nottingham NGI 7AP. Tel: 0115-952 7000. *Frequencies:* MW 1260 kHz (Leicester); 999 kHz (Nottingham); 945 kHz (Derby)

GEMINI, c/o Curzon House, Southernhay West, Exeter. *Frequencies:* 97/96.4/103 FM

GREAT NORTH RADIO, Newcastle upon Tyne NE99 IBB. Tel: 0191-496 0377. *Frequencies:* MW 1152/1170 kHz (Tyne and Wear); 1170 kHz (Teeside)

GREAT YORKSHIRE GOLD, 900 Herries Road, Sheffield S6 IRH. Tel: 0114-285 2121; PO Box 3000, Forster Square, Bradford BD1 5NE. Tel: 01274-731521; Commercial Road, Hull HUI 2SG. Tel: 01482-25141. *Frequencies:* MW 1548/1305/990 kHz (S. Yorks., N. Midlands); 1278/1530 kHz (W. Yorks.); 1161 kHz (Humberside)

GWR FM (EAST), PO Box 2000, Swindon SN4 7EX. Tel: 01793-440300. *Frequencies:* 96.5 FM (Marlborough); 97.2 FM (Swindon); 102.2 FM (West Wilts)

GWR FM (WEST), PO Box 2000, Bristol BS99 7SN. Tel: 0117-984 3200. *Frequency:* 96.3/103.0 FM

HALLAM FM, Radio House, 900 Herries Road, Hillsborough, Sheffield S6 IRH. Tel: 0114-285 3333. *Frequencies:* 97.4 FM (Sheffield); 96.1 FM (Rotherham); 102.9 FM (Barnsley); 103.4 FM (Doncaster)

HEARTLAND FM, Lower Oakfield, Pitlochry, Perthshire PH16 2DS. Tel: 01796-474040. *Frequency:* 97.5 FM

HEREWARD RADIO, Queensgate Centre, Peterborough PEI IXJ. Tel: 01733-460460. *Frequency:* 102.7 FM

HORIZON RADIO, Broadcast Centre, Crownhill, Milton Keynes, Bucks. MK8 0AB. Tel: 01908-269111. *Frequency:* 103.3 FM

INVICTA FM AND SUPERGOLD, Radio House, John Wilson Business Park, Whitstable, Kent CT5 3QX. Tel: 01227-772004. *Frequencies:* MW 1242/603 kHz, 102.8/95.9/97.0/96.1/103.1 FM

ISLAND FM, 12 Westerbrook, St Sampsons, Guernsey, Channel Islands. Tel: 01481-42000. *Frequency:* 93.7/104.7 FM

ISLE OF WIGHT RADIO, Dodnor Park, Newport, Isle of Wight PO30 5XE. Tel: 01983-822557. *Frequency:* MW 1242 kHz

JFM, 26–27 Castlereagh Street, London WIH 5YR. Tel: 0171-706 4100. *Frequency:* 102.2 FM

KCBC (Kettering), Unit 1, Centre 2000, Robinson Close, Telford Way Industrial Estate, Kettering, Northants. NNI6 8PU. Tel: 01536-412413. *Frequency:* MW 1584 kHz

KISS 100 FM, Kiss House, 80 Holloway Road, London N7 8JG. Tel: 0171-700 6100. *Frequency:* 100.0 FM

KISS 102, PO Box 102, Manchester M60 1GJ. Tel: 0161-228 0102. *Frequency:* 102 FM

KL.FM, 18 Blackfriars Street, King's Lynn, Norfolk PE30 1NN. Tel: 01553-772777. *Frequency:* 96.7 FM

LANTERN RADIO, Light House, 17 Market Place, Bideford, N. Devon EX39 2DR. Tel: 01237-424444. *Frequency:* 96.2 FM

LEICESTER SOUND FM, Granville House, Granville Road, Leicester LE1 7RW. Tel: 0116-255 1616. *Frequency:* 103.2 FM

LINCS FM, Witham Park, Waterside South, Lincoln LN5 7JN. Tel: 01522-549900. *Frequency:* 102.2 FM

LONDON FIRST AND LONDON EXTRA, 72 Hammersmith Road, London W14 8YE. Tel: 0171-333 0400. *Frequency:* 1152 kHz

LONDON GREEK RADIO, Florentia Village, Vale Road, London N4 1TD. Tel: 0181-800 8001. *Frequency:* 103.3 FM

LONDON NEWS RADIO, 72 Hammersmith Road, London W14 8YE. Tel: 0171-603 2400. *Frequency:* 97.3 FM

MAGIC 828, PO Box 2000, Leeds LS3 1LR. Tel: 0113-245 2299. *Frequency:* MW 828 kHz

MARCHER COAST FM, 41 Conwy Road, Colwyn Bay, Clwyd. Tel: 01492-534555. *Frequency:* 96.3 FM

MARCHER GOLD, The Studios, Mold Road, Wrexham, Clwyd LL11 4AF. Tel: 01978-752202. *Frequencies:* MW 1260 kHz

MAX AM, Forth House, Forth Street, Edinburgh EH1 3LF. Tel: 0131-556 9255. *Frequency:* MW 1548 kHz

MELLOW 1557, 21–23 Walton Road, Frinton-on-Sea, Essex CO13 0AA. Tel: 01255-675303. *Frequency:* MW 1557 kHz

MELODY RADIO, 180 Brompton Road, London SW3 1HF. Tel: 0171-584 1049. *Frequency:* 104.9 FM

MERCIA FM AND MERCIA CLASSIC GOLD, Hertford Place, Coventry CV1 3TT. Tel: 01203-868200. *Frequencies:* MW 1359 kHz; 97.0/102.9 FM

MERCURY EXTRA AM, Broadfield House, Brighton Road, Crawley, W. Sussex RH11 9TT. Tel: 01293-519161. *Frequencies:* MW 1476/1521 kHz

METRO FM, Newcastle upon Tyne NE99 1BB. Tel: 0191-488 3131. *Frequencies:* 97.1/103.0 FM

MFM, The Studios, Mold Road, Wrexham, Clwyd LL11 4AF. Tel: 01978-752202. *Frequencies:* 103.4/97.1 FM

MINSTER FM, PO Box 123, Dunnington, York YO1 5ZX. Tel: 01904-488888. *Frequency:* 104.7 FM

MIX 96, Friars Square Studios, 11 Bourbon Street, Aylesbury, Bucks. HP20 2PZ. Tel: 01296-399396. *Frequency:* 96.2 FM

MORAY FIRTH RADIO, PO Box 271, Inverness IV3 6SF. Tel: 01463-224433. *Frequencies:* MW 1107 kHz, 97.4 FM

NEVIS RADIO, Inverlochy, Fort William, Inverness-shire PH33 6LU. Tel: 01397-700007. *Frequency:* 96.6 FM

96.7 BCR, Russell Court Building, Claremont Street, Lisburn Road, Belfast BT9 6JX. Tel: 01232-438500. *Frequency:* 96.7 FM

NORTHANTS RADIO, Broadcast Centre, The Enterprise Park, Boughton Green Road, Northampton NN2 7AH. Tel: 01604-792411. *Frequencies:* MW 1557 kHz, 96.6 FM

NORTH-EAST COMMUNITY RADIO, Inverurie, Town House, Kintore, Aberdeenshire AB51 0US. Tel: 01467-632878. *Frequency:* 102.1 FM

NORTHSOUND RADIO, 45 Kings Gate, Aberdeen AB2 6BL. Tel: 01224-632234. *Frequencies:* MW 1035 kHz, 96.9/103 FM

OCEAN FM, Radio House, Whittle Avenue, Segensworth West, Fareham, Hants. PO15 5PA. Tel: 01489-589911. *Frequencies:* 97.5/96.7 FM

ORCHARD FM, Haygrove House, Shoreditch, Taunton TA3 7BT. Tel: 01823-338448. *Frequencies:* 102.6/97.1 FM

PICCADILLY RADIO LTD, 127-131 The Piazza, Piccadilly Plaza, Manchester M1 4AW. Tel: 0161-236 9913. *Frequencies:* MW 1152 kHz, 103.0 FM

PIRATE FM, Carn Brea Studios, Wilson Way, Redruth, Cornwall TR15 3XX. Tel: 01209-314400. *Frequencies:* 102.2/102.8 FM

PLYMOUTH SOUND LTD, Earl's Acre, Plymouth PL3 4HX. Tel: 01752-27272. *Frequencies:* MW 1152 kHz, 97.0 FM

POWERFM, Radio House, Whittle Avenue, Segensworth West, Fareham, Hants. PO15 5PA. Tel: 01489-589911. *Frequency:* 103.2 FM.

THE PULSE, PO Box 3000, Bradford BD1 5NE. Tel: 01274-731521. *Frequencies:* 97.5/102.5 FM

Q102.9, The Old Waterside Railway Station, Duke Street, Waterside, Londonderry BT47 1DH. Tel: 01504-44449. *Frequency:* 102.9 FM

Q103 (Cambridge and Newmarket), The Vision Park, Chivers Way, Histon, Cambridge CB4 4WW. Tel: 01223-235255. *Frequencies:* 103.0/97.4 FM

Q96, 26 Lady Lane, Paisley PA1 2LG. Tel: 0141-887 9630. *Frequency:* 96.3 FM

RADIO BORDERS, Tweedside Park, Galashiels TD1 3TD. Tel: 01896-759444. *Frequencies:* 96.8/97.5/103.1/103.4 FM

RADIO BROADLAND, St George's Plain, 47–49 Colegate, Norwich NR3 1DB. Tel: 01603-630621. *Frequencies:* MW 1152 kHz, 102.4 FM

RADIO CEREDIGION, Yr Hen Ysgol Gymraeg, Ffordd Alexandra, Aberystwyth, Dyfed SY23 1PE. Tel: 01970-627999. *Frequencies:* 103.3/96.6 FM

RADIO CITY GOLD, PO Box 967, Liverpool L69 1TQ. Tel: 0151-227 5100. *Frequency:* MW 1548 kHz

RADIO HARMONY, Ringway House, Hill Street, Coventry CV1 4AN. Tel: 01203-525656. *Frequency:* 102.6 FM

RADIO MALDWYN, The Studios, The Park, Newtown, Powys SY16 2NZ. Tel: 01686-623555. *Frequency:* MW 756 kHz

RADIO MERCURY (EAST), Broadfield House, Brighton Road, Crawley, W. Sussex. Tel: 01293-519161. *Frequency:* 102.7 FM

RADIO MERCURY (WEST), The Friary, Guildford, Surrey GU1 4YX. Tel: 01428-61019. *Frequencies:* 96.4/97.1 FM

RADIO TAY, PO Box 123, 6 North Isla Street, Dundee DD1 9UF. Tel: 01382-200800. *Frequencies:* MW 1161 kHz, 102.8 FM (Dundee); 1584 kHz, 96.4 FM (Perth)

RADIOWAVE, 965 Mowbray Drive, Blackpool, Lancs. FY3 7JR. Tel: 01253-304965. *Frequency:* 96.5 FM

RADIO WYVERN, The Hollies, Barbourne Terrace, Worcester WR1 3JZ. Tel: 01905-612212. *Frequencies:* MW 954 kHz, 97.6 FM (Hereford); 1530 kHz, 102.8 FM (Worcester)

RAM FM, The Market Place, Derby DE1 3AA. Tel: 01332-292945. *Frequency:* 102.8 FM

RED DRAGON FM, West Canal Wharf, Cardiff CF1 5XJ. Tel: 01222-384041. *Frequencies:* 97.4/103.2 FM

RED ROSE GOLD and RED ROSE ROCK FM, PO Box 999, St Paul's Square, Preston, Lancs. PR1 1XR. Tel: 01772-556301. *Frequencies:* MW 999 kHz, 97.4 FM

RTM, 19 Tavy Bridge, Thamesmead, London SE2 9UG. Tel: 0181-311 3112. *Frequency:* 103.8 FM

ST ALBANS AND WATFORD BROADCASTING COMPANY, c/o G. Hunter, Bushey Hall School, Watford, Herts. WD2 3AB. Tel: 01582-666001. *Frequency:* 96.6 FM

SEVERN SOUND, Broadcast Centre, 67 Southgate Street, Gloucester GL1 2DQ. Tel: 01452-423791. *Frequencies:* MW 774 kHz, 103.0/102.4 FM

SGR COLCHESTER, Abbeygate Two, 9 Whitewell Road, Colchester CO2 7DE. Tel: 01206-575859. *Frequency:* 96.1 FM

SGR-FM (BURY), PO Box 250, Bury St Edmunds, Suffolk IP33 IAD. Tel: 01284-702622. *Frequencies:* MW 1251 kHz, 96.4 FM

SGR-FM (IPSWICH), Radio House, Alpha Business Park, Whitehouse Road, Ipswich IP1 5AR. Tel: 01473-461000. *Frequencies:* MW 1170 kHz, 97.1 FM

SIBC, Market Street, Lerwick, Shetland ZE1 0JN. Tel: 01595-5299. *Frequency:* 96.2 FM

SIGNAL CHESHIRE, Regent House, Heaton Lane, Stockport SK4 1BX. Tel: 0161-480 5445. *Frequencies:* 104.9/96.4 FM

SIGNAL ONE AND SIGNAL GOLD, Studio 257, Stoke Road, Stoke-on-Trent ST4 2SR. Tel: 01782-747047. *Frequencies:* MW 1170 kHz, 102.6/96.9 FM

603 RADIO, Churchill Studios, Churchill Road, Cheltenham, Glos. GL53 7EP. Tel: 01242-255023. *Frequency:* MW 603 kHz

SOUTH COAST RADIO, Radio House, Whittle Avenue, Segensworth West, Fareham, Hants. PO15 5PA. Tel: 01489-589911; Radio House, PO Box 2000, Brighton BN41 2SS. Tel: 01273-430111. *Frequencies:* MW 1170/1557/1323 kHz

SOUTHERN FM, Radio House, PO Box 2000, Brighton BN41 2SS. Tel: 01273-430111. *Frequencies:* 103.5 FM (Brighton); 96.9 FM (Newhaven); 102.4 FM (Eastbourne); 102.0 FM (Hastings)

SOUTH WEST SOUND, Campbell House, Bankend Road, Dumfries DG1 4TH. Tel: 01387-50999. *Frequency:* 97.2 FM

SPECTRUM INTERNATIONAL RADIO, Endeavour House, Brent Cross, London NW2 1JT. Tel: 0181-905 5000. *Frequency:* MW 558 kHz

SPIRE FM, City Hall Studios, Malthouse Lane, Salisbury, Wilts. Tel: 01722-416644. *Frequency:* 102.0 FM

STAR FM, The Observatory, Slough, Berks. SL1 1LH. Tel: 01753-551016. *Frequency:* 101.6 FM

STRAY FM, Stray Studios, PO Box 972, Station Parade, Harrogate HG1 5YF. Tel: 01423-522972. *Frequency:* 97.2 FM

SUNRISE EAST MIDLANDS, Granville House, Granville Road, Leicester LE1 7RW. Tel: 0116-254 3002. *Frequency:* MW 1260 kHz

SUNRISE FM, 30 Chapel Street, Little Germany, Bradford BD1 5DN. Tel: 01274-735043. *Frequency:* 103.2 FM

SUNRISE RADIO, Sunrise House, Sunrise Road, Southall, Middx. UB2 4AU. Tel: 0181-574 6666. *Frequency:* MW 1413 kHz

SUNSHINE 855, Sunshine House, Waterside, Ludlow, Shropshire SY8 1PE. Tel: 01584-873795. *Frequency:* MW 855 kHz

SUPA AM, 730 Pershore Road, Selly Park, Birmingham B29 7NJ. Tel: 0121-472 1000. *Frequency:* 1296 kHz

SWANSEA SOUND, Victoria Road, Gowerton, Swansea SA4 3AB. Tel: 01792-893751. *Frequencies:* MW 1170 kHz, 96.4 FM

TEN 17, Latton Bush Centre, Southern Way, Harlow, Essex CM18 7BU. Tel: 01279-432415. *Frequency:* 101.7 FM

TFM RADIO, Yale Crescent, Thornaby, Stockton-on-Tees, Cleveland TS17 6AA. Tel: 01642-615111. *Frequency:* 96.6 FM

1332 THE WORLD'S GREATEST MUSIC STATION, Queensgate Centre, Peterborough PE1 1XJ. Tel: 01733-460460. *Frequency:* MW 1332 kHz

TOUCH AM, PO Box 99, Cardiff CF1 5YJ. Tel: 01222-237878. *Frequencies:* MW 1359 kHz (Cardiff); 1305 kHz (Newport)

TRENT-FM, 29–31 Castle Gate, Nottingham NG1 7AP. Tel: 0115-952 7000. *Frequencies:* 96.2/96.5 FM

TURKISH RADIO (UK) LTD, 93 Westbury Avenue, London N22 6SA. Tel: 0181-889 6677. *Frequency:* 1584 kHz

2CR RADIO, 5 Southcote Road, Bournemouth BH1 3LR. Tel: 01202-294881. *Frequencies:* MW 828 kHz, 102.3 FM

210 CLASSIC GOLD RADIO, PO Box 2020, Reading, Berks. RG3 5RZ. Tel: 01734-413131. *Frequency:* MW 1431 kHz

2 TEN FM, PO Box 210, Reading, Berks. RG3 5RZ. Tel: 01734-413131. *Frequency:* 97.0 FM (Reading); 102.9 FM (Basingstoke and Andover)

VIKING FM, Commercial Road, Hull HU1 2SG. Tel: 01482-25141. *Frequency:* 96.9 FM

WABC, 267 Tettenhall Road, Wolverhampton WV6 0DQ. Tel: 01902-757211. *Frequencies:* MW 990 kHz (Wolverhampton); 1017 kHz (Shrewsbury and Telford)

WEAR FM, Forster Building, Chester Road, Sunderland SR1 3SD. Tel: 0191-515 2103. *Frequency:* 103.4 FM

WESSEX FM, Radio House, Trinity Street, Dorchester, Dorset DT1 1DJ. Tel: 01305-250333. *Frequency:* 97.2 FM

WEST SOUND RADIO, Radio House, 54 Holmston Road, Ayr KA7 3BE. Tel: 01292-283662. *Frequencies:* MW 1035 kHz, 96.7/97.5 FM

WEY VALLEY 102, Prospect Place, Mill Lane, Alton, Hants. GU34 2SY. Tel: 01420-544444. *Frequency:* 102 FM

XTRA-AM, Radio House, Aston Road North, Birmingham B6 4BX. Tel: 0121-359 4481. *Frequencies:* MW 1152 kHz (Birmingham); 1359 kHz (Coventry)

YORKSHIRE COAST RADIO, PO Box 962, Scarborough, N. Yorks. YO12 5YX. Tel: 01723-500962. *Frequency:* 96.2/103.1 FM

ASSOCIATION OF INDEPENDENT RADIO COMPANIES, 46 Westbourne Grove, London W2 5SH. Tel: 0171-727 2646. *Director,* B. West

## COMPLAINTS

The Broadcasting Complaints Commission considers and adjudicates upon complaints of unjust or unfair treatment or unwarranted infringement of privacy in sound or television programmes broadcast by the BBC, S4C, the Independent Television Commission, the Radio Authority or their licensees. This function extends to all sound, television and cable advertisements and teletext transmissions, and programmes broadcast by the BBC's World Services.

THE BROADCASTING COMPLAINTS COMMISSION, Grosvenor Gardens House, 35-37 Grosvenor Gardens, London SW1W 0BS. Tel: 0171-630 1966. *Chairman,* Canon P. Pilkington; *Secretary,* R. M. Hargreaves

# The Press

The newspaper and periodical press in the UK is large and diverse, catering for a wide variety of views and interests. There is no state control or censorship of the press, though it is subject to the laws on publication and the Press Complaints Commission (*see* below) was set up by the industry as a means of self-regulation.

The press is not state-subsidized and receives few tax concessions. The income of most newspapers and periodicals is derived largely from sales and from advertising; the press is the largest advertising medium in Britain.

## PRESS SELF-REGULATION

When the report of the Committee on Privacy and Related Matters, chaired by David Calcutt, QC, was published in June 1990, the then Home Secretary (David Waddington) said that the Government would review the performance of a non-statutory Press Complaints Commission after 18 months of operation to determine whether statutory measures were required. The Press Complaints Commission began work on 1 January 1991, and in July 1992 the then Secretary of State for National Heritage (David Mellor) asked Sir David Calcutt, QC, to conduct the review. The *Calcutt Review of Press Self-Regulation* was presented to Parliament by the then Secretary of State for National Heritage (Peter Brooke) on 14 January 1993 (for summary, *see* Whitaker's Almanack 1994). The Government's response to the review will be given in a White Paper, which is expected in late 1994.

## THE PRESS COMPLAINTS COMMISSION
1 Salisbury Square, London EC3Y 8AE
Tel 0171-353 1248

The Press Complaints Commission was founded by the newspaper and magazine industry in January 1991 to replace the Press Council (established in 1953). It is a voluntary, non-statutory body set up to operate the press's self-regulation system, and funded by the industry through the Press Standards Board of Finance.

The Commission's objects are to consider, adjudicate, conciliate, and resolve complaints of unfair treatment by the press; and to ensure that the press maintains the highest professional standards with respect for generally recognized freedoms, including freedom of expression, the public's right to know, and the right of the press to operate free from improper pressure. The Commission judges newspaper and magazine conduct by a code of practice drafted by editors, agreed by the industry and ratified by the Commission. The code of practice is now incorporated into the employment contracts of many journalists and is increasingly included in the contracts of editors.

Seven of the Commission's members are editors of national, regional and local newspapers and magazines, and nine, including the chairman, are drawn from other fields. One member has been appointed Privacy Commissioner with special powers to investigate complaints about invasion of privacy.

*Chairman*, Lord McGregor of Durris
*Members*, Ms J. Brown; Ms I. Burton; Lady Elizabeth Cavendish, LVO; The Lord Colnbrook, KCMG, PC; Baroness Dean of Thornton-le-Fylde; Dame Mary Donaldson, GBE; Sir David English; B. Hitchen; G. Isaaman; Dr A. Macintyre; G. McKechnie; K. Parker; Prof. R. Pinker (*Privacy Commissioner*); P. Preston; Prof. L. Rees, FRCP, FRCPath
*Director*, M. Bolland

## NEWSPAPERS

Newspapers are usually financially independent of any political party, though most adopt a political stance in their editorial comments, usually reflecting proprietorial influence. Ownership of the national and regional daily newspapers is concentrated in the hands of large corporations whose interests cover publishing and communications. There are strict rules on cross-media ownership to prevent undue concentration of newspaper ownership.

There are 15 daily national papers and 10 Sunday national papers, about 80 regional daily papers, and several hundred local papers that are published weekly or twice-weekly. Scotland, Wales and Northern Ireland all have at least one daily and one Sunday national paper.

Newspapers are usually published in either broadsheet or tabloid format. The 'quality' daily papers, i.e. those providing detailed coverage of a wide range of public matters, have a broadsheet format. The tabloid papers take a more popular approach and are more illustrated.

### NATIONAL DAILY NEWSPAPERS

DAILY EXPRESS, Ludgate House, 245 Blackfriars Road, London SE1 9UX. Tel: 0171-928 8000
DAILY MAIL, Northcliffe House, 2 Derry Street, London W8 5TT. Tel: 0171-938 6000
DAILY MIRROR, Holborn Circus, London EC1P 1DQ. Tel: 0171-353 0246
DAILY SPORT, 19 Great Ancoats Street, Manchester M60 4BT. Tel: 0161-236 4466
DAILY STAR, Ludgate House, 245 Blackfriars Road, London SE1 9UX. Tel: 0171-928 8000
DAILY TELEGRAPH, 1 Canada Square, Canary Wharf, London E14 5DT. Tel: 0171-538 5000
THE EUROPEAN, Orbit House, 5 New Fetter Lane, London EC4A 1AP. Tel: 0171-822 2020
FINANCIAL TIMES, 1 Southwark Bridge, London SE1 9HL. Tel: 0171-873 3000
THE GUARDIAN, 119 Farringdon Road, London EC1R 3ER. Tel: 0171-278 2332
THE INDEPENDENT, 1 Canada Square, Canary Wharf, London E14 5AP.
MORNING STAR, 1-3 Ardleigh Road, London N1 4HS. Tel: 0171-254 0033
RACING POST, 112-120 Coombe Lane, London SW20 0BA. Tel: 0181-879 3377
THE SCOTSMAN, 20 North Bridge, Edinburgh EH1 1YT. Tel: 0131-225 2468
THE SPORTING LIFE, Orbit House, 1 New Fetter Lane, London EC4A 1AR. Tel: 0171-822 2119
THE SUN, 1 Virginia Street, London E1 9XR. Tel: 0171-782 4000
THE TIMES, 1 Pennington Street, London E1 9XN. Tel: 0171-782 5000

TODAY, 1 Virginia Street, London E1 9BD. Tel: 0171-782 4600

## REGIONAL DAILY NEWSPAPERS

*Aberdeen:* PRESS AND JOURNAL, and EVENING EXPRESS, PO Box 43, Lang Stracht, Mastrick, AB9 8AF
*Barrow-in-Furness:* NORTH-WEST EVENING MAIL, Newspaper House, Abbey Road, LA14 5QS
*Bath:* BATH EVENING CHRONICLE, 33–34 Westgate Street, BA1 1EW
*Basildon:* EVENING ECHO, Newspaper House, Chester Hall Lane, SS14 3BL
*Belfast:* BELFAST TELEGRAPH, 124–144 Royal Avenue, BT1 1EB; IRISH NEWS AND BELFAST MORNING NEWS, 113–117 Donegall Street, BT1 2GE; NEWS LETTER, 51–59 Donegall Street, BT1 2GB
*Birmingham:* THE BIRMINGHAM POST, and BIRMINGHAM EVENING MAIL, 28 Colmore Circus, Queensway, B4 6AX
*Blackburn:* LANCASHIRE EVENING TELEGRAPH, Newspaper House, High Street, BB1 1HT
*Blackpool:* WEST LANCASHIRE EVENING GAZETTE, PO Box 20, Preston New Road, FY4 4AU
*Bolton:* BOLTON EVENING NEWS, Newspaper House, Churchgate, BL1 1DE
*Bournemouth:* EVENING ECHO, Richmond Hill, BH2 6HH
*Bradford:* TELEGRAPH AND ARGUS, Hall Ings, BD1 1JR
*Brighton:* EVENING ARGUS, Argus House, Crowhurst Road, Hollingbury, BN1 8AR
*Bristol:* BRISTOL EVENING POST, and WESTERN DAILY PRESS, Temple Way, BS99 7HD
*Burton-on-Trent:* BURTON MAIL, 65–68 High Street, DE14 1LE
*Cambridge:* CAMBRIDGE EVENING NEWS, 51 Newmarket Road, CB5 8EJ
*Cardiff:* SOUTH WALES ECHO, and WESTERN MAIL, Thomson House, Havelock Street, CF1 1WR
*Carlisle:* EVENING NEWS AND STAR, Newspaper House, Dalston Road, CA2 5UA
*Cheltenham:* GLOUCESTERSHIRE ECHO, 1 Clarence Parade, GL50 3NZ
*Colchester:* EVENING GAZETTE, Oriel House, 43–44 North Hill, CO1 1TZ
*Coventry:* COVENTRY EVENING TELEGRAPH, Corporation Street, CV1 1FP
*Darlington:* NORTHERN ECHO, Priestgate, DL1 1NF
*Derby:* DERBY EVENING TELEGRAPH, Northcliffe House, Meadow Road, DE1 2DW
*Dundee:* COURIER AND ADVERTISER, and EVENING TELEGRAPH AND POST, 2 Albert Square, DD1 9QJ
*Edinburgh:* EVENING NEWS, 20 North Bridge, EH1 1YT
*Exeter:* EXPRESS AND ECHO, Heron Road, Sowton, EX2 7NF
*Glasgow:* DAILY RECORD, 40 Anderston Quay, G3 8DA; HERALD, and EVENING TIMES, 195 Albion Street, G1 1QP; SCOTTISH DAILY EXPRESS, Park House, Park Circus Place, G3 6AF
*Gloucester:* THE GLOUCESTERSHIRE CITIZEN, St John's Lane, GL1 2AY
*Greenock:* GREENOCK TELEGRAPH, 2 Crawford Street, PA15 1LH
*Grimsby:* GRIMSBY EVENING TELEGRAPH, 80 Cleethorpe Road, DN31 3EH
*Guernsey:* GUERNSEY EVENING PRESS AND STAR, PO Box 57, Braye Road, Vale
*Halifax:* EVENING COURIER, PO Box 19, Courier Buildings, King Cross Street, HX1 2SF
*Hartlepool:* HARTLEPOOL MAIL, Clarence Road, TS24 8BU

*Huddersfield:* HUDDERSFIELD DAILY EXAMINER, PO Box A26, Queen Street South, HD1 2TD
*Hull:* HULL DAILY MAIL, Blundell's Corner, Beverley Road, HU3 1XS
*Ipswich:* EAST ANGLIAN DAILY TIMES, and EVENING STAR, 30 Lower Brook Street, IP4 1AN
*Jersey:* JERSEY EVENING POST, PO Box 582, Five Oaks, St Saviour
*Kettering:* NORTHAMPTONSHIRE EVENING TELEGRAPH, Northfield Avenue, NN16 9TT
*Leeds:* YORKSHIRE EVENING POST, and YORKSHIRE POST, PO Box 168, Wellington Street, LS1 1RF
*Leicester:* LEICESTER MERCURY, St George Street, LE1 9FQ
*Lincoln:* LINCOLNSHIRE ECHO, Brayford Wharf East, LN5 7AT
*Liverpool:* DAILY POST, and LIVERPOOL ECHO, PO Box 48, Old Hall Street, L69 3EB
*London:* THE EVENING STANDARD, 2 Derry Street, W8 5EE
*Maidstone:* KENT TODAY, Messenger House, New Hythe Lane, Larkfield, ME20 6SG
*Manchester:* MANCHESTER EVENING NEWS, 164 Deansgate, M60 2RR
*Middlesbrough:* EVENING GAZETTE, Gazette Buildings, Borough Road, TS1 3AZ
*Newcastle upon Tyne:* EVENING CHRONICLE, and THE JOURNAL, Thomson House, Groat Market, NE1 1ED
*Newport:* SOUTH WALES ARGUS, Cardiff Road, Maesglas, NP9 1QW
*Northampton:* CHRONICLE AND ECHO, Upper Mounts, NN1 3HR
*Norwich:* EASTERN DAILY PRESS, and EASTERN EVENING NEWS, Prospect House, Rouen Road, NR1 1RE
*Nottingham:* EVENING POST, PO Box 99, Forman Street, NG1 4AB
*Nuneaton:* EVENING NEWS, Newspaper House, Whatacre Road East, CV11 6BY
*Oldham:* EVENING CHRONICLE, 172 Union Street, OL1 1EQ
*Oxford:* OXFORD MAIL, Newspaper House, Osney Mead, OX2 0EJ
*Paisley:* PAISLEY DAILY EXPRESS, 195 Albion Street, Glasgow G1 1QP
*Peterborough:* PETERBOROUGH EVENING TELEGRAPH, New Priestgate House, 57 Priestgate, PE1 1JW
*Plymouth:* WESTERN MORNING NEWS, and EVENING HERALD, 17 Brest Road, Derriford Business Park, PL6 5AA
*Portsmouth:* THE NEWS, The News Centre, Hilsea, PO2 9SX
*Preston:* LANCASHIRE EVENING POST, Oliver's Place, Fulwood, PR2 4ZA
*Reading:* EVENING POST, 8 Tessa Road, RG1 8NS
*Scarborough:* SCARBOROUGH EVENING NEWS, 17–23 Aberdeen Walk, YO11 1BB
*Scunthorpe:* SCUNTHORPE EVENING TELEGRAPH, Telegraph House, Doncaster Road, DN15 7RE
*Sheffield:* THE STAR, York Street, S1 1PU
*South Shields:* SHIELDS GAZETTE, Chapter Row, NE33 1BL
*Southampton:* SOUTHERN EVENING ECHO, 45 Above Bar, SO9 7BA
*Stoke-on-Trent:* EVENING SENTINEL, Sentinel House, Etruria, ST1 5SS
*Sunderland:* SUNDERLAND ECHO, Echo House, Pennywell Estate, SR4 9ER
*Swansea:* SOUTH WALES EVENING POST, Adelaide Street, SA1 1QT
*Swindon:* EVENING ADVERTISER, Newspaper House, 100 Victoria Road, SN1 3BE
*Telford:* SHROPSHIRE STAR, Ketley, TF1 4HU

*Torquay:* HERALD EXPRESS, Harmsworth House, Barton Hill Road, TQ2 8JN

*Weymouth:* DORSET EVENING ECHO, 57 St Thomas Street, DT4 8EU

*Wolverhampton:* EXPRESS AND STAR, 51–53 Queen Street, WV1 3BU

*Worcester:* EVENING NEWS, Hylton Road, WR2 5JX

*Wrexham:* EVENING LEADER, Mold Business Park, Wrexham Road, CH7 1XY

*York:* YORKSHIRE EVENING PRESS, PO Box 29, 76–86 Walmgate, YO1 1YN

## WEEKLY NEWSPAPERS

AL MAJALLA, Arab Press House, 184 High Holborn, London WC1V 7AP. Tel: 0171-831 8181

ASIAN TIMES, 3rd Floor, Tower House, 141–149 Fonthill Road, London N4 3HF. Tel: 0171-281 1191

CARIBBEAN TIMES, 3rd Floor, Tower House, 141–149 Fonthill Road, London N4 3HF. Tel: 0171-281 1191

THE GUARDIAN WEEKLY, 119 Farringdon Road, London EC1R 3ER. Tel: 0171-278 2332

THE INDEPENDENT ON SUNDAY, 1 Canada Square, Canary Wharf, London E14 5AP.

INDIA TIMES, Suites F and G, 2nd Floor, Liberty Shopping Centre, 14 South Road, Southall, Middx. UB1 1RT. Tel: 0181-843 1605

THE MAIL ON SUNDAY, Northcliffe House, 2 Derry Street, London W8 5TS. Tel: 0171-938 6000

NEWS OF THE WORLD, 1 Virginia Street, London E1 9XR. Tel: 0171-782 4000

THE OBSERVER, Chelsea Bridge House, Queenstown Road, London SW8 4NN. Tel: 0171-627 0700

THE PEOPLE, Holborn Circus, London EC1P 1DQ. Tel: 0171-353 0246

SCOTLAND ON SUNDAY, 20 North Bridge, Edinburgh EH1 1YT. Tel: 0131-225 2468

SUNDAY EXPRESS, Ludgate House, 245 Blackfriars Road, London SE1 9UX. Tel: 0171-928 8000

SUNDAY MAIL, 40 Anderston Quay, Glasgow G3 8DA. Tel: 0141-248 7000

SUNDAY MIRROR, Holborn Circus, London EC1P 1DQ. Tel: 0171-353 0246

SUNDAY NEWS, 51–59 Donegall Street, Belfast BT1 2GB. Tel: 01232-244441

SUNDAY POST, Courier Place, Dundee DD1 9QJ. Tel: 01382-23131

SUNDAY SPORT, Marten House, 39–47 East Road, London N1 6AH. Tel: 0171-251 2544

SUNDAY TELEGRAPH, Peterborough Court at South Quay, 181 Marsh Wall, London E14 9SR. Tel: 0171-538 5000

THE SUNDAY TIMES, 1 Pennington Street, London E1 9XN. Tel: 0171-782 5000

THE VOICE, 370 Coldharbour Lane, London SW9 8PL. Tel: 0171-737 7377

WALES ON SUNDAY, Thomson House, Havelock Street, Cardiff CF1 1WR. Tel: 01222-583583

WEEKLY NEWS, Courier Place, Dundee, Angus DD1 9QJ. Tel: 01382-23131

WEEKLY TELEGRAPH, 1 Canada Square, Canary Wharf, London E14 5DT. Tel: 0171-538 6298

## RELIGIOUS PAPERS

*Alt.* = Alternate; *M.* = Monthly; *Q.* = Quarterly; *W.* = Weekly

BAPTIST TIMES, PO Box 54, 129 The Broadway, Didcot, Oxon OX11 8XB. *W.*

CATHOLIC HERALD, Herald House, Lamb's Passage, Bunhill Row, London EC1Y 8TQ. *W.*

CHALLENGE: THE GOOD NEWS PAPER, Revenue Buildings, Chapel Road, Worthing, W. Sussex BN11 1BQ. *M.*

CHRISTIAN HERALD, Herald House, 96 Dominion Road, Worthing, W. Sussex BN14 8JP. *W.*

CHRISTIAN SCIENCE MONITOR, Monitor House, 20 Beulah Road, London SW19 3SU. *W.*

CHURCH OF ENGLAND NEWS, 12–13 Clerkenwell Green, London EC1R 0DP. *W.*

CHURCH OF IRELAND GAZETTE, 36 Bachelor's Walk, Lisburn, Co. Antrim, BT28 1XN. *W.*

CHURCH TIMES, 33 Upper Street, London N1 0PN. *W.*

ENGLISH CHURCHMAN, 22 Lesley Avenue, Canterbury, Kent CT1 3LF. *Alt. W.*

THE FRIEND, Drayton House, 30 Gordon Street, London WC1H 0BQ. *W.*

THE INQUIRER, Essex Hall, 1–6 Essex Street, London WC2R 3HY. *Alt. W.*

JEWISH CHRONICLE, 25 Furnival Street, London EC4A 1JT. *W.*

JEWISH GAZETTE, 27 Bury Old Road, Prestwich, Manchester M25 8EY. *W.*

JEWISH TELEGRAPH, Telegraph House, 11 Park Hill, Bury Old Road, Prestwich, Manchester M25 8HH. *W.*

LIFE AND WORK, Church of Scotland, 121 George Street, Edinburgh EH2 4YN. *M.*

METHODIST RECORDER, 122 Golden Lane, London EC1Y 0TL. *W.*

ORTHODOX OUTLOOK, 37 Salop Road, Welshpool, Powys SY21 7GA. *Alt. M.*

PRESBYTERIAN HERALD, Church House, Fisherwick Place, Belfast BT1 6DW. *Ten times a year.*

QUAKER MONTHLY, Friends House, Euston Road, London NW1 2BJ. *M.*

REFORM, 86 Tavistock Place, London WC1H 9RT. *Eleven times a year.*

SIKH MESSENGER, 43 Dorset Road, London SW19 3EZ. *Q.*

THE TABLET, 1 King Street Cloisters, Clifton Walk, London W6 0QZ. *W.*

THE UNIVERSE, 1st Floor, St James Building, Oxford Street, Manchester M1 6FP. *W.*

THE WAR CRY, 101 Queen Victoria Street, London EC4P 4EP. *W.*

## PERIODICALS

There are about 6,700 periodicals published in Britain. These are classified as consumer, i.e. general interest, or as trade, professional or academic.

### CONSUMER PERIODICALS

*Alt.* = Alternate; *M.* = Monthly; *Q.* = Quarterly; *W.* = Weekly

AMATEUR PHOTOGRAPHER, King's Reach Tower, Stamford Street, London SE1 9LS. *W.*

ANGLING TIMES, Bretton Court, Bretton, Peterborough PE3 8DZ. *W.*

ANNABEL, 80 Kingsway East, Dundee, Angus DD4 8SL. *M.*

THE ANTIQUE COLLECTOR, National Magazine House, 72 Broadwick Street, London W1V 2BP. *M.*

APOLLO MAGAZINE, 29 Chesham Place, London SW1X 8HB. *M.*

ARENA, 3rd Floor, Block A, Exmouth House, Pine Street, London ECIR OJL. *Alt. M.*

THE ARTIST, Caxton House, 63–65 High Street, Tenterden, Kent TN30 6BD. *M.*

ASTRONOMY NOW, Intra House, 193 Uxbridge Road, London W12 9RA. *M.*

ATHLETICS WEEKLY, Bretton Court, Bretton, Peterborough PE3 8DZ. *W.*

AUTOCAR AND MOTOR, 38–42 Hampton Road, Teddington, Middx. TW11 OJE. *W.*

BBC GARDENER'S WORLD, 101 Bayham Street, London NW1 OAG. *M.*

BBC GOOD FOOD, 101 Bayham Street, London NW1 OAG. *M.*

BBC WILDLIFE MAGAZINE, Woodlands, 80 Wood Lane, London W12 OTT. *M.*

BELFAST GAZETTE (*Official*), 129 IDB House, 64 Titchester Street, Belfast BT1 4PS. *W.*

BELLA, 2nd Floor, Shirley House, 25–27 Camden Road, London NW1 9LL. *W.*

BEST, 10th Floor, Portland House, Stag Place, London SW1E 5AU. *W.*

BIRDS, RSPB, The Lodge, Sandy, Beds. SG19 2DL. *Q.*

BIRD WATCHING, Bretton Court, Bretton, Peterborough PE3 8DZ. *M.*

BOXING NEWS, PO Box 300, London SW15 5QF. *W.*

BRIDES & SETTING UP HOME, Vogue House, Hanover Square, London W1R OAD. *Alt. M.*

THE BURLINGTON MAGAZINE, 6 Bloomsbury Square, London WC1A 2LP. *M.*

CAMPING & CARAVANNING, Greenfields House, Westwood Way, Coventry CV4 8JH. *M.*

CAR, Bushfield House, Orton Centre, Peterborough PE2 5UW. *M.*

CAT WORLD, 10 Western Road, Shoreham-by-Sea, W. Sussex BN43 5WD. *M.*

CHAT, King's Reach Tower, Stamford Street, London SE1 9LS. *W.*

CITY LIMITS, 3rd Floor, 115 Shaftesbury Avenue, London WC2H 8ED. *W.*

CLASSICAL MUSIC, 241 Shaftesbury Avenue, London WC2H 8EH. *Alt. W.*

CLASSIC AND SPORTSCAR, 60 Waldegrave Road, Teddington, Middx. TW11 8LG. *M.*

CLOTHES SHOW MAGAZINE, 101 Bayham Street, London NW1 OAG. *M.*

COARSE ANGLER, 281 Ecclesall Road, Sheffield S11 8NX. *M.*

COIN NEWS, 105 High Street, Honiton, Devon EX14 8PE. *M.*

COMPANY MAGAZINE, 72 Broadwick Street, London W1V 2BP. *M.*

COMPETITORS JOURNAL, PO Box 300, London SW15 5QF. *Alt. W.*

COMPUTER AND VIDEO GAMES, Priory Court, 30–32 Farringdon Road, London ECIR 3AU. *M.*

COSMOPOLITAN, National Magazine House, 72 Broadwick Street, London W1V 2BP. *M.*

COUNTRY HOMES AND INTERIORS, King's Reach Tower, Stamford Street, London SE1 9LS. *M.*

COUNTRY LIFE, King's Reach Tower, Stamford Street, London SE1 9LS. *W.*

COUNTRY LIVING, National Magazine House, 72 Broadwick Street, London W1V 2BP. *M.*

THE COUNTRYMAN, Link House, Dingwall Avenue, Croydon, Surrey CR9 2TA. *Alt. M.*

CRICKETER INTERNATIONAL, Beech Hanger, Ashurst, Tunbridge Wells, Kent TN3 9ST. *M.*

CYCLING WEEKLY, King's Reach Tower, Stamford Street, London SE1 9LS. *W.*

THE DALESMAN, Stable Courtyard, Broughton Hall, Skipton, N. Yorks. BD23 3AE. *M.*

DALTONS WEEKLY, CI Tower, St George's Square, New Malden, Surrey KT3 4JA. *W.*

DANCE AND DANCERS, 214 Panther House, 38 Mount Pleasant, London WCIX OAP. *M.*

DANCING TIMES, Clerkenwell House, 45–47 Clerkenwell Green, London ECIR OEB. *M.*

DOGS TODAY, 10 Sheet Street, Windsor, Berks. SL4 1BG. *M.*

DOG WORLD, 9 Tufton Street, Ashford, Kent TN23 1QN. *W.*

THE ECOLOGIST, Agriculture House, Bath Road, Sturminster Newton, Dorset DT10 1DU. *Alt. M.*

THE ECONOMIST, 25 St James's Street, London SW1A 1HG. *W.*

EDINBURGH GAZETTE (*Official*), HMSO, PO Box 276, London SW8 5DT. *Twice a week.*

ELLE, 20 Orange Street, London WC2H 7ED. *M.*

EMPIRE, 42–48 Great Portland Street, London W1N 5AH. *M.*

ESQUIRE, 72 Broadwick Street, London W1V 2BP. *M.*

ESSENTIALS, 57–59 Long Acre, London WC2E 9JL. *M.*

EVERYWOMAN, 34 Islington Green, London N1 8DU. *M.*

EXCHANGE AND MART, Link House, West Street, Poole, Dorset BH15 1LL. *W.*

THE FACE, 3rd Floor, Block A, Exmouth House, Pine Street, London ECIR OJL. *M.*

FAMILY CIRCLE, King's Reach Tower, Stamford Street, SE1 9LS. *M.*

FHM, 9–11 Curtain Road, London EC2A 3LT. *M.*

THE FIELD, 10 Sheet Street, Windsor, Berks. SL4 1BG. *M.*

FILM REVIEW, 9 Blades Court, Deodar Road, London SW15 2NU. *M.*

GARDEN NEWS, Apex House, Oundle Road, Peterborough PE2 9NP. *W.*

GAY TIMES, Worldwide House, 116–134 Bayham Street, London NW1 OBA. *M.*

GEOGRAPHICAL MAGAZINE, 80 Wood Lane, London W12 OTT. *M.*

GIBBONS STAMP MONTHLY, 5 Parkside, Christchurch Road, Ringwood, Hants. BH24 3SH. *M.*

GOLF ILLUSTRATED WEEKLY, Advance House, 37–39 Millharbour, London E14 9TX. *W.*

GOLF WORLD, Advance House, 37–39 Millharbour, London E14 9TX. *M.*

GOOD HOLIDAY MAGAZINE, 1–2 Dawes Court, 93 High Street, Esher, Surrey KT10 9QD. *Q.*

GOOD HOUSEKEEPING, National Magazine House, 72 Broadwick Street, London W1V 2BP. *M.*

GQ, Vogue House, Hanover Square, London W1R OAD. *M.*

GRAMOPHONE, 177–179 Kenton Road, Harrow, Middx. HA3 OHA. *M.*

GRANTA, 2–3 Hanover Yard, Noel Road, London N1 8BE. *Q.*

GUIDING, 17–19 Buckingham Palace Road, London SW1W OPT. *M.*

HANSARD, *see* Parliamentary Debates.

HARPERS AND QUEEN, National Magazine House, 72 Broadwick Street, London W1V 2BP. *M.*

HELLO!, 69–71 Upper Ground, London SE1 9PQ. *W.*

HOMES AND GARDENS, King's Reach Tower, Stamford Street, London SE1 9LS. *M.*

HORSE AND HOUND, King's Reach Tower, Stamford Street, London SE1 9LS. *W.*

HOUSE AND GARDEN, Vogue House, Hanover Square, London W1R OAD. *M.*

HOUSE BEAUTIFUL, National Magazine House, 72 Broadwick Street, London W1V 2BP. *Ten times a year.*

i-D MAGAZINE, 44 Earlham Street, London WC2H 9LA. *M.*

IDEAL HOME, King's Reach Tower, Stamford Street, London SE1 9LS. *M.*

ILLUSTRATED LONDON NEWS, 20 Upper Ground, London SE1 9PF. *Alt. M.*

IN BRITAIN, Greater London House, Hampstead Road, London NW1 7QQ. *M.*

INVESTORS CHRONICLE, Greystoke Place, Fetter Lane, London EC4A IND. *W.*

IRISH POST, Uxbridge House, 464 Uxbridge Road, Hayes, Middx. UB4 0SP. *W.*

JAZZ JOURNAL INTERNATIONAL, 1–5 Clerkenwell Road, London EC1M 5PA. *M.*

JUST SEVENTEEN, 20 Orange Street, London WC2H 7ED. *W.*

LABOUR RESEARCH, 78 Blackfriars Road, London SE1 8HF. *M.*

THE LADY, 39–40 Bedford Street, London WC2E 9ER. *W.*

LAND AND LIBERTY, 177 Vauxhall Bridge Road, London SW1V IEU. *Alt. M.*

LITERARY REVIEW, 51 Beak Street, London W1R 3LF. *M.*

LIVING, King's Reach Tower, Stamford Street, London SE1 9LS. *M.*

LONDON GAZETTE (*Official*) Room 413, HMSO, 51 Nine Elms Lane, London SW8 5DR. *Five times a week.*

LONDON REVIEW OF BOOKS, Tavistock House South, Tavistock Square, London WC1H 9JZ. *Alt. W.*

LONDON WEEKLY ADVERTISER, 137 George Lane, London E18 1AJ. *W.*

MAJESTY, 26–28 Hallam Street, London W1N 5LF. *M.*

MARIE CLAIRE, 2 Hatfields, London SE1 9PG. *M.*

ME, 57–59 Long Acre, London WC2E 9JL. *W.*

MELODY MAKER (MM), King's Reach Tower, Stamford Street, London SE1 9LS. *W.*

METEOROLOGICAL MAGAZINE, HMSO, PO Box 276, London SW8 5DT. *M.*

MIZZ, King's Reach Tower, Stamford Street, London SE1 9LS. *Alt. W.*

MODEL BOATS, Argus House, Boundary Way, Hemel Hempstead, Herts. HP2 7ST. *M.*

MONEYWISE, Berkeley Square House, Berkeley Square, London W1X 6AB. *M.*

MORE!, 20 Orange Street, London WC2H 7ED. *Alt. W.*

MOTHER AND BABY, Victory House, 14 Leicester Place, London WC2H 7BP. *M.*

MOTOR CYCLE NEWS, 20–22 Station Road, Kettering, Northants. NN15 7HH. *W.*

MOTORING NEWS, Standard House, Bonhill Street, London EC2A 4DA. *W.*

MOTOR SPORT, Standard House, Bonhill Street, London EC2A 4DA. *M.*

MY WEEKLY, 80 Kingsway East, Dundee DD4 8SL. *W.*

NATIONAL STUDENT EXTRA, PO Box 5, Glossop, Derbys. SK13 8PT. *Alt. M.*

NATURE, 4 Little Essex Street, London WC2R 3LF. *W.*

NEEDLECRAFT, Beauford Court, 30 Monmouth Street, Bath BA1 2BW. *M.*

NEW DIY, Link House, Dingwall Avenue, Croydon, Surrey CR9 2TA. *M.*

NEW INTERNATIONALIST, 55 Rectory Road, Oxford OX4 1BW. *M.*

NEW MUSICAL EXPRESS (NME), King's Reach Tower, Stamford Street, London SE1 9LS. *W.*

NEW SCIENTIST, King's Reach Tower, Stamford Street, London SE1 9LS. *W.*

NEW STATESMAN AND SOCIETY, Foundation House, Perseverance Works, 38 Kingsland Road, London E2 8DQ. *W.*

NEWSWEEK INTERNATIONAL, 25 Upper Brook Street, London W1Y 2AB. *W.*

NEW WOMAN, 20 Orange Street, London WC2H 7ED. *M.*

19, King's Reach Tower, Stamford Street, London SE1 9LS. *M.*

OK!, Northern and Shell Tower, City Harbour, London E14 9GL. *Thirteen times a year.*

THE OLDIE, 26 Charlotte Street, London W1P 1HJ. *M.*

OPERA, 1A Mountgrove Road, London N5 2LU. *M.*

OPERA NOW, 241 Shaftesbury Avenue, London WC2H 8EH. *M.*

OPTIONS, King's Reach Tower, Stamford Street, London SE1 9LS. *M.*

OUR DOGS, 5 Oxford Road, Station Approach, Manchester M60 1SX. *W.*

PARENTS, Victory House, 14 Leicester Place, London WC2H 7BP. *M.*

PARLIAMENTARY DEBATES (COMMONS) (Hansard), HMSO, PO Box 276, London SW8 5DT. *Daily or weekly during Session.*

PARLIAMENTARY DEBATES (LORDS) (Hansard), HMSO, PO Box 276, London SW8 5DT. *Daily or weekly during Session.*

PEOPLE'S FRIEND, 80 Kingsway East, Dundee DD4 8SL. *W.*

PLAYS AND PLAYERS, 18 Friern Park, London N12 9DA. *M.*

POETRY REVIEW, 22 Betterton Street, London WC2H 9BU. *Q.*

PONY, 296 Ewell Road, Surbiton, Surrey KT6 7AQ. *M.*

PRACTICAL BOAT OWNER, Westover House, West Quay Road, Poole, Dorset BH15 1JG. *M.*

PRACTICAL CARAVAN, 38–42 Hampton Road, Teddington, Middx. TW11 0JE. *M.*

PRACTICAL GARDENING, Apex House, Oundle Road, Peterborough PE2 9NP. *M.*

PRACTICAL PARENTING, King's Reach Tower, Stamford Street, London SE1 9LS. *M.*

PRACTICAL PHOTOGRAPHY, Apex House, Oundle Road, Peterborough PE2 9NP. *M.*

PRIMA, 9th Floor, Portland House, Stag Place, London SW1E 5AU. *M.*

PRIVATE EYE, 6 Carlisle Street, London W1V 5RG. *Alt. W.*

PROGRESS (*Braille type*), RNIB, Orton, Southgate, Peterborough PE2 0XU. *M.*

THE PUZZLER, Glenthorne House, Hammersmith Grove, London W6 0LG. *M.*

Q, Meed House, 21 John Street, London W1N 2BP. *M.*

RACING CALENDAR, The Jockey Club, Weatherbys, Sanders Road, Wellingborough, Northants. NN8 4BX. *W.*

RADIO TIMES, 80 Wood Lane, London W12 0TT. *W.*

RAILWAY MAGAZINE, King's Reach Tower, Stamford Street, London SE1 9LS. *M.*

RAILWAY MODELLER, Peco Publications, Beer, Seaton, Devon EX12 3NA. *M.*

READER'S DIGEST, Berkeley Square House, Berkeley Square, London W1X 6AB. *M.*

RIDING, Corner House, Foston, Grantham, Lincs. NG32 2JU. *M.*

RUGBY LEAGUER, Martland Mill, Martland Mill Lane, Wigan, Lancs. WN5 0LX. *W.*

RUGBY WORLD AND POST, Weirbank, Bray on Thames, Maidenhead, Berks. SL6 2ED. *M.*

SCOTS MAGAZINE, 2 Albert Square, Dundee DD1 9QJ. *M.*

SCOTTISH FIELD, 7th Floor, The Plaza Tower, East Kilbride, Glasgow G74 1LW. *M.*

SCOUTING, Baden-Powell House, Queen's Gate, London SW7 5JS. *M.*

SEA ANGLER, Bretton Court, Bretton, Peterborough PE3 8DZ. *M.*

SHE, National Magazine House, 72 Broadwick Street, London WIV 2BP. *M.*

SHOOT, King's Reach Tower, Stamford Street, London SEI 9LS. *W.*

SHOOTING TIMES AND COUNTRY MAGAZINE, 10 Sheet Street, Windsor, Berks. SL4 1BG. *W.*

SKY MAGAZINE, 5th Floor, Mappin House, 4 Winsley Street, London W1N 7AR. *M.*

SLIMMING MAGAZINE, Victory House, 14 Leicester Place, London WC2H 7BP. *Ten times a year.*

SMASH HITS, Meed House, 21 John Street, London W1N 2BP. *Alt. W.*

THE SPECTATOR, 56 Doughty Street, London WC1N 2LL. *W.*

THE STRAD, 7 St John's Road, Harrow, Middx. HA1 2EE. *M.*

TATLER, Vogue House, Hanover Square, London W1R 0AD. *Ten times a year.*

TENNIS WORLD, The Spendlove Centre, Enstone Road, Charlbury, Chipping Norton, Oxon. OX7 3PQ. *M.*

THIS ENGLAND, Alma House, 73 Rodney Road, Cheltenham, Glos. GL50 1HT. *Q.*

TIME INTERNATIONAL, Time Life Building, 153 New Bond Street, London W1Y 0AA. *W.*

TIME OUT, Tower House, Southampton Street, London WC2E 7HD. *W.*

THE TIMES EDUCATIONAL SUPPLEMENT, Priory House, St John's Lane, London EC1M 4BX. *W.*

THE TIMES HIGHER EDUCATION SUPPLEMENT, Priory House, St John's Lane, London EC1M 4BX. *W.*

THE TIMES LITERARY SUPPLEMENT, Priory House, St John's Lane, London EC1M 4BX. *W.*

TRIBUNE, 308 Gray's Inn Road, London WC1X 8DY. *W.*

TROUT AND SALMON, Bretton Court, Bretton, Peterborough PE3 8DZ. *M.*

TRUE ROMANCES, 2–4 Leigham Court Road, London SW16 2PD. *M.*

TRUE STORY, 2–4 Leigham Court Road, London SW16 2PD. *M.*

TV TIMES, King's Reach Tower, Stamford Street, London SE1 9LS. *W.*

VACHER'S PARLIAMENTARY COMPANION, 113 High Street, Berkhamsted, Herts. HP4 2DJ. *Q.*

VANITY FAIR, Vogue House, Hanover Square, London W1R 0AD. *M.*

VIZ COMIC, The Boat House, Crabtree Lane, London SW6 6LU. *Alt. M.*

VOGUE, Vogue House, Hanover Square, London W1R 0AD. *M.*

VOX, King's Reach Tower, Stamford Street, London SE1 9LS. *M.*

WEATHER, 104 Oxford Road, Reading RG1 7LJ. *M.*

WELSH NATION, 51 Cathedral Road, Cardiff CF1 9HD. *Alt. M.*

WHICH?, 2 Marylebone Road, London NW1 4DX. *M.*

WOMAN, King's Reach Tower, Stamford Street, London SE1 9LS. *W.*

WOMAN AND HOME, King's Reach Tower, Stamford Street, London SE1 9LS. *M.*

WOMAN'S JOURNAL, King's Reach Tower, Stamford Street, London SE1 9LS. *M.*

WOMAN'S OWN, King's Reach Tower, Stamford Street, London SE1 9LS. *W.*

WOMAN'S REALM, King's Reach Tower, Stamford Street, London SE1 9LS. *W.*

WOMAN'S WEEKLY, King's Reach Tower, Stamford Street, London SE1 9LS. *W.*

WORLD OF INTERIORS, Vogue House, Hanover Square, London W1R 0AD. *Eleven times a year.*

YACHTING MONTHLY, King's Reach Tower, Stamford Street, London SE1 9LS. *M.*

## TRADE, PROFESSIONAL AND ACADEMIC PERIODICALS

*Alt.* = Alternate; *M.* = Monthly; *Q.* = Quarterly; *W.* = Weekly

ACCOUNTANCY, Institute of Chartered Accountants, 40 Bernard Street, London WC1N 1LD. *M.*

ACCOUNTANCY AGE, 32–34 Broadwick Street, London W1A 2HG. *W.*

ACCOUNTANTS' MAGAZINE, Institute of Chartered Accountants of Scotland, 27 Queen Street, Edinburgh EH2 1LA. *Alt. M.*

THE ACTUARY, Garrets Building, Cathles Road, London SW12 9LD. *M.*

AGRICULTURE AND EQUIPMENT INTERNATIONAL, Yew Tree House, Horne, Horley, Surrey RH6 9JP. *Alt. M.*

ANTIQUARIES JOURNAL, Oxford University Press, Walton Street, Oxford OX2 6DP. *Annual.*

ANTIQUE DEALER AND COLLECTORS' GUIDE, PO Box 805, London SE10 8TD. *M.*

ANTIQUES TRADE GAZETTE, 17 Whitcomb Street, London WC2H 7PL. *W.*

ARCHITECTS' JOURNAL, 33–39 Bowling Green Lane, London EC1R 0DA. *W.*

ARCHITECTURAL REVIEW, 33–39 Bowling Green Lane, London EC1R 0DA. *M.*

ARMED FORCES DEFENCE INTERNATIONAL, 21 Hawley Road, London NW1 8RP.

THE AUTHOR, Society of Authors, 84 Drayton Gardens, London SW10 9SB. *Q.*

THE BANKER, Greystoke Place, Fetter Lane, London EC4A 1ND. *M.*

BANKING WORLD (Chartered Institute of Bankers), Greater London House, Hampstead Road, London NW1 7QQ. *M.*

THE BIOCHEMIST, The Biochemist Society, 59 Portland Place, London W1N 3AJ. *Alt. M.*

BIOLOGIST, Institute of Biology, 20 Queensberry Place, London SW7 2DZ. *Five times a year.*

THE BOOKSELLER, 12 Dyott Street, London WC1A 1DF. *W.*

BRAIN, Oxford University Press, Walton Street, Oxford OX2 6DP. *Alt. M.*

BREWING AND DISTILLING INTERNATIONAL, Southbound House, 163 Burton Road, Burton-on-Trent, Staffs. DE14 3DP. *M.*

BRITISH BAKER, Maclaren House, 19 Scarbrook Road, Croydon CR9 1QH. *W.*

BRITISH DENTAL JOURNAL, BMA House, Tavistock Square, London WC1H 9JR. *Alt. W.*

BRITISH FOOD JOURNAL, MCB University Press Ltd, 60–62 Toller Lane, Bradford BD8 9BY. *Ten times a year.*

BRITISH JEWELLER & WATCHBUYER, Wentworth House, Wentworth Street, Peterborough PE1 1DS. *M.*

BRITISH JOURNAL FOR THE PHILOSOPHY OF SCIENCE, Oxford University Press, Walton Street, Oxford OX2 6DP. *Q.*

BRITISH JOURNAL OF PHOTOGRAPHY, 58 Fleet Street, London EC4Y 1JU. *W.*

BRITISH JOURNAL OF PSYCHIATRY, Royal College of Psychiatrists, 17 Belgrave Square, London SW1X 8PG. *M.*

BRITISH JOURNAL OF PSYCHOLOGY, British Psychological Society, 13A Church Lane, London N2 8DX. *Q.*

BRITISH JOURNAL OF SOCIAL WORK, Oxford University Press, Walton Street, Oxford OX2 6DP. *Six times a year.*

BRITISH MEDICAL JOURNAL, British Medical Association, BMA House, Tavistock Square, London WC1H 9JR. *W.*

BRITISH PRINTER, Maclean Hunter House, Chalk Lane, Cockfosters Road, Barnet, Herts. EN4 0BU. *M.*

BRITISH TAX REVIEW, South Quay Plaza, 183 Marsh Wall, London E14 9FT. *Alt. M.*

BRITISH VETERINARY JOURNAL, 24–28 Oval Road, London NW1 7DX. *Alt. M.*

BUILDING, Builder House, 1 Millharbour, London E14 9RA. *W.*

BUILDING TRADE & INDUSTRY, 131–133 Duckmoor Road, Ashton Gate, Bristol BS3 2BH. *M.*

BUSINESS CONNECTIONS, Node Court, Drivers End, Codicote, Hitchin, Herts. SG4 8TR. *Q.*

BUSINESS EDUCATION TODAY, 128 Long Acre, London WC2E 9AN. *M.*

CABINET MAKER AND RETAIL FURNISHER, PO Box 20, Sovereign Way, Tonbridge, Kent TN9 1RW. *W.*

CAMPAIGN, 22 Lancaster Gate, London W2 3LY. *W.*

CARPET AND FLOORCOVERINGS REVIEW, PO Box 20, Sovereign Way, Tonbridge, Kent TN9 1RW. *Alt. W.*

CATERER AND HOTELKEEPER, Quadrant House, The Quadrant, Sutton, Surrey SM2 5AS. *W.*

CHEMIST AND DRUGGIST, PO Box 20, Sovereign Way, Tonbridge, Kent TN9 1RW. *W.*

CHEMISTRY AND INDUSTRY, 14 Belgrave Square, London SW1X 8PS. *Alt. W.*

CHEMISTRY IN BRITAIN, Royal Society of Chemistry, Burlington House, Piccadilly, London W1V 0BN. *M.*

CHILD EDUCATION, Villiers House, Clarendon Avenue, Leamington Spa, Warks. CV32 5PR. *M.*

CLASSICAL QUARTERLY, Oxford University Press, Walton Street, Oxford OX2 6DP. *Twice a year.*

CLASSICAL REVIEW, Oxford University Press, Walton Street, Oxford OX2 6DP. *Twice a year.*

COMPUTER SHOPPER, 19 Bolsover Street, London W1P 7HJ. *M.*

COMPUTER WEEKLY, Quadrant House, The Quadrant, Sutton, Surrey SM2 5AS. *W.*

COMPUTING, VNU House, 32–34 Broadwick Street, London W1A 2HG. *W.*

CONSTRUCTION NEWS, 100 Avenue Road, London NW3 3TP. *W.*

CONSTRUCTION WEEKLY, Morgan-Grampian House, Calderwood Street, London SE18 6QH. *W.*

CONTAINERISATION INTERNATIONAL, National Magazine House, 72 Broadwick Street, London W1V 2BP. *M.*

CONTRACT JOURNAL, Quadrant House, The Quadrant, Sutton, Surrey SM2 5AS. *W.*

CONTROL AND INSTRUMENTATION, Morgan-Grampian House, 30 Calderwood Street, London SE18 6QH. *M.*

CRAFTS MAGAZINE, Crafts Council, 44A Pentonville Road, London N1 9BY. *Alt. M.*

CRIMINOLOGIST, East Row, Little London, Chichester, W. Sussex PO19 1PG. *Q.*

DAIRY FARMER AND DAIRY BEEF PRODUCER, Fenton House, Wharfedale Road, Ipswich IP1 4LG. *M.*

DAIRY INDUSTRIES INTERNATIONAL, Wilmington House, Church Hill, Wilmington, Dartford, Kent DA2 7EF. *M.*

THE DENTIST, 20 Leas Road, Guildford, Surrey GU1 4QT. *M.*

DESIGN, The Design Council, 28 Haymarket, London SW1Y 4SU. *M.*

DESIGN WEEK, St Giles House, 49–50 Poland Street, London W1V 4AX. *W.*

DIRECTOR, Institute of Directors, Mountbarrow House, 6–20 Elizabeth Street, London SW1W 9RB. *M.*

ECONOMIC JOURNAL, 108 Cowley Road, Oxford OX4 1JF. *Alt. M.*

EDUCATION, 21–27 Lamb's Conduit Street, London WC1N 3NJ. *W.*

ELECTRICAL AND RADIO TRADING, Quadrant House, The Quadrant, Sutton, Surrey SM2 5AS. *W.*

ELECTRICAL REVIEW, Quadrant House, The Quadrant, Sutton, Surrey SM2 5AS. *Alt. W.*

ELECTRICAL TIMES, Quadrant House, The Quadrant, Sutton, Surrey SM2 5AS. *Ten times a year.*

ELECTRONIC ENGINEERING, Morgan-Grampian House, 30 Calderwood Street, London SE18 6QH. *M.*

ENERGY MANAGEMENT, Maclean Hunter House, Chalk Lane, Cockfosters Road, Barnet, Herts. EN4 0BU. *Alt. M.*

THE ENGINEER, Morgan-Grampian House, 30 Calderwood Street, London SE18 6QH. *W.*

ENGINEERING, The Design Council, 28 Haymarket, London SW1Y 4SU. *Eleven times a year.*

ENGLISH HISTORICAL REVIEW, Longman House, Burnt Mill, Harlow, Essex CM20 2JE. *Q.*

ENGLISH TODAY, Cambridge University Press, The Edinburgh Building, Shaftesbury Road, Cambridge CB2 2RU. *Q.*

THE ENVIRONMENTALIST, PO Box 81, Northwood, Middx. HA6 3DN. *Q.*

EQUITY JOURNAL, Guild House, Upper St Martin's Lane, London WC2H 9EG. *Q.*

ESTATES GAZETTE, 151 Wardour Street, London W1V 4BN. *W.*

FAIRPLAY INTERNATIONAL SHIPPING WEEKLY, 20 Ullswater Crescent, Ullswater Business Park, Coulsdon, Surrey CR5 2HR. *W.*

FARMERS WEEKLY, Quadrant House, The Quadrant, Sutton, Surrey SM2 5AS. *W.*

FASHION WEEKLY, 67 Clerkenwell Road, London EC1R 5BH. *W.*

FIRE, Queensway House, 2 Queensway, Redhill, Surrey RH1 1QS. *M.*

FIRE PREVENTION, 140 Aldersgate Street, London EC1A 4HX. *Ten times a year.*

FISH, Institute of Fisheries Management, 151 Cove Road, Farnborough, Hants. GU14 0HQ. *Q.*

FISH TRADER, Queensway House, 2 Queensway, Redhill, Surrey RH1 1QS. *M.*

FLIGHT INTERNATIONAL, Quadrant House, The Quadrant, Sutton, Surrey SM2 5AS. *W.*

FOOD TRADE REVIEW, Station House, Hortons Way, Westerham, Kent TN16 1BZ. *M.*

FORESTRY AND BRITISH TIMBER, PO Box 20, Sovereign Way, Tonbridge, Kent TN9 1RW. *M.*

FOUNDRY TRADE JOURNAL, Queensway House, 2 Queensway, Redhill, Surrey RH1 1QS. *Alt. W.*

FROZEN AND CHILLED FOODS, Queensway House, 2 Queensway, Redhill, Surrey RH1 1QS. *M.*

FUEL, Linacre House, Jordan Hill, Oxford OX2 8DP. *M.*

GARDEN TRADE NEWS, Apex House, Oundle Road, Peterborough PE2 9NP. *M.*

GAS WORLD INTERNATIONAL, PO Box 105, 25–31 Ironmonger Row, London EC1V 3PN. *Q.*

GEOGRAPHY, Geographical Association, 343 Fulwood Road, Sheffield S10 3BP. *Q.*

GEOLOGICAL MAGAZINE, Cambridge University Press, The Edinburgh Building, Shaftesbury Road, Cambridge CB2 2RU. *Alt. M.*

GLASS AND GLAZING PRODUCTS, 19 Scarbrook Road, Croydon CR9 1QH. *M.*

GREECE AND ROME, Oxford University Press, Walton Street, Oxford OX2 6DP. *Twice a year.*

THE GROCER, Broadfield Park, Crawley, West Sussex RH11 9RT. *W.*

GROWER, Warwick House, Azalea Drive, Swanley, Kent BR8 8HY. *W.*

HAIRDRESSERS' JOURNAL INTERNATIONAL, Quadrant House, The Quadrant, Sutton, Surrey SM2 5AS. *W.*

THE HEALTH SERVICE JOURNAL, 4 Little Essex Street, London WC2R 3LF. *W.*

HEALTH VISITOR, BMA House, Tavistock Square, London WC1H 9JR. *M.*

HEATING, VENTILATING AND PLUMBING, PO Box 13, Hereford House, Bridle Path, Croydon CR9 4NL. *M.*

HISTORY TODAY, 20 Old Compton Street, London W1V 5PE. *M.*

INDEPENDENT RETAILER, 14 Pierpoint Street, Worcester WR1 1TA. *M.*

INDUSTRIAL EXCHANGE AND MART, Link House, West Street, Poole, Dorset BH15 1LL. *W.*

INDUSTRIAL RELATIONS JOURNAL, 108 Cowley Road, Oxford OX4 1JF. *Q.*

INTERNATIONAL AFFAIRS, Cambridge University Press, The Edinburgh Building, Shaftesbury Road, Cambridge CB2 2RU. *Q.*

JANE'S DEFENCE WEEKLY, Sentinel House, 163 Brighton Road, Coulsdon, Surrey CR5 2NH. *W.*

THE JOURNALIST, National Union of Journalists, Acorn House, 314 Gray's Inn Road, London WC1X 8DP. *M.*

JOURNAL OF ALTERNATIVE AND COMPLEMENTARY MEDICINE, Mariner House, 53A High Street, Bagshot, Surrey GU19 5AH. *M.*

JOURNAL OF THE BRITISH ASTRONOMICAL ASSOCIATION, Burlington House, Piccadilly, London W1V 9AG. *Alt. M.*

JOURNAL OF THE CHEMICAL SOCIETY, Thomas Graham House, Science Park, Milton Road, Cambridge CB4 4WF. *Irregular.*

JUSTICE OF THE PEACE, East Row, Little London, Chichester, W. Sussex PO19 1PG. *W.*

THE LANCET, 42 Bedford Square, London WC1B 3SL. *W.*

LAW QUARTERLY REVIEW, South Quay Plaza, 183 Marsh Wall, London E14 9FT. *Q.*

THE LAW REPORTS, 3 Stone Buildings, Lincoln's Inn, London WC2A 3XN. *M.*

LAW SOCIETY GAZETTE, 50 Chancery Lane, London WC2A 1SX. *W.*

LEATHER, PO Box 20, Sovereign Way, Tonbridge, Kent TN9 1RW. *M.*

LIBRARY ASSOCIATION RECORD, 7 Ridgmount Street, London WC1E 7AE. *M.*

LLOYD'S LOADING LIST, Collwyn House, Sheepen Place, Colchester, Essex CO3 3LP. *W.*

LLOYD'S SHIPPING INDEX, Collwyn House, Sheepen Place, Colchester, Essex CO3 3LP. *W.*

LOCAL GOVERNMENT CHRONICLE, 33–39 Bowling Green Lane, London EC1R 0DA. *W.*

MACHINERY AND PRODUCTION ENGINEERING, Franks Hall, Franks Lane, Horton Kirby, Dartford, Kent DA4 9LL. *Alt. W.*

MACHINERY MARKET, 6 Blyth Road, Bromley, Kent BR1 3RX. *W.*

MANAGEMENT ACCOUNTING, Chartered Institute of Management Accountants, 63 Portland Place, London W1N 4AB. *M.*

MANAGEMENT TODAY, 32 Lancaster Gate, London W2 3LY. *M.*

MANUFACTURING CHEMIST, Morgan-Grampian House, 30 Calderwood Street, London SE18 6QH. *M.*

MARKETING, 22 Lancaster Gate, London W2 3LY. *W.*

MARKETING WEEK, St Giles House, 49–50 Poland Street, London W1V 4AX. *W.*

MATERIALS RECLAMATION WEEKLY, Maclaren House, 19 Scarbrook Road, Croydon CR9 1QH. *W.*

MATERIALS WORLD, Institute of Materials, 1 Carlton House Terrace, London SW1Y 5DB. *M.*

MEAT TRADES' JOURNAL, Maclaren House, 19 Scarbrook Road, Croydon, Surrey CR9 1QH. *W.*

MEDIA WEEK, 33–39 Bowling Green Lane, London EC1R 0DA. *W.*

METALS INDUSTRY NEWS, Queensway House, 2 Queensway, Redhill, Surrey RH1 1QS. *Q.*

MIND, Oxford University Press, Walton Street, Oxford OX2 6DP. *Q.*

MINING JOURNAL, 60 Worship Street, London EC2A 2HD. *W.*

MOTOR TRANSPORT, Quadrant House, The Quadrant, Sutton, Surrey SM2 5AS. *W.*

MUNICIPAL JOURNAL, 32 Vauxhall Bridge Road, London SW1V 2SS. *W.*

MUNICIPAL REVIEW AND AMA NEWS, 35 Great Smith Street, London SW1P 3BJ. *Ten times a year.*

MUSEUMS JOURNAL, Museums Association, 42 Clerkenwell Close, London EC1R 0PA. *M.*

THE MUSICAL TIMES, 7 St John's Road, Harrow, Middx. HA1 2EE. *M.*

MUSIC AND LETTERS, Oxford University Press, Walton Street, Oxford OX2 6DP. *Q.*

MUSIC WEEK, 8th Floor, Ludgate House, 245 Blackfriars Road, London SE1 9UR. *W.*

NOTES AND QUERIES, Oxford University Press, Walton Street, Oxford OX2 6DP. *Q.*

NUCLEAR ENGINEERING INTERNATIONAL, Quadrant House, The Quadrant, Sutton, Surrey SM2 5AS. *M.*

NURSING TIMES & NURSING MIRROR, 4 Little Essex Street, London WC2R 3LF. *W.*

OFF-LICENCE NEWS, Broadfield Park, Crawley, W. Sussex RH11 9RT. *W.*

OPTICIAN, Quadrant House, The Quadrant, Sutton, Surrey SM2 5AS. *W.*

OPTOMETRY TODAY, 11 Somerset Place, Glasgow G3 7JT. *Alt. W.*

PACKAGING WEEK, PO Box 20, Sovereign Way, Tonbridge, Kent TN9 1RW. *W.*

PAPER, PO Box 20, Sovereign Way, Tonbridge, Kent TN9 1RW. *M.*

PC PLUS, Beauford Court, 30 Monmouth Street, Bath BA1 2BW. *M.*

PERSONAL COMPUTER WORLD, 32–34 Broadwick Street, London W1A 2HG. *M.*

PERSONNEL MANAGEMENT (Institute of Personnel Management), 17 Britton Street, London EC1M 5NQ. *M.*

PHARMACEUTICAL JOURNAL, 1 Lambeth High Street, London SE1 7JN. *W.*

PHILOSOPHY, Cambridge University Press, The Edinburgh Building, Shaftesbury Road, Cambridge CB2 2RU. *Q.*

THE PHOTOGRAPHER, Fox Talbot House, Amwell End, Ware, Herts. SG12 9HN. *M.*

PHYSICS WORLD, Techno House, Redcliffe Way, Bristol BS1 6NX. *M.*

PLUMBING AND HEATING NEWS, Peterson House, Northbank, Berryhill Industrial Estate, Droitwich, Worcs. WR9 9BL. *M.*

POLICE REVIEW, South Quay Plaza 2, 183 Marsh Wall, London E14 9FS. *W.*

THE PRACTITIONER, Morgan-Grampian House, Calderwood Street, London SE18 6QH. *M.*

PRINTING WORLD, PO Box 20, Sovereign Way, Tonbridge, Kent TN9 IRW. *W.*

PROBATION JOURNAL, 3–4 Chivalry Road, London SW11 IHT. *Q.*

PROFESSIONAL CARE OF MOTHER AND CHILD, Media Medica, 1 The Chambers, Chapel Street, Chichester, W. Sussex PO19 IDL. *M.*

THE PSYCHOLOGIST, The British Psychological Society, St Andrews House, 48 Princess Road East, Leicester LE1 7DR. *M.*

QUARRY MANAGEMENT, 7 Regent Street, Nottingham NG1 5BY. *M.*

RAILWAY GAZETTE INTERNATIONAL, Quadrant House, The Quadrant, Sutton, Surrey SM2 5AS. *M.*

RATING & VALUATION REPORTER, 4 Breams Buildings, London EC4A IAQ. *M.*

RETAIL NEWSAGENT, Robert Taylor House, 11 Angel Gate, City Road, London EC1V 2PT. *W.*

RETAIL WEEK, 19 Scarbrook Road, Croydon CR9 IQH. *W.*

REVIEW OF ENGLISH STUDIES, Oxford University Press, Walton Street, Oxford OX2 6DP. *Q.*

RUSI JOURNAL, Royal United Services Institute for Defence Studies, Whitehall, London SW1A 2ET. *Alt. M.*

SHIPPING WORLD & SHIPBUILDER, 4 Hubbard Road, Houndsmill, Basingstoke, Hants. RG21 2UH. *M.*

SHOE & LEATHER NEWS, 19 Scarbrook Road, Croydon, Surrey CR9 IQH. *M.*

SMALLHOLDER, High Street, Stoke Ferry, King's Lynn, Norfolk PE33 9SF. *M.*

SOCIOLOGICAL REVIEW, 108 Cowley Road, Oxford OX4 IJF. *Q.*

SOLICITORS' JOURNAL, 21–27 Lamb's Conduit Street, London WC1N 3NJ. *W.*

SPORTS RETAILING, 147 Temple Chambers, Temple Avenue, London EC4Y ODT. *M.*

THE STAGE AND TELEVISION TODAY, 47 Bermondsey Street, London SE1 3XT. *W.*

STRUCTURAL ENGINEER, 11 Upper Belgrave Street, London SW1X 8BH. *Alt. W.*

SURVEYOR, Quadrant House, The Quadrant, Sutton, Surrey SM2 5AS. *W.*

TAXATION PRACTITIONER, Tolley House, 2 Addiscombe Road, Croydon, Surrey CR9 5AF. *M.*

TAXI, Taxi House, 7–11 Woodfield Road, London W9 2BA. *Alt. W.*

THE TEACHER, National Union of Teachers, Hamilton House, Mabledon Place, London WC1H 9BD. *Eight times a year.*

TEACHING HISTORY, 59A Kennington Park Road, London SE11 4JH. *Q.*

TELEVISION, Quadrant House, The Quadrant, Sutton, Surrey SM2 5AS. *M.*

TEXTILE HORIZONS, 33 Bedford Place, London WC1B 5JX. *M.*

TEXTILE MONTH, 76 Kirkgate, Bradford, W. Yorkshire BD1 ITB. *M.*

TOBACCO, Queensway House, 2 Queensway, Redhill, Surrey RH1 IQS. *Alt. M.*

TOWN AND COUNTRY PLANNING, 17 Carlton House Terrace, London SW1Y 5AS. *M.*

TOWN PLANNING REVIEW, PO Box 147, Liverpool L69 3BX. *Q.*

TOY TRADER, 171–173 High Street, Rickmansworth, Herts WD3 ISN. *M.*

TRADE MARKS JOURNAL, Patent Office, 25 Southampton Buildings, London WC2A IAY. *W.*

THE TRADER, Link House, West Street, Poole, Dorset BH15 ILL. *M.*

TRAVEL TRADE GAZETTE (UK & IRELAND), Morgan-Grampian House, Calderwood Street, London SE18 6QH. *W.*

TTJ-TIMBER TRADES JOURNAL, PO Box 20, Sovereign Way, Tonbridge, Kent TN9 IRW. *W.*

UK PRESS GAZETTE, Maclean Hunter House, Chalk Lane, Cockfosters Road, Barnet, Herts. EN4 OBU. *W.*

WEEKLY LAW REPORTS, 3 Stone Buildings, Lincoln's Inn, London WC2A 3XN. *W.*

WOODCARVING, 166 High Street, Lewes, E. Sussex BN7 IXU. *Alt. M.*

WORLD'S FAIR, 2 Daltry Street, Oldham OL1 4BB. *W.*

---

## NEWS AGENCIES IN LONDON

---

News agencies provide general, business, sport and television news to a variety of subscribers including the press, other media, and industrial, commercial, financial and business users.

THE ASSOCIATED PRESS LTD (AP), 12 Norwich Street, London EC4A 4BP. Tel: 0171-353 1515.

CENTRAL PRESS FEATURES LTD, 20 Spectrum House, 32–34 Gordon House Road, London NW5 ILP. Tel: 0171-284 1433.

EXTEL FINANCIAL LTD, Fitzroy House, 13–17 Epworth Street, London EC2A 4DL. Tel: 0171-251 3333.

HAYTERS, 4–5 Gough Square, London EC4A 3DE. Tel: 0171-353 0971.

PARLIAMENTARY AND EEC NEWS SERVICE, 19 Douglas Street, London SW1P 4PA. Tel: 0171-233 8283.

PRESS ASSOCIATION, 85 Fleet Street, London EC4P 4BE. Tel: 0171-353 7440.

REUTERS LTD, 85 Fleet Street, London EC4P 4AJ. Tel: 0171-250 1122.

TWO-TEN COMMUNICATIONS LTD, 210 Old Street, London EC1V 9UN. Tel: 0171-490 8111.

UNITED PRESS INTERNATIONAL (UK) LTD, 2 Greenwich View, Millharbour, London E14 9NN. Tel: 0171-538 0932.

# Book Publishers

More than 15,000 firms, individuals and societies have published one or more books in recent years. The list which follows is a selective one comprising, in the main, those firms whose names are most familiar to the general public. A fuller list, *Publishers in the United Kingdom and Their Addresses*, containing some 2,500 names and addresses is published annually in March by the publishers of *Whitaker's Almanack*.

ADDISON-WESLEY PUBLISHERS, Finchampstead Road, Wokingham, Berks. RG11 2NZ. Tel: 01734-794000
ALLAN (IAN), Coombelands House, Coombelands Lane, Addlestone KT15 1HY. Tel: 01932-855909
ALLEN (J. A.), 1 Lower Grosvenor Place, London SW1W 0EL. Tel: 0171-834 0090
ANAYA PUBLISHERS, 50 Osnaburgh Street, London NW1 3ND. Tel: 0171-383 2997
APPLE PRESS, 6 Blundell Street, London N7 9BH. Tel: 0171-700 6700
ARGUS BOOKS, Argus House, Boundary Way, Hemel Hempstead, Herts. HP2 7ST. Tel: 01442-66551
ARMADA BOOKS, 77 Fulham Palace Road, London W6 8JB. Tel: 0181-741 7070
ARMS & ARMOUR PRESS, 41 Strand, London WC2N 5JE. Tel: 0171-839 4900
ARNOLD (EDWARD), 338 Euston Road, London NW1 3BH. Tel: 0171-873 6000
ARROW BOOKS, 20 Vauxhall Bridge Road, London SW1V 2SA. Tel: 0171-973 9700
ATHLONE PRESS, 1 Park Drive, London NW11 7SG. Tel: 0181-458 0888
AURUM PRESS, 25 Bedford Avenue, London WC1B 3AT. Tel: 0171-637 3225
AUTOMOBILE ASSOCIATION, Norfolk House, Priestly Road, Basingstoke, Hants., RG24 9NY. Tel: 01256-491524
BAILLIÈRE TINDALL, 24 Oval Road, London NW1 7DX. Tel: 0171-267 4466
BANTAM BOOKS, 61 Uxbridge Road, London W5 5SA. Tel: 0181-579 2652
BARRIE & JENKINS, 20 Vauxhall Bridge Road, London SW1V 2SA. Tel: 0171-973 9690
BARTHOLOMEW, 77 Fulham Palace Road, London W6 8JB. Tel: 0181-741 7070
BATSFORD (B. T.), 4 Fitzhardinge Street, London W1H 0AH. Tel: 0171-486 8484
BBC BOOKS, 80 Wood Lane, London W12 0TT. Tel: 0181-576 2570
BLACK (A. & C.), 35 Bedford Row, London WC1R 4JH. Tel: 0171-242 0946
BLACKIE CHILDREN'S BOOKS, 27 Wrights Lane, London W8 5TZ. Tel: 0171-938 2200
BLACKWELL PUBLISHERS, 108 Cowley Road, Oxford OX4 1JF. Tel: 01865-791100
BLANDFORD PRESS, 41 Strand, London WC2N 5JE. Tel: 0171-839 4900
BLOOMSBURY PUBLISHING, 2 Soho Square, London W1V 5DE. Tel: 0171-494 2111
BODLEY HEAD, 20 Vauxhall Bridge Road, London SW1V 2SA. Tel: 0171-973 9730
BOXTREE, 21 Broadwall, London SE1 9PL. Tel: 0171-928 9696
BOYARS (MARION), 24 Lacy Road, London SW15 1NL. Tel: 0181-788 9522
BRIMAX BOOKS, 4 Studlands Park Industrial Estate, Exning Road, Newmarket, Suffolk CB8 7AU. Tel: 01638-664611

BRITISH MUSEUM PRESS, 46 Bloomsbury Street, London WC1B 3QQ. Tel: 0171-323 1234
BUTTERWORTH & Co., Borough Green, Sevenoaks TN15 8PH. Tel: 01732-884567
CADOGAN BOOKS, London House, Parkgate Road, London SW11 4NQ. Tel: 0171-738 1961
CALDER PUBLICATIONS, 9–15 Neal Street, London WC2H 9TU. Tel: 0171-497 1741
CAMBRIDGE UNIVERSITY PRESS, The Edinburgh Building, Cambridge CB2 2RU. Tel: 01223-312393
CANONGATE PRESS, 14 Frederick Street, Edinburgh EH2 2HB. Tel: 0131-220 3800
CAPE (JONATHAN), 20 Vauxhall Bridge Road, London SW1V 2SA. Tel: 0171-973 9730
CASSELL, 41 Strand, London WC2N 5JE. Tel: 0171-839 4900
CAVENDISH PUBLISHING, The Glass House, Wharton Street, London WC1X 9PX. Tel: 0171-278 8000
CENTURY PUBLISHING CO., *see* Random House UK
CHAMBERS, 24 Great Titchfield Street, London, W1P 7AD. Tel: 0171-631 0878
CHANCELLOR PRESS, 81 Fulham Road, London SW3 6RB. Tel: 0171-581 9393
CHAPMAN & HALL, 2 Boundary Row, London SE1 8HN. Tel: 0171-865 0066
CHAPMAN (GEOFFREY), 41 Strand, London WC2N 5JE. Tel: 0171-839 4900
CHAPMANS PUBLISHERS, 5 Upper St Martin's Lane, London WC2H 9EA. Tel: 0171-240 3444
CHATTO & WINDUS, 20 Vauxhall Bridge Road, London SW1V 2SA. Tel: 0171-973 9740
CHIVERS PRESS, Windsor Bridge Road, Bath BA2 3AX. Tel: 01225-335336
CHURCH HOUSE PUBLISHING, Church House, Great Smith Street, London SW1P 3NZ. Tel: 0171-340 9011
CHURCHILL LIVINGSTONE, 1–3 Baxter's Place, Leith Walk, Edinburgh EH1 3AF. Tel: 0131-556 2424
COLLINS (WILLIAM), *see* HarperCollins Publishers
CONSTABLE & Co., 3 The Lanchesters, 162 Fulham Palace Road, London W6 9ER. Tel: 0181-741 3663
CONSUMERS' ASSOCIATION, 2 Marylebone Road, London NW1 4DF. Tel: 0171-486 5544
CORGI BOOKS, 61 Uxbridge Road, London W5 5SA. Tel: 0181-579 2652
DARTON, LONGMAN & TODD, 1 Spencer Court, 140 Wandsworth High Street, London SW18 4JJ. Tel: 0181-875 0155
DAVID & CHARLES, Brunel House, Newton Abbot, Devon TQ12 4PU. Tel: 01626-61121
DEAN & SON, 81 Fulham Road, London SW3 6RB. Tel: 0171-581 9393
DENT (J. M.) & SONS, 5 Upper St Martin's Lane, London WC2H 9EA. Tel: 0171-240 3444
DEUTSCH (ANDRE), 106 Great Russell Street, London WC1B 3LJ. Tel: 0171-580 2746
DORLING KINDERSLEY, 9 Henrietta Street, London WC2E 8PS. Tel: 0171-836 5411
DOUBLEDAY, 61 Uxbridge Road, London W5 5SA. Tel: 0181-579 2652
DUCKWORTH & Co., 48 Hoxton Square, London N1 6PB. Tel: 0171-729 5986
EBURY PRESS, 20 Vauxhall Bridge Road, London SW1V 2SA. Tel: 0171-973 9690
ELEMENT BOOKS, The Old School House, The Courtyard, Bell Street, Shaftesbury, Dorset SP7 8BP. Tel: 01747-851448

ELLIOT RIGHT WAY BOOKS, Kingswood Building, Kingswood, Tadworth, Surrey KT20 6TD. Tel: 01737-832202

ELSEVIER SCIENCE, The Boulevard, Langford Lane, Kidlington, Oxon. OX5 1GB. Tel: 01865-843000

ENCYCLOPAEDIA BRITANNICA INTERNATIONAL, Carew House, Station Approach, Wallington, Surrey SM6 0DA. Tel: 0181-669 4355

EPWORTH PRESS, c/o SCM Press, 26 Tottenham Road, London N1 4BZ. Tel: 0171-249 7262

EVANS BROS, 2A Portman Mansions, Chiltern Street, London W1M 1LE. Tel: 0171-935 7160

EVERYMAN, see Orion Publishing Group

EVERYMAN'S LIBRARY, 79 Berwick Street, London W1V 3PF. Tel: 0171-287 0035

FABER & FABER, 3 Queen Square, London WC1N 3AU. Tel: 0171-465 0045

FLAMINGO, see HarperCollins Publishers

FONTANA, 77 Fulham Palace Road, London W6 8JB. Tel: 0181-741 7070

FOULIS (G. T.), Sparkford, Yeovil, Somerset BA22 7JJ. Tel: 01963-440635

FOULSHAM (W.) & CO., Yeovil Road, Slough SL1 4JH. Tel: 01753-526769

FOURTH ESTATE, 289 Westbourne Grove, London W11 2QA. Tel: 0171-727 8993

FRENCH (SAMUEL), 52 Fitzroy Street, London W1P 6JR. Tel: 0171-387 9373

GAIA BOOKS, 20 High Street, Stroud GL5 1AS. Tel: 01453-752985

GIBBONS (STANLEY), 5 Parkside, Christchurch Road, Ringwood, Hants. BH24 3SH. Tel: 01425-472363

GINN & CO., Prebendal House, Parson's Fee, Aylesbury, Bucks. HP20 2QZ. Tel: 01296-394442

GOLLANCZ (VICTOR), 41 Strand, London WC2N 5JE. Tel: 0171-839 4900

GOWER PUBLISHING CO., Croft Road, Aldershot, Hants. GU11 3HR. Tel: 01252-331551

GRAFTON BOOKS, 77 Fulham Palace Road, London W6 8JB. Tel: 0181-741 7070

GRANTA BOOKS, 2 Hanover Yard, London N1 8BE. Tel: 0171-704 9776

GUINNESS PUBLISHING, 33 London Road, Enfield, Middx. EN2 6DJ. Tel: 0181-367 4567

HALE (ROBERT), 45 Clerkenwell Green, London EC1R 0HT. Tel: 0171-251 2661

HAMILTON (HAMISH), 27 Wrights Lane, London W8 5TZ. Tel: 0171-416 3100

HAMLYN (PAUL), 81 Fulham Road, London SW3 6RB. Tel: 0171-581 9393

HARCOURT BRACE, 24 Oval Road, London NW1 7DX. Tel: 0171-267 4466

HARPERCOLLINS PUBLISHERS, 77 Fulham Palace Road, London W6 8JB. Tel: 0181-741 7070

HARRAP, 24 Great Titchfield Street, London W1P 7AD. Tel: 0171-631 0878

HARVESTER WHEATSHEAF, Campus 400, Maylands Avenue, Hemel Hempstead HP2 7EZ. Tel: 01442-881900

HAYNES (J. H.), Sparkford, Yeovil, Somerset BA22 7JJ. Tel: 01963-440635

HEADLINE BOOK PUBLISHING, see Hodder Headline

HEINEMANN (WILLIAM), 81 Fulham Road, London SW3 6RB. Tel: 0171-581 9393

HERBERT PRESS, 46 Northchurch Road, London N1 4EJ. Tel: 0171-254 2379

HIPPO BOOKS, 7 Pratt Street, London NW1 0AE. Tel: 0171-284 4474

HMSO, PO Box 276, London SW8 5DT. Tel: 0171-873 0011

HODDER & STOUGHTON, see Hodder Headline

HODDER HEADLINE, 338 Euston Road, London NW1 3BH. Tel: 0171-873 6000

HOGARTH PRESS, 20 Vauxhall Bridge Road, London SW1V 2SA. Tel: 0171-973 9740

HUTCHINSON, see Random House UK

JARROLD PUBLISHING, Whitefriars, Norwich NR3 1TR. Tel: 01603-763300

JORDAN PUBLISHING, 21 St Thomas Street, Bristol BS1 6JS. Tel: 0117-923 0600

JOSEPH (MICHAEL), 27 Wrights Lane, London W8 5TZ. Tel: 0171-416 3200

KEGAN PAUL INTERNATIONAL, PO Box 256, London WC1B 3SW. Tel: 0171-580 5511

KINGFISHER BOOKS, 24 Great Titchfield Street, London W1P 7AD. Tel: 0171-631 0878

KINGSWAY PUBLICATIONS, Lottbridge Drove, Eastbourne BN23 6NT. Tel: 01323-410930

KOGAN PAGE, 120 Pentonville Road, London N1 9JN. Tel: 0171-278 0433

LADYBIRD BOOKS, Beeches Road, Loughborough LE11 2NQ. Tel: 01509-268021

LAROUSSE, 24 Great Titchfield Street, London W1P 7AD. Tel: 0171-631 0878

LASCELLES (ROGER), 47 York Road, Brentford, Middx TW8 0QP. Tel: 0181-847 0935

LAWRENCE & WISHART, 144A Old South Lambeth Road, London SW8 1XX. Tel: 0171-820 9281

LENNARD PUBLISHING, Windmill Cottage, Mackerye End, Harpenden AL5 5DR. Tel: 01582-715866

LETTS OF LONDON, 37 Connaught Street, London W2 2AZ. Tel: 0171-258 0204

LINCOLN (FRANCES), 4 Torriano Mews, Torriano Avenue, London NW5 2RZ. Tel: 0171-284 4009

LION PUBLISHING, Peter's Way, Oxford OX4 5HG. Tel: 01865-747550

LITTLE, BROWN & CO., Brettenham House, Lancaster Place, London WC2E 7EN. Tel: 0171-911 8000

LONGMAN GROUP, Burnt Mill, Harlow, Essex CM20 2JE. Tel: 01279-426721

LUND HUMPHRIES, 1 Russell Gardens, London NW11 9NN. Tel: 0181-458 6314

LUTTERWORTH PRESS, PO Box 60, Cambridge CB1 2NT. Tel: 01223-350865

MACDONALD & EVANS, 128 Long Acre, London WC2E 9AN. Tel: 0171-379 7383

McGRAW-HILL, Shoppenhangers Road, Maidenhead, Berks. SL6 2QL. Tel: 01628-23432

MACMILLAN PUBLISHERS, 4 Little Essex Street, London WC2R 3LF. Tel: 0171-836 6633

MACRAE (JULIA), 20 Vauxhall Bridge Road, London SW1V 2SA. Tel: 0171-973 9750

MAMMOTH, 38 Hans Crescent, London SW1X 0LZ. Tel: 0171-581 9393

MANDALA, see HarperCollins Publishers

MANDARIN, 81 Fulham Road, London SW3 6RB. Tel: 0171-581 9393

METHUEN LONDON, 81 Fulham Road, London SW3 6RB. Tel: 0171-581 9393

MILLS & BOON, 18 Paradise Road, Richmond, Surrey TW9 1SR. Tel: 0181-948 0444

MINERVA PRESS, 2 Old Brompton Road, London SW7 3DQ. Tel: 0171-225 3113

MITCHELL BEAZLEY, 81 Fulham Road, London SW3 6RB. Tel: 0171-581 9393

MOWBRAY, 41 Strand, London WC2N 5JE. Tel: 0171-839 4900

MURRAY (JOHN), 50 Albemarle Street, London W1X 4BD. Tel: 0171-493 4361

NATIONAL CHRISTIAN EDUCATION COUNCIL, Robert
Denholm House, Nutfield, Redhill RH1 4HW. Tel: 01737-
822411

NELSON (THOMAS), Mayfield Road, Walton-on-Thames
KT12 5PL. Tel: 01932-252211

NEW ENGLISH LIBRARY, see Hodder Headline

NISBET & CO., 78 Tilehouse Street, Hitchin, Herts.
SG5 2DY. Tel: 01462-438331

NOVELLO & CO., 8 Frith Street, London W1V 5TZ. Tel:
0171-434 0066

OCTOPUS BOOKS, 81 Fulham Road, London SW3 6RB. Tel:
0171-581 9393

OLIVER & BOYD, Longman House, Burnt Mill, Harlow,
Essex CM20 2JE. Tel: 01279-426721

O'MARA (MICHAEL) BOOKS, 9 Lion Yard, Tremadoc
Road, London SW4 7NQ. Tel: 0171-720 8643

ORCHARD BOOKS, 96 Leonard Street, London EC2A 4RH.
Tel: 0171-739 2929

ORION PUBLISHING GROUP, 5 Upper St Martin's Lane,
London WC2H 9EA. Tel: 0171-240 3444

OWEN (PETER), 73 Kenway Road, London SW5 0RE. Tel:
0171-373 5628

OXFORD UNIVERSITY PRESS, Walton Street, Oxford
OX2 6DP. Tel: 01865-56767

PAN BOOKS, Cavaye Place, London SW10 9PG. Tel: 0171-
373 6070

PELHAM BOOKS, 27 Wrights Lane, London W8 5TZ. Tel:
0171-416 3200

PENGUIN BOOKS, Bath Road, Harmondsworth, Middx.
UB7 0DA. Tel: 0181-759 1984

PERGAMON PRESS, The Boulevard, Langford Lane,
Kidlington, Oxon OX5 1GB. Tel: 01865-843000

PHAIDON PRESS, 2 Kensington Square, London W8 5EP.
Tel: 0171-361 1234

PHARMACEUTICAL PRESS, 1 Lambeth High Street,
London SE1 7JN. Tel: 0171-735 9141

PHILIP (GEORGE), 81 Fulham Road, London SW3 6RB.
Tel: 0171-581 9393

PIATKUS BOOKS, 5 Windmill Street, London W1P 1HF. Tel:
0171-631 0710

PICADOR, see Pan Books

PICCADILLY PRESS, 5 Castle Road, London NW1 8PR. Tel:
0171-267 4492

PINTER PUBLISHERS, 25 Floral Street, London WC2E 9DS.
Tel: 0171-240 9233

PITKIN PICTORIALS, Healey House, Dene Road,
Andover, Hants. SP10 2AA. Tel: 01264-334303

PITMAN PUBLISHING, 128 Long Acre, London WC2E 9AN.
Tel: 0171-379 7383

QUARTET BOOKS, 27 Goodge Street, London W1P 1FD.
Tel: 0171-636 3992

QUILLER PRESS, 46 Lillie Road, London SW6 1TN. Tel:
0171-499 6529

RANDOM HOUSE UK, 20 Vauxhall Bridge Road, London
SW1V 2SA. Tel: 0171-973 9000

READER'S DIGEST, 25 Berkeley Square, London W1X 6AB.
Tel: 0171-629 8144

RELIGIOUS & MORAL EDUCATION PRESS, St Mary's
Works, St Mary's Plain, Norwich NR3 3BH. Tel: 01603-
615995

ROUGH GUIDES, 1 Mercer Street, London WC2H 9QJ. Tel:
0171-379 3329

ROUTLEDGE, 11 New Fetter Lane, London EC4P 4EE. Tel:
0171-583 9855

ST ANDREW PRESS, 121 George Street, Edinburgh
EH2 4YN. Tel: 0131-225 5722

SCM PRESS, 26 Tottenham Road, London N1 4BZ. Tel:
0171-249 7262

SCRIPTURE UNION, 130 City Road, London EC1V 2NJ. Tel:
0171-782 0013

SECKER & WARBURG, 81 Fulham Road, London SW3 6RB.
Tel: 0171-581 9393

SERPENT'S TAIL PUBLISHING, 4 Blackstock Mews,
London N4 2BT. Tel: 0171-354 1949

SEVERN HOUSE, 9 Sutton High Street, Sutton SM1 1DF. Tel:
0181-770 3930

SHELDON PRESS, Holy Trinity Church, Marylebone Road,
London NW1 4DU. Tel: 0171-387 5282

SIDGWICK & JACKSON, Cavaye Place, London SW10 9PG.
Tel: 0171-373 6070

SIMON & SCHUSTER, Campus 400, Maylands Avenue,
Hemel Hempstead HP2 7EZ. Tel: 01442-881900

SINCLAIR-STEVENSON, 81 Fulham Road, London
SW3 6RB. Tel: 0171-581 9393

SOUVENIR PRESS, 43 Great Russell Street, London
WC1B 3PA. Tel: 0171-580 9307

SPCK, Holy Trinity Church, Marylebone Road, London
NW1 4DU. Tel: 0171-387 5282

SPON (E. & F. N.), 2 Boundary Row, London SE1 8HN.
Tel: 0171-865 0066

STEPHENS (PATRICK), Sparkford, Yeovil BA22 7JJ. Tel:
01963-440635

SWEET & MAXWELL, 183 Marsh Wall, London E14 9FT.
Tel: 0171-538 8686

THAMES & HUDSON, 30 Bloomsbury Street, London
WC1B 3QP. Tel: 0171-636 5488

THORSONS, 77 Fulham Palace Road, London W6 8JB. Tel:
0181-741 7070

TIMES BOOKS, 77 Fulham Palace Road, London W6 8JB.
Tel: 0181-741 7070

UNIVERSITY OF WALES PRESS, 6 Gwennyth Street,
Cardiff CF2 4YD. Tel: 01222-231919

VIKING, 27 Wrights Lane, London W8 5TZ. Tel: 0171-938
2200

VIRAGO PRESS, 42 Gloucester Crescent, London NW1 7PD.
Tel: 0171-916 6066

VIRGIN PUBLISHING, 33–34 Grand Union Centre, 332
Ladbroke Grove, London W10 5AH. Tel: 0181-968 7554

WALKER BOOKS, 87 Vauxhall Walk, London SE11 5HJ. Tel:
0171-793 0909

WARD LOCK, 41 Strand, London WC2N 5JE. Tel: 0171-839
4900

WARD LOCK EDUCATIONAL CO., 1 Christopher Road,
East Grinstead, W. Sussex RH19 3BT. Tel: 01342-318980

WARNE (FREDERICK), see Penguin Books

WATTS (FRANKLIN), 96 Leonard Street, London
EC2A 4RH. Tel: 0171-739 2929

WEIDENFELD & NICOLSON, 5 Upper St Martin's Lane,
London WC2H 9EA. Tel: 0171-240 3444

WHITAKER (J.), 12 Dyott Street, London WC1A 1DF. Tel:
0171-836 8911

WILEY (JOHN) & SONS, Baffins Lane, Chichester, W.
Sussex PO19 1UD. Tel: 01243-779777

WISDEN (JOHN), 25 Down Road, Merrow, Guildford
GU1 2PY. Tel: 01483-570358

# Annual Reference Books

If the address of the editorial office of a publication differs from the address to which orders should be sent, the address given is usually the one for orders

ADVERTISER'S ANNUAL, East Grinstead House, East Grinstead, W. Sussex RH19 1XA. 3 vol. £170.00

ALLIED DUNBAR INVESTMENT AND SAVINGS GUIDE, PO Box 88, Harlow, Essex CM19 5SR. £19.99

ALLIED DUNBAR TAX HANDBOOK, PO Box 88, Harlow, Essex CM19 5SR. £19.99

ANNUAL ABSTRACT OF STATISTICS, PO Box 276, London SW8 5DT. (Feb.) £23.00

ANNUAL REGISTER OF WORLD EVENTS, PO Box 88, Harlow, Essex CM19 5SR. £92.00

ANTIQUE SHOPS OF BRITAIN, GUIDE TO THE, 5 Church Street, Woodbridge, Suffolk IP12 1DS. £14.95

ART SALES INDEX, 1 Thames Street, Weybridge, Surrey KT13 8JG. £95.00

ART WORLD DIRECTORY, 20 Prescott Place, London SW4 6BT. (Jan.) £19.50

ASSOCIATION OF CONSULTING ENGINEERS DIRECTORY OF MEMBERS FIRMS, Alliance House, 12 Caxton Street, London SW1H 0QL. £10.00

ASTRONOMICAL ALMANAC, HMSO, PO Box 276, London SW8 5DT. (Dec.) £19.00

ATHLETICS ANNUAL, 10 Sheet Street, Windsor, Berks. SL4 1BG. (May) £13.95

AUTOMOBILE YEAR, Waldenbury, North Common, North Chailey, Lewes, E. Sussex BN8 4DR. £29.95

BAILY'S HUNTING DIRECTORY, 10 Sheet Street, Windsor, Berks. SL4 1BG. (Nov.) £29.95

BANKER'S ALMANAC AND YEAR BOOK, East Grinstead House, East Grinstead, W. Sussex RH19 1XE. (Feb.) 3 vol. £239.00

BENEDICTINE AND CISTERCIAN MONASTIC YEAR BOOK, Ampleforth Abbey, York YO6 4EN. (Dec.) £1.75

BENN'S MEDIA DIRECTORY, PO Box 20, Sovereign Way, Tonbridge, Kent TN9 1RQ. 3 vol. £297.00

BIRMINGHAM POST AND MAIL YEAR BOOK AND WHO'S WHO, 137 Newhall Street, Birmingham B3 1SF. (Sept.) £23.90

BPIF SERVICES AND LIST OF MEMBERS, 11 Bedford Row, London WC1R 4DX. £90.00

BRASSEY'S DEFENCE YEAR BOOK, PO Box 87, Osney Mead, Oxford OX2 0DT. £40.00

BRITAIN: AN OFFICIAL HANDBOOK, HMSO, PO Box 276, London SW8 5DT. (Jan.) £21.00

BRITANNICA BOOK OF THE YEAR, Carew House, Station Approach, Wallington, Surrey SM6 0DA. (May) £60.00

BRITISH CLOTHING INDUSTRY YEAR BOOK, 11 The Swan Courtyard, Charles Edward Road, Yardley, Birmingham B26 1BU. £55.00

BRITISH EXPORTS, East Grinstead House, East Grinstead, W. Sussex RH19 1XB. £140.00

BRITISH MUSIC YEARBOOK, 241 Shaftesbury Avenue, London WC2H 8EH. £16.00

BRITISH PERFORMING ARTS YEAR BOOK, 241 Shaftesbury Avenue, London WC2H 8EH. (Jan.) £18.95

BRITISH PLASTICS AND RUBBER DIRECTORY, Catalyst House, 159 Clapham High Street, London SW4 7SS. £10.00

BROWN'S NAUTICAL ALMANACK DAILY TIDE TABLES, 4–10 Darnley Street, Glasgow G41 2SD. (Sept.) £34.50

BUILDING AND CONSTRUCTION INDEX, PO Box 20, Sovereign Way, Tonbridge, Kent TN9 1RQ. (May) £55.00

BUILDING SOCIETIES YEAR BOOK, South Quay Plaza, 183 Marsh Wall, London E14 9FS. £60.00

BUSES YEARBOOK, 39 Milton Park, Abingdon, Oxon OX14 4TD. £10.99

BUTTERWORTHS LAW DIRECTORY AND LEGAL SERVICES DIRECTORY, Borough Green, Sevenoaks, Kent TN15 8PH. (Feb.) 2 vol. £47.00

CARPET ANNUAL, PO Box 20, Sovereign Way, Tonbridge, Kent TN9 1RQ. £72.00

CATERING BUYERS GUIDE, PO Box 20, Sovereign Way, Tonbridge, Kent TN9 1RQ. (Jan.) £60.00

CATHOLIC DIRECTORY OF ENGLAND AND WALES, 18 Crosby Road North, Liverpool L22 4QF. £17.50

CHARITIES DIGEST, 501–505 Kingsland Road, London E8 4AU. £15.95

CHEMICAL INDUSTRY, EUROPE, PO Box 20, Sovereign Way, Tonbridge, Kent TN9 1RQ. £75.00

CHEMIST AND DRUGGIST DIRECTORY, PO Box 20, Sovereign Way, Tonbridge, Kent TN9 1RQ. £89.00

CHRISTIES' REVIEW OF THE SEASON, 1 Langley Lane, London SW8 1TH. (Nov.) £30.00

CHURCH OF ENGLAND YEAR BOOK, Church House, Great Smith Street, London SW1P 3NZ. (Jan.) £18.50

CHURCH OF SCOTLAND YEAR BOOK, 121 George Street, Edinburgh EH2 4YN. (Sept.) £9.95

CITY OF LONDON DIRECTORY AND LIVERY COMPANIES GUIDE, Seatrade House, 42–48 North Station Road, Colchester, Essex CO1 1RB. £19.00, £17.00

CIVIL SERVICE YEAR BOOK, HMSO, PO Box 276, London SW8 5DT. (Feb.) £19.50

COMMONWEALTH UNIVERSITIES YEAR BOOK, 36 Gordon Square, London WC1H 0PF. (July) 4 vol. £145.00

COMMONWEALTH YEAR BOOK, HMSO, PO Box 276, London SW8 5DT. (May) £23.00

COMPUTER USERS' YEAR BOOK, 32–34 Broadwick Street, London W1A 2HG. 4 vol. £151.50

CONCRETE YEAR BOOK, Thomas Telford House, 1 Heron Quay, London E14 9XF. £55.00

CURRENT LAW YEAR BOOK, Cheriton House, North Way, Andover, Hants. SP10 5BE. £115.00

DEBRETT'S PEOPLE OF TODAY, 73–77 Britannia Road, PO Box 357, London SW6 2JY. (April) £93.50

DIPLOMATIC SERVICE LIST, HMSO, PO Box 276, London SW8 5DT. (April) £18.95

DIRECTORY OF DIRECTORS, East Grinstead House, East Grinstead, W. Sussex RH19 1XE. (April) 2 vol. £179.00

DIRECTORY OF FURTHER EDUCATION, Bateman Street, Cambridge CB2 1LZ. (June) £51.95, £46.95

DIRECTORY OF HIGHER EDUCATION, Bateman Street, Cambridge CB2 1LZ. (June) £51.95, £46.95

DIRECTORY OF OFFICIAL ARCHITECTURE AND PLANNING, PO Box 88, Harlow, Essex CM19 5SR. £68.00

DIY TRADE BUYERS GUIDE, PO Box 20, Sovereign Way, Tonbridge, Kent TN9 1RQ. £62.00

DOD'S PARLIAMENTARY COMPANION, Hurst Green, Etchingham, E. Sussex TN19 7PX. £70.00

EDUCATION AUTHORITIES' DIRECTORY AND ANNUAL, Derby House, Bletchingley Road, Merstham, Surrey RH1 3DN. (Jan.) £60.00, £50.00

EDUCATION YEAR BOOK, PO Box 88, Harlow, Essex CM19 5SR. £72.00

ELECTRICAL AND ELECTRONICS TRADES DIRECTORY, Michael Faraday House, Six Hills Way, Stevenage, Herts. SG1 2AY. (Feb.) £72.00

ELECTRICITY SUPPLY HANDBOOK, Quadrant House, The Quadrant, Sutton, Surrey SM2 5AS. (Feb.) £37.50

EUROPA WORLD YEAR BOOK, 18 Bedford Square, London WC1B 3JN. 2 vol. £310.00

EUROPEAN FOOD TRADES DIRECTORY, 32 Vauxhall Bridge Road, London SW1V 2SS. 2 vol. £135.00

EUROPEAN GLASS DIRECTORY AND BUYER'S GUIDE, 2 Queensway, Redhill, Surrey RH1 1QS. £83.00

FLIGHT INTERNATIONAL DIRECTORY, PO Box 1315, Potters Bar, Herts. EN6 1PU. 2 vol. £44.00, £45.00

FROZEN AND CHILLED FOODS YEAR BOOK, 2 Queensway, Redhill, Surrey RH1 1QS. £69.20

FURNISHING TRADE, DIRECTORY TO THE, PO Box 20, Sovereign Way, Tonbridge, Kent TN9 1RQ. £95.00

GAS INDUSTRY DIRECTORY, PO Box 20, Sovereign Way, Tonbridge, Kent TN9 1RQ. (Oct.) £79.00

GIBBONS' STAMPS OF THE WORLD CATALOGUE, 5 Parkside, Christchurch Road, Ringwood, Hants. BH24 3SH. (Oct.) 3 vol. £19.95, £19.95, £17.95

GOOD FOOD GUIDE, Bath Road, Harmondsworth, West Drayton, Middx. UB7 0DA. £14.99

GOOD HOTEL GUIDE, Brunel Road, Houndmills, Basingstoke, Hants. RG21 2XS. £12.99

GOVERNMENT AND MUNICIPAL BUYERS GUIDE, PO Box 20, Sovereign Way, Tonbridge, Kent TN9 1RQ. (Jan.) £55.00

GRADUATE STUDIES, Bateman Street, Cambridge CB2 1LZ. (July) £99.75

GUINNESS BOOK OF ANSWERS, 33 London Road, Enfield EN2 6DJ. £13.99

GUINNESS BOOK OF RECORDS, 33 London Road, Enfield EN2 6DJ. (Oct.) £14.99

HEALTH CARE BUYERS GUIDE, PO Box 20, Sovereign Way, Tonbridge, Kent TN9 1RQ. £72.00

HISTORIC HOUSES, CASTLES AND GARDENS IN GREAT BRITAIN AND IRELAND, East Grinstead House, East Grinstead, W. Sussex RH19 1XA. (March) £7.80

HOLLIS PRESS AND PR ANNUAL, Contact House, Lower Hampton Road, Sunbury-on-Thames TW16 5HG. (Oct.) £85.00

HOSPITALS AND HEALTH SERVICES YEARBOOK AND DIRECTORY OF HOSPITAL SUPPLIERS, 39 Chalton Street, London NW1 1JD. £90.00

HUTCHINS' PRICED SCHEDULES, 33 Station Road, Bexhill-on-Sea, E. Sussex TN40 1RG. £45.00

INDEPENDENT SCHOOLS YEAR BOOK, PO Box 19, Huntingdon, Cambs. PE19 3SF. £22.99

INSURANCE DIRECTORY AND YEAR BOOK, 58 Fleet Street, London EC4Y 1JU. (Jan.) 4 vol. £295.00

INTERNATIONAL PAPER DIRECTORY, PHILLIPS', PO Box 20, Sovereign Way, Tonbridge, Kent TN9 1RQ. £110.00

INTERNATIONAL WHO'S WHO, 18 Bedford Square, London WC1R 4JH. (Sept.) £140.00

INTERNATIONAL YEARBOOK AND STATESMEN'S WHO'S WHO, East Grinstead House, East Grinstead, W. Sussex RH19 1XE. (April) £155.00

JANE'S ALL THE WORLD'S AIRCRAFT, Sentinel House, 163 Brighton Road, Coulsdon, Surrey CR5 2NH. (Oct.) £160.00

JANE'S ARMOUR AND ARTILLERY, Sentinel House, 163 Brighton Road, Coulsdon, Surrey CR5 2NH. (Nov.) £160.00

JANE'S CONTAINERIZATION DIRECTORY, Sentinel House, 163 Brighton Road, Coulsdon, Surrey CR5 2NH. (Nov.) £175.00

JANE'S FIGHTING SHIPS, Sentinel House, 163 Brighton Road, Coulsdon, Surrey CR5 2NH. £160.00

JANE'S HIGH SPEED MARINE CRAFT AND AIR CUSHION VEHICLES, Sentinel House, 163 Brighton Road, Coulsdon, Surrey CR5 2NH. £175.00

JANE'S INFANTRY WEAPONS, Sentinel House, 163 Brighton Road, Coulsdon, Surrey CR5 2NH. (Aug.) £160.00

JANE'S NAVAL WEAPON SYSTEMS, Sentinel House, 163 Brighton Road, Coulsdon, Surrey CR5 2NH. £250.00

JANE'S WORLD RAILWAYS, Sentinel House, 163 Brighton Road, Coulsdon, Surrey CR5 2NH. £175.00

JEWISH YEAR BOOK, 25 Furnival Street, London EC4A 1JT. (Jan.) £18.50

KELLY'S BUSINESS DIRECTORY, East Grinstead House, East Grinstead, W. Sussex RH19 1XB. £159.00

KEMPE'S ENGINEERS YEAR BOOK, PO Box 20, Sovereign Way, Tonbridge, Kent TN9 1RQ. £99.00

KEMP'S INTERNATIONAL MUSIC BOOK, 12 Felix Avenue, London N8 9TL. £30.00

KIME'S INTERNATIONAL LAW DIRECTORY, PO Box 88, Harlow, Essex CM19 5SR. (Dec.) £48.00

LAXTON'S BUILDING PRICE BOOK, East Grinstead House, East Grinstead, W. Sussex RH19 1XE. 2 vol. £87.50

LIBRARY ASSOCIATION YEARBOOK, 7 Ridgmount Street, London WC1E 7AE. (June) £35.00

LLOYD'S LIST OF SHIPOWNERS, 71 Fenchurch Street, London EC3M 4BS. (Sept.) £115.00

LLOYD'S MARITIME DIRECTORY, Sheepen Place, Colchester CO3 3LP. (Jan.) £140.00

LLOYD'S NAUTICAL YEAR BOOK, Sheepen Place, Colchester CO3 3LP. (Sept.) £37.50

LLOYD'S REGISTER OF SHIPS, 71 Fenchurch Street, London EC3M 4BS. (July). 3 vol. £425.00

LYLE'S OFFICIAL ANTIQUES PRICE GUIDE, Glenmayne, Galashiels TD1 3NR. £16.95

LYLE'S OFFICIAL PAINTINGS PRICE GUIDE, Glenmayne, Galashiels TD1 3NR. £16.95

MACMILLAN AND SILK CUT NAUTICAL ALMANACK, Brunel Road, Houndmills, Basingstoke, Hants. RG21 2XS. £24.99

MAGISTRATES' COURT GUIDE, Borough Green, Sevenoaks, Kent TN15 8PH. £19.50

MEDICAL ANNUAL, Falcon House, Queen Square, Lancaster LA1 1RN. £29.60

MEDICAL DIRECTORY, PO Box 88, Harlow, Essex CM19 5SR. (April) 3 vol. £155.00

MEDICAL REGISTER, 44 Hallam Street, London W1N 6AE. (March) 3 vol. £90.00

MIDDLE EAST AND NORTH AFRICA, 18 Bedford Square, London WC1B 3JN. (Oct.) £145.00

MILLER'S ANTIQUES PRICE GUIDE, The Cellars, 5 High Street, Tenterden, Kent TN30 6BN. £19.99

MINING ANNUAL REVIEW, PO Box 10, Edenbridge, Kent TN8 5NE. £60.00

MINING INTERNATIONAL YEAR BOOK, PO Box 88, Harlow, Essex CM19 5SR. (June) £150.00

MOTOR INDUSTRY OF GREAT BRITAIN WORLD AUTOMOTIVE STATISTICS, Forbes House, Halkin Street, London SW1X 7DS. (Oct.) £75.00

MOTOR SHIP DIRECTORY, Quadrant House, The Quadrant, Sutton, Surrey SM2 5AS. £80.00

MUNICIPAL YEARBOOK AND PUBLIC SERVICES DIRECTORY, 32 Vauxhall Bridge Road, London SW1V 2SS. (Dec.) 2 vol. £140.00

MUSEUMS AND GALLERIES IN GREAT BRITAIN AND IRELAND, East Grinstead House, East Grinstead, W. Sussex RH19 IXA. (Oct.) £7.20

NAUTICAL ALMANAC, HMSO, PO Box 276, London SW8 5DT. (Oct.) £17.50

PACKAGING INDUSTRY DIRECTORY, PO Box 20, Sovereign Way, Tonbridge, Kent TN9 IRQ. £72.00

PEARS CYCLOPEDIA, 27 Wright's Lane, London W8 5TZ. £14.99

PHOTOGRAPHY YEAR BOOK, Queensborough House, 2 Claremont Road, Surbiton, Surrey KT6 4QU. £19.95

POLYMERS, PAINT AND COLOUR YEAR BOOK, 2 Queensway, Redhill, Surrey RHI IQS. £88.60

PORTS OF THE WORLD, Sheepen Place, Colchester, Essex CO3 3LP. £130.00

PRINTING TRADES DIRECTORY, PO Box 20, Sovereign Way, Tonbridge, Kent TN9 IRQ. £88.00

PUBLIC AUTHORITIES DIRECTORY, 122 Minories, London EC3N INT. (Jan.) £75.00

PUBLIC SERVICES YEARBOOK, Cheriton House, North Way, Andover, Hants SP10 5BE. (April) £19.99

PUBLISHING, DIRECTORY OF, Artillery House, Artillery Row, London SWIP IRT. (Oct.) £50.00

RAC EUROPEAN HOTEL GUIDE, PO Box 100, RAC House, Lansdowne Road, Croydon CR9 2JA. (Jan.) £9.99

RAC HOTEL GUIDE, PO Box 100, RAC House, Lansdowne Road, Croydon CR9 2JA. (Nov.) £15.99, £12.99

RAILWAY DIRECTORY AND YEAR BOOK, Quadrant House, The Quadrant, Sutton, Surrey SM2 5AS. (Dec.) £80.00

REGIONAL TRENDS, PO Box 276, London SW8 5DT. (July) £27.00

RETAIL DIRECTORY OF THE UNITED KINGDOM, 32 Vauxhall Bridge Road, London SWIV 2SS. £139.00

RIBA DIRECTORY OF PRACTICES, Royal Institute of British Architects, 39 Moreland Street, London ECIV 8BB. (Oct.) £49.50

ROTHMANS FOOTBALL YEAR BOOK, 39 Milton Park, Abingdon, Oxon. OX14 4TD. (Aug.) £27.50, £16.99

ROTHMAN'S RUGBY LEAGUE YEAR BOOK, 39 Milton Park, Abingdon, Oxon OX14 4TD. (Sept.) £15.99

ROTHMAN'S RUGBY UNION YEAR BOOK, 39 Milton Park, Abingdon, Oxon OX14 4TD. (Sept.) £15.99

ROYAL AND ANCIENT GOLFER'S HANDBOOK, Brunel Road, Houndmills, Basingstoke, Hants. RG21 2XS. (April) £40.00, £17.99

ROYAL SOCIETY YEAR BOOK, 6 Carlton House Terrace, London SWIY 5AG. (Feb.) £16.50

RUFF'S GUIDE TO THE TURF AND SPORTING LIFE ANNUAL, Orbit House, I New Fetter Lane, London EC4A IAR. (Jan.) £55.00

SALVATION ARMY YEAR BOOK, 117–121 Judd Street, London WCIH 9NN. (April) £10.75, £5.50

SCOTTISH CURRENT LAW YEAR BOOK, 21 Alva Street, Edinburgh EH2 4PS. £115.00

SCOTTISH LAW DIRECTORY, 59 George Street, Edinburgh EH2 2LQ. £32.00

SELL'S AEROSPACE EUROPE, PO Box 20, Sovereign Way, Tonbridge, Kent TN9 IRQ. £63.00

SELL'S PRODUCTS AND SERVICES DIRECTORY, PO Box 20, Sovereign Way, Tonbridge, Kent TN9 IRQ. (June) £76.00

SHEET METAL INDUSTRIES YEAR BOOK, 2 Queensway, Redhill, Surrey RHI IQS. £65.00

SOCIAL SERVICES YEAR BOOK, PO Box 88, Harlow, Essex CMI9 5SR. (April) £72.00

SOCIAL TRENDS, PO Box 276, London SW8 5DT. (Jan.) £27.00

SOLICITORS AND BARRISTERS DIRECTORY, 50 Chancery Lane, London WC2A ISX. £50.00

SPON'S ARCHITECTS' AND BUILDERS' PRICE BOOK, 2–6 Boundary Row, London SEI 8HN. £62.00

SPON'S MECHANICAL AND ELECTRICAL SERVICES PRICE BOOK, 2–6 Boundary Row, London SEI 8HN. £67.50

STATESMAN'S YEARBOOK, Brunel House, Houndmills, Basingstoke, Hants. RG21 2XS. (Aug.) £42.00

STOCK EXCHANGE OFFICIAL YEAR BOOK, Brunel House, Houndmills, Basingstoke, Hants. RG21 2XS. £199.00

STONE'S JUSTICES' MANUAL, Borough Green, Sevenoaks, Kent TNI5 8PH. 3 vol. (May) £175.00

TANKER REGISTER, 12 Camomile Street, London EC3A 7BP. (April) £145.00

TIMBER TRADE ADDRESS BOOK, PO Box 20, Sovereign Way, Tonbridge, Kent TN9 IRQ. £52.00

TRAINING DIRECTORY, 120 Pentonville Road, London NI 9JN. £25.00

TRAVEL TRADE GAZETTE DIRECTORY, PO Box 20, Sovereign Way, Tonbridge, Kent TN9 IRQ. (March) £65.00

UK KOMPASS REGISTER, East Grinstead House, East Grinstead, W. Sussex RH19 IXD. 5 vol. £865.00

UNITED KINGDOM MINERALS YEARBOOK, British Geological Survey, Keyworth, Nottingham NGI2 5GG. £30.00

UNITED REFORMED CHURCH YEAR BOOK, 86 Tavistock Place, London WCIH 9RT. (Sept.) £8.50, £7.50

UNIT TRUST YEAR BOOK, 7th Floor, 50–64 Broadway, London SWIH ODB. (March) £120.00

UNIVERSITY AND COLLEGE ENTRANCE, 14 Cooper's Row, London EC3N 2BH. (June) £12.00

VETERINARY ANNUAL, Osney Mead, Oxford OX2 OEL. £60.00

WATER SERVICES YEAR BOOK, 2 Queensway, Redhill, Surrey RHI IQS. (Oct.) £65.00

WHITAKER'S ALMANACK, 12 Dyott Street, London WCIA IDF. (Nov.) £40.00, £25.00

WHITAKER'S BOOKS IN PRINT, 12 Dyott Street, London WCIA IDF. (Jan.) 5 vol. £250.00

WHITAKER'S CONCISE ALMANACK, 12 Dyott Street, London WCIA IDF. (Nov.) £9.95

WHITAKER'S PUBLISHERS IN THE UNITED KINGDOM AND THEIR ADDRESSES, 12 Dyott Street, London WCIA IDF. (March) £9.95

WHO OWNS WHOM?, Holmers Farm Way, High Wycombe, Bucks. HPI2 4UL. 2 vol. £325.00

WHO'S WHO, 35 Bedford Row, London WCIR 4JH. £90.00

WILLING'S PRESS GUIDE, East Grinstead House, East Grinstead, W. Sussex RH19 IXE. (Feb.) 2 vol. £145.00

WISDEN CRICKETERS' ALMANACK, 13–14 Eldon Way, Lineside Estate, Littlehampton, W. Sussex BN17 7HE. (April) £22.50, £20.00

WORLD HOTEL DIRECTORY, PO Box 88, Harlow, Essex CMI9 5SR. £96.00

WORLD INSURANCE, PO Box 88, Harlow, Essex CMI9 5SR. £135.00

WORLD MINERAL STATISTICS, British Geological Survey, Keyworth, Notts. NGI2 5GG. (Sept.) 2 vol. £70.00

WORLD OF LEARNING, 18 Bedford Square, London WCIB 3JN. (Jan.) 2 vol. £190.00

WORLD SHIPPING DIRECTORY, PO Box 96, Coulsdon, Surrey CR5 2TE. £99.00

WRITERS' AND ARTISTS' YEAR BOOK, 35 Bedford Row, London WCIR 4JH. (Sept.) £9.99

# Employers' and Trade Associations

At 31 December 1993 there were 123 employers' associations listed by the Certification Officer (*see* page 295). Most national employers' associations are members of the Confederation of British Industry (CBI). For ACAS, the Certification Office, the Commission for Racial Equality, the Equal Opportunities Commission, the Health and Safety Commission, the Industrial Tribunals and Review Bodies, *see* Index.

## CONFEDERATION OF BRITISH INDUSTRY
Centre Point, 103 New Oxford Street, London WC1A 1DU
Tel 0171-379 7400

The Confederation of British Industry was founded in 1965 and is an independent non-party political body financed by industry and commerce. It exists primarily to ensure that the Government understands the intentions, needs and problems of British business. It is the recognized spokesman for the business viewpoint and is consulted as such by the Government.

The CBI represents, directly and indirectly, some 250,000 companies, large and small, from all sectors.

The governing body of the CBI is the 400-strong Council, which meets monthly in London under the chairmanship of the President. It is assisted by some 27 expert standing committees which advise on the main aspects of policy. There are 13 regional councils and offices covering the administrative regions of England, Wales, Scotland and Northern Ireland. There is also an office in Brussels.
*President*, Sir Bryan Nicholson
*Director-General*, H. Davies
*Secretary*, M. W. Hunt

## ASSOCIATIONS

ADVERTISING ASSOCIATION, Abford House, 15 Wilton Road, London SW1V 1NJ. Tel: 0171-828 2771. *Director-General*, A. Brown
AEROSPACE COMPANIES LTD, SOCIETY OF BRITISH, 29 King Street, London SW1Y 6RD. Tel: 0171-839 3231. *Director*, Sir Barry Duxbury, KCB, CBE
APPAREL AND TEXTILE CONFEDERATION, BRITISH, British Apparel and Textile Centre, 7 Swallow Place, London W1R 7AA. Tel: 0171-408 0020. *Director-General*, J. R. Wilson
BAKERS, FEDERATION OF, 20 Bedford Square, London WC1B 3HF. Tel: 0171-580 4252. *Director*, A. Casdagli, CBE
BANKERS' ASSOCIATION, BRITISH, 10 Lombard Street, London EC3V 9EL. Tel: 0171-623 4001. *Director-General*, The Lord Inchyra
BLIND AND DISABLED INC., NATIONAL ASSOCIATION OF INDUSTRIES FOR THE, Triton House, 43A High Street South, Dunstable, Beds. LU6 3RZ. Tel: 01582-606796. *Hon. Secretary*, G. J. Entwistle
BREWERS' AND LICENSED RETAILERS' ASSOCIATION, 42 Portman Square, London W1H 0BB. Tel: 0171-486 4831. *Director*, R. W. Simpson
BRUSH MANUFACTURERS' ASSOCIATION, BRITISH, Brooke House, 4 The Lakes, Bedford Road, Northampton NN4 7YD. Tel: 01604-22023. *Secretary*, A. N. Nisbet

BUILDING EMPLOYERS' CONFEDERATION, 82 New Cavendish Street, London W1M 8AD. Tel: 0171-580 5588. *Director-General*, I. A. Deslandes
BUILDING MATERIAL PRODUCERS, NATIONAL COUNCIL OF, 26 Store Street, London WC1E 7BT. Tel: 0171-323 3770. *Director-General*, N. M. Chaldecott, OBE
CHAMBER OF SHIPPING LTD, Carthusian Court, 12 Carthusian Street, London EC1M 6EB. Tel: 0171-417 8400. *Director-General*, Adm. Sir Nicholas Hunt, GCB, LVO
CHEMICAL INDUSTRIES ASSOCIATION LTD, Kings Buildings, Smith Square, London SW1P 3JJ. Tel: 0171-834 3399. *Director-General*, J. C. L. Cox
CLOTHING INDUSTRY ASSOCIATION LTD, BRITISH, British Apparel and Textile Centre, 7 Swallow Place, London W1R 7AA. Tel: 0171-408 0020. *Director*, J. R. Wilson
DAIRY TRADE FEDERATION, 19 Cornwall Terrace, London NW1 4QP. Tel: 0171-486 7244. *Director-General*, J. P. Price
ELECTROTECHNICAL AND ALLIED MANUFACTURERS' ASSOCIATIONS, FEDERATION OF BRITISH (BEAMA), Leicester House, 8 Leicester Street, London WC2H 7BN. Tel: 0171-437 0678. *Director-General*, J. G. Gaddes
ENGINEERING EMPLOYERS' FEDERATION, Broadway House, Tothill Street, London SW1H 9NQ. Tel: 0171-222 7777. *Director-General*, G. R. Mackenzie, F.Eng.
FARMERS' UNION, NATIONAL (NFU), 22 Long Acre, London WC2E 9LY. Tel: 0171-235 5077. *Director-General*, D. Evans, CBE
FARMERS' UNION OF SCOTLAND, NATIONAL, Rural Centre-West Mains, Ingliston, Newbridge, Midlothian EH28 8LT. Tel: 0131-335 3111. *Chief Executive*, T. J. Brady
FARMERS' UNION, ULSTER, Dunedin, 475–477 Antrim Road, Belfast BT15 3DA. Tel: 01232-370222. *Director-General*, A. MacLaughlin
FINANCE AND LEASING ASSOCIATION, 18 Upper Grosvenor Street, London W1X 9PB. Tel: 0171-491 2783. *Director*, N. A. D. Grant, CBE
FOOD AND DRINK FEDERATION, 6 Catherine Street, London WC2B 5JJ. Tel: 0171-836 2460. *Director-General*, M. P. Mackenzie
FREIGHT TRANSPORT ASSOCIATION LTD, Hermes House, 157 St John's Road, Tunbridge Wells, Kent TN4 9UZ. Tel: 01892-526171. *Director-General*, D. C. Green
INSURERS, ASSOCIATION OF BRITISH, 51 Gresham Street, London EC2V 7HQ. Tel: 0171-600 3333. *Director-General*, M. Boléat
KNITTING INDUSTRIES' FEDERATION LTD, 53 Oxford Street, Leicester LE1 5XY. Tel: 0116-254 1608. *Director*, J. P. Harrison
LEATHER CONFEDERATION, BRITISH, Leather Trade House, Kings Park Road, Moulton Park, Northampton NN3 1JD. Tel: 01604-494131. *Chief Executive*, Dr K. T. W. Alexander
LEATHER PRODUCERS' ASSOCIATION, Leather Trade House, Kings Park Road, Moulton Park, Northampton NN3 1JD. Tel: 01604-494131. *National Secretary*, J. Purvis
MANAGEMENT CONSULTANCIES ASSOCIATION, 11 West Halkin Street, London SW1X 8JL. Tel: 0171-235 3897. *Executive Director*, B. O'Rorke
MARINE INDUSTRIES FEDERATION, BRITISH, Meadlake Place, Thorpe Lea Road, Egham, Surrey TW20 8HE. Tel: 01784-473377. *Executive Chairman*, A. V. Beechey

MARKET TRADERS' FEDERATION, NATIONAL, Hampton House, Hawshaw Lane, Hoyland, Barnsley S74 OHA. Tel: 01226-749021. *General Secretary*, D. E. Feeny

MASTER BUILDERS, FEDERATION OF, Gordon Fisher House, 14–15 Great James Street, London WCIN 3DP. Tel: 0171-242 7583. *Director-General*, J. D. Maiden

MOTOR MANUFACTURERS AND TRADERS LTD, SOCIETY OF, Forbes House, Halkin Street, London SWIX 7DS. Tel: 0171-235 7000. *Chief Executive*, Sir Hal Miller

NEWSPAPER PUBLISHERS ASSOCIATION LTD, 34 Southwark Bridge Road, London SEI 9EU. Tel: 0171-928 6928. *Director*, D. Pollock

NEWSPAPER SOCIETY, Bloomsbury House, 74–77 Great Russell Street, London WCIB 3DA. Tel: 0171-636 7014. *Director*, D. Nisbet-Smith

OFFICE SYSTEMS AND STATIONERY FEDERATION, BRITISH, 6 Wimpole Street, London WIM 8AS. Tel: 0171-637 7692. *Director*, D. F. Hall

PAPER FEDERATION, THE, Papermakers House, Rivenhall Road, Westlea, Swindon SN5 7BD. Tel: 01793-886086. *Director-General*, W. J. Bartlett

PASSENGER TRANSPORT UK, CONFEDERATION OF, Sardinia House, 52 Lincoln's Inn Fields, London WC2A 3LZ. Tel: 0171-831 7546. *Director-General*, Mrs V. Palmer, OBE

PLASTICS FEDERATION, BRITISH, 5 Belgrave Square, London SWIX 8PD. Tel: 0171-235 9483. *Director*, D. R. Jones

PORTS FEDERATION, BRITISH, Africa House, 64–78 Kingsway, London WC2B 6AH. Tel: 0171-242 1200. *Director*, D. Whitehead

PRINTING INDUSTRIES FEDERATION, BRITISH, 11 Bedford Row, London WCIR 4DX. Tel: 0171-242 6904. *Director-General*, G. C. Stanley

PRIVATE MARKET OPERATORS, ASSOCIATION OF, 4 Worrygoose Lane, Rotherham S60 4AD. Tel: 01709-700072. *Secretary*, D. J. Glasby

PROPERTY FEDERATION, BRITISH, 35 Catherine Place, London SWIE 6DY. Tel: 0171-828 0111. *Director-General*, W. McKee

PUBLISHERS ASSOCIATION, THE, 19 Bedford Square, London WCIB 3HJ. Tel: 0171-580 6321. *Chief Executive*, C. Bradley

RADIO COMPANIES LTD, ASSOCIATION OF INDEPENDENT, Radio House, 46 Westbourne Grove, London W2 5SH. Tel: 0171-727 2646. *Chief Executive*, B. West

RETAIL CONSORTIUM, BRITISH, Bedford House, 69–79 Fulham High Street, London SW6 3JW. Tel: 0171-371 5185. *Director-General*, J. N. W. May

RETAIL NEWSAGENTS, NATIONAL FEDERATION OF, Yeoman House, Sekforde Street, London ECIR OHD. Tel: 0171-253 4225. *Chief Executive*, R. P. Frost

ROAD FEDERATION, BRITISH, Pillar House, 194–202 Old Kent Road, London SEI 5TG. Tel: 0171-703 9769. *Director*, R. Diment

ROAD HAULAGE ASSOCIATION LTD, Roadway House, 35 Monument Hill, Weybridge, Surrey KT13 8RN. Tel: 01932-841515. *Director-General*, D. B. H. Colley, CB, CBE

RUBBER MANUFACTURERS' ASSOCIATION LTD, BRITISH, 90 Tottenham Court Road, London WIP OBR. Tel: 0171-580 2794. *Director*, W. R. Pollock

SPORT AND ALLIED INDUSTRIES FEDERATION LTD, BRITISH, 23 Brighton Road, Croydon CR2 6EA. Tel: 0181-681 1242. *Chief Executive*, L. F. Standen

TIMBER GROWERS' ASSOCIATION, 5 Dublin Street Lane South, Edinburgh EHI 3PX. Tel: 0131-538 7111. *Chief Executive*, P. H. Wilson

TIMBER MERCHANTS' ASSOCIATION, BRITISH, Stocking Lane, Hughenden Valley, High Wycombe, Bucks. HP14 4JZ. Tel: 01494-563602. *Secretary*, R. T. Allcorn

TIMBER TRADE FEDERATION, Clareville House, 26–27 Oxendon Street, London SWIY 4EL. Tel: 0171-839 1891. *Director-General*, P. G. Harris

UK OFFSHORE OPERATORS ASSOCIATION LTD, 3 Hans Crescent, London SWIX OLN. Tel: 0171-589 5255. *Director-General*, Dr H. W. D. Hughes, OBE

UK PETROLEUM INDUSTRY ASSOCIATION LTD, 9 Kingsway, London WC2B 6XH. Tel: 0171-240 0289. *Director-General*, D. Parker

# Trade Unions

At 31 December 1993 there were 287 trade unions listed by the Certification Officer (*see* page 295). In 1992 8,928,902 people were members of listed trade unions, compared with 9,489,034 in 1991. Over 80 per cent of trade union members belong to unions affiliated to the TUC (*see* below).

The Central Arbitration Committee arbitrates in industrial disputes between trade unions and employers, and determines disclosure of information complaints. The Commissioner for the Rights of Trade Union Members provides assistance to individuals taking action against their trade union when they have not been afforded their statutory rights or when specific union rules have been breached.

For ACAS, the Certification Office, the Commission for Racial Equality, the Equal Opportunities Commission, the Health and Safety Commission, the Industrial Tribunals and Review Bodies, *see* Index.

THE CENTRAL ARBITRATION COMMITTEE, 39 Grosvenor Place, London SW1X 7BD. Tel: 0171-210 3737/8. *Chairman*, Prof. Sir John Wood, CBE; *Secretary*, S. Gouldstone

THE COMMISSIONER FOR THE RIGHTS OF TRADE UNION MEMBERS, 1st Floor, Bank Chambers, 2A Rylands Street, Warrington, Cheshire WA1 1EN. Tel: 01925-415771. *Commissioner*, Mrs G. Rowlands

---

## TUC-AFFILIATED TRADE UNIONS

---

### TRADES UNION CONGRESS (TUC)
Congress House, 23–28 Great Russell Street, London WC1B 3LS
Tel 0171-636 4030

The Trades Union Congress, founded in 1868, is an independent association of trade unions. Its main job is to help unions achieve together things which they could not do alone. It draws up common policies and promotes and publicizes them. It makes representations to government, to employers and, increasingly, to international bodies such as the European Union. The TUC also carries out research, campaigns and a programme of trade union education. Resolving disputes between unions is another task it undertakes. TUC representatives sit on many public bodies at national and international level.

The governing body of the TUC is the annual Congress. Between Congresses, business is conducted by a General Council, which meets five times a year, and an Executive Committee, which meets monthly. The full-time staff is headed by the General Secretary who is elected by Congress and is a permanent member of the General Council.

Affiliated unions (in 1993–4) totalled 68 with an aggregate membership of 7,298,262.
*President* (1994–5), J. Knapp (RMT)
*General Secretary*, J. Monks, *elected* 1993

### SCOTTISH TRADES UNION CONGRESS
16 Woodlands Terrace, Glasgow G3 6DF
Tel 0141-332 4946

The Congress was formed in 1897 and acts as a national centre for the trade union movement in Scotland. In 1994 it consisted of 51 unions with a membership of 740,328 and 41 directly affiliated Trades Councils.

The Annual Congress in April elects a 36-member General Council on the basis of eight industrial sections.
*Chairperson*, W. Queen
*General Secretary*, C. Christie

AFFILIATED UNIONS *as at 1 September 1994* (Number of members in parenthesis)

AMALGAMATED ENGINEERING AND ELECTRICAL UNION (AEEU) (835,019), Hayes Court, West Common Road, Bromley, Kent BR2 7AU. Tel: 0181-462 7755. *General Secretary*, G. H. Laird, CBE

ASSOCIATED METALWORKERS' UNION (AMU) (1,450), 92 Worsley Road North, Worsley, Manchester M28 5QW. Tel: 01204-793245. *General Secretary*, R. Marron

ASSOCIATED SOCIETY OF LOCOMOTIVE ENGINEERS AND FIREMEN (ASLEF) (17,386), 9 Arkwright Road, London NW3 6AB. Tel: 0171-431 0275. *Secretary*, L. Adams

ASSOCIATION OF FIRST DIVISION CIVIL SERVANTS (11,000), 2 Caxton Street, London SW1H 0QH. Tel: 0171-222 6242. *General Secretary*, Ms E. Symons

ASSOCIATION OF UNIVERSITY TEACHERS (34,000), United House, 9 Pembridge Road, London W11 3JY. Tel: 0171-221 4370. *General Secretary*, D. Triesman

BAKERS, FOOD AND ALLIED WORKERS' UNION (31,110), Stanborough House, Great North Road, Stanborough, Welwyn Garden City, Herts. AL8 7TA. Tel: 01707-260150. *General Secretary*, J. R. Marino

BANKING, INSURANCE AND FINANCE UNION (143,000), Sheffield House, 1B Amity Grove, London SW20 0LG. Tel: 0181-946 9151. *General Secretary*, L. A. Mills

BRITISH ACTORS' EQUITY ASSOCIATION (41,592), Guild House, Upper St Martin's Lane, London WC2H 9EG. Tel: 0171-379 6000. *General Secretary*, I. McGarry

BRITISH AIR LINE PILOTS ASSOCIATION, THE (5,218), 81 New Road, Harlington, Hayes, Middx. UB3 5BG. Tel: 0181-476 4000. *General Secretary*, C. Darke

BRITISH ASSOCIATION OF COLLIERY MANAGEMENT, THE (7,057), 17 South Parade, Doncaster, S. Yorks. DN1 2DN. Tel: 01302-349152. *General Secretary*, M. Gillespie

BROADCASTING, ENTERTAINMENT, CINEMATOGRAPH AND THEATRE UNION (BECTU) (30,062), 111 Wardour Street, London W1V 4AY. Tel: 0171-437 8506. *General Secretary*, R. Bolton

CARD SETTING MACHINE TENTERS' SOCIETY (88), 48 Scar End Lane, Staincliffe, Dewsbury, W. Yorks. WF12 4NY. Tel: 01924-400206. *Secretary*, A. Moorhouse

CERAMIC AND ALLIED TRADES UNION, THE (22,373), Hillcrest House, Garth Street, Hanley, Stoke-on-Trent ST1 2AB. Tel: 01782-272755. *General Secretary*, A. W. Clowes

CHARTERED SOCIETY OF PHYSIOTHERAPY, THE (25,480), 14 Bedford Row, London WC1R 4ED. Tel: 0171-242 1941. *Secretary*, T. Simon

CIVIL AND PUBLIC SERVICES ASSOCIATION, THE (132,743), 160 Falcon Road, London SW11 2LN. Tel: 0171-924 2727. *General Secretary*, B. Reamsbottom

COMMUNICATION MANAGERS' ASSOCIATION (14,293), Hughes House, Ruscombe Road, Twyford, Reading RG10 9JD. Tel: 01734-342300. *General Secretary*, T. L. Deegan

EDUCATIONAL INSTITUTE OF SCOTLAND, THE (48,629), 46 Moray Place, Edinburgh EH3 6BH. Tel: 0131-225 6244. *General Secretary*, J. B. Martin

ELECTRICAL AND PLUMBING INDUSTRIES UNION (5,100), Park House, 64–66 Wandsworth Common North Side, London SW18 2SH. Tel: 0181-874 0458. *General Secretary*, J. Aitkin

ENGINEERING AND FASTENER TRADE UNION (240), 42 Galton Road, Warley, West Midlands, B67 5JU. Tel: 0121-429 2594. *General Secretary*, J. Burdis

ENGINEERS' AND MANAGERS' ASSOCIATION (35,917), Flaxman House, Gogmore Lane, Chertsey, Surrey KT16 9JS. Tel: 01932-564131. *General Secretary*, D. A. Cooper

FILM ARTISTES' ASSOCIATION (1,200) 61 Marloes Road, London W8 6LE. Tel: 0171-937 4567. *General Secretary*, R. Hodges

FIRE BRIGADES UNION, THE (52,080), Bradley House, 68 Coombe Road, Kingston upon Thames, Surrey KT2 7AE. Tel: 0181-541 1765. *General Secretary*, K. Cameron

GENERAL UNION OF ASSOCIATIONS OF LOOM OVERLOOKERS, THE (490), 9 Wellington Street, St Johns, Blackburn, Lancs. BB1 8AF. Tel: 01254-51760. *President*, D. J. Rishton

GMB (formerly GENERAL, MUNICIPAL, BOILERMAKERS AND ALLIED TRADES UNION) (834,835), 22–24 Worple Road, London SW19 4DD. Tel: 0181-947 3131. *General Secretary*, J. Edmonds

GRAPHICAL, PAPER AND MEDIA UNION (223,687), Keys House, 63–67 Bromham Road, Bedford MK40 2AG. Tel: 01234-351521. *General Secretary*, A. D. Dubbins

HOSPITAL CONSULTANTS AND SPECIALISTS ASSOCIATION, THE (2,300), 1 Kingsclere Road, Overton, Basingstoke, Hants. RG25 3JA. Tel: 01256-771777. *Chief Executive*, S. J. Charkham

INLAND REVENUE STAFF FEDERATION (57,907), Douglas Houghton House, 231 Vauxhall Bridge Road, London SW1V 1EH. Tel: 0171-834 8254. *General Secretary*, C. Brooke

INSTITUTION OF PROFESSIONALS, MANAGERS AND SPECIALISTS (86,346), 75–79 York Road, London SE1 7AQ. Tel: 0171-928 9951. *General Secretary*, W. Brett

IRON AND STEEL TRADES CONFEDERATION, THE (50,000), Swinton House, 324 Gray's Inn Road, London WC1X 8DD. Tel: 0171-837 6691. *General Secretary*, D. K. Brookman

MANUFACTURING, SCIENCE AND FINANCE UNION (MSF) (516,000), Park House, 64–66 Wandsworth Common North Side, London SW18 2SH. Tel: 0181-871 2100. *General Secretary*, R. Lyons

MILITARY AND ORCHESTRAL MUSICAL INSTRUMENT MAKERS' TRADE SOCIETY (48), 2 Whitehouse Avenue, Borehamwood, Herts. WD6 1HD. Tel: 0181-952 7711. *General Secretary*, F. McKenzie

MUSICIANS' UNION (33,500), 60–62 Clapham Road, London SW9 0JJ. Tel: 0171-582 5566. *General Secretary*, D. Scard

NATFHE (THE UNIVERSITY AND COLLEGE LECTURERS UNION), (76,742), 27 Britannia Street, London WC1X 9JP. Tel: 0171-837 3636. *General Secretary*, J. Akker

NATIONAL ASSOCIATION OF COLLIERY OVERMEN, DEPUTIES AND SHOTFIRERS (1,902), Simpson House, 48 Nether Hall Road, Doncaster DN1 2PZ. Tel: 01302-368015. *Secretary*, P. McNestry

NATIONAL ASSOCIATION OF CO-OPERATIVE OFFICIALS (3,697), Coronation House, Arndale Centre, Manchester

M4 2HW. Tel: 0161-834 6029. *General Secretary*, L. W. Ewing

NATIONAL ASSOCIATION OF LICENSED HOUSE MANAGERS (9,881), 9 Coombe Lane, London SW20 8NE. Tel: 0181-947 3080. *General Secretary*, J. Madden

NATIONAL ASSOCIATION OF PROBATION OFFICERS (7,900), 3–4 Chivalry Road, London SW11 1HT. Tel: 0171-223 4887. *Secretary*, Ms J. McKnight

NATIONAL ASSOCIATION OF SCHOOLMASTERS AND UNION OF WOMEN TEACHERS (NAS/UWT) (138,381), 5 King Street, London WC2E 8HN. Tel: 0171-379 9499. *General Secretary*, N. de Gruchy

NATIONAL COMMUNICATIONS UNION (122,068), Greystoke House, 150 Brunswick Road, London W5 1AW. Tel: 0181-998 2981. *General Secretary*, A. I. Young

NATIONAL LEAGUE OF THE BLIND AND DISABLED, THE (2,264), 2 Tenterden Road, London N17 8BE. Tel: 0181-808 6030. *General Secretary*, M. A. Barrett (*until end Sept. 1994*)

NATIONAL UNION OF CIVIL AND PUBLIC SERVANTS (NUCPS) (112,080), 124–130 Southwark Street, London SE1 0TU. Tel: 0171-928 9671. *General Secretary*, J. Sheldon

NATIONAL UNION OF DOMESTIC APPLIANCES AND GENERAL OPERATIVES, THE (2,402), 6–8 Imperial Buildings, Corporation Street, Rotherham, S. Yorks. S60 1PB. Tel: 01709-382820. *General Secretary*, A. McCarthy

NATIONAL UNION OF INSURANCE WORKERS (12,519), 27 Old Gloucester Street, London WC1N 3AF. Tel: 0171-405 6798. *General Secretary*, K. Perry

NATIONAL UNION OF JOURNALISTS (NUJ) (23,149), Acorn House, 314–320 Gray's Inn Road, London WC1X 8DP. Tel: 0171-278 7916. *General Secretary*, J. Foster

NATIONAL UNION OF KNITWEAR, FOOTWEAR AND APPAREL TRADES (49,910), The Grange, 108 Northampton Road, Earls Barton, Northampton NN6 0JH. Tel: 01604-810326. *General Secretary*, Mrs H. McGrath

NATIONAL UNION OF LOCK AND METAL WORKERS (4,300), Bellamy House, Wilkes Street, Willenhall, W. Midlands WV13 2BS. Tel: 01902-366651. *General Secretary*, R. Ward

NATIONAL UNION OF MARINE, AVIATION AND SHIPPING TRANSPORT OFFICERS, THE (18,500), Oceanair House, 750–760 High Road, London E11 3BB. Tel: 0181-989 6677. *General Secretary*, B. Orrell

NATIONAL UNION OF MINEWORKERS (NUM) (18,227), Miners' Offices, 2 Huddersfield Road, Barnsley, S. Yorks. S70 2LS. Tel: 01226-284006. *President*, A. Scargill

NATIONAL UNION OF RAIL, MARITIME AND TRANSPORT WORKERS (RMT) (80,000), Unity House, Euston Road, London NW1 2BL. Tel: 0171-387 4771. *General Secretary*, J. Knapp

NATIONAL UNION OF TEACHERS (NUT) (168,708), Hamilton House, Mabledon Place, London WC1H 9BD. Tel: 0171-388 6191. *General Secretary*, D. McAvoy

NORTHERN CARPET TRADES' UNION (692), 22 Clare Road, Halifax, W. Yorks. HX1 2HX. Tel: 01422-360492. *General Secretary*, K. Edmondson

POWER LOOM CARPET WEAVERS' AND TEXTILE WORKERS' UNION, THE (1,800), 148 Hurcott Road, Kidderminster, Worcs. DY10 2RL. Tel: 01562-823192. *General Secretary*, R. White

PRISON OFFICERS' ASSOCIATION, THE (27,737), Cronin House, 245 Church Street, London N9 9HW. Tel: 0181-803 0255. *General Secretary*, D. Evans

ROSSENDALE UNION OF BOOT, SHOE AND SLIPPER OPERATIVES, THE (1,643), Taylor House, 7 Tenterfield

Street, Waterfoot, Rossendale, Lancs. BB4 7BA. Tel: 01706-215657. *General Secretary*, M. Murray
SCOTTISH PRISON OFFICERS' ASSOCIATION (4,132) 21 Calder Road, Edinburgh EH11 3PF. Tel: 0131-443 8175. *General Secretary*, D. Turner
SCOTTISH UNION OF POWER-LOOM OVERLOOKERS (60), 3 Napier Terrace, Dundee DD2 2SL. Tel: 01382-612196. *Secretary*, J. D. Reilly
SHEFFIELD WOOL SHEAR WORKERS' UNION (13), 50 Bankfield Road, Malin Bridge, Sheffield S6 4RD. Tel: 01742-333688. *Secretary*, J. H. R. Cutler
SOCIETY OF RADIOGRAPHERS (12,815), 14 Upper Wimpole Street, London WIM 8BN. Tel: 0171-935 5726. *General Secretaries*, P. Smith and W. Town (*acting*)
SOCIETY OF TELECOM EXECUTIVES (22,000), 1 Park Road, Teddington, Middx. TW11 0AR. Tel: 0181-943 5181. *General Secretary*, S. Petch
TRANSPORT AND GENERAL WORKERS' UNION (TGWU) (949,107), Transport House, Smith Square, London SW1P 3JB. Tel: 0171-828 7788. *General Secretary*, W. Morris
TRANSPORT SALARIED STAFFS' ASSOCIATION (39,234), Walkden House, 10 Melton Street, London NW1 2EJ. Tel: 0171-387 2101. *General Secretary*, R. A. Rosser
UNION OF COMMUNICATION WORKERS, THE (UCW) (165,212), UCW House, Crescent Lane, London SW4 9RN. Tel: 0171-622 9977. *General Secretary*, A. Johnson
UNION OF CONSTRUCTION, ALLIED TRADES AND TECHNICIANS (UCATT) (135,878), UCATT House, 177 Abbeville Road, London SW4 9RL. Tel: 0171-622 2442. *Secretary*, G. Brumwell
UNION OF SHOP, DISTRIBUTIVE AND ALLIED WORKERS (USDAW) (299,495), Oakley, 188 Wilmslow Road, Fallowfield, Manchester M14 6LJ. Tel: 0161-224 2804. *Secretary*, D. G. Davies
UNION OF TEXTILE WORKERS (1,660), Foxlowe, Market Place, Leek, Staffs. ST13 6AD. Tel: 01538-382068. *General Secretary*, A. Hitchmough
UNISON (1,450,000), 1 Mabledon Place, London WC1H 9AJ. Tel: 0171-388 6609. *General Secretary*, A. Jinkinson
UNITED ROAD TRANSPORT UNION (16,800), 76 High Lane, Chorlton, Manchester M21 1FD. Tel: 0161-881 6245. *General Secretary*, D. Higginbottom
WRITERS' GUILD OF GREAT BRITAIN, THE (1,690), 430 Edgware Road, London W2 1EH. Tel: 0171-723 8074. *General Secretary*, Ms A. Gray

MERGERS, ETC, 1993–4

The Electrical, Electronics, Telecommunications and Plumbing Union (EETPU) section of the Amalgamated Engineering and Electrical Union (AEEU) reaffiliated with the TUC in September 1993.

The National Union of Scalemakers merged with the MSF in December 1993.

The Furniture, Timber and Allied Trade Union merged with the GMB on 1 January 1994.

---

## NON-AFFILIATED TRADE UNIONS

---

ASSOCIATION OF CAREER TEACHERS, Hillsborough, Castledine Street, Loughborough, Leics. LE11 2DX. Tel: 01509-214617. *General Secretary*, Miss R. Yaffé
BRITISH DENTAL ASSOCIATION (15,500), 64 Wimpole Street, London WIM 8AL. Tel: 0171-935 0875. *Chief Executive*, J. M. G. Hunt

NATIONAL ASSOCIATION OF HEAD TEACHERS (NAHT), 1 Heath Square, Boltro Road, Haywards Heath, W. Sussex RH16 1BL. Tel: 01444-458133. *General Secretary*, D. Hart, OBE
NATIONAL SOCIETY FOR EDUCATION IN ART AND DESIGN (1,990), The Gatehouse, Corsham Court, Corsham, Wilts. SN13 0BZ. Tel: 01249-714825. *General Secretary*, J. H. M. Steers
PATTERN WEAVERS SOCIETY, 38 St Paul's Road, Kirkheaton, Huddersfield HD5 0EY. Tel: 01484-424988. *General Secretary*, K. Bradley
RETAIL BOOK, STATIONERY AND ALLIED TRADES EMPLOYEES' ASSOCIATION, 8–9 Commercial Road, Swindon SN1 5RB. Tel: 01793-615811. *General Secretary*, J. Windust
ROYAL COLLEGE OF MIDWIVES (36,000), 15 Mansfield Street, London WIM 0BE. Tel: 0171-580 6523. *General Secretary*, Mrs J. Allison
SCOTTISH SECONDARY TEACHERS' ASSOCIATION (7,200), 15 Dundas Street, Edinburgh EH3 6QG. Tel: 0131-556 5919. *General Secretary*, A. M. Lamont
SECONDARY HEADS ASSOCIATION (8,400), 130 Regent Road, Leicester LE1 7PG. Tel: 0116-247 1797. *General Secretary*, J. Sutton
SOCIETY OF AUTHORS (5,600), 84 Drayton Gardens, London SW10 9SB. Tel: 0171-373 6642. *General Secretary*, M. Le Fanu
SOCIETY OF CHIROPODISTS AND PODIATRISTS, 53 Welbeck Street, London WIM 7HE. Tel: 0171-486 3381. *General Secretary*, J. G. C. Trouncer

# National Academies of Scholarship

## THE BRITISH ACADEMY (1901)
20–21 Cornwall Terrace, London NW1 4QP
Tel 0171-487 5966

The British Academy is an independent, self-governing learned society for the promotion of historical, philosophical and philological studies. It supports advanced academic research in the humanities and social sciences, and is a channel for the Government's support of research in those disciplines. The Humanities Research Board is responsible for the administration of the majority of the Academy's grant programmes.

The Fellows are scholars who have attained distinction in one of the branches of study that the Academy exists to promote. Candidates must be nominated by existing Fellows. At 1 June 1994 there were 605 Fellows, 13 Honorary Fellows, and 298 Corresponding Fellows overseas.

*President,* Sir Keith Thomas, PBA
*Vice Presidents,* Prof. D. N. Winch, FBA; Prof. T. B. Wiseman, FBA
*Treasurer,* Dr E. A. Wrigley, FBA
*Foreign Secretary,* Prof. J. B. Trapp, FBA
*Publications Officer,* Prof. D. E. Luscombe, FBA
*Chairman, Humanities Research Board,* Prof. J. D. Laver, FBA
*Secretary,* P. W. H. Brown

## THE ROYAL ACADEMY (1768)
Burlington House, London W1V 0DS
Tel 0171-439 7438

The Royal Academy of Arts is an independent, self-governing society devoted to the encouragement and promotion of the fine arts.

Membership of the Academy is limited to 80 Royal Academicians, all being painters, engravers, sculptors or architects. Candidates are nominated and elected by the existing Academicians. There is also a limited class of honorary membership and there were 10 honorary members as at mid-1994.

*President,* Sir Philip Dowson, CBE, PRA
*Treasurer,* Sir Philip Powell, CH, OBE, RA
*Keeper,* Prof. N. Adams, RA
*Secretary,* P. Rodgers

## THE ROYAL ACADEMY OF ENGINEERING (1976)
29 Great Peter Street, London SW1P 3LW
Tel 0171-222 2688

The Royal Academy of Engineering was established as the Fellowship of Engineering in 1976. It was granted a Royal Charter in May 1983 and its present title in 1992. It is an independent, self-governing body whose object is the pursuit, encouragement and maintenance of excellence in the whole field of engineering, in order to promote the advancement of the science, art and practice of engineering for the benefit of the public.

Election to the Fellowship is by invitation only from nominations supported by the body of Fellows. Fellows are chosen from among chartered engineers of all disciplines. At July 1994 there were 976 Fellows, 12 Honorary Fellows and 58 Foreign Members. The Duke of Edinburgh is the Senior Fellow and the Duke of Kent is a Royal Fellow.

*President,* Sir William Barlow, FEng
*Senior Vice-President,* B. W. Manley, CBE, FEng
*Vice-Presidents,* Dr A. Denton, FEng; R. J. Margetts, FEng; Dr A. M. Neville, CBE, MC, FEng, FRSE
*Hon. Treasurer,* D. Hanson
*Hon. Secretaries,* R. H. Rooley, FEng (*Civil Engineering*); D. G. Jefferies, CBE, FEng (*Electrical Engineering*); Dr A. A. Denton, FEng (*International Activities*); P. C. Ruffles, FEng (*Mechanical Engineering*); G. Clerehugh, OBE, FEng (*Process Engineering*); Sir Gordon Higginson, FEng (*Education, Training and Competence to Practise*)
*Executive Secretary,* J. R. Appleton.

## THE ROYAL SCOTTISH ACADEMY (1838)
The Mound, Edinburgh EH2 2EL
Tel 0131-225 6671

The Scottish Academy was founded in 1826 to arrange exhibitions for contemporary paintings and to establish a society of fine art in Scotland. The Academy was granted a Royal Charter in 1838.

Members are elected from the disciplines of painting, sculpture, architecture and printmaking. Elections are from nominations put forward by the existing membership. At mid-1994 there were 9 Senior Academicians, 36 Academicians, 44 Associates, three non-resident Associates and 22 Honorary Members.

*President,* W. J. L. Baillie, PRSA
*Secretary,* I. McKenzie Smith, RSA
*Treasurer,* J. Morris, RSA
*Librarian,* P. Collins, RSA
*Administrative Secretary,* A. Mathewson

## ROYAL SOCIETY (1660)
6 Carlton House Terrace, London SW1Y 5AG
Tel 0171-839 5561

The Royal Society is the United Kingdom's national academy of science. It is an independent, self-governing body under a Royal Charter, promoting and advancing all fields of physical and biological sciences, of mathematics and engineering, medical and agricultural sciences, their applications and place in society.

Election to Fellowship of the Royal Society is limited to those distinguished for original scientific work. Each year up to 40 new Fellows and six Foreign Members are elected from the most distinguished scientists. In addition, the Council can recommend for election members of the Royal family and, on average, one person each year for conspicuous service to the cause of science. At June 1994, there were 1,150 Fellows and 110 Foreign Members.

*President,* Sir Michael Atiyah, OM, FRS
*Treasurer,* Prof. J. H. Horlock, F.Eng, FRS
*Biological Secretary,* Prof. P. J. Lackmann, FRS

*Physical Secretary,* Prof. J. S. Rowlinson, FRS
*Foreign Secretary,* Dr A. L. McLaren, DBE, FRS
*Executive Secretary,* Dr P. T. Warren

---

THE ROYAL SOCIETY OF EDINBURGH (1783)
22–24 George Street, Edinburgh EH2 2PQ
Tel 0131-225 6057

---

The Royal Society of Edinburgh is Scotland's premier learned society. The Society was founded by Royal Charter in 1783 for 'the advancement of Learning and Useful Knowledge', and its principal role is the promotion of scholarship in all its branches. It provides a forum for broadly-based interdisciplinary activity in Scotland, including organizing public lectures, conferences and specialist research seminars; providing advice to Parliament and government; administering a range of research fellowships held in Scotland; and publishing learned journals.

Fellows are elected by ballot after being nominated by at least four existing Fellows. At 31 May 1994 there were 1,047 Ordinary Fellows and 69 Honorary Fellows.

*President,* Dr T. L. Johnston
*Treasurer,* The Lord Balfour of Burleigh
*General Secretary,* Prof. V. B. Proudfoot
*Executive Secretary,* Dr W. Duncan

# Royal Academicians

*Senior Academician

| | |
|---|---|
| 1991 | Abrahams, Ivor |
| 1991 | Ackroyd, Norman |
| 1972 | Adams, Norman |
| 1988 | Aitchison, Craigie |
| 1991 | Armfield, Diana |
| 1991 | Ayres, Gillian, OBE |
| 1991 | Bellany, John, CBE |
| 1992 | Berg, Adrian |
| 1976 | Blackadder, Elizabeth, OBE |
| 1981 | Blake, Peter, CBE |
| 1975 | *Blamey, Norman |
| 1978 | Blow, Sandra |
| 1975 | Bowey, Olwyn |
| 1981 | Bowyer, William |
| 1972 | Brown, Ralph |
| 1972 | Butler, James |
| 1975 | *Cadbury-Brown, H. T., OBE |
| 1984 | Camp, Jeffery |
| 1970 | *Casson, Sir Hugh, CH, KCVO |
| 1993 | Caulfield, Patrick |
| 1989 | Christopher, Ann |
| 1976 | Clarke, Geoffrey |
| 1973 | Clatworthy, Robert |
| 1972 | Coker, Peter |
| 1972 | Cooke, Jean |
| 1994 | Cragg, Tony |
| 1993 | Craxton, John |
| 1991 | Cullinan, Edward, CBE |
| 1974 | Cuming, Frederick |
| 1992 | Cummins, Gus |
| 1983 | Dannatt, Trevor |
| 1969 | *de Grey, Sir Roger, KCVO |

| | |
|---|---|
| 1976 | Dickson, Jennifer |
| 1985 | Dowson, Sir Philip, CBE |
| 1991 | Draper, Kenneth |
| 1968 | Dunstan, Bernard |
| 1986 | Eyton, Anthony |
| 1992 | *Fedden, Mary |
| 1991 | Flanagan, Barry, OBE |
| 1991 | Foster, Sir Norman |
| 1985 | Fraser, Donald Hamilton |
| 1991 | Freeth, Peter |
| 1992 | *Frost, Terry |
| 1972 | *Gore, Frederick, CBE |
| 1977 | Green, Anthony |
| 1994 | Grimshaw, Nicholas |
| 1970 | Hayes, Colin |
| 1990 | *Herman, Josef, OBE |
| 1991 | Hockney, David |
| 1984 | *Hogarth, Paul, OBE |
| 1992 | Hopkins, Michael, CBE |
| 1991 | Howard, Ken |
| 1991 | Hoyland, John |
| 1991 | Huxley, Paul |
| 1991 | Jacklin, Bill |
| 1991 | *Jellicoe, Sir Geoffrey |
| 1986 | Jones, Allen |
| 1986 | Kenny, Michael |
| 1991 | Kiff, Ken |
| 1988 | King, Phillip, CBE |
| 1991 | Kitaj, R. B. |
| 1974 | Kneale, Bryan |
| 1991 | Koralek, Paul, CBE |
| 1991 | *Lasdun, Sir Dennis, CBE |
| 1991 | Lawson, Sonia |

| | |
|---|---|
| 1986 | Levene, Ben |
| 1991 | McComb, Leonard |
| 1993 | MacCormac, Richard, CBE |
| 1956 | *Machin, Arnold, OBE |
| 1979 | *Manasseh, Leonard, OBE |
| 1985 | *Martin, Sir Leslie |
| 1985 | *Medley, Robert, CBE |
| 1991 | Mistry, Dhruva |
| 1994 | Moon, Mick |
| 1992 | Neiland, Brendan |
| 1979 | Paolozzi, Sir Eduardo, CBE |
| 1988 | Partridge, John, CBE |
| 1983 | *Pasmore, Victor, CH, CBE |
| 1989 | Phillips, Tom |
| 1977 | Powell, Sir Philip, CH, OBE |
| 1973 | *Roberts-Jones, Ivor, CBE |
| 1984 | Rogers, Sir Richard |
| 1991 | Rooney, Michael |
| 1969 | *Rosoman, Leonard, OBE |
| 1989 | Sandle, Michael |
| 1969 | *Soukop, Willi |
| 1986 | Stephenson, Ian |
| 1988 | Sutton, Philip |
| 1991 | Tilson, Joe |
| 1979 | Tindle, David |
| 1991 | Titchell, John |
| 1992 | Tucker, William |
| 1965 | *Ward, John, CBE |
| 1965 | *Weight, Carel, CBE |
| 1989 | Whishaw, Anthony |
| 1974 | *Williams, Kyffin, OBE |
| 1991 | Wilson, Colin St J. |
| 1991 | Wragg, John |

# The Research Councils

The Government funds basic and applied civil science research mostly through the six research councils, which are supported by the Office of Public Service and Science (OPSS) at the Cabinet Office. The councils conduct research through their own establishments (listed below) and by supporting selected research, study and training in universities and other higher education establishments. They also receive income for research commissioned by government departments and the private sector.

## BIOTECHNOLOGY AND BIOLOGICAL SCIENCES RESEARCH COUNCIL

HEADQUARTERS, Polaris House, North Star Avenue, Swindon SN2 IUH. Tel: 01793-413200

BABRAHAM INSTITUTE
*Director of Research*, Dr R. G. Dyer, Babraham Hall, Babraham, Cambridge CB2 4AT. Tel: 01223-832312

INSTITUTE FOR ANIMAL HEALTH
*Director of Research*, Prof. F. J. Bourne, PH.D., Compton, Newbury, Berks. RG16 0NN. Tel: 01635-578411
BBSRC AND MRC NEUROPATHOGENESIS UNIT, Ogston Building, West Mains Road, Edinburgh EH9 3JF. Tel: 0131-667 5204/5. *Head*, vacant
COMPTON LABORATORY, Compton, Newbury, Berks. RG16 0NN. Tel: 01635-578411. *Head of Division in Charge*, Dr P. Jones
PIRBRIGHT LABORATORY, Ash Road, Pirbright, Woking, Surrey GU24 0NF. Tel: 01483-232441. *Head*, Dr A. I. Donaldson

INSTITUTE OF ARABLE CROPS RESEARCH
*Director of Research*, Prof. B. Miflin, Rothamsted Experimental Station, Harpenden, Herts. AL5 2JQ. Tel: 01582-763133
BROOM'S BARN EXPERIMENTAL STATION, Higham, Bury St Edmunds, Suffolk IP28 6NP. Tel: 01284-810363. *Head*, Prof. T. H. Thomas, PH.D., D.SC.
LONG ASHTON RESEARCH STATION, Long Ashton, Bristol BS18 9AF. Tel: 01275-392181. *Head*, Prof. P. R. Shewry
ROTHAMSTED EXPERIMENTAL STATION, Harpenden, Herts. AL5 2JQ. Tel: 01582-763133. *Head*, Prof. B. Miflin.

INSTITUTE OF FOOD RESEARCH
*Director of Research*, Prof. A. D. B. Malcolm, Earley Gate, Whiteknights Road, Reading RG6 2EF. Tel: 01734-357055
NORWICH LABORATORY, Norwich Research Park, Colney Lane, Norwich NR4 7UA. Tel: 01603-56122. *Head*, Prof. P. S. Belton
READING LABORATORY, Earley Gate, Whiteknights Road, Reading RG6 2EF. Tel: 01734-357000. *Head*, vacant

INSTITUTE OF GRASSLAND AND ENVIRONMENTAL RESEARCH
*Director of Research*, Prof. C. J. Pollock, Plas Gogerddan, Aberystwyth, Dyfed SY23 3EB. Tel: 01970-828255

ABERYSTWYTH RESEARCH CENTRE, Plas Gogerddan, Aberystwyth, Dyfed SY23 3EB. Tel: 01970-828255. *Head*, Prof. D. Wilson, PH.D.
NORTH WYKE RESEARCH STATION, Okehampton, Devon EX20 2SB. Tel: 01837-82558. *Head*, Prof. R. J. Wilkins, PH.D.

JOHN INNES CENTRE
*Director of Research*, Prof. R. B. Flavell, John Innes Institute, Colney Lane, Norwich NR4 7UH. Tel: 01603-52571
NITROGEN FIXATION LABORATORY, University of Sussex, Brighton BN1 9RQ. Tel: 01273-678252. *Head*, Prof. B. E. Smith, PH.D.

ROSLIN INSTITUTE
*Director of Research*, Prof. G. Bulfield, Roslin, Midlothian EH25 9PS. Tel: 0131-440 2726

SILSOE RESEARCH INSTITUTE
*Director of Research*, Prof. B. J. Legg, Wrest Park, Silsoe, Bedford MK45 4HS. Tel: 01525-860000

## SCOTTISH AGRICULTURAL AND BIOLOGICAL RESEARCH INSTITUTES

HANNAH RESEARCH INSTITUTE, Ayr KA6 5HL. Tel: 01292-76013. *Director*, Prof. M. Peaker
MACAULAY LAND USE RESEARCH INSTITUTE, Craigiebuckler, Aberdeen AB9 2QJ. Tel: 01224-318611. *Director*, Prof. T. J. Maxwell, PH.D.
MOREDUN RESEARCH INSTITUTE, 408 Gilmerton Road, Edinburgh EH17 7JH. Tel: 0131-664 3262. *Director*, Prof. I. D. Aitken, PH.D.
ROWETT RESEARCH INSTITUTE, Greenburn Road, Bucksburn, Aberdeen AB2 9SB. Tel: 01224-712751. *Director*, Prof. W. P. T. James, CBE
SCOTTISH AGRICULTURAL STATISTICS SERVICE, University of Edinburgh, James Clerk Maxwell Building, The King's Buildings, Mayfield Road, Edinburgh EH9 3JZ. Tel: 0131-650 4900. *Director*, R. A. Kempton
SCOTTISH CROP RESEARCH INSTITUTE, Invergowrie, Dundee DD2 5DA. Tel: 01382-562731. *Director*, Prof. J. Hillman, PH.D., FRSE

## ECONOMIC AND SOCIAL RESEARCH COUNCIL

HEADQUARTERS, Polaris House, North Star Avenue, Swindon SN2 IUJ. Tel: 01793-413000

RESEARCH CENTRES
CAMBRIDGE GROUP FOR THE HISTORY OF POPULATION AND SOCIAL STRUCTURE, 27 Trumpington Street, Cambridge CB2 1QA. Tel: 01223-333186. *Director*, Dr R. Schofield
CENTRE FOR BUSINESS RESEARCH, Department of Applied Economy, University of Cambridge, Cambridge CB3 9DE. Tel: 01223-335248. *Director*, A. Hughes

CENTRE FOR ECONOMIC PERFORMANCE, London School of Economics, Houghton Street, London WC2A 2AE. Tel: 0171-955 7048. *Director,* Prof. R. Layard

CENTRE FOR EDUCATIONAL SOCIOLOGY, University of Edinburgh, 7 Buccleuch Place, Edinburgh EH8 9LW. Tel: 0131-650 4190. *Director,* Prof. D. Raffe

CENTRE FOR HOUSING RESEARCH, University of Glasgow, 25 Bute Gardens, Hillhead, Glasgow G12 8LE. Tel: 0141-339 8855. *Director,* Prof. D. MacLennan, PH.D.

CENTRE FOR MICRO-ECONOMIC ANALYSIS OF FISCAL POLICY, Institute for Fiscal Studies, 7 Ridgmount Street, London WC1E 7AE. Tel: 0171-636 3784. *Director,* Prof. R. Blundell

CENTRE FOR RESEARCH IN DEVELOPMENT INSTRUCTION AND TRAINING, Department of Psychology, University of Nottingham, Nottingham NG7 2RD. Tel: 0115-951 5312. *Director,* Prof. D. J. Wood

CENTRE FOR RESEARCH IN ETHNIC RELATIONS, University of Warwick, Gibbet Hill Road, Coventry CV4 7AL. Tel: 01203-523523. *Director,* Prof. Z. Layton-Henry

CENTRE FOR SCIENCE TECHNOLOGY, ENERGY AND ENVIRONMENTAL POLICY, Science Policy Research Unit, University of Sussex, Mantell Building, Falmer, Brighton BN1 9RF. Tel: 01273-686758. *Director,* Prof. M. Gibbons

CENTRE FOR SOCIAL AND ECONOMIC RESEARCH ON THE GLOBAL ENVIRONMENT, School of Environmental Sciences, University of East Anglia, Norwich NR4 7TJ. Tel: 01603-593176. *Director,* Prof. R. K. Turner

CENTRE FOR SOCIAL WORK RESEARCH, University of Stirling, Stirling FK9 4LA. Tel: 01786-467724. *Director,* Prof. J. Cheetham

CENTRE FOR THE STUDY OF AFRICAN ECONOMIES, St Cross Building, Manor Road, Oxford OX1 3UL. Tel: 01865-271084. *Director,* Prof. P. Collier

FINANCIAL MARKETS GROUP, London School of Economics, Houghton Street, London WC2A 2AE. Tel: 0171-955 7002. *Director,* Prof. D. Webb

HUMAN COMMUNICATION RESEARCH CENTRE, University of Edinburgh, 2 Buccleuch Place, Edinburgh EH8 9LW. Tel: 0131-650 4444. *Director,* Prof. K. Stenning

INDUSTRIAL RELATIONS RESEARCH UNIT, School of Industrial and Business Studies, University of Warwick, Gibbet Hill Road, Coventry CV4 7AL. Tel: 01203-523523. *Director,* Prof. K. Sisson

JOINT UNIT FOR THE STUDY OF SOCIAL TRENDS, Social and Community Planning Research, 35 Northampton Square, London EC1V 0AX. Tel: 0171-250 1866. *Director,* Prof. R. Jowell

MRC/ESRC SOCIAL AND APPLIED PSYCHOLOGY UNIT, Department of Psychology, University of Sheffield, Sheffield S10 2TN. Tel: 0114-275 6600. *Director,* Prof. P. Warr

NORTHERN IRELAND ECONOMIC RESEARCH CENTRE, 46–48 University Road, Belfast BT7 1NJ. Tel: 01232-325594. *Director,* Dr G. Gudgin

RESEARCH CENTRE IN MICRO-SOCIAL CHANGE, University of Essex, Wivenhoe Park, Colchester, Essex CO4 3SQ. Tel: 01206-872957. *Director,* Prof. J. Gershuny

TRANSPORT STUDIES UNIT, University of Oxford, Oxford OX2 6NB. Tel: 01865-274715. *Director,* Dr P. Goodwin

RESOURCE CENTRES

CENTRE FOR ECONOMIC POLICY RESEARCH, 25–28 Old Burlington Street, London W1X 1LB. Tel: 0171-734 9110. *Director,* Prof. R. Portes

ESRC DATA ARCHIVE, University of Essex, Wivenhoe Park, Colchester, Essex CO4 3SQ. Tel: 01206-872001. *Director,* Prof. D. Lievesley

INTERNATIONAL BIBLIOGRAPHY FOR THE SOCIAL SCIENCES RESOURCE CENTRE, London School of Economics, Houghton Street, London WC2A 2AE. Tel: 0171-405 7686. *Director,* Ms L. Brindley

QUALITATIVE DATA ARCHIVAL RESOURCE CENTRE, University of Essex, Wivenhoe Park, Colchester, Essex CO4 3SQ. Tel: 01206-873333. *Director,* Prof. P. Thompson

## ENGINEERING AND PHYSICAL SCIENCES RESEARCH COUNCIL

HEADQUARTERS, Polaris House, North Star Avenue, Swindon, Wilts. SN2 1ET. Tel: 01793-444000

DARESBURY AND RUTHERFORD APPLETON LABORATORIES (DRAL)
*Director,* Dr P. R. Williams (based at Didcot)

DARESBURY LABORATORY, Keckwick Lane, Daresbury, Warrington, Cheshire WA4 4AD. Tel: 01925-603000. *Head,* Dr R. W. Newport

RUTHERFORD APPLETON NUCLEAR PHYSICS LABORATORY, Chilton, Didcot, Oxon. OX11 0QX. Tel: 01235-821900. *Head,* Dr T. G. Walker

## MEDICAL RESEARCH COUNCIL

HEADQUARTERS, 20 Park Crescent, London W1N 4AL. Tel: 0171-636 5422

NATIONAL INSTITUTE FOR MEDICAL RESEARCH, The Ridgeway, Mill Hill, London NW7 1AA. Tel: 0181-959 3666. *Director,* J. Skehel, PH.D., FRS

CLINICAL SCIENCES CENTRE, Royal Postgraduate Medical School, Du Cane Road, London W12 0NN. Tel: 0181-743 7117. *Director of Research,* vacant

LABORATORY OF MOLECULAR BIOLOGY, Hills Road, Cambridge CB2 2QH. Tel: 01223-248011. *Director,* Prof. Sir Aaron Klug, SC.D., FRS

RESEARCH UNITS

ANATOMICAL NEUROPHARMACOLOGY UNIT, Mansfield Road, Oxford OX1 3TH. Tel: 01865-271865. *Hon. Director,* Prof. A. D. Smith, D.Phil.

APPLIED PSYCHOLOGY UNIT, 15 Chaucer Road, Cambridge CB2 2EF. Tel: 01223-355294. *Director,* A. D. Baddeley, PH.D., FRS

BBSRC/MRC NEUROPATHOGENESIS UNIT, Ogston Building, West Mains Road, Edinburgh EH9 3JF. Tel: 0131-667 5204. *Director,* vacant

BIOCHEMICAL AND CLINICAL MAGNETIC RESONANCE UNIT, University Department of Biochemistry, South Parks Road, Oxford OX1 3QU. Tel: 01865-275274. *Hon. Director,* Prof. G. K. Radda, CBE, D.Phil., FRS

BIOSTATISTICS UNIT, Institute of Public Health, University Forvie Site, Robinson Way, Cambridge CB2 2SR. Tel: 01223-330366. *Hon. Director,* Prof. N. E. Day, PH.D.

BLOOD GROUP UNIT, University College, London, Wolfson House, 4 Stephenson Way, London NW1 2HE. Tel: 0171-388 7752. *Director,* P. Tippett, OBE, Ph.D.

BRAIN METABOLISM UNIT, University Department of Pharmacology, 1 George Square, Edinburgh EH8 9JZ. Tel: 0131-650 3543. *Director,* Prof. G. Fink, MD, D.Phil., FRSE

CELL MUTATION UNIT, University of Sussex, Falmer, Brighton BN1 9RR. Tel: 01273-678123. *Director*, Prof. B. A. Bridges, Ph.D., FIBiol.

CELLULAR IMMUNOLOGY UNIT, Sir William Dunn School of Pathology, Oxford OX1 3RE. Tel: 01865-275594. *Director (acting)*, D. W. Mason

CHILD PSYCHIATRY UNIT, Institute of Psychiatry, De Crespigny Park, Denmark Hill, London SE5 8AF. Tel: 0171-703 5411. *Hon. Director*, Prof. Sir Michael Rutter, CBE, FRS, MD, FRCP, FRCPsych.

CLINICAL ONCOLOGY AND RADIOTHERAPEUTICS UNIT, MRC Centre, Hills Road, Cambridge CB2 2QH. Tel: 01223-245133. *Hon. Director*, Prof. N. M. Bleehen, CBE, FRCP, FRCR

COGNITIVE DEVELOPMENT UNIT, 4 Taviton Street, London WC1H 0BT. Tel: 0171-387 4692. *Director*, Prof. J. Morton, ph.d.

COLLABORATIVE CENTRE, 1–3 Burtonhole Lane, Mill Hill, London NW7 1AD. Tel: 0181-906 3811. *Director*, C. C. G. Hentschel, ph.d.

CYCLOTRON UNIT, MRC Clinical Sciences Centre, RPMS Hammersmith Hospital, Du Cane Road, London W12 0NN. Tel: 0181-740 3162. *Director (acting)*, T. Jones, D.SC., MD

DUNN NUTRITION UNIT, Downhams Lane, Milton Road, Cambridge CB4 1XJ. Tel: 01223-426356. *Director*, R. G. Whitehead, CBE, ph.d.

ENVIRONMENTAL EPIDEMIOLOGY UNIT, Southampton General Hospital, Southampton SO9 4XY. Tel: 01703-777624. *Director*, Prof. D. J. P. Barker, MD, ph.d, FRCP, FRCOG

EPIDEMIOLOGY AND MEDICAL CARE UNIT, Wolfson Institute of Preventive Medicine, St Bartholomew's Medical College, Charterhouse Square, London EC1M 6BQ. Tel: 0171-982 6000. *Director*, Prof. T. W. Meade, CBE, DM, FRCP

EPIDEMIOLOGY UNIT (SOUTH WALES), Llandough Hospital, Penarth, South Glamorgan CF64 2XW. Tel: 01222-711404. *Director*, P. C. Elwood, MD, FRCP

EXPERIMENTAL EMBRYOLOGY AND TERATOLOGY UNIT, St George's Hospital Medical School, Cranmer Terrace, London SW17 0RE. Tel: 0181-672 9944 ext. 56309. *Director*, Prof. D. G. Whittingham, D.SC., FRCVS, FIBiol.

HUMAN BIOCHEMICAL GENETICS UNIT, The Galton Laboratory, University College London, Wolfson House, 4 Stephenson Way, London NW1 2HE. Tel: 0171-387 7050. *Director*, Prof. D. A. Hopkinson, MD

HUMAN GENETICS UNIT, Western General Hospital, Crewe Road, Edinburgh EH4 2XU. Tel: 0131-332 2471. *Director*, Prof. H. J. Evans, ph.d., FIBiol., FRCPE, FRCSE, FRSE

HUMAN MOVEMENT AND BALANCE UNIT, Institute of Neurology, National Hospital for Neurology and Neurosurgery, Queen Square, London WC1 3BG. Tel: 0171-837 3611. *Hon. Director*. Prof. C. D. Marsden, D.SC., FRCP, FRS

IMMUNOCHEMISTRY UNIT, University Department of Biochemistry, South Parks Road, Oxford OX1 3QU. Tel: 01865-275354. *Director*, K. B. M. Reid, ph.d.

INSTITUTE OF HEARING RESEARCH, University of Nottingham, Nottingham NG7 2RD. Tel: 0115-922 3431. *Director*, Prof. M. P. Haggard, ph.d.

MEDICAL SOCIOLOGY UNIT, 6 Lilybank Gardens, Glasgow G12 8QQ. Tel: 0141-357 3949. *Director*, Prof. S. Macintyre, ph.d.

MOLECULAR HAEMATOLOGY UNIT, Institute of Molecular Medicine, John Radcliffe Hospital, Headington, Oxford OX3 9DU. Tel: 01865-222359. *Hon.*

*Director*, Prof. Sir David Weatherall, MD, FRCP, FRCPath., FRS

MOLECULAR IMMUNOPATHOLOGY UNIT, MRC Centre, University Medical School, Hills Road, Cambridge CB2 2QH. Tel: 01223-245133. *Hon. Director*, Prof. P. J. Lachmann, ph.d., SC.D., FRCP, FRCPath., FRS

MRC/ESRC SOCIAL AND APPLIED PSYCHOLOGY UNIT, Dept. of Psychology, University of Sheffield, Sheffield S10 2TN. Tel: 0114-275 6600. *Director*, Prof. P. B. Warr, ph.d.

MRC LABORATORIES, THE GAMBIA, PO Box 273, Banjul, The Gambia, W. Africa. *Director*, B. M. Greenwood, CBE, MD, FRCP

MRC LABORATORIES, JAMAICA, University of the West Indies, Mona, Kingston 7, Jamaica. *Director*, Prof. G. R. Serjeant, CMG, MD, FRCP

MUSCLE AND CELL MOTILITY UNIT, Division of Biomedical Sciences, King's College London, 26–29 Drury Lane, London WC2B 5RL. Tel: 0171-836 8851. *Hon. Director*, Prof. R. M. Simmons, ph.d.

NEUROCHEMICAL PATHOLOGY UNIT, Newcastle General Hospital, Westgate Road, Newcastle upon Tyne NE4 6BE. Tel: 0191-273 5251. *Director*, Prof. J. A. Edwardson, ph.d.

PROTEIN FUNCTION AND DESIGN UNIT, Department of Chemistry, University of Cambridge, Lensfield Road, Cambridge CB2 1EW. Tel: 01223-336341. *Hon. Director*, Prof. A. R. Fersht, ph.d., FRS

PROTEIN PHOSPHORYLATION UNIT, Department of Biochemistry, Medical Sciences Institute, University of Dundee, Dundee DD1 4HN. Tel: 01382-307238. *Hon. Director*, Prof. P. Cohen, ph.d., FRS, FRSE

RADIOBIOLOGY UNIT, Chilton, Didcot, Oxon. OX11 0RD. Tel: 01235-834393. *Director*, Prof. G. E. Adams, D.SC.

REPRODUCTIVE BIOLOGY UNIT, Centre for Reproductive Biology, 37 Chalmers Street, Edinburgh EH3 9EW. Tel: 0131-229 2575. *Director*, Prof. D. W. Lincoln, D.SC., FRSE

SOCIAL AND COMMUNITY PSYCHIATRY UNIT, Institute of Psychiatry, De Crespigny Park, Denmark Hill, London SE5 8AF. Tel: 0171-703 5411. *Director*, Prof. J. P. Leff, MD, FRCPsych.

TOXICOLOGY UNIT, Hodgkin Building, University of Leicester, PO Box 138, Lancaster Road, Leicester LE1 9HN. Tel: 0116-252 5600. *Director*, L. Smith, ph.d.

TUBERCULOSIS AND RELATED INFECTIONS UNIT, MRC Clinical Sciences Centre, RPMS, Hammersmith Hospital, Du Cane Road, London W12 0NN. Tel: 0181-740 3161. *Director*, Prof. J. Ivanyi, MD, ph.d.

UK HUMAN GENOME MAPPING PROJECT RESOURCE CENTRE, Sanger Centre, Hinxton Hall, Hinxton, Cambridge CB10 1RQ. *Manager*, K. Gibson, ph.d.

VIROLOGY UNIT, Institute of Virology, Church Street, Glasgow G11 5JR. Tel: 0141-330 4017. *Hon. Director*, Prof. J. H. Subak-Sharpe, CBE, ph.d., FRSE

---

## NATURAL ENVIRONMENT RESEARCH COUNCIL

---

HEADQUARTERS, Polaris House, North Star Avenue, Swindon SN2 1EU. Tel: 01793-411500

BRITISH ANTARCTIC SURVEY, Madingley Road, Cambridge CB3 0ET. Tel: 01223-61188. *Director*, Dr D. J. Drewry

BRITISH GEOLOGICAL SURVEY, Nicker Hill, Keyworth, Nottingham NG12 5GG. Tel: 0115-936 3100. *Director*, Dr P. Cook

CENTRE FOR ECOLOGY AND HYDROLOGY
*Director (acting)*, Prof. B. Wilkinson

INSTITUTE OF FRESHWATER ECOLOGY, The Ferry
House, Far Sawrey, Ambleside, Cumbria LA22 OLP. Tel:
015394-42468. *Director*, Prof. J. G. Jones
INSTITUTE OF HYDROLOGY, Maclean Building,
Crowmarsh Gifford, Wallingford, Oxon. OX10 8BB. Tel:
01491-838800
INSTITUTE OF TERRESTRIAL ECOLOGY, Bush Estate,
Penicuik, Midlothian EH26 0QB. Tel: 0131-445 4343
INSTITUTE OF TERRESTRIAL ECOLOGY, Monks Wood,
Abbots Ripton, Huntingdon PE17 2LS. Tel: 014873-381/8.
*Director*, Dr T. M. Roberts
INSTITUTE OF VIROLOGY AND ENVIRONMENTAL
MICROBIOLOGY, Mansfield Road, Oxford OX1 3SR. Tel:
01865-512361. *Director*, Prof. D. H. L. Bishop

CENTRE FOR COASTAL AND MARINE SCIENCE
*Director (acting)*, Dr B. Bayne

PLYMOUTH MARINE LABORATORY, Prospect Place, The
Hoe, Plymouth PL1 3DH; Citadel Hill, Plymouth PL1 2PB.
Tel: 01752-222772. *Assistant Director*, Dr P. N. Claridge
PROUDMAN OCEANOGRAPHIC LABORATORY, Bidston,
Birkenhead L43 7RA. Tel: 0151-653 8633. *Director*, Dr
B. S. McCartney
DUNSTAFFNAGE MARINE LABORATORY, PO Box 3,
Oban, Argyll PA34 4AD. Tel: 01631-62244. *Director*, Prof.
J. B. L. Matthews

SOUTHAMPTON OCEANOGRAPHY CENTRE
*Director*, Dr J. Shephard

INSTITUTE OF OCEANOGRAPHIC SCIENCES, Deacon
Laboratory, Wormley, nr. Godalming, Surrey GU8 5UB.
Tel: 0142868-4141. *Director*, Dr C. Summerhayes
JAMES RENNELL CENTRE FOR OCEAN CIRCULATION,
Gamma House, Chilworth Research Centre, Chilworth,
Southampton SO1 7NS. Tel: 01703-766184. *Head of Centre*,
Dr R. Pollard
RESEARCH VESSEL SERVICES, No. 1 Dock, Barry,
S. Glamorgan. Tel: 01446-737451. *Head*, Dr C. Fay

SEA MAMMAL RESEARCH UNIT, c/o British Antarctic
Survey (*see* above). Tel: 01223-311354. *Head*, J. Harwood,
PH.D.
UNIT OF AQUATIC BIOCHEMISTRY, Stirling University,
FK9 4LA. Tel: 01786-73171. *Director*, Prof. J. R. Sargent
UNIT OF COMPARATIVE PLANT ECOLOGY, Department
of Animal and Plant Biology and Ecology, Sheffield
University, Sheffield S10 2TN. Tel: 0114-276 8555. *Head
of Unit*, Prof. J. P. Grime
NERC UNIT FOR THEMATIC INFORMATION SYSTEMS,
Department of Geography, Reading University,
Whiteknights, PO Box 227, Reading RG6 2AB. Tel:
01734-318741. *Officer in Charge*, Prof. R. Gurney

CENTRE FOR POPULATION BIOLOGY, Imperial College,
Silwood Park, Ascot, Berks. SL5 7PY. Tel: 01344-294223.
*Director*, Prof. J. Lawton

---

## PARTICLE PHYSICS AND ASTRONOMY
## RESEARCH COUNCIL

HEADQUARTERS, Polaris House, North Star Avenue,
Swindon SN2 1SZ. Tel: 01793-442000

THE OBSERVATORIES
*Director*, Prof. A. Boksenberg, FRS

ROYAL GREENWICH OBSERVATORY, Madingley Road,
Cambridge CB3 OEZ. Tel: 01223-374700

ROYAL OBSERVATORY, EDINBURGH, Blackford Hill,
Edinburgh EH9 3HJ. Tel: 0131-668 8100

# Research Associations

The following industrial and technological research bodies
are members of the Association of Independent Research
and Technology Organizations (AIRTO), PO Box 330,
Cambridge CB5 8DU. Tel: 01223-467831

ADVANCED MANUFACTURING TECHNOLOGY
RESEARCH INSTITUTE, Hulley Road, Macclesfield,
Cheshire SK10 2NE. Tel: 01625-425421. *Chief Executive*,
N. A. Eldred
AIRCRAFT RESEARCH ASSOCIATION LTD, Manton Lane,
Bedford MK41 7PF. Tel: 01234-350681. *Chief Executive*,
Dr J. E. Green
BHR GROUP LTD (BRITISH HYDRO-MECHANICS
RESEARCH GROUP), Cranfield, Bedford MK43 0AJ. Tel:
01234-750422. *Chief Executive*, I. Cooper
BIBRA TOXICOLOGY INTERNATIONAL, Woodmansterne
Road, Carshalton, Surrey SM5 4DS. Tel: 0181-643 4411.
*Director*, Dr S. E. Jaggers
BRITISH GLASS, Northumberland Road, Sheffield S10 2UA.
Tel: 0114-268 6201. *Research Director*, Dr G. J. Copley
BRITISH LEATHER CONFEDERATION, Leather Trade
House, Kings Park Road, Moulton Park, Northants. NN3
1JD. Tel: 01604-494131. *Technical Director*, Dr
K. Alexander
BRITISH MARITIME TECHNOLOGY LTD, Orlando House,
1 Waldegrave Road, Teddington, Middx. TW11 8LZ. Tel:
0181-943 5544. *Chief Executive*, D. Goodrich
BRITISH TEXTILE TECHNOLOGY GROUP, Wira House,
West Park Ring Road, Leeds LS16 6QL. Tel: 0113-259
1999. *Chief Operating Officer*, A. King
BUILDING SERVICES RESEARCH AND INFORMATION
ASSOCIATION, Old Bracknell Lane West, Bracknell,
Berks. RG12 7AH. Tel: 01344-426511. *Chief Executive*,
G. J. Baker
CAMBRIDGE CONSULTANTS LTD (*Product and process
development of technology applications in business*), Science
Park, Milton Road, Cambridge CB4 4DW. Tel: 01223-
420024. *Managing Director*, Dr J. P. Auton
CAMBRIDGE REFRIGERATION TECHNOLOGY (CRT),
140 Newmarket Road, Cambridge CB5 8HE. Tel: 01223-
65101. *Technical Director*, R. D. Heap
CAMPDEN FOOD AND DRINK RESEARCH ASSOCIATION,
Chipping Campden, Glos. GL55 6LD. Tel: 01386-840319.
*Director-General*, Prof. C. Dennis
CERAM RESEARCH LTD (*Ceramics*), Queen's Road,
Penkhull, Stoke-on-Trent ST4 7LQ. Tel: 01782-45431.
*Chief Executive*, Dr N. E. Sanderson
CIRIA (THE CONSTRUCTION INDUSTRY RESEARCH
AND INFORMATION ASSOCIATION), 6 Storey's Gate,
London SW1P 3AU. Tel: 0171-222 8891. *Director-General*,
Dr P. L. Bransby
CUTLERY AND ALLIED TRADES RESEARCH
ASSOCIATION, Henry Street, Sheffield S3 7EQ. Tel: 0114-
2769736. *Director of Research*, R. C. Hamby
EA TECHNOLOGY, Capenhurst, Chester CH1 6ES. Tel:
0151-339 4181. *Managing Director*, Dr S. F. Exell
ERA TECHNOLOGY LTD (*Electronic and electrical
engineering*), Cleeve Road, Leatherhead, Surrey KT22 7SA.
Tel: 01372-374151. *Chief Executive*, M. J. Withers
FLOUR MILLING AND BAKING RESEARCH
ASSOCIATION, Chorleywood, Herts. WD3 5SH. Tel:
01923-284111. *Director-General*, Dr A. D. B. Malcolm
FURNITURE INDUSTRY RESEARCH ASSOCIATION,
Maxwell Road, Stevenage, Herts. SG1 2EW. Tel: 01438-
313433. *Director and Chief Executive*, Dr
C. A. Aitkenhead

INTERNATIONAL RESEARCH AND DEVELOPMENT LTD (*Electronics and mechanical and electrical engineering*), Fossway, Newcastle upon Tyne NE6 2YD. Tel: 0191-265 0451. *General Manager*, W. Carpenter

LEATHERHEAD FOOD RESEARCH ASSOCIATION, Randalls Road, Leatherhead, Surrey KT22 7RY. Tel: 01372-376761. *Director*, Dr M. P. J. Kierstan

MOTOR INDUSTRY RESEARCH ASSOCIATION, Watling Street, Nuneaton, Warks. CV10 0TU. Tel: 01203-348541. *Managing Director*, J. R. Wood

THE NATIONAL COMPUTING CENTRE LTD, Oxford Road, Manchester M1 7ED. Tel: 0161-228 6333. *Chief Executive*, N. Banister

PAINT RESEARCH ASSOCIATION, 8 Waldegrave Road, Teddington, Middx. TW11 8LD. Tel: 0181-977 4427. *Managing Director*, J. A. Bernie

PERA INTERNATIONAL (*Multi-disciplinary research, design, development and consultancy*), Melton Mowbray, Leics. LE13 0PB. Tel: 01664-501501. *Director-General*, R. A. Armstrong

PIRA INTERNATIONAL (*Paper and board, printing, publishing and packaging*), Randalls Road, Leatherhead, Surrey KT22 7RU. Tel: 01372-376161. *Managing Director*, B. W. Blunden, OBE

RAPRA TECHNOLOGY LTD (*Polymer materials*), Shawbury, Shrewsbury SY4 4NR. Tel: 01939-250383. *Chief Executive*, Dr M. Copley

RICARDO AEROSPACE LTD, Bowling Hill, Chipping Sodbury, Bristol BS17 6JX. Tel: 01454-325288. *Managing Director*, J. Baker

SATRA FOOTWEAR TECHNOLOGY CENTRE, Satra House, Rockingham Road, Kettering, Northants. NN16 9JH. Tel: 01536-410000. *Chief Executive*, Dr R. E. Whittaker

SIRA LTD (*Instrumentation and systems technology*), South Hill, Chislehurst, Kent BR7 5EH. Tel: 0181-467 2636. *Managing Director*, R. A. Brook

SMITH SYSTEM ENGINEERING LTD, Surrey Research Park, Guildford, Surrey GU2 5YP. Tel: 01483-442000. *Chairman*, Dr B. G. Smith

SPRING RESEARCH AND MANUFACTURERS' ASSOCIATION, Henry Street, Sheffield S3 7EQ. Tel: 01742-760771. *Director*, D. Saynor

TIMBER RESEARCH AND DEVELOPMENT ASSOCIATION, Stocking Lane, Hughenden Valley, High Wycombe, Bucks. HP14 4ND. Tel: 01494-563091. *Director*, Dr C. J. Gill

THE WELDING INSTITUTE (TWI), Abington Hall, Abington, Cambridge CB1 6AL. Tel: 01223-891162. *Chief Executive*, A. B. M. Braithwaite, OBE

WRC (WATER RESEARCH) PLC, Henley Road, Medmenham, PO Box 16, Marlow, Bucks. SL7 2HD. Tel: 01491-571531. *Managing Director*, Dr J. Moss

# Sports Bodies

Bodies which are the governing body for their sport are indicated by *

*Sports Councils*

THE SPORTS COUNCIL, 16 Upper Woburn Place, London WC1H 0QP. Tel: 0171-388 1277. *Director-General (acting)*, D. Casey

SCOTTISH SPORTS COUNCIL, Caledonia House, South Gyle, Edinburgh EH12 9DQ. Tel: 0131-317 7200. *Chief Executive*, F. A. L. Alstead, CBE

SPORTS COUNCIL FOR WALES, Sophia Gardens, Cardiff CF1 9SW. Tel: 01222-397571. *Chief Executive*, L. Tatham

SPORTS COUNCIL FOR NORTHERN IRELAND, House of Sport, Upper Malone Road, Belfast BT9 5LA. Tel: 01232-381222. *Chief Executive*, E. McCartan

CENTRAL COUNCIL OF PHYSICAL RECREATION, Francis House, Francis Street, London SW1P 1DE. Tel: 0171-828 3163. *General Secretary*, P. Lawson

*Alpine Skiing*

*BRITISH SKI FEDERATION, 258 Main Street, East Calder, Livingston, West Lothian EH53 0EE. Tel: 01506-884343. *Chief Executive*, M. Jardine

*Angling*

*NATIONAL FEDERATION OF ANGLERS, Halliday House, Egginton Junction, Derbys. DE65 6GU. Tel: 01283-734735. *Chief Administration Officer*, K. E. Watkins

*Archery*

*GRAND NATIONAL ARCHERY SOCIETY, 7th Street, National Agricultural Centre, Stoneleigh, Kenilworth, Coventry CV8 2LG. Tel: 01203-696631. *Chief Executive*, J. S. Middleton

*Association Football*

*THE FOOTBALL ASSOCIATION, 16 Lancaster Gate, London W2 3LW. Tel: 0171-262 4542. *Chief Executive*, R. H. G. Kelly

FOOTBALL LEAGUE LTD, 319 Clifton Drive South, Lytham St Annes, Lancs. FY8 1JG. Tel: 01253-729421. *Secretary*, J. D. Dent

*SCOTTISH FOOTBALL ASSOCIATION, 6 Park Gardens, Glasgow G3 7YF. Tel: 0141-332 6372. *Chief Executive*, J. Farry

SCOTTISH FOOTBALL LEAGUE, 188 West Regent Street, Glasgow G2 4RY. Tel: 0141-248 3844. *Secretary*, P. Donald

*FOOTBALL ASSOCIATION OF WALES, Plymouth Chambers, 3 Westgate Street, Cardiff CF1 1DD. Tel: 01222-372325. *Secretary*, A. E. Evans

*IRISH FOOTBALL ASSOCIATION, 20 Windsor Avenue, Belfast BT9 6EE. Tel: 01232-669458. *General Secretary*, D. I. Bowen

IRISH FOOTBALL LEAGUE, 96 University Street, Belfast BT7 1HE. Tel: 01232-242888. *Secretary*, H. Wallace

*Athletics*

*BRITISH ATHLETIC FEDERATION, 225A Bristol Road, Edgbaston, Birmingham B5 7UB. Tel: 0121-440 5000. *Executive Chairman*, Prof. P. F. Radford

AMATEUR ATHLETIC ASSOCIATION OF ENGLAND, 225A Bristol Road, Edgbaston, Birmingham B5 7UB. Tel: 0121-440 5000. *Executive Chairman*, Prof. P. F. Radford

SCOTTISH ATHLETICS FEDERATION, Caledonia House, South Gyle, Edinburgh EH12 9DQ. Tel: 0131-317 7320. *Administrator*, N. F. Park

ATHLETICS ASSOCIATION OF WALES, Morfa Athletics Stadium, Upper Bank, Landore, Swansea, W. Glamorgan SA1 7DF. Tel: 01792-456237. *National Administrator*, Mrs B. Currie

NORTHERN IRELAND AMATEUR ATHLETIC FEDERATION, 106 Cumberland Road, Dundonald, Belfast BT16 0BB. Tel: 01232-887007. *Secretary*, J. Allen

*Badminton*

*BADMINTON ASSOCIATION OF ENGLAND LTD, National Badminton Centre, Bradwell Road, Loughton Lodge, Milton Keynes MK8 9LA. Tel: 01908-568822. *Chief Executive*, Miss A. Smillie

*SCOTTISH BADMINTON UNION, Cockburn Centre, 40 Bogmoor Place, Glasgow G51 4TQ. Tel: 0141-445 1218. *Chief Executive*, Miss A. Smillie

*WELSH BADMINTON UNION, Fourth Floor, 3 Westgate Street, Cardiff CF1 1DD. Tel: 01222-222082. *Chief Executive*, L. Williams

*Baseball*

*BRITISH BASEBALL FEDERATION, 66 Belvedere Road, Hessle, N. Humberside HU13 9JJ. Tel: 01482-643551. *Secretary*, K. Macadam

*Basketball*

*ENGLISH BASKETBALL ASSOCIATION, 48 Bradford Road, Stanningley, Leeds LS28 6DF. Tel: 0113-236 1166. *Chief Executive*, D. Ransom

*SCOTTISH BASKETBALL ASSOCIATION, Caledonia House, South Gyle, Edinburgh EH12 9DQ. Tel: 0131-317 7260. *Technical Director*, K. Johnston

*BASKETBALL ASSOCIATION OF WALES, Connies House, Rhymney River Bridge Road, Cardiff CF3 7YZ. Tel: 01222-454395. *Administrator*, F. M. Daw

*Billiards*

*WORLD PROFESSIONAL BILLIARDS AND SNOOKER ASSOCIATION, 27 Oakfield Road, Clifton, Bristol BS8 2AT. Tel: 0117-974 4491. *Company Secretary*, M. D. Blake

*WORLD LADIES BILLIARDS AND SNOOKER ASSOCIATION, 3 Sywell Grove, Elm, Wisbech, Cambs. PE14 0BN. Tel: 01945-860545. *Secretary*, Ms M. Fisher

*Bobsleigh*

*BRITISH BOBSLEIGH ASSOCIATION, Springfield House, 7 Woodstock Road, Coulsdon, Surrey CR5 3HS. Tel: 01737-555152. *Secretary*, P. Pruszynski

*Bowls*

*BRITISH ISLES BOWLING COUNCIL, 28 Woodford Park, Lurgan, Co. Armagh BT66 7HA. Tel: 01762-322036. *Hon. Secretary*, W. A. Gracey

*BRITISH ISLES INDOOR BOWLING COUNCIL, 9 Highlights Lane, Barry, S. Glamorgan CF6 5AA. Tel: 01446-733978. *Secretary*, J. R. Thomas

*BRITISH ISLES WOMEN'S BOWLING COUNCIL, 2 Case Gardens, Seaton, Devon EX12 2AP. Tel: 01297-21317. *Hon. Secretary*, Ms N. Colling

*BRITISH ISLES WOMEN'S INDOOR BOWLS COUNCIL, 16 Windsor Crescent, Radyr, Cardiff CF4 8AE. Tel: 01222-842391. *Hon. Secretary*, Ms J. Johns

*ENGLISH BOWLING ASSOCIATION, Lyndhurst Road, Worthing, W. Sussex BN11 2AZ. Tel: 01903-820222. *Secretary*, D. Johnson
*ENGLISH WOMEN'S BOWLING ASSOCIATION, 2 Case Gardens, Seaton, Devon EX12 2AP. Tel: 01297-21317. *Hon. Secretary*, Ms N. Colling

*Boxing*
*AMATEUR BOXING ASSOCIATION OF ENGLAND LTD, Crystal Palace National Sports Centre, London SE19 2BB. Tel: 0181-778 0251. *Secretary*, C. Brown
*BRITISH BOXING BOARD OF CONTROL LTD, Jack Petersen House, 52A Borough High Street, London SE1 1XW. Tel: 0171-403 5879. *General Secretary*, J. Morris
*BRITISH AMATEUR BOXING ASSOCIATION, 96 High Street, Lochee, Dundee DD2 3AY. Tel: 01382-611412. *Chief Executive*, F. Hendry

*Canoeing*
*BRITISH CANOE UNION, John Dudderidge House, Adbolton Lane, West Bridgford, Nottingham NG2 5AS. Tel: 0115-982 1100. *Director*, P. Owen

*Chess*
*BRITISH CHESS FEDERATION, 9A Grand Parade, St Leonard's-on-Sea, E. Sussex TN38 0DD. Tel: 01424-442500. *General Manager*, Mrs G. White

*Clay Pigeon Shooting*
*CLAY PIGEON SHOOTING ASSOCIATION, 107 Epping New Road, Buckhurst Hill, Essex IG9 5TQ. Tel: 0181-505 6221. *Director*, E. Orduna

*Cricket*
*CRICKET COUNCIL, Lord's, London NW8 8QZ. Tel: 0171-286 4405. *Chairman*, D. R. W. Silk; *Secretary*, A. C. Smith
MCC, Lords, London NW8 8QN. Tel: 0171-289 1611. *President*, The Hon. Sir Oliver Popplewell; *Secretary*, R. Knight
TEST AND COUNTY CRICKET BOARD, Lord's, London NW8 8QZ. Tel: 0171-286 4405. *Chairman* (1994–5), D. R. W. Silk; *Chief Executive*, A. C. Smith

*Croquet*
*CROQUET ASSOCIATION, c/o The Hurlingham Club, Ranelagh Gardens, London SW6 3PR. Tel: 0171-736 3148. *Secretary*, L. W. D. Antenen

*Cycling*
*BRITISH CYCLING FEDERATION, 36 Rockingham Road, Kettering, Northants. NN16 8HG. Tel: 01536-412211. *Chief Executive*, J. Hendry
*ROAD TIME TRIALS COUNCIL, 77 Arlington Drive, Pennington, Leigh, Lancs. WN7 3QP. Tel: 01942-603976. *National Secretary*, P. Heaton

*Diving*
*GREAT BRITAIN DIVING FEDERATION, PO Box 222, Batley, W. Yorks. WF17 8XD. Tel: 01924-422322. *Director of Administration*, J. Cryer

*Equestrianism*
*BRITISH EQUESTRIAN FEDERATION, British Equestrian Centre, Stoneleigh Park, Kenilworth, Warks. CV8 2LR. Tel: 01203-696697. *Director-General*, vacant

*Eton Fives*
*ETON FIVES ASSOCIATION, Welches, Bentley, Farnham, Surrey GU10 5HZ. Tel: 01420-22107. *Hon. Secretary*, M. P. Powell

*Fencing*
*AMATEUR FENCING ASSOCIATION, 1 Barons Gate, 33–35 Rothschild Road, London W4 5HT. Tel: 0181-742 3032. *Secretary*, Miss G. Kenneally

*Gliding*
*BRITISH GLIDING ASSOCIATION, Kimberley House, Vaughan Way, Leicester LE1 4SE. Tel: 0116-253 1051. *Secretary*, B. Rolfe

*Golf*
*ROYAL AND ANCIENT GOLF CLUB, St Andrews, Fife KY16 9JD. Tel: 01334-472112. *Secretary*, M. F. Bonallack, OBE
*LADIES' GOLF UNION, The Scores, St Andrews, Fife KY16 9AT. Tel: 01334-475811. *Administrator*, Mrs E. A. Mackie

*Greyhound Racing*
*NATIONAL GREYHOUND RACING CLUB LTD, 24–28 Oval Road, London NW1 7DA. Tel: 0171-267 9256. *Senior Stipendiary Steward*, F. Melville

*Gymnastics*
*BRITISH AMATEUR GYMNASTICS ASSOCIATION, Ford Hall, Lilleshall National Sports Centre, nr. Newport, Shropshire TF10 9NB. Tel: 01952-820330. *General Secretary*, D. Minnery

*Hockey*
*HOCKEY ASSOCIATION, Norfolk House, 102 Saxon Gate West, Milton Keynes MK9 2EP. Tel: 01908-241100. *Chief Executive*, S. P. Baines
*ALL ENGLAND WOMEN'S HOCKEY ASSOCIATION, 51 High Street, Shrewsbury SY1 1ST. Tel: 01743-233572. *Executive Director*, Miss T. Morris
*SCOTTISH HOCKEY UNION, 48 The Pleasance, Edinburgh EH8 9TJ. Tel: 0131-650-8170. *Chairman*, Mrs E. Raistrick
*WELSH HOCKEY ASSOCIATION, 1 White Hart Lane, Caerleon, Gwent NP6 1AB. Tel: 01633-420326. *Secretary*, J. G. Williams
*WELSH WOMEN'S HOCKEY ASSOCIATION, Welsh Hockey Office, Deeside Leisure Centre, Chester Road West, Deeside, Clwyd CH5 1SA. Tel: 01244-811825. *President*, Miss A. Ellis, MBE

*Horseracing*
*BRITISH HORSERACING BOARD, 42 Portman Square, London W1H 0EN. Tel: 0171-396 0011. *Chief Executive*, R. T. Ricketts
THE JOCKEY CLUB, 42 Portman Square, London W1H 0EN. Tel: 0171-486 4921. *Senior Steward*, Sir Thomas Pilkington, Bt.

*Ice Hockey*
*BRITISH ICE HOCKEY ASSOCIATION, Second Floor Offices, 517 Christchurch Road, Boscombe, Bournemouth BH1 4AG. Tel: 01202-303946. *General Secretary*, D. Pickles

*Ice Skating*
*NATIONAL SKATING ASSOCIATION OF THE UNITED KINGDOM LTD, 15–27 Gee Street, London EC1V 3RE. Tel: 0171-253 3824. *President*, C. J. L. Jones, OBE

*Judo*
*BRITISH JUDO ASSOCIATION, 7A Rutland Street, Leicester LE1 1RB. Tel: 0116-255 9669. *Office Manager*, Ms S. Startin

*Lacrosse*
*ENGLISH LACROSSE UNION, 70 High Road, Rayleigh, Essex SS6 7AD. Tel: 01268-770758. *Hon. Secretary*, R. Balls
*ALL ENGLAND WOMEN'S LACROSSE ASSOCIATION, 4 Western Court, Bromley Street, Digbeth, Birmingham B9 4AN. Tel: 0121-773 4422. *Administrator*, Ms A. Chesses

*Lawn Tennis*
*LAWN TENNIS ASSOCIATION, The Queen's Club, London W14 9EG. Tel: 0171-381 7000. *Secretary*, J. C. U. James

*Lugeing*
*GREAT BRITAIN LUGE ASSOCIATION, Mortimer House, Holmer Road, Hereford HR4 9SB. Tel: 01432-353539. *General Secretary*, J. G. Evans

*Martial Arts*
MARTIAL ARTS DEVELOPMENT COMMISSION, PO Box 381, Erith, Kent DA8 1TF. Tel: 01322-431 440. *Office Administrator*, Mrs E. Jewell

*Motor Sports*
*AUTO-CYCLE UNION, ACU House, Wood Street, Rugby, Warks. CV21 2YX. Tel: 01788-540519. *Chief Executive*, D. R. Barnfield
*RAC MOTOR SPORTS ASSOCIATION LTD, Motor Sports House, Riverside Park, Colnbrook, Slough SL3 0HG. Tel: 01753-681736. *Chief Executive*, J. R. Quenby
*SCOTTISH AUTO CYCLE UNION LTD, Block 2, Unit 6, Whiteside Industrial Estate, Bathgate, West Lothian EH48 2RX. Tel: 01506-630262. *Secretary*, A. M. Brownlie

*Mountaineering*
*BRITISH MOUNTAINEERING COUNCIL, Crawford House, Precinct Centre, Booth Street East, Manchester M13 9GH. Tel: 0161-273 5835. *General Secretary*, D. Walker

*Multi-Sport Bodies*
BRITISH OLYMPIC ASSOCIATION, 1 Wandsworth Plain, London SW18 1EH. Tel: 0181-871 2677. *General Secretary*, R. Palmer, OBE
COMMONWEALTH GAMES COUNCIL FOR ENGLAND, 1 Wandsworth Plain, London SW18 1EH. Tel: 0181-877 3346. *General Secretary*, Ms A. Hogbin
COMMONWEALTH GAMES FEDERATION, Walkden House, 3–10 Melton Street, London NW1 2EB. Tel: 0171-383 5596. *Hon. Secretary*, D. Dixon, CVO
BRITISH UNIVERSITIES SPORTS ASSOCIATION, 11 Allcock Street, Birmingham B9 4DY. Tel: 0121-766 8855. *Chief Executive*, G. Gregory-Jones

*Netball*
*ALL ENGLAND NETBALL ASSOCIATION, Netball House, 9 Paynes Park, Hitchin, Herts. SG5 1EH. Tel: 01462-442344. *Chief Executive*, Mrs E. M. Nicholl
*SCOTTISH NETBALL ASSOCIATION, Kelvin Hall Sports Complex, Argyle Street, Glasgow G3 8AW. Tel: 0141-334 3650. *Administrator*, Ms M. Spence
*WELSH NETBALL ASSOCIATION, 82 Cathedral Road, Cardiff CF1 9LN. Tel: 01222-237048. *Chairman*, Mrs P. J. Lane

*Orienteering*
*BRITISH ORIENTEERING FEDERATION, Riversdale, Dale Road North, Darley Dale, Matlock, Derbyshire DE4 2HX. Tel: 01629-734042. *Manager*, Mrs H. Gregson

*Polo*
*HURLINGHAM POLO ASSOCIATION, Winterlake, Kirtlington, Kidlington, Oxon. OX5 3HG. Tel: 01869-350044. *Secretary*, J. W. M. Crisp

*Rackets and Real Tennis*
*TENNIS AND RACKETS ASSOCIATION, c/o The Queen's Club, Palliser Road, London W14 9EQ. Tel: 0171-386 3447. *Chief Executive*, Brig. A. D. Myrtle, CB, CBE

*Rifle Shooting*
*NATIONAL RIFLE ASSOCIATION, Bisley Camp, Brookwood, Woking GU24 0PB. Tel: 01483-797777. *Chief Executive*, Col. C. A. Ewing, OBE
*NATIONAL SMALL-BORE RIFLE ASSOCIATION, Lord Roberts House, Bisley Camp, Brookwood, Woking GU24 0NP. Tel: 01483-476969. *Secretary*, Lt.-Col. J. D. Hoare

*Rowing*
*AMATEUR ROWING ASSOCIATION LTD, The Priory, 6 Lower Mall, London W6 9DJ. Tel: 0181-748 3632. *Senior Administrative Officer*, Mrs R. Napp
HENLEY ROYAL REGATTA, Regatta Headquarters, Henley-on-Thames, Oxon. RG9 2LY. Tel: 01491-572153. *Secretary*, R. S. Goddard
SCOTTISH AMATEUR ROWING ASSOCIATION, 134 Newton Street, Greenock PA16 8SJ. Tel: 01475-22996. *Secretary*, Mrs M. Pow
*WELSH AMATEUR ROWING ASSOCIATION, 15 Kingfisher Close, St Mellons, Cardiff CF3 0DD. Tel: 01222-777389. *Hon. Secretary*, M. Nhatiw

*Rugby Fives*
*RUGBY FIVES ASSOCIATION, The Old Forge, Sutton Valence, Maidstone, Kent ME17 3AW. Tel: 01622-842278. *General Secretary*, M. F. Beaman

*Rugby League*
*RUGBY FOOTBALL LEAGUE, 180 Chapeltown Road, Leeds LS7 4HT. Tel: 0113-262 4637. *Chief Executive*, M. P. Lindsay
*BRITISH AMATEUR RUGBY LEAGUE ASSOCIATION, West Yorkshire House, 4 New North Parade, Huddersfield HD1 5JP. Tel: 01484-544131. *Chief Executive*, M. F. Oldroyd

*Rugby Union*
*RUGBY FOOTBALL UNION, Twickenham TW1 1DZ. Tel: 0181-892 8161. *Secretary*, D. E. Wood
*SCOTTISH RUGBY UNION, Murrayfield, Edinburgh EH12 5PJ. Tel: 0131-346 5000. *Chief Executive*, I. A. L. Hogg
*WELSH RUGBY UNION, Cardiff Arms Park, PO Box 22, Westgate Street, Cardiff CF1 1JL. Tel: 01222-390111. *Secretary*, E. H. Jones.
*IRISH RUGBY FOOTBALL UNION, 62 Lansdowne Road, Dublin 4, Republic of Ireland. Tel: 00 353-16-684601. *Secretary*, P. J. O'Donoghue
RUGBY FOOTBALL UNION FOR WOMEN (ENGLAND), 33 Rice Mews, St Thomas, Exeter EX2 9AY. Tel: 01392-221754. *Secretary*, Ms S. Eakers
SCOTTISH WOMEN'S RUGBY UNION, 11 Bavelaw Crescent, Penicuik, Midlothian EH26 9AX. Tel: 01968-673355. *Secretary*, Ms M. Sharp
WELSH WOMEN'S RUGBY UNION, 40 Wolseley Street, Pillwenlly, Gwent NP9 2HP. Tel: 01633-220249. *Secretary*, Ms F. Margerison
IRISH WOMEN'S RUGBY UNION, 31 Ashley Drive, Belfast BT9 7BE. Tel: 01232-664363. *Secretary*, Ms J. Hall

*Snooker*
*WORLD PROFESSIONAL BILLIARDS AND SNOOKER ASSOCIATION, 27 Oakfield Road, Clifton, Bristol BS8 2AT. Tel: 0117-974 4491. *Company Secretary*, M. D. Blake
*WORLD LADIES BILLIARDS AND SNOOKER ASSOCIATION, 3 Felsted Avenue, Wisbech, Cambs. PE13 3SL. Tel: 01945-589589. *Chairman*, Ms M. Fisher

*Speedway*

*SPEEDWAY CONTROL BOARD, ACU Headquarters, Wood Street, Rugby, Warks. CV21 2YX. Tel: 01788-560648. *Manager*, G. Reeve

*Squash Rackets*

*SQUASH RACKETS ASSOCIATION, Westpoint, 33–34 Warple Way, London W3 0RG. Tel: 0181-746 1616. *Chairman*, C. Grimley

*SCOTTISH SQUASH, Caledonia House, South Gyle, Edinburgh EH12 9DQ. Tel: 0131-317 7343. *Secretary*, N. Brydon

*WELSH SQUASH RACKETS FEDERATION, 7 Kymin Terrace, Penarth, South Glamorgan CF6 1AP. Tel: 01222-704096. *Chairman*, D. Gadsby

BRITISH SQUASH PROFESSIONALS' ASSOCIATION, 16 Station Road, Chingford, London E4 7BE. Tel: 0181-523 7019. *Chief Executive*, C. Walker

*Swimming*

*AMATEUR SWIMMING ASSOCIATION, Harold Fern House, Derby Square, Loughborough, Leics. LE11 0AL. Tel: 0116-223 0431. *Director of Operations*, D. Sparkes

*SCOTTISH AMATEUR SWIMMING ASSOCIATION, Holmhills Farm, Greenlees Road, Cambuslang, Glasgow G72 8DT. Tel: 0141-641 8818. *Administration Manager*, Mrs E. Mackenzie

*WELSH AMATEUR SWIMMING ASSOCIATION, Wales Empire Pool, Wood Street, Cardiff CF1 1PP. Tel: 01222-342201. *Hon. General Secretary*, P. Rees

*BRITISH SUB-AQUA CLUB, Telfords Quay, Ellesmere Port, South Wirral, Cheshire L65 4FY. Tel: 0151-357 1951. *Chairman*, H. Painter

*Table Tennis*

*ENGLISH TABLE TENNIS ASSOCIATION, Queensbury House, Havelock Road, Hastings TN34 1HF. Tel: 01424-722525. *Chief Executive*, vacant

*Volleyball*

*ENGLISH VOLLEYBALL ASSOCIATION, 27 South Road, West Bridgford, Nottingham NG2 7AG. Tel: 0115-981 6324. *National Director*, G. Bulman

*SCOTTISH VOLLEYBALL ASSOCIATION, 48 The Pleasance, Edinburgh EH8 9TJ. Tel: 0131-556 4633. *Director*, N. S. Moody

*WELSH VOLLEYBALL ASSOCIATION, 70 Swakeleys Road, Ickenham, Uxbridge, Middlesex UB10 8BD. Tel: 01895-673369. *Secretary*, B. Goodman

*Walking*

*RACE WALKING ASSOCIATION. Hufflers, Heard's Lane, Shenfield, Brentwood, Essex CM15 0SF. Tel: 01277-220687. *Hon. Secretary*, P. J. Cassidy

*Water Skiing*

*BRITISH WATER SKI FEDERATION, 390 City Road, London EC1V 2QA. Tel: 0171-833 2855. *Executive Officer*, Ms G. Hill

*Weightlifting*

*BRITISH AMATEUR WEIGHTLIFTERS ASSOCIATION, 3 Iffley Turn, Oxford OX4 4DU. Tel: 01865-778319. *Hon. Secretary*, W. Holland, OBE

*Wrestling*

*BRITISH AMATEUR WRESTLING ASSOCIATION, 41 Great Clowes Street, Salford, Manchester M7 9RQ. Tel: 0161-832 9209. *Development and Public Relations Officer*, R. Tomlinson

*Yachting*

*ROYAL YACHTING ASSOCIATION, RYA House, Romsey Road, Eastleigh, Hants. SO50 9YA. Tel: 01703-629962. *Secretary-General*, R. Duchesne, OBE

# Clubs

ROYAL THAMES YACHT CLUB (1775), 60 Knightsbridge, London SW1X 7LF. Tel: 0171-235 2121. *Secretary*, Capt. D. Goldson, RN (retd)

ST STEPHEN'S CONSTITUTIONAL CLUB (1870), 34 Queen Anne's Gate, London SW1H 9AB. Tel: 0171-222 1382. *Secretary*, L. D. Mawby

SAVAGE CLUB (1857), 1 Whitehall Place, London SW1A 2HD. Tel: 0171-930 8118. *Hon. Secretary*, D. Stirling

SAVILE CLUB (1868), 69 Brook Street, London W1Y 2ER. Tel: 0171-629 5462. *Secretary*, N. Storey

SKI CLUB OF GREAT BRITAIN (1903), 118 Eaton Square, London SW1W 9AF. Tel: 0171-245 1033. *Chief Executive*, Ms I. Grimsey

THAMES ROWING CLUB (1860), Embankment, Putney, London SW15 1LB. Tel: 0181-788 0798. *Hon. Secretary*, Mrs N. S. Powell

TRAVELLERS' CLUB (1819), 106 Pall Mall, London SW1Y 5EP. Tel: 0171-930 8688. *Secretary*, M. S. Allcock

TURF CLUB (1868), 5 Carlton House Terrace, London SW1Y 5AQ. Tel: 0171-930 8555. *Secretary*, J. Rigby, OBE

UNITED OXFORD AND CAMBRIDGE UNIVERSITY CLUB (1972), 71 Pall Mall, London SW1Y 5HD. Tel: 0171-930 5151. *General Secretary*, G. R. Buchanan

UNIVERSITY WOMEN'S CLUB (1886), 2 Audley Square, London W1Y 6DB. Tel: 0171-499 2268. *Secretary*, J. Robson

VICTORIA CLUB (1863), 1 North Court, Great Peter Street, London SW1P 3LL. Tel: 0171-222 2357. *Secretary*, Ms H. David

VICTORY SERVICES CLUB (1907), 63–79 Seymour Street, London W2 2HF. Tel: 0171-723 4474. *General Manager*, G. F. Taylor

WHITE'S CLUB (1693), 37–38 St James's Street, London SW1A 1JG. Tel: 0171-493 6671. *Secretary*, D. C. Ward

WIG AND PEN CLUB (1908), 229–230 Strand, London WC2R 1BA. Tel: 0171-583 7255. *Administrator*, J. Reynolds

## CLUBS OUTSIDE LONDON

*Bath:* BATH AND COUNTY CLUB (1865), Queens Parade, Bath, BA1 2NJ. Tel: 01225-423732. *Secretary*, Mrs G. M. Jones

*Birmingham:* BIRMINGHAM CLUB (1872), Winston Churchill House, 8 Ethel Street, Birmingham B2 4BG. Tel: 0121-643 3357. *Hon. Secretary*, T. R. Pepper

ST PAUL'S CLUB (1859), 34 St Paul's Square, Birmingham B3 1QZ. Tel: 0121-236 1950. *Hon. Secretary*, E. A. Fellowes

*Bishop Auckland:* THE CLUB (1868), 1 Victoria Avenue, Bishop Auckland, Co. Durham DL14 7JH. Tel: 01388-603219. *Hon. Secretary*, R. Kellett

*Blackburn:* DISTRICT AND UNION CLUB (1849), Northwood, 1 West Park Road, Blackburn BB2 6DE. Tel: 01254-51474. *Hon. Secretary*, B. Haydock

*Bristol:* CLIFTON CLUB (1882), 22 The Mall, Clifton, Bristol BS8 4DS. Tel: 0117-973 5527. *Secretary*, M. H. Titcomb

*Cambridge:* AMATEUR DRAMATIC CLUB (1855), ADC Theatre, Park Street, Cambridge CB5 8AS. Tel: 01223-359547. *Secretary*, M. Mitchell

THE UNION (1815), Bridge Street, Cambridge CB2 1UB. Tel: 01223-61521. *Chief Clerk*, B. Thoday

*Canterbury:* KENT AND CANTERBURY CLUB (1868), The Elms, 17 Old Dover Road, Canterbury CT1 3JB. Tel: 01227-462181. *Secretary*, H. V. Brown, LVO, QPM, CPM

*Cheltenham:* NEW CLUB (1874), Montpellier Parade, Cheltenham GL50 1UD. Tel: 01242-523285. *Hon. Secretary*, N. S. Parrack

*Chichester:* THE REGNUM CLUB (1862), 45A South Street, Chichester, W. Sussex PO19 1DS. Tel: 01243-780219. *Chairman*, M. Pearson

*Durham:* COUNTY CLUB (1890), 52 Old Elvet, Durham. Tel: 0191-384 1679. *Secretary*, Mrs C. Arnot

DURHAM UNION SOCIETY (1842), 24 North Bailey, Durham DH1 3EP. Tel: 0191-384 3724. *Secretary*, Mrs E. M. Hardcastle

*Guildford:* COUNTY CLUB, 158 High Street, Guildford GU1 3HJ. Tel: 01483-575370. *Hon. Secretary*, R. W. D. Hemingway

*Henley-on-Thames:* LEANDER CLUB (1818), Henley-on-Thames, Oxon. RG9 2LP. Tel: 01491-575782. *Hon. Secretary*, J. Beveridge

PHYLLIS COURT CLUB (1906), Marlow Road, Henley, Oxon. RG9 2HT. Tel: 01491-574366. *Secretary*, D. M. Brockett

*Hove:* HOVE CLUB (1882), 28 Fourth Avenue, Hove, E. Sussex BN3 2PJ. Tel: 01273-730872. *Secretary*, J. C. Ager, RD

*Leamington:* TENNIS COURT CLUB (1846), 50 Bedford Street, Leamington, Warks. CV32 5DT. Tel: 01926-424977. *Hon. Secretary*, O. D. R. Dixon

*Leeds:* LEEDS CLUB (1850), 3 Albion Place, Leeds LS1 6JL. Tel: 0113-242 1591. *Manager*, Mrs C. Myers

*Leicester:* LEICESTERSHIRE CLUB (1873), 9 Welford Place, Leicester LE1 6ZH. Tel: 0116-254 0399. *Hon. Secretary*, G. C. Jones

*Liverpool:* THE ATHENAEUM (1797), Church Alley, Liverpool L1 3DD. Tel: 0151-709 7770. *Permanent Secretary*, B. B. P. Kinsman

*Macclesfield:* OLD BOYS' AND PARK GREEN CLUB, 7 Churchside, Macclesfield, Cheshire SK10 1HG. Tel: 01625-423292. *Hon. Secretary*, Dr P. R. Baker, MBE

*Manchester:* ST JAMES'S CLUB, St James's House, Charlotte Street, Manchester M1 4DZ. Tel: 0161-236 2235. *Hon. Secretary*, R. H. C. Nichols

*Newcastle upon Tyne:* NORTHERN CONSTITUTIONAL CLUB (1882), 37 Pilgrim Street, Newcastle upon Tyne NE1 6QE. Tel: 0191-232 0884. *Hon. Secretary*, J. L. Browne

*Northampton:* NORTHAMPTON AND COUNTY CLUB (1873), George Row, Northampton NN1 1DF. Tel: 01604-32962. *Secretary*, J. Green

*Norwich:* NORFOLK CLUB (1770), 17 Upper King Street, Norwich NR3 1RB. Tel: 01603-610652. *Secretary*, A. J. M. Williamson

*Nottingham:* NOTTINGHAM AND NOTTS UNITED SERVICES CLUB (1920), Newdigate House, Castle Gate, Nottingham NG1 6AF. Tel: 0115-947 2138. *Hon. Secretary*, A. C. Ready

*Oxford:* FREWEN CLUB (1869), 98 St Aldate's, Oxford OX1 1BT. Tel: 01865-243816. *Hon. Secretary*, B. R. Boyt

VINCENT'S CLUB (1863), 1A King Edward Street, Oxford OX1 4HS. Tel: 01865-722984. *Steward*, H. Dean

*Paignton:* PAIGNTON CLUB (1882), The Esplanade, Paignton, Devon TQ4 6ED. Tel: 01803-559682. *Hon. Secretary*, P. Grafton

*Shrewsbury:* SALOP CLUB (1974), The Old House, Dogpole, Shrewsbury SY1 1EP. Tel: 01743-362182. *Secretary*, J. W. Rouse

*Stourbridge:* STOURBRIDGE OLD EDWARDIAN CLUB (1898), Drury Lane, Stourbridge, West Midlands DY8 1BL. Tel: 01384-395635. *Hon. Secretary*, J. V. Sanders

*Teddington:* ROYAL CANOE CLUB (1866), Trowlock Island, Teddington, Middx. TW11 9QZ. Tel: 0181-977 5269. *Hon. Secretary,* Mrs J. S. Evans

*York:* YORKSHIRE CLUB (1839), 17 Museum Street, York YO1 2DW. Tel: 01904-624116. *Hon. Secretary,* D. E. Gabbitas

## WALES

*Cardiff:* CARDIFF AND COUNTY CLUB (1866), Westgate Street, Cardiff CF1 1DA. Tel: 01222-220846. *Hon. Secretary,* Cdr. J. E. Payn, RD

## SCOTLAND

*Aberdeen:* ROYAL NORTHERN AND UNIVERSITY CLUB (1854/1889, amal. 1979), 9 Albyn Place, Aberdeen AB1 1YE. Tel: 01224-583292. *Secretary,* Miss R. A. Black

*Ayr:* AYR COUNTY CLUB (1872), Savoy Park Hotel, Ayr KA7 2XA. Tel: 01292-266112. *Hon. Secretary,* G. Hay

*Edinburgh:* CALEDONIAN CLUB (1825), 32 Abercromby Place, Edinburgh EH3 6QE. Tel: 0131-557 2675. *Secretary,* Ms F. Fowler

NEW CLUB (1787), 86 Princes Street, Edinburgh EH2 2BB. Tel: 0131-226 4881. *Secretary,* A. D. Orr Ewing

*Glasgow:* GLASGOW ART CLUB (1867), 135 Wellington Street, Glasgow G2 2XE. Tel: 0141-248 3904. *Secretary,* L. J. McIntyre

ROYAL SCOTTISH AUTOMOBILE CLUB (1899), 11 Blythswood Square, Glasgow G2 4AG. Tel: 0141-221 3850. *Secretary,* J. C. Lord

WESTERN CLUB (1825), 32 Royal Exchange Square, Glasgow G1 3AB. Tel: 0141-221 2016. *Secretary,* D. H. Gifford

## NORTHERN IRELAND

*Belfast:* ULSTER REFORM CLUB (1885), 4 Royal Avenue, Belfast BT1 1DA. Tel: 01232-323411. *Secretary,* Miss M. P. Mackintosh

*Londonderry:* NORTHERN COUNTIES CLUB (1880), 24 Bishop Street, Londonderry BT48 6PP. Tel: 01504-262012. *Hon. Secretary,* N. Dykes

## CHANNEL ISLANDS

*Guernsey:* UNITED CLUB (1870), Pier Steps, St Peter Port, Guernsey GY1 2LF. Tel: 01481-725722. *Secretary,* G. D. E. Chaloner

*Jersey:* VICTORIA CLUB (1853), Beresford Street, St Helier, Jersey JE2 4WN. Tel: 01534-23381. *Secretary,* Miss C. Rynd

## YACHT CLUBS

*Bembridge:* BEMBRIDGE SAILING CLUB (1886), Embankment Road, Bembridge, IOW, PO35 5NR. Tel: 01983-872237. *Hon. Secretary,* C. W. Barstow

*Birkenhead:* ROYAL MERSEY YACHT CLUB (1844), Bedford Road East, Rock Ferry, Birkenhead, Merseyside L42 1LS. Tel: 0151-645 3204. *Hon. Secretary,* A. Tetley

*Bridlington:* ROYAL YORKSHIRE YACHT CLUB (1847), 1 Windsor Crescent, Bridlington, N. Humberside YO15 3HX. Tel: 01262-672041. *Secretary,* J. H. Evans

*Burnham-on-Crouch:* ROYAL CORINTHIAN YACHT CLUB (1872), Burnham-on-Crouch, Essex CM0 8AX. Tel: 01621-782105. *Hon. Secretary,* K. W. Bushell

*Chichester:* CHICHESTER YACHT CLUB (1965), Chichester Yacht Basin, Birdham, Chichester, W. Sussex PO20 7EJ. Tel: 01243-512918

*Cowes:* ROYAL YACHT SQUADRON (1815), The Castle, Cowes, IOW, PO31 7QT. Tel: 01983-292191. *Secretary,* Maj. R. P. Rising, RM

ROYAL LONDON YACHT CLUB (1838), The Parade, Cowes, IOW, PO31 7QS. Tel: 01983-299727. *Secretary,* Lt.-Col. R. J. Freeman-Wallace (retd)

*Dover:* ROYAL CINQUE PORTS YACHT CLUB (1872), 5 Waterloo Crescent, Dover, Kent CT16 1LA. Tel: 01304-206262. *Secretary,* Mrs S. Relf

*Fishbourne:* ROYAL VICTORIA YACHT CLUB (1844), Fishbourne Lane, Ryde, IOW, PO33 4EU. Tel: 01983-882325. *Hon. Secretary,* Ms H. Vrba

*Fowey:* ROYAL FOWEY YACHT CLUB (1881), Whitford Yard, Fowey, Cornwall PL23 1BH. Tel: 01726-833573. *Hon. Secretary,* E. P. Warren

*Harwich:* ROYAL HARWICH YACHT CLUB (1843), Woolverstone, Ipswich IP9 1AT. Tel: 01473-780319. *Secretary,* I. A. Murdoch

*Kingswear:* ROYAL DART YACHT CLUB (1866), Priory Street, Kingswear, Dartmouth, Devon TQ6 0AB. Tel: 01803-752496. *Hon. Secretary,* Dr N. Baxter

*Leigh-on-Sea:* ESSEX YACHT CLUB (1890), HQS Bembridge, Foreshore, Leigh-on-Sea, Essex SS9 1BD. Tel: 01702-78404. *Hon. Secretary,* A. Manning

*London:* THE CRUISING ASSOCIATION (1908), Ivory House, St Katharine Dock, London E1 9AT. Tel: 0171-481 0881. *General Secretary,* Mrs L. Hammett

ROYAL CRUISING CLUB (1880), c/o Royal Thames Yacht Club, 60 Knightsbridge, London SW1X 7LF. Tel: 01276-65946. *Hon. Secretary,* P. Price

ROYAL THAMES YACHT CLUB (1775), 60 Knightsbridge, London SW1X 7LF. Tel: 0171-235 2121. *Secretary,* Capt. D. Goldson, RN (retd)

*Lowestoft:* ROYAL NORFOLK AND SUFFOLK YACHT CLUB (1859), Royal Plain, Lowestoft, Suffolk NR33 0AQ. Tel: 01502-566726. *Hon. Secretary,* A. Donovan

*Lymington:* ROYAL LYMINGTON YACHT CLUB (1922), Bath Road, Lymington, Hants SO41 9SE. Tel: 01590-672677. *Secretary,* Gp Capt J. D. Hutchinson (retd)

*Plymouth:* ROYAL WESTERN YACHT CLUB (1827), Queen Anne's Battery, Plymouth PL4 0TW. Tel: 01752-660077. *Secretary,* Maj. J. Lewis, RM

ROYAL PLYMOUTH CORINTHIAN YACHT CLUB (1877), Madeira Road, Plymouth PL1 2NY. Tel: 01752-664327. *Hon. Secretary,* V. J. De Boo

*Poole:* EAST DORSET SAILING CLUB (1875), 352 Sandbanks Road, Poole, Dorset BH14 8HY. Tel: 01202-706111. *Hon. Secretary,* Ms H. Knott

PARKSTONE YACHT CLUB (1895), Pearce Avenue, Parkstone, Poole, Dorset BH14 8EH. Tel: 01202-743610. *Secretary,* D. E. Norman

POOLE HARBOUR YACHT CLUB (1949), 38 Salterns Way, Lilliput, Poole, Dorset BH14 8JR. Tel: 01202-707321. *Secretary,* J. N. J. Smith

POOLE YACHT CLUB (1865), New Harbour Road West, Hamworthy, Poole, Dorset BH15 4AQ. Tel: 01202-672687. *Secretary/Manager,* Miss L. Clark

*Portsmouth:* ROYAL NAVAL CLUB AND ROYAL ALBERT YACHT CLUB (1867), 17 Pembroke Road, Portsmouth PO1 2NT. Tel: 01705-824491. *Secretary,* Cdr. N. J. Stone, OBE

*Ramsgate:* ROYAL TEMPLE YACHT CLUB (1857), 6 Westcliff Mansions, Ramsgate, Kent CT11 9HY. Tel: 01843-591766. *Hon. Secretary,* G. F. Randell

*Southampton:* ROYAL AIR FORCE YACHT CLUB (1932),
Riverside House, Rope Walk, Hamble, Southampton
SO31 4HD. Tel: 01703-452208. *Secretary,* Miss
A. R. Prees
ROYAL SOUTHAMPTON YACHT CLUB, 1 Channel Way,
Ocean Village, Southampton SO1 1XE. Tel: 01703-223352.
*President,* Cdre C. R. Basche
ROYAL SOUTHERN YACHT CLUB (1837), Rope Walk,
Hamble, Southampton SO31 4HB. Tel: 01703-453271.
*Secretary,* Mrs J. A. Atkins
*Torquay:* ROYAL TORBAY YACHT CLUB (1863), Beacon
Hill, Torquay, Devon TQ1 2BQ. Tel: 01803-292006. *Hon.*
*Secretary,* J. N. Carleton-Stiff, TD
*Westcliff-on-Sea:* THAMES ESTUARY YACHT CLUB (1895),
3 The Leas, Westcliff-on-Sea, Essex SS0 7ST. Tel: 01702-
345967. *Hon. Secretary,* D. Howard
*Weymouth:* ROYAL DORSET YACHT CLUB (1875),
11 Custom House Quay, Weymouth, Dorset DT4 8BG.
Tel: 01305-786258. *Secretary,* Mrs K. Mead
*Windermere:* ROYAL WINDERMERE YACHT CLUB (1860),
Fallbarrow Road, Bowness-on-Windermere,
Windermere, Cumbria LA23 3DJ. Tel: 015394-43106.
*Hon. Secretary,* M. C. Bentley
*Yarmouth:* ROYAL SOLENT YACHT CLUB (1878),
Yarmouth, IOW, PO41 0NS. Tel: 01983-760256.
*Secretary,* Mrs S. Tribe

## WALES

*Beaumaris:* ROYAL ANGLESEY YACHT CLUB (1802),
6–7 Green Edge, Beaumaris, Gwynedd LL58 8BY. Tel:
01248-810295. *Hon. Secretary,* V. G. Keep
*Caernarfon:* ROYAL WELSH YACHT CLUB (1847), Porth-
Yr-Aur, Caernarfon, Gwynedd LL55 1SW. Tel: 01286-
672599. *Hon. Secretary,* G. Tecwyn Evans
*Penarth:* PENARTH YACHT CLUB (1880). The Esplanade,
Penarth, S. Glamorgan CF64 3AU. Tel: 01222-708196.
*Hon. Secretary,* R. S. McGregor
*Swansea:* BRISTOL CHANNEL YACHT CLUB (1875),
744 Mumbles Road, Mumbles, Swansea SA3 4EL. Tel:
01792-366000. *Hon. Secretary,* B. G. T. Rees

## SCOTLAND

*Dundee:* ROYAL TAY YACHT CLUB (1885), 34 Dundee
Road, Broughty Ferry, Dundee DD5 1LX. Tel: 01382-
77516. *Hon. Secretary,* Dr G. R. Foster
*Edinburgh:* ROYAL FORTH YACHT CLUB (1868), Middle
Pier, Granton Harbour, Edinburgh EH5 1HF. Tel: 0131-
552 8560. *Hon. Secretary,* A. R. Woods
*Glasgow:* ROYAL WESTERN YACHT CLUB (1875),
Lochaber, 20 Barclay Drive, Helensburgh,
Dunbartonshire G84 9RB. Tel: 01436-672088. *Hon.*
*Secretary,* D. G. M. Watson
*Oban:* ROYAL HIGHLAND YACHT CLUB (1881), West
Manse House, Kilchrenan, Taynuilt, Argyll PA35 1HG.
Tel: 018663-213. *Secretary,* Mrs J. D. Carr
*Rhu:* ROYAL NORTHERN AND CLYDE YACHT CLUB
(1824, amal. 1978), Rhu, Helensburgh, Dunbartonshire
G84 8NG. Tel: 01436-820322. *Hon. Secretary,* B. C. Staig

## NORTHERN IRELAND

*Bangor:* ROYAL ULSTER YACHT CLUB (1866), 101 Clifton
Road, Bangor, Co. Down BT20 5HY. Tel: 01247-270568.
*Hon. Secretary,* N. D. Brooks

## CHANNEL ISLANDS

*Jersey:* ROYAL CHANNEL ISLANDS YACHT CLUB (1862),
Le Boulevard, Bulwarks, St Aubin, Jersey. Tel: 01534-
41023. *Hon. Secretary,* D. C. Dale

# Societies and Institutions

Although this section is arranged in alphabetical order, organizations are usually listed by the keyword in their title. The date in parenthesis after the organization's title is the year of its foundation.

ABBEYFIELD SOCIETY, 186–192 Darkes Lane, Potters Bar, Herts. EN6 1AB. Tel: 01707-644845. Housing for elderly people. *Chief Executive*, F. Murphy

ACCOUNTANTS, CHARTERED ASSOCIATION OF CERTIFIED (1904), 29 Lincoln's Inn Fields, London WC2A 3EE. Tel: 0171-242 6855. *Secretary*, Mrs A. L. Rose

ACCOUNTANTS, INSTITUTE OF COMPANY (1974), 40 Tyndalls Park Road, Bristol BS8 1PL. Tel: 0117-973 8261. *Director-General*, B. T. Banks

ACCOUNTANTS, INSTITUTE OF FINANCIAL (1916), Burford House, 44 London Road, Sevenoaks, Kent TN13 1AS. Tel: 01732-458080. *Chief Executive*, J. M. Dean

ACCOUNTANTS IN ENGLAND AND WALES, INSTITUTE OF CHARTERED (1880), PO Box 433, Chartered Accountants' Hall, Moorgate Place, London EC2P 2BJ. Tel: 0171-920 8100. *Secretary*, A. J. Colquhoun

ACCOUNTANTS IN IRELAND, INSTITUTE OF CHARTERED (1888), Chartered Accountants House, 87–89 Pembroke Road, Dublin 4. Tel: 00 353-1-6680400/01232-321600. *Director*, R. F. Hussey

ACCOUNTANTS OF SCOTLAND, THE INSTITUTE OF CHARTERED (1854), 27 Queen Street, Edinburgh EH2 1LA. Tel: 0131-225 5673. *Chief Executive*, P. W. Johnston

ACCOUNTING TECHNICIANS, ASSOCIATION OF (1980), 154 Clerkenwell Road, London ECIR 5AD. Tel: 0171-837 8600. *Secretary*, J. Hanson

ACE STUDY TOURS (formerly Association for Cultural Exchange), Babraham, Cambridge CB2 4AP. Tel: 01223-835055. *General Secretary*, P. B. Barnes

ACTION RESEARCH (1952), Vincent House, North Parade, Horsham, W. Sussex RH12 2DP. Tel: 01403-210406. *Director-General*, Mrs A. Luther

ACTORS' BENEVOLENT FUND (1882), 6 Adam Street, London WC2N 6AA. Tel: 0171-836 6378. *General Secretary*, Mrs R. Stevens

ACTORS' CHARITABLE TRUST (1896), 19–20 Euston Centre, London NW1 3JH. Tel: 0171-608 6212. *Administrative Secretary*, Ms A. Stewart

ACTORS' CHURCH UNION (1899), St Paul's Church, Bedford Street, London WC2E 9ED. Tel: 0171-836 5221. *Senior Chaplain*, Canon W. Hall

ACTUARIES, INSTITUTE OF (1848), Staple Inn Hall, High Holborn, London WCIV 7QJ. Tel: 0171-242 0106. *Secretary-General*, A. G. Tait

ACTUARIES IN SCOTLAND, THE FACULTY OF (1856), 40 Tristle Street, Edinburgh EH2 1EN. Tel: 0131-220 4555. *Secretary*, W. W. Mair

ADMINISTRATIVE MANAGEMENT, INSTITUTE OF (1915), 40 Chatsworth Parade, Petts Wood, Orpington, Kent BR5 1RW. Tel: 01689-875555. *Chief Executive*, Prof. G. Robinson

ADULT SCHOOL ORGANIZATION, NATIONAL (1899), MASU Centre, Gaywood Croft, Cregoe Street, Birmingham B15 2ED. Tel: 0121-622 3400. *General Secretary*, W. J. Scarle

ADVERTISING BENEVOLENT SOCIETY, NATIONAL (1913), 199–205 Old Marylebone Road, London NW1 5QP. Tel: 0171-723 8028. *Director*, Mrs D. Larkin

ADVERTISING, INSTITUTE OF PRACTITIONERS IN (1927), 44 Belgrave Square, London SWIX 8QS. Tel: 0171-235 7020. *Director-General*, N. Phillips

ADVERTISING STANDARDS AUTHORITY (1962), Brook House, 2–16 Torrington Place, London WCIE 7HN. Tel: 0171-580 5555. *Director-General*, Mrs M. Alderson

AERONAUTICAL SOCIETY, ROYAL (1866), 4 Hamilton Place, London WIV 0BQ. Tel: 0171-499 3515. *Director*, R. J. Kennett

AFRICAN INSTITUTE, INTERNATIONAL (1926), SOAS, Thornhaugh Street, Russell Square, London WCIH 0XG. Tel: 0171-323 6035. *Hon. Director*, Prof. D. Parkin

AFRICAN MEDICAL AND RESEARCH FOUNDATION, 2nd Floor, 8 Bourdon Street, London WIX 9HX. Tel: 0171-409 3230. *Executive Director*, A. Heroys

AGE CONCERN ENGLAND (1940), Astral House, 1268 London Road, London SW16 4ER. Tel: 0181-679 8000. *Director-General*, Ms S. Greengross

AGE CONCERN NORTHERN IRELAND (1976), 3 Lower Crescent, Belfast BT7 1NR. Tel: 01232-245729. *Director*, C. J. Common

AGE CONCERN SCOTLAND (1943), 54A Fountainbridge, Edinburgh EH3 9PT. Tel: 0131-228 5656. *Director*, Ms M. O'Neill

AGE CONCERN WALES, 4th Floor, 1 Cathedral Road, Cardiff CF1 9SD. Tel: 01222-371566. *Director*, R. W. Taylor

AGED POOR SOCIETY, *see* ST JOSEPH'S SOCIETY FOR THE RELIEF OF THE AGED POOR

AGEING, CENTRE FOR POLICY ON (1947), 25–31 Ironmonger Row, London ECIV 3QP. Tel: 0171-253 1787. *Director*, Ms K. Herbst, PH.D.

AGEING, RESEARCH INTO (1978), Baird House, 15–17 St Cross Street, London ECIN 8UN. Tel: 0171-404 6878. *Director*, Mrs H. McGarry

AGRICULTURAL BENEVOLENT INSTITUTION, ROYAL (1860), Shaw House, 27 West Way, Oxford OX2 0QH. Tel: 01865-724931. *Chief Executive*, Brig. A. G. Staniforth, CBE

AGRICULTURAL BENEVOLENT INSTITUTION, ROYAL SCOTTISH (1897), Ingliston, Edinburgh, EH28 8NB. Tel: 0131-333 1023. *Director*, I. C. Purves-Hume

AGRICULTURAL ENGINEERS ASSOCIATION (1875), Samuelson House, Paxton Road, Orton Centre, Peterborough PE2 5LT. Tel: 01733-371381. *Director-General*, J. Vowles

AGRICULTURAL SOCIETY, EAST OF ENGLAND, East of England Showground, Peterborough PE2 6XE. Tel: 01733-234451. *Chief Executive*, T. Gibson, OBE

AGRICULTURAL SOCIETY OF ENGLAND, ROYAL (1838), National Agricultural Centre, Stoneleigh Park, Warks. CV8 2LZ. Tel: 01203-696969. *Chief Executive*, C. Runge

AGRICULTURAL SOCIETY OF THE COMMONWEALTH, ROYAL (1957), 55 Sleaford Street, London SW8 5AB. Tel: 0171-978 1301. *Hon. Secretary*, F. R. Francis, LVO, MBE

AGRICULTURAL SOCIETY, ROYAL ULSTER (1826), The King's Hall, Balmoral Show Grounds, Belfast BT9 6GW. Tel: 01232-665225. *Chief Executive*, W. H. Yarr, OBE

AIR LEAGUE, THE (1909), 4 Hamilton Place, London WIV OBQ. Tel: 0171-491 0470. *Secretary-General*, Air Cdre J. C. Atkinson, CBE

ALCOHOLICS ANONYMOUS (1947), PO Box 1, Stonebow House, Stonebow, York YO1 2NJ. Tel: 01904-644026. *General Secretary*, J. Keeney

ALEXANDRA ROSE DAY (1912), 1 Castelnau, Barnes, London SW13 9RP. Tel: 0181-748 4824. *National Director*, Mrs G. Greenwood

ALLOTMENT AND LEISURE GARDENERS LIMITED, NATIONAL SOCIETY OF (1930), Hunters Road, Corby, Northants. NN17 1JE. Tel: 01536-266576. *National Secretary*, G. W. Stokes

ALMSHOUSES, NATIONAL ASSOCIATION OF (1946), Billingbear Lodge, Wokingham, Berks. RG11 5RU. Tel: 01344-52922. *Director*, D. M. Scott

ALZHEIMER'S DISEASE SOCIETY (1979), Gordon House, 10 Greencoat Place, London SW1P 1PH. Tel: 0171-306 0606. *Executive Director*, H. Cayton

AMNESTY INTERNATIONAL (1961), 99–119 Rosebery Avenue, London EC1R 4RE. Tel: 0171-814 6200. *Director*, D. Bull

ANAESTHETISTS OF GREAT BRITAIN AND IRELAND, ASSOCIATION OF (1932), 9 Bedford Square, London WC1B 3RA. Tel: 0171-631 1650. *Hon. Secretary*, Dr R. S. Vaughan

ANCIENT BUILDINGS, SOCIETY FOR THE PROTECTION OF (1877), 37 Spital Square, London E1 6DY. Tel: 0171-377 1644. *Secretary*, P. Venning, FSA

ANCIENT MONUMENTS SOCIETY (1924), St Ann's Vestry Hall, 2 Church Entry, London EC4V 5HB. Tel: 0171-236 3934. *Secretary*, M. J. Saunders

ANGLO-ARAB ASSOCIATION (1961), The Arab British Centre, 21 Collingham Road, London SW5 ONU. Tel: 0171-373 8414. *Executive Director*, A. Lee

ANGLO-BELGIAN SOCIETY (1982), 45 West Common, Haywards Heath, W. Sussex RH16 2AJ. Tel: 01444-452183. *Hon. Secretary*, Mrs A. M. Woodhead

ANGLO-BRAZILIAN SOCIETY (1943), 32 Green Street, London W1Y 3FD. Tel: 0171-493 8493. *Secretary*, C. H. Seaward, CBE

ANGLO-DANISH SOCIETY (1924), 25 New Street Square, London EC4A 3LN Tel: 01753-884846. *Chairman*, Sir Andrew Stark, KCMG, CVO

ANGLO-NORSE SOCIETY (1918), 25 Belgrave Square, London SW1X 8QD. Tel: 0171-235 7151. *Chairman*, Dame Gillian Brown, DCVO, CMG

ANIMAL CONCERN (SCOTLAND) (1988), 62 Old Dumbarton Road, Glasgow G3 8RE. Tel: 0141-334 6014. *Organizing Secretary*, J. F. Robins

ANIMAL HEALTH TRUST (1942), PO Box 5, Newmarket, Suffolk CB8 7DW. Tel: 01638-661111. *Director*, A. J. Higgins, PH.D.

ANTHROPOLOGICAL INSTITUTE, ROYAL (1843), 50 Fitzroy Street, London W1P 5HS. Tel: 0171-387 0455. *Director*, J. C. M. Benthall

ANTHROPOSOPHICAL SOCIETY IN GREAT BRITAIN (1923), Rudolf Steiner House, 35 Park Road, London NW1 6XT. Tel: 0171-723 4400. *General Secretary*, N. C. Thomas

ANTIQUARIES OF LONDON, SOCIETY OF (1717), Burlington House, Piccadilly, London W1V OHS. Tel: 0171-734 0193. *General Secretary*, D. M. Evans, FSA

ANTIQUARIES OF SCOTLAND, SOCIETY OF (1780), Royal Museum of Scotland, Queen Street, Edinburgh EH2 1JD. Tel: 0131-225 7534, ext. 327. *Director*, Mrs F. Ashmore

ANTIQUE DEALERS' ASSOCIATION, BRITISH (1918), 20 Rutland Gate, London SW7 1BD. Tel: 0171-589 4128. *Secretary-General*, Mrs E. J. Dean

ANTI-SLAVERY INTERNATIONAL FOR THE PROTECTION OF HUMAN RIGHTS (1839), Unit 4, Stableyard, Broomgrove Road, London SW9 9TL. Tel: 0171-924 9555. *Director*, Miss L. Roberts

ANTI-VIVISECTION: BRITISH UNION FOR THE ABOLITION OF VIVISECTION (1898), 16A Crane Grove, London N7 8LB. Tel: 0171-700 4888. *Executive Director*, vacant

ANTI-VIVISECTION SOCIETY, NATIONAL (1875), 261 Goldhawk Road, London W12 9PE. Tel: 0181-846 9777. *Director*, Ms J. Creamer

APOSTLESHIP OF THE SEA (1920), Stella Maris, 66 Dock Road, Tilbury, Essex RM18 7BX. Tel: 01375-845641. *National Director*, Revd J. Maguire

APOTHECARIES OF LONDON, SOCIETY OF (1617), Black Friars Lane, London EC4V 6EJ. Tel: 0171-236 1189. *Registrar*, A. M. Wallington-Smith

ARBITRATORS, CHARTERED INSTITUTE OF (1915), 24 Angel Gate, City Road, London EC1V 2RS. Tel: 0171-837 4483. *Secretary*, K. R. K. Harding

ARCHAEOLOGICAL ASSOCIATION, CAMBRIAN (1846), The Laurels, Westfield Road, Newport, Gwent NP9 4ND. Tel: 01633-262449. *General Secretary*, Dr J. M. Hughes

ARCHAEOLOGICAL INSTITUTE, ROYAL (1843), c/o Society of Antiquaries of London, Burlington House, Piccadilly, London W1V OHS. *Secretary*, J. G. Coad, FSA

ARCHAEOLOGY, COUNCIL FOR BRITISH (1944), Bowes Morrell House, 111 Walmgate, York YO1 2UA. Tel: 01904-671417. *Director*, R. K. Morris

ARCHITECTS, ROYAL INSTITUTE OF BRITISH (1834), 66 Portland Place, London W1N 4AD. Tel: 0171-580 5533. *President*, Dr F. Duffy; *Director-General*, Dr A. Reid

ARCHITECTS AND SURVEYORS INSTITUTE (1926), 15 St Mary Street, Chippenham, Wilts. SN15 3JN. Tel: 01249-444505. *Chief Executive*, B. A. Hunt

ARCHITECTS BENEVOLENT SOCIETY (1850), 66 Portland Place, London W1N 4AD. *Hon. Secretary*, R. J. Double

ARCHITECTS IN SCOTLAND, ROYAL INCORPORATION OF (1922), 15 Rutland Square, Edinburgh EH1 2BE. Tel: 0131-229 7545. *Secretary*, C. A. McKean, FRSA

ARCHITECTS REGISTRATION COUNCIL OF THE UNITED KINGDOM (1931), 73 Hallam Street, London W1N 6EE. Tel: 0171-580 5861. *Registrar*, D. W. Smart

ARCHITECTURAL ASSOCIATION INC. (1847), 34–36 Bedford Square, London WC1B 3ES. Tel: 0171-636 0974. *Secretary*, E. Le Maistre

ARCHITECTURAL HERITAGE FUND, THE (1976), 27 John Adam Street, London WC2N 6HX. Tel: 0171-925 0199. *Secretary*, Lady Weir

ARCHIVISTS, SOCIETY OF (1947), Information House, 20–24 Old Street, London EC1V 9AP. Tel: 0171-253 5087. *Executive Secretary*, P. S. Cleary

ARK ENVIRONMENTAL FOUNDATION, THE (1988), 8 Bourdon Street, London W1X 9HX. Tel: 0171-409 2638. *Director*, Miss R. Orosz

ARLIS/UK AND IRELAND, THE ART LIBRARIES SOCIETY (1969). *Administrator*, Ms S. French, 18 College Road, Bromsgrove, Worcs. B60 2NE. Tel: 01527-579298

ARMY BENEVOLENT FUND (1944), 41 Queen's Gate, London SW7 5HR. Tel: 0171-584 5232. *Controller*, Maj.-Gen. G. M. G. Swindells, CB

ARMY CADET FORCE ASSOCIATION (1930), E Block, Duke of York's HQ, London SW3 4RR. Tel: 0171-730 9733/4. *General Secretary*, Brig. R. B. MacGregor-Oakford, CBE, MC

ART, ROYAL CAMBRIAN ACADEMY OF (1882), Crown Lane, Conwy, Gwynedd LL32 8BH. Tel: 01492-593413. *Curator and Secretary*, Ms V. Macdonald

ART COLLECTIONS FUND, NATIONAL (1903), Millais House, 7 Cromwell Place, London SW7 2JN. Tel: 0171-225 4800. *Director*, D. Barrie

ARTHRITIS AND RHEUMATISM COUNCIL FOR RESEARCH (1936), Copeman House, St Mary's Court, St Mary's Gate, Chesterfield, Derbys. S41 7TD. Tel: 01246-558033. *General Secretary*, J. Norton

ARTHRITIS CARE (1949), 18 Stephenson Way, London NW1 2HD. Tel: 0171-916 1500. *Secretary*, J. R. Collins

ARTISTS' GENERAL BENEVOLENT INSTITUTION (1814) AND ARTISTS' ORPHAN FUND (1871), Burlington House, Piccadilly, London W1V 0DJ. Tel: 0171-734 1193. *Secretary*, Ms A. Dance

ARTISTS, FEDERATION OF BRITISH, 17 Carlton House Terrace, London SW1Y 5BD. Tel: 0171-930 6844. *Chairman*, J. Walton

ARTS, NATIONAL CAMPAIGN FOR THE (1984), Francis House, Francis Street, London SW1P 1DE. Tel: 0171-828 4448. *Director*, Ms J. Edwards

ART WORKERS' GUILD (1884), 6 Queen Square, London WC1N 3AR. Tel: 0171-837 3474. *Secretary*, H. Krall

ASIAN FAMILY COUNSELLING SERVICE (1985), 74 The Avenue, London W13 8LB. Tel: 0181-997 5749. *National Director*, Mrs R. Atma

ASLIB, The Association for Information Management (1924), Information House, 20–24 Old Street, London EC1V 9AP. Tel: 0171-253 4488. *Chief Executive*, R. Bowes

ASTHMA CAMPAIGN, NATIONAL (1927), Providence House, Providence Place, London N1 0NT. Tel: 0171-226 2260. *Chief Executive*, M. Letts

ASTRONOMICAL ASSOCIATION, BRITISH (1890), Burlington House, Piccadilly, London W1V 9AG. Meetings at 23 Savile Row, London W1X 1AB. *Assistant Secretary*, Miss P. M. Barber

ASTRONOMICAL SOCIETY, ROYAL (1820), Burlington House, Piccadilly, London W1V 0NL. Tel: 0171-734 3307. *President*, Prof. Sir Martin Rees, FRS; *Executive Secretary*, J. E. Lane

ATS/WRAC BENEVOLENT FUNDS (1964), PO Box 212, Guildford, Surrey GU2 6ZD. Tel: 01252-355562. *Secretaries*, Mrs A. H. S. Matthews; Lt.-Col. D. Dunn

AUDIT BUREAU OF CIRCULATIONS LTD (1931), Black Prince Yard, 207–209 High Street, Berkhamsted, Herts. HP4 1AD. Tel: 01442-870800. *Secretary*, J. Beadell

AUTHORS, SOCIETY OF (1884), 84 Drayton Gardens, London SW10 9SB. Tel: 0171-373 6642. *General Secretary*, M. Le Fanu, OBE

AUTOMOBILE ASSOCIATION (1905), Norfolk House, Priestley Road, Basingstoke, Hants. RG24 9NY. Tel: 01256-20123. *Director-General*, S. Dyer

AVICULTURAL SOCIETY (1894), c/o Bristol Zoological Gardens, Clifton, Bristol BS8 3HA. *Hon. Secretary*, G. R. Greed

AYRSHIRE CATTLE SOCIETY OF GREAT BRITAIN AND IRELAND (1877), 1 Racecourse Road, Ayr KA7 2DE. Tel: 01292-267123. *General Secretary*, S. J. Thomson

BACK PAIN ASSOCIATION, NATIONAL (1968), 16 Elm Tree Road, Teddington, Middlesex TW11 8ST. Tel: 0181-977 5474. *Executive Director*, Maj.-Gen. M. P. J. Hunt, OBE, FRSA

BALTIC AIR CHARTER ASSOCIATION (1949), 6 The Office Village, Romford Road, London E15 4EA. Tel: 0181-519 3909. *Hon. Executive*, D. Shepherd

BALTIC EXCHANGE, THE (1903), St Mary Axe, London EC3A 8BH. Tel: 0171-623 5501. *Chief Executive*, J. Buckley

BALTIC EXCHANGE CHARITABLE SOCIETY (1978), 14–20 St Mary Axe, London EC3A 8BH. Tel: 0171-369 1643. *Secretary*, D. A. Painter

BALZAN FOUNDATION – PRIZE, INTERNATIONAL (1956), Piazzetta U. Giordano 4, Milan 20122, Italy. Awards prizes for literature; moral sciences and the arts; physical, mathematical and natural sciences; medicine; humanity, peace and brotherhood. *Secretary-General*, Dr F. M. Tedeschi

BANKERS, CHARTERED INSTITUTE OF (1879), 10 Lombard Street, London EC3V 9AS. Tel: 0171-623 3531. *Chief Executive*, G. Shreeve

BANKERS IN SCOTLAND, CHARTERED INSTITUTE OF (1875), 19 Rutland Square, Edinburgh EH1 2DE. Tel: 0131-229 9869. *Chief Executive*, Dr C. W. Munn

BAPTIST MISSIONARY SOCIETY (1792), Baptist House, PO Box 49, 129 Broadway, Didcot, Oxon. OX11 8XA. Tel: 01235-512077. *General Secretary*, Revd R. G. S. Harvey

BAR ASSOCIATION FOR LOCAL GOVERNMENT AND THE PUBLIC SERVICE (1945), c/o Milton Keynes Borough Council, Civic Offices, 1 Saxon Gate East, Milton Keynes MK9 3HG. Tel: 01908-682205. *Chairman*, P. G. Stivadoros

BARNARDO'S (1866), Tanners Lane, Barkingside, Ilford, Essex IG6 1QG. Tel: 0181-550 8822. *Senior Director*, R. Singleton

BARONETAGE, STANDING COUNCIL OF THE (1898), The Church House, Bibury, Cirencester, Glos. GL7 5NR. *Hon. Secretary*, R. B. Snow, ISO

BARRISTERS' BENEVOLENT ASSOCIATION (1873), 14 Gray's Inn Square, London WC1R 5JP. Tel: 0171-242 4761. *Secretary*, Mrs A. Ashley

BEECHAM TRUST, SIR THOMAS (1946), Denton House, Denton, Harleston, Norfolk IP20 0AA. Tel: 01986-788780. *Secretary*, Shirley, Lady Beecham

BEE-KEEPERS' ASSOCIATION, BRITISH (1874), National Agricultural Centre, Stoneleigh Park, Kenilworth, Warks. CV8 2LZ. Tel: 01203-696679. *General Secretary*, J. K. Law

BIBLE SOCIETY, BRITISH AND FOREIGN (1804), Stonehill Green, Westlea, Swindon SN5 7DG. Tel: 01793-513713. *Executive Director*, N. Crosbie

BIBLIOGRAPHICAL SOCIETY (1892), British Library, Great Russell Street, London WC1B 3DG. Tel: 0171-323 7567. *Hon. Secretary*, Dr M. M. Foot

BIBLIOGRAPHICAL SOCIETY, EDINBURGH (1890), c/o New College Library, Mound Place, Edinburgh EH1 2LU. Tel: 0131-650 8956. *Hon. Secretary*, Dr M. C. T. Simpson

BIOCHEMICAL SOCIETY (1911), 59 Portland Place, London WIN 3AJ. Tel: 0171-580 5530. *Executive Secretary,* G. D. Jones

BIOLOGICAL ENGINEERING SOCIETY (1960), Royal College of Surgeons, Lincoln's Inn Fields, London WC2A 3PN. Tel: 0171-242 7750. *Hon. Secretary,* Dr R. E. Trotman

BIOLOGY, INSTITUTE OF (1950), 20–22 Queensberry Place, London SW7 2DZ. Tel: 0171-581 8333. *General Secretary,* Dr. R. H. Priestley

BIRMINGHAM AND MIDLAND INSTITUTE (1854) and PRIESTLEY LIBRARY (1779), Margaret Street, Birmingham B3 3BS. Tel: 0121-236 3591. *Administrator,* J. Hunt

BIRTHDAY TRUST FUND, NATIONAL (1928), 27 Sussex Place, London NWI 4RG.Tel: 0171-706 3903. For extension of maternity services

BLIND, GUIDE DOGS FOR THE, *see* GUIDE DOGS FOR THE BLIND ASSOCIATION

BLIND PEOPLE, ACTION FOR (1857), 14–16 Verney Road, London SE16 3DZ. Tel: 0171-732 8771. *Director,* S. Remington

BLIND, NATIONAL LIBRARY FOR THE (1882), Cromwell Road, Bredbury, Stockport, Cheshire SK6 2SG. Tel: 0161-494 0217. *Director-General,* A. Leach

BLIND, ROYAL LONDON SOCIETY FOR THE (1838), 105 Salusbury Road, London NW6 6RH. Tel: 0171-624 8844. *Chief Executive,* P. Talbot

BLIND, ROYAL NATIONAL COLLEGE FOR THE (1872), College Road, Hereford HRI IEB. Tel: 01432-265725. *Principal,* C. Housby-Smith, PH.D.

BLIND, ROYAL NATIONAL INSTITUTE FOR THE, *see* ROYAL NATIONAL INSTITUTE FOR THE BLIND

BLIND, ROYAL SCHOOL FOR THE, *see* SEEAbility

BLOOD TRANSFUSION ASSOCIATION, SCOTTISH NATIONAL (1940), Erskine House, 68–73 Queen Street, Edinburgh EH2 4NH. *Secretary,* P. C. Taylor

BLOOD TRANSFUSION SERVICE, NATIONAL (1948), National Directorate, Gateway House, Piccadilly South, Manchester M60 7LP. Tel: 01923-212121. *Chief Executive,* J. Adey

BLUE CROSS (1897), Shilton Road, Burford, Oxon. OXI8 4PF. Tel: 01993-822651. *Secretary,* A. Kennard, MBE

BODLEIAN, FRIENDS OF THE (1925), Bodleian Library, Oxford OXI 3BG. Tel: 01865-277022/234. *Secretary,* G. Groom

BOOKSELLERS ASSOCIATION OF GREAT BRITAIN AND IRELAND (1895), Minister House, 272 Vauxhall Bridge Road, London SWIV IBA. Tel: 0171-834 5477. *Chief Executive,* T. E. Godfray

BOOK TRADE BENEVOLENT SOCIETY (1967), Dillon Lodge, The Retreat, Kings Langley, Herts. WD4 8LT. Tel: 01923-263128. *Executive Secretary,* Mrs A. R. Brown

BOOK TRUST (1986), Book House, 45 East Hill, London SWI8 2QZ. Tel: 0181-870 9055. *Chief Executive,* B. Perman

BORN FREE FOUNDATION, THE (1984), Cherry Tree Cottage, Coldharbour, Dorking, Surrey RH5 6HA. Tel: 01306-712091. *Director,* W. Travers

BOTANICAL SOCIETY OF THE BRITISH ISLES (1836), The Natural History Museum, Cromwell Road, London SW7 5BD. Tel: 0171-938 9026. *Hon. General Secretary,* Mrs M. Briggs, MBE

BOTANICAL SOCIETY OF SCOTLAND, c/o Royal Botanic Garden, Inverleith Row, Edinburgh EH3 5LR. Tel: 0131-552 7171. *Hon. General Secretary,* R. Galt

BOY SCOUTS ASSOCIATION, *see* SCOUT ASSOCIATION

BOYS' BRIGADE (1883), Felden Lodge, Felden, Hemel Hempstead HP3 OBL. Tel: 01442-231681. *Brigade Secretary,* S. Jones.

BOYS' CLUBS OF NORTHERN IRELAND (1940), 2nd Floor, 38 Dublin Road, Belfast BT2 7HN. Tel: 01232-241924. *General Secretary,* K. Culbert

BREWING, INSTITUTE OF (1886), 33 Clarges Street, London WIY 8EE. Tel: 0171-499 8144. *Chief Executive,* P. W. E. Istead

BRIDEWELL ROYAL HOSPITAL (1553), Witley, Godalming, Surrey GU8 5SG. Tel: 01428-682371. *Registrar,* Mrs J. Benyon

BRITAIN-NEPAL SOCIETY (1960), 3C Gunnersbury Avenue, London W5 3NH. *Hon. Secretary*

BRITAIN-RUSSIA CENTRE (1959), 14 Grosvenor Place, London SWIX 7HW. Tel: 0171-235 2116. *Director,* I. Elliot

BRITISH AND FOREIGN SCHOOL SOCIETY (1808), Richard Mayo Hall, Eden Street, Kingston upon Thames, Surrey KTI IHZ. Tel: 0181-546 2379. *Secretary,* S. M. A. Banister

BRITISH INSTITUTE IN EASTERN AFRICA (1959), 1 Kensington Gore, London SW7 2AR. Tel: 0171-584 4653. *London Secretary,* Mrs J. Moyo

BRITISH INSTITUTE OF ARCHAEOLOGY AT ANKARA (1948), 31–34 Gordon Square, London WCIH OPY. Tel: 0171-388 2361. *London Secretary,* Ms G. Coulthard

BRITISH INSTITUTE OF PERSIAN STUDIES (1961), 63 Old Street, London ECIV 9HK. Tel: 0171-490 4404. *Secretary,* Ms V. Curtis, PH.D

BRITISH INTERPLANETARY SOCIETY (1933), 27–29 South Lambeth Road, London SW8 ISZ. *Executive Secretary,* Ms S. A. Jones

BRITISH ISRAEL WORLD FEDERATION (1919), 8 Blades Court, Deodar Road, London SW15 2NU. Tel: 0181-877 9010. *Secretary,* A. E. Gibb

BRITISH LEGION, ROYAL (1921), 48 Pall Mall, London SWIY 5JY. Tel: 0171-973 0633. *General Secretary,* Lt.-Col. P. C. E. Creasy, OBE, FCIS

BRITISH LEGION SCOTLAND, ROYAL (1921), New Haig House, Logie Green Road, Edinburgh EH7 4HR. Tel: 0131-557 2782. *General Secretary,* Maj.-Gen. J. D. MacDonald, CB, CBE

BRITISH MEDICAL ASSOCIATION (1832), BMA House, Tavistock Square, London WCIH 9JP. Tel: 0171-387 4499. *Chairman,* Dr A. Macara; *Secretary,* Dr E. M. Armstrong

BRITISH NATIONAL PARTY (1982), PO Box 117, Welling, Kent DAI6 3DW. Tel: 0181-316 4721. *Chairman,* J. Tyndall

BRITISH RED CROSS (1870), 9 Grosvenor Crescent, London SWIX 7EJ. Tel: 0171-235 5454. *Director-General,* M. R. Whitlam

BRITISH SCHOOL OF ARCHAEOLOGY IN JERUSALEM (1919), 21 Buccleuch Place (Top Flat), University of Edinburgh, Edinburgh EH8 9LN. Tel: 0131-650 3975. *President,* P. R. S. Moorey, PH.D., FBA

BRITISH TECHNOLOGY GROUP INTERNATIONAL PLC, 101 Newington Causeway, London SEI 6BU. Tel: 0171-403 6666. *Chief Executive,* I. A. Harvey

BTCV (British Trust for Conservation Volunteers) (1970), 36 St Mary's Street, Wallingford, Oxon. OX10 0EU. Tel: 01491-839766. *Chief Executive,* T. Flood

Buddhist Society, The (1924), 58 Eccleston Square, London SW1V 1PH. Tel: 0171-834 5858. *General Secretary,* R. C. Maddox

Budgerigar Society, The (1925), 49–53 Hazelwood Road, Northampton NN1 1LG. Tel: 01604-24549. *General Secretary,* A. C. Crook

Building, Chartered Institute of (1834), Englemere, Kings Ride, Ascot, Berks. SL5 8BJ. Tel: 01344-23355. *Chief Executive,* K. Banbury

Building Engineers, Association of (1925), Jubilee House, Billing Brook Road, Weston Favell, Northampton NN3 8NW. Tel: 01604-404121. *Chief Executive,* B. D. Hughes

Building Services Engineers, Chartered Institution of (1897), Delta House, 222 Balham High Road, London SW12 9BS. Tel: 0181-675 5211. *Secretary,* A. V. Ramsay

Building Societies Association (1936), 3 Savile Row, London W1X 1AF. Tel: 0171-437 0655. *Director-General,* A. Coles

Business and Professional Women UK Ltd (1938), 23 Ansdell Street, London W8 5BN. Tel: 0171-938 1729. *General Secretary,* Mrs R. Bangle

Business Archives Council (1934), 4 Maguire Street, London SE1 2NQ. Tel: 0171-407 6110. *Secretary-General,* W. S. Quinn-Robinson

Cadet Force Association, Combined (1952), 'E' Block, The Duke of York's HQ, London SW3 4RR. Tel: 0171-730 9733. *Secretary,* Brig. R. B. MacGregor-Oakford, CBE, MC

CAFOD (Catholic Fund for Overseas Development) (1962), Romero Close, Stockwell Road, London SW9 9TY. Tel: 0171-733 7900. *Director,* J. Filochowski

Calouste Gulbenkian Foundation (1956), 98 Portland Place, London W1N 4ET. Tel: 0171-636 5313. *Director,* B. Whitaker

Cambridge Preservation Society (1929), Wandlebury Ring, Gog Magog Hills, Babraham, Cambridge CB2 4AE. Tel: 01223-243830. *Secretary,* G. Brewster

Cameron Fund, The (1971), Tavistock House North, Tavistock Square, London WC1H 9JP. Tel: 0171-388 0796. *Secretary,* Mrs J. Martin

Campaign for Nuclear Disarmament (CND) (1958), 162 Holloway Road, London N7 8DQ. Tel: 0171-700 2393. *General Secretary,* G. Lefley

Cancer Relief Macmillan Fund (1911), Anchor House, 15–19 Britten Street, London SW3 3TZ. Tel: 0171-351 7811. *Chief Executive,* D. Scott, OBE

Cancer Research Campaign, 10 Cambridge Terrace, London NW1 4JL. Tel: 0171-224 1333. *Director-General,* D. de Peyer

Cancer Research Fund, Imperial (1902), PO Box 123, Lincoln's Inn Fields, London WC2A 3PX. Tel: 0171-242 0200. *Secretary,* Miss M. J. Craggs

Cancer Research, Institute of, Royal Cancer Hospital, 17A Onslow Gardens, London SW7 3AL. Tel: 0171-352 8133. *Chief Executive,* Prof. P. Garland

Cancer United Patients, British Association of (BACUP) (1985), 3 Bath Place, Rivington Street, London EC2A 3JR. Tel: 0171-696 9003. *Chief Executive,* A. Watson

Carers National Association (1988), 20–25 Glasshouse Yard, London EC1A 4JS. Tel: 0171-490 8818. *Director,* Ms J. Pitkeathley, OBE

Carnegie Dunfermline Trust (1903), Abbey Park House, Dunfermline, Fife KY12 7PB. Tel: 01383-723638. *Secretary,* W. C. Runciman

Carnegie Hero Fund Trust (1908). Abbey Park House, Dunfermline, Fife KY12 7PB. Tel: 01383-723638. *Secretary,* W. C. Runciman

Carnegie United Kingdom Trust (1913), Comely Park House, Dunfermline, Fife KY12 7EJ. Tel: 01383-721445. *Secretary,* C. J. Naylor, OBE

Cathedrals Fabric Commission for England (1949), 83 London Wall, London EC2M 5NA. Tel: 0171-638 0971. *Secretary,* Dr. R. Gem

Catholic Central Library (1914), St Francis Friary, 47 Francis Street, London SW1P 1QR. Tel: 0171-834 6128

Catholic Enquiry Centre (1954), 120 West Heath Road, London NW3 7TY. Tel: 0181-455 9871. *Director,* Revd M. Loughlin

Catholic Marriage Advisory Council (1946), Clitherow House, 1 Blythe Mews, Blythe Road, London W14 0NW. Tel: 0171-371 1341. *Chief Executive,* Mrs M. Corbett

Catholic Record Society (1904), c/o 114 Mount Street, London W1Y 6AH. *Hon. Secretary,* Miss R. Rendel

Catholic Truth Society (1868), 192 Vauxhall Bridge Road, London SW1V 1PD. Tel: 0171-834 4392. *General Secretary,* D. Murphy

Catholic Union of Great Britain (1872), St Maximilian Kolbe House, 63 Jeddo Road, London W12 9EE. Tel: 0181-749 1321. *President,* The Lord Craigmyle; *Hon. Secretary,* Mrs J. Stuyt, MBE

Cattle Breeders' Association, National, Lawford Grange, Lawford Heath, Rugby, Warks. CV23 9HG. Tel: 01788-565264. *Secretary,* R. W. Kershaw-Dalby

Cattle Breeder's Club Ltd, British (1945), 16A Swan Street, Loughborough, Leics. LE11 0BL. Tel: 01509-261810. *Secretary,* M. J. Peasnall

Central and Cecil Housing Trust (1926), 2 Priory Road, Kew, Richmond, Surrey TW9 3DG. Tel: 0181-940 9828/9. *Secretary,* G. Brighton

Central Bureau for Educational Visits and Exchanges (1948), Seymour Mews House, Seymour Mews, London W1H 9PE. Tel: 0171-486 5101. *Director* A. H. Male

Chadwick Trust (1895), Department of Civil and Environmental Engineering, University College London, Gower Street, London WC1E 6BT. Tel: 0171-380 7327. For the promotion of health and prevention of disease. *Secretary to the Trustees,* I. K. Orchardson PH.D.

Chantrey Bequest (1875), Royal Academy of Arts, Burlington House, Piccadilly, London W1V 0DS. Tel: 0171-439 7438. *Secretary,* P. Rodgers

Charities Aid Foundation (1974), 48 Pembury Road, Tonbridge, Kent TN9 2JD. Tel: 01732-771333. *Executive Director,* M. Brophy

Chartered Secretaries and Administrators, Institute of (1891), 16 Park Crescent, London W1N 4AH. Tel: 0171-580 4741. *Chief Executive and Secretary,* M. J. Ainsworth

CHEMICAL ENGINEERS, INSTITUTION OF (1922), The Davis Building, 165–171 Railway Terrace, Rugby, Warks. CV21 3HQ. Tel: 01788-578214. *Chief Executive and Secretary,* Dr. T. J. Evans

CHEMISTRY, ROYAL SOCIETY OF, Burlington House, Piccadilly, London W1V OBN. Tel: 0171-437 8656. *Secretary-General,* Dr. J. S. Gow, FRSE

CHESHIRE (LEONARD) FOUNDATION, *see* LEONARD CHESHIRE FOUNDATION

CHESS FEDERATION, BRITISH (1904), 9A Grand Parade, St Leonards-on-Sea, E. Sussex TN38 ODD. Tel: 01424-442500. *General Manager,* Mrs G. White

CHEST, HEART AND STROKE ASSOCIATION, *see* STROKE ASSOCIATION, THE

CHIEF EMERGENCY PLANNING OFFICERS' SOCIETY (1966), Emergency Planning Department, County Hall, Trowbridge, Wilts. BA14 8JE. Tel: 01243-777917. *Hon. Secretary,* J. D. Williams

CHILDBIRTH TRUST, NATIONAL (1956), Alexandra House, Oldham Terrace, London W3 6NH. Tel: 0181-992 8637. *Director,* vacant

CHILDMINDING ASSOCIATION, NATIONAL (1977), 8 Masons Hill, Bromley, Kent BR2 9EY. Tel: 0181-464 6164. *Director,* Mrs J. Burnell

CHILDREN'S SOCIETY, THE (1881), Edward Rudolf House, Margery Street, London WC1X OJL. Tel: 0171-837 4299. *Director,* I. Sparks

CHINA ASSOCIATION, THE (1889), Swire House, 59 Buckingham Gate, London SW1E 6AJ. Tel: 0171-821 3220. *Executive Director,* Brig. B. G. Hickey, OBE, MC

CHIROPODISTS AND PODIATRISTS, SOCIETY OF (1945), 53 Welbeck Street, London W1M 7HE. Tel: 0171-486 3381. *General Secretary,* J. G. C. Trouncer

CHIROPRACTIC ASSOCIATION, BRITISH (1925), 29 Whitley Street, Reading, Berks. RG2 OEG. Tel: 01734-757557. *Executive Director,* Miss S. Wakefield

CHOIRS SCHOOLS ASSOCIATION (1921), Wells Cathedral, Wells, Somerset BA5 2ST. Tel: 01749-672117. *Hon. Secretary,* J. S. Baxter

CHRISTIAN ACTION, 125 Kennington Road, London SE11 6SF. Tel: 0171-735 2372. *Hon. Director,* Revd Canon E. James

CHRISTIAN AID (1945), PO Box 100, London SE1 7RT. Tel: 0171-620 4444. *Director,* Revd M. H. Taylor

CHRISTIAN EDUCATION COUNCIL, NATIONAL (1809), 1020 Bristol Road, Selly Oak, Birmingham B29 6LB. Tel: 0121-472 4242. *Executive Officer,* Revd J. Gear

CHRISTIAN EDUCATION MOVEMENT (1965), Royal Buildings, Victoria Street, Derby DE1 1GW. Tel: 01233-296655. *General Secretary,* Revd Dr. S. Orchard

CHRISTIAN EVIDENCE SOCIETY (1870), St Stephen's House, St Stephen's Crescent, Brentwood, Essex CM13 2AT. Tel: 01277-214623. *Administrator,* Mrs G. M. Ryeland

CHRISTIAN KNOWLEDGE, SOCIETY FOR PROMOTING (SPCK) (1698), Holy Trinity Church, Marylebone Road, London NW1 4DU. Tel: 0171-387 5282. *General Secretary,* P. Chandler

CHRISTIANS AND JEWS, COUNCIL OF (1942), 1 Dennington Park Road, London NW6 1AX. Tel: 0171-794 8178. *Executive Director,* M. Latham

CHURCH ARMY (1882), Independents Road, London SE3 9LG. Tel: 0181-318 1226. *Chief Secretary,* Capt. P. Johanson

CHURCH BUILDING SOCIETY, INCORPORATED (1818), Fulham Palace, London SW6 6EA. Tel: 0171-736 3054. *Secretary,* Capt. R. H. C. Heptinstall, RN

CHURCH EDUCATION CORPORATION, Bedgebury School, Goudhurst, Cranbrook, Kent TN17 2SH. Tel: 01580-211630. *Secretary,* Col. C. G. Champion

CHURCH HOUSE, THE CORPORATION OF (1888), Dean's Yard, London SW1P 3NZ. Tel: 0171-222 5261. *Secretary,* C. D. L. Menzies

CHURCH LADS' AND CHURCH GIRLS' BRIGADE (1891), 2 Barnsley Road, Wath upon Dearne, Rotherham, S. Yorks. S63 6PY. Tel: 01709-876535. *General Secretary,* J. S. Cresswell

CHURCH MISSIONARY SOCIETY (1799), 157 Waterloo Road, London SE1 8UU. Tel: 0171-928 8681. *General Secretary,* Rt. Revd M. Nazir-Ali

CHURCH MUSIC, ROYAL SCHOOL OF (1927), Addington Palace, Croydon CR9 5AD. Tel: 0181-654 7676. *Chief Executive,* R. Lawrence

CHURCH OF ENGLAND PENSIONS BOARD (1926), 7 Little College Street, London SW1P 3SF. Tel: 0171-222 2091. *Secretary,* R. G. Radford

CHURCH UNION (1859), Faith House, 7 Tufton Street, London SW1P 3QN. *General Secretary,* A. Leggatt

CHURCHES, COUNCIL FOR THE CARE OF (1921), 83 London Wall, London EC2M 5NA. Tel: 0171-638 0971. *Secretary,* Dr. T. Cocke

CHURCHES FOR BRITAIN AND IRELAND, COUNCIL OF (1942), Inter-Church House, 35–41 Lower Marsh, London SE1 7RL. Tel: 0171-620 4444. *General Secretary,* Revd J. P. Reardon

CHURCHES, FRIENDS OF FRIENDLESS (1957), St Ann's Vestry Hall, 2 Church Entry, London EC4V 5HB. Tel: 0171-236 3934. *Hon. Director,* M. Saunders

CHURCHES MAIN COMMITTEE (1941), Fielden House, Little College Street, London SW1P 3JZ. Tel: 0171-222 4984. *Secretary,* D. Taylor Thompson, CB

CHURCHES TOGETHER IN ENGLAND (1990), Inter-Church House, 35-41 Lower Marsh, London SE1 7RL. Tel: 0171-620 4444. *General Secretary,* Canon M. Reardon

CHURCHES TOGETHER IN SCOTLAND, ACTION OF (1990), Scottish Churches House, Kirk Street, Dunblane FK15 OAJ. Tel: 01786-823588. *General Secretary,* Revd M. Craig

CHURCHILL SOCIETY (1990), 18 Grove Lane, Ipswich IP4 1NR. Tel: 01473-221607. *Founder,* N. H. Rogers

CITIZENS' ADVICE BUREAUX, NATIONAL ASSOCIATION OF (1931), Myddelton House, 115–123 Pentonville Road, London N1 9LZ. Tel: 0171-833 2181. *Chief Executive,* Ms A. Abraham

CITY PAROCHIAL FOUNDATION (1891), 6 Middle Street, London EC1A 7PH. Tel: 0171-606 6145. *Clerk,* T. Cook

CIVIC TRUST, THE (1957), 17 Carlton House Terrace, London SW1Y 5AW. Tel: 0171-930 0914. *Director,* M. C. Bradshaw

CIVIL DEFENCE AND DISASTER STUDIES, INSTITUTE OF (1938), Bell Court House, 11 Blomfield Street, London EC2M 7AY. Tel: 0171-588 3700. *Hon. General Secretary,* Lt.-Col. R. L. Mole

CIVIL ENGINEERS, INSTITUTION OF (1818), Great George Street, London SW1P 3AA. Tel: 0171-222 7722. *Secretary,* R. S. Dobson, OBE

CIVIL LIBERTIES, NATIONAL COUNCIL FOR, *see* LIBERTY

CLASSICAL ASSOCIATION (1903), Department of Classics, University of Keele, Keele, Newcastle under Lyme, Staffs. ST5 5BG. Tel: 01782-583049. *Hon. Treasurer,* R. Wallace

CLEAN AIR AND ENVIRONMENTAL PROTECTION, NATIONAL SOCIETY FOR (1899), 136 North Street, Brighton BN1 1RG. Tel: 01273-326313. *Secretary-General,* Dr T. Crossett

CLERGY ORPHAN CORPORATION (1749), 57B Tufton Street, London SW1P 3QL. Tel: 0171-222 1812. *Secretary,* Miss J. Buncher

CLERKS OF WORKS OF GREAT BRITAIN INC., INSTITUTE OF (1882), 41 The Mall, London W5 3TJ. Tel: 0181-579 2917/8. *Secretary,* A. P. Macnamara

COACHING CLUB (1871), West Compton House, West Compton, Shepton Mallet, Somerset BA4 4PD. Tel: 01749-890633. *Secretary,* D. H. Clarke

COMMERCE, BRITISH CHAMBERS OF (1860), 9 Tufton Street, London SW1P 3QB. Tel: 0171-222 1555. *Director-General,* R. G. Taylor, CBE

COMMERCE, ASSOCIATION OF SCOTTISH CHAMBERS OF, 30 George Square, Glasgow G2 1EQ. Tel: 0131-539 0017. *Director,* A. Moore

COMMERCE AND INDUSTRY, LONDON CHAMBER OF (1881), Swan House, 33 Queen Street, London EC4R 1AP. Tel: 0171-248 4444. *Chief Executive,* S. G. Sperryn

COMMERCE AND MANUFACTURERS, EDINBURGH CHAMBER OF (1786), 3 Randolph Crescent, Edinburgh EH3 7UD. Tel: 0131-225 5851. *Chief Executive,* I. Brown

COMMERCE AND MANUFACTURERS, GLASGOW CHAMBER OF (1783), 30 George Square, Glasgow G2 1EQ. Tel: 0141-204 2121. *Chief Executive,* G. Runcie

COMMERCE, CANADA UNITED KINGDOM CHAMBER OF (1921), 3 Regent Street, London SW1Y 4NZ. Tel: 0171-930 7711. *Executive Director,* G. F. Bacon

COMMERCIAL AND INDUSTRIAL EDUCATION, BRITISH ASSOCIATION FOR (BACIE) (1919), 35 Harbour Exchange Square, Off Marsh Wall, London E14 9GE. Tel: 0171-987 8989. *Director,* B. V. Murphy

COMMERCIAL TRAVELLERS' BENEVOLENT INSTITUTION (1849), Gable End, Mill Hill Road, Arnesby, Leics. LE8 3WG. Tel: 0116-247 8647. *Secretary,* M. N. Bown

COMMISSIONAIRES, THE CORPS OF (1859), Market House, 85 Cowcross Street, London EC1M 6BP. Tel: 0171-490 1125. *Managing Director,* C. J. Salt

COMMONWEALTH TRUST (linking the Royal Commonwealth Society and the Victoria League for Commonwealth Friendship), Commonwealth House, 18 Northumberland Avenue, London WC2N 5BJ. Tel: 0171-930 6733. *Director-General,* Maj.-Gen. Sir David Thorne, KBE

COMPLEMENTARY AND ALTERNATIVE MEDICINE, COUNCIL FOR (1985), 179 Gloucester Place, London NW1 6DX. Tel: 0171-724 9103. *Secretary,* Ms C. Daglish

COMPLEMENTARY MEDICINE, INSTITUTE FOR (1856), PO Box 194, 15 Tavern Quay, London SE16 1QZ. Tel: 0171-237 5165. *Director,* A. Baird

COMPOSERS' GUILD OF GREAT BRITAIN (1945), 34 Hanway Street, London W1P 9DE. Tel: 0171-436 0007. *General Secretary,* Ms H. Rosenblatt

COMPUTER SOCIETY, BRITISH (1957), 1 Sanford Street, Swindon SN1 1HJ. Tel: 01793-417417. *Chief Executive,* G. Kirkpatrick

CONSERVATION OF HISTORIC AND ARTISTIC WORKS, INTERNATIONAL INSTITUTE FOR (1950), 6 Buckingham Street, London WC2N 6BA. Tel: 0171-839 5975. *Secretary-General,* D. Bomford

CONSULTANTS BUREAU, BRITISH (1965), 1 Westminster Palace Gardens, 1–7 Artillery Row, London SW1P 1RJ. Tel: 0171-222 3651. *Director,* Maj.-Gen. T. A. Boam, CB, CBE

CONSULTING ECONOMISTS' ASSOCIATION, INTERNATIONAL (1986), 1C Barnes High Street, London SW13 9LB. Tel: 0181-876 2299. *Chairman,* P. Prynn

CONSULTING ENGINEERS, ASSOCIATION OF (1913), Alliance House, 12 Caxton Street, London SW1H 0QL. Tel: 0171-222 6557. *Chief Executive,* H. C. Woodrow

CONSULTING SCIENTISTS, ASSOCIATION OF (1958), Westgate House, 39-41 Romsey Road, Winchester, Hants. SO22 5BE. Tel: 01962-869128. *Hon. Secretary,* B. A. Richardson

CONSUMERS' ASSOCIATION (1957), c/o The Association for Consumer Research, 2 Marylebone Road, London NW1 4DF. Tel: 0171-830 6000. *Director,* Dr J. Beishon

CONTEMPORARY APPLIED ARTS (1948), 43 Earlham Street, London WC2H 9LD. Tel: 0171-836 6993. *Director,* Ms M. La Trabe-Bateman

CONVEYANCERS, COUNCIL FOR LICENSED (1986), 16 Glebe Road, Chelmsford, Essex CM1 1QG. Tel: 01245-349599. *Director,* Mrs V. Eden

CO-OPERATIVE PARTY, 342 Hoe Street, London E17 9PX. Tel: 0181-520 3580. *Secretary,* P. Clarke

CO-OPERATIVE STUDIES, PLUNKETT FOUNDATION FOR (1919), 23 Hanborough Business Park, Long Hanborough, Oxford OX8 8LH. Tel: 01993-883636. *Director,* E. Parnell

CO-OPERATIVE UNION LTD (1869), Holyoake House, Hanover Street, Manchester M60 0AS. Tel: 0161-832 4300. *Chief Executive,* D. L. Wilkinson

CO-OPERATIVE WHOLESALE SOCIETY LTD (CWS) (1863), PO Box 53, New Century House, Manchester M60 4ES. Tel: 0161-834 1212. *Chief Executive,* D. Skinner

COPYRIGHT COUNCIL, BRITISH (1953), 29–33 Berners Street, London W1P 4AA. *Secretary,* G. V. Adams

CORONERS' SOCIETY OF ENGLAND AND WALES (1846), 44 Ormond Avenue, Hampton, Middx. TW12 2RX. Tel: 0181-979 6805. *Hon. Secretary,* Dr. J. D. K. Burton, CBE

CORPORATE TREASURERS, ASSOCIATION OF (1979), 12 Devereux Court, London WC2R 3JJ. Tel: 0171-936 2354. *Secretary,* Ms G. Pierpoint

CORPORATE TRUSTEES, ASSOCIATION OF (1974), The Glen House, 43 Surrey Road, Westbourne, Bournemouth, Dorset BH4 9HR. Tel: 01202-761112. *Secretary,* R. J. Payne

CORRESPONDENCE COLLEGES, ASSOCIATION OF BRITISH (1955), 6 Francis Grove, London SW19 4DT. Tel: 0181-544 9559. *Secretary,* Mrs H. Owen

CORRYMEELA COMMUNITY (1965), Corrymeela House, 8 Upper Crescent, Belfast BT7 1NT. Tel: 01232-325008. *Director,* Revd T. Williams

COTTON GROWING ASSOCIATION, BRITISH (1904), Knowle Hill Park, Fairmile Lane, Cobham, Surrey KT11 2PD. Tel: 01932-861000. *Managing Director,* P. R. Walters

COUNCIL FOR THE PROTECTION OF RURAL ENGLAND, *see* RURAL

COUNSEL AND CARE (1954), Twyman House, 16 Bonny Street, London NW1 9PG. Tel: 0171-485 1550. *General Manager*, J. Smith

COUNTRY HOUSES ASSOCIATION (1955), 41 Kingsway, London WC2B 6UB. Tel: 0171-836 1624. *Chief Executive*, R. D. Bratby

COUNTRY LANDOWNERS ASSOCIATION (1907), 16 Belgrave Square, London SW1X 8PQ. Tel: 0171-235 0511. *Director-General*, J. Anderson

COUNTY CHIEF EXECUTIVES, ASSOCIATION OF (1974), PO Box 9, Shire Hall, Warwick CV34 4RR. Tel: 01926-412559. *Hon. Secretary*, I. G. Caulfield

COUNTY COUNCILS, ASSOCIATION OF (1890), Eaton House, 66A Eaton Square, London SW1W 9BH. Tel: 0171-201 1500. *Secretary*, R. G. Wendt

COUNTY EMERGENCY PLANNING OFFICERS' SOCIETY, *see* CHIEF EMERGENCY PLANNING

COUNTY SECRETARIES, SOCIETY OF (1974), Director of Business Services, Bedfordshire County Council, County Hall, Cauldwell Street, Bedford MK42 9AP. Tel: 01234-228911. *Hon. Secretary*, R. C. Wilkinson

COUNTY SURVEYORS' SOCIETY (1884), Director of Planning and Highways, Wiltshire County Council, County Hall, Trowbridge BA14 8JD. Tel: 01225-713301. *Hon. Secretary*, D. T. Gardner

COUNTY TREASURERS, SOCIETY OF (1903), PO Box 4, County Hall, Chelmsford, Essex CM1 1JZ. Tel: 01245-431000. *Hon. Secretary*, K. D. Neale

CRAFTS COUNCIL (1971), 44A Pentonville Road, London N1 9BY. Tel: 0171-278 7700. *Director*, T. Fora

CRISIS (1967), 7 Whitechapel Road, London E1 1DU. Tel: 0171-377 0489. *Director*, M. Scothern

CROSSLINKS (1922), 251 Lewisham Way, London SE4 1XF. Tel: 0181-691 6111. *General Secretary*, Canon J. M. Ball

CRUEL SPORTS, THE LEAGUE AGAINST (1924), 83 Union Street, London SE1 1SG. Tel: 0171-403 6155. *Executive Director*, J. Barrington

CRUELTY TO ANIMALS, SOCIETY FOR THE PREVENTION OF, *see* ROYAL and SCOTTISH

CRUELTY TO CHILDREN, SOCIETY FOR THE PREVENTION OF, *see* NATIONAL and ROYAL SCOTTISH

CRUSE – BEREAVEMENT CARE (1959), 126 Sheen Road, Richmond, Surrey TW9 1UR. Tel: 0181-940 4818. *Director*, R. Pearce

CURWEN INSTITUTE (1875), 5 Bigbury Close, Styvechale, Coventry CV3 5AJ. Tel: 01203-413010. *General Secretary*, vacant

CWMNI URDD GOBAITH CYMRU (1922), Swyddfa'r Urdd, Aberystwyth, Dyfed SY23 1EN. Tel: 01970-623744. *Director*, J. E. Williams

CYCLISTS' TOURING CLUB (1878), Cotterell House, 69 Meadrow, Godalming, Surrey GU7 3HS. Tel: 01483-417217. *Director*, A. Harlow

CYMMRODORION, THE HONOURABLE SOCIETY OF (1751), 30 Eastcastle Street, London W1N 7PD. Tel: 0171-631 0502. *Hon. Secretary*, D. L. Jones

CYSTIC FIBROSIS TRUST (1964), Alexandra House, 5 Blyth Road, Bromley BR1 3RS. Tel: 0181-464 7211. *Executive Director*, G. J. Edkins

CYTUN (CHURCHES TOGETHER IN WALES) (1990), 21 St Helen's Road, Swansea SA1 4AP. Tel: 01792-460876. *General Secretary*, Revd N. A. Davies

DAIRY FARMERS, ROYAL ASSOCIATION OF BRITISH (1876), 55 Sleaford Street, London SW8 5AB. Tel: 0171-627 2111. *Chief Executive*, P. M. Gilbert

DAIRY TECHNOLOGY, SOCIETY OF (1943), 72 Ermine Street, Huntingdon, Cambs. PE18 6EZ. Tel: 01480-450741. *National Secretary*, Mrs R. Gale

DATA (DESIGN AND TECHNOLOGY ASSOCIATION), 16 Wellesbourne House, Walton Road, Wellesbourne, Warks. CV35 9JB. Tel: 01789-470007. *Chairman*, R. V. Peacock, OBE, PH.D

D-DAY AND NORMANDY FELLOWSHIP (1968), 9 South Parade, Southsea, Hants. PO5 2JB. Tel: 01705-812180. *Hon. Secretary*, Mrs L. R. Reed

DEAF, COMMONWEALTH SOCIETY FOR THE (1959), Dilke House, Malet Street, London WC1E 7JA. Tel: 0171-631 5311. *Chairman*, C. Holborow, OBE, TD, MD, FRCS

DEAF ASSOCIATION, BRITISH (1890 *formerly* BRITISH DEAF AND DUMB ASSOCIATION), 38 Victoria Place, Carlisle CA1 1HU. Tel: 01228-48844. *Chief Executive*, Ms E. Wincott

DEAF CHILDREN, ROYAL SCHOOL FOR (1792), Victoria Road, Margate, Kent CT9 1NB. Tel: 01843-227561. *Secretary*, D. E. Downs

DEAF PEOPLE, FOLEY HOUSE RESIDENTIAL HOME FOR (1851), Foley House, 115 High Garrett, Braintree, Essex CM7 5NU. Tel: 01376-326652. *Director*, Mrs N. Hartard

DEAF PEOPLE, ROYAL ASSOCIATION IN AID OF (1841), 27 Old Oak Road, London W3 7HN. Tel: 0181-743 6187. *General Secretary*, B. Edmond

DEAF PEOPLE, ROYAL NATIONAL INSTITUTE FOR (1911), 105 Gower Street, London WC1E 6AH. Tel: 0171-387 8033. *Chief Executive*, S. Etherington

DEFENCE STUDIES, ROYAL UNITED SERVICES INSTITUTE FOR (1831), Whitehall, London SW1A 2ET. Tel: 0171-930 5854. *Director*, Gp. Capt. D. Bolton

DEMOCRATIC LEFT (1991), 6 Cynthia Street, London N1 9JF. Tel: 0171-278 4443. *Secretary*, Ms N. Temple.

DENTAL ASSOCIATION, BRITISH (1880), 64 Wimpole Street, London W1M 8AL. Tel: 0171-935 0875. *Chief Executive*, J. M. G. Hunt

DENTAL COUNCIL, GENERAL (1956), 37 Wimpole Street, London W1M 8DQ. Tel: 0171-486 2171. *Registrar*, N. T. Davies, MBE

DENTAL HOSPITALS OF THE UNITED KINGDOM, ASSOCIATION OF (1942), Birmingham Dental Hospital, St Chad's Queensway, Birmingham B4 6NN. Tel: 0121-236 8611. *Hon. Secretary*, Mrs P. Harrington

DESIGN AND INDUSTRIES ASSOCIATION (1915), Suite 142, Business Design Centre, 52 Upper Street, London N1 0QH. Tel: 0171-288 6212. *President*, Sir Graham Hills

DESIGNERS FOR INDUSTRY, FACULTY OF ROYAL (1936), RSA, 8 John Adam Street, London WC2N 6EZ. Tel: 0171-930 5115. *Secretary*, C. Lucas

DESIGNERS, CHARTERED SOCIETY OF (1930), 29 Bedford Square, London WC1B 3EG. Tel: 0171-631 1510. *Director*, B. Lymbery

DIABETIC ASSOCIATION, BRITISH (1934), 10 Queen Anne Street, London W1M 0BD. Tel: 0171-323 1531. *Director-General*, M. Cooper

DICKENS FELLOWSHIP (1902), Dickens House, 48 Doughty Street, London WC1N 2LF. Tel: 0171-405 2127. *Hon. General Secretary*, E. Preston

DIRECTORS, INSTITUTE OF (1903), 116 Pall Mall, London SW1Y 5ED. Tel: 0171-839 1233. *Director-General*, T. Melville Ross

DIRECTORS OF PUBLIC HEALTH, ASSOCIATION OF (1982), Walsall Health Authority, Litchfield House, 27–31 Litchfield Street, Walsall, West Midlands WS1 1TE. Tel: 01922-720255. *Hon. Secretary*, Dr. S. Ramaiah

DIRECTORY PUBLISHERS ASSOCIATION (1970), 93A Blenheim Crescent, London W11 2EQ. Tel: 0171-221 9089. *Secretary*, Ms R. Pettit

DISPENSING OPTICIANS, ASSOCIATION OF BRITISH (1925), 6 Hurlingham Business Park, Sulivan Road, London SW6 3DU. Tel: 0171-736 0088. *Registrar*, D. S. Baker

DISTRESSED GENTLEFOLKS' AID ASSOCIATION (1897), Vicarage Gate House, Vicarage Gate, London W8 4AQ. Tel: 0171-229 9341. *General Secretary*, N. B. M. Clack

DISTRICT COUNCILS, ASSOCIATION OF (1974), 26 Chapter Street, London SW1P 4ND. Tel: 0171-233 6868. *Secretary*, G. Filkin

DISTRICT SECRETARIES, ASSOCIATION OF (1974), 9 Margaret Road, Bishopsworth, Bristol BS13 9DQ. Tel: 0117-964 7299. *Hon. Secretary*, E. Richards

DITCHLEY FOUNDATION, Ditchley Park, Enstone, Chipping Norton, Oxon. OX7 4ER. Tel: 01608-677346. *Director*, Sir Michael Quinlan, GCB

DOMESTIC SERVANTS' BENEVOLENT INSTITUTION (1846), Royal Bank of Scotland PLC, 7 Burlington Gardens, London W1A 3DD. *Secretary*, A. J. Gibson

DOWNS SYNDROME ASSOCIATION (1970), 155 Mitcham Road, London SW17 9PG. Tel: 0181-682 4001. *Director*, Ms A. Khan

DOWSERS, BRITISH SOCIETY OF (1933), Sycamore Barn, Hastingleigh, Ashford, Kent TN25 5HW. Tel: 01233-750253. *Secretary*, M. D. Rust

DRAINAGE AUTHORITIES, ASSOCIATION OF (1937), The Mews, 3 Royal Oak Passage, High Street, Huntingdon, Cambs. PE18 6EA. Tel: 01480-411123. *Secretary*, D. Noble

DRINKING FOUNTAIN AND CATTLE TROUGH ASSOCIATION, METROPOLITAN (1859), 105 Wansunt Road, Bexley, Kent DA5 2DN. Tel: 01322-528062. *Secretary*, D. R. W. Randall

DRIVING SOCIETY, BRITISH (1957), 27 Dugard Place, Barford, Warwick CV35 8DX. Tel: 01926-624420. *Secretary*, Mrs J. M. Dillon

DRUG DEPENDENCE, INSTITUTE FOR THE STUDY OF (1968), Waterbridge House, 32–36 Loman Street, London SE1 0EE. Tel: 0171-928 1211. *Director*, Ms A. Bradley

DUKE OF EDINBURGH'S AWARD SCHEME (1956), Gulliver House, Madeira Walk, Windsor, Berks. SL4 1EU. Tel: 01753-810753. *Director*, Maj.-Gen. M. F. Hobbs, CBE

DYERS AND COLOURISTS, SOCIETY OF (1884), Perkin House, PO Box 244, 82 Grattan Road, Bradford BD1 2JB. Tel: 01274-725138. *General Secretary*, J. D. Watson

DYSLEXIA INSTITUTE (1972), 133 Gresham Road, Staines, Middx TW18 2AJ. Tel: 01784-463851. *Executive Director*, Mrs E. J. Brooks

EARLY CHILDHOOD EDUCATION, BRITISH ASSOCIATION FOR (1923), 111 City View House, 463 Bethnal Green Road, London E2 9QY. Tel: 0171-739 7594. *Secretary*, Mrs B. Boon

ECCLESIASTICAL HISTORY SOCIETY (1961), Department of Medieval History, University of Glasgow, Glasgow G12 8QQ. Tel: 0141-339 8855 ext. 4087. *Secretary*, M. J. Kennedy

ECCLESIOLOGICAL SOCIETY (1839), Underedge, Back Lane, Hathersage, Derbys. S30 1AR. Tel: 01742-768555 ext. 4719/01433-650833. *Hon. Secretary*, Prof. K. H. Murta

EDITORS, GUILD OF (1946), Bloomsbury House, 74–77 Great Russell Street, London WC1B 3DA. Tel: 0171-636 7014. *Secretary*, Ms V. L. Hird

EDUCATION OFFICERS, SOCIETY OF (1971), 3–6 Alfred Place, London WC1E 7EB. Tel: 0171-612 6388. *General Secretary*, J. Hendy

EDUCATION OFFICERS' SOCIETY, COUNTY (1889), Education Department, County Hall, West Bridsford, Nottingham NG2 7QP. Tel: 0115-982 3823. *Hon. Secretary*, P. J. Housden

EDUCATIONAL RESEARCH IN ENGLAND AND WALES, NATIONAL FOUNDATION FOR (1946), The Mere, Upton Park, Slough SL1 2DQ. Tel: 01753-574123. *Director*, Ms C. Burstall, PH.D., D.SC.

EGYPT EXPLORATION SOCIETY (1882), 3 Doughty Mews, London WC1N 2PG. Tel: 0171-242 1880. *Secretary*, Dr P. A. Spencer

ELECTORAL REFORM SOCIETY, 6 Chancel Street, London SE1 0UU. Tel: 0171-928 1622. *President*, Baroness Seear, PC; *Office Manager*, P. Stock

ELECTRICAL ENGINEERS, INSTITUTION OF (1871), Savoy Place, London WC2R 0BL. Tel: 0171-240 1871. *Secretary*, J. C. Williams, PH.D., FEng.

ELGAR FOUNDATION (1973), 23 Meadow Hill Road, King's Norton, Birmingham B38 8DE. Tel: 0121-458 2747. *Secretary to the Trustees*, J. G. Hughes

ELGAR SOCIETY (1951), 20 Geraldine Road, Malvern, Worcs. WR14 3PA. Tel: 01684-568822. *Secretary*, Mrs C. Holt

ENERGY ASSOCIATION, BRITISH (1924), 34 St James's Street, London SW1A 1HD. Tel: 0171-930 1211. *Director*, M. Jefferson.

ENERGY, INSTITUTE OF (1927), 18 Devonshire Street, London W1N 2AU. Tel: 0171-580 7124. *Secretary*, J. E. H. Leach

ENERGY SAVING TRUST (1992), 11–12 Buckingham Gate, London SW1E 6LB. Tel: 0171-931 8401. *Chief Executive*, Dr E. Lees

ENGINEERING COUNCIL, THE (1981), 10 Maltravers Street, London WC2R 3ER. Tel: 0171-240 7891. *Public Affairs Director*, R. Kirby

ENGINEERING DESIGNERS, INSTITUTE OF (1945), Courtleigh, Westbury Leigh, Westbury, Wilts. BA13 3HB. Tel: 01373-822801. *Secretary*, M. J. Osborne

ENGINEERING INDUSTRIES ASSOCIATION (1941), 16 Dartmouth Street, London SW1H 9BL. Tel: 0171-222 2367. *Director*, Col. W. T. Williams

ENGINEERS, INSTITUTION OF BRITISH (1928), Royal Liver Building, 6 Hampton Place, Brighton BN1 3DD. Tel: 01273-734274. *Secretary*, Mrs D. Henry

ENGINEERS, SOCIETY OF (INCORPORATED) (1854), Guinea Wiggs, Nayland, Colchester, Essex CO6 4NF. Tel: 01206-263332. *Secretary*, Mrs C. A. Wright

ENGLISH ASSOCIATION, THE (1906), University of Leicester, 128 Regent Road, Leicester LE1 7PA. Tel: 0116-252 5927. *Secretary*, Ms H. Lucas

ENGLISH FOLK DANCE AND SONG SOCIETY (1932), Cecil Sharp House, 2 Regent's Park Road, London NW1 7AY. Tel: 0171-485 2206. *Chief Officer*, J. Ripley

ENGLISH PLACE-NAME SOCIETY (1923), Grey College, Durham DH1 3LG. Tel: 0191-374 2960. *Hon. Director,* V. Watts

ENGLISH-SPEAKING UNION OF THE COMMONWEALTH, THE (1918), Dartmouth House, 37 Charles Street, London W1X 8AB. Tel: 0171-493 3328. *Director-General,* Mrs V. Mitchell

ENTOMOLOGICAL SOCIETY OF LONDON, ROYAL (1833), 41 Queen's Gate, London SW7 5HR. Tel: 0171-584 8361. *Registrar,* G. G. Bentley

ENVIRONMENTAL HEALTH OFFICERS, INSTITUTION OF (1883), 16 Great Guildford Street, London SE1 0ES. Tel: 0171-928 6006. *Secretary,* T. Brunt

ENVIRONMENT COUNCIL (1969), 21 Elizabeth Street, London SW1W 9RP. Tel: 0171-824 8411. *Chief Executive,* S. Robinson

EPILEPSY ASSOCIATION, BRITISH (1949), Anstey House, 40 Hanover Square, Leeds LS3 1BE. Tel: 0113-243 9393. *Chief Executive,* T. J. O'Leary

EPILEPSY, NATIONAL SOCIETY FOR (1892), Chalfont St Peter, Gerrards Cross, Bucks. SL9 0RJ. Tel: 01494-873991. *Chief Executive,* Col. D. W. Eking

EQUESTRIAN FEDERATION, BRITISH (1972), British Equestrian Centre, Stoneleigh Park, Kenilworth, Warks. CV8 2LR. Tel: 01203-696697. *Director-General,* vacant

ESPERANTO ASSOCIATION OF BRITAIN (1977), 140 Holland Park Avenue, London W11 4UF. Tel: 0171-727 7821. *General Secretary,* M. McClelland

ESTATE AGENTS, NATIONAL ASSOCIATION OF (1962), Arbon House, 21 Jury Street, Warwick CV34 4EH. Tel: 01926-496800. *Chief Executive,* H. Dunsmore-Hardy

ESTATE AGENTS, OMBUDSMAN FOR CORPORATE (1990), PO Box 1114, Salisbury, Wilts. SP1 1YQ. Tel: 01722-333306. *Ombudsman,* T. D. Quayle, CB

EUGENICS SOCIETY, *see* GALTON INSTITUTE

EVANGELICAL ALLIANCE (1846), Whitefield House, 186 Kennington Park Road, London SE11 4BT. Tel: 0171-582 0228. *General Director,* Revd C. R. Calver

EVANGELICAL LIBRARY, THE (1928), 78A Chiltern Street, London W1M 2HB. Tel: 0171-935 6997. *Librarian,* S. J. Taylor

EXECUTIVES ASSOCIATION OF GREAT BRITAIN LTD (1929), Suite 87–89, The Hop Exchange, 24 Southwark Street, London SE1 1TY. Tel: 0171-403 3653. *Secretary,* Lt.-Col. J. J. Langdon-Mudge

EXPORT, INSTITUTE OF (1935), Export House, 64 Clifton Street, London EC2A 4HB. Tel: 0171-247 9812. *Director-General,* I. J. Campbell

EX-SERVICES LEAGUE, BRITISH COMMONWEALTH (1921), 48 Pall Mall, London SW1Y 5JG. Tel: 0171-973 0633. *Secretary-General,* Brig. M. J. Doyle, MBE

EX-SERVICES MENTAL WELFARE SOCIETY (1919), Broadway House, The Broadway, London SW19 1RL. Tel: 0181-543 6333. *Director,* Brig. A. K. Dixon

FABIAN SOCIETY (1884), 11 Dartmouth Street, London SW1H 9BN. Tel: 0171-222 8877. *General Secretary,* S. Crine

FAIR ISLE BIRD OBSERVATORY TRUST (1948), Burkle, Fair Isle, Shetland ZE2 9JU. Tel: 0135-12284. *Secretary,* Ms C. Ross-Smith

FAMILY HISTORY SOCIETIES, FEDERATION OF (1974), The Benson Room, Birmingham and Midland Institute, Margaret Street, Birmingham B3 3BS. *Administrator,* Mrs P. A. Saul

FAMILY MEDIATION AND CONCILIATION SERVICES, THE NATIONAL ASSOCIATION OF (1982), 9 Tavistock Place, London WC1H 9SN. Tel: 0171-383 5993. *Director,* Ms T. Fisher

FAMILY PLANNING ASSOCIATION (1939), 27–35 Mortimer Street, London W1N 7RJ. Tel: 0171-636 7866. *Director,* Mrs D. E. Massey

FAMILY WELFARE ASSOCIATION (1869), 501–505 Kingsland Road, London E8 4AU. Tel: 0181-254 6251. *Director,* Ms L. Berry

FAUNA AND FLORA PRESERVATION SOCIETY (1903), 1 Kensington Gore, London SW7 2AR. Tel: 0171-823 8899. *Director,* M. Rose

FELLOWSHIP HOUSES TRUST (1937), Clock House, 192 High Road, Byfleet, Surrey KT14 7RN. Tel: 01932-343172. *Secretary,* Mrs A. J. Elliot

FIELD ARCHAEOLOGISTS, INSTITUTE OF (1982), University of Birmingham, Edgbaston, Birmingham B15 2TT. Tel: 0121-471 2788. *General Secretary,* F. M. Walls

FIELD SPORTS SOCIETY, BRITISH (1930), 59 Kennington Road, London SE1 7PZ. Tel: 0171-928 4742. *Director,* P. Smith

FIELD STUDIES COUNCIL (1943), Preston Montford, Montford Bridge, Shrewsbury SY4 1HW. Tel: 01743-850674. *Director,* A. D. Thomas

FILM CLASSIFICATION, BRITISH BOARD OF (1912), 3 Soho Square, London W1V 5DE. Tel: 0171-439 7961. *Director,* J. Ferman

FIRE ENGINEERS, INSTITUTION OF (1918), 148 New Walk, Leicester LE1 7QB. Tel: 0116-255 3654. *General Secretary,* D. Evans

FIRE PROTECTION ASSOCIATION (1946), 140 Aldersgate Street, London EC1A 4HX. Tel: 0171-606 3757. *Director,* A. S. Kidd

FIRE SERVICES ASSOCIATION, BRITISH (1949), 86 London Road, Leicester LE2 0QR. Tel: 0116-254 2879. *General Secretary,* D. Stevens

FIRE SERVICES NATIONAL BENEVOLENT FUND (1943), Marine Court, Fitzalan Road, Littlehampton, W. Sussex BN17 5NF. Tel: 01903-717185. *General Manager,* C. W. Pile

FLAG INSTITUTE, THE (1971), 10 Vicarage Road, Chester CH2 3HZ. Tel: 01244-351335. *Director,* W. G. Crampton

FLEET AIR ARM OFFICERS ASSOCIATION (1957), 94 Piccadilly, London W1V 0BP. Tel: 0171-499 0360. *Chairman,* Capt. A. A. Hensher, MBE, RN

FOLKLORE SOCIETY, c/o University College, Gower Street, London WC1E 6BT. Tel: 0171-387 5894. *Hon. Secretary,* T. W. Brown

FOOD FROM BRITAIN (1983), 301–344 Market Towers, New Covent Garden Market, London SW8 5NQ. Tel: 0171-720 2144. *Chairman,* G. John, CBE

FOOD SCIENCE AND TECHNOLOGY, INSTITUTE OF (1964), 10 Cambridge Court, 210 Shepherd's Bush Road, London W6 7NL. Tel: 0171-603 6316. *Executive Secretary,* Ms H. G. Wild

FORCES HELP SOCIETY AND LORD ROBERTS WORKSHOPS (1899), 122 Brompton Road, London SW3 1JE. Tel: 0171-589 3243. *Comptroller and Secretary,* Col. A. W. Davis, OBE

FOREIGN PRESS ASSOCIATION IN LONDON (1888), 11 Carlton House Terrace, London SW1Y 5AJ. Tel: 0171-930 0445. *Secretary,* Ms D. Crole

FORENSIC SCIENCE SOCIETY, THE (1959), Clarke House, 18A Mount Parade, Harrogate, N. Yorks HG1 1BX. Tel: 01423-506068. *Hon. Secretary,* Dr A. R. W. Forrest

FORENSIC SCIENCES, BRITISH ACADEMY OF (1959), Anaesthetic Unit, The London Hospital Medical College, Turner Street, London E1 2AD. Tel: 0171-377 9201. *Secretary-General,* Dr P. J. Flynn

FORESTERS, INSTITUTE OF CHARTERED (1982), 22 Walker Street, Edinburgh EH3 7HR. *Secretary,* Mrs M. W. Dick

FORESTRY ASSOCIATION, COMMONWEALTH (1921), c/o Oxford Forestry Institute, South Parks Road, Oxford OX1 3RB. Tel: 01865-275072. *Chairman,* P. J. Wood

FORESTRY SOCIETY OF ENGLAND, WALES AND NORTHERN IRELAND, ROYAL (1882), 102 High Street, Tring, Herts. HP23 4AF. Tel: 01442-822028. *Director,* J. E. Jackson, PH.D.

FORESTRY SOCIETY, ROYAL SCOTTISH (1854), 62 Queen Street, Edinburgh EH2 4NA. Tel: 0131-228 8142. *Director,* M. Osborne

FOUNDRYMEN, INSTITUTE OF BRITISH (1904), Bordesley Hall, The Holloway, Alvechurch, Birmingham B48 7QA. Tel: 01527-596100. *Secretary,* G. A. Schofield

FRANCO-BRITISH SOCIETY (1924), Room 623, Linen Hall, 162–168 Regent Street, London W1R 5TB. Tel: 0171-734 0815. *Executive Secretary,* Mrs M. Clarke

FREE CHURCH FEDERAL COUNCIL (1940), 27 Tavistock Square, London WC1H 9HH. Tel: 0171-387 8413. *General Secretary,* Revd D. Staple

FREEDOM ASSOCIATION (1975), 35 Westminster Bridge Road, London SE1 7JB. Tel: 0171-928 9925. *Office Manager,* Mrs P. North

FREEMASONS, GRAND LODGE OF ANTIENT FREE AND ACCEPTED MASONS OF SCOTLAND (1736), Freemasons' Hall, 96 George Street, Edinburgh EH2 3DH. Tel: 0131-225 5304. *Grand Master Mason of Scotland,* The Lord Burton; *Grand Secretary,* C. M. McGibbon

FREEMASONS, UNITED GRAND LODGE OF ENGLAND (1717), Freemasons' Hall, Great Queen Street, London WC2B 5AZ. Tel: 0171-831 9811. *Grand Master,* HRH The Duke of Kent, KG, GCMG, GCVO; *Grand Secretary,* Cdr. M. B. S. Higham

FREEMEN OF ENGLAND AND WALES (1966), 10 Wyngate Road, Hale, Altrincham, Cheshire WA15 0LZ. Tel: 0161-904 9304. *Secretary,* R. J. M. Bishop

FREEMEN'S GUILDS:

*City of Coventry Freemen's Guild* (1946), 5 Adare Drive, Styvechale, Coventry CV3 6AD. Tel: 01203-501801. *Hon. Clerk,* J. H. Bradbury

*Guild of Freemen of the City of London* (1908), PO Box 153, 40A Ludgate Hill, London EC4M 7DE. Tel: 0171-223 7638. *Clerk,* Col. D. Ivy

*Gild of Freemen of the City of York* (1953), 29 Albemarle Road, York YO2 1EW. Tel: 01904-653698. *Hon. Clerk,* R. Lee

FRIENDLY SOCIETIES, NATIONAL CONFERENCE OF (1887), Rayex House, Aldermanbury Square, London EC2V 7HR. Tel: 0171-606 1881. *General Secretary,* Miss M. Poole

FRIENDS OF CATHEDRAL MUSIC (1956), c/o Addington Palace, Croydon, Surrey CR9 5AD. *Secretary,* V. Waterhouse

FRIENDS OF THE CLERGY CORPORATION, THE (1972), 27 Medway Street, London SW1P 2BD. Tel: 0171-222 2288. *Secretary,* J. M. Greany

FRIENDS OF THE EARTH (1971), 26–28 Underwood Street, London N1 7JQ. Tel: 0171-490 1555. *Director,* C. Secrett

FRIENDS OF THE ELDERLY AND GENTLEFOLK'S HELP (1905), 42 Ebury Street, London SW1W 0LZ. Tel: 0171-730 8263. *Chief Executive,* Mrs S. Levett

FRIENDS OF THE NATIONAL LIBRARIES (1931), c/o The British Library, London WC1B 3DG. Tel: 0171-323 7559. *Hon. Secretary,* Mrs A. Payne, FSA

FURNITURE HISTORY SOCIETY (1964), 1 Mercedes Cottages, St John's Road, Haywards Heath, W. Sussex RH16 4EH. Tel: 01444-413845. *Membership Secretary,* Dr B. Austen

GALLIPOLI ASSOCIATION (1915), Earlydene Orchard, Earlydene, Ascot, Berks. SL5 9JY. Tel: 01344-26523. *Hon. Secretary,* J. C. Watson Smith

GALTON INSTITUTE, THE (formerly The Eugenics Society) (1907), 19 Northfields Prospect, London SW18 1PE. Tel: 0181-874 7257. *General Secretary,* Mrs L. Brooks

GAMBLERS ANONYMOUS (1954), PO Box 88, London SW10 0EU. Tel: 0181-741 4181

GAME CONSERVANCY TRUST, THE (1969), Fordingbridge, Hants. SP6 1EF. Tel: 01425-652381. *Director-General,* G. R. Potts, PH.D., D.SC.

GARDEN HISTORY SOCIETY (1965), 5 The Knoll, Hereford HR1 1RU. Tel: 01432-354479. *Hon. Membership Secretary,* Mrs A. Richards

GARDENERS' ASSOCIATION, THE GOOD (1968), Pinetum, Churcham, Glos. GL2 8AD. Tel: 01452-750402. *Hon. Director,* R. Shewell-Cooper

GARDENERS' ROYAL BENEVOLENT SOCIETY, THE (1839), Bridge House, 139 Kingston Road, Leatherhead, Surrey KT22 7NT. Tel: 01372-373962. *Chief Executive,* C. R. C. Bunce

GAS CONSUMERS COUNCIL (1986), 6th Floor, Abford House, 15 Wilton Road, London SW1V 1LT. Tel: 0171-931 0977. *Director,* I. W. Powe

GAS ENGINEERS, INSTITUTION OF (1863), 21 Portland Place, London W1N 3AF. Tel: 0171-636 6603. *Secretary,* D. J. Chapman

GEMMOLOGICAL ASSOCIATION OF GREAT BRITAIN (1931), 1st Floor, 27 Greville Street, London EC1N 8SU. Tel: 0171-404 3334. *Director,* R. R. Harding

GENEALOGICAL RESEARCH, IRISH (1936), c/o The Irish Club, 82 Eaton Square, London SW1W 9AJ. Tel: 0171-235 4164. *Hon. Secretary,* Mrs S. Welsh

GENEALOGISTS AND RECORD AGENTS, ASSOCIATION OF (1968), 29 Badgers Close, Horsham, W. Sussex RH12 5RU. *Secretaries*

GENEALOGISTS, SOCIETY OF (1911), 14 Charterhouse Buildings, Goswell Road, London EC1M 7BA. Tel: 0171-251 8799. *Director,* A. J. Camp

GENERAL PRACTITIONERS, ROYAL COLLEGE OF (1952), 14 Princes Gate, London SW7 1PU. Tel: 0171-581 3232. *Secretary,* Dr W. Reith

GENTLEPEOPLE, GUILD OF AID FOR (1904), 10 St Christopher's Place, London W1M 6HY. Tel: 0171-935 0641. *Secretary*

GEOGRAPHICAL ASSOCIATION, 343 Fulwood Road, Sheffield S10 3BP. Tel: 0114-267 0666. *Senior Administrator,* Miss F. Soar

GEOGRAPHICAL SOCIETY, ROYAL (1830), 1 Kensington Gore, London SW7 2AR. Tel: 0171-589 5466. *President,* The Earl Jellicoe, KBE, DSO, MC, FRS, PC; *Director,* Dr J. Hemming, CMG

GEOGRAPHICAL SOCIETY, ROYAL SCOTTISH (1884), Graham Hills Building, 40 George Street, Glasgow G1 1QE. Tel: 0141-552 3330. *Director,* A. B. Cruickshank

GEOLOGICAL SOCIETY (1807), Burlington House, Piccadilly, London W1V 0JU. Tel: 0171-434 9944. *Executive Secretary,* R. M. Bateman

GEOLOGISTS' ASSOCIATION (1858), Burlington House, Piccadilly, London W1V 9AG. Tel: 0171-434 9298. *Executive Secretary,* Ms S. Stafford

GEORGIAN GROUP (1937), 37 Spital Square, London E1 6DY. Tel: 0171-377 1722. *Secretary,* N. Burton

GIFTED CHILDREN, NATIONAL ASSOCIATION FOR (1966), Park Campus, Boughton Green Road, Northampton NN2 7AL. Tel: 01604-792300. *Executive Director,* M. Short

GILBERT AND SULLIVAN SOCIETY (1924), 1A Tower Lane, Bearsted, Maidstone, Kent ME14 4JJ. *Hon. Secretary,* Miss B. Dove

GINGERBREAD, AN ASSOCIATION FOR ONE PARENT FAMILIES (1970), 35 Wellington Street, London WC2E 7BN. Tel: 0171-240 0953. *Chief Executive,* K. Murphy

GIRL GUIDES, *see* GUIDE ASSOCIATION

GIRLS' BRIGADE, THE, Girls' Brigade House, 62 Foxhall Road, Didcot, Oxon. OX11 7BQ. Tel: 01235-510425. *Brigade Secretary,* Mrs S. Bunting

GIRLS' FRIENDLY SOCIETY AND TOWNSEND FELLOWSHIP (1875), 126 Queens Gate, London SW7 5LQ. Tel: 0171-589 9628. *General Secretary,* Mrs H. Crompton

GIRLS' VENTURE CORPS AIR CADETS (1964), Redhill Aerodrome, Kings Mill Lane, South Nutfield, Redhill RH1 5JY. Tel: 01737-823345. *Corps Director,* Mrs M. Rowland

GLASS ENGRAVERS, GUILD OF (1975), 19 Wildwood Road, London NW11 6UL. Tel: 0181-731 9352. *Secretary,* Mrs G. Plant

GLASS TECHNOLOGY, SOCIETY OF (1916), Thornton, 20 Hallam Gate Road, Sheffield S10 5BT. Tel: 0114-266 3168. *Administration Manager,* Miss J. Costello

GLIDING ASSOCIATION, BRITISH (1930), Kimberley House, Vaughan Way, Leicester LE1 4SE. Tel: 0116-253 1051. *Secretary,* B. Rolfe

GOAT SOCIETY, BRITISH (1879), 34–36 Fore Street, Bovey Tracey, Newton Abbot, Devon TQ13 9AD. Tel: 01626-833168. *Secretary,* Ms S. Knowles

GRAPHIC FINE ART, SOCIETY OF (1919), 9 Newburgh Street, London W1V 1LH. *Secretary,* Ms J. Caesar

GRAPHOLOGISTS, BRITISH INSTITUTE OF (1983), 24–26 High Street, Hampton Hill, Middx. TW12 1PD. *Chairman,* Dr C. Molander

GREEK INSTITUTE (1969), 34 Bush Hill Road, London N21 2DS. Tel: 0181-360 7968. *Director,* Dr K. Tofallis

GREEN PARTY, THE (1973), 10 Station Parade, Balham High Road, London SW12 9AZ. Tel: 0181-673 0045. *Office Manager,* J. Bishop

GREENPEACE UK (1971), Canonbury Villas, London N1 2PN. Tel: 0171-354 5100. *Executive Director,* The Lord Melchett

GROCERS ASSOCIATION, BRITISH INDEPENDENT (1890), Federation House, 17 Farnborough Street, Farnborough, Hants. GU14 8AG. Tel: 01252-515001. *National Secretary,* D. Eastwood

GUIDE ASSOCIATION (1910), 17–19 Buckingham Palace Road, London SW1W 0PT. Tel: 0171-834 6242. *Chief Commissioner,* Mrs J. Garside; *Chief Executive,* Ms H. Williams

GUIDE DOGS FOR THE BLIND ASSOCIATION (1931), Hillfields, Burghfield, Reading RG7 3YG. Tel: 01734-835555. *Director-General,* J. C. Oxley

GULBENKIAN FOUNDATION, *see* CALOUSTE GULBENKIAN FOUNDATION

HAEMOPHILIA SOCIETY, THE (1950), 123 Westminster Bridge Road, London SE1 7HR. Tel: 0171-928 2020. *Director of Services and Development,* G. Barker

HAKLUYT SOCIETY (1846), c/o Map Library, The British Library, Great Russell Street, London WC1B 3DG. Tel: 01986-788359. *Joint Hon. Secretaries,* Dr W. F. Ryan; Mrs S. Tyacke

HANSARD SOCIETY FOR PARLIAMENTARY GOVERNMENT, THE (1944), St Philips Building North, Sheffield Street, London WC2A 2EX. Tel: 0171-955 7478. *Director,* D. Harris

HARD OF HEARING, BRITISH ASSOCIATION OF THE (1948), 7–11 Armstrong Road, London W3 7JL. Tel: 0181-743 1110. *Director,* C. J. Meyer, OBE

HARVEIAN SOCIETY OF EDINBURGH (1782), Department of Medicine, The Royal Infirmary, Edinburgh EH3 9YW. Tel: 0131-229 2477, ext. 3166. *Joint Secretaries,* A. B. MacGregor; Dr A. D. Toft

HARVEIAN SOCIETY OF LONDON (1831), Lettson House, 11 Chandos Street, London W1M 0EB. Tel: 0171-580 1043. *Executive Secretary,* M. Griffiths, TD

HEALTH AUTHORITIES AND TRUSTS, NATIONAL ASSOCIATION OF (1974), Birmingham Research Park, Vincent Drive, Birmingham B15 2SQ. Tel: 0121-471 4444. *Director,* P. Hunt, OBE

HEALTH CARE ASSOCIATION, BRITISH (1931), 24A Main Street, Garforth, Leeds LS25 1AA. Tel: 0113-232 0903. *National Secretary,* Mrs C. Bell

HEALTH EDUCATION, INSTITUTE OF (1962), 14 High Elm Road, Hale Barns, Altrincham, Cheshire WA15 0HS. Tel: 0161-980 8276. *Hon. Secretary,* L. Baric, PH.D.

HEALTH, GUILD OF (1904), Edward Wilson House, 26 Queen Anne Street, London W1M 9LB. Tel: 0171-580 2492. *General Secretary,* Revd A. Lynn

HEALTH SERVICES MANAGEMENT, INSTITUTE OF (1902), 39 Chalton Street, London NW1 1JD. Tel: 0171-388 2626. *Director,* R. Rowden

HEART FOUNDATION, BRITISH (1963), 14 Fitzhardinge Street, London W1H 4DH. Tel: 0171-935 0185. *Director-General,* Maj.-Gen. L. F. H. Busk, CB

HEDGEHOG PRESERVATION SOCIETY, BRITISH (1982), Knowbury House, Knowbury, Ludlow, Shropshire SY8 3LQ. Tel: 01584-890287. *Founder,* Maj. A. H. Coles

HELLENIC STUDIES, SOCIETY FOR THE PROMOTION OF (1879), 31–34 Gordon Square, London WC1H 0PP. Tel: 0171-387 7495. *Secretary,* Dr L. Rodley

HELP THE AGED (1960), St James's Walk, Clerkenwell Green, London EC1R 0BE. Tel: 0171-253 0253. *Director-General,* Col. J. Mayo, OBE

HERALDIC AND GENEALOGICAL STUDIES, INSTITUTE OF (1961), 79–82 Northgate, Canterbury, Kent CT1 1BA. Tel: 01227-768664. *Registrar,* J. Palmer

HERALDRY SOCIETY, THE (1947), 44–45 Museum Street, London WCIA ILY. Tel: 0171-430 2172. *Secretary*, Mrs M. Miles, MBE

HERPETOLOGICAL SOCIETY, BRITISH (1947), c/o Zoological Society of London, Regent's Park, London NWI 4RY. Tel: 0181-452 9578. *Secretary*, Mrs M. Green

HIGHWAYS AND TRANSPORTATION, INSTITUTION OF (1930), 3 Lygon Place, Ebury Street, London SWIW OJS. Tel: 0171-370 5245. *Secretary*, Dr M. R. Cragg

HISPANIC AND LUSO BRAZILIAN COUNCIL (1943), Canning House, 2 Belgrave Square, London SWIX 8PJ. Tel: 0171-235 2303. *Director-General*, Sir Michael Simpson-Orlebar, KCMG

HISTORICAL ASSOCIATION, THE (1906), 59A Kennington Park Road, London SEII 4JH. Tel: 0171-735 3901. *Secretary*, Mrs M. Stiles

HISTORICAL SOCIETY, ROYAL (1868), University College London, Gower Street, London WCIE 6BT. Tel: 0171-387 7532. *Executive Secretary*, Mrs J. N. McCarthy

HOMOEOPATHIC ASSOCIATION, BRITISH (1902), 27A Devonshire Street, London WIN IRJ. Tel: 0171-935 2163. *General Secretary*, Mrs E. Segall

HONG KONG ASSOCIATION (1961), Swire House, 59 Buckingham Gate, London SWIE 6AJ. Tel: 0171-821 3220. *Executive Director*, Brig. B. G. Hickey, OBE, MC

HOROLOGICAL INSTITUTE, BRITISH (1858), Upton Hall, Upton, Newark, Notts. NG23 5TE. Tel: 01636-813795. *Secretary*, W. M. G. Evans

HOROLOGICAL SOCIETY, ANTIQUARIAN (1953), New House, High Street, Ticehurst, Wadhurst, E. Sussex TN5 7AL. Tel: 01580-200155. *Secretary*, Mrs M. A. Collins

HORSE SOCIETY, BRITISH (1947) (incorporating The Pony Club), British Equestrian Centre, Stoneleigh Park, Kenilworth, Warks. CV8 2LR. Tel: 01203-696697. *Chief Executive*, Col. T. Eastwood

HOSPITAL FEDERATION, INTERNATIONAL (1947), 4 Abbot's Place, London NW6 4NP. Tel: 0171-372 7181. *Director-General*, Dr E. N. Pickering

HOSPITAL SATURDAY FUND, THE (1873), 24 Upper Ground, London SEI 9PQ. Tel: 0171-928 6662. *Chief Executive*, K. R. Bradley

HOSPITAL SAVING ASSOCIATION, THE, Hambleden House, Andover, Hants. SPIO ILQ. Tel: 01264-353211. *General Secretary*, J. A. Young

HOSPITALITY ASSOCIATION, BRITISH (1907), 40 Duke Street, London WIM 6HR. Tel: 0171-499 6641. *Chief Executive*, R. Lees, CB, MBE

HOTEL, CATERING AND INSTITUTIONAL MANAGEMENT ASSOCIATION (1971), 191 Trinity Road, London SW17 7HN. Tel: 0181-672 4251. *Chief Executive*, J. Logie

HOUSE OF ST BARNABAS-IN-SOHO (1846), 1 Greek Street, London WIV 6NQ. Tel: 0171-437 1894. For homeless women in London. *Director*, D. G. Saunders

HOUSING, CHARTERED INSTITUTE OF, Octavia House, Westwood Business Park, Westwood Way, Coventry CV4 8JP. Tel: 01203-694433. *Director*, P. McGurk

HOUSING AID SOCIETY, CATHOLIC (1956), 209 Old Marylebone Road, London NWI 5QT. Tel: 0171-723 7273. *Director*, Ms R. Rafferty

HOUSING AND TOWN PLANNING COUNCIL, NATIONAL (1900), 14–18 Old Street, London ECIV 9AB. Tel: 0171-251 2363. *Director*, Ms A. Holmes

HOUSING ASSOCIATION FOR OFFICERS' FAMILIES (1916), Alban Dobson House, Green Lane, Morden, Surrey SM4 5NS. Tel: 0181-648 0335. *General Secretary*, J. B. Holt

HOVERCRAFT SOCIETY, THE (1971), 24 Jellicoe Avenue, Alverstoke, Gosport, Hants. POI2 2PE. Tel: 01705-601310. *Chairman*, M. J. Cox

HOWARD LEAGUE FOR PENAL REFORM (1866), 708 Holloway Road, London NI9 3NL. Tel: 0171-281 7722. *Director*, Ms F. Crook

HUGUENOT SOCIETY OF GREAT BRITAIN AND IRELAND (1885), The Huguenot Library, University College, Gower Street, London WCIE 6BT. Tel: 0171-380 7094. *Hon. Secretary*, Mrs M. Bayliss

HUMANE RESEARCH TRUST (1974), Brook House, 29 Bramhall Lane South, Bramhall, Stockport, Cheshire SK7 2DN. Tel: 0161-439 8041. *Chairman*, K. Cholerton

HUMANIST ASSOCIATION, BRITISH (1963), 47 Theobald's Road, London WCIX 8SP. Tel: 0171-430 0908. *Administrator*, Mrs J. M. Woodman

HYDROGRAPHIC SOCIETY (1972), c/o University of East London, Longbridge Road, Dagenham, Essex RM8 2AS. Tel: 0181-597 1946. *Hon. Secretary*, V. J. Abbott

HYMN SOCIETY OF GREAT BRITAIN AND IRELAND (1936), St Nicholas Rectory, Glebe Fields, Curdworth, Sutton Coldfield, W. Midlands B76 9ES. *Secretary*, Revd M. Garland

IMMIGRATION ADVISORY SERVICE (1970), 190 Great Dover Street, London SEI 4YB. Tel: 0171-357 7511. *Chief Executive*, K. Best

INDEPENDENT BRITAIN, CAMPAIGN FOR AN (1976), 81 Ashmole Street, London SW8 INF. Tel: 0181-340 0314. *Hon. Secretary*, Sir Robin Williams, Bt.

INDEPENDENT SCHOOL BURSARS' ASSOCIATION (1933), Woodlands, Closewood Road, Denmead, Waterlooville, Hants PO7 6JD. Tel: 01705-264506. *Secretary*, D. J. Bird

INDEPENDENT SCHOOLS CAREERS ORGANIZATION (1942), 12A–18A Princess Way, Camberley, Surrey GUI5 3SP. Tel: 01276-21188. *Director*, G. W. Searle

INDEPENDENT SCHOOLS INFORMATION SERVICE (ISIS) (1972), 56 Buckingham Gate, London SWIE 6AG. Tel: 0171-630 8793. *Director*, D. J. Woodhead

INDEPENDENT SCHOOLS JOINT COUNCIL (1974), Grosvenor Gardens House, 35–37 Grosvenor Gardens, London SWIW OBS. Tel: 0171-630 0144. *General Secretary*, Dr A. G. Hearnden, OBE

INDEXERS, SOCIETY OF (1957), 38 Rochester Road, London NWI 9JJ. Tel: 0171-916 7809. *Secretary*, Mrs C. Troughton

INDUSTRIAL EDITORS, BRITISH ASSOCIATION OF, (1949), 3 Locks Yard, High Street, Sevenoaks, Kent, TNI3 ILT. Tel: 01732-459331. *Director*, A. F. Brobyn

INDUSTRIAL MARKETING RESEARCH ASSOCIATION (IMRA) (1963), 11 Bird Street, Lichfield, Staffs. WS13 6PW. Tel: 01543-263448. *Executive Officer*, M. Berry

INDUSTRIAL SOCIETY, THE (1918), Robert Hyde House, 48 Bryanston Square, London WIH 7LN. Tel: 0171-262 2401. *Director*, T. Morgan

INDUSTRY AND PARLIAMENT TRUST, 1 Buckingham Place, London SWIE 6HR. Tel: 0171-976 5311. *Director*, F. R. Hyde-Chambers

INDUSTRY CHURCHES FORUM (formerly Industrial Christian Fellowship) (1877), 86 Leadenhall Street, London EC3A 3DH. Tel: 0171-283 6120. *Director,* Revd R. Holloway

INDUSTRY TRAINING ORGANIZATIONS, NATIONAL COUNCIL OF (1988), 5 George Lane, Royston, Herts. SG8 9AR. Tel: 01763-247285. *Administrator,* Mrs C. Armstrong

INFANT DEATHS, FOUNDATION FOR THE STUDY OF (1971), 35 Belgrave Square, London SW1X 8QB. Tel: 0171-235 0965/1721 (Cot death helpline). *Secretary-General,* Mrs J. Epstein

INFORMATION SCIENTISTS, INSTITUTE OF (1958), 44–45 Museum Street, London WC1A 1LY. Tel: 0171-831 8003. *Executive Secretary,* Mrs S. A. Carter

INNER WHEEL CLUBS IN GREAT BRITAIN AND IRELAND, ASSOCIATION OF (1934), 51 Warwick Square, London SW1V 2AT. Tel: 0171-834 4600. *General Secretary,* Miss J. Dobson

INSOLVENCY, SOCIETY OF PRACTITIONERS OF (1990), 18–19 Long Lane, London EC1A 9HE. Tel: 0171-600 3375. *General Secretary,* R. M. Stancombe

INSURANCE AND INVESTMENT BROKERS' ASSOCIATION, BRITISH, BIIBA House, 14 Bevis Marks, London EC3A 7NT. Tel: 0171-623 9043. *Director-General,* Mrs I. R. Rooley

INSURANCE BROKERS REGISTRATION COUNCIL, 15 St Helen's Place, London EC3A 6DS. Tel: 0171-588 4387. *Registrar,* Miss E. J. Rees

INSURANCE INSTITUTE, CHARTERED (1897), 20 Aldermanbury, London EC2V 7HY. Tel: 0171-606 3835. *Director-General,* Prof. D. E. Bland

INSURERS, ASSOCIATION OF BRITISH (1985), 51 Gresham Street, London EC2V 7HQ. *Director-General,* M. Boléat

INTERCON (INTERCONTINENTAL CHURCH SOCIETY) (1823), 175 Tower Bridge Road, London SE1 2AQ. Tel: 0171-407 4588. *General Secretary,* Deaconess P. K. L. Schmiegelow

INTERNATIONAL AFFAIRS, ROYAL INSTITUTE OF (1920), Chatham House, 10 St James's Square, London SW1Y 4LE. Tel: 0171-957 5700. *Director,* Sir Laurence Martin

INTERNATIONAL FRIENDSHIP LEAGUE (1931), 3 Creswick Road, London W3 9HE. Tel: 0181-992 0221. *Secretary,* Mrs B. Macdonald

INTERNATIONAL LAW ASSOCIATION (1873), Charles Clore House, 17 Russell Square, London WC1B 5DR. Tel: 0171-323 2978. *Hon. Secretary-General,* B. Mauleverer, QC

INTERNATIONAL POLICE ASSOCIATION (British Section) (1950), 1 Fox Road, West Bridgford, Nottingham NG2 6AJ. Tel: 0115-981 3638. *Chief Executive Officer,* A. F. Carter

INTERNATIONAL STUDENTS HOUSE (1962), 229 Great Portland Street, London W1N 5HD. Tel: 0171-631 3223. *Secretary,* P. Anwyl

INTERNATIONAL TIN RESEARCH INSTITUTE (1932), Kingston Lane, Uxbridge, Middx. UB8 3PJ. Tel: 01895-272406. *Director,* Dr B. T. K. Barry

INTERSERVE (1852), 325 Kennington Park Road, London SE11 4QH. Tel: 0171-735 8227. *General Director,* R. Clark

INTER VARSITY CLUBS, ASSOCIATION OF (1946), 2nd Floor, Grosvenor House, 94–96 Grosvenor Street, Manchester M1 7HL. Tel: 0161-273 2316. *Secretary,* D. Bousfield

INVALID CHILDREN'S AID NATIONWIDE (I CAN)(1888), 10 Bowling Green Lane, London EC1R 0BD. Tel: 0171-253 9111. *Director,* B. J. Jones

INVALIDS-AT-HOME (1966), 17 Lapstone Gardens, Kenton, Harrow HA3 0EB. *Executive Officer,* Ms S. Lomas

INVISIBLES, BRITISH (1983), 6th Floor, Windsor House, 39 King Street, London EC2V 8DQ. Tel: 0171-600 1198. *Director-General,* Mrs A. Wright

INVOLVEMENT AND PARTICIPATION ASSOCIATION (1884), 42 Colebrook Row, London N1 8AF. Tel: 0171-354 8040. *Director,* B. C. Stevens

IRAN SOCIETY (1936), 2 Belgrave Square, London SW1X 8PJ. Tel: 0171-235 5122. *Hon. Secretary,* A. D. Ashmole

JACQUELINE DU PRÉ MUSIC BUILDING APPEAL (1988), The Development and Alumnae Office, St Hilda's College, Oxford OX4 1DY. Tel: 01865-276828.

JAPAN ASSOCIATION, THE (1950), Swire House, 59 Buckingham Gate, London SW1E 6AJ. Tel: 0171-821 3220. *Executive Director,* Brig. B. G. Hickey, OBE, MC

JERUSALEM AND THE MIDDLE EAST CHURCH ASSOCIATION, THE (1887), 1 Hart House, The Hart, Farnham, Surrey GU9 7HA. Tel: 01252-726994. *Secretary,* Mrs V. Wells

JEWISH HISTORICAL SOCIETY OF ENGLAND (1893), 33 Seymour Place, London W1H 5AP. Tel: 0171-723 4404. *Hon. Secretary,* C. M. Drukker

JEWISH YOUTH, ASSOCIATION FOR (1899), 128 East Lane, Wembley, Middx. HA0 3NL. Tel: 0181-908 4747. *Executive Director,* M. Shaw

JEWS, CHURCH'S MINISTRY AMONG THE (1809), 30C Clarence Road, St Albans, Herts. AL1 4JJ. Tel: 01727-833114. *General Director,* Revd Dr W. Riggans

JOURNALISTS, THE CHARTERED INSTITUTE OF (1883), 2 Dock Offices, Surrey Quays, Lower Road, London SE16 2XL. Tel: 0171-252 1187. *General Secretary,* C. T. Underwood

JUSTICE (British Section of the International Commission of Jurists) (1957), 59 Carter Lane, London EC4V 5AQ. Tel: 0171-353 5180. *Director,* Ms A. Owers

JUSTICES' CLERKS' SOCIETY (1839), The Law Courts, Petters Way, Yeovil, Somerset BA20 1SW. Tel: 01935-21912. *Hon. Secretary,* L. G. C. Cramp

KING EDWARD'S HOSPITAL FUND FOR LONDON (THE KING'S FUND) (1897), 2 Palace Court, London W2 4HS. Tel: 0171-727 0581. *Director,* Dr R. J. Maxwell, CBE

KING GEORGE'S FUND FOR SAILORS (1917), 8 Hatherley Street, London SW1P 2YY. Tel: 0171-932 0000. *Director-General,* Capt. M. J. Appleton, RN

KIPLING SOCIETY, THE (1927), PO Box 68, Haslemere, Surrey GU27 2YR. Tel: 01428-652709. *Hon. Secretary,* N. Entract

LADIES IN REDUCED CIRCUMSTANCES, SOCIETY FOR THE ASSISTANCE OF (1886), Lancaster House, 25 Hornyold Road, Malvern, Worcs. WR14 1QQ. Tel: 01684-574645. *Secretary*

LANDSCAPE INSTITUTE (1929), 6–7 Barnard Mews, London SW11 1QU. Tel: 0171-738 9166. *Registrar,* P. R. Broadbent, OBE

LAND-VALUE TAXATION AND FREE TRADE, INTERNATIONAL UNION FOR, 177 Vauxhall Bridge Road, London SW1V 1EU. Tel: 0171-834 4266. *President,* Mrs B. P. Sobrielo

LANGUAGE LEARNING, ASSOCIATION FOR (1990), 16 Regent Place, Rugby CV21 2PN. Tel: 01788-546443. *General Secretary*, Mrs C. Wilding

LAW REPORTING FOR ENGLAND AND WALES, INCORPORATED COUNCIL OF (1865), 3 Stone Buildings, Lincoln's Inn, London WC2A 3XN. Tel: 0171-242 6471. *Secretary*

LEAGUE OF THE HELPING HAND (1908), Baileys, Church Street, Charlbury, Oxford OX7 3PR. *Secretary*, Mrs I. Goodlad

LEAGUE OF WELLDOERS (1893), 119–133 Limekiln Lane, Liverpool L5 8SN. Tel: 0151-207 1984. *Warden and Secretary*, K. H. Stanton

LEATHER AND HIDE TRADES' BENEVOLENT INSTITUTION (1860), 60 Wickham Hill, Hurstpierpoint, Hassocks, W. Sussex BN6 9NP. Tel: 01273-843488. *Secretary*, Mrs G. M. Stapleton, MBE

LEGAL EXECUTIVES, INSTITUTE OF (1892), Kempston Manor, Kempston, Bedford MK42 7AB. Tel: 01234-841000. *Secretary-General*, L. A. Evans

LEONARD CHESHIRE FOUNDATION (1955), 26–29 Maunsel Street, London SW1P 2QN. Tel: 0171-828 1822. *Director-General*, J. Stanford

LEPROSY MISSION, THE (England and Wales) (1874), Goldhay Way, Orton Goldhay, Peterborough PE2 5GZ. Tel: 01733-370505. *Executive Director*, Revd J. A. Lloyd, PH.D

LEUKAEMIA RESEARCH FUND (1962), 43 Great Ormond Street, London WC1N 3JJ. Tel: 0171-405 0101. *Executive Director*, D. L. Osborne

LIBERAL PARTY (1877; relaunched 1989), Gayfere House, 22 Gayfere Street, London SW1 3HP. Tel: 0171-233 2124. *Secretary-General*, N. Ashton

LIBERTY (NATIONAL COUNCIL FOR CIVIL LIBERTIES) (1934), 21 Tabard Street, London SE1 4LA. Tel: 0171-403 3888. *General Secretary*, A. Puddephatt

LIBRARY ASSOCIATION (1877), 7 Ridgmount Street, London WC1E 7AE. Tel: 0171-636 7543. *Chief Executive*, R. Shimmon

LIFEBOATS, *see* ROYAL NATIONAL LIFEBOAT INSTITUTION

LIGHT HORSE BREEDING SOCIETY, NATIONAL (1885), 96 High Street, Edenbridge, Kent TN8 5AR. Tel: 01732-866277. *Secretary*, G. W. Evans

LINGUISTS, INSTITUTE OF (1910), 24A Highbury Grove, London N5 2EA. Tel: 0171-359 7445. *Director*, Ms E. H. F. Ostarhild

LINNAEAN SOCIETY OF LONDON, THE (1788), Burlington House, Piccadilly, London W1V 0LQ. Tel: 0171-434 4479. *President*, Prof. B. G. Gardiner; *Executive Secretary*, Dr J. C. Marsden

LIONS CLUBS INTERNATIONAL (British Isles and Ireland) (1949), 257 Alcester Road South, Kings Heath, Birmingham B14 6BT. Tel: 0121-441 4544. *General Secretary*, P. Jay

LLOYD'S OF LONDON, 1 Lime Street, London EC3M 7HA. Tel: 0171-623 7100. *Chief Executive*, P. J. Middleton

LLOYD'S PATRIOTIC FUND (1803), Lloyd's, Lime Street, London EC3M 7HA. Tel: 0171-326 5377. *Secretary*, Miss B. A. Lowden

LOCAL AUTHORITY CHIEF EXECUTIVES, SOCIETY OF (1974), Kensington Town Hall, Hornton Street, London W8 7NX. Tel: 0171-938 3400. *Hon. Secretary*, A. Taylor

LOCAL COUNCILS, NATIONAL ASSOCIATION OF (1947), 109 Great Russell Street, London WC1B 3LD. Tel: 0171-637 1865. *Secretary*, J. Clark

LOCAL GOVERNMENT INTERNATIONAL BUREAU (1913), *also* COUNCIL OF EUROPEAN MUNICIPALITIES AND REGIONS (British Section) and INTERNATIONAL UNION OF LOCAL AUTHORITIES (British Section) (1951), 35 Great Smith Street, London SW1P 3BJ. Tel: 0171-222 1636. *Secretary-General*, P. N. Bongers

LOCAL HISTORY, BRITISH ASSOCIATION FOR (1843), 24 Lower Street, Harnham, Salisbury, Wilts. SP2 8EY. Tel: 01722-320115. *Secretary*, M. Cowan

LONDON APPRECIATION SOCIETY (1932), 17 Manson Mews, London SW7 5AF. *Hon. Secretary*, H. L. B. Peers, PH.D.

LONDON BOROUGHS ASSOCIATION (1964), College House, Great Peter Street, London SW1P 3LN. Tel: 0171-799 2477. *Secretary*, J. Hall

LONDON CITY MISSION (1835), 175 Tower Bridge Road, London SE1 2AH. Tel: 0171-407 7585. *General Secretary*, Revd J. McAllen

LONDON COURT OF INTERNATIONAL ARBITRATION (1892), 12 Carthusian Street, London EC1B 6EB. Tel: 0171-417 8228. *Registrar*, B. W. Vigrass, OBE, VRD

LONDON FLOTILLA (1937), Marden Rise, 81 Lower Road, Fetcham, Leatherhead, Surrey KT22 9HG. Tel: 01372-453059. *Hon. Secretary*, Lt. Cdr. P. A. G. Norman, RD, RNR

LONDON LIBRARY, THE (1841), 14 St James's Square, London SW1Y 4LG. Tel: 0171-930 7705. *Librarian*, A. S. Bell

LONDON MAGISTRATES' CLERKS' ASSOCIATION (1889), c/o Marlborough Street Magistrates' Court, 21 Great Marlborough Street, London W1A 4EY. Tel: 0171-287 4525, ext. 3842. *Hon. Secretary*, K. W. Burman

LONDON PLAYING FIELDS SOCIETY, THE (1890), Boston Manor Playing Field, Boston Gardens, Brentford, Middx. TW8 9LR. Tel: 0181-560 3667. *Secretary*, D. Northwood

LONDON SOCIETY, THE (1912), 4th Floor, Senate House, Malet Street, London WC1E 7HU. Tel: 0171-580 5537. *Hon. Secretary*, Mrs B. Jones

LORD'S DAY OBSERVANCE SOCIETY, THE (1831), 6 Sherman Road, Bromley, Kent BR1 3JH. Tel: 0181-313 0456. *General Secretary*, J. G. Roberts

LOTTERIES COUNCIL, THE (1979), c/o Community Publishing (Avon) Ltd, PO Box 215, Pamwell House, Pennywell Road, Bristol BS99 7QX. Tel: 0117-954 1111. *Hon. Secretary*, P. Broderick

LUNG FOUNDATION, BRITISH (1985), 8 Peterborough Mews, London SW6 3BL. Tel: 0171-371 7704. *Director (acting)*, Ms H. Lamont

MAGISTRATES' ASSOCIATION, THE (1920), 28 Fitzroy Square, London W1P 6DD. Tel: 0171-387 2353. *Secretary*, Ms S. Dickson

MAILING PREFERENCE SERVICE (1983). To limit direct mail: Freepost 22, London W1E 7EZ. Business: 5 Reef House, London SW11 3UF. Tel: 0171-738 1625. *Chief Executive*, Ms K. Beckett

MAIL USERS' ASSOCIATION (1976), Pharos House, Wye Valley Business Park, Hay-on-Wye, Hereford HR3 5PG. Tel: 01497-821357. *Chairman*, L. K. Morelli

MALAYSIAN RUBBER PRODUCERS' RESEARCH ASSOCIATION (1938), Tun Abdul Razak Laboratory, Brickendonbury, Hertford SG13 8NL. Tel: 01992-584966. *Director*, Dr C. S. L. Baker

MALCOLM SARGENT CANCER FUND FOR CHILDREN (1968), 14 Abingdon Road, London W8 6AF. Tel: 0171-937 4548. *Chief Executive*, Ms S. Darley, OBE

MANAGEMENT, INSTITUTE OF (1992), 3rd Floor, 2 Savoy Court, Strand, London WC2R OEZ. Tel: 0171-497 0580. *Director-General*, R. Young

MANAGEMENT AND PROFESSIONAL STAFFS, ASSOCIATION OF (1972), Parkgates, Bury New Road, Prestwich, Manchester M25 8JX. Tel: 0161-773 8621. *Executive Secretary*, A. J. Casey

MANAGEMENT SERVICES, INSTITUTE OF, 1 Cecil Court, London Road, Enfield, Middx. EN2 6DD. Tel: 0181-366 1261. *Secretary*, F. O'Connolly

MANIC DEPRESSION FELLOWSHIP (1983), 8–10 High Street, Kingston upon Thames, Surrey KT1 1EY. Tel: 0181-974 6550. *Director*, Ms M. Fulford

MANORIAL SOCIETY OF GREAT BRITAIN (1906), 104 Kennington Road, London SE11 6RE. Tel: 0171-735 6633. *Hon. Chairman*, R. A. Smith

MANPOWER SOCIETY (1969), 39 Apple Tree Walk, Climping, Littlehampton, W. Sussex BN17 5QN. Tel: 01903-731728. *Administrator*, Mrs H. Gale

MARIE CURIE CANCER CARE (1948), 28 Belgrave Square, London SW1X 8QG. Tel: 0171-235 3325. *Scottish Office*, 21 Rutland Street, Edinburgh EH1 2AH. Tel: 0131-229 8332. *Director-General*, Maj.-Gen. M. E. Carleton-Smith, CBE

MARINE ARTISTS, ROYAL SOCIETY OF (1939), 17 Carlton House Terrace, London SW1Y 5BD. Tel: 0171-930 6844. *Secretary*, D. Curtis

MARINE BIOLOGICAL ASSOCIATION OF THE UK (1884), Citadel Hill, Plymouth PL1 2PB. Tel: 01752-222772. *Secretary*, Dr M. Whitfield

MARINE ENGINEERS, INSTITUTE OF (1889), The Memorial Building, 76 Mark Lane, London EC3R 7JN. Tel: 0171-481 8493. *Secretary*, J. E. Sloggett

MARINE SCIENCE, THE SCOTTISH ASSOCIATION FOR (1914), PO Box 3, Oban, Argyll PA34 4AD. Tel: 01631-62244. *Secretary*, Prof. J. B. L. Matthews, FRSE

MARINE SOCIETY, THE (1756), 202 Lambeth Road, London SE1 7JW. Tel: 0171-261 9535. *General Secretary*, Lt. Cdr. R. M. Frampton

MARIO LANZA EDUCATIONAL FOUNDATION (1976), 7 Lionsfield Avenue, Allesley Village, Coventry CV5 9GN. *Hon. Secretary*, Miss P. Barron

MARKET AUTHORITIES, NATIONAL ASSOCIATION OF BRITISH (1948), 19 Derwent Avenue, Milnrow, Rochdale, Lancs. OL16 3UD. Tel: 01695-623860. *Secretary*, J. Edwards

MARKETING, CHARTERED INSTITUTE OF (1911), Moor Hall, Cookham, Maidenhead, Berks. SL6 9QH. Tel: 01628-524922. *Director-General*, S. Cuthbert

MARK MASTER MASONS, GRAND LODGE OF (1856), Mark Masons' Hall, 86 St James's Street, London SW1A 1PL. Tel: 0171-839 5274. *Grand Master*, HRH Prince Michael of Kent, KCVO; *Grand Secretary*, P. G. Williams

MASONIC BENEVOLENT INSTITUTION, ROYAL (1842), 20 Great Queen Street, London WC2B 5BG. Tel: 0171-405 8341. *Chief Executive*, Ms J. Reynolds

MASONIC BENEVOLENT INSTITUTIONS IN IRELAND, 17–19 Molesworth Street, Dublin 2. Tel: 00 353-1-679 6799. *Secretary*, M. R. McWilliam

MASONIC TRUST FOR GIRLS AND BOYS (1985), 31 Great Queen Street, London WC2B 5AG. Tel: 0171-405 2644. *Secretary*, Lt.-Col. J. C. Chambers

MASTERS OF WINE, INSTITUTE OF (1955), Five Kings House, 1 Queen Street Place, London EC4R 1QS. Tel: 0171-236 4427. *Executive Director*, D. F. Stevens

MATERNAL AND CHILD WELFARE, NATIONAL ASSOCIATION FOR (1911), 40–42 Osnaburgh Street, London NW1 3ND. Tel: 0171-383 4115. *Administrator*, Mrs F. N. Kapadia

MATERIALS, INSTITUTE OF (1985), 1 Carlton House Terrace, London SW1Y 5DB. Tel: 0171-839 4071. *Secretary*, Dr J. A. Catterall

MATERNITY ALLIANCE, THE (1980), 15 Britannia Street, London WC1X 9JP. Tel: 0171-837 1265. *Chair*, A. Phillips

MATHEMATICAL ASSOCIATION (1871), 259 London Road, Leicester LE2 3BE. Tel: 0116-270 3877. *Executive Secretary*, Ms H. Whitby

MATHEMATICS AND ITS APPLICATIONS, INSTITUTE OF (1964), Catherine Richards House, 16 Nelson Street, Southend-on-Sea SS1 1EF. Tel: 01702-354020. *Registrar*, Dr A. M. Lepper

ME ASSOCIATION (1976), Stanhope House, High Street, Stanford-le-Hope, Essex SS17 0HA. Tel: 01375-642466. *Chief Executive*, Ms V. Airs

MEASUREMENT AND CONTROL, INSTITUTE OF, 87 Gower Street, London WC1E 6AA. Tel: 0171-387 4949. *Secretary*, M. Yates

MECHANICAL ENGINEERS, INSTITUTION OF (1847), 1 Birdcage Walk, London SW1H 9JJ. Tel: 0171-222 7899. *Director-General*, Dr R. Pike

MEDIC-ALERT FOUNDATION, 12 Bridge Wharf, 156 Caledonian Road, London N1 9UU. Tel: 0171-833 3034. *Chief Executive*, Mrs M. B. Evans

MEDICAL COUNCIL, GENERAL (1858), 44 Hallam Street, London W1N 6AE. Tel: 0171-580 7642. *Registrar*, F. Scott

MEDICAL SOCIETY OF LONDON (1773), Lettsom House, 11 Chandos Street, London W1M OEB. Tel: 0171-580 1043. *Registrar*, M. Griffiths, TD

MEDICAL WOMEN'S FEDERATION (1917), Tavistock House North, Tavistock Square, London WC1H 9HX. *Hon. Secretary*, Dr I. Weinreb

MEMORIAL FUND FOR DISASTER RELIEF, Europa House, 13–17 Ironmonger Row, London EC1V 3QN. Tel: 0171-250 1700. *Director*, D. Childs

MENCAP (THE ROYAL SOCIETY FOR MENTALLY HANDICAPPED CHILDREN AND ADULTS) (1946), 123 Golden Lane, London EC1Y ORT. Tel: 0171-454 0454. *Chief Executive*, F. Heddell

MENTAL AFTER CARE ASSOCIATION (1879), 25 Bedford Square, London WC1B 3HW. Tel: 0171-436 6194. *Director*, B. G. Garner

MENTAL HEALTH FOUNDATION, THE (1949), 37 Mortimer Street, London W1N 7RS. Tel: 0171-580 0145. *Director-General*, Ms J. McKerrow

MERCHANT NAVY WELFARE BOARD (1948), 19–21 Lancaster Gate, London W2 3LN. Tel: 0171-723 3642. *General Secretary*, Capt. D. A. Parsons

METAL TRADES BENEVOLENT SOCIETY, ROYAL (1843), Brooke House, 4 The Lakes, Bedford Road, Northampton NN4 7YD. Tel: 01604-22023. *General Secretary*, A. N. Nisbet

METEOROLOGICAL SOCIETY, ROYAL (1850), 104 Oxford Road, Reading, Berks. RG1 7LJ. Tel: 01734-568500. *Executive Secretary*, R. P. C. Swash

METROPOLITAN AND CITY POLICE ORPHANS FUND (1870), 30 Hazlewell Road, London SW15 6LH. Tel: 0181-788 5140. *Secretary*, R. Duff-Cole, BEM

METROPOLITAN AUTHORITIES, ASSOCIATION OF (1974), 35 Great Smith Street, London SW1P 3BJ. Tel: 0171-222 8100. *Secretary*, R. Brooke

METROPOLITAN HOSPITAL-SUNDAY FUND (1872), 40 High Street, Teddington, Middx. TW11 8EW. Tel: 0181-977 4154. *Secretary*, D. A. B. Lynch

MIDDLE EAST ASSOCIATION, THE (1961), Bury House, 33 Bury Street, London SW1Y 6AX. Tel: 0171-839 2137. *Director-General*, J. R. Grundon

MIDWIVES, ROYAL COLLEGE OF (1881), 15 Mansfield Street, London W1M 0BE. Tel: 0171–580 6523. *General Secretary*, Mrs J. Allison

MIGRAINE ASSOCIATION, BRITISH (1958), 178A High Road, West Byfleet, Surrey KT14 7ED. Tel: 01932-352468. *Director*, Mrs J. Liddell

MIGRAINE TRUST (1965), 45 Great Ormond Street, London WC1N 3HD. Tel: 0171-278 2676. *Director*, Ms A. Rush

MILITARY HISTORICAL SOCIETY, National Army Museum, Royal Hospital Road, London SW3 4HT. Tel: 0181-460 7341. *Hon. Secretary*, J. Gaylor

MIND (NATIONAL ASSOCIATION FOR MENTAL HEALTH), 22 Harley Street, London W1N 2ED. Tel: 0171-673 0741. *Director*, Ms J. Clements

MINERALOGICAL SOCIETY (1876), 41 Queen's Gate, London SW7 5HR. Tel: 0171-584 7516. *Hon. General Secretary*, Dr G. M. Manby

MINES OF GREAT BRITAIN, FEDERATION OF SMALL, 29 King Street, Newcastle under Lyme, Staffs. ST5 1ER. Tel: 01782-614618. *Secretary*, R. W. Bladen

MINIATURE PAINTERS, SCULPTORS AND GRAVERS, ROYAL SOCIETY OF (1895), Burwood House, 15 Union Street, Wells, Somerset BA5 2PU. Tel: 01749-674472. *Executive Secretary*, Mrs S. M. Burton

MINING AND METALLURGY, THE INSTITUTION OF (1892), 44 Portland Place, London W1N 4BR. Tel: 0171-580 3802. *Secretary*, M. J. Jones

MINING ENGINEERS, INSTITUTION OF (1889), Danum House, South Parade, Doncaster, S. Yorks. DN1 2DY. Tel: 01302-320486. *Secretary*, Dr G. J. M. Woodrow

MISSING PERSONS HELPLINE, NATIONAL (1992), Roebuck House, 284–286 Upper Richmond Road West, London SW14 7JE. Tel: 0181-392 2000. *Chairman*, D. Winn

MISSION TO DEEP SEA FISHERMEN, ROYAL NATIONAL (1881), 43 Nottingham Place, London W1M 4BX. Tel: 0171-487 5101. *Chief Executive*, A. D. Marsden

MISSIONS TO SEAMEN, THE (1856), St Michael Paternoster Royal, College Hill, London EC4R 2RL. Tel: 0171-248 5202. *Secretary-General*, Revd Canon G. Jones

MODERN CHURCHPEOPLE'S UNION (1898), St Martin's Vicarage, 25 Birch Grove, London W3 9SP. Tel: 0181-992 2333. *General Secretary*, Revd N. Henderson

MONUMENTAL BRASS SOCIETY (1887), 57 Leeside Crescent, London NW11 0HA. *Hon. Secretary*

MORAVIAN MISSIONS, LONDON ASSOCIATION IN AID OF (1817), Moravian Church House, 5–7 Muswell Hill, London N10 3TH. Tel: 0181-883 3409. *Secretary*, Revd F. Linyard

MOTHERS' UNION, THE (1876), Mary Sumner House, 24 Tufton Street, London SW1P 3RB. Tel: 0171-222 5533. *Chief Executive*, Mrs A. Ridler

MOTOR INDUSTRY, INSTITUTE OF THE, Fanshaws, Brickendon, Hertford SG13 8PQ. Tel: 01992-511521. *Secretary*, F. W. Janes

MOUNTBATTEN MEMORIAL TRUST (1979), 1 Grosvenor Crescent, London SW1X 7EF. Tel: 0171-235 5231. *Director*, J. Boyd-Brent

MOUNTBATTEN TRUST, THE EDWINA (1960), 1 Grosvenor Crescent, London SW1X 7EF. Tel: 0171-235 5231. *Secretary*, J. Boyd-Brent

MULTIPLE SCLEROSIS SOCIETY (1953), 25 Effie Road, London SW6 1EE. Tel: 0171-736 6267. *General Secretary*, J. Walford

MUNICIPAL ENGINEERS, ASSOCIATION OF, Institution of Civil Engineers, 1–7 Great George Street, London SW1P 3AA. Tel: 0171-222 7722. *Director*, K. J. Marchant

MUSEUMS ASSOCIATION (1889), 42 Clerkenwell Close, London EC1R 0PA. Tel: 0171-250 1836. *Director*, M. Taylor

MUSIC HALL SOCIETY, BRITISH (1963), Brodie and Middleton Ltd, 68 Drury Lane, London WC2B 5SP. Tel: 0171-836 3289/80. *Hon. Secretary*, Mrs J. D. Masterton

MUSICIANS BENEVOLENT FUND (1921), 16 Ogle Street, London W1P 7LG. Tel: 0171-636 4481. *Secretary*, Ms H. Faulkner

MUSICIANS, INCORPORATED SOCIETY OF (1882), 10 Stratford Place, London W1N 9AE. Tel: 0171-629 4413. *Chief Executive*, N. Hoyle

MUSICIANS OF GREAT BRITAIN, ROYAL SOCIETY OF (1738), 10 Stratford Place, London W1N 9AE. Tel: 0171-629 6137. *Administrator*, Mrs M. Gibb

MUSIC INFORMATION CENTRE, BRITISH (1967), 10 Stratford Place, London W1N 9AE. Tel: 0171-499 8567. *Administrator*, R. Montgomery

MUSIC SOCIETIES, NATIONAL FEDERATION OF (1935), Francis House, Francis Street, London SW1P 1DE. Tel: 0171-828 7320. *Director*, R. Jones

NABC – CLUBS FOR YOUNG PEOPLE (1925), 369 Kennington Lane, London SE11 5QY. Tel: 0171-793 0787. *National Director*, D. James

NACRO (NATIONAL ASSOCIATION FOR THE CARE AND RESETTLEMENT OF OFFENDERS) (1966), 169 Clapham Road, London SW9 0PU. Tel: 0171-582 6500. *Director*, Ms V. Stern

NATIONAL BENEVOLENT INSTITUTION (1812), 61 Bayswater Road, London W2 3PG. Tel: 0171-723 0021. *Secretary*, Gp Capt D. St J. Homer, MVO

NATIONAL COUNCIL FOR VOLUNTARY ORGANIZATIONS (1919), Regent's Wharf, 8 All Saints Street, London N1 9RL. Tel: 0171-713 6161. *Director*, Ms J. Weleminsky

NATIONAL COUNCIL OF WOMEN OF GREAT BRITAIN (1895), 36 Danbury Street, London N1 8JU. Tel: 0171-354 2395. *President*, Ms J. Clark

NATIONAL EXTENSION COLLEGE (1963), 18 Brooklands Avenue, Cambridge CB2 2HN. Tel: 01223-316644. *Director*, R. Morpeth

NATIONAL FRONT (1967), PO Box 2269, London E6 3RF. Tel: 0181-471 6872. *Chairman*, I. Anderson

NATIONAL LISTENING LIBRARY, 12 Lant Street, London SE1 1QH. Tel: 0171-407 9417. *Executive Director*, G. A. Hepworth

NATIONAL SOCIETY, THE, (1811), Church House, Great Smith Street, London SW1P 3NZ. Tel: 0171-222 1672. For promoting religious education. *General Secretary*, G. Duncan

NATIONAL SOCIETY FOR THE PREVENTION OF CRUELTY TO CHILDREN (NSPCC) (1884), 67 Saffron Hill, London ECIN 8RS. Tel: 0171-242 1626. *Director,* C. Brown

NATIONAL TRUST, THE (1895), 36 Queen Anne's Gate, London SWIH 9AS. Tel: 0171-222 9251. *Chairman,* Lord Chorley; *Director-General,* Sir Angus Stirling

NATIONAL TRUST FOR SCOTLAND (1931), 5 Charlotte Square, Edinburgh EH2 4DU. Tel: 0131-226 5922. *Chairman,* R. C. Tyrrel; *Director,* Rear-Adm. D. Dow, CB

NATIONAL UNION OF STUDENTS (1922), Nelson Mandela House, 461 Holloway Road, London N7 6LJ. Tel: 0171-272 8900. *National President,* J. Murphy

NATIONAL VIEWERS' AND LISTENERS' ASSOCIATION (1964), All Saints House, High Street, Colchester COI IUG. Tel: 01206-561155. *Chairman,* Revd G. Stevens

NATIONAL WOMEN'S REGISTER (1960), 9 Bank Plain, Norwich, Norfolk NR2 4SL. Tel: 01603-765392. *National Organizer,* Ms J. Ross

NATION'S FUND FOR NURSES (1917), 3 Albemarle Way, London ECIV 4JB. Tel: 0171-490 1808. *Administrator,* Mrs P. Bagnall

NATURALISTS' ASSOCIATION, BRITISH (1905), I Bracken Mews, Chingford, London E4 7UT. *Hon. Membership Secretary,* Mrs Y. H. Griffiths

NATURE CONSERVATION, ROYAL SOCIETY FOR, *see* RSNC

NAUTICAL RESEARCH, SOCIETY FOR (1911), c/o National Maritime Museum, Greenwich, London SEIO 9NF. *Hon. Secretary,* D. G. Law

NAVAL, MILITARY AND AIR FORCE BIBLE SOCIETY (1780), Radstock House, 3 Eccleston Street, London SWIW 9LZ. Tel: 0171-730 2155 ext. 242. *General Secretary,* Lt.-Cdr. J. M. Hines

NAVAL ARCHITECTS, ROYAL INSTITUTION OF (1860), 10 Upper Belgrave Street, London SWIX 8BQ. Tel: 0171-235 4622. *Secretary,* J. Rosewarn

NAVIGATION, ROYAL INSTITUTE OF (1947), I Kensington Gore, London SW7 2AT. Tel: 0171-589 5021. *Director,* Gp Capt D. W. Broughton, MBE

NAVY RECORDS SOCIETY (1893), Barclays de Zoete Wedd Ltd, Ground Floor, Minster House, 12 Arthur Street, London EC4R 9AB. *Hon. Secretary,* A. J. McMillan

NCH ACTION FOR CHILDREN (1869), 85 Highbury Park, London N5 IUD. Tel: 0171-226 2033. *Principal and Chief Executive,* T. White, CBE

NEEDLEWORK, ROYAL SCHOOL OF (1872), Apartment 12A, Hampton Court Palace, East Molesey, Surrey KT8 9AU. Tel: 0181-943 1432. *Principal,* Mrs E. Elvin

NEWCOMEN SOCIETY (1920), The Science Museum, London SW7 2DD. Tel: 0171-589 1793. For the study of the history of engineering and technology. *Executive Secretary,* C. Ellam

NEWSPAPER PRESS FUND (1864), Dickens House, 35 Wathen Road, Dorking, Surrey RH4 IJY. Tel: 01306-887511. *Director,* P. W. Evans

NEWSVENDORS' BENEVOLENT INSTITUTION (1839), PO Box 306, Dunmow, Essex CM6 IHY. Tel: 01371-874198. *Director,* B. Buckingham

NOISE ABATEMENT SOCIETY (1959), PO Box 8, Bromley, Kent BR2 OUH. *Chairman,* J. Connell, OBE

NON-SMOKERS, NATIONAL SOCIETY OF, *see* QUIT

NORWOOD CHILD CARE (1795), Norwood House, Harmony Way, Victoria Road, London NW4 2DR. Tel: 0181-203 3030. *Executive Director,* S. Brier

NOTARIES' SOCIETY (1907), 7 Lower Brook Street, Ipswich IP4 IAF. Tel: 01473-214762. *Secretary,* A. G. Dunford

NUCLEAR ENERGY SOCIETY, BRITISH (1962), 1–7 Great George Street, London SWIP 3AA. Tel: 0171-839 9838. *Executive Officer,* P. Bacos

NUFFIELD FOUNDATION (1943), 28 Bedford Square, London WCIB 3EG. Tel: 0171-631 0566. *Director,* R. Hazell

NUFFIELD PROVINCIAL HOSPITALS TRUST (1939), 59 New Cavendish Street, London WIM 7RD. Tel: 0171-485 6632. *Secretary,* Dr M. Ashley-Miller

NUMISMATIC SOCIETY, BRITISH (1903), c/o Hunterian Museum, Glasgow University, Glasgow GI2 8DQ. Tel: 0141-330 4221. *Hon. Secretary,* Dr J. D. Bateson

NUMISMATIC SOCIETY, ROYAL (1836), c/o Department of Coins and Medals, The British Museum, Great Russell Street, London WCIB 3DG. Tel: 0171-323 8585. *Hon. Secretaries,* J. E. Cribb; R. G. Bland

NURSES' NATIONAL HOME, RETIRED (1934), Riverside Avenue, Bournemouth BH7 7EE. Tel: 01202-396418. *Chairman,* G. J. Rowlett

NURSES, ROYAL NATIONAL PENSION FUND FOR, Burdett House, 15 Buckingham Street, London WC2N 6ED. Tel: 0171-839 6785. *General Manager,* V. G. West

NURSING, MIDWIFERY AND HEALTH VISITING, UK CENTRAL COUNCIL FOR, 23 Portland Place, London WIN 3AF. Tel: 0171-637 7181. *Registrar and Chief Executive,* C. Ralph

NURSING, MIDWIFERY AND HEALTH VISITING, ENGLISH NATIONAL BOARD FOR, Victory House, 170 Tottenham Court Road, London WIP OHA. Tel: 0171-388 3131. *Chief Executive Officer,* A. P. Smith

NURSING, MIDWIFERY AND HEALTH VISITING, WELSH NATIONAL BOARD FOR, Floor 13, Pearl Assurance House, Greyfriars Road, Cardiff CFI 3AG. Tel: 01222-395535. *Chief Executive,* D. A. Ravey

NURSING, MIDWIFERY AND HEALTH VISITING FOR SCOTLAND, NATIONAL BOARD FOR, 22 Queen Street, Edinburgh EH2 INT. Tel: 0131-226 7371. *Chief Executive,* Mrs E. Mitchell

NURSING, MIDWIFERY AND HEALTH VISITING FOR NORTHERN IRELAND, NATIONAL BOARD FOR, RAC House, 79 Chichester Street, Belfast BTI 4JE. Tel: 01232-238152. *Chief Executive,* Dr O. D'A. Slevin

NURSING, ROYAL COLLEGE OF (1916), 20 Cavendish Square, London WIM OAB. Tel: 0171-409 3333. *General Secretary,* Miss C. Hancock

NUTRITION FOUNDATION, BRITISH (1967), High Holborn House, 52–54 High Holborn, London WCIV 6RQ. Tel: 0171-404 6504. *Director-General,* Dr B. A. Wharton

NUTRITION SOCIETY (1941), 10 Cambridge Court, 210 Shepherds Bush Road, London W6 7NJ. Tel: 0171-602 0228. *Hon. Secretary,* Dr R. F. Grimble

OBSTETRICIANS AND GYNAECOLOGISTS, ROYAL COLLEGE OF (1929), 27 Sussex Place, London NWI 4RG. Tel: 0171-262 5425. *Secretary,* P. A. Barnett

OCCUPATIONAL PENSIONS ADVISORY SERVICE (1982), II Belgrave Road, London SWIV IRB. Tel: 0171-233 8080. *Chief Executive,* D. Hall

OCCUPATIONAL SAFETY AND HEALTH, INSTITUTION OF (1946), The Grange, Highfield Drive, Wigston, Leicester LE18 1NN. Tel: 0116-257 1399. *Chief Executive*, J. R. Barrell

OFFICERS' ASSOCIATION, THE (1920), 48 Pall Mall, London SW1Y 5JY. Tel: 0171-930 0125. *General Secretary*, Brig. P. D. Johnson

OFFICERS' PENSIONS SOCIETY LTD (1946), 68 South Lambeth Road, London SW8 1RL. Tel: 0171-820 9988. *General Secretary*, Maj.-Gen. Sir Laurence New, CB, CBE

OIL PAINTERS, ROYAL INSTITUTE OF (1883), 17 Carlton House Terrace, London SW1Y 5BD. Tel: 0171-930 6844. *Secretary*, B. Bennett

OILSEED, OIL AND FEEDINGSTUFFS TRADES BENEVOLENT ASSOCIATION, c/o Baltic Exchange, 14–20 St. Mary Axe, London EC3A 8BH. Tel: 0171-369 1643. *Secretary*, D. A. Painter

ONE PARENT FAMILIES, NATIONAL COUNCIL FOR, 255 Kentish Town Road, London NW5 2LX. Tel: 0171-267 1361. *Director*, Miss S. Slipman, OBE

OPEN-AIR MISSION, THE (1853), 19 John Street, London WC1N 2DL. Tel: 0171-405 6135. *Secretary*, A. J. Greenbank

OPEN SPACES SOCIETY (1865), 25A Bell Street, Henley-on-Thames, Oxon. RG9 2BA. Tel: 01491-573535. *General Secretary*, Miss K. Ashbrook

OPERATIC AND DRAMATIC ASSOCIATION, NATIONAL (1899), NODA House, 1 Crestfield Street, London WC1H 8AU. Tel: 0171-837 5655. *General Administrator*, M. Thorburn

OPSIS (National Association for the Education, Training and Support of Blind and Partially Sighted People) (1992), Albany House, 5 New Street, Salisbury, Wilts. SP1 2PH. Tel: 01722-410234. *Secretary-General*, Sir Anthony Walker, KCB

OPTICAL COUNCIL, GENERAL (1958), 41 Harley Street, London W1N 2DJ. Tel: 0171-580 3898. *Registrar*, R. Wilshin

OPTOMETRISTS, BRITISH COLLEGE OF, 10 Knaresborough Place, London SW5 0TG. Tel: 0171-373 7765. *General Secretary*, P. D. Leigh

ORDERS AND MEDALS RESEARCH SOCIETY (1942), 123 Turnpike Link, Croydon CR0 5NU. Tel: 0181-680 2701. *General Secretary*, N. G. Gooding

ORIENTAL CERAMIC SOCIETY, THE (1921), 30B Torrington Square, London WC1E 7LJ. Tel: 0171-636 7985. *Secretary*, Mrs J. Martin

ORNITHOLOGISTS' CLUB, SCOTTISH (1936), 21 Regent Terrace, Edinburgh EH7 5BT. Tel: 0131-556 6042.

ORNITHOLOGISTS' UNION, BRITISH (1858), c/o Natural History Museum, Akeman Street, Tring, Herts. HP23 6AP. Tel: 01442-890080. *Administrative Secretary*, Mrs G. Bonham

ORNITHOLOGY, BRITISH TRUST FOR (1932) National Centre for Ornithology, The Nunnery, Thetford, Norfolk IP24 2PU. Tel: 01842-750050. *Director of Services*, A. Elvin

ORTHOPAEDIC ASSOCIATION, BRITISH (1918), c/o The Royal College of Surgeons, 35–43 Lincoln's Inn Fields, London WC2A 3PN. Tel: 0171-405 6507. *Hon. Secretary*, I. J. Leslie, FRCS

OSTEOPATHIC MEDICINE, LONDON COLLEGE OF, 8–10 Boston Place, London NW1 6QH. Tel: 0171-262 1128/5250. *Secretary*, W. R. MacDonald

OSTEOPATHS, GENERAL COUNCIL AND REGISTER OF (1936), 56 London Street, Reading, Berks. RG1 4SQ. Tel: 01734-576585. *Secretary*, Lt.-Col. G. P. Blaker

OSTEOPOROSIS SOCIETY, NATIONAL (1986), PO Box 10, Radstock, Bath BA3 3YB. Tel: 01761-432472. *General Secretary*, Miss H. Wollacott

OUTWARD BOUND TRUST LTD (1941), Chestnut Field, Regent Place, Rugby, Warks. CV21 2PJ. Tel: 01788-560423. *Director*, I. L. Fothergill

OVERSEAS DEVELOPMENT INSTITUTE (1960), Regent's College, Inner Circle, Regent's Park, London NW1 4NS. Tel: 0171-487 7413. *Director*, Dr J. Howell

OVERSEAS SERVICE PENSIONERS' ASSOCIATION (1960), 138 High Street, Tonbridge, Kent TN9 1AX. Tel: 01732-363836. *Secretary*, D. LeBreton, CBE

OVERSEAS SETTLEMENT (1925), Church of England Board for Social Responsibility, Great Smith Street, London SW1P 3NZ. Tel: 0171-222 9011. *Administration Secretary*, Miss P. J. Hallett

OXFAM (1942), 274 Banbury Road, Oxford OX2 7DZ. Tel: 01865-312140. *Director*, D. Bryer

OXFORD PRESERVATION TRUST (1927), 10 Turn Again Lane, St Ebbes, Oxford OX1 1QL. Tel: 01865-242918. *Secretary*, Mrs M. Haynes

OXFORD SOCIETY (1932), 41 Wellington Square, Oxford OX1 2JF. Tel: 01865-270088. *Secretary*, Dr H. A. Hurren

PAEDIATRIC ASSOCIATION, BRITISH (1928), 5 St Andrew's Place, London NW1 4LB. Tel: 0171-486 6151. *Hon. Secretary*, Dr R. MacFaul

PAINTER-PRINTMAKERS, ROYAL SOCIETY OF (1880), Bankside Gallery, 48 Hopton Street, London SE1 9JH. Tel: 0171-928 7521. *Secretary*, Ms J. Dixley

PAINTERS IN WATER COLOURS, ROYAL INSTITUTE OF (1831), 17 Carlton House Terrace, London SW1Y 5BD. Tel: 0171-930 6844. *Secretary*, R. Spurrier

PALAEONTOGRAPHICAL SOCIETY (1847) c/o British Geological Survey, Keyworth, Nottingham NG12 5GG. *Secretary*, S. P. Tunnicliff

PALAEONTOLOGICAL ASSOCIATION (1957), c/o British Antarctic Survey, High Cross, Madingley Road, Cambridge CB3 0ET. Tel: 01223-251443. *Secretary*, Dr J. A. Crame

PARENTS AT WORK (1985), 77 Holloway Road, London N7 8JZ. Tel: 0171-700 5771. *Director*, Mrs L. Daniels

PARKINSON'S DISEASE SOCIETY (1969), 22 Upper Woburn Place, London WC1H 0RA. Tel: 0171-383 3513. *Chief Executive*, M. Whelan

PARLIAMENTARY AND SCIENTIFIC COMMITTEE (1939), 16 Great College Street, London SW1P 3RX. Tel: 0171-222 7085. *Secretary*, A. Butler

PASTORAL PSYCHOLOGY, GUILD OF (1936), PO Box 1107, London W3 6ZP. Tel: 0181-993 8366. *Administrator*, Mrs N. Stanley

PATENT AGENTS, CHARTERED INSTITUTE OF (1882), Staple Inn Buildings, High Holborn, London WC1V 7PZ. Tel: 0171-405 9450. *Secretary*, M. C. Ralph

PATENTEES AND INVENTORS, INSTITUTE OF (1919), Suite 505a, Triumph House, 189 Regent Street, London W1R 7WF. Tel: 0171-242 7812. *Secretary*, R. Magnus

PATHOLOGISTS, ROYAL COLLEGE OF, 2 Carlton House Terrace, London SW1Y 5AF. Tel: 0171-930 5863. *Secretary*, K. Lockyer

PATIENTS ASSOCIATION (1963), 18 Victoria Park Square, London E2 9PF. *Director*, Mrs L. Lamont

PEACE COUNCIL, NATIONAL (1908), 88 Islington High Street, London N1 8EG. Tel: 0171-354 5200. *Co-ordinators*, L. McLeod, D. Thompson, Ms L. Peck

PEAK AND NORTHERN FOOTPATHS SOCIETY (1894), 15 Parkfield Drive, Tyldesley, Manchester M29 8NR. Tel: 0161-790 4383. *Hon. General Secretary*, D. Taylor

PEARSON'S HOLIDAY FUND, PO Box 123, Bishops Waltham, Southampton, Hants SO32 IZE. Tel: 01489-893260. *General Secretary*, R. Heasman

PEDESTRIANS ASSOCIATION (1929), 126 Aldersgate Street, London EC1A 4JQ. Tel: 0171-490 0750. *Chairman*, Ms F. Lawson

PEN, INTERNATIONAL (1921), 9–10 Charterhouse Building, Goswell Road, London EC1M 7AT. Tel: 0171-253 4308. World association of writers. *International Secretary*, A. Blokh

PENSION FUNDS LTD, NATIONAL ASSOCIATION OF (1923), 12–18 Grosvenor Gardens, London SW1W 0DH. Tel: 0171-730 0585. *Director-General*, M. A. Elton

PEOPLE'S DISPENSARY FOR SICK ANIMALS (PDSA) (1917), Whitechapel Way, Priorslee, Telford, Shropshire TF2 9PQ. Tel: 01952-290999. *Director-General*, M. R. Curtis, MBE

PERFORMING RIGHT SOCIETY LTD (1914), 29–33 Berners Street, London W1P 4AA. Tel: 0171-580 5544. *General Manager*, J. Axon

PERIODICAL PUBLISHERS ASSOCIATION LTD (1913), Imperial House, 15–19 Kingsway, London WC2B 6UN. Tel: 0171-379 6268. *Chief Executive*, I. Locks

PESTALOZZI CHILDREN'S VILLAGE TRUST (1959), Sedlescombe, Battle, E. Sussex TN33 0RR. Tel: 01424-870444. *Director*, M. Phillips

PETROLEUM, INSTITUTE OF (1913), 61 New Cavendish Street, London W1M 8AR. Tel: 0171-467 7100. *Director-General*, I. Ward

PHARMACEUTICAL SOCIETY OF GREAT BRITAIN, ROYAL (1841), 1 Lambeth High Street, London SE1 7JN. *Secretary and Registrar*, J. Ferguson

PHARMACOLOGICAL SOCIETY, BRITISH (1931), 16 Angel Gate, City Road, London EC1V 2PT. Tel: 0171-417 0113. *Hon. General Secretary*, Dr J. Maclagan

PHILOLOGICAL SOCIETY (1842), School of Oriental and African Studies, University of London, Thornhaugh Street, London WC1H 0XG. Tel: 0171-323 6318. *Hon. Secretary*, Prof. R. J. Hayward

PHILOSOPHY, ROYAL INSTITUTE OF (1925), 14 Gordon Square, London WC1H 0AG. Tel: 0171-387 4130. *Director*, Prof. A. Phillips Griffiths

PHOTOGRAPHY, BRITISH INSTITUTE OF PROFESSIONAL (1901), Fox Talbot House, Amwell End, Ware, Herts. SG12 9HN. Tel: 01920-464011. *Chief Executive*, A. M. Berkeley

PHYSICAL RECREATION, CENTRAL COUNCIL OF (1935), Francis House, Francis Street, London SW1P 1DE. Tel: 0171-828 3163. *General Secretary*, P. Lawson

PHYSICIANS, ROYAL COLLEGE OF (1518), 11 St Andrew's Place, London NW1 4LE. Tel: 0171-935 1174. *Secretary*, D. B. Lloyd

PHYSICIANS AND SURGEONS OF GLASGOW, ROYAL COLLEGE OF (1599), 234–242 St Vincent Street, Glasgow G2 5RJ. Tel: 0141-221 6072. *Hon. Secretary*, Dr B. Williams

PHYSICIANS OF EDINBURGH, ROYAL COLLEGE OF (1681), 9 Queen Street, Edinburgh EH2 1JQ. Tel: 0131-225 7324. *Secretary*, Dr J. St J. Thomas

PHYSICS, INSTITUTE OF (1874), 47 Belgrave Square, London SW1X 8QX. Tel: 0171-235 6111. *Chief Executive*, Dr A. Jones

PHYSIOLOGICAL SOCIETY (1876), PO Box 506, Oxford OX1 3XE. Tel: 01865-798498. *Hon. Secretary*, Dr C. A. R. Boyd

PHYSIOTHERAPY, CHARTERED SOCIETY OF (1894), 14 Bedford Row, London WC1R 4ED. Tel: 0171-242 1941. *Secretary*, T. Simon

PIG ASSOCIATION, BRITISH (1884), 7 Rickmansworth Road, Watford, Herts. WD1 7HE. Tel: 01923-234377. *Chief Executive*, G. E. Welsh

PILGRIM TRUST, THE (1930), Fielden House, Little College Street, London SW1P 3SH. Tel: 0171-222 4723. *Secretary*, Hon. A. Hoyer Millar

PILGRIMS OF GREAT BRITAIN, THE (1902), Savoy Hotel, London WC2R 0EU. *Hon. Secretary*, M. P. S. Barton

PLANT ENGINEERS, INSTITUTION OF, 77 Great Peter Street, London SW1P 2EZ. Tel: 0171-233 2855. *Secretary-General*, R. S. Pratt

PLAYING FIELDS ASSOCIATION, NATIONAL (1925), 25 Ovington Square, London SW3 1LQ. Tel: 0171-584 6445. *Director*, Ms E. Davies

POETRY SOCIETY, THE (1909), 22 Betterton Street, London WC2H 9BU. Tel: 0171-240 4810. *Director and General Secretary*, C. Green

POLICY STUDIES INSTITUTE (1978), 100 Park Village East, London NW1 3SR. Tel: 0171-387 2171. *Director*, Ms P. Meadows

POLIO FELLOWSHIP, BRITISH (1939), Bell Close, West End Road, Ruislip, Middx. HA4 6LP. Tel: 01895-675515. *General Secretary*, M. Drake

POLITE SOCIETY, THE (1986), 6 Norman Avenue, Henley-on-Thames, Oxon. RG9 1SG. Tel: 01491-572794. *Hon. Secretary*, Miss G. Mackenzie

PORTRAIT PAINTERS, ROYAL SOCIETY OF (1891), 17 Carlton House Terrace, London SW1Y 5BD. Tel: 0171-930 6844. *Secretary*, J. Stultiens

POST OFFICE USERS' NATIONAL COUNCIL (1970), Waterloo Bridge House, Waterloo Road, London SE1 8UA. Tel: 0171-928 9458. *Secretary*, K. Hall

PRAYER BOOK SOCIETY, THE (1975), St James Garlickhythe, Garlick Hill, London EC4V 2AL. Tel: 0181-958 8769. *Hon. Secretary*, Mrs. M. Thompson

PRECEPTORS, COLLEGE OF (1846), Coppice Row, Theydon Bois, Epping, Essex CM16 7DN. Tel: 01992-812727. *Chief Executive Officer*, T. Wheatley

PRE-SCHOOL PLAYGROUPS ASSOCIATION, 61–63 Kings Cross Road, London WC1X 9LL. Tel: 0171-833 0991. *Chief Executive Officer*, Ms M. Lochrie

PRESS UNION, COMMONWEALTH (1909), Studio House, 184 Fleet Street, London EC4A 2DU. Tel: 0171-242 1056. *Director*, R. MacKichan

PREVENTION OF ACCIDENTS, THE ROYAL SOCIETY FOR THE (1916), Cannon House, The Priory Queensway, Birmingham B4 6BS. Tel: 0121-200 2461. *Chief Executive*, A. Edwards

PRINCESS LOUISE SCOTTISH HOSPITAL (Erskine Hospital) (1916), Bishopton, Renfrewshire PA7 5PU. Tel: 0141-812 1100. For disabled ex-servicemen and women. *Commandant*, Col. W. K. Shepherd

PRINCESS ROYAL TRUST FOR CARERS (1990), 16 Byward Street, London EC3R 5BA. Tel: 0171-480 7788. *Chief Executive*, Dr E. Nelson

PRINCE'S SCOTTISH YOUTH BUSINESS TRUST, THE (1989), 6th Floor, Mercantile Chambers, 53 Bothwell Street, Glasgow G2 6TS. Tel: 0141-248 4999. *Director*, D. W. Cooper

PRINCE'S TRUST, THE (1976) and THE ROYAL JUBILEE TRUSTS (1935, 1977), 8 Bedford Row, London WC1R 4BA. Tel: 0171-430 0524. *Director*, T. Shebbeare

PRINCE'S YOUTH BUSINESS TRUST, THE, 5 Cleveland Place, London SW1Y 6JJ. Tel: 0171-925 2900. *Chief Executive*, J. White

PRINTERS' CHARITABLE CORPORATION (1827), Victoria House, Harestone Valley Road, Caterham, Surrey CR3 6HY. Tel: 01883-345331. *Director*, H. J. Court

PRINTING HISTORICAL SOCIETY (1964), St Bride Institute, Bride Lane, London EC4Y 8EE. *Hon. Secretary*, J. H. Bowman

PRINTING, INSTITUTE OF (1961), 8 Lonsdale Gardens, Tunbridge Wells, Kent TN1 1NU. Tel: 01892-538118. *Secretary-General*, D. Freeland

PRISONERS ABROAD (1978), 72–82 Rosebery Avenue, London EC1R 4RR. Tel: 0171-833 3467. *Director*, Ms J. Johnstone

PRISON VISITORS, NATIONAL ASSOCIATION OF (1922), 46B Hartington Street, Bedford MK41 7RP. Tel: 01234-359763. *General Secretary*, Mrs A. G. McKenna

PRIVATE LIBRARIES ASSOCIATION (1957), Ravelston, South View Road, Pinner, Middx. HA5 3YD. *Hon. Secretary*, F. Broomhead

PROCURATORS IN GLASGOW, ROYAL FACULTY OF (1600), 12 Nelson Mandela Place, Glasgow G2 1BT. Tel: 0141-552 3422. *Clerk*, A. J. Campbell

PROFESSIONAL CLASSES AID COUNCIL (1921), 10 St Christopher's Place, London W1M 6HY. Tel: 0171-935 0641. *Secretary*

PROFESSIONAL ENGINEERS, UK ASSOCIATION OF (1969), Hayes Court, West Common Road, Bromley BR2 7AU. Tel: 0181-462 7755. *National Secretary*, J. M. Dalgleish

PROFESSIONAL FOOTBALLERS' ASSOCIATION, 2 Oxford Court, Bishopsgate, Manchester M2 3WQ. Tel: 0161-236 0575. *Chief Executive*, G. Taylor

PROFESSIONS SUPPLEMENTARY TO MEDICINE, THE COUNCIL FOR, Park House, 184 Kennington Park Road, London SE11 4BU. Tel: 0171-582 0866. *Registrar*, R. Pickis

PROTECTION OF THE UNBORN CHILD, SOCIETY FOR THE (1967), 7 Tufton Street, London SW1P 3QN. Tel: 0171-222 5845. *National Director*, Mrs P. Bowman

PROTESTANT ALLIANCE, THE (1845), 77 Ampthill Road, Flitwick, Bedford MK45 1BD. Tel: 01525-712348. *General Secretary*, Dr S. J. Scott-Pearson

PSORIASIS ASSOCIATION (1968), 7 Milton Street, Northampton NN2 7JG. Tel: 01604-711129. *National Secretary*, Mrs L. Henley

PSYCHIATRISTS, ROYAL COLLEGE OF (1971), 17 Belgrave Square, London SW1X 8PG. Tel: 0171-235 2351. *Secretary*, Mrs V. Cameron

PSYCHICAL RESEARCH, SOCIETY FOR (1882), 49 Marloes Road, London W8 6LA. Tel: 0171-937 8984. *Secretary*, Ms E. O'Keefe

PSYCHOLOGICAL SOCIETY, BRITISH (1901), St Andrews House, 48 Princess Road East, Leicester LE1 7DR. Tel: 0116-254 9568. *Executive Secretary*, C. V. Newman, PH.D.

PUBLIC FINANCE AND ACCOUNTANCY, CHARTERED INSTITUTE OF (1885), 3 Robert Street, London WC2N 6BH. Tel: 0171-895 8823. *Director*, N. P. Hepworth, OBE

PUBLIC HEALTH AND HYGIENE, ROYAL INSTITUTE OF (1937), 28 Portland Place, London W1N 4DE. Tel: 0171-580 2731. *Secretary*, Gp Capt. R. A. Smith

PUBLIC RELATIONS, INSTITUTE OF (1948), The Old Trading House, 15 Northburgh Street, London EC1V 0PR. Tel: 0171-253 5151. *Executive Director*, J. B. Lavelle

PUBLIC TEACHERS OF LAW, SOCIETY OF (1908), All Souls College, Oxford OX1 4AL. Tel: 01865-279338. *Hon. Secretary*, Prof. P. B. H. Birks

PURCHASING AND SUPPLY, CHARTERED INSTITUTE OF (1967), Easton House, Easton on the Hill, Stamford, Lincs. PE9 3NZ. Tel: 01780-56777. *Director-General*, P. Thomson

PURE WATER ASSOCIATION, NATIONAL (1960), Meridan, Cae Goody Lane, Ellesmere, Shrops. SY12 9DW. Tel: 01691-623015. *Secretary*, N. Brugge

QUAKER SOCIAL RESPONSIBILITY AND EDUCATION, Friends House, Euston Road, London NW1 2BJ. Tel: 0171-387 3601. *General Secretary*, Ms B. Smith

QUALITY ASSURANCE, INSTITUTE OF, PO Box 712, 61 Southwark Street, London SE1 1SB. Tel: 0171-401 7227. *Secretary-General*, D. Campbell

QUARRIER'S HOMES (1871), Bridge of Weir, Renfrewshire PA11 3SA. Tel: 01505-612224. *Director*, G. E. Lee

QUARRYING, INSTITUTE OF (1917), 7 Regent Street, Nottingham NG1 5BS. Tel: 0115-941 1315. *Secretary*, M. J. Arthur

QUEEN ELIZABETH'S FOUNDATION FOR DISABLED PEOPLE (1967), Leatherhead Court, Leatherhead, Surrey KT22 0BN. Tel: 01372-842204. *Director*, M. B. Clark, PH.D.

QUEEN VICTORIA CLERGY FUND (1897), Church House, Dean's Yard, London SW1P 3NZ. Tel: 0171-222 5261. *Secretary*, C. D. L. Menzies

QUEEN VICTORIA SCHOOL (1908), Dunblane, Perthshire FK15 0JY. Tel: 01786-822288. *Headmaster*, B. Raine

QUEEN'S ENGLISH SOCIETY, THE (1972), 104 Drive Mansions, Fulham Road, London SW6 5JH. Tel: 0171-371 7530. *Hon. Membership Secretary*, M. Plumbe

QUEEN'S NURSING INSTITUTE (1887), 3 Albemarle Way, London EC1V 4JB. Tel: 0171-490 4227. *Director*, Mrs P. Bagnall

QUEKETT MICROSCOPICAL CLUB (1865). *Hon. Business Secretary*, B. Scott, 237 Petts Hill, Northolt, Middx. UB5 4NR

QUIT (NATIONAL SOCIETY OF NON-SMOKERS) (1926), Victory House, 170 Tottenham Court Road, London W1P 0HA. Tel: 0171-388 5775. *Director*, P. McCabe

RADAR (ROYAL ASSOCIATION FOR DISABILITY AND REHABILITATION) (1977), 12 City Forum, 250 City Road, London EC1V 8AF. Tel: 0171-250 3222. *Director*, B. Massie, OBE

RADIOLOGISTS, ROYAL COLLEGE OF (1934), 38 Portland Place, London W1N 3DG. Tel: 0171-636 4432. *Secretary*, A. J. Cowles

RADIOLOGY, BRITISH INSTITUTE OF (1897), 36 Portland Place, London W1N 4AT. Tel: 0171-580 4085. *Chief Executive*, Ms M. A. Piggott

RAILWAY AND CANAL HISTORICAL SOCIETY, 17 Clumber Crescent North, The Park, Nottingham NG7 1EY. Tel: 0115-941 4844. *Hon. Secretary,* G. H. R. Gwatkin

RAILWAY BENEVOLENT INSTITUTION (1858), Pullman House, Railway Technical Centre, London Road, Derby DE24 8UP. Tel: 01332-264082. *Director,* R. B. Boiling

RAINER FOUNDATION (1876), 89 Blackheath Hill, London SE10 8TJ. Tel: 0181-694 9497. Provides community-based services for young people who are homeless, offending or in difficulty with their families. *Director,* Dr R. Kay

RAMBLERS' ASSOCIATION (1935), 1–5 Wandsworth Road, London SW8 2XX. Tel: 0171-582 6878. *Director,* A. Mattingly

RANFURLY LIBRARY SERVICE (1954), 2 Coldharbour Place, 39–41 Coldharbour Lane, London SE5 9NR. Tel: 0171-733 3577. *Director,* Mrs S. Harrity

RARE BREEDS SURVIVAL TRUST (1973), National Agricultural Centre, Kenilworth, Warks. CV8 2LG. Tel: 01203-696551. *Executive Director,* L. Alderson

RATHBONE SOCIETY, THE (1919), 1st Floor, The Excalibur Building, Whitworth Street, Manchester M1 6EZ. Tel: 0161-236 5358. Advice Line: 0161-236 1877. Helps people with learning difficulties. *Chief Executive,* Ms A. Weinstock, CBE

RECORD SOCIETY, SCOTTISH (1897), Department of Scottish History, University of Glasgow, Glasgow G12 8QH. Tel: 0141-339 8855, ext. 5682. *Hon. Secretary,* J. Kirk, PH.D.

RECORDS ASSOCIATION, BRITISH (1932), 18 Padbury Court, London E2 7EH. Tel: 0171-729 1415. *Secretary,* T. Harris

RED CROSS SOCIETY, BRITISH, *see* BRITISH RED CROSS

RED POLL CATTLE SOCIETY (1888), The Market Hill, Woodbridge, Suffolk IP12 4LU. Tel: 01394-380643. *Secretary,* P. Ryder-Davies

REFRIGERATION, INSTITUTE OF (1899), Kelvin House, 76 Mill Lane, Carshalton, Surrey SM5 2JR. Tel: 0181-647 7033. *Secretary,* M. J. Horlick

REFUGEE COUNCIL, BRITISH (1981), Bondway House, 3–9 Bondway, London SW8 1SJ. Tel: 0171-582 6922. *Director,* A. Dubs

REGIONAL STUDIES ASSOCIATION (1965), Wharfdale Projects, 15 Micawber Street, London N1 7TB. Tel: 0171-490 1128. *Director,* Mrs S. Hardy

REGULAR FORCES EMPLOYMENT ASSOCIATION (1885), 25 Bloomsbury Square, London WC1A 2LN. Tel: 0171-637 3918. *General Manager,* Maj.-Gen. M. F. L. Shellard, CBE

RELATE: NATIONAL MARRIAGE GUIDANCE (1938), Herbert Gray College, Little Church Street, Rugby, Warks. CV21 3AP. Tel: 01788-573241. *Director,* D. French

RENT OFFICERS, INSTITUTE OF (1966), Beaufort House, Hamble Lane, Bursledon, Southampton SO3 8BR. Tel: 01703-403716. *Hon. Secretary,* A. E. Corcoran

RESEARCH DEFENCE SOCIETY (1908), 58 Great Marlborough Street, London W1V 1DD. Tel: 0171-287 2818. *Executive Director,* Dr M. Matfield

RESIDENTS' ASSOCIATIONS, NATIONAL UNION OF (1921). *Hon. General Secretary,* Mrs B. Reith, 35 Clement Way, Upminster, Essex RM14 2NX

RETIREMENT PENSIONS ASSOCIATIONS, NATIONAL FEDERATION OF (1938), 14 St Peter Street, Blackburn BB2 2HD. Tel: 01254-52606. *General Secretary,* R. Stansfield

REVENUES, RATING AND VALUATION, INSTITUTE OF (1882), 41 Doughty Street, London WC1N 2LF. Tel: 0171-831 3505. *Director,* C. Farrington

RICHARD III SOCIETY (1924), 4 Oakley Street, London SW3 5NN. *Secretary,* Miss E. M. Nokes

ROAD SAFETY OFFICERS, INSTITUTE OF (1971), 31 Heather Grove, Hollingworth, via Hyde, Cheshire SK14 8JL. Tel: 0161-474 4876. *Secretary,* B. Wilkinson

ROAD TRANSPORT ENGINEERS, INSTITUTE OF (1945), 22 Greencoat Place, London SW1P 1PR. Tel: 0171-630 1111. *Chief Executive,* A. F. Stroud

ROMAN STUDIES, SOCIETY FOR PROMOTION OF (1910), 31–34 Gordon Square, London WC1H 0PP. Tel: 0171-387 8157. *Secretary,* Dr H. M. Cockle

ROTARY INTERNATIONAL IN GREAT BRITAIN AND IRELAND (1914), Kinwarton Road, Alcester, Warks. B49 6BP. Tel: 01789-765411. *Secretary,* G. S. Large

ROUND TABLES OF GREAT BRITAIN AND IRELAND, NATIONAL ASSOCIATION OF (1927), Marchesi House, 4 Embassy Drive, Calthorpe Road, Edgbaston, Birmingham B15 1TP. Tel: 0121-456 4402. *General Secretary,* R. H. Renold

ROYAL AFRICAN SOCIETY (1901), 18 Northumberland Avenue, London WC2N 5BJ. Tel: 0171-930 1662. *Secretary,* Mrs L. Allan

ROYAL AIR FORCE BENEVOLENT FUND (1919), 67 Portland Place, London W1N 4AR. Tel: 0171-580 8343. *Controller,* Air Chief Marshal Sir Roger Palin, KCB, OBE

ROYAL AIR FORCES ASSOCIATION (1943), 43 Grove Park Road, London W4 3RX. Tel: 0181-994 8504. *Secretary-General,* J. G. Hargreaves, CBE

ROYAL ALEXANDRA AND ALBERT SCHOOL (1758), Gatton Park, Reigate, Surrey RH2 0TW. Tel: 01737-642576. *Secretary,* Capt. A. J. Walsh, RN

ROYAL ALFRED SEAFARERS' SOCIETY (1865), Weston Acres, Woodmansterne Lane, Banstead, Surrey SM7 3HB. Tel: 01737-352231. *General Secretary,* A. R. Quinton

ROYAL ARMOURED CORPS WAR MEMORIAL BENEVOLENT FUND (1946), c/o RHQ RTR, Bovington Camp, Wareham, Dorset BH20 6JA. Tel: 01929-403331. *Secretary,* Maj. R. Clooney (retd)

ROYAL ARTILLERY ASSOCIATION, Old Royal Military Academy, Artillery House, Woolwich, London SE18 4DN. Tel: 0181-319 4052. *General Secretary,* Lt.-Col. M. J. Darmody

ROYAL ASIATIC SOCIETY (1823), 60 Queen's Gardens, London W2 3AF. Tel: 0171-724 4741/2. *Secretary,* Miss L. Collins

ROYAL BRITISH LEGION, *see* BRITISH LEGION, ROYAL

ROYAL CALEDONIAN SCHOOLS (1815), Aldenham Road, Bushey, Watford, Herts. WD2 3TS. Tel: 01923-226642. *Master,* Capt. D. F. Watts, RN

ROYAL CELTIC SOCIETY (1820), 23 Rutland Street, Edinburgh EH1 2RN. Tel: 0131-228 6449. *Secretary,* J. G. Cameron, WS

ROYAL CHORAL SOCIETY (1871), c/o Cazenove & Co., 12 Tokenhouse Yard, London EC2R 7AN. Tel: 0171-972 9442. *Administrator,* G. Tonge

ROYAL ENGINEERS ASSOCIATION, RHQ Royal Engineers, Brompton Barracks, Chatham, Kent ME4 4UG. Tel: 01634-847005. *Controller,* Lt.-Col. J. W. Ray

ROYAL ENGINEERS, INSTITUTION OF (1875), Brompton Barracks, Chatham, Kent ME4 4UG. Tel: 01634-842669. *Secretary*, Col. R. I. Reive, OBE

ROYAL HIGHLAND AND AGRICULTURAL SOCIETY OF SCOTLAND (1784), Royal Highland Centre, Ingliston, Edinburgh EH28 8NF. Tel: 0131-333 2444. *Secretary*, J. R. Good

ROYAL HORTICULTURAL SOCIETY (1804), PO Box 313, 80 Vincent Square, London SW1P 2PE. Tel: 0171-834 4333. *Secretary*, D. P. Hearn

ROYAL HOSPITAL AND HOME, PUTNEY (1854), West Hill, London SW15 3SW. Tel: 0181-788 4511. *Chief Executive*, Brig. V. J. Beauchamp

ROYAL HUMANE SOCIETY (1774), Brettenham House, Lancaster Place, London WC2E 7EP. Tel: 0171-836 8155. *Secretary*, Maj. A. J. Dickinson

ROYAL INSTITUTION, THE (1799), 21 Albemarle Street, London W1X 4BS. Tel: 0171-409 2992. *Director*, Prof. P. Day, FRS

ROYAL LIFE SAVING SOCIETY UK (1891), Mountbatten House, Studley, Warks. B80 7NN. Tel: 01527-853943. *Director*, Ms C. J. Godsall

ROYAL LITERARY FUND (1790), 144 Temple Chambers, Temple Avenue, London EC4Y ODA. Tel: 0171-353 7150. *Secretary*, Mrs F. M. Clark

ROYAL MEDICAL BENEVOLENT FUND (1836), 24 King's Road, London SW19 8QN. Tel: 0181-540 9194. *Secretary*, Mrs G. A. R. Wells

ROYAL MEDICAL SOCIETY (1737), Students Centre, 5/5 Bristo Square, Edinburgh EH8 9AL. Tel: 0131-650 2672. *Secretary*, Mrs P. E. Strong

ROYAL MICROSCOPICAL SOCIETY (1839), 37–38 St Clements, Oxford OX4 1AJ. Tel: 01865-248768. *Administrator*, P. B. Hirst

ROYAL MUSICAL ASSOCIATION (1874), Faculty of Music, St Aldates, Oxford OX1 1DB. Tel: 01865-276137. *Secretary*, E. West

ROYAL NATIONAL INSTITUTE FOR THE BLIND (1868), 224 Great Portland Street, London W1N 6AA. Tel: 0171-388 1266. *Director-General*, I. Bruce

ROYAL NATIONAL LIFEBOAT INSTITUTION (1824), West Quay Road, Poole, Dorset BH15 1HZ. Tel: 01202-671133. *Director*, Lt.-Cdr. B. Miles, CBE, RD

ROYAL NAVAL AND ROYAL MARINES CHILDREN'S TRUST (1834), HMS *Nelson*, Portsmouth, PO1 3HH. Tel: 01705-817435. *Secretary*, Mrs M. Bateman

ROYAL NAVAL ASSOCIATION (1950), 82 Chelsea Manor Street, London SW3 5QJ. Tel: 0171-352 6764. *General Secretary*, Capt. J. W. Rayner, RMR

ROYAL NAVAL BENEVOLENT SOCIETY (1739), 1 Fleet Street, London EC4Y 1BD. Tel: 0171-353 4080. *Secretary*, Cdr P. J. F. Moore, RN

ROYAL NAVAL BENEVOLENT TRUST (1922), Castaway House, 311 Twyford Avenue, Portsmouth, Hants. PO2 8PE. Tel: 01705-660296. *General Secretary*, Lt.-Cdr. D. C. Lawrence (retd)

ROYAL NAVY OFFICERS, ASSOCIATION OF (1920), 70 Porchester Terrace, London W2 3TP. Tel: 0171-402 5231. *Secretary*, Lt.-Cdr. I. M. P. Coombes

ROYAL OVER-SEAS LEAGUE (1910), Over-Seas House, Park Place, St James's Street, London SW1A 1LR. Tel: 0171-408 0214. *Director-General*, R. F. Newell

ROYAL PATRIOTIC FUND CORPORATION (1854), Golden Cross House, Duncannon Street, London WC2N 4JR. Tel: 0171-930 9370. *Secretary*, Brig. T. G. Williams, CBE

ROYAL PHILATELIC SOCIETY, THE (1869), 41 Devonshire Place, London W1N 1PE. Tel: 0171-486 1044. *Hon. Secretary*, Prof. B. Jay

ROYAL PHOTOGRAPHIC SOCIETY (1853), Milsom Street, Bath BA1 1DN. Tel: 01225-462841. *Secretary*, A. Knowles

ROYAL PINNER SCHOOL FOUNDATION, 110 Old Brompton Road, London SW7 3RB. Tel: 0171-373 6168. *Secretary*, D. Crawford

ROYAL SAILORS' RESTS (1876), 2A South Street, Gosport, Hants. PO12 1ES. Tel: 01705-589551. *General Secretary*, A. A. Lockwood

ROYAL SCOTTISH SOCIETY FOR PREVENTION OF CRUELTY TO CHILDREN (1884), Melville House, 41 Polwarth Terrace, Edinburgh EH11 1NU. Tel: 0131-337 8539. *Chief Executive*, A. M. M. Wood, OBE

ROYAL SIGNALS INSTITUTION (1950), 56 Regency Street, London SW1P 4AD. Tel: 0171-414 8421. *Secretary*, Col. A. N. de Bretton-Gordon

ROYAL SOCIETY FOR ASIAN AFFAIRS (1901), 2 Belgrave Square, London SW1X 8PJ. Tel: 0171-235 5122. *Secretary*, Miss M. FitzSimons, MBE

ROYAL SOCIETY FOR THE ENCOURAGEMENT OF ARTS, MANUFACTURES AND COMMERCE (RSA) (1754), 8 John Adam Street, London WC2N 6EZ. Tel: 0171-930 5115. *Director*, P. Cowling

ROYAL SOCIETY FOR THE PREVENTION OF CRUELTY TO ANIMALS (RSPCA) (1824), Causeway, Horsham, W. Sussex RH12 1HG. Tel: 01403-264181. *Director-General*, P. R. Davies, CB

ROYAL SOCIETY FOR THE PROTECTION OF BIRDS (1889), The Lodge, Sandy, Beds. SG19 2DL. Tel: 01767-680551. *Chief Executive*, Ms B. Young

ROYAL SOCIETY OF HEALTH, THE (1876), RSH House, 38 St George's Drive, London SW1V 4BH. Tel: 0171-630 0171. *Chief Executive*, A. J. Byrne

ROYAL SOCIETY OF LITERATURE (1823), 1 Hyde Park Gardens, London W2 2LT. Tel: 0171-723 5104. *Secretary*, Ms M. Parham

ROYAL SOCIETY OF MEDICINE (1805), 1 Wimpole Street, London W1M 8AE. Tel: 0171-290 2900. *Executive Director*, Dr J. T. Green

ROYAL SOCIETY OF ST GEORGE (1894), Dartmouth House, 37 Charles Street, London W1X 8AB. Tel: 0171-499 5430. *Chairman*, Lt.-Col. R. Bury, OBE, TD

ROYAL STAR AND GARTER HOME FOR DISABLED SAILORS, SOLDIERS AND AIRMEN (1916), Richmond, Surrey TW10 6RR. Tel: 0181-940 3314. *Chief Executive*, I. Lashbrooke

ROYAL STATISTICAL SOCIETY (1834), 25 Enford Street, London W1H 2BH. Tel: 0171-723 5882. *Executive Secretary*, I. Goddard

ROYAL TANK REGIMENT BENEVOLENT FUND (1919), RHQ RTR Centre, Bovington Camp, Wareham, Dorset BH20 6JA. Tel: 01929-403331. *Regimental Secretary*, Maj. R. Clooney (retd)

ROYAL TELEVISION SOCIETY (1927), Holborn Hall, 100 Gray's Inn Road, London WC1X 8AL. Tel: 0171-430 1000. *Executive Director*, M. Bunce

ROYAL UNITED KINGDOM BENEFICENT ASSOCIATION (1863), 6 Avonmore Road, London W14 8RL. Tel: 0171-602 6274. *Director*, W. Rathbone

RSNC (ROYAL SOCIETY FOR NATURE CONSERVATION, NATIONAL OFFICE OF THE WILDLIFE TRUSTS) (1912), The Green, Witham Park, Lincoln LN5 7JR. Tel: 01522-544400. *Chief Executive,* T. S. Cordy

RURAL ENGLAND, COUNCIL FOR THE PROTECTION OF (CPRE) (1926), Warwick House, 25 Buckingham Palace Road, London SW1W 0PP. Tel: 0171-976 6433. *Director,* Ms F. Reynolds

RURAL SCOTLAND, ASSOCIATION FOR THE PROTECTION OF (1926), 3rd Floor, Gladstone's Land, 483 Lawnmarket, Edinburgh EH1 2NT. Tel: 0131-225 7012/3. *Director,* Mrs E. J. Garland

RURAL WALES, CAMPAIGN FOR THE PROTECTION OF (1928), Tŷ Gwyn, 31 High Street, Welshpool, Powys SY21 7JP. Tel: 01938-552525. *Director,* Dr N. Caldwell

SAILORS' FAMILIES' SOCIETY, THE (1821), Newland, Hull HU6 7RJ. Tel: 01482-42331. *General Secretary,* G. J. Powell

SAILORS' SOCIETY, BRITISH (1818), 3 Orchard Place, Southampton, S09 7SS. Tel: 01703-337333. *General Secretary,* G. Chambers

ST DEINIOL'S LIBRARY (1902), Hawarden, Deeside, Clwyd CH5 3DF. Tel: 01244-532350. *Warden and Chief Librarian,* Revd Dr P. J. Jagger

ST DUNSTAN'S, PO Box 4XB, 12–14 Harcourt Street, London W1A 4XB. Tel: 0171-723 5021. For men and women blinded in the Services. *Secretary,* G. B. J. Frost

ST JOHN AMBULANCE (1887), 1 Grosvenor Crescent, London SW1X 7EF. Tel: 0171-235 5231. *Executive Director,* T. Gauvain

ST JOSEPH'S SOCIETY FOR THE RELIEF OF THE AGED POOR (1708), St Joseph's House, 42 Brook Green, London W6 7BW. Tel: 0171-603 9817. *Secretary,* S. Dolan

SALES AND MARKETING MANAGEMENT, INSTITUTE OF (1966), Georgian House, 31 Upper George Street, Luton LU1 2RD. Tel: 01582-411130. *Director-General,* K. Williams

SALMON AND TROUT ASSOCIATION (1903), Fishmongers' Hall, London Bridge, London EC4R 9EL. Tel: 0171-283 5838. *Director,* C. W. Poupard

SALTIRE SOCIETY (1936), 9 Fountain Close, 22 High Street, Edinburgh EH1 1TF. Tel: 0131-556 1836. *Administrator,* Mrs K. Munro

SAMARITANS, THE (1953), 10 The Grove, Slough SL1 1QP. Tel: 01735-532713. Telephone numbers in local telephone directories. *Chief Executive,* S. Armson

SAMUEL PEPYS CLUB (1903), 26 Gloucester Street, Faringdon, Oxon. SN7 7HY. *Secretary,* P. L. Gray

SANE: THE MENTAL HEALTH CHARITY (1986), 199–205 Marylebone Road, London NW1 5QP. Tel: 0171-724 6520. *Saneline:* 0171-724 8000. *Chief Executive,* Ms M. Wallace, MBE

SAVE BRITAIN'S HERITAGE (1975), 68 Battersea High Street, London SW11 3HX. Tel: 0171-228 3336. *Secretary,* Miss E. Phillips

SAVE THE CHILDREN FUND, THE (1919), Mary Datchelor House, 17 Grove Lane, London SE5 8RD. Tel: 0171-703 5400. *Director-General,* N. J. Hinton, CBE

SCHIZOPHRENIA FELLOWSHIP, NATIONAL (1970), 28 Castle Street, Kingston upon Thames, Surrey KT1 1SS. Tel: 0181-547 3937. *Chief Executive,* B. Mehta

SCHOOL LIBRARY ASSOCIATION (1937), Liden Library, Barrington Close, Liden, Swindon SN3 6HF. Tel: 01793-617838. *Executive Secretary,* Ms V. Fea

SCHOOLMASTERS, SOCIETY OF (1798), West Lodge, Seaborough, Beaminster, Dorset DT8 3QY. Tel: 01308-868439. *Secretary,* Mrs E. Nicholson

SCHOOLMISTRESSES AND GOVERNESSES BENEVOLENT INSTITUTION (1843), Queen Mary House, Manor Park Road, Chislehurst, Kent BR7 5PY. Tel: 0181-468 7997. *Director,* L. I. Baggott

SCIENCE AND LEARNING, SOCIETY FOR THE PROTECTION OF (1933), 20–21 Compton Terrace, London N1 2UN. *Secretary,* Ms E. Fraser

SCIENCE, BRITISH ASSOCIATION FOR THE ADVANCEMENT OF (1831), 23 Savile Row, London W1X 1AB. Tel: 0171-494 3326. *Executive Secretary,* Dr P. Briggs

SCIENCE EDUCATION, ASSOCIATION FOR (1963), College Lane, Hatfield, Herts. AL10 9AA. Tel: 01707-267411. *General Secretary,* Dr D. S. Moore

SCOPE (formerly The Spastics Society) (1952), 12 Park Crescent, London W1N 4EQ. Tel: 0171-636 5020. *Chief Executive,* Ms A. Robinson

SCOTCH WHISKY ASSOCIATION, THE (1919), 20 Atholl Crescent, Edinburgh EH3 8HF. Tel: 0131-229 4383. *Director-General,* H. Morison

SCOTTISH CHIEFS, THE STANDING COUNCIL OF (1952), Hope Chambers, 52 Leith Walk, Edinburgh EH6 5HW. Tel: 0131-554 6321. *General Secretary,* G. A. Way of Plean

SCOTTISH CHURCH HISTORY SOCIETY (1922), St Serf's Manse, 1 Denham Green Terrace, Edinburgh EH5 3PG. Tel: 0131-552 4059. *Hon. Secretary,* Revd Dr P. H. Donald

SCOTTISH CORPORATION, ROYAL (1611), 37 King Street, London WC2E 8JS. Tel: 0171-240 3718. *Chief Executive,* Wg Cdr. A. Robertson

SCOTTISH COUNTRY DANCE SOCIETY, ROYAL (1923), 12 Coates Crescent, Edinburgh EH3 7AF. Tel: 0131-225 3854. *Secretary,* Mrs J. A. Moore

SCOTTISH GENEALOGY SOCIETY (1953), Library and Family History Centre, 15 Victoria Terrace, Edinburgh EH1 2JL. Tel: 0131-220 3677. *Hon. Secretary,* Miss J. P. S. Ferguson

SCOTTISH HISTORY SOCIETY (1886), Department of Scottish History, University of Edinburgh, Edinburgh EH8 9YL. Tel: 0131-650 4030/2. *Hon. Secretary,* Dr E. P. D. Torrie

SCOTTISH LANDOWNERS' FEDERATION (1906), 25 Maritime Street, Edinburgh EH6 5PW. Tel: 0131-555 1031. *Director,* S. Fraser

SCOTTISH LAW AGENTS SOCIETY, 79 West Regent Street, Glasgow G2 2AW. Tel: 0141-332 5537. *Secretary,* D. C. Clapham

SCOTTISH NATIONAL INSTITUTION FOR THE WAR BLINDED (1915), PO Box 500, Gillespie Crescent, Edinburgh EH10 4HZ. Tel: 0131-229 1456. *Secretary,* J. B. M. Munro

SCOTTISH NATIONAL WAR MEMORIAL (1927), The Castle, Edinburgh EH1 2YT. Tel: 0131-226 7393. *Secretary,* Lt.-Col. I. Shepherd

SCOTTISH SOCIETY FOR THE PREVENTION OF CRUELTY TO ANIMALS (1839), 19 Melville Street, Edinburgh EH3 7PL. Tel: 0131-225 6418. *Chief Executive,* J. Morris, CBE

SCOTTISH SOCIETY FOR THE PROTECTION OF WILD BIRDS (1927), Foremount House, Kilbarchan, Renfrewshire PA10 2EZ. Tel: 01505-702419. *Secretary*, Dr J. A. Gibson

SCOTTISH WILDLIFE TRUST (1964), Cramond House, Kirk Cramond, Cramond Glebe Road, Edinburgh EH4 6NS. Tel: 0131-312 7765. *Director*, D. J. Hughes Hallett

SCOUT ASSOCIATION, THE (1907), Baden-Powell House, Queen's Gate, London SW7 5JS. Tel: 0171-584 7030. *Chief Scout*, W. G. Morrison, CBE; *Chief Executive Commissioner*, A. E. N. Black, OBE

SCRIBES AND ILLUMINATORS, SOCIETY OF (1921), c/o The Art Workers Guild, 6 Queen Square, London WC1N 3AR

SCRIPTURE GIFT MISSION INCORPORATED (1888), Radstock House, 3 Eccleston Street, London SW1W 9LZ. Tel: 0171-730 2155. *International Director*, R. Kennedy

SCRIPTURE UNION (1867), 130 City Road, London EC1V 2NJ. Tel: 0171-782 0013. *General Director*, G. D. Q. Carr

SCULPTORS, ROYAL SOCIETY OF BRITISH (1904), 108 Old Brompton Road, London SW7 3RA. Tel: 0171-373 5554. *President*, Ms P. Davidson Davis

SEA CADETS (1895), 202 Lambeth Road, London SE1 7JF. Tel: 0171-928 8978. *General Secretary*, Cdr G. J. A. Shaw, OBE (retd)

SEAMEN'S BOYS' HOME, BRITISH (1863), Berry Head Road, Brixham, Devon TQ5 9AE. Tel: 01803-882129. *Secretary*, Capt. E. M. Marks, RD, RNR

SEAMEN'S CHRISTIAN FRIEND SOCIETY (1846), 48 South Street, Alderley Edge, Cheshire SK9 7ES. Tel: 01625-590010. *General Secretary*, M. J. Wilson

SEAMEN'S PENSION FUND, ROYAL (1919), 65 High Street, Ewell, Epsom, Surrey KT17 1RX. Tel: 0181-393 3064. *Secretary*, D. Barker

SECULAR SOCIETY LTD, NATIONAL (1866), 702 Holloway Road, London N19 3NL. Tel: 0171-272 1266. *General Secretary*, T. Mullins

SEEABILITY (formerly Royal School for the Blind) (1799), 56–66 Highlands Road, Leatherhead, Surrey KT22 8NR. Tel: 01372-373086. *Chief Executive*, R. M. Perkins

SELDEN SOCIETY (1887), Faculty of Laws, Queen Mary and Westfield College, Mile End Road, London E1 4NS. Tel: 0171-975 5136. To encourage the study and advance the knowledge of the history of English law. *Secretary*, V. Tunkel

SENSE (THE NATIONAL DEAF-BLIND AND RUBELLA ASSOCIATION) (1955), 11–13 Clifton Terrace, London N4 3SR. Tel: 0171-272 7774. *Chief Executive*, R. Clark

SHAFTESBURY HOMES AND *Arethusa* (1843), 3 Rectory Grove, London SW4 0EG. Tel: 0171-720 8709. *Director*, Capt. N. C. Baird-Murray, CBE, RN

SHAFTESBURY SOCIETY, THE (1844), 18–20 Kingston Road, London SW19 1JZ. Tel: 0181-542 5550. Cares for physically and mentally handicapped, elderly and socially deprived people. *Chief Executive*, G. Holloway

SHELLFISH ASSOCIATION OF GREAT BRITAIN (1904), Fishmongers' Hall, London Bridge, London EC4R 9EL. Tel: 0171-283 8305. *Director*, E. Edwards, OBE, Ph.D.

SHELTER (THE NATIONAL CAMPAIGN FOR HOMELESS PEOPLE) (1966), 88 Old Street, London EC1V 9HU. Tel: 0171-253 0202. *Director*, vacant

SHERLOCK HOLMES SOCIETY OF LONDON (1951), 3 Outram Road, Southsea, Hants. PO5 1QP. Tel: 01705-812104. *Hon. Secretary*

SHIPBROKERS, INSTITUTE OF CHARTERED (1911), 3 Gracechurch Street, London EC3V 0AT. Tel: 0171-283 1361. *Secretary*, J. H. Parker

SHIRE HORSE SOCIETY (1878), East of England Showground, Peterborough PE2 6XE. Tel: 01733-390696. *Secretary*, T. Gibson, OBE

SHRIEVALTY ASSOCIATION (1971), Express Buildings, 17–29 Upper Parliament Street, Nottingham NG1 2AQ. Tel: 0115-935 0350. *Secretary*, R. Bullock

SIGHT SAVERS (Royal Commonwealth Society for the Blind) (1950), Grosvenor Hall, Bolnore Road, Haywards Heath, W. Sussex RH16 4BX. Tel: 01444-412424. *Executive Director*, D. Porter

SIMPLIFIED SPELLING SOCIETY (1908), Clare Hall, Chapel Lane, Chigwell, Essex IG7 6JJ. Tel: 0181-501 0405. *Chairman*, C. J. H. Jolly

SIR OSWALD STOLL FOUNDATION (1916), 446 Fulham Road, London SW6 1DT. Tel: 0171-385 2110. *Director*, R. C. Brunwin

SMALL BUSINESSES, FEDERATION OF (1974), Parliamentary Office, 140 Lower Marsh, London SE1 7AE. Tel: 0171-928 9272. *National Chairman*, J. Harris

SMALL FARMERS' ASSOCIATION, THE (1979), PO Box 18, Woodbridge, Suffolk IP13 0QP. *Chairman*, J. Morford

SOCIALIST PARTY OF GREAT BRITAIN (1904), 52 Clapham High Street, London SW4 7UN. Tel: 0171-622 3811. *General Secretary*, A. Buick

SOCIAL WORKERS, BRITISH ASSOCIATION OF (1970), 16 Kent Street, Birmingham B5 6RD. Tel: 0121-622-3911. *General Secretary*, D. N. Jones

SOLDIERS' AND AIRMEN'S SCRIPTURE READERS ASSOCIATION, THE (1838), Havelock House, Barrack Road, Aldershot, Hants. GU11 3NP. Tel: 01252-310033. *General Secretary*, Lt.-Col. M. Hitchcott

SOLDIERS', SAILORS' AND AIRMEN'S FAMILIES ASSOCIATION (SSAFA) (1885), 19 Queen Elizabeth Street, London SE1 2LP. Tel: 0171-403 8783. *Controller*, Maj.-Gen. C. R. Grey, CBE

SOLDIERS' WIDOWS, ROYAL CAMBRIDGE HOME FOR (1851), 82–84 Hurst Road, East Molesey, Surrey KT8 9AH. Tel: 0181-979 3788. *Superintendent*, Mrs I. O. Yarnell

SOLICITORS IN THE SUPREME COURTS OF SCOTLAND, SOCIETY OF (1784), 2 Abercromby Place, Edinburgh EH3 6JZ. Tel: 0131-556 4070. *Secretary*, A. R. Brownlie, OBE

SOROPTIMIST INTERNATIONAL OF GREAT BRITAIN AND IRELAND (1923), 127 Wellington Road South, Stockport SK1 3TS. Tel: 0161-480 7686. *Executive Officer*, Ms K. Heward

SOS SOCIETY, THE, *see* 2CARE

SOUTH AMERICAN MISSIONARY SOCIETY (1844), Allen Gardiner House, Pembury Road, Tunbridge Wells, Kent TN2 3QU. Tel: 01892-538647. *General Secretary*, Rt. Revd D. Evans

SOUTH WALES INSTITUTE OF ENGINEERS (1857), Empire House, Mount Stuart Square, Cardiff CF1 6DN. Tel: 01222-481726. *Hon. Secretary*, R. E. Lindsay

SPEAKERS CLUBS, THE ASSOCIATION OF (1971), 28 High Street, Auchterarder PH3 1DF. Tel: 01764-662457. *National Secretary*, D. Williams

SPINA BIFIDA AND HYDROCEPHALUS, ASSOCIATION FOR (ASBAH), 42 Park Road, Peterborough PE1 2UQ. Tel: 01733-555988. *Executive Director*, A. Russell

SPORTS MEDICINE, INSTITUTE OF (1963), Burlington House, Piccadilly, London W1V 0LQ. Tel: 0171-287 5269. *Hon. Secretary*, Dr W. T. Orton

SPURGEON'S CHILD CARE (1867), 30 Mill Street, Bedford MK40 3HD. Tel: 01234-261843. *Director*, D. C. Culwick

STANDING CONFERENCE OF NATIONAL AND UNIVERSITY LIBRARIES (SCONUL) (1950), 102 Euston Street, London NW1 2HA. Tel: 0171-387 0317. *Secretary*, Miss G. M. Pentelow

STATISTICIANS, INSTITUTE OF, *see* ROYAL STATISTICAL SOCIETY

STATUTE LAW SOCIETY (1968), Onslow House, 9 The Green, Richmond, Surrey TW9 1PU. Tel: 0181-940 0017. *Hon. Secretary*, N. Frudd

STEWART SOCIETY (1899), 17 Dublin Street, Edinburgh EH1 3PG. Tel: 0131-557 6824. *Hon. Secretary*, Mrs M. Walker

STRATEGIC PLANNING SOCIETY, THE (1967), 17 Portland Place, London W1N 3AF. Tel: 0171-636 7737. *Office Manager*, Mrs J. Mainee

STRATEGIC STUDIES, INTERNATIONAL INSTITUTE FOR (1958), 23 Tavistock Street, London WC2E 7NQ. Tel: 0171-379 7676. *Director*, Dr J. Chipman

STROKE ASSOCIATION, THE (1899), CHSA House, Whitecross Street, London EC1Y 8JJ. Tel: 0171-490 7999. *Director-General*, Dr S. McLauchlan

STRUCTURAL ENGINEERS, INSTITUTION OF (1908), 11 Upper Belgrave Street, London SW1X 8BH. Tel: 0171-235 4535. *Secretary*, Dr J. W. Dougill

STUDENT CHRISTIAN MOVEMENT (1889), 186 St Paul's Road, Balsall Heath, Birmingham B12 8LZ. Tel: 0121-440 3000. *General Secretary*

SUFFOLK HORSE SOCIETY (1878), The Market Hill, Woodbridge, Suffolk IP12 4LU. Tel: 01394-380643. *Secretary*, P. Ryder-Davies

SURGEONS OF EDINBURGH, ROYAL COLLEGE OF (1505), Nicolson Street, Edinburgh EH8 9DW. Tel: 0131-556 6206. *Secretary*, I. B. MacLeod, FRCSEd.

SURGEONS OF ENGLAND, ROYAL COLLEGE OF (1800), 35–43 Lincoln's Inn Fields, London WC2A 3PN. Tel: 0171-405 3474. *Secretary*, R. H. E. Duffett

SURVEYORS, ROYAL INSTITUTION OF CHARTERED (1868), 12 Great George Street, London SW1P 3AD. Tel: 0171-334 3701. *Chief Executive*, M. Pattison

SURVIVAL INTERNATIONAL (1969), 310 Edgware Road, London W2 1DY. Tel: 0171-723 5535. *Director*, S. Corry

SUZY LAMPLUGH TRUST (1986), 14 East Sheen Avenue, London SW14 8AS. Tel: 0181-392 1839. *Executive Secretary*, P. Lamplugh

SWEDENBORG SOCIETY (1810), 20–21 Bloomsbury Way, London WC1A 2TH. Tel: 0171-405 7986. *Secretary*, Ms M. G. Waters

TALKING BOOKS FOR THE HANDICAPPED AND HOSPITAL PATIENTS, *see* NATIONAL LISTENING LIBRARY

TAVISTOCK INSTITUTE, THE (1947), 30 Tabernacle Street, London EC2A 4DE. Tel: 0171-417 0407. *Secretary*, N. Barnes

TAXATION, INSTITUTE OF (1930), 12 Upper Belgrave Street, London SW1X 8BB. Tel: 0171-235 9381. *Secretary*, R. J. Ison

TEACHERS AND LECTURERS, ASSOCIATION OF (1978), 7 Northumberland Street, London WC2N 5DA. Tel: 0171-930 6441. *General Secretary*, P. Smith

TEACHERS OF HOME ECONOMICS AND TECHNOLOGY, NATIONAL ASSOCIATION OF (1896), Hamilton House, Mabledon Place, London WC1H 9BJ. Tel: 0171-387 1441. *Secretary*, G. Thompson

TEACHERS OF MATHEMATICS, ASSOCIATION OF (1952), 7 Shaftesbury Street, Derby DE3 8YB. Tel: 01332-346599. *Hon. Secretary*, Ms M. Gorman

TEACHERS OF THE DEAF, BRITISH ASSOCIATION OF (1977). *Hon. Secretary*, Mrs A. Underwood, 41 The Orchard, Leven, Beverley, N. Humberside HU17 5QA. Tel: 01964-544243

TEACHERS' UNION, ULSTER (1919), 94 Malone Road, Belfast BT9 5HP. Tel: 01232-662216. *General Secretary*, D. Allen

TELECOMMUNICATIONS USERS' ASSOCIATION (1965), 48 Percy Road, London N12 8BU. Tel: 0181-445 0996. *Executive Chairman*, W. E. Mieran

TEMPERANCE SOCIETIES:

*British National Temperance League* (1834), Westbrook Court, Sharrow Vale Road, Sheffield S11 8YZ. Tel: 0114-267 9976. *Executive Director*, A. Willis

*Church of England National Council for Social Aid*, 38 Ebury Street, London SW1W 0LU. Tel: 0171-730 6175. *General Secretary*, Revd E. W. F. Agar

*National United Temperance Council* (1880), 176 Blackfriars Road, London SE1 8ET. Tel: 0171-928 1538. *General Secretary*, Revd B. Kinman

*Order of the Sons of Temperance* (1855), Friendly Society, 5 Ashbourne Road, Derby DE22 3FQ. Tel: 01332-41672. *Secretary*, D. Newbury

*Royal Naval Temperance Society* (1876) (auxiliary of Royal Sailors' Rests), 2A South Street, Gosport, Hants. PO12 1ES. Tel: 01705-589551. *General Secretary*, A. A. Lockwood

*United Kingdom Alliance* (1863), 176 Blackfriars Road, London SE1 8ET. Tel: 0171-928 1538. *General Secretary*, Revd B. Kinman

TEMPLETON FOUNDATION (1973), 18 Eastgate Gardens, Taunton, Somerset TA1 1RD. Tel: 01823-324522. *UK Representative*, Mrs N. Pearse

TERRENCE HIGGINS TRUST (1982), 52–54 Grays Inn Road, London WC1X 8JU. Tel: 0171-831 0330. *Helpline*, 0171-242 1010. *Chairman*, N. Partridge

TERRITORIAL, AUXILIARY AND VOLUNTEER RESERVE ASSOCIATIONS, COUNCIL OF (1908), Centre Block, Duke of York's HQ, London SW3 4SG. Tel: 0171-730 6122. *Secretary*, Maj.-Gen. W. A. Evans, CB

TEXTILE INSTITUTE, THE (1910), International HQ, 10 Blackfriars Street, Manchester M3 5DR. Tel: 0161-834 8457. *Chief Executive*, R. G. Denyer

THEATRE RESEARCH, SOCIETY FOR (1948), c/o The Theatre Museum, 1E Tavistock Street, London WC2E 7PA. *Joint Hon. Secretaries*, Ms E. Cottis; Ms F. Dann

THEATRES TRUST, THE (1976), 22 Charing Cross Road, London WC2H 0HR. Tel: 0171-836 8591. *Director*, J. Earl

THEATRICAL FUND, ROYAL (1839), 11 Garrick Street, London WC2E 9AR. Tel: 0171-836 3322. *Secretary*, Mrs R. M. Oliver

THEOSOPHICAL SOCIETY IN ENGLAND (1875), 50 Gloucester Place, London W1H 3HJ. Tel: 0171-935 9261. *General Secretary*, Mrs L. Storey

THISTLE FOUNDATION, THE (1945), 27A Walker Street, Edinburgh EH3 7HX. Tel: 0131-225 7282. *Director*, P. Croft

THOMAS CORAM FOUNDATION FOR CHILDREN (formerly The Foundling Hospital) (1739), 40 Brunswick Square, London WC1N 1AZ. Tel: 0171-278 2424. *Director and Secretary*, Dr C. Hanvey

TIDY BRITAIN GROUP, THE (1953), The Pier, Wigan WN3 4EX. Tel: 01942-824620. *Director-General*, Prof. G. Ashworth, CBE

TOC H (1915), Headquarters, 1 Forest Close, Wendover, Aylesbury, Bucks. HP22 6BT. Tel: 01296-623911. *Director*, M. Lyddiard

TOURIST BOARD, ENGLISH, Thames Tower, Black's Road, London W6 9EL. Tel: 0181-846 9000. *Chief Executive*, J. East

TOURIST BOARD, NORTHERN IRELAND, St Anne's Court, 59 North Street, Belfast BT1 1ND. Tel: 01232-231221. *Chief Executive*, I. G. Henderson

TOURIST BOARD, SCOTTISH (1969), 23 Ravelston Terrace, Edinburgh EH4 3EU. Tel: 0131-332 2433. *Chief Executive*, D. D. Reid

TOURIST BOARD, WALES, Brunel House, 2 Fitzalan Road, Cardiff CF2 1UY. *Chief Executive*, P. Loveluck

TOWN AND COUNTRY PLANNING ASSOCIATION (1899), 17 Carlton House Terrace, London SW1Y 5AS. Tel: 0171-930 8903. *Director*, D. Hall, MBE

TOWN PLANNING INSTITUTE, ROYAL (1914), 26 Portland Place, London W1N 4BE. Tel: 0171-636 9107. *Secretary-General*, D. Fryer

TOWNSWOMEN'S GUILDS (1929), Chamber of Commerce House, 75 Harborne Road, Birmingham B15 3DA. Tel: 0121-456 3435. *National Secretary*

TOYNBEE HALL, The Universities' Settlement in East London (1884), 28 Commercial Street, London E1 6LS. Tel: 0171-247 6943. *Chief Executive*, A. Prescott

TRADE MARK AGENTS, INSTITUTE OF (1934), Canterbury House, 2–6 Sydenham Road, Croydon CR0 9XE. Tel: 0181-686 2052. *Secretary*, Mrs M. J. Tyler

TRADING STANDARDS ADMINISTRATION, INSTITUTE OF (1881), 4–5 Hadleigh Business Centre, 351 London Road, Hadleigh, Essex SS7 2BT. Tel: 01702-559922. *Chief Executive*, A. J. Street

TRANSLATION AND INTERPRETING, INSTITUTE OF (1986), 377 City Road, London EC1V 1NA. Tel: 0171-713 7600. *Chairman*, R. Fletcher

TRANSPORT ADMINISTRATION, INSTITUTE OF (1944), 32 Palmerston Road, Southampton SO14 1LL. Tel: 01703-631380. *Director*, Wg Cdr. P. F. Green

TRANSPORT, CHARTERED INSTITUTE OF (1919), 80 Portland Place, London W1N 4DP. Tel: 0171-636 9952. *Director*, A. M. J. Pomeroy

TRANSPORT CONSULTATIVE COMMITTEE, CENTRAL (1948), 1st Floor, Golden Cross House, Duncannon Street, London WC2N 4JF. Tel: 0171-839 7338. *Secretary*, M. Patterson

TRAVEL AGENTS, ASSOCIATION OF BRITISH (ABTA) (1950), 55–57 Newman Street, London W1P 4AH. Tel: 0171-637 2444. *President*, C. Trigger

TREE COUNCIL (1974), 35 Belgrave Square, London SW1X 8XN. Tel: 0171-235 8854. *Director*, R. Osborne

TREE FOUNDATION, INTERNATIONAL (formerly Men of the Trees) (1922), Sandy Lane, Crawley Down, W. Sussex RH10 4HS. Tel: 01342-712536. *Chairman*, J. Caunce

TROPICAL MEDICINE AND HYGIENE, ROYAL SOCIETY OF (1907), Manson House, 26 Portland Place, London W1N 4EY. Tel: 0171-580 2127. *Hon. Secretaries*, Dr D. C. Barker; Dr W. R. C. Weir

TURNER SOCIETY (1975), BCM Box Turner, London WC1N 3XX. *Chairman*, E. Shanes

2CARE (formerly The SOS Society) (1929), 13 Harwood Road, London SW6 4QP. Tel: 0171-371 0118. Residential homes for the elderly, and psychiatric rehabilitation centres. *Chief Executive*, Miss E. C. R. O'Sullivan

UFAW (UNIVERSITIES FEDERATION FOR ANIMAL WELFARE) (1926), 8 Hamilton Close, South Mimms, Potters Bar, Herts. EN6 3QD. Tel: 01707-658202. *Chief Executive*, Sir Michael Simmons

UNITED NATIONS ASSOCIATION OF GREAT BRITAIN AND NORTHERN IRELAND (1945), 3 Whitehall Court, London SW1A 2EL. Tel: 0171-930 2931. *Director*, M. C. Harper

UNITED REFORMED CHURCH HISTORY SOCIETY (1972), 86 Tavistock Place, London WC1H 9RT. Tel: 0171-916 2020. *Hon. Secretary*, Revd Dr S. Orchard

UNITED SOCIETY FOR CHRISTIAN LITERATURE (1799), Robertson House, Leas Road, Guildford, Surrey GU1 4QW. Tel: 01483-577877. *General Secretary*, Dr A. Marriage

UNITED SOCIETY FOR THE PROPAGATION OF THE GOSPEL (USPG) (1701), Partnership House, 157 Waterloo Road, London SE1 8XA. Tel: 0171-928 8681. *Secretary*, Canon P. Price

UNIVERSITIES OF THE UNITED KINGDOM, COMMITTEE OF VICE-CHANCELLORS AND PRINCIPALS OF THE (1918), 29 Tavistock Square, London WC1H 9EZ. Tel: 0171-387 9231. *Secretary*, T. U. Burgner

UNIVERSITY AND COLLEGE LECTURERS, ASSOCIATION OF (1973), 104 Albert Road, Southsea, Hants. PO5 2SN. Tel: 01705-818625. *Chief Executive*, Ms C. Cheesman

VALUERS AND AUCTIONEERS, INCORPORATED SOCIETY OF (1968), 3 Cadogan Gate, London SW1X 0AS. Tel: 0171-235 2282. *Chief Executive*, H. Whitty

VEGAN SOCIETY, THE (1944), 7 Battle Road, St Leonards-on-Sea, E. Sussex TN37 7AA. Tel: 01424-427393. *General Secretary*, R. Farhall

VEGETARIAN SOCIETY OF THE UNITED KINGDOM LTD, Parkdale, Dunham Road, Altrincham, Cheshire WA14 4QG. Tel: 0161-928 0793. *Director*, P. J. Lloyd

VENEREAL DISEASES, MEDICAL SOCIETY FOR THE STUDY OF (1922), c/o Royal Society of Medicine, 1 Wimpole Street, London W1M 8AE. Tel: 0171-290 2968. *Hon. Secretary*, Dr T. McManus

VERNACULAR ARCHITECTURE GROUP (1953), 16 Falna Crescent, Coton Green, Tamworth, Staffs. B79 8JS. Tel: 01827-69434. *Hon. Secretary*, R. Meeson

VETERINARY ASSOCIATION, BRITISH (1881), 7 Mansfield Street, London W1M 0AT. Tel: 0171-636 6541. *Chief Executive*, J. H. Baird

VETERINARY SURGEONS, ROYAL COLLEGE OF, 32 Belgrave Square, London SW1X 8QP (1844). *Registrar*, Mr P. E. Woolley, OBE

VICTIM SUPPORT (NATIONAL ASSOCIATION OF VICTIM SUPPORT SCHEMES) (1979), Cranmer House, 39 Brixton Road, London SW9 6DZ. Tel: 0171-735 9166. *Director*, Ms H. Reeves, OBE

VICTORIA CROSS AND GEORGE CROSS ASSOCIATION, 2 Ripley Courtyard, Old Admiralty Building, Whitehall, London SW1A 2BE. Tel: 0171-930 3506. *Chairman,* Col. B. S. T. Archer, GC, OBE

VICTORIA INSTITUTE, THE (Philosophical Society of Great Britain), Latchett Hall, Latchett Road, London E18 1DL. Tel: 0181-505 5224. *Hon. Treasurer,* B. H. T. Weller

VICTORIAN SOCIETY (1958), 1 Priory Gardens, Bedford Park, London W4 1TT. Tel: 0181-994 1019. *Director,* Dr W. Filmer-Sankey

VICTORY (SERVICES) ASSOCIATION LTD AND CLUB (1907), 63–79 Seymour Street, London W2 2HF. Tel: 0171-723 4474. *General Manager,* G. F. Taylor

VIKING SOCIETY FOR NORTHERN RESEARCH (1892), Department of Scandinavian Studies, University College, Gower Street, London WC1E 6BT. Tel: 0171-380 7176. *Hon. Secretaries,* Prof. M. P. Barnes; Dr J. Jesch

VOLUNTARY ORGANIZATIONS, NATIONAL COUNCIL FOR (1919), Regent's Wharf, 8 All Saints Street, London N1 9RL. Tel: 0171-713 6161. *Director (acting),* S. Hebditch

VSO (VOLUNTARY SERVICE OVERSEAS) (1958), 317 Putney Bridge Road, London SW15 2PN. Tel: 0181-780 2266. *Director,* D. Green

WAR ON WANT (1952), 37–39 Great Guildford Street, London SE1 0ES. Tel: 0171-620 1111. *Director,* G. Alhadeff

WATER AND ENVIRONMENTAL MANAGEMENT, INSTITUTION OF (1987), 15 John Street, London WC1N 2EB. Tel: 0171-831 3110. *Executive Director,* T. Bispham

WATERCOLOUR SOCIETY, ROYAL (1804), Bankside Gallery, 48 Hopton Street, London SE1 9JH. Tel: 0171-928 7521. *President,* L. Worth; *Secretary,* Ms J. Dixey

WELDING INSTITUTE, THE, Abington Hall, Cambridge CB1 6AL. Tel: 01223-891162. *Chief Executive,* A. B. M. Braithwaite

WELLBEING (1964), 27 Sussex Place, London NW1 4SP. Tel: 0171-262 5337. *Director,* Mrs R. Barnes

WELLCOME TRUST (1936), The Wellcome Building, 183 Euston Road, London NW1 2BE. Tel: 0171-611 8000. *Director,* Dr B. Ogilvie

WELLS SOCIETY, H. G. (1961). *Hon. Secretary,* Dr S. Hardy, English Department, Nene College, Moulton Park, Northampton NN2 7AL. Tel: 01604-735500, ext. 2133

WESLEY HISTORICAL SOCIETY (1893), 34 Spiceland Road, Northfield, Birmingham B31 1NJ. Tel: 0121-475 4914. *General Secretary,* Dr E. D. Graham

WEST LONDON MISSION (1887), 19 Thayer Street, London W1M 5LJ. Tel: 0171-935 6179. *Superintendent,* Revd D. S. Cruise

WESTMINSTER FOUNDATION FOR DEMOCRACY (1992), Clutha House, 10 Storey's Gate, London SW1P 3AY. Tel: 0171-976 7565. *Chief Executive,* Ms D. Warwick

WILDFOWL AND WETLANDS TRUST (1946), The New Grounds, Slimbridge, Gloucester GL2 7BT. Tel: 01453-890333. *Director-General,* Dr M. Owen

WILLIAM MORRIS SOCIETY AND KELMSCOTT FELLOWSHIP (1918), Kelmscott House, 26 Upper Mall, London W6 9TA. Tel: 0171-741 3735. *Hon. Secretary,* D. Baker

WINE AND SPIRIT ASSOCIATION OF GREAT BRITAIN AND NORTHERN IRELAND (*c.* 1825), Five Kings House, 1 Queen Street Place, London EC4R 1XX. *Director,* P. Lewis

WOMEN, SOCIETY FOR PROMOTING THE TRAINING OF (1859), The Rectory, Main Street, Great Casterton, Stamford, Lincs. PE9 4AP. Tel: 01780-64036. *Hon. Secretary,* Revd B. Harris

WOMEN ARTISTS, SOCIETY OF (1855), Westminster Gallery, Westminster Central Hall, Storey's Gate, London SW1H 9NU. *President,* Prof. B. Tate

WOMEN GRADUATES, BRITISH FEDERATION OF (1907), 4 Mandeville Courtyard, 142 Battersea Park Road, London SW11 4NB. Tel: 0171-498 8037. *Secretary,* Mrs A. B. Stein

WOMEN'S ENGINEERING SOCIETY (1920), Imperial College of Science and Technology, Department of Civil Engineering, Imperial College Road, London SW7 2BU. Tel: 0171-594 6025. *Secretary,* Mrs C. MacGillivray

WOMEN'S INSTITUTES, NATIONAL FEDERATION OF (1915), 104 New Kings Road, London SW6 4LY. Tel: 0171-371 9300. *General Secretary,* Ms H. Mayall

WOMEN'S INSTITUTES OF NORTHERN IRELAND, FEDERATION OF (1932), 209–211 Upper Lisburn Road, Belfast BT10 0LL. Tel: 01232-301506. *General Secretary,* Mrs I. A. Sproule

WOMEN'S INTERNATIONAL LEAGUE FOR PEACE AND FREEDOM (British Section) (1915), 157 Lyndhurst Road, Worthing, W. Sussex BN11 2DG. Tel: 01903-205161. *Chair,* Ms C. Lowden

WOMEN'S NATIONWIDE CANCER CONTROL CAMPAIGN (1964), Suna House, 128–130 Curtain Road, London EC2A 3AR. Tel: 0171-729 4688. *Helpline,* 0171-729 2229. *Administrator,* Ms J. Harding

WOMEN'S ROYAL NAVAL SERVICE BENEVOLENT TRUST (1942), 311 Twyford Avenue, Portsmouth, Hants. PO2 8PE. Tel: 01705-655301. *General Secretary,* Mrs J. Russell

WOMEN'S ROYAL VOLUNTARY SERVICE (WRVS), 234–244 Stockwell Road, London SW9 9SP. Tel: 0171-416 0146. *National Chairman,* Mrs E. Toulson

WOMEN'S RURAL INSTITUTES, SCOTTISH (1917), 42 Heriot Row, Edinburgh EH3 6ES. Tel: 0131-225 1724. *General Secretary,* Mrs A. Peacock

WOMEN'S TRANSPORT SERVICE (1907), Mercury House, Duke of York's HQ, London SW3 4RX. Tel: 0171-730 2058. *Corps Commander,* Mrs A. Whitehead

WOODLAND TRUST, THE (1972), Autumn Park, Dysart Road, Grantham, Lincs. NG31 6LL. Tel: 01476-74297. *Chief Executive Director,* J. D. James

WOOD PRESERVING ASSOCIATION, BRITISH (1930), 6 The Office Village, 4 Romford Road, London E15 4EA. Tel: 0181-519 2588. *Director,* Dr C. R. Coggins

WORKERS' EDUCATIONAL ASSOCIATION, Temple House, 9 Upper Berkeley Street, London W1H 8BY. Tel: 0171-402 5608. *General Secretary,* R. Lochrie

WORLD EDUCATION FELLOWSHIP (1921), 33 Kinnaird Avenue, London W4 3SH. Tel: 0181-994 7258. *General Secretary,* Mrs R. Crommelin

WORLD ENERGY COUNCIL (1924), 34 St James's Street, London SW1A 1HD. Tel: 0171-930 3966. *Secretary-General,* I. D. Lindsay

WORLD MISSION, COUNCIL FOR (1977), Livingstone House, 11 Carteret Street, London SW1H 9DL. Tel: 0171-222 4214. *General Secretary,* D. P. Niles, PH.D.

WORLD SHIP SOCIETY (1946), 101 The Everglades, Hempstead, Gillingham, Kent ME7 3PZ. Tel: 01634-372015. *Secretary,* J. Poole

WORLD SOCIETY FOR THE PROTECTION OF ANIMALS (1981), 2 Langley Lane, London SW8 ITJ. Tel: 0171-793 0540. *Chief Executive*, A. Dickson

WORLD-WIDE EDUCATION SERVICE LTD (WES) (1888), Canada House, 272 Field End Road, Eastcote, Ruislip, Middx. HA4 9NA. Tel: 0181-866 4400. *Head of Consultancy*, Mrs T. Mulder-Reynolds

WRITERS TO HM SIGNET, SOCIETY OF (1532), 16 Hill Street, Edinburgh EH2 3LD. Tel: 0131-226 6703. *Clerk*, A. M. Kerr

WWF UK (World Wide Fund for Nature) (1961), Panda House, Weyside Park, Godalming, Surrey GU7 IXR. Tel: 01483-426444. *Director*, Dr R. Pellew

YEOMANRY BENEVOLENT FUND (1902), 10 Stone Buildings, Lincoln's Inn, London WC2A 3TG. Tel: 0171-831 6727. *Secretary*, Mrs C. W. Chrystie

YORKSHIRE AGRICULTURAL SOCIETY (1837), Great Yorkshire Showground, Hookstone Oval, Harrogate, N. Yorks HG2 8PW. Tel: 01423-561536. *Chief Executive*, R. Keigwin

YORKSHIRE SOCIETY, THE (1812), 35 Waldorf Heights, Camberley, Surrey GU17 9JH. Tel: 01276-36342. Educational trust making grants to students of all ages. *Secretary*, G. G. Prince, TD

YOUNG FARMERS' CLUBS, NATIONAL FEDERATION OF, The YFC Centre, National Agricultural Centre, Stoneleigh Park, Kenilworth, Warks. CV8 2LG. Tel: 01203-696544. *Secretary*, T. Shields

YOUNG MEN'S CHRISTIAN ASSOCIATION (YMCA) (1844), National Council of YMCAs, 640 Forest Road, London E17 3DZ. Tel: 0181-520 5599. *National Secretary*, N. Nightingale

YOUNG WOMEN'S CHRISTIAN ASSOCIATION OF GREAT BRITAIN (YWCA) (1855), 52 Cornmarket Street, Oxford OXI 3EJ. Tel: 01865-726110. *Chief Executive*, Ms G. Tishler

YOUTH ACTION, NORTHERN IRELAND (1944), Hampton, Glenmachan Park, Belfast BT4 2PJ. Tel: 01232-760067. *Director*, P. Graham

YOUTH CLUBS UK (1911), 11 St Bride Street, London EC4A 4AS. Tel: 0171-353 2366. *Chief Executive*, D. Stickels

YOUTH HOSTELS ASSOCIATION (ENGLAND AND WALES) (1930), Trevelyan House, 8 St Stephens Hill, St Albans, Herts. ALI 2DY. Tel: 01727-855215. *Chief Executive*, C. Logan

YOUTH HOSTELS ASSOCIATION OF NORTHERN IRELAND (1931), 22 Donegall Road, Belfast BTI2 5JN. Tel: 01232-324733. *Hon. Secretary*, N. O'Reilly

YOUTH HOSTELS ASSOCIATION, SCOTTISH (1931), 7 Glebe Crescent, Stirling FK8 2JA. Tel: 01786-451181. *General Secretary*, J. Martin

ZOOLOGICAL SOCIETY, NORTH OF ENGLAND (1934), Chester Zoo, Upton by Chester, Chester CH2 ILH. Tel: 01244-380280. *Director*, Dr M. Brambell

ZOOLOGICAL SOCIETY OF LONDON (1826), Regent's Park, London NWI 4RY. Tel: 0171-722 3333. *President*, Dr M. W. Holdgate, CB, FRS; *Clerk to the Council*, P. H. Denton

ZOOLOGICAL SOCIETY OF SCOTLAND, ROYAL (1913), Scottish National Zoological Park, Edinburgh Zoo, Corstorphine Road,Edinburgh EH12 6TS. Tel: 0131-334 9171. *Director*, Prof. R. J. Wheater, OBE, FRSE

## LOCAL HISTORY AND ARCHAEOLOGICAL SOCIETIES

### ENGLAND

*Bedfordshire:* SOUTH BEDFORDSHIRE ARCHAEOLOGICAL SOCIETY. *Hon. Secretary*, D. H. Kennett, 27 Lords Lane, Bradwell, Great Yarmouth, Norfolk NR31 8NY

*Berkshire:* BERKSHIRE ARCHAEOLOGICAL SOCIETY. *Hon. Secretary*, L. J. Over, 43 Laburnham Road, Maidenhead, Berks. SL6 4DE. Tel: 01628-31225

NEWBURY DISTRICT FIELD CLUB. *President*, 4 Coombe Cottages, Coombe Road, Compton, Berks. RG16 ORQ. Tel: 01635-579076

*Buckinghamshire:* BUCKINGHAMSHIRE ARCHAEOLOGICAL SOCIETY. *Hon. Secretary*, Dr R. P. Hagerty, County Museum, Church Street, Aylesbury, Bucks. HP20 2QP. Tel: 01296-20984

*Cambridgeshire:* CAMBRIDGE ANTIQUARIAN SOCIETY. *Hon. Secretary*, Dr M. Hesse, 39 Highsett Hills Road, Cambridge CB2 INZ. Tel: 01223-355515

*Cheshire:* CHESTER ARCHAEOLOGICAL SOCIETY. *Secretary*, Dr D. J. P. Mason, FSA, Ochr Cottage, Porch Lane, Hope Mountain, Caergwrle, Clwyd LLI2 9LS. Tel: 01978-760834

*Cornwall:* CORNWALL ARCHAEOLOGICAL SOCIETY. *Hon. Secretaries*, Mr and Mrs B. Hammond, 7 Porthmeor Road, Holmbush, St Austell, Cornwall PL25 3LT. Tel: 01726-74763

*Cumberland and Westmorland:* CUMBERLAND AND WESTMORLAND ANTIQUARIAN AND ARCHAEOLOGICAL SOCIETY. *Hon. Secretary*, R. Hall, 2 High Tenterfell, Kendal, Cumbria LA9 4PG. Tel: 01539-814405

*Derbyshire:* DERBYSHIRE ARCHAEOLOGICAL SOCIETY. *Hon. Secretary*, I. Mitchell, 159 Draycott Road, Sawley, Long Eaton, Nottingham NGI0 3BX. Tel: 0115-972 9029

*Devonshire:* DEVON ARCHAEOLOGICAL SOCIETY, Royal Albert Memorial Museum, Queen Street, Exeter EX4 3RX. Tel: 01392-265858. *Hon. Secretary*, H. Bishop

*Dorset:* DORSET NATURAL HISTORY AND ARCHAEOLOGICAL SOCIETY, Dorset County Museum, Dorchester, Dorset DTI IXA. Tel: 01305-262735. *Secretary*, R. Peers

*Durham:* DURHAM AND NORTHUMBERLAND ARCHITECTURAL AND ARCHAEOLOGICAL SOCIETY. *Hon. Secretary*, A. Lloyd-Wallis, 53 Brook Terrace, Darlington, Co. Durham DL3 6PJ. Tel: 01325-359772

*Essex:* ESSEX SOCIETY FOR ARCHAEOLOGY AND HISTORY, Hollytrees Museum, High Street, Colchester COI IUG. *Secretary*, N. P. Wickendon

*Gloucestershire:* BRISTOL AND GLOUCESTERSHIRE ARCHAEOLOGICAL SOCIETY. *Hon. Secretary*, D. J. H. Smith, FSA, 22 Beaumont Road, Gloucester GL2 OEJ. Tel: 01452-302610

*Hampshire:* HAMPSHIRE FIELD CLUB AND ARCHAEOLOGICAL SOCIETY. *Hon. Secretary*, D. Allen, Andover Museum, 6 Church Close, Andover SPIO IDP. Tel: 01264-366283

*Herefordshire:* WOOLHOPE NATURALISTS' FIELD CLUB. *Hon. Secretary*, J. W. Tonkin, FSA, Chy an Whyloryon, Wigmore, Leominster, Herefordshire HR6 9UD. Tel: 01568-86356

*Hertfordshire:* EAST HERTFORDSHIRE ARCHAEOLOGICAL SOCIETY. *Hon. Secretary*, Mrs M. C. Readman, 1 Marsh Lane, Stanstead Abbots, Ware, Herts. SG12 8HH. Tel: 01920-870664

ST ALBANS AND HERTFORDSHIRE ARCHITECTURAL AND ARCHAEOLOGICAL SOCIETY. *Hon. Secretary*, B. E. Moody, 24 Rose Walk, St Albans, Herts. AL4 9AF

*Isle of Wight:* ISLE OF WIGHT NATURAL HISTORY AND ARCHAEOLOGICAL SOCIETY. *Hon. Secretary*, Mrs T. Goodley, Island Countryside Centre, Rylstone Gardens, Shanklin, IOW PO37 6RG. Tel: 01983-867016

*Kent:* KENT ARCHAEOLOGICAL SOCIETY. *Hon. General Secretary*, A. Moffatt, Three Elms, Woodlands Lane, Shorne, Gravesend, Kent DA12 3HH

*Leicestershire:* LEICESTERSHIRE ARCHAEOLOGICAL AND HISTORICAL SOCIETY, The Guildhall, Leicester LE1 5FQ. Tel: 0116-270 3031. *Hon. Secretary*, Dr A. D. McWhirr

*London and Middlesex:* CITY OF LONDON ARCHAEOLOGICAL SOCIETY. *Hon. Secretary*, Ms M. Andrews, 19 Hawes Road, Bromley, Kent BR1 3JS. Tel: 0171-832 7367

LONDON AND MIDDLESEX ARCHAEOLOGICAL SOCIETY. *Hon. Secretary*, M. Curtis, 34 Alexander Road, London SW19 7JZ. Tel: 0181-879 7109

*Norfolk:* NORFOLK AND NORWICH ARCHAEOLOGICAL SOCIETY. *Hon. General Secretary*, R. Bellinger, 30 Brettingham Avenue, Norwich NR4 6XG. Tel: 01603-55913

*Northumberland and Tyne and Wear:* SOCIETY OF ANTIQUARIES OF NEWCASTLE UPON TYNE, Black Gate, Castle Garth, Newcastle upon Tyne NE1 1RQ. Tel: 0191-261 5390. *Secretary*, D. Cutts

SUNDERLAND ANTIQUARIAN SOCIETY. *Hon. Secretary*, Mrs V. M. Stevens, 16 Grizedale Court, Seaburn Dene, Sunderland SR6 8JP. Tel: 0191-548 7541

*Oxfordshire:* OXFORDSHIRE ARCHITECTURAL AND HISTORICAL SOCIETY, Research Laboratory for Archaeology, 6 Keble Road, Oxford OX1 3QJ. *Hon. Secretary*, Dr A. Millard

*Shropshire:* SHROPSHIRE ARCHAEOLOGICAL AND HISTORICAL SOCIETY. *Chairman*, J. B. Lawson, Westcott Farm, Pontesbury, Shrewsbury SY5 0SQ. Tel: 01743-790531

*Somerset:* SOMERSET ARCHAEOLOGICAL AND NATURAL HISTORY SOCIETY, Taunton Castle, Taunton, Somerset TA1 4AD. Tel: 01823-272429. *Hon. Secretary*, B. Watkin

*Staffordshire:* CITY OF STOKE-ON-TRENT MUSEUM ARCHAEOLOGICAL SOCIETY, City Museum and Art Gallery, Hanley, Stoke-on-Trent ST1 3DW. Tel: 01782-502907. *Chairman*, E. E. Royle

*Suffolk:* SUFFOLK INSTITUTE OF ARCHAEOLOGY AND HISTORY. *Hon. Secretary*, E. A. Martin, Oak Tree Farm, Finborough Road, Hitcham, Ipswich IP7 7LS. Tel: 01449-741266

*Surrey:* SURREY ARCHAEOLOGICAL SOCIETY, Castle Arch, Guildford, Surrey GU1 3SX. Tel: 01483-32454. *Hon. Secretaries*, Mr and Mrs K. D. Graham

*Sussex:* SUSSEX ARCHAEOLOGICAL SOCIETY, Bull House, 92 High Street, Lewes, E. Sussex BN7 1XH. Tel: 01273-486260. *Chief Executive*, J. Manley

*Warwickshire:* BIRMINGHAM AND WARWICKSHIRE ARCHAEOLOGICAL SOCIETY, c/o Birmingham and Midland Institute, Margaret Street, Birmingham B3 3BS. Tel: 01789-488726. *Hon. Secretary*, A. J. Wilson

*Wiltshire:* WILTSHIRE ARCHAEOLOGICAL AND NATURAL HISTORY SOCIETY, The Museum, 41 Long Street, Devizes, Wilts SN10 1NS. Tel: 01380-727369. *Secretary*, G. G. Brown

*Worcestershire:* WORCESTERSHIRE ARCHAEOLOGICAL SOCIETY. Queen Elizabeth House, Trinity Street, Worcester WR1 2PW. Tel: 01905-722369. *Hon. Chairman*, T. J. Bridges

*Yorkshire:* YORKSHIRE ARCHAEOLOGICAL SOCIETY. *Hon. Secretary*, N. Cookson, PH.D., Claremont, 23 Clarendon Road, Leeds LS2 9NZ. Tel: 0113-245 7910

HALIFAX ANTIQUARIAN SOCIETY. *Hon. Secretary*, J. A. Hargreaves, 7 Hyde Park Gardens, Haugh Shaw Road, Halifax, W. Yorks HX1 3AH. Tel: 01422-352126

THORESBY SOCIETY. *Hon. Secretary*, B. Harrison, Claremont, 23 Clarendon Road, Leeds LS2 9NZ

## SCOTLAND

AYRSHIRE ARCHAEOLOGICAL AND NATURAL HISTORY SOCIETY. *Hon. Secretary*, Dr T. Mathews, 10 Longlands Park, Ayr KA7 4RJ. Tel: 01292-441915

DUMFRIESSHIRE AND GALLOWAY NATURAL HISTORY AND ANTIQUARIAN SOCIETY. *Hon. Secretary*, Mrs J. Muir, North Wing, Carzield House, Kirmahoe, Dumfriesshire DG1 1SY. Tel: 01387-710216

HAWICK ARCHAEOLOGICAL SOCIETY. *Hon. Secretary*, I. W. Landles, Orrock House, Stirches Road, Hawick, Roxburghshire TD9 7HF. Tel: 01450-75546

INVERNESS FIELD CLUB. *Hon. Secretary*, Miss I. McLean, 6 Drumblair Crescent, Inverness IV2 4RG

## WALES

*Dyfed:* CEREDIGION ANTIQUARIAN SOCIETY. *Hon. Secretary*, Mrs M. Burdett-Jones, Skomer, Llanbadarn Road, Aberystwyth, Dyfed SY23 3QW. Tel: 01970-612342

*Gwynedd:* ANGLESEY ANTIQUARIAN SOCIETY. *Hon. Secretary*, S. C. G. Caffell, 1 Fronheulog Sling, Tregarth, Bangor LL57 4RD

*Powys:* POWYSLAND CLUB. *Hon. Secretary*, Miss P. M. Davies, Llygad y Dyffryn, Llanidloes, Powys SY18 6JD

## CHANNEL ISLANDS

SOCIÉTÉ JERSIAISE, ARCHAEOLOGICAL SECTION, La Hougue Bie Museum, Grouville, Jersey. Tel: 01534-58314. *Hon. Secretary*, Dr R. A. H. Nichols

# International Organizations

## ASSOCIATION OF SOUTH EAST ASIAN NATIONS
70 A. Jl. Sisingamangaraja Kebayoran Baru, Jakarta Selatan, PO Box 2072, Jakarta, Indonesia

Formed in 1967, the main aims of the Association of South East Asian Nations (ASEAN) are the acceleration of economic growth, social progress and cultural development, the promotion of collaboration and mutual assistance in matters of common interest, and the continuing stability of the South East Asian region.

The heads of government of the member countries are the highest authority and give directions to ASEAN as and when necessary. The main policy-making body is the annual meeting of foreign ministers of the member countries. The members are Brunei, Indonesia, Malaysia, the Philippines, Singapore and Thailand. Laos and Vietnam were granted observer status in 1992.

In 1992 it was agreed to create an ASEAN free trade area within 15 years. Progress towards this began in January 1993 with the beginning of the implementation of a common preferential tariff. In 1993 it was decided to establish the ASEAN regional forum on security. The new security forum is to be based on preventive diplomacy to prevent potential conflicts in the Asia-Pacific area.

*Secretary-General*, Dato' Ajit Singh (*Malaysia*)

## BANK FOR INTERNATIONAL SETTLEMENTS
Centralbahnplatz 2, 4002 Basle, Switzerland

The objectives of the Bank for International Settlements (founded in 1930) are to promote the co-operation of central banks; to provide facilities for international financial operations; and to act as trustee or agent in international financial settlements entrusted to it. The London agent is the Bank of England, and the Governor of the Bank of England is a member of the Board of Directors, in which administrative control is vested.

*Chairman of the Board of Directors and President of the Bank for International Settlements*, Dr W. F. Duisenberg (*Netherlands*)

## CAB INTERNATIONAL
Wallingford, Oxon. OX10 8DE Tel: 01491-832111

CAB International (formerly the Commonwealth Agricultural Bureau) was founded in 1929. The organization generates, disseminates and applies scientific knowledge in support of sustainable development, with an emphasis on agriculture, forestry, human health and the management of natural resources, and with particular attention to the needs of developing countries. It consists of four institutes and five editorial divisions. The organization is owned by 36 countries, each represented on an Executive Council. A Governing Board was appointed in 1990 to provide expert guidance to management on policy issues. The functions of CABI's four institutes are to provide identification, diagnostic, bio-systematic and management support for the control of pests and diseases of crops and livestock. Each institute and editorial division acts as an effective clearing house for the collection, collation and dissemination of information in its particular branch of agricultural science.

*Director-General*, J. Gilmore (*acting*)

## CARIBBEAN COMMUNITY AND COMMON MARKET
PO Box 10827, Georgetown, Guyana

The Caribbean Community and Common Market (CARICOM) was established in 1973 with three objectives: economic co-operation through the Caribbean Common Market; the co-ordination of foreign policy among the independent member states; the provision of common services and co-operation in functional matters such as health, education and culture, communications and industrial relations. The supreme organ is the Conference of Heads of Government, which determines policy, takes strategic decisions and is responsible for resolving conflicts and all matters relating to the founding treaty. The second most important organ is the Caribbean Community Council, consisting of ministers of government with special responsibility for CARICOM affairs, which is responsible for the operational planning, resource allocation, development and smooth running of the Common Market and for the settlement of any problems arising out of its functioning. The principal administrative arms are the Secretariat, based in Guyana and the Bureau of the Conference.

The 13 member states are Antigua and Barbuda, The Bahamas (which is not a member of the Common Market), Barbados, Belize, Dominica, Grenada, Guyana, Jamaica, Montserrat, St Christopher and Nevis, St Lucia, St Vincent and the Grenadines, and Trinidad and Tobago. The British Virgin Islands and the Turks and Caicos Islands are associate members. The Dominican Republic, Haiti, Mexico, Puerto Rico, Suriname and Venezuela have observer status.

*Secretary-General*, Edwin W. Carrington

## THE COMMONWEALTH

The Commonwealth is a free association of 51 sovereign independent states together with their associated states and dependencies. All of the states were formerly parts of the British Empire, or League of Nations (later UN) mandated territories.

The status and relationship of member nations were first defined by the Inter-Imperial Relations Committee of the 1926 Imperial Conference, under the chairmanship of Lord Balfour, when the six existing dominions (Australia, Canada, the Irish Free State, Newfoundland, New Zealand and South Africa) were described as 'autonomous Communities within the British Empire, equal in status, in no way subordinate one to another in any aspect of their domestic or external affairs, though united by a common allegiance to the Crown and freely associated as Members of the British Commonwealth of Nations'. This formula was given legal substance by the Statute of Westminster 1931.

This concept of a group of countries owing allegiance to a single Crown changed in 1949 when India decided to become a republic. Her continued membership of the Commonwealth was agreed by the other members on the basis of her 'acceptance of The King as the symbol of the free association of its independent member nations and as such the head of the Commonwealth'. This paved the way for other republics to join the association in due course. Member nations agreed at the time of the accession of Queen Elizabeth II to recognize Her Majesty as the new Head of the Commonwealth. However, the position is not vested in the British Crown.

## THE MODERN COMMONWEALTH

With the membership of India and Pakistan in 1947, Ceylon (later Sri Lanka) in 1948 and Ghana in 1957, the character of the Commonwealth changed fundamentally. The grouping of all-white dominions gave way to a modern, multi-racial association of equal, sovereign nations and their peoples as Britain granted independence to almost all of her colonies in Africa, Asia, the Caribbean and the Pacific. Virtually all of these newly-independent countries joined the Commonwealth.

In its modern form, the Commonwealth increasingly focused its attention on promoting development and on helping to end racial inequality in southern Africa. The Commonwealth played an important role in the resolution of the Rhodesian crisis ending with the independence of Zimbabwe, strongly supported the independence of Namibia, and from the late 1970s took concerted action, including sporting and economic sanctions, against the South African government over its policy of apartheid.

## THE HARARE DECLARATION

As progress was made towards ending apartheid and introducing democracy in South Africa, the Commonwealth set itself new goals at its heads of government meeting in Harare, Zimbabwe, in 1991. Outlined in the Harare Commonwealth Declaration, these goals include the promotion of the Commonwealth's fundamental political values, such as democracy, the rule of law, good government and human rights; the promotion of equality for women; the provision of universal access to education; the promotion of sustainable development and the alleviation of poverty; action against disease and illegal drugs; help for small Commonwealth states; and support of the UN in the quest for international consensus on key issues.

At the heads of government meeting in Cyprus in 1993 the goals and principles of the Harare Declaration were transformed into membership rules for the Commonwealth for new members and for the four remaining non-democratic members (Nigeria, Sierra Leone, Uganda and Malawi). South Africa was invited to rejoin the Commonwealth after the April 1994 multi-racial election and Cameroon invited to join when it has fulfilled the Harare principles. The Commonwealth aims for all its 51 members to be democracies by the 1995 heads of government meeting.

## MEMBERSHIP

Membership of the Commonwealth involves acceptance of the association's basic principles and is subject to the approval of existing members. The membership currently stands at 51. (The date of joining the Commonwealth is shown in parenthesis.)

| | |
|---|---|
| Antigua and Barbuda (1981) | Brunei (1984) |
| Australia (1931) | *Canada (1931) |
| The Bahamas (1973) | Cyprus (1961) |
| Bangladesh (1972) | Dominica (1978) |
| Barbados (1966) | The Gambia (1965) |
| Belize (1981) | Ghana (1957) |
| Botswana (1966) | *Grenada (1974) |

| | |
|---|---|
| Guyana (1966) | *St Vincent and the |
| India (1947) | Grenadines (1979) |
| *Jamaica (1962) | Seychelles (1976) |
| Kenya (1963) | Sierra Leone (1961) |
| Kiribati (1979) | Singapore (1965) |
| Lesotho (1966) | *Solomon Islands (1978) |
| Malawi (1964) | South Africa (1931) |
| Malaysia (1957) | Sri Lanka (1948) |
| The Maldives (1982) | Swaziland (1968) |
| Malta (1964) | Tanzania (1961) |
| Mauritius (1968) | Tonga (1970) |
| Namibia (1990) | Trinidad and Tobago (1962) |
| Nauru (1968) | *Tuvalu (1978) |
| *New Zealand (1931) | Uganda (1962) |
| Nigeria (1960) | *United Kingdom |
| Pakistan (1947) | Vanuatu (1980) |
| *Papua New Guinea (1975) | Western Samoa (1970) |
| *St Christopher and Nevis | Zambia (1964) |
| (1983) | Zimbabwe (1980) |
| *St Lucia (1979) | *Realms of Queen Elizabeth II |

Nauru and Tuvalu are special members, with the right to participate in all functional Commonwealth meetings and activities, but not to attend meetings of Commonwealth heads of government.

*Countries which have left the Commonwealth*
Fiji (1987)
Republic of Ireland (1949)
Pakistan (1972, rejoined 1989)
South Africa (1961, rejoined 1994)

Of the 51 member states, 16 have Queen Elizabeth II as head of state, 30 are republics, and five are indigenous monarchies.

In each of the realms where Queen Elizabeth II is head of state (except for the United Kingdom), she is personally represented by a Governor-General, who holds in all essential respects the same position in relation to the administration of public affairs in the realm as is held by Her Majesty in Britain. The Governor-General is appointed by The Queen on the advice of the government of the state concerned.

## INTERGOVERNMENTAL AND OTHER LINKS

The main forum for consultation is the Commonwealth heads of government meetings held biennially to discuss international developments and to consider co-operation among members. New Zealand is the venue of the October 1995 meeting. Decisions are reached by consensus, and the views of the meeting are set out in a communiqué. There are also annual meetings of finance ministers and frequent meetings of ministers and officials in many other fields, such as education, health, labour, law, women's affairs, agriculture, youth and science. Intergovernmental links are complemented by the activities of some 300 Commonwealth non-governmental organizations linking professionals, sportsmen and sportswomen, and interest groups, forming a 'people's Commonwealth'. The Commonwealth Games take place every four years.

Assistance to other Commonwealth countries normally has priority in the bilateral aid programmes of the association's developed members (Australia, Britain, Canada and New Zealand), who direct some 30 per cent of their aid to other member countries. Developing Commonwealth nations also assist their poorer partners, and many Commonwealth voluntary organizations promote development.

Many of the smaller Commonwealth countries are party to the Lomé Convention, which accords preferential access to the European Community (EC) for developing countries of Africa, the Caribbean and the Pacific, and provides for them to receive EC aid.

## COMMONWEALTH SECRETARIAT

The Commonwealth has a secretariat, established in 1965 in London, which is funded by all member governments. This is the main agency for multilateral communication between member governments on issues relating to the Commonwealth as a whole. It promotes consultation and co-operation, disseminates information on matters of common concern, organizes meetings including the biennial summits, co-ordinates Commonwealth activities, and provides technical assistance for economic and social development through the Commonwealth Fund for Technical Co-operation.

The Commonwealth Foundation, also based in London, was established by Commonwealth governments in 1966 as an autonomous body with a board of governors representing Commonwealth governments that fund the Foundation. It promotes and funds exchanges and other activities aimed at strengthening the skills and effectiveness of professionals and non-government organizations. It also promotes culture, rural development, social welfare and the role of women.

COMMONWEALTH SECRETARIAT, Marlborough House, Pall Mall, London SW1Y 5HX. Tel: 0171-839 3411. *Secretary-General*, Chief Emeka Anyaoku (Nigeria)

COMMONWEALTH FOUNDATION, Marlborough House, Pall Mall, London SW1Y 5HY. Tel: 0171-930 3783. *Director*, Dr Humayun Khan (Pakistan)

COMMONWEALTH INSTITUTE, Kensington High Street, London W8 6NQ. Tel: 0171-603 4535. *Director-General*, S. Cox

## COMMONWEALTH OF INDEPENDENT STATES

The Commonwealth of Independent States (CIS) is a multilateral grouping of sovereign states which were formerly constituent republics of the USSR. The formation of the CIS was agreed by Russia, Ukraine and Belorussia on 8 December 1991. On 20 December the remaining republics, apart from the Baltic states and Georgia, joined the CIS and the USSR formally ceased to exist on 26 December 1991. Georgia joined in December 1993. Azerbaijani and Moldovan membership effectively lapsed, because of non-ratification, until September 1993 and April 1994 respectively. Membership of the CIS now consists of all the former Soviet republics apart from the Baltic states (twelve in total).

The CIS acts as a co-ordinating mechanism for foreign, defence and economic policies, and is a forum for addressing those problems which have specifically arisen from the break-up of the USSR. The affairs of the CIS are addressed in more than 50 inter-state, intergovernmental co-ordinating and consultative statutory bodies and not by central institutions. The two supreme CIS bodies were formed in January 1992: the Council of Heads of State, and the Council of Heads of Government. The Council of Heads of State is the highest organ of the CIS and meets not less than twice yearly; it is chaired by the heads of state of the members in (Russian) alphabetical order. The Council of Heads of Government meets not less than once every three months and carries out the co-ordination of military and economic activity in the Commonwealth. Other important bodies are: the Council of Heads of Collective Security (Defence Ministers); the Joint Staff for co-ordinating the CIS member states military co-operation; the CIS Inter-Parliamentary Assembly; the Economic Arbitration Court and the Co-ordinating Consultative Committee. Administrative support is provided by the Executive Secretariat based in Minsk. The chairmanship of CIS statutory bodies rests with Russia in 1994 and Tajikistan in 1995.

### OPERATION

In practice the CIS did not in 1992 and the first half of 1993 work as well as had been hoped and became a mechanism for attempting to ameliorate conflicts between the former republics of the USSR. However, it failed to solve the underlying political reasons for these conflicts, the organization being constantly undermined by divisions between republics over issues such as: the Armenia–Azerbaijan war over Nagorno-Karabakh; Ukrainian nuclear weapons; the Black Sea Fleet; the pace of economic reform; the control of oil, gas and natural resources; inter-state debts; the separatist conflict with ethnic Russians in Moldavia; and Russian support for the Abkhazian separatists in Georgia.

In January 1993 seven states (Russia, Armenia, Belarus, Kazakhstan, Uzbekistan, Tajikistan, Kyrgyzstan) attempted to increase economic and defence co-operation with the signing in Minsk of the CIS Charter which formally established CIS functions and the obligations of member states. It was not, however, until the summer of 1993 that the CIS began to function and co-ordinate more effectively, with Russia using its economic power, aid, natural resources and military influence to force and entice some of the other former Soviet republics to curb their attempts at economic or military independence. Since September 1993 Azerbaijan, Georgia and Moldova have joined or rejoined the CIS and Russia has pacified conflicts in Georgia and Tajikistan on its own terms. Economic and monetary co-operation have increased with the signing of a Treaty on Economic Union (24 September 1993) and the creation of a Free Trade Zone (signed 15 April 1994), while defence co-operation has increased with the entering into force after ratification of the Treaty on Collective Security (signed 15 May 1992) and an agreement on joint CIS defence forces for Tajikistan under Russian command and control.

### DEFENCE CO-OPERATION

On becoming member states of the CIS, the 11 original states agreed to recognize their existing borders, respect one another's territorial integrity and reject the use of military force or other forms of coercion to settle disputes between them. Agreement was also reached on fulfilling all the international treaty obligations of the former USSR, and on a unified central control for nuclear weapons and other strategic forces, together with the establishment of CIS joint armed forces. However, implementation of these agreements has proved problematic because of disputes and even open warfare between republics.

The CIS states agreed on a central CIS command for all nuclear weapons, and when President Gorbachev resigned in December 1991 he handed control of nuclear weapons to the CIS commander-in-chief Marshal Shaposhnikov. All tactical nuclear weapons had been transferred to the Russian republic by May 1992. An agreement was reached with the USA in May 1992 by the four republics with strategic nuclear weapons (Russia, the Ukraine, Belarus, Kazakhstan) on implementing the strategic arms reduction talks (START) treaty previously signed by the USA and USSR. Under this agreement the Ukraine, Belarus and Kazakhstan agreed to eliminate all their strategic nuclear weapons over a seven-year period and Russia has agreed to reduce its strategic nuclear weapons over the same period to such an extent that there will be a 38 per cent reduction in the overall former Soviet arsenal. The USA (Oct. 1992), Kazakhstan (July 1992), Russia (Nov. 1992), Belarus (Feb. 1993) and finally Ukraine (Feb. 1994) have ratified the START I treaty. The Treaty became effective in March 1994 when Ukraine began transferring its strategic nuclear weapons to Russia for disposal and reprocessing, in return for US aid for dismantlement and for the highly enriched uranium of the warheads, and fuel-grade uranium for Ukraine's civilian nuclear reactors.

At the non-nuclear level and at the level of defence co-operation generally, the situation remained confused in 1992 and early 1993. While all member states formed their own defence ministries and armed forces aimed at independent military action, a CIS high command and joint armed forces were also established in early 1992 and the Treaty on Collective Security signed in May 1992 by six member states. Nine CIS states also agreed in June 1992 on the establishment of joint peacemaking forces to intervene in CIS conflicts. Deployment of these forces is conditional on consensus in the Council of Heads of State. Forces have been deployed in Moldova and Tajikistan.

However, the fear and resentment of Russian domination by some states (Ukraine, Moldova, Turkmenistan) frustrated the defence co-operation efforts of the remaining members and led to the downgrading in August 1993 of the CIS high command into the Joint Staff for military co-operation. The member states interested in further defence co-operation led by Russia have since summer 1993 engaged in a series of bilateral and multilateral agreements under the supervision of the Council of Heads of Collective Security (established August 1993). Russia established bilateral defence agreements with Tajikistan, Turkmenistan, Kyrgyzstan, Armenia and Georgia, together with multilateral agreements on a common air defence system, joint CIS armed forces to protect the former USSR borders of the Central Asian states, and joint peacekeeping forces in Tajikistan. Russia has gradually increased its influence since mid 1993, converting the bilateral and multilateral agreements into CIS ones under the umbrella of the Treaty on Collective Security, and forced several states into military co-operation. The effect has been to legitimize the stationing of Russian forces and peacekeeping troops in ten of the other 11 states (not Ukraine) and grant Russian forces control of virtually all of the former USSR's external borders. Only Ukraine and Moldova remain outside the defence co-operation framework and have not signed the Treaty on Collective Security.

ECONOMIC CO-OPERATION

As it became clear that the Soviet Union was disintegrating in October 1991, nine republics signed a treaty forming an economic community, and were joined by two other republics in November 1991. The principles of the treaty were embodied within the CIS and formed the basis of its economic co-operation in 1992 and the first half of 1993. Members agreed to refrain from economic actions that would damage each other and to co-ordinate economic and monetary policies. A Co-ordinating Consultative Committee, an economic arbitration court and an inter-state bank were established. A single monetary unit, the rouble, was originally agreed upon by all member states, and the members recognized that the basis of recovery for their economies was private ownership, free enterprise and competition. Throughout 1992 and early 1993 economic co-operation failed to function effectively because of the differing pace of economic reform in member states and the introduction of separate currencies by member states.

Russia effectively forced the collapse of the rouble zone in July 1993 by withdrawing all pre-1993 roubles and forcing the remaining states using roubles to accept Russian monetary control or introduce their own currencies, which all did apart from Tajikistan. The resulting economic collapse of the non-Russian economies led to renewed interest in economic co-operation and the signing of a Treaty on

Economic Union in September 1993. The eleven CIS members who have signed the Treaty (Ukraine is an associate member of the Economic Union) are committed to a common market without internal barriers to trade, common fiscal policies and an eventual currency union with currencies semi-fixed against the rouble. Belarus has withdrawn its currency and rejoined Russia and Tajikistan in the rouble zone. As the first step to a common market, the creation of a Free Trade Zone has been agreed involving the lifting of customs duties.

Originally the main advantage of economic co-ordination by the CIS members was the granting of large amounts of aid by Western countries and international organizations, which made it clear that economic aid was dependent on CIS co-ordination in accepting responsibility for the former USSR's debt, abiding by all the former USSR's international obligations (such as nuclear and conventional arms reductions), and having a secure, central control and command of nuclear weapons. As a result of CIS co-ordination members have gained extensive grants, loans, credits, trade agreements and technological, business and planning expertise and guidance.

CONFERENCE ON SECURITY AND CO-OPERATION IN EUROPE
Kärntner Ring 5–7, A-1010 Vienna, Austria

The Conference on Security and Co-operation in Europe (CSCE) was launched in 1975 under the Helsinki Final Act, which established agreements between NATO members, Warsaw Pact members, and neutral and non-aligned European countries covering security in Europe; economic, scientific, technological and environmental co-operation; and humanitarian principles and co-operation. Further conferences were held at Belgrade (1977–8), Madrid (1980–3), Vienna (1986–9) and Helsinki (1992).

With the end of the Cold War, it was decided that the CSCE should be revitalized to provide a new security framework for Europe. The Charter of Paris for a New Europe was signed on 21 November 1990, committing members to support for multi-party democracy, free-market economics, the rule of law, and human rights. The signatories also undertook to enhance political consultation, agreeing to regular meetings of heads of government, ministers and officials. The CSCE held its first institutionalized Heads of State and Government summit in Helsinki in December 1992, at which they adopted the Helsinki Document 1992. This declares the CSCE to be a regional organization in the sense of Chapter VIII of the UN Charter and defines the structures of the organization. The summit also appointed a High Commissioner on National Minorities.

Three structures have been established: the Council of Foreign Ministers as a central forum for regular political consultations which meets at least once a year; the Committee of Senior Officials (CSO) which prepares work for the Council, carries out its decisions and is responsible for the overview, management and co-ordination of CSCE activities; and the Permanent Committee, which is responsible for the day-to-day operational tasks of the CSCE. The chairmanship of the Council, CSO and Permanent Committee rotates among participating states with the CSO meeting in Prague and the Permanent Committee in Vienna. The CSCE is also underpinned by four permanent institutions; a Secretariat and a Forum for Security Co-operation (Vienna), an Office for Democratic Institutions and Human Rights (Warsaw), and an office of the High Commissioner on National Minorities (The Hague). There is also a documentation and conference centre in Prague. The European Assembly of member parliamentarians has also formed, with a secretariat based in Copenhagen. In June 1991 the CSCE agreed upon new crisis prevention mechanisms to prevent violent conflict between and within member countries. In an attempt to put these mechanisms into place, the CSCE has established monitoring missions in areas of potential or actual conflict.

The CSCE has 53 participating states: Albania, Armenia, Austria, Azerbaijan, Belarus, Belgium, Bosnia-Hercegovina, Bulgaria, Canada, Croatia, Cyprus, Czech Republic, Denmark, Estonia, Finland, France, Georgia, Germany, Greece, Hungary, Iceland, Ireland, Italy, Kazakhstan, Kyrgyzstan, Latvia, Liechtenstein, Lithuania, Luxembourg, Malta, Moldova, Monaco, the Netherlands, Norway, Poland, Portugal, Romania, the Russian Federation, San Marino, Slovakia, Slovenia, Spain, Sweden, Switzerland, Tajikistan, Turkey, Turkmenistan, UK, Ukraine, USA, Uzbekistan, the Vatican and Yugoslavia (suspended from activities July 1992). The Former Yugoslav Republic of Macedonia is an observer.

*Chair of the Council and CSO (1994)*, Italy
*Secretary-General of the CSCE*, Wilhelm Hoÿnck (*Germany*)
*Director of the Office for Democratic Institutions and Human Rights*, Audrey Glover (*UK*)
*CSCE High Commissioner on National Minorities*, Max van der Stoel (*Netherlands*)

## THE COUNCIL OF EUROPE
67075 Strasbourg, France

The Council of Europe was founded in 1949. Its aim is to achieve greater unity between its members to safeguard their European heritage and to facilitate their economic and social progress through discussion and common action in economic, social, cultural, educational, scientific, legal and administrative matters, and in the maintenance and furtherance of pluralist democracy, human rights and fundamental freedoms.

The 32 members are Austria, Belgium, Bulgaria, Cyprus, Czech Republic, Denmark, Estonia, Finland, France, Germany, Greece, Hungary, Iceland, the Republic of Ireland, Italy, Liechtenstein, Lithuania, Luxembourg, Malta, Netherlands, Norway, Poland, Portugal, Romania, San Marino, Slovakia, Slovenia, Spain, Sweden, Switzerland, Turkey and the UK. 'Special guest status' has been granted to Albania, Belarus, Bosnia-Hercegovina, Croatia, Latvia, Macedonia (Former Yugoslav Republic of), Moldova, the Russian Federation and Ukraine.

The organs are the Committee of Ministers, consisting of the foreign ministers of member countries, who meet twice yearly, and the Parliamentary Assembly of 234 members, elected or chosen by the national parliaments of member countries in proportion to the relative strength of political parties. There is also a Joint Committee of Ministers and Representatives of the Parliamentary Assembly.

The Committee of Ministers is the executive organ of the Council. The majority of its conclusions take the form of international agreements (known as European Conventions) or recommendations to governments. Decisions of the Ministers may also be embodied in partial agreements to which a limited number of member governments are party. Member governments accredit Permanent Representatives to the Council in Strasbourg, who are also the Ministers' Deputies. The Committee of Deputies meets every month to transact business and to take decisions on behalf of Ministers.

The Parliamentary Assembly holds three week-long sessions a year at which it debates reports on matters of concern and reports received annually from the other European organizations and certain agencies of the United Nations. Its 13 permanent committees meet once or twice between each public plenary session of the Assembly. The Standing Conference of Local and Regional Authorities of Europe each year brings together mayors and municipal councillors in the same numbers as the members of the Parliamentary Assembly.

One of the principal achievements of the Council of Europe is the European Convention on Human Rights (1950) under which was established the European Commission and the European Court of Human Rights. Because of an increasing workload, the Committee of Ministers decided in 1993 to merge the European Commission and European Court of Human Rights into a single permanent body. The reorganized European Court of Human Rights sits usually in chambers of seven judges and exceptionally as a grand chamber of 17 judges. Litigants must still exhaust legal processes in their own country before bringing cases before the court.

Among the other conventions and agreements which have been concluded are the European Social Charter, the European Cultural Convention, the European Code of Social Security, and conventions on extradition, the legal status of migrant workers, torture prevention, conservation, and the transfer of sentenced prisoners. Most recently the specialized bodies of the Venice Commission and Demosthenes have been set up to assist in developing legislative, administrative and constitutional reforms in central and eastern Europe.

Non-member states take part in certain Council of Europe activities on a regular or *ad hoc* basis; thus the Holy See participates in all the educational, cultural and sports activities. The European Youth Centre is an educational residential centre for young people from all over Europe and further afield. The European Youth Foundation provides youth organizations with funds for their international activities.

*Secretary-General*, Daniel Tarschys (*Sweden*)
*Permanent UK Representative*, His Excellency Roger Beetham, *apptd* 1993

## THE ECONOMIC COMMUNITY OF WEST AFRICAN STATES
6 King George V Road, PMB 12745, Lagos, Nigeria

The Economic Community of West African States (ECOWAS) was founded at a summit of West African heads of government at Lagos in 1975, and came into operation in January 1977. It aims to promote the cultural, economic and social development of West Africa through mutual co-operation. At the 1993 heads of government summit in Benin a revised ECOWAS Treaty was signed which also makes the prevention and control of regional conflicts an aim of ECOWAS. The Treaty also provides for the establishment of a regional parliament, an economic and social council, and a court of justice.

Measures undertaken by ECOWAS include the gradual elimination of barriers to the movement of goods, people and services between member states and the improvement of regional telecommunications and transport.

The supreme authority of ECOWAS is vested in the annual summit of heads of government of all 16 member states. A Council of Ministers, two from each member state, meets biannually to monitor the organization and make recommendations to the summit. ECOWAS operates through a Secretariat, headed by the Executive Secretary. In addition there is a financial controller, an external auditor, the Disputes Tribunal and the Defence Council.

A Fund for Co-operation, Compensation and Development, situated at Lomé, Togo, finances development projects and provides compensation to member states who have suffered losses as a result of ECOWAS's policies, particularly in relation to trade liberalization.

In 1989–90 ECOWAS attempted to mediate in the Liberian civil war and sent an ECOWAS Monitoring Group (ECOMOG) peacekeeping force of 15,000 troops to the country in 1990. The force, led by Nigerian units with troops from Senegal, Gambia, Ghana, Guinea and Sierra Leone, succeeded in establishing an interim government and preventing further conflict in 1991, but fighting broke out again in late 1992 and continued into 1993. ECOMOG forces remain in the country until a peace agreement reached early in 1994 is implemented.

*Executive Secretary*, Dr Abbas Bundu

## THE EUROPEAN BANK FOR RECONSTRUCTION AND DEVELOPMENT
1 Exchange Square, London EC2A 2EH

The foundation of a European Bank for Reconstruction and Development (EBRD) was proposed by President Mitterrand of France in 1989 and the charter of the EBRD was signed by 40 countries, the European Commission and the European Investment Bank on 29 May 1990. The EBRD was inaugurated in London on 15 April 1991.

The aim of the EBRD is to assist the transformation of the states of central and eastern Europe (Albania, Bulgaria, Czech Republic, Estonia, Hungary, Latvia, Lithuania, Poland, Romania, Slovakia, the republics of the former USSR and Yugoslavia) from centrally-planned economies to free market economies, with particular regard for strengthening democratic institutions, and respect for human rights and the environment. The EBRD provides technical assistance, training and investment in: the upgrading of infrastructure; the creation of modern financial systems; nuclear safety; tourism; the exploitation of natural resources; and the restructuring of state industries. The EBRD's assistance is weighted towards the private sector; no more than 40 per cent of its investment can be made in state-owned concerns. It works in co-operation with its members, private companies, and international organizations, such as the OECD, the IMF, the World Bank and the UN specialized agencies.

The EBRD has an initial subscribed capital of 10 billion ECU. The major subscribers are: the USA, 10 per cent; Britain, France, Germany, Italy and Japan, 8.5 per cent each; central and eastern European states, 11.9 per cent. In 1993 the EBRD approved 91 projects, totalling ECU 2,280m; the total number of projects approved since its establishment is 196 in 19 states.

The EBRD has 59 members. The highest authority is the Board of Governors; each member appoints one Governor and one alternate. The Governors delegate most powers to a 23-member Board of Directors; the Directors are responsible for the EBRD's operations and are appointed by the Governors for three-year terms. The Governors also elect the President of the Board of Directors, who acts as the Bank's president, for a four-year term. A Secretary-General liaises between the Directors and EBRD staff.

*President of the Board of Directors*, Jacques de Larosière
(*France*)
*UK Executive Director*, Robert Graham-Harrison
*Secretary-General*, Bart le Blanc (*Netherlands*)

## EUROPEAN FREE TRADE ASSOCIATION
9–11 rue de Varembé, 1211 Geneva 20, Switzerland

The European Free Trade Association (EFTA) was established on 3 May 1960, by Austria, Denmark, Norway, Portugal, Sweden, Switzerland and the UK. EFTA was subsequently joined by Finland, Iceland and Liechtenstein. Denmark and the UK left EFTA in 1972 and Portugal in 1985 to join the EC.

The first objective of EFTA was to establish free trade in industrial goods between members; this was achieved in 1966. Its second objective was the creation of a single market in western Europe and in 1972 EFTA signed a free trade agreement with the EC covering trade in industrial goods; the remaining tariffs on industrial products were finally abolished in 1984.

Exploratory talks on the free movement of goods, services, capital and labour throughout the EC–EFTA area led to negotiations on the establishment of a European Economic Area (EEA) encompassing all 19 EC and EFTA countries. These concluded with the signing of the EEA Agreement on 2 May 1992 in Oporto, Portugal. The EEA was intended to enter into force at the same time as the EC single market in 1993. This proved impossible when the Swiss electorate rejected ratification of the EEA Agreement in a referendum in December 1992. The remaining six EFTA states and the EC negotiated a protocol to the EEA Agreement which was signed in March 1993. The protocol provides for the adjustment of contributions by the EFTA states to the EC cohesion funds after Switzerland's withdrawal. The EEA Agreement entered into force on 1 January 1994 for the six remaining countries (except Liechtenstein which must first adapt its customs union with Switzerland) after its ratification by all 18 states.

The EEA is controlled by regular ministerial meetings and by a joint EU-EFTA committee and will develop alongside EU legislation. Apart from single market measures, there will also be co-operation in education, research and development, consumer policy and tourism. An EFTA Court of Justice has been established in Geneva and an EFTA Surveillance Authority in Brussels to supervise the implementation of the EEA Agreement.

Austria, Sweden, Finland and Norway have negotiated membership of the EU, with a possible entry date of 1 January 1995. Switzerland's EU application is being reassessed in the light of the rejection of the EEA Agreement.

EFTA has expanded its relations with other non-EU states in recent years and free trade agreements have been signed with Turkey (December 1991), Israel (September 1992), Poland and Romania (December 1992), Bulgaria and Hungary (March 1993), Czech Republic and Slovakia (April 1993). In addition, EFTA has signed declarations of economic co-operation with Estonia, Latvia and Lithuania (December 1991), Slovenia (May 1992) and Albania (December 1992).

The Council of EFTA is the principle organ of the Association. It generally meets once a week at the level of heads of the permanent national delegations to the EFTA Secretariat in Geneva and twice a year at ministerial level. The chairmanship of the Council rotates every six months. Each state has a single vote and recommendations must normally be unanimous; decisions of the Council are binding on member countries.

*Secretary-General*, Georg Reisch (*Austria*)

EUROPEAN ORGANIZATION FOR NUCLEAR
RESEARCH (CERN)
CH-1211 Geneva 23, Switzerland

The Convention establishing the European Organization for
Nuclear Research (CERN) came into force in 1954. The
organization promotes European collaboration in high
energy physics of a purely scientific nature. It is not
concerned with research of a military nature.

The member countries are Austria, Belgium, Czech
Republic, Denmark, Finland, France, Germany, Greece,
Hungary, Italy, Netherlands, Norway, Poland, Portugal,
Slovak Republic, Spain, Sweden, Switzerland and the UK.
The following have observer status: Israel, the Russian
Federation, Turkey, Yugoslavia (suspended), the EC Com-
mission and UNESCO.

The Council is the highest policy-making body and is
made up of two delegates from each member state. There is
also a Committee of the Council comprising a single delegate
from each member state (who is also a Council member) and
the chairmen of the scientific policy and finance advisory
committees. The Council is chaired by a President who is
elected by the Council in Session. The Council also elects the
Director-General, the person responsible for the internal
organization of CERN. The Director-General heads a
workforce of approximately 3,000, including physicists,
craftsmen, technicians and administrative staff. At present
over 6,000 physicists use CERN's facilities.

The member countries contribute to the budget directly
in proportion to their net national revenue. The 1994 budget
was SFr 940 million.

*President of the Council*, Prof. Hubert Carien (*France*)
*Director-General* (1994–9), Prof. Christopher Llewellyn-
Smith (*UK*)

EUROPEAN SPACE AGENCY
8–10 rue Mario Nikis, 75738 Paris, France

The European Space Agency (ESA) was set up on 31 May
1975. It was formed from two earlier space organizations –
the European Space Research Organization (ESRO) and the
European Launcher Development Organization (ELDO). Its
aims include the advancement of space research and
technology, the implementation of a long-term European
space policy and the co-ordination of national space
programmes.

The member countries are Austria, Belgium, Denmark,
France, Germany, Republic of Ireland, Italy, Netherlands,
Norway, Spain, Sweden, Switzerland and the United Kingdom. Finland is an associate member and Canada a co-
operating state.

The agency is directed by a Council composed of the
representatives of the member states, and its chief officer is
the Director-General.

*Director-General*, Jean-Marie Luton, *apptd* 1990

THE EUROPEAN UNION

The beginnings of the European Community (EC) lie in the
desire following the Second World War to replace the
European system of competing nation states with a new
union. In May 1951 Robert Schuman, the French Foreign
Minister of the time, proposed that France and West

Germany pool their coal and steel industries under an
independent, supranational authority. They were joined by
Belgium, Luxembourg, the Netherlands and Italy, and the
Treaty of Paris was signed in 1951, establishing the European
Coal and Steel Community (ECSC) in 1952.

The success of the ECSC led to discussions in 1955
between the foreign ministers of its six member states on
proposals for further moves towards European economic
integration. As a result of these discussions the Treaty of
Rome, establishing the European Economic Community,
was signed on 25 March 1957. A second treaty founding the
European Atomic Energy Community (EURATOM) was
signed on the same day; this pledged the six signatories to
co-operate in research into nuclear science, particularly in
relation to nuclear energy.

The Treaty of Rome was intended to create a customs
union to remove all obstacles to the free movement of capital,
goods, people and services between member states. It also
established a common external trade policy and common
policies for agriculture and fisheries. Other articles of the
treaty refer to preventing the distortion of competition within
the Common Market; the co-ordination of economic policies;
the harmonization of social policy sufficient to enable the
functioning of the Common Market; the creation of a
European Social Fund to increase employment and raise
living standards; and the association of overseas countries
and territories with the Community to increase mutual trade
and to assist their economic and social development.

In addition, the Treaty of Rome established the Community's institutional structure; the Commission, the Council of
Ministers, the Economic and Social Committee, the European
Investment Bank, the Parliament, and the Court of Justice.
Whereas the Parliament and Court of Justice were common
to all three Communities from 1958, each Community had
its own executive body and Council of Ministers. The three
separate executive bodies and Councils of Ministers were
merged in 1967.

In May 1969, the heads of government of the Six decided
both to widen and to deepen the Community. Accordingly,
the Council of Ministers agreed in 1970 that from 1975 the
Community would have its own revenue, independent of
national contributions; this would be derived from customs
duties and agricultural import levies collected at the EC
external frontier, and a proportion of national receipts from
VAT.

In June 1970, the Six invited Britain, Denmark, Ireland
and Norway to open negotiations on their applications to
join the EC. The four countries signed a Treaty of Accession
in Brussels on 22 January 1972; Norway subsequently
withdrew its application after conducting a referendum on
entry. The enlarged Community of the Nine came into
existence on 1 January 1973.

During the 1970s the EC sought to strengthen the
democracies of southern Europe; this led to the admission of
Greece to the EC on 1 January 1981, and Portugal and Spain
on 1 January 1986. Following a plebiscite, Greenland
negotiated its withdrawal from the EC and left in 1986. The
unification of Germany brought the former German Democratic Republic into the EC in October 1990. Andorra joined
the customs union on 1 July 1991, but does not participate in
other EC institutions.

The Maastricht Treaty, which became effective on 1
November 1993, established the European Union composed
of three pillars: the European Community; one pillar to co-
ordinate foreign and security policies; and one pillar to co-
ordinate justice and interior affairs.

ENLARGEMENT AND EXTERNAL RELATIONS (*see also* EFTA entry)

The EC Single Market programme spurred other European non-member states to open negotiations with the EC on some form of preferential access for their goods, services, labour and capital to the Single Market, or failing this, to open negotiations on EC membership. Principal among these states were the members of the European Free Trade Association (EFTA) who opened negotiations with the EC on extending the Single Market to the EFTA states by the formation of the European Economic Area (EEA) encompassing all 19 EC and EFTA states. An agreement on this was reached and signed in May 1992 with the operation of the EEA due to begin on 1 January 1993. The subsequent rejection of ratification of the EEA by the Swiss electorate in December 1992 necessitated negotiations on, and agreement to, a protocol to the EEA Agreement by the EC and the remaining six EFTA states which was reached in March 1993. The EEA came into effect on 1 January 1994 after ratification by 17 member states (Liechtenstein must adapt its customs union with Switzerland). The EFTA states will provide a 'cohesion fund' for the poorer regions of the EC of some 500 million ECU in grants and 1.5 billion ECU in loans.

Despite the EEA negotiations, five of the EFTA states have also applied for EC membership. The EC opened membership negotiations with Austria, Finland, Norway and Sweden on 1 February 1993, and at the EC Copenhagen summit of June 1993, agreement was reached on a target date of 1 January 1995 for EC membership for the four countries. Accession negotiations with the four were successfully completed on 1 March 1994 with the resulting Accession Treaty being ratified by Austria in a parliamentary vote on 5 May 1994 and a referendum on 12 June 1994 in preparation for the 1 January 1995 accession date.

The procedure for accession to the EC is laid down in the Treaty of Rome; states have to be European and stable democracies governed by the rule of law with free market economies. When a state applies for membership, its application is studied by the Commission, which produces an opinion. If the opinion is positive, negotiations may be opened leading to an Accession Treaty which must be approved by all member state governments, the European Parliament, all member state parliaments and the applicant state's government and parliament.

*Other applicants:* Morocco (applied 1987/rejected 1987); Turkey (applied April 1987/negative opinion Dec. 1989); Cyprus (applied June 1990/rejected June 1993); Malta (applied July 1990/negative opinion June 1993); Switzerland (applied May 1992/no opinion yet); Hungary (applied April 1994/no opinion yet); Poland (applied April 1994/no opinion yet).

The EC has also signed association agreements with several states; these include a commitment to eventual membership. Long standing agreements exist with Turkey (Dec. 1974), Malta (April 1971) and Cyprus (Dec. 1972). Since the end of the Cold War and the emergence of democratic, free market states in eastern Europe, new association agreements (Europe agreements) have been signed with Poland (Dec. 1991), Hungary (Dec. 1991), Romania (Feb. 1993), Bulgaria (March 1993), and the Czech Republic (Oct. 1993) and the Slovak Republic (Oct. 1993). These new agreements commit the EC to long-term political and economic integration with eastern European states and liberalization of trade with the states in the 1993–5 period (although free trade in agriculture and the free movement of labour has been excluded). Meanwhile, partnership and co-operation agreements have been signed with Ukraine (March

1994) and Russia (June 1994) which are based on improving political and economic co-operation and mutual trade concessions but exclude any possibility of membership.

EUROPEAN COMMUNITY BUDGET 1994

| | Billion ECU* | As % of total |
|---|---|---|
| Agriculture | 37.5 | 51 |
| Regional and Social | 23.4 | 32 |
| Foreign Aid | 4.2 | 6 |
| Administration | 3.9 | 5 |
| Research and Development | 2.6 | 3.5 |
| Industry, Internal Market, Education | 1.8 | 2.5 |
| TOTAL | 73.4 | 100 |

*1 ECU = £0.79 as at 16 September 1994

EC BUDGET BY MEMBER STATE 1992 (*billion ECU*\*)

| | Contributions | | Receipts | Net Contributor (−)/ Recipient (+) |
|---|---|---|---|---|
| Germany | 19.0 | (28.6%) | 10.0 | −9.0 |
| France | 12.8 | (19.3%) | 11.3 | −1.5 |
| Italy | 9.9 | (14.9%) | 10.5 | +0.6 |
| UK | 8.6 | (12.9%) | 5.6 | −3.0 |
| Spain | 5.8 | (8.7%) | 8.7 | +2.9 |
| Netherlands | 3.9 | (5.9%) | 3.8 | −0.1 |
| Belgium | 2.7 | (4.1%) | 4.3 | +1.6 |
| Denmark | 1.3 | (1.9%) | 1.8 | +0.5 |
| Greece | 0.9 | (1.4%) | 4.8 | +3.9 |
| Portugal | 0.9 | (1.4%) | 2.0 | +1.1 |
| Ireland | 0.5 | (0.8%) | 2.9 | +2.4 |
| Luxembourg | 0.1 | (0.2%) | 0.8 | +0.7 |
| TOTAL† | 66.4 | (100.1%) | 66.5 | |

*1 ECU = £0.79 as at 16 September 1994
†Figures not precise because of rounding
Under the Maastricht Treaty the EC budget will rise from 1.2 per cent of Community GDP in 1992 to 1.27 per cent by 1997

THE COMMON AGRICULTURAL POLICY

The Treaty of Rome established the Common Agricultural Policy (CAP) to increase agricultural production, to provide a fair standard of living for farmers and to ensure the availability of food at reasonable prices. This aim is achieved by a number of mechanisms: Import Levies (the EC sets a target price for a particular product in the Community, the world price is monitored and if it falls below the guide price, an import levy can be imposed equivalent to the difference between the two); Intervention Purchase (if the price of a product falls below the level indicated by the Council, member states must purchase supplies of the product, provided that they are of suitable quality); Export Subsidies (the EC pays a food exporter a subsidy equivalent to the difference between the price at which the product is bought in the EC and the lower sale price on the world market).

These measures had the required aim of stimulating production but also placed increasing demands on the EC budget. To surmount this problem, the EC created the system of co-responsibility levies; farm payments to the EC by volume of product sold. This system was supplemented by national quotas for particular products, such as milk. The increase in the number of EC members and the greater use of modern technology has further increased production and exacerbated EC budgetary problems; CAP now accounts for over 50 per cent of EC expenditure. Radical reforms were agreed at the end of May 1992, based on the reduction of target prices for cereals, beef and dairy produce. These are being reduced by 29 per cent, 15 per cent and 5 per cent respectively, and the amount of money spent by the EC on the three mechanisms will fall. Production is expected to fall also because EC prices will be much closer to world price levels. Reforms were also introduced in 1988 emphasising set aside, whereby farmers are given direct grants to take land out of production as a means of reducing surpluses. Originally aimed at cereal farmers, who were allowed to set aside between 15 per cent and 100 per cent of their land, the set aside reforms were extended in 1993 for another five years and to every farm in the EC, which must set aside at least 15 per cent of their land.

Under the Uruguay round agreement of GATT reached in December 1993, the EC must, over a six year period from 1 January 1995: reduce its import levies by 36 per cent; reduce its domestic subsidies by 20 per cent; reduce its export subsidies by 36 per cent in value; and reduce its subsidized exports by 21 per cent in volume.

## EUROPEAN POLITICAL CO-OPERATION

The framework for European political co-operation (EPC) dates from an initiative at the Hague summit in 1969. In the resultant Luxembourg Report (1970), EC foreign ministers decided to harmonize and co-ordinate their foreign policy positions and achieve common actions where possible. Although the Single European Act obliged EC members to consult each other on foreign policy and the Commission participates in deliberations, EPC is an inter-governmental system operating parallel to, but outside, the Community.

The EPC system is headed by the European Council, which provides general lines of policy. Specific policy decisions are taken by the Council of Foreign Ministers, which meets at least four times a year. The foreign minister of the state holding the EC presidency initiates action, manages EPC and represents it abroad. He is supported by a secretariat based in Brussels and is advised by the past and future holders of the presidency, forming a so-called troika. The Council of Ministers is supported by the Political Committee which meets each month, or within 48 hours if there is a crisis, to prepare for ministerial discussions. A group of correspondents, designated diplomats in each member's foreign ministry, provides day-to-day contact.

## THE EUROPEAN MONETARY SYSTEM

The European monetary system (EMS) began operation on 13 March 1979 with three main purposes. The first purpose is to establish monetary stability in Europe, initially in exchange rates between EC member state currencies, and in the longer term to be part of a wider stabilization process, overcoming inflation and budget and trade deficits. The second purpose is to overcome the constraints resulting from the interdependence of EC economies, and the third is to aid the long-term process of European monetary integration. From its beginning all EC member state currencies have been members of the EMS (the Belgian and Luxembourg francs are one single currency).

The EMS has three components: the ECU; the Exchange Rate Mechanism (ERM); and the Credit Mechanisms. The ECU is a monetary unit, the value of which is calculated as a basket of set amounts of each Community currency. The relative weighting given to each currency in the ECU basket is proportional to the size of an EC member's economy and the state's share of EC trade. The German Deutsche Mark (DM) has the largest weighting of 32 per cent. The ECU is used for officially fixing the central rates in the ERM and as a means of settlement among central banks in the EMS.

The Exchange Rate Mechanism is the central component of the EMS. Officially all member currencies of the ERM have a central rate against the ECU, the anchor of the mechanism. In practice, the Deutsche Mark has become the anchor currency, with all other currencies' central rates expressed against the DM. Central banks are obliged to maintain their currencies within set margins (either 2.25 per cent above or below, or 6 per cent above or below) of their central rate by intervening in the foreign currency markets. Currencies may be revalued or devalued by up to 10 per cent by agreement with all other ERM members.

To do this, central banks co-ordinate their actions and can use the Credit Mechanisms to borrow money from each other and from the Central European Monetary Co-operation Fund where they each deposit 20 per cent of their reserves. Financial assistance is available to central banks over very short-term, short-term and medium-term periods.

Five currencies (Deutsche Mark, French franc, Belgian franc, Dutch guilder, Danish krone) joined the ERM with 2.25 per cent fluctuation margins, and two currencies (Irish punt and Italian lira) with 6 per cent margins in March 1979. Subsequently the punt and lira reduced to 2.25 per cent margins. The Spanish peseta (Oct. 1989), UK pound sterling (Oct. 1990) and Portuguese escudo (April 1992) joined the ERM with 6 per cent margins. The pound and the lira were forced out of the mechanism by speculation in September 1992. Speculation forced the widening of the fluctuation margins to 15 per cent from 1 August 1993 for six of the remaining ERM member currencies (the Deutsche Mark and Dutch Guilder remain within 2.25 per cent margins). By April 1994 the French franc, Belgian franc, Irish punt, Danish krone were informally operating within 2.25 per cent fluctuation margins again.

## THE SINGLE MARKET

Throughout the 1970s and early 1980s, EC members became increasingly concerned at the slow growth of the European economy. Although tariffs and quotas had been removed between member states, the EC was still separated into a number of national markets by a series of non-tariff barriers. It was to overcome these internal barriers to trade that the concept of the Single Market was developed. The measures to be undertaken were outlined in the Cockfield report (1985) and codified in the Single European Act (SEA), signed in 1986 and which came into force in 1987.

The SEA includes articles removing obstacles that distort the internal market: the elimination of frontier controls; the mutual recognition of professional qualifications; the harmonization of product specifications, largely by the mutual recognition of national standards; open tendering for public procurement contracts; the free movement of capital; the harmonization of VAT and excise duties; and the reduction of state aid to particular industries. The SEA changed the legislative process within the EC, particularly with the introduction of qualified majority voting in the Council of Ministers for some policy areas, and the introduction of the assent procedure in the European Parliament, requiring the approval of an absolute majority of MEPs for other policy areas. The SEA also extends EC competence into the fields of technology, the environment, regional policy, monetary policy and external policy. The Single Market came into effect on 1 January 1993, at which time some 90–95 per cent of the necessary legislation had been agreed and passed by all member parliaments. The Single Market is expected to result in at least a 5 per cent increase in the collective GNP of EC member states. The full implementation of the elimination of frontier controls between member states has, however, been repeatedly delayed.

## THE MAASTRICHT TREATY

The impetus given to the EC by the Single European Act and Single Market led to further moves towards European integration. Inter-governmental conferences on political and economic and monetary union began in December 1990 and culminated at the Maastricht European Council in December 1991, where a new Treaty on European Union, divided into an Economic and Monetary Union section and a Political Union section was agreed. After a long and acrimonious ratification process in the 12 member states, which involved its rejection in the first of two Danish referendums, the Maastricht Treaty came into force on 1 November 1993.

The Maastricht Treaty established a European Union (EU) composed of three 'pillars'. The first pillar is the existing European Community (EC) with its established institutions and decision-making processes. The second and third 'pillars' are new and have decision-making processes based on the Council of Ministers with minimal roles for the other institutions. The second 'pillar' deals with a common foreign and security policy and is based on the continuing European Political Co-operation framework (*see* above). The Maastricht Treaty enshrines moves towards common foreign and defence policies with the WEU eventually becoming the defence component of the EU. The third 'pillar' deals with justice and interior affairs; the Council of Ministers will co-ordinate policies on asylum, immigration, conditions of entry, cross-border crime, drug trafficking and international terrorism.

A common European citizenship for the nationals of all EU member states was established by the Maastricht Treaty. The Treaty also introduced into the EC the principle of subsidiarity whereby decisions are taken at the most appropriate level: national, regional or local. The Treaty extends EC competence into the areas of environmental policy; industrial policy; consumer affairs and protection; health; education and training. The use of qualified majority voting in the Council of Ministers is extended to cover areas previously covered by unanimity. The power of the European Parliament is significantly increased by the Maastricht Treaty, with greater control over the budget and the Commission. The use of the co-operation procedure is extended to new policy areas, but most importantly the Treaty establishes a new co-decision procedure whereby the European Parliament can, for the first time, override decisions of the Council of Ministers.

The Treaty lays down a timetable and criteria for Economic and Monetary Union (EMU) and an eventual single currency. Stage three of EMU, with irreversibly locked exchange rates for a majority of the EU currencies which have converged sufficiently, will begin by 31 December 1996. A European Central Bank will be established by 1 July 1998 and a single currency will be introduced by 1 January 1999. A special protocol was agreed allowing the UK to 'opt out' of a single currency if it so wishes in January 1999. Denmark also secured an 'opt out' from the single currency, European citizenship, common defence policy, and justice and interior affairs 'pillar' in order to obtain approval of Maastricht ratification in a second referendum. A separate protocol to the Maastricht Treaty on social policy was adopted by 11 member states but not the UK. The Maastricht Treaty is to be reviewed at a series of inter-governmental conferences in 1996–7.

## THE LEGISLATIVE PROCESS

The core of the EC policymaking process is a dialogue between the Commission, which initiates and implements policy, and the Council of Ministers, which takes policy decisions. A degree of democratic control is exercised by the European Parliament.

The original EC legislative process is known as the consultative procedure. The Commission drafts a proposal which it submits to the Council and to the Parliament. The Council then consults the ESC and the Parliament; the Parliament may request that amendments are made. With or without these amendments, the proposal is then adopted by the Council and becomes law.

Under the Single European Act, changes were made to the EC legislative process, particularly in strengthening the role of the Parliament by the introduction of the co-operation procedure. The Parliament now has a second reading of proposals in some fields, and after the second reading its rejection of a proposal can only be overturned by a unanimous decision of the Council. The Maastricht Treaty extends the scope of the co-operation procedure, which now applies to: Single Market laws and harmonization; trans-European networks; development policy; the social fund; and some aspects of the following: transport; environment; research; social policy; competition policy.

The SEA introduced the assent procedure, whereby an absolute majority of the whole of the Parliament's MEPs must vote to approve laws in certain fields before they are passed. Issues covered by the assent procedure include foreign treaties; accession treaties; international agreements with budgetary implications; citizenship; residence rights; the CAP; regional and structural funds.

The Maastricht Treaty introduced the co-decision procedure; if, after the Parliament's second reading of a proposal, the Council and Parliament fail to agree, a conciliation committee of the two will reach a compromise. If a compromise is not reached, the Parliament can reject the legislation by the vote of an absolute majority of its members. This procedure applies in the areas of education and training; health; consumer protection; culture; research frameworks; general environment programmes.

The Council issues the following legislation: (a) Regulations, which are binding in their entirety and directly applicable to all member states; they do not need to be incorporated into national law to come into effect; (b) Directives, which are less specific, binding as to the result to be achieved but leaving the method of implementation open to member states; a directive thus has no force until it is incorporated into national law; (c) Decisions, which are also binding but are addressed solely to one or more member states or individuals in a member state; (d) Recommendations; (e) Opinions, which are merely persuasive.

## THE COUNCIL OF THE EUROPEAN UNION
170 rue de la Loi, 1048 Brussels, Belgium

The Council of the European Union (Council of Ministers) consists of ministers from the government of each of the member states. It formally comprises the foreign ministers of the member states but in practice the minister depends on the subject under discussion; i.e. when EC environment matters are under discussion, the meeting is informally known as the Environment Council. Council decisions are taken by qualified majority vote (in which members' votes are weighted) or by unanimity. Council meetings are prepared by the Committee of Permanent Representatives (COREPER) of the member states, which acts as the 'gatekeeper' between national governments and the supranational EC, often negotiating on proposals with the Commission during the legislative process.

Unanimity votes are taken on issues such as taxation; budgets; foreign policy; the accession of new members; European Parliament electoral law; rights of free movement and residence; and some environment and transport policies. Qualified majority votes are taken on Single Market laws and harmonization; environment policy; health and safety; transport policy; overseas aid; research and development; culture; consumer protection; education and training; the development of a single currency; social policy. Germany, France, Italy and the UK have ten votes each, Spain eight; the Netherlands, Greece, Belgium and Portugal five votes each; Denmark and Ireland three votes each; and Luxembourg two votes, making a total of 76 votes. For a proposal to pass it must receive 54 votes, 23 votes are necessary to block a proposal. Following enlargement in 1995 there will be a total of 90 votes and a proposal must receive 64 votes for it to be passed; 27 votes against will block a proposal.

The European Council, comprising the heads of government of the member states, meets three times a year to provide overall policy direction. The presidency of the EC is held in rotation for six-month periods, setting the agenda for and chairing all Council meetings. The presidency serves an important function since the incumbent nation has an opportunity to pursue its own policy priorities. The European Council holds a summit in the country holding the presidency at the end of its period in office. The holders of the presidency for the years 1994–6 (dependent on enlargement) are:

1994 Greece; Germany
1995 France; Spain
1996 Italy; Ireland

OFFICE OF THE UNITED KINGDOM PERMANENT REPRESENTATIVE TO THE EUROPEAN COMMUNITIES
Rond-point Robert Schuman 6, 1040 Brussels, Belgium
*Ambassador and UK Permanent Representative,* Sir John Kerr, KCMG, *apptd* 1990

## THE EUROPEAN COMMISSION
200 rue de la Loi, 1049 Brussels, Belgium

The Commission consists of 17 Commissioners, two each from France, Germany, Italy, Spain and the UK, and one each from the remaining member states. The members of the Commission are appointed for four-year renewable terms by the agreement of the member states; the present Commission came into office on 1 January 1993 for a two-year term in order that from 1 January 1995 the five-year term will run concurrently with the term of the European Parliament. The President and Vice-Presidents are appointed from among the Commissioners for two-year terms, also renewable. The Commissioners pledge sole allegiance to the EC. The Commission initiates and implements EC legislation and is the guardian of the EC treaties. It is the exponent of Community-wide interests rather than the national preoccupations of the Council. Each Commissioner is supported by advisers and oversees whichever of the 23 departments, known as Directorates-General (DGs), is assigned to him. Each Directorate-General is headed by a Director-General.

COMMISSIONERS *as at July 1994 (until 1 Jan. 1995)*

*President*

*Secretariat-General; Forward Studies Unit; Inspectorate-General; Legal Services; Monetary Affairs; Spokesman's Service; Joint Interpreting and Conference Service; Security Office,* Jacques Delors (France) (from 1 Jan. 1995, Jacques Santer (Luxembourg))

*Vice-Presidents*

*Economic and Financial Affairs, Monetary Matters, Credit and Investments, Statistical Office,* Henning Christophersen (*Denmark*)
*Co-operation and Development, Lomé Convention, Humanitarian Aid,* Manuel Marin (*Spain*)

*Members*

*Industrial Affairs, Information and Telecommunications Technology,* Martin Bangemann (*Germany*)

*External Economic Affairs (North America, Japan, China, CIS, Europe, including Central and Eastern Europe), Commercial and Trade Policy,* Sir Leon Brittan (*UK*)
*Budgets, Financial Control, Fraud Prevention, Cohesion Fund,* Peter Schmidhuber (*Germany*)
*Energy and Euratom Supply Agency, Transport,* Marcelino Oreja (*Spain*)
*Customs, Taxation, Consumer Policy,* Christiane Scrivener (*France*)
*Regional Policy, Relations with the Committee of the Regions,* Bruce Millan (*UK*)
*Science, Research and Development, Joint Research Centre, Human Resources, Education, Training and Youth,* Antonio Ruberti (*Italy*)
*Competition, Personnel and Administration,* Karel Van Miert (*Belgium*)
*External Political Relations, Common Foreign and Security Policy, Enlargement Negotiations,* Hans van den Broek (*Netherlands*)
*Relations with the European Parliament, Openness, Communication and Information, Culture and Audiovisual, Office for official publications,* João de Deus Pinheiro (*Portugal*)
*Social Affairs and Employment, Relations with the Economic and Social Committee, Immigration, Interior and Judicial Affairs,* Padraig Flynn (*Ireland*)
*Agriculture and Rural Development,* Rene Steichen (*Luxembourg*)
*Environment, Nuclear Safety and Civil Protection, Fisheries,* Ioannis Paleokrassas (*Greece*)
*Internal Market, Financial Institutions, Institutional Questions, Small and Medium-sized Enterprises,* Raniero Vanni d'Archirafi (*Italy*)
*Secretary-General,* D. Williamson (UK)

## THE EUROPEAN PARLIAMENT

The European Parliament originated as the Common Assembly of the ECSC; it acquired its present name in 1962. Members (MEPs) were initially appointed from the membership of national parliaments. Direct elections to the Parliament were first held in 1979. Elections to the Parliament are held on differing bases throughout the EC; British MEPs are elected on a first-past-the-post system, except in Northern Ireland which uses proportional representation. The latest elections were held in June 1994.

In line with the Edinburgh summit agreement of December 1992, the Parliament expanded at the 1994 election to 567 seats from the previous 518 to include representatives from the former East Germany and concurrent increases in other member states' representatives. The allocation of seats is: Germany 99 (81 at 1989 elections); UK, France, Italy 87 each (81); Spain 64 (60); the Netherlands 31 (25); Belgium, Greece, Portugal 25 each (24); Denmark 16 (16); Ireland 15 (15); Luxembourg 6 (6). MEPs serve on 19 committees, which scrutinize draft EC legislation and the activities of the Commission. Plenary sessions are held in Strasbourg, committees meet in Brussels and the Secretariat's headquarters is in Luxembourg.

The EP has gradually expanded its influence within the EC through the Single European Act, with its introduction of the co-operation procedure, and the Maastricht Treaty, with its extension of the co-operation procedure and the introduction of the co-decision procedure (*see* Legislative Process). It has general powers of supervision over the Commission, and consultation and co-decision with the Council; it votes to approve a newly appointed Commission and can dismiss it at any time by a two-thirds majority. Under the Maastricht Treaty it has the right to be consulted on the appointment of the new Commission and can veto its appointment. It can reject the EC budget as a whole, alter non-compulsory expenditure not specified in the EC primary legislation, and can question the Commission's management of the budget and call in the Court of Auditors. Although the EP cannot directly initiate legislation, its reports can spur the Commission into action. The EP is to appoint an Ombudsman to whom citizens can complain about EC institutions.

The Parliament's organization is deliberately biased in favour of multi-national political groupings, with recognition of a political grouping in the parliament (which entitles it to offices, funding, representation on committees and influence in debates and legislation) being easier for multi-national groups. A political grouping with members from only one country needs a minimum of 26 members for recognition, whereas one with members from two countries needs 21 members, a grouping with members from three countries needs 16 members, and a grouping with members from four or more countries needs only 13 members.

PARLIAMENT , Palais de l'Europe, 67006 Strasbourg Cedex, France; 97–113 rue Belliard, 1040 Brussels, Belgium
SECRETARIAT , Centre Européen, Kirchberg, 2929 Luxembourg
*President*, Klaus Hänsch (Germany)
(For a full list of British MEPs, *see* pages 274–5)

## THE ECONOMIC AND SOCIAL COMMITTEE
2 rue Ravenstein, 1000 Brussels, Belgium

The Economic and Social Committee is an advisory and consultative body. The ESC has 189 members, who are nominated by member states. It is divided into three groups; employers; workers; and other interest groups such as consumers, farmers and the self-employed. It issues opinions on draft EC legislation and can bring matters to the attention of the Commission, Council and Parliament; it has a key role in providing specialist and technical input.
*President*, Susanne Tiemann *(Germany)*

## THE COURT OF AUDITORS
12 rue A. De Gasperi, L-1615 Luxembourg

The Court of Auditors, established in October 1977, is responsible for the audit of the legality and regularity as well as of the sound financial management of the resources managed by the European Communities and Community bodies. The Court may also submit observations on specific questions and deliver opinions. The Court draws up an annual report and a statement of assurance on the accounts and underlying operations of the Communities. It has 12 members appointed for six-year terms by the Council of Ministers following consultation with the European Parliament.
*President*, André Middelhoek *(Netherlands)*

## COURT OF JUSTICE OF THE EUROPEAN COMMUNITIES
L-2925 Luxembourg

The European Court superseded the Court of Justice of ECSC and is common to the three European Communities. It exists to safeguard the law in the interpretation and application of the Community treaties, to decide on the legality of decisions of the Council of Ministers or the Commission, and to determine violations of the Treaties. Cases may be brought to it by the member states, the Community institutions, firms or individuals. Its decisions are directly binding in the member countries. The 13 judges and six advocates-general of the Court are appointed for renewable six-year terms by the member governments in concert. During 1993, 204 new cases were lodged at the court and 203 judgments were delivered.

EUROPEAN PARLIAMENT POLITICAL GROUPINGS

|  | PES | EPP | ELDR | EUL | FE | EDA | Green | ERA | EN | Ind. | Total |
|---|---|---|---|---|---|---|---|---|---|---|---|
| Belgium | 6 | 7 | 6 | – | – | – | 2 | 1 | – | 3 | 25 |
| Denmark | 3 | 3 | 5 | – | – | – | 1 | – | 4 | – | 16 |
| Germany | 40 | 47 | – | – | – | – | 12 | – | – | – | 99 |
| Greece | 10 | 9 | – | 4 | – | 2 | – | – | – | – | 25 |
| Spain | 22 | 30 | 2 | 9 | – | – | – | 1 | – | – | 64 |
| France | 15 | 13 | 1 | 7 | – | 14 | – | 13 | 13 | 11 | 87 |
| Ireland | 1 | 4 | 1 | – | – | 7 | 2 | – | – | – | 15 |
| Italy | 18 | 12 | 7 | 5 | 27 | – | 4 | 2 | – | 12 | 87 |
| Luxembourg | 2 | 2 | 1 | – | – | – | 1 | – | – | – | 6 |
| Netherlands | 8 | 10 | 10 | – | – | – | 1 | – | 2 | – | 31 |
| Portugal | 10 | 1 | 8 | 3 | – | 3 | – | – | – | – | 25 |
| UK | 63 | 19 | 2 | – | – | – | – | – | 2 | 1 | 87 |
| TOTAL | 198 | 157 | 43 | 28 | 27 | 26 | 23 | 19 | 19 | 27 | 567 |

| PES | Party of European Socialists (including British Labour Party, Northern Ireland Social Democratic and Labour Party, Italian Democratic Left Party) Socialist, Social Democratic and Labour parties |
| EPP | European People's Party (including British Conservative Party, Northern Ireland Official Unionist Party, Spanish Popular Party, Irish Fine Gael) Christian Democrats and Conservatives |
| ELDR | European Liberal Democratic and Reformist Group (including British Liberal Democratic Party, Italian Northern League, Portuguese Social Democrats) centre and liberal parties |
| EUL | Confederal Group of the European United Left (French, Greek, Spanish and Portuguese Communist Parties, Italian Refounded Communist Party, some Spanish regionalists) |

| FE | Forza Europa (Forza Italia Party) |
| EDA | European Democratic Alliance (French Gaullists, Irish Fianna Faíl, Greek Political Spring Party, Portuguese Centre Party) |
| Green | Green and Ecologist parties |
| ERA | European Radical Alliance (Scottish National Party, French Radicals of the Left, Italian Radical Party, Belgian Flemish and Spanish regionalists) |
| EN | Europe of the Nations Group (French Other Europe Group, Dutch and Danish Euro-sceptics) |
| Ind. | Independents (Italian National Alliance, French National Front, Belgian Vlaams Blok, Northern Ireland Democratic Unionist Party) |

Composition of the Court, in order of precedence, with effect from 7 October 1993:
O. Due (*President*); G. F. Mancini (*President of the 2nd and 6th Chambers*); M. Darmon (*First Advocate-General*); J. C. Moitinho De Almeida (*President of the 3rd and 5th Chambers*); M. Diez De Velasco (*President of the 4th Chamber*); D. A. O. Edward (*President of the 1st Chamber*); C. N. Kakouris; C. O. Lenz (*Advocate-General*); R. Joliet; F. A. Schockweiler; G. C. Rodriguez Iglesias; F. Grevisse; M. Zuleeg; W. van Gerven (*Advocate-General*); F. G. Jacobs (*Advocate-General*); G. Tesauro (*Advocate-General*); P. J. G. Kapteyn; C. Gulman (*Advocate-General*); J. L. Murray; R. Grass (*Registrar*)

COURT OF FIRST INSTANCE
L-2925 Luxembourg

Established by a Council decision of 24 October 1988, under powers conferred by the Single European Act, the Court of First Instance started to exercise its functions at the end of October 1989. It had jurisdiction to hear and determine certain categories of cases brought by natural or legal persons, in particular cases brought by European Community officials, or cases on competition law. By a Council decision of 8 June 1993 the court had its jurisdiction enlarged to hear and determine all actions brought by natural or legal persons with the exemption of those concerned with anti-dumping matters. During 1993, 145 new cases were lodged at the court and 47 judgments were delivered.

Composition of the Court, in order of precedence, for the judicial year 1993–4:
J. L. Cruz Vilaca (*President*); M. R. Schintgen (*President of the 1st Chamber*); C. P. Briët (*President of the 4th Chamber*); R. García-Valdecasas y Fernandez (*President of the 3rd Chamber*); A. Kalogeropoulos (*President of the 5th Chamber*); D. P. M. Barrington; A. Saggío; H. Kirschner; B. Vesterdorf; J. Biancarelli; K. Lenaerts; C. W. Bellamy; H. Jung (*Registrar*)

THE EUROPEAN INVESTMENT BANK
100 Boulevard Konrad Adenauer, L-2950 Luxembourg

The European Investment Bank (EIB) was set up in 1958 under the terms of the Treaty of Rome to finance capital investment projects promoting the balanced development of the European Community.

It grants long-term loans to private and public enterprises, public authorities and financial institutions, to finance projects which further the economic development of less advanced regions (Assisted Areas); improvement of European communications; environmental protection; attainment of the Community's energy policy objectives; modernization of enterprises, co-operation between undertakings in the different member states, and the activities of small and medium-sized enterprises.

EIB activities have also been extended outside member countries as part of the Community's development co-operation policy, under the terms of different association or co-operation agreements with 12 countries in the Mediterranean region, six in central and eastern Europe, 30 in Latin America and Asia, and, under the Lomé Conventions, 70 in Africa, the Caribbean and the Pacific. The Bank has also been asked to extend its activity to Albania, Estonia, Latvia, Lithuania and Slovenia.

The Bank's total financing operations in 1993 amounted to 19,611 million ECU, of which 17,724 million was for investment in the European Community and 1,887 million for investment outside the Community. Between 1989 and 1993 the EIB had made available a total of 9,865 million ECU for investment in the UK.

The members of the European Investment Bank are the 12 member states of the Community, who have all subscribed to the Bank's capital of 57,600 million ECU. The bulk of the funds required by the Bank to carry out its tasks are borrowed on the capital markets of the Community and non-member countries, and on the international market.

As it operates on a non-profit-making basis, the interest rates charged by the EIB reflect the cost of the Bank's borrowings and closely follow conditions on world capital markets.

The Board of Governors of the European Investment Bank consists of one government minister nominated by each of the member countries, usually the finance minister, who lay down general directives on the policy of the Bank and appoint members to the Board of Directors (21 nominated by the member states, one by the Commission of the European Communities), which takes decisions on the granting and raising of loans and the fixing of interest rates. A Management Committee, composed of the Bank's President and six Vice-Presidents, also appointed by the Board of Governors, is responsible for the day-to-day operations of the Bank. The President and Vice-Presidents also preside as Chairman and Vice-Chairmen at meetings of the Board of Directors.
*President*, Sir Brian Unwin, KCB
*Vice-Presidents*, Lucio Izzo; Alain Prate; José de Oliveira Costa; Wolfgang Roth; Corneille Bruck; Hans Duborg
UK OFFICE: 68 Pall Mall, London SWIY 5ES Tel: 0171-839 3351

NEW INSTITUTIONS AND AGENCIES

The Maastricht Treaty, together with the Brussels Council summit of October 1993, established a number of new institutions and agencies:
THE COMMITTEE OF THE REGIONS, Brussels
THE EUROPEAN MONETARY INSTITUTE, Frankfurt
THE EUROPEAN DRUGS AGENCY (EUROPOL), The Hague
THE EUROPEAN MEDICINE EVALUATION AGENCY, London
THE EUROPEAN TRADEMARK OFFICE, Alicante
THE EUROPEAN AGENCY FOR HEALTH AND SAFETY AT WORK, Bilbao
THE EUROPEAN OFFICE FOR VETERINARY AND PLANT HEALTH INSPECTION, Dublin
THE EUROPEAN DRUGS OBSERVATORY, Lisbon
THE EUROPEAN FOUNDATION FOR TRAINING, Turin
THE EUROPEAN CENTRE FOR THE DEVELOPMENT OF VOCATIONAL TRAINING, Salonika
THE EUROPEAN ENVIRONMENT AGENCY, Copenhagen
THE EUROPEAN TRANSLATION AGENCY, Luxembourg

EUROPEAN COMMUNITY INFORMATION

The Commission maintains offices in:
LONDON, 8 Storey's Gate, London SWIP 3AT. Tel: 0171-973 1992
EDINBURGH, 9 Alva Street, Edinburgh EH2 4HP. Tel: 0131-225 2058
CARDIFF, 4 Cathedral Road, Cardiff CFI 9SG. Tel: 01222-371631
BELFAST, Windsor House, 9–15 Bedford Street, Belfast BT2 7EG. Tel: 01232-240708
DUBLIN, 39 Molesworth Street, Dublin 2
WASHINGTON, 2100 M Street NW (Suite 707), Washington DC 20037

NEW YORK, 1 Dag Hammarskjöld Plaza, 254 East 47th Street, New York, NY 10017
OTTAWA, Inn of the Provinces, Office Tower (Suite 1110), 350 Sparks Street, Ontario, KIR 7SA
CANBERRA, 18 Alakana Street, Yarralumia, ACT 2600, and a number of other cities

UK EUROPEAN PARLIAMENT INFORMATION OFFICE
2 Queen Anne's Gate, London SW1H 9AA. Tel: 0171-222 0411

There are European Information Centres, set up to give information and advice to small businesses, in 24 British towns and cities. A number of universities maintain European Documentation Centres.

## FOOD AND AGRICULTURE ORGANIZATION OF THE UNITED NATIONS
Viale delle Terme di Caracalla, 00100 Rome, Italy

The Food and Agriculture Organization (FAO) is a specialized UN agency, established on 16 October 1945. It assists rural populations by raising levels of nutrition and living standards, and by encouraging greater efficiency in food production and distribution. In addition, it collects, analyses and disseminates information on agriculture and natural resources. FAO also advises governments on national agricultural policy and planning; its Investment Centre, together with the World Bank and other financial institutions, helps to prepare development projects. FAO's field programme covers a range of activities, including strengthening crop production, rural and livestock development, and conservation.

FAO's top priorities are sustainable agriculture, rural development and food security. The Organization attempts to ensure the availability of adequate food supplies, stability in the flow of supplies and the securing of access to food by the poor. FAO keeps a special watch on areas where famine can occur. The Office for Special Relief Operations channels emergency aid from governments and other agencies, and assists in rehabilitation. The Technical Co-operation Programme provides schemes for countries facing agricultural crises.

FAO had 170 members (169 states and the EU) and one associate member (Puerto Rico) as at January 1994. It is governed by a biennial conference of all its members which sets the forthcoming programme and budget. The budget for 1994-5 was US$673,000,000, funded by member countries in proportion to their gross national products. FAO also receives substantial additional funding from the UN Development Programme, donor governments and other institutions.

The Conference elects a Director-General and a 49-member Council, which governs between conferences. The Regular and Field Programmes are administered by a Secretariat, headed by the Director-General. Five regional offices help administer the Field Programme.
*Director-General*, Jacques Diouf (*Senegal*)
*UK Representative*, D. Sands Smith, British Embassy, Rome

## GENERAL AGREEMENT ON TARIFFS AND TRADE
Centre William Rappard, 154 rue de Lausanne, 1211 Geneva 21, Switzerland

Under an initiative of the UN Economic and Social Council, a committee met in 1947 to draft the charter of a new international trade organization. The charter was never ratified and the General Agreement on Tariffs and Trade (GATT), intended as an interim arrangement with effect from January 1948, became the only regime for the regulation of world trade. Never formalized, GATT has evolved rules and procedures to adapt to changing circumstances. The contracting parties number 123, and a further 13 apply its rules *de facto*; GATT thus covers nearly 90 per cent of world trade.

GATT is dedicated to the expansion of non-discriminatory international trade. It provides a common code of conduct and a forum for the discussion and solution of international trade problems, and for multilateral negotiations to reduce tariffs and other trade barriers. Special attention is given to assisting the trade of developing countries, which are exempted from some GATT provisions.

Extensions of free trade are made progressively via 'rounds' of multilateral negotiations. Eight have been completed: Geneva (1947); Annecy (1948); Torquay (1950); Geneva (1956); Dillon (1960-1); Kennedy (1964-7); Tokyo (1973-9); Uruguay (1986-94). The average duties on manufactured goods have been reduced from 40 per cent in the 1940s to 5 per cent.

The Uruguay Round, originally scheduled to be completed in 1990, was successfully concluded in Geneva on 15 December 1993. The final agreements, including the establishment of a World Trade Organization (WTO) to supersede GATT and implement the Uruguay Round agreement, were signed by trade ministers from the 123 negotiating states and the EU on 15 April 1994 in Marrakesh, Morocco. After ratification by all contracting parties the Final Act of the Uruguay Round will take effect on 1 January 1995, its measures taking until 2002 to be implemented fully. Apart from establishing the WTO, the Uruguay Round also extended GATT coverage for the first time to agriculture, textiles and clothing, services, and intellectual property rights. Tariffs on imported goods are to be reduced to an average of 3 per cent, with peak tariffs being specifically targeted. State subsidies to industries are to be reduced, export-boosting subsidies outlawed, and public procurement contracts opened up. The WTO will enforce GATT rules with a strengthened trade compliance and enforcement mechanism. The most important effects of the Uruguay Round will be in agriculture, where domestic and export subsidies, import duties and subsidized export volumes are all to be reduced by between 20 and 36 per cent.

The most authoritative body of GATT is the Session of Contracting Parties, which usually meets once a year, and comprises senior officials from the 123 member governments. Early in the Uruguay Round it was also agreed that at least once every two years governments participating in the Session would be represented at ministerial level. In the period between the meetings of the Session, the Council of Representatives meets about nine times a year to act on routine and urgent matters. The work and decision-making process of these two bodies is supported by several specialist standing committees, which regularly meet to examine, discuss and negotiate the various aspects of international trade policies and practices. *Ad hoc* working parties are also established to consider specific issues, as well as panels to examine and rule upon trade disputes. The committees overseeing the non-tariff agreements reached in the Tokyo Round report to the Contracting Parties Session only.

The International Trade Centre, founded in 1964 to help developing countries with export expansion, is operated jointly with the UN Conference on Trade and Development.
*Director-General*, Peter Sutherland (*Ireland*)
*Permanent UK Representative*, N. C. R. Williams, CMG, 37-39 rue de Vermont, 1211 Geneva 20

## INTERNATIONAL ATOMIC ENERGY AGENCY
Vienna International Centre, Wagramerstrasse 5,
PO Box 100, 1400 Vienna, Austria

The International Atomic Energy Agency (IAEA) was established in 1957 as a consequence of the UN International Conference on the Peaceful Uses of Atomic Energy held the previous year. Although it operates under the aegis of, and reports annually to, the UN, the IAEA is not a specialized agency.

The IAEA aims to accelerate and enlarge the contribution of atomic energy to peace, health and prosperity, and to ensure that any assistance provided by it or under its supervision is not used for military purposes. It establishes atomic energy safety standards and offers services to its member states for the safe operation of their nuclear facilities and for radiation protection. It is the central point for the International Convention on early notification of a nuclear accident. The IAEA also encourages research and training in nuclear power. It is additionally charged with drawing up safeguards and verifying their use in accordance with the Nuclear Non-Proliferation Treaty (NPT) 1968, the Treaty for the Prohibition of Nuclear Weapons in Latin America (Tlatelolco Treaty) 1968 and the Treaty on a South Pacific Nuclear Free Zone (Rarotonga Treaty). Together with the Food and Agriculture Organization and the World Health Organization, the IAEA established an International Consultative Group on Food Irradiation in 1983.

In line with its responsibilities with regard to the Nuclear Non-Proliferation Treaty, the IAEA has for the past few years attempted to verify that the North Korean nuclear programme is non-military. This led North Korea in 1993–4 to withdraw from and then suspend its withdrawal from the NPT and then to impede, restrict and negate IAEA verification and inspection efforts. In June 1994 the IAEA informed the UN Security Council that North Korea was in violation of its treaty obligations by attempting to produce nuclear weapons and suspended all technical aid to North Korea. North Korea formally resigned from the IAEA on 14 June 1994.

The IAEA had 121 members as at May 1994. A General Conference of all its members meets annually to decide policy, a programme and a budget (1994, US$200 million), as well as electing a Director-General and 35-member Board of Governors. The Board meets four times a year to execute policy which is implemented by the Secretariat under a Director-General.
*Director-General*, Hans Blix (*Sweden*)
*Permanent UK Representative*, C. Hulse, Jaurésgasse 12, 1030 Vienna, Austria

## INTERNATIONAL CIVIL AVIATION ORGANIZATION
1000 Sherbrooke Street West, Montreal, Quebec, Canada H3A 2R2

The International Civil Aviation Organization (ICAO) was founded with the signing of the Chicago Convention on International Civil Aviation in December 1944, and became a specialized agency of the United Nations in 1947. It sets international technical standards and recommended practices for all areas of civil aviation, including airworthiness, air navigation, traffic control and pilot licensing. It encourages uniformity and simplicity in ground regulations and operations at international airports, including immigration and customs control. The ICAO also promotes regional air navigation, plans for ground facilities, and collects and distributes air transport statistics world-wide. It is dedicated to improving safety and to the orderly development of civil aviation throughout the world.

The ICAO had 183 members as at 20 February 1994. It is governed by an assembly of all its members which meets at least once every three years. A Council of 33 members is elected, taking into account the leading air transport nations as well as ensuring representation of less developed countries. The Council elects the President, appoints the Secretary-General and supervises the organization through subsidiary committees, serviced by a Secretariat.
*President of the Council*, Dr Assad Kotaite (*Lebanon*)
*Secretary-General*, Dr Philippe Rochat (*Switzerland*)
*UK Representative*, D. S. Evans, CMG, Suite 928, 1000 Sherbrooke Street West, Montreal, Quebec, Canada H3A 3G4

## INTERNATIONAL CONFEDERATION OF FREE TRADE UNIONS
Boulevard Emile Jacqmain 155 B1, B-1210 Brussels, Belgium

Formed in 1949 the International Confederation of Free Trade Unions (ICFTU) was created to promote free trade unionism world-wide. It aims to establish, maintain and promote free trade unions, and to promote peace with economic security and social justice.

Affiliated to the ICFTU are 174 individual unions and representative bodies in 124 countries and territories. On 3 December 1993 there were 120 million members.

The supreme authority of the organization is the Congress which convenes at least every four years. It is composed of delegates from the affiliated trade union organizations. The Congress elects an Executive Board of 49 members which meets not less than once a year. The Board establishes the budget and receives suggestions and proposals from affiliates as well as acting on behalf of the Confederation. The Congress also elects the General Secretary.
*General Secretary*, Enzo Friso
*UK Affiliate*, TUC, Congress House, 23–28 Great Russell Street, London WC1B 3LS. Tel: 0171-636 4030

## INTERNATIONAL CRIMINAL POLICE ORGANIZATION
50 quai Achille Lignon, 69006 Lyon, France

The International Criminal Police Commission (Interpol) was set up in 1923 to establish an international criminal records office and to harmonize extradition procedures. In 1956 a revised constitution was adopted and the organization adopted its present name. On 1 January 1994 the organization comprised 174 member states.

Interpol's aims are to ensure and promote mutual assistance between all criminal police authorities, and to support government agencies concerned with combating crime, whilst respecting the national sovereignty of members. Interpol is financed by annual contributions from the governments of member states.

Interpol's policy is decided by the General Assembly which meets annually; it is composed of delegates appointed by the member states. The 13-member Executive Committee is elected by the General Assembly from among the member states' delegates, and is chaired by the President, who has a

four-year term of office. The permanent administrative organ is the General Secretariat, headed by the Secretary-General, who is appointed by the General Assembly.
*Secretary-General*, Raymond Kendall, QPM *(UK)*
UK OFFICE, NCIS-Interpol, Spring Gardens, Tinworth Street, London SE11 5EH
*UK Representative*, A. Pacey, CBE, QPM

## INTERNATIONAL ENERGY AGENCY
Chateau de la Muette, 2 rue André-Pascal, 75775 Paris, France

The International Energy Agency (IEA), founded in November 1974, is an autonomous agency within the framework of the Organization for Economic Co-operation and Development (OECD). The IEA had 23 member countries at January 1994.

The IEA's objectives include improvement of energy supply and demand worldwide, increased efficiency, development of alternative energy sources and the promotion of relations between oil producing and oil consuming countries. The IEA also maintains an emergency system to alleviate the effects of severe oil supply disruptions.

The main decision-making body is the Governing Board composed of senior energy officials from member countries. Various standing groups and special committees exist to facilitate the work of the Board. The IEA Secretariat, with a staff of energy experts, carries out the work of the Governing Board and its subordinate bodies. The Executive Director is appointed by the Board.
*Executive Director*, Mrs Helga Steeg *(Germany)*

## INTERNATIONAL FUND FOR AGRICULTURAL DEVELOPMENT
107 Via del Serafico, 00142 Rome, Italy

The establishment of the International Fund for Agricultural Development (IFAD) was proposed by the 1974 World Food Conference and IFAD began operations as a UN specialized agency in December 1977. Its purpose is to mobilize additional funds for agricultural and rural development projects in developing countries that benefit the poorest rural populations. The organization's lending policy is based on using its resources to support projects which: raise food production; provide employment and additional income for poor farmers; reduce malnutrition; and improve food distribution systems.

IFAD had 157 members as at June 1994. Membership is divided into three categories: category I, with 22 members, the developed countries (OECD); category II, with 12 members, the oil-exporting developing countries (OPEC); category III, with 123 members, the remaining developing countries. The three groups have equal voting rights in IFAD's governing structure. All powers are vested in a Governing Council of all member countries. It elects an 18-member Executive Board (with 17 alternate members) responsible for IFAD's operations. The Council elects a President who is also chairman of the Board. He is assisted by a Vice-President and three Assistant Presidents.

At the end of June 1994 IFAD's loan portfolio comprised commitments of US$3,900 million for 370 approved projects in 100 developing countries. The operational budget for 1993 was US$122.4 million. IFAD has a staff of 105 professionals and 154 support staff.
*President*, Fawzi H. Al-Sultan *(Kuwait)*

## INTERNATIONAL LABOUR ORGANIZATION
4 route des Morillons, 1211 Geneva 22, Switzerland

The International Labour Organization (ILO) was established in 1919 as an autonomous body of the League of Nations and became the UN's first specialized agency in 1946. The ILO aims to increase productive labour, improve working conditions and raise living standards. It sets minimum international labour standards through the drafting of international conventions. Member countries are obliged to submit these to their domestic authorities for ratification, and thus undertake to bring their domestic legislation in line with the conventions. Members must report to the ILO periodically on how these regulations are being implemented. The ILO also runs a technical assistance programme in developing countries, and conducts research and disseminates information on labour. Through its World Employment Programme, it is attempting to reduce unemployment in developing countries by assisting national and international efforts to provide productive work. It is also developing an international programme to improve working conditions.

The ILO had 170 members as at June 1994. It is composed of the International Labour Conference, the Governing Body and the International Labour Office. The Conference of members meets annually, and is attended by national delegations comprising two government delegates, one worker delegate and one employer delegate. It formulates international labour conventions and recommendations, provides a forum for discussion of world labour and social problems, and approves the ILO's programme and budget (1994–5, US$466,500,000). Additional project funding is provided by the UN Development Programme, the UN Fund for Population Activities and other sources.

The 56-member Governing Body, composed of 28 government, 14 worker and 14 employer members, acts as the ILO's executive council. Ten governments, including Britain, hold seats on the Governing Body because of their industrial importance. There are also various regional conferences and advisory committees. The International Labour Office acts as a secretariat and as a centre for operations, publishing and research.

In 1960 the ILO established the International Institute for Labour Studies in Geneva as a think-tank on labour and social policy.
*Director-General*, Michel Hansenne *(Belgium)*
UK OFFICE, Vincent House, Vincent Square, London SW1P 2NB. Tel: 0171-828 6401

## INTERNATIONAL MARITIME ORGANIZATION
4 Albert Embankment, London SE1 7SR

The International Maritime Organization (IMO) was established as a UN specialized agency in 1948. Due to delays in treaty ratification it did not commence operations until 1958. Originally it was called the Inter-Governmental Maritime Consultative Organization (IMCO) but changed its name in 1982.

The IMO fosters inter-governmental co-operation in technical matters relating to international shipping, especially with regard to safety at sea. It is also charged with preventing and controlling marine pollution caused by shipping and facilitating marine traffic. The IMO is responsible for calling maritime conferences and drafting marine conventions.

Additionally, it provides technical aid to countries wishing to develop their activities at sea.

The IMO had 149 members as at May 1994. It is governed by an Assembly comprising delegates of all its members. It meets biennially to make policy, decide the budget (1994–5, £34 million), vote on specific recommendations on pollution and maritime safety and elect the Council. The Council fulfils the functions of the Assembly between sessions and appoints the Secretary-General. It consists of 32 members; eight from the world's largest shipping nations, eight from the nations most dependent on seaborne trade, and 16 other members to ensure a fair geographical representation. The Maritime Safety Committee, working through various sub-committees, makes reports and recommendations to the Council and the Assembly. There are a number of other specialist subsidiary committees, including one for marine environmental protection.

The IMO acts as the secretariat for the London Dumping Convention (1972) which regulates the disposal of land-generated waste at sea.

*Secretary-General,* William A. O'Neil (*Canada*)

## INTERNATIONAL MOBILE SATELLITE ORGANIZATION
99 City Road, London ECIY IAX

Inmarsat (the International Mobile Satellite Organization) was founded in July 1978 as the International Maritime Satellite Organization and began operations on 1 February 1982. Inmarsat operates a system of satellites to provide global mobile communications at sea, in the air and on land. Inmarsat satellite terminals are used world-wide on ships, in aircraft and on land for global telephone, facsimile, telex, e-mail data, as well as maritime safety and distress communications.

Inmarsat comprises three bodies: the Assembly, the Council and the Directorate. The Assembly is composed of representatives of all member countries, each with one vote. It meets every two years to review activities and objectives, and to make recommendations to the Council. The Council is the main decision-making body and consists of representatives of the 18 members with the largest investment shares. Four others who represent the interests of developing countries are elected to the Council on the basis of geographical representation. The Council meets at least three times a year and oversees the activities of the directorate, the permanent staff of Inmarsat.

As at June 1994 there were 75 member countries.

*Director-General,* Olof Lundberg (*Sweden*)

## INTERNATIONAL MONETARY FUND
700 19th Street NW, Washington DC 20431, USA

The International Monetary Fund (IMF) was established on 22 July 1944, at the UN Monetary and Financial Conference held at Bretton Woods, New Hampshire. Its Articles of Agreement entered into force on 27 December 1945, and the IMF began operations in May 1946. The IMF exists to promote international monetary co-operation, the expansion of world trade, and exchange stability, and to eliminate foreign exchange restrictions. The IMF advises members on their economic and financial policies; promotes policy co-ordination among the major industrial countries; and gives technical assistance in central banking, balance of payments accounting, taxation, and other financial matters. The IMF

serves as a forum for members to discuss important financial and monetary issues and seeks the balanced growth of international trade and, through this, high levels of employment, income and productive capacity. As at April 1994 the IMF had 178 members.

Upon joining the IMF, a member is assigned a 'quota', based on the member's relative standing in the world economy and its balance of payments position, that determines its capital subscription to the Fund, its access to IMF resources, its voting power, and its share in the allocation of Special Drawing Rights (SDRs). Quotas are reviewed every five years and adjusted accordingly. With the coming into effect of the Ninth General Review of quotas, which increased quotas by 50 per cent, total Fund quotas increased to SDR 144.8 billion at the end of April 1994 (from SDR 91.2 billion at the end of April 1992). The SDR, an international reserve asset issued by the IMF, is calculated daily on a basket of usable currencies and is the IMF's unit of account; on 31 March 1994, SDR 1 equalled US\$1.41260. SDRs are allocated at intervals to supplement members' reserves and thereby improve international financial liquidity.

IMF financial resources derive primarily from members' capital subscriptions, which are equivalent to their quotas. In addition, the IMF is authorized to borrow from official lenders. It may also draw on a line of credit of SDR 18.5 billion from various countries under the so-called General Arrangements to Borrow (GAB). Periodic charges are also levied on financial assistance. At the end of March 1993, total outstanding IMF credits amounted to SDR 29.5 billion; borrowings amounted to SDR 24.3 billion.

The IMF is not a bank and does not lend money; it provides temporary financial assistance by selling a member's SDRs or other members' currencies in exchange for the member's own currency. The member can then use the purchased currency to alleviate its balance of payments difficulties. The IMF's credit under its regular facilities is made available to members in tranches or segments of 25 per cent of quota. For first credit tranche purchases, members are required to demonstrate reasonable efforts to overcome their balance of payments difficulties. There are no performance criteria and the total amount is repaid in three and a quarter to five years. Upper credit tranche purchases are normally associated with stand-by arrangements. These typically cover periods of one to two years. They focus on macroeconomic policies aimed at overcoming balance of payment difficulties and are required to meet certain performance criteria. Repurchases are made in three and a quarter to five years.

The IMF supports long-term efforts at economic reform and transformation, such as the re-establishment of market economies in the countries of eastern Europe and the former Soviet Union. In addition, the IMF supports medium-term programmes under the extended Fund facility, which generally runs for three years (sometimes up to four years) and is aimed at overcoming balance of payments difficulties stemming from macroeconomic and structural problems. Members experiencing a temporary balance of payments shortfall have access to the compensatory and contingency financing facility. The IMF also offers credits to low-income countries engaged in economic reform through its structural adjustment facility and enhanced structural adjustment facility. As of 31 March 1994, SDR 4.3 billion has been disbursed under arrangements with 44 countries. Under its buffer stock financing facility, the IMF provides resources to help members' contributions to approved buffer stocks. In April 1993, the IMF adopted a new temporary facility, the systemic transformation facility, designed to extend financial assistance to members experiencing severe disruptions in their trade and payments arrangements due to a shift from significant reliance on trading at nonmarket prices to multilateral, market-based trade.

The IMF is headed by a Board of Governors, comprising representatives of all members, which meets annually. The Governors delegate powers to 24 Executive Directors, five appointed and 19 elected. The Executive Directors operate the Fund on a daily basis under a Managing Director, whom they elect. The appointed directors represent France, Germany, Japan, UK and USA.

*Managing Director*, Michel Camdessus (*France*)
*UK Executive Director*, Huw Evans, Room 11-120, IMF, 700 19th Street NW, Washington DC 20431

## INTERNATIONAL RED CROSS AND RED CRESCENT MOVEMENT
17 avenue de la Paix, 1211 Geneva, Switzerland

The International Red Cross and Red Crescent Movement is composed of three elements. The International Committee of the Red Cross (ICRC) is the founding body of the Red Cross and was formed in 1863. It is a neutral intermediary negotiating between warring factions, working throughout the world to protect and assist victims of armed conflict. It also ensures the application of the Geneva Conventions with regard to prisoners of war and detainees.

The International Federation of Red Cross and Red Crescent Societies, founded in 1919, is the body which exists to contribute to the development of the humanitarian activities of national societies, to co-ordinate their relief operations for victims of natural disasters, and to care for refugees outside areas of conflict. There are national Red Cross and Red Crescent Societies in 161 countries with a global membership of 250 million.

The International Conference of the Red Cross and Red Crescent meets every four years, bringing together delegates of the ICRC, the International Federation and the national societies, as well as representatives of nations bound by the Geneva Conventions.

*President of the ICRC*, Cornelio Sommaruga
BRITISH RED CROSS, 9 Grosvenor Crescent, London SW1X 7EJ. *Director-General*, Michael R. Whitlam

## INTERNATIONAL TELECOMMUNICATIONS SATELLITE ORGANIZATION
3400 International Drive NW, Washington DC 20008–3098, USA

Formed in 1964, the International Telecommunications Satellite Organization (Intelsat) owns and operates the worldwide commercial communications satellite system. The system is composed of a network of 20 satellites and more than 2,000 antennas which link together over 180 countries, territories and dependencies.

Intelsat provides international telephone services; international television services; the Intelsat Business Service (IBS); Intelnet (a digital service designed for data collection and distribution); domestic telecommunications services and the Vista service providing telecommunications to remote communities.

Each of the 132 member states contributes to the capital costs of the organization in proportion to its investment share. The investment share is based on the relative usage of the system by member countries.

There is a four-tier hierarchy. The Assembly of Parties to the agreement meets every two years to consider long-term objectives and is composed of representatives of the member governments. The Meeting of Signatories annually considers the financial, technical and operational aspects of the system. The Board of Governors has 27 members; the executive organ is the permanent staff of Intelsat and is headed by a Director-General who reports to the Board of Governors.

*Director-General*, Irving Goldstein (*USA*)

## INTERNATIONAL TELECOMMUNICATION UNION
Place des Nations, 1211 Geneva 20, Switzerland

The International Telecommunication Union (ITU) was founded in Paris in 1865 as the International Telegraph Union and became a UN specialized agency in 1947. It promotes international co-operation and sets standards and regulations for telecommunications operations of all kinds. It assists the development of telecommunications and provides technical assistance to developing countries. The ITU allocates the radio frequency spectrum and registers radio frequency assignments in order to avoid harmful interference between radio stations of different countries. It also collects and disseminates telecommunications information.

The ITU had 180 members as at 11 May 1993. The supreme authority is the Plenipotentiary Conference, composed of representatives of all the members, which meets not less than once every five years. It elects the Administrative Council of 43 members which meets annually to supervise the Union and set the budget (1993, SFr 154 million). The Conference also elects the Secretary-General, who heads the General Secretariat. Four other permanent bodies include the International Frequency Registration Board, the Telecommunications Development Bureau and two consultative committees, one for radio, and one for telephone and telegraph.

*Secretary-General*, Dr P. Tarjanne (*Finland*)

## LEAGUE OF ARAB STATES
Maidane Al-Tahrir, Cairo, Egypt

The purpose of the League of Arab States (founded 1945) is to ensure co-operation among member states and protect their independence and sovereignty, to supervise the affairs and interests of Arab countries, to control the execution of agreements concluded among the member states, and to promote the process of integration among them. The League considers itself a regional organization and has observer status at the United Nations.

Member states are Algeria, Bahrain, Comoros, Djibouti, Egypt, Iraq, Jordan, Kuwait, Lebanon, Libya, Mauritania, Morocco, Oman, Palestine, Qatar, Saudi Arabia, Somalia, Sudan, Syria, Tunisia, United Arab Emirates and the Republic of Yemen.

Member states participate in various specialized agencies of the League whose role is to develop specific areas of co-operation between Arab states. These include: the Arab Organization for Mineral Resources; the Arab Monetary Fund; the Arab Satellite Communications Organization; the Arab Academy of Maritime Transport; the Arab Bank for Economic Development in Africa; the Arab League Educational, Cultural and Scientific Organization; and the Council of Arab Economic Unity.

*Secretary-General*, Dr Ahmed Esmat Abdel-Meguid (*Egypt*)
UK OFFICE, 52 Green Street, London W1Y 3RH

## NORDIC COUNCIL
Tyrgatan 7, Box 19506, Stockholm 10432, Sweden

The Nordic Council was established in March 1952 as an advisory body on economic and social co-operation, comprising parliamentary delegates from Denmark, Iceland, Norway and Sweden. It was subsequently joined by Finland (1955), and representatives from the Faröes (1970), the Åland Islands (1970), and Greenland (1984).

Co-operation is regulated by the Treaty of Helsinki signed in 1962. This was amended in 1971 to create the Nordic Council of Ministers, which discusses all matters except defence and foreign affairs. Matters are given preparatory consideration by a Committee of Co-operation Ministers' Deputies and joint committees of officials. Decisions of the Council of Ministers, which are taken by consensus, are binding, although if ratification by member parliaments is required, decisions only become effective following parliamentary approval. The Council of Ministers is advised by the Nordic Council, to which it reports annually. There are Ministers for Nordic Co-operation in every member government.

The Nordic Council, comprising 87 voting delegates nominated from member parliaments and about 80 non-voting government representatives, meets twice a year in plenary sessions. The full Council chooses an eleven-member Praesidium, comprising two delegates from each sovereign member and one party group-nominated delegate, which conducts business between sessions. A Secretariat, located in Stockholm and headed by a Secretary-General, liaises with the Council of Ministers and provides administrative support, as well as acting as a publishing house and information centre. The Council of Ministers has a separate Secretariat, based in Copenhagen.

SECRETARIAT TO THE NORDIC COUNCIL, Tyrgatan 7, s-10432 Stockholm, Sweden
*Secretary-General*, Anders Wenström (*Sweden*)
SECRETARIAT OF NORDIC COUNCIL OF MINISTERS, Store Strandgade 18, 1255 Copenhagen K, Denmark
*Secretary-General*, Per Stenback (*Finland*)

## NORTH ATLANTIC TREATY ORGANIZATION
Brussels 1110, Belgium

The North Atlantic Treaty (Treaty of Washington) was signed on 4 April 1949 by the foreign ministers of 12 nations: Belgium, Canada, Denmark, France, Iceland, Italy, Luxembourg, the Netherlands, Norway, Portugal, the UK and USA. Greece and Turkey acceded to the Treaty in 1952, the Federal Republic of Germany in 1955 (the reunited Germany acceded in October 1990), and Spain in 1982. The North Atlantic Treaty has been the framework for a defensive political and military alliance designed to provide common security for its members through co-operation and consultation in political, military, economic, scientific and other non-military fields. Since the end of the Cold War in 1990, the Alliance has adapted its structures and policies to meet new security challenges, including contributing to peacekeeping operations and co-operating closely with the countries of central and eastern Europe. The Alliance is now committed to promoting security and stability throughout Europe and to playing a major role in support of UN and CSCE operations. NATO is involved in supporting the UN peacekeeping effort in the former Yugoslavia, supplying a naval force to monitor compliance with the UN embargo, a

headquarters for the UNPROFOR II force in Bosnia-Hercegovina, and aircraft to monitor and enforce the UN air exclusion zone over Bosnia-Hercegovina and to protect and defend UN personnel and UN-designated safe areas under attack.

The North Atlantic Council, chaired by the Secretary-General, is the highest authority of the Alliance and is composed of permanent representatives of the 16 member countries. It meets at ministerial level (foreign ministers) at least twice a year. The permanent representatives (ambassadors) head national delegations of advisers and experts. Defence matters are dealt with by the Defence Planning Committee (DPC), composed of representatives of all member countries, except France. The DPC also meets at ministerial level (defence ministers) at least twice a year. Nuclear matters are dealt with in the Nuclear Planning Group (NPG), composed of representatives of all countries except for France (Iceland being an observer). The NPG meets regularly at Permanent Representatives level and twice a year at ministerial level (defence ministers). The NATO Secretary-General chairs the Council, the DPC and the NPG.

The Council and DPC are forums for confidential and constant inter-governmental consultation and are the main decision-making bodies within the North Atlantic Alliance. They are assisted by an International Staff, divided into five divisions: Political Affairs; Defence Planning and Policy; Defence Support; Infrastructure, Logistics and Civil Emergency Planning; Scientific and Environmental Affairs.

The senior military authority in NATO, under the Council and DPC, is the Military Committee composed of the Chief of Defence Staffs of each member country, except France and Iceland. The Military Committee, which is assisted by an integrated international military staff, also meets in permanent session with permanent military representatives and is responsible for making recommendations to the Council and DPC on measures considered necessary for the common defence of the NATO area and for supplying guidance on military matters to the major NATO commanders. The Chairman of the Military Committee, elected for a period of two to three years, represents the committee on the Council.

The strategic area covered by the North Atlantic Treaty is divided between two major NATO commands (MNCs), European and Atlantic; and three major subordinate commands (MSCs) within Allied Command Europe, South, Central and North-West. There is also a Regional Planning Group (Canada and the United States).

The major NATO commanders are responsible for the development of defence plans for their respective areas, for the determination of force requirements and for the deployment and exercise of the forces under their command. The major NATO commanders report to the Military Committee. By 1995 the reorganized NATO force structure will consist of three components: the Allied Rapid Reaction Corps of four divisions, with air and sea components (the majority of which will be British forces); the main defence force of four corps (one Danish-German, one Dutch-German, two US-German); and the augmentation forces of reserves and territorials.

In 1990 NATO heads of state and government redefined the goals and strategy of the organization in the light of the end of the Cold War. A Declaration of Peace and Co-operation was issued in November 1991 and a new strategic concept was published, introducing major changes in the organization of NATO forces and overall reductions of around 30 per cent. The new strategic concept also provides for a reduced dependence on nuclear weapons; greater mobility, flexibility and adaptability of forces; greater use of multinational formations; active involvement in international crisis management and peace-keeping operations; increased co-ordination and co-operation with international institutions such as the CSCE and WEU; and a streamlining of NATO's military command structure.

A North Atlantic Co-operation Council (NACC) was established in 1991 within a framework of dialogue and partnership between the member countries of the Alliance and states of eastern Europe and the former Soviet Union. The NACC has 38 member states and one observer (Finland). Its role is to facilitate closer official and informal ties on security and related issues between the members. It focuses on the particular areas of peacekeeping, defence planning, defence industry conversion, defence management and force structuring, and the democratic concepts of civilian-military relations. An NACC *ad hoc* group on co-operation in peacekeeping has also been established with participation by the 38 NACC members, together with Austria, Finland and Sweden.

The potential for destabilizing conflicts in central and eastern Europe has, however, led to the states of eastern Europe and the former Soviet Union being dissatisfied with the level of security and co-operation offered by NATO through the NACC and at its Brussels summit of January 1994 NATO launched its Partnerships for Peace (PFP) programme, inviting eastern European and former Soviet states to become official partners of the NATO Alliance. The PFP programme offers gradual progress towards full membership of NATO. The 21 partner states have representative offices in the NATO headquarters at Brussels and a Partnership Co-ordination Cell has been established at NATO military headquarters (SHAPE) at Mons. Partner states will be involved in NATO military planning, joint military exercises and eventually NATO peacekeeping operations, as well as receiving aid and advice towards meeting their partnership commitments of transparent military budgets and democratic civilian control of their armed forces. NATO will consult with any partner state which perceives a direct threat to its security.

*Secretary-General and Chairman of the North Atlantic Council, of the DPC and of the NPG,* vacant
*UK Permanent Representative on the North Atlantic Council,* Sir John Weston, KCMG
*Chairman of the Military Committee,* Field Marshal Sir Richard Vincent, GBE, KCB, DSO (*UK*)
*Supreme Allied Commander, Europe,* Gen. George Joulwan (*US*)
*Supreme Allied Commander, Atlantic,* Adm. Paul D. Miller (*US*)

## ORGANIZATION FOR ECONOMIC CO-OPERATION AND DEVELOPMENT
2 rue André-Pascal, 75116 Paris

Formed on 30 September 1961, the Organization for Economic Co-operation and Development (OECD) replaced the Organization for European Economic Co-operation. The OECD is the instrument for international co-operation among industrialized member countries on economic and social policies. Its objectives are to assist its member governments in the formulation and co-ordination of policies designed to achieve high, sustained economic growth while maintaining financial stability, to contribute to world trade on a multilateral basis and to stimulate members' aid to developing countries.

The following countries belong to the OECD: Australia, Austria, Belgium, Canada, Denmark, Germany, Finland, France, Greece, Iceland, Republic of Ireland, Italy, Japan, Luxembourg, Mexico, the Netherlands, New Zealand, Norway, Portugal, Spain, Sweden, Switzerland, Turkey, UK and USA. The OECD is considering membership applications from the Czech Republic, the Slovak Republic, Poland and Hungary.

The Council is the supreme body of the organization. Composed of one representative for each member country, it meets at permanent representative level under the chairmanship of the Secretary-General, or at ministerial level (usually once a year) under the chairmanship of a minister elected annually. Decisions and recommendations are adopted by mutual agreement of all members of the Council. Fourteen members of the Council are chosen annually to form an executive committee to assist the Council. However, most of the OECD's work is undertaken in over 200 specialized committees and working parties. Five autonomous or semi-autonomous bodies are related in varying degrees to the Organization: the Nuclear Energy Agency, the International Energy Agency, the Development Centre, the Centre for Educational Research and Innovation, and the European Conference of Ministers of Transport. These bodies, the committees and the Council are serviced by an international Secretariat headed by the Secretary-General of the Organization.

*Secretary-General,* Jean-Claude Paye (*France*)
*UK Permanent Representative,* Keith MacInnes, 19 rue de Franqueville, Paris 75116

## ORGANIZATION OF AFRICAN UNITY
PO Box 3243, Addis Ababa, Ethiopia

The Organization of African Unity (OAU) was established in 1963 and has 53 members (Morocco suspended its participation in 1985 in protest at the Polisario-proclaimed Saharan Arab Democratic Republic (SADR), representing Western Sahara, being admitted as a member). It aims to further African unity and solidarity, to co-ordinate political, economic, social and defence policies, and to eliminate colonialism in Africa.

The chief organs are: the Assembly of heads of state or government, which is the supreme organ of the OAU and meets once a year to consider matters of common African concern and to co-ordinate the Organization's policies; the Council of foreign ministers, which is the Organization's executive body responsible for the implementation of the Assembly's policies, and which meets twice a year; and the Commission of Mediation, Conciliation and Arbitration which promotes the peaceful settlement of disputes between member countries. The main administrative body is the General Secretariat, based in Addis Ababa, headed by a Secretary-General who is elected by the Assembly for a four-year term.

Substantial budgetary arrears due to delays in the payment of national contributions has meant that the OAU continually faces difficulties in furthering its aims. In June 1991 the Assembly adopted an African Economic Community Treaty which envisages establishment of the Economic Community after ratification by two-thirds of the OAU's membership. In June 1993 a mechanism was created for conflict prevention, management and resolution, and a peace fund was established.

*Secretary-General,* Salim Ahmed Salim (*Tanzania*)

## ORGANIZATION OF AMERICAN STATES
17th Street and Constitution Avenue NW, Washington
DC 20006, USA

Originally founded in 1890 for largely commercial purposes, the Organization of American States (OAS) adopted its present name and charter in 1948. The charter was later amended by the Protocol of Buenos Aires (1967) and the Protocol of Cartagena de Indias (1985). Its aims are to strengthen the peace and security of the continent; to promote and consolidate representative democracy with due respect for the principle of non-intervention; to prevent possible causes of difficulties and to ensure the pacific settlement of disputes that may arise among the member states; to provide for common action on the part of those states in the event of aggression; to seek the solution of political, judicial and economic problems that may arise among them; to promote, by co-operative action, their economic, social and cultural development; and to achieve an effective limitation of conventional weapons that will make it possible to devote the largest amount of resources to the economic and social development of the member states. The OAS is a regional organization within the United Nations.

Policy is determined by the annual General Assembly. Meetings of ministers of foreign affairs consider urgent problems, and advise in cases of armed attack and threats to peace. A Permanent Council, comprised of one representative from each member state, meets at OAS headquarters throughout the year. The General Secretariat based in Washington DC is the central administrative organ of the OAS. Other organs promoting OAS aims are the Inter-American Juridical Committee, the Inter-American Commission on Human Rights, the Inter-American Economic and Social Council, and the Inter-American Council for Education, Science and Culture.

The 35 member states are Antigua and Barbuda, Argentina, Bahamas, Barbados, Belize, Bolivia, Brazil, Canada, Chile, Colombia, Costa Rica, Cuba, Dominica, Dominican Republic, Ecuador, Grenada, Guatemala, Guyana, Haiti, Honduras, Jamaica, Mexico, Nicaragua, Panama, Paraguay, Peru, St Christopher and Nevis, St Lucia, St Vincent and the Grenadines, El Salvador, Suriname, Trinidad and Tobago, Uruguay, USA and Venezuela.
*Secretary-General*, Dr César Gaviria Trujillo (*Colombia*)

## ORGANIZATION OF ARAB PETROLEUM EXPORTING COUNTRIES
PO Box 108 Maglis Al-Shaab, 11516 Cairo, Egypt.

The Organization of Arab Petroleum and Exporting Countries (OAPEC) was founded in 1968. The objectives of the organization are to promote co-operation in economic activities; to safeguard members' interests; to unite efforts to ensure the flow of oil to consumer markets; and to create a favourable climate for the investment of capital and expertise.
The Ministerial Council is composed of oil ministers from the member countries and meets twice a year to determine policy, to direct activities and to approve the budgets and accounts of the General Secretariat and the Judicial Tribunal. The Judicial Tribunal is composed of seven part-time judges who rule on disputes between member countries and disputes between countries and oil companies. The executive organ of OAPEC is the General Secretariat.

The member countries of OAPEC are Algeria, Bahrain, Egypt, Iraq, Kuwait, Libya, Qatar, Saudi Arabia, Syria and the United Arab Emirates. Tunisia's membership has been inactive since 1987.
*Secretary-General*, Abdel-Aziz A. Al-Turki

## ORGANIZATION OF THE ISLAMIC CONFERENCE
PO Box 178, Jeddah 21411, Saudi Arabia

The Organization of the Islamic Conference (OIC) was established in May 1971 with the purpose of generating solidarity and co-operation among all the Islamic countries of the world. It also has the specific aims of co-ordinating efforts to safeguard the Muslim Holy Places; supporting the Palestine cause and the formation of a Palestinian state; assisting member states to maintain their independence; co-ordinating the views of member states in international forums such as the UN; improving co-operation in the economic, cultural and scientific fields.

The OIC has three central organs, supreme among them the Conference of the Heads of State which meets once every three years to discuss issues of importance to Islamic states. The Conference of Foreign Ministers meets annually to prepare reports for the Conference of Heads of State and to fulfil the Organization's aims. The General Secretariat, based in Jeddah, carries out administrative tasks. It is headed by a Secretary-General who is elected by the Conference of Foreign Ministers for a non-renewable four-year term.

In addition to this structure, the OIC has several subsidiary bodies and specialized bodies. These include the Islamic Solidarity Fund, to aid Islamic institutions in member countries, and the Islamic Development Bank, to finance development projects in poorer member states. An Islamic Court of Justice is also planned. The Organization runs various offices to organize the economic boycott of Israel.

The achievement of the Organization's aims has often been prevented by political rivalry and conflicts between member states, such as the Iran-Iraq war and the Iraqi invasion of Kuwait. Egypt's membership was suspended from 1979 to 1984 because of its peace treaty with Israel. Saudi Arabia, as the Organization's main source of funding, exercises great influence within the Organization. Since 1991 the Organization has become more united and has spoken out against violence against Muslims in India, the Occupied Territories and Bosnia-Hercegovina. In July 1993 the OIC summit in Islamabad agreed to offer 7,600 troops to the UN to protect Muslim areas of Bosnia-Hercegovina.

The Organization has 50 members (49 sovereign Muslim states in Africa, the Middle East, central and south-east Asia and Europe, plus the Palestine Liberation Organization) and two observers, Mozambique and Turkish Northern Cyprus. It has an annual budget of £5 million.
*Secretary-General*, Hamid Algabid (*Niger*)

## ORGANIZATION OF THE PETROLEUM EXPORTING COUNTRIES
Obere Donaustrasse 93, 1020 Vienna, Austria

The Organization of the Petroleum Exporting Countries (OPEC) was created in 1960 as a permanent intergovernmental organization with the aims of unifying and co-ordinating the petroleum policies of members and determining the best means of protecting their interests, individually and collectively. Since 1982 OPEC has attempted (only partially successfully) to impose overall production limits and member state production quotas in an attempt to maintain stable oil prices. In the third quarter of 1994 the overall production quota was 24,520,000 barrels per day.

The supreme authority is the Conference of Ministers of Oil, Mines and Energy of member countries which meets at least twice a year and formulates policy. The Board of Governors, nominated by member countries, directs the management of OPEC and implements Conference resolutions. The Secretariat, based in Vienna, carries out executive functions under the direction of the Board of Governors.

The 12 member countries are Algeria, Gabon, Indonesia, Iran, Iraq, Kuwait, Libya, Nigeria, Qatar, Saudi Arabia, UAE and Venezuela. Ecuador withdrew from OPEC in 1992.

*Secretary-General*, Dr Subroto (*Indonesia*)

## SOUTH PACIFIC COMMISSION
BP D5, Nouméa Cedex, New Caledonia

The South Pacific Commission is a technical assistance agency with programmes in agriculture and plant protection, fisheries and marine resources, community health, socio-economic and statistical services, and community education services. The organization is run by a management committee headed by the Secretary-General. The other committee members are the Director of Services and the Director of Programmes.

The South Pacific Commission (SPC) was established in February 1947 following the signing of the Canberra Agreement by the governments of Australia, France, the Netherlands, New Zealand, the UK and the USA. The aim was to promote the economic and social stability of the islands in the region. The SPC now numbers 27 member states and territories, including the five remaining founder states (the Netherlands has withdrawn) in which no programmes are run, and the other 22 states and territories of Melanesia, Micronesia and Polynesia.

Since 1967 the South Pacific Conference has met annually to discuss and adopt the SPC's work programme, to adopt the budget and to nominate the officers of the Commission.

*Secretary-General*, Ati George Sokomanu (*Vanuatu*)
*Director of Programmes*, Mafaitu'uga Vaasatia Poloma Komiti (*W. Samoa*)
*Director of Services*, Fusi Vave Caginavanua (*Fiji*)

## THE UNITED NATIONS
UN Plaza, New York, NY 10017, USA

The United Nations is a voluntary association of states, dedicated through signature of the UN Charter to the maintenance of international peace and security and the solution of economic, social and political problems through international co-operation. The UN is not a world government and has no right of intervention in the essentially domestic affairs of states.

The UN was founded as a successor to the League of Nations and inherited many of its procedures and institutions. The name 'United Nations' was first used in the Washington Declaration of January 1942 to describe the 26 states which had allied to fight the Axis powers. The UN Charter developed from discussions at the Moscow Conference of the foreign ministers of China, the United Kingdom, the USA and Soviet Union in October 1943. Further progress was made at Dumbarton Oaks, Washington, between August and October 1944 during talks involving the same states.

The role of the Security Council was formulated at the Yalta Conference in January 1945. The Charter was formally drawn up by 50 allied nations at the San Francisco Conference between April and 26 June 1945, when it was signed. Following ratification the UN came into effect on 24 October 1945, which is celebrated annually as United Nations Day. The UN flag is light blue with the UN emblem centred in white.

The principal organs of the UN are the General Assembly, the Security Council, the Economic and Social Council, the Trusteeship Council, the Secretariat and the International Court of Justice. The Economic and Social Council and the Trusteeship Council are auxiliaries, charged with assisting and advising the General Assembly and Security Council. The official languages used are Arabic, Chinese, English, French, Russian and Spanish. Deliberations at the International Court of Justice are in English and French only.

### MEMBERSHIP

Membership is open to all countries which accept the Charter and its principle of peaceful co-existence. New members are admitted by the General Assembly on the recommendation of the Security Council. The original membership of 51 states has grown to 184:

| | |
|---|---|
| Afghanistan | *Czech Republic |
| Albania | *Denmark |
| Algeria | Djibouti |
| Andorra | Dominica |
| Angola | *Dominican Republic |
| Antigua and Barbuda | *Ecuador |
| *Argentina | *Egypt |
| Armenia | Equatorial Guinea |
| *Australia | Eritrea |
| Austria | Estonia |
| Azerbaijan | *Ethiopia |
| The Bahamas | Federated States of Micro- |
| Bahrain | nesia |
| Bangladesh | Fiji |
| Barbados | Finland |
| *Belarus | *France |
| *Belgium | Gabon |
| Belize | Gambia |
| Benin | Georgia |
| Bhutan | Germany |
| *Bolivia | Ghana |
| Bosnia-Hercegovina | *Greece |
| Botswana | Grenada |
| *Brazil | *Guatemala |
| Brunei | Guinea |
| Bulgaria | Guinea-Bissau |
| Burkina | Guyana |
| Burundi | *Haiti |
| Cambodia | *Honduras |
| Cameroon | Hungary |
| *Canada | Iceland |
| Cape Verde | *India |
| Central African Rep. | Indonesia |
| Chad | *Iran |
| *Chile | *Iraq |
| *China | Ireland, Republic of |
| *Colombia | Israel |
| Comoros | Italy |
| Congo | Jamaica |
| *Costa Rica | Japan |
| Côte d'Ivoire | Jordan |
| Croatia | Kazakhstan |
| *Cuba | Kenya |
| Cyprus | Korea, D.P.Rep. (North) |

Korea, Rep. of (South)
Kuwait
Kyrgyzstan
Laos
Latvia
*Lebanon
Lesotho
*Liberia
Libya
Liechtenstein
Lithuania
*Luxembourg
Macedonia (The Former
   Yugoslav Republic of)
Madagascar
Malawi
Malaysia
The Maldives
Mali
Malta
Marshall Islands
Mauritania
Mauritius
*Mexico
Moldova
Monaco
Mongolia
Morocco
Mozambique
Myanmar (Burma)
Namibia
Nepal
*Netherlands
*New Zealand
*Nicaragua
Niger
Nigeria
*Norway
Oman
Pakistan
*Panama
Papua New Guinea
*Paraguay
*Peru
*Philippines
*Poland
Portugal
Qatar
Romania

*Russian Federation
Rwanda
St Christopher and Nevis
St Lucia
St Vincent and the Grena-
   dines
*El Salvador
San Marino
São Tomé and Príncipe
*Saudi Arabia
Senegal
Seychelles
Sierra Leone
Singapore
*Slovak Republic
Slovenia
Solomon Islands
Somalia
*South Africa
Spain
Sri Lanka
Sudan
Suriname
Swaziland
Sweden
*Syria
Tajikistan
Tanzania
Thailand
Togo
Trinidad and Tobago
Tunisia
*Turkey
Turkmenistan
Uganda
*Ukraine
United Arab Emirates
*United Kingdom
*United States of America
*Uruguay
Uzbekistan
Vanuatu
*Venezuela
Vietnam
Western Samoa
Yemen
*Yugoslavia (suspended)
Zaire
Zambia
Zimbabwe

*Original member (i.e. from 1945). From 25 October 1971 'China' was taken to mean the People's Republic of China. Czechoslovakia was an original member in 1945 and a member until 31 December 1992. The successor states of the Czech Republic and the Slovak Republic were admitted as members in January 1993.

The Russian Federation took over the membership of the Soviet Union in the Security Council and all other UN organs on 24 December 1991. Belarus (formerly Belorussia) and the Ukraine on becoming independent sovereign states continued their existing memberships of the UN, both having been granted separate UN membership in 1945 as a concession to the Soviet Union.

OBSERVERS

Permanent observer status is held by the Vatican City State and Switzerland. The Palestine Liberation Organization has special observer status.

NON-MEMBERS

A number of countries are not members, usually due to their small size and limited financial resources. Notable exceptions include Switzerland, which follows a policy of absolute neutrality, and Taiwan, which was replaced by the People's Republic of China in October 1971. The others are: Kiribati; Nauru; Tonga; Tuvalu; Vatican City State.

THE GENERAL ASSEMBLY
UN Plaza, New York, NY 10017, USA

The General Assembly is the main deliberative organ of the UN. It consists of all members, each entitled to five representatives but having only one vote. The annual session begins on the third Tuesday of September, when the President is elected, and usually continues until mid-December. Special sessions are held on specific issues and emergency special sessions can be called within 24 hours.

The Assembly is empowered to discuss any matter within the scope of the Charter, except when it is under consideration by the Security Council, and to make recommendations. Under the 'uniting for peace' resolution, adopted in 1950, the Assembly may also take action to maintain international peace and security when the Security Council fails to do so because of a lack of unanimity of its permanent members. Important decisions, such as those on peace and security, the election of officers, the budget, etc., need a two-thirds majority. Others need a simple majority. The Assembly has effective power only over the internal operations of the UN itself; external recommendations are not legally binding.

The work of the General Assembly is divided among seven main committees, on each of which every member has the right to be represented: Disarmament and related security questions (assisted by a Special Political Committee); Economic and Financial; Social, Humanitarian and Cultural; Decolonization (including non-self governing territories); Administrative and Budgetary; Legal. In addition, the General Assembly appoints ad hoc committees to consider special issues, such as human rights, peacekeeping, disarmament and international law. All committees consider items referred to them by the Assembly and recommend draft resolutions to its plenary meeting.

The Assembly is assisted by a number of functional committees. The General Committee co-ordinates its proceedings and operations, while the Credentials Committee verifies the credentials of representatives. There are also two standing committees, the Advisory Committee on Administration and Budgetary Questions and the Committee on Contributions, which suggests the scale of members' payments to the UN.
*President of the General Assembly* (1993), Samuel Insanally (*Guyana*)

The Assembly has created a large number of specialized bodies over the years, which are supervised jointly with the Economic and Social Council. They are supported by UN and voluntary contributions from governments, non-governmental organizations and individuals. These organizations include:

THE CONFERENCE ON DISARMAMENT (CD)
Palais des Nations, 1211 Geneva 10, Switzerland
Established by the UN as the Committee on Disarmament in 1962, the CD is the single multilateral disarmament negotiating forum. The present title of the organization was adopted in 1984. There were 39 members as at 1 June 1991.

The Conference holds three regular sessions per year, from January to March, May to June, and July to August. The work of the Conference is conducted both in public plenary meetings and in private ad hoc committees set up

with the consent of all members to deal with specific items of the agenda. After 25 years of negotiations, a Chemical Weapons Convention was finally agreed and opened for signing in Paris on 14 January 1993. The Convention will come into force six months after it has been ratified by 65 states. It bans the use, production, stockpiling and transfer of all chemical weapons. All US and Russian weapons must be destroyed within 15 years of the Convention entering into force and all other states' weapons must be destroyed within ten years.
*Secretary-General,* HE Miljan Komatina
*UK Representative,* Miss T. A. H. Solesby, CMG, 37–39 rue de Vermont, 1211 Geneva 10, Switzerland

THE UNITED NATIONS CHILDREN'S FUND (UNICEF)
3 UN Plaza, New York, NY 10017, USA
Established in 1947 to assist children and mothers in the immediate post-war period, UNICEF now concentrates on developing countries. It provides primary health-care and health education. In particular, it conducts programmes in oral hydration, immunization against leading diseases, child growth monitoring, and the encouragement of breast-feeding. Its operations are often conducted in co-operation with the World Health Organization (WHO).
*Executive Director,* James Grant (*USA*)

THE UNITED NATIONS DEVELOPMENT PROGRAMME (UNDP)
1 UN Plaza, New York, NY 10017, USA
Established in 1966 from the merger of the UN Expanded Programme of Technical Assistance and the UN Special Fund, UNDP is the central funding agency for economic and social development projects around the world. Much of its annual expenditure is channelled through UN specialized agencies, governments and non-governmental organizations.
*Administrator,* James G. Speth (*USA*)

THE UNITED NATIONS HIGH COMMISSIONER FOR REFUGEES (UNHCR)
Centre William Rappard, 154 rue de Lausanne, PO Box 2500, 1211 Geneva 2, Switzerland
Established in 1951 to protect the rights and interests of refugees, it organizes emergency relief and longer-term solutions, such as voluntary repatriation, local integration or resettlement.
*High Commissioner,* Sadako Ogata (*Japan*)
UK OFFICE, 76 Westminster Palace Gardens, London SW1P 1RL. Tel: 0171-222 3065

THE UN RELIEF AND WORKS AGENCY FOR PALESTINE REFUGEES IN THE NEAR EAST (UNRWA)
Vienna International Centre, Wagramerstrasse 5, PO Box 100, 1400 Vienna, Austria
Established in 1949 to bring relief to the Palestinians displaced by the Arab-Israeli conflict.
*Commissioner-General,* Ilter Turkman (*Turkey*)

THE UNITED NATIONS HIGH COMMISSIONER FOR HUMAN RIGHTS
Established in 1993 to secure respect for, and prevent violations of human rights by engaging in dialogue with governments and international organizations. Responsible for the co-ordination of all UN human rights activities.
*High Commissioner,* José Ayala Lasso (*Ecuador*)

*Other bodies include:*
THE UN CENTRE FOR HUMAN SETTLEMENTS (Habitat), PO Box 30030, Nairobi, Kenya
THE UN COMMISSION FOR TRADE AND DEVELOPMENT (UNCTAD), Palais des Nations, 1211 Geneva 10, Switzerland

THE DEPARTMENT OF HUMANITARIAN AFFAIRS (DHA), Palais des Nations, 1211 Geneva 10, Switzerland
THE UN ENVIRONMENT PROGRAMME (UNEP), PO Box 30552, Nairobi, Kenya
THE UN POPULATION FUND (UNFPA), 220 East 42nd Street, New York, NY 10017, USA
THE UN INSTITUTE FOR THE ADVANCEMENT OF WOMEN (INSTRAW), PO Box 21747, Santo Domingo, Dominican Republic
THE UN UNIVERSITY (UNU), Toho Seimei Building, 15–1, Shibuya, 2-Chome, Shibuya-ku, Tokyo 150, Japan
THE WORLD FOOD COUNCIL (WFC), Via delle Terme di Caracalla, 00100 Rome, Italy
THE WORLD FOOD PROGRAMME (WFP), Via delle Terme di Caracalla, 00100 Rome, Italy

BUDGET OF THE UNITED NATIONS
The budget adopted for the biennium 1994–5 was US$2,580.2 million. The scale of assessment contributions of 88 UN members is set at the minimum 0.01 per cent. The ten largest assessments are: USA, 25 per cent; Japan, 11.38; Russian Federation, 9.99; Germany, 9.36; France, 6.25; UK, 4.86; Italy, 3.99; Canada, 3.09; Spain, 1.95; Netherlands, 1.65.

THE SECURITY COUNCIL
UN Plaza, New York, NY 10017, USA

The Security Council is the senior arm of the UN and has the primary responsibility for maintaining world peace and security. It consists of 15 members, each with one representative and one vote. There are five permanent members, China, France, the Russian Federation, UK and USA, and ten non-permanent members. Each of the non-permanent members is elected for a two-year term by a two-thirds majority of the General Assembly and is ineligible for immediate re-election. Five of the elective seats are allocated to Africa and Asia, one to eastern Europe, two to Latin America and two to western Europe and remaining countries. Procedural questions are determined by a simple majority vote. Other matters require a majority inclusive of the votes of the permanent members; they thus have a right of veto. The abstention of a permanent member does not constitute a veto. The presidency rotates each month by state in (English) alphabetical order. Parties to a dispute, other non-members and individuals can be invited to participate in Security Council debates but are not permitted to vote. In 1994 the ten non-permanent members were: Brazil, Djibouti, New Zealand, Pakistan, Spain (*term expires 31 December 1994*); Argentina, Czech Republic, Nigeria, Oman, Rwanda (*term expires 31 December 1995*).
   The Security Council is empowered to settle or adjudicate in disputes or situations which threaten international peace and security. It can adopt political, economic and military measures to achieve this end. Any matter considered to be a threat to or breach of the peace or an act of aggression can be brought to the Security Council's attention by any member state or by the Secretary-General. The Charter envisaged members placing at the disposal of the Security Council armed forces and other facilities which would be co-ordinated by the Military Staff Committee, composed of military representatives of the five permanent members. The Security Council is also supported by a Committee of Experts, to advise on procedural and technical matters, and a Committee on Admission of New Members. Owing to superpower disunity, the Security Council has rarely played the decisive role set out in the Charter; the Military Staff Committee was effectively suspended from 1948 until 1990, when a meeting was convened during the Gulf Crisis on the formation and control of UN-supervised armed forces.

At an extraordinary meeting of the Security Council on 31 January 1992 attended by heads of government, plans were laid to transform the UN in light of the changed post-Cold War world. The Secretary-General was asked to draw up a report on transforming the UN's peacekeeping ability. The report was produced in June 1992 and centred on the establishment of a UN army composed of national contingents on permanent standby, as envisaged at the time of the UN's formation.

### PEACEKEEPING FORCES

The Security Council has established a number of peace-keeping forces since its foundation, comprising contingents provided mainly by neutral and non-aligned UN members. In mid-1994 there were 17 peacekeeping operations deploying some 71,000 military and civilian police personnel from 70 countries at an annual cost of US$3,200 million.

Current forces include: the UN Truce Supervision Organization (UNTSO), 1948, Israel; the UN Military Observer Group in India and Pakistan (UNMOGIP), 1949; the UN Peacekeeping Force in Cyprus (UNFICYP), 1964; the UN Disengagement Observer Force (UNDOF), 1974, Golan Heights, Syria; the UN Interim Force in Lebanon (UNIFIL), 1978; the UN Iraq-Kuwait Observation Mission (UNIKOM), 1991; UN Angola Verification Mission II (UNAVEM II), 1991; UN Observer Mission in El Salvador (ONUSAL), 1991; the UN Mission for the Referendum in Western Sahara (MINURSO), 1991; the UN Protection Force (UNPROFOR), 1992, Croatia, Bosnia-Hercegovina, Federal Republic of Yugoslavia and the former Yugoslav Republic of Macedonia; the UN Operation in Mozambique (ONUMOZ), 1992; the UN Operation in Somalia II (UNOSOM II), 1993; the UN Observer Mission Uganda-Rwanda (UNOMUR), 1993; the UN Observer Mission in Georgia (UNOMIG), 1993; the UN Observer Mission in Liberia (UNOMIL), 1993; the UN Mission in Haiti (UNMIH), 1993; the UN Assistance Mission for Rwanda (UNAMIR), 1993.

### THE ECONOMIC AND SOCIAL COUNCIL
UN Plaza, New York, NY 10017, USA

The Economic and Social Council is responsible under the General Assembly for the economic and social work of the UN and for the co-ordination of the activities of the 15 specialized agencies and other UN bodies. It makes reports and recommendations on economic, social, cultural, educational, health and related matters, often in consultation with non-governmental organizations, passing the reports to the General Assembly and other UN bodies. It also drafts conventions for submission to the Assembly and calls conferences on matters within its remit.

The Council consists of 54 members, 18 of whom are elected annually by the General Assembly for a three-year term. Each has one vote and can be immediately re-elected on retirement. A President is elected annually and is also eligible for re-election. One substantive session is held annually and decisions are reached by simple majority vote of those present.

The Council has established a number of standing committees on particular issues and several commissions. Commissions include: Statistical, Human Rights, Social Development, Sustainable Development, Status of Women, Crime Prevention and Criminal Justice, Narcotic Drugs, Science and Technology for Development, and Population; and Regional Economic Commissions for Europe, Asia and the Pacific, Western Asia, Latin America and Africa.

### THE TRUSTEESHIP COUNCIL
UN Plaza, New York, NY 10017, USA

The Trusteeship Council supervises the administration of territories within the UN Trusteeship system inherited from the League of Nations. It now consists of the USA, the only remaining administrator, and the four other permanent members of the Security Council. Meetings are held annually and decisions reached by a majority vote of those present. Ten of the original eleven trusteeships have now progressed towards independence or merged with neighbouring states. With the termination of the trust status for the Federated States of Micronesia in December 1990, only the Republic of Palau now remains within the system.

### THE SECRETARIAT
UN Plaza, New York, NY 10017, USA

The Secretariat services the other UN organs and is headed by a Secretary-General elected by a majority vote of the General Assembly on the recommendation of the Security Council. He is assisted by an international staff, chosen to represent the international character of the organization. The Secretary-General is charged with bringing to the attention of the Security Council any matter which he considers poses a threat to international peace and security. He may also bring other matters to the attention of the General Assembly and other UN bodies and may be entrusted by them with additional duties. As chief administrator to the UN, the Secretary-General is present in person or via representatives at all meetings of the other five main organs of the UN. He may also act as an impartial mediator in disputes between member states.

The power and influence of the Secretary-General has, to a large extent, been determined by the character of the office-holder and by the state of relations between the superpowers. The thaw in these relations since the mid-1980s has increased the effectiveness of the UN, particularly in its attempts to intervene in international disputes. It helped to end the Iran-Iraq war and sponsored peace in Central America. Following Iraq's invasion of Kuwait in 1990 the UN took its first collective security action since the Korean War. UN action to protect the Kurds in northern Iraq has widened its legal authority by breaching the prohibition on its intervention in the essentially domestic affairs of states. Currently the UN is involved in peacekeeping, aid distribution and negotiations in the former Yugoslavia; and is addressing the global problems of AIDS and environmental destruction.

*Secretary-General*, Boutros Boutros-Ghali (*Egypt*)
*Under-Secretaries-General*:
  *Africa, Asia and the Middle East*, James Jonah (*Sierra Leone*)
  *Political Affairs*, Marrack Goulding (*UK*)
  *Peacekeeping Operations*, Kofi Annan (*Ghana*)
  *Development Support and Management Services*, Ji Chaozhu (*China*)
  *Legal Affairs*, Hans Axel Valdemar-Corell (*Sweden*)
  *Humanitarian Affairs*, Peter Hansen (*Denmark*)
  *Administration and Management*, Joseph Connor (*USA*)
  *Policy Co-ordination and Sustainable Development*, Nitin Desai (*India*)
  *Economic and Social Information and Policy Analysis*, Jean-Claude Milleron (*France*)

*Former Secretaries-General*
| 1946–53 | Trygve Lie (*Norway*) |
| 1953–61 | Dag Hammarskjöld (*Sweden*) |
| 1961–71 | U Thant (*Burma*) |
| 1971–81 | Kurt Waldheim (*Austria*) |

1981–91   Javier Pérez de Cuéllar (*Peru*)
1992–    Boutros Boutros-Ghali (*Egypt*)

## INTERNATIONAL COURT OF JUSTICE
The Peace Palace, 2517 KJ The Hague, The Netherlands

The International Court of Justice is the principal judicial organ of the UN. The Statute of the Court is an integral part of the Charter and all members of the UN are *ipso facto* parties to it. The Court is composed of 15 judges, elected by both the General Assembly and the Security Council for nine-year terms which are renewable. Judges may deliberate over cases in which their country is involved. If no judge on the bench is from a country which is a party to a dispute under consideration, that party may designate a judge to participate *ad hoc* in that particular deliberation. If any party to a case fails to adhere to the judgment of the Court, the other party may have recourse to the Security Council.

*President*, Mohammed Bedjaoui (*Algeria*) (2000)
*Vice-President*, Stephen M. Schwebel (*USA*) (1997)
*Judges*, Geza Herczegh (*Hungary*) (1994); Bola Ajibola (*Nigeria*) (1994); Roberto Ago (*Italy*) (1997); Sir Robert Jennings (*UK*) (2000); Shigeru Oda (*Japan*) (1994); Ni Zhengyu (*China*) (1994); Jens Evensen (*Norway*) (1997); Nikolai K. Tarassov (*Russian Federation*) (1997); Gilbert Guillaume (*France*) (2000); Mohammed Shahabuddeen (*Guyana*) (1997); Andrés Aguilar Mawdsley (*Venezuela*) (2000); Christopher G. Weeramantry (*Sri Lanka*) (2000); and Raymond Ranjeva (*Madagascar*) (2000)

### UN WAR CRIMES TRIBUNAL FOR THE FORMER YUGOSLAVIA

On 27 May 1993 the Security Council voted to establish a war crimes tribunal for the former Yugoslavia. This tribunal court will hear cases covering grave breaches of the Geneva Conventions and crimes against humanity. The Court was inaugurated in November 1993 in the Hague with 11 member judges elected by the UN General Assembly from 11 states, and with two trial chambers and an appeal court. The court will be unable to force suspects to stand trial and will not be empowered to pass verdicts in the absence of suspects. It is, however, entitled to put suspects under an 'act of accusation' which will prevent them from leaving their own country.
*President*, Antonio Cassese (*Italy*)

## SPECIALIZED AGENCIES

Fifteen independent international organizations, each with its own membership, budget and headquarters, carry out their responsibilities in co-ordination with the UN under agreements made with the Economic and Social Council. An entry for each appears elsewhere in the International Organizations section. They are as follows: the Food and Agriculture Organization of the UN; International Civil Aviation Organization; International Fund for Agricultural Development; International Labour Organization; International Maritime Organization; the International Monetary Fund; International Telecommunications Union; UN Educational, Scientific and Cultural Organization; UN Industrial Development Organization; Universal Postal Union; World Bank (International Bank for Reconstruction and Development, International Development Agency, International Finance Corporation); World Health Organization; World Intellectual Property Organization; and World Meteorological Organization. The International Atomic Energy Agency and the General Agreement on Tariffs and Trade are linked to the UN but are not specialized agencies.

### UK MISSION TO THE UNITED NATIONS
845 Third Avenue, New York, NY 10022, USA
*Permanent Representative to the United Nations and Representative on the Security Council*, Sir David Hannay, KCMG, *apptd* 1990
*Deputy Permanent Representative*, S. J. Gomersall

### UK MISSION TO THE OFFICE OF THE UN AND OTHER INTERNATIONAL ORGANIZATIONS IN GENEVA
37–39 rue de Vermont, 1211 Geneva 20, Switzerland
*Permanent UK Representative*, N. C. R. Williams, CMG *apptd* 1993
*Deputy Permanent Representatives*, E. G. M. Chaplin, OBE (*Head of Chancery*); Miss A.E.Stoddart (*Economic Affairs*)

### UK MISSION TO THE INTERNATIONAL ATOMIC ENERGY AGENCY, THE UN INDUSTRIAL DEVELOPMENT ORGANIZATION AND THE UNITED NATIONS OFFICE AT VIENNA
Jaurésgasse 12, 1030 Vienna, Austria
*Permanent UK Representative*, C. Hulse, CMG, OBE *apptd* 1993
*Deputy Permanent Representative*, S. H. Innes

### UN OFFICE AND INFORMATION CENTRE
Ship House, 20 Buckingham Gate, London SW1E 6LB
Tel 0171-630 1981

## UNITED NATIONS EDUCATIONAL, SCIENTIFIC AND CULTURAL ORGANIZATION
7 place de Fontenoy, 75352 Paris 07SP, France

The United Nations Educational, Scientific and Cultural Organization (UNESCO) was established on 4 November 1946, the consequence of an international conference held in London in 1945. It promotes collaboration among its member states in education, science, culture and communication. It aims to further a universal respect for human rights, justice and the rule of law, without distinction of race, sex, language or religion, in accordance with the UN Charter.

UNESCO runs a number of programmes to improve education and extend access to it. It provides assistance to ensure the free flow of information and its wider and better balanced dissemination without any obstacle to freedom of expression, and to maintain cultural heritage in the face of development. It fosters research and study in all areas of the social sciences.

UNESCO had 181 member states as at July 1994. There are three associate members. The General Conference, consisting of representatives of all the members, meets biennially to decide the programme and the budget (1992–3, US$444,704,000). It elects the 51-member Executive Board, which supervises operations, and appoints a Director-General. The Director-General heads a Secretariat responsible for carrying out the organization's programmes. In most member states national commissions liaise with UNESCO to execute its programme.

The UK withdrew from UNESCO in 1985. It was granted observer status in 1986.

*Director-General*, Federico Mayor Zaragoza (*Spain*)

## UNITED NATIONS INDUSTRIAL DEVELOPMENT ORGANIZATION
Vienna International Centre, Wagramerstrasse 5,
PO Box 300, 1400 Vienna, Austria

The United Nations Industrial Development Organization (UNIDO) was established as an organ of the UN General Assembly in 1966, replacing the Centre for Industrial Development. It became a UN specialized agency in 1986 with the aim of promoting the industrialization of developing countries, with special emphasis upon the manufacturing sector. To this end it provides technical assistance and advice, as well as help with planning.

UNIDO had 165 members as at January 1994. It is funded by the UN Development Programme, other UN bodies, governments and non-governmental organizations. A General Conference of all the members meets biennially to discuss policy, set a budget (1993–4, US$196,310,300) and elect the Industrial Development Board. This executive body is composed of 33 members from developing countries, 15 from developed countries and five from centrally planned economies. There is a subsidiary Programme and Budget Committee. A Secretariat administers UNIDO under a Director-General, appointed by the Conference.

*Director-General*, Mauricio de Maria y Campos (*Mexico*)
*Permanent UK Representative*, C. Hulse, CMG, OBE, British
   Embassy, Vienna

## UNIVERSAL POSTAL UNION
Weltpoststrasse 4, 3000 Berne 15, Switzerland

The Universal Postal Union (UPU) was established by the Convention of Berne 1874, taking effect from July 1875, and became a UN specialized agency in 1947. The UPU exists to form a single postal territory of all member countries, for the reciprocal exchange of correspondence without discrimination. It also assists and advises on the improvement of postal services.

The UPU had 187 members as at March 1994. A Universal Postal Congress of all the members meets every five years to review the Convention and to elect a 40-member Executive Council (including one member from the host country) which continues the UPU's work between Congresses. The Congress also elects a 35-member Consultative Council for Postal Studies which meets annually to address specific matters. The Council, together with the Swiss government, supervises the International Bureau, a secretariat headed by a Director-General.

Funding is provided by members according to a scale of contributions drawn up by the Congress. The Council sets the annual budget (1994, SFr 33,907,630) within a five-year figure decided by the Congress.

*Director-General*, A. C. Botto de Barros (*Brazil*)

## WESTERN EUROPEAN UNION
4 rue de la Régence, 1000 Brussels, Belgium

The Western European Union (WEU) originated as the Brussels Treaty Organization (BTO). This was established under the Treaty of Brussels, signed in 1948 by Belgium, France, Luxembourg, the Netherlands and UK, to provide collective self-defence and economic, cultural and social collaboration amongst its signatories. With the collapse of the European Defence Community and the decision of NATO to incorporate the Federal Republic of Germany into the Western security system, the BTO was modified to become the WEU in 1954 with the admission of West Germany and Italy.

Owing to the overlap with NATO and the Council of Europe, the Union became largely defunct. From the late 1970s onwards efforts were made to add a security dimension to the EC's European Political Co-operation. Opposition to these efforts from Denmark, Greece and Ireland led the remaining EC countries, all WEU members, to decide to reactivate the Union in 1984. Members committed themselves to harmonizing their views on defence and security and developing a European security identity, while bearing in mind the importance of transatlantic relations. Portugal and Spain joined the WEU in 1988, and Greece became a full member in 1992.

After much debate about the future of the WEU, the EC Maastricht Treaty designated the WEU as the future defence component of the EU. WEU foreign ministers agreed in the Petersberg Declaration 1992 to assign forces to WEU command for 'peacemaking' operations in Europe. On 20 November 1992 the WEU's role as the common security dimension of the EU was enhanced when WEU ministers signed a declaration with remaining European NATO members to give them various forms of WEU membership. Greece became a full member, Ireland and Denmark observer members and Iceland, Norway and Turkey became associate members. On 9 May 1994 the WEU reached agreements with nine eastern European states, Estonia, Latvia, Lithuania, Poland, Czech Republic, Slovak Republic, Hungary, Romania and Bulgaria, under which they all became associate members.

The WEU acts in accordance with positions adopted within the Atlantic Alliance, and relations between the WEU and NATO are developing on the basis of transparency and complementarity. WEU foreign ministers stated in the Luxembourg Declaration (November 1993) that the WEU is ready to participate in the future work of the NATO Alliance as its European pillar, and to co-operate to prevent the duplication of WEU and NATO actions.

Building on past experience of joint actions in the Gulf (1989–90), the WEU operates a naval patrol force in the Adriatic Sea and an embargo enforcement mission on the River Danube as part of the European peace initiatives in the former Yugoslavia.

The formation of a 'Eurocorps' based on the Franco-German brigade under the umbrella of the WEU was announced in May 1992. The 'Eurocorps' was inaugurated in Strasbourg in November 1993 and will be fully operational by October 1995 with a strength of 40,000–50,000 comprising French, German, Belgian, Luxembourg and Spanish forces.

A Council of Ministers (foreign and defence) meets biannually in the capital of the presiding country; the presidency rotates biannually. A Permanent Council of the signatories' Brussels ambassadors meets regularly in Brussels. Associate members have the right to attend Permanent Council meetings. An Enlarged Council of political directors and member defence officials were created in 1986. Both the Enlarged Council and the Permanent Council are chaired by the Secretary-General and serviced by the Secretariat. The Assembly of the WEU is composed of 108 parliamentarians of member states and meets twice annually in Paris to debate matters within the scope of the Brussels Treaty.

*Presidency* (1994), Portugal, United Kingdom
*Secretary-General*, Dr Willem van Eekelen (*Netherlands*)
*UK Representative on the Permanent Council*, Sir John
   Weston, KCMG

ASSEMBLY, 43 avenue du Président Wilson, 75775 Paris Cedex 16, France

---

## THE WORLD BANK
1818 H Street NW, Washington DC 20433, USA

---

The World Bank, more formally known as the International Bank for Reconstruction and Development (IBRD), is a specialized agency of the UN, and developed from the international monetary and financial conference held at Bretton Woods, New Hampshire, in 1944. Determined to avoid the financial chaos and depression of the inter-war years, 44 nations established the IBRD in December 1945, to encourage economic growth in developing countries through the provision of loans and technical assistance to their respective governments. The IBRD now has 176 members.

The Bank is owned by the governments of member countries and its capital is subscribed by its members. It finances its lending primarily from borrowing in world capital markets, and derives a substantial contribution to its resources from its retained earnings and the repayment of loans. The interest rate on its loans is calculated in relation to its cost of borrowing. Loans generally have a grace period of five years and are repayable within 20 years. The loans made by the Bank since its inception to 30 June 1993, totalled US$312,970.8 million to 110 countries. Subscribed capital is US$152,248 million.

Originally directed towards post-war reconstruction in Europe, the Bank has subsequently turned towards assisting less-developed countries with the establishment of two affiliates, the International Finance Corporation (IFC) in 1956 and the International Development Association (IDA) in 1960. The IFC aids developing member countries by promoting the growth of the private sector of their economies and by helping to mobilize domestic and foreign capital for this purpose. The IFC's subscribed share capital was US$2,050 million at 30 June 1993. It is also empowered to borrow up to two and half times the amount of its unimpaired subscribed capital and accumulated earnings for use in its lending programme. At 30 June 1993, the IFC had committed financing totalling more than US$12,400 million in about 98 countries.

The IDA performs the same function as the World Bank but primarily to less developed countries and on terms that bear less heavily on their balance of payments than IBRD loans. Eligible countries typically have a per capita gross national product of less than US$765 (1991). Funds (called credits to distinguish them from IBRD loans) come mostly in the form of subscriptions and contributions from the IDA's richer members and transfers from the net income of the IBRD. The terms for IDA credits, which bear no interest and are made to governments only, are ten-year grace periods and 35- or 40-year maturities. By 30 June 1993, the IDA had extended development credits totalling US$77,816.4 million to 90 countries.

The IBRD and its affiliates are financially and legally distinct but share headquarters. The IBRD is headed by a Board of Governors, consisting of one Governor and one alternate Governor appointed by each member country. Twenty-four Executive Directors exercise all powers of the Bank except those reserved to the Board of Governors. The President, elected by the Executive Directors, conducts the business of the Bank, assisted by an international staff. Membership in both the IFC (154 members) and the IDA (150 members) is open to all IBRD countries. The IDA is administered by the same staff as the Bank; the IFC has its

own personnel but draws on the IBRD for administrative and other support. All share the same President.

In 1988 a third affiliate, the Multilateral Investment Guarantee Agency (MIGA) was formed. MIGA encourages foreign investment in developing states by providing investment guarantees to potential investors and advisory services to developing member countries. At 30 June 1993 102 countries were members of MIGA.

*President (IBRD, IFC, IDA, MIGA)*, L. Preston (*USA*)
*UK Executive Director*, H. Evans, Room 11-120, IMF, 700 19th Street NW, Washington DC 20431
EUROPEAN OFFICE, 66 avenue d'Iena, 75116 Paris, France
JAPAN OFFICE, Kokusai Building 1-1, Marunouchi 3-Chomse, Chiyoda-ku, Tokyo 100, Japan
UK OFFICE, New Zealand House, Haymarket, London SW1Y 4TQ

---

## THE WORLD COUNCIL OF CHURCHES
PO Box 2100, 1211 Geneva 2, Switzerland

---

The World Council of Churches (WCC) was constituted in Amsterdam in 1948 to promote unity among the many different Christian churches. The 324 member churches of the WCC have adherents in more than 100 countries. With the exception of Roman Catholicism, virtually all Christian traditions are included in the WCC membership.

The policies of the Council are determined by delegates of the member churches meeting in Assembly, about every seven years; the seventh Assembly was held in Canberra, Australia, in February 1991. More detailed decisions are taken by a 151-member Central Committee which is elected by the Assembly and meets, with the eight WCC Presidents, annually. The Central Committee in turn appoints a smaller Executive Committee and also nominates commissions to guide the various programmes.

*General Secretary*, Dr Konrad Raiser (*Germany*)

---

## WORLD HEALTH ORGANIZATION
20 avenue Appia, 1211 Geneva 27, Switzerland

---

The UN International Health Conference held in 1946 established the World Health Organization (WHO) as a UN specialized agency, with effect from 1948. It is dedicated to attaining the highest possible level of health for all. It collaborates with member governments, UN agencies and other bodies to develop health standards, control communicable diseases and promote all aspects of family and environmental health. It seeks to raise the standards of health teaching and training, and promotes research through collaborating research centres world-wide. Its other services include the *International Pharmacopoeia*, epidemiological surveillance, and the collation and publication of statistics. WHO activities are orientated to achieving 'Health for all by the year 2000', i.e. a level of health allowing the world's citizens to lead socially and economically productive lives.

WHO had 187 members as at May 1994. It is governed by the annual World Health Assembly of members which meets to set policy, approve the budget (1994-5, US$1,800 million), appoint a Director-General, and adopt health conventions and regulations. It also elects 31 members who designate one health-qualified person to serve in a personal capacity on the Executive Board. The Board effects the programme, suggests initiatives and is empowered to deal

with emergencies. A Secretariat, headed by the Director-General, supervises the health activities of six regional offices.
*Director-General*, Dr H. Nakajima (*Japan*)

## WORLD INTELLECTUAL PROPERTY ORGANIZATION
34 chemin des Colombettes, 1211 Geneva 20, Switzerland

The World Intellectual Property Organization (WIPO) was established in 1967 by the Stockholm Convention, which entered into force in 1970. In addition to that Convention, WIPO administers 17 treaties, the principal ones being the Paris Convention for the Protection of Industrial Property and the Berne Convention for the Protection of Literary and Artistic Works. WIPO became a UN specialized agency in 1974.

WIPO promotes the protection of intellectual property throughout the world through co-operation among states, and the administration of various 'Unions', each founded on a multilateral treaty and dealing with the legal and administrative aspects of intellectual property.

Intellectual property comprises two main branches: industrial property (inventions, trademarks, industrial designs and appellations of origin); and copyright (literary, musical, photographic, audiovisual and artistic works, etc.). WIPO also assists creative intellectual activity and facilitates technology transfer, particularly to developing countries. It administers various conventions, most importantly the Berne and Paris Conventions.

WIPO had 147 members as at 1 April 1994. The biennial session of all its governing bodies sets policy, a programme and a budget (1994–5, SFr 230,000,000). WIPO has three governing bodies: the General Assembly, the Conference and the Co-ordination Committee. The Assembly appoints, instructs and supervises a Director-General, who heads the International Bureau (secretariat). The Co-ordination Committee represents the organizations of the Berne and Paris Conventions.

A separate International Union for the Protection of New Varieties of Plants (UPOV), established by convention in 1961, is linked to WIPO. It has 24 members.
*Director-General*, Dr Arpad Bogsch (*USA*)

## WORLD METEOROLOGICAL ORGANIZATION
41 avenue Giuseppe Motta, PO Box 2300, 1211 Geneva 20, Switzerland

The World Meteorological Organization (WMO) was established as a UN specialized agency in 1950, succeeding the International Meteorological Organization which had been founded in 1873. It facilitates co-operation between the world-wide network of meteorological, climatological and related hydrological and geophysical observation services, standardizes meteorological observations and data, and assists training and research. It also fosters collaboration between meteorological and hydrological services, and furthers the application of meteorology to aviation, shipping, agriculture, etc.

The WMO had 170 member states and five member territories, as at 30 June 1994. The supreme authority is the World Meteorological Congress of member states and member territories, which meets every four years to determine general policy, make recommendations and set a budget (1992–5, SFr 236,100,000). It also elects 26 members of the 36-member Executive Council, the other members being the President and three Vice-Presidents of the WMO, and the Presidents of the six Regional Associations. The Council supervises the implementation of Congress decisions, initiates studies and makes recommendations on matters needing international action. The WMO functions through six Regional Meteorological Associations and eight technical commissions. Each of the Regional Associations has responsibility for co-ordinating meteorological activities within its region. The technical commissions study meteorological problems, lay down the necessary methodologies and procedures, and make recommendations to the Executive Council and Congress. The Secretariat is headed by a Secretary-General, appointed by the Congress.
*Secretary-General*, G. O. P. Obasi (*Nigeria*)

# Countries of the World

The total population of the world in mid-1990 was estimated at 5,292 million, compared with 3,019 million in 1960 and 2,070 million in 1930.

| Continent, etc. | Area sq. miles '000 | Area sq. km '000 | Estimated population mid-1990 |
|---|---|---|---|
| Africa | 11,704 | 30,313 | 642,000,000 |
| North America[1] | 8,311 | 21,525 | 276,000,000 |
| Latin America[2] | 7,933 | 20,547 | 448,000,000 |
| Asia[3] | 10,637 | 27,549 | 3,113,000,000 |
| Europe[4] | 1,915 | 4,961 | 498,000,000 |
| Former USSR | 8,649 | 22,402 | 289,000,000 |
| Oceania[5] | 3,286 | 8,510 | 26,500,000 |
| TOTAL | 52,435 | 135,807 | 5,292,000,000 |

[1] Includes Greenland and Hawaii
[2] Mexico and the remainder of the Americas south of the USA
[3] Includes European Turkey, excludes former USSR
[4] Excludes European Turkey and former USSR
[5] Includes Australia, New Zealand and the islands inhabited by Micronesian, Melanesian and Polynesian peoples
*Source: UN Demographic Yearbook 1990 (pub. 1992)*

A United Nations report (*The Future Growth of World Population*) in 1958 stated that the population of the world had increased since the beginning of the 20th century at an unprecedented rate: in 1850 it was estimated at 1,094 million and in 1900 at 1,500 million, an increase of 42 per cent in 50 years. By 1925 it had risen to 1,907 million (23 per cent in 25 years) and by 1950 it had reached 2,500 million, an increase of 31 per cent in 25 years. Levels of population and the trend in distribution of the population by continents as forecast for the year 2000 were:

| Continents, etc. | Estimated population | per cent |
|---|---|---|
| Africa | 517,000,000 | 8.2 |
| North America | 312,000,000 | 5.0 |
| Latin America[1] | 592,000,000 | 9.4 |
| Asia (excluding USSR) | 3,870,000,000 | 61.8 |
| Europe (including USSR) | 947,000,000 | 15.1 |
| Oceania | 29,000,000 | 0.5 |
| TOTAL | 6,267,000,000 | 100 |

[1] Mexico and the remainder of the Americas south of USA

No complete survey of many countries has yet been achieved and consequently accurate area figures are not always available. Similarly, many countries have not recently, or have never, taken a census. The areas of countries given below are derived from estimated figures published by the United Nations. The conversion factors used are:
(i) to convert square miles to square km, multiply by 2·589988
(ii) to convert square km to square miles, multiply by 0·3861022

Population figures for countries are derived from the most recent estimates available. Accurate and up-to-date data for the populations of capital cities are scarce, and definitions of cities' extent differ. The figures given below are the latest estimates available, and where it is known that the figure applies to an urban agglomeration this is indicated.

\* latest census figure
Ψ seaport
*u.a.* urban agglomeration

## AFRICA

| COUNTRY/TERRITORY | AREA sq. miles | AREA sq. km | POPULATION | CAPITAL | POPULATION OF CAPITAL |
|---|---|---|---|---|---|
| Algeria | 919,595 | 2,381,741 | 25,660,000 | Ψ Algiers | 3,250,000 |
| Angola | 481,354 | 1,246,700 | 10,303,000 | Ψ Luanda | 3,000,000 |
| Benin | 43,484 | 112,622 | 4,889,000 | Ψ Porto Novo | 208,258 |
| Botswana | 224,607 | 581,730 | 1,348,000 | Gaborone | 137,174 |
| Burkina | 105,869 | 274,200 | 9,242,000 | Ouagadougou | 441,514 |
| Burundi | 10,747 | 27,834 | 5,620,000 | Bujumbura | 215,243 |
| Cameroon | 183,566 | 475,442 | 12,239,000 | Yaoundé | 635,670 |
| Cape Verde Islands | 1,557 | 4,033 | 382,000 | Ψ Praia | 57,748\* |
| Central African Republic | 240,535 | 622,984 | 3,127,000 | Bangui | 473,817 |
| Chad | 495,755 | 1,284,000 | 5,819,000 | Ndjaména | 402,000 |
| Comoros | 838 | 2,171 | 570,000 | Moroni | 17,267\* |
| Congo | 132,047 | 342,000 | 2,346,000 | Brazzaville | 596,200\* |
| Côte d'Ivoire | 124,503 | 322,463 | 12,464,000 | Ψ Abidjan | 3,500,000 |
| Djibouti | 8,494 | 22,000 | 520,000 | Ψ Djibouti | 340,700 |
| Egypt | 386,662 | 1,001,449 | 54,688,000 | Cairo | 14,000,000 |
| Equatorial Guinea | 10,830 | 28,051 | 356,000 | Ψ Malabo | 30,418 |
| Eritrea | 36,170 | 93,679 | 3,500,000 | Asmara | 275,000 |
| Ethiopia | 471,778 | 1,221,900 | 49,883,000 | Addis Ababa | 1,793,000 |
| Gabon | 103,347 | 267,667 | 1,212,000 | Ψ Libreville | 251,000 |
| Gambia | 4,361 | 11,295 | 884,000 | Ψ Banjul (*u.a.*) | 109,986 |
| Ghana | 92,100 | 238,537 | 15,509,000 | Ψ Accra (*u.a.*) | 1,781,100 |
| Guinea | 94,926 | 245,857 | 5,931,000 | Ψ Conakry | 763,000 |
| Guinea-Bissau | 13,948 | 36,125 | 984,000 | Ψ Bissau | 109,214\* |

| Country/Territory | AREA sq. miles | sq. km | Population | Capital | Population of Capital |
|---|---|---|---|---|---|
| Kenya | 224,961 | 582,646 | 25,905,000 | Nairobi | 1,400,000 |
| Lesotho | 11,720 | 30,355 | 1,826,000 | Maseru | 288,951* |
| Liberia | 43,000 | 111,369 | 2,705,000 | Ψ Monrovia | 425,000 |
| Libya | 679,362 | 1,759,540 | 4,509,000 | Ψ Tripoli | 1,000,000 |
| Madagascar | 226,669 | 587,041 | 11,493,000 | Antananarivo | 1,250,000 |
| Malawi | 45,747 | 118,484 | 8,556,000 | Lilongwe | 233,973* |
| Mali | 478,791 | 1,240,000 | 9,507,000 | Bamako | 658,275 |
| Mauritania | 397,955 | 1,030,700 | 2,036,000 | Nouakchott | 850,000 |
| Mauritius | 790 | 2,045 | 1,092,384 | Ψ Port Louis | 143,444 |
| Mayotte (Fr.) | 144 | 372 | 94,410 | Mamoundzou | 12,000 |
| Morocco | 172,414 | 446,550 | 27,575,000 | Ψ Rabat | 1,494,000 |
| Western Sahara | 102,703 | 266,000 | 183,000 | Laayoune | 96,784* |
| Mozambique | 309,495 | 801,590 | 16,084,000 | Ψ Maputo | 1,150,000 |
| Namibia | 318,261 | 824,292 | 1,837,000 | Windhoek | 110,000 |
| Niger | 489,191 | 1,267,080 | 7,984,000 | Niamey | 410,000 |
| Nigeria | 356,669 | 923,768 | 112,163,000 | Abuja | 378,671 |
| Réunion (Fr.) | 969 | 2,510 | 598,000 | St Denis | 122,000 |
| Rwanda | 10,169 | 26,338 | 7,491,000 | Kigali | 156,000 |
| St Helena (UK) | 47 | 122 | 5,644 | Ψ Jamestown | 1,332 |
| Ascension Island | 34 | 88 | 1,117 | Ψ Georgetown | — |
| Tristan da Cunha | 38 | 98 | 295 | Ψ Edinburgh | — |
| São Tomé and Príncipe | 372 | 964 | 124,000 | Ψ São Tomé | 25,000 |
| Senegal | 75,750 | 196,192 | 7,533,000 | Ψ Dakar | 1,000,000 |
| Seychelles | 108 | 280 | 68,000 | Ψ Victoria | 24,324 |
| Sierra Leone | 27,699 | 71,740 | 4,260,000 | Ψ Freetown | 470,000 |
| Somalia | 246,201 | 637,657 | 7,691,000 | Ψ Mogadishu | 1,000,000 |
| South Africa | 471,445 | 1,221,031 | 40,049,000 | Pretoria (u.a.) | 822,925 |
| | | | | Ψ Cape Town (u.a.) | 1,911,521 |
| Sudan | 967,500 | 2,505,813 | 25,941,000 | Khartoum (u.a.) | 3,000,000 |
| Swaziland | 6,704 | 17,363 | 817,000 | Mbabane | 38,290 |
| Tanzania | 364,900 | 945,087 | 28,359,000 | Dodoma | 88,474 |
| Togo | 21,925 | 56,785 | 3,643,000 | Ψ Lomé | 366,476 |
| Tunisia | 63,170 | 163,610 | 8,362,000 | Ψ Tunis | 1,394,749 |
| Uganda | 91,259 | 236,036 | 19,517,000 | Kampala (u.a.) | 750,000 |
| Zaire | 905,567 | 2,345,409 | 36,672,000 | Kinshasa | 2,778,281* |
| Zambia | 290,586 | 752,614 | 8,780,000 | Lusaka (u.a.) | 1,000,000 |
| Zimbabwe | 150,804 | 390,580 | 10,019,000 | Harare | 681,000 |

## AMERICA

*North America*

| Country/Territory | AREA sq. miles | sq. km | Population | Capital | Population of Capital |
|---|---|---|---|---|---|
| Canada | 3,849,646 | 9,970,537 | 27,296,859 | Ottawa (u.a.) | 313,987* |
| Greenland (Den.) | 840,004 | 2,175,600 | 55,117 | Ψ Godthab | 8,425 |
| Mexico | 761,605 | 1,972,547 | 87,836,000 | Mexico City (u.a.) | 14,987,051 |
| St Pierre and Miquelon (Fr.) | 93 | 242 | 6,300 | Ψ St Pierre | — |
| United States | 3,787,318 | 9,809,108 | 259,681,000 | Washington DC | 585,221 |

*Central America and the West Indies*

| Country/Territory | AREA sq. miles | sq. km | Population | Capital | Population of Capital |
|---|---|---|---|---|---|
| Anguilla (UK) | 35 | 91 | 8,800* | The Valley | 1,400 |
| Antigua and Barbuda | 170 | 440 | 65,962 | Ψ St John's | 30,000 |
| Aruba (Neth.) | 75 | 193 | 59,000 | Ψ Oranjestad | 20,000 |
| Bahamas | 5,380 | 13,935 | 258,000 | Ψ Nassau | 171,000* |
| Barbados | 166 | 431 | 255,000 | Ψ Bridgetown | 7,466 |
| Belize | 8,867 | 22,965 | 205,000 | Belmopan | 3,739 |
| Bermuda (UK) | 20 | 53 | 58,460 | Ψ Hamilton | 1,617 |
| Cayman Islands (UK) | 100 | 259 | 29,700 | Ψ George Town | 15,000 |
| Costa Rica | 19,575 | 50,700 | 3,000,000 | San José (u.a.) | 1,068,206 |
| Cuba | 42,804 | 110,861 | 10,736,000 | Ψ Havana | 2,096,000 |
| Dominica | 290 | 751 | 72,000 | Ψ Roseau | 15,850 |
| Dominican Republic | 18,816 | 48,734 | 7,321,000 | Ψ Santo Domingo (u.a.) | 1,313,172* |
| Grenada | 133 | 344 | 84,000 | Ψ St George's | 10,000 |
| Guadeloupe (Fr.) | 687 | 1,779 | 386,600 | Ψ Basse-Terre | 14,000 |
| Guatemala | 42,042 | 108,889 | 9,745,000 | Guatemala City | 1,675,589 |
| Haiti | 10,714 | 27,750 | 6,625,000 | Ψ Port au Prince | 1,000,000 |

| Country/Territory | Area sq. miles | Area sq. km | Population | Capital | Population of Capital |
|---|---|---|---|---|---|
| Honduras | 43,277 | 112,088 | 4,915,900 | Tegucigalpa | 670,100 |
| Jamaica | 4,244 | 10,991 | 2,460,700 | Ψ Kingston (u.a.) | 696,300 |
| Martinique (Fr.) | 425 | 1,102 | 359,800 | Ψ Fort de France | 101,540 |
| Montserrat (UK) | 38 | 98 | 11,000 | Ψ Plymouth | 2,500 |
| Netherlands Antilles (Neth.) | 371 | 961 | 189,000 | Ψ Willemstad | 50,000 |
| Nicaragua | 50,193 | 130,000 | 3,999,000 | Managua | 615,000 |
| Panama | 29,762 | 77,082 | 2,370,000 | Ψ Panama City | 1,063,565 |
| Puerto Rico (USA) | 3,435 | 8,897 | 3,336,000 | Ψ San Juan (u.a.) | 437,745 |
| St Christopher and Nevis | 101 | 261 | 44,000 | Ψ Basseterre | 15,000 |
| St Lucia | 238 | 616 | 153,000 | Ψ Castries | 56,000 |
| St Vincent and the Grenadines | 150 | 388 | 117,000 | Ψ Kingstown | 33,694 |
| El Salvador | 8,124 | 21,041 | 5,376,000 | San Salvador | 497,644 |
| Trinidad and Tobago | 1,981 | 5,130 | 1,253,000 | Ψ Port of Spain | 59,649 |
| Turks and Caicos Is. (UK) | 166 | 430 | 12,400 | Ψ Grand Turk | 3,700 |
| Virgin Islands: | | | | | |
| British (UK) | 59 | 153 | 16,108* | Ψ Road Town | 3,983* |
| US (USA) | 132 | 342 | 101,809 | Ψ Charlotte Amalie | 11,756 |
| *South America* | | | | | |
| Argentina | 1,068,302 | 2,766,889 | 32,370,298* | Ψ Buenos Aires | 2,955,002 |
| Bolivia | 424,165 | 1,098,581 | 6,440,000* | La Paz | 1,115,000* |
| Brazil | 3,286,488 | 8,511,965 | 150,368,000 | Brasilia | 1,803,478 |
| Chile | 292,258 | 756,945 | 13,386,000 | Santiago | 5,443,000 |
| Colombia | 439,737 | 1,138,914 | 33,613,000 | Bogotá | 5,000,000 |
| Ecuador | 109,484 | 283,561 | 10,851,000 | Quito | 1,387,887 |
| Falkland Islands (UK) | 4,700 | 12,173 | 2,121 | Ψ Stanley | 1,643 |
| French Guiana (Fr.) | 35,135 | 91,000 | 114,900 | Ψ Cayenne | 41,000 |
| Guyana | 83,000 | 214,969 | 800,000 | Ψ Georgetown | 187,056 |
| Paraguay | 157,048 | 406,752 | 4,397,000 | Asunción (u.a.) | 729,307 |
| Peru | 496,225 | 1,285,216 | 22,465,000 | Lima (u.a.) | 6,483,901 |
| South Georgia (UK) | 1,580 | 4,092 | — | | |
| Suriname | 63,037 | 163,265 | 429,000 | Ψ Paramaribo (u.a.) | 182,100 |
| Uruguay | 68,037 | 176,215 | 3,116,802 | Ψ Montevideo | 1,383,660 |
| Venezuela | 352,144 | 912,050 | 20,226,000 | Caracas (u.a.) | 2,784,000 |

## ASIA

| Country/Territory | Area sq. miles | Area sq. km | Population | Capital | Population of Capital |
|---|---|---|---|---|---|
| Afghanistan | 250,000 | 647,497 | 16,430,000 | Kabul | 2,000,000 |
| Bahrain | 240 | 622 | 516,000 | Ψ Manama | 108,684* |
| Bangladesh | 55,598 | 143,998 | 108,000,000 | Dhaka | 6,537,308 |
| Bhutan | 18,147 | 47,000 | 650,000 | Thimphu | 15,000 |
| Brunei | 2,226 | 5,765 | 260,863 | Bandar Seri Begawan | 46,229 |
| Cambodia | 69,898 | 181,035 | 8,442,000 | Ψ Phnom Penh | 920,000 |
| China[1] | 3,705,408 | 9,596,961 | 1,171,000,000 | Beijing (Peking) (u.a.) | 10,860,000 |
| Hong Kong (UK) | 416 | 1,074 | 5,900,000 | Ψ Victoria | — |
| India | 1,269,346 | 3,287,590 | 846,302,688 | Delhi | 8,375,188 |
| Indonesia | 735,358 | 1,904,569 | 187,765,000 | Ψ Jakarta | 7,885,519 |
| Iran | 636,296 | 1,648,000 | 55,762,000 | Tehran | 6,042,584 |
| Iraq | 167,925 | 434,924 | 19,581,000 | Baghdad | 3,205,665 |
| Israel[2] | 8,019 | 20,770 | 5,090,000 | Tel Aviv | 1,781,500 |
| Japan | 145,834 | 377,708 | 123,921,000 | Tokyo (u.a.) | 11,935,700 |
| Jordan | 37,738 | 97,740 | 4,145,000 | Amman | 1,270,000 |
| Kazakhstan | 1,049,155 | 2,716,626 | 16,963,600 | Alma Ata | 1,500,000 |
| Korea, DPR (North) | 46,540 | 120,538 | 23,193,000 | Pyongyang | 2,000,000 |
| Korea, Rep. of (South) | 38,025 | 98,484 | 43,268,000 | Seoul | 10,920,000 |
| Kuwait | 6,880 | 17,818 | 1,000,000 | Ψ Kuwait (city) | 400,000 |
| Kyrgyzstan | 76,642 | 198,501 | 4,500,000 | Biskek | 616,000 |
| Laos | 91,429 | 231,800 | 4,262,000 | Vientiane | 120,000 |
| Lebanon | 4,015 | 10,400 | 2,745,000 | Ψ Beirut | 702,000 |
| Macao (Port.) | 6 | 16 | 479,000 | Ψ Macao | — |
| Malaysia | 127,317 | 329,749 | 18,333,000 | Kuala Lumpur | 1,103,200 |
| Maldives | 115 | 298 | 238,000 | Ψ Malé | 46,334 |
| Mongolia | 604,250 | 1,565,000 | 2,156,000 | Ulan Bator | 600,500 |
| Myanmar (Burma) | 261,218 | 676,552 | 42,561,000 | Ψ Yangon (Rangoon) (u.a.) | 3,973,872 |
| Nepal | 54,342 | 140,747 | 19,605,000 | Kathmandu | 300,000 |

| COUNTRY/TERRITORY | AREA sq. miles | sq. km | POPULATION | CAPITAL | POPULATION OF CAPITAL |
|---|---|---|---|---|---|
| Oman | 82,030 | 212,457 | 1,559,000 | Ψ Muscat | 400,000 |
| Pakistan | 307,374 | 746,045 | 115,524,000 | Islamabad (u.a.) | 350,000 |
| Philippines | 115,831 | 300,000 | 62,868,000 | Ψ Manila | 1,876,195 |
| Qatar | 4,247 | 11,000 | 381,000 | Ψ Doha | 220,000 |
| Saudi Arabia | 830,000 | 2,149,640 | 16,929,294 | Riyadh | 2,000,000 |
| Singapore | 247 | 639 | 2,818,200 | — | — |
| Sri Lanka | 25,332 | 65,610 | 17,243,000 | Ψ Colombo | 1,963,000 |
| Syria | 71,498 | 185,180 | 12,993,000 | Damascus | 1,378,000 |
| Tajikistan | 55,251 | 143,100 | 5,513,400 | Dushanbe | 595,000 |
| Taiwan | 13,800 | 35,742 | 20,894,522 | Taipei | 2,719,659 |
| Thailand | 198,457 | 514,000 | 56,923,000 | Ψ Bangkok | 5,876,000 |
| Turkey[3] | 301,382 | 780,576 | 60,777,000 | Ankara | 3,236,626 |
| Turkmenistan | 188,456 | 488,100 | 3,809,000 | Ashkhabad | 398,000 |
| United Arab Emirates | 32,278 | 83,600 | 2,173,000 | Abu Dhabi | 450,000 |
| Uzbekistan | 172,742 | 447,229 | 21,206,000 | Tashkent | 2,073,000 |
| Vietnam | 127,242 | 329,556 | 71,267,000 | Hanoi | 2,150,000 |
| Yemen | 203,850 | 527,696 | 12,302,000 | Sana'a | 427,150 |

[1] Including Tibet
[2] Including East Jerusalem, the Golan Heights and Israeli citizens on the West Bank
[3] Including Turkey in Europe

## EUROPE

| COUNTRY/TERRITORY | sq. miles | sq. km | POPULATION | CAPITAL | POPULATION OF CAPITAL |
|---|---|---|---|---|---|
| Albania | 11,099 | 28,748 | 3,331,000 | Tirana | 239,381 |
| Andorra | 180 | 468 | 58,000 | Andorra La Vella | 22,205 |
| Armenia | 11,306 | 29,271 | 3,645,000 | Erevan | 1,119,000 |
| Austria | 32,374 | 83,849 | 8,000,000 | Vienna | 1,539,848* |
| Azerbaijan | 33,436 | 86,565 | 7,409,900 | Baku | 1,757,000 |
| Belarus | 80,300 | 207,897 | 10,260,000 | Minsk | 1,589,000 |
| Belgium | 11,781 | 30,513 | 10,054,559 | Brussels (u.a.) | 960,324* |
| Bosnia–Hercegovina | 19,735 | 51,129 | 4,100,000 | Sarajevo | 447,000 |
| Bulgaria | 42,823 | 110,912 | 8,982,000 | Sofia | 1,114,925 |
| Croatia | 21,823 | 56,538 | 4,760,344 | Zagreb | 950,000 |
| Cyprus | 3,572 | 9,251 | 725,000 | Nicosia | 181,000 |
| Czech Republic | 30,372 | 78,664 | 10,302,000 | Prague | 1,215,076 |
| Denmark | 16,629 | 43,069 | 5,180,614 | Ψ Copenhagen (u.a.) | 1,339,395 |
| Faroe Islands | 540 | 1,399 | 47,287 | Ψ Thorshavn | 10,726 |
| Estonia | 17,413 | 45,082 | 1,526,177 | Talinn | 452,840 |
| Finland | 137,851 | 337,032 | 5,029,000 | Ψ Helsinki | 492,200 |
| France | 211,208 | 547,026 | 56,893,000 | Paris (u.a.) | 9,318,800 |
| Georgia | 26,911 | 69,673 | 5,401,000 | Tbilisi | 1,211,000 |
| Germany | 137,738 | 365,755 | 81,075,000 | Berlin | 3,437,900 |
| Gibraltar (UK) | 2 | 6 | 28,848 | Ψ Gibraltar | — |
| Greece | 50,944 | 131,944 | 10,256,464 | Athens (u.a.) | 3,096,775 |
| Hungary | 35,919 | 93,030 | 10,278,000 | Budapest | 2,004,000 |
| Iceland | 39,768 | 103,000 | 264,922 | Ψ Reykjavik (u.a.) | 100,185 |
| Ireland, Republic of | 27,136 | 70,283 | 3,525,719 | Ψ Dublin | 478,389 |
| Italy | 116,304 | 301,225 | 57,052,000 | Rome (u.a.) | 2,693,383 |
| Latvia | 24,695 | 63,935 | 2,606,000 | Riga | 874,500 |
| Liechtenstein | 61 | 157 | 29,868 | Vaduz | 4,995 |
| Lithuania | 26,173 | 67,761 | 3,724,000 | Vilnius | 579,000 |
| Luxembourg | 998 | 2,586 | 395,200 | Luxembourg | 75,800 |
| Macedonia | 9,925 | 25,713 | 2,034,000 | Skopje | 448,229 |
| Malta | 122 | 316 | 366,541 | Ψ Valletta | 9,149 |
| Moldova | 13,912 | 36,018 | 4,359,000 | Kishinev | 665,000 |
| Monaco | 0.4 | 1 | 28,000 | Monaco-Ville | 1,234 |
| Netherlands | 15,770 | 40,844 | 15,240,000 | Ψ Amsterdam (u.a.) | 1,034,562 |
| Norway[1] | 125,181 | 324,219 | 4,299,167 | Ψ Oslo | 473,344 |
| Poland | 120,725 | 312,677 | 38,300,000 | Warsaw | 1,655,063 |
| Portugal[2] | 35,553 | 92,082 | 9,862,700 | Ψ Lisbon | 2,128,000 |
| Romania | 91,699 | 237,500 | 22,760,449 | Bucharest | 2,064,474 |
| Russia[3] | 6,593,391 | 17,070,289 | 148,704,300 | Moscow | 8,967,000 |
| San Marino | 23 | 61 | 24,000 | San Marino | — |
| Slovak Republic | 18,932 | 49,035 | 5,274,335 | Bratislava | 440,421 |
| Slovenia | 7,816 | 20,251 | 2,020,000 | Ljubljana | 268,000 |

| COUNTRY/TERRITORY | AREA sq. miles | sq. km | POPULATION | CAPITAL | POPULATION OF CAPITAL |
|---|---|---|---|---|---|
| Spain[4] | 194,897 | 504,782 | 38,872,268 | Madrid (u.a.) | 4,947,555 |
| Sweden | 173,732 | 449,964 | 8,635,000 | Ψ Stockholm (u.a.) | 669,485 |
| Switzerland | 15,943 | 41,293 | 6,833,750 | Berne | 135,600 |
| Ukraine | 233,090 | 603,700 | 52,100,000 | Kiev | 2,577,000 |
| United Kingdom[5] | 94,248 | 244,101 | 56,467,000* | Ψ London (u.a.) | 6,679,699 |
| England | 50,351 | 130,410 | 46,382,050* | — | — |
| Wales | 8,015 | 20,758 | 2,811,865* | Ψ Cardiff | 290,000 |
| Scotland | 30,420 | 78,789 | 4,998,567* | Ψ Edinburgh | 418,914 |
| Northern Ireland | 5,461 | 14,144 | 1,577,836* | Ψ Belfast (u.a.) | 287,100 |
| Vatican City State | 0.2 | 0.44 | 1,000 | Vatican City | — |
| Yugoslavia, Fed. Rep. of | 39,506 | 102,350 | 10,410,000 | Belgrade | 1,455,000 |

[1] Excludes Svalbard and Jan Mayen Islands (approx. 24,101 sq. miles (62,422 sq. km) and 3,000 population)
[2] Includes Madeira (314 sq. miles) and the Azores (922 sq. miles)
[3] Includes Russia in Asia
[4] Includes Balearic Islands, Canary Islands, Ceuta and Melilla
[5] Excludes Isle of Man (221 sq. miles (572 sq. km), 69,788* population), and Channel Islands (75 sq. miles (194 sq. km), 142,949* population)

## OCEANIA

| | AREA sq. miles | sq. km | POPULATION | CAPITAL | POPULATION OF CAPITAL |
|---|---|---|---|---|---|
| Australia | 2,967,909 | 7,686,848 | 17,746,600 | Canberra | 296,400 |
| Norfolk Island | 14 | 36 | 1,912 | Ψ Kingston | — |
| Fiji | 7,055 | 18,274 | 776,000 | Ψ Suva | 69,665 |
| French Polynesia (Fr.) | 1,544 | 4,000 | 206,000 | Ψ Papeete | 24,200 |
| Guam (USA) | 212 | 549 | 132,152 | Agaña | — |
| Kiribati | 281 | 728 | 68,000 | Tarawa | 17,921 |
| Marshall Islands | 70 | 181 | 45,569 | Majuro | 20,000 |
| Micronesia, Fed. States of | 271 | 701 | 101,000 | Palikir | — |
| Nauru | 8 | 21 | 9,000 | Ψ Nauru | — |
| New Caledonia (Fr.) | 7,358 | 19,058 | 167,000 | Ψ Noumea | 65,000 |
| New Zealand | 103,736 | 268,676 | 3,494,300 | Ψ Wellington (u.a.) | 325,682 |
| Cook Islands | 91 | 236 | 18,300 | Avarua | — |
| Niue | 100 | 259 | 2,239 | Alofi | — |
| Ross Dependency[1] | 286,696 | 750,310 | — | — | — |
| Tokelau | 5 | 12.9 | 1,700 | — | — |
| Northern Mariana Islands (USA) | 184 | 476 | 43,555 | Saipan | 39,090 |
| Palau (USA) | 192 | 497 | 15,105 | Koror | 10,493 |
| Papua New Guinea | 178,260 | 461,691 | 3,772,000 | Ψ Port Moresby | 173,500 |
| Pitcairn Islands (UK) | 1.9 | 5 | 65 | — | — |
| Samoa, Eastern (USA) | 76 | 197 | 46,773 | Ψ Pago Pago | 3,075 |
| Solomon Islands | 10,983 | 28,446 | 328,723 | Ψ Honiara | 40,000 |
| Tonga | 270 | 699 | 94,000 | Ψ Nuku'alofa | 30,000 |
| Tuvalu | 10 | 25 | 9,000 | Ψ Funafuti | 2,856 |
| Vanuatu | 4,706 | 12,190 | 163,000 | Ψ Port Vila | 19,400 |
| Wallis and Futuna Islands (Fr.) | 106 | 274 | 13,705 | Ψ Mata-Utu | — |
| Western Samoa | 1,097 | 2,842 | 162,000 | Ψ Apia | 36,000 |

[1] Includes permanent shelf ice

## THE ANTARCTIC

The Antarctic is generally defined as the area lying within the Antarctic Convergence, the zone where cold northward-flowing Antarctic sea water sinks below warmer southward-flowing water. This zone is at about latitude 50° S. in the Atlantic Ocean and latitude 55°–62° S. in the Pacific Ocean. The continent itself lies almost entirely within the Antarctic Circle, an area of about 14.25 million square km (5.5 million square miles), 99 per cent of which is permanently ice-covered. The average thickness of the ice is 2,450 m (7,100 ft) but in places exceeds 4,500 m (14,500 ft). Some mountains protrude, the highest being Vinson Massif, 4,897 m (16,067 ft). The ice amounts to some 30 million cubic km (7.2 million cubic miles) and represents more than 90 per cent of the world's fresh water.

Along one-third of the Antarctic coastline, land-ice flowing outwards forms extensive ice shelves, fragments of which break off to form tabular icebergs, leaving ice-cliffs up to 50 m (150 ft) high. Much of the sea freezes in winter, forming fast ice which breaks up in summer and drifts north as pack ice.

The most conspicuous physical features of the continent are its high inland plateau (much of it over 3,000 m (10,000 ft)), the Transantarctic Mountains (which together with the large embayments of the Weddell Sea and Ross Sea mark the approximate boundary between East and West Antarctica), and the mountainous Antarctic Peninsula and off-lying islands which extend northwards towards South America. The continental shelf averages about 32 km (20 miles) in width (half the global mean, and in places it is non-existent) and reaches exceptional depths (390–780 m (1,300–2,600 ft), which is three to six times the global mean).

### CLIMATE

On land, summer temperatures range from just below freezing around the coast to −34° C (about −30° F) on the plateau, and in winter from −20° C (about −4° F) on the coast to −65° C (about −85° F) inland. Over a large area the maxima do not exceed −15° C (+5° F).

Precipitation is scanty over the plateau but amounts to 25–76 cm (10–30 in) (water equivalent) along the coast and some scientific stations are permanently buried by snow. Some rain falls over the more northerly areas in summer. Gravity winds on the plateau slopes and cyclonic storms further north can both exceed 160 km/h (100 m.p.h.) and gusts have been known to reach 240 km/h (150 m.p.h.). Visibility can be reduced to zero in blizzards.

### FLORA AND FAUNA

Although a small number of flowering plants, ferns and clubmosses occur on the sub-Antarctic islands, only two (a grass and a pearlwort) extend south of 60° S. Antarctic vegetation is dominated by lichens and mosses, with a few liverworts, algae and fungi. Most of these occur around the coast or on islands, but lichens and some mosses also occur inland.

The only land animals are tiny insects and mites with nematodes, rotifers, and tardigrades in the mosses, but large numbers of seals, penguins and other sea-birds go ashore to breed in the summer. The emperor penguin is the only species which breeds ashore throughout the winter. By contrast, the Antarctic seas abound with life, a wide variety of invertebrates (including krill) and fish providing food for the seals, penguins and other birds, and a residual population of whales.

On 26 May 1994 the International Whaling Commission agreed to establish a whale sanctuary around Antarctica in which commercial whaling will be banned for ten years. The sanctuary will cover all sea areas south of 60°S. latitude, apart from the south-west Atlantic and south-east Pacific where it will be south of 40°S. latitude.

### POTENTIAL RESOURCES

In the 180 years from Captain James Cook's circumnavigation of the Antarctic in 1772–5 to the mid-1950s, expeditions to the Antarctic made major contributions to geographical and scientific knowledge of the area.

Increasing pressure on the world's food and mineral supplies has stimulated interest in the potential resources even in the extremely hostile polar environment. Minerals may be present in great variety but not in commercially exploitable concentrations in accessible localities. There are indications that off-shore hydrocarbons may be present but mostly below great depths of stormy, ice-infested seas.

Currently, the chief interest is in marine protein, including the shrimp-like krill already fished commercially by Japan and Poland. Research to ensure rational management of stocks of this organism is being continued by international groups, but it is estimated that they could sustain a yield equal to the present total annual world fish catch.

### THE ANTARCTIC TREATY

The International Geophysical Year 1957–8 gave great impetus to Antarctic research, increasing the number of stations from 17 to 44 and the number of nations involved in research from four to 12 by 1957. The co-operative scientific effort proved so fruitful that the 12 nations involved (Argentina, Australia, Belgium, Chile, France, Japan, New Zealand, Norway, South Africa, the USSR, the UK and the USA) pledged themselves to promote scientific and technical co-operation unhampered by politics, and the Antarctic Treaty was signed by the 12 states in 1959.

The 12 signatories to the treaty agreed to establish free use of the Antarctic continent for peaceful scientific purposes; to freeze all territorial claims and disputes in the Antarctic; to ban all military activities in the area; and to prohibit nuclear explosions and the disposal of radioactive waste. Since then additional agreements have been reached to promote conservation and restrict tourism, waste disposal and pollution.

The Antarctic Treaty was defined as covering areas south of latitude 60° S., excluding the high seas but including the ice shelves, and came into force in 1961. It has since been signed by a further 28 states, 14 of which are active in the Antarctic and have therefore been accorded consultative status, bringing the number of consultative parties to 26. In 1991 a protocol to the treaty was adopted by the signatory states which introduced a range of measures to protect Antarctica's environment and prohibit mineral exploitation and mining for at least 50 years.

### TERRITORIAL CLAIMS

Under the provisions of the Antarctic Treaty of 1959 all territorial claims and disputes were frozen without the acceptance or denial of the claims of the various claimants. The US and Soviet governments also made it clear that although they had not made any specific territorial claims, they did not relinquish the right to make such claims.

Seven states have made claims in the Antarctic: Argentina claims the part of Antarctica between 74° W. and 25° W.;

Chile that part between 90° W. and 53° W.; Britain claims the British Antarctic Territory, an area of 1,810,000 sq. km (700,000 sq. miles) between 20° and 80° W. longitude; France claims Adélie Land, 432,000 sq. km (166,800 sq. miles) between 136° and 142° E.; Australia claims the Australian Antarctic Territory, 6,120,000 sq. km (2,320,000 sq. miles) between 160° and 45° E. longitude excluding Adélie Land; Norway claims Queen Maud Land between 20° W. and 45° E.; and New Zealand claims the Ross Dependency, 450,000 sq. km (175,000 sq. miles) between 160° E. and 150° W. longitude. The Argentinian, British and Chilean claims overlap while the part of the continent between 90° W. and 150° W. is unclaimed by any state.

SCIENTIFIC RESEARCH

There are over 40 permanently occupied stations operated by the following nations: Argentina (6), Australia (4), Brazil (1), Chile (3), China (2), France (4), Germany (1), India (1), Japan (2), New Zealand (2), Poland (1), Russia (5), South Africa (3), South Korea (1), Uruguay (1), UK (5), USA (3, including one at the South Pole).

The staff of these stations and summer field-workers are the only people present on the continent and off-lying islands. There are no indigenous inhabitants.

## LARGEST CITIES OF THE WORLD

In most cases figures refer to urban agglomerations.

| | Population | | Population |
|---|---|---|---|
| Mexico City, Mexico | 14,987,051 | Moscow, Russia | 8,967,000 |
| Cairo, Egypt | 14,000,000 | Delhi, India | 8,375,188 |
| Ψ Shanghai, China | 12,760,000 | Ψ Jakarta, Indonesia | 7,885,519 |
| Ψ Bombay, India | 12,571,720 | Ψ New York, USA | 7,322,564 |
| Tokyo, Japan | 11,718,720 | Ψ Istanbul, Turkey | 7,309,190 |
| Seoul, South Korea | 10,920,000 | Ψ Karachi, Pakistan | 7,183,000 |
| Ψ Calcutta, India | 10,916,272 | Manila, Philippines | 6,720,050 |
| Beijing, China | 10,860,000 | Ψ London, UK | 6,679,699 |
| São Paulo, Brazil | 10,063,110 | Rio de Janeiro, Brazil | 6,603,388 |
| Paris, France | 9,318,800 | Dhaka, Bangladesh | 6,537,308 |

# Currencies of the World

AND EXCHANGE RATES AGAINST £ STERLING

Franc CFA = Franc de la Communauté financière africaine
Franc CFP = Franc des Comptoirs français du Pacifique

| COUNTRY/TERRITORY | MONETARY UNIT | AVERAGE RATE TO £ 27 August 1993 | AVERAGE RATE TO £ 2 September 1994 |
|---|---|---|---|
| Afghanistan | Afghani (Af) of 100 puls | Af 2115.75 | Af 4014.40 |
| Albania | Lek (Lk) of 100 qindarka | Lk 165.99 | Lk 154.400 |
| Algeria | Algerian dinar (DA) of 100 centimes | DA 29.787 | DA 59.5468 |
| American Samoa | Currency is that of USA | US$ 1.5005 | US$ 1.5448 |
| Andorra | French and Spanish currencies in use | — | — |
| Angola | New Kwanza (Kz) of 100 lwei | Kz 5996.70 | Kz 146577.5 |
| Anguilla | East Caribbean dollar (EC$) of 100 cents | EC$ 4.07 | EC$ 4.1688 |
| Antigua and Barbuda | East Caribbean dollar (EC$) of 100 cents | EC$ 4.07 | EC$ 4.1688 |
| Argentina | Peso of 10,000 australes | Pesos 1.5107 | Pesos 1.5107 |
| Armenia | Dram of 100 Couma | Roubles 0.8720 | — |
| Aruba | Aruban florin | Florins 2.7011 | Florins 2.7638 |
| Australia | Australian dollar ($A) of 100 cents | $A 2.2625 | $A 2.0804 |
| Austria | Schilling of 100 Groschen | Schilling 17.555 | Schilling 17.0657 |
| Azerbaijan | Manat of 100 gopik | Roubles 0.8720 | — |
| Bahamas | Bahamian dollar (B$) of 100 cents | B$ 1.5005 | B$ 1.5448 |
| Bahrain | Bahrain dinar (BD) of 1,000 fils | BD 0.5689 | BD 0.5824 |
| Bangladesh | Taka (Tk) of 100 paisa | Tk 59.58 | Tk 61.0177 |
| Barbados | Barbados dollar (BD$) of 100 cents | BD$ 3.0351 | BD$ 3.1054 |
| Belarus | Rouble of 100 kopeks | Roubles 0.8720 | Roubles 1.0821 |
| Belgium | Belgian franc (or frank) of 100 centimes (centiemen) | Francs 53.25 | Francs 49.6638 |
| Belize | Belize dollar (BZ$) of 100 cents | BZ$ 3.0180 | BZ$ 3.0880 |
| Benin | Franc CFA | Francs 437.375 | Francs 826.440 |
| Bermuda | Bermuda dollar of 100 cents | $ 1.5005 | $ 1.5448 |
| Bhutan | Ngultrum of 100 chetrum (Indian currency is also legal tender) | Ngultrum 47.2619 | Ngultrum 48.4588 |
| Bolivia | Boliviano ($b) of 100 centavos | $b 6.5113 | $b 7.2140 |
| Bosnia-Hercegovina | Dinar of 100 paras | Dinars 158.445 | — |
| Botswana | Pula (P) of 100 thebe | P 3.7416 | P 4.2208 |
| Brazil | Real of 100 centavos | BRC 139.025 | Real 1.3687 |
| British Virgin Islands | US dollar (US$) (£ sterling and EC$ also circulate) | US$ 1.5005 | US$ 1.5448 |
| Brunei | Brunei dollar of 100 sen (fully inter-changeable with Singapore currency) | $ 2.4107 | $ 2.3168 |
| Bulgaria | Lev of 100 stotinki | Leva 39.55 | Leva 87.5216 |
| Burkina | Franc CFA | Francs 437.375 | Francs 826.440 |
| Burundi | Burundi franc of 100 centimes | Francs 366.50 | Francs 382.60 |
| Cambodia | Riel of 100 sen | Riel 5432.40 | Riel 5404.00 |
| Cameroon | Franc CFA | Francs 437.375 | Francs 826.440 |
| Canada | Canadian dollar (C$) of 100 cents | C$ 1.9770 | C$ 2.1115 |
| Cape Verde | Escudo Caboverdiano of 100 centavos | Esc 111.96 | Esc 130.337 |
| Cayman Islands | Cayman Islands dollar (CI$) of 100 cents | CI$ 1.2827 | CI$ 1.2661 |
| Central African Republic | Franc CFA | Francs 437.375 | Francs 826.440 |
| Chad | Franc CFA | Francs 437.375 | Francs 826.440 |
| Chile | Chilean peso of 100 centavos | Pesos 616.80 | Pesos 642.693 |
| China | Renminbi Yuan of 10 jiao or 100 fen | Yuan 8.6655 | Yuan 13.2138 |
| Christmas Island | Currency is that of Australia | $A 2.2625 | $A 2.0804 |
| Cocos (Keeling) Islands | Currency is that of Australia | $A 2.2625 | $A 2.0804 |
| Colombia | Colombian peso of 100 centavos | Pesos 1218.92 | Pesos 1266.23 |
| Comoros | Franc CFA/Franc | Francs 437.375 | Francs 612.837 |
| Congo | Franc CFA | Francs 437.375 | Francs 826.440 |
| Cook Islands | Currency is that of New Zealand | NZ$ 2.7325 | NZ$ 2.5527 |
| Costa Rica | Costa Rican colón (₡) of 100 céntimos | ₡ 216.82 | ₡ 242.779 |
| Côte d'Ivoire | Franc CFA | Francs 437.375 | Francs 826.440 |

| Country/Territory | Monetary Unit | Average Rate to £ 27 August 1993 | Average Rate to £ 2 September 1994 |
|---|---|---|---|
| Croatia | Kuna of 100 lipas | Dinars 6713.70 | Kuna 8.9762 |
| Cuba | Cuban peso of 100 centavos | Pesos 1.1429 | Pesos 1.1694 |
| Cyprus | Cyprus pound (C£) of 100 cents | C£ 0.7703 | C£ 0.7400 |
| Czech Republic | Koruna (Kčs) of 100 haléřu | Kčs 44.268 | Kčs 43.6830 |
| Denmark | Danish krone of 100 øre | Kroner 10.3075 | Kroner 9.5243 |
| Djibouti | Djibouti franc of 100 centimes | Francs 265.75 | Francs 274.400 |
| Dominica | East Caribbean dollar (EC$) of 100 cents | EC$ 4.07 | EC$ 4.1688 |
| Dominican Republic | Dominican Republic peso (RD$) of 100 centavos | RD$ 19.617 | RD$ 20.2882 |
| Ecuador | Sucre of 100 centavos | Sucres 2791.65 | Sucres 3223.87 |
| Egypt | Egyptian pound (£E) of 100 piastres or 1,000 millièmes | £E 4.9695 | £E 5.2322 |
| Equatorial Guinea | Franc CFA | Francs 437.375 | Francs 826.440 |
| Eritrea | Ethiopian currency is in use | EB 7.4621 | EB 8.4766 |
| Estonia | Kroon of 100 sents | Kroons 20.05 | Kroons 19.4760 |
| Ethiopia | Ethiopian birr (EB) of 100 cents | EB 7.4621 | EB 8.4766 |
| Falkland Islands | Falkland pound of 100 pence | *at parity with £ sterling* | *at parity with £ sterling* |
| Faroe Islands | Currency is that of Denmark | Kroner 10.3075 | Kroner 9.5243 |
| Fiji | Fiji dollar (F$) of 100 cents | F$ 2.3040 | F$ 2.2315 |
| Finland | Markka (Mk) of 100 penniä | Mk 8.770 | Mk 7.7933 |
| France | Franc of 100 centimes | Francs 8.7475 | Francs 8.2644 |
| French Guiana | Currency is that of France | Francs 8.7475 | Francs 8.2644 |
| French Polynesia | Franc CFP | Francs 159.50 | Francs 148.566 |
| Gabon | Franc CFA | Francs 437.375 | Francs 826.440 |
| Gambia | Dalasi (D) of 100 butut | D 14.0337 | D 14.9768 |
| Georgia | Georgian Coupon | Roubles 0.8720 | — |
| Germany | Deutsche Mark (DM) of 100 Pfennig | DM 2.5000 | DM 2.4101 |
| Ghana | Cedi of 100 pesewas | Cedi 995.00 | Cedi 1505.40 |
| Gibraltar | Gibraltar pound of 100 pence | *at parity with £ sterling* | *at parity with £ sterling* |
| Greece | Drachma of 100 leptae | Drachmae 354.875 | Drachmae 368.655 |
| Greenland | Currency is that of Denmark | Kroner 10.3075 | Kroner 9.5243 |
| Grenada | East Caribbean dollar (EC$) of 100 cents | EC$ 4.07 | EC$ 4.1688 |
| Guadeloupe | Currency is that of France | Francs 8.7475 | Francs 8.2644 |
| Guam | Currency is that of USA | US$ 1.5005 | US$ 1.5448 |
| Guatemala | Quetzal (Q) of 100 centavos | Q 8.7109 | Q 8.8369 |
| Guinea | Guinea franc of 100 centimes | Francs 1225.75 | Francs 1508.01 |
| Guinea-Bissau | Guinea-Bissau peso of 100 centavos | Pesos 7545.00 | Pesos 18983.5 |
| Guyana | Guyana dollar (G$) of 100 cents | G$ 190.13 | G$ 217.395 |
| Haiti | Gourde of 100 centimes | Gourdes 18.108 | Gourdes 29.3360 |
| Honduras | Lempira of 100 centavos | Lempiras 10.5175 | Lempiras 13.7416 |
| Hong Kong | Hong Kong dollar (HK$) of 100 cents | HK$ 11.6438 | HK$ 11.9364 |
| Hungary | Forint of 100 fillér | Forints 143.14 | Forints 165.736 |
| Iceland | Icelandic króna (Kr) of 100 aurar | Kr 106.64 | Kr 105.31 |
| India | Indian rupee (Rs) of 100 paisa | Rs 47.2619 | Rs 48.4588 |
| Indonesia | Rupiah (Rp) of 100 sen | Rp 3182.00 | Rp 3361.61 |
| Iran | Rial | Rials 2310.00 | Rials 2682.50 |
| Iraq | Iraqi dinar (ID) of 1,000 fils | ID 0.4690 | ID 0.4800 |
| Ireland, Republic of | Punt (IR£) of 100 pence | IR£ 1.0700 | IR£ 1.0086 |
| Israel | Shekel of 100 agora | Shekels 4.34 | Shekels 4.6645 |
| Italy | Lira of 100 centesimi | Lire 2391.75 | Lire 2432.83 |
| Jamaica | Jamaican dollar (J$) of 100 cents | J$ 36.216 | J$ 51.7240 |
| Japan | Yen of 100 sen | Yen 156.00 | Yen 153.541 |
| Jordan | Jordanian dinar (JD) of 1,000 fils | JD 1.0472 | JD 1.0798 |
| Kazakhstan | Tenge | Roubles 0.8720 | — |
| Kenya | Kenya shilling (Ksh) of 100 cents | Ksh 98.537 | Ksh 84.0399 |
| Kiribati | Australian dollar ($A) of 100 cents | $A 2.2625 | $A 2.0804 |
| Korea, North | Won of 100 jun | Won 3.2444 | Won 3.3196 |
| Korea, South | Won of 100 jeon | Won 1221.325 | Won 1236.96 |
| Kuwait | Kuwaiti dinar (KD) of 1,000 fils | KD 0.4500 | KD 0.4607 |
| Kyrgyzstan | Som | Roubles 0.8720 | — |
| Laos | Kip (K) of 100 at | K 1086.48 | K 1111.68 |
| Latvia | Lats of 100 santimes | Lats 0.9374 | Lats 0.8481 |
| Lebanon | Lebanese pound (L£) of 100 piastres | L£ 2606.15 | L£ 2580.51 |

| Country/Territory | Monetary Unit | Average Rate to £ 27 August 1993 | Average Rate to £ 2 September 1994 |
|---|---|---|---|
| Lesotho | Loti (M) of 100 lisente | M 5.0550 | M 5.5260 |
| Liberia | Liberian dollar (L$) of 100 cents | L$ 1.5005 | L$ 1.5448 |
| Libya | Libyan dinar (LD) of 1,000 dirhams | LD 0.4470 | LD 0.4717 |
| Liechtenstein | Swiss franc of 100 rappen (or centimes) | Francs 2.2075 | Francs 2.0260 |
| Lithuania | Litas | Roubles 0.8720 | Litas 6.1760 |
| Luxembourg | Luxembourg franc (LF) of 100 centimes (Belgian currency is also legal tender) | LF 53.25 | LF 49.6638 |
| Macao | Pataca of 100 avos | Pataca 12.0790 | Pataca 12.3275 |
| Macedonia, Former Yugoslav Rep. | Dinar of 100 paras | Dinars 158.445 | — |
| Madagascar | Franc malgache (FMG) of 100 centimes | FMG 2859.15 | FMG 5430.25 |
| Malawi | Kwacha (K) of 100 tambala | K 6.5755 | K 12.4717 |
| Malaysia | Malaysian dollar (ringgit) (M$) of 100 sen | M$ 3.8305 | M$ 3.9415 |
| Maldives | Rufiyaa of 100 laaris | Rufiyaa 18.0705 | Rufiyaa 17.9104 |
| Mali | Franc CFA | Francs 437.375 | Francs 826.440 |
| Malta | Maltese lira (LM) of 100 cents or 1,000 mils | LM 0.5837 | LM 0.5731 |
| Marshall Islands | Currency is that of USA | US$ 1.5005 | US$ 1.5448 |
| Martinique | Currency is that of France | Francs 8.7475 | Francs 8.2644 |
| Mauritania | Ouguiya (UM) of 5 khoums | UM 171.74 | UM 189.047 |
| Mauritius | Mauritius rupee of 100 cents | Rs 27.17 | Rs 27.5218 |
| Mayotte | Currency is that of France | Francs 9.7475 | Francs 8.2644 |
| Mexico | Peso of 100 centavos | Pesos 4.6970 | Pesos 5.2283 |
| Moldova | Leu | Roubles 0.8720 | — |
| Monaco | French franc of 100 centimes | Francs 8.7475 | Francs 8.2644 |
| Mongolia | Tugrik of 100 möngö | Tugriks 603.60 | Tugriks 617.600 |
| Montserrat | East Caribbean dollar (EC$) of 100 cents | EC$ 4.07 | EC$ 4.1688 |
| Morocco | Dirham (DH) of 100 centimes | DH 13.9065 | DH 13.9873 |
| Mozambique | Metical (MT) of 100 centavos | MT 6165.34 | MT 9680.70 |
| Myanmar (Burma) | Kyat (K) of 100 pyas | K 9.4750 | K 8.9904 |
| Namibia | Namibian dollar of 100 cents | R 5.0550 | — |
| Nauru | Australian dollar ($A) of 100 cents | $A 2.2625 | $A 2.0804 |
| Nepal | Nepalese rupee of 100 paisa | Rs 69.2405 | Rs 76.0420 |
| Netherlands | Gulden (guilder) or florin of 100 cents | Guilders 2.8100 | Guilders 2.7041 |
| Netherlands Antilles | Netherlands Antilles guilder of 100 cents | Guilders 2.7010 | Guilders 2.7638 |
| New Caledonia | Franc CFP | Francs 159.50 | Francs 148.566 |
| New Zealand | New Zealand dollar (NZ$) of 100 cents | NZ$ 2.7325 | NZ$ 2.5527 |
| Nicaragua | Córdoba (C$) of 100 centavos | C$ 9.3340 | C$ 10.5526 |
| Niger | Franc CFA | Francs 437.375 | Francs 826.440 |
| Nigeria | Naira (N) of 100 kobo | N 37.725 | N 33.9845 |
| Niue | Currency is that of New Zealand | NZ$ 2.7325 | NZ$ 2.5527 |
| Norfolk Island | Currency is that of Australia | $A 2.2625 | $A 2.0804 |
| Northern Mariana Islands | Currency is that of USA | US$ 1.5005 | US$ 1.5448 |
| Norway | Krone of 100 øre | Kroner 10.8775 | Kroner 10.5718 |
| Oman | Rial Omani (OR) of 1,000 baiza | OR 0.5810 | OR 0.5948 |
| Pakistan | Pakistan rupee of 100 paisa | Rs 45.1340 | Rs 47.2993 |
| Palau | Currency is that of USA | US$ 1.5005 | US$ 1.5448 |
| Panama | Balboa of 100 centésimos (US notes are also in circulation) | Balboa 1.5005 | Balboa 1.5448 |
| Papua New Guinea | Kina (K) of 100 toea | K 1.4745 | K 1.4212 |
| Paraguay | Guaraní (Gs) of 100 céntimos | Gs 2640.75 | Gs 2945.18 |
| Peru | New Sol of 100 cénts | New Sol 3.0655 | New Sol 3.4865 |
| Philippines | Philippine peso (P) of 100 centavos | P 41.70 | P 40.7043 |
| Poland | Złoty of 100 groszy | Złotys 29680.0 | Złotys 35506.1 |
| Portugal | Escudo (Esc) of 100 centavos | Esc 255.20 | Esc 247.191 |
| Puerto Rico | Currency is that of USA | US$ 1.5005 | US$ 1.5448 |
| Qatar | Qatar riyal of 100 dirhams | Riyals 5.4930 | Riyals 5.6202 |
| Réunion | Currency is that of France | Francs 8.7475 | Francs 8.2644 |
| Romania | Leu (Lei) of 100 bani | Lei 1218.77 | Lei 2616.00 |
| Russia | Rouble of 100 kopeks | Roubles 0.8720 | Roubles 1.0821 |
| Rwanda | Rwanda franc of 100 centimes | Francs 214.10 | Francs 216.20 |
| St Christopher and Nevis | East Caribbean dollar (EC$) of 100 cents | EC$ 4.07 | EC$ 4.1688 |

| Country/Territory | Monetary Unit | Average Rate to £ 27 August 1993 | Average Rate to £ 2 September 1994 |
|---|---|---|---|
| St Helena | St Helena pound (£) of 100 pence | *at parity with £ sterling* | *at parity with £ sterling* |
| St Lucia | East Caribbean dollar (EC$) of 100 cents | EC$ 4.07 | EC$ 4.1688 |
| St Pierre and Miquelon | Currency is that of France | Francs 8.7475 | Francs 8.2644 |
| St Vincent and the Grenadines | East Caribbean dollar (EC$) of 100 cents | EC$ 4.07 | EC$ 4.1688 |
| El Salvador | El Salvador colón (₡) of 100 centavos | ₡ 13.1358 | ₡ 13.5100 |
| San Marino | Italian currency is in circulation | Lire 2391.75 | Lire 2432.83 |
| São Tomé and Príncipe | Dobra of 100 centavos | Dobra 362.16 | Dobra 1060.02 |
| Saudi Arabia | Saudi riyal (SR) of 20 qursh or 100 halala | SR 5.6342 | SR 5.7935 |
| Senegal | Franc CFA | Francs 437.375 | Francs 826.440 |
| Seychelles | Seychelles rupee of 100 cents | Rs 7.7410 | Rs 7.6737 |
| Sierra Leone | Leone (Le) of 100 cents | Le 829.95 | Le 903.240 |
| Singapore | Singapore dollar (S$) of 100 cents | S$ 2.4107 | S$ 2.3168 |
| Slovak Republic | Koruna (Kčs) of 100 haléřu | Kčs 48.93 | Kčs 48.5255 |
| Slovenia | Tolar (SIT) of 100 stotin | Tolars 180.1980 | Tolars 186.886 |
| Solomon Islands | Solomon Islands dollar (SI$) of 100 cents | SI$ 4.8005 | SI$ 5.0392 |
| Somalia | Somali shilling of 100 cents | Shillings 3931.30 | Shillings 4045.28 |
| South Africa | Rand (R) of 100 cents | R 5.0550 | R 5.5260 |
| Spain | Peseta of 100 céntimos | Pesetas 203.60 | Pesetas 200.200 |
| Sri Lanka | Sri Lankan rupee of 100 cents | Rs 73.2010 | Rs 76.0712 |
| Sudan | Sudanese dinar (SD) of 10 pounds | SD 19.6170 | SD 48.0184 |
| Suriname | Suriname guilder of 100 cents | Guilders 2.6935 | Guilders 282.737 |
| Swaziland | Lilangeni (E) of 100 cents (South African currency also in circulation) | E 5.0550 | E 5.5260 |
| Sweden | Swedish krona of 100 öre | Kronor 12.0725 | Kronor 11.8205 |
| Switzerland | Swiss franc of 100 rappen (or centimes) | Francs 2.2075 | Francs 2.0260 |
| Syria | Syrian pound (S£) of 100 piastres | S£ 32.4435 | S£ 31.6520 |
| Taiwan | New Taiwan dollar (NT$) of 100 cents | T$ 40.675 | NT$ 40.5312 |
| Tajikistan | Rouble of 100 kopeks | Roubles 0.8720 | Roubles 1.0821 |
| Tanzania | Tanzanian shilling of 100 cents | Shillings 656.40 | Shillings 810.986 |
| Thailand | Baht of 100 satang | Baht 37.7375 | Baht 38.6265 |
| Togo | Franc CFA | Francs 437.375 | Francs 826.440 |
| Tokelau | Currency is that of New Zealand | NZ$ 2.7325 | NZ$ 2.5527 |
| Tonga | Pa'anga (T$) of 100 seniti | T$ 2.2625 | T$ 2.0804 |
| Trinidad and Tobago | Trinidad and Tobago dollar (TT$) of 100 cents | TT$ 8.3540 | TT$ 8.6078 |
| Tunisia | Tunisian dinar of 1,000 millimes | Dinars 1.5370 | Dinars 1.5266 |
| Turkey | Turkish lira (TL) of 100 kurus | TL 17582.74 | TL 52676.1 |
| Turkmenistan | Manat | Roubles 0.8720 | — |
| Turks and Caicos Islands | US dollar (US$) | US$ 1.5005 | US$ 1.5448 |
| Tuvalu | Australian dollar ($A) of 100 cents | $A 2.2625 | $A 2.0804 |
| Uganda | Uganda shilling of 100 cents | Shillings 1785.70 | Shillings 1397.32 |
| Ukraine | Karbovanets (Ka) | Roubles 0.8720 | Ka 31668.5 |
| United Arab Emirates | UAE dirham of 100 fils | Dirham 5.5160 | Dirham 5.6759 |
| United Kingdom | Pound sterling (£) of 100 pence | £ 1.00 | £ 1.00 |
| United States of America | US dollar (US$) of 100 cents | US$ 1.5005 | US$ 1.5448 |
| Uruguay | New Uruguayan peso of 100 centésimos | Pesos 6.1115 | Pesos 8.1755 |
| Uzbekistan | Sum | Roubles 0.8720 | — |
| Vanuatu | Vatu of 100 centimes | Vatu 183.20 | Vatu 175.329 |
| Vatican City State | Italian currency is legal tender | Lire 2391.75 | Lire 2432.83 |
| Venezuela | Bolívar (Bs) of 100 céntimos | Bs 143.10 | Bs 262.276 |
| Vietnam | Dông of 10 hào or 100 xu | Dông 16063.30 | Dông 16965.5 |
| Virgin Islands (US) | Currency is that of USA | US$ 1.5005 | US$ 1.5448 |
| Wallis and Futuna Islands | Franc CFP | Francs 159.50 | Francs 148.566 |
| Western Samoa | Tala (WS$) of 100 sene | WS$ 3.88 | WS$ 3.8991 |
| Republic of Yemen | Yemeni dinar (YD) of 1,000 fils | YD 0.6804 | YD 0.6884 |
|  | Riyal of 100 fils | Riyals 24.8985 | Riyals 88.30 |
| Yugoslavia, Federal Rep. | Dinar of 100 paras | Dinars 158.445 | — |
| Zaïre | Zaïre of 100 makuta | Zaïre 8943300 | Zaïre 1992.50 |
| Zambia | Kwacha (K) of 100 ngwee | K 663.96 | K 1049.92 |
| Zimbabwe | Zimbabwe dollar (Z$) of 100 cents | Z$ 9.7765 | Z$ 12.6376 |

# Time Zones

Standard time differences from the Greenwich meridian

+ hours ahead of GMT
− hours behind GMT
* varies from standard time at some part of the year (Summer Time or Daylight Saving Time)
h hours
m minutes

| | h | m |
|---|---|---|
| Afghanistan | + 4 | 30 |
| *Albania | + 1 | |
| Algeria | + 1 | |
| *Andorra | + 1 | |
| Angola | + 1 | |
| Anguilla | − 4 | |
| Antigua and Barbuda | − 4 | |
| Argentina | − 3 | |
| *Jujuy | − 4 | |
| *Mendoza | − 4 | |
| Armenia | + 4 | |
| Aruba | − 4 | |
| Ascension Island | 0 | |
| *Australia | +10 | |
| Broken Hill area (NSW) | + 9 | 30 |
| Northern Territory | + 9 | 30 |
| *South Australia | + 9 | 30 |
| Western Australia | + 8 | |
| *Austria | + 1 | |
| Azerbaijan | + 4 | |
| *Azores | − 1 | |
| *Bahamas | − 5 | |
| Bahrain | + 3 | |
| Bangladesh | + 6 | |
| Barbados | − 4 | |
| *Belarus | + 2 | |
| *Belgium | + 1 | |
| Belize | − 6 | |
| Benin | + 1 | |
| *Bermuda | − 4 | |
| Bhutan | + 6 | |
| Bolivia | − 4 | |
| Botswana | + 2 | |
| Brazil | | |
| Acre | − 5 | |
| *eastern, including all coast and Brasilia | − 3 | |
| *western | − 4 | |
| British Indian Ocean Territory | + 5 | |
| Diego Garcia | + 6 | |
| British Virgin Islands | − 4 | |
| Brunei | + 8 | |
| *Bulgaria | + 2 | |
| Burkina | 0 | |
| Burundi | + 2 | |
| Cambodia | + 7 | |
| Cameroon | + 1 | |
| Canada | | |
| *Alberta | − 7 | |
| *British Columbia | − 8 | |
| British Columbia NE | − 7 | |
| *Labrador | − 4 | |
| *Manitoba | − 6 | |
| *New Brunswick | − 4 | |
| *Newfoundland | − 3 | 30 |
| *Northwest Territories east of 63° W. | − 4 | |

| | h | m |
|---|---|---|
| west of 63° W. | − 5 | |
| eastern | − 5 | |
| central | − 6 | |
| mountain | − 7 | |
| western | − 8 | |
| *Nova Scotia | − 4 | |
| Ontario | | |
| *east of 90° W. | − 5 | |
| west of 90° W. | − 5 | |
| *Prince Edward Island | − 4 | |
| *Quebec | | |
| east of 63° W. | − 4 | |
| west of 63° W. | − 5 | |
| *Saskatchewan | − 6 | |
| *Yukon | − 8 | |
| *Canary Islands | 0 | |
| Cape Verde | − 1 | |
| Cayman Islands | − 5 | |
| Central African Republic | + 1 | |
| Chad | + 1 | |
| *Chile | − 4 | |
| China | + 8 | |
| Christmas Island (Indian Ocean) | + 7 | |
| Cocos Keeling Islands | + 6 | 30 |
| Colombia | − 5 | |
| Comoros | + 3 | |
| Congo | + 1 | |
| Cook Islands | − 10 | |
| Costa Rica | − 6 | |
| Côte d'Ivoire | 0 | |
| *Cuba | − 5 | |
| *Cyprus | + 2 | |
| *Czech Republic | + 1 | |
| *Denmark | + 1 | |
| Djibouti | + 3 | |
| Dominica | − 4 | |
| Dominican Republic | − 4 | |
| Ecuador | − 5 | |
| *Egypt | + 2 | |
| Equatorial Guinea | + 1 | |
| *Estonia | + 2 | |
| Ethiopia | + 3 | |
| *Falkland Islands | − 4 | |
| *Faroe Islands | 0 | |
| Fiji | +12 | |
| *Finland | + 2 | |
| *France | + 1 | |
| French Guiana | − 3 | |
| French Polynesia | −10 | |
| Marquesas Islands | − 9 | 30 |
| Gabon | + 1 | |
| The Gambia | 0 | |
| *Georgia | + 3 | |
| *Germany | + 1 | |
| Ghana | 0 | |
| *Gibraltar | + 1 | |
| *Greece | + 2 | |
| Greenland | | |
| *Angmagssalik and west coast | − 3 | |
| Danmarkshavn | − 1 | |
| *Scoresby Sound | − 1 | |
| Thule area | − 4 | |
| Grenada | − 4 | |
| Guadeloupe | − 4 | |
| Guam | + 10 | |
| Guatemala | − 6 | |

| | h | m |
|---|---|---|
| Guinea | 0 | |
| Guinea-Bissau | 0 | |
| Guyana | − 4 | |
| *Haiti | − 5 | |
| Honduras | − 6 | |
| Hong Kong | + 8 | |
| *Hungary | + 1 | |
| Iceland | 0 | |
| India | + 5 | 30 |
| Indonesia | | |
| Bali | + 8 | |
| Irian Jaya | + 9 | |
| Java | + 7 | |
| Kalimantan (south and east) | + 8 | |
| Kalimantan (west and central) | + 7 | |
| Molucca Islands | + 9 | |
| Sulawesi | + 8 | |
| Sumatra | + 7 | |
| Timor | + 8 | |
| *Iran | + 3 | 30 |
| *Iraq | + 3 | |
| *Ireland, Republic of | 0 | |
| *Israel | + 2 | |
| *Italy | + 1 | |
| Jamaica | − 5 | |
| Japan | + 9 | |
| *Jordan | + 2 | |
| *Kazakhstan | + 6 | |
| Kenya | + 3 | |
| Kiribati | | |
| Banaba | +12 | |
| Gilbert Islands | +12 | |
| Kiritimati Island | −10 | |
| Phoenix Islands | −11 | |
| Korea, North | + 9 | |
| Korea, South | + 9 | |
| Kuwait | + 3 | |
| *Kyrgyzstan | + 5 | |
| Laos | + 7 | |
| *Latvia | + 2 | |
| *Lebanon | + 2 | |
| Lesotho | + 2 | |
| Liberia | 0 | |
| Libya | + 2 | |
| *Liechtenstein | + 1 | |
| *Lithuania | + 2 | |
| *Luxembourg | + 1 | |
| Macao | + 8 | |
| Madagascar | + 3 | |
| *Madeira | 0 | |
| Malawi | + 2 | |
| Malaysia | + 8 | |
| Maldives | + 5 | |
| Mali | 0 | |
| *Malta | + 1 | |
| Marshall Islands | +12 | |
| Ebon Atoll | −12 | |
| Martinique | − 4 | |
| Mauritania | 0 | |
| Mauritius | + 4 | |
| Mexico | − 6 | |
| central | − 7 | |
| western | − 8 | |
| Micronesia | | |
| Caroline Islands | +10 | |
| Kosrae | +11 | |

| | h | m | | h | m |
|---|---|---|---|---|---|
| Pohnpei | +11 | | *Spain | + 1 | |
| *Moldova | + 2 | | Sri Lanka | + 5 | 30 |
| *Monaco | + 1 | | Sudan | + 2 | |
| *Mongolia | + 8 | | Suriname | − 3 | |
| Montserrat | − 4 | | Swaziland | + 2 | |
| Morocco | 0 | | *Sweden | + 1 | |
| Mozambique | + 2 | | *Switzerland | + 1 | |
| Myanmar | + 6 | 30 | *Syria | + 2 | |
| Namibia | + 2 | | Taiwan | + 8 | |
| Nauru | +12 | | Tajikistan | + 5 | |
| Nepal | + 5 | 45 | Tanzania | + 3 | |
| *Netherlands | + 1 | | Thailand | + 7 | |
| Netherlands Antilles | − 4 | | Togo | 0 | |
| New Caledonia | +11 | | Tonga | +13 | |
| *New Zealand | +12 | | Trinidad and Tobago | − 4 | |
| Nicaragua | − 5 | | Tristan da Cunha | 0 | |
| Niger | + 1 | | Tunisia | + 1 | |
| Nigeria | + 1 | | *Turkey | + 2 | |
| Norfolk Island | +11 | 30 | Turkmenistan | + 5 | |
| *Norway | + 1 | | *Turks and Caicos Islands | − 5 | |
| Oman | + 4 | | Tuvalu | +12 | |
| Pakistan | + 5 | | Uganda | + 3 | |
| Palau | + 9 | | *Ukraine | + 2 | |
| Panama | − 5 | | United Arab Emirates | + 4 | |
| Papua New Guinea | +10 | | *Uruguay | − 3 | |
| *Paraguay | − 4 | | United States | | |
| Peru | − 5 | | *Alaska, east of | | |
| Philippines | + 8 | | 169° 30′ W. | − 9 | |
| *Poland | + 1 | | *Aleutian Islands, west | | |
| *Portugal | + 1 | | of 169° 30′ W. | −10 | |
| Puerto Rico | − 4 | | eastern time | − 5 | |
| Qatar | + 3 | | *central time | − 6 | |
| Réunion | + 4 | | Hawaii | −10 | |
| *Romania | + 2 | | *mountain time | − 7 | |
| *Russia | | | *Pacific time | − 8 | |
| Zone 0 | + 2 | | Uzbekistan | + 5 | |
| Zone 1 | + 3 | | *Vanuatu | +11 | |
| Zone 2 | + 4 | | *Vatican City State | + 1 | |
| Zone 3 | + 5 | | Venezuela | − 4 | |
| Zone 4 | + 6 | | Vietnam | + 7 | |
| Zone 5 | + 7 | | Virgin Islands (US) | − 4 | |
| Zone 6 | + 8 | | Western Samoa | −11 | |
| Zone 7 | + 9 | | Yemen | + 3 | |
| Zone 8 | +10 | | *Yugoslav republics | + 1 | |
| Zone 9 | +11 | | Zaire | | |
| Zone 10 | +12 | | East | + 2 | |
| Rwanda | + 2 | | West | + 1 | |
| St Helena | 0 | | Zambia | + 2 | |
| St Kitts and Nevis | − 4 | | Zimbabwe | + 2 | |
| St Lucia | − 4 | | | | |
| *St Pierre and Miquelon | − 3 | | | | |
| St Vincent and the | | | | | |
| Grenadines | − 4 | | | | |
| El Salvador | − 6 | | | | |
| Samoa, American | −11 | | | | |
| *San Marino | + 1 | | | | |
| São Tomé and Príncipe | 0 | | | | |
| Saudi Arabia | + 3 | | | | |
| Senegal | 0 | | | | |
| Seychelles | + 4 | | | | |
| Sierra Leone | 0 | | | | |
| Singapore | + 8 | | | | |
| *Slovak Republic | + 1 | | | | |
| Solomon Islands | +11 | | | | |
| Somalia | + 3 | | | | |
| South Africa | + 2 | | | | |
| South Georgia | − 2 | | | | |

*Source:* reproduced with permission from data produced by HM Nautical Almanac Office. Copyright of the Science and Engineering Research Council

# Countries of the World: A–Z

SOURCES: sources of statistical data specific to one country are credited in that country's entry. Sources of statistical data used throughout the Countries of the World section include *UN Demographic Yearbook, UN Statistical Yearbook* (pub. UN), *UNESCO Statistical Yearbook* (pub. UNESCO), *World Bank Atlas, World Bank World Tables* (pub. World Bank), *World Mineral Statistics* (pub. British Geological Survey), *The Military Balance* (pub. IISS).

Other sources of information include the Foreign and Commonwealth Office Research Department and the diplomatic representatives and information offices in London of overseas countries, whom Whitaker's wishes to thank for their assistance.

## AFGHANISTAN
*Da Afghanistan Jamhuriat*

Afghanistan is bounded on the west by Iran, on the south by Pakistan, on the north by Tajikistan, Uzbekistan and Turkmenistan, and on the east by Pakistan and China. Its ancient name was Aryana, by which title it is referred to by Strabo, the Greek geographer who lived in the first century BC. The estimated area is 250,000 sq. miles (647,497 sq. km).

Mountains, chief among which are the Hindu Kush, cover three-quarters of the country, the elevation being generally over 4,000 feet. There are three great river basins, the Oxus, Helmand, and Kabul. The climate is dry, with extreme temperatures.

POPULATION – The population is 16,430,000 (1991 UN estimate). It is estimated that 3.5 million refugees fled to Pakistan and two million to Iran during the Soviet occupation. About 1.5 million have returned since 1992. The population is very mixed. The most numerous race is the Pushtuns who form around half of the population and predominate in the south and west, the Tajiks, a Persian-speaking people, Uzbeks and Turkomans in the north, Hazaras in the centre, Baluchis in the south-west and Nuristanis, who live near the Chitral border. All are Sunni Muslims, except the Hazaras and Kizilbashes, who belong to the Shia sect.

CAPITAL – Kabul (1,424,400 in 1988 but much reduced since due to fighting). The chief commercial centres are Kabul and Kandahar (225,500). Other provincial capitals are (UN estimates) Herat (177,300), Mazar-i-Sharif (130,600), Jalalabad (55,000).
CURRENCY – Afghani (Af) of 100 puls.
FLAG – Three horizontal stripes of green, white, black with the national arms in the centre in gold.
NATIONAL ANTHEM – Soroud-e-Melli.
NATIONAL DAY – 19 August.

## GOVERNMENT

The constitutional monarchy, introduced by the 1964 constitution, was overthrown by a coup in 1973. The country was ruled by presidential decree until February 1977 when a constitution was approved by a *Loya Jerga* (Grand Tribal Council). Mohammad Daoud was elected President but was overthrown in 1978 by the armed forces and power was handed to the People's Democratic Party of Afghanistan (PDPA). In December 1979 Soviet troops invaded Afghanistan and installed Babrak Karmal as head of state. Armed Islamic resistance groups, the mujahidin, aided by western arms and Arab finance, fought a brutal war against Soviet and Afghan armed forces. A peace agreement in April 1988 led to the withdrawal of Soviet troops, which was completed by February 1989.

Following widespread defections from the armed forces to the Islamic resistance groups, President Najibollah (who had replaced Karmal in 1986) was forced to step down in April 1992 and was replaced initially by an army-dominated council of his former colleagues. However, anti-government forces overran Kabul on 25 April, bringing to an end the war against the Soviet and Afghan armed forces in which an estimated one million people died. Afghanistan was declared an Islamic state and the Homeland Party (formerly the PDPA) was dissolved.

A new government was installed under Sebghatullah Mujaddedi, previously leader of a Pakistan-based government-in-exile. Mujaddedi was interim President until June 1992 when he was succeeded by Burnahuddin Rabbani, who was meant to serve for a four-month period until a permanent President could be elected by the coalition of seven former Pakistan-based Sunni Muslim mujahidin groups and three former Iran-based Shia Muslim groups. However, the ten groups could not agree on a new President and renewed fighting broke out in the Kabul area in December 1992 between the rival groups. The fighting was mainly between forces of the Hezb-i-Islami of Gulbardin Hekmatyar (mainly Pushtun) supported by the Shia Hezb-i-Wahdat forces, trying to force their way into Kabul, which was controlled by the militia of Ahmad Shah Massoud of the Jamiat-i-Islami party supported by fellow Tajik and Uzbek forces from the north. Fighting continued until March 1993, during which time thousands were killed in artillery and rocket attacks. Interim President Rabbani was elected for a two-year term on 30 December 1992 by a *Loya Jerga* but this was rejected by Hekmatyar and the Hezb-i-Wahdat. After negotiations a peace agreement was signed on 7 March 1993 under which Rabbani would remain President until June 1994, Hekmatyar would become Prime Minister of a transitional government until elections, to be held by June 1994, and Massoud would resign as Defence Minister. Hekmatyar finally entered Kabul on 17 June 1993 where he was sworn in with his new coalition government by President Rabbani.

The peace agreement collapsed in October 1993 and renewed fighting broke out for control of Kabul and the government between the forces of Hekmatyar and those of Rabbani and Massoud. The fighting intensified in January 1994 when the Uzbek militia leader and former Afghan armed forces General Rashid Dostum, allied his forces with Hekmatyar's and fighting spread throughout the north of the country towards Dostum's base at Mazar-i-Sharif. Hekmatyar's and Dostum's forces were finally forced out of Kabul by Rabbani and Massoud's militia at the end of June 1994, by which time artillery, missile and air attacks had destroyed most of Kabul and forced most of the city's population to flee to the surrounding countryside.

President Rabbani refused to resign in June 1994 and remains in office, but effectively the transitional government is inoperative and increasingly power is exercised at regional and local level by ethnic and militia leaders. The warfare since April 1992 has become a battle to reassert the traditional Pushtun political dominance of the past 250 years, which has been broken by Rabbani and Massoud's Tajiks and Uzbeks; it has left 13,500 dead and 80,000 injured.

*President of the Islamic State of Afghanistan*, Prof. Burhanuddin Rabbani, *elected*, 30 December 1992

EMBASSY OF THE ISLAMIC STATE OF AFGHANISTAN
31 Prince's Gate, London SW7 1QQ
Tel 0171-589 8891

*Ambassador Extraordinary and Plenipotentiary*, new appointment awaited
*Minister-Counsellor and Chargé d'Affaires*, N. Ahmad Wali Masud

BRITISH EMBASSY
Karte Parwan, Kabul
Tel: Kabul 30511/3
Staff were withdrawn from post in February 1989. Ambassador is now resident in Islamabad.

LOCAL GOVERNMENT
The country is divided into 32 provinces. At present, only a few have governors appointed by the new government in Kabul.

JUDICIARY
The constitution introduced in 1965 provided for the creation of a legal code, and for the complete separation of executive and judiciary, but was abolished in July 1973. In late 1976 and early 1977 new penal and civil codes were published.

Few major changes were made to the operation of the judicial system by the 1987 constitution and subsequent amendments under the Najibollah regime. The new government in Kabul has, however, announced its intention to introduce Islamic law.

DEFENCE
Before the fall of the Najibollah government, the army numbered about 50,000, supplemented by other security agencies and irregular militias. A small air force was also maintained. After the fall of the Najibollah government the Afghan army disintegrated, with large numbers defecting to local mujahidin groups. The Northern Army Command, however, was formed into the National Islamic Movement of the Uzbek militia leader General Dostum and numbers around 65,000 men. The Jamiat-i-Islami forces of Rabbani and Massoud number some 60,000 men, while Hekmatyar's Hezb-i-Islami forces number some 50,000. Five other Sunni Muslim mujahidin groups formerly based in Peshawar have forces of some 113,000 personnel and the Shia Hezb-i-Wahdat coalition of forces have some 126,000 men under arms. The former Afghan Air Force has been divided between Dostum's and Rabbani's forces.

ECONOMY
The economy has been devastated by the political upheavals of the last 15 years. Agriculture and sheep raising have been the principal industries. There are generally two crops a year, one of wheat (the staple food), barley or lentils, the other of rice, millet, maize and dal. Sugar beet and cotton are grown. Afghanistan is rich in fruits. Sheep, including the Karakuli, and transport animals are bred. Silk, woollen and hair cloths and carpets are manufactured. Salt, silver, copper, coal, iron, lead, rubies, lapis lazuli, gold, chrome, barite, uranium, and talc are found.

TRADE
Trade is currently limited but in the past exports have been mainly Persian lambskins (Karakul), dried fruits, nuts, cotton, raw wool, carpets, spice and natural gas, while the imports are chiefly oil, cotton yarn and piece goods, tea, sugar, machinery and transport equipment.

| Trade with UK | 1992 | 1993 |
|---|---|---|
| Imports from UK | £4,926,000 | £5,915,000 |
| Exports to UK | 4,676,000 | 4,310,000 |

COMMUNICATIONS
Main roads run from Kabul to Kandahar, Herat, Maimana via Mazari-Sharif and Faizabad via Khanabad. The road from Kabul to the north was shortened by the completion in 1964 of the Salang pass. Roads cross the border with Pakistan at Chaman and via the Khyber Pass, and there are roads from Herat to the borders of Central Asia and Iran. A network of minor roads fit for motor traffic in fine weather links up all important towns and districts.

In 1982 the Afghan and Uzbek shores of the River Oxus were linked by a road and rail bridge which joins the Afghan port of Hairatan and the Uzbek port of Termez. A network of internal air services operates between the main towns.

CULTURE
The principal languages of the country are Dari (a form of Persian) and Pushtu, although a number of minority languages are also spoken in various provinces. All schoolchildren learn both Persian and Pushtu. Education is free and nominally compulsory, elementary schools having been established in most centres; there are secondary schools in large urban areas and four universities, in Kabul (established 1932), Jalalabad (established 1962), Balkh and Herat (both established 1988).

---

# ALBANIA
*Republika Shqipërisë*

---

Situated on the Adriatic Sea, Albania is bounded on the north by Montenegro, on the east by Serbia and Macedonia and on the south by Greece. The area of the republic is estimated at 11,099 sq. miles (28,748 sq. km), with a population (1991 UN estimate) of 3,331,000. After many years as an officially atheist country, the Albanian population is now estimated to be 50 per cent Muslim, 18 per cent Orthodox and 13 per cent Roman Catholic.

CAPITAL – Tirana, population (1989) 239,381.
CURRENCY – Lek (Lk) of 100 qindarka.
FLAG – Black two-headed eagle on a red field.
NATIONAL DAY – 11 January.

GOVERNMENT
Albania was under Turkish suzerainty from 1468 until 1912, when independence was declared. After a period of unrest, a republic was declared in 1925, and in 1928 a monarchy. The King went into exile in 1939 when the country was occupied by the Italians; Albania was liberated in November 1944. Elections in 1945 resulted in a Communist-controlled Assembly; the King was deposed in absentia and a republic declared in January 1946.

From 1946 to 1991 Albania was a one-party, Communist state. In March 1991 multiparty elections were held and were won by the Socialist Party (the renamed Party of Labour). Following labour unrest, a coalition government was formed in June 1991.

In December 1991 the Democratic Party withdrew from the government and a non-party government was established which continued in office until new elections were held in March 1992. These elections were won overwhelmingly by the Democratic Party, which formed a coalition government with the much smaller Social Democrat and Republican parties. In April 1992 the Democratic Party leader Dr Sali Berisha was elected by parliament as Albania's first non-Communist President.

CONSTITUTION

A Human Rights Law, part of a new constitution, was approved in principle by the parliament in March 1993. The government in June 1993 published a draft constitution which defines Albania as a parliamentary republic with guaranteed individual freedoms. The draft is being scrutinized by parliament.

HEAD OF STATE
*President*, Dr Sali Berisha, *elected* April 1992

COUNCIL OF MINISTERS *as at June 1994*
*Prime Minister*, Aleksander Meksi
*Deputy Chairman of the Council of Ministers responsible for economic reform*, Bashkim Kopliku (DP)
*Minister without Portfolio*, Rexhep Uka (DP)
*General Secretary*, Vullnet Ademi (SDP)
*Finance*, Pirro Dishnica (DP)
*Foreign Affairs*, Alfred Serreqi (DP)
*Justice*, Kudred Cela (Ind)
*Industry, Mining and Energy Sources*, Abdyl Xhaja (Ind)
*Trade and Industry*, Selim Belortaja (DP)
*Defence*, Safet Zhulali (DP)
*Transport and Communications*, Fatos Bitncka (RP)
*Construction, Housing and Territory Adjustments*, Ilir Manushi (DP)
*Health and Environmental Protection*, Maksim Cikuli (DP)
*Education*, Xhezair Teliti (Ind)
*Culture, Youth and Sports*, Dhimiter Anagnosti (DP)
*Tourism*, Edmond Spaho (Ind)
*Labour, Emigration, Social Assistance and Political Persecutors*, Dashamir Shehu (DP)
*Chairman of the Committee of Science and Technology*, Maskim Konomi (DP)
*Chairman of the Control Commission*, Blerim Cela (DP)
*Public Order*, Agron Musaraj (DP)
*Agriculture and Food*, Hassan Halili (DP)

DP Democratic Party; Ind Independent; SDP Social Democrat Party; RP Republican Party.

EMBASSY OF THE REPUBLIC OF ALBANIA
6 Wilton Court, 59 Ecclestone Square, London SW1V 1PH
Tel 0171-976 5295

*Ambassador Extraordinary and Plenipotentiary*, His Excellency Pavli Qesku, apptd 1993

BRITISH AMBASSADOR – His Excellency Sir Patrick Fairweather, KCMG, resident in Rome
*Chargé d'Affaires*, S. Nash (resident in Tirana). Tel: 873 144 5564

DEFENCE

Albania has a total active armed forces strength of some 73,000 personnel (22,400 conscripts). Conscripts serve for a term of 18 months. The Army has a strength of 60,000 (20,000 conscripts) with some 900 main battle tanks, 105 armoured reconnaissance vehicles and armoured personnel carriers and 210 artillery pieces.
   The Navy has a strength of 2,000 (1,000 conscripts) with two submarines and some 45 patrol and coastal craft. The Air Force has a strength of 11,000 personnel (1,400 conscripts) with some 112 combat aircraft of Chinese and Soviet manufacture.

ECONOMY

Much of the country is mountainous and nearly a half is covered by forest. There are fertile areas along the Adriatic coast and the Koritza Basin and there have been land reclamation and irrigation programmes. The main crops are wheat, maize, sugar-beet, potatoes and fruit.
   There has been some privatization of small and medium-sized enterprises. The principal industries are agricultural product processing, textiles, oil products and cement. Exports include crude oil, minerals (bitumen, chrome, nickel, copper), tobacco, fruit and vegetables. The government is now committed to economic reform, privatization and the creation of a market economy. Most agriculture has been privatized and land redistributed, with a consequent increase in production.
   Since April 1992 the government has introduced severe economic measures, stringently cut the budget to reduce deficits and has brought down inflation to around 30 per cent per year from 40 per cent a month in early 1992. The currency has stabilized, with industrial output continuing to fall, but at a slow rate after a fall of 60 per cent in 1991-2. Commerce and the service sectors have expanded, and agricultural production increased in 1993 by 11 per cent. The country is now self-sufficient in food production, producing 470,000 tonnes of wheat in 1993 after most land had been privatized. Remittances from overseas workers remain an important source of revenue. Albania has received $1 billion in aid from Western donors.

| Trade with UK | 1992 | 1993 |
| --- | --- | --- |
| Imports from UK | £2,763,000 | £5,406,000 |
| Exports to UK | 290,000 | 465,000 |

# ALGERIA
*Al-Jumhuriya al-Jazairiya ad-Dimuqratiya ash-Shabiya*

Algeria lies between 8° 45′ W. and 12° E. longitude, 27° 6′ N. to a southern limit about 19° N. and has an area of 919,595 sq. miles (2,381,741 sq. km). The population (1987 census) was 22,971,558. A 1991 UN estimate gives a figure of 25,660,000.

CAPITAL – ΨAlgiers, population 3,250,000 (approx). It is one of the principal ports of the Mediterranean as well as an important industrial centre. Other towns include ΨOran; Constantine; ΨAnnaba; Blida; Setif; Sidi-Bel-Abbès; Tlemcen; ΨMostaganem; ΨSkikda; ΨBejaia and Tizi Ouzou.
CURRENCY – Algerian dinar (DA) of 100 centimes.
FLAG – Divided vertically green and white with a red crescent and star over all in the centre.
NATIONAL ANTHEM – Qassaman.
NATIONAL DAY – 1 November.

GOVERNMENT

Algiers surrendered to a French force in 1830, and Algeria was annexed to France in 1842. From 1881 the three northern departments of Algiers, Oran and Constantine formed an integral part of France. The Southern Territories of the Sahara, formerly a separate colony, became an integral part of Algeria on the attainment of independence. An armed rebellion against French rule led by the Muslim Front de

Liberation Nationale (FLN) broke out in 1954. French control of Algeria came to an end when President de Gaulle declared Algeria independent on 3 July 1962; by October 1963 all agricultural land held by foreigners had been expropriated and by 1965 more than 80 per cent of the French population had left Algeria.

Ben Bella was elected President of the republic in September 1963, but was deposed; a Council of the Revolution presided over by Col. Boumediène assumed power in June 1965. A new constitution was established by referendum in November 1976, and in December 1976 President Boumediène was elected for a six-year term of office. Following President Boumediène's death in December 1978, Chadli Bendjedid was elected President in February 1979.

A new constitution was agreed by referendum in February 1989 which moved Algeria away from a one-party socialist system to a more pluralist system. Local elections in June 1990 were won by the opposition Islamic Salvation Front (FIS). Following extensive unrest, the government declared a state of siege in June 1991 and postponed multiparty elections until the end of the year.

The first round of the legislative elections was held in December 1991 with the FIS emerging as the clear winner. However before the second round of the elections was held, President Bendjedid resigned and the elections were abandoned. A Higher Committee of State (HCS) was formed, backed by the armed forces, to govern the country. The former FLN veteran Mohammed Boudiaf returned from 25 years in exile to head the HCS. The HCS declared a state of emergency in February 1992, which was extended indefinitely in February 1993, and the FIS was banned in March 1992 but continues its activities underground. Clashes between security forces and fundamentalists of the FIS and the Armed Islamic Group (GIA) continued, and in June 1992 President Boudiaf was assassinated by suspected FIS supporters.

Throughout late 1993 the HCS and armed forces attempted unsuccessfully to reach agreement with non-Islamic political parties on a common anti-Islamic front. A national reconciliation conference in January 1994 was boycotted by the FIS and other political parties, but nevertheless it appointed General Lamine Zeroual as President to replace the HCS, which disbanded itself. The conflict between the government and armed fundamentalists continues, with some 3,000 dead, tens of thousands detained and hundreds sentenced to death. Since November 1993 the armed fundamentalists have targeted expatriates, killing 30 and forcing 70,000 (out of a total 100,000) to leave the country.

HEAD OF STATE
*President*, Gen. Lamine Zeroual, *appointed* January 1994

GOVERNMENT *as at July 1994*

*Prime Minister*, Mokdad Sifi
*National Defence*, The President
*Foreign Affairs*, Mohamed Salah Dembri
*Interior*, Abderrahmane Meziane Cherif
*Finance*, Ahmed Benbitour
*Justice*, Muhamed Teguia
*Communications*, Mohamed Benamar Zerhouni
*National Education*, Amar Sakhri
*Higher Education*, Boubakeur Benbouzid
*War Veterans*, Said Abadou
*Industrial Restructuring*, Mourad Benachnhou
*Energy and Industry*, Amar Makhloufi
*Equipment*, Cherif Rahmani
*Commerce*, Saci Aziza
*Agriculture*, Noureddine Bahbouh
*Religious Affairs*, Sassi Lamouri

*Housing*, Mohamed Maghlaoui
*Health and Population*, Yahia Kaidoum
*Labour and Social Affairs*, Mohamed Laichoubi
*Vocational Training*, Hacene Laskri
*Culture*, Slimane Chikh
*Youth and Sport*, Sid Ali Lebib
*Post and Telecommunications*, Tahar Allane
*Transport*, Muhamed Arezki Isli
*Small Enterprises*, Redha Hamiani
*Tourism*, Mohamed Bensalem

ALGERIAN EMBASSY
54 Holland Park, London W11 3RS
Tel 0171-221 7800

*Ambassador Extraordinary and Plenipotentiary*, His Excellency Ali Lakhdari, apptd 1992

BRITISH EMBASSY
7 Chemin des Glycines,
BP43, Alger-Gare 16000, Algiers
Tel: Algiers 605038

*Ambassador Extraordinary and Plenipotentiary*, His Excellency Christopher Donald Crabbie, apptd 1994
*Cultural Attaché and British Council Representative*, D. Munro, 6 Avenue Souidani Boudjemaa, Algiers

DEFENCE

Algeria has a total active armed forces strength of 121,700 personnel, of which 65,000 are conscripts. Conscripts serve only in the Army and for a period of 18 months.

The Army has a strength of 105,000 (65,000 conscripts) with 960 main battle tanks, 1,375 armoured personnel carriers and armoured infantry fighting vehicles, 120 reconnaissance vehicles, 700 artillery pieces and 895 air defence guns.

The Navy has a strength of 6,700 in four main bases. It is equipped with two submarines, three frigates and 22 patrol and coastal vessels. The Air Force has a strength of 10,000 personnel with 193 combat aircraft and 58 armed helicopters.

In addition, there are 41,000 personnel in the paramilitary Gendarmerie and National Security Forces. Russia maintains 500 military advisers in the country.

ECONOMY

Development in Algeria was from 1965 to 1989 regulated by a series of national development plans. During this period the FLN pursued the eastern European socialist economic model, with heavy industries run by large state conglomerates central to the economy, and state control of most sectors. The 1985–9 Plan concentrated on housing, water supply, agriculture, food and processing industries. Agrarian reform started in 1987. The 4,000 state farms have been broken up into 23,000 units. Following riots in October 1988, economic reform was speeded up and now includes the industrial and financial sectors. The aim is to decentralize planning and devolve management. The private sector is also receiving official encouragement. In April 1994 the government finally accepted full economic reform and liberalization under a reform programme agreed with the IMF to gain US$1 billion necessary for balance of payments support.

Algeria's main industry is the hydrocarbons industry. Oil and natural gas are pumped from the Sahara to terminals on the coast before being exported; the gas is first liquefied at liquefaction plants at Skikda and Arzew, although pipelines serve Libya and Italy direct.

Other major industries being developed include a steel industry, motor vehicles, building materials, paper making, chemical products and metal manufactures. Most major industrial enterprises are still under state control.

| Trade with UK | 1992 | 1993 |
|---|---|---|
| Imports from UK | £38,130,000 | £56,162,000 |
| Exports to UK | 162,560,000 | 187,081,000 |

Algeria's exports are worth around $12 billion annually, mainly from crude oil and liquefied natural gas. Principal imports from the United Kingdom are capital plant, equipment for industrial use and foodstuffs. The country's external debt is nearly $26 billion with a current debt service ration of 75 per cent. Algeria needs US$9 billion annually to service its foreign debt for which it is negotiating with the IMF.

## COMMUNICATIONS

Algeria has a rapidly expanding network of roads and railways. Considerable sums are also being spent on the development of the state airline, the national shipping company and telecommunications.

## ANDORRA
*Principat d'Andorra*

A small, neutral principality formed by a treaty in 1278, Andorra is situated on the southern slopes of the Pyrenees between Spain and France. It is surrounded by mountains of 6,500 to 10,000 feet. It has an approximate area of 175 sq. miles (468 sq. km), and population (UN estimate 1991) of 58,000, less than one-quarter of whom are native Andorrans. The official language of the country is Catalan, but French and Spanish (Castilian) are also spoken. The established religion is Roman Catholicism.

CAPITAL – Andorra la Vella (population 22,205).
CURRENCY – French francs and Spanish pesetas are both in use.
FLAG – Three vertical bands, blue, yellow, red; Andorran coat of arms frequently imposed on central (yellow) band but not essential.
NATIONAL DAY – 8 September.

## GOVERNMENT

Andorra has a unicameral legislature of 28 members known as the Consell General de las Valls d'Andorra (Valleys of Andorra General Council). Fourteen members are elected on a national list basis and fourteen in seven dual-member constituencies based on Andorra's seven parishes. The Council appoints the head of the executive government, who designates the members of his government.

A new constitution was promulgated on 4 May 1993 under which Andorra is an independent, democratic parliamentary co-principality, with the state's sovereignty being vested in the people rather than in the two co-princes as before. The constitution enables Andorra to establish an independent judiciary for the first time and to carry out its own foreign policy, whilst its people may now join trade unions and political parties. The two co-princes, the President of the French Republic and the Spanish Bishop of Urgel, remain heads of state but with drastically reduced powers, now only able to veto treaties with France and Spain which affect the state's borders and security. Andorra was admitted to UN membership on 28 July 1993. The co-princes are represented by Permanent Delegates of whom one is the French Prefect of the Pyrenees Orientales Department at Perpignan and

the other is the Spanish Vicar-General of the Diocese of Urgel. They are in turn represented in Andorra la Vella by two resident Viguiers known as the Viguier Français and the Viguier Episcopal. The first elections under the new constitution were held in December 1993, and on 20 January 1994 Oscar Ribas Reig was elected as the head of the first sovereign government of Andorra with the support of 15 of the members of the General Council.

*Viguier Français*, Jean-Pierre Courtois
*Viguier Episcopal*, Francesc Badia

EXECUTIVE COUNCIL *as at June 1994*
*President*, Oscar Ribas Reig
*Foreign Affairs*, Antoni Armengol
*Finance*, Josep Casal Casal
*Agriculture, Commerce and Industry*, Modest Baro Moles
*Public Services*, Joan Albert Teixe
*Tourism and Sport*, Xavier Espot Miro
*Labour, Health and Social Welfare*, Bibiana Rossa Torres
*Sindic (President) of General Council*, Jordi Farras

HM CONSUL-GENERAL, M. Perceval, apptd 1992
(resident in Barcelona, Spain). Tel 3-322 2151

## ECONOMY

The Budget is expressed in pesetas. The estimated national revenue (1989) was US$895 million, with a per capita income of US$17,596.

Potatoes are produced in the highlands and tobacco in the valleys. The mountain slopes have been developed for skiing, and it is estimated that 10 million tourists visit the valleys during the year. The economy is largely based on tourism, banking, commerce, tobacco, construction and forestry; a third of the country is classified as forest, in which pine, fir, oak, birch and box-tree predominate. Andorra has negotiated a customs union with the European Community which came into force on 1 July 1991. Andorra's very low consumer taxes enticed 12,000,000 shopping tourists to the state in 1992. The economy is now diversifying rapidly into offshore financial services.

| Trade with UK | 1992 | 1993 |
|---|---|---|
| Imports from UK | £13,071,000 | £18,680,000 |
| Exports to UK | 19,000 | 89,000 |

## COMMUNICATIONS

A good road into the valleys from Spain is open all year round, and that from France is closed only occasionally in winter. An airport at Seo d'Urgell just outside Andorra provides very limited air connections. There are two radio stations in Andorra, one privately owned and one operated by a French government corporation. Both pay dues to the Council of the Valleys.

## ANGOLA
*República de Angola*

Angola, which has an area of 481,354 sq. miles (1,246,700 sq. km), lies on the western coast of Africa. To the north and east lies Zaïre, to the east Zambia and to the south Namibia. The enclave of Cabinda is separated from the rest of Angola by Zaïre and also borders on the Congo. Its population in 1991 was estimated by the UN at 10,303,000.

CAPITAL – ΨLuanda, population estimate 1993, 3 million.
CURRENCY – New Kwanza (Kz) of 100 lwei.

FLAG – Red and black with a yellow star, machete and cog-wheel.

NATIONAL ANTHEM – Angola Avante.

NATIONAL DAY – 11 November (Independence Day).

## GOVERNMENT

After a Portuguese presence of five centuries, and an anti-colonial war since 1961, Angola became independent on 11 November 1975 in the midst of civil war. Soviet-Cuban military assistance to the Popular Movement for the Liberation of Angola (MPLA) enabled it to defeat its rivals early in 1976. However, the MPLA government remained under pressure from the UNITA guerrilla movement (led by Dr Jonas Savimbi) which by the mid 1980s was operating freely. In August 1988 it was announced that a ceasefire between South African, Cuban and Angolan forces had taken place pending talks on withdrawal of South African troops from Angola. In December 1988 an agreement providing for the withdrawal of the 50,000 Cuban troops by July 1991 was signed in New York. In May 1991 a peace agreement was signed between the government and UNITA. Multiparty presidential and legislative elections took place in September 1992. In the legislative elections the MPLA won 129 seats, UNITA 70 seats and minor parties 21 seats out of a total of 220. In the first round of the presidential election, MPLA leader President Dos Santos won 49.5 per cent of the vote to Savimbi's 40 per cent, necessitating a second round. However, no second round was held as Savimbi and UNITA refused to accept the election results. Rising tension led to outbreaks of fighting throughout November and December 1992 and a return to civil war in January 1993.

Fierce fighting has continued throughout 1993 and 1994, with UNITA having gained control of around two-thirds of the country, including most of the south, west, north-west and central highlands, and around one-third of the population. UNITA controls virtually all the diamond-producing areas, while the government controls most oil-producing areas. The fighting has increasingly concentrated in the central high-lands where UNITA has besieged the government-held cities of Kuito, Luena, Menongue and Malange, necessitating a massive UN food airlift. With the resumption of the civil war the UN reduced its personnel in the country from 700 to around 100, and since October 1993 has presided over peace talks in the Zambian capital Lusaka.

The MPLA, formerly but no longer a Marxist-Leninist party, was the sole legal party until early 1991 when a multi-party system was adopted. The constitution declares Angola to be a democratic state and provides for a President, who appoints a Council of Ministers to assist him, and a National Assembly. The present MPLA-dominated government also includes several minor parties and was sworn in after the elections in November 1992.

### SECESSION

In the northern enclave of Cabinda, the Front for the Liberation of the Cabinda Enclave (FLEC) has been fighting for independence against government forces since 1975, and has a strength of some 600, armed with light arms. Cabinda is rich in oil and is separated from the rest of Angola by Zaire.

HEAD OF STATE
*President,* Jose Eduardo Dos Santos

COUNCIL OF MINISTERS *as at June 1994*

*Prime Minister,* Dr Marcolino Jose Carlos Moco
*Defence,* Pedro Tonho Pedale
*Interior,* Santana Andre Pitra
*Foreign,* Dr Venancio de Silva Moura

*Territorial Administration,* Anibal Lopes Rocha
*Finance,* Alvaro Craveiro
*Oil,* Albina Pereira Africano
*Industry,* Dr Idalino Manuel Mendes
*Agriculture and Rural Development,* Isaac Maria dos Anjos
*Fisheries,* Maria Monteiro Jardin
*Geology and Mines,* Jose Antonio Dias
*Public Works and Urbanization,* Dr Mateus de Brito Junior
*Transport and Communications,* Dr Andre Luis Brandao
*Trade and Tourism,* Dr Emanuel Moreira Carneiro
*Health,* Dr Martinho Sanches Epalanga
*Education,* Dr Joao Manuel Bernardo
*Planning,* Jose Pedro de Morais
*Assistance and Social Reintegration,* Albino Malunga
*Culture,* vacant
*Youth and Sports,* José Rocha de Castro
*Justice,* Dr Paulo Chipilika
*Public Administration, Employment and Social Security,* Dr Antonio Costa Neto
*Governor of Luanda,* Justino Fernandes

EMBASSY OF ANGOLA
98 Park Lane, London W1Y 3TA
Tel 0171-495 1752

*Ambassador Extraordinary and Plenipotentiary,* His Excellency António DaCosta Fernandes, apptd 1993

BRITISH EMBASSY
Rua Diogo Caõ 4 (Caixa Postal 1244), Luanda
Tel: Luanda 392991/8

*Ambassador Extraordinary and Plenipotentiary,* His Excellency Anthony Richard Thomas, apptd 1993

## DEFENCE

Under the 1991 peace agreement, the armed forces of the governing MPLA and the opposition UNITA movement were to have merged to form a 50,000 strong National Army shortly after the elections of September 1992. To this end, large proportions of both government and UNITA forces were in UN containment camps or had been demobilized by September 1992. However, with the return to civil war after the elections, both sides have remobilized.

Government active armed forces number some 45,000. The Army has some 35,000 personnel with 200 main battle tanks, 200 armoured infantry fighting vehicles and armoured personnel carriers and 350 artillery pieces. The Navy has a strength of 4,000 with 13 patrol and coastal craft. The Air Force has a strength of 6,000 personnel with 81 combat aircraft and 40 armed helicopters. In addition the government can call on 20,000 paramilitary internal security police. UNITA forces number some 40,000. Equipment numbers include about 80 main battle tanks and numerous captured artillery, mortar and anti-aircraft guns.

## ECONOMY

Angola has valuable oil and diamond deposits and exports of these two commodities account for over 90 per cent of total exports.

Principal agricultural crops are cassava, maize, bananas, coffee, palm oil and kernels, cotton and sisal. Coffee, sisal, maize and palm oil are exported; exports also include mahogany and other hardwoods from the tropical rain forests in the north of the country.

The government is attempting to reform the socialist economy by free market reforms but is making little progress, with high inflation and a collapsing economy, together with the loss of most diamond-producing areas to UNITA.

| Trade with UK | 1992 | 1993 |
|---|---|---|
| Imports from UK | £64,371,000 | £27,512,000 |
| Exports to UK | 144,324,000 | 21,202,000 |

## ANTIGUA AND BARBUDA
*State of Antigua and Barbuda*

Antigua and Barbuda comprises the islands of Antigua (108 sq. miles (279 sq. km)), Barbuda (62 sq. miles (160 sq. km)) 25 miles north of Antigua, and Redonda (¼ sq. mile (1.2 sq. km)) 25 miles south-west of Antigua. Antigua is part of the Leeward Islands in the eastern Caribbean and lies 17° 3′ N. and 61° 48′ W. It is distinguished from the rest of the Leeward group by its absence of high hills and forest, and a drier climate than most of the West Indies. Barbuda, formerly a possession of the Codrington family, is very flat, mainly scrub-covered, with a large lagoon.

POPULATION – The total population (official census 1991) is 65,962; Antigua had a population of 64,562, Barbuda 1,400, and Redonda was uninhabited.

CAPITAL – ΨSt John's. Population, 30,000. The town of Barbuda is Codrington.

CURRENCY – East Caribbean dollar (EC$) of 100 cents.

FLAG. – Red with an inverted triangle divided black over blue over white, with a rising gold sun on the white band.

NATIONAL ANTHEM – Fair Antigua and Barbuda.

NATIONAL DAY – 1 November (Independence Day).

### GOVERNMENT

Antigua was first settled by the English in 1632, and was granted to Lord Willoughby by Charles II. Antigua became internally self-governing in 1967 and fully independent on 1 November 1981, as a constitutional monarchy with The Queen as Head of State, represented by the Governor-General. There is a Senate of 17 appointed members and a House of Representatives elected every five years. The Attorney-General may be appointed.

The Antigua Labour party won the general election of 8 March 1994 and a fifth successive term of office with 11 seats in the House of Representatives compared to five seats for the United Progressive Party.

*Governor-General,* His Excellency Sir James Carlisle, GCMG

CABINET *as at June 1994*

*Prime Minister, Foreign Affairs, Social Affairs,* Hon. Lester Bird
*Justice, Legal Affairs and Attorney-General,* Hon. Clare Roberts
*Finance and Social Security,* Hon. Molwyn Joseph
*Home Affairs and Health,* Hon. Hilroy Humphreys
*Education, Youth, Sports, Community Development,* Hon. Dr Rodney Williams
*Agriculture, Fisheries, Commerce, Industry and Consumer Affairs,* Hon. John St Luce
*Tourism, Culture and Environment,* Hon. Bernard Percival
*Labour, Civil Service, Co-operatives,* Hon. Adolphus Freeland
*Public Utilities, Communications, Transportation and Energy,* Hon. Robin Yearwood
*Housing, Leader of the Senate,* Sen. Hon. Henderson Simon

HIGH COMMISSION FOR ANTIGUA AND BARBUDA
15 Thayer Street, London WIM 5LD
Tel 0171-486 7073

*High Commissioner,* His Excellency James Thomas, CMG, apptd 1987

BRITISH HIGH COMMISSION
11 Old Parham Road (PO 483), St John's
Tel: St John's 462 0008/9

*High Commissioner,* His Excellency Emrys Thomas Davies, CMG, resident at Bridgetown, Barbados
*Resident Representative,* R. G. Baylis, MVO (*Acting High Commissioner*)

### ECONOMY

Tourism is the main sector of the economy. Tourism and related services account for 60 per cent of GDP and employ 40 per cent of the workforce; Antigua was one of the first Caribbean islands to attract tourists.

For many years sugar was the dominant crop but is no longer produced. Agricultural production includes livestock, sea island cotton, mixed market gardening and fishing.

| FINANCE | 1992* | 1993* |
|---|---|---|
| Revenue | EC$251,331,799 | EC$255,893,891 |
| Expenditure (recurrent) | 278,084,340 | 306,663,306 |
| *estimated | | |

| Trade with UK | 1992 | 1993 |
|---|---|---|
| Imports from UK | £16,528,000 | £17,752,000 |
| Exports to UK | 2,511,000 | 2,524,000 |

## ARGENTINA
*República Argentina*

Argentina occupies the greater portion of the southern part of the South American continent, and extends from Bolivia to Cape Horn, a total distance of nearly 2,300 miles; its greatest breadth is about 930 miles. It is bounded on the north by Bolivia, on the north-east by Paraguay, Brazil and Uruguay, on the south-east and south by the Atlantic, and on the west by Chile, from which it is separated by the Cordillera de los Andes. On the west the mountainous Cordilleras, with their plateaux, extend from the northern to the southern boundaries; on the east are the great plains.

Argentina has an area of 1,068,302 sq. miles (2,766,889 sq. km.), with a population (census 1991) of 32,370,298.

CAPITAL – ΨBuenos Aires, population (1990), metropolitan area 2,955,002; with suburbs, 10,881,381. Other large towns are: ΨRosario (1,071,384), Córdoba (1,134,086), ΨLa Plata (630,260), ΨMar del Plata (503,779), San Miguel de Tucumán (603,331), ΨSanta Fé (329,814) and Mendoza (706,909).

CURRENCY – Peso of 10,000 australes.

FLAG – Horizontal bands of blue, white, blue; gold sun in centre of white band.

NATIONAL ANTHEM – Oid Mortales! (Hear, oh mortals!).

NATIONAL DAY – 25 May.

### GOVERNMENT

The estuary of La Plata was discovered in 1515 by Juan Díaz de Solís, but it was not until 1536 that Pedro de Mendoza founded Buenos Aires. This city was abandoned and later re-founded by Don Juan de Garay in 1580. Spain ruled the territory from the 16th century until 1810, when Spanish rule was defied. In 1816, after a long campaign of liberation conducted by General José de San Martín, the independence of Argentina was declared by the Congress of Tucumán.

In 1946 Juan Domingo Perón became President until overthrown in 1955. There followed eighteen years of political and economic instability, and eventually in 1973, Perón was recalled from exile. Elected President he died within a year and was succeeded by his widow, Vice-President María Estela Martínez de Perón. However, warring factions in the Perónist movement and increasing terrorist activity eventually led to a coup by the armed forces in 1976. A Junta, consisting of the three commanders of the armed forces, was established, with one of their number as President. Following the Falkland Islands defeat in 1982 the President, Gen. Galtieri, resigned and the Army appointed Gen. Bignone as President. Elections for a civilian government to replace the military one were held in 1983 and a civilian President was elected. Presidential elections in May 1989 were won by the Justicialist Party (Perónist) candidate Carlos Menem.

Executive power is vested in the President who appoints the Cabinet and is elected for a single six-year term by an electoral college. The legislature consists of a 46-member (two for each province) Senate and a 259-member Chamber of Deputies. A third of the Senate is elected every three years and half of the Chamber of Deputies is elected every two years. Senators serve for a nine-year term and Deputies for a four-year term. After the most recent elections in October 1993 the Justicialist Party held 126 seats in the Chamber of Deputies and the Radical Civic Union 83 seats. In April 1994 elections were held to a 305-seat constitutional assembly which, at President Menem's instigation, will debate and amend the 1853 constitution by late 1994, principally to allow two presidential terms of four years rather than one of six years.

The republic is divided into 23 provinces and one federal district (Buenos Aires).

## HEAD OF STATE
*President*, Dr Carlos Saúl Menem, *took office* 8 July 1989

## CABINET *as at June 1994*

*Interior*, Dr Carlos Ruckauf
*Foreign Affairs*, Dr Guido Di Tella
*Labour*, Armando Caro-Figueroa
*Economy and Public Works*, Dr Domingo Cavallo
*Education*, Jorge Alberto Rodriguez
*Defence*, Dr Oscar Camillión
*Health and Social Welfare*, Dr Alberto Mazza
*Justice*, Jorge Maiorano

## EMBASSY OF THE ARGENTINE REPUBLIC
53 Hans Place, London SW1X 0LA
Tel 0171-584 6494

*Ambassador Extraordinary and Plenipotentiary*, His Excellency Mario Cámpora, apptd 1991

## BRITISH EMBASSY
Dr Luis Agote 2412, 1425 Buenos Aires
Tel: Buenos Aires 803-7070/1

*Ambassador Extraordinary and Plenipotentiary*, His Excellency Sir Peter Hall, KBE, CMG, apptd 1994
*Deputy Ambassador, Minister and Consul-General*, David Reddaway, CMG
*Defence and Military Attaché*, Col. R. J. Lawson
*First Secretary (Commercial)*, H. M. McIntosh, CBE
*Cultural, Attaché and British Council Representative*, Harold Fish, OBE, Martcelo T. de Alvear 590, 1058 Buenos Aires

## BRITISH CHAMBER OF COMMERCE, Av. Corrientes 457,
10 piso, 1043 Buenos Aires

## ECONOMY

The Menem government introduced a successful economic reform programme in April 1991 which has involved the privatization of most state-owned industries, widespread deregulation, exchange-rate stabilization and lower trade barriers. This has led to increased foreign investment (US$17 billion in 1993) and much lower inflation (9 per cent annually in 1993-4), which has transformed the economy (average growth of 8 per cent since 1991).

Argentina's foreign debt in 1993 was calculated at US$19,200 million in principal (not including interest charges). A debt reduction plan was agreed in April 1993 with creditors to reduce the cost of servicing the foreign debt by one-third. Large-scale privatization has brought the government US$9 billion in receipts, retired a larger amount of foreign debt and enabled the introduction of a balanced budget in February 1994, but unemployment increased to 18 per cent in 1994.

## AGRICULTURE
Of a total land area of approximately 700 million acres, farms occupy about 425 million. About 60 per cent of the farmland is pasture, 10 per cent annual crops, 5 per cent permanent crops and the remaining 25 per cent forest and wasteland. A large proportion of the land is still held in large estates devoted to cattle raising but the number of small farms is increasing. The principal crops are wheat, maize, oats, barley, rye, linseed, sunflower seed, alfalfa, sugar, fruit and cotton. Argentina is pre-eminent in the production of beef, mutton and wool, and pastoral and agricultural products provide about 85 per cent of Argentina's exports.

## MINERAL PRODUCTION
Oil is found in various parts of the republic and the production of oil is of first importance to Argentina's industries. Total petroleum output for 1991 was 484,000 b.p.d. There is a refinery in San Lorenzo (Santa Fé province). Natural gas is also produced in a number of provinces.

Coal, lead, zinc, tungsten, iron ore, sulphur, mica and salt are the other chief minerals being exploited. There are small worked deposits of beryllium, manganese, bismuth, uranium, antimony, copper, kaolin, arsenate, gold, silver and tin. Coal is produced at the Rio Turbio mine in the province of Santa Cruz. The output of other materials is not large but greater attention is now being paid to the development of these natural resources, especially copper for which the Government and private companies are carrying out exploration.

## INDUSTRIES
Meat-packing is one of the principal industries; flour-milling, sugar-refining, and the wine industry are also important. In recent years progress has been made by the textile, plastic and machine tool industries and engineering, especially in the production of motor vehicles and steel manufactures.

| *Trade with UK* | 1992 | 1993 |
|---|---|---|
| Imports from UK | £118,746,000 | £179,259,000 |
| Exports to UK | 124,603,000 | 141,143,000 |

## COMMUNICATIONS

There are 25,386 miles of railways, which are state property. Plans are in hand for complete re-organization of the railways in order to improve their operating efficiency and reduce a very large financial deficit. The combined national and provincial road network totals approximately 137,000 miles of which 23,180 miles are surfaced. There are air services between Argentina and all the neighbouring republics, Europe, Asia, Canada, the USA and South Africa.

## DEFENCE

Total active armed forces number some 70,800 personnel (18,100 conscripts). Conscripts serve between seven and 14 months. Reserves total 377,000 (Army 250,000; Navy 77,000; Air Force 50,000).

The Army numbers 40,400, including about 13,400 conscripts with 265 main battle tanks, 165 light tanks, 585 armoured infantry fighting vehicles and armoured personnel carriers, 375 artillery pieces and 43 helicopters.

The Navy consists of 1 aircraft carrier (in store), 6 destroyers, 7 frigates, 4 submarines, 6 minesweepers, 13 patrol and coastal craft, 42 combat aircraft and 13 armed helicopters. Strength is 28,500, including 3,500 conscripts and 4,000 marines. The Air Force has a strength of 8,900 (1,200 conscripts) with 180 combat aircraft, 11 armed helicopters and 10 air defence artillery batteries. In addition, there is a paramilitary gendarmerie of some 18,000 personnel under Ministry of Defence control.

Argentina currently deploys one 895-strong infantry battalion with UN forces in Croatia and one 373-strong infantry battalion with UN forces in Cyprus.

## EDUCATION

Education is compulsory for the seven grades of primary school (6 to 13). Secondary schools (14 to 17+) are available in and around Buenos Aires and in most of the important towns in the interior of the country. Most secondary schools are administered by the Central Ministry of Education in Buenos Aires, while primary schools are administered by the Central Ministry or by Provincial Ministries of Education. Private schools, of which there are many, are also loosely controlled by the Central Ministry. The total number of universities is over 50 with 24 national, 25 private and a small number of provincial universities.

## CULTURE

Spanish is the language of the republic and the literature of Spain is accepted as an inheritance by the people. There is little indigenous literature before the break from Spain, but all branches have flourished since the latter half of the nineteenth century. About 450 daily newspapers are published in Argentina, including seven major ones in the city of Buenos Aires. The English language newspaper is the *Buenos Aires Herald* (daily). There are several other foreign language newspapers.

---

# ARMENIA
*Haikakan Hanrapetoutioun*

---

Armenia has an area of 11,306 sq. miles (29,800 sq. km) and lies between the Black and Caspian Seas, occupying the south-western part of the Caucasus region of the former Soviet Union. It is bordered on the east and south-west by Azerbaijan, on the north by Georgia, on the south by Iran and on the west by Turkey. It is a very mountainous country consisting of several vast tablelands surrounded by ridges.

CLIMATE – Continental, dry and cold, but the Araks valley has a long, hot and dry summer.

POPULATION – The population (1992 official estimate) is 3,645,000, concentrated in the low-lying part of Armenia, the Aras valley and the Erevan hollow. Armenians form 93 per cent of the population, Kurds 1.7 per cent and Russians 1.6 per cent. Azerbaijanis formed 2.6 per cent of the population, but most fled or were expelled after the outbreak of the conflict with Azerbaijan. There are also Ukranians, Greeks and Assyrians. The Armenian diaspora numbers some 5,300,000, including 1,500,000 in the former Soviet states, 1,000,000 in the USA and 400,000 in France.

LANGUAGE – Armenian is the official language, though Russian is widely spoken and understood.

RELIGION – Armenian Orthodox Christian (Armenian Church centred in Etchmiadzin). Armenia adopted Christianity as its official religion in AD 301, the first state in the world to do so.

CAPITAL – Erevan. Population 1,199,000 (1989).

CURRENCY – Dram of 100 louma.

FLAG – Three horizontal stripes of red, blue and orange.

NATIONAL DAY – 27 May (Independence Day).

## GOVERNMENT

Armenia was an ancient society, first mentioned in the ninth century BC. In 95 BC the country was first united, stretching from the Caspian to the Black Seas and southwards to the Mediterranean. Divided between the Persian and Byzantine Empires in AD 387, the country was conquered in the 11th century by the Seljuk Turks and the Mongols. In the 16th century most of Armenia was incorporated into the Ottoman Empire. In 1639 the country was divided again, the easternmost portions, now the republic of Armenia, becoming part of the Persian Empire. In 1828 eastern Armenia became part of the Russian Empire while western Armenia remained under Ottoman rule. The Ottomans launched pogroms against the Armenians from 1894 onwards, and in 1915 to 1918 massacred 1,500,000 Armenians.

After the 1917 Russian revolution, Armenia declared its independence as a republic on 27 May 1918, but was crushed and divided between Turkish and Soviet forces in 1920. On 29 November 1920 Armenia was proclaimed a Soviet Socialist Republic. The Soviet government was overthrown by a nationalist revolt in 1921 but reinstated by the Red Army a few months later. In early 1922 Armenia acceded to the USSR.

Gorbachev's reform policies slowly filtered through to Armenia in 1987 when demonstrations against pollution caused by Soviet industrialization in the republic and against local Communist Party corruption became political. The focus of political opposition to Communist rule was support for the self-determination of the autonomous region of Nagorny-Karabakh in Azerbaijan which was predominantly Armenian populated. Throughout 1988–90 the Soviet authorities were perceived as supporting Azerbaijan over Nagorny-Karabakh, and an Armenian nationalist movement evolved which swept to power in national elections in mid-1990. The new non-Communist government supported Nagorno-Karabakh Armenians in their conflict with Azerbaijan and loosened links with the rest of the Soviet Union. In a referendum in September 1991, 99 per cent of the electorate voted for independence. Armenia declared independence from the Soviet Union on 23 September 1991 and was admitted to membership of the UN in March 1992.

The political situation in Armenia is dominated by the war with Azerbaijan and the effects of the 1988 earthquake. The earthquake, which devastated much of the country, left thousands homeless and industry badly affected, and Armenia has neither the money nor the expertise to complete the rebuilding process.

The war with Azerbaijan over the disputed region of Nagorny-Karabakh, the Armenian-populated enclave in Azerbaijan, simmered from February 1988 and erupted into all-out war in May 1992, when Armenian forces breached Azerbaijan's defences to form a land bridge to Nagorny-Karabakh. By the end of summer 1992 all of Nagorny-Karabakh was under Armenian control. Continued victories over Azeri forces in late 1992 and 1993 culminated in victories in April 1993 at Kelbadzher, July 1993 at Agdam, August 1993 at Fizuli and September 1993 at Kabatli. All

Azeri territory that separated Nagorny-Karabakh from Armenia and all mountainous Azeri territory around Nagorny-Karabakh are now under Armenian control, an estimated 10 per cent of Azeri territory. Armenia claims this territory as historically Armenian land arbitrarily given to Azerbaijan by Stalin in 1921–2.

Since 1988 Azerbaijan has imposed an economic blockade on Armenia which is almost total as the neighbouring states of Turkey and Iran generally support Azerbaijan. Fighting in Georgia in 1993 and 1994 cut all remaining land supply routes and the gas pipeline from Russia, which now sends gas via Iran. The severe economic crisis led the President to declare a state of emergency on 15 December 1992, and to replace the government in February 1993 for failing to implement economic reforms.

Armenia is divided into 37 Administrative Districts.

HEAD OF STATE
*President*, Levon Ter-Petrosyan, *elected* 16 October 1991

CABINET *as at July 1994*
*Prime Minister*, Grant Bagratyan
*Deputy Prime Minister*, Vigen Chitechan
*Minister of State (Industry and Energy)*, Sepuh Taschan
*Minister of State (Agriculture and Food)*, Gagik Shakhbazyan
*Minister of State (Border Regions)*, Vasgen Sarkisiyan
*Ministers of State*: Rafael Bagoan; Armenak Kasarian; Gagik Martirosian
*Defence*, Serge Sarkissian
*Interior*, Vano Siradegyan
*Higher Education and Science*, Vardkes Gnuni
*Public Health*, Ara Babloyan
*Foreign Affairs*, Vagan Papazian
*Culture*, Akop Akopyan
*Light Industry*, Rudolf Teymurazan
*Material Resources*, Vagan Melkonyan
*Environmental Protection*, Karine Danielyan
*Industry*, Ashot Safaryan
*Education*, Gaik Kazaryan
*Food*, David Zadoyan
*Communications*, Grigor Pokhpatyan
*Agriculture*, Ashot Voskahyan
*Construction*, Felix Pirumiyan
*Trade*, Tigran Grigoryan
*Transport*, Genrikh Kochinyan
*Labour*, Ashot Yesayan
*Finance*, Levon Barhudaryan
*Economics*, Armen Egiazaran
*Engineering and Fuel*, Miron Shishmaniyan
*Justice*, Vage Stepanyan
*Procurator-General*, Artavazd Gevorkyan

*Chairman of the Supreme Soviet*, Babken Ararktsyan

EMBASSY OF THE REPUBLIC OF ARMENIA
25 Cheniston Gardens, London w8 6TG
Tel 0171-938 5345
*Ambassador Extraordinary and Plenipotentiary*, His Excellency Prof. Armen Sarkissian, apptd 1993
BRITISH AMBASSADOR – His Excellency Sir Brian Fall, KCMG, resident at Moscow

DEFENCE

Armenia maintains an army of some 20,000 regular personnel, including conscripts who serve 18-month terms, and paramilitary forces of some 1,000. Both these forces are heavily involved in supplying and supporting the Nagorno-Karabakh armed volunteers who engage in the majority of fighting with Azeri forces. The Nagorno-Karabakh forces

number 20,000 personnel equipped with light and medium weapons and artillery, while Armenian forces supply small numbers of tanks and helicopters. The regular army has some 160 main battle tanks, 440 armoured personnel carriers and infantry fighting vehicles, 260 artillery pieces and 20 armed helicopters.

Russia maintains 4,500 army personnel in Armenia.

ECONOMY

Armenia has a strong agricultural sector in low-lying areas, where industrial and fruit crops are grown. Grain is grown in the hills and the country is also noted for its wine. There are large copper ore and molybdenum deposits and other minerals. The Armenian economy has been crippled by a trade blockade by Azerbaijan, through which supplies of oil and gas used to come. The severe energy crisis caused the government to announce its intention to reopen the republic's nuclear power station, which had been closed since the 1988 earthquake; in January 1993 the single remaining fuel supply, the gas pipeline from Russia through Georgia, was destroyed by sabotage. Rationing was introduced in December 1992 to combat food shortages and the supply of electricity and water is erratic. The President has appealed for international aid.

| *Trade with UK* | 1993 |
| --- | --- |
| Imports from UK | £5,346,000 |
| Exports to UK | 18,000 |

CULTURE

The Armenian alphabet was established in AD 391 and had a fully written form in the fifth century. Major writers include the poets Frick (13th century), Naapet Kuchat (16th century) and Saat-Nova (18th century). The composer Aram Khachaturian (1903–78) was Armenian.

# AUSTRALIA
## *The Commonwealth of Australia*

AREA AND POPULATION*

| *States and Territories* | *Area (sq. km)* | Resident population 31 December 1993p |
| --- | --- | --- |
| New South Wales (NSW) | 801,600 | 6,023,500 |
| Queensland (Qld.) | 1,727,200 | 3,155,400 |
| South Australia (SA) | 984,000 | 1,466,500 |
| Tasmania (Tas.) | 67,800 | 472,100 |
| Victoria (Vic.) | 227,600 | 4,468,300 |
| Western Australia (WA) | 2,525,500 | 1,687,300 |
| Australian Capital Territory (ACT) | 2,400 | 299,400 |
| Northern Territory (NT) | 1,346,200 | 170,500 |
| *Total* | 7,682,300 | 17,746,600 |

* estimated
p preliminary

POPULATION OF ABORIGINAL AND TORRES STRAIT ISLANDER ORIGIN *as at June 1991*

| | Number | % of state population |
| --- | --- | --- |
| New South Wales | 68,941 | 1.20 |
| Queensland | 67,012 | 2.32 |

| South Australia | 16,238 | 1.14 |
| Tasmania | 8,886 | 1.90 |
| Victoria | 16,570 | 0.39 |
| Western Australia | 41,792 | 2.54 |
| Australian Capital Territory | 1,772 | 0.63 |
| Northern Territory | 39,918 | 24.01 |
| *Total* | 261,129 | 1.53 |

BIRTHS, DEATHS, MARRIAGES AND DIVORCES *year ended 30 June*

| | 1991 | 1992 | 1993p |
|---|---|---|---|
| Births | 261,158 | 255,624 | 265,590 |
| Deaths | 119,571 | 120,838 | 121,776 |
| Marriages | 114,796 | 113,524 | 113,706 |
| Divorces† | 45,630 | 45,665 | 48,324 |

† year ended 31 December
p preliminary

MIGRATION *year ended 30 June*

| | 1991 | 1992 | 1993 |
|---|---|---|---|
| Permanent arrivals | 121,690 | 107,390 | 76,330 |
| Permanent departures | 31,130 | 29,120 | 27,910 |

## GEOGRAPHY

Australia, including Tasmania, comprises a land area of 7,682,300 sq. km lying between latitudes 10°41′ S. (Cape York) and 43°39′ S. (South East Cape, Tasmania) and longitudes 113°09′ E. (Steep Point) and 153°39′ E. (Cape Byron). The latitudinal distance between Cape York and South East Cape is about 3,680 km and the longitudinal distance between Steep Point and Cape Byron is about 4,000 km. The latitudinal distance between Cape York and the most southerly point on the mainland South Point, Wilson's Promontory, is about 3,180 km.

Australia has three major landforms: the western plateau, the interior lowlands and the eastern uplands. The western half of the continent consists mainly of a great plateau of altitude 300–600 metres. The interior lowland includes the channel country of south-west Queensland (drainage to Lake Eyre) and the Murray-Darling river system to the south. The eastern uplands consist of a broad belt of varied width extending from north Queensland to Tasmania and composed largely of tablelands, ranges and ridges with only limited mountain areas above 1,000 metres. The highest point is Mt. Kosciusko (2,228 m) and the lowest, Lake Eyre (−15 m).

Climatic conditions range from the alpine to the tropical. Two-thirds of the continent is arid or semi-arid although good rainfalls (over 800 mm annually) occur in the northern monsoonal belt and along the eastern and southern highland regions. Fifty per cent of the area of Australia has a medium rainfall of less than 300 mm per year and 80 per cent has less than 600 mm. The effectiveness of the rainfall is greatly reduced by marked alternations of wet and dry seasons, unreliability from year to year, high temperatures and high potential evaporation.

FEDERAL CAPITAL – Canberra, in the Australian Capital Territory. Estimated population at 30 June 1992 was 296,400. It has been the seat of government since 1927 and the location of most government department headquarters. The Australian Capital Territory was surrendered by New South Wales to the Commonwealth Government on 1 January 1911.

CURRENCY – Australian dollar ($A) of 100 cents.

FLAG – The British Blue Ensign with five stars of the Southern Cross in the fly and the white Commonwealth Star of seven points beneath the Union Jack.

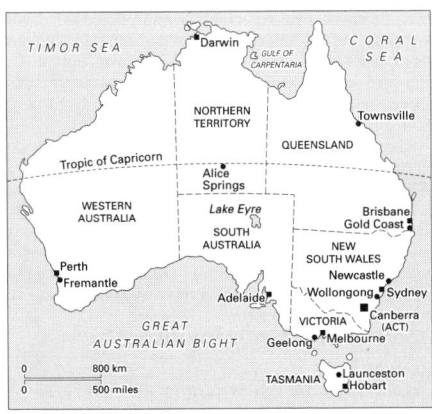

NATIONAL ANTHEM – Advance Australia Fair.
NATIONAL DAY – 26 January (Australia Day).

## GOVERNMENT

The continent of Australia was discovered in the 18th century and was colonized by the British, initially as a penal colony.

The Commonwealth of Australia was inaugurated on 1 January 1901. The government is that of a federal Commonwealth within the British Commonwealth, the executive power being vested in the Sovereign (through the Governor-General), assisted by a federal government. Under the constitution the federal government has acquired and may acquire certain defined powers as surrendered by the States, residuary legislative power remaining with the States. The right of a State to legislate on any matter is not abrogated except in connection with matters exclusively under federal control, but where a State law is inconsistent with a law of the Commonwealth the latter prevails to the extent of the inconsistency.

The 1993 Native Title Act restores land rights to the Aborigines which were lost after British settlement, by establishing a system of tribunals that may give land title to indigenous people who can show customary use over the land.

GOVERNOR-GENERAL AND STAFF

*Governor-General*, His Excellency the Hon. Bill Hayden, AC, *assumed office*, 16 February 1989
*Official Secretary*, R. D. Sturkey
*Deputy Official Secretary*, Ms J. Hall

CABINET *as at June 1994*

*Prime Minister*, Hon. Paul Keating
*Deputy Prime Minister, Housing and Regional Development*, Hon. Brian Howe
*Leader of the Government in the Senate and Foreign Affairs*, Senator Hon. Gareth Evans, QC
*Deputy Leader of the Government in the Senate and Defence*, Senator Hon. Robert Ray
*Treasurer*, Hon. Ralph Willis
*Finance*, Hon. Kim Beazley
*Employment, Education and Training*, Hon. Simon Crean
*Health and Human Services*, Hon. Dr Carmen Lawrence
*Environment, Sport and Territories*, Senator Hon. John Faulkner
*Trade*, Senator Hon. Robert McMullan
*Immigration and Ethnic Affairs*, Senator Hon. Nick Bolkus
*Primary Industries and Energy*, Senator Hon. Robert Collins

*Industry, Science and Technology,* Senator Hon. Peter Cook
*Communications, Tourism and the Arts,* Hon. Michael Lee
*Industrial Relations and Transport,* Hon. Laurence Brereton
*Attorney-General,* Hon. Michael Lavarch
*Social Security,* Hon. Peter Baldwin

JUNIOR MINISTERS

*Resources,* Hon. David Beddall
*Development Co-operation and Pacific Island Affairs,* Hon. Gordon Bilney
*Aboriginal and Torres Strait Islander Affairs,* Hon. Robert Tickner
*Schools, Vocational Education and Training,* Hon. Ross Free
*Consumer Affairs,* Hon. Jeannette McHugh
*Family Services,* Senator Hon. Rosemary Crowley
*Defence Science and Personnel,* Hon. Gary Punch
*Veterans' Affairs,* Hon. Con Sciacca
*Assistant Treasurer,* Hon. George Gear
*Justice,* Hon. Duncan Kerr
*Small Business, Customs and Construction,* Senator Hon. Christopher Schacht
*Administrative Services,* Hon. Frank Walker
*Special Minister of State,* Hon. Gary Johns

AUSTRALIAN HIGH COMMISSION
Australia House, Strand, London WC2B 4LA
Tel 0171-379 4334

*High Commissioner,* His Excellency The Hon. Neal Blewett, apptd 1994
*Deputy High Commissioner,* D. Goss
*Ministers,* I. Wilcock (*Political*); R. Murray (*Economic*); D. Richard (*Commercial*)
*Defence Adviser and Head of Defence Staff,* Cdre G. P. Kable
*Consul-General,* Ms J. Harrhy (*Manchester*)

BRITISH HIGH COMMISSION
Commonwealth Avenue, Yarralumla, Canberra, ACT 2600
Tel: Canberra (6) 270 6666

*High Commissioner,* His Excellency Sir Brian Barder, KCMG, apptd 1991
*Deputy High Commissioner, Head of Chancery,* D. W. Fall
*Counsellor,* T. H. Byrne (*Director, Trade Promotion*)
*Defence and Naval Adviser and Head of British Defence Liaison Staff,* Cdre B. J. Adams
*Consuls-General,* J. C. Durham, LVO (*Brisbane*); S. D. R. Brown (*Melbourne*); A. J. Abott (*Perth*); R. S. Reeve (*Sydney*)
*Cultural Adviser and British Council Representative,* J. Potts, OBE, Edgecliff Centre, 203–233 New South Head Road (PO Box 88), Edgecliff, Sydney, NSW 2027

LEGISLATURE

Parliament consists of The Queen, the Senate and the House of Representatives. The constitution provides that the number of members of the House of Representatives shall be, as nearly as practicable, twice the number of Senators. Members of the Senate are elected for six years by universal suffrage, half the members retiring every third year. Each of the six States returns an equal number of 12 Senators, and the Australian Capital Territory and the Northern Territory two each. The House of Representatives, similarly elected for a maximum of three years, contains members proportionate to the population, with a minimum of five members for each State. There are now 148 members in the House of Representatives, including one member for the Northern Territory and two for the Australian Capital Territory.

*President of the Senate,* Senator Hon. Kerry Sibraa
*Speaker, House of Representatives,* Hon. Stephen Martin

JUDICATURE

The constitution of the Commonwealth of Australia established a High Court, composed of a Chief Justice and six Justices appointed by the Governor-General on the advice of the government. The High Court exercises jurisdiction over all matters arising from the constitution, all matters arising between the States and between residents of different States, matters to which the Commonwealth of Australia is a party, and treaties and foreign representatives in Australia. The High Court also hears appeals from the Federal Court and from the Supreme Courts of States and Territories.

The Federal Court of Australia was established in 1977 and has jurisdiction over important industrial and bankruptcy matters and also acts as a court of appeal from State and Territory Courts in relation to Federal matters.

*Chief Justice of the High Court of Australia,* Hon. Sir Anthony Mason, AC, KBE
*Chief Justice of the Federal Court of Australia,* Hon. M. E. J. Black
*Chief Justice of the Australian Capital Territory,* Hon. J. A. Miles

DEFENCE

A single Department of Defence was created in 1973, though the separate identities of the three services have been retained. The Chief of Defence Force Staff is responsible for command of the Defence Force through the three Service Chiefs of Staff and is also the principal military adviser to the Minister. The Secretary to the Department of Defence is responsible to the Minister for Defence for advice on policy, resources and organization. Total defence expenditure was $A9,886 million in 1992–3.

The total active armed forces number 63,200 personnel, with reserves numbering 29,400 personnel. All service is voluntary. The Army has a strength of 28,600 and is organized into one regular and one reservist division (reserves number 26,200). In addition, there is a regular northern command of one air defence, one aviation and one SAS regiment. The regular division is composed of one mechanized and two infantry brigades with reconnaissance, artillery, engineer and aviation regiments, whereas the reservist division is composed of 14 infantry battalions with similar support regiments. Equipment includes 103 main battle tanks, 785 armoured personnel carriers and armoured infantry fighting vehicles, 355 artillery pieces, 22 aircraft and 125 helicopters, of which 25 are armed.

The Navy has a personnel strength of 15,300 with a further 1,600 reservists, and has four main bases at Sydney, Cockburn Sound, Cairns and Darwin. It has five submarines, three destroyers, eight frigates and 18 patrol and coastal craft with 15 armed helicopters.

The Air Force has a strength of 19,300, together with 1,600 reserves, and 157 combat aircraft organized into two ground attack/reconnaissance, three air defence, two maritime reconnaissance and seven transport squadrons with training and support units.

One Army infantry company and one Air Force detachment are stationed in Malaysia. US Navy and Air Force personnel numbering 400 are stationed at communications facilities in Australia.

## FINANCE

COMMONWEALTH GOVERNMENT FINANCE

Outlays and revenue of the Commonwealth Government were ($Amillion):

|  | 1992–3 | 1993–4 |
|---|---|---|
| Current outlays | 105,511 | 113,636 |
| Capital outlays | 3,917 | 1,191 |
| Total revenue | 94,858 | 100,920 |

STATE GOVERNMENT FINANCE 1992–3* ($A million)

|  | Outlay (current and capital) | Revenue and grants received | Net Financing Requirement |
|---|---|---|---|
| NSW | 23,740 | 23,059 | 318 |
| Victoria | 18,654 | 16,558 | 1,716 |
| Queensland | 11,470 | 12,471 | −1,105 |
| S. Australia | 6,995 | 6,139 | 697 |
| W. Australia | 7,440 | 6,760 | 682 |
| Tasmania | 2,239 | 2,084 | 164 |
| NT | 1,473 | 1,408 | 120 |
| ACT | 1,275 | 1,262 | −26 |
| Total | 73,286 | 69,741 | 2,566 |

* preliminary

BANKING

In April 1994 the trading banks had total liabilities of $A345,172 million including total deposits of $A370,431 million securities.

## ECONOMY

AGRICULTURE – In 1992, 60.6 per cent of land area consisted of agricultural establishments, the remainder being urban areas, state forests, mining leases and unoccupied land. Crop-growing areas constituted up to 3.52 per cent of the total agricultural establishments, emphasizing the relative importance of the livestock industries in Australia (sheep in the warm, temperate, semi-arid lands and beef cattle in the tropics).

The wide range of climatic and soil conditions has resulted in a diversity of crops. Generally, cereal crops (excluding rice and sorghum) are grown in all States over wide areas, while other crops are confined to specific locations in a few States. However, scanty or erratic rainfall, limited potential for irrigation and unsuitable soils or topography have restricted intensive agriculture.

GROSS VALUE OF AGRICULTURAL COMMODITIES 1992–3p

|  | $A million |
|---|---|
| Crops | 10,654.3 |
| Livestock slaughterings and other disposals | 6,074.7 |
| Livestock products | 5,218.4 |
| Total agriculture | 21,959.9 |

p preliminary

LIVESTOCK NUMBERS at 31 March 1992

|  | Thousands |
|---|---|
| Cattle | 23,880 |
| Sheep | 148,203 |
| Pigs | 2,792 |
| Poultry | 55,743 |

GROSS VALUE OF CROPS 1992–3p

|  | $A million |
|---|---|
| Cereals for grain | 4,081.7 |
| Cotton | 766.4 |
| Crops for hay | 120.8 |
| Fruit and nuts | 1,689.9 |
| Legumes for grain | 435.3 |
| Nursery production | 568.6 |
| Oilseeds | 92.6 |
| Peanuts | 34.1 |
| Sugar cane for crushing | 807.3 |
| Tobacco | 66.0 |
| Vegetables | 1,398.5 |
| Pastures and grasses | 593.0 |
| Total crops | 10,654.3 |

p preliminary

MINES AND MINERALS – Significant mineral resources include bauxite, coal, copper, crude petroleum, gems, gold, ilmenite, iron ore, lead, limestone, manganese, nickel, rutile, salt, silver, tin, tungsten, uranium, zinc and zircon. Recently, geological exploration has significantly increased mineral resources and a number of oilfields are in production.

In 1991–2 the total value of all minerals produced was $A25,985 million. In 1991–2 mine production of black coal was 218,262,000 tonnes, crude oil (including condensate) was 31,309 megalitres and natural gas 22,564 gigalitres. Production of principal metals in 1991 was (tonnes):

| Iron ore | 117,000,000 |
|---|---|
| Copper | 311,000 |
| Lead | 531,000 |
| Gold | 234 |

MANUFACTURES – In 1990–1 there were in Australia 40,653 manufacturing establishments, employing 961,800 persons; wages paid amounted to $A27,706 million; and turnover $A171,874 million.

## TRADE

Of Australia's total exports in the year 1992–3, the largest category was coal worth $A7,538m. This was followed by gold, $A4,315m; iron ore concentrates, $A2,895m; and meat of bovine animals, $A2,991m.

The largest category of Australia's imports was road vehicles, worth $A3,195m. This was followed by aircraft and associated equipment, $A1,697m; office and automatic data processing machines, $A2,323m; petrol and oils, $A2,258m; parts and accessories for office machinery, $A1,591m; paper and pulp, $A1,419m.

|  | 1991–2 | 1992–3 |
|---|---|---|
| Imports | $A50,984m | $A59,577m |
| Exports | 55,027m | 60,778m |

In 1992–3, 25 per cent of Australia's total exports went to Japan. The USA received 8 per cent, Republic of Korea 7, Singapore 6, New Zealand 6, Taiwan 4, UK 4, Hong Kong 4 and China 4.

Of Australia's total imports in 1992–3, 22 per cent came from the USA, 19 from Japan, 6 Germany, 6 UK, 5 New Zealand, 4 Taiwan and 4 China.

| Trade with UK | 1992 | 1993 |
|---|---|---|
| Imports from UK | £1,376,737,000 | £1,598,359,000 |
| Exports to UK | 1,013,680,000 | 996,153,000 |

## COMMUNICATIONS

RAILWAYS – There are six government-owned railway systems, operated by the State Rail Authority of NSW, Victorian Railways, Queensland Government Railways, Western Australian Government Railways, the State Transport Authority of Southern Australia, and the Australian National Railways Commission. The ANRC incorporates the former Commonwealth Railways system, and the Tasmanian and non-metropolitan South Australian railways (urban rail services in Southern Australia remain the responsibility of the State Transport Authority). In 1990 there were 35,486 route-kilometres open.

In 1990–1 there were 410.6 million rail passenger journeys on government railways and 188.56 million tonnes of goods and livestock carried.

MOTOR VEHICLES – At 30 June 1992, there were 9,954,500 motor vehicles registered in Australia and 292,400 motor cycles.

CIVIL AVIATION – Figures for domestic and overseas services in 1992 are as follows:

|  | Domestic | Overseas |
|---|---|---|
| Paying passengers | 20,198,197 | 9,302,052 |
| Freight (tonnes) | 124,991 | 405,870 |

SHIPPING – Total arrivals and departures of vessels engaged in overseas trade at the various Australian ports in 1989–90 were: arrivals 15,521 (362,030,000 deadweight tonnes); departures 15,372 (527,223,000 deadweight tonnes).

BROADCASTING AND TELEVISION – On 30 June 1991, the Australian Broadcasting Corporation operated 410 stations. Privately owned commercial broadcasting stations totalled 203. On 30 June 1991, 511 national and 563 commercial television and translator stations were in operation.

## THE NORTHERN TERRITORY

The Northern Territory has a total area of 519,770 sq. miles (1,346,200 sq. km), and lies between 129°–138° E. longitude and 11°–26° S. latitude. The estimated population in the Northern Territory at 30 June 1993 was 175,000, of which about a quarter are Aboriginals.

### GOVERNMENT

The administration was taken over by the Commonwealth on 1 January 1911 from the State of South Australia. The Northern Territory (Self-Government) Act 1978 established the Northern Territory as a body politic as from 1 July 1978, with Ministers having control over and responsibility for Territory finances and the administration of the functions of government as specified by the federal government by regulations made pursuant to the Act. Proposed laws passed by the Legislative Assembly in relation to a transferred function require the assent of the Administrator. Proposed laws in all other cases may be assented to by the Administrator or reserved by the Administrator for the Governor-General's pleasure. The Governor-General may disallow any laws assented to by the Administrator within six months of the Administrator's assent.

The Northern Territory has federal representation, electing one member to the House of Representatives and two members to the Senate.

SEAT OF ADMINISTRATION – Darwin

*Administrator*, His Hon. the Honourable Austin Asche, AC, QC

*Chief Minister*, Hon. Marshall Perron

*Chief Justice of the Supreme Court of the Northern Territory*, Hon. B. F. Martin

### ABORIGINAL LANDS

Various Aboriginal Land Trusts hold title to land previously called Reserves, totalling about one-fifth of the Northern Territory. The Aboriginal Land Rights (NT) Act of 1976 provides for the investigation and determination of Aboriginal traditional claims to vacant Crown land or land already owned by or on behalf of Aboriginals. Successful land claims to date have increased Aboriginal ownership to 34 per cent of the Northern Territory and a further 13 per cent is the subject of claims.

A number of major Aboriginal communities previously administered by church mission societies and the federal government are now controlled by the Aboriginal people through local Aboriginal Councils. A recent phenomenon is the voluntary movement of some Aboriginals to their traditional homeland areas where they feel that their culture will be better preserved.

### ECONOMY

Northern Territory's economy is based on the exploitation of its natural resources of minerals, land and fisheries and on tourist attractions. Following the introduction of a number of government measures designed to expand and diversify primary production, the Territory's agricultural and horticultural industries are also beginning to contribute an increasing amount to Territory rural output. The beef cattle industry continues to be the major user of pastoral lands.

Mining and energy resource development has played a major part in the development of the Northern Territory and in 1991 the total value of production was $A1.83 billion. The Territory is a leading uranium producer and contains 20 per cent of the western world's low-cost uranium reserves. Large scale production of zinc-lead concentrate is planned to commence in 1994. In 1991 more than one million tonnes of manganese was sold, with a total value of about $A165 million. Gold production for 1991 was estimated at $A298 million. The value ex mines of bauxite sales exceeded $A128 million and alumina production was valued at $A566 million. The value of oil and gas production for 1991 was $A566 million.

Tourism is a major growth industry and generates over $A490 million annually.

### COMMUNICATIONS

The Northern Territory has three main ports; Darwin, managed by the Darwin Port Authority, and the private mining ports of Gove and Groote Eylandt.

The standard gauge rail link between Southern Australia and Alice Springs was officially opened in October 1980. The link between Alice Springs and Darwin is provided by a fully co-ordinated rail-road service.

The main population centres are linked by the Stuart Highway, which connects Alice Springs to Darwin via Tennant Creek and Katherine. Of special interest to the Northern Territory is the operation of 'road trains'. These are massive trucks hauling two or three trailers, having a net capacity of about 100 tonnes and measuring up to 45 metres in length.

## EXTERNAL TERRITORIES

### ASHMORE AND CARTIER ISLANDS

Ashmore Islands (known as Middle, East and West Islands) and Cartier Island are situated in the Indian Ocean some 850 km and 790 km west of Darwin respectively. The islands lie at the outer edge of the continental shelf. They are small and low and are composed of coral and sand. Turtles are plentiful at certain times of the year and beche-de-mer is abundant. The islands are uninhabited.

Great Britain took formal possession of the Ashmores in 1878 and Cartier was annexed in 1909. In 1931 the islands were placed under the authority of the Commonwealth of Australia, and were accepted in 1933 under the name of the Territory of Ashmore and Cartier Islands. The territory was annexed to the Northern Territory of Australia until 1978, when administration of Ashmore and Cartier Islands became a direct responsibility of the Commonwealth Government. In 1983 Ashmore Reef was declared a national nature reserve.

In accordance with an agreement between the governments of Indonesia and Australia, Indonesian fishermen who have traditionally plied the area may engage in limited fishing activity within the territory but are prohibited from taking any products from the nature reserve. They can land to collect water from West Island.

THE AUSTRALIAN ANTARCTIC TERRITORY

The Australian Antarctic Territory was established in 1933 by an Order in Council which placed under the government of the Commonwealth of Australia all the islands and territories, other than Adélie Land, which are situated south of the latitude 60° S. and lying between 160° E. longitude and 45° E. longitude. The Order came into force in 1936. The territory is administered by the Antarctic Division of the Department of the Environment, Sport and Territories, which, since 1948, has organized yearly expeditions to Antarctica, known as Australian National Antarctic Research Expeditions (ANARE).

Scientific research is carried out at Mawson Station (opened 1954) in MacRobertson Land, Davis Station (opened 1957) in Princess Elizabeth Land and Casey Station (opened 1969). Since 1948 ANARE has operated a station on Macquarie Island, a dependency of Tasmania, situated at 54° 29′ S. and 158° 56′ E., about 900 miles north of the Antarctic Continent. Summer stations have been established at Cape Denison, Commonwealth Bay in the Bunger Hills, the Larsemann Hills, the Prince Charles Mountains, and on Heard Island.

CHRISTMAS ISLAND

Christmas Island was administered as part of the Colony of Singapore until 1957. In 1958 it became an Australian territory. It is situated in the Indian Ocean about 1,408 km NW of North West Cape in Western Australia, and has an area of 135 sq. km. Population (1991 census) is 1,275, largely consisting of employees of Phosphate Resources NL, and employees of the Christmas Island Administration, the Christmas Island Shire Council, and their families. There is no indigenous population.

The island is densely wooded and had extensive deposits of phosphates, the extraction of which has traditionally been the major economic activity. The deposits of low grade phosphate ore are now being extracted by a private mining company, Phosphate Resources NL. Alternative economic development is being encouraged. The principal current development is a hotel complex.

On 1 July 1992 the Australian Government introduced major reforms to the laws of the island with the application of the Western Australian legal regime.

The Administrator is responsible to the Australian Minister for the Environment, Sport and Territories in Canberra. The Christmas Island Shire Council has nine elected members. The Council is responsible for municipal functions and services on the island.

*Administrator*, M. Grimes

COCOS (KEELING) ISLANDS

The Cocos (Keeling) Islands are two separate atolls (North Keeling Island and, 24 km to the south, the main atoll) comprising some 27 small coral islands with a total area of about 14 sq. km, situated in the Indian Ocean in latitude 12° 5′ S. and longitude 96° 53′ E. The main islands of the southern atoll are West Island (the largest, about 9 km from north to south) on which are the administrative centre, the aerodrome, and the Australia-based employees of government departments; Home Island, where the Cocos Malay community live; Direction Island, Horsburgh and South Island.

The islands were declared a British possession in 1857. All land in the islands was granted to George Clunies-Ross and his heirs by Queen Victoria in 1886. In 1955 the islands, which had been governed through the British colonies of Ceylon (from 1878), the Straits Settlements (1886) and Singapore (1903), were accepted as a Territory of Australia. In 1978 the Australian Government purchased all Clunies-Ross land and property interests except for the family home and grounds. In 1979 ownership of the kampong area of Home Island was transferred to the Cocos (Keeling) Islands Council, the local government body established in 1979. Title to most of the remaining land purchased from Clunies-Ross in 1978 was transferred to the Council in 1984. In 1993 the federal government purchased the last of the remaining grounds.

The Cocos (Keeling) Islands Act 1955 provided the legal framework for the political and administrative arrangements in the territory. On 6 April 1984 the Cocos community, in a UN supervised Act of Self-Determination, chose to integrate with Australia. The Government's major commitment was that living standards would reach comparable mainland levels by 1994. The Commonwealth Grants Commission monitors the progress. The Territories Law Reform Act 1992 provides for the modernization of the territory's legal regime through the extension of all Commonwealth laws and the introduction of state-type laws based on those of Western Australia.

The territory has a limited economic base at present. In 1986–7 the copra industry suffered severe losses and in 1987 ceased production. Tourism is being developed as a growth area with construction of a new resort due to be completed towards the end of 1993.

A weekly air charter service operates between Perth, the Cocos (Keeling) Islands and Christmas Island. Population (30 June 1991), 647. The islands are administered by the Australian Government through the Department of the Environment, Sport and Territories in Canberra.

*Administrator*, John Read

CORAL SEA ISLANDS TERRITORY

The Coral Sea Islands Territory lies east of Queensland between the Great Barrier Reef and longitude 156° 06′ E., and between latitudes 12° and 24° S. It comprises scattered islands, spread over a sea area of 780,000 sq. km. The islands are formed mainly of coral and sand, and most are extremely small, with no permanent fresh water. There is a manned meteorological station in the Willis Group but the remaining islands are uninhabited. Large populations of sea birds nest and breed in the area, and two national nature reserves were designated in the Territory in 1982.

The Australian Government bases its claim to the islands on numerous acts of sovereignty since early this century and enacted the Coral Sea Islands Act 1969 which declares the islands a territory of the Commonwealth of Australia. The Department of the Environment, Sport and Territories, Canberra, is responsible for the administration of the territory.

HEARD ISLAND AND McDONALD ISLANDS

The Heard and McDonald islands, about 4,100 km southwest of Fremantle, comprise all the islands and rocks lying between 52° 30′ and 53° 30′ S. latitude and 72° and 74° 30′ E. longitude. Sovereignty over the islands was transferred by the UK to the Commonwealth of Australia in 1947. The Heard Island and McDonald Islands Act 1953 provides for the government of the islands as one territory. Under this Act the law operating there is that of the Australian Capital Territory. The islands are administered by the Department of the Environment, Sport and Territories. Under the

Environment Protection and Management Ordinance 1987, a permit system regulates entry to the territory and a range of activities there.

## NORFOLK ISLAND

Norfolk Island is situated in the South Pacific Ocean at latitude 29° 02′ S. and longitude 167° 57′ E., being about 1,676 km north-east of Sydney and 1,063 km north of Auckland. It is about 8 km long by 5 km wide, with an area of 3,455 hectares. The climate is mild and subtropical. Resident population at the 1991 census was 1,912.

The island, discovered by Captain Cook in 1774, served as a penal colony from 1788 to 1814 and 1825 to 1855. In 1856, 194 descendants of the *Bounty* mutineers accepted an invitation to leave Pitcairn and settle on Norfolk Island, which led to Norfolk Island becoming a separate settlement under the jurisdiction of the Governor of New South Wales. In 1897 Norfolk Island became a dependency of NSW, and in 1914 a territory of Australia. From that date, Norfolk Island has been regarded as an integral part of Australia.

In 1979 Norfolk Island gained a substantial degree of self-government, enabling the island to run its affairs to the greatest practical extent. Wide powers are exercised by a nine-member Legislative Assembly. The Act preserves the Commonwealth's responsibility for Norfolk Island as a territory under its authority, with the Minister for the Environment, Sport and Territories as the responsible Minister.

The island is a popular tourist resort, and a large proportion of the population depends on tourism and its ancillaries for employment. In 1992–3 there were 27,376 tourist arrivals on the Island. Regular air services operate from mainland Australia and New Zealand.

The seat of government and administration offices are in Kingston.

*Administrator*, A. G. Kerr

---

## AUSTRALIAN STATES

---

## NEW SOUTH WALES

The State of New South Wales is situated entirely between the 28th and 38th parallels of S. latitude and 141st and 154th meridians of E. longitude, and comprises an area of 309,433 sq. miles (801,427 sq. km) (exclusive of 939 sq. miles of Australian Capital Territory which lies within its borders). POPULATION – Preliminary estimated resident population at 30 June 1993 was 6,008,600.

STATE CAPITAL – ΨSydney, the largest city in Australia, stands on the shores of Port Jackson. Sydney Harbour extends inland for 21 km; the total area of water is about 55 sq. km. The preliminary estimated resident population in 1993 of the Sydney statistical division was 3,719,000. The Newcastle and Wollongong statistical subdivisions contain populations of 455,680 and 250,090 respectively.

TOWNS – The populations of other principal municipalities are: Albury 41,160, Dubbo 35,410, Greater Taree 43,220, Hastings 52,450, Lismore 43,920, Shoalhaven 74,560, Tamworth 36,380, Wagga Wagga 56,070.

### GOVERNMENT

New South Wales was first colonized as a British possession in 1788, and after progressive settlement a partly elective legislature was established in 1843. In 1855 responsible government was granted, the present constitution being founded on the Constitution Act of 1902. New South Wales

federated with the other States of Australia in 1901. The executive authority of the State is vested in a Governor (appointed by the Crown), assisted by a Council of Ministers.

*Governor of New South Wales*, His Excellency Rear-Adm. Peter Sinclair, AO, RAN, *assumed office* August 1990
*Lt.-Governor and Chief Justice of NSW,* The Hon. Mr Justice Gleeson, AC
*Premier*, Hon. John Fahey

NEW SOUTH WALES GOVERNMENT OFFICE IN LONDON, 75 King William Street, London EC4N 7HA

### LEGISLATURE

The Legislative Council consists of 42 members, elected by popular vote, and the Legislative Assembly consists of 99 members elected for a maximum period of four years.
*President of the Legislative Council,* Hon. M. Willis, MLC
*Speaker, Legislative Assembly,* Hon. K. R. Rozzoli, MP

### JUDICATURE

The judicial system includes a Supreme Court, Industrial Commission, District Court, Land and Environment Court, Compensation Court, and Local Courts (Magistrates).
*Chief Justice, Supreme Court,* The Hon. Mr Justice Gleeson, AC
*President, Court of Appeal,* Hon. Mr Justice Kirby, AC, CMG

### EDUCATION

Education is compulsory between the ages of six and 15 years. It is non-sectarian and free at all government schools. The enrolment in 1993 in 2,184 government and 851 non-government schools was 1,052,096. The nine universities, together with advanced education colleges, had an enrolment of 174,000 in 1993. Students enrolled in technical and further education colleges in 1992 numbered 418,065.

### ECONOMY

A large area is suitable for sheep-raising, the principal breed of sheep being the merino, which was introduced in 1797.

The principal minerals are coal, lead, zinc, gold, rutile, copper and zircon. The total value of minerals extracted in 1991–2 was $A4,582 million. The average number of persons employed in the mining industry during 1991–2 was 18,277. In 1992–3, 84,211,000 tonnes of coal were produced.

In 1990–1 there were 9,715 manufacturing establishments (employing four or more persons). The number of persons employed at 30 June 1991 was 330,000.

### LORD HOWE ISLAND

Lord Howe Island, which is part of New South Wales, is situated 702 kilometres north-east of Sydney, in 31° 33′ 4″ S. latitude and 159° 4′ 26″ E. longitude. Area 6.37 sq. miles (16.5 sq. km.). Population, 1993, 350. The island is of volcanic origin with Mount Gower reaching an altitude of 866 m. The affairs of the Island are administered by the Lord Howe Island Board.

## QUEENSLAND

This State, situated in 9° 14′–29° S. latitude and 138°–153° 30′ E. longitude, comprises the whole north-eastern portion of the Australian continent. Queensland possesses an area of 666,798 sq. miles (1,727,000 sq. km).

POPULATION – At 30 June 1993 the estimated resident population numbered 3,116,150.

STATE CAPITAL – ΨBrisbane is situated on the Brisbane River, which is navigable by large vessels to the city, over 23 km from Moreton Bay. The estimated resident population of the Brisbane statistical division at 30 June 1993 was

1,421,610. This area includes the cities of Brisbane (777,280), Ipswich (77,042), Logan (154,102) and Redcliffe (49,307). CITIES – Other cities with population over 40,000 at 30 June 1993, are: ΨTownsville 87,651; Gold Coast 141,794; Toowoomba 88,133; ΨRockhampton 61,631; ΨCairns 42,487; ΨCaloundra 58,213; ΨThuringowa 43,439.

GOVERNMENT

Queensland was constituted a separate colony with responsible government in 1859, having previously formed part of New South Wales. The executive authority is vested in a Governor (appointed by the Crown), aided by an Executive Council of 18 members.
*Governor of Queensland*, Her Excellency Mrs Mary Marguerite Leneen Forde, AC
*Premier*, Hon. W. K. Goss

AGENT-GENERAL'S OFFICE IN LONDON, 392 Strand, London WC2R 0LZ. *Agent-General*, R. T. Anderson

LEGISLATURE

Parliament consists of a Legislative Assembly of 89 members, elected by all persons aged 18 years and over. The Assembly, as at 30 June 1994, was composed of: Australian Labor Party, 54; National Party of Australia, 26; Liberal Party of Australia, 9.
*Speaker*, Hon. D. Fouras
*Chairman of Committees*, H. Palaszczuk
*Leader of the Opposition*, R. E. Borbidge

JUDICATURE

There are a Supreme Court; District Courts; Children's Courts; an Industrial Court; a Land Court and a Medical Assessment Tribunal; a Planning and Environment Court; the Industrial Conciliation and Arbitration Commission; Inferior Courts at all the principal towns, presided over by Stipendiary Magistrates; a Small Claims Tribunal; Small Debts Court and a Licensing Court.
*Chief Justice, Supreme Court*, Hon. J. M. Macrossan, AC

EDUCATION

Education is compulsory, secular and free between the ages of five and 15. At July 1993, there were 1,008 government primary schools, 71 primary/secondary, and 185 secondary schools with 260,493 primary students, and 143,770 secondary students.

Post-secondary education involves technical and further education (TAFE) and higher education. During 1992, 173,283 students were enrolled in TAFE courses, excluding 104,512 enrolled in adult education courses. At 30 April 1993 there were 53,937 full-time, 24,739 part-time, and 15,279 external students enrolled in higher education courses.

ECONOMY

Total Queensland-sawn timber produced in 1992–3 amounted to 640,927 cubic metres (gross volume measure).

There are rich deposits of both metal and non-metal ores. Coal is mined extensively in central Queensland and on a lesser scale in the Ipswich district.

In 1992–3 there were 6,573 establishments with four or more workers, employing 122,400 persons, with a turnover of $A22,837 million. Much of the production was the processing of foodstuffs, minerals and chemical, petroleum and coal products. Included in other factory production were the products from engineering, transport equipment, timber, basic and fabricated metal, cement, paper and textile mills and oil refineries.

In recent years the economy has diversified from its original basis of agriculture and mining into high technology manufacturing and tourism. The labour force was 1.57 million strong in June 1994.

SOUTH AUSTRALIA

The State of South Australia is situated between 26° and 38° S. latitude and 129° and 141° E. longitude, the total area being 380,070 sq. miles (984,376 sq. km).
POPULATION – At 30 June 1993, the resident population was estimated to be 1,461,721.
STATE CAPITAL – ΨAdelaide, the chief city and capital, estimated resident population on 30 June 1993, 1,070,240 inclusive of suburbs. Other centres (with 1992 populations) are: ΨWhyalla (25,416); ΨMt Gambier (22,439); ΨPort Pirie (14,817); ΨPort Augusta (14,747).

GOVERNMENT

South Australia was proclaimed a British province in 1836, and in 1851 a partially elective legislature was established. The present constitution rests upon a law of 24 October 1856, the executive authority being vested in a Governor appointed by the Crown, aided by a Council of 13 Ministers.
*Governor of South Australia*, Her Excellency the Hon. Dame Roma Mitchell, AC, DBE, *assumed office 1991*
*Lt.-Governor*, The Hon. Dr Basil Hetzel, AC, *assumed office 1992*
*Premier*, Hon. Dean Craig Brown

AGENT-GENERAL'S OFFICE IN LONDON, South Australia House, 50 Strand, London WC2N 5LW. *Agent-General*, G. Walls

LEGISLATURE

Parliament consists of a Legislative Council of 22 members elected for eight years, one half retiring every four years; and a House of Assembly of 47 members, elected for a maximum duration of four years. Election is by ballot, with universal adult suffrage for both the Legislative Council and the House of Assembly.

The representation in the House of Assembly is 36 Liberals and 11 Labor.
*President of the Legislative Council*, Hon. H. P. K. Bruce
*Speaker of the House of Assembly*, Hon. G. Gunn

JUDICATURE

The Supreme Court is presided over by the Chief Justice and 13 Puisne Judges.

EDUCATION

Education at the primary and secondary level is available at government schools controlled by the Education Department and at non-government schools, most of which are denominational. In 1993 there were 677 government schools with 184,620 students, and 184 independent schools with 62,607 students. Tertiary education is available through universities, and technical and further education colleges.

The three universities had, in 1993, a total enrolment of 44,445 students, of which 26,471 were full-time.

TASMANIA

Tasmania is an island state of Australia situated in the Southern ocean off the south-eastern extremity of the mainland. It is separated from the Australian mainland by Bass Strait and incorporates King Island and the Furneaux group of islands which are in the Strait. It lies between 40° 38'–43° 39' S. latitude and 144° 36'–148° 23' E. longitude, and has an area of 26,383 sq. miles (68,331 sq. km). Macquarie Island, situated at 54° 30' S. and 158° 57' E., about 900 miles north of the Antarctic Continent, is a dependency of Tasmania.

POPULATION – The estimated resident population at 30 June 1993 was 471,450.

STATE CAPITAL – ΨHobart, founded 1804. Population (30 June 1993) (metropolitan area), 193,250. Other towns (with population at 30 June 1993) are ΨLaunceston (metropolitan area), 97,460), ΨBurnie-Devonport (79,030).

GOVERNMENT

The island was first settled by a British party from New South Wales in 1803, becoming a separate colony in 1825. In 1851 a partly elective legislature was inaugurated, and in 1856 responsible government was established. In 1901 Tasmania became a State of the Australian Commonwealth. Executive authority is vested in a Governor appointed by the Crown, but is exercised by Cabinet Ministers responsible to the legislature, of which they are members.
*Governor of Tasmania*, His Excellency Gen. Sir Phillip
    Bennett, AC, KBE, DSO
*Premier*, Hon. Raymond J. Groom

LEGISLATURE

Parliament consists of a Legislative Council of 19 members, elected for six years (three retiring annually, in rotation, except in every sixth year, when four retire), and a House of Assembly of 35 members, elected by proportional representation for four years in five seven-member constituencies. All Tasmanians of 18 years and over who have resided continuously in the State for at least six months may vote in elections to both houses. Elections for the Assembly are held every four years.

The election of February 1992 resulted in a victory for the Liberal Party, with 19 Liberal, 11 Labor and 5 Tasmanian Green members of the House of Assembly. The state of the parties in the Legislative Council following the election was Independent 17, Liberal 1, Labor 1.
*President of the Legislative Council*, Hon. E. J. C. Stopp
*Speaker of the House of Assembly*, Hon. G. R. Page

JUDICATURE

The Supreme Court of Tasmania, with civil, criminal, ecclesiastical, admiralty and matrimonial jurisdiction, was established in 1823. Local Courts are held before Commissioners who are legal practitioners. Courts of General Sessions, constituted by a chairman who is a Justice of the Peace and at least one other Justice, are established in the municipalities and Courts of Petty Sessions are constituted by Magistrates sitting alone, or by two or more justices. A single justice may hear and determine certain matters.
*Chief Justice, Supreme Court*, Hon. Sir Guy Green, KBE

EDUCATION

Government schools are of three main types: primary, secondary and secondary colleges. On 1 July 1993 there were 64,727 students enrolled in 237 government schools. There were also 65 independent schools with an enrolment of 21,034. The University of Tasmania with campuses in Hobart and Launceston, had 8,015 full-time students and 3,603 part-time students in 1993.

ECONOMY

Tasmania, the smallest Australian state, produces the most electrical energy per head of population. Most of it is derived from water power, with a total installed generator capacity of 2,435,000 kW at 30 June 1993. By reason of its low-cost electricity, Tasmania has large plants producing ferro-manganese and newsprint. A large aluminium plant is

situated at Bell Bay and Tasmania is the source of the bulk of Australian requirements of zinc and fine papers.

The quantity of timber (excluding firewood) of various species cut in 1992–3 was 4,223,700 cubic metres, including 3,350,600 cubic metres for woodchip and wood-pulp.

The chief ores mined are those containing copper, tin, iron, silver, zinc and lead.

The chief manufactures for export are refined metals, preserved fruit and vegetables, butter, cheese, meat, seafood, textiles, paper, confectionery, wood chips and sawn timber. As at 30 June 1992, 858 manufacturing establishments employed 23,500 persons.

VICTORIA

The State of Victoria comprises the south-east corner of Australia, at the part where its mainland territory projects furthest into the southern latitudes; it lies between 34°–39° S. latitude and 141°–150° E. longitude. Its area is 87,876 sq. miles (227,600 sq. km).

POPULATION – The estimated resident population at 30 June 1993 was 4,462,100.

STATE CAPITAL – ΨMelbourne had a resident population at 30 June 1993 estimated at 3,080,800. Other urban centres are ΨGeelong 180,000; Ballarat 90,000; Bendigo 67,000.

GOVERNMENT

Victoria was originally known as the Port Phillip District of New South Wales and was created a separate colony in 1851, with a partially elective legislature. In 1855 responsible government was conferred. The executive authority is vested in a Governor, appointed by the Crown, aided by an Executive Council of Ministers.
*Governor of Victoria*, His Excellency the Hon. Richard E.
    McGarvie, *assumed office* 23 April 1992
*Lt.-Governor*, The Hon. Sir John McIntosh Young, KCMG,
    AO, *apptd* 1974
*Premier*, Hon J. G. Kennett

AGENT-GENERAL'S OFFICE IN LONDON, Victoria House, Melbourne Place, Strand, London WC2B 4LG.
    *Agent-General*, K. C. Crompton

LEGISLATURE

Parliament consists of a Legislative Council of 44 members, elected for the 22 Provinces for two terms of the Legislative Assembly, one half retiring every four years at a general election; and a Legislative Assembly of 88 members, elected for a maximum duration of four years. Voting is compulsory.

The state of parties in the Legislative Council (July 1994) is Liberal Party 24, Australian Labour Party 14, National Party 6. The state of parties in the Legislative Assembly (elected 3 October 1992) is Liberal Party 52, Australian Labour Party 27, National Party 9.
*President of the Legislative Council*, Hon. Bruce Chamberlain
*Speaker of the Legislative Assembly*, Hon. John Delzoppo

JUDICATURE

There is a Supreme Court with a Chief Justice and 25 Puisne Judges, a County Court and Magistrates' Courts.
*Chief Justice, Supreme Court*, Hon. Mr Justice John Phillips
*Chief Judge, County Court*, Hon. G. R. D. Waldron, AO

EDUCATION

State education is compulsory, secular and free between the ages of six and 15. At 30 June 1993 there were 2,016 schools, attended by 539,926 students. In addition there were 677 non-government schools with 252,148 students. Victoria has 29 technical and further education colleges and eight universities with 32 campuses.

ECONOMY

Minerals raised include oil and natural gas, brown coal, limestone, clays and stone for construction material. Production of brown coal in 1991-2 was 48,884m tonnes.

In 1965 natural gas was discovered in commercial quantities in the offshore waters of the Gippsland Basin in eastern Victoria and in 1966-7 three valuable oilfields were located in the same general area. These fields are still the largest yet found in Australia. Production from Victorian natural gas and crude oil fields in 1991-2 was 16,935 megalitres of crude oil and 6,668 million cubic metres of natural gas.

At 30 June 1991 there were 8,976 manufacturing establishments in which total employees numbered 308,555. The main manufacturing sectors are textiles, clothing and footwear, paper, automotive and transport products, chemicals, fabricated metals and food and beverages.

WESTERN AUSTRALIA

Western Australia includes all that portion of the continent west of 129° E. longitude, the most westerly point being in 113° 9′ E. longitude and from 13° 44′ to 35° 8′ S. latitude. Its area is 975,920 sq. miles (2,527,621 sq. km).

POPULATION – At 30 June 1993 the estimated resident population was 1,676,400.

STATE CAPITAL – ΨPerth, on the north bank of the Swan River estuary, 12 miles from Fremantle. Estimated resident population (30 June 1993) of Perth statistical division, including the port of ΨFremantle, 1,221,300.

GOVERNMENT

Western Australia was first settled by the British in 1829, and in 1870 it was granted a partially elective legislature. In 1890 responsible government was granted, and the administration vested in a Governor, a Legislative Council, and a Legislative Assembly. The present constitution rests upon the Constitution Act 1889, the Constitution Acts Amendment Act 1899, and amending Acts. The executive is vested in a Governor appointed by the Crown and aided by a Council of responsible Ministers.

*Governor of Western Australia*, His Excellency the Hon. Sir Francis Burt, AC, KCMG, QC

*Lt.-Governor and Administrator*, The Hon. D. K. Malcolm, AC

*Premier*, Hon. Richard Court

AGENT-GENERAL'S OFFICE IN LONDON, Western Australia House, 115 Strand, London WC2R 0AJ. *Agent-General (acting)*, G. Stokes

LEGISLATURE

Parliament consists of a Legislative Council and a Legislative Assembly, elected by adult suffrage subject to qualifications of residence and registration. The qualifying age for electors for both the Legislative Council and Legislative Assembly is 18 years. There are 34 members in the Legislative Council elected for a period of four years. The Legislative Assembly has 57 members, who are elected for a term of four years. The Legislative Assembly (elected 6 February 1993) is composed of Liberal Party 26, Australian Labor Party 24, National Party of Australia 6, Independent Liberal 1.

*President of the Legislative Council*, Hon. C. E. Griffiths

*Speaker of the Legislative Assembly*, Hon. J. Clarko

JUDICATURE

*Chief Justice*, Hon. D. K. Malcolm, AC

*Senior Puisne Judge*, Hon. W. P. Pidgeon

EDUCATION

In 1993 there were 766 government and 249 non-government primary and secondary school campuses with 222,451 and 74,288 full-time students respectively. The principal higher education institutions are the University of Western Australia (12,795 enrolments in 1994), Murdoch University (8,830), Curtin University (20,617) and Edith Cowan University (17,216).

ECONOMY

There were 3,696 manufacturing establishments operating in the State at 30 June 1992. The total number of persons employed (including working proprietors) by these establishments at the end of June 1992 was 62,100.

The forests contain some of the finest hardwoods in the world. The total quantity of sawn timber produced during 1992-3 was 3,081,000 cubic metres.

The State has large deposits of a wide range of minerals, many of which are being mined or are under development for production. The ex-mine value of all minerals (excluding construction materials) produced during 1991-2 was $A11,988,398,000.

AUSTRIA
*Republik Österreich*

Austria is a country of central Europe bounded on the north by the Czech Republic and the Slovak Republic, on the south by Italy and Slovenia, on the east by Hungary, on the north-west by Germany and on the west by Switzerland and Liechtenstein. Its area is 32,367 sq. miles (83,855 sq. km), and its population is 8,000,000 (official estimate 1994). The predominant religion is Roman Catholicism.

CAPITAL – Vienna, on the Danube, population 1,539,848 (census 1991). Other larger towns are Graz (237,810), Linz (203,044), Innsbruck (118,112), Salzburg (143,978), and Klagenfurt (89,415).

CURRENCY – Schilling of 100 Groschen.

FLAG – Three equal horizontal stripes of red, white, red.

NATIONAL ANTHEM – Land der Berge, Land am Strome (Land of mountains, land on the river).

NATIONAL DAY – 26 October.

GOVERNMENT

The Republic of Austria comprises nine provinces (Vienna, Lower Austria, Upper Austria, Salzburg, Tyrol, Vorarlberg, Carinthia, Styria and Burgenland) and was established in 1918 on the break-up of the Austro-Hungarian Empire. In March 1938, as a result of the *Anschluss*, Austria was incorporated into the *Deutsches Reich* under the name *Ostmark*. After the liberation of Vienna in 1945, the Republic of Austria was reconstituted within the frontiers of 1937 and a freely-elected government took office in December 1945. The country was divided at this time into four zones occupied respectively by the UK, USA, USSR and France, while Vienna was jointly occupied by the four Powers. In 1955 the Austrian State Treaty was signed in Vienna by the foreign ministers of the four Powers and of Austria. This treaty recognized the re-establishment of Austria as a sovereign, independent and democratic state, having the same frontiers as on 1 January 1938.

Austria applied for European Community membership in July 1989 and successfully completed accession negotiations on 1 March 1994. Accession to the European Union on 1 January 1995 was ratified in a 140-35 parliamentary vote on

5 May 1994 and a 67 per cent vote in a referendum on 12 June 1994.

There is a national assembly of 183 Deputies. After the elections of 7 October 1990, the Socialists formed a coalition with the People's Party. The state of the parties in the Nationalrat (Lower House) as at July 1994 was: Socialist Party (Social Democrat), 80; People's Party (Conservative), 60; Freedom Party (Liberal-Nationalist), 28; Green, 10; Liberal Forum, 5. In the Bundesrat (Upper House) in March 1990 the People's Party held 30 seats, the Socialist Party 29 and the Freedom Party 5.

HEAD OF STATE
*President of the Republic of Austria*, Dr Thomas Klestil, *took office* 8 July 1992

CABINET *as at July 1994*

*Chancellor*, Dr Franz Vranitzky (SPÖ)
*Vice-Chancellor, Science and Research*, Dr Erhard Busek (ÖVP)
*Federalism and Administrative Reform*, Juergen Weiss (ÖVP)
*Women's Affairs*, Johanna Dohnal (SPÖ)
*Foreign Affairs*, Dr Alois Mock (ÖVP)
*Economic Affairs*, Dr Wolfgang Schüssel (ÖVP)
*Employment and Social Affairs*, Josef Hesoun (SPÖ)
*Finance*, Ferdinand Lacina (SPÖ)
*Health, Consumer Protection and Sport*, Christa Krammer (SPÖ)
*Interior*, Dr Franz Löschnak (SPÖ)
*Justice*, Dr Nikolaus Michalek (Ind.)
*Defence*, Dr Werner Fasslabend (ÖVP)
*Agriculture and Forestry*, Dr Franz Fischler (ÖVP)
*Environment, Youth and Family Affairs*, Maria Rauch-Kallat (ÖVP)
*Education and Arts*, Dr Rudolf Scholten (SPÖ)
*Public Economy and Transport*, Viktor Klima (SPÖ)
*Ministers of State*, Brigitte Ederer (SPÖ) (*European Questions*); Dr Peter Kostelka (SPÖ) (*Public Service*); Dr Johannes Ditz (ÖVP) (*Finance*); Dr Maria Fekter (ÖVP) (*Economic Affairs, Construction and Tourism*)
SPÖ Socialists; ÖVP People's Party (Conservatives).

AUSTRIAN EMBASSY
18 Belgrave Mews West, London SW1X 8HU
Tel 0171-235 3731

*Ambassador Extraordinary and Plenipotentiary*, His Excellency Dr Georg Hennig, LVO, apptd 1993
*Minister-Counsellor*, Dr Hebert Krauss
*Defence Attaché*, Brig. H. Rüdiger Sulzgruber
*Consul-General*, G. R. Widor
*Commercial Counsellor and Trade Commissioner*, Dr Gerhard Kernthaler

BRITISH EMBASSY
Jaurèssgasse 12, 1030 Vienna
Tel: Vienna 7131575/9

*Ambassador Extraordinary and Plenipotentiary*, His Excellency Terence Wood, CMG, apptd 1992
*Deputy Ambassador, Counsellor and Consul-General*, J. W. Forbes-Meyler, OBE
*Defence Attaché*, Lt.-Col. P. W. L. Hughes, MBE
*First Secretary (Commercial)*, P. J. W. Le Breton

BRITISH CONSULAR OFFICES – There is a consular office at *Vienna*, and Honorary Consulates at *Bregenz, Graz, Innsbruck* and *Salzburg*.

BRITISH COUNCIL REPRESENTATIVE, David Handforth, Schenkenstrasse 4, 1010 Vienna

## EDUCATION

Education is free and compulsory between the ages of six and 15 and there are good facilities for secondary, technical and professional education. There are 12 state-maintained universities and six colleges of art with a combined registered student population of 202,821.

## CULTURE

The language of Austria is German, but the rights of the Slovene- and Croat-speaking minorities in Carinthia, Styria and Burgenland are protected.

## COMMUNICATIONS

Internal communications in Austria are partly restricted because of the mountainous nature of the country, although there has been an extensive programme to increase the number of motorways (*Autobahn*), many of which are tunnelled through the mountains. There is a network of 1,532 km of *Autobahn* between major cities which also links up with the West German and Italian networks. The railways in Austria (ÖBB) are state-owned and in 1991 had 5,782 km of track, 57.4 per cent of which is electrified. Of the 425 km of waterways, 350 km are navigable and there is considerable trade through the Danube ports by both local and foreign shipping. There are six commercial airports catering for 7,444,102 passengers in 1991.

In 1991 there were 3,370,000 telephones, 677 radio and 963 television transmitters. There are four national radio and two national television channels, together with three national and twelve regional newspapers which have a combined daily circulation of 2,560,000.

## DEFENCE

The total active strength of the armed forces numbers 52,000 (25,000 conscripts). In addition, there are some 119,000 reserves ready at 72 hours notice. Conscripts serve for six months and then either for an extra two months or they can choose to undertake two months refresher training over a 15-year period. Each year 66,000 reservists undergo refresher training.

The Army has an active strength of 46,000 (19,500 conscripts) with 170 main battle tanks, 465 armoured personnel carriers, 230 artillery pieces and some 765 anti-tank heavy guns. The Air Force has an active strength of 6,000 (2,400 conscripts) with 54 combat aircraft of Swedish manufacture. Austria deploys one infantry battalion of 347 troops with UN forces in Cyprus and one infantry battalion of 451 troops on the Golan Heights in Syria.

## ECONOMY

The origin of Gross Domestic Product in 1992 was as follows (Schilling billion):

| | |
|---|---|
| Agriculture and forestry | 50.1 |
| Manufacturing and mining | 525.9 |
| Energy and water supply | 55.6 |
| Construction | 153.6 |
| Commerce, hotels, restaurants | 333.7 |
| Transport and communications | 126.3 |
| Asset management | 350.4 |
| Other services and producers | 248.5 |
| Import duties and other items | 184.5 |

The total value of GDP in 1992 was Schilling 2,028.6 billion.

Austria is self-sufficient in agricultural production, with some 273,000 agricultural units. The arable land produces wheat, rye, barley, oats, maize, potatoes, sugar beet, turnips, and miscellaneous crops. Many varieties of fruit trees flourish and the vineyards produce excellent wine. The pastures support horses, cattle and pigs and large numbers of chickens are also produced. Timber forms a valuable source of Austria's indigenous wealth, about 45 per cent of the total land area consisting of forest areas. Coniferous species predominate (75 per cent of afforested area).

In 1991–2, 19,175,000 foreign tourists visited Austria. Foreign exchange receipts from tourism were a major contribution to the balance of payments.

| FINANCE | 1991 | 1992 |
|---|---|---|
| *Federal Budget* (Schilling) | | |
| Revenue | 549,259m | 584,200m |
| Expenditure | 644,768m | 675,065m |
| Gross Budget Deficit | 95,509m | 90,865m |

Austria's total federal public debt in 1992 was Schilling 992 billion.

TRADE

Main exports are processed goods (iron and steel, other metal goods, textiles, paper and cardboard products), machinery and transport equipment, other finished goods (including clothing), raw materials, chemical products and foodstuffs. Main imports are machinery and transport equipment, processed goods, chemical products, foodstuffs, fuel and energy.

| | 1991 | 1992 |
|---|---|---|
| Imports | Schilling 592,000m | 594,000m |
| Exports | 480,000m | 488,000m |

Over 80 per cent of trade is with other European countries, EC countries accounting for about 67 per cent, eastern Europe for about 10 per cent and EFTA members for 8 per cent. By far the most important trading partner is Germany, with which around 41 per cent of Austrian trade is conducted.

| *Trade with UK* | 1992 | 1993 |
|---|---|---|
| Imports from UK | £795,107,000 | £911,611,000 |
| Exports to UK | 948,894,000 | 971,124,000 |

## AZERBAIJAN
*Azarbaijchan Respublikasy*

Azerbaijan has an area of 33,436 sq. miles (86,600 sq. km) and occupies the eastern part of the Caucasus region of the former Soviet Union, on the shore of the Caspian Sea. It is bordered on the south by Iran, on the west by Armenia and on the north by Georgia and Russia. The north-eastern part of the republic is taken up by the south-eastern end of the main Caucasus ridge, its south-western part by the smaller Caucasus hills, and its south-eastern corner by the spurs of the Talysh Ridge. Its central part is a depression irrigated by the River Kura and the lower reaches of its tributary the Araks. Azerbaijan has 64 administrative districts and also includes the Nakhichevan Autonomous Republic, which is geographically separated from the rest of Azerbaijan by Armenia and borders on Iran and Turkey, and the Nagorno-Karabakh Autonomous Province.

CLIMATE – Sheltered by the mountains from the humid west winds blowing from the Black Sea, Azerbaijan has a continental climate.

POPULATION – According to a 1993 estimate, Azerbaijan has a population of 7,400,900, of which 83 per cent are Azeris, 6 per cent Russians and 6 per cent Armenians. There are also Kurds, Jews, Georgians and Turks. There are more Azeris in Iran than in Azerbaijan.

The population is predominantly Shia Muslim although it was heavily secularized during the Soviet era. Azeri in the

Latin script was adopted as the official language in December 1992. Closely related to Turkish, Azeri was previously written in the Russian script.

CAPITAL – ΨBaku. Population 1,757,000 (1989).
CURRENCY – Manat of 100 gopik.
FLAG – Three horizontal stripes of blue, red and green with a white crescent and eight-pointed star in the centre.
NATIONAL DAY – 28 May (Independence Day).

GOVERNMENT

The territory that is now Azerbaijan was fought over many times between the ninth and first centuries BC, being successively part of the Assyrian, Persian, Median and Greek empires. With the influx of Huns and Khazars in the first century BC, the Turkic Azerbaijani people evolved and formed an independent state. The country was invaded by the Arab Caliphates in the seventh century AD and under their 300-year rule Islam was introduced and became the dominant religion. In the 16th century Azerbaijan was again invaded by Persia, when it became a Persian province. The country was divided during the Russo-Persian wars of the early 19th century, the northern portion (the present-day Azerbaijan) becoming part of the Russian Empire and the southern portion remaining Persian and subsequently Iranian.

Azerbaijan was heavily industrialized as part of the Russian Empire, with railways, commercial shipping on the Caspian Sea, and, most importantly, the oil industry. In the late 19th and early 20th centuries Baku was the most important oil-producing centre in the world. Following the Russian Revolution of 1917, a Soviet government was set up in Azerbaijan in 1918. This was overthrown by Allied forces a few months later but when Allied forces withdrew in 1920, the Soviet government was restored and Azerbaijan acceded to the USSR in 1922.

In January 1990, the Azerbaijani Popular Front took power from the local Communist Party and declared independence from the Soviet Union, partly because of the Soviet government's decision in 1989 to take control of the Nagorno-Karabakh region away from Azerbaijan and to impose direct rule upon it to stop Azeri-Armenian fighting there. Soviet troops overthrew the Popular Front regime the day after it took power and re-installed the Communist regime under President Ayaz Mutalibov. This government declared Azerbaijan's independence from the Soviet Union in August 1991 and gained UN membership for Azerbaijan in March 1992. Mutalibov overwhelmingly won the presidential election held in September 1991, but he was forced to resign by widespread civil unrest at his perceived pro-Moscow stance and the poor conduct of the war with Armenia. At the presidential election in June 1992 the Popular Front leader Abulfaz Elchibey was elected and pledged to withdraw from the CIS and align his country more closely with Turkey.

Azerbaijan withdrew from the CIS in October 1992 when its parliament (Milli Majlis) rejected membership. The war with Armenia, however, continued to go badly in the winter of 1992–3, culminating in Armenian forces breaking out of Nagorny-Karabakh and capturing all Azeri territory between Armenia and Nagorny-Karabakh. The defeat, in April 1993, led to political crisis. President Elchibey declared a state of emergency but discontent with his rule grew in parliament and the military. A military rebellion against the Popular Front government broke out in June and the military rebels marched on Baku and overthrew President Elchibey and his Popular Front government. The former Azerbaijani Communist Party General Secretary Heidar Aliyev took over the presidency and the rebel leader Col. Guseinov the premiership. The new regime was confirmed in office in a referendum in August and Aliyev won presidential elections on 3 October 1993 with 99 per cent of the vote. The government has reversed the previous policy of close relations with Turkey and replaced them, mainly for economic reasons, with closer relations with Russia, rejoining the CIS in September 1993.

Meanwhile, the war with the Nagorno-Karabakh and Armenian forces has continued throughout 1993 and 1994, with further Azeri defeats. By December 1993 Armenian forces controlled some 20 per cent of Azeri territory, although Azeri offensives between December 1993 and February 1994 pushed back Armenian forces until they controlled only 10 per cent of the country. Between 500,000 and one million Azeris have been displaced by the fighting. The CSCE and Russia have sought to broker peace.

HEAD OF STATE

*President,* Heidar Aliyev, *assumed office* 18 June 1993, *elected* 3 October 1993

GOVERNMENT *as at July 1994*

*Prime Minister,* Col. Surat Husseinov
*Deputy Prime Ministers,* Abbas Abbasov; Asker Mamedov;
    Elchin Efendiev; Samed Sadyhov
*Foreign Affairs,* Gasan Gasanov
*Interior,* Vagif Novrusov
*Housing and Communal Services,* Suddgedin Abdullaev
*Culture,* Byul-byul Polad
*Material Resources,* Faruh Zeinalov
*Land Improvement and Water Conservancy,* Salekh
    Gadzhiyev
*Local Industry,* Agabba Abdulaev
*Education,* Lidiya Rasulova
*National Security,* Nariman Imanov
*Defence,* Mamedrafi Mamedov
*Information,* Cabir Rustamhanly
*Communications,* Sirus Abbasbeily
*Agriculture and Foodstuffs,* Muzamil Abdullaev
*Trade,* Rizvan Guseinov
*Economics,* Samed Sadyhov
*Justice,* Ilyas Ismailov
*Procurator-General,* Ali Omarov

AZERBAIJANI EMBASSY

*Ambassador Extraordinary and Plenipotentiary,* His
    Excellency Mahmud Mamed-Kuliyev, apptd 1994

BRITISH EMBASSY

c/o Stary Intourist Hotel Room 214, Baku
Tel: Baku 926 307/6

*Ambassador Extraordinary and Plenipotentiary,* His
    Excellency Thomas Young, apptd 1993

DEFENCE

The total active strength of the armed forces is 42,600 personnel, with conscripts serving 17-month terms. The army has a strength of 38,900, with 285 main battle tanks, 840 armoured personnel carriers and infantry fighting vehicles, 330 artillery pieces and 23 armed helicopters. The Navy is based at Baku, with a share of the former Soviet Caspian Fleet Flotilla, comprising one frigate and 14 patrol and coastal combatants, together with 2,100 personnel. The Air Force is 1,600 strong with 47 combat aircraft. All forces, together with some 30,000 paramilitary personnel, are engaged in the conflict around Nagorny-Karabakh, where they face a force some 20,000 strong.

ECONOMY

The Azerbaijani economy has been devastated by the war and the attempt to resettle up to one million refugees.

Inflation reached an annual rate of 600 per cent in 1994 while privatization plans and oil exploration contracts are stalled.

Azerbaijani industry is dominated by oil and natural gas extraction and related chemical and engineering industries centred on Baku and Sumgait and the large oil deposits in the Caspian Sea. The republic is also rich in mineral resources, with iron, copper, lead and salt. A large power station on the Araks was completed in 1969, in conjunction with Iran. Azerbaijan is also important as a cotton-growing area and a silkworm breeding area.

| Trade with UK | 1993 |
|---|---|
| Imports from UK | £2,965,000 |
| Exports to UK | 823,000 |

CULTURE

Azerbaijan was the birthplace of the prophet Zoroaster, who founded one of the first monotheistic religions in the world. The country has witnessed a succession of three religions; Zoroastrianism, Christianity and Islam.

Azeri is one of the Turkic languages. In the 18th and 19th centuries Azerbaijani literature produced the poets and dramatists Vagif, Vazekhi, Zakir, Akhundov and Vezirov, who all introduced ideas of progressive Russian culture.

---

THE BAHAMAS
*The Commonwealth of The Bahamas*

---

The Bahama Islands are an archipelago lying in the North Atlantic Ocean between 20° 55′–25° 22′ N. latitude and 72° 35′–79° 35′ W. longitude. They extend from the coast of Florida on the north-west almost to Haiti on the south-east. The group consists of 700 islands, of which 30 are inhabited and 2,400 cays comprising an area of more than 5,832 sq. miles. The population (UN estimate 1991) is 258,000. The principal islands include: Abaco, Acklins, Andros, Berry Islands, Bimini, Cat Island, Crooked Island, Eleuthera, Exumas, Grand Bahama, Harbour Island, Inagua, Long Island, Mayaguana, New Providence (on which is located the capital, Nassau), Ragged Island, Rum Cay, San Salvador and Spanish Wells. San Salvador was the first landfall in the New World of Christopher Columbus on 12 October 1492.

CAPITAL – ΨNassau, population (census 1990) 171,000.
CURRENCY – Bahamian dollar (B$) of 100 cents.
FLAG – Horizontal stripes of aquamarine, gold and
    aquamarine, with a black equilateral triangle on the hoist.
NATIONAL ANTHEM – March on, Bahamaland.
NATIONAL DAY – 10 July (Independence Day).

GOVERNMENT

The Bahamas were settled by British subjects when the islands were deserted. The ownership of The Bahamas was taken over in 1782 by the Spanish, but the Treaty of Versailles in 1783 restored them to the British. The Bahamas gained independence on 10 July 1973. The Head of State is HM Queen Elizabeth II, represented in the islands by a Governor-General. There is a Senate of 16 members and an elected House of Assembly of 49 members. A general election was held on 19 August 1992 and won by the Free National Movement, ending five successive election victories for the Progressive Liberal Party since independence. The Free National Movement won 33 seats in the House of Assembly and the Progressive Liberal Party 16 seats.

*Governor-General*, His Excellency Sir Clifford Darling, apptd 1992

CABINET *as at June 1994*

*Prime Minister and Minister of Finance and Planning*, Hon. Hubert A. Ingraham
*Attorney-General, Minister of Justice and Foreign Affairs*, Hon. Orville A. Turnquest
*Public Works and Utilities*, Hon. Frank H. Watson
*Social Services, National Insurance and Housing*, Hon. Janet W. Bostwick
*Labour, Human Resources and Training*, Hon. Maurice E. Moore
*Health and Environment*, Hon. Ivy L. Dumont
*Education and Culture*, Hon. Cornelius A. Smith
*Tourism*, Hon. Brent Symonette
*Agriculture and Fisheries*, Hon. Tennyson R. G. Wells
*Public Safety and Immigration*, Hon. Arlington G. Butler
*Youth and Personal Development and Leader of the House of Assembly*, Hon. Algernon Allen
*Transport and Communication*, Hon. Theresa M. Moxey

*President of the Court of Appeal*, Kenneth Henry
*Chief Justice*, J. C. Gonsalves-Sabola

BAHAMAS HIGH COMMISSION
Bahamas House, 10 Chesterfield Street, London WIX 8AH
Tel 0171-408 4488

*High Commissioner*, His Excellency Arthur A. Foulkes, apptd 1992

BRITISH HIGH COMMISSION
PO Box N-7516, Nassau
Tel: Nassau 325-7471/2/3

*High Commissioner*, His Excellency Brian Attewell, apptd 1992

ECONOMY

Tourism is the economic mainstay of The Bahamas, employing about two-thirds of the labour force. It provides about two-thirds of government revenue and about half the country's foreign exchange earnings. The second main industry is international banking and trust business. The Bahamas' absence of any direct taxation and internal stability have enabled the country to become one of the world's leading offshore financial centres. Confidence in both the tourist and financial industries dropped, however, after widespread allegations of corruption during the 25 years of PLP government surfaced in 1992 and 1993.

Agricultural production is mainly of fresh vegetables, fruit, meat and eggs for the domestic market, and crawfish, mostly for export. Reserves of aragonite, limestone and salt are being commercially exploited. Freeport is the country's leading industrial centre, with a pharmaceutical and chemicals plant, an oil trans-shipment and storage terminal, and port and bunkering facilities. There are also a brewery and a rum distillery on New Providence.

| FINANCE | 1989p | 1990p |
|---|---|---|
| Public revenue | B$448.1m | B$489.1m |
| Expenditure | 561.6m | 532.1m |
| p provisional | | |

TRADE

The imports are chiefly foodstuffs, manufactured articles, building materials, vehicles and machinery, chemicals and petroleum. The chief exports are rum, petroleum, hormones, salt, crawfish and aragonite.

| Trade with UK | 1992 | 1993 |
|---|---|---|
| Imports from UK | £24,532,000 | £41,662,000 |
| Exports to UK | 38,178,000 | 25,163,000 |

EDUCATION

Education is compulsory between the ages of five and 14. More than 59,500 students are enrolled in Ministry of Education and independent schools in New Providence and the Family Islands.

COMMUNICATIONS

The main ports are Nassau (New Providence), Freeport (Grand Bahama), Mathew Town (Inagua). International air services are operated from Abaco, Bimini, Eleuthera, Exuma, Grand Bahama and New Providence. About 50 smaller airports and landing strips facilitate services between the islands, the services being mainly provided by Bahamasair, the national carrier. There are roads on the larger islands, and roads are under construction on the smaller islands. There are no railways. Wireless and telephone services are in operation to all parts of the world.

---

## BAHRAIN
*Dawlet al-Bahrein*

---

Bahrain consists of a group of low-lying islands situated about half-way down the Gulf, some 20 miles off the east coast of Arabia. The largest of these, Bahrain island itself, is about 30 miles long and 10 miles wide at its broadest. The capital, Manama, is situated on the north shore of this island. The second largest, Muharraq, with the town and Bahrain International Airport, is connected to Manama by a causeway 1½ miles long. Bahrain is connected by causeway to Saudi Arabia's Eastern Province.

CLIMATE – The climate is humid all the year round, with rainfall of about 3 inches, concentrated in the mild winter months, December to March; in summer, May to October, temperatures can exceed 110°F (44°C).

POPULATION – The population (1991 UN estimate) is 516,000, of whom 68.4 per cent are Bahraini. About 40 per cent of the Bahrainis are Sunni Muslims, the remaining 60 per cent being Shias; the ruling family and many of the most prominent merchants are Sunnis.

CAPITAL – ΨManama, population (1981 census) 108,684. In 1990, it was estimated that 32 per cent of Bahrain's population lives in Manama.

CURRENCY – Bahrain dinar (BD) of 1,000 fils.
FLAG – Red, with vertical serrated white bar next to staff.
NATIONAL DAY – 16 December.

GOVERNMENT

Bahrain has been a fully independent state since 1971. Government takes the form of a constitutional monarchy, in which traditional consultative procedures continue to play an important role. The 1973 constitution provides for a National Assembly but this was dissolved in 1975. In December 1992 the Amir announced plans to set up a consultative council, which was established with 30 members in January 1993 and dominated by the business community.

HEAD OF STATE

*HH The Amir of Bahrain*, Shaikh Isa bin Sulman Al Khalifa, GCMG, *born* 1932; *acceded* 16 December 1961
*Crown Prince (and C.-in-C., Bahrain Defence Force)*, HE Shaikh Hamad bin Isa Al Khalifa, KCMG

CABINET *as at June 1994*

*Prime Minister*, HE Shaikh Khalifa bin Sulman Al Khalifa
*Foreign Affairs*, Shaikh Mohammed bin Mubarak Al Khalifa
*Defence*, Maj.-Gen. Shaikh Khalifa bin Ahmed Al Khalifa
*Justice and Islamic Affairs*, Shaikh Abdullah bin Khalid Al
  Khalifa
*Development and Industry, and Cabinet Affairs*, Yusuf
  Ahmad Shirawi
*Education*, Dr Ali Fakhro
*Health*, Jawad Salim Al-Arayyed
*Transportation*, Ibrahim Mohammed Humaidan
*Interior*, Shaikh Mohammed bin Khalifa Al Khalifa
*Information*, Tariq Abdulrahman Al Moayed
*Labour and Social Affairs*, Shaikh Isa bin Alibin Hamad al-
  Khalifa
*Works, Power and Water*, Majid Jawad Al-Jishi
*Housing*, Shaikh Khalid bin Abdullah Al Khalifa
*Finance and National Economy*, Ibrahim Abdul Karim
*Commerce and Agriculture*, Habib Ahmed Kassim
*Minister of State, Legal Affairs*, Dr Hussain Al-Baharna

EMBASSY OF THE STATE OF BAHRAIN
98 Gloucester Road, London SW7 4AU
Tel 0171-370 5132/3/4/5

*Ambassador Extraordinary and Plenipotentiary*, His
  Excellency Karim Ebrahim Al Shakar, apptd 1990

BRITISH EMBASSY
21 Government Avenue, Manama 306, PO Box 114
Tel: Manama 534404

*Ambassador Extraordinary and Plenipotentiary*, His
  Excellency Hugh Tunnell, apptd 1992

BRITISH COUNCIL REPRESENTATIVE, J. Wright, OBE,
  AMA Centre, PO Box 452, Manama 356

## ECONOMY

The largest sources of revenue are oil production and
refining. The Bahrain field, discovered in 1932, is wholly
owned by the Bahrain National Oil Co. The Sitra refinery
derives about 70 per cent of its crude oil by submarine
pipeline from Saudi Arabia. Bahrain also has a half share
with Saudi Arabia in the profits of the offshore Abu Sa'afa
field. A reservoir of unassociated gas has recently been
developed on Bahrain island.

Heavy industry is currently limited to the Aluminium
Bahrain (ALBA) smelter, the Gulf Petrochemical Industries
Co. (GPIC) producing ammonia and methanol, the Gulf
Aluminium Rolling Mill (GARMCO), and the Arab Shipbuilding and Repair Yard (ASRY), operating dry dock
facilities up to 500,000 tons. There are a number of small to
medium-size industrial units.

The state has developed as a financial centre. Apart from
commercial banks, led by the National Bank of Bahrain, the
Standard Chartered Bank, the British Bank of the Middle
East and the Bank of Bahrain and Kuwait, many international
banks have been licensed as offshore banking units; there are
also money brokers and merchant banks.

| Trade with UK | 1992 | 1993 |
|---|---|---|
| Imports from UK | £167,104,000 | £151,093,000 |
| Exports to UK | 49,702,000 | 51,712,000 |

## COMMUNICATIONS

Bahrain International airport is one of the main air traffic
centres of the Gulf; it is the headquarters of Gulf Air, and a
stopping point on routes between Europe and Australia and
the Far East for other airlines. A causeway linking Bahrain
to Saudi Arabia was opened in November 1986.

A world-wide telephone and telex service, by satellite and
cable, is operated by Bahrain Telecommunications Company.

# BANGLADESH
*Ghana Praja Tantri Bangladesh*

The People's Republic of Bangladesh consists of the territory
which was formerly East Pakistan (the old province of East
Bengal and the Sylhet district of Assam), covering an area of
55,598 sq. miles (143,998 sq. km) in the region of the
Gangetic delta.

The country is crossed by a network of rivers, including
the eastern arms of the Ganges, the Jamuna (Brahmaputra)
and the Meghna, flowing into the Bay of Bengal. The climate
is tropical and monsoon; hot and extremely humid during
the summer, and mild and dry during the short winter. The
rainfall is heavy, varying from 50 inches to 135 inches in
different districts and the bulk of it falls during monsoon
season from June to September.

POPULATION – The population (1991 census) was
108,000,000. The faith of 88 per cent of the population is
Islam and 10.5 per cent Hinduism. Islam has been
constitutionally declared the state religion of Bangladesh.

The state language is Bengali. Use of Bengali is compulsory
in all government departments. English, however, is understood and is used widely as an unofficial second language.

CAPITAL – Dhaka, population (1991 census) 6,537,308.
CURRENCY – Taka (Tk) of 100 poisha.
FLAG – Red circle on a bottle-green ground.
NATIONAL ANTHEM – Amar Sonar Bangla.
NATIONAL DAY – 26 March (Independence Day).

## GOVERNMENT

Prior to becoming East Pakistan, the territory had been part
of British India. It acceded to Pakistan in October 1947,
which became a republic on 23 March 1956.

By a proclamation of 26 March 1971, Bangladesh purported
to secede from the central government, and a government-
in-exile, led by Sheikh Mujibur Rahman of the Awami
League, was set up which formally declared independence
on 17 April. Bangladesh achieved its independence on 16
December 1971, following the conclusion of the Indo-
Pakistan war. Pakistan and Bangladesh accorded one another
mutual recognition in February 1974.

In 1975 the constitution was amended and a one-party
presidential system was introduced, with Prime Minister
Sheikh Rahman assuming the presidency under martial law.
A presidential election was held in June 1978 and President
Zia was elected. He lifted martial law and introduced a multiparty presidential system of government. Zia was assassinated
in May 1981 in an unsuccessful coup. He was replaced by
Justice Abdus Sattar, who won a presidential election in
October 1981 but was overthrown in 1982 in a coup led by
the then Chief of Army Staff, Gen. Ershad. Following
parliamentary elections held in May 1986, which were
boycotted by several opposition parties, a civilian cabinet was
appointed and Gen. Ershad was elected as President in
October 1986. Further elections, again boycotted by the
opposition, were held in March 1988. Popular unrest forced
Gen. Ershad's resignation in December 1990. A caretaker
government was formed and parliamentary elections were
held in February 1991. The Bangladesh Nationalist Party
(BNP) won the largest number of seats and, after a series of
by-elections, gained a parliamentary majority. The BNP
leader, Begum Khaleda Zia, was sworn in as Prime Minister

on 19 March 1991. On 6 August 1991, Parliament approved a constitutional amendment reverting Bangladesh to parliamentary rule after 16 years of presidential government. Under the new system, the parliament elected BNP nominee Abdur Rahman Biswas as President.

HEAD OF STATE
*President*, Abdur Rahman Biswas, *sworn in* 8 October 1991

CABINET *as at June 1994*
*Prime Minister, Defence, Establishment, Cabinet Division*,
  Begum Khaleda Zia
*Law, Justice and Parliamentary Affairs*, Mirza Golam Hafiz
*Education*, Zamiruddin Sircar
*Agriculture, Irrigation, Flood Control and Water Resources*,
  Maj.-Gen. Majedul Haque (retd.)
*Foreign Affairs*, A. S. M. Mustafizur Rahman
*Finance*, Saifur Rahman
*Local Government, Rural Development and Co-operatives*,
  Abdus Salam Talukder
*Communication*, Col. Oli Ahmed (retd.)
*Commerce*, M. Shamsul Islam
*Post and Telecommunications*, Tariqul Islam
*Health and Family Welfare*, Chowdhury Kamal Ibne Yusuf
*Food*, Mir Shawkat Ali
*Information*, Nazmul Huda
*Home*, Abdul Matin Chowdhury
*Religious Affairs*, Keramat Ali
*Shipping*, M. K. Anwar
*Jute*, A. S. M. Hannan Shah
*Environment and Forest*, Col. Akbar Hossain (retd.)
*Power, Energy and Mineral Resources*, Dr. Khandakar
  Mosharraf Hossain
*Works*, Rafiqul Islam Miah
*Labour and Manpower*, Abdul Mannan Bhuiyan
*Fisheries and Livestock*, Abdullah Al-Noman
*Planning*, A. M. Zahiruddin Knan

BANGLADESH HIGH COMMISSION
28 Queen's Gate, London SW7 5JA
TEL 0171–584  0081/2/3/4
*High Commissioner*, His Excellency Dr A. F. M. Yusuf,
  apptd 1992
*Deputy High Commissioner*, M. M. Hossain
*Defence Adviser*, Brig. S. Huda
*Minister*, M. M. Reza *(Economic)*

BRITISH HIGH COMMISSION
United Nations Road, Baridhara Dhaka
PO Box 6079, Dhaka-12
Tel: Dhaka 882705
*High Commissioner*, His Excellency Peter James Fowler,
  CMG, apptd 1993
*Deputy High Commissioner*, J. R. Nicols
*Defence Adviser*, Col. E. D. Powell-Jones, OBE
*First Secretary (Economic)*, P. D. Grant

BRITISH COUNCIL REPRESENTATIVE, K. Burd, OBE,
  5 Fuller Road (PO Box 161), Dhaka 1000

EDUCATION

Primary education is free and planned to be universal by the year 2000. There are 48,146 primary schools, mostly managed by the Government. There are 10,575 secondary schools and 997 colleges offering general and technical education. There are 13 universities including one for engineering and technology, one for agriculture and another for Islamic education and research. In 1991 the literacy rate was estimated to be 32.4 per cent (38.9 per cent male and 25.5 per cent female).

COMMUNICATIONS

Principal seaports are Chittagong and Mongla. The Bangladesh Shipping Corporation has been set up by the Government to operate the Bangladesh merchant fleet. The principal airports are Dhaka (Zia International) and Chittagong. The international airline, Bangladesh Biman, serves Europe, the Middle East, South and South-East Asia, and an internal network.

There are about 6,880 miles of roads in Bangladesh; 4,724 miles are metalled. There are 2,798 miles of railway track.

Radio Bangladesh is the main national broadcasting service. A television service was introduced in 1965 and colour transmissions began in 1980.

ECONOMY

Since 1991 the BNP government has been implementing an IMF economic reform plan which has delivered stable prices and inflation and brought down the budget deficit from 8 per cent of GDP in 1989 to 5.3 per cent in 1993.

Bangladesh is a principal producer of raw jute. Other agricultural products are rice, tea, oil seeds, pulses and sugar cane. The chief industries are jute, cotton, tea, leather, pharmaceuticals, fertilizer, sugar, prawn fishing, natural gas and garment manufacture. Remittances sent home by Bangladeshi workers abroad have been of considerable support to the economy in recent years.

Bangladesh is a major recipient of bilateral and multilateral development aid. The total aid pledged for 1993 from international donors formed into a consortium led by the World Bank is US$2,150 million.

| *Trade with UK* | 1992 | 1993 |
| --- | --- | --- |
| Imports from UK | £39,355,000 | £54,274,000 |
| Exports to UK | 94,952,000 | 140,114,000 |

## BARBADOS

Barbados, the most easterly of the Caribbean islands, is situated in 13° 14′ N. latitude and 59° 37′ W. longitude. The island has a total area of 166 sq. miles (430 sq. km), the land rising in a series of tablelands marked by terraces to the highest point, Mt Hillaby (1,116 ft). It is nearly 21 miles long by 14 miles broad. The climate is equable with annual average temperature 26.6°C (79.8°F) and rainfall varying from a yearly average of 75 inches in the high central district to 50 inches in some of the low-lying coastal areas.

POPULATION – The population of Barbados (1991 UN estimate) was 255,000. There are eleven administrative areas (parishes): St Michael, Christ Church, St Andrews, St George, St James, St John, St Joseph, St Lucy, St Peter, St Philip and St Thomas.

CAPITAL – ΨBridgetown (population, estimated April 1980, 7,466) in the parish of St Michael. There are other towns, Oistins in Christ Church, Holetown in St James and Speightstown in St Peter.

CURRENCY – Barbados dollar (BD$) of 100 cents.
FLAG – Three vertical stripes, dark blue, gold and dark blue, with a trident head on gold stripe.
NATIONAL ANTHEM – In Plenty and in Time of Need.
NATIONAL DAY – 30 November (Independence Day).

GOVERNMENT

The first inhabitants of Barbados were Arawak Indians but the island was uninhabited when first settled by the British in 1627. It was a Crown Colony from 1652 until it became an independent state within the Commonwealth on 30 November 1966. The legislature consists of the Governor-General, a Senate and a House of Assembly. The Senate comprises 21 Senators appointed by the Governor-General, of whom 12 are appointed on the advice of the Prime Minister, two on the advice of the Leader of the Opposition and seven by the Governor-General at his/her discretion to represent religious, economic or social interests in the Island or such other interests as the Governor-General considers ought to be represented. The House of Assembly comprises 28 members elected every five years by adult suffrage. The last general election took place on 22 January 1991 and seats in the House of Assembly were distributed as follows: Democratic Labour Party 18, Barbados Labour Party 10. The Prime Minister dissolved the National Assembly on 19 June 1994 after losing a parliamentary vote of no confidence.

*Governor-General*, Her Excellency Dame Nita Barrow, GCMG, DA, apptd 1990

CABINET *as at June 1994*

*Prime Minister, Civil Service*, Rt. Hon. L. Erskine Sandiford
*Deputy Prime Minister, Leader of the House of Assembly, Minister of International Transport, Telecommunications and Immigration, Transport and Works*, Hon. Philip M. Greaves, QC
*Minister of State, Prime Minister's Office, Leader of the Senate*, Sen. Hon. L. V. Harcour Lewis
*Attorney-General and Caricom Affairs*, Hon. Maurice A. King, QC
*Health and Foreign Affairs*, Hon. Brandford M. Taitt
*Housing and Lands, Community Development and Culture*, Hon. E. Evelyn Greaves
*Finance and Economic Affairs*, Hon. David Thompson
*Labour, Consumer Affairs and the Environment*, Hon. Carl D. Clarke
*Tourism and Sports*, Hon. Wesley W. Hall
*Justice and Public Safety*, Hon. Keith Simmons
*Education*, Hon. Cyril V. Walker
*Agriculture, Food and Fisheries*, Hon. David Bowen
*Trade, Industry and Commerce*, Hon. Warwick O. Franklin

BARBADOS HIGH COMMISSION
1 Great Russell Street, London WC1B 3JY
Tel 0171-631 4975
*High Commissioner*, His Excellency Austin Sealey, apptd 1991
*Deputy High Commissioner*, O. O. Eversley, OBE
*First Secretary*, W. Gooding

BRITISH HIGH COMMISSION
Lower Collymore Rock, PO Box 676, Bridgetown C
Tel: Bridgetown 436 6694
*High Commissioner*, His Excellency Richard Thomas, CMG, apptd 1994
*Deputy High Commissioner*, J. A. Noakes
*Defence Adviser*, Col. C. S. Faith, OBE
*First Secretary (Chancery)*, A. Ffrench Blake, OBE

JUDICATURE

There is a Supreme Court of Judicature consisting of a High Court and a Court of Appeal. In certain cases a further appeal lies to the Judicial Committee of the Privy Council. The Chief Justice and Puisne Judges are appointed by the Governor-General on the recommendation of the Prime Minister and after consultation with the Leader of the Opposition.

*Chief Justice*, The Hon. Sir Denys Williams, KCMG

ECONOMY

The economy of the island is based on tourism, sugar and light manufacturing. In 1990, 432,092 tourists visited Barbados and 362,611 cruise ship passengers. Chief exports are sugar and its by-products, chemicals, electronic components and clothing.

| FINANCE | 1992–3* |
|---|---|
| Current revenue | BD$1,077,900,000 |
| Current expenditure | 1,248,800,000 |
| Deficit | 170,500,000 |
| *estimated | |

| *Trade with UK* | 1992 | 1993 |
|---|---|---|
| Imports from UK | £21,027,000 | £28,229,000 |
| Exports to UK | 22,306,000 | 25,079,000 |

EDUCATION

Primary and secondary education is free in government schools. There are 105 primary schools, 21 government secondary schools and 15 approved government secondary schools.

COMMUNICATIONS

Barbados has some 965 miles of roads, of which about 917 miles are asphalted. The Grantley Adams International airport is situated at Seawell, 12 miles from Bridgetown, and frequent scheduled services connect Barbados with the major world air routes. Bridgetown, the only port of entry, has a deep-water harbour with berths for eight ships, but oil is pumped ashore at Spring Gardens and at an Esso installation on the West Coast. Barbados has a colour television service, three radio broadcasting services, and a wired broadcasting service.

# BELARUS
*Respublika Belarus*

Belarus (formerly Byelorussia) has an area of 80,300 sq. miles (207,600 sq. km) and is situated in the western part of the European area of the former USSR. It is bordered on the north by Latvia and Lithuania, on the east by Russia, on the south by the Ukraine and on the west by Poland. The republic is mostly a plain with many lakes, swamps and marshy areas. The main rivers are the upper reaches of the Dnieper, of the Niemen and of the Western Dvina. The republic is divided into six provinces (Brest, Gomel, Grodno, Minsk, Mogilev and Vitebsk).

CLIMATE – Continental with mild, humid winters and relatively cool and rainy summers. The autumns are damp and springs sunny. The climate is changeable due to the occasional influence of Atlantic sea air.

POPULATION – The population (1990 official estimate) is 10,260,000, of which 78 per cent are Belarusians, 13 per cent Russians, 4 per cent Poles and 3 per cent Ukrainians, with smaller numbers of Jews and Lithuanians. Most of the population are Roman Catholics, with a large minority of Russian Orthodox.

Belarusian is one of the Slavonic family of languages, more specifically part of the eastern group which includes Russian and Ukrainian. The alphabet is similar to the Russian one. Russian remains the dominant language.

CAPITAL – Minsk. Population 1,589,000 (1989). The city is the administrative centre of the CIS. Other important cities are Gomel, Vitebsk, Brest and Grodno.

CURRENCY – Rouble of 100 kopeks. (The zaichik currency coupon has been withdrawn under the monetary union agreement with Russia.)
FLAG – Three horizontal stripes of white, red, white.
NATIONAL ANTHEM – The former Soviet national anthem but with the words omitted.
NATIONAL DAY – 27 July (Independence Day).

## GOVERNMENT

In the early ninth century AD the Kievan Rus state was a unified state encompassing all the Russian, Ukrainian and Belarusian populations. After being absorbed into Lithuania in the 13th and 14th centuries, the Belarusian nationality, language and culture flourished until it came under Polish rule in the mid-16th century. Two hundred years of Polish rule followed until Belarus was re-absorbed into the Russian Empire.

Much of Belarus was under German control at the time of the Russian revolution and it was not until German forces withdrew that a Byelorussian Soviet Socialist Republic was declared on 1 January 1919. Western Belarus was ceded to Poland after the Soviet defeat in the Polish-Soviet war of 1919–20, and was not recovered until Soviet forces occupied the area under the 1939 Nazi-Soviet Pact. Belarus was devastated by the German invasion in the Second World War with 200 towns, 9,000 villages and 75 per cent of industry destroyed. Resistance to the Nazi occupation was strong, with 25 per cent of the population killed and hundreds of thousands deported. Virtually all of Belarus had to be rebuilt after the war.

Belarus issued a Declaration of State Sovereignty on 27 July 1990 and then declared its independence from the Soviet Union after the failed coup in Moscow in August 1991. Its independence from the USSR was recognized by the EC and USA in January 1992; as the Soviet republic of Byelorussia it had been a member of the UN since 1945.

After the failed Moscow coup, the Belarusian leader Nikolai Dementei was ousted because of his involvement with the coup leaders. He was replaced by Stanislav Shushkevich at the head of an informal coalition of Communists and democrats. Belarus was one of the three CIS founding members.

Throughout 1992 and 1993 parliament and the government remained under the control of former Communists who thwarted the economic and political reform efforts of Shushkevich and his democratic nationalist allies. Shushkevich was forced to resign in January 1994 after losing a no-confidence vote in the Supreme Soviet. Police General Mecheslav Grib was elected by the Supreme Soviet to replace Shushkevich as head of state and immediately aligned himself with the conservative government in pursuing closer political, economic and trade links with Russia and the CIS, to which Belarus' centrally-planned economy is tied. Belarus reached agreement with Russia on a monetary union in January 1994, which came into force in April, under which Belarus has re-entered the rouble zone, replaced its currency and subordinated its central bank to Russia's in order to get access to cheap supplies of Russian raw materials.

A new constitution came into effect on 30 March 1994 under which a directly elected President serving a maximum of two five-year terms was instituted. The President appoints the cabinet and directs government policy. Elections to a 260-seat Supreme Soviet are to be held on 31 December 1994. The first direct presidential election was held in July 1994 and won by maverick populist Alexander Lukashenko, who promised to purge corruption and form even closer relations with Russia. The Prime Minister and cabinet resigned on 12 July 1994 and the President had yet to appoint a new government at the time of going to press.

HEAD OF STATE
*President*, Alexander Lukashenko, *elected*, 10 July 1994

EMBASSY OF THE REPUBLIC OF BELARUS
1 St Stephens Crescent, London W2 5QT
Tel 0171-225 4568

*Ambassador Extraordinary and Plenipotentiary*, His Excellency Uladzimir Syanko, apptd 1994

BRITISH EMBASSY
UL Sacharova 26, Minsk 220034
Tel: Minsk 3474

*Ambassador Extraordinary and Plenipotentiary*, His Excellency John Everard, apptd 1993

## DEFENCE

Belarus has on its territory 80 SS-25 Intercontinental Ballistic Missiles which it is obliged to return to Russia for destruction under the terms of the START 1 Treaty, which it ratified in February 1993 along with the Nuclear Non-Proliferation Treaty.

The total active armed forces number some 102,600 personnel (which is being reduced to 90,000) with a term of conscription of 18 months. The Army has 50,500 personnel 3,280 main battle tanks, 3,710 armoured infantry fighting vehicles and armoured personnel carriers and 1,590 artillery pieces. The Air Force has 29,700 personnel (including 15,600 Air Defence) with 415 combat aircraft and 95 attack helicopters. In addition there are 8,000 parliamentary border guards. Russia maintains some 35,000 Air Force personnel in Belarus, with 272 combat aircraft.

## ECONOMY

The collapse of the Soviet centrally planned economic system has hit Belarusian industry badly. Belarus had many factories manufacturing products such as tractors, textiles and metal workings from raw materials sent from the rest of the former USSR. However, the republic cannot afford to pay market prices for the raw materials, causing factories to close. It is hoped that the monetary union agreement with Russia will enable Belarus to gain access to cheap Russian raw materials, oil and gas. Before the agreement was reached, Belarus had begun to experience hyper-inflation of over 50 per cent. Belarus is exchanging its zaichik currency at a one to one rate for Russian roubles.

Belarusian agriculture, based on the meat and dairy industries, is in better shape and will cushion the republic from the worst of any food shortages, but rationing for some goods has been enforced since late 1992. The economy is still dependent on Russian fuel supplies but the peat industry is also being developed to make Belarus as self-sufficient as possible in fuel.

| *Trade with UK* | 1993 |
|---|---|
| Imports from UK | £10,506,000 |
| Exports to UK | 4,105,000 |

## BELGIUM
*Royaume de Belgique*

A kingdom of western Europe, with a total area of 11,781 sq. miles (30,513 sq. km), Belgium is bounded on the north by the Netherlands, on the south by France, on the east by

Germany and Luxembourg, and on the west by the North Sea. Belgium has a frontier of 898 miles, and a seaboard of 41 miles. The Meuse and its tributary, the Sambre, divide it into two distinct regions, that in the west being generally level and fertile, while the tableland of the Ardennes, in the east, has for the most part a poor soil. The polders near the coast, which are protected by dykes against floods, cover an area of 193 sq. miles. The highest hill, Signal de Botranges, rises to a height of 2,276 feet, but the mean elevation of the whole country does not exceed 526 feet. The principal rivers are the Scheldt and the Meuse.

POPULATION – The population (1991) was 10,054,559: Greater Brussels 960,324; Flanders 5,767,856; Wallonia 3,326,379, of whom 67,584 are German-speaking. The majority of Belgians are Roman Catholics.

CAPITAL – Brussels, has a population (1991) of 960,324. Other towns are ΨAntwerp, the chief port (467,875); ΨGhent (230,466); Liège (195,201); Charleroi (206,928); Bruges (117,150); ΨOstend (68,370); Malines (75,514).
CURRENCY – Belgian franc of 100 centimes (centiemen).
FLAG – Three vertical bands, black, yellow, red.
NATIONAL ANTHEM – La Brabançonne.
NATIONAL DAY – 21 July (Accession of King Leopold I, 1831).

## GOVERNMENT

The kingdom formed part of the Low Countries (Netherlands) from 1815 until 14 October 1830, when a National Congress proclaimed its independence. On 4 June 1831, Prince Leopold of Coburg was chosen as the hereditary king. The separation from the Netherlands and the neutrality and inviolability of Belgium were guaranteed by a Conference of the European Powers, and by the Treaty of London (19 April 1839), the famous 'scrap of paper', signed by Austria, France, Great Britain, Prussia, The Netherlands, and Russia. On 4 August 1914 the Germans invaded Belgium, in violation of the terms of the treaty. The kingdom was again invaded by Germany on 10 May 1940 and was occupied by Nazi troops until liberated by the Allies in September 1944.

### CONSTITUTION

According to the constitution of 1831 the form of government is a constitutional representative and hereditary monarchy with a bicameral legislature, consisting of the King, the Senate and the Chamber of Deputies. The parliamentary term is four years.

Since 1968 separatist and regionalist political tension between the Dutch-speaking Flemish population and the French-speaking Walloons has grown considerably. This led to constitutional amendments in 1971, 1980, 1988 and 1993 intended to devolve power to the regions. The 1993 constitutional amendments, which will be implemented in stages until late 1995, explicitly states that Belgium is a federal state. The package devolves many traditional powers from the national government to the community and regional governments. The national government retains competence only in the areas of foreign and defence policy, the national budget and monetary policy, social security, and the judiciary, legal and penal systems. The King loses his power to dissolve parliament and the Senate loses mosts of its power, becoming a limited revising chamber secondary to the Chamber of Representatives. The Senate is reduced (in 1995) from 184 to 71 seats, of which 40 are directly elected (25 Flemish and 15 French), 21 indirectly elected (10 from Flemish Community Council, 10 from Francophone Community Council and one from Germanophone Community Council), and 10 co-opted by the Flemish and Francophone Communities. The Chamber of Representatives is reduced (in 1995) from 212 to 150 seats and the national government is limited to 15 ministers.

The last general election was held on 24 November 1991. The results were as follows (seats):

*Chamber of Deputies:* CVP 39; PS 35; SP 28; VLD (Flemish Liberals and Democrats) 26; PRL (Liberal Reform Party (Francophone)) 20; PSC 18; Vlaams Blok (Flemish Nationalist Party) 12; VU (Flemish People's Union) 10; Ecolo (Francophone Ecology Party) 10; Agalev (Flemish Environmental Party) 7; FDF (Francophone Democratic Front) 3; ROSSEM 3; National Front (FN/NF) 1.

*Senate:* CVP 20; PS 18; SP 14; VLD 13; PRL 9; PSC 9; Vlaams Blok 5; VU 5; Ecolo 6; Agalev 5; ROSSEM 1; FDF 1. Besides these directly elected representatives the Senate also includes 51 members who are elected by the Provincial Councils and 26 who are co-opted in the proportions of the directly elected seats.

### HEAD OF STATE

*HM The King of the Belgians,* King Albert II, *born* 6 June 1934; *succeeded* 9 August 1993, after the death of his elder brother, King Baudouin, on 31 July 1993; *married* 2 July 1959, Donna Paola Ruffo di Calabria, and has *issue* Prince Philippe (*see* below); Princess Astrid Josephine-Charlotte Fabrizia Elisabeth Paola Marie, *b.* 5 June 1962; Prince Laurent, *b.* 20 October 1963

*Heir,* HRH Prince Philippe Léopold Louis Marie, *born* 15 April 1960

### CABINET *as at June 1994*

*Prime Minister,* Jean-Luc Dehaene (CVP)
*Deputy Prime Minister, Transport and Public Enterprises,* Elio di Rupo (PS)
*Deputy Prime Minister, Foreign Affairs,* Willy Claes (SP)
*Deputy Prime Minister, Justice, Economic Affairs,* Melchoir Wathelet (PSC)
*Finance,* Philippe Maystadt (PSC)
*Social Affairs,* Magda de Galan (PS)
*Scientific Policy,* Jean-Maurice Dehousse (PS)
*Foreign Trade and European Affairs,* Robert Urbain (PS)
*Small and Medium-Sized Enterprises and Agriculture,* André Bourgeois (CVP)
*Defence,* Leo Delcroix (CVP)
*Social Integration, Public Health and the Environment,* Jacques Santkin (PS)
*Pensions,* Freddy Willockx (SP)
*Internal Affairs and the Civil Service,* Louis Tobback (SP)

*Employment and Equality*, Miet Smet (CVP)
*Budget*, Herman van Rompuy (CVP)
*Development Co-operation*, Erik Derycke (SP)

CVP Christian Social Party (Flemish); PS Socialist Party (Francophone); SP Socialist Party (Flemish); PSC Christian Social Party (Francophone)

BELGIAN EMBASSY
103 Eaton Square, London SW1W 9AB
Tel 0171-235 5422
*Ambassador Extraordinary and Plenipotentiary*, new appointment awaited
*Minister-Counsellor*, M. Den Doncker
*Military, Naval and Air Attaché*, Capt. P. Lavaert
*First Secretary (Economic)*, C. Peeters

BRITISH EMBASSY
rue d'Arlon 85, 1040 Brussels
Tel: Brussels 287 6211
*Ambassador Extraordinary and Plenipotentiary*, His Excellency John W. D. Gray, CMG, apptd 1993
*Deputy Ambassador, Counsellor and Consul-General*, N. M. McCarthy, OBE
*Counsellor (Commercial/Economic)*, N. R. Jarrold
*Defence and Military Attaché*, Col. J. M. Craster
BRITISH CONSULAR OFFICES – There are offices at *Brussels, Antwerp* and *Liège.*
BRITISH COUNCIL REPRESENTATIVE TO BELGIUM AND LUXEMBOURG – Dr Malcolm Cooper, rue Joseph II 30, 1040 Brussels
BRITISH CHAMBER OF COMMERCE FOR BELGIUM AND LUXEMBOURG (INC.), 30 rue Joseph II, 1040 Brussels

REGIONAL GOVERNMENT

The constitutional amendment packages of 1980, 1988 and 1993 make provision for four levels of sub-national government in Belgium: Community; Regional; Provincial; and Communal.

There are four defined communities in Belgium: Flemish; Francophone; Brussels; Germanophone. Each community has its own assembly with powers and competence in the areas of language, culture, media, sport, tourism, education, social welfare and public health. The assemblies each elect their own community government. At this level, Flanders is covered by the Flemish Community Assembly; Brussels is covered by its Joint Community Commission as well as the Flemish and Francophone Community Assemblies; most of Wallonia is covered by the Francophone Community Assembly and the remainder of Wallonia in the German-speaking communities of Eupen and Malmedy (ceded by Germany under the Versailles Treaty 1919) is covered by the Germanophone Community Assembly.

At regional level, Belgium is divided into the regions of Wallonia, Brussels and Flanders. Each region has its own assembly and government with powers and competences over areas such as the environment, housing, energy, employment, transport, agriculture, regional economic policy and foreign trade. The Wallonia regional assembly will be directly elected with 75 members by 1995, the Brussels regional assembly is already directly elected with 75 members, and the Flemish regional assembly will have 118 directly elected members and six nominated by the Flemish in Brussels.

There are nine provinces in Belgium, of which four are French-speaking and in Wallonia (Hainault, Liège, Luxembourg and Namur) and four are Dutch-speaking and in Flanders (Antwerp, East Flanders, West Flanders, Limbourg). Brabant is Dutch-speaking in the north and French-speaking in the south and is due to be divided into two new

provinces by 1995. In addition, Belgium has 589 communes as the lowest level of local government.

The main consequence of the constitutional amendments has been the increase in political power of the regional governments at the expense of both the community and national levels. As a result the Francophone Community Assembly and Government is gradually losing power to the Walloon and Brussels regional governments, whilst the Flemish have amalgamated their community and regional governments to form one increasingly powerful Flanders government.

An Arbitration Court was set up in 1984 to resolve conflicts between laws made by the various legislative bodies.

*Minister-President of the Flemish Government*, Luc Van den Brande (CVP)
*Minister-President of the Walloon Regional Government*, Robert Collignon (PS)

DEFENCE

The total active armed forces number some 80,700 (28,600 conscripts) with 146,000 reservists who have served within the last three years. Conscripts serve for eight months. In July 1992 the government announced its intention to end conscription by the end of 1994 and reduce the armed forces to 43,000 personnel.

The Army has a strength of 54,000 (23,300 conscripts) with 360 main battle tanks, 133 light tanks, 2,020 armoured personnel carriers and armoured infantry fighting vehicles, 375 artillery pieces and 60 helicopters. The Army is organized into one armoured and two mechanized infantry brigades, one paratroop-commando regiment and various support units.

The Navy has a strength of 4,400 (1,000 conscripts) with three frigates and 13 mine warfare vessels. The Air Force is 17,300 strong (4,300 conscripts) with 122 combat aircraft and another 74 in store.

Belgium maintains an army corps of 19,000 troops in Germany as part of its NATO commitment. It also maintains 700 troops in Croatia and 100 in Bosnia as part of the UN forces. In Belgium there are the headquarters of NATO and SHAPE and the Western European Union Military Planning Cell, as well as 1,900 US personnel.

ECONOMY

Belgium is a manufacturing country. With no natural resources except coal, production of which has now ceased, industry is based largely on the processing for re-export of imported raw materials. Gross Domestic Product in 1993 was BFr. 7,137 billion. Principal industries are steel and metal products, chemicals and petrochemicals, textiles, glass, and foodstuffs.

In an attempt to meet the Maastricht Treaty criteria for economic and monetary union, the government in late 1993 introduced an austerity package to try to reduce Belgium public debt of 140 per cent of GDP, which is the highest in the developed world.

FINANCE

| *Budget* | 1988 | 1989 |
| --- | --- | --- |
| Revenue | BFr.1,505,500m | BFr.1,037,000m |
| Expenditure | 1,901,600m | 1,409,600m |

TRADE

External trade figures relate to Luxembourg as well as Belgium since the two countries formed an economic union in 1921.

|              | 1991              | 1992              |
|--------------|-------------------|-------------------|
| Total imports | BFr.4,120,000m   | BFr.4,024,000m    |
| Total exports | 4,024,000m       | 3,768,000m        |

*Trade with UK (Belgium and Luxembourg)*

|               | 1992          | 1993          |
|---------------|---------------|---------------|
| Imports from UK | £5,714,150,000 | £6,597,146,000 |
| Exports to UK  | 5,741,401,000  | 6,270,295,000  |

## CULTURE

Belgium is divided between those who speak Dutch (the Flemings) and those who speak French (the Walloons). Dutch is recognized as the official language in the northern areas and French in the southern (Walloon) area and there are guarantees for the respective linguistic minorities. Brussels is officially bi-lingual. There is a small German-speaking area (Eupen and Malmedy) along the German border, east of Liège.

The literature of France and the Netherlands is supplemented by an indigenous Belgian literary activity, in both French and Dutch. Maurice Maeterlinck (1862–1949) was awarded the Nobel Prize for Literature in 1911. Emile Verhaeren (1855–1916) was a poet of international standing. Of contemporary Belgian writers, perhaps the most celebrated was Georges Simenon (1903–89). There are 39 daily newspapers in Belgium (23 in French, 15 in Dutch and one in German).

## EDUCATION

Nursery schools provide free education for the 2½ to 6 age group. There are over 8,000 primary schools (6 to 12 years) of which approximately 5,000 are administered by the local Communities. The remainder are free institutions (predominantly Roman Catholic). There are more than 1,100 secondary schools offering a general academic education slightly over half of which are free institutions (predominantly Roman Catholic but subsidized by the state) and the remainder official institutions. The official school leaving age is 18.

## COMMUNICATIONS

The railways are operated by the Belgian National Railways. The Belgian National Light Railways (SNCV) also operates regular bus routes.

Ship canals include Ghent-Terneuzen (18 miles, of which half is in Belgium and half in the Netherlands) which permits the passage to Ghent of ships up to 60,000 tons; the Canal of Willebroek Rupel-Brussels (20 miles, by which ships drawing 18 ft reach Brussels from the sea; opened in 1922); and Bruges (from Zeebrugge on the North Sea to Bruges, 6¼ miles). The Albert Canal (79 miles), links Liège with Antwerp; it was completed in 1939 and accommodates barges up to 1,350 tons. The River Meuse from the Dutch to the French frontiers, the River Sambre between Namur and Monceau, the River Scheldt from Antwerp to Ghent and the Brussels-Charleroi Canal are being widened or deepened to take barges up to 1,350 tons. Most of the maritime trade of Belgium is carried in foreign shipping.

In 1986 there were 14,260 km of trunk roads, of which about 1,550 km were motorways.

The Belgian national airline Sabena operates regular services between Brussels and European centres, as well as intercontinental services world-wide.

# BELIZE

Belize lies on the east coast of Central America, bounded on the north and north-west by Mexico, and on the west and south by Guatemala. The total area (including offshore islands) is about 8,867 sq. miles (22,965 sq. km.). The climate is sub-tropical, with a mean annual temperature of 20°C, but is tempered by sea breezes. There are two dry seasons, the main one from February to May and the other (the Maugre season) from August to September. The country is occasionally affected by hurricanes.

The coastal areas are mostly flat and swampy with many islets but the country rises gradually towards the interior, which is mainly forest. The northern and western districts are hilly, and in the south the Maya Mountains and the Cockscombs form the backbone of the country, reaching a height of 3,700 feet at Victoria Peak.

POPULATION – The population is 205,000 (1993 census), of which the main racial groups are: Mestizo (Maya-Spanish), 44 per cent; Creole, 30 per cent; Maya, 11 per cent; plus a number of East Indian and Spanish descent. The races are now heavily inter-mixed. The majority of the population is Christian, about 58 per cent Catholic and 34 per cent Protestant. The official language and language of instruction is English. Spanish is also widely spoken and English Creole is the vernacular. There are also Garifuna and Maya speakers.

CAPITAL – Belmopan (1993 census 3,739). The largest city and the former capital is ΨBelize City (population, 1993 census 46,342). Other towns are Corozal (7,420), San Ignacio (9,417), Dangriga (6,761), Orange Walk (11,573).

CURRENCY – Belize dollar (BZ$) of 100 cents. The Belize dollar is tied to the US dollar, BZ$2 = US$1.

FLAG – Blue ground with red band along top and bottom edges, and in centre a white disc containing the coat of arms surrounded by a green garland.

NATIONAL ANTHEM – Land of the Free.

NATIONAL DAY – 21 September (Independence Day).

## GOVERNMENT

The early history of Belize is little known, although the numerous ruins in the area indicate that it was heavily populated by the Maya Indians. The first British settlement was established in 1638 but was subject to repeated attacks by the Spanish, who claimed sovereignty over the area, until the decisive defeat of Spanish forces by the Royal Navy and settlers in the battle of St George's Caye in 1798. In 1871 the area was recognized by Britain as a colony and called British Honduras. In 1973 the colony was officially renamed Belize, and was granted independence on 21 September 1981. The long-standing territorial dispute with Guatemala, which had delayed independence earlier, was provisionally resolved in November 1992 when the Guatemalan Congress and Supreme Court voted to recognize Belize and establish diplomatic relations. Guatemala still retains its claim, subject to arbitration by the International Court of Justice.

Following the Guatemalan decision to recognize Belize, the United Kingdom announced in February 1993 its decision to withdraw its Army and Royal Air Force garrison as no longer necessary to defend Belize against the Guatemalan threat. Most of the 1,800 strong garrison will be withdrawn by the end of 1994 leaving only a small jungle-warfare training school. The subsequent Guatemalan constitutional crisis and overthrow of President Serrano in May and June 1993 caused concern in Belize over the new Guatemalan government's policy towards Belize.

Queen Elizabeth II is head of state, represented in Belize by a Governor-General, who is a citizen of the country. There is a National Assembly, comprising a House of Representatives (29 members elected for five years) and a Senate (nine members appointed by the Governor-General). Executive power is vested in the Cabinet, which is responsible to the National Assembly.

The National Assembly was dissolved in June 1993 and in the ensuing elections the People's United Party government was defeated by the United Democratic Party.

*Governor-General*, His Excellency Sir Colville Norbert Young, GCMG, apptd 17 November 1993.

THE CABINET *as at July 1994*

*Prime Minister and Minister of Finance and Defence*, Rt. Hon. Manuel Esquivel
*Deputy PM, Attorney-General, Minister of Foreign Affairs and Economic Development*, Hon. Dean Barrow
*Natural Resources*, Hon. Edwardo Juan
*Agriculture*, Hon. Russell Garcia
*Tourism and Environment*, Hon. Henry Young
*Home Affairs*, Hon. Elito Urbina
*Energy and Communications*, Hon. Joseph Cayetano
*Health and Sports*, Hon. Ruben Campos
*Education, Public Service and Labour*, Hon. Elodio Aragon
*Housing, Urban Development, Co-operatives and Local Government*, Hon. Hubert Elrington
*Trade and Industry*, Hon. Salvador Fernandez
*Youth Development and Human Resources*, Hon. Philip Goldson
*Works*, Hon. Melvin Hulse
*Ministers of State:*
*Housing, Urban Development, Co-operatives, Local Government*, Hon. Michael Finnegan
*Youth Development and Human Resources*, Hon. Faith Babb
*Works*, Hon. Wilfred Dennis Usher

BELIZE HIGH COMMISSION
10 Harcourt House, 19A Cavendish Square, London WIM 9AD
Tel 0171-499 9728

*High Commissioner*, Her Excellency Dr Ursula Barrow, apptd 1993

BRITISH HIGH COMMISSION
PO Box 91, Belmopan
Tel: Belmopan 22146/7

*High Commissioner*, His Excellency David McKilligin, CMG, apptd 1991

ECONOMY

About 30 per cent of the population is engaged in agriculture. Corn (maize), rice, red kidney beans, root crops and fruit are the main food crops, although main agricultural exports are sugar, bananas and citrus products. The country is more or less self-sufficient in fresh beef, pork and poultry, but processed meat and dairy products are imported. About 25 per cent of timber production (mostly mahogany) is exported, and there is a large US market for lobster, conch and scale fish. Tourism is also a valuable source of income.

| FINANCE | 1990–1 |
|---|---|
| Revenue | BZ$215.8m |
| Expenditure | 205.8m |
| Surplus | 10.0m |

| TRADE | 1992 | 1993 |
|---|---|---|
| Total imports | BZ$548.3m | BZ$545.3m |
| Total exports | 231.1m | 228.6m |

| Trade with UK | 1992 | 1993 |
|---|---|---|
| Imports from UK | £11,072,000 | £16,642,000 |
| Exports to UK | 32,157,000 | 37,405,000 |

EDUCATION

Education is compulsory from six to 14 years of age. In 1992 primary education was provided by 241 schools, most of which are government aided. Enrolment totalled 48,612. Secondary education is provided by 40 secondary and post-secondary institutions with an enrolment of 10,647. A University College of Belize has been established. The Government also offers scholarships for students to go abroad. There is an extra-mural faculty of the University of the West Indies, with a resident tutor.

COMMUNICATIONS

There is a government-operated radio service and three privately-owned radio stations. However, there is no official television service in the country. An automatic telephone service operated by Belize Telecommunications Ltd covers the whole country.

The principal airport is at Belize City and various airlines operate international flights to the USA and other Central American states. The main port is also Belize City, where construction of deep water quays was recently completed. Several inland waterways are also navigable. There are 1,865 miles of road, including four main highways, but there is no railway system.

BENIN
*République du Benin*

A republic situated in West Africa, between 2° and 3° W. and 6° and 12° N., Benin (formerly known as Dahomey) has a short coastline of 78 miles on the Gulf of Guinea but extends northwards inland for 437 miles. It is flanked on the west by Togo, on the north by Burkina and Niger and on the east by Nigeria. It is divided into four main regions running horizontally; a narrow sandy coastal strip, a succession of inter-communicating lagoons, a clay belt and a sandy plateau in the north. It has an area of 43,484 sq. miles (122,622 sq. km), and a population of 4,889,000 (UN 1991 estimate). The official language is French. Although poor in resources, Benin is one of the most heavily populated areas in West Africa, with a high standard of education.

CAPITAL – ΨPorto Novo, population (1982 estimate) 208,258. Principal commercial town and port, ΨCotonou (487,020).
CURRENCY – Franc CFA of 100 centimes.
FLAG – Two horizontal stripes of yellow over red with a vertical green band in the hoist.
NATIONAL DAY – 30 November.

GOVERNMENT

The first treaty with France was signed by one of the kings of Abomey in 1851 but the country was not placed under French administration until 1892. Benin became an independent republic within the French Community in December 1958; full independence outside the Community was proclaimed on 1 August 1960. In October 1963 a popular revolution led to the fall of the government and the Army held power until a civilian government was formed. In subsequent years successive governments were overthrown by the military after only short terms in office until a coup d'état in October 1972 brought to power a Marxist-Leninist military government, headed by Lt.-Col. Kerekou.

In response to mounting unrest, the government agreed to drop Marxism-Leninism as the official ideology in December 1989. Following a 'National Conference of Active Forces of the Nation,' the constitution was revoked in March 1990 and the country's official name was changed from the People's Republic of Benin to the Republic of Benin. The Revolutionary National Assembly (legislature) was dissolved and replaced by a High Council of the Republic (HCR). This, in conjunction with a new 15-member civilian government, is implementing a political transition programme; a new pluralistic constitution was adopted by referendum in December 1990. Legislative and presidential elections were held in February and March 1991. Nicéphore Soglo was sworn in as the new President on 4 April 1991 and appointed a provisional government. The lack of a clear majority in the legislature for the Union for the Triumph of Democratic Renewal coalition of President Soglo has meant the government has had to rely on an unstable alliance of independents in the 64-member National Assembly.

HEAD OF STATE
*President and Head of the Armed Forces,* HE Nicéphore Soglo, *elected,* March 1991

CABINET *as at June 1994*
*The President*
*Minister of State and National Defence,* Desire Vieyra
*Interior, Public Security and Territorial Administration,* Antoine Alabi Gbegan
*Foreign Affairs and Co-operation,* Robert Dossou
*Finance,* Paul Dossou
*Planning and Economic Reconstruction,* Robert Tagnon
*Rural Development,* Mama Adamou N'Diaye
*Public Works and Transport,* Lazare Kpatokpa
*Industry, Small and Medium Enterprises,* Rigobert Ladikpo
*Energy, Mines and Hydraulic Resources,* Aurelien Houessou
*Culture and Communications,* Marius Francisco
*National Education,* Karim Dramane
*Youth and Sports,* Alassance Idriss
*Civil Service and Administrative Reform,* Timothee Adahui
*Labour, Employment and Social Welfare,* Kapuoe Koumourade Osseni
*Public Health,* Véronique Lawson
*Environment, Housing and Town Planning,* Roger Ahoyo
*Parliamentary Relations and Government Spokesman,* Theodore Holo
*Commerce and Tourism,* Yacoumo Kpatashi
*Justice and Legislation,* Yves Yéhouessi

EMBASSY OF THE REPUBLIC OF BENIN
87 Avenue Victor Hugo, 75116 Paris, France
Tel: Paris 45009882

*Ambassador Extraordinary and Plenipotentiary,* His Excellency Richard Adjaho
HONORARY CONSULATE, 16 The Broadway, Stanmore, Middlesex HA7 4DW. Tel: 081–954 8800. *Honorary Consul,* L. Landau

BRITISH AMBASSADOR, His Excellency Sir Christopher MacRae KCMG, resident at Lagos, Nigeria

ECONOMY

In early 1994 the IMF approved a three-year enhanced structural adjustment facility credit of US$72.6m to underpin economic reforms.

The principal exports are cotton, palm products, groundnuts, shea-nuts, and coffee. Small deposits of gold, iron and chrome have been found; oil production started in 1983.

| Trade with UK | 1992 | 1993 |
|---|---|---|
| Imports from UK | £16,788,000 | £31,014,000 |
| Exports to UK | 1,564,000 | 1,436,000 |

# BHUTAN
*Druk-yul*

Bhutan is a small Himalayan kingdom situated between Tibet (to the north) and India (to the west, south and east). The total area is about 18,147 sq. miles (47,000 sq. km), with a mountainous northern region which is infertile and sparsely populated, a central zone of upland valleys where most of the population and cultivated land is found, and in the south the densely forested foothills of the Himalayas, which are mainly inhabited by Nepalese settlers and indigenous tribespeople.

POPULATION – The population is estimated at 650,000, about 80 per cent of whom are Buddhists. The remainder (mostly the Nepali Bhutanese) are Hindu. The official language, for administrative and religious purposes, is Dzongkha, a variant of Tibetan, which functions as a lingua franca amongst a variety of languages and dialects. From 1990 it has been government policy to make the study of Dzongkha compulsory in schools. However, Nepali remains a recognized language and English remains the medium of instruction and the working language of the administration.

CAPITAL – Thimphu, population estimate (1987) 15,000.
CURRENCY – Ngultrum (Nu) of 100 chetrums. Indian currency is also legal tender.
FLAG – Saffron yellow and orange-red divided diagonally, with dragon device in centre.
NATIONAL DAY – 17 December.

GOVERNMENT

In 1949 a treaty was concluded with the Government of India under which the Kingdom of Bhutan agreed to be guided by the advice of the Government of India in regard to its external relations. It has its own diplomatic representatives and is a member of the UN and other international and regional organizations. It also receives from the Government of India an annual payment of Rs500,000 as compensation for portions of its territory annexed by the British Government in India in 1864.

Bhutan has a 150-member National Assembly which meets twice a year. The ten-member Royal Advisory Council, nominated by the King and the National Assembly, acts as a consultative body when the National Assembly is not in session. The King is also assisted by a Council of Ministers. There are no political parties.

In April 1994 the King intensified measures protecting the national culture and language from Nepali encroachment. These measures, introduced less severely over the past few years, together with the granting of citizenship only to Nepalis settled in Bhutan before 1958, has led to an exodus of ethnic Nepalis from the south of the country to Nepal, where about 80,000 live in camps. A low-level insurgency has been waged in the south of the country against the King's policies by ethnic Nepalis since 1990.

HEAD OF STATE
*HM The King of Bhutan,* Jigme Singye Wangchuk, *born* 11 November 1955; *succeeded his father,* July 1972; *crowned,* 2 June 1974

*Heir*, Crown Prince Jigme Gesar Namgyal Wangchuk, *designated*, 31 October 1988

COUNCIL OF MINISTERS *as at 30 June 1994*
*Chairman of Council of Ministers*, HM The King
*HM Representative in Ministry of Finance*, HRH Ashi Sonam Chhoden Wangchuk
*HM Representative in Ministry of Agriculture*, HRH Ashi Dorji W. Wangchuk
*Home Affairs*, HRH Namgyel Wangchuk
*Finance*, Dorji Tshering
*Foreign Affairs*, Dawa Tshering
*Communications, Social Services and Tourism*, Dr T. Tobgyel
*Trade and Industries*, Om Pradhan
*Planning*, Chenkhap Dorji
*Deputy Minister of Defence, Chief Operations Officer of Royal Bhutan Army*, Maj.-Gen. Lam Dorji
*Speaker of the National Assembly, Chief Justice*, Sangye Penjor

## ECONOMY

The seventh five-year plan (1992–7) envisages a doubling of internal revenues to Nu2,000m. Economic emphasis is on the infrastructure, especially roads and telecommunications, and hydro-electric power.

The economy is based on agriculture and animal husbandry, which engage over 90 per cent of the workforce in what is largely a self-sufficient rural society. The principal food crops are rice, wheat, maize and barley. Vegetables and fruit are also produced. Bhutan is the world's largest producer of cardamom, which forms its principal export to countries other than India. Agriculture is, however, limited by the country's mountainous topography and 60 per cent forest cover. The mountains contain rich deposits of limestone, gypsum, dolomite and graphite and small amounts of coal, which are exported to India. A modest industrial base is being developed. A distillery and cement, chemicals and food processing plants are in production; a forestry industries complex is being expanded. Tourism and postage stamps are increasingly important sources of foreign exchange.

### TRADE

Over 90 per cent of foreign trade is with India. Principal exports are agricultural products, timber, cement and coal; main imports are textiles, cereals and consumer goods. Bhutan's airline, Druk Air, flies between Paro, New Delhi and Calcutta.

| Trade with UK | 1992 | 1993 |
|---|---|---|
| Imports from UK | £15,505,000 | £2,263,000 |
| Exports to UK | 237,000 | 1,642,000 |

## BOLIVIA
*República de Bolivia*

Bolivia extends between 10° and 23° S. latitude and 57° 30′ and 69° 45′ W. longitude. It has an area estimated at 424,165 sq. miles (1,098,581 sq. km). Bolivia is without a coastline, having been deprived of the ports of Tocopilla, Cobija, Mejillones and Antofagasta by the Pacific War of 1879–84.

The chief topographical feature is the great central plateau over 500 miles in length, at an average altitude of 12,500 feet above sea level, between the two great chains of the Andes, which traverse the country from south to north. The total length of the navigable rivers is about 12,000 miles, the principal rivers being the Itenez, Beni, Mamore and Madre de Dios.

POPULATION – The population (1992 census) was 6,440,000. The official language of the country is Spanish, but many of the Indian inhabitants (about two-thirds of the population) speak Quechua or Aymará, the two linguistic groups being more or less equal in numbers. Roman Catholicism was the state religion until disestablishment in 1961.

CAPITAL – La Paz (population, 1,115,000). Other large centres are Cochabamba (512,000), Oruro (183,000), Santa Cruz (694,000), Potosí (112,000), Sucre, the legal capital and seat of the judiciary (131,000) and Tarija (90,000).
CURRENCY – Boliviano ($b) of 100 centavos.
FLAG – Three horizontal bands; red, yellow, green.
NATIONAL ANTHEM – Bolivianos, El Hado Propicio (Oh Bolivia, our long-felt desires).
NATIONAL DAY – 6 August (Independence Day).

## GOVERNMENT

Bolivia won its independence from Spain in 1825 after a war of liberation led by Simon Bolivar (1783–1830), from whom the country derives its name. From 1964 to 1982 Bolivia was ruled by military juntas until civilian rule was restored. The constitution provides for a directly elected executive President who appoints the Cabinet. The legislature (Congress) consists of a 27-member Senate and a 130-member Chamber of Deputies. Both the President and Congress are elected for four-year terms.

Congressional and presidential elections were held in June 1993 with Gonzalo Sánchez of the opposition National Revolutionary Movement (MNR) winning the largest share of the vote in the presidential election but as no candidate won more than 50 per cent, the new President was chosen by Congressional vote in August, when Gonzalo Sánchez was elected. The MNR emerged as the largest party in Congress, winning 52 out of 130 seats, and formed a government in coalition with the Civic Solidarity Union (20 seats) and the Free Bolivia Movement (7 seats).

### HEAD OF STATE
*President of the Republic*, Gonzalo Sánchez de Lozada, *inaugurated* 5 August 1993
*Vice President*, Victor Hugo Cardenas

CABINET *as at June 1994*
*Foreign Affairs and Worship*, Antonio Araníbar Quiroga
*Interior*, Germán Quiroga Gómez
*National Defence*, Raúl Tovar Píerola
*Presidency*, Carlos Sánchez Verzaín
*Economic Development and Finance*, Fernando Alvaro Cassio
*Education and Culture*, Fernando Romero Moreno
*Labour*, Reynaldo Peters Arzabe
*Human Development*, Enrique Ipiña Melgar
*Information*, Ernesto Machicado
*Justice*, René Blattman
*Privatization*, Alfonso Revollo
*Sustainable Development*, José Guillermo Sandoval

BOLIVIAN EMBASSY
106 Eaton Square, London SW1W 9AD
Tel 0171–235 2257/4248

*Ambassador Extraordinary and Plenipotentiary*, new appointment awaited

BRITISH EMBASSY
Avenida Arce 2732–2754, (Casilla 694) La Paz
Tel: La Paz 357424

*Ambassador Extraordinary and Plenipotentiary*, His
Excellency Richard Michael Jackson, CVO, apptd 1991
*Deputy Ambassador, Consul and First Secretary
(Commercial)*, I. Davies

There is an Honorary Consulate at *Santa Cruz.*

## EDUCATION

Elementary education is compulsory and free and there are
secondary schools in urban centres. Provision is also made
for higher education; in addition to St Francisco Xavier's
University at Sucre, founded in 1624, there are seven other
universities, the largest being the University of San Andres
at La Paz, and ten private universities.

## DEFENCE

Bolivia has a total active armed forces of some 33,500
personnel (20,000 conscripts). Conscription is selective and
lasts for 12 months.

The Army is 25,000 strong (18,000 conscripts) with 36
light tanks, 132 armoured personnel carriers and reconnaissance vehicles and 100 artillery pieces. Although Bolivia is
landlocked, it operates a navy of 4,500 on Lake Titicaca and
its many rivers. It has some 10 patrol craft and six battalions
of marines numbering 2,000 troops. The Air Force has a
strength of 4,000 personnel (2,000 conscripts) with 52
combat aircraft and 10 armed helicopters. In addition, there
are some 30,000 paramilitary National Police personnel.

## ECONOMY

Mining, natural gas, petroleum and agriculture are the
principal industries. The ancient silver mines of Potosí are
now worked chiefly for tin, but gold, partly dug and partly
washed, is obtained on the Eastern Cordillera of the Andes.
The tin output, together with other minerals (copper,
antimony, lead, zinc, asbestos, wolfram, bismuth salt and
sulphur), provides over one-third of Bolivia's exports. Small
quantities of oil are produced for internal consumption, and
gas (currently providing about a quarter of Bolivia's export
income) is piped to Argentina; there are plans to build a
pipeline to São Paulo, Brazil. Bolivia's agricultural produce
consists chiefly of rice, barley, oats, wheat, sugar-cane, maize,
cotton, indigo, rubber, cacao, potatoes, cinchona bark,
medicinal herbs, brazil nuts etc.

The economy deteriorated badly in the late 1970s and
early 1980s, with disappointing petroleum reserves, a large
external debt, and the collapse of world tin prices in 1985. In
the mid-1980s free market economic reforms were introduced
by the government with privatization of most state-owned
firms and the encouragement of foreign investment. Tin
prices began to increase once more from April 1989, but
most of the tin industry remains uneconomic or has closed
down. Many workers took to growing coca which has now
become a significant export.

The peso was replaced in January 1987 with the Boliviano
of 1,000,000 old pesos in a successful effort to stem
hyperinflation and had brought the inflation rate down to 9
per cent in 1993. The economy and currency have stabilized
and the foreign debt is being repaid. Gross Domestic Product
in 1992 was US$5,994 m. The new government is committed
to continuing the reforms.

## TRADE

Mineral exports represent about 35 per cent of total trade.
Bolivia has now developed its own smelters and is exporting

metals. The chief imports are wheat and flour, iron and steel
products, machinery, vehicles and textiles.

| Trade with UK | 1992 | 1993 |
|---|---|---|
| Imports from UK | £17,640,000 | £7,997,000 |
| Exports to UK | 10,404,000 | 13,144,000 |

## COMMUNICATIONS

There are 2,200 miles of railways in operation including the
lines from Corumbá to Santa Cruz (312 miles). There is
direct railway communication to the sea at Antofagasta (32
hours), Arica (10 hours), and Mollendo (2 days), and also to
Buenos Aires (3½ days). Communication with Peru is by road
from La Paz via Copacabana and thence to the railhead at
Puno. In July 1993 Bolivia and Peru signed an agreement
granting Bolivia a concession of 162 hectares at the southern
Peruvian port of Ilo for 98 years to construct a free trade
zone.

Commercial aviation in Bolivia is conducted by the
national airline, Lloyd Aereo Boliviano and Transporte
Aereo Militar between the major towns, and Lloyd Aereo
Boliviano and a number of foreign airlines provide interna-
tional flights to the USA, South and Central America and
Europe.

There are about 10,950 miles of telegraphs, and microwave
telephone communications between La Paz, Santa Cruz,
Cochabamba, Oruro and Sucre. Most other towns have radio/
telephone communication with the main cities. There are
nine principal daily newspapers.

---

# BOSNIA-HERCEGOVINA

---

Bosnia-Hercegovina is bounded by Serbia on the east,
Montenegro on the south-east and Croatia on the north and
west, apart from a narrow 20 km coastline on the Adriatic at
Neum. It has an area of 19,735 sq. miles (51,129 sq. km.).
The population is 4.1 million, of whom some 43 per cent are
Muslims, 32 per cent Serbs and 17 per cent Croats.

CAPITAL – Sarajevo, population (1981) 447,000. Other
major cities include Tuzla, Banja Luka, Zenica, Vitez and
Mostar.

FLAG – White flag bearing a blue shield with a white
diagonal and six gold fleurs-de-lys.

## GOVERNMENT

The country was settled by Slavs in the seventh century and
conquered by the Ottoman Turks in 1463. Ruled by the
Turks for over 400 years, the country came under Austro-
Hungarian control in 1878 under the Treaty of Berlin.
Austria-Hungary's annexation of Bosnia-Hercegovina in
1908 was never accepted by Serbia because of the large
ethnic Serb population in the country, and the assassination
of the heir to the Austro-Hungarian throne in Sarajevo by an
ethnic Serb precipitated the First World War. Bosnia-
Hercegovina became part of the Kingdom of Serbs, Croats
and Slovenes' (renamed Yugoslavia in 1929) under the
Versailles Treaty of 1919, and was occupied by German and
Axis forces between 1941 and 1945, when there was heavy
resistance by partisans in the mountains. At the end of the
war Bosnia-Hercegovina came under Communist rule as part
of the Federal Republic of Yugoslavia, which collapsed with
the secession of Slovenia and Croatia in 1991.

While the war in Croatia (July 1991–January 1992)
continued, Bosnia-Hercegovina declared its independence
from Yugoslavia on 15 October 1991, and this was affirmed

in a referendum on 1 March 1992. Bosnia-Hercegovina was recognized as an independent state by the EC and USA in April 1992 and admitted to UN membership in May 1992. Independence was supported by the ethnic Muslims and Croats but rejected by the ethnic Serbs, who formed 32 per cent of the population and wanted to form a Greater Serbia with the Serbian republic. Fighting between Muslims and Serbs broke out in March 1992 and the predominantly Serbian Federal Yugoslav Army (JNA) intervened against the poorly-armed Muslims. By May 1992 Serbian forces had overrun the majority of the republic and Croat forces much of the rest, leaving the legitimate Bosnian Muslim government forces besieged in the capital Sarajevo, the central area of the republic, and a few other cities. By May intense international pressure forced Serbia to withdraw the JNA from Bosnia, but the JNA handed over most of its weapons to Bosnian Serb forces. At the end of May the UN imposed a total trade embargo and economic sanctions on Serbia and Montenegro, but the war in Bosnia continued throughout the summer. As evidence of 'ethnic cleansing' and Serb-run concentration camps emerged in August 1992, the UN authorized the use of troops to keep Sarajevo airport open for relief flights, and then forced all the warring participants and their backers to attend a peace conference in London at the end of August. For events since August 1992, *see* The War *below*.

Results of the elections held in November and December 1990 for the 240-seat bicameral Assembly were: the (Muslim) Party of Democratic Action 86 seats, the (Serbian) Democratic Party 72, and the Croat Democratic Union 44.

In December 1990 Alija Izetbegović (Muslim) was elected President at the head of a seven-man collective presidency formed of three Muslims, two ethnic Serbs and two ethnic Croats. Throughout the war Izetbegovic has held this office although it was originally to be rotated among the collective. The ethnic Serb and ethnic Croat representatives resigned in 1992 and 1993, leaving the presidency effectively representing only the Muslim and mixed population of Bosnia-Hercegovina. The Bosnian Serb leadership under Radovan Karadzic declared their own 'Republic of Srpska' in August 1992 with its capital at Pale, and the Bosnian Croats established the 'Republic of Herceg-Bosna' in August 1993 with its capital at Mostar. The Bosnian (Muslim) government has remained in Sarajevo.

After a Muslim-Croat cease-fire was agreed on 23 February 1994, the Bosnian (Muslim), Bosnian Croat and Croatian governments signed the Washington agreement on 1 March 1994 which provided for a Bosnian Muslim-Croat Federation and a confederation of this entity with Croatia. Under the Federation constitution, a federal presidency, government and constituent assembly have been established, while the mainly Muslim (Republican) presidency and government also remain. The Federation is based on a cantonal system, each canton having authority over the police, education, housing, public services, broadcasting and culture. The federal government has authority in the fields of foreign affairs, defence, trade and the economy. A Constitutional Court with Muslim, Croat and international judges is to be established. Four of the eight cantons have a Muslim majority, two a Croat majority and two Muslim-Croat parity. A federal government of 17 ministers has been established and a Bosnian Croat president and Muslim vice-president were elected by the Constituent Assembly on 31 May 1994 to serve for six months until federal elections can be held.

The Confederation of the Federation with Croatia is to be based on economic co-operation, a common market and defence co-operation. The highest body is to be the Confederation Council, with the chair rotating annually between the Federation and Croatia.

*President: (Republican)*, Alija Izetbegovic, *elected*, December 1990; *(Federation)*, Kresimir Zubak, *elected*, 31 May 1994
*Vice President (Republican and Federation)*, Ejup Ganic, *elected*, 31 May 1994
*Prime Minister (Republican and Federation)*, Haris Silajdzic

EMBASSY OF THE REPUBLIC OF BOSNIA-HERCEGOVINA
40–41 Conduit, London WIR 9FB
Tel 0171-743 3758
*Chargé D'Affairs*, Dr Muharem Krzic

BRITISH EMBASSY
Sarajevo
*Ambassador Extraordinary and Plenipotentiary*, His
  Excellency Robert Barnett, apptd 1994

THE WAR

At the time of the August 1992 London Conference 70 per cent of Bosnia was controlled by Bosnian Serb forces and a further 20 per cent by Bosnian Croat forces. The mainly Muslim forces of the Bosnian government were in an uneasy alliance with Croatian and Bosnian Croat forces, who were trying to cut Serbian supply lines to Serb enclaves in Croatia. The London Conference was initially judged a success when all sides signed an agreement to end the war, respecting Bosnia's international boundaries and rejecting the use of force to gain land. However, the signatures soon proved worthless as it became clear that the Bosnian Serbs would not give up the land that they had gained and that the Muslims would not settle for peace without winning back land.

Fierce Muslim-Bosnian Serb fighting in the second half of 1992 in central and eastern Bosnia forced Western nations to deploy troops under UN auspices to secure humanitarian aid supplies as winter began in October. These added to the aid airlifts into besieged Sarajevo begun in July.

After months of negotiations with the warring factions, the joint EC-UN peace negotiating team reconvened the peace conference in Geneva in January 1993 and presented the Owen-Vance peace plan. The plan was composed of three parts: a set of constitutional principles; a means to, and timetable for the end of hostilities; and a map delineating ten autonomous provinces, of which three were Serb, three Croat, three Muslim and one mixed (Sarajevo). The plan was accepted by the Bosnian Croats, partly accepted by the Muslim government, but rejected by the Bosnian Serbs. Over the next four months the EC-UN negotiating team pressured the Muslims and Bosnian Serbs to accept the plan, which the Muslims eventually did. The Bosnian-Serb leader Radovan Karadzic eventually signed the peace plan on 2 May at an emergency peace conference in Athens after continued Western diplomatic pressure and military threats, and after the UN imposed total trade and diplomatic isolation in April 1993 on the rump Yugoslav state (a naval blockade had been imposed in November 1992). The Bosnian Serb Parliament, however, rejected the plan and defied the international community, which shrank from military engagement. On 22 May the USA, EC and Russia agreed on the 'Joint Action Programme' for future peace negotiations, its basis being the acceptance of territorial gain by force.

Meanwhile, in the first half of 1993 fighting had continued, with Bosnian Serb forces renewing their attacks on the Muslim enclaves in eastern Bosnia and heavy fighting breaking out between Croats and Muslims in central Bosnia and Mostar. As Bosnian Serb forces starved and shelled the Muslim enclaves in the east, the pressure on Western governments to intervene grew. In February, US Air Force planes began dropping supplies to the beleaguered enclaves; in April the UN evacuated and demilitarized Srebrenica; and

Areas Held
Serbs
Croats
Muslims

0 _____ 150 km

0 _____ 100 miles

in early May it declared the Muslim enclaves of Srebrenica and Zepa, Gorazde and Foca, Tuzla, Bihac and Sarajevo UN 'safe areas', which moderated Serb attacks. The Muslims, meanwhile, began to gain the upper hand over the Croats in central Bosnia, taking Zenica and Travnik.

The refusal of the West to intervene militarily led to increased fighting in the summer of 1993, with continued Muslim successes against Bosnian Croat forces in central Bosnia and Bosnian Serb strangulation and heavy shelling of Sarajevo. The West put pressure on the Muslim government to accept the new peace proposals based on partition of the country but it would not accept. As the Bosnian Serbs were poised to attempt to take Sarajevo in early August, NATO issued an ultimatum to the Bosnian Serbs to withdraw from the heights around Sarajevo or face air strikes. The Bosnian Serbs complied, giving an impetus to the peace process throughout the rest of 1993. The Muslim government and forces reluctantly agreed to the principle of the ethnic division of Bosnia, leading to a dramatic drop in Muslim-Serb fighting as their confrontation lines became static, and a concentration of fighting in central Bosnia between the Muslims and Croats, which greatly inhibited aid distribution. The peace process collapsed in December 1993 over the amount of land to be given to each ethnic group, Muslim demands for access to the Adriatic Sea and Sava river, the status of international administrations for Sarajevo and Mostar and the Muslim enclaves in eastern Bosnia.

With the collapse of the peace process, Muslim-Serb fighting increased in January 1994 with Bosnian Serb shelling of Srebrenica, Sarajevo and Tazla airport. A Bosnian-Serb artillery attack on 5 February on a Sarajevo market in which 60 were killed and 200 injured caused international outrage and led NATO to issue a further ultimatum to the Bosnian Serbs to withdraw all heavy artillery from a 12 mile (20 km) zone around Sarajevo, or hand over the weapons to UN forces, or face sustained air strikes. The Bosnian Serbs complied after intervention by the Russian government which sent troops to Sarajevo. A ceasefire around Sarajevo came into effect on 10 February 1994 and was holding, with minor infringements, in July 1994. Meanwhile, Bosnian Croat and Muslim forces ended hostilities on 25 February 1994, reforming their alliance of 1992 and early 1993, and formed a Federation. March saw the lifting of the sieges of Maglaj and Mostar, the opening of Tuzla airport for relief flights, the deployment of a further 5,000 UN troops to consolidate and patrol the Muslim-Croat cease-fire, and the partial lifting of the siege of Sarajevo.

However, in April the Bosnian Serbs launched assaults on the eastern Muslim-held enclave of Gorazde. Despite NATO air strikes on Bosnian Serb forces, virtually all of the enclave had fallen before Russia, NATO and the UN forced the Bosnian Serbs to withdraw their artillery. The attack forced NATO to widen its use of air strikes to all UN-designated safe areas and galvanized the USA, Russia, Britain, France and Germany to form the International Contact Group (ICG) to co-ordinate all peace efforts. This was given added impetus by Muslim offensives in May demonstrating that the arms embargo was becoming less effective as the Muslims gained more armaments through Croatia. On 10 June 1994 the ICG brought about a one-month ceasefire between the Muslim-Croat Federation and the Bosnian Serbs which lessened the extent of fighting. On 6 July the ICG presented its peace plan to the warring factions, concentrating on a map giving 51 per cent of Bosnian territory to the Muslim-Croat Federation and 49 per cent to the Bosnian Serbs. The Muslims and Bosnian Serbs have been told to accept or reject the plan within 14 days.

At July 1994 the situation was finely balanced. The ICG has made it clear to the warring parties that this is the last chance for peace: if the Muslims reject the plan the UN sanctions on the rump Yugoslav state will be eased and lifted; if the Bosnian Serbs reject the plan the arms embargo will be lifted and the US will arm the Bosnian Muslims; if the fighting continues the UK and France will withdraw their UN troops and the remaining UN troops would follow. Both sides have yet to respond.

| Trade with UK | 1993 |
|---|---|
| Imports from UK | £3,494,000 |
| Exports to UK | 70,000 |

## BOTSWANA
*The Republic of Botswana*

Botswana (formerly the British Protectorate of Bechuanaland) lies between 18° and 26° S. latitude and 20° and 28° W. longitude and is bounded by South Africa on the south and east, by Zimbabwe, the rivers Zambezi and Chobe (Linyanti) on the north and north-east, and by Namibia on the west. Botswana has a total area of 224,607 sq. miles (581,730 sq. km). The climate of the country is generally sub-tropical, but varies considerably with latitude and altitude.

A plateau at a height of about 4,000 feet divides Botswana into two main topographical regions. To the east of the plateau streams flow into the Marico, Notwani and Limpopo rivers; to the west lies a flat region comprising the Kgalagadi Desert, the Okavango Swamps and the Northern State Lands area. Large areas of the country support only herds of game. Elephant numbers have been estimated at 55,000–60,000.

POPULATION – Botswana has a population (UN estimate 1991) of 1,348,000. The eight principal Botswana tribes are Bakgatla, Bakwena, Bangwaketse, Bamalete, Bamangwato, Barolong, Batawana and Batlokwa. The principal languages in use are Setswana and English.

CAPITAL – Gaborone, estimated population (1991) 137,174. Other centres are Francistown (60,000), Lobatse (25,000), and Selebi-Phikwe (46,000).

CURRENCY – Pula (P) of 100 thebe.

FLAG – Light blue with a horizontal black stripe fimbriated in white across the centre.

NATIONAL ANTHEM – Fatshe La Rona.
NATIONAL DAY – 30 September.

## GOVERNMENT

On 30 September 1966, Bechuanaland became a republic within the Commonwealth under the name Botswana. The President of Botswana is head of state and is elected by an absolute majority in the National Assembly. He appoints as Vice President a member of the National Assembly who is his principal assistant and leader of government business in the National Assembly. The Assembly consists of the President, 34 members elected every five years on a basis of universal adult suffrage, four specially elected members, the Attorney-General (non-voting) and the Speaker. Presidential and legislative elections are held every five years. There is also a 15-member House of Chiefs which considers legislation affecting the constitution and chieftaincy matters.

HEAD OF STATE
*President*, His Excellency Dr Q. K. J. Masire, *sworn in* 10 October 1989 for a second five-year term

CABINET *as at June 1994*
*Vice President, Finance and Development Planning*, Festus Mogae
*Presidential Affairs, Public Administration*, Lt.-Gen. Mompati Merafhe
*Local Government, Lands and Housing*, Chapson Butale
*External Affairs*, Dr Gaositwe Chiepe
*Mineral Resources and Water*, Archibald Mogwe
*Commerce and Industry*, Ponatshego Kedikilwe
*Agriculture*, Kebatlamang Morake
*Works and Communications*, David Magang
*Health*, Bahiti Temane
*Education*, Ray Molomo
*Home Affairs*, Patrick Balopi
*Assistant Ministers: Finance*, E. Setlhomo Masisi; *Local Government and Lands*, M. Mokgothu, Geoffrey Oteng; *Agriculture*, Roy Blackbeard

BOTSWANA HIGH COMMISSION
6 Stratford Place, London WIN 9AE
Tel 0171-499 0031
*High Commissioner*, His Excellency Alfred Uyapo Majaye Dube, apptd 1993

BRITISH HIGH COMMISSION
Private Bag 0023, Gaborone
Tel: Gaborone 352841
*High Commissioner*, His Excellency John Edwards, CMG, apptd 1992

BRITISH COUNCIL REPRESENTATIVE, T. A. Jones, MBE
(*Cultural Attaché*)

## ECONOMY

Botswana is predominantly a pastoral country. The national herd is normally around 3 million cattle and 1 million sheep and goats but recent drought conditions have reduced the number of cattle to around 2.5 million.

Cattle rearing accounts for about 85 per cent of agricultural output and livestock products, particularly beef, are a major source of foreign exchange earnings. The government has a number of programmes to improve land use and cattle and crop production, and schemes to provide financial assistance for farmers.

Mineral extraction and processing is now the major source of income for the country following the opening of large mines for diamonds and copper-nickel. Botswana is one of the largest producers of diamonds in the world, with diamonds accounting for some 80 per cent of export revenue since they were discovered in the early 1970s. Large deposits of coal have been discovered and are being mined on a small scale. Much of the country has yet to be fully prospected. Manufacturing industry is growing and will continue to do so as communications improve but it is still a small sector of the economy. The economy expanded by an average 9 per cent a year in the 1980s.

| FINANCE | 1990–1 | 1991–2e |
|---|---|---|
| Revenue | P3,318m | P3,183m |
| Expenditure | 2,899m | 3,318m |

e estimate

TRADE
Principal exports are diamonds, copper-nickel matte, and beef and beef products.

| | 1989p | 1990 |
|---|---|---|
| Imports | P2,136m | P3,483m |
| Exports | 3,613m | 3,262m |

p preliminary

| Trade with UK | 1992 | 1993 |
|---|---|---|
| Imports from UK | £19,999,000 | £20,555,000 |
| Exports to UK | 27,446,000 | 26,051,000 |

## EDUCATION

There are over 654 primary schools (enrolment approx. 308,840), 176 community junior secondary schools (enrolment approx. 48,624) and 23 government and government-aided senior secondary schools (enrolment 19,308). There are four teacher training establishments (total enrolment 1,365), two colleges of education (enrolment 340), one polytechnic with 558 students and the University of Botswana with 2,862 undergraduates. Further expansion of the technical education system is planned via a network of vocational training centres.

## COMMUNICATIONS

The railway from Cape Town to Zimbabwe passes through eastern Botswana. The main roads in the country are the north–south road, which closely follows the railway, and the road running east–west that links Francistown and Maun. A new road from Nata to Kazungula provides a direct link to Zambia from Botswana. Air services are provided on a scheduled basis between the main towns.

---

## BRAZIL
*República Federativa do Brasil*

Brazil, discovered in 1500 by Portuguese navigator Pedro Alvares Cabral, is bounded on the north by the Atlantic Ocean, the Guianas, Colombia and Venezuela; on the west by Peru, Bolivia, Paraguay, and Argentina; on the south by Uruguay; and on the east by the Atlantic Ocean. Brazil extends between 5° 16′ N. and 33° 45′ S. latitude and 34° 45′ and 73° 59′22″ W. longitude. The country has an area of 3,286,488 sq. miles (8,511,965 sq. km), with a population (official estimate 1990) of 150,368,000.

The northern states of Amazonas and Pará are mainly wide, low-lying, forest-clad plains. The central states of Mato Grosso are principally plateau land and the eastern and southern states are traversed by successive mountain ranges interspersed with fertile valleys. The principal ranges are

Serra do Mar, the Serra da Mantiqueira and the Serra do Espinhaco along the east coast.

The River Amazon with a total length of some 4,000 miles has tributaries which are themselves great rivers, and flows from the Peruvian Andes to the Atlantic. Its principal northern tributaries are the Rio Branco, Rio Negro, and Japurá; its southern tributaries are the Juruá, Purus, Madeira and Tapajós, while the Xingú meets it within 200 miles of its outflow into the Atlantic. The Tocantins and Araguaia flow northwards from Mato Grosso and Goiás to the Gulf of Pará. The Parnaiba flows from Piaui into the Atlantic. The São Francisco rises in the South of Minas Gerais and flows to the eastern coast. The Paraguai, rising in the south-west of Mato Grosso, flows through Paraguay to its confluence with the Paraná, which rises in the mountains of that name and divides Brazil from Paraguay.

CAPITAL – Brasilia (inaugurated on 21 April 1960). Population (1990 estimate) 1,803,478. Other important centres are São Paulo (10,063,110); the former capital ΨRio de Janeiro (6,603,388); Belo Horizonte (2,114,429); ΨRecife (1,287,623); ΨSalvador (1,804,438); ΨPorto Alegre (1,272,121); ΨFortaleza (1,582,414); and Belem (1,116,578).

CURRENCY – Real of 100 centavos.

FLAG – Green with a yellow lozenge containing a blue sphere studded with white stars, and crossed by a white band with the motto *Ordem e Progresso*.

NATIONAL ANTHEM – Ouviram do Ipirangas Margens Placidas (From peaceful Ypiranga's banks).

NATIONAL DAY – 7 September (Independence Day).

## GOVERNMENT

Brazil was colonized by Portugal in the early part of the 16th century, and in 1822 became an independent empire under Dom Pedro, son of the refugee King Joao VI of Portugal. On 15 November 1889, Dom Pedro II, second of the line, was dethroned and a republic was proclaimed. In 1985 Brazil returned to democratic rule after two decades of military government.

The Federative Republic of Brazil is made up of the federal district and 26 states. The constitution of October 1988 draws on the same conceptual basis as that of the United States, and envisages an equal distribution of power between the executive, the legislature and the judiciary. The President, who heads the executive, is directly elected for a single four-year term. The Congress consists of a Senate (three senators per state elected for an eight-year term) and a Chamber of Deputies which is elected every four years. The number of deputies per state depends upon the state's population. Each state has a Governor, and a Legislative Assembly with a four-year term.

President Fernando Collor de Mello, who came to power in 1990, was suspended in September 1992 by the Chamber of Deputies because of alleged corruption. He resigned on 29 December 1992 after being indicted by the Senate on 2 December 1992. The Vice-President Itamar Franco was immediately sworn in for the remainder of the five-year term. The next presidential and Congressional elections are scheduled for late 1994.

HEAD OF STATE
*President*, Itamar Franco, *sworn in* 29 December 1992
*Vice President*, vacant

CABINET *as at June 1994*
*Justice*, Alexandre Martins Dupeyrat
*Labour*, Henríque Calvacanti

*Communications*, Djalma Bastos de Moraes
*Interior*, vacant
*Mines and Energy*, Aluizio Alves
*Health*, Henrique Santillo
*Education and Sports*, Murillo Hingel
*Army*, Gen. Zenildo Gonzago Lucena
*Navy*, Adm. Ivan Serpa
*Air Force*, Air Chief Marshal Lélio Viana Lobo
*Culture*, Jeronimo Mascardo de Souza
*Social Welfare*, Leonor Franco
*Agriculture*, Silval Guazzeli
*Science and Technology*, José Israel Vargas
*Environment*, Mozart Abreu
*Planning*, Beni Veras
*Finance*, Rubens Ricupero
*Foreign*, Celso Amorim
*Transport*, Gen. Rubens Bayma Denys
*Brazilian Amazon*, vacant
*Industry, Commerce and Tourism*, Elcio Alvares
*Administration*, Rouildo Canhim
*Armed Forces' Chief of Staff*, Adm. Arnaldo Pereira

BRAZILIAN EMBASSY
32 Green Street, London WIY 4AT
Tel 0171-499 0877

*Ambassador Extraordinary and Plenipotentiary*, His Excellency Rubens Antonio Barbosa, apptd 1994
*Minister-Counsellors*, M. E. C. Costa; E. dos Santos
*Defence Attachés*, Capt. O. S. de Almeída (*Naval*); Col. A. A. Filho (*Army*); Gp Capt J. Saito (*Air*)

There is also a Brazilian Consulate-General in *London* and honorary consular offices at *Cardiff* and *Glasgow*.

BRITISH EMBASSY
Setor de Embaixadus Sul, Quadra 801, Conjunto K, 70.408 Brasilia DF
Tel: Brasilia 225-2710

*Ambassador Extraordinary and Plenipotentiary*, His Excellency Peter Heap, CMG, apptd 1992
*Deputy Ambassador, Consul-General*, P. R. Jenkins
*Defence Attaché*, Col. D. Farrant
*First Secretary (Economic)*, P. B. Yaghmourian

There are British Consulates-General at *Rio de Janeiro* and *São Paulo*.

BRITISH COUNCIL REPRESENTATIVE, Patric Early. OBE, SCRN, 708/9 Bloco F Nos 1/3 (Caixa Postal 6104), 70740-780 Brasilia DF. Regional directors in *Recife, Rio de Janeiro* and *São Paulo*

BRITISH AND COMMONWEALTH CHAMBER OF COMMERCE IN SÃO PAULO, Rua Barão de Itapetininga 275, 7th Floor, 01042, São Paulo (*Postal Address*, PO Box 1621, 01000 São Paulo) and Rua Real Grandeza 99, 22281 Rio de Janeiro

## ECONOMY

Since the return to civilian rule in 1985 successive Brazilian governments have attempted to introduce economic and financial plans to curb high inflation and large budget deficits. During 1994 Brazil has undergone its most radical and successful plan so far. In February 1994 Finance Minister Cardoso forced the government and Congress to agree to the first balanced budget in 20 years and create a US$16 billion social emergency fund as the first stage to financial stability. An interim currency pegged to the US dollar, known as the Real Unit Value, was introduced in March 1994 as the second stage. In July 1994 a new non-inflationary currency, the real, was introduced. In April 1994 Brazil signed an agreement to reschedule its US$52,000 m debt to 750 foreign commercial banks.

There are large and valuable mineral deposits including iron ore (hematite), manganese, bauxite, beryllium, chrome, nickel, tungsten, cassiterite, lead, gold, monazite (containing rare earths and thorium) and zirconium. Diamonds and precious and semi-precious stones are also found. The iron ore deposits of Minas Gerais are exceeded by those of the Amazon region, principally in the Carajás areas where deposits are estimated at 35,000 million tonnes. Mining operations began in February 1985.

Electric power production in 1990 was 50,000 m Kwh. In the same year, the total output of steel was 25,055 million tonnes and production of oil was 27.9 million cubic metres. The main agriculture products are coffee, cassava, maize, soya, rice, wheat, black beans, potatoes, cotton, cocoa, tobacco and peanuts.

| FINANCE | 1990 | 1991 |
|---|---|---|
| Revenue | Cr$3,146,420m | Cr$52,809,946m |
| Expenditure | 3,146,420m | 52,809,946m |

### TRADE

Principal imports are fuel and lubricants, machinery, mineral products, chemicals, wheat, metals and metal manufactures. Principal exports are coffee, iron ore, soya, meat, steel and orange juice. In 1987 the Brazilian automobile industry produced 730,992 vehicles. Of these, 339,900 vehicles were exported.

| | 1989 | 1990 |
|---|---|---|
| Total imports | US$18,263 m | US$20,661 m |
| Total exports | 34,382 m | 31,413 m |

| Trade with UK | 1992 | 1993 |
|---|---|---|
| Imports from UK | £273,106,000 | £415,070,000 |
| Exports to UK | 885,632,000 | 903,531,000 |

### DEFENCE

The total strength of the active armed forces is 296,000 (133,500 conscripts). Conscripts serve for 12 months and there are 400,000 reservists subject to immediate recall.

The Army has a strength of 196,000, of which 126,500 are conscripts. Equipment consists of 520 light tanks, 300 reconnaissance vehicles, 845 armoured personnel carriers, 840 artillery pieces and 51 helicopters.

The Navy has a strength of 50,000 personnel (2,000 conscripts) including 15,000 marines with one aircraft carrier, four submarines, six destroyers, 13 frigates and 28 patrol and coastal craft, together with some 13 armed helicopters.

The Air Force is 50,700 strong (5,000 conscripts). It deploys 326 combat aircraft and eight armed helicopters. In addition there is the 243,000 strong Public Security Forces paramilitary unit.

### EDUCATION

Primary education is compulsory and is the responsibility of state governments and municipalities. At this level approximately 12 per cent attend private schools. Secondary education is largely the responsibility of state and municipal governments, although a small number of very old foundations (the Pedro II Schools) remain under direct federal control. Over 33 per cent of all pupils at this level attend private schools. Higher education is available in federal, state, municipal and private universities and faculties.

### CULTURE

Portuguese is the language of the country, but Italian, Spanish, German, Japanese and Arabic are also spoken by minorities, and newspapers of considerable circulation are produced in those languages.

Public libraries have been established in urban centres and there is a flourishing national press with widely circulated daily and weekly newspapers.

### COMMUNICATIONS

In 1990 there were 1,670,148 km of highways. The route-length of railways in 1990 was 30,129 km. Internal air services are highly developed. There are 21,944 miles of navigable inland waterways. Rio de Janeiro and Santos are the two leading ports.

---

## BRUNEI
*Negara Brunei Darussalam*

---

Brunei is situated on the north-west coast of the island of Borneo, total area of 2,226 sq. miles (5,765 sq. km). The population is 260,863 (1991), of whom 68 per cent are of Malay, 18 per cent Chinese and 5 per cent other indigenous races. The country has a humid tropical climate.

CAPITAL – Bandar Seri Begawan, with a population of 46,229 (1991).

CURRENCY – Brunei dollar (B$) of 100 sen. It is fully interchangeable with the currency of Singapore.

FLAG – Yellow with diagonal stripes of white over black and the arms in red all over the centre.

NATIONAL ANTHEM – Allah Selamatkan Sultan (O God, long live our Majesty the Sultan).

NATIONAL DAY – 23 February.

### GOVERNMENT

In 1959 the Sultan of Brunei promulgated the first written constitution, which provides for a Privy Council, a Council of Ministers and a Legislative Council. On 1 January 1984 Brunei resumed full independence from Britain. A ministerial system of government was established at independence, the seven ministers being appointed by the Sultan and responsible to him. The Sultan presides over the Privy Council and the Council of Ministers. The Legislative Council was disbanded in February 1984. The Sultan effectively rules by decree since a state of emergency has been in effect since a revolt in November 1962.

HEAD OF STATE

*HM The Sultan of Brunei*, HM Sultan Haji Hassanal Bolkiah Mu'izzaddin Waddaulah, Sultan and Yang Di-Pertuan, GCB, *acceded* 1967, *crowned* 1 August 1968

THE COUNCIL OF MINISTERS *as at June 1994*
*Prime Minister, Minister of Defence*, HM The Sultan
*Foreign Affairs*, HRH Prince Mohammed
*Finance*, HRH Prince Jefri
*Special Adviser to the Sultan and Minister for Home Affairs*, Pehin Dato Haji Isa
*Education*, Pehin Dato Abdul Aziz
*Law*, Pengiran Bahrin
*Industry and Primary Resources*, Pehin Dato Abdul Rahman
*Religious Affairs*, Pehin Dato Mohammed Zain
*Development*, Pengiran Dato Dr Ismail
*Culture, Youth and Sports*, Pehin Dato Haji Hussein

*Health,* Dato Dr Johar
*Communications,* Dato Haji Zakaria

BRUNEI DARUSSALAM HIGH COMMISSION
19–20 Belgrave Square, London SWIX 8PG
Tel 0171-581 0521

*High Commissioner,* His Excellency Dato Kassim Daud, apptd 1993

BRITISH HIGH COMMISSION
Hong Kong and Shanghai Bank Building (3rd Floor), Jalan Pemancha, PO Box 2197 Bandar Seri Begawan
Tel: Bandar Seri Begawan 222231

*High Commissioner,* His Excellency Ivan Callan, CMG, apptd 1994

BRITISH COUNCIL REPRESENTATIVE, Susan Mathews, PO Box 3049, Bandar Seri Begawan 1930

## ECONOMY

The economy is based on the extraction and production of oil and natural gas from large onshore and offshore fields by Brunei Shell Petroleum, and the liquification of natural gas at the plant at Lamut. Royalties and taxes from these operations form the bulk of government revenue and have enabled the construction of free health, education and welfare services. The country has eight hospitals, 350 schools and one university. Brunei's main road connects the capital with Kuala Belait in the centre of the oil fields. Brunei International Airport has been extensively redeveloped and expanded, and Royal Brunei Airlines operates scheduled flights to the UK, Australia and throughout the Far East. Radio Television Brunei broadcasts one colour television and three radio channels from the capital.

| FINANCE | | 1991 |
|---|---|---|
| Revenue | | B$2,686m |
| Expenditure | | 2,760m |

| *Trade with UK* | 1992 | 1993 |
|---|---|---|
| Imports from UK | £211,384,000 | £324,432,000 |
| Exports to UK | 126,365,000 | 307,552,000 |

## BULGARIA
*Republika Bulgaria*

Bulgaria is bounded on the north by Romania, on the west by Serbia and Macedonia, on the east by the Black Sea, and on the south by Greece and Turkey. The total area is 42,823 sq. miles (110,912 sq. km), with a UN estimated population of 8,982,000 in 1991. The largest religion of the Bulgarians is the Greek Orthodox Church.

The language is Bulgarian, a Southern Slavonic tongue closely allied to Serbo-Croat and Russian with local admixtures of modern Greek, Albanian and Turkish words. The alphabet is Cyrillic.

CAPITAL – Sofia, population (1992), 1,114,925, at the foot of the Vitosha mountains, the capital and commercial centre is on the main railway line to Istanbul, 338 miles from the Black Sea port of ΨVarna (308,432); ΨBourgas (195,686) is also a Black Sea port. Other important trading and industrial centres are Plovdiv (341,058), Rousse (170,038), Pleven (130,812), Stara Zagora (150,518), Sliven (106,212) and Dobrich (104,494).
CURRENCY – Lev of 100 stotinki.
FLAG – 3 horizontal bands, white, green, red.
NATIONAL DAY – 3 March.

## HISTORY

A principality of Bulgaria was created by the Treaty of Berlin (1878) and in 1885 Eastern Roumelia was added to the principality. In 1908 the country was declared an independent kingdom. In 1912–13 a successful war of the Balkan League against Turkey increased the size of the kingdom, but in August 1913 a short campaign against the remaining members of the League reduced the acquired area and led to the surrender of Southern Dobrudja to Romania. In October 1915, Bulgaria entered the war on the side of the Central Powers by declaring war on Serbia. Involved in the defeats of 1918, Bulgaria made an unconditional surrender to the Allied Powers in September 1918, and in November 1919 signed the Treaty of Neuilly, which ceded to the Allies the Thracian territories (later handed over to Greece) and some territory on the western frontier to Yugoslavia.

Nazi troops entered the country in March 1941, and occupied Black Sea ports. In August 1944 the government declared Bulgaria to be neutral in the Russo-German war and sought terms of peace from Britain and the USA. The Soviet Union refused to recognize the so-called neutrality until Bulgaria declared war on Germany on 7 September. The armistice with the Allies was signed on 28 October 1944. The peace treaty with Bulgaria was signed on 22 February 1947 and came into force on 15 September 1947. It recognized the return of Southern Dobrudja to Bulgaria.

On 9 September 1944 a coup d'état gave power to the Fatherland Front, a coalition of Communists, Agrarians, Social Democrats, and officers and intellectuals. In August 1945, the main body of Agrarians and Social Democrats left the government. On 8 September 1946 a referendum was held which led to the abolition of the monarchy and the setting up of a republic.

The post-war period was dominated by the Communist Party (BCP), led by Todor Zhivkov. After he was forced to resign in November 1989, further leadership changes and reforms culminated, in January 1990, in the National Assembly voting to abolish the BCP's constitutional guarantee of power. Multiparty elections to a 400-seat Grand National Assembly (parliament) were held in June 1990. The BCP, renamed the Bulgarian Socialist Party in April, emerged as the majority party. A BSP-dominated government formed in September 1990 was brought down two months later by a combination of industrial strikes and opposition pressure. A multiparty government was formed in December 1990 which began to implement a radical programme of economic and political reform.

## GOVERNMENT

A new constitution, enshrining democracy, the free market and a directly elected presidency, was adopted by the Grand National Assembly on 12 July 1991.

Parliamentary elections were held on 13 October 1991, the Union of Democratic Forces (UDF) emerging as the largest party in the new National Assembly. The UDF formed a new government under Filip Dimitrov which took office in November with the support of the ethnic Turkish Movement for Rights and Freedom Party (MRF), and declared its priorities to be the economic stabilization of the country and strong anti-inflationary policies.

Dimitrov's UDF government fell after only one year when it was defeated in a parliamentary vote of no confidence in October 1992 over charges of allowing sanctions against Serbia to be broken. After a period of instability, the President appointed as Prime Minister Lyuben Berov, who successfully formed a government in December 1992 of non-party technocrats with the support of the MRF, some of the BSP and the Alternative Social Liberal Party (UDF members expelled from the UDF for supporting the government's formation).

HEAD OF STATE
*President*, Zhelyu Zhelev, *elected* 1 August 1990, *re-elected* 19 January 1992
*Vice-President*, vacant

COUNCIL OF MINISTERS *as at July 1994*
*Prime Minister*, Lyuben Berov
*Trade*, Kiril Bonev
*Transport and Communications*, Kiril Ermenkov
*Foreign Affairs*, Stanislav Daskalov
*Agriculture*, Georgi Tanev
*Environment*, Valentin Bossevski
*Finance*, Stoyan Alexandrov
*Defence*, Valentin Alexandrov
*Internal Affairs*, Victor Mihailov
*Justice*, Peter Korndzhev
*Industry*, Roumen Bikov
*Territorial Development, Housing and Construction*, Hristo Totev
*Education and Science*, Marin Todorov
*Public Health*, Tancho Gougalov
*Social Affairs*, Yordan Hirstozkov
*Culture*, Ivailo Znepolski

*Speaker of the National Assembly*, Aleksandar Yordanov

EMBASSY OF THE REPUBLIC OF BULGARIA
186–188 Queen's Gate, London SW7 5HL
Tel 0171–584 9400/9433/3144
*Ambassador Extraordinary and Plenipotentiary*, vacant
*Deputy Ambassador*, Z. Radoukov
*Consul-General*, B. Zaimov
*Head of Trade*, D. Georgiev

BRITISH EMBASSY
Boulevard Vassil Levski 65–67, Sofia 1000
Tel: Sofia 885361/2
*Ambassador Extraordinary and Plenipotentiary*, His Excellency Richard Thomas, CMG, apptd 1989
*Deputy Ambassador, Consul and First Secretary*, J. Buchanan
*Defence Attaché*, Col. R. A. F. Pearson, MVO
*First Secretary (Commercial)*, J. C. Northover

BRITISH COUNCIL REPRESENTATIVE
David Stokes, 7 Tulovo Street, 1504, Sofia

DEFENCE

Bulgaria has a total active armed forces strength of 99,000 including 60,000 conscripts. Conscripts serve for 18 months. The Army has a strength of 52,000 personnel, including 33,300 conscripts. Equipment includes 2,200 main battle tanks, 1,050 armoured infantry fighting vehicles and armoured personnel carriers and 1,680 artillery pieces.

The Navy has a strength of 3,000 personnel (2,000 conscripts), one frigate, two submarines, 23 patrol and coastal craft and ten armed helicopters. The Air Force has a strength of 22,000 (16,000 conscripts), 275 combat aircraft and 44 armed helicopters.

In addition, there are 34,000 paramilitary border guards, security police and railway and construction troops.

EDUCATION

Free basic education is compulsory for children from seven to 15 years inclusive. Government policy emphasizes the need to democratize the education system, to remove the former ideological basis and to encourage private education. There are three universities (at Sofia, Plovdiv and Veliko Turnovo), an American University and 21 higher educational establishments.

ECONOMY

Until 1939 Bulgaria was a predominantly agricultural country, but subsequently pursued an elaborate programme of industrialization. About 90 per cent of the country's agriculture was turned over to co-operatives, and a smaller proportion mechanized. The principal crops are wheat, maize, beet, tomatoes, tobacco, oleaginous seeds, fruit, vegetables and cotton. The livestock includes cattle, sheep, goats, pigs, horses, asses, mules and water buffaloes. Land is currently being handed over to its previous owners.

There is a substantial engineering industry and considerable production of ferrous and non-ferrous metals. There are mineral deposits of varying importance. Bulgaria's heavy industry includes a steel plant near Sofia and the steel mill at Pernik, the chemical complex at Devnia, the petro-chemical plant at Bourgas and various other chemical and metallurgical works situated around the country. The Soviet-designed nuclear power station at Kozlodui, comprising four reactors, each with a capability of producing 800 million kilowatt-hours and a fifth, 1,000 MW unit, accounts for over 40 per cent of Bulgaria's electrical generating capacity.

In November 1992 the government initiated a plan to privatize 92 major companies by the end of 1992 as the first stage in a mass privatization programme. The second stage was launched in August 1993 when 500 medium to large-sized enterprises were approved for privatization under a plan entitling all adults to a certificate to exchange for shares. The mining, power and defence industries are to remain under state control.

TRADE

Political and economic developments in eastern Europe since 1989 have significantly altered the pattern of foreign trade. In 1988, 79 per cent of Bulgaria's foreign trade was within the CMEA, including approximately 57 per cent with the former Soviet Union. Now over 38 per cent of exports by value go to developed industrial countries, some 35 per cent to the former CMEA and 26 per cent to developing countries. In 1992 trade with the European Community states grew rapidly to overtake trade with former Soviet states. In March 1993 Bulgaria signed an Association Agreement with the EC under which EC duties on Bulgarian industrial goods will be abolished by the end of 1994 and levies on agricultural goods will be significantly lowered.

The principal imports are fuels, minerals and metals, engineering goods and industrial equipment. The principal exports are agricultural produce, engineering goods and industrial equipment, industrial consumer goods, chemicals and fuels, minerals and metals.

| Trade with UK | 1992 | 1993 |
| --- | --- | --- |
| Imports from UK | £59,932,000 | £84,229,000 |
| Exports to UK | 49,780,000 | 76,218,000 |

# BURKINA FASO
*République Populaire de Burkina*

Burkina Faso (formerly Upper Volta) is an inland savanna state in West Africa, situated between 9° and 15°N. latitude and 2°E. and 5°W. longitude, with an area of 105,869 sq. miles (274,200 sq. km). It has common boundaries with Mali on the west, Niger and Benin on the east and Togo, Ghana and the Côte d'Ivoire on the south.

POPULATION – The population (UN estimate 1991) is 9,242,000. The largest tribe is the Mossi whose king, the Moro Naba, still wields a certain moral influence. The official language is French.

CAPITAL – Ouagadougou (441,514). Other principal towns; Bobo-Dioulasso (228,668) and Koudougou (30,000).

CURRENCY – Franc CFA.

FLAG – Equal bands of red over green, with a yellow star in centre.

NATIONAL DAY – 11 December.

## GOVERNMENT

Burkina Faso was annexed by France in 1896 and between 1932 and 1947 was administered as part of the Colony of the Ivory Coast. It decided on 11 December 1958 to remain an autonomous republic within the French Community; full independence outside the Community was proclaimed on 5 August 1960.

The 1960 constitution provided for a presidential form of government with a single chamber National Assembly, but in January 1966 the Army assumed power. A new constitution allowing for a partial return to civilian rule but with the Army still in effective control was adopted in 1970, but in 1974 this was suspended. Full legislative and presidential elections were held again in 1978.

Following a number of military coups, Capt. Blaise Compaoré took power in October 1987, also by coup. A new constitution was adopted by referendum on 2 June 1991. Presidential elections were held in December 1991 and won by Capt. Compaoré in the face of a boycott by the main opposition parties, who were unhappy with the new constitution. Opposition parties then boycotted the legislative elections held in May 1992, which were consequently won by Compaoré's Organization for Popular Democracy-Labour Movement (ODP-MT) party, which formed the government in coalition with several smaller parties.

HEAD OF STATE
*President*, Blaise Compaoré, *assumed office*, October 1987, *elected* December 1991

COUNCIL OF MINISTERS *as at July 1994*

*Prime Minister*, Roch Marc Christian Kabore
*Minister of State, Defence*, Kanidoua Naboho
*Minister of State, Integration and African Solidarity*, Herman Yameogo
*Presidential Special Envoy*, Salif Diallo
*Economy, Finance and Planning*, Zéphirín Diabre
*Foreign Affairs*, Ablasse Oudraogo
*Territorial Administration*, Vincent Kabre
*Public Works, Housing and Urban Areas*, Joseph Kabore
*Industry, Commerce and Mines*, Souley Mohamed
*Secondary and Higher Education, Scientific Research*, Mélégué Traore
*Justice*, Yarga Larba
*Culture, Communications, Government Spokesman*, Claude Somda
*Water*, Joseph Ouedraogo
*Employment, Works and Social Security*, Ardiouma Ouedraogo
*Transport*, Ouala Koutiebou
*Parliamentary Relations*, Thomas Sanon
*Primary Education and Literacy*, Alice Tiendrebeogo
*Environment and Tourism*, Anatole Tiendrebeogo

*Agriculture and Animal Husbandry*, Jean-Paul Sawadogo
*Civil Service and Administrative Reform*, Juliette Bonkoungou
*Health*, Christophe Dabire
*Youth and Sport*, Ibrahim Traore
*Social Action and the Family*, Akila Belembaogo

EMBASSY OF BURKINA FASO
16 Place Guy d'Arezzo, 1060 Brussels, Belgium
Tel: Brussels 3459911

*Ambassador Extraordinary and Plenipotentiary*, His Excellency Salifou Rigobert Kongo, apptd 1992, resident in Brussels
HONORARY CONSULATE, 5 Cinnamon Row, Plantation Wharf, London SW11 3TW. Tel: 0171–738 1800. *Honorary Consul*, S. G. Singer

BRITISH AMBASSADOR, Her Excellency Margaret Rothwell, CMG resident at Abidjan, Côte d'Ivoire

## ECONOMY

The 1988 Budget totalled Franc CFA 90,300 million. The principal industry is the rearing of cattle and sheep and the chief exports are livestock, groundnuts, millet and sorghum. Small deposits of gold, manganese, copper, bauxite and graphite have been found. Trade in 1991 was valued at imports, CFA 149,704m, exports, CFA 77,843m.

| Trade with UK | 1992 | 1993 |
|---|---|---|
| Imports from UK | £5,612,000 | £5,077,000 |
| Exports to UK | 423,000 | 477,000 |

## BURUNDI
*République de Burundi*

Situated on the east side of Lake Tanganyika, Burundi has an area of 10,747 sq. miles (27,834 sq. km) and a population (UN estimate 1991) of 5,620,000. The majority of the population are of the Hutu ethnic group (83 per cent), but power and army control has traditionally rested in the hands of the minority Tutsi ethnic group (15 per cent). Official languages are Kirundi, a Bantu language, and French. Kiswahili is also used.

CAPITAL – Bujumbura (formerly Usumbura), with 215,243 (1987 estimate) inhabitants. Kitega (18,000 inhabitants) is the only other sizeable town.

CURRENCY – Burundi franc of 100 centimes.

FLAG – Divided diagonally by a white saltire into red and green triangles; on a white disc in the centre three red six-pointed stars edged in green.

NATIONAL DAY – 1 July.

## GOVERNMENT

Formerly a Belgian trusteeship under the United Nations, Burundi became independent as a constitutional monarchy on 1 July 1962. However, the monarchy was overthrown in 1966 and the country became a republic. Attempts by the ethnic Hutu majority to overthrow Tutsi rule resulted in defeat and ethnic massacres in 1965, 1969, 1972 and 1988, with an estimated 100,000 killed in 1972. In 1976 the government was overthrown and a Supreme Revolutionary Council took power. In 1980 the SRC was replaced by a political bureau and central committee as part of a process of political normalization, which continued with elections to the

National Assembly. In September 1987 the government was overthrown by a Military Committee of National Redemption led by Maj. Pierre Buyoya. Against a background of continuing Tutsi-Hutu violence, the ruling National Unity and Progress party (UPRONA) of President Buyoya attempted to introduce multiparty non-tribal politics in 1991-2. This was approved by national referendum in March 1992, together with a directly elected President serving five-year terms.

Presidential elections were held on 1 June 1993 and won by the opposition Front for Democracy in Burundi (FRO-DEBU) leader Melchior Ndadaye with 60 per cent of the vote. Ndadaye, being a Hutu, brought to an end the political dominance of the minority Tutsi. This was confirmed on 29 June 1993 when FRODEBU won 65 seats and UPRONA only 16 seats in legislative elections to the 81-seat National Assembly. FRODEBU formed a government on 10 July 1993 but despite the attempt at non-tribal politics, clearly became identified as an ethnic Hutu party and UPRONA as an ethnic Tutsi party.

In an attempt to restore Tutsi power, the Tutsi-dominated army launched an attempted coup on 21 October 1993 in which President Ndadaye and six cabinet ministers were killed. The remainder of the government survived and regained control in December but two months of ethnic fighting left 50,000-100,000 dead and 500,000, mainly Hutu, refugees in neighbouring states. The National Assembly elected Cyprien Ntaryamira (Hutu) as President in January 1994, but he was killed in a rocket attack on the plane of President Habyarimana of Rwanda in April 1994. FRODEBU and UPRONA agreed to form a coalition government in February 1994 with a Tutsi as Prime Minister and this government reached agreement in April 1994 on disarming all tribal militias to restore political stability.

HEAD OF STATE
*Acting President (Parliamentary Speaker)*, Sylvestre Ntibantunganya

COUNCIL OF MINISTERS *as at July 1994*

*Prime Minister*, Anatole Kanyenkiko
*Minister of State, Development Planning and Reconstruction*, Bernard Ciza
*Minister of State, Foreign Affairs and Co-operation*, Jean-Marie Ngendahayo
*Minister of State, Interior and Public Security*, Leonard Nyangoma
*Finance*, Salvator Toyi
*National Defence*, Col. Gedeon Fyiroko
*Justice*, Fulgence Bakana
*Territorial Administration*, Jean-Baptiste Manwangari
*Agriculture and Livestock*, Pierre-Claver Nahimana
*Primary Education and Adult Literacy*, Nicephore Ndimurukundo
*Secondary and Higher Education*, Liboire Ngendahayo
*Labour and Professional Training*, Venerand Bakevyumusaya
*Civil Service*, Marguerite Bukuru
*Communal Development*, Ambroise Niyonsaba
*Commerce and Industry*, Joseph Nzeyimana
*Small and Medium-Sized Businesses and Tourism*, Onesime Ciza
*Energy and Mines*, Ernest Kabushemeye
*Transport, Ports and Telecommunications*, Schadrack Niyonkuru
*Public Works and Equipment*, Leonidas Nyamwana
*Territorial and Environmental Management*, Salvator Ntihabose

*Communications and Government Spokesman*, Cyriaque Simbizi
*Human Rights and Refugees*, Issa Ngendakumana
*Public Health*, Jean Minani
*Social Welfare*, Emilienne Minani
*Culture, Youth and Sports*, Alphonse Rugambarara
*Relations with the National Assembly and Institutional Reform*, Gaetan Nikobamye

EMBASSY OF THE REPUBLIC OF BURUNDI
Square Marie Louise 46, 1040 Brussels, Belgium
Tel: Brussels 2304535

*Ambassador Extraordinary and Plenipotentiary*, His Excellency Balthazar Habonimana, apptd 1992 (resident in Brussels)
BRITISH AMBASSADOR, His Excellency Roger Westbrook, CMG, resident at Kinshasa, Zaire

ECONOMY

The chief crop is coffee, representing about 80 per cent of Burundi's export earnings. Cotton is the second most important crop. Mineral, tea, hide and skin exports are also important.

| Trade with UK | 1992 | 1993 |
|---|---|---|
| Imports from UK | £2,581,000 | £2,267,000 |
| Exports to UK | 1,526,000 | 1,968,000 |

# CAMBODIA

Situated between Thailand and the south of Vietnam and extending from the border with Laos in the north to the Gulf of Thailand, Cambodia covers an area of 69,898 sq. miles (181,035 sq. km). Fifty per cent of the total land area is forest or jungle. Around the Tonlé Sap lake in the centre of the country and along the Mekong river, which traverses the country, there is ample fertile land for the support of the population in times of peace. The climate is tropical monsoon with a rainy season from May to October.

POPULATION – The population (UN estimate 1991) is 8,442,000. The state religion is Buddhism of the 'Little Vehicle'. This was suppressed by the Khmer Rouge but there has been some revival recently. There were also small Muslim and Christian communities, but many members of them died or fled the country during Khmer Rouge rule.
LANGUAGE – The national language is Khmer.

CAPITAL – Phnom Penh, population 920,000 (1993 estimate).
CURRENCY – Riel of 100 sen.
FLAG – Three horizontal stripes of blue, red, blue, with the blue of double width and containing a representation of the temple of Angkor in white.
NATIONAL ANTHEM – Nokoreach.
NATIONAL DAY – 9 November (Independence Day).

HISTORY

Once a powerful kingdom, which, as the Khmer Empire, flourished between the tenth and 14th centuries, Cambodia became a French protectorate in 1863 and was granted independence within the French Union as an Associate State in 1949. Full independence was proclaimed on 9 November 1953. From 1955 the political life of the country was dominated by Prince Norodom Sihanouk, first as king, then as head of government after he had abdicated in favour of his father and finally (following his father's death in 1960) as head of state. On 18 March 1970, during his absence from the country, Prince Sihanouk was deposed as head of state

attacks on UN peace-keeping troops, leading the UN Security Council to impose economic sanctions on the Khmer Rouge. The Khmer Rouge failed to register to take part in the multiparty elections and SOC government forces launched an offensive against them in late January 1993. Despite this, UNTAC stabilized the country to such an extent that between January and early April 1993 95 per cent of the Cambodian electorate was able to register to vote. All 330,000 refugees in Thailand were also repatriated to Cambodia under UNTAC supervision by 30 March 1993.

## GOVERNMENT

Multiparty elections under UNTAC supervision were held on 23–28 May 1993 for 120 seats in a National Assembly. The Royalist FUNCINPEC party led by Prince Sihanouk's son Prince Ranariddh won 45 per cent of the vote and 58 seats and the Cambodian People's Party (CPP) (the former ruling SOC party) won 38 per cent of the vote and 51 seats. Prince Sihanouk brokered a coalition government agreement in June between FUNCINPEC and the CPP under which he became head of state and FUNCINPEC and CPP leaders Prince Ranariddh and Hun Sen became co-chairmen of the coalition government. This agreement was accepted by UNTAC and officially approved by the new National Assembly on 1 July. The National Assembly adopted a new constitution on 21 September under which Cambodia became a pluralist liberal democracy with a constitutional monarchy. On 23 September the new constitution was promulgated, marking the end of the UNTAC mission and the restoration of Cambodian sovereignty. The same day Prince Sihanouk was elected king by a seven-member Council of the Throne made up of religious and political leaders, and he appointed a new government. Legislative power is vested in the National Assembly, executive power in the Royal Government, with the King having the power only to make appointments and declare a state of emergency, in consultation with the government.

The Khmer Rouge remain unreconciled to the new government and continue their guerrilla and sabotage campaign, mainly in the north and east of the country, where they control some 10 per cent of territory along the border with Thailand. In July 1994 the Royal Government outlawed the Khmer Rouge, which responded by declaring a provisional government in the territory it holds.

### HEAD OF STATE

*HM The King of Cambodia*, Norodom Sihanouk, *elected by the Council of the Throne*, 23 September 1993

### ROYAL GOVERNMENT *as at July 1994*

*First Prime Minister*, Prince Norodom Ranariddh
*Second Prime Minister*, Hun Sen
*Vice-Prime Ministers*, Prince Norodom Sereivut (*Foreign Affairs and International Co-operation*); Sar Kheng (*Interior*)
*State Minister, Rehabilitation and Development*, Keat Chhon
*State Minister, Inspection*, Ung Phan
*State Minister, Cultural Affairs and Urbanization*, Van Molivan
*State Minister, Justice*, Chem Snguon
*State Minister, Finance and Economy*, Sam Rangsi
*State Minister, Public Works and Transport*, Ing Kiet
*Ministers in the Office of the Council of Ministers*, Sok An; Veng Sereivut
*Agriculture, Forestry, Wildlife and Fisheries*, Kong Sam-ol
*Interior*, Yu Hokkri
*Education, Youth Affairs and Sports*, Ing Huot
*Press*, Ieng Muli
*Tourism*, Veng Sereivut

by a vote of the National Assembly. A republic was declared on 9 October 1970 and the name of the country changed to the Khmer Republic.

In April 1970 a civil war began between Communist insurgents and government forces. In April 1975 Phnom Penh fell to the North Vietnamese-backed Khmer Rouge. A new constitution was promulgated in 1976 and elections to a People's Representative Assembly were held in March. A government led by Pol Pot, the leader of the Khmer Rouge (Communist) party, was appointed and the state was renamed Democratic Kampuchea. During the years of Khmer Rouge rule hundreds of thousands of Cambodians fled into exile and an estimated one million were killed in the 'killing fields'.

In December 1978 Vietnamese troops invaded Cambodia and captured Phnom Penh on 7 January 1979. The following day the Cambodian National United Front for National Salvation established a People's Revolutionary Council, recognized by Vietnam, USSR and by other, chiefly Soviet-aligned, countries. The state was renamed The People's Republic of Kampuchea (PRK); in April 1989 it became the State of Cambodia (SOC).

With support from the Vietnamese army the PRK gained control of most of the country, containing the challenge from the guerrilla forces of the Coalition Government of Democratic Kampuchea (CGDK), which was formed in June 1982 by the Khmer Rouge and two non-Communist groups. Following the withdrawal of Vietnam's fighting units in 1989, the resistance forces regained ground inside Cambodia.

In September 1990, the SOC and the CGDK established a Supreme National Council to embody Cambodian sovereignty and to help implement a peace settlement. A temporary ceasefire began on 1 May 1991, became permanent on 23 June and the peace agreements were finally signed on 23 October 1991. In mid-March 1992 the United Nations Transitional Authority for Cambodia (UNTAC) began to implement the peace agreement and take over the administration of the country from the SOC government in the run-up to elections. UNTAC was hampered throughout 1992 and early 1993 by Khmer Rouge attacks and SOC obstructiveness; the Khmer Rouge refused to disarm their forces and mounted

*National Defence*, Tie Banh
*Trade*, Va Huot
*Industry, Minerals and Energy*, Pu Sothirak
*Planning*, Chea Chanto
*Public Health*, Chhea Thang
*Chairman of the National Assembly*, Chea Sim

BRITISH EMBASSY
29, Street 75, Phnom Penh
Tel: Phnom Penh 855 2327124
*Ambassador Extraordinary and Plenipotentiary*, His Excellency Paul Redicliffe, apptd 1994

ECONOMY

Cambodia has an economy based on agriculture, fishing and forestry, the bulk of its people being rice-growing farmers. In addition to rice, which is the staple crop, the major products are rubber, livestock, maize, timber, pepper, palm sugar, fresh and dried fish, kapok, beans, soya and tobacco. Rice and rubber used to be the main exports though production was brought to a standstill by the hostilities. Following the Khmer Rouge victory, the populations of Phnom Penh and other towns were forcibly evacuated to the country to work on the land, and re-establish the plantations producing such crops as cotton, rubber and bananas. Following the Vietnamese invasion of 1978 the towns were repopulated and commerce revived; currency was reintroduced. Factories, in particular textile mills, iron smelting works and cement works were put back in production. The UNTAC presence boosted the economy, at least in the short term, and particularly in Phnom Penh.

Cambodia is heavily dependent on foreign aid pledges to rebuild its economy and large amounts have been pledged since the 1991 Paris peace agreements: US$880 m was pledged in 1992; US$119 m in September 1993, and Cambodia's debts to the IMF were paid off; US$486 m was pledged in March 1994. However, foreign investors have been unenthusiastic because of insecurity, corruption, and the lack of a firm legal basis for business. In July 1994 a new investment law was passed.

| Trade with UK | 1992 | 1993 |
|---|---|---|
| Imports from UK | £1,238,000 | £3,113,000 |
| Exports to UK | 4,000 | 711,000 |

COMMUNICATIONS

The country had over 5,000 kilometres of roads, of which nearly half were hard-surfaced and passable in the rainy season, although now in a state of disrepair. There are two railways, one from Phnom Penh to the Thai border; the other from Phnom Penh to Kampot and Sihanoukville (Kompong Som), but operations and repairs are hindered by occasional Khmer Rouge attacks. Phnom Penh is on a river capable of receiving ships of up to 2,500 tons all the year round. The deep water port at Sihanoukville (Kompong Som) on the Gulf of Thailand can receive ships up to 10,000 tons. The port is linked to Phnom Penh by a modern highway.

EDUCATION

In the years preceding the civil war considerable efforts were devoted to the development of education, and new schools, colleges and technical institutes had been established. Until April 1975 there was a Buddhist University in Phnom Penh, and several residential teachers' training colleges were in operation. However, most of the country's educated élite died under the Khmer Rouge regime, which closed all institutions of higher education. The university was re-opened in 1988.

---

CAMEROON
*République du Cameroun*

---

Cameroon lies on the Gulf of Guinea between Nigeria to the west, Chad and the Central African Republic to the east and Congo and Gabon and Equatorial Guinea to the south. It has an area of 183,569 sq. miles (475,442 sq. km).

POPULATION – The population is 12,239,000 (UN estimate 1991). French and English are both official languages and enjoy equal status, and the government's declared long-term objective is to achieve complete bilingualism and biculturalism.

CAPITAL – Yaoundé, population estimate (1986) 653,670.
Ψ Douala (1,029,736) is the commercial centre.
CURRENCY – Franc CFA of 100 centimes.
FLAG – Vertical stripes of green, red and yellow with single five-pointed yellow star in centre of red stripe.
NATIONAL ANTHEM – O Cameroun, Berceau de Nos Ancêtres (O Cameroun, thou cradle of our forefathers).
NATIONAL DAY – 20 May.

GOVERNMENT

The whole territory was administered by Germany from 1884 to 1916. From 1916 to 1959, the former East Cameroon was administered by France as a League of Nations (later UN) trusteeship. On 1 January 1960 it became independent as the Republic of Cameroon. The republic was joined on 1 October 1961 by the former British-administered trust territory of the Southern Cameroons, after a plebiscite held under United Nations auspices. Cameroon became a federal republic with separate East and West Cameroon state governments. After a plebiscite held in May 1972, Cameroon became a unitary republic and a one-party state.

After extensive unrest, multiparty elections were promised by the end of 1991. These were finally held in March 1992, although they were boycotted by two of the main opposition parties. The ruling People's Democratic Movement emerged just short of a majority in the parliament and formed a coalition government with a small opposition party, the Movement for the Defence of the Republic.

Presidential elections were held on 11 October 1992 and won by the incumbent President Paul Biya with 40 per cent of the vote. The results were, however, disputed by the runner-up Fru Ndi and two opposition parties, together with foreign observers who accused the authorities of widespread malpractice. Opposition parties tried unsuccessfully to persuade the Supreme Court to annul the election result, after which violent opposition protests continued until December. On 27 November a new coalition government was formed with the two parties of the previous government being joined by the Union for Democracy and Progress and the Union of Peoples of Cameroon. In May 1993 President Biya published a draft bill on constitutional reform providing for a Council of State, Senate and a Constitutional Court but rejecting a return to a federal state. However, there has been no progress towards finalizing a new constitution.

In March 1994 Cameroon took Nigeria to the International Court of Justice after Nigerian forces occupied the oil-rich Bakassi peninsula on the border of the two states.

HEAD OF STATE
*President, Prime Minister and Commander in Chief of the Armed Forces*, His Excellency Paul Biya, *acceded*

6 November 1982, *elected* 14 January 1984, *re-elected* 24 April 1988, 10 October 1992, *sworn in* 3 November 1992

MINISTRY *as at July 1994*

*Deputy Prime Minister, Territorial Administration,* Gilbert Andze
*Deputy Prime Minister, Housing and Town Planning,* Hamadou Mustapha
*Minister of State, Posts and Telecommunications,* Dakolle Daissala
*Minister of State, Planning and Regional Development,* Augustin Frederic Kodock
*Minister of State, Communications,* Augustin Koutchou Kouomegni
*Defence,* Edouard Akame Mfoumou
*External Relations,* Ferdinand Leopold Oyono
*Justice,* Douala Moutome
*Animal Husbandry and Fisheries,* Hamadjoda Adjoudji
*Higher Education,* Titus Edzoa
*Public Health,* Joseph Mbede
*Labour and Social Insurance,* Simon Mbila
*Industrial and Commercial Development,* Patrice Ambassad Mandeng
*Finance,* Antoine Ntsimi
*Public Service and Administrative Reforms,* Sali Dairou
*Women and Social Affairs,* Yaou Aissatou
*Agriculture,* Stephen Njinyan
*Public Works,* Jean-Baptiste Bokam
*Technical and Scientific Research,* Dr Ayuk Takem
*Tourism,* Pierre Souman
*Environment and Forests,* Dr Bava Djingoer
*Youth and Sports,* Bernard Massoua
*National Education,* Dr Robert Mboppe
*Mines, Water Resources and Energy,* Jean Bosco Samgba
*Transport,* Issa Bakary Tchiroma
*Culture,* Joseph-Marie Bipoun

EMBASSY OF THE REPUBLIC OF CAMEROON
84 Holland Park, London WII 3SB
Tel 0171-727 0771/3

*Ambassador Extraordinary and Plenipotentiary,* His Excellency Dr Gibering Bol-Alima, apptd 1987

BRITISH EMBASSY
Avenue Winston Churchill, BP 547 Yaoundé
Tel: Yaoundé 220545

*Ambassador Extraordinary and Plenipotentiary,* His Excellency William E. Quantrill, apptd 1991
There is also a British Consulate at *Douala.*

BRITISH COUNCIL REPRESENTATIVE, Harley Brookes, Immeuble Christo, Avenue Charles de Gaulle (BP 818), Yaoundé

## ECONOMY

The main economic emphasis is on agricultural development, through encouraging small-scale peasant agriculture and through the development of large-scale agro-industrial complexes, with the aim of making the country agriculturally self-sufficient and a major food exporter.

Principal products are cocoa, coffee, bananas, cotton, timber, groundnuts, aluminium, rubber and palm products. There is an aluminium smelting plant at Edéa with an annual capacity of 50,000 tons. Oil is now also one of Cameroon's principal products with an estimated production of 7.31 million tonnes during 1989.

In 1993 President Biya's government was increasingly accused of economic incompetence and most foreign donors suspended aid after an IMF structural adjustment plan lapsed

in 1992. The IMF agreed to resume support of an improved economic reform programme with a US$114 million standby credit in March 1994.

| TRADE | 1987 | 1988 |
|---|---|---|
| Total imports | CFA526,186m | CFA378,726m |
| Total exports | 487,849m | 468,683m |

| Trade with UK | 1992 | 1993 |
|---|---|---|
| Imports from UK | £19,156,000 | £16,565,000 |
| Exports to UK | 6,495,000 | 17,878,000 |

# CANADA

## AREA AND POPULATION

| Provinces or Territories (with official contractions) | Area (sq. miles) | Population estimate 1993 |
|---|---|---|
| Alberta (Alta.) | 255,290 | 2,662,300 |
| British Columbia (BC) | 365,946 | 3,535,100 |
| Manitoba (Man.) | 250,946 | 1,116,000 |
| New Brunswick (NB) | 28,355 | 750,900 |
| Newfoundland and Labrador (Nfld.) | 156,648 | 581,000 |
| Nova Scotia (NS) | 21,425 | 923,000 |
| Ontario (Ont.) | 412,579 | 10,746,000 |
| Prince Edward Island (PEI) | 2,185 | 131,600 |
| Quebec (Que.) | 594,857 | 7,208,800 |
| Saskatchewan (Sask.) | 251,865 | 1,003,100 |
| Yukon Territory (YT) | 186,660 | 32,000 |
| Northwest Territories (NWT) | 1,322,902 | 62,900 |
| Total | 3,849,658 | 28,753,100 |

Area figures include land and water area

## BIRTHS, DEATHS AND MARRIAGES, 1991

| Province | Births | Deaths | Marriages |
|---|---|---|---|
| Alberta | 42,776 | 14,451 | 18,612 |
| British Columbia | 45,612 | 23,977 | 23,691 |
| Manitoba | 17,282 | 8,943 | 7,032 |
| New Brunswick | 9,497 | 5,469 | 4,521 |
| Newfoundland | 7,166 | 3,798 | 3,480 |
| Nova Scotia | 12,016 | 7,255 | 5,845 |
| Ontario | 151,478 | 72,917 | 72,938 |
| Prince Edward Island | 1,885 | 1,188 | 876 |
| Québec | 97,310 | 49,121 | 28,922 |
| Saskatchewan | 15,304 | 8,098 | 5,923 |
| Yukon | 568 | 114 | 196 |
| NW Territories | 1,634 | 237 | 215 |
| Total | 402,528 | 195,568 | 172,251 |

Canada's birth rate per 1,000 population (1991) 14.9; death rate 7.2; marriage rate 6.4. Divorces were 77,031 in 1991.

Of the total immigration of 252,537 in 1992, 14,722 were from the Caribbean, 7,512 from the United Kingdom and Ireland, and 7,155 from the United States of America.

## MOTHER TONGUES OF THE POPULATION 1991

*Single Responses*
| | |
|---|---|
| English | 16,516,180 |
| French | 6,505,565 |
| Non-official languages | 3,549,305 |
| Cree | 77,355 |
| Inuktitut | 24,030 |
| Ojibway | 21,225 |

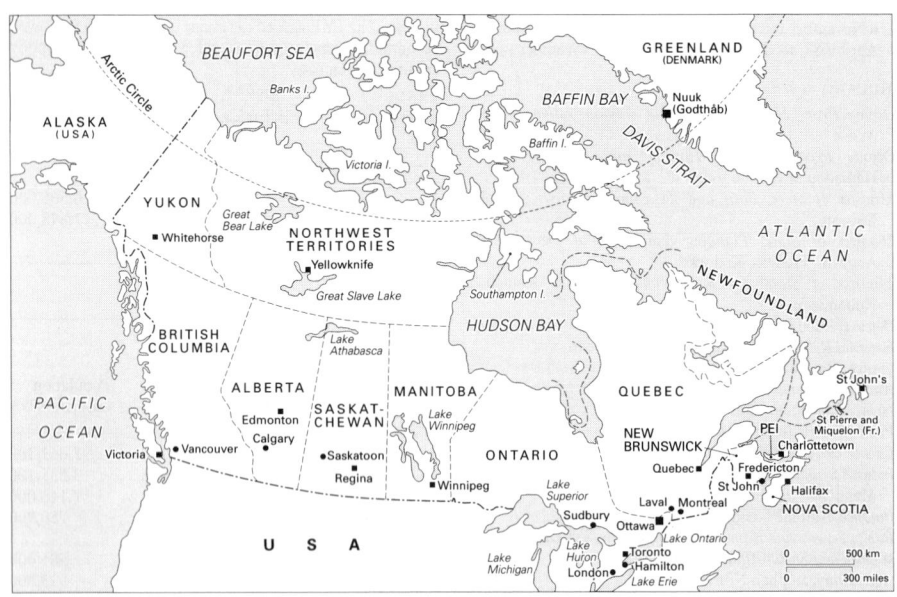

## PHYSIOGRAPHY

Canada occupies the whole of the northern part of the North American continent (with the exception of Alaska), from 49° N. latitude to the North Pole, and from the Pacific to the Atlantic Ocean. In eastern Canada, the southernmost point is Middle Island in Lake Erie, at 41° 41′.

The relief of Canada is dominated by the mountain ranges running north and south on the west side of the continent, by the pre-Cambrian shield on the east, with, in between, the northern extension of the North American Plain. From the physiographic point of view Canada has six main divisions. These are: Appalachian-Acadian region, the Canadian shield, the St Lawrence-Great Lakes lowland, the interior plains, the Cordilleran region and the Arctic archipelago.

The great Canadian shield comprises more than half the area. The interior as a whole is an undulating, low plateau (general level 1,000 to 1,500 feet), with water or muskeg-filled depressions separated by irregular hills and ridges, 150 to 200 feet in elevation. The flat relief of the St Lawrence-Great Lakes lowland varies from 500 feet in the east to 1,700 feet south of Georgian Bay. The interior plains, comprising the Pacific provinces, slope eastward and northward a few feet per mile. The descent from west to east is made from 5,000 feet to less than 1,000 feet in three distinct levels, with each new level being marked by an eastward facing conteau or scarp.

Five fairly well-developed topographic divisions mark out the Cordilleran region of western Canada. These are: coastal ranges, largely above 5,000 feet with deep fjords and glaciated valleys; the interior plateau, around 3,500 feet and comparatively level; the Selkirk ranges, largely above 5,000

feet; the Rocky Mountains with their chain of 10,000 to 12,000 feet peaks; the Peace River or Tramontane region with its rolling diversified country.

The Arctic archipelago, with its plateau-like character has an elevation between 500 and 1,000 feet, though in Baffin Land and Ellesmere Island the mountain ranges rise to 8,500 and 9,500 feet. Two tremendous waterway systems, the St Lawrence and the Mackenzie, providing thousands of miles of water highway, occupy a broad area of lowland with their dominant axis following the edge of the shield.

The climate of the eastern and central portions presents greater extremes than in corresponding latitudes in Europe, but in the south-western portion of the prairie region and the southern portions of the Pacific slope the climate is milder. Spring, summer and autumn are of about seven to eight months' duration, and the winter four to five months.

FEDERAL CAPITAL – Ottawa, on the south bank of the Ottawa river, 111 miles west of Montreal and 247 miles north-east of Toronto. Ottawa is connected with Lake Ontario by the Rideau Canal. The city was chosen as the capital of the Province of Canada in 1857 and was later selected as the Dominion capital. Ottawa contains the Parliament Buildings, the Public Archives, Royal Mint, the National Art Gallery and the Dominion Observatory. The city population was 313,987 at the census of 1991; and the population of the metropolitan area of Ottawa–Hull was estimated at 994,300 in 1993.

CURRENCY – Canadian dollar (C$) of 100 cents.

FLAG – Red maple leaf with 11 points on white square, flanked by vertical red bars one-half the width of the square.

NATIONAL ANTHEM – O Canada.

NATIONAL DAY – 1 July (Dominion Day).

## GOVERNMENT

Canada was originally discovered by Cabot in 1497 but its history dates from 1534, when the French took possession of the country. The first permanent settlement at Port Royal (now Annapolis), Nova Scotia, was founded in 1605, and

Quebec was founded in 1608. In 1759 Quebec was captured by British forces under General Wolfe and in 1763 the whole territory of Canada became a possession of Great Britain by the Treaty of Paris 1763. Nova Scotia was ceded in 1713 by the Treaty of Utrecht, the Provinces of New Brunswick and Prince Edward Island being subsequently formed out of it. British Columbia was formed into a Crown colony in 1858, having previously been a part of the Hudson Bay Territory, and was united to Vancouver Island in 1866.

The constitution of Canada had its source in the British North America Act of 1867 which formed a Dominion, under the name of Canada, of the four provinces of Ontario, Quebec, New Brunswick and Nova Scotia; to this federation the other provinces have subsequently been admitted. Under this Act, Canada came into being on 1 July 1867, and the Statute of Westminster 1931 removed all limitations with regard to the legislative autonomy of Canada and the provinces, except that the British North America Act could be amended in important respects only by Acts of the British Parliament. Provinces admitted since 1867 are: Manitoba (1870), British Columbia (1871), Prince Edward Island (1873), Alberta and Saskatchewan (1905) and Newfoundland (1949).

The election of a separatist Parti Quebecois government in Quebec in 1976 led to a referendum in 1980 on whether the province should conduct negotiations with the federal government on a new 'sovereignty-association'; the proposal was rejected.

Agreement was reached in November 1981 between the federal and provincial governments (except Quebec) to patriate the constitution so that it was amendable only in Canada. The inclusion in the constitution of a Charter of Rights was also agreed. At the request of the Canadian Parliament, legislation was passed at Westminster and the constitution formally patriated on 17 April 1982.

To reconcile Quebec to the new constitution the Canadian federal government and the ten provincial governments signed the Meech Lake Accord on 3 June 1987. This transferred certain powers to the provinces and specifically recognized Quebec as 'a distinct society'. The provincial legislatures of Manitoba and Newfoundland refused to approve the Accord by the deadline for its ratification in 1990. In September 1992 agreement on a new federal constitution called the Charlottetown Accord was reached between the federal government and the provincial governments. The agreement guaranteed Quebec a special status within Canada as a 'distinct society' and reserved 25 per cent of seats in the House of Commons for the province. The Senate was also to be reformed to ensure each province had an equal number of seats and that it was directly elected. The Charlottetown Accord was put to a national referendum on 26 October 1992 but was rejected by 54 per cent to 46 per cent nationally and by six provinces including Quebec. Canada now remains in constitutional limbo with no constitutional discussions taking place at the moment. The rejection of the accord was a major factor leading to the resignation of Prime Minister Brian Mulroney and his replacement by Kim Campbell, who was sworn in with her new cabinet on 25 June 1993. The Progressive Conservative Party government was defeated by the Liberal Party in the Federal general election on 25 October 1993.

Executive power is vested in a Governor-General appointed by the Sovereign on the advice of the Canadian Ministry, and aided by a Privy Council.

GOVERNOR-GENERAL
*Governor-General and Commander-in-Chief,* His Excellency the Rt. Hon. Ramon John Hnatyshyn, PC, CC, CMM, CD, QC
*Secretary to the Governor-General,* J. A. LaRocque, CVO

CABINET *as at July 1994*
*Prime Minister,* Rt. Hon. Jean Chrétién
*Deputy Prime Minister, Environment,* Hon. Sheila Copps
*Justice, Attorney-General,* Hon. Allan Rock
*Finance, Regional Development,* Hon. Paul Martin
*External Affairs,* Hon. André Ouellet
*Defence, Veteran's Affairs,* Hon. David Collenette
*Treasury Board President, Infrastructure,* Hon. Arthur Eggleton
*Agriculture and Agri-Food,* Hon. Ralph Goodale
*Government Leader in the Senate, Literacy,* Hon. Joyce Fairburn
*Atlantic Opportunities and Public Works,* Hon. David Dingwall
*International Trade,* Hon. Roy MacLaren
*Western Economic Diversification and Human Resources Development,* Hon. Lloyd Axworthy
*National Revenue,* Hon. David Anderson
*Fisheries and Oceans,* Hon. Brian Tobin
*Immigration and Citizenship,* Hon. Sergio Marchi
*Solicitor-General, Government Leader in the House of Commons,* Hon. Herbert Gray
*Transport,* Hon. Douglas Young
*Indian Affairs and Northern Development,* Hon. Ron Irwin
*Health,* Hon. Diane Marleau
*Natural Resources,* Hon. Anne McLellan
*Industry,* Hon. John Manley
*Intergovernmental Affairs and Public Services Renewal,* Hon. Marcel Massé

CANADIAN HIGH COMMISSION
Macdonald House, 1 Grosvenor Square, London W1X 0AB
Tel 0171–629 9492
*High Commissioner,* His Excellency Frederik Eaton, apptd 1991
*Deputy High Commissioner,* Serge April
*Ministers,* J. Wright *(Political and Public Affairs);* R. Burchill *(Commercial/Economic)*
*Minister-Counsellor,* G. Schroh *(Immigration)*
*Defence Adviser,* Brig.-Gen. D. M. Dean
*Counsellor,* R. Picard *(Cultural Affairs);* R. D. Merner, G. Parsons, W. G. Hughes *(Commercial)*

BRITISH HIGH COMMISSION
80 Elgin Street, Ottawa K1P 5K7
Tel: Ottawa 237 1530
*High Commissioner,* His Excellency Sir Nicholas Bayne KCMG, apptd 1992
*Deputy High Commissioner,* B. H. Dinwiddy
*Counsellors,* W. B. McCleary *(Economic and Commercial);* A. E. Lewis
*Defence and Military Adviser,* Brig. A. P. Naughton
*First Secretary,* R. V. Welborn *(Management and Consular)*
There are also Consulates-General at *Montreal, Toronto,* and *Vancouver* and Consulates at *Halifax, St John's* and *Winnipeg*

BRITISH COUNCIL DIRECTOR, J. Harniman, OBE *(Cultural Attaché)*

BRITISH COUNCIL REPRESENTATIVE IN QUEBEC, S. Dawbarn, c/o British Consulate-General, 1155 University Street, Montreal, Quebec H3B 3A7

LEGISLATURE
Parliament consists of a Senate and a House of Commons. The Senate consists of 107 members, nominated by the Governor-General (age limit 75), the seats being distributed between the various provinces. Each Senator must be at least 30 years old, a resident in the province for which he is appointed, a natural-born or naturalized subject of The

Queen, and the owner of a property qualification amounting to $4,000. The Speaker of the Senate is chosen by the government of the day.

The House of Commons has 295 members and is elected every five years at longest. Representation by provinces is at present: Newfoundland 7, Prince Edward Island 4, Nova Scotia 11, New Brunswick 10, Quebec 75, Ontario 99, Manitoba 14, Saskatchewan 14, Alberta 26, British Columbia 32, Yukon 1, Northwest Territories 2.

The state of the parties in the Senate as at June 1994 was Progressive Conservatives 53, Liberals 45, Independent 5, Vacant 3.

The state of parties in the House of Commons as at June 1994, was Liberals 178, Bloc Quebecois 54, Reform Party 52, New Democracy 8, Progressive Conservatives 2, Independents 1.

*Speaker of the Senate,* Hon. Guy Charbonneau, QC

*Speaker of the House of Commons,* Hon. Gilbert Parent, MP

## JUDICATURE

The judicature is administered by judges following the civil law in Quebec province and common law in other provinces. Each province has its Court of Appeal. All superior, county and district court Judges are appointed by the Governor-General, the others by the Lieutenant-Governors of the provinces.

The highest federal court is the Supreme Court of Canada, which exercises general appellate jurisdiction throughout Canada in civil and criminal cases, and which usually holds three sessions each year. There is one other federally constituted court, the Federal Court of Canada, which has jurisdiction on appeals from its trial division, from federal tribunals and reviews of decisions and references by federal boards and commissions. The trial division has jurisdiction in claims by or against the Crown, its officers or servants or federal bodies. It also deals with inter-provincial and federal-provincial disputes.

SUPREME COURT OF CANADA

*Chief Justice of Canada,* Rt. Hon. A. Lamer, PC

FEDERAL COURT OF CANADA

*Chief Justice,* vacant
*Associate Chief Justice,* Hon. J. A. Jerome

## FINANCE

Federal government gross general revenue and expenditure was:

|  | 1992–3 | 1993–4* |
|---|---|---|
| Total Revenue | C$132,668m | C$131,069m |
| Total Expenditure | 171,006m | 176,459m |
| *estimated |  |  |

| DEBT | 1991–2 | 1992–3 |
|---|---|---|
| Gross Public Debt | C$476,610m | C$514,722m |
| Net Public Debt | 420,951m | 460,778m |

## DEFENCE

The Minister of National Defence has the control and management of the Canadian armed forces and all matters relating to national defence establishments and works for the defence of Canada. The Canadian forces are organized into National Defence Headquarters and four major commands reporting to the Chief of the Defence Staff. The four commands are: *Mobile Command; Maritime Command; Air Command; Canadian Forces Communications Command.* All Canadian forces left Europe in 1994.

National defence expenditure for the year 1993 was C$11,960 million. The Canadian armed forces number 78,100 personnel. The Canadian Armed Forces are an all-volunteer force.

Land forces comprise some 20,000 personnel organized into three infantry brigade groups together with independent airborne, artillery and engineer units. Equipment includes 115 main battle tanks, 370 reconnaissance vehicles, 1,405 armoured personnel carriers and 330 artillery pieces.

Maritime forces number 12,500 personnel with four destroyers, 13 frigates, three submarines and 12 patrol and coastal craft. Air forces number 20,600 personnel with 198 combat aircraft and 128 armed helicopters. Organization is into five air defence, four maritime reconnaissance, three anti-submarine warfare, 11 helicopter and six transport squadrons.

In addition, there are 25,000 personnel assigned to Communications Command or are not identified in any of the above three services.

## EDUCATION

Education is under the control of the provincial governments, the cost of the publicly controlled schools being met by local taxation, aided by provincial grants. In 1992–3 there were 16,063 elementary and secondary schools with 5,287,730 pupils. Of these, 1,515 were private schools with 256,140 pupils; 383 federal schools with 55,600 pupils and 19 special schools for the blind and deaf with 2,330 pupils.

In 1992–3 there were 69 degree-granting universities with a full-time enrolment of 572,900, as well as 348,400 students in 203 other post-secondary, non-university institutions.

## ECONOMY

About 7.3 per cent of the total land area of Canada is farmed land. Over 60 per cent of this is under cultivation, the remainder being predominantly classified as unimproved pasture. More than 80 per cent of the land now cultivated is found in the prairie region of western Canada.

Farm cash receipts from the sale of farm products in 1993 were C$23,697m. Livestock and animal products contributed C$12,163m; field crops C$8,852m; grain and oilseed C$5,500m.

In July 1993 the livestock included 13,405,800 cattle, 10,906,600 pigs, 949,100 sheep and lambs and 21,937,000 chickens (layers).

Canada in 1992–3 produced pelts valued at C$36m. Wildlife pelts made up 40.1 per cent of the total, with a value of C$14m.

The marketed value of fish catches in 1992 was C$2,928m (preliminary).

About 43 per cent of the total land area is considered as inventoried forest area. The value of shipments and other revenue from forestry-related industries in 1991 was: logging $7,701.9m; sawmill and planing mill products $7,728.3m; shingle and shake $213.6m; veneer and plywood $857.5m; and paper and allied products $21,003m.

In 1992, Canada was the world's largest producer of zinc, nickel, potash and uranium, the second largest of asbestos, cadmium and elemental sulphur. The country is also rich in many other minerals, including gold, silver, copper, lead, molybdenum, platinum group metals, gypsum, cobalt, titanium concentrates, and aluminium. The total value of mineral production in 1993 was C$36,062.2m.

Production of gold was 157,554,000 kg in 1992 and of silver 1,147,000 kg. Uranium production in 1992 was 9,057,000 kg.

## TRADE

Merchandise imports into Canada in 1993 were valued at C$169,460m and merchandise exports (including re-exports) at C$186,681m. The main exports in 1993 were passenger automobiles and chassis, motor vehicle parts (except engines), trucks, truck tractors and chassis, wood pulp and similar pulp, newsprint paper, softwood lumber, crude petroleum, office machines and equipment, other telecommunications and related equipment (excluding televisions, radio sets, phonographs), wheat and natural gas.

Trade with the USA accounts for about 76.7 per cent of total trade in merchandise, although efforts are being made to develop alternative markets.

| Trade with UK | 1992 | 1993 |
|---|---|---|
| Imports from UK | £1,582,124,000 | £1,843,814,000 |
| Exports to UK | 1,897,115,000 | 1,854,312,000 |

## COMMUNICATIONS

The total track of railways in operation on 31 December 1991, was 85,563 km. In 1991 freight transportation was 261 billion tonne-kilometres, and the balance of property accounts at end 1991 was C$18,635m.

The registered shipping on 1 January 1991 including inland vessels, was 43,787 vessels with gross tonnage 4,956,845. The volume of international shipping handled at Canadian ports in 1991 was 168,030,334 metric tonnes loaded and 65,863,148 metric tonnes unloaded.

The bulk of canal shipping in Canada is handled through the two sections of the St Lawrence Seaway, which provide access to the Great Lakes for ocean-going ships. In 1992, transits on the Montreal-Lake Ontario section numbered 2,493 for a total of 31,400,000 cargo tonnes; transits in the Welland Canal section numbered 3,140 for a total of 33,200,000 cargo tonnes. Principal commodities carried were iron ore, wheat, corn, barley, soybeans, manufactured iron and steel, coal and salt.

*Source:* for financial and economic statistics, Statistics Canada

## YUKON TERRITORY

The area of the Territory is 205,346 sq. miles (531,842 sq. km), with a population (1991 census) of 27,797. Minerals, government and tourism are the chief industries, followed closely by transportation, communications and other utilities industry.

SEAT OF GOVERNMENT – Whitehorse, population (1991 census) 17,925.

The Yukon Act 1970, as amended, provides for the administration of the Territory by a Commissioner acting under instructions given by the Governor-in-Council or the Minister of Indian Affairs and Northern Development. Legislative powers, analogous to those of a provincial government, are exercised by a Legislative Assembly of 17 members elected from electoral districts in the Territory. The Executive Council of the Assembly consists of the government leader as chairman and five elected members.

*Commissioner,* J. K. McKinnon
*Premier,* Hon. John Ostashek

## NORTHWEST TERRITORIES

The area of the Northwest Territories is 1,322,900 sq. miles (3,426,389 sq. km), with a population (1991 census) of 57,649. The chief industry is mining, with a total value of $637,294,000 in 1992. Lead, zinc, gold, silver, oil exploration and natural gas contributed about 19 per cent of the 1992 GDP of the Northwest Territories.

The Northwest Territories are subdivided into the regions of Baffin, Fort Smith, Inuvik, Keewatin, Kitikmeot.

SEAT OF GOVERNMENT – Yellowknife, population (1991 census) 15,179.

The Northwest Territories Act 1979, as amended, provides for a Legislative Assembly of 24 elected members, of which the Executive Council under the chairmanship of the government leader is the senior decision-making body of the government in the Territory.

In November 1992 a referendum was held in the Northwest Territories which approved a plan to divide the Territories into two and to establish in one part a self-governing autonomous Inuit (Eskimo) populated territory known as Nunavat. Nunavat will be established in the east of the Northwest Territories and will comprise the present regions of Baffin, Keewatian and Kitikmeot. An agreement to establish Nunavat with self-government phased in over six years up to 1999 was signed in the new territory's capital Iqaluit on Baffin Island by the federal Prime Minister Brian Mulroney on 1 June 1993. The territory will have its own government and legislature, though neither will have the status of their provincial equivalents. It has a population of some 22,000, of which 80 per cent are Inuit, and covers some 850,000 sq. miles (2,201,500 sq. km). The agreement has yet to be ratified by the Federal Parliament.

*Commissioner,* D. L. Norris
*Government Leader,* Hon. Dennis Patterson

## CANADIAN PROVINCES

## ALBERTA

The Province of Alberta has an area of 661,185 sq. km (255,285 sq. miles), including about 6,485 sq. miles of water (16,796 sq. km), with a population (1 July 1993) of 2,662,300.

CAPITAL – Edmonton, city population (1993) 626,999, metropolitan area, 839,924. Other centres are Calgary (727,719), Lethbridge (64,938), Red Deer (59,826), Medicine Hat (43,807), St Albert (44,195).

### GOVERNMENT

The Government is vested in a Lieutenant-Governor and Legislative Assembly composed of 83 members, elected for five years. At a provincial election held on 15 June 1993, the Progressive Conservative Party took 51 seats and the Liberal Party 32 seats.

*His Hon. The Lt.-Governor,* The Hon. Gordon Towers
*Premier, President of Executive Council,* Hon. Ralph Klein

AGENT-GENERAL'S OFFICE IN LONDON, Alberta House, 1 Mount Street, London WIY 5AA. *Agent-General,* Geoff Davey

### JUDICATURE

*Chief Justice, Court of Appeal,,* Hon. C. A. Fraser
*Chief Justice, Court of Queen's Bench of Alberta,* Hon. W. K. Moore
*Associate Chief Justice,* Hon. A. H. Wachowich

### ECONOMY

The total GDP at factor cost in 1993 amounted to C$74,188 million. Preliminary estimates for mineral production in 1993 came to C$18,642 million. Of this total, crude oil amounted to C$9,016 million, and natural gas and its by-products to C$8,744 million.

The total value of manufacturing shipments (1993) was C$21,275 million. Number of manufacturing establishments 2,827 (1990), total employees 96,200 (1993). The leading industrial products are refined petroleum and coal products, meat and meat products, chemicals and chemical products, fabricated metal products, non-metallic mineral products and primary metals.

### FINANCE

| Budgetary Estimates | 1992–3 | 1993–4 |
|---|---|---|
| Revenue | C$13,218m | C$14,324m |
| Expenditure | 16,911 | 16,004 |
| Deficit | 3,773 | 1,680 |

## BRITISH COLUMBIA

British Columbia has a total area estimated at 952,263 sq. km (367,669 sq. miles), with a population of 3,535,100 (July 1993).

PROVINCIAL CAPITAL – ΨVictoria, metropolitan population (1993) 305,244. Other principal cities are ΨVancouver (metropolitan population (1993) 1,713,595), Prince George, Kamloops, Kelowna and Nanaimo.

### GOVERNMENT

The government consists of a Lieutenant-Governor and an Executive Council together with a Legislative Assembly of 75 members.

The New Democratic Party formed a government after a general election on 17 October 1991. The present standing in the Assembly is New Democratic Party 51, Liberal Party 15, Reform Party 4, Social Credit Party 2, Progressive Democratic Alliance 2, Independent 1.

*His Hon. The Lt.-Governor*, The Hon. Dr David See-Chai Lam

*Premier*, Hon. Mike Harcourt

AGENT-GENERAL'S OFFICE IN LONDON, British Columbia House, 1 Regent Street, London SW1Y 4NS.
*Agent-General*, Paul King

### JUDICATURE

*Chief Justice, Court of Appeal*, Hon. A. McEachern
*Chief Justice, Supreme Court*, Hon. W. A. Esson
*Associate Chief Justice*, Hon. D. H. Campbell

| FINANCE | 1993–4 | 1994–5 |
|---|---|---|
| Estimated revenue | C$17,681m | C$18,732m |
| Estimated expenditure | 18,965m | 19,630m |

### ECONOMY

Manufacturing activity is based largely on the processing of the output of the logging, mineral, fishing and agriculture industries. The principal manufacturing centres are Vancouver, New Westminster, Victoria, North Vancouver, Kelowna and Prince George. Service industries generate 72 per cent of total of provincial GDP and are the largest employer, accounting for over 76 per cent of total employment. British Columbia is the leading province of Canada in the quantity and value of its timber and sawmill products. Mining, the second most important non-service economic activity, is based on copper, zinc, lead, iron concentrates, molybdenum, coal, natural gas, crude petroleum, asbestos, gold and silver. Molybdenum production is approximately 95 per cent of the Canadian total.

The production levels for important industries for 1993 were as follows:

| Lumber | 33,935,000 cu. metres |
|---|---|
| Paper | 3,120,000 tonnes |
| Pulp | 4,040,000 tonnes |
| Coal | 19,264,000 tonnes |
| Natural gas | 17,398,700,000 cu. metres |

Solid mineral production for 1993 is estimated to be valued at C$2,282 million.

The most important agricultural products are livestock, eggs and poultry, fruits and dairy products. Salmon accounts for approximately 60 per cent of the value of fisheries. Other species include halibut, herring, sole, cod, flounder, perch, tuna and shellfish. In 1993 farm cash receipts were valued at C$1,427 million.

The economy is dependent upon markets outside the province for the disposal of most of its industrial products. An estimated 55–60 per cent of production is exported to foreign markets. Manufacturing shipments in 1993 were valued at C$26,892 million.

### TRANSPORT

The province has deep water harbours which are well serviced by railways and modern highways. Vancouver has one of the finest natural harbours in the world, servicing a variety of vessels, including large bulk cargo carriers. Vancouver is also the base for regular scheduled air routes to other parts of Canada, the United States, Europe, Mexico, South America, Hawaii, Fiji, Australia, Japan, Hong Kong and the Middle East.

## MANITOBA

Manitoba, originally the Red River settlement, is the central province of Canada. The province has a considerable area of prairie land but also has 645 kilometres (401 miles) of coastline on Hudson Bay, large lakes and rivers covering an area of 101,592 sq. km (39,225 sq. miles) and pre-Cambrian rock which covers about three-fifths of the province. The total area is 649,947 sq. km (250,946 sq. miles), with a population (1993 estimate) of 1,116,000.

PROVINCIAL CAPITAL – Winnipeg, population 652,355 (1991). Other cities are Brandon (38,567), Thompson (14,977), Portage la Prairie (13,186).

### GOVERNMENT

The Lieutenant-Governor is The Queen's personal representative in Manitoba. There is a Legislative Assembly of 57 members, of which the Executive Council of Ministers are all members.

The Progressive Conservatives formed a majority government after a general election held on 11 September 1990. The standing in the House at 30 September 1993 was: Progressive Conservatives 29, New Democratic Party 21, Liberal 7.

*His Hon. The Lt.-Governor*, The Hon. W. Yvon Dumont
*Premier*, Hon. Gary A. Filmon

### JUDICATURE

*Chief Justice, Court of Appeal*, Hon. Richard J. Scott
*Chief Justice, Queen's Bench Division*, Hon. B. Hewak
*Associate Chief Justices*, Hon. J. J. Oliphant (*QBD*),
   Hon. G. W. Mercier (*Family Division*)

### ECONOMY

The projected revenue in the fiscal year 1994–5 was C$5,065 million while expenditures were forecast at C$5,361 million.

Of the total land area, 19,126,517 acres are in occupied farms. The gross value of agriculture production in 1993 was estimated at C$2,286 million.

Manufacturing enterprises employed about 55,000 persons on average in 1990. The chief manufacturing centres are Winnipeg, Brandon, Selkirk and Portage la Prairie. The largest manufacturing industry is the food and beverage industry, followed by transportation equipment and primary metal industries.

## NEW BRUNSWICK

New Brunswick is situated between 45°–48° N. latitude and 63° 47′–69° W. longitude and comprises an area of 73,439 sq. km (28,355 sq. miles), with a population (July 1993) of 750,900. It was first colonized by British subjects in 1761, and in 1783 by inhabitants of New England who had been dispossessed of their property in consequence of their loyalty to the British Crown.

PROVINCIAL CAPITAL – Fredericton, population (1991), 71,869. Other cities are ΨSaint John (124,981); Moncton (106,503); Bathurst (36,167); Edmundston (22,478); Campbellton (17,183).

### GOVERNMENT

Government is administered by a Lieutenant-Governor, an Executive Council, and a Legislative Assembly of 58 members elected by the people. The present Legislative Assembly of the Province was elected on 23 September 1991 and has 58 members; 44 from the Liberal Party, 6 from the Confederation of Regions (COR), 5 from the Progressive Conservative Party, 1 from the New Democratic Party and 2 independents.
*Her Hon. The Lt-Governor*, The Hon. Margaret McCain
*Premier*, Hon. Frank McKenna

### JUDICATURE

*Chief Justice, Court of Appeal*, Hon. W. Hoyt
*Chief Justice, Queen's Bench Division*, Hon. G. A. Richard

### ECONOMY

The estimated revenue for the year ending 31 March 1993 was C$3,968,402,629 and ordinary expenditure, $4,085,972,887.

New Brunswick's largest manufacturing group, in terms of shipments, is the paper and allied industries, followed by the food and wood industries. Together these industries accounted in 1993 for 48.1 per cent of the total value of manufacturing shipments of C$6,389 million. Saint John has an ice-free port and is the principal manufacturing centre of the province.

Farms numbered 3,252 and averaged 285 acres each in 1991. Dairy products and potatoes are the leading agricultural products. Both industries together accounted for 51.9 per cent of total farm cash receipts in 1993. Farm cash receipts in 1993 totalled C$286,000,000.

Fishing is an important industry, employing about 7,700 fishermen. The chief commercial fish are lobsters, herring, tuna, crab and cod. Landings reached 115,483 tonnes valued at C$103,118,000 in 1993.

Extensive zinc, lead and copper deposits are being mined in the north-eastern part of the province, with New Brunswick being the largest producer of zinc in Canada. A lead smelter, fertilizer plant and port facilities have been constructed at Belledune. Canada's only primary antimony producer is located at Lake George. There is exploration and development near Sussex and Salt Springs, where potash production continues to escalate. A potash terminal has been built at the port of Saint John. Coal is mined at Grand Lake and exploration for other deposits is being undertaken. Total mineral production was valued at C$781,663,000 in 1993.

Tourism is of increasing value to the economy.

## NEWFOUNDLAND AND LABRADOR

The Island of Newfoundland is situated between 46° 37′–51° 37′ N. latitude and 52° 44′–59° 30′ W. longitude, on the north-east side of the Gulf of St Lawrence, and is separated from the North American continent by the Straits of Belle Isle on the north-west and by Cabot Strait on the south-west. The island is about 510 km long and 508 km broad and is triangular in shape. It comprises an area of 111,390 sq. km (43,008 sq. miles), with a population (1993 estimate) (inclusive of Labrador) of 581,000.

Labrador forms the most easterly part of the North American continent, and extends from Point St Charles, at the north-east entrance to the Straits of Belle Isle on the south, to Cape Chidley, at the eastern entrance to Hudson's Straits on the north. It has an area of 294,328 sq. km (113,641 sq. miles), with a population (1991 census) of 30,375. Labrador is noted for its cod fisheries and also possesses valuable salmon, herring, trout and seal fisheries.

PROVINCIAL CAPITAL – ΨSt John's (population 1991 census, Greater St John's 171,859) is North America's oldest city, and thus of historical interest. It is the seat of the provincial legislature, the site of most provincial and federal government offices and the principal port for the island of Newfoundland. Newfoundland's second city of Corner Brook (population 1991 census, 22,410) is situated on the west coast.

### GOVERNMENT

The government is administered by a Lieutenant-Governor, aided by an Executive Council and a Legislative Assembly of 52 members elected for a term of five years. A general election was held on 3 May 1993. The standings in the current House of Assembly are: Liberals 35; Progressive Conservatives 16; New Democrats 1.
*His Hon. The Lt.-Governor*, The Hon. Frederick W. Russell
*Premier*, Hon. Clyde Wells

### JUDICATURE

*Chief Justice, Court of Appeal*, Hon. Noel H. A. Goodridge
*Chief Justice, Trial Division*, Hon. T. A. Hickman

### ECONOMY

The estimated gross capital and current account revenues for 1994–5 are C$3,274,552,000 and the gross current and capital account expenditures C$3,521,222,100.

The main primary industries are fishing, forestry and mining. In 1993 shipments of fish products were valued at C$480 million. In 1993 newsprint shipments from the three pulp and paper mills were valued at C$419 million, mining plus structural materials shipments were estimated at C$728 million, of which C$637 million was from the two iron ore mines in Labrador. Total manufacturing shipments were valued at C$1,317 million in 1993. The hydro-electric plant on the Churchill river is the largest underground plant in the world, with a capacity of 5,225,000 kW.

Over 139 wells have been drilled off Newfoundland since 1965. Discovery of oil was made in 1979 on the Grand Banks. Oil production is expected to begin in the 1990s, with a peak production of 110,000 barrels of oil a day. In 1993 offshore exploration expenditure was approximately C$100,000

### TRANSPORT

The island portion of the province utilizes the Trans-Canada Highway and other roadways to access most communities. There is a coastal boat service that operates on the southern portion of the island and on the coast of Labrador linking otherwise isolated communities. The Quebec-North shore and Labrador Railway is operated in Labrador, linking the interior with Sept-Iles, Quebec. The island is connected to mainland Canada by a ferry service that runs from Sydney, Nova Scotia, to Port Aux Basques and Argentia.

## NOVA SCOTIA

Nova Scotia is a peninsula between 43° 25′–47° N. latitude and 59° 40′–66° 25′ W. longitude, and is connected to New Brunswick by a low fertile isthmus about 28 km wide. It comprises an area of 55,490 sq. km (21,425 sq. miles), including 2,650 sq. km of lakes and rivers and 10,424 km of shoreline. No place is more than 56 km from the Atlantic Ocean. Population (July 1993 estimate) 923,000.

Cape Breton Island has been part of Nova Scotia since 1819. It is the centre of the steel manufacturing and coal mining industries, and is also noted for its lakes and coastal scenery, making it a tourist attraction in Canada.

PROVINCIAL CAPITAL – ΨHalifax, including the neighbouring city of Dartmouth, has a population of 182,253. The harbour, ice-free all year round, is the main Atlantic winter port of Canada. Other cities and towns include ΨSydney (26,063), ΨGlace Bay (19,501).

GOVERNMENT

The government consists of a Lieutenant-Governor and a 52-member elected Legislative Assembly, from which the Executive Council is selected. The state of the parties in June 1994 was Liberals 41, Independent 8, New Democratic Party 3.

The Lieutenant-Governor represents The Queen and is appointed by the Governor-in-Council.
*His Hon. The Lt.-Governor*, The Hon. Jim Kinley
*Premier*, Hon. Dr John Savage
*Speaker of the House of Assembly*, Hon. Paul MacEwan

JUDICATURE

*Chief Justice, Court of Appeal*, Hon. L. O. Clarke
*Chief Justice, Supreme Court*, Hon. Constance R. Glube

ECONOMY

The revenue for the fiscal year ending 31 March 1994 was C$3,500,700,000 and expenditure was C$3,872,700,000.

Manufacturing constitutes the most important goods-producing sector of the economy. Manufacturing plants provide employment for 10.6 per cent of the labour force. Electric power in Nova Scotia is supplied by the Nova Scotia Power Corporation. The Corporation's generating stations, which are predominantly coal fired, have a capacity of 2,129,300 kilowatts.

Canada's first offshore oil well went into production on 6 June 1992. Total production was valued at C$131,649,000 in 1993.

The total value of mineral production in 1993 (preliminary) was estimated at C$530 million. Dollar value of coal production was C$222 million, and salt production C$58 million.

A total of 402,407 tonnes of fish and shellfish was harvested in 1993 for a landed value of C$474.3 million.

Forest land covers 73 per cent of the land area and most is privately owned. Forest-based industries employed an average of 8,700 in 1993, and contributed C$800 million to the Nova Scotia economy.

Between 15 May and 31 October 1993, about 1.08 million visitors spent about C$440 million in the province.

## ONTARIO

Ontario contains a total area of 1,068,472 sq. km (412,578 sq. miles), with a population (1993 estimate) of 10,746,000.

PROVINCIAL CAPITAL – ΨToronto (metropolitan, census 1991, 3,893,046) has a wide range of manufacturing and service industries and is a centre of education, business and finance. Other major urban areas are: Ottawa, the national capital (313,987); ΨHamilton (599,760), with iron and steel industry, metal fabrication, machinery, electrical and chemical industries; London (381,522), a business and manufacturing centre; ΨWindsor (262,075); Kitchener (356,421) and Sudbury (157,613).

GOVERNMENT

The government is vested in a Lieutenant-Governor and a Legislative Assembly of 130 members elected for five years. As at 21 June 1993, there were 71 New Democrats, 34 Liberals, 21 Progressive Conservatives, 3 Independents, and one vacant seat. The last elections were held on 6 September 1990.
*His Hon. The Lt.-Governor*, The Hon. Henry N. R. Jackman.
*Premier*, Hon. Bob Rae

JUDICATURE

*Chief Justice, Court of Appeal*, Hon. C. L. Dubin
*Chief Justice, General Division*, Hon. F. W. Callaghan
*Chief Justice, Provincial Division*, Hon. Sidney B. Linden

ECONOMY

Ontario has the highest total of agricultural production in Canada with a gross value of C$6,030 million and a total net farm income of C$1,180 million.

Productive forested lands cover 39.9 million hectares. Paper and allied industries are by far the most important sector of Ontario's forest industry.

Ontario's natural resources include 30 basic minerals, such as copper, iron ore, zinc, sulphur, gold, nickel and platinum. Total value of the mineral production in 1992 was estimated at C$4,800 million.

Total electrical energy generated in Ontario in 1992 was 136,972 million kW.

Ontario is the chief manufacturing province in Canada, producing 50 per cent of all manufactured goods. During 1992 Ontario's exports totalled C$82,233 million.

## PRINCE EDWARD ISLAND

Prince Edward Island lies in the southern part of the Gulf of St Lawrence, between 46°–47° N. latitude and 62°–64° 30′ W. longitude. It is about 225 km in length, and from 6 to 64 km in breadth; its area is 5,659 sq. km (2,185 sq. miles), and its population (1993 estimate) 131,600.

PROVINCIAL CAPITAL – ΨCharlottetown (30,436), on the shore of Hillsborough Bay, which forms a good harbour.

GOVERNMENT

The government is vested in a Lieutenant-Governor, an Executive Council, and Legislative Assembly of 32 members elected for a term of up to five years, 16 as Councillors and 16 as Assemblymen. After the election of 29 March 1993 there were 31 Liberals and 1 Progressive Conservative.
*Her Hon. The Lt.-Governor*, The Hon. Marion L. Reid
*Premier*, Hon. Catherine S. Callbeck
*Speaker of the Legislative Assembly*, Hon. Nancy Guptill

JUDICATURE

*Chief Justice, Appeal Division*, Hon. Norman H. Carruthers
*Chief Justice, Trial Division*, Hon. K. R. MacDonald

ECONOMY

The ordinary revenue of the province in 1992–3 was C$679.5 million and the expenditure C$763 million.

Approximately 46 per cent of the total area of the province is farmland. The value of farm cash receipts in 1993 was

C$235.2 million, of which 42 per cent was from the sale of potatoes. Dairy, beef and hogs are also important agriculture products.

Fish landings were valued at C$70.4 million in 1993 of which 72 per cent was of lobster.

The total value of manufacturing shipments was C$455.6 million in 1993, of which 70.6 per cent was in the food products industry.

A major summer economic activity is tourism. Non-resident tourists spent C$121.5 million in the province in 1993.

EDUCATION

A university and a college of applied arts and technology were established in 1969, estimated full- and part-time enrolment for 1992–3 being 3,638 (University of Prince Edward Island), and 5,286 for the college of applied arts and technology (Holland College).

QUEBEC

Quebec contains an area estimated at 1,540,667 sq. km (594,855 sq. miles) with a population (1993 estimate) of 7,208,800.

PROVINCIAL CAPITAL – ΨQuebec. Population (1991 census) 167,517; historic city visited annually by thousands of tourists, and one of the great seaport towns of Canada. ΨMontreal (1,017,666) is the commercial centre. Other important cities are Laval (314,398); Sherbrooke (76,429); Montreal-Nord (85,516); La Salle (73,804); Longueuil (129,874) and Gatineau (92,284).

GOVERNMENT

The government of the province is vested in a Lieutenant-Governor, a Council of Ministers and a National Assembly of 125 members elected for five years. At 25 June 1994, there were 78 Liberals, 33 Parti Quebecois, 1 Equality member, 5 Independents and 8 vacant seats.

*His Honour The Lt.-Governor*, The Hon. Martial Asselin
*Prime Minister*, Hon. Daniel Johnson

AGENT-GENERAL'S OFFICE IN LONDON, 59 Pall Mall, London SW1Y 5JH. *Agent-General*, Harold Mailhot

JUDICATURE

*Chief Justice, Court of Appeal*, Hon. Claude Bisson
*Chief Justice, Superior Court*, Hon. Lawrence Poitras

ECONOMY

The revenue for the year 1992–3 was C$35,444,607,000; expenditure amounted to C$40,376,973,000.

The principal manufacturing centres are Montreal, Montreal East, Quebec, Trois-Rivières, Sherbrooke, Shawinigan Drummondville and Lachine. Forest lands cover 655,382 sq. km, of which 536,053 sq. km are productive.

Total estimated value of shipments in the manufacturing industries in 1993 was C$74,169 million. Value of 1993 shipments in the chief industries was accounted for by food, C$10,344 million; paper and allied industries, C$7,075m; primary metal industries, C$6,003m, and transport equipment, C$6,796m.

In 1993 total farm receipts were:

| | |
|---|---|
| Crops | C$793,052,000 |
| Livestock and livestock products | 2,626,143,000 |
| Other farm receipts | 505,803,000 |

In 1992 70,429 tonnes of fish, to the value of C$88,882,000 were landed.

Minerals to the value of C$2,555,765,000 were mined in 1993. This included copper, C$196,322,000; asbestos, C$209,860,000; and gold, C$619,946,000.

SASKATCHEWAN

Saskatchewan lies between Manitoba to the east and Alberta to the west and has an area of 652,324 sq. km (251,864 sq. miles) (of which the land area is 570,269 sq. km, or 220,182 sq. miles), with a population (estimated 1993) of 1,003,100. Saskatchewan extends along the Canada–USA boundary for 632 km (393 miles) and northwards for 1,224 km (761 miles). Its northern width is 440 km (276 miles).

PROVINCIAL CAPITAL – Regina. Population (1991 census), 179,178. Other cities: Saskatoon (186,058), Moose Jaw (33,593); Prince Albert (34,181) and Yorkton (15,315).

GOVERNMENT

The government is vested in the Lieutenant-Governor, with a Legislative Assembly of 66 members. There is an Executive Council of 18 members. The Legislative Assembly is elected for five years and the state of the parties in June 1994 was: New Democratic Party 53; Progressive Conservative 10; Liberal 3.

*Her Hon. The Lt.-Governor*, The Hon. Sylvia O. Fedoruk
*Premier*, Hon. Roy Romanow, QC

JUDICATURE

*Chief Justice, Court of Appeal*, Hon. E. D. Bayda
*Chief Justice, Queen's Bench*, Hon. D. K. MacPherson
*Chief Judge, Provincial Court*, Hon. B. P. Carey

FINANCE

Consolidated Fund and Heritage combined revenue for year ending March 1994 is C$4,631,800,000 and expenditure C$4,928,142,000.

CAPE VERDE
*República de Cabo Verde*

Cape Verde, off the west coast of Africa, consists of two groups of islands, Windward (Santo Antão, São Vicente, Santa Luzia, São Nicolau, Boa Vista and Sal) and Leeward (Maio, São Tiago, Fogo and Brava) with a total area of 1,557 sq. miles (4,033 sq. km). The population (UN estimate 1991) was 382,000, the majority of whom are Roman Catholic.

CAPITAL – ΨPraia, population (1980) 57,748.
CURRENCY – Escudo Caboverdiano of 100 centavos.
FLAG – Blue with three horizontal stripes of white, red, white near the bottom; over all on these near the hoist a ring of ten yellow stars.
NATIONAL DAY – 5 July (Independence Day).

GOVERNMENT

The islands, colonized c.1460, achieved independence from Portugal on 5 July 1975 under the nationalist party of Guinea Bissau and Cape Verde. A federation of the islands with Guinea Bissau was planned (till 1879 Guinea-Bissau and the islands were a single administrative unit) but this was dropped following the 1980 coup in Guinea Bissau.

The republic was a one-party (the PAICV) state until the constitution was amended in September 1990. Multiparty elections, held in January 1991, were won by the opposition Movement for Democracy (MPD) which won 56 seats in the 79-seat National Assembly. The Independent António Mascarenhas Monteiro was elected as President in February 1991.

HEAD OF STATE
*President*, António Mascarenhas Monteiro, *assumed office*, 22 March 1991

COUNCIL OF MINISTERS *as at August 1994*
*Prime Minister and Minister of Defence*, Carlos Veiga
*Justice*, Pedro Monteiro Freire
*Economic Co-ordination*, José Veiga
*Foreign Affairs*, Manuel Chantre
*Fisheries, Agriculture and Rural Animation*, Helena Semedo
*Infrastructure and Transport*, Teofilo Silva
*Health*, João Medina
*Education and Sport*, Manuel Faustino
*Culture and Communication*, Ondina Ferreira
*Tourism, Industry and Commerce*, João Higino do Rosário
*Employment, Youth and Social Promotion*, José António Mendes
*Presidency of the Council of Ministers*, Mario Silva
*Finance*, Alpio Fernandes

EMBASSY OF THE REPUBLIC OF CAPE VERDE
44 Konninginnegracht, 2514 AD, The Hague,
The Netherlands
Tel: The Hague 3469623
*Ambassador Extraordinary and Plenipotentiary*, new appointment awaited
BRITISH AMBASSADOR, His Excellency Alan E. Furness, CMG, resident at Dakar, Senegal
There is a British Consulate on *São Vicente*.

## ECONOMY

The islands have little rain and agriculture is mostly confined to irrigated inland valleys, the chief products being bananas and coffee (for export), maize, sugarcane and nuts. Fish and shellfish are important exports. Salt is obtained on Sal, Boa Vista and Maio; volcanic rock is also mined for export.

In January 1993 the government announced a programme of reform to institute a change to a market economy and to privatize most industry within four years.

The main ports are Praia and Mindelo, and there is an international airport on Sal.

| Trade with UK | 1992 | 1993 |
|---|---|---|
| Imports from UK | £2,990,000 | £3,539,000 |
| Exports to UK | 409,000 | 123,000 |

## CENTRAL AFRICAN REPUBLIC
*République Centrafricaine*

The Central African Republic lies just north of the Equator between Cameroon, Chad, the southern part of Sudan, and Zaire. The republic has an area of 240,535 sq. miles (622,984 sq. km), and a population (UN estimate 1991) of 3,127,000.

CAPITAL – Bangui, near the border with Zaire, population (1984 estimate) 473,817.
CURRENCY – Franc CFA of 100 centimes.
FLAG – Four horizontal stripes, blue, white, green, yellow, crossed by central vertical red stripe with a yellow five-pointed star in top left-hand corner.
NATIONAL DAY – 1 December.

## GOVERNMENT

On 1 December 1958 the French colony of Ubanghi Shari elected to remain within the French Community and adopted the title of the Central African Republic. It became fully independent on 17 August 1960. The first President of the Central African Republic, David Dacko, held office from 1960 until 1966, when he was replaced by the then Col. Bokassa after a coup d'état. On 4 December 1976, President Bokassa proclaimed himself Emperor and a new constitution was introduced, the country being known as the Central African Empire. On 20 September 1979 Bokassa was deposed by David Dacko in a bloodless coup and the country reverted to a republic.

President Dacko surrendered power in September 1981 to Gen. André Kolingba in a bloodless coup. In September 1985 President Kolingba dissolved the Military Committee for National Recovery (CMRN) and appointed a civilian-dominated cabinet. In November 1986 a referendum was held which approved a new constitution and the establishment of a one-party state.

Strikes and unrest occurred throughout 1991 and 1992 as opposition groupings and unions pressed for multiparty politics. Multiparty presidential and legislative elections were held on 25 October 1992 but were annulled by the Supreme Court due to sabotage and irregularities. President Kolinga formed a coalition government in December 1992 and another in February 1993 in which opposition parties participated. A National Provisional Council for the Republic (CNPRR) was established in February as the transitional legislature to monitor compliance with the constitution during the transition period until presidential and legislative elections were held in August and September 1993. The presidential election was won by Ange-Felix Patasse, whose Central African People's Liberation Party (MPLC) emerged as the largest party in the National Assembly with 34 of the 85 seats. The MPLC formed a coalition government with three other former opposition parties in October 1993.

HEAD OF STATE
*President*, Ange-Felix Patasse, *elected* 19 September 1993

COUNCIL OF MINISTERS *as at August 1994*
*Prime Minister*, Jean-Luc Mandaba
*Finance, Planning and International Co-operation*, Emmanuel Dokouna
*National Defence and War Veterans*, Jean Mette-Yapende
*Interior and National Security*, Jean-Claude Dobanga
*Foreign and Francophone Affairs*, Prof. Simon Bedaya-Ngaro
*Justice and Law Reform*, Jacques Mbosso
*Education, Research and Technology*, Etienne Goyemide
*Public Health and Population*, Zanife Touambona
*Resources and Minerals*, Charles Massi
*Agriculture and Stockbreeding*, Gabriel Badekara
*Water, Forests, Hunting, Fishing, Tourism and Environment*, Martin Gbafolo
*Industry, Commerce and Crafts*, Leon Ododou
*Civil Service, Employment, Social Security and Training*, Fidele Ogbami
*Communication, Post and Telecommunications*, Joseph-Vermond Tehendo
*Transport, Public Works, Housing and Territorial Administration*, Olivier Gabirault
*Youth, Sport, Art and Culture*, Albert Ndode
*Women's Affairs and Social Action*, Marie-Noelle Koyara
*Relations with Parliament*, Gerard Gaba

EMBASSY OF THE CENTRAL AFRICAN REPUBLIC
30 rue des Perchamps, 75016, Paris
Tel: Paris 42244256
*Ambassador Extraordinary and Plenipotentiary*, His Excellency Auguste Magba, apptd 1993

BRITISH AMBASSADOR, His Excellency William Ernest Quantrill, resident at Yaoundé, Cameroon
*Honorary Consul*, A. G. Perreard, PO Box 728, Bangui

## ECONOMY

In an effort to revive an ailing economy, the government launched a structured adjustment programme in 1986, streamlining the civil service, increasing tax revenues, and reducing price controls. The IMF approved a US$23 million credit to support economic reform in March 1994. Cotton, diamonds, coffee and timber are the major exports.

| Trade with UK | 1992 | 1993 |
|---|---|---|
| Imports from UK | £656,000 | £1,487,000 |
| Exports to UK | 100,000 | 53,000 |

## CHAD REPUBLIC
*Republique du Tchad*

Situated in north-central Africa, the Chad Republic extends from 23° to 7° N. latitude and is flanked by Niger and Cameroon on the west, by Libya on the north, by the Sudan on the east and by the Central African Republic on the south. It has an area of 495,755 sq. miles (1,284,000 sq. km) and a population (UN estimate 1991) of 5,819,000.

CAPITAL – Ndjaména, south of Lake Chad (402,000).
CURRENCY – Franc CFA of 100 centimes.
FLAG – Vertical stripes, blue, yellow and red.
NATIONAL DAY – 13 April.

## GOVERNMENT

Chad became a member state of the French Community in 1958, and was proclaimed fully independent on 11 August 1960. The constitution was suspended in April 1975 when President Tombalbaye was killed in a military coup by Gen. Felix Malloum, who was overthrown in February 1979. A Transitional Government of National Unity was replaced in June 1982 by the government of Hissène Habré. Fighting between Chad and Libya over the Aouzou strip was ended by a ceasefire in September 1987 and in September 1990 Chad and Libya presented their territorial claims for the Aouzou strip to the International Court of Justice, which in February 1994 awarded jurisdiction over the whole of the strip to Chad. On 30 may 1994 Libya withdrew the last of its forces, which had occupied the strip since June 1973.

In December 1990 Idriss Déby launched a successful coup and the Habré government fell. Déby announced that he would adopt a multiparty system in Chad and allowed the legalization of an increasing number of political parties in 1991 and 1992. After repeated delays a sovereign national conference was held from January to April 1993. The conference produced a charter which provided for a transitional period of one year in which to write a new constitution and hold multiparty elections. Conference delegates elected a Higher Transitional Council (CST) of 57 members to serve as the transitional legislature and appointed a transitional government in conjunction with President Déby. In April 1994 the CST extended the transitional period by one year to give the President and government sufficient time to organize elections. The CST also adopted an electoral timetable including a constitutional referendum in December 1994, legislative elections in January 1995 and presidential elections in March 1995.

HEAD OF STATE
*President*, Idriss Déby, *took power*, December 1990

TRANSITIONAL GOVERNMENT *as at August 1994*
*Prime Minister*, Dr Kassire Delwa Coumakoye
*National Defence, War Veterans and Victims*, Ali Absakine
*Foreign Affairs*, Ahmat Abderamane Haggar
*Interior and Security*, Abderamane Izzo Miskine
*Justice*, Loum Hinoussou Laina
*Agriculture and Environment*, Mahamat Adoum Kaloboune
*Planning and Co-operation*, Nour Mariam Mahamat
*Public Works and Transport*, Esaie Tchakna
*Civil Service and Labour*, Salibou Garba
*Livestock and Water Resources*, Mahamat Ahmat Soukou
*Communications, Posts and Telecommunications, Government Spokesman*, Koumtog Laoteggue Guelnodji
*Mines, Energy and Petroleum*, Mahamat Garfa
*Economy and Tourism*, Ouardougou Bolou
*Education, Culture, Youth and Sports*, Mahamat Saleh Alabo
*Social and Women's Affairs*, Mamadou Mahamat Regui
*Finance and Computer Science*, Patake Albert Pahimi
*Public Health*, Salomon Ngarbaye Tombalaye
*Government Secretary-General*, Carmele Soukat Ngarmbatina

EMBASSY OF THE REPUBLIC OF CHAD
Boulevard Lambermont 52, 1030 Brussels, Belgium
Tel: Brussels 2151975

*Ambassador Extraordinary and Plenipotentiary*, His Excellency Ramadane Barma, apptd 1994
BRITISH AMBASSADOR, His Excellency William E. Quantrill, resident at Yaoundé, Cameroon
*Honorary Consul*, E. Abtour, BP877, Avenue Charles de Gaulle, Ndjaména

## ECONOMY

About 90 per cent of the workforce is occupied in agriculture, fishing and forestry. There is an oilfield in Kanem and salt is mined around Lake Chad, but the most important activities are cotton growing (mostly in the south) and animal husbandry (in central areas). Raw cotton and meat are the main exports.

| Trade with UK | 1992 | 1993 |
|---|---|---|
| Imports from UK | £1,359,000 | £2,006,000 |
| Exports to UK | 1,604,000 | 1,471,000 |

## CHILE
*República de Chile*

A state of South America lying between the Andes and the shores of the South Pacific, Chile extends coastwise from just north of Arica to Cape Horn, between 17° 15′ and 55° 59′ S. latitude and 66° 30′ and 75° 48′ W. longitude. The extreme length of the country is about 2,800 miles, with an average breadth, north of 41°, of 100 miles. The disputed boundary with Argentina in the Beagle Channel was settled by a treaty ratified in 1985. The total area of Chile is 292,258 sq. miles (756,945 sq. km).

The great chain of the Andes runs along its eastern limit, with a general elevation of 5,000 to 15,000 feet above sea level. The chain lowers considerably towards its southern extremity. There are no rivers of great size, and none of them is of much service as a navigable highway. In the north the country is arid.

Among the island possessions of Chile are the Juan Fernandez group (three islands) about 360 miles distant from Valparaiso. One of these islands is the reputed scene of Alexander Selkirk's (Robinson Crusoe) shipwreck. Easter

Island (27° 8' S. and 109° 28' W.), about 2,000 miles distant in the South Pacific Ocean, contains stone platforms and hundreds of stone figures, the origin of which has not yet been determined. The area of the island is about 45 sq. miles (116.5 sq. km).

POPULATION – The population (UN estimate 1991) is 13,386,000. There are four main groups: indigenous Araucanian Indians, Fuegians, and Changos; Spanish settlers and their descendants; mixed Spanish Indians; and European immigrants. As a result of extensive intermarriage only the few remaining indigenous Indians and some originally Bolivian Indians in the north are racially separate. The main religion is Roman Catholicism.

CAPITAL – Santiago, population (1993 estimate) 5,443,000 (Greater Santiago). Other large towns are: ΨValparaiso (608,000), Concepción (311,000), Temuco (249,000), ΨAntofagasta (110,000), Chillán (79,461), ΨTalcahuano (75,643), Talca (75,354), ΨValdivia (70,000), ΨIquique (50,000), ΨPunta Arenas (50,000). Punta Arenas, on the Straits of Magellan, is the southernmost city in the world.

CURRENCY – Chilean peso of 100 centavos.

FLAG – Two horizontal bands, white, red; in top sixth a white star on blue square, next staff.

NATIONAL ANTHEM – Canción Nacional de Chile.

NATIONAL DAY – 18 September (National Anniversary).

## GOVERNMENT

Chile was discovered by Spanish adventurers in the 16th century and remained under Spanish rule until 1810, when a revolutionary war, culminating in the Battle of Maipu (5 April 1818), achieved the independence of the nation.

At a general election held in September 1970, the Marxist candidate Dr Allende was elected President by a narrow margin. After industrial unrest and widespread violence, Allende was overthrown on 11 September 1973 by leaders of the armed forces and national police.

After a national plebiscite, the constitution of 1925 was replaced early in 1981 and Gen. Pinochet was sworn in as President, to serve until 1989. Pinochet was defeated in a plebiscite in October 1988 regarding his term of office being extended for a further eight years. He resisted calls for his resignation. Another plebiscite in July 1989 was held on changes to the 1981 constitution. Presidential and congressional elections were held in December 1989, beginning the transition to full democracy. Gen. Pinochet remains Commander-in-Chief of the Armed Forces until 1997, before which he cannot be removed under the 1989 constitutional changes unless a two-thirds majority in both chambers of Congress agree to his removal. This has led to continued political friction between the government and armed forces as Pinochet's nine nominees in the Senate and conservative parties ensure he cannot be removed or the constitution changed to remove him, nor can alleged human right abuses by his regime be investigated.

Presidential and legislative elections were held in December 1993. Eduardo Frei won the presidential election and his ruling Coalition for Democracy (centre and centre-left parties) won 70 Chamber of Deputies seats and 22 of the Senate seats. At Frei's wish a joint session of Congress in February 1994 reduced the presidential term from eight to six years with no possibility of re-election.

Executive power is held by the President, legislative power is exercised by a Congress which comprises a Senate of 47 Senators (38 elected and nine appointed) and a Chamber of Deputies of 120 elected members.

Chile is divided into 12 regions and the Metropolitan Area.

HEAD OF STATE

*President of the Republic*, Eduardo Frei Ruíz-Tagle, *elected* 11 December 1993, *sworn in* 11 March 1994

CABINET *as at July 1994*

*Interior*, Germán Correa
*Foreign Affairs*, Carlos Figueroa
*Defence*, Eduardo Perez
*Economy*, Alvaro García
*Finance*, Eduardo Aninat
*Education*, Ernesto Schiefelbein
*Justice*, María Soledad Alvear
*Public Works*, Ricardo Lagos
*Agriculture*, Emiliano Ortega
*National Properties*, Adriana del Piano
*Labour*, Jorge Arrate
*Public Health*, Carlos Massad
*Mining*, Benjamin Teplizky
*Housing*, Edmundo Ilermosilla
*Transport and Communication*, Narciso Irureta
*General Secretary of Government*, Victor Manuel Rebolledo
*General Secretary of Presidency*, Genaro Arriagada
*Central Planning*, Luis Maira
*Business*, Felipe Sandoval
*Women's Affairs*, Josefina Bilbao
*Energy*, Alejandro Jadresic

EMBASSY OF CHILE
12 Devonshire Street, London WIN 2DS
Tel 0171-580 6392
*Ambassador Extraordinary and Plenipotentiary*, His Excellency Herrán Errázuriz, apptd 1993
*Minister-Counsellor*, L. del Solar.
*Military Attaché*, Brig. J. Arangua.
*Counsellor*, F. Hafemann (*Economic*).

BRITISH EMBASSY
Avenae El Bosque Norte 0125
Casilla 72-D, Santiago 9
Tel: Santiago 2239166
*Ambassador Extraordinary and Plenipotentiary*, His Excellency Frank B. Wheeler, CMG, apptd 1993
*Counsellor, Head of Chancery and Consul-General*, P. L. Hunt
*Defence, Naval and Military Attaché*, Capt. R. A. Rowley, OBE, RN
*First Secretary (Commercial)*, J. W. Ayres
BRITISH CONSULAR OFFICES – There are British Consular Offices at *Antofagasta, Arica, Concepción, Santiago, Punta Arenas, Valparaiso.*
BRITISH COUNCIL REPRESENTATIVE – Robin Evans (*Cultural Attaché*), Eliodoro Yañez 832, Casilla 115 Correa 55, Santiago
The Council supplies books to the libraries of the Instituto Chileno-Britanico in *Santiago, Viña del Mar/Valparaiso* and *Concepción.*
BRITISH-CHILEAN CHAMBER OF COMMERCE, Av. Suecia 155-C, Casilla 536, Santiago

## ECONOMY

During the late 1970s and 1980s Chile embraced free market reforms under the military regime, with large-scale privatization and deregulation, and became the most successful economy in Latin America. The economy has grown by 50 per cent in ten years, with economic growth averaging 6 per cent a year in 1989–93. In 1993 inflation was down to 12 per cent from 30 per cent in 1990, unemployment is 4 per cent, and the country has attracted considerable foreign investment.

Cereals, legumes, sugar beet, vegetables, fruit, tobacco, hemp and vines are grown extensively (especially in the central zone) and livestock accounts for nearly 40 per cent of agricultural production. Sheep farming predominates in the extreme south. There are large timber tracts in the central and southern zones of Chile, some types of which are exported, along with wood derivatives such as cellulose and pulp. Industrial-scale fishing makes Chile the fifth largest nation in terms of catch. The principal end product is fish meal.

The mineral wealth is considerable, the country being particularly rich in copper-ore, iron-ore and nitrates and having in the north the only commercial production of nitrate of soda (Chile saltpetre) from natural resources in the world. There are large deposits of high grade sulphur, but mostly around extinct volcanoes in the Andes Cordillera, difficult of access. Oil and natural gas are produced in the Magallanes area from on- and off-shore wells, but domestic production, now declining, covers less than 30 per cent of total oil requirement and imported crude oil is refined at Concon and San Vicente. There is a steel plant at Huachipato, near Concepción.

Provisional production figures for 1993 were:

| | |
|---|---|
| Coal (tonnes) | 1,580,692 |
| Copper (tonnes) | 2,115,936 |
| Crude oil (cu. metres) | 825,100 |
| Natural gas (cu. metres) | 4,136,200 |

Industry is based on the processing of mineral, forestry, fish and agricultural products, and the manufacture of consumer goods.

| FINANCE | 1987 | 1988 |
|---|---|---|
| Total revenue | US$8,469.8 m | US$8,967.1 m |
| Total expenditure | 8,421.6 m | 9,452.4 m |

Foreign debt at 28 February 1994 was US$20,066 million, including Central Bank obligations with the IMF of US$438 million.

TRADE

The principal exports are metallic and non-metallic minerals, timber products, metal products, fish products, vegetables, fruit and wool. The principal imports are sugar and other food products, industrial raw materials, machinery, equipment and spares, oil fuels, lubricants and transportation equipment.

| | 1992 | 1993 |
|---|---|---|
| Total imports | US$10,125.5 m | US$9,416.2 m |
| Total exports | 9,670.2 m | 10,771.4 m |
| *Trade with UK* | 1992 | 1993 |
| Imports from UK | £125,832,000 | £141,773,000 |
| Exports to UK | 205,737,000 | 246,826,000 |

COMMUNICATIONS

Shipping had a virtual monopoly in the coastwide trade, though with the improvement of the roads an increasing share of internal transportation is moving by road and rail.

A railway line (*the Longitudinal*) runs from La Calera, just north of Santiago, to Iquique. Another rail line runs from Valparaiso through La Calera and Santiago to Puerto Montt. With the completion of a section of 435 miles from Corumba, Brazil, to Santa Cruz, Bolivia, the Trans-Continental Line will link the Chilean Pacific port of Arica with Rio de Janeiro on the Atlantic. Another line from Antofagasta to Salta (Argentina) was opened in 1948.

Chile is served by over 20 international airlines. Domestic traffic is carried by Linea Aerea Nacional (LAN) and LADECO, which also operate internationally, and smaller regional carriers.

Chile's road system is about 65,000 kilometres in length.

DEFENCE

Military service is compulsory for one or two years but not all those who are liable are required. Recruitment for the Navy is mostly voluntary, but there are some conscripts.

The total active armed forces strength is 91,800, including 31,000 conscripts. The Army consists of 54,000 personnel (27,000 conscripts) with 170 main battle tanks, 160 light tanks, 200 reconnaissance vehicles, 560 armoured personnel carriers and 160 artillery pieces.

Naval strength is 25,000 (3,000 conscripts) with six destroyers, four frigates, four submarines and 17 patrol and coastal craft together with seven combat aircraft and 21 armed helicopters. There are 3,000 marines and 1,500 coast guard personnel. The Air Force numbers 12,800 personnel (1,000 conscripts) with 117 combat aircraft.

There is a paramilitary Carabineros police force of 31,000 personnel.

EDUCATION

Elementary education is free and compulsory. There are eight universities (three in Santiago, two in Valparaiso, one each in Antofagasta, Concepción and Valdivia).

CULTURE

Spanish is the language of the country, with admixtures of local words of Indian origin. Recent efforts have reduced illiteracy. The Nobel Prize for Literature was awarded in 1945 to Gabriela Mistral, for Chilean verse and prose, and in 1971 to the poet Pablo Neruda. There are over 100 newspapers and a large number of periodicals.

# CHINA
*Zhonghua Renmin Gongheguo – The People's Republic of China*

The area of China is 3,705,408 sq. miles, (9,596,961 sq. km). A nationwide census (the fourth) was held in July 1990, which recorded a total population of 1,130 million. The estimated population for 1992 was 1,171 million.

POPULATION OF THE PROVINCES (1991 estimates)

| | |
|---|---|
| Anhui | 57,610,000 |
| Beijing | 10,940,000 |
| Fujian | 30,790,000 |
| Gansu | 22,850,000 |
| Guangdong | 64,390,000 |
| Guangxi Zhuang Autonomous Region | 43,240,000 |
| Guizhou | 33,150,000 |
| Hainan | 6,740,000 |
| Hebei | 62,200,000 |
| Heilongjiang | 35,750,000 |
| Henan | 87,630,000 |
| Hubei | 55,120,000 |
| Hunan | 62,090,000 |
| Jiangsu | 68,440,000 |
| Jiangxi | 38,650,000 |
| Jilin | 25,090,000 |
| Liaoning | 39,900,000 |
| Nei Monggol Autonomous Region | 21,840,000 |
| Ningxia Hui Autonomous Region | 4,800,000 |
| Qinghai | 4,540,000 |

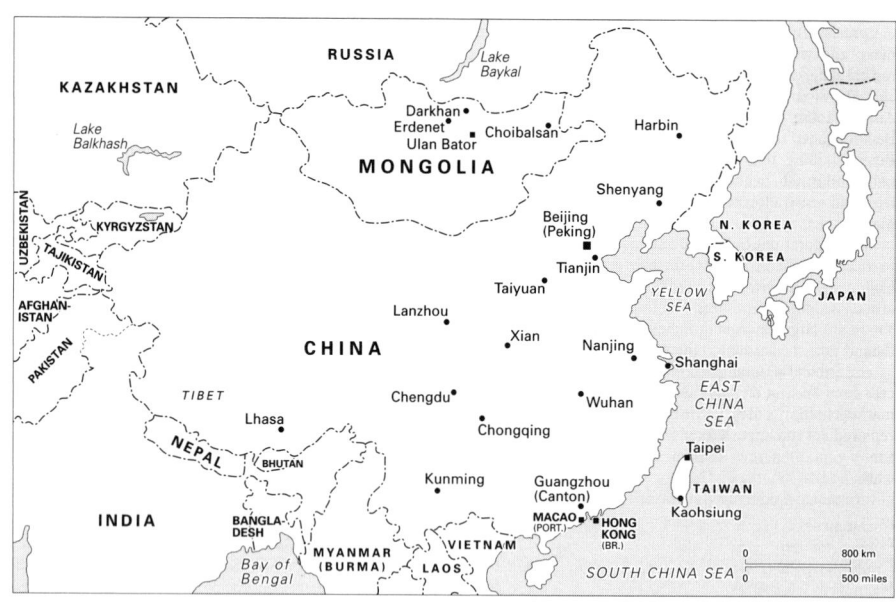

| | | | |
|---|---|---|---|
| Shaanxi | 33,630,000 | | |
| Shandong | 85,700,000 | | |
| Shanghai | 13,400,000 | | |
| Shanxi | 29,420,000 | | |
| Sichuan | 108,970,000 | | |
| Tianjin | 9,090,000 | | |
| Tibet Autonomous Region | 2,260,000 | | |
| Xinjiang Uygur Autonomous Region | 15,550,000 | | |
| Yunnan | 37,820,000 | | |
| Zhejiang | 42,020,000 | | |
| Armed Forces | 2,700,000 | | |

China is anxious to control the growth of the population and has introduced stringent policies intended to result in a population of 1,250 million by the year 2000. About 6 per cent of the population belong to around 55 ethnic minorities. Among the largest are the Zhuang of Guangxi, the Uygurs of Xinjiang, the Tibetans and the Mongols.

CAPITAL – Beijing (Peking), population (metropolitan area, 1990) 10,860,000 (excluding temporary residents).

MAJOR CITIES – Population of major cities in 1989 was:

| | | | |
|---|---|---|---|
| ΨShanghai* | 12,670,000 | Harbin | 2,800,000 |
| Tianjin | 5,700,000 | Chengdu | 2,780,000 |
| Shenyang | 4,500,000 | Xian | 2,710,000 |
| Wuhan | 3,710,000 | Nanjing | 2,470,000 |
| Guangzhou | | Taiyuan | 1,900,000 |
| (Canton) | 3,540,000 | Kunming | 1,500,000 |
| Chongqing | 2,960,000 | Lanzhou | 1,480,000 |

*metropolitan area

CURRENCY – The currency is called Renminbi (RMB). The unit of currency is the yuan of 10 jiao or 100 fen.

FLAG – Red, with large gold five-point star and four small gold stars in crescent, all in upper quarter next staff.

NATIONAL ANTHEM – March of the Volunteers.

NATIONAL DAY – 1 October (Founding of People's Republic).

## GOVERNMENT

China was ruled over by successive imperial dynasties for over 20 centuries until the party of reform forced the Emporer to abdicate on 10 October 1911 and declared a republic. However, the new government, formed by the Chinese National People's Party (the Kuomintang), the emergent Chinese Communist Party (CCP) after 1918, and more traditional factions were unable to provide a central unifying force or philosophy to replace the monarchy and Confucianism, or to agree on the basis for further reform. After the 1911 revolution warlords thrived and in the 1930s Japanese expansionist ambitions were irresistible, so that by the end of the 1930s Japan occupied Manchuria and all the important northern and coastal areas of China. Japan's occupation was ended by its defeat by the allies in 1945.

The Communists' initial co-operation with the Kuomintang ended in 1927, though it was revived by opposition to Japan in the late 1930s, but the Kuomintang government was unable to suppress the CCP. The CCP had successfully politicized the rural population, setting up a 'Soviet Republic' in Kiangsi in the early 1930s, but they were forced out of the area by the Kuomintang and began the 'Long March' to Shenshi in 1934. The Communists established control over large areas of China in the early 1940s and in 1945 succeeded in reoccupying most of the areas which Japan had occupied. Civil war lasted until 1949 when the CPP, led by Mao Zedong (Mao Tse-tung), inaugurated the Chinese People's Republic, and the Kuomintang under Chiang K'ai-shek went into exile in Taiwan. Diplomatic recognition of the People's Republic was accorded by many countries, though others, led by USA, continued to recognize the Chiang Kai-shek regime as the rightful government of China until 1971, when the People's Republic took over China's membership of the United Nations from Taiwan.

### RECENT EVENTS

Following the deaths of Mao Zedong and Zhou En-lai in 1976, the disgraced Deng Xiaoping was recalled and in 1977 was elected Vice-Chairman of the CCP, becoming the dominant force within the party by eliminating leftist influence, rehabilitating fallen leaders and adjusting Maoist policies to permit economic liberalization. The Congresses of 1982 and 1987 reaffirmed Deng's policies, and in 1987 most of the revolutionary generation were replaced in the top posts by younger, more liberal supporters of reform.

Student-led pro-democracy demonstrations throughout April and May 1989 and centred on Tiananmen Square in Beijing, ended on 3–4 June when the army took control of Beijing, killing thousands of protesters. Political control swung into the hands of the hardline elements of the leadership, who adopted policies of recentralization based on Marxist ideology, while simultaneously pledging commitment to reform under the influence of Deng. Deng retired from his last official post as Chairman of the Central Military Commission in November 1989 but is still the ultimate arbiter on policy decisions. At Deng's instigation during 1992 the emphasis again switched to economic reform and the power of the hardline elements went into decline again.

The 14th Party Congress in October 1992 endorsed Deng's calls for faster, bolder economic reforms and his 'socialist market economy'. Most of the remaining conservatives were replaced by moderate economic reformers. However, the summer of 1993 saw the Chinese economy overheating, which led to unrest in the provinces. In July 1993 the government introduced a programme to reduce inflation and growth by cutting government spending and raising interest rates. A degree of central control was reasserted over the free-market coastal regions in an attempt to prevent a repitition of the political unrest of 1989.

Further austerity measures and economic reforms were introduced in November 1993 and January 1994 to combat rising inflation and peasant protests. Most importantly, the central government has raised its proportion of tax revenues from 30 per cent to 60 per cent, reducing the economic influence of provincial governments, who were able to block Beijing's control of the economy.

## CONSTITUTION

A new constitution was adopted in December 1982, under which the National People's Congress is the highest organ of state power. It is elected for a term of five years and is supposed to hold one session a year. It is empowered to amend the constitution, make laws, select the President and Vice-President and other leading officials of the state, approve the national economic plan, the state budget and the final state accounts, and to decide on questions of war and peace. The State Council is the highest organ of the state administration. It is composed of the Premier, the Vice-Premiers, the State Councillors, heads of Ministries and Commissions, the Auditor-General and the Secretary-General. Command over the armed forces is vested in the Central Military Commission.

Deputies to Congresses at the primary level are 'directly elected' by the voters 'through a secret ballot after democratic consultation'. This is now extended to county level. These Congresses elect the deputies to the Congress at the next higher level. Deputies to the National People's Congress are elected by the People's Congresses of the provinces, autonomous regions and municipalities directly under the central government, and by the armed forces.

Local government is conducted through People's Governments at provincial, municipal and county levels. Autonomous regions, prefectures and counties exist for national minorities and are described as self-governing. The system prevailing is that found elsewhere, i.e. People's Congresses and People's Governments. Beijing, Shanghai and Tianjin continue to come directly under the central government.

## HEAD OF STATE

*President of the People's Republic of China,* Jiang Zemin, *elected* April 1993

*Vice President,* Rong Yiren

*Chairman of the Standing Committee of the Eighth National People's Congress,* Qiao Shi

*Chairman of the Central Military Commission,* Jiang Zemin

## STATE COUNCIL *as at August 1994*

*Premier,* Li Peng

*Vice-Premiers,* Qian Qichen; Li Lanqing; Zhu Rongji; Zou Jiahua

*State Councillors,* Li Tieying; Chi Haotian; Song Jian; Li Guixian; Ismail Amat; Peng Peiyun; Luo Gan; Chen Junsheng

## MINISTERS

*Agriculture,* Liu Jiang

*Chemical Industry,* Gu Xiulian

*Civil Affairs,* Doje Cering

*Coal Industry,* Wang Senhao

*Communications,* Huang Zhendong

*Construction,* Hou Jie

*Culture,* Liu Zhongde

*Electronics Industry,* Hu Qili

*Finance,* Liu Zhongli

*Foreign Affairs,* Qian Qichen

*Foreign Trade and Economic Co-operation,* Wu Yi

*Forestry,* Xu Youfang

*Geology and Mineral Resources,* Song Ruixiang

*Internal Trade,* Zhang Haoruo

*Justice,* Xiao Yang

*Labour,* Li Boyong

*Machine Building Industry,* He Guangyuan

*Metallurgical Industry,* Liu Qi

*National Defence,* Chi Haotian

*Personnel,* Song Defu

*Posts and Telecommunications,* Wu Jichuan

*Public Health,* Chen Minzhang

*Public Security,* Tao Siju

*Radio, Film and Television,* Sun Jiazheng

*Railways,* Han Zhubin

*State Security,* Jia Chunwang

*Supervision,* Cao Qingze

*Water Resources,* Niu Maosheng

## MINISTERS IN CHARGE OF STATE COMMISSIONS

*Economics and Trade,* Wang Zhongyu

*Education,* Zhu Kaixuan

*Family Planning,* Peng Peiyun

*Nationalities Affairs,* Ismail Amat

*Physical Culture and Sports,* Wu Shaozu

*Planning,* Chen Jinhua

*Restructuring Economy,* Li Tieying

*Science, Technology and Industry for National Defence,* Ding Henggao

*Science and Technology,* Song Jian

*Auditor-General,* Guo Zhenqian

*Secretary-General,* Luo Gan

*President of the People's Bank of China,* Zhu Rongji

## THE CHINESE COMMUNIST PARTY

*General Secretary,* Jiang Zemin

*Politburo Standing Committee,* Jiang Zemin; Li Peng; Qiao Shi; Li Ruihuan; Zhu Rongji; Liu Huaqing; Hu Jutao

*Politburo of the Central Committee*, Tian Jiyun; Qiao Shi; Jiang Zemin; Li Tieying; Li Ruihuan; Liu Huaqing; Zhu Rongji; Hu Jintao; Ding Guangen; Qian Qichen; Chen Xitong; Jiang Chunyun; Li Lanqing; Wei Jianxing; Wu Bangguo; Xie Fei; Yang Baibing; Zou Jiahua; Li Peng (*full members*); Wen Jiabao; Wang Hanbin (*alternate members*)

*Secretariat of the Central Committee*, Jiang Zemin; Ding Guangen; Hu Jintao; Wei Jiangxing; Ren Jianxin; Wen Jiabao (*full members*)

*Discipline Inspection Commission*, Wei Jianxing (*Secretary*); Xu Qing; Hou Zongbin; Chen Zuolin; Wang Deying (*Deputy Secretaries*)

*Membership*, 52,000,000 (1993)

EMBASSY OF THE PEOPLE'S REPUBLIC OF CHINA
49–51 Portland Place, London WIN 3AH
Tel 0171–636 9375/5726

*Ambassador Extraordinary and Plenipotentiary*, His Excellency Ma Yuzhen, apptd 1991
*Minister-Counsellor*, Lin Zhongming (*Commercial*)
*Defence Attaché*, Maj.-Gen. Han Kaihe
*Cultural Attaché*, Wang Guilin
*Consul-General*, Xiao Houde

BRITISH EMBASSY
11 Guang Hua Lu, Jian Guo Men Wai, Beijing 100 600
Tel: Beijing 5321961/5

*Ambassador*, His Excellency Sir Robin McLaren, KCMG, apptd 1991
*Minister, Consul-General and Deputy Head of Mission*, P. A. McLean
*Counsellors*, N. Cox (*Political*); A. Kerfoot (*Commercial*); Dr T. Craig-Cameron (*Cultural, and British Council Representative*); J. Smith-Laittan (*Head of China Trade Unit*) (resides at Hong Kong)
*Defence, Military and Air Attaché*, Col. K. O. Winfield
There is also a Consulate-General in *Shanghai*.

## ARMED FORCES

All three military arms in China are parts of the People's Liberation Army (PLA). The size of this body has not been formally given, but it is estimated that China has approximately 3,030,000 personnel under arms (1,275,000 conscripts), with a further 12 million (or perhaps many more) reserves who take part in militia activities. Military service for all men between the ages of 18 and 40 is compulsory. Conscripts serve three years in the Army, four years in the Air Force and the Navy. The rank structure, abolished in 1965, was reinstated in 1988.

China has 14 intercontinental and 90 intermediate range land-based, and 12 submarine-launched nuclear ballistic missiles. The Army has a strength of 2,300,000 (around 1,100,000 conscripts), with some 8,000 main battle tanks, 2,000 light tanks, 2,800 armoured personnel carriers and 14,500 artillery pieces. Organization is in ten armoured, five artillery and 78 infantry divisions, together with 30 engineer regiments and one airborne corps.

The Navy has a strength of 260,000 (40,000 conscripts), 47 submarines, 18 destroyers, 38 frigates, 870 patrol and coastal craft, one marine brigade of 5,000 men, 880 combat aircraft and 65 armed helicopters. The Air Force numbers 470,000 (160,000 conscripts) and some 4,970 combat aircraft of mainly Chinese manufacture.

## EDUCATION

The Cultural Revolution of 1966 to 1969 caused considerable disruption to the educational system and since 1976 attempts have been made to raise academic standards. Primary education lasts five years, and enrolment (1991) was 121,642,000 including kindergarten. Secondary education lasts five years (three years in junior middle school and two years in senior middle school). There were 52,268,000 middle school pupils in 1991. There are over 1,000 universities, colleges and institutes with an enrolment (1991) of 2 million students. In May 1985 the Central Committee of the Party announced the abolition of free higher education except for teacher training, and the aim of providing all children with junior secondary education within ten years. There are 220 million illiterates; efforts are being made to expand secondary education, particularly in the rural areas.

## CULTURE

RELIGION – The indigenous religions are Confucianism (which includes ancestor worship), Taoism (originally a philosophy rather than a religion) and, since its introduction in the first century AD, Buddhism. There are also Muslims (officially estimated at about 12 million) and Christians (unofficially estimated at about 50 million). Religious freedoms, severely curtailed during the Cultural Revolution, are reviving slightly under more liberal policies. Ethnic unrest in Buddhist Tibet and Muslim Xinjiang could threaten such liberalization.

LANGUAGE – The Chinese language has many dialects, notably Cantonese, Hakka, Amoy, Foochow, Changsha, Nanchang, Wu (Shanghai) and the northern dialect. The Common Speech or *Putonghua* (often referred to as Mandarin) is based on the northern dialect. The Communists have promoted it as the national language and it is taught throughout the country. As *Putonghua* encourages the use of the spoken language in writing, the old literary style and ideographic form of writing has fallen into disuse.

Since 1956 simplified characters have been introduced to make reading and writing easier and there are now over 2,000 simplified characters in use. In 1956 all Chinese newspapers and most books began to appear with the characters printed horizontally from left to right, instead of reading vertically from right to left, as previously.

In 1958 the National People's Congress adopted a system of romanization, known as pinyin, using 25 of the letters of the Latin alphabet (not v). This has been used within the country largely for assisting schoolchildren and others to learn the pronunciation of characters in *Putonghua*, and is now used for Chinese names in foreign-language publications.

LITERATURE – Chinese literature is one of the richest in the world. Paper has been employed for writing and printing for nearly 2,000 years. The Confucian classics which formed the basis of the traditional Chinese culture date from the Warring States period (fourth to third centuries BC) as do the earliest texts of the rival tradition, Taoism. Histories, philosophical and scientific works, poetry, literary and art criticism, novels and romances survive from most periods. Many have been translated into English. With the spread of literacy in the 20th century, particularly since 1949, traditional literature has been largely superseded by modern works of a popular kind and by the classics of Marxism and modern developments from them.

The most important among the newspapers and magazines are the *People's Daily* and the twice-monthly *Qiushi*, which replaced *Red Flag* as the CCP's mouthpiece in August 1989.

## ECONOMY

In 1982 China set itself the aim of quadrupling the 1980 gross agricultural and industrial output value by the year 2000. The focus of its reform programme was switched to industry in 1984. Reforms have been introduced to make the industrial sector more efficient by narrowing the scope of central planning and broadening enterprise decision-making, material incentives and the role of the market. Since 1984 this has led to an explosion in manufacturing, concentrated in China's coastal regions, where the central government has devolved economic decision-making to provincial governments. Foreign direct investment, especially from Hong Kong and Taiwan, has mushroomed and, with low tax rates and wage levels, enabled the construction of a significant industrial base and transport infrastructure. In the coastal regions the economy has become a free market in all but name, with several stock markets and Shanghai's emergence as a financial centre. China's foreign trade over the past ten years has grown enormously and now it runs a substantial deficit. In 1993-4 the economy has overheated as it grew at 13.4 per cent per year, leading to inflation of 23 per cent in urban areas in 1993.

The latest economic reforms announced in November 1993 in the 'Grand Blueprint' of the Communist Party will effectively make China a market economy over the next few years. The Central Bank is to be reorganized on a Western model; market pricing is to be extended from goods to labour, property and financial markets; small firms are to be privatized and larger ones made joint stock companies or given independent boards; a social security system is to be established and paid for by a tax on wages; a housing market is to be established; and the government is to use macroeconomic instruments, rather than administrative orders, to run the economy. The currency should become fully convertible in 1995.

At present, China is still essentially an agricultural and pastoral country. Agricultural policies designed to give greater incentives to the rural population have meant that the responsibility for agricultural production has been devolved down to individual households, whereas previously work was generally assigned on a collective basis.

Cereals, with peas and beans, are grown in the northern provinces, and rice, tea and sugar in the south. Rice is the staple food of the inhabitants. Cotton (mostly in valleys of the Yangtze and Yellow Rivers), tea (in the west and south), with hemp, jute and flax, are the most important crops. Livestock is raised in large numbers. Silkworm culture is one of the oldest industries. Cottons, woollens and silks are manufactured in large quantities.

The mineral wealth of the country is great. Coal, iron ore, tin, antimony, wolfram, bismuth and molybdenum are abundant. Oil is produced in several northern provinces, particularly in Heilongjiang and Shandong, and off-shore deposits are being sought in co-operation with western and Japanese companies.

The State Statistical Bureau valued the Gross Domestic Product in 1993 at Yuan 3,138 billion, a 13.4 per cent increase over 1992. The total value of agricultural output rose by 4 per cent over the 1992 figure to Yuan 665 billion. The total value of industrial output rose by 21.1 per cent to Yuan 1,416 billion in 1993.

## TRADE

Foreign trade and external economic relations have grown enormously in the past ten years and China now runs a substantial deficit. Total exports in 1993 rose 8 per cent to US$91 billion, while imports rose 29 per cent to US$104 billion. The principal exports are animals and animal products, oil, textiles, ores, metals, tea and manufactured goods. The principal imports are motor vehicles, machinery, chemical fertilizer, plants, aircraft, books, paper and paper-making materials, chemicals, metals and ores, and dyes.

| Trade with UK | 1992 | 1993 |
|---|---|---|
| Imports from UK | £429,865,000 | £739,484,000 |
| Exports to UK | 953,583,000 | 1,327,128,000 |

## COMMUNICATIONS

Over half of the country consists of tableland and mountainous areas where communications and travel are difficult but the communications network now covers most of the country. There are more than 53,400 kilometres of railway lines and some 1,041,100 kilometres of highway (1991). In addition, internal civil aviation has been developed, with routes now totalling more than 471,900 kilometres.

In the past the principal means of communication east to west were by the rivers, the most important of which are the Yangtze (Changjiang) (3,400 miles long), the Yellow River (Huanghe) (2,600 miles long) and the West River (Xihe) (1,650 miles). These, together with the network of canals connecting them, are still much used but their overall importance has declined. Coastal port facilities are being improved and the merchant fleet expanded.

Postal services and telecommunications have been developed in recent years and it is claimed that 95 per cent of all rural townships are on the telephone and that postal routes reach practically every production brigade headquarters.

## TIBET

Tibet is a plateau seldom lower than 10,000 feet, which forms the northern frontier of India (boundary imperfectly demarcated), from Kashmir to Burma, but is separated therefrom by the Himalayas. The area is estimated at 463,000 square miles with a population of 2,260,000 in 1991.

From 1911 to 1950, Tibet was virtually an independent country though its status was never officially so recognized. In October 1950 Chinese Communist forces invaded eastern Tibet. In May 1951 an agreement was reached whereby the Chinese army was allowed entry into Tibet. A Communist military and administrative headquarters was set up. In 1954 the government of India recognized that Tibet was an integral part of China in return for the right to maintain trade and consular representation there.

A series of revolts against Chinese rule over several years culminated in March 1959 in a rising in Lhasa. Fighting continued for several days before the rebellion was suppressed by Chinese troops and military rule imposed. The Dalai Lama fled to India where he and his followers were granted political asylum. In March 1959 the Tibetan government was replaced by the Preparatory Committee for the Tibetan Autonomous Region, originally set up in 1955 with the Dalai Lama as Chairman, which administered Tibet until it became an Autonomous Region of China in September 1965.

In December 1964 the Dalai Lama was declared to be a traitor, and both he and the Panchen Lama were dismissed. This move marked the end of the period of co-operation by the Chinese government with the traditional religious authorities and the eclipse of the latter. The Panchen Lama was rehabilitated as an official of the CPPCC, but died in 1989. The Chinese have invited the Dalai Lama to return from exile, but suggested negotiations between the Chinese and the Dalai Lama have failed to materialize. Martial law was declared in Tibet in 1989 after serious unrest, and sporadic outbursts of unrest continue, the most recently in May 1993. The Dalai Lama was awarded the Nobel Peace Prize in 1990.

## COLOMBIA
*República de Colombia*

Colombia lies in the extreme north-west of South America, having a coastline on both the Caribbean Sea and Pacific Ocean. It is situated between 4° 13′ S. to 12° 30′ N. latitude and 68° to 79° W. longitude, with an area of 440,714 sq. miles (1,141,748 sq. km).

The country is divided into a coastal region in the north and west and extensive plains in the east by the Cordillera de los Andes. The eastern range of the Colombian Andes consists of a series of vast tablelands. This temperate region is the most densely peopled portion of the country. The principal rivers are the Magdalena, Guaviare, Cauca, Atrato, Caquetá, Putumayo and Patia.

POPULATION – The population (UN estimate 1991) is 33,613,000. The language is Spanish and Roman Catholicism is the established religion.

CAPITAL – Bogotá, population (1990 estimate) 5,000,000. Other centres are Medellin (2,400,000); Cali (1,800,000); ΨBarranquilla (1,400,000); ΨCartagena (700,000), the major port on the Caribbean; Bucaramanga (350,000); ΨBuenaventura (130,000), the major port on the Pacific.

CURRENCY – Colombian peso of 100 centavos.

FLAG – Broad yellow band in upper half, surmounting equal bands of blue and red.

NATIONAL ANTHEM – Oh gloria inmarcesible.

NATIONAL DAY – 20 July (National Independence Day).

## GOVERNMENT

The Colombian coast was visited in 1502 by Columbus, and in 1536 a Spanish expedition under Jiménez de Quesada penetrated to the interior and established a government. The country remained under Spanish rule until the revolt of the Spanish-American colonies of 1810–24. In 1819 Simón Bolívar (1783–1831) established the Republic of Colombia, consisting of the territories now known as Colombia, Panama, Venezuela and Ecuador. In 1829–30 Venezuela and Ecuador withdrew from the association of provinces, and in 1831 the remaining territories were formed into the Republic of New Granada. The name was changed to the Granadine Confederation in 1858, to the United States of Colombia in 1861 and to the Republic of Columbia in 1866. In 1903 Panama seceded from Colombia and became a separate republic.

During the early 1950s Colombia suffered a period of virtual civil war between the supporters of the traditional political parties, the Conservatives and the Liberals. From 1957 to 1974 the country was governed under the 'National Front' agreement with the presidency alternating between the two parties every four years and ministerial posts being shared equally by the parties. The alternation of the presidency ended in 1974 and parity in appointments in 1978. Thereafter, the constitution lays down that government portfolios and administrative appointments shall be divided among the two majority parties in Congress in an adequate and equitable manner.

Elections to a constitutional convention were held in November 1990, in which the former guerrilla movement M19 gained 30 per cent of the vote and a new constitution was promulgated in July 1991. Congressional elections to the Senate and House of Representatives were last held on 13 March 1994 and saw the re-emergence of the traditional parties. The Liberal Party won 89 out of 163 House of Representative seats, with the Social Conservative Party (PSC) winning 56 seats and M19 two seats. In the Senate elections the Liberal Party won 52 out of 102 seats, the PSC 21 seats and M19 one seat. In the second round of the presidential election on 19 June 1994 the Liberal candidate Ernesto Samper narrowly defeated the PSC candidate.

INSURGENCY

Colombia is dogged by insurgency from left-wing guerrillas and from the drugs cartels now centred on Cali. Over the 1989–94 period the government has reached peace agreements with four left-wing guerrilla groups, including M19 and in April 1994 the Current of Socialist Revolution (CRS), and these guerrillas have disarmed. The National Liberation Army (ELN) and the Revolutionary Armed Forces of Columbia (FARC) groups remain active and disrupted the 1994 elections. The security threat from the Medellin drugs cartel has effectively been defeated with the death of Pablo Escobar, the cartel leader, in December 1993. The Cali cartel remains strong. In November 1992 a state of emergency was introduced after FARC guerrillas killed over 100 people and peace talks suspended in March 1992 have not restarted.

HEAD OF STATE
*President*, Dr Ernesto Samper-Pizano, *elected*, 19 June 1994

CABINET *as at July 1994*

*Interior*, Fabío Villegas Ramirez
*Foreign Affairs*, Noení Sanin Posada
*Finance and Public Credit*, Rudolf Hommes Rodríguez
*Justice*, Andrés González
*National Defence*, Rafael Pardo Rueda
*Transport*, Jorge Bendeck Olivella
*Labour and Social Security*, José Elias Melo-Acosta
*Agriculture*, José Antonio Ocampo
*Health*, Juan Luis Londoño
*Mines and Energy*, Guido Nule Amin
*Communications*, William Jarmillo Gómez
*National Education*, Maruja Pachón de Villamizar
*Economic Development*, Mauricio Cardenas
*Foreign Trade*, Juan Manuel Santos Calderón

COLOMBIAN EMBASSY
Flat 3A, 3 Hans Crescent, London SWIX OLR
Tel 0171–589 9177/5037

*Ambassador Extraordinary and Plenipotentiary*, His
  Excellency Luis Prieto-Ocampo, apptd 1993

BRITISH EMBASSY
Torre Propaganda Sancho, Calle 98 No. 9–03 Piso 4,
Bogotá
Tel: Bogota 2185111

Ambassador Extraordinary and Plenipotentiary, His
  Excellency Arthur L. Coltman, apptd 1994

There are British Consular Offices at *Barranquilla, Bogotá,
  Cali* and *Medellin*.

BRITISH COUNCIL REPRESENTATIVE, W. Campbell,
  Calle 87 No. 12–79, Bogotá DE
COLOMBO-BRITISH CHAMBER OF COMMERCE, Apartado
  Aereo 054 728, Calle 106 No. 25-41, Bogotá DE

DEFENCE

The Colombian armed forces have been occupied in recent years in fighting the armed groups of the Medellin and Cali drugs cartels and some 5,000 remaining active guerrillas. The total active strength of the armed forces is 140,000 personnel (40,000 conscripts). Service is compulsory and lasts between one and two years.

The Army's strength is some 120,000 (38,000 conscripts) with 12 light tanks, 124 reconnaissance vehicles, 155 armoured personnel carriers and 130 artillery pieces. The Navy, with 13,000 personnel including 8,000 marines and 500 conscripts, has five frigates, 26 patrol and coastal craft and two submarines. The Air Force, with 7,000 personnel (1,900 conscripts), has a strength of 92 combat aircraft and 61 armed helicopters. There is also a paramilitary police force of 85,000 personnel.

## ECONOMY

Much of Colombia's natural resources in coal, natural gas and hydro-electricity are largely unexploited. Development of coal is being given priority but no new hydro projects are likely to be started for the next four to five years. Annual coal production is about 12.5 million tonnes, essentially for export. Proven coal reserves stand at 16,000 million tonnes. Estimated natural gas reserves are 3,788,000 million cu. ft, with daily use at 381,772 million BTU. Proven crude oil reserves stand at 2,000 million barrels. Colombia is again a net exporter of oil. In 1991 exports averaged 472,000 b.p.d. In 1993 large oil reserves were found under the eastern plains which are estimated to be worth US$3 billion per year when exploited.

The hydrocarbon sector accounts for over half of the mining output with precious metals (gold, platinum and silver) and iron ore accounting for the remainder. Other mineral deposits include nickel (a processing plant started operating in 1982), bauxite, copper, gypsum, limestone, phosphates, sulphur and uranium. Colombia is also the world's largest producer of emeralds and has deposits of other precious and semi-precious stones.

Because of the range of climate, a wide variety of crops can be grown, and the country is close to self-sufficiency in food. The principal agricultural product is coffee and other major cash crops are sugar, bananas, cut flowers and cotton. Cattle are raised in large numbers, and meat and cured skins and hides are also exported.

The government has encouraged diversification to reduce dependence on coffee as the major export and this has led to the growth of new export-orientated industries, particularly textiles, paper products and leather goods. Stimulus to the economy has been provided by loans from the World Bank and IADB for project development, particularly in the power sector (in which hydroelectric projects have predominated) and for telecommunications.

Since the late 1980s the government has introduced trade liberalization and privatization measures which have effectively freed foreign exchange transactions, increased foreign competition, ended protectionism and brought down inflation. In 1993 GDP growth was 5 per cent and unemployment 8 per cent.

### TRADE

Colombia's principal exports are petroleum and derivatives, coffee, bananas, cut flowers, clothing and textiles, ferro-nickel and coal. Principal trading partners are USA, the EC and Latin America.

| Trade with UK | 1992 | 1993 |
|---|---|---|
| Imports from UK | £75,340,000 | £104,592,000 |
| Exports to UK | 126,097,000 | 176,094,000 |

## COMMUNICATIONS

The Andes make surface transport difficult so air transport is used extensively. There are daily air services between Bogotá and all the principal towns, as well as daily services to the USA, frequent services to other countries in South America, and to Europe. The 'Atlantic Railway' links the departmental lines running down to the River Magdalena, and completes the connection between Bogotá and Santa Marta. Although the railways are in a poor state, there are about 2,600 miles of rail in use at present. The total road network (1985) consists of 105,201 km of roads of all types, of which 21,800 km are classified as main trunk and transversal roads.

Large appropriations have been made for modernization of the country's telecommunication system. There are 485 radio stations (1983) and three national television channels with several regional ones.

## CULTURE

State education is free. Great efforts have been made in reducing illiteracy and estimates (1990) put the literacy rate at 87 per cent of those over ten years of age. In addition to the National University with headquarters at Bogotá there are 26 other universities. There is a flourishing press in urban areas and a national literature supplements the rich inheritance from the time of Spanish colonial rule.

# THE COMOROS
*Republique Fédérale Islamique des Comores*

The Comoro archipelago includes the islands of Great Comoro, Anjouan, Mayotte and Moheli and certain islets in the Indian Ocean with an area of 838 sq. miles (2,171 sq. km) and a population (UN estimate 1991) of 570,000, most of whom are Muslim.

CAPITAL – Moroni, on Great Comoro (pop. 17,267).
CURRENCY – Comorian franc of 100 centimes. The Comoros also use the Franc CFA of 100 centimes.
FLAG – Green with a white crescent and four white stars in the centre, tilted towards the lower fly.
NATIONAL DAY – 6 July (Independence Day).

## GOVERNMENT

The islanders voted for independence from France in December 1974 and three islands became independent on 6 July 1975. The island of Mayotte was against independence and has remained under French administration.

A new constitution was adopted by referendum in 1992 which provides for a President directly elected for a five-year term which is renewable once only; an elected 42-member legislative assembly with a four-year term; a 15-member Senate (five from each island) chosen by an electoral college for six-year terms; and the appointment of a Prime Minister from the largest party in the legislative assembly. On 10 May 1992 President Djohar appointed a government of national unity to govern until elections were held in November. These, however, proved inconclusive and the instability following an uprising by rebel soldiers in October 1992 continued. President Djohar appointed two governments during the course of 1993 but instability continued until another legislative election was held in December 1993. This was marked by violence and allegations of rigging but brought stability as President Djohar's RDR party gained an absolute majority with 22 out of 42 seats.

Each island is administered by a Governor, assisted by up to four Commissioners whom he appoints, and has an elected Legislative Council.

### HEAD OF STATE
*President*, Said Mohamed Djohar, *sworn in* 20 March 1990

GOVERNMENT *as at July 1994*
*Prime Minister and Public Services*, Mohamed Abdou Madi
*Interior and Decentralization*, Ahmed Houmadi
*Finance and Budget*, Ahmed el Harif Hamidi
*Foreign Affairs and Co-operation*, Said Mohammed Sagaf
*Economy, Industry, Crafts and Planning*, Ahmed Bourhane
*Public Works, Urbanization, Housing and Energy*, Moussa
  Toybou
*Production*, Idarousse Athoumane.
*National Education and Teaching*, Ibrahim Hissani
*Public Health*, Attoumane Boinaissa
*Transport and Tourism*, Ahmed Said Issilam
*Justice and Islamic Affairs*, Mouslim Ben Moussa
*Information, Culture, Youth, Sport, Posts and*
  *Telecommunications, Government Spokesman and*
  *Relations with Parliament*, Houmed Mdahoma M'Saidie
*Social Affairs, Employment and Labour*, Sittou Raghadat
  Mohammed

BRITISH AMBASSADOR, His Excellency Peter Smith,
  resident at Antananarivo, Madagascar

BRITISH CONSULATE
PO Box 986, Moroni
*Honorary Consul*, J. de Jaeger

ECONOMY

The most important products are vanilla, copra, cloves and
essential oils, which are the principal exports; cacao, sisal and
coffee are also cultivated. Great Comoro is well forested and
produces some timber.

| Trade with UK | 1992 | 1993 |
|---|---|---|
| Imports from UK | £279,000 | £440,000 |
| Exports to UK | 194,000 | 8,000 |

## CONGO
*République du Congo*

The Congo lies on the Equator between Gabon on the west
and Zaire on the east, the River Congo and its tributary the
Ubangui forming most of the eastern boundary of the state.
It has a short Atlantic coastline. The area of the Republic of
Congo is 132,047 sq. miles (342,000 sq. km), with a
population of 2,346,000 (UN estimate 1991).

CAPITAL – Brazzaville (600,000); Ψ Pointe Noire
(350,000).
CURRENCY – Franc CFA of 100 centimes.
FLAG – Divided diagonally into green, yellow and red
bands.
NATIONAL DAY – 15 August.

GOVERNMENT

Formerly the French colony of Middle Congo, the Congo
became a member state of the French Community on 28
November 1958 and fully independent on 17 August 1960.
In 1968, conduct of affairs was assumed by a National
Council of army officers. The Parti Congolais du Travail
(PCT) was created in 1969 and the People's Republic of the
Congo was established. After popular pressure, the PCT
abandoned its monopoly of power and renounced Marxism
in July 1990. A transitional government was formed in
January 1991 and a national conference convened in February.
The national conference suspended the constitution, strip-
ping President Sassou-Nguesso of all powers and forming
itself into the Higher Council of the Republic (CSR). In

December 1991 the CSR adopted a new multiparty constitution with a directly-elected President and bicameral parliament, the President appointing the Prime Minister from the
majority party in parliament. The new constitution was
approved by a referendum in March 1992 and a transitional
government formed in May 1992 to govern the country until
the presidential and legislative elections in July and August
1992. The PCT was heavily defeated by the Pan-African
Union for Social Democracy (UPADS), which emerged as
the largest party in both the Senate and the National
Assembly.
  In September 1992 President Lissouba appointed a
coalition government, but this failed to gain a majority in the
National Assembly and was brought down by the PCT-led
opposition in November. To break the deadlock, Lissouba
called fresh elections which were held in May and June 1993
and won by the UPADS. The results were disputed by
opposition groups and violence broke out between the armed
forces and armed supporters of the URD-PCT opposition
alliance. Agreement was reached in August on a rerun of 11
seats in the 125-seat National Assembly, the majority of
which were won by the URD-PCT. With UPADS still
retaining a parliamentary majority, fighting between the
armed forces and URD-PCT militias again broke out in
November and lasted until February 1994, when it was
agreed to call in an international panel to examine the 1993
election results.

HEAD OF STATE
*President*, Pascal Lissouba, *elected* 16 August 1992

CABINET *as at July 1994*
*Prime Minister*, Jacques-Joachim Yhombi Opango
*Minister of State, Development*, Claude Dacosta
*Minister of State, Socio-Cultural Development*, Maurice-
  Stephane Bongho-Nouarra
*Minister of State, Interior, Security, Regional Development*,
  Martin M'Beri
*Minister of State, National Defence*, Gen. Raymond Ngollo
*Minister of State, Justice and Administration*, Aime Matsika
*Foreign and Francophone Affairs and Co-operation*, Benjamin
  Bounkoulou
*Economy and Finance*, N'Guila Moungounga Nkombo
*Planning*, Clement Mouamba
*Communications, Posts, Telecommunications and Government*
  *Spokesman*, Albertine Massala
*Industrial Development, Mines and Energy*, Jean Itadi
*Equipment and Public Works*, Lambert Galibali
*Agriculture and Animal Husbandry*, Gregoire Lefouoba
*Civil Service and Administrative Reform*, Jean-Prosper Koyo
*Transport and Civil Aviation*, Maurice Mouamba
*Commerce and Small and Medium-sized Enterprises*, Marius
  Mouambenga
*Health and Social Welfare*, Jean-Roger Ekoundzola
*Labour and Social Security*, Anachet Tsomambet
*Hydraulic Resources*, Benoit Koukebene
*Tourism and Environment*, François Tchitchele
*Water, Forestry and Fisheries*, Rigobert Ngouolali
*Education*, Noutete Tangui
*Human Rights*, Gabriel Matsiola

EMBASSY OF THE REPUBLIC OF CONGO
37 bis rue Paul Valery, 75116 Paris, France
Tel: Paris 45006057

*Ambassador Extraordinary and Plenipotentiary*, His
  Excellency Alphonse Niangoula, apptd 1993

HONORARY CONSULATE, Livingstone House, 11 Carteret
Street, London SW1H 9DJ. Tel: 0171-222 7575. *Honorary
Consul and Head of Mission*, L. Muzzu

BRITISH CHARGÉ D'AFFAIRS, (resident in Zaire)
There is an Honorary Consulate in *Pointe Noire.*

## ECONOMY

Congo has its own oil deposits, producing about 8 million tonnes annually. It also produces lead, zinc and gold. The principal agricultural products are timber, cassava, sugar cane and yams. Imports are mainly of machinery.

| Trade with UK | 1992 | 1993 |
|---|---|---|
| Imports from UK | £8,680,000 | £12,408,000 |
| Exports to UK | 2,813,000 | 4,807,000 |

---

## COSTA RICA
*República de Costa Rica*

---

Costa Rica extends across the Central American isthmus between 8° 17′ and 11° 10′ N. latitude and from 82° 30′ to 85° 45′ W. longitude. It has an area of 19,575 sq. miles (50,700 sq. km). The republic lies between Nicaragua and Panama, and between the Caribbean Sea and the Pacific Ocean. The coastal lowlands have a tropical climate but the interior plateau, with a mean elevation of 4,000 feet, enjoys a temperate climate.

POPULATION – The population (1991 estimate) is 3,064,000, mainly of European origin. The language is Spanish.

CAPITAL – San José, population (estimate 1989) 1,068,206; Alajuela (519,351); Cartago (328,259); Heredia (235,700); Guanacaste (234,962); ΨPuntarenas (326,163); ΨLimón (209,731). (Populations are of provinces, cantons and districts.)

CURRENCY – Costa Rican colón (₡) of 100 céntimos.

FLAG – Five horizontal bands, blue, white, red, white, blue (the red band twice the width of the others with emblem near staff).

NATIONAL ANTHEM – Himno Nacional de Costa Rica.

NATIONAL DAY – 15 September.

## GOVERNMENT

For nearly three centuries (1530–1821) Costa Rica was part of the Spanish American dominions. In 1821 the country obtained its independence, although from 1824 to 1839 it was one of the United States of Central America.

On 1 December 1948, the Army was abolished, the President declaring it unnecessary. Executive power is vested in the President, who is head of state and government, with legislative power vested in the 57-member Legislative Assembly. Under the constitution both the President and the members of the Legislative Assembly are elected for a single four-year term and may not be re-elected. The main political parties are the Social Christian Unity Party (PUSC) and the National Liberation Party (PLN). The last presidential and legislative elections were held on 6 February 1994 when PLN candidate José Maria Figueres won the presidential election, and the PLN won 28 seats and the PUSC 25 seats in the Legislative Assembly.

HEAD OF STATE
*President,* José Maria Figueres Olsen, *took office,* 8 May 1994
*Vice-Presidents,* Rodrigo Oreamuno; Sandra Piszk

MINISTERS *as at August 1994*

*Minister for the Presidency,* Elias Soley
*Foreign Affairs,* Dr Fernando Naranjo

*Interior,* Maureen Clarke
*Justice,* Enrique Castillo
*Finance,* Fernando Herrero
*Agriculture,* Marío Carvajal
*Economy, Industry and Commerce,* Marcos Vargas
*Foreign Trade,* Jose Rossi
*Environment,* Rene Castro
*Rural Development,* Roberto Solorzano
*Special Projects,* Dr Longino Soto
*National Co-ordination,* Sergio Quiros
*Public Works and Transport,* Bernardo Arce
*Education,* Marvin Herrera
*Health,* Dr German Weinstoke
*Culture, Youth and Sports,* Arnoldo Mora
*Labour,* Farid Ayales
*Planning,* Leonardo Garnier
*Housing,* Edgar Arroyo
*Security,* Juan Diego Castro
*Science and Technology,* Roberto Dobles
*Information,* Florisabel Rodriguez
*Tourism,* Carlos Roesch

COSTA RICAN EMBASSY
2nd Floor, 36 Upper Brook Street, London W1Y 1PE
Tel 0171-495 3985
*Ambassador Extraordinary and Plenipotentiary,* new appointment awaited

BRITISH EMBASSY
Apartado 815, Edificio Centro Colon (11th Floor), San José 1007
Tel: San José 215566
*Ambassador Extraordinary and Plenipotentiary and Consul-General,* Her Excellency Mary Louise Croll, apptd 1992

## ECONOMY

Agriculture is the chief industry and the principal products are coffee, bananas, sugar and cattle (for meat). Other crops are cocoa, rice, maize, potatoes, hemp, pineapple, casava, ginger, chaw chaw, melon and flowers. Industrial activity is principally in the manufacturing sector and manufactured goods include foodstuffs, textiles and clothing, plastic goods, pharmaceuticals, fertilizers and electrical equipment. Tourism is of growing importance and became the main source of foreign exchange revenue in 1992.

| FINANCE | 1993 |
|---|---|
| Revenue | ₡168,000m |
| Expenditure | 187,000m |

TRADE
The chief exports are manufactured goods and other products, coffee, bananas, cocoa and sugar. The chief imports are machinery, including transport equipment, manufactures, chemicals, fuel and mineral oils and foodstuffs.

| | 1992 | 1993 |
|---|---|---|
| Total imports | US$2,461.7m | US$2,936.8m |
| Total exports | 1,828.4m | 2,064.3m |

| Trade with UK | 1992 | 1993 |
|---|---|---|
| Imports from UK | £28,774,000 | £18,473,000 |
| Exports to UK | 17,559,000 | 41,286,000 |

## COMMUNICATIONS

The chief ports are Limón on the Atlantic coast, through which passes most of the coffee exported, and Caldera on the Pacific coast, currently under construction. The railway system is nationalized. About 500 miles of railroad are open.

LACSA is the national airline, operating flights throughout Central and South America, the Caribbean and USA, besides internal flights to local airports by SANSA.

## CÔTE D'IVOIRE
*République de Côte d'Ivoire*

Côte d'Ivoire is situated on the Gulf of Guinea between 5° and 10° N. latitude and 3° and 8° W. longitude. It is flanked on the west by Guinea and Liberia, on the north by Mali and Burkina, and on the east by Ghana. It has an area of 124,503 sq. miles (322,463 sq. km). The climate is equatorial in the south and west, which are mainly forested; tropical in the centre and east, which are savannah regions with trees; dry and tropical in the north, which is a grassy savannah region. The population of 12,464,000 (UN estimate 1991) is divided into a large number of ethnic and tribal groups. The official language is French. Some 39 per cent of the population is Muslim, 28 per cent Christian (mainly Roman Catholic) and 17 per cent maintain traditional beliefs.

CAPITAL – Yamoussoukro has been the political and administrative capital since 1983. The economic and financial capital remains Abidjan (population 3,500,000), which is also the largest city and main port.
CURRENCY – Franc CFA of 100 centimes.
FLAG – Three vertical stripes, orange, white and green.
NATIONAL ANTHEM – L'Abidjanaise.
NATIONAL DAY – 7 December.

### GOVERNMENT

Although French contact was made in the first half of the 19th century, Côte d'Ivoire became a colony only in 1893 and was finally pacified in 1912. It decided on 5 December 1958 to remain an autonomous republic within the French Community; full independence outside the Community was proclaimed on 7 August 1960.

Côte d'Ivoire has a presidential system of government modelled on that of the United States and the French Fifth Republic. The single-chamber National Assembly has 175 members. Although the constitution provides for a multiparty system, it was not until May 1990 that any party other than the ruling PDCI party was authorized. The PDCI won multiparty elections held in November 1990 amid allegations of electoral fraud; opposition protests continue. After having been President since independence in 1960, President Houphouët-Boigny died on 7 December 1993 and was replaced as President by the parliamentary speaker Henri Konan-Bédié who will serve until new elections in October 1995.

HEAD OF STATE
*President*, Henri Konan-Bédié, *took office* 7 December 1993

CABINET *as at August 1994*
*Prime Minister, Minister of Economy and Finance*, Daniel Kablan Duncan
*Relations with Parliament*, Ahoua N'Guetta Timothee
*National Integration*, Laurent Dona-Fologo
*Defence*, Leon Konan Koffi
*Foreign Affairs*, Amara Essy
*Interior*, Emile Constant Bombet
*Justice*, Faustin Kouame
*Higher Education and Scientific Research*, Salíou Toure
*Agriculture and Animal Resources*, Lambert Kouassi Konan
*Raw Materials*, Alain Gauze

*National Education*, Píerre Kipre
*Environment and Tourism*, Lancine Gon Coulibaly
*Industry and Commerce*, Ferdinard Kacou Angora
*Mines and Energy*, Mohamed Lamine Fadika
*Health and Social Affairs*, Maurice Kakou Guikahue
*Communication*, Daniele Boni-Claverie
*Equipment, Transport and Telecommunciations*, Ezan Akele
*Construction and Town Planning*, Albert Kakou Tiapani
*Employment and Civil Service*, Achi Atsain
*Security*, Gaston Ouassenan Kone
*Culture*, Bernard Zadi Zaourou
*Women and the Family*, Albertine Gnanazan Hipie
*Youth and Sports*, Komenan Zakpa

EMBASSY OF THE REPUBLIC OF CÔTE D'IVOIRE
2 Upper Belgrave Street, London SW1X 8BJ
Tel 0171–235 6991
*Ambassador Extraordinary and Plenipotentiary*, His Excellency Gervais Yao Attoungbre, apptd 1989

BRITISH EMBASSY
Immeuble Les Harmonies, 01 BP 2581, Abidjan 01
Tel: Abidjan 226850

*Ambassador Extraordinary and Plenipotentiary*, Her Excellency Margaret I. Rothwell, CMG, apptd 1990
*Deputy Head of Mission, First Secretary (Commercial), Consul*, D. R. Flanagan

### ECONOMY

Côte D'Ivoire became wealthy in the 1970s because of the high prices of its two principal export earners, coffee and cocoa. Since 1987, however, the economy has shrunk considerably as its exports have deteriorated in competitiveness and its rivals have devalued their currencies while the franc CFA has remained pegged to the French franc. In March 1994 Côte D'Ivoire had a relatively large foreign debt for US$15,600m incurred by the infastructure programmes of the 1970s and 1980s. An economic reform programme for the 1994–6 period has received US$467m in credit support from the IMF.

The principal exports are coffee, cocoa, timber, palm oil, rubber, pineapples, bananas, and cotton. There are a few deposits of diamonds and minerals including manganese and iron.

|  | 1988 | 1989 |
|---|---|---|
| Imports | US$1,907m | US$1,781m |
| Exports | 2,354m | 2,588m |

| *Trade with UK* | 1992 | 1993 |
|---|---|---|
| Imports from UK | £29,480,000 | £33,411,000 |
| Exports to UK | 53,022,000 | 67,424,000 |

## CROATIA

Croatia is bounded by Slovenia, Hungary, the rump Federal Yugoslav state and Bosnia-Hercegovina; it includes the Adriatic coastline of Istria and Dalmatia and has an area of 21,823 sq. miles (56,538 sq. km). It is divided into three major geographic regions: the Pannonían region in the north has a moderate continental climate with abundant arable land and forests and is traversed by the Sava, Drava and Danube rivers. The central mountain belt has three main plateaus with areas of forest and grazing land. The Adriatic coast region has 1,185 islands and islets and 1,104 miles (1,778 km) of coastline. It has a sunny, Mediterranean climate with arable land in the hinterland areas.

POPULATION – The population (1991 census) was 4,760,344, of which some 78 per cent were ethnic Croats, 12 per cent ethnic Serbs, 2 per cent Yugoslavs and 1 per cent Muslims. The remaining minorities were Hungarians, Italians, Albanians, Czechs, Ukrainians and Jews. Croatia is host to some 500,000 refugees from Bosnia-Hercegovina.

About 77 per cent of the population is Roman Catholic, 11 per cent Serbian Orthodox and 1 per cent Muslim. The majority language is Croatian in the Latin script. Ethnic Serbs use Serbian in the Cyrillic script.

CAPITAL – Zagreb, population (1991 estimate) 950,000.
  Other major cities are Split (200,000), Rijeka (200,000) and Osijek (160,000).
CURRENCY – Kuna of 100 lipas.
FLAG – Three horizontal stripes of red, white, blue, with the national arms over all in the centre.
NATIONAL ANTHEM – Lijepa naša domovina (Our Beautiful Homeland).
NATIONAL DAY – 30 May (Statehood Day).

## HISTORY

Croatia was part of the Austro-Hungarian Empire from 1526 to 1918. On 29 October 1918 the Croatian parliament declared Croatia independent and soon after Croatia joined with Slovenia, Bosnia-Hercegovina, Serbia and Montenegro to form the 'Kingdom of Serbs, Croats and Slovenes' (renamed Yugoslavia in 1929). Independence was confirmed and accepted by the Allied Powers at Versailles in 1919. From 1941 to 1945 Yugoslavia was occupied by the Axis powers, with Italy and Hungary annexing parts of Croatia and a pro-Nazi Croat puppet state being established in the remainder of Croatia and Bosnia-Hercegovina. The armed extremists of this puppet state, known as Ustashe, engaged in fierce fighting with Serbian royalists and Communist partisans, together with pro-Allied Croat partisans, leaving a bitterness that has re-emerged 46 years later.

At the end of the war Yugoslavia was re-established as a federal republic under Communist rule but following the death of the wartime partisan leader Josep Tito in 1980 Yugoslavia gradually disintegrated. Efforts by the federal presidency and international mediators to end intercommunal conflict and negotiate a new federal or confederal structure for the country failed in 1991. On 25 June 1991 Slovenia and Croatia both informed Belgrade of their independence from Yugoslavia. Fighting began immediately as the Federal Yugoslav Army (JNA) intervened against local defence forces to prevent the disintegration of the federation.

Croatia contained an ethnic Serb minority comprising 12 per cent of the population. These ethnic Serbs, with JNA support, refused to accept Croatia's independence and formed themselves into armed groups. Fighting erupted in July 1991 between Croat defence forces and armed Serbs, and by September 1991 had escalated into war between Croatia and Serbia, which had taken over control of the JNA.

The war in Croatia continued until January 1992 when the EC and the UN were able to bring about a ceasefire that held. The JNA and Serb forces had secured control of virtually all ethnic Serb areas in Croatia and the two sides were not able to carry on the fighting. Four UN Protected Areas, Northern and Southern Krajina and Eastern and Western Slavonia, were created from the Serb-controlled areas in Croatia and 16,000 UN troops arrived to police the areas. The JNA withdrew from Croatia but the ethnic Serb forces refused to disarm, apart from placing their heaviest artillery under UN control.

## GOVERNMENT

In April and May 1990 the first free, democratic elections were held in Croatia and were won overwhelmingly by the Croatian Democratic Union (HDZ) of Dr Franjo Tudjman. A new constitution was adopted by parliament in December 1990 and in a national referendum in May 1991, 94 per cent of those who voted (the referendum was boycotted by many ethnic Serbs) voted in favour of independence from Yugoslavia. The Croatian parliament and government, declared independence on 30 May 1991. The EC recognized Croatia's independence on 15 January 1992 and it was admitted to the UN in May 1992.

Executive power is vested in a President and government. The President appoints the Prime Minister and, on the proposal of the Prime Minister and subject to confirmation by the Chamber of Deputies, appoints other government members. The President is directly elected for five-year terms. Legislative power is vested in the bicameral parliament which consists of the 63-member Chamber of Districts and the 138-member Chamber of Deputies. The state of the parties in August 1994 in the Chamber of Deputies is: Croatian Democratic Union (HDZ) 69; Croatian Independent Democrats Party (HND) 16; Croatian Social Liberal Party (HSLS) 14; Party of Democratic Change (SDP) 11; ethnic Serb and regionalist parties 9; Independants 6; Others 13.

### SECESSION

During 1992 the situation in the UN protected areas remained tense. Fighting restarted in January 1993, centring on the bridge at Maslenica linking central Croatia to the Adriatic coast, and on Zemunik airport near Zadar. Croat forces managed to regain control of both facilities and ethnic Serb forces regained their heavy weapons from UN control before a ceasefire was signed in April. Sporadic fighting continued from June to September 1993, with the ethnic Serbs using artillery to destroy the Maslenica bridge. Despite having voted in 1993 to establish a separate 'Republic of Serbian Krajina' (RSK) and to unite with Serbia, in January 1994 the ethnic Serbs voted in elections for a separate RSK parliament and President, the latter election being won by Milan Martic.

In April 1994 a ceasefire agreement was reached under which forces and heavy weapons have been withdrawn out of range of the front lines. The Croation government maintains that the UN should force the ethnic Serbs forces to disarm.

### LOCAL GOVERNMENT

Croatia is divided into 21 counties (each county elects three members to the Chamber of Districts) and 102 districts. Counties are composed of groups of districts and function both as units of local government and as regional offices for the central administration.

### JUDICIAL SYSTEM

The constitution provides for a Supreme Court as the highest judicial body and a Constitutional Court. The Supreme Court consists of 15 members and the Constitutional Court of 11 members, all 26 of whom are elected by the Chamber of Districts for eight-year terms.

### HEAD OF STATE
*President*, Franjo Tudjman, *elected* May 1990, *re-elected* 2 August 1992

### CABINET *as at August 1994*

*Prime Minister*, Nikica Valentic.
*Deputy Prime Minister, Foreign Affairs*, Mate Granic.

*Deputy Prime Ministers*, Ivica Kostic; Vladimir Šelas; Borislav Skegro
*Defence*, Gojko Susak
*Interior*, Ivan Jarnjak
*Finance*, Zoran Jasic
*Construction and Environmental Protection*, Zlatko Tomcic
*Health*, Andrija Hebrang
*Industry, Shipbuilding and Energy*, Nadan Vidoševic
*Education and Culture*, Vesna Girardi-Jurkic
*Agriculture and Forestry*, Ivan Tarnaj
*Shipping, Transport and Communications*, Ivica Mudrinic
*Justice and Administration*, Ivica Crnic
*Labour and Social Welfare*, Ivan Parac
*Tourism and Trade*, Niko Bulic
*Science*, Branko Jeren
*Ministers without Portfolio*, Cedomir Pavlovic; Ivan Majdak; Zlatko Matesa; Juraj Njavro
*President of the Chamber of Deputies*, Nedjeljko Mihanovic

EMBASSY OF THE REPUBLIC OF CROATIA
c/o 5th Floor, 18–21 Germain Street, London SW1Y 6HP
Tel 0171-434 2946
*Ambassador Extraordinary and Plenipotentiary*, new appointment awaited

BRITISH EMBASSY
Ilica 12/II, PO Box 454, 4100 Zagreb.
Tel: Zagreb 424888

*Ambassador Extraordinary and Plenipotentiary*, His Excellency Gavin Hewitt, apptd 1994

There are British Consulates in *Split* and *Dubrovnik*.

BRITISH COUNCIL DIRECTOR, I. Stewart, PO Box 55, Ilica 12/1, Zagreb 41001.

## DEFENCE

Croatia had to build up its armed forces rapidly to survive the 1991–2 war with ethnic Serb and federal forces (JNA) and then to support ethnic Croat forces in Bosnia-Hercegovina. It salvaged as much equipment as was possible from former JNA forces in the republic but most was taken back to Serbia or given to ethnic Serb forces in Croatia. At present the armed forces number some 103,300 active and 180,000 reserve personnel. A conscription term of ten months is in operation. Croatia remains constrained by the UN arms embargo on the former Yugoslavia.

The Army has some 95,000 active personnel, with 200 main battle tanks, 200 armoured personnel carriers and 150 artillery pieces. The Air Force has some 4,300 active personnel, mainly air defence forces, with some 20 aircraft and helicopters. The Navy has some 4,000 active personnel with one submarine and 11 patrol and coastal combatants. Paramilitary personnel include 40,000 armed police and 1,000 members of the nationalist Croatian Party of Rights (HSP) armed wing (HOS).

Opposing ethnic Serb forces number 40,000–50,000 personnel, with 200 main battle tanks, 100 armoured personnel carriers and 500 artillery pieces. The UN deploys 15,400 troop in Croatia.

## ECONOMY

Large areas of Croatia's most productive farmland were destroyed by the war or remain under Serb control. The tourist industry has been decimated by the war and by the continuing fighting in neighbouring Bosnia. Shipbuilding and fishing are major industries on the Adriatic coast. Inland there is a light manufacturing sector, food-processing industries, bauxite deposits, thermal mineral springs, hydro-electric potential, and agriculture based on grain, horticulture, livestock and tobacco. Serb control of large amounts of Croatia has seriously disrupted hydro-electric supplies and transport and communications links.

| Trade with UK | 1993 |
|---|---|
| Imports from UK | £42,645,000 |
| Exports to UK | 30,627,000 |

# CUBA
*Republica de Cuba*

Cuba, the largest island in the Caribbean, lies between 74° and 85° W. longitude, and 19° and 23° N. latitude, with a total area of 42,804 sq. miles (110,861 sq. km). The country is divided into 14 provinces. The population (1991 UN estimate) was 10,736,000.

CAPITAL – ΨHavana, population estimate (1989) 2,096,000; other towns are ΨSantiago (405,000), Santa Clara (194,000), Camagüey (283,000), Holgüin (228,000), Guantánamo (200,000) and ΨCienfuegos (123,600).
CURRENCY – Cuban peso of 100 centavos.
FLAG – Five horizontal bands, blue and white (blue at top and bottom) with red triangle, close to staff, charged with five-point star.
NATIONAL ANTHEM – Al Combate, Corred Bayameses (To battle, men of Bayamo).
NATIONAL DAY – 1 January (Day of Liberation).

## GOVERNMENT

The island of Cuba was visited by Columbus on 27 October 1492, and was then believed to be part of India. Early in the 16th century the island was conquered by the Spanish, and for almost four centuries remained under Spanish rule. Separatist agitation culminated in the closing years of the 19th century in open warfare. In 1898 the government of the USA intervened and demanded the evacuation of Cuba by the Spanish forces. A short Spanish–American war led to the abandonment of the island, which came under American military rule from 1899 until 1902, when an autonomous government was inaugurated with an elected President, and a legislature of two houses.

A revolution led by Dr Fidel Castro overthrew the government of Gen. Batista on 1 January 1959. In October 1965 the Communist Party of Cuba was formed to succeed the United Party of the Socialist Revolution; it is the only authorized political party. A new Socialist Constitution came into force in 1976 and indirect elections to the National Assembly of People's Power were subsequently held. The first direct elections to the 589-member National Assembly were held in February 1993; all candidates were officially approved by the Community Party and ran for election unopposed. The fourteen provincial assemblies were elected in the same manner. On 15 March 1993 the National Assembly re-elected Fidel Castro as President of the Council of State for a five-year term.

*President of Council of State and Head of Government*, Dr Fidel Castro Ruz, *appointed* 2 November 1976

COUNCIL OF STATE *as at July 1994*
*President*, Dr Fidel Castro Ruz
*First Vice-President*, Raúl Castro Ruz

*Vice-Presidents,* Juan Almeida Bosque; José Ramón Machado Ventura; Abelardo Colome Ibarra; Carlos Lage Dávila; Esteban Lazo Hernandez
*Secretary,* José M. Miyar Barrueco

COUNCIL OF MINISTERS *as at July 1994*
*President,* Dr Fidel Castro Ruz
*First Vice-President,* Raúl Castro Ruz
*Vice-Presidents,* Dr Carlos Rafael Rodríguez; Pedro Miret Prieto; José Ramón Fernández Alvarez; Osmany Cienfuegos Gorriarán; Antonio Rodriguez Maurell; Jaime Crombet Hernández-Baquero; Aldofo Diaz Suárez; Lionel Soto Prieto
*Secretary,* Carlos Lage Dávila
*Ministers,* Alfredo Jordan Morales (*Agriculture*); Marcos J. Portal Leon (*Basic Industry*); Gen. Silvano Colás Sanchez (*Communications*); Homero Crabb (*Construction*); José M. Cañete Alvarez (*Construction Materials Industry*); Armando Enrique Hart Davalos (*Culture*); Manuel Vila Sosa (*Domestic Trade*); Antonio Rodríguez Maurell (*Economy and Planning*); Luis Ignacio Gomez Gutierrez (*Education*); José Luis Rodríguez García (*Finance and Prices*); Jorge A. Fernandez Cuervo-Vinent (*Fishing*); Alejandro Roca Iglesias (*Food Industry*); Ernesto Meléndez Bachs (*Foreign Investment and Economic Co-operation*); Roberto Robaina (*Foreign Relations*); Ricardo Cabrisas Ruiz (*Foreign Trade*); Fernando Vecino Alegret (*Higher Education*); Gen. Abelardo Colomé Ibarra (*Interior*); Ignacio González Planas (*Iron and Steel, Machine and Electronics Industries*); Carlos Amat Fores (*Justice*); Francisco Linares Calvo (*Labour and Social Security*); Eddie Fernandez Boada (*Light Industry*); Julio Jesus Teja Pérez (*Public Health*); Raul Castro Ruz (*Revolutionary Armed Forces*); Rosa Elena Simeón Negrín (*Science, Technology and Environment*); Nelson Torres Perez (*Sugar Industry*); Osmany Cienfuegos Gorriarán (*Tourism*); Gen. Senén Casas Regueiro (*Transport*); Jose Alberto Naranjo Morales; Joaqin Benavides Rodrioguez (*Ministers without Portfolio*)
*President of the National Assembly,* Ricardo Alarcón de Quesada
*President of the National Bank,* Hector Rodríguez Llompart

EMBASSY OF THE REPUBLIC OF CUBA
167 High Holborn, London WC1V 6PA
Tel 0171-240 2488

*Ambassador Extraordinary and Plenipotentiary,* Her Excellency Maria A. Flores, apptd 1990

BRITISH EMBASSY
Edificio Bolívar, Cárcel 101-103, e Morro y Prado, Apartado 1069, Havana.
Tel: Havana 33 8071

*Ambassador Extraordinary and Plenipotentiary,* His Excellency Philip McLean, apptd 1994

DEFENCE

Cuba has a total active armed forces strength of 175,000 personnel, including 74,500 conscripts who serve for two years. In addition, there are 135,000 ready reserves who serve for 45 days per year and a territorial militia of 1,300,000 personnel. Paramilitary Ministry of Interior personnel number 19,000.

The Army numbers 145,000 (60,000 conscripts) and uses reservists to man many units. Equipment includes 1,575 main battle tanks, 50 light tanks, 100 reconnaissance vehicles and 1,600 armoured infantry fighting vehicles and armoured personnel carriers. The Navy has a strength of 13,500 (8,500 conscripts) with three frigates, three submarines and 28

patrol and coastal craft, together with two marine battalions. The Air Force has 15,000 personnel (6,000 conscripts) with 140 combat aircraft and 85 armed helicopters of Soviet manufacture.

The last former Soviet combat personnel left Cuba on 3 July 1993, but Russian military advisers remain to operate military intelligence facilities. The United States has 2,300 naval personnel at Guantanamo Bay Naval Base, which has been leased since before the 1959 revolution.

ECONOMY

After coming to power the government carried out a programme of land reform and nationalization; by 1968 virtually all land and industrial and commercial enterprises had been nationalized. With the end of Cuba's privileged trading relationships with the Soviet bloc since 1989–91 the economy has deteriorated sharply. GDP fell by 24 per cent in 1991 and 15 per cent in 1992. Economic difficulties have forced the government to introduce free-market economic reforms to prevent the worsening of food, fuel and mechanical spare parts shortages. In July 1993 the government legalized the holding of US dollars by private individuals in an attempt to gain hard currency reserves for the state. Following protests and riots against food and energy shortages in August 1993, individual private enterprise and small businesses were allowed again, and state farms began to be transformed into co-operatives run by private individuals. In May 1994 the National Assembly approved austerity measures, including reducing subsidies to loss-making state industries, price rises for selected goods and services, and the selective introduction of an income tax system.

Partially successful efforts are being made to diversify the economy, although sugar is still its mainstay and principal source of foreign exchange. In 1989–90 the harvest was 8.04 million tons but this dropped in 1992–3 to 4.4m tons owing to a lack of fuel and spare parts. Domestic oil production is rising and reached 1.3m tonnes in 1993, enough for 40 per cent of domestic demand. Production of nickel is also rising, reaching 45,000 tonnes in 1993.

The tourism industry has expanded since 1986. In 1993 544,000 tourists visited Cuba, generating US$700 million in gross income.

The total foreign debt stands at US$16,000 million.

TRADE

Cuba's exports dropped from US$8.1 billion in 1989 to US$1.7 billion in 1993. Imports have declined by 73 per cent since 1989. Trade between Cuba and the former socialist economies of Europe totalled US$830 million in 1992, only 7 per cent of pre-1989 levels. A new Russian-Cuban trade deal was signed in November 1992 under which Russia promised to buy limited quantities of sugar in return for selling oil at world prices. The US total trade and economic embargo remains in force.

Principal exports are sugar, nickel, seafood, citrus fruits, tobacco and rum.

| Trade with UK | 1992 | 1993 |
|---|---|---|
| Imports from UK | £28,345,000 | £14,009,000 |
| Exports to UK | 12,979,000 | 8,000,000 |

There are 12,700 km of railway track, of which 5,000 km are in public service. In 1986 there were 13,247 km of road. At present scheduled international air services run to North, Central and South American countries and Europe.

CULTURE

Spanish is the language of the island. English, formerly widely understood, is now spoken less. Education is compulsory and free. In 1964 illiteracy was officially declared to be completely eliminated. The press and broadcasting and television are under the control of the government.

---

# CYPRUS
*Kypriaki Dimokratia/Kibris Cumhuriyeti*

---

Cyprus, with an area of 3,572 sq. miles (9,251 sq. km), is the third largest island in the Mediterranean Sea. Its greatest length is 140 miles and greatest breadth 60 miles, situated at 35°N. latitude and 33° 30′E. longitude. It is about 40 miles from the nearest point of Asia Minor.

The climate is Mediterranean, with a hot dry summer and a variable warm winter.

POPULATION – In 1994 the population was estimated at 725,000. There are two major communities, Greek Cypriots (580,000, or 81.6 per cent) and Turkish Cypriots (135,800, or 18.4 per cent), and minorities of Armenians, Maronites and others.

CAPITAL – Nicosia, near the centre of the island, with a population of 181,000 (in the government-controlled area); the other principal towns are ΨLimassol, ΨFamagusta, ΨLarnaca, Paphos and Kyrenia.

CURRENCY – Cyprus pound (C£) of 100 cents.

FLAG – White with a gold map of Cyprus above a wreath of olive.

NATIONAL ANTHEM – Ode to Freedom.

NATIONAL DAY – 1 October (Independence Day).

## GOVERNMENT

Cyprus came under British administration from 1878, and was formally annexed to Britain in November 1914 on the outbreak of war with Turkey. From 1925 to 1960 it was a Crown Colony. Following the launching in April 1955 of an armed campaign by EOKA in support of union with Greece, a state of emergency was declared in November 1955 which lasted for four years. After a meeting between the Prime Ministers of Greece and Turkey, a conference was held in London and an agreement was signed on 19 February 1959 between the United Kingdom, Greece, Turkey, and the Greek and Turkish Cypriots which provided that Cyprus would be an independent republic.

The island became an independent republic on 16 August 1960. The constitution provided for a Greek Cypriot President and a Turkish Cypriot Vice-President elected for a five-year term by the Greek and Turkish communities respectively. The House of Representatives, elected for five years by universal suffrage of each community separately, was to consist of 35 Greek and 15 Turkish members. The 1960 constitution proved unworkable in practice and led to intercommunal troubles. The UN Peace-Keeping Force in Cyprus (UNFICYP) was set up in March 1964; its mandate was last renewed on 15 June 1994 for six months. Increasing frustration at the obstinate attitudes of both communities towards any solution to the island's division led to the withdrawal of the Danish contingent in December 1992 and the Canadian contingent in summer 1993. The remaining 1,400 troops are British, Austrian and Argentinian.

## DIVISION

In July 1974, mainland Greek officers of the Greek Cypriot National Guard under instructions from the military junta in Athens launched a coup d'état against President Makarios and installed a former EOKA member, Nikos Sampson, in his place. Turkey, reserving to itself the right to maintain constitutional order and the independence and territorial integrity of the island, invaded Northern Cyprus and occupied over a third of the island. In February 1975 a 'Turkish Federated State of Cyprus' under Rauf Denktash was declared in this area, its constitution being approved by referendum in July 1975. In November 1983 a 'Declaration of Statehood' was issued which purported to establish the 'Turkish Republic of Northern Cyprus'. The declaration was condemned by the UN Security Council and only Turkey has recognized the new 'state'. In May 1985 a referendum in the north of Cyprus approved a constitution for the 'Turkish Republic of Northern Cyprus'. In June 1985 Denktash was elected President of the 'state' and a general election was held. Denktash was re-elected in April 1990 and general elections were held in May 1990 and December 1993.

Since 1974 attempts to reach a settlement have focused on intercommunal talks under the auspices of the UN. In June 1992 a UN plan for a bizonal bi-communal federal state, with the Turkish community having a veto over all the important decisions of the government and parliament, was approved by the UN Security Council and in principle by the Greek community but not by the Turkish because of the loss of land involved.

A general election was held for the House of Representatives (expanded to 56 Greek Cypriot and 24 vacant Turkish Cypriot seats) in May 1991, resulting in the parties gaining the following number of seats: Democratic Rally-Liberal Party 20; AKEL (Communist) 18; Democratic Party (Centre) 16; EDEK (Socialist) 2. The last presidential election was held in February 1993 when Glafcos Clerides of the Democratic Rally-Liberal Party defeated the Communist-supported independent incumbent George Vassiliou.

Cyprus applied for EC membership in 1990 but in June 1993 the EC Commission issued a negative opinion on the application, stating that the division of the island must be resolved before entry into the EC.

*President*, Glafcos Clerides, *elected* 14 February 1993

COUNCIL OF MINISTERS *as at August 1994*

*Foreign Affairs*, Alecos Michaelides
*Interior*, Dinos Michaelides
*Finance*, Phaedros Economides
*Education and Culture*, Claire Angelidou
*Justice and Public Order*, Alecos Evangelou
*Defence*, Costas Eliades
*Communications and Works*, Adamos Adamides
*Health*, Manolis Christofides
*Commerce and Industry*, Stelias Kiliaris
*Labour and Social Insurance*, Andreas Moushouttas
*Agriculture, Environment and Natural Resources*, Costas Petrides

CYPRUS HIGH COMMISSION
93 Park Street, London W1Y 4ET
Tel 0171-499 8272

*High Commissioner*, new appointment waited
*Deputy High Commisioner*, C. Ioannou
*Counsellor*, A. Georghiades (*Commerce*)

BRITISH HIGH COMMISSION
Alexander Pallis Street (PO Box 1978), Nicosia
Tel: Nicosia 2-473131

*High Commissioner*, His Excellency David Christopher Madden, apptd 1994
*Counsellor and Deputy High Commissioner*, C. B. Jennings
*Defence Adviser*, Col. J. A. Anderson
*First Secretary (Commercial)*, P. J. Newman

BRITISH COUNCIL REPRESENTATIVE, Robert Frost, PO Box 5654, 3 Museum Street, Nicosia

## BRITISH SOVEREIGN AREAS

The UK retained full sovereignty and jurisdiction over two areas of 99 square miles in all: Akrotiri–Episkopi–Paramali and Dhekelia–Pergamos–Ayios Nicolaos–Xylophagou. This includes use of roads and other facilities. The British Administrator of these areas is appointed by The Queen and is responsible to the Secretary of State for Defence. The combined total of army and RAF personnel stationed in the areas is 4,100.

*Administrator of the British Sovereign Areas*, Maj.-Gen. A. G. H. Harley

## ECONOMY

Although agriculture still occupies a prime position in the Cyprus economy it is unlikely to expand further. Main products are citrus fruits, grapes and vine products, potatoes and other vegetables. Manufacturing, construction, distribution and other service industries are other major employers. Tourism is the main growth industry with over 1.2 million long-stay tourists producing C£573 million in foreign exchange earnings in 1991. Over 5,000 foreign firms and individuals have registered as offshore companies in Cyprus, which supports Cyprus's claim to be a centre for Middle East trade.

Britain continues to be the country's most important trading partner, taking some 35 per cent of its exports in 1992 and supplying 12 per cent of its imports. Cyprus is seeking to diversify its export markets and until recently sold almost half its exports to the Middle East. However, these traditional markets are drying up, and Cyprus is looking more towards Europe. A Customs Union between Cyprus and the EC came into force in January 1988.

### TRADE

There is a large visible trade deficit (C£743.6 million in 1993), which is offset by invisible earnings, particularly from tourism. The current account in 1993 showed a deficit of C£80.9m.

|  | 1992 |
|---|---|
| Imports | C£1,294.2m |
| Exports (including | |
| re-exports) | 406.9m |

| Trade with UK | 1992 | 1993 |
|---|---|---|
| Imports from UK | £221,910,000 | £235,930,000 |
| Exports to UK | 144,746,000 | 136,217,000 |

## CZECH REPUBLIC
*Česká Republika*

The Czech Republic, composed of Bohemia and Moravia, has an area of 30,441 sq. miles (78,664 sq. km). Bohemia is surrounded by mountain ranges while Moravia is composed of lands which stretch to the Danubian basin. The republic is bordered by Poland in the north-east, by Germany in the west and north-west, by Austria in the south and by Slovakia in the south-east.

POPULATION – The population (1991 census) is 10,302,000, of which 95 per cent is Czech and 3 per cent Slovak. The majority of the population are Roman Catholic, with a small Protestant minority. Czech is the official language.

CAPITAL – Prague (Praha) on the Vltava (Moldau), with a population (1991) of 1,215,076. Other major cities are Brno (Brün) (391,093), Ostrava (331,241) and Plzeň (174,676).

CURRENCY – Koruna (Kc) or Czech crown of 100 Haléřů (Heller).

FLAG – White over red horizontally with a blue triangle extending from the hoist to the centre of the flag. (The Czech Republic retained the former Czechoslovak federal flag.)

NATIONAL ANTHEM – Kde Domov Můj (Where is my Motherland).

NATIONAL DAY – 28 October.

## HISTORY

The land which is now the Czech Republic came under the rule of the Habsburg dynasty in 1526 and remained part of the Austro-Hungarian Empire until 1918. Austrian attempts to Germanize the Czech lands in the 18th and 19th centuries led to the rise of Czech nationalism in the late 19th century. The independence of Czechoslovakia was proclaimed on 28 October 1918 following an amalgamation of Bohemia, Moravia, Slovakia and Ruthenia and was confirmed by the Versailles Peace Conference in 1919.

The inter-war democratic Czechoslovak state was forced to cede the ethnic German Sudetenland to Nazi Germany on 30 September 1938 after the Munich Agreement. German forces invaded the Czech Republic in March 1939 and incorporated it into Germany while Slovakia became a puppet state. The Czech Republic was liberated by Soviet and American forces in May 1945. The pre-war democratic Czechoslovak state was re-established in 1945, having ceded Ruthenia to the Soviet Union, with the Communist Party in a very strong political position. The Communists took power in a coup in February 1948 and remained in power until November 1989.

In 1968 the Czechoslovak Communist Party under Alexander Dubček embarked on a political and economic reform programme (the Prague Spring). The reforms were suppressed following the invasion by Soviet, Polish, East German, Hungarian and Bulgarian troops on the night of 20 August 1968, and were abandoned when Gustáv Husák became leader of the Communist Party in April 1969.

Opposition to Communist Party rule gathered pace in the late 1980s and mass protests in November 1989 led to the resignation of the Communist Party Central Committee. The Communist Party was forced to concede its monopoly of power and on 10 December a new government was appointed in which only half the ministers were Communist Party members. Gustáv Husák resigned as President and was replaced by the dissident writer Václav Havel. Free elections were held in June 1990 in which the Communist Party was destroyed as a political force.

## GOVERNMENT

Legislative elections were held in early June 1992 which returned the Civic Democratic Party and the Movement for a Democratic Slovakia as the dominant parties in the Czech and Slovak republics respectively. Talks between Czech and Slovak leaders on continuing the federation broke down because of the insistence of Vladimir Meciar, the Slovak leader, on a declaration of Slovak sovereignty. Meciar agreed with the Czech leader Vaclav Klaus on forming an interim transitional government for the federation with much reduced powers, and this was sworn in on 1 July 1992. In the second half of 1992 Klaus and Meciar agreed on the separation of the Czech and Slovak republics into two sovereign states, which took effect on 1 January 1993. The former federal state's institutions, assets, property and debts were divided in the ratio 2:1 Czech to Slovak republics.

The elections of June 1992 had returned the Civic Democratic Party (ODS) as the largest party in the Czech parliament, and on 1 July 1992 it had formed a coalition government with three other centre-right parties. This government was sworn in as the government of the Czech Republic on 1 January 1993, with former federal President Havel being elected as Czech President on 26 January 1993.

The Czech constitution vests legislative power in the bicameral parliament, comprising a 200-member Chamber of Deputies elected for a four-year term and an 81-member Senate elected for a six-year term, one-third being renewed every two years. The President is elected by parliament for a five-year term. Executive power is held by the Prime Minister and Council of Ministers. A two-thirds majority in parliament is necessary to amend the constitution, and federal laws remain in place unless superseded by Czech ones. A Constitutional Court has been established at Brno comprising 15 judges nominated by the President for ten-year terms with Senate approval.

HEAD OF STATE
*President*, Vaclav Havel, *elected* 26 January 1993, *sworn in* 2 February 1993

COUNCIL OF MINISTERS *as at July 1994*

*Prime Minister*, Vaclav Klaus (ODS)
*Deputy Prime Minister, Finance*, Ivan Kocarnik (ODS)
*Deputy Prime Minister, Agriculture*, Josef Lux (KDU-CSL)
*Deputy Prime Minister*, Jan Kalvoda (ODA)
*Foreign Affairs*, Josef Zieleniec (ODS)
*Industry and Trade*, Vladimir Dlouhy (ODA)
*Economy*, Karel Dyba (ODS)
*Health*, Ludek Rubas (ODS)
*Interior*, Jan Ruml (ODS)
*Culture*, Pavel Tigrid (KDU-CSL)
*Education*, Ivan Pilip (KDS)
*Labour and Social Affairs*, Jindrich Vodicka (ODS)
*State Control*, Igor Nemec (ODS)
*Privatization*, Jiri Skalicky (ODA)
*Environment*, Frantisek Benda (KDS)
*Justice*, Jiri Novak (ODS)
*Economic Competition*, Stanislav Belehradek (KDU-CSL)
*Defence*, Antonin Baudys (KDU-CSL)
*Transport*, Jan Strasky (ODS)

ODS Civic Democratic Party; KDU-CSL Christian Democratic Union–Czech People's Party; ODA Civic Democratic Alliance; KDS Christian Democratic Party.

EMBASSY OF THE CZECH REPUBLIC
26–30 Kensington Palace Gardens, London w8 4QY
Tel 0171-243 1115

*Ambassador Extraordinary and Plenipotentiary*, His Excellency Karel Kühnl, apptd 1993
*Chargé d'Affaires and First Secretary*, Peter Hrdlička
*Military Attaché*, Maj.-Gen. S. Thurnvald
*Counsellor*, J. Žabža

BRITISH EMBASSY
Thunovská 14, 125 50 Prague
Tel: Prague 533347

*Ambassador Extraordinary and Plenipotentiary*, His Excellency Sir Michael Burton, KCVO, CMG, apptd 1994
*Counsellor and Deputy Head of Mission*, C. M. T. Elmes
*Defence and Military Attaché*, Col. W. E. Nowosielski-Slopowron
*First Secretary (Commercial)*, J. Cummins, MBE
*First Secretary (Management) and Consul*, D. J. Jackson
*Cultural Attaché*, W. Jefferson, OBE (*British Council Director*)

ECONOMY

Under Communist rule industry was state-owned and nearly all agricultural land was cultivated by state or co-operative farms. An economic reform programme began in 1990 to produce a free-market economy, and the government of the Czech Republic has continued to follow the policies of the former federal government. This has necessitated a restrictive monetary policy to stem inflation and a restructuring of manufacturing industry to be internationally competitive, and these were major reasons for the break with Slovakia. As a result, foreign investment (US$2,053m in 1990–3) and private enterprises have grown and reliance on trade with the former Soviet bloc countries has declined. Unemployment has risen but is still low by west European standards (4 per cent), and a trade-liberalizing association agreement with the EU is in operation.

Privatization of state enterprises began in May 1993 with the transfer of 60 per cent of productive capacity to private ownership. Privatization of some 700 medium-sized enterprises began in January 1994 and by the end of 1994 about 80 per cent of the economy will have been privatized. The state continues to own and subsidize a few enterprises, such as the national airline and parts of the Skoda engineering group. Overall output has dropped by 25 per cent since 1990 but began to grow in 1993 as did GDP. The budget and current account remain in surplus and foreign debt is small.

A customs union between the Czech and Slovak Republics is in place but separate currencies were introduced in February 1993 following speculation. In April 1993 the Prague Stock Exchange reopened after 50 years and new western-style bankruptcy laws came into operation.

The Czech Republic is not rich in minerals, although significant quantities of coal and lignite are mined. Principal agricultural products are sugar-beet, potatoes and cereal crops; the timber industry is also very important. Having been the major industrial area of the Austro-Hungarian Empire, the country has long been industrialized, and machinery, industrial consumer goods and raw materials are major exports.

| *Trade with UK\** | 1992 | 1993 |
|---|---|---|
| Imports from UK | £208,912,000 | £287,568,000 |
| Exports to UK | 170,268,000 | 245,265,000 |

\* 1992 figures refer to Czechoslovakia, 1993 figures to the Czech Republic

CULTURE

The Reformation gave a widespread impulse to Czech literature, the writings of Jan Hus (martyred in 1415 as a religious and social reformer) familiarizing the people with Wyclif's teaching. This impulse endured to the close of the 17th century when Jan Amos Komensky or Comenius (1592–1670) was expelled from the country. Under Austrian rule and with the persistent pursuit of Germanization, there was a period of stagnation until the national revival in the 19th century. Authors of international reputation include Jaroslav Hašek (1883–1923), Jaroslav Seifert (1901–86, Nobel Prize for Literature, 1985), Václav Havel (b. 1936) and Milan Kundera (b. 1929).

EDUCATION

Education is compulsory and free for all children from the ages of six to 16. There are three universities in the Czech Republic, of which the most famous is Charles University in Prague (founded 1348), the others being situated at Brno and Olomouc. In addition there are a considerable number of other institutions of university standing, technical colleges, agricultural colleges, etc.

# DENMARK
*Kongeriget Danmark*

Denmark is a kingdom of northern Europe, consisting of the islands of Zealand, Funen, Lolland, etc., the peninsula of Jutland, the outlying island of Bornholm in the Baltic, and the Faröes and Greenland. Denmark is situated between 54° 34′ and 57° 45′ N. latitude and 8° 4′–15° 12′ E. longitude, with an area of 16,629 sq. miles (43,069 sq. km), and a population (official estimate 1993) of 5,180,614.

CAPITAL – ΨCopenhagen, population (1992) 464,566; Greater Copenhagen 1,339,395; ΨAarhus 204,139; ΨOdense 140,886; ΨAalborg 114,970; ΨEsbjerg 72,205; ΨRanders 55,358.
CURRENCY – Danish krone (Kr) of 100 øre.
FLAG – Red, with white cross.
NATIONAL ANTHEMS – Kong Kristian and Det er et yndigt land.
NATIONAL DAY – 5 June (Constitution Day).

## GOVERNMENT

Under the Constitution of the Kingdom of Denmark Act 1953, the legislature consists of one chamber, the *Folketing*, of not more than 179 members, including two for the Faröes and two for Greenland. The voting age is 18 with voting based on a proportional respresentation system with a 2 per cent minimum for parliamentary representation.

A coalition government led by Poul Schlüter was formed in December 1990 after the general election on 12 December. The government resigned on 14 January 1993 after a judicial enquiry stated that it had lied over measures to prevent Tamil refugees from entering Denmark. On 25 January a new coalition government of the Social Democrat, Centre Democrat, Social Liberal and Christian People's Party was sworn in. The state of the parties in the Folketing is: Social Democrat Party (SD) 71; Conservatives (C) 31; Liberals (L) 31; Socialist People's Party (SP) 15; Progress Party (P) 12; Centre Democrat Party (CD) 8; Social Liberal Party (SL) 7; Christian People's Party (CP) 4.

## HEAD OF STATE

*HM The Queen of Denmark*, Queen Margrethe II, KG, *born* 16 April 1940, *succeeded* 14 January 1972, *married* 10 June 1967, Count Henri de Monpezat (Prince Henrik of Denmark), and *has issue* Crown Prince Frederik (*see* below); Prince Joachim, *born* 7 June 1969
*Heir*, HRH Crown Prince Frederik, *born* 26 May 1968

## CABINET *as at August 1994*

*Prime Minister*, Poul Nyrup Rasmussen (SD)
*Industry*, Mimi Jakobsen (CD)
*Economic Affairs*, Marianne Jelved (SL)
*Energy*, Jann Sjursen (CP)
*Finance*, Mogens Lykketoft (SD)
*Foreign Affairs*, Niels Helveg Petersen (SL)
*Agriculture and Fisheries*, Bjoern Westh (SD)
*Environment*, Svend Auken (SD)
*Communications and Tourism*, Helge Mortensen (SD)
*Education*, Ole Vig Jensen (SL)
*Housing, Nordic Collaboration and Baltic Affairs*, Flemming Kofod-Svensdsen (CP)
*Development Co-operation*, Helle Degn (SD)
*Interior*, Birthe Weiss (SD)
*Labour*, Jytte Andersen (SD)
*Taxation*, Ole Stovad (SD)
*Defence*, Hans Haekkerup (SD).

*Cultural Affairs*, Jytte Hilden (SD)
*Health*, Torben Lund (SD)
*Transport*, Jan Trøjborg (SD)
*Justice*, Erling Olsen (SD)
*Social Affairs*, Yvonne Herløv Andersen (CD)
*Ecclesiastical Affairs and Research*, Arne Oluf Anderson (CD)

ROYAL DANISH EMBASSY
55 Sloane Street, London SW1X 9SR
Tel 0171-333 0200
*Ambassador Extraordinary and Plenipotentiary*, His Excellency Rudolph Thorning-Petersen, apptd 1989
*Minister*, Mrs A. Hugau
*Counsellor (Commercial)*, Jorgen Gulev
*Defence Attaché*, Capt. S. Lund

BRITISH EMBASSY
36–40 Kastelsvej, DK-2100 Copenhagen Ø
Tel: Copenhagen 35 264600
*Ambassador Extraordinary and Plenipotentiary*, His Excellency Hugh J. Arbuthnott, CMG, apptd 1993
*Counsellor and Deputy Head of Mission*, P. S. Astley, LVO
*Counsellor (Economic/Commcercial)*, A. M. Layden
*Defence Attaché*, Cmdr. R. Kirkwood, RN
*First Secretary (Management) and Consul*, B. Robertson
There are Consulates at Aabenraa, Aalborg, Aarhus, Esbjerg, Fredericia, Herning, Odense, Rønne (Bornholm); at *Tórshavn* (Faröe Islands); and *Nuuk* (Godtháb) (Greenland).

BRITISH COUNCIL REPRESENTATIVE, Len Tyler, Gammel Mont 123, 1117 Copenhagen K

## DEFENCE

Total active armed forces number 27,700 (9,100 conscripts). Conscripts serve for nine to 12 months. Reserves number 70,000 personnel.

Army personnel number 16,900 (7,700 conscripts) but major use is made of the 54,000 reservists to reinforce peacetime units. Equipment includes 460 main battle tanks, 640 armoured personnel carriers and 565 artillery pieces.

The Navy has 4,500 personnel (700 conscripts) with three frigates, five submarines, 35 patrol and coastal craft and eight armed helicopters.

The Air Force numbers 6,300 personnel (700 conscripts) with 73 combat aircraft of US and Swedish manufacture. Denmark deploys a 975-strong infantry battalion with UN forces in Croatia.

## EDUCATION

Education is free and compulsory. Special schools are numerous, commercial, technical and agricultural predominating. There are universities at Copenhagen (founded in 1479), Aarhus (1928), Odense (1966), Roskilde (1972) and Aalborg (1974).

## LANGUAGE AND LITERATURE

The Danish language is akin to Swedish and Norwegian. Danish literature, ancient and modern, embraces all forms of expression, familiar names being Hans Christian Andersen (1805–75), Søren Kierkegaard (1813–55) and Karen Blixen (1885–1962). Some 47 newspapers are published in Denmark; nine daily papers are published in Copenhagen.

## ECONOMY

Of the labour force, in 1991 6 per cent was engaged in agriculture, fishing, forestry, etc.; 26 per cent in manufacturing, building and construction; 21 per cent in the retailing, transport, financial and insurance service sectors and 31 per cent in public services. The chief agricultural products are pigs, cattle, dairy products, poultry and eggs, seeds, cereals and sugar beet; manufactures are mostly based on imported raw materials but there are also considerable imports of finished goods. Denmark is self-sufficient in oil and natural gas after off-shore discoveries in recent years.

FINANCE

| Budget Estimates | 1993 | 1994 |
|---|---|---|
| Revenue | Kr307,414m | Kr334,533m |
| Expenditure | 351,359m | 388,901m |

Denmark's balance of payments on current account showed a deficit for 1993 of Kr28,700 million (1992, Kr28,100 million). The foreign debt in 1993 was Kr214,000 million.

TRADE

The principal imports are industrial raw materials, consumer goods, construction inputs, machinery, raw materials, vehicles and textile products. The chief exports are miscellaneous manufactured articles, agricultural and dairy products.

| | 1990 | 1991 |
|---|---|---|
| Total imports | Kr240,555m | Kr255,764m |
| Total exports | 283,437m | 309,440m |

| Trade with UK | 1992 | 1993 |
|---|---|---|
| Imports from UK | £1,560,607,000 | £1,574,963,000 |
| Exports to UK | 2,384,964,000 | 2,046,184,000 |

## COMMUNICATIONS

Mercantile marine (ships above 250 gross tonnage) at the beginning of 1993, totalled 634 ships. In 1985 there was 2,471 km of state-owned railway and 494 km of privately-owned railway systems.

## THE FARÖES

The Faröes, or Sheep Islands have an area of 540 sq. miles (1,399 sq. km) and a population (1992) of 47,287. The capital is Tórshavn.

Since 1948 the Faröes have had a degree of home rule. The islands are governed by a *Løgting* of 26 members and a *Landsstyre* of four members which deals with special Faröes affairs, and send two representatives to the *Folketing* at Copenhagen. The Faröes are not part of the EU.

The main industries are agriculture, fishing, fish-farming, whaling and the public sector; tourism is growing in importance.

*Prime Minister*, Marita Petersen

| Trade with UK | 1992 | 1993 |
|---|---|---|
| Imports from UK | £7,755,000 | £7,767,000 |
| Exports to UK | 44,303,000 | 52,601,000 |

## GREENLAND

Greenland has a total area of 2,175,600 sq. km, of which about 16 per cent is ice-free, and a population (1993) of 55,117. It is divided into three provinces (West, North and East). The capital is Nuuk (Godthåb)).

Greenland attained a status of internal autonomy on 1 May 1979 and a government (*Landsstyre*) was established. It has a *Landsting* of 17 members and sends two representatives to the *Folketing* at Copenhagen. Following a plebiscite Greenland negotiated its withdrawal from the EC, but without discontinuing relations with Denmark, and left on 1 February 1985.

Mineral and oil prospecting revealed deposits of lead, zinc, iron ore, oil, gas and uranium. Commercial exploitation of these resources has already begun. The traditional industries of fishing, sealing, whaling and reindeer herding remain the most important sectors of the economy, together with public services and administration. The trade of Greenland is mainly under the management of the Grønlands Handel. The United States of America has acquired certain rights to maintain air bases in Greenland.

*Premier*, Lars Emil Johansen

| Trade with UK | 1992 | 1993 |
|---|---|---|
| Imports from UK | £1,034,000 | £2,209,000 |
| Exports to UK | 3,098,000 | 5,904,000 |

# DJIBOUTI
*Jumhouriyya Djibouti*

Djibouti is situated on the north-east coast of Africa (i.e. the Horn of Africa) and has an area of 8,494 sq. miles (22,000 sq. km.). The climate is harsh and much of the country is semi-arid desert. It has a population (1991 census) of 520,000.

CAPITAL – Ψ Djibouti, population (1991) 340,700.
CURRENCY – Djibouti franc of 100 centimes.
FLAG – Blue over green with white triangle in the hoist containing a red star.
NATIONAL DAY – 27 June (Independence Day).

## GOVERNMENT

Formerly French Somaliland and then the French Territory of the Afars and the Issas, the Republic of Djibouti became independent on 27 June 1977. The sole legal party was formerly the *Rassemblement Populaire pour le Progrès* (RPP), the Popular Rally for Progress. A new multiparty constitution was adopted by referendum in September 1992 and subsequent multiparty elections held on 18 December were won by the ruling RPP with 77 per cent of the vote and all 65 seats in the Chamber of Deputies. President Aptidon was re-elected for a fourth six-year term in 1993. However, less than half the electorate voted in either election and the Front for the Restoration of Unity and Democracy (FRUD) boycotted both.

## INSURGENCY

Armed FRUD rebels, their support based among ethnic Afars (most of the population is either Afar or Issas), have been fighting the government since late 1991 in protest at the concentration of political power in the hands of the Somali-speaking Issas at the expense of the nomadic Afars. FRUD gained control of most of the country in 1992 but in 1993 was driven back into the north by government forces.

## HEAD OF STATE

*President*, Hassan Gouled Aptidon, *elected* 1977, *re-elected* 1981, 1987 and 9 May 1993

### CABINET *as at July 1994*

*Prime Minister*, Barkat Gourad Hamadou
*Justice and Islamic Affairs*, Moumin Bahdon Farah
*Foreign Affairs*, Abdou Bolok Abdou
*Interior and Decentralization*, Idriss Harbi Farah
*National Defence*, Ahmed Boulaleh Barre
*Finance*, Ahmed Aden Youssouf
*Ports and Shipping*, Moussa Bouraleh Robleh
*Economy and Commerce*, Mohamed Ali Mohamed
*National Education*, Ahmed Guire Waberi
*Youth and Sports and Culture*, Mohamed Ibrahim Mohamed
*Public Health and Social Affairs*, Mohamed Said Saleh
*Civil Service and Administrative Reform*, Ougoureh Hassan Ibrahim
*Public Works, Construction and Housing*, Atteyeh Ismael Waiss
*Industry, Energy and Mines*, Ali Mahamade Houmed
*Planning, Regional Development, Environment and Co-operation*, Mohamed Moussa Chehem
*Transport, Tourism and Telecommunications*, Ahmed Waberi Guedi
*Labour and Professional Organizations*, Ibiro Ahmed Hamadou
*Agriculture and Rural Development*, Omar Chirdon Abass

### EMBASSY OF THE REPUBLIC OF DJIBOUTI

26 rue Emile Ménier, 75116 Paris, France
Tel: Paris 47274922

*Ambassador Extraordinary and Plenipotentiary*, His Excellency Ahmed Omar Farah, apptd 1991

BRITISH AMBASSADOR, His Excellency Duncan Christopher, resides at Addis Ababa, Ethiopia

BRITISH CONSULATE
PO Box 81, 9–11 Rue de Geneve, Djibouti
*Honorary Consul*, P. Lieven

The French continue to maintain army, navy and air force bases in Djibouti, with a total strength of 4,000 personnel. Djibouti has an excellent port, an international airport, and a railway line runs to Addis Ababa.

| Trade with UK | 1992 | 1993 |
|---|---|---|
| Imports from UK | £25,472,000 | £21,601,000 |
| Exports to UK | 58,000 | 1,146,000 |

# DOMINICA
*The Commonwealth of Dominica*

Dominica, the loftiest of the Lesser Antilles, lies in the Windward Group, between 15° 12' and 15° 39' N. latitude and 61° 14' and 61° 29' W. longitude, 95 miles south of Antigua. It is about 29 miles long and 16 broad comprising an area of 289 sq. miles (748.5 sq. km). The island is of volcanic origin and very mountainous, and the soil is very fertile. The temperature varies, according to the altitude, from 13° to 29°C. The population is 72,000 (1991 UN estimate).

CAPITAL – ΨRoseau, on the south-west coast, population 15,850. The other principal town is Portsmouth, population 3,620.
CURRENCY – East Caribbean dollar (EC$) of 100 cents.
FLAG – Green ground with a cross overall of yellow, black and white stripes, and in the centre a red disc charged with a Sisserou parrot in natural colours within a ring of ten green stars.
NATIONAL ANTHEM – Isle of Beauty.
NATIONAL DAY – 3 November (Independence Day).

## GOVERNMENT

The island was discovered by Columbus in 1493, when it was a stronghold of the Caribs, who remained virtually the sole inhabitants until the French established settlements in the 18th century. It was captured by the British in 1759 but passed back and forth between France and Britain until 1805, after which British possession was not challenged. From 1871 to 1939 Dominica was part of the Leeward Islands Colony, then from 1940 the island was a unit of the Windward Islands group. Internal self-government from 1967 was followed on 3 November 1978 by independence as a republic.

Executive authority is vested in the President, who is elected by the House of Assembly for not more than two terms of five years. Parliament consists of the President and the House of Assembly (representatives elected by universal adult suffrage) and nine Senators, five of whom are appointed on the advice of the Prime Minister and the other four on the advice of the Leader of the Opposition. Parliament has a life of five years.

At the general election of May 1990, the Dominica Freedom Party won 11 seats, the Dominica United Workers' Party 6, and the Labour Party of Dominica 4.

## HEAD OF STATE

*President*, His Excellency Crispin Sorhaindo, OBE, *elected* 4 October 1993, *took office* 25 October 1993

### CABINET *as at July 1994*

*Prime Minister, Minister of Finance and Economic Affairs, Information and Public Relations*, Dame Eugenia Charles, DBE
*Attorney-General and Minister of Legal Affairs*, Hon. Jenner Armour
*External Affairs and OECS Unity*, Hon. Brian Alleyne
*Trade, Industry and Tourism*, Hon. Charles Maynard
*Education and Sports*, Hon. Rupert Sorhaindo sen
*Community Development and Social Affairs*, Hon. Henry George
*Health and Social Security*, Hon. Allan Guye
*Labour and Immigration*, Hon. Heskeith Alexander
*Communications, Works and Housing*, Hon. Alleyne Carbon
*Agriculture*, Hon. Maynard Joseph
*Minister without Portfolio, Prime Minister's Office*, Hon. Dermott Southwell
*Parliamentary Secretary in the Ministry of Agriculture, Trade, Industry and Tourism*, Hon. Ossie Walsh
*Parliamentary Secretary in the Ministry of Communications, Works and Housing*, Hon. Clem Shillingford

HIGH COMMISSION FOR THE COMMONWEALTH OF DOMINICA
1 Collingham Gardens, London SW5 0HW
Tel 0171-370 5194/5
*High Commissioner*, His Excellency Ashworth Elwin, apptd 1992

BRITISH HIGH COMMISSIONER, His Excellency Richard Thomas, CMG, resides at Bridgetown, Barbados

BRITISH CONSULATE
PO Box 6, Roseau
*Honorary Consul*, J. Calvert

ECONOMY
Agriculture is the principal occupation, with tropical and citrus fruits the main crops. Products for export are bananas, lime juice, lime oil, bay oil, copra and rum. Forestry, fisheries and agro-processing are being encouraged. The only commercially exploitable mineral is a pumice, used chiefly for building purposes. Manufacturing consists largely of the processing of agricultural products.

| FINANCE | 1991–2 |
| --- | --- |
| Recurrent revenue | EC$144.5m |
| Recurrent expenditure | 98.8m |

| TRADE | 1990 |
| --- | --- |
| Imports | EC$318.3m |
| Exports | 148.5m |

| *Trade with UK* | 1992 | 1993 |
| --- | --- | --- |
| Imports from UK | £8,559,000 | £10,226,000 |
| Exports to UK | 21,870,000 | 23,534,000 |

## DOMINICAN REPUBLIC
*República Dominicana*

The Dominican Republic, the eastern part of the island of Hispaniola, is the oldest settlement of European origin in America. The western part of the island forms the republic of Haiti. The island lies between Cuba on the west and Puerto Rico on the east and the Dominican Republic covers an area of 18,816 sq. miles (48,734 sq. km). The climate is tropical in the lowlands and semi-tropical to temperate in the higher altitudes.

The population (1991 UN estimate) is 7,321,000. Spanish is the language of the republic.

CAPITAL – Ψ Santo Domingo, population of the Capital District (1981 census) 1,313,172. Other centres, with populations (1981 census): Santiago de los Caballeros (550,372); La Vega (385,043); San Francisco De Macoris (235,544); San Juan (239,957); San Cristóbal (446,132).
CURRENCY – Dominican Republic peso (RD$) of 100 centavos.
FLAG – Divided into blue and red quarters by a white cross.
NATIONAL ANTHEM – Quisqueyanos Valientes, Alcemos (Brave men of Quisqueya, let's raise our song).
NATIONAL DAY – 27 February (Independence Day 1844).

GOVERNMENT

Santo Domingo was discovered by Columbus in December 1492, and remained a Spanish colony until 1821. In 1822 it was subjugated by the neighbouring Haitians who remained in control until 1844, when the Dominican Republic was proclaimed. The country was occupied by American marines from 1916 until 1924. From 1930 until 30 May 1961 (when he was assassinated) Gen. Rafael Trujillo ruled the country.

President Juan Bosch held office from December 1962 to September 1963, when he was deposed by a military junta. A left-wing revolt in favour of ex-President Bosch in April 1965 developed into civil war lasting until September the same year when Bosch's supporters were defeated by the arrival of US troops and a provisional President was elected.

In November 1966 a new constitution was introduced. The last presidential election was held on 16 May 1994 and won by the incumbent President Balaguer amid allegations of violence, intimidation and vote-rigging.

Executive power is vested in the President, who is elected by direct vote and serves for four years. The President forms his cabinet without reference to the Congress. Legislative power is exercised by the Congress, which has a term of four years concurrent with the presidency. The Congress comprises the Senate of 27 senators, one for each province and one for Santo Domingo, and the Chamber of Deputies, which has 120 members, one for each 50,000 inhabitants in each province, with the provision that no province has less than two members. Judicial power is exercised by the Supreme Court of Justice.

HEAD OF STATE
*President*, Dr Joaquin Balaguer, *took office*, 16 August 1986, re-elected 1990, 16 May 1994
*Vice-President*, Carlos Morales Troncoso

CABINET *as at July 1994*
*Presidency*, Rafael Bello Andino
*Finance*, Florencío Lorenzo Silva
*Foreign Affairs*, Juan Aristides Guzman
*Education and Culture*, Jacqueline Malagón
*Agriculture*, Victor Hernández
*Labour*, Rafael Alburquerque
*Public Health and Social Welfare*, Dr Miguel A. Strepan
*Industry and Trade*, Arturo Martinez Moya
*Sports, Physical Education and Recreation*, Cristobal Marte Tourism, Luis Taveras
*Interior and Police*, Dr Atilio Guzmán Fernandez
*Armed Forces*, Lt.-Gen. Constantino Mato Villanueva
*Without Portfolio*, Domingo Gutiérrez

EMBASSY OF THE DOMINICAN REPUBLIC
17 rue La Fontaine, 75016 Paris, France
Tel: Paris 45018881
*Ambassador Extraordinary and Plenipotentiary*, new appointment awaited

HONORARY CONSULATE
6 Queen's Mansions, Brook Green, London W6 7EB
Tel 0171–602 1885
*Honorary Consul*, vacant
There are also Consular Offices at *Birmingham, Cardiff, Grimsby* and *Plymouth*.

BRITISH AMBASSADOR, His Excellency John Gerrard Flynn, CMG, resident at Caracas, Venezuela

BRITISH CONSULATE
Abraham Lincoln 552, Santo Domingo DR
Tel: Santo Domingo 5015 5010
*Honorary Consul*, M. Tejeda, MBE

COMMUNICATIONS

There are over 4,000 miles of roads in the republic. There is a direct road from Santo Domingo to Port-au-Prince, the capital of Haiti, but that part of it in the border area has fallen into disuse. The frontier has been closed since September 1967, except for that section crossed by the main road linking the two capitals. A telephone system connects practically all the principal towns of the republic and there is a telegraph service to all parts of the world. There are more than 90 commercial broadcasting stations and six television stations.

The republic is served by two national and six foreign airlines, and an international airport 18 miles to the east of the capital is in operation. Another has been built near Puerto Plata on the north coast.

# ECONOMY

Since 1990 the government has successfully reduced inflation from 100 per cent to 3 per cent per annum and has increased output substantially. Large amounts of foreign debt have been paid off but unemployment remains high at 25 per cent.

Sugar, coffee, cocoa, and tobacco are the most important crops. Other products are peanuts, maize, rice, bananas, molasses, salt, cement, ferro-nickel, gold, silver, cattle, sisal products, honey and chocolate. There is a growing number of light industries producing beer, tinned foodstuffs, glass products, textiles, soap, cigarettes, construction materials, plastic articles, shoes, papers, paint, rum, matches, peanut oil and other products.

## TRADE

The chief imports are machinery, food stuffs, iron and steel, cotton textiles and yarns, mineral oils (including petrol), motor vehicles, chemical and pharmaceutical products, electrical equipment and accessories, construction material, paper and paper products, and rubber and rubber products. The chief exports are sugar, coffee, cocoa, tobacco, chocolate, molasses, bauxite, ferro-nickel and gold. Tobacco and tobacco manufactures are the principal exports to the UK.

|         | 1992        | 1993        |
|---------|-------------|-------------|
| Imports | RD$2,174.6m | RD$2,115.5m |
| Exports | 562.4m      | 530.4m      |

| Trade with UK  | 1992        | 1993        |
|----------------|-------------|-------------|
| Imports from UK | £16,668,000 | £24,316,000 |
| Exports to UK  | 19,792,000  | 21,645,000  |

---

# ECUADOR
*Republica del Ecuador*

---

Ecuador is an equatorial state of South America, extending from 1° 38′ N. to 4° 50′ S. latitude, and between 75° 20′ and 81° W. longitude, comprising an area of about 109,484 sq. miles (283,561 sq. km). The republic extends across the Western Andes, the highest peaks in Ecuador being Chimborazo (20,408 ft) and Ilinza (17,405 ft) in the Western Cordillera; and Cotopaxi (19,612 ft) and Cayambe (19,160 ft) in the Eastern Cordillera. Ecuador is watered by the Upper Amazon, and by the rivers Guayas, Mira, Santiago, Chone, and Esmeraldas on the Pacific coast. There are extensive forests.

POPULATION – The population (UN estimate 1991) is 10,851,000, mostly descendants of the Spanish, aboriginal Indians, and Mestizoes. Spanish is the principal language but Quechua is also a recognized language and is spoken by the majority of the Indian population.

CAPITAL – Quito, population (1991 estimate) 1,387,887; Ψ Guayaquil (1,531,229) is the chief port; Cuenca (332,117).

CURRENCY – Sucre of 100 centavos.

FLAG – Three horizontal bands, yellow, blue and red (the yellow band twice the width of the others); emblem in centre.

NATIONAL DAY – 10 August (Independence Day).

# GOVERNMENT

The former kingdom of Quito was conquered by the Incas of Peru in the latter part of the 15th century. Early in the 16th century Pizarro's conquests led to the inclusion of the present territory of Ecuador in the Spanish Vice-royalty of Quito. The independence of the country was achieved in a revolutionary war which culminated in the battle of Mount Pichincha on 24 May 1822.

After seven years of military rule, Ecuador returned to democracy in 1979. The present constitution, introduced in 1978, provides for an elected President and Vice-President who serve for a four-year term. Neither may stand for re-election. There is a unicameral National Congress with 77 members elected every four years, 12 of whom are elected on a national basis and the rest by the provinces. The Chamber meets for two months every year (August to October) but can be convoked at any time for extraordinary sessions. Four Legislative Commissions meet through the year. Voting is compulsory for all literate and (since 1980) voluntary for all illiterate citizens over the age of 18. The republic is divided into 21 provinces.

In the May 1992 legislative election no party or coalition gained a majority but a loose agreement between various right-wing and centre-right parties enabled President Ballén to introduce a programme of free market economic reform, financial liberalization and privatization. This, together with reduction in state spending, has caused serious social unrest throughout late 1992 and 1993.

HEAD OF STATE
*President*, Sixto Durán Ballén, *elected* 5 July 1992, *sworn in* 10 August 1992
*Vice-President*, Alberto Dahik Garzozi

CABINET *as at August 1994*
*Government Affairs*, Roberto Dunn Barreira
*Foreign Affairs*, Dr Diego Paredes
*Interior*, Marcelo Santos Vera
*National Defence*, Jose Gallardo Roman
*Education and Culture*, Rosalia Arteaga
*Finance and Public Credit*, César Robalino Gonzaga
*Public Works and Communications*, Pedro Lopez Torres
*Energy and Mines*, Francisco Acosta Coloma
*Industry, Commerce, Integration and Fisheries*, José Vincente Maldonado
*Labour*, Alfredo Corral Borrero
*Agriculture and Livestock*, Mariano Gonzalez
*Public Health*, Patricio Abdad Herrera
*Social Welfare*, Alberto Cárdenas Davalos
*Information and Tourism*, Armando Espinel Elizalde
*Housing and Urban Development*, Francisco Albornoz
*Secretary-General of the Administration*, Carlos Larreategui

EMBASSY OF ECUADOR
Flat 3B, 3 Hans Crescent, London SWIX OLS
Tel 0171-584 8084

*Ambassador Extraordinary and Plenipotentiary*, His Excellency Patricio Maldonado, apptd 1994

BRITISH EMBASSY
Av. Gonzalez Suarez, 111 (Casilla 314), Quito
Tel: Quito 560670

*Ambassador Extraordinary and Plenipotentiary*, His Excellency Richard Lavers, apptd 1993

There are British Consular Offices at *Cuenca, Galapagos* and *Guayaquil.*

BRITISH COUNCIL REPRESENTATIVE, Anthony Deyes, Av. Amazonas 1646, Orellana (Casilla 17078829), Quito. There is also an English Language Teaching Centre at Guayaquil.

## ECONOMY

Agriculture is the most important sector of the economy, supporting nearly 50 per cent of the population (particularly the poorest) and contributing 14.5 per cent of GDP and 19.5 per cent of exports. The main products for export are fish (mainly shrimps, tuna and sardines), bananas, which provide a third of agricultural exports, cocoa and coffee. Other important crops are sugar, corn, soya, rice, cotton, African palm (for oil), vegetables, fruit and timber, the temperate crops being produced mostly in the highlands.

The economy was transformed by the discovery in 1972 of major oil fields in the Oriente area, and oil accounted for two-thirds of export earnings by 1981, but the fall in the price of oil has reduced economic growth. The oil deposits in the Oriente are estimated at between 10,000 and 15,000 million barrels, and further exploration and development is taking place. The oil is evacuated by a trans-Andean pipeline to the port of Balao (near Esmeraldas City). Ecuador withdrew from OPEC in September 1992 in order to raise its production to 385,000 barrels per day by the end of 1992. The total foreign debt is estimated at US$12,500m.

### TRADE

Import permits are required for all merchandise and these are issued by the Central Bank of Ecuador. Manufactured goods and machinery are the main imports.

|  | 1991 |
| --- | --- |
| Imports | US$2,207m |
| Exports | 2,851m |

| Trade with UK | 1992 | 1993 |
| --- | --- | --- |
| Imports from UK | £33,064,000 | £48,269,000 |
| Exports to UK | 15,657,000 | 19,855,000 |

## COMMUNICATIONS

There are 23,256 km of permanent roads and 5,044 km of roads which are only open during the dry season. There are about 750 miles of railway. Ten commercial airlines operate international flights, linking Ecuador with major foreign cities and there are internal services between all important towns. Two daily newspapers are published at Quito and four at Guayaquil.

## DEFENCE

The total active armed forces number some 58,000 personnel, with a further 100,000 reserves. The Army has a strength of 50,000 personnel with 150 light tanks, 160 armoured personnel carriers and reconnaissance vehicles and 70 artillery pieces. The Air Force has a strength of 3,500 personnel with 83 combat aircraft. The Navy is 4,500 strong (including 1,500 marines) and has two submarines, two frigates and 12 patrol and coastal combatants.

## EDUCATION

As a result of an intensive national education programme more than 75 per cent of the population are now literate. Elementary education is free and compulsory. There are ten universities (three at Quito, three at Guayaquil, and one each at Cuenca, Machala, Loja and Portoviejo), polytechnic schools at Quito and Guayaquil and eight technical colleges in other provincial capitals.

## GALÁPAGOS ISLANDS

The Galápagos (Giant Tortoise) Islands, forming the province of the Archipelago de Colón, were annexed by Ecuador in 1832. The archipelago lies in the Pacific, about 500 miles from the mainland. There are 12 large and several hundred smaller islands with a total area of about 3,000 sq. miles, an estimated population (1982) of 6,119. The capital is San Cristobal, on Chatham Island. Although the archipelago lies on the equator, the temperature of the surrounding water is well below equatorial average owing to the Antarctic Humboldt Current. The province consists for the most part of National Park Territory, where unique marine birds, iguanas, and the giant tortoises are conserved. There is some local subsistence farming; the main industry, apart from tourism, is tuna and lobster fishing.

---

## EGYPT
*Al-Jumhuriyat Misr al-Arabiya*

Egypt comprises Egypt proper, the peninsula of Sinai and a number of islands in the Gulf of Suez and Red Sea, of which the principal are Jubal, Shadwan, Gafatin and Zeberged (or St John's Island). This territory lies between 22° and 32° N. latitude and 24° and 37° E. longitude. The northern boundary is the Mediterranean, and Egypt borders the Sudan in the south and Libya in the west. The east boundary follows a line drawn from Rafa on the Mediterranean (34° 15′ E. longitude.) to the head of the Gulf of 'Aqaba. The total area of Egypt is 386,662 sq. miles (1,001,449 sq. km).

The country is mainly flat but there are mountainous areas in the south-west, along the Red Sea coast and in the south of the Sinai peninsula, rising in some places to peaks of over 6,000 ft. The highest mountain is Mt Catherina (8,668 ft). Most of the land is desert and the Nile valley and delta were the only fertile areas until the opening of the Aswam Dam allowed areas of desert to be reclaimed by irrigation and fertilization.

West of the Nile Valley is the Western desert, containing some depressions whose springs irrigate small areas known as oases, of which the principal are Kharga, Dakhla, Farafra, Baharia and Siwa. The Eastern Desert between the Nile and the mountains along the Red Sea coast is mostly plateaux dissected by wadis (dry water-courses), with occasional wells and springs.

POPULATION – The population (UN estimate 1991) is 54,688,000. The largest, or 'Egyptian' element, is a Hamito-Semite race, known in the rural districts as *Fellahin* (*fellâh*, ploughman or tiller of the soil). A second element is the *Bedouin*, or nomadic Arabs of the Western and Arabian deserts, of whom about one-seventh are real nomads, and the remainder semi-sedentary tent-dwellers on the outskirts of the cultivated end of the Nile Valley and the Fayüm. The third element is the *Nubian* of the Nile Valley between Aswân and Wadi-Halfa of mixed Arab and Negro blood. Over 90 per cent of the population are Muslims of the Sunni denomination, and most of the rest Coptic Christians.

CAPITAL – Cairo (population, 1986 estimate, 14,000,000), stands on the Nile about 14 miles from the head of the delta. Its oldest part is the fortress of Babylon in old Cairo, with its Roman bastions and Coptic churches. The earliest Arab building is the Mosque of 'Amr, dating from AD 643, and the most conspicuous is the Citadel, built by Saladin towards the end of the 12th century and containing in its walls the Mosque of Mohamed Ali built in the 19th century.

Other cities and towns are: ΨAlexandria (population, 1986 estimate, 5,000,000), founded 332 BC by Alexander the Great, was for over 1,000 years the capital of Egypt and a centre of Hellenic culture which vied with Athens itself. Its great *pharos* (lighthouse), 480 feet high, with a lantern burning resinous wood, was one of the Seven Wonders of the World; Ismailia (400,000); ΨPort Said (285,000); Mansura (120,000); Asyût (300,000); Faiyûm (180,000); Tanta (150,000); Mahalla el Kubra (130,000); ΨSuez; Ψ Damietta (100,000).

CURRENCY – Egyptian pound (£E) of 100 piastres and 1,000 millièmes.

FLAG – Horizontal bands of red, white and black, with an eagle in the centre of the white band.

NATIONAL DAY – 23 July (Anniversary of Revolution in 1952).

## HISTORY

The unification of the kingdoms of Lower and Upper Egypt under the Pharaohs c.3100 BC marked the establishment of the Egyptian state, with Memphis as its capital. Egypt was ruled for nearly 2,800 years by a succession of Pharaonic dynasties (31 in all), which built the pyramids at Gizeh. A period of Hellenic rule began in 332 BC, after the conquest of Egypt by Alexander the Great, followed by a period of rule by Rome (30 BC to AD 324) and then by the Byzantine Empire. In AD 640 Egypt was subjugated by Arab Muslim invaders, becoming a province of the Eastern Caliphate. In 1517 the country was incorporated in the Ottoman Empire, under which it remained until early in the 19th century. A British Protectorate over Egypt lasted from 1914 to 1922, when Sultan Ahmed Fuad was proclaimed King of Egypt. In June 1953 the monarchy was deposed and Egypt became a republic.

In 1956, as a result of Egypt's trade agreements with Communist countries, Britain and USA withdrew offers of financial aid and in retaliation President Nasser seized the assets of the Suez Canal Company. Egyptian occupation of the Canal Zone while repulsing an Israeli attack was used as a pretext for military action by Britain and France in support of their Suez Canal Company interests. A ceasefire and Anglo-French withdrawal were negotiated by the UN.

The Israeli invasion of 1956 overran the Sinai peninsula but six months later Israel withdrew and a UN peace-keeping force was established in the area. However, mounting tension culminated in a second invasion of Sinai (the Six Day War of June 1967) and occupation of the peninsula by Israel. Egypt's attempt to recapture the territory (the Yom Kippur War of October 1973) was unsuccessful but Sinai was returned to Egypt in April 1982, under the treaty of 1979 which resulted from the Camp David talks and formally terminated a 31-year-old state of war between the two countries. The treaty with Israel caused Egypt to be ostracized by the rest of the Arab world until 1990 when its participation in the Gulf War helped to rehabilitate it in the Arab world.

Militant Muslim fundamentalists re-emerged in March 1992 declaring war on the government and carrying out attacks on Coptic Christians, tourists and the security forces. Attacks have continued in 1993-4 and are concentrated in Upper Egypt and the Cairo area. The two main terrorist groups, the Gama'a el-Islamiya and Egyptian Islamic Jihad, extended their campaign in February 1994 by ordering all foreigners to leave the country or face violent attacks. The government has reacted vigorously to the armed campaign with the arrest of some 2,800 militants. By summer 1994 400 militants and security force personnel had been killed and some 50 militants sentenced to death by military courts.

## GOVERNMENT

The constitution of 1971 provides for an executive President who appoints ministers to the government. The President determines policy which the Council of Ministers implements. The legislature consists of the People's Assembly (454 members, 444 of whom are elected, the remaining ten nominated by the President). The Shura Council, or Consultative Assembly (258 members) has an advisory role. Religious courts were abolished in 1956 and their functions transferred to the national court system.

The ruling National Democratic Party won general elections, boycotted by the major opposition parties, held in November and December 1990. President Mubarak was nominated by the legislature to run unopposed for a third six-year term in July 1993, and was elected in October.

HEAD OF STATE
*President*, Muhammad Hosni Mubarak, *elected* 13 October 1981, *re-elected* 1987, 13 October 1993

COUNCIL OF MINISTERS *as at July 1994*
*Prime Minister and International Co-operation*, Dr Atef Muhammad Naguib Sidqi
*Deputy PM and Minister of Planning*, Dr Kamal Ahmed al-Ganzuri
*Deputy PM and Minister of Agriculture, Animal Wealth, Fisheries and Land Reclamation*, Dr Yussif Amin Wali
*Defence and Military Production*, Field Marshal Mohammed Hussein Tantawi
*Foreign Affairs*, Amre Moussa
*Economy and Foreign Trade*, Mohamed Mahmoud Baioumi
*Finance*, Dr Muhammad Ahmed el-Razzaz
*Interior*, Maj.-Gen. Hassan al-Alfi
*Oil*, Dr Hamdy El Bambi
*Tourism*, Mamdouh Beltagui
*Justice*, Farouq Saif al-Nasr
*Culture*, Farouq Hosni
*Industry and Mineral Resources*, Ibrahim Abdel-Wahed
*Supply and Internal Trade*, Dr Mohammed Galal Abdul-Dahab.
*Public Works and Water Resources*, Mohammed Abdel-Hadi Radi
*Manpower and Vocational Training*, Ahmed Ahmed El-Amawi
*Education*, Dr Hussein Kamal Baha El-Din
*Transport, Communications and Civil Aviation*, Suliman Metwalli Suliman
*Health*, Dr Ali El-Makhzangi
*Information*, Muhammad Safwat al-Sharif
*Cabinet Affairs and Administrative Development*, Ahmed Radwan Gomaa
*Religious Affairs (Waqfs)*, Dr Muhammad Ali Mahgoub
*Social Affairs and Social Insurance*, Dr Amal Abdul Rahim Osman
*Electricity and Energy*, Mohammad Mahir Osman Abaza
*Public Business*, Dr Atef Mohamed Ebeid
*Housing and Public Utilities*, Mohammed Salaheddin Hasaballah
*Local Government*, Dr Mahmmoud Sherif

EMBASSY OF THE ARAB REPUBLIC OF EGYPT
26 South Street, London W1Y 8EL
Tel 0171-499 2401

*Ambassador Extraordinary and Plenipotentiary*, His Excellency Mohamed I. Shaker, apptd 1988
*Minister Plenipotentiary, Deputy Chief of Mission*, Dr Mamdouh Shawky
*Minister Plenipotentiary and Consul-General*, Hassan Salem
*Minister Plenipotentiary*, Ahmed Abdel Hameed Nafeh
*Defence Attaché*, Comm. Nour Eldin Negm
*Minister Plenipotentiary (Commercial)*, Amr Osman El Menshawi
*Cultural Attaché*, Dr Omar B. Salman

BRITISH EMBASSY
Ahmed Ragheb Street, Garden City, Cairo
Tel: Cairo 354–0850
*Ambassador Extraordinary and Plenipotentiary*, His
  Excellency Christopher Long, CMG, apptd 1992
*Counsellor and Deputy Head of Mission*, A. F. Goulty
*Counsellor*, J. B. MacPherson
*Defence and Military Attaché*, Col. G. N. R. Sayle, OBE
*First Secretary and Consul*, A. M. M. Sheldon
*First Secretary (Commercial)*, I. S. Lockhart, MBE
There are British consular offices at *Luxor*, *Suez* and *Port
Said*, and a Consulate-General at *Alexandria*.

BRITISH COUNCIL REPRESENTATIVE, Howard
  Thompson, OBE, 192 Sharia el Nil, Agouza, Cairo. There
  is also a library in *Alexandria*.

## DEFENCE

The armed forces number some 430,000 active personnel
(272,000 conscripts). Selective conscription for three-year
terms operate. Equipment is from a wide range of Soviet,
US, Chinese, French and UK manufacture.

The Army numbers 310,000 (200,000 conscripts) with
3,165 main battle tanks, 4,045 armoured infantry fighting
vehicles and armoured personnel carriers, and 1,300 artillery
pieces. It is organized into four armoured and eight
mechanized divisions, together with a further 32 independent
brigades.

The Navy has 20,000 personnel (12,000 conscripts) with
one destroyer, four frigates, two submarines, 39 patrol and
coastal craft, and 17 armed helicopters. The Air Force has
100,000 personnel (60,000 conscripts) with 546 combat
aircraft and 74 armed helicopters. These are organized into
seven ground attack, 16 air defence and two reconnaissance
squadrons.

There are also 370,000 paramilitary Security Forces and
National Guard personnel.

## ECONOMY

Egypt's foreign debt to western governments stood at US$14
billion in mid-1994, having been reduced from US$20 billion
the previous year by write-offs tied to an IMF economic and
financial reform programme. Economic growth has improved
under the programme to 2.4 per cent of GDP in 1993–4,
while inflation stood at 7.3 per cent a year in April 1994.

Despite increasing industrialization, agriculture remains
the most important economic activity, employing over 45
per cent of the labour force and contributing to 17 per cent
of the country's exports. Agricultural output has been
increased as a result of land reclamation programmes and
the introduction of more efficient methods of irrigation,
fertilization and increasing mechanization. Egypt is still a
net importer of foodstuffs, especially grain, and a food
security programme has been set up with the aim of achieving
self-sufficiency.

The main cash crop is cotton, of which Egypt is one of the
world's main producers. Other important summer crops are
maize, rice and sugar cane. Important winter crops are wheat
and beans. Citrus fruit and other fruits and vegetables are
also grown.

With its considerable reserves of petroleum and natural
gas in Sinai, the Nile delta and the Western Desert, and the
hydro-electric power produced by the Aswan and High
Dams, Egypt is self-sufficient in energy. Electricity has been
provided to almost all of the country and there are plans to
extend the natural gas network to all major cities.

The production of petroleum provides Egypt with its
major export (60–65 per cent of total exports), and supports

a refining industry. Steel production is another important
heavy industry. The major manufacturing industries are food
processing, motor cars and electrical goods, chemical
products and yarns and textiles.

## TRADE

The main imports are wheat, flour, wood and trucks. The
main exports are crude petroleum, cotton, cotton yarn,
oranges, rice and cotton textiles.

| Trade with UK | 1992 | 1993 |
|---|---|---|
| Imports from UK | £252,271,000 | £337,105,000 |
| Exports to UK | 137,008,000 | 188,355,000 |

## COMMUNICATIONS

The road and rail networks link the Nile valley and delta
with the main development areas to east and west of the
river. The Suez Canal was reopened in 1975 and a two-stage
development project begun to widen and deepen the canal
to allow the passage of larger shipping and to permit two-
way traffic. Port Said and Suez have been reconstructed and
the port of Alexandria is being improved.

---

## EQUATORIAL GUINEA
*República de Guinea Ecuatorial*

---

Equatorial Guinea (formerly Spanish Guinea) consists of the
island of Biogo (formerly Macias Nguema), in the Bight of
Biafra about 20 miles from the west coast of Africa, Pagalu
Island (formerly Annobon) in the Gulf of Guinea, the Corisco
Islands (Corisco, Elobey Grande and Elobey Chico) and Rio
Muni, a mainland area between Cameroon and Gabon. It
has a total area of 10,830 sq. miles (28,051 sq. km), and a
population (UN estimate 1991) of 356,000.

CAPITAL – ΨMalabo on the island of Bioco, population
  (1983 estimate) 30,418. ΨBata is the principal town and
  port of Rio Muni.
CURRENCY – Franc CFA of 100 centimes.
FLAG – Three horizontal bands, green over white over red;
  blue triangle next staff; coat of arms in centre of white
  band.
NATIONAL DAY – 12 October.

## GOVERNMENT

Formerly colonies of Spain, the territories now forming the
Republic of Equatorial Guinea were constituted as two
provinces of Metropolitan Spain in 1959, became autonomous
in 1963 and fully independent in 1968.

In August 1979 President Macias was deposed by a
revolutionary military council headed by his nephew Col.
Obiang Nguema. The first parliamentary elections since
1968 were held in August 1983, under a constitution approved
by a referendum in August 1982. Elections to the National
Assembly took place in July 1988, but all candidates were
nominated by the President and elected unopposed.

The introduction of a multiparty political system was
approved by a referendum in November 1991, and since then
ten opposition parties have been legalized to operate
alongside the ruling Equatorial Guinea Democratic Party
(PDGE). A National Pact was agreed and signed in March
1993 but when legislative elections were held on 22 November
1993 they were boycotted by most of the electorate and
opposition parties because the President was alleged to have
taken control of the electoral boards and rigged the election.

The PDGE won 68 out of 80 National Assembly seats and formed a government. A Presidential election is due in 1995.

HEAD OF STATE
*President of the Supreme Military Council and Minister of Defence*, Brig.-Gen. Teodoro Obiang Nguema Mbasogo, *took office*, August 1979, *re-elected* June 1989

MINISTERS *as at August 1994*
*Prime Minister*, Silvestre Siale Bileka
*Deputy Prime Minister, Economics and Finance*, Anatolio Ndong Mba
*Justice and Religion*, Francisco Javier Mbengono
*Public Works, Housing and Town Planning*, Alejandro Envoro Ovono
*Education and Science*, Ricardo Mangue Obama Nfube
*Labour and Social Security*, Constantino Congue
*Industry, Energy, Small and Medium-sized Enterprises*, Severino Obiang Bengono
*Mines and Hydrocarbons*, Juan Olo Nseng
*Agriculture, Fishing and Food*, Alfredo Mokudi Nanga
*Health and Environment*, Bemabe Ngore
*Social Affairs and Women*, Balbina Nchama Nvo
*Culture, Tourism and Francophone Affairs*, Agustin Nse Nfumu
*Relations with Parliament*, Mariano Nsue Nguema
*Foreign Affairs and Co-operation*, Feliciano Nsue Mangue

EMBASSY OF THE REPUBLIC OF EQUATORIAL GUINEA
6 Rue Alfred de Vigny, 75008, Paris
Tel: Paris 47664433

*Ambassador Extraordinary and Plenipotentiary*, new appointment awaited

BRITISH AMBASSADOR, His Excellency William Ernest Quantrill, resident at Yaoundé, Cameroon

BRITISH CONSULATE
World Bank Compound, Apartado 801, Malabo
Tel: Malabo 2400
*Honorary Consul*, vacant

## ECONOMY

The chief products are cocoa, coffee and wood (which is exported almost entirely from Rio Muni). Production has declined and except for cocoa there is little commercial agriculture and the economy is now heavily dependent on outside aid, principally from Spain. Oil and gas deposits exist but remain largely unexploited. Equatorial Guinea entered the 'Franc zone' in 1985.

| Trade with UK | 1992 | 1993 |
|---|---|---|
| Imports from UK | £1,357,000 | £1,237,000 |
| Exports to UK | 40,000 | 6,000 |

# ERITREA

Eritrea is bordered to the north and north-west by Sudan, to the south and south-west by Ethiopia, to the south-east by Djibouti and in the north-east and east borders on the Red Sea. Included in its territory are the Dahlak Islands group in the Red Sea. It has an area of 36,170 sq. miles (93,679 sq. km) and rises from a long, narrow, low-lying coastal strip to highlands in the centre and north which are 2,000–3,000 m high (6,500–9,800 ft) and are an extension of the Ethiopian highlands.

POPULATION – The population is 3,500,000 (1991 official estimate). About 50 per cent are Coptic Christian and 50 per cent Muslim. The majority of highlanders are Christian and the majority of lowlanders are Muslim.

The two main languages in use for business and taught in schools are English and Arabic. There are also nine indigenous language groups: Afar; Bilen; Hadareb; Kunama; Nara; Rashida; Saho; Tigre; Tigrinya.

CAPITAL – Asmara (275,000) in the central highlands.
ΨMassawa and ΨAssab are the two main ports and major towns in the country.
CURRENCY – The Ethiopian birr of 100 cents remains in use at present.
FLAG – Divided into three triangles; the one based on the hoist is red and bears a gold olive wreath; the upper triangle is green and the lower one light blue.
NATIONAL DAY – 24 May (Independence Day).

## GOVERNMENT

Eritrea was colonized by Italy in the late 19th century and it was from Eritrea that Italian forces launched their invasion of Abyssinia (Ethiopia) in 1936. After the Italian defeat in East Africa in 1941 by British and Commonwealth forces, Eritrea became a British protectorate. This lasted until 15 September 1952 when, according to the wishes of the UN, Eritrea was federated with Ethiopia but retained a high degree of political autonomy. The Ethiopian Emperor Haile Selassie eroded Eritrea's autonomy and in 1962 incorporated it as a province of Ethiopia. The incorporation provoked widespread resistance and an armed campaign for independence began which gathered momentum in the 1970s and 1980s, first against Emperor Haile Selassie's forces and from 1974 against the Soviet and Cuban-supported Mengistu regime.

In May 1991 the Mengistu government was brought down by the defeat of its armed forces by the Eritrean People's Liberation Front (EPLF) and its allies the Ethiopian People's Revolutionary Democratic Front (EPRDF). In July 1991 the new EPRDF-led government in Ethiopia agreed to an Eritrean referendum on independence which was held in April 1993. In the referendum, over 99 per cent of the electorate voted for independence. Independence was declared on 24 May 1993.

At independence the provisional government became the transitional government of Eritrea and is to govern the country for a maximum of four years while a new constitution is drafted. At the end of the transition period multiparty elections are to be held. During the transition period legislative power is vested in the National Assembly and executive power in the State Council appointed and chaired by the President. In early 1994 the EPLF transformed itself into a political party, the People's Front for Democracy and Justice (PFDJ), and the National Assembly voted to agree that for the remainder of the transition period it will comprise of 75 PFDJ central council members and 75 elected members. The government is committed to repatriating the remaining 500,000 of the 700,000 refugees who fled to Sudan during the war.

HEAD OF STATE
*President, Chairman of the National Assembly*, Issaias Afewerki, *elected by National Assembly* 22 May 1993

STATE COUNCIL *as at August 1994*
*Chairman*, The President
*Local Government*, Mahmoud Ahmed Sherifo
*Internal Affairs*, Ali Said Abdella
*Defence*, Mesfin Hafos
*Justice*, Fozia Hashim
*Foreign Affairs*, Petros Soloman

*Culture and Information*, Baraki Gebresalassie
*Finance and Development*, Haile Weldetensae
*Trade and Industry*, Ekuba Abraha
*Agriculture*, Tesfai Ghermazien
*Marine Resources*, Saleh Meki
*Construction*, Abraha Asfaha
*Energy, Mining and Water Resources*, Testay Gebraselassie
*Education*, Uthman Salih Muhammed
*Health*, Sebhat Ephrem
*Transport*, Giorgis Tekle Mikael
*Tourism*, Worku Tesfa Mikael

EMBASSY OF THE STATE OF ERITREA
Rue de Merode 216, 1060 Brussels, Belgium
Tel: Brussels 534 9563
*Ambassador Extraordinary and Plenipotentiary*, His
    Excellency Ato Ghebremichael Mengistu, apptd 1993

CONSULATE
96 White Lion Street, London N1 9PF
Tel: 0171 713 0096

BRITISH AMBASSADOR, His Excellency Duncan
    Christopher, resides at Addis Ababa, Ethiopia

BRITISH COUNCIL DIRECTOR – Simon Bush, PO Box
    997, Asmara

ECONOMY

The Eritrean economy was devastated by the war of
independence and the scorched earth policy of the retreating
Ethiopian forces. Since 1991 the government has directed all
its efforts into rebuilding the country's industry, agriculture
and infrastructure, especially in the highlands, where the
Ethiopian army uprooted nearly all the trees, leading to
serious erosion. Some 22 million tree seedlings are being
grown for planting. As the traditional agricultural and
industrial sectors producing sorghum, livestock, salt, cement,
fish, hides and potash are rebuilt, the government has
directed large parts of the population into infrastructure
rebuilding schemes in return for daily food aid. The focus of
the rebuilding programme are the ports of Massawa and
Assab, the roads from the ports to Ethiopia, and the railway
from Massawa to Sudan via Asmara. Before 1962 Eritrea was
one of the most industrialized areas of Africa and some
industry remains, producing textiles and footwear. The
government hopes to base the rebuilding of the economy on
the return of well-educated exiles, international aid and
investment, the development of tourism along the coast, and
the diversification of the economy away from agriculture.
The reconstruction programme has, however, been hampered severely by the failure of the main grain crop in the
highlands in late 1993, caused by a lack of rain. Food
shortages in late 1993 and early 1994 were met by foreign
aid from Western donors.

---

ESTONIA
*The Republic of Estonia*

---

Estonia is situated in northern Europe on the eastern coast
of the Baltic Sea. To the north lies the Gulf of Finland, to the
east the Russian Federation, and to the south Latvia. Estonia
lies between 57°30′ and 59°49′N., and between 21°46′ and
28°13′E. and has an area of 17,458 sq. miles (45,125 sq. km).
It includes 1,500 islands in the Baltic Sea and the Gulf of
Riga. Forests cover roughly 20 per cent of the country, which
also has many lakes. The climate is mild and maritime.
POPULATION – The population is 1,526,177 (1992 estimate),
of which 61.5 per cent are Estonian, 30.3 per cent Russian,

3.1 per cent Ukrainian, 1.8 per cent Belarussian. The religion
of the majority is Lutheran, with Russian Orthodox and
Baptist minorities.
    Estonian is the first language of 61.5 per cent and Russian
of 33.3 per cent. Estonian belongs to the Finno-Ugri language
group and is related to Finnish and Hungarian.

CAPITAL – Tallinn (population 452,840). Other cities are
    Tartu (109,133); Narva (80,491); Kohtla-Järve (56,141);
    Pärnu (52,085).
CURRENCY – Kroon (Crown) of 100 sent.
FLAG – Three horizontal stripes of blue, black, white.
NATIONAL ANTHEM – Mu Isamaa, mu õnn ja rõõm (My
    Fatherland).
NATIONAL DAY – 24 February (Independence Day).

HISTORY

Estonia, a former province of the Russian Empire, declared
its independence from Russia on 24 February 1918. A war of
independence was fought against the German army until
November 1918, and then against Soviet forces until the
peace treaty of Tartu was signed on 2 February 1920. By this
treaty the Soviet Union recognized Estonia's independence.
    The Soviet Union annexed Estonia in 1940 under the
terms of the Molotov-Ribbentrop pact with Germany. Estonia
was invaded and occupied when Germany invaded the Soviet
Union during the Second World War. In 1944 the Soviet
Union recaptured the country from Germany and confirmed
its annexation, though this was never accepted as legal by
most states.
    Under mounting public pressure, the Estonian Supreme
Soviet in November 1989 declared the republic to be
sovereign and its 1940 annexation by the Soviet Union to be
illegal. In February 1990 the leading role of the Communist
Party was abolished, and following multiparty elections in
March 1990 the Supreme Soviet inaugurated a period of
transition to independence. Full independence was supported
by an overwhelming majority in a referendum held in March
1991 and was declared on 20 August 1991. The State Council
of the Soviet Union recognized the independence of Estonia
on 10 September 1991.

GOVERNMENT

Under the 1992 constitution, legislative power is exercised
by the unicameral *Riigikogu* of 101 members elected by
proportional representation every four years. The President
is elected for a five-year term by the Riigikogu by a two-
thirds majority or, if no candidate receives this majority after
three rounds of voting, the President is elected by an electoral
body composed of Riigikogu members and local government
officials. Executive authority is vested in a Prime Minister
and government formed from a governing majority within
the parliament.
    Presidential and legislative elections were held in Septem-
ber 1992 on the basis of special provisions different from the
1992 constitution. The President was directly elected in the
first instance and only elected by the Riigikogu when no
candidate secured over 50 per cent of the vote. The President
was elected for a four-year term and the Riigikogu for a
three-year one. This was to enable newly-naturalized citizens
to be able to vote for representatives in national elections in
a shorter period of time. A conservative governing coalition
was formed from the Pro Patria National Coalition Party,
the Estonian Rural Centre Party, the Estonian Social
Democratic Party and the Estonia National Independence
Party.
    The vast majority of the ethnic Russian population was
unable to vote in either election as the government had

decreed that only citizens of pre-1940 Estonia and their descendants were eligible to vote. Tensions with the ethnic Russian population and Russia over citizenship remain. In June 1993 a citizenship law was introduced under which applicants must pass language tests in the Estonia language to gain citizenship by naturalization. After advice from international organizations, the citizenship law was amended in July 1993 to make it less discriminatory against ethnic Russians. The Estonian government declared illegal a referendum in July 1993 in the two mainly ethnic Russian cities of Narva and Sillamäe in which the populations voted for autonomy.

Estonia is divided into six towns and 15 districts for local administration purposes.

HEAD OF STATE
*President*, Lennart Meri, *elected* 5 October 1992

GOVERNMENT *as at August 1994*
*Prime Minister*, Mart Laar
*Justice*, Urmas Arumäe
*Defence*, Enn Tupp
*Finance*, Andres Lipstok
*Economy*, Toivo Jürgenson
*Interior*, Heiki Arike
*Foreign Affairs*, Juri Luik
*Social Services*, Marju Lauristin
*Culture and Education*, Peeter Olesk
*Agriculture*, Jaan Leetsar
*Transport and Communications*, Andi Meister
*Environment*, Andres Tarand
*Energy*, Arvo Niitenberg
*Reforms*, Liia Hänni
*Citzenship and Immigration*, vacant

EMBASSY OF THE REPUBLIC OF ESTONIA
16 Hyde Park Gate, London SW7 5DG
Tel 0171-589 3428
*Ambassador Extraordinary and Plenipotentiary*, His
   Excellency Riivo Sinijärv, apptd 1993

BRITISH EMBASSY
Kentmanni 20, Tallinn EE0100
Tel: Tallinn 313353
*Ambassador Extraordinary and Plenipotentiary*, His
   Excellency Charles De Chassiron, apptd 1994

## DEFENCE

Since independence Estonia has formed a small army of three infantry and two support battalions with a total number of 2,500 active personnel. A term of conscription of 12 months is in operation, with reserve forces numbering 6,000 militia, and a Navy is being formed. In addition there are 2,000 (1,200 conscripts) paramilitary border guards. Russia still maintains 2,500 army and air force personnel in Estonia, although these are being gradually withdrawn. On various occasions in 1992-4 President Yeltsin has threatened to suspend the withdrawal because of the alleged discrimination against ethnic Russians. An agreement on the full withdrawal of Russian forces by 31 August 1994 was reached in July 1994 under which the Estonian government guaranteed the welfare status of Russian military pensioners living in Estonia.

## ECONOMY

Estonia's economy was greatly affected by the collapse of the centralized Soviet economic system. Over the past three years the government has introduced reforms to transform the economy into one based on market economic principles

with privatization and restructuring. To this end, and to support a strong and fully convertible currency, the IMF provided credits worth US$40m in August 1992 and US$32m in October 1993. Having in 1992 established a stable currency linked to the Deutsche Mark, the economy has stabilized and output is recovering from the fall experienced in 1990-2. The process of privatization, started in 1992, has gained momentum and the privatization agency advertises internationally lists of enterprises that are up for auction. However, Estonia is still dependent on foreign fuel supplies, mainly natural gas, and this has been used as a weapon by President Yeltsin when he has threatened to suspend gas supplies to Estonia.

Agriculture and dairy-farming are a major sector of the Estonian economy, the main products being rye, oats, barley, flax, potatoes, meat, milk, butter and eggs.

Light industry is the other major area of the economy, concentrating on textiles, clothing and footwear, forestry, wood and paper products, and food and fish processing. Some heavy industry exists, concentrated in chemicals and the manufacture of power equipment.

## TRADE

Although Estonia signed a free trade deal with Russia in September 1992, it has greatly reduced its trade with the former Soviet states. In 1993 only 30 per cent of Estonian exports went to CIS states while 49 per cent went to EU and EFTA states. Imports in 1992 came from Finland (26 per cent), CIS (22 per cent), Sweden (7 per cent), Germany (6 per cent).

| Trade with UK | 1992 | 1993 |
|---|---|---|
| Imports from UK | £5,593,000 | £8,043,000 |
| Exports to UK | 10,418,000 | 20,039,000 |

## COMMUNICATIONS

Freedom of the press is guaranteed in the constitution, and the state monopoly on television and radio ended soon after independence. The remaining state-owned newspapers and broadcasting channels are editorially independent and in the process of being privatized. As at 6 January 1993 the government had granted 15 radio and nine television broadcasting licences. Russian-language news and programmes are provided on Estonian Television. There are five Estonian and three Russian-language daily newspapers.

## EDUCATION

Estonia has a three-tier education system, consisting of primary level (nine years), secondary level (three years) and university level (four to six years).

---

# ETHIOPIA
*Ityopia*

---

Ethiopia is in north-eastern Africa, bounded on the north-west by the Sudan, on the south by Kenya, on the east by Djibouti and Somalia, and on the north-east by Eritrea. The area is 435,608 sq. miles (1,128,221 sq. km). Eritrea became independent of Ethiopia on 24 May 1993.

A large central plateau (average height, 6,000-7,000 ft) rises to nearly 15,000 ft at Ras Dashan in the north. The plateau drops to the Nile basin in the west, to the Ogaden desert in the east and Eritrea and the Red Sea in the north. In the east (Ogaden) the land is mostly desert. The chief river is the Blue Nile, issuing from Lake Tana; the Atbara and many other tributaries of the Nile also rise in the Ethiopian highlands.

POPULATION – The population (UN estimate 1991) is 49,883,000. About one-third are of Semitic origin (Amharas and Tigrayans) and the remainder mainly Oromos (about 40 per cent of the population), Somalis and Afar. Those of Semitic origin and many of the Oromos, are Christians of the Ethiopian Orthodox Church, whose current Patriarch is Abuna Paulos Gebre-Yohannis. The Afar people, who inhabit Wollo, Hararghe and Bale provinces, and the Somalis, in the south-east, as well as some Oromos are Muslim. The Falashas, adherents of Judaism, formerly found principally in Gonder and Tigray provinces, were airlifted to Israel in 1984–5 and 1991.

There are 15 major ethnic groups which speak a total of 70 languages, of which the most widely used is Amharic.

CAPITAL – Addis Ababa (population, 1989 estimate, 1,739,130). Dire Dawa is the most important commercial centre after Addis Ababa. There are ancient architectural remains at Aksum, Gondar, Lalibela and elsewhere.

CURRENCY – Ethiopian birr (EB) of 100 cents.

FLAG – Three horizontal bands: green, yellow, red.

NATIONAL ANTHEM – Ityopya, Ityopya Kidemi.

NATIONAL DAY – 28 May.

## GOVERNMENT

The basic Hamitic culture was heavily influenced by Semitic immigration from Arabia in the centuries about the time of Christ. Christianity was introduced in the fourth century. The empire expanded sporadically, attaining a zenith in the sixth century under the Axum rulers, but subsequently was checked by Islamic expansion from the east. Modern Ethiopia dates from 1855 when Theodore succeeded in establishing supremacy over the various tribes. The last Emperor was Haile Selassie who reigned from 1930, though in exile from 1936–41 during the Italian occupation. After considerable military and civil unrest the armed forces assumed power in September 1974 and deposed the Emperor. After ten years of military rule, a Workers' Party on the Soviet model was formed in September 1984, with Mengistu Haile Mariam as General Secretary.

The civilian government of the People's Democratic Republic of Ethiopia was established under a new constitution in 1987 with Lt.-Col. Mengistu as President. Armed insurgencies by the Eritrean People's Liberation Front (EPLF) and the Ethiopian People's Revolutionary Democratic Front (EPRDF), originating in Tigray, brought down Mengistu's government in May 1991. An estimated one million people died in the civil war or from famine and government massacres during the Mengistu regime. At a national conference held in July 1991, an 87-member Council of Representatives was formed, comprising the EPRDF and a number of other opposition groups. The transitional government drew up plans dividing Ethiopia into 14 regions based as closely as possible on the different ethnic groups that were recognized, with these councils having a great amount of power devolved to them. Elections to the regional councils were held on 21 June 1992. Resentment at the end of the traditional Amharic political dominance caused by the Tigrayan-led EPRDF has caused social unrest.

The central government in Addis Ababa remains in control of foreign affairs, defence and economic policy. In early 1994 the central government devolved more power to the regions and in effect introduced a federal system whereby each regional administration may use its own local language, courts and schools. The Council of Representatives agreed on a draft federal constitution in April 1994, and the June election to a constituent assembly which will approve the new constitution was won by the EPRDF and its allies. The transitional government remains in power and has successfully introduced freedom of speech and established an independent judiciary.

HEAD OF STATE
*President*, Meles Zenawi, *elected by the Council of Representatives* 21 July 1991

TRANSITIONAL GOVERNMENT *as at June 1994*

*Prime Minister*, Tamirat Layne
*Justice*, Mehitema Solomon
*Information*, Dima Nego
*Foreign Affairs*, Seyoum Mesfin
*Health*, Dr Adanech Kidane Mariam
*Education*, Ibsa Gutema
*Industry*, Bekele Tadessa
*Interior*, Kuma Demeksa
*Mines and Energy*, Isedin Ali
*Commerce*, Yosef Kamalo
*State Farms*, Hassan Abdella
*Defence*, Seye Abraha
*Agriculture and Environmental Protection*, Zegeye Asfaw
*Housing and Construction*, Aragaw Tiruneh
*Culture and Sports*, Lieule Selassie Timamo
*Labour and Social Affairs*, Dr Legaso Gidada
*Transport*, Belachaw Mekbib
*Finance*, Alemayehu Dhaba

EMBASSY OF ETHIOPIA
17 Prince's Gate, London SW7 1PZ
Tel 0171–589 7212/3/4/5

*Ambassador Extraordinary and Plenipotentiary*, His Excellency Dr Solomon Gidada, apptd 1992
*Counsellor*, Laine Kahsu (*Commercial*)

BRITISH EMBASSY
Fikre Mariam Abatechan Street (PO Box 858), Addis Ababa
Tel: Addis Ababa 1612354

*Ambassador Extraordinary and Plenipotentiary*, His Excellency Duncan R. Christopher, apptd 1994
*Deputy Ambassador and First Secretary*, C. O. Pigott
*First Secretary*, A. J. Barber

BRITISH COUNCIL REPRESENTATIVE, Michael Sargent, Artistic Building, Adwa Avenue (PO Box 1043), Addis Ababa

## ECONOMY

The post-Mengistu government has engaged in a programme of free-market economic reform. Government spending has been brought under control and inflation was reduced to 12.9 per cent in 1992. The currency has been devalued, the civil service drastically reduced and the army halved in size. Western states have responded with debt relief and loans and the IMF approved a three-year loan of US$70m in October 1992 to support economic reform.

Thousands of peasant farmers resettled by the Mengistu regime in barren areas have returned to their own areas. Farms remain in state ownership but farmers have been granted security of tenure for life and agricultural policy is now market-based. Agriculture accounts for approximately 40 per cent of GDP, 85 per cent of exports and 80 per cent of total employment. The major food crops are teff, maize, barley, sorghum, wheat, pulses and oil seeds. Coffee, the principal export crop, generates over 50 per cent of the country's export earnings. Famine conditions, which attracted world attention in 1984–5, recurred for a short period and to a lesser extent in 1992. However, agricultural liberalization has led to dramatic progress in food production and produced a record harvest of 7.7 million tonnes of grain and pulses in 1993.

Manufacturing industry accounts for less than 9 per cent of GDP and is heavily dependent on agriculture. Ethiopia's known, but as yet largely unexploited, natural resources include gold, platinum, copper and potash. Traces of oil and natural gas have been found.

TRADE

The chief imports by value are machinery and transport equipment, manufactured goods and chemicals (from UK); the principal exports by value being coffee, oil seeds, hides and skins, and pulses.

| Trade with UK | 1992 | 1993 |
|---|---|---|
| Imports from UK | £53,312,000 | £57,660,000 |
| Exports to UK | 13,216,000 | 13,011,000 |

COMMUNICATIONS

A network of roads has been built in rural areas and links the major cities with each other, with the Sudanese and Kenyan borders and through Eritrea to the Red Sea coast. The Ethiopian and Eritrean governments negotiated an agreement in 1992 which guarantees Ethiopia access to the Red Sea via the ports of Assab and Massawa. Transport links suffered during the secessionist wars and under the heavy burden of famine relief traffic.

There is a railway link from Addis Ababa to Djibouti although this has been vulnerable to guerrilla activity. Ethiopian Airlines maintains regular services from Addis Ababa to many provincial towns. External services are operated throughout Africa and to Europe.

DEFENCE

Ethiopia's military forces (over 300,000 men) failed to contain the rebel forces and were disbanded by the post-Mengistu government. The EPRDF forces, numbering some 100,000, became the national army. Equipment includes 350 main battle tanks and 200 armoured personnel carriers and infantry fighting vehicles. The Air Force has 38 combat aircraft and 18 armed helicopters.

EDUCATION

Elementary education is provided by government schools in the main centres of population; there are also mission schools. Government secondary schools are found mainly in Addis Ababa, but also in most of the provincial capitals. The National University (founded 1961) co-ordinates the institutions of higher education (University College, Engineering, Building and Theological Colleges in Addis Ababa, and Public Health Centre in Gondar, etc.). There is a separate university at Alemaya (agricultural).

Amharic was the official language of instruction, with English as the first foreign language and main language of instruction from secondary level upwards. Arabic is taught in Koran schools; and Ge'ez (the ancient Ethiopic) in Christian church schools. Language policy is now under review by the post-Mengistu government.

---

# FIJI
*Matanitu Ko Viti - Republic of Fiji*

---

Fiji is made up of about 332 islands and over 500 islets (including numerous atolls and reefs) in the South Pacific Ocean, about 1,100 miles north of New Zealand. About 100 islands are permanently inhabited. The group extends 300 miles from east to west and 300 north to south between 15° 45' and 21° 10' S. latitude and 176° E. and 178° W. longitude. Its gross area is 7,055 sq. miles (18,274 sq. km). The International Date Line has been diverted to the east of the island group. The largest islands are Viti Levu and Vanua Levu. The main groups of islands are Lomaiviti, Lau and Yasawas. Most of the larger islands are mountainous with sharp peaks and crags, but also have conspicuous areas of flat land and many of the rivers have built extensive deltas. The climate is tropical without extremes of heat and temperatures rarely exceed 32°C or fall below 15°C.

POPULATION – The population (census 1986) was 715,373, comprising 48.6 per cent Indians, 46.2 per cent Fijians, and 5.2 per cent other races. A UN estimate (1991) gives a total figure of 776,000. Since the 1987 coup many ethnic Indians have left and by 1994 Melanesian Fijians formed the largest population group.

CAPITAL – ΨSuva, on the island of Viti Levu. Population (1986) 69,665.

CURRENCY – Fiji dollar (F$) of 100 cents.

FLAG – Light blue ground with Union flag in top left quarter and the shield of Fiji in the fly.

NATIONAL ANTHEM – God Bless Fiji.

NATIONAL DAY – 10 October (Fiji Day).

GOVERNMENT

Fiji was a British colony from 1874 until 10 October 1970 when it became an independent state and a member of the Commonwealth.

A coalition of the left under Dr Timoci Bavadra defeated the Alliance Party of Ratu Sir Kamisese Mara in a general election on 12 April 1987. The new government, drawing its support mainly from the Indian population, was overthrown in a military coup on 14 May by Lt.-Col. Sitiveni Rabuka. In the wake of the constitutional crisis an Advisory Council was set up as an interim government to consider constitutional reform. A second coup occurred on 25 September 1987. On 7 October Rabuka declared Fiji to be a republic; the Governor-General resigned on 15 October and Fiji's Commonwealth membership lapsed. In December another interim government was formed to work for a resolution to the political crisis.

A new constitution, promulgated in 1990, established the political dominance of the Melanesian community within the judiciary and a bicameral parliament; an amnesty was granted to participants in the 1987 coups. The bicameral parliament consists of a Senate of 34 members appointed by the President, of which 24 seats are reserved for Melanesian Fijians, one for the Polynesian island of Rotuma and nine for other races. The House of Representatives has a total of 70 seats; 37 reserved for Melanesians, 27 for Indians, one for Rotuma, and five for other races (European and Chinese). The presidency and the premiership can only be held by Melanesians. The President is elected by the (Melanesian) Great Council of Chiefs. The Fijian Political Party led by Rabuka won the general elections of May 1992 and February 1994 and has formed a coalition government with the General Voters Party.

HEAD OF STATE
*President*, Ratu Sir Kamisese Mara, GCMG, KBE, *elected* 10 January 1994, *inaugurated* 18 January 1994

CABINET *as at August 1994*
*Prime Minister, Minister for Foreign Affairs and External Trade*, Maj.-Gen. Sitiveni Rabuka, OBE

*Lands, Mineral Resources and Energy*, Ratu Timoci Vesikula
*Attorney-General and Minister for Justice*, Kelemedi Bulewa
*Education, Women, Culture, Science and Technology*, Miss
Taufa Vakatale
*Finance and Public Enterprise*, Paul Manueli, OBE
*Agriculture, Fisheries and Forests*, Ratu Ovini Bokini
*Infrastructure and Public Works, Transport, Information,
Broadcasting and Telecommunications*, Ratu Jo Dimuri
*Fijian Affairs*, Adi Samanunu Talakuli Cokobau
*Health, Social Welfare, Housing, Urban Development and
Environment*, Lt.-Col. Jonetani Kaukimoce
*Commerce, Industry, Civil Aviation and Tourism*, Harold
Powell
*National Planning, Regional Development and Multi-ethnic
Affairs*, Ratu Jo Nacola
*Home Affairs, Immigration, Labour and Industrial Relations,
Youth Employment and Sports*, Beranado Vunibobo

EMBASSY OF THE REPUBLIC OF FIJI
34 Hyde Park Gate, London SW7 5BN
Tel 0171-584 3661

*Ambassador Extraordinary and Plenipotentiary*, His
Excellency Brig.-Gen. Ratu Epeli Nailatikau, LVO, OBE,
apptd 1988

BRITISH EMBASSY
Victoria House, 47 Gladstone Road, PO Box 1355, Suva
Tel: Suva 311033

*Ambassador Extraordinary and Plenipotentiary*, His
Excellency Timothy David, apptd 1992
*Deputy Ambassador, Consul and First Secretary*, D. J. Noble

## ECONOMY

The economy is primarily agrarian. The principal cash crop
is sugar cane, which is the main export, followed by coconuts,
ginger and copra. A variety of other fruit, vegetables and
root crops are also grown, and self-sufficiency in rice is a
major aim. Forestry, fishing and beef production are being
encouraged in order to diversify the economy. The processing
of agricultural, marine and timber products are the main
industries, along with gold mining. A policy of tax concessions
for export-oriented manufacturing has encouraged expansion
of the garment industry. Tourism is also a major factor in the
economy, second only to sugar as a money-earner.

| FINANCE | 1991 | 1992 |
|---|---|---|
| Public income | F$564m | F$551m |
| Public expenditure | 551m | 601m |

TRADE

The chief imports are foodstuffs, machinery, mineral fuels,
chemicals, beverages, tobacco and manufactured articles.
Chief exports are sugar, coconut oil, gold, lumber, garments,
molasses, ginger and canned fish.

| | 1992 | 1993 |
|---|---|---|
| Total Imports | F$962m | F$938m |
| Total Exports | 665m | 653m |
| *Trade with UK* | 1992 | 1993 |
| Imports from UK | £7,656,000 | £8,299,000 |
| Exports to UK | 79,189,000 | 86,688,000 |

## COMMUNICATIONS

Fiji is one of the main aerial crossroads in the Pacific,
providing services to New Zealand, Australia, Tonga,
Western Samoa, Vanuatu, the Solomon Islands, Kiribati,
Tuvalu, New Caledonia and American Samoa. Fiji has three
ports of entry, at Suva, Lautoka and Levuka.

# FINLAND
*Suomen Tasavalta*

Finland is situated on the Gulfs of Finland and Bothnia, with
a total area of 137,851 sq. miles (337,032 sq. km), of which
65 per cent is forest, 8 per cent cultivated land and 9 per cent
lakes. The population (1991 UN estimate) is 5,029,000;
population density is 15 inhabitants per square km. The
population is predominantly Lutheran.

The Åland archipelago (Ahvenanmaa), a group of small
islands at the entrance to the Gulf of Bothnia, covers about
572 square miles, with a population (December 1985) of
23,600 (95.2 per cent Swedish-speaking). The islands have a
semi-autonomous status.

CAPITAL – ΨHelsinki (Helsingfors), population (1990)
492,200; other towns are Tampere (Tammerfors),
172,560; ΨTurku (Åbo), 159,180; Espoo (Esbo), 172,629;
Vantaa (Vanda), 154,933; ΨOulu (Oleåborg), 97,329;
Lahti (Lahtis), 94,467; ΨPori (Björneborg), 78,365.
CURRENCY – Markka (Mk) of 100 penniä.
FLAG – White with blue cross.
NATIONAL DAY – 6 December (Independence Day).

## GOVERNMENT

Finland was part of the Swedish Empire from the middle
ages until it was ceded to Russia in 1809 and became an
autonomous grand duchy of the Russian Empire. The
country became independent after the Russian revolution of
1917, but defeats by the Soviet Union in the 'Winter War'
1939–40 and during the Second World War 1941–4 forced
Finland to cede around one-eighth of its land to the Soviet
Union under the Treaty of Paris 1947. The ceded land
included Finland's access to the Arctic Ocean and to Lake
Ladoga. The Treaty of Paris also forced Finland to
demilitarize its border with the Soviet Union, to enter into a
barter trade agreement with its neighbour and to adopt a
stance of neutrality. These terms lasted until the demise of
the Soviet Union in 1991.

Under the constitution there is a single chamber, the
*Eduskunta*, composed of 200 members elected by universal
suffrage. The legislative power is vested in the Eduskunta
and the President. The highest executive power is held by
the President who is elected for a period of six years. The
first direct elections for the presidency were held in 1994,
the President having been elected by an electoral college
before then.

The present government took office in April 1990, the
first government for 25 years not to include left-wing parties.
The four parties in the coalition are the National Coalition
Party (conservative), the Centre Party, the Swedish People's
Party of Finland, and the Finnish Christian Union Party.

Finland applied for membership of the European Community on 18 March 1992 and negotiations opened with the
EC on Finland's application in January 1993 and were
completed on 1 March 1994. Finland is to hold a parliamentary
vote and national referendum on membership in late 1994,
before accession on 1 January 1995.

HEAD OF STATE
*President*, Martti Ahtisaari, *elected* 6 February 1994,
*inaugurated* 1 March 1994

CABINET *as at August 1994*
*Prime Minister*, Esko Aho (CP)
*Deputy Prime Minister, Foreign Trade* Pertti Salolainen
(NCP)

*Foreign Affairs,* Heikki Haavisto (CP)
*Social Affairs and Health,* Jorma Huuhtanen (CP)
*Labour,* Ilkka Kanerva (NCP)
*Transport and Communications,* Ole Norrback (SPP)
*Defence,* Elisabeth Rehn (SPP)
*Trade and Industry,* Seppo Kääriäinen (CP)
*Justice,* Anneli Jäätteenmäki (CP)
*Interior,* Mauri Pekkarinen (CP)
*Finance,* Iiro Viinanen (NCP)
*Education,* Olli-Pekka Heinonen (NCP)
*Cultural Affairs,* Tytti Isohookana-Asunmaa (CP)
*Environment,* Sirpa Pietikäinen (NCP)
*Housing,* Pirjo Rusanen, (NCP)
*Development Co-operation,* Toimi Kankaanniemi (FCU)
*Agriculture and Forestry,* Mikko Pesälä (CP)

NCP National Coalition Party; CP Centre Party; FCU Finnish Christian Union; SPP Swedish People's Party

EMBASSY OF FINLAND
38 Chesham Place, London SW1W 8HW
Tel 0171–235 9531

*Ambassador Extraordinary and Plenipotentiary,* His
    Excellency Leif Blomquist, apptd 1991
*Minister,* L. Korpinen
*Counsellor (Commercial),* Olli Anttila
*Defence Attaché,* Lt.-Col. R. Noopila
*Consul,* Mrs T. Gallen-Kallela

BRITISH EMBASSY
Itäinen Puistotie 17, 00140 Helsinki
Tel: Helsinki 661293

*Ambassador Extraordinary and Plenipotentiary,* His
    Excellency Neil Smith, CMG, apptd 1989
*Deputy Ambassador and Counsellor (Commercial),* N. A.
    Thorne
*First Secretary and Consul,* N. J. Kelly
*Defence Attaché,* Lt.-Col. S. W. L. Strickland

There are British Consular offices at *Helsinki, Jyväskylä,
Kotka, Kuopio, Oulu, Pori, Tampere, Turku, Vaasa* and
*Mariehamn.*

BRITISH COUNCIL REPRESENTATIVE, Tuija Talvitie,
    Hakaniemenkatu 2, 00530 Helsinki

## DEFENCE

By the terms of the peace treaty of 1947 with the UK and
USSR, the Army is limited to a force not exceeding 34,400.
The Navy is limited to a total of 10,000 tons displacement
with personnel not exceeding 4,500. The Air Force, including
naval air arm, is limited to 60 machines with a personnel not
exceeding 3,000. Bombers or aircraft with bomb-carrying
facilities are expressly forbidden.

The total active armed forces number some 32,800
personnel including 24,100 conscripts, who serve for 8–11
months. However, total mobilization strength is based on the
700,000 reservists, who are obliged to undergo between 40
and 100 days training up to age 50; 30,000 reservists
undergo training each year.

The Army has a strength of 27,300 (21,600 conscripts)
with 230 main battle tanks, 840 armoured infantry fighting
vehicles and armoured personnel carriers, and 700 artillery
pieces. The Navy has 2,500 personnel (1,000 conscripts)
with 23 patrol and coastal craft and 13 mine warfare vessels.
The Air Force has 3,000 personnel (1,500 conscripts) and
112 combat aircraft. There are also 4,400 Ministry of Interior
Frontier Guards.

Finland deploys with UN forces abroad: one infantry
battalion in Lebanon; one infantry battalion on the Golan

Heights; 296 troops in Croatia; 135 troops in the Former
Yugoslav Republic of Macedonia.

## EDUCATION

Primary education (co-educational comprehensive school) is
compulsory for children from seven to 16 years, and free of
charge. In the autumn of 1986, there were 678,463 in
comprehensive schools and 113,117 in vocational institutions
of senior level. There are 21 universities or other schools of
academic level.

## CULTURE

There are two official languages in Finland: 93.6 per cent of
the population speak Finnish as their first language, 6.2 per
cent Swedish (1986). The remaining 0.2 per cent speak other
languages (mainly Lapps who number about 2,500 and live
in the far north). Both Finnish and Swedish are used for
administration and education; newspapers, books, plays and
films appear in both languages.There is a vigorous modern
literature. F. E. Sillanpää, who died in 1964, was awarded the
Nobel prize for Literature in 1939. In 1988 there were 103
daily newspapers (12 Swedish).

## ECONOMY

Finland is a highly industrialized country producing a wide
range of capital and consumer goods. Timber and the
products of the timber-based industries remain the backbone
of the economy, but the importance of metal-working,
shipbuilding and engineering has grown. The textile industry
is well developed and the glass, ceramics and furniture
industries enjoy international reputations. Other important
industries are rubber, plastics, chemicals and pharmaceuticals, footwear, foodstuffs and electronic equipment.

The Finnish economy has been adversely affected by
declining trade with the former Soviet bloc, together with the
world-wide economic recession. Unemployment rose to 19
per cent in 1993 while inflation in 1992 was 2.1 per cent. The
government has introduced austerity measures, raising taxes
and reducing health and social welfare spending and the
large overseas development budget.

### TRADE

The principal imports are raw materials, machinery and
manufactured goods. The value of exports in 1992 was
dominated by wood and paper products (38 per cent) and
metal and engineering products (33 per cent). The special
barter-trade relationship with the former Soviet Union
collapsed in 1991 and exports to the countries of the former
Soviet Union fell from 20 per cent of the total in the early
1980s to 4 per cent in 1992.

| Trade with UK | 1992 | 1993 |
|---|---|---|
| Imports from UK | £994,656,000 | £1,129,722,000 |
| Exports to UK | 1,676,575,000 | 1,904,694,000 |

## COMMUNICATIONS

There are 9,000 kilometres of railroad, railway connections
with Sweden and Russia, and passenger boat connections
with Sweden, Germany, Poland, Russia and the Baltic States.
There are also passenger/cargo services between Britain and
Helsinki, Kotka and other Finnish ports. External civil air
services are maintained by most European airlines. The
merchant fleet at the end of 1986 totalled 1,900,000 tons
gross.

# FRANCE
*La République Française*

France extends from 42° 20′ to 51° 5′ N. latitude, and from 7° 85′ E. to 4° 45′ W. longitude. Its area is estimated at 211,208 sq. miles (547,026 sq. km), divided into 95 departments, including the island of Corsica, in the Mediterranean off the west coast of Italy. The principal rivers are the Seine, Loire, Garonne and Rhône. The population, according to the 1991 official estimates, is 56,893,000 (Metropolitan France), and 58,353,000 when overseas departments are included.

POPULATION OF THE REGIONS 1991
*Names of Departments in brackets*

| | |
|---|---:|
| Alsace (Bas-Rhin, Haut-Rhin) | 1,631,000 |
| Aquitaine (Dordogne, Gironde, Landes, Lot-et-Garonne, Pyrénées-Atlantiques) | 2,808,000 |
| Auvergne (Allier, Cantal, Haute-Loire, Puy-de-Dôme) | 1,318,000 |
| Basse-Normandie (Calvados, Manche, Orne) | 1,394,000 |
| Bourgogne (Côte-d'Or, Nièvre, Saône-et-Loire, Yonne) | 1,611,000 |
| Bretagne (Côtes-du-Nord, Finistère, Ille-et-Vilaine, Morbihan) | 2,804,000 |
| Centre (Cher, Eure-et-Loir, Indre, Indre-et-Loire, Loir-et-Cher, Loiret) | 2,387,000 |
| Champagne-Ardenne (Ardennes, Aube, Marne, Haute-Marne) | 1,347,000 |
| Corse (Corse-du-Sud, Haute-Corse) | 250,000 |
| Franche-Comté (Doubs, Haute-Saône, Jura, Territoire-de-Belfort) | 1,103,000 |
| Haute-Normandie (Eure, Seine-Maritime) | 1,743,000 |
| Île-de-France (Essonne, Hauts-de-Seine, Seine-et-Marne, Seine-St-Denis, Val-de-Marne, Val-d'Oise, Ville de Paris, Yvelines) | 10,740,000 |
| Languedoc-Roussillon (Aude, Gard, Hérault, Lozère, Pyrénées-Orientales) | 2,137,000 |
| Limousin (Corrèze, Creuse, Haute-Vienne) | 721,000 |
| Lorraine (Meurthe-et-Moselle, Meuse, Moselle, Vosges) | 2,302,000 |
| Midi-Pyrénées (Ariège, Aveyron, Haute-Garonne, Gers, Lot, Hautes-Pyrénées, Tarn, Tarn-et-Garonne) | 2,445,000 |
| Nord-Pas-de-Calais (Nord, Pas-de-Calais) | 3,967,000 |
| Pays de la Loire (Loire-Atlantique, Maine-et-Loire, Mayenne, Sarthe, Vendée) | 3,071,000 |
| Picardie (Aisne, Oise, Somme) | 1,817,000 |
| Poitou-Charentes (Charente, Charente-Maritime, Deux-Sèvres, Vienne) | 1,599,000 |
| Provence-Alpes-Côte d'Azur (Alpes-de-Haute-Provence, Alpes-Maritimes, Bouches-du-Rhône, Hautes-Alpes, Var, Vaucluse) | 4,305,000 |
| Rhône-Alpes (Ain, Ardèche, Drôme, Isère, Loire, Rhône, Savoie, Haute-Savoie) | 5,394,000 |

CAPITAL – Paris, on the Seine. Population (census 1990) 2,152,400 (city); 9,318,800 (incl. suburbs).
The largest conurbations (populations 1990) are ΨMarseille (1,231,000); Lyon (1,262,000); Toulouse (650,000); Lille (959,000); ΨBordeaux (696,000); Nice (516,000); Nantes (496,000); Toulon (437,000); Grenoble (404,000).
The chief towns of Corsica are ΨAjaccio (58,315) and ΨBastia (52,446).
CURRENCY – French franc of 100 centimes.
FLAG – The tricolour, three vertical bands, blue, white, red (blue next to flagstaff).

NATIONAL ANTHEM – La Marseillaise.
NATIONAL DAY – 14 July (Bastille Day 1789).

## HISTORY

There are dolmens and menhirs in Brittany, prehistoric remains and cave drawings in Dordogne and Ariège, and throughout France various megalithic monuments erected by primitive tribes, predecessors of Iberian invaders from Spain (now represented by the Basques), Ligurians from northern Italy and Celts or Gauls from the valley of the Danube. Julius Caesar found Gaul 'divided into three parts' and described three political groups; Aquitanians south of the Garonne, Celts between the Garonne and the Seine and Marne, and Belgae from the Seine to the Rhine. Roman remains are plentiful throughout France in the form of aqueducts, arenas, triumphal arches, etc. The celebrated Norman and Gothic cathedrals, including Notre Dame in Paris, and those of Chartres, Reims, Amiens (where Peter the Hermit preached the First Crusade for the recovery of the Holy Sepulchre), Bourges, Beauvais, Rouen, etc., have survived invasions and bombardments with only partial damage, and many of the Renaissance and the 17th- and 18th-century chateaux survived the French Revolution.

## CULTURE

French is the official language. The work of the French Academy, founded by Richelieu in 1635, has established *le bon usage*, equivalent to 'The Queen's English' in Britain. French authors have been awarded the Nobel Prize for Literature on twelve occasions, including R. F. A. Sully-Prudhomme (1901), Anatole France (1921), André Gide (1947), François Mauriac (1952), Albert Camus (1957), Jean Paul Sartre (1964) and Claude Simon (1985).

## GOVERNMENT

The legislature consists of the National Assembly of 577 deputies (555 for Metropolitan France and 22 for the overseas departments and territories) and the Senate composed of 321 Senators (296 for Metropolitan France, 13 for the overseas departments and territories and 12 for French citizens abroad). One-third of the Senate is indirectly elected every three years.
The normal session of the legislature is confined to five and a half months each year and it may also meet in extraordinary session for 12 days at the request of the Prime Minister or a majority of the Assembly.

The Prime Minister is appointed by the President, as is the Council of Ministers on the Prime Minister's recommendation. They are responsible to the legislature, but as the executive is constitutionally separate from the legislature, ministers may not sit in the legislature and must hand over their seats to a substitute.

A Constitutional Council is responsible for supervising all elections and referenda and must be consulted on all constitutional matters and before the President of the Republic assumes emergency powers. In the event of the presidency falling vacant for any reason, the President of the Senate assumes the position until a presidential election, which must be held within 35 days.

The state of the parties in the Senate at August 1994 was: Rassemblement pour la république (RPR) 90; Socialists 70; Centrist Union 66; UDF-Republican Party 47; Democratic and European Rally (RDE) 22; Communists 15; Independents 10.

At the last elections to the National Assembly in March 1993 the Socialist government was decisively beaten by the right-wing alliance of the Gaullist Rassemblement pour la république (RPR) and the Union pour la démocratie française (UDF) parties. At August 1994 the state of parties was: RPR 256; UDF 215; Socialists (PS) and allies 58; other right-wing parties 23; Communists (PCF) 23; Independent 1; vacant 1.

HEAD OF STATE

*President of the French Republic,* François Mitterrand, *elected* 10 May 1981, *re-elected* 8 May 1988

COUNCIL OF MINISTERS *as at August 1994*

*Prime Minister,* Edouard Balladur (RPR)
*Minister of State, Social Affairs, Health and Urban Affairs,* Simone Veil (Ind.)
*Minister of State, Interior and Administrative Reform,* Charles Pasqua (RPR)
*Minister of State, Justice,* Pierre Méhaignerie (UDF)
*Minister of State, Defence,* François Léotard (UDF)
*Foreign Affairs,* Alain Juppé (RPR)
*National Education,* François Bayrou (UDF)
*Economy,* Edmond Alphandéry (UDF)
*Industry and Foreign Trade,* Gérard Longuet (UDF)
*Public Works, Transport and Tourism,* Bernard Bosson (UDF)
*Businesses and Enterprise,* Alain Madelin (UDF)
*Labour, Employment and Vocational Training,* Michel Giraud (RPR)
*Culture and Francophone Affairs,* Jacqus Tourbon (RPR)
*Budget, Government Spokesperson,* Nicolas Sarkozy (RPR)
*Agriculture and Fisheries,* Jean Puech (UDF)
*Higher Education and Research,* François Fillon (RPR)
*Environment,* Michel Barnier (RPR)
*Civil Service,* André Rossinot (UDF)
*Housing,* Hervé de Charette (UDF)
*Co-operation,* Michel Roussin (RPR)
*Overseas Departments and Territories,* Dominique Perben (RPR)
*Youth and Sports,* Michèle Alliot-Marie (RPR)
*Communications,* vacant
*Veterans and War Victims,* Phillipe Mestre (UDF)

*President of the Senate,* René Monory
*President of the National Assembly,* Phillipe Séguin

FRENCH EMBASSY
58 Knightsbridge, London SW1X 7JT
Tel 0171-201 1000

*Ambassador Extraordinary and Plenipotentiary,* His Excellency Jean Gueguinou, apptd 1993
*Counsellors,* P. Bossiere; Richard Narich

*Defence Attaché,* Contre-Amiral P. Garibal
*Cultural Attaché,* M. Lummaux
*Consul-General,* G. Gautier
*Head of Commerce/Trade,* M. Murcia

BRITISH EMBASSY
35 rue du Faubourg St Honoré, 75383 Paris Cedex 08
Tel: Paris 42 66 91 42

*Ambassador Extraordinary and Plenipotentiary,* His Excellency Sir Christopher Mallaby, GCVO, KCMG, apptd 1993
*Minister,* J. R. Young, CMG
*Defence and Air Attaché,* Air Cdre C. R. Adams, AFC
*Counsellor, Director of Trade Promotion and Investment,* R. A. Kealy, CMG
*First Secretary and Consul-General,* M. E. Hunt

BRITISH CONSULAR OFFICES. – *at Bordeaux, Biarritz, Toulouse, Lille, Boulogne, Calais, Dunkirk, Lyon, Marseille, Nice, Paris, Cherbourg, Le Havre, Nantes and St Malo in* Metropolitan France, *and overseas in Cayenne (French Guiana), Papeete (French Polynesia), Fort de France (Martinique), Pointe à Pitre (Guadeloupe) and St Denis (Réunion).*

BRITISH COUNCIL REPRESENTATIVE, D. Ricks, OBE, 9 rue de Constantine, 75007 Paris
FRANCO-BRITISH CHAMBER OF COMMERCE, 8 rue Cimarosa, 75116 Paris. *President,* R. Lyon. *Vice-President,* B. Cordery, OBE

DEFENCE

The total active armed forces number some 411,600 personnel (190,400 conscripts). Conscripts serve for ten months. Reserves total 379,800. Strategic nuclear forces consist of 80 submarine-launched ballistic missiles on five nuclear-powered submarines, 18 land-based intermediate range ballistic missiles, 15 (with a further 13 in store) nuclear-capable Mirage IVP aircraft and 45 Mirage 2000N aircraft, both with medium-range nuclear air-to-surface missiles.

The Army has a strength of 242,800 (138,000 conscripts) with 15 Hadès short-range nuclear missile launchers, 1,010 main battle tanks, 4,915 armoured personnel carriers and armoured infantry fighting vehicles, 1,435 artillery pieces and 683 helicopters. Organization is into three armoured and one motorized infantry divisions; the Rapid Action Force of four lightly armoured and air-mobile divisions; the Foreign Legion of nine regiments; 11 marine infantry regiments; and one armoured division assigned to Eurocorps, together with French elements of the Franco-German brigade.

The Navy has a strength of 65,600 (19,700 conscripts) with 38 Super Etendard aircraft (with 19 in store), capable of carrying short-range nuclear air-to-surface missiles, 14 submarines, two aircraft carriers, one cruiser, four destroyers, 35 frigates, 69 other combat aircraft and 40 armed helicopters.

The Air Force has a strength of 90,600 (32,700 conscripts) and some 796 combat aircraft. The Air Force is organized into an air defence command of four squadrons; a tactical command of 11 ground attack, 11 air defence, three reconnaissance, two early warning and one helicopter squadrons; an air transport command of 19 transport and five helicopter squadrons; a training command.

France deploys 52,300 armed forces personnel abroad; 16,000 in Germany; 21,600 in French Overseas Departments and Territories; 8,550 in former French colonies in Africa; and 6,150 on UN and peacekeeping duties.

In 1993 the French government announced a planned reduction in the armed forces over the following five years of 25 per cent.

## EDUCATION

The educational system is highly centralized and is administered by the Ministry of National Education. Local administration comprises 25 Territorial Academies, with inspecting staff for all grades, and Departmental Councils presided over by the *Préfet*, and charged especially with primary education. Education is compulsory, free and secular from six to 16. Schools may be single-sex or co-educational. Primary education is given in nursery schools, primary schools and *collèges d'enseignement général* (four-year secondary modern course); secondary education in *collèges d'enseignement technique, collèges d'enseignement secondaire* and *lycées* (seven-year course leading to one of the five *baccalauréats*). Special schools are numerous.

There are many *grandes écoles* in France which award diplomas in many subjects not taught at university, especially applied science and engineering. Most of these are state institutions but have a competitive system of entry, unlike the universities. There are universities in 24 towns in France, two or three in some major provincial towns, and 13 in Paris and the immediate surrounding district.

In 1991-2 enrolment in pre-school and primary schools was 6,668,600; in secondary schools 5,877,400, and in post-secondary education 1,840,300.

In 1993 the government gave German official parity with French in Alsace schools.

## COMMUNICATIONS

The length of roads in use at the end of 1991 was 888,440 km, of which 7,080 km were motorways.

The railroad system in France is extensive. The length of lines open for traffic at the end of 1991 was 33,446 km, of which 12,828 km were electrified.

The French mercantile marine consisted in 1992 of 216 ships of over 100 tons gross, of which 30 were passenger vessels (234,000 tons gross), 56 tankers (2,058,000 tons gross) and 130 cargo vessels (1,432,000 tons gross).

## ECONOMY

Government expenditure (ordinary and capital) in the 1993 general budget was F1,369,900 million, of which the largest components were: Local government F287,500 million, education F281,800 million, defence F245,600 million, and equipment, housing and transport F117,200 million. In 1993 the budget deficit was equivalent to 4 per cent of GDP, which itself declined by 0.8 per cent as France was in recession, leading to an unemployment rate of 12.7 per cent in 1994.

In May 1993 the new conservative government announced the privatization of all public sector companies apart from those in the telecommunications, utilities and gaming sectors. The programme is espected to generate F300,000 million over five years. By mid 1994 total or majority holdings in Banque National de Paris, Rhône-Poulenc (chemicals), Elf Aquitaine (oil) and UAP (insurance) had been sold. Holdings in Renault, Air France, Aérospatiale, Crédit Lyonnais and a further 13 companies are to follow.

In January 1994 the government established the independence of the central bank, the Banque de France, with the formation of a nine-member monetary policy council to define and implement monetary policy independent of the government.

Approximately 30,581,000 hectares of land is used for agricultural purposes; 15,216,000 hectares is forested. Production in 1992 included wheat, 32,507,300 tonnes; maize, 14,886,000 tonnes; barley, 10,476,300 tonnes; and potatoes 4,252,700 tonnes.

Viniculture is extensive, regions famous for their wines including Bordeaux, Burgundy and Champagne. Production of wine in 1992 was 6,500,000 tonnes. Cognac, liqueurs and cider are also important products.

France produces its own oil, the greater part coming from fields in the Landes area, but is a net importer of crude oil, for processing by its important oil-refining industry. Natural gas is produced in the foothills of the Pyrenees. Electricity production was 441,400m kW in 1991.

France's heavy industries include oil-refining and the production of iron and steel, and aluminium. In 1992 production of steel was 16,000,000 tonnes and cement 24,990,000 tonnes. Other important industries produce chemicals, tyres, aluminium, textiles, paper products and processed food. Engineering products include motor vehicles, and television and radio sets.

## TRADE

The principal imports are raw materials for the heavy and manufacturing industries (e.g. oil, minerals, chemicals), machinery and precision instruments, agricultural products and vehicles. Raw materials, semi-manufactured and manufactured goods are also the principal exports. Other member countries of the EC are France's main trading partners.

|  | 1991 | 1992 |
|---|---|---|
| Imports | F1,251,298m | F1,217,760m |
| Exports | 1,221,108m | 1,248,312m |

| Trade with UK | 1992 | 1993 |
|---|---|---|
| Imports from UK | £11,486,695,000 | £11,440,344,000 |
| Exports to UK | 12,215,890,000 | 12,847,093,000 |

## OVERSEAS DEPARTMENTS

Greater powers of self-government were granted to French Guiana, Guadeloupe, Martinique and Réunion in 1982. These former colonies had enjoyed departmental status since 1947 and the status of regions of France since 1974. Their directly-elected Assemblies operate in parallel with the existing, indirectly constituted Regional Councils. The French government is represented by a Prefect in each.

FRENCH GUIANA – Situated on the north-eastern coast of South America, French Guiana is flanked by Suriname on the west and by Brazil on the south and east. Area, 34,749 sq. miles (90,000 sq. km). Population (1990) 114,900. Capital, ΨCayenne (41,000). Under the administration of French Guiana is a group of islands (St Joseph, Ile Royal and Ile du Diable), known as Iles du Salut. Captain Dreyfus was imprisoned on Devil's Isle from 1894 to 1899.

*Prefect,* J.-F. Cordet

| Trade with UK | 1993 |
|---|---|
| Imports from UK | £4,807,000 |
| Exports to UK | 259,000 |

GUADELOUPE – A number of islands in the Leeward Islands group of the West Indies, consisting of the two main islands of Guadeloupe (or Basse-Terre) and Grande-Terre, with the adjacent islands of Marie-Galante, La Désirade and Îles des Saintes, and the islands of St Martin and St Barthélemy over 150 miles to the north-west. Area, 687 sq. miles (1,779 sq. km). Population (1990) 386,600. Capital ΨBasse Terre (14,000) in Guadeloupe. Other towns are ΨPointe à Pitre (26,000) in Grande-Terre and ΨGrand Bourg (6,611) in Marie-Galante.

*Prefect,* A. Froute

| Trade with UK | 1993 |
|---|---|
| Imports from UK | £7,693,000 |
| Exports to UK | 62,000 |

MARTINIQUE – An island situated in the Windward Islands group of the West Indies, between Dominica in the north and St Lucia in the south. Area, 425 sq. miles (1,102 sq. km). Population (1990) 359,800. Capital ΨFort de France (101,540). Other towns are ΨTrinité (11,214) and ΨMarin (6,104).
*Prefect*, M. Morin

| Trade with UK | 1993 |
|---|---|
| Imports from UK | £26,078,000 |
| Exports to UK | 133,000 |

RÉUNION – Réunion, which became a French possession in 1638, lies in the Indian Ocean, about 569 miles east of Madagascar and 110 miles south-west of Mauritius. Area, 969 sq. miles (2,510 sq. km). Population (1990) 598,000. Capital, St Denis (122,000). Other towns are Saint-Paul (71,669) and Saint-Pierre (58,846). The smaller, uninhabited islands of Bassas da India, Europa, Îles Glorieuses, Juan de Nova and Tromelin are administered from Réunion.
*Prefect*, H. Fournier

| Trade with UK | 1993 |
|---|---|
| Imports from UK | £13,283,000 |
| Exports to UK | 5,453,000 |

## TERRITORIAL COLLECTIVITÉS

MAYOTTE – Area, 144 sq. miles (372 sq. km). Population (1991 census) is 94,410. Capital, Mamoundzou (12,000). Part of the Comoros Islands group, Mayotte remained a French dependency when the other three islands became independent as the Comoros Republic in 1975. Since 1976 the island has been a *collectivité territoriale*, an intermediate status between Overseas Department and Overseas Territory.
*Prefect*, A. Weil

| Trade with UK | 1993 |
|---|---|
| Imports from UK | £10,646,000 |
| Exports to UK | 209,000 |

ST PIERRE AND MIQUELON – Area 93 sq. miles (242 sq. km). Population (1990) 6,300. Two small groups of islands off the coast of Newfoundland. Became a *collectivité territoriale* in 1985.
*Prefect*, R. Maurice

| Trade with UK | 1993 |
|---|---|
| Imports from UK | £1,075,000 |
| Exports to UK | — |

## OVERSEAS TERRITORIES

FRENCH POLYNESIA – Five archipelagos in the south Pacific, comprising the Society Islands (Windward Islands group includes Tahiti, Moorea, Makatea, Mehetia, Tetiaroa, Tubuai Manu; Leeward Islands group includes Huahine, Raiatea, Tahaa, Bora-Bora, Maupiti), the Tuamotu Islands (Rangiroa, Hao, Turéia, etc.), the Gambier Islands (Mangareva, etc.), the Tubuai Islands (Rimatara, Rurutu, Tubuai, Raivavae, Rapa, etc.) and the Marquesas Islands (Nuku-Hiva, Hiva-Oa, Fatu-Hiva, Tahuata, Ua Huka, etc.). Area, 1,544 sq. miles (4,000 sq. km). Population (1990 UN estimate) 206,000. Capital, ΨPapeete (24,200) in Tahiti. Economy based on tourism and exports of copra, coffee, vanilla, citrus fruits and cultured pearls.
*Government Representative*, M. Jau

| Trade with UK | 1993 |
|---|---|
| Imports from UK | £3,873,000 |
| Exports to UK | 46,000 |

NEW CALEDONIA – A large island in the western Pacific,

700 miles east of Queensland. Dependencies are the Isles of Pines, the Loyalty Islands (Mahé, Lifou, Urea, etc.), the Bélep Archipelago, the Chesterfield Islands, the Huon Islands and Walpole. New Caledonia was discovered in 1774 and annexed by France in 1854; from 1871 to 1896 it was a convict settlement. A referendum in 1987 on the question of independence for New Caledonia was boycotted by the indigenous Kanaks, and New Caledonia therefore voted to remain French. However, a new independence referendum has been promised for 1998. Area, 7,358 sq. miles (19,058 sq. km). Population (1990 UN estimate) 167,000. Capital ΨNoumea (65,000). It is one of the world's largest producers of nickel.
*Government Delegate*, A. Christnacht

| Trade with UK | 1993 |
|---|---|
| Imports from UK | £7,744,000 |
| Exports to UK | 2,431,000 |

SOUTHERN AND ANTARCTIC TERRITORIES – Created in 1955 from former Réunion dependencies, the territory comprises the islands of Amsterdam (25 sq. miles) and St Paul (2.7 sq. miles), the Kerguelen Islands (2,700 sq. miles) and Crozet Islands (116 sq. miles) archipelagos and Adélie Land (116,800 sq. miles) in the Antarctic continent. The only population are members of staff of the scientific stations.

WALLIS AND FUTUNA ISLANDS – Two groups of islands (the Wallis Archipelago and the Îles de Hoorn) in the central Pacific, north-east of Fiji. Area, 106 sq. miles (274 sq. km). Population (1990 census) 13,705. Capital, Mata-Utu on Uvea, the main island of the Wallis group.
*Supreme Administrator*, M. Legix.

| Trade with UK | 1993 |
|---|---|
| Imports from UK | £10,000 |
| Exports to UK | — |

## THE FRENCH COMMUNITY

The constitution of the Fifth French Republic, promulgated in 1958, envisaged the establishment of a French Community of States. A number of the former French states in Africa have seceded from the Community but for all practical purposes continue to enjoy the same close links with France as those that remain formally members. Most former French African colonies are closely linked to France by financial, technical and economic agreements.

*Source:* for statistical data: *L'Annuaire Statistique de la France 1993*; *Tableaux de l'Economie Française 1993-4.*

---

# GABON
*République Gabonaise*

---

Gabon lies on the Atlantic coast of Africa at the Equator and is flanked on the north by Equatorial Guinea and Cameroon, and on the east and south by Congo. It has an area of 103,347 sq. miles (267,667 sq. km) and a population (UN estimate 1991) of 1,212,000.

CAPITAL – ΨLibreville (251,000).
CURRENCY – Franc CFA of 100 centimes.
FLAG – Horizontal bands, green, yellow and blue.
NATIONAL ANTHEM – La Concorde.
NATIONAL DAY – 17 August.

## GOVERNMENT

Gabon elected on 28 November 1958 to remain an autonomous republic within the French Community and was proclaimed fully independent on 17 August 1960. The constitution provides for an executive President directly elected for a seven-year term, who appoints the Council of Ministers. There is a unicameral National Assembly comprising 120 members.

Following widespread unrest, a national conference was called in March 1990 and forced President Bongo to legalize opposition parties. Several rounds of multiparty elections were held in September, October and November 1990 and eventually won by the ruling Parti democratique gabonais (PDG), amid allegations of fraud. The PDG formed a coalition government with several opposition parties but retained the most important portfolios. Opposition parties left the government in June 1991 in protest at the dominating power of the PDG. Multiparty presidential elections were held in December 1993 and won by the incumbent, President Bongo of the PDG, amid widespread accusations of fraud, which led to riots in Libreville and the principal opposition candidate Mba Abessole forming a rival government.

HEAD OF STATE

*President*, El Hadj Omar Bongo, *assumed office*, December 1967, *re-elected*, 1973, 1979, 1986 and 5 December 1993

COUNCIL OF MINISTERS *as at August 1994*

*Prime Minister*, Casimir Oyé Mba
*Minister of State, Engineering and Construction*, Zacharie Myboto
*Minister of State, Communication, Posts and Telecommunications*, Jacques Adiahenot
*Justice*, Dr Serge Mba Bekale
*Foreign Affairs and Co-operation*, Jean Ping
*Trade, Industry and Scientific Research*, Patrice Nziengui
*National Defence, Public Security and Immigration*, Gen. Idriss Ngari
*Interior and Local Collectives*, Antoine Mboumbou-Miyakou.
*Civil Service and Administrative Reform*, Pierre-Claver Zeng Ebome
*Finance, Budget and State Holdings*, Marcel Doupamby Matoka
*Planning, Economy and Privatization*, Andre-Dieudonne Berre
*Social Affairs, Family and Solidarity*,Victor Mapangou Moucani Muetsa
*Mines, Energy and Hydraulic Resources*, Paul Toungui
*National Education, Professional Training and Government Spokesperson*, Paulette Missambo
*Public Health*, Jerome Ngoua Bekale
*Labour and Human Resources*, Jean-Remy Pendy Bouyiki
*Agriculture and Rural Development*, Emmanuel Ondo Methogo.
*Forests and Environment*, Eugene Kakou Mayaza
*Arts, Culture and Popular Education, in charge of Human Rights*, Lazare Digombe
*Youth and Sports*, Yolande Bike
*Higher Education*, Rene Ndemezo Obiang
*Tourism, National Parks and Transport*, Martin Fidele Magnaga
*Small and Medium-Sized Enterprises*, Pierre Nziengui Mabilat
*Shipping*, Joachim Mahotes Magouindi
*Housing, Land Registry and Town Planning*, Emmanuel Akoghe Mba

EMBASSY OF THE REPUBLIC OF GABON
27 Elvaston Place, London SW7 5NL
Tel 0171–823 9986

*Ambassador Extraordinary and Plenipotentiary*, His Excellency Vincent Boulé, apptd 1991

BRITISH CHARGÉ D'AFFAIRS, Kaye Oliver, resident in Kinshasha, Zaire

ECONOMY

Gabon's economy remains heavily dependent on oil and, to a much lesser extent, other mineral resources, including manganese and uranium. Gabon has considerable timber reserves (particularly Okoumé) with 80 per cent of the country still forested, although production has stagnated in recent years.

The economy, which experienced considerable growth in real terms from the mid-1970s onwards, has since 1986 been adversely affected by the fall in oil prices. Revenue is expected to increase in the 1990s following major oil exploitation at Rabi-Kounga. Gabon is a full member of OPEC. The IMF approved a US$85 million credit in March 1994.

| Trade with UK | 1992 | 1993 |
| --- | --- | --- |
| Imports from UK | £19,703,000 | £21,887,000 |
| Exports to UK | 3,456,000 | 6,065,000 |

THE GAMBIA
*The Republic of the Gambia*

The Gambia takes its name from the Gambia River, which it straddles for over 200 miles inland from the west coast of Africa. It is a narrow strip, surrounded by Senegal, except at the coast, lying between 13° 10'–13° 45' N. and 13° 90'–16° 50' W. The area is 4,361 sq. miles (11,295 sq. km), of which one-fifth is the river. The climate is typically Sahelian, with a dry season between October and May and heavy rainfall during the months of July and August (32–40 inches a year).
POPULATION – The population comprises mainly Wolof, Mandinka and Fula peoples who originally migrated there from the north and east. Population (UN estimate 1991) was 884,000.

CAPITAL – ΨBanjul. Population (1983 census) of the island of Banjul was 44,536, and of adjacent Kombo St Mary district 102,858. Total population of Banjul/Kombo St Mary, 147,394.
CURRENCY – Dalasi (D) of 100 butut.
FLAG – Horizontal stripes of red, blue and green, separated by narrow white stripes.
NATIONAL ANTHEM – For The Gambia, Our Homeland.
NATIONAL DAY – 18 February (Independence Day).

HISTORY

The Gambia River basin was part of the region dominated in the tenth to 16th centuries by the Songhai and Mali kingdoms centred on the upper Niger. The first recorded Europeans to reach the Gambia River were the Portuguese in 1447. English merchants began to trade along the river from 1588. Merchants from France, Courland (now part of Latvia) and the Netherlands also established trading posts there. In 1816 the British stationed a garrison on an island at the river mouth which became the capital of a small British-administered colony, initially under the Governor of Sierra Leone. In 1889 France agreed that the British rights along the upper river should extend 10 km on either bank. British administration was extended from the Colony to this Protectorate. The Gambia became independent within the Commonwealth on 18 February 1965, and a republic on 24 April 1970.

The Gambia's relationship with Senegal has always been an important factor in political and economic policy. Moves towards a closer association were accelerated after an abortive coup in The Gambia in 1981 was put down with the help of Senegalese troops. In 1982 the Senegambia Confederation was formally instituted but following disagreements it was dissolved in 1989. A treaty of friendship and co-operation was signed with Senegal in 1991.

## GOVERNMENT

The constitution is democratic and parliamentary, with an executive President elected for five years. The House of Representatives has 35 elected members, five elected Chiefs Representatives and up to eight nominated members plus the Attorney-General (ex-officio). The Vice-President and other ministers are appointed by the President. Parliament must be dissolved after five years.

The last general elections were held in April 1992. In July 1994 junior army officers launched a military coup in protest at not being paid and at government corruption, which was blamed for squandering foreign aid. The President and some of his government fled to Senegal and the army officers formed a ruling military council. At the time of going to press the coup leader, Lt. Yayah Jammeh, had assumed the presidency and the ruling military council was in the process of forming a military-civilian government.

HEAD OF STATE
*President, Chairman of the Ruling Military Council*, Lt.
  Yayah Jammeh, *took power*, 23 July 1994
*Vice-President*, Lt. Sana Sabally

RULING MILITARY COUNCIL *as at August 1994*
Lt. Yayah Jammeh, Lt. Sana Sabally, Lt. Edward Singhateh,
  Lt. Sadibou Hydara, Lt. Yankuba Touray

GAMBIA HIGH COMMISSION
57 Kensington Court, London W8 5DG
Tel 0171-937 6316

*High Commissioner*, His Excellency Mohammadou
  N. Bobb, apptd 1992

BRITISH HIGH COMMISSION
48 Atlantic Road, Fajara (PO Box 507), Banjul
Tel: Banjul 95133

*High Commissioner*, His Excellency Michael Hardie, OBE,
  apptd 1993

## COMMUNICATIONS

There is an international airport at Yundum, 17 miles from Banjul, with scheduled services flying to other West African states and to the UK and Belgium. Banjul is the main port. Internal communication is by road and river. There is no railway system. There are three broadcasting stations and a UHF telephone service linking Banjul with the principal towns in the provinces. There is no television service.

## EDUCATION

There are 24 secondary schools (eight high and 16 technical) with a total enrolment of 15,635 students. Two high schools provide A-level education. Gambia College provides post-secondary courses in education, agriculture, public health and nursing. There are seven vocational training institutions with a total enrolment of 1,400. Higher education and advanced training courses are taken outside The Gambia, currently by over 200 students.

## ECONOMY

Most of the population (75 per cent) depend for their livelihood on agriculture, which contributes 40 per cent of

GDP. The chief product, groundnuts, is also the most important export item, forming over 80 per cent of domestic exports. Other crops are rice, millet, sorghum, maize and cotton. Fishing and livestock industries are being developed. Thirty per cent of the country's basic food requirements are imported. There are no significant deposits of minerals.

Manufactures are limited to groundnut processing, minor metal fabrications, paints, furniture, soap and bottling. Tourism is developing quickly. Trade through The Gambia, re-exporting imported goods to neighbouring countries, is an important element in the economy.

| FINANCE | 1990–1* |
|---|---|
| Recurrent Revenue | D623,000,000 |
| Recurrent Expenditure | 633,000,000 |
| *estimate. | |

Over 80 per cent of capital expenditure comes from external aid grants and loans. In 1987–8 there was a GDP growth rate of 5.4 per cent.

| TRADE | 1987–8 | 1988–9 |
|---|---|---|
| Total imports | D844,900,000 | D940,000,000 |
| Total exports | 576,600,000 | 311,400,000 |
| *Trade with UK* | 1992 | 1993 |
| Imports from UK | £20,092,000 | £23,714,000 |
| Exports to UK | 3,118,000 | 5,617,000 |

# GEORGIA
*Sakartvelos Respublika*

Georgia has an area of 26,911 sq. miles (69,700 sq. km) and occupies the north-western part of the Caucasus region of the former Soviet Union. It is bordered on the north by Russia, on the south-east by Azerbaijan, on the south by Armenia, on the south-west by Turkey, and on the west by the Black Sea. Georgia contains the two autonomous republics of Abkhazia and Adjaria and the autonomous province of South Ossetia. The latter was abolished by Georgian law in December 1990 but this was not recognized by the Soviet government.

Georgia is very mountainous, with the Greater Caucasus in the north and the Lesser Caucasus in the south. The relatively low-lying land between these two ranges is divided into western and eastern Georgia by the Surz Ridge. Western Georgia has a mild and damp climate, eastern Georgia is more continental and dry. The Black Sea shore and the Rioni lowland are subtropical.

POPULATION – According to a 1990 estimate, Georgia has a population of 5,456,000, of which 70 per cent are Georgian, 8 per cent are Armenian, 6 per cent Russian, 6 per cent Azerbaijani and 3 per cent Ossetians, together with smaller groups of Abkhazians, Greeks, Ukrainians, Jews and Kurds. Most of the population are adherents of the Georgian Orthodox Church. There is also a small Muslim minority.

Georgian, Russian and Armenian are most commonly in use. Georgian is one of the oldest languages in the world to have been continually in use, the alphabet having emerged in the third century BC.

CAPITAL – Tbilisi. Population 1,260,000 (1989). Other
  major cities are Sukhumi (capital of Abkhazia) (125,000)
  and Batumi (150,000).
CURRENCY – The Georgian coupon, introduced in April
  1993. In August 1993 Georgia left the rouble zone but is
  expected to re-enter it soon.

FLAG – Cherry red with a canton in the upper hoist divided black over white.

NATIONAL DAY – 26 May (Independence Day).

## GOVERNMENT

The Georgians are an ancient people who formed two states, Colchis and Iberia, on the edge of the Black Sea around 1000 BC. After centuries of invasions by Arabs, Turks and Khazars, Georgia entered its 'Golden Age' in the 12th century AD when trade, irrigation and communications were greatly developed. Invasions by the Khazars and Mongols led to the division of Georgia into several kingdoms and principalities. These Georgian states struggled against the Turkish and the Persian Empires from the 16th to the 18th centuries, gradually turning to the Russian Empire for protection and support. Eastern Georgia signed a treaty of alliance with Russia which recognized Russian supremacy in 1783 and joined the Russian Empire in 1801, followed soon after by Western Georgia.

In the late 19th century nationalist and Marxist movements formed in Georgia and competed for the very limited political influence possible under autocratic Russian rule. One of the most prominent Marxist activists was Iosif Dzhugashvili (Josef Stalin). After the Russian revolution of 1917, a nationalist government came to power in Georgia supported by allied intervention forces. In 1921 Soviet forces occupied Tbilisi, leading to a Communist takeover. In 1922 Georgia joined the Soviet Union as part of the Transcaucasian Soviet Socialist Republic.

In March 1990 the Georgian Supreme Soviet declared illegal the treaties of 1921–2 by which Georgia had joined the Soviet Union. The Communist Party's monopoly on power was abolished in 1990 and in multiparty elections held in October and November 1990 the nationalist leader Zviad Gamsakhurdia was elected President. Georgia declared its independence from the Soviet Union in May 1991 and this was recognized internationally in 1992.

### CIVIL WAR

After independence the increasingly dictatorial attitude of Gamsakhurdia alienated much of the population and by late 1991 armed opposition to Gamsakhurdia's government had begun. By the end of December 1991 there was civil war in Tbilisi between supporters and opponents of President Gamsakhurdia. The President was overthrown and fled in January 1992 and a military council took power until March 1992, when a state council was appointed with the former Soviet foreign minister Eduard Shevardnadze as its chairman. Fighting continued throughout 1992 and 1993 between the Government and supporters of Gamsakhurdia, and also Abkhazian separatists. In October 1992 Eduard Shevard-

nadze was elected head of state and Chairman of the Parliament, and a loose alliance of pro-Shevardnadze parties gained a majority in parliament and formed a government. No voting took place in Abkhazia or South Ossetia.

Gamsakhurdia returned to western Georgia in September 1993 to ferment rebellion after the poor conduct of the war against Abkhazian separatists, together with economic chaos and deprivations, caused the government to resign in August 1993. President Shevardnadze assumed full executive powers at the head of an emergency council, but failed to prevent the advance of the rebels from western Georgia because most government forces were engaged in Abkhazia. Shevardnadze was forced to accept Russian armaments and troops in October to defeat the rebellion and in return agreed to join the CIS. The rebels were eventually defeated in November and forced into Abkhazia. Russian influence in Georgia was further increased by the signing of a ten-year Treaty of Friendship and Co-operation in February 1994 under which Russia has gained a decisive say in Georgian economic policy and maintains three major military bases in the country. The Georgian parliament ratified CIS membership on 1 March 1994.

### SECESSION

The status of South Ossetia and Abkhazia remains unresolved. The deployment of a joint Russian-Georgian-Ossetian peacekeeping force in June 1992 ended the campaign by South Ossetian separatists. Abkhazian separatists defeated Georgian forces in September 1993, leading to the deployment of Russian peacekeepers under the May 1994 ceasefire.

### HEAD OF STATE
*President, Chairman of the Supreme Soviet,* Eduard Shevardnadze, *elected* 11 October 1992

CABINET *as at August 1994*

*Prime Minister,* Otar Patsatsiya
*Deputy Prime Ministers,* Amiran Kadagishvili; Zurab Kadagishvili; Nicolaz Lekishvili; Avtandil Margiani; Tamas Nadareishvili; Irakly Menagarishvili; Temur Basilia
*Defence,* Lt.-Gen. Vardiko Nadibaidze
*National Security,* Igor Georgadse
*Industry,* Vladimir Kereselidse
*State Property,* Avtandil Silagadse
*Economics,* Mikhail Djibuty
*Finance,* David Yakobidse
*Communications,* Pridon Indjia
*Agriculture and Food,* Georgy Kvesitadse
*Environment,* Shota Adamia
*Education,* Tamas Kvachantiradse
*Culture,* David Magradse
*Public Health,* Avtandil Jorbenadse
*Foreign Affairs,* Alexander Chikvaidse
*Interior,* Shota Kviraga
*Justice,* Tevdore Ninidse
*Social Welfare and Labour,* Vaja Gudjavidse
*Trade,* Zurab Zankaliani

BRITISH AMBASSADOR, His Excellency Sir Brian Fall, KCMG, resident in Moscow, Russia

### ECONOMY

The Georgian economy has been brought to the brink of collapse by the war in Abkhazia and the ending of former Soviet trading relationships. Although Georgia has deposits of coal, they have not been exploited and it is desperately short of energy supplies. Barter deals with Turkmenistan and Kazakhstan for natural gas in return for tea, wine and citrus fruit ended in 1994, with Georgia now having to pay with hard currency that it does not possess. Shevardnadze is attempting to agree barter deals for Azeri and Iranian oil and for an Azeri pipeline to the Black Sea. It is hoped that the closer economic relations with Russia will yield cheap supplies of grain and oil. A large proportion of Georgian production is stolen by black marketers, whilst the tourist industry on the Black Sea coast has been destroyed by the fighting. Georgia will soon replace its inflationary currency, the coupon, with the stronger Russian rouble when it re-enters the rouble zone. The only productive sector of the economy at present is agriculture, with a concentration on viniculture, tea and tobacco-growing and citrus fruits.

| Trade with UK | 1993 |
|---|---|
| Imports from UK | £9,166,000 |
| Exports to UK | 283,000 |

# GERMANY
*Bundesrepublik Deutschland - Federal Republic of Germany*

The area of the Federal Republic is approximately 138,000 sq. miles (357,050 sq km). The estimated population of the Federal Republic (March 1993) was 81,075,000, of whom 65,400,000 live in the former West and 15,700,000 in the former East Germany. There were 10.1 live births per 1,000 inhabitants in the Federal Republic in 1992 (11.3 in West and 5.4 in East). In West Germany in 1987 there were 25.4 million Protestants, 26.2 million Roman Catholics, and 1.6 million Muslims. The number of Jews was estimated to be 30,000 in 1993.

CAPITAL – Berlin. By decision of the Bundestag, the seat of government is to be transferred from Bonn, West Germany's post-war provisional capital, to the historical capital, Berlin. The move was originally scheduled for completion by 1998 but in 1993 was postponed for budgetary reasons until 2000. The *Bundesrat* (upper house) will remain in Bonn.

The population of the principal cities and towns in the Federal Republic in 1991 was:

| Berlin | 3,437,900 | Düsseldorf | 576,700 |
|---|---|---|---|
| Hamburg | 1,660,700 | Bremen | 552,300 |
| Munich | 1,236,500 | Duisberg | 536,700 |
| Cologne | 995,500 | Hanover | 514,400 |
| Frankfurt am | | Leipzig | 507,800 |
| Main | 647,200 | Nuremberg | 494,900 |
| Essen | 626,100 | Dresden | 488,000 |
| Dortmund | 599,900 | Chemnitz | 296,300 |
| Stuttgart | 583,700 | Bonn | 294,300 |

CURRENCY – Deutsche Mark (DM) of 100 Pfennig.
FLAG – Horizontal bars of black, red and gold.
NATIONAL ANTHEM – Einigkeit und Recht und Freiheit (Unity and right and freedom).
NATIONAL DAY – 3 October (Anniversary of 1990 Unification).

## HISTORY

The term 'deutsch' (German) probably began to be used in the eighth century and initially described the language spoken in the eastern part of the Frankish realm which reached its apogee in Charlemagne's reign, and subsequently the term was transferred from the language to its speakers, and ultimately to the region they lived in. The first German realm was the Holy Roman Empire, established in AD 962 when Otto I of Saxony was crowned Emperor. The Empire endured until 1806, but from as early as the 12th century the achievement of a national state was prevented by territorial fragmentation into small principalities and dukedoms, the gradually increasing autonomy of their rulers weakening the central power.

The Holy Roman Empire was replaced by a loose association of the individual sovereign states known as the German Confederation, which survived until 1866 when it was dissolved and replaced by the Prussian-dominated North German Federation. Prussia had translated its earlier economic predominance into political hegemony by the annexation of the duchies of Schleswig and Holstein from Denmark in 1864 and a decisive defeat of Austria in 1866 (the Seven Weeks' War) which ended Austrian influence over German politics. After the Franco-Prussian War of 1870–1 resulted in the defeat of France and the cession of Alsace and part of Lorraine, the south German principalities united with the northern federation to form a second German Empire, the King of Prussia being proclaimed Emperor in 1871.

Germany's defeat in the 1914–18 War led to the abdication of the Emperor and the princes, and the country became a republic. The 1919 Treaty of Versailles returned Alsace–Lorraine to France, large areas in the east of the country were lost to the newly created state of Poland, and all German colonies placed under the administration of other countries. The world economic crisis of 1929 led to the collapse of the Weimar Republic and the subsequent rise to power of the National Socialist movement of Adolf Hitler, who became Chancellor in 1933.

After concluding a Treaty of Non-Aggression with the Soviet Union in August 1939, Germany invaded Poland (1 September 1939), thus precipitating the Second World War, which lasted until 1945. Hitler committed suicide on 30 April 1945. On 8 May 1945, the unconditional surrender of all German forces was accepted by representatives of the Western Allied and Soviet Supreme Commanders.

### THE POST-WAR PERIOD

After the surrender, the Four Powers (France, UK, USA, USSR) assumed supreme authority in Germany. Policy was agreed at the Potsdam Conference (July/August 1945) between the UK, USA and USSR. Germany was divided into

American, French, British and Soviet zones of occupation. Supreme authority was exercised by the Commanders-in-Chief, each in his own zone of occupation and, in matters affecting Germany as a whole, jointly through the Control Council comprising the four Commanders. Berlin was placed under the joint administration of the four occupying powers. However, quadripartite control failed when differences with the USSR over the implementation of the Potsdam Agreement could not be resolved; and against a background of growing international tension, the USSR withdrew from the Control Council in March 1948. The rift divided Germany *de facto* into east and west.

The Federal Republic of Germany (FRG) was created out of the three Western zones in 1949 when, following general elections, a federal government took office in Bonn. A Communist government was meanwhile established in the Soviet zone (henceforth the German Democratic Republic (GDR)). The Bonn/Paris Conventions in May 1955 terminated the occupation regime in West Germany and restored federal German autonomy subject to the reservation of Three Power rights and responsibilities relating to Berlin and to Germany as a whole, including the reunification of Germany and a peace settlement. The GDR became an ostensibly sovereign state in the same year.

In August 1961 the Soviet zone was sealed off, and the Berlin Wall was built along the zonal boundary, partitioning the western sectors of the city from the eastern.

Soviet-initiated reform in eastern Europe during the late 1980s led to unrest in the GDR. The mass exodus of its citizens via the open borders to the west culminated in the opening of the Berlin Wall in November 1989 and the collapse of Communist government there. The 'Treaty on the Final Settlement with respect to Germany', concluded between the FRG, GDR and the four former occupying powers on 12 September 1990, unified Germany with effect from 3 October 1990 as a fully sovereign state and NATO member occupying the territory of the former two Germanies and Berlin. Economic and monetary union preceded formal union on 1 July 1990. Unification is constitutionally the accession of Berlin and the five re-formed *Länder* of the GDR to the FRG, which remains in being. The first government of the new Germany took office in January 1991 following all-German elections on 2 December 1990.

## GOVERNMENT

The Basic Law provides for a President, elected by a Federal Convention electoral college for a five-year term, a lower house (*Bundestag*) of 662 members elected by direct universal suffrage for a four-year term of office, and an upper house (*Bundesrat*) composed of 79 delegates of the *Länder*, without a fixed term of office.

Post-reunification elections were held for the Bundestag on 2 December 1990. The distribution of seats at July 1994 is:

Christian Democratic Union, 267
Social Democrats, 239
Free Democrats, 79
Christian Social Union, 51
Democratic Socialists, 17
The Greens/Alliance 90, 8
Republicans, 1

HEAD OF STATE
*Federal President*, Professor Roman Herzog, *born* 1934, *elected* 23 May 1994, *sworn in* 1 July 1994

CABINET *as at August 1994*

*Federal Chancellor*, Dr Helmut Kohl (CDU)

*Foreign Affairs and Deputy Chancellor*, Dr Klaus Kinkel (FDP)
*Federal Chancellery*, Friedrich Böhl (CDU)
*Interior*, Manfred Kanther (CDU)
*Economy*, Günter Rexrodt (FDP)
*Justice*, Sabine Leutheusser-Schnarrenberger (FDP)
*Finance*, Dr Theodor Waigel (CSU)
*Agriculture*, Jochen Borchert (CSU)
*Labour and Social Affairs*, Dr Norbert Blüm (CDU)
*Defence*, Volker Rühe (CDU)
*Health*, Horst Seehofer (CSU)
*Women and Youth*, Dr Angela Merkel (CDU)
*Family and Elderly*, Hannelore Rönsch (CDU)
*Transport*, Matthias Wissmann (CDU)
*Environment*, Dr Klaus Töpfer (CDU)
*Posts and Telecommunications*, Wolfgang Bötsch (CSU)
*Housing and Construction*, Dr Irmgard Adam-Schwätzer (FDP)
*Research*, Paul Krüger (CDU)
*Education*, Dr Karl-Hans Laerman (FDP)
*Economic Co-operation*, Carl-Dieter Spranger (CSU)

CDU Christian Democratic Union; CSU Christian Social Union; FDP Free Democratic Party.

EMBASSY OF THE FEDERAL REPUBLIC OF GERMANY
23 Belgrave Square, London SW1X 8PZ
Tel 0171-235 5033/824 1300

*Ambassador Extraordinary and Plenipotentiary*, His Excellency Dr Peter Hartmann, KBE, apptd 1993
*Minister*, Dr Friedrich Kroneck
*Minister-Counsellor*, Gerhard Kunz
*First Counsellors*, Dr R. W. Ehni (*Cultural Affairs*); B. Westphal (*Economic Affairs*)
*Defence Attaché*, Rear-Adm. K. M. Reichert

BRITISH EMBASSY
Friedrich-Ebert-Allee 77, 53113 Bonn 1
Tel: Bonn 23 40 61

*Ambassador Extraordinary and Plenipotentiary*, His Excellency Sir Nigel Broomfield, KCMG, apptd 1993
*Minister*, J. A. Shepherd, CMG
*Defence Attaché*, Col. P. P. Rawlens, MBE
*Counsellor (Economic)*, D. S. Broucher
*Counsellor (Management and Consular)*, P. V. Rollitt

BRITISH CONSULATE-GENERAL
Yorck Strasse 19, 40476 Düsseldorf

*Consul-General and Director-General of Trade and Investment Promotion*, A. C. Hunt, CMG

BRITISH EMBASSY OFFICE, BERLIN
Unter den Linden 32/34, 0-10117 Berlin
Tel: Berlin 220 2431
International Trade Centre, Georgenstrasse, 35, 0-1080 Berlin

*Minister and Head of Mission*, R. J. Spencer, CMG
*Counsellor, Deputy Head of Mission*, D. L. Corner.
*First Secretary (Economic)*, P. Bateman

There are British Consulates-General at *Berlin, Düsseldorf, Frankfurt, Hamburg, Munich* and *Stuttgart* and Consulates at *Bremen, Hanover, Kiel* and *Nuremberg.*

BRITISH COUNCIL REPRESENTATIVE, K. Dobson, Hahnenstrasse 6, 50667 Köln. Offices at *Berlin, Leipzig, Hamburg* and *Munich* and British Council libraries at all five centres.

BRITISH CHAMBER OF COMMERCE, Neumarkt 14, D-5000 Köln 1. *Director*, Herr Heumann

## THE LANDER

The distribution of the population among the *Länder* at the end of 1991 was:

| | |
|---|---|
| Baden-Württemberg | 9.9m |
| Bavaria | 11.5m |
| Berlin | 3.4m |
| Brandenburg | 2.6m |
| Bremen | 0.7m |
| Hamburg | 1.7m |
| Hesse | 5.8m |
| Lower Saxony | 7.4m |
| Mecklenburg–Western Pomerania | 1.9m |
| North Rhine-Westphalia | 17.4m |
| Rhineland-Palatinate | 3.8m |
| Saarland | 1.1m |
| Saxony | 4.7m |
| Saxony-Anhalt | 2.8m |
| Schleswig-Holstein | 2.6m |
| Thuringia | 2.6m |

The Ministers-President (Prime Ministers) of the *Länder* governments in July 1994, were:

*Baden-Württemberg* – Erwin Teufel (CDU)
*Bavaria* – Edmund Stoiber (CSU)
*Berlin* – Eberhard Diepgen (CDU) (*Governing Mayor*)
*Brandenburg* – Manfred Stolpe (SPD)
*Bremen* – Klaus Wedemeier (*Mayor*) (SPD)
*Hamburg* – Henning Voscherau (*First Mayor*) (SPD)
*Hesse* – Hans Eichel (SPD)
*Lower Saxony* – Gerhard Schröder (SPD)
*Mecklenburg-Western Pomerania* – Berndt Seite (CDU)
*North Rhine-Westphalia* – Johannes Rau (SPD)
*Rhineland-Palatinate* – Rudolf Scharping (SPD)
*Saarland* – Oskar Lafontaine (SPD)
*Saxony* – Kurt Biedenkopf (CDU)
*Saxony-Anhalt* – Reinhard Höppner (SPD)
*Schleswig-Holstein* – Heidi Simonis (SPD)
*Thuringia* – Bernhardt Vogel (CDU)

## JUDICATURE

Judicial authority is exercised by the Federal Constitutional Court, the Federal courts provided for in the Basic Law and the courts of the Länder. The death sentence has been abolished.

## DEFENCE

Under the terms of the Treaty of Unification the German armed forces are to be reduced from the 1993 active total of 408,200 (176,300 conscripts) to 370,000 by the end of 1994, at which time the last of the former Soviet armed forces will leave Germany. The term of conscription is 12 months. Germany is in the process of absorbing the former GDR armed forces, for which a separate total is shown for the army as the Eastern Command remains a non-NATO force.

The Army has a strength of 287,000 including 140,400 conscripts, 69,100 territorials and 38,700 Eastern Command. It deploys 4,775 main battle tanks, 2,600 artillery pieces, 6,620 armoured personnel carriers and infantry fighting vehicles, and 712 helicopters. In addition, former GDR equipment in store includes 1,790 main battle tanks, 4,500 armoured personnel carriers, 1,175 artillery pieces and 90 helicopters. The Field Army of 170,300 personnel is organized into six armoured, four armoured infantry, one airborne and one mountain division. The Territorial Army is organized into eight infantry regiments and eleven motorized infantry battalions. The Navy has a strength of 31,200 including 6,900 conscripts, with 20 submarines, 14 principal surface combatants and 115 aircraft and 19 armed helicopters. The Air Force has a strength of 90,000 including 29,000 conscripts, with 617 combat aircraft. Organization is in three commands: tactical command with one early warning, two reconnaissance, seven air defence and 15 ground attack squadrons; transport command with four wings; and training command.

There remain some 215,700 NATO personnel in Germany (USA 123,400; UK 53,600; Belgium 19,000; France 16,000; Netherlands 3,700). The number is to be reduced to around 110,000 by 2000; all remaining Russian forces left on 31 August 1994.

During 1993 both the Constitutional Court and the Bundestag agreed that German armed forces may operate outside Germany and the NATO area in UN and other peacekeeping operations for the first time since 1945. In 1994 the Constitutional Court ruled that German forces could serve in armed peacemaking missions. The wish to fulfil a stronger international role means that by August 1994 German personnel had been engaged in UN operations in Somalia and Cambodia, in NATO AWACS aircraft over the former Yugoslavia, and in NATO and WEU patrols in the Adriatic enforcing the UN blockade against the rump Yugoslav state.

## ECONOMY

Despite the division of Germany, which cut off from the West the main food-producing areas of eastern Germany and some of the principal centres of light industry, West Germany became the main industrial power in Europe. It is the most economically powerful member of the European Union.

Unification costs have, however, severely strained federal resources, increasingly weakened by apparent structural problems. Capital transfers from West to East Germany amount to around DM 140 billion per annum, some 5 per cent of GDP, under a massive government investment programme. After a mini-boom generated by new East German demand in 1990 and 1991, Germany entered its most severe recession since the war. Real GDP fell in the West by 1.9 per cent in 1993. The first budgetary and trade deficits in the West for over ten years have resulted in tax increases, rising interest rates and serious inflationary pressures. In March 1993 a 'Solidarity Pact' agreement was reached by federal and länder governments, opposition parties, and employers and trade unions, to take effect from 1995 onwards. The pact lays down the basis of future funding transfers to the East based on a 7.5 per cent rise in income taxes, wage restraint in the West, more private investment in the East, and the distribution of the funding burden between the federal and länder governments. The 'Solidarity Pact' was supplemented in August 1993 by reductions of DM 77,000 million in Western social security payments for the 1994–6 period, and in 1994 by a petrol tax levy on private motorists. In 1993 federal GNP stood at DM 3,108,400m (West 2,832,900m; East 275,500m).

As East Germany struggles to adapt to free market conditions, output has fallen to 40 per cent of pre-unification levels. The sudden loss of established East European trading outlets following the introduction of the Deutsche Mark, and the rapid rise of East German labour costs without corresponding increases in productivity, were largely responsible for this. Unemployment reached 15 per cent in 1993 but is much higher if job creation schemes and part-time working are taken into account. Inflation at 8.8 per cent in 1993 was twice that in West Germany and industrial growth of 6 per cent was less than expected. However, in early 1994 the West German economy began to pull out of recession and growth in East Germany reached 8 per cent in

1994. East German inflation fell to 3 per cent in 1994 but unemployment continued to rise, reaching 8.5 per cent in the West and 16 per cent in the East.

INDUSTRIAL PRODUCTION

Germany has a predominantly industrial economy. Principal industries are coal mining, iron and steel production, machine construction, the electrical industry, the manufacture of steel and metal products, chemicals and textiles, and the processing of foodstuffs. The index of industrial net production adjusted for irregularities of the calendar (1985 = 100) is as follows:

| West Germany | 1992 | 1993 |
|---|---|---|
| Mining | 79.3 | 70.9 |
| Manufacturing industry | 119.8 | 110.6 |
| Basic materials | 113.3 | 109.6 |
| Capital goods | 121.9 | 107.7 |
| Consumer goods | 119.8 | 112.8 |
| Foodstuffs | 127.4 | 125.1 |
| Power (electricity and gas) | 116.2 | 114.3 |
| Construction | 135.7 | 132.4 |
| *Total industry* | 119.4 | 111.6 |

Annual production figures were ('000 tonnes):

| All Germany | 1992 | 1993 |
|---|---|---|
| Hard coal | 65,906 | 58,282 |
| Brown coal | 241,745 | 221,748 |
| Crude petroleum | 3,304 | 3,051 |
| Pig iron | 27,586 | 26,322 |
| Rolled steel | 28,959 | 29,717 |
| Petrol | 25,329 | 26,733 |
| Cement | 37,194 | 36,801 |
| Passenger vehicles (units) | 4,160,000 | 3,285,000 |

AGRICULTURE

In 1992 total area of farmland was 11.5 million hectares, of which 7.3 million hectares (West Germany) and 4.2 million (East Germany) were arable land. Forest areas cover 10.4 million hectares. Crop yields were ('000 tonnes):

| West Germany | 1991 | 1992 |
|---|---|---|
| Rye | 1,856.8 | 1,467.3 |
| Wheat | 11,840.4 | 11,312.2 |
| Barley | 9,428.5 | 8,571.1 |
| Oats | 1,582.2 | 1,170.8 |
| Potatoes | 7,481.6 | 8,554.7 |
| Sugar beet | 19,837.7 | 24,845.1 |
| Colza and rape | 2,012.6 | 1,552.7 |

| East Germany | 1991 | 1992 |
|---|---|---|
| Rye | 1,467.3 | 873.2 |
| Wheat | 4,770.0 | 4,229.5 |
| Barley | 5,065.1 | 3,625.4 |
| Oats | 284.8 | 143.3 |
| Potatoes | 2,719.5 | 2,342.3 |
| Sugar beet | 6,088.0 | 6,248.6 |
| Colza and rape | 959.7 | 1,064.1 |

Milk production in 1992 was 27,851,000 tonnes. Total yield of fisheries in 1992 was 211,763 tonnes, valued at DM240,556,000.

LABOUR

Labour figures, in annual averages, were:

| West Germany | 1992 | 1993 |
|---|---|---|
| Employment | 29,141,000 | 28,652,000 |
| Unemployed | 1,808,000 | 2,270,000 |
| Short-time workers | 283,000 | 767,000 |

| East Germany | 1992 | 1993 |
|---|---|---|
| Unemployed | 1,170,000 | 1,149,000 |
| Short-time workers | 370,000 | 181,000 |

In 1993 the unemployment rate in the West was 8.2 per cent and in the East was 15.8 per cent.

FINANCE

*All Germany*

| | 1993 | 1994p |
|---|---|---|
| Expenditure | DM458 billion | DM478 billion |
| Revenue | 392 billion | 408 billion |

p planned

TRADE *(All Germany)*

| | 1992 | 1993 |
|---|---|---|
| Total imports | DM637,546m | DM544,843m |
| Total exports | 671,203m | 603,973m |

Main trading partners in 1993 were (figures shown as percentage of total trade):

| | Imports | Exports |
|---|---|---|
| France | 11.2 | 11.7 |
| Netherlands | 8.3 | 7.4 |
| Italy | 8.1 | 7.2 |
| UK | 6.1 | 7.7 |
| Belgium/Luxembourg | 5.7 | 6.6 |
| USA | 7.4 | 7.7 |
| Japan | 6.3 | 2.6 |

| Trade with UK | 1992 | 1993 |
|---|---|---|
| Imports from UK | £15,060,073,000 | £15,093,481,000 |
| Exports to UK | 19,034,628,000 | 18,793,316,400 |

COMMUNICATIONS

At the end of 1991 the state-owned railways of the Federal Republic (*Deutsche Bundesbahn and Reichsbahn*) measured 41,525 km of which 16,285 km were electrified, and the privately owned railways totalled approximately 2,807 km. In 1991 the railways handled 418.5 million tonnes of goods. State railways rolling stock included, in 1991, 3,891 electric locomotives, 7,516 diesel locomotives and 314,325 goods wagons.

Classified roads measured 226,282 km (West and East) in 1992, of which motorways were 10,955 km. The total number of motor vehicles registered at the end of 1992 was 46.7 million.

Ocean-going shipping under the German flag in December 1991, amounted to 5,996,000 tons gross. Inland waterways were 6,929 km long in 1991.

SOCIAL WELFARE

There is compulsory insurance against sickness, accident, old age and unemployment. Children's allowances, child rearing benefits and parental leave of absence are available in respect of all children. Pension schemes for widows and orphans of public servants are in operation. Public assistance is given to persons unable to earn their living, or with insufficient income to maintain a decent standard of living.

EDUCATION

School attendance is compulsory for all children and juveniles between the ages of six and 18 and comprises nine years full-time compulsory education at primary and main schools and three years of compulsory vocational education on a part-time basis. In 1991 there were 25,017 primary and main schools (*Grund und Hauptschulen*) with 4,832,539 pupils. Secondary modern schools (*Realschulen*) numbered 3,666 with 1,039,081 pupils. There were 3,901 other general secondary schools (*Gymnasien* including *Gesamtschulen*) with 2,300,655 pupils.

There were also 3,367 special schools (*Sonderschulen*) for physically and mentally handicapped and socially maladjusted children with 344,006 pupils.

The secondary school leaving examination (*Abitur*) entitles the holder to a place of study at a university or another institution of higher education.

Children below the age of 18 who are not attending a general secondary or a full-time vocational school have compulsory day-release at a vocational school. In 1991 there were 3,295 full- and part-time vocational schools (*Berufsschulen*) with 1,816,469 pupils and 259 vocational extension schools (*Berufsaufbauschulen*) with 7,938 pupils, 1,992 full-time vocational schools (*Berufsfachschulen*) with 248,856 pupils, 1,150 schools for secondary technical studies (*Fachoberschulen/Fachgymnasien*) with 215,120 students.

In 1992–3 there were a total of 1,827,229 students at institutions of higher education, of whom 1,214,715 were attending universities. The largest universities are in Munich, Berlin, Hamburg, Bonn and Cologne.

## CULTURE

Modern (or New High) German has developed from the time of the Reformation to the present day, with differences of dialect in Austria, Alsace and the German-speaking cantons of Switzerland.

The literary language is usually regarded as having become fixed by Luther and Zwingli at the Reformation, since which time many great names occur in all branches, notably philosophy, from Leibnitz (1646–1716) to Kant (1724–1804), Fichte (1762–1814), Schelling (1775–1854) and Hegel (1770–1831); drama from Goethe (1749–1832) and Schiller (1759–1805) to Gerhart Hauptmann (1862–1946); and poetry, Heine (1797–1856). Seven German authors have received the Nobel Prize for Literature: Theodor Mommsen (1902), R. Eucken (1908), P. Heyse (1909), Gerhart Hauptmann (1912), Thomas Mann (1929), N. Sachs (1966) and Heinrich Böll (1972).

# GHANA
*The Republic of Ghana*

Ghana (formerly known as the Gold Coast) is situated on the Gulf of Guinea, between 3° 07′ W. and 1° 14′ E. longitude (about 334 miles), and extends 441 miles north from Cape Three Points (4° 45′ N.) to 11° 11′ N. It is bounded on the north by Burkina, on the west by Côte d'Ivoire, on the east by Togo, and on the south by the Atlantic Ocean. Although a tropical country, Ghana is cooler than many countries within similar latitudes. It has a total area of 92,099 sq. miles (238,537 sq. km).

POPULATION – The population (UN estimate 1991) was 15,509,000. Most Ghanaians are Sudanese Negroes, although Hamitic strains are common in northern Ghana. The official language is English. The principal indigenous language group is Akan, of which Twi and Fanti are the most commonly used. Ga, Ewe and languages of the Mole-Dagbani group are common in certain regions. Most Ghanaians are Christians, although there is a substantial Muslim minority in the north.

CAPITAL – ΨAccra. Population of the Greater Accra Region (including Tema) was (1990 estimate) 1,781,100. Other towns are Kumasi, Tamale, ΨSekondi-Takoradi, ΨCape Coast, Sunyani, Ho, Koforidua, Tarkwa and ΨWinneba.

CURRENCY – Cedi of 100 pesewas.

FLAG – Equal horizontal bands of red over gold over green; five-point black star on gold stripe.

NATIONAL ANTHEM – Hail the Name of Ghana.

NATIONAL DAY – 6 March (Independence Day).

## GOVERNMENT

There is no recorded history of the Gold Coast region before the coming of Europeans in the 15th century. The constituent parts of the state came under British administration at various times, the original Gold Coast Colony (the coastal and southern areas) being constituted in 1874; Ashanti in 1901; and the Northern Territories Protectorate in 1901. The territory of Trans-Volta-Togoland, part of the former German colony of Togo, was mandated to Britain by the League of Nations after the First World War, and remained under British administration as a United Nations Trusteeship after the Second World War. After a plebiscite in May 1956, under the auspices of the United Nations, the territory was integrated with the Gold Coast Colony. The former Gold Coast Colony and associated territories became the independent state of Ghana on 6 March 1957 and adopted a republican constitution in 1960.

Since 1966 Ghana has experienced long periods of military rule (1966–9, 1972–9, 1982–92) divided by short-lived civilian governments. A coup in 1979 led to the formation of an Armed Forces Revolutionary Council chaired by Flt. Lt. Jerry Rawlings. Civilian rule was restored in 1979 but overthrown on 31 December 1981, when another coup brought Flt. Lt. Rawlings back to power.

A referendum in April 1992 approved a new multiparty constitution, with political parties being allowed to form legally from May 1992. The National Democratic Congress (NDC) was established as a political party from the ruling Provisional National Defence Council. Flt. Lt. Rawlings won the presidential election in November 1992 and the National Democratic Congress won parliamentary elections in December 1992. The parliamentary election was boycotted by most opposition parties and most of the electorate, who protested that Rawlings should not have been able to stand for the presidency; only 29 per cent of the electorate voted when the NDC won 189 of the 200 parliamentary seats. The Fourth Republic was declared on 7 January 1993 and a new government nominated by the President was approved by parliament and sworn in by the President in March 1993. As executive President, Flt. Lt. (retd) Rawlings also chairs the cabinet. The presidential term is four years, renewable only once.

HEAD OF STATE

*President*, Flt. Lt. (retd) Jerry John Rawlings, *took power* 31 December 1981, *elected* 3 November 1992
*Vice-President*, Kow Nkensen Arkaah

CABINET *as at August 1994*

The President
The Vice-President
*Defence*, Mahama Iddrisu
*Finance and Economic Planning*, Dr Kwesi Botchwey
*Foreign Affairs, Acting Attorney-General and Justice*, Dr Obed Asamoah
*Information*, Kofi Quakyi
*Parliamentary Affairs*, J. H. Owusu-Acheampong
*Interior*, Col. (retd) E. M. Osei-Owusu
*Trade and Industries*, Emma Mitchell
*Transport and Communications*, Edward Salia
*Mines and Energy*, Richard Kwame Peprah
*Education*, Harry Sawyerr
*Local Government and Rural Development*, Kwamena Ahwoi
*Food and Agriculture*, Ibrahim Adam
*Employment and Social Welfare*, David Boateng
*Environment*, Christine Amoaka-Nuamah
*Health*, Commodore (retd) S. G. Obimpeh
*Lands and Forestry*, Dr Kwabena Adjei

*Speaker of the Legislature,* Justice Daniel Annan

GHANA HIGH COMMISSION
104 Highgate Hill, London N6 5HE
Tel 0181-342 8686

*High Commissioner,* His Excellency K. K. S. Dadzie, apptd
1994
*Deputy High Commissioner,* Johnson Osei-Hwedieh
*Defence Adviser,* Brig. H. W. K. Agbevey
*Counsellor,* A. K. Budu-Amoako (*Trade*)

BRITISH HIGH COMMISSION
PO Box 296, Osu Link, Accra
Tel: Accra 221665

*High Commissioner,* His Excellency David Walker, CVO,
apptd 1992
*Deputy High Commissioner,* M. J. Greenstreet
*Defence Adviser,* Lt.-Col. T. E. Hawkins, MBE
*First Secretary (Management/Consular),* D. J. Walker
*First Secretary (Commercial),* S. S. Strong

BRITISH COUNCIL REPRESENTATIVE, T. Cowin, Liberia
Road (PO Box 771), Accra. There is also an office in
*Kumasi.*

## ECONOMY

Agriculture forms the basis of Ghana's economy, employing
70 per cent of the working population. Crops include cocoa,
which is the largest single source of revenue, rice, cassava,
fruits such as avocado pears, oranges and pineapples, pulses
such as groundnuts, corn, millet, oil palms, yams, maize and
vegetables. Livestock is raised in the uncultivated areas.
Attempts are being made to diversify agricultural production,
with cash crops being extensively cultivated for export and
to provide raw materials for local industry.

Fishing is important in coastal areas and in the Volta itself.
About 80 per cent of home supply is obtained from sea
fisheries, and production from the Volta Lake and other
inland fisheries is increasing to meet demand, which at
present exceeds production.

The area within a 60-mile radius of Dunkwa produces 90
per cent of Ghana's mineral exports. Manganese production
ranks among the world's highest and gold, industrial
diamonds and bauxite are also produced. Some 30,000
persons are employed by the mining companies.

Small-scale traditional industries include tailoring, gold-
smithing and carpentry. Priority has been given in recent
years to the establishment of a number of 'pioneer industries'
including timber products, vehicle and refrigerator assembly,
cigarettes, boatbuilding, food processing, cotton textiles,
clothing, footwear, printing and other light industries. A
modern industrial complex is growing in the Accra-Tema
area.

Since 1966 the Volta Dam at Akosombo has generated
hydro-electric power for the processing of bauxite and fed a
power transmission network for the Accra-Kumasi-Takoradi
area. Electricity is exported to Togo and Benin.

Under the Economic Recovery Programme (ERP) in place
since 1983, the Ghanian economy has achieved a growth rate
of 6 per cent a year for the past decade and paid off a large
proportion of its foreign debt; debt servicing had fallen to 30
per cent of export earnings in 1991. IMF and World Bank
support for the ERP's free market and deregulatory
restructuring has gained Ghana US$3,600m in soft loans and
grants in the past decade and enabled the diversification of
agricultural and industrial products.

## TRADE

Principal exports are cocoa, timber and gold. Principal
imports are road vehicles, manufacturing equipment, petroleum and raw materials.

| Trade with UK | 1992 | 1993 |
| --- | --- | --- |
| Imports from UK | £174,098,000 | £214,081,000 |
| Exports to UK | 81,881,000 | 71,814,000 |

## COMMUNICATIONS

The Kotoka Airport at Accra is an international airport and
Ghana Airways Corporation is the national airline. There are
also internal airports at Takoradi, Kumasi, Sunyani, and
Tamale.

There are 20,000 miles of motorable roads, of which 2,335
miles are bituminized. There are 600 miles of railway,
linking Accra and the principal ports of Takoradi and Tema
with their hinterlands, the mining centres and with each
other.

Takoradi Harbour consists of seven quay berths – one is
leased specially for manganese exports. Tema Harbour has
ten berths for larger ocean-going vessels and the largest dry
dock on the West African coast. An oil berth has also been
built to serve the Ghaip refinery which has been constructed
at Tema.

---

# GREECE
*Elliniki Dimokratia*

---

Greece is a maritime state in the south-east of Europe,
bounded on the north by Albania, the Former Yugoslav
Republic of Macedonia and Bulgaria, on the south and west
by the Ionian and Mediterranean seas, and on the east by
Turkey. It has an estimated area of 50,944 sq. miles (131,944
sq. km).

The main areas of Greece are: Macedonia (which includes
Mt Athos and the island of Thasos), Thrace (including the
island of Samothrace), Epirus, Thessaly, Continental Greece
(which includes the island of Euboea and the Sporades) and
the Peloponnese (or Morea). The main island groups are the
Sporades (of which the largest is Skyros), the Dodecanese or
Southern Sporades (Rhodes, Astypalaia, Karpathos, Kassos,
Nisyros, Kalymnos, Leros, Patmos, Kos, Symi, Khalki,
Tilos), the Cyclades (about 200, including Syros, Andros,
Tinos, Mykonos, Naxos, Paros, Santorini, Milos and Serifos),
the Ionian Islands (Corfu, Paxos, Levkas, Ithaca, Cephalonia,
Zante and Cerigo), the Aegean Islands (Chios, Lesbos,
Limnos and Samos). In Crete from about 3000 to 1400 BC a
flourishing civilization existed which spread its influence
throughout the Aegean, and the ruins of the palace of Minos
at Knossos afford evidence of astonishing comfort and luxury.

POPULATION – The population at the 1991 census was
10,256,464. Over 97 per cent of the people are adherents of
the Greek Orthodox Church, which is the state religion, all
others being tolerated and free from interference. The
Church of Greece recognizes the spiritual primacy of the
Ecumenical Patriarch of Constantinople, but is otherwise a
self-governing body administered by the Holy Synod under
the presidency of the Archbishop of Athens and All Greece.
It has no jurisdiction over the Church of Crete, which has a
degree of autonomy under the Ecumenical Patriarch, nor
over the monastic community of Mount Athos and the
Church in the Dodecanese, both of which come directly
under the Ecumenical Patriarch.

CAPITAL – Athens, population (including ΨPiraeus and
suburbs), 3,096,775 (1991 census). Other large towns are

(1991) ΨThessaloniki (Salonika) (739,998); ΨPatras (172,763); ΨVolos (115,732); Larissa (113,426); and ΨKavalla (58,576).
Larger towns in the islands are: in Crete, ΨHeraklion (127,600), ΨCanea (65,519), and ΨRethymnon (23,595); ΨCorfu (36,901); ΨRhodes (43,619); ΨSyros Hermoupolis (16,008); ΨMytilene in Lesbos (25,440); Ψ Chios (27,405).
CURRENCY – Drachma of 100 leptae.
FLAG – Blue and white stripes with a white cross on a blue field in the canton.
NATIONAL ANTHEM – Imnos Eis Tin Eleftherian (Hymn to Freedom).
NATIONAL DAY – March 25 (Independence Day).

## GOVERNMENT

Greece was under Turkish rule from the mid 15th century until a war of independence (1821–2) led to the establishment of a Greek kingdom in the Peloponnese in 1829. There was a civil war between monarchist and Communist groups from 1946 to 1949, and tension between right-wing and more radical groups continued after 1949. In 1967 right-wing elements in the army seized power and established a military regime (the 'Greek Colonels'). The King went into voluntary exile in 1967; in 1973 the monarchy was abolished and a republic established.

Unrest in Athens in 1973–4 intensified after the government was implicated in the overthrow of Archbishop Makarios, President of Cyprus, in July 1974, and led the Colonels to surrender power. Konstantinos Karamanlis (Prime Minister 1955–63) returned from exile to form a provisional government, and the first elections for ten years were held in November 1974. The constitutional position of the King, who was still in exile, remained unsettled until 8 December, when the restoration of the monarchy was rejected by 69.2 per cent to 30.8 per cent and Greece became a republic.

A new constitution came into force in 1975. In 1986 the powers of the presidency were greatly reduced, with most executive power transferred to the government and the President becoming a ceremonial figure. The unicameral 300-member Chamber of Deputies is elected for a four-year term by universal adult suffrage under a system of proportional representation, with 3 per cent of the vote needed for parliamentary representation.

The most recent general election was held on 10 October 1993 with the Panhellenic Socialist Party (PASOK) winning 170 seats, the New Democracy Party (Christian Democrats) 111 seats, the Political Spring Party ten seats and the Communist Alliance nine seats. In February 1994 the government imposed a trade embargo on and sealed its border with the Former Yugoslav Republic of Macedonia over its alleged territorial claim on northern Greece.

HEAD OF STATE
*President of the Hellenic Republic*, Constantine Karamanlis, *elected* 4 May 1990

CABINET *as at August 1994*

*Prime Minister*, Andreous Papandreou
*Minister to the PM*, Anastasios Peponis
*Foreign Affairs*, Karolos Papoulias
*Interior*, Apostolos Tsokhatsopoulos
*National Defence*, Gerasimos Arsenis
*Justice*, Georgios Kouvelakis
*National Economy, Finance*, Yannos Papantoniou
*Merchant Marine*, Georgios Katsifaras
*Agriculture*, Georgios Moraitis

*Labour*, Evangelos Yiannopoulos
*Health and Social Security*, Dimitris Kremastinos
*Education and Religious Affairs*, Dimitris Fatouros
*Culture*, Thanos Mikroutsikos
*Public Order*, Stelios Papathemelis
*Macedonia and Thrace*, Konstantinos Triaridis
*Environment and Public Works*, Kostas Laliotis
*Industry, Commerce, Energy and Technology*, Kostas Simitis
*Transport and Communications*, Ioannis Charalambous
*Aegean*, Kostas Skandalidis

EMBASSY OF GREECE
1A Holland Park, London W11 3TP
Tel 0171-229 3850
*Ambassador Extraordinary and Plenipotentiary*, His Excellency Elias Gounaris, apptd 1993
*Deputy Ambassador*, A. Scopelitis
*Defence Attaché*, Capt. I. Theofanides
*Consul-General*, G. Costoulas
*Counsellor*, Miss A. Missa-Kerkentzes (*Economic Affairs*)

There are Honorary Consulates at *Belfast, Birmingham, Edinburgh, Falmouth, Glasgow, Leeds* and *Southampton*.

BRITISH EMBASSY
1 Ploutarchou Street, 10675 Athens
Tel: Athens 7236211
*Ambassador Extraordinary and Plenipotentiary*, His Excellency Oliver Miles, CMG, apptd 1993
*Deputy Head of Mission, Counsellor and Consul-General*, C. J. Denne, CMG
*Defence and Military Attaché*, Brig. N. M. Prideaux
*First Secretary (Commercial)*, N. J. G. Bowie

BRITISH CONSULAR OFFICES – There are British Consular Offices at *Athens, Corfu, Patras, Samos, Rhodes, Salonika, Heraklion* (Crete), *Syros* and *Volos*.

BRITISH COUNCIL, 17 Plateia Philikis Etairias (PO Box 3488), Kolonaki Square, Athens 10210. *Representative*, Dr J. L. Munby, OBE (*Counsellor, Cultural Affairs*).
There is also an office at *Salonika* and British Council libraries at both centres.

BRITISH-HELLENIC CHAMBER OF COMMERCE, 25 Vas. Sofias Avenue, GR-106 74 Athens. Tel: 72 10 361

## DEFENCE

The total active armed forces number some 159,300 personnel (122,300 conscripts). The strength of the Army is 113,000, including 100,000 conscripts; in addition there are some 34,000 in the National Guard. Equipment includes 2,640 main battle tanks, 2,310 armoured personnel carriers and armoured infantry fighting vehicles, and 1,245 artillery pieces. The Navy consists of 19,500 men (7,900 conscripts) and is equipped with ten submarines and eight destroyers and seven frigates with 12 armed helicopters. The Air Force consists of 26,800 men (14,400 conscripts) and has a total of 384 combat aircraft. National service is between 19 and 23 months.

Greece maintains 2,250 army personnel in Cyprus. There is also a paramilitary Gendarmerie of 26,500 personnel. Some 850 US personnel are stationed in Greece.

## COMMUNICATIONS

The 2,650 km of Greek railways are state-owned, with the exception of the Athens–Piraeus Electric Railway. Greek roads total over 35,500 km, of which about 25 per cent are classified as national highways and just under 30,000 km are classified as provincial roads. The road connection with Albania was reopened in 1985.

In March 1994 the Greek mercantile fleet numbered 1,864 ships over 100 tons gross with a total tonnage of 53,778,128 tons gross. Athens has direct airline links with Australasia, North America, most countries in Europe, Africa and the Middle East.

## EDUCATION

Education is free and compulsory from the age of six to 15 and is maintained by state grants. There are ten universities, Athens, Thessaloniki, Patras, Thrace, Ioannina, Piraeus, Aegean, Ionian, Thessaly and Crete. There are several other institutes of higher learning, mostly in Athens.

## ECONOMY

The 1989–93 New Democracy government followed an IMF-recommended austerity programme of privatization and reduction of the overmanned public sector. This has been partially reversed by the PASOK government, which has ended privatization. Despite significant European Union capital transfers the economy remains in poor shape with inflation at 12 per cent, the budget deficit 13 per cent of GDP, public debt at 120 per cent of GDP, large-scale tax evasion and a huge black economy.

Though there has been a substantial measure of industrialization, agriculture still employs about a quarter of the working population. The most important agricultural products are tobacco, wheat, cotton, sugar, rice, fruit (olives, peaches, vines, oranges, lemons, figs, almonds and currant-vines). Exports of fresh fruit and vegetables are an important contributor to the economy and have considerable growth potential. Currants are one of the main exports.

The principal minerals are nickel, bauxite, iron ore, iron pyrites, manganese magnesite, chrome, lead, zinc and emery, and prospecting for petroleum is being carried on. Oil refineries are in operation near Athens and at Salonika, where there is also a petro-chemical plant.

The chief industries are textiles (cotton, woollen and synthetics), chemicals, cement, glass, metallurgy, shipbuilding, domestic electrical equipment and footwear, the production of aluminium, nickel, iron and steel products, tyres, chemicals, fertilizers and sugar (from locally-grown beet). Food processing and ancillary industries have also grown up throughout the country.

The development of the country's electric power resources, irrigation and land reclamation schemes, and the exploitation of lignite resources for fuel and industrial purposes are also being carried out. Tourism has developed rapidly, with 9.9 million visitors in 1993.

| TRADE | 1991 | 1992 |
|---|---|---|
| Total imports | US$19,104m | US$19,902m |
| Total exports | 6,797m | 6,008m |

| Trade with UK | 1992 | 1993 |
|---|---|---|
| Imports from UK | £770,742,000 | £875,698,000 |
| Exports to UK | 372,191,000 | 310,186,000 |

## CULTURE

Greek civilization emerged c. 1300 BC and the poems of Homer, the blind poet of Chios, which were probably current c. 800 BC, record the ten-year struggle between the Achaeans of Greece and the Phrygians of Troy (1194 to 1184 BC).

The spoken language of modern Greece is descended from the Common Greek of Alexander's empire. *Katharevousa*, a conservative literary dialect evolved by Adamantios Corais (Diamant Coray) (1748–1833) and used for official and technical matters, has been phased out. Novels and poetry are mostly in *dimotiki*, a progressive literary dialect which owes much to John Psycharis (1854–1929). The poets Solomos, Palamas, Cavafis and Sikelianos have won a European reputation. Giorgis Seferis (1963) and Odysseus Elytis (1979) have won the Nobel Prize for Literature.

# GRENADA
*The State of Grenada*

Grenada is situated between 12°13′–11° 58′ N. latitude and 61° 20′–61° 35′ W. longitude, and is about 90 miles north of Trinidad, 68 miles south-south-west of St Vincent, and about 120 miles south-west of Barbados. The island is about 21 miles in length and 12 miles in breadth, with an area of 133 sq. miles (344 sq. km). Also a part of Grenada are some of the Grenadines islets, the largest of which is Carriacou, 13 square miles in area. The country is mountainous.

POPULATION – The population is estimated at 84,000 (1991 UN estimate).

CAPITAL – ΨSt George's (population 10,000) lies on the south-west coast, and possesses a good harbour.

CURRENCY – East Caribbean dollar (EC$) of 100 cents.

FLAG – Divided diagonally into yellow and green triangles within a red border containing six yellow stars, a yellow star on a red disc in the centre and a nutmeg on the green triangle in the hoist.

NATIONAL DAY – 7 February (Independence Day).

## GOVERNMENT

Grenada was discovered by Columbus in 1498, and named Conception. It was originally colonized by the French and was ceded to Great Britain by the Treaty of Versailles in 1783. It became an Associated State in 1967 and an independent nation within the Commonwealth on 7 February 1974.

The government was overthrown in 1979 by the New Jewel Movement and a People's Revolutionary Government was set up. In October 1983 disagreements within the PRG led to violence and the death of the Prime Minister, whose government was replaced by a Revolutionary Military Council. These events prompted the intervention of Caribbean and US forces. The Governor-General installed an advisory council to act as an interim government until a general election was held in December 1984. A phased withdrawal of US forces was completed by June 1985.

The Queen is head of state and is represented by a Governor-General. Legislative power is vested in a bicameral parliament consisting of an elected 15-member House of Representatives and a nine-member Senate appointed by the Governor-General. The most recent general election was held in March 1990.

*Governor-General*, His Excellency Sir Reginald Palmer, GCMG, apptd 1993

CABINET *as at August 1994*

*Prime Minister, Minister for External Affairs, Finance and Planning, National Security, Home Affairs, Personnel and Management Services, Carriacou and Petit Martinique Affairs*, Rt. Hon. Nicholas Brathwaite, OBE
*Agriculture, Forestry, Fisheries, Energy, Trade, Industry*, Hon. George Brizan
*Attorney-General, Minister for Legal Affairs, Local Government*, Dr the Hon. Francis Alexis
*Tourism, Civil Aviation, Social Development, Youth Affairs, Sports and Culture*, Sen. Tillman Thomas
*Health, Housing, the Environment*, Hon. Phinsley St Louis
*Labour, Co-operatives, Social Security, Community Development*, Hon. Edzel Thomas
*Education, Information*, Sen. the Hon. Carlyle Glean
*Minister of State (Finance)*, Hon. Michael Andrews

GRENADA HIGH COMMISSION
1 Collingham Gardens, London SW5 0HW
Tel 0171–373 7808/9/0
*High Commissioner*, new appointment awaited.

BRITISH HIGH COMMISSION
14 Church Street, St George's
Tel: St George's 3222
*High Commissioner*, His Excellency Emrys Davies, CMG, resides at Bridgetown, Barbados
*Resident Representative*, A. H. Drury (*Acting High Commissioner*)

## JUDICIARY

Justice is administered by the Grenada Supreme Court, which is composed of a High Court of Justice and a two-tier Court of Appeals, and by Magistrates' Courts. The final court of appeal remains the UK Privy Council.

## ECONOMY

The economy is principally agrarian, with cocoa, nutmegs and bananas the major crops. Fruit and vegetables are grown and a little livestock raised for domestic consumption. The fishing industry is being developed. Manufacturing is mostly confined to processing agricultural products and to the production of textiles, concrete, aluminium and handicrafts.

Tourism has prospered since the opening in 1984 of the Point Salines International Airport. A hotel expansion programme is taking place. The number of cruise ship calls to Grenada in 1993 was 382, bringing 200,061 visitors out of a total of 300,602 tourists.

TRADE

In 1993 total exports amounted to US$20.4 million, of which 84 per cent were agricultural products, mainly nutmeg, cocoa, bananas and mace. Total imports were US$118.4 million, mainly machinery and manufactured goods. The total external debt in 1993 was US$66.4 million.

| Trade with UK | 1992 | 1993 |
|---|---|---|
| Imports from UK | £5,546,000 | £6,628,000 |
| Exports to UK | 3,519,000 | 3,919,000 |

# GUATEMALA
*República de Guatemala*

Guatemala, in Central America, is situated in 13° 45' to 17° 49' N. latitude and 88° 12' 49" to 92°13' 43" W. longitude and has an area of 42,042 sq. miles (108,889 sq. km). The country is traversed from west to east by mountains containing several volcanic summits rising to 13,000 feet above sea level; earthquakes are frequent. There are numerous rivers. The climate is hot and malarial near the coast, temperate in the higher regions.

POPULATION – The population (estimate 1992) is 9,745,000. Spanish is the language of the country, but 40 per cent of the population speak an Indian language.

CAPITAL – Guatemala City, population estimate (1990), 1,675,589. Quezaltenango has a population of over 100,000. Other towns are ΨPuerto Barrios (23,000), Mazatenango (21,000), and Antigua (30,000).

CURRENCY – Quetzal (Q) of 100 centavos.

FLAG – Three vertical bands, blue, white, blue; coat of arms on white stripe.

NATIONAL ANTHEM – Guatemala Feliz (Guatemala be praised).

NATIONAL DAY – 15 September.

## GOVERNMENT

Guatemala was under Spanish rule from 1524 to 1821 when it became independent. It formed part of the Confederation of Central America from 1823 to 1839, when the Confederation dissolved.

After a series of military coups in 1963, 1982 and 1983, civilian rule was restored with the election of a Constituent Assembly in 1984 and the promulgation of a new constitution in June 1985.

In May 1993 President Serrano partially suspended the constitution, dissolved Congress and the Supreme Court and declared that he would rule by decree until a new constitution was drafted to combat state corruption. However, following widespread international and domestic criticism, he failed to gain the support of political and business leaders and, most crucially, of the Army. The military effectively ousted Serrano on 1 June when he fled the country. On 5 June the former Human Rights Ombudsman, Ramiro de Léon Carpio, was elected by Congress as the new President to serve out Serrano's term to January 1996.

President de Léon continued the attempt to end political corruption and in November 1993 forced Congress and the Supreme Court to dissolve themselves and to agree to constitutional changes, which were ratified by a referendum in January 1994. Legislative elections to a smaller 80-seat Congress will be held in the latter half of 1994, the Congress will elect 13 Supreme Court judges, and the presidential term was reduced from five to four years.

The republic is divided into 22 departments.

INSURGENCY

Since 1960 the armed forces have been engaged in fighting the insurgency by the left-wing, mainly Mayan Indian, guerrillas of the Guatemalan Revolutionary National Unity Movement (URNG). Some 100,000 have been killed in the fighting, which reached its peak in the Army's 1979–82 counter-insurgency campaign. Government-URNG negotiations began in April 1991 and have continued fitfully since, leading to a reduction in fighting and an agreement in 1993 on the return of 45,000 refugees in Mexico. In March 1994 a human rights accord was reached allowing for the establishment of a UN observer mission in the country. Peace talks continue and the URNG has shrunk to around 2,000 guerrillas.

HEAD OF STATE
*President,* Ramiro de Léon Carpio, *elected by Congress* 5 June 1993
*Vice-President,* Arturo Herbruger Asturias

GOVERNMENT *as at August 1994*
*The President,*
*The Vice-President,*
*Foreign Affairs,* Maritza Ruíz de Vielman
*Interior,* Danilo Parinello Blanco
*Defence,* Gen. Mario Enríquez Morales
*Finance,* Ana Ordoñez de Molina
*Economy and Foreign Trade,* Eduardo González Castillo
*Communications and Public Works,* Jorge Erdmenger la Fuente
*Education,* Celestino Tay Coyoy
*Energy and Mines,* José Luis Terrón
*Agriculture,* Luis del Valle García
*Labour and Social Work,* Gladys Morfín Mansilla
*Health,* Gustavo Hernández Polanco
*Attorney-General,* Acisclo Valladares

EMBASSY OF GUATEMALA
13 Fawcett Street, London SW10 9HN
Tel 0171-351 3042

*Ambassador Extraordinary and Plenipotentiary,* His Excellency Edmundo Nanne, apptd 1992

BRITISH EMBASSY
Centro Financiero Torre II (7th Floor), Seventh Avenue 5-10, Zone 4, Guatemala City
Tel: Guatemala City 321601

*Ambassador Extraordinary and Plenipotentiary,* His Excellency Justin Nason, OBE, apptd 1990
There is also a consulate at *Puerto Barrios.*

FINANCE
The central government revenue in 1992 was Quetzales 5,483 million, and expenditure Quetzales 5,756 million.

TRADE
The principal export is coffee, other articles being manufactured goods, sugar, bananas, cotton, beef and essential oils. The chief imports are petroleum, vehicles, machinery and foodstuffs.
   The chief seaports are San José de Guatemala and Champerico on the Pacific and Santo Tomás de Castilla and Puerto Barrios on the Atlantic side.

|  | 1992 |
|---|---|
| Imports (f.o.b.) | US$2,531m |
| Exports (f.o.b.) | 1,380m |

| Trade with UK | 1992 | 1993 |
|---|---|---|
| Imports from UK | £20,779,000 | £25,966,000 |
| Exports to UK | 10,611,000 | 16,708,000 |

## GUINEA
*République de Guinée*

Formerly part of French West Africa, Guinea has a coastline on the Atlantic Ocean between Guinea-Bissau and Sierra Leone, and in the interior is adjacent to Senegal, Mali, Côte d'Ivoire, Liberia and Sierra Leone. The area is 94,926 sq. miles (245,857 sq. km). The population (UN estimate 1991) is 5,931,000, mostly of the Fullah, Malinké and Soussou tribes.

CAPITAL – ΨConakry (763,000). Other towns are Kankan, which is connected with Conakry by a railway, Kindia, N'Zérékoré, Mamou, Siguiri and Labé.
CURRENCY – Guinea franc of 100 centimes.
FLAG – Three vertical stripes of red, yellow and green.
NATIONAL DAY – 2 October (Anniversary of Proclamation of Independence).

## GOVERNMENT
Guinea was separated from Senegal in 1891 and administered by France as a separate colony until 1958. On 2 October 1958 Guinea became an independent republic.
   M. Sékou Touré assumed office as head of the new government, and was elected President in 1961. President Sékou Touré died in March 1984; a few days later there was a military coup. Guinea was ruled by a military government directed by a Military Committee for National Recovery (CMRN). A new constitution, providing for the end of military rule and the introduction of a two-party system within five years, was approved by referendum in December 1990.
   In January 1991 the CMRN was dissolved and a mixed civilian-military Transitional Committee for National Recovery (CTRN) was established. This appointed a new government in February 1991. Disturbances throughout 1991 led by trade unions and opposition parties caused the government to announce in October that a full multiparty system would be introduced in April 1992. Forty opposition parties have been legalized since April 1992. A presidential election was held on 19 December 1993 and won by the incumbent President Conté with 51 per cent of the vote amid opposition claims of electoral fraud. Legislative elections have yet to be held.

HEAD OF STATE
*President and Minister of Defence,* Maj. Gen. Lansana Conté, *took power* 3 April 1984, *elected* 19 December 1993

COUNCIL OF MINISTERS *as at August 1994*
*Foreign Affairs and Co-operation,* Maj. Ibrahima Sylla
*Minister at the Presidency in charge of National Defence,* Maj. Abdourahmane Diallo
*Interior and Security,* René Alseny Gomez
*Planning and Finance,* Soriba Kaba
*Justice,* Salifou Sylla
*Agriculture and Animal Resources,* Ibrahima Sory Sow
*Natural Resources, Energy and Environment,* Toumani Dakoum Sako
*Territorial Development,* Maj. Ibrahima Diallo
*Higher Educational and Scientific Research,* Charles Pascal Tollo
*Public Health and Social Affairs,* Madigbe Fofana
*Communication,* Capt. Jean-Claude Fassou
*Youth, Culture, Arts and Sports,* Assifat Dorank
*Administrative Reform, Civil Service and Labour,* René Loua Passou
*Industry, Small- and Medium-sized Enterprises,* Mamadou Boyé Barry
*Commerce, Transport and Tourism,* Nantenin Camara
*Vocational Training,* Diallo Aicha Bah

EMBASSY OF THE REPUBLIC OF GUINEA
51 rue de la Faisanderie, 75061 Paris, France
Tel: Paris 47048148

*Ambassador Extraordinary and Plenipotentiary*, His Excellency Lamine Kamara, apptd 1994

BRITISH CONSULATE
BP 834 Conakry, Guinea

*British Ambassador*, His Excellency Alan Furness, CMG resident at Dakar, Senegal

## ECONOMY

The principal products of Guinea are bauxite, alumina, iron-ore, palm kernels, millet, rice, coffee, bananas, pineapples and rubber. At Sangaredi in the mountainous hinterland, where the rivers Senegal, Gambia and Niger have their sources, large deposits of bauxite are mined. Deposits of iron ore, gold, diamonds and uranium have also been discovered. Principal imports are cotton goods, manufactured goods, tobacco, petroleum products, sugar, rice, flour and salt; exports, bauxite, alumina, iron-ore, diamonds, coffee, hides, bananas, palm kernels and pineapples.

| *Trade with UK* | 1992 | 1993 |
|---|---|---|
| Imports from UK | £7,965,000 | £11,059,000 |
| Exports to UK | 239,000 | 593,000 |

## GUINEA-BISSAU
*República da Guiné-Bissau*

Guinea-Bissau, formerly Portuguese Guinea, lies in Western Africa, between Senegal and Guinea; it has an area of 13,948 sq. miles (36,125 sq. km), and a population (UN estimate 1991) of 984,000. The main ethnic groups are the Balante, Malinké, Fulani, Mandjako and Pepel.

CAPITAL – ΨBissau, population (census 1979) 109,486, is also the chief port.

CURRENCY – Guinea-Bissau peso of 100 centavos.

FLAG – Horizontal bands of yellow over green with vertical red band in the hoist charged with a black star.

NATIONAL DAY – 24 September (Independence Day).

## GOVERNMENT

Guinea-Bissau achieved independence on 24 September 1974. Following a coup led by Maj. (now Brig.-Gen.) Vieira in November 1980, the Assembly was suspended and a Revolutionary Council was established. Under a new constitution adopted in April 1984, the Revolutionary Council became a 15-member Council of State and an Assembly of 150 members was set up. The ruling African Party for the Independence of Guinea and Cape Verde (PAIGC) voted to introduce a multiparty system in January 1991. Ten opposition parties have been legalized since November 1991. Legislative elections to a new 100-seat legislature were held on 3 July 1994 and won by the PAIGC, which took 64 seats. In the first round of the presidential election held on the same day, Brig.-Gen. Vieira failed to gain 50 per cent of the vote. At the time of going to press the second round had yet to be held.

HEAD OF STATE
*Chairman of the Council of State , C.-in-C. of the Armed Forces*, Brig.-Gen. João Bernardo Vieira, *took power* November 1980, *elected for a five-year term*, June 1989

COUNCIL OF MINISTERS *as at July 1994*
*Prime Minister*, Carlos Correia
*Foreign Affairs and Co-operation*, Bernadino Cardoso
*Justice*, Manadou Saliu Djalo Pires

*Territorial Administration*, Manuel Mane
*Finance*, Flinto Barros
*Rural Development and Agriculture*, Mario Cabral
*Fisheries*, Eduardo Fernandes
*Natural Resources*, Joao Cardosa
*Commerce and Industry*, Assumane Mane
*Health*, Henriqueta Godinho Gomes
*National Education, Culture and Sport*, Fernando Delfim da Silva
*Social and Women's Affairs*, Francisca Perreira
*Public Works*, Alberto Lina Gomes
*Transport and Communications*, Luis Olivera Sanca
*Administrative Reform and the Civil Service*, Malam Bacai Sanha
*Defence*, Samba Lamine Mane
*Interior*, Abubacar Balde

EMBASSY OF THE REPUBLIC OF GUINEA-BISSAU
94 Rue St Lazare, Paris, France
Tel: Paris 45261851

*Ambassador Extraordinary and Plenipotentiary*, new appointment awaited

BRITISH CONSULATE
Mavegro Int., CP100, Bissau

*British Ambassador*, His Excellency Alan Furness, CMG, resident at Dakar, Senegal

## ECONOMY

The country produces rice, coconuts, groundnuts and palm oil products. Cattle are raised, and there are bauxite deposits in the south.

| *Trade with UK* | 1992 | 1993 |
|---|---|---|
| Imports from UK | £1,117,000 | £1,260,000 |
| Exports to UK | 4,000 | 9,000 |

## GUYANA
*The Co-operative Republic of Guyana*

Guyana, the former colony of British Guiana, which includes the counties of Demerara, Essequibo and Berbice, is situated on the north-east coast of South America, bordering Venezuela, Brazil and Suriname. It has a total area of 83,000 sq. miles (214,969 sq. km).

There is a narrow alluvial coastal belt ten to 40 miles deep. Much of this is below sea level and is drained and irrigated by canals constructed by the Dutch. A mountainous area of dense rain forest lies behind the coastland, and reaches its highest point at Mount Roraima (9,000 ft) on the junction of the Guyana–Brazil–Venezuela borders. In the south-west lies the open savanna country of the Rupununi. The country is intersected by numerous large rivers. The most notable of many waterfalls are the Kaieteur Fall on the Potaro River, the Horse Shoe Falls on the Essequibo and the Marina Fall on the Ipobe River.

The two dry seasons normally last from mid February to end April, and from mid August to end November. Temperatures are lower and rainfall higher on the coast than in the interior.

THE POPULATION – The population (UN estimate 1991) is 800,000.

CAPITAL – ΨGeorgetown. Estimated population, including environs, 185,000. Other towns are: Linden (29,000); ΨNew Amsterdam (23,000); Corriverton (17,000).

CURRENCY – Guyana dollar (G$) of 100 cents.

FLAG – Green with a yellow, white-bordered triangle based on the hoist and surmounted by a red, black-bordered triangle.

NATIONAL ANTHEM – Dear Land of Guyana.

NATIONAL DAYS – 26 May (Independence Day); 23 February (Republic Day).

## GOVERNMENT

Guyana became independent on 26 May 1966, with a Governor-General appointed by The Queen. It became a republic on 23 February 1970. The Independence constitution was replaced by a new constitution promulgated in 1980. It provides for an Executive President who serves a five-year term, a National Assembly of 65 members, and a National Congress of Local Democratic Organs responsible for local government. The Supreme Congress of the People consists of all members of these two assemblies. The electoral system is a proportional representation or 'single list' system, each voter casting his vote for a party list of candidates. The voting age is 18.

A general election was scheduled for the end of 1991 but was not held until 5 October 1992 because of the failure to establish proper electoral machinery and voter registration lists. In the presidential election Dr Cheddi Jagan defeated the incumbent Desmond Hoyte and in the legislative election Jagan's People's Progressive Party (PPP) defeated the People's National Congress (PNC) which had governed since independence. In the National Assembly the state of the parties at August 1994 was: PPP 36; PNC 26; Working People's Alliance 2; United Force 1.

HEAD OF STATE
*Executive President,* Dr Cheddi Bharrat Jagan, *elected* 5 October 1992, *sworn in* 9 October 1992

CABINET *as at August 1994*
*The Executive President*
*Prime Minister and Senior Minister of Public Works, Communications, and Regional Development,* Samuel Hinds
*Attorney-General and Minister of Legal Affairs,* Bernard De Santos
*Senior Ministers:*
*Agriculture,* Reepu Daman Persaud
*Finance,* Asgar Ally
*Foreign Affairs,* Clement Rohee
*Health,* Gail Teixeira
*President's Office,* vacant
*Education and Cultural Development,* Dale Bisnauth
*Labour, Human Services and Social Security,* Henry Jeffrey
*Home Affairs,* Feroze Mohamed
*Trade, Industry and Tourism,* Shree Chand
*Ministers:*
*Public Works, Communications and Regional Development,* Harripersaud Nokta
*Agriculture,* Clinton Collymore
*Labour, Human Services and Social Security,* Indra Chandarpaul
*Amerindian Affairs,* Vibert D'Souza
*President's Office,* George Fung-On

GUYANA HIGH COMMISSION
3 Palace Court, Bayswater Road, London W2 4LP
Tel 0171-229 7684

*High Commissioner,* His Excellency Laleshwar Singh, apptd 1993

BRITISH HIGH COMMISSION
44 Main Street (PO Box 10849), Georgetown
Tel: Georgetown 65881/4

*High Commissioner,* His Excellency David J. Johnson, apptd 1993

## JUDICATURE

The Supreme Court of Judicature consists of a Court of Appeal and a High Court. There are also Courts of Summary Jurisdiction. The Court of Appeal consists of the Chancellor as President, the Chief Justice and Justices of Appeal.

The High Court consists of the Chief Justice, as President, and nine Puisne Judges. It is a court with unlimited jurisdiction in civil matters and exercises exclusive jurisdiction in probate, divorce and admiralty, and certain other matters.
*Chancellor,* K. M. George
*Chief Justice,* Aubrey Bishop

## ECONOMY

The economy is based almost entirely on the main export items of sugar, rice, bauxite and alumina. Diamonds and gold are also mined, timber and rum are produced. There is some cattle ranching in the savanna country, and oil deposits have been found there. The fishing industry is being expanded. Industry is fairly small-scale. Much emphasis is now being placed on eco-tourism.

| Trade with UK | 1992 | 1993 |
| --- | --- | --- |
| Imports from UK | £20,242,000 | £34,218,000 |
| Exports to UK | 78,742,000 | 75,001,000 |

## COMMUNICATIONS

Georgetown and New Amsterdam are the principal ports, though bauxite ships also sail to Linden, on the River Demerara, and Everton, on the River Berbice. There are no public railways and the few roads are confined mainly to the coastal areas. Air transport is the easiest form of communication between the coast and the interior.

There is a state-owned radio broadcasting station which operates two channels and a fledgling television service.

## EDUCATION

The government assumed total control of the education system in September 1976 and made education free from nursery to university level. The government trains teachers for primary and secondary schools at its own institutions.

Approximately 1,800 students were enrolled at the University of Guyana in degree programmes and certificate and diploma courses in 1990.

There are several technical and vocational institutions, as well as some 30 adult education schools (with an enrolment of 13,500). There are also a number of technical and vocational institutions not under the aegis of the Ministry of Education.

---

## HAITI
*République d'Haiti*

---

The Republic of Haiti occupies the western third of the island of Hispaniola. The area, including off-shore islands, is 10,714 sq. miles (27,750 sq. km), of which about three-quarters is mountainous. The climate is tropical with comparatively little difference in the temperatures between the summer (March–October) and the winter (November–February). Humidity is high, especially in the autumn.

POPULATION – The population (UN estimate 1991) is 6,625,000. Both French and Creole are regarded as official

languages. French is the language of the government and the press but it is only spoken by the educated minority. The usual language of the people is Creole.

CAPITAL – Ψ Port-au-Prince. Population estimated at about 1 million. Other centres are: Ψ Cap Haitien (54,691); Gonaives (36,736); Les Cayes (27,222); Jérémie (25,117); St Marc (20,504); Jacmel (16,449); Ψ Port de Paix (21,733).
CURRENCY – Gourde of 100 centimes.
FLAG – Horizontally blue over red.
NATIONAL ANTHEM – La Dessalinienne.
NATIONAL DAY – 1 January.

## GOVERNMENT

Haiti was a French colony under the name of Saint-Domingue from 1697. The slave population revolted in 1791 under the leadership of Toussaint L'Ouverture, who was born a slave and made himself Governor-General of the colony. He capitulated to the French in 1802 and died in captivity in 1803. Resistance was continued by Jean Jacques Dessalines, also a former slave, who declared the colony independent on

1 January 1804, and adopted the name Haiti, an aboriginal word meaning mountainous. Dessalines became Emperor of Haiti but was assassinated in 1806.

Haiti was under US military occupation from 1915 to 1934. Dr François 'Papa Doc' Duvalier was elected in 1957 and became life President in 1964. On his death in 1971 he was succeeded by his son Jean-Claude 'Baby Doc' Duvalier who continued his father's method of maintaining power by the use of the brutal 'Totons Macoutes' militia to terrorize the population. Jean-Claude Duvalier fled to France in February 1986 in the face of sustained popular unrest. Five years of political instability and military government followed until Father Jean-Bertrand Aristide, leader of the National Front for Change and Democracy, won a free presidential election in 1990.

Father Aristide launched an anti-corruption campaign, removing from power the last supporters of the Duvalier dictatorships and purging the military leadership. This led to a military coup in September 1991 which ousted Aristide, who escaped to the USA. The Organization of American States imposed a trade embargo on Haiti to force the military to accept the return of Aristide as President, but without immediate result.

Efforts to resolve the situation continued throughout 1992 and 1993, led by UN and OAS special envoy Dante Caputo. As the military continued to refuse to accept Aristide's return despite international pressure, the UN imposed limited sanctions, including an embargo on oil and arms supplies and freezing the military élite's assets abroad in June 1993. These measures led to the opening of negotiations between the military government and Aristide which culminated in the Governor's Island Agreement of 3 July 1993. The agreement provided for the return of Aristide as President by 30 October 1993; the nomination by Aristide of a new Prime Minister; an amnesty for those involved in the coup; the resignation of the military high command; and the creation of a new police and military force after training by foreign forces.

Aristide's nominee for Prime Minister Robert Malval was confirmed by the Haitian parliament in August and in return the UN lifted its oil embargo. However, the internal situation began to deteriorate in September with the intimidation and murder of Aristide supporters by the military and attachés (successors to the Tontons Macoutes). In October the military regime reneged on the Governor's Island Agreement, preventing the deployment of US and Canadian troops to train a new police force and refusing to resign. Consequently, the UN Security Council reimposed sanctions and imposed a naval blockade.

The situation in Haiti remains tense, with human rights abuses, the murder of the Justice Minister, the resignation of Malval, and thousands attempting to flee the country. In May 1994 the military regime installed Emile Jonaissant as provisional President and the UN imposed a total trade, economic and travel ban on Haiti. The continued resistance of the military regime to international pressure to resign and restore President Aristide, and the murder of 3,000 pro-democracy activists since Aristide's overthrow, led the UN Security Council on 31 July 1994 to authorize the use of all means including force to oust the military regime and restore President Aristide. At the time of going to press preparations for an invasion were being made by the USA and provisional President Jonaissant had declared a state of siege.

**President,** Jean-Bertrand Aristide, elected 16 December 1990, *sworn in* 7 February 1991 *(remains constitutional President)*

The London Embassy of the Republic of Haiti closed on 30 March 1987.

BRITISH AMBASSADOR, His Excellency Derek Milton CMG, resident at Kingston, Jamaica

## ECONOMY

UN sanctions have led to a sharp decline in economic activity, with industry particularly badly hit by the shortage of fuel.

Agricultural production declined after the ending of the colonial plantation scheme. Measures had been taken with the aim of a gradual restoration of productivity. The main project was a scheme for the irrigation of more than 70,000 acres of the Artibonite valley.

Coffee accounts for about 32 per cent of total exports. Cocoa is the second largest export earner. Corn, sorghum and rice are also grown. Increased production of tropical fruits and vegetables is being encouraged.

Export assembly industries accounted for about 30 per cent of the total manufacturing industry in Haiti, employing an estimated 40,000 people but many have been relocated as a result of the unstable political climate. Items such as leather goods, textiles, electronic components and sports equipment are manufactured, using imported raw materials, for re-export. Principal imports are raw materials for the export assembly sector, foodstuffs, machinery, vehicles, mineral oils and textiles.

| *Trade with UK* | 1992 | 1993 |
|---|---|---|
| Imports from UK | £7,212,000 | £10,199,000 |
| Exports to UK | 762,000 | 932,000 |

## COMMUNICATIONS

The main roads are asphalted and secondary roads are fair. Internal air services are maintained between the capital and the principal provincial towns. International air-services (before UN sanctions) connected Port-au-Prince with the USA and other Caribbean and South American cities. The principal towns and villages are connected by telephone and/or telegraph. The telephone company is state owned (51 per cent) and the service both in Port-au-Prince and between urban areas had been improved. There are several commercial radio stations and two television stations at Port-au-Prince. However, recently all services have been considerably disrupted, together with telephone and telegraph services, by UN sanctions.

## EDUCATION

Education is free but estimates of illiteracy are as high as 85 per cent.

## HOLY SEE, *see* VATICAN CITY STATE

---

## HONDURAS
*Republica de Honduras*

---

Honduras, in Central America, lies between 13° and 16° 30′ N. latitude and 83° and 89° 41′ W. longitude, with a seaboard of about 375 miles on the Caribbean Sea and an outlet, consisting of a small strip of coast 63 miles in length, on the Pacific. Its neighbours are Guatemala, Nicaragua and El Salvador. The area is approximately 43,277 sq. miles (112,088 sq. km). The country is very mountainous, being traversed by the Cordilleras, with peaks rising to 1,500 and 2,400 metres above sea level. Rainfall is seasonal, May to October being wet and November to April dry.

POPULATION – The population, 4,915,900 (1991 estimate), is of mixed Spanish and Indian blood. The Garifunas in northern Honduras are of West Indian origin. The language of the country is Spanish, although English is the first language of many in the islands and on the north coast.

CAPITAL – Tegucigalpa, population (1991 estimate) 670,100; other towns are San Pedro Sula (325,900), ΨLa Ceiba (77,100), ΨPuerto Cortes (32,500), Choluteca (63,200) and ΨTela (24,000).

CURRENCY – Lempira of 100 centavos.

FLAG – Three horizontal bands, blue, white, blue (with five blue stars on white band).

NATIONAL ANTHEM – Tu Bandera Es Un Lampo De Cielo (Your flag is a heavenly light).

NATIONAL DAY – 15 September.

## GOVERNMENT

Discovered and settled by the Spanish in the 16th century, Honduras formed part of the Spanish American dominions until 1821 when independence was proclaimed. Under military government from 1972, Honduras returned to civilian rule in 1981 with an executive Presidency, a 148-seat unicameral Congress, and a multi-party system based on the Liberal Party and the National Party. The last presidential and legislative elections were held on 28 November 1993 and won by the Liberal Party, which formed a new government in January 1994.

The country is divided into 18 departments, one of which, Gracias a Dios, is now the home of thousands of Miskito Indian refugees from Nicaragua.

## HEAD OF STATE

*President of the Republic*, Carlos Roberto Reina, *elected*, 28 November 1993, *sworn in* 27 January 1994
*Vice-Presidents*, Walter López Reyes; Juan de la Cruz Avelar; Guadalupe Jerezano

## CABINET *as at August 1994*

*Interior and Justice*, Efraín Moncada Silva
*Foreign Affairs*, Dr Ernesto Paz Aguilar
*Defence*, Gen. Reynolds Andino Flores
*Education*, Zenobia Rodas de Léon Gómez
*Finance*, Juan Ferrera
*Economic Planning*, Guillermo Molina Chocano
*Communications and Public Works*, German Aparicio
*Health*, Dr Enrique Samayoa
*Labour and Social Security*, Cecilio Zavala Méndez
*Natural Resources*, Dr Ramon Villeda Bermúdez
*Culture*, Rodolfo Pastor Fasquelle
*Economy*, Delmer Urbizo Panting
*Environment*, Carlos Medina
*Director of National Agrarian Institute*, Ubodoro Arriaga Iraheta
*President of the Central Bank of Honduras*, Dr Hugo Noé Pino

EMBASSY OF HONDURAS
115 Gloucester Place, London WIH 3PJ
Tel 0171–486 4880

*Ambassador Extraordinary and Plenipotentiary*, new appointment awaited

BRITISH EMBASSY
Apartado Postal 290, Tegucigalpa
Tel: Honduras 32–0612/18

*Ambassador Extraordinary and Plenipotentiary*, His Excellency Patrick Morgan, apptd 1992
There is a British Consulate in *San Pedro Sula*.

## ECONOMY

Three-quarters of the country is covered by pine forests. Agriculture is mainly confined to the fertile coastal plain on the Caribbean and the extensive valleys in the Comayagua and Olancho regions of the interior. A vast tropical forest called the Mosquitia covers the area from the coast to the border with Nicaragua and provides valuable reserves of timber. Lead, zinc and silver are mined on a small scale.

## TRADE

The chief exports are coffee, bananas and timber, the most important woods being pine, mahogany and cedar. Cattle raising and the exporting of frozen meat is an important industry, and exports of shrimps and lobsters are increasing. Other products are tobacco, beans, maize, rice, cotton, palm oil, sugar cane, cement and tropical fruits.

|         | 1990          | 1991     |
|---------|---------------|----------|
| Imports | Lempiras 1,342.6m | 1,332.1m |
| Exports | 997.1m        | 985.8m   |

| *Trade with UK* | 1992       | 1993        |
|-----------------|------------|-------------|
| Imports from UK | £6,101,000 | £14,124,000 |
| Exports to UK   | 13,255,000 | 12,313,000  |

## EDUCATION

Primary and secondary education is free, primary education being compulsory, and the government has launched a campaign to eradicate illiteracy.

## COMMUNICATIONS

There are about 1,004 km of railway in operation, chiefly to serve the banana plantations and the Caribbean ports. There are 17,947 km of roads, of which 2,383 km are paved, excluding some 250 km of new major highways recently inaugurated. Improvements are being made and new roads built. There are 33 smaller airstrips and four international airports, Tegucigalpa, San Pedro Sula, La Ceiba and Roatan (Bay Island).

The chief ports are Puerto Cortes, Tela and La Ceiba on the north coast, through which passes the bulk of the trade with the United States and Europe. Puerto Castilla is being developed as a deep-water container port, and San Lorenzo is also experiencing rapid growth.

# HUNGARY
*Magyar Köztársaság*

The area of Hungary is 35,919 sq. miles (93,030 sq. km) with a population (1993) of 10,278,000. There are minorities of gypsies (4.8 per cent), ethnic Germans (1.9 per cent) and Slovaks (0.9 per cent). About two-thirds of the population are Roman Catholic and the remainder mostly Calvinist.

CAPITAL – Budapest, on the Danube; population (1992) 2,004,000. Other large towns are: Miskolc (192,000); Debrecen (215,000); Szeged (177,000) and Pécs (169,000).
CURRENCY – Forint of 100 fillér.
FLAG – Red, white, green (horizontally).
NATIONAL ANTHEM – Isten Aldd Meg A Magyart (God Bless the Hungarians).
NATIONAL DAYS – 15 March, 20 August, 23 October.

## GOVERNMENT

Hungary, reconstituted a kingdom in 1920 after having been declared a republic on 17 November 1918, joined the Anti-Comintern Pact in February 1939 and entered the Second World War on the side of Germany in 1941. On 20 January 1945 a Hungarian provisional government of liberation signed an armistice under the terms of which the frontiers of Hungary were withdrawn to the limits existing in 1937.

After the liberation, a coalition of the Smallholder, National Peasant, Social Democrat and Communist parties carried out major land reform, and mines, heavy industry, banks and schools were nationalized. By 1949 the Communists had succeeded in gaining a monopoly of power and by 1952 practically the entire economy had been 'socialized'. The Party formulated policy and the function of the government was mainly executive.

The period from July 1956 to the outbreak of the national revolution on 23 October was marked by growing ferment in intellectual circles and increased discord within the Party. The withdrawal of Soviet troops from the country and free elections were among the demands put forward. Fighting broke out on the night of 23 October between demonstrators, who had been joined by large numbers of factory workers, and the State Security Police. Soviet forces intervened in strength early the next morning. By 30 October Soviet troops had withdrawn from Budapest and on 3 November an all-party coalition government under Imre Nagy was formed. This government was overthrown and the revolution suppressed as the result of a renewed attack by Soviet forces on Budapest in the early hours of 4 November. The formation of a new Hungarian Revolutionary Worker Peasant Government under the leadership of Mr Kádár was announced.

From 1968 the government gradually introduced economic reforms and some political liberalization. Kádár was forced to resign in May 1989. In October 1989 the National Assembly (*Országgyűlés*) approved an amended constitution which described Hungary as an independent, democratic state. The National Assembly is elected on a proportional representation basis with a five per cent threshold for representation.

Multiparty elections took place in March and April 1990 and were won by the (conservative) Hungarian Democratic Forum.

The last general election was held in May 1994 and won by the former ruling Communist Party, reconstituted as the Hungarian Socialist Party. as voters showed their dissatisfaction at the fall in living standards since 1990. A coalition government of the Hungarian Socialist Party and the Alliance of Free Democrats was sworn in on 15 July 1994. The government has promised to continue market economic reforms but with significantly increased welfare support and guarantees. The composition of the National Assembly in August 1994 was: Hungarian Socialist Party (HSP) 209, Alliance of Free Democrats (AFD) 69, Hungarian Democratic Forum 38, Independent Smallholders Party 26, Christian Democratic People's Party 22, Federation of Young Democrats 20.

Hungary applied for European Union membership on 1 April 1994.

HEAD OF STATE
*President,* Árpád Göncz, *sworn in* 3 August 1990

CABINET *as at August 1994*

*Prime Minister,* Gyula Horn (HSP)
*Deputy Prime Minister, Interior,* Gábor Kuncze (AFD)
*Agriculture,* László Lakos (HSP)
*Justice,* Pál Vastagh (HSP)
*Industry and Trade,* László Pál (HSP)
*Transport, Telecommunications and Water Management,*
   Károly Lotz (AFD)
*Foreign Affairs,* László Kovács (HSP)
*Defence,* György Keleti (HSP)
*Environment and Regional Policy,* Ferenc Baja (HSP)
*Labour,* Magda Kósa (HSP)
*Education and Culture,* Gábor Fodor (AFD)
*Public Welfare,* Pál Kovács (HSP)
*Finance,* László Békesi (HSP)
*Minister without Portfolio,* Béla Katona (HSP)

HSP Hungarian Socialist Party; AFD Alliance of Free Democrats

EMBASSY OF THE REPUBLIC OF HUNGARY
35 Eaton Place, London SW1X 8BY
Tel 0171–235 4048/7191

*Ambassador Extraordinary and Plenipotentiary,* His
   Excellency Tibor Antalpéter, apptd 1990
*Minister Plenipotentiary,* József Hajgató
*Counsellors,* I. Gerelyes (*Consul*); G. Odze (*Press*);
   J. Hámori, M. Szegvári (*Commercial*); J. G. Turi (*Culture*)
*Defence and Military Attaché,* Col. P. Szücs

BRITISH EMBASSY
Harmincad Utca 6, Budapest V
Tel: Budapest 266–2888

*Ambassador Extraordinary and Plenipotentiary,* His
   Excellency Sir John Birch, KCVO, CMG, apptd 1989
*Counsellor and Deputy Head of Mission,* H. Pearce, CVO
*Defence and Military Attaché,* Col. W. Ibbetson
*First Secretary (Commercial),* D. Taylor
*First Secretary (Management) and Consul,* S. MacTaggart,
   LVO

BRITISH COUNCIL DIRECTOR, Dr John Grote, OBE,
H-1068 Benczur Utca 26, Budapest VI

DEFENCE

Hungary has a total armed forces active strength of 78,000 (including 52,000 conscripts). Conscripts serve for 12 months. The Army has a strength of 60,500 (40,000 conscripts) with 1,331 main battle tanks, 1,680 armoured personnel carriers and armoured infantry fighting vehicles and 790 artillery pieces. The Air Force has a strength of 17,500 (12,000 conscripts), 91 combat aircraft (with a further 43 in store) and 39 attack helicopters. As Hungary is landlocked it has no navy but the Army maintains a small Danube Flotilla with six mine countermeasure vessels. In addition there are 15,900 paramilitary border guards.

ECONOMY

Since 1968 the Hungarian economy had been allowed more decentralized decision-making than most eastern European countries, although central control in vital areas such as the allocation of fuels and raw materials remained. The conservative government embarked upon the privatization of state-owned concerns, the deregulation of the command economy and the return of nationalized land to its former owners. In 1992 the IMF suspended a three-year loan arrangement of US$1,621m because of Hungary's inability to meet required criteria, especially in terms of the budget deficit. To combat this, the parliament in July 1993 approved a harsh austerity budget and devalued the forint to meet IMF criteria to restart the loan. In response the IMF in the second half of 1993 agreed a total credit of US$1,178m to support Hungary's economic reform programme for 1993–4.

The economy has found the transition to a market economy and the loss of export markets in the former Soviet Union and former Yugoslavia difficult. The budget deficit reached 6.2 per cent of GDP in 1994, with GDP falling substantially in 1991–3, and unemployment at 12 per cent and inflation at 22 per cent in mid-1994. Privatization and the establishment of small businesses has proved successful, aided by large-scale foreign investment.

Industrialization has made considerable progress in the last decade and now produces 37 per cent of national income. Industry is mainly based on imported raw materials but Hungary has its own coal (mostly brown), bauxite, considerable deposits of natural gas (some not yet under full exploitation), some iron ore and oil. Output figures in 1993 were (1,000 tons): coal 14,121; aluminium 6,328; rolled steel 1,835; crude oil 1,709. Natural gas production totalled 5,325 million cubic metres.

Agriculture still occupies an important place in the economy. In 1993, 6 per cent of the land area was owned by state farms and 47 per cent was within co-operative farms. Co-operative farms will remain a feature of Hungarian agriculture. Production is concentrated on maize, wheat, sugar beet, barley, rye and oats. GDP per capita in 1993 was US$3,500.

| TRADE (Forints) | 1992 | 1993 |
|---|---|---|
| Imports | 878,200m | 1,162,500m |
| Exports | 843,600m | 819,900m |

| Trade with UK | 1992 | 1993 |
|---|---|---|
| Imports from UK | £161,510,000 | £205,692,000 |
| Exports to UK | 117,636,000 | 152,209,000 |

## EDUCATION

There are five types of schools under the Ministry of Education: kindergartens for age three to six, general schools for age six to 14 (compulsory), vocational schools (15–18), secondary schools (15–18), universities and adult training schools (over 18).

## CULTURE

Magyar, or Hungarian, is one of the Finno-Ugrian languages. Hungarian literature began to flourish in the second half of 16th century. Among the greatest writers of the 19th and 20th centuries are Mihály Vörösmarty (1800–55), Sándor Petöfi (1823–49), János Arany (1817–82), Imre Madách (1823–64), Kálmán Mikszáth (1847–1910), Endre Ady (1877–1918), Attila József (1905–37), Mihály Babits (1883–1941), Dezsö Kosztolányi (1885–1936), Gyula Illyes (1902–83), János Pilinszky (1921–81) and Sándov Weöres (1913–89).

---

# ICELAND
*Island*

---

Iceland is a large volcanic island in the North Atlantic Ocean, extending from 63° 23' to 66° 33' N. latitude, and from 13° 22' to 24° 35' W. longitude, with an estimated area of 39,768 sq. miles (103,000 sq. km). The population was 264,922 on 1 December 1993. Some 92.6 per cent of the population are members of the (Lutheran) Church of Iceland.

CAPITAL – ΨReykjavík, population (1 December 1992), 100,185. Other centres are ΨAkureyri, Kópavogur, ΨHafnarfjördur, Keflavík, Westmann Islands, Akranes, Isafjördur and ΨSiglufjördur.

CURRENCY – Icelandic króna (Kr) of 100 aurar.

FLAG – Blue, with white-bordered red cross.

NATIONAL ANTHEM – O Gud Vors Lands (Our Country's God).

NATIONAL DAY – 17 June.

## GOVERNMENT

Iceland was uninhabited before the ninth century, when settlers came from Norway. For several centuries a form of republican government prevailed, with an annual assembly of leading men called the *Althing*, but in 1241 Iceland became subject to Norway, and later to Denmark. During the colonial period, Iceland maintained its cultural integrity but a deterioration in the climate, together with frequent volcanic eruptions and outbreaks of disease, led to a serious fall in the standard of living and to a decline in the population to little more than 40,000. In the 19th century a struggle for independence began which led to home rule under the Danish Crown in 1918, and to independence as a republic in 1944.

The parliamentary (*Althing*) elections in April 1991 gave the Independence Party 26 seats, Progressives 13, Social Democratic Party 10, People's Alliance 9 and Women's Alliance 5.

HEAD OF STATE

*President,* Vigdís Finnbogadóttir, *born* 1930, *elected* 29 June 1980, *re-elected,* 1984, 1988 and June 1992

CABINET *as at August 1994*

*Prime Minister, Minister for the Statistical Bureau of Iceland,* David Oddsson (IP)
*Foreign Affairs and Trade,* Jón Baldvin Hannibalsson (SDP)
*Finance,* Fridrik Sophusson (IP)
*Fisheries, Justice and Ecclesiastical Affairs,* Thorsteinn Pálsson (IP)
*Education and Culture,* Ólafur Einarsson (IP)
*Social Affairs,* Jóhanna Sigurthardóttir (SDP)
*Health and Social Security,* Gudmundur Arni Stefánsson (SDP)
*Commerce, Industry and Nordic Co-operation,* Sighvatur Björgvinsson (SDP)
*Agriculture and Communications,* Halldór Blöndal (IP)
*Environmental Affairs,* Össur Skarphedinsson (SDP)

IP Independence Party; SDP Social Democrat Party

EMBASSY OF ICELAND
1 Eaton Terrace, London SW1W 8EY
Tel 0171-730 5131/2

*Ambassador Extraordinary and Plenipotentiary,* His Excellency Helgi Ágústsson, GCVO, apptd 1989

BRITISH EMBASSY
Laufásvegur 49, 101 Reykjavík
Tel: Reykjavík 15883/4

*Ambassador Extraordinary and Plenipotentiary and Consul-General,* His Excellency Michael S. Hone, OBE, apptd 1993

BRITISH CONSULAR OFFICES – There are Consular Offices at *Akureyri* and *Reykjavík.*

## CULTURE

The ancient Norraena (or Northern tongue) has close affinities to Anglo-Saxon and as spoken and written in Iceland today differs little from that introduced into the island in the ninth century. There is a rich literature with two distinct periods of development, from the mid-11th to the late 13th century and from the early 19th century to the present.

## ECONOMY

Iceland has considerable resources of hydro-electric and geothermal energy. It is estimated that exploited water power (4,000 Gigawatt hours/a) represents only about 9 per cent of that economically exploitable, whereas only 5 per cent of the estimated 80,000 Gigawatt hours/a of available geothermal power has so far been harnessed. Heavy industry includes an aluminium smelter, a nitrogen fertilizer factory, a diatomite plant and a ferro-silicone plant.

In 1990 Iceland had a total labour force of 124,739, of which 17.6 per cent was engaged in government services, 14.9 in restaurants and hotels, 12.5 per cent in manufacturing and 11.8 per cent in fishing and fish processing.

As a member of the European Free Trade Association (EFTA), Iceland has become a member of the European Economic Area (EEA) which extends most of the provisions of the EC's single market to EFTA states.

TRADE

The principal exports are frozen fish fillets, salt fish, stock fish, fresh fish on ice, frozen scampi, fishmeal and oil, skins and aluminium; imports consist of almost all the necessities of life, the chief items being petroleum products, transport equipment, textiles, foodstuffs, animal feeds, timber, and alumina.

|  | 1991 | 1992 |
|---|---|---|
| Exports | Kr129,207m | Kr126,669m |
| Imports | 147,937m | 138,669m |

| *Trade with UK* | 1992 | 1993 |
|---|---|---|
| Imports from UK | £92,127,000 | £146,891,000 |
| Exports to UK | 239,510,000 | 249,705,000 |

## COMMUNICATIONS

At 1 January 1992, the mercantile marine consisted of 1,107 registered vessels (187,217 gross tons), of which 1,000 (140,349 gross tons) are decked fishing vessels. There are regular shipping services between Reykjavík and Felixstowe, Humber ports and the Continent.

A regular air service is maintained between Glasgow and London and Reykjavík. There are also air services to Scandinavia, USA, Germany, France and Luxembourg.

Road communications are adequate in summer but greatly restricted by snow in winter. Only roads in town centres and key highways are metalled, the rest being of gravel, sand and lava dust. The climate and terrain make first-class surfaces for highways out of the question. There are no railways.

---

## INDIA
*The Republic of India*

---

India has an area of 1,269,346 sq. miles (3,287,590 sq. km), composed of three well-defined regions: the mountain range of the Himalayas, the Indo–Gangetic plain, and the southern peninsula. The main mountain ranges are the Himalayas in the north (over 29,000 feet) and the Western and Eastern Ghats (over 8,000 feet). Major rivers include the Ganges, Indus, Krishna, Godavari and Mahanadi.

There are four seasons: the cold season (December–March); the hot season (April–May); the rainy season (June–September); and the season of the retreating south-west monsoon (October–November). Temperatures vary over the whole country, between averages of about 10°C and 33°C, reaching over 38°C in some parts during the hot season. There are similar variations in rainfall, from only a few inches a year falling in the western Thar Desert to over 400 inches in Meghalaya.

POPULATION – India is the second most populous country in the world. The population at the 1991 census was 846,302,688, of which more than 20 per cent was urban. The majority of the population is Hindu (82.6 per cent), the rest being Muslim (11.4 per cent), Christian (2.4 per cent), Sikh (2.0 per cent) and Buddhist (0.7 per cent) and Jain (0.5 per cent).

The official languages are Hindi in the Devanagari script and English, though 17 regional languages also are recognized for adoption as official state languages.

CAPITAL – Delhi (population in 1991 was 8,375,188). Populations of other principal cities (1991 figures) were Ahmedabad 3,297,655; Bangalore 4,086,548; ΨBombay (Mumbai) 12,571,720; ΨCalcutta 10,916,272; Hyderabad 4,280,261; Kanpur 2,111,284; Lucknow 1,642,134; ΨMadras 5,361,468; Pune 2,485,014.

CURRENCY – Indian rupee (Rs) of 100 paisa.

FLAG – A horizontal tricolour with bands of deep saffron, white and dark green in equal proportions. In the centre of the white band appears an Asoka wheel in navy blue.

NATIONAL ANTHEM – Jana-gana-mana.

NATIONAL DAY – 26 January (Republic Day).

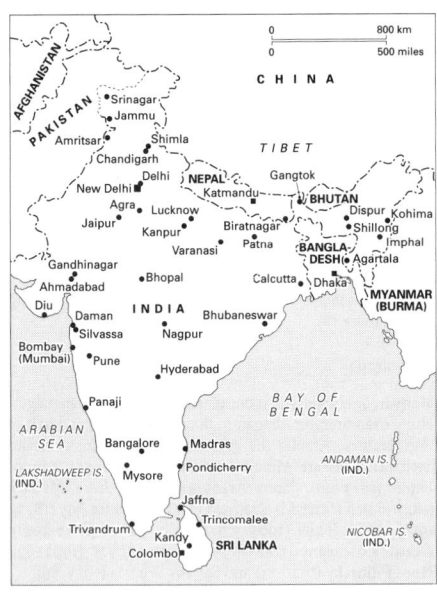

## HISTORY

The Indus civilization was fully developed by *c*.2500 BC but collapsed *c*.1750 BC, subsequently being replaced by an Aryan civilization spread from the west. The first Arab invasions of the north-west began in the seventh century and Muslim, Hindu and Buddhist states developed until the establishment of the Mogul dynasty in 1526. The British East India Company established settlements throughout the 17th century; clashes with the French and native princes led to the British government taking control of the company in 1784 and gradually gaining control of the whole subcontinent. The separate dominions of India and Pakistan became independent within the Commonwealth on 15 August 1947 and India became a republic in 1950.

India and Pakistan have fought three major wars since independence in 1947–8, 1965 and 1971. Since 1985 they have continued a low-level war at altitude for control of the Siachen glacier in Kashmir.

## GOVERNMENT

Under the 1950 constitution, executive power is vested in the President, who is elected for a five-year term by an electoral college consisting of the elected members of the Union and State legislatures. He appoints the Prime Minister and, on the latter's advice, the ministers, and can dismiss them. The Council of Ministers is collectively responsible to the *Lok Sabha* (lower house). The Vice-President is ex-officio chairman of the *Rajya Sabha* (upper house).

Legislative power rests with the President, the Rajya Sabha (which has 245 members) and the Lok Sabha (which has 545 members). Twelve members of the Rajya Sabha are nominated by the President, the rest are indirectly elected representatives of the State and Union Territories. They hold office for six years. The 530 members of the Lok Sabha representing the States are directly elected by universal adult franchise, and 15 representatives of the Union Territories are chosen, for a maximum term of five years. Subject to the provisions of the constitution, the Union Parliament can make laws for the whole of India and the State legislatures for their respective units.

India has been ruled by the Congress (I) Party for all but four years (March 1977–January 1980, November 1989–June 1991) since independence. The Congress (I) Party has been led by members of the Nehru-Gandhi dynasty for most of the post-independence period: Prime Ministers Jawaharlal Nehru (1947–64), Indira Gandhi (1966–1977, 1980–84) and Rajiv Gandhi (1984–89). Indira Gandhi was assassinated by Sikh extremists seeking an independent Sikh state in Punjab who continue their insurgency, but at a lower level than in the early 1980s. Her son Rajiv was assassinated by Sri Lankan Tamils. Inter-communal violence between Hindus and Muslims swept India in 1992–3 following the destruction of the mosque at Ayodhya by Hindu fundamentalists; about 1,200 were killed and 5,000 injured.

The last parliamentary elections to the Lok Sabha were held in June 1991 and won by Congress (I) which formed a government with the support of independents.

## SECESSION

The Hindu Maharaja of the state of Kashmir signed his state's instrument of accession to India in October 1947, two months after India and Pakistan became independent. This was not accepted by Pakistan, on the basis that the majority of the state's population was Muslim, and the UN Security Council ordered a plebiscite on this question of whether Kashmir should accede to India or Pakistan, but this has never been held. After three Indian-Pakistani wars over the state, a line of control was agreed under the 1972 Simla agreement (China has also occupied some of Kashmir since the 1962 Sino-Indian war). The line of control has not been accepted by a significant part of the Muslim population, who since 1989 have formed armed groups fighting either for unification with Pakistan or Kashmiri independence. The armed groups have waged a campaign of violence against the Hindu population of Kashmir and against the 400,000 Indian troops in the state. India claims that the rebels are armed and supplied by Pakistan.

## HEAD OF STATE

*President of the Republic of India*, Dr Shankar Dayal Sharma, elected 16 July 1992
*Vice-President*, K. R. Narayanan, *elected* 19 August 1992

COUNCIL OF MINISTERS *as at August 1994*

*Prime Minister, Minister of Personnel, Public Grievances and Pensions, Science and Technology, Electronics, Atomic Energy, Rural Development, Non-Conventional Energy Sources, Law, Justice and Company Affairs, Space, Ocean Development, Defence and Industry*, P. V. Narasimha Rao
*Finance*, Dr Manmohan Singh
*Agriculture*, Balram Jakhar
*Human Resources Development*, Arjun Singh
*Urban Development*, Sheila Kaul
*Railways*, C. K. Jaffer Sharief
*Power*, N. K. P. Salve
*Civil Supplies, Consumer Affairs and Public Distribution*, A. K. Antony
*Home Affairs*, S. B. Chavan
*External Affairs*, Dinesh Singh
*Welfare*, Sitarem Kesri
*Health and Family Welfare*, B. Shankaranand
*Water Resources and Parliamentary Affairs*, V. C. Shukla
*Civil Aviation and Tourism*, Ghulam Nabi Azad
*Commerce*, Pranab Mukerjee
*Fertilizers and Chemicals*, Ram Lakhan Singh Yadav
In addition there are 12 ministers of state (independent charge), 28 ministers of state and three deputy ministers, making a total of 59 in the Council of Ministers.

INDIAN HIGH COMMISSION
India House, Aldwych, London WC2B 4NA
Tel 0171–836 8484

*High Commissioner*, His Excellency Dr L. M. Singhvi, apptd 1991
*Deputy High Commissioner*, K. V. Rajan
*Minister*, M. P. Bezbaruah (*Economic*); R. Banerji (*Consular*), G. Gandhi (*Culture*)
*Military Adviser*, Brig. B. S. Malik

BRITISH HIGH COMMISSION
Chanakyapuri, New Delhi 1100–21.
Tel: New Delhi 601371

*High Commissioner*, His Excellency Sir Nicholas Fenn, KCMG, apptd 1991
*Deputy High Commissioner and Minister*, H. N. H. Synnott
*Deputy High Commissioners*, T. D. Curran (*Bombay*); A. B. N. Morey, CBE (*Calcutta*); S. H. Palmer (*Madras*)
*Defence and Military Adviser*, Brig. R. A. Draper, OBE
*Counsellor (Economic and Commercial)*, J. E. Holmes
*Minister for Cultural Affairs and British Council Representative in India*, C. W. Perchard, OBE.
Offices also at *Bombay*, *Calcutta* and *Madras*. There are British Council libraries at these four centres and British libraries at *Ahmedabad, Bangalore, Bhopal, Hyderabad, Lucknow, Patna, Pune, Ranchi* and *Trivandrum*.

## STATES AND TERRITORIES OF THE UNION

There are 25 States and seven Union Territories. Each State is governed by a Governor, who is appointed by the President and holds office for five years, and by a Council of Ministers. All States have a Legislative Assembly, and some have also a Legislative Council, elected directly by adult suffrage for a maximum period of five years.

The Union Territories are administered, except where otherwise provided by Parliament, by the President acting through an Administrator or Lieutenant-Governor, or other authority appointed by him.

| (Capital in parenthesis) | Area (sq. km) | Population (1991 census) |
| --- | --- | --- |
| STATES | | |
| Andhra Pradesh (Hyderabad) | 275,100 | 66,304,854 |
| Arunachal Pradesh (Itanagar) | 83,700 | 858,392 |
| Assam (Dispur) | 78,400 | 22,414,322 |
| Bihar (Patna) | 173,900 | 86,374,465 |
| Goa (Panaji) | 3,700 | 1,168,622 |
| Gujarat (Gandhinagar) | 196,000 | 41,309,582 |
| Haryana (Chandigarh) | 44,200 | 16,463,648 |
| Himachal Pradesh (Shimla) | 55,700 | 5,170,877 |
| Jammu and Kashmir* (Srinagar/Jammu) | 222,200 | 5,987,389 |
| Karnataka (Bangalore) | 191,800 | 44,977,201 |
| Kerala (Trivandrum) | 38,900 | 29,011,237 |
| Madhya Pradesh (Bhopal) | 443,500 | 66,135,862 |
| Maharashtra (Bombay) | 307,700 | 78,937,187 |
| Manipur (Imphal) | 22,300 | 1,826,714 |
| Meghalaya (Shillong) | 22,400 | 1,774,778 |
| Mizoram (Aizawl) | 21,100 | 686,217 |
| Nagaland (Kohima) | 16,600 | 1,209,549 |
| Orissa (Bhubaneswar) | 155,700 | 31,659,736 |
| Punjab (Chandigarh) | 50,400 | 20,190,795 |
| Rajasthan (Jaipur) | 342,200 | 44,005,990 |
| Sikkim (Gangtok) | 7,100 | 405,550 |
| Tamil Nadu (Madras) | 130,100 | 55,638,318 |

* The area figure includes those parts occupied by Pakistan and China, which are claimed by India, but the population figure excludes the population of these areas, where the census was not taken. The state's capital is at Srinagar in summer and Jammu in winter.

| (Capital in parenthesis) | Area (sq. km) | Population (1991 census) |
|---|---|---|
| Tripura (Agartala) | 10,500 | 2,744,827 |
| Uttar Pradesh (Lucknow) | 294,400 | 139,112,287 |
| West Bengal (Calcutta) | 88,800 | 67,982,732 |
| UNION TERRITORIES | | |
| Andaman and Nicobar Is. | | |
| (Port Blair) | 8,200 | 280,661 |
| Chandigarh | 114 | 642,015 |
| Dadra and Nagar Haveli | | |
| (Silvassa) | 500 | 138,477 |
| Daman and Diu | 112 | 101,586 |
| Delhi | 1,500 | 9,420,644 |
| Lakshadweep (Kavaratti) | 30 | 51,681 |
| Pondicherry | 500 | 807,785 |

JUDICATURE

The Supreme Court consists of the Chief Justice and not more than 25 other judges, appointed by the President. It is the highest court in respect of all constitutional matters and the final Court of Appeal and is situated in New Delhi. Each state or group of states also has a High Court with a hierarchy of subordinate courts. The judges of the High Court of a state are appointed by the President.

*Chief Justice*, M. N. Venkatachaliah

DEFENCE

The supreme command of the armed forces is vested in the President. Administrative and operational control resides in the Army, Navy and Air Headquarters under the supervision of the Ministry of Defence. Total active armed forces strength numbers 1,265,000. Service is voluntary. India exploded its first nuclear weapon in 1974 and is since believed to have acquired a stockpile of nuclear arms. In 1993–4 India successfully test-fired its intermediate-range 'Prithvi' and 'Agni' ballistic missiles.

The Army has five commands, Southern, Eastern, Northern, Western and Central, and a total strength of some 1,100,000, with some 3,400 main battle tanks of Soviet and indigenous manufacture; 1,450 armoured infantry fighting vehicles and armoured personnel carriers; 3,580 artillery pieces and 200 helicopters. The Army is organized into 11 corps and deploys two armoured, one mechanized, ten mountain and 22 infantry divisions, with a further 27 independent brigades.

The Indian Navy has a strength of 55,000 personnel and consists of two aircraft carriers, 15 submarines, five destroyers, 17 frigates and 40 patrol and coastal craft. A naval aviation wing deploys some 64 combat aircraft and 75 armed helicopters. India has started building her own naval craft.

The Indian Air Force has a strength of some 110,000 with 707 combat aircraft and 36 armed helicopters. It is organized into 23 ground attack, 17 air defence, eight maritime attack, four reconnaisance, two attack helicopters and 23 transport squadrons.

In addition, there are 1,422,000 personnel in 12 paramilitary organizations.

ECONOMY

Agriculture is the chief industry, supporting about 70 per cent of the population, and providing nearly 32 per cent of GDP. The area under cultivation has been increased by irrigation schemes but most holdings are less than five acres. Production has grown by 3 per cent each year since 1951, remaining slightly ahead of the 2 per cent increase necessary to keep pace with the rising population. Food crops occupy three-quarters of the total cropped area and production of food grains amounted to 167 million tonnes in 1991–2. There are three main crop seasons each year, in which different crops are grown. The main food crops are rice, cereals (principally wheat) and pulses. The major cash crops include sugar cane, jute, cotton and tea. Other products include oil seeds, spices, groundnuts, soya bean, tobacco, rubber and coffee. Livestock is raised, principally for dairy purposes or for the hides: cattle (an estimated 181 million), goats (71 million), sheep (45.7 million) and pigs (10 million). In 1992–3 milk production was 58.6m tonnes, egg production reached 22 billion, wool production 44,000 tonnes and fish caught totalled 4.1m tonnes.

India's major industries are based on the exploitation and processing of her mineral resources, principally coal, oil and iron, and on the production of textiles. The coal industry reached an output in 1991–2 of 244 million tonnes. Production of crude oil from the main fields in Assam and from offshore drilling was about 30.4 million tonnes in 1991–2. Steel production is mainly in the hands of the public sector, with five public and one private sector integrated steel plants producing 12 million tonnes of ingot steel in 1991–2. The engineering industry, heavy and light, is also primarily in the hands of the public sector, but is increasingly being privatized.

The manufacture of paper, cement, pharmaceuticals, chemicals, fertilizers, petrochemicals, motor vehicles and commercial vehicles has been expanded. Other principal manufactures are those derived from agricultural products, textiles, jute goods, sugar, leather, which along with tea, tobacco, rubber, fish, and iron ore and concentrates are India's major exports.

Faced with the need to obtain loans from the World Bank and assistance from the IMF, India abandoned centralized planning in July 1991 after 40 years and introduced liberalized free market reforms. Subsidies are being cut, state corporations privatized and the economy opened up to foreign competition and investment. To take India into the international trading system proper, a budget was passed in 1993 which floated the rupee, cut interest rates and dismantled protectionist structures. The budget was in line with IMF proposals and prompted foreign and international donors to pledge US$7,400m to support economic reforms in 1993–4. The reforms have been successful, producing US$5,000m in foreign investment since 1991, a fall in inflation from 17 to 6 per cent, a 21 per cent increase in exports, a rise in foreign currency reserves from US$1,000 million to US$13,000 million, an average GDP growth of 4 per cent per year, and improved agricultural efficiency and industrial growth.

FINANCE

The budget estimates for 1994–5 placed total expenditure at Rs 1,517,000 million. Total revenue (excluding States' shares) was Rs 1,457,000 million.

| Trade with UK | 1992 | 1993 |
|---|---|---|
| Imports from UK | £945,541,000 | £1,129,998,000 |
| Exports to UK | 862,131,000 | 1,088,837,000 |

COMMUNICATIONS

The International Airports Authority manages five international airports: Palam (Delhi), Sahar (Bombay), Dum Dum (Calcutta), Meenambakkam (Madras) and Trivandrum. The other 88 aerodromes are controlled and operated by the Civil Aviation Department of the Government. The national airlines are Indian Airlines (internal) and Air India (international).

The railways are grouped into nine administrative zones, Southern, Central, Western, Northern, North-Eastern,

North-East Frontier, Eastern, South-Eastern and South-Central with a total track length of 62,458 km, about 17 per cent of which is electrified. The total length of the road network is 1,998,434 km of which 964,072 km is surfaced.

The chief seaports are Bombay, Calcutta, Haldia, Madras, Mormugao, Cochin, Visakhapatnam, Kandla, Paradip, Mangalore and Tuticorin. There are 139 minor working ports with varying capacity. On 31 December 1992, 430 ships totalling 6,275,000 gross tons were on the Indian Register.

# INDONESIA
*Republik Indonesia*

Indonesia is situated between 6° N. and 11° S. latitude and between 95° and 141° E. longitude, and comprises the islands of Java, Madura, Sumatra, the Riouw-Lingga archipelago, the islands of Bangka and Billiton, part of the island of Borneo (Kalimantan), Sulawesi (formerly Celebes) Island, the Molucca Islands, the islands of Bali, Lombok, Sumbawa, Sumba, Flores, Timor and others comprising the provinces of East and West Nusa Tenggara and the western half of the island of New Guinea (Irian Jaya), with a total area of 735,358 sq. miles (1,904,569 sq. km), and a population (UN estimate 1991) of 187,765,000.

CAPITAL – ΨJakarta (population 7,885,519). Other important centres are: (Java) ΨSurabaya (2,027,913), ΨSemarang (1,026,671), Bandung (1,462,637); (Sumatra) Palembang (787,187), Medan (1,378,955); (Sulawesi) ΨUjung Pandang (formerly *Makassar*) (709,038); (Kalimantan) Banjarmasin (381,286), ΨPontianak (304,778), ΨBalikpapan (280,675); (Moluccas) Ambon (208,898); (Bali) Denpasar, Singaraja (for whole island 2,174,105); (Nusa Tenggara) Kupang (329,371); (Irian Jaya) Jayapura (107,164).
CURRENCY – Rupiah (Rp) of 100 sen.
FLAG – Equal bands of red over white.
NATIONAL ANTHEM – Indonesia Raya (Great Indonesia).
NATIONAL DAY – 17 August (Anniversary of Proclamation of Independence).

## GOVERNMENT

From the early part of the 17th century much of the Indonesian archipelago was under Dutch rule. Following the Second World War, during which the archipelago was occupied by the Japanese, a strong nationalistic movement manifested itself and after sporadic fighting all the former Dutch East Indies except western New Guinea became independent as Indonesia on 27 December 1949. Western New Guinea became part of Indonesia in 1963 under the name West Irian (now Irian Jaya), this interpretation being confirmed in an 'Act of Free Choice' in July 1969, of which the United Nations took note in November 1969.

Following a three-week period of unrest and violent student demonstrations in 1966 the Minister of the Army, Gen. Suharto, took over effective political power in 1966. Gen. Suharto was appointed President in March 1968 and has been reappointed by the People's Consultative Assembly (composed of the House of People's Representatives together with 500 government appointees) at each presidential election since. The House of People's Representatives is composed of 400 elected members and 100 military appointees. The military has effectively ruled since 1966 through its political organization Golkar.

In the general election of June 1992, Golkar obtained 281 seats, the Muslim United Development Party 63 seats and the Indonesian Democratic Party 56 seats.

### SECESSION

Apart from East Timor (see page 909), there are two armed secessionist movements based on ethnic and nationalist groups fighting perceived Javanese domination of the country. In Western New Guinea (Irian Jaya) government forces are fighting the Papua Independent Organization (OPM) guerrillas who claim the 1969 referendum was flawed and rigged. In northern Sumatra the Free Aceh Movement is active.

### HEAD OF STATE

*President*, Gen. Suharto, *appointed Acting President* March 1967; *confirmed as President* 28 March 1968, *re-elected,* 1973, 1978, 1983, 1988 and March 1993
*Vice-President*, Try Sutrisno, *elected* March 1993

CABINET *as at August 1994*

*Co-ordinating Ministers,* Gen. (retd) Soesilo Soedarman *(Political and Security Affairs)*; Saleh Afiff *(Economy, Finance, Industry and Development Supervision)*; Maj.-Gen. Azwar Anas *(Public Welfare)*; Ir Hartarto *(Industrial and Trade Affairs)*
*Ministers,* Lt.-Gen. (retd) Yogi Memet *(Internal Affairs)*; Ali Alatas *(Foreign Affairs)*; Gen. Edi Sudrajat *(Defence and Security)*; Utoyo Usman *(Justice)*; Mr Harmoko *(Information)*; Mar'ie Muhammad *(Finance)*; Satrio Yudono *(Trade)*; Tungki Arinibowo *(Industry)*; Sjarifuddin Baharsyah *(Agriculture)*; Lt.-Gen. Ida Bagus Sujana *(Mines and Energy)*; Radinal Mochtar *(Public Works)*; Haryanto Danudirto *(Communications)*; Abdul Latief *(Manpower)*; Siswono Yudohusodo *(Transmigration)*; Joop Ave *(Tourism, Posts and Telecommunications)*; Wardiman Joyonegoro *(Education and Culture)*; Dr Suyudi *(Health)*; Tarmizi Taher *(Religious Affairs)*; Prof. Endang Suweno *(Social Affairs)*; Jamaludin Suryohadikasumo *(Forestry)*; Subiakto Cakrawerdaya *(Co-operatives and Small Businesses)*; Dr Murdiono *(Minister and State Secretary)*
In addition there are 14 ministers of state.

INDONESIAN EMBASSY
38 Grosvenor Square, London WIX 9AD
Tel 0171–499 7661

*Ambassador Extraordinary and Plenipotentiary,* His Excellency Junus Habibie, apptd 1993
*Minister,* Herijanto Soeprapto *(Deputy Chief of Mission)*
*Minister Counsellor,* N. M. Koro *(Commercial)*
*Defence Attaché,* Col. J. P. Mandas

BRITISH EMBASSY
Jalan M. H. Thamrin 75, Jakarta 10310
Tel: Jakarta 330904

*Ambassador Extraordinary and Plenipotentiary,* His Excellency Graham Burton, apptd 1994
*Deputy Ambassador, Counsellor and Consul-General,* J. C. R. Gray
*Counsellor (Commercial/Development),* P. J. Bacon
*Defence Attaché,* Col. B. G. Nicholson, OBE

BRITISH CONSULAR OFFICES – There are British Consular Offices at *Jakarta, Medan* and *Surabaya.*
BRITISH COUNCIL REPRESENTATIVE, A. Webster, S Widjojo Centre, Jalan Jenderal Sudirman 71, Jakarta 12190.
There are also libraries at *Bandung* and *Medan.*
INDONESIA BRITAIN ASSOCIATION, c/o R. A. M. Ramsay, Lippo Life Building, 7th Floor, Jl. HR Rasuna Said, Jakarta 12910

## DEFENCE

The armed forces have a total active strength of 270,900 with selective conscription of two years. The Army has a strength of 202,900 with some 155 light tanks, 735 armoured personnel carriers, 180 artillery pieces and 39 helicopters. The Navy has 44,000 personnel (including 12,000 marines), two submarines, 17 frigates, 45 patrol and coastal craft, 18 combat aircraft and 25 armed helicopters. The Air Force has 24,000 personnel and some 80 combat aircraft of US and British manufacture organized into three ground attack, one air defence, two counter-insurgency, one maritime reconnaissance, three helicopter and four training squadrons. There are 215,000 paramilitary police personnel.

## ECONOMY

Nearly 70 per cent of the population is engaged in agriculture and related production. Copra, kapok, nutmeg, pepper and cloves are produced, mainly by smallholders; palm oil, sugar, fibres and cinchona are produced by large estates. Rubber, tea, coffee and tobacco are produced by both in large quantities. Rice is a staple food and the islands of Java, Sulawesi and Sumatra are important producers. Production has risen rapidly in recent years and the country is now self-sufficient.

Oil and liquefied natural gas are the most important assets, the export of which constitutes around 80 per cent of export earnings. However, dependence on these has made the economy vulnerable to depressed international markets and weak oil prices. Timber is the second largest foreign exchange earner after oil. Strenuous efforts have been made to develop non-oil exports, and in real terms their value continues to rise.

Indonesia is rich in minerals, particularly tin, of which the country is the world's third biggest producer; coal, nickel and bauxite are the other principal mineral products. There are also considerable deposits of gold, silver, manganese phosphates and sulphur. Aid to Indonesia is channelled through the Indonesian Consultative Group (ICG). Indonesia received about US$4.8 billion in 1992–3.

Indonesia is aiming to diversify its economy to reduce dependence on crude oil, with particular emphasis on agriculture, heavy engineering (shipbuilding) and high technology (aerospace).

*Trade with UK*

Principal exports to the United Kingdom are rubber, timber, non-ferrous metals, clothing, tea, coffee, spices, vegetable oils and fats, and crude oil for refinement. Imports from the United Kingdom are mainly of machinery, transport equipment, electrical equipment and chemicals.

|                | 1992 | 1993 |
|----------------|------|------|
| Imports from UK | £312,756,000 | £331,094,000 |
| Exports to UK | 536,057,000 | 700,535,000 |

## COMMUNICATIONS

There are railway systems in Java and Sumatra linking the main towns. There are about 50,000 miles of roads.

Sea communications are maintained by the state-run shipping companies Djakarta-Lloyd (ocean-going) and Pelni (coastal and inter-island) and other small concerns. Transport by small craft on the rivers of the larger islands plays an important part in trade.

Air services are operated by Garuda Indonesian Airways and other local airlines, and Jakarta is served by various international services.

# EAST TIMOR

The territory of East Timor comprises the eastern half of the mountainous island of Timor, together with an enclave on the north coast of western Timor. The island is the largest and most easterly of the Lesser Sundas group and is situated across the Timor Sea from Darwin in northern Australia. East Timor was a Portuguese colony from 1702 until Portuguese control collapsed in 1974-5 following the 1974 coup in Portugal. An independence war against Portuguese rule waged by the Marxist Fretilin (Revolutionary Front for an Independent East Timor) developed into a civil war between Fretilin and local conservative forces in autumn 1975. After gaining control, Fretilin declared East Timor independent on 27 November 1975 and this was recognized by Portugal. Indonesian forces invaded East Timor on 7 December 1975, claiming that they had been invited by non-Fretilin forces. In July 1976 Indonesia declared East Timor its 27th province.

Since 1975 the East Timorese people have resisted integration with Indonesia and Fretilin have waged an armed campaign for independence. Resistance has left 200,000 East Timorese dead through starvation or killings by the Indonesian army. About 150,000 Muslims have been settled in East Timor to dilute resistance from the predominantly Roman Catholic population (80 per cent in 1975). The United Nations refuses to accept Indonesia's annexation of East Timor and considers Portugal to exercise sovereignty still. The international community was outraged by the massacre of pro-independence demonstrators in the capital, Dili, in November 1991. Fighting between Fretilin and the Indonesian army continues, with Fretilin numbering about 800 guerrillas, armed with light weapons and based in the island's mountainous interior. Fretilin's leader, Xanana Gusmao, was captured and jailed by the Indonesians in 1993.

# IRAN
*Jomhori-e-Islami-e-Iran*

Iran has an area of 636,296 sq. miles (1,648,000 sq. km). It is mostly an arid tableland, encircled, except in the east, by mountains, the highest in the north rising to 18,934 ft. The central and eastern portion is a vast salt desert.

POPULATION – The population (UN estimate 1991) is 55,762,000. The Iranians are mostly Shia Muslims but among them are Zoroastrians, Bahais, Sunni Muslims and Armenian and Assyrian Christians. Emigration has much reduced the once substantial Jewish community.

Persian or Farsi, the language of Iran and of some other areas formerly under Persian rule, is an Indo-European tongue with many Arabic elements added; the alphabet is mainly Arabic, with writing from right to left. Among the great names in Persian literature are those of Abu'l Kásim Mansúr, or Firdausi (AD 939-1020), Omar Khayyám, the astronomer-poet (died AD 1122), Muslihu'd-Din, known as Sa'di (born AD 1184), and Shems-ed-Din Muhammad, or Hafiz (died AD 1389).

CAPITAL – Tehran, population (1990 UN estimate) 6,042,584. Other large towns are Tabriz, Isfahan, Meshed, Shiraz, Resht, Kerman, Hamadan, Yazd, Kermanshah and Ahwaz.
CURRENCY – Rial.
FLAG – Three horizontal stripes of green, white, red, with the slogan *Allahu Akbar* repeated 22 times along the edges of the green and red stripes, and the national emblem in the centre.

NATIONAL ANTHEM – Sorood-e Jomhoori-e Eslami.
NATIONAL DAY – 11 February.

## GOVERNMENT

Iran was ruled from the end of the 18th century by Shahs of the Qajar dynasty. After the war of 1914-18, the subsequent troubles and the signature of the Soviet-Iranian Treaty of 1921, a vigorous Prime Minister, Reza Khan, re-established general order. In 1925 the last representative of the Qajar dynasty, Sultan Ahmed Shah, was deposed in his absence by the National Assembly, which handed over the government to Prime Minister Reza Khan. Reza Khan was elected Shah in December 1925 by the Constituent Assembly and took the title Reza Shah Pahlavi. In 1941 Reza Shah abdicated in favour of the Crown Prince, who ascended the throne under the title of Mohammed Reza Shah Pahlavi.

Following widespread and persistent opposition to his regime, the Shah departed from Iran in January 1979. Ayatollah Khomeini, the main spiritual leader of the Shia Muslims, returned from exile on 1 February. Following a national referendum, Iran was declared an Islamic Republic on 1 April 1979. A new constitution, providing for a President, Prime Minister and Consultative Assembly, and also for overall leadership by Ayatollah Khomeini, was approved by referendum in December 1979. The government's severe measures suppressed violent opposition. In June 1989 Khomeini died and President Khamenei was appointed Leader of the Islamic Republic. Rafsanjani was elected President in July 1989, and the post of prime minister was abolished. In April 1992 elections to the Majlis (consultative assembly), candidates supporting President Rafsanjani were overwhelmingly elected, winning over 200 of the 270 seats. However, in the June 1993 presidential elections, President Rafsanjani received only 63 per cent of the vote (compared with 94 per cent in 1989) and only 56 per cent of the electorate voted. This reflects growing discontent with economic hardship caused by free market economic reforms which have been introduced by Rafsanjani and Nourbakhsh.

Iran was at war with Iraq following the Iraqi invasion of Iran in September 1980. International efforts to end the fighting resulted in a ceasefire in August 1988. In August 1990 Iraq accepted Iran's conditions for settling the conflict, including a return to the 1975 border, but a formal peace treaty has not been signed.

*Leader of the Islamic Republic*, Ayatollah Seyed Ali Khamenei, *appointed* June 1989
*President*, Hojjatoleslam Ali Akbar Hashemi Rafsanjani, *elected* 28 July 1989, *re-elected* 11 June 1993
*Vice-President (Economic Affairs)*, Mohsen Nourbakhsh, *appointed by the President*, 16 August 1993

CABINET *as at August 1994*

*Agriculture*, Issa Kalantari
*Commerce*, Yahya Al-Eshaq
*Construction Crusade*, Gholam Reza Forouzesh
*Defence*, Mohammed Forouzandeh
*Economy and Finance*, Mohammed Khan
*Education*, Mohammad Ali Najafi
*Culture and Higher Education*, Dr Hashemi Golpeygani
*Energy*, Bizhan Namdar Zanganeh
*Islamic Culture and Guidance*, Mostafa Mir-Salim
*Foreign Affairs*, Ali Akbar Velayati
*Health*, Ali Reza Marandi
*Heavy Industries*, Mohammad Hadi Nezhad-Hosseinian
*Housing and Urban Development*, Abbas Ahmad Akhundi
*Industries*, Mohammad Reza Nematzadeh
*Intelligence*, Ali Fallahian
*Interior*, Ali Mohammad Besharati

*Justice*, Mohammad Esmail Shoushtari
*Labour and Social Affairs*, Hossein Kamali
*Mines and Metals*, Mohammad Hossein Mahloujchi
*Oil*, Gholamreza Aghazadeh
*Posts, Telephones and Telegraphs*, Mohammad Gharrazi
*Roads and Transport*, Akbar Torkan
*Co-operatives*, Gholem Reza Shafei

EMBASSY OF THE ISLAMIC REPUBLIC OF IRAN
16 Prince's Gate, London SW7 1PX
Tel 0171-584 8101

*Chargé d'Affaires*, G. Ansari.

BRITISH EMBASSY
143 Ferdowsi Avenue, PO Box 11365–4474, Tehran 11344
Tel: Tehran 675011

*Counsellor and Chargé d'Affaires*, Jeffrey R. James, apptd
   1993
*First Secretary (Commercial)*, M. A. Hilton

### DEFENCE

Since the end of the war with Iraq the Iranian armed forces have been significantly reduced in size and now number 473,000 active personnel. The conscription term is 24 months, with conscripts serving almost exclusively in the Army. The Army has a strength of 320,000 (including 250,000 conscripts) with one special forces, four armoured and seven infantry divisions, some 700 main battle tanks, 1,030 armoured personnel carriers and armoured infantry fighting vehicles, 2,300 artillery pieces and 300 helicopters.

The Navy is 18,000 strong, with two submarines, three destroyers, five frigates, 33 patrol and coastal craft, and nine armed helicopters. The Air Force has 15,000 personnel, with some 293 combat aircraft. However, only around 50 per cent of these are serviceable due to the US armaments embargo, in operation since 1979.

The Islamic Revolutionary Guards Corps numbers some 120,000, of which 100,000 are ground and 20,000 naval forces.

### EDUCATION

Since 1943 primary education has been compulsory and free. There are 22 universities in Iran (eight in Tehran, 14 in the provinces). The educational system has been reformed following the revolution. The literacy rate is 74.1 per cent.

### ECONOMY

The economy has been badly affected by the fall in world oil prices in the past few years, which has exacerbated the hardship caused by the loss of subsidies on all but the most basic foodstuffs following free market reforms. In 1994 the total foreign debt reached US$30,000m with inflation at 30 per cent per month.

Agriculture suffered from a lack of investment during the Iran–Iraq war, but output is rising. An attempt is being made to reduce Iran's dependence on food imports. Wheat is the principal crop; other important crops are barley, rice, cotton, sugar beet, fruit, nuts and vegetables. Wool is also a major product. There are extensive forests in the north and west, the conservation of which is a continuing problem.

Apart from oil, the principal industrial products are carpets, textiles, sugar, cement and other construction materials, ginned cotton, vegetable oil and other food products, leather and shoes, metal manufactures, pharmaceuticals, motor vehicles, fertilizers and plastics. Industrial output was severely curtailed by the 1979 revolution, as a result of which many industrialists left the country, and by

the Iran–Iraq war, but the private sector is now being encouraged again and prospects for industry are reasonable.

The oilfields, which lie in south-western Iran, were nationalized in 1951. From 1957 until the 1979 revolution a consortium of eight foreign oil companies was responsible for the production, refining and sale of oil but in July 1979 the National Iranian Oil Company assumed full control of the oil industry. In addition to that extracted from the onshore wells, oil is also produced from a number of off-shore oilfields. Oil production is around 3.6 million b.p.d., of which some 2.5 million b.p.d. is exported. Iran is a member of OPEC.

| FINANCE | 1994–5 |
|---|---|
| Revenue | Rials 30,048,000m |
| Expenditure | 30,048,900m |

TRADE

Over 80 per cent of Iran's export earnings come from oil, but an effort is being made to increase non-oil exports. The level of finance for imports depends largely on the international oil price and Iran has recently had a deficit in foreign trade partly because of the depressed state of world oil prices. Tighter import controls were introduced in 1994.

Imports are mainly industrial and agricultural machinery, motor vehicles and motor vehicle components for assembly, iron and steel (including manufactures), electrical machinery and goods, meat, various other foods, and certain textile fabrics and yarns.

The principal exports, apart from oil, are cotton, carpets, dried fruit, nuts, hides and skins, mineral ores, wool, gums, caviare, cumin seed and spices. Germany and Japan are Iran's leading suppliers.

| *Trade with UK* | 1992 | 1993 |
|---|---|---|
| Imports from UK | £568,113,000 | £496,555,000 |
| Exports to UK | 164,512,000 | 244,851,000 |

### COMMUNICATIONS

Tehran is at the centre of a network of highways linking the capital with other major towns, the ports and the frontiers with Turkey, Armenia, Azerbaijan, Turkmenistan, Afghanistan and Pakistan, and with the Caspian Sea.

The Trans-Iranian Railway runs from Bandar Turcoman, on the Caspian Sea, via Tehran to Bandar Khomeini, on the Persian Gulf. Other lines link Tehran with Tabriz and with Mashad. There are also railways from Tabriz to Julfa and from Zahedan to Quetta, and a branch line from Ahwaz to Khorramshahr. An extension from Qom to Kerman is now in operation, as is one from Bandar Turcoman to Gorgan. The Iranian rail system is linked to the Turkish system via Van, and is to be linked also to Turkmenistan.

There is an international airport at Tehran (Mehrabad), and airports at all the major provincial centres. The national airline, Iranair, is government-owned and operates international and domestic routes.

---

# IRAQ
*Al-Jumhouriya al-'Iraqia*

Iraq extends between 37½° to 48½° E. longitude, and 37½° to 30° N. latitude, from Turkey on the north and north-east to the Gulf on the south and south-east, and from Iran on the east to Syria and the Arabian Desert on the west. In January 1993 the border between Iraq and Kuwait was formally demarcated, moving a few hundred metres northwards and giving part of the port of Umm Qasr to Kuwait. The area of

Iraq is 167,925 sq. miles (434,924 sq. km), of which 37 per cent is desert. The rivers Euphrates and Tigris traverse the country. The Euphrates (1,700 miles) rises near Erzurum in Turkey and flows through Turkey, Syria and Iraq to its outflow on the Gulf. The River Tigris (1,150 miles from its source to the Euphrates) rises in the Taurus mountains in Turkey and flows through Iraq to its junction with the Euphrates at Qurna, 70 miles from the Gulf.

POPULATION – The population at the census of October 1987 was 16,278,316. A 1991 UN estimate gives a figure of 19,581,000.

The official language is Arabic. Minority languages include Kurdish (about 15 per cent), Turkic and Aramaic.

CAPITAL – Baghdad. Population of the governorate (census 1977) 3,205,645. Other towns of importance are Ψ Basra, Mosul and Kirkuk.

CURRENCY – Iraqi dinar (ID) of 1,000 fils.

FLAG – Three horizontal stripes of red, white, black; on the white stripe three stars and the slogan *Allahu Akbar* all in green.

NATIONAL DAY – 17 July (Revolution Day).

## HISTORY

In 1944 excavations at Tell Hassuna, near Shura (on the Tigris in north Iraq) unearthed abundant traces of culture dating back to 5000 BC. Excavations in 1948 at Tel Abu Shahrain, south of 'Ur of the Chaldees', confirm Eridu's claim to be the most ancient city of the Sumerian world. Hillah, the ancient city on the left bank of the Shatt el Hillah, a branch of the Euphrates, about 70 miles south of Baghdad, is near the site of Babylon and of the 'house of the lofty-head' or 'gate of the god' (Tower of Babel). Mosul governorate covers a great part of the ancient kingdom of Assyria, the ruins of Ninevah, the Assyrian capital, being visible on the banks of the Tigris, opposite Mosul. Qurna, at the junction of the Tigris and Euphrates, is traditionally supposed to be the site of the Garden of Eden.

Under the Treaty of Lausanne (1923), Turkey renounced sovereignty over Mesopotamia. A provisional government was set up in November 1920, and in August 1921 the Emir Faisal was elected King of Iraq. The country was a monarchy until July 1958, when King Faisal II was assassinated. From 1958 Iraq has been under the rule of the Ba'ath Party.

Iraq invaded Iran in September 1980 and was at war with Iran until 1988. A cease-fire began in August 1988 and in August 1990 Iraq accepted Iran's conditions for peace, including a return to the 1975 border, but a formal peace treaty has not been signed.

Iraq invaded Kuwait on 2 August 1990 and declared Kuwait a province of Iraq. The UN Security Council declared the annexation void. After months of diplomatic attempts to secure an Iraqi withdrawal from Kuwait, an alliance of NATO and Middle East countries launched an offensive in January 1991 and liberated Kuwait in February 1991.

## GOVERNMENT

According to the provisional constitution, the highest state authority is the Revolutionary Command Council (RCC), which elects the President from among its own members. The President appoints the Council of Ministers. Legislative authority is shared by the RCC and the 250-member National Assembly, which is elected every four years by universal adult suffrage. Following general elections in April 1989 the Arab Ba'ath Socialist Party holds the majority of the Assembly seats, the remainder being held by the state-sponsored National Progressive Patriotic Front.

Iraqi attacks on Kurdish armed forces and civilian populations in northern Iraq in early 1991 led the UN Security Council to establish Kurdish safe havens in northern Iraq and an air exclusion zone above the 36th parallel patrolled by US, British and French aircraft based in Turkey. A similar zone was established below the 32nd parallel in August 1992 to stop Iraqi aircraft bombing the Shia refugees in the southern Iraqi marshes. Throughout 1991–3 Iraq violated the air exclusion zones, provoking retaliatory air strikes by allied forces.

The regime also obstructed the work of UN weapons inspection teams who have overseen the destruction of Iraqi weapons of mass destruction since April 1991. In retaliation, the UN Security Council voted in October 1992 to seize all Iraqi assets in foreign banks and use the money to compensate Gulf war victims, finance UN weapons inspection teams and fund relief operations to Kurdish and Shia areas. In January and June 1993 the USA destroyed an Iraqi nuclear weapons plant and the headquarters of the Iraqi intelligence service in retaliation for, respectively, Iraqi refusals to allow UN weapons inspection teams entry and an Iraqi attempt to murder ex-President Bush.

Since late 1993 the economic hardship caused by sanctions and the oil embargo has led to several assassination attempts on Saddam Hussein, an attempted coup, and government reshuffles. The regime has co-operated increasingly with UN weapons inspection teams in an attempt to have economic sanctions lifted. In November 1993 the regime agreed to the destruction of all its weapons of mass destruction and the means of manufacturing them. In February 1994 all remaining plutonium and enriched uranium was removed by the UN; in March all remaining chemical and biological weapons were destroyed; in June all nuclear, chemical and biological weapons and missile production facilities were destroyed; and in July a nationwide network of cameras and sensors was installed to ensure production of weapons was not restarted. Iraq, however, continues its claim to, and refuses to accept the sovereignty and independence of, Kuwait and so UN sanctions remain in place.

### SECESSION

Following the allied victory in Kuwait in February 1991, rebellion against the government broke out in both Kurdish northern Iraq and Shi'ite southern Iraq. Although the revolt was suppressed by the end of April, the plight of the resultant Kurdish refugees led western governments to set up a security zone in northern Iraq to protect them. Allied forces were withdrawn in July. Saddam Hussein withdrew his administration from Kurdish-dominated areas of northern Iraq in October 1991 and imposed an economic embargo on the territory. The Kurds have since established a *de facto* administration with its capital at Arbil and control over certain northern areas, which have a population of 3.5 million. In May 1992 the Kurds voted in free elections for a 100-seat parliament and a 'political leader'. The Kurdish Democratic Party (KDP) and the Patriotic Union of Kurdistan (PUK) both gained 50 seats and a Kurdish government was formed in July with party leaders Masoud Barzani and Jalal Talabani as joint leaders of the territory and Fuad Masum, later replaced by Kosrat Abdullah Rasul, as Prime Minister. The Iraqi economic embargo has caused great hardship, and the neighbouring states of Syria, Iran and Turkey have been reluctant to trade with the Kurdish administration as they all have their own Kurdish minorities. Continued fuel and food shortages and land disputes led to fighting for most of 1994 between KDP and PUK forces.

*President, Chairman of the Revolutionary Command Council, Prime Minister*, Saddam Hussein, *assumed office* 16 July 1979
*Vice Presidents*, Taha Yassin Ramadhan; Taha Mohieddin Maaruf

REVOLUTIONARY COMMAND COUNCIL
*Chairman*, Saddam Hussein
*Vice-Chairman*, Izzat Ibrahim
*Head of the Presidential Office*, Hatim Hamdan al-Azawi
*Members*, Taha Yassin Ramadhan; Tariq Aziz; Hassan Ali; Mohammed Hamza al-Zubeidi; Gen. Ali Hassan al-Majeedi; Mizban Khider Hadi; Taha Mohieddin Maaruf

CABINET *as at August 1994*
*Prime Minister*, Saddam Hussein
*Deputy Prime Ministers*, Tariq Aziz; Taha Mohieddin Maaruf; Mohammed Hamza al-Zubeidi
*Interior*, Wathban Ibrahim al-Hassan
*Defence*, Gen. Ali Hassan al-Majeed
*Foreign Affairs*, Mohammed Saaed al-Sahhaf
*Finance*, Ahmad Hussein al-Khodair
*Culture and Information*, Hamad Youssef Hammadi
*Justice*, Shabib al-Maliki
*Agriculture and Irrigation*, Karim Hassan Rida
*Industry and Minerals*, Lt.-Gen. Hussein Kamil Hassan
*Oil*, Safa Hadi Jawad al-Habubi
*Education*, Hikmat Abdullah al-Bazzaz
*Labour and Social Affairs*, Latif Nassif Jassem
*Health*, Umeed Madhat Mubarak
*Planning*, Samal Majid Faraj
*Higher Education and Scientific Research*, Humam Abdel-Khaliq Ghafuras
*Housing and Construction*, Mahmoud Diyab Al-Ahmad
*Transport and Communications*, Ahmed Murtada Ahmed Khalil
*Religious Endowments and Religious Affairs*, Abdul-Muneim Ahmed Saleh
*Trade*, Muhammed Mahdi Salih

IRAQI DIPLOMATIC MISSION IN LONDON
Since Iraq's breach of diplomatic relations with Britain in February 1991, the Jordanian Embassy has handled Iraqi interests in this country.

BRITISH DIPLOMATIC REPRESENTATION
The British Embassy was closed in January 1991. Since the breach of diplomatic relations, the Russian Embassy has handled British interests in Iraq.

DEFENCE

The Iraqi armed forces were decimated in the defeat by the allied coalition which drove them from Kuwait but remained strong enough to suppress the Kurdish and Shi'ite rebellions. Estimates of the size and strength of the armed forces are vague but total active personnel is in the region of 382,000, from a pre-war total of one million. Reservists number 650,000 personnel, of whom around 100,000 are on permanent recall to the Army. Conscripts serve for between 18 and 24 months.
The Army has a strength of around 350,000, with around 2,200 main battle tanks (5,300 pre-war); 4,200 reconnaissance vehicles, armoured personnel carriers and armoured infantry fighting vehicles (6,300 pre-war); 1,730 artillery pieces (3,150 pre-war) and 120 armed helicopters. The Army is organized into seven Republican Guard and 22 regular divisions with 15 specialized counterinsurgency brigades.

The Navy has a strength of around 2,000 with one frigate, 14 patrol and coastal craft and five mine warfare vessels. The Air Force has a strength of around 30,000 with some 320 combat aircraft and a further 115 still in Iran, where they were flown during the war. The allies destroyed 135 aircraft. In addition, there are 24,800 paramilitary frontier guards and security troops.
Since the end of the war, UN weapons inspection teams have destroyed or dismantled nuclear, chemical and biological weapons, Scud missiles and their launchers, and the Superguns. By mid 1994 it was believed that all these weapons and their means of production had been destroyed and a long-term monitoring operation was under way to ensure production did not restart.
In opposition to Iraqi forces there are some 57,000 armed Kurdish guerrillas, with a further 36,000 support personnel. These are armed with captured Iraqi tanks, artillery and mortars, and a proliferation of small arms. There is also a brigade-sized armed Shia opposition force based in Iran.

ECONOMY

In August 1990, the UN imposed economic sanctions on Iraq, including a world-wide ban on its oil exports. Sanctions were modified in August 1991 to allow the sale of 20 per cent of pre-war oil production; the proceeds are to be allocated to a special UN account for the purchase of food and other essential supplies, and for the funding of war reparations, but Iraq has refused to make use of this. The sanctions have caused considerable economic hardships.
Apart from the revenues to be derived from oil, agricultural development makes a valuable contribution to the wealth of the country and two harvests can usually be gathered in a year. Production fluctuates from year to year according to rainfall. The Government's concern with agricultural development is shown in the large financial allocations made to the sector. Salinity and soil erosion, caused by a high water table, inadequate irrigation and drainage and traditional farming methods, are the major problems now being addressed by development planners.
Increasing industrialization is taking place but industrial production has been greatly reduced because of war damage and sanctions.
Iraq's major industry is oil production. It was nationalized in 1972 and accounts for approximately 98 per cent of the total government revenue and 45 per cent of GNP. Production was some 3.5 million barrels per day in 1979 but the effects of war damage on the Basra terminals and the closure of the trans-Syria pipeline reduced production until new pipelines were built via Turkey and Saudi Arabia (both closed since August 1990).

TRADE

The principal imports are normally iron and steel, cement and other building materials, mechanical and electrical machinery, motor vehicles, textiles and clothing, essential foodstuffs, grain, tinned foods and raw industrial materials. The chief exports are normally crude petroleum, dates, raw wool, raw hides and skins and raw cotton.

| Trade with UK | 1992 | 1993 |
|---|---|---|
| Imports from UK | £34,023,000 | £11,956,000 |
| Exports to UK | 311,000 | 39,000 |

COMMUNICATIONS

The port of Basra has not been used since the outbreak of hostilities with Iran in September 1980. Continuous dredging of the Shatt-al-Arab has also been suspended by hostilities and the channel has seriously silted. The port of Um Qasr on the Kuwaiti border, which was developed for freight and sulphur handling and includes a container terminal, was opened in late 1993. All external borders, except that of Jordan, are closed to Iraqi traffic.

There is an international airport at Baghdad. Iraqi Airways provided flights between Baghdad and London, and other international airlines operated to Europe. Iraqi Republican Railways provided regular passenger and goods services between Basra, Baghdad and Mosul. There is also a metre gauge rail line connecting Baghdad with Khanaqin, Kirkuk and Arbil.

Iraqi communications were greatly affected by the Gulf War; large numbers of bridges were destroyed and the railway system extensively disrupted.

## IRELAND

Ireland lies in the Atlantic Ocean between 51° 26' and 55° 21' N. latitude and 5° 25' and 10° 30' W. longitude. It is separated from Scotland by the North Channel and from Wales by the Irish Sea and St George's Channel. The area of the island is 32,588 sq. miles (84,402 sq. km). The greatest length of the island, from north-east to south-west (Torr Head to Mizen Head), is 302 miles, and the greatest breadth, from east to west (Dundrum Bay to Annagh Head), is 174 miles. On the north coast of Achill Island (Co. Mayo) are the highest cliffs in the British Isles, 2,000 feet sheer above the sea.

The island is mostly a central plain, with an elevation 50 to 350 ft above mean sea level, with isolated mountain ranges near the coastline. The principal mountains, with their highest points, are the Sperrin Mountains (Sawel 2,240 ft), Co. Tyrone; the Mountains of Mourne (Slieve Donard 2,796 ft), Co. Down; the Wicklow Mountains (Lugnaquilla 3,039 ft); the Derryveagh Mountains (Errigal 2,466 ft), Co. Donegal; the Connemara Mountains (Twelve Pins 2,695 ft), Co. Galway; Macgillicuddy's Reeks (Carrantuohill 3,414 ft, the highest point in Ireland); the Galtee Mountains (3,018 ft), Co. Tipperary, and the Knockmealdown (2,609 ft) and Comeragh Mountains (2,470 ft), Co. Waterford.

The principal river of Ireland (and the longest in the British Isles) is the Shannon (240 miles), rising in Co. Cavan and draining the central plain. The Slaney flows into Wexford Harbour, the Liffey to Dublin Bay, the Boyne to Drogheda, the Lee to Cork Harbour, the Blackwater to Youghal Harbour, and the Suir, Barrow and Nore to Waterford Harbour.

The principal hydrographic feature is the loughs, of which Lough Neagh (150 sq. miles) in the north-east is the largest in Ireland and the British Isles, others being the Shannon chain of Allen, Boderg, Forbes, Ree and Derg, and the Erne chain of Gowna, Oughter, Lower Erne, and Erne; Melvin, Gill, Gara and Conn in the north-west; and Corrib and Mask (joined by a hidden channel) in the west. In Co. Kerry, to the east of Macgillicuddy's Reeks, are the famous lakes of Killarney.

EARLY HISTORY – Although little is known about the earliest inhabitants of Ireland, there are traces of neolithic man throughout the island; a grave containing a polished stone axehead assigned to 2500 BC was found at Linkardstown, Co. Carlow, in 1944, and the use of bronze implements appears to have become known about the middle of the 17th century BC. In the later Bronze Age a Celtic race of Goidels appears to have invaded the island, and in the early Iron Age Brythons from South Britain are believed to have effected settlements in the south-east, while Picts from North Britain

established similar settlements in the north. Towards the close of the Roman occupation of Britain, the dominant tribe in the island was that of the Scoti, who afterwards established themselves in Scotland.

*Hibernia* was visited by Roman merchants but never by Roman legions, and little is known of the history of the country until the invasions of Northmen (Norwegians and Danes) towards the close of the eighth century AD. The outstanding events in the encounters with the Northmen are the Battle of Tara (980), at which the Hy Neill king Maelsechlainn II defeated the Scandinavians of Dublin and the Hebrides under the king Amlaib Cuarán; and the Battle of Clontarf (1014) by which the Scandinavian power was completely broken.

After Clontarf the supreme power was disputed by the O'Briens of Munster, the O'Neills of Ulster, and the O'Connors of Connaught, with varying fortunes. In 1152 Dermod MacMurrough (Diarmit MacMurchada), the deposed king of Leinster, sought assistance in his struggle with Rauidhri O'Connor (the high king of Ireland) from Henry II of England. Henry authorized him to obtain armed support in England for the recovery of his kingdom, and Dermod enlisted the services of Richard de Clare, the Norman Earl of Pembroke afterwards known as Strongbow, who landed at Waterford in 1170 with 200 knights and 1,000 other troops for the reconquest of Leinster, where he eventually settled after marriage with Dermod's daughter.

In 1172 Henry II himself landed in Ireland. He received homage from the Irish kings and established his capital at Dublin. The invaders subsequently conquered most of the island and a feudal government was created. In the 14th and 15th centuries, the Irish recovered most of their lands, while many Anglo-Irish lords became virtually independent, royal authority being confined to the Pale, a small district round Dublin. Though, under Henry VII, Sir Edward Poynings, as Lord Deputy, had passed at the Parliament of Drogheda (1494) the act later known as Poynings' Law, subordinating the Irish legislature to the Crown, the Earls of Kildare retained effective power until Henry VIII began the reconquest of Ireland in 1534. Parliament in 1541 recognized him as King of Ireland and by 1603 English authority was supreme.

# REPUBLIC OF IRELAND
*Poblacht Na hEireann*

The Republic of Ireland has a land area of 27,136 sq. miles (70,283 sq. km), divided into four provinces of 26 counties: Leinster (Carlow, Dublin, Kildare, Kilkenny, Laoighis, Longford, Louth, Meath, Offaly, Westmeath, Wexford and Wicklow); Munster (Clare, Cork, Kerry, Limerick, Tipperary and Waterford); Connacht (Galway, Leitrim, Mayo, Roscommon and Sligo); and part of Ulster (Cavan, Donegal and Monaghan).

POPULATION – The population of the Republic in 1991 census was 3,525,719. Figures also showed 49,473 births, 15,732 marriages and 31,673 deaths in 1992 (provisional).

At the census of 1991 religious adherence was: Roman Catholic, 3,228,327; Church of Ireland, 89,187; Presbyterians, 13,199; Methodists, 5,037; Others, 189,969.

The Irish language, being the national language, is the first official language. The English language is recognized as a second official language.

CAPITAL – ΨDublin (*Baile Atha Cliath*) is a city and county borough on the River Liffey at the head of Dublin Bay. In April 1991 the population (1991 census) was 478,389.

Other county boroughs, with their population figures at the 1991 census, are ΨCork (127,253); ΨLimerick (52,083); ΨWaterford (40,328); and Ψ Galway (50,853).

FLAG – Equal vertical stripes of green, white and orange.

NATIONAL ANTHEM – Amhrán na BhFiann (The Soldier's Song).

NATIONAL DAY – 17 March (St Patrick's Day).

## GOVERNMENT

The 1937 constitution declares the national territory to be the whole island of Ireland, its islands and territorial seas, but that, pending the reintegration of the national territory, laws enacted by Parliament shall have the like area and extent of application as those of the Irish Free State, which did not include the six counties of Northern Ireland.

The President (*Uachtarán na hEireann*) is directly elected for a term of seven years, and is eligible for a second term. The President is aided and advised by a Council of State.

The National Parliament (*Oireachtas*) consists of the President and two Houses: a House of Representatives (*Dáil Éireann*) and a Senate (*Seanad Éireann*). Dáil Éireann is composed of 166 members elected by adult suffrage on a basis of proportional representation by means of the single transferable vote. The voting age is 18 years. The term of each Dáil is five years. Seanad Éireann is composed of 60 members, of whom 11 are nominated by the Taoiseach and 49 are elected; six by institutions of higher education, and 43 from panels of candidates established on a vocational basis.

The executive authority is exercised by the government subject to the constitution. The government is responsible to the Dáil, meets and acts as a collective authority, and is collectively responsible for the departments of state administered by the Ministers. The Taoiseach is appointed by the President on the nomination of the Dáil. The other members of the government are appointed by the President on the nomination of the Taoiseach with the previous approval of the Dáil. The Taoiseach appoints a member of the government to be his deputy (the *Tánaiste*).

The last general election was on 25 November 1992. The composition of the Dáil Eireann in August 1994 was: Fianna Fáil 66; Fine Gael 46; Labour 33; Progressive Democrats 9; Democratic Left 5; Independent 7. The present coalition government was formed by the Fianna Fail Party (FF) and the Labour Party (L) in January 1993.

HEAD OF STATE
*President*, Mary Robinson, *assumed office* 3 December 1990

CABINET *as at August 1994*
*Taoiseach*, Albert Reynolds (FF)
*Tánaiste, Minister for Foreign Affairs*, Dick Spring (L)
*Finance*, Bertie Ahern (FF)
*Employment and Enterprise*, Ruairi Quinn (L)
*Justice*, Maire Geoghegan-Quinn (FF)
*Agriculture, Forestry and Food*, Joe Walsh (FF)
*Social Welfare*, Michael Woods (FF)
*Environment*, Michael Smith (FF)
*Health*, Brendan Howlin (L).
*Education*, Niamh Breatnach (L)
*Defence and Marine*, David Andrews (FF)
*Transport, Energy and Communications*, Brian Cowen (FF)
*Tourism and Trade*, Charlie McCreevy (FF)
*Equality and Law Reform*, Mervyn Taylor (L)
*Arts, Culture and the Gaeltacht*, Michael Higgins (L)

IRISH EMBASSY
17 Grosvenor Place, London SW1X 7HR
TEL 0171-235 2171

*Ambassador Extraordinary and Plenipotentiary*, His Excellency Joseph Small, apptd 1991
*Counsellor*, J. Timbs (*Economic and Commercial*)

BRITISH EMBASSY
31 Merrion Road, Dublin 4
Tel: Dublin 2695211

*Ambassador Extraordinary and Plenipotentiary*, His Excellency David E. S. Blatherwick, CMG, OBE, apptd 1991
*Counsellor and Deputy Head of Mission*, J. A. Dew
*Defence Attaché*, Col. S. D. Lambe
*First Secretary (Commercial)*, J. F. Pepper

BRITISH COUNCIL REPRESENTATIVE, Harold Fish, 22 Lower Mount Street, Dublin 2

## JUDICIAL SYSTEM

The judicial system comprises courts of first instance and a court of final appeal called the Supreme Court (*Cúirt Uachtarach*). The courts of first instance include a High Court (*Ard-Chúirt*) and courts of local and limited jurisdiction, with a right of appeal as determined by law. The High Court alone has original jurisdiction to consider the question of the validity of any law having regard to the provisions of the constitution. The Supreme Court has appellate jurisdiction from decisions of the High Court.

*Chief Justice*, Hon. Thomas A. Finlay
*President of the High Court*, Hon. Liam Hamilton
*Attorney-General*, Harold Whelehan

## DEFENCE

There is a Permanent Defence Force in which enlistment is voluntary. The minimum term of enlistment is five years, followed by seven years in the Reserve Defence Force. Enlistment in the Reserve Defence Force is also voluntary; minimum term of enlistment is three years. The defence estimate for the year ending 31 December 1994 provides for an expenditure of IR£354,229,000.

The total active armed forces number 13,000 personnel with 16,100 reserves. The Army has a strength of 11,200 personnel with 14 light tanks, 51 reconnaissance vehicles, 72 armoured personnel carriers and 60 artillery pieces. It is organized into 12 infantry battalions, one light tank squadron and three field artillery regiments, with attendant reconnaissance, air defence support and engineer units. The Navy has a strength of 1,000, with seven patrol and coastal vessels. The Air Corps has a strength of 800, with 16 combat aircraft and 15 armed helicopters.

Ireland deploys an infantry battalion of 679 troops with UN forces in South Lebanon.

## ECONOMY

Although industry has expanded greatly since Ireland's entry into the European Community in 1973, agriculture remains of great importance to the economy; in 1992, 13 per cent of the workforce was employed in agriculture. The main crops are wheat, barley, potatoes, sugar beat, oats and turnips. Animal products, dairy products and livestock, especially pigs and cows, are major exports. Agriculture has benefited considerably from the EC Common Agricultural Policy and support funds, which have been used to modernize farming methods and machinery, but agriculture has suffered from the drift of the rural population to urban areas and abroad.

Industry has recently overtaken agriculture as the most important sector of the economy, benefiting from significant European investment. The traditional brewing, spirits and food-processing sectors have expanded and have been joined by the manufacture of textiles, chemical, pharmaceuticals, electronics, office machinery and transportation equipment. Waterford glass and crystal has gained a world-wide reputation. Tourism is the most important part of the service sector and in recent years has provided substantial revenue, with over three million visitors in 1992.

The difficulties posed by the lack of energy resources have been transformed over the past 15 years by the discovery of the Kinsale Head and Ballycotton natural gas fields off the south coast, which now supply all the country's natural gas needs, and by the opening of seven government-funded milled peat power-generating stations which use the country's large peat resources. Hydro-electric power from the Shannon barrage and other schemes is also important but Ireland still must import significant quantities of oil and coal for power generation.

Metal content of ores raised (1993) was lead, 44,600 tonnes; zinc, 193,700 tonnes; silver 13,100,000 grammes. An estimated 15,400 persons were employed in the fisheries in 1993. Total value of all fish landed in 1993 was IR£98.25 million.

## FINANCE

|  | 1993 | 1994 |
|---|---|---|
| Total current revenue | IR£10,140m | IR£10,846m |
| Total current expenditure | 10,519 | 11,115 |

The gross debt at end 1991 was IR£25,377.7 million.

| TRADE | 1992 |
|---|---|
| Imports | IR£13,194,772,000 |
| Exports | 16,628,836,000 |
| Trade balance | 3,434,064,000 |

| Trade with UK | 1992 | 1993 |
|---|---|---|
| Imports from UK | £5,739,613,000 | £6,421,450,000 |
| Exports to UK | 5,070,124,000 | 5,125,285,000 |

## EDUCATION

Primary education is directed by the state, with the exception of 79 private primary schools with an enrolment of 8,280 in

1992–3. There were 3,326 state-aided primary schools with an enrolment of 521,531.

In 1992–3 there were 467 recognized secondary schools with 221,167 pupils under private management (mainly religious orders), and 248 vocational schools with 92,003 pupils. Vocational schools are controlled by 38 statutory local Vocational Education Committees. There were 16 state comprehensive schools in 1992–3 with a total enrolment of 9,218 students, and 54 community schools with an enrolment of 35,959 students. There were also other miscellaneous second-level schools and the total full-time enrolment at second-level for 1992–3 was 362,230.

Third-level education is catered for by seven university colleges, and also by third-level courses offered by the technical colleges and regional technical colleges and other miscellaneous third-level institutions. There were 84,140 full-time third-level students in 1992–3, of whom 46,540 were attending university courses.

The estimated state expenditure on education in 1994, excluding administration and inspection, is: first-level IR£628,675,000; second-level IR£697,049,000. The vote for third-level education amounted to IR£363,347,000.

## COMMUNICATIONS

In the year ended 31 December 1992, there were 1,944 km of railway operated by *Iarnród Eireann*; the receipts were IR£83,396,000 and expenditure IR£172,238,000.

In 1992 road motor vehicles carried 237,915,000 passengers, the gross receipts being IR£164,486,000.

In 1992 the number of ships with cargo which arrived at Irish ports was 12,109 (33,857,000 net registered tons); of these 2,080 (5,473,000 net registered tons) were of Irish nationality.

Shannon Airport, Co. Limerick, is on the main transatlantic air route. In 1993 the airport handled 1,709,981 passengers. Dublin Airport serves the cross-channel and European services operated by the Irish national airline Aer Lingus and other airlines. In 1993 the airport handled 5,938,126 passengers. Cork Airport serves the cross-channel and European services operated by Aer Lingus and other airlines. In 1993 the airport handled 732,242 passengers.

---

# ISRAEL
*Medinat Israel*

---

Israel lies on the western edge of Asia at the eastern extremity of the Mediterranean Sea, between 29° 30′ to 33° 15′ N. latitude and 34° 15′ to 35° 40′ E. longitude. It is bordered by Lebanon on the north, Syria on the north-east, Jordan and the West Bank on the east and the Gaza Strip and the Egyptian province of Sinai on the south-west. The area is estimated at 8,019 sq. miles (20,770 sq. km).

Israel comprises: the hill country of Galilee, together with parts of Judea and Samaria, rising in places to heights of nearly 4,000 ft; the coastal plain from the Gaza strip to north of Acre, including the plain of Esdraelon running from Haifa Bay to the south-east, and cutting in two the hill region; the Negev, a semi-desert triangular-shaped region, extending from a base south of Beersheba, to an apex at the head of the Gulf of Aqaba; and parts of the Jordan valley, including the Hula region, Tiberias and the south-western extremity of the Dead Sea.

The principal river is the Jordan, which rises from three main sources in Israel, the Lebanon and Syria, and flows through the Hula valley, Lake Tiberias/Kinneret (Sea of Galilee) and the Jordan Valley into the Dead Sea, falling

1,517 ft from Hulata to the Dead Sea. The other principal rivers are the Yarkon and Kishon. The Dead Sea is a lake (shared between Israel, the West Bank and Jordan), 1,286 ft below sea-level; it has no outlet, the surplus being carried off by evaporation. The highest mountain peak is Mount Meron, 3,962 ft above sea-level, near Safad, Upper Galilee.

The climate is variable, modified by altitude and distance from the sea. Summer is hot, tempered by sea-breezes. The winter is the rainy season lasting from November to March.

POPULATION – The population (estimate 1992) including East Jerusalem and Jewish settlers in the Occupied Territories is 5,090,000. Of these 4,175,000 are Jewish (82 per cent); 700,000 are Arab Muslims (13.8 per cent); 130,000 Christians (2.5 per cent), of which 90 per cent are Arab, and 85,000 Druze (1.7 per cent). During the upheavals of 1948–9 a large number of Arabs left the country as refugees and settled in neighbouring countries and the Occupied Territories.

Since independence Israel has had a policy of granting an immigration visa to every Jew who expresses his desire to settle in Israel. Between 1948 and 1992, 2.3 million immigrants had entered Israel from over 100 different countries.

Hebrew and Arabic are the official languages. Arabs are entitled to transact all official business with government departments in Arabic, and provision is made in the *Knesset* for the simultaneous translation of all speeches into Arabic.

CAPITAL – Most of the government departments are in Jerusalem, population (1993 estimate) 556,400. A resolution proclaiming Jerusalem as the capital of Israel was adopted by the *Knesset* in 1950. It is not, however, recognized as the capital by the United Nations because East Jerusalem is part of the Occupied Territories captured in 1967. The United Nations and international law continues to reject the Israeli annexation of East Jerusalem and considers the pre-1950 capital Tel Aviv (population, with district, 1,781,500) to remain the capital. Other principal towns (1990) are ΨHaifa and district (432,900) and Beersheba and district (122,000).

CURRENCY – New Shekel of 100 agora.

FLAG – White, with two horizontal blue stripes, the Shield of David in the centre.

NATIONAL ANTHEM – Hatikvah (The Hope).

## GOVERNMENT

The Ottoman Empire province of Palestine was captured by British forces in 1917, the same year that the British Government issued the Balfour Declaration which 'viewed with favour the establishment of a national home for the Jewish people in Palestine'. The Balfour Declaration's terms were enshrined in Britain's League of Nations mandate over Palestine, leading to steady Jewish immigration in the inter-war years and a post-1945 flood by Nazi concentration camp survivors. The Arab Palestinian population revolted against Jewish immigration from 1936 onwards, while Jewish groups conducted a terrorist campaign against the British administration from 1945 onwards.

In May 1947 Britain announced its withdrawal from Palestine with effect from May 1948, handing over to the UN responsibility for solving the conflict between Arabs and Jews. Both sides ignored the UN partition plan; on the withdrawal of British forces on 14 May 1948 the State of Israel was proclaimed and the first Arab-Israeli war began. By the time of the January 1949 cease-fire Israeli forces controlled all of the former mandate territory apart from the West Bank (and East Jerusalem) and the Gaza Strip, which

had come under Jordanian and Egyptian administration respectively.

During the 1967 Six-Day War Israel captured the West Bank and the Gaza Strip, together with Sinai from Egypt and the Golan Heights from Syria, and annexed East Jerusalem. Israel held onto its gains in the 1973 Yom Kippur War. The Golan Heights were annexed in 1981; Sinai was returned to Egypt in April 1982 in accordance with the 1979 Israeli-Egyptian peace treaty, and the South Lebanon Security Zone was established after the 1982–5 invasion of Lebanon. The annexations of East Jerusalem and the Golan Heights remain unrecognized internationally.

Israel is a sovereign democratic republic with executive power vested in a Prime Minister and Cabinet, and legislative power in a unicameral legislature (*Knesset*) of 120 members elected on a proportional representation basis for a maximum term of four years. The President is head of state and is elected by the Knesset for a maximum of two five-year terms. The present government coalition of the Labour, Meretz and Shas parties came to power after the general election of June 1992.

The peace process started in October 1991 in Madrid and led to agreements with the Palestine Liberation Organization (*see* page 918), and with Jordan on 14 September 1993. A framework agreement for peace with Jordan was signed on 25 July 1994. Direct telephone links have been established, the first border crossing has opened, and negotiations on water rights, border demarcation, environmental and economic co-operation continue.

HEAD OF STATE
*President of Israel*, Ezer Weizmann, *elected* 24 March 1993, *inaugurated* 13 May 1993

CABINET *as at August 1994*

Prime Minister, Defence, Interior and Religious Affairs,
Yitzhak Rabin (L)
Deputy Prime Minister, Foreign Affairs, Shimon Peres (L)
Deputy Prime Minister, Transport, Yisrael Kessar (L)
Energy, Infrastructure and Police, Moshe Shachal (L)
Communications, Science and Technology, Shulamit
Aloni (M)
Health, Ephraim Sneh (L)
Industry and Trade, Michael Harish (L)
Finance, Avraham Shochat (L)
Economics, Shimon Shetreet (L)
Agriculture, Yaacov Tsur (L)
Immigration Absorption, Yair Tsaban (M)
Tourism, Uzi Baram (L)
Justice, David Libai (L)
Education and Culture, Amnon Rubinstein (M)
Housing, Binyamin Ben-Eliezer (L)
Environment, Yossi Sarid (L)
Labour and Social Affairs, Ora Namir (L)

L Labour Party; M Meretz

EMBASSY OF ISRAEL
2 Palace Green, Kensington, London W8 4QB
Tel 0171-957 9500
Ambassador Extraordinary and Plenipotentiary, His
Excellency Moshe Raviv, apptd 1993
Minister Plenipotentiary, G. Meir
Defence Attaché, Brig.-Gen. A. Nevo
Minister, M. Hacohen (Consular)
Counsellor, S. Maoz (Economic).

BRITISH EMBASSY
192 Hayarkon Street, Tel Aviv 63405
Tel: Tel Aviv 5249171

Ambassador Extraordinary and Plenipotentiary, His
Excellency Robert A. Burns, CMG, apptd 1992
Counsellor, Consul-General and Deputy Ambassador,
C. J. White
Defence and Military Attaché, Col. J. R. Andrew, OBE
First Secretary (Commercial), P. A. Connolly
There are British consular offices in Tel Aviv and Eilat and a
Consulate-General in East Jerusalem (Occupied Territories).

BRITISH COUNCIL REPRESENTATIVE, P. Sandiford, OBE,
140 Hayarkon Street, PO Box 3302, Tel Aviv 61032.
There are also libraries in West Jerusalem and Nazareth.

ISRAEL-BRITISH CHAMBER OF COMMERCE,
76 IBN Guirol Street, Tel Aviv 64162

## DEFENCE

The Israeli defence forces have a total active strength of
176,000 (including 139,500 conscripts). Since its inception,
however, Israel has based its defence capabilities on a large
and highly-trained reserve, which numbers at present
430,000 personnel. Conscripts serve for periods of four years
(officers), three years (men) or two years (women). Reserves
serve for one month a year and are eligible for call-up until
age 54 (men) and age 24 or marriage (women). Israel is
widely believed to have a nuclear capacity of around 100
warheads which could be delivered by aircraft and Jericho I
and II missiles.
The Army has an active strength of 134,000 (114,700
conscripts) and a strength of 598,000 on mobilization, with
some 3,960 main battle tanks, 9,400 armoured personnel
carriers and 1,784 artillery pieces. The Army is organized
into three regular armoured and three regular infantry
divisions, with a further four regular mechanized infantry

brigades. Reserve units comprise nine armoured divisions,
one air mobile division and ten infantry and four artillery
brigades.
The Navy has an active strength of 10,000 (3,000
conscripts) and 20,000 on mobilization, with three submarines and 63 patrol and coastal craft. The Air Force has a
strength of 32,000 (21,800 conscripts) and 37,000 on
mobilization, with some 662 combat aircraft of US and home
manufacture and 93 armed helicopters. The Air Force
comprises 16 ground attack/air defence and four ground
attack squadrons, together with one transport wing and
reconnaissance, airborne early warning, tanker and training
units. There is also a paramilitary force of 6,000 border
police.

## EDUCATION AND CULTURE

Education for all children from six to 16 years is free and
compulsory. The law also provides for working youth age
16-18, who for some reason have not completed their
education, to be exempted from work in order to do so.
There are seven universities including two engineering and
technological institutes.
Important historic sites in Israel include: *Jerusalem* – the
Church of the Holy Sepulchre, the Al Aqsa Mosque and
Dome of the Rock standing on the remains of the Temple
Mount of Herod the Great of which the Western (wailing)
Wall is a fragment, the Church of the Dormition and the
Coenaculum on Mount Zion, Ein Karem, Church of the
Visitation, Church of St John the Baptist; *Galilee* – the Sea,
Church and Mount of the Beatitudes, ruins of Capernaum
and other sites connected with the life of Christ; *Mount Tabor*
– Church of the Transfiguration; *Nazareth* – Church of the
Annunciation, and other Christian shrines associated with
the childhood of Christ; There are also numerous sites dating
from biblical and medieval days, such as Ascalon, Caesarea,
Atlit, Massada, Megiddo and Hazor.

## COMMUNICATIONS

Israel State Railways serves Haifa, Tel Aviv, Jerusalem, Lod,
Nahariya, Beersheba, Dimona, Ashdod and intermediate
stations. In 1986 the total railway network amounted to
528 km. There were 12,823 km of paved road in 1986.
Israel's merchant marine had reached a total of 2,805,000
tons deadweight by December 1985. The chief ports are
Haifa and Ashdod on the Mediterranean, and Eilat on the
Red Sea; Acre has an anchorage for small vessels.
In 1986, 3,098,000 passengers passed through Ben Gurion
airport, of which 230,146 arrived by charter flight.

## ECONOMY

Government expenditure in 1992 was 101,000 million new
Shekels at market prices. GNP at market prices was 181,700
million new Shekels in 1993.
The country is generally fertile and climatic conditions
vary so widely that crops range from the temperate to the
subtropical. Water supply for irrigation is the principal
limiting factor to greater production. The area under
cultivation is 1.1 million acres, of which 0.6 million is under
irrigation. Agriculture accounts for 5 per cent of GNP and 4
per cent of exports.
The famous 'Jaffa' orange is produced in large quantities
for export, along with other high-profit and specialized
glasshouse crops, such as flowers, tomatoes and strawberries.
Olives are cultivated, mainly for the production of oil. The
main winter crops are wheat, barley and various kinds of
pulses, while in summer sorghum, millet, maize, sesame and
summer pulses are grown. Large areas of seasonal vegetables

and summer fruits are planted. Beef, cattle and poultry farming have been developed and the production of mixed vegetables and dairy produce has greatly increased. Tobacco and medium staple cotton are now grown. Fishing production (mostly from fish farms) was 12,200 tons in 1993.

In value polished diamonds account for about 23 per cent of Israel's total exports. Amongst the most important industries are textiles, foodstuffs, chemicals (mainly fertilizers and pharmaceuticals). Metal-working and science-based industries are highly sophisticated and technologically advanced. These include the aircraft and military industries. Other important manufacturing industries include plastics, rubber, cement, glass, paper and oil refining. Industry accounts for 30 per cent of GNP and 60 per cent of exports.

TRADE

The principal imports are foodstuffs, crude oil, machinery and vehicles, iron, steel and manufactures thereof, and chemicals. The principal exports are metal machinery, electronic goods, chemicals, rubber, plastics, textiles, food and beverages, minerals, citrus produce and polished diamonds.

|         | 1993       |
|---------|------------|
| Imports | US$31,000m |
| Exports | 22,900m    |

| Trade with UK   | 1992         | 1993         |
|-----------------|--------------|--------------|
| Imports from UK | £586,236,000 | £876,330,000 |
| Exports to UK   | 485,078,000  | 550,200,000  |

## PALESTINIAN AUTONOMOUS AREAS

The total area is 2,406 sq. miles (6,231 sq. km). The area which is fully autonomous is 159 sq. miles (412 sq. km) of which the Gaza Strip is 136 sq. miles (352 sq. km) and the Jericho enclave 23 sq. miles (60 sq. km). The partially autonomous area is the remainder of the West Bank, some 2,247 sq miles (5,819 sq. km). The UN and the international community also recognize East Jerusalem as part of the Occupied Territories.

POPULATION – (1992 estimate) 1,635,000, of whom 660,000 live in Gaza Strip, 40,000 in Jericho, and 935,000 in the remainder of the West Bank. In addition there are 120,000 Jewish settlers in the West Bank and 4,000 in the Gaza Strip who remain under Israeli administration and jurisdiction. Some 90 per cent of Palestinians are Muslim (the vast majority Sunni) and 10 per cent are Christians.

CAPITAL – Although Palestinians claim East Jerusalem as their capital, the administrative capital has been established in Gaza City (120,000). Other major towns are Khan Yunis and Rafah in the Gaza Strip and Nablus, Hebron, Jericho, Ramallah and Bethlehem on the West Bank.

FLAG – Three horizontal stripes of black, white, green with a red triangle based on the hoist (the PLO flag).

GOVERNMENT

Israel captured the Gaza Strip, East Jerusalem and the West Bank during the 1967 Six-Day War and annexed East Jerusalem. After the war the Israeli government began to establish security settlements in the Occupied Territories and religious groups later established further settlements. Palestinian resistance to Israeli rule was led by the Palestine Liberation Organization (PLO) established in 1964, which carried out armed attacks, bombings and aircraft hijackings against Israeli targets around the world. Frustration at continued Israeli occupation led to the start of the *intifada* in 1987, a campaign of sustained unrest in the Occupied

Territories. When the 1991 Madrid peace process stalled, Israeli and PLO officials engaged in secret negotiations in Norway in 1993 leading to the signing of the 'Declaration of Principles on Interim Self-Government Arrangements' on 13 September 1993. Under this agreement the PLO renounced terrorism and recognized Israeli's right to exist in secure borders, while Israel recognized the PLO as the legitimate representatives of the Palestinian people.

The Declaration of Principles established a timetable for progress towards a final settlement: negotiations leading to an Israeli military withdrawal from the Gaza Strip and Jericho by 13 April 1994, when power was to be transferred to a nominated Palestinian National Authority (PNA); elections to a new PNA, which will also exercise control over six policy areas in the rest of the West Bank (culture, tourism, health, education, social welfare, direct taxation), and the Israeli military administration dissolved by 13 July 1994; negotiations on a permanent settlement, including Jewish settlers and East Jerusalem, to begin by 13 April 1996; and a permanent settlement to be in place by 13 April 1999. The timetable slipped, with the Israeli military not finally withdrawing from the Gaza Strip and Jericho until 18 May 1994, when the five-year period of interim self-government under the PNA began. The Israeli military remains responsible for all Jewish settlements and road links in the Gaza Strip and Jericho, while the 9,000 Palestinian policemen are responsible for security and law and order for the majority of the Gaza Strip and Jericho. In the rest of the West Bank and at border crossings with Jordan and Egypt the Israeli military remains in full control and the PNA only exercises authority in the six policy areas. At the time of going to press, elections to the PNA had not been held and were not planned to be held until late 1994 so the Israeli military administration in the West Bank remained. The PNA is to be allowed to issue stamps, travel documents, raise taxes, set customs duties and gain an international dialling code.

*President of the Palestinian National Authority*, Yasser Arafat

## ITALY
*Repubblica Italiana*

Italy consists of a peninsula, the large islands of Sicily and Sardinia, the island of Elba and about 70 other small islands. It is bounded on the north by Switzerland and Austria, on the south by the Mediterranean Sea, on the east by the Adriatic Sea and Slovenia, and on the west by France and the Ligurian and Tyrrhenian Seas. The total area is about 116,304 sq. miles (301,225 sq. km).

The peninsula is for the most part mountainous, but between the Apennines, which form its spine, and the east coastline are two large fertile plains: Emilia/Romagna in the north and Apulia in the south. The Alps form the northern limit of Italy, dividing it from France, Switzerland, Austria and Slovenia. Mont Blanc (15,771 ft), the highest peak, is in the French Pennine Alps, but partly within the Italian borders are Monte Rosa (15,217 ft), Matterhorn (14,780 ft) and several peaks from 12,000 to 14,000 ft. The chief rivers are the Po (405 miles), which flows through Piedmont, Lombardy and the Veneto, and the Adige (Trentino and Veneto) in the north, the Arno (Florentine plain) and the Tiber (flowing through Rome to Ostia).

POPULATION – The population (UN estimate 1991) was 57,052,000.

LANGUAGE – Italian is a Romance language derived from Latin. It is spoken in its purest form in Tuscany, but there are numerous dialects, showing variously French, German,

Spanish and Arabic influences. Sard, the dialect of Sardinia, is accorded by some authorities the status of a distinct Romance language.

CAPITAL – Rome. Population of the commune (1991 census) 2,693,383. The Eternal City was founded, according to legend, by Romulus in 753 BC. It was the centre of Latin civilization and capital of the Roman Republic and Roman Empire. In the 1991 census the population of the communes of the principal cities and towns was Milan 1,371,008; ΨNaples 1,054,601; Turin 961,916; ΨGenoa 675,639; Bologna 404,322; Florence 402,316; *Sicily*, ΨPalermo 697,162; *Sardinia*, ΨCagliari 203,254.

CURRENCY – Lira of 100 centesimi.
FLAG – Vertical stripes of green, white and red.
NATIONAL ANTHEM – Inno di Mameli.
NATIONAL DAY – 2 June.

## HISTORY

Italian unity was accomplished under the House of Savoy, after a struggle from 1848 to 1870, in which Mazzini (1805–72), Garibaldi (1807–82) and Cavour (1810–61) were the principal figures. It was completed when Lombardy was ceded by Austria in 1859 and Venice in 1866, and through the evacuation of Rome by the French in 1870. In 1871 the King of Italy entered Rome, and that city was declared to be the capital.

The fascist regime came to power in 1922 under Benito Mussolini, known as *Il Duce* (The Leader), who was Prime Minister from 1922 until 25 July 1943, when the fascist regime was abolished. Mussolini was captured by Italian partisans while attempting to escape across the Swiss frontier and killed on 28 April 1945.

In fulfilment of a promise given in April 1944 that he would retire when the Allies entered Rome, a decree was signed in June 1944, by King Victor Emmanuel III under which Prince Umberto, his son, became Lieutenant-General of the Realm. The King remained head of the House of Savoy and retained the title King of Italy until his abdication in May 1946, when he was succeeded by the Crown Prince. A general election was held in June 1946, together with a referendum on the future of the monarchy. The result showed a majority in favour of replacing the monarchy with a republic and the royal family left the country.

## GOVERNMENT

The 1947 constitution provides for the election of the President by an electoral college which consists of the two houses of the parliament (the Chamber of Deputies and the Senate) sitting in joint session, together with three delegates from each region (one in the case of the Valle d'Aosta). The President, who must be over 50 years of age, holds office for seven years. He has numerous carefully defined powers, the main one of which is the right to dissolve one or both houses after consultation with the Speakers. Members of both houses were elected wholly by proportional representation until the voting system was altered in 1993. Now 75 per cent (232) of the 315 elected seats in the Senate are elected on a first-past-the-post basis and the remaining elected seats are filled by proportional representation. In addition there are 11 life senators, who are past presidents and prime ministers. In the Chamber of Deputies 75 per cent (472) of seats are elected on a first-past-the-post basis, and 25 per cent (158) by proportional representation, with a 4 per cent of the vote minimum for parliamentary representation.

Political instability (50 governments since 1947) and widespread political and business corruption, often with Mafia links, led to public disillusion with the major political parties, whose support collapsed in the April 1992 general election, which produced a great increase in support for Northern League and anti-Mafia parties. Disillusionment with the established parties was confirmed in regional and local elections when the governing parties lost most of their local power and the Northern League, Democratic Left and anti-Mafia La Rête parties progressed. Meanwhile, thousands of politicians and businessmen have been arrested by magistrates in the so-called 'clean hands' investigation into corruption and Mafia links that began in Milan in February 1992.

Between 1992 and 1994 the political and economic systems have been transformed to increase political stability, improve the economy and reduce corruption. In addition to constitutional reform, governments have acted to privatize state industries, to reduce the budget deficit and inflation with an austerity budget, to reorganize and reduce the civil service, and to reorganize and increase democracy in local government.

Following the Ciampi government's resignation in January 1994 the first general election under the new electoral system, on 27–28 March, resulted in victory for the right-wing Freedom Alliance composed of the new Forza Italia party, the Northern League and the National Alliance (based on the neo-fascist MSI party). The Freedom Alliance won 366 seats in the Chamber of Deputies compared to the left-wing Progressive Alliance's 213 seats and the Centre Coalition's 46 seats. The Forza Italia leader, and millionaire businessman, Silvio Berlusconi formed a government and took power on 20 May 1994 after bringing the small Centre Union and Centre Christian Democrats into the coalition in order to gain a majority in the Senate.

HEAD OF STATE
*President of the Italian Republic,* Oscar Luigi Scalfaro, *elected* 25 May 1992

COUNCIL OF MINISTERS *as at August 1994*

*Prime Minister,* Silvio Berlusconi (FI)
*Deputy Prime Minister, Post and Telecommunications,* Giuseppe Tatarella (NA)
*Deputy Prime Minister, Interior,* Roberto Maroni (NL)
*Foreign,* Antonio Martino (FI)

*Defence*, Cesare Previti (FI)
*Justice*, Alfredo Biondi (FI)
*Treasury*, Lamberto Dini (Ind.)
*Budget*, Giancarlo Pagliarini (NL)
*Finance*, Giulio Tremonti (Ind.)
*Education*, Francesco D'Onofrio (CU)
*Health*, Raffaele Costa (CU)
*Public Works*, Roberto Radice (FI)
*Agriculture*, Adriana Poli Bortone (NA)
*Labour*, Clemente Mastella (CCD)
*European Union and Regional Affairs*, Domenico Comino (NL)
*Foreign Trade*, Giorgio Bernini (FI)
*Transport*, Publio Fiori (NA)
*Industry*, Vito Gnutti (NL)
*Cultural Affairs*, Domenico Fisichella (NA)
*Environment*, Altero Matteoli (NA)
*Family*, Antonio Guidi (FI)
*University and Science*, Stefano Pedesta (NL)
*Relations with Parliament*, Giuiano Ferrara (FI)
*Public Administration*, Giuliano Urbani (FI)
*Institutional Reforms*, Francesco Speroni (NL)
*Italians Abroad*, Sergio Berlinguer (Ind.)

FI Forza Italia; NL Northern League; NA National Alliance; CU Centre Union; CCD Centre Christian Democrats; Ind. Independent.

ITALIAN EMBASSY
14 Three Kings Yard, Davies Street, London WIY 2EH
Tel 0171-312 2200

*Ambassador Extraordinary and Plenipotentiary,* His Excellency Count Giacomo Attolico, apptd 1991
*Minister-Counsellor*, A. Armellini
*Defence Attaché,* Adm. M. Maguolo
*Cultural Attaché,* Prof. F. Villari
*Consul-General,* L. Brofferio
*First Counsellor*, G. Ardizzone (*Commercial*)

There are also consular offices in *Bedford, Edinburgh* and *Manchester.*

BRITISH EMBASSY
Via XX Settembre 80A, 00187 Rome
Tel: Rome 482-5441

*Ambassador Extraordinary and Plenipotentiary,* His Excellency Sir Patrick Fairweather, KCMG, apptd 1992
*Minister,* D. H. Colvin, CMG
*Defence and Military Attaché,* Brig. J. H. Thoyts
*Director-General for British Trade Development in Italy and Consul-General,* P. H. Wetton, CMG (*Milan*)
*Counsellor (Economic and Commercial)*, T. G. Paxman

BRITISH CONSULAR OFFICES – There are Consulates-General at *Milan* and *Naples* and Consulates offices at *Rome, Genoa, Florence, Venice, Trieste, Bari* and *Turin.*

BRITISH COUNCIL REPRESENTATIVE, K. Hunter, OBE, Palazzo del Drago, Via Quattro Fontane 20, 00184 Rome. There are British Council Offices at *Milan, Bologna* and *Naples,* each with a library.

BRITISH CHAMBER OF COMMERCE, Via San Paolo 7, 20121 Milan.

DEFENCE

Total active armed forces personnel number some 344,600 (including 207,900 conscripts who serve for 12 months). Reserves number 584,000, with an obligation to age 25 or 45 (Air Force), 45 (Army), 39 or 73 (Navy).
The Army has a strength of 223,300 (165,000 conscripts), with some 1,210 main battle tanks, 3,835 armoured personnel

carriers, 1,250 artillery pieces, 60 aircraft and 335 helicopters. Organization consists of a Field Army and Territorial Defence forces. The Field Army has three corps with a total of three mechanized, four mountain, one armoured cavalry and two armoured brigades, seven artillery regiments, two armoured cavalry, five anti-aircraft and four aviation battalions. Territorial Defence forces comprise eight mechanized and one airborne brigades, a Rapid Intervention Force of two brigades, and one infantry, five armoured cavalry, four engineer and one artillery regiments.
The Navy has a strength of 43,600 (including 16,400 conscripts), with eight submarines, one helicopter carrier, one cruiser, four destroyers and 22 frigates with 30 armed helicopters. The Air Force has a strength of 77,700 (26,500 conscripts) with 385 combat aircraft. Organization is into six air defence, ten ground attack, three transport, one reconnaissance, two maritime reconnaissance, one electronic warfare, two communications and six training squadrons.
In addition to the regular armed forces there is the paramilitary Carabinieri, who are part of the Ministry of Defence and number 111,800, with 179 armoured personnel carriers and 85 helicopters. There are several NATO bases in Italy with 13,000 US armed forces personnel stationed in the country, together with 128 aircraft and support forces from Britain, France, the Netherlands, Turkey and USA for operations over the former Yugoslavia.

ECONOMY

The Amato and Ciampi governments of 1992–4 introduced economic reforms to lessen corruption and reduce the budget deficit and national debt. In October 1992 the government significantly reduced public expenditure by reforming the bloated pensions system, civil service and health service. In March 1993 further welfare reductions were made, privatization began and the tradition of annual wage indexation to inflation was ended. This was followed in April by the referendum in which the electorate voted for reforming the state's participation in industry, and in July the government announced the beginning of large-scale privatization. One of the economy's major problems is the large budget deficit which in 1993 was 10.5 per cent of GDP. Two successive austerity budgets in May and December 1993 will reduce the budget deficit to 8.7 per cent of GDP in 1995. The national debt remains high at 125 per cent of GDP, as does unemployment at 11.5 per cent in 1994. Privatization has proceeded, with the IMI banking group, banks Credito Italiano and Banca Commerciale Italiana, and INA insurance transferred to the private sector.
The state-owned sector of Italian industry is still important, dominated by the holding companies IRI (mechanical, steel, airlines), ENI (petro-chemicals) and ENEL (electricity). Industry (including construction) accounted for 30.2 per cent of gross domestic product in 1991. Industry is centred around the cities of Milan (steel, machine tools, motor cars), Turin (motor cars, steel, roller bearings, textiles), Rome (light industries), Venice (shipbuilding, paper, mechanical equipment, electrical goods, woollens), Bologna/Florence (food industry, footwear and textiles, reproduction furniture, glassware, pottery, ceramics), Naples, Bari (valves, vehicle bodies, tyres), Taranto (steel, oil refining), Trieste (shipbuilding), Cagliari (aluminium production, petrochemicals).
Italy is generally poor in mineral resources but since the war deposits of natural methane gas and small deposits of oil have been discovered mainly south of Sicily and rapidly exploited. Production of lignite has also increased. Other minerals produced in significant quantities include iron ores and pyrites, mercury (over one-quarter of the world

production), lead, zinc and aluminium. Marble is a traditional product of the Massa Carrara district.

Agriculture accounted for 3.8 per cent of gross domestic product in 1991. Agricultural production is concentrated in Tuscany, Emilia and Romagna, Sicily and the whole of the southern third of the country. The principal products are wine, tobacco, citrus fruits, tomatoes, almonds, sugar beat, wheat and maize.

In 1987 an estimated 52 million foreign tourists visited Italy, spending an estimated L15,782,808 million. Tourism is centred on Rome, Florence, Venice, the Alps, Sicily, the Adriatic coast and the Bay of Naples. The commercial and banking services are concentrated in Rome and in Milan, where the stock market is located.

## TRADE

The balance of trade in 1988 showed a deficit of 12,875 billion lire, compared with 11,143 billion lire in 1987. The main markets for Italian exports in 1987 were the OECD countries, which accounted for almost 80 per cent of the total, and the EC markets with 56 per cent of the total. Imports came principally from Germany, France and the USA.

| Trade with UK | 1992 | 1993 |
|---|---|---|
| Imports from UK | £6,146,719,000 | £5,761,242,000 |
| Exports to UK | 6,769,218,000 | 6,467,666,000 |

## COMMUNICATIONS

The main railway system is state-run by the *Ferrovia dello Stato*. A network of motorways (*autostrade*) covers the country, built and operated mainly by the IRI state holding company and ANAS, the state highway authority. Alitalia, the principal international and domestic airline, is also state-controlled by the IRI group. Other smaller companies, including ATI (an Alitalia subsidiary) and Air Mediterranea, operate on domestic routes. The Italian mercantile marine totalled 7,587,117 tons in December 1985. Genoa is the major port, handling about one-third of Italy's foreign trade.

## CULTURE

Florence, the capital of Tuscany, was one of the greatest cities in Europe from the 11th to the 16th centuries, and the cradle of the Renaissance. Under the Medici family in the 15th century flourished many of the greatest names in Italian art, including Filippo Lippi, Botticelli, Donatello and Brunelleschi, and in the 16th century Michelangelo and Leonardo da Vinci.

Italian literature (in addition to Latin literature, which is the common inheritance of western Europe) is one of the richest in Europe, particularly in its golden age (Dante, 1265–1321; Petrarch, 1304–74; Boccaccio, 1313–75) and in the Renaissance (Ariosto, 1474–1533; Machiavelli, 1469–1527; Tasso, 1544–95). Notable in modern Italian literature are Manzoni (1785–1873), Carducci (1835–1907) and Gabriele d'Annunzio (1864–1938). The Nobel Prize for Literature has been awarded to Italian authors on five occasions: G. Carducci (1906), Signora G. Deledda (1926), Luigi Pirandello (1934), Salvatore Quasimodo (1959) and Eugenio Montale (1975).

In 1987, there were 72 daily newspapers published in Italy, of which 14 were published in Rome and seven in Milan.

## EDUCATION

Education is free and compulsory between the ages of six and 14; this comprises five years at primary school and three

in the 'middle school', of which there are about 8,000. Pupils who obtain the middle school certificate may seek admission to any 'senior secondary school', which may be a lyceum with a classical or scientific or artistic bias, or an institute directed at technology (of which there are eight different types), trade or industry (including vocational schools), or teacher-training. Courses at the lyceums and technical institutes usually last for five years and success in the final examination qualifies for admission to university. In 1990–1 there were 3,056,000 students at elementary school, 2,266,000 at middle school and 2,861,000 at senior secondary school.

There are 35 state and 14 private universities, some of ancient foundation; those at Bologna, Modena, Parma and Padua were started in the 12th century. University education is not free, but entrants with higher qualifications are charged reduced fees according to a sliding scale. In 1990–1 there were 1,381,000 students at university.

In general, schools, lyceums and universities are financed by local taxation and central government grants.

## ISLANDS

PANTELLERIA ISLAND (part of Trapani Province) in the Sicilian Narrows, has an area of 31 sq. miles and a population of 9,601.

THE PELAGIAN ISLANDS (Lampedusa, Linosa and Lampione) are part of the province of Agrigento and have an area of 8 sq. miles, population 4,811.

THE TUSCAN ARCHIPELAGO (including Elba), area 293 sq. km, population 31,861.

PONTINE ARCHIPELAGO, including Ponza, area 10 sq. km, population 2,515.

FLEGREAN ISLANDS, including Ischia, area 60 sq. km, population 51,883.

CAPRI.

EOLIAN ISLANDS, including Lipari, area 116 sq. km, population 18,636.

TREMITI ISLANDS, area 3 sq. km, population 426.

# JAMAICA

Jamaica is situated in the Caribbean Sea south of the eastern extremity of Cuba and lies between 17° 43′ and 18° 32′ N. latitude and 76° 11′ and 78° 21′ W. longitude. It is 4,244 sq. miles (10,991 sq. km) in area and is divided into three counties (Surrey, Middlesex and Cornwall) and 14 parishes. The island consists mainly of coastal plains, divided by the Blue Mountain range in the east, and the hills and limestone plateaux which occupy the central and western areas of the interior. The central chain of the Blue Mountains is over 6,000 feet above sea level, and the Blue Mountain Peak is 7,402 feet.

POPULATION – The population (UN estimate 1992) was 2,460,700.

CAPITAL – The seat of government is ΨKingston, the largest town and seaport (estimated population of the corporate area of Kingston and St Andrew in 1982, 696,300). Other main towns are ΨMontego Bay, Ocho Rios, Spanish Town, Mandeville and May Pen.

CURRENCY – Jamaican dollar (J$) of 100 cents.

FLAG – Gold diagonal cross forming triangles of green at top and bottom, triangles of black at hoist and in fly.

NATIONAL ANTHEM – Jamaica, Land We Love.

NATIONAL DAY – First Monday in August (Independence Day).

## GOVERNMENT

The island was discovered by Columbus in 1494, and occupied by the Spanish from 1509 until 1655 when a British expedition under Admiral Penn and General Venables attacked the island, which capitulated after a token resistance. In 1670 it was formally ceded to England by the Treaty of Madrid. Jamaica became an independent state within the Commonwealth on 6 August 1962.

HM Queen Elizabeth II is the head of state, represented in Jamaica by the Governor-General. The legislature consists of a Senate of 21 nominated members and a House of Representatives consisting of 60 members elected by universal adult suffrage.

At the general election of 30 March 1993, the People's National Party won 52 seats and the Jamaica Labour Party won 8.

*Governor-General*, His Excellency Howard Felix Hanlon Cooke, *apptd* 1991

CABINET *as at 15 August 1994*

*Prime Minister, Defence*, Rt. Hon. Percival J. Patterson, QC
*Deputy Prime Minister, Agriculture*, Hon. Seymour Mullings
*Industry, Tourism and Commerce*, Sen. the Hon. Carlyle Dunkley
*Public Utilities, Mining and Energy*, Hon. Robert Pickersgill
*Public Service and the Environment*, Hon. Easton Douglas
*Foreign Affairs and Foreign Trade*, Hon. Dr Paul Robertson
*Education and Culture*, Hon. Burchell Whiteman
*Health*, Hon. Desmond Leakey
*Labour and Welfare*, Hon. Portia Simpson
*Construction*, Hon. O. D. Ramtaillie
*Local Government, Youth and Sports*, Hon. John Junior
*National Security and Justice*, Hon. K. D. Knight
*Minister without Portfolio in the Office of the Prime Minister*, Sen. the Hon. Dr Peter Phillips
*Legal Affairs*, Hon. David Coore
*Water and Transport*, Hon. Horace Clarke
*Finance and Planning*, Hon. Omar Davies

JAMAICAN HIGH COMMISSION
1–2 Prince Consort Road, London SW7 2BZ
Tel 0171–823 9911

*High Commissioner*, His Excellency Derek Heaven, apptd 1994
*Deputy High Commissioners*, Mrs M. Roberts; J. K. Pringle, CBE (*Trade*)
*Minister-Counsellor*, S. H. Parris (*Consular Affairs*)
*Defence Adviser*, Col. T. D. Lewis

BRITISH HIGH COMMISSION
PO Box 575, Trafalgar Road, Kingston 10
Tel: Kingston 926 9050

*High Commissioner*, His Excellency Derek Francis Milton, CMG, apptd 1989
*Deputy High Commissioner*, A. White
*Defence Adviser*, Col. J. J. Dumas, OBE
*First Secretary (Management/Consular)*, J. McLeod

BRITISH COUNCIL REPRESENTATIVE IN THE CARIBBEAN, Andrew Norris, 3rd Floor, PCMB Building, 64 Knutsford Boulevard, Kingston 5.

## JUDICATURE

*Chief Justice and Keeper of Records*, Hon. Carl Rattray
*President of the Court of Appeal*, Hon. B. M. Carey
*Judges of the Court of Appeal*, Hons. M. L. Wright; I. X. Forte; H. E. Downer; U. D. Gordon

## ECONOMY

Since 1989 the PNP government has introduced economic reforms including the abolition of price subsidies, the removal of foreign exchange controls and the introduction of a 10 per cent consumption tax. The IMF in December 1992 approved a credit facility of US$153m for a three-year period. Jamaica is a popular tourist resort, attracting 1,563,097 visitors during 1992. Actual foreign exchange receipts from tourism amounted to US$850m in 1992.

Alumina, bananas, bauxite and sugar are the four major Jamaican exports. Earnings from sugar in 1992 amounted to US$82.5m, bauxite and alumina US$560m and bananas US$39.6m. Less traditional exports include garments, processed food products, limestone and ornamental horticultural products.

| FINANCE | 1990 | 1991 |
| --- | --- | --- |
| Revenue | US$2,401.6m | US$908m |
| Expenditure | 2,537.5m | 1,091.7m |

| TRADE | 1991 | 1992 |
| --- | --- | --- |
| Merchandise imports | US$1,828.6m | US$1,692.8m |
| Merchandise exports | 1,150.7m | 1,052.8m |

| Trade with UK | 1992 | 1993 |
| --- | --- | --- |
| Imports from UK | £43,521,000 | £56,257,000 |
| Exports to UK | 127,051,000 | 121,623,000 |

## COMMUNICATIONS

There are several excellent harbours, Kingston being the principal port. The island has 2,944 miles of main roads and 7,264 miles of subsidiary roads.

There are two international airports, the Norman Manley International Airport on the south coast serving Kingston, and Sangster Airport on the north coast serving the major tourist areas. In addition there are licensed aerodromes at Port Antonio, Ocho Rios, Mandeville and Negril. There are 16 privately owned, seven public and two military airstrips. Air Jamaica, the national airline, operates international services; Trans-Jamaica Airlines operates scheduled internal services.

## JAPAN
*Nihon Koku – Land of the Rising Sun*

Japan consists of four large islands: *Honshū* (or Mainland) 88,839 sq. miles (230,448 sq. km), *Shikoku*, 7,231 sq. miles (18,757 sq. km), *Kyūshū*, 16,170 sq. miles (42,079 sq. km), *Hokkaido*, 30,265 sq. miles (78,508 sq. km), and many small islands situated in the north Pacific Ocean between 128° 6' and 145° 49' E. longitude and between 26° 59' and 45° 31' N. latitude, with a total area of 145,834 sq. miles (377,708 sq. km).

The coastline is deeply indented, so that few places are far from the sea. The interior is very mountainous, and crossing the mainland from the Sea of Japan to the Pacific is a group of volcanoes, mainly extinct or dormant. Mount Fuji, the most sacred mountain of Japan, is 12,370 ft high and has been dormant since 1707, but there are other volcanoes which are active, including Mount Aso in Kyūshū. There are frequent earthquakes, mainly along the Pacific coast near the Bay of Tokyo. Japan proper extends from a sub-tropical climate in the south to cool temperate in the north. Snowfalls are frequent on the western slopes of Hokkaidō and Honshū, but the Pacific coasts are warmed by the Japan current. There is a plentiful rainfall and the rivers are short and swift-flowing, offering abundant opportunities for the supply of hydro-electric power.

POPULATION – The population (1991 UN estimate) is 123,921,000. The principal religions are Mahayana Buddhism and Shinto. About 1 per cent of Japanese are Christians.

CAPITAL – Tokyo, population (December 1989) 11,718,720. The other chief cities had the following populations:
Ψ Osaka (2,633,000); Ψ Nagoya (2,152,000);
Ψ Yokohama (3,197,000); Kyoto, the ancient capital (1,471,000); Ψ Kobé (1,464,000); Kita-Kyushu (1,034,000); Ψ Sapporo (1,652,000); Ψ Kawasaki (1,159,000); Ψ Fukuoka (1,220,000).

CURRENCY – Yen of 100 sen.

FLAG – White, charged with sun (red).

NATIONAL ANTHEM – Kimigayo.

NATIONAL DAY – 23 December (the Emperor's Birthday).

## GOVERNMENT

According to Japanese tradition, Jimmu, the first Emperor of Japan, ascended the throne on 11 February 660 BC. Under the *Meiji* constitution (1889), the monarchy is hereditary in the male heirs of the Imperial house.

After the unconditional surrender to the allied nations (14 August 1945), Japan was occupied by Allied forces under General MacArthur. A Japanese peace treaty conference held in San Francisco in September 1951 led to 48 nations signing the treaty, which became effective on 28 April 1952. Japan then resumed her status as an independent power.

A new constitution came into force in 1947. Legislative authority rests with the Diet, which is bicameral, consisting of a 511-member House of Representatives and a 252-member House of Councillors, both houses being composed of elected members. The House of Councillors, whose powers are subordinate to the House of Representatives, elects half its members every three years. Executive authority is vested in the Cabinet which is responsible to the legislature.

The conservatives governed Japan almost without interruption from the Second World War until 1993. During the 1990s growing public disgust over political corruption led to a loss of support for the Liberal Democratic Party (LDP) and in 1992 a group of LDP MPs broke away to form the Japan New Party (JNP). After attempts at political reform to end corruption continually failed, the LDP government was brought down by its own rebel MPs in a no confidence notion in the Diet on 18 June 1993. Before the subsequent general election, two new groups of LDP MPs broke away to form the Japan Renewal Party (JRP) (Shinseito) and the Sakigate (Harbinger) Party and support for the new parties caused the LDP to lose its majority at the election on 18 July. After the election the three new parties formed a coalition with the opposition Komeito, Social Democratic (SDPJ), Democratic Socialist (DSP) and United Social Democratic (USDP) (Shaminren) parties, and the new government was sworn in on 9 August 1993.

The seven-party coalition government led by Morihiro Hosokawa (JNP) was unable to push anti-corruption and electoral reforms bills through the Diet undiluted because of LDP control of the House of Councillors. Eventually a compromise was reached with the LDP and in January 1994 laws were passed to limit corporate donations to individual MPs' funds and to ban them after five years, and to dilute the first-past-the-post electoral system (from the next election) with 200 MPs elected by proportional representation while 300 seats remain first-past-the-post. After corruption scandals and coalition manoeuvrings the governments of Hosokawa and his successor Tsutoma Hata were brought down and the LDP returned to power in June 1994 in coalition with the SDPJ and Sakigate parties, with SDPJ leader Tomiichi

Murayama becoming Japan's first socialist Prime Minister. In August 1994 the strength of the parties in the House of Representatives was: Liberal Democratic Party 206; Kaishin (Innovation) (JRP/JNP/DSP) 130; Social Democratic Party 74; Komeito 52; Japan Communist Party 15; Sakigate 15; United Social Democratic Party 4; Independents 15.

In June 1994 the strength of the parties in the House of Councillors was: Liberal Democratic Party 95; Japan Socialist Party 68; Komeito 24; Other, 21; Rengo 12; Japan Communist Party 11; Democratic Socialist Party 7.

HEAD OF STATE

*His Imperial Majesty The Emperor of Japan*, Emperor Akihito, *born* 23 December 1933; *succeeded* 8 January 1989; *enthroned* 12 November 1990; *married* 10 April 1959, Miss Michiko Shoda, and has *issue*: the Crown Prince; Prince Akishino, *born* 30 November 1965, and Princess Sayako, *born* 18 April 1969

*Heir*, HRH Crown Prince Naruhito Hironomiya, *born* 23 February 1960, *married* 9 June 1993 Miss Masako Owada

CABINET *as at August 1994*

*Prime Minister*, Tomiichi Murayama (SDPJ)
*Deputy PM, Foreign Affairs*, Yohei Kono (LDP)
*Justice*, Isao Maeda (LDP)
*Finance*, Masayoshi Takemura (Sakigate)
*Education*, Kaoru Yosano (LDP)
*Health and Welfare*, Shoichi Ide (Sakigate)
*Agriculture, Forestry and Fisheries*, Taichiro Okawara (LDP)
*International Trade and Industry*, Ryutaro Hashimoto (LDP)
*Transport*, Shizuka Kamei (LDP)
*Posts and Telecommunications*, Shun Oide (SDPJ)
*Labour*, Manso Hamamoto (SDPJ)
*Construction*, Koken Nosaka (SDPJ)
*Home Affairs*, Hiromu Nonaka (LDP)

MINISTERS OF STATE

*Chief Cabinet Secretary*, Kozo Igarashi (SDPJ)
*Director-General of Management and Co-ordination Agency*, Tsuruo Yamaguchi (SDPJ)
*Director-General of Hokkaido and Okinawa Development Agencies*, Sadatoshi Ozato (LDP)
*Director-General of the Defence Agency*, Tokuichiro Tamazawa (LDP)
*Director-General of Science and Technology Agency*, Makiko Tanaka (LDP)
*Director-General of Environment Agency*, Shin Sakarai (LDP)
*Director-General of the Economic Planning Agency*, Masahiko Komura (LDP)
*Director-General of National Land Agency*, Kiyoshi Ozawa (LDP)
SDJP Social Democratic Party of Japan; LDP Liberal Democratic Party.

EMBASSY OF JAPAN
101–104 Piccadilly, London W1V 9FN
Tel 0171-465 6500

*Ambassador Extraordinary and Plenipotentiary*, His Excellency Hiroaki Fujii, apptd 1994
*Ministers*, Sadaaki Numata; Takayuki Kimura; Keisuke Takanishi (*Commercial*); Yoshihiko Matsuo (*Financial*); Kyoji Komachi (*Consul-General*)
*Defence Attaché*, Capt. Kazuo Tohyama
*Counsellor (Culture)*, Haruhisa Takeuchi

BRITISH EMBASSY
No. 1 Ichiban-cho, Chiyoda-ku, Tokyo 102
Tel: Tokyo 3265-5511

*Ambassador Extraordinary and Plenipotentiary*, His Excellency Sir John Boyd, KCMG, apptd 1992

*Ministers*, A. C. Thorpe, CMG (*Deputy Head of Mission*); J. E. W. Kirby (*Financial*)

*Counsellors*, D. A. Warren (*Commercial*); M. A. Price, LVO (*Management and Consul-General*)

*Defence and Naval Attaché*, Capt. A. P. Masterson-Smith

There are British Consulates General at *Tokyo* and *Osaka*, and Honorary Consulates at *Fukuoka, Hiroshima* and *Nagoya*.

BRITISH COUNCIL REPRESENTATIVE, Michael Barrett, OBE, 2 Kagurazaka 1-Chome, Shinjuku-ku, Tokyo 162. There is also an office and library in *Kyoto*.

BRITISH CHAMBER OF COMMERCE, No. 16 Kowa Building, 1–9–20 Akasaka, Minato-ku, Tokyo 107

## ECONOMY

Owing to the mountainous nature of the country less than 20 per cent of its area can be cultivated and only 14 per cent is used for agriculture; 67 per cent is wooded. The forest land includes Cryptomeria japonica, Pinus massoniana, Zeikowaskeaki, and Paulownia imperialis, in addition to camphor trees, mulberry, vegetable wax tree and a lacquer tree which furnishes the celebrated lacquer of Japan. The soil is only moderately fertile but intensive cultivation secures good crops. Tobacco, tea, potato, rice, maize, wheat and other cereals are all cultivated. Rice is the staple food of the people, about 13,124,000 tonnes being produced in 1990. Fruit is abundant, including the mandarin, persimmon, loquat and peach. European fruits such as apples, strawberries, pears, grapes and figs are also produced. There is a small-scale beef industry and pigs and chickens are widely reared.

The country has mineral resources, including gold, silver, copper, lead, zinc, iron chromite, white arsenic, coal, sulphur, petroleum, salt and uranium. However, iron ore, coal and crude oil are among the principal imports to supply deficiencies at home.

Japan is one of the most highly industrialized nations in the world, with the whole range of modern light and heavy industries, including steel, aerospace, computers, office machinery, motor vehicles, electronics, metals, machinery, chemicals, textiles (cotton, silk, wool and synthetics), cement, pottery, glass, rubber, lumber, paper, oil refining and shipbuilding.

The labour force of Japan in 1992 (average) was 64,360,000, of which around 2.1 per cent were unemployed. Of the total labour force, over 15 per cent are over 65 and this rate is increasing. Industrial, manufacturing and services workers numbered 59,422,000 and agricultural, forestries and fisheries workers 4,267,000 in 1990. In the same year primary industry accounted for 2.4 per cent of GDP, manufacturing, mining and construction for 36.9 per cent of GDP, and services for 60.7 per cent. Japan's GDP in US$2,940,365m in 1990 made its economy the second largest in the world.

### FINANCE

The budget for the financial year 1993 for revenue and expenditure on the general account was Yen 72,355,000 million.

### TRADE

Being deficient in natural resources, Japan has had to develop a complex foreign trade. Principal imports in 1988 consisted of mineral oils (20.5 per cent), raw materials (8.7 per cent) e.g. metal ores and scrap, timber, foodstuffs (15.5 per cent), e.g. wheat and sugar, machinery (14.2 per cent), chemicals (7.9 per cent) and textiles (5.7 per cent).

Principal exports consist of non-electric machinery (21.2 per cent), motor vehicles (18.4 per cent), electric machinery

and appliances (18.4 per cent), steel (5.8 per cent), chemicals (4.5 per cent), textile goods (2.6 per cent) and ships (1.5 per cent).

|  | 1992 |
|---|---|
| Total imports | US$232,698m |
| Total exports | 339,762m |

| Trade with UK | 1992 | 1993 |
|---|---|---|
| Imports from UK | £2,226,986,000 | £2,653,575,000 |
| Exports to UK | 7,443,723,000 | 8,536,146,000 |

## COMMUNICATIONS

There were 1,104,667 km of road in 1991 and 44,297 km of railroad (steam and electric) in 1984. Shinkansen (bullet train) tracks are currently being expanded. Japan National Railways was privatized in 1987 and is known as Japan Railways (JR). There are six regional companies and one goods company. The opening in 1988 of the Seikan rail tunnel and the Seto Ohashi rail bridge means that the four major islands are now linked for the first time.

The merchant fleet had a shipping capacity of 26.4 million gross tons and 10,063 vessels in 1991, making it the largest in the world in terms of number of vessels and third in terms of tonnage.

## DEFENCE

After the unconditional surrender of August 1945 the Imperial Army and Navy were disarmed and disbanded. Although the constitution prohibits the maintenance of armed forces, internal security forces came into being in 1950 and 1952. In 1954 the mission of the forces was extended to include the defence of Japan against direct and indirect aggression. Legislation passed in 1992 allows a maximum of 2,000 troops to take part in UN peacekeeping missions overseas, limited to non-front line activities.

The defence budget for 1992 was Yen 4,552,000 million. The total active armed forces strength is 237,700. The Ground Self-Defence Force (GSDF) has a strength of 149,900 and is organized into five regional armies, totalling 13 divisions, one of which is an armoured division, together with two composite, one airborne, one artillery, two air defence, five engineer and one helicopter brigades. Equipment includes 1,200 main battle tanks, 885 armoured personnel carriers, 1,010 artillery pieces and 72 attack helicopters. Equipment is now largely manufactured in Japan.

The Maritime Self-Defence Force (MSDF) has a strength of 43,100 personnel, with 17 submarines and 62 destroyers and frigates, 93 combat aircraft and 75 armed helicopters.

The Air Self-Defence Force (ASDF) has a strength of 44,700 personnel with 440 combat aircraft of US and Japanese manufacture organized into ten air defence, four ground attack, five transport, one airborne early warning, one reconnaissance and ten training squadrons.

The USA at present stations 43,100 personnel in Japan: Army 1,900; Navy 7,300; Marines 18,300; Air Force 15,600.

## EDUCATION

Education at elementary (six-year course) and lower secondary (three-year course) schools is free, compulsory and co-educational. The (three-year) upper secondary schools are attended by 95.4 per cent of the age group. They have courses in general, agricultural, commercial, technical, mercantile marine, radio communication and home economics education, etc.

Of the population aged between 18 and 21, 38.9 per cent were enrolled in higher education in 1992. There are two- or three-year junior colleges and four-year universities. Some of the universities have graduate schools. In 1991 there were 1,106 universities and junior colleges, the vast majority of which are privately maintained. The most prominent universities are the seven state universities of Tokyo, Kyoto, Tohoku (Sendai), Hokkaido (Sapporo), Kyushu (Fukuoka), Osaka and Nagoya, and the two private universities of Keio and Waseda.

## CULTURE

Japanese is said to be one of the Uro-Altaic group of languages and remained a spoken tongue until the fifth to seventh centuries AD, when Chinese characters came into use. Japanese who have received school education (99.8 per cent of the population) can read and write the Chinese characters in current use (about 1,800 characters) and also the syllabary characters called Kana. English is the best known foreign language. It is taught in all middle and high schools and universities. There are 125 daily newspapers in Japan.

# JORDAN
*Al-Mamlaka al Urduniya al-Hashemiyah*

The Hashemite Kingdom of the Jordan, which covers 37,738 sq. miles (97,740 sq. km), is bounded on the north by Syria, on the west by Israel, on the south by Saudi Arabia and on the east by Iraq. Since the hostilities of June 1967, that part of the country lying to the west of the River Jordan has been under Israeli occupation.

POPULATION – The population on the East Bank of the Jordan (1991 UN estimate) was 4,145,000. The majority of the population are Sunni Muslims and Islam is the religion of the state; freedom of belief is, however, guaranteed by the constitution.

CAPITAL – Amman, population (1994 estimate) 1,270,000.
CURRENCY – Jordanian dinar (JD) of 1,000 fils.
FLAG – Three horizontal stripes of black, white, green and a red triangle based on the hoist, containing a seven-pointed white star.
NATIONAL ANTHEM – Long Live the King.
NATIONAL DAY – 25 May (Independence Day).

## HISTORY

After the defeat of Turkey in the First World War, the Amirate of Transjordan was established in the area east of the River Jordan as a state under British mandate. The mandate was terminated after the Second World War and the Amirate, still ruled by its founder, the Amir Abdullah, became the Hashemite Kingdom of Jordan. Following the 1948 war between Israel and the Arab states, that part of Palestine remaining in Arab hands (the West Bank and East Jerusalem, but excluding Gaza) was incorporated into the Hashemite Kingdom. King Abdullah was assassinated in 1951; his son Talal ruled briefly but abdicated in favour of King Hussein in 1952.

The West Bank has been under Israeli occupation since its capture from Jordan in the 1967 war, with East Jerusalem annexed by Israel in 1967. In 1988 Jordan severed its legal and administrative ties with the occupied West Bank, but did not formally renounce sovereignty over the area. As a result of the wars of 1948–9 and 1967 there are about one million Palestinian refugees and displaced persons living in East Jordan, about 200,000 of whom live in refugee and displaced persons camps established by the UN Relief and Works Agency (UNRWA). In addition there are some 300,000 entirely self-supporting Palestinian members of the East Jordanian community.

## GOVERNMENT

The 1952 constitution provides for a senate of 40 members (all appointed by the King) and an elected House of Representatives. Until 1988, the House of Representatives had 60 members representing both the East and West Banks. Legislation passed in 1989 stipulated that in future elections seats would be contested on the East Bank only. The first parliamentary elections since 1967 to the new 80-member House of Representatives took place in November 1989.

The King appoints the members of the Council of Ministers. Crown Prince Hassan normally acts as regent when King Hussein is away from Jordan. In June 1991 a new national charter was agreed between the King and political parties in a National Conference in which the ban on political parties, imposed in 1957 after a left-wing coup attempt, was lifted in return for allegiance to the monarchy. The first multiparty parliamentary elections since 1956 were held in November 1993 with traditionalists and centrists winning 59 seats and the Islamic Action Front 16 seats.

The Middle East peace process started in Madrid in October 1991 achieved success for Jordan when an agreement on a 'common agenda' for peace was signed with Israel in September 1993. Intensive bilateral negotiations continued throughout 1993–4 with Israel agreeing to return two narrow strips of territory in the Arava desert seized in 1967 and a border commission being established. On 25 July 1994 King Hussein and the Israeli Prime Minister signed a framework agreement for peace which ended the state of war existing since 1948 and established negotiations on co-operation in trade, water resources, telephone and electricity services, as well as granting Jordan a special role in overseeing Muslim holy sites in Jerusalem. The first Israeli-Jordanian border crossing was opened between Eilat and Aquaba on 8 August 1994.

HEAD OF STATE

*His Majesty The King of the Jordan*, King Hussein, GCVO, *born* 14 November 1935, *succeeded* on the abdication of his father, King Talal, 11 August 1952, *assumed constitutional powers*, 2 May 1953, on coming of age
*Crown Prince*, Prince Hassan, third son of King Talal of Jordan, *born* 1947, *appointed Crown Prince*, 1 April 1965

COUNCIL OF MINISTERS *as at August 1994*

*Prime Minister and Minister of Defence and Foreign Affairs,*
  Dr Abdul Salam Al-Majali
*Deputy PM,* Thogan al-Hindawi
*Agriculture,* Mansour bin Tareef
*Communications and Posts,* Hasham Dabbas
*Culture,* Jumaa' Hammad
*Education,* Abdul Raouf al-Rawabdeh
*Finance,* Sammi Gammouh
*Health,* Aref Batayneh
*Information,* Dr Jawad Anani
*Interior,* Salameh Hammad
*Justice,* Hisham al-Tal
*Labour,* Khaled al-Ghzawi
*Municipal and Rural Affairs,* Tawfiq Kheishan
*Planning,* Hisham al-Khatib
*Public Works and Housing,* Dr Adul Razak al-Nsour
*Religious Affairs,* Abdul al-Abbadi
*Social Development,* Mohammed al-Sqour
*Supply,* Abdullah al-Qdah
*Tourism and Antiquities,* Muhammed al-Idwan
*Trade and Industry,* Dr Rima Khalef

*Water and Irrigation*, Saleh Irsheidat
*Youth*, Fawaz Abu al-Ghanam
*Energy and Minerals*, Talal Ereikat
*Higher Education*, Rateb al-Saoud
*Transport*, Samir Kawar

EMBASSY OF THE HASHEMITE KINGDOM OF JORDAN
6 Upper Phillimore Gardens, London W8 7HB
Tel 0171-937 3685
*Ambassador Extraordinary and Plenipotentiary*, His
   Excellency Fouad Ayoub, apptd 1991
*Minister Counsellor*, Abdullah Madadha
*Defence Attaché*, Brig. A. Maytah
*Consul*, S. N. Faris, MBE
*Head of Commerce*, B. Khasawneh
*Jordan Information Bureau*: 11–12 Buckingham Gate,
   London SW1E 6LB. Tel: 0171-630 9277

BRITISH EMBASSY
Abdoun (PO Box 87), Amman
Tel: Amman 823100
*Ambassador Extraordinary and Plenipotentiary, His*
   Excellency Peter R. M. Hinchcliffe, CMG, CVO, apptd
   1994
*Counsellor*, J. W. Watt (*Deputy Head of Mission and Consul-
   General*)
*Defence Attaché*, Col. B. A. C. Duncan, MBE
*First Secretary*, D. G. Tunstall (*Management*)
BRITISH COUNCIL REPRESENTATIVE, David Burton,
   Rainbow Street (PO Box 634), Jebel Amman, Amman
   11118

DEFENCE

The total active armed forces strength is 100,600 personnel,
with selective conscription of two-year terms in operation.
Reserves number a further 35,000. The Army has a strength
of 90,000, with 1,160 main battle tanks, 150 reconnaissance
vehicles, 1,160 armoured personnel carriers and armoured
infantry fighting vehicles, and 495 artillery pieces.
   The Navy has 600 personnel in its Aquaba base with five
patrol craft. The Air Force has a strength of 10,000 personnel
with 106 combat aircraft and 24 armed helicopters. In
addition, there is a paramilitary civil militia of 200,000
personnel.

ECONOMY

The main agricultural areas are the Jordan Valley, the hills
overlooking the valley, and the flatter country to the south of
Amman and around Madaba and Irbid. However, several
large farms, which depend for irrigation on water pumped
from deep aquifers, have been established in the southern
desert area. The rest of the country is desert and semi-desert.
The principal crops are wheat, barley, vegetables, olives and
fruit (mainly grapes and citrus fruits). Agricultural production
has increased considerably in recent years due to improvements in production and irrigation techniques, and exports
are increasing.
   Important industrial products are raw phosphates (1993,
4.2 million tons) and potash (1993, 1.4 million tons), most of
which is exported, together with fertilizers and pharmaceuticals. The Trans-Arabian oil pipeline (Tapline) runs through
north Jordan from Saudi Arabia to the Lebanese port of
Sidon. A branch pipeline, together with oil trucked by road
from Iraq, feeds a refinery at Zerqa (production 1993, 2.8
million tons) which meets most of Jordan's requirements for
refined petroleum products. Sufficient reserves of natural gas
have been discovered in the north-east to produce electricity
for the national grid (generators were commissioned in May

1989). Despite extensive efforts no significant reserves of oil
have been found.
   Tourism has steadily developed with hotels in Amman,
Aqaba, Zerka Ma'in and on the shores of the Dead Sea. The
peace agreement with Israel has enabled planning to begin
of new coastal resorts spanning the border between Aquaba
and Israel.

| *Trade with UK* | 1992 | 1993 |
|---|---|---|
| Imports from UK | £110,859,000 | £140,083,000 |
| Exports to UK | 20,743,000 | 21,520,000 |

COMMUNICATIONS

The trunk road system is good. Amman is linked to Aqaba,
Damascus, Baghdad and Jeddah by roads which are of
considerable importance in the overland trade of the Middle
East.
   The former Hejaz Railway runs from Syria through Jordan,
and is used mainly for freight between Amman and
Damascus. The Aqaba railway carries phosphate rock from
the mines of al Hasa and al Abiad to Aqaba. A total of 2,583
vessels called at Aqaba in 1988, and 20,096,200 tons of cargo
were handled.
   The Royal Jordanian Airline operates from Amman to
Aqaba and has an extensive network of routes to the Middle
East, Europe, North America and the Far East.

KAZAKHSTAN
*Kazak Respublikasy*

Kazakhstan has an area of 1,049,155 sq. miles (2,717,300 sq.
km) and occupies the northern part of what was Soviet
Central Asia. It stretches from the Volga and the Caspian
Sea in the west to the Altai and Tienshan mountains in the
east. It is bordered on the west by the Caspian Sea and
Russia, on the south by Turkmenistan, Uzbekistan and
Kyrgyzstan, on the east by China and on the north by Russia.
Kazakhstan is a country of arid steppes and semi-deserts, flat
in the west, hilly in the east and mountainous in the south-
east (Southern Altai and Tienshan mountains). The main
rivers are the Irtysh, the Ural, the Syr-Darya and the Ili. The
climate is continental and very dry.
   POPULATION – According to 1994 estimates, the population
is 16,963,600, of which 43 per cent are Kazakhs, 36 per cent
Russians, 5 per cent Ukrainians and 4 per cent ethnic
Germans. There are also smaller numbers of Tatars, Uzbeks,
Koreans and Belarussians. The Russian population is
concentrated in the north of the country, where it forms a
significant majority, and in Alma-Ata. By the end of 1995 all
non-Kazakh residents will have to decide whether to acquire
Kazakh citizenship or not.
   The majority of ethnic Kazakhs are Sunni Muslims, and
this is the main religion of the republic. Kazakh (one of the
Turkic languages) became the official language in January
1993 and Russian was given a special status as the 'social
language between peoples'. Otherwise each ethnic group
uses its own language (e.g. Kazakh 43 per cent, Russian 36
per cent).

CAPITAL – Alma-Ata (Almaty). Population 1,500,000
   (1994). The Kazakh parliament in July 1994 voted to
   move the capital to the central town of Akmola, but no
   date for the move has been given. The other major city is
   Chimkent, population 400,000 (1992).
CURRENCY – Tenge.

FLAG – Dark blue with a sun and a soaring eagle in the centre all in gold, and a red vertical ornamentation stripe near the hoist.

NATIONAL DAY – 16 December (Republic Day).

## HISTORY

For centuries Kazakhstan was inhabited by nomadic tribes before being invaded by Ghenghiz Khan and incorporated into his empire in 1218. After his empire disintegrated feudal towns emerged based on large oases. These towns affiliated and established a Kazakhstan state in the late 15th century which engaged in almost continuous warfare with the marauding Khanates on its southern border. After appealing to Russia for aid and protection, in 1731 Kazakhstan acceded to the Russian Empire under a voluntary act of accession.

The First World War brought privation to Kazakhstan as livestock and agricultural produce was requisitioned, leading to an uprising in 1916 against the conscription of male Kazakhs. After the 1917 Russian revolution, Kazakhstan came under the control of White Russian forces before they were driven from Kazakhstan in 1919. On 26 August 1920 a constitution was signed under which Kazakhstan became a Soviet Socialist Republic. Under Soviet rule in the 1920s and 1930s there was rapid industrial development and the traditional nomadic way of life disappeared. The Kazakhs suffered greatly in the Stalinist purges, the merchant and religious classes being murdered and thousands dying in the desert on forced collective farms. Other nationalities, such as Tatars and Germans, were forceably transported to Kazakhstan by Stalin.

## GOVERNMENT

Kazakhstan was the last of the former USSR republics to declare its independence (16 December 1991).

Under the constitution adopted on 28 January 1993, executive power is vested in the President and government. The President must be a Kazakh speaker and has the power to appoint the Prime Minister, deputy prime ministers, the foreign, defence and interior ministers and all ambassadors. The parliament does not have the power to impeach the President and the President cannot dissolve parliament. The legislature is the 177-member Supreme Kenges.

Elections to a new Supreme Kenges were held on 7 March 1994 and won by the presidential party SNEK-People's Unity Party (SNEK-PUP) which is derived from the former Kazakh Communist Party and supported by most ethnic Kazakhs. SNEK-PUP gained a majority in the Supreme Kenges despite claims of fraud by the ethnic Russian-supported LAD party which were supported by international election observers.

President Nazarbaev has maintained a delicate balance between ethnic Kazakhs and Russians, though tensions between the two nationalities remain below the surface and the January 1993 language compromise is disliked by many Kazakhs and Russians. Ethnic Russians dominate the state's economy and the north of the country, and Nazarbaev knows he needs their co-operation for the country's successful development. The Russians understand that Nazarbaev restrains any anti-Russian feelings in the country and the majority have accepted his presidency. Islamic groups have, however, called for the repatriation of Russians, many of whom have emigrated to Russia as the economic situation has worsened during the transition to a market economy. The ethnic-Russian LAD party has also called for the north of the country to secede. Nazarbaev has signed important agreements with Russia regarding the space launch site centre at Baikonur, which Russia will rent for 20 years at

US$115 million per year, and the nuclear testing ground at Semipalatinsk.

HEAD OF STATE
*President*, Nursultan Nazarbaev, *elected* 1 December 1991

CABINET *as at August 1994*
*Prime Minister*, Sergei Tereshchenko
*First Deputy Prime Minister*, Kazhageldin Akezhan Magzhan Ulu
*Deputy Prime Ministers*, Tulegeu Zhukeyev; Salibeck Karibzhanov; Asygat Zhabagin; Galym Abelsiitov; Syzdk Abishev; Sergei Kulagin
*Foreign Affairs*, Kanat Saudabayev
*Interior*, Vladimir Shumov
*Defence*, Sagadat Nurmagambetov
*Environment and Ecology*, Svyatoslav Mevedev
*Oil and gas*, vacant
*Justice*, Galikhan Yerzhanov
*Industry and Trade*, vacant
*Economy*, Beysenbaye Izteleulov
*Finance*, Erkembay Derbisov
*Power Engineering and Coal Industry*, vacant
*Education*, Shaisultan Shayakhmetov
*Motor Roads*, Shamil Bekbulatov
*Transport and Communications*, vacant
*Labour*, Sayat Beisenov
*Science and New Technologies*, Galym Abelsiitov
*Press*, Altenbek Sarsenbayev
*Tourism, Physical Culture and Sport*, Karatai Turysov
*Health*, Vasily Devyakto
*Culture*, Erkegali Rakhmadiev
*Social Protection*, Zaure Kadyrova
*Agriculture*, Bakhtash Tursunbaye
*Forestry*, Alexander Amanbayer

BRITISH EMBASSY
U1 Furmanova 173, Alma-Ata
Tel: Alma-Ata 506191
*Ambassador*, His Excellency Noel Jones, apptd 1993

## DEFENCE

Kazakhstan retains close defence relations with Russia but in 1993-4 has established its own armed forces from forces that were formerly under joint CIS control with Russia. The CIS mutual defence treaty of August 1993, to which Kazakhstan is a signatory, retains a common air defence force, while Kazakh forces also take part in the CIS peacekeeping force along the Tajikistan-Afghanistan border. Kazakhstan ratified the Start 1 Treaty in July 1992 and the Nuclear Non-Proliferation Treaty in December 1993. In March 1994, when the Start 1 Treaty came into effect, Kazakhstan began to transfer its strategic nuclear forces of 104 SS-18 intercontinental ballistic missiles and 40 nuclear-capable Tu-95H bombers to Russia.

The army numbers some 44,000 personnel with 1,400 main battle tanks, 1,500 artillery pieces and 50 attack helicopters. The Caspian Sea Flotilla, which Kazakhstan shares with Russia and Turkmenistan, operates under Russian command. The air force has a strength of 195 combat aircraft, while the CIS air defence forces based in Kazakhstan have 90 combat aircraft.

## ECONOMY

In March 1993 the government announced a privatization programme for 1993-6 under which most state-owned enterprises (37 large and 3,500 medium-sized enterprises) are to be sold by means of a voucher system. Outside the programme, small businesses and retail outlets have been sold at auction since 1992. Foreign investment from western states has been significant since 1992, with US$500 million invested so far. Foreign aid pledged in 1993–4 has reached US$1,000 million, including US$396 million from the USA to dismantle nuclear weapons and US$255 million from the IMF to aid the transformation to a market economy. The economy has been weakened by the less preferential trading links to other CIS states since the end of the Soviet Union, with GDP falling each year since 1991.

Kazakhstan is very rich in minerals, with copper, lead, gold, uranium, chromium, silver, zinc, iron ore, coal, oil and natural gas. In 1993 production of coal was 60 million tonnes and iron ore was 20 million tonnes, while reserves of gold were estimated at 60 million tonnes. The oil and gas industry, concentrated in the west of the country, is being expanded by western investment, which is also being used to explore two large fields in the Caspian Sea, Karachaganak (gas) and Tengiz (oil). Oil production in 1993 was 470,000 barrels per day with estimated reserves of 35,000 million barrels. Industry is dominated by food processing and mining and metals production, and textiles, steel and tractors are also produced. The main centres of the metal industry are in the Altai mountains, in Chimkent, north of the Balkhash Lake and in central Kazakhstan.

Agriculture, including stock-raising, is highly developed, particularly in the central and south-west of the republic. Grain is grown in the north and north-east, and cotton and wool produced in the south and south-east. A record grain crop was grown in 1992 and 1.5 million tonnes of meat produced in 1993.

| Trade with UK | 1993 |
| --- | --- |
| Imports from UK | £14,943,000 |
| Exports to UK | 57,915,000 |

## KENYA
*Jamhuri ya Kenya*

Kenya is bisected by the equator and extends approximately from 4° N. to 4° S. latitude and from 34° E. to 41° E. longitude. The Indian Ocean and Somalia lie to the east and Ethiopia and Sudan in the north and north-west. To the west lie Uganda and Lake Victoria and to the south Tanzania. The total area is 224,961 sq. miles (582,646 sq. km), including 5,171 square miles of water. The country is divided into eight provinces (Central, Coast, Eastern, Nairobi, Nyanza, North Eastern, Rift Valley, Western).

POPULATION – The population is 25,905,000 (1991 UN estimate). The main tribal groups are the Kikuyu, Luhya, Luo, Kalenjin, Kamba and Masai. The official languages are Swahili, which is generally understood throughout Kenya, and English; numerous indigenous languages are also spoken.

CAPITAL – Nairobi, population 1,400,000 (1989 estimate).
CURRENCY – Kenya shilling (Ksh) of 100 cents.
FLAG – Horizontally black, red and green with the red fimbriated in white, and with a shield and crossed spears all over in the centre.
NATIONAL ANTHEM – Kenya, Land of the Lion.
NATIONAL DAY – 12 December (Independence Day).

## GOVERNMENT

Kenya became an independent state and a member of the British Commonwealth on 12 December 1963 and a republic in 1964. In 1982 the government introduced amendments to the constitution and election law making the country a one-

party state. The Kenya African National Union (KANU) was the sole legal political organization until December 1991 when the government yielded to internal and international pressure and introduced a multiparty democracy through parliamentary legislation.

Multiparty presidential and legislative elections were held in December 1992 which were won by President Moi and KANU respectively, amid opposition claims that the elections were not free and fair which were supported by the Commonwealth observers monitoring the election. In the unicameral National Assembly of 200 seats, KANU has 107 seats (95 elected and 12 nominated by the President) and the three major opposition parties have 85 seats between them. KANU formed a new government on 13 January 1993 and parliament reopened on 22 March 1993 but was boycotted by two of the main opposition parties for three months. In May the government reached agreement with the IMF and World Bank on anti-corruption and economic reform measures and the IMF resumed aid to Kenya, suspended in November 1991. Ethnic clashes in the Rift Valley since 1991 between the largest tribe, the Kikuyus, who mainly support opposition parties, and the smaller government supporting tribes of the Kalenjin, Masai and Pokot have left some 1,500 dead.

HEAD OF STATE
*President and C.-in-C. Armed Forces*, Hon. Daniel T. arap Moi, *took office* 14 October 1978, *re-elected* for a fourth five-year term on 29 December 1992

CABINET *as at August 1994*
*The President*
*Vice-President and Minister for Planning and National Development*, Hon. Prof. George Saitoti
*Foreign Affairs*, Hon. Stephen Musyoka
*Finance*, Hon. Wycliffe Mudavadi
*Agriculture, Livestock Development and Marketing*, Hon. Simon Nyachae
*Land Reclamation, Regional and Water Development*, Hon. Darius Mbela
*Environment and Natural Resources*, Hon. John Sambu
*Transport and Communication*, Hon. Dalmas Otieno
*Energy*, Hon. John Kyalo
*Commerce and Industry*, Hon. Kirugi M'mukindia
*Tourism and Wildlife*, Hon. Katana Ngala
*Health*, Hon. Joshua Angatia
*Local Government*, Hon. William Ntimana
*Home Affairs and National Heritage*, Hon. Francis Lotodo
*Lands and Urban Planning*, Hon. Jackson Mulinge
*Labour and Manpower Development*, Hon. Phillip Masinde
*Information and Broadcasting*, Hon. Johnstone Makau
*Cultural and Social Services*, Hon. Hussein Mohamed
*Co-operative Development*, Hon. Kamwithi Munyi
*Public Works and Housing*, Hon. Jonathan N'geno
*Research and Technical Training*, Hon. Zachary Onyonka
*Attorney-General*, Hon. Amos Wako

KENYA HIGH COMMISSION
45 Portland Place, London WIN 4AS
Tel 0171-636 2371
*High Commissioner, His Excellency* Joseph K. A. Ruto, apptd 1993
*Defence Attaché*, Col. E. Sifuma
*Commercial Attaché*, C. Mkangi

BRITISH HIGH COMMISSION
Bruce House, Standard Street, PO Box 30465 Nairobi
Tel: Nairobi 335944
*High Commissioner, His Excellency* Sir Kieran Prendergast, KCVO, CMG, apptd 1992

Deputy High Commissioner, R. A. Pullen
Defence and Military Adviser, Col. P. R. Bell
First Secretary (Commercial), D. L. Littlefield
First Secretary (Consular), A. Summers
There are consular offices in Nairobi, Mombasa and Malindi.

BRITISH COUNCIL REPRESENTATIVE, Bill Harvey, (PO Box 40751) ICEA Building, Kenyatta Avenue, Nairobi. There are offices at Kisumu and Mombasa.

## ECONOMY

Agriculture provides about 52 per cent of total export earnings (excluding processed oil products). The great variation in altitude and ecology provide conditions under which a wide range of crops can be grown. These include wheat, barley, pyrethrum, coffee, tea, sisal, coconuts, cashew nuts, cotton, maize and a wide variety of tropical and temperate fruits and vegetables. The total area of well-farmed land on which concentrated mixed farming can be practised is small and the remainder is arid or semi-arid country but population pressure and the need to increase agricultural production for export has led to attempts to develop such areas.

Prospecting and mining are carried on in some parts of the country, the principal minerals produced being soda ash, salt and limestone. Hydro-electric power has been developed, particularly on the Upper Tana River. Kenya is now almost self-sufficient in electric power generation but the connection with Owen Falls in Uganda is still in being.

There has been considerable industrial development over the last 15 years and Kenya has a wide variety of industries processing agricultural produce and manufacturing an increasing range of products from local and imported raw materials. New industries have recently come into being such as steel, textile mills, dehydrated vegetable processing and motor tyre manufacture as well as many smaller schemes which have added to the country's already considerable consumer goods. There is an oil refinery in Mombasa supplying both Kenya and Uganda, and a fuel pipeline now connects Mombasa and Nairobi.

## TRADE

Principal exports are coffee and tea, which account for 33 per cent of total export earnings. Also exported are fruit, vegetables, and crude animal and vegetable material. Petroleum products account for about 37 per cent of imports; other imports are manufactured goods, particularly machinery, transport equipment, metals, pharmaceuticals and chemicals.

| Trade with UK | 1992 | 1993 |
|---|---|---|
| Imports from UK | £139,865,000 | £152,208,000 |
| Exports to UK | 138,397,000 | 172,680,000 |

## COMMUNICATIONS

The Kenya Railways Corporation has 1,700 miles of railway open to traffic. There are also 39,000 miles of road, of which 5,000 are bitumen surfaced. Trans-border links with Tanzania were reopened in 1985 with rail services for freight and steamer services for passengers and freight.

The principal port is Mombasa, operated by the Kenya Ports Authority. International air services operate from airports at Nairobi and Mombasa.

# KIRIBATI
Ribaberikin Kiribati

Kiribati, the former Gilbert Islands, became an independent republic in 1979. Kiribati comprises 36 islands, the Gilberts Group (17) including Banaba (formerly Ocean Island), the Phoenix Islands (8), and the Line Islands (11), which are situated in the south-west central Pacific around the point at which the International Date Line cuts the Equator. The total land area of 281 sq. miles (728 sq. km) is spread over some 2 million square miles of ocean. Few of the atolls are more than half a mile in width or more than 12 feet high. The vegetation consists mainly of coconut palms, breadfruit trees and pandanus. The population (UN estimate 1991) is 66,000, and predominantly Christian.

CAPITAL – Tarawa, population estimated at 17,921.
CURRENCY – Kiribati uses the Australian dollar ($A) of 100 cents.
FLAG – Red, with blue and white wavy lines in base, and in the centre a gold rising sun and a flying frigate bird.
NATIONAL ANTHEM – Teirake Kain Kiribati (Stand Kiribati).
NATIONAL DAY – 12 July (Independence Day).

## GOVERNMENT

The President is head of state as well as head of government and is elected nationally. There is an elected House of Assembly of 41 members. Executive authority is vested in the Cabinet. The government of President Teannaki was brought down in May 1994 by a no confidence vote in the House of Assembly. A Council of State will administer the country until new elections in late 1994.

HEAD OF STATE
President, HE Teatao Teannaki
Vice-President, Hon. Taomati T. Iuta

HONORARY CONSULATE
c/o Faith House, 7 Tufton Street, London SW1P 3QN
Tel 0171-222 6952

Honorary Consul, M. Chandler, CBE.

BRITISH HIGH COMMISSIONER, His Excellency Timothy David, apptd 1994, resident at Suva, Fiji.

## ECONOMY

Most people still practise a semi-subsistence economy, the main staples of their diet being coconuts and fish.

Estimated recurrent revenue for 1988 was $A24.9m. The principal imports are foodstuffs, consumer goods, machinery and transport equipment. The principal exports are copra and fish. Total value of exports in 1990 was $A3,681,000.

| Trade with UK | 1992 | 1993 |
|---|---|---|
| Imports from UK | £571,000 | £327,000 |
| Exports to UK | 2,000 | 2,000 |

## COMMUNICATIONS

Air communication exists between most of the islands and is operated by Air Tungaru, a statutory corporation. Air Marshall Islands operates a weekly service between Majuro, Tarawa, Funafuti and Nandi, and Air Nauru between Tarawa, Nauru and Nandi. Inter-island shipping is operated by a statutory corporation, the Shipping Corporation of Kiribati.

SOCIAL WELFARE

The government maintains a teacher training college and a secondary school. Five junior secondary schools are maintained by missions. Throughout the republic there are about a hundred primary schools. The total enrolment of children of school age is about 16,000.

The Marine Training School at Tarawa trains seamen for service with overseas shipping lines.

There is a general hospital at Tarawa. The other inhabited islands have dispensaries.

# KOREA

Korea is situated between 124° 11″ and 130° 57′ E. longitude, and between 33° 7′ and 43° 1″ N. latitude. It has an area of 84,565 sq. miles (219,022 sq. km), with a population (UN estimate 1991) of 65,461,000. The southern and western coasts are fringed with innumerable islands, of which the largest, forming a province of its own, is Cheju.

LANGUAGE AND LITERATURE

Despite the great cultural influence of the Chinese, Koreans have developed and preserved their own cultural heritage. The Korean language is of the Ural-Altaic Group. Its script, Hangul, was invented in the 15th century; prior to this Chinese characters alone were used.

HISTORY

The last native dynasty (Yi) ruled from 1392 until 1910, in which year Japan formally annexed Korea. The country remained part of the Japanese Empire until the defeat of Japan in 1945, when it was occupied by troops of the USA and the USSR, the 38th parallel being fixed as the boundary between the two zones of occupation.

The US government endeavoured to reach agreement with the Soviet government for the creation of a Korean government for the whole country and the withdrawal of all Russian and American troops. These efforts met with no success, and in September 1947 the US government laid the question of the future of Korea before the General Assembly of the United Nations. The Assembly in November 1947 resolved that elections should be held in Korea for a National Assembly under the supervision of a temporary commission formed for that purpose by the United Nations and that the National Assembly when elected should set up a government. The Soviet government refused to allow the Commission to visit the Russian-occupied zone and in consequence it was only able to discharge its function in that part of Korea which lies south of the 38th parallel.

A general election was held on 10 May 1948, and the first National Assembly met in Seoul on 31 May. The Assembly passed a constitution on 12 July and on 15 August 1948 the republic was formally inaugurated and American military government came to an end. Meanwhile, in the Russian-occupied zone north of the 38th parallel the Democratic People's Republic had been set up with its capital at Pyongyang. A Supreme People's Soviet was elected in September 1948, and a Soviet-style constitution adopted.

THE KOREAN WAR

The country remained effectively divided into two along the line of the 38th parallel until June 1950, when North Korean forces invaded South Korea. In response to Security Council recommendations that United Nations members should furnish assistance to repel the attack, 16 nations, including the USA and the UK, came to the aid of the Republic of Korea. China entered the war on the side of North Korea in November 1950. The fighting was ended by an armistice agreement signed on 27 July 1953. By this agreement (which was not signed by the representatives of the Republic of Korea), the line of division between North and South Korea remained in the neighbourhood of the 38th parallel.

Talks between North and South Korea on the reunification of the country have taken place intermittently. A non-aggression accord was signed between the North and South in December 1991 and an agreement on the denuclearization of the Korean peninsula was reached in February 1992. In June 1994 agreement was reached on a July summit of North and South Korean Presidents but Kim Il-sung died before it could take place.

# REPUBLIC OF KOREA
*Daehanminkuk*

The Republic of Korea has been officially recognized by the governments of the USA, France, United Kingdom, and most other countries but, until recently, not by any Communist bloc country. Since 1989 diplomatic relations have been established with all eastern European countries, including the then Soviet Union, and in 1992 with the People's Republic of China, which required the breaking of diplomatic relations with Taiwan.

POPULATION – The population (UN estimate 1991) is 43,268,000. There is freedom of religion. Buddhism has the most followers (13 million) followed by Protestantism (8 million) and Confucianism (4.7 million). Catholics number 2.2 million.

CAPITAL – Seoul, population (1993) 10,920,000. Other main centres are Ψ Pusan (3,654,097), Taegu (2,165,954) and Ψ Inchon (1,526,435).

CURRENCY – Won of 100 jeon.

FLAG – White with a red and blue yin-yang in the centre, surrounded by four black trigrams.

NATIONAL ANTHEM – Aegukka.

NATIONAL DAY – 15 August (Independence Day).

GOVERNMENT

Following extensive political unrest in 1987, a new constitution was adopted in 1988. The President, who is head of state, chief of the executive and Commander-in-Chief of the Armed Forces, is directly elected for a single term of five years. He appoints the Prime Minister with the consent of the National Assembly, and members of the State Council (Cabinet) on the recommendation of the Prime Minister. The President is also empowered to take wide-ranging measures in an emergency, including the declaration of martial law, but must obtain the agreement of the National Assembly. The National Assembly of 299 members is directly elected for a four-year term.

The most recent elections to the National Assembly were held in March 1992. The ruling Democratic Liberal Party (DLP) lost its parliamentary majority, winning 149 out of 299 seats, but then regained a majority by persuading independent members to join the party. In the most recent presidential election of December 1992, long-time opposition leader Kim Young-sam was victorious as the Democratic Liberal Party candidate (he had merged his opposition party with the DLP in 1990). On 26 February 1993 he named the first wholly civilian government in 32 years. In 1993–4 the government of President Kim Young-sam has implemented an anti-corruption programme against the bureaucracy, and armed forces, and also has begun the deregulation of the economy with plans for mass privatization and tax cuts. Since the 1960s South Korea has followed the Japanese model of a government-business partnership controlling the economy.

HEAD OF STATE

*President*, Kim Young-sam, *elected* 18 December 1992, *took office* 25 February 1993

CABINET *as at August 1994*

*Prime Minister*, Lee Yung-duk
*Deputy Prime Minister, Economic Planning Board*, Chong Chae-sok
*Deputy Prime Minister, National Unification*, Lee Hong-ku
*Foreign Affairs*, Han Seung-joo
*Home Affairs*, Choe Hyong-u
*Finance*, Hong Jae-young
*Justice*, Kim Doo-hee
*Defence*, Yi Pong-tae
*Education*, Kim Suk-hui
*Agriculture and Fisheries*, Choi In-kee
*Environment*, Pak Yun-hun
*Trade and Industry*, Kim Chui-Soo
*Construction*, Kim U-sok
*Health and Social Affairs*, So Sang Mok
*Labour*, Nam Chae-hui
*Transport*, O Myong
*Communications*, Yoon Dong-yoon
*Culture and Sports*, Lee Min-sub
*Information*, Oh In-hwan
*Government Administration*, Hwang Yong-ha
*Science and Technology*, Kim Si-joong
*Patriot's and Veteran's Administration*, Yi Chung-kil
*First Minister for Political Affairs*, So Chon-won
*Second Minister for Political Affairs*, Kwon Young-ja
*Director, National Security Planning Agency*, Kim Duck

EMBASSY OF THE KOREAN REPUBLIC
4 Palace Gate, London W8 5NF
Tel 0171–581 0247

*Ambassador Extraordinary and Plenipotentiary*, His Excellency Chang-Hee Roe, apptd 1993
*Defence Attaché*, Capt. Jang Kil Joo
*Consul*, Han Gon Lee
*Commercial Attaché*, Young Sang Yoo

BRITISH EMBASSY
No. 4, Chung-Dong, Chung-Ku, Seoul 100
Tel: Seoul 735–7341/3

*Ambassador Extraordinary and Plenipotentiary*, His Excellency Thomas George Harris, apptd 1994
*Counsellor (Economic), Consul-General and Deputy Ambassador*, T. C. Holmes
*Defence and Military Attaché*, Brig. C. D. Parr, OBE
*First Secretary (Commercial)*, A. C. Stephens

There is an Honorary British Consul at *Pusan*.

BRITISH COUNCIL REPRESENTATIVE, T. White, MBE, Anglican Church Annex, 3–7 Chung Dong, Choong-ku, Seoul 100–120. There is also an office at Pusan.

BRITISH CHAMBER OF COMMERCE, c/o Chartered Bank, 1st and 2nd Floors, Samsung Building, 50, 1-Ka Ulchi Ro, Chung-Ku, Seoul.

DEFENCE

The Republic of Korea has total active armed forces of 633,000 personnel. Conscripts serve for 26 months (army)

or 30 months (navy and air force) and then in reserve forces until age 33. Reserves number some 4,500,000 personnel.

The army has a strength of 520,000 active personnel, with 1,800 main battle tanks, 3,550 armoured personnel carriers and armoured infantry fighting vehicles, 4,540 artillery pieces and 135 armed helicopters. The regular army is organized into nine corps with a total of three mechanized infantry and 19 infantry divisions together with two infantry and ten special forces brigades. The reserves comprise 23 infantry divisions.

The navy has a strength of 60,000 (19,000 conscripts) including 25,000 marines, with four submarines, nine destroyers and 29 frigates, 120 patrol and coastal craft, 15 combat aircraft and 47 armed helicopters. The air force has a strength of 53,000, with 445 combat aircraft, almost all of US manufacture, organized into eight ground attack, four air defence, one counter-insurgency, one reconnaissance and three transport squadrons.

The USA maintains 35,500 personnel in the Republic of Korea divided into 26,000 army and 9,500 air force personnel.

EDUCATION

Primary education is compulsory for six years from the age of seven. Secondary and higher education is extensive. The national illiteracy rate is among the lowest in Asia.

ECONOMY

The soil is fertile but arable land is limited by the mountainous nature of the country. Staple agricultural products are rice, barley and other cereals, beans, tobacco and hemp. Fruit-growing and sericulture are also practised. Ginseng, a medicinal root much used by both the Chinese and Koreans, forms a useful source of revenue. The fishing industry is a major contributor to both food supply and exports.

The Republic of Korea is deficient in mineral resources, except for deposits of coal on the east coast and tungsten. There are some prospects of discovering oil in the sea between Korea and Japan.

Rapid industrialization has taken place since the 1960s on the basis of the model of the Japanese income-doubling plan concentrating on expanding exports. Major industries now include shipbuilding, construction, iron and steel, textiles, electrical and electronic goods, footwear, passenger vehicles and railway rolling stock. The 1994–8 five-year economic plan includes the liberalization of foreign exchange rates and capital markets, the deregulation of interest rates and the easing of regulations on foreign exchange holdings by companies.

FINANCE

The budget for 1994 totals Won 43,250,000 million. From 1962 a series of successful five-year plans resulted in real economic growth averaging around 10 per cent a year. However, growth fell to 8.5 per cent in 1991 and to 4.8 per cent in 1992, the lowest figure since 1980. Annual per capita GNP is US$6,749 (1992).

| TRADE | 1990 | 1991 |
|---|---|---|
| Imports | US$65,091m | US$76,561m |
| Exports | 63,236m | 69,581m |

| Trade with UK | 1992 | 1993 |
|---|---|---|
| Imports from UK | £654,060,000 | £769,380,000 |
| Exports to UK | 933,946,000 | 1,077,735,000 |

## COMMUNICATIONS

In 1989 there were 37,493 km of paved road. Seoul and Pusan have subway systems and there are national railway and airline systems. Korean Air operates regular flights to Europe, the United States, the Middle East and South East Asia. Pusan and Inchon are the major ports with Pusan serving the industrial areas of the south-east. Inchon, 28 miles from Seoul, serves the capital, but development and operation at Inchon are hampered by a tidal variation of 9–10 metres.

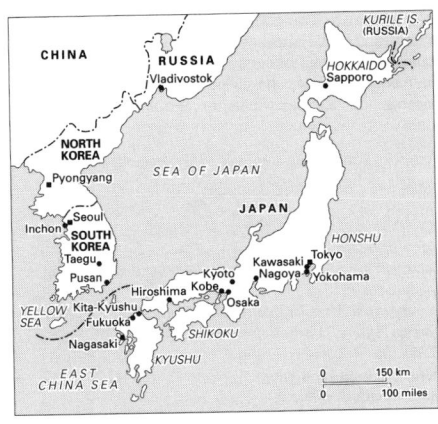

## DEMOCRATIC PEOPLE'S REPUBLIC OF KOREA
*Chosun Minchu-chui Inmin Kongwa-guk*

The area of North Korea is 46,540 sq. miles (120,538 sq. km), with a population of 22,193,000 (UN estimate 1991).

CAPITAL – Pyongyang, approximate population, 2,000,000.
CURRENCY – Won of 100 chon.
FLAG – Red with white fimbriations and blue borders at top and bottom; a large red star on a white disc near the hoist.
NATIONAL ANTHEM – A Chi Mun Bin No Ra I Gang San (Shine bright, oh dawn, on this land so fair).
NATIONAL DAY – 8 September.

## GOVERNMENT

The constitution of the Democratic People's Republic of Korea provides for a Supreme People's Assembly, presently consisting of 687 deputies, which is elected every five years by universal suffrage. The Assembly elects a President, and the Central People's Committee. In turn, the Central People's Committee directs the Administrative Council which implements the policy formulated by the Committee. The Administrative Council (51 members), formally the government of North Korea, includes the Prime Minister and various ministers. In practice, however, the country is ruled by the Korean Workers' Party which elects a Central Committee; this in turn appoints a Politburo. The senior ministers of the Administrative Council are all members of the Communist Central Committee and the majority are also members of the Politburo. Kim Il-sung, who had been head of the state, party and military since the country's inception in 1948, died on 8 July 1994. Five days later his son Kim Jong-il was appointed to the same posts by the Korean Workers' Party. The President is usually elected by the Supreme People's Assembly for five-year terms.

In 1992–4 North Korea's attempts to develop nuclear weapons in secret have brought it into conflict with western countries. As a signatory of the Nuclear Non-Proliferation Treaty (NPT), North Korea is legally required to open its nuclear facilities to inspection by the International Atomic Energy Authority (IAEA). After repeatedly blocking special inspections of its facility at Yongbyon, in April 1993 North Korea was reported to the UN Security Council, which ordered it to allow special inspections. It refused and announced its decision to withdraw from the NPT by 12 June 1993. After negotiations with the USA, it announced on 11 June that the country would remain in the NPT and allow partial IAEA inspections. After continued negotiations with the USA and IAEA in late 1993 and early 1994 North Korea allowed IAEA inspectors to visit all seven nuclear sites in March 1994 but limited the scope of the inspections and refused to allow regular inspections. In May 1994 the IAEA informed the UN Security Council that North Korea was in violation of the NPT by attempting to reprocess plutonium for nuclear weapons. A crisis ensued with North Korea announcing its withdrawal from the IAEA in June and international pressure for sanctions until, after Kim Il-sung's death, an agreement was reached by the USA and North Korea in August. Under the agreement North Korea will remain a party to the NPT, will switch from its present graphite nuclear reactors to a US-supplied light-water reactor unsuitable for the production of weapons grade plutonium, and will forgo the reprocessing of spent fuel rods. In return the USA will establish diplomatic relations and move to full political and diplomatic relations.

### HEAD OF STATE
*President, Commander-in-Chief, General-Secretary of the Party*, Kim Jong-il, appointed 13 July 1994
*Vice-Presidents*, Kim Yong-ju; Kim Pyong-sik

*Politburo of the Central Committee*, Kim Jong-il; Marshal O Chin-u (*full members and members of the presidium*); Kim Yong-ju; Yi Chong-ok; Pak Song-chol; Kim Yong-nam; Kye Ung-tae; Kang Song-san; So Yun-sok; Chon Pyong-ho; Choe Kwang; Han Song-yong (*full members*); Kang Hui-won; Kim Pok-sin; Hong Si-hak; Hong Song-nam; Choe Tae Pok; Kim Chol-man; Choe Yong-nim; Ying Hyong-sop; Yon Hyong-muk; Hong Sok-hyong (*alternate members*)
*Secretariat of the Central Committee*, Kim Jong-il (*General Secretary*); Kim Chong-il; Hwang Chang-yop; So Kwan-hui; Pak Nam-ki; Kim Chung-nin; Kye Ung-tae; Chon Pyong-ho; Choe Tae-pok; Han Song-yong; Yun Ki-pok; Kim Yong-sun; Kim Kuk-tae; Kim Ki-nam
*Premier of Administrative Council*, Kang Song-San, appointed 11 December 1992

## DEFENCE

It is believed that North Korea has manufactured a very small number of nuclear weapons or has the technology and raw materials to do so. In 1993 the Rodong 1 intermediate range missile with a range of 1,000 km and the ability to carry nuclear, chemical or biological weapons was successfully tested.

The total active armed forces number remains high, at 1,127,000 personnel, and is a destabilizing factor in the region. Conscripts serve for three to four years (air force), five to eight years (army) or five to ten years (navy), followed by service in the reserves to age 40 and the Red Guard to age 60.

The army has an active strength of 1,000,000 personnel, with 3,700 main battle tanks, 3,000 armoured personnel carriers and 9,080 artillery pieces. Personnel are organized into one armoured, one artillery, one special forces, four mechanized and eight infantry corps. Reserves number 1,200,000 divided into 23 infantry divisions and six infantry brigades. The navy is 45,000 strong, with 25 submarines, three frigates and 387 patrol and coastal vessels. The air force has a strength of 82,000 personnel, with 730 combat aircraft and 50 armed helicopters, organized into three bomber, seven ground attack, and 10 air defence regiments, with attendant transport and training units. In addition, paramilitary troops of the Ministry of Public Security number 115,000 personnel.

## ECONOMY

North Korea is rich in minerals and industry has been developed, but the economy stagnated for many years because of poor planning and a shortage of foreign exchange. Since the collapse of the Soviet Union in 1991, the economy has been in crisis because of the ending of barter trade, severe fuel shortages and the end of Soviet aid. Industrial output has collapsed and the economy shrank for three years, with agricultural production also badly affected. Most industry is operating at only one-third of capacity.

| Trade with UK | 1992 | 1993 |
|---|---|---|
| Imports from UK | £7,426,000 | £5,928,000 |
| Exports to UK | 334,000 | 249,000 |

## KUWAIT
*Dowlat al- Kuwait*

Kuwait extends along the shore of the Persian Gulf from Iraq to Saudi Arabia, with an area of 6,880 sq. miles (17,818 sq. km). In 1993 the UN decided on the border dispute between Kuwait and Iraq, moving the border some few hundred metres northwards and Kuwait has since begun digging a trench system along its border.

Kuwait has a dry, desert climate with a summer season extending from April to September. The mean temperature varies between 29–45°C in summer, and 8–18°C in winter. Humidity rarely exceeds 60 per cent except in July and August.

POPULATION – At the 1985 census the population was 1,695,128, of which about 40 per cent were Kuwaiti citizens, the remainder being other Arabs, Iranians, Indians and Pakistanis. The total European and American population was about 12,500. The Iraqi occupation of Kuwait led to a substantial emigration of nationals and foreign residents. The population was estimated to have returned to over one million in January 1992, including 425,000 foreigners. It is the government's intention to keep the proportion of foreigners down to 40 per cent.

Islam is the official religion, though religious freedom is constitutionally guaranteed. The official language is Arabic, and English is widely spoken as a second language.

CAPITAL – Ψ Kuwait, population (excluding suburbs) 400,000.
CURRENCY – Kuwaiti dinar (KD) of 1,000 fils.
FLAG – Three horizontal stripes of green, white and red, with black trapezoid next to staff.
NATIONAL DAY – 25 February.

## GOVERNMENT

Although Kuwait had been independent for some years, the 'exclusive agreement' of 1899 between the Sheikh of Kuwait and the British Government was formally abrogated by an exchange of letters dated 19 June 1961. Iraq invaded Kuwait on 2 August 1990 and was liberated in February 1991 by an alliance of western and Arab forces.

Under the constitution legislative power is vested in the Amir and the 50-member National Assembly, and executive power in the Amir and the Cabinet. The sixth National Assembly was dissolved in July 1986 and was replaced by the National Council, a partially elected, partially appointed body with much narrower powers, in April 1990. Elections to this, held in June 1990, were boycotted by the opposition. Elections for a new National Assembly were held on 5 October 1992. The electorate consists of all Kuwaiti male nationals over 21 whose families have lived in the Emirate since before 1921.

HEAD OF STATE
HH The Amir of Kuwait, Sheikh Jabir al-Ahmad al Jabir Al-Sabah, *born* 1928, acceded 1 January 1978
Crown Prince, HH Sheikh Saad al-Abdullah al-Salim al-Sabah

CABINET *as at August 1994*
*Prime Minister*, HH The Crown Prince
*First Deputy Prime Minister and Minister for Foreign Affairs*, Sheikh Sabah al-Ahmad al-Jabir al-Sabah
*Second Deputy Prime Minister, Finance*, Nasir al-Rowdhan
*Education and Higher Education*, Dr Ahmad al-Rubie
*Defence*, Sheikh Ahmad Hamoud al-Jabir al-Sabah
*Interior*, Sheikh Ali Sabah al-Salim al-Sabah
*Information*, Sheikh Saoud Nasir al-Sabah
*Social Affairs and Labour*, Ahmed Khalid al-Kulaib
*Communications, Electricity and Water*, Jasim Muhammed al-Awn
*Public Health*, Dr Abdul Rahman Saleh al-Mehilan
*Public Works and Housing*, Habib Jawhar Hayat
*Oil*, Abdel-Mohsen al-Mudej
*Awqaf and Islamic Affairs*, Dr Ali Fahd al-Zumai
*Commerce and Industry*, Hilal Meshari al-Mutairi
*Planning and Cabinet Affairs*, Abdul-Aziz al-Dakheel
*Justice and Administrative Affairs*, Mishari Jassim al-Anjari

*Speaker of the National Assembly*, Ahmad Abdul-Aziz al-Saadoun

EMBASSY OF THE STATE OF KUWAIT
45–46 Queen's Gate, London SW7 5JN
Tel 0171-589 4533

*Ambassador Extraordinary and Plenipotentiary*, His Excellency Khaled al-Duwaisan, apptd 1993
*Counsellor*, Jasem Mubarak Al-Mubaraki
*Attachés*, Abdul-Rahman Saleh Al-Radi (*Consular Affairs*); Dr Jasem Karam (*Cultural*)

BRITISH EMBASSY
PO Box 2 Safat, 13001 Safat, Kuwait
Tel: Kuwait 2403334/6

*Ambassador Extraordinary and Plenipotentiary*, His Excellency William Hugh Fullerton, CMG, apptd 1992
*Counsellor and Deputy Ambassador*, F. X. Gallagher, OBE
*First Secretaries*, J. Bentley (*Management and Consul*); C. R. Winter, MBE (*Commercial*)
*Defence Attaché*, Col. C. J. Squires

BRITISH COUNCIL REPRESENTATIVE, A. Broderick, 2 al Arabi Street (PO Box 345), 13004 Safat, Mansouriyah.

## SOCIAL WELFARE

The government invested its considerable oil revenues in comprehensive social services. Education and medical treatment are free. Kuwait University was opened in 1966, and in 1987-8 had 15,602 students. In 1987-8 there were over 489,000 pupils at government and private schools. These numbers have declined along with the total population since the Iraqi invasion and a number of schools did not re-open after Kuwait's liberation.

## COMMUNICATIONS

Kuwait's ports and airport were damaged during the Iraqi occupation, but have re-opened since liberation. There is a network of dual-carriageway roads and more are under construction. Telecommunications and postal services are conducted by the government. Its earth satellite station and telecommunications network were severely damaged during the Iraqi occupation but domestic and international telephone services have been fully restored. The 1993 UN border demarcation line gave part of the port of Umm Qasr to Kuwait.

## ECONOMY

Despite the desert terrain, 8.4 per cent of land is under cultivation, fruit and vegetables being the main crops. Shrimp fishing is becoming important.

The oil industry was brought into government ownership in 1975. Since reorganization in 1980, the national industry has been run by the Kuwait Petroleum Corporation. The centre of oil production is at Burgan, south of Kuwait City. Oil is also lifted in the Kuwait/Saudi Arabia Partitioned Zone (Wafra) south of the state. Oil is exported through a specially constructed port at Mina al Ahmadi.

Oil installations were extensively damaged during the Iraqi occupation. Oil exports were resumed in July 1991 and production (including output from the neutral zone) reached 2,000,000 barrels per day in December 1993, in line with the quota allocated to it by OPEC (compared to a production capacity of 2,200,000 barrels per day before the Iraqi invasion). Kuwait is anxious to expand production and unhappy that the quota is not closer to its capacity of 2,500,000 barrels per day.

### ENERGY, ETC

Before the Iraqi invasion Kuwait had six power stations capable of generating 7,200 MW of electricity. Associated desalination capacity, on which the country largely depends for water, was 118 million gallons a day; reserves stored up to 2,000 million barrels. All six power stations were damaged during the Iraqi occupation. Essential services were restored after liberation but it will take several years and substantial investment to restore electricity and water distillation capacity to pre-invasion levels.

### FINANCE

Expected revenue for the financial year 1994-5 was KD2,537m and expenditure KD4,390m. Oil revenues constitute about 90 per cent of total revenue. There are a large number of investment banks, in some of which the government holds equity. The banking system is controlled by the Central Bank of Kuwait.

### TRADE

Oil constitutes Kuwait's major export. Non-oil exports, mainly to Asian countries and the Indian sub-continent, have included chemical fertilizers, ammonia and other chemicals, metal pipes, shrimps and building materials. Re-exports to neighbouring states traditionally accounted for a major proportion of non-oil exports but were brought to a halt by the Iraqi invasion. Major trading partners are Japan, the USA and Western Europe.

| Trade with UK | 1992 | 1993 |
| --- | --- | --- |
| Imports from UK | £262,288,000 | £311,669,000 |
| Exports to UK | 127,226,000 | 236,480,000 |

# KYRGYZSTAN
*Kyrgyz Respublikasy*

Kyrgyzstan has an area of 76,642 sq. miles (198,500 sq. km) and occupies the central eastern part of the former Soviet Central Asia. The republic's name was changed from Kirghizia in December 1990. It is bordered on the north by Kazakhstan, on the east by China, on the south and south-west by Tajikistan and on the west by Uzbekistan. Kyrgyzstan is a mountainous country, the major part being covered by the ridge of the Central Tienshan, while the mountains of the Pamir-Altai system occupy its southern part. There are a number of spacious mountain valleys, the Alai, Susamyr and others. Kyrgyzstan is divided into six administrative regions.

POPULATION – According to a 1994 estimate the population is 4,500,000, of which 52.4 per cent are Kirghiz (Turkic origin), 21.5 per cent are Russian and 12.9 per cent Uzbek, with smaller numbers of Ukrainians, Germans, Tatars and Kazakhs. The majority of the population is concentrated in plains lying at the foot of the mountains. Islam is the main religion.

Kirghiz is a Turkic language which was given an alphabet in the 1930s and became the official language after independence. Russian is an equal official language in the fields of science, industry and the health service. Kirghiz is most widely spoken (52.4 per cent), then Russian (21.5 per cent) and Uzbek (12.9 per cent).

CAPITAL – Bishkek. Population 616,000 (1989 census).
CURRENCY – Som (introduced on 10 May 1993 at rate of 1:200 against the Rouble).
FLAG – Red with a rayed sun containing a representation of a yurt, all in gold.
NATIONAL DAY – 31 August (Independence Day).

## GOVERNMENT

The Kirghiz people were first mentioned in Chinese chronicles in the second millenium BC. They are a merger of two ethnic groups, a Turkic-speaking people driven into the area by the Mongols from the River Yenisei area of Central Asia, and indigenous peoples who spoke a similar language. After a long period under Mongol, Chinese and Persian rule, the Kirghiz became part of the Russian Empire in the 1860s and 1870s. Kyrgyzstan became part of the Soviet Union in 1920 and underwent some industrialization.

Kyrgyzstan declared independence from the Soviet Union just after the failed Moscow coup on 31 August 1991. A new constitution was adopted on 5 May 1993 by the Uluk Kenesh (parliament) which requires the country's adherence to moral and international principles of law and human rights and to the values of Islam. President Akaev transferred the role of head of government from himself to the Prime Minister. Agreement was also reached on the terms of office of the President and Uluk Kenesh, which are to expire in 1995.

Ethnic tensions between the rural nomadic Kirghiz, the urban Russians and the wealthy Uzbeks who own many businesses and form the majority in the second largest town of Osh, are never far from the surface. Fighting over land between ethnic Kirghiz and Uzbeks in Osh in 1991 left over 500 dead. By presidential decree the sphere of official usage of the Russian language has been expanded to encourage Russians to remain, and a treaty on dual citizenship has been signed with Russia. The government is also committed to the fair representation of ethnic Russians in the civil service.

President Akaev has had difficulty in introducing economic reforms because of obstruction by the bureaucracy, and the Uluk Kenesh continues to clash with the President over the free market reforms enshrined in the constitution. The President won a resounding victory in a referendum on his plans for greater free market reforms held on 31 January 1994, and to help him democratic groups have formed the Republican Party to contest the strength of Communists in the Uluk Kenesh.

HEAD OF STATE
*President,* Askar Akaev, *elected* 12 October 1991

GOVERNMENT *as at August 1994*
*Prime Minister,* Apas Jumagulov
*First Deputy Prime Minister,* Almanat Mutabrimov
*Deputy Prime Ministers,* Osmanakul Ibraimov; Dgungalbek Amanbaev; Essengul Omuraliev; Andrey Iordan; Yan Fisher
*Interior,* Abdybek Sutalinov
*Foreign Affairs,* Rosa Otunbayeva
*Communications,* Emil Bektenov
*Economics and Finance,* Kamchibek Shakirov
*Justice,* Mukar Cholponbaev
*Agriculture,* Galal Asanov
*Education,* Askar Kakeev
*Defence,* Myrsykan Subanov
*Transport,* Sykdykbek Ablesov
*Culture,* Cholponbek Basarbaev
*Health,* Naken Kasiyev
*Labour and Social Affairs,* Zafar Hakimov
*Water Conservancy and Land Improvement,* Meirazhdin Zulpuyev
*Chairman of the Uluk Kenesh,* Medetkan Shereimkulov

BRITISH AMBASSADOR, His Excellency Noel Jones; resident at Alma-Ata.

ECONOMY

The government introduced Kyrgyzstan's own currency in May 1993 to break the link with the depreciating rouble, the cause of high inflation in 1992 and early 1993. The IMF provided a US$62 million credit to support the currency reform and a loan of US$26 million to support the pace of privatization. By the end of 1993 the government planned to have privatized 35 per cent of state-owned enterprises. The President and government have also made the Central Bank independent of government and parliamentary control. However, the country needs direct foreign investment desperately and has had most of its trading links with other Central Asian republics reduced because of their refusal to accept payments in Soms, although this has been ameliorated by the signing of an economic union agreement with Kazakhstan and Uzbekistan in February 1994. Subsidized goods supplies from Russia have also been reduced.

Agriculture is the major sector of the economy with sugar beet, cotton and sheep being the main products. Industry is concentrated in the food-processing, textiles, timber and mining fields. Hydro-electric power is abundant and Kyrgyzstan has reserves of gold, coal, mercury and uranium, although only gold has so far been exploited and is the country's largest export.

| Trade with UK | 1993 |
|---|---|
| Imports from UK | £7,629,000 |
| Exports to UK | 331,000 |

CULTURE

Until the 1930s the Kirghiz language had an oral tradition of literature which included the epic poem *Manas,* which tells the history of the Kirghiz people. Internationally, one of the best-known writers of the former Soviet Union is the Kirghiz writer Chingiz Aitmatov (1928–).

# LAOS
*Satharanarath Pasathipatai Pasason Lao*

Laos is in the northern part of Indo-China, with China and Vietnam on the north and east, Myanmar (Burma) and Thailand on the west, and Cambodia to the south. The area of the country is 91,429 sq. miles (231,800 sq. km), with a population (UN estimate 1991) of 4,262,000.

CAPITAL – Vientiane, population (estimated 1984) 120,000.
CURRENCY – Kip (K) of 100 at.
FLAG – Blue background with a central white circle, framed by two horizontal red stripes.
NATIONAL DAY – 2 December.

GOVERNMENT

The kingdom of Lane Xang, the Land of a Million Elephants, was founded in the 14th century but broke up at the beginning of the 15th century into the separate kingdoms of Luang Prabang and Vientiane and the Principality of Champassac, which together came under French protection in 1893. In 1945 the Japanese executed a coup and suppressed the French administration. In 1947 Laos became a constitutional monarchy under King Sisvang Vong, and an independent sovereign state in 1953. The next 22 years in Laos were marked by power struggles and civil war, eventually won by the North Vietnamese-backed Pathet Lao, a Communist-dominated organization.

The Lao People's Democratic Republic was proclaimed in December 1975 following victory by the Pathet Lao and the abdication of the King. A President and Council of Ministers were installed, and a 45-member Supreme People's Council was appointed to draft a constitution, which was approved in 1991. The Lao People's Revolutionary Party (LPRP) is the sole legal political organization. A general election to the 85-member National Assembly established by the 1991 constitution was held on 20 December 1992; all the candidates were approved by the LPRP. The President, Prime Minister and Council of Ministers were confirmed in their posts by the National Assembly on 22 February 1993.

HEAD OF STATE
*President,* Nouhak Phonmsavan, *elected by Supreme People's Assembly* 25 November 1992

COUNCIL OF MINISTERS *as at August 1994*
*Prime Minister,* Gen. Khamtai Siphandone
*Deputy PM and President of State Committee for Planning and Co-operation,* Khamphoui Keoboualapha
*Deputy Prime Minister,* Phoun Sipaseut
*National Defence and Supreme Commander of the Lao People's Army,* Lt.-Gen. Choummali Sayasone
*Minister, and Head of the Office of the Council of Ministers,* Phao Bounnaphon

*Foreign Affairs*, Somsavat Lengsavat
*Interior*, Asang Laoli
*Justice*, Khamouane Boupha
*Health*, Vannareth Rasapho
*Agriculture and Forestry*, Sisavat Keobounphan
*Industry*, Soulivong Dalavong
*Communications, Transport, Posts and Construction*,
  Bouathong
*Finance*, Khamsay Souphanouvang
*Education*, Phimmasone
*Commerce*, Sompadith Volasane
*Information and Culture*, Osakan Thammatheva
*Governor of the National Bank*, Boutsabong Souvannavong
*Labour and Social Welfare*, Thongloun Sisoulith
*Head of the President's Office*, Thongdam Chanthapon
*President of the Supreme People's Assembly*, Samane Vignaket

EMBASSY OF THE LAO PEOPLE'S DEMOCRATIC
REPUBLIC
74 Avenue Raymond-Poincaré 75116 Paris
Tel: Paris 45530298

*Ambassador Extraordinary and Plenipotentiary*, His
  Excellency Phoune Khammounheuang, apptd 1993

BRITISH AMBASSADOR, His Excellency Christian Adams,
CMG, resident at Bangkok, Thailand

## ECONOMY

A 'new economic management' programme was introduced
in 1986 which began the liberalization of the Laotian
economy, with greater autonomy for state enterprises, the
relaxation of price controls and the encouragement of private
business and investors. These reforms have produced a
market-orientated economic system which has led to significant economic growth of 5 per cent annually and a decline in
inflation from 68 per cent in 1989 to 12 per cent in 1993. The
economy is dominated by the agricultural sector, which
contributed 59 per cent of real GDP in 1992, when 1.5
million tons of paddy rice was produced. Although Laos has
a major balance of payments problem, exports have recently
been increasing.

Although Laos is one of the poorest states in the world,
there is potential for increased hydro-electric power exports
to Thailand and there are unexploited deposits of iron ore,
gold, bauxite and lignite. Foreign capital investment in
necessary infrastructure began with the 1994 opening of the
Friendship Bridge over the Mekong river border with
Thailand which links road routes from Singapore to China.
Hydro-electric power is the main export, followed by wood.

| *Trade with UK* | 1992 | 1993 |
|---|---|---|
| Imports from UK | £656,000 | £1,486,000 |
| Exports to UK | 201,000 | 87,000 |

## LATVIA
*The Republic of Latvia*

The republic of Latvia is situated in northern Europe on the
eastern coast of the Baltic sea. To the north lies Estonia, to
the south Lithuania and Belarus, and to the east the Russian
Federation. The area is 63,935 sq. km (24,695 sq. miles).
Latvia is low-lying with occasional chains of hills. Forests
cover more than 20 per cent of the total territory. The
climate is continental and temperate, influenced by maritime
winds.

POPULATION – The population is 2,606,000 (1993) of which
53 per cent is Latvian, 33.8 per cent Russian, 4.5 cent

Belarussian, small Ukrainian and Polish minorities. The
main religions are Lutheran, Roman Catholic and Russian
Orthodox.

The majority (53 per cent) have Latvian as their first
language and 33.8 per cent Russian. Education is now in
Latvian and Russian. Public sector employees must pass
language tests in Latvian to a level commensurate with the
nature of their employment. The right of minorities to use
their mother tongue has been acknowledged.

CAPITAL – Riga (population (1993) 874,500). Other major
cities are: Daugavpils (124,900); Liepaja (108,300);
Jelgava (72,300); Jurmala (60,100); and Ventspils
(48,800).

CURRENCY – Lats of 100 santimes.

FLAG – Crimson, with a white horizontal stripe across the
centre.

NATIONAL ANTHEM – Dievs, sveti Latviju (God bless
Latvia).

NATIONAL DAY – 18 November (Independence Day 1918).

## HISTORY

Latvia came under the control of the German Teutonic
Knights at the end of the 13th century. During the next few
centuries the country endured sporadic invasions by the
Swedes, Poles and Russians. By 1795 Latvia was entirely
under Russian control. On 18 November 1918 Latvia declared
its independence and this was confirmed by the Versailles
Treaty in 1919. Several years of fighting with the new Soviet
Union ensued until a peace treaty was signed under which
the Soviet Union renounced all claims to Latvian territory.

The Soviet Union annexed Latvia in 1940 under the terms
of the Molotov-Ribbentrop pact with Germany. Latvia was
invaded and occupied when Germany invaded the Soviet
Union during the Second World War. In 1944 the Soviet
Union recaptured the country from Germany and confirmed
its annexation, though this was never accepted as legal by
most states.

In October 1988 the Popular Front of Latvia was formed
to campaign for greater sovereignty and democracy for
Latvia. The Popular Front convincingly won elections to the
Latvian Supreme Council in 1989, and on 4 May 1990 the
Supreme Council declared the independent republic of Latvia
to be, *de jure*, still in existence. Agitation in Latvia against
Soviet rule led in 1990 and early 1991 to clashes between
independence supporters and Latvian Communists and the
Soviet military. Violence reached a peak in January 1991 with
deaths caused by Soviet Interior Ministry troops and attacks
on Baltic border posts. A national referendum was held in
March 1991 in which 73 per cent of voters declared in favour
of independence, and this was declared on 21 August 1991.
The State Council of the Soviet Union recognized the
independence of Latvia on 10 September 1991.

## GOVERNMENT

Democratic government and a unicameral parliament were
restored after multiparty elections in June 1993. The 1922
constitution was restored in July 1993 and the laws of the
pre-war republic are gradually being restored. Executive
authority is vested in a Prime Minister and Cabinet of
Ministers. Legislative power is exercised by the unicameral
parliament (Saeíma) which consists of 100 deputies elected
for three-year terms by proportional representation with a 4
per cent threshold for parliamentary representation. The
deputies elect a President of State, who in turn appoints
the Prime Minister. The Prime Minister appoints, and the
Saeíma approves, the Cabinet of Ministers. The electorate
has, however, been restricted to those whose forefathers lived

in Latvia before 1940, which means that two-thirds of the ethnic Russian population has been unable to vote and this has caused tension with the Russian government.

After the June 1993 general election eight political parties are represented in the Saeíma. No party had a clear majority, but a coalition of the 'Latvian Way' and 'Peasants' Union' held 48 seats and formed a government. This government, led by Valdis Birkavs, resigned in July 1994 after the Peasants' Union withdrew its support and at the time of going to press a new government had still to be formed.

HEAD OF STATE

*President,* Guntis Ulmanis, *elected* 7 July 1993

EMBASSY OF THE REPUBLIC OF LATVIA
72 Queensborough Terrace, London W2 3SP
Tel 0171-727 1698

*Ambassador Extraordinary and Plenipotentiary,*
His Excellency Jānis Lūsis, apptd 1992

BRITISH EMBASSY
3rd Floor, Elizabetes Iela 2, LV-1340 Riga 226010
Tel: Riga 320 737

*Ambassador Extraordinary and Plenipotentiary,* His
Excellency Richard Ralph, CVO, apptd 1993

BRITISH COUNCIL DIRECTOR, Susan Maingay (*Cultural Attaché*)

DEFENCE

Since independence Latvia has sought to form its own armed forces. Total active armed forces number some 5,000 personnel with conscripts serving for 18 months. Ground forces are formed into eight border guard, one infantry and one reconnaissance battalions. The army reserve of the Home Guard numbers 16,000 personnel. The navy is 300 strong, with five patrol craft. The air force is 60 strong, with a few transport aircraft and helicopters.

In May 1994 Russia and Latvia reached agreement on the withdrawal on all remaining Russian forces in Latvia by 31 August 1994 except for those stationed at the anti-ballistic missile early-warning radar at Skrunda which will continue to operate for four years.

ECONOMY

Since independence Latvia has pressed ahead with transition from a command economy to a market economy system. It has also attempted to achieve economic independence from the rest of the former Soviet Union. The government has initiated a privatization process which has made many industrial facilities available for purchase both by Latvian and foreign private investors. By the end of 1993 20 per cent of economic production and 40 per cent of agricultural production had been privatized.

Latvia is an agricultural exporter, specializing in cattle and pig breeding, dairy farming and crops, including sugar beet, flax, cereals and potatoes. Natural resources include limestone, gypsum, peat and timber.

Industry was organized to contribute to the centralized Soviet command economy and is specialized in certain areas. These include the production of electric and diesel trains, telephones, telephone exchange equipment, food processing, agricultural machinery, and timber and paper products.

Tourism is being developed, capitalizing on its beach resorts, nature reserves and parks. Latvia is also geographically well-placed for the development of transport services.

TRADE

The Russian Federation remains the most important trading partner for Latvia. In 1993 46 per cent of exports went to the CIS, 24 per cent to the European Union, 9 per cent to EFTA states, 6 per cent to Lithuania and Estonia; 38 per cent of imports came from the CIS, 17 per cent from the EU, 13 per cent from Lithuania and Estonia, 11 per cent from EFTA states. The main imports are oil and energy, and the main exports are artificial fibres, meat, dairy products and rolled ferrous metals.

| *Trade with UK* | 1992 | 1993 |
|---|---|---|
| Imports from UK | £7,782,000 | £15,823,000 |
| Exports to UK | 25,859,000 | 69,254,000 |

COMMUNICATIONS

Latvia has a reasonably well-developed railway (2,397 km) and road (18,834 km) system, along which a significant proportion of exports from CIS republics are transported to western Europe. Latvia is also being developed as a transportation route from Scandinavia to central and southern Europe. Several warm-water ports exist, of which two, Riga and Ventspils, are developed for commercial transport. The national airline, Latvijas Aviolinijas, operates regular flights to Russia, Scandinavia and London.

CULTURE

The Latvian language belongs to the Baltic branch of the Indo-European languages, and as such is distinct from Russian. The Latin alphabet is used. Independent Latvian literature appeared in the 19th century and played a role in the fight for independent in 1918.

There are 15 higher education institutions, of which four are universities.

---

LEBANON
*Al-Jumhouriya al-Lubnaniya*

---

Lebanon forms a strip about 120 miles long and between 30 and 35 miles wide along the Mediterranean littoral. It extends from the Israel frontier in the south to the Nahr al Kebir (15 miles north of Tripoli) in the north; its eastern boundary runs down the Anti-Lebanon range and then down the great central depression, the *Beqa'a,* from which flow the rivers Orontes and Litani. It is divided into five districts, North Lebanon, Mount Lebanon, Beirut, South Lebanon and Beqaa. The seaward slopes of the mountains have a Mediterranean climate and vegetation. The inland range of Anti-Lebanon has the characteristics of steppe country. The area is 4,015 sq. miles (10,400 sq. km).

POPULATION – The population (UN estimate 1991) was 2,745,000. It is a mixture of Christians, Muslims and Druses. Arabic is the official language, and French and English are also widely used.

CAPITAL – Ψ Beirut (population 702,000). Other towns are Ψ Tripoli (175,000), Zahlé (46,800), Ψ Sidon (24,740), Ψ Tyre (14,000).

CURRENCY – Lebanese pound (L£) of 100 piastres.

FLAG – Horizontal bands of red, white and red with a green cedar of Lebanon in the centre of the white band.

NATIONAL ANTHEM – Kulluna Lil Watan Lil'ula Lil'alam (We all belong to the homeland).

NATIONAL DAY – 22 November.

GOVERNMENT

Lebanon became an independent state in September 1920, administered under French mandate until 22 November 1943. Powers were transferred to the Lebanese government from January 1944 and French troops were withdrawn in 1946.

In April 1975, fighting broke out in Beirut between members of the predominantly Christian Phalangist Party and predominantly Muslim militias, later supported by Palestinian guerrillas based in Lebanon. In the autumn of 1976 the Arab Deterrent Forces, composed mainly of Syrian troops, imposed a ceasefire but fighting began again subsequently and continued until the end of the civil war in 1990. In March 1978 Israeli forces invaded but withdrew some months later, handing over their positions, except for a belt in the south, to the UN Interim Force in Lebanon (UNIFIL). In the summer of 1982 Israeli forces again invaded the country, penetrating as far as Beirut. Following negotiations, Palestinian officials and fighters left Beirut for various Arab countries. Although the bulk of Israeli troops withdrew from southern Lebanon in 1985, a buffer zone controlled by the Israeli-backed South Lebanon Army (SLA), a Christian militia was established along the Israeli-Lebanon border. Syrian forces are deployed in west Beirut and in the north and the east of the country.

The Taif Accord 'for national conciliation', drawn up by an Arab League-appointed committee, gained the approval of a majority of Lebanese MPs in October 1989, but was rejected by Gen. Aoun, who insisted on an immediate Syrian troop withdrawal. Following an outbreak of fighting between Gen. Aoun and the dominant Christian militia, the Lebanese government acted with the backing of Syrian troops to oust Gen. Aoun in October 1990. A new government, which included the main militia leaders, was formed in December 1990. Since then the government has moved to clear the militias from the Greater Beirut area and has restored its authority throughout the former Christian enclave. The Lebanese Army moved into surrounding areas during 1991–2, extending the control of the government to virtually all areas not under Syrian (Beqa'a valley) and Israeli (South Lebanon Security Zone) control and disarming all the militias apart from Hezbollah and the SLA. Since July 1992 the Army has been enforcing the government's policy of retaking all public buildings from the militias. In August 1993 the Lebanese Army began deploying in southern villages alongside UNIFIL forces but has not disarmed Hezbollah forces, who are financed, armed and trained by Syria and Iran to continue fighting against Israel and the SLA. This fighting has continued throughout 1993–4.

The first parliamentary elections since 1972 were held between August and October 1992. The 128-seat unicameral parliament was directly elected by universal suffrage and divided equally between Christians and Muslims. The polls were widely boycotted in Christian areas because of the continuing presence of Syrian troops, in breach of the Taif Accord. A government was formed under Prime Minister Rafiq Hariri in October 1992 which has focused on the economy and reconstruction.

In October 1991 Lebanon began to participate in the bilateral sessions of the Middle East peace talks, but so far has, with Syria, boycotted the multilateral rounds.

HEAD OF STATE

*President of the Republic of Lebanon*, Elias Hrawi, *took office* 25 November 1989

CABINET *as at August 1994*

*Prime Minister and Finance*, Rafiq Hariri
*Deputy PM*, Michel Murr
*Foreign and Expatriate Affairs*, Fares Bouez
*Justice*, Bahij Tabbara
*Health and Social Affairs*, Marwan Hamadeh
*Defence*, Mohsen Dalloul

*Labour*, Abdullah al-Amin
*Posts and Telecommunications*, Muhammad Ghaziri
*Education and Fine Arts*, Mikhail Daher
*State*, Jean Obeid; Fuad Sinyurah
*Economy and Trade*, Hagop Demerdjian
*Information*, Michel Samaha
*Agriculture*, Abdel Kortas
*Public Works and Transport*, Muhammad Mortada
*Industry and Oil,* Assaad Rizk
*Municipal and Rural Affairs*, Suleiman Franjieh
*Refugee Affairs*, Walid Jumblatt
*Interior*, Beshara Merhej
*Housing and Co-operatives*, Mohammad Abu Hamdan
*Tourism*, Nicolas Fattoush
*Water and Electricity Resources*, Elie Hobeika
*National Assembly Speaker*, Nabih Berri

LEBANESE EMBASSY
21 Kensington Palace Gardens, London W8 4QM
Tel 0171–229 7265/6

*Ambassador Extraordinary and Plenipotentiary*, His Excellency Mahmoud Hammoud, apptd 1990
*Consular Section*, 15 Palace Gardens Mews, London W8.
Tel: 0171–727 6696

BRITISH EMBASSY
Shamma Building, Raouché, Ras Beirut, Beirut
Tel: Beirut 812849

*Ambassador Extraordinary and Plenipotentiary*, Her Excellency Maeve Fort, CMG, apptd 1992

ECONOMY

A ten-year plan has been initiated to repair war damage and to restore Lebanon's position as a regional financial services and light industrial centre. The 1993–2002 reconstruction plan is estimated to cost US$12,900m in total, of which US$7,600m is to come from foreign loans and grants and US$5,300m from budget surpluses. It is to concentrate on rebuilding housing, transport, utilities, services, education and health services, and aiding industry and agriculture.

Economic recovery has, however, been slower than hoped and the foreign debt is projected to rise to 84 per cent of GDP in 1995 before falling to 39 per cent in 2002. A plan to reconstruct the commercial centre of Beirut has been started, with the issue in January 1994 of US$650 million shares in the US$1,800 million Solidère company which will reconstruct the 400-acre site. The government has also obtained US$1,600 million in loans and grants for its national reconstruction programme, mainly from Arab states and international agencies.

Fruits are the most important products and include citrus fruit, apples, grapes, bananas and olives. There is some light industry, mostly for the production of consumer goods, but most factories are still in need of reconstruction because of the civil war.

TRADE

Principal imports are gold and precious metals, machinery and electrical equipment, textiles and yarns, vegetable products, iron and steel goods, and motor vehicles. There had been a gradual decline in the overall amount of imports, as a result of continued instability.

Principal exports include gold and precious metals, fruits and vegetables, textiles, building materials, furniture, plastic goods, foodstuffs, tobacco and wine.

At one time there was a considerable transit trade through Beirut into the Arab hinterland. Lebanon is the terminal for two oil pipe lines, one formerly belonging to the Iraq

Petroleum Company, debouching at Tripoli, the other belonging to the Trans Arabian Pipeline Company, at Sidon. These lines have not functioned for some years.

| Trade with UK | 1992 | 1993 |
|---|---|---|
| Imports from UK | £91,868,000 | £136,372,000 |
| Exports to UK | 10,405,000 | 11,436,000 |

## COMMUNICATIONS

The railways are not functioning as a result of the civil war. There is an international airport at Beirut, served by the national carrier MEA, Air France, Cyprus Air and other Arab and European airlines. An internal service operates from Beirut to Tripoli.

## ARCHAEOLOGY

Lebanon has some important historical remains, notably Baalbek (Heliopolis) which contains the ruins of first- to third-century Roman temples and Jbeil (Byblos), one of the oldest continuously inhabited towns in the world, and ancient Tyre.

## EDUCATION

There are six universities in Beirut, the American and the French universities established in the last century, and the Lebanese National University, the Beirut University College, the Kaslik Saint Esprit University and the Arab University, with the University of Balamond situated near Tripoli. There are several institutions for vocational training, and there is a good provision throughout the country of primary and secondary schools, among which are a great number of private schools. Education at all levels has been severely disrupted by the civil war.

## LESOTHO
*'Muso oa Lesotho*

Lesotho is a landlocked mountainous state entirely surrounded by the Republic of South Africa. Of the total area of 11,720 sq. miles (30,355 sq. km), about one-third, in the west and south, is classed as lowlands, being between 5,000 and 6,000 ft. above sea level. The remaining two-thirds are classed as foothills and highlands, rising to 11,425 ft. The population (UN estimate 1991) is 1,826,000.

CAPITAL – Maseru, population (1986 census) 288,951.
CURRENCY – Loti (M) of 100 lisente.
FLAG – Diagonally white over blue over green with the white of double width, and an assegai and knobkerrie on a Basotho shield in brown in the upper hoist.
NATIONAL ANTHEM – Pina ea Sechaba.
NATIONAL DAY – 4 October (Independence Day).

## GOVERNMENT

Lesotho (formerly Basutoland) became a constitutional monarchy within the Commonwealth on 4 October 1966. The independence constitution was suspended in January 1970 and the country was governed by a Council of Ministers headed by Leabua Jonathan until the establishment of a nominated National Assembly in April 1974.

Jonathan's government was overthrown in January 1986, and executive and legislative powers were conferred upon the King, to be advised by the Military Council and Council of Ministers led by Maj.-Gen. Justin Lekhanya. In March

1990 King Moshoeshoe II's powers were formally revoked and vested in the Chairman of the Council of Ministers. In November 1990 the King was deposed and replaced by his son, who assumed the title of Letsie III. Maj.-Gen. Lekhanya was overthrown in a coup in April 1991 led by Col. Elias Ramaema. Elections promised for 1992 were eventually held on 27 March 1993 and the Basotho Congress Party (BCP) won all 65 seats in the new National Assembly. The BCP government led by Ntsu Mokhele was sworn in on 2 April 1993, at which time King Letsie III swore allegiance to a new multiparty democratic constitution and the Military Council was dissolved.

Significant sections of the military remained opposed to the BCP government and launched two unsuccessful coup attempts in January and February 1994 which were defeated after heavy fighting in which the Deputy Prime Minister was killed. On 17 August 1994 King Letsie III and sections of the military launched a coup attempt and announced the dismissal of the government and the dissolution of parliament until new elections. The government, however, refused to leave office and at the time of going to press the constitutional crisis continued.

The country is divided into ten administrative districts. In each district there is a district secretary who co-ordinates all government activity in the area, working in co-operation with hereditary chiefs.

HEAD OF STATE
*King*, HM King Letsie III, *acceded* November 1990

COUNCIL OF MINISTERS *as at August 1994*
*Prime Minister, Minister of Defence and Public Service*, Dr Ntsu Mokhele
*Deputy Prime Minister, Finance, Economic Planning*, vacant
*Foreign Affairs*, Molapo Qhobela
*Trade, Industry, Tourism, Sports and Culture*, Shakhane Robong Mokhehle
*Agriculture, Co-operatives and Marketing*, Ntsukunyane Mphanya
*Home Affairs*, Lesao Lehohla
*Education and Training, Manpower Development and Youth Affairs*, Pakalitha Mosisili
*Health and Social Welfare*, Dr Khauhelo Ralitapole
*Natural Resources*, Tseliso Makhakhe
*Works, Transport, Post and Telecommunications*, David Mochochoko
*Information and Broadcasting*, Mpho Malie
*Justice, Human Rights, Law and Constitutional Affairs*, Kelebone Maope
*Employment and Labour*, Not'si Molopo

HIGH COMMISSION FOR THE KINGDOM OF LESOTHO
7 Chesham Place, London SW1X 8HN
Tel 0171-235 5686

*High Commissioner*, His Excellency M. K. Tsekoa, apptd 1989

BRITISH HIGH COMMISSION
PO Box 521, Maseru 100
Tel: Maseru 313961

*High Commissioner*, His Excellency James Roy Cowling, apptd 1992

BRITISH COUNCIL REPRESENTATIVE, P. Thompson, Hobson's Square, PO Box 429, Maseru 100

## JUDICIARY

The Lesotho courts of law consist of the court of appeal, the High Court, magistrates' courts, judicial commissioners' court, central and local courts. Magistrates' and higher courts administer the laws of Lesotho. They also adjudicate appeals from the judicial commissioners' and subordinate courts. *Chief Justice*, Hon. J. L. Kheola

## ECONOMY

The economy of Lesotho is based on agriculture and animal husbandry, and the adverse balance of trade (mainly consumer and capital goods) is offset by the earnings of the large numbers of the population who work in South Africa. Apart from some diamonds, Lesotho has few natural resources and only small-scale industrial development. The Lesotho National Development Corporation was set up to promote the development of industry, mining, trade and tourism. Work has commenced on the Highlands Water Scheme designed to provide water for the Vaal industrial zone in South Africa. Drilling is being carried out for oil. A National Park has been established at Sehlabathebe in the Maluti mountains. A number of light manufacturing and processing industries have recently been established.

### FINANCE

The main sources of revenue are customs and excise duty. Estimates of expenditure and revenue (1986) are recurrent revenue M241.2 million; recurrent expenditure M265.3 million; capital revenue M144 million; capital expenditure M198 million.

| Trade with UK | 1992 | 1993 |
|---|---|---|
| Imports from UK | £2,725,000 | £908,000 |
| Exports to UK | 4,159,000 | 2,343,000 |

## EDUCATION

Most schools are mission-controlled, the government providing grants for salaries and buildings. There are over 1,000 primary and over 100 secondary schools; few areas lack a school and there is a high literacy rate of about 70 per cent. Increasing emphasis is being laid on agricultural and vocational education. The National University of Lesotho at Roma, whose history dates back to 1945, was established as a university in 1975.

## COMMUNICATIONS

A tarred road links Maseru to several of the main lowland towns, and this is being extended in the south of the country. The mountainous areas are linked by tarred, gravelled and earth roads and tracks. Roads link border towns in South Africa with the main towns in Lesotho. Maseru is also connected by rail with the main Bloemfontein–Natal line of the South African Railways. Scheduled international air services are operated daily between Maseru and Johannesburg and other scheduled international flights are to Gabarone, Harare, Manzini and Maputo. There are around 30 airstrips. Internal scheduled services are operated by Lesotho Airways Corporation.

The telephone network is fully automated in all urban centres. Radio telephone communication is used extensively in the remote rural areas.

## LIBERIA
*Republic of Liberia*

An independent republic of West Africa, occupying that part of the coast between Sierra Leone and the Côte d'Ivoire which is between the rivers Mano in the north-west and Cavalla in the south-east, a distance of about 350 miles, with an area of about 43,000 sq. miles (111,369 sq. km), and extending to the interior to latitude 8° 50', a distance of 150 miles from the seaboard. It was founded by the American Colonization Society in 1822 as a colony for freed American slaves, and has been recognized since 1847 as an independent state. The population at the census of 1974 was 1,481,524; a 1991 UN estimate put the figure at 2,705,000. The official language is English. Over 16 ethnic languages are spoken.

CAPITAL – Ψ Monrovia, population estimate (1984) 425,000. Other ports are Ψ Buchanan, Ψ Greenville (Sinoe) and Ψ Harper (Cape Palmas).
CURRENCY – Liberian dollar (L$) of 100 cents.
FLAG – Alternate horizontal stripes (five white, six red), with five-pointed white star on blue field in upper corner next to flagstaff.
NATIONAL ANTHEM – All Hail, Liberia, Hail.
NATIONAL DAY – 26 July.

## GOVERNMENT

William V. S. Tubman, President since 1944, died in 1971 and was succeeded by Dr Tolbert. The constitution was suspended following a military coup on 12 April 1980 during which Tolbert was killed. M/Sgt. Samuel Doe assumed power as chairman of a military council. A new constitution was endorsed by a referendum in July 1984. Doe and his party, the National Democratic Party of Liberia (NDPL) won the elections held in October 1985, amid allegations of electoral fraud, and a civilian government was formally installed in January 1986.

### CIVIL WAR

A rebel incursion launched in December 1989 by the National Patriotic Front of Liberia (NPFL) led by Charles Taylor developed into a full-scale civil war in 1990. A five-nation ECOWAS peacekeeping force (known as ECOMOG) landed in Monrovia in an effort to end the conflict but in September 1990 President Doe was killed, having refused to step down. The Interim Government of National Unity (IGNU) was formed in August 1990 in The Gambia and arrived in Monrovia in November. A ceasefire agreement was signed in Bamako, Mali in November 1990 but proved ineffective and the political impasse continued. A further agreement to establish a ceasefire and confine troops to barracks under ECOMOG supervision broke down in October 1992 when the NPFL attempted to seize Monrovia. In response ECOMOG was enlarged to 10,000 personnel (and in February 1993 to 15,000) and assumed a more offensive role, launching a full-scale offensive against NPFL forces and driving them out of Monrovia's suburbs. By March 1993 the NPFL had been driven back into eastern parts of Liberia and peace negotiations between the warring factions had begun. Under UN-sponsored negotiations a peace agreement was signed in Cotonou, Benin on 25 July 1993 which brought about a ceasefire on 1 August. Interim President Amos Sawyer was due to be replaced within one month by a five-member Council of State to govern the country during a seven-month transitional period, together with a 35-member transitional legislature including members from all three factions. The Council of State and the transitional legislature did not actually take power until March 1993 owing to problems in deploying peacekeeping forces; multiparty elections to a new legislature are due in late 1994.

### COUNCIL OF STATE *as at August 1994*

*Chairman*, David Kpormakor (IGNU)
*First Deputy Chairman*, Thomas Ziah (ULIMO)

*Second Deputy Chairman*, Issac Moussa (NPFL)
*Members*, Phillip Banks (IGNU); Mohammed Sheriff (ULIMO)
IGNU Interim Government of National Unity; ULIMO United Liberation Movement for Democracy; NPFL National Patriotic Front of Liberia.

EMBASSY OF THE REPUBLIC OF LIBERIA
2 Pembridge Place, London w2 4xB
Tel 0171-221 1036

*Minister Plenipotentiary*, George Bardell Cooper (*Maritime Affairs*)
*Chargé d'Affaires*, Ishmael Grant

BRITISH EMBASSY
The British Embassy in Monrovia was closed in March 1991.

## ECONOMY

In December 1990 the UN launched an appeal for $13.8m in emergency aid to finance the enormous task of reconstruction. Of the country's 2.5 million population, about 750,000 are refugees in neighbouring countries and it is estimated that up to 150,000 have died. Liberia is receiving relief aid from a number of countries including the United Kingdom, the EU and various international agencies.

TRADE
Before the civil war began principal exports were iron ore, crude rubber, timber, uncut diamonds, palm kernels, cocoa and coffee, but the civil war has resulted in the suspension of most economic activity.

| Trade with UK | 1992 | 1993 |
|---|---|---|
| Imports from UK | £8,766,000 | £9,549,000 |
| Exports to UK | 4,654,000 | 56,000 |

## COMMUNICATIONS

The artificial harbour and free port of Monrovia was opened in 1948. There are nine ports of entry, including three river ports. Robertsfield International Airport is under NPFL control and not yet in use. Spriggs Payne airfield, on the outskirts of Monrovia, normally used for internal flights, is currently being used for flights to other West African countries.

---

# LIBYA
*Al-Jamahiriya Al-Arabiya*
*Al-Libiya Al-Shabiya Al-Ishtirakiya Al-Uthma*

---

Libya, on the Mediterranean coast of Africa, is bounded on the east by Egypt and Sudan, on the south by Chad and Niger, and on the west by Algeria and Tunisia. It consists of the three former provinces of Tripolitania, Cyrenaica and the Fezzan, with an area of 679,362 sq. miles (1,759,540 sq. km) and a population (UN estimate 1992) of 4,509,000. The people of Libya are principally Arab with some Berbers in the west and some Tuareg tribesmen in the Fezzan. Islam is the official religion of Libya, but other religions are tolerated. The official language is Arabic.

Vast sand and rock deserts, almost completely barren, occupy the greater part of Libya. The southern part of the country lies within the Sahara Desert. There are few rivers and as rainfall is irregular outside parts of Cyrenaica and Tripolitania, good harvests are rare.

The ancient ruins in Cyrenaica, at Cyrene, Ptolemais (Tolmeta) and Apollonia, are outstanding, as are those at Leptis Magna, 70 miles east, and at Sabratha, 40 miles west of Tripoli. An Italian expedition found in the south-west of the Fezzan a series of rock-paintings more than 5,000 years old.

CAPITAL – ΨTripoli, population estimate (1991) 1,000,000. The principal towns are: ΨBenghazi (500,000); ΨMisurata (200,000); Sirte (100,000).
CURRENCY – Libyan dinar (LD) of 1,000 dirhams.
FLAG – Libya uses a plain emerald green flag.
NATIONAL DAY – 1 September.

## GOVERNMENT

Libya was occupied by Italy in 1911–12 in the course of the Italo-Turkish War, and under the Treaty of Ouchy 1912 the sovereignty of the province was transferred by Turkey to Italy. In 1939 the four provinces of Libya (Tripoli, Misurata, Benghazi and Derna) were incorporated in the national territory of Italy as *Libia Italiana*. After the Second World War Tripolitania and Cyrenaica were placed provisionally under British and the Fezzan under French administration, and in conformity with a resolution of the UN General Assembly in November 1949, Libya became on 24 December 1951 the first independent state to be created by the United Nations. The monarchy was overthrown by a revolution in September 1969 and the country was declared a republic. It was ruled by the Revolutionary Command Council (RCC) under the leadership of Colonel Muammar Gadhafi.

In March 1977 a new form of direct democracy, the 'Jamahiriya' (state of the masses) was promulgated and the official name of the country was changed to Socialist People's Libyan Arab Jamahiriya. At local level authority is now vested in about 1,500 Basic and 14 Municipal People's Congresses which appoint Popular Committees to execute policy. Officials of these congresses and committees, together with representatives from unions and other organizations, form the General People's Congress, which normally meets for about a week each year. In addition, a number of extraordinary sessions are held throughout the year. This is the highest policy-making body in the country.

The General People's Congress appoints its own General Secretariat and the General People's Committee, whose members head the 13 government departments which execute policy at national level. The Secretary of the General People's Committee has functions similar to those of a Prime Minister.

Since a reorganization in March 1979 neither Col. Gadhafi nor his former RCC colleagues have held formal posts in the administration. Gadhafi continues to hold the ceremonial title 'Leader of the Revolution'.

*Leader of the Revolution and Supreme Commander of the Armed Forces*, Col. Muammar al-Gadhafi.

SECRETARIAT OF THE GENERAL PEOPLE'S CONGRESS *as at August 1994*

*Secretary*, Zanati Muhammad al-Zanati
*Assistant Secretary*, Abu Zayd Umar Durdah
*Secretary (Affairs of People's Congresses)*, Ali al-Sha'iri
*Secretary (Affairs of People's Committees)*, Mahmud al-Hitki
*Secretary (Trade Unions)*, Ali al-Shamikh
*Secretary (Women's Affairs)*, Salmah Rashid
*Secretary (Foreign Affairs)*, Sa'ad Mujbir

GENERAL PEOPLE'S COMMITTEE

*Secretary*, Abd al-Majid al-Qa'ud
*Foreign Liaison*, Omar al-Muntasir
*Unity*, Jum'a al-Mahdi al-Fazzani
*Justice and Public Security*, Mohammed Mahmud al-Hijazi

*Agrarian Reform and Land Reclamation*, Dr Isa Abd al-Kafi al-Sayd
*Information and Culture*, Mohammed Ahmad Ibrahim
*Marine Resources*, Miftah Muhammad Ka'aybah
*Industry*, Fathi bin Shatwan
*Energy*, Abdullah Salem al-Badri
*Planning and Finance*, Dr Muhammad Bayt al Mal
*Education and Scientific Research*, Ma'tug Muhammad Ma'tug
*Health and Social Security*, Dr Baghdadi Ali al-Mahmudi
*Utilities and Housing*, Mubarak Abdullah al-Shamikh
*Supervision and Follow-up*, Mahmud Badji
*Economy and Trade*, Tahir al-Jihimi
*Transport and Communications*, Izz al-Din al-Hinshiri

LIBYAN DIPLOMATIC MISSION IN LONDON

Since the break of diplomatic relations with Libya in April 1984, the Royal Embassy of Saudi Arabia has handled Libyan interests in Britain.

BRITISH EMBASSY

British interests are currently handled by the British Interests Section of the Italian Embassy, Sharia Uahran 1 (PO Box 4206), Tripoli.

DEFENCE

Libya has a total active armed forces of some 70,000, with selective conscription of two years. The army has a strength of 40,000, with 2,300 main battle tanks, 2,670 armoured infantry fighting vehicles and armoured personnel carriers, and some 1,070 artillery pieces. The navy has a strength of 8,000 personnel, with five submarines, three frigates, 39 patrol and coastal vessels, and 30 armed helicopters. The air force has some 22,000 personnel, with 409 combat aircraft and 45 armed helicopters. Paramilitary forces number 3,000 personnel, with some tanks and armoured personnel carriers.

Russia maintains 1,000 advisers in Libya and the air force has some Syrian pilots and North Korean instructors.

As part of the UN economic sanctions imposed since April 1992 a total arms embargo is in place against Libya.

ECONOMY

Economic sanctions were imposed on Libya in April 1992 under UN Security Council Resolution 748 following Libya's failure to hand over to the USA or Britain two suspects in the bombing of a Pan-Am flight over Lockerbie, Scotland, in 1988. The UN imposed additional sanctions in December 1993, including freezing assets abroad and restricting imports of spare parts and equipment for the oil and aviation sectors.

Agriculture is confined mainly to the coastal areas of Tripolitania and Cyrenaica, where barley, wheat, olives, almonds, citrus fruits and dates are produced, and to the areas of the oases, many of which are well supplied with springs supporting small fertile areas. Among the important oases are Jaghbub, Ghadames, Jofra, Sebha, Murzuq, Brak, Ghat, Jalo and the Kufra group in the south-east.

The main industry is oil and gas production. There are pipelines from Zelten to the terminal at Mersa Brega, from Dahra to Ras-es-Sider, from Amal to Ras Lanuf, and from the Intisar field to Zuetina. In 1994 average production of crude oil has been about 1.38 million barrels per day. A major petrochemical complex has been built at Ras Lanuf where a refinery and ethylene plant began operations in 1985. The construction of an iron and steel plant at Misurata has been completed. Economic constraints have delayed some projects, particularly since Libya decided in 1983 to go ahead with a major irrigation scheme, the 'Great Man-Made River'.

Libya has technical assistance agreements with a number of countries, and also employs large numbers of foreign labourers and experts.

TRADE

Exports from Libya are dominated by crude oil, but some wool, cattle, sheep and horses, olive oil, and hides and skins are also exported. Principal imports are foodstuffs, including sugar, tea and coffee, and most construction materials and consumer goods. After the revolution the private sector was virtually eliminated and Libya became a state trading country with imports controlled by state monopolies. In early 1988, however, reforms were implemented which have allowed a small private sector to be re-established.

| Trade with UK | 1992 | 1993 |
| --- | --- | --- |
| Imports from UK | £228,274,000 | £274,051,000 |
| Exports to UK | 162,900,000 | 156,542,000 |

COMMUNICATIONS

The coastal road running from the Tunisian frontier through Tripoli to Benghazi, Tobruk and the Egyptian border serves the main population centres. Main roads also link the provincial centres, and the oil-producing areas of the south with the coastal towns.

There are airports at Tripoli and Benghazi (Benina), Tobruk, Mersa Brega, Sebha, Ghadames and Kufra regularly used by commercial airlines, and military airfields near Tobruk, near Tripoli and at Al Watiya, south of Zuara. Since April 1992 a UN embargo on air links with Libya has been in force.

# LIECHTENSTEIN
*Fürstentum Liechtenstein*

Liechtenstein is a principality on the Upper Rhine, between Vorarlberg (Austria) and Switzerland, with an area of 61 sq. miles (158 sq. km), and a population in 1992 of 29,868. The language of the principality is German.

CAPITAL – Vaduz, population (1992) 4,995.
CURRENCY – Swiss franc of 100 rappen (or centimes).
FLAG – Equal horizontal bands of blue over red; gold crown on blue band near staff.
NATIONAL ANTHEM – Oben am Jungen Rhein (High on the Rhine).
NATIONAL DAY – 15 August.

GOVERNMENT

The Patriotic Union and Progressive Citizen's parties have governed the country in coalition since 1938. There is a threshold of 8 per cent for parties to gain representation in the Landtag. At the general election on 24 October 1993 the Progressive Citizens' Party won 11 seats, the Patriotic Union Party 13 seats and the Free List (Environmentalist) grouping, 1 seat.

HEAD OF STATE

*HRH The Prince of Liechtenstein*, Hans Adam II, *born* 14 February 1945; *succeeded* 13 November 1989; *married* 30 July 1967, Countess Marie Kinsky; and has *issue*: Prince Alois (*see* below); Prince Maximilian, *b.* 16 May 1969; Prince Constantin, *b.* 15 March 1972; Princess Tatjana, *b.* 10 April 1973
*Heir*, HRH Prince Alois, *b.* 11 June 1968, *m.* 1993 Duchess Sophie of Bavaria

MINISTRY *as at August 1994*
*Prime Minister*, Dr Mario Frick (*Head of Government 'Presidium', Finance, Justice*)
*Deputy PM*, Thomas Büchel (*Interior, Agriculture, Forestry and Environment, Education*).
*Government Councillors*, Cornelia Gassner-Matt (*Construction*), Andrea Willi (*Foreign Affairs, Culture, Youth and Sport*), Michael Ritter (*Economy, Family, Welfare, Health*)

DIPLOMATIC REPRESENTATION
Liechtenstein is represented in diplomatic and consular matters in the United Kingdom by the Swiss Embassy.

BRITISH CONSUL-GENERAL, T. Bryant, CMG, Dufourstrasse 56, 8008 Zürich.

## ECONOMY

The main industries are high and ultra-high vacuum engineering, semi-conductor industry, roller bearings, fastenings and securing systems, artificial teeth, heating and hot water equipment, synthetic fibres, woollen and homespun fabrics.

In May 1991 Liechtenstein became a member of the European Free Trade Association, and as such is a party to the European Economic Area (EEA) Agreement with the EU, which came into force on 1 January 1994. In December 1992 in separate referenda, Switzerland voted against EEA membership while Liechtenstein voted in favour. Liechtenstein has a customs union with Switzerland which will need to be renegotiated in light of the EEA votes.

| FINANCE | 1992 | 1993 |
|---|---|---|
| Revenue | F426,805,387 | F449,165,116 |
| Expenditure | 430,531,696 | 441,383,850 |

## LITHUANIA
*Lietuva*

Lithuania lies on the eastern coast of the Baltic Sea between 53° 54′ and 56° 27′ N., and 20° 56′ and 26° 51′ E. To the north lies Latvia, to the east and south lies Belarus, to the south-west lie Poland and the Kaliningrad region of the Russian Federation. The area is 25,170 sq. miles (65,200 sq. km).

The country lies in the middle and lower basin of the river Nemunas. Along the coast is a lowland plain which rises inland to form uplands in east and central Lithuania. These uplands, the Middle Lowlands, give way to the Baltic Highlands in east and south-east Lithuania; the highest point is 294 m (965 ft). The country has a network of rivers and over 2,800 lakes, which mainly lie in the east of the country. The climate varies between maritime and continental.

POPULATION – The total population of Lithuania is 3,724,000 (1994). The main ethnic groups are: 80.6 per cent Lithuanian, 8.7 per cent Russian, 7.1 per cent Polish, 1.6 per cent Belarussian, 1.1 per cent Ukrainian. The majority are Roman Catholic, with Russian Orthodox and Lutheran minorities.

Lithuanian is the state language, spoken by 80 per cent, with Russian, Polish and Belarussian minorities.

CAPITAL – Vilnius (population 579,000). Other major cities are Kaunas (419,000), Klaipéda (203,000), Siauliai (147,000).

CURRENCY – Litas.

FLAG – Three horizontal stripes of yellow, green, red.

NATIONAL ANTHEM – Tautiška Giesmé (The National Song).

NATIONAL DAY – 16 February (Independence Day).

## HISTORY

The first independent Lithuanian state emerged as the Kingdom of Lithuania in 1251, and over the next few centuries acted as a buffer state between Germans to the west and Mongols and Tartars to the east. After forming a joint Commonwealth and Kingdom with Poland in 1561, Lithuania was taken over by the Russian Empire in the partitions of Poland that occurred in 1772, 1792 and 1795.

Lithuania declared its independence from the Russian Empire on 16 February 1918 and then fought against German and Soviet forces until its independence was recognized by the Versailles Treaty in 1919 and the peace treaty signed with the Soviet Union on 12 July 1920. The Soviet Union annexed Lithuania in 1940 under the terms of the Molotov-Ribbentrop pact with Germany. Lithuania was invaded and occupied when Germany invaded the Soviet Union during the Second World War. In 1944 the Soviet Union recaptured the country and confirmed its annexation, though this was never accepted as legal by most states.

In December 1989 public pressure forced the Lithuanian Communist Party to agree to multiparty elections, which were held in February 1990. These were won by the nationalist Sajudis movement, and the Supreme Council (parliament) declared the restoration of the independence of Lithuania on 11 March 1990. Clashes occurred throughout 1990 between the Lithuanian population and Soviet military forces, culminating in January 1991 with the killing of Lithuanians at the television centre in Vilnius. Over 90 per cent of the population voted for independence in a referendum in February 1991. The State Council of the Soviet Union recognized the independence of Lithuania on 10 September 1991.

## GOVERNMENT

Under the constitution approved in 1992, executive authority is vested in the government, consisting of the Prime Minister, who is appointed by the President with the approval of the Seimas, and ministers appointed upon the recommendation of the Prime Minister. The government is accountable to the Seimas, and presidential powers are under strict parliamentary control.

Legislative power is exercised by the Seimas, which is a one-chamber parliament of 141 members elected for four-year terms. Seventy-one members are elected in first-past-the-post constituencies and 70 by proportional representation, with a 4 per cent threshold for representation. The constitution bans an alignment of Lithuania with any post-Soviet eastern alliance.

In the two-round parliamentary elections of October and November 1992, a majority of seats in the Seimas were won by the Lithuanian Democratic Labour Party (DLP) (the former Lithuanian Communist Party), which formed a government under Bronislovas Lubys. The DLP leader Algirdas Brazauskas was elected as Chairman of the Seimas and acting President of Lithuania until direct presidential elections, which he won in February 1993. The Sajudis leader and former Chairman of the Supreme Council, (President) Vytautas Landsbergis, became leader of the opposition in Parliament. On 10 March 1993 President Brazauskas appointed as Prime Minister Adolfas Šleževičius, who formed a new government on 16 March. In August 1994 the state of the parties in the Seimas was: DLP 73; Sajudis 30; Christian Democratic Party 18; Social Democratic Party 8; others 12.

LOCAL GOVERNMENT

Lithuania is divided into 11 cities and 44 rural districts. Each has a municipal council elected by the local population for a period of five years.

HEAD OF STATE

*President*, Algirdas Brazauskas, *elected* 14 February 1993 for a five-year term

GOVERNMENT *as at August 1994*

*Prime Minister*, Adolfas Šleževičius
*Agriculture*, Rimantis Karazija
*Housing and Urban Development*, Julius Laiconas
*Communication and Information*, Gintautas Žintelis
*Culture*, Dainlus Trinkūnas
*Economics*, Aleksandras Vasiliauskas
*Education and Science*, Vladislavas Domarkas
*Energy*, Algimantas Stasiukynas
*Finance*, Eduardas Vilkelis
*Foreign Affairs*, Povilas Gylys
*Forestry*, Gintautas Kovalčikas
*Health*, Jurkis Bredíkis
*Industry and Trade*, Kazimieras Klimašauskas
*Interior*, Romasis Vaitiekunas
*Justice*, Jonas Prapiestis
*Social Security*, vacant
*Transportation*, Jonas Birziskis
*Defence*, Linas Linkevičius
*Environment Protection*, Bronius Bradauskas
*Government Reform*, Laurynas Stankevičius

EMBASSY OF THE REPUBLIC OF LITHUANIA
17 Essex Villas, London W8 7BP
Tel 0171-938 2481

*Ambassador Extraordinary and Plenipotentiary*, His Excellency Raimundas Rajeckas, apptd 1994

BRITISH EMBASSY
2 Antakalnio, Gatve, PO Box 863, 2055 Vilnius

*Ambassador Extraordinary and Plenipotentiary*, His Excellency Michael Peart, LVO, apptd 1991

JUDICIAL SYSTEM

The judicial system comprises the Constitutional Court (consisting of nine judges appointed for terms of nine years), the Supreme Court, Court of Appeal, district and local courts. For the investigation of administrative, labour, family and other litigations, specialized courts may be established pursuant to law. Supreme legal supervision is exercised by the Prosecutor-General of the republic and by local prosecutors under his supervision.

DEFENCE

Lithuania has gradually developed its defence forces since independence from the Soviet Union. Total active armed forces personnel stands at 9,800. Authorized conscription for 12 month terms operates and the reserve National Guard numbers a further 11,000 personnel. The army has an active strength of 4,300 personnel organized into a rapid reaction brigade. The navy numbers 250 personnel with two frigates and seven patrol and coastal craft. The air force has 250 personnel, whilst the paramilitary border guard numbers 5,000. The last Russian troops withdrew on 31 August 1993.

ECONOMY

The economy is basically an agricultural one that was heavily and rapidly industrialized by the Soviet Union in the 1940s

and 1950s. The transition of the economy from a centralized system to a free-market one has taken place against the background of a decline in GDP in 1992 of 35 per cent. The major obstacles met by the programme of privatization begun in September 1991 concern the restitution of agricultural land ownership and large state-owned industrial enterprises that need fundamental technological renovation, but progress in the sale of small enterprises has been quick and successful. By the end of 1993 nearly all housing and agricultural enterprises had been privatized.

Agriculture and forestry are still major sectors of the economy, the chief products being beef, pork, rye, oats, wheat, flax, barley, sugar beet and potatoes. The main industries are chemicals and petrochemicals, food processing, wood products, building materials, textiles, leather goods, machinery, machine tools and household appliances. Lithuania is capitalizing on its clean beaches and picturesque countryside to develop a tourism industry attractive to western visitors.

TRADE

Lithuania's main trading partners remain the republics of the former Soviet Union, although trade with western states is increasing. The Lithuanian economy is still heavily dependent on Russian supplies of oil, gas and metals.

| Trade with UK | 1992 | 1993 |
| --- | --- | --- |
| Imports from UK | £54,869,000 | £13,746,000 |
| Exports to UK | 6,085,000 | 143,377,000 |

COMMUNICATIONS

Lithuania has a relatively well-developed railway system of some 1,240 miles (2,000 km) running east-west and north-south and linking the major towns with Vilnius and Klaipéda, the main international port. Vilnius has an international airport and there are smaller ones at Kaunas, Palanga and Siauliai.

CULTURE

Lithuanian culture and literature are closely linked to the national liberation movements of the 19th and early 20th centuries, and the underground literature of the Soviet occupation era. In 1991 there were 1,749 public libraries, 15 state archives, 53 museums, 13 theatres and 523 cinemas in Lithuania. The country has national television and radio stations and several privately-owned radio stations.

SOCIAL WELFARE

Lithuania re-established a national education system in 1990. There are 2,147 schools of general education with 517,000 pupils (1991). Education begins at age 6–7 years, with the system comprising elementary schools (four years), nine-year schools (five years), and secondary schools (three years). The language of instruction is predominantly Lithuanian, but there are also Russian and Polish schools. There are 108 vocational schools and 65 colleges. Lithuania has six universities and eight other institutes of higher education. Vilnius University, founded in 1579, is one of the oldest universities in eastern Europe.

In 1991 there were 202 hospitals with 45,900 beds, 16,800 physicians and 44,000 paramedical personnel. A national social security system exists which comprises compulsory state social insurance, and social benefits provided by the state. The retirement age is 60 years for men and 55 years for women.

# LUXEMBOURG
*Grand-Duché de Luxembourg*

Luxembourg is a Grand Duchy in western Europe, bounded by Germany, Belgium and France. The area is 998 sq. miles (2,586 sq. km), the population of 395,200 (1993) is nearly all Roman Catholic. The country is well wooded, with many deer and wild boar. The official language is Letzeburgesch (Luxembourgish) but most speak French and German, which are the languages of administration.

CAPITAL – Luxembourg, population (1993) 75,800, is a dismantled fortress.
CURRENCY – Luxembourg franc (LF) of 100 centimes. Belgian currency is also legal tender. The Luxembourg franc has at present the same value as the Belgian franc.
FLAG – Three horizontal bands, red, white and blue.
NATIONAL ANTHEM – Ons Hémécht (Our homeland).
NATIONAL DAY – 23 June.

## GOVERNMENT

Established as an independent state under the sovereignty of the King of the Netherlands as Grand Duke by the Congress of Vienna in 1815, Luxembourg formed part of the Germanic Confederation from 1815 to 1866, and was included in the German 'Zollverein'. In 1867 the Treaty of London declared it a neutral territory. On the death of the King of the Netherlands in 1890 it passed to the Duke of Nassau.

The territory was invaded and overrun by the Germans at the beginning of the war in 1914 but was liberated in 1918. By the Treaty of Versailles 1919, Germany renounced its former agreements with Luxembourg and in 1921 an economic union was made with Belgium. The Grand Duchy was again invaded and occupied by Germany in 1940, and liberated in 1944.

The constitution of the Grand Duchy was modified in 1948 and the stipulation of permanent neutrality was abandoned. Luxembourg is now a signatory of the Brussels and North Atlantic Treaties, and also a member of the European Union. Luxembourg is a member of the Belgium-Netherlands-Luxembourg Customs Union (Benelux 1960).

There is a Chamber of 60 Deputies, elected by universal suffrage for five years. Legislation is submitted to the Council of State. A general election was held on 12 June 1994 and at the time of going to press a new government had yet to be formed.

HEAD OF STATE
*HRH The Grand Duke of Luxembourg*, Grand Duke Jean, KG, *born* 5 January 1921; *succeeded* (on the abdication of his mother) 12 November 1964; *married*, 9 April 1953, Princess Joséphine-Charlotte of Belgium, and has *issue*, three sons and two daughters
*Heir*, HRH Prince Henri, *born* 16 April 1955, *married* 14 February 1981, Maria Teresa Mestre, and has *issue*, Prince Guillaume, *b.* 11 November 1981; Prince Felix, *b.* 3 June 1984; Prince Louis, *b.* 3 August 1986; Princess Alexandra, *b.* 2 February 1991; Prince Sébastien, *b.* 16 April 1992.

EMBASSY OF LUXEMBOURG
27 Wilton Crescent, London SW1X 8SD
Tel 0171-235 6961

*Ambassador Extraordinary and Plenipotentiary*, His Excellency Joseph Weyland, apptd 1993

BRITISH EMBASSY
14 Boulevard F. D. Roosevelt, L-2450 Luxembourg Ville
Tel: Luxembourg 229864

*Ambassador Extraordinary and Plenipotentiary*, His Excellency John N. Elam, CMG, apptd 1994

## DEFENCE

Luxembourg has a total active armed forces strength of 800 personnel organized into one light infantry battalion. For legal reasons, NATO's squadron of 18 E-3A Sentry airborne early warning aircraft is registered in Luxembourg. The paramilitary gendarmerie number 560 personnel.

## ECONOMY

The Grand Duchy possesses an important iron and steel industry and is an important financial centre. Government revenue for 1994 was estimated at LF 133 million, expenditure LF 135 million.

*Trade with UK*
(Belgium and Luxembourg)

|  | 1992 | 1993 |
|---|---|---|
| Imports from UK | £5,714,150,000 | £6,597,146,000 |
| Exports to UK | 5,741,401,000 | 6,270,295,000 |

# MACEDONIA (FORMER YUGOSLAV REPUBLIC OF)

Macedonia is a mountainous landlocked republic situated in the southern Balkans and bordered on the north by the Federal Republic of Yugoslavia (Serbia), on the east by Bulgaria, on the south by Greece and on the west by Albania. It has an area of 9,925 sq. miles (25,713 sq. km).
POPULATION – According to the 1991 census the population is 2,034,000, of whom 64.6 per cent are Macedonian, 21 per cent Albanian, 4.8 per cent ethnic Turks, 2.7 per cent gypsies and 2.2 per cent Serbs, with smaller numbers of ethnic Greeks and Bulgars. The Albanian minority claims that it accounts for up to 40 per cent of the population.
Macedonian Orthodox Christianity is the majority religion, with a Muslim minority. The main language is Macedonian (a south Slavic language), with Albanian a minority language. Macedonian is written in the Cyrillic script.

CAPITAL – Skopje, population (1991 census) of 448,229. Other major towns are Bitola (84,002), Prilep (70,152) and Kumanova (69,231).
CURRENCY – Macedonian Denar.
FLAG – Red with a gold star of sixteen rays in the centre.
NATIONAL ANTHEM – Today over Macedonia.

## GOVERNMENT

From the ninth to the 14th centuries AD Macedonia was ruled alternately by the Bulgars and the Byzantine Empire. In the middle of the 14th century the area was conquered by the Turks and remained under the Ottoman Empire for over 500 years. After the defeat of Turkey in the two Balkan wars of 1912–13 the geographical area of Macedonia was divided, the major part becoming Serbian (the areas of the present-day Macedonia) and the remainder given to Greece and Bulgaria. In 1918 on the formation of the Kingdom of the Serbs, Croats and Slovenes (later Yugoslavia), Serbian Macedonia was incorporated into Serbia as South Serbia. When Yugoslavia was reconstituted in 1944 as a Communist federal republic under President Tito, Macedonia became a constituent republic.

Multiparty elections were held in November and December 1990 for the 120-seat assembly which produced the first non-Communist government since the Second World War.

The electorate overwhelmingly approved Macedonian sovereignty and independence in a referendum on 8 September 1991 and Macedonia declared its independence from Yugoslavia on 18 September 1991. A new constitution was adopted in November 1991 and then amended at the EC's request to make it clear that Macedonia had no territorial claim on its neighbours. Macedonia applied for EC recognition in December 1991 but was refused because of Greece's objections to the state's name, flag and currency which, according to the Greek government, amounted to a territorial claim on the Greek province of Macedonia. The peaceful withdrawal of the Yugoslav Army (JNA) from Macedonia was completed in April 1992.

The inability of the government to secure Macedonia's international recognition, the consequent blocking of international aid, trade and investment, and the effect on the economy of UN trade sanctions against Serbia and Montenegro, caused the downfall of the government in July 1992. A new coalition government of the Social Democratic Alliance, Democratic Prosperity-People's Democratic Party, Reform Forces of Macedonia and Socialist parties was formed on 4 September 1992 and confirmed by a majority in the National Assembly. Tensions between Macedonia and its neighbours grew in late 1992, with Greece imposing a virtual economic blockade and Albania alleging discrimination against ethnic Albanians. Fearing conflict over Macedonia, western states and the UN intervened, sending 700 UN peacekeepers to Macedonia in December 1992 and a further 300 in July 1993 to man border posts with Serbia and Albania. Eventually Macedonia gained UN membership on 8 April 1993 following a compromise with Greece by which it is temporarily known as the 'Former Yugoslav Republic of Macedonia' (FYROM).

Following the FYROM compromise Greece reopened its border to Macedonian trade in September 1993, but reimposed its economic blockade and embargo in February 1994 after the majority of EU states established diplomatic relations with Macedonia in December 1993. Greece has been taken to the European Court of Justice by the European Commission over its unilateral embargo. The economic crisis caused by the embargo has heightened ethnic tensions and led the government increasingly to allow the breaking of sanctions across the Serbian border in return for oil supplies.

HEAD OF STATE
*President*, Kiro Gligorov, *elected by the National Assembly* 27 January 1991

GOVERNMENT *as at August 1994*

*Prime Minister*, Branko Crvenkovski
*Deputy Prime Minister and acting Foreign Minister*, Stevo Crvenkovski
*Deputy Prime Ministers*, Jovan Andonov; Becir Zuta
*Interior*, Ljubomir Danailov-Frckovski
*Defence*, Vlado Popovski
*Justice*, Tuse Gosev
*Economy*, Petrus Stefanov
*Finance*, Dzevdet Hajredini
*Health*, Jovan Tofovski
*Science*, Aslan Selmani
*Education and Physical Culture*, Dimitar Bajaldziev
*Development*, Sofia Todorova
*Urbanism, Civil Engineering, Traffic and Environment*, Antoni Pesev
*Agriculture and Forestry*, Eftim Ancev
*Labour and Social Policy*, Ilijaz Sabriu
*Culture*, Guner Ismail
*Ministers without Portfolio*, Jane Miljovski; Ljube Trpevski; Servet Avziu; Gordana Siljanovska

EMBASSY OF THE FORMER YUGOSLAV REPUBLIC OF MACEDONIA
6th Floor, Kingsway House, 103 Kingsway, London WC2B 6QX
Tel 0171-404 6558
*Ambassador Extraordinary and Plenipotentiary*, His Excellency Risto Nikovski, apptd 1994

BRITISH EMBASSY
Veljko Vlahovíc 26, 9100 Skopje
Tel: Skopje 116 772
*Ambassador Extraordinary and Plenipotentiary*, His Excellency Tony Millson, apptd 1994

ECONOMY

Economic activity in Macedonia has been decimated by the implementation of UN trade sanctions against the rump Yugoslav Federal Republic (Serbia and Montenegro), with which Macedonia previously conducted 60 per cent of its trade. The Greek economic blockade has deprived Macedonia of most of its oil supplies and industry has survived on imports from Turkey and Bulgaria via the one remaining major transportation route, the road from the Bulgarian port of Burgas to Skopje. Macedonia is attempting to transform its economy to a market-orientated one and introduce large scale privatization under an IMF stabilization programme which began in early 1994 with loans totalling US$97 million. Foreign debt, mostly inherited from the former Yugoslavia, stands at US$846 million, although western donors have paid off debts to the World Bank. In early 1994 unemployment was 28 per cent and annual inflation 253 per cent. Output and GDP have fallen significantly since 1990. Foreign investment has been minimal because of the lack of international recognition.

In 1991 41.2 per cent of the country GDP was produced by industry and mining and 14 per cent by agriculture. Mineral resources include nickel, lead, zinc, manganese and iron ore. The main industrial sectors are basic metal industries, chemicals, textiles and food processing. Important agricultural crops are wheat, tobacco, rice, wine, lamb, cotton and sugar beet.

| *Trade with UK* | 1993 |
|---|---|
| Imports from UK | £47,612,000 |
| Exports to UK | 41,005,000 |

## MADAGASCAR
*Repoblika n'i Madagaskar*

Madagascar lies 240 miles off the east coast of Africa and is the fourth largest island in the world. It has an area of 226,669 sq. miles (587,041 sq. km), and a population (UN estimate 1991) of 11,493,000. The people are of mixed Malayo-Polynesian, Arab and African origin. There are sizeable French, Chinese and Indian communities. The official languages are Malagasy and French.

CAPITAL – Antananarivo, population estimate 1,250,000. Other main towns are the chief port Ψ Toamasina (230,000); Ψ Mahajanga (200,000); Fianarantsoa (300,000); Ψ Antsiranana (220,000).
CURRENCY – Franc Malgache (Malagasy franc) (FMG) of 100 centimes.
FLAG – Equal horizontal bands of red (above) and green, with vertical white band by staff.
NATIONAL DAY – 26 June (Independence Day).

# GOVERNMENT

Madagascar (known from 1958 to 1975 as the Malagasy republic) became a French protectorate in 1895, and a French colony in 1896 when the former queen was exiled. Republican status was adopted on 14 October 1958, and independence was proclaimed on 26 June 1960.

The post-independence civilian government was replaced by a military government in January 1975 and the following month martial law was declared. A Supreme Council of the Revolution under Capitaine de Frégate (subsequently Admiral) Didier Ratsiraka was established in June 1975.

After six months of strikes and agitation against his one-party socialist rule, President Ratsiraka in November 1991 relinquished executive power to a new Prime Minister, Guy Razanamasy. However, the President retained his official position and the main opposition grouping, the Forces Vives, established a rival government led by Albert Zafy. In December 1991 a transitional government including Forces Vives and Razanamasy supporters was formed to draft a new constitution which, after continued instability and Ratsiraka attempting to regain executive power, was approved by referendum in August 1992. Presidential elections were held in two rounds in November 1992 and February 1993, Albert Zafy emerging victorious with 67 per cent of the vote. He became the first President of the Third Republic, which also come into being at the same time. A legislative election held in June 1993 was won by Zafy's Forces Vives and allied parties, with Forces Vives member Francisque Ravony being elected Prime Minster by parliament in August 1993. The new constitution declares Madagascar to be a unitary state and reduces the executive powers of the President.

HEAD OF STATE
*President*, Professor Albert Zafy, *elected* 10 February 1993

COUNCIL OF MINISTERS *as at August 1994*
*Prime Minister*, Francisque Ravony
*Agriculture and Rural Development*, Emmanuel Rakotovahiny
*Foreign Affairs*, Jacques Sylla
*Civil Service, Labour and Social Legislation*, Henri Rakotovololona
*Economy, Town Planning and Social Recovery*, Tovonanahary Rabetsitonta
*Industrial Promotion and Tourism*, Herizo Razafimahaleo
*Interior and Decentralization*, Charles Clement Severin
*Energy and Mining*, Bruno Betiana
*Transport and Meteorology*, Daniel Ramaromisa
*Finance and Budget*, Jose Yvon Raserijaona
*Regional Planning*, Henri Raoul Mahatovo
*Culture and Communications*, Tsilavina Ralaindimby
*Research and Development*, Roger Andrianasolo
*Public Works*, Royal Raoelfils
*Promotion of Commerce and Craftsmanship*, Frederic Manelo Anony
*Police*, Bertin Razafindrazaka
*Armed Forces*, Gen. Charles Rabenja
*National Education*, Falgence Fanony
*Public Health*, Damasy Andriambo

EMBASSY OF THE REPUBLIC OF MADAGASCAR
4 avenue Raphael, 75016 Paris, France
Tel: Paris 45046211

*Ambassador Plenipotentiary and Extraordinary*, new appointment awaited

HONORARY CONSULATE OF THE REPUBLIC OF MADAGASCAR
16 Lanark Mansions, Pennard Road, London W12 8DT
Tel 0181-746 0133

*Honorary Consul*, Stephen Hobbs.

BRITISH EMBASSY
1st Floor, Immeuble 'Ny Havana', Cite de 67 Ha, BP 167, Antananarivo
Tel: Antananarivo 277 49

*Ambassador Extraordinary and Plenipotentiary*, His Excellency Peter John Smith, apptd 1992

# ECONOMY

The island's economy is still largely based on agriculture, which accounts for three-quarters of its exports. Development plans have placed emphasis on increasing agricultural and livestock production, the improvement of communications, the exploitation of mineral deposits and the creation of small industries.

| Trade with UK | 1992 | 1993 |
|---|---|---|
| Imports from UK | £8,690,000 | £5,418,000 |
| Exports to UK | 6,000,000 | 10,747,000 |

# MALAWI
*Dziko La Malawi*

Malawi lies in south-eastern Africa. Its neighbours are Tanzania to the north-east, Zambia to the west, and Mozambique, which surrounds the southern part of the country. Much of the eastern border of Malawi is formed by Lake Malawi (formerly Lake Nyasa), which covers nearly half of the north of the country. The valley of the River Shire runs south from the lake, its watershed with the Zambezi lying on the western border with Mozambique and its tributary, the Ruo, with lakes Chinta and Chirwa lying on the eastern border with Mozambique. The north and centre are plateaux, and the south highlands. The total area is 45,747 sq. miles (118,484 sq. km).

POPULATION – The population (census 1987) was 7,982,607. According to a UN estimate (1991), the population was 8,556,000. The official languages are Chichewa and English.

CAPITAL – Lilongwe, population (1987) 223,973. The city of Blantyre in the south, incorporating Blantyre and Limbe (population (1987) 331,588), is the major commercial and industrial centre. Other main centres are: Mzuzu, Thyolo, Mulanje, Mangochi, Salima, Dedza and Zomba, the former capital.
CURRENCY – Kwacha (K) of 100 tambala.
FLAG – Horizontal stripes of black, red and green, with rising sun in the centre of the black stripe.
NATIONAL ANTHEM – O God Bless Our Land of Malawi.
NATIONAL DAY – 6 July (Independence Day).

# GOVERNMENT

Malawi (formerly Nyasaland) assumed internal self-government on 1 February 1963, and became independent on 6 July 1964. It became a republic on 6 July 1966.

There is a Cabinet consisting of the President and other ministers. The Parliament consists of 177 members, each elected by universal suffrage. The Parliament, which usually meets three times a year, is presided over by a Speaker. A new multiparty constitution ending the idea of the Life Presidency and reducing presidential powers came into effect on 17 May 1994. The constitution is subject to changes during a 12-month discussion period from May 1994.

During late 1991 and the first half of 1992 the Life President Hastings Banda, who had ruled since independence, came under increasing international and internal pressure to move towards a multiparty democratic system of government. In May 1992 aid donors tied new loans to improvements in the country's human rights record and moves to multiparty democracy. A referendum was held on the adoption of a multiparty democracy in June 1993 and 63 per cent of voters approved the adoption of a multiparty system. President Banda and the Malawi Congress Party refused to resign but parliament passed a law to amend the constitution to allow multiparty politics and Banda announced a political amnesty to allow exiles to return. Multiparty presidential and legislative elections were held in May 1994 and won by Bakili Muluzi and his United Democratic Front (UDF) respectively. Foreign and multilateral aid has since been restored. In August 1994 the state of the parties in parliament was United Democratic Front (UDF) 84 seats, Malawi Congress Party (MCP) 55 seats, Alliance for Democracy (AFORD) 36 seats.

HEAD OF STATE
*President*, Bakili Muluzi, *elected* 17 May 1994, *sworn in*, 21 May 1994
*Vice-President*, Justin Malewezi

CABINET *as at August 1994*

The President
The Vice President
*Finance*, Aleka Banda
*Commerce, Industry and Tourism*, Harry Thomson
*External Affairs*, Edward Bwanali
*Economic Planning and Development*, Tim Mangwazu
*Information and Broadcasting*, Brown James Mpinganjira
*Home Affairs*, Peter Fachi
*Defence*, Cassim Chilampha
*Education, Science and Technology*, Sam Mpasu
*Justice and Attorney-General*, Wehnam Nakanga
*Transport and Communications*, Collins Chizumila
*Agriculture and Livestock Development*, Dr John Nankumba
*Health and Environment*, Dr George Mtafu
*Local Government and Rural Development*, James Makhumula
*Works, Supplies and Water Development*, Patrick Mbewe
*Lands and Housing*, Alhaji Shaiba Itimu
*Energy and Mining*, Rolph Patel
*Youth, Sports and Culture*, Zililo Chibambo
*Labour and Manpower Development*, George Kanyanya

MALAWI HIGH COMMISSION
33 Grosvenor Street, London WIX ODE
Tel 0171-491 4172/7

*High Commissioner*, new appointment awaited

BRITISH HIGH COMMISSION
PO Box 30042, Lilongwe 3
Tel: Lilongwe 782400

*High Commissioner*, His Excellency John Francis Martin, CMG, apptd 1993

BRITISH COUNCIL REPRESENTATIVE, James Kennedy, PO Box 30222, Lilongwe 3. There is also a library at *Blantyre*.

EDUCATION

Primary education is the responsibility of local authorities in both urban and rural areas, although policy, curricula and inspection are the responsibility of the Ministry of Education and Culture. The Ministry is also responsible for secondary schools, technical education and primary teacher training. Religious bodies, with government assistance, still play an important part in these fields. The University of Malawi was opened in 1965 and has five constituent colleges.

COMMUNICATIONS

A single-track railway runs from Mchinji on the Zambian border, through Lilongwe and Salima on Lake Malawi (itself served by two passenger and a number of cargo boats) through to Blantyre. The route south to the Mozambique port of Beira has been severed by the Mozambican civil war, but the route to Nacala in Mozambique is open again. There are 12,215 km of roads in Malawi of which about 21.8 per cent are bituminized. There is an international airport 26 km from Lilongwe, which handles regional and inter-continental flights.

ECONOMY

The economy is largely agricultural, with maize the main subsistence crop. Tobacco, sugar, tea, groundnuts and cotton are the main cash crops and principal exports. There are two sugar mills and total production in 1989 was 157 million kg. A number of light manufacturing industries have been established, mainly in agricultural processing, clothing/textiles and building materials.

| *Trade with UK* | 1992 | 1993 |
|---|---|---|
| Imports from UK | £23,880,000 | £18,021,000 |
| Exports to UK | 22,107,000 | 21,714,000 |

## MALAYSIA
*Persekutuan Tanah Malaysia*

Malaysia, comprising the 11 states of peninsular Malaya plus Sabah and Sarawak, forms a crescent well over 1,000 miles long between 1° and 7° N. latitude and 100° and 119° E. longitude. It occupies two distinct regions, the Malay peninsula which extends from the isthmus of Kra to the Singapore Strait, and the north-west coastal area of the island of Borneo. Each is separated from the other by the South China Sea. The total area of Malaysia is about 127,317 sq. miles (329,749 sq. km).

The year is commonly divided into the south-west and north-west monsoon seasons. Rainfall averages about 100 inches throughout the year. The average daily temperature varies from 21° C to 32° C, though in higher areas temperatures are lower and vary widely.

POPULATION – The population was 16,921,300 (1988 census), 18,333,000 UN estimate (1991). The principal racial groups are the Malays, the Chinese and those of Indian and Sri Lankan origin, as well as the indigenous races of Sarawak and Sabah. Bahasa Malaysia (Malay) is the sole official language, but English, various dialects of Chinese, and Tamil are also widely spoken. There are a few indigenous languages widely spoken in Sabah and Sarawak.

Islam is the official religion of Malaysia, each ruler being the head of religion in his state, though the heads of state of Sabah and Sarawak are not heads of the Muslim religion in their states. The Yang di-Pertuan Agung is the head of religion in Melaka and Penang. The constitution guarantees religious freedom.

CAPITAL – Kuala Lumpur was proclaimed federal territory in 1974. Its population (1985) is 1,103,200.
CURRENCY – Malaysian dollar (ringgit) (M$) of 100 sen.
FLAG – Equal horizontal stripes of red (seven) and white (seven); 14-point yellow star and crescent in blue canton.
NATIONAL ANTHEM – Negara-Ku.
NATIONAL DAY – 31 August (*Hari Kebangsaan*).

## GOVERNMENT

The Federation of Malaya became an independent country within the Commonwealth on 31 August 1957. On 16 September 1963 the Federation was enlarged by the accession of the states of Singapore, Sabah (formerly British North Borneo) and Sarawak, and the name of Malaysia was adopted from that date. On 9 August 1965 Singapore seceded from the Federation.

The constitution was designed to ensure the existence of a strong federal government and also a measure of autonomy for the state governments. It provides for a constitutional Supreme Head of the Federation (HM the *Yang di-Pertuan Agung*) and a Deputy Supreme Head (HRH *Timbalan Yang di-Pertuan Agung*) to be elected for a term of five years by the rulers from among their number. The Malay rulers are either chosen or succeed to their position in accordance with the custom of the particular state. In other states of Malaysia, choice of the head of state is at the discretion of the Yang di-Pertuan Agung after consultation with the Chief Minister of the state.

The Federal Parliament consists of two houses, the Senate and the House of Representatives. The Senate (*Dewan Negara*) consists of 68 members, under a President (*Yang di-Pertua Dewan Negara*), 26 elected by the Legislative Assemblies of the States (two from each) and 42 appointed by the Yang di-Pertuan Agung. The House of Representatives (*Dewan Rakyat*) consists of 180 members elected by universal adult suffrage with a common electoral roll.

The constitution provides that each state shall have its own constitution not inconsistent with the federal constitution, with the ruler or Governor acting on the advice of an Executive Council appointed on the advice of the Chief Minister and a single-chamber Legislative Assembly. The Legislative Assemblies are fully elected on the same basis as the Federal Parliament.

Dr Mahathir Muhammad won a third term in office in a general election held on 21 October 1990.

### HEAD OF STATE

*Supreme Head of State*, HM Tuanku Jaafar Ibni Al-Marhum Tuanku Abdul Rahman (Yang Dipertuan Besar of Negeri Sembilan), *sworn in* 26 April 1994.

*Deputy Supreme Head of State*, HRH Sultan Salahuddin Abdul Aziz Shah Al-Haj ibni Almarhum Sultan Hishamuddin Alam Shah Al-Haj (Sultan of Selangor)

### CABINET *as at August 1994*

*Prime Minister, Minister of Home Affairs*, Hon. Datuk Seri Dr Mahathir Muhammad

*Deputy Prime Minister, Minister for Finance*, Hon Datuk Seri Anwar Ibrahim

*Transport*, Hon. Datuk Seri Dr Ling Liong Sik

*Energy, Telecommunications and Posts*, Hon. Datuk Seri S. Samy Vellu

*Primary Industries*, Hon. Datuk Seri Dr Lim Keng Yaik

*Works*, Hon. Datuk Leo Moggie Anak Irok

*International Trade and Industry*, Hon. Datuk Seri Rafidah Aziz

*Education*, Hon. Datuk Dr Haji Sulaiman bin Haji Daud

*Agriculture*, Hon. Datuk Seri Sanusi bin Junid

*Rural Development*, Senator Datuk Haji Annuar bin Musa

*Domestic Trade and Consumer Affairs*, Hon. Datuk Haji Abu Hassan bin Haji Omar

*Health*, Hon. Datuk Lee Kim Sai

*Foreign Affairs*, Hon. Datuk Abdullah bin Haji Ahmad Badawi

*Defence*, Hon. Datuk Sri Haji Mohd Najib bin Tun Haji Abdul Razak

*Information*, Hon. Datuk Mohamed bin Rahmat

*Culture, Arts and Tourism*, Hon. Datuk Sabbaruddin bin Chik

*National Unity and Community Development*, Hon. Datuk Napsiah binti Omar

*Public Enterprises*, Hon. Datuk Dr Mohammad Yusof bin Haji Mohamed Nor

*Human Resources*, Hon. Datuk Lim Ah Lek

*Science, Technology and Environment*, Hon. Datuk Law Hieng Ding

*Housing and Local Government*, Hon. Datuk Dr Ting Chew Peh

*Land and Co-operative Development*, Hon. Osu bin Haji Sukam

*Justice*, Hon. Datuk Syed Hamid bin Syed Jaafar Albar

*Youth and Sports*, Haji Abdul Ghani bin Othman.

*Prime Minister's Department*, Hon. Datuk Abang Abu Bakar bin Datu Bandar Abang Haji Mustapha

NOTE: Tunku/Tengku, Tun, Tan Sri, and Datuk are titles. Tunku/Tengku is equivalent to Prince. Tun denotes membership of a high order of Malaysian chivalry and Tan Sri and Datuk (Datuk Seri in Perak and Datu in Sabah) are each the equivalent of a knighthood. The wife of a Tun is styled Toh Puan, that of a Tan Sri is styled Puan Sri and of a Datuk, Datin. The honorific Tuan or Encik is equivalent to Mr and the honorific Puan is equivalent to Mrs.

MALAYSIAN HIGH COMMISSION
45 Belgrave Square, London SW1X 8QT
Tel 0171-235 8033

*High Commissioner*, His Excellency Dato Kamarudin Abu, apptd 1992
*Deputy High Commissioner*, Muhammad Noh
*Attaché*, Col. Muhammad Yunus (*Defence*); Nasir Ahmad (*Immigration*)
*Commissioner*, Bahar Ahmad (*Trade*)

BRITISH HIGH COMMISSION
185 Jalan Ampang (PO Box 11030), 50450 Kuala Lumpur
Tel: Kuala Lumpur 03-2482122

*High Commissioner*, His Excellency David Moss, CMG, apptd 1994
*Deputy High Commissioner and Counsellor (Commercial/Economic)*, B. E. Cleghorn
*Defence Adviser*, Col. J. L. Seddon-Brown

BRITISH COUNCIL REPRESENTATIVE, Dr G. Howell, CBE, PO Box 10539, Jalan Bukit Aman, Kuala Lumpur 50916. There are also offices at *Johore Bahru, Kota Kinabalu* (Sabah) and *Kuching* (Sarawak), and a library in *Penang*.

## STATES

The 13 states of the Federation of Malaysia (state capitals in brackets) and their populations at the 1988 census are:

| | |
|---|---|
| ΨJohore (Johore Bahru) | 2,007,300 |
| Kedah (Alor Setar) | 1,353,500 |
| Kelantan (Kota Bahru) | 1,150,400 |
| ΨMelaka (Melaka) | 560,700 |
| Negri Sembilan (Seremban) | 694,100 |
| ΨPahang (Kuantan) | 1,001,200 |
| ΨPenang (Georgetown) | 1,103,200 |
| Perak (Ipoh) | 2,143,200 |
| Perlis (Kangar) | 179,700 |
| ΨSabah (Kota Kinabalu) | 1,371,000 |
| ΨSarawak (Kuching) | 1,591,000 |
| ΨSelangor (Shah Alam) | 1,878,300 |
| ΨTerengganu (Kuala Terengganu) | 705,200 |

The two federal territories and their population at the 1988 census are:

Kuala Lumpur ⎤
Labuan          ⎦ 1,182,700

| Trade with UK | 1992 | 1993 |
|---|---|---|
| Imports from UK | £635,857,000 | £964,985,000 |
| Exports to UK | 1,103,782,000 | 1,396,413,000 |

## JUDICATURE

The judicial system consists of a Supreme Court and two High Courts, one in peninsular Malaysia and one for Sabah and Sarawak. The Supreme Court comprises a President, the two Chief Justices of the High Courts and other judges. It possesses appellate, original and advisory jurisdiction.

Each of the High Courts consists of a Chief Justice and not less than four other judges. In peninsular Malaysia the subordinate courts consist of the sessions courts and the magistrates' courts. In Sabah/Sarawak the magistrates' courts constitute the subordinate courts.

## DEFENCE

Total active armed forces personnel number 114,500, with volunteer service in operation. The Army has a strength of 90,000 personnel, with 26 light tanks, 388 reconnaissance vehicles, 700 armoured personnel carriers and 200 artillery pieces. Reserve army personnel number 55,000. The Royal Malayasian Navy has a strength of 12,000, with four frigates, 37 patrol and coastal craft and 12 armed helicopters. The Royal Malaysian Air Force has a strength of 77 combat aircraft and 12,500 personnel.

The paramilitary police field force has a strength of 18,000 personnel in 21 battalions, together with marine police and air wing units. Border scouts in North Borneo number 1,200.

Australia maintains an infantry company and an air force detachment in the country.

## ECONOMY

From being an agriculturally-based economy reliant on raw materials exports at independence, Malaysia has undergone an industrialization programme beginning with clothing, textiles and rubber goods, to which have been added electronics, office equipment, cars, household appliances, semi-conductors, food processing and chemicals. Under the New Economic Policy of 1970–90, the economy grew at an average rate of 6.7 per cent a year. The National Development Policy 1990–2000 is seen as the second stage in making Malaysia a fully-developed industrial state by 2020. In 1993 44 per cent of GDP was produced by services, 30 per cent by manufacturing and 16 per cent by agriculture.

| FINANCE | 1992 | 1993* |
|---|---|---|
| Revenue | M$38,106m | M$41,231m |
| Expenditure | 42,414m | 41,036m |
| *estimated | | |

## TRADE

Malaysia is the largest exporter of natural rubber, tin, palm oil and tropical hardwoods. Other major export commodities are manufactured and processed products, petroleum, oil, and other minerals, palm kernel oil, tea and pepper. Exports of major commodities were (1993): manufactured goods 71 per cent, agricultural products 13 per cent, minerals, oil and gas 9 per cent. Imports consist mainly of machinery and transport equipment, manufactured goods, foods, mineral fuels, chemicals and inedible crude materials.

| | 1992 | 1993 |
|---|---|---|
| Imports (c.i.f.) | M$105,805m | M$113,639m |
| Exports (f.o.b.) | 104,608m | 120,225m |
| *estimated | | |

## THE MALDIVES
*Divehi Jumhuriya*

The Maldives are a chain of coral atolls some 400 miles to the south-west of Sri Lanka, stretching north for about 600 miles from just south of the Equator. There are about 20 coral atolls comprising over 1,200 islands, 202 of which are inhabited. Total area of the islands is 115 sq. miles (298 sq. km). No point in the entire chain of islands is more than 8 feet above sea-level.

POPULATION – The population of the islands (official estimate 1993) is 238,000. The people are Sunni Muslims and the Maldivian (Dhivehi) language is akin to Elu or old Sinhalese.

CAPITAL – ΨMalé, population (1985) 46,334. There is an international airport at Malé.

CURRENCY – Rufiyaa of 100 laaris.

FLAG – Green field bearing a white crescent, with wide red border.

NATIONAL ANTHEM – Qawmee Salaam.

NATIONAL DAY – 26 July.

## GOVERNMENT

Until 1952 the islands were a sultanate under the protection of the British Crown. Internal self-government was achieved in 1948 and full independence in 1965. The Maldives became a special member of the Commonwealth in 1982 and a full member in 1985.

The Maldives form a republic which is elective. There is a legislature, the *Citizens' Majlis*, with representatives elected from all the atolls. The life of the Majlis is five years. The government consists of a Cabinet, which is responsible to the Majlis.

HEAD OF STATE
*President*, His Excellency Maumoon Abdul Gayoom, *elected* 1978, *re-elected* 1983, 1989, 1 October 1993.

CABINET *as at August 1994*
*Defence and National Security*, The President
*Foreign Affairs*, Hon. Fathulla Jameel
*Justice*, Hon. Mohamed Rasheed Ibrahim
*Home Affairs and Sports*, Hon. Umar Zahir
*Finance*, Hon. Ismail Fathy
*Education*, Hon. Abdulla Hameed
*Health and Welfare*, Hon. Mohammed Yoosuf
*Fisheries and Agriculture*, Hon. Abbas Ibrahim
*Atolls Administration*, Hon. Mohammed Latheef
*Trade and Industries*, Hon. Ahmed Mujuthaba
*Tourism*, Hon. Abdulla Jameel
*Public Works and Labour*, Hon. Abdulla Kamaludeen
*Planning and Environment*, Hon. Ismail Shafeen
*Transport and Shipping*, Ahmed Zahir
*Minister at the President's Office and Acting Attorney-General*, Hon. Mohamed Zahir Hussain

BRITISH HIGH COMMISSIONER, His Excellency Edward Field, CMG, resides at Colombo, Sri Lanka

## ECONOMY

The vegetation of the islands is coconut palms with some scrub. Hardly any cultivation of crops is possible and nearly all food to supplement the basic fish diet has to be imported. The principal industry is fishing and considerable quantities of fish are exported to Japan. Dried fish is exported to Sri Lanka, where it is a delicacy. The tourist industry is expanding rapidly (241,000 visitors in 1993). The Maldives National Ship Managment Ltd (MNSML) has a fleet of nine merchant ships.

| Trade with UK | 1992 | 1993 |
|---|---|---|
| Imports from UK | £4,261,000 | £4,968,000 |
| Exports to UK | 8,174,000 | 8,996,000 |

# MALI
*République du Mali*

Mali, an inland state in north-west Africa, has an area of 478,791 sq. miles (1,240,000 sq. km), and a population (UN estimate 1991) of 9,507,000. The principal rivers are the Niger and the Senegal.

CAPITAL – Bamako (1987 census, 658,275). Other towns are Gao, Kayes, Mopti, Sikasso, Segou and Timbuktu (all regional capitals).

CURRENCY – Franc CFA of 100 centimes.

FLAG – Vertical stripes of green (by staff), yellow and red.

NATIONAL DAY – 22 September.

## GOVERNMENT

Formerly the French colony of Soudan, the territory elected on 24 November 1958 to remain an autonomous republic within the French Community. It associated with Senegal in the Federation of Mali which was granted full independence on 20 June 1960. The Federation was effectively dissolved in August 1960 by the secession of Senegal. The title of the Republic of Mali was adopted in September 1960.

The regime of Modibo Keita was overthrown in 1968 by a group of army officers who formed a National Liberation Committee and appointed a Prime Minister. Moussa Traoré assumed the functions of head of state. A new civil constitution came into being in 1979.

After several months of pro-reform protests and strikes, often leading to riots, President Traoré was overthrown in March 1991 by troops led by Lt.-Col. Toure. A joint civilian/military National Reconciliation Committee, later replaced by the Transitional Committee for the Salvation of the People, suspended the constitution and dissolved the Mali People's Democratic Union (UPDM), formerly the sole party. A transitional government was formed in April. A new constitution was approved by a national conference in August 1991 and by a national referendum in January 1992. The new constitution provided for a multiparty political system, and legislative elections were held in February and March 1992 with the Alliance for Democracy in Mali (ADEMA) emerging victorious. Alpha Konare, the ADEMA leader, won the presidential elections in April 1992 and appointed a Prime Minister and Cabinet in June dominated by ADEMA members. The Prime Minister and government resigned in April 1993 after political unrest in Bamako led by students. On 12 April the President appointed a new cabinet, again dominated by ADEMA, but this was replaced by another ADEMA-dominated cabinet in February 1994.

HEAD OF STATE
*President*, Alpha Oumar Konare, *elected* 28 April 1992, *sworn in* 8 June 1992

CABINET *as at August 1994*

*Prime Minister*, Ibrahim Boubacar Keita

*Minister of State, Defence*, Dioncounda Traore
*Mines, Energy and Hydraulics*, Cheickna Seydou Diawara
*Civil Service, Labour and Employment*, Mohammed Ag Erlaf
*Foreign Affairs, Malians Abroad and African Integration*, Sy Kadiatou Sow
*Finance and Commerce*, Soumeyla Cisse
*Youth and Sports*, Boubacar Coulibaly
*Tourism and Crafts*, Fatou Haidara
*Health, Solidarity and Pensioners*, Modibo Sidibe
*Territorial Administration and Security*, Lt.-Col. Sada Samake
*Equipment and Training*, Bakary Konimba Traore
*Primary Education*, Adama Sammassekou
*Rural Development and Environment*, Dr Boubarcar Sy
*Justice*, Boubacar Gaoussou Dairra
*Secondary and Higher Education and Scientific Research*, Moustapha Dicko
*Culture and Communications*, Cheickna Kamissoko

EMBASSY OF THE REPUBLIC OF MALI
Avenue Molière 487, 1060 Brussels, Belgium
Tel: Brussels 3457432

*Ambassador Extraordinary and Plenipotentiary*, His Excellency N'Tiji Traoré, apptd 1993; resident at Brussels

BRITISH AMBASSADOR, His Excellency Alan Furness, CMG, resident at Dakar, Senegal
There is a Consulate in Bamako.

## ECONOMY

Mali's principal exports are gold, groundnuts (raw and processed), cotton fibres, meat and dried fish. Mali rejoined the CFA Franc Zone in 1984. In March 1994 the IMF approved a US$41 million credit to support free market economic reforms.

| Trade with UK | 1992 | 1993 |
|---|---|---|
| Imports from UK | £11,101,000 | £9,455,000 |
| Exports to UK | 2,061,000 | 1,561,000 |

# MALTA
*Repubblika Ta'Malta*

Malta lies in the Mediterranean Sea, 58 miles (93 km) from Sicily and about 180 miles (288 km) from the African coast. It is about 17 miles (27 km) in length and 9 miles (14.5 km) in breadth, and has an area of 94.9 sq. miles (246 sq. km). Malta includes also the adjoining islands of Gozo (area 25.9 sq. miles (67 sq. km)), Comino and minor islets.

POPULATION – The estimated population in January 1994 was 366,541. The Maltese are mainly Roman Catholic. The Maltese language is of Semitic origin and held by some to be derived from the Carthaginian and Phoenician tongues. Maltese and English are the official languages of administration and Maltese is the official language in all the courts of law and the language of general use in the islands.

CAPITAL – ΨValletta. Population (census 1993), 9,149. Valletta Grand Harbour is very deep and large vessels can anchor alongside the shore. It is an important port of call and ship-repairing centre.

CURRENCY – Maltese lira (LM) of 100 cents and 1,000 mils.

FLAG – Two equal vertical stripes, white at the hoist and red at the fly. A representation of the George Cross is carried edged with red in the canton of the white stripe.

NATIONAL ANTHEM – L-Innu Malti.

NATIONAL DAYS – 31 March (Freedom Day); 8 September (Lady of Victories); 7 June; 21 September (Independence Day); 13 December (Republic Day).

## GOVERNMENT

Malta was in turn held by the Phoenicians, Carthaginians, Romans and Arabs. In 1090 it was conquered by Count Roger of Normandy and in 1530 it was handed over to the Knights of St John, who made it a stronghold of Christianity. In 1565 it sustained the famous siege, when the Turks were successfully withstood by Grandmaster La Valette. The Knights fortified the islands and built Valletta before being expelled by Napoleon in 1798. The Maltese rose against the French garrison soon afterwards and the island was subsequently blockaded by the British fleet. The Maltese people freely requested the protection of the British Crown in 1802 on condition that their rights and privileges would be preserved and respected. The islands were finally annexed to the British Crown by the Treaty of Paris 1814.

Malta was again closely besieged in the Second World War. From June 1940 to the end of the war, 432 members of the garrison and 1,540 civilians were killed by enemy aircraft, and about 35,000 houses were destroyed or damaged. The island was awarded the George Cross for gallantry on 15 April 1942.

On 21 September 1964 Malta became an independent state within the Commonwealth, and on 13 December 1974 a republic within the Commonwealth.

Elections are held for the unicameral Parliament of 65 members every five years by a system of proportional representation. Seats are obtained by the highest number of votes in the respective districts. The party with the highest number of votes forms the government, with extra members being co-opted if necessary.

Malta applied for EC membership in 1990 but in June 1993 the Commission issued a negative opinion on its application, principally because of its small size.

HEAD OF STATE
*President*, Dr Ugo Mifsud Bonnici, *took office* 4 April 1994

CABINET *as at August 1994*
*Prime Minister*, Hon. Dr Edward Fenech Adami
*Deputy PM and Minister of Foreign Affairs*, Hon. Prof. Guido De Marco
*Education and Human Resources*, Hon. Michael Falzon
*Home Affairs and Social Development*, Hon. Dr Louis Galea
*Economic Services*, Hon. Dr G. Bonello Du Puis
*Environment*, Hon. Dr Francis Zammit Dimench
*Food, Agriculture and Fisheries*, Hon. Censu Galea
*Social Security*, Hon. Dr George Hyzler
*Justice*, Hon. Dr Joseph Fenech
*Youth and the Arts*, Hon. Dr Michael Refalo
*Transport, Communications and Technology*, Dr Michael Frendo
*Gozo*, Hon. Anton Tabone
*Finance*, Hon. John Dalli

MALTA HIGH COMMISSION
16 Kensington Square, London W8 5HH
Tel 0171-938 1712

*High Commissioner*, His Excellency Saviour Stellini, apptd 1991

BRITISH HIGH COMMISSION
7 St Anne Street, Floriana (PO Box 506)
Tel: Floriana 233134/7

*High Commissioner*, His Excellency Sir Peter Wallis, KCVO, CMG, apptd 1991

BRITISH COUNCIL REPRESENTATIVE, Anne Bradley, c/o British High Commission

## EDUCATION

In 1993 there were 65 government kindergarten centres with 7,850 pupils, 81 government primary schools with 23,847 pupils and 40 secondary and post-secondary schools and new lyceums, with a total of 21,964 pupils.

The government also runs 21 technical/trade schools (with an enrolment of 5,593 students). Schools of art, music, secretarial studies, catering, nursing and dramatic art are sponsored by the government. Tertiary education is available at the University of Malta, which had 4,886 students in 1993. There are a number of private schools. All state education is free.

## ECONOMY

Agriculture plays a significant role in the economy. There are 3,000 full-time and 13,000 part-time farmers. Crops are principally vegetables, fruit (especially grapes), flowers and cuttings.

The island's leading industry is the state-owned Malta Drydocks, employing about 3,329 people. The main port of Grand Harbour handled traffic of 1.75 million tonnes in 1993. Malta Freeport was opened in 1990 in the southern port of Marsaxlokk and comprises a container distribution centre, an oil products terminal and warehouse facilities.

At the end of 1993 manufacturing firms employed some 31,394 people. Industries include food processing, textiles and clothing, plastics and chemical products, electronic equipment and components. The gross output of the manufacturing industry in 1993 was LM708.9 million, of which LM475.6 million were export sales.

Tourism has assumed primary importance, with 1,063,213 tourists visiting the island in 1993, and Marsamxett Harbour has been further developed by the extension of a yacht centre. The number of cruise liners calling at the Grand Harbour has increased considerably. Gross income from this industry stood at LM233.2 million in 1993.

| FINANCE | 1992 | 1993 |
| --- | --- | --- |
| Revenue | LM395,036,000 | LM428,310,000 |
| Expenditure | 388,032,000 | 428,298,000 |

TRADE

The principal imports for home consumption are foodstuffs (mainly wheat, meat and bullocks, milk and fruit), fodder, beverages and tobacco, fuels, chemicals, textiles and machinery (industrial, agricultural and transport). The chief domestic exports are processed food, electronics, textiles, and other manufactures.

| | 1992 | 1993 |
| --- | --- | --- |
| Imports | LM747,770,000 | LM830,920,000 |
| Exports | 490,903,000 | 518,325,000 |

| Trade with UK | 1992 | 1993 |
| --- | --- | --- |
| Imports from UK | £164,489,000 | £206,113,000 |
| Exports to UK | 51,332,000 | 62,961,000 |

# MARSHALL ISLANDS
*Republic of the Marshall Islands*

The Republic of the Marshall Islands consists of 29 atolls and five islands in the central Pacific Ocean lying between 4° and 19° N., and 160° and 175° E. The islands and atolls are scattered over 1,294,500 sq. km (500,000 sq. miles), forming two parallel chains running north-west to south-east: the Ratak (Sunrise) chain and the Ralik (Sunset) chain. The total land area is 70 sq. miles (181 sq. km). The largest atoll is Kwajalein in the Ralik chain. The atolls are coral and the islands are volcanic. None of the islands rises more than a few metres above sea level.

The climate is hot and humid with little seasonal variation in temperature. The typhoon season lasts from December to March.

POPULATION – The population of the Marshall Islands is 45,569 (1990). There is an annual rate of increase of 4.29 per cent and over half the population is under 15. About 60 per cent of the population is concentrated on the two atolls of Majuro and Kwajalein. The population is 99 per cent Micronesian. Marshallese and English are the official languages.

The population is Christian, primarily Protestant but with a substantial Catholic minority. The principal Protestant denomination is the United Church of Christ.

CAPITAL – Majuro (population 20,000). The other major town is Ebeye (9,200).

CURRENCY – US Dollar.

FLAG – Blue with a diagonal ray divided white over orange running from the lower hoist to the upper fly; in the canton a white sun.

NATIONAL DAY – 21 October (Compact Day).

## GOVERNMENT

The Marshall Islands were claimed by Spain in 1592 but were left undisturbed by the Spanish Empire for 300 years. In 1886 the Marshall Islands formally became a German protectorate. On the outbreak of the First World War in 1914, Japan took control of the islands on behalf of the Allied powers, and after the war administered the territory as a League of Nations mandate. During the Second World War United States armed forces took control of the islands from the Japanese after intense fighting. In 1947 the USA entered into agreement with the UN Security Council to administer the Micronesia area, of which the Marshall Islands are a part, as the UN Trust Territory of the Pacific Islands.

The islands became internally self-governing in 1979, and the US Trusteeship administration came to an end on 21 October 1986, when a Compact of Free Association between the USA and the Republic of the Marshall Islands came into effect. By this agreement the USA recognized the Republic of the Marshall Islands as a fully sovereign and independent state. The UN Security Council terminated the UN Trust Territory of the Pacific in relation to the Marshall Islands and recognized its independence in December 1990.

The Republic of the Marshall Islands is a democracy based on a parliamentary system of government. Under the 1979 constitution, the executive is under the leadership of the President, who is elected by the Nitijela from among its members. The President serves for a four-year term. The legislature has two chambers, the Council of Iroij of 12 members and the Nitijela of 33 members. The Nitijela is the law-making chamber, to which the President and government are accountable. The Council of Iroij has an advisory role.

There are 24 local government districts, each of which usually consists of an elected council, a mayor and appointed local officials.

## HEAD OF STATE

*President*, Hon. Amata Kabua, *elected* 1979, *re-elected* 1984, 1988, 1992

THE GOVERNMENT *as at August 1994*

*Finance*, Hon. Ruben Zackras
*Foreign Affairs*, Hon. Tom Kijiner
*Transport and Communications*, Hon. Kunio Lemari
*Resources and Development*, Hon. Amsa Jonathan
*Education*, Hon. Phillip Muller
*Social Services*, Hon. Christopher Loeak
*Public Works*, Hon. Antonio Eliu
*Health and Environment*, Hon. Henchi Balos
*Justice*, Hon. Luckner Abner
*Internal Affairs*, Hon. Brenson Wase

BRITISH AMBASSADOR, His Excellency Timothy David, resident at Suva, Fiji

## JUDICIARY

There are four court levels; the Supreme Court; the High Court; the district and community courts; and the traditional rights courts. Trial is by jury. Jurisdiction of the traditional rights courts is limited to cases involving titles or land rights and other disputes arising from customary law and traditional practice.

## DEFENCE

The Republic of the Marshall Islands has no defence forces. The Compact of Free Association places full responsibility for defence of the Marshall Islands on the USA. The US Department of Defence controls islands within Kwajalein Atoll where it has a missile test range.

## ECONOMY

The economy is a mixture of subsistence and a service-based sector. About half the working population is engaged in agriculture and fishing, with coconut oil and copra production comprising 90 per cent of total exports. The service sector is based in Majuro and Ebeye and concentrated in banking and insurance, construction, transportation and tourism. Direct US aid under the Compact accounts for two-thirds of the islands budget. The islands charge large foreign (mainly Japanese) fishing fleets licences for fishing tuna in the waters around the islands. Japanese fleets pay some US$3 million a year. The USA and Japan are the major trading partners.

The GDP was (1988) US$68 million and GDP per head (1988) was US$1,600.

| Trade with UK | 1992 | 1993 |
|---|---|---|
| Imports from UK | £553,000 | £1,666,000 |
| Exports to UK | — | — |

## COMMUNICATIONS

Air Marshall Islands provides air services within the islands and to Hawaii. Continental Air Micronesia serves Majuro and Kwajalein with flights to Hawaii and Guam. Majuro also has shipping links to Hawaii, Australia, Japan and throughout the Pacific.

## CULTURE

The Marshallese culture revolves around a complex clan system of matrilineal structure. The social structure and system of land tenure are closely related. The sea has traditionally been the major source of food and thoroughfare among the atolls, and remains important to the Marshallese culture.

SOCIAL WELFARE

The state school system provides education up to age 18, but only 25 per cent of students proceed beyond elementary level because of inadequate resources.

Majuro and Ebeye have hospitals run by the government with aid from the US Public Health Service. Each outer island community has a health assistant.

## MAURITANIA
*République Islamique de Mauritanie*

Mauritania lies on the north-west coast of Africa. It is bounded on the south by Senegal, on the east by Mali, and on the north by Morocco, Algeria and the Western Sahara. The area is 397,955 sq. miles (1,030,700 sq. km). The population (UN estimate 1991) is 2,036,000. The official languages are French and Arabic.

CAPITAL – Nouakchott (850,000).
CURRENCY – Ouguiya of 5 khoums.
FLAG – Yellow star and crescent on green ground.
NATIONAL DAY – 28 November.

GOVERNMENT

Mauritania elected on 28 November 1958 to remain within the French Community as an autonomous republic. It became fully independent on 28 November 1960. In 1972 Mauritania left the Franc Zone.

Mauritania and Morocco took possession of the Western Sahara territory in February 1976 when Spain formally relinquished it and in April 1976 agreed on a new frontier dividing the territory between them. In August 1979, Mauritania relinquished all claim to the southern sector of the Western Sahara after a three-year war against the Polisario front guerrilla army.

After a military coup in 1978, Mauritania was ruled by a Military Committee for National Salvation (CMSN). Having previously rejected reform, in April 1991 President Taya announced a political amnesty and a referendum on the constitution, followed by multiparty elections for a reconvened Senate and National Assembly. The constitution was approved by a large majority in July. Multiparty elections to the Senate and National Assembly were held in March 1992 and won by the Republican Democratic and Social Party (PRDS) led by President Taya. The President appointed a cabinet of PRDS members in April 1992 but the legitimacy of the new government was undermined by the boycotting of the elections by the main opposition grouping, the Union of Democratic Forces (UDF). Conflict continues between the Arab-dominated government and the African minority in the south of the country.

HEAD OF STATE
*President*, Col. Maaouya Ould Sidi Ahmed Taya, *took power* 12 December 1984, *elected* 17 January 1992

CABINET *as at August 1994*

*Prime Minister*, Sidi Mohammed Ould Boubaker
*Foreign Affairs and Co-operation*, Mohammed Salem Ould Lekhel
*Defence*, Col. Ahmed Ould Minnih
*Justice*, Adema Samba Sow
*Interior, Posts and Telecommunications*, Lemrabet Cheikh Ahmed
*Finance*, Kan Acheikh
*Planning*, Taki Ould Sidi

*Fisheries and Maritime Economy*, Mohamed Lemine Salem Ould Dah
*Commerce, Handicrafts and Industry*, Cheikh Malainine Ould Ch'bih
*Mines*, Sidi Mohammed Fall
*Rural Development and Environment*, Sghaier Ould M'bareck
*Health and Social Affairs*, Mohammed Ould Lamar
*Culture and Islamic Orientation*, Limam Ould Tagaddi
*Relations with Parliament*, Rachid Ould Saleh
*Civil Service, Labour, Youth and Sports*, Abdallahi Ould Abdi
*Equipment and Transport*, Diagana Moussa
*Education and Literacy*, Cheikh Ould Ali

EMBASSY OF THE ISLAMIC REPUBLIC OF MAURITANIA
5 rue de Montevideo, Paris XVIe, France
Tel: Paris 45048854

*Ambassador Extraordinary and Plenipotentiary*, His Excellency Muhammad Al-Hanchi Ould Muhammad Saleh, apptd 1989, resident at Paris

BRITISH AMBASSADOR, His Excellency Sir Allan Ramsay, KBE, CMG, resident at Rabat, Morocco

ECONOMY

Mauritania's main source of potential wealth lies in rich deposits of iron ore around Zouérate, in the north of the country.

In October 1992 Mauritania agreed a four-year economic restructuring programme with the IMF to reduce inflation and the country's external debt. In late 1992 the IMF announced a US$47 million loan to support the government's economic and financial reform programme up to September 1995, with a further US$23 million loan announced in January 1994.

| Trade with UK | 1992 | 1993 |
|---|---|---|
| Imports from UK | £3,407,000 | £8,418,000 |
| Exports to UK | 12,757,000 | 15,071,000 |

## MAURITIUS

Mauritius is an island group lying in the Indian Ocean, 550 miles east of Madagascar, between 57° 17′ and 57° 46′ E. longitude and 19° 58′ and 20° 33′ S. latitude. Mauritius and Rodrigues with the other outer islands comprise an area of 790 sq. miles (2,045 sq. km).

Mauritius enjoys a sub-tropical maritime climate, with a wide range of rainfall and temperature resulting from the mountainous nature of the island. Humidity is high throughout the year.

POPULATION – The population (1992 estimate, excluding Rodrigues and the outer islands) was 1,092,384, made up of Asiatic races (Hindus 52.6 per cent, Muslims 16.5 per cent), and persons of European (mainly French) extraction, mixed and African descent (28.3 per cent). English is the official language but French may be used in the National Assembly and lower law courts. However, Creole is the most commonly used language and several Indian languages are also used.

CAPITAL – ΨPort Louis, population (1992) 143,444; other centres are Beau Bassin-Rose Hill (94,890); Curepipe (75,262); Vacoas-Phoenix (92,846) and Quatre Bornes (75,262).
CURRENCY – Mauritius rupee of 100 cents.
FLAG – Red, blue, yellow and green horizontal stripes.

## GOVERNMENT

NATIONAL ANTHEM – Glory to thee, Motherland.
NATIONAL DAY – 12 March.

Mauritius was discovered in 1511 by the Portuguese; the Dutch visited it in 1598 and named it Mauritius after Prince Maurice of Nassau. From 1638 to 1710 it was held as a small Dutch colony and in 1715 the French took possession but did not settle it until 1721. Mauritius was taken by a British force in 1810 and became a Crown Colony. Mauritius became an independent state within the Commonwealth on 12 March 1968 and a republic on 12 March 1992.

The President is head of state and is elected by the members of the National Assembly. The Prime Minister, appointed by the President, is the member of the National Assembly who appears to the President best able to command the support of the majority of members of the Assembly. Other ministers are appointed by the President acting in accordance with the advice of the Prime Minister.

The National Assembly has a normal term of five years and consists of 62 elected members (the island of Mauritius is divided into 20 three-member constituencies and Rodrigues returns two members), and eight specially-elected members. Of the latter, four seats go to the 'best loser' of whichever communities in the island are under-represented in the Assembly after the general election and the four remaining seats are allocated on the basis of both party and community.

At the general election held on 15 September 1991, the ruling alliance of the Mouvement Socialiste Militant (MSM), Mouvement Militant Mauricien (MMM) and the Mouvement Travailliste Democrate (MTD) gained 57 of the 62 seats available and formed the government.

HEAD OF STATE
*President*, Cassam Uteem, *elected by National Assembly* June 1992

COUNCIL OF MINISTERS *as at August 1994*

*Prime Minister, Minister of Defence and Internal Security, Attorney-General, Information, Internal and External Communications and the Outer Islands,* Rt. Hon. Sir Anerood Jugnauth, KCMG, QC
*Deputy PM, Minister for Economic Planning and Development,* Hon. Dr Paramhamsa Nababsing
*External Affairs,* Hon. Ahmud Swalay Kasenally
*Finance,* Hon. Ramakrishna Sithanen
*Education and Science,* Hon. Armoogum Parsuramen
*Trade and Shipping,* Hon. Anil Kumar Bachoo
*Energy, Water Resources and Postal Services,* Hon. Mahyendrah Utchanah
*Housing, Lands and Town and Country Planning,* Hon. Louis Darga
*Social Security and National Solidarity,* Hon. Karl Auguste Offman
*Women's Rights, Child Development and Family Welfare,* Hon. Sheilabhai Bappoo
*Youth and Sports,* Hon. Michael Glover
*Rodrigues,* Hon. Serge Clair
*Co-operatives and Handicrafts,* Hon. Jagdishwar Goburdhun
*Agriculture and Natural Resources,* Hon. Keertee Coomar Ruhee
*Industry and Industrial Technology,* Hon. Jean Claude Raoul de l'Estrac
*Works,* Hon. Dwarkanath Gungah
*Local Government,* Hon. Premdut Koonjoo
*Civil Service Affairs and Employment,* Hon. Ashok Kumar Jugnauth
*Environment and Quality of Life,* Hon. Ahmud Khodabux

*Manpower Resources, Vocational and Technical Training,* Hon. Ramduthsing Jaddoo
*Health,* Hon. Jean Regis Finette
*Fisheries and Marine Resources,* Hon. Mathieu Ange Laclé
*Tourism,* Hon. Noe Ah-Quret Lee Cheong Lem
*Arts, Culture, Leisure and Reform Institutions,* Hon. Mookhesswur Choonee
*Labour and Industrial Relations,* Hon. Dharmanand Fokeer

MAURITIUS HIGH COMMISSION
32–33 Elvaston Place, London SW7 5NW
Tel 0171-581 0294
*High Commissioner,* His Excellency Babooram Mahadoo, apptd 1992

BRITISH HIGH COMMISSION
Les Cascades Building, Edith Cavell Street, Port Louis (PO Box 1063)
Tel: Port Louis 1361
*High Commissioner,* His Excellency John Clive Harrison, apptd 1993

BRITISH COUNCIL REPRESENTATIVE, M. Bootle, PO Box III, Foondun Building, 2nd Floor, Royal Road, Rose Hill.

## EDUCATION

Primary and secondary education are free and primary education is compulsory. In 1992 some 92 per cent of children aged 5–18 were in education, with 129,738 children at 283 primary schools. At secondary level there were a total of 83,591 students attending 122 secondary schools; fees and teachers' salaries in the private secondary schools are paid by government. There are a number of training facilities offering vocational training. The Institute of Education is responsible for training primary and secondary schoolteachers and for curriculum development. The University of Mauritius had 1,858 students in 1992–3. Estimated expenditure on education in 1992–3 was Rs.1,440,200,000.

## ECONOMY

About 55 per cent of the total sugar crop is produced on plantations, while smaller owners (cultivating less than ten acres) cultivate about 24 per cent of the land under cane. Tea and tobacco are also grown commercially but on a smaller scale than sugar. Production in 1993 was: sugar, 562,026 tonnes; tea (manufactured), 5,931 tonnes; tobacco (leaves), 1,015 tonnes. In 1993 production of molasses, mainly for export, was 162,000 tonnes. Other products include alcohol, rum, denatured spirits, perfumed spirits and vinegar.

The bulk of the island's requirements in manufactured products still has to be imported. However, the Mauritius Export Processing Zone (MEPZ) scheme, introduced in 1971, has attracted investment from overseas and the number of export-orientated enterprises has risen from ten in 1971 to 536 at the end of 1993, employing 85,621 people. The biggest firms are in clothing manufacture, particularly woollen knitwear, but the range of goods produced includes toys, plastic products, leather goods, diamond cutting and polishing, watches, television sets and telephones.

Tourism is a major source of income for Mauritius, with an estimated 374,630 tourists in 1993. Earnings from tourism in 1993 are estimated to be Rs.5,300 million. The neighbouring French island of Réunion is the most important source of tourists, followed closely by mainland France.

## FINANCE

The main sources of government revenue are private and company income tax, customs and excise duties, mainly on imports but also on sugar exports.

|                               | 1993-4     | 1994-5*    |
|-------------------------------|-----------|-----------|
| Public revenue                | Rs.12,937m | Rs.13,800m |
| Public expenditure (recurrent) | 13,250m    | 14,290m    |
| * estimate                    |           |           |

TRADE

Most foodstuffs and raw materials have to be imported from abroad. Apart from local consumption (about 36,500 tonnes a year), the sugar produced is exported, mainly to Britain.

|               | 1991       | 1992       |
|---------------|-----------|-----------|
| Total imports | Rs.24,650m | Rs.25,265m |
| Total exports | 18,672m    | 20,572m    |

| Trade with UK  | 1992        | 1993        |
|----------------|------------|------------|
| Imports from UK | £59,892,000 | £73,335,000 |
| Exports to UK   | 272,610,000 | 281,362,000 |

COMMUNICATIONS

Port Louis, on the north-west coast, handles the bulk of the island's external trade. A bulk sugar terminal capable of handling the total crop began operating in 1980. The international airport is located at Plaisance in the south-east of the island about five miles from Mahébourg. There are five daily newspapers and 15 weeklies, mostly in French, and two Chinese daily papers and one weekly paper. The Mauritius Broadcasting Corporation has a monopoly of radio broadcasting in the country; television was introduced in 1965. There is a satellite communications ground station near Port Louis.

RODRIGUES AND DEPENDENCIES

Rodrigues, formerly a dependency but now part of Mauritius, is about 350 miles east of Mauritius, with an area of 40 square miles. Population (1992) 34,493. Cattle, salt fish, sheep, goats, pigs, maize and onions are the principal exports. The island is administered by an Island Secretary.
*Island Secretary*, R. Gajeelee

The islands of Agalega and St Brandon are dependencies of Mauritius. Total population (1989) 500. Other small islands, formerly Mauritian dependencies, have since 1965 constituted the British Indian Ocean Territory (*see* British Dependent Territories section).

---

MEXICO
*Estados Unidos Mexicanos*

---

Mexico occupies the southern part of North America, with an extensive seaboard to both the Atlantic and Pacific Oceans, extending from 14° 33' to 32° 43' N. latitude and 86° 46' to 117° 08' W. longitude. It covers an area of 761,605 sq. miles (1,972,547 sq. km).

The Sierra Nevada, known in Mexico as the Sierra Madre, and Rocky Mountains continue south from the northern border with the USA, running parallel to the west and east coasts. The interior consists of an elevated plateau between the two ranges. In the west is the peninsula of Lower California, separated from the mainland by the Gulf of California. The main rivers are the Rio Grande del Norte, which forms part of the northern boundary and is navigable for about 70 miles from its mouth in the Gulf of Mexico, and the Rio Grande de Santiago, the Rio Balsas and Rio Papaloapan.

POPULATION – At the 1990 census, the total population was 81,140,922; a 1991 UN estimate gives a figure of 87,836,000.

Spanish is the official language of Mexico and is spoken by about 95 per cent of the population. In addition, there are five basic groups of Indian languages (Náhuatl, Maya, Zapotec, Otomí, Mixtec) and 59 dialects derived from them. The poet Octavio Paz won the Nobel Prize for Literature in 1991.

CAPITAL – Mexico City, population of metropolitan area (1990 census) 14,987,051. Other cities (1990 census) are:

| Guadalajara | 2,846,000 | Puebla        | 1,454,526 |
|-------------|-----------|---------------|-----------|
| Monterrey   | 2,521,697 | León          | 956,070   |
| Torréon     | 876,456   | Ciudad Juarez | 797,679   |
| Toluca      | 827,339   | Tijuana       | 742,686   |

CURRENCY – Peso of 100 centavos.

FLAG – Three vertical bands in green, white, red, with the Mexican emblem (an eagle on a cactus devouring a snake) in the centre.

NATIONAL ANTHEM – Mexicanos, Al Grito De Guerra (Mexicans, to the war cry).

NATIONAL DAY – 16 September (Proclamation of Independence).

HISTORY

The present Mexico and Guatemala were once the centre of a civilization which flowered in the periods from AD 500 to 1100 and 1300 to 1500 and collapsed before the little army of Spanish adventurers under Hernán Cortés in the years following 1519. Pre-Columbian Mexico was divided between different but connected Indian cultures, each of which has left distinctive archaeological remains. The best-known of these are Chichén Itzá, Uxmal, Bonampak and Palenque, in Yucatán and Chiapas (Maya); Teotihuacon, renowned for the Pyramid of the Sun in the Valley of Mexico (Teotihuacáno); Monte Albán and Mitla, near Oaxaca (Zapotec); El Tajín in the state of Veracruz (Totonac); and Tula in the state of Hidalgo (Toltec). The last and most famous Indian culture, the Aztec, based on Tenochitlán, suffered more than the others from the Spanish and very few Aztec monuments remain.

After the conquest, the Spanish appointed a Viceroy to rule their new dominions, which they called New Spain. The country was largely converted to Christianity and a distinctive colonial civilization, representing a marriage of Indian and Spanish traditions, developed. In 1810 a revolt began against Spanish rule. This was finally successful in 1821, when a precarious independence was proclaimed.

Friction with the United States in Texas led to the war of 1845-8, at the end of which Mexico was forced to cede the northern provinces of Texas, California and New Mexico. In 1862 Mexican insolvency led to invasion by French forces which installed Archduke Maximilian of Austria as Emperor. The empire collapsed with the execution of the Emperor in 1867 and the austere reformer Juárez restored the republic. Juárez's death was followed by the dictatorship of Porfirio Diaz, which saw an enormous increase in foreign, particularly British and American, investment in the country. In 1910 began the Mexican Revolution which reformed the social structure and the land system, curbed the power of foreign companies and ushered in the independent industrial Mexico of today. In 1986 Mexico joined GATT and began a liberalization programme of privatization and administrative reform.

GOVERNMENT

Under the constitution of 1917 (as subsequently amended), Congress consists of a Senate of 64 members, elected for six years, and of a Chamber of Deputies, at present numbering

500, elected for three years. Presidents, who wield full executive powers, are elected for six years; they cannot be re-elected.

There are nine registered political parties, of which the largest and most influential is the Partido Revolucionario Institucional (PRI) which for more than 60 years has constituted the governing party despite constant allegations of electoral fraud. The main opposition parties are Partido de Acción Nacional (PAN) and Partido de la Renovación Democratica (PRD). In June 1992 the state of the parties in the Chamber of Deputies was: PRI 320, PAN 89, PRD and allied parties 91.

Since he took office in 1988 President Salinas de Gortari has reformed Mexico's political, economic and social systems. Market economic reforms have brought about significant economic growth, whilst political reform has reduced corruption and the autocratic control by the PRI. However, certain areas of the country and sections of the population remain untouched by the reforms, and there was an armed revolt of peasant Indians in the southern state of Chiapas in January 1994. The revolt highlighted continuing charges against the PRI of corruption and fraud at national and local level and these continued up to the 21 August 1994 presidential and Congressional elections. Although fraud and irregularities in the elections were confirmed, they were considered to be on a much smaller scale than in the past. PRI candidate Ernesto Zedillo won the presidential election with 50 per cent of the vote and will take office on 1 December 1994.

The country is divided into 31 states and the federal district of Mexico City.

### HEAD OF STATE

*President*, Carlos Salinas de Gortari, *elected*, 4 June 1988, *took office*, 1 December 1988

### CABINET *as at August 1994*

*Interior*, Dr Jorge Carpizo McGregor
*Foreign Affairs*, Manuel Tello Macías
*Finance and Public Credit*, Dr Pedro Aspe Armella
*Defence*, Gen. Antonio Riviello Bazán
*Navy*, Adm. Luis Carlos Ruano Angulo
*Energy, Mines and Parastatal Industries*, Emilio Lozoya Thalman
*Trade and Industrial Development*, Dr Jaime Serra Puche
*Agriculture and Water Resources*, Carlos Hank González
*Communications and Transport*, Emilio Gamboa Patrón
*Education*, José Angel Pescador Osuna
*Social Development*, Carlos Rojas Gutíerrez
*Health*, Dr Jesús Kumate Rodríguez
*Labour and Social Security*, Manuel Gomezperalta Damirón
*Agrarian Reform*, Victor Cervera Pacheco
*Tourism*, Jesús Silva Herzog
*Fisheries*, Guillermo Jiménez Morales
*Attorney-General*, Humberto Benítez Trevino
*Attorney-General of Federal District*, Ernesto Santillana Santillana
*Comptroller-General*, María Elena Vazquez Nava
*Mayor of Mexico City*, Manuel Aguilera Gómez

### MEXICAN EMBASSY

42 Hertford Street, London W1Y 7TF
Tel 0171-499 8586

*Ambassador Extraordinary and Plenipotentiary*, His Excellency Dr Juan José De Olloqui, apptd 1993
*Chargé D'Affairs*, Tomas Peñaloza
*Military Attaché*, Gen. Rafael Ramos-Padilla
*Consul-General*, M. Brito
*Counsellor*, F. Estandia (*Commercial*)

### BRITISH EMBASSY

Calle Río Lerma 71, Colonia Cuauhtémoc,
06500 Mexico City
Tel: Mexico City 207 20 89

*Ambassador Extraordinary and Plenipotentiary*, His Excellency Sir Roger Hervey, KCVO, CMG, apptd 1992
*Deputy Ambassador and Counsellor*, G. Berg
*Defence Attaché*, Col. S. R. Daniell
*First Secretary (Commercial)*, J. F. Thompson

There are British Consular Offices at *Mexico City, Acapulco, Cancun, Guadalajara, Mérida, Monterrey, Tampico, Tijuana, Veracruz*, and *Cuidad Juarez*.

BRITISH CONSULAR REPRESENTATIVE, Frank Edwards, Maestro Antonio Caso 127, Col. San Rafael (PO Box 30-588), Mexico 06470 DF.

BRITISH CHAMBER OF COMMERCE, British Trade Centre, Rio de la Plata 30, Col. Cuauhtemoc, CP 06500, Mexico City DF, *Manager*, Stephen Grant.

## COMMUNICATIONS

Veracruz, Tampico and Coatzacoalcos are the chief ports on the Atlantic, and Guaymas, Mazatlán, Puerto Lázaro Cárdenas, Acapulco, Salina Cruz and Puerto Madero on the Pacific. Work is proceeding on the reorganization and re-equipment of the whole system. Total track length of the railways was 240,186 km in 1990. Mexico City may be reached by at least three highways from the United States, and from the south from Yucatán as well as on two principal highways from the Guatemalan border.

There are 1,113 airports and landing fields in Mexico, of which 18 are equipped to handle long-distance flights. There are 166 airline companies, including two of the major, now private, national airlines, Mexicana de Aviación and Aero-méxico.

Teléfonos de México, now privatized, controls about 98 per cent of all telephone services.

## ECONOMY

In 1991 26 per cent of GDP was produced by commerce, 23 per cent by manufacturing, 33.6 per cent by services, 5 per cent by construction, 7.4 per cent by agriculture, 3.5 per cent by mining and 1.5 per cent by public utilities. Direct foreign investment at the end of 1991 was a cumulative US$33.9 billion, of which over 60 per cent was American. Privatization has been successful, with only 208 public enterprises remaining in 1991 (1,155 in 1982). Inflation has been reduced from 160 per cent to 8 per cent per annum, the foreign debt has been reduced, and spending on social programmes increased by 85 per cent since 1988. Agriculture has been reformed to allow communal farmers to buy and sell their own plots. In 1993 the budget surplus was US$6,000 million, or 1.1 per cent of GDP.

The principal crops are maize, beans, rice, wheat, sugar cane, coffee, cotton, tomatoes, chili, tobacco, chick-peas, groundnuts, sesame, alfalfa, vanilla, cocoa and many kinds of fruit. The maguey, or Mexican cactus, yields several fermented drinks, mezcal and tequila (distilled) and pulque (undistilled). Another species of the same plant supplies sisal-hemp (henequen). The forests contain mahogany, rosewood, ebony and chicle trees. Agriculture employs an estimated 20 per cent of the working population.

The principal industries are mining and petroleum, although there has been considerable expansion of both light and heavy industries. Exports of manufactured goods now average about 56 per cent of total exports. The steel industry expanded steadily until recently and current production is around 7.9m tons. In 1991, 989,000 motor vehicles were produced of which 365,000 were for export.

The mineral wealth is great, and principal minerals are gold, silver, copper, lead, zinc, quicksilver, iron and sulphur. Substantial reserves of uranium have been found. Mexico produces 25 per cent of the world's supply of fluorspar.

Oil exports were 1.37 million barrels per day in 1991. Daily production of natural gas is approximately 3 billion cubic feet. Oil reserves have increased substantially due to discoveries in the Gulf of Campeche. A refinery at Tula is the nation's largest; and new refineries in Monterrey, State of Nuevo Leon, and Salina Cruz, State of Oaxaca, are under construction.

## TRADE

Major imports include computers, auto assembly material, electrical parts, auto and truck parts, powdered milk, corn and sorghum, transport, sound-recording and power-generating equipment, chemicals, industrial machinery, pharmaceuticals and specialized appliances. Principal exports include oil, automobiles, auto engines, fruits and vegetables, shrimps, coffee, computers, cattle, glass, iron and steel pipes, and copper. The main trading partners are the USA (65.6 per cent), EC (15 per cent), Latin America (5.2 per cent) and Japan (5 per cent). The North American Free Trade Agreement, to which Mexico is a signatory, came into effect on 1 January 1994.

| Trade with UK | 1992 | 1993 |
|---|---|---|
| Imports from UK | £291,334,000 | £335,872,000 |
| Exports to UK | 152,205,000 | 165,743,000 |

## DEFENCE

Supreme command is vested in the President, exercised through the Ministries of Defence (for army and air force) and Marine. The total armed forces number some 175,000, including 60,000 conscripts. Conscription is decided by lottery and is for a one-year period. The Army has a strength of 130,000 (including 60,000 conscripts), with some 350 reconnaissance vehicles, 110 armoured personnel carriers, 120 artillery pieces.

The Navy has a strength of 37,000 personnel, including 8,000 marines, with three destroyers, 102 patrol and coastal vessels, and nine combat aircraft. The Air Force is 8,000 strong, with 101 combat aircraft and 25 armed helicopters.

## EDUCATION

Education is divided into primary, secondary and superior levels. In 1990 there were 18,061,000 in the first level, 6,599,000 in the second and 1,236,000 in the third.

---

# FEDERATED STATES OF MICRONESIA

---

The Federated States of Micronesia comprise more than 600 islands extending 2,900 km (1,800 miles) across the archipelago of the Caroline Islands in the western Pacific Ocean. The islands are located between the Equator and 9° N., and 138° and 168° E. Pohnpei island is 4,670 km (2,900 miles) south-west of Honolulu and 1,610 km (1,100 miles) south-east of Guam. The area is 700 sq. km (270 sq. miles). The islands vary geologically from mountainous islands to low coral atolls. The climate is tropical. Storms are common between August and December, and typhoons between July and November.

POPULATION – The population (1991 UN estimate) is 101,000: Pohnpei 31,000; Chuuk (formerly Truk) 52,000;

Yap 12,000; Kosrae 6,500. The population is Micronesian and predominantly Christian.

English (official) and eight other languages are used in different parts of the Federated States: Yapese, Ulithian, Woleaian, Ponapean, Nukuoran, Kapingamarangi, Trukese and Kosraen.

CAPITAL – The federal capital is Palikir, on Pohnpei island.
FLAG – United Nations blue with four white stars in the centre.

## HISTORY

The Spanish Empire claimed sovereignty over the Caroline Islands until 1899, when Spain withdrew from her Pacific territories and sold her possessions in the Caroline Islands to Germany. The Caroline Islands became a German protectorate until the outbreak of the First World War in 1914, when Japan took control of the islands on behalf of the Allied powers. After the war Japan continued to administer the territory under a League of Nations mandate. During the Second World War, United States armed forces took control of the islands from the Japanese. In 1947 the USA entered into agreement with the UN Security Council to administer the Micronesia area, of which the Federated States of Micronesia were a part, as the UN Trust Territory of the Pacific Islands.

The US Trusteeship administration came to an end on 3 November 1986, when a Compact of Free Association between the USA and the Federated States of Micronesia came into effect. By this agreement the USA recognized the Federated States of Micronesia as a fully sovereign and independent state. The independence of the Federated States of Micronesia was recognized by the UN in December 1990.

## GOVERNMENT

The Federated States of Micronesia is a federal republic of four constituent states: Chuuk, Kosrae, Pohnpei, Yap. The constitution separates the executive, legislative and judicial branches. There is a bill of rights and provision for traditional rights.

The executive comprises a federal President and Vice-President, both of whom must be chosen from amongst the four nationally-elected senators. There is a one-chamber legislature of 14 members, four members elected on a nation-wide basis and ten members elected from congressional districts apportioned by population.

HEAD OF STATE
*President*, Bailey Olter (Pohnpei)
*Vice-President*, Jacob Nina (Kosrae)

BRITISH AMBASSADOR, His Excellency Timothy David, resident at Suva, Fiji

LOCAL GOVERNMENT
Each of the constituent states has its own government and legislative system.
Pohnpei: *population*, 31,000; *capital*, Kolonia; *Governor*, Rasio Moses
Chuuk (Truk): *population*, 52,000; *capital*, Moen; *Governor*, Sasao Gouland
Yap: *population*, 12,000; *capital*, Colonia; *Governor*, Petrus Tun
Kosrae: *population*, 6,500; *capital*, Lelu; *Governor*, Yosivo George

## JUDICIARY

The judiciary is headed by the Supreme Court, which is divided into trial and appellate divisions. Below this, each state has its own judicial system.

## DEFENCE

The Compact of Free Association places full responsibility for the defence of the Federated States of Micronesia on the USA.

## ECONOMY

The economy is dependent mainly on subsistence agriculture and government spending. Copra and fish are the two main exports. The majority of the working population is engaged in government administration, subsistence farming, fishing, copra production and the growing tourist industry.

| Trade with UK | 1993 |
| --- | --- |
| Imports from UK | £116,000 |
| Exports to UK | 27,000 |

## CULTURE

Each of the four states has an indigenous culture, and these differ considerably from one another. Recognition of the role of traditional leaders and customs is common to all, though Kosrae has no traditional leaders.

---

## MOLDOVA
*Republica Moldovenească*

Moldova has an area of 13,912 sq. miles (33,700 sq. km) and occupies the extreme south-western corner of the former USSR. To the north, east and south-east it is bordered by the Ukraine, and to the west by Romania. The border with Romania is formed by the Pruth (Prut) river, but the main river of the republic is the Dniester, navigable along its whole course. The northern part of the republic consists of flat steppe lands, in the centre there are woody hills, and in the south low-lying steppe lands. Forests skirt the Dniester. The climate is moderate.

POPULATION – The population (official estimate 1994) is 4,359,000, of which 65 per cent are Moldovan, 14.2 per cent Ukrainian and 13 per cent Russian, together with smaller numbers of Gagauz (ethnic Turks), Jews and Bulgarians. Most of the population are adherents of the Romanian Orthodox Church.

LANGUAGE – Moldovan 65 per cent, Ukranian 14.2 per cent, Russian 13 per cent. Moldovan was made the official language (written in the Latin script) in 1989 but the use of Russian and Ukrainian in official business is permitted.

CAPITAL – Kishinev. Population 665,000 (1989 census).

CURRENCY – Leu (plural lei) which replaced the rouble in November 1993.

FLAG – Vertical stripes of blue, yellow, red, with the national arms in the centre.

NATIONAL DAY – 27 August (Independence Day).

## GOVERNMENT

A Moldovan feudal state was established in the 14th century when Slavic tribes who had previously lived under Roman and Byzantine rule integrated with Slavic tribes from further east. In the 15th century a Moldovan principality was formed which entered into military and political alliances with Muscovy before being conquered and absorbed into the Turkish Empire in the 16th century. Moldova became the site of many Russo-Turkish battles and skirmishes in the 18th century before the area between the Dniester and Prut rivers (later known as Bessarabia) was annexed to the Russian Empire by the Bucharest Peace Treaty 1812.

After the Russian Revolution in 1917, Bessarabia was under the control of White Russian forces and was annexed to Romania under the Versailles Peace Treaty 1919. In 1924 the Moldavian Autonomous Soviet Socialist Republic (ASSR) was established on the east bank of the Dniester river as part of Soviet Ukraine. In August 1940 the Soviet Union forced Romania to cede Bessarabia to the Soviet Union and the Moldavian Soviet Socialist Republic was formed from the fusion of the majority of Bessarabia (the southernmost parts were incorporated into the Ukraine) with the Moldavian ASSR.

When Moldova (formerly Moldavia) declared its independence from the USSR in August 1991, the majority ethnic Romanian (Moldovan) population expressed a wish to rejoin Romania. This alienated the ethnic Ukrainian and Russian populations, who form a majority east of the Dniester. After failed negotiations and several armed clashes, the Ukrainian and Russian populations declared their independence from Moldova as the Transdniester republic in December 1991. The Moldovan government refused to recognize this and throughout the first half of 1992 a war was waged between government forces and Transdniester forces, who were supported by the 30,000-strong former Soviet 14th Army stationed in Transdniester and by Cossack volunteers from Russia.

A mainly Russian CIS peacekeeping force (later changed to a joint Russian-Moldovan-Transdniester force) was deployed in July 1992 and a ceasefire has held since August 1992. Although no final political solution has been reached on the future of the Transdniester republic and a state of armed truce remains, the Moldovan government in February 1994 agreed to a CSCE plan for the Transdniester area to have a high degree of autonomy within Moldova but no independent or federal status. Negotiations on the CSCE plan continue, while the Russian and Moldovan governments agreed in August 1994 on the withdrawal of the 14th Army over a three-year period. The idea of reunification with Romania was defeated by a 90 per cent vote against in a national referendum on 6 March 1994, following which the Moldovan parliament in April 1994 voted to ratify the CIS agreement and joined the organization.

The Moldovan Popular Front government which came to power in the 1990 legislative elections to the 380-seat Supreme Soviet was replaced in July 1992 by a government of national accord led by the Peasant Democratic Party, which began an economic reform programme in 1993. The former Communists of the Agrarian Democratic Party were brought back to power in the legislative election of February 1994 and formed a coalition government with the Socialist Party.

HEAD OF STATE
*President*, Mircea Snegur, *elected* 8 December 1991

GOVERNMENT *as at August 1994*

*Prime Minister*, Andrei Sangeli
*First Deputy PMs*, Michail Koshkodan; Nickolai Andronati
    (*Industry*)
*Minister of State*, Gheorghe Gusac
*National Economy*, Valerian Boboutac
*Agriculture and Foodstuffs*, Vitali Gorincioi
*Industry*, Grigore Trifoi
*Transport*, Nicolai Alinov

*Information, Science and Communications,* Ion Cassian
*Public Health,* Timofei Mosneaga
*Culture,* Mihail Cebotari
*Justice,* Vasile Sturza
*Internal Affairs,* Maj.-Gen. Constantin Antoci
*Foreign Affairs,* Mihai Popov
*National Security,* Col. Vasile Calmoi
*Defence,* Maj.-Gen. Pavel Creanga
*Finance,* Valeriu Chitan
*Education,* Pavel Gauges
*Relations with Parliament,* Victor Pascas
*Utilities,* Mihai Severovan
*Social Protection,* Dumitru Nidelcu
*Privatization,* Ceslav Ciobanu
*Power Engineeering,* Valentin Chumak

BRITISH AMBASSADOR, His Excellency Sir Brian Fall, KCMG, resident at Moscow

## ECONOMY

The main sector of the economy is agriculture, especially viniculture, fruit-growing and market gardening. Industry is small and concentrated east of the Dniester. Severe drought in 1992, the severance of most trading ties with former Soviet republics, war damage and reductions in Russian fuel deliveries paralysed the economy in 1992–4. Entry into the CIS and its economic union in April 1994 should, however, improve trading ties with other former Soviet republics and increase Russian fuel supplies. An economic reform pro-gramme began in summer 1993 and is being supported by IMF credits of some US$135 million.

| *Trade with UK* | 1993 |
|---|---|
| Imports from UK | £2,243,000 |
| Exports to UK | 325,000 |

## MONACO
*Principauté de Monaco*

A small principality on the Mediterranean, with land frontiers joining France at every point, Monaco is divided into the districts of Monaco-Ville, La Condamine, Fontvielle and Monte Carlo. The principality comprises a narrow strip of land about two miles long with an area of approx. 195 hectares, and approximately 28,000 inhabitants (1990).

CAPITAL – Monaco-Ville, population (1982) 1,234.
CURRENCY – Monaco uses the French franc of 100 centimes as legal tender.
FLAG – Two equal horizontal stripes, red over white.
NATIONAL ANTHEM – Hymne Monegasque.
NATIONAL DAY – 19 November.

## GOVERNMENT

The principality, ruled by the Grimaldi family since the late 13th century, was abolished during the French Revolution and re-established in 1815 under the protection of the kingdom of Sardinia. In 1861 Monaco came under French protection.
The 1962 constitution, which can be modified only with the approval of the National Council, maintains the traditional hereditary monarchy and guarantees freedom of association, trade union freedom and the right to strike. Legislative power is held jointly by the Prince and a unicameral, 18-member National Council elected by universal suffrage. Executive power is exercised by the Prince and a four-member Council of Government, headed by a Minister of State. The judicial code is based on that of France. Monaco became a member of the United Nations in 1993.

HEAD OF STATE
*HSH The Prince of Monaco,* Prince Rainier III Louis-Henri-Maxence Bertrand, *born* 31 May 1923, *succeeded* 9 May 1949; *married* 19 April 1956, Miss Grace Patricia Kelly (died 14 September 1982) and *has issue* Prince Albert (*see* below); Princess Caroline Louise Marguerite, *born* 23 January 1957; and Princess Stephanie Marie Elisabeth, *born* 1 February 1965
*Heir,* HRH Prince Albert Alexandre Louis Pierre, *born* 14 March 1958

*President of the Crown Council,* Jean-Charles Marquet
*President of the National Council,* Dr Jean-Louis Campora
*Minister of State,* Jacques Dupont, *appointed* 1991

CONSULATE-GENERAL OF MONACO
4 Cromwell Place, London SW7 2JE
Tel 0171-225 2679
*Consul-General,* I. B. Ivanovic.

BRITISH CONSUL-GENERAL, John Illman, apptd 1990, resident at Marseilles, France

## ECONOMY

The whole available ground is built over so that there is no cultivation, though there are some notable public and private gardens. The economy is based on real estate revenues, the financial sector and tourism (over 250,000 visitors a year). Monaco has a small harbour (30 ft alongside quay) and the import duties are the same as in France.

## MONGOLIA
*State of Mongolia*

Mongolia is a large and sparsely populated country to the north of China. Its area is 604,250 sq. miles (1,565,000 sq. km). Its population (1992 estimate) is 2,156,000; this total constitutes only part of the Mongolians of Asia, a number of whom are to be found in China and in the neighbouring regions of the Russian Federation, especially the Mongolian Buryat Autonomous Region.
Mongolia, which is almost nowhere below 1,000 metres above sea level, forms part of the central Asiatic plateau and rises towards the west in the mountains of the Mongolian Altai and Hangai ranges. The Hentai range, situated to the north-east of the capital Ulan Bator, is less high. The Gobi region covers much of the southern half of the country and contains sand deserts interspersed with semi-desert. There are several long rivers and many lakes, but good water is scarce as much of the lake water is salty. The climate is harsh, with a short mild summer giving way to a long winter when temperatures can drop as low as − 50°C.

CAPITAL – Ulan Bator (Ulaanbaator), population (1993) 600,500.
CURRENCY – Tugrik of 100 möngö.
FLAG – Vertical tri-colour red, blue, red and in the hoist the traditional Soyombo symbol in gold.
NATIONAL DAY – 11 July.

## GOVERNMENT

Mongolia, under Genghis Khan the conqueror of China and much of Asia, was for many years a buffer state between

Tsarist Russia and China, although it was under general Chinese suzerainty. The outbreak of the Chinese Revolution in 1911 led to a declaration of autonomy under Chinese suzerainty which was confirmed by the Sino-Russian Treaty of Kiakhta (1915) but cancelled by a unilateral Chinese declaration in 1919. Later the country became a battleground of the Russian civil war, and Soviet and Mongolian troops occupied Ulan Bator in 1921; this was followed by another declaration of independence. In 1924 the Soviet Union in a treaty with China again recognized the latter's sovereignty over Mongolia, but this was never properly exercised because of China's preoccupation with internal affairs and later by the war with Japan. The Mongolian People's Republic was formally established in 1924. Under the Yalta Agreement, Chiang Kai-shek agreed to a plebiscite, held in 1945, in which the Mongolians declared their desire for independence and this was formally recognized by China.

The Mongolian People's Revolutionary Party (MPRP) was the sole political party from 1924 to 1990. Demonstrations in favour of political and economic reform began in December 1989 and led to changes in the MPRP leadership in March 1990. The MPRP's constitutionally guaranteed monopoly of power was subsequently relinquished, and the introduction of a multiparty system was approved by the Great People's Hural (parliament). The MPRP won the first multiparty elections, held in July 1990. Since then, and following Moscow's lead, Mongolia has embarked on a programme of political and economic reforms.

A new constitution was approved in January 1992 which enshrines the concepts of democracy, a mixed economy, free speech, and neutrality in foreign affairs. The Great and Little Hurals were abolished, and a new unicameral Great Hural became the legislative body of the country. Elections were held in June 1992 which were won by the MPRP with 57 per cent of the vote and 71 out of 76 seats. The country's first direct presidential election was held in June 1993 and won by the incumbent Punsalmaagiyn Orchirbat who stood as an opposition candidate after the MPRP refused to endorse him as its candidate.

The last remaining former Soviet armed forces personnel were withdrawn in late 1992.

The country and three city districts (Ulan Bator, Darkhan and Erdenet) are divided into 21 *aimaks* (provinces) and beneath these into 258 *somons* (districts), and these form the basis of the state organization of the country.

HEAD OF STATE
*President*, Punsalmaagiyn Ochirbat, *elected* June 1993

CABINET *as at August 1994*

*Prime Minister*, Puntsagiyn Jasray
*Deputy PM, Administration*, Lhamsurengiyn Enebish
*Deputy PM*, Choyjilsurengiyn Purevdorj
*Defence*, Maj.-Gen. Shagalyn Jadambaa
*Minister of State and Chairman of National Development
    Board*, Chultemiyn Ulaan
*Agriculture and Food*, Tseveenjavyn Oold
*Foreign Relations*, Tserenpiliyn Gombosuren
*Culture*, Nambaryn Enhbayar
*Demography and Labour*, Erdeniyn Gormbojav
*Finance*, Dalrain Davaasambun
*Energy, Geology and Minerals*, Byambyn Jigjid
*Law*, Narnsraijavyn Luvsanjav
*Infrastructure Development*, Razdakyn Sandalhaan
*Science and Education*, Nadmidyn Olziihutag
*Trade and Industry*, Tsevegmediyn Tsogt
*Health*, Pagvajavyn Nyamdavaa
*Nature and the Environment*, Zambyn Batjargal
*Chairman of the Great Hural*, Natsagiyn Bagabandi

EMBASSY OF MONGOLIA
7 Kensington Court, London W8 5DL
Tel 0171-937 0150

*Ambassador Extraordinary and Plenipotentiary*, His
    Excellency Choisurengyn Baatar, apptd 1991

BRITISH EMBASSY
30 Enkh Taivny Gudamzh (PO Box 703), Ulan Bator 13
Tel: Ulan Bator 358133

*Ambassador Extraordinary and Plenipotentiary*, His
    Excellency Ian Sloane, apptd 1994

ECONOMY

Traditionally the Mongolians led a nomadic life tending flocks of sheep, goats, horses, cows and camels. With the coming of the Communist regime and especially after 1952, great efforts were made to settle the population, but a proportion still live nomadically or semi-nomadically in the traditional *ger* (circular tent). The pastoral population was collectivized at the end of the 1950s into huge *negdels* (co-operatives) and state farms which have hastened the process of settlement, but within these the herdsmen and their families still move with their *gers* from pasture to pasture as the seasons change. Total livestock was 25 million in 1993. The semi-desert areas of the Gobi region provide pasture for sheep, goats, camels, horses and some cattle.

In the steppe areas to the north of the Gobi pasturage is better and livestock more abundant. Even further north, in the better-watered provinces, grain, fodder and vegetable crops are grown.

Membership of the Communist bloc brought Mongolia considerable quantities of aid from other socialist countries, especially from the Soviet Union, but this ended in 1990. In June 1993 the IMF approved a US$31 million loan to Mongolia to aid its economic restructuring after Mongolia had allowed the tugrik to float freely. Western aid donors pledged some US$150 million in aid for 1993–4 in September 1993 and Japan provided a loan of US$90 million at the same time. In April 1994 Mongolia signed a treaty of friendship and mutual assistance with China to gain aid and economic and technological co-operation. The country has been experiencing transitional problems in its attempt to establish a market economy, such as food and fuel shortages, inflation, and unemployment.

Although the economy remains predominantly based on the herds of animals, factories have started up and the coal and electricity industries are being developed to provide an industrial base. A joint Mongolian/Soviet enterprise for copper and molybdenum mining was opened in 1978 at Erdenet. Coal production had risen to 8.04 m tons by 1990.

Ulan Bator and Darkhan are the main seats of industry. Industries include lime, cement and building materials, a flour mill and a power station. Choibalsan is also being developed industrially.

Mongolia's fundamental difficulty is its very small population and labour force, and its basic infasructure. Communication is still difficult in the country as there are very few tarmac roads and horses are still the characteristic means of transport for the rural population. The trans-Mongolian railway links Mongolia with both China and Russia.

TRADE

Foreign trade was formerly dominated by the Soviet Union and other eastern bloc countries. Following the collapse of the CMEA, trade with western countries, Japan and South Korea is increasing. Since January 1991, trade is in hard currency, causing particular strain. The principal exports are animal by-products (especially wool, hides and furs) and cattle.

| Trade with UK | 1992 | 1993 |
|---|---|---|
| Imports from UK | £1,698,000 | £1,659,000 |
| Exports to UK | 2,166,000 | 2,284,000 |

## MOROCCO
### Al-Mamlaka Al-Maghrebia

Morocco is situated in the north-west of the African continent between 27° 40′ and 36° N. latitude and 1° and 13° W. longitude with an area estimated at 172,414 sq. miles (446,550 sq. km). It is traversed in the north by the Rif mountains and, in a south-west to north-east direction, by the Middle Atlas, the High Atlas, the Anti-Atlas and the Sarrho ranges. Much of the country is desert. The north-westerly point of Morocco is the peninsula of Tangier dominated by the Jebel Mousa which, with the rocky eminence of Gibraltar, was known to the ancients as the Pillars of Hercules, the western gateway of the Mediterranean.

POPULATION – The population (1990 estimate) is 27,575,000. Arabic is the official language. Berber is the vernacular, mainly in the mountain regions. French and Spanish are also spoken, mainly in the towns. Islam is the state religion.

CAPITAL – ΨRabat, population (including Salé) 1,494,000. Regional capitals, with municipal population figures as at 1991, are: ΨCasablanca (2,990,000); Marrakesh (644,000); Fez (719,000); Oujda (646,000); Meknes (484,000); ΨAgadir (420,000).

CURRENCY – Dirham (DH) of 100 centimes.

FLAG – Red, with green pentagram (the Seal of Solomon).

NATIONAL DAY – 3 March (Anniversary of the Throne).

## GOVERNMENT

Morocco became an independent sovereign state in 1956, following joint declarations made with France on 2 March 1956 and with Spain on 7 April 1956. The Sultan of Morocco, Sidi Mohammad ben Youssef, adopted the title of King Mohammad V.

The 1992 constitution states that Morocco is a democratic constitutional monarchy. The King nominates the Prime Minister and, on the latter's recommendation, appoints the members of the Council of Ministers. The government is responsible both to parliament and to the King. The unicameral legislature (Chamber of Representatives) has 333 members, 222 elected by direct universal suffrage (including five representing overseas workers) and 111 members elected by electoral colleges representing local government, industry, agriculture, professional and trade union groups. It may call votes of no confidence in the government.

Effective political power remains with the King despite the constitutional changes of October 1992 enhancing the Prime Minister's and legislature's powers. Legislative elections were held in June–September 1993, with the centre-right four-party Entente National coalition winning 154 seats and the leftist six-party Bloc Democratique winning 120 seats. After both coalitions had been unable to form a government, King Hassan appointed a government of technocrats and independents in November 1993.

### HEAD OF STATE
*HM The King of Morocco*, King Hassan II (Moulay Hassan Ben Mohammed), *born* 9 July 1929; *acceded* 3 March 1961
*Heir*, HRH Crown Prince Sidi Mohamed, *born* 21 August 1963

CABINET *as at August 1994*

*Prime Minister, Minister of Foreign Affairs and Co-operation*, Abdellatif Filali

*Minister of State*, Moulay Ahmed Alaoui

*Minister of State, Interior and Information*, Driss Basri

*Justice*, Mohammed Idrissi Alami Machichi

*National Education*, Mohammed Knidri

*Public Health*, Dr Abderrahim Harouchi

*Religious Endowments and Islamic Affairs*, Abdelkebir Alaoui M'Daghri

*Public Works, Vocational and Executive Training*, Mohamed Hassad

*Finance*, Mohamed Sagou

*Transport*, Rachidi El-Rhezouani

*Energy and Mines*, Abdelatif Gurraoui

*Youth and Sport*, Driss Alaoui M'Daghri

*Sea Fisheries and the Merchant Marine*, Mustapha Sahel

*Secretary-General of the Government*, Abdessadek Rabiaa

*Culture*, Allal Sinaceur

*Housing*, Driss Toulali

*Posts and Telecommunications*, Abdeslam Ahizoune

*Agriculture and Agricultural Reform*, Abdelaziz Meziane Belfkih

*Trade, Industry and Privatization*, Driss Jettou

*Employment and Social Affairs*, Rafiq Haddaoui

*Handicrafts, Foreign Investments and Foreign Trade*, Mourad Charif

*Tourism*, Serge Berdugo

*Ministers-Delegate*, Ahmed El Ouardi (*Moroccans Abroad*); Mohammed Mouaatassim (*Relations with Parliament*); Omar Azziman (*Human Rights*); Aziz Hasbi (*Administrative Affairs*); Abderrahmane Sbai; Omar Kabbaj; Abderrahmane Saidi

EMBASSY OF THE KINGDOM OF MOROCCO
49 Queen's Gate Gardens, London SW7 5NE
Tel 0171-581 5001/4

*Ambassador Extraordinary and Plenipotentiary*, His Excellency Khalil Haddaoui, apptd 1991

BRITISH EMBASSY
17 Boulevard de la Tour Hassan (BP 45), Rabat
Tel: Rabat 20905/6

*Ambassador Extraordinary and Plenipotentiary*, His Excellency Sir Allan Ramsay, KBE, CMG, apptd 1992
There is a British Consulate-General/Commercial Office at Casablanca, an office of the Embassy at Tangier and an Honorary Consulate at Agadir.

BRITISH COUNCIL REPRESENTATIVE, John Weston, BP 427, 36 rue Tanger, Rabat
BRITISH CHAMBER OF COMMERCE, 1st Floor, 185 Boulevard Zerktouni, Casablanca. Tel: 256920

## DEFENCE

The armed forces have a total active strength of 195,500, including authorized conscripts who serve 18-month terms. Total reserves number some 150,000 personnel. The Army has a strength of some 175,000 (100,000 conscripts), the majority of which has been deployed in southern Morocco and Western Sahara fighting the Polisario Front. It is equipped with 285 main battle tanks, 105 light tanks, 345 reconnaissance vehicles, 870 armoured infantry fighting vehicles and armoured personnel carriers, and 280 artillery pieces.

The Navy has a strength of 7,000, with one frigate, and 29 patrol and coastal combatant craft, together with a marine battalion. The Air Force has a strength of 13,500, with 93 combat aircraft and 24 armed helicopters. In addition, there are a paramilitary Gendarmerie Royale of 10,000 and an Auxiliary Force of 30,000 paramilitaries.

Morocco deploys some 2,000 troops in the United Arab Emirates and 360 in Equatorial Guinea. The UN has some 330 personnel in Western Sahara pending the referendum. Polisario deploys some 4,000 front line and 5,000 support troops in Western Sahara with Algerian-supplied and captured Moroccan tanks, armoured personnel carriers, anti-tank and anti-aircraft weapons.

## ECONOMY

Morocco's main sources of wealth are agricultural and mineral. The latest development plan (1987 onwards) emphasizes social improvement, industrial development, agriculture, fisheries and tourism.

Agriculture employs more than 40 per cent of the working population and accounts for about 36 per cent of exports. The main agricultural exports are fruit and vegetables, with cereals and sugar beet being produced and sheep reared for domestic consumption. Cork and wood-pulp are the most important commercial forest products. Esparto grass is also produced. There is a fishing industry and substantial quantities of canned fish, mainly sardines and fishmeal, are exported.

For a developing country Morocco has a large industrial sector, which accounts for some 70 per cent of exports (including mineral exports). The main sectors are chemicals, textiles and leather goods, food processing and cement production. Manufacturing industries are centred in Casablanca, Fez, Tangier and Safi.

Morocco's mineral exports are phosphates, fluorite, barite, manganese, iron ore, lead, zinc, cobalt, copper and antimony. Morocco possesses nearly three-quarters of the world's estimated reserves of phosphates. There are oil refineries at Mohammedia and Sidi Kacem handling about four million tonnes of crude oil per year, but no significant quantities of hydrocarbons have been found.

Tourism is of increasing importance to the economy, with development concentrated in Agadir and Marrakesh. In 1992, 3,252,062 foreign tourists visited Morocco and tourism accounted for 3–4 per cent of GDP. Workers remittances of some US$1,959 million in 1993 are also very important to the economy.

## TRADE

Morocco's main imports are petroleum products, motor vehicles, building materials, agricultural and other machinery, chemical products, sugar, green tea and other foodstuffs. The EU, led by France and Spain, is Morocco's largest trading partner. The main exports are textiles, phosphates and phosphoric acid, fertilizers, citrus fruits, and fish and seafoods.

|  | 1992 | 1993 |
|---|---|---|
| Imports | US$7,389m | US$6,643m |
| Exports | 3,995m | 3,680m |

| Trade with UK | 1992 | 1993 |
|---|---|---|
| Imports from UK | £123,301,000 | £168,303,000 |
| Exports to UK | 123,232,000 | 182,378,000 |

## COMMUNICATIONS

Railroads cover 1,175 miles (1,893 km), linking the major towns. An extensive network of 9,880 miles (15,900 km) of well-surfaced roads covers all the main towns. There are air services between Casablanca, Tangier, Agadir (seasonal), Marrakesh and London, and also between Tangier and Gibraltar connecting with London. Royal-Air-Maroc operates internal services and services to 36 states in Europe, Africa and Asia.

In 1984 there were seven Arabic and five French daily newspapers.

## EDUCATION

There are government primary, secondary and technical schools. In 1991 there were 4,890 government schools with a total of 3,608,757 pupils. At Fez there is a theological university of great repute in the Muslim world. There is a secular university at Rabat. A total of 206,725 students studied at 13 universities in 1991. Schools for special denominations, Jewish and Catholic, are permitted and may receive government grants. American schools operate in Rabat and Casablanca.

## WESTERN SAHARA

Formerly the Spanish Sahara, the territory was split between Morocco and Mauritania in 1976 after Spain withdrew in December 1975. In 1976 the Polisario Front (Frente Popular para la Liberacíon de Saguia y Río de Oro) declared Western Sahara to be an independent state, the Saharan Arab Democratic Republic, and formed a government led by Bouchraya Bayoune which remains in exile. The Polisario Front has been recognized as the legitimate government of Western Sahara by over 70 states and the Organization of African Unity. In 1979 Mauritania renounced its claim to its share of the territory, which was added by Morocco to its area. Morocco's annexation has been opposed by Polisario guerrillas, who want the territory to become an independent state.

In 1988, Morocco and the Polisario Front accepted a UN peace plan under which a ceasefire came into effect in September 1991, and a referendum to determine the future of the area was to have been held in January 1992. The referendum has not yet been held as the Moroccan government and the Polisario guerrillas have not agreed on the referendum terms or who should be eligible to vote. The UN Security Council intervened to break the impasse, passing resolution 809 (March 1993) which stipulates that the referendum should be a straight choice between independence or integration with Morocco. UN Security Council resolution 907 (March 1994) mandated the UN to establish a new voter registration list by means of a voter identification commission. The new list is to be ready by late summer 1994 and a referendum on the territory's future is due to be held by the end of 1994. This has been accepted by Polisario.

---

# MOZAMBIQUE
*República de Moçambique*

---

Mozambique lies on the east coast of Africa, and is bounded by Swaziland in the south, South Africa in the south and west, Zimbabwe in the west, Zambia and Malawi in the north-west and Tanzania in the north. It has an area of 309,495 sq. miles (801,590 sq. km), with a population (1991 UN estimate) of 16,084,000. The official language is Portuguese.

CAPITAL – Ψ Maputo, estimated population (1990), 1,150,000. Other main ports are Ψ Beira and Ψ Nacala.
CURRENCY – Metical (MT) of 100 centavos.
FLAG – Horizontally green, black, yellow with white fimbriations; a red triangle based on the hoist containing the national emblem.
NATIONAL DAY – 25 June (Independence Day).

## GOVERNMENT

Mozambique, discovered by Vasco de Gama in 1498 and colonized by Portugal, achieved complete independence from Portugal on 25 June 1975. The country was a Marxist one-party (Frelimo) state until a multiparty system was adopted in 1990, enshrining freedom of association and the free market. The legislative assembly has between 200 and 250 members.

Following two years of negotiations in Rome, the (Frelimo) Mozambican government and rebel Mozambican National Resistance (Renamo) signed a peace agreement in August 1992 which ended 16 years of civil war. Under the peace agreement the Frelimo government and Renamo troops were to have assembled at designated points around the country within one month of parliamentary ratification of the peace accord (which occurred on 9 October 1992) and to have handed over their weapons to UN monitors within six months. The majority of troops were to be demobilized and the remainder integrated to form a 30,000-strong Army and police force. However, the process was soon behind schedule, with arguments over demobilization and the late arrival of UN forces. The UN Operation for Mozambique (ONUMOZ) was approved by the Security Council on 16 December 1992, but the first of 6,000 UN troops and civilian police only arrived in May 1993. Multiparty presidential and legislative elections planned for June 1993 have been postponed to the end of October 1994. The demobilization of government and Renamo forces took palce between January and August 1994 and the formation of the new unified Mozambican Defence Armed Forces (FADM) is under way. Meanwhile, voter registration began on 1 June 1994 and the majority of the 1.3 million refugees in neighbouring states have been repatriated.

HEAD OF STATE
*President,* Joaquim Alberto Chissano, *sworn in* November 1986

COUNCIL OF MINISTERS *as at August 1994*
*Prime Minister,* Mario da Graca Machungo
*Foreign Affairs,* Pascoal Mocumbi
*National Defence,* Alberto Joaquim Chipande
*Co-operation,* Jacinto Veloso
*Minister in the Presidency,* Feliciano Gundana
*State Administration,* Aguiar Jonassane Reinaldo Mazula
*Education,* Aniceto dos Muchangos
*Interior,* Manuel Antonio
*Minister without Portfolio,* Mariano de Araujo Matsinha
*Transport and Communications,* Armando Emilio Guebuza
*Finance,* Eneas Da Conceicao Comiche
*Health,* Dr Leonardo Simao
*Information,* Rafael Maguni
*Construction and Water,* Joao Salomao
*Trade,* Daniel Gabriel Tembe
*Agriculture,* Alexandre Jose Zandamela
*Industry and Energy,* Octavio Muthemba
*Mineral Resources,* John Kachamila
*Justice,* Ossumane Ali Dauto
*Culture,* Jose Mateus Katupha
*Labour,* Teodato Mondim Da Silva Hunguana

EMBASSY OF THE REPUBLIC OF MOZAMBIQUE
21 Fitzroy Square, London W1P 5HJ
Tel 0171-383 3800

*Ambassador Extraordinary and Plenipotentiary,* His
Excellency Armando Alexandre Panguene, apptd 1988

BRITISH EMBASSY
Av. Vladimir I Lenine 310, CP 55, Maputo
Tel: Maputo 420111/2/5/6/7

*Ambassador Extraordinary and Plenipotentiary,* His
Excellency Richard J. Edis, CMG, apptd 1992

BRITISH COUNCIL REPRESENTATIVE, Gail Liesching, PO
Box 4178, Maputo

## ECONOMY

The basis of the economy is subsistence agriculture, but there is an industrial sector based mainly in Beira and Maputo. After giving priority to the development of collective farms and state enterprises in all sectors, the government is now encouraging the private sector and foreign investment, particularly in agriculture and consumer goods production. An IMF economic reform programme is being followed, with subsidies on basic foods having been removed. There are substantial coal deposits in Tete province and an offshore gas field at Pande. Mozambique has a range of aid and co-operation agreements with a number of countries and following the signing of the peace accord US$520 million in aid has been pledged for reconstruction. An agreement of non-aggression and good neighbourliness with South Africa was signed in 1984 (the Nkomati Accord), and in June 1994 a joint Mozambican-South African Chamber of Commerce was formed.

TRADE
Main exports are sugar, cashew nuts, prawns, copra, cotton, tea and sisal.

| Trade with UK | 1992 | 1993 |
|---|---|---|
| Imports from UK | £17,008,000 | £21,717,000 |
| Exports to UK | 2,593,000 | 1,568,000 |

## MYANMAR
*Pyidaungsu Myanma Naingngandaw - Union of Myanmar*

Myanmar (Burma) forms the western portion of the Indo-Chinese part of Asia, lying between 9° 58′ and 28° N. latitude and 92° 11′ and 101° 9′ E. longitude, with an extreme length of approximately 1,200 miles and an extreme width of 575 miles. It has a sea coast on the Bay of Bengal to the south and west, and a frontier with Bangladesh along the Naaf River and with India to the north-west. In the north and east the country borders China and there is a short frontier with Laos in the east, while the long finger of Tenasserim stretches southwards along the west coast of the Malay peninsula, forming a frontier with Thailand to the east. The total area is 261,218 sq. miles (676,552 sq. km).

Mountains enclose the Union on three sides. The principal river systems are the Kaladan-Lemro in Arakan, the Irrawaddy-Chindwin and the Sittang in central Myanmar, and the Salween which flows through the Shan Plateau.

POPULATION – The population (UN estimate 1991) is 42,561,000. The indigenous inhabitants are of similar racial types and speak languages of the Tibeto-Burman, Mon-Khmer and Thai groups. The three important non-indigenous elements are Indians, Chinese and those from Bangladesh. Burmese is the official language, but minority languages include Shan, Karen, Chin, Kayah and the various Kachin dialects. English is spoken in educated circles.

Buddhism is the religion of 85 per cent of the people, with 5 per cent Animists, 4 per cent Muslims, 4 per cent Hindus and less than 3 per cent Christians.

CAPITAL – ΨYangon (Rangoon). Population (1983):
Yangon District 3,973,872; city population 2,458,712.
The other major cities are Mandalay, population (1983):

Mandalay district 4,580,923; city 532,985; Mawlamyine (Moulmein) 219,991 and Pathein (Bassein) 144,092. Pagan, on the Irrawaddy, contains many sacred buildings.

CURRENCY – Kyat (K) of 100 pyas.

FLAG – Red, with a canton of dark blue, inside which are a cogwheel and two rice ears surrounded by 14 white stars.

NATIONAL DAY – 4 January.

## GOVERNMENT

The Union of Burma (the name was officially changed to the Union of Myanmar in June 1989) became an independent republic outside the British Commonwealth on 4 January 1948 and remained a parliamentary democracy for 14 years. In 1962 the army took power and suspended the parliamentary constitution. A Revolutionary Council of senior officers under Gen. Ne Win took measures to create a socialist state.

After months of popular demonstrations and rioting and a series of presidents during the summer of 1988, Gen. Saw Maung, leader of the armed forces, assumed power in September 1988. The People's Assembly, the Council of State and the Council of Ministers were abolished and replaced by the State Law and Order Restoration Council (SLORC). The constitution was effectively abrogated.

A People's Assembly Election Law was published in March 1989 committing the SLORC to hold multiparty elections. These were held on 27 May 1990, resulting in a majority for the National League for Democracy (NLD) even though its leader Aung San Suu Kyi had been under house arrest since July 1989. The SLORC refused to transfer power to a civilian government and large numbers of NLD MPs and supporters were detained. Others fled to the border areas with Thailand where they established an exile government led by Sein Wim, which is known as the National Coalition Government of the Union of Burma (NCGUB). However, following the replacement of Saw Maung by Than Shwe as SLORC Chairman and Prime Minister in April 1992, the government announced that it would begin a dialogue with some elements of the opposition. A Constitutional Convention of delegates appointed by the SLORC to discuss a future constitution convened in January 1993, was almost immediately adjourned, reopened in February and was adjourned again in April after the majority of the delegates refused to accept the leading role in politics demanded by the armed forces. The talks continue but progress has been minimal, with the next round expected to begin in autumn 1994. The SLORC has released about 2,000 political detainees but many, including Aung San Suu Kyi (who won the Nobel Peace Prize in 1991) and other senior leaders, remain in detention or under house arrest.

Myanmar is comprised of seven states (Chin, Kachin, Kayin (Karen), Kayah, Mon, Rakhine, Shan) and seven divisions (Irrawaddy, Magwe, Mandalay, Pegu, Yangon (Rangoon), Sagaing, Tenasserim).

### INSURGENCY

Since independence in 1948 the central government has fought various armed insurgent groups formed from ethnic minorities seeking greater autonomy or independence. The largest insurgent forces were based on the Kachin, Karen and Wa ethnic groups but the Shan, Mon, Arakan and Chin ethnic minorities have also formed armed groups. In 1989 ethnic Wa insurgents signed an agreement with the government ending their insurgency, but in 1990 the fleeing NLD and pro-democracy supporters allied themselves to the remaining ethnic insurgent groups to form the Democratic Alliance of Burma (DAB) based at Mannerplaw near the Thai border, which is also the NCGUB base. The Kachin

Independence Army signed a ceasefire agreement with the government in February 1994 leaving the 5,000 strong Karen National Union as the largest force in the DAB.

CABINET *as at August 1994*

*Chairman of SLORC, Prime Minister and Minister of Defence*, Gen. Than Shwe

*Deputy Prime Ministers*, Vice-Adm. Maung Maung Khin; Lt.-Gen. Tin Tun

*Agriculture*, Maj.-Gen. Myint Aung

*Border Areas*, Maj.-Gen. Maung Thint

*Communications, Posts and Telegraphs*, U Soe Tha

*Construction*, U Khin Maung Yin

*Co-operatives*, U Than Aung

*Culture*, Lt.-Gen. Aung Ye Kyaw

*Education*, Col. Pe Thein

*Energy*, U Khin Maung Thein

*Finance and Revenue*, Brig.-Gen. Win Tin

*Foreign Affairs*, U Ohn Gyaw

*Forestry*, Lt.-Gen. Chit Swe

*Health*, Rear-Adm. Than Nyunt

*Home*, Maj.-Gen. Mya Thinn

*Hotels and Tourism*, Maj.-Gen. Kyaw Ba

*Industry*, Lt.-Gen. Sein Aung

*Information*, Brig.-Gen. Myo Thant

*Labour*, Maj.-Gen. Aye Thoung

*Livestock Breeding and Fisheries*, Brig.-Gen. Maung Maung

*Mines*, Maj.-Gen. Kyaw Min

*Office of the Prime Minister*, Brig.-Gen. Lun Maung

*Planning and Finance*, Brig.-Gen. Abel

*Rail and Transportation*, U Win Sein

*Religious Affairs*, Maj.-Gen. Myo Nyunt

*Social Welfare*, Brig.-Gen. Thaung Myint

*Trade*, Maj.-Gen. Tun Kyi

*Transport*, Maj.-Gen. Thein Win

EMBASSY OF THE UNION OF MYANMAR
19A Charles Street, Berkeley Square, London WIX 8ER
Tel 0171-629 6966

*Ambassador Extraordinary and Plenipotentiary*, His Excellency U Hla Maung, apptd 1992

BRITISH EMBASSY
80 Strand Road (Box No. 638), Rangoon
Tel: Rangoon 95300

*Ambassador Extraordinary and Plenipotentiary*, His Excellency Julian Hartland-Swann, CMG, apptd 1990

*Cultural Attaché and British Council Representative*, Chris Harrison

## ECONOMY

The chief sources of revenue are profits on state trading, taxes and duties; the chief heads of expenditure are defence, education and police. The budget estimates for 1992–3 were: revenue K53,867 million; expenditure, K57,203 million.

Three-quarters of the population depend on agriculture; the chief products are rice, oilseeds (sesamum and groundnut), maize, millet, cotton, beans, wheat, grain, tea, sugarcane, tobacco, jute and rubber.

Myanmar is rich in minerals, including petroleum, lead, silver, tungsten, zinc, tin, wolfram and gemstones. Of these, petroleum products are the most important. Oil is produced from oilfields in Myanaung, Prome and Shwepyitha and at Chauk, Yenangyaung, Mann, and Letpando. Production of crude oil in 1991–2 totalled 5,500,000 US barrels. There are refineries at Chauk, the main oilfield, Syriam and Mann. There has been a steady decline in oil production in recent years and the country is no longer self-sufficient. Onshore exploration continues. There has also been some offshore oil exploration on a small scale. Major reserves of natural gas have been discovered in the Martaban Gulf, which Myanmar is hoping to develop.

All industrial activity of any size is in the public sector. Under development plans, projects completed or under construction with overseas financial and technical assistance include the production of cement, bricks and tiles, sheet glass, steel sections, jute bags and twine, cotton yarns and cloth, pharmaceuticals, sugar, paper, plywood, urea fertilizers, soda ash, tractors and tyres; also a hydro-electric scheme and various irrigation works.

A new ministry was established in 1992 with the task of attracting 500,000 tourists; less than 10,000 visited in 1991.

In 1993 the military government began to open the economy to foreign investment, signing 50 joint ventures in the fields of oil and gas exploration, hotel construction and forestry. Mild economic liberalization has so far failed to gain the country IMF loans.

| Trade with UK | 1992 | 1993 |
|---|---|---|
| Imports from UK | £9,145,000 | £19,274,000 |
| Exports to UK | 5,046,000 | 9,100,000 |

## EDUCATION

The literacy rate is high compared to other Asian countries. Most children attend primary school, and about four million are currently enrolled; in middle and high schools, enrolment is about 11 million. There are five universities, at Yangon (Rangoon), Mandalay, Taunggyi, Sagaing and Mawlamyine (Moulmein). Under the universities are three affiliated degree colleges and the Workers' College, Yangon. There are also 14 two-year colleges affiliated to the universities, spread throughout the country.

Vocational training is provided at 16 teachers' training institutes, seven government technical institutes, 14 technical high schools, 15 agricultural institutes and schools, and 34 vocational schools for weaving, handicrafts, etc.

## COMMUNICATIONS

The Irrawaddy and its chief tributary, the Chindwin, are important waterways, the main stream being navigable 900 miles from its mouth and carrying much traffic. The chief seaports are Yangon (Rangoon), Mawlamyine (Moulmein), Akyab (Sittwe) and Pathein (Bassein).

The railway network covers 2,764 route miles, extending to Myitkyina, on the Upper Irrawaddy. There were 2,452 miles of highways and 11,767 miles of other main roads in 1982–3. The airport at Mingaladon, about 13 miles north of Yangon (Rangoon), only handles limited international air traffic.

## NAMIBIA
*The Republic of Namibia*

Namibia stretches from the southern border of Angola (17° 23′ S. latitude) to the northern (Orange River) border of the Northern Cape region of South Africa; and from the Atlantic Ocean in the west to Botswana in the east. In addition the Caprivi Strip in the north-west of the country borders on Zambia and Zimbabwe. The average rainfall over 70 per cent of the country is below 400 mm a year.

Namibia has an area of 318,261 sq. miles (824,292 sq. km), including the area of Walvis Bay (434 sq. miles). Previously

a British and South African colony separate from German South West Africa and later Namibia, Walvis Bay was governed from August 1992 by the joint South African-Namibian Walvis Bay Administrative Body until 28 February 1994, when South Africa renounced its claim to sovereignty over the enclave and it became part of Namibia.

POPULATION – The population was estimated by the UN at 1,837,000 in 1991. The main population groups are: Ovambo (587,000), Kavango (110,000), Damara (89,000), Herero (89,000), Whites (78,000), Nama (57,000), Coloured (48,000), Caprivians (44,000), Bushmen (34,000), Rehoboth Baster (29,000), Tswana (7,000). English is the official language, with Afrikaans, German and local languages also in use.

CAPITAL – Windhoek (population, 1987 estimate, 110,000). Other major towns are Grootfontein, ΨWalvis Bay, ΨLüderitz, Karasburg and Keetmanshoop.

CURRENCY – Namibian Dollar of 100 cents, introduced in September 1993 at parity to South African rand (the previous currency).

FLAG – Divided diagonally blue, red and green with the red fimbriated in white; a gold twelve-rayed sun in the upper hoist.

NATIONAL DAY – 21 March (Independence Day).

## HISTORY

The German protectorate of South West Africa from 1880 to 1915, Namibia was administered until the end of 1920 by the Union of South Africa. Under the terms of the Treaty of Versailles, the territory was entrusted to South Africa with full powers of administration and legislation over the territory. After the dissolution of the League of Nations and in the absence of a trusteeship agreement, South Africa informed the United Nations that it would continue to administer South West Africa.

In 1971 the International Court of Justice at The Hague delivered a majority opinion that the continued presence of South Africa was illegal, and that it was to withdraw its administration from Namibia immediately, putting an end to its occupation of the territory. The South African government rejected this opinion, but accepted the principle that the territory should attain independence. In 1977 five Western members of the UN Security Council drew up a plan, later incorporated into Security Council Resolution 435, for a peaceful settlement. Implementation of Resolution 435 began in April 1989 and elections for 72 seats in Namibia's first nationally elected body took place under UN supervision on 7–11 November 1989. The South West Africa People's Organization (SWAPO) won 41 seats, the Democratic Turnhalle Alliance 21 seats, the United Democratic Front 4 seats, Action Christian National 3, Namibia Patriotic Front 1, Federal Convention of Namibia 1, and Namibia National Front 1.

Independence was declared on 21 March 1990. Namibia joined the Commonwealth upon independence.

## GOVERNMENT

Constitutionally defined as a multiparty, secular, democratic republic, Namibia has an executive President as head of state who exercises the functions of government with the assistance of a Cabinet headed by a Prime Minister. The President is directly elected for a maximum of two five-year terms. Legislative authority lies with the National Assembly, which is the lower house of a bicameral parliament; an upper house (National Council) representing regional councils was elected in November 1992 and inaugurated in January 1993. Each of the thirteen regional councils appoints two representatives to the National Council. The main function of the National Council is to review and consider legislation from the National Assembly. Under a system of proportional representation, elections to the National Assembly are to take place every five years (there will be 96 seats contested at the next election), or earlier if decided by the President. Members of the National Council hold their seats for six years.

HEAD OF STATE
President, Dr Sam Nujoma, elected, 16 February 1990

CABINET as at August 1994
Prime Minister, Hon. Hage Geingob
Home Affairs, Hon. Hifikepunye Pohamba
Foreign Affairs, Hon. Theo-Ben Gurirab
Defence, Hon. Peter Mueshihange
Finance, Hon. Gerhard Hanekom
Education and Culture, Hon. Nahas Angula
Information and Broadcasting, Hon. Ben Amathila
Health and Social Services, Hon. Dr Nicky Iyambo
Labour, Public Service and Human Resource Development,
   Hon. Hendrik Witbooi
Mines and Energy, Hon. Andimba Toivo Ya Toivo
Justice, Hon. Ngarikutuke Tjiriange
Regional and Local Government and Housing, Hon. Libertine
   Amathila
Agriculture, Water and Rural Development, Hon. Nangolo
   Mbumba
Trade and Industry, Hon. Hidipo Hamutenya
Environment and Tourism, Hon. Nico Bessinger
Works, Transport, and Communication, Hon. Marco
   Hausiku
Lands, Resettlement and Rehabilitation, Hon. Richard
   Kapelwa
Youth and Sport, Hon. Pendukeni Iithana
Fisheries and Marine Resources, Hon. Helmut Angula
State Security, Hon. Peter Tshirumbu

HIGH COMMISSION OF THE REPUBLIC OF NAMIBIA
6 Chandos Street, London WIM OLQ
Tel 0171-636 6244

High Commissioner, His Excellency Veiccoh K. Nghiwete,
   apptd 1991

BRITISH HIGH COMMISSION
116 Robert Mugabe Avenue, Windhoek 9000
Tel: Windhoek 223022

High Commissioner, His Excellency Henry George Hogger,
   apptd 1992

BRITISH COUNCIL REPRESENTATIVE, J. Utley, PO Box
24224, 74 Bülowstrasse, Windhoek 9000

ECONOMY

Mining (mainly diamonds and uranium), agriculture and fisheries account for over 40 per cent of Namibia's GDP. Most of the labour force is employed in the agricultural sector. Large deposits of diamonds along the coast and offshore along the sea bed are estimated at between 1,500 and 3,000 million carats. Walvis Bay and Lüderitz are the main ports.

| Trade with UK | 1992 | 1993 |
|---|---|---|
| Imports from UK | £6,730,000 | £6,214,000 |
| Exports to UK | 16,766,000 | 23,641,000 |

# NAURU
*The Republic of Nauru*

Nauru is an island 8.2 sq. miles (21 sq. km) in area, situated in 166° 55′ E. longitude and 0° 32′ S. of the Equator. It had a population (census May 1983) of 8,042: Nauruans 4,964; other Pacific Islanders 2,134; Asians 682; Caucasians 262. The UN estimated a total population of 9,000 in 1991. About 43 per cent of Nauruans are adherents of the Nauruan Protestant Church and there is a Roman Catholic Mission on the island. The main languages are English and Nauruan.

CURRENCY – Nauru uses the Australian dollar ($A) of 100 cents as legal tender.
FLAG – Twelve-point star (representing the 12 original Nauruan tribes) below a gold bar (representing the Equator), all on a blue ground.
NATIONAL DAY – 31 January (Independence Day).

GOVERNMENT

From 1888 until the First World War Nauru was administered by Germany, in 1920 becoming a British Empire-mandated territory under the League of Nations administered by Australia. A trusteeship superseding the mandate was approved in 1947 by the UN and Nauru continued to be administered by Australia until it became independent on 31 January 1968. It was announced in November 1968 that a special form of membership of the Commonwealth had been devised for Nauru at the request of its government.

Parliament has eighteen members including the Cabinet and Speaker. Voting is compulsory for all Nauruans over 20 years of age, except in certain specified instances. Elections are held every three years. The Cabinet is chosen by the President, who is elected by the Parliament from amongst its members, and comprises not fewer than five nor more than six members including the President.

HEAD OF STATE
President and Minister for External Affairs, Island
   Development and Industry, Civil Aviation Authority and
   the Public Service, His Excellency Hon. Bernard
   Dowiyogo

CABINET as at August 1994
Internal Affairs, Works and Community Services and Minister
   Assisting the President, Hon. Vinson Detenamo
Finance, Hon. Vinci Clodumar
Education, Hon. Nimes Ekewona
Justice, Hon. Derog Gioura
Health, Hon. Ludwig Scotti

BRITISH HIGH COMMISSIONER, His Excellency Timothy
   David, resides at Suva, Fiji

JUDICIARY

A Supreme Court of Nauru is presided over by the Chief Justice. The District Court, which is subordinate to the Supreme Court, is presided over by a Resident Magistrate. Both the Supreme Court and the District Court are courts of record. The Supreme Court exercises both original and appellate jurisdiction.

ECONOMY

The only fertile areas are the narrow coastal belt and local requirements of fruit and vegetables are mostly met by imports. The economy is heavily dependent on the extraction of phosphate, of which the island has one of the world's richest deposits. About 1.5 million tonnes of phosphate are mined each year, providing employment for over 1,000 people. The industry has been run since 1970 by the Nauru Phosphate Corporation. Considerable investments have been made abroad with the royalties on phosphate exports to provide for a time when production declines. In August 1993 an agreement was signed with Australia for compensation to cover damage caused by phosphate mining during the Australian mandate and trusteeship periods. The compensation package is worth some £50 million (a portion of which will be paid by the UK government), composed of a £33 million gift and a 20-year package of health and education programmes.

The Nauru Pacific Line owns six ships; the government-owned Air Nauru operates air services throughout the Pacific region and to Australia, New Zealand, Japan, Singapore and the Philippines.

| Trade with UK | 1992 | 1993 |
|---|---|---|
| Imports from UK | £904,000 | £185,000 |
| Exports to UK | 1,000 | 35,000 |

### SOCIAL SERVICES

Nauru has a hospital service and other medical and dental services. There is also a maternity and child welfare service.

Education is available in nine primary and two secondary schools on the island with a total enrolment of about 1,600 pupils receiving primary education and 500 secondary education.

---

# NEPAL

---

Nepal lies between India and the Tibet Autonomous Region of China on the slopes of the Himalayas, and includes Mount Everest (29,078 ft). It has a total area of 54,342 sq. miles (140,747 sq. km).

The southern region, the Terai, was covered with jungle but has been more widely cultivated recently. It forms about 23 per cent of the total land area and nearly 44 per cent of the population live there. The central belt of the country is hilly, but with many fertile valleys, leading up to the snowline at about 16,000 feet. The hills account for 42 per cent of the area of the country and about 48 per cent of the population. The remainder of the country, the Himalayan region, consists of high mountains which are sparsely inhabited. The country is drained by three great river systems rising within and beyond the Himalayan mountain ranges and eventually flowing into the Ganges in India.

POPULATION – The population (UN estimate 1991) was 19,605,000. The inhabitants are of mixed stock, with Mongolian characteristics prevailing in the north and Indian in the south. The official religion is Hinduism: 89.5 per cent of the population are Hindus and 6 per cent are Buddhist. Gautama Buddha was born in Nepal.

CAPITAL – Kathmandu, population (1989) 300,000. Other towns of importance are Biratnagar (94,000), Lalitpur (81,000) and Bhaktapur (50,500), and Pokhara (48,500).

CURRENCY – Nepalese rupee of 100 paisa.

FLAG – Double pennant of crimson with blue border on peaks; white moon with rays in centre of top peak; white quarter sun, recumbent in centre of bottom peak.

NATIONAL ANTHEM – May Glory Crown Our Illustrious Sovereign.

NATIONAL DAY – 18 February (National Democracy Day).

### GOVERNMENT

Nepal was originally divided into numerous hill clans and petty principalities, but emerged as a nation in the middle of the 18th century when it was unified by the warrior Raja of Gorkha, Prithvi Narayan Shah, who founded the present Nepalese dynasty. In 1846 power was seized by Jung Bahadur Rana after a massacre of nobles, and he was the first of a line of hereditary Rana Prime Ministers who ruled Nepal for 104 years. During this time the role of the monarchs was mainly ceremonial.

In 1950–1 a revolutionary movement achieved its aim of breaking the hereditary power of the Ranas and restoring the monarchy to its former position. After ten years, during which various parties and individuals tried their hand at government, King Mahendra proscribed all political parties and assumed direct powers in 1960, with the object of leading a united country to democracy. In 1962 he introduced a new constitution embodying a tiered, partyless system of panchyat (council) democracy.

Mass agitation for political reform led in April 1990 to the lifting of the ban on political parties and the abolition of the panchyat system. A new constitution was promulgated in November 1990 establishing a multiparty, parliamentary system of government and a constitutional monarchy. The King retained joint executive power with the Council of Ministers. A bicameral legislature was set up, consisting of a 205-member House of Representatives and a 60-member National Council, including ten royal nominees. Elections, held on 12 May 1991, were won by the Nepali Congress Party, which formed a government. The Congress government was brought down by a no-confidence vote in July 1994 on charges that the economy had worsened and corruption increased during its rule. The government resigned and the King dissolved parliament, calling fresh elections for November 1994.

HEAD OF STATE
*HM The King of Nepal*, King Birendra Bir Bikram Shah Dev, *born* 28 December 1945; *succeeded* 31 January 1972; *crowned* 24 February 1975; *married*, February 1970, HM Queen Aishwatya Rajya Laxmi Devi Shah
*Heir*, HRH Crown Prince Dipendra Bir Bikram Shah Dev, *born* 27 June 1971

ROYAL NEPALESE EMBASSY
12A Kensington Palace Gardens, London W8 4QU
Tel 0171-229 1594/6231
*Ambassador Extraordinary and Plenipotentiary*, His Excellency Surya Prasad Shrestha, apptd 1992
*Counsellor*, Madhab Prasad Khanal

BRITISH EMBASSY
Lainchaur Kathmandu, PO Box 106
Tel: Kathmandu 410583
*Ambassador Extraordinary and Plenipotentiary*, His Excellency Timothy George, CMG, apptd 1990

BRITISH COUNCIL REPRESENTATIVE, Sarah Evans, (PO Box 640), Kantipath, Kathmandu

### ECONOMY

The budget for the fiscal year 1993–4 is estimated at NRs. 35,513.9 million, of which NRs. 12,888 million was allocated to regular and NRs. 22,625.9 million to development expenditures. Revenue was estimated at NRs. 16,424.5 million, foreign aid and grants NRs. 4,328.5 million, and domestic borrowing NRs. 1,820 million.

In October 1992 the IMF approved a three-year loan of US$49 million to support Nepal's medium-term economic reform programme. In February 1993 the rupee was floated and made fully convertible.

Nepal exports carpets, jute, handicrafts, garments, hides and skins, medicinal herbs, cardamom, pulses, tea, etc., and imports textiles, machinery and parts, transport equipment, medicine, construction materials etc. Tourism is the single largest commercial earner of foreign exchange.

| Trade with UK | 1992 | 1993 |
|---|---|---|
| Imports from UK | £6,300,000 | £11,920,000 |
| Exports to UK | 5,888,000 | 6,440,000 |

## COMMUNICATIONS

The total length of roads in Nepal in 1987–8 was 6,525 km. Most of the major roads have been built since the 1960s, often with aid from India and China. Kathmandu is connected by road with India and Tibet. Internally, the road network links Kathmandu to Kodari and Pokhara, and Pokhara to Sunauli. A road between Mugling and Naryanghat has further improved communications between Kathmandu and the Terai. The East–West Highway (Mahendra Raj Marg) running along the entire length of the country is complete except for the Banbasa-Mahakali section.

Royal Nepal Airlines operates an extensive network of domestic flights, and there are international flights to Europe, the Middle East and throughout Asia.

Telecommunication services, both domestic and international, are available. Nepal television was introduced in 1984.

## THE NETHERLANDS
*Koninkrijk der Nederlanden*

The kingdom of the Netherlands is a maritime country of western Europe, situated on the North Sea, in 50° 46′ to 53° 34′ N. latitude and 3° 22′ to 7° 14′ E. longitude, consisting of 12 provinces (Eastern and Southern Flevoland being amalgamated to form the twelfth province) and containing a total area of 15,770 sq. miles (40,844 sq. km).

The land is generally flat and low, intersected by numerous canals and connecting rivers. The principal rivers are the Rhine, Maas, Yssel and Scheldt.

POPULATION – The population (1991 estimate) is 15,240,000. The language is Dutch, a West Germanic language of Saxon origin closely akin to Old English and Low German. It is spoken in the Netherlands and the northern part of Belgium (Flanders). It is also used in the Netherlands Antilles.

CAPITAL – ΨAmsterdam, population 1,031,000 (urban agglomeration), 713,407 (city) (1992).

SEAT OF GOVERNMENT – The Hague (Den Haag or, in full, 's-Gravenhage), population 445,287 (1992). Other principal cities (1992) ΨRotterdam 589,707; Utrecht, 232,705; Eindhoven, 193,966; Haarlem 149,788; Groningen 169,387; Tilburg 160,618.

CURRENCY – Netherlands guilder of 100 cents.

FLAG – Three horizontal bands of red, white and blue.

NATIONAL ANTHEM – Wilhelmus.

## GOVERNMENT

In 1815 the Netherlands became a constitutional kingdom under King William I, a descendant of the house of Orange-Nassau which had taken a leading part in the affairs of the nation since the 16th century.

The States-General consists of the *Eerste Kamer* (First Chamber) of 75 members, elected for four years by the Provincial Council; and the *Tweede Kamer* (Second Chamber) of 150 members, elected for four years by voters of 18 years and upwards. Members of the *Tweede Kamer* are paid. The most recent election to the Second Chamber was held on 3 May 1994 and resulted in a new three-party centre-left coalition of the Labour Party, People's Party and Democrats 66.

HEAD OF STATE

HM The Queen of the Netherlands, Queen Beatrix Wilhelmina Armgard, KG, GCVO, *born* 31 January 1938; *succeeded* 30 April 1980, upon the abdication of her mother Queen Juliana; *married* 10 March 1966, HRH Prince Claus George Willem Otto Frederik Geert of the Netherlands, Jonkheer van Amsberg; and has *issue*, Prince Willem (*see below*); Prince Johan Friso, *b.* 25 September 1968; Prince Constantijn Christof, *b.* 11 October 1969

*Heir*, HRH Prince Willem Alexander, *b.* 27 April 1967

CABINET *as at August 1994*

*Prime Minister, Minister of General Affairs*, Wim Kok (PvdA)

*Deputy PM and Minister of Home Affairs*, H. Dijkstal (VVD)

*Deputy PM and Foreign Affairs*, H. A. F. van Mierlo (D66)

*Finance*, G. Zalm (VVD)

*Development Co-operation*, J. Pronk (PvdA)

*Defence*, J. J. C. Voorhoeve (VVD)

*Economic Affairs*, G. J. Wijers (D66)

*Justice*, W. Sorgdrager (D66)

*Agriculture, Nature Management and Fisheries*, J. van Aartsen (VVD)

*Education, Culture and Science*, Prof. Dr J. M. M. Ritzen (PvdA)

*Social Affairs and Employment*, A. P. W. Melkert (PvdA)

*Transport and Public Works*, A. Jorritsma-Lebbink (VVD)

*Housing, Physical Planning and Environment*, M. De Boer (PvdA).

*Welfare, Health and Sport*, Dr E. Borst-Eilers (D66)

VVD People's Party for Freedom and Democracy; D66 Democrats 66; PvdA Labour Party

ROYAL NETHERLANDS EMBASSY
38 Hyde Park Gate, London SW7 5DP
Tel 0171–584 5040

*Ambassador Extraordinary and Plenipotentiary*, His
Excellency Joop Hoekman, apptd 1990
*Ministers Plenipotentiary*, M. H. R. Loudon; A. J. Quanjer
(*Economic*)
*Consul-General*, G. J. Schulten
*Defence, Naval and Air Attaché*, Capt. Willem F. L. van
Leeuwen

BRITISH EMBASSY
Lange Voorhout 10, The Hague, 2514 ED
Tel: The Hague 364 5800

*Ambassador Extraordinary and Plenipotentiary*, His
Excellency Sir David Miers, KBE, CMG, apptd 1993
*Counsellors*, P. S. Dimond (*Deputy Head of Mission*);
C. W. Robins (*Commercial*)
*Defence and Naval Attaché*, Capt. H. W. Rickard, RN
*Consul-General*, D. H. Doble (*resides at Amsterdam*)

There is a Consulate-General at Amsterdam, a Consulate at
Willemstad (*Curaçao*) and a Vice-Consulate at
Philipsburg (*St Maarten*) (both Netherlands Antilles).

BRITISH COUNCIL REPRESENTATIVE, Iain Frater,
Keizersgracht 343, 1016 EH Amsterdam

NETHERLANDS-BRITISH CHAMBER OF COMMERCE, The
Dutch House, 307–308 High Holborn, London WC1V 7LS

UK OFFICE IN THE HAGUE, Holland Trade House,
Bezuidenhoutseweg 181, 2594 AH The Hague

## ECONOMY

Of a total GNP of US$279.1 billion in 1990, industry
accounted for around 31 per cent, agriculture for 4 per cent
and services 65 per cent. Excluding the construction industry,
the index of industrial production in the Netherlands (1980 =
100) was 109 in 1989. Inflation was 3.7 per cent in 1992.

The chief agricultural products are potatoes, wheat, rye,
barley, sugar beet, cattle, pigs, milk and milk products,
cheese, butter, poultry, eggs, beans, peas, vegetables, fruit,
flower bulbs, plants and cut flowers and there is an important
fishing industry.

Among the principal industries are engineering, electronics, nuclear energy, petro-chemicals and plastics, road
vehicles, aircraft and defence equipment, shipbuilding repair,
steel, textiles of all types, electrical appliances, metal ware,
furniture, paper, cigars, sugar, liqueurs, beer, clothing etc.

| FINANCE | 1991 |
| --- | --- |
| Budget Revenue | Guilders 176,327m |
| Budget Expenditure | 170,666m |

## TRADE

The Dutch are traditionally a trading nation. Trade, banking
and shipping are of particular importance to the economy.
The geographical position of the Netherlands, at the mouths
of the Rhine, Meuse and Scheldt, brings a large volume of
transit trade to and from the interior of Europe to Dutch
ports.

Principal trading partners are Germany, Belgium/
Luxembourg and France.

| | 1991 | 1992 |
| --- | --- | --- |
| Imports | Guilders 118,194m | Guilders 117,526m |
| Exports | 124,862m | 126,119m |

| *Trade with UK* | 1992 | 1993 |
| --- | --- | --- |
| Imports from UK | £8,484,040,000 | £7,909,232,000 |
| Exports to UK | 9,908,795,000 | 8,535,619,000 |

## DEFENCE

The armed forces are almost entirely committed to NATO.
Total armed forces number some 74,600, which includes
30,050 conscripts and 2,600 women. In addition there are
150,300 reservists. There is compulsory military service of
12–15 months. In January 1993 the government announced
plans to reduce the term of conscription from 1994 from 12–
15 months to nine months and to abolish it in 1998.

The Army has a strength of 43,300 (24,700 conscripts)
with 743 main battle tanks, 2,745 armoured infantry fighting
vehicles and armoured personnel carriers, 650 artillery pieces
and 85 armed helicopters.

The Navy has a strength of 14,900, including 830 naval
air arm, 3,250 marines and 1,650 conscripts. It maintains a
force of five submarines, four destroyers, 13 frigates with
mine warfare, amphibious and support ships, 13 combat
aircraft and 22 armed helicopters. The Air Force has a
strength of 12,000 (3,300 conscripts), with some 185 combat
aircraft, all of which are variants of the US-manufactured
F16.

As part of its NATO commitment, the Netherlands
maintains 3,700 Army personnel in Germany and is the base
for HQ Allied Forces Central Europe, and for 2,700 US
personnel. One frigate, marine and aircraft detachments are
deployed in the Netherlands Antilles; 925 troops are
deployed with UN forces in Croatia and Bosnia; 30 aircraft
are deployed in Italy for NATO operations over Bosnia.

There is also a paramilitary Royal Military Constabulary
of 3,600 personnel (400 conscripts).

## EDUCATION

Primary and secondary education is given in both denominational and state schools. Attendance at primary school is
compulsory.

The principal universities are at Leiden, Utrecht, Groningen, Amsterdam (two), Nijmegen, Maastricht and Rotterdam, and there are technical universities at Delft, Eindhoven,
Enschede and Wageningen (agriculture).

## COMMUNICATIONS

The total extent of navigable rivers including canals, was
5,046 km at 1 January 1992, and of metalled roads
104,831 km. In 1992 the total length of the railway system
amounted to 2,780 km, of which 1,939 km were electrified.
The mercantile marine in 1992 consisted of 410 ships of total
2,890,000 gross registered tons. The total of kilometres
flown by KLM (Royal Dutch Airlines) in 1991–2 was 188
million km.

There are six national papers, four of which are morning
papers, and there are many regional daily papers.

## OVERSEAS TERRITORIES

ARUBA

Aruba covers an area of 75 sq. miles (193 sq. km) with a
population (1994) of 71,000. The island of Aruba was from
1828 part of the Dutch West Indies and from 1845 part of
the Netherlands Antilles. On 1 January 1986 it became a
separate territory within the Kingdom of the Netherlands.
The 1983 Constitutional Conference agreed that Aruba's
separate status would last for ten years from 1986, after which
the island would become fully independent. In March 1994
this decision was changed and it was decided that Aruba will
retain its separate status within the Kingdom of the
Netherlands.

*Governor*, F. B. Tromp
*Prime Minister*, Nelson Oduber

CAPITAL – ΨOranjestad (population 20,000); and Sint Nicolaas (17,000).
CURRENCY – Aruban florin.

ECONOMY – The economy of Aruba is based largely on tourism. In 1993 there were 562,034 tourists.

| Trade with UK | 1992 | 1993 |
|---|---|---|
| Imports from UK | £27,292,000 | £41,930,000 |
| Exports to UK | 4,495,000 | 80,000 |

## NETHERLANDS ANTILLES

The Netherlands Antilles comprise the islands of Curaçao, Bonaire, part of St Martin, St Eustatius, and Saba in the West Indies. The islands cover an area of 308 sq. miles (800 sq. km) with a population (UN 1991 estimate) of 189,000. The Netherlands Antilles, which have a 22-member federal parliament, are largely self-governing under the terms of the Realm Statute which took effect in 1954.
*Governor*, Dr Jaime Saleh
*Prime Minister*, Miguel Pourier

CAPITAL – ΨWillemstad (on Curaçao) (pop. 50,000).
CURRENCY – Netherlands Antilles guilder of 100 cents.

ECONOMY – The economy of the Netherlands Antilles is based on small manufacturing industries. The soil is too poor to permit large-scale agriculture and most products for consumption and industrial raw materials must be imported.

| Trade with UK | 1992* | 1993* |
|---|---|---|
| Imports from UK | £19,920,000 | £17,024,000 |
| Exports to UK | 7,261,000 | 28,871,000 |
| *Curaçao | | |

---

# NEW ZEALAND

## AREA AND POPULATION

| Islands | Area (sq. miles) | Population at 31 March 1993 |
|---|---|---|
| North Island | 44,281 | 2,604,200 |
| South Island | 58,093 | 890,100 |
| Other islands | 1,362 | |
| Total | 103,736 | 3,494,300 |

| Territories | | |
|---|---|---|
| Tokelau | 5 | 1,700 (a) |
| Niue | 100 | 2,239 |
| Cook Islands | 93 | 18,300 (b) |
| Ross Dependency | 175,000 | |

(a) 1994
(b) 1991

Of the total population of New Zealand, some 79 per cent is of European stock, 13 per cent Maori and 5 per cent other Pacific Islanders.

The main religion is Christianity. In 1991 the principal denominations were Anglican 22.1 per cent, Presbyterian 16.3 per cent, Roman Catholic 15 per cent, Methodist 4.2 per cent, Baptist 2.1 per cent.

## GEOGRAPHY

New Zealand consists of a number of islands in the South Pacific Ocean, and has also administrative responsibility for the Ross Dependency in Antarctica. The two larger islands, North Island and South Island, are separated by a relatively narrow strait. The remaining islands are very much smaller and are dispersed over a considerable expanse of ocean. The boundaries, inclusive of the most outlying islands and dependencies, range from 33° to 53° S. latitude, and from 162° E. longitude to 173° W. longitude.

Much of the North and South Islands is mountainous. The principal range is the Southern Alps, extending the entire length of the South Island and having its culminating point in Mount Cook (12,349 ft). The North Island mountains include several volcanoes, two of which are active. Of the numerous glaciers in the South Island, the Tasman (18 miles long by 1¼ wide), the Franz Josef and the Fox are the best known. The North Island is noted for its hot springs and geysers. The more important rivers include the Waikato (270 miles in length), Wanganui (180), and Clutha (210). lakes include Taupo, 234 sq. miles in area; Wakatipu, 113; and Te Anau, 133.

New Zealand includes, in addition to North and South Islands: Chatham Islands (Chatham, Pitt, South East Islands and some rocky islets, combined area, 965 sq. km (373 sq. miles), largely uninhabited); Stewart Island (area 1,746 sq. km (674 sq. miles), largely uninhabited; the Kermadec Group (Raoul or Sunday, Macaulay, Curtis Islands, L'Esperance, and some islets; population 9–10, all government employees at a meteorological station); Campbell Island, used as a weather station; the Three Kings (discovered by Tasman on the Feast of the Epiphany); Auckland Islands; Antipodes Group; Bounty Islands; Snares Islands and Solander.

New Zealand has a temperate marine climate, but with abundant sunshine. The mean temperature ranges from 15°C in the north to about 9°C in the south. Rainfall in the North Island ranges from 35 to 70 inches and in the South Island from 25 to 45 inches.

CAPITAL – ΨWellington, in the North Island. Population (March 1991 census) of Wellington urban area, 325,682. Other large urban areas; ΨAuckland 885,600; ΨChristchurch 307,200; ΨDunedin 109,500; Hamilton 148,625; Ψ Napier-Hastings 110,200.
CURRENCY – New Zealand dollar (NZ$) of 100 cents.
FLAG – Blue ground, with Union Flag in top left quarter, four five-pointed red stars with white borders on the fly.
NATIONAL ANTHEM – God Save The Queen/God Defend New Zealand.
NATIONAL DAY – 6 February (Waitangi Day).

## GOVERNMENT

The discoverers and first colonists of New Zealand were Polynesian people, ancestors of the Maori of today. Whether there was a single colonization or many is not known but the ninth century is generally considered to be the date of the first settlement. By the 13th or 14th century early exploration was over and there were well-established Maori settlements. The first European to discover New Zealand was a Dutch navigator, Abel Tasman, who sighted the coast in 1642 but did not land. It was the British explorer James Cook who circumnavigated New Zealand and landed in 1769. Largely as a result of increased British emigration, the country was annexed by the British government in 1840. The British Lieutenant-Governor, William Hobson, proclaimed sovereignty over the North Island by virtue of the Treaty of Waitangi, signed by him and many Maori chiefs, and over the South Island and Stewart Island by right of discovery.

In 1841 New Zealand was, by letters patent, created a separate colony distinct from New South Wales. In 1907 the designation was changed to 'The Dominion of New Zealand'. The constitution rests upon the Constitution Act 1852 and other Imperial statutes. A 1986 Constitution Act brought a number of statutory constitutional provisions. The Statute of Westminster was formally adopted by New Zealand in 1947.

The executive authority is entrusted to a Governor-General appointed by the Crown and aided by an Executive Council, within a unicameral legislature, the House of Representatives.

The House of Representatives consists of 99 members elected for three years. There are four Maori electorates. In a referendum in 1992 the electorate voted in favour of electoral reform and the introduction of a mixed-member proportional representation system to replace the first-past-the-post system.

Following the general election of 6 November 1993, the state of the parties in the House of Representatives was National 50, Labour 45, The Alliance 2, New Zealand First 2.

GOVERNOR-GENERAL
*Governor-General and Commander-in-Chief of New Zealand,* Her Excellency Dame Catherine Tizard, GCMG, DBE, *sworn in* November 1990

THE EXECUTIVE COUNCIL *as at August 1994*
The Governor-General
*Prime Minister, Minister in Charge of the New Zealand Security Intelligence Service,* Rt. Hon. J. B. Bolger.
*Deputy PM, Minister of Foreign Relations and Trade, Foreign Affairs, Pacific Island Affairs, Leader of the House,* Rt. Hon. D. C. McKinnon
*Health,* Hon. Jenny Shipley
*Finance,* Rt. Hon. W. F. Birch
*Attorney-General,* Hon. Paul East
*Agriculture and Forestry,* Hon. John Falloon
*Employment,* Hon. Wyatt Creech
*Commerce, Industry and Trade Negotiations, State-Owned Enterprises, Railways,* Hon. Philip Burdon
*Environment, Research, Science and Technology,* Hon. Simon Upton
*Local Government, Tourism, Recreation and Sport,* Hon. John Banks
*Social Welfare, Senior Citizens,* Hon. Peter Gresham
*Defence, Interior,* Hon. Warren Cooper
*Justice, Disarmament and Arms Control, Culture,* Hon. Douglas Graham
*Education,* Hon. Dr Lockwood Smith
*Labour,* Hon. Doug Kidd
*Housing, Customs,* Hon. Murray McCully
*Conservation,* Hon. Denis Marshall
*Police, Maori Affairs,* Hon. John Luxton
*Transport, Communications, Broadcasting, Statistics,* Hon. Maurice Williamson
*Insurance, Radio and Television,* Hon. Bruce Cliffe
*Speaker of the House of Representatives,* Hon. Robin Gray

NEW ZEALAND HIGH COMMISSION
New Zealand House, Haymarket, London SW1Y 4TQ
Tel 0171–930 8422

*High Commissioner,* His Excellency John Collinge, apptd 1994
*Deputy High Commissioner,* M. Chilton
*Minister,* J. Charles (*Commercial*)
*Head, Defence Staff,* Cdre J. Peddie
*First Secretary,* Ms S. Craig (*Cultural Affairs*)
*Consul-General,* N. E. Parkes

BRITISH HIGH COMMISSION
44 Hill Street (PO Box 1812), Wellington 1
Tel: Wellington 4726-049

*High Commissioner,* His Excellency Robert Alston, CMG, apptd 1994
*Deputy High Commissioner,* A. Heath

*Counsellor,* A. W. Turquet
*Defence Adviser,* Gp Capt D. Angela
*First Secretary,* M. Capes (*Commercial*)
*Consul-General and Director of Trade Promotion,* J. F. Holding (*resides at Auckland*)
There is a Consulate-General at Auckland and a Consulate in Christchurch.

BRITISH COUNCIL REPRESENTATIVE, D. J. F. King (*Cultural Attaché*)
BRITISH CHAMBER OF COMMERCE FOR AUSTRALIA AND NEW ZEALAND, PO Box 141, Manuka, ACT 2603, Australia; UK OFFICE, Suite 615, 6th Floor The Linen Hall, 162–168 Regent Street, London W1R 5TB.

JUDICATURE

The judicial system comprises a High Court, a Court of Appeal and district courts having both civil and criminal jurisdiction.
*Chief Justice,* Rt. Hon. Sir Thomas Eichelbaum, GBE, PC.
*President, Court of Appeal,* Rt. Hon. Sir Robin Cooke, KBE.

DEFENCE

In 1994 the total active number of armed forces personnel is 10,800, with a further 8,500 reserves. The Army has a strength of 4,800 personnel, with 26 light tanks, 76 armoured personnel carriers and 44 artillery pieces. The Navy has a strength of 2,300, with four frigates, eight patrol and support craft, and six armed helicopters. The Air Force has a strength of 3,700 personnel with 38 combat aircraft. A support unit of 20 troops is maintained in Singapore. In 1994 250 troops were dispatched to serve under UK command with UN forces in Bosnia-Hercegovina.

FINANCE

Revenue and expenditure, including the National Roads Fund, for year ended 30 June 1993 was: revenue NZ$ 29,874 million, expenditure 31,468 million. Taxation receipts in 1992–3 for all purposes amounted to NZ$25,812 million (an average of NZ$7,387 per head of population). Total net expenditure 1992–3 was NZ$31,468 million, of which the principal items were social services NZ$10,702 million, education NZ$4,545 million, administration NZ$4,393 million, debt services NZ$4,257 million and health NZ$4,058 million.

ECONOMY

Since 1984 economic reforms under both Labour and National Party governments have changed the economy from a highly regulated, nationalized and protected economy with a large welfare state to an economy at the forefront of market economics. Finance market deregulation, privatization, VAT reform, the introduction of private sector principles in the civil service, the ending of agricultural subsidies and the near elimination of import tariffs have all occurred. The Reserve Bank has been made independent, with a contract to keep inflation below 2 per cent, centralized wage-bargaining ended and widespread means-testing introduced throughout the welfare state.

GROSS VALUE OF AGRICULTURAL PRODUCTION
*to year ended March* (NZ$ million)

| | 1990–1 | 1991–2 |
|---|---|---|
| *Gross output* | 8,216 | 9,027 |
| Sheep | 885 | 833 |
| Wool | 832 | 783 |
| Cattle | 1,376 | 1,422 |
| Dairy products | 1,641 | 2,203 |

| Fruit, nuts, oilseeds | 694 | 821 |
|---|---|---|
| Agricultural services | 648 | 665 |
| Sales of live animals | 671 | 701 |

AGRICULTURAL AND PASTORAL PRODUCTION

| | 1992 | 1993 |
|---|---|---|
| ‡Meat, metric tons | 1,142,000 | 1,098,000 |
| *Wool, metric tons | 221,000 | 193,000 |
| †Butter, metric tons | 271,000 | 267,000 |
| †Cheese, metric tons | 137,000 | 143,000 |

*Year ended 30 June
†Year ended 31 May
‡Year ended 30 September

Livestock on farms at 30 June 1992 included 3,500,000 dairy cattle, 4,700,000 beef cattle and 1,700,000 deer and goats. Sheep numbered 52,600,000.

The output of sawn timber for 1992 was 2,300,000 cubic metres, of which 2,200,000 cubic metres represented exotic varieties, mainly radiata pine.

Non-metallic minerals such as coal, clay, limestone and dolomite are both economically and industrially more important than metallic ones. Coal output in 1993 was 2,900,000 tonnes. Of the metals, the most important are gold and ironsand. Natural gas deposits in Taranaki are being used for electricity generation and as a premium fuel. Hydro-electric power is used to generate 96 per cent of the country's electricity.

| TRADE | 1992 | 1993 |
|---|---|---|
| Imports (v.f.d.) | NZ$14,215m | NZ$15,980m |
| Exports (f.o.b.) | 17,891m | 19,006m |

New Zealand's largest trading partners are Australia, Japan, USA and the UK. New Zealand exports to the UK include butter and cheese, wool, lamb, hides, skins and leather.

| Trade with UK | 1992 | 1993 |
|---|---|---|
| Imports from UK | £264,830,000 | £332,897,000 |
| Exports to UK | 429,363,000 | 496,357,000 |

EDUCATION

Schools are free and attendance is compulsory between the ages of six and 15. In 1991 there were 403,435 pupils attending public primary schools, and 12,649 pupils attending registered private primary schools. The secondary education of boys and girls is carried on in 314 state secondary schools and 21 registered private secondary schools. The total number of pupils receiving full-time secondary education in July 1992 was 227,912. There were seven universities with a total of 93,182 students in 1992.

COMMUNICATIONS

The national railway system is owned and operated by the privately-owned New Zealand Rail Ltd. In March 1993, there were 4,251 route km of railway in operation. At 31 March 1993 there were 2,379,417 licensed motor vehicles operating on the road network of 93,322 km.

During 1991-2 the vessels entered from overseas ports numbered 3,282 (gross tonnage 27,983,000) and those cleared for overseas 3,298 (gross tonnage 27,508,000).

Domestic flights in 1990 carried 4,502,000 passengers and 47,700 tonnes of freight. International flights carried 3,129,000 passengers, 134,074 tonnes of freight and 5,082 tonnes of mail.

TERRITORIES

TOKELAU (OR UNION ISLANDS)

Tokelau is a group of atolls, Fakaofo, Nukunonu and Atafu, with a total land area of 5 sq. miles and a population of 1,700

(1994), which was proclaimed part of New Zealand as from 1 January 1949. A council of Faipule, composed of one elected representative from each atoll, was established in August 1992 to govern Tokelau when the council of elders (General Fono) was not in session. The position of Ulu-o-Tokelau (Prime Minister) was also established in 1992 and is rotated among the three Faipale members annually. New Zealand provides substantial aid ($4.55 million in year ended 30 June 1993), to meet administrative, social, economic and development requirements. Administrative responsibility for Tokelau lies with the Administrator but in January 1994 his powers were delegated to the General Fono and Council of Faipale. Tokelau receives revenue from the granting of fishing rights in its economic zone.

*Administrator*, Lindsay Watt
Ulu-o-Tokelau (1995) Lepaio Simi

THE ROSS DEPENDENCY

The Ross Dependency, placed under the jurisdiction of New Zealand in 1923, is defined as all the Antarctic islands and territories between 160° E. and 150° W. longitude which are situated south of the 60° S. parallel, including Edward VII Land and portions of Victoria Land. Since 1957 a number of research stations have been established in the Dependency.

ASSOCIATED STATES

COOK ISLANDS

Included in the boundaries of New Zealand since June 1901, the Cook Islands group consists of the islands of Rarotonga, Aitutaki, Mangaia, Atiu, Mauke, Mitiaro, Manuae, Takutea, Palmerston, Penrhyn or Tongareva, Manihiki, Rakahanga, Suwarrow, Pukapuka or Danger, and Nassau. The total population of the group was 18,300 in 1991.

The chief industries are tourism, financial services and the production of fruit juice, clothing, copra, bananas, citrus fruit and pulp, and black pearls. The New Zealand Government continues to give financial aid to the Cook Islands.

The Queen has a representative on the islands, as does the New Zealand government. Since 1965, the islands have been in free association with New Zealand and enjoyed complete internal self-government, executive power being in the hands of a Cabinet consisting of the Prime Minister and 12 other ministers. There is a 25-member Legislative Assembly. The New Zealand citizenship of the Cook Islanders is embodied in the constitution.

*HM Representative*, Apenera Short, OBE
*New Zealand High Commissioner*, Darryl Dunn
*Prime Minister*, Sir Geoffrey Henry

NIUE

The population of Niue was 2,239 at the November 1991 census. A New Zealand High Commissioner is stationed at Niue, which since 1974 has been self-governing in free association with New Zealand. New Zealand is responsible for external affairs and defence, and continues to give financial aid. Executive power is in the hands of a Premier and a Cabinet of three drawn from the Assembly of 20 members. The Assembly is the supreme legislative body.

*New Zealand High Commissioner*, W. Searell

---

# NICARAGUA
*República de Nicaragua*

---

Nicaragua is the largest state of Central America, with a long seaboard on both the Atlantic and Pacific Oceans, situated between 10° 45′ and 15° N. latitude and 83° 40′ and 87° 38′ W. longitude, containing an area of 50,193 sq. miles (130,000 sq. km).

POPULATION – There is a population (UN estimate 1991) of 3,999,000, of whom about three-quarters are of mixed blood. Another 15 per cent are white, mostly of pure Spanish descent, and the remaining 10 per cent are West Indians or Indians. The latter group includes the Misquitos, who live on the Atlantic coast. The official language is Spanish and the majority are Roman Catholic, although the English language and the Moravian Church are widespread on the Atlantic coast.

CAPITAL – Managua, population 615,000. Other centres are León, 158,577; Granada, 72,640; Masaya, 78,308; Chinandega, 144,291.

CURRENCY – Córdoba (C$) of 100 centavos.

FLAG – Horizontal stripes of blue, white and blue, with the Nicaraguan coat of arms in the centre of the white stripe.

NATIONAL DAY – 15 September.

NATIONAL ANTHEM – Salve A Ti Nicaragua (Hail, Nicaragua).

## GOVERNMENT

The eastern coast of Nicaragua was touched by Columbus in 1502, and in 1518 was overrun by Spanish forces. It formed part of the Spanish Captaincy-General of Guatemala until 1821, when its independence was secured. In 1927 Augusto Cesar Sandino began a guerrilla war against the occupation of Nicaragua by US Marines, which continued until they were expelled in 1933. Sandino was assassinated by Anastasio Somoza, director of the National Guard, and in 1936 Somoza assumed the Presidency. He was succeeded in power by his sons Luis and Anastasio Somoza, until 1979 when the family and the National Guard were overthrown by guerrillas of the Sandinista National Liberation Front (FSLN).

After ten years in power and a ten-year civil war against US-backed Contra guerillas, the Sandinistas lost their parliamentary majority in elections held in February 1990. A coalition of former opposition parties, Unión Nacional de Opositora (UNO) gained 51 seats to the Sandinistas' 39 seats in the 92-seat National Assembly and formed a government, with UNO leader Violeta Chamorro becoming President. With the defeat of the Sandinistas, the civil war came to an end and the new government began to transform the Sandinistas' socialist economy into a free-market one. President Chamorro and the UNO found that they had to compromise with the still-powerful Sandinistas, who controlled the trade unions, and to leave the armed forces and police under Sandinista control. Resentment among the UNO coalition at having to compromise with the Sandinistas came to a head in December 1992 when UNO deputies tried to topple Chamorro from power. In response Chamorro ordered the police to seize the National Assembly and negotiated a new governing majority in the National Assembly of 39 Sandinistas and nine loyal centrist UNO deputies. In January 1993 Sandinistas entered the government and the remaining 42 UNO deputies and Vice-President Godoy were forced into opposition. A further 19 UNO deputies formed the Democratic Christian Union (UDC) in January 1994, which joined the governing coalition of Sandinistas and centrists and enabled constitutional reforms to be passed affecting civil and political rights, the national economy, legislature and defence.

In the north of the country from late 1992 to early 1994 government forces fought against re-armed Contra and Sandinista groups disgruntled at the lack of land and jobs. The last of the groups disarmed in April 1994 after offers of jobs in police forces. The government has initiated negotia-

tions with political, business and church leaders to try to strengthen democracy and national security further through reforms to the judiciary and the executive.

HEAD OF STATE
*President, Minister of Defence*, Violeta Barrios de Chamorro, inaugurated 25 April 1990
*Vice-President*, Virgilio Godoy

COUNCIL OF MINISTERS *as at August 1994*
*Minister to the Presidency*, Antonio Lacayo
*External Relations*, Ernesto Leal
*Interior*, Alfredo Mendieta
*Finance*, Emilio Pereira
*Foreign Co-operation*, Erwin Krugger
*Construction and Transport*, Pablo Vigil
*Health*, Martha Pereira
*Agriculture*, Roberto Rondón Sacasa
*Labour*, Francisco Rosales
*Economy and Planning*, Pablo Pereira
*Education*, Humberto Belli Pereira
*Tourism*, Fernando Guzman
*Environment and Natural Resources*, Jaime Iucer Barquero

EMBASSY OF NICARAGUA
8 Gloucester Road, London SW7 4PP
Tel 0171–584 4365

*Ambassador Extraordinary and Plenipotentiary*, new appointment awaited

BRITISH EMBASSY
PO Box A-169, El Reparto 'Los Robles', Primera Etapa, Entrada Principal de la Carretera a Masaya, Managua, Nicaragua.
Tel: Managua 780014

*Ambassador and Consul-General*, His Excellency John Howard Culver, apptd 1992

## DEFENCE

Under the Sandinista government of 1979–80, Nicaragua maintained armed forces of over 120,000 personnel. Since 1990, active armed forces have fallen to 15,200 and service is now voluntary. The Army has 13,500 personnel, with 130 main battle tanks, 22 light tanks, 80 reconnaissance vehicles, 119 armoured personnel carriers and 156 artillery pieces. The Navy has a strength of 500, with 21 patrol and coastal vessels. The Air Force has 1,200 personnel and 16 combat aircraft and two armed helicopters.

## ECONOMY

Since the end of the civil war the UNO government has begun to transform the Sandinistas' socialist economy into a free-market one. An agreement was reached with the IMF in April 1994 providing US$662 million in credits to stabilize the economy and refinance some debt.

The country is mainly agricultural. The major crops are peanuts, cotton, coffee (30 per cent of total export earnings), sugar cane, tobacco, sesame and bananas. Beans, rice, maize and ipecacuanha, livestock and timber production are also important. However, fishing, forestry, grain and cattle production are still recovering from the civil war in the main growing areas. Nicaragua possesses deposits of gold and silver.

## TRADE

Considerable quantities of foodstuffs are imported as well as cotton goods, jute, iron and steel, machinery and petroleum products. The chief exports are peanuts, sesame seed, cotton, coffee, beef, gold, sugar, cottonseed and bananas.

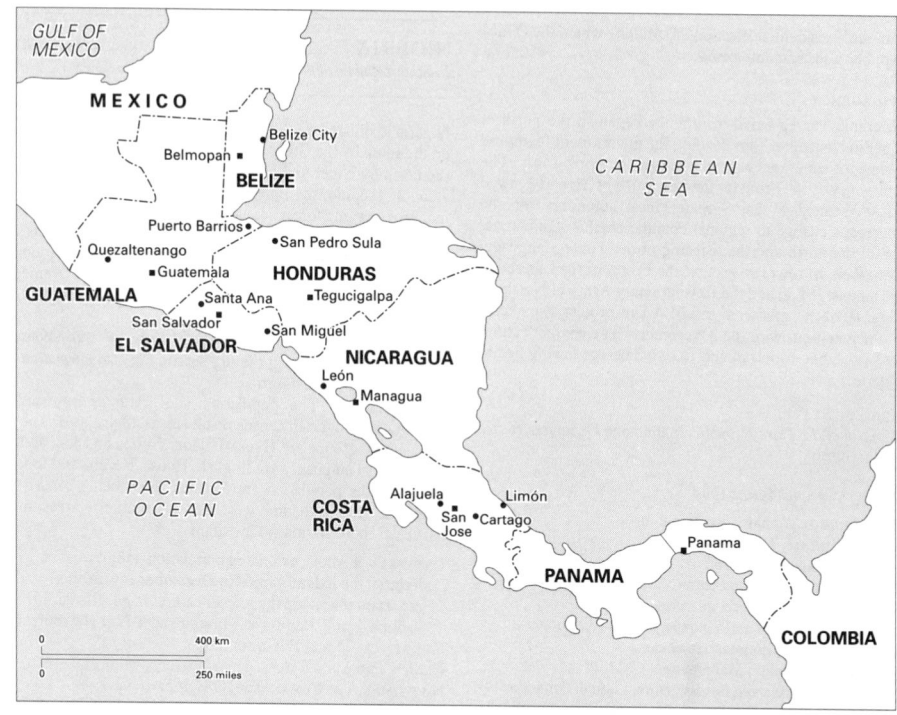

| Trade with UK | 1992 | 1993 |
|---|---|---|
| Imports from UK | £7,297,000 | £4,369,000 |
| Exports to UK | 3,452,000 | 1,857,000 |

## COMMUNICATIONS

Transport, except on the Pacific slope, is still difficult but many new roads have been opened. The Inter-American Highway runs between the Honduras and the Costa Rican borders; the inter-oceanic highway runs from the Corinto on the Pacific coast via Managua to Rama, where there is a natural waterway to Bluefields on the Atlantic. The country's main airport is at Managua. The chief port is Corinto on the Pacific. There are 252 miles of railway, all on the Pacific side of the country. There are 51 radio stations and five television stations in Managua. An automatic telephone system has been installed in major cities.

There are four daily newspapers published at Managua, apart from the official Gazette (*La Gaceta*). There are universities at León and Managua.

---

## NIGER
*République du Niger*

---

Situated in central west Africa, between 12° and 24° N. and 0° and 16° E., Niger has common boundaries with Algeria and Libya in the north, Chad in the east, Nigeria and Benin in the south, Mali and Burkina in the west. It has an area of about 489,191 sq. miles (1,267,000 sq. km). Apart from a small region along the Niger Valley in the south-west near the capital, the country is entirely savanna or desert.

POPULATION – The population (UN estimate 1991) is 7,984,000. The main ethnic groups are the Hausa (54 per cent) in the south, the Songhai and Djerma in the south-west, the Fulani, the Beriberi–Manga, and the nomadic Tuareg in the north. The official language is French.

CAPITAL – Niamey, population 410,000.
CURRENCY – Franc CFA of 100 centimes.
FLAG – Three horizontal stripes, orange, white and green with an orange disc in the middle of the white stripe.
NATIONAL DAY – 18 December.

## GOVERNMENT

The first French expedition arrived in 1891 and the country was fully occupied by 1914. It decided on 18 December 1958 to remain an autonomous republic within the French Community; full independence outside the Community was proclaimed on 3 August 1960.

The 1960 constitution provided for a presidential system of government and a single-chamber National Assembly. In April 1974 Lt.-Col. Seyni Kountché seized power, suspended the constitution, dissolved the National Assembly, and suppressed all political organizations. He set up a Supreme Military Council with himself as President. President Kountché died in 1987 and was succeeded peacefully by his cousin, Col. Ali Saibou, who restored a measure of normal political life.

In August 1991, a national conference of all groups voted to suspend the constitution and stripped President Saibou of all powers. A transitional government held office until a legislative election was held in February 1993. The former ruling party, the National Movement for a Development Society (MNSD), emerged as the largest party, with 29 seats in the 83-seat National Assembly. The opposition Alliance of Forces for Change (AFC) gained 50 seats, however, and formed the government. Mahamane Ousmane of the AFC won the presidential election in March, when the Third Republic also came into being.

## INSURGENCY

An ethnic Tuareg-based insurgency began in the north of Niger in November 1991, leading the government to impose a state of emergency in the north in April 1992. The insurgency by the Front for the Liberation of Aïr and Azawad (FLAA) aimed to gain greater local autonomy for the Tuaregs, a change to regional boundaries, the demilitarization of the north and the teaching of the Tuareg language, Tamashek. In 1993 two groups, the Front for the Liberation of Tamoust (FLT) and the Revolutionary Army of Northern Niger (RANN) split from the FLAA in protest at its entry into negotiations with the government. The conflict continues, with some 100 dead and 10,000 Tuaregs having fled to Algeria.

## HEAD OF STATE

*President of the Third Republic*, Mahamane Ousmane, *elected* March 1993

## MINISTERS *as at August 1994*

*Prime Minister*, Mahamadou Issoufou
*National Defence*, Tahirou Amadou
*Interior*, Ousmane Oumarou
*Foreign Affairs and Co-operation*, Abdourahamane Hama
*Finance and Planning*, Abdallah Boureima
*Commerce, Transport and Tourism*, Souley Abdoulaye
*Mines and Energy*, Foumakoye Gado
*Public Health*, Koulou Mahamane
*Equipment, Housing and Infrastructure*, Laouali Amadou
*Social Development, Population and Promotion of Women*, Ali Mariama
*Industry*, Effad Emoud
*National and Higher Education and Research*, Garba Djibo
*Civil Service and Employment*, Salissou Madougou
*Relations with Parliament and Government Spokesman*, Diallo Moctar
*Communications, Culture, Youth and Sport*, Hassoumi Massaoudou
*Justice*, Kandine Mallam Adam
*Agriculture and Animal Breeding*, Sadjo Djoulde
*Water Resources and Environment*, Billo Soumana
*Administrative Reform and Decentralization*, Iba Hamed Ibrahim

EMBASSY OF THE REPUBLIC OF NIGER
154 rue de Longchamp, 75116, Paris
Tel: Paris 45048060

*Ambassador Extraordinary and Plenipotentiary*, His Excellency Sandi Yacouba, apptd 1990

BRITISH AMBASSADOR, Her Excellency Margaret Rothwell, CMG, resident at Abidjan, Côte d'Ivoire

## ECONOMY

The cultivation of groundnuts and the production of livestock are the main industries and provide two of the main exports. A company formed by the government, the French Atomic Energy Authority and private interests is exploiting uranium deposits at Arlit, and this is the main export. There is also some oil exploration which has found signs of oil in the eastern desert. Gold deposits exist north-west of Niamey.

| Trade with UK | 1992 | 1993 |
|---|---|---|
| Imports from UK | £24,634,000 | £5,317,000 |
| Exports to UK | 1,151,000 | 3,495,000 |

## NIGERIA
*Federal Republic of Nigeria*

Nigeria is situated on the west coast of Africa. It is bounded on the south by the Gulf of Guinea, on the west by Benin, on the north by Niger and on the east by Cameroon. It has an area of 356,669 sq. miles (923,768 sq. km). A belt of mangrove swamp forest lies along the entire coastline. North of this there is a zone of tropical rain forest and oil-palms. North of the rain forest, the country rises and the vegetation changes to open woodland and savanna. In the extreme north the country is semi-desert. The Niger, Benue, and Cross are the main rivers.

The climate is tropical. The rainy season is from about April to October. During the dry season the cool *harmattan* wind blows from the desert.

POPULATION – The population (UN estimate 1991) is 112,163,000 (Nigerian census result (1991) 88,514,501). The main ethnic groups are Hausa/Fulani, Yoruba and Ibo, and the principal languages are English, Hausa, Yoruba and Ibo. Over half the population are Muslim, these being concentrated in the north and west. In the southern areas in particular there are many Christians.

CAPITAL – ΨAbuja, estimated population 378,671, declared the federal capital in December 1991. Other important towns are the former capital Lagos, Ibadan, Kaduna, Kano, Benin City, Enugu and ΨPort Harcourt.

CURRENCY – Naira (N) of 100 kobo.

FLAG – Three equal vertical bands, green, white and green.

NATIONAL ANTHEM – Arise, O Compatriots.

NATIONAL DAY – 1 October (Independence Day).

## GOVERNMENT

The Federation of Nigeria attained independence as a member of the Commonwealth on 1 October 1960 and became a republic in 1963. Originally regional in structure, the Federation is now divided into 30 states and the Federal Capital Territory.

In 1966 the military took power; in 1979 civil rule was restored after elections at national and state level. After similar elections in 1983 the new administration was removed by the military on 31 December, this regime itself being overthrown in August 1985. A 28-member Armed Forces Ruling Council (AFRC) was sworn in on 30 August and governed in conjunction with a Council of Ministers until January 1993, when the AFRC and Council of Ministers were replaced by a National Defence and Security Council (NDSC) and a civilian Transitional Council respectively to govern the country until a handover to civilian government. A presidential election was held on 11 June and is generally believed to have been won by Chief Moshood Abiola of the SDP but the military government refused to release the results and had the election declared invalid. The military tried to organize a new election but widespread rioting and support for Chief Moshood Abiola prevented this. The military government resigned on 26 August, handing power to the Transitional Council.

Continued strikes in support of Abiola and a High Court ruling that the interim government was illegal threatened to bring down the government, and led Defence Minister Gen. Sanni Abacha to launch a military coup on 17 November 1993 and install himself as head of state. A (military) Provisional Ruling Council and (civilian) Federal Executive Council has been established to govern the country until a new constitution is passed and political activity restored. Widespread strikes and pro-democracy demonstrations

continue in support of Chief Moshood Abiola, who returned from exile in June 1994 to establish a rival government, for which he has been arrested and put on trial for treason.

## HEAD OF STATE

*Chairman of the Provisional Ruling Council and Federal Executive Council, Commander-in-Chief of the Armed Forces*, Gen. Sanni Abacha, *took power* 17 November 1993

**FEDERAL EXECUTIVE COUNCIL** *as at August 1994*
*Chairman, Minister of Defence*, Gen. Sanni Abacha
*Vice-Chairman*, Lt.-Gen. D. O. Diya
*Federal Capital Territory*, Lt.-Gen. J. Oseni
*Education*, Dr Iyorchia Ayu
*Industries*, Bamanga Tukur
*Works and Housing*, Lateef Jakande
*Finance*, Dr Kalu Idika Kalu
*Petroleum Resources*, Don Etiebet
*Power and Steel*, Bashir Dalhatu
*Health and Human Resources*, Dr Sarki Tafida
*Foreign Affairs*, Babagana Kingibe
*Interior*, Alex Ibru
*Communications*, Abubaker Rimi
*Labour and Productivity*, Dr Samuel Ogbemudia
*Agriculture*, Adama Ciroma
*Information*, Prof. Jerry Gana
*Justice and Attorney-General*, Dr Olu Onagoruwa
*Commerce and Tourism*, Chief Mehford Okilo
*Transport and Aviation*, Chief E. Babatope
*Water Resources*, Isa Mohammed
*Science and Technology*, Dr Lazarus Unagu
*Police Affairs*, Solomon Lar
*Local Government*, Mohammed Anka
*National Planning*, Chief S. B. Daniyan
*Establishment Management Services*, Mobolaji Osomo

## NIGERIA HIGH COMMISSION
9 Northumberland Avenue, London WC2 5BX
Tel 0171–839 1244

*High Commissioner*, His Excellency Alhaji, Abubakar Alhaji, KBE, apptd 1992
*Deputy High Commissioner*, T. A. B. Sodipo
*Ministers*, M. L. Abubakar; A. A. Ella; A. K. Sambo; A. I. Imohe
*Defence Attaché*, Brig.-Gen. D. Mohammed
*Information Attaché*, O. Oyawale
*Head of Commerce/Trade*, B. A. Ameh

## BRITISH HIGH COMMISSION
Shehu Shangari Way (North), Maitama, Abuja
Tel: Abuja 5232011
11 Eleke Crescent, Victoria Island, Lagos
Tel: Lagos 619531
*High Commissioner*, His Excellency John Thorold Masefield, CMG, apptd 1994
*Deputy High Commissioner and Minister-Counsellor*, R. S. Gorham
*Defence Adviser*, Col. A. C. Taylor
*Counsellor (Economic and Commercial)*, E. A. Burner
There are liaison offices at Kano, Port Harcourt and Ibadan.

**BRITISH COUNCIL REPRESENTATIVE**, P. MacKenzie-Smith, 11 Kingsway Road, Ikoyi (PO Box 3702), Lagos. Branch offices at *Enugu, Ibadan, Kaduna* and *Kano City*.

## DEFENCE

Nigeria has a total active armed forces of some 78,800 personnel, all of whom are volunteers. The Army is 62,000 strong, with 157 main battle tanks, 100 light tanks, 330 reconnaissance vehicles, 380 armoured personnel carriers and 450 artillery pieces. The Navy has 7,300 personnel, with two frigates, 53 patrol and coastal vessels and two armed helicopters. The Air Force numbers 9,500 personnel, with 95 combat aircraft and 15 armed helicopters. Nigeria deploys 10,000 personnel in Liberia as part of the ECOMOG peacekeeping force, 800 troops in Sierra Leone, and a 70-strong training unit in the Gambia.

## EDUCATION

A programme was introduced in 1976 intended to achieve universal primary education. There are 37 universities (24 federal, 12 state and one military).

## COMMUNICATIONS

The Nigerian railway system, which is controlled by the Nigerian Railway Corporation, has 2,178 route miles of lines. The principal international airlines operate from Lagos, Kano and Port Harcourt. A network of internal air services connects the main centres. The principal seaports are served by a number of shipping lines, including the Nigerian National Line. A nationwide television and radio network is being developed, with each state eventually having its own television and radio station.

## ECONOMY

Nigeria was a predominantly agricultural country until the early 1970s when oil became the principal source of export revenue (over 90 per cent). Since 1981 oil revenues have fallen to half their peak level and austerity measures such as import curbs and payments restrictions were introduced in 1982. Recent governments have attempted to stimulate greater self-reliance in the economy by encouraging non-oil exports and the use of local rather than imported raw materials. Even so the country has a large foreign debt of US$30,000 million which has been unserviced for two years. The 1993 budget deficit was US$3,750 million, equivalent to 15 per cent of GDP, while inflation in 1993 was 100 per cent. The recent strikes have severely affected the oil industry, restricting output and exports.

  Three oil refineries are in operation at Port Harcourt, Warri and Kaduna, and steel plants at Warri and Ajaokuta. Other projects include natural gas liquifaction, petrochemicals, fertilizers, power stations and irrigation schemes.

Tin and calumbite mining on the Jos plateau, textiles and coal mining are also important.

TRADE

The principal exports are oil, groundnuts, palm products, tin, cocoa, rubber and timber.

| Trade with UK | 1992 | 1993 |
|---|---|---|
| Imports from UK | £622,630,000 | £634,688,000 |
| Exports to UK | 168,274,000 | 112,375,000 |

# NORWAY
*Kongeriket Norge*

Norway is a kingdom in the northern and western part of the Scandinavian peninsula, 1,752 km in length, its greatest width about 430 km. The length of the coastline is 2,650 km, and the frontier between Norway and the neighbouring countries is 2,542 km. It comprises an area of 149,405 sq. miles (386,958 sq. km), of which Svalbard and Jan Mayen have a combined area of 24,355 sq. miles (63,080 sq. km).

The coastline is deeply indented with numerous fjords and fringed with rocky islands. The surface is mountainous, consisting of elevated and barren tablelands separated by deep and narrow valleys. At the North Cape the sun does not appear to set from the second week in May to the last week in July, causing the phenomenon known as the Midnight Sun; conversely, there is no apparent sunrise from about 18 November to 23 January. During the long winter nights are seen the Northern Lights or Aurora Borealis.

POPULATION – The population (1993) is 4,299,167. The Norwegian language in both its present forms is closely related to other Scandinavian languages. Independence from Denmark (1814) and resurgent nationalism led to the development of 'new Norwegian' based on dialects, which now has equal official standing with 'bokmål', in which Danish influence is more obvious. This was formed in the time of the Reformation, and Ludvig Holberg (1684–1754) is regarded as the father of Norwegian literature, though the modern period begins with the writings of Henrik Wergeland (1808–45). Some of the famous names are Henrik Ibsen (1828–1906), Bjørnstjerne Bjørnson (1832–1910), Nobel Prizewinner in 1903, and the novelists Jonas Lie (1833–1908), Alexander Kielland (1849–1906), Knut Hamsun (1859–1952) and Sigrid Undset (1882–1949), the latter two also Nobel Prizewinners. Old Norse literature is among the most ancient and richest in Europe.

CAPITAL – ΨOslo (including Aker), population (1993) 473,344. Other towns are ΨTrondheim 139,660; ΨBergen 215,967; ΨStavanger 99,764; ΨKristiansand 66,398; ΨDrammen 52,062; ΨTromsø 52,459.

CURRENCY – Krone of 100 øre.

FLAG – Red, with white-bordered blue cross.

NATIONAL ANTHEM – Ja, Vi Elsker Dette Landet (Yes, we love this country).

NATIONAL DAY – 17 May (Constitution Day).

GOVERNMENT

The kingdom of Norway was founded in AD 872. From 1397 to 1814 Norway was united with Denmark and from 1814 with Sweden. The union with Sweden was dissolved on 7 June 1905 when Norway regained complete independence. Under the 1814 constitution, the 165-member *Storting* elects one-quarter of its members to constitute the *Lagting* (Upper Chamber), the other three-quarters forming the *Odelsting* (Lower Chamber).

A minority Labour government replaced the centre-right coalition government which collapsed in October 1990 because of a dispute over whether to apply for membership of the European Community. The minority Labour government was returned to power in the general election held on 13 September 1993. The state of the parties as at August 1994 was Labour 67, Centre Party 32, Conservatives 28, Christian Democrats 13, Socialist Left 13, Progress Party 10, Liberal Party 1. The Storting voted in November 1992 to apply to join the European Community. Negotiations with the EC concluded on 1 March 1994 with a proposed accession date of 1 January 1995, subject to parliamentary and national referendum ratifications.

HEAD OF STATE

*HM The King of Norway*, King Harald V, GCVO, *born* 21 February 1937; *succeeded*, 17 January 1991, on death of his father King Olav V; *married* 29 August 1968, Sonja Haraldsen, and has *issue*, Prince Haakon Magnus (*see below*), and Princess Martha Louise, *born* 22 September 1971

*Heir*, HRH Crown Prince Haakon Magnus, *born* 20 July 1973

CABINET *as at August 1994*

*Prime Minister*, Gro Harlem Brundtland
*Foreign Affairs*, Björn Tore Godal
*Industry, Petroleum and Energy*, Jens Stoltenberg
*Defence*, Jorgen Kosmo
*Local Government and Labour*, Gunnar Berge
*Government Administration*, Nils Olav Totland
*Agriculture*, Gunhild Øyangen
*Justice*, Grete Faremo
*Fisheries*, Jan Henry Olsen

*Environment*, Thorbjørn Berntsen
*Transport and Communications*, Kjell Opseth
*Health and Social Affairs*, Hill Marta Solberg
*Church, Education and Research*, Gudmund Hernes
*Trade and Shipping*, Grete Knudsen
*Family and Consumer Affairs*, Grete Berget
*Cultural Affairs*, Åse Kleveland
*Finance*, Sigbjørn Johnsen
*Development Co-operation*, Kari Nordheim Larsen

ROYAL NORWEGIAN EMBASSY
25 Belgrave Square, London SW1X 8QD
Tel 0171-235 7151

*Ambassador Extraordinary and Plenipotentiary*, His
Excellency Tom Vraalsen, apptd 1994
*Minister*, Truls Hanevold
*Defence Attaché*, Col. P. J. Aunaas
*First Secretary*, Inger Brusell (*Consular*)
*Counsellor*, T. Gulli (*Commercial*)

BRITISH EMBASSY
Thomas Heftyesgate 8, 0244 Oslo
Tel: Oslo 22 55 24 00

*Ambassador Extraordinary and Plenipotentiary*, His
Excellency Mark Elliott, CMG, apptd 1994
*Counsellor*, E. J. Hughes (*Deputy Head of Mission and
Consul-General*)
*First Secretary*, S. M. Williams (*Economic and Commercial*)
*Defence and Naval Attaché*, Cdr. G. S. Pearson, RN

BRITISH CONSULAR OFFICES – There is a British
Consular Office at *Oslo* and Honorary Consulates at
*Bergen, Tromsø, Alesund, Kristiansund* (North), *Stavanger,
Trondheim, Kristiansand* (South), *Haugesund* and *Harstad*.

BRITISH COUNCIL REPRESENTATIVE – Rosalind Olsen,
Fridtjof Nansens Plass 5, 0160, Oslo 1

## DEFENCE

Norway is a member of NATO and the headquarters of
Allied Forces Northern Europe is situated near Oslo. The
total active armed forces number some 29,400 (18,800
conscripts), Reserve forces number some 298,000. The
Army has a strength of 12,900 (10,000 conscripts), with 260
main battle tanks, 340 armoured infantry fighting vehicles
and armoured personnel carriers, and 405 artillery pieces.
Most of the army is deployed in the north of the country.
The Navy has a strength of 8,300, including 4,500 conscripts,
with 12 submarines, five frigates, and 30 patrol and coastal
combatants. The Air Force has a strength of 8,200 (4,300
conscripts), with 85 combat aircraft, mainly US manufactured
F16s. The period of compulsory national service is 15 months
(without refresher training) in the Navy and 12 months (with
refresher training) in the Army and Air Force. Norway
deploys 866 troops with UN forces in Lebanon and 287 in
the former Yugoslavia.

## ECONOMY

The cultivated area is about 10,016 sq. km, 3.5 per cent of
total surface area. Forests cover nearly 25 per cent; the rest
consists of highland pastures or uninhabitable mountains.
The chief agricultural products are grain, potatoes, root
vegetables, milk, furs and timber.

The Gulf Stream causes the sea temperature to be higher
than the average for the latitude. It brings shoals of herring
and cod into the fishing grounds and the quantity of fish
caught by Norwegian fishing vessels is greater than that of
any other European country except Russia. In 1989 the total
catch amounted to 1,788,000 tonnes.

The chief industries are manufactures, agriculture and
forestry, fisheries, mining, production of metals and ferro-
alloys, and shipping. Industries providing both manufactured
products and services for the development of North Sea oil
and gas resources are also important. In 1992 106,103,000
tons of crude oil were produced, of which 92,546,000 tons
were exported. Manufactures are aided by great resources of
hydro-electric power. Actual production in 1991 amounted to
110,950 GWh. In 1992, the total workforce was 2,004,000 of
which 5.5 per cent were employed in agriculture, forestry
and fishing, 23.2 per cent in industry, construction and
mining, and 71.3 per cent in services.

| FINANCE | 1992 |
|---|---|
| Total revenue | K353,443,000,000 |
| Total expenditure | 436,905,000,000 |

### TRADE

The chief imports are raw materials, motor vehicles,
chemicals, motor spirit, fuel and other oils; coal, ships and
machinery; and manufactures of silk, cotton and wool.
Exports consist chiefly of crude oil and gas, manufactured
goods, fish and fish products (as canned fish, whale oils),
pulp, paper, iron ore and pyrites, nitrate of lime, stone,
calcium carbide, aluminium, ferro-alloys, zinc, nickel,
cyanamides, etc. Norway's major trading partners are the
UK, Sweden, Germany, the Netherlands, Denmark and the
USA.

| | 1992 |
|---|---|
| Total imports | K251,748m |
| Total exports | 303,034m |

| Trade with UK | 1992 | 1993 |
|---|---|---|
| Imports from UK | £1,419,570,000 | £1,519,473,000 |
| Exports to UK | 3,861,771,000 | 4,170,275,000 |

## EDUCATION

Education from seven to 16 is free and compulsory in the
'basic schools'. The majority of the pupils receive post-
compulsory schooling at 'upper secondary' schools, colleges
of education (19), regional colleges akin to polytechnics (12),
universities (four) and other university-level specialist institutions. In 1991–2 there were 68,249 students at universities
and university-level institutions.

## COMMUNICATIONS

The total length of railways open at the end of 1992 was
4,027 km, excluding private lines. There are 89,135 km of
public roads in Norway (including urban streets). At the end
of 1992, 2,958,454 road motor vehicles were registered.
Scheduled internal air services are operated by Scandinavian
Airlines System (SAS) on behalf of Det Norske Luftfartselskap
(DNL), by Braathens South American and Far East
Airtransport (SAFE), and by Wideróes Flyveselskap AS.
The mercantile marine in 1990 consisted of 1,516 vessels of
23,607,000 gross tons (vessels above 100 gross tons,
excluding fishing boats, floating whaling factories, tugs,
salvage vessels, icebreakers and similar types of vessel).

In 1991 there were 148 daily newspapers.

## TERRITORIES

### SVALBARD

The Svalbard archipelago lies between 74° and 81° N. and
between 10° and 35° E., with an estimated area of 24,295 sq.
miles. The archipelago consists of the main island Spitsbergen
(15,200 sq. miles), North East Land, the Wiche Islands,
Barents and Edge Islands, Prince Charles Foreland, Hope

Island, Bear Island and many islands in the neighbourhood of the main group. South Cape is 355 miles from the Norwegian coast. Transit from Tromsø to Green Harbour takes two to three days.

The sovereignty of Norway over the archipelago was recognized by other nations in 1920 and in 1925 Norway assumed sovereignty. The inhabitants are mainly engaged in coal-mining, but the islands are also visited by hunters for seals, foxes and polar bears.

### JAN MAYEN ISLAND

Jan Mayen, an island in the Arctic Ocean (70° 49′ to 71° 9′ N. and 7° 53′ to 9° 5′ W.) was joined to Norway by law in 1930.

### NORWEGIAN ANTARCTIC TERRITORIES

BOUVET ISLAND (54° 26′ S. and 3° 24′ E.) was declared a dependency of Norway in 1930.
PETER THE FIRST ISLAND (68° 48′ S. and 90° 35′ W.), was declared a dependency of Norway in 1931.
PRINCESS RAGNHILD LAND (from 70° 30′ to 68° 40′ S. and 24° 15′ to 33° 30′ E.) has been claimed as Norwegian since 1931.
QUEEN MAUD LAND – In 1939 the Norwegian Government declared the area between 20° W. and 45° E., adjacent to Australian Antarctica, to be Norwegian territory.

## OMAN
*The Sultanate of Oman*

Oman lies at the eastern corner of the Arabian peninsula, bordered on the west by Yemen, Saudi Arabia and the UAE. To the north lies the Gulf of Oman and to the east the Arabian Sea, giving a coastline of nearly 1,000 miles. Sharjah and Fujairah (UAE) separate the main part of Oman from the northernmost part of the state, a peninsula extending into the Strait of Hormuz. The area has been estimated at 115,830 sq. miles (300,000 sq. km).

The north and the south of Oman are divided by nearly 400 miles of desert. The Batinah, the coastal plain, is fertile. The Hajjar is a mountain spine running from north-west to south-east and for the most part barren, but valleys penetrate the central massif which are irrigated by wells or a system of underground canals called *falajs* which tap the water table. The two plateaus leading from the western slopes of the mountains descend to the Empty Quarter of the Arabian Desert. Dhofar, the southern province, is the only part of the Arabian peninsula to be touched by the south-west monsoon. Temperatures are more moderate than in the north.
POPULATION – The population (UN estimate 1991) is 1,559,000. The inhabitants of the north are mostly Arab, though there are large communities of Hindus, Khojas and Baluch, in addition to Omanis of Zanzibari origin, especially around Salalah. However, in the mountains the inhabitants are either of pure Arab descent or belong to tribes of pre-Arab origin, the Qarra and Mahra, who speak their own dialects of Semitic origin.

CAPITAL – Ψ Muscat, estimated population 400,000. The commercial centre has grown around Mutrah, three miles away and the main port, and Ruwi. The main towns on the northern coast are Ψ Sur, Ψ Barka and Ψ Sohar. The main town of Dhofar is Salalah.
CURRENCY – Rial Omani (OR) of 1,000 baiza.
FLAG – Red with a white panel in the upper fly and a green one in the lower fly; in the canton the national emblem in white.
NATIONAL DAY – 18 November.

### GOVERNMENT

A State Consultative Council established in 1981 was replaced by Sultanic decree in 1991 by a Majlis A' shura, or State Advisory Council. This body, meeting twice a year, consists of a representative from each of the 59 wilayats, or governorates, of the Sultanate. The Council has the right to review legislation, question ministers and make policy proposals. Effective political power remains with the Sultan, who rules by decree and is advised by the Cabinet, which he appoints.

### HEAD OF STATE

*HM The Sultan of Oman*, Sultan HM Qaboos Bin-Said, *succeeded* on deposition of Sultan Said bin Taimur, 23 July 1970

### COUNCIL OF MINISTERS *as at August 1994*

*Prime Minister, Minister of Foreign Affairs, Defence and Finance*, The Sultan
*Personal Representative of HM The Sultan*, HH Sayyid Thuwainy bin Shihab Al Said
*Deputy PM for Security and Defence*, HH Sayyid Fahr bin Taimur al Said
*Deputy PM for Legal Affairs*, HH Sayyid Fahad bin Mahmood al Said
*Deputy PM for Financial and Economic Affairs*, HE Qais bin Abdul Munem al Zawawi
*Minister of State and Governor of Dhofar*, HE Sayyid Mussellam bin Ali Al Busaidi
*Minister of State and Governor of Muscat*, HE Sayyid Al Mutassim bin Hamoud Al Busaidi
*National Heritage and Culture*, HH Sayyid Faisal bin Ali al Said
*Agriculture and Fisheries*, HE Mohammed bin Abdallah bin Zaher al Hinai
*Electricity and Water*, HE Shaikh Mohammed bin Ali Al Qatabi
*Water Resources*, HE Hamed bin Said Al Aufi
*Justice, Awqaf and Islamic Affairs*, HE Hamoud bin Abdullah Al Harthi
*Health*, HE Dr Ali bin Mohammed bin Moosa
*Petroleum and Minerals*, HE Said bin Ahmed bin Said al Shanfari
*Housing*, HE Malik bin Suleiman al Ma'amari
*Civil Services*, HE Ahmed bin Abdul Nabi Macki
*Communications*, HE Salim bin Abdullah Al Ghazali
*Education and Youth Affairs*, HE Saud bin Ibrahim bin Saud al-Busa'di
*Higher Education*, HE Yahya bin Mahfoodh al Manthri
*Interior*, HE Sayyid Badr bin Sa'oud bin Hareb al Busaidi
*Information*, HE Abdul Aziz bin Mohammed al Rowas
*Regional Municipalities and Environment*, HE Shaikh Amer bin Shuwain al Hosni
*Minister of State for Foreign Affairs*, HE Yousuf bin Alawi bin Abdullah
*Commerce and Industry*, HE Maqbool bin Ali bin Sultan
*Social Affairs and Labour*, HE Ahmed bin Mohammed bin Salim Al Isa'ee
*Posts, Telegraphs and Telephones*, HE Ahmed bin Sweidan al Baluchi
*Secretary-General at the Ministry of Defence*, HE Saif bin Hamad al Batashi
*Diwan of Royal Court*, HE Sayyid Saif bin Hamed bin Sa'oud
*Palace Office Affairs*, HE Gen. Ali bin Majid Al Ma'amari

EMBASSY OF THE SULTANATE OF OMAN
167 Queen's Gate, London SW7 5HE
Tel 0171-225 0001

*Ambassador Extraordinary and Plenipotentiary*, His
  Excellency Abdulla bin Mohammed Al-Dhahab, apptd
  1990
*First Secretary and Deputy Head of Mission*, Mahmood bin
  Mohamed Al-Raeesy
*Military Attaché*, Capt. Mohammed bin Ali Al-Farsi

BRITISH EMBASSY
PO Box 300, Muscat
Tel: Muscat 738501/5

*Ambassador Extraordinary and Plenipotentiary*, His
  Excellency Richard John Muir, CMG, apptd 1994
*Counsellor*, N. J. Guckian (*Deputy Head of Mission*)
*Defence Attaché*, Brig. P. A. Goddard
*First Secretary (Commercial)*, P. Nessling
*Consul*, G. H. Davies

BRITISH COUNCIL REPRESENTATIVE, Clive Bruton,
PO Box 73, Muscat, Oman. There are also offices at
*Salalah* and *Sohar*.

## DEFENCE

The total active armed forces strength is 36,700 personnel.
Service is voluntary. The Army has a strength of 20,000
personnel, with 73 main battle tanks, 43 light tanks and 96
artillery pieces. The Navy has 3,500 personnel, and 12 patrol
and coastal vessels. The Air Force has 3,500 personnel and
55 combat aircraft. The Royal Household has 6,000
personnel formed into a Royal Guard brigade, two special
forces regiments, the Royal Yacht Squadron and the Royal
Flight. In addition there is the paramilitary home guard
(*Firqat*) of 3,500 personnel. Some 3,700 hired and seconded
personnel (many British) serve in the Omani armed forces.

## ECONOMY

Although there is considerable cultivation in the fertile areas
and cattle are raised on the mountains, the backbone of the
economy is the oil industry. Petroleum Development (Oman)
Ltd (owned 60 per cent by Oman Government and 34 per
cent by Shell) began exporting oil in 1967. Concessions (off
and on shore) are held by several major international
companies. The current level of oil production is about
650,000 barrels per day, planned to increase to 700,000.
  A gas turbine power station operates at Rusail, where
there is also a 200-plot industrial estate. There is a power
station and a desalination plant near Muscat and flour, animal
feed, cement and copper production facilities.

### TRADE

Trade is mainly with the UAE, UK, Japan, the Netherlands,
USA, Germany, France and India. Chief imports are
machinery, cars, building materials, food and telecommunications equipment.

| Trade with UK | 1992 | 1993 |
|---|---|---|
| Imports from UK | £240,695,000 | £305,592,000 |
| Exports to UK | 83,106,000 | 82,664,000 |

## SOCIAL WELFARE

For many years the Sultanate was a poor country but the
advent of oil revenues and the change of regime in 1970 led
to the initiation of a wide-ranging development programme,
especially concerned with health, education and communications. There are now nearly 50 hospitals with around 3,400
beds; 823 schools, with 387,000 pupils, were in operation in
1992.

## COMMUNICATIONS

Port Qaboos at Matrah has eight deep-water berths which
have been constructed as part of the harbour facilities. A
modern telecommunications service to the main population
centres and an international service are operated by the
General Telecommunications Organization. There are good
tarmac roads linking most main population centres of the
country with the coast and with the towns of the UAE, though
only a trunk road links the north and south of Oman.

---

# PAKISTAN
*Islami Jamhuriya-e-Pakistan*

---

Pakistan is situated in the north-west of the Indian sub-
continent, bordered by Iran, Afghanistan, China, the disputed
territory of Kashmir, and India. It covers a total area of
803,950 sq. km. Running through Pakistan are five great
rivers, the Indus, Jhelum, Chenab, Ravi and Sutlej. The
upper reaches of these rivers are in Kashmir, and their
sources in the Himalayas.

POPULATION – The census in 1981 showed a population
figure of 83,780,000 (1991 UN estimate, 115,524,000). Of
these, about 95 per cent are Muslims, 3.5 per cent Christians,
about 1 per cent Hindus, and 0.5 per cent Buddhists.

CAPITAL – Islamabad, population 350,000. ΨKarachi
  (estimated population 7,183,000) is the largest city and
  seaport; Lahore has a population of 4,072,000.
CURRENCY – Pakistan rupee of 100 paisa.
FLAG – Green with a white crescent and star, and a white
  vertical strip in the hoist
NATIONAL ANTHEM – Quami Tarana.
NATIONAL DAYS – 23 March (Pakistan Day), 14 August
  (Independence Day).

## GOVERNMENT

Pakistan was constituted as a Dominion under the Indian
Independence Act 1947, becoming a republic on 23 March
1956. Until 1972 Pakistan consisted of two geographical
units, West and East Pakistan, which were separated by
about 1,100 miles of Indian territory. Relations between the
main parties in East and West Pakistan broke down in 1971
over East Pakistan's insistance on complete autonomy. Civil
war broke out on 25 March 1971 and continued until
December 1971 when a ceasefire was arranged, and the
independence of East Pakistan as Bangladesh was proclaimed
in April 1972.
  The armed forces under Gen. Zia-ul-Haq assumed power
in 1977 and martial law was in force from July 1977 to March
1985. Gen. Zia declared himself President in September
1978. Zia was killed in a plane crash in August 1988. The
Pakistan People's Party won the election to the National
Assembly and Benazir Bhutto became Prime Minister. In
August 1990, the President dissolved the National Assembly
and dismissed the Bhutto cabinet. Elections were held on 24
October 1990 and won by the Islamic Democratic Alliance,
led by Mian Muhammad Nawaz Sharif.
  In late 1992 and early 1993 a power struggle between
President Ishaq Khan and Prime Minister Sharif developed,
in which the Army eventually intervened in July 1993, forcing
both Khan and Sharif to resign and replacing them with a
caretaker President and Cabinet until new elections were
held on 6 October 1993. These were won by the Pakistan
People's Party (PPP) and Benazir Bhutto resumed the
premiership. The PPP and allies gained majorities in the
National Assembly and in the provincial assemblies of

the Punjab, Sind and North-West Frontier, with no party controlling the Baluchistan provincial assembly, and the PPP's Farooq Leghari was elected President by an electoral college of the National and provincial assemblies.

HEAD OF STATE
*President*, Farooq Ahmad Khan Leghari, *elected* 13 November 1993

FEDERAL CABINET *as at August 1994*
*Prime Minister, Minister of Finance*, Benazir Bhutto
*Defence*, Aftab Shahban Mirani
*Foreign Affairs*, Aseff Ahmad Ali
*Industries and Production*, Muhammad Asghar
*Interior*, Maj.-Gen. Nasirullah Khan Babar
*Kashmir and Northern Affairs*, Muhammad Afzal Khan
*Law, Justice and Parliamentary Affairs*, Sayed Iqbal Haider
*Social Welfare*, Dr Sher Afghan Khan Niazi
*Petroleum and Natural Resources*, Anwar Saifullah Khan
*Information and Broadcasting*, Khalid Ahmad Khan Kharal
*Education*, Khurshid Ahmed Shah
*Works*, Makhdoom Mohammed Amin Fahin
*Food, Agriculture and Livestock*, Mohammed Yousef Talpur
*Water and Power*, Ghulam Mustafa Khar
*Commerce*, Chaudhry Ahmed Mukhtar
*Population Welfare*, Julius Salik
*Economic Adviser*, V. A. Jafarey

HIGH COMMISSION FOR PAKISTAN
35–36 Lowndes Square, London SW1X 9JN
Tel 0171–235 2044
*High Commissioner*, His Excellency Wajid Shamsul Hassan, apptd 1994
*Minister and Deputy High Commissioner*, M. J. Naim
*Minister*, K. Shafi
*Consul-General*, M. Nisar
*Defence and Naval Attaché*, Cdre M. J. Akhtar
*Counsellor*, M. A. Tahir (*Commercial*)

BRITISH HIGH COMMISSION
Diplomatic Enclave, Ramna 5, PO Box 1122, Islamabad
Tel: Islamabad 822131/5
*High Commissioner*, His Excellency Sir Christopher MacRae, KCMG, apptd 1994
*Deputy High Commissioners*, A. J. F. Caie (*Islamabad*); E. W. Callway (*Karachi*)
*Counsellor (Economical and Comercial)*, S. N. Evans, OBE
*Counsellor*, T. A. Willasey-Wilsey
*Defence and Military Adviser*, Brig. I. McLeod, OBE, MC

There is a British Deputy High Commission at *Karachi* and a Consulate at *Lahore*.

BRITISH COUNCIL REPRESENTATIVE, Peter Elborn, OBE, PO Box 1135, Islamabad. There are offices at *Karachi, Lahore* and *Peshawar*.

DEFENCE

In July 1993 the former Pakistani Army Chief-of-Staff Gen. Aslam Beg confirmed that since 1987 Pakistan has had the capability to construct nuclear weapons at short notice and that Pakistan would use this capability if its conventional forces faced defeat in a war with India. In August 1994 former Prime Minister Nawaz Sharif stated that Pakistan had constructed a nuclear weapon. Pakistan has Chinese manufactured M11 (range 185 miles) and M9 (range 370 miles) missiles capable of delivering nuclear warheads.

Pakistan has a total armed forces active strength of 577,000 personnel, with a further 313,000 reserves. The Army has a strength of 510,000 personnel, with 2,000 main battle tanks,

800 armoured personnel carriers, 2,090 artillery pieces and 20 attack helicopters. The Navy has 22,000 personnel, with six submarines, three destroyers, 11 frigates, 18 patrol and coastal vessels, four combat aircraft and ten armed helicopters. The Air Force has 45,000 personnel, and 393 combat aircraft of French, Chinese and US manufacture. In addition, there are 275,000 paramilitary personnel in four organizations.

EDUCATION

Education consists of five years of primary education (five to nine years), three years of middle or lower secondary (general or vocational), two years of upper secondary, two years of higher secondary (intermediate) and two to five years of higher education in colleges and universities. Education is free to upper secondary level.

COMMUNICATIONS

The main seaport is Karachi. The main airports are Karachi, Islamabad, Lahore, Peshawar and Quetta. Pakistan International Airlines operates air services between the principal cities within the country as well as abroad. Post and telegraph facilities are available to every country in the world.

ECONOMY

Pakistan's economy is based on agriculture. The principal crops are cotton, rice, wheat, sugar cane, maize and tobacco. Pakistan has one of the longest irrigation systems in the world. The total area irrigated is 33 million acres. There are large deposits of rock salt.

Pakistan also produces hides and skins, leather, wool, fertilizers, paints and varnishes, soda ash, paper, cement, fish, carpets, sports goods, surgical appliances and engineering goods, including switchgear, transformers, cables and wires.

An agreement was reached in November 1993 with the IMF for a three-year loan of US$1,300 million in return for the implementation of an austerity and structural adjustment programme. The programme has led to the lowering of the foreign debt, reductions in inflation and in the budget deficit (7 per cent of GDP in 1993). Privatization begun under Sharif's government has continued, with 32 major firms sold in the first half of 1993.

TRADE

Principal imports are petroleum products, machinery, fertilizers, transport equipment, edible oils, chemicals and ferrous metals. Principal exports are raw cotton, cotton yarn and cloth, carpets, rice, petroleum products, synthetic textiles, leather, and fish.

| Trade with UK | 1992 | 1993 |
|---|---|---|
| Imports from UK | £311,771,000 | £338,581,000 |
| Exports to UK | 273,324,000 | 324,335,000 |

---

PANAMA
*República de Panamá*

---

Panama lies on the isthmus of that name which connects North and South America. The area is 29,762 sq. miles (77,082 sq. km), the population (census 1990) 2,315,047. Spanish is the official language.

CAPITAL – ΨPanama City, population (1990) 1,064,221.

CURRENCY – Balboa of 100 centésimos. US$ notes are also in circulation.

FLAG – Four quarters; white with blue star (top, next staff), red (in fly), blue (below, next staff) and white with red star.

NATIONAL ANTHEM – Alcanzamos Por Fin La Victoria (Victory is ours at last).

NATIONAL DAY – 3 November.

## GOVERNMENT

After a revolt in 1903, Panama declared its independence from Colombia and established a separate government. After 1968, control of Panama was increasingly taken over by Gen. Omar Torrijos, commander of the National Guard, following a military coup. In 1978 Gen. Torrijos withdrew from the government, and Dr Aristides Royo was elected President by the Assembly of Representatives.

An attempt in February 1988 by President Delvalle to remove Gen. Noriega as Commander of the Defence Forces failed. Noriega ousted Delvalle and replaced him with Manuel Solis Palma. Presidential elections were held in May 1989 but Noriega annulled the results, which appeared to give victory to the opposition and on 15 December he assumed power formally as head of state. On 20 December US troops invaded Panama to oust Noriega. Guillermo Endara, believed to have won the May elections, was installed as President. In December 1991 the Legislative Assembly approved a change to the constitution which abolished the armed forces.

Legislative power is vested in a unicameral Legislative Assembly of 67 members; executive power is held by the President, assisted by an elected Vice-President and an appointed Cabinet. Elections are held every five years under a system of universal and compulsory adult suffrage. The last presidential election was held on 8 May 1994 and won by Ernesto Pérez Balladares of the Democratic Revolutionary Party (PRD). At the time of going to press he had yet to appoint his cabinet.

HEAD OF STATE
*President*, Ernesto Pérez Balladares, *elected* 8 May 1994, *sworn in* 1 September 1994

EMBASSY OF THE REPUBLIC OF PANAMA
48 Park Street, London W1Y 3PD
Tel 0171–409 2255

*Ambassador Extraordinary and Plenipotentiary*, His Excellency Teodoro F. Franco, apptd 1990

BRITISH EMBASSY
Torre Swiss Bank, Calle 53 (Apartado 889) Zona 1, Panama City, Panama 1
Tel: Panama City 69-0866

*Ambassador Extraordinary and Plenipotentiary*, His Excellency Thomas Malcomson, apptd 1992

There is a British consular office at *Panama City*.

## ECONOMY

The soil is moderately fertile, but nearly one-half of the land is uncultivated. The chief crops are bananas, sugar, coconuts, cacao, coffee and cereals. The shrimping industry plays an important role in the economy. In 1992 tourism became the principal foreign currency earner, ahead of bananas. A railway joins the Atlantic and Pacific oceans.

Education is compulsory and free from seven to 15 years.

## TRADE

Imports are mostly manufactured goods, machinery, lubricants, chemicals and foodstuffs. Exports are bananas, petroleum products, shrimps, sugar, meat and fishmeal.

| Republic of Panama | 1988 | 1989 |
| --- | --- | --- |
| Imports | US$712.3m | US$796.0m |
| Exports | 283.0m | 297.3m |

| Colon Free Zone | | |
| --- | --- | --- |
| Imports | US$1,843m | US$243.8m |
| Exports | 2,119m | 249.9m |

| Trade with UK† | 1992 | 1993 |
| --- | --- | --- |
| Imports from UK | £42,178,000 | £53,367,000 |
| Exports to UK | 7,025,000 | 12,674,000 |

† Including Colon Free Zone

## THE PANAMA CANAL ZONE

With effect from 1 October 1979 the Canal Zone (647 sq. miles) was disestablished, with all areas of land and water within the Zone reverting to Panama. By the 1977 treaty with the USA, the USA is allowed the use of operating bases for the Panama Canal, together with several military bases, but the Republic of Panama is sovereign in all such areas. Control of the Canal will revert to Panama at noon on 31 December 1999.

## DEPENDENCIES

Taboga Island (area 4 sq. miles) is a popular tourist resort some 12 miles from the Pacific entrance to the Panama Canal.

Tourist facilities have also been developed in the Las Perlas Archipelago in the Gulf of Panama, particularly on the island of Contadora.

There is a penal settlement at Guardia on the island of Coiba (area 19 sq. miles) in the Gulf of Chiriqui.

# PAPUA NEW GUINEA

Papua New Guinea extends from the Equator to Cape Baganowa in the Louisiade Archipelago at 11° S. latitude and from the border with Irian Jaya to 160° E. longitude. The total area is 178,260 sq. miles, (461,691 sq. km), of which approximately 152,420 sq. miles form the mainland on the island of New Guinea. The country has many island groups, principally the Bismarck Archipelago, a portion of the Solomon Islands, the Trobriands, the D'Entrecasteaux Islands and the Louisade Archipelago. The main islands of the Bismarck Archipelago are New Britain, New Ireland and Manus. Bougainville is the largest of the Solomon Islands within Papua New Guinea.

Papua New Guinea lies within the tropics and has a typically monsoonal climate. Temperature and humidity are uniformly high throughout the year.

POPULATION – The population in 1991 (UN estimate) was 3,772,000.

CAPITAL – ΨPort Moresby. Estimated population (1990), 173,500. Other major towns are Lae, Rabaul, Madang, Wewak, Goroka and Mount Hagen.

CURRENCY – Kina (K) of 100 toea.

FLAG – Divided diagonally red (fly) and black (hoist); on the red a soaring Bird of Paradise in yellow and on the black five white stars of the Southern Cross.

NATIONAL ANTHEM – Arise All You Sons.
NATIONAL DAY – 16 September (Independence Day).

## GOVERNMENT

New Guinea was sighted by Portuguese and Spanish navigators in the early 16th century, but remained largely isolated from the rest of the world. In 1884 a British Protectorate, British New Guinea, was proclaimed over the southern coast of New Guinea (Papua) and the adjacent islands, which were annexed outright in 1888. In 1906 the Territory of British New Guinea was placed under the authority of Australia.

In 1884 Germany had formally taken possession of certain northern areas, later to be known as the Trust Territory of New Guinea. In 1914 the German areas were occupied by Australian troops and remained under military administration until 1921, when they became a League of Nations mandate administered by Australia. New Guinea was administered under the mandate and Papua under the Papua Act until the invasion by the Japanese in 1942 when the civil administration was suspended until the surrender of the Japanese in 1945.

From 1970 there was a gradual assumption of powers by the Papua New Guinea government, culminating in formal self-government in December 1973. Papua New Guinea achieved full independence within the Commonwealth on 16 September 1975.

Elections are held every five years. The Parliament comprises 109 elected members, 20 from regional electorates, the remainder from open electorates. There are 19 provinces, which have their own provincial governments with certain legislative and administrative powers.

### SECESSION

Bougainville witnessed separatist tensions at the time of independence and in 1989 a secessionist movement, the Bougainville Revolutionary Army (BRA), began an insurrection on Bougainville. In March 1990 the Papua New Guinean security forces withdrew from the island and the BRA declared an independent republic in May 1990. In January 1991, a peace accord was signed between the two sides; the question of Bougainville's future status was deferred. However, fighting has continued, with Papua New Guinea security forces returning to the island in October 1992. Raids by Papua New Guinean forces on islands in the Solomons chain to destroy supply routes to the rebels led to protests by the Solomon Islands government and clashes between Papuan and Solomon Islands patrol boats in April 1993. By late 1993 Papua New Guinean security forces were in control of the island's port and airport and the capital Arawa.

*Governor-General*, His Excellency Sir Wiwa Korowi, GCMG, appointed 18 November 1991

### NATIONAL EXECUTIVE COUNCIL *as at August 1994*

*Prime Minister*, Rt. Hon. Paias Wingti
*Deputy PM and Minister of Foreign Affairs and Trade*, Rt. Hon. Sir Julius Chan, GCMG, KBE
*Provincial Affairs and Village Development*, John Nilkare, CMG
*Works*, Albert Karo, CBE
*Transport*, Roy Yaki
*Fisheries*, Iairo Lasaro
*Public Services*, John Orea
*Lands*, Sir Albert Kipalan, KBE, CMG
*Finance and Planning*, Masket Iangalio
*Mining and Petroleum*, John Kaputin, CBE
*Forests*, Tim Neville
*State*, Michael Ogio, CBE

*Justice*, Philemon Embel
*Agriculture and Livestock*, Roy Evara
*Environment and Conservation*, Parry Zeipi
*Commerce and Industry*, David Mai
*Labour and Employment*, Castan Maibawa
*Defence*, Paul Tohian
*Education*, Andrew Baing
*Health*, Francis Koimanrea
*Housing*, John Jaminan
*Home Affairs*, Andrew Posai
*Communications*, Martin Thompson
*Energy and Science*, Thomas Pelika
*Police*, Stanley Pil
*Culture*, Matthew Yago
*Tourism and Civil Aviation*, Avusi Tanao
*Correctional Services*, John Kamb

PAPUA NEW GUINEA HIGH COMMISSION
3rd Floor, 14 Waterloo Place, London SW1R 4AR
Tel 0171-930 0922/7

*High Commissioner*, His Excellency Noel Levi, CBE, apptd 1991

BRITISH HIGH COMMISSION
PO Box 4778, Boroko, Port Moresby
Tel: Port Moresby 251677

*High Commissioner*, His Excellency John Westgarth Guy, OBE, apptd 1991

## COMMUNICATIONS

Air Niugini (the national airline) operates regular air services to other countries in the region. Internal air services are operated by Air Niugini, Douglas Airways, and Talair. Several shipping companies operate cargo services to Australia, Europe, the Far East and USA. There are very limited cargo and passenger services between Papua New Guinea main ports, outports, plantations and missions. Road communications are very limited, the most important road being that linking Lae with the populous highlands. Papua New Guinea is linked by international cable to Australia, Guam, Hong Kong, Kota Kinabalu, the Far East and USA. Telecommunications are widely available.

## ECONOMY

Until the 1970s the Papua New Guinea economy was based almost entirely on agriculture, principally copra, cocoa, tea, coffee, palm oil, rubber, groundnuts, spices and timber. A variety of commercial agricultural developments co-exist with the traditional rural economy.

There are extensive mineral deposits throughout Papua New Guinea, including copper, gold, silver, nickel, chromite, bauxite and possibly commercial deposits of oil and gas. In 1972, Bougainville Copper Pty Ltd (BCL) began mining in the North Solomons province, producing copper, silver and gold. The Bougainville copper mine closed indefinitely in May 1989 because of the unrest on the island. The most important new development is the exploitation of large copper and gold deposits on the Ok Tedi, in the Western province.

Industry includes processing of primary products, and brewing, bottling and packaging, paint, plywood, and metal manufacturing and the construction industries.

| *Trade with UK* | 1992 | 1993 |
|---|---|---|
| Imports from UK | £6,469,000 | £10,858,000 |
| Exports to UK | 41,020,000 | 53,690,000 |

# PARAGUAY
*República del Paraguay*

Paraguay is an inland subtropical state of South America, situated between Argentina, Bolivia and Brazil. The area is estimated at 157,048 sq. miles (406,752 sq. km). Paraguay is a country of grassy plains and forested hills. In the angle formed by the Paraná-Paraguay confluence are extensive marshes, one of which, known as Neembucú (or endless) is drained by Lake Ypoa, a large lagoon south-east of the capital. The Chaco, lying between the rivers Paraguay and Pilcomayo and bounded on the north by Bolivia, is a flat plain, rising uniformly towards its western boundary to a height of 1,140 feet; it suffers much from floods and still more from drought, but the building of dams and reservoirs has converted part of it into good pasture for cattle raising.

POPULATION – The population (1991 UN estimate) is 4,397,000. Spanish is the official language of the country but outside the larger towns Guarani, the language of the largest single group of original Indian inhabitants, is widely spoken, and is also an official language.

CAPITAL – Asunción, population (1985 census) 729,307; other centres are Ciudad del Este (98,491); Encarnación (31,445); Concepción (25,607); P. Juan Caballero (41,475).

CURRENCY – Guaraní (Gs) of 100 céntimos.

FLAG – Three horizontal bands, red, white, blue with the National seal on the obverse white band and the Treasury seal on the reverse white band.

NATIONAL ANTHEM – Paraguayos, Republica O Muerte (Paraguayans, republic or death).

NATIONAL DAY – 15 May.

## GOVERNMENT

In 1535 Paraguay was settled as a Spanish possession. In 1811 it declared its independence from Spain.

The constitution provides for a two-chamber legislature consisting of a 45-member Senate and an 80-member Chamber of Deputies. Deputies are elected on a regional basis, the number of seats allocated to each regional department being directly proportional to the department's population. Voting is compulsory for all citizens over 18. The President is elected for a single five-year term and may not be re-elected. The Vice-President may only put himself forward for presidential elections if he resigns his post six months before the election. The President appoints the Cabinet, which exercises all the functions of government.

Gen. Alfredo Stroessner, dictator from 1954, was over-thrown by Gen. Andrés Rodriguez in February 1989. Gen. Rodriguez was elected President in May 1989. In May 1991, the first free municipal elections were held, and elections to the parliament were held in December 1991. Amendments to the constitution came into effect in June 1992. Presidential and legislative elections were held on 9 May 1993. The presidential election was won by Juan Carlos Wasmosy of the ruling Colorado Party (ANR-PC), which also won 20 of the 45 Senate seats and 40 of the 80 Chamber of Deputies seats. The opposition Authentic Radical Liberal Party (PLRA) and National Encounter (EN) won, respectively, 17 and eight Senate, and 32 and eight Chamber seats, depriving the Colorado Party of a majority in the legislature. After his inauguration, President Wasmosy moved to subjugate the military to civilian control.

HEAD OF STATE

*President*, Juan Carlos Wasmosy, *elected* 9 May 1993, *sworn in* 15 August 1993

CABINET *as at August 1994*

*Foreign Affairs*, Luis Maria Ramirez Boetther
*Interior*, Carlos Podesta
*Finance*, Crispiniano Sandoval
*Education*, Nicanor Duarte Frutos
*Agriculture and Livestock*, Arseuio Vascoucellos
*Public Works and Communications*, Carlos Facetti
*National Defence*, Hugo Estigarribia Elizeche
*Public Health and Social Welfare*, Candido Nunez Leon
*Justice and Labour*, Juan Manuel Morales
*Industry and Commerce*, Ubaldo Scavone

EMBASSY OF PARAGUAY

Braemar Lodge, Cornwall Gardens, London SW7 4AQ
Tel 0171-937 1253

*Ambassador Extraordinary and Plenipotentiary*, His Excellency Antonio Espinoza, apptd 1990

BRITISH EMBASSY

Calle Presidente Franco 706 (PO Box 404), Asunción
Tel: Asunción 444472

*Ambassador Extraordinary and Plenipotentiary and Consul-General*, His Excellency Michael A. C. Dibben, apptd 1991

ECONOMY

President Rodriguez introduced an economic liberalization programme which has been continued by the Wasmosy government. About three-quarters of the population are engaged in agriculture and cattle raising. Cassava, sugar cane, soya, corn, cotton and wheat are the main agricultural products. The forests contain many varieties of timber which find a good market abroad.

Paraguay's rivers give it considerable hydroelectric capacity. There is a hydroelectric power station at Acaray which exports surplus power to Argentina and Brazil. Joint hydroelectric projects have been undertaken with Brazil, on a hydroelectric dam at Itaipú, and with Argentina, at Yacyretá.

TRADE

The chief imports are machinery; fuels and lubricants; transport and accessories; and drinks and tobacco. The chief exports are soya bean; cotton fibres; meat; and coffee.

| *Trade with UK* | 1992 | 1993 |
| --- | --- | --- |
| Imports from UK | £34,149,000 | £35,797,000 |
| Exports to UK | 2,514,000 | 3,113,000 |

COMMUNICATIONS

There are direct shipping services to Asunción from Europe and the USA, and river steamer services for internal transport and to Argentina. Eight airlines operate services from Asunción. There are 27,741 km (1990) of asphalted roads in Paraguay, connecting Asunción with São Paulo (26 hours) via the Bridge of Friendship and Foz de Yguazú, and with Buenos Aires (24 hours) via Puerto Pilcomayo, and about 4,050 miles of earth roads in fairly good condition, but liable to be closed or to become impassable in wet weather. A 1,000 km road links Asunción with the Bolivian border. Rail services, with train ferries, provide internal and international links. Four daily and five weekly newspapers are published in Asunción.

EDUCATION

Education is free and compulsory. In 1990 there were 4,641 government primary schools with 694,972 pupils and 27,477 teachers. There were 809 secondary schools with 155,339 pupils and 8,112 teachers. The National University in Asunción had 20,343 students in 1984. The Catholic University had 10,971 students.

# PERU
*República del Peru*

Peru is a maritime republic of South America, situated between 0° 00′ 48″ and 18° 21′ 00″ S. latitude and between 68° 39′ 27″ and 81° 20′ 13″ W. longitude. The area is 496,225 sq. miles (1,285,216 sq. km). The country is traversed throughout its length by the Andes, running parallel to the Pacific coast. There are three main regions, the Costa, west of the Andes, the Sierra or mountain ranges of the Andes, which include the Punas or mountainous wastes below the region of perpetual snow, and the Montaña or Selva, which is the vast area of jungle stretching from the eastern foothills of the Andes to the eastern frontiers of Peru. The coastal area, lying upon and near the Pacific, is not tropical though close to the Equator, being cooled by the Humboldt Current.

POPULATION – The population (1992 estimate) is 22,465,000. Spanish, the language of the original Spanish stock from which the governing and professional classes are mainly recruited, was formerly the only official language of the country. However, in 1979 Quechua and Aymará also became official languages. Quechua and Aymará are spoken by more than half the population of the country.

CAPITAL – Metropolitan Lima (including ΨCallao), population census (1993) 6,483,901. Other major cities are: Arequipa (820,471) and Trujillo (508,715).

CURRENCY – Nuevo Sol 100 cents.

FLAG – Three vertical stripes of red, white, red.

NATIONAL ANTHEM – Somos Libres, Seámoslo Siempre (We are free, let us remain so forever).

NATIONAL DAY – 28 July (Anniversary of Independence).

## GOVERNMENT

Peru was conquered in the early 16th century by Francisco Pizarro (1478–1541). He subjugated the Incas (the ruling caste of the Quechua Indians), who had started their rise to power some 500 years earlier, and for nearly three centuries Peru remained under Spanish rule. A revolutionary war of 1821–4 established its independence, declared on 28 July 1821. A military junta ruled Peru from October 1968 until July 1980 when civilian government was restored. In April 1992 President Fujimori, faced with increasing terrorist violence, with the support of the armed forces suspended the constitution, dissolved Congress and began to govern with absolute powers. A programme of market-orientated economic reform, new measures in the anti-terrorist war, and a streamlining of the executive, legislative and judicial institutions was undertaken. On 22 November 1992 a legislative general election was held to an 80-seat Democratic Constituent Congress (CCD) which was installed as an interim legislature and constituent assembly to write a new constitution. Parties supporting Fujimori's suspension of the constitution gained a majority in the CCD. In January 1993 the 1979 constitution was re-established and the CCD declared Fujimori constitutional head of state. The CCD produced a new constitution which was passed in a national referendum held on 30 October 1993. The constitution, promulgated in December 1993, provides for: the President to be able to serve two terms rather than one, as previously;

the introduction of the death penalty for terrorists; the formation of a new 120-member unicameral Congress.

## INSURGENCY

Since the late 1970s the government has faced violence from drug organizations and insurgencies from two leftist guerrilla movements, the Maoist Sendero Luminoso (Shining Path) and the Movimiento Revolucionario Tapac Amaru (MRTA). Some areas of the country remain under states of emergency, but the capture of the leaders of both groups in 1992 and President Fujimori's anti-terrorist clampdown in 1992–4 has drastically reduced the size and resources of both groups and reduced violence considerably. The Shining Path continues to launch attacks on security forces and the country's infrastructure and has engaged in mass intimidation and execution campaigns in rural areas, with fighting so far having left 25,000 dead.

## HEAD OF STATE

*President of the Republic*, Alberto Fujimori, *assumed office 28 July 1990*

*CABINET as at August 1994*

*Prime Minister and Minister of Foreign Affairs*, Efraín Goldenberg Schreiber
*Economy and Finance*, Jorge Camet Dickman
*Interior*, Gen. Juan Briones Dávilla
*Justice*, Dr Fernando Vega Santa Gadea
*Defence*, Gen. Victor Malca Villanueva
*Education*, Jorge Trelles Montero
*Health*, Jaime Oyanguren
*Labour and Social Promotion*, Augusto Antoniolli Vásquez
*Agriculture*, Absalon Vásquez Villanueva
*Energy and Mines*, Daniel Hokama Tokahiki
*Transport and Communications, Housing and Construction*, Dante Córdova Blanco
*Fisheries*, Jaime Augustin Sobero Taira
*Industry, Commerce, Tourism and Integration*, Liliana Canale Novella
*Minister of the Presidency*, Raúl Vittor Alfaro

EMBASSY OF PERU
52 Sloane Street, London SW1X 9SP
Tel 0171–235 1917/2545/3802

*Ambassador Extraordinary and Plenipotentiary*, His Excellency Arturo Garcia, apptd 1992

BRITISH EMBASSY
Natalio Sánchez 125, Piso 12, Plaza Washington (PO Box 854), Lima 100.
Tel: Lima 334735

*Ambassador Extraordinary and Plenipotentiary*, His Excellency Keith Haskell, CMG, CVO, apptd 1990
*First Secretary (Commercial)*, R. G. Church (*Deputy Head of Mission and Consul*)

There is a British Consular Office at *Lima* and Honorary Consulates in *Arequipa, Cusco, Iquitos, Piura* and *Trujillo*.

BRITISH COUNCIL REPRESENTATIVE, J. Harvey, PO Box No. 14-0114, Calle Alberto Lynch 110, San Isidro, Lima 27

## ECONOMY

Since 1990 President Fujimori's government has launched a radical free-market restructuring programme which has rebuilt the country's foreign exchange reserves from virtually zero, reduced inflation from 7,600 per cent per year in 1990 to 30 per cent in 1994, cut subsidies and import tariffs, freed interest rates, privatized most state firms, and seen the economy grow by 6 per cent of GDP in 1993. Foreign investment has been encouraged and in June 1993 US$900 million was gained in credits from foreign donors. In March 1993 Peru cleared its arrears with the World Bank and IMF of US$1,700 million, enabling it to gain access to a new IMF loan of US$1,395 million over three years. The total foreign debt in 1993 stood at US$21,000 million.

The chief products of the coastal belt are cotton, sugar and petroleum. There are large tracts of land suitable for cultivation and stock-raising (cattle, sheep, llamas, alpacas and vicuñas) on the eastern slopes of the Andes, and in the mountain valleys maize, potatoes and wheat are grown. The jungle area is a source of timber and petroleum. Other major crops are fruit, vegetables, rice, barley, grapes and coffee. The mountains contain rich mineral deposits and mineral exports include lead, zinc, copper, iron ore and silver. Peru is normally the world's largest exporter of fishmeal.

TRADE

The principal imports are machinery and chemicals and pharmaceutical products. The chief exports are minerals and metals, fishmeal, sugar, cotton and coffee.

| Trade with UK | 1992 | 1993 |
|---|---|---|
| Imports from UK | £30,775,000 | £33,031,000 |
| Exports to UK | 91,804,000 | 126,482,000 |

COMMUNICATIONS

In recent years the coastal and sierra zones have been opened up by means of roads and air routes. There is air communication, as well as communication by protracted land routes, with the tropical and eastern zones which lie east of the Andes towards the borders of Brazil. The Andean Highway forms a link between the Pacific, the Amazon and the Atlantic. The Pan-American Highway runs along the Peruvian coast connecting it with Ecuador and Chile. The Inter-Ocean Corridor linking the port of Matarani and Buenos Aires will be opened soon.

The railway is administered by the government. There is also steam navigation on the Ucayali and Huallaga, and in the south on Lake Titicaca. Air services are maintained throughout Peru, and many international services call at Lima.

DEFENCE

The armed forces have a total active strength of 115,000 (65,500 conscripts), with selective conscription of some two years duration. The Army has a strength of 75,000 (50,000 conscripts) and is heavily engaged in combating the Shining Path and MRTA guerrilla movements. It has 300 main battle tanks, 110 light tanks, 425 reconnaissance and armoured personnel carriers and 248 artillery pieces. The Navy has some 25,000 personnel (13,500 conscripts), divided into the Pacific, Lake Titicaca and Amazon River force areas. It has a strength of nine submarines, two cruisers, ten destroyers and frigates, seven patrol and coastal vessels, seven combat aircraft and 14 armed helicopters. The Air Force has a strength of 15,000 personnel (2,000 conscripts), with 96 combat aircraft and 15 armed helicopters. In addition there is the paramilitary National Police, 60,000 strong, who also play a major role in counter-insurgency operations.

EDUCATION

Education is compulsory and free between five and 16.

# THE PHILIPPINES
*República ng Pilipinas*

The Philippines are situated between 21° 20′–4° 30′ N. latitude and 116° 55′–126° 36′ E. longitude, and are about 500 miles from the south-east coast of the continent of Asia. The total land area of the country is 115,831 sq. miles (300,000 sq. km). There are eleven larger islands and 7,079 other islands. The principal islands are:

|  | sq. miles |  | sq. miles |
|---|---|---|---|
| Luzon | 40,422 | Mindoro | 3,759 |
| Mindanao | 36,538 | Leyte | 2,786 |
| Samar | 5,050 | Cebu | 1,703 |
| Negros | 4,906 | Bohol | 1,492 |
| Palawan | 4,550 | Masbate | 1,262 |
| Panay | 4,446 |  |  |

Other groups are the Sulu islands (capital, Jolo), Babuyanes and Batanes; the Calamian islands; and Kalayaan Islands.

POPULATION – The population (UN estimate 1991) is 62,868,000. The inhabitants are basically of Malay stock, with a considerable admixture of Spanish and Chinese blood in many localities. The Chinese minority is estimated at 500,000, with smaller numbers of Spanish, American and Indian. About 90 per cent are Christian, predominantly Roman Catholics. Most of the remainder are Muslims, in the south, and indigenous animists, mainly in Luzon and parts of Mindanao.

The official languages are Filipino and English. Filipino is based on Tagalog, one of the Malay–Polynesian languages and is spoken by 29.66 per cent of the total number of households (and understood by nearly 90 per cent of the population), but local languages and dialects are strong and Cebuano is spoken by 24.2 per cent of total households. English, which is the language of government and of instruction in secondary and university education, is spoken by at least 44 per cent of the population. Spanish, which ceased to be an official language in 1973, is now spoken by a very small minority. Eighty-nine per cent of the population are literate.

CAPITAL – Ψ Manila, on the island of Luzon, estimated population (1990) City area 1,876,195; Manila with suburbs (incl. Quezon City, Pasay City, Caloocan City, Makati, Parañaque, San Juan Mandaluyong, Malabon, Valenzuela, Peteros, Las Piñas, Taguig, Muntinlupa and Navotas) 6,720,050. The next largest cities are (1989 estimate) Ψ Cebu (613,184), Ψ Davao (819,525), Ψ Iloilo (287,711), Ψ Zamboanga (433,328), and Bacolod (328,648).

CURRENCY – Philippine peso (P) of 100 centavos.

FLAG – Equal horizontal bands of blue (above) and red; gold sun with three stars on a white triangle next staff.

NATIONAL ANTHEM – Bayang Magiliw.

NATIONAL DAY – 12 June (Independence Day 1898).

GOVERNMENT

The Portuguese navigator Magellan came to the Philippines in 1521 and was killed by the natives of Mactan, a small island near Cebu. In 1565 Spain undertook the conquest of the country, which was named Filipinas after Philip II of Spain, then heir apparent. In 1762 Manila was occupied by a British force but in 1764 it was restored to Spain. In 1896 the Filipinos revolted against Spanish rule and declared their independence on 12 June 1898. In the Spanish–American War of 1898, Manila was captured by American troops with the help of Filipinos and the islands were ceded to the USA by the Treaty of Paris 1898. Despite a rebellion against US rule between 1899 and 1902, the Americans remained in control of the country until 1946. The Republic of the Philippines came into existence on 4 July 1946.

Ferdinand Marcos was President from 1965 to 1986. Although he gained a majority of votes in the official count of a presidential election in February 1986, the election was marred by widespread electoral abuse and his rival, Mrs Corazon Aquino, launched a campaign of non-violent civil disturbance which gained wide support. On 25 February Marcos, his family and aides left for Hawaii. Mrs Aquino took over as President and survived seven coup attempts.

A new constitution was approved by referendum in February 1987 and came into force in July. Legislative authority is vested in a bicameral elected Congress comprising a House of Representatives of up to 250 members and a 24-member Senate. Fidel Ramos was elected President on 11 May 1992 and has overcome the problems that plagued President Aquino, namely military coup attempts and legislative obstructiveness.

## INSURGENCY

There is unrest in some of the islands due to insurgency. Muslim insurgents, the Moro National Liberation Front (MNLF) have since 1968, operated in central and western Mindanao and the Sulu archipelago. The Communist New People's Army (NPA), has maintained a presence in eastern Mindanao, Negros, Samar, Bicol, the mountains of northern Luzon, and Bataan. The effectiveness of the MNLF has been declining for several years. In November 1993 the government and the MNLF signed an interim ceasefire agreement including a three-year cessation of hostilities while negotiations continue. The strength and activity of the NPA has also been declining and in December 1993 a government-NPA ceasefire was agreed. The NPA maintains 12,000 armed personnel and the MNLF 3,300 but the most active insurgents are now 4,500 who broke away from the MNLF and 1,000 in the Islamic fundamentalist Abu Sayyaf group.

## HEAD OF STATE

*President,* Fidel V. Ramos, *assumed office* 30 June 1992
*Vice-President,* Joseph Estrada

## CABINET SECRETARIES *as at August 1994*

*Foreign Affairs,* Roberto Romulo
*Finance,* Roberto de Ocampo
*Justice,* Franklin Drilon
*Agriculture,* Roberto Sebastian
*Public Works and Highways,* Gregorio Vigilar
*Education, Culture and Sport,* Ricardo Gloria
*Labour and Employment,* Nieves Confesor
*National Defence,* Renato de Villa
*Health,* Dr Juan Flavier
*Trade and Industry,* Rizalino Navarro
*Social Welfare and Development,* Corazon de Leon
*Agrarian Reform,* Ernesto Garilao
*Interior and Local Government,* Rafael Alunan
*Tourism,* Vicente Carlos
*Environment and Natural Resources,* Angel Alcala
*Budget and Management,* Salvador Enriquez
*Transport and Communications,* Jesus Garcia
*Science and Technology,* William Padolina
*Director-General, National Economic and Development Authority,* Cielito Habito
*Energy,* Delfin Lazaro

## EMBASSY OF THE PHILIPPINES

9A Palace Green, London W8 4QE
Tel 0171-937 1600/9

*Ambassador Extraordinary and Plenipotentiary,* His Excellency Jesus P. Tambunting, apptd 1993
*Minister-Counsellor,* George B. Reyes
*Defence Attaché,* Col. C. P. Garcia
*First Secretary and Consul,* E. C. Castro
*Commercial Counsellor,* P. Sales

## BRITISH EMBASSY

Locsin Building, 6752 Ayala Avenue, Corner Makati Avenue, 1226 Makati, Metro Manila (PO Box 2927 MCPO) Tel: Manila 816-7116

*Ambassador Extraordinary and Plenipotentiary,* His Excellency Alan Montgomery, CMG, apptd 1992
*Deputy Ambassador,* D. B. Merry
*Defence Attaché,* Col. J. L. Seddon-Brown (*resides at Kuala Lumpur*)
*First Secretary,* C. B. Glynn (*Commercial*)

BRITISH COUNCIL REPRESENTATIVE, N. Bisset, 7, 3rd Street, New Manila, PO Box AC 168, Cubao, Quezon City, Metro Manila.

## DEFENCE

The Philippine armed forces number 106,500 active personnel with a further 131,000 reserves, and have been engaged for some years in combating insurgent forces. The Army has an active strength of 68,000 personnel, with 41 light tanks, 370 armoured personnel carriers and armoured infantry fighting vehicles and 240 artillery pieces. The Navy has 23,000 personnel, including 8,500 marines, and deploys one frigate, 42 patrol and coastal vessels, eight combat aircraft and ten marine battalions. The Air Force has some 15,500 personnel, with 53 combat aircraft and 106 armed helicopters. The paramilitary Philippine National Police number 45,000 personnel and there is a part-time militia of 62,000 personnel.

## EDUCATION

Secondary and higher education is extensive and there are 37 private universities recognized by the government, including the Dominican University of Santo Tomas (founded in 1611). There are also 296 state-supported colleges and universities, including the University of the Philippines, founded 1908.

## COMMUNICATIONS

The highway system covered 161,709 kilometres in 1985. The Philippine National Railway used to operate 1,282 km of track, but a greater part of this is now being rebuilt. There are 94 ports of entry in the Philippines and 164,404 vessels of various types totalling 50,467,000 tons are engaged in inter-island traffic. There are 82 national airports and 137 privately operated airports. Philippine Air Lines have regular flights throughout the Far East, to the USA and Europe, in addition to inter-island services.

## ECONOMY

The Philippines has been bypassed by the economic growth of most of the rest of south-east Asia since the 1960s, mainly because of the incompetence and corruption of Marcos' rule. President Ramos has restored economic growth, which was 2 per cent in 1993, and concentrated on closing the electricity generation gap.

The Philippines is a predominantly agricultural country, the chief products being rice, coconuts, maize, coffee, sugarcane, abaca (manila hemp), fruits, tobacco and lumber. There is, however, an increasing number of manufacturing industries and it is the policy of the government to diversify its economy. There are also deposits of nickel, iron, copper, gold and silver.

TRADE

Principal exports are sugar, coconut oil, copper concentrate, lumber and copra, together with increasingly important manufactured exports such as electronics products and clothing. The major trading partners are the USA, Japan, Taiwan and Hong Kong.

|  | 1992 |  |
|---|---|---|
| Total imports | US$10,580m | |
| Total exports | 7,150m | |

| Trade with UK | 1992 | 1993 |
|---|---|---|
| Imports from UK | £204,962,000 | £306,146,000 |
| Exports to UK | 240,732,000 | 276,820,000 |

# POLAND
*Rzeczpospolita Polska*

Poland adjoins Germany in the west, the boundary being formed by the rivers Oder and Neisse, the Czech Republic and Slovakia in the south, and Belarus, Ukraine, Lithuania and the Kaliningrad region of Russia in the east. To the north is the Baltic Sea. The country has an area of 120,725 sq. miles (312,677 sq. km), and a population (official estimate 1991) of 38,300,000. Roman Catholicism is the religion of 95 per cent of the inhabitants.

CAPITAL – Warsaw, on the Vistula, population (1989) 1,655,063. Other large towns are Lódź (851,690); Kraków (748,356); Wroclaw (642,234); Poznan (588,715); Gdansk (464,649); Szczecin (412,000); Katowice (367,041); Bydgoszcz (380,385).
CURRENCY – Zloty of 100 groszy.
FLAG – Equal horizontal stripes of white (above) and red.
NATIONAL ANTHEM – Jeszcze Polska Nie Zginela (Poland has not yet been destroyed).
NATIONAL DAY – 3 May.

## GOVERNMENT

The Polish Commonwealth ceased to exist in 1795 after three successive partitions in 1772, 1793 and 1795, in which Prussia, Russia and Austria shared. The Republic of Poland, reconstituted within the limits of the old Polish Commonwealth, was proclaimed at Warsaw in November 1918, and its independence guaranteed by the signatories of the Treaty of Versailles.

German forces invaded Poland on 1 September 1939; on 17 September, Russian forces invaded eastern Poland, and on 21 September 1939 Poland was declared by Germany and Russia to have ceased to exist. At the end of the war a coalition government was formed in which the Polish Workers' Party played a large part. In December 1948, the Polish Workers' Party and the Polish Socialist Party fused in the new Polish United Workers' Party (PUWP). A new constitution modelled on the Soviet constitution was adopted in July 1952, and was modified in February 1976.

Strikes in July and August 1980 over steep rises in food prices forced the government to agree to allow independent trade unions, the right to strike, the easing of censorship and other political and economic demands. The independent trade union movement Solidarity, led by Lech Walesa, became a powerful force but many of its leaders, including Walesa, were detained and union activity suspended when martial law was declared in December 1981. Initially there was some passive resistance to martial law, which was suspended in December 1982 and finally lifted in July 1983.

A wave of strikes resulted in talks between Walesa and the PUWP early in 1989. By April plans for political and economic reforms had been drawn up. Multiparty parliamentary elections were held in the summer of 1989, following which the PUWP ceased to be the ruling party. The post-Communist governments have rapidly introduced a market economy but political divisions, economic difficulties and a fragmented Parliament of over 20 parties led to a succession of short-lived governments in the early 1990s. Elections were held on 19 September 1993 and resulted in six parties gaining representation in the 460-seat Sejm: Democratic Left Alliance (SLD) 171 seats; Polish Peasant Party (PSL) 132 seats; Freedom Union (UW) 74 seats; Labour Union (UP) 41 seats; Confederation for an Independent Poland (KPN) 22 seats; Reform Bloc 16 seats; German minority parties 4 seats. In the 100-member Senate the results were: SLD 37; PSL 36; Solidarity 10; UW 4; others 13. The former Communist SLD returned to power after four years by forming a coalition government with the PSL and UP parties, as a result of the electorate's backlash against the hardships caused by economic reform. The government has promised to increase subsidies to industry, increase welfare spending and reduce unemployment.

Disagreement over a post-Communist constitution ended in November 1992 when President Walesa signed a 'small constitution' approved by the parliament which defines the division of powers between the President and government. The President has the right to be consulted over the appointment of the foreign, defence and finance ministers. There is a 5 per cent threshold for representation for parties in the Sejm and 8 per cent for alliances (except for minority groups). The Senate is elected on a provincial basis. Poland presented its application for membership to the European Union on 8 April 1994.

HEAD OF STATE
*President*, Lech Walesa, *elected* 9 December 1990 *for a five-year term*

COUNCIL OF MINISTERS *as at August 1994*
*Prime Minister*, Waldemar Pawlak (PSL)
*Deputy Prime Minister (Economy) and Finance*, Prof. Grzegorz Kolodko (Ind)
*Deputy Prime Minister (Social Policy) and Justice*, Wlodzimierz Cimoszewícz (SLD)
*Deputy Prime Minister (State Administration) and Education*, Aleksander Luczak (PSL)
*Head of the Council of Minister's Office*, Michal Strak (PSL)
*Foreign Affairs*, Andrzej Olechowski (Ind)
*Internal Affairs*, Andrzej Milczanowski (Ind)
*National Defence*, Adm. Piotr Kolodziejczyk (Ind)
*Head of the Central Planning Office*, Miroslaw Pietrewicz (PSL)
*Foreign Economic Relations*, Leslaw Podkanski (PSL)
*Agriculture*, Andrzej Smietanko (PSL)
*Transport and Maritime Economy*, Boguslaw Liberadzki (Ind)
*Environment Protection, Natural Resources and Forestry*, Stanislaw Zelichowski (PSL)
*Labour and Social Policy*, Leszek Miller (SLD)
*Culture*, Kazimierz Dejmak (PSL)
*Health*, Prof. Jacek Zochowski (SLD)
*Industry and Trade*, Marek Pol (UP)
*Regional Planning and Construction*, Barbara Blida (SLD)
*Communication*, Andrzej Zielinski (Ind)
*Privatization*, Wieslaw Kaczmarek (SLD)

*Head of Scientific Research Committee,* Witold Karczewski (Ind)

PSL Polish Peasant Party; SLD Democratic Left Alliance; UP Labour Union; Ind Independent

EMBASSY OF THE REPUBLIC OF POLAND
47 Portland Place, London WIN 3AG
Tel 0171–580 4324/9

*Ambassador Extraordinary and Plenipotentiary,* His Excellency Ryszard Stemplowski, apptd 1994
*Defence Attaché,* Cdr. R. Szlegier
*Consul-General,* Dr J. Kochanowski
*Minister,* R. Szuniewicz *(Commercial)*

BRITISH EMBASSY
No. 1 Aleja Róz, 00-556 Warsaw
Tel: Warsaw 6281001

*Ambassador Extraordinary and Plenipotentiary,* His Excellency Michael J. Llewellyn-Smith, CMG, apptd 1991
*Counsellor,* R. A. E. Gordon, OBE *(Deputy Head of Mission)*
*Defence and Air Attaché,* Gp. Capt. H. H. Moses, MBE
*First Secretary (Commercial),* A. J. Gooch

BRITISH COUNCIL REPRESENTATIVE, Ed Pugh, Al. Jerozolimskie 59, 00–697 Warsaw

## DEFENCE

The total active armed forces number 287,500 personnel (162,400 conscripts) with a further 465,500 reserves. Conscripts serve in all services for 18 months. The Army numbers 188,500 (106,700 conscripts) with 2,545 main battle tanks, 590 reconnaissance vehicles, 2,115 armoured infantry fighting vehicles and armoured personnel carriers and 1,775 artillery pieces. The Navy has a strength of 19,200 including 10,400 conscripts, with three submarines, one destroyer, one frigate, 21 patrol and coastal vessels, 36 combat aircraft and 14 armed helicopters. The Air Force is 79,800 strong (45,300 conscripts), with 468 combat aircraft and 30 attack helicopters. The Paramilitary Border Guards and Police Prevention Units number 24,400 personnel (1,400 conscripts). The last Russian troops left in September 1993.

## EDUCATION

Elementary education (ages seven to 15) is compulsory and free. Secondary education is optional and free. There are universities at Kraków, Warsaw, Poznan, Lódź, Wroclaw, Lublin and Toruń and a considerable number of other towns.

## CULTURE

Polish is a western Slavonic tongue, the Latin alphabet being used. Major writers include Henryk Sienkiewicz (1846–1916), Nobel Prizewinner for Literature in 1905; Boleslaw Prus (1847–1912); Stanislaw Reymont (1868–1925), Nobel Prizewinner in 1924; Czeslaw Milosz, Nobel Prizewinner in 1980.

The state monopoly on radio and television broadcasting ended in October 1992.

## ECONOMY

Mines, petroleum resources, water, gas and electricity services, banks, textile factories and large retail stores were nationalized in 1946. Until recently over 99 per cent of Polish industry was stated to be 'socialized', but 68 per cent of agricultural land was privately farmed. Legislation passed in July 1990 provided for 80 per cent of the economy to be transferred from the state to the private sector. In 1991 the IMF and western banks suspended co-operation and lending because the government had exceeded agreed budget deficit

and inflation limits. The IMF-prescribed 'shock therapy' treatment for the economy was resumed in 1992 with reforms to allow bankruptcy and the ending of state subsidies to reduce the budget deficit. After the passing of a budget in March 1993, which kept the deficit to 5.5 per cent of GDP, and a mass privatization bill for 600 state-owned firms, passed by parliament in April, the IMF and the banks provided more credit to enable reforms to continue.

The transition to a market economy has been painful, with unemployment in 1994 reaching 17 per cent. Privatization continues, and GDP and industrial output grew in 1993 by 4 and 7 per cent respectively. The budget deficit fell from 5 per cent of GDP in 1993 to 4.2 per cent in 1994. Agreements were also reached in 1994 to cancel 30 per cent of Poland's US$33,000 million debt to foreign governments and 42.5 per cent of US$8,800 million debt to western banks. Some 60 per cent of the workforce is now employed in the private sector and 50 per cent of Poland's GDP is produced by the private sector.

| *Trade with UK* | 1992 | 1993 |
|---|---|---|
| Imports from UK | £605,586,000 | £717,802,000 |
| Exports to UK | 356,173,000 | 449,320,000 |

# PORTUGAL
*República Portuguesa*

Portugal occupies the western part of the Iberian Peninsula, covering an area of 34,317 sq. miles (88,880 sq. km). It lies between 36° 58′ and 42° 12″ N. latitude and 6° 11′ 48″ and 9° 29′ 45″ W. longitude. It is 362 miles in length from north to south, and averages about 117 miles in breadth from east to west.

POPULATION – The population (census 1991) is 9,862,700 (including the Azores and Madeira). The language is Portuguese, a Romance language with admixtures of Arabic and other idioms.

CAPITAL – ΨLisbon, population estimate (1989) 2,128,000. ΨOporto 1,683,000.

CURRENCY – Escudo (Esc) of 100 centavos.

FLAG – Divided vertically into unequal parts of green and red with the national emblem over all on the line of division.

NATIONAL ANTHEM – A Portuguesa.

NATIONAL DAY – 10 June.

## GOVERNMENT

From the 12th century until 1910 Portugal was a monarchy, but in 1910 an armed rising in Lisbon drove King Manuel II into exile and a republic was set up. A period of great political instability ensued until eventually the military stepped in and abolished political parties in 1926. The constitution of 1933 gave formal expression to the corporative 'Estado Novo' (New State) which was personified by Dr Salazar, Prime Minister 1932–68. Dr Caetano succeeded Salazar as Prime Minister in 1968 but his failure to liberalize the regime or to conclude the wars in the African colonies resulted in his government's overthrow by a military coup on 25 April 1974. There was great political turmoil between April 1974 and July 1976 but with the failure of an attempted coup by the extreme left in November 1975 the situation became more stable.

Under the 1976 constitution, amended in 1982 and 1989, the President, elected for a five-year term by universal adult suffrage, appoints the Prime Minister and, on the latter's recommendation, the members of the Council of Ministers.

Legislative authority is vested in the 230-member Assembly of the Republic, elected by a system of proportional representation every four years. The President retains certain limited powers to dismiss the government, dissolve the Assembly or veto laws.

In the general election held on 6 October 1991, the Social Democratic Party (PSD) won 135 seats; the Socialist Party (PS) 72 seats; the Communist Party (PCP) 17 seats, the Christian Democrats (CDS) 5 seats and the National Solidarity Party 1 seat.

HEAD OF STATE

*President of the Republic*, Dr Mario Soares, *elected* 1986, re-elected 13 January 1991

COUNCIL OF MINISTERS *as at August 1994*

*Prime Minister*, Prof. Anibal Cavaco Silva
*Minister of the Presidency, Defence*, Joaquim Fernando Nogueira
*Justice*, Dr Alvaro Laborinho Lucio
*Parliamentary Affairs*, Luis Marques Mendes
*Finance*, Eduardo Catroga
*Planning and Territorial Administration*, Luis Valente de Oliveira
*Home Affairs*, Manuel Dias Loureiro
*Foreign*, José Durão Barroso
*Agriculture*, António Duarte Silva
*Industry and Energy*, Luis Mira Amaral
*Education*, Manuela Ferreira Leite
*Public Works, Transport and Communications*, Joaquim Ferreira do Amaral
*Health*, Paulo Mendo
*Labour and Social Security*, José Falcão e Cunha
*Commerce and Tourism*, Fernando Faria de Oliveira
*Environment and Natural Resources*, Teresa Gouveia
*Sea*, Eduardo de Azevedo Soares

PORTUGUESE EMBASSY
11 Belgrave Square, London SW1X 8PP
Tel 0171-235 5331

*Ambassador Extraordinary and Plenipotentiary*, His Excellency Antonio Vaz-Pereira, GCVO, apptd 1989
*Minister-Plenipotentiary*, Francisco Seixas-da-Costa, CMG
*Minister-Plenipotentiary and Consul-General*, J. D. Ortigão, CMG
*Defence Attaché*, Col. A. M. A. dos Santos, CBE
*Counsellor*, J. A. Pereira, LVO (*Economic*)

BRITISH EMBASSY
35-37 Rua de S. Domingos à Lapa, 1200 Lisbon
Tel: Lisbon 3961191

*Ambassador Extraordinary and Plenipotentiary*, His Excellency John Wall, CMG, LVO, apptd 1993
*Deputy Ambassador, Counsellor*, A. F. Smith
*Defence Attaché*, Cdr. R. Wykes-Sneyd, AFC
*First Secretaries*, C. Gibson (*Commercial*); D. J. Ferguson (*Consul*)

There are British Consulates in *Oporto, Portimão, Funchal* (Madeira), *Ribeira Grande* (Azores) and *Macao*

BRITISH COUNCIL REPRESENTATIVE, Patrick Jackson, Rua de Sao Marçal 174, 1294 Lisbon. There are also offices at *Cascais, Coimbra* and *Oporto*.
BRITISH PORTUGUESE CHAMBER OF COMMERCE, Rua da Estrela 8, 1200 Lisbon and Rua Sa de Bandeira 784-20E, Frente, 4000 Oporto.

DEFENCE

The armed forces have a total active strength of 50,700 (17,600 conscripts) with reserves of 210,000. Conscripts serve four to 18 months. The present strength of the Army is 27,200 (15,000 conscripts), with 210 main battle tanks, 480 armoured personnel carriers and reconnaissance vehicles, and 175 artillery pieces. The Navy consists of 12,500 personnel (800 conscripts), including 1,850 marines, manning three submarines, 11 frigates and 30 patrol and coastal vessels. The strength of the Air Force is 11,000 (1,800 conscripts), including 1,800 paratroops, with 105 combat aircraft plus helicopters and transport and training aircraft. The paramilitary National Republican Guard, Public Security Police and Border Security Force number a total of 49,800 personnel.

Lisbon is the base of the NATO Iberian Atlantic Command and the USA maintains 1,500 personnel in mainland Portugal and on the Azores.

EDUCATION

Education is free and compulsory for nine years from the age of six. Secondary education is mainly conducted in state lyceums, commercial and industrial schools, but there are also private schools. There are also military, naval, technical, polytechnic and other special schools. There are universities at Coimbra (founded in 1290), Oporto, Lisbon, Braga, Aveiro, Vila Real, Faro, Evora and in the Azores.

COMMUNICATIONS

There are international airports at Lisbon and Oporto, and at Faro in the Algarve. Four morning and one evening daily newspapers are published in Lisbon and four morning newspapers in Oporto, and six main weekly newspapers.

ECONOMY

The chief agricultural products are cork, potatoes, maize, wheat, rice, vegetables, olives, olive oil, figs, citrus fruits, almonds, timber, port wine and table wines. There are extensive forests of pine, cork, eucalyptus and chestnut covering about 20 per cent of the total area of the country. The principal mineral products are pyrites, wolfram, uranium, iron ores, copper and sodium and calcium minerals.

The country is moderately industrialized. The principal manufactures are textiles, clothing and footwear, machinery (including electric machinery and transport equipment), pulp and paper, pharmaceuticals, foodstuffs, chemicals, fertilizers, wood, cork, furniture, cement, glassware and pottery. There are a modern steelworks and two large shipbuilding and repair yards at Lisbon and Setúbal, working mainly for foreign shipowners. There are several hydro-electric power stations and a new thermal power station.

TRADE

The principal imports are cereals, meat, raw and semi-manufactured iron and steel, industrial machinery, chemicals, crude oil, motor vehicles and raw materials for textiles. The principal exports are textiles, footwear, timber, pulp, automotive parts, cork, electrical and other machinery, and chemicals.

|  | 1991 | 1992 |
|---|---|---|
| Total imports | Esc3,811,076,000m | Esc4,087,577,000m |
| Total exports | 2,354,083,000m | 2,475,202,000m |

| *Trade with UK* | 1992 | 1993 |
|---|---|---|
| Imports from UK | £1,164,098,000 | £1,325,193,000 |
| Exports to UK | 1,170,815,000 | 1,189,352,000 |

## AUTONOMOUS REGIONS

Madeira and The Azores are two administratively autonomous regions of Portugal, having locally elected assemblies and governments.

### MADEIRA

Madeira is a group of islands in the Atlantic Ocean about 520 miles south-west of Lisbon, and consists of Madeira, Porto, Santo and three uninhabited islands (Desertas). The total area is 314 sq. miles (813 sq. km), with a population of 271,400 (1989). ΨFunchal in Madeira, the largest island (270 sq. miles), is the capital (population 44,111); Machico (10,905).

### THE AZORES

The Azores are a group of nine islands (Flores, Corvo, Terceira, São Jorge, Pico, Faial, Graciosa, São Miguel and Santa Maria) in the Atlantic Ocean, with a total area of 922 sq. miles (2,387 sq. km), and a population of 255,100 (1989). ΨPonta Delgada, on São Miguel, is the capital of the group (population 137,700). Other ports are ΨAngra, in Terceira (55,900) and ΨHorta (16,300).

## OVERSEAS TERRITORY

### MACAO

Macao, situated at the mouth of the Pearl River, comprises a peninsula and the islands of Coloane and Taipa, having an area of six sq. miles (15.5 sq. km), with a population (UN estimate 1990) of 479,000. Macao became a Portuguese colony in 1557; in a Sino-Portuguese treaty of 1887 China recognized Portugal's sovereignty over Macao. Following the Sino-British Joint Declaration on Hong Kong in 1984, Sino-Portuguese negotiations on the transfer of administration began in 1986 and an agreement on the transfer of the administration of Macao to the Chinese authorities was signed on 13 April 1987. Macao will become a 'special administrative region' (SAR) of China when transferred on 20 December 1999. The final session of the Macao SAR Basic Law Drafting Committee was held in Beijing in January 1993 and approved the Basic Law which will serve as Macao's constitution after 1999.

Macao is subject to Portuguese constitutional law but otherwise enjoys autonomy. The Governor is appointed by the Portuguese President and there is a 23-member legislative assembly, which has a three-year term. The assembly comprises seven members appointed by the Governor; eight directly elected, and eight indirectly elected by business associations.

Macao's major industry is textile manufacturing which accounts for 62 per cent of all exports. Most government revenue, however, comes from gambling, which attracts many Hong Kong and Chinese visitors. Port Macao is served by British, Portuguese and Dutch shipping lines and has regular services to Hong Kong, some 35 miles away.

*Governor*, Rocha Vieira.

| Trade with UK | 1992 | 1993 |
|---|---|---|
| Imports from UK | £8,473,000 | £12,835,000 |
| Exports to UK | 36,306,000 | 37,141,000 |

## QATAR
*Dawlat Qatar*

The state of Qatar covers the peninsula of Qatar from approximately the northern shore of Khor al Odaid to the eastern shore of Khor al Salwa. The area is about 4,247 sq. miles (11,000 sq. km).

POPULATION – The population (UN estimate 1991) is 381,000. Most of the population is concentrated in the urban district of Doha. Only a small minority still pursue the traditional life of the semi-nomadic tribesmen and fisherfolk.

CAPITAL – ΨDoha, population (estimated) 220,000. Other towns include Khor, Dukhan, Wakra and ΨUmm Said.

CURRENCY – Qatar riyal of 100 dirhams.

FLAG – White and maroon, white portion nearer the mast; vertical indented line comprising 17 angles divides the colours.

NATIONAL DAY – 3 September.

## GOVERNMENT

Qatar was one of nine independent emirates in the Gulf in special treaty relations with the UK until 1971, when the special treaty relations were terminated. On 2 April 1970 a provisional constitution for Qatar was proclaimed, providing for the establishment of a Council of Ministers and for the formation of a Consultative Council to assist the Council of Ministers in running the affairs of the state. There are no political parties or legislature.

HEAD OF STATE
*HH Amir of Qatar*, Sheikh Khalifa bin Hamad Al Thani, GCMG, GCB, *assumed power* 22 February 1972
*Heir*, HH Sheikh Hamad bin Khalifa Al Thani, KCMG

COUNCIL OF MINISTERS *as at August 1994*
*Prime Minister*, The Amir
*Minister of Defence and Commander-in-Chief of Armed Forces*, HH Sheikh Hamad bin Khalifa Ali Thani, KCMG
*Interior*, HE Sheikh Abdullah bin Khalifa Al Thani
*Finance, Economy and Trade*, HE Sheikh Mohammed bin Khalifa Al-Thani
*Foreign Affairs*, HE Sheikh Hamad bin Jassem bin Jabr Al-Thani
*Education*, HE Abdulaziz Abdullah Turki
*Justice*, HE Sheikh Ahmed bin Saif Al Thani
*Minister of State for Defence Affairs* HE Sheikh Hamad bin Abdulah Al-Thani
*Endowments and Islamic Affairs*, HE Sheikh Abdullah bin Khalid Al-Thani
*Municipal Affairs and Agriculture*, HE Sheikh Ahmed bin Hamad Al-Thani
*Labour, Social Affairs and Housing*, HE Abdulrahman Saad Al Dirham
*Communications and Transport*, HE Abdulla bin Saleh Al Manna
*Public Health*, HE Sheikh Hamad bin Suhaim Al-Thani
*Information and Culture*, HE Dr Hamad Abdulaziz Al-Kawari
*Amiri Diwan Affairs*, HE Dr Issa Ghanim Al Kawari
*Electricity and Water*, HE Ahmed Mohamed Ali Al-Subaie
*Energy and Industry*, HE Abdulla Bin Hamad Al-Attiyah

EMBASSY OF THE STATE OF QATAR
1 South Audley Street, London W1Y 5DQ
Tel 0171–493 2200

*Ambassador Extraordinary and Plenipotentiary*, His Excellency Ali Al-Jaidha, apptd 1993

BRITISH EMBASSY
PO Box 3, Doha
Tel: Doha 421991

*Ambassador Extraordinary and Plenipotentiary*, His Excellency Patrick F. Wogan, CMG, apptd 1993.

*First Secretary*, F. G. Geere (*Commercial*)

BRITISH COUNCIL REPRESENTATIVE, J. Shorter, Ras
Abu Aboud Road (PO Box 2992), Doha

## ECONOMY

Although Qatar is a desert country, there are gardens and smallholdings near Doha and to the north, and encouragement is being given to the development of agriculture.

The Qatar General Petroleum Corporation is the state-owned company controlling Qatar's interests in oil, gas and petrochemicals. The corporation is responsible for Qatar's oil production onshore and offshore. The production level for Qatar agreed in OPEC is currently 364,000 b.p.d. Explorations continue for further oil. The large reserves of natural gas in the North Field came into production in September 1991. A 50,000 b.p.d. oil refinery was commissioned in 1984 to increase domestic refinery capacity.

Current industries include a steel mill, a fertilizer plant, a cement factory, a petrochemical complex and two natural gas liquids plants. With the exception of the cement works at Umm Bab, all these industries are at Umm Said, about 30 miles south of Doha. Qatar is also expanding its infrastructure, including electrical generation and water distillation, roads, houses, and government buildings, although reduced demand for crude oil in international markets has led to a downturn in the economy and a slower rate of development than hitherto.

| *Trade with UK* | 1992 | 1993 |
|---|---|---|
| Imports from UK | £118,114,000 | £143,021,000 |
| Exports to UK | 10,142,000 | 20,464,000 |

## COMMUNICATIONS

Regular air services provided by Gulf Air and Qatar Airways connect Qatar with the other Gulf states, the Middle East, the Indian sub-continent, Africa and Europe. The Qatar Broadcasting Service transmits on medium, shortwave, and VHF. Regular television transmissions in colour began in 1974 and a second channel opened in 1982.

## ROMANIA
*România*

Romania is a republic of south-eastern Europe, formerly the classical *Dacia* and *Scythia Pontica*. The area is 91,699 sq. miles (237,500 sq. km).

POPULATION – The population (1992 census) is 22,760,449. Romanians number 21,559,910 (88 per cent), there is a Hungarian minority of 1,714,000 (7.9 per cent), a dwindling German minority of 359,000 (1.6 per cent) and 227,000 Gypsies (1.1 per cent). The leading religion is that of the Romanian Orthodox Church; the Roman Catholic and some Protestant denominations are of importance numerically.

Romanian is a Romance language with many archaic forms and with admixtures of Slavonic, Turkish, Magyar and French words. There is a wealth of folk-songs and folklore, transmitted orally through many centuries and collected in the 19th century. The government and Hungarian minority groups reached agreement on increasing the provision of education in Hungarian in July 1993.

CAPITAL – Bucharest, on the Dimbovita, population (1992 census) 2,064,474.

Other large towns are:

| | | | |
|---|---|---|---|
| Braşov | 323,835 | Ψ Galati | 325,788 |
| Constanţa | 350,476 | Craiova | 303,520 |
| Cluj-Napoca | 328,008 | Ploieşti | 252,073 |
| Iasi | 342,994 | Ψ Brăila | 234,706 |
| Timişoara | 334,278 | | |

CURRENCY – Leu (*plural* Lei) of 100 bani.
FLAG – Three vertical bands, blue, yellow, red.
NATIONAL ANTHEM – Desteapta-te, romane.
NATIONAL DAY – 1 December.

## GOVERNMENT

Romania has its origin in the union of the Danubian principalities of Wallachia and Moldavia under the Treaty of Paris 1856. Although under nominal Turkish suzerainty, the principalities achieved effective unification and independence in 1859 when Alexander Cuza had himself proclaimed ruler of both principalities. The new country adopted the name Romania in 1862. Cuza was deported and replaced by Prince Karl von Hohenzollern in 1864. By the Treaty of Berlin 1878 the principality was recognized as an independent state, and part of the Dobrudja (which had been occupied by the Romanians) was incorporated; on 27 March 1881 it was recognized as a kingdom. The First World War and the break-up of Austria-Hungary added Bessarabia, the Bukovina, the Banat and Crisana-Maramures, these additions of territory being confirmed by treaty in 1919. Transylvania was acquired from Hungary under the Treaty of Trianon 1920. In June 1940, in compliance with an ultimatum from USSR, Bessarabia and Northern Bukovina were ceded to the Soviet Union, and in August 1940 Romania ceded to Bulgaria the portion of southern Dobrudja taken from Bulgaria in 1913.

In 1947 King Michael abdicated and Romania became 'The Romanian People's Republic' in December 1947. The leading political force from the Second World War until 1989 was the Romanian Communist Party. A revolution in December 1989 led to the overthrow of Nicolae Ceauşescu, President since 1967. A provisional government was formed which abolished the leading role of the Communist Party and held free elections in May 1990. A new constitution was introduced in 1991 and formally makes Romania a multi party democracy and endorses human rights and a market economy. There is a Senate of 143 members and a 341-member Assembly of Deputies (of which 13 seats are reserved for ethnic minorities other than Hungarians).

New presidential and parliamentary elections took place in September and October 1992. President Ilieseu was re-elected and his Democratic National Salvation Front (DNSF), renamed the Social Democracy Party of Romania (PSDR) in July 1993, gained the largest number of seats in both houses of parliament and formed a minority government with the support of nationalist parties and the ex-Communists. Throughout 1992-4 the government remained antagonistic to economic reform because it included many members of the Ceauşescu regime. The worsening economic situation caused the PSDR to search for political support and in March 1994 it formed a majority coalition government with the nationalist Party of Romanian National Unity (PRNU), the Greater Romanian Party (GRP) and the ex-Communist Socialist Labour Party (SLP).

HEAD OF STATE
*President of the Republic*, Ion Iliescu, *elected* May 1990, *re-elected* 11 October 1992

GOVERNMENT *as at August 1994*

*Prime Minister*, Nicolae Vacaroiu
*Minister of State, Foreign Affairs*, Teodor Melescanu

*Minister of State, Finance,* Florin Georgescu
*Minister of State, Labour and Social Security,* Dan Popescu
*Minister of State, Economic Reform and Strategy,* Mircea Cosea
*Defence,* Gheorghe Tinca
*Industry,* Dumitru Popescu.
*Interior,* Ioan Taracila
*Justice,* Iosif Chiuzbaian
*Communications,* Andrei Chirica
*Parliamentary Relations,* Valer Dorneanu
*Public Works,* Marin Cristea
*Research and Technology,* Doru Palade
*Education,* Liviu Maior
*Culture,* Marie Sorescu
*Agriculture and Food Industry,* Ioan Oancea
*Environment, Forestry and Water,* Aurel Ilie
*Health,* Iulian Mincu
*Tourism,* Matei Dan
*Trade,* Christian Ionescu
*Transport,* Aurel Novac
*Youth and Sports,* Alexandru Mironev

EMBASSY OF ROMANIA
Arundel House, 4 Palace Green, London W8 4QD
Tel 0171-937 9666
*Ambassador Extraordinary and Plenipotentiary,* His Excellency Sergiu Celac, apptd 1990
*Defence Attaché,* Lt.-Col. Vasile Huica
*Counsellor,* M. Diaconu (*Economic*)
*Third Secretary,* A. Gheorghe (*Consular*)

BRITISH EMBASSY
24 Strada Jules Michelet, 70154 Bucharest
Tel: Bucharest 3120 303/4/5/6

*Ambassador Extraordinary and Plenipotentiary,* His Excellency Andrew Bache, CMG, apptd 1992
*Counsellor, Deputy Head of Mission,* C. J. Ingham
*Defence, Naval and Military Attaché,* Lt.-Col. P. G. Davies
*First Secretary (Commercial),* W. J. Preston

BRITISH COUNCIL REPRESENTATIVE – C. C. Henning, Calea Dorobantilor 14, Bucharest

DEFENCE

Romania has a total active armed forces strength of 203,100 personnel (125,000 conscripts) with a further 427,000 reserves. Conscripts serve 12 months (Army and Air Force) and 18 months (Navy). The Army has a strength of 161,000 (105,000 conscripts) with 2,870 main battle tanks, 412 assault guns, 2,930 armoured infantry fighting vehicles and armoured personnel carriers and 2,040 artillery pieces. The Navy has a strength of 19,000 personnel (10,000 conscripts) including 1,000 coastal defence and a marine division of 5,000. It deploys one submarine, one destroyer, five frigates and 88 patrol and coastal vessels. The Air Force has 23,100 personnel (10,000 conscripts) with 469 combat aircraft and 220 armed helicopters. Paramilitary Border Guards, Construction Troops and Gendarmerie number 43,000 personnel (11,700 conscripts).

ECONOMY

Wallachia, Moldavia and Transylvania are among the most fertile areas in Europe, and agriculture and sheep and cattle raising are the principal industries of Romania. The principal cereal crops are vegetables, flax and hemp. Vines and fruits are also grown. The forests of the mountainous regions are extensive, and the timber industry is important. Collectivization of agriculture was achieved in the spring of 1962. Since December 1989 agricultural workers have sold their produce on the open market and since 1991 private ownership of plots up to 10 hectares in size has been permitted. Allocation of land and distribution of ownership certificates is still taking place, though in some areas it is virtually complete.

There are plentiful supplies of natural gas, together with various mineral deposits including coal, iron ore, bauxite, lead, zinc, copper and uranium in quantities which allow a substantial part of the requirements of industry to be met from local resources. Production of crude oil was 6,600,000 tonnes in 1992.

The economy faced increasing problems from the late 1970s as a result of over-investment in energy-intensive heavy industry and neglect of agriculture. The effects of these policies were aggravated by the international recession and by high interest rates, and Romania was severely in debt by the early 1980s. The Ceauşescu government aimed to completely repay Romania's foreign debt by reducing borrowing, cutting imports and increasing exports. After the 1989 revolution the government pursued only a limited programme of economic reform and liberalization, because of the opposition of the large ex-Communist element of the PSDR. Subsidies for fuel, food and other goods continued, as did those for uneconomic state firms, wages were indexed to prices and privatization delayed. In early 1994, after inflation had reached over 300 per cent annually and unemployment 10 per cent, the government and parliament agreed to an IMF austerity package to gain loans of US$700 million. Most consumer subsidies and price controls have since been lifted, interest and exchange rates have been freed and the free-marketing restructuring of state enterprises has begun. In July 1994 the government announced a mass privatization programme, with foreign ownership of up to 100 per cent permitted.

TRADE

Imports are chiefly semi-manufactured goods, raw materials, fuel, machinery and metals. Exports consist principally of maize, wheat, barley, oats, petroleum, timber, cattle, meat, machines and industrial equipment.

| *Trade with UK* | 1992 | 1993 |
|---|---|---|
| Imports from UK | £64,388,000 | £93,843,000 |
| Exports to UK | 62,814,000 | 93,289,000 |

EDUCATION

Education is free and nominally compulsory. There are state universities in seven cities, 66 private universities, six polytechnics, two commercial academies, and five agricultural colleges.

COMMUNICATIONS

In 1990 there were 11,348 km of railway open for traffic. The mercantile marine had a gross tonnage of 12,140,000 tons in 1990. The principal ports are Constanta (on the Black Sea), Sulina (on the Danube Estuary), Galati, Braila, Giurgiu and Turnu Severin. The Danube and the Black Sea are linked by a canal completed in 1984.

RUSSIA
*Rossiiskaya Federatsiya – Russian Federation*

Russia has an area of 6,593,391 sq. miles (17,075,400 sq. km) and occupies three-quarters of the land area of the former Soviet Union. In the west it is bordered by Norway, the Gulf of Finland, Finland, Estonia, Latvia, Belarus and

the Ukraine; the Kaliningrad enclave borders Lithuania and Poland. To the south Russia is bordered in Europe by Georgia, Azerbaijan, the Black Sea and the Caspian Sea, and in Asia by Kazakhstan, China, Mongolia and North Korea. In the east it meets the North Pacific (where its nearest point is only a few miles from Japan), and the Bering Strait (where its nearest point is only a few miles from Alaska). To the north is the Arctic Ocean and the Barents Sea.

The Russian Federation comprises 89 members: 49 regions (Amur, Archangel, Astrakhan, Belgorod, Bryansk, Chelyabinsk, Chita, Irkutsk, Ivanovo, Kaliningrad, Kaluga, Kamchatka, Kemerovo, Kirov, Kostroma, Kurgan, Kursk, Leningrad, Lipetsk, Magadan, Moscow, Murmansk, Nizhny Novgorod, Novgorod, Novosibirsk, Omsk, Orel, Orenburg, Penza, Perm, Pskov, Rostov, Ryazan, Sakhalin, Samara, Saratov, Smolensk, Sverdlovsk, Tambov, Tomsk, Tula, Tver, Tyumen, Ulyanovsk, Vladimir, Volgograd, Vologda, Voronezh, Yaroslavl); six autonomous territories (Altai, Khabarovsk, Krasnodar, Krasnoyarsk, Primorye, Stavropol); 21 republics (Adygeia, Altai, Bashkortostan, Buryatia, Chechen, Chuvash, Daghestan, Ingush, Kabardin-Balkar, Kalmykia, Karachaevo-Cherkess, Karelia, Khakassia, Komi, Mari-El, Mordovia, North Ossetia, Sakha, Tatarstan, Tyva, Udmurt); ten autonomous areas (Agin-Buryat, Chukot, Evenki, Khanty-Mansi, Komi-Permyak, Koryak, Nenets, Taimyr, Ust-Ordyn-Buryat, Yamalo-Nenets); two cities of federal status (Moscow, St Petersburg); and one autonomous Jewish region (Birobijan).

There are three principal geographic areas: a low-lying flat western area stretching eastwards up to the Yenisei and divided in two by the Ural ridge; the eastern area between the Yenisei and the Pacific, consisting of a number of tablelands and ridges; and a southern mountainous area. Russia has a very long coast-line, including the longest Arctic coastline in the world (about 17,000 miles). The most important rivers are the Volga, the Northern Dvina and the Pechora, the Neva, the Don and the Kuban in the European part, and in the Asiatic part, the Ob, the Irtysh, the Yenisei, the Lena and the Amur, and, further north, Khatanga, Olenek, Yana, Indigirka, Kolyma and Anadyr. Lakes are abundant, particularly in the north-west. The huge Baikal Lake in eastern Siberia is the deepest lake in the world. There are also two large artificial water reservoirs within the Greater Volga canal system, the Moscow and Rybinsk 'Seas'.

Climatically, Russia extends from Arctic and tundra belts to the subtropical in the south.

POPULATION – The 1994 estimate gave a population of 148,704,300, of which about 82 per cent are Russian, 4 per cent Tatar and 3 per cent Ukrainian. There are another 12 minorities with populations of over half a million and more than 100 nationalities in total.

The Russian Orthodox Church is the predominant religion, though the Tatars are Muslims and there are Jewish communities in Moscow and St Petersburg.

LANGUAGE AND ARTS – Russian is a branch of the Slavonic family of languages and is written in the Cyrillic script.

Before the westernization of Russia under Peter the Great (1682–1725), Russian literature consisted mainly of folk ballads (byliny), epic songs, chronicles and works of moral theology. The 18th and 19th centuries saw the development of poetry and fiction. Poetry reached its zenith with Alexander Pushkin (1799–1837), Mikhail Lermontov (1814–41), Alexander Blok (1880–1921), the 1958 Nobel Prize laureate Boris Pasternak (1890–1960), Vladimir Mayakovsky (1893–1930) and Anna Akhmatova (1888–1966). Fiction is associated with the names of Nikolai Gogol (1809–52), Ivan Turgenev (1818–83), Fedor Dostoyevsky (1821–81), Leo Tolstoy (1828–1910), Anton Chekhov (1860–1904), Maxim Gorky (1868–1936), Ivan Bunin (1870–1953), Mikhail Bulgakov (1891–1940), Mikhail Sholokhov (1905–84) and Alexander Solzhenitsyn (b. 1918).

Great names in music include Glinka (1804–57), Borodin (1833–87), Mussorgsky (1839–81), Rimsky-Korsakov (1844–1908), Rubinstein (1829–94), Tchaikovsky (1840–93), Rachmaninov (1873–1943), Skriabin (1872–1915), Prokofiev (1891–1953), Stravinsky (1882–1971), Shostakovich (1906–75) and Alfred Schnittke (b. 1934).

CAPITAL – Moscow. Population 8,967,000 (1989).

Moscow, founded about 1147, became the centre of the rising Moscow principality and in the 15th century the capital of the whole of Russia (Muscovy). In 1325 it became the seat of the Metropolitan of Russia. In 1703 Peter the Great transferred the capital to St Petersburg, but on 14 March 1918 Moscow was again designated as the capital. ΨSt Petersburg (from 1914 to 1924 Petrograd and from 1924 to 1991 Leningrad) has a population of 5,020,000 (1989).

Other towns with populations (1990) exceeding one
million are:

| | |
|---|---|
| Nizhny-Novgorod (Gorky) | 1,438,000 |
| Novosibirsk (Novonikolayevsk) | 1,436,000 |
| Yekaterinburg (Sverdlovsk) | 1,367,000 |
| Samara (Kuibyshev) | 1,257,000 |
| Omsk | 1,148,000 |
| Chelyabinsk | 1,143,000 |
| Ufa | 1,083,000 |
| Perm (Molotov) | 1,091,000 |
| Kazan | 1,094,000 |
| Rostov-on-Don | 1,020,000 |

CURRENCY – Rouble of 100 kopeks.
FLAG – Three horizontal stripes of white, blue, red.
NATIONAL DAY – 12 June (Independence Day).

## HISTORY

The Gregorian calendar was not introduced until 14 February
1918. For the events surrounding the 1917 revolutions the
dates given here are the Gregorian calendar dates in use in
the rest of the world at the time, with the dates in the Julian
calendar (os) in parenthesis.

Russia was formally created from the principality of
Muscovy and its territories by Tsar Peter I (The Great)
(1682–1725), who initiated its territorial expansion, introduced western ideas of government and state organization
and founded St Petersburg. By the end of Peter the Great's
reign, the Baltic territories (modern-day Estonia and Latvia)
had been annexed from Sweden and Russia had become the
dominant military power of north-eastern Europe. In the
18th century the partitions of Poland and wars with Turkey
brought the territories of modern-day Lithuania, Belarus, the
Ukraine and the Crimea under Russian control, and the
colonization of Siberia east of the Urals began in earnest.
Russia overran the Caucasus region (modern-day Armenia,
Azerbaijan and Georgia) in the early 19th century, seized
Finland from Sweden in 1809 and Bessarabia from Turkey
in 1812. Throughout the remainder of the 19th century
Russia subdued and annexed the independent Muslim states
which formed the five Central Asian republics.

It was as a multinational empire covering a huge
geographical area, in which the monarch and nobility held
almost absolute power (an ineffectual parliament, the Duma,
was created in 1905), that the Russian Empire entered the
First World War in 1914. Discontent caused by autocratic
rule, the poor conduct of the military campaign and wartime
privation led to a revolution which broke out on 12 March
(27 February os) 1917. Tsar Nicholas II abdicated three days
later and a provisional government was formed; a republic
was proclaimed on 14 September (1 September os) 1917. A
political power struggle ensued between the provisional
government and the Bolshevik Party which controlled the
Soviets (councils) set up by workers, soldiers and peasants.
This led to a second revolution on 7 November (25 October
os) 1917 in which the Bolsheviks, led by Lenin, seized power.

The Bolshevik (Communist) Party withdrew from the
First World War under the Treaty of Brest-Litovsk (March
1918), surrendering large areas of territory. Armed resistance
to Communist rule developed into an all-out civil war between
'red' Bolshevik forces and 'white' monarchist and anti-
Communist forces which lasted until the end of 1922. During
the civil war, Russia had been declared a Soviet Republic and
other Soviet republics had been formed in the Ukraine,
Byelorussia and Transcaucasia. These four republics merged
to form the Union of Soviet Socialist Republics (USSR) on 30
December 1922.

The Nazi-Soviet pact of August 1939 and the Second
World War resulted in further territorial expansion, regain-
ing much of the territory lost in or after 1918, as well as
extending Soviet influence to the countries of eastern Europe
liberated by Soviet troops. The USSR lost 26 million
combatants and civilians in the war.

After an internal Communist Party power struggle
following Lenin's death in 1924, Joseph Stalin emerged in
1928 as the undisputed party leader. He initiated a series of
reorganizations of the USSR, introduced a policy of rapid
industrialization under a system of five-year plans, brought
all sectors of industry under government control, abolished
private ownership and enforced the collectivization of
agriculture. He eliminated potential political opponents
through purges and show trials, and total political repression
lasted until his death in 1953.

Repression lessened under Khruschev and Brezhnev, but
the Communist Party remained dominant in all walks of life.
This was the state of affairs when Mikhail Gorbachev became
Soviet leader in March 1985. Gorbachev introduced the
policies of perestroika (complete restructuring) and glasnost
(openness) in order to revamp the economy, which had
stagnated since the 1970s, to root out corruption and
inefficiency, and to end the Cold War and its attendant arms
race. Private ownership was allowed, individual expression
and limited private enterprise were tolerated, political
prisoners released and the guaranteed leading role of the
Communist Party abolished. The political openness and the
retreat from total control by the Communist Party unleashed
ethnic and nationalist tensions. Events came to a head on 19
August 1991 when a coup was attempted against Soviet
President Gorbachev by hardline elements of the Communist
Party, the armed forces and the state security service (KGB)
in order to reimpose Communist control on the USSR. The
coup was defeated by reformist and democratic political
groupings supported by the majority of the population, who
took to the streets of Moscow and other large cities under the
leadership of Russian President Yeltsin. The coup leaders
were arrested and imprisoned, and Mikhail Gorbachev
returned to Moscow. However, it became clear that effective
political power was in the hands of the republican leaders,
especially Russian President Yeltsin, and the Soviet Union
began to break up as the constituent republics declared their
independence. Mikhail Gorbachev resigned as Soviet President on 25 December 1991 and on 26 December 1991 the
USSR formally ceased to exist.

## GOVERNMENT

Russia was recognized as an independent state by the EC
and USA in January 1992, and it inherited the Soviet Union's
seat at the UN on 24 December 1991.

A new Russian Federal Treaty was signed on 13 March
1992 between the central government and the autonomous
republics. However, the Chenchen republic had declared its
'independence' in November 1991 after a nationalist coup in
the republic and refused to sign the Treaty. Tatarstan also
refused to sign the Treaty and declared its 'independence'.
In November 1992 President Yeltsin imposed direct rule in
the autonomous republics of Ingush and North Ossetia after
Ingush forces attacked North Ossetia; a state of emergency
was declared by President Yeltsin in the two autonomous
republics in March 1993; it remains in place in the Ingush
republic. In February 1994 Tatarstan signed its own
agreement with the Federal government on the basis of
being a 'state united with Russia'. In 1994 a civil war has
developed in the Chenchen republic with opposition forces
fighting against the dictatorial nationalist regime.

Throughout 1992–3 President Yeltsin's government and
reformist political groups faced opposition to constitutional
and economic reform from the bureaucracy, some

of the military, influential heads of major state enterprises and the Supreme Soviet and the Congress of People's Deputies, led by its speaker Ruslan Khasbulatov. Negotiations between Yeltsin and Khasbulatov in January and February 1993 led to a compromise but in March 1993 the Congress of Deputies rejected the power-sharing deal and President Yeltsin imposed direct 'special rule' on 20 March, confirmed a referendum for 25 April and ordered the armed forces to refrain from entering the crisis. The constitutional court declared Yeltsin's special rule illegal and an emergency session of the Supreme Soviet narrowly voted against impeaching the President. This defeat of the parliamentary hardliners was confirmed by the overwhelming victory of President Yeltsin in the April referendum on continuing socio-economic reform.

Throughout the summer of 1993, however, the parliamentary hardliners continued to block government policy on economic reform and stalemate ensued. Eventually the stalemate was broken and events came to a head on 21 September when President Yeltsin dissolved parliament and called new elections. The hardline parliamentary forces led by Khasbulatov and Rutskoi declared the move a coup d'état, formed a rival government and occupied the White House. After several days of fighting in Moscow between parliamentary and government forces, the parliamentary hardline forces attempted a coup which was put down by the army. After the hardline defeat, President Yeltsin's government suspended the constitutional court, clamped down on broadcasting and press organizations that had supported the coup attempt, and held new elections in all 89 regions and republics. Elections to the new Federal Assembly were held on 12 December 1993, the same day as the constitutional referendum, and resulted in the pro-reform Russia's Choice bloc emerging as the largest party in the State Duma, but the anti-reform neo-fascist Liberal Democratic Party gained the largest share of the vote in the proportional representation section. The strong showing of the anti-reform Communist and Agrarian parties and the splintered nature of the resulting parliament led to a more centrist government being formed and the ending of radical economic reforms. The state of the major parties in the State Duma as at August 1994 was: Russia's Choice 103; Liberal Democratic Party 66; Communist Party 62; Agrarian Party 47; Yabloko 33; Party of Unity and Accord 27; Women of Russia 25; Democratic Party 21; Civic Union 18.

## CONSTITUTION

The present constitution came into force on 22 December 1993 after approval in a national referendum. It enshrines the right to private ownership and the freedoms of press, speech, association, worship and travel, and states that Russia is a multiparty democracy. The President is given strong powers under the constitution, being head of state, head of government, head of Security Council and commander-in-chief of the armed forces. The President is pre-eminent in foreign and defence policies and may declare war on foreign states or declare a state of emergency or martial law in Russia (subject to confirmation by the Federation Council). He may chair cabinet meetings, determine basic government policy, veto parliamentary legislation, issue decrees and directives, call referendums, dismiss the government, nominate senior judges, the prosecutor-general and the Central Bank Governor. The President nominates the Prime Minister and Deputy Prime Ministers, who must be approved by the State Duma. If the President's nominees are rejected once or twice by the State Duma he may ignore it; on the third rejection he may dismiss the State Duma and call new elections. The President is directly elected for a maximum of two four-year terms, and may only be impeached on the grounds of treason

or serious crime after rulings in both the Supreme and Constitutional Courts and two-thirds majorities in both houses of parliament. The Prime Minister takes over from the President in the event that he is unable to fulfil his duties.

Legislative power is vested in the Federal Assembly, comprising the Federation Council (upper house) of 178 members, two elected by each of the 89 members of the Russian Federation; the State Duma (lower house) of 450 members, of which 225 are elected by constituencies on a first-past-the-post basis and 225 by proportional representation, with a 5 per cent threshold for representation. The Federation Council maintains jurisdiction over central-local government matters, and its approval is needed for economic and defence legislation to be passed. The State Duma, elected for four-year terms, oversees government appointments, has the power to reject the government's fiscal and monetary policies, may pass votes of no confidence in the government (which the President may ignore on the first vote), and cannot be dissolved less than one year after its election. In addition there is the Constitutional Court composed of judges appointed for life to protect and interpret the constitution. The main clauses of the constitution may only be changed with the agreement of the President and with a three-quarters vote in the Federation Council, a two-thirds vote in the State Duma, and the agreement of two-thirds of the Russian Federation's 89 members. A transitional period is in operation with the present Federal Assembly having a two-year term, and President Yeltsin a five-year term until June 1996.

HEAD OF STATE
*President*, Boris Yeltsin, *elected* 12 June 1991

GOVERNMENT *as at August 1994*
*Prime Minister*, Viktor Chernomyrdin
*First Deputy PM*, Oleg Saskovets
*Deputy PMs*, Anatoly Chubais (*Privatization*); Alexandr Zaverukha (*Agriculture*); Alexander Shokhin (*Economy and CIS relations*); Yuri Yarov
*Foreign Affairs*, Andrei Kozyrev
*Defence*, Marshal Pavel Grachev
*Interior*, Lt.-Gen. Viktor Yerin
*Justice*, Yuri Kalmykov
*Education*, Yevgeny Tkachenko
*Labour*, Gennady Melikyan
*Ecology and Natural Resources*, Viktor Danilov-Danilyan
*Public Health*, Eduard Nechaev
*Communications*, Vladimir Bulgak
*Transport*, Vitaly Yefimov
*Fuel and Energy*, Yuri Shafranik
*Agriculture and Foodstuffs*, Viktor Khlystun
*Railways*, Gennady Fadeyev
*Culture and Tourism*, Yevgeny Sidorov
*Nuclear Power*, Viktor Mikhailov
*Science, Technology and Higher Education*, Boris Saltykov
*Social Security*, vacant
*Security*, Nikolai Golushko
*Civil Defence*, Sergei Shoiga
*Foreign Economic Relations*, Oleg Davydov
*Finance*, Sergei Dubinin (*acting*)

*Speaker of the Federation Council*, Vladimir Shumeiko
*Speaker of the State Duma*, Ivan Rybkin

EMBASSY OF THE RUSSIAN FEDERATION
13 Kensington Palace Gardens, London W8 4QX
Tel 0171-229 3628

*Ambassador Extraordinary and Plenipotentiary*, His Excellency Boris Pankin, apptd 1991
*Minister-Counsellor*, Aleksandr Kudinov

*Defence Attaché*, Lt.-Gen. V. N. Pronin
*Trade Representative*, N. B. Teliatnikov.

BRITISH EMBASSY
Moscow 72, Sosiiskaya Naberezhnaya 14
Tel: Moscow 230 6333

*Ambassador Extraordinary and Plenipotentiary*, His
  Excellency Sir Brian Fall, KCMG, apptd 1992. (Also non-
  resident Ambassador to Armenia, Georgia, Moldova and
  Turkmenistan)
*Minister and Deputy Head of Mission*, F. N. Richards, CVO
*Minister-Counsellor*, G. D. G. Murrell, CMG, OBE
*Defence and Air Attaché*, Air Cdre P. J. Wilkinson
*Counsellors (Commercial)*, D. J. Gowan (*Moscow*);
  G. E. Mearns (*St Petersburg*)
*Consuls-General*: J. Daly (*Moscow*); S. D. Jack (*St Petersburg*)
There is a British Consulate-General in St Petersburg.

BRITISH COUNCIL DIRECTOR, M. Evans, Ulyanovskaya
  Ulitsa, Dom 1, Moscow 109189. There is also an office at
  St Petersburg.

DEFENCE (*see also* CIS entry, pages 752–3)

Since the demise of the Soviet Union the Russian armed
forces have been considerably reduced but remain some of
the most powerful in the world. The total active armed forces
number some 2,030,000 personnel (including 950,000
conscripts serving for 18 or 24-month periods and 165,000
Ministry of Defence staff). Reserves number 2,400,000
personnel.

  The Strategic Nuclear Forces are centrally controlled,
number 194,000 personnel and have: 788 nuclear missiles in
52 submarines; 1,204 inter-continental ballistic missiles based
on land; 170 long-range nuclear bombers; 100 anti-ballistic
missiles with related satellites, radar and long-range early
warning systems.

  The Navy has a strength of 290,000 personnel (including
180,000 conscripts, 60,000 naval aviation, 12,000 naval
infantry and 17,500 coastal defence and artillery personnel).
It deploys: 153 tactical submarines; one fixed-wing and three
V/STOL aircraft carriers; 29 cruisers; 24 destroyers; 114
frigates; 163 patrol and coastal craft; 211 mine warfare vessels;
and 650 support ships. Naval Aviation has 910 combat
aircraft and 240 armed helicopters whilst the infantry and
coastal defence forces deploy 1,320 main battle tanks, 4,390
armoured vehicles and 1,385 artillery pieces. The Navy is
organized into four fleets: Northern, Baltic, Pacific and Black
Sea (control of which has yet to be agreed with Ukraine); and
one flotilla (Caspian Sea) operated jointly with Kazakhstan
and Turkmenistan.

  The Army numbers 1,000,000 personnel (450,000
conscripts) organized into 99 divisions and 132 brigades.
Equipment includes: 25,000 main battle tanks; 51,000
armoured infantry fighting vehicles and armoured personnel
carriers; 23,700 artillery pieces; 800 surface-to-surface
missiles; 1,500 attack helicopters. The Air Force has a
strength of 381,000 personnel (including 185,000 conscripts)
with some 1,800 ground attack aircraft, 3,400 air defence
fighters, 350 transport aircraft, 345 reconnaissance aircraft
and 1,700 training aircraft. Paramilitary forces number
220,000, including 100,000 KGB and 120,000 internal
security troops.

  The Russian withdrawal from eastern Europe was completed on 31 August 1994 when the last troops left Eastern
Germany. On the same day the last combat troops left
Estonia and Latvia, leaving behind 600 in Latvia to operate
and then dismantle the Skrunda radar base over five and a
half years, and 200 in Estonia to dismantle the Paldiski
nuclear submarine base by summer 1995. In the rest of the

CIS, Russia maintains a joint air defence force with the five
Central Asian republics and also deploys forces in Armenia
(5,000), Georgia (20,000), Moldova (30,000), Tajikistan
(8,500), Turkmenistan (34,000), Belarus (30,000).

ECONOMY

Under the Soviet regime, an essentially agricultural economy
in 1917 was transformed by the early 1960s into the second
strongest industrial power in the world. However, by the late
1960s and early 1970s the concentration of resources on the
military-industrial complex was causing the civilian economy
to stagnate. This was exacerbated by the bureaucratic
inefficiency of the centrally planned economic system and
the extremely poor distribution system. It was in an attempt
to solve the problems of the centrally planned economic
system that Gorbachev introduced economic restructuring
(*perestroika*). After attempts to reform the economy within
the restraints of the centrally planned system had failed, an
increasing number of free market reforms were introduced,
including the legalization of small private businesses in
August 1990, the reduction of state control over the economy
in October 1990, and denationalization and privatization
measures in July 1991. In May 1992 the great majority of
state subsidies were abolished and price liberalization was
introduced. The first stage of mass privatization of state
industries began in October 1992 and the central distribution
system was abolished with effect from 1 January 1993.

  However, the abolition of central planning before a fully
free market system was in place, and continued argument
over reform between radicals and centrists in the government
in 1992–4 resulted in economic confusion. Economic reform
and the continuation of western aid were thrown into doubt
in January 1993 when Prime Minister Chernomyrdin
signalled the re-introduction of price controls on some goods;
but President Yeltsin returned to economic reform policies
soon afterwards. By the end of the first stage of mass
privatization in June 1994 an estimated 35–40 per cent of
enterprises had been privatized (about 85,000); 45 per cent
of the workforce worked in the private sector, which produced
40 per cent of GDP; and an estimated 40 million Russians
owned shares. This added to the 30,000 small enterprises
and shops and 184,000 agricultural holdings privatized in
1992. On 27 October 1993 President Yeltsin issued a decree
allowing the unrestricted buying and selling of land for the
first time since 1917. The second stage of mass privatization
was launched on 1 July 1994.

  While privatization has been a success, the restructuring
of state industries and enterprises has not, because of the
continued obstruction of economic reform. In January 1992
the radical reform government introduced economic 'shock
therapy' to end hyperinflation and restore government
reserves by liberalizing prices and restructuring firms to end
their reliance on state subsidies. The result would have been
reduced inflation and money supply levels, the stabilization
of production levels and improved budget and trade positions.
Shock therapy was only partially implemented in 1992–4
because of parliamentary control over the Central Bank until
summer 1993 and parliamentary insistence on large budget
deficits to support credits to enterprises which were bankrupt.
The result has been that industrial production fell further (18
per cent in 1992, 15.5 per cent in 1993), hyperinflation (900
per cent 1993) lasted longer and the rouble fell further (90
per cent against the US dollar 1992–4) than necessary. By
early 1994 the economic situation stabilized with industrial
output growing, inflation at 8 per cent a month, a budget
deficit of 6 per cent of GDP, and a trade surplus of
US$20, 900 million for 1993, which had helped to raise

government foreign currency reserves to US$10,000 million. GDP in 1993 was 170,320,000 million roubles.

Russia has received large-scale international aid in 1993–4. In April 1993 a major rescheduling of Russia's US$80 billion foreign debt was announced, which saved US$15 billion in repayments; in June 1994 a further US$7 billion was rescheduled. The G7 summit in Tokyo in April pledged aid of US$43 billion for structural reform and rouble stabilization, conditional on political and economic reforms. Since 1992 the IMF has provided US$4,000 million under its systemic transformation facility to bring about a market economy.

Russia has some of the richest mineral deposits in the world. Coal is mined in the Kuznetsk area, in the Urals, south of Moscow, in the Donets basin and in the Pechora area in the north. Oil is produced in the northern Caucasus, between the Volga and the Urals, and in western Siberia, which also has large deposits of natural gas. Coal and gas deposits in Siberia and the far east (especially Yakutia) are currently being developed. The Ural mountains contain high-quality iron ore, manganese, copper, aluminium, gold, platinum, precious stones, salt, asbestos, pyrites, coal, oil, etc. Iron ore is also mined near Kursk, Tula, Lipetsk, in several areas in Siberia and in the Kola Peninsula. Non-ferrous metals are found in the Altai, in eastern Siberia, in the northern Caucasus, in the Kuznetsk basin, in the far east and in the far north.

The vast area and the great variety in climatic conditions cause great differences in the structure of agriculture from north to south and from west to east. In the far north reindeer breeding, hunting and fishing are predominant. Further south, timber industry is combined with grain growing. In the southern half of the forest zone and in the adjacent forest-steppe zone, the acreage under grain crops is larger and the structure of agriculture more complex. Between the Volga and the Urals cericulture is predominant (particularly summer wheat), followed by cattle breeding. Beyond the Urals is another important grain-growing and stock-breeding area in the southern part of the western Siberian plain. The southern steppe zone is the main wheat granary of Russia, containing also large acreages under barley, maize and sunflowers. In the extreme south cotton is cultivated. Vine, tobacco and other southern crops are grown on the Black Sea shore of the Caucasus.

Moscow and St Petersburg are still the two largest industrial centres in the country, but new industrial areas have been developed in the Urals, the Kuznetsk basin, Siberia and the far east. Most of the oil produced in the former USSR came from Russia; half the annual output comes from Tyumen Oblast in western Siberia. All industries are represented in Russia, including iron and steel and engineering.

## TRADE

Foreign trade in 1993 was worth US$76,200 million, the main trading partners being other CIS states, the USA, Germany, Japan, UK, France and Italy.

*Trade with UK*
(1992 CIS12; 1993 Russia)

|  | 1992 | 1993 |
|---|---|---|
| Imports from UK | £456,554,000 | £551,873,000 |
| Exports to UK | 673,346,000 | 822,125,000 |

## COMMUNICATIONS

The European area of Russia is well served by railways, St Petersburg and Moscow being the two main focal points of rail routes. The centre and south have a good system of north-south and east-west lines, but the eastern part (the

Volga lands), traversed by trunk lines between Europe and Asia, lacks north-south routes. In Asia, there are still large areas, notably in the far north and Siberia, with few or no railways. In the northern part of European Russia, the North Pechora Railway has been completed, while in the far east a second Trans-Siberian line (the Baikal-Amur Railway) is partially in use; it follows a more northerly alignment than the earlier Trans-Siberian and terminates in the Pacific port of Sovetskaya Gavan.

The most important ports (Taganrog, Rostov and Novo-rossiisk) lie around the Black Sea and the Sea of Azov. The northern ports (St Petersburg, Murmansk and Archangel) are, with the exception of Murmansk, icebound during winter. Several ports have been built along the Arctic Sea route between Murmansk and Vladivostok and are in regular use every summer. The far eastern port of Vladivostok, the Pacific naval base of Russia, is kept open by icebreakers all the year round.

Inland waterways, both natural and artificial, are of great importance in the country, although some of them are icebound in winter (from two and a half months in the south to six months in the north). The great rivers of European Russia flow outwards from the centre, linking all parts of the plain with the chief ports, an immense system of navigable waterways which carried about 690 million tons of freight in 1988. They are supplemented by a system of canals which provide a through traffic between the White, Baltic, Black and Caspian Seas. The most notable are the White Sea-Baltic Canal, the Moscow-Volga Canal and the Volga-Don Canal linking the Baltic and the White Seas in the north to the Caspian Sea, the Black Sea and the Sea of Azov in the south.

# RWANDA
*Republika y'u Rwanda*

Rwanda, formerly part of the Belgian-administered trustee-ship of Ruanda-Urundi, has an area of 10,169 sq. miles (26,338 sq. km), and a population (UN estimate 1991) of 7,491,000, mainly of the Hutu tribe (90 per cent), with Tutsi (9 per cent) and Twa (Pigmy) (1 per cent) minorities.

CAPITAL – Kigali (156,000).
CURRENCY – Rwanda franc of 100 centimes.
FLAG – Three vertical bands, red, yellow and green with letter R on yellow band.
NATIONAL DAY – 1 July.

## GOVERNMENT

The majority Hutu population rebelled against Tutsi feudal rule (under the Belgian colonial authority) in 1959–61, leading to the massacre of thousands of Tutsis. Large numbers fled into exile in Uganda. A referendum held in September 1961 showed the majority of the population were opposed to the retention of the monarchy, which was abolished in October 1961. Rwanda became an independent republic on 1 July 1962, with Gregoire Kayibanda as head of state. He was deposed in 1973 and replaced by a military government under Maj.-Gen. Juvénal Habyarimana, who established a one-party state.

Armed Tutsi exiles repeatedly attempted to invade Rwanda in the 1960s and 1970s but were defeated by the Hutu army, leading to a series of massacres of Tutsis remaining in the country and continued Hutu-Tutsi conflict which left hundreds of thousands dead over a period of 30 years. In October 1990 Rwanda was invaded by the Rwandan Patriotic Front of exiled Tutsis and moderate

Hutus who were sufficiently strong to force the one-party MRND (National Revolutionary Movement for Development) government to end its monopoly of power and introduce a multiparty constitution in 1991. After the government reneged on a 1992 peace agreement, the RPF advanced on the capital Kigali and forced the government to restart negotiations, which led to the August 1993 Arusha peace accord. The accord provided for a transitional period under a broad-based government including the RPF until 1995 elections, with UN forces in the country throughout the period.

The transitional period was proceeding, albeit with a degree of inter-racial violence, when President Habyarimana, who had retained the interim presidency, died in a plane crash on 6 April 1994 widely believed to have been caused by a rocket attack by extremist sections of the Hutu army. The Hutu army and armed militia, the 'interahamwe' then carried out a pre-planned act of genocide against the Tutsi minority and moderate Hutus; 500,000 people were massacred in three months. The civil war restarted and the RPF gradually put an end to the massacres as it took control of the country, forcing the defeated government forces and 2.5 million Hutu refugees into Zaire, Burundi and Tanzania, while another 1.9 million Hutus fled to the French 'safe zone' in the south-west. On 18 July 1994 the RPF declared victory in the civil war and established a broad-based government of national unity in which moderate Hutus were given the presidency and premiership and the RPF took eight of the 22 seats. At the time of going to press an estimated 50,000 Hutu refugees had died from disease in camps in Zaire, from which the refugees were prevented from returning to Rwanda by extremist Hutu army and militia elements, and western forces had arrived in Rwanda to co-ordinate and secure relief supplies.

HEAD OF STATE
President, Pasteur Bizimungu, sworn in 19 July 1994
Vice-President, Paul Kagane

GOVERNMENT OF NATIONAL UNITY as at August 1994
The President
The Vice-President
Prime Minister, Faustin Twagiramungu
Deputy PM, Alexis Kanyarungwe

ECONOMY

Coffee, tea and sugar are grown. Tin, hides, bark of quinine and extract of pyrethrum flowers are also exported.

In 1987 total imports were valued at US$351.7m; total exports, US$112.3m. Coffee accounted for 90 per cent of export earnings in 1989.

| Trade with UK | 1992 | 1993 |
|---|---|---|
| Imports from UK | £1,552,000 | £3,337,000 |
| Exports to UK | 2,582,000 | 1,892,000 |

---

# ST CHRISTOPHER AND NEVIS
*The Federation of St Christopher and Nevis*

---

The state of St Christopher and Nevis is located at the northern end of the eastern Caribbean. It comprises the islands of St Christopher (St Kitts) (68 sq. miles) and Nevis (36 sq. miles). The central area of St Christopher, 17° 18′ N. and 62° 48′ W., is forest-clad and mountainous, rising to 3,792 ft. Mount Liamuiga. Nevis, 17° 10′ N. and 62° 35′ W., is separated from the southern tip of St Christopher by a strait two miles wide and is dominated by Nevis Peak, 3,232 ft. The combined population (UN estimate 1991) was 44,000.

CAPITAL – ΨBasseterre (estimated population, 15,000).
   Chief town of Nevis is ΨCharlestown (population 1,200),
   which is a port of entry.
CURRENCY – East Caribbean dollar (EC$) of 100 cents.
FLAG – Three diagonal bands, green, black and red; each
   colour separated by a stripe of yellow. Two white stars on
   the black band.
NATIONAL ANTHEM – Oh Land of Beauty.
NATIONAL DAY – 19 September (Independence Day).

GOVERNMENT

St Christopher was the first island in the British West Indies to be colonized (1623). The Territory of St Christopher and Nevis became a State in Association with Britain in 1967. The State of St Christopher and Nevis became an independent nation on 19 September 1983.

Under the constitution, The Queen is head of state, represented in the islands by the Governor-General. There is a central government with a ministerial system, the head of which is the Prime Minister of St Christopher and Nevis, and a National Assembly located on St Christopher. The National Assembly is composed of the Speaker, three senators (nominated by the Prime Minister and the Leader of the Opposition) and 11 elected representatives. On Nevis there is a Nevis Island Administration, the head being styled Premier of Nevis, and a Nevis Island Assembly of five elected and three nominated members.

*Governor-General*, His Excellency Sir Clement Athelston Arrindell, GCMG, GCVO, QC, apptd 1983

CABINET *as at August 1994*

*Prime Minister and Minister of Finance, Home Affairs, Caricom Affairs and Foreign Affairs*, Rt. Hon. Dr Kennedy A. Simmonds
*Deputy PM, Education, Youth and Community Affairs, Communications, Works and Public Utilities*, Hon. Sydney E. Morris
*Agriculture, Lands, Housing and Development*, Hon. Hugh C. Heyliger
*Health, Labour and Women's Affairs*, Hon. Constance Mitcham
*Trade, Industry and Tourism*, Hon. Joseph Parry
*Minister in Ministry of Agriculture*, Hon. Alpheus M. Roberts
*Attorney-General*, Hon. S. W. Tapley Seaton, CVO
*Minister in the Office of the Prime Minister*, Hon. Uriel Swanston

ST KITTS HIGH COMMISSION
10 Kensington Court, London W8 5DL
Tel 0171-937 9522

*High Commissioner for the Eastern Caribbean States*, His Excellency Aubrey Hart, apptd 1994

BRITISH HIGH COMMISSIONER, His Excellency Emrys Davies, CMG, resident at Bridgetown, Barbados

## ECONOMY

The economy of the islands has been based on sugar for over three centuries. Tourism (88,264 visitors in 1992) and light industry, concentrating on brewing and food processing, are now being developed. The economy of Nevis centres on small peasant farmers, but a sea-island cotton industry is being developed for export.

| FINANCE | 1991 | 1992 |
|---|---|---|
| Revenue | EC$93,300,000 | EC$108,900,000 |
| Expenditure | 97,500,000 | 105,000,000 |

| Trade with UK | 1992 | 1993 |
|---|---|---|
| Imports from UK | £6,074,000 | £8,735,000 |
| Exports to UK | 7,052,000 | 8,996,000 |

## COMMUNICATIONS

Basseterre is a port of registry and has deep water harbour facilities. Golden Rock airport, on St Kitts, can take most large jet aircraft; Newcastle airstrip on Nevis can take small aircraft and has night landing facilities. The sea ferry route from Basseterre to Charlestown is 11 miles.

---

# ST LUCIA

---

St Lucia, the second largest of the Windward group, situated in 13° 54' N. latitude and 60° 50' W. longitude, is 27 miles

in length, with an extreme breadth of 14 miles. It comprises an area of 238 sq. miles (616 sq. km), with a population (1991 UN estimate) of 153,000. It is mountainous, its highest point being Mt Gimie (3,145 ft) and for the most part it is covered with forest and tropical vegetation.

CAPITAL – ΨCastries (population 1989, 56,000).
CURRENCY – East Caribbean dollar (EC$) of 100 cents.
FLAG – Blue, bearing in centre a device of yellow over black over white triangles having a common base.
NATIONAL ANTHEM – Sons and Daughters of Saint Lucia.
NATIONAL DAY – 22 February (Independence Day).

## GOVERNMENT

Possession of St Lucia was fiercely disputed and it constantly changed hands between the British and the French. It became independent within the Commonwealth on 22 February 1979. The head of state is The Queen, represented in the island by a St Lucian Governor-General, and there is a bicameral legislature. The Senate has 11 members, six appointed by the ruling party, three by the Opposition and two by the Governor-General. The House of Assembly, which has a life of five years, has 17 elected Members and a Speaker, who may be elected from outside the House.

*Governor-General*, His Excellency Sir Stanislaus James, KCMG, OBE

CABINET *as at August 1994*

*Prime Minister, Minister of Finance, Planning, Development, Information and Broadcasting*, Rt. Hon. John G. M. Compton
*Deputy PM and Minister of Home Affairs, Foreign Affairs, Trade and Industry*, Hon. George Mallet
*Communications, Works and Transport*, Hon. Gregory Avril
*Tourism, Public Utilities and National Mobilization*, Hon. Romanus Lansiquot
*Youth, Community Development, Social Affairs, Sports and Co-operatives*, Hon. Desmond Braithwaite
*Attorney-General and Minister for Legal Affairs*, Hon. Senator Lorraine Williams
*Agriculture, Lands, Fisheries and Forestry*, Hon. Ira D'Auvergne
*Education, Culture and Labour*, Hon. Louis George
*Health and Local Government*, Hon. Stephenson King
*Minister of State, Housing, Urban Development and Renewal*, Hon. Senator Michael Pilgrim
*Minister of State, Youth, Sports and Co-operatives*, Hon. Edward Innocent
*Minister of State, Trade and Industry*, Hon. Rufus Bousquet

ST LUCIA HIGH COMMISSION
10 Kensington Court, London W8 5DL
Tel 0171-937 9522

*High Commissioner for the Eastern Caribbean States*, His Excellency Aubrey Hart, apptd 1994

OFFICE OF THE BRITISH HIGH COMMISSION
Columbus Square, PO Box 227, Castries
Tel: Castries 4522484

*High Commissioner*, His Excellency Emrys Davies, CMG, resident at Bridgetown, Barbados
*Resident Representative*, P. T. Rouse, MBE

## ECONOMY

The economy is mainly agrarian, with manufacturing based on the processing of agricultural products. Principal crops are bananas, coconuts, cocoa, mangoes, avocado pears, breadfruit, spices, root crops such as cassava and yams, and citrus fruit. Attempts are being made to diversify the economy, in particular through greater industrialization. Tourism is also of increasing importance, with 204,000 visitors to the island in 1989.

TRADE

The principal exports are bananas, coconut products (copra, edible oils, soap), cardboard boxes, beer, and textile manufactures. The chief imports are flour, meat, machinery, building materials, motor vehicles, cotton piece goods, petroleum and fertilizers.

| Trade with UK | 1992 | 1993 |
|---|---|---|
| Imports from UK | £19,586,000 | £19,559,000 |
| Exports to UK | 53,820,000 | 53,663,000 |

## ST VINCENT AND THE GRENADINES

The territory of St Vincent includes certain of the Grenadines, a chain of small islands stretching 40 miles across the Caribbean Sea between Grenada and St Vincent, some of the larger of which are Bequia, Canouan, Mayreau, Mustique, Union Island, Petit St Vincent and Prune Island. The whole territory extends 150 sq. miles (388 sq. km). The main island, St Vincent, is situated between 13° 6' and 14° 35' N. latitude and 61° 6' and 61° 20' W. longitude. The island has an area of 133 sq. miles (344 sq. km), and a population (1991 UN estimate) of 117,000.

CAPITAL – ΨKingstown, estimated population 33,694.
CURRENCY – East Caribbean dollar (EC$) of 100 cents.
FLAG – Three vertical bands, of blue, yellow and green, with three green diamonds in the shape of a 'V' mounted on the yellow band.
NATIONAL ANTHEM – St Vincent, Land So Beautiful.
NATIONAL DAY – 27 October (Independence Day).

### GOVERNMENT

St Vincent was discovered by Christopher Columbus in 1498. It was granted by Charles I to the Earl of Carlisle in 1627 and after subsequent grants and a series of occupations alternately by the French and English, it was finally restored to Britain in 1783. St Vincent achieved full independence within the Commonwealth as St Vincent and the Grenadines on 27 October 1979.

The Queen is head of state, represented by a Governor-General. The House of Assembly consists of 15 elected members and four Senators appointed by the government and two by the Opposition. It is presided over by a Speaker elected by the House from within or without it. All 15 seats were won by the governing New Democratic Party at the election held on 16 May 1989.

*Governor-General*, His Excellency Sir David Jack, GCMG, MBE, *sworn in* 20 September 1989.

CABINET *as at August 1994*

*Prime Minister, Minister of Finance and Planning*, Rt. Hon. James Mitchell
*Deputy Prime Minister, Attorney-General and Minister of Justice and Information*, Hon. Parnell Campbell, CVO
*Culture, Education, Youth and Women's Affairs*, Hon. John Horne
*Agriculture, Industry and Labour*, Hon. Allan Cruickshank
*Foreign Affairs and Tourism*, Hon. Alpian Allen
*Health and the Environment*, Hon. Yvonne Gibson
*Trade and Consumer Affairs*, Hon. Bernard Wyllie

*Housing, Local Government, Community Development*, Hon. Louis Jones
*Communications and Works*, Hon. Jeremiah Scott
*Ministers of State*, Hon. Stephanie Browne (*Communications and Works*); Monty Roberts (*PM's Office*).

ST VINCENT AND THE GRENADINES HIGH COMMISSION
10 Kensington Court, London W8 5DL
Tel 0171-937 9522

*High Commissioner for the Eastern Caribbean States*, His Excellency Aubrey Hart, apptd 1994

BRITISH HIGH COMMISSION
Granby Street (PO Box 132), Kingstown
Tel: St Vincent 4571701

*High Commissioner*, His Excellency Emrys Davies, CMG, resident at Bridgetown, Barbados
*Resident Representative*, A. Ferguson

### ECONOMY

This is based mainly on agriculture but tourism (155,068 visitors in 1992) and manufacturing industries have been expanding. The main products are bananas, arrowroot, coconuts, cocoa, spices and various kinds of food crops. The main imports are foodstuffs (meat, rice, beverages), textiles, lumber, cement and other building materials, fertilizers, motor vehicles and fuel.

| Trade with UK | 1992 | 1993 |
|---|---|---|
| Imports from UK | £9,469,000 | £7,959,000 |
| Exports to UK | 26,546,000 | 25,891,000 |

## EL SALVADOR
*República de El Salvador*

El Salvador extends along the Pacific coast of Central America for 160 miles, with an area of 8,124 sq. miles (21,041 sq. km). The surface of the country is very mountainous, many of the peaks being extinct volcanoes. Much of the interior has an average altitude of 2,000 feet. The climate varies from tropical to temperate. There is a wet season from May to October, and a dry season from November to April. Earthquakes have been frequent, the most recent being in October 1986.

POPULATION – The population (1991 estimate) was 5,376,000. The language is Spanish.

CAPITAL – San Salvador (497,644, 1989 estimate). Estimated population of metropolitan area, 2,000,000. Other towns are Santa Ana (417,000), San Miguel (157,838), Ψ La Union (Cutuco), Ψ La Libertad and Ψ Acajutia.
CURRENCY – El Salvador colón (₡) of 100 centavos.
FLAG – Three horizontal bands, sky blue, white, sky blue; coat of arms on white band.
NATIONAL ANTHEM – Saludemos La Patria Orgullosos (Let us proudly hail the Fatherland).
NATIONAL DAY – 15 September.

### GOVERNMENT

El Salvador was conquered in 1526 by Pedro de Alvarado, and formed part of the Spanish vice-royalty of Guatemala until 1821. It is divided into 14 Departments.

Decades of military rule ended in March 1982 when a Constituent Assembly was elected. Subsequent presidential and parliamentary elections were boycotted by the FMLN

(Farabundo Martí National Liberation Front) guerrilla movement. Conflict between the guerrillas and the government continued throughout the 1980s until negotiations culminated in a peace plan signed in January 1992. A ceasefire took effect on 1 February and began a nine-month transition period which ended in December 1992 when the FMLN finished its disarmament and became a political party. A 'Truth Commission', established under UN auspices to investigate and report on human rights abuses in the 1980–91 period, reported in March 1993. The report caused a political crisis when it declared that 15 senior army commanders should be removed by the government. The government was reluctant to do so but came under economic pressure from the USA, which withheld aid for reconstruction until the officers were dismissed on 1 July 1993.

The UN Observer Mission in El Salvador (ONUSAL) monitored the 1992–4 transition process, overseeing the final destruction of FMLN arms in August 1993 and the presidential, parliamentary and local elections held in March and April 1994. Armando Calderon Sol of the ruling right-wing ARENA party won the presidential election, defeating the FMLN's Ruben Zamora. ARENA won 39 of the Legislative Assembly's 84-seats and formed a government with other right-wing parties; the FMLN won 21 seats.

HEAD OF STATE

*President*, Armando Calderón Sol, *assumed office* 1 June 1994
*Vice-President*, Enrique Borgo Bustamante

CABINET *as at August 1994*

*Minister of the Presidency*, The Vice President
*Foreign Affairs*, Dr Oscar Alfredo Santamaría
*Planning*, Ramón González
*Interior*, Dr Roberto Angulo Samayoa
*Justice*, Dr Rubén Antonio Mejía Peña
*Economy*, Enrique Cordova
*Education*, Cecilia Gallardo de Cano
*Defence*, Col. Humberto Corado Figueroa
*Labour and Social Security*, Dr Juan Sifontes
*Agriculture*, Carlos Mejía Alférez
*Public Health*, Dr Eduardo Interiano
*Public Works*, Jorge Sansivirini
*Treasury*, Ricardo Montenegro

EMBASSY OF EL SALVADOR
5 Great James Street, London WC1N 3DA
Tel 0171-430 2141

*Ambassador Extraordinary and Plenipotentiary*, His Excellency Dr Ernesto Trígueros Alcaine, apptd 1994

BRITISH EMBASSY
PO Box 1591, San Salvador
Tel: San Salvador 981763

*Ambassador Extraordinary and Plenipotentiary*, His Excellency Michael H. Connor, apptd 1992

ECONOMY

El Salvador has received substantial aid to rebuild the country's war-damaged infrastructure and services. The USA has written off 75 per cent of El Salvador's debt and in May 1993 the IMF agreed a standby credit facility for El Salvador of US$49 million over 10 months.

The principal cash crops are coffee, cotton, sugarcane and shrimps. However, cotton and sugar production have decreased as a result of the civil war. Also cultivated are maize, sesame, indigo, rice, balsam, etc. In the lower altitudes towards the east, sisal is produced and used in the manufacture of coffee and cereal bags. The Salvadorean Coffee Company, sugar exports and the banking system are being privatized.

Existing factories make textiles, clothing, constructional steel, furniture, cement and household items. In 1989 GDP amounted to US$4,808 million (US$874 per capita).

TRADE

Chief exports are coffee, cotton, sugar, shrimps, sisal, balsam, meat, towels, hides and skins. The chief imports are chemicals, fertilizers, pharmaceutical goods, petroleum, manufactured goods, industrial and electronic machinery and equipment, vehicles and consumer goods.

| *Trade with UK* | 1992 | 1993 |
| --- | --- | --- |
| Imports from UK | £15,002,000 | £15,160,000 |
| Exports to UK | 7,890,000 | 8,895,000 |

EDUCATION

The illiteracy rate has risen to 68.1 per cent (1985) since 1980 when the figure was 30.5 per cent. Primary education is nominally compulsory, but the number of schools and teachers available is too small to enable education to be given to all children of school age.

COMMUNICATIONS

The Executive Autonomous Port Commission (CEPA) administers the ports of Cutuco, La Union, Acajutla, and the railways through FENADESAL. There is a railway line between San Salvador and Guatemala City and Puerto Barrios on the Caribbean coast but it is subject to interruption. The roads are paved and in good condition but some bridges are temporary structures following guerrilla action. There are good roads between Acajutla and the capital (60 miles), and between the capital and Guatemala City. The Pan-American Highway from the Guatemalan frontier follows this route and continues to the Honduran frontier. The El Salvador international airport can receive jet aircraft with daily flights to other Central American capitals, Mexico, and five US cities. There are 100 broadcasting stations and six television stations. Five daily newspapers are published in San Salvador and four in the provinces.

---

# SAN MARINO
*Repubblica di San Marino*

---

San Marino is a small republic in the hills near Rimini, on the Adriatic, founded, it is said, by a pious stonecutter of Dalmatia in the fourth century. The republic resisted Papal claims and those of neighbouring dukedoms during the 15th to 18th centuries, and its integrity and sovereignty is recognized and respected by Italy. The area is approximately 23 sq. miles (61 sq. km.) and the population (1994) is 24,399.

CITY – San Marino, on the slope of Monte Titano, has three towers, a fine church and Government palace, a theatre and museums.

CURRENCY – San Marino and Italian currencies are in circulation.

FLAG – Two horizontal bands, white, blue (with coat of arms of the republic in centre).

NATIONAL DAY – 3 September.

The republic is governed by a State Congress of ten members, under the presidency of two heads of state, who are elected at six-monthly intervals. The Great and General Council, a legislative body of 60 members, is elected by universal suffrage for a term of five years. A Council of Twelve forms in certain cases a Supreme Court of Justice. A coalition government of the Christian Democratic Party and the Socialist Party took office in March 1992, and was returned in the general election of 31 May 1993.

The principal products are wine, cereals, and cattle, and the main industries are tourism, ceramics, lime, concrete, cotton yarns, colour and paints.

HEADS OF STATE
*Regents*, Two 'Capitani Reggenti'

CONSULATE-GENERAL IN LONDON
166 High Holborn, London WCIV 6TT
Tel 0171-836 7744
*Consul-General*, The Lord Forte
BRITISH CONSUL-GENERAL, M. Holmes, OBE, resident at Florence, Italy

## SÃO TOMÉ AND PRÍNCIPE
*República Democrática de São Tomé e Príncipe*

The islands of São Tomé and Príncipe are situated in the Gulf of Guinea, off the west coast of Africa. They have an area of 372 sq. miles (964 sq. km), and a population (UN estimate 1991) of 124,000.

CAPITAL – Ψ São Tomé (25,000).
CURRENCY – Dobra of 100 centavos.
FLAG – Horizontal stripes of green, yellow, green, the yellow of double width and bearing two black stars; and a red triangle in the hoist.
NATIONAL DAY – 12 July (Independence Day).

## GOVERNMENT

The islands became independent on 12 July 1975. A multi-party constitution was approved by referendum in August 1990. The Movement for the Liberation of São Tomé and Príncipe (MLSTP), which had been the sole legal party since independence, was defeated by the opposition Democratic Convergence Party (PCD) in legislative elections held on 20 January 1991. Miguel Trovoada, an independent, was elected President on 3 March 1991. The President dismissed governments in 1992 and 1994 because of mounting criticism of economic reforms. A legislative election has been called for late 1994.

HEAD OF STATE
*President and Commander-in-Chief of the Armed Forces*,
Miguel Trovoada, *elected* 3 March 1991

COUNCIL OF MINISTERS *as at August 1994*

*Prime Minister, Defence*, Alberto Carvalho
*Economy and Finance*, Helder Soares de Barros
*Justice*, Alberto Paulino
*Education*, Alberto Neto
*Health*, Fernando Silveira
*Príncipe*, Sylvestre Umbelina

EMBASSY OF THE DEMOCRATIC REPUBLIC OF SÃO TOMÉ AND PRÍNCIPE
42 avenue Brugman, Brussels 1060, Belgium
Tel: Brussels 3475375
*Ambassador Extraordinary and Plenipotentiary*, new appointment awaited

HONORARY CONSULATE
42 North Audley Street, London WIA 4PY
Tel 0171-499 1995
*Honorary Consul*, W. S. Wilder

BRITISH CONSULATE
c/o Hull Blythe (Angola) Ltd, BP 15, São Tomé
*British Ambassador*, His Excellency Anthony Thomas, resident at Luanda, Angola
*Honorary Consul*, J. Gomes

TRADE
Cacao is the main product.

| Trade with UK | 1992 | 1993 |
|---|---|---|
| Imports from UK | £1,154,000 | £3,433,000 |
| Exports to UK | 4,000 | — |

## SAUDI ARABIA
*Al Mamlaka al Arabiya as-Sa'udiyya*

Saudi Arabia comprises almost the whole of the Arabian peninsula, with the exception of Yemen in the extreme south, Oman and the UAE in the south-east and Qatar in the east. In the north-west it borders Jordan and in the north-east Iraq and Kuwait, while to the west lies the Red Sea and to the east the Gulf. The Nejd ('plateau'), now the Central Province, extends over the centre of the peninsula, including the Nafud and Dahna deserts. The Hejaz ('the boundary'), now the Western Province, extends along the Red Sea coast to Asir and contains the holy towns of Mecca (Makkah) and Medina (Madinah). Asir ('inaccessible') is named for its mountainous terrain, and, with the coastal plain of the Tihama, lies along the southern Red Sea coast from the Hejaz to the border with Yemen. It is the only region to enjoy substantial rainfall. The east and south-east of the country are lower-lying and largely desert. The total area is about 830,000 sq. miles (2,149,640 sq. km), with a population (1992 census) of 16,929,294. Islam is the only permitted religion.

Mecca, about 60 km east of Jeddah, is the birthplace of the Prophet Muhammad, and contains the Great Mosque, within which is the Kaaba or sacred shrine of the Muslim religion. This is the focus of the annual Hajj ('pilgrimage'). Medina (Al-Madinah) Al Munawwarah ('The City of Light'), some 300 km north of Mecca, is celebrated as the first city to embrace Islam and as the Prophet Muhammad's burial place.

CAPITAL – Riyadh, population (1992) about 2 million.
Other major centres are Jeddah (estimated population 1.5 million), Buraydah, Dammam, Hofuf, Mecca, Medina and Tabuk.
CURRENCY – Saudi riyal (SR) of 20 qursh or 100 halala.
FLAG – Green oblong, white Arabic device in centre: 'There is no God but God and Muhammad is the Prophet of God,' and a white scimitar beneath the lettering.
NATIONAL ANTHEM – Long live our beloved King.

## GOVERNMENT

In the 18th century Nejd was an independent state governed from Diriya and the stronghold of the Wahhabis, a puritanical Islamic sect. It subsequently fell under Turkish rule; in 1913 Abdul Aziz Ibn Saud threw off Turkish rule and captured Turkish province of Al Hasa. In 1920 he captured the Asir and in 1921 the Jebel Shammar territory of the Rashid family. In 1925 he completed the conquest of the Hejaz. Great Britain recognized Abdul Aziz Ibn Saud as an independent ruler, King of the Hejaz and of Nejd and its Dependencies, in 1927. The name was changed to the Kingdom of Saudi Arabia in September 1932.

Saudi Arabia is a hereditary monarchy, ruled by the sons and grandsons of Abdul Aziz Ibn Saud, in accordance with

*Petroleum and Mineral Resources*, Hisham Nazer
*Planning*, Abdul Wahab al-Attar
*Labour and Social Affairs*, Dr Mohamed Ali al-Faiz
*Information*, Ali Sha'er
*Health*, Faisal bin Abdul Aziz al Hejailan
*Islamic Affairs, Awqafs and Guidance*, Abdul Mohsen Al-Turki
*Pilgrimage*, Dr Mahmoud Safr
*Education*, Dr Abdul Aziz Al-Abdullah al-Khuwaiter
*Higher Education*, Khalid al-Angari
*Posts, Telegraphs and Telecommunications*, Dr Alawi Darwish Kayyal
*Industry and Electricity*, Abdul Aziz al-Zamil
*Chairman of the Consultative Council*, Sheikh Mohammed bin Ibrahim al Jubeir
*Chairman of the Board of Grievances*, Sheikh Nasir bin Hamad al-Rashid
*Chairman of the Supreme Judicial Council*, Sheikh Salih Bin Muhammad al-Lihaydan
*Grand Mufti of Saudi Arabia*, Sheikh Abdul Aziz bin Baz
*Royal Court Adviser*, Sheikh Abdul Wahhab Ahmad Abdul Wasi

the Sharia law of Wahhabi Islam. The line of succession passes from brother to brother according to age, although several sons of Ibn Saud renounced their right to the throne. All sons and grandsons of Ibn Saud must be consulted before a new King accedes the throne.

In 1992 King Fahd announced a new Basic Law based on Sharia law and including rules to protect personal freedoms. A consultative council (*Majlis-al-Shura*) of 60 members appointed by the King was set up to share power with, and question the government, and to make recommendations to the King. The Majlis-al-Shura began meeting in September 1993 and debates government policy in the areas of the budget, defence, foreign and social affairs. Members of the ruling Al-Saud family are excluded from membership of the Council, which has a four-year term and takes decisions by majority vote. Cabinet ministers have terms of four years, with the possibility of a two-year extension.

In 1993 the country's provinces were reorganized into 13 regions, each with a governor appointed by the King and an assembly of prominent local citizens to advise the governor on local government issues.

HEAD OF STATE
*Custodian of the Two Holy Mosques and HM The King of Saudi Arabia*, King Fahd bin Abdul Aziz Al Saud, *born* 1921, *ascended the throne* 1 June 1982
*HRH Crown Prince*, Prince Abdullah bin Abdul Aziz Al Saud

COUNCIL OF MINISTERS *as at August 1994*
*Prime Minister*, HM The King
*First Deputy Prime Minister and Commander of the National Guard*, HRH The Crown Prince
*Second Deputy Prime Minister, Defence and Aviation*, HRH Prince Sultan bin Abdul Aziz Al Saud
*Public Works and Housing*, HRH Prince Mit'ab bin Abdul Aziz Al Saud
*Interior*, HRH Prince Naif bin Abdul Aziz Al Saud
*Foreign Affairs*, HRH Prince Saud al-Faisal bin Abdul Aziz
*Finance and National Economy*, Muhammad Aba al-Khail
*Agriculture and Water*, Dr Abdul Rahman bin Abdul Aziz bin Hassan Al al-Shaikh
*Municipal and Rural Affairs*, Muhammad al-Shaikh
*Justice*, Dr Abdallah bin Ibrahim al-Shaikh
*Commerce*, Dr Sulaiman al-Solaim
*Communications*, Dr Hussain Mansouri

ROYAL EMBASSY OF SAUDI ARABIA
30 Charles Street, London WIX 7PM
Tel 0171-917 3000

*Ambassador Extraordinary and Plenipotentiary*, His Excellency Dr Ghazi Algosaibi, apptd 1992
*Minister-Counsellor*, Dr Mohammed Rajah Al-Hussainy
*Defence Attaché*, Brig. A. H. Al-Bassam
*Cultural Attaché*, A. M. Al-Nasser
*Commercial Attaché*, M. A. Al-Sheddi

BRITISH EMBASSY
PO Box 94351, Riyadh 11693
Tel: Riyadh 488 0077

*Ambassador Extraordinary and Plenipotentiary*, His Excellency The Hon. David Gore-Booth, CMG, apptd 1993
*Counsellors*, J. S. Laing, CMG (*Deputy Head of Mission and Consul-General*); C. M. J. Sugar (*Commercial*); J. H. Bunney
*Defence and Military Attaché*, Brig. M. J. Lance
*First Secretary and Consul*, T. C. Lamb

CONSUL-GENERAL, L. E. Walker, OBE, LVO, PO Box 393, Jeddah 21411. There is also a trade office in Dhahran/Al Khobar (PO Box 88, Dhahran Airport 31932).

BRITISH COUNCIL REPRESENTATIVE, Clive Mogford, Olaya Main Road, Al Mousa Centre, Tower B (PO Box 58012), Riyadh 11594. There are also offices in *Jeddah*, *Dammam* and *Jubail*.

DEFENCE

Total active armed forces number 158,000 personnel, service being voluntary. The Army numbers 68,000 personnel, with 700 main battle tanks, 3,080 armoured infantry fighting vehicles and armoured personnel carriers and 460 artillery pieces. The Navy has 11,000 personnel including two battalions of 1,500 marines. It deploys eight frigates, 29 patrol and coastal combatants and 20 armed helicopters. The Air Force has 22,000 personnel, including 4,000 air defence forces, and deploys 296 combat aircraft of US and UK manufacture. The National Guard, which is directly under royal command, has 57,000 active personnel and 20,000 tribal levies, with 1,100 armoured personnel carriers and 70 artillery pieces. In addition, the paramilitary Frontier Force and Coast Guard number 15,000 personnel. Saudi Arabia is base to the Gulf Co-operational Council Peninsula Shield Force of 5,000 troops. The USA, UK and France station aircraft and support units in the country to patrol the air exclusion zone in southern Iraq.

## ECONOMY

Saudi Arabia's revenue has been lower since the drop in world oil prices from the mid-1980s onwards, and in the 1990s this has caused some economic distress as financial reserves have been used up to meet budget deficits. In addition the country has had the cost of the 1990–1 Gulf War, estimated at US$60,000 million. The 1993 budget was in deficit by US$7,500 million, or 6.5 per cent of GDP, and this led to spending cuts of 20 per cent in 1994 to achieve a balanced budget.

Outside the manufacturing centres which have grown up around many towns, most of the population are engaged in agriculture. The productivity of traditional dryland farming is supplemented by irrigation.

The principal industry is oil extraction and processing. Oil was first found in commercial quantities in 1938. About 97 per cent of the total is extracted by the Arabian–American Oil Company. Aramco's 66-year lease will terminate in 1999 but the company was effectively nationalized in 1980.

The government actively encourages the establishment of manufacturing industries in the country. Industries have developed in the fields of construction materials, metal fabrication, simple machinery and electrical equipment, food and beverages, chemicals and plastics. Investment in industrial gases, intermediate petrochemicals, light engineering and machinery is encouraged.

Two industrial centres have been established at Jubail and Yanbu, financed by the state agency Saudi Arabian Basic Industries Corporation. Linked by gas and oil pipelines, both have petrochemical complexes producing ethylene and methanol; six of the seven plants on-stream are joint ventures with American and Japanese companies.

The state agency Petromin operates three domestic refineries, two lubricant plants and three export refineries. Total refining capacity is approximately 1,950,000 b.p.d.

### TRADE

Oil remains the main source of receipts in the balance of payments. The leading suppliers of imports are USA, Japan, Germany, the UK, Italy and France and the chief customers for exports are Japan, France, USA and Singapore. There is a total ban on the importation of alcohol, pork products, firearms, and items regarded as non-Islamic or pornographic.

| Trade with UK | 1992 | 1993 |
|---|---|---|
| Imports from UK | £1,967,625,000 | £1,826,121,000 |
| Exports to UK | 963,607,000 | 1,274,480,000 |

## COMMUNICATIONS

There are few railway lines. They principally connect the oilfields to the ports and the capital. Metalled roads connect all the cities and main towns. The principal port on the Gulf is Dammam which has 39 berths and an annual capacity of 9.1 million tons. Jeddah is the centre of commercial traffic on the Red Sea and has 51 piers, giving an annual capacity of 17 million tons.

The government-owned Saudi Arabian Airlines (Saudia) operate scheduled services to 22 domestic airports. There are international airports at Dhahran, Jeddah and Riyadh. Work on the new King Fahd International Airport in Eastern Province has yet to be completed. Saudia have an extensive overseas operation, and a large number of international airlines operate into the country. Telecommunications are being rapidly expanded.

## EDUCATION

With the exception of a few schools for expatriate children, all schools are government-supervised and segregated for boys and girls. There are universities in Jeddah, Mecca, Riyadh (branches in Abha and Qassim), Dammam (branch at Hofuf) and Dhahran, and there are Islamic universities in Medina and Riyadh. There is great emphasis on vocational training, provided at 24 literacy and artisan skill training centres and 21 more advanced industrial, commercial and agricultural education institutes. Education in government-owned institutes is free at all levels.

# SENEGAL
*République du Sénégal*

Senegal lies on the west coast of Africa between Mauritania in the north, Mali in the east, and Guinea-Bissau and Guinea in the south. It entirely surrounds the Gambia, except for its sea-coast. Senegal has an area of 75,750 sq. miles (196,192 sq. km), and a population (UN estimate 1991) of 7,533,000.

CAPITAL – Ψ Dakar (1,000,000).
CURRENCY – Franc CFA of 100 centimes.
FLAG – Three vertical bands, green, yellow and red; a green star on the yellow band.
NATIONAL DAY – 4 April.

## GOVERNMENT

Formerly a French colony, Senegal elected in 1958 to remain within the French Community as an autonomous republic. It became independent as part of the Federation of Mali in June 1960 and seceded to form the Republic of Senegal in September 1960. A border dispute with Mauritania was defused in early 1992 when the border was reopened and diplomatic relations restored. There is an insurgent separatist movement (Movement of Democratic Forces of Casamance (MFDC)) in the southern Casamance region. A ceasefire between the government and MFDC was signed in July 1993 but a political agreement has still to be reached.

In 1963 a new constitution was approved giving executive powers to the President. There are 16 officially recognized political parties. A general election for the National Assembly of 120 seats (70 elected by proportional representation and 50 on a majority basis) is held every five years.

President Diouf was re-elected in the first round of presidential elections in February 1993 with 58.4 per cent of the vote. The legislative election in May 1993 was won by the ruling Parti Socialiste (PS), which secured 84 seats, with the Parti Démocratique Sénégalais winning 27 seats, and other parties nine seats.

HEAD OF STATE
*President*, Abdou Diouf, *installed* 1981, *re-elected* 1988, 21 February 1993

GOVERNMENT *as at August 1994*

*Prime Minister*, Habib Thiam
*Minister of State*, Moustapha Niasse (*Foreign Affairs and Expatriates*); Robert Sagna (*Agriculture*); Ousmane Dieng (*Presidency*); Djibo Ka (*Interior*)
*Justice*, Jacques Baudin
*Armed Forces*, Madieng Dieng
*Economy, Finance and Planning*, Papa Sakho
*Environment and Protection of Nature*, Abdoulaye Bathily
*Urban Planning and Housing*, Amath Dansokho
*National Education*, André Sonko

Energy, Mines and Industry, Alasane N'Diaye
Modernization and Technology, Magued Diouf
Communications, Abdoulaye Kane
Culture, Coura Ba Thiam
Health and Social Welfare, Assane Diop
Employment, Labour and Professional Training, Serigne Diop
Commerce and Handicrafts, Cheikh Kane
Women, Children and Family Welfare, Ndioro N'Diaye
Equipment and Land Transport, Landing Sone
Youth and Sports, Ousmane Paye
Fisheries and Sea Transport, Abdourahmane Sow
Tourism and Air Transport, Tidiane Sylla
Water Resources, Mamadou Faye
Towns, Daour Cisse

EMBASSY OF THE REPUBLIC OF SENEGAL
11 Phillimore Gardens, London W8 7QG
Tel 0171–937 0925/6

Ambassador Extraordinary and Plenipotentiary, His
Excellency Gabriel Alexandre Sar, apptd 1993

BRITISH EMBASSY
BP 6025, Dakar
Tel: Dakar 237392

Ambassador Extraordinary and Plenipotentiary, His
Excellency Alan Furness, CMG, apptd 1993

BRITISH COUNCIL REPRESENTATIVE, Donald Munro,
34–36 Blvd. de la Republique, Immeuble Sonatel, BP
6232, Dakar

TRADE

Senegal's principal exports are groundnuts (raw and processed) and phosphates. Tourism is also of growing
importance as a revenue earner.

| Trade with UK | 1992 | 1993 |
|---|---|---|
| Imports from UK | £13,345,000 | £14,615,000 |
| Exports to UK | 3,519,000 | 4,012,000 |

---

# SEYCHELLES
The Republic of Seychelles

---

Seychelles, in the Indian Ocean, consists of 115 islands with a
total land area of 176 sq. miles (456 sq. km), spread over
400,000 sq. miles of ocean. There is a relatively compact
granitic group, 32 islands in all, with high hills and mountains
(highest point about 2,972 ft), of which Mahé is the largest
and most populated (90 per cent of the population live on
Mahé); and the outlying coralline group, for the most part
only a little above sea-level. Although only 4° S. of the
Equator, the climate is pleasant though tropical.
POPULATION – The population is 68,000 (1991 UN
estimate).

CAPITAL – ΨVictoria (population, 1987, 24,324), on Mahé.
CURRENCY – Seychelles rupee (Rs) of 100 cents.
FLAG – Red over green, divided by wavy white band.
NATIONAL ANTHEM – Fyer Seselwa (Proud Seychellois).
NATIONAL DAY – 5 June.

GOVERNMENT

Proclaimed French territory in 1756, the Mahé group was
settled as a dependency of Mauritius from 1770, was captured
by a British ship in 1794, and changed hands several times
between 1803 and 1814, when it was finally assigned to Great

Britain. In 1903 these islands, together with the coralline
group, were formed into a separate colony. On 29 June 1976,
the islands became an independent republic within the
Commonwealth. A coup d'état took place in 1977. Seychelles
was a one-party state from 1979 until 1991, when a multiparty
democratic system was proposed by the President. A new
constitution was adopted in a referendum in June 1993.
Under the new constitution multiparty politics was institutionalized, a National Assembly of 33 members (22 elected
by constituencies, 11 by proportional representation) was
established and the presidential mandate was set at five
years, renewable three times. In presidential and legislative
elections held in July 1993, President René was re-elected
and the Seychelles People's Progressive Front formed a
government after winning 27 of the National Assembly seats,
to the Democratic Party's five.

HEAD OF STATE
President, France Albert René, assumed office 5 June 1977;
elected 1979; re-elected 1984, 1989, 27 July 1993

COUNCIL OF MINISTERS as at August 1994
Finance, Communications and Defence, James Michel
Administration and Manpower, Joseph Belmont
Industry, Esme Jumeau
Environment, Economic Planning and Foreign Affairs,
    Danielle de St Jorre
Health, Ralph Adam
Agriculture and Fisheries, Jacquelin Dugasse
Employment and Social Affairs, William Herminie
Tourism and Transport, Simone Testa
Local Government, Youth and Sports, Sylvette Frichot
Education and Culture, Patrick Pillay
Community Development, Dolor Ernesta

SEYCHELLES HIGH COMMISSION
Box No. 4PE, 2nd Floor, Eros House, 111 Baker Street,
London WIM 1FE
Tel 0171-224 1660

High Commissioner, His Excellency John P. Mascarenhas,
apptd 1993

BRITISH HIGH COMMISSION
Victoria House, PO Box 161 Victoria, Mahé
Tel: Victoria 225225

High Commissioner, His Excellency John Sharland, apptd
1991

ECONOMY

The economy is based on tourism, fishing, small-scale
agriculture and manufacturing, and the re-export of fuel for
aircraft and ships. Deep sea tuna fishing by foreign fleets
under licence, improved trans-shipment and other port
facilities at Victoria, exports from a tuna canning factory and
the export of fresh and frozen fish, attract growing revenues.

TRADE
The principal imports are foodstuffs, beverages, tobacco,
mineral fuels, manufactured items, building materials,
machinery and transport equipment.

| | 1989 | 1990 |
|---|---|---|
| Imports | Rs.925,771,000 | Rs.991,500,000 |
| Exports | 67,789,000 | 73,200,000 |
| Re-exports | 109,407,000 | 131,200,000 |

| Trade with UK | 1992 | 1993 |
|---|---|---|
| Imports from UK | £12,352,000 | £17,821,000 |
| Exports to UK | 2,891,000 | 6,598,000 |

# SIERRA LEONE
## The Republic of Sierra Leone

Sierra Leone, with a total land area of 27,699 sq. miles (71,740 sq. km), is on the west coast of Africa, between Guinea and Liberia.

POPULATION – 1991 UN estimate, 4,260,000. The south is inhabited by peoples whose languages fall into the Mende group; the north by the Temne and smaller groups such as the Limba, Loko, Koranko and Susu.

CAPITAL – ΨFreetown (population, 1985 census, 470,000).
CURRENCY – Leone (Le) of 100 cents.
FLAG – Three horizontal stripes of leaf green, white and cobalt blue.
NATIONAL ANTHEM – High We Exalt Thee, Realm of the Free.
NATIONAL DAY – 27 April (Independence Day).

## GOVERNMENT

In the late 18th century a project was begun to settle destitute Africans from England on Freetown peninsula. In 1808 the settlement was declared a Crown colony and became the main base in West Africa for enforcing the 1807 Act outlawing the slave trade. The colony was also used as a settlement for Africans from North America and the West Indies, and Africans rescued from slave ships also settled there. In 1896 a Protectorate was declared over the hinterland.

In 1951 a new constitution was set up that united the colony of Freetown and the Protectorate and on 27 April 1961 Sierra Leone became a fully independent state within the Commonwealth. In 1971 a republican constitution was adopted and Dr Siaka Stevens became the first Executive President. In 1978 Sierra Leone became a one-party state, following approval by Parliament and a referendum. In September 1991 a new multiparty constitution was adopted and an interim government formed until a general election could be held. This government was overthrown because of alleged corruption by a coup on 29 April 1992. Captain Valentine Strasser became head of state, the House of Representatives was dissolved and all political activity was suspended. A cabinet was appointed to govern the country until promised multiparty elections. In July 1992 Strasser abolished the cabinet and appointed a Council of State Secretaries to co-ordinate the day-to-day running of government. This is subordinate to a military Supreme Council of State (SCS). The military government has announced a timetable to put an elected civilian government in power by the end of 1995.

### HEAD OF STATE
*President, Chairman of the SCS, Minister of Defence*, Capt. Valentine Strasser, *sworn in* 3 May 1992

### SUPREME COUNCIL OF STATE *as at August 1994*
*Chairman*, Capt. Valentine Strasser
*Vice-Chairman*, Lt. Julius Bio
*Labour, Energy, Power, Trade and Industry, State Enterprises, Lands, Housing and Environment*, Lt. Samuel Kambo
*Transport, Communications, Tourism, Mines and Works*, Lt. Charles M'Bayo

### COUNCIL OF STATE SECRETARIES *as at August 1994*
*Chief Secretary of State*, Lt. Julius Bio
*Youth, Sports and Social Mobilization*, Lt. Charles M'Bayo
*Chairman's Office*, Col. (retd) S. B. Jumu
*Finance, Development and Economic Planning*, Dr John Karimu

*Foreign Affairs*, Lt. Kargbo Karifa
*Transport and Communications*, Arnold Bishop-Gooding
*Agriculture and Forestry*, Lt.-Col. A. K. Sesay
*Mineral Resources*, Capt. Reginald Glover
*Trade, Industry and State Enterprises*, Dr Alusine Fofana
*Works*, Lt.-Col. J. P. Gbondo
*Information, Broadcasting and Culture*, Hindolo Trye
*Labour, Energy and Power*, Ales Browne
*Education*, Bassie Bangura
*Justice*, Franklyn Kargbo
*Health and Social Services*, Lt.-Col. A. A. Gibril
*Lands, Housing and Environment*, Lt.-Col. S. F. Koroma
*Interior and Rural Development*, Col. (retd) A. Kamara
*Tourism*, Maj. (retd) Gabriel Turay
*Eastern Region*, Lt. S. Nyuma
*Northern Region*, Maj. Fallah Sewah
*Southern Region*, Lt. Idris Kamara

SIERRA LEONE HIGH COMMISSION
33 Portland Place, London WIN 3AG
Tel 0171-636 6483/4/5/6

*High Commissioner*, His Excellency Prof. Cyril Foray, apptd 1993

BRITISH HIGH COMMISSION
Standard Bank of Sierra Leone Building, Lightfoot Boston Street, Freetown
Tel: Freetown 223961-5

*High Commissioner*, His Excellency Ian McCluney, CMG, apptd 1993

BRITISH COUNCIL REPRESENTATIVE, Peter Hilken, PO Box 124, Tower Hill, Freetown

## ECONOMY

The military government has cracked down on corruption, liberalized the foreign exchange system and reduced inflation from 120 per cent to 25 per cent. The government's economic and financial reform programme for 1994–6 has been approved by the IMF, which has provided a credit of US$163 million to support it.

On the Freetown peninsula, farming is largely confined to the production of cassava and crops such as maize and vegetables for local consumption. In the hinterland the principal agricultural product is rice, which is the staple food of the country, and cash crops such as cocoa, coffee, palm kernels and ginger.

The economy depends largely on mineral exports; mainly diamonds, gold, bauxite and rutile. Diamond exports provided Le1,254.5m in 1989. Total imports for 1989 were to the value of Le10,901.8m and exports were Le8,269.5m.

| Trade with UK | 1992 | 1993 |
| --- | --- | --- |
| Imports from UK | £15,450,000 | £20,169,000 |
| Exports to UK | 9,424,000 | 16,219,000 |

## COMMUNICATIONS

Since the phasing out of the railway system in 1974 the road network has been developed considerably and there are now 5,000 miles of roads in the country, over 2,000 miles being surfaced. A bridge has been constructed over the Mano River linking Sierra Leone and Liberia.

The Freetown international airport is situated at Lungi. The main port is Freetown, which has one of the largest natural harbours in the world, and where there is a deep water quay. There are smaller ports at Pepel, Bonthe and Niti.

Radio is operated by the government. Broadcasts are made in several of the indigenous languages, in addition to English and French.

## EDUCATION

In 1989 there were 2,554 primary schools in Sierra Leone and 201 secondary schools. Technical education is provided in the two government technical institutes, situated in Freetown and Kenema, in two trade centres and in the technical training establishments of the mining companies. Teacher training is carried out at the University of Sierra Leone, six colleges in the provinces and in the Milton Margai Training College near Freetown.

---

## SINGAPORE

---

Singapore consists of the island of Singapore and 59 islets, covering a total area of 244 sq. miles (639 sq. km). Singapore island is 26 miles long and 14 miles in breadth and is situated just north of the Equator off the southern extremity of the Malay peninsula, from which it is separated by the Straits of Johore. A causeway crosses the three-quarters of a mile to the mainland. The climate is hot and humid. Rainfall averages 240 cm a year and temperature ranges from 24° to 32° C (76°–89° F).

POPULATION – In 1992 the population was 2,818,200, which comprised 2,187,200 (77.6 per cent) Chinese, 399,400 (14.2 per cent) Malays, 199,600 (7.1 per cent) Indians (including those of Pakistani, Bangladeshi and Sri Lankan origin) and 32,000 (1.1 per cent) from other ethnic groups. Malay, Mandarin, Tamil and English are the official languages. At least eight Chinese dialects are used.

CURRENCY – Singapore dollar (S$) of 100 cents.

FLAG – Horizontal bands of red over white; crescent with five five-point stars on red band near staff.

NATIONAL ANTHEM – Majulah Singapura.

NATIONAL DAY – 9 August.

## GOVERNMENT

Singapore, where Sir Stamford Raffles first established a trading post under the East India Company in 1819, was incorporated with Penang and Malacca to form the Straits Settlements in 1826. The Straits Settlements became a Crown colony in 1867. Singapore fell into Japanese hands in 1942 and civil government was not restored until 1946, when it became a separate colony. Internal self-government was introduced in 1959. Singapore became a state of Malaysia when the Federation was enlarged in September 1963, but left Malaysia and became an independent sovereign state within the Commonwealth on 9 August 1965. Singapore adopted a republican constitution from that date. There is a Cabinet collectively responsible to an 87-member (81 elected and six nominated by the President) Parliament. In November 1991 the constitution was amended to provide for a directly-elected President with enlarged powers and the ability to veto government decisions in certain instances relating to the budget, financial reserves and the appointment of senior civil servants. The President appoints the Prime Minister and, on his advice, the members of the Cabinet.

After the general election of 31 August 1991 the People's Action Party (PAP) had 77 seats in Parliament. The Singapore Democratic Party (SDP) won three seats and the Workers' Party won one seat.

HEAD OF STATE
*President*, Ong Teng Cheong, *elected* 28 August 1993

CABINET *as at August 1994*
*Prime Minister*, Goh Chok Tong
*Senior Minister, PM's Office*, Lee Kuan Yew, GCMG, CH
*Deputy PM, Foreign, Trade, Defence*, Lee Hsien Loong
*Trade and Industry*, Yeo Cheow Tong
*Education*, Lee Yock Suan
*Environment and Communications*, Mah Bow Tan
*Law and Foreign Affairs*, Prof. S. Jayakumar
*Finance*, Dr Richard Hu Tsu Tau
*Labour*, Lee Boon Yang
*Muslim Affairs and Community Development*, Abdullah Tarmugi
*Health, Information and The Arts*, George Yeo
*Home Affairs*, Wong Kan Seng
*National Development*, Lim Hng Kiang
*Without Portfolio*, Lim Boon Heng

HIGH COMMISSION FOR THE REPUBLIC OF SINGAPORE
9 Wilton Crescent, London SW1X 8SA
Tel 0171-235 8315

*High Commissioner*, His Excellency Abdul Aziz Mahmood, apptd 1988
*Counsellor (Defence Procurement)*, Col. Hung Khiang Puah
*First Secretary*, Miss J. Kang *(Commercial)*

BRITISH HIGH COMMISSION
Tanglin Road, Singapore 1024
Tel: Singapore 4739333

*High Commissioner*, His Excellency Gordon Duggan, apptd 1990
*Deputy High Commissioner and Counsellor (Economic/Commercial)*, P. W. Ford
*Defence Adviser*, Gp Capt P. G. Wildman

BRITISH COUNCIL REPRESENTATIVE, J. Davies, 30 Napier Road, Singapore 1025

## ECONOMY

Historically Singapore's economy was based on the sale and distribution of raw materials from surrounding countries and on entrepot trade in finished products. However, manufacturing industries have been established, including ship building and repairing, iron and steel, textiles, footwear, wood products, micro-electronics, televisions, computers, office machinery, audio equipment, scientific instruments, detergents, confectionery, pharmaceuticals, petroleum products, etc. Singapore has also become a financial centre with 131 commercial banks and 75 merchant banks and an oil-refining centre.

| FINANCE (estimates) | 1991 | 1992 |
| --- | --- | --- |
| Revenue | S$19,570m | S$17,219m |
| Expenditure | 13,860m | 12,270m |

| TRADE | 1991 | 1992 |
| --- | --- | --- |
| Total imports | S$114,000m | S$117,529m |
| Total exports | 102,000m | 103,351m |

| Trade with UK | 1992 | 1993 |
| --- | --- | --- |
| Imports from UK | £1,145,058,000 | £1,429,660,000 |
| Exports to UK | 1,192,803,000 | 1,615,210,000 |

## COMMUNICATIONS

Singapore is one of the largest and busiest seaports in the world, with deep water wharves and ship repairing facilities. Ships also anchor in the roads, unloading into lighters. In 1992, the total volume of cargo handled was 238,500,000 tonnes. More than 600 shipping lines use the port, with 81,000 ship arrivals in 1992.

The international airport is at Changi, in the east of the island, with Singapore Airlines operating flights to 40 countries. There are 67 km of metric gauge railway connected to the Malaysian rail system by the causeway across the Straits of Johore, and 2,976 km of roads.

There are nine radio and three television channels operated by the Singapore Broadcasting Corporation in the four official languages, and three private broadcasting stations.

---

## SLOVAKIA
*Slovenská Republika - The Republic of Slovakia*

---

Slovakia has an area of 18,940 sq. miles (49,035 sq. km). It is situated in central Europe and is bordered to the north by Poland, to the east by the Ukraine, to the south by Hungary, to the south-west by Austria and to the west by the Czech Republic. The Tatry (Tatras) mountains in the centre and north of the country reach heights of 2,600 m (8,530 ft). The major river is the Váh which flows from the Tatry mountains to join the Danube at the Hungarian border. The climate is continental.

POPULATION – The population (1991) is 5,274,335, of which 85.7 per cent are ethnic Slovaks, 10.8 per cent ethnic Hungarians, 1.4 per cent Gypsy, 1.1 per cent Czech, with smaller numbers of Ruthenians, Ukrainians and Germans. The population is mainly Christian, some 60 per cent Roman Catholic and 6 per cent Protestant.

The main languages are Slovak (85.7 per cent), Hungarian (10.8 per cent), Czech (1.1 per cent). Slovak is the official language but the law safeguards the right to use minority languages in dealing with public authorities in areas where the minority forms 20 per cent or more of the population.

CAPITAL – Bratislava, on the Danube, population (1991) 440,421. Other major cities are: Košice (238,454); Žilina (97,537); Prešov (89,000); Banská Bystríca (78,321).

CURRENCY – Slovak Koruna (SK) (Crown).

FLAG – Three horizontal stripes of white, blue, red with the arms all over near the hoist.

NATIONAL ANTHEM – Nad Tatrou sa blýska (Storm over the Tatras).

NATIONAL DAYS – 8 May (Liberation from fascism); 5 July (Day of the Slav Missionaries); 29 August (Slovak National Uprising).

GOVERNMENT   *(see also Czech Republic)*

At the end of the 11th century Slovakia became part of the Hungarian state when the Magyars gained control of the area. After the Hungarians were defeated at the battle of Moháč in 1526, most of Hungary (including part of Slovakia) was occupied by the Turks, with the remainder of Hungary and Slovakia being incorporated into the Austrian Empire. With the establishment of the Austro-Hungarian monarchy in 1867, Slovakia again came under Hungarian control. The attempted Magyarization of Slovakia gave impetus to the national revival which had begun in 1848–9, and when the First World War came many Slovaks fought with the allies. Amalgamated into the republic of Czechoslovakia on 28 October 1918, Slovakia became independent in March 1939 as a Nazi puppet state when Germany invaded the Czech lands. Slovakia was liberated by Soviet forces in 1945 and returned to Czechoslovakia. The formation of a federal republic between the Czech lands and Slovakia was the only Prague Spring reform to survive the Soviet invasion of 1968. Following the collapse of Communist rule at federal and republic level in 1989, nationalist feeling grew even stronger

and the Czech and Slovak republics began to negotiate the dissolution of the federation into two sovereign states in 1992. Dissolution took effect on 1 January 1993.

The constitution vests legislative power in the National Council of 150 members elected for a four-year term. The President is elected for a five-year term by the National Council; executive power is held by the Prime Minister and Cabinet. Minority rights are enshrined in the constitution but discrimination is claimed by the ethnic Hungarian population.

A coalition government of the Movement for a Democratic Slovakia (HZDS) and Slovak National Party (SNS) was sworn in on 12 January 1993 but lost its majority in the National Council when the SNS left the government. Increasing criticism of the economic policy and authoritarian style of the HZDS government led ten HZDS members to break away and form a new party which, in alliance with three other parties, brought down the government by a parliamentary no-confidence vote in March 1994. The four-party coalition then formed a government which was approved by President Kovac on 16 March 1994. Legislative elections are planned for October 1994.

HEAD OF STATE
*President*, Michal Kovac, *elected* 15 February 1993

COUNCIL OF MINISTERS *as at August 1994*
*Prime Minister*, Jozef Moravčik (DEUS)
*Deputy Prime Ministers*, Roman Kovač (DEUS); Ivan Šimko (KDH) *(Legislation)*; Brigita Schmögnerová (SDL) *(Economy)*
*Foreign Affairs*, Eduard Kukan (Ind.)
*Economy*, Peter Magvaši (Ind.)
*Finance*, Rudolf Filkus (DEUS)
*Labour, Social Welfare and the Family*, Julius Brocka (KDH)
*Environment*, Juraj Hraško (SDL)
*Administration and Privatization*, Milan Janicina (NDS)
*Transport, Communications and Public Works*, Mikulaš Dzurínda (KDH)
*Agriculture*, Pavel Koncoš (SDL)
*Culture*, Lubomir Roman (Ind.)
*Education and Science*, Lubomir Harach (Ind.)
*Health*, Tibor Šagat (Ind.)
*Interior*, Ladislav Pittner (KDH)
*Justice*, Milan Hanzel (Ind.)
*Defence*, Pavol Kanis (SDL)

DEUS Democratic Union of Slovakia; SDL Party of the Democratic Left; KDH Christian Democratic Movement; NDS National Democratic Party; Ind. Independent

*Chairman, Slovak National Council*, Ivan Gašparovič.

EMBASSY OF THE SLOVAK REPUBLIC
25 Kensington Palace Gardens, London W8 4QY
Tel 0171-243 0803

*Ambassador Extraordinary and Plenipotentiary*, His Excellency Dr Jan Vilikovsky, apptd 1992

BRITISH EMBASSY 4th Floor, Grosslingova 35, 81109 Bratislava
Tel: Bratislava 364459
*Chargé d'Affaires*, Michael Bates

BRITISH COUNCIL DIRECTOR, Rosemary Hillhorst, PO Box 68, Panska 17, 81499 Bratislava

ECONOMY

From independence until mid-1994 Slovakia faced substantial economic difficulties because of the structure of its economy, reliant of state-subsidized heavy industries, and the ambivalent attitude to reform of the HZDS government. The HZDS faced increasing problems in 1993 as output, exports and foreign currency reserves fell and unemployment and inflation increased. In July 1993 the Slovak Crown was devalued by 10 per cent in return for an IMF loan of US$89 million. Privatization policies were continued, though at a slower rate than in the Czech Republic. Firms have been privatized by a voucher system, transfer, public auction, restoration to former owners, or transformation into joint-stock companies.

In mid-1994, however, the economic situation stabilized as the new government, more committed to reform, speeded up the privatization process and launched a second round of privatization. The budget has been brought into surplus, as has the trade balance, while the foreign debt is being reduced and foreign exchange reserves have increased significantly. Unemployment and inflation have been reduced and foreign investment is increasing and beginning to offset the loss of subsidies from the former Czechoslovak federation. Natural resources include brown coal, natural gas, iron ore, antimony, lead, zinc and magnesite.

| Trade with UK | 1993 |
|---|---|
| Imports from UK | £10,628,000 |
| Exports to UK | 2,392,000 |

# SLOVENIA
*Republike Slovenije*

Slovenia is a small mountainous state which was the most northerly of the former Yugoslav republics. It has an area of 7,819 sq. miles (20,251 sq. km) and is bordered on the north by Austria, on the north-east by Hungary, on the east and south by Croatia and on the west by Italy. The two major rivers are the Sava and the Drava. There is a short coastline in the south-west 25 miles (40 km) in length on the Adriatic. The climate is a mixture of Mediterranean, continental and alpine.

POPULATION – The population (1992) is 2,020,000 and is mostly Slovenian. There are small Hungarian (0.5 per cent) and Italian (0.1 per cent) minorities, together with a Romany population. Slovenia has also taken in 100,000–150,000 refugees from the former Yugoslavia.

The main religion is Roman Catholicism. Slovene is the official language, together with Hungarian and Italian in ethnically mixed regions.

CAPITAL – Ljubljana, population (1991) 268,000. Other major towns (1991) are: Maribor (105,400); Celje (42,000); Kranj (37,100) and ΨKoper (24,600), the only port.

CURRENCY – Slovene Tolar (SIT) of 100 stotin.

FLAG – Three horizontal stripes of white, blue, red, with the arms in the upper hoist.

NATIONAL ANTHEM – Zdravljica (A Toast).

NATIONAL DAY – 25 June (Independence Day).

## GOVERNMENT

The area that is now Slovenia came under the control of the Habsburg Empire in the 15th century and remained so until the defeat of the Austro-Hungarian Empire in 1918. On 27 October 1918 Slovenia became part of the state of Slovenes, Croats and Serbs (later Yugoslavia) and this was confirmed by the Versailles Treaty 1919. Slovenia was reduced in size, however, by the Italian annexation of the western third of the country and the Austrian annexation of parts of the north.

In 1941 Yugoslavia was invaded by German forces and Slovenia was divided between Germany, Italy and Hungary. Slovenia was reformed as a constituent republic of the federal Yugoslav state in May 1945. After a dispute with Italy and nine years of international administration, the Adriatic coast and hinterland were returned to Slovenia in 1954 and Italy retained Trieste.

Slovenian fears of Serbian dominance led the Slovene Assembly in 1989 to amend the republican constitution to lay the basis of a sovereign state. In a referendum in December 1990, 88 per cent of the electorate voted for independence, which was declared on 25 June 1991. A ten-day war with the Yugoslav National Army followed before the Army called off hostilities and withdrew.

A new constitution was adopted in December 1991. Executive power is vested in the Prime Minister and Cabinet of Ministers. Legislative authority is held by the bicameral National Assembly, composed of the 90-member State Chamber (lower house) and 40-member State Council (upper house). The State Chamber is elected on a proportional representation basis, with one seat each reserved for the Italian and Hungarian minorities. The State Council has 22 elected and 18 appointed members. Presidential and legislative elections were held on 6 December 1992, with incumbent President Milan Kučan being re-elected and the Liberal Democratic Party emerging as the largest party in parliament. A coalition government led by the Liberal Democrats was formed in January 1993.

HEAD OF STATE
*President,* Milan Kučan, *elected* April 1990, *re-elected for a five-year term* 6 December 1992

CABINET *as at August 1994*

*Prime Minister,* Janez Drnovšek (LDS)
*Deputy PM, Foreign Affairs,* Lojze Peterle (SKD)
*Finance,* Mitja Gaspari (LDS)
*Economy, Development,* Davorin Kračun (LDS)
*Education and Sports,* Slavko Gaber (LDS)
*Justice,* Miha Kozinc (LDS)
*Internal Affairs,* Andrej Šter (SKD)
*Transport and Communications,* Igor Umek (SKD)
*Agriculture and Forestry,* Jože Osterc (SKD)
*Health,* Božidar Voljč (ZS)
*Science and Technology,* Rado Bohinc (ZL)
*Labour, Family and Social Affairs,* Jožica Puhar (ZL)
*Culture,* Sergij Pelhan (ZL)
*Economic Activities,* Maks Tajnikar (ZL)
*Environment,* Dr Pavle Gantar (LDS)
*Defence,* Jelko Kacin (LDS)

LDS Liberal Democratic Party; SKD Slovenian Christian Democrats; ZL United List; ZS Greens.

EMBASSY OF SLOVENIA
11–15 Wigmore Street, London W1H 9LA
Tel 0171-495 7775

*Ambassador Extraordinary and Plenipotentiary,* His Excellency Matjaž Šinkovec, apptd 1992

BRITISH EMBASSY
4th Floor, Trg Republike 3, 61–000 Ljubljana
Tel: Ljubljana 157191

*Ambassador Extraordinary and Plenipotentiary,* His Excellency Gordon Johnston, apptd 1992

BRITISH COUNCIL REPRESENTATIVE – Roger Woodham, MBE, Stefanova I/III, 61000 Ljubljana

## ECONOMY

Although still with problems, Slovenia's economy has emerged as the most stable of the former Yugoslav economies and the least affected by the end of central planning. Although it has lost its captive export market and cheap supplies of raw materials from Serbia, the country is one of the richest of the former Communist countries. Small trade surpluses were recorded in 1992 and 1993, with foreign currency reserves of US$1.9 billion in early 1994 and foreign debt at US$1.7 billion. Inflation has been gradually reduced to around 20 per cent and the tolar is stable and convertible, while GDP grew in 1993 and early 1994.

In 1993 GDP was US$12,000 million of which agriculture, forestry and fishing produced 5 per cent. The main products are potatoes, wheat, corn, apples, wine, meat and milk. Mining and manufacturing produced 55 per cent of GDP, the major sectors being metal-working, electronics, textiles, chemicals, glass products, food-processing and iron ore mining. Tourism (worth US$750 million in 1993) and transport are major export earners, with 1,400,000 tourists visiting in 1991. Foreign investment is being attracted, with US$1,200 million invested by the end of 1993.

Important road and rail communications cross the country from west to east (Milan–Ljubljana–Budapest), and north to south (Munich–Ljubljana–Zagreb–Belgrade–Athens). There are international airports at Ljubljana, Maribor and Portoroz (Adriatic Coast). The port of Koper is an important shipment point for goods from Austria, Hungary and the Czech Republic.

| Trade with UK | 1993 |
|---|---|
| Imports from UK | £56,713,000 |
| Exports to UK | 53,344,000 |

## EDUCATION

Education is compulsory and free between the ages of seven and 19. There are 842 primary schools (age seven–15), 149 secondary or middle schools (age 15–19), 26 colleges and two universities (Ljubljana and Maribor).

---

# SOLOMON ISLANDS

---

Forming a scattered archipelago of mountainous islands and low-lying coral atolls, the Solomon Islands stretches about 900 miles in a south-easterly direction from the Shortland Islands to the Santa Cruz islands. The archipelago covers an area of about 249,000 sq. miles, with a land area of 10,938 sq. miles (28,446 sq. km), between 155° 30′ and 170° 30′E. longitude and 5° 10′ and 12° 45′S. latitude. The six biggest islands are Choiseul, New Georgia, Santa Isabel, Guadalcanal, Malaita and Makira. They are characterized by thickly-forested mountain ranges intersected by deep, narrow valleys.

POPULATION – The total population was 328,723 at the 1991 census. English is the official language; there are over 80 local languages.

CAPITAL – ΨHoniara, population (1991) 40,000.
CURRENCY – Solomon Islands dollar (SI$) of 100 cents.
FLAG – Blue over green divided by a diagonal yellow band, with five white stars in the top left quarter.
NATIONAL ANTHEM – God Bless our Solomon Islands.
NATIONAL DAY – 7 July (Independence Day).

## GOVERNMENT

The origin of the present Melanesian inhabitants is uncertain. European discovery of the islands began in the mid-16th century and continued intermittently for about 300 years, when the inauguration of sugar plantations in Queensland and Fiji (which created a need for labour) and the arrival of missionaries and traders led to increased European interest in the region. Great Britain declared a Protectorate in 1893 over the Southern Solomons, adding the Santa Cruz group in 1898 and 1899. The islands of the Shortland groups were transferred from Germany to Great Britain by treaty in 1900.

The Solomon Islands achieved internal self-government in 1976, and became independent in July 1978. The Solomon Islands is a constitutional monarchy, The Queen being represented locally by the Governor-General. Legislative power is vested in a unicameral National Parliament of 47 members, elected for a four-year term. Executive authority is exercised by the Cabinet. A four-party National Coalition government took power after winning 24 of the 47 seats in the legislative election of 26 May 1993.

*Governor-General*, His Excellency Moses Pitakaka, apptd 1994

CABINET *as at August 1994*

*Prime Minister*, Hon. Francis Billy Hilly
*Deputy Prime Minister, Foreign Affairs*, Hon. Francis Saemala
*Agriculture and Fisheries*, Hon. Edmond Adresen
*Commerce, Employment and Trade*, Hon. Revd Michael Maeliau
*Development Planning*, Hon. George Kejoa
*Culture, Sports and Tourism*, Hon. Michael Maena
*Education and Training*, Rt. Hon. Ezekiel Alebua
*Finance*, Hon. Andrew Nori
*Health and Medical Services*, Hon. Nathaniel Waena
*Home Affairs*, Hon. Alpha Kimata
*Justice*, Hon. Jackson Piasi
*Provincial Government and Rural Development*, Hon. Oliver Zapo
*Post and Communication*, Hon. John Masuota
*Transport, Works and Utilities*, Hon. Edward Hunuehu
*Lands and Housing*, Hon. Francis Orodani
*Forestry, Environment and Conservation*, Hon. Joses Tuhanuku
*Energy, Minerals and Mines*, Hon. Hilda Kari
*Sports, Youth and Women*, Hon. Alfred Maetia

HIGH COMMISSION OF THE SOLOMON ISLANDS
Boulevard St Michel 101, 1040 Brussels
Tel: Brussels 2732 7085

*High Commissioner*, His Excellency Lindsay F. Misros, apptd 1993

HONORARY CONSULATE
19 Springfield Road, London SW19 7AL
Tel 0181-946 5552

*Honorary Consul*, new appointment awaited

BRITISH HIGH COMMISSION
Soltel House, Mendana Avenue (PO Box 676), Honiara
Tel: Honiara 21705/6

*High Commissioner*, His Excellency Raymond F. Jones, OBE, apptd 1991

## COMMUNICATIONS

Solomon Airlines operates international services to other Pacific states and Australia. Air Niugini flies from Port

Moresby to Honiara. There are about 52 miles of secondary and minor roads in the urban areas of Honiara, Auki and Gizo. In the rural areas there are some 800 miles of road, including those in private plantations, forestry areas and roads built and maintained by councils. Telekom, a company jointly owned by Cable and Wireless and the Solomon Islands government, operates the international and domestic telephone circuits from a ground station in Honiara via the Intelsat Pacific Ocean communication satellite.

## TRADE

The main imports are foodstuffs, consumer goods, machinery and transport materials. Principal exports are timber, fish, copra, and palm oil. Fisheries exports for 1992 totalled SI$88.1m, timber SI$110.4m and copra SI$22.7m. Other exports include cocoa and marine shells.

| Trade with UK | 1992 | 1993 |
|---|---|---|
| Imports from UK | £606,000 | £1,681,000 |
| Exports to UK | 5,691,000 | 2,339,000 |

# SOMALIA
*Jamhuuriyadda Diimoqraadiga ee Soomaaliya*

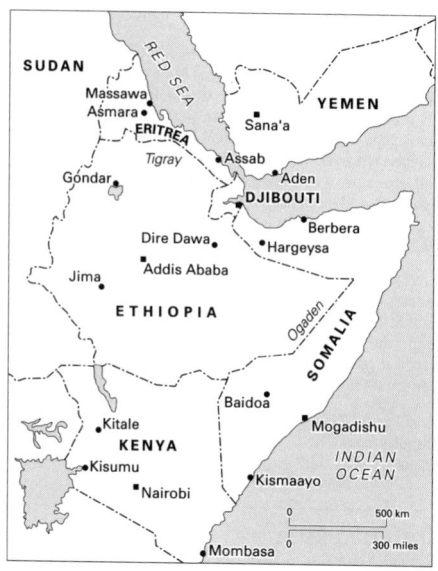

Somalia occupies part of the north-east horn of Africa, with a coastline on the Indian Ocean extending from the boundary with Kenya (2° S. latitude) to Cape Guardafui (12° N.), and on the Gulf of Aden to the boundary with Djibouti. Somalia is bounded on the west by Djibouti, Ethiopia and Kenya and covers an area of about 246,201 sq. miles (637,657 sq. km). The population, of which a large proportion is nomadic, is 7,691,000 (UN estimate 1991).

CAPITAL – Ψ Mogadishu, population (estimated 1987), 1,000,000. Other towns are Hargeisa (20,000), Boroma (65,000), ΨKisimayu (60,000), ΨBerbera (15,000) and Burao (15,000).

CURRENCY – Somali shilling of 100 cents.

FLAG – Five-pointed white star on blue ground.

NATIONAL DAY – under review.

## GOVERNMENT

British rule in Somaliland lasted from 1887 until 1960, except for a short period in 1940–1 when the Protectorate was occupied by Italian forces. Somalia, formerly an Italian colony, was occupied by British forces in 1941. In 1950 it was placed under Italian administration by a resolution of the UN; this trusteeship lasted until the British protectorate and the trust territory became independent as the Somali Democratic Republic on 1 July 1960. In 1969, the armed forces took over the government and a Revolutionary Council under Siad Barre assumed control of the country.

Siad Barre was overthrown in January 1991 by rebel movements. One group, the United Somali Congress, took control in Mogadishu and formed an interim administration in February 1991 with the USC leader, Ali Mahdi Mohammed, as president. However, the USC government failed to establish its authority over the other, clan-based movements, the Somali Salvation Democratic Front (SSDF), the Somali Patriotic Movement (SPM) and the Somali Democratic Movement (SDM). In the north of the country, the Somali National Movement (SNM) refused to participate in negotiations and formed a government under SNM leader Abourahman Ahmed Ali.

Fighting erupted in the summer of 1991 between supporters of Ali Mahdi Mohammed and supporters of the Somali National Alliance (SNA) of Gen. Mohammed Aideed. The fighting degenerated into civil war in 1991, devastating Mogadishu and large parts of the south of the country. The UN intervened in April 1992 with food aid to prevent starvation. In August 1992 the UN Security Council approved the dispatch of the UN Operation in Somalia (UNOSOM) force to protect relief convoys, while the USA initiated an emergency food airlift. However, the UN force proved ineffective in securing aid distribution routes from the armed factions. On 9 December 1992, with UN authority, a US-led United Task Force (UNITAF) launched a military intervention to create a safe environment for the delivery of aid. Distribution routes were secured by the end of December and UNITAF turned its attention to confiscating and destroying the weapons of the armed factions, which provoked clashes with armed gunmen in the Mogadishu area in early 1993.

On 4 May 1993 UNITAF handed over to a 28,000 strong UN force (UNOSOM II) mandated to maintain a secure environment and promote political reconciliation. Heavy fighting between Gen. Aideed's SNA forces and UN troops attempting to destroy the SNA's weapons, arrest Aideed and broker a political settlement took place between June and November 1993, and left 90 UN troops and 2,000 Somalis dead. From November onwards the UN has focused its efforts on political reconciliation between the various Somali factions, but this has remained elusive despite a March 1994 ceasefire agreement between Gen. Aideed and Ali Mahdi Mohammed. With the withdrawal of US and other western troops from the UN operation in March 1994, the remaining UN troops of around 20,000 are composed mainly of troops from India, Pakistan and Egypt. The Somali factions have taken advantage of this; fighting has broken out again and attacks on UN troops have increased. Political authority remains in the hands of clan leaders; there is no national government. About 350,000 are believed to have died from starvation or in the fighting.

SOMALI DIPLOMATIC REPRESENTATION, The Embassy closed in January 1992.

BRITISH DIPLOMATIC REPRESENTATION, The British Embassy in Mogadishu closed in January 1991.

## SECESSION

Civil war broke out in May 1988 between the government and the opposition Somali National Movement (SNM) in the north of the country. With the downfall of Siad Barre, the SNM took control of the north-west (the former British Somaliland Protectorate) and in May 1991 declared unilateral independence as the 'Somaliland Republic'. A government and legislature was formed which elected Mohamed Ibrahim Egal as President in May 1993.

## ECONOMY

Livestock raising is the main occupation and there is a modest export trade in livestock, skins and hides. Italy, the Gulf States and Saudi Arabia import the bulk of the banana crop, the second biggest export. Due to UN aid and pacification of the countryside, the havest improved from 10 per cent of normal in 1992 to 50 per cent in 1993.

| Trade with UK | 1992 | 1993 |
|---|---|---|
| Imports from UK | £3,436,000 | £3,540,000 |
| Exports to UK | 118,000 | 246,000 |

## SOUTH AFRICA
*Republiek van Suid-Afrika*

South Africa occupies the southernmost part of the African continent from the courses of the Limpopo, Marico, Molopo, Nosop and Orange Rivers (34° 50′ 22″ S.) to the Cape of Good Hope, with the exception of Lesotho, Swaziland and the extreme south of Mozambique. It has a total area of 471,445 sq. miles (1,221,031 sq. km) and borders on Namibia in the north-west, Botswana and Zimbabwe in the north, Mozambique and Swaziland in the north-east, and Lesotho, which it completely surrounds. To the west, east and south lie the south Atlantic and southern Indian Oceans. Some 1,192 miles (1,920 km) to the south-east of Capetown lie Prince Edward and Marion Islands, part of South Africa since 1947.

Ranges of hills run parallel to the coast along much of the southern and eastern coastline, rising in steps towards the interior. Most of the ranges are of no great height, the exception being the Drakensberg (11,000 ft) running south-west to north-east in the east of the country. Between the ranges of hills and in the interior in the north-east are plateaux, such as the Great Karoo in the south. In the north and centre are grassy plains with occasional hills or kopjes. The Orange, with its tributary the Vaal, is the principal river, rising in the Drakensberg and flowing into the Atlantic near the border with Namibia. The Limpopo, or Crocodile River, in the north, rises in the Transvaal and flows into the Indian Ocean through Mozambique. Most of the remaining rivers are furious torrents after rain, with partially dry beds at other seasons.

The climate is subtropical, dry and sunny moderated by the warm temperate winds from the Atlantic and Indian Oceans. Moist hot air masses from the Indian Ocean are the chief source of rainfall for most of the country.

POPULATION – The official population estimate for 1993, excluding Bophuthatswana, Ciskei, Transkei and Venda, was 32,589,000, comprising 23,016,000 Blacks, 5,149,000 Whites, 3,402,000 Coloureds, and 1,022,000 Asians. The population of the four homelands (now reincorporated into South Africa) was 7,460,000, which was overwhelmingly black, giving a total estimated population of 40,049,000.

LANGUAGE – The interim constitution designates 11 official languages: Afrikaans; English; Ndebele; Sesotho sa Leboa;

Sesotho; Si Swati (Swazi); Tsonga; Tswana; Venda; Xhosa; Zulu. Afrikaans and English are to remain the languages of record although any citizen may correspond official business in his own language. Afrikaans is descended from old Dutch and is the language of the Afrikaner and Coloured populations.

CAPITAL – The administrative seat of the government is Pretoria, PWV; population (1985 estimate) 822,925; the seat of the legislature is ΨCape Town, Western Cape, population (1985) 1,911,521; the seat of the judiciary is Bloemfontein, Orange Free State (232,984).
Other large towns (1985 figures) are Johannesburg, PWV (1,609,408); Ψ Durban, Kwazulu/Natal, the largest seaport (634,301); Ψ Port Elizabeth, Eastern Cape (651,993); Ψ East London, Eastern Cape (167,992); and Pietermaritzburg, Kwazulu Natal (192,417).

CURRENCY – Rand (R) of 100 cents.

FLAG – Divided red over blue by a horizontal white-fimbriated green Y; in the hoist a black triangle fimbriated in yellow.

NATIONAL ANTHEMS – Die Stem Van Suid-Afrika (The Call of South Africa); Nkosi Sikelel'i Afrika (God Bless Africa).

NATIONAL DAY – 31 May.

## HISTORY

The colony of the Cape of Good Hope was founded by the Dutch at Cape Town in 1652 and remained a Dutch colony until Britain took possession of it in 1795. Restored to Dutch rule in 1803, it was again taken by Britain in 1806 and this was confirmed by the London Convention of 1814. Increasing Anglicization of the colony led to the movement of a large proportion of the descendants of Dutch settlers (known as Boers) north-eastwards in the years following 1834. This 'Great Trek' led to the foundation of the Orange Free State and Transvaal republics by the Boers, which were recognized by Britain in 1853–4. Natal was annexed to Cape Colony and the British in 1844 and then formed as a separate colony in 1856, to which Zululand was added in 1897 after the British victory in the Zulu wars. Transvaal and the Orange Free State (renamed the Orange River Colony) became British colonies after the Boer defeat in the Second Boer War 1899–1902. The self-governing colonies of the Cape of Good Hope, Natal, the Transvaal and the Orange River Colony became united in 1910 under the name of the Union of South Africa. Independence within the Commonwealth was gained in 1931 under the Statute of Westminster. South Africa left the Commonwealth and became a republic on 31 May 1961, largely as a result of international condemnation of apartheid and of the Sharpeville massacre.

From 1948, when the Afrikaner National Party came to power, South Africa's social and political structure was based on apartheid, a policy of racial segregation. Opposition protests culminated in the Sharpeville massacre in 1960; the African National Congress and other opposition groups were subsequently banned. A new wave of opposition climaxed in 1976 with uprisings in Soweto, in which hundreds were shot dead. In 1984 renewed rioting in the black townships and continuing unrest led to the declaration of a state of emergency in July 1985 in 36 districts, and nationwide from 12 June 1986; it was renewed annually until 1990.

As part of its policy of apartheid, the government established a number of black 'homelands'. Six areas (Gazankulu, Lebowa, KwaNdbele, KaNgwane, Qwaqwa and KwaZulu) were designated as self-governing states. A further four (Bophuthatswana, Ciskei, Transkei and Venda) were regarded as independent republics by the South African government but never recognized as such by the UN.

## MOVES TO DEMOCRACY

The first moves to reform apartheid came into effect in September 1984, when a new constitution extended the franchise to the Coloured and Indian populations. Coloured and Indians elected members to a three-house parliament, Coloured and Indian houses being added to the existing white chamber. However, whites retained effective political power and blacks remained excluded.

In September 1989, F. W. de Klerk became President of South Africa and accelerated the process of reform. In February 1990, the ban on the ANC and restrictions on other anti-apartheid groups were lifted; Nelson Mandela, the main ANC political detainee, was released. In 1991 the laws implementing apartheid were effectively abolished. In March 1992 a referendum amongst the white electorate on continued political reform and a new constitution reached by negotiation was approved by 69 per cent to 31 per cent.

Negotiations continued between various groups to establish a non-racial democracy. These negotiations led to the opening in Johannesburg on 20 December 1991 of the Convention on a Democratic South Africa (CODESA) talks between the government, the ANC, the Inkatha Freedom Party and other political, business and church groups. The talks took place against an escalating level of violence involving mainly ANC and Inkatha supporters, but also the security forces, white extremists and Pan-Africanist Congress (PAC) supporters. After the Boipatong massacre in June 1992 the ANC withdrew from the talks, which broke down. Violence, strikes and campaigns of mass action escalated, culminating in the massacre at Bisho, Ciskei, in September 1992.

The continuing violence led the government and the ANC to resume negotiations on 25 September. Agreements were reached in January and February 1993 on establishing an interim multiracial administration in the latter half of 1993 and on the formation of a five-year coalition government after the multiracial election. On 1 April full CODESA negotiations resumed, attended for the first time by the right-wing Conservative Party and by the PAC. Progress towards the establishment of a Transitional Executive Council (TEC) in June 1993 was disrupted by the assassination of the senior ANC member Chris Hani by white extremists on 10 April. Negotiations reached an impasse in June with white right-wing extremists uniting to form the Afrikaner Volksunie to fight for an independent Afrikaner state and hundreds dying in ANC-Inkatha violence. In July the Conservative Party and Inkatha and some homelands leaders left the talks in protest at the refusal of the government and ANC to grant in an interim constitution a degree of regional autonomy that could not be removed when a full constitution was agreed.

The remaining CODESA delegations agreed on 7 September 1993 upon the formation of the multiparty TEC which, together with the independent media and electoral commissions, became effective in December 1993. An interim constitution was agreed on 17 November and adopted by parliament on 22 December. The TEC was boycotted and the interim constitution rejected by the powerful Freedom Alliance (FA) composed of Inkatha, the homeland governments of KwaZulu, Ciskei and Boputhatswana, and the Afrikaner Volksfront (AVF), itself composed of the Conservative Party, the neo-Nazi AWB and the Afrikaner Volksunie. Throughout late 1993 and early 1994 the government and ANC were involved in intense negotiations with the FA and its constituent parts to accept the interim constitution and take part in the April general election. Meanwhile ANC–Inkatha violence continued in Natal and Johannesburg and Afrikaner right-wing violence increased.

The Ciskei government agreed to the interim constitution and elections in January 1994 and the Boputhatswana government was overthrown by the SADF in March 1994 after the AWB had attempted to take control in the homeland. After amendments to the interim constitution Inkatha and the majority of the Afrikaner Volksunie (renamed the Freedom Front) agreed to take part in the elections some eight days before they began.

## GOVERNMENT

The interim constitution establishes South Africa as a democratic multiparty state which will be governed by the interim constitution for a period of two to five years. The final constitution will be decided by the Constituent Assembly (composed of the National Assembly and Senate) by two-thirds majorities in both houses by 27 April 1996. If that is not achieved, it will be approved by a 60 per cent vote in a national referendum, and if that fails it will wait until after the 1999 general election for approval.

Under the interim constitution the ten homelands have been reincorporated in South Africa. Executive power is vested in a President and Cabinet, with the President elected by parliament; at least two deputy Presidents appointed by parties with over 20 per cent of the vote; and a Cabinet and government of national unity to last five years composed of all parties gaining over 5 per cent of the vote. Legislative power is vested in a bicameral parliament, a directly elected 400-member National Assembly elected by proportional representation, and an indirectly elected 90 member Senate composed of ten members elected by each of the nine regional legislatures.

The four former provinces (Cape Province, Natal, Orange Free State, Transvaal) have been replaced by nine new regions (Western Cape, Northern Cape, Eastern Cape, Orange Free State, North-West, KwaZulu/Natal, Pretoria-Witwatersrand-Vereeniging (PMV), Northern Transvaal, Eastern Transvaal). Each region has its own Prime Minister, a legislature of between 30 and 100 seats elected by proportional representation, and its own constitution. At local government level, new multiracial municipal councils have their seats allocated on a 30 per cent white, 30 per cent non-white and 40 per cent non-racial basis.

The interim constitution also establishes a constitutional court of 11 members to adjudicate in disputes between the three tiers of government, to interpret and certify amendments to the constitution and to protect all rights and freedoms.

In the country's first multiracial general election held on 27–29 April 1994 the results were (National Assembly seats): African National Congress (ANC) 62.7 per cent (252), National Party (NP) 20.4 per cent (82), Inkatha Freedom Party (IFP) 10.5 per cent (43), Freedom Front (FF) 2.2 per cent (9), Democratic Party (DP) 1.7 per cent (7), Pan Africanist Congress (PAC) 1.3 per cent (5), African Christian Democratic Party 0.4 per cent (2).

HEAD OF STATE
*President*, Nelson Rolihlahla Mandela, *elected by parliament* 9 May 1994, *sworn in* 10 May 1994
*First Deputy President*, Thabo Mbeki (ANC)
*Second Deputy President*, Frederick de Klerk (NP)

CABINET *as at August 1994*
*Justice*, Dullah Omar (ANC)
*Defence*, Joe Modise (ANC)
*Safety and Security*, Sydney Mufamadi (ANC)
*Education*, Sibusiso Bhengu (ANC)
*Trade, Industry and Tourism*, Trevor Manuel (ANC)
*Foreign Affairs*, Alfred Nzo (ANC)
*Labour*, Tito Mboweni (ANC)
*Post, Telecommunications and Broadcasting*, Pallo Jordan (ANC)
*Health*, Nkosazana Zuma (ANC)
*Transport*, Mac Maharaj (ANC)
*Provincial Affairs and Constitutional Development*, Roelf Meyer (NP)
*Land Affairs*, Derek Hanekom (ANC)
*Public Enterprises*, Stella Sigcau (ANC)
*Public Services and Administration*, Zola Skweyiya (ANC)
*Housing*, Joe Slovo (ANC)
*Public Works*, Jeff Radebe (ANC)
*Correctional Services*, Sipho Mzimela (IFP)
*Finance*, Christo Liebenberg (NP)
*Agriculture*, Kraai Van Niekerk (NP)
*Sports and Recreation*, Steve Tshwete (ANC)
*Home Affairs*, Mangosuthu Buthelezi (IFP)
*Water and Forestry*, Kader Asmal (ANC)
*Environmental Affairs*, Dawie de Villiers (NP)
*Mines and Energy*, Pik Botha (NP)
*Welfare and Population Development*, Abe Williams (NP)
*Arts, Culture, Science and Technology*, Ben Ngubane (IFP)
*Reconstruction and Development*, Jay Naidoo (ANC)
In addition there are 13 deputy ministers, of whom nine are ANC, three are NP and one is IFP.

HIGH COMMISSION OF THE REPUBLIC OF SOUTH AFRICA
South Africa House, Trafalgar Square, London WC2N 5DP
Tel 0171-930 4488

*High Commissioner*, His Excellency K. D. S. Durr, apptd 1991
*Deputy High Commissioner*, G. J. Grobler
*Minister (Trade)*, P. M. Pullen
*Counsellors*, B. H. Knoefel; S. Morkel; W. G. Chisholm; D. J. Cloete; T. Eygelaar (*Consul-General*)
*Defence Attaché*, G. A. Hallowes
*First Secretary*, Miss A. Reesburg (*Cultural*)

BRITISH HIGH COMMISSION
255 Hill Street, Pretoria 0002
Tel: Pretoria 4333121
91 Parliament Street, Cape Town 8001 (January–June)
Tel: Cape Town 4617220

*High Commissioner*, His Excellency Sir Anthony Reeve, KCMG, apptd 1991
*Counsellor, Deputy High Commissioner*, Dr D. Carter
*Counsellor (Political)*, A. Hardie, OBE
*Defence Attaché*, Brig. J. W. Palmer, CBE

*Consul-General and Director of Trade Promotion* (*Johannesburg*), P. Longworth

There is a British Consulate-General at *Johannesburg* (PO Box 10101, Johannesburg 2000), Consulates at *Cape Town* and *Durban*, and Honorary Consuls at *Port Elizabeth* and *East London*.

*Cultural Attaché and British Council Representative*, Les Phillips, 76 Juta Street, (PO Box 30637), Braamfontein 2017, Johannesburg. There is also an office in Cape Town.

DEFENCE

The armed forces are engaged in the formation of a new South African National Defence Force (SANDF) from the merger of the South African Defence Forces (SADF), the Umkhonto we Sizwe (MK) armed wing of the ANC, the Azanian People's Liberation Army (APLA) of the PAC, and the defence forces of the four former independent homelands. White conscription is being phased out and the SANDF will be a fully professional force.

The total active armed forces strength of the former SADF numbers 67,500 (35,400 white conscripts). Total reserves number 635,000 personnel. The active Army strength is 47,000 personnel, of whom 18,000 are full-time professionals (13,000 white, 5,000 other races) and 29,000 National Service conscripts. Equipment includes 250 main battle tanks, 1,700 reconnaissance vehicles, 3,160 armoured personnel carriers and infantry fighting vehicles and 550 artillery pieces.

The Navy has a strength of 4,500 (900 conscripts) with three submarines and 12 patrol and coastal combatants. The Air Force has a strength of 10,000 (3,000 conscripts) with 245 combat aircraft and 14 armed helicopters. In addition the paramilitary South African Police number 110,000 personnel, with 37,000 reserves. MK forces number 6,000 personnel, the APLA 200 and the former homeland defence forces 7,000 personnel.

COMMUNICATIONS

There are international airports at Johannesburg (Jan Smuts), Durban (Louis Botha) and Cape Town (D. F. Malan). South African Airways operates international services to Europe, South America, the Far East, Africa, Australia and the USA, and it is the principal operator of domestic flights. The largest sea-port is Durban, Natal. Other major ports are Cape Town, Port Elizabeth, East London, Saldanha Bay and Mossel Bay in Cape Province and Richards Bay, Natal. The national railway system, and most long-distance passenger and freight road transport are run by independent companies. The six landlocked states of Botswana, Lesotho, Swaziland, Zimbabwe, Zambia and Malawi make extensive use of South African Railways for foreign trade.

ECONOMY

The South African economy has suffered in recent years from recession, industrial unrest, drought, the fall in world gold price and foreign disinvestment. With the end of financial sanctions the new government is hoping that investors will return in their previous numbers. The price of gold has recovered somewhat and the drought ended but industrial unrest continues because of black workers' increased expectations. An austerity programme launched in 1985 brought the national debt down to 70 per cent of GDP and enabled the government in September 1993 to announce the repayment of the US$5,000 million foreign debt over an eight-year period. The first budget of the new government in June 1994 envisaged expenditure of £24,000 million and revenue of £19,000 million, with a one-off 5 per cent levy on corporations and wealthy individuals. Although the budget was well-received, subsequent argument over the cost of the ANC's social and economic reconstruction programme, including increased-spending on education, health care, new homes and electrification, led to a run on the rand and a crisis in foreign exchange and gold reserves, necessitating an IMF loan which the ANC-led government is loath to agree to because of the conditions which would be attached.

Mining is of great importance, producing 10.3 per cent of GDP in 1991 and minerals to the value of R39,376 million. The principal minerals produced are gold, coal, diamonds, copper, iron ore, manganese, lime and limestone, uranium, platinum, fluorspar, andalusite, zinc, zirconium, vanadium, titanium, nickel, lead and chrome ore. South Africa is the world's largest producer of gold, chrome ore, manganese and vanadium, and has the world's largest reserves of chrome ore, manganese, vanadium and andalusite.

Agriculture, forestry and fishing account for about 5 per cent of GDP. Over 50 per cent of land is pasture so livestock farming is widespread and meat and wool important products. Principal crops are maize, sugar-cane, fruits and vegetables, wheat, sorghum, sunflower seed and groundnuts. Cotton is widely grown because of its suitability to the climate, and viticulture is also widespread.

Industries, concentrated most heavily around Johannesburg, Pretoria and the major ports, process foodstuffs, metals and non-metallic mineral products, produce oil from coal, and also produce beverages and tobacco, motor vehicles, chemicals and chemical products, machinery, textiles and clothing, and paper and paper products. Manufacturing industry contributed 24.6 per cent of GDP in 1993.

Energy production is based upon coal and natural gas and the production of synthetic liquid fuel from coal. One nuclear power station is in operation and others are planned. South Africa exports electricity through its electric grid connections to all states in southern Africa.

TRADE

Principal exports are gold, base metals and metal products, coal, diamonds, food (especially fruit), chemicals, machinery and transport equipment, and wool. Principal imports are machinery, chemicals, motor vehicles, metals and metal products, food, inedible raw materials and textiles.

American and EC sanctions, in place since 1986, were lifted in July 1991 and January 1992 respectively. The longer-standing UN finance, oil and arms embargoes were lifted in October 1993, December 1993 and April 1994 respectively.

| Trade with UK | 1992 | 1993 |
|---|---|---|
| Imports from UK | £1,078,697,000 | £1,124,424,000 |
| Exports to UK | 865,328,000 | 998,437,000 |

# SPAIN
*España*

Spain occupies most of the Iberian Pensinsula, between 36° and 43° 45′ N., and 4° 25′ E. and 9° 20′ W. It is bounded on the south and east by the Mediterranean, on the west by the Atlantic and Portugal, and on the north by the Bay of Biscay and France. It comprises a total area of 194,897 sq. miles (504,782 sq. km), with a population (1991 census) of 38,872,268.

The interior of the Iberian peninsula consists of an elevated tableland surrounded and traversed by mountain ranges: the Pyrenees, the Cantabrian Mountains, the Sierra Guadarrama,

Sierra Morena, Sierra Nevada, Montes de Toledo, etc. The principal rivers are the Duero, the Tajo, the Guadiana, the Guadalquivir, the Ebro and the Miño.

CAPITAL – Madrid, population (1991) 4,947,555. Other large cities are ΨBarcelona (4,654,407), ΨValencia (2,117,972), Seville (1,619,703), Alicante (1,292,563), ΨMálaga (1,160,843), Bilbao (1,179,148); Murcia (1,045,601).

CURRENCY – Peseta of 100 céntimos.

FLAG – Three horizontal stripes of red, yellow, red, with the yellow of double width.

NATIONAL ANTHEM – Marcha Real Española.

NATIONAL DAY – 12 October.

## GOVERNMENT

Spain was a monarchy until 1931, when King Alfonso XIII left the country and a republic was proclaimed. A provisional government, drawn from the various republican and Socialist parties, was formed. In July 1936 a counter-revolution broke out in military garrisons in Spanish Morocco and spread throughout Spain. The principal leader was Gen. Franco, leader of the Military-Fascist fusion, or *Falange*. Civil war ensued until March 1939, when the Popular Front governments in Madrid and Barcelona surrendered to the Nationalists (as Gen. Franco's followers were then named). Gen. Franco became President and ruled the country until his death in 1975, when, according to his wishes, he was succeeded as head of state by Prince Juan Carlos of Bourbon (grandson of Alfonso XIII) and Spain again became a monarchy.

Under the 1978 constitution there is a bicameral *Cortes* comprising a 350-member Congress of Deputies elected for four years by universal adult suffrage, and a Senate consisting of directly elected representatives of the provinces, islands, autonomous regions, and Ceuta and Melilla. At the general election on 6 June 1993, PSOE (Spanish Socialist Workers' Party) won 159 seats; the PP (Popular Party) 141; the (Communist) United Left Party 18; Catalan Nationalists 17; Basque Nationalists (PNV) 5; others 10. The PSOE formed a minority government with the support of the Catalan and Basque nationalists in July.

## REGIONS

Since the promulgation of the 1978 constitution, 17 autonomous regions have been established, with their own parliaments and governments. These are Andalucia, Aragon, Asturias, Balearics, the Basque country, Canaries,

Castilla-La Mancha, Castilla-Leon, Cantabria, Cataluña, Extremadura, Galicia, Madrid, Murcia, Navarre, La Rioja and Valencia. The Basque terrorist group ETA has waged a terrorist campaign for 20 years against the Spanish state to gain independence for the Basque country.

HEAD OF STATE

*HM The King of Spain*, King Juan Carlos I de Borbón y Borbón, KG, GCVO, *born* 5 January 1938, *acceded to the throne*, 22 November 1975, *married* 14 May 1962, Princess Sophie of Greece *and has issue*, Infante Felipe (*see below*); Infanta Elena Maria Isabel Dominga, *born* 20 December 1963; and Infanta Cristina Federica Victoria Antonia, *born* 13 June 1965

*Heir*, HRH The Prince of the Asturias (Infante Felipe Juan Pablo Alfonso y Todos los Santos), *born* 30 January 1968

CABINET *as at August 1994*

*Prime Minister*, Felipe González Márquez
*Deputy PM*, Narcís Serra Serra
*Foreign Affairs*, Javier Solana Madariaga
*Justice*, Juan Alberto Belloch
*Defence*, Julián García Vargas
*Economy and Finance*, Pedro Solbes Mira
*Interior*, Juan Alberto Belloch
*Public Works and Town Planning and Transport*, José Borrell Fontelles
*Education and Science*, Gustavo Pertierra
*Labour and Social Security*, José Griñán Martínez
*Industry*, Juan Eguiagaray Ucelay
*Trade and Tourism*, Javier Gómez Navarro
*Agriculture, Food and Fisheries*, Luis Maria Atienza
*Public Administration*, Jerónimo Saavedra Acevedo
*Culture*, Carmen Alboroch
*Health and Consumer Affairs*, Angeles Amador Millán
*Relations with the Cortes and Government Secretariat*, Alfredo Pérez Rubalcaba
*Social Affairs*, Cristina Alberdi Alonso

SPANISH EMBASSY

24 Belgrave Square, London SW1X 8SB
Tel 0171-235 5555

*Ambassador Extraordinary and Plenipotentiary*, His Excellency Don Alberto Aza Arias, apptd 1993
*Minister-Plenipotentiary*, The Marqués de Torregrosa
*Defence Attaché*, Capt. J. M. Ryan
*Minister*, Dr D. de Lario (*Cultural*)
*Minister*, Don L. E. Valera (*Consul*)
*Counsellor*, J. G. Valverde (*Commercial*)

BRITISH EMBASSY

Calle de Fernando el Santo, 16, 28010 Madrid
Tel: Madrid 319 0200

*Ambassador Extraordinary and Plenipotentiary*, His Excellency Anthony David Brighty, CMG, CVO, apptd 1994
*Minister, Deputy Ambassador*, E. Jones Parry
*Counsellors*, D. Ridgway, OBE (*Commercial*); A. Longrigg, CMG (*Economic and Community Affairs*); D. C. Ankerson
*Defence and Naval Attaché*, Capt. J. Gozzard RN
*Consuls-General*, D. R. McIntyre (*Madrid*); M. Perceval (*Barcelona*); M. McLoughlin (*Bilbao*)

There are Consulates-General in *Madrid, Barcelona, Bilbao*; Consulates in *Tenerife, Alicante, Seville, Malaga, Palma de Mallorca, Las Palmas*; Vice-Consulates in *Ibiza* and *Menorca*; Honorary Consulates in *Santander, Tarragona, Vigo*.

BRITISH COUNCIL REPRESENTATIVE, B. Vale, CBE, Paseo del General Martinez, Campos 31, 2800 Madrid.

There are offices in *Barcelona, Bilbao, Granada, Las Palmas, Palma, Segovia, Seville* and *Valencia*.

BRITISH CHAMBER OF COMMERCE, Plaza de Santa Barbara 10, 1st Floor, 28004 Madrid; Paseo de Gracia 11, Barcelona 7; Alameda de Mazarredo 5, Bilbao 1.

DEFENCE

The armed forces have a total active strength of 200,700 (133,500 conscripts) with a nine-month period of conscription. The Army has 138,900 personnel (100,000 conscripts), with 1,150 main battle tanks, 440 reconnaissance vehicles, 2,000 armoured personnel carriers, 825 artillery pieces, and 28 combat helicopters. The Army is organized into eight regional commands and a General Reserve Force.

The Spanish Navy has a strength of 32,000 (18,000 conscripts), including 7,000 marines, and consists of eight submarines, one V/STOL aircraft carrier, 15 frigates, 28 patrol and coastal combatants, 28 armed helicopters and 21 Harrier aircraft. The Air Force has a strength of 29,860 (15,500 conscripts) and has 150 combat aircraft. The paramilitary Guardia Civil with 66,000 personnel (3,000 conscripts) operates as a gendarmerie in rural areas under the control of the Ministry of Defence and has been actively engaged in combating Basque terrorism.

Spain deploys an infantry battalion group of 1,220 troops with UN forces in Bosnia. The USA maintains 3,400 naval and 500 air force personnel in Spain.

ECONOMY

The expansion of the Spanish economy and accession to the EC have led to changes in Spanish agriculture. It accounts for over 5 per cent of GDP and employs over 13 per cent of the working population. The country is generally fertile, and fruits such as olives, oranges, lemons, almonds, pomegranates, bananas, apricots, tomatoes, peppers, cucumbers and grapes are cultivated. Other agricultural products include wheat, barley, oats, rice, hemp and flax. The vine is cultivated widely; in the south-west, Jerez, sherry and tent wines are produced. The fishing industry is important.

Spain's mineral resources of coal, iron, wolfram, copper, zinc, lead and iron ores are variously exploited. Output of coal in 1988 was 15.5 million tonnes; output of steel (1988) 11.9 million tonnes.

The principal industrial goods are cars, steel, ships, manufactured goods, textiles, chemical products, footwear and other leather goods. Tourism is a major industry; in 1993 an estimated 57,259,000 tourists visited Spain.

TRADE

The principal imports are cotton, tobacco, cellulose, timber, coffee and cocoa, food products, fertilizers, dyes, machinery, motor vehicles and agricultural tractors, wool and petroleum products. The principal exports include cars, petroleum products, iron ore, cork, salt, vegetables, fruits, wines, olive oil, potash, mercury, pyrites, tinned fruit and fish, tomatoes and footwear. The balance of payments on current account showed a deficit of Pesetas 2,000,000 million in 1993, when reserves stood at US$45,300 million.

|  | 1993 |
|---|---|
| Imports | Pesetas 10,000,000m |
| Exports | 7,600,000m |

| *Trade with UK* | 1992 | 1993 |
|---|---|---|
| Imports from UK | £4,405,290,000 | £4,124,367,000 |
| Exports to UK | 2,938,716,000 | 3,044,042,000 |

*Excluding the Canary Islands, Ceuta and Melilla

## EDUCATION

Education is free for those aged six to 18, and compulsory up to the age of 14. Private schools (30 per cent of primary and 60 per cent of secondary schools) have to fulfill certain criteria to receive government maintenance grants. There are 33 public sector universities, the oldest of which, Salamanca, was founded in 1218. Other ancient foundations are Valladolid (1346), Barcelona (1430), Zaragoza (1474), Santiago (1495), Valencia (1500), Seville (1505), Madrid (1508), Granada (1531), Oveido (1604). Private universities are Deusto in Bilbao, Navarra in Pamplona, one in Madrid and one in Salamanca. Student numbers in the universities in 1989–90 totalled 1,067,874.

## CULTURE

Castilian is the language of more than three-quarters of the population of Spain. Basque, said to have been the original language of Iberia, is spoken in Vizcaya, Guipuzcoa and Alava. Catalan is spoken in Provençal Spain, and Galician, spoken in the north-western provinces, is akin to Portuguese. The governments of these regions actively encourage use of their local languages.

The literature of Spain is one of the oldest and richest in the world, the *Poem of the Cid*, the earliest of the heroic songs of Spain, having been written about 1140. The outstanding writings of its golden age are those of Miguel de Cervantes Saavedra (1547–1616), Lope Felix de Vega Carpio (1562–1635) and Pedro Calderón de la Barca (1600–81). The Nobel Prize for Literature has five times been awarded to Spanish authors: J. Echegaray (1904), J. Benavente (1922), Juan Ramón Jimenez (1956), Vicente Aleixandre (1977) and Camilo José Cela (1989).

## ISLANDS

The Balearic Isles form an archipelago off the east coast of Spain. There are four large islands (Majorca, Minorca, Ibiza and Formentera), and seven smaller (Aire, Aucanada, Botafoch, Cabrera, Dragonera, Pinto and El Rey). The total area is 1,935 sq. miles (5,011 sq. km), with a population of 685,088. The archipelago forms a province of Spain, the capital being ΨPalma in Majorca, pop. 304,422.

The Canary Islands are an archipelago in the Atlantic, off the African coast, consisting of seven islands and six mostly uninhabited islets. The total area is 2,807 sq. miles (7,270 sq. km), with a population of 1,444,626. The Canary Islands form two provinces of Spain: Las Palmas, comprising Gran Canaria, Lanzarote (38,500), Fuerteventura (19,500) and the islets of Alegranza, Roque del Este, Roque del Oeste, Graciosa, Montaña Clara and Lobos, with seat of administration at ΨLas Palmas (366,454) in Gran Canaria; and Santa Cruz de Tenerife, comprising Tenerife, La Palma (76,000), Gomera (31,829), and Hierro (10,000), with seat of administration at ΨSanta Cruz in Tenerife, population estimate 190,784.

Isla de Faisanes is an uninhabited Franco-Spanish condominium, at the mouth of the Bidassoa in La Higuera bay.

ΨCeuta is a fortified post on the Moroccan coast, opposite Gibraltar. The total area is 5 sq. miles (13 sq. km), with a population of 70,864.

ΨMelilla is a town on a rocky promontory of the Rif coast, connected with the mainland by a narrow isthmus. Population 58,449. Ceuta and Melilla are parts of Metropolitan Spain.

## OVERSEAS TERRITORIES

Spanish settlements on the Moroccan seaboard are:
*Peñon de Alhucemas*, a bay including six islands, population 366

*Peñon de la Gomera* (or *Peñon de Velez*), a fortified rocky islet, population 450
*The Chaffarinas* (or Zaffarines), a group of three islands near the Algerian frontier, population 610

---

## SRI LANKA
*Sri Lanka Prajatantrika Samajawadi Janarajaya*

---

Sri Lanka (formerly Ceylon) is an island in the Indian Ocean, off the southern tip of India and separated from it by the narrow Palk Strait. Situated between 5° 55′ and 9° 50′ N. latitude and 79° 42′ and 81° 52′ E. longitude, it has an area of 25,332 sq. miles (65,610 sq. km), including 33 sq. miles of inland water. Forests, jungle and scrub cover the greater part of the island. In areas over 2,000 ft above sea level grasslands (*patanas* or *talawas*) are found. One of the highest peaks in the central massif is Adam's Peak (7,360 ft), a place of pilgrimage for Buddhists, Hindus and Muslims.

The climate is warm throughout the year, with a high relative humidity. The two main monsoon seasons are mid-May to September (south-west) and November to March (north-east).

POPULATION – The population (1991 estimate) was 17,243,000, of which 74 per cent were Sinhalese, 12.6 per cent Sri Lankan Tamils, 5.6 per cent Indian Tamils, 7.1 per cent Sri Lankan Moors and 0.7 per cent Burghers, Malays and others. The religion of the majority is Buddhism (69.3 per cent), then Hinduism (15.5 per cent); Islam (7.6 per cent), and Christianity (7.5 per cent). The national languages are Sinhalese, Tamil and English.

CAPITAL – ΨColombo, population (1991) 1,963,000. Other principal towns are ΨJaffna (876,000), Kandy (1,251,000), ΨGalle (946,000), and ΨTrincomalee (316,000).
CURRENCY – Sri Lankan rupee (Rs) of 100 cents.
FLAG – On a dark red field, within a golden border, a golden lion passant holding a sword in its right paw, and a representation of a *bo*-leaf, issuing from each corner; and to its right, two vertical stripes of saffron and green also placed within a golden border, to represent the minorities of the country.
NATIONAL ANTHEM – Namo Namo Matha (We all stand together).
NATIONAL DAY – 4 February (Independence Commemoration Day).

## GOVERNMENT

The Portuguese landed in Ceylon in the early 16th century and founded settlements, eventually conquering much of the country. Portuguese rule lasted 150 years; in 1658 it gave way to that of the Dutch East India Company until 1796. The maritime provinces of Ceylon were ceded by the Dutch to the British in 1798, becoming a British Crown Colony in 1802. With the annexation of the Kingdom of Kandy in 1815, all Ceylon came under British rule.

Ceylon became a self-governing state and a member of the British Commonwealth on 4 February 1948. A republican constitution was adopted in 1972 and the country was renamed Sri Lanka (meaning 'Resplendent Island'). In 1978 a new constitution introduced a system of proportional representation. Legislative power is exercised by the National State Assembly, executive power being exercised by the President.

Eight provincial councils were set up in 1988 in an attempt to diffuse ethnic tension. The Northern-Eastern council is controlled by the Eelam People's Revolutionary Liberation Front, the other seven councils by the United National Party. In the south of the country during the 1980s 100,000 people were killed in fighting between government forces and Sinhalese armed extremists.

In the general election of 16 August 1994 the ruling United National Party was defeated by the opposition People's Alliance led by Chandrika Bandaranaike Kumaratunga. The People's Alliance won 105 seats; the United National Party 94 seats; and other parties, mainly Muslim and moderate Tamils, 26 seats. At the time of going to press Chandrika Bandaranaike had been sworn in as Prime Minister and was in the process of forming a government with the support of moderate Tamil and Muslim parties. Presidential elections are scheduled for late 1994.

SECESSION

The Tamil Tigers guerrilla group has been fighting Sri Lankan forces for control of the Tamil majority areas in the north and east of the country since 1983. They were suppressed by Indian peacekeepers in 1987–90 but grew in strength after the Indians left. They are now virtually confined to the Jaffna peninsula by Sri Lankan forces, but a Tamil suicide bomber assassinated President Premadasa on 1 May 1993. Some 30,000 have been killed in 11 years of fighting, including 1,000 in November 1993 when the Tamil Tigers' attempt to break out of the Jaffna peninsula was defeated by government forces. The new People's Alliance government has expressed a wish to negotiate a political settlement including autonomy for the Tamil areas, and relaxed the embargo on the Jaffna peninsula in August 1994

HEAD OF STATE

*President*, His Excellency Dingiri Banda Wijetunge, *elected and sworn in by parliament* 7 May 1993

*Prime Minister*, Chandrika Bandaranaike Kumaratunga, *sworn in* 20 August 1994

HIGH COMMISSION FOR THE DEMOCRATIC SOCIALIST REPUBLIC OF SRI LANKA
13 Hyde Park Gardens, London W2 2LU
Tel 0171-262 1841

*High Commissioner*, His Excellency Gen. S. C. Ranatunga, apptd 1993
*Deputy High Commissioner*, G. S. Munasinghe
*Minister-Counsellors*, Mrs S. Rajapakse (*Consular*); K. J. Weerasinghe (*Economic*)
*First Secretary*, N. De Silva Gunatilleke (*Defence*)

BRITISH HIGH COMMISSION
Galle Road 190, Kollupitiya (PO Box 1433), Colombo 3
Tel: Colombo 437336

*High Commissioner*, His Excellency Edward John Field, CMG, apptd 1991
*Deputy High Commissioner*, R. P. Nash, LVO
*Defence Adviser*, Lt.-Col. D. G. Wheelan, RM
*First Secretary* (*Commercial*), I. M. Dallas

BRITISH COUNCIL REPRESENTATIVE, Peter Ellwood, 49 Alfred House Gardens, PO Box 753, Colombo 3. Library also in *Kandy*.

ECONOMY

The staple products of the island are tea, rubber, copra, spices and gems. There is increasing emphasis on local production of food, especially rice, and plans for the large-scale production of sugar cane, cotton and citrus fruits.

Factories are established for the manufacture or processing of ceramic ware, vegetable oils and by-products, paper,

tobacco, tanning and leather goods, plywood, cement, chemicals, sugar, flour, salt, textiles, ilmenite, tiles, tyres, fertilizers, clothing, jewellery and hardware and there is a petroleum refinery.

| Trade with UK | 1992 | 1993 |
|---|---|---|
| Imports from UK | £103,214,000 | £126,243,000 |
| Exports to UK | 93,045,000 | 142,478,000 |

COMMUNICATIONS

There are over 15,660 miles of roads in Sri Lanka and a government-run railway system with 984 miles of lines. A satellite earth station at Padukka provides telecommunication links world-wide. The principal airports are at Katunayake, 19 miles north of Colombo, and Ratmalana, nine miles south of the capital. Air Lanka operates on 76 flights weekly to the Gulf States, the Maldives, western Europe and throughout the Far East.

SUDAN
*Al-Jamhuryat es-Sudan Al-Democratia*

Sudan lies in north-east Africa, between 22° and 3°36′ N. latitude, and 21° 49′ and 38° 35′ E. longitude. To the north lies Egypt, to the east the Red Sea, Eritrea and Ethiopia, to the south Kenya, Uganda and Zaire, and to the west the Central African Republic, Chad, and Libya. The area is about 967,500 sq. miles (2,505,813 sq. km).

The White Nile, as the Bahr el Jebel, flows through Sudan from Nimule to Wadi Halfa. The Blue Nile flows from Lake Tana on the Ethiopian plateau through Sudan to join the White Nile at Khartoum. The next confluence of importance is at Atbara where the main Nile is joined by the River Atbara. Between Khartoum and Wadi Halfa lie five of the six cataracts.

POPULATION – The population is 25,941,000 (UN estimate 1991). Arab and Nubian peoples populate the north and centre, Nilotic and Negro peoples the south. Arabic is the official language and Islam the state religion, although the Nilotics of the Bahr el Ghazal and Upper Nile valleys are generally Animists or Christians.

CAPITAL – Khartoum. The combined population of Khartoum, Khartoum North and Omdurman (excluding refugees and displaced people) is estimated at 3,000,000.
CURRENCY – Sudanese Dinar of 10 pounds.
FLAG – Three horizontal stripes of red, white and black with a green triangle next to the hoist.
NATIONAL ANTHEM – Nahnu Djundullah (We are the army of God).
NATIONAL DAY – 1 January (Independence Day).

GOVERNMENT

The Anglo-Egyptian Condominium over Sudan was established in 1899 and ended when the Sudan House of Representatives, on 19 December 1955, declared Sudan a fully independent sovereign state. A republic was proclaimed on 1 January 1956, and was recognized by Great Britain and Egypt. Sudan was under military rule from 1958 to 1964; under the rule of a revolutionary council headed by Col. Gaafar Mohamed El Nimeri from 1969 until April 1985 when the army command deposed Nimeri; and experienced a third military coup in June 1989 when the civilian government, in power since 1986, was overthrown by Brig.-Gen. Omar Hassan Ahmad al-Bashir. The constitution was suspended and parliament was replaced by a 15-member ruling junta

(Revolutionary Command Council) who exercised control over a cabinet. The ruling junta appointed Gen. al-Bashir as head of state on 16 October 1993 and then dissolved itself, paving the way for presidential and legislative elections in 1995.

The government has developed close relations with Iran and is believed by western states to support international terrorism and have Iranian Revolutionary Guards' bases on its territory. Supported by the National Islamic Front (NIF), the government has since 1989 turned Sudan into an Islamic state. In August 1993 the USA placed Sudan on a list of countries sponsoring terrorism and suspended all trade apart from humanitarian goods.

## SECESSION

Nearly 17 years of insurrection in the southern provinces ended in 1972 with the signing of an agreement recognizing southern regional autonomy within the Sudanese state. However, insurrection broke out again in 1983 and since then there has been civil war in the regions of Eastern and Western Equatoria in the south of the country between government forces and the Christian and Animist majority in the area, organized into the Sudan People's Liberation Army (SPLA). Although the Islamic government has officially stated that it is not attempting to introduce Sharia law in the south, the Sharia affects the two million Christians in northern areas. In 1991–2 the SPLA split into three factions based on different tribal groups: SPLA-Torit; SPLA-Nasir; SPLA-United. The SPLA lost the control that it had exercised over most of the south to government forces because of fighting between the SPLA factions. By early 1994 government forces controlled most of the towns and roads in the region and launched the largest offensive since 1983 against the secessionist forces. The SPLA factions have resorted to guerrilla tactics. The warfare has left an estimated one million dead, including 300,000 who died in the war-induced famine in 1988. Some three million refugees have fled the fighting, either to the north, to neighbouring states or to the far south near the Ugandan border.

## HEAD OF STATE

*President, Minister of Defence,* Lt.-Gen. Omar Hassan Ahmad al-Bashir, *appointed* 16 October 1993
*Vice-President,* George Kengor Arop

CABINET *as at September 1994*

*Prime Minister and Minister of Interior,* Maj.-Gen. Zubir Mohammed Saleh
*Presidential Affairs,* Lt.-Col. Tayib Ibrahim Mohammed Khayr
*Federal Administration,* Dr Ali al-Hajj Muhammad
*Foreign Affairs,* Dr Hassein Suleiman Abu Saleh
*Justice and Attorney-General,* Abdel-Aziz Shiddo
*Culture and Information,* Abdel-Basit Sahdarat
*Planning and Investment,* Mohammed Khair al-Zubeir
*Agriculture and Natural Resources,* Abdul-Gasim Shammo
*Peace and Development,* Mubarak Gismallah
*Local Government and Co-ordination of Provincial Affairs,* Natali Yanku Ambu
*Irrigation,* Yacoub Abu Shura Musa
*Energy and Mining,* Salah al-Din Karrar
*Industry and Commerce,* Dr Taj Al Sir Mustafa Abdel-Salaam
*Social Planning,* Ali Osman Muhammad Taha
*Housing, Construction and Public Utilities,* Osman Abdoul Gadir Abdul Latif
*Education and Scientific Research,* Dr Ibrahim Ahmed Omer
*Tourism and Communications,* Maj.-Gen. Ibrahim Nayil Idam

*Labour and Administrative Reform,* Gen. Dominic Kassiano
*Health,* Lt.-Col. Galwuk Deng

EMBASSY OF THE REPUBLIC OF THE SUDAN
3 Cleveland Row, London SW1A 1DD
Tel 0171-839 8080

*Ambassador Extraordinary and Plenipotentiary,* new appointment awaited

BRITISH EMBASSY
(PO Box 801), Khartoum
Tel: Khartoum 70760

*Chargé d'Affaires,* J. M. Crane

BRITISH COUNCIL REPRESENTATIVE, A. Thomas, 14 Abu Sinn Street (PO Box 1253), Khartoum.

## ECONOMY

Agriculture provides employment for over half the labour force and contributes over one-third of GDP. It is based on large and medium-sized public sector irrigation projects with small-scale private irrigation schemes providing mostly fruit and vegetables. Mechanized and traditional agriculture is practised in areas of sufficient rainfall. The principal grain crops are *dura* (great millet) and wheat, the staple food of the population. Sesame and groundnuts are other important food crops, which also yield an exportable surplus, and a promising start has been made with castor seed. The principal export crop is cotton, both long-staple cotton and short and medium-staple cotton. Sudan also produces the bulk of the world's supply of gum arabic. Sugar is an increasingly important crop, although Sudan still has to achieve self sufficiency in its production.

Livestock is the mainstay of the nomadic Arab tribes of the desert and the Negro tribes of the swamp and wooded grassland country in the south. Production has, however, been affected by drought, famine and civil war.

The manufacturing sector contributes less than 8 per cent to GDP and provides employment for 4 per cent of the work force. The main manufacturing enterprises are food processing, textiles, shoes, cigarettes and batteries.

Sudan's voting rights at the IMF were suspended in August 1993 after its persistent failure to fulfil its obligations regarding overdue amounts of US$1,600 million. Sudan is in danger of losing its IMF membership after the government's refusal to negotiate an arrears strategy.

## TRADE

The principal exports are cotton, livestock, gum arabic and other agricultural produce. The chief imports are petroleum goods and other raw materials, machinery and equipment, transport and equipment, medicines and chemicals.

| Trade with UK | 1992 | 1993 |
|---|---|---|
| Imports from UK | £52,304,000 | £45,399,000 |
| Exports to UK | 5,250,000 | 8,174,000 |

## COMMUNICATIONS

The railway system, adversely affected by the civil war, has a route length of about 3,200 miles. Nile river services between Khartoum and Juba have been interrupted by the southern insurrection. Port Sudan is the country's main seaport. Sudan Airways fly services from Khartoum to other parts of the Sudan and to other African states, Europe and the Middle East.

## EDUCATION

School education is free for most children but not compulsory, beginning with six years primary education, followed by three years secondary education at general secondary schools, the more academic higher secondary schools or vocational schools. The medium of instruction is Arabic. English is no longer taught in schools since new Arabization legislation came into effect in 1991.

Khartoum University has ten faculties. There is a branch of Cairo University in Khartoum, an Islamic University at Omdurman and universities at Wad Medani and Juba. In addition to the universities there are various technical post-secondary institutes as well as professional and vocational training establishments.

## SURINAME
*Republiek Suriname*

Suriname is situated on the north coast of South America and is bounded by the Atlantic in the north, French Guiana in the east, Brazil in the south and Guyana in the west. It has an area of 63,037 sq. miles (163,265 sq. km), with a population (UN 1991 estimate) of 429,000.

CAPITAL – ΨParamaribo, population (1971) 110,000.
CURRENCY – Suriname guilder of 100 cents.
FLAG – Horizontal stripes of green, white, red, white, green, with a five-pointed yellow star in the centre.
NATIONAL DAY – 25 November.

## GOVERNMENT

Formerly known as Dutch Guiana, Suriname remained part of the Netherlands West Indies until 25 November 1975, when it achieved complete independence from the Netherlands. The civilian government was ousted in 1980 by the military who appointed a predominantly civilian government in 1982. According to the 1987 constitution, a National Assembly of 51 members elects the President. The Army remains the 'vanguard of the people'.

President Shankar was overthrown in a military coup, instigated by Lt.-Col. Desi Bouterse, in December 1990; Johan Kraag, a supporter of Bouterse, was installed as President. Elections to the National Assembly were held in May 1991. The New Front for Democracy and Development, a coalition comprising opposition groups, won 30 of the 51 seats, but failed to gain the necessary two-thirds majority to appoint the President. In September 1991 a special sitting of a United People's Assembly elected New Front leader Ronald Venetiaan as President and he formed a government which amended the constitution in April 1992 to limit the power of the military. In August 1992 the government and the two largest guerrilla groups signed a peace agreement under which the guerrillas will be integrated into the police force.

HEAD OF STATE
*President*, Dr Ronald Venetiaan, *elected* 7 September 1991

CABINET *as at August 1994*
*Vice-President, Prime Minister*, Jules Ajodhia
*Labour*, Jack Kross
*Foreign Affairs*, Subhas Mungra
*Defence*, Siegfried Gilds.
*Finance*, Humphrey Hildenberg
*Economics*, Richard Kalloe
*Justice and Police*, Soeshiel Girjasing
*Natural Resources*, Franco Demon
*Education*, Gerard Hiwat
*Public Works*, Radj Koemar Randjietsingh
*Planning and Development*, Edwin Sedoc

*Regional Affairs*, Rufus Nooitmeer
*Agricultural and Fisheries*, S. Setroredjo
*Transport, Communications and Tourism*, John Defares
*Public Health*, Mohamed Khudabux
*Interior*, J. Sisal
*Social Affairs*, W. Soemita

EMBASSY OF THE REPUBLIC OF SURINAME
2 Alexander Gogelweg, The Hague, The Netherlands
Tel: The Hague 3650844
*Ambassador Extraordinary and Plenipotentiary*, new appointment awaited

BRITISH AMBASSADOR, His Excellency D. J. Johnson, resident at Georgetown, Guyana
BRITISH CONSULATE, c/o VSH United Buildings, Van't Hogerhuystraat, PO Box 1300, Paramaribo. *Honorary Consul*, J. J. Healy, MBE

## ECONOMY

Suriname has large timber resources. Rice and sugar cane are the main crops. Bauxite is mined, and is the principal export. In 1987, GDP amounted to US$1,080 million. Principal trading partners are the Netherlands, USA and Norway.

| Trade with UK | 1992 | 1993 |
| --- | --- | --- |
| Imports from UK | £11,521,000 | £6,289,000 |
| Exports to UK | 11,531,000 | 14,232,000 |

## SWAZILAND
*Umbuso we Swatini*

Swaziland is a small, land-locked country surrounded by South Africa on its northern, western and southern borders and by Mozambique to the east. The broken mountainous Highveld along the western border, with an average altitude of 4,000 ft, is densely forested, mainly with conifers and eucalyptus; the Middleveld, averaging about 2,000 ft, is a mixed farming area including cotton and pineapples; and the Lowveld in the east was mainly scrubland until the introduction of large sugar-cane plantations. Four rivers, the Komati, Usutu, Mbuluzi and Ngwavuma, flow from west to east. The total area of Swaziland is 6,704 sq. miles (17,363 sq. km), and the population (UN estimate 1991) is 817,000.

CAPITAL – Mbabane (population 1986, 38,290). Other main townships are Manzini (estimated population, 30,000), Big Bend, Mhlambanyati, Mhlume, Nhlangano, Pigg's Peak and Simunye.
CURRENCY – Lilangeni (E) of 100 cents. South African currency is also in circulation. Swaziland is a member of the Common Monetary Area and its unit of currency *Emalangeni* (singular *Lilangeni*) has a par value with the South African rand.
FLAG – Blue with a wide crimson horizontal band bordered in yellow across the centre, bearing a shield and two spears horizontally.
NATIONAL ANTHEM – Ingoma Yesive.
NATIONAL DAY – 6 September (Independence Day).

## GOVERNMENT

The Kingdom of Swaziland came into being on 25 April 1967 under a self-government constitution and became an independent kingdom, headed by HM Sobhuza II, in membership of the Commonwealth on 6 September 1968.

A new government system was introduced in 1978 and amended in 1992–3 under which the King, assisted by his appointed Cabinet, holds considerable executive, legislative and judicial authority. In addition, there is a bicameral legislative body comprising a Senate and a House of Assembly. Each of the 55 traditional *Tinkhundla* (chieftaincies) are directly elected and become members of the House of Assembly. The King appoints ten members to the House of Assembly, making 65 in all, who then elect ten members of their own number to the Senate. To these are added 20 senators appointed by the King, bringing the full membership of the Senate to 30. All political parties are banned under the 1978 constitution.

HEAD OF STATE
*King of Swaziland*, HM King Mswati III, *inaugurated* 25 April 1986

CABINET *as at August 1994*

*Prime Minister*, Rt. Hon. Prince Mbilini
*Deputy Prime Minister*, Hon. Dr Sishayi Nxumalo
*Foreign Affairs*, Hon. Solomon Dlamini
*Justice*, Hon. Chief Maweni Simelane
*Home Affairs*, Hon. Prince Sobandla
*Finance*, Hon. Issac Shabangu
*Education*, Hon. Prince Khuzulwandle
*Works and Construction*, Hon. Prince Mahlalengangeni
*Health*, Hon. Dr Derrick von Wissel
*Agriculture and Co-operatives*, Hon. Chief Dambuza Lukhele
*Commerce and Industry*, Hon. Muntu Mswane
*Labour and Public Service*, Hon. Albert Shabangu
*Natural Resources*, Hon. Arthur Khoza
*Housing and Urban Development*, Hon. John Carmichael
*Economic Planning and Development*, Hon. Themba Masuku
*Transport and Communications*, Hon. Ephraem Magagula
*Broadcasting, Information and Tourism*, Hon. Prince Phinda

KINGDOM OF SWAZILAND HIGH COMMISSION
58 Pont Street, London SW1X OAE
Tel 0171–581 4976/8

*High Commissioner*, His Excellency Revd Percy S. Mngomezulu, apptd 1994

BRITISH HIGH COMMISSION
Allister Miller Street, Mbabane
Tel: Mbabane 42581

*High Commissioner*, His Excellency Richard Gozney, apptd 1993

BRITISH COUNCIL REPRESENTATIVE, James Kennedy (*Cultural Attaché*)

ECONOMY

In the 1989–90 budget, total expenditure, including debt repayment, was projected at E447 million. A surplus of E12.5 million was predicted due to increase in revenue. Manufacturing was announced to have replaced agriculture as the dominant sector in 1988.

| Trade with UK | 1992 | 1993 |
| --- | --- | --- |
| Imports from UK | £3,226,000 | £2,887,000 |
| Exports to UK | 40,101,000 | 42,187,000 |

COMMUNICATIONS

Swaziland's railway is about 150 miles long and connects with the Mozambique port of Maputo and the South African railway network to Richards Bay. A rail line to the north-west border provides a link to Komatipoort. Most passenger and goods traffic is carried by privately-owned motor transport services. There are scheduled air services by Royal Swazi National Airways to southern and eastern Africa. International telecommunications and television services are provided through a satellite earth station, and there is also a national telephone network.

# SWEDEN
*Konungariket Sverige*

Sweden occupies the eastern area of the Scandinavian peninsula in north-west Europe and comprises 24 local government districts (*Län*), with a total area of 173,732 sq. miles (449,964 sq. km), and population of 8,635,000 (1991 UN estimate). The state religion is Lutheran Protestant, to which over 95 per cent officially adhere.

CAPITAL – ΨStockholm. Population (1988): City 669,485; Greater Stockholm, 1,471,242; ΨGothenburg (Göteborg) (430,765); ΨMalmö (231,575); Uppsala (161,828).
CURRENCY – Swedish krona of 100 öre.
FLAG – Yellow cross on a blue ground.
NATIONAL ANTHEM – Du Gamla, Du Fria (Thou ancient, thou freeborn).
NATIONAL DAY – 6 June (Day of the Swedish Flag).

GOVERNMENT

Sweden is a constitutional monarchy, with the monarch retaining purely ceremonial functions as head of state. Under the Act of Succession 1809 (with amendments) the throne is hereditary in the House of Bernadotte. The constitution is based upon the Act of Succession 1974, which amended the 1809 Act and removed from the monarch the roles of appointing the Prime Minister and signing parliamentary bills into law. A 1979 amendment vested the succession in the monarch's eldest child irrespective of sex.

Executive power is vested in the Prime Minister and Council of Ministers. There is a unicameral legislature (*Riksdag*) of 349 members elected by universal suffrage on a proportional representation basis for three years. The Council of Ministers (*Statsråd*) is responsible to the *Riksdag*. In the general election held on 15 September 1991, the following seats were won: Social Democrats 138; Moderates 80; Liberals 33; Centre 31; Christian Democrats 26; New Democracy 25; Left Party 16. A general election was about to be held at the time of going to press in September 1994.

Sweden applied for European Community membership in July 1991 and negotiations on entry were successfully concluded on 1 March 1994. The Accession Treaty to the European Union must be ratified by parliament and in a national referendum on 13 November 1994 for accession on 1 January 1995.

HEAD OF STATE
*HM The King of Sweden*, Carl XVI Gustaf, KG, *born* 30 April 1946, *succeeded* 15 September 1973, *married* 19 June 1976 Fräulein Silvia Renate Sommerlath and has *issue*, Crown Princess Victoria (*see below*); Prince Carl Philip Edmund Bertil, Duke of Värmland, *born* 13 May 1979; Princess Madeleine Thérèse Amelie Josephine, Duchess of Hälsingland and Gästrikland, *born* 10 June 1982
*Heir*, HRH Crown Princess Victoria Ingrid Alice Désirée, Duchess of Västergötland, *born* 14 July 1977

COUNCIL OF MINISTERS *as at August 1994*
*Prime Minister*, Carl Bildt (M)
*Deputy Prime Minister, Minister of Social Affairs*, Bengt
   Westerberg (L)
*Justice*, Gun Hellsvik (M)
*Foreign Affairs*, Baroness Margaretha of Ugglas (M)
*Defence*, Anders Björck (M)
*Transport and Communications*, Mats Odell (CD)
*Finance*, Anne Wibble (L)
*Education*, Per Unckel (M)
*Agriculture*, Karl Erik Olsson (C)
*Labour*, Börje Hörnlund (C)
*Industry and Commerce*, Per Westerberg (M)
*Public Administration*, Inger Davidsson (CD)
*Environment*, vacant
*Culture*, Birgit Friggebo (L)
*Constitutional and Civil Law*, Reidunn Laurén (Ind)
*International Development Co-operation and Human Rights
   Issues*, Alf Svensson (CD)
*European Affairs and Foreign Trade*, Ulf Dinkelspiel (M)
*Health and Social Security*, Bo Könberg (L)
*Fiscal Affairs and Financial Markets*, Bo Lundgren (M)
*Schools and Adult Education*, Beatrice Ask (M)
*Physical Planning*, Görel Thurdin (C)

M Moderate Party; L Liberal Party; C Centre Party;
CD Christian Democrat Party

SWEDISH EMBASSY
11 Montagu Place, London WIH 2AL
Tel 0171-917 6400

*Ambassador Extraordinary and Plenipotentiary*, His
   Excellency Lennart Eckerberg, KCMG, apptd 1991·
*Minister Plenipotentiary*, R. Ängeby
*Defence and Naval Attaché*, Cdr. Count Gustaf Taube
*Consul-General*, G. Naessén
*Trade Commissioner*, A. Lundwall

BRITISH EMBASSY
Skarpögatan 6–8, S115 93 Stockholm
Tel: Stockholm 671 9000

*Ambassador Extraordinary and Plenipotentiary*, His
   Excellency Robert Cormack, CMG, apptd 1991
*Counsellor (Political) and Consul-General*, Dr V. Caton
*Counsellor (Economic and Commercial)*, A. R. Murray
*Defence and Air Attaché*, Wg Cdr. P. McCullum

There are British Consular Offices at *Stockholm* and
*Gothenburg*, and Honorary Consulates at *Luleå, Gothenburg,
Malmö* and *Sundsvall.*

BRITISH COUNCIL REPRESENTATIVE, Ann Hellström,
   Strandagen 57A, S-111 523 Stockholm
BRITISH-SWEDISH CHAMBER OF COMMERCE, Grevgatan
   34, 11453 Stockholm.

## ECONOMY

Following the election of a centre-right government in 1991
there has been drastic change in the Swedish socio-economic
system. Free market economic policies of privatization,
deregulation, the ending of state subsidies, trade union
legislation, and welfare and spending cuts have been
introduced. Austerity packages were introduced in November
1992 and April 1993 to overcome budget deficits, improve
competitiveness and stabilize the currency. The restructuring
of industry, together with the world recession, caused
unemployment to rise to 9.5 per cent (together with a further
4 per cent on workfare schemes) in 1994 and manufacturing
output to fall 15 per cent between 1989 and 1992. The 1993
budget deficit remained high at 13 per cent of GDP, with the

national debt reaching 71 per cent of GDP in the same year.
Further cuts and reductions in the public sector, local
government, and the welfare state are being undertaken to
reduce the unsustainable levels of public spending.

Industrial prosperity is based on natural resources: forests,
mineral deposits and water power. The forests cover about
half the total land surface and sustain timber, finished wood
products, pulp and paper milling industries. The mineral
resources include iron ore, lead, zinc, sulphur, granite,
marble, precious and heavy metals (the latter not exploited)
and extensive deposits of low grade uranium ore. Industries
based on mining are important but it is the general
engineering industry that provides the basis of Sweden's
exports, especially specialized machinery and systems, motor
vehicles, electrical and electronic equipment, plastics and
chemical industries. The relative importance of agriculture
has declined and in 1993 only 3 per cent of the labour force
was engaged in farming, compared to 24.5 per cent in
mining, manufacturing and construction, 36.6 per cent in
services and 31 per cent in government.

Apart from water power (hydroelectricity supplies 15 per
cent of energy needs) Sweden has no significant indigenous
resources of conventional hydrocarbon fuels and relies for 50
per cent of its energy needs upon imported oil and coal.
Around half of Sweden's electricity is generated by nuclear
power but as a result of a referendum in 1980 the nuclear
programme is to be discontinued by 2010. However, this
decision is now being debated once more and could be
reversed. Small supplies of natural gas are imported from
Denmark into southern Sweden, with the pipeline being
extended to Gothenburg.

| FINANCE | 1991–2 | 1992–3 |
| --- | --- | --- |
| Revenue | Kronor 464,632m | Kronor 419,125m |
| Expenditure | 470,107m | 489,457m |

TRADE
About 45 per cent of industrial output is exported, mainly in
the form of cars, trucks, machinery, electrical and communications equipment. Sweden conducts 70 per cent of its trade
with the rest of EFTA and the EU.

| | 1991 | 1992 |
| --- | --- | --- |
| Imports | Kronor 301,290m | Kronor 289,923m |
| Exports | 332,790m | 326,008m |

| *Trade with UK* | 1992 | 1993 |
| --- | --- | --- |
| Imports from UK | £2,438,972,000 | £2,892,123,000 |
| Exports to UK | 3,283,739,000 | 3,622,621,000 |

## COMMUNICATIONS

The total length of railroads is 11,745 km. The road network
is over 400,000 km in length. The mercantile marine
amounted in 1985 to 2,619,625 gross tonnage. Regular
domestic air traffic is maintained by the Scandinavian
Airlines System and by Linjeflyg. Regular European and
inter-continental air traffic is maintained by the Scandinavian
Airlines System.

## DEFENCE

Sweden has a policy of non-alignment in peace and neutrality
in war, and it maintains a 'total defence' which includes
peacetime organizations for civil, economic and psychological
defence. All men aged 18–47 are eligible for conscription,
with the initial term being seven to 15 months for the Army
and Navy and eight to 12 months for the Air Force. Men are
obliged to serve in the reserves until age 47 with a
commitment to five periods of refresher training.

The armed forces have a total active strength of 64,800
(36,600 conscripts), with reserves of 729,000 (Army

586,000; Navy 66,000; Air Force 77,000). The Army has an active strength of 43,500 (27,000 conscripts), and on mobilization a strength of 630,000. Equipment includes 630 main battle tanks, 210 light tanks, 505 armoured infantry fighting vehicles, 715 artillery pieces and 20 combat helicopters. The Navy has 12 submarines, 41 patrol and coastal vessels, 28 mine warfare craft, six coast artillery brigades, 14 combat helicopters and a strength of 9,800 (4,100 conscripts). The Air Force has modern supersonic aircraft of Swedish manufacture forming a standing force of 481 combat aircraft and a modern air defence radar system. The Air Force has a strength of 11,500 (5,500 conscripts). Sweden deploys some 495 troops in Lebanon, 153 in Macedonia and 97 in Croatia with UN forces.

## CULTURE

Swedish belongs, with Danish and Norwegian, to the North Germanic language group. Swedish literature dates back to King Magnus Eriksson, who codified the old Swedish provincial laws in 1350. With his translation of the Bible, Olaus Petri (1493-1552) formed the basis for the modern Swedish language. Literature flourished during the reign of Gustavus III, who founded the Swedish Academy in 1786. Notable Swedish writers include Almquist (1795-1866), Strindberg (1849-1912) and Lagerlöf (1858-1940), Nobel Prizewinner in 1909. Contemporary authors include Lagerquist (1891-1974), Nobel Laureate in 1951, Martinson (1904-78) and Johnson (1900-76), Nobel Laureates jointly in 1974. The Swedish scientist Alfred Nobel (1833-96) founded the Nobel Prizes for literature, science and peace.

## EDUCATION

The state system provides nine years' free and compulsory schooling from the age of seven to 16 in the comprehensive elementary schools. Over 90 per cent continue into further education of two to four years' duration in the upper secondary schools and a unified higher education system administered in six regional areas containing one of the universities: Uppsala (founded 1477); Lund (1668); Stockholm (1878); Gothenburg (1887); Umeå (1963) and Linköping (1967). At present there are 33 institutions of higher education including three technical universities in Stockholm, Gothenburg and Luleå, and the Karolinska Institute in Stockholm, which specializes in medicine and dentistry.

## SWITZERLAND
*Schweizerische Eidgenossenschaft - Confédération Suisse - Confederazione Svizzera*

Switzerland, the Helvetia of the Romans, lies in central Europe, situated between 45° 50′ and 47° 48′ N. latitude and 5° 58′ and 10° 30′ E. longitude. It comprises a total area of 15,943 sq. miles (41,293 sq. km), with a population (1991 census) of 6,833,750. Of the total population in 1991, 46.1 per cent was Roman Catholic, 40 per cent Protestant, 5 per cent other religions and 8.9 per cent without religion. The official languages are German, French, Italian and Romansch.

Switzerland is the most mountainous country in Europe. The Alps, from 5,000 to 15,217 ft in height, occupy its southern and eastern frontiers and the chief part of its interior; the Jura mountains rise in the north-west. The Alps occupy 61 per cent, and the Jura mountains 12 per cent of the country. The highest peak, Mont Blanc, Pennine Alps (15,782 ft) is partly in France and Italy; Monte Rosa (15,217

ft) and Matterhorn (14,780 ft) are partly in Switzerland and partly in Italy. The highest wholly Swiss peaks are Dufourspitze (15,203 ft), Finsteraarhorn (14,026), Aletschhorn (13,711), Jungfrau (13,671), Mönch (13,456), Eiger (13,040), Schreckhorn (13,385), and Wetterhorn (12,150) in the Bernese Alps, and Dom (14,918), Weisshorn (14,803) and Breithorn (13,685). The Swiss lakes include Lakes Maggiore, Zürich, Lucerne, Neuchâtel, Geneva, Constance, Thun, Zug, Lugano, Brienz and the Walensee. There are also many artificial lakes.

CAPITAL – Berne, population (1991 census) 135,600 (city).
  Other large towns are (1991) Zürich (345,200), Basle (173,800), Geneva (169,600), Lausanne (124,800), Winterthur (86,800), St Gallen (74,500), Lucerne (60,500).
CURRENCY – Swiss franc of 100 centimes or rappen.
FLAG – Square and red, bearing a couped white cross.
NATIONAL ANTHEM – Trittst im Morgenrot Daher (Radiant in the morning sky).
NATIONAL DAY – 1 August.

## GOVERNMENT

Switzerland is a federal republic. There are 20 cantons and six half cantons (three cantons have been subdivided), making 26 in all. Each canton has its own government.

The federal government consists of the Federal Assembly of two chambers, a National Council (*Nationalrat*) of 200 members, and a States Council (*Ständerat*) of 46 members. Members of the National Council are elected for four years, elections taking place in October. The executive power is in the hands of a Federal Council (*Bundesrat*) of seven members, elected for four years by the Federal Assembly and presided over by the President of the Confederation. Each year the Federal Assembly elects from the Federal Council the President and the Vice-President. Not more than one of the same canton may be elected a member of the Federal Council; however, there is a tradition that Italian and French-speaking areas should between them be represented on the Federal Council by at least two members.

The Federal Council voted in 1992 to apply for European Community membership. The European Economic Area (EEA) Treaty between the EC and EFTA, which extends the provisions of the EC single internal market to EFTA states, was defeated in a national referendum on 6 December 1992. Switzerland will consequently be the only EFTA state outside the EEA.

FEDERAL COUNCIL

*President of the Swiss Confederation* (1994) *and Head of Finance*, Otto Stich
*Vice-President* (1994) *and Head of Defence*, Kaspar Villiger
*Transport, Communications and Energy*, Adolf Ogi
*Foreign Affairs*, Flavio Cotti
*Public Economy*, Jean-Pascal Delamuraz
*Home Affairs*, Ruth Dreifuss
*Justice and Police*, Arnold Koller

EMBASSY OF SWITZERLAND
16-18 Montagu Place, London W1H 2BQ
Tel 0171-723 0701

*Ambassador Extraordinary and Plenipotentiary*, His Excellency Franz E. Muheim, apptd 1989
*Minister*, R. Reich
*Defence Attaché*, Maj.-Gen. G. de Loës
*Consul-General*, E. Jaun
*Counsellor*, J. de Watteville (*Economic and Financial*)

There is a Swiss Consulate-General in *Manchester*.

BRITISH EMBASSY
Thunstrasse 50, 3005 Berne
Tel: Berne 3525021/6

Ambassador Extraordinary and Plenipotentiary, His
Excellency David Beattie, CMG, apptd 1992
Counsellor and Deputy Head of Mission, I. Knight-Smith
Consul-General and Director of British Export Promotion,
T. Bryant (Zurich)
Consul-General, P. J. Priestley (Geneva)
Defence Attaché, Lt.-Col. W. R. Thatcher

BRITISH COUNCIL DIRECTOR, Caroline Morrissey,
Thunstrasse 50, PO Box 265, Berne 15

BRITISH CONSULAR OFFICES – There is a Consular
section at the Embassy in Berne; Consulates-General at
Zürich and Geneva and Consular offices at Lugano, Valais
and Montreux. The Directorate of British Export
Promotion in Switzerland is in the Consulate-General
Office, Dufourstrasse 56, 8008 Zürich.

BRITISH-SWISS CHAMBER OF COMMERCE, Freiestrasse
155, 8032 Zürich

SWISS-BRITISH SOCIETIES: Berne, President, Dr
H. Beriger; Zürich, President, J.-P. Müller; Basle,
President, Dr C. Grey

## DEFENCE

All Swiss males must undertake military service in the Army
or the Air Corps, which is part of the Army. The total active
armed forces number some 1,800 regulars with 28,000 each
year for recruit training. Conscription takes the form of 17
weeks recruit training at age 20 and 30 weeks of regular
reservist refresher training up to age 42, with some 390,000
reservists attending training each year. The Army has a
strength on mobilization of 565,000 with 785 main battle
tanks, 1,285 armoured personnel carriers and armoured
infantry fighting vehicles, and 1,180 artillery pieces. The Air
Corps has a strength on mobilization of 60,000 with 241
combat aircraft. In addition, there are the paramilitary civil
defence forces, with 300,000 fully-trained personnel.

## ECONOMY

Agriculture is followed chiefly in the valleys and the central
plateau, where cereals, flax, hemp, and tobacco are produced,
and fruits and vegetables as well as grapes are grown.
Dairying and stock-raising are the principal industries, about
3,000,000 acres being under grass for hay and 2,000,000
acres pasturage. The forests cover about one-quarter of the
whole surface.
   The chief manufacturing industries comprise engineering
and electrical engineering, metal-working, chemicals and
pharmaceuticals, textiles, watchmaking, woodworking, foodstuffs and footwear. Banking, insurance and tourism are
major industries.

| FINANCE | 1989* | 1990 |
|---|---|---|
| Revenue | SFr28,031m | SFr30,324m |
| Expenditure | 27,555m | 29,850m |
| *estimate | | |

## TRADE

The principal imports are machinery, electrical and electronic
equipment, textiles, motor vehicles, non-ferrous metals,
chemical elements, clothing, food, medicinal and pharmaceutical products. The principal exports are machinery,
chemical elements, non-ferrous metals, watches, electrical
and electronic equipment, textiles, dyeing, tanning and
colouring equipment.

| | 1990 | 1991 |
|---|---|---|
| Total imports | SFr96,611m | SFr95,032m |
| Total exports | 88,257m | 87,946m |

| †Trade with UK | 1992 | 1993 |
|---|---|---|
| Imports from UK | £1,844,610,000 | £2,273,423,000 |
| Exports to UK | 3,918,936,000 | 4,721,923,000 |
| †Including Liechtenstein | | |

## COMMUNICATIONS

There were in 1990, 5,031 km of railway tracks (Swiss
Federal Railways, 2,990 km; privately owned railways
2,041 km). At the end of 1990 the total length of motorways
was 1,495 km. The merchant marine consisted at June 1990
of 20 vessels with a total gross tonnage of 287,487 tonnes. In
1989, goods handled at Basle Rhine ports amounted to
8,845,162 tonnes. In 1990, 163 lake and river vessels
(excluding the Rhine) transported 12 million passengers and
500 tonnes of freight. Swiss airlines have a network covering
348,762 km (1990) and in 1990 carried 17,100,000 passengers. Swissair, the national airline, flies to and from the
airports at Zürich, Geneva and Basle.
   The Swiss electorate voted in a February 1994 referendum
for a ban on foreign lorries using alpine roads, which will be
phased in over ten years. From 2005 onwards foreign lorries
will have to use two new north-south road-rail tunnels.

## EDUCATION

Education is controlled by cantonal and communal authorities. Primary education is free and compulsory. School age
varies, generally seven to 14, with secondary education from
age 12 to 15. Special schools make a feature of commercial
and technical instruction. Universities are Basle (founded
1460), Berne (1834), Fribourg (1889), Geneva (1873),
Lausanne (1890), Zürich (1832), and Neuchâtel (1909), the
technical universities of Lausanne and Zürich and the
economics university of St Gall.

## CULTURE

There are four national languages: French, German, Italian
and Romansch. German is the dominating language in 19 of
the 26 cantons; French in Fribourg, Jura, Geneva, Neuchâtel,
Valais and Vaud; Italian in Ticino; and Romansch in parts of
the Grisons.
   Many modern authors, alike in the German school and in
the Suisse Romande, have achieved international fame. Karl
Spitteler (1845–1924) and Hermann Hesse (1877–1962) were
awarded the Nobel Prize for Literature, the former in 1919,
the latter in 1946.

## SYRIA
Al-Jamhouriya Al-Arabia as-Souriya

Syria is in the Levant, bounded by the Mediterranean and
Lebanon on the west, Israel and Jordan on the south-west,
Iraq on the east and Turkey on the north. It has an estimated
area of 71,498 sq. miles (185,180 sq. km). The Orontes flows
northwards from the Lebanon range across the northern
boundary to Antakya (Antioch, Turkey). The Euphrates
crosses the northern boundary near Jerablus and flows
through north-eastern Syria to the boundary of Iraq.
POPULATION – The population (UN estimate 1991) is
12,993,000, most of whom are Muslim. Arabic is the principal
language, but Kurdish, Turkish and Armenian are spoken

among significant minorities and a few villages still speak Aramaic, the language spoken by Christ and the Apostles. English has taken over from French as the main foreign language.

The region is rich in historical remains. Damascus (Dimishq ash-Sham) is said to be the oldest continuously inhabited city in the world (although Aleppo disputes this claim), having existed as a city for over 4,000 years. The city contains the Omayed Mosque, the Tomb of Saladin, and the 'street which is called Straight' (Acts 9:11), while to the north-east is the Roman outpost of Dmeir and further east is Palmyra. On the Mediterranean coast at Amrit are ruins of the Phoenician town of Marath, and also ruins of Crusaders' fortresses at Markab, Sahyoun, and Krak des Chevaliers. At Tartous the cathedral of Our Lady of Syria, built by the Knights Templars in the 12th and 13th centuries, has been restored as a museum. One of the oldest alphabets in the world has been discovered at Ugarit (Ras Shamra), a Phoenician village near the port of Latakia. Hittite cities dating from 2000 to 1500 BC, have been explored on the west bank of the Euphrates at Jerablus and Kadesh.

CAPITAL – Damascus, population (1990 estimate) 1,378,000. Other important towns are Aleppo, Homs and Hama, and the principal port is ΨLatakia.
CURRENCY – Syrian pound (S£) of 100 piastres.
FLAG – Red over white over black horizontal bands, with two green stars on central white band.
NATIONAL DAY – 17 April.

## GOVERNMENT

Once part of the Ottoman Empire, following the First World War Syria came under French mandate. Syria became an independent republic during the Second World War; the first independently elected Parliament met in August 1943, but foreign troops were in part occupation until April 1946. Syria remained an independent republic until 1958, when it became part of the United Arab Republic. It seceded from the United Arab Republic in September 1961.

A new constitution was promulgated in 1973. This declared that Syria is a democratic, popular socialist state, and that the Arab Socialist Renaissance (Ba'ath) Party, which has been the ruling party since 1963, is the leading party in the state and society. Elections to the 250-seat People's Council in May 1990 resulted in a large majority for the Ba'ath Party, which won 134 seats; its National Progressive Front allies (Arab Socialist Union, Socialist Unionist Movement, Arab Socialist Party, Syrian Communist Party) together won 32 seats, and Independents won 84.

HEAD OF STATE
*President*, Lt.-Gen. Hafez el Assad, *assumed office* 14 March 1971, *re-elected*, 1978, 1985, 3 December 1991
*Vice-Presidents*, Abdul Halim Khaddam, Rifaat Al Assad, Zuhair Mashariqa

MINISTERS *as at August 1994*
*Prime Minister*, Mahmoud Al Zubi
*Deputy PM and Minister for Defence*, Gen. Mustafa Tlass
*Deputy PM for Public Services*, Rashid Akhtarini
*Deputy PM for Economic Affairs*, Dr Salim Yassin
*Education*, Ghassan Halabi
*Higher Education*, Salha Sankar
*Interior*, Mohammad Harbah
*Transport*, Mufeed Abdul-Karim
*Information*, Mohammad Salman
*Local Administration*, Yahya Abu Asali
*Supply and Internal Trade*, Nadin Akkash
*Economy and Foreign Trade*, Mohammad al-Imadi

*Culture*, Najah al-Attar
*Foreign Affairs*, Farooq al-Shara
*Tourism*, Amin Abul-Shamat
*Health*, Iyad al-Shatti
*Waqfs (Religious Endowments)*, Abdel-Majid Tarabulsi
*Irrigation*, Abd ar-Rahman Madani
*Electricity*, Munib Daher
*Oil and Mineral Resources*, Nadir Nabulsi
*Construction*, Majid Ezzou Rhaibani
*Housing and Utilities*, Hosam al-Safadi
*Agriculture and Agrarian Reform*, As'ad Mustafa
*Finance*, Khaled al-Mahayni
*Industry*, Ahmad Nezamuldin
*Communications*, Redwan Martini
*Justice*, Abdullah Tulbah
*Presidential Affairs*, Wahib Fadil
*Labour and Social Affairs*, Ali Khalil

EMBASSY OF THE SYRIAN ARAB REPUBLIC
8 Belgrave Square, London SW1X 8PH
Tel 0171-245 9012

*Ambassador Extraordinary and Plenipotentiary*, His Excellency Mohammed Khodor, apptd 1991

BRITISH EMBASSY
Quartier Malki, 11 rue Mohammad Kurd Ali, Imm. Kotob, Damascus (PO Box 37)
Tel: Damascus 712561

*Ambassador Extraordinary and Plenipotentiary*, His Excellency Adrian John Sindall, CMG, apptd 1994

BRITISH COUNCIL REPRESENTATIVE, Dr Peter Clark, OBE, Ground Floor, Tasheen Tabaa' Building, Abd Almalek Bin Marwan Street, Malki, PO Box 33105 Al Jalla, Damascus.

## DEFENCE

The total active armed forces have a strength of 408,000. There is a conscription period of 30 months, with a reserve commitment to age 45; reserves number 400,000 personnel. The Army has a strength of 300,000 (130,000 conscripts, 50,000 mobilized reservists), with 4,500 main battle tanks, 500 reconnaissance vehicles, 3,800 armoured personnel carriers and infantry fighting vehicles and 2,230 artillery pieces. The Navy has a strength of 8,000 personnel, with three submarines, two frigates, 32 patrol and coastal combatants and 25 armed helicopters. The Air Force (including the Air Defence Command) has a strength of some 100,000, with 639 combat aircraft and 100 armed helicopters of Soviet manufacture, together with 22 Air Defence brigades with surface-to-air missiles. Syria maintains a force of some 30,000 men in Lebanon and within Syria has some 4,500 men of the Palestinian Liberation Army and 500 advisers from the former Soviet Union.

## ECONOMY

Agriculture is the principal source of production; wheat and barley are the main cereal crops, but the cotton crop is the highest in value. Tobacco is grown in the maritime plain in Sahel, the Sahyoun and the Djebleh district of Latakia. Large areas are coming under cultivation in the north-east of the country as a result of irrigation from the Thawra dam. There are an increasing number of light assembly plants as Syria's industrialization programme develops. Skins and hides, leather goods, wool and silk, textiles, cement, vegetable oil, glass, soap, sugar, plastics and copper and brass utensils are produced. Oil has been found at Karachuk and other parts in the north-eastern corner of the country and production of high quality reserves is proceeding in the region of Deir ez Zor. Syria produces nearly 400,000 barrels per day at present. A pipeline has been built to the Mediterranean port of Banias, via Homs. Two oil refineries are in production at Homs and Banias. Syria also has gas reserves, deposits of phosphate and rock salt, and produces asphalt.

## TRADE

The principal imports are foodstuffs (fruit, vegetables, cereals, meat and dairy products, tea, coffee and sugar), mineral and petroleum products, yarn and textiles, iron and steel manufactures, machinery, chemicals, pharmaceuticals, fertilizers and timber. Exports include raw cotton, oil, cereals, fruit, phosphates, cement, livestock and dairy products, other foodstuffs, textiles and raw wool.

| Trade with UK | 1992 | 1993 |
| --- | --- | --- |
| Imports from UK | £64,598,000 | £74,551,000 |
| Exports to UK | 53,211,000 | 105,311,000 |

## EDUCATION

Education is under state control and although a few of the schools are privately owned, they all follow a common syllabus. Elementary education is free at state schools and is compulsory from the age of seven. Secondary education is not compulsory and is free only at the state schools. Because of the shortage of places, entry to the state schools is competitive. There are universitites at Damascus, Aleppo, Tishrin, Latakia and the Ba'ath University, Homs. Approximately 10 per cent of all students receive scholarships, and the rest pay fees.

## COMMUNICATIONS

Although railway lines run from Damascus to both Beirut and Amman, train services go only to Amman as much of the Lebanese line has been dismantled. A track has been opened connecting Homs with Damascus. A track links Homs, Hamah, Aleppo, Deir ez Zor and Qamishliye to the Iraq frontier. Branch lines connect the ports of Tartous and Latakia to the system and another line runs from Aleppo down the Euphrates valley to Deir ez Zor and thence north to Qamishliye, with a branch going to the Euphrates dam. All the principal towns in the country are connected by roads which vary from modern dual carriageways to narrow country lanes. An internal air service operates between all major towns. The main international airport is at Damascus and there are also flights from Aleppo.

There are three daily newspapers and several periodicals in Arabic published in Damascus, and also a daily newspaper in English.

## TAIWAN (REPUBLIC OF CHINA)
*Chung-hua Min-kuo*

An island of some 13,800 sq. miles (35,742 sq. km) in the China Sea, Taiwan, formerly Formosa, lies 90 miles east of the Chinese mainland in 21° 45′ to 25° 56′ N. latitude. The eastern part of the main island is mountainous and forested. Mt Morrison (Yu Shan) (13,035 ft) and Mt Sylvia (Tz'ukaoshan) (12,972 ft) are the highest peaks. The western plains are watered by many rivers.

Territories include the Pescadores Islands (50 sq. miles), some 35 miles west of Taiwan, as well as Quemoy (68 sq. miles) and Matsu (11 sq. miles) which are only a few miles from the mainland.

POPULATION – The population (1993) is 20,894,522, almost entirely Chinese. About two million mainlanders came to the island with Chiang Kai-shek in 1947–9. Mandarin Chinese has been the official language since 1949. Now Taiwanese, spoken by 85 per cent of the population, is growing in importance.

CAPITAL – Taipei, population (1990) 2,719,659. Other towns are ΨKaohsiung (1,386,723); Tainan (667,622); Taichung (730,376); and ΨKeelung (348,672).
CURRENCY – New Taiwan dollar (NT$) of 100 cents.
FLAG – Red, with blue quarter at top next staff, bearing a 12-point white sun.
NATIONAL DAY – 10 October.

## GOVERNMENT

Settled for centuries by the Chinese, the island was administered by Japan from 1895 to 1945. Gen. Chiang Kai-shek withdrew to Taiwan in 1949, towards the end of the war against the Communist regime in mainland China, after which the territory continued under his presidency until his death in 1975. Martial law was lifted in 1987 after 38 years.

In 1991, President Lee announced that the 'period of Communist rebellion' on the Chinese mainland was over, recognizing *de facto* the People's Republic of China. The announcement also ended emergency measures which had frozen political life on Taiwan since 1949. In 1991–2 power shifted away from mainlanders to native Taiwanese with the forcible retirement of the 'Senior Parliamentarians' who had retained their seats since being elected on the mainland in 1948. The new parliament, the Legislative Yuan, gained control of the budget, of law-making and of the appointment of the Prime Minister. A general election to the Legislative Yuan in December 1992 was won by the Nationalist Kuomintang (KMT) with 96 of the 161 seats; the opposition Democratic Progressive Party won 50 seats, and independents and minor parties the remaining 15 seats. During 1993–4 the KMT has been weakened by defections by mainlanders and their descendants who wish to retain the claim on the mainland and by Taiwanese who wish to declare independence. The first direct election to the presidency will be held in 1996.

HEAD OF STATE
*President*, Lee Teng-hui, *elected* 1988, *re-elected* 20 May 1990
*Vice-President*, Li Yuan-zu

EXECUTIVE YUAN *as at August 1994*
*Prime Minister*, Lien Chan
*Deputy PM*, Hsu Li-teh
*Secretary-General*, Li Hou-kao
*Interior*, Wu Po-hsiung
*Foreign Affairs*, Frederick Chien Fu
*Finance*, Lin Chen-kuo
*Education*, Kuo Wei-fan
*Economic Affairs*, P. K. Chiang
*Justice*, Ma Ying-jeou
*National Defence*, Sun Chen
*Transportation and Communications*, Liu Chao-shiuan
*Ministers without Portfolio*, Chiu Hung-ta; Shirley Kuo Wan-jung; Wang Chau-ming; Hsia Han-min; Huang Shih-cheng

*Chairs of Councils:*
*Mainland Affairs*, Huang Kun-hui
*Atomic Energy*, Hsu Yih-yun
*Research*, Sun Te-hsiung
*Agriculture*, Sun Ming-hsien
*Labour Affairs*, Chao Shou-po

*Economic Planning and Development*, Hsiao Wan-chang
*Overseas Chinese Affairs*, Chang Hsiao-yen
*Youth*, Yin Shih-hao
*Science*, Kuo Nan-hung
*Culture*, Shen Hsueh-yung
*Mongolian and Tibetan Affairs*, Chang Chun-yi
*Health*, Chang Po-ya

## DEFENCE

The total active armed forces number 442,000 personnel, with conscripts serving for two-year terms. Reserves number 1,657,500 with an obligation until the age of 30. The Army is 312,000 strong with 510 main battle tanks, 905 light tanks, 1,175 armoured infantry fighting vehicles and armoured personnel carriers, 1,375 artillery pieces and 112 helicopters. The Navy has a strength of 60,000, including 30,000 marines, with four submarines, 22 destroyers, 11 frigates, 98 patrol and coastal combatants, 32 combat aircraft and 32 armed helicopters. The Air Force has 70,000 personnel, with 484 combat aircraft. Paramilitary security groups under Ministry of Defence control number 25,000 personnel.

## ECONOMY

Over the past 30 years Taiwan has transformed itself from a mainly agricultural country to one of the fastest growing industrial economies in Asia. A series of six-year plans has expanded the industrial base; important sectors are steel, shipbuilding, chemicals, cement, machinery, plastic and rubber goods, electrical equipment and textiles. In 1990–3 economic growth averaged 6 per cent and inflation 3.5 per cent. GNP in 1993 was US$220,129 million. Continued trade surpluses have led to one of the largest foreign exchange reserves of any country in the world (US$86,632 million in mid-1992).

The soil is very fertile, producing sugar, rice, sweet potatoes, tea, bananas, pineapples and tobacco. Mineral resources are meagre. Taiwan produces one-tenth of its coal needs and some natural gas. There are important fisheries. The principal seaports are ΨKeelung and ΨKaohsiung situated in the north and south of the island.

### TRADE

The principal exports are electronic goods, machinery, metal goods, textiles, plastic products and toys and games. The main imports are oil, chemicals, machinery and natural resources. The main trading partners are the USA, Japan, Hong Kong, Germany, UK, Canada.

| Trade with UK | 1992 | 1993 |
|---|---|---|
| Imports from UK | £545,422,000 | £667,765,000 |
| Exports to UK | 1,393,718,000 | 1,617,418,000 |

# TAJIKISTAN
*Respublika i Tojikiston*

Tajikistan has an area of 55,251 sq. miles (143,100 sq. km) and occupies the extreme south-east of former Soviet Central Asia. It is bordered on the west and north-west by Uzbekistan, on the north-east by Kyrgyzstan, on the east by China and on the south by Afghanistan. The republic includes the Gorno-Badakhstan Autonomous Province and the Kulyab, Kurgan-Tyubinsk and Khodzhent Provinces. The country is mountainous with the Pamir highlands in the east and the high ridges of the Pamir-Altai system in the centre. Plains are formed by wide stretches of the Syr-Darya valley in the north and of the Amu-Darya in the south. The country has areas prone to earthquakes, and a continental climate.

POPULATION – The population (1989 census) is 5,093,000, of which 62 per cent are Tajiks, 23 per cent Uzbeks and 8 per cent Russians, with smaller numbers of Tatars, Kirghiz, Germans and Ukrainians. The estimated population in 1994 was 5,513,400. The poeple are predominantly Sunni Muslim. The main languages are Tajik (62 per cent), Uzbek (23 per cent), Russian (8 per cent). Tajik is close to the Farsi spoken in Iran.

CAPITAL – Dushanbe. Population 595,000 (1989).

CURRENCY – Rouble of 100 kopeks.

FLAG – Three horizontal stripes of red, white and green with the white of double width and charged with a crown and seven stars, all in gold.

NATIONAL DAY – 9 September (Independence Day).

## GOVERNMENT

The area that is now Tajikistan had a highly developed culture when it was invaded and conquered by Alexander the Great in the fourth century BC. The area remained under Greek and Greco-Persian rule for 200 years until the Kingdom of Kusha was established, based on Bacharia (Bukhara). Tajikistan was invaded by the Arabs in the seventh century AD and by the Samanid Persians in the ninth century AD. The Tajik cities of Bukhara and Samarkand became two of the most important cultural and educational centres in the Islamic world.

The Tajiks lived under the control of various feudal emirates until the area which is now Tajikistan was subsumed within the Russian Empire in 1868. At the time of the Russian revolution in 1917 the central Asian emirates attempted to re-establish their independence. Soviet power was re-established in northern Tajikistan by 1 April 1918, when the Turkestan Soviet Socialist Republic was formed, and the Bukhara emirate was overthrown by Soviet forces in 1920. In 1924 the Tajikistan Autonomous Soviet Socialist Republic was formed as part of the Uzbek Republic before Tajikistan was given full republican status within the Soviet Union in 1929. Stalin deprived the Tajiks of Bukhara and Samarkand, which remained in Uzbekistan, and during Soviet rule 1,000,000 Uzbeks and 800,000 Russians were settled in Tajikistan.

Tajikistan declared independence from the Soviet Union on 9 September 1991 and became a UN member on 2 March 1992. Tension between President Nabiev's supporters and the opposition Islamic and democratic groups led to demonstrations and armed clashes in the capital Dushanbe in 1992 and Nabiev was forced to resign on 7 September 1992 as he tried to flee the capital. The Islamic-Democratic alliance formed a government in September but civil war broke out as forces loyal to the former Communist regime rebelled against the new government. By early November pro-Communist forces controlled virtually all the country and the Islamic-Democratic forces were driven out of Dushanbe on 11 December. The Supreme Soviet installed Imamoli Rakmanov as its Speaker and head of state. Fighting continued in the mountainous east and south of the country, but by March 1993 the Islamic-Democratic forces had been defeated by government and Russian Army units and driven across the border into Afghanistan. However, fighting restarted in July between Russian and Tajik government forces and the Afghan-based rebels, leading to the establishment of a CIS peacekeeping force on the Tajik-Afghan border to contain continuing rebel attacks. Throughout 1993–4 fighting has continued along the border and there have been terrorist attacks inside Tajikistan. Negotiations between the government and opposition began in April 1994 in Moscow.

Since March 1994 a constitutional committee has been preparing a new democratic constitution which will be put to parliament and the electorate for ratification. The People's Party of Tajikistan was formed in April 1994 as the ruling party; other political parties are still banned at the moment. Administratively Tajikistan is divided into two regions and one autonomous region.

HEAD OF STATE

*Acting President, Chairman of the Supreme Soviet*, Imomali Rakmonov, *elected by Supreme Soviet* 19 November 1992

GOVERNMENT *as at August 1994*

*Prime Minister*, Abdujalil Samadov
*First Deputy PMs*, Abdumalik Abdullojanov (*Ambassador to Moscow*); Rahimjon Ghafarov
*Deputy PMs*, Jura Shokirov; Rustam Mirzoyev (*Economy*); Bozgul Khayrulloyev (*Education*)
*Interior*, Yakub Salimov
*Foreign Affairs*, Rashid Olimov
*Culture*, Ato Khodjayev
*Defence*, Maj.-Gen. Aleksandr Shlyapnikov
*Security*, Maj.-Gen. Saidamin Gafurov
*Industry*, Shavkat Umarov
*Finance*, Mahmad Yunusov
*Justice*, Shavkat Ishmoilev
*Agriculture*, Habiballo Tabarov
*Foreign Economic Relations*, Izatullo Hayoyev
*Communications*, Ibrahim Usmanov
*Transport*, Fariddun Muhiddinov
*Trade and Material Resources*, Khakim Saliyev
*Press and Information*, Bobokhon Makhmadov
*Health*, Alamkhon Ahmedov
*Environmental Protection*, Sadullo Hairulloev
*Land Improvement and Water Conservancy*, Vokhid Shafov
*Social Security*, Abdusayer Jaburov
*Construction*, Odil Ochilov
*Chair of State Property Committee*, Davlatov
*Administrator of the Council of Ministers*, Ramazan Mirzoyev

BRITISH AMBASSADOR, His Excellency Alexander Paul Bergne, OBE, apptd 1994, resident in Tashkent, Uzbekistan

## ECONOMY

In January 1994 Tajikistan entered into a monetary union with Russia and exchanged its old roubles for post-1993 new Russian roubles. Effectively monetary control was handed over to the Russian central bank and a large amount of economic sovereignty to the Russian government in exchange for a US$100 million loan from Russia. This was needed to prevent an economic collapse caused by 40 per cent of the budget being spent on the civil war. The economy is being reformed and privatization undertaken in order to attract foreign investment.

Agriculture is the major sector of the economy, concentrating on cotton-growing and cattle-breeding. Tajikistan also has rich mineral deposits of lead, zinc and oil and is a source of uranium. Industry specializes in the production of clothing and textiles.

| *Trade with UK* | 1993 |
|---|---|
| Imports from UK | £19,486,000 |
| Exports to UK | 157,000 |

## TANZANIA
*Jamhuri ya Muungano wa Tanzania*

Tanzania comprises Tanganyika, on the mainland of east Africa between 1° and 11° 45′ S. latitude and 29° 20′ and 40° 38′ E. longitude, and the island of Zanzibar. The mainland part is bounded on the north by Kenya and Uganda; on the south by Mozambique; on the south-west by Lake Malawi, Malawi and Zambia; on the west by Rwanda, Burundi and Zaire; and on the east by the Indian Ocean. Tanzania has an area of 364,900 sq. miles (945,087 sq. km). The greater part of the country is occupied by the central African plateau from which rise, among others, Mt Kilimanjaro (19,340 ft), the highest point on the continent of Africa, and Mt Meru (14,974 ft). The Serengeti National Park covers an area of 6,000 sq. miles in the Arusha, Mwanza and Mara Regions.

Zanzibar was formerly ruled by the Sultan of Zanzibar and was a British Protectorate until 10 December 1963. It consists of the islands of Zanzibar, Pemba and Latham. The area is 2,461 sq. km, and the population (1992 estimate), is 687,634. ΨZanzibar (population, 133,000) is the chief town and seaport of the island.

POPULATION – The total population was (UN estimate 1991) 28,359,000. Africans form a large majority, with European, Asian, and other non-African minorities. The African population consists mostly of tribes of mixed Bantu race. Swahili is the national and official language. The use of English is widespread both for educational and government purposes.

CAPITAL – Dodoma (population 88,474, 1988 estimate). The economic and administrative centre is ΨDar es Salaam (population 1,096,000, 1985 estimate). Other towns (1985 population) are ΨTanga (172,000), Mwanza (252,000), Mbeya (194,000).

CURRENCY – Tanzanian shilling of 100 cents.

FLAG – Green (above) and blue; divided by diagonal black stripe bordered by gold, running from bottom (next staff) to top (in fly).

NATIONAL ANTHEM – Mungu Ibariki Afrika (God Bless Africa).

NATIONAL DAY – 26 April (Union Day).

## GOVERNMENT

Tanganyika became an independent state and a member of the British Commonwealth on 9 December 1961, and a republic within the Commonwealth on 9 December 1962. On 10 December 1963, Zanzibar became an independent state within the Commonwealth and on 26 April 1964, Tanganyika united with Zanzibar to form the United Republic of Tanzania.

There are a President and two Vice-Presidents, one the President of Zanzibar and the other the Prime Minister. If the President comes from Zanzibar the Prime Minister will be the First Vice-President and must come from Tanganyika. If the President comes from Tanganyika the President of Zanzibar will be the First Vice-President. The President may only serve two terms.

The National Assembly contains 255 members, of whom 130 are elected from mainland constituencies and 50 from Zanzibar, 25 are ex-officio, 15 nominated and 35 indirectly elected. The Speaker may either be elected from among the members or be an additional member. Constituency members are elected by popular vote at a general election held at a maximum of five-yearly intervals.

Although Zanzibar has its own President, government and House of Representatives, Tanganyika is governed by the government of the Union. Overall policy has been decided by the Chama Cha Mapinduzi (CCM), which was the sole party until 1992, when President Mwinyi and the CCM leadership agreed to amend the constitution to allow multiparty politics. In June 1992 President Mwinyi endorsed a bill legalizing multiparty politics, with the stipulation that all parties must be active in both the mainland and in Zanzibar and that parties must not be formed on tribal or racial grounds.

*President of the United Republic,* HE Hon. Ali Hassan Mwinyi, *elected* 1985; *re-elected* 28 October 1990
*First Vice-President of the United Republic and Prime Minister,* Hon. John Malecela
*Second Vice-President of the United Republic and President of Zanzibar,* HE Dr Salmin Amour

CABINET *as at August 1994*

*The President (also Minister of Defence)*
*The First Vice-President and Prime Minister*
*The Second Vice-President*
*Deputy Prime Minister and Home Affairs,* Hon. Augustine Mrema
*Foreign Affairs and International Co-operation,* Hon. Joseph Rwegasira
*Agriculture, Livestock and Co-operatives,* Hon. Jackson Makweta
*Education, Culture, Communications and Transport,* Hon. Prof. Phillemon Sarungi
*Works,* Hon. Nalaila Kiula
*Energy, Minerals and Water,* Hon. Jakaya Kikwete
*Finance,* Hon. Prof. Kighoma Malima
*Health,* Hon. Amran Mayagila
*Industry and Trade,* Hon. Cleopa D. Msuya
*Information and Broadcasting,* Hon. Dr William Shija
*Labour and Youth,* Hon. Ahmed Hassan
*Community Development, Women and Children,* Hon. Anna Makinda
*Tourism, Natural Resources, Environment,* Hon. Juma Omar Juma
*Science, Technology and Higher Education,* Hon. Benjamin Mkapa
*Minister without Portfolio,* Hon. K. Ngombale Mwiru

HIGH COMMISSION FOR THE UNITED REPUBLIC OF TANZANIA
43 Hertford Street, London W1Y 7TF
Tel 0171-499 8951/2/3/4

*High Commissioner,* His Excellency Ali S. Mchumo, apptd 1991

BRITISH HIGH COMMISSION
Hifadhi House, Samora Avenue (PO Box 9200), Dar es Salaam
Tel: Dar es Salaam 29601-5

*High Commissioner,* His Excellency Roger Westbrook, CMG, apptd 1992

BRITISH COUNCIL REPRESENTATIVE, Robert Sykes, Ohio Samora Avenue (PO Box 9100), Dar es Salaam

ECONOMY

The economy is based mainly on the production and export of primary produce and the growing of foodstuffs for local consumption. The islands of Zanzibar and Pemba produce a large part of the world's supply of cloves and clove oil; and coconuts, coconut oil and copra are also produced. The mainland's chief export crops are coffee, cotton, sisal, tea, tobacco, cashew nuts and diamonds. The most important minerals are diamonds. Hides and skins are another valuable export. Industry is largely concerned with the processing of raw material for either export or local consumption. There are also secondary manufacturing industries, including factories for the manufacture of leather and rubber footwear, knitwear, razor blades, cigarettes and textiles, and a wheat flour mill.

| *Trade with UK* | 1992 | 1993 |
|---|---|---|
| Imports from UK | £78,545,000 | £108,943,000 |
| Exports to UK | 21,140,000 | 25,633,000 |

EDUCATION

The school system is administered in Swahili but the government is making efforts to improve English standards for the purposes of secondary and higher education. All Tanzanian secondary schools are expected to include practical subjects in the basic course. For higher education Tanzanian students go to the University of Dar es Salaam, Sokoine University of Agriculture in Morogoro, other African universities, or to universities and colleges outside Africa.

COMMUNICATIONS

The main ports are Dar es Salaam, Tanga, Mtwara, Zanzibar, Mkoani and Wete, in addition to Mwanza, Musoma and Bukoba on Lake Victoria and Kigoma on Lake Tanganyika. Coastal shipping services connect the mainland to Zanzibar, and lake services are operated on Lake Tanganyika and Lake Malawi with neighbouring countries. The principal international airports are Dar es Salaam and Kilimanjaro. Other airports include Zanzibar, Arusha, Mwanza and Tanga. There are two railway systems; one connecting Dar es Salaam to Zambia, and the second having two main lines running from Dar es Salaam, one to northern Tanzania and Kenya and the other to Lake Tanganyika and Victoria.

# THAILAND
*Prathes Thai*

Thailand, formerly known as Siam, has an area of 198,457 sq. miles (514,000 sq. km). It has a common boundary with Malaysia in the south, is bounded on the west by Myanmar (Burma) and on the north-east and east by Laos and Cambodia. Thailand is divided geographically into four: the centre is a plain; to the north-east there is a plateau area and to the north-west mountains. The south of Thailand consists of a narrow mountainous peninsula. The principal rivers are the Chao Phraya in the central plains, and the Mekong on the northern and north-eastern borders.

POPULATION – The population (UN estimate 1991) is 56,923,000. The principal language is Thai, a monosyllabic, tonal language of the Indo-Chinese linguistic family, with a vocabulary strongly influenced by Sanskrit and Pali. It is written in an alphabetic script derived from ancient Indian scripts. Significant minorities speak Chinese (in urban areas), Lao (in the north-east), Khmer (in the east) and Malay (in the far south).

The principal religion is Buddhism (94.37 per cent), with 3.95 per cent Muslims, 0.53 per cent Christians and 1.15 per cent other religions.

CAPITAL – ΨBangkok, at the mouth of the River Chao Phraya, population (1990) 5,876,000. Other centres are

Chiang Mai, Phitsanuloke, Chon Buri, Korat, Khon Kaen, Surat Thani, Hat Yai and ΨPhuket.
CURRENCY – Baht of 100 satang.
FLAG – Five horizontal bands, red, white, dark blue, white, red (the blue band twice the width of the others).
NATIONAL ANTHEM – Pleng Chart.
NATIONAL DAY – 5 December (The King's Birthday).

## GOVERNMENT

Thailand became a constitutional monarchy in 1932. The 1978 constitution (as amended) provides for a National Assembly consisting of a 270-member Senate appointed by the monarch and a 360-member House of Representatives elected by universal adult suffrage for a term of four years. Following a military coup in February 1991, a new constitution was approved in December 1991 under which the military would appoint the members of the Senate and so enshrine its place in Thai politics. Parties aligned with the military won the general election in March 1992, but opposition to the military-controlled government grew and mass demonstrations held in Bangkok from 17 to 20 May eventually, with the help of the King, forced the government from power. Military power was curbed and the interim government sacked military chiefs. Parliamentary elections in September 1992 resulted in a majority for 'democratic parties', i.e. those not allied with the military. Chuan Leekpai became Prime Minister at the head of a five-party governing coalition which held 193 of the House of Representatives seats in August 1994. The new government is committed to the reduction of the political power of the military.

HEAD OF STATE
*HM The King of Thailand*, King Bhumibol Adulyadej, *born* 1927; *succeeded his brother*, 9 June 1946; *married* Princess Sirikit Kitiyakara, 28 April 1950; *crowned* 5 May 1950; and has *issue*, Princess Ubolratana, *born* 6 April 1951; Crown Prince Vajiralongkorn (*see below*); Princess Maha Chaki Sirindhorn, *born* 2 April 1955; Princess Chulabhorn, *born* 4 July 1957
*Heir*, HRH Crown Prince Vajiralongkorn, *born* 28 July 1952

GOVERNMENT *as at August 1994*
*Prime Minister*, Chuan Leekpai
*Deputy PMs*, Banyat Banthatthan; Amnuai Wirawan; Bunchu Rotchanasathian; Suphachai Phanitchaphak
*Ministers in the Prime Minister's Office*, Theotphong Chaiyanan; Sawit Phothiwihok; Surasak Thiamprasoet; Col. Chinnawut Sunthonsina
*Defence*, Gen. Wichit Sukmak
*Finance*, Tharin Nimmanhemin
*Foreign Affairs*, Sqn. Ldr. Prasong Sonsiri
*Agriculture and Co-operatives*, Niphon Phromphan
*Communications*, Col. Winai Somphong
*Commerce*, Uthai Phimchaichon
*Interior*, Gen. Chaovalit Yongchaiyuth
*Justice*, Sawai Patano
*Science, Technology and Environment*, Phisan Munlasatsathan
*Education*, Samphan Thongsamak
*Public Health*, Arthit Urairat
*Industry*, Maj.-Gen. Sanan Khachonprasat
*University Affairs*, Suthep Attakor
*Labour and Social Welfare*, Phaitoon Kaewthong

ROYAL THAI EMBASSY
29–30 Queen's Gate, London SW7 5JB
Tel 0171-589 2944

*Ambassador Extraordinary and Plenipotentiary*, His Excellency Tongchan Jotikasthira, apptd 1991

*Minister and Deputy Head of Mission*, V. Snidvongs
*Defence Attaché*, Capt. S, Kolasastraseni
*Minister Counsellor*, P. Phonthirasuwan (*Commercial*)

BRITISH EMBASSY
Wireless Road, Bangkok 10330
Tel: Bangkok 253 01919

*Ambassador Extraordinary and Plenipotentiary*, His Excellency Charles C. Adams, CMG, apptd 1992
*Deputy Ambassador and Counsellor*, R. T. Fell
*Defence Attaché*, Col. J. L. Longman
*First Secretary (Commercial)*, D. J. Hawkes, MBE
*Consul*, J. C. Sharpe, CBE
There is a British Consulate at *Chang Mai*

BRITISH COUNCIL REPRESENTATIVE, Dr P. Moss, 428 Rama I Road, Siam Square Soi 2, Pathumwan, Bangkok 10330. There is also an office in Chiang Mai
BRITISH CHAMBER OF COMMERCE, BP Building 18th Floor, Unit 1810, 54 Asoke Road (Sukhumvit 21) Bangkok 10110

## DEFENCE

Total active armed forces number 295,000 personnel, with conscription terms of two years. Reserves number a further 500,000 personnel. The Army numbers 190,000 (80,000 conscripts) with 200 main battle tanks, 510 light tanks, 970 armoured personnel carriers, 409 artillery pieces and four attack helicopters. The Navy has 62,000 personnel, with nine frigates, 63 patrol and coastal combatants, 29 combat aircraft, eight armed helicopters and a marine division of seven regiments. The Air Force has 43,000 personnel, with 156 combat aircraft. Six paramilitary forces, including three police forces, have a total strength of 141,700 personnel.

## ECONOMY

The agricultural sector provides just under half the national income and employs 67.5 per cent of the labour force. Rice remains the most important crop, accounting for 60 per cent of the area planted. The other main crops are sugar, maize, sorghum, cassava, rubber, tobacco, kenaf and jute. In recent years the production of livestock and poultry, especially pigs and chickens for export, has gained importance. There is a large fishing industry with more than 20,000 vessels registered. Fish and prawn farming is popular in many inland areas. A ban on hardwood export has resulted in the decline of the forestry industry.

Onshore oil and offshore gas were discovered in the late 1970s; crude oil production began in 1983. The predicted surplus of natural gas has led the government to designate an area on the east coast as the future centre of the petrochemical industry. Another energy resource is lignite, which is found mainly in the north and is being used increasingly for electricity production. Mineral resources are mainly tin, tungsten, lead, antimony and iron. Among these tin is the most important. In addition, a zinc refinery was opened in 1984.

Since 1960 the government has actively promoted industrial investment by means of tax relief and other incentives to local and foreign investors; in 1985, 74.6 per cent of this investment was in Thai projects. Initially industries established under this scheme were import-substituting but the emphasis has shifted now to export-oriented industries. Important sectors are transportation vehicles and equipment, construction materials, brewing, petroleum refining, electrical appliances. Manufacturing now accounts for about 21.8 per cent of the national income. The service sector is large, the banking system contributing greatly to the economy, and since 1982 tourism has been the main foreign exchange earner.

In 1993 the economy grew by 7.5 per cent, inflation was 3.2 per cent, the government budget had a surplus of 2.3 per cent of GDP and foreign currency reserves stood at US$25,500 million.

## TRADE

Thailand's main exports are rice, tapioca and tapioca products, garments, rubber, integrated circuit boards, precious stones, pearls and other ornaments, maize, canned sea food, fabrics, sugar and tin. Main imports are crude oil, chemicals and pharmaceuticals, electrical and non-electrical machinery and spare parts, industrial machinery, iron and steel, diesel oil and other fuel oil, vehicle and transport equipment.

|  | 1992 | 1993 |
|---|---|---|
| Total imports | Bhat 1,020 600m | Bhat 1,151,000m |
| Total exports | 815,400m | 909,000m |
| | | |
| *Trade with UK* | 1992 | 1993 |
| Imports from UK | £476,368,000 | £659,376,000 |
| Exports to UK | 641,886,000 | 770,677,000 |

## EDUCATION

Primary education is compulsory and free, and secondary education in government schools is free. Private universities and colleges are playing an increasing role in higher education. Out of 43 universities and other similar higher institutes of learning, 21 are private.

## COMMUNICATIONS

The road network, totalling 46,047 km in 1991, reaches all parts of the country. Most of the smaller towns and bigger villages are now served by paved roads. Navigable waterways have a length of about 1,100 km in the dry season and 1,600 km in the wet season. About 4,450 km of state-owned railways were open to traffic in 1989. Main lines run from Bangkok to the Cambodian border, the ferry terminal on the River Mekong opposite Vientiane, Chiang Mai and to Hat Yai, whence lines run down both sides of the Malay peninsula to Singapore. A new line to Sattahip on the east coast is being constructed. Bangkok is the international airport, though airports at Chiang Mai, Phuket and Hat Yai also receive international flights. Most major provincial towns have airports. The THAI airline is state-owned.

There are two important ports in the country. Bangkok, which is a river port, can serve vessels up to 27 ft draught. The deep-sea port at Sattahip caters for larger vessels. Phuket and Songkhla deep-water ports have already been completed and are the first to be managed privately under a ten-year concession. Construction of Laem Chabang deep-water port started in 1988.

---

## TOGO
*Républic Togolaise*

---

Togo is situated in West Africa between 0° and 2° W. and 6° and 11° N., with a coastline 35 miles long on the Gulf of Guinea. It extends northwards inland for 350 miles and is flanked on the west by Ghana, on the north by Burkina and in the east by Benin. It has an area of 21,925 sq. miles (56,785 sq. km), and a population (UN estimate 1991) 3,643,000, including people of several African races. The official language is French; Ewe is spoken by about 47 per cent.

CAPITAL – ΨLomé, population (1983) 366,476.
CURRENCY – Franc CFA of 100 centimes.
FLAG – Five alternating green and yellow horizontal stripes; a quarter in red at top next staff bearing a white star.
NATIONAL DAY – 13 January (National Liberation Day).

## GOVERNMENT

The first President of Togo, Sylvanus Olympio, was assassinated in 1963. His successor was overthrown by an army coup d'état in 1967 and the army commander Lt.-Col. (later Gen.) Eyadéma named himself President. President Eyadéma came under increasing popular pressure to introduce reforms in 1990 and in October the Rassemblement du peuple togolais (RPT), the sole legal party, approved plans for a new constitutional conference after pro-democracy riots. Riots broke out again in March 1991 in protest at the slow pace of reform, and in April the government was forced to concede a political amnesty, the introduction of a multiparty constitution and a national conference. In August 1991 the national conference stripped President Eyadéma of all powers, banned the RPT and elected Kokou Koffigoh as Prime Minister of an interim government. The national conference set a date of 9 February 1992 for a referendum on a new constitution.

However, from the second half of 1991 onwards the political situation became progressively more unstable. Troops loyal to President Eyadéma three times attempted to overthrow the Koffigoh government (October, November and December 1991) but were frustrated by pro-democracy supporters. Continued political violence in 1992 between the army and pro-democracy groups and among rival opposition parties forced the postponement of the referendum until September 1992, when a new multiparty constitution was agreed. In November Eyadéma, who had regained the position of head of state in August 1992, ordered the Army to crush civil unrest and a general strike against his rule. In February 1993, as political violence continued, Koffigoh and Eyadéma agreed on the formation of a crisis government, which the national conference and the Collective Democratic Opposition-2 (COD-2) declared illegal.

President Eyadéma won a presidential election in August 1993 that was boycotted by opposition parties and declared rigged by international monitors. Legislative elections to the 81-seat National Assembly were held in February 1994 and won by the opposition alliance of the Action Committee for Renewal (CAR) (36 seats) and the Togolese Union for Democracy (UTD) (7 seats), while the RPT and allied parties won 38 seats. However, Eyadéma persuaded UTD leader Edem Kodjo to form a coalition UTD-RPT government in April 1994, the RPT retaining a majority of cabinet seats.

HEAD OF STATE
*President*, Gen. Gnassingbé Eyadéma, *assumed office*, 14 April 1967; *re-elected* 1986, August 1993

GOVERNMENT *as at August 1994*
*Prime Minister*, Edem Kodjo
*Economy and Finance*, Elome Dadzie
*Foreign Affairs and Co-operation*, Boumbera Alassounouma
*Planning and Territorial Development*, Yandjia Yentchabre
*Equipment*, Tchamdja Andjo
*Justice*, Kagni Gabriel
*Territorial Administration and Security*, Seyi Memene
*Communications and Culture*, Atsutse Agbobli
*Tourism, Rural Development and Environment*, Yao Do Felli

*Health and National Solidarity*, Afatbao Amédomé
*Social Welfare, Civil Service, Labour and Employment*, Kpandja Fare
*National Defence*, Alfa Abalo
*Industry and State Companies*, Payadowa Boukpessi
*Youth and Sport*, Kouami Agbogboli Ihou
*National Education and Scientific Research*, Komlavi Seddoh
*Commerce and Transport*, Dedevi Michele Ekue
*Interior and Decentralization*, Kodjo Sagbo
*Human Rights, Rehabilitation and Relations with Parliament*, Djovi Gally
*Mines, Energy and Water Resources*, Anato Agbodouhoue
*Technical Education and Vocational Training*, Bamouhi Baba

EMBASSY OF TOGO – The Embassy of Togo closed in September 1991

BRITISH AMBASSADOR, His Excellency David Walker, CVO, resident in Accra, Ghana
There is a Consulate (BP 20050) and a Commercial Office (BP 80607) in Lomé.

ECONOMY

Although the economy remains largely agricultural, exports of phosphates have superseded agricultural products as the main source of export earnings. Other exports include palm kernels, copra and manioc. The production of phosphates entirely for export was taken over completely by the government in February 1974.

| Trade with UK | 1992 | 1993 |
|---|---|---|
| Imports from UK | £7,658,000 | £4,769,000 |
| Exports to UK | 4,066,000 | 901,000 |

## TONGA
*Kingdom of Tonga*

Tonga, or the Friendly Islands, comprises a group of islands situated in the southern Pacific some 450 miles east-south-east of Fiji, with an area of 270 sq. miles (699 sq. km), and population (1991 UN estimate) of 94,000. The largest island, Tongatapu, was discovered by Tasman in 1643. Most of the islands are of coral formation, but some are volcanic (Tofua, Kao and Niuafoou or 'Tin Can' Island). The limits of the group are between 15° and 23° 30′ S., and 173° and 177° W.

CAPITAL – ΨNuku'alofa (population estimate 30,000), on Tongatapu.
CURRENCY – Pa'anga (T$) of 100 seniti.
FLAG – Red with a white canton containing a couped red cross.
NATIONAL ANTHEM – E, 'Otua Mafimafi (Oh, Almighty God Above).
NATIONAL DAY – 4 June (Independence Day).

GOVERNMENT

The Kingdom of Tonga is an independent constitutional monarchy within the Commonwealth. Prior to 4 June 1970 it had been a British-protected state for 70 years. The constitution provides for a government consisting of the Sovereign, an appointed privy council, a cabinet, a legislative assembly and a judiciary. The 30-member legislative assembly comprises the King, the 11-member-privy council, nine hereditary nobles elected by their peers, and nine popularly elected representatives who hold office for three years. The most recent election took

place on 4 February 1993 and six of the nine seats were won by candidates wishing to reduce the power of the King and nobles and to strengthen democracy.

HEAD OF STATE
*King of Tonga*, HM King Taufa'ahau Tupou IV, GCMG, GCVO, KBE, *acceded* 16 December 1965
*Heir*, HRH Crown Prince Tupouto'a

CABINET *as at August 1994*
*Prime Minister, Minister of Agriculture, Fisheries, Forests, and Marine*, Baron Vaea of Houma
*Deputy Prime Minister, Minister of Education, Works and Civil Aviation*, Hon. Dr S. Langi Kavaliku
*Labour, Commerce and Industry*, Hon. Tutoatasi Fakafanva
*Police, Prisons and Fire Services*, Hon. George 'Akau'ola
*Health*, Hon. Dr S. Tapa
*Foreign Affairs and Defence*, HRH Crown Prince Tupouto'a
*Finance*, Hon. J. Cecil Cocker
*Attorney-General, Justice*, Hon. Tevita P. Tupou
*Minister without Portfolio*, Hon. Ma'afu Tuku'i'aulahi
*Minister of Lands, Survey, and Natural Resources*, Hon. Dr S. Ma'afu Tupou
*Governor of Ha'apai*, Hon. Fakafanua
*Governor of Vava'u*, Hon. Tu'i'afitu

TONGA HIGH COMMISSION
36 Molyneux Street, London W1H 6AB
Tel 0171-724 5828

*High Commissioner*, His Excellency Sione Kité, apptd 1992

BRITISH HIGH COMMISSION
PO Box 56, Nuku'alofa
Tel: Nuku'alofa 21020

*High Commissioner*, His Excellency Andrew James Morris, apptd 1994

ECONOMY

The economy is primarily agricultural; the main crops are coconuts, bananas, vanilla, yams, taro, cassava, groundnuts, squash pumpkins and other fruits. Fish is an important staple food, though recent shortfalls have led to canned fish being imported. Industry is based on the processing of agricultural produce, and the manufacture of foodstuffs, clothing and sports equipment.

TRADE

The principal exports are copra, other coconut products, tropical root crops, bananas, knitwear, leather goods and fibreglass boats.

| | 1989 |
|---|---|
| Total imports | T$68,334,194 |
| Total exports | 11,517,597 |

| Trade with UK | 1992 | 1993 |
|---|---|---|
| Imports from UK | £482,000 | £1,463,000 |
| Exports to UK | 294,000 | 55,000 |

## TRINIDAD AND TOBAGO
*The Republic of Trinidad and Tobago*

Trinidad, the most southerly of the West Indian islands, lies seven miles off the north coast of Venezuela. The island is situated between 10° 2′ and 11° 12′ N. latitude and 60° 30′ and 61° 56′ W. longitude, and is about 50 miles in length by 37 miles in width, with an area of 1,864 sq. miles (4,827 sq.

km). Two mountain systems, the Northern and Southern Ranges, stretch across almost its entire width and a third, the Central Range, lies diagonally across its middle portion; otherwise the island is mostly flat.

Tobago lies between 11° 9′ and 11° 21′ N. latitude and between 60° 30′ and 60° 50′ W. longitude, 19 miles north-east of Trinidad. The island is 32 miles long at its widest point, and 11 wide, and has an area of 116 sq. miles (300 sq. km).

Corozal Point and Icacos Point, the north-west and south-west extremities of Trinidad, enclose the Gulf of Paria. West of Corozal Point lie several islands, of which Chacachacare, Huevos, Monos and Gaspar Grande are the most important.

The climate is tropical. There is a dry season from January to May, and a wet season from June to December broken by a short dry season (the *Petite Careme*) in September and October.

POPULATION – The population (UN estimate 1991) was 1,253,000; Tobago's population is about 45,000.

CAPITAL – ΨPort of Spain (population, 1985, 59,649) is the administrative centre of the islands. San Fernando (population 34,300) is emerging as the industrial centre of Trinidad. The main town of Tobago is ΨScarborough.

CURRENCY – Trinidad and Tobago dollar (TT$) of 100 cents.

FLAG – Black diagonal stripe bordered with white stripes, running from top by staff, all on a red field.

NATIONAL DAYS – 31 August (Independence Day); 24 September (Republic Day).

## GOVERNMENT

Trinidad was discovered by Columbus in 1498, was colonized in 1532 by the Spaniards, capitulated to the British in 1797, and was ceded to Britain under the Treaty of Amiens 1802. Tobago was discovered by Columbus in 1498. Dutch colonists arrived in 1632; Tobago subsequently changed hands numerous times until it was ceded to Britain by France in 1814 and amalgamated with Trinidad in 1888.

The Territory of Trinidad and Tobago became an independent state and a member of the British Common-wealth on 31 August 1962, and a republic in 1976. The President is elected for five years by all members of the Senate and the House of Representatives. The House of Representatives has 36 members, elected by universal adult suffrage, and the Senate has 31, of whom 16 are appointed on the advice of the Prime Minister, six on the advice of the Leader of the Opposition and nine at the discretion of the President. Legislation was passed in September 1980 which afforded Tobago a degree of self-administration through the 15-member Tobago House of Assembly.

The most recent general election on 16 December 1991 was won by the People's National Movement, which took 21 out of 36 seats and formed a government.

### HEAD OF STATE

*President*, His Excellency Noor Mohammed Hassanali, *elected* 1987, *re-elected* February 1992

### CABINET *as at August 1994*

*Prime Minister*, Hon. Patrick Manning
*Finance and Tourism*, Hon. Wendell Mottley
*Attorney-General*, Hon. Keith Sobion
*Energy and Energy Industries*, Hon. Barry Barnes
*Trade and Industry*, Hon. Kenneth Valley
*National Security*, Hon. Russel Huggins
*Foreign Affairs*, Hon. Ralph Maraj
*Sport and Youth Affairs*, Hon. Jean Pierre
*Consumer Affairs and Social Services*, Hon. Linda Baboolal

*Local Government, Works and Transport*, Hon. Colm Imbert
*Education*, Hon. Augustus Ramrekersingh
*Health*, Hon. John Eckstein
*Public Utilities*, Hon. Morris Marshall
*Planning and Development*, Hon. Lenny Saith
*Labour and Co-operatives*, Hon. Kenneth Collis
*Community Development, Culture and Women's Affairs*, Hon. Joan Yuille-Williams
*Agriculture, Lands and Marine Resources*, Hon. Dr Keith Rowley
*Housing and Settlements*, Hon. Dr Vincent Lasse
*Social Development*, Camille Robinson-Regis

HIGH COMMISSION OF THE REPUBLIC OF TRINIDAD AND TOBAGO
42 Belgrave Square, London SW1X 8NT
Tel 0171-245 9351

*High Commissioner*, His Excellency Rabindranath Permanand, apptd 1993

BRITISH HIGH COMMISSION
19 St Clair Ave, St Clair, Port of Spain
Tel: Port of Spain 6222748

*High Commissioner*, His Excellency Richard Neilson, CMG, LVO, apptd 1994

## ECONOMY

Trinidad and Tobago's main source of revenue is from oil. Production of domestic crude was 55 million barrels in 1990. Trinidad has large reserves of natural gas, and reserves are estimated to be in the region of 100 years at the current rates of production. An integrated steel plant, an anhydrous ammonia plant and a methanol plant have been constructed at Point Lisas. An industrial complex is developing around San Fernando.

Fertilizers, tyres, clothing, soap, furniture and foodstuffs are manufactured locally while motor vehicles, radios, TV sets, and electro-domestic equipment are assembled from parts, mainly from Japan. The main agricultural products are sugar, cocoa, coffee and teak.

| TRADE | 1991 | 1992 |
|---|---|---|
| Imports | TT$7,084.8m | TT$6,081.1m |
| Exports | 8,436.4m | 7,942.9m |

| Trade with UK | 1992 | 1993 |
|---|---|---|
| Imports from UK | £59,083,000 | £70,700,000 |
| Exports to UK | 35,187,000 | 43,077,000 |

## EDUCATION

Education is free at all state-owned and government-assisted denominational schools and certain faculties at the University of the West Indies. In addition there are various private teaching establishments. Attendance is compulsory for children aged six to 12 years, after which attendance at free secondary schools is determined by success in the common entrance examination at 11 years. There are three technical institutes, two teachers' training colleges, and one of the three branches of the University of the West Indies is located in Trinidad. A medical teaching complex at Mt Hope operates in collaboration with the University of the West Indies.

## COMMUNICATIONS

There are some 6,436 km of all-weather roads in Trinidad and Tobago. The only general cargo port is Port of Spain but there are specialized port facilities elsewhere for crude oil, refinery products, sugar, bauxite and cement. Regular shipping services call and many inter-island craft use the port. Another rapidly growing port is at Port Lisas where new industries powered by local natural gas are located. International scheduled airlines, including the national airline, Trinidad and Tobago Airways (BWIA) Corporation, use Piarco International Airport, Port of Spain. The airline also flies between Piarco and Crown Point Airport in Tobago.

Three commercial broadcasting stations and one commercial television station operate in Trinidad and Tobago. The internal telephone system and the external telephone and telegraph connections are operated by partly state-owned companies.

---

## TUNISIA
*Al-Djoumhouria Attunusia*

Tunisia lies between Algeria and Libya and extends southwards to the Sahara Desert, with a total area of 164,150 sq. km, and a population (UN estimate 1991) of 8,362,000.

CAPITAL – Ψ Tunis had a population (1984) of 1,394,749. The ruins of ancient Carthage lie a few miles from the city. Other towns of importance are: Ψ Sfax (577,992); Ψ Sousse (322,491); Ψ Bizerta (394,670); Kairouan; Gabes; Menzel Bourguiba.

CURRENCY – Tunisian dinar of 1,000 millimes.

FLAG – Red with a white disc containing a red crescent and star.

NATIONAL ANTHEM – Himat Al Hima.

NATIONAL DAY – 20 March.

## GOVERNMENT

A French Protectorate from 1881 to 1956, Tunisia became an independent sovereign state on 20 March 1956. In 1957 the Constituent Assembly abolished the monarchy and elected M. Bourguiba President of the Republic. In March 1975 the National Assembly proclaimed M. Bourguiba as President for life but he was deposed on 7 November 1987 and succeeded by President Zine el-Abidine Ben Ali. Presidential and legislative elections were held in April 1989. The Rassemblement Constitutionnel Democratique (RCD) won all 141 seats in the National Assembly, which were contested by seven parties; President Ben Ali was elected with 99 per cent of the vote. Electoral changes enacted in September 1993 provide for opposition parties to be represented in the National Assembly; the Assembly has been expanded to 163 seats, 19 of which are reserved, on a proportional basis, for those parties not winning any of the 144 first-past-the-post seats. Presidential and legislative elections held in March 1994 were won by President Ben Ali, the only candidate, and the RCD, which won all 144 constituency seats.

The country is divided into 23 regions (*gouvernorats*) each administered by a governor.

HEAD OF STATE
*President*, Zine el-Abidine Ben Ali, *took office* 7 November 1987, *elected* 2 April 1989, *re-elected* 21 March 1994

CABINET *as at August 1994*

*Prime Minister*, Hamed Karoui
*Minister of State, Interior*, Abdallah Kallel
*Justice*, Sadok Chaabane
*Director of Presidential Office*, Mohamed el Jeri
*Foreign Affairs*, Habib ben Yahia
*Defence*, Abdelaziz Ben Dhia
*Economy*, Sadok Rabah
*Finance*, Nouri Zorgati

*Planning and Regional Development*, Mustapha Nabli
*International Co-operation and Development*, Mohammed Ghannouchi
*Agriculture*, Mohammed Ben Rajab
*Public Estates*, Mustapha Bouaziz
*Equipment and Housing*, Ali Chaouch
*Transport*, Tahar Haj Ali
*Tourism and Handicrafts*, Mohamed Jegham
*Communications*, Habib Lazreg
*Education and Science*, Mohamed Charfi
*Culture*, Mongi Bousnina
*Health*, Hedi Henni
*Social Affairs*, Mohamed Fadhel Khelil
*Environment, Town and Country Planning*, Mohamed Mehdi Melika
*Professional Training and Employment*, Moncer Rouissi
*Youth and Childhood Welfare*, Abderrahim Zouari
*Secretary-General of the Government*, Ridha Grira
*Religious Affairs*, Ali Chebbi

TUNISIAN EMBASSY
29 Prince's Gate, London SW7 1QG
Tel 0171-584 8117

*Ambassador Extraordinary and Plenipotentiary*, His Excellency Mohamed Lessir, apptd 1992

BRITISH EMBASSY
5 Place de la Victoire, Tunis 1015 RP
Tel: Tunis 1341444

*Ambassador Extraordinary and Plenipotentiary and Consul-General*, His Excellency Michael Tait, CMG, LVO, apptd 1992
*First Secretary*, B. England (*Deputy Head of Mission*)
There is a Consulate at *Sfax*.

BRITISH COUNCIL REPRESENTATIVE, C. Stevenson (*Cultural Attaché*)

## ECONOMY

The valleys of the northern region support large flocks and herds and contain rich agricultural areas in which wheat, barley, and oats are grown. Vines and olives are extensively cultivated. Some oil has been discovered and crude oil production in 1989 was 4.8 million tons. Gas has also been discovered off the east coast but exploitation is not viable at present. Tourists numbered almost three million in 1989 and tourism is the main foreign exchange earner.

TRADE

The chief exports are crude oil, phosphates, olive oil, finished textiles, and fruit. The chief imports are machinery and equipment, foodstuffs, petroleum products, and textiles. France remains the main trading partner.

Tunisia became an associate of the EC early in 1969 and signed a new agreement with the EC in 1976.

| Trade with UK | 1992 | 1993 |
|---|---|---|
| Imports from UK | £50,685,000 | £62,210,000 |
| Exports to UK | 48,445,000 | 39,383,000 |

---

## TURKEY
*Türkiye Cumhuriyeti*

Turkey lies partly in Europe and partly in Asia. The total area is 814,578 sq. km, of which 790,200 sq. km is in Asia and 24,378 sq. km is in Europe. Turkey in Europe consists of Eastern Thrace, including the cities of Istanbul and Edirne, and is separated from Asia by the Bosporus at Istanbul and by the Dardanelles (about 40 miles in length with a width varying from one to four miles), the political neighbours being Greece and Bulgaria on the west. Turkey in Asia comprises the whole of Asia Minor or Anatolia and extends from the Aegean Sea to the western boundaries of Georgia, Armenia and Iran, and from the Black Sea to the Mediterranean and the northern boundaries of Syria and Iraq.

POPULATION – Population at the 1990 census was 56,473,035. The 1991 UN estimate is 60,777,000. Islam ceased to be the state religion in 1928 but 98.99 per cent of the population are Muslim. The main religious minorities, which are concentrated in Istanbul and on the Syrian frontier, are Greek Orthodox, Armenian, Syriani Christian, and Jewish.

CAPITAL – Ankara (Angora), in Asia, population (1990) 3,236,626. Ankara (or Ancyra) was the capital of the Roman Province of *Galatia Prima*, and a marble temple (now in ruins), dedicated to Augustus, contains the *Monumentum (Marmor) Ancyranum*, inscribed with a record of the reign of Augustus Caesar.

Ψ Istanbul (7,309,190), in Europe, is the former capital. The Roman city of Byzantium, it was selected by Constantine the Great as the capital of the Roman Empire about AD 328 and renamed Constantinople. Istanbul contains the celebrated church of St Sophia, which, after becoming a mosque, was made a museum in 1934. It also contains Topkapi, former palace of the Ottoman Sultans, which is also a museum. Other cities are Ψ Izmir (2,649,770); Adana (1,934,907); Bursa (1,603,137); Gaziantep (1,140,549); and Konya (1,750,303).

CURRENCY – Turkish lira (TL) of 100 kurus.

FLAG – Red, with white crescent and star.

NATIONAL ANTHEM – Istiklal Marşi (The Independence March).

NATIONAL DAY – 29 October (Republic Day).

## GOVERNMENT

On 29 October 1923 the National Assembly declared Turkey a republic and elected Gazi Mustafa Kemal (later known as Kemal Ataturk) President. In 1945 a multiparty system was introduced but in 1960 the government was overthrown by the armed forces. A new constitution was adopted in 1961 and, after a general election, a civilian government took office. Civilian governments remained in power until September 1980 when mounting problems with the economy and terrorism led to a military takeover.

A new constitution, extending the powers of the President, was approved in 1982. It provided for the separation of powers between the legislature, executive and judiciary, and the holding of free elections to the unicameral Grand National Assembly, which now has 450 members elected every five years. Following the general election in November 1983 the military leadership handed over power to a civilian government. The last election was held in October 1991. Süleyman Demirel, leader of the True Path Party, formed a coalition government with the Social Democrat Populist Party. President Özal died on 17 April 1993 leading to the election by parliament of Süleyman Demirel as President. Tansu Çiller was elected party chairman by the True Path Party and formed a government which was sworn in on 25 June by President Demirel, when Çiller became the first woman Turkish Prime Minister.

Turkey is divided for administrative purposes into 76 *il* with subdivisions into *ilçe* and *nahiye*. Each *il* has a governor (*vali*) and elective council.

### SECESSION

Since 1984 Turkey has been fighting armed guerrillas of the Marxist Kurdish Workers Party (PKK) in the south-east of the country where Kurds are the majority population. The PKK has an estimated strength of 10,000 operating from bases in Lebanon and Syria, with the latter giving tacit support and finance. The south-east remains under martial law and about 10,500 have died in the ten years of warfare. Since the end of a two month PKK ceasefire in May 1993 the Turkish army has attempted to destroy the PKK by launching land and air raids against PKK bases in Syria and northern Iraq. The PKK has unsuccessfully attempted to gain the Kurdish population's support by intimidating and executing those who oppose it.

### HEAD OF STATE

*President*, Süleyman Demirel, *elected by parliament for a seven-year term*, 16 May 1993

GOVERNMENT *as at August 1994*

*Prime Minister*, Prof. Tansu Çiller (DYP)
*Deputy Prime Minister*, Murat Karayalçin (SHP)
*Ministers of State*, Necmettin Cevheri; Yildirim Aktuna; Mehmet Gazioğlu; Bekir Sami Daçe; Ali Şevki Erek; Nafiz Kurt; Aykon Doğan; Mehmet Ali Yilmaz; Abdulbaki Ataç; Nurhan Tekinel; Şükrü Erdem (DYP); Ibrahim Tez; Türkan Akyol; Mehmet Kahraman; Erman Şahin (SHP)
*Justice*, Mehmet Seyfi Oktay (SHP)
*National Defence*, Mehmet Gölhan (DYP)
*Interior*, Nahit Menteşe (DYP)
*Foreign Minister*, Prof. Mumtaz Soysal (SHP)
*Finance and Customs*, Ismet Atilla (DYP)
*Education*, Nevzat Ayaz (DYP)
*Public Works and Housing*, Prof. Onur Kumbaracibaşi (SHP)
*Health*, Kazim Dinç (DYP)
*Communications*, Mehmet Köstepen (DYP)
*Labour and Social Security*, Mehmet Moğultay (SHP)
*Trade and Industry*, Tahir Köse (SHP)
*Agriculture and Rural Affairs*, Refaiddin Şahin (DYP)
*Energy and Natural Resources*, Veysel Atasoy (DYP)
*Culture*, Fikri Sağlar (SHP)
*Tourism*, Prof Abdulkadir Ateş (SHP)
*Forestry*, Hasan Ekinci (DYP)
*Environment*, Riza Akçali (DYP)

DYP True Path Party; SHP Social Democrat Populist Party

### TURKISH EMBASSY

43 Belgrave Square, London SW1X 8PA
Tel 0171-235 5252

*Ambassador Extraordinary and Plenipotentiary*, His Excellency Candemir Önhon, apptd 1991
*Minister Counsellor*, Cinar Aldemir
*Defence Attaché*, Col. I. Tanel
*Consul-General*, A. Ünlütürk
*Counsellor*, T. F. Baran (*Commercial*)

### BRITISH EMBASSY

Sehit Ersan Caddesi 46/A, Cankaya, Ankara
Tel: Ankara 4686230

*Ambassador Extraordinary and Plenipotentiary*, His Excellency John Goulden, CMG, apptd 1992
*Counsellor, Deputy Head of Mission*, N. A. Ling
*First Secretary*, D. T. Healy (*Commercial*)
*Defence and Military Attaché*, Brig. The Hon. S. J. T. Coleridge
*Consul-General* (*Istanbul*), M. E. Cook

BRITISH CONSULAR OFFICES, There is a Consulate-General at *Istanbul*, a Vice-Consulate at *Izmir* and Honorary Consulates at *Antalya, Bodrum, Iskenderun, Mersin* and *Marmaris*.

BRITISH COUNCIL REPRESENTATIVE, David Marler, OBE, Kirklangic Sokak 9, Gazi Osman Pasa, Ankara 06700. There is also a centre and library at *Istanbul*.

BRITISH CHAMBER OF COMMERCE OF TURKEY INC., Mesrutiyet Caddessi No. 34, Tepebasi Beyoğlu, Istanbul (*postal address*, PO Box 190 Karaköy, Istanbul).

## EDUCATION

Education is free, secular and compulsory at primary level. There are elementary, secondary and vocational schools. There are 27 universities in Turkey, including six in Istanbul, five in Ankara, two in Izmir, and one each in Erzurum and Trabzon.

## CULTURE

Turkish was written in Arabic script until 1926 when a version of the Roman alphabet reflecting Turkish phonetics was substituted for use in official correspondence and in 1928 for universal use, with Arabic numerals as used throughout Europe. The revolution of 1908 led to the introduction of native literature free from foreign influences and adapted to the understanding of the people.

The leading Turkish newspapers are centred in Istanbul and Ankara, although most provincial towns have their own daily papers. There are foreign language papers in French, Greek, Armenian and English and numerous magazines and weeklies.

## ECONOMY

Agricultural production accounts for some 16 per cent of GDP at constant factor prices. About 50 per cent of the working population are in the rural sector. The principal crops are wheat, barley, rice, tobacco, sugar beet, tea, olives, grapes, figs and hazelnuts. With the exception of wheat, which is mostly grown on the arid central Anatolian plateau, most of the crops are grown on the fertile littoral. Tobacco, sultana and fig cultivation is centred around Izmir, where substantial quantities of cotton are also grown. The main cotton area is in the Cukurova plain around Adana. The forests which lie between the littoral plain and the Anatolian plateau contain beech, pine, oak, elm, chestnut, lime, plane, alder, box, poplar and maple. In 1990 28 per cent of the land area was forest.

After agriculture, Turkey's most important industry is based on the considerable mineral wealth which is, however, comparatively unexploited. The main export minerals are chromite and boron. Production in 1990 was (tons):

| | |
|---|---|
| Coal | 5,628,000 |
| Lignite | 46,892,000 |
| Crude petroleum | 3,753,000 |
| Crude iron | 4,928,000 |
| Boron minerals | 2,062,000 |

The bulk of the country's requirements in sugar, cotton, woollen and silk textiles, and cement, is produced locally. Other industries include vehicle assembly, paper, glass and glassware, iron and steel, leather and leather goods, sulphur refining, canning and rubber goods, soaps and cosmetics, pharmaceutical products, and prepared foodstuffs.

Steep rises in oil prices from 1973 onwards led to a succession of economic crises culminating in January 1980 in the introduction of an economic stability programme. Exports have since risen dramatically, topping US$11,846 million in 1988, but since 1988 imports have risen dramatically too, creating a significant trade gap. Inflation remains high (60 per cent in 1993). GNP growth for 1992 was 5.2 per cent and unemployment remains high. The total foreign debt in 1992 stood at US$54,700 million and the budget deficit in 1993 was equivalent to 9 per cent of GDP.

The government of Tansu Çiller has announced radical measures to deregulate, liberalize and transform the economy. The government effectively gained the power to issue decrees to run the economy without parliamentary approval in June 1992. A large-scale privatization programme is under way, which is designed to raise some US$26,000 million in revenue. An austerity package of price rises, new taxes and job cuts in state industries was introduced in April 1994 to curb inflation and reduce the budget deficit. At the same time a standby agreement was reached with the IMF for loans of US$690 million over three years in return for a devaluation of the lira by 28 per cent.

## FINANCE

| | 1990 |
|---|---|
| Estimated expenditure | TL64,400.4 billion |
| Estimated revenue | 53,860.0 billion |

## TRADE

The main imports are machinery, crude oil and petroleum products, iron and steel, vehicles, medicines and dyes, chemicals, fertilizers and electrical appliances. Agricultural commodities (cotton, tobacco, fruits, nuts, livestock) represent 47 per cent of total exports. Other exports are minerals, textiles, glass and cement.

| | 1989 | 1991 |
|---|---|---|
| Total imports | US$15,762.6m | US$22,302m |
| Total exports | 11,627.3m | 12,959m |

| *Trade with UK* | 1992 | 1993 |
|---|---|---|
| Imports from UK | £691,738,000 | £1,046,504,000 |
| Exports to UK | 457,000,000 | 532,007,000 |

## DEFENCE

The armed forces have a total active strength of 480,000 (390,000 conscripts), with a term of conscription of 15 months. Reserves number 1,104,000 with commitment to age 46. The Army has an active strength of 370,000 (320,000 conscripts) with 4,835 main battle tanks, 2,950 armoured personnel carriers and 2,520 artillery pieces. The Navy has 50,000 personnel (40,000 conscripts) including 4,000 marines, with 15 submarines, 11 destroyers, eight frigates, 45 patrol and coastal craft, 21 combat aircraft and 15 armed helicopters. The Air Force has a strength of 60,000 (30,000 conscripts), with 539 combat aircraft. Paramilitary Gendarmerie and National Guard forces number 70,000 active and 50,000 reserve personnel.

Between 150,000 and 200,000 troops are stationed in the south-east of the country fighting Kurdish guerrillas.

Since its invasion of Cyprus in 1974, Turkey has maintained forces in the north of the island and at present has 30,000 men in two infantry divisions stationed there. Turkey has also deployed an air force detachment of 18 aircraft to Italy for NATO operations over Bosnia.

As a member of NATO, Turkey is host to the Headquarters Allied Land Forces South-Eastern Europe and the Sixth Allied Tactical Air Force Headquarters. US (2,100 personnel), UK (260 personnel) and French (110 personnel) Air Force detachments are based at Incirlik airbase in southern Turkey to patrol the air exclusion zone over northern Iraq.

## COMMUNICATIONS

The rail network is run by the State Railways Administration. The total length of lines in operation (1989) is 10,369 km. At the end of 1988 there were 59,128 km of roads (31,149 of which were national). The Bosporus is spanned by two bridges; plans are being drawn up for a third fixed link between the two continents. By the end of 1988 the number of ships over 18 gross tons was 3,805. The state airline (THY) operates all internal services and has services to Europe, the Far East, Africa, North America and the Middle East. Most of the leading European airlines operate services to Istanbul and some also to Ankara.

## TURKMENISTAN
*Turkmenostan Respublikasy*

Turkmenistan has an area of 188,456 sq. miles (488,100 sq. km) and occupies the extreme south of the former Soviet Central Asia between the Caspian Sea and the Amu-Darya river. To the west it is bordered by the Caspian Sea, to the south by Iran, to the south-east by Afghanistan, to the east and north by Uzbekistan and to the north-west by Kazakhstan. The republic comprises five regions: Ashkhabad; Chardjou; Krasnovodsk; Mary; and Tashauz. The country is a low-lying plain fringed by hills in the south. Ninety per cent of the plain is taken up by the Obe Kara-Kum (Black Sands) desert. The climate is hot and dry.
POPULATION – The population (1989 census) is 3,523,000, of which 72 per cent are Turkomans, 9.5 per cent Russians and 9 per cent Uzbeks, together with smaller numbers of Kazakhs, Tatars, Ukrainians and Armenians. A 1994 estimate put the population at 3,809,000. Most of the population are Sunni Muslims. The main languages are Turkmenian (72 per cent), Russian (9 per cent), Uzbek (9 per cent). Turkmenian is one of the Turkic languages.

CAPITAL – Ashkhabad. Population 398,000 (1989).
CURRENCY – Manat.
FLAG – Green with a vertical carpet pattern near the hoist in black, white and wine-red; in the upper hoist a crescent and five stars, all in white.
NATIONAL DAY – 27 October (Independence Day).

## GOVERNMENT

Situated at the cross-roads of Central Asia, the area that is now Turkmenistan has been invaded and occupied by many empires: Persian; Greek under Alexander the Great; Parthian; Mongol. A Turkmenian nation was established in the 15th century but remained riven with dissent and divided between warring emirates. From the early 19th century until 1886 Turkmenistan was gradually incorporated into the Russian Empire. Soviet control over Turkmenistan was established on 30 April 1918 when it became an Autonomous Soviet Socialist Republic. The banks, cotton refineries and oil and gas fields were nationalized before a civil war broke out in July 1918, sparked by the intervention of British troops from Iran and India. The war ended in 1920 with the withdrawal of the interventionist forces and Turkmenistan became a full republic of the Soviet Union in February 1925.
Turkmenistan declared its independence from the Soviet Union on 27 October 1991 and gained UN membership on 2 March 1992. The constitution passed on 18 May 1992 makes the President head of state and government and provides for a bicameral legislature of the existing Supreme Soviet (renamed the *Majlis*) and a 60-member (50 directly elected

and ten appointed) supervisory upper house, the *Khalk Maslakhaty* (People's Council).
The autocratic government of President Niyazov has prevented any effective political opposition or free press through harassment and the continuation of Soviet authoritarianism. The political leadership has rejected political pluralism and instead a cult of personality has developed around President Niyazov. The Supreme Soviet voted on 30 December 1993 to extend the term of President Niyazov to 2002 and this was confirmed by a 99.99 per cent vote in a referendum on 15 January 1994. The Communist Party, renamed the Democratic Party, remains in power.
In 1991-2 there were fears of inter-ethnic tension and conflict with Russia because the constitution abolished the use of Russian as the official language of inter-ethnic communication. However, these fears have failed to materialize and in 1993-4 Turkmenistan's relations with Russia and the CIS improved. In 1992 joint Turkmen–Russian armed forces of 34,000 army and air force personnel were established and remain in operation. In late 1993 Turkmen–Russian agreements were signed allowing Russian troops to protect the borders with Iran and Afghanistan; Russian citizens to undergo military training in Turkmenistan; Turkmen officers to train in Russia; and Turkmenistan to bear the cost of Russian forces in the country. Agreement on dual citizenship for ethnic Russians in Turkmenistan was also reached. In December 1993 Turkmenistan signed the CIS charter to become a full CIS member and in January 1994 became a member of the CIS economic union.

*President,* Saparmurad Niyazov, *elected* 27 October 1990, *re-elected* 21 June 1992, *appointed head of government* 18 May 1992, *elected by referendum for an eight-year term* 15 January 1994

COUNCIL OF MINISTERS *as at August 1994*
*Prime Minister,* The President
*Deputy PMs,* Orasgeldy Ajdogdyev; Jumageldy Amansahatov; Jorakuly Babakulyev; Kurban Orazov; Sapargeldy Motaev; Batir Sarjaev; Pirkuli Odeev; Valerij Otcherzov; Redjepmanet Pukhanov; Matkarim Rajapov; Reedjep Saparov; Boris Shihmuradov; Abad Irzayeva
*Interior,* Kurbanmukhamed Kasymov
*Foreign Affairs,* Hakberdy Attaev
*Defence,* Dangatar Kopekov
*Trade,* Halnazar Agakhanov
*Economy and Finance,* Muhamed Abalakov
*Justice,* Tagandurdy Khallyev
*Culture and Tourism,* Geldymurad Nurmukhamedov
*Health,* Aksoltan Atayeva
*State Property,* Matkarim Rajapov
*Communications,* Amanmurad Djummiev
*Oil and Gas,* Nazar Suynov
*Agriculture,* Payzgeldi Meredov
*Social Affairs,* Nedirmamed Alavov
*Labour,* Bayramnur Soyunov.
*Construction,* Nury Orazmukhamedov
*Transport,* Kakadjan Achilov
*Education,* Rejepdurdye Garaev
*Water Conservancy,* Amannazar Ilamanov

BRITISH AMBASSADOR, His Excellency Sir Brian Fall, KCMG, resident at Moscow

## ECONOMY

The large reserves of natural gas and the foreign revenue that they earn make the country economically viable and have enabled the government to maintain low stable prices for all basic commodities and utilities.

Cotton cultivation, stock-raising and mineral extraction are the principal industries, together with the natural gas production and the long-established silk industry. Some fisheries exist along the Caspian sea coast. Arable land is irrigated by the Niyazov canal, which cuts through the Kara Kum desert. There are estimated reserves of some 700 million tonnes of oil and 8,000,000 million cubic metres of natural gas. Natural gas is exported to Ukraine and western Europe.

Agreements have been reached with Iran to build rail links so that the Persian Gulf and Mediterranean can be reached.

| *Trade with UK* | 1993 |
|---|---|
| Imports from UK | £14,619,000 |
| Exports to UK | 25,000 |

---

## TUVALU

Tuvalu comprises nine coral atolls situated in the south-west Pacific around the point at which the International Date Line cuts the Equator. The total land area is about 10 sq. miles. Few of the atolls are more than 12 ft above sea level or more than half a mile in width. The vegetation consists mainly of coconut palms.

POPULATION – The resident population in 1985 was 8,229, but it is estimated that about 1,500 Tuvaluans work overseas, mostly in Nauru, or as seamen. The UN estimated that the population was 9,000 in 1991. The people are almost entirely Polynesian. The principal languages are Tuvaluan and English. The entire population is Christian and is predominantly Protestant.

CAPITAL – ΨFunafuti, estimated population 2,856. The capital has a grass strip airfield from which a service operates regularly to Fiji and Kiribati, and is also the only port.

CURRENCY – Tuvalu uses the Australian dollar ($A) of 100 cents as legal tender. In addition there are Tuvalu dollar and cent coins in circulation.

FLAG – Blue ground with Union Flag in top left quarter and nine five-pointed gold stars in the fly.

NATIONAL ANTHEM – Tuvalu Mo Te Atua (Tuvalu for the Almighty).

NATIONAL DAY – 1 October (Independence Day).

### GOVERNMENT

Tuvalu, formerly the Ellice Islands, formed part of the Gilbert and Ellice Islands Colony until 1 October 1975, when separate constitutions came into force. Separation from the Gilbert Islands was implemented on 1 January 1976. On 1 October 1978 Tuvalu became a fully independent state within the Commonwealth.

The constitution provides for a Prime Minister and four other Ministers, who must be members of the 12-member elected Parliament. The Prime Minister presides at meetings of the Cabinet, which consists of the five Ministers, and is attended by the Attorney-General. Local government services are provided by elected Island Councils.

*Governor-General*, His Excellency the Rt. Hon. Sir Toaripi Lauti, KCMG

CABINET *as at August 1994*

*Prime Minister, Foreign Affairs and Economic Planning*, Hon. Kamuta Latasi
*Deputy Prime Minister, Natural Resources, Home Affairs and Rural Development*, Hon. Otinielu Tausi

*Labour, Works and Communications*, Hon. Hovati Lele
*Health and Human Resource Development*, Hon. Faimalaga Luka
*Finance, Trade, Commerce, Public Corporations*, Koloa Talake

BRITISH HIGH COMMISSIONER, His Excellency Timothy David, resides at Suva, Fiji

### SOCIAL WELFARE

There are eight primary schools in Tuvalu and a church secondary school run jointly with the Government. A maritime training school caters for 60 boys a year. There is a 30-bed hospital at Funafuti. All islands are served by a dispensary and a primary school.

### ECONOMY

Most people still practise a subsistence economy, the main staples of the diet being coconuts and fish. The main imports are foodstuffs, consumer goods and building materials. The only export is copra, though philatelic sales provide a major source of revenue and handicraft sales are increasing. However, Tuvalu is almost entirely dependent on foreign aid.

| *Trade with UK* | 1992 | 1993 |
|---|---|---|
| Imports from UK | £170,000 | £74,000 |
| Exports to UK | — | 1,000 |

---

## UGANDA
*Republic of Uganda*

---

Uganda is situated in eastern Africa, flanked by Zaire, Sudan, Kenya and on the south by Tanzania and Rwanda. Large parts of Lakes Victoria, Edward and Albert (Mobuto) are within its boundaries, as are Lakes Kyoga, Kwania, George and Bisina (formerly Salisbury) and the course of the River Nile from its outlet from Lake Victoria to the Sudan border at Nimule. Uganda has an area of 91,259 sq. miles (236,036 sq. km) (water and swamp 16,400 sq. miles) and a population (1991 UN estimate) of 19,517,000. The official language is English. The main local vernaculars are of Bantu, Nilotic and Hamitic origins. Ki-Swahili is generally understood.

Despite its tropical location, the climate is tempered by its situation some 3,000 ft above sea level, and well over that altitude in the highlands of the Western and Eastern Regions. Uganda has three National Parks and a fourth (Lake Mburo) has been designated.

CAPITAL – Kampala (estimated population of Greater Kampala, 1990, 750,000). Other principal towns are Jinja (45,000), Mbale (28,000) and Masaka (29,000).

CURRENCY – Uganda shilling of 100 cents.

FLAG – Six horizontal stripes of black, yellow, red, with a white disc in the centre containing the badge of a crested crane.

NATIONAL ANTHEM – Oh Uganda.

NATIONAL DAY – 9 October (Independence Day).

### GOVERNMENT

Uganda became an independent state within the Commonwealth on 9 October 1962, after some 70 years of British rule. A republic was instituted in 1967, under an executive President assisted by a Cabinet of Ministers.

Early in 1971 an army coup took place and Maj.-Gen. Idi Amin, the army commander, proclaimed himself head of state. In 1979, following risings and military intervention by Tanzania, President Amin was overthrown. Dr Milton Obote became President in 1980 but was ousted by a military coup in 1985. A military council was installed but the National Resistance Movement led by Yoweri Museveni captured Kampala in January 1986, securing control of the rest of the country in the following few months. Yoweri Museveni was sworn in as President in January 1986; subsequently a National Resistance Council (NRC) was appointed to draw up a constitution. A draft constitution was published in February 1993. Elections to a constituent assembly to amend the draft constitution were held in March 1994, the assembly having 214 elected and 66 appointed seats. The National Resistance Movement won the majority of the seats; the assembly plans to debate the draft constitution until late 1994, when presidential and parliamentary elections will be held. The ban on political party activity in the interest of stability will continue to the year 2000.

HEAD OF STATE
*President,* Yoweri Museveni, *sworn in* 29 January 1986
*Vice-President,* Dr Samson Kisseka

CABINET *as at August 1994*

*Defence,* The President
*Internal Affairs,* The Vice-President
*Prime Minister,* George Cosma Adyebo
*First Deputy PM,* Eriya Kategaya
*Second Deputy PM and Minister for Foreign Affairs,* Paul Ssemogerere
*Third Deputy PM and Attorney-General,* Abu Bakar Mayanja
*Finance and Economic Planning,* Joshua Mayanja-Nkangi
*Agriculture, Animal Industry and Fisheries,* Mrs Victoria Ssekitoleko
*Commerce, Industry and Co-operatives,* Richard Kaijuka
*Local Government,* Jaberi Bidandi-Ssali
*Educational and Sports,* Amanya Mushega
*Public Services,* Sam Sebagereka
*Information,* Paul Etiang
*Lands, Housing and Urban Development,* Dr E. T. Adriko
*Labour and Social Affairs,* Ateke Ejalu
*Works, Transport and Communications,* Dr Ruhakana-Rugunda
*Tourism, Wildlife and Antiquities,* James Wapakabulo
*Health,* James Makumbi
*Water, Energy, Minerals and Environmental Protection,* Henry Kajura
*Women in Development, Culture and Youth,* Wandira Kazibwe

UGANDA HIGH COMMISSION
Uganda House, 58–59 Trafalgar Square, London WC2N 5DX
Tel 0171–839 5783

*High Commissioner,* His Excellency Prof. George Kirya, apptd 1990
*Financial Attaché,* A. Bamweyana
*Commercial Attaché,* R. Lubwama-Kebba

BRITISH HIGH COMMISSION
10–12 Parliament Avenue, PO Box 7070, Kampala
Tel: Kampala 257054/9

*High Commissioner,* His Excellency Edward Clay, CMG, apptd 1993
*Deputy High Commissioner,* J. O. Atkinson
*Defence Adviser,* Lt.-Col. E. A. M. Graham
*First Secretary (Commercial),* P. L. D. Byrde

BRITISH COUNCIL REPRESENTATIVE, Roger Wilkins
*(Cultural Attaché)*

EDUCATION

Education is a joint undertaking by the government, local authorities and voluntary agencies. In 1988 Uganda had an estimated 7,905 primary schools with 2,638,100 children, 774 secondary schools with 240,834 students; and 7,291 students in various technical training institutions. There are four universities, Makerere University in Kampala, the Uganda Martyrs University, and at Mbale and Mbarara.

COMMUNICATIONS

There is an international airport at Entebbe, and eight other airfields around the country. Having no sea coast, Uganda is dependent upon rail and road links to Mombasa and Dar es Salaam for its trade. Over 5,000 km of the country's roads are currently being rehabilitated. A railway network joins the capital to the western, eastern and northern centres.

ECONOMY

Since 1988 the government has been successful in implementing an IMF recovery programme. The civil service and army have been reduced in size, foreign investment encouraged, and property returned to Asians expelled by Idi Amin. Annual growth since 1988 has averaged 6 per cent, inflation has been reduced to 3 per cent a year and aid donors in June 1993 gave £550 million of aid.

The principal export earner is coffee, over 90 per cent of all exports. Attempts are being made to increase production of tobacco, cocoa, cotton and tea for export. Hydro-electricity is produced from the Owen Falls power station, some of which is exported to Kenya. The principal food crops are plantains, bananas, cassava, sweet potatoes, potatoes, maize and sorghum; livestock raising and inshore fishing are also important.

| Trade with UK | 1992 | 1993 |
|---|---|---|
| Imports from UK | £26,682,000 | £30,439,000 |
| Exports to UK | 9,398,000 | 7,601,000 |

# UKRAINE
*Ukraina*

Ukraine has an area of 233,090 sq. miles (603,700 sq. km) and lies in the south-west of the European part of the former Soviet Union. It is bordered on the north by Belarus and Russia, on the east by Russia, on the south by the Black Sea, on the south-west by Romania and Moldova and on the west by Hungary, Slovakia and Poland. The area of the present Ukraine is larger than that of the Ukrainian Soviet Republic formed in 1917–19 because of the westward territorial expansion of the former Soviet Union in the 1939–45 period and the addition of the Crimea from Russia in 1954. The Ukraine now consists of 24 regions: Cherkassy, Chernigov, Chernovtsy, Dnepropetrovsk, Donetsk, Ivano-Frankovsk, Kharkov, Kherson, Khmelnitsky, Kiev, Kirovograd, Lugansk, Lvov, Nikolayev, Odessa, Poltava, Rovno, Sumy, Ternopol, Transcarpathia, Vinnitsa, Volhynia, Zaporozhye and Zhitomir, and one autonomous republic, Crimea.

Most of the Ukraine forms a plain with small elevations. The Carpathian mountains lie in the south-western part of the republic. The main rivers are the Dnieper with its tributaries, the Southern Bug and the Northern Donets (a tributary of the Don). The climate is moderate with relatively mild winters (particularly in the south-west) and hot summers.

POPULATION – The population (1989 census) was 51,471,000, of which 73 per cent are Ukrainian and 22 per cent Russian, with smaller numbers of Jews, Belarussians, Moldovans, Tatars, Poles, Hungarians and Greeks. The 1994 estimate put the population at 52,100,000.

The two main religions are Roman Catholicism and Orthodox. The Orthodox rite is divided between the Russian Orthodox Church with its Patriarch in Moscow and the Autocephalous Orthodox Church of the Ukraine with its own Patriarch in Kiev. There are also large numbers of Reformed Protestants in the Transcarpathian region and a sizeable Jewish community in Kiev.

The main languages are Ukrainian (73 per cent) and Russian (22 per cent). Ukrainian is an Eastern Slavonic language related to Russian and Belarussian.

CAPITAL – Kiev. Population 2,577,000 (1989). Other major cities (1990) are Kharkov (1,611,000); Dnepropetrovsk (1,179,000); ΨOdessa (1,115,000); Donetsk (1,110,000).
CURRENCY – Coupons called Karbovanets were introduced in November 1992 and are fully convertible to the rouble.
FLAG – Two horizontal stripes of blue over yellow.
NATIONAL DAY – 24 August (Independence Day).

## GOVERNMENT

The earliest Russian state was formed in the middle reaches of the Dnieper River with its capital at Kiev in the ninth century AD. The state united the two large Slav states of Kiev and Novgorod and established the first common Russian language and nationality. The state lasted until Kiev fell to the Mongols in 1240. For the next four centuries the Ukraine was invaded and ruled by Tatars, Turks, Poles, Hungarians and Lithuanians. In 1648 the Ukrainians threw off Polish rule to become independent and increasingly allied with Russia (formerly Muscovy). During the reign of Catherine the Great of Russia (1763–96) the Ukraine and the Crimea came under Russian control.

By the time of the Treaty of Brest-Litovsk in March 1918, most of the Ukraine had been occupied by German and Austrian forces. The Treaty forced the Soviet government in Moscow to cede parts of western Ukraine to Germany and Austria-Hungary and accept the independence of the remainder. After the defeat of Germany in 1918, the Ukraine became a battleground in the Russian civil war before the imposition of Soviet rule in 1922. The Ukraine became a constituent republic of the USSR on 30 December 1922. The 1920s saw the collectivization of agriculture, which led to a famine in which millions died, and the Stalinist purges caused thousands more to be killed. The Ukraine was again devastated in the Second World War and millions of Ukrainians died. The country was rebuilt and heavily industrialized in the post-war period.

The Ukraine declared itself independent of the Soviet Union, subject to a referendum, after the failed Moscow coup in August 1991. The referendum was held on 1 December 1991 and 90 per cent of the electorate voted for independence. Simultaneously, the former Ukrainian Communist leader Leonid Kravchuk was elected President of the Republic. Political power in the Ukraine in 1991-4 rested with the former Communists, led by the President, in loose alliance with the Rukh nationalist party. This has limited political and economic change, although Leonid Kuchma, Prime Minister 1992-3, began to introduce economic reforms in December 1992, with privatization and the partial liberalization of price controls. Kuchma resigned in September 1993 after the Supreme Council obstructed his reform programme and President Kravchuk effectively took over the government. Economic chaos due to strikes forced the President to call early legislative and presidential elections.

The legislative elections, by a first-past-the-post system, to the 450-seat Supreme Council in March and April 1994 resulted in a majority for Communist and allied candidates, plus 'independents' who were mainly agricultural and industrial managers tied to the status quo. In the June 1994 presidential election Kuchma defeated President Kravchuk. At the time of going to press a government had yet to be formed because of a power struggle between President Kuchma and the Supreme Council over who controlled the government.

The relationship with Russia and ethnic Russians in the Ukraine remains central to events. The situation of the Crimea with its ethnic Russian majority has caused concern, as the Crimean parliament voted to make the Crimea an autonomous republic in September 1991, which was accepted by Kiev, but then voted for independence in May 1992, which was not accepted and was suspended. A Russian nationalist, Yuri Meshkov, was elected President of Crimea in January 1994 and the Crimean parliament in May 1994 restored the suspended 1992 constitution declaring sovereignty. In the legislative and presidential elections in 1994 the western regions of Ukraine voted for nationalist and reformist candidates while the eastern regions voted for Communist and allied ones. A referendum in the Donbass region of eastern Ukraine in favour of closer economic ties with Russia and making Russian an official language was overwhelmingly passed, as was one in the Crimea in favour of dual Russian–Ukrainian citizenship.

HEAD OF STATE
*President*, Leonid Kuchma, *elected* 13 July 1994

UKRAINIAN EMBASSY
78 Kensington Park Road, London W11 2PL
Tel 0171-727 6312

*Ambassador Extraordinary and Plenipotentiary*, His Excellency Prof. Sergui Komisarenko, apptd 1992
*Minister-Counsellor*, Prof. M. Bilooussov
*Counsellor (Economic and Commercial)*, Dr B. Savchuk

BRITISH EMBASSY
252025 Kiev Desyatinna 9
Tel: Kiev 228 0504

*Ambassador Extraordinary and Plenipotentiary*, His Excellency Simon N. Hemans, CMG, CVO, apptd 1992
*Consul-General and Deputy Head of Mission*, R. T. Jenkins
*Defence Attaché*, Capt. C. A. M. Parrish, OBE, RN
*First Secretary (Commercial)*, R. C. Cook

BRITISH COUNCIL REPRESENTATIVE – John Day, 9/1 Bessarabska Ploshcha, Flat 9, Kiev 252004.

## DEFENCE

Since the demise of the Soviet Union, Russia and Ukraine have clashed over defence issues. All strategic nuclear weapons were placed under a central CIS command in December 1991, but on the abolition of the central command in July 1993 the government claimed possession of all nuclear weapons on its territory. Despite international pressure, the Supreme Council only ratified the START I Treaty in February 1994 and has yet to ratify the Nuclear Non-Proliferation Treaty.

Under a January 1994 USA–Russia–Ukraine Treaty, the Ukrainian nuclear arsenal will be transferred to Russia for dismantling over a seven-year period. This includes all the warheads in Ukraine's 166 inter-continental ballistic missiles and carried by its 42 nuclear-capable bombers (some 1,800 warheads in total). In return Ukraine has received a territorial guarantee by Russia, a cancellation of a large part of its debt to Russia, and nuclear security guarantees from Russia and the USA. Ukraine will also receive lower grade uranium from Russia for use in its power stations; economic and technical aid from the USA; US$300 million from the USA to pay for dismantling the weapons; and US$1,000 million to buy some of the enriched uranium from the warheads. The first warheads were transferred to Russia in March 1994.

Negotiations between Ukraine and Russia continue over the division of the former Soviet Black Sea Fleet. In April 1994 agreement was reached on a 80:20 Russian: Ukrainian division of ships, with Russia paying Ukraine compensation for its smaller share, but negotiations remain deadlocked over control of the Fleet base at Sevastopol. The Fleet remains under joint Russian–Ukrainian control, with a strength of 48,000 personnel (including 2,000 marines), 21 submarines, one helicopter carrier, four cruisers, seven destroyers, 23 frigates, 244 combat aircraft and 85 combat helicopters.

The total armed forces number 438,000 personnel (including 47,000 central staff but excluding navy), with conscripts serving 18 months. The army numbers 217,000 personnel, with 5,700 main battle tanks, 8,050 armoured personnel carriers and armoured infantry fighting vehicles, 3,020 artillery pieces and 220 attack helicopters. The air force and air defence forces have 171,000 personnel, with some 1,340 combat aircraft and 2,400 surface-to-air missiles. The paramilitary National Guard and Border Guard number 72,000 personnel.

## ECONOMY

Throughout 1991–4 the Communist-led government and legislature have obstructed economic reform and economic mismanagement has resulted. The economy has come close to collapse because of hyperinflation caused by the printing of money to support uneconomic enterprises and to pay strikers' wage demands. Industrial output and GDP have fallen considerably, while Russia has threatened to cut all oil and gas supplies as Ukraine cannot pay in hard currency. Ukraine has joined the CIS economic union as an associate member and is likely to seek full membership for access to better trading relations with Russia. In March 1994 Ukrainian debt to other CIS states was US$3,426 million, of which US$2,703 million was to Russia.

The southern part of the country contains a coal-mining and iron and steel industrial area which was the largest in the former Soviet Union. The Ukraine also contains engineering and chemical industries and ship-building yards on the Black Sea coast. Ukrainian agricultural production is good with large areas under cultivation with wheat, cotton, flax and sugar beet; stock-raising is very important. There are large deposits of coal and salt in the Donets Basin, of iron ore in Krivoy Rog and near Kerch in the Crimea, of manganese in Nikopol, and of quicksilver in Nikitovka.

The major ports are Odessa, Nikolayev, Kerch and Sevastopol.

| Trade with UK | 1993 |
|---|---|
| Imports from UK | £73,091,000 |
| Exports to UK | 12,462,000 |

# UNITED ARAB EMIRATES
*Al-Imarat Al-Arabiya Al-Muttahida*

The United Arab Emirates are situated in the south-east of the Arabian peninsula. Six of the emirates lie on the shore of the Gulf between the Musandam peninsula in the east and the Qatar peninsula in the west while the seventh, Fujairah, lies on the Gulf of Oman. The climate varies between hot and humid in May to September and mild with erratic rainfall in October to April. The approximate area is 32,278 sq. miles (83,600 sq. km), and the population (1992 estimate) is 2,173,000. The official language is Arabic, and English is widely spoken. The established religion is Islam.

CAPITAL – Abu Dhabi. Population (city) 450,000.
CURRENCY – UAE dirham (Dh) of 100 fils.
FLAG – Horizontal stripes of green over white over black with vertical red stripe in the hoist.
NATIONAL DAY – 2 December.

## GOVERNMENT

The United Arab Emirates (formerly the Trucial States) is composed of seven emirates (Abu Dhabi, Ajman, Dubai, Fujairah, Ras al-Khaimah, Sharjah and Umm al-Qaiwain) which came together as an independent state on 2 December 1971 when they ended their individual special treaty relationships with the British Government (Ras al-Khaimah joined the other six on 10 February 1972). On independence the Union Government assumed full responsibility for all internal and external affairs apart from some internal matters that remained the prerogative of the individual emirates.

Overall authority lies with the Supreme Council of the seven emirate rulers, each of whom also governs in his own territory. The President and Vice-President are elected every five years by the Supreme Council from among its members. The President appoints the Council of Ministers. A 40-member Federal National Council, drawn proportionately from each emirate and composed of appointees of the rulers, studies draft laws referred to it by the Council of Ministers. Each emirate also has its separate government, with Abu Dhabi having an executive council chaired by the Crown Prince.

HEAD OF STATE
*President*, HH Sheikh Zayed bin Sultan al-Nahyan (*Abu Dhabi*), *elected* 1971, *re-elected* 1976, 1981, 1986, October 1991
*Vice-President*, HH Sheikh Maktoum bin Rashid al-Maktoum (*Dubai*), *elected* October 1991

SUPREME COUNCIL *as at August 1994*
*President*, HH Sheikh Zayed bin Sultan al-Nahyan (*Abu Dhabi*)
*Vice-President*, HH Sheikh Maktoum bin Rashid al-Maktoum (*Dubai*)
HH Sheikh Sultan bin Mohammed al-Qassimi (*Sharjah*)
HH Sheikh Saqr bin Mohammed al-Qassimi (*Ras Al-Khaimah*)
HH Sheikh Hamid bin Mohammed al-Sharqi (*Fujairah*)
HH Sheikh Humaid bin Rashid al-Nuaimi (*Ajman*)
HH Sheikh Rashid bin Ahmed al-Mualla (*Umm al-Qaiwain*)

COUNCIL OF MINISTERS *as at August 1994*
*The President*
*Prime Minister*, The Vice-President
*Deputy Prime Minister*, Sheikh Sultan bin Zayed al-Nahyan
*Finance and Industry*, Sheikh Hamdan bin Rashid al-Maktoum
*Defence*, Lt.-Gen. Sheikh Mohammed bin Rashid al-Maktoum
*Interior*, Lt.-Gen. Dr Mohammed Saeed al-Badi
*Foreign Affairs*, Rashid Abdullah al-Nuaimi
*Communications*, Mohammed Saeed al-Mulla
*Planning*, Sheikh Humaid bin Ahmed al-Mu'alla
*Islamic Affairs and Endowments*, Sheikh Mohammed bin Ahmed al Khazraji

*Water and Electricity*, Humaid bin Nasser al-Owais
*Economy and Commerce*, Saeed Ghobash
*Agriculture and Fisheries*, Saeed al-Ragabani
*Labour and Social Affairs*, Saif al-Jarwan
*Information and Culture*, Khalfan bin Mohammed al-Roumi
*Education*, Hamad Abdul Rahman al-Madfa
*Higher Education*, Sheikh Nahyan bin Mubarak al-Nahyan
*Justice*, Dr Abdullah bin Omran Taryam
*Health and Environment*, Ahmed bin Saeed al-Badi
*Petroleum and Mineral Resources*, vacant
*Public Works and Housing*, Rakkad bin Salem bin Rakkad
*Youth and Sports*, Sheikh Faisal bin Khaled al-Qassimi
*Minister of State for Cabinet Affairs*, Saeed al-Ghaith
*Minister of State for Financial and Industrial Affairs*, Ahmed bin Humaid al-Tayer
*Minister of State for Foreign Affairs*, Sheikh Hamdan bin Zayed al-Nahyan
*Minister of State for Supreme Council Affairs*, Sheikh Mohammed bin Saqr al-Qassimi

EMBASSY OF THE UNITED ARAB EMIRATES
30 Prince's Gate, London SW7 1PT
Tel 0171–581 1281

*Ambassador Extraordinary and Plenipotentiary*, His Excellency Easa Saleh Al-Gurg, CBE, apptd 1991
*Minister-Plenipotentiary*, Khalid Abdul-Latif Al-Bassam
*Military Attaché*, Lt.-Col. M. A. M. Al-Mehrizi
*Cultural Attaché*, A. A. M. Al-Marri

BRITISH EMBASSIES
PO Box 248, Abu Dhabi
Tel: Abu Dhabi 326600

*Ambassador Extraordinary and Plenipotentiary*, His Excellency Anthony David Harris, LVO, apptd 1994
*First Secretary, Consul and Deputy Head of Post*, S. O. Cobb
*First Secretary (Commercial)*, P. J. McGuinness
*Defence Attaché*, Lt.-Col. C. J. Copeland

BRITISH COUNCIL REPRESENTATIVE, Abu Dhabi, David Latta (*Cultural Attaché*). There is also an office at Al Ain.

PO Box 65, Dubai
Tel: Dubai 521070

*Counsellor and Consul-General*, C. E. J. Wilton
*Deputy Head of Post, Consul and First Secretary (Commercial)*, J. C. Fisher

BRITISH COUNCIL REPRESENTATIVE, A. Mackay, PO Box 1636, Dubai

DEFENCE

The Ministry of Defence and general headquarters are located in Dubai. The armed forces of the emirates were merged in 1976, although Dubai still retains some independent units. The total active armed forces strength is 57,500, of which around 30 per cent are hired or seconded foreign nationals. The Army is 53,000 strong including 12,000 Dubai forces, and is equipped with 125 main battle tanks, 76 light tanks, 160 reconnaissance vehicles, 445 armoured personnel carriers and armoured infantry fighting vehicles and 238 artillery pieces. The Navy has a strength of 2,000 personnel, with 19 patrol and coastal vessels. The Air Force is 2,500 strong, including 700 Dubai forces, with 79 combat aircraft and 19 armed helicopters. Some 2,000 Moroccan troops are stationed in the UAE.

ECONOMY

The UAE is the Gulf's third largest oil producer after Saudi Arabia and Iran, producing 3 million barrels per day (bpd)

in 1993, and with oil reserves of 200,000 million barrels and gas reserves of 200,000,000 million cubic feet. Oil production in 1993 accounted for 40 per cent of GDP. Other important sectors of the economy are government, re-exporting, construction, manufacturing (aluminium, cement, chemicals, fertilizers, ship repair); finance and insurance services, and transport and communications. Tourism is growing in importance. Agricultural production (vegetables, dates, fruit, milk, eggs, poultry, flowers, olives, animal husbandry) has increased significantly due to large-scale water desalination and irrigation projects. There is no personal or corporate taxation apart from on oil companies and foreign banks. Fourteen major ports, of which nine are modern container terminals, handled 35 million tonnes of cargo in 1993. Six international airports (Dubai, Abu Dhabi, Sharjah, Ras al-Khaimah, Fujairah, Al Ain) are in operation. Oil revenues over the past 30 years have enabled the government to invest heavily in education, health and social services, housing, transport and communications infrastructure, and agriculture.

| TRADE | | 1993 |
| --- | --- | --- |
| Exports | | Dhs 85,200m |
| Imports | | 67,700m |
| | | |
| *Trade with UK* | 1992 | 1993 |
| Imports from UK | £926,557,000 | £1,314,578,000 |
| Exports to UK | 331,928,000 | 251,453,000 |

SOCIAL WELFARE

In 1993 there were 300,000 pupils studying at the 500 government schools, where education is free; some 150,000 (many expatriates) attended 300 private schools. The Emirates University at Al Ain (Abu Dhabi) had 10,900 students in 1993, and the three Colleges of Technology (Abu Dhabi, Dubai, Al Ain) had 1,800 students. There are 29 government and six private hospitals, 96 government health centres and 500 private clinics with a total of 4,300 beds.

ABU DHABI

Abu Dhabi is by far the largest emirate, with an area of 30,888 sq. miles (80,000 sq. km) stretching from Khor al-Odaid in the west to the borders with Dubai in the Jebel Ali area. It includes six villages in the Buraimi oasis, the other three being part of the Sultanate of Oman, and a number of settlements in the Liwa oasis system. Following negotiations with Saudi Arabia, some adjustment of the border has now been made in the Khor al-Odaid region, but the agreement has not yet been ratified. The population of the Emirate (1990) is 889,000

The Abu Dhabi government controls oil, gas and petrochemical operations in the emirate through the Supreme Petroleum Council. This body in turn issues instructions to the Abu Dhabi National Oil Company (ADNOC) which has majority shareholdings in the oil operating and gas treatment companies, and in oil industry-related companies covering drilling, refining, distribution, chemical manufacture and investment. Production began offshore in 1962 and onshore in 1963. Crude oil production in 1990 was approximately 1.65 million barrels per day. With its oil wealth the emirate has seen a period of growth (which is currently slowing down), in Abu Dhabi, Al-Ain in the Buraimi oasis and in the new petro-chemical city at Ruwais.

AJMAN AND UMM AL-QAIWAIN

Ajman and Umm al-Qaiwain are the smallest emirates in area; they have populations (1990) of 92,000 and 21,000 respectively. Both lie on the Gulf coast although Ajman has two inland enclaves at Manama and Masfut. Exploration work continues in both emirates for oil and gas but so far only Umm al-Qaiwain has experienced any success, with the offshore discovery of natural gas, but the field has yet to be commercially developed. The discovery of onshore gas in nearby Sharjah has increased hopes of similar discoveries in both Ajman and Umm al-Qaiwain.

## DUBAI

Dubai is the second largest emirate both in size and in population, which is (1990) 559,000. The town of Dubai is the main port for the UAE. Dubai's prosperity was established by this trade long before the discovery of oil in 1966; production began in 1969. The producer in Dubai's offshore oilfields is Dubai Petroleum Company, operated by CONOCO. Production is in excess of 350,000 b.p.d. In 1982 an extensive gas and condensate field was discovered onshore. A small amount of condensate is produced from the onshore Margam field. Oil income has been used to finance Dubai's infrastructure. The port of Jebel Ali, at the heart of an industrial complex, and its immediate area is a free trade zone which is expected to attract more industry.

## FUJAIRAH

Fujairah, with a population (1990) of 76,000, is the most remote of the seven emirates, lying on the Gulf of Oman coast and only connected by a metal road to the rest of the country. Largely agricultural, its population is spread between the slopes of the inland Hajar mountain range and the town of Fujairah itself, together with a number of smaller settlements on the comparatively fertile plain on the coast. Although exploration work continues, there have been no hydrocarbon discoveries in the emirate. However, there are some chrome and other mineral deposits.

## RAS AL-KHAIMAH

Ras al-Khaimah has a population (1990) of 159,000, of whom more than half live in the town. An ancient sea-port, near to which archaeological remains have been found, Ras al-Khaimah is the most agricultural of the emirates, producing vegetables, dates, fruit and tobacco. In 1982 oil and gas were discovered offshore and this field currently produces approximately 5,000 b.p.d. An industrial area has been developed to the north of the emirate, and the infrastructure has been developed. It is hoped that more industry will be attracted to the emirate.

## SHARJAH

Sharjah, with a population (1990) of 377,000, has declined from its former position as principal town in the area. Oil production began in 1974 and gas discoveries were made in 1982; production now stands at about 55,000 b.p.d. Sharjah is connected by metalled roads to all the other northern emirates. A container port has been constructed on the Gulf of Oman at Khor Fakkan. A free trade zone has been established.

# UNITED STATES OF AMERICA

The United States of America occupies nearly all of the North American continent between the Atlantic and Pacific Oceans, in 25° 07′ to 49° 23′ N. latitude and 66° 57′ to 124° 44′ W. longitude, its northern boundary adjoining Canada and the southern boundary Mexico. The separate state of Alaska reaches a latitude of 71′ 23″ N., at Point Barrow. The coastline has a length of about 2,069 miles on the Atlantic, 7,623 miles on the Pacific, 1,060 miles on the Arctic, and 1,631 miles on the Gulf of Mexico.

The principal river is the Mississippi-Missouri-Red (3,710 miles long), traversing the whole country to its mouth in the Gulf of Mexico; its main affluents are the Yellowstone, Platte, Arkansas, and Ohio rivers. The chain of the Rocky Mountains separates the western portion of the country from the remainder. West of these, bordering the Pacific coast, the Cascade Mountains and Sierra Nevada form the outer edge of a high tableland, consisting in part of stony and sandy desert and partly of grazing land and forested mountains, and including the Great Salt Lake, which extends to the Rocky Mountains. In the eastern states large forests still exist, the remnants of the forests which formerly extended over all the Atlantic slope. The highest point is Mount McKinley (20,320 ft) in Alaska, and the lowest point of dry land is in Death Valley (Inyo, California), 282 ft below sea-level.

## AREA AND POPULATION

| | Total land area 1990 (sq. miles) | Population census 1990 |
|---|---|---|
| The United States (a) | 3,536,338 | 248,709,873 |
| Outlying areas under US jurisdiction | 4,220 | 3,862,431 |
| *Territories* | 4,204 | 3,862,238 |
| Puerto Rico | 3,427 | 3,522,037 |
| Guam | 210 | 133,152 |
| US Virgin Islands | 134 | 101,809 |
| American Samoa | 77 | 46,773 |
| Northern Mariana Is. | 179 | 43,345 |
| Palau | 177 | 15,122 |
| Other possessions | 16 | 193 |
| Population abroad (b) | – | 925,845 |
| TOTAL | 3,540,558 | 253,498,149 |

(a) the 50 states and the Federal District of Columbia
(b) excludes US citizens temporarily abroad on business

The total population was estimated at 259,681,000 on 1 January 1994

RESIDENT POPULATION BY RACE 1990 (Thousands)

| | |
|---|---|
| White | 199,686.1 |
| Black | 29,986.1 |
| *American Indian | 1,959.2 |
| Chinese | 1,645.5 |
| Filipino | 1,406.8 |
| Japanese | 847.6 |
| Asian Indian | 815.4 |
| Korean | 798.8 |
| Vietnamese | 614.5 |
| Other Asian | 780.0 |
| Pacific Islander | 365.0 |
| All other races | 9,804.8 |
| †Hispanic origin | 22,354.1 |
| Cuban | 1,043.9 |
| Mexican | 13,495.9 |
| Puerto Rican | 2,727.8 |
| Other Hispanic | 5,086.4 |
| TOTAL | 248,709.9 |

* Includes Eskimo and Aleut
† Persons of Hispanic origin may be of any race

## IMMIGRATION

From 1820 to 1993, 60,699,450 immigrants were admitted to the United States. Total number of immigrants in 1993 was 904,292, of which 355,301 came from North and Central America (126,561 from Mexico), 358,047 from Asia and 158,254 from Europe.

## VITAL STATISTICS

In 1993 (provisional figures) live births were 4,039,000, a rate of 15.7 per 1,000 of population. Deaths were 2,268,000, a rate of 8.8 per 1,000 of population. In 1993 marriages were 2,334,000, a rate of 9.0 per 1,000 of population. Divorces were approximately 1,187,000, a rate of 4.6 per 1,000 of population.

## LARGEST CITIES 1992 estimate

| | |
|---|---|
| ΨNew York, NY | 7,311,966 |
| ΨLos Angeles, California | 3,489,779 |
| ΨChicago, Illinois | 2,768,483 |
| ΨHouston, Texas | 1,690,180 |
| ΨPhiladelphia, Pennsylvania | 1,552,572 |
| ΨSan Diego, California | 1,148,851 |
| Dallas, Texas | 1,022,497 |
| Phoenix, Arizona | 1,012,230 |
| ΨDetroit, Michigan | 1,012,110 |
| San Antonio, Texas | 966,437 |

Ψ seaport

## CAPITAL

The federal capital is the City of Washington in the District of Columbia. It is situated on the west central edge of Maryland, opposite the state of Virginia, on the left bank of the Potomac at its confluence with the Anacostia. The area of the District of Columbia (with which the City of Washington is considered co-extensive) is 61 sq. miles, with a resident population (mid-1992 estimate) of 585,221. The population of the metropolitan area in 1992 was estimated at 4,360,349. The District of Columbia is governed by an elected mayor and City Council.

CURRENCY – The dollar ($) of 100 cents.
FLAG – 13 stripes and 50 stars in nine horizontal rows of six and five alternately.
NATIONAL ANTHEM – The Star-Spangled Banner.
NATIONAL DAY – 4 July (Independence Day).

## GOVERNMENT

The United States of America is a federal republic consisting of 50 states and the federal District of Columbia and of organized territories. Of the present 50 states, 13 are original states, seven were admitted without previous organization as territories, and 30 were admitted after such organization.

By the constitution of 17 September 1787 (to which amendments were added in 1791, 1798, 1804, 1865, 1868, 1870, 1913, 1920, 1933, 1951, 1961, 1964, 1967, 1971 and 1992), the government of the United States is entrusted to three separate authorities: the executive (the President and Cabinet), the legislature (Congress) and the judicature.

The President is indirectly elected every four years. There is also a Vice-President, who, should the President die, becomes President for the remainder of the term. The tenure of the presidency is limited to two terms.

The President, with the consent of the Senate, appoints the Cabinet officers and all the chief officials. He makes recommendation of a general nature to Congress, and when laws are passed by Congress he may return them to Congress with a veto. But if a measure so vetoed is again passed by both Houses of Congress by two-thirds majority in each House, it becomes law, notwithstanding the objection of the President. The President must be at least 35 years of age and a native citizen of the United States.

### Presidential elections

Each state elects (on the first Tuesday after the first Monday in November of the year preceding the year in which the presidential term expires) a number of electors, equal to the whole number of Senators and Representatives to which the state may be entitled in the Congress. The electors for each state meet in their respective states on the first Monday after the second Wednesday in December following, and

## THE STATES OF THE UNION

| STATE (with date and *order* of admission) | LAND AREA sq. m. | POPULATION (1990 census) | CAPITAL | GOVERNOR (term of office in years, and expiry year) | |
|---|---|---|---|---|---|
| Alabama (Ala.) (1819) *(22)* | 50,750 | 4,040,587 | Montgomery | Jim Folsom, jun. (*D*) | (4 – 1995) |
| Alaska (1959) *(49)* | 570,374 | 550,043 | Juneau | Walter Hickel (*I*) | (4 – 1994) |
| Arizona (Ariz.) (1912) *(48)* | 113,642 | 3,665,228 | Phoenix | Fife Symington (*R*) | (4 – 1995) |
| Arkansas (Ark.) (1836) *(25)* | 52,075 | 2,350,725 | Little Rock | Jim Guy Tucker (*D*) | (4 – 1995) |
| California (Calif.) (1850) *(31)* | 155,973 | 29,760,021 | Sacramento | Pete Wilson (*R*) | (4 – 1995) |
| Colorado (Colo.) (1876) *(38)* | 103,729 | 3,294,394 | Denver | Roy Romer (*D*) | (4 – 1995) |
| Connecticut (Conn.)§(1788) *(5)* | 4,845 | 3,287,116 | Hartford | Lowell Weicker (*I*) | (4 – 1995) |
| Delaware (Del.) § (1787) *(1)* | 1,955 | 666,168 | Dover | Tom Carper (*D*) | (4 – 1997) |
| Florida (Fla.) (1845) *(27)* | 53,997 | 12,937,926 | Tallahassee | Lawton Chiles (*D*) | (4 – 1995) |
| Georgia (Ga.) § (1788) *(4)* | 57,919 | 6,478,216 | Atlanta | Zell Miller (*D*) | (4 – 1995) |
| Hawaii (1959) *(50)* | 6,423 | 1,108,229 | Honolulu | John D. Waihee III (*D*) | (4 – 1994) |
| Idaho (1890) *(43)* | 82,751 | 1,006,749 | Boise | Cecil D. Andrus (*D*) | (4 – 1995) |
| Illinois (Ill.) (1818) *(21)* | 55,593 | 11,430,602 | Springfield | Jim Edgar (*R*) | (4 – 1995) |
| Indiana (Ind.) (1816) *(19)* | 35,870 | 5,544,159 | Indianapolis | Evan Bayh (*D*) | (4 – 1997) |
| Iowa (1846) *(29)* | 55,875 | 2,776,755 | Des Moines | Terry Branstad (*R*) | (4 – 1995) |
| Kansas (Kan.) (1861) *(34)* | 81,823 | 2,477,574 | Topeka | Joan Finney (*D*) | (4 – 1995) |
| Kentucky (Ky.) (1792) *(15)* | 39,732 | 3,685,296 | Frankfort | Brereton C. Jones (*D*) | (4 – 1996) |
| Louisiana (La.) (1812) *(18)* | 43,566 | 4,219,973 | Baton Rouge | Edwin Edwards (*D*) | (4 – 1996) |
| Maine (Me.) (1820) *(23)* | 30,865 | 1,227,928 | Augusta | John R. McKernan, jun. (*R*) | (4 – 1995) |
| Maryland (Md.) § (1788) *(7)* | 9,775 | 4,781,468 | Annapolis | William D. Schaefer (*D*) | (4 – 1995) |
| Massachusetts (Mass.) § (1788) *(6)* | 7,838 | 6,016,425 | Boston | William Weld (*R*) | (4 – 1995) |
| Michigan (Mich.) (1837) *(26)* | 56,809 | 9,295,297 | Lansing | John Engler (*R*) | (4 – 1995) |
| Minnesota (Minn.) (1858) *(32)* | 79,617 | 4,375,099 | St Paul | Arne Carlson (*R*) | (4 – 1995) |
| Mississippi (Miss.) (1817) *(20)* | 46,914 | 2,573,216 | Jackson | Kirk Fordice (*R*) | (4 – 1996) |
| Missouri (Mo.) (1821) *(24)* | 68,898 | 5,117,073 | Jefferson City | Mel Carnahan (*D*) | (4 – 1997) |
| Montana (Mont.) (1889) *(41)* | 145,556 | 799,065 | Helena | Marc Raciot (*R*) | (4 – 1997) |
| Nebraska (Neb.) (1867) *(37)* | 76,878 | 1,578,385 | Lincoln | Ben Nelson (*D*) | (4 – 1995) |
| Nevada (Nev.) (1864) *(36)* | 109,806 | 1,201,833 | Carson City | Robert J. Miller (*D*) | (4 – 1995) |
| New Hampshire (NH) § (1788) *(9)* | 8,969 | 1,109,252 | Concord | Steve Merrill (*R*) | (2 – 1995) |
| New Jersey (NJ) § (1787) *(3)* | 7,419 | 7,730,188 | Trenton | Christine Whitman (*R*) | (4 – 1998) |
| New Mexico (NM) (1912) *(47)* | 121,365 | 1,515,069 | Santa Fé | Bruce King (*D*) | (4 – 1995) |
| New York (NY) § (1788) *(11)* | 47,224 | 17,990,455 | Albany | Mario M. Cuomo (*D*) | (4 – 1995) |
| North Carolina (NC) § (1789) *(12)* | 48,718 | 6,628,637 | Raleigh | James B. Hunt, jun. (*D*) | (4 – 1997) |
| North Dakota (ND) (1889) *(39)* | 68,994 | 638,800 | Bismarck | Edward Schafer (*R*) | (4 – 1997) |
| Ohio (1803) *(17)* | 40,953 | 10,847,115 | Columbus | George Voinovich (*R*) | (4 – 1995) |
| Oklahoma (Okla.) (1907) *(46)* | 68,679 | 3,145,585 | Oklahoma City | David Walters (*D*) | (4 – 1995) |
| Oregon (Ore.) (1859) *(33)* | 96,003 | 2,842,321 | Salem | Barbara Roberts (*D*) | (4 – 1995) |
| Pennsylvania (Pa.) § (1787) *(2)* | 44,820 | 11,881,643 | Harrisburg | Robert P. Casey (*D*) | (4 – 1995) |
| Rhode Island (RI) § (1790) *(13)* | 1,045 | 1,003,464 | Providence | Bruce Sundlun (*D*) | (2 – 1993) |
| South Carolina (SC) § (1788) *(8)* | 30,111 | 3,486,703 | Columbia | Carroll A. Campbell, jun. (*R*) | (4 – 1995) |
| South Dakota (SD) (1889) *(40)* | 75,896 | 696,004 | Pierre | Walter D. Miller (*R*) | (4 – 1995) |
| Tennessee (Tenn.) (1796) *(16)* | 41,220 | 4,877,185 | Nashville | Ned R. McWherter (*D*) | (4 – 1995) |
| Texas (1845) *(28)* | 261,914 | 16,986,510 | Austin | Ann Richards (*D*) | (4 – 1995) |
| Utah (1896) *(45)* | 82,168 | 1,722,850 | Salt Lake City | Mike Leavitt (*R*) | (4 – 1997) |
| Vermont (Vt.) (1791) *(14)* | 9,249 | 562,758 | Montpelier | Howard Dean (*D*) | (2 – 1995) |
| Virginia (Va.) § (1788) *(10)* | 39,598 | 6,187,358 | Richmond | George Allen (*R*) | (4 – 1998) |
| Washington (Wash.) (1889) *(42)* | 66,581 | 4,866,692 | Olympia | Mike Lowry (*D*) | (4 – 1997) |
| West Virginia (W. Va.) (1863) *(35)* | 24,087 | 1,793,477 | Charleston | Gaston Caperton (*D*) | (4 – 1997) |
| Wisconsin (Wis.) (1848) *(30)* | 54,314 | 4,891,769 | Madison | Tommy Thompson (*R*) | (4 – 1995) |
| Wyoming (Wyo.) (1890) *(44)* | 97,705 | 453,588 | Cheyenne | Michael Sullivan (*D*) | (4 – 1995) |
| Dist. of Columbia (DC) (1791) | 61 | 606,900 | — | † | |

### OUTLYING TERRITORIES AND POSSESSIONS

| | | | | | |
|---|---|---|---|---|---|
| American Samoa | 77 | 46,773 | Pago Pago | A. P. Lutati (*D*) | (4 – 1997) |
| Guam | 210 | 133,152 | Agaña | Joseph Ada (*R*) | (4 – 1995) |
| Northern Mariana Islands | 179 | 43,345 | Saipan | Froilan C. Tenorio (*D*) | (4 – 1998) |
| Palau | 177 | 15,122 | Koror | — | |
| Puerto Rico | 3,427 | 3,522,037 | San Juan | Dr Pedro J. Rossello (*PNP*) | (4 – 1997) |
| US Virgin Islands | 134 | 101,809 | Charlotte Amalie | Alexander Farrelly (*D*) | (4 – 1995) |

§The 13 original states
*D* Democratic Party; *I* Independent; *PNP* New Progressive Party; *R* Republican Party
†The capital territory is governed by Congress through a Commissioner and City Council

vote for a President by ballot. The ballots are then sent to Washington, and opened on 6 January by the President of the Senate in the presence of Congress. The candidate who has received a majority of the whole number of electoral votes cast is declared President for the ensuing term. If no one has a majority, then from the highest on the list (not exceeding three) the House of Representatives elects a President, the votes being taken by states, the representation from each state having one vote. A presidential term begins at noon on 20 January.

*President of the United States*, William Jefferson Blythe IV Clinton, *born* 19 August 1946, *sworn in* 20 January 1993. Democrat

*Vice-President*, Albert Gore, jun., *born* 31 March 1948, *sworn in* 20 January 1993

THE CABINET *as at August 1994*

*Secretary of State*, Warren Christopher
*Secretary of the Treasury*, Lloyd Bentsen
*Secretary of Defence*, William Perry
*Attorney-General*, Janet Reno
*Secretary of the Interior*, Bruce Babbit
*Secretary of Agriculture*, Mike Espy
*Secretary of Commerce*, Ron Brown
*Secretary of Labour*, Robert Reich
*Secretary of Health and Human Services*, Donna Shalala
*Secretary of Housing and Urban Development*, Henry Cisneros
*Secretary of Transportation*, Federico Pena
*Secretary of Energy*, Hazel O'Leary
*Secretary of Education*, Richard Riley
*Secretary of Veterans' Affairs*, Jesse Brown
*Ambassador to the UN*, Madeleine Albright
*US Trade Representative*, Mickey Kantor
*Administrator, Environmental Protection Agency*, Carol Browner
*Director, Office of Management and Budget*, Alice Rivlin (*acting*)
*National Security Adviser*, Anthony Lake
*White House Chief of Staff*, Leon Panetta

Other senior positions:
*Director of CIA*, James Woolsey
*Director, Office of National Drug Control Policy*, Lee Brown
*Director of FBI*, Louis Freeh
*Chairman, Federal Reserve Board of Governors*, Alan Greenspan

UNITED STATES EMBASSY
24 Grosvenor Square, London WIA IAE
Tel 0171-499 9000

*Ambassador Extraordinary and Plenipotentiary*, The Honourable Adm. William J. Crowe jun., apptd 1994
*Minister*, T. E. Deal
*Defence and Naval Attaché*, Capt. J. E. Hart
*Minister-Counsellors*, T. H. Gewecke (*Economic*); M. F. O'Brien (*Cultural*); N. S. Baskey, jun. (*Consular*); K. P. Moorefield (*Commercial*)

BRITISH EMBASSY
3100 Massachusetts Avenue NW, Washington DC 20008
Tel: Washington DC 462 1340

*Ambassador Extraordinary and Plenipotentiary*, His Excellency Sir Robin Renwick, KCMG, apptd 1991
*Ministers*, H. P. Evans (*Economic*); S. Webb (*Defence Equipment*); J. Q. Greenstock, CMG; W. Marsden, CMG; P. Lo, E. B. Wiggam (*Hong Kong Economic and Trade Affairs*)
*Head of British Defence Staff and Defence Attaché*, Rear-Adm. D. A. Blackburn, LVO, RN

*Counsellor*, H. Parkinson (*Management and HM Consul-General*)
*Consul-General* (*New York*) *and Director-General of Trade and Investment*, A. J. Hunter, CMG
*Cultural Attaché and British Council Representative*, D. J. Evans

BRITISH CONSULATES-GENERAL – Atlanta, Boston, Chicago, Houston, Los Angeles, New York and San Francisco.
BRITISH CONSULATES – Anchorage, Charlotte, Cleveland, Dallas, Denver, Kansas City, Miami, New Orleans, Norfolk, Philadelphia, Portland, St Louis, Seattle and Puerto Rico.
BRITISH-AMERICAN CHAMBER OF COMMERCE, 275 Madison Avenue, New York 10016; UK OFFICE, Suite 201, High Holborn, London WCIV 6RR

## THE CONGRESS

Legislative power is vested in two houses, the Senate and the House of Representatives. The Senate has 100 members, two Senators from each state, elected for the term of six years, and each Senator has one vote. Representatives are chosen in each state, by popular vote, for two years.

The House of Representatives consists of 435 Representatives, a resident commissioner from Puerto Rico and a delegate each from American Samoa, the District of Columbia, Guam and the Virgin Islands.

Members of the 103rd Congress were elected on 3 November 1992. The 103rd Congress is constituted as follows:

*Senate* – Democrats 56; Republicans 44; total 100
*House of Representatives* – Democrats 256; Republicans 178; Independent 1; total 435 (15 June 1994)

*President of the Senate*, The Vice-President
*Speaker of the House of Representatives*, Thomas S. Foley, Washington
*Secretary of the Senate*, Martha S. Pope, *District of Columbia*
*Clerk of the House of Representatives*, Donnald K. Anderson, *California*

## THE JUDICATURE

The federal judiciary consists of three sets of federal courts: the Supreme Court at Washington DC, consisting of a Chief Justice and eight Associate Justices, with original jurisdiction in cases where a state is a party to the suit, and with appellate jurisdiction from inferior federal courts and from the judgments of the highest courts of the states; the United States Courts of Appeals, dealing with appeals from district courts and from certain federal administrative agencies, and consisting of 168 circuit judges within 13 circuits; the 94 United States district courts served by 575 district court judges.

THE SUPREME COURT
US Supreme Court Building, Washington DC 20543

*Chief Justice*, William H. Rehnquist, *Arizona*, apptd 1986

*Associate Justices*
John Paul Stevens, *Illinois*, apptd 1975
Sandra Day O'Connor, *Arizona*, apptd 1981
Antonin Scalia, *Virginia*, apptd 1986
Anthony M. Kennedy, *California*, apptd 1988
David H. Souter, *New Hampshire*, apptd 1990
Clarence Thomas, *Georgia*, apptd 1991
Ruth Ginsburg, *DC*, apptd 1993
Stephen Breyer, *Massachusetts*, apptd 1994

*Clerk of the Supreme Court*, William K. Suter

CRIMINAL STATISTICS *Number of offences*

| | 1991 | 1992 |
|---|---|---|
| Murder and non-negligent manslaughter | 24,703 | 23,760 |
| Forcible rape | 106,593 | 109,062 |
| Robbery | 687,732 | 672,478 |
| Aggravated assault | 1,092,739 | 1,126,974 |
| Burglary | 3,157,150 | 2,979,884 |
| Larceny – theft | 8,142,228 | 7,915,199 |
| Thefts of motor vehicles | 1,661,738 | 1,610,834 |
| *Total* | 14,872,883 | 14,438,191 |

DEFENCE

Each military department is separately organized and functions under the direction, authority and control of the Secretary of Defence. The Air Force has primary responsibility for the Department of Defence space development programmes and projects.

*Secretary of Defence (in the Cabinet)*, Dr William Perry
*Chairman, Joint Chiefs of Staff*, Gen. John Shalikashvili

STRENGTHS *as at 30 June 1994*
The US Army had a strength of 557,546. The strength of the Navy was 479,276 active duty personnel. The strength of the Marine Corps was 173,726 active duty personnel. The Air Force had 433,091 officers and airmen on active duty.

DEPLOYMENT
Under strategic command the USA has 480 submarine-launched ballistic missiles, 818 inter-continental ballistic missiles and 238 heavy nuclear-capable bombers, together with multiple intelligence satellites, radars and early warning systems throughout the world. The Army deploys 15,120 main battle tanks, 900 light tanks, 34,785 armoured infantry fighting vehicles and armoured personnel carriers, 6,470 artillery pieces, 404 aircraft and 1,660 armed helicopters. The Navy deploys 23 strategic (SLBM) submarines, 87 tactical submarines, 12 aircraft carriers, 52 cruisers, 38 destroyers, 59 frigates, 28 patrol and coastal combatants, 214 amphibious and support ships, 1,690 combat aircraft and 475 armed helicopters. The Marine Corps has 237 main battle tanks, 1,940 armoured vehicles, 1,050 artillery pieces, 550 combat aircraft and 96 armed helicopters. The Air Force deploys 226 long-range and 3,451 tactical combat aircraft and 3,360 transport, tanker and training aircraft. The major deployments of US personnel overseas are: Germany (123,400); UK (16,950); Italy (12,900); Mediterranean (17,500); Japan (43,100); South Korea (35,500); Panama (10,200).

FINANCE

BUDGET

| | 1992 | 1993 |
|---|---|---|
| Total receipts | $1,090.5 bn | $1,153.2 bn |
| Total outlay | 1,380.8 bn | 1,408.1 bn |
| Defence | 298.4 bn | 290.6 bn |
| Social security | 287.6 bn | 304.6 bn |
| Income security | 196.9 bn | 207.9 bn |
| Debt interest | 199.4 bn | 198.9 bn |

SOCIAL WELFARE EXPENDITURE 1991

| | Total | Per capita |
|---|---|---|
| Social insurance | $561,178 m | $2,185 |
| Education | 277,124 m | 1,083 |
| Public aid | 180,411 m | 705 |
| Health and medical | 69,365 m | 271 |
| Veterans' programmes | 32,857 m | 126 |
| Other social welfare | 19,780 m | 77 |
| Housing | 21,523 m | 84 |
| TOTAL | 1,162,239 m | 4,531 |

PUBLIC DEBT
At the end of September 1992 the total gross federal debt stood at US$4,002,815 million.

ECONOMY

GROSS DOMESTIC PRODUCT BY INDUSTRY 1991

| | US$ millions |
|---|---|
| *Private industries* | 4,992,795 |
| Agriculture, forestry, fisheries | 108,630 |
| Mining | 91,841 |
| Construction | 223,394 |
| Manufacturing | 1,026,182 |
| Transportation and public utilities | 506,017 |
| Wholesale trade | 375,133 |
| Retail trade | 532,075 |
| Finance, insurance, and real estate | 1,039,707 |
| Services | 1,089,816 |
| *Government and government enterprises* | 720,600 |
| Statistical discrepancy | 9,575 |
| TOTAL | 5,722,970 |

AGRICULTURE
The total number of farms in 1994 was 2,040,410, with a total area of land in farms of 974,800,000 acres, and an average acreage per farm of 478 acres. The total number of people employed on farms during the week of 10–16 April 1994 was 2,919,000, of whom 456,000 were unpaid workers, 803,000 hired workers and 240,000 agricultural service workers. Principal crops are corn for grain, soybeans, wheat hay, cotton, tobacco, grain sorghums, potatoes, oranges and barley.

Livestock on farms on 1 January 1993 and 1994 was:

| | 1993 | 1994 |
|---|---|---|
| Cattle | 100,611,000 | 101,749,000 |
| Milk cows | 9,838,000 | 9,638,000 |
| Sheep and lambs | 10,013,000 | 9,079,000 |
| Hogs and pigs | 58,116,000 | 57,938,000 |
| Chickens | 367,015,000 | 377,529,000 |

Gross income from farming in 1993 was US$194,500 million, of which cash receipts from marketing were US$181,800 million and government payments US$12,700 million. Cash income from all crops in 1993 was US$84,100 million and from livestock and livestock products US$90,300 million.

MINERALS
The value of non-fuel raw mineral production in 1992 totalled an estimated US$32,012 million compared with US$31,038 million in 1991. Mineral exports in 1992 were valued at US$23,234 million, and imports at US$34,426 million.

| *Production* ('000 metric tons) | 1991 | 1992 |
|---|---|---|
| Iron ore | 56,775 | 55,569 |
| Phosphate rock | 48,096 | 46,965 |
| Zinc ore | 518 | 523 |
| Refined copper | 1,631 | 1,765 |
| Refined lead | 466 | 397 |

ENERGY
Production in 1992 was 67.72 quadrillion BTU, principally coal, natural gas and crude oil. Coal accounted for over half of energy exports of 5.03 quadrillion BTU. Imports were 19.45 quadrillion BTU, of which crude oil was 16.35 quadrillion BTU, to meet consumption of 81.14 quadrillion BTU (quadrillion = $10^{15}$).

LABOUR

The civilian labour force was 129,839,000 in June 1993. Unemployment was estimated at 9,252,000 in June 1993 (7.1 per cent) (7.8 per cent in June 1992).

| TRADE | 1991 | 1992 |
|---|---|---|
| *General imports* | | |
| c.i.f. value | US$510,168m | US$553,335m |
| customs value | 488,453 | 532,665 |
| *Exports and re-exports* | | |
| †f.a.s. value | 421,853 | 447,471 |
| *Trade balance* | | |
| f.a.s. exports: c.i.f. | | |
| imports | −88,315 | −105,864 |
| f.a.s. exports: customs | | |
| imports | −65,723 | −84,501 |

† excluding military aid

Principal sources of imports were Asian countries (of which Japan contributed 41 per cent), north and central America (of which Canada 68 per cent), Europe (of which EC countries 83 per cent). Principal destinations for exports and re-exports were Asian states (of which Japan took 34 per cent), north and central America (of which Canada 63 per cent), Europe (of which EC 83 per cent).

| *Trade with UK* | 1992 | 1993 |
|---|---|---|
| Imports from UK | £12,225,877,000 | £15,354,306,000 |
| Exports to UK | 13,711,323,000 | 16,357,928,000 |

COMMUNICATIONS

Revenue, etc., of Class I line-haul railroads (US$ thousands):

| | 1990 | 1991 |
|---|---|---|
| Operating revenue | | |
| Total | 28,370,000 | 27,845,000 |
| Freight | 24,471,000 | 26,949,000 |
| Passenger | 941,900 | 962,300 |
| Total operating expenses | 24,652,000 | 28,061,000 |
| Railroad track (miles) | 239,000 | 234,000 |
| Average number of | | |
| employees | 216,000 | 206,000 |

In 1992 there were 3.9 million miles of public roads and streets, of which 3.12 million miles were in rural areas and 785,160 miles were in urban areas. Surfaced roads and streets account for 58.8 per cent of the total. An estimated total of US$80,012 million was spent in 1992 on roads and streets in the United States. In 1992 there were 39,235 deaths caused by motor vehicle accidents. The death rate per 100 million vehicle-miles of travel was 1.75 in 1992 compared with 1.91 in 1991.

The ocean-going merchant marine on 1 January 1994 consisted of 564 vessels of 1,000 gross tons and over, of which 367 were privately-owned and 197 were government-owned ships. There were 157 ships in the National Defence Reserve Fleet of inactive government-owned vessels.

According to preliminary figures, domestic and international scheduled airlines in 1993 carried 486,392,067 passengers over 489,205,481,000 revenue passenger miles. Air cargo ton-miles were distributed as follows: freight and express 16,511,821,308; and air mail 2,356,686,931. Total operating revenues of all US scheduled airlines were US$83,688,100,322 in 1993. Total operating expenses rose to US$82,248,136,900 in 1993. Scheduled operations showed a net operating loss of US$1,439,963,423 in 1993, compared with a net operating loss of US$2,163,647,000 in 1992.

EDUCATION

All the states and the District of Columbia have compulsory school attendance laws. In general, children are obliged to attend school from seven to 16 years of age. In the autumn of 1993, 48,824,000 children were enrolled in regular elementary and secondary day schools, of whom 5.47 million or 11.2 per cent attended private schools.

During the 1991–2 school year, the average daily attendance in regular public elementary and secondary day schools was 38,960,783. In the 1992–3 school year 2,255,000 students graduated from regular public high schools and 257,000 graduated from private high school. In addition an estimated 457,000 received high school equivalency certificates. Public school teachers numbered 2,458,000, with an average salary of US$35,027.

Most of the revenue for public elementary and secondary school purposes comes from federal, state, and local governments. Less than 2.7 per cent comes from gifts and from tuition and transportation fees. Revenue receipts during 1991–2 amounted to US$234,500 million; 6.6 per cent from the federal government, 46.4 per cent from state governments, and 44.3 per cent from local sources. Estimated current expenditure in the 1991–2 school year was US$211,200 million; for sites, buildings, furniture and equipment expenditures, US$20,800 million; for interest on school debt US$5,200 million.

HIGHER EDUCATION

In the autumn of 1993, total enrolment in universities, colleges, professional schools, and two-year schools numbered 14,600,000.

During 1991–2 the major fields for bachelor's degrees were business and management (256,603), social sciences (133,974), education (108,006) and engineering (77,541). First-profession degrees in law (38,848) and medicine (15,243) predominated. Master's degrees were heavily concentrated in education (92,668) and business and management (84,642). The most popular fields of study for doctorates were education (6,864) and engineering (5,499). Total expenditures for colleges and universities during the 1991–2 academic year were US$177,200 million.

Among the better-known universities are: *Harvard*, founded at Cambridge, Mass. in 1636, and named after John Harvard of Emmanuel College, Cambridge, England, who bequeathed to it his library and a sum of money in 1638; *Yale*, founded at New Haven, Connecticut, in 1701; *Princeton*, NJ, founded 1746.

US TERRITORIES, ETC

Responsibility for territorial affairs generally is centred in the Office of the Assistant Secretary, Territorial and International Affairs, Department of the Interior, Washington DC.

As well as the territories mentioned below, the USA also exercises sovereignty over the following:

Johnston Atoll – two small islands, less than 1 sq. mile in area, to the south-west of Hawaii; administered by the US Air Force.

Midway Islands – two islands (area, 3 sq. miles), at the western end of the Hawaiian chain; administered by the US Navy.

Wake Islands – area about 3 sq. miles and average elevation of less than 3 metres, lying about 2,300 miles west of Hawaii; administered by the US Air Force.

Certain small guano islands, rocks or keys, considered as appertaining to the USA.

## THE COMMONWEALTH OF PUERTO RICO

Puerto Rico (Rich Port) is an island of the Greater Antilles group in the West Indies, and lies between 17° 50′ and 18° 30′ N. latitude and 65° 30′ and 67° 15′ W. longitude, with a total area of 3,427 sq. miles (8,875 sq. km), and a population (1994 estimate) of 3,600,000. The 1990 census put the population at 3,522,037. The majority of the inhabitants are of Spanish descent, and Spanish and English are the official languages.

Puerto Rico was discovered in 1493 by Columbus and explored by Ponce de Léon in 1508. It was a Spanish possession until 1898, when the USA took formal possession as a result of the Spanish-American War.

The 1952 constitution establishes the Commonwealth of Puerto Rico with full powers of local government. The Legislative Assembly consists of two elected houses; the Senate of 27 members and the House of Representatives of 51 members. The term of the Legislative Assembly is four years. The Governor is popularly elected for a term of four years. Residents of Puerto Rico are US citizens. Puerto Rico is represented in Congress by a Resident Commissioner, elected for a term of four years, who has a seat in the House of Representatives but not a vote, although he has a right to vote on those committees of which he is a member. A plebiscite on the future constitutional status of Puerto Rico was held on 14 November 1993 in which 48 per cent voted to maintain the existing Commonwealth status, 46 per cent voted for full US statehood and 4 per cent for independence. The existing Commonwealth status continues which gives Puerto Rico the benefit of a common market with the USA and leaves it without the burden of federal taxes.

Preliminary 1994 figures for the Commonwealth government's budget were receipts, US$12,627 million. Manufacturing added US$13,183 million to net Commonwealth income in 1993 (preliminary figures), trade US$3,834 million, finance, insurance and real estate US$4,000 million and agriculture US$468 million. Principal crops are sugar cane, coffee, vegetables, fruits and tobacco. Most valuable areas of manufacturing are chemicals and allied products, metal products and machinery, and food processing.

CAPITAL – ΨSan Juan, population of the municipality (1990), 437,745; Other major towns are: Bayamón (220,262); ΨPonce (187,749); and Carolina (177,806).

*Governor*, Dr Pedro J. Rossello

| TRADE | 1992 | 1993 |
|---|---|---|
| Total Imports | US$19,677m | US$19,133m |
| Total Exports | 21,051m | 19,791m |

| *Trade with UK* | 1992 | 1993 |
|---|---|---|
| Imports from UK | £156,118,000 | £188,417,000 |
| Exports to UK | 103,463,000 | 107,113,000 |

## GUAM

Guam, the largest of the Mariana Islands in the north Pacific Ocean, lies in 13° 26′ N. latitude and 144° 39′ E. longitude and has an area of about 210 sq. miles (544 sq. km). The population (1990 estimate) is 133,152, mostly of Chamorro stock mingled with Filipino and Spanish blood. The Chamorro language belongs to the Malayo-Polynesian family, but with considerable admixture of Spanish. Chamorro and English are the official languages and most residents are bilingual.

Guam was occupied by the Japanese in December 1941 but was recaptured by US forces in 1944. Under the Organic

Act of Guam 1950, Guam has statutory powers of self-government, and Guamanians are US citizens. A 21-member unicameral legislature is elected biennially. The Governor and Lieutenant-Governor are popularly elected. A non-voting Delegate is elected to serve in the US House of Representatives. There is also a District Court of Guam, with original jurisdiction in cases under federal law.

Guam's two main sources of revenue are tourism and US military spending.

CAPITAL – Agaña. Port of entry, ΨApra.

*Governor*, Joseph F. Ada
*Lt.-Governor*, Frank Blas

## AMERICAN SAMOA

American Samoa consists of the islands of Tutuila, Anu'u, Ofu, Olesega, Ta'u, Rose and Swains Islands, with a total area of 77 sq. miles (199 sq. km). Tutuila, the largest of the group, has an area of 52 sq. miles and a magnificent harbour at Pago Pago. The remaining islands have an area of about 24 sq. miles. The population (1990 estimate) is 46,773. Tuna and copra are the chief exports.

American Samoans are US nationals, but some have acquired citizenship through service in the United States armed forces or other naturalization procedure. The 1960 constitution grants American Samoa a measure of self-government, with certain powers reserved to the US Secretary of the Interior. There is a bicameral legislature with popularly elected Representatives and Governors and a popularly elected Governor. A non-voting Delegate is elected to serve in the US House of Representatives.

SEAT OF GOVERNMENT – Fagatogo.

*Governor*, A. P. Lutali
*Lt.-Governor*, Tauese P. Sunia

## THE VIRGIN ISLANDS

The US Virgin Islands were purchased from Denmark and proclaimed US territory in 1917. The total area of the islands is 134 sq. miles (347 sq. km), with a population (1990) of 101,809. There are three main islands, St Thomas (28 sq. miles), St Croix (84 sq. miles), St John (20 sq. miles) and about 50 small islets or cays, mostly uninhabited.

Under the provisions of the Revised Organic Act of the Virgin Islands 1954, legislative power is vested in the Legislature, a unicameral body composed of 15 senators popularly elected for two-year terms. The Governor is popularly elected. Virgin Islanders are US citizens. A non-voting Delegate is elected to serve in the US House of Representatives. A referendum is to take place at a future date to determine the future political status of the islands.

CAPITAL – ΨCharlotte Amalie on St Thomas. Population (1980) 11,756.

*Governor*, Alexander Farrelly
*Lt.-Governor*, Derek M. Hodge

| *Trade with UK* | 1993 |
|---|---|
| Imports from UK | £5,311,000 |
| Exports to UK | 488,000 |

## NORTHERN MARIANA ISLANDS

The land area of the Northern Mariana Islands is 179 sq. miles (464 sq. km) with an estimated population (1990) of 43,345. The USA administered the islands as part of a UN Trusteeship until the trusteeship agreement was terminated in 1986 bringing fully into effect a 1976 congressional law establishing a commonwealth of the Northern Mariana

Islands. Most of the residents became US citizens. There is a popularly elected bicameral legislature and a popularly elected Governor.

SEAT OF GOVERNMENT – Saipan.
Population (1990 estimate) 39,090.

*Governor*, Froilan C. Tenorio
*Lt.-Governor*, Benjamin M. Manglona

## REPUBLIC OF PALAU

Palau consists of more than 200 Pacific Ocean islands, of which eight are permanently inhabited. The Palau archipelago stretches over 400 miles. The land area is 177 sq. miles (458 sq. km), with an estimated population of 15,122. The major island is Koror with a population of 10,493.

Since 1981 Palau has had a bicameral legislature, consisting of a House of Delegates of 16 members and a Senate of 14 members. The President and Vice-President are directly elected. Palau and the USA signed a Compact of Free Association in August 1982, but this repeatedly failed to gain the three-quarters majority in a referendum needed for it to come into effect. The necessary majority was changed to a simple majority in three-quarters of Palau's 16 divisions in November 1992 and this majority was gained in a referendum on 9 November, making implementation of the Compact of Free Association possible once procedural issues and law suits by opponents of the Compact have been resolved. When the Compact comes into effect, Palau will become an independent sovereign state and the US-administered UN Trust Territory of the Pacific Islands, of which Palau is the only remaining part, will end. The USA is responsible for financial support, and for the defence of Palau for 50 years.

*President*, Kuniwo Nakamura
*Vice-President*, Tommy Remengesau, jun.

## THE PANAMA CANAL

As a result of the Panama Canal Treaty 1977, the Canal Zone was disestablished, with all jurisdiction over the former Canal Zone reverting to Panama with effect from 1 October 1979. Under the treaty, the United States is allowed the use of operating areas for the Panama Canal, together with several military bases, although the Republic of Panama is sovereign in all such areas. The Panama Canal Commission, an arm of the US Government, will continue to operate the canal until noon on 31 December 1999.

In the fiscal year 1993, the total number of transits by ocean-going commercial traffic was 12,086; canal net tons totalled 186,407,529; cargo tons totalled 157,703,910.

## URUGUAY
*República Oriental del Uruguay*

Uruguay is situated on the east coast of the Rio de la Plata in South America, in 30° to 35° S. latitude and 53° 15′ to 57° 42′ W. longitude, with an area of 68,037 sq. miles (176,215 sq. km). The country consists mainly of undulating grassy plains. The principal river is the Rio Negro (with its tributary the Yi), flowing from north-east to south-west into the Rio Uruguay. The climate is temperate.

POPULATION – The population (1992) is 3,116,802, predominantly of Spanish and Italian descent. Spanish is the official language. Many Uruguayans are Roman Catholics. There is no established church.

CAPITAL – Ψ Montevideo, population (1992) 1,383,660. Other centres are Salto, Ψ Paysandu, Mercedes, Minas, Melo, Rivera and Punta del Este.
CURRENCY – New Uruguayan peso of 100 centésimos.
FLAG – Four blue and five white horizontal stripes surcharged with sun on a white ground in the top corner, next flagstaff.
NATIONAL ANTHEM – Orientales, La Patria O La Tumba (Uruguayans, the fatherland or death).
NATIONAL DAY – 25 August (Declaration of Independence, 1825).

## GOVERNMENT

Uruguay (or the *Banda Oriental*, as the territory lying on the eastern bank of the Uruguay River was then called) resisted all attempted invasions of the Portuguese and Spanish until the early 17th century; 100 years later the Portuguese settlements were captured by the Spanish. From 1726 to 1814 the country formed part of Spanish South America. In 1814 the armies of the Argentine Confederation captured the capital and annexed the province; afterwards it was annexed by Portugal and became a province of Brazil. In 1825, the country threw off Brazilian rule. This action led to war between Argentina and Brazil which was settled by the mediation of the United Kingdom, Uruguay being declared an independent state in 1828. In 1830 a republic was inaugurated.

Under the constitution the President appoints a council of 11 ministers and a Secretary (Planning and Budget Office), and the Vice-President presides over Congress. The Congress consists of a Chamber of 99 deputies and a Senate of 30 members (plus the Vice-President), elected for five years by proportional representation. General elections held in 1984 marked the return to civilian rule after 11 years of presidential rule with military support. The first fully free presidential and legislative elections since 1971 were held in 1989, and were won by the Partido Nacional Blanco.

The republic is divided into 19 Departments each with a mayor, a chief of police and a Departmental Council.

HEAD OF STATE
*President*, Dr Luis Alberto Lacalle, took office 1 March 1990
*Vice-President*, Dr Gonzalo Aguirre Ramírez

CABINET *as at September 1994*

*Interior*, Raúl Iturria
*Foreign Affairs*, Dr Sergío Abreu
*Economy and Finance*, Dr Ignacío De Posadas
*Transport and Public Works*, Juan C. Raffo
*Public Health*, Guillermo Garcia Costa
*Labour and Social Security*, Dr Ricardo Reilly
*Livestock, Agriculture and Fisheries*, Pedro Saravia
*Education and Culture*, Antonio Mercader
*National Defence*, Dr Daniel Martins
*Industry and Energy*, Dr Eduardo Ache
*Tourism*, José Villar
*Housing, Territorial Regulation and Environment*, Hugo Romay
*Secretary, Planning and Budget Office*, Carlos Alfredo Cat

EMBASSY OF THE ORIENTAL REPUBLIC OF URUGUAY
2nd Floor, 140 Brompton Road, London SW3 1HY
Tel 0171-584 8192; *Consulate* 0171-589 8735

*Ambassador Extraordinary and Plenipotentiary*, His Excellency Juan Enrique Fischer, apptd 1993

BRITISH EMBASSY
Calle Marco Bruto 1073, Montevideo 11300 (PO Box 16024)
Tel: Montevideo 623650

*Ambassador Extraordinary and Plenipotentiary*, His
Excellency Robert Hendrie, apptd 1994

There is a British Consular Office at *Montevideo*.

BRITISH-URUGUAYAN CHAMBER OF COMMERCE,
Avenida Labertador Brig. Gen., Lavalleja 1641, P2-OF
201, Montevideo

## ECONOMY

The economy is based on agriculture, primarily livestock.
There are just over 9 million cattle and just under 24 million
sheep. Wheat, barley, maize, linseed, sunflower seed and
rice are cultivated. In addition to wool, meat packing, other
foodstuffs (citrus, wine, beer), fishing and textile industries
are of importance.

Industrial development continues and, in addition to the
greatly augmented textile industry, includes tyres, sheet-
glass, three-ply wood, cement, leather-curing, beet-sugar,
plastics, household consumer goods, edible oils and the
refining of petroleum and petroleum products. There are
some ferrous minerals, not extracted at present. Non-ferrous
exploited minerals include clinker, dolomite, marble and
granite.

The external debt in 1993 was US$4,200 million. Central
Bank reserves (1992) were US$1,711 million, while GNP was
(1991) US$9,480,000m, inflation (1992) 58.9 per cent,
unemployment (1992) 8.3 per cent and budget deficit (1992)
was 0.7 per cent of GDP.

| FINANCE | 1991 | 1992 |
|---|---|---|
| Revenue | US$1,839,075m | US$1,990,373m |
| Expenditure | 1,800,733m | 1,959,930m |

TRADE

The major exports are meat and by-products, wool and by-
products, hides and bristle and agricultural products. The
principal imports are raw materials, construction materials,
oils and lubricants, automotive vehicles, kits and machinery.
Principal trading partners are Brazil, USA and Argentina.

| | 1991 | 1992 |
|---|---|---|
| Total exports | US$1,604,700 m | US$1,702,500 m |
| Total imports | 1,636,400 m | 2,058,000 m |
| *Trade with UK* | 1992 | 1993 |
| Imports from UK | £31,462,000 | £45,674,000 |
| Exports to UK | 49,492,000 | 47,394,000 |

## COMMUNICATIONS

There are about 11,300 km of national highways, and
2,993 km of standard gauge railway in use. Passenger rail
services were cancelled in 1988 and services are now limited
to cargo transport; services are state-run. A state-owned
airline, PLUNA, provides international services, and internal
passenger and limited freight services are provided by
TAMU, another state-owned airline, using principally
military aircraft and personnel. The international airport of
Carrasco lies 12 miles outside Montevideo. The River
Uruguay is navigable from its estuary to Salto, 200 miles
north, and the Negro is also navigable for a considerable
distance.

Six daily newspapers are published in Montevideo and
most of them are distributed throughout the country.

## EDUCATION

Primary and secondary education is compulsory and free,
and technical and trade schools and evening courses for adult
education are state controlled. The university at Montevideo

(founded in 1849) has ten faculties and a new university has
been built at Salto.

---

## UZBEKISTAN
*Ozbekiston Respublikasy*

---

Uzbekistan has an area of 172,742 sq. miles (447,400 sq.
km) and occupies the south-central part of former Soviet Central
Asia, lying between the high Tienshan Mountains and the
Pamir highlands in the east and south-east and sandy
lowlands in the west and north-west. It is bordered by the
north by Kazakhstan and the Aral Sea, on the east by
Kyrgyzstan and Tajikistan, on the south by Afghanistan and
Turkmenistan, and on the west by Kazakhstan. Uzbekistan
consists of the Kara-Kalpak Autonomous Republic and
12 regions: Andizhan, Bokhara, Dzhizak, Ferghana, Kash-
kadar, Khorezm, Namangan, Navoi, Samarkand, Surkhan-
Darya, Syr-Darya and Tashkent. Most of the country is a
plain with huge waterless deserts, and several large oases
which form the main centres of population and economic
life. The climate is continental and dry.

POPULATION – The population (1989 census) is 19,810,000,
of which 71 per cent are Uzbeks, 8 per cent Russians, 5 per
cent Tajiks and 4 per cent Kazakhs, with smaller numbers of
Tatars, Kara-Kalpaks, Koreans, Ukrainians and Kirghiz.
The 1994 estimate put the population at 21,206,000. The
predominant religion is Sunni Muslim. Islam is tolerated
within strict bounds; it is allowed to play no part in politics.

The principal language is Uzbek (71 per cent) with Russian
(8 per cent), Tajik (5 per cent) and Kazakh (4 per cent).
Uzbek is one of the Turkic group of languages. In June 1994
the government approved a six-year programme for the
transfer of the Uzbek language to a Latin script.

CAPITAL – Tashkent. Population 2,073,000 (1992).
Samarkand (388,000) contains the Gur-Emir
(Tamerlane's Mausoleum) completed 1400 by Ulugbek,
Tamerlane's astronomer grandson.

CURRENCY – Sum (Som) of 100 tiyin.

FLAG – Three horizontal stripes of blue, white, green, with
the white fimbriated in red; on the blue near the hoist a
crescent and twelve stars, all in white.

NATIONAL DAY – 1 September (Independence Day).

## GOVERNMENT

Between the sixth and fourth centuries BC the area that is
now Uzbekistan was under the control of the Persians and
then Alexander the Great. In the 14th century the area
became the centre of a great Muslim empire under Tamerlane
and then his grandson Ulugbek, following whose murder the
state disintegrated. By the beginning of the 19th century
three independent Khanates, Khiva, Kokand and Bukhara,
existed in what is now Uzbekistan. These were gradually
annexed to the Russian Empire by the middle of the 19th
century. In November 1917 a Communist revolution broke
out in Tashkent and parts of Uzbekistan were included in the
Turkestan Soviet Republic at its formation in 1918. The
remainder of Uzbekistan was under the rule of the
independent states of Khiva and Bukhara, which had re-
emerged in 1918, until they were defeated by the Red Army
and Soviet rule was established throughout the area in 1921.
Under Soviet rule a massive land irrigation programme was
implemented to allow the cultivation of cotton.

Uzbekistan declared its independence from the Soviet
Union on 1 September 1991 after the failed Moscow coup. Its
independence was confirmed in a referendum on 29

December and recognized internationally. A new constitution was adopted by the Supreme Soviet in December 1992 under which the President and government hold executive power. The President may serve a maximum of two five-year terms and has the power to dissolve the 500-member Supreme Soviet. The Supreme Soviet may not remove or impeach the President. The last parliamentary elections were held on 24 March 1990.

The government of President Karimov is formed by the former Communist Party, which has renamed itself the People's Democratic Party. Despite the constitutionally guaranteed freedom of religion and thought and respect for human rights and multiparty democracy, censorship is still widely used and little political opposition is tolerated. The main opposition party, Birlik (Unity) nationalist party, has been continually banned since the introduction of the multi-party constitution in December 1992. Uzbek forces have been deployed in Tajikistan since late 1992 to help maintain the government and defeat the Islamic forces.

Uzbek nationalism has caused violent clashes with Tajiks in the Ferghana valley in recent years. The ability to speak Uzbek is now a condition of appointment to government posts, and those not able to speak it are being dismissed. This has severely disrupted the civil service and public sector, mostly staffed by ethnic Russians. President Karimov is attempting to form close ties with Turkey in the cultural and business spheres, and in 1994 began to strengthen economic ties with Russia again.

HEAD OF STATE
*President*, Islam Karimov, *elected* 29 December 1991

CABINET *as at August 1994*
*Chairman of the Cabinet*, The President
*Prime Minister*, Abdulkhashim Mutalov
*First Deputy Prime Minister, Agro-industrial Complex*, Ismail Djurabekov
*Deputy PMs*, Erkin Samandarov (*Social Development, Science and Culture*); Kayim Khakkulov (*Industry, Fuel and and Power*); Bakhtiyar Khamidov (*Finance and Economy*); Utkir Sultanov (*Foreign Economic Relations*); Viktor Chzhen (*Local Industry*); Kazim Tulyaganov; Anatoli Voznenko; Mukhmmadjon Karabayev; Rakhim Radjabov; Tulkin Mirijakubov
*Interior*, Zokirjon Almatov
*Foreign Affairs*, Sadik Safaev
*Defence*, Maj.-Gen. Rustam Akhmedov
*Justice*, Mukhamad-Bobur Malikov
*Health*, Shavkat Karimov
*Education*, Djura Yuldashev
*Industry and Construction*, Inom Iskanderov
*Agriculture*, Norbek Kayumov
*Communications*, Kamilzhan Rakhimov
*Labour*, Alikhan Atajanov
*Roads*, Rustam Yunusov
*Higher Education*, Jura Abdullayev
*Public Utilities*, Viktor Mikhailov
*Culture*, Naim Gaibov
*Land Improvement*, Rim Giniyatullin
*Social Security*, Sanobar Khodjayeva
*Power Engineering*, Marat Tashpulatov
*Construction*, Kudratilla Makhamadaliyev
*Bread*, Rakhmatull Akhmedov

BRITISH EMBASSY
13 Ulitsa Akakademik Nurmakhamedov Street, District Yakkasaraiskiy, Raion, Tashkent 700100
Tel: Tashkent 533685
*Ambassador Extraordinary and Plenipotentiary*, His Excellency Alexander Paul Bergne, OBE, apptd 1993

## ECONOMY

Uzbekistan is attempting to integrate its economy with that of Kazakhstan, with which it signed an economic agreement in January 1994 to allow the free circulation of goods, services and capital and the co-ordination of credit and finance policies, budgets, taxation and customs duties. Uzbekistan is also a member of the CIS economic union and in March 1994 signed an economic treaty with Russia to provide for mutually convertible currencies and enhance private business links.

Uzbekistan's economy is based on intensive agricultural production, and especially cotton production, made possible by extensive irrigation schemes. In addition there are some agricultural and textile machinery plants and several chemical combines. Large and previously underdeveloped mineral resources have begun to be exploited; these include gold, natural gas, oil, copper, lead, zinc and coal. A sizeable oilfield was discovered in the Ferghana Valley in 1992. The Muruntao mine is the largest open-cast gold mine in the world, producing 75 million tonnes per year. Foreign direct investment of US$2,000 million has been pledged in the fields of mining, exploration and vehicle assembly plants.

| *Trade with UK* | 1993 |
| --- | --- |
| Imports from UK | £8,363,000 |
| Exports to UK | 282,000 |

## VANUATU
*Ripablik Blong Vanuatu*

Vanuatu is situated in the South Pacific Ocean, between 13° and 21° S. and 166° and 170° E. It includes 13 large and some 70 small islands, of coral and volcanic origin, including the Banks and Torres Islands in the north, and has a total land area of 4,706 sq. miles (12,190 sq. km). The principal islands are Vanua Lava, Espiritu Santo, Maewo, Pentecost, Ambae, Malekula, Ambrym, Epi, Efate, Erromango, Tanna and Aneityum. Most islands are mountainous and there are active volcanoes on several. The climate is oceanic tropical, moderated by the south-east trade winds which blow between May and October. At other times winds are variable and cyclones may occur.

POPULATION – The population (1989 census) is 142,900. The 1991 UN estimate is 163,000. About 95 per cent are Melanesian, the rest being mostly Micronesian, Polynesian and European. The national language is Bislama, but English and French are also official languages.

SEAT OF ADMINISTRATION – ΨPort Vila, Efate, population (1989) 19,400. The only other town is Luganville (population, 1989, 6,900), on Espiritu Santo.
CURRENCY – Vatu of 100 centimes.
FLAG – Red over green with a black triangle in the hoist, the three parts being divided by fimbriations of black and yellow, and in the centre of the black triangle a boar's tusk overlaid by two crossed fern leaves.
NATIONAL ANTHEM – Nasonal sing sing blong Vanuatu.
NATIONAL DAY – 30 July (Independence Day).

## GOVERNMENT

Vanuatu, the former Anglo-French Condominium of the New Hebrides, became an independent republic within the Commonwealth on 30 July 1980. Parliament consists of 46 members elected for a term of four years. A Council of Chiefs advises on matters of custom. Executive power is held by the Prime Minister (elected from and by parliament) and a Council of Ministers who are responsible to parliament. The

President is elected for a five-year term by the presidents of the 11 regional councils and the members of parliament.

HEAD OF STATE

*President*, His Excellency Jean-Marie Leye, *elected* 2 March 1994

COUNCIL OF MINISTERS *as at August 1994*

*Prime Minister and Minister of Foreign Affairs, Public Service, Planning and Statistics, Police, Media and Language Services*, Hon. Maxime Carlot Korman
*Deputy Prime Minister and Minister for Justice, Culture and Women's Affairs*, Hon. Sethy John Regenvanu
*Home Affairs*, Hon. Charlie Nako
*Finance, Commerce and Industry*, Hon. Willie Jimmy
*Economic Affairs and Tourism*, Hon. Serge Vohor
*Transport, Public Works, Ports and Marine and Urban Water Supply*, Hon. Amos Bangabiti
*Natural Resources*, Hon. Paul Telukluk
*Education*, Hon. Romain Batick
*Health and Rural Water Supply*, Hon. Hilda Lini
*Agriculture, Livestock, Forestry and Fisheries*, Hon. Onneyn Tahi
*Postal Services, Telecommunications and Meteorology*, Dr Edward Tambisari

*Chief Justice*, Charles Vaudin D'Imecourt
*Attorney-General (acting)*, Julian Marc Ala

HIGH COMMISSIONER TO GREAT BRITAIN, vacant, resident at Port Vila, Vanuatu

BRITISH HIGH COMMISSION
PO Box 567, Port Vila
Tel: Vila 23100

*High Commissioner*, His Excellency Thomas Duggin, apptd 1992

ECONOMY

Most of the population is employed on plantations or in subsistence agriculture. Subsistence crops include yams, taro, manioc, sweet potato and breadfruit; principal cash crops are copra, cocoa and coffee. Large numbers of cattle are kept on the plantations and beef is the second largest export. Principal exports are copra, meat (frozen, tinned and chilled), timber and cocoa.
Tourism is an important revenue earner, and the absence of direct taxation has led to growth in the finance and associated industries.

| Trade with UK | 1992 | 1993 |
|---|---|---|
| Imports from UK | £569,000 | £220,000 |
| Exports to UK | 448,000 | 1,484,000 |

VATICAN CITY STATE
*Stato della Città del Vaticano*

The office of the ecclesiastical head of the Roman Catholic Church (Holy See) is vested in the Pope, the Sovereign Pontiff. For many centuries the Sovereign Pontiff exercised temporal power but by 1870 the Papal States had become part of unified Italy. The temporal power of the Pope was in suspense until the treaty of 1929 which recognized the full and independent sovereignty of the Holy See in the City of the Vatican. The area of the Vatican City is 108 acres and its population in 1989 was about 1,000.

CURRENCY – Italian currency is legal tender.

FLAG – Square flag; equal vertical bands of yellow (next staff), and white; crossed keys and triple crown device on white band.

NATIONAL DAY – 22 October (Inauguration of present Pontiff).

*Sovereign Pontiff*, His Holiness Pope John Paul II (Karol Wojtyla), *born* at Wadowice (Krakow, Poland), 18 May 1920, *elected* Pope in succession to Pope John Paul I, 16 October 1978
*Secretary of State*, Cardinal Angelo Sodano, *appointed* December 1990

APOSTOLIC NUNCIATURE
54 Parkside, London SW19 5NE
Tel 0181–946 1410

*Apostolic Nuncio*, His Excellency Archbishop Luigi Barbarito, apptd 1986

BRITISH EMBASSY TO THE HOLY SEE
91 Via Condotti, I–00187 Rome
Tel: Rome 678 9462

*Ambassador Extraordinary and Plenipotentiary*, His Excellency Andrew Eustace Palmer, CMG, CVO, apptd 1991

| Trade with UK | 1992 | 1993 |
|---|---|---|
| Imports from UK | £966,000 | £869,000 |
| Exports to UK | 2,000 | 53,000 |

VENEZUELA
*Republica de Venezuela*

Venezuela is a South American republic, situated approximately between 0° 45′ S. and 12° 12′ N. latitude and 59° 45′ and 73° 09′ W. longitude. It has a total area of 352,144 sq. miles (912,050 sq. km) and is bounded on the north by the Caribbean Sea, west by Colombia, east by Guyana, and south by Brazil. Included in the area of the republic are 72 islands off the coast, with a total area of about 14,650 sq. miles, the largest being Margarita (area, about 400 sq. miles), which is politically associated with Tortuga, Cubagua and Coche to form the state of Nueva Esparta. The mountains are the Eastern Andes and Maritime Andes, running south-west to north-east. The main range is known as the Sierra Nevada de Merida, and contains Pico Bolivar (16,411 ft) and Picacho de la Sierra (15,420 ft). The principal river is the Orinoco, with innumerable affluents, the main river exceeding 1,600 miles in length. The upper waters of the Orinoco are united with those of the Rio Negro (a Brazilian tributary of the Amazon) by a natural river or canal, known as the Casiquiare. The coastal regions contain many lagoons and lakes, of which Maracaibo (area 8,296 square miles) is the largest lake in South America. The climate is tropical, except where modified by altitude or tempered by sea breezes.

POPULATION – The population (UN estimate 1991) is 20,226,000, of which 67 per cent are Mestizo, 21 per cent white, 10 per cent black and 2 per cent Indian. Spanish is the language of the country. About 96 per cent of the population is Roman Catholic.

CAPITAL – Caracas, population 2,784,000. Other principal towns are Ψ Maracaibo (1,364,000), Barquisimeto (602,000), Valencia (903,000), Maracay (354,000), San Cristobal (230,000), Cumaná (212,000) and Ciudad Guayana (536,506).

CURRENCY – Bolivar (BS) of 100 céntimos.

FLAG – Three horizontal stripes of yellow, blue, red with an arc of seven white stars on the blue stripe.

NATIONAL ANTHEM – Gloria Al Bravo Pueblo (Glory to the brave people).
NATIONAL DAY – 5 July.

## GOVERNMENT

Venezuela gained independence from Spain in 1830. Under the 1961 constitution, executive power is held by the President, who also appoints the Council of Ministers. Legislative power is exercised by a bicameral National Congress, comprising a 201-member Chamber of Deputies and a Senate of 49 elected members plus the former presidents of constitutional governments as life members. The President and National Congress are directly elected for concurrent five-year terms.

Carlos Andrés Pérez of the (Social Democratic) Democratic Action (AD) party won the December 1988 presidential election and the AD emerged as the largest party in both houses in the Congressional elections. President Pérez's government successfully introduced a series of free market economic reforms which led to impressive economic growth but increasing social problems. Two military coup attempts in 1992 were defeated but President Pérez resigned in May 1993 after the Supreme Court indicted him on corruption charges. Former President Rafael Caldera won the ensuing presidential election in December 1993 but his National Convergence coalition of 17 parties failed to gain majorities in either house of Congress, where the traditional AD and COPEI (Social Christian) parties remained strong. President Caldera took office with his new government in February 1994 and announced an economic austerity programme and the revival of privatization.

Venezuela is divided into 20 states, two federal territories and a federal district.

### HEAD OF STATE
*President*, Rafael Caldera Rodríguez, *elected* 5 December 1993, *sworn in* 2 February 1994

### COUNCIL OF MINISTERS *as at August 1994*
*Interior*, Ramón Escobar Salom
*Foreign Affairs*, Miguel Angel Burelli
*Finance*, Julio Sosa Rodríguez
*Defence*, Rafael Angel Montero
*Transport and Communications*, Ciro Zaa
*Urban Development*, Francisco Gonzalez
*Energy and Mines*, Erwin José Arrieta
*Environment and Natural Resources*, Roberto Pérez Lecuna.
*Health and Social Security*, Carlos Walter
*Agriculture and Livestock*, Ciro Añez Fonseca
*Education*, Antonio Luis Cardenas
*The Family*, Mercedes Pulido
*Justice*, Ruben Creixems
*Presidential Secretariat*, Andres Caldera
*Decentralization*, José Guillermo Andueza
*Culture*, Oscar Sambrano
*Co-ordination and Planning*, Luis Carlos Palacios
*Minister, Guyana Corporation of Venezuela*, Alfredo Gruber
*Development and Foreign Trade*, Alberto Poleto
*Federal District Governor*, Asdrubal Aguiar
*Labour and Employment*, Juan Garrido
*National Economic Reform*, Asdrubal Baptista
*Information*, Guillermo Alváraz
*Higher Education, Science and Technology*, Guido Arnal Arroyo
*Investment Fund*, Carlos Bernardez
*Youth*, Pilarica Iribarren
*State Reform*, Ricardo Combellas

VENEZUELAN EMBASSY
1 Cromwell Road, London SW7 2HW
Tel 0171-584 4206/7
*Ambassador Extraordinary and Plenipotentiary*, His Excellency Dr Ignacio Arcaya, apptd 1992
*Defence Attaché*, Capt. Juan B. Leoni
*Cultural Attaché*, A. Montes

BRITISH EMBASSY
Apartado 1246, Caracas 1010-A
Tel: Caracas 9934111
*Ambassador Extraordinary and Plenipotentiary*, His Excellency John G. Flynn, CMG, apptd 1993
*Counsellor*, M. Hickson, LVO (*Deputy Head of Mission*)
*Consul*, P. P. Haggar
*First Secretary (Commercial)*, C. Dresser

There are British Consular Offices at *Caracas, Maracaibo, Margarita* and *Mérida*.

BRITISH COUNCIL REPRESENTATIVE, Paul de Quincey, Apartado 65131, Caracas 1065

BRITISH-VENEZUELAN CHAMBER OF COMMERCE, Apartado 5713, Caracas 1010. Torre Británica, Piso 10, Letra E, Av. José Félix Sosa, Altamira Sur, Caracas 1060

## DEFENCE

The total active armed forces strength is 75,000 personnel, including 18,000 conscripts, who serve for two years (Army and Air Force) or 30 months (Navy). Conscription is selective. The Army has 34,000 personnel, with 70 main battle tanks, 161 light tanks, 290 armoured personnel carriers, 127 artillery pieces and six attack helicopters. The Navy has 11,000 personnel, including 6,000 marines, with two submarines, six frigates, six patrol and coastal vessels, four combat aircraft and eight armed helicopters. The Air Force is 7,000 strong, with 141 combat aircraft and 27 armed helicopters. The National Guard has 23,000 internal security personnel, with 229 armoured infantry fighting vehicles and armoured personnel carriers, mortar, aircraft, helicopters and inshore patrol craft.

## EDUCATION

Education is free and compulsory between the ages of five and 14. There are ten universities in Venezuela, five in Caracas and the others in Maracaibo, Mérida, Valencia, Cumaná and Barquisimeto.

## ECONOMY

The government of President Caldera, despite introducing an austerity budget, has promised to moderate the free market reforms which provided impressive GDP growth in 1990-2 but saw recession in 1993-4. The oil industry accounted for 21.3 per cent of GNP in 1992, manufacturing 16.8 per cent, commerce 11.7 per cent, government 8.7 per cent and construction 7.4 per cent. In 1993 inflation was 45.9 per cent, unemployment 8 per cent and the budget deficit US$3,500 million.

Products of the tropical forest region include orchids, wild rubber, timber, mangrove bark, balata gum and tonka beans. Agricultural products include corn, bananas, cocoa beans, coffee, cotton, rice, maize, sugar, sesame, groundnuts, potatoes, tomatoes, other vegetables, sisal and tobacco. There is an extensive beef and dairy farming industry. Despite substantial improvements in agriculture, Venezuela is heavily reliant upon food imports, which constitute about 60 per cent of total consumption.

The principal industry is that of petroleum, which in 1988 contributed 81 per cent of Venezuela's foreign exchange income and 52 per cent of government revenues. Daily production in the oilfields (nationalized 1976) has steadily declined since 1973 in line with Venezuela's conservation policies. There are eight refineries. The Orinoco heavy oil belt is being developed; estimates put recoverable resources at 70,000 million barrels in the Orinoco region.

Aluminium is the second highest source of foreign exchange after petroleum. The Venezuelan state holds the majority stake in both the principal producing companies, Venalum and Alcasa, and is moving towards a consolidation of the industry. Rich iron ore deposits in eastern Venezuela have been developed. The government-owned steel mill at Matanzas uses local iron ore and obtains its electric power from hydro-electric installations on the Caroni River. A mill at Ciudad Guayana produces centrifugally-cast iron pipe. Other industry includes a wide variety of manufacturing and component assembly, principally petrochemicals, gold, diamonds, clothing and foodstuffs.

## TRADE

Apart from oil the main exports are bauxite, iron ore, agricultural products and basic manufactures. The main imports are machinery and transport equipment, chemicals and foodstuffs. Some 50 per cent of trade is conducted with the USA.

|                | 1992        | 1993        |
|----------------|-------------|-------------|
| Total imports  | US$11,240m  | US$11,013m  |
| Total exports  | 14,000m     | 14,226m     |
| *Trade with UK* | 1992       | 1993        |
| Imports from UK | £188,895,000 | £226,769,000 |
| Exports to UK  | 138,425,000 | 125,492,000 |

## COMMUNICATIONS

There are about 93,471 km of roads, 29,954 km of them paved. The state has now acquired all but a very few of the railway lines, whose total length is only some 363 km. Road and river communications have made railways of negligible importance in Venezuela except for carrying iron ore in the south-east, though the government is expanding the network.

The Orinoco is navigable for ocean-going ships (up to 40 ft draught) for 150 miles upstream, by large steamers for 700 miles, and by smaller vessels some 900 miles upstream. There are seven Venezuelan airlines which between them have a comprehensive network of internal and international flights. There are ten television stations, one of which is government controlled.

---

# VIETNAM
*Công Hòa Xã Hôi Chu Nghĩa Viêt Nam*

Vietnam has an area of 127,242 sq. miles (329,556 sq. km), and an estimated population (1993) of 71,267,000. It is bordered on the north by China and the west by Laos and Cambodia.

CAPITAL – Hanoi, population (1993) 2,150,000. Other cities are Ho Chi Minh City (3,169,000) and Hai Phong (456,000).

CURRENCY – Dông of 10 hao or 100 xu.

FLAG – Red, with yellow five-point star in centre.

NATIONAL ANTHEM – Tien Quan Ca (The troops are advancing).

NATIONAL DAY – 2 September.

## GOVERNMENT

Following the end of the war in Vietnam in 1975, North and South Vietnam were reunified in 1976 under the name of the Socialist Republic of Vietnam. The national flag, anthem and capital of North Vietnam were adopted, and Saigon was renamed Ho Chi Minh City. Effective power lies with the Vietnamese Communist Party (VCP), its highest executive body being the Central Committee, elected by a Party Congress on a national basis. The Politburo and the Secretariat of the Central Committee exercise the real power.

A new constitution was adopted in June 1992 which reaffirmed Communist Party rule but also formalized free market economic reforms. The constitution increased the powers of the President and replaced the Council of Ministers by a Prime Minister and Cabinet. A new National Assembly of 365 members was elected in August 1992 and convened in September when it elected Le Duc Anh as President and, in October, approved the composition of the new government headed by Vo Van Kiet.

HEAD OF STATE
*President,* Le Duc Anh, *elected by National Assembly,* 23 September 1992
*Vice President,* Nguyen Thi Binh

CABINET *as at August 1994*
*Prime Minister,* Vo Van Kiet
*First Deputy PM,* Phan Van Khai
*Deputy PM,* Nguyen Kanh; Tran Duc Luong
*National Defence,* Doan Khue
*Foreign Affairs,* Nguyen Manh Cam
*Interior,* Bui Thien Ngo
*Chairman, Office of the Government,* Le Xuah Trinh
*Chairman, State Planning Commission,* Do Quoc Sam
*Chairman, State Inspectorate,* Nguyen Ky Cam
*Chairman, Ethnic Minorities and Mountain Region Commission,* Hoang Duc Nghi
*Chairman, State Commission for Co-operation and Investment,* Dau Ngoc Xuan
*Chairman, Government Organization and Personnel Commission,* Phan Ngoc Tuong
*Chairman, National Population Committee,* Mai Ky
*Finance,* Ho Te
*Governor, State Bank,* Cao Sy Kiem
*Commerce and Tourism,* Le Van Triet
*Labour, War Invalids and Social Affairs,* Tran Dinh Hoan
*Construction,* Ngo Xuan Loc
*Communications and Transport,* Bui Danh Luu
*Heavy Industry,* Tran Lum
*Energy,* Thai Phung Ne
*Light Industry,* Dang Vu Chu
*Agriculture,* Nguyen Cong Tan
*Forestry,* Nguyen Quang Ha
*Water Conservancy,* Nguyen Canh Dinh
*Marine Products,* Nguyen Tan Trinh
*Culture and Information,* Tran Hoan
*Public Health,* Nguyen Trong Nhan
*Education and Training,* Tran Hong Quan
*Justice,* Nguyen Dinh Loc
*Population and Family Planning,* Mai Ky
*Children,* Tran Thi Thanh Thanh
*Ministers without Portfolio,* Phan Van Tiem; Ha Quang Du

VIETNAMESE COMMUNIST PARTY
*Politburo of the Central Committee,* Do Muoi (*General Secretary*); Le Duc Anh; Vo Van Kiet; Dao Duy Tung; Doan Khue; Vu Oanh; Le Phuoc Tho; Pham Van Khai; Bui Thien Ngo; Nong Duc Manh; Pham The Duyet; Nguyen Duc Binh; Vo Tran Chi; Nguyen Manh Cam; Le

Kha Phieu; Do Quang Thang; Nguyen Ha Phan (*full members*)

EMBASSY OF THE SOCIALIST REPUBLIC OF VIETNAM
12–14 Victoria Road, London W8 5RD
Tel 0171–937 1912/8564

*Ambassador Extraordinary and Plenipotentiary*, His Excellency Huynh Ngoc An, apptd 1994

BRITISH EMBASSY
16 Pho Ly Thuong Kiet, Hanoi
Tel: Hanoi 25 2349

*Ambassador Extraordinary and Plenipotentiary*, His Excellency Peter Williams, CMG, apptd 1990
There is also a Consulate-General in Ho Chi Minh City.

BRITISH COUNCIL REPRESENTATIVE, Muriel Kirton (*Cultural Attaché*)

## DEFENCE

Total active armed forces number 857,000 personnel, with conscripts serving between two and three years. Reserves number three to four million. The Army has 700,000 personnel, with 1,300 main battle tanks, 600 light tanks, 1,500 armoured infantry fighting vehicles and armoured personnel carriers and 2,940 artillery pieces. The Navy is 42,000 strong, including 30,000 naval infantry, and deploys seven frigates and 55 patrol and coastal vessels. Air Force strength is 15,000, with 240 combat aircraft and 20 armed helicopters. The Air Defence Force has 100,000 personnel, with surface-to-air missiles.

## ECONOMY

Vietnam experienced considerable economic difficulties following the imposition of socialist reforms in the south after 1975. These were exacerbated by significant reductions in western aid as a result of Vietnam's invasion and occupation of Cambodia, border hostilities with China, and the allocation of resources to military expenditure. The economy has also been adversely affected by the sharp decrease in aid from the former Soviet Union. However, economic reforms, known as 'Doi Moi' liberalization, were instituted after the Sixth Party Congress (1986) and have had significant success. Inflation has been brought down to 4 per cent a year in 1994; the exchange rate has been rationalized, subsidies removed, much greater private economic activity allowed and average economic growth of 7 per cent a year in 1991–3 attained. The state's share of control has fallen to 60 per cent of industry, 40 per cent of services and 2 per cent of agriculture, which is now mainly run by family farms. This has led to a significant improvement in agricultural production, with Vietnam becoming a major rice exporter.

Foreign investment has been actively encouraged, with US$5,300 million invested in 1988–93. This level is growing since the USA dropped its opposition to IMF and World Bank loans and aid to Vietnam in July 1993 and ended its trade embargo in February 1994. International aid donors, the IMF and the World Bank in November 1993 approved a loan and grant package of US$1,860 million to support economic reform. A bankruptcy law has been passed, which has led to increasing unemployment and fears for social stability. Oil production (mainly offshore) has increased to 110,000 barrels per day and large natural gas reserves have been found offshore, though these are also claimed by China.

| Trade with UK | 1992 | 1993 |
|---|---|---|
| Imports from UK | £21,373,000 | £16,950,000 |
| Exports to UK | 11,921,000 | 22,104,000 |

## WESTERN SAMOA
*Malotuto'atasi o Samoa i Sisifo*

Western Samoa lies in the south Pacific Ocean between 13° and 15° S. latitude and 171° and 173° W. longitude. It consists of the islands of Savai'i (662 sq. miles), Upolu, Apolima, Manono, Fanuatapu, Namua, Nuutele, Nuulua and Nuusafee, and has an area of 435 sq. miles (1,714 sq. km). All the islands are mountainous. Upolu, the most fertile, contains the harbours of Apia and Saluafata, and Savai'i the harbours of Asau and Salelologa.

POPULATION – The population (1989 census) was 162,000, the largest numbers being on Upolu (114,980) and Savai'i (43,150); a 1990 UN estimate put the figure at 164,000. The Samoans are a Polynesian people, though the population also includes other Pacific Islanders, Euronesians, Chinese and Europeans. The main languages are Samoan and English. The islanders are Christians of different denominations.

CAPITAL – ΨApia, on Upolu (population, 1989 census, 36,000). Robert Louis Stevenson died and was buried at Apia in 1894.

CURRENCY – Tala (WS$) of 100 sene.

FLAG – Red with a blue canton bearing five white stars of the Southern Cross.

NATIONAL ANTHEM – The Banner of Freedom.

NATIONAL DAY – 1 June (Independence Day).

## GOVERNMENT

Formerly administered by New Zealand (latterly with internal self-government), Western Samoa became fully-independent on 1 January 1962. The state was treated as a member country of the Commonwealth until its formal admission on 28 August 1970.

The 1962 constitution provides for a head of state to be elected by the 49-member legislative assembly, the *Fono*, for a five-year term. Initially two of the four Paramount chiefs jointly held the office of head of state for life. When one of the chiefs died in April 1963, Malietoa Tanumafili II became head of state for life. The head of state's functions are analogous to those of a constitutional monarch. Executive government is carried out by a Cabinet of Ministers.

Suffrage was made universal following a referendum held in 1990. After elections held on 7 March 1991, the seats in the *Fono* were: Human Rights Protection Party 30; Samoan National Development Party 16; Independents 3.

*Head of State*, HH Malietoa Tanumafili II, GCMG, CBE, *since 15 April 1963*
*Deputy Head of State*, Hon. Mataafa Faasuamaleaui Puela

CABINET *as at August 1994*
*Prime Minister, Minister for Foreign Affairs*, Hon. Tofilau Eti Alesana
*Finance*, Hon. Tuilaepa Sailele
*Justice*, Hon. Fuimanono Lotomau
*Education*, Hon. Fiame Naomi
*Health*, Hon. Sala Vaimili Uili II
*Post and Telecommunications*, Hon. Toi Aukuso
*Agriculture*, Hon. Misa Telefoni
*Public Works*, Hon. Leafa Vitale
*Lands and Environment*, Hon. Faasooatuloa Pati
*Civil Aviation*, Hon. Jack Netzler
*International Affairs*, Hon. Polataïvao Fosi
*Sports and Culture*, Hon. Pule Lameko

WESTERN SAMOA HIGH COMMISSION
Avenue Franklin D. Roosevelt 123, 1050 Brussels
Tel: Brussels 6608454

*High Commissioner*, His Excellency Afamasaga Toleafoa,
apptd 1990

BRITISH HIGH COMMISSIONER, His Excellency David
Moss, CMG, resident at Wellington, New Zealand
There is an Honorary Consulate (PO Box 2029) in Apia.

## ECONOMY

Agriculture is the basis of the economy, the principal cash
crops (and exports) being coconuts (copra), cocoa and
bananas. Other agricultural exports include coffee, timber,
tropical fruits and seeds. Efforts are being made to develop
fishing on a commercial scale. Manufacturing is very small
in scope and concerned largely with processing agricultural
products, but is being encouraged by the government.
Tourism is increasing rapidly.

| Trade with UK | 1992 | 1993 |
|---|---|---|
| Imports from UK | £471,000 | £1,297,000 |
| Exports to UK | 12,000 | 23,000 |

## REPUBLIC OF YEMEN
*Al-Jamhuriya Al-Yamaniya*

Yemen lies in the extreme south-west of the Arabian
peninsula. Bounded on the west by the Red Sea, on the north
by Saudi Arabia, on the east by Oman and on the south by
the Gulf of Aden, Yemen has an estimated area of 203,850 sq.
miles (527,969 sq. km) and a population (1991 UN estimate)
of 12,302,000. Included in the state are the offshore islands
of Perim and Kamaran in the Red Sea, and Socotra in the
Gulf of Aden. The highlands and central plateau, and
the highest portions of the maritime range in the south,
form the most fertile part of Arabia, with abundant but
irregular rainfall. The north is largely composed of mountains
and desert, and rainfall is generally scarce.

CAPITAL – Sana'a, population (1986) 427,150. Ψ Aden
  (270,000) is the other main city and the former capital of
  South Yemen.
CURRENCY – Yemeni dinar (YD) of 1,000 fils and Riyals of
  100 fils are both legal tender (1 Dinar = 26 Riyals). The
  Dinar is being phased out.
FLAG – Horizontal bands of red, white and black.
NATIONAL DAY – 22 May.

## GOVERNMENT

Turkish occupation of North Yemen (1872–1918) was
followed by the rule of the Hamid al-Din dynasty until a
revolution in 1962 overthrew the monarchy and the Yemen
Arab Republic was declared. The People's Republic of South
Yemen was set up in 1967 when the British government
ceded power to the National Liberation Front, bringing to
an end 129 years of British rule in Aden and some years of
protectorate status in the hinterland. Negotiations towards
merging the two states began in 1979 and unification was
proclaimed on 22 May 1990. The constitution was approved
by referendum in May 1991. A five-member Presidential
Council comprising former senior government figures of the
separate states was formed for the period of transition.
  A general election for the House of Representatives took
place on 27 April 1993. Of the total of 301 seats, 122 were
won by the General People's Congress (GPC, former ruling

party in the North), 62 by the Islamic Islah (Alliance for
reform) party and 56 by the Yemini Socialist Party (YSP,
former ruling party in the South). The three parties formed
a coalition government and the House of Representatives
asked the Presidential Council to remain in office.
  Continued political tensions and a power struggle between
the former Northern and Southern Yemen elites in mid-
1993, coupled with arguments over the distribution of oil
revenues and the alleged assassination of Southern ministers
led YSP leaders to withdraw to Aden in August 1993. A
reconciliation pact signed in February 1994 by President
Saleh and Vice-President al-Beedh was never implemented
and, after sporadic clashes, a civil war broke out on 5 May
1994 between the unmerged Northern and Southern forces.
The Southern leadership declared secession on 20 May but
fled when Aden was captured by victorious Northern forces
on 7 July, bringing the civil war to an end. The post-war
government is likely to exclude all but a token YSP presence.

*President*, Gen. Ali Abdullah Saleh, *since* 22 May 1990
*Vice President*, vacant
*Members of Presidential Council*, Abdul Majid Zindani;
  Abdel Aziz Abdel Ghani

COUNCIL OF MINISTERS *as at August 1994*

*Prime Minister*, Faraj bin Ghanem
*First Deputy PM*, Dr Hassan Mohammed Makki
*Deputy PMs*, Brig.-Gen. Mujahid Yahya Abu Shawarib;
  Abdul-Wahhab al-Anisi; Abdul Qadir Ba Jammal
*Construction*, Abdullah Hussayn al-Kurshumi
*Foreign Affairs*, Muhammad Salim Basindwah
*Industry*, Dr Mohammed Said al-Attar
*Oil and Mineral Resources*, Faisal Othman Shamlan
*Supply and Trade*, Dr Abdul-Rahman Abdul-Qadir Bafadl
*Local Administration*, Muhammad Hasan Dammaj
*Electricity and Water Resources*, vacant
*Civil Service and Administrative Reform*, Yahya Husain al-
  Arashi
*Planning and Development*, Dr Abdul-Karim al-Iryani
*Communications*, Ahmad Mohammed al-Anisi
*Legal Affairs*, Abdul-Salam Khalid
*Waqfs (Religious Affairs) and Guidance*, Ghalib Abdul-Kafi
  al-Qirshi
*Social Security and Labour*, Abdullah al-Battani
*Culture*, vacant
*Youth and Sports*, Dr Mohammed Ahmad al-Kabab
*Education*, Dr Abu Bakr al-Qirbi
*Justice*, Abdullah Ahmad Ghanim
*Information*, Hasan Ahmad al-Lawzi
*Transport*, vacant
*Fisheries*, Fadhl Muhsin Abdullah
*Housing and Urban Planning*, vacant
*Finance*, Alawi Salih al-Salami
*Public Health*, Dr Najib Ghanim
*Agriculture*, Sadiq Amin Abu Ras
*Interior*, Yahya Muhammad al-Mutawakkil
*Defence*, Brig.-Gen. Abdrubbo Mansur Hadi
*Speaker of the House of Representatives*, Shaikh Abdullah bin
  Husain al-Ahmar

EMBASSY OF THE REPUBLIC OF YEMEN
57 Cromwell Road, London SW7 2ED
Tel 0171–584 6607

*Ambassador Extraordinary and Plenipotentiary*, His
  Excellency Dr Shaya Mohsin Mohamed Zindani, apptd
  1991

BRITISH EMBASSY
PO Box 1287, Sana'a
Tel: Sana'a 1215630

Ambassador Extraordinary and Plenipotentiary, His
Excellency Robert Gordon, apptd 1993

BRITISH COUNCIL REPRESENTATIVE, A. Lewis, As-
Sabain Street No. 7 (PO Box 2157), Sana'a

## ECONOMY

The civil war has seriously damaged the country's economy,
already weakened since 1991 by the loss of US$2,000 million
in annual remittances from 800,000 Yemini workers in
Saudi Arabia, who were sent home because of Yemen's
support for Iraq in the Gulf War. However, the war had little
effect on oil production, which averages 180,000 barrels per
day (bpd) from the Marib field and 150,000 bpd from the
Masila field, on stream since August 1993. The refinery at
Aden was damaged in the war and is working at reduced
capacity. Despite the production of oil Yemen remains one
of the poorest states in the world.

Agriculture is the main occupation of the inhabitants. This
is largely of a subsistence nature, sorghum, sesame and
millets being the chief crops, with wheat and barley widely
grown at the higher elevations. Exports include cotton,
coffee, hides and skins.

| Trade with UK | 1992 | 1993 |
|---|---|---|
| Imports from UK | £78,409,000 | £85,484,000 |
| Exports to UK | 56,871,000 | 16,065,000 |

## YUGOSLAVIA
Federativna Republika Jugoslavije – Federal Republic of
Yugoslavia

The area of the two remaining Yugoslav republics (Serbia
and Montenegro) is 39,506 sq. miles (102,350 sq. km). The
rump Federal Yugoslav state, which is not internationally
recognized as the successor state to the former Socialist
Federal Republic of Yugoslavia, is bordered to the north by
Hungary, to the east by Romania and Bulgaria, to the south
by the Former Yugoslav Republic of Macedonia, to the
south-west by Albania and the Adriatic Sea, and to the west
by Bosnia-Hercegovina and Croatia. The climate is continental. Montenegro and southern Serbia are extremely mountainous, while the north is dominated by the low-lying plains
of the Danube. The major rivers are: the Danube, which
flows through the north of Serbia to Romania and Bulgaria;
the Sava which flows eastwards from Bosnia to join the
Danube at Belgrade; and the Morava which flows from the
extreme south to join the Danube in the north.

POPULATION – The last (federal) estimate of 1988 gave a
population of 10,410,000, of which 66 per cent are Serbs and
Montenegrins, 18 per cent Albanian, 8 per cent Muslim, 4
per cent Hungarian, with smaller numbers of Yugoslavs (no
ethnic group), Croats and Bulgarians. The majority religion
is Serbian Orthodox, with significant Muslim and small
Roman Catholic minorities.

The main language is Serbian (Serbo-Croat) (74 per cent),
with Albanian and Hungarian minorities. Serbo-Croat is a
South Slav language written in the Cyrillic script.

CAPITAL – (federal and Serbian) Belgrade, on the Danube
(population 1,455,000). Other major cities are (1981):
Novi Sad (257,685); Niš (230,711); Priština (210,040);
Kragujevac (164,823); Subotica (154,611); Podgorica
(132,290), the capital of Montenegro.
CURRENCY – Dinar of 100 paras.
FLAG – Three horizontal stripes of blue, white, red.

NATIONAL ANTHEM – Hej, Slaveni, Jošte Živi Reð Naših
Dedova (Oh! Slavs, our ancestors' words still live).
NATIONAL DAY – 29 November.

## GOVERNMENT

Serbia emerged from the rule of the Byzantine Empire in the
13th century to form a large and prosperous state in the
Balkans. Defeat by the Turks in 1389 led to almost 500 years
of Turkish rule. After gaining autonomy within the Ottoman
Empire in 1815, Serbia became fully independent in 1878
and a kingdom in 1881. Montenegro was part of the Serbian
state before it was conquered by the Turks in 1355; it became
independent in 1851. At the end of the First World War
Serbia and Montenegro joined with the former Austro-
Hungarian provinces of Slovenia, Croatia and Bosnia-
Hercegovina to form the 'Kingdom of Serbs, Croats and
Slovenes' which was proclaimed on 1 December 1918 under
the rule of the Serbian royal house. The state was renamed
Yugoslavia in 1929. In 1941–5 Yugoslavia was occupied by
Axis forces which were fought by Communist and royalist
Chetnik partisans supplied by Allied forces. In 1945 with the
defeat of Nazi Germany, Yugoslavia was reformed as a
Communist federal republic under the presidency of partisan
leader Josip Tito.

Increasing pressure from the non-Serbian nationalities for
more political power were met by Tito in the post-war period
by new constitutions in 1963 and 1974 which devolved power
to the republics (Slovenia, Croatia, Bosnia-Hercegovina,
Serbia, Montenegro, Macedonia). Tito died in 1980 and the
delicate political balance of a rotating federal presidency was
unable to contain the gradually growing nationalist movements after his death. The Catholic, western-looking, more
prosperous republics of Slovenia and Croatia began to break
away from the other predominantly Orthodox and Muslim
Balkan republics; Communism was widely rejected. Efforts
by the federal presidency and international mediators to end
inter-communal conflict and negotiate a new federal or
confederal structure for the country failed in 1991. On 25
June 1991 Slovenia and Croatia declared their independence
from Yugoslavia. Intervention by the Federal Yugoslav
Army (JNA) against local defence forces to prevent the
disintegration of the Yugoslav federation failed and within
two months the ethnically homogeneous Slovenia had
negotiated its independence.

The situation in Croatia differed because its ethnic Serb
minority comprised 12 per cent of the population. These
ethnic Serbs refused to accept Croatia's independence and
fighting began in July 1991 between Croat Defence Forces
and Serbian guerrillas backed by the JNA. By September

1991 this had escalated into war between Croatia and Serbia. In October the last vestiges of the power of the Federation ended when the federal presidency was usurped by Serbia and its ally Montenegro. The war in Croatia continued until January 1992 when, after constant attempts, the EC and the UN were able to bring about a ceasefire that held.

Bosnia-Hercegovina declared its independence from Yugoslavia on 15 October 1991, and this was affirmed in a referendum on 1 March 1992. Independence was supported by the ethnic Muslims and Croats but rejected by the ethnic Serbs, who formed 33 per cent of the population and wanted to form a Greater Serbia with the Serbian republic. Fighting between Muslims and Serbs broke out on 2 March 1992 and the JNA intervened against the poorly-armed Muslims. In May 1992, after intense international pressure, the JNA withdrew to Serbia and Montenegro.

On 27 April 1992 the two remaining republics of the former Socialist Federal Republic of Yugoslavia, Serbia and Montenegro, announced the formation of a new Yugoslav federation, which they invited Serbs in Croatia and Bosnia-Hercegovina to join. The new federation remains unrecognized internationally because of continued ethnic Serb aggression in Bosnia, and is seen as a Serbian attempt to inherit the rights of the former federation. Continued Serbian aid and supplies to the ethnic Serb forces in the Bosnian war has led to increasing international pressure and the imposition by the UN in May 1992 of a trade embargo, economic sanctions and a ban on air and sporting links. In April 1993 a total blockade was imposed.

In October 1993 the UN Security Council imposed the condition that ethnic-Serb held territories in Croatia must be integrated into Croatia before sanctions on the rump Yugoslav state would be lifted. In July 1994 after the Bosnian Serbs had rejected the International Contact Group's (ICG's) peace plan and map for Bosnia-Hercegovina, the ICG announced that new sanctions (including a ban on all Serbian officials and military travelling abroad; a directive to neighbouring states to erect physical barriers at their borders; permission for countries to sell frozen Yugoslav property; a ban on Danube river traffic stopping at Serbian ports; and a ban on all traffic crossing Yugoslav borders) would be implemented if the Bosnian Serbs did not agree to the plan. In an attempt to stave off these sanctions, President Milosevic has severed all political and economic ties to the Bosnian Serb leadership and closed the Yugoslav-Bosnian border to all trade except food and medicines.

The Federal Republic has a bicameral parliament with a 138-seat lower house, the Chamber of Citizens, and a 40-seat (20 Serbian, 20 Montenegrin) upper house, the Chamber of Republics. Executive power is vested in a Federal President and government but has effectively been usurped by the authoritarian Serbian Socialist (former Communist) Party leader and Serbian President Slobodan Milosevic. The last federal legislative elections were held in December 1992 and were universally considered flawed and unfair. The Serbian Socialist Party emerged as the largest party in the federal legislature and formed a coalition government with the extreme nationalist Serbian Radical Party. This government was replaced in March 1993 by a coalition of the Serbian Socialist Party and the Democratic Party of Socialists of Montenegro.

HEAD OF STATE

*Federal President*, Zoran Lilic, *elected by parliament* 25 June 1993

FEDERAL GOVERNMENT *as at August 1994*

*Prime Minister*, Radoje Kontic
*Deputy Prime Ministers*, Asim Telacevic; Jovan Zebic (*Finance*); Nikola Sainovic (*Economic Reform*); Vladislav Jovanovic (*Foreign Affairs*); Zeljko Simic

*Interior*, Djordje Blagojevic
*Defence*, Pavle Bulatovic
*Justice*, Zoran Stojanovic
*Economics*, Tomislav Simovic
*Foreign Economic Relations*, Milorad Unkovic
*Transport and Communications*, Blagoje Lucic
*Labour, Health and Social Policy*, Velibor Popovic
*Education and Culture*, Slavko Gordic
*Science and Technology*, Milan Dimitrijevic
*Information*, Slobodan Ignjatovic
*Environment*, Slobodanka Djordan
*Trade*, Miroslav Ivanisevic
*Agriculture*, Kiviljko Lovre
*Sport*, Zoran Bingulac
*Human and Minority Rights*, Margit Savovic
*Without Portfolio*, Tomislav Rajicevic

EMBASSY OF YUGOSLAVIA
5 Lexham Gardens, London W8 5JU
Tel 0171-370 6105

*Chargé d'Affairs*, R. Bogojevic
*Defence Attaché*, Cdr. M. Ladicorbic
*Consul-General*, R. Jengic
*Second Secretary*, L. Raspopovic (*Economic*)

BRITISH EMBASSY
General Ždanova 46, 11000 Belgrade
Tel: Belgrade 645055

*Chargé d'Affaires, Counsellor and Consul-General*, I. A. Roberts
*Counsellor*, M. J. Robinson
*Defence and Military Attaché*, Col. A. M. Moody
*First Secretary* (*Economic*), vacant

BRITISH COUNCIL REPRESENTATIVE, J. McGrath, Generala Ždanova 34-Mazanin (Post Fah 248), 11001 Belgrade

MONTENEGRO

Montenegro has an area of 5,331 sq. miles (13,812 sq. km) and a population of 615,000, of whom 62 per cent are Montenegrins, 14.5 per cent Muslims, 6.5 per cent Albanians and 3 per cent Serbs. The capital is Podgorica with a population (1981) of 132,290. The Democratic Party of Socialists (former Communists) won multiparty elections in December 1992 for the 85-seat republican assembly and formed a government.

*President*, Momir Bulatovic, *elected* 11 January 1993
*Prime Minister*, Milo Djukanović

SERBIA

Serbia has a total area of 34,175 sq. miles (88,538 sq. km) and a total population of 9.3 million, of whom 66 per cent are Serbs. The capital is Belgrade with a population (1981) of 1,455,000. It includes the provinces of Kosovo (population 1.6 million), of great historic importance to Serbs, and Vojvodina (population 2 million); the autonomy of both was ended in September 1990. Kosovo, with its capital at Priština, is predominantly Albanian (90 per cent). In defiance of the Serbian authorities, ethnic Albanians held parliamentary and presidential elections in May 1992, which were won respectively by the Democratic League of Kosovo and its leader Ibrahim Rugova. Tension between Albanians and Serbs remains very high. Vojvodina, with its capital at Novi Sad, has a large Hungarian minority (21 per cent).

The Socialist Party of Serbia (SPS) (formerly the Communists) emerged as the largest party in multiparty elections for the 250-seat National Assembly, held in December 1992 and formed a coalition government with the extreme nationalist Serbian Radical Party (SRS). The coalition broke down in

September 1993 when the SRS called for a parliamentary vote of no confidence in the government, forcing President Milosevic to dissolve parliament. In the ensuing parliamentary election on 19 December 1993 the SPS gained 123 seats; Depos 45 seats; SRS 39 seats; Democratic Party 29 seats; Democratic Party of Serbia 7 seats; Democratic Community of Hungarians in the Vojvodina 5 seats; Albanian coalition 2 seats. The SPS, three seats short of a majority, formed a minority government in March 1994, and has unsuccessfully sought the support of centrist opposition parties.

*President*, Slobodan Milosevic, *elected* 20 December 1992
*Prime Minister*, Mirko Marjanovic

## ECONOMY

Since 1991 the economy has been devastated by the wars in Croatia and Bosnia-Hercegovina, by the UN economic sanctions and trade embargo, and because of the lack of free-market reforms. Most factories have closed. Only the country's agricultural self-sufficiency has kept it alive. In 1993 hyperinflation became rampant because the government continued to print money to finance the wars and subsidize industries. By December 1993 inflation had reached 21,000 per cent a month, the tax system had collapsed, output was one-third of pre-war levels, industry was working at one-quarter of capacity and the dinar had been devalued ten times. In January 1994 a successful economic stabilization package was introduced with a new superdinar pegged at one-to-one parity with the Deutsche Mark. This reduced monthly inflation from 313 million per cent in January to 1 per cent in February. The package is based on the use of state and private individuals' gold and foreign currency reserves to maintain the value of the dinar, an increasingly leaky economic embargo which is allowing in significant amounts of goods and supplies, and an economy based on barter rather than money. Industrial production remains extremely low and unemployment high, and it is doubtful how long the package can be maintained.

| Trade with UK | 1992 | 1993 |
|---|---|---|
| Imports from UK | £123,061,000 | £3,652,000 |
| Exports to UK | 123,797,000 | 2,000 |

## ZAIRE
*République du Zaïre*

Situated between 12° and 31° E. longitude and 5° N. and 13° S. latitude, Zaire comprises an area of 905,567 sq. miles (2,345,409 sq. km). Apart from the coastal district in the west which is fairly dry, the rainfall averages between 60 and 80 inches. The average temperature is about 27°C, but in the south the winter temperature can fall nearly to freezing point. Extensive forest covers the central districts.

POPULATION – The population was 34,671,607 at the 1985 census. A 1991 UN estimate put it at 36,672,000. It is composed almost entirely of Bantu groups, divided into semi-autonomous tribes. Minorities include Sudanese, Nilotes, Pygmies and Hamites, as well as refugees from Angola.

Swahili, a Bantu dialect with an admixture of Arabic, is the nearest approach to a common language in the east and south, while Lingala is the language of a large area along the river and in the north, and Kikongo of the region between Kinshasa and the sea. French is the language of administration.

CAPITAL – Kinshasa (formerly Leopoldville), population (1985 census) 2,778,281. Principal towns, Lubumbashi (formerly Elisabethville) (403,623); Kisangani (formerly Stanleyville) (310,705); Likasi (146,394); Kananga (601,239); Ψ Matadi (143,598); and Mbandaka (134,495).

CURRENCY – Zaïre of 100 makuta.

FLAG – Dark brown hand and torch with red flame in yellow roundel on green background.

NATIONAL DAY – 24 November.

## GOVERNMENT

The state of the Congo, founded in 1885, became a Belgian colony in 1908 and was administered by Belgium until independence in 1960. Mobutu Sésé Seko, formerly commander-in-chief of the Congolese National Army, came to power in a coup in 1965 and was elected President in 1970. Legislative power was vested in a unicameral National Legislative Council, elected for a five-year term by compulsory direct and universal suffrage with candidates proposed by the sole legal political party, Mouvement Populaire de la Révolution (MPR).

Following mounting tension, political reforms were announced in April 1990 and President Mobutu called a National Conference to draft a new constitution in April 1991. The conference convened in August but the government refused to grant it sovereign status, causing the main opposition parties to form a 'Sacred Union' to bring down the transitional government. Mobutu accepted an opposition-dominated government under Prime Minister Etienne Tshisekedi in October 1991. His attempts to replace this with MPR-dominated governments failed and the National Conference confirmed the Tshisekedi government as the legitimate one in August 1992.

In 1992–4 President Mobutu and the opposition have been locked in a power struggle. In December 1992 the National Conference adopted a draft constitution and elected an interim legislature, the High Council of the Republic (HCR). Throughout 1993 the Tshisekedi government attempted to transfer the President's powers to the HCR, while President Mobutu unsuccessfully attempted to dismiss the HCR and Tshisekedi government, and then used the Army to intimidate them while a rival pro-Mobutu government was established. A constitutional limbo existed until January 1994 when President Mobutu dissolved the pro-Mobutu government and the HCR and endorsed the formation of a new High Council of the Republic–Parliament of Transition (HCR–PT) with a mandate of choosing a new Prime Minister. On 9 April 1994 President Mobutu promulgated a Transitional Constitutional Act endorsed by the HCR–PT which regulates a 15-month period of transition to democracy. During the 15-month period the HCR–PT will oversee the activities of a transitional government while a constitutional referendum and presidential and legislative elections are held. On 17 June President Mobutu appointed Kengo Wa Dondo as Prime Minister after he had been elected by the HCR–PT; Tshisekedi's candidacy was excluded, leading to opposition unrest.

There are 11 regions, each under a Governor and provincial administration: Bas-Zaire (provincial capital, Matadi); Bandundu (Bandundu); Equateur (Mbandaka); Haut-Zaire (Kisangani); Kinshasa (Kinshasa); Maniema (Kindu); Nord-Kivu (Goma); Sud-Kivu (Bukavu); Shaba (Katanga) (Lubumbashi); East Kasai (Mbuji-Mayi); West Kasai (Kananga).

SECESSION

Since 1992 ethnic Katangans have been forcing ethnic Kasai mineworkers and their families out of the southern region of Shaba (Katanga) in a wave of ethnic violence which is a repeat of the Katanga secessionist war in 1960. In December 1993 the Governor of Shaba declared total autonomy from the rest of Zaire and announced the reversion of the region's name to Katanga.

HEAD OF STATE

*President of the Republic and National Security*, Marshal Mobutu Sésé Séko, *assumed office* 25 November 1965; *elected* 5 November 1970; *re-elected* 1977, 28 July 1984, *remained in power when term ended* 1991

CABINET *as at August 1994*

*Prime Minister*, Leon Kengo Wa Dondo
*Deputy Prime Ministers*, Gustave Malumba Mbangula (*Interior*); Adm. Mavua Mudima (*National Defence*); Kamanda Wa Kamanda (*Justice and Institutional Reform*); Mozagba Ngbuka (*International Co-operation*)
*Foreign Affairs*, Lunda Bululu
*Press and Information*, Masegabio Nzanzu
*Planning*, Kiawama Kia Kiziki
*Finance*, Pay Pay Wa Syakassighe
*Budget*, Bahati Lukwebo
*Agriculture*, Landu Kavidi
*National Economy, Industry and Small and Medium-sized Enterprises*, Katanga Mukumadi
*Mines*, Mutombo Bakafwa
*Energy*, Kisanga Kabongelo
*Public Works, Territorial Administration and Housing*, Mwando Nsimba
*Transport and Communication*, Nyindu Kitenge
*Foreign Trade*, Jibi Ngoy
*Land Affairs*, Mangwanda Gifugu
*Education*, Sekimonyo Wa Magangu
*Social Affairs*, Soki Fuani Eyenga
*Labour and Social Welfare*, Omba Pene Djunga
*Civil Service*, Bolenge Mekesombo
*Posts and Telecommunications*, Pierre Lumbi
*Environment, Conservation and Tourism*, Kisimba Ngoy
*Sport and Leisure*, Bofassa Djema
*Culture and Arts*, Lukonzala Munyangwa
*Without Portfolio*, Assea Mindre

EMBASSY OF THE REPUBLIC OF ZAIRE
26 Chesham Place, London SW1X 8HH
Tel 0171-235 6137

*Ambassador Extraordinary and Plenipotentiary*, new appointment awaited

BRITISH EMBASSY
Avenue des Trois 'Z', Gombe, Kinshasa
Tel: Kinshasa 34775

*Chargé d'Affaires and Consul*, J. G. Lindsay

There are British Consulates at *Lubumbashi, Goma* and *Kisangani*.

ECONOMY

The cultivation of oil palms is widespread, palm oil being the most important agricultural cash product though it is no longer exported. Coffee, rubber, cocoa and timber are the most important agricultural exports. The production of cotton, pyrethrum and copal is increasing. The country is rich in minerals, particularly Shaba (Katanga) province. Copper is widely exploited, and industrial diamonds and cobalt are also produced. Oil deposits are exploited off the Zaïre estuary and reef-gold is mined in the north-east of the country.

There is a wide variety of small secondary industries, the main products being foodstuffs, beverages, tobacco, textiles, leather, wood products, cement and building materials, metallurgy, small river craft and bicycles. There are reserves

of hydro-electric power and the Inga dam on the river Zaïre supplies electricity to Matadi, Kinshasa and Shaba.

TRADE

The chief exports are copper, crude oil, coffee, diamonds, rubber, cobalt, gold, cassiterite, zinc and other metals.

| Trade with UK | 1992 | 1993 |
| --- | --- | --- |
| Imports from UK | £16,820,000 | £16,941,000 |
| Exports to UK | 3,022,000 | 7,138,000 |

COMMUNICATIONS

There are approximately 20,500 km of roads (earth-surfaced) of national importance, and 6,000 km of railways. The country has four international and 40 principal airports.

---

ZAMBIA
*Republic of Zambia*

---

Zambia lies on the plateau of Central Africa between 22° and 33° 33′ E. longitude and 8° 15′ and 18° S. latitude. It has an area of 290,586 sq. miles (752,614 sq. km) and a population (UN estimate, 1991) of 8,780,000. With the exception of the valleys of the Zambezi, the Luapula, the Kafue and the Luangwa rivers, and the Luano valley, elevations vary from 3,000 to 5,000 feet above sea level, but in the north-east the plateau rises to occasional altitudes of over 6,000 feet. Although Zambia lies within the tropics, and fairly centrally in the African land mass, its elevation relieves it from extremely high temperatures and humidity.

CAPITAL – Lusaka, population (1989 estimate) 1 million. Other centres are Livingstone, Kabwe, Chipata, Mazabuka, Mbala, Kasama, Solwezi, Mongu, Mansa, Ndola, Luanshya, Mufulira, Chingola, Chililabombwe, Kalulushi and Kitwe, the last six towns being the main centres on the copper belt.
CURRENCY – Kwacha (K) of 100 ngwee.
FLAG – Green with three small vertical stripes, red, black and orange (next fly); eagle device on green above stripes.
NATIONAL ANTHEM – Stand and Sing of Zambia, Proud and Free.
NATIONAL DAY – 24 October (Independence Day).

GOVERNMENT

Northern Rhodesia came under British rule in 1889. It achieved internal self-government when the Federation of Rhodesia and Nyasaland was dissolved in 1963 and became an independent republic within the Commonwealth on 24 October 1964 under the name of Zambia.

The country was a one-party state (the United National Independence Party) from 1973 until 1990, when pressure from opposition groups led to multiparty legislative and presidential elections in October 1991. The Movement for Multiparty Democracy (MMD) won 125 of the 150 seats in parliament, and the MMD candidate Frederick Chiluba defeated Kaunda, who had ruled since independence, in the presidential election. The MMD government has begun the transformation of the state-controlled economy into a free market system with the sale and privatization of large sectors of the economy. Aid and investment have poured into the country, foreign exchange controls have been removed, the Kwacha floated and prices freed. A state of emergency was in force between March and May 1993 after the discovery of a coup plot by UNIP. Continued allegations of corruption by government ministers led first to the resignation of 15 MMD MPs from the party and then ministerial resignations, under pressure from foreign aid donors in 1993-4.

*President*, Frederick J. Chiluba, *elected* 31 October 1991
*Vice-President*, vacant.

CABINET *as at August 1994*
*Defence*, Benjamin Mwila
*Foreign Affairs*, Remmy Mushota
*Finance*, Ronald Penza
*Home Affairs*, Chitalou Sampa
*Local Government and Housing*, Ben Mwiinga
*Health*, Michael Sata
*Education*, Alfeyo Hambayi
*Commerce, Trade and Industry*, Dipak Patel
*Community Development and Social Welfare*, Dr Kabunda Kayongo
*Labour and Social Security*, Newstead Zimba
*Communications, Transport and Public Works*, William Harrington
*Energy and Water Development*, Edith Nawakwi
*Agriculture, Food and Fisheries*, Simon Zukas
*Lands*, Dr Chuulu Kalima
*Legal Affairs*, Dr Ludwig Sondashi
*Environment and Natural Resources*, Dawson Lupunga
*Information and Broadcasting*, Kelly Walubita
*Mines and Mineral Development*, Paul Kapinga
*Technical Education and Vocational Training*, Gabriel Maka
*Sport, Youth and Child Development*, Amusa Mwanamwabwa
*Tourism*, Gen. Christon Tembo
*Works and Supply*, Andrew Kashita
*Minister without Portfolio*, Brig.-Gen. Godfrey Miyanda

HIGH COMMISSION FOR THE REPUBLIC OF ZAMBIA
2 Palace Gate, London W8 5NG
Tel 0171-589 6655

*High Commissioner*, His Excellency Love Mtesa, apptd 1992
*Deputy High Commissioner*, A. M. Mwale
*Consul-General*, M. C. Mwanambale
*First Secretary*, J. Chikwenda (*Information/Tourism*)

BRITISH HIGH COMMISSION
Independence Avenue (PO Box 50050), 15 101 Ridgeway, Lusaka
Tel: Lusaka 251133

*High Commissioner*, His Excellency Patrick Nixon, CMG, OBE, apptd 1993
*Deputy High Commissioner*, B. S. Jones, LVO
*First Secretary (Commercial/Consular)*, K. A. Neill

BRITISH COUNCIL REPRESENTATIVE, Adrian Greer, Heroes Place, Cairo Road (PO Box 34571), Lusaka. There is also a library in *Ndola*.

## ECONOMY

The free market economic reforms introduced since 1991 by the MMD government have revolutionized the economy, which had been highly regulated and protected from competition. Price subsidies and tariffs have been lowered or abolished and public sector wages frozen but inflation and interest rates have increased, causing hardships. Increased imports have affected manufacturing and agricultural production.

Principal products are maize, sugar, groundnuts, cotton, livestock, vegetables and tobacco. Mineral production was valued at K8,390 million in 1987, of which copper production (of 483,100 tonnes) accounted for K6,870 million.

GDP (current prices) was K18,079.8 million in 1987. GDP per capita (current prices) was K2,486.9. Following the reforms initiated by the government, the US government wrote off K59,000 million of debt in April 1993.

| Trade with UK | 1992 | 1993 |
|---|---|---|
| Imports from UK | £65,127,000 | £73,548,000 |
| Exports to UK | 7,279,000 | 12,056,000 |

## ZIMBABWE
*Republic of Zimbabwe*

Zimbabwe, the former Southern Rhodesia, lies south of the Zambezi river and borders Zambia and Mozambique on the north, South Africa and Botswana on the south and west, and Mozambique on the east. It has a total area of 150,804 sq. miles (390,580 sq. km), and a population (UN estimate 1991) of 10,019,000.

CAPITAL – Harare (formerly Salisbury) situated on the Mashonaland plateau, population (July 1983) 681,000. Bulawayo is the largest town in Matabeleland, population (July 1983) 429,000. Other centres are Chitungwiza, Mutare, Gweru, Kadoma, Kwe Kwe, Masvingo and Hwange.
CURRENCY – Zimbabwe dollar (Z$) of 100 cents.
FLAG – Seven horizontal stripes of green, yellow, red, black, red, yellow, green; a white, black-bordered, triangle based on the hoist containing the national emblem.
NATIONAL ANTHEM – Ngaikomberarwe Nyika Ye Zimbabwe (Blessed be the country of Zimbabwe).
NATIONAL DAY – 18 April (Independence Day).

## GOVERNMENT

Southern Rhodesia was granted responsible government in 1923. An illegal declaration of independence on 11 November 1965 was finally terminated on 12 December 1979. Following elections in February 1980 the country became independent on 18 April 1980 as the Republic of Zimbabwe, a member of the British Commonwealth.

The independence constitution was amended in 1987, making the presidency an executive post. The President is popularly elected for a six-year term, appoints the Cabinet and can veto parliamentary bills. The legislature became unicameral in 1990 and the House of Assembly has 150 members, 120 elected, 20 appointed by the President and ten appointed by traditional chiefs. A merger agreement between the ZANU (PF) and ZAPU parties was signed in 1987 with a view to the eventual creation of a one-party state. The new party is known as ZANU-PF. The latest general election was held in March 1990 and ZANU-PF won 116 of the 120 elective seats.

The country is divided into eight provinces: Manicaland, Masvingo, Matabeleland North, Matabeleland South, Midlands, Mashonaland West, Central and East.

HEAD OF STATE
*Executive President*, Hon. Robert Gabriel Mugabe, *elected* 30 December 1987, *re-elected* March 1990

CABINET *as at August 1994*
The President
*Vice-Presidents*, Hon. Simon Muzenda; Hon. Dr Joshua Nkomo
*Senior Minister, National Affairs, Employment Creation and Co-operatives*, Hon. Didymus Mutasa

*Senior Minister, Economic Ministries*, Hon. Dr Bernard
 Chidzero
*Foreign Affairs*, Hon. Dr Nathan Shamuyarira
*Justice, Legal and Parliamentary Affairs*, Hon. Emmerson
 Munangagwa
*Defence*, Hon. Moven Mahachi
*Higher Education*, Hon. Dr Stanslous Mudenge
*Education and Culture*, Hon. Dr Witness Mangwende
*Home Affairs*, Hon. Dumiso Dabengwa
*Public Construction and National Housing*, Hon. Enos
 Chikowore
*Lands, Agriculture and Water Resources*, Hon. Kumbirai
 Kangai
*Information, Posts and Telecommunications*, Hon. David
 Karimanzira
*Labour, Public Service and Social Welfare*, Hon. John
 Nkomo
*Industry and Commerce*, vacant
*Mines*, Hon. Dr Eddison Zvogbo
*Transport and Energy*, Hon. Dennis Norman
*Health and Child Welfare*, Hon. Dr Timothy Stamps
*Environment and Tourism*, Hon. Herbert Murerwa
*Attorney-General*, Hon. Patrick Chinamasa

HIGH COMMISSION OF THE REPUBLIC OF ZIMBABWE
Zimbabwe House, 429 Strand, London WC2R 0SA
Tel 0171-836 7755

*High Commissioner*, His Excellency Dr Ngoni Togarepi
 Chideya, apptd 1993
*Minister-Counsellors*, G. P. Chanesta; J. Mupamhanga
*Defence Adviser*, Lt.-Col. E. Zabanyana
*Counsellor*, S. Undenge (*Commercial*)

BRITISH HIGH COMMISSION
Stanley House, Jason Moyo Avenue (PO Box 4490), Harare
Tel: Harare 793781

*High Commissioner*, His Excellency Richard Dales, CMG,
 apptd 1992
*Deputy High Commissioner*, R. S. Dewar
*Defence Adviser*, Col. A. McNeil
*First Secretaries*, M. K. Page (*Commercial*); P. S. Covill
 (*Consular*)

BRITISH COUNCIL REPRESENTATIVE, P. L. Elborn, OBE,
 23 Jason Moyo Avenue (PO Box 664), Harare. There is
 also a library at Bulawayo.

## ECONOMY

Ten years of socialism and central planning in 1980–90,
coupled with a period of drought, brought the economy to
crisis point before free market economic reforms were
introduced in 1990 under the auspices of a World Bank-
enhanced structural adjustment programme. This has involved the removal of food subsidies, the floating of the
currency, opening the market to imports, and reducing
subsidies. The programme has been partly implemented but
the civil service and armed forces have not been reduced,
leading to a budget deficit of around 10 per cent of GDP
(1993). The foreign debt is £2,300 million and costs one-
third of export revenue to service. The compulsory purchase
of white-owned commercial farms by the government in
1993–4 has caused a scandal as the land has been given to
senior government officials rather than the landless black
peasants it was intended for, and the farmers given
compensation in worthless government bonds. This policy
means agricultural production is set to decline.
 The country is endowed with minerals, water, forests,
wildlife and other resources. The agricultural sector is well-
developed and employs 70 per cent of the workforce. Tobacco

remains the most important crop in terms of export and
maize the most important for domestic consumption. Other
crops include wheat, cotton, and sugar. Beef is exported to
the EU.
 The manufacturing sector is very dependent on the
agricultural sector for raw materials. Industry is also
dependent on imports e.g. fuel oil, steel products and
chemicals, as well as heavy machinery and items of transport.
The mining sector, although contributing a relatively small
portion to GDP, is important to the economy as a foreign
exchange earner. Almost all mineral production is exported.
Gold is the most important mineral, others are asbestos,
silver, nickel, copper, chrome ore, tin, iron ore and cobalt.
There is a successful ferro-chrome industry and a substantial
steel works which has been heavily subsidized by government.

| Trade with UK | 1992 | 1993 |
|---|---|---|
| Imports from UK | £100,856,000 | £83,114,000 |
| Exports to UK | 86,254,000 | 121,500,000 |

## EDUCATION

Since independence, a policy of free primary education and
accelerated expansion at secondary level has resulted in
rapidly expanding enrolment. Over 80 per cent of schools
are government-aided schools. The University of Zimbabwe
was founded in 1955.

# British Dependent Territories

## ANGUILLA

Anguilla is a flat coralline island, about 16 miles in length, three and a half miles in breadth at its widest point and its area is about 35 sq. miles (91 sq. km). It lies approximately 18° N. latitude and 63° W. longitude, to the north of the Leeward Islands group. The island is covered with low scrub and fringed with white coral-sand beaches. The climate is pleasant, with temperatures in the range of 24-30°C throughout the year.

POPULATION – The population (1992 census) is 8,960.
CAPITAL – The Valley (population 1,400).
CURRENCY – East Caribbean dollar (EC$) of 100 cents.
FLAG – British Blue Ensign with the shield of arms in the fly.

### GOVERNMENT

Anguilla has been a British colony since 1650. For most of its history it has been linked administratively with St Christopher, but three months after the Associated State of Saint Christopher (St Kitts)-Nevis-Anguilla came into being in 1967, the Anguillans repudiated government from St Kitts. A Commissioner was installed in 1969 and in 1976 Anguilla was given a new status and separate constitution. Final separation from St Kitts and Nevis was effected on 19 December 1980 and Anguilla reverted to a British dependency. A new constitution was introduced in 1982, providing for a Governor, an Executive Council comprising four elected Ministers and two ex-officio members (the Attorney-General and Permanent Secretary, Finance), and an 11-member legislative House of Assembly presided over by a Speaker.

The 1982 Constitution (Amendment) Order 1990 came into operation on 30 May 1990. Among the new constitutional provisions are a Deputy Governor (who replaces the Permanent Secretary (Finance) in the Executive Council and the Legislature), a Parliamentary Secretary, Leader of Opposition and Deputy Speaker.

*Governor*, His Excellency Alan Shave, CVO, OBE, *apptd* 1992
*Deputy Governor*, Henry McCrory, LVO, OBE, *apptd* 1991

EXECUTIVE COUNCIL *as at June 1994*

*Chief Minister and Minister of Lands, Agriculture and Fisheries*, Hon. Hubert Hughes
*Social Services*, Hon. Edison Baird
*Communications, Public Utilities and Works*, Hon. Albert Hughes
*Finance and Economic Development*, Hon. Victor Banks
*Attorney-General*, Hon. Kurt De Freitas

### ECONOMY

Low rainfall limits agricultural output and export earnings are mainly from sales of lobsters. Tourism has developed rapidly in recent years and accounts for most of the island's economic activity. In 1993 there were 37,658 tourists and a further 73,692 day visitors.

| FINANCE | 1992 | 1993 |
| --- | --- | --- |
| Revenue | EC$34,810,000 | EC$36,554,029 |
| Expenditure | 31,895,000 | 34,183,714 |

| TRADE WITH UK | 1992 | 1993 |
| --- | --- | --- |
| Imports from UK | £1,064,000 | £1,501,000 |
| Exports to UK | 12,000 | 118,000 |

## ASCENSION
— *see* St Helena

## BERMUDA

The Bermudas, or Somers Islands, are a cluster of about 100 small islands (about 20 of which are inhabited) situated in the west of the Atlantic Ocean, in 32° 18′ N. latitude and 64° 46′ W. longitude, the nearest point of the mainland being Cape Hatteras in North Carolina, about 570 miles distant. The total area is approximately 20.59 sq. miles (53 sq. km), which includes 2.3 sq. miles leased to the USA.

POPULATION – The civil population (1993) is 59,549.
CAPITAL – ΨHamilton (population 1993, 2,000).
CURRENCY – Bermuda dollar of 100 cents.
FLAG – British Red Ensign with the shield of arms in the fly.

### GOVERNMENT

The colony derives its name from Juan Bermudez, a Spaniard, who sighted it before 1515. No settlement was made until 1609 when Sir George Somers, who was shipwrecked there on his way to Virginia, colonized the islands.

Internal self-government was introduced on 8 June 1968. There is a Senate of 11 members and an elected House of Assembly of 40 members. The Governor retains responsibility for external affairs, defence, internal security and the police, although administrative matters for the police service have been delegated to the Minister of Home Affairs.

The last general election was held on 5 October 1993. The United Bermuda Party holds 22 seats, and the Progressive Labour Party 18 seats.

*Governor and Commander-in-Chief*, His Excellency The Lord Waddington, GCVO, PC, QC, *apptd* 1992
*Deputy Governor*, Peter Willis

CABINET *as at June 1994*

*Premier*, Hon. Sir John Swan, KBE
*Deputy Premier and Minister of Labour and Home Affairs*, Hon. J. Irving Pearman
*Health, Social Services and Housing*, Hon. Quinton Edness
*Environment*, Senator Hon. Gerald D. E. Simons
*Education*, Dr the Hon. Clarence Terceira
*Youth, Sport and Recreation*, Hon. Pamela Gordon
*Works and Engineering*, Hon. Leonard O. Gibbons
*Tourism*, Hon. C. V. Jim Woolridge
*Transport*, Hon. Maxwell Burgess
*Finance*, Dr the Hon. David Saul
*Management and Technology*, Senator Dr the Hon. E. Grant Gibbons
*Human Affairs and Information*, Hon. C. Jerome Dill
*Community and Cultural Affairs*, Hon. Wayne L. Furbert

*President of the Senate*, Hon. A. S. Jackson, MBE
*Speaker of the House of Assembly*, Hon. Ernest DeCouto
*Chief Justice*, Hon. Austin Ward, QC

## ECONOMY

The islands' economic structure is based on tourism, the major industry, and international company business, attracted by the low level of taxation and sophisticated telecommunications system. In 1993 a total of 374,497 visitors arrived by air and cruise ship.

Locally manufactured concentrates, perfumes, cut flowers and pharmaceuticals are the colony's leading exports. Little food is produced except vegetables and fish, other foodstuffs being imported.

| FINANCE | 1992–3 | 1993–4 |
|---|---|---|
| Public revenue | $342,409,000 | $352,510,000 |
| Public expenditure | 329,901,000 | 331,750,000 |

| TRADE WITH UK | 1992 | 1993 |
|---|---|---|
| Imports from UK | £27,040,000 | £23,344,000 |
| Exports to UK | 5,773,000 | 1,687,000 |

## COMMUNICATIONS

One daily and three weekly newspapers are published in Bermuda. Three commercial companies operate radio and television services, including a cable-television system which started service in July 1988. The Bermuda Telephone Company and Cable and Wireless provide telecommunications links to more than 140 countries.

## EDUCATION

Free elementary education was introduced in 1949. Free secondary education was introduced in 1965 for those children in the aided and maintained schools who were below the upper limit of the statutory school age of 16 (from 1969 onwards).

## THE BRITISH ANTARCTIC TERRITORY

The British Antarctic Territory was designated in 1962 and consists of the areas south of 60°S. latitude which were previously included in the Falkland Islands Dependencies. The territory lies between longitudes 20° and 80°W., south of latitude 60°S. and includes the South Orkney Islands, the South Shetland Islands, the mountainous Antarctic Peninsula (highest point Mount Jackson, 13,620 ft, in Palmer Land) and all adjacent islands, and the land mass extending to the South Pole. The territory has no indigenous inhabitants and the British population consists of the scientists and technicians who man the British Antarctic Survey stations. The number averages about 60 to 70 in winter, but increases considerably in the summer months with the arrival of field workers. Argentina, Brazil, Chile, China, Korea (South), Poland, USA, Russia and Uruguay also have scientific stations in the territory.

The first two British Antarctic Survey stations were established in the South Shetland Islands in 1944, and by 1956 the number of stations had risen to 12. Due to the completion of field work in some areas and increased mobility, the number has now been reduced to five. These are Signy (Signy Island, South Orkney Islands), Faraday (Argentine Islands, Graham Coast), Rothera (Adelaide Island), Halley (Caird Coast) and, in summer only, Fossil Bluff (George VI Sound). Fifteen other stations have been established but are at present unoccupied.

The territory is administered by a Commissioner, resident in London.

*Commissioner* (non-resident), Peter M. Newton, *apptd* 1992

## THE BRITISH INDIAN OCEAN TERRITORY

The British Indian Ocean Territory was established by an Order in Council in 1965 and included islands formerly administered from Mauritius and the Seychelles. After the independence of both, the territory was redefined in 1976 as comprising only the islands of the Chagos Archipelago.

The Chagos Archipelago consists of six main groups of islands situated on the Great Chagos Bank and covering some 21,000 sq. miles (54,389 sq. km). The largest and most southerly of the Chagos Islands is Diego Garcia, a sand cay with a land area of about 17 sq. miles approximately 1,100 miles east of Mahé, used as a joint naval support facility by Britain and USA.

The other main island groups of the archipelago, Peros Banhos (29 islands with a total land area of 4 sq. miles) and Salomon (11 islands with a total land area of 2 sq. miles) are uninhabited. The islands have a typical tropical maritime climate, with average temperatures between 25° C and 29° C in Diego Garcia, and rainfall in the whole archipelago of 90–100 inches a year.

FLAG – Divided horizontally into blue and white wavy stripes, with the Union Flag in the canton and a crowned palm-tree over all in the fly.

*Commissioner*, David Ross MacLennan, *apptd* 1994
*Administrator*, D. H. Cairns

| TRADE WITH UK | 1992 | 1993 |
|---|---|---|
| Imports from UK | £2,087,000 | £701,000 |
| Exports to UK | 26,000 | 28,000 |

## THE BRITISH VIRGIN ISLANDS

The Virgin Islands are a group of islands at the eastern extremity of the Greater Antilles, divided between Great Britain and the USA. Those of the group which are British number 46, of which 11 are inhabited, and have a total area of about 59 sq. miles, (153 sq. km). The principal are Tortola, the largest (situated in 18° 27′ N. lat. and 64° 40′ W. long., area, 21 sq. miles), Virgin Gorda (8¼ sq. miles), Anegada (15 sq.miles) and Jost Van Dyke (3½ sq. miles).

Apart from Anegada, which is a flat coral island, the British Virgin Islands are hilly, being an extension of the Puerto Rico and the US Virgin Islands archipelago. The highest point is Sage Mountain on Tortola which rises to a height of 1,780 feet.

The islands lie within the trade winds belt and possess a sub-tropical climate. The average temperature varies from 22°–28° C in winter to 26°–31° C in summer. Average annual rainfall is 53 inches.

POPULATION – The 1991 census showed a total population of 16,108: Tortola (13,225); Virgin Gorda (2,431); Anegada (162); Jost Van Dyke (140); and other islands (144).

CAPITAL – ΨRoad Town, on the south-east of Tortola. Population 3,983.

CURRENCY – The US dollar (US$) of 100 cents is legal tender.

FLAG – British Blue Ensign with the shield of arms in the fly.

## GOVERNMENT

Under the 1977 constitution the Governor, appointed by the Crown, remains responsible for defence and internal security, external affairs and the civil service but in other matters acts in accordance with the advice of the Executive Council. The Executive Council consists of the Governor as Chairman, one ex-officio member (the Attorney-General), the Chief Minister and three other ministers. The Legislative Council consists of a Speaker chosen from outside the Council, one ex-officio member (the Attorney-General), and nine elected members returned from nine one-member electoral districts.

*Governor,* His Excellency Peter Alfred Penfold, OBE, *apptd 1992*
*Deputy Governor,* E. Georges, OBE

THE EXECUTIVE COUNCIL *as at 30 June 1994*

*Chairman,* The Governor
*Chief Minister and Minister of Finance,* Hon. H. Lavity Stoutt
*Natural Resources and Labour,* Hon. Ralph O'Neal, OBE
*Communications and Works,* Hon. Terrance Lettsome
*Health, Education and Welfare,* Hon. Louis Walters, MBE
*Attorney-General,* Hon. Dancia Penn

*Puisne Judge (resident),* Justice Ephraim Georges

ECONOMY

Tourism is the main industry but the financial centre is growing steadily in importance. Other industries include a rum distillery, three stone-crushing plants and factories manufacturing concrete blocks and paint. The major export items are fresh fish, gravel, sand, fruit and vegetables; exports are largely confined to the US Virgin Islands. Chief imports are building materials, machinery, cars and beverages.

| FINANCE | 1991 | 1992 |
|---|---|---|
| Revenue | US$51,175,000 | US$60,538,000 |
| Expenditure | 50,938,000 | 56,024,000 |

| TRADE WITH UK | 1992 | 1993 |
|---|---|---|
| Imports from UK | £4,097,000 | £2,597,000 |
| Exports to UK | 139,000 | 1,316,000 |

COMMUNICATIONS

The principal airport is on Beef Island, linked by bridge to Tortola, and an extended runway of 3,600 ft enables larger aircraft to call. There is a second airfield on Virgin Gorda and a third on Anegada. There are direct shipping services to the United Kingdom and the United States and fast passenger services connect the main islands by ferry.

# THE CAYMAN ISLANDS

The Cayman Islands, between 79° 44′ and 81° 26′ W. and 19° 15′ and 19° 46′ N., consist of three islands, Grand Cayman, Cayman Brac, and Little Cayman, with a total area of 100 sq. miles (259 sq. km). About 150 miles south of Cuba, the islands are divided from Jamaica, 180 miles to the south-east, by the Cayman Trench, the deepest part of the Caribbean. The nearest point on the US mainland is Miami in Florida, 450 miles to the north. Cooled by trade winds, the annual average temperature and rainfall are 27.2° C and 50.7 inches respectively.

POPULATION – Population (estimate 1992) 29,700, of which the vast majority live on Grand Cayman.
CAPITAL – ΨGeorge Town, in Grand Cayman, population (estimate 1992) 15,000.
CURRENCY – Cayman Islands dollar (CI$) of 100 cents, which is fixed at CI$ = US$1.20.

FLAG – British Blue Ensign with the arms on a white disc in the fly.

GOVERNMENT

The colony derives its name from the Carib word for the crocodile, 'caymanas', which appeared in the log of the first English visitor to the Cayman Islands, Sir Francis Drake. Although tradition has it that the first settlers arrived in 1658, the first recorded settlers arrived in 1666–71. The first recorded permanent settlers followed the first land grant by Britain in 1734. The islands were placed under direct control of Jamaica in 1863. When Jamaica became independent in 1962, the islands opted to remain under the British Crown.

The constitution provides for a Governor, a Legislative Assembly and an Executive Council, and effectively allows a large measure of self-government. Unless there are exceptional reasons, the Governor accepts the advice of Executive Council, which comprises three official members and five others elected from the 15 elected members of the Assembly. The official members also sit in the Assembly. The Governor has responsibility for the police, civil service, defence and external affairs. The Governor handed over the presidency of the Legislative Assembly to the Speaker in 1991. The normal life of the Assembly is four years, with a general election next due in November 1996.

*Governor,* His Excellency Michael E. J. Gore, CVO, CBE, *apptd 1992*

EXECUTIVE COUNCIL *as at 30 June 1994*

*President,* The Governor
*Chief Secretary,* Hon. J. L. Hurlston, CVO, MBE
*Attorney-General,* Hon. R. H. Coles
*Financial Secretary,* Hon. G. A. McCarthy, OBE
*Minister for Tourism, Environment and Planning,* Hon. T. C. Jefferson, OBE
*Minister for Community Development, Sports, Youth Affairs and Culture,* Hon. W. M. Bush
*Minister for Education and Aviation,* Hon. T. M. Bodden, CBE
*Minister for Health, Drug-abuse Prevention and Rehabilitation,* Hon. A. S. Eden
*Minister for Communications, Works and Agriculture,* Hon. J. McLean
*Speaker of Legislative Assembly,* Mrs S. I. McLaughlin, MBE

LONDON OFFICE
Cayman Islands Government Office, 100 Brompton Road, London SW3 1EX
Tel 0171–581 9418
*Government Representative,* T. Russell, CMG, CBE

ECONOMY

With a complete absence of direct taxation, the Cayman Islands have become successful over the past 25 years as an offshore financial centre. With representation from 62 countries, there were, at the end of 1993, 537 banks and trust companies, of which local offices were maintained by 84. In addition, there were 352 licensed insurance companies and 29,298 registered companies at the end of 1993. Tourism, with an emphasis on scuba diving, has also been developed successfully. There were 287,277 visitors by air and 605,715 cruise ship callers in 1993.

The two industries support a heavy imbalance in trade resulting from the need to import most of what is consumed and used on the islands, and have created a thriving local economy in which the GNP reached US$669.6m (US$25,300 per capita) in 1991. Import duty and fees from financial centre operations have provided revenue enabling the government to undertake heavy investment in education (which is provided free to all 4–16 year olds), health and other social programmes.

| FINANCE | 1993 | 1994* |
|---|---|---|
| Revenue | CI$158.3m | CI$158.1m |
| Expenditure | 151.8m | 157.1m |
| *estimated | | |

| TRADE | 1991 | 1992 |
|---|---|---|
| Total imports | CI$222.9m | CI$253.5m |
| Total exports | 2.5m | 3.7m |

| TRADE WITH UK | 1992 | 1993 |
|---|---|---|
| Imports from UK | £6,173,000 | £7,136,000 |
| Exports to UK | 2,497,000 | 1,268,000 |

# FALKLAND ISLANDS

The Falkland Islands, the only considerable group in the South Atlantic, lie about 300 miles east of the Straits of Magellan, between 52° 15′–53° S. latitude and 57° 40′–62° W. longitude. They consist of East Falkland (area 2,610 sq. miles; 6,759 sq. km), West Falkland (2,090 sq. miles; 5,413 sq. km) and over 100 small islands. Mount Usborne (E. Falkland), the loftiest peak, rises 2,312 feet above the level of the sea. The islands are chiefly moorland.

The climate is cool. At Stanley the mean monthly temperature varies between 9° C in January and 2° C in July.
POPULATION – The population, excluding the British garrison, was 2,121 at 5 March 1991.
CHIEF TOWN – ΨStanley, population (1991) 1,643. Stanley is about 8,103 miles distant from England .
CURRENCY – Falkland pound of 100 pence.
FLAG – British Blue Ensign with the arms on a white disc in the fly.

## GOVERNMENT

The Falklands were sighted first by Davis in 1592, and then by Hawkins in 1594; the first known landing was by Strong in 1690. A settlement was made by France in 1764; this was subsequently sold to Spain, but the latter country recognized Great Britain's title to a part at least of the group in 1771. After Argentina declared independence from Spain, the Argentine government in 1820 proclaimed its sovereignty over the Falklands and a settlement was founded in 1826. The settlement was destroyed by the Americans in 1831. In 1833 occupation was resumed by the British for the protection of the seal-fisheries, and the islands were permanently colonized as the most southerly organized colony of the British Empire. Argentina continued to claim sovereignty over the islands (known to as las Islas Malvinas), and in pursuance of this claim invaded the islands on 2 April 1982 and also occupied South Georgia. A naval and military force dispatched from Great Britain recaptured South Georgia on 25 April and after landing at San Carlos Bay on 21 May, recaptured the islands from the Argentines, who surrendered on 14 June 1982. A British naval and military garrison of some 2,000 personnel remains in the area. A military zone of 55 miles (previously 80) remains around the islands within which Argentinian naval and air forces may not intrude.

Under the 1985 constitution, the Governor is advised by an Executive Council consisting of three elected members of the Legislative Council and two ex-officio members, the Chief Executive and the Financial Secretary. The Legislative Council consists of eight elected members and the same two ex-officio members.

*Governor and Chairman of the Executive Council*, His Excellency David Everard Tatham, CMG, *apptd* 1992
*Chief Executive*, R. Sampson
*Financial Secretary*, D. F. Howatt
*Commander, British Forces, Falkland Islands*, Air Cdre P. G. Johnson, OBE
*Attorney-General*, D. G. Lang, QC

LONDON OFFICE
Falkland Islands Government Office, Falkland House, 14 Broadway, London SW1H 0BH
Tel 0171-222 2542
*Government Representative*, Miss S. Cameron

## ECONOMY

The economy was formerly based solely on agriculture, principally sheep-farming with a little dairy farming for domestic requirements and crops for winter fodder. After the 1982 war the UK government provided some £46 million to restore the economy. The 36 large estates were also divided into some 90 smaller ones with occupier-owners in place of the previously mainly absentee landlords. Since the establishment of an interim conservation and management fishing zone around the islands and the consequent introduction on 1 February 1987 of a licensing regime for vessels fishing within the 200 mile zone, the economy has diversified and income from the associated fishing activities, mainly for illex squid, is now the largest source of revenue. The dramatic increase in government revenue from fishing licences has led to the establishment of a substantial health, education and welfare system with a well-equipped hospital in Stanley, free education until the age of 16 and further education in the UK paid for by the Falklands government. The islands are now self-financing except for defence. Chief imports are provisions, alcoholic beverages, timber, clothing and hardware. Tourism is a small but expanding industry. Most important, the British Geological Survey in 1993 announced a 200 mile oil exploration zone around the islands. Early seismic surveys suggest substantial reserves capable of producing 500,000 barrels per day.

| FINANCE | 1991–2 | 1992–3 |
|---|---|---|
| Public revenue | £40,300,000 | £40,500,000 |
| Expenditure | 39,100,000 | 34,500,000 |

| TRADE WITH UK | 1992 | 1993 |
|---|---|---|
| Imports from UK | £13,100,000 | £10,380,000 |
| Exports to UK | 3,091,000 | 4,317,000 |

# GIBRALTAR

Gibraltar is a rocky promontory, 2¾ miles in length, three-quarters of a mile in breadth, with a total area of 2¼ sq. miles. It is 1,396 ft high at its greatest elevation, near the southern extremity of Spain, with which it is connected by a low isthmus. It is about 14 miles from the opposite coast of Africa. The town stands at the foot of the promontory on the west side.
POPULATION – The population at the end of 1992 was 28,848.
CURRENCY – Gibraltar pound of 100 pence.
FLAG – White with a red stripe along the lower edge; over all a red castle with a key hanging from its gateway.

## GOVERNMENT

Gibraltar was captured in 1704, during the war of the Spanish Succession, by a combined Dutch and English force under Sir George Rooke, and was ceded to Great Britain by the Treaty of Utrecht 1713. Several attempts have been made to retake it, the most celebrated being the great siege of 1779 to 1783, when General Eliott, afterwards Lord Heathfield, held it for three years and seven months against a combined French and Spanish force. The Treaty of Utrecht stipulates that if Britain ever relinquishes its colonial rights over Gibraltar then the colony would return to Spain. In 1967 a referendum was held in Gibraltar on the colony's status in which 12,000 voted to remain a British Dependent Territory and 44 voted to join Spain. Spain closed the border with Gibraltar from 1969 to 1985 and refused to engage in any trade.

The constitution of Gibraltar, approved in 1969, made formal provision for certain domestic matters to devolve on a local government of Ministers appointed from among elected members of the House of Assembly. The House of Assembly consists of an independent Speaker, 15 elected members, the Attorney-General and the Financial and Development Secretary.

The Governor retains responsibility for external affairs, defence, internal security and financial security, while the local government is responsible for other domestic matters. However, the Gibraltar government has recently been agitating for more local autonomy and responsibility, especially in the colony's relations with the EC. Gibraltar is part of the EC (with the UK government responsible for enforcing EC directives affecting Gibraltar) but is not a fully-fledged member and, for example, its citizens cannot vote in European Parliament elections. In 1993 the Gibraltar government took the UK and Spanish governments to the European Court of Justice over a 1987 Anglo-Spanish agreement to exclude Gibraltar's airport from the EC's air liberalization directive of the EC Single Market Programme but the case was defeated.

*Governor and Commander-in-Chief*, His Excellency Field Marshal Sir John Chapple, GCB, CBE
*Flag Officer, Gibraltar, and Admiral Superintendent, HM Naval Base, Gibraltar*, Rear-Adm. J. T. Sanders, OBE
*Deputy Governor*, A. Carter
*Financial and Development Secretary*, B. Traynor
*Attorney-General*, J. Blackburn Gittings
*Chief Justice*, A. Kneller
*Chief Minister*, Joe Bossano
*Speaker*, Mayor R. J. Peliza, OBE

## ECONOMY

Gibraltar enjoys the advantages of an extensive shipping trade and is a popular shopping centre. The chief sources of revenue are the port dues, the rent of the Crown estate in the town, and duties on consumer items. The free port tradition of Gibraltar is still reflected in the low rates of import duty. The gradual change from a fortress city to a holiday centre has led to a flourishing tourist trade. A financial services industry is expanding, based on Gibraltar's status as an offshore financial centre. However, many jobs have been lost over the past few years as a result of reductions in the British naval and military presence.

A total of 4,881 merchant ships (63.6 million gross registered tons aggregate) entered the port during 1992. There are 49.9 km of roads.

| FINANCE | 1991–2 | 1992–3 |
| --- | --- | --- |
| Revenue | £86,700,000 | £72,735,000 |
| Expenditure | 83,683,000 | 77,916,000 |

| TRADE | 1991 | 1992 |
| --- | --- | --- |
| Total imports | £219,100,000 | £262,300,000 |
| Total exports | 12,900,000 | 35,400,000 |

| Trade with UK | 1992 | 1993 |
| --- | --- | --- |
| Imports from UK | £82,238,000 | £103,402,000 |
| Exports to UK | 4,059,000 | 3,693,000 |

## EDUCATION

Education is compulsory and free for children between the ages of four and 15 whose parents are ordinarily resident in Gibraltar. Scholarships are available for higher education in Britain. The total enrolment in government schools was 5,649 in December 1993.

## HONG KONG

Hong Kong, consisting of more than 230 islands and of a portion of the mainland (Kowloon and the New Territories) on the south-east coast of China, is situated at the eastern side of the mouth of the Pearl River, between 22° 9′ and 22° 37′ N. latitude and 113° 52′–114° 30′ E. longitude. The total area of the territory (including recent reclamation) is 416 sq. miles (1,077 sq. km).

The island of Hong Kong is about 11 miles (18 km) long and from two to five miles (three to eight km) broad, with a total area of 29 sq. miles (80 sq. km); at the eastern entrance to the harbour it is separated from the mainland by a narrow strait.

The climate is sub-tropical, tending towards the temperate for nearly half the year. The mean monthly temperature ranges from 16° C to 29° C. The average annual rainfall is 2,214 mm, of which nearly 80 per cent falls between May and September. Tropical cyclones occur between May and November, causing high winds and heavy rain.

POPULATION – Population at the beginning of 1993 was 6.0 million.

CAPITAL – ΨVictoria, situated on the island of Hong Kong.

CURRENCY – Hong Kong dollar (HK$) of 100 cents.

FLAG – British Blue Ensign with the arms on a white disc in the fly.

## GOVERNMENT

The island of Hong Kong was first occupied by Great Britain in January 1841 and formally ceded by the Treaty of Nanking in 1842. Kowloon was acquired by the Peking Convention of 1860 and the New Territories, consisting of a peninsula in the southern part of the Guangdong province together with adjacent islands, by a 99-year lease signed on 9 June 1898.

Hong Kong is administered by the Hong Kong government, at the head of which is the Governor. The Governor governs aided by an Executive Council and a Legislative Council. The Executive Council consists of three ex-officio members (the Chief Secretary, the Financial Secretary and the Attorney-General) together with 10 other members, including one member who is an official and appointed by the Governor with the approval of the British Foreign Secretary. The Legislative Council consists of 60 members, of whom three are ex-officio members and 57 are non-official members. Of these 57 non-official members, 18 are appointed by the Governor, 21 are elected by functional constituencies by corporate voting and 18 are elected by direct election. The President of the Legislative Council is a non-official member elected to that office by the non-official members.

The first direct elections for 18 of the 60 Legislative Council seats were held in September 1991. It is planned that 20 members of the Legislative Council will be directly elected in 1995.

There is also an Urban Council which provides services relating to public health and sanitation, culture and recreation in the urban area. The Urban Council consists of 40 members, of which 15 are directly elected from district constituencies, 15 appointed by the Governor and 10 are representative members from the urban district boards. A Regional Council was also set up in 1986 to provide similar services in the New Territories. Of the 36 Regional Council seats, 12 are directly elected, 12 are appointed by the Governor and nine are elected as representatives of the nine district boards within the Regional Council area. The remaining three are ex-officio members, being the chairman and the two vice-chairmen of the Heung Yee Kuk (a statutory advisory body which represents the indigenous population of the New Territories). Direct elections to the Urban and Regional Councils were held for the first time in May 1991 and the next elections are due to be held in March 1995 with an increased number of elected seats and the abolition of the appointed membership. Both Councils are financially autonomous.

### HANDOVER TO CHINA

Under the terms of the Joint Declaration of the British and Chinese governments, which came into force on 27 May 1985, Hong Kong will become, with effect from 1 July 1997, a Special Administrative Region of the People's Republic of China. However, the social and economic systems in the SAR will remain unchanged for 50 years. The British and Chinese governments have, since the entry into force of the agreement, been involved in consultations on the implementation of the agreement via the Joint Liaison Group.

China is demanding an increasing voice in Hong Kong affairs as the handover approaches. This has led to increasing friction between the British and Hong Kong authorities on one side and the Chinese government on the other. Central to the acrimonious disputes in 1992–4 has been the plan for an extension of democracy in Hong Kong presented by the Governor to the Legislative Council in October 1992. By the 1995 Legislative Council elections, when these reforms will come into effect, there will effectively be 39 directly-elected members out of 60 (20 directly-elected, 10 elected by electoral college, nine by large functional constituencies), together with 21 indirectly-elected members elected by larger electorates than previously.

The plan outraged the Chinese government which believes it agreed in the 1985 Joint Declaration to only 20 directly-elected seats on the Legislative Council and 40 appointed (or pliant pro-Beijing) members. In an attempt to derail the democracy reform package, the Chinese government suspended meetings of the Joint Liaison Group and talks on the new airport in late 1992, and launched a propaganda campaign against Governor Patten. Meanwhile, the Executive Council passed the reform package without amendment in February 1993. The Governor then suspended the presentation of the reform package to the Legislative Council for debate to enable UK-Chinese discussions on the issue to begin in April 1993. The Chinese government approved the re-opening of the Joint Liaison Group meetings and talks on the new airport, which began in June 1993. In July the Chinese officially established a shadow government for Hong Kong, known as the preparatory work subcommittee of the Chinese parliament and headed by foreign minister Qian Qichen.

After 17 rounds of fruitless negotiations between the UK and Chinese governments and no progress in the Joint Liaison Group meeting, Governor Patten presented his reform package to the Legislative Council in two parts in December 1993. The first, and less controversial, part was approved by the Legislative Council in February 1994 and includes: a reduction in the voting age from 21 to 18; the introduction of single member constituencies; and the replacement of appointed seats on the Regional and Urban Councils by elected seats in the 1994–5 elections. The second part of the reform package was passed by the Legislative Council on 30 June 1994 and includes: the establishment of nine new functional Legislative Council constituencies with an electorate of 2.5 million; the establishment of ten Legislative Council seats indirectly elected by the directly-elected Regional and Urban Councils; the replacement of corporate voting by individual voting in the 21 existing functional constituencies.

The Chinese government continues to refuse to accept the democracy reform package and says that it will dismantle all the elected councils and replace them with its own arrangements after it assumes sovereignty. Meanwhile, it has adopted flexible positions on 'non-political' issues, allowing the Joint Liaison Group to reach agreement on the stationing of Chinese defence forces in Hong Kong after 1 July 1997.

*Governor*, His Excellency The Rt. Hon. Christopher Patten, sworn in 9 July 1992
*Chief Justice*, The Hon. Sir Ti Liang Yang

CIVIL ESTABLISHMENT *as at June 1994*

*\*Chief Secretary*, Hon. Mrs Anson Chan, CBE
*Commander, British Forces*, Maj.-Gen. B. Dutton, CBE
*\*Financial Secretary*, Hon. Sir Hamish McLeod, KBE
*\*Attorney-General*, Hon. J. F. Mathews, CMG
*Civil Service*, Hon. Michael Sze, ISO
*Planning, Environment and Lands*, Hon. A. G. Eason
*Transport*, Hon. Haider Barma Man-kin
*Education and Manpower*, Hon. Michael Leung
*Economic Services*, Hon. Gordon Siu
*Home Affairs*, Hon. Michael M. Y. Suen
*Health and Welfare*, Hon. Mrs Elizabeth C. L. Wong-Chien, ISO
*Security*, Hon. A. P. Asprey, OBE, AE
*Financial Services and Economic Analysis*, Hon. Michael Cartland
*Recreation and Culture*, Hon. James So, CBE
*Trade and Industry*, Hon. Chau Tak-hay
*Works*, Hon. James Blake
*Political Adviser*, Robert Peirce
*Commissioner of Police*, Li Kwan-ha
*\*ex-officio member of the Executive and Legislative Councils*

BRITISH COUNCIL REPRESENTATIVE, T. Buchanan, Easey Commercial Building, 225 Hennessy Road, Wanchai, Hong Kong.

LONDON OFFICE
Hong Kong Government Office, 6 Grafton Street, London W1X 3LB
Tel 0171-499 9821

*Commissioner*, Sir David Ford, KBE, LVO, *apptd* 1993.

### ECONOMY

Over the past 30 years Hong Kong has become one of the world's major trade, manufacturing and financial centres. It has an advanced employment structure, with three-quarters of its workforce employed in services. In 1993–4 it had an unemployment rate of 2 per cent; an annual inflation rate of

8.5 per cent; GDP growth rate of 5.5 per cent (1993); and a budget surplus (1994) of HK$15 billion. Increasingly tied economically to China, Hong Kong firms are the largest investors in China and China has invested some HK$20 billion in Hong Kong, which is also the main trade and investment entry point into China.

The manufacturing sector is important in Hong Kong's economy, contributing about 13.2 per cent to the GDP and accounting for about 19.7 per cent of total employment. Up to 80 per cent of Hong Kong's manufacturing output is eventually exported.

Hong Kong's manufacturing industries produce light consumer goods, such as electronics, plastics, electrical products, watches and clocks, which accounted for 28 per cent of Hong Kong's total domestic exports in 1993. The corresponding share of textiles and clothing, Hong Kong's traditional leading industries, was 40 per cent in 1993.

Diversification in terms of products and markets continues to be the main feature of recent industrial development, as are industrial partnerships with overseas companies. The economy of Hong Kong is based on export rather than the domestic market.

| FINANCE | 1992–3 | 1993–4 |
|---|---|---|
| Public revenue | HK$135,311m | HK$164,412m |
| Public expenditure | 113,332m | 149,307m |

TRADE

In 1993, the total value of visible trade (including domestic exports, re-exports and imports) amounted to 250 per cent of the GDP. Hong Kong's visible trade account had in 1993 a deficit of HK$26,347 million. Taking visible and invisible trade together, there was a combined surplus of HK$31,959 million, compared with HK$13,420 million in 1992. In 1993, Hong Kong's principal customers for its domestic products, in order of value of trade, were China, USA, Germany, Singapore, the United Kingdom, Japan and Taiwan. China was its principal supplier.

| | 1992 | 1993 |
|---|---|---|
| Total exports | HK$924,953m | HK$1,046,250m |
| Total imports | 955,295m | 1,072,597m |
| *Trade with UK* | 1992 | 1993 |
| Imports from UK | £1,612,934,000 | £2,170,115,000 |
| Exports to UK | 2,397,362,000 | 2,997,774,000 |

COMMUNICATIONS

Hong Kong, one of the world's finest natural harbours, possesses excellent wharves. The Kwai Chung container terminal has 20 berths. A pier at the Ocean Terminal can accommodate large liners and cargo vessels up to 290 metres length and 10 metres draught. The Marine Department provides and maintains 76 mooring buoys within the port for ships to work cargo in the stream. Available dockyard facilities include six floating drydocks, the largest being capable of docking vessels up to 150,000 tonnes deadweight. In 1993 some 331,005 ocean-going and river-trade vessels called at Hong Kong and loaded and discharged more than 118 million tonnes of cargo. To cope with increasing demand two new container terminals are being constructed at Stonecutters Island and at South-East Tsing Yi Island. The first two berths are in operation and the whole terminal should be completed by the end of 1995.

Hong Kong International Airport, Kai Tak, situated to the east of the Kowloon peninsula, is regularly used by over 57 international airlines, providing over 2,598 frequent scheduled passenger and cargo services each week. During 1993, over 135,092 aircraft on international flights arrived and departed, carrying 24.5 million passengers and 1,140,000 tonnes of freight. A new international airport is being built on reclaimed land off Lantau Island at Chek Lap Kok and is planned to become operational by 1997.

EDUCATION

In the school year 1993–4 there were 1,869 day schools with 1,128,545 pupils. Free education for children up to the age of 15 was made compulsory in 1979. Post-secondary education is provided by three universities, two polytechnics, the Hong Kong Baptist College and four approved post-secondary colleges. The Open Learning Institute of Hong Kong provides university education to about 15,500 students. There are also seven technical institutes and four teacher-training colleges.

---

## MONTSERRAT

Situated in 16° 45′ N. latitude and 61° 15′ W. longitude, 27 miles south-west of Antigua, Montserrat is about 11 miles long and seven miles wide, with an area of 38 sq. miles (98 sq. km). Fertile and green, it is volcanic with several hot springs. About two-thirds of the island is mountainous, the rest capable of cultivation.

POPULATION – Population (estimate 1991) was 11,000.
CHIEF TOWN – ΨPlymouth, population 2,500.
CURRENCY – East Caribbean dollar (EC$) of 100 cents.
FLAG – British Blue Ensign with the shield of arms in the fly.

GOVERNMENT

Discovered by Columbus in 1493, Montserrat became a British colony in 1632. The first settlers were predominantly Irish indentured slaves from St Kitts. Montserrat was captured by the French in 1664, 1667 and 1782 but the island reverted to Britain within a few years on each occasion and was finally assigned to Great Britain in 1783.

A ministerial system was introduced in Montserrat in 1960. The Executive Council is presided over by the Governor and is composed of four elected members (the Chief and three other Ministers) and two ex-officio members (the Attorney-General and the Financial Secretary). The four Ministers are appointed from the members of the political party holding the majority in the Legislative Council. The Legislative Council consists of the Speaker, two ex-officio members (the Attorney-General and the Financial Secretary), two nominated unofficial members and seven elected members.

*Governor*, His Excellency Frank Savage, LVO, OBE, *apptd* 1993

EXECUTIVE COUNCIL *as at July 1994*

*President*, The Governor
*Chief Minister and Minister of Finance and Economic Development*, Hon. Reuben T. Meade
*Communications and Works*, Hon. Nowell Tuitt
*Agriculture, Trade and the Environment*, Hon. Charles T. Kirnon
*Education, Health, Community Services and Labour*, Hon. Lazelle Howes
*Attorney-General*, Hon. Gertel Thom
*Financial Secretary*, Hon. C. T. John, OBE

*Speaker of the Legislative Council*, Dr the Hon. H. A. Fergus, OBE

## ECONOMY

The economy is dominated by tourism, related construction activities and offshore business services. There is some light industry and efforts are being made to increase agricultural exports and establish an agro-processing industry.

| FINANCE | 1991 | 1992 |
|---|---|---|
| Revenue | EC$44,443,000 | EC$39,273,000 |
| Expenditure | 39,216,000 | 39,056,000 |

| TRADE WITH UK | 1992 | 1993 |
|---|---|---|
| Imports from UK | £1,854,000 | £2,141,000 |
| Exports to UK | 143,000 | 65,000 |

## PITCAIRN ISLANDS

Pitcairn, a small volcanic island 1.9 sq. miles (5 sq. km) in area, is the chief of a group of islands situated about midway between New Zealand and Panama in the South Pacific Ocean at longitude 130° 06′ W. and latitude 25° 04′ S. The island rises in cliffs to a height of 1,100 feet and access from the sea is possible only at Bounty Bay, a small rocky cove, and then only by surf boats. The other three islands of the group (Henderson lying 105 miles east-north-east of Pitcairn, Oeno lying 75 miles north-west and Ducie lying 293 miles east) are all uninhabited. Henderson Island is occasionally visited by the Pitcairn Islanders to obtain supplies of 'miro' wood which is used for their carvings. Oeno is visited for excursions of about a week's duration every two years or so.

Mean monthly temperatures vary between 66°F (19°C) in August and 75°F (24°C) in February and the average annual rainfall is 80 inches. With an equable climate, the island is very fertile and produces both tropical and sub-tropical trees and crops.

POPULATION – At 31 December 1993 the population was 53. Since 1887 the islanders have all been adherents of the Seventh-day Adventist Church.

FLAG – British Blue Ensign with the arms in the fly.

## GOVERNMENT

First settled in 1790 by the Bounty mutineers and their Tahitian companions, Pitcairn was left uninhabited in 1856 when the entire population was resettled on Norfolk Island. The present community are descendants of two parties who, not wishing to remain on Norfolk, returned to Pitcairn in 1859 and 1864 respectively.

Pitcairn became a British settlement under the British Settlement Act 1887, and was administered by the Governor of Fiji from 1952 until 1970, when the administration was transferred to the British High Commission in New Zealand and the British High Commissioner was appointed Governor. The local Government Ordinance of 1964 provides for a Council of ten members of whom six are elected.

*Governor of Pitcairn, Henderson, Ducie and Oeno Islands*, His Excellency Robert John Alston, CMG (*British High Commissioner to New Zealand*)
*Island Magistrate and Chairman of Island Council*, J. Warren
*Education Officer and Government Adviser*, Mrs P. Foley

## ECONOMY

The islanders live by subsistence gardening and fishing, and their limited monetary needs are satisfied by the manufacture of wood carvings and other handicrafts which are sold to passing ships and to a few overseas customers. Other than small fees charged for gun and driving licences there are no taxes and government revenue is derived almost solely from the sale of postage stamps and income from investments. Communication with the outside world is maintained by cargo vessels travelling between New Zealand and Panama which call at irregular intervals, and by means of a satellite service providing telephone, telex and fax facilities.

## SOCIAL WELFARE

Education is compulsory between the ages of five and 15. Secondary education in New Zealand is encouraged by the Administration which provides scholarships and bursaries for the purpose. Medical care is provided by a registered nurse when a doctor is not present.

## ST HELENA AND DEPENDENCIES

## ST HELENA

Probably the best known of all the solitary islands in the world, St Helena is situated in the South Atlantic Ocean, 955 miles south of the Equator, 702 south-east of Ascension, 1,140 from the nearest point of the African continent, 1,800 from the coast of South America, 1,694 from Cape Town, in 15° 55′ S. latitude and 5° 42′ W. longitude. It is 10½ miles long, 6¼ broad, and encloses an area of 47 sq. miles (122 sq. km).

St Helena is of volcanic origin, and consists of numerous rugged mountains, the highest rising to 2,700 feet (820 m), interspersed with picturesque ravines. Although within the tropics, the south-east trade winds keep the temperature mild and equable.

POPULATION – The population (1987) is 5,644.
CAPITAL– ΨJamestown. Population (1987) 1,332.
CURRENCY – St Helena pound (£) of 100 pence.
FLAG – British Blue Ensign with the shield of arms in the fly.

## GOVERNMENT

St Helena was discovered by the Portuguese navigator, Juan da Nova Castella, in 1502 (probably on St Helena's Day) and remained unknown to other European nations until 1588. It was used as a port of call for vessels of all nations trading to the East until it was annexed by the Dutch in 1633. It was never occupied by them, however, and the English East India Company seized it in 1659. In 1834 it was ceded to the British Crown. During the period 1815 to 1821 the island was lent to the British government as a place of exile for the Emperor Napoleon Bonaparte who died in St Helena on 5 May 1821. It was formerly an important station on the route to India, but its prosperity decreased after the construction of the Suez Canal.

The government of St Helena is administered by a Governor, with the aid of a Legislative Council, consisting of a Speaker, three ex-officio members (Chief Secretary, Financial Secretary and Attorney-General) and 12 elected members. Five committees of the Legislative Council are reponsible for general oversight of the activities of government departments and have in addition a wide range of statutory and administrative functions. The Governor is also assisted by an Executive Council of the three ex-officio members and the chairmen of the Council committees.

*Governor*, His Excellency A. N. Hoole, OBE, *apptd* 1991
*Chief Secretary*, J. G. Perrott
*Financial Secretary*, R. Perrott, OBE
*Attorney-General*, D. Jeremiah

*Deputy Secretary*, E. C. Yon
*Chief Medical Officer*, Dr J. L. Sharp
*Chief Agriculture and Forestry Officer*, C. Lomas
*Chief Education Officer*, B. George
*Chief Engineer*, D. Johnston
*Chief Social Services and Employment Officer*, J. Young
*Chief Personnel Officer*, S. I. Ellick
*Chief Development Officer*, R. I. Ellick
*Chief Finance Officer*, D. H. Wade
*Chief Justice*, G. W. Martin, OBE

ECONOMY

Since the collapse of the New Zealand flax industry in 1965, the only significant export is that of canned and frozen fish. The other exports are a small amount of high quality coffee and cottage industry products (including lace, decorative woodwork and beadwork). St James's Bay, on the north-west of the island, possesses a good anchorage. There is as yet no airport or airstrip.

| FINANCE | 1991–2 | 1992–3 |
| --- | --- | --- |
| Local revenue | £4,384,626 | £3,545,407 |
| Budgetary | 3,424,000 | 3,526,100 |
| Recurrent expenditure | 6,756,049 | 6,816,429 |
| Development aid | 1,397,531 | 1,614,478 |

| TRADE | 1991–2 | 1992–3 |
| --- | --- | --- |
| Total imports | £6,543,088 | £6,100,400 |
| Total exports | 90,095 | 169,525 |

| Trade with UK | 1992 | 1993 |
| --- | --- | --- |
| Imports from UK | £7,336,000 | £6,564,000 |
| Exports to UK | 691,000 | 412,000 |

## ASCENSION

The small island of Ascension lies in the South Atlantic (7° 56′ S., 14° 22′ W.) some 700 miles north-west of the island of St Helena. It is a rocky peak of purely volcanic origin. The highest point (Green Mountain), some 2,817 ft, is covered with lush vegetation and has a farm of some ten acres, producing vegetables and livestock. The island is famous for turtles, which land on the beaches from January to May to lay their eggs. It is also a breeding area for the sooty tern, or wideawake, large numbers of which settle on the south-western coastal section every tenth month to hatch their eggs. Other wildlife on the island includes feral donkeys and cats, rabbits and francolin partridge. All wildlife except rabbits and cats is protected by law. The ocean surrounding the island contains shark, barracuda, tuna, bonito and many other fish.

POPULATION – The resident population in March 1994 totalled 1,159, of whom 807 were from St Helena, 198 from the UK and 154 from the USA. The residents consist of the employees and families of the British organizations, of the contractors of the US Air Force (Computer Sciences Raytheon) and of the St Helena government.

British forces returned to the island in April 1982 in support of operations in the Falkland Islands. At present there are over 100 RAF personnel on the island supporting the air link to the Falklands.

CAPITAL – Georgetown.

## GOVERNMENT

Ascension is said to have been discovered by Juan da Nova Castella on Ascension Day 1501 and two years later was visited by Alphonse d'Albuquerque, who gave the island its present name. It was uninhabited until the arrival of Napoleon in St Helena in 1815 when a small British naval garrison was stationed on the island. It remained under the

supervision of the Board of Admiralty until 1922, when it was made a dependency of St Helena by letters patent.

The British Foreign Secretary appoints the Administrator who is responsible to the Governor resident in St Helena. There is a small police force and post office. The British organizations through Ascension Island Services (AIS) provide and operate various common services for the island (school, hospital, public works etc).

*Administrator*, Brian Connelly, *apptd* 1991

COMMUNICATIONS

Cable and Wireless PLC operates the international telephone and cable services and maintains an internal telephone service. The BBC opened its Atlantic relay station broadcasting to Africa and South America in 1967.

## TRISTAN DA CUNHA

Tristan da Cunha is the chief island of a group of islands in the South Atlantic which lies in latitude 37° 6′ S. and longitude 12° 2′ W., some 1,320 miles (2,124 km) south-south-west of St Helena, about 1,500 miles (2,414 km) west of the Cape of Good Hope, and 3,600 miles (5,794 km) north-east of Cape Horn. Tristan da Cunha has an area of 38 sq. miles (98 sq. km). Inaccessible Island lies 20 miles west and has an area of 4 sq. miles (11 sq. km), and the three Nightingale Islands lie 20 miles south of Tristan da Cunha and have an area of three-quarters of a sq. mile (2 sq. km). Gough Island lies some 250 miles south-south-east of Tristan da Cunha in latitude 40° 20′ S. and longitude 9° 44′ W. and has an area of 35 sq. miles (91 sq. km).

All the islands are volcanic and steep-sided with cliffs or narrow beaches. Tristan itself has a single volcanic cone rising to 6,760 feet (2,060 m) and a narrow north-western coastal plain on which the settlement of Edinburgh is situated.

Inaccessible Island is a lofty mass of rock with sides two miles in length; the island is the resort of penguins and sea-fowl. Cultivation was started in 1937 but has been abandoned.

The Nightingale Islands are three in number, of which the largest is one mile long and three-quarters of a mile wide, and rises in two peaks, 960 and 1,105 feet above sea level respectively. The smaller islands, Stoltenhoff and Middle Isle, are little more than huge rocks. Seals, innumerable penguins, and vast numbers of sea-fowl visit these islands.

Gough Island (or Diego Alvarez) is about eight miles long and four miles broad. It is the resort of penguins and sea-elephants and has valuable guano deposits.

Gough and Inaccessible islands are nature reserves and access is strictly limited.

CLIMATE – The islands have a warm-temperate oceanic climate which is damp and windy and supports forest and scrub. Rainfall averages 66 inches a year on the coast of Tristan da Cunha.

POPULATION – Population in 1992 was 295, in the settlement of Edinburgh on Tristan da Cunha. In addition, there is a meteorological station maintained on Gough Island by the South African government and manned by South Africans. Inaccessible Island and the Nightingale Islands are uninhabited.

CAPITAL – Edinburgh.

CURRENCY – Pound sterling.

HISTORY

Tristan da Cunha was discovered in 1506 by a Portuguese admiral (Tristão da Cunha) after whom it was named. It was the resort of British and American sealers from the middle of the 18th century, and in 1760 a British naval officer visited the group of islands and gave his name to Nightingale Island.

On 14 August 1816 the group was annexed to the British Crown and a garrison was placed on Tristan da Cunha, but this force was withdrawn in 1817. Corporal William Glass remained at his own request with his wife and two children. This party, with five others, formed a settlement. In 1827 five women from St Helena, and afterwards others from Cape Colony, joined the party.

Due to its position on a main sailing route the colony thrived, with an economy based on whaling, sealing and barter with passing ships. However, with the replacement of sail by steam in the late 19th century, a period of decline set in, with no regular calls by shipping.

In October 1961, a volcano, believed to have been extinct for thousands of years, erupted and the danger of further volcanic activity led to the evacuation of inhabitants to the United Kingdom. An advance party returned to Tristan da Cunha in the spring of 1963, and subsequently the main body of the islanders returned to the island.

GOVERNMENT

In 1938 Tristan da Cunha and the neighbouring islands of Inaccessible, Nightingale and Gough were made dependencies of St Helena and this remains their status today. They are administered by the Foreign and Commonwealth Office through a resident Administrator, with headquarters at the settlement of Edinburgh. Under a new constitution introduced in 1985, the Administrator is advised by an Island Council of eight elected members, of whom one must be a woman, and three appointed members. There is universal suffrage at 18.

*Administrator*, Philip Johnson, *apptd* 1992

ECONOMY

The main industries on the island are crayfish fishing, fish-processing and agriculture, with the shore-based fishing industry having been developed with the construction of the boat harbour in 1967 and the re-establishment of the crayfish-freezing factory in 1966. There are no taxes on Tristan, with income being derived from the fishing company, and the sales of stamps and handicrafts. Apart from the fishing industry, the other main employer is the Administration itself. There is one hospital, opened in 1971, and a school opened in 1975 catering for those up to age 15.

COMMUNICATIONS

The island is isolated and scheduled visits are restricted to about six calls a year by fishing vessels from Cape Town and an annual call of the RMS *St Helena* from the UK. A wireless station on the island is in daily contact with Cape Town and a radio-telephone service was established in 1969, the same year that electricity was introduced to all the islanders' homes. A satellite system providing direct dialling telephone and fax facilities was installed in November 1992.

## SOUTH GEORGIA AND THE SOUTH SANDWICH ISLANDS

South Georgia is an island 800 miles east-south-east of the Falkland group, with an area of 1,450 sq. miles. The population comprises an army unit and a civilian harbour master at King Edward Point, and staff of the British Antarctic Survey at Bird Island, in the north-west of South Georgia.

The South Sandwich Islands lie some 470 miles south-east of South Georgia. The group is a chain of uninhabited,

actively volcanic islands about 150 miles long, with a wholly Antarctic climate.

The present constitution came into effect on 3 October 1985. It provides for a Commissioner who, for the time being, shall be the officer administering the government of the Falkland Islands.

In May 1993 the UK government decreed an extension of Crown sovereignty and jurisdiction from 12 miles around South Georgia and the South Sandwich Islands to 200 miles around each in order to preserve marine stocks.

*Commissioner for South Georgia and the South Sandwich Islands*, David Everard Tatham, CMG, *apptd* 1992

## TURKS AND CAICOS ISLANDS

The Turks and Caicos Islands are situated between 21° and 22° N. latitude and 71° and 72° W. longitude, about 100 miles north of the Dominican Republic and 50 miles south-east of the Bahamas of which they are geographically an extension. There are over 30 islands, of which eight are inhabited, covering an estimated area of 166 sq. miles (430 sq. km). The principal island is Grand Turk.

The islands lie in the trade wind belt. The average temperature varies from 24°–27° C in the winter to 29°–32° C in the summer and humidity is generally low. Average rainfall is 21 inches per annum.

POPULATION – The population in 1990 was estimated to be 12,400 (Grand Turk 3,700).

FLAG – British Blue Ensign with the shield of arms in the fly.

## GOVERNMENT

A new constitution was introduced in 1988, and amended in 1993, which provides for an Executive Council and a Legislative Council. The Executive Council is presided over by the Governor and comprises the Chief Minister and five elected Ministers, together with the ex-officio Chief Secretary and Attorney-General.

At the general election of 3 April 1991, the People's National Party won eight seats and the People's Democratic Movement five seats in the Legislative Council.

*Governor*, His Excellency Martin Bourke, *apptd* 1993

EXECUTIVE COUNCIL *as at 15 June 1994*
*President*, The Governor
*Chief Secretary*, Hon. R. Cousins
*Attorney-General*, Hon. L. D. Ballantyre
*Chief Minister*, Hon. W. Misick
*Other Ministers*, Hon. A. Durham; Hon. A. Smith; Hon. R. Hall; Hon. M. Misick; Hon. Mrs E. Saunders

ECONOMY

| FINANCE | 1991–2 | 1992–3* |
|---|---|---|
| Local revenue | US$26,874,684 | US$25,839,825 |
| Expenditure | 26,019,039 | 28,563,752 |
| *estimate | | |

The most important industries are fishing, tourism and offshore finance.

| TRADE WITH UK | 1992 | 1993 |
|---|---|---|
| Imports from UK | £722,000 | £758,000 |
| Exports to UK | 1,127,000 | 528,000 |

# Events of the Year

## 1 September 1993 to 31 August 1994

### SEPTEMBER 1993

**6.** More than 700 inmates rioted at Wymott Prison, Lancs., destroying much of the prison. The TUC conference opened in Brighton. **10.** Violence broke out during an anti-racism demonstration outside the Royal London Hospital in east London, where an Asian youth who had been the victim of a racist attack was critically ill. **16.** The British National Party won its first local council seat in a by-election on the Isle of Dogs, east London. **19.** The Liberal Democrat Party annual conference opened in Torquay. **27.** The Labour Party annual conference opened in Brighton; on the 28th the conference approved a one-member-one-vote system of selecting prospective parliamentary candidates. **28.** The Labour MP George Foulkes resigned as a defence spokesman; he was later fined £1,000 for assaulting a policeman and £50 for being drunk and disorderly at Westminster in July 1993.

### OCTOBER 1993

**1.** Five people suffered minor injuries when three small IRA bombs exploded in Finchley Road, London. **4.** Four small IRA bombs exploded in Highgate and Hornsey, London. A British freelance cameraman was shot dead in fighting in Moscow (*see* page 1101). **5.** The Conservative Party conference opened in Blackpool. The *Daily Mirror* published leaked extracts from Lady Thatcher's memoirs which indicated that she had a low opinion of John Major; she later issued a statement supporting him as leader of the Conservative Party and as Prime Minister. **6.** At the Conservative Party conference the Home Secretary (Michael Howard) announced 27 new measures designed to combat rising crime, including the abolition of a suspect's right to silence; the Social Security Secretary (Peter Lilley) announced measures to tackle benefit fraud and welfare payments to foreigners. **8.** At the Conservative Party conference the Prime Minister launched a campaign to take Britain 'back to basics'. Small IRA bombs exploded at two locations in north London. Viscount Linley married the Hon. Serena Stanhope at St Margaret's Church, Westminster. **13.** Heavy rain caused flooding in many parts of England and Wales. **16.** About 75 people were injured when anti-racist demonstrators clashed with police near the headquarters of the British National Party in south London. **18.** The Queen arrived in Cyprus for a seven-day visit during which she presided over a meeting of the Commonwealth Heads of Government. **19.** The Armed Forces Minister (Jeremy Hanley) announced that the Women's Royal Naval Service would be integrated into the Navy from 1 November 1993. **20.** British Coal announced a review of all 30 mines still in production. In the annual Shadow Cabinet election, only three women were elected, in spite of a new rule requiring MPs to vote for at least four women; on 21 October John Smith reshuffled the Shadow Cabinet. **24.** A small IRA bomb exploded near Reading station, Berks. **25.** The president of Sinn Fein, Gerry Adams, was banned from entering Britain under the Prevention of Terrorism Act. A small IRA bomb exploded near Dorton, Bucks. **28.** The Home Secretary announced reforms in the structure, pay and conditions of the police; many of the recommendations of the Sheehy Report (*see* Whitaker's Almanack 1994) were rejected. **29.** A small IRA bomb exploded in Kensington, London. The House of Commons voted in favour of the ordination of women as priests; the House of Lords passed the legislation on 2 November. Queens Moat Houses announced a pre-tax loss of £1,040.5 million for 1992.

### NOVEMBER 1993

**4.** Kurdish separatists attacked five Turkish offices in London with petrol bombs; a woman was seriously injured. **5.** About 250,000 civil servants staged a one-day strike in protest at the Government's market testing and privatization policies. **7.** The *Sunday Mirror* published photographs taken by a hidden camera of the Princess of Wales exercising in a gymnasium in London. On 8 November the Princess instructed her solicitors to sue Mirror Group Newspapers. MGN withdrew from the Press Complaints Commission after the chairman (Lord McGregor of Durris) called on readers and advertisers to boycott the paper, but rejoined on 10 November. The Prince of Wales started a six-day official tour of Saudi Arabia, Kuwait, Abu Dhabi and Dubai. **9.** The Supreme Head of State of Malaysia arrived in Britain for a four-day state visit. **11.** Five-year-old Laura Davies, who had undergone two multiple organ transplants, died in Pittsburgh, USA. The Transport Secretary (John MacGregor) announced that the Channel Tunnel high-speed rail link would not open until 2002. **15.** The CBI annual conference opened in Harrogate. **17.** The annual rate of inflation fell to 1.4 per cent. **18.** The state opening of Parliament took place. Unemployment figures for October showed a fall of 49,000 to 2,855,100, the biggest monthly fall for more than four years. **21.** Seven-year-old Dean Parker was mauled to death by a dog in Middlesbrough. **22.** Six people died in road accidents caused by heavy snowfalls throughout Britain. **24.** More than 20,000 commuters had to be rescued from tunnels after a major power failure on the London Underground. **30.** The Chancellor of the Exchequer (Kenneth Clarke) presented his first Budget to the House of Commons (*see* pages 1160–2).

## DECEMBER 1993

**1.** The electronics group Ferranti called in receivers. **3.** The Princess of Wales announced that she would be reducing the extent of her public duties from the end of 1993. **8.** Baroness Thatcher told the Scott inquiry on the export of defence equipment to Iraq that she had not been told officially that export policy had been relaxed in 1988. President de Klerk was received in audience at Buckingham Palace, the first South African leader to meet The Queen since 1961. **8.** Sir Edward Heath arrived in Iraq to plead for the release of three Britons, Paul Ride, Michael Wainwright and Simon Dunn, who had been imprisoned for alleged illegal entry into the country; they were released on 9 December. **8–9.** At least 14 people died in accidents as hurricane-force winds hit many parts of Britain. **13.** Alan Clark, the former Trade and Defence Minister, said in evidence to the Scott inquiry that the relaxation of controls on the export of defence equipment to Iraq should have been announced in Parliament. **14.** A small IRA bomb exploded on the railway line between Woking and West Byfleet, Surrey. The Government suspended implementation of restrictions on the number of days British fishermen can spend at sea pending a decision of the European Court on whether the restrictions complied with EC law. **16.** Two small IRA bombs were found and detonated on the main London to Southampton railway line in Surrey. **20.** Six sick and injured children and a wounded man were flown to Britain from Bosnia for treatment. Four IRA incendiary devices exploded in London. **22.** The Prime Minister visited Northern Ireland. **25.** A Minister of State at the Department of the Environment, Tim Yeo, admitted that he was the father of an illegitimate baby born in July 1993 as a result of an extra-marital affair. A 59–year-old British woman gave birth to twins in London after being implanted with a test-tube embryo in Italy. **29.** The Archbishop of Canterbury (Dr George Carey) cancelled plans to visit Khartoum after the Sudanese Government said that he could do so only under its auspices; he flew to rebel-held southern Sudan as a guest of the Sudanese Anglican Church. On 30 December the British ambassador in Khartoum was expelled, and on 4 January 1994 the Sudanese ambassador in Britain was expelled. **30.** The New Year Honours list, including 70 people honoured as a result of being nominated by members of the public, was published. Torrential rain caused flooding in parts of southern and south-west England.

## JANUARY 1994

**5.** Tim Yeo resigned his ministerial post after officials in his local constituency party failed to support him; on 8 January he admitted that he had fathered an illegitimate daughter in 1967. The Education Secretary (John Patten) accepted all the proposals of a report by Sir Ron Dearing which recommended severe cuts in the structure of the national curriculum. **6.** The Prime Minister defended his 'back to basics' policy and said that it was not a crusade about personal morality. **7–12.** Rain and melting snow caused severe flooding in parts of southern and south-west England. **8.** Alan Duncan, MP, resigned as parliamentary private secretary to Brian Mawhinney, the Health Minister, over allegations that he had used a legal loophole to buy a cut-price council house. **9.** Lord Caithness resigned as a Minister of State at the Department of Transport after the suicide of his wife. **10–11.** The Prime Minister attended a NATO summit in Brussels called by President Clinton to discuss the possible future membership of the former Communist states of eastern Europe. **12.** Before giving evidence to the Scott inquiry, Lord Howe criticized the procedures being used to question witnesses. **13.** After a four-year investigation into Westminster City Council's 'designated sales' housing policy, the district auditor published a provisional report describing the policy as unlawful and unauthorized and accusing the council's former leaders of gerrymandering. On 27 January Dr Michael Dutt, one of the former councillors criticized in the report, committed suicide. **14.** The Duchess of Kent was received into the Roman Catholic Church. **15.** Downing Street denied allegations in two newspapers that the Prime Minister had made a disparaging comment about right-wing Cabinet ministers at a dinner. The Queen broke a bone in her left wrist in a riding accident at Sandringham. **16.** Four Romanian stowaways were found dead in a container on a ship in Felixstowe, Suffolk. **17.** In evidence to the Scott inquiry the Prime Minister said that he had not been involved in formulating policy on defence exports to Iraq and did not know the guidelines had been relaxed. **18.** The Labour MP George Galloway met President Hussein of Iraq in Baghdad; he later received a severe reprimand from the Opposition chief whip for being absent from the House of Commons without permission, and apologized for any offence he may have caused by appearing to praise the Iraqi president. **19.** The Ministry of Defence released files relating to the massacre of British prisoners of war by the German SS in Wormhoudt, northern France, in 1940. **23.** The Prince of Wales left London for a 12–day official visit to Australia and New Zealand. **24.** The Transport Secretary announced final plans for the high-speed rail link between London and the Channel Tunnel. **26.** A man firing a starting pistol ran on to a stage in Sydney, Australia, where the Prince of Wales was about to give a speech; the man was overpowered and arrested. **27.** The House of Commons public accounts committee published a report which said that recent civil service reforms had been accompanied by serious failures in financial and administrative control and accountability. IRA firebombs exploded in three shops in Oxford Street, London, causing extensive damage. **28.** Paul Goodall, a British aid worker, was shot dead by an armed gang in Bosnia. The former Chancellor Norman Lamont denied that he had called the Prime Minister 'weak and hopeless' in an interview with *The Times*. An IRA firebomb exploded in a shop in Oxford Street, London, causing minor damage. Lord Templeman, the chairman of the City Churches Commission, announced a plan to replace the 22 parishes in the City of London with four larger parishes, leaving 24 churches redundant. **31.** Rover, the last British-owned major car manufacturer, was sold to the German firm BMW for £800 million. Honda later announced that it would sell its 20 per cent stake in Rover.

FEBRUARY 1994

**4.** The Chief Secretary to the Treasury (Michael Portillo) apologized after attacking standards of public life and education in countries other than Britain in a speech to students at Southampton University. **5.** A half-naked man using a motorized parachute landed on the roof of Buckingham Palace. **6.** A man tried to spray the Prince of Wales with an aerosol can in Auckland, New Zealand. **7.** Stephen Milligan, the Conservative MP for Eastleigh, was found dead at his home in London; he had died from asphyxiation while engaging in a form of sexual gratification involving self-strangulation and the inhalation of stimulants. **9.** The Conservative MP Mark Robinson and the Labour MP Tony Worthington were kidnapped by gunmen in Somalia; they escaped on 10 February. Mr Worthington later resigned as an Opposition foreign affairs spokesman because he had gone on the trip without permission. The Labour MP Bryan Gould said that he would be resigning his seat and returning to his native New Zealand in September 1994. **11.** The report of the inquiry headed by Sir Cecil Clothier, QC, into the circumstances in which a nurse, Beverley Allitt, killed four children and injured a further nine at Grantham and Kesteven Hospital in 1991 was published. **12.** The Conservative MP Hartley Booth resigned as parliamentary private secretary to Douglas Hogg, the Foreign Office Minister, after admitting that he had had an affair with his former House of Commons research assistant. The Foreign Office advised all Britons in Serbia, Bosnia and Montenegro to leave. **15.** The Prime Minister and President Yeltsin held talks in Moscow. A woman climber was rescued after 41 hours in sub-zero temperatures in the Cairngorms. An earthquake registering 4.0 on the Richter scale hit Norfolk. **16.** British Steel was fined £28.8 million by the EC Commission for its part in a price-fixing cartel. Seven hundred police and 300 court officials ejected more than 300 people protesting against the

construction of the M11 link road from three barricaded houses in Wanstead, east London. **18.** The Queen and the Duke of Edinburgh left Britain for a three-week tour of eight nations in the West Indies and Central America. **19.** Seven shops in London were damaged by IRA firebombs. **21.** After a debate in the House of Commons MPs defeated a motion to lower the age of consent for homosexuals to 16 but agreed to lower it to 18; about ten gay rights protesters were arrested after angry scenes outside the House of Commons and in Whitehall. In evidence to the Scott inquiry, the Chancellor of the Exchequer (Kenneth Clarke) defended his decision when Home Secretary in 1992 to sign public interest immunity certificates to restrict evidence in the Matrix Churchill trial. **22.** The General Synod of the Church of England promulged the canon permitting the ordination of women as priests. **23.** Five retired or suffragan Church of England bishops and 570 clergy opposed to women priests signed a declaration accepting the full authority of the Roman Catholic Church. **24.** The report of an official inquiry into the murder of Jonathan Zito by Christopher Clunis, a paranoid schizophrenic, in December 1992 was published; it criticized medical staff, police and social workers, and recommended increased supervision of mental patients discharged from hospital and the provision of more psychiatric beds. The Health Secretary announced an extra £10 million for community mental health services in London. The Armed Forces Minister announced that the Women's Royal Air Force would be integrated into the RAF from 1 April 1994. **25.** Malaysia imposed a trade embargo on Britain in response to allegations in the British press of corruption among Malaysian politicians after £234 million of British aid to the Pergau dam project in the 1980s was linked to a £1 billion arms deal. The Foreign Secretary later admitted that the two deals had at one stage been 'incorrectly' linked by the then Defence Secretary, George Younger. **28.** In evidence to the Scott inquiry, the President of the Board of Trade (Michael Heseltine) said that he had been unwilling to sign a public interest immunity certificate for documents relevant to the Matrix Churchill trial, that he had only done so after being told by the Attorney-General (Sir Nicholas Lyell) that it was his ministerial duty, and that Sir Nicholas had broken a promise to him to pass on his reservations to the trial judge. The Prime Minister began two days of talks with President Clinton in the USA.

MARCH 1994

**1.** The Russian federal counter-espionage service said that a senior manager in the arms industry had admitted spying for Britain. A political counsellor at the British Embassy in Moscow was subsequently expelled from Russia, and on 1 April Britain expelled a diplomat from the Russian Embassy in London in retaliation. **2.** The Princess Royal started a four-day official visit to Vietnam. **8.** The Minister of Public Service and Science (William Waldegrave) said that in exceptional circumstances it was acceptable for a minister to lie to the House of Commons. **9.** MPs voted to renew the Prevention of Terrorism Act and to set up a select committee on Northern Ireland. Four IRA mortar bombs were fired at Heathrow Airport, London, from the car park of an airport hotel; two of the bombs landed on the north runway but none exploded. **10.** Britain agreed to send 905 more troops to Bosnia to monitor a new Muslim-Croat cease-fire. **11.** Four more IRA mortar bombs were fired at Heathrow Airport; they landed near Terminal Four but none exploded. **12.** Thirty-two women became the first female priests in the Church of England when they were ordained in a service at Bristol Cathedral. **13.** Four more IRA mortar bombs were fired at Heathrow Airport; one landed on the roof of Terminal Four but none exploded. Sir Peter Harding resigned as chief of the defence staff after newspaper reports of an extra-marital affair. **15.** A small IRA bomb was found on the railway line near Sevenoaks, Kent. **19.** A British soldier was killed when he stepped on a land-mine in Stari Vitez, Bosnia. **21.** The Minister for Public Service and Science launched the first National Science Week. **24.** Sir Nicholas Lyell, the Attorney-General, acknowledged in evidence to the Scott inquiry that he had not read the papers relating to the Matrix Churchill trial; he said that there were circumstances in which ministers were not obliged to sign public interest immunity certificates, but that this did not apply to the papers in question. **25.** Five British soldiers who had been missing for three weeks were found alive in Low's Gully on Mount Kinabalu, Borneo. **26.** After several weeks of arguing that the veto on decisions by the EC Council of Ministers should remain at 23 votes following the enlargement of the Community in 1995, the Foreign Secretary agreed to a solution which conceded the principle of an increase from 23 to 27. On 29 March the Cabinet approved the decision, but in the House of Commons the Conservative MP Tony Marlow called for the Prime Minister's resignation.

APRIL 1994

**6.** A resolution allowing the ordination of women as priests was passed by the House of Bishops and the House of Laity of the governing body of the Anglican Church in Wales, but failed to win the required two-thirds majority in the House of Clergy and was therefore defeated. **7.** A letter bomb exploded at the headquarters of the British National Party in London. **12.** The Labour MP Bob Cryer was killed in a car crash. **14.** The Labour MP Ann Clwyd began a sit-in underground at Tower Colliery, the last pit in south Wales, in an attempt to stop its closure; on 19 April miners voted to accept closure rather than lose redundancy payments. **15.** An SAS soldier was killed in Bosnia when Bosnian Serbs attacked Gorazde. **21.** The Cheltenham and Gloucester Building Society announced that it had agreed, subject to approval, to a take-over by Lloyds Bank. **23.** Sir Norman Fowler

announced that he would resign as chairman of the Conservative Party after the European elections in June 1994. **29.** A British soldier was killed when his vehicle hit an anti-tank mine in Bosnia.

MAY 1994

**2.** A Conservative MP, David Evans, called on the Prime Minister to sack at least six Cabinet ministers and the Conservative Party chairman. **5.** In local council elections in England, Wales and Scotland, the Conservatives lost control of 18 councils, Labour gained control of four and the Liberal Democrats gained control of nine; the British National Party lost its only council seat. The Rotherham by-election took place. **6.** The Queen and President Mitterrand opened the Channel Tunnel. **7.** The Conservative MP Michael Brown resigned as a junior government whip after the *News of the World* alleged that he had a homosexual relationship with a 20-year-old student. **9.** The Education Secretary published proposals for a new, shorter national curriculum. **10.** The Duke of Edinburgh and the Foreign Secretary attended the inauguration in Pretoria of Nelson Mandela as president of South Africa. The Social Security Minister, Nicholas Scott, apologized in the House of Commons for misleading the House about his department's involvement in drafting amendments used to talk out a disability rights bill on 6 May. A House of Commons committee voted to reject the proposed CrossRail underground link through London. **11.** The Secretary of State for National Heritage (Peter Brooke) announced plans for a family day in Hyde Park on 14 August to commemorate the 50th anniversary of D-Day, instead of a proposed 'dazzling entertainment' in the park in July which was abandoned because of criticism by D-Day veterans. On 10 June the event was cancelled altogether. **12.** The leader of the Labour Party, John Smith, died after suffering a heart attack at his home in London; proceedings in both Houses of Parliament and at the Scottish Conservative Party conference in Inverness were suspended as a mark of respect. The party's deputy leader, Margaret Beckett, took over as acting leader. An earthquake registering 3.1 on the Richter scale hit central England. **16.** The Prince of Wales left Britain for a four-day official visit to St Petersburg. **17.** President Mugabe of Zimbabwe arrived in Britain for a four-day state visit. Lloyd's of London announced a £2.05 billion loss for 1991. **25.** The contract to run the national lottery, due to start in November 1994, was awarded to the Camelot consortium. The government's Chief Medical Officer (Dr Kenneth Calman) said that there was no evidence of an increase in the incidence of the flesh-eating disease necrotizing fasciitis, in spite of a cluster of cases in Gloucestershire which had caused public anxiety. **26.** In the Atlantic a Trident ballistic missile was test-fired from a British submarine for the first time. Britain lifted the arms embargo imposed on Israel in 1982. **27.** The Prince of Wales took the salute for the last Queen's Birthday Parade in Berlin before the withdrawal of British troops from the city. The Prime Minister said that the presence of beggars on the streets was offensive and unjustified.

## JUNE 1994

**1.** Iran expelled a British diplomat from Teheran, alleging that he had links with terrorist groups; the Foreign Office disclosed that an Iranian diplomat in London had been expelled for distributing forged letters designed to discredit British policy in Bosnia. **4.** A memorial service to mark the 50th anniversary of D-Day was held at the American military cemetery at Madingley, Cambs.; the Prime Minister and President Clinton attended. The Queen attended a D-Day commemoration banquet for heads of state at Portsmouth Guildhall. **5.** A drumhead service of thanksgiving and remembrance led by the Archbishop of Canterbury to mark the 50th anniversary of D-Day was held on Southsea Common, Portsmouth; it was attended by The Queen, other members of the royal family and heads of state and government from allied countries. The Queen, on board *Britannia*, reviewed a fleet of allied ships in the Solent and there was a flypast of Second World War and modern aircraft. **6.** The Queen, the Duke of Edinburgh, the Prime Minister and President Mitterrand of France attended a commemorative service at the Bayeux war cemetery. The Queen and other heads of state attended a memorial service followed by a flypast and fleet salute at Omaha beach, Normandy. A parade of British D-Day veterans was held on the beach at Arromanches, Normandy, in front of The Queen and other members of the royal family. Two Britons, Kim Housego and David Mackie, were kidnapped by fundamentalist Islamic guerrillas in the Himalayas; they were released unharmed on 23 June. **8.** Alec Kellaway, the Liberal Democrat candidate in the Newham North East by-election on 9 June, said that he had rejoined the Labour Party. **9.** In the UK elections to the European Parliament Labour won 62 seats, the Conservatives 18, the Liberal Democrats two, and the Scottish National Party two. By-elections also took place in Eastleigh, Newham North East, Barking, Dagenham and Bradford South. **13.** Train services were disrupted after a small IRA bomb exploded outside Stevenage station, Herts. **15.** Signal staff in the Rail, Maritime and Transport Union (RMT) held the first of a series of 24–hour strikes over pay. **16.** The Episcopal Church in Scotland voted to permit the ordination of women as priests. **27.** A British soldier was shot dead by a Bosnian Serb sniper in Gorazde, Bosnia. **29.** A documentary about the Prince of Wales was shown on television to mark the 25th anniversary of his investiture. **30.** The Monklands East by-election took place. The Government published a consultative document on the future of the Post Office.

## JULY 1994

**1.** The Prince of Wales attended a garden party at Caernarfon Castle to mark the anniversary of his investiture. **5.** The King and Queen of Norway arrived in Britain for a four-day state visit. **8.** The Transport Secretary (John MacGregor) announced that the Government would proceed with plans for the proposed underground CrossRail link in London. **10.** Two Conservative MPs, David Tredinnick and Graham Riddick, were suspended as parliamentary private secretaries after the *Sunday Times* alleged that they had each accepted £1,000 to table a parliamentary question on behalf of a reporter posing as a businessman. **12.** Police seized a van containing two tons of IRA explosives at Heysham, Lancs.; it had arrived on a ferry from Warrenpoint, Northern Ireland. **14.** The Secretary of State for Defence (Malcolm Rifkind) announced more defence cuts under the *Front Line First* defence costs study (see page 392). **15.** Lady Sarah Armstrong-Jones married Daniel Chatto at the church of St Stephen Walbrook in London. **15.** The Conservative MP Tim Devlin said that he had resigned as parliamentary private secretary to the Attorney-General over defence cuts; the Whips' office said he had been sacked. **17.** The Australian Government said that two Britons and an Australian kidnapped in Cambodia in April 1994 had probably been murdered by the Khmer Rouge. **20.** A Cabinet reshuffle was announced. The House of Commons foreign affairs select committee published its report on the Pergau dam affair. **21.** Tony Blair was elected leader of the Labour Party and John Prescott was elected deputy leader. **22.** Three people including a Briton, Mark Slater, were kidnapped by the Khmer Rouge in Cambodia. **26.** The Ministry of Defence said that it had overspent by £800 million on the Trident nuclear missile programme. Signal staff in the RMT held the first of a series of 48–hour strikes. **27.** A British soldier was killed in an attack by Bosnian Serbs near Sarajevo. **30.** The *Guardian* published parts of a leaked letter sent in mid-July by the then Chief Secretary to the Treasury (Michael Portillo) to the President of the Board of Trade (Michael Heseltine) which criticized the level of spending at the Department of Trade and Industry.

## AUGUST 1994

**2–12.** More than 600 British soldiers arrived in Rwanda to help in the UN relief operation. **4.** A Gallup opinion poll gave Labour a record 33½ per cent lead over the Conservatives. **5.** The Royal Navy boarded a Cornish fishing boat, *Charisma*, involved in the 'tuna war' in the Bay of Biscay, and impounded its nets; they were later found to be slightly longer than the maximum permitted under EC regulations. **11.** The Employment Secretary (Michael Portillo) withdrew a scheme favouring the employment of disabled workers, saying he was required to do so by a new EC directive; EC officials said that this was not the directive's intention, and Opposition politicians criticized Mr Portillo for not arguing for the scheme's retention. **13.** A small IRA bomb exploded in Bognor Regis, W. Sussex; a second device was found in Brighton and destroyed in a controlled explosion.

The Queen and the Duke of Edinburgh arrived in Canada on a ten-day official tour. **16.** A British soldier was killed while clearing mines in Bosnia. **21.** The *News of the World* published allegations that the Princess of Wales had made nuisance phone calls to an art dealer; the Princess gave an interview to the *Daily Mail* in which she denied making the calls. **22.** An IRA bomb was found and defused in a litter bin in Regent Street, London.

## ACCIDENTS AND DISASTERS

### SEPTEMBER 1993

**6.** Six people were killed and six others injured in Sowerby Bridge, West Yorks., when a lorry crashed into a van, pushing it into a newsagent's shop and two houses. A goods train derailed at 2 a.m. and destroyed much of Maidstone East station, Kent; the driver was later charged with driving with excess alcohol in his blood. **12.** A woman onlooker was killed and four people were injured when a controlled explosion was used to demolish two blocks of flats in Glasgow. **22.** At least 44 people were killed when a train was derailed on a bridge and plunged into a swamp in Alabama, USA. **27.** A school bus driver was killed and 58 children injured in a collision with an articulated lorry near York. **30.** An estimated 22,000 people were killed and at least 130,000 left homeless when an earthquake registering between 6.0 and 6.4 on the Richter scale hit Maharashtra state, India.

### OCTOBER 1993

**4.** A minibus driver was killed and 19 people were injured when two buses collided near High Wycombe, Bucks. **26–4 November.** A British film director was killed and thousands of people were left homeless by bush fires in southern California.

### NOVEMBER 1993

**4.** All 296 passengers and crew survived when a China Airlines jumbo jet skidded into Hong Kong harbour when landing at Kai Tak airport in a storm. **10.** Nine American tourists and a British driver were killed and 36 people were injured when a coach crashed on the M2 near Faversham, Kent. **18.** Eleven schoolchildren and their teacher were killed when a minibus crashed into a motorway maintenance vehicle on the M40 in Warwickshire; two more children died later. **21.** A plane crashed in southern Macedonia, killing 115 people.

### JANUARY 1994

**3.** A Russian airliner crashed after take-off from Irkutsk, Siberia, killing 120 people. **3–10.** Bush fires in New South Wales, Australia, spread to the suburbs of Sydney, killing at least five people and destroying hundreds of homes. **17.** At least 44 people were killed and about 2,000 injured when an earthquake registering 6.6 on the Richter scale hit Los Angeles,

USA; in the following days the city was shaken by hundreds of after-shocks, including one on 20 March registering 5.3 on the Richter scale. **30.** Five British doctors and their French guide were killed by an avalanche while skiing near Tignes in the French Alps.

### FEBRUARY 1994

**3.** Twenty-seven people were drowned when the Greek-registered cargo ship *Christinaki* sank in the Atlantic 285 miles south-west of Land's End. **16.** At least 127 people were killed and 1,000 injured when an earthquake registering 6.5 on the Richter scale hit Indonesia. **23.** At least 110 people were killed when a disused dam burst and buried a gold mine housing complex in mud near Virginia, South Africa. **26.** A man's body was found on Ben Nevis; he was the fifteenth climber to die in the Scottish Highlands since the beginning of 1994.

### MARCH 1994

**8.** At least 63 people were killed and 370 injured when a commuter train was derailed east of Durban, South Africa. **14.** At least 15 people were killed and 29 injured after a collision between an oil tanker and a freighter in the Bosporus near Istanbul. **17.** Thirty-two people were killed when a Hercules transport plane crashed in Nagorno Karabakh, Azerbaijan. **23.** All 75 people aboard a Russian airbus were killed when it crashed in the Altai mountains, Siberia; the subsequent investigation revealed that the pilot's teenage son had been at the controls when the plane crashed. Twenty-three people were killed and about 60 injured when a US air force fighter plane and a transport plane collided in mid-air and crashed on to Pope air force base in North Carolina, USA. **24.** Six British tourists, including four members of the same family, and a Romanian pilot were killed when their helicopter crashed during a sightseeing flight near Brasov, Romania. A gas explosion killed up to 41 people and left hundreds homeless in New Jersey, USA. **27.** At least 42 people were killed when tornadoes hit the south-eastern states of the USA.

### APRIL 1994

**1.** A nine-year-old boy was killed when a steel gantry fell on to a water-chute ride at a funfair at Porthcawl, south Wales. **4.** Three people were killed when a KLM plane en route from Amsterdam to Cardiff crash-landed at Schiphol Airport, Amsterdam. **26.** A China Airlines airbus crashed and exploded on landing at Nagoya airport, Japan, killing 261 people.

### MAY 1994

**3.** At least 100 people were killed when a cyclone hit the south-east coast of Bangladesh. **5.** A woman and a baby girl were killed in a fire in a hostel in Scarborough, North Yorks., which was in breach of fire regulations. **15.** Two Cub Scouts and their Scout leader were killed and three other children were seriously injured when their minibus collided with a coach near Hopperton, North Yorks. **23.** At least 250 Muslim pilgrims were crushed to death during a ceremony near Mecca, Saudi Arabia.

## JUNE 1994

**2.** Nineteen senior intelligence and security officers from the army and the RUC, six civil servants from the Northern Ireland Office and four crew members were killed when a Chinook helicopter taking them from Belfast to Inverness crashed in thick fog on the Mull of Kintyre, western Scotland. **3.** Tidal waves triggered by an earthquake registering 5.9 on the Richter scale killed at least 128 people in East Java. **6.** One hundred and sixty people were killed when a Chinese airliner crashed after take-off from Xian, China. **7.** At least 1,000 people were killed and thousands left homeless by an avalanche caused by an earthquake registering 6.4 on the Richter scale in south-west Colombia. **8–22.** At least 700 people were killed and 14,000 injured in flooding caused by heavy rain in southern and eastern China.

## JULY 1994

**2.** Thirty-seven people were killed when an aircraft crashed in North Carolina, USA. **5–13.** At least 28 people died in severe flooding caused by a tropical storm in Georgia, Alabama and northern Florida, USA. **6.** At least 13 firefighters were killed by bush fires in Colorado, USA. **14–20.** Over 580 people were killed in monsoon floods in India. **24.** Twenty-six people were injured when lightning struck an oil refinery near Pembroke, Dyfed, causing a series of explosions and a large fire.

## AUGUST 1994

**1.** A fire destroyed books and archives at Norwich Central Library. **5.** A 14–year-old boy was killed when he fell from a big wheel at a funfair in Manningtree, Essex. At least 45 people were killed when a transport plane carrying military officers crashed in eastern Siberia. **10.** All 160 passengers and crew survived when a Korean Airlines jet crash-landed at Cheju airport, South Korea. **13.** At least 57 people were injured when an InterCity train collided with a runaway diesel engine in Edinburgh. **18.** At least 164 people were killed in an earthquake in north-west Algeria. **21.** Over 300 people were feared drowned when a river ferry sank near Chandpur, Bangladesh. All 44 people on board a Royal Air Maroc plane were killed when the pilot committed suicide by crashing it into a mountain near Agadir, Morocco. **23.** At least 700 people were killed when a typhoon hit Zhejiang province, China. **25.** More than 100 passengers and crew were rescued from the *Sally Star* Channel ferry about eight miles off Ramsgate after fire broke out in its engine room.

## ARTS, SCIENCE AND MEDIA

### SEPTEMBER 1993

**1.** The new British Sky Broadcasting multi-channel satellite television service was launched. **3.** The Radio Authority announced the allocation of local radio licences in London from October 1994; LBC lost its licence to London News Radio. **19.** The playwright Alan Ayckbourn was presented with a Lifetime Achievement Award by the Writers' Guild. **20.** Salman Rushdie's 1981 novel *Midnight's Children* was named the best of the books to have won the Booker Prize since its inception in 1969.

### OCTOBER 1993

**5.** A papal encyclical on morality, *Veritatis Splendor*, was published. **10.** *Vita and Virginia* opened in London, the first West End play to open on a Sunday. **11.** William Nygaard, the Norwegian publisher of *The Satanic Verses*, was shot and seriously wounded in Oslo. **19.** At the British Fashion Awards John Rocha was named Designer of the Year. **20.** In the European Court of Justice the rock singer Phil Collins won the right to seek an injunction in Germany banning further sales of a pirated recording of one of his concerts.

### NOVEMBER 1993

**1.** National Library Week began. **8.** Five paintings and a sculpture by Picasso were stolen from the Modern Museum, Stockholm. **9.** The actors' union Equity voted to lift its ban on the sale of British television and radio programmes involving Equity members to South Africa. **13.** The pop star Michael Jackson, who had been accused of sexual abuse by a child in the USA, cut short his world tour to seek treatment for an addiction to painkillers. **23.** Rachel Whiteread was awarded the Turner prize for contemporary art for a series of works in concrete including the internal cast of a house in the East End of London. The house was demolished on 11 January 1994. Ms Whiteread was also awarded the K Foundation award for the worst body of art produced in the year. Five British television programmes won International Emmy awards in New York; Richard Dunn, the chief executive of Thames Television, was awarded the International Emmy Founders' Award. **24.** The National Heritage Secretary (Peter Brooke) announced a relaxation in the rules on ownership of ITV companies. President Clinton met Salman Rushdie at the White House, Washington DC. **29.** Carlton Communications made an agreed bid of £758 million for Central TV.

### DECEMBER 1993

**1.** The English Shakespeare Company announced that it would abandon its touring activities and concentrate on education work because of funding cuts. **2.** The space shuttle *Endeavour* blasted off from Cape Canaveral on a mission to repair the Hubble space telescope. **5.** The Arts Council's music advisory panel recommended that funding to the London Philharmonic Orchestra and the Royal Philharmonic Orchestra should be phased out over three years rather than withdrawn immediately. **9.** A Greek vase from the late sixth century BC was sold for more than £2.2 million at Sotheby's. **15.** The Arts Council announced that it would continue to fund all four London orchestras in 1994–5. The Council's music director, Kenneth Baird, resigned. **21.** The daughter of the sculptor Henry Moore lost a High Court action against the trustees of the Henry Moore Foundation in which she had claimed ownership of his later works.

JANUARY 1994

**6.** Thirty-five artists, critics and art historians signed a letter to the London *Evening Standard* calling for the resignation of the paper's art critic, Brian Sewell, because of his hostility to modern art; Mr Sewell was later named arts journalist of the year in the British Press Awards. **7.** The chairman of the Arts Council's music panel, Bryan Magee, resigned. **10.** The *Eagle* comic ceased publication.

FEBRUARY 1994

**2.** The Health and Safety Executive issued a prohibition order on research work involving genetically engineered viruses at the Department of Cancer Studies at Birmingham University, which had been closed in December 1993 because of inadequate safety standards. **7.** The High Court granted an injunction sought by the Attorney-General to stop the opening of a West End musical based on the life of Robert Maxwell on the grounds that it might prejudice the future trial of Robert Maxwell's sons. **16.** Patty and Michael Hopkins won the 1994 RIBA Gold Medal for Architecture. **25.** Granada took over London Weekend Television with a £765 million hostile bid; on 9 March Greg Dyke resigned as chief executive of LWT. **28.** Matthew Epstein resigned as general director of Welsh National Opera, criticizing the Government for causing the under-funding of the company.

MARCH 1994

**15.** The Prince of Wales launched *Perspectives on Architecture*, a magazine published by his Institute of Architecture. **18.** A consortium led by Mirror Group Newspapers took control of the *Independent* and the *Independent on Sunday* newspapers. **28.** BBC Radio Five Live went on the air. **30.** The London radio station LBC went into receivership.

APRIL 1994

**8.** Kurt Cobain, the lead singer of the rock band Nirvana, was found dead at his home in Seattle, USA. **10.** Natalie Clein won the BBC Young Musician of the Year competition. **14.** Sir John Gielgud celebrated his 90th birthday. On 17 April it was announced that the Globe Theatre, Shaftesbury Avenue, would be renamed the Gielgud Theatre in his honour. An Iron Age sword was stolen from Peterborough Museum. An organized group of hecklers hostile to contemporary music booed at the end of a performance of Sir Harrison Birtwistle's opera *Gawain* at the Royal Opera House. **20.** Barbra Streisand gave her first concert in Britain for 28 years at Wembley Arena, London. **22.** The Labour Party accused the BBC of succumbing to political pressure after the Corporation postponed the broadcast of a *Panorama* programme alleging corruption in Westminster City Council. **26.** The British Library bought the sole surviving complete copy of William Tyndale's 1526 translation of the New Testament from the Bristol Baptist College for £1 million. **28.** The Tate Gallery announced plans for a Gallery of Modern Art at the former Bankside power station.

MAY 1994

**9.** The Secretary of State for Scotland (Ian Lang) rejected a proposal by the trustees of the National Galleries of Scotland to establish a National Gallery of Scottish Art in Glasgow. **10.** Prince Edward complained to the Press Complaints Commission about an alleged intrusion into his privacy over photographs taken of him with his girlfriend, Sophie Rhys Jones, at Balmoral, which were published by tabloid newspapers. **24.** Journalists and production staff at the BBC staged a 24-hour strike in protest at proposals affecting their pay and working conditions; another 24-hour strike was held on 9 June. **26.** The Home Secretary (Michael Howard) announced plans to require the British Board of Film Classification to take into account the harm a video might cause to children before awarding a certificate. A volume of music by Purcell fetched £276,500 at Sotheby's. **27.** Alexander Solzhenitsyn returned to Russia after 20 years in exile in the USA. **28.** The new opera house at Glyndebourne opened.

JUNE 1994

**2.** Talk Radio UK was awarded the franchise to run Britain's third national independent radio station. **22.** The *Daily Telegraph* cut its cover price to 30p. **24.** *The Times* cut its cover price to 20p. Stephen Hyatt left Addenbrooke's Hospital, Cambridge, three months after a pioneering six-organ transplant operation.

JULY 1994

**6.** A 3,000-year-old Assyrian bas-relief found at a school in Dorset was sold for £7.7 million at Christie's. **9.** Mark Tully, the BBC's South Asia correspondent, resigned after being told by the Corporation not to criticize it in public. **17–22.** Parts of the comet Shoemaker-Levy 9 collided with Jupiter. **18.** A 62-year-old Italian woman gave birth in Rome by Caesarian section after *in vitro* fertilization. **29.** Two Turner paintings were stolen from the Schirn Kunsthalle in Frankfurt, Germany, while on loan from the Tate Gallery. **31.** The *Independent* newspaper cut its cover price to 30p.

## AUGUST 1994

**1.** Elvis Presley's daughter Lisa Marie confirmed that she had married the pop star Michael Jackson in May 1994. **17.** The Director of the National Galleries of Scotland, Timothy Clifford, apologized to John Paul Getty II for saying in an interview that Mr Getty's donation of £1 million to the appeal to keep Canova's statue *The Three Graces* in the UK was motivated by a grudge against his late father; Mr Getty later withdrew his threat to rescind the donation. **18.** The *Endeavour* space shuttle launch was aborted at the last second at Cape Canaveral after a high-pressure fuel pump overheated. **26.** A 62–year-old man was given a permanent artificial heart in a pioneering operation at Papworth Hospital, Cambs.

## CRIMES AND LEGAL AFFAIRS

## SEPTEMBER 1993

**24.** Mark Lee and Ricky Lee were sentenced at the Central Criminal Court to life imprisonment for murdering an Asian minicab driver and dumping his body in the Thames in east London in February 1993. **25.** A Briton, Andrew McGarrity, was sentenced to 52 years' imprisonment in Thailand for drug trafficking. **28.** Syed Ziaudinn Ali Akbar, a senior official of the collapsed Bank of Credit and Commerce International (BCCI), was sentenced at the Central Criminal Court to six years' imprisonment after pleading guilty to 16 charges of false accounting involving more than £500 million.

## OCTOBER 1993

**5.** Two members of the INLA, Eamonn O'Donnell and Sean Cruickshank, were sentenced at Newcastle Crown Court to 20 years' and 15 years' imprisonment respectively for planting nine incendiary devices in shops in Leeds in June 1992. **7.** The case against three retired detectives accused of tampering with evidence in the prosecution of the Birmingham Six in 1975 collapsed at the Central Criminal Court when Mr Justice Garland ruled that a fair trial would not be possible. A 17–year-old joyrider, Carl Sherwood, who hit and killed a 13–year-old girl with the car he had stolen in January 1993, was sentenced at Stafford Crown Court to seven years' detention after admitting manslaughter. Leslie Bailey, who was serving a life sentence for the murder and rape of three boys, was found strangled in his cell at Whitemoor prison, Cambs. **12.** Lord Justice Woolf described the Government's plans to imprison more offenders and impose longer sentences as 'short-sighted and irresponsible'. **13.** Paul Dandy accepted record compensation of £70,000 from West Midlands police for wrongful arrest and malicious prosecution for armed robbery in 1987; the case led to the disbanding of the West Midlands serious crime squad. Gunther Parche, who stabbed the tennis star Monica Seles in the back at a tournament in Hamburg in April 1993, received a two-year suspended jail sentence. **15.** An armed bank robber was shot dead by police in Holloway, north London. **19.** Austen Donnellan, a former London University student, was acquitted at the Central Criminal Court of raping a fellow student in December 1992. Patrick Kelly, an Irish lorry driver arrested in London in November 1992 when a 3.2–ton bomb was found in his lorry, was sentenced at the Central Criminal Court to 25 years' imprisonment for attempted murder and conspiracy to cause an explosion. **20.** A policeman was shot dead in Clapham, south London, while investigating a shooting incident in which another man had been killed. **28.** Two High Court judges rejected a claim by the Church Society that the General Synod of the Church of England had exceeded its powers in voting for the ordination of women as priests.

## NOVEMBER 1993

**4.** A woman and her four-year-old daughter were found murdered at their home in Plumstead, London. The rock star Elton John was awarded £350,000 damages in the High Court over an article published by the *Sunday Mirror* in December 1992 which said that he suffered from an eating disorder. **18.** The Home Secretary obtained a court order preventing members of the Prison Officers' Association from taking strike action. The former Pakistan bowler Sarfraz Nawaz withdrew a libel action against England cricketer Allan Lamb, who had accused him of ball-tampering, at the High Court in London. Michael Smith was sentenced at the Central Criminal Court to 25 years' imprisonment for passing military secrets from the Hirst Research Centre to the Russians between 1990 and 1992. **19.** Sandra Wignall and her two accomplices were sentenced at the Central Criminal Court to life imprisonment for the murder of her husband in September 1992. **21.** George Heron was cleared at Leeds Crown Court of murdering seven-year-old Nikki Allan in Sunderland in October 1992; the judge had ruled that his taped confession was not admissible as evidence because of the nature of the police questioning. **22.** Two Department of Transport vehicle inspectors were shot dead at a garage in Stockport. **24.** Two 11–year-old boys, Robert Thompson and Jon Venables, were convicted at Preston Crown Court of the murder of two-year-old James Bulger in Liverpool in February 1993; they were ordered to be detained at Her Majesty's pleasure. **25.** Police sergeant Stephen Jones was sentenced at Caernarvon Crown Court to life imprisonment for the murder of his wife Madallin in January 1993. **26.** Roger Levitt, whose financial services group collapsed in 1990 with debts of £34 million, was sentenced at Southwark Crown Court to 180 hours' community service after admitting fraudulent trading with intent to defraud his creditors. **30.** Fifteen-year-old Peter Lomas, who admitted starting a fire at Littlewoods in Chesterfield in May 1993 in which two people died, was ordered at Nottingham Crown Court to be detained at Her Majesty's pleasure.

## DECEMBER 1993

**8.** A committee headed by the Lord Chancellor (Lord Mackay of Clashfern) decided that solicitors should have audience rights in the higher courts from spring 1994. **10–11.** A man held ten people hostage at gunpoint in a dental surgery in Hay-on-Wye, Powys; the siege ended when four of the hostages overpowered the gunman after he fell asleep. **13.** An 18-year-old joyrider, Robert Hoe, was sentenced at Teesside Crown Court to four years in a young offenders' institution for causing the deaths of two children in Middlesbrough in April 1993. **16.** Two INLA members, Martin McMonagle and Liam Heffernan, were sentenced at the Central Criminal Court to 25 years' and 23 years' imprisonment respectively for conspiracy to cause explosions. **17.** Jean Powell, Glyn Powell and Bernadette McNeilly were sentenced at Manchester Crown Court to life imprisonment for the torture and murder of 16-year-old Suzanne Capper in December 1992; 17-year-old Anthony Dudson was ordered to be detained at Her Majesty's pleasure and two others were sentenced to 15 years' and 12 years' imprisonment respectively. **20.** Colin Ireland was sentenced at the Central Criminal Court to life imprisonment for murdering five homosexual men in London between March and June 1993.

## JANUARY 1994

**6.** Peter Malkin, who kidnapped his son Oliver, a ward of court, in November 1993 for the third time in three years, returned to Britain from Egypt; his son was reunited with his mother in Brittany. On 7 January Mr Malkin was sentenced to 18 months' imprisonment for contempt of court. **14.** The Prime Minister discontinued his libel action against the magazine *Scallywag* over allegations of a relationship with the caterer Clare Latimer after the magazine undertook not to repeat the allegations. **21.** Lorena Bobbitt was cleared in Virginia, USA, of maliciously wounding her husband when she cut off his penis in June 1993 after he had allegedly raped her; the jury accepted her plea of temporary insanity. **25.** The *Eastenders* actress Gillian Taylforth lost a High Court libel action brought against the *Sun* newspaper for alleging that she and her fiancé had oral sex in their car on a motorway slip road in June 1992. The pop star Michael Jackson reached an out-of-court settlement with a 14-year-old boy who had accused him of sexual abuse; the singer said that the settlement did not constitute an admission of guilt. Derek Fleming was sentenced at Leeds Crown Court to life imprisonment for the murder of his 23-year-old daughter Linda in January 1993. **26.** A factory executive, Terence Maidens, was shot dead at his home in Nuneaton, Warks., by a man wearing a crash helmet. **28.** Grant Price, who went missing from a car park in Gosport, Hants., on 22 January, was found stabbed to death on a beach at Lymington.

## FEBRUARY 1994

**9.** Police sergeant Derek Robertson was stabbed to death during a robbery at a sub-post office in Croydon. **10.** Pairic MacFhloinn, Denis Kinsella and John Kinsella were sentenced at the Central Criminal Court to 35 years', 25 years' and 20 years' imprisonment respectively for bombing a gasworks in Warrington in February 1993. **12.** The Munch painting *The Scream* was stolen from the National Art Museum, Oslo; it was found undamaged on 7 May. **17.** Paul Weddle was sentenced at Teesside Crown Court to life imprisonment and Philip English was ordered to be detained at Her Majesty's pleasure after being convicted of murdering police sergeant Bill Forth in March 1993. **24.** A thief broke into the Prince of Wales's private apartment at St James's Palace, London. **26.** Eleven men were killed and 13 seriously injured when an arsonist set fire to a private cinema club showing sex films in London; a man was later charged with the murders. **26 February–9 March.** The remains of 16-year-old Heather West, who went missing in 1987, and two other young women were found buried in the garden of 25 Cromwell Street, Gloucester. The remains of six more young women were found under the cellar and bathroom of the house. Frederick and Rosemary West, Heather West's parents, were subsequently charged with the murders.

## MARCH 1994

**6.** An 85-year-old woman was stabbed to death near Wimborne Minster, Dorset; a 13-year-old boy was later charged with her murder. **9.** Two policemen were shot when they stopped a motorcyclist in Brixton, south London. **14.** Christine Leung, who was paralysed in a car accident in 1989, was awarded record damages of £3.4 million in the High Court. **17.** Stephen Doyle was sentenced at Preston Crown Court to 15 years' imprisonment for the attempted murder of WPC Leslie Harrison in December 1992. Ten young men were sentenced at Newcastle upon Tyne Crown Court to a total of 58 years' imprisonment for throwing bricks at a police car and severely injuring PC John Robinson in February 1993. **21.** Susan Whybrow and Dennis Saunders, who were convicted in March 1991 of conspiring to murder Mrs Whybrow's husband, were cleared in a retrial at the Central Criminal Court. **22.** Duncan Gray, a former employee of the Royal Household, was charged with stealing a painting and other items from Buckingham Palace. **23.** Stephen Young was sentenced at Hove Crown Court to life imprisonment for the murders of Harry and Nicola Fuller in Wadhurst, East Sussex in February 1993. Wallace Smith was sentenced at the Central Criminal Court to six years' imprisonment for a £100 million banking fraud. **28.** Twelve-year-old Nicola Conroy was stabbed to death and two other pupils were injured when an armed man broke into a classroom in Hall Garth School, Middlesbrough; the man was overpowered by two teachers and arrested. **29.** Two High Court judges ruled that the presumption that a child aged between ten and 14 cannot commit a criminal act unless it can be proved that the child knew the act to be seriously wrong was outdated and nonsensical.

## APRIL 1994

**7.** The first televised trial in Britain was broadcast by BBC Scotland. **10.** The remains of Frederick West's first wife Catherine were found buried in a field in Kempley, Glos.; he was charged with her murder. **12.** An elderly couple were murdered in their home in Hounslow, London; two teenage girls were then taken to the couple's flat and sexually assaulted. A man was later arrested and charged with the crimes. **13.** Sarah Alesworth was found battered to death at her home in Aylesbury, Bucks.; on 14 April her father, a doctor, was arrested in France. In the High Court two Lloyd's Names who sustained large losses in the insurance market won compensation of at least £1 million against their former agents. **17.** Arsonists caused damage estimated at £1 million to schools and other buildings in Stockport. **20.** Heirlooms were stolen from Abbotsford in the Scottish Borders, the former home of Sir Walter Scott. **21.** The conviction of Paul Hill, one of the Guildford Four, for the murder of a former British soldier in Belfast in 1974 was quashed at the Court of Appeal in Belfast. West Midlands police said that insufficient evidence had been found to support further criminal proceedings relating to the Birmingham pub bombings by the IRA in 1974. **28.** Aldrich Ames, the former head of the Soviet branch of CIA counter-intelligence, was sentenced in Washington DC to life imprisonment for selling secrets to the Soviet Union for £1.6 million.

## MAY 1994

**1.** Karen Reed was shot dead at her home in Woking, Surrey; she had been mistaken for her sister, the wife of an Armenian political killer. **3.** Mark Cleary, who was sentenced to life imprisonment in 1986 for the murder of ten-year-old Wayne Keeton, was cleared by the Court of Appeal. **5.** The remains of Frederick West's eight-year-old daughter Charmaine, who went missing in 1972, were found under a floor at his former home in Midland Road, Gloucester; he was charged with her murder. **7.** A Roman Catholic priest was found shot dead in Co. Clare, Ireland; on 8 May a woman and her three-year-old son were found shot dead nearby. **13.** Two Englishmen, Patrick Hayes and Jan Taylor, were each sentenced at the Central Criminal Court to 30 years' imprisonment for IRA bomb attacks in Britain. Eddie Browning, who was sentenced to life imprisonment in 1989 for the murder of Marie Wilks on the M50 in 1988, was released after the Court of Appeal quashed his conviction. Jewellery and other items worth £150,000 were stolen from Floors Castle in the Scottish Borders. **14.** Jewellery, ornaments and a collection of Fabergé eggs were stolen from Luton Hoo, Beds. **18.** The American fashion designer Ralph Lauren was fined £250,000 in a commercial court in Paris for copying

a dress design by the French couturier Yves Saint Laurent. **19.** Robert Black was sentenced at Newcastle Crown Court to ten terms of life imprisonment for the abduction and murder of three young girls between 1982 and 1986. **20.** David Bond was sentenced at Nottingham Crown Court to life imprisonment for the murder of Deborah Buxton in April 1993. **23.** Colin James was sentenced at Reading Crown Court to life imprisonment for the murder of his business partner David Martin in December 1992. **25.** Antiques and heirlooms were stolen from Scone Palace, Perthshire. **26.** Gordon Foxley, a former Ministry of Defence official, was sentenced to four years' imprisonment for accepting bribes worth £1.3 million from overseas companies between 1979 and 1984; he was also ordered to pay £1.5 million under a confiscation order. **27.** Sam Kulasingham and Prem Sivalingham, who were convicted in 1988 of murdering three people in a firebomb attack in London in 1986, were released after the Court of Appeal quashed their convictions. In the High Court the BBC was ordered to pay libel damages of £60,000 and costs estimated at £1.5 million to the American drugs company Upjohn over allegations in a *Panorama* programme in October 1991 that the firm had deliberately concealed adverse side-effects of its sleeping pill Halcion.

## JUNE 1994

**2.** The Ministry of Defence confirmed that Josephine Green, a former Royal Navy nurse who was sacked when she became pregnant by a Roman Catholic priest in 1984, had been awarded compensation of more than £350,000 at an industrial tribunal in Exeter; this was the highest sum awarded in a series of pregnancy dismissal compensation claims against the MOD. The report of an inquiry commissioned by the Government in 1991 into sexual abuse allegations was published; it found no evidence to substantiate the existence of satanic sexual abuse. **2.** Silver worth thousands of pounds was stolen from the Bowes Museum, Co. Durham. **6.** A British businessman, Jeremy Lowndes, was sentenced by a court in Spain to nine years' imprisonment for the murder of his wife Carmel at their Spanish villa in July 1992. **8.** The European Court of Justice ruled that the British Government had failed to provide adequate protection for employees when privatizing and contracting-out public services. The remains of a young pregnant woman were found in Fingerpost field, Kempley, Glos.; Frederick West was charged with the murder. **9.** Three suspected IRA members, Paul Hughes, Donna Maguire and Sean Hick, were acquitted at a court in Dusseldorf of the murder of Maj. Michael Dillon-Lee in 1990. **12.** Five members of a paedophile ring were convicted at Swansea Crown Court; they were later sentenced to between five and 15 years' imprisonment each. **17.** Three pupils were seriously injured when a man using a fire extinguisher as a flame thrower attacked a class sitting exams at Sullivan Upper Grammar School in Holywood,

Northern Ireland. **18.** The actor and former American football player O. J. Simpson was arrested in California, USA, after a police car chase which was shown live on television; he was charged with the murder of his former wife and a male friend of hers. **21.** The pop star George Michael lost a High Court action against his record company, Sony, in which he claimed that his lack of control over the way his work was exploited amounted to an unreasonable restraint of trade. **22.** Eight British tourists were injured in a series of bomb attacks on the Mediterranean coast of Turkey; one of them died on 26 June. The Crown Prosecution Service said that insufficient evidence had been found to support further criminal proceedings relating to the murder of PC Keith Blakelock in 1985. **24.** A 13–year-old boy was cleared at a youth court in the Isle of Wight of raping a 12–year-old girl. **25.** Two people were killed when a train was derailed by a concrete slab placed on the line in Greenock, Ayrshire. **30.** The report of the four-year inquiry headed by Sir John May into the case of the Guildford Four was published; it said the acquittals were justified but that no individuals could be held responsible for the miscarriage of justice.

JULY 1994

**1.** A four-hour-old baby, Abbie Humphries, was abducted from the maternity ward at Queen's Medical Centre, Nottingham, by a woman posing as a nurse. On 16 July the baby was found unharmed at a house in Nottingham; a woman was charged with the abduction. **3.** The body of three-year-old Rosie Palmer, who went missing on 30 June, was found in a house near her home in Hartlepool, Cleveland; a man was later charged with her murder. **4.** Brian Vale was convicted at the Central Criminal Court of the manslaughter of Dr Ann Mead; he was later sentenced to life imprisonment. The Department of Trade and Industry confirmed that Lord Archer was the subject of an official inquiry into alleged insider dealing; on 28 July the Department said that no further action would be taken against him. A High Court jury awarded Mr and Mrs John Walker and their yachting company £1.485 million in libel damages against the magazine *Yachting World* and IPC Magazines over an article critical of their revolutionary trimaran *Blue Nova*. **14.** The European Court of Justice ruled that Carole Webb, who was sacked in 1987 when she became pregnant two weeks after being recruited to cover for an employee on maternity leave, had been the victim of unlawful sex discrimination. The Director of Public Prosecutions announced that no British soldiers would be charged in connection with allegations of war crimes committed during the Falklands War in 1982. Glen Ashby, who had been convicted of murder, was hanged in Trinidad before his final appeal against the sentence had been heard and in defiance of the Judicial Committee of the Privy Council. **21.** A bag stolen from a train in Reading, Berks., was found to contain more than 15 lb of high explosives apparently

intended to be used in an IRA attack in Britain. **26.** Fourteen people were injured when a car bomb exploded outside the Israeli embassy in London. Two detectives in the Metropolitan Police were cleared at the Central Criminal Court of fabricating evidence against Winston Silcott, who was convicted and then cleared of murdering PC Keith Blakelock in 1985. **28.** Derek Treadaway, who served nine years in prison after being convicted of armed robbery in 1982, was awarded £50,000 damages in the High Court.

AUGUST 1994

**2.** A man killed himself after shooting and wounding a policeman and taking a man hostage after an armed robbery at a jeweller's in London. **8.** Roderick Newall was sentenced in Jersey to life imprisonment for the murder of his parents in October 1987; his brother Mark was sentenced to six years' imprisonment for helping to dispose of the bodies. **13.** Fifteen-year-old Richard Everitt was stabbed to death in Somers Town, London. **14.** Illich Ramirez Sanchez, known as Carlos the Jackal, who was wanted in connection with 83 terrorist murders since 1972, was arrested in Sudan and extradited to France. **18.** A verdict of suicide was recorded on the death of Alan Conner, who hanged himself on 9 August, leaving a note admitting the rape and murder of Sandra Parkinson in Devon on 19 July. Three men were charged in Kaliningrad, Russia, with attempting to sell radioactive material. **22.** An Englishman, Sean McNulty, was sentenced at the Central Criminal Court to 25 years' imprisonment for conspiring to plant the IRA bombs which exploded on Tyneside in June 1993. **24.** Four firebombs planted by animal rights activists exploded in shops on the Isle of Wight.

---

# ENVIRONMENT

---

SEPTEMBER 1993

**26.** Eight people left a 'biosphere' (a sealed, artificial ecosystem) in the Arizona desert in which they had lived for two years.

OCTOBER 1993

**5.** China broke the world-wide nuclear testing moratorium and carried out an underground test in north-west China. **8.** In a High Court test case, British Nuclear Fuels was cleared of causing cancer in two children whose fathers worked at the Sellafield nuclear reprocessing plant in Cumbria. **17.** The Department of the Environment published *The Countryside Survey 1990*, which showed a widespread loss of hedges and wild flowers in Britain since 1984. **20.** A Health and Safety Executive report was published which showed that children whose fathers worked at Sellafield and who lived in Seascale ran a risk 14 times the national average of developing leukaemia and non-Hodgkin's lymphoma.

DECEMBER 1993

**11.** Seventeen EC directives on the quality of drinking and bathing water were amended or withdrawn, allowing broad general standards to be applied at national level. **15.** The Environment Secretary (John Gummer) announced that the THORP nuclear reprocessing plant at Sellafield could start operating early in 1994; environmental groups said that they would mount a legal challenge to the decision.

JANUARY 1994

**20.** The Department of Transport's investigation into the wreck of the oil tanker *Braer* off Shetland in January 1993 was published; it accused the tanker's captain of serious dereliction of duty. **25.** The Government published the Sustainable Development Strategy in response to the 1992 Rio Earth Summit.

FEBRUARY 1994

**7.** The Environment Secretary announced that government policy would in future favour new shops in town centres rather than large out-of-town developments. **17.** The Government said that it would accept the ban on dumping low- and intermediate-level radioactive waste at sea adopted at the consultative meeting of the London Convention in November 1993.

MARCH 1994

**1.** A report by the Health and Safety Commission criticized the safety level of the nuclear reactors at Sellafield, Cumbria. **4.** A High Court judge ruled that the Government had not acted illegally in granting approval for the THORP nuclear reprocessing plant at Sellafield to start operating. **24.** The EC agreed a complete ban on exports of toxic waste to developing countries.

APRIL 1994

**16.** A chemical leak from a factory in Wem, Shropshire, polluted water supplies to nearly 250,000 people in Worcestershire and Gloucestershire. **25.** Fires in the Galapagos Islands which had been threatening the colonies of giant tortoises on Isabela Island were brought under control.

MAY 1994

**17.** The report of the Donaldson inquiry into shipping safety standards and marine pollution by ships was published. Thousands of fish were killed when caustic soda leaked into the River Ellen, Cumbria. **26.** The International Whaling Commission voted to establish a whale sanctuary in Antarctica; Japan voted against the proposal and Norway refused to take part in the vote.

JUNE 1994

**3.** The Prime Minister announced the UK's ratification of the 1992 Rio summit's biodiversity convention. **10.** Seven protesters were arrested for obstructing workmen clearing trees at Solsbury Hill, near Bath,

to make way for a bypass. **14.** The Environment Secretary signed a protocol in Oslo in which Britain agreed to reduce its sulphur dioxide emissions by 80 per cent, based on 1980 levels, by 2010.

JULY 1994

**15.** The National Heritage Secretary (Peter Brooke) announced that all churches and chapels in England and Wales would be brought under listed building control. **28.** More than 12,000 fish were killed in the Old River Nene, Cambs., by an overflow from Anglian Water's sewerage system during heavy rain.

AUGUST 1994

**30.** At least 100,000 fish were killed in a slurry spillage into the River Camel, near Camelford, Cornwall.

## NORTHERN IRELAND AFFAIRS

SEPTEMBER 1993

**1.** A prison officer was shot dead by the UVF in Belfast. A Roman Catholic man was shot dead by UFF in Belfast. **3.** A Roman Catholic man was shot dead by the UFF in Belfast. **7.** A Roman Catholic man was shot dead by the UFF in Belfast. **15.** A Roman Catholic man was shot dead by the IRA in Lisburn, Co. Antrim.

OCTOBER 1993

**12.** A Roman Catholic man was shot dead and five others injured by the UVF in Belfast. **15.** A Roman Catholic man was shot dead by the UDA in Belfast. **17.** A Protestant man was shot dead by the IRA in Belfast. **21.** A director of a building company which carried out work for the security forces was shot dead by the IRA in Glengormley, Co. Antrim. **23.** Ten people were killed and 59 injured when an IRA bomb exploded without warning in the Shankill Road, Belfast; one of the bombers died in the explosion. A Roman Catholic man was shot by the UFF in Belfast; he died on 25 October. **25.** A Roman Catholic man was shot dead by the UVF in Belfast. **26.** Two Roman Catholic men were shot dead and five were injured when two UDA gunmen fired on a group of workers at a council depot in Belfast. A soldier was arrested and later charged with attempted murder after opening fire on a group of mourners outside the home of Thomas Begley, the IRA bomber killed on 23 October. **28.** The Irish Government issued a six-point statement on the political future of Northern Ireland, including the principle that any constitutional change would require the consent of the Unionist majority. Two Roman Catholic men were shot dead by the UVF in Bleary, Co. Down. **29.** The Prime Minister (John Major) and the Irish Taoiseach (Albert Reynolds) said after an EC summit in Brussels that Sinn Fein could be invited to talks on the political future of Northern Ireland if the IRA were to

RUSSIA
President Yeltsin's attempt to dissolve the Russian parliament led to street battles in Moscow in
September–October 1993 before the army crushed opposition to the President (*Rex Features*)

SOUTH AFRICA
Violence flared in advance of the country's first multi-racial elections in April 1994 but the elections passed off peacefully (*Associated Press/Rex Features*)

RWANDA
Thousands fled to Zaïre to escape ethnic violence triggered by the assassination of the president in April 1994
(*Rex Features*)

ITALY
The right-wing Freedom Alliance led by Silvio Berlusconi swept to power in the March 1994 general election amid high expectations (*Rex Features*)

BOSNIA
Serb shelling of Sarajevo's main market killed 68 in February 1994 and prompted a tougher international attitude towards the Bosnian Serbs (*Rex Features*)

LT.-GEN. SIR MICHAEL ROSE TAKES THE TRAM
The cease-fire and demilitarization of Sarajevo from February 1994 allowed a resumption of normal life
(*Popperfoto*)

PALESTINIAN AUTONOMY
Yasser Arafat, chairman of the PLO, returned from exile when Palestinian self-government was established in the Gaza Strip and Jericho in July 1994 (*Rex Features*)

MIDDLE EAST
Israel and Jordan signed a peace agreement in July 1994 (*Rex Features*)

NORTH KOREA
President Kim Il-sung (right) died in July 1994 in the midst of an international crisis over North Korea's production of nuclear weapons. He was succeeded by his son, Kim Jong-il (left) (*Associated Press*)

NORTHERN IRELAND
The level of sectarian violence rose in 1994 as the 25th anniversary approached of the deployment of troops on the streets (*Phillip Hollis*)

NORTHERN IRELAND
The Prime Minister (centre) and the Taoiseach (right) issued a joint declaration of a framework for peace talks at Downing Street in December 1993 (*Rex Features*)

NORTHERN IRELAND
Hopes of a peaceful settlement in Northern Ireland rose when the IRA announced 'a complete cessation of military operations' on 31 August 1994 (*Crispin Rodwell (FSP)*)

INVESTITURE ANNIVERSARY
*Charles: the Private Man, the Public Role*, broadcast in June 1994, proved controversial when the Prince appeared to admit to adultery (*Central TV*)

LABOUR PARTY LEADERSHIP
Tony Blair (right) was elected leader of the Labour Party after John Smith's sudden death in May 1994 (*Rex Features*)

D-DAY ANNIVERSARY
The 50th anniversary of D-Day was commemorated in June 1994 by events such as a parade of British veterans at Arromanches beach, Normandy (*Brian Smith*)

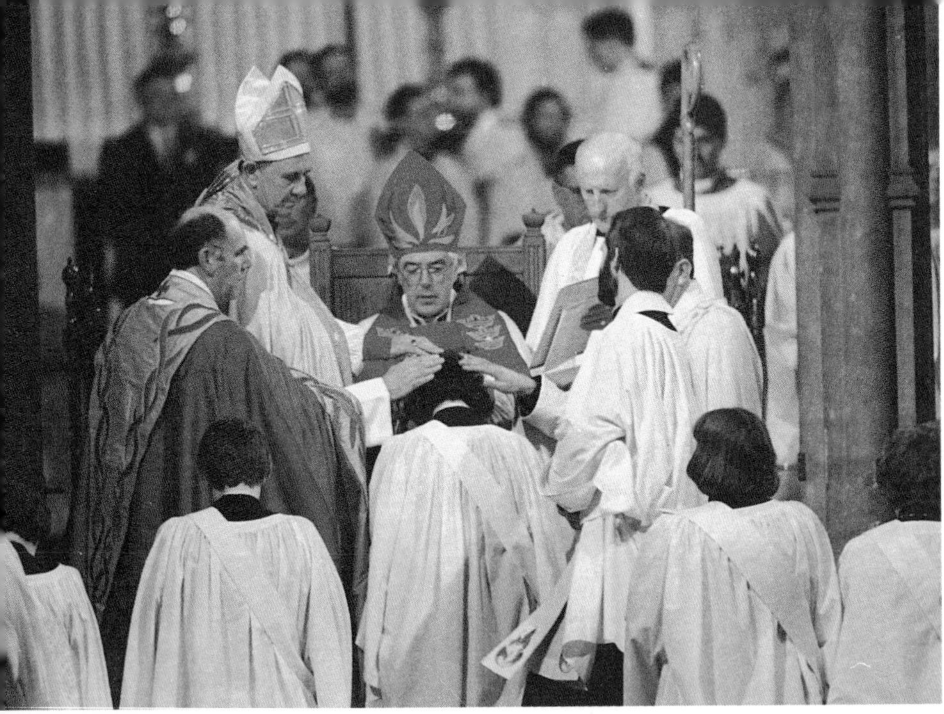

WOMEN PRIESTS
The ordination of the first women priests in the Church of England took place at Bristol Cathedral in March 1994 (*Rex Features*)

JUPITER
The collision of fragments of the comet Shoemaker-Levy 9 with Jupiter in July 1994, seen from the *Galileo* spacecraft (left) and looking towards the planet's south pole (*Rex Features*)

OBITUARIES
Deaths included (left to right): (top) Richard Nixon, Sir Matt Busby, Derek Jarman, Federico Fellini; (bottom) Brian Redhead, Dennis Potter, Jackie Onassis, Brian Johnston (*Rex Features/Allsport*)

DEATH CRASH
The Formula 1 racing driver Ayrton Senna was killed during the San Marino grand prix in May 1994 (*Popperfoto*)

CRICKET TRIALS AND TRIUMPHS
The England captain Mike Atherton was at the centre of a ball-tampering controversy in July 1994. The West Indies and Warwickshire batsman Brian Lara set world records for run-scoring in April and June 1994 (*Allsport*)

renounce violence, but that there could be no talks with those who use, threaten or support violence. They rejected an initiative based on talks between the SDLP leader (John Hume) and the president of Sinn Fein (Gerry Adams). **30.** Seven people were killed and 11 injured when two UFF gunmen opened fire in a pub in Greysteel, Co. Londonderry; five men were later charged with the murders. **31.** A police constable was shot by the IRA in Newry, Co. Down; he died on 2 November.

NOVEMBER 1993

**24.** A huge consignment of arms and explosives destined for the UVF was seized aboard a Polish container ship by customs officials at Teesport. **27.** The Government admitted, following press revelations, that it had been communicating regularly with the IRA through secret intermediaries. **29.** The Government published the messages exchanged with the IRA since February 1993. The leader of the Democratic Unionists, Ian Paisley, was 'named' by the Speaker and expelled from the House of Commons for five days after accusing the Secretary of State for Northern Ireland (Sir Patrick Mayhew) of lying about the Government's contacts with the IRA. **30.** A Roman Catholic man was shot dead by the UFF in Belfast.

DECEMBER 1993

**2.** A soldier was shot dead by the IRA at Keady, Co. Armagh. **3.** The Prime Minister and the Irish Taoiseach held talks in Dublin. **5.** A man and a 15-year-old boy, both Roman Catholics, were shot dead by the UFF in Belfast. **7.** A Roman Catholic man was shot dead by the UFF in Belfast. **12.** Two policemen were shot dead by the IRA in Fivemiletown, Co. Tyrone. **13.** A Protestant man was shot dead by the UFF in Belfast. **14.** An elderly woman died of a heart attack when a 1,000 lb bomb was discovered in Belfast; the bomb was later defused. **15.** The Prime Minister and the Irish Taoiseach issued a joint declaration on an agreed framework providing the starting point for a peace process designed to culminate in a political settlement in Northern Ireland; they confirmed that all democratically mandated parties could be involved in talks as long as they committed themselves to ending permanently the use of, or support for, paramilitary violence (the Downing Street declaration). The Prime Minister later said that if the IRA were to agree a permanent cessation of violence, Sinn Fein could be involved in talks within three months. **16.** The president of Sinn Fein said that his organization was committed to peace but needed time to consider the Anglo-Irish declaration. **19.** A 500 lb IRA bomb exploded on the outskirts of Londonderry. **30.** A soldier was shot dead by an IRA sniper in Crossmaglen, Co. Armagh.

JANUARY 1994

**1.** IRA firebombs exploded in Belfast. **11.** The Irish Government lifted its ban on broadcasting interviews

with Sinn Fein and other paramilitary groups. **27.** Two Roman Catholic men were shot dead, one in Belfast and one in Ballymena, Co. Antrim. **30.** After being banned for 20 years, Gerry Adams, the president of Sinn Fein, was granted a USA visa to attend a conference on Northern Ireland in New York.

FEBRUARY 1994

**10.** Dominic McGlinchey, a former leader of the INLA, was shot dead at Drogheda, Co. Louth. **17.** A police officer was killed and two others injured when their vehicle was hit by an IRA rocket in Belfast. **24.** A man was shot dead by the INLA in Belfast. **26.** At Sinn Fein's annual conference in Dublin, Gerry Adams repeated a request for the British Government to clarify details of the Downing Street declaration. **28.** The Ulster Unionists said that they would not take part in talks involving the Government of the Irish Republic, and launched *A Blueprint for Stability*, which called for a devolved assembly and a Bill of Rights.

MARCH 1994

**10.** An off-duty RUC officer was shot dead by the IRA in Belfast. **11.** A Roman Catholic man was killed by a UVF booby-trap bomb in Portadown, Co. Armagh. **13.** The IRA issued a statement requesting clarification of the Downing Street declaration and urging the British Government to move from its current 'negative stance'. **19.** A RUC officer was seriously injured when an army helicopter was shot down by an IRA missile in Crossmaglen, Co. Armagh. **30.** The IRA announced a three-day cease-fire from midnight on 5 April and again requested clarification of the Downing Street declaration; the Prime Minister, on a visit to Belfast, said that only a permanent cease-fire could lead to talks and that the Downing Street declaration was not negotiable.

APRIL 1994

**6.** The chairman of Sinn Fein (Tom Hartley) delivered a letter to 10 Downing Street requesting clarification of the Downing Street declaration. On 7 April the Prime Minister again refused to offer clarification; he denied that the Government had caused a stalemate and called on the IRA to renounce violence. **7.** A Protestant woman was shot dead by a loyalist gang in Belfast after being mistaken for a Roman Catholic. On 12 April the UVF shot dead a Protestant man who they claimed had been responsible for the killing. **12.** The Northern Ireland Secretary said in New York that the IRA did not have to surrender in order to join talks on the future of Northern Ireland. **14.** The wife of a former Sinn Fein councillor was shot dead in Belfast. **16.** The Irish Taoiseach outlined a plan for a united Ireland in which Ulster politicians would be guaranteed 30 per cent of government posts; this was rejected in principle by the Ulster Unionists. **20.** A policeman was killed when an IRA mortar bomb hit his vehicle in Londonderry. **24.** Two Protestant men were shot dead by the IRA in Garvagh, Co. Londonderry. **25.** In Belfast IRA gunmen murdered one man and knee-capped 16 others who they alleged had been involved in drug dealing. **26.** A Roman Catholic taxi driver was shot dead by the UFF in Belfast. **27.** A Protestant man was shot dead by the INLA in Belfast. **28.** A Roman Catholic man was shot dead by the UVF in Belfast. **29.** The IRA shot dead a man who they alleged was a RUC informer, and dumped his body near Newry, Co. Down.

MAY 1994

**3.** A Protestant man was shot dead by the INLA in Belfast. **8.** An elderly Roman Catholic woman was shot dead by the UVF in Greystone, Co. Tyrone. **12.** A Roman Catholic man was shot dead by the UFF in Belfast. **13.** A Protestant man was killed by an IRA booby-trap bomb in Lurgan, Co. Armagh. **14.** A soldier was killed in an IRA rocket attack on the RUC station at Keady, Co. Armagh. **17.** Two Roman Catholic men were shot dead by the UVF in Belfast. **18.** A 17–year-old Roman Catholic man was shot dead by a loyalist gunman in Armagh city centre. **19.** The British Government published a response to 20 questions submitted by Sinn Fein, via the Irish Government, requesting clarification of the Downing Street declaration; the British response said that the permanent cessation of violence was the only precondition for negotiation, and included the promise that a referendum could be held in Northern Ireland on the issue of a united Ireland. **21.** A member of the Royal Irish Regiment was shot dead by the IRA in Armagh. **22.** A Roman Catholic man was shot dead by loyalist gunmen at a Sinn Fein fund-raising event in Dublin; a bomb left by the gunmen failed to explode. **23.** A security guard was shot dead by the IRA in Belfast.

JUNE 1994

**10.** A Roman Catholic man was shot dead by the UVF in Belfast. **16.** Two Protestant men were killed and two others injured by INLA gunmen in Belfast. Laurence Maguire, a member of the UVF, was sentenced at Belfast Crown Court to five terms of life imprisonment for ordering sectarian murders and other terrorist offences. **17.** A Roman Catholic taxi driver was shot dead by the UVF in Carrickfergus, Co. Antrim. A Protestant man was shot dead in Newtownabbey, Co. Antrim. **18.** Six Roman Catholic men were shot dead by the UVF as they watched a World Cup football match on television in Loughinisland, Co. Down.

JULY 1994

**11.** Ray Smallwoods, a spokesman for the Ulster Democratic Party, was shot dead by the IRA in Lisburn, Co. Antrim. A member of the UVF who had been shot by the IRA on 20 June died. In Magherafelt, Co. Londonderry, the home of the Democratic Unionist MP William McCrea was sprayed with gunfire. **12.** An RAF helicopter made a crash landing after being hit by an IRA mortar bomb in Newtown-

hamilton, south Armagh. **17.** The body of a woman was found near Roslea, Co. Fermanagh; she had been shot by the IRA as an alleged police informer. **22.** A Roman Catholic man was shot dead by loyalist gunmen in Belfast. **24.** At a conference in Letterkenny, Co. Donegal, Sinn Fein endorsed some parts of the Downing Street declaration but said it did not deal adequately with some central issues and contained negative and contradictory elements. **26.** The leader of the Democratic Unionist Party, Ian Paisley, refused to join talks on the political future of Northern Ireland because of his objections to the Downing Street declaration. **29.** Forty-six people were injured in an IRA mortar bomb attack on an RUC station in Newry, Co. Down. **31.** Two Protestant men were shot dead by the IRA in Belfast.

AUGUST 1994

**7.** A pregnant Roman Catholic woman was shot dead by the UVF at her home in Co. Tyrone. **8.** A part-time member of the Royal Irish Regiment was shot dead in Crossgar, Co. Down. **10.** A Roman Catholic man was shot dead in Belfast. **11.** A Roman Catholic man was shot dead by the UFF in Lurgan, Co. Armagh. **14.** A Roman Catholic man was shot dead by the UFF in Belfast. **31.** The IRA announced a complete cessation of military operations from midnight.

## SPORT

SEPTEMBER 1993

**1.** Ffyona Campbell became the first woman to walk the length of Africa. **2.** Terry Venables sold his shares in Tottenham Hotspur football club and resigned from the board. **3.** A record aggregate score for a first-class cricket match in England was set by Essex and Sussex at Hove when they scored a total of 1,808 runs. **5.** Wayne Rainey, the world 500 cc motorcycling champion, was left paralysed after a crash during the Italian grand prix at Misano. **6.** Marseille football club, the European Cup holders, was banned from the 1993–4 competition by UEFA after allegations of bribery involving the club. **13.** Andy Roxburgh resigned as manager of the Scotland football team. **15.** About 100 Welsh football supporters were arrested in Belgium before Cardiff City's match against Liège. **19.** Viv Richards played his last game of first-class cricket. Nigel Mansell won the IndyCar world series championship. **23.** The International Olympic Committee announced that the Olympic Games in 2000 would be held in Sydney, Australia. **24.** Alain Prost announced that he would retire from Formula One motor-racing at the end of the season.

OCTOBER 1993

**2.** Lennox Lewis retained his WBC world heavyweight title when he beat Frank Bruno in a fight in Cardiff. **6.** Michael Jordan announced his retirement from basketball. **12.** About 190 British football fans were arrested after clashes with police in Amsterdam. **13.** More than 1,000 British football fans were arrested in Rotterdam before England's World Cup match against Holland. **21.** Garry Kasparov beat Nigel Short to win the PCA World Chess Championship in London.

## NOVEMBER 1993

**3.** At least 160 Manchester United fans were deported from Turkey after violent clashes with police in Istanbul before the club's European Cup match against Galatasaray. **7.** A man parachuted into the boxing ring during the world heavyweight championship fight between Riddick Bowe and Evander Holyfield in Las Vegas; he was later charged with dangerous flying. **13.** David Gower announced his retirement from cricket. **17.** The England football team failed to qualify for the 1994 World Cup finals. A man was killed when a marine distress flare was fired into a stand at the World Cup qualifying match between Wales and Romania at Cardiff Arms Park; two men were later charged with murder. Craig Brown was appointed manager of the Scotland football team. **23.** Graham Taylor resigned as manager of the England football team. **27.** The England rugby union team beat New Zealand for the first time in ten years. **28.** Seventeen-year-old Ronnie O'Sullivan became the youngest winner of a ranking snooker tournament when he won the UK Championship. **29.** Peter Swales resigned as chairman of Manchester City football club.

## DECEMBER 1993

**3.** Karen Pickering became Britain's first woman world swimming champion when she won the 200 metres freestyle race at the short-course championships in Palma, Majorca. **12.** Linford Christie was named BBC Sports Personality of the Year. **21.** The International Cricket Council announced that for an initial period of three years all Test matches would be umpired jointly by one home official and one from an international panel of umpires. **24.** The Football Association cleared the Wimbledon striker John Fashanu of misconduct over an elbow blow that caused a severe facial injury to the Tottenham Hotspur captain Gary Mabbutt on 24 November.

## JANUARY 1994

**7.** The American ice skater Nancy Kerrigan was hit on the knee by a man wielding a crowbar after a practice session in Detroit; four men including the ex-husband and the bodyguard of Ms Kerrigan's chief skating rival, Tonya Harding, were later charged in connection with the assault. Ms Harding denied any involvement, and was allowed to skate at the Winter Olympics in February after threatening to sue the US Olympic Committee if she were debarred (*see also* 25 February and 16 March). **8.** Jayne Torvill and Christopher Dean won the British ice dance championships in Sheffield after a ten-year absence

from competitive skating. The athletics journalist Cliff Temple committed suicide; it was later reported that Andy Norman, the promotions officer of the British Athletic Federation, about whom Temple had written a critical article, had threatened Temple that he would spread rumours that Temple had sexually harrassed women athletes (*see also* 8 April). **10.** A fight broke out between Michael Bentt and Herbie Hide at a press conference at a London hotel to publicize their WBO title fight on 19 March; the fighters were later fined £10,000 each by the British Boxing Board of Control. **28.** Terry Venables was appointed coach of the England football team. Graeme Souness resigned as manager of Liverpool football club; Roy Evans was later appointed in his place. John Toshack was appointed technical director of the Wales football team. **29.** Ulrike Maier, the former world champion skier, was killed after falling in a World Cup downhill race in Garmisch-Partenkirchen, Germany. **30.** Fourteen-year-old Peter Leko became the world's youngest-ever chess grand master.

## FEBRUARY 1994

**4.** Francis Lee became chairman of Manchester City football club. **8.** The Indian bowler Kapil Dev broke the world record for taking Test wickets with his 432nd Test wicket in the match against Sri Lanka in Ahmedabad. **12.** The Winter Olympics opened in Lillehammer, Norway. Colin Jackson equalled the world indoor record of 7.36 seconds for the 60 metres hurdles. **16.** Bryan Hamilton was appointed manager of the Northern Ireland football team. **17.** Birmingham City football club was fined £55,000 by the Football League and ordered to pay £75,000 compensation to Southend United for luring away Barry Fry as manager in December 1993. **21.** At the Winter Olympics in Lillehammer, Jayne Torvill and Christopher Dean won only bronze medals in the ice dance competition, provoking criticism of the standard of judging. **24.** The British Horseracing Board cancelled the season's four remaining jump races on all-weather surfaces after the death of the 13th horse to die on all-weather tracks in eight weeks. **25.** Nancy Kerrigan won the silver medal in the women's figure-skating competition at the Winter Olympics; Tonya Harding finished eighth.

## MARCH 1994

**1.** The champion National Hunt jockey Richard Dunwoody was suspended for 14 days after causing 'intentional interference' in a race at Nottingham. **2.** The England cricket team suffered their worst-ever defeat in a one-day international when they were beaten by 165 runs by the West Indies. Jayne Torvill and Christopher Dean announced their retirement from competitive skating. **4.** The millionaire businessman Fergus McCann took over control of Celtic football club, which was on the brink of receivership. **9.** Ray Illingworth was appointed chairman of the England cricket selectors. **10.** The Winter Paralympics opened in Lillehammer, Norway. **16.** John Toshack resigned as technical director of the Wales football team after only one match in charge. On 17 March his deputy Mike Smith, a former Wales manager, was appointed in his place. Tonya Harding admitted at a court hearing in Portland, Oregon, that she had hindered the prosecution over the attack on Nancy Kerrigan; she resigned from the US Figure Skating Association, was put on probation, fined $100,000 and sentenced to 500 hours' community service. **19.** Geoff Cooke resigned as manager of the England rugby union team; he was replaced by Jack Rowell. The defeated WBO heavyweight champion Michael Bentt was advised never to fight again after being taken to hospital following his match against Herbie Hide. **22.** The Manchester United striker Eric Cantona was sent off for the second time in four days in a match against Arsenal at Highbury. **24.** Frank Dick resigned as director of British athletics coaching. **29.** Graham Taylor was appointed manager of Wolverhampton Wanderers football club. **30.** The England cricket team was all out for 46 against the West Indies, the lowest total by an England side in a Test match since 1887.

## APRIL 1994

**1.** Robin Knox-Johnston and Peter Blake set a new round-the-world record of 74 days, 22 hours, 17 minutes and 22 seconds in their yacht *Enza*. **6.** The Football Association cancelled a friendly match between England and Germany in Berlin on 20 April, the anniversary of the birth of Hitler, because of fears of violent demonstrations. The Pakistani squash international Mir Zaman Gul was disqualified from the British Open championships after head-butting an opponent. **8.** Andy Norman was sacked from his post of promotions officer of the British Athletics Federation. **12.** Alec Stewart became the first England batsman to score two centuries in a Test against the West Indies. On 13 April England won the match, the first Test defeat suffered by the West Indies in Barbados since 1935. Curtly Ambrose was later fined £1,000 for hitting a stump out of the ground at the end of the match. **18.** The West Indian batsman Brian Lara achieved the highest-ever individual Test score when he made 375 in the match against England in Antigua. **20.** The Premier League commission fined Everton £125,000 for indirectly inducing Mike Walker to leave Norwich City to manage Everton in January 1994. **21.** During the world snooker championships in Sheffield, the defending champion Stephen Hendry suffered a hairline fracture of his left arm in an accident in his hotel room; he went on to win the tournament for the third year in succession. **22.** Evander Holyfield lost his world heavyweight boxing titles to Michael Moorer; on 26 April he announced his retirement because of a heart condition. **24.** The England women's rugby union team won the World Cup final in Edinburgh. **28.** The boxer Bradley Stone died two days after suffering brain damage in a British super-bantamweight boxing contest against Richie Wenton in London. The Trinidadian and Leicestershire

cricketer Phil Simmons made the highest-ever debut score in professional cricket when he was 247 not out. **30.** The Austrian driver Roland Ratzenberger was killed during a practice session for the San Marino Grand Prix at Imola. Wigan achieved the rugby league championship and Cup double for the fifth year in succession when they won the Challenge Cup for the seventh successive time at Wembley. On 4 May the Wigan coach, John Dorahy, was sacked for gross misconduct

## MAY 1994

**1.** Ayrton Senna, three times world motor-racing champion, was killed when his car crashed in the San Marino grand prix at Imola. **4.** Malcolm Arnold was appointed national track and field coach for British athletics. **6.** The jockey Steve Wood was killed after falling from his horse during a race at Lingfield Park. **7.** Lennox Lewis retained his WBC heavyweight boxing title when he beat Phil Jackson in Atlantic City, USA. Mike Golding set a new world record of 167 days, 7 hours, 42 minutes for sailing non-stop west-bound around the world in his yacht *Group 4*. **10.** MPs voted to lift restrictions on betting on Sundays, paving the way for Sunday racing from 1995. **11.** The Australian cricket captain Allan Border announced his retirement. **13.** The International Motoring Federation announced a radical package of safety measures for Formula One racing; a modified version of the package was announced on 3 June after drivers and teams threatened to strike. **14.** Manchester United completed the league and Cup double when they won the FA Cup final. **15.** The former Pakistan captain Imran Khan resigned from the cricket committee of the International Cricket Council after the publication of his autobiography, in which he admitted ball-tampering in 1981. **17.** The Wales rugby union team set a new record of points scored in a senior international when they beat Portugal 102–11 in Lisbon. **17.** The US Court of Appeal ruled that the US court which awarded Butch Reynolds $27.4 million in December 1992 against the International Amateur Athletic Federation over his suspension for drug abuse in 1990 had no jurisdiction over the IAAF, whose headquarters were then in London; the award was therefore revoked. **18.** Two Derby County footballers were assaulted by Millwall fans in two pitch invasions during the first division play-off match at the New Den; crowd trouble continued after the match.

## JUNE 1994

**3.** Brian Lara set a new world record of seven centuries in eight innings when he scored 101 not out for Warwickshire at Edgbaston. On 6 June in the same innings he set a new world record for an individual first-class score with 501 not out, and a new world record of 390 runs scored by an individual in one day. **7.** The England rugby union player Tim Rodber and the Eastern Province player Simon Tremain were sent off for fighting in a match in Port Elizabeth, South Africa. **10.** Paul Elliott, the former

Chelsea footballer, lost a High Court action against the former Liverpoool player Dean Saunders in which he had sought damages for what he claimed was a deliberate foul which had caused an injury which ended his career in 1992. **14.** The Football Association fined Tottenham Hotspur £600,000, banned the club from the FA Cup in 1995 and ordered it to start the 1994–5 Premiership with 12 points deducted after finding it guilty of making undisclosed payments to players in the late 1980s. After an appeal the fine was increased to £1.5 million and the points deduction reduced to six. **17.** The football World Cup finals began in Chicago. **24.** Seventeen-year-old Alex Kelly set a new world record by taking ten wickets for no runs in 27 deliveries in a cricket match in the Durham County Junior League. **25.** The Ireland football manager Jack Charlton was fined £10,000 and banned from the touchline for one match for abusing FIFA officials at a World Cup match in Florida, USA. **26.** The British women's athletics team qualified for the World Cup for the first time when they finished second in the European Cup. **30.** Diego Maradona, the captain of Argentina, was suspended by FIFA after failing a drugs test at the World Cup finals. He was later suspended for 15 months and fined £10,000.

JULY 1994

**2.** Martina Navratilova played her last match at Wimbledon in the Ladies' Singles final. The Colombian footballer Andres Escobar, who scored an own goal during the World Cup finals, was shot dead in Medellin. **3.** Nigel Mansell returned to Formula One motor racing for the French Grand Prix. **6–7.** Two stages of the Tour de France cycle race were held in Kent and Sussex. **6.** Leroy Burrell set a new world record of 9.85 seconds for the 100 metres. The House of Commons national heritage select committee recommended that satellite and cable television channels should not be allowed exclusive access to big sporting events, and that events sponsored by tobacco companies should not be shown on television. **13.** The British cyclist Chris Boardman retired during the 11th stage of the Tour de France, having led the race for the first three days. **15.** The Norwich City footballer Chris Sutton was sold to Blackburn Rovers for a record £5 million. **17.** Brazil won the football World Cup for a record fourth time; the result of the final was decided for the first time by a penalty shoot-out. **21–25.** The South African cricket team played its first Test in England for 24 years. On 23 July the match referee cleared the England captain, Mike Atherton, of ball-tampering after examining film footage of an alleged incident. On 24 July the chairman of the England selectors, Ray Illingworth, fined Atherton £2,000 after he admitted having dirt in his pocket and not telling the whole truth to the referee. On 25 July the referee said Atherton had been 'foolish in the extreme' but he did not propose to take any further action. **25.** The South African rugby forward Johan le Roux was banned from international rugby until March 1996 for biting the

New Zealand captain Sean Fitzpatrick on the ear in a Test in Wellington on 23 July. **26.** The racing driver Michael Schumacher was suspended for two races and the Benetton Ford team was fined £330,000 by the International Motor Sport Federation (FIA) for failing to obey the instructions of officials at the British Grand Prix on 10 July. **29.** Tottenham Hotspur football club signed the German striker Jurgen Klinsmann for £2 million. **31.** The racing driver Jos Verstappen and five members of the Benetton Ford crew suffered minor burns when Verstappen's car burst into flames during a refuelling stop at the German grand prix.

AUGUST 1994

**1.** Dick Best was sacked as coach of the England rugby union team and replaced by Jack Rowell. **7.** The British sprinter Solomon Wariso was sent home from the European Championships after a drugs test at an earlier meeting proved positive. **12.** Sally Gunnell became the first woman to hold world, Olympic, Commonwealth and European titles and the world record at the same time when she won the 400 metres hurdles at the European Championships. **15.** The world 4,000 metres pursuit cycling champion, Graeme Obree, was disqualified from the 1994 world championships in Palermo because of his riding style. **17.** The vice-president of the Commonwealth Games Federation, Arthur Tunstall, apologized after saying that the participation of disabled athletes in the Commonwealth Games was an embarrassment. **18.** The Queen opened the Commonwealth Games in Victoria, Canada. The South African batsman Jonty Rhodes suffered concussion after being hit on the head by a ball in the Test match at the Oval. **19.** Mike Atherton was fined £1,250 for dissent after being given out in the Test against South Africa at the Oval. **23.** The 14-year-old gymnast Annika Reeder became the youngest-ever Commonwealth Games gold medallist. **24.** The English athletes Diane Modahl and Paul Edwards were flown home from the Commonwealth Games after recording positive drugs tests at previous meetings. **28.** Horace Dove-Edwin was stripped of his Commonwealth Games 100 metres silver medal after testing positive for drugs. Michael Schumacher won the Belgian Grand Prix but was disqualifed because his car contravened technical regulations.

APPOINTMENTS AND RESIGNATIONS

In addition to those mentioned above, the following appointments, resignations, etc., were announced:

1993

10 September: Norman Willis retired as general secretary of the TUC

1 December: Richard Giordano was appointed chairman of British Gas

1994

5 January: Lt.-Gen. Sir Michael Rose was appointed commander of the UN forces in Bosnia

21 January: Kelvin MacKenzie was appointed managing director of British Sky Broadcasting; he was replaced as editor of the *Sun* newspaper by Stuart Higgins

17 February: Anthony Everitt resigned as secretary-general of the Arts Council

4 March: David Spedding was appointed head of MI6 from September 1994

14 April: David Banks was appointed editorial director of Mirror Group Newspapers; he was replaced as editor of the *Daily Mirror* by Colin Myler

22 June: Sir Harrison Birtwistle was appointed to the newly-created Henry Purcell Chair of composition at King's College, London

1 July: Andrew Knight resigned as chairman of News International and was replaced by Rupert Murdoch; John Witherow was appointed acting editor of the *Sunday Times* during the temporary posting of the editor, Andrew Neil, to New York; Tessa Hilton was appointed editor of the *Sunday Mirror*

26 July: Andreas Whittam Smith resigned as editor of the *Independent*; he was replaced by Ian Hargreaves

2 August: Kelvin MacKenzie resigned as managing director of British Sky Broadcasting

25 August: Eve Pollard resigned as editor of the *Sunday Express*; she was replaced by Brian Hitchen, editor of the *Daily Star*

26 August: Malcolm Reilly resigned as coach of the Great Britain rugby league team; he was replaced by Ellery Hanley

---

AFRICA

---

SEPTEMBER 1993

5. Somali gunmen ambushed and killed seven Nigerian UN troops in the capital Mogadishu. UN helicopters attacked and destroyed a Somali militia base from which mortars had been fired at Mogadishu airport. 7. The constitutional negotiations in South Africa reached agreement on establishing a multiracial Transitional Executive Council to govern alongside the white government until legislative elections in April 1994. 8. In Johannesburg 19 black commuters were killed by gunmen. 9. One hundred Somalis were killed in Mogadishu by UN helicopters repelling an attack by 300 Somali militiamen on a Pakistani UN unit, which led to a street battle in Mogadishu. 21. US special forces captured four senior aides of the Somali warlord Gen. Aideed in a raid in Mogadishu. A total of 31 black commuters and hostel dwellers were killed in three separate attacks around Johannesburg. 23. A joint sitting of the three houses of South Africa's parliament voted by 211 to 36 to approve the draft bill to establish a Transitional Executive Council, giving the country's blacks a share

of political power for the first time. 24. The USA, EC, Commonwealth and other countries began lifting remaining sanctions against South Africa, apart from the arms embargo. 26. Three US soldiers were killed in Somalia when their helicopter was shot down by gunmen loyal to Gen. Aideed.

OCTOBER 1993

3. Over 200 Somalis and 15 US troops were killed in a UN raid on supporters of Gen. Aideed in Mogadishu. 7. President Clinton of the USA ordered the dispatch of 5,300 US reinforcements to Somalia. 14. An American serviceman held hostage in Somalia was released by Gen. Aideed after 11 days in captivity. A Polish immigrant, Janusz Walus, and a former MP, Clive Derby-Lewis, were found guilty in Johannesburg of murdering the South African Communist Party leader Chris Hani in April 1993.

NOVEMBER 1993

10. The Nigerian High Court ruled that the military-appointed interim government of President Ernest Shonekan was illegal. 16. The UN Security Council voted to suspend the search for Gen. Aideed until an independent investigation of fighting in Mogadishu had been concluded. 17. South African negotiators approved a non-racial interim constitution under which the country will be governed until a permanent constitution is drafted by a new multi-racial parliament. The Defence Minister Gen. Sani Abacha replaced Ernest Shonekan as Nigerian head of state and government in what was effectively a *coup d'état*. 25. A new, predominantly-civilian Nigerian government was announced.

DECEMBER 1993

2. Multiparty constitutional negotiators agreed to reincorporate into South Africa the four nominally independent homelands of Transkei, Boputhatswana, Venda and Ciskei in April 1994. 7. The Transitional Executive Council was inaugurated in Cape Town. President Félix Houphouët-Boigny of Côte d'Ivoire died in office and was replaced by the parliamentary speaker Henri Konan-Bédié pending a presidential election. The Presidential Council in Malawi was dissolved and President Hastings Banda resumed his powers as head of state two weeks after brain surgery. 9. In Algeria Islamic fundamentalists killed eight members of an elite anti-terrorist force. 12. Peace talks in Addis Ababa between rival Somali factions collapsed. 15. Islamic fundamentalists in Algeria killed 12 expatriate workers. 22. The South African parliament voted by 236 to 46 to endorse the interim constitution.

JANUARY 1994

2. The Archbishop of Canterbury ended his controversial tour of rebel-held Christian southern Sudan, which had taken place against the wishes of the government. 16. The Pan Africanist Congress announced the suspension of its armed struggle against the South African government and said that it would take part in the April elections. 24. The

Lesotho government appealed for South African military aid and international help as rebel soldiers fought with troops loyal to the government in an attempted military coup. **30.** The Algerian Higher Committee of State disbanded itself after appointing Defence Minister Gen. Lamine Zeroual as President. **31.** Talks between the South African government, the ANC and the Freedom Alliance collapsed without agreement on the Freedom Alliance's participation in the multi-racial elections. US marines shot dead five Somalis in Mogadishu after gunmen opened fire on a diplomatic convoy.

**FEBRUARY 1994**
**10.** The Afrikaner Volksfront announced its decision to boycott South Africa's multi-racial elections in April after negotiations over its demand for an Afrikaner state collapsed. **12.** The Freedom Alliance, the Inkatha Freedom Party, the Afrikaner Volksfront and the Boputhatswana and Ciskei independent homeland governments, missed the deadline to register for South Africa's April multi-racial elections. **27.** The leader and nine members of the Armed Islamic Group attempting to overthrow the Algerian government were killed in a gun battle with security forces in Algiers. **28.** South Africa transferred sovereignty of the enclave of Walvis Bay to Namibia.

**MARCH 1994**
**2.** The South African parliament approved amendments to the country's interim constitution to increase regional powers in an attempt to persuade the Freedom Alliance to register for April's multi-racial elections. **4.** The Inkatha Party and the Afrikaner Volksfront registered for the multi-racial elections, on condition that international mediators negotiate amendments to the interim constitution. **5.** The Afrikaner Volksfront leader Gen. Constand Viljoen was forced to withdraw his grouping's registration for April's election by the Volksfront council. **7.** In Liberia a five-member coalition government was sworn in. **10.** The President of the nominally independent homeland of Boputhatswana in South Africa, Lucas Mangope, fled the homeland after sections of the homeland security forces joined rioting demonstrators demanding the right to vote in April's multi-racial elections. **11.** South African army units took control of Boputhatswana after the homeland defence force had driven out armed white extremists brought in by President Mangope to restore him to power. The Afrikaner Volksfront split, Gen. Constand Viljoen leading a faction called the Freedom Front to register for the April elections. **13.** The South African government and the Transitional Executive Council jointly took control of Boputhatswana, deposing President Mangope and appointing interim administrators. **21.** President Ben Ali won Tunisia's presidential election; the ruling Constitutional Democratic Party won 144 seats in elections for the National Assembly. **22.** The President of the nominally independent homeland of Ciskei, Brig. Oupa Gqozo, relinquished power to the South African

Defence Force and two administrators after a mutiny by the homeland police. **25.** The last US troops left Somalia. **28.** A running battle in Johannesburg between 15,000 Inkatha supporters, ANC security guards and South African security forces left 53 people dead and 220 injured. **31.** President de Klerk declared a state of emergency in the province of Natal and the KwaZulu homeland.

**APRIL 1994**
**3.** Fighting between supporters of the ANC and Inkatha in Natal over the Easter weekend left 40 people dead. **5.** South Africa's Independent Electoral Commission recommended that the country's multi-racial elections should be postponed in the KwaZulu homeland because of violence and intimidation. **6.** Presidents Juvenal Habyarimara of Rwanda and Cyprien Ntaryanura of Burundi were killed when their plane was shot down by a rocket at Kigali airport. **7.** Rwandan troops went on the rampage in Kigali and murdered the Prime Minister Agathe Uwilingiyimana, 11 Belgian UN peacekeeping troops and 17 Rwandan priests. **9.** French, Belgian and US troops arrived in Rwanda and Burundi to evacuate westerners from Rwanda as fighting continued in Kigali and thousands were massacred. **11.** The Algerian government resigned after failing to end the Islamic fundamentalist insurgency. **12.** The Rwandan Patriotic Front, dominated by the minority Tutsi tribe, entered Kigali and fought the Hutu-dominated army for control of the city, forcing the government to flee south. **14.** The seven-man mediation team led by Lord Carrington and Dr Henry Kissinger left South Africa after two days when the ANC and Inkatha failed to agree on their terms of reference. **14.** The Deputy Prime Minister of Lesotho was killed and four other ministers taken hostage in an army mutiny in Maseru. **19.** Chief Mangosutha Buthelezi, the leader of Inkatha, called off Inkatha's boycott of South Africa's multi-racial elections after securing guarantees for the future of the Zulu monarchy. **22.** The UN Security Council voted to withdraw most of the UNAMIR peacekeeping force from Rwanda and leave 270 UN troops in the country to assist in mediating a cease-fire between government and rebel forces. **24.** A car bomb exploded in Johannesburg killing nine people. **25.** A number of bombs, believed to have been planted by white right-wingers, exploded in Transvaal and Cape Province killing 12 people and injuring 65. **26.** The first day of voting in South Africa's first multi-racial elections began. **29.** Over 250,000 Rwandan refugees fled into neighbouring Tanzania to escape the fighting and massacres by the majority Hutu tribe. The South African multi-racial elections ended.

**MAY 1994**
**6.** The results of the South African elections were announced. **9.** The new multi-racial South African parliament was sworn in and elected Nelson Mandela President. **10.** Nelson Mandela was inaugurated as President of South Africa at a ceremony in Pretoria

attended by royalty and politicians from around the world. **17.** The UN Security Council voted to send 5,500 peacekeeping troops to Rwanda, of whom 650 were to be sent immediately and the remainder after Security Council approval of a detailed report on how the troops would operate. Malawi's first multiparty presidential and legislative elections since independence were won by the opposition United Democratic Front, and the UDF leader Chakufwa Chihana defeated President Hastings Banda. **22.** The Rwandan Patriotic Front captured Kigali airport and the main army barracks. **24.** President Mandela opened the first session of South Africa's multi-racial parliament. **29.** The Rwandan Patriotic Front captured more of Kigali and advanced on Gitarama.

JUNE 1994

**13.** The Rwandan Patriotic Front captured Gitarama. **17.** The Rwandan Patriotic Front broke through government lines to rescue Tutsi refugees and return them to rebel-held areas. **22.** The UN Security Council approved the dispatch of 2,600 French troops to Rwanda as peacekeepers, despite opposition from the Rwandan Patriotic Front which accused France of supporting Hutu supremacy in Rwanda. **23.** The Nigerian opposition leader Chief Moshood Abiola was arrested in Lagos after proclaiming himself President; he is believed to have won the June 1993 presidential election subsequently cancelled by the government. **28.** French troops rescued 35 European and African nuns in a raid on a Rwandan government camp.

JULY 1994

**4.** The Rwandan Patriotic Front captured the centre of Kigali and the town of Butare. **5.** The South African finance minister Derek Keys announced his resignation, with effect from October 1994; he will be replaced by Christo Lieberberg. **6.** Gunmen opened fire on taxis near Johannesburg, killing 11. The Rwandan Patriotic Front announced that it had formed a government with Hutu opposition parties, and that it had agreed not to attack the French security zone in the south-west. **11.** Two mass graves were discovered in Kibuye, Rwanda, containing the bodies of an estimated 10,000 Tutsis. **14.** The Rwandan Patriotic Front captured Ruhengeri, forcing the government to flee. **17.** Thousands of Hutus and the remnants of Rwanda's army fled to the Zaïrean town of Goma as the Rwandan Patriotic Front captured Gisenyi. **18.** The Rwandan Patriotic Front announced a cease-fire, declared victory in the civil war and appointed a government of national unity led by Hutu moderates. **19.** Thousands of Hutus fled from the French security zone to Zaïre. **22.** The US government launched an airlift of food, water and medicines to the estimated 1.8 million Hutu refugees in Zaïre to combat a cholera outbreak. **23.** President Sir Alaji Dawda Jawara and the Gambian government were overthrown in a military coup. **28.** Chief Moshood Abiola went on trial for treason in Nigeria;

several pro-democracy demonstrators outside the court were killed by police.

AUGUST 1994

**2.** British troops started to arrive in Kigali to support relief operations for refugees returning from Zaïre. **3.** In Lagos unions and pro-democracy supporters enforced a general strike, demanding the release of Chief Moshood Abiola; three people died in rioting. Islamic fundamentalists killed five French consular officials and policemen in a car bomb attack on the French Embassy compound in Algiers. **15.** Thousands of Hutus fled from south-west Rwanda to Zaïre after French troops began to withdraw from the security zone they had established in the area. **17.** King Letsie III, the constitutional monarch of Lesotho, led a coup against his government and indicated he would return the throne to his deposed father, King Moshoeshoe III. **20.** Zaïrean troops closed the border with Rwanda to prevent more Hutu refugees entering the town of Bukava.

## THE AMERICAS

SEPTEMBER 1993

**7.** President Clinton announced a plan to save $108 billion over five years by reducing the civil service by 250,000 personnel. **10.** The Senate passed a bill to allow the armed services to continue discharging homosexuals, rejecting President Clinton's policy of removing the ban on homosexuals serving in the US military.

OCTOBER 1993

**11.** US troops were prevented from docking at Port-au-Prince, Haiti, after Haiti's military regime reneged on an agreement with the UN to prepare for the return of deposed President Aristide. **18.** The UN Security Council reimposed sanctions on Haitian assets abroad, while US and Canadian warships enforced the economic embargo on the country. **26.** In the Canadian general election the Conservative government was defeated by the Liberal Party.

NOVEMBER 1993

**14.** In a plebiscite on the island's future, Puerto Rico rejected US statehood. **17.** The US House of Representatives approved the North American Free Trade Agreement. The Senate ratified the agreement on 21 November and the Mexican Senate ratified it on 23 November. **24.** The US Congress passed the 'Brady' bill on gun control.

DECEMBER 1993

**2.** Pablo Escobar, the leader of the Medellin cocaine cartel wanted for drug trafficking and terrorism, was shot dead by Colombian police in Medellin. A state of emergency was imposed by the government in St Christopher and Nevis after supporters of the opposition Labour Party rioted following the reappointment of a government of the People's Action

Party after the 30 November general election. **5.** Rafael Caldera was elected President of Venezuela. **11.** Eduardo Frei was elected President of Chile. **15.** The US Defence Secretary Les Aspin resigned with effect from 20 January. **16.** The Haitian Prime Minister Robert Malval resigned after his government had failed to secure the return of ousted President Aristide. **28.** A pro-Aristide slum area of the Haitian capital Port-au-Prince was burned down by pro-military forces in retaliation for the killing of two military officials.

JANUARY 1994

**1.** The North American Free Trade Agreement (NAFTA) between Canada, the United States and Mexico came into force. Rebels, mainly Mayan Indians, calling themselves the Zapatista National Liberation Army seized five towns in southern Mexico to protest at rural poverty and discrimination over land holdings; after five days of fighting which left 150 dead, the rebels lost control of the five towns to the Mexican army and retreated into the mountains. **9.** Bombs which exploded in Mexico City and Acapulco were blamed on the Zapatista rebels. **12.** President Clinton gave in to intense pressure and ordered the US Attorney-General to appoint an independent special prosecutor to investigate the President's dealings with a failed bank and the Whitewater property development in Arkansas while he was state governor. **17.** An earthquake hit Los Angeles. **24.** President Clinton appointed the Deputy Secretary of Defence William Perry as Defence Secretary after three nominees had rejected the post.

FEBRUARY 1994

**3.** President Clinton lifted the US trade embargo against Vietnam. **20.** Representatives of the Zapatista National Liberation Army began negotiations with Mexican government officials.

MARCH 1994

**1.** Four Jewish rabbinical students were seriously injured in New York in a gun attack, believed to have been carried out by an Arab immigrant in retaliation for the Hebron mosque massacre. **2.** Mexican government negotiators and representatives of the Zapatista National Liberation Army agreed a package of reforms and the end of the armed rebellion in the southern state of Chiapas. **5.** Bernard Nussbaum, the White House counsel and a personal friend of President and Mrs Clinton, was forced to resign over unethical conduct regarding the independent special prosecutor's investigation of the Whitewater scandal. **8.** The Labour Party retained power in the Antiguan general election; Lester Bird took over the premiership from his father Dr Vere Bird. **14.** Webster Hubbell, the US Associate Attorney-General and a personal friend of President Clinton, resigned over criticism of his performance. **18.** The US Senate voted 98–0 to hold public hearings on President Clinton's Whitewater property dealings; this decision was confirmed by the House of Representatives four days later. **23.** The presidential candidate of the ruling

Mexican Institutional Revolutionary Party, Luis Donaldo Colosio, was assassinated in Tijuana.

APRIL 1994

**25.** Armando Calderon Sol of the right-wing Arena party won El Salvador's presidential election.

MAY 1994

**6.** Paula Jones, a former Arkansas state employee, launched a legal action against President Clinton for allegedly making unwarranted sexual propositions to her while he was Governor of Arkansas. **6.** The UN Security Council voted to tighten sanctions on Haiti's military regime from 22 May in order to enforce the return of President Aristide. **8.** Ernesto Perez Balladares of the Democratic Revolutionary Party won Panama's presidential election. **24.** Four Muslim fundamentalists were each sentenced to 240 years in prison after being convicted of the bombing of the World Trade Centre in New York in February 1993. **25.** US warships fired warning shots across the bows of ships attempting to break the trade embargo on Haiti. **31.** Dan Rostenkowski, the chairman of the influential US House of Congress Ways and Means Committee, was indicted on 17 counts of corruption.

JUNE 1994

**12.** President and Mrs Clinton were questioned by the Whitewater special prosecutor Robert Fiske on events surrounding the death of deputy White House counsel Vincent Foster in 1993. **19.** Ernesto Samper of the ruling Liberal Party won Colombia's presidential election. **27.** President Clinton dismissed his White House Chief of Staff Thomas McLarty and replaced him with Leon Panetta.

JULY 1994

**11.** The Haitian military government ordered the expulsion within 48 hours of the UN-OAS observer mission in Haiti. **26.** Congressional hearings into the Whitewater affair opened in Washington DC; White House counsel Lloyd Cutler admitted that presidential officials had shown poor judgement in their investigation. **31.** The UN Security Council approved the use of all necessary means, including force, to oust the Haitian military regime.

AUGUST 1994

**5.** Robert Fiske was replaced as the Whitewater special prosecutor by Kenneth Starr. **6.** Riots in the Cuban capital Havana in protest at food shortages and emigration restrictions were quelled by militias. **17.** The US Deputy Treasury Secretary Roger Altman resigned after his impropriety in briefing the White House on a confidential investigation into the Whitewater affair was exposed in the Whitewater congressional hearings. **19.** President Clinton ended automatic asylum in the USA for Cubans after record numbers had been allowed by the Cuban government to flee to Florida in small boats and on rafts. **21.** President Clinton's crime bill, including tighter gun control measures, was passed by the House of Representatives ten days after being defeated in an earlier vote. The bill was passed in the Senate on the 26th.

## ASIA

SEPTEMBER 1993
**7.** India and China agreed to reduce troop numbers in the disputed border area and respect the cease-fire line of the 1962 war. **24.** Prince Sihanouk was elected King of Cambodia by the seven-member Council of the Throne after he had promulgated the new constitution drawn up by the National Assembly.

OCTOBER 1993
**6.** The Pakistan People's Party led by Benazir Bhutto emerged as the largest party in parliament after the Pakistani general election. **17.** Indian troops surrounded the Hazratbal mosque in Kashmir after it had been taken over by armed Muslim separatists. **19.** Benazir Bhutto was sworn in as Prime Minister of Pakistan after she won a parliamentary election for the post.

NOVEMBER 1993
**10.** The British government warned China that if an agreement on proposed democratic reforms in Hong Kong was not reached within weeks, Britain would unilaterally implement the reforms. **11.** Tamil rebels overran a Sri Lankan military base on the Jaffna lagoon. **13.** The national and provincial assemblies elected Farooq Leghari of the Pakistan People's Party as President of Pakistan. **14.** Sri Lankan government forces retook the military base on Jaffna lagoon. **16.** Muslim militants ended their month-long occupation of the Hazratbal mosque in Kashmir and surrendered to Indian security forces. **18.** The Japanese coalition government forced four bills to end political corruption through the lower house of parliament.

DECEMBER 1993
**2.** Governor Patten of Hong Kong announced that, after 17 rounds of unsuccessful talks with the Chinese government, he would put the more modest portion of his democratic reform proposals before the Legislative Council for discussion and voting. **15.** The Hong Kong government tabled its bill on political reforms in the Legislative Council. **16.** The South Korean Prime Minister Hwang In-sung resigned after accepting the blame for the failure to prevent rice imports into South Korea under the GATT agreement; Lee Hoi Chang replaced him.

JANUARY 1994
**6.** Eighty people were killed and 2,500 wounded in six days of heavy fighting in the Afghan capital Kabul between militias loyal to President Rabbani's government and those loyal to Gen. Rashid Dostum. **20.** The International Atomic Energy Agency (IAEA) stated that North Korea was seeking to impose unacceptable limitations on international inspection of its nuclear sites. **21.** The political reform bills of the Japanese coalition government were rejected by the upper house of parliament. **29.** The Japanese coalition government reached agreement with the opposition Liberal Democratic Party on the political reform bills, which were passed by both houses of parliament.

FEBRUARY 1994
**4.** Sultan Tuanku Juafar Abdul Rahman was elected to serve as Malaysia's head of state from April 1994. **23.** The Hong Kong Legislative Council passed the electoral reform bill abolishing appointed seats on the regional and urban councils and introducing single-seat constituencies.

MARCH 1994
**1.** Khmer Rouge guerrillas retook their second most important base at Anlong Veng from the Cambodian army. IAEA inspectors arrived in North Korea after receiving permission from the government to inspect its seven declared nuclear sites. **16.** The IAEA inspectors had to abandon their inspection after obstruction by officials. **22.** The IAEA stated that it was unable to verify that North Korea had not diverted nuclear material for military purposes.

APRIL 1994
**3.** IAEA inspectors announced that they had concluded that North Korea had doubled its capacity to produce plutonium for the production of nuclear weapons. **8.** The Japanese Prime Minister Morihiro Hosokawa announced his resignation over alleged personal financial misdealings in the 1980s. **18.** Two Hong Kong political groups in the Legislative Council, the United Democrats and the Meeting Point Group, announced their merger to form the Democratic Party. **20.** Khmer Rouge guerrillas recaptured their headquarters at Pailin four weeks after it had been captured by the Cambodian army. **25.** Tsutomu Hata of the Japan Renewal Party was elected Prime Minister; afterwards the Social Democrat Party announced its withdrawal from the seven-party coalition government. Hata formed a minority government three days later.

MAY 1994
**29.** IAEA inspectors left North Korea after its government refused to allow monitoring of the removal of spent fuel rods from its nuclear sites.

JUNE 1994
**2.** The IAEA informed the UN Security Council that North Korea was in violation of its international treaty obligations not to construct nuclear weapons. **9.** North Korea threatened military retaliation against South Korea and Japan if they enforced proposed UN sanctions over its nuclear weapons programme. **10.** The governing body of the IAEA voted to suspend technical aid to North Korea after it barred nuclear inspections. **13.** North Korea announced its withdrawal from the IAEA, heightening tension and leading South Korea to mobilize its reservists. **15.** Former US President Jimmy Carter visited North

Korea in an attempt to diffuse the international crisis over its nuclear weapons production. **21.** Britain and China resumed negotiations over the transfer of power in Hong Kong. **22.** North Korea agreed to a US demand to freeze its nuclear weapons programme and allow international inspectors to remain in North Korea, in return for discussions with the USA on security, political and economic issues. **25.** The Japanese minority government resigned. **26.** In Kabul forces loyal to President Rabbani defeated forces loyal to Prime Minister Hekmatyar. **29.** The Hong Kong Legislative Council passed the final part of Governor Patten's democratic reform programme. **29.** The Japanese parliament elected Social Democratic Party leader Tomiichi Murayama as Prime Minister of a coalition government.

JULY 1994

**8.** President Kim Il-sung of North Korea died from a heart attack, leading to the cancellation of US-North Korean talks. **13.** Kim Jong-il, the son of President Kim Il-sung, was appointed as North Korea's President, party chief and military commander.

AUGUST 1994

**12.** The USA and North Korea reached an agreement under which North Korea will change its graphite nuclear reactors for a US-supplied light-water system less suited to producing weapons grade plutonium, in return for compensation; North Korea will remain a party to the Nuclear Non-Proliferation Treaty; and the USA and North Korea will establish diplomatic relations. **17.** The opposition People's Alliance won the Sri Lankan general election. **23.** The former Pakistani Prime Minister Mian Nawaz Sharif stated that Pakistan possessed a nuclear weapon.

## AUSTRALASIA AND THE PACIFIC

SEPTEMBER 1993

**17.** The Prime Minister of Australia, Paul Keating, had an audience with The Queen at Balmoral at which he outlined his plans for Australia to become a republic by 2001.

NOVEMBER 1993

**6.** New Zealand was left with a hung parliament after a general election in which the ruling National Party lost its majority but remained the largest party. A referendum approved changing the electoral system from first-past-the-post to proportional representation. **17.** The counting of expatriate votes in the New Zealand general election led to the National Party gaining a one-seat majority in parliament. **29.** The Fijian government was brought down in a parliamentary vote of no confidence over the 1994 budget.

DECEMBER 1993

**16.** The President of Fiji, Ratu Sir Penaia Ganilau, died of a blood disorder. **22.** The Australian

parliament passed the Native Title Bill to restore native land rights to Aborigines who had lost them 200 years earlier.

JANUARY 1994

**9.** Sydney was cut off from the rest of Australia by bush fires which burned for several days and devastated suburbs to the north and south of the city. **12.** The Great Council of Chiefs of Fiji elected Ratu Sir Kanisese Mara as President. **26.** The Prince of Wales escaped unhurt after a man shot a firing pistol at him during a celebration of Australia Day in Sydney.

FEBRUARY 1994

**25.** A parliamentary election in Fiji was won by the Fijian Political Party.

MARCH 1994

**2.** Jean-Marie Leye was elected President of Vanuatu.

## EUROPE

SEPTEMBER 1993

**19.** In the Polish general election the Democratic Left Alliance emerged as the largest party in parliament.

OCTOBER 1993

**10.** The Panhellenic Socialist Movement (PASOK) won the Greek general election. **18.** President Walesa nominated the Peasant Party leader Waldemar Pawlak as Prime Minister of Poland after Hanna Suchocka's government resigned. **19.** A Spanish air force general was shot dead in Madrid by Basque separatists. **29.** The Italian Senate passed a bill abolishing the immunity from prosecution of members of the Italian parliament in response to the continuing national corruption scandal.

NOVEMBER 1993

**4.** Members of the radical Kurdistan Worker's Party (PKK) attacked Turkish embassies, banks, newspaper, travel and airline offices in Britain, Germany, Denmark, Switzerland, Austria and France. **21.** In the first round of local elections for town and city councils in Italy the established Christian Democratic Party was defeated by coalitions of the broad left led by the former Communist Party and by the right-wing Northern League and neo-Fascist MSI party. **26.** Belgium was paralysed by a general strike called to protest at the government austerity plan, introduced to reduce the enormous public debt.

DECEMBER 1993

**5.** In the second round of local elections in Italy left-wing parties led by the Democratic Left Party emerged victorious over the Northern League and neo-Fascist MSI party. **8.** Two German neo-Nazis were sentenced to life imprisonment and ten years respectively for the murder of three Turks in an arson attack in Mölln near Hamburg in November 1992. **12.** The Hungarian Prime Minister Jozsef Antall died of heart failure; the Interior Minister Peter Boross was appointed acting Prime Minister. **23.** The Northern League withdrew its 55 members from the lower house of the Italian parliament in an attempt to force the President to call a general election.

JANUARY 1994

**1.** The European Economic Area Agreement, extending most of the single market provisions of the EC to six of the seven EFTA states, came into operation. **16.** The Italian President dissolved parliament and called a general election for 27 March. **18.** The former Bulgarian Communist dictator Todor Zhivkov was sentenced to seven years in jail for embezzlement. **27.** The former Italian Prime Minister and Socialist Party leader Bettino Craxi was ordered by a Milan judge to stand trial for corruption.

FEBRUARY 1994

**4.** Rioting French fishermen demanding an increase in subsidies destroyed cars and shops and burnt down the regional court in street battles with police. **6.** Martti Ahtisaari was elected President of Finland in the country's first direct election for President. **20.** Swiss voters approved in a referendum the banning, phased over ten years, of foreign lorries from Alpine roads, forcing lorries to use two new road-rail tunnels from 2005 onwards. **28.** The collapse of public sector wage negotiations led to a series of strikes across Germany.

MARCH 1994

**11.** The Slovak government was brought down by a vote of no confidence. **14.** A five-party coalition government was formed in Slovakia with Jozef Moravcik as Prime Minister. **28.** The right-wing Freedom Alliance, comprising Forza Italia, the Northern League and the National Alliance, won the Italian general election, with a clear majority in the lower house of parliament.

APRIL 1994

**28.** The Italian President asked Silvio Berlusconi, the leader of the right-wing Freedom Alliance, to form a government.

MAY 1994

**3.** The coalition government in the Netherlands lost its parliamentary majority in the general election and the Prime Minister Ruud Lubbers resigned. **9.** Poland, Hungary, the Czech Republic, the Slovak Republic, Romania, Bulgaria, Estonia, Latvia and Lithuania became associate members of the Western European Union. **11.** The Italian government led by Silvio Burlusconi was sworn in. **23.** The Christian Democrat candidate Roman Herzog was elected President of Germany. **29.** The Socialist Party won the most seats in the Hungarian general election.

JUNE 1994

**26.** The Hungarian Socialist Party formed a coalition government with the Alliance of Free Democrats Party.

JULY 1994

**1.** Roman Herzog was sworn in as President of Germany. **12.** The German constitutional court ruled that German forces might take part in armed missions outside the NATO area, subject on each occasion to parliamentary approval. **29.** The former Italian Prime Minister Bettino Craxi was sentenced *in absentia* to eight and a half years in jail for fraud. **29.** A Spanish army general was killed in a car bomb attack by Basque separatists.

AUGUST 1994

**31.** The last Russian troops left eastern Germany. All but 800 of the remaining Russian troops left Estonia and Latvia.

COMMONWEALTH OF INDEPENDENT STATES

SEPTEMBER 1993

**1.** The Russian President Boris Yeltsin issued a decree suspending Vice-President Rutskoi and Deputy Prime Minister Shumeiko, who had accused each other of corruption. **3.** President Yeltsin and President Kravchuk of the Ukraine agreed that Ukraine would transfer its nuclear weapons to Russia for dismantling and sell its share of the Black Sea fleet to Russia, in return for enriched uranium for its nuclear power stations and a reduction in its debt to Russia. **3.** The Russian parliament voted to overrule President Yeltsin's dismissal of Vice-President Rutskoi and to refer the issue to the Constitutional Court. **14.** President Eduard Shevardnadze of Georgia agreed to retract his resignation, announced earlier in the day, after the Georgian parliament agreed to his conditions of declaring a state of emergency and dissolving itself for three months. **16.** Abkhazian rebels in Georgia reneged on an August ceasefire and launched a new offensive against the Abkhazian capital Sukhumi. **16.** President Yeltsin reappointed the leading economic reformer Yegor Gaidar to the cabinet as First Deputy Prime Minister responsible for economics. **20.** The Azerbaijani parliament voted to rejoin the CIS. **21.** President Yeltsin announced the dissolution of the Russian parliament and called elections to a new parliament for December. The parliament responded by attempting to suspend President Yeltsin and swearing in Vice-President Rutskoi as acting President, together with a new cabinet. **22.** Abkhazian rebels brought down two Georgian aeroplanes in two days near Sukhumi. **23.** The Congress of People's Deputies voted to impeach President Yeltsin after he called a presidential election for June 1994. **24.** President Yeltsin ordered armed troops to surround the White House, the Russian parliament building in Moscow. Nine CIS member states signed an economic union agreement at a summit meeting in Moscow; the other two, Ukraine and Turkmenistan, became associate members. **25.** The Ukrainian parliament accepted the resignation of Prime Minister Leonid Kuchma and his government and called parliamentary elections for March 1994. **27.** Abkhazian rebels defeated Georgian government forces and captured Sukhumi, forcing President Shevardnadze to retreat. **28.** Demonstrators supporting the besieged Russian parliament clashed with police in Moscow and blocked the ring road before being dispersed.

### OCTOBER 1993

**2.** Street battles occurred in central Moscow between supporters of the parliament and police and interior ministry troops. In Georgia armed supporters of former President Gamsakhurdia took control of the port of Poti. **3.** In Moscow armed supporters of the Russian parliament broke the siege of the White House and attacked the Mayor's office, the television station and news agencies. President Yeltsin declared a state of emergency and ordered the army into the city to put down the rebellion. **4.** Four army divisions with tanks and heavy weaponry entered Moscow, defeated the supporters of the parliament, severely damaging the parliament building, and captured the main opposition leaders, former Vice-President Aleksandr Rutskoi and the parliament's chairman Ruslan Khasbulatov. Some 171 people were killed and 600 injured in the two days of fighting. **5.** President Yeltsin banned all political parties and newspapers which had supported the rebellion, had 1,452 hardliners arrested and declared a state of emergency in Moscow. **6.** Acting President Heidar Aliyev was elected President of Azerbaijan. **8.** President Shevardnadze announced that Georgia would join the CIS. **10.** President Yeltsin issued a decree ordering all Russia's regional councils to subordinate themselves to local administrations and ordering elections to all the councils to be held simultaneously with parliamentary elections. **17.** The state of emergency was lifted in Moscow. Rebels loyal to former President Gamsakhurdia captured the western Georgian town of Samtredia from government forces. **20.** Georgian government troops launched a counter-attack against rebel forces and captured the towns of Khoni and Mameti. **22.** Sixteen leaders of the former Russian parliament, including Aleksandr Rutskoi and Ruslan Khasbulatov, were formally charged with an armed attempt to remove the President. **25.** Georgian forces recaptured the port of Poti. **27.** President Yeltsin issued a decree allowing the unrestricted buying and selling of land for the first time since 1917.

### NOVEMBER 1993

**4.** A joint Russian-Ukrainian amphibious and marine task force from the Black Sea fleet landed at Poti to aid Georgian government forces and to secure communications links to Armenia and Azerbaijan. **7.** Georgian government forces captured the rebel capital of Zugdidi and forced rebels loyal to former

President Gamsakhurdia into the secessionist province of Abkhazia. **9.** President Yeltsin published a new constitution, to be put to the electorate in a referendum on 12 December.

### DECEMBER 1993

**12.** The federal parliamentary election in Russia resulted in a defeat for the policies and parties of radical economic reform; the main pro-reform party, Russia's Choice, emerged as the largest of 11 parties in the State Duma but with only 70 out of 450 seats. **23.** President Yeltsin and President Niyazov of Turkmenistan signed an agreement allowing Russian troops to protect Turkmenistan's borders with Iran and Afghanistan. **31.** Former President Gamsakhurdia of Georgia committed suicide after the defeat of his rebellion in western Georgia.

### JANUARY 1994

**16.** President Niyazov of Turkmenistan was confirmed in office until the year 2002 in a national referendum. **20.** The Russian Prime Minister Victor Chernomyrdin announced a new government of moderate reformers and conservatives. **26.** President Shushkevich of Belarus was dismissed by a vote of no confidence in the Communist-dominated parliament, which had opposed his plans for economic reform; he was replaced on 28 January by Mecheslav Grib. **31.** Yuri Meshkov was elected President of the Ukrainian autonomous republic of the Crimea and called for a referendum on Crimean independence.

### FEBRUARY 1994

**3.** President Yeltsin and President Shevardnadze signed a treaty under which Russia would gain a decisive say over Georgian economic policy, would train and arm the Georgian army, and would keep three military bases in Georgia. **23.** The Russian State Duma voted to pardon and release the leaders of the August 1991 and October 1993 coup attempts. **27.** The Agrarian Democratic Party won the Moldovan general election.

### MARCH 1994

**1.** The Georgian parliament ratified the country's membership of the CIS. **3.** Russia began to reduce gas supplies to Ukraine and Belarus in an attempt to force them to pay debts for past gas supplies of £600 million and £160 million respectively. **5.** Ukraine began the transfer of its nuclear weapons to Russia for dismantling. **6.** In a referendum 95 per cent of the population of Moldova voted to remain independent and rejected unification with Romania. **11.** The Russian Supreme Court ordered a retrial of the plotters of the August 1991 attempted coup, who had been released in an amnesty a month earlier. **27.** In referendums in the largely Russian-populated regions of the Donbass and Crimea in Ukraine, the electorates voted in favour of greater devolution of political power, making Russian an official language, and closer economic relations with Russia.

APRIL 1994

**4.** The Georgian government and the Abkhazian separatists signed a UN-mediated cease-fire agreement. **10.** Ukrainian soldiers stormed part of the Odessa naval base of the Black Sea fleet, injuring civilian and military personnel, and arrested Russian naval officers after a ship of the fleet had sailed to Sevastopol against Ukrainian wishes.

MAY 1994

**14.** The Georgian government and Abkhazian rebels signed a cease-fire agreement. **20.** The parliament of the Ukrainian autonomous republic of the Crimea voted to restore a suspended 1992 constitution declaring the Crimea to be sovereign. The Ukrainian parliament ordered the Crimean parliament to rescind its declaration within ten days. **27.** The dissident Alexander Solzhenitsyn returned to Russia after 20 years in exile.

JULY 1994

**1.** The second stage of the Russian mass privatization scheme was launched. **10.** Alexander Lukashenko won the Belarussian presidential election. Former Prime Minister Leonid Kuchma won the Ukrainian presidential election.

AUGUST 1994

**19.** Seven Russian troops and about 50 Tajik Muslim rebels were killed when the rebels attempted to cross the border from their Afghanistan bases.

## THE FORMER YUGOSLAVIA

SEPTEMBER 1993

**1.** The Bosnia-Hercegovina peace negotiations in Geneva collapsed after the Bosnian Serb and Bosnian Croat delegations refused Muslim demands for more land. **11.** The Croatian capital Zagreb came under rocket attack from ethnic Serb-controlled areas in Krajina in retaliation for the shelling of ethnic Serb-controlled areas in Croatia by Croat forces. **16.** Bosnian Muslim and Serb leaders signed an agreement in Geneva which included the closure of detention camps and the establishment of working groups to deal with border disputes. Heavy fighting between Bosnian Muslim and Bosnian Croat forces continued in central Bosnia as the two sides sought control of the area around Vitez. **20.** Peace negotiations aboard HMS *Invincible* ended after all sides refused to make further concessions. Heavy fighting in central and southern Bosnia continued as Muslim forces attempted to relieve the siege of the Muslim enclave of east Mostar. **29.** The Bosnian parliament rejected the latest Geneva peace plan until there were further Bosnian Serb withdrawals.

OCTOBER 1993

**7.** Mass graves containing the bodies of 576 Muslims massacred by Bosnian Croats were discovered near Mostar. **20.** President Milosevic of Serbia called a parliamentary election for 19 December after the government collapsed because of economic chaos. **23.** The rebel Muslim leader Fikret Abdic, who controlled part of the Bihac enclave in defiance of the Bosnian government, signed a peace agreement with the Bosnian Serb leader Radovan Karadzic and President Milosevic in Belgrade. **25.** Heavy fighting between Bosnian Muslim and Bosnian Croat forces around the central Bosnian town of Vares caused aid supplies to the Muslim-held Tuzla region to be suspended.

NOVEMBER 1993

**1.** Fighting broke out around Vares after Bosnian Croats massacred Muslims in the village of Stupni Do. **3.** Bosnian Croat forces and civilians abandoned Vares to advancing Muslim forces and fled through Bosnian Serb lines to Croatia. **9.** Shelling by Bosnian Croat forces destroyed the 16th-century bridge in Mostar. **10.** Seven people were killed in the Bosnian capital Sarajevo by Serb shelling and sniping. **24.** British troops replaced civilian UN drivers and escorted the first aid convoys into central Bosnia for a month. **29.** The Presidents of Serbia, Croatia and Bosnia-Hercegovina, together with the leaders of Bosnia's Croats and Serbs, agreed to reopen Bosnia-Hercegovina peace negotiations on the basis of an EC plan for a gradual suspension of UN sanctions against Serbia in return for the ceding of land to the Bosnian Muslims by the Bosnian Serbs.

DECEMBER 1993

**2.** Peace negotiations between the warring Bosnian factions ended in Geneva without progress. **14.** Bosnian Serb forces launched an offensive throughout Bosnia-Hercegovina against both Muslim- and Croat-held areas. **18.** Relief agencies evacuated 90 wounded Bosnian adults and children for treatment in Europe and the USA. **19.** In the Serbian general election the Socialist Party won 123 seats in parliament, three short of a majority. **23.** Peace talks in Brussels on the Bosnian conflict ended without agreement. Sarajevo came under heavy Bosnian Serb bombardment which killed six people. **27.** Heavy shelling of Sarajevo over two days killed 12 people and severed electricity and water supplies. **28.** The UNHCR evacuated 950 people from Sarajevo.

JANUARY 1994

**3.** Shelling of Sarajevo by Bosnian Serbs left 15 dead. **4.** The USA announced that it was doubling the number of nightly air drops of food and medicine to besieged Muslim communities in eastern Bosnia-Hercegovina. **6.** Lt.-Gen. Sir Michael Rose was appointed commander of UN forces in Bosnia-Hercegovina following the resignation the previous day of Lt.-Gen. Francis Briquemont of Belgium. Heavy bombardment of and fighting in Sarajevo left eight people dead. **11.** At the NATO heads of government summit in Brussels, NATO leaders agreed to use air strikes against Bosnian Serb forces if UN troops were prevented from relieving Canadian troops in the Srebrenica enclave or from opening

Tuzla airport. **14.** Two offensives were launched in central Bosnia: Bosnian Serbs attempted to encircle the Muslim-held Tuzla region; Bosnian Muslim forces succeeded in dividing the Croat-held Lasva valley. **18.** The UN announced that Gen. Jean Cot, the commander of UN forces in the former Yugoslavia, would leave his command early at the end of March after he criticized the ineffectiveness of UN forces in the conflict. **19.** The Federal Yugoslav Republic and Croatia signed an agreement on mutual limited recognition. **20.** The European Parliament voted to demand the dismissal of Lord Owen from his position as EC negotiator because of the lack of success in ending the conflict. **22.** Six Muslim children were killed by shelling in Sarajevo. **28.** One British aid worker was shot dead and two others wounded when their vehicle was hijacked near Zenica, Bosnia.

FEBRUARY 1994

**1.** Dutch UN troops entered the besieged Muslim town of Srebrenica in eastern Bosnia to relieve Canadian troops. The UN Secretary-General announced that Gen. Bertrand de Lapresle would replace Gen. Jean Cot as UN commander in the former Yugoslavia. **3.** Bosnian Serb forces allowed a UN convoy through a checkpoint outside Sarajevo after they were given an ultimatum by Lt.-Gen. Sir Michael Rose. **5.** Bosnian Serb shelling of the main market in Sarajevo killed 68. **9.** NATO issued an ultimatum to Bosnian Serb forces to remove all their artillery, mortars and tanks at least 12½ miles (20 km) from the centre of Sarajevo or to hand them over to the UN within ten days from midnight on the 20th, and to cease all attacks on the city in the meantime or face air strikes. Lt.-Gen. Sir Michael Rose brokered a separate cease-fire in Sarajevo and Bosnian Serbs agreed to withdraw their artillery or place it under UN control. **10.** The cease-fire in and around Sarajevo came into effect at midday. **11.** Bosnian Serb forces and the forces of the mainly Muslim government in and around Sarajevo began to hand over artillery pieces and mortars to the UN. **17.** Bosnian Serb forces began a mass withdrawal of heavy weapons from the NATO exclusion zone around Sarajevo after the Bosnian Serb leader Radovan Karadzic reached agreement with the Russian Deputy Foreign Minister Vitali Churkin on the deployment of 400 Russian troops in Sarajevo. Bosnian Serb forces launched artillery and tank attacks on the Muslim-held Bihac enclave in north-west Bosnia. **20.** The UN stated that Bosnian Serb forces had effectively complied with the NATO ultimatum. **25.** A cease-fire came into force at midday between Bosnian Muslim and Bosnian Croat forces throughout Bosnia-Hercegovina. **26.** A joint Bosnian Serb-Bosnian Croat force launched artillery and infantry assaults on the besieged Muslim enclave of Maglaj in northern Bosnia. **28.** Four Bosnian Serb aircraft were shot down by US aircraft after they violated the UN air exclusion zone over Bosnia and bombed Muslim-held areas.

MARCH 1994

**1.** Bosnian Muslim and Croat negotiators in Washington signed a peace agreement based on a federation of Muslim- and Croat-held areas in Bosnia-Hercegovina and a confederation of these areas of Bosnia with Croatia. **5.** UN forces in central Bosnia began patrolling cease-fire lines agreed by Bosnian Muslim and Croat forces and monitoring storage sites for heavy weapons. **7.** Muslim and Croat commanders in central Bosnia signed cease-fire maps and completed the withdrawal or handing over of heavy weapons to UN troops. **10.** Bosnian Serb forces prevented a UN aid convoy from reaching the besieged Muslim town of Maglaj and continued to shell the town. **18.** Agreements on a draft constitution for a federation of Muslims and Croats in Bosnia-Hercegovina and on a confederation of the federation with Croatia were signed by President Tudjman of Croatia, President Izetbegovic of Bosnia, Prime Minister Silajdzic of Bosnia and the Bosnian Croat representative Kresimir Zubak. **19.** The second British soldier to die in Bosnia, Cpl. Barney Warburton, was killed by a mine in Vitez. **20.** British UN troops escorted the first aid convoy for nine months into Maglaj after Bosnian Serb forces withdrew from part of their siege lines. **22.** The first flight for two years landed at Tuzla airport. **23.** The front lines around Sarajevo were opened for the first time since the beginning of the siege for restricted travel. **24.** The parliament of the self-proclaimed Bosnian Serb republic refused to join the Muslim-Croat federation in Bosnia and called for international recognition of their republic. **30.** The Croatian government and representatives of the Krajina Serbs signed a cease-fire agreement. Bosnian Serb forces launched an offensive against the Muslim-held enclave of Gorazde in eastern Bosnia.

APRIL 1994

**4.** Croatian and Krajina Serb forces began the withdrawal agreed under their cease-fire. **5.** Bosnian Serb forces broke through the Muslim defence of the Gorazde enclave and captured several villages. **6.** Bosnian Serbs captured half of the Gorazde enclave and prevented Lt.-Gen. Sir Michael Rose from entering the enclave; Bosnian Serb leaders announced that they were ready to come to cease-fire talks to cover the whole of Bosnia. **7.** Continued Bosnian Serb bombardment of Gorazde led to the cancellation of planned peace talks. **10.** Two NATO aircraft bombed Bosnian Serb forces around Gorazde and halted their advance. **11.** Bosnian Serb forces continued to bombard Gorazde and reimposed an aid blockade on Sarajevo after a second NATO air strike on Bosnian Serb artillery in the Gorazde area. **12.** Bosnian Serb forces took hostage UN monitors and aid workers throughout Bosnia in retaliation for the NATO air strikes of the previous two days. **14.** Bosnian Serb forces took hostage more UN monitors, bringing the total to 45, and attempted to remove heavy weapons from a UN compound near Sarajevo. **15.** Bosnian

Serb forces launched an all-out offensive on Gorazde in which a British SAS soldier with the UN force was killed and all the strategic points in the enclave captured. **16.** A British Sea Harrier was shot down over Gorazde by Bosnian Serb forces as it took part in unsuccessful attempts to bomb advancing Bosnian Serb forces. **18.** Bosnian Serb forces reneged on a cease-fire agreement negotiated by the Russian envoy Vitaly Churkin, captured the eastern part of Gorazde and shelled Muslim refugees in the centre and west of the town. **19.** Bosnian Serb forces stormed a heavy weapons collection point outside Sarajevo and took 18 anti-aircraft weapons; later they returned 13 weapons and began the release of over 100 UN soldiers and personnel held hostage. **21.** Bosnian Serb infantry entered Gorazde after three days of shelling. **22.** NATO issued an ultimatum to the Bosnian Serbs to cease all attacks on Gorazde immediately and to remove all heavy weapons and infantry from within a 3 km radius of the town centre. They were also ordered to withdraw all heavy weapons from within 12½ miles of the remaining UN safe areas of Tuzla, Bihac, Srebrenica and Zepa by midnight on 26 April. **23.** Gorazde came under severe bombardment from Bosnian Serb forces, leading to an argument between NATO, which requested an air strike, and the UN, which rejected it. **24.** Bosnian Serb forces withdrew to a 3 km radius of Gorazde town centre, ended their shelling of the town, and allowed in a UN convoy. **25.** A second UN convoy reached Gorazde. **29.** A British officer was killed and two British soldiers wounded by a land-mine near Gornji Vakuf, Bosnia.

**MAY 1994**
**1.** Danish UN peacekeeping troops destroyed Bosnian Serb artillery positions and an ammunition dump after they were fired upon by Bosnian Serb artillery whilst guarding Tuzla airport. **5.** The UN withdrew the permission that the Secretary-General's representative Yasushi Akashi had given to the Bosnian Serbs to move a tank column through the Sarajevo heavy weapons exclusion zone. **5.** Bosnian Serb forces allowed 150 British UN peacekeeping troops into Gorazde after blockading them for four days. **17.** The French government announced that it would withdraw 2,500 of its 6,000 peacekeeping troops by the end of 1994. **23.** Bosnian government forces launched their two most effective offensives for many months, capturing land around Tesanj and Kamenica from Bosnian Serb forces. **31.** The Bosnian Croat leader Kresimir Zubak was elected by the Bosnian parliament as the President of the Muslim-Croat Federation of Bosnia-Hercegovina, with the Muslim Ejup Ganic as Vice-President.

**JUNE 1994**
**6.** Peace negotiations began in Geneva after Bosnian Serb forces had complied with Bosnian government demands to withdraw from the two-mile exclusion zone around Gorazde. **8.** Leaders of the Bosnian Muslim-Croat federation and of the Bosnian Serbs

signed a one-month cease-fire, which came into effect on the 9th. **23.** The twin parliaments of Bosnia and the Muslim-Croat federation elected the Bosnian prime minister as prime minister of the federation. **27.** A British soldier was killed in Gorazde by a sniper.

**JULY 1994**
**6.** The foreign ministers of the USA, Britain, France, Germany and Russia (the International Contact Group) presented their peace plan and map for the division of Bosnia-Hercegovina to the warring factions. **12.** The Bosnian Serbs and Muslims agreed to extend their month-long cease-fire by a further month. **20.** The Bosnian factions presented their answers to the International Contact Group's peace plan; the Muslim-Croat federation accepted the plan but the Bosnian Serbs effectively rejected it. **22.** Mostar came under the control of European Union administrators as part of the Muslim-Croat federation agreement. **25.** The UN Secretary-General recommended to the UN Security Council that all UN peacekeepers should be withdrawn from Bosnia-Hercegovina. **27.** One British soldier was killed and one wounded in a Bosnian Serb attack on a UN convoy near Sarajevo as the Bosnian Serbs partly reimposed the siege of the city. **30.** The foreign ministers of the International Contact Group decided to tighten sanctions against the Yugoslav Federal Republic and to strengthen the protection of Muslim enclaves in eastern Bosnia.

**AUGUST 1994**
**3.** The Bosnian Serb assembly voted to hold a referendum on the peace plan. **4.** The Serbian President Slobodan Milosevic closed the Yugoslav-Bosnian border and severed all political and economic links with the Bosnian Serbs. **5.** NATO aircraft destroyed a Bosnian Serb anti-tank gun after Bosnian Serb forces withdrew weapons from a UN depot near Sarajevo; the weapons were returned the next day. **9.** Bosnian government forces defeated the forces of the rebel Muslim leader Fikret Abdic in the Bihac enclave. **11.** President Clinton announced that if the Bosnian Serbs did not accept the peace plan by 15 October, he would press the UN to lift the arms embargo on the Bosnian government. **16.** Bosnian Serb forces cut water supplies to Sarajevo. **19.** The Bosnian government took control of the Bihac enclave. **28.** The Bosnian Serb population voted in a referendum to reject the International Contact Group peace plan and map.

---

## EUROPEAN UNION

**SEPTEMBER 1993**
**20.** A crisis meeting of EC foreign, finance, trade and agriculture ministers held in Brussels in an attempt to prevent crises both in the GATT negotiations and in the EC, ended with a compromise

agreement to negotiate clarifications and interpretations of the 1992 Blair House agricultural agreement with the USA.

OCTOBER 1993

**12.** Germany ratified the Maastricht Treaty. **29.** At a special summit in Brussels the 12 EC heads of government agreed that the European Monetary Institute (the future European Central Bank) should be located in Frankfurt, and confirmed that economic and monetary union should be achieved by 1997 or 1999.

NOVEMBER 1993

**1.** The Maastricht Treaty on European Union came into force throughout the European Community. **16.** The EC Court of Auditors published its annual report, which stated that fraud and poor management cost the EC £125 million in 1992.

DECEMBER 1993

**11.** A two-day heads of government summit ended in Brussels with partial agreement to support President Delors's White Paper on infrastructure and information technology spending in the Community. **21.** The EC Commission reduced its number of Vice-Presidents from six to two as required under the Maastricht Treaty.

JANUARY 1994

**1.** The European Monetary Institute, based in Frankfurt, came in to operation. Greece assumed the presidency of the Council of Ministers.

FEBRUARY 1994

**16.** The Europol Drugs Agency was established in the Hague.

MARCH 1994

**1.** Austria, Finland and Sweden completed negotiations on their terms of accession to the European Union (EU). **4.** The European Parliament used for the first time powers introduced by the Maastricht Treaty to force the Council of Ministers to form a committee to agree a compromise to varying budgets for research programmes. **16.** Norway agreed the terms of its accession to the EU. **29.** Member governments agreed to a compromise on the voting structure of the Council of Ministers after enlargement; a veto will require 27 votes instead of the present 23, but if 23 to 26 votes oppose a measure, a delay will ensue before the measure is voted on again in which every effort will be made to reach a compromise.

APRIL 1994

**1.** Hungary applied for membership of the EU. **7.** Poland applied for membership of the EU. **13.** The European Commission began legal action in the European Court of Justice against the Greek government to force it to end its blockade of the former Yugoslav republic of Macedonia.

MAY 1994

**4.** The European Parliament voted to approve the accession to the EU of Austria, Finland, Norway and Sweden. **5.** The Austrian parliament approved the country's accession to the EU.

JUNE 1994

**9.** Elections to the European Parliament were held in some member states; the other states held their elections on the 12th. **12.** The Austrian electorate voted in favour of joining the European Union. **14.** The European Union signed a partnership and co-operation agreement with Ukraine. **24.** At the heads of government summit in Corfu, Austria, Finland, Norway and Sweden signed the instrument of accession. **25.** The UK government vetoed the appointment of the Belgian Prime Minister Jean-Luc Dehaene as President of the European Commission.

JULY 1994

**1.** Germany took over the presidency of the European Union. **15.** Heads of government agreed on the appointment of the Luxembourg Prime Minister Jacques Santer as President of the European Commission from January 1995. **19.** The first session of the new European Parliament opened in Strasbourg. **21.** The European Parliament endorsed the nomination of Jacques Santer as European Commission President.

## THE MIDDLE EAST

SEPTEMBER 1993

**5.** President Saddam Hussein of Iraq reshuffled his cabinet and dismissed the Prime Minister after his failure to foresee a coup attempt. **8.** Aryeh Deri, the Israeli Interior Minister and leader of the Shas religious party, resigned after the Supreme Court stated that he should be dismissed for corruption. **9.** Israel and the Palestine Liberation Organization (PLO) officially exchanged letters under which the PLO recognized the right of the state of Israel to exist, renounced violence, promised to end the *intifada* and pledged to remove offending articles from the PLO charter, while Israel recognized the PLO as the representative of the Palestinian people. Israel allowed 189 of the 400 Palestinian deportees stranded in southern Lebanon for nine months to return to the Occupied Territories. **13.** Israel and the PLO signed a 'Declaration of Principles' peace accord at a ceremony at the White House in Washington. **14.** Israeli and Jordanian officials initialled a set of principles for a formal peace treaty. **23.** The Israeli Knesset voted 61 to 50 with eight abstentions to approve the peace agreement with the PLO. **27.** A team of 50 weapons inspectors arrived in Iraq to test Iraq's promise to destroy its nuclear, chemical, biological and ballistic missile weapons and to establish a long-term monitoring system.

OCTOBER 1993

**3.** President Mubarak of Egypt was elected for a third six-year term in an election in which he was the only candidate. **11.** The PLO central council ratified the peace accords with Israel by 63 votes to eight with 11 abstentions. **13.** Israel and the PLO began discussions on implementing the peace accord and on the Israeli withdrawal from the Gaza Strip and Jericho. **30.** Eight Islamic fundamentalists were sentenced to death in Egypt for their part in a terror campaign. **31.** A UN weapons team ended its inspection of Iraq's military programmes and stated that no evidence had been found of any Iraqi violation of the UN ban on building weapons of mass destruction.

NOVEMBER 1993

**1.** Jewish settlers in the West Bank attacked a Palestinian refugee camp at Jalazoun and blocked main roads to prevent Palestinians passing close to Jewish settlements after attacks on them by members of the fundamentalist Hamas movement. **2.** Israeli-PLO negotiations on implementing the peace agreement were suspended after the PLO negotiators stated that the Israelis were intent on redeploying their forces rather than withdrawing them. **9.** In Jordan's first parliamentary election since 1956 traditionalist and centrist supporters of King Hussein took 59 of the 80 seats in the lower house of parliament. **11.** The UN Security Council voted to impose new sanctions on Libya, including freezing its overseas assets and limiting its imports of oil industry equipment, because of Libya's refusal to surrender two suspects in the Lockerbie bombing case. **16.** Hezbollah guerrillas launched an offensive against the Israeli security zone in southern Lebanon. **25.** Violence by Palestinians erupted in the Gaza Strip after the killing of armed members of Hamas by Israeli security forces. **30.** The Israeli army suspended its search for Islamic and PLO militants in the Occupied Territories in an attempt to end violent clashes.

DECEMBER 1993

**1.** The new UN sanctions against Libya took effect. **10.** Jewish settlers in the West Bank shot dead three Palestinians in revenge for the killing of two settlers by the Hamas movement. **13.** Israel failed to meet the deadline set by the peace accord with the PLO to begin withdrawing its forces from the Gaza Strip and Jericho, after the peace negotiations failed to reach agreement on the control of border crossings, defining the Jericho area and the security of Jewish settlements. **15.** Israel allowed the return to the Occupied Territories of the remaining Palestinians deported to southern Lebanon in 1992. **20.** Six Islamic fundamentalists were hanged in Cairo for terrorist attacks.

JANUARY 1994

**16.** At a meeting in Geneva with President Clinton, President Assad of Syria stated that Syria would return to the Middle East peace negotiations and was ready to establish normal relations with Israel.

FEBRUARY 1994

**7.** Four Israeli soldiers were killed by Hezbollah guerrillas in southern Lebanon; Israel retaliated with air strikes. **9.** The PLO chairman Yasser Arafat and the Israeli Foreign Minister Shimon Peres signed a partial agreement on the issues still to be agreed before the Israeli withdrawal from the Gaza Strip and Jericho. **25.** Violence between Palestinians and Israeli security forces erupted throughout the Occupied Territories after a Jewish settler shot dead 30 Palestinians in a mosque in Hebron. **26.** The PLO suspended peace negotiations with Israel until all Israeli settlers in the Occupied Territories were disarmed and some settlements were dismantled; Syria, Lebanon and Jordan suspended peace negotiations with Israel two days later. **27.** The Israeli government approved a limited crackdown on militant Jewish settlers. Nine people were killed when a bomb exploded during mass in a Maronite Catholic church in Jounieh, Lebanon.

MARCH 1994

**1.** The Israeli government released 500 Palestinian prisoners in an attempt to persuade the PLO to reopen negotiations on implementing the peace accord. **13.** The Israeli government outlawed two Jewish extremist groups, Kach and Kahane Chai, one of whose members had perpetrated the Hebron mosque massacre. **17.** Two Islamic militants were hanged in Egypt for attempting to kill President Mubarak, and nine were sentenced to death for attempting to murder the Prime Minister in November 1993. **18.** Syria, Jordan and Lebanon announced the resumption of peace negotiations with Israel after the UN Security Council condemned the Hebron mosque massacre and called for an international presence in the Occupied Territories to protect Palestinians. **28.** Undercover Israeli troops killed six Palestinian activists of the Fatah organization in the Gaza Strip. **31.** Israeli and PLO negotiators signed a security accord on the deployment of observers in Hebron and agreed to resume talks on the peace accord.

APRIL 1994

**3.** Israel and the PLO resumed negotiations on implementing the peace accord. **5.** Fifty PLO officials returned from exile to the Gaza Strip and Jericho to begin the establishment of an autonomous Palestinian authority. **6.** A Palestinian car bomber killed himself and nine Israelis in Afula. **13.** The deadline for Israeli forces to withdraw from the Gaza Strip and Jericho and for the transfer of powers to a nominated Palestinian authority passed without Israeli-PLO agreement on the completion of the Israeli withdrawal. Six Israelis were killed in Hadera by a suicide bomber of the Hamas movement. **14.** Two US fighter planes patrolling the air exclusion zone over northern Iraq shot down two US army helicopters which they had mistakenly identified as Iraqi aircraft; the helicopters were carrying 26 UN personnel, including two British officers, and Iraqi Kurdish leaders. **27.** Fighting broke out in northern Yemen between rival army units of the former states of North Yemen and South Yemen after political tension between the former ruling parties of the two states.

**MAY 1994**

**2.** Israel, the PLO, Norway, Denmark and Italy signed an agreement to deploy an international group of observers from Norway, Denmark and Italy in Hebron. **4.** The Israeli Prime Minister Yitzhak Rabin and the PLO chairman Yasser Arafat signed the Cairo accords detailing the implementation of the September 1993 Declaration of Principles and enabling the first phase of Palestinian autonomy to begin. **5.** Civil war broke out in Yemen between the armed forces of the former North Yemen and South Yemen after months of unsuccessful negotiations over alleged inequitable political and economic arrangements. **6.** The Yemeni civil war intensified, with southern missile attacks on the northern capital of Sana'a and a northern armoured advance towards Aden. **11.** Israel began its military withdrawal from the Palestinian autonomous areas of the Gaza Strip and Jericho and the transfer of civil administration to the Palestinians. **13.** Israel handed over security and administrative control of the Palestinian autonomous area of Jericho to Palestinian police and officials, and the first joint Israeli-Palestinian patrols of the area's main road began. **18.** Israeli forces completed their withdrawal from the Palestinian autonomous area of the Gaza Strip and redeployed to Israel and to Jewish settlements in the strip. **20.** Two Israeli soldiers were killed by Islamic militants at a checkpoint on the Israel-Gaza Strip border. **20.** The South Yemeni leadership announced its secession from the united state of Yemen and the independence of South Yemen as the Democratic Republic of Yemen.

**JUNE 1994**

**2.** Israeli aircraft bombed a Hezbollah camp in Lebanon, killing 45. **5.** Jordan resumed peace negotiations with Israel. **14.** A UN weapons inspection team completed the destruction of Iraq's main chemical weapons plant at Muthanna.

**JULY 1994**

**1.** The PLO chairman Yasser Arafat was welcomed by 200,000 Palestinians when he arrived in the Gaza Strip after 27 years in exile. **5.** Yasser Arafat flew to the Palestinian autonomous area of Jericho and swore in members of the Palestinian National Authority. **6.** Northern Yemeni forces entered Aden after capturing all other areas under southern Yemeni control. **7.** Northern Yemeni forces captured Aden as southern leaders fled the country, bringing the civil war to an end. **16.** Palestinian police and Israeli border guards exchanged gunfire after thousands of Palestinian workers had been prevented from travelling from the Gaza Strip to Israel. **19.** Israeli and Jordanian officials agreed to start continuous peace negotiations on 8 August. **25.** King Hussein of Jordan and the

Israeli Prime Minister Yitzhak Rabin signed a peace declaration in Washington DC.

**AUGUST 1994**

**8.** The first border crossing between Israel and Jordan was opened. **10.** Yasser Arafat and Yitzhak Rabin held their first summit and agreed to open negotiations on the extension of Palestinian authority throughout the West Bank. **15.** Palestinian security forces in the Gaza Strip arrested 40 suspected Hamas militants after attacks on Israelis in the area. **29.** Israel and the PLO signed an agreement to extend Palestinian control in education, health, culture, social welfare, taxation and tourism to the rest of the West Bank.

# INTERNATIONAL RELATIONS

**SEPTEMBER 1993**

**8.** The USA and Russia signed a military co-operation agreement. **15.** The UN General Assembly elected the 11 judges to serve on the international war crimes tribunal for the former Yugoslavia. **23.** The International Olympic Committee awarded the 2000 Olympic Games to Sydney, Australia. **27.** The Uruguay round of GATT talks remained unresolved after US government refused to negotiate or clarify the 1992 Blair House agricultural agreement with EC negotiators.

**OCTOBER 1993**

**25.** The biennial Commonwealth heads of government summit in Cyprus ended with agreement to invite South Africa to rejoin the Commonwealth after multi-racial elections; to promote democracy in the remaining non-democratic Commonwealth states; to invite Cameroon to join when it becomes sufficiently democratic; and denounced the Turkish occupation of northern Cyprus.

**NOVEMBER 1993**

**17.** The 11 judges of the UN war crimes tribunal for the former Yugoslavia were sworn in during the inaugural session.

**DECEMBER 1993**

**15.** The Uruguay round of GATT negotiations was successfully concluded hours before the deadline with an agreement between the USA and the EC over the audiovisual, textile, agricultural and services sectors. **30.** Israel and the Vatican signed an agreement in Jerusalem establishing full diplomatic relations between the two states.

**JANUARY 1994**

**4.** Lithuania formally requested membership of NATO. **11.** The NATO heads of government summit in Brussels endorsed President Clinton's 'Partnership for Peace' plan inviting the states of eastern Europe into closer military relationships with NATO without them becoming members. **14.** The Presidents of Russia, the Ukraine and the USA signed treaties agreeing to retarget their long-range nuclear missiles away from each other's cities and to dismantle and destroy Ukraine's nuclear weapons in exchange for security guarantees, US$1 billion in compensation, and reprocessed nuclear fuel for Ukraine's nuclear power stations.

FEBRUARY 1994
**3.** The International Court of Justice in the Hague rejected Libyan claims to the Aouzou strip and stated that the area should remain part of Chad. **11.** Trade talks between the USA and Japan ended without agreement in Washington. **14.** A Bosnian Serb accused of killing Muslim prisoners at detention camps in Bosnia-Hercegovina was arrested in Munich. **15.** Russia and the UK signed an agreement in Moscow to retarget their nuclear weapons away from each other's countries and to conduct a series of joint military exercises.

APRIL 1994
**4.** The UN Secretary-General (Boutros Boutros Ghali) rejected a Russian request to have Russian peacekeeping troops in the CIS designated UN peacekeeping forces. **15.** The Final Act of the Uruguay round of GATT was signed by over 100 states in Marrakash, Morocco.

MAY 1994
**25.** The United Nations lifted its only remaining sanction on South Africa, that on armaments. South Africa became a member of the Organization of African Unity. **26.** President Clinton renewed China's most favoured nation trading status despite acknowledging that it had not fulfilled any of the human rights conditions set by the US government a year ago. The International Whaling Commission agreed to establish a whale sanctuary around Antarctica which would include a ban on commercial whaling in the area for ten years.

JUNE 1994
**1.** South Africa rejoined the Commonwealth. **10.** China exploded an underground nuclear device in contravention of the international nuclear test moratorium. **22.** Russia joined NATO's Partnership for Peace programme. **23.** South Africa resumed its seat at the UN.

JULY 1994
**10.** The G7 summit in Naples ended without significant agreement on economic issues but admitted Russia to form the G8 on political issues.

# Wedding Anniversaries

| | | | |
|---|---|---|---|
| First | Cotton | Fourteenth | Ivory |
| Second | Paper | Fifteenth | Crystal |
| Third | Leather | Twentieth | China |
| Fourth | Fruit and Flower | Twenty-fifth | Silver |
| Fifth | Wood | Thirtieth | Pearl |
| Sixth | Sugar/Iron | Thirty-fifth | Coral |
| Seventh | Wool | Fortieth | Ruby |
| Eighth | Bronze/Electrical appliances | Forty-fifth | Sapphire |
| Ninth | Copper/Pottery | Fiftieth | Gold |
| Tenth | Tin | Fifty-fifth | Emerald |
| Eleventh | Steel | Sixtieth | Diamond |
| Twelfth | Silk and Fine Linen | Seventieth | Platinum |
| Thirteenth | Lace | | |

# Obituaries

## 1 SEPTEMBER 1993 – 31 AUGUST 1994

Acton, Sir Harold, CBE, historian and aesthete, aged 89 – 27 February 1994

Adams, Daisy, oldest person in Britain, aged 113 – 8 December 1993

Ailsa, 7th Marquess, OBE, landowner, aged 68 – 7 April 1994

Aldrich, Ronnie, musical arranger and director, aged 77 – 30 September 1993

Alexander of Potterhill, Lord, PH.D., general secretary of Association of Education Committees 1945–77, aged 87 – 8 September 1993

Allen, David, research astronomer, aged 47 – 26 July 1994

Ameche, Don, American film actor, aged 85 – 6 December 1993

Anderson, Lindsay, film and stage director, aged 71 – 30 August 1994

Ansell, Colonel Sir Michael, CBE, DSO, chairman of British Show Jumping Association 1945–64, president of St Dunstan's 1977–86, show director of the Royal International and Horse of the Year shows, aged 88 – 17 February 1994

Antall, Jozsef, prime minister of Hungary since 1990, aged 61 – 12 December 1993

Ardwick, Lord, journalist and politician, aged 84 – 18 August 1994

Armstrong, Sir Thomas, principal of the Royal Academy of Music 1955–68, aged 96 – 26 June 1994

Aylestone, Lord (Herbert Bowden), CH, CBE, PC, Labour chief whip 1955–64, Leader of the House of Commons 1964–6, Secretary of State for Commonwealth Affairs 1966–7 and chairman of the Independent Broadcasting Authority 1967–75, aged 89 – 30 April 1994

Baldwin, Geoffrey, GC, PH.D., explosives expert, aged 82 – 2 May 1994

Barrault, Jean-Louis, French actor-manager, aged 83 – 22 January 1994

Beit, Sir Alfred, Bt., art collector, Conservative MP for St Pancras South-East 1931–45, aged 91 – 12 May 1994

Benjamin, Louis, theatrical impresario, aged 71 – 20 June 1994

Bessborough, 10th Earl, Conservative junior minister 1963–4, 1970, aged 80 – 5 December 1993

Blanch, Rt. Revd Lord (Stuart), PC, Archbishop of York 1975–83, aged 76 – 3 June 1994

Blanchflower, Danny, footballer, aged 67 – 9 December 1993

Blum, Maitre Suzanne, formerly lawyer for the Duke and Duchess of Windsor, aged 95 – 23 January 1994

Borotra, Jean, Basque tennis player, aged 95 – 17 July 1994

Boyce, James, MP, Labour MP for Rotherham since 1992, aged 46 – 25 January 1994

Boyden, James, Labour MP for Bishop Auckland 1959–79, aged 82 – 26 September 1993

Bradbury, 2nd Baron, aged 80 – 31 March 1994

Bruce-Mitford, Rupert, archaeologist, aged 79 – 10 March 1994

Burgess, Anthony, novelist, essayist and composer, aged 76 – 22 November 1993

Burr, Raymond, American actor, aged 76 – 12 September 1993

Busby, Sir Matt, CBE, manager and general manager of Manchester United FC 1945–71 and president since 1980, aged 84 – 20 January 1994

Calman, Mel, cartoonist, aged 62 – 10 February 1994

Canetti, Elias, author and Nobel laureate 1981, aged 89 – 14 August 1994

Carew, 6th Baron, CBE, chairman of the Royal British Legion 1963–6, aged 89 – 27 June 1994

Carr, J. L., author and publisher, aged 81 – 26 February 1994

Chatt, Joseph, CBE, FRS, chemist, aged 79 – 19 May 1994

Christison, General Sir Philip, Bt., GBE, CB, DSO, MC, aged 100 – 21 December 1993

Clegg, Sir Walter, Conservative MP for North Fylde, later Wyre 1966–87, aged 73 – 15 April 1994

Clemo, Jack, poet, novelist and essayist, aged 78 – 25 July 1994

Cobain, Kurt, American rock singer, aged 28 – 8 April 1994

Compton, Sir Edmund, GCB, KBE, first Parliamentary Commissioner for Administration (Ombudsman) 1967–71, aged 87 – 11 March 1994

Connor, Kenneth, MBE, comic actor, aged 75 – 28 November 1993

Conrad, William, American actor and director, aged 73 – 11 February 1994

Corbet, Freda, London councillor 1934–64, Labour MP for North West Camberwell 1945–74 (February), aged 92 – 1 November 1993

Cotten, Joseph, American actor, aged 88 – 6 February 1994

Cottesloe, 4th Baron, GBE, TD, chairman of the Arts Council 1960–5 and of the South Bank Theatre Board 1962–77, aged 94 – 22 April 1994

Crawley, Aidan, MBE, Labour MP for Buckingham 1945–51, Conservative MP for West Derbyshire 1962–8, first editor-in-chief of ITN and founding chairman of London Weekend Television, aged 85 – 3 November 1993

Cross, Sir Barry, CBE, FRS, physiologist, aged 69 – 27 April 1994

Cross, Joan, CBE, opera singer, aged 93 – 12 December 1993

Cryer, Robert (Bob), MP, Labour MP for Keighley 1974–83 and for Bradford South since 1987, and MEP for Sheffield 1984–9, aged 59 – 12 April 1994

Curry, John, OBE, former Olympic and world champion ice skater, aged 44 – 15 April 1994

Cusack, Cyril, Irish actor-manager, aged 82 – 7 October 1993

Cushing, Peter, OBE, actor, aged 81 – 11 August 1994

Daryngton, 2nd Baron, aged 85 – 5 April 1994

Delfont, Lord, theatrical impresario, aged 84 – 28 July 1994

Del Mar, Norman, CBE, conductor and music writer, aged 74 – 6 February 1994

de Mille, Agnes, American choreographer, aged 88 – 7 October 1993

de Vere White, Terence, Irish novelist, biographer and critic, aged 82 – 17 June 1994

Donaldson, Frances (Lady Donaldson of Knightsbridge), author, aged 87 – 27 March 1994

Downes, Ralph, CBE, organist, aged 89 – 24 December 1993

Elliot of Harwood, Baroness, DBE, chairman of the Consumer Council 1963–8, aged 90 – 3 January 1994

Ellis, Raymond, Labour MP for Derbyshire North East 1979–87, aged 70 – June 1994

Feldberg, Wilhelm, CBE, FRS, head of the Division of Physiology and Pharmacology, National Institute for Medical Research, London 1949–67, aged 92 – 23 October 1993

Fellini, Federico, Italian film-maker, aged 73 – 31 October 1993

Fitch, Admiral Sir Richard, KCB, Second Sea Lord 1986–8, aged 64 – 15 February 1994

Foote, Maj.-Gen. Robert, VC, CB, DSO, aged 88 – 22 November 1993

Gage, 7th Viscount, aged 61 – 30 November 1993

Galpern, Lord, Labour MP for Glasgow Shettleston 1959–79, aged 90 – 23 September 1993

Gamsakhurdia, Zviad, president of Georgia 1990–2, aged 54 – 31 December 1993

Ganilau, Ratu Sir Penaia, GCMG, KCVO, KBE, DSO, governor-general of Fiji 1983–7 and president of Fiji since 1987, aged 75 – 15 December 1993

Gebler Davies, Stan, Irish journalist, aged 50 – 23 June 1994

Gilliat, Sidney, screenwriter and film director, aged 86 – 31 May 1994

Ginsburg, David, Labour and then SDP MP for Dewsbury 1959–83, aged 73 – 18 March 1994

Goldsworthy, Lt.-Cdr. Leon, GC, DSC, GM, aged 85 – 7 August 1994

Graves, 8th Baron (Peter Graves), actor, aged 82 – 6 June 1994

Griffiths, Sir Roy, deputy chairman of the National Health Service Policy Board, aged 67 – 28 March 1994

Grimond, Lord (Jo), TD, PC, leader of the Liberal Party 1956–67, aged 80 – 24 October 1993

Haldeman, H. R. (Harry), White House chief of staff under President Nixon and a leading figure in the Watergate scandal, aged 67 – 12 November 1993

Hall, Adelaide, American jazz singer, aged 92 – 7 November 1993

Hambro, Jocelyn, MC, former chairman of Hambros Bank and J. O. Hambro & Co., aged 75 – 19 June 1994

Hannigan, Rt. Revd James, Roman Catholic Bishop of Wrexham since 1987, aged 65 – 6 March 1994

Harkness, Jack, OBE, rose grower, aged 75 – 18 June 1994

Hartman, Dame Marea, DBE, manager of the British athletics team 1956–78 and president of the AAA, aged 74 – 29 August 1994

Harvey of Prestbury, Lord, CBE, Conservative MP for Macclesfield 1945–71, aged 88 – 5 April 1994

Hay, Prof. Denys, FBA, historian, aged 78 – 14 June 1994

Headley, 5th Baron, aged 91 – 23 February 1994

Hepple, Norman, RA, portrait painter, aged 85 – 3 January 1994

Higgins, Rt. Hon. Sir John (Eoin), judge of the High Court of Northern Ireland since 1984, aged 66 – 2 September 1993

Hindlip, 5th Baron, aged 81 – 19 December 1993

Hirshfield, Lord, accountant and founder and chairman of Trades Union Unit Trust Managers 1961–83, aged 80 – 6 December 1993

Hodgkin, Prof. Dorothy, OM, FRS, scientist, discoverer of the structure of penicillin and insulin, winner of the Nobel prize for chemistry 1964, aged 84 – 29 July 1994

Honecker, Erich, general secretary of the Communist Party of East Germany 1971–89 and East German head of state 1976–89, aged 81 – 29 May 1994

Houphouet-Boigny, Felix, president of the Côte d'Ivoire since 1960, aged 88 – 7 December 1993

Hovsepian-Mehr, Revd Haik, superintendent of the Assemblies of God churches in Iran, aged 49 – 20 January 1994, from unknown causes

Hunter of Newington, Lord, MBE, FRCP, vice-chancellor of Birmingham University 1968–81, aged 78 – 24 March 1994

Huntingfield, 6th Baron, linguist, aged 78 – 1 May 1994

Inchcape, 3rd Earl, chairman and chief executive of Inchcape PLC 1958–82, chairman of P & O 1973–83, aged 76 – 17 March 1994

Innocent, Harold, actor, aged 60 – 12 September 1993

Ionesco, Eugene, Romanian-born French playwright, aged 81 – 28 March 1994

Jackson, Norman, VC, aged 74 – 26 March 1994

Jarman, Derek, film director, aged 52 – 19 February 1994

Jarred, Mary, opera singer, aged 94 – 12 December 1993

John-Mackie, Lord, Labour MP for Enfield East 1959–74 and junior Agriculture minister, chairman of the Forestry Commission 1976–9, farmer, aged 84 – 25 May 1994

Johnston, Brian, CBE, MC, cricket commentator, broadcaster and writer, aged 81 – 5 January 1994

Kim Il Sung, head of state of North Korea since 1948, aged 82 – 8 July 1994

King, Evelyn, Labour MP for Penryn and Falmouth 1945–50, Conservative MP for South Dorset 1964–79, and headmaster, aged 86 – 14 April 1994

Lazar, Irving 'Swifty', American literary and talent agent, aged 86 – 30 December 1993

Leicester, 6th Earl, farmer and cattle-breeder, aged 84 – 19 June 1994

Leighton, Ron, MP, Labour MP for Newham North East since 1979, aged 64 – 28 February 1994

Lessore, Helen, OBE, RA, painter, aged 86 – 6 May 1994

Lewis, Admiral Sir Andrew, KCB, aged 75 – 8 November 1993

Lindsay of Birker, 2nd Lord, former professor of Far Eastern studies, aged 84 – 13 February 1994

Lorimer, Hew, CBE, RSA, sculptor, aged 86 – 1 September 1993

Loughlin, Charles, Labour MP for West Gloucestershire 1959–74, aged 79 – October 1993

Loy, Myrna, American actress, aged 88 – 14 December 1993

Lutoslawski, Witold, Polish composer and conductor, aged 81 – 7 February 1994

Luyt, Sir Richard, GCMG, KCVO, DCM, Governor of British Guiana 1964–6, vice-chancellor of the University of Cape Town 1968–80, aged 78 – 12 February 1994

Lyon, Alex, Labour MP for York 1966–83 and junior minister, aged 61 – 30 September 1993

McManus, Mark, actor, aged 59 – 6 June 1994

Mais, Lord, GBE, TD, ERD, structural engineer, Lord Mayor of London 1972–3, aged 82 – 28 November 1993

Mancini, Henry, film music composer, aged 70 – 14 June 1994

Mar (13th) and Kellie (15th), Earl of, aged 72 – 22 December 1993

Marchamley, 3rd Baron, aged 72 – June 1994

Maude of Stratford-upon-Avon, Lord, TD, PC, journalist and former Conservative MP and junior minister, aged 81 – 9 November 1993

Maxwell, The Hon. Lord (Peter), Senator of the College of Justice 1973–88, aged 74 – 2 January 1994

Mercouri, Melina, Greek Minister of Culture and former film actress, aged 68 – 6 March 1994

Methuen, 6th Baron, aged 68 – 24 August 1994

Milford, 2nd Baron, aged 91 – 30 November 1993

Milligan, Stephen, MP, Conservative MP for Eastleigh since 1992, aged 45 – 7 February 1994

Monsell, 2nd Viscount, aged 88 – 28 November 1993

Moores, Sir John, CBE, founder of the Littlewoods Organization and chairman 1924–77 and 1980–2, aged 97 – 25 September 1993

Moya, Hidalgo, architect, aged 74 – 3 August 1994

Muggeridge, Kitty, author, aged 90 – 11 June 1994

Murray of Newhaven, Lord, KCB, PH.D., chairman of the Universities Grants Committee 1953–63, aged 90 – 10 October 1993

Ndadaye, Melchior, president of Burundi since July 1993, aged 40 – assassinated 21 October 1993

Nixon, Richard, president of the USA 1969–74, aged 81 – 22 April 1994

Normanby, 4th Marquess, KG, CBE, landowner, aged 81 – 30 January 1994

Northesk, 13th Earl, landowner and farmer, aged 67 – 26 January 1994

Norton, 7th Baron, OBE, aged 78 – October 1993

Novotna, Jarmila, Czech-born soprano, aged 86 – 9 February 1994

Nugent of Guildford, Lord, PC, Conservative MP for Guildford 1950–66 and junior minister, aged 86 – 16 March 1994

Onassis, Jacqueline Kennedy, American First Lady 1961–3, aged 64 – 19 May 1994

O'Neill, Thomas (Tip), Speaker of the US House of Representatives 1977–86, aged 81 – 6 January 1994

Palmer, Arthur, Labour MP for Wimbledon 1945–50, Cleveland 1952–9, Bristol Central (later Bristol North East) 1964–83, aged 82 – 14 August 1994

Park, George, Labour MP for Coventry North East 1974–87, aged 79 – 8 May 1994

Parkin, Leonard, former ITN newscaster, aged 64 – 20 September 1993

Pauling, Linus, American chemist and winner of the Nobel prize for chemistry 1954 and the Nobel peace prize 1963, aged 93 – 19 August 1994

Peppard, George, American film and television actor, aged 65 – 8 May 1994

Perry, Frances, MBE, horticulturist, aged 86 – 11 October 1993

Phillimore, 4th Baron, architect, aged 83 – 29 March 1994

Phoenix, River, American film actor, aged 23 – 31 October 1993

Plunkett, Roy, American inventor of Teflon, aged 83 – 12 May 1994

Popp, Lucia, Czech-born opera singer, aged 54 – 16 November 1993

Porritt, Lord, GCMG, GCVO, CBE, surgeon, and governor-general of New Zealand 1967–72, aged 93 – 1 January 1994

Potter, Dennis, television dramatist, aged 59 – 7 June 1994

Price, Vincent, American film actor, aged 82 –
25 October 1993

Quennell, Sir Peter, writer and editor, aged 88 –
27 October 1993

Redhead, Brian, broadcaster and journalist, and
presenter of Radio Four's *Today* programme
since 1975, aged 64 – 23 January 1994

Reid, Sir Robert, CBE, chairman of the British Rail
Board 1983–90, aged 72 – 17 December 1993

Revelstoke, 4th Baron, landowner, aged 83 – 18 July
1994

Rey, Fernando, Spanish film actor, aged 76 –
9 March 1994

Richardson, General Sir Charles, GCB, CBE, DSO,
deviser of the El Alamein deception plan,
aged 85 – 7 February 1994

Richardson, Jo, MP, Labour MP for Barking since
1974 and party spokeswoman for women's rights
1983–92, aged 70 – 1 February 1994

Roberts, Ernest, Labour MP for Hackney North and
Stoke Newington 1979–87, aged 82 – 29 August
1994

Robinson, Kenneth, broadcaster and satirist,
aged 68 – 26 March 1994

Roden, 9th Earl, aged 83 – 18 October 1993

Rogerson, Sydney, GC, aged 78 – 23 September
1993

Savalas, Telly, American actor, aged about 70 –
23 January 1994

Saveen, Albert, ventriloquist, aged 79 –14 April
1994

Schwinger, Julian, American physicist and Nobel
laureate, aged 76 – 16 July 1994

Scott, Lt.-Col. Sir James, Bt., Lord Lieutenant of
Hampshire since 1982, aged 69 – 2 November
1993

Scott, Terry, comedian and actor, aged 67 – 26 July
1994

Selvon, Samuel, West Indian novelist and short-
story writer, aged 70 – 16 April 1994

Senna, Ayrton, Brazilian Formula One motor-racing
driver, world champion 1988, 1990 and 1991,
aged 34 – 1 May 1994 in San Marino grand prix

Sharp of Grimsdyke, Lord, CBE, chairman of Cable
and Wireless 1980–90, aged 77 – 2 May 1994

Shelton, Anne, OBE, singer, aged 70 – 31 July 1994

Shore, Dinah, American singer and actress,
aged 76 – 24 February 1994

Simon, 2nd Viscount, CMG, chairman of the Port of
London Authority 1958–71, aged 91 –
5 December 1993

Smith, Arnold, CH, OC, first secretary-general of the
Commonwealth, 1965–75, aged 75 – 7 February
1994

Smith, Rt. Hon. John, QC, MP, Labour MP for
Monklands East since 1970 and Leader of the
Opposition since 1992, aged 55 – 12 May 1994

Springer, Sir Hugh, GCMG, GCVO, governor-general
of Barbados 1984–90, aged 80 – 14 April 1994

Stack, Air Chief Marshal Sir Neville, KCB, CVO, CBE,
AFC, aged 74 – 26 January 1994

Stewart, Andy, Scottish entertainer, aged 59 –
11 October 1993

Swann, Donald, composer and pianist, aged 70 –
23 March 1994

Symons, Patrick, RA, painter, aged 68 – 30 October
1993

Synge, Prof. Richard, FRS, biochemist and winner of
Nobel prize for chemistry 1952, aged 79 –
18 August 1994

Tanaka, Kakuei, Japanese politician, aged 75 –
16 December 1993

Tedder, 2nd Baron, FRSE, chemist, aged 67 –
18 February 1994

Thomson, Air Chief Marshal Sir John, GCB, CBE,
AFC, recently appointed C.-in-C. Allied Forces
North-Western Europe, aged 53 – 10 July 1994

Thorneycroft, Lord, CH, PC, Conservative MP
1938–66, President of the Board of Trade
1951–7, Chancellor of the Exchequer 1957–8,
Minister of Defence 1962–4 and party chairman
1975–81, aged 84 – 4 June 1994

Tilney, Sir John, TD, Conservative MP for Liverpool
Wavertree 1950–74, aged 86 – 26 April 1994

Tranmire, Lord, KBE, MC, PC, former Conservative
MP and minister, aged 90 – 17 January 1994

Travers, Bill, actor and conservationist, aged 72 –
29 March 1994

Tweedie, Jill, journalist and author, aged 59 –
12 November 1993

Twiss, Admiral Sir Frank, KCB, KCVO, DSC,
Gentleman Usher of the Black Rod, House of
Lords 1970–8, aged 83 – 26 January 1994

Vickers, Baroness (Joan), DBE, Conservative MP for
Plymouth Devonport 1955–74, aged 86 – 23 May
1994

Wain, John, CBE, novelist, poet, critic, aged 69 –
24 May 1994

Wanamaker, Sam, HON. CBE, American actor,
director, and founder of the Shakespeare Globe
Trust, aged 74 – 18 December 1993

Watford, Gwen, actress, aged 66 – 6 February 1994

Westmorland, 15th Earl, GCVO, Master of the Horse
1978–91, aged 69 – 8 September 1993

Wigglesworth, Prof. Sir Vincent, CBE, FRS, biologist,
aged 94 – 12 February 1994

Wilkins, Lt.-Gen. Sir Michael, KCB, OBE, Lieutenant
Governor of Guernsey since 1990, aged 61 –
25 April 1994

Wimborne, 3rd Viscount, aged 54 – 17 December
1993

Winn, Anona, MBE, radio quiz panellist, singer and
actress, aged 86 – 2 February 1994

Wörner, Manfred, secretary-general of NATO since
1988, aged 59 – August 1994

Zappa, Frank, rock musician, aged 52 –
4 December 1993

Zetterling, Mai, Swedish-born film actress and
director, aged 68 – 17 March 1994

# Archaeology

In archaeology the most significant finds are often those which are the most ordinary in appearance. So it is with the part of a shin bone found in December 1993, the discovery of which was announced in May 1994. The interest in this part of a tibia derives from the fact that it is estimated to be about half a million years old and is related to the hominid jaw found in 1907 at Mauer, near Heidelberg in Germany. Belonging neither to modern man, *Homo sapiens sapiens*, nor to *Homo erectus*, the bone will help specialists considering the date at which humans left Africa for Europe; it is suggested that this may have happened nearer to a million years ago, rather than two million years ago as was previously thought. Found at Boxgrove, near Chichester, the bone and the context in which it was found also suggest that, contrary to previously-held views, early man may have been able to live through the earliest Ice Age (the Anglian) known from British evidence.

In *British Archaeological News* for June 1994 it is reported that 'According to Dr Chris Stringer of the Natural History Museum, the length and thickness of the left shin bone suggests a male about 6 ft tall weighing over 12 stone, similar in build to other hominids known from Africa but far sturdier than the later Neanderthal Man or modern humans. Boxgrove Man's bone was dated by its stratigraphic relationship with animal bones, in particular those of the watervole *Arvicola terrestris cantiana* known to have lived shortly before the onset of the Anglian Ice Age *c.*478,000 years ago. It was preserved in calcium-rich lagoonal silts – the site was near the sea at the time – and was found last year in a small test-shaft surrounded by flint cutting tools, the bones of rhinoceros, elephant, deer, bear, mink and vole. Mark Roberts, director of the site, said the rest of the skeleton could be found when the area around the shaft is fully excavated next year. Boxgrove, near Chichester is one of the most important archaeological sites in the world. Excavations, funded for ten years by English Heritage, have produced numerous Lower Palaeolithic stone tools and animal bones but the shin bone is the first hominid fossil to be found. Although over 3,000 Palaeolithic sites are known in Britain, human bones are very rare. After the Boxgrove fossil, the next oldest are three skull fragments of archaic *Homo sapiens* found at Swanscombe in Kent, *c.*400,000–300,000 years old; and a Neanderthal adult molar and juvenile mandible, *c.*225,000 years old, from Pontnewydd in Clwyd.'

## A41 BY-PASS

The reconstruction of about twelve miles of the A41 from the M25 at Watford to the dual carriageway at Tring bypassing Kings Langley and Berkhamsted allowed the Hertfordshire Archaeological Trust to investigate the route and the results are summarized in *Current Archaeology* (number 136, 1993). Along the twelve miles of the new road seven separate sites were found and investigated. The initial investigations were carried out by cutting trenches with mechanical excavators, rather than relying upon geophysical surveys or air photographs; the former were unlikely to be helpful because the subsoil was clay with flints, while the latter showed nothing along the line of the road. Equally the usefulness of field walking was called into doubt. 'More important perhaps is the argument that field walking is biased: the hard fired pottery of the later Iron Age and Roman periods tends to survive, while the more fragile pottery of the Neolithic, Bronze and early Iron Ages may well be destroyed by a single ploughing. Usually this is offset by picking up struck flint, but since the geology itself consists of flint nodules, scatters of worked flint were difficult to locate.'

In the event the methodology adopted by the Hertfordshire Archaeological Trust paid dividends, not least in the discovery of substantial Neolithic remains. In the words of *Current Archaeology*, 'A new Neolithic village has been discovered along the line of a new road in Hertfordshire. Neolithic villages are not supposed to exist in Hertfordshire: the heavy clay land north of London was thought to be far too intractable for prehistoric man before the Iron Age.' The site was at Rucklers Lane and was associated with another to the north known as Apsley, both being perhaps part of the same complex. As yet it is difficult to interpret the nature of the site from the large number of pits and postholes but there is no doubt about the significance of the objects excavated. 'Some eight hundred pottery sherds were retrieved from 126 features out of some 1,000 excavated ranging from the Neolithic through to the earliest Iron Age. Stone tools included five leaf-shaped arrowheads recovered from one of the large parallel ditches, while a large number of hollow flakes, scrapers and many flint blades were retrieved from both excavations. The flint was very much a local product with the majority of flakes and tools derived from nodules picked up locally on the surface. Consequently the flints tended to be of poor quality, though beautifully worked. Flint knapping was taking place on the site, for hammer stones with evidence of hammering were discovered alongside cores and waste material. There is little evidence of "imported flint". Thus the Rucklers Lane and Apsley sites as a whole remain enigmatic; though the origins may have been ceremonial, there was also clearly evidence for occupation.'

There was a second important Neolithic site and that was near Bottom House Lane. According to *Current Archaeology* 'This is a site that appears to be totally without parallel, for its main component consists of over 40 parallel ditches running east-west across the road corridor – ditch after ditch after ditch. It appears that only three or four of these ditches were open at any one time and these were many times recut. In an early phase a causewayed entrance can be traced running through the ditches at an angle. Later, the entrance was deliberately blocked with smaller ditches dug across the causeways, though these too were backfilled. A later phase of ditch-digging shows a similar set of causeways again running at an angle across the open ditches. At least six broad phases of ditch digging and remodelling were identified, and it would seem that at least three or four ditches were open at any one time. Do they represent a linear monument? Or are they one side of some form of enclosure? ... The ditches are associated with plain Neolithic bowls and flint was knapped on-site. After the ditches had been filled a series of pits were dug over the area containing fragments of Peterborough pottery. One large pit contained a nearly complete vessel. Over 2,500 features were excavated in all, dating through to the late Bronze and early Iron Ages. In its final phase a series of four, six, eight and twelve posted structures were built across the site, which provides a useful *terminus post quem.*'

## Snettisham

Snettisham in Norfolk is synonymous with the discovery of gold torques, or neckrings, made of twisted strands of gold and worn as status symbols during the Iron Age. However, what may not be realized is how many of these treasure hoards have been discovered at this site. Following the first discovery in the course of ploughing in 1948, further finds were made in 1950, 1964, 1968, 1973 and 1990. Subsequently two seasons of archaeological excavations were undertaken in the area by the British Museum and the results were explained in a display at the British Museum and the National Museum of Wales in 1993 and 1994 as well as being reported in *Current Archaeology* (number 135, 1993). In addition to the gold torques, metal ingots and coins, there were also examples of torques made of silver, a metal rarely used in the Iron Age in Britain.

In the course of the British Museum excavations, a V-shaped ditch was found which was 'dated to the fourth century AD by an early fourth century coin and some late Roman sherds of the type normally dated after AD 375.' Following further investigations the ditch it became, in the words of *Current Archaeology* 'apparent that it forms an enclosure 20 acres in extent. Five sides have been traced, but it appears to be open on the remaining side where there was marshy ground formed by an inlet to the Wash. Only one entrance has been located on the west, and the ditches on either side of this entrance were fully excavated in the expectation that here if anywhere dated material would be found. In this they were not disappointed, for a number of sherds of pottery were found in the primary silt dating to the late first

century AD – Neronian/Flavian. What was this enclosure? The hoards lay towards the centre of the enclosure, as if it was intended to bound them, but the filling dated 150 years after the hoards. Did some memory of the hoards still survive? Was it conceivably kept open for 150 years before any filling accumulated? It is tempting to see it as being the enclosure of a temple, for the Romans sometimes erected temples over Iron Age ritual sites. However there is no trace of a temple, nor is there any indication of the offerings which would normally be made. Forty Roman coins have been recovered in the course of the excavations but the majority (28) are second century AD, and a few are even of the fourth. The size of the enclosure is also unexpected for it covered 20 acres – the size of a medium-size Romano-British small town. However there is no trace of any occupation. Does the enclosure acknowledge the presence of the treasure, as if some folk memory still remained that this has once been a ritual site?'

The coins recovered from the site are the most important evidence for the dating of the hoards. There are some 234 coins, some found within five of the hoards. The coins are all Celtic and are either Gallo-Belgic imports dating to around 70 BC and therefore demonstrating that the hoard discovered in 1948 cannot have been buried by refugees fleeing from Julius Caesar's invasion. The other coins are made from tin and seem to have been used as small change; although often dated towards the end of the Iron Age there was an earlier class 'and the Snettisham examples belong to this early phase, dating to the first century BC. The evidence of the coins therefore is that the hoards were all deposited at the same time, around 70 BC.' Despite this reassessment as a result of the British Museum excavations, 'The Snettisham treasure remains a mystery.' As *Current Archaeology* says, 'we must accept that they are local work and represent local taste and standards. Is this a prehistoric treasury – perhaps the royal treasury of the ruling house of Iceni or their predecessors in this part of the world? Whatever it may be, it emphasizes the surprising wealth of this part of the world in the Iron Age.'

## Salt

The need to construct a new sewage treatment works by Anglian Water Services Ltd led to the discovery of a salt production site at Tetney in Lincolnshire which was excavated by Colin Palmer-Brown of Lindsey Archaeological Services. The particular significance of the site lies in its date; the Bronze Age was suggested by the pottery and this was confirmed by a radio-carbon sampling which gave a date 'centring on 805 BC, thus confirming the late Bronze Age date. It would appear therefore that we have at Tetney one of the earliest salterns so far recorded in this country', writes Colin Palmer-Brown in *Current Archaeology* (number 136, 1993). The principle behind the saltern was that sea-water was trapped in a pool from which, over the summer months, the sea-water would evaporate leaving behind salt-impregnated mud. This mud would then have been heated and the clay separated from the salt. The site produced two major categories of pottery, one thick-walled and the other thin; it may be that these reflect two different parts of the process. The director of the excavation asks in *Current Archaeology*: 'When did salt-making begin? The earliest evidence for European salt-production is on the Neolithic sites in Poland. Bronze Age sites have already been discovered in England, firstly at Mucking in Essex, and more recently at Brean Down in Somerset (Middle Bronze Age) and at Fenn Creek in Essex (12th–15th centuries BC). However, unlike Fenn Creek and Brean Down, enough information was gathered at Tetney to allow us to reconstruct the whole process, from the original procurement through washing, filtration, and evaporation; we were fortunate that the area excavated was large enough and preservation good enough. It is more than another catalogue of briquetage and it is certainly the earliest saltern recorded in Lincolnshire. It surely deserves to stand beside the flint mines and the copper mines as being among the earliest evidence for industry in Britain.'

LONDON'S AMPHITHEATRE

One of the most important discoveries of the last decade was that of a Roman amphitheatre in London in 1988. Following the demolition of existing buildings, excavations were undertaken in 1993–4 by the Museum of London Archaeology Service under the direction of Nicholas Bateman. The results of the excavation, when concluded and evaluated, will reveal much about the history of London in the area of the Guildhall, especially in those centuries between the end of Roman rule and the first documented appearance of the Guildhall towards the middle of the 12th century. However, from Nicholas Bateman's wide-ranging article in *Current Archaeology* (number 137, 1994) may be noted recent developments in understanding London's Roman amphitheatre. For example, it is apparent that the masonry amphitheatre 'dates from around AD 120, but replaced an earlier and smaller timber version, probably dating from around AD 70, for which there was also clear evidence'. The report in *Current Archaeology* continues: 'the amphitheatre was constructed in what must originally have been a shallow valley through which ran a small stream, one of the upper branches of the Walbrook. The Roman architects chose a natural depression which was enlarged by digging out the arena area and dumping the spoil all around it. The resulting bank was used as a base for the tiers of timber seating which rose around the arena. The rivetting wall around the arena, and the walls flanking the entrance-way, were built of brick and ragstone. It is likely that they were only some 12–14 feet high, with the rest of the structure, and in particular the whole arrangement for the seating, being made of timber, like the well-known carving of an amphitheatre on Trajan's

Column. No traces of an outer wall have been discovered, so it is assumed that this was built of timber not masonry. On either side of the entrance-way were two rectangular chambers with doorways leading out into the arena . . . in the southern room a stone threshold which lead out into the arena had slots in its upper surface. These may represent the base of a sliding trapdoor, which could suggest that the room was used as a pen for animals. Apart from gladiatorial combat the most popular form of shows involved fights with wild animals. This is the first excavation of a British amphitheatre from which large quantities of bones have been recovered. We are just starting to examine these but already it is clear that at least one bull and a bear met their fates in the arena. Of equal interest is the statistically high number of disarticulated human bones – which had not been carefully or respectfully buried. In addition, cut into the dumped deposits beneath the timber seating were at least two Roman burials. The later levels contained a considerable number of bones of sheep and cows; could this imply that in its later life the amphitheatre was used as a market?'

The environmental conditions are such that much important information may be extracted. For example, it is recorded in *Current Archaeology* that 'The particularly impressive preservation of wood on the site has allowed the rare survival of features such as door-frames and gateways. Most impressive of all were the drains which ran through the amphitheatre and channelled water away to the Walbrook stream. Not only the sides, but also the timber lids to these drains survived, and at one point along the main drain there was a silt trap; a timber rivetted tank about a metre square designed to trap water-borne silts and capable of being cleaned out regularly.'

The amphitheatre, which it has been calculated held about 8,000 spectators, was in existence for a long period of time. 'There was no evidence for any period of disuse or abandonment during the lifetime of the amphitheatre; surfaces were relaid one on top of the other, drains were repaired, till the very end. The latest deposits all contain very frequent coins of the 340–70 period. This makes the amphitheatre almost the only building in the western part of the city known to have been still in use in the fourth century. If this is the case it will be of crucial importance to an understanding of late Roman London. After all, you cannot have an amphitheatre without people to sit in it or money to run it. The arena was eventually abandoned and soon afterwards the masonry walls were robbed. The stone may have been removed to provide material for the building of the bastions added to the city wall, or the completion of the wall along the riverside, all of which took place in the late fourth century. In the 'Dark Ages' the area, like the rest of Roman London, appears to have been abandoned.

CULT OF THE HEAD

Further work on the results of the late Iron Age royal burial at St Albans investigated in 1992 suggest that the temple which existed at the site from about AD 50 to the third century might have been the centre of a pagan 'cult of the head'. The evidence for this is reported by Rosalind Niblett, the director of the excavation, in *British Archaeological News* (April 1994). She notes that the 52 deep pits lying outside the precinct of the tomb and its related pagan temple 'contained a "surprisingly large" number of face urns-pots with human heads as decoration – and also two real heads. One, a horse's head, was deliberately laid on the bottom of a pit. The other was a human head with several deep cut-marks, suggesting its owner may have been killed. The evidence is paralleled by a similar collection of heads – real, ceramic, or stone-buried in pits as offerings at several Iron Age shrines on the Continent.'

It is further suggested that this pagan 'cult of the head' might have been so popular that it had an influence on the later Christian story of St Alban. 'In the earliest account of the saint's death, St Alban is said to have been taken to a hill "across a river, 500 paces from the town" – an accurate description of the site of the Iron Age burial – and beheaded. Although beheading was a normal form of execution for Roman citizens, the account of the execution may have been coloured by the early Church's desire to make the pagan head cult Christian'. According to a later medieval tradition, the saint's executioner went blind during the execution – and Celtic head cults were possibly associated with poor sight. A similar head cult at a pagan sanctuary site in Gaul was associated with a later shrine devoted to the healing of eyes.

## HODDOM

Trial excavations under the auspices of Historic Scotland were organized at the important site of Hoddom in Dumfries and Galloway. It is reported in *Current Archaeology* (number 135, 1993) that 'Hoddom is one of the great "lost" monasteries of Scotland. In the sixth century and again in the eighth century it was among the most important monasteries in the country; but in the 12th century it lost its importance. It all concerns the story of St Mungo'. Otherwise known as St Kentigern, St Mungo's death was recorded in 612: he is better known as the patron saint of Glasgow. Hoddom was the site most associated with St Mungo in the early Christian period and certainly there was a major Northumbrian monastery there in the eighth century AD as demonstrated from photographs of now destroyed carved stones. 'However in the 12th century when many other ancient monasteries were revived, Hoddom was not; Glasgow at the time was rising in importance and it is tempting to suggest that they would not have taken kindly to any other church which could put in a rival claim to their great patron, St Mungo. Today, therefore, Hoddom is almost forgotten. The church survived as the parish church till the end of the Middle Ages, but since then it has been merely a burial ground, isolated and lonely in the midst of fields on the other side of the River

Annan from Hoddom Castle and two miles from Ecclefechan.'

The recent excavations in advance of quarrying for gravel extraction revealed a large boundary ditch, a large number of timber buildings, including ovens, and a kiln used as a corn-drier or malt-house. It is reported in *Current Archaeology* that 'so far these buildings would all seem to fit into the Anglian monastery of the seventh and eighth centuries.' In addition to these and other features, a particularly interesting stone building was found which was named 'Mungo's chapel' by the press. It is reported that 'This was much better built than anything else on the site, being constructed from Roman masonry, presumably robbed from the Roman fort at Birrens only four miles away. Indeed two fragments of inscriptions were included, one with the letters VMIN visible (equals NUMINI, to the divinity of the Emperor(?)) while the other, even more fragmentary, mentions 'VIII AVG' and 'XXII PR', a reference to the legions VIII Augusta and XXII Primigenia which served together in Upper Germany. This building therefore could be described as sub-Roman, for it was constructed of squared sandstone blocks, even if clay-bonded.' Preceding the boundary ditch to the north, the radio-carbon date calibrates to around AD 600. 'The really enigmatic feature however is the curving passage that leads away from the south-west corner of the building, entered through a narrow gap in the wall, 30 cm wide. This resembles to some extent a souterrain, but this is probably misleading, and it may perhaps have been more of a drain. If so, could the building have been a baptistry?' While there are still questions of interpretation to be answered, not least over the location of the building, it would appear to date to an earlier phase than the Anglian monastery: could it be therefore part of the sixth-century monastery, the monastery founded by St Mungo?'

## CANTERBURY CATHEDRAL

The decision to refloor the nave of Canterbury Cathedral, last refloored in 1787, gave the Canterbury Archaeological Trust the opportunity to investigate the location of the Anglo-Saxon cathedral, about which very little was known. The work is described in *Current Archaeology* (number 136, 1993) and it is noted that 'As excavations continued along the west and east ends of the nave and along the north aisle, additional masonry fragments combined to form a ground plan for one of the largest Anglo-Saxon cathedrals in England, and a structure ranking amongst the great cathedrals of northern Europe! The walls of the final phase of the Anglo-Saxon church lay parallel to the Norman cathedral, but the latter had evidently been built just five metres to the south so as to avoid the earlier foundations.' In due course four main phases of Anglo-Saxon work were distinguished.

The earliest of these phases had cut into the 'dark earth' which sealed a Romano-British street and the church appears to have been set diagonally across the street itself. The question still to be answered is whether this church is that of St Augustine as recorded in Bede's chronicle. In the second phase 'the early church was demolished, and a large basilican-style cathedral was constructed. This phase comprised massive aisle foundations; two cross-walls towards the east end of the nave perhaps represent the foundations for a central tower and quire area. The south wall lay in the present south aisle, whilst its matching north wall must lie outside the present cathedral, in the cloister area. On the west end was a squared narthex or perhaps an oratory (later rebuilt as part of a large *westwerk*). It appears that the central tower partly respected the plan of the first phase nave – retaining the "heart" of the original cathedral.' The third phase appears to be a rebuild, as demonstrated 'by an offset string course on the south wall', while the final fourth phase 'at the very end of the Saxon period saw a major reconstruction at the west end. At this time westwerks were the fashion through northern Europe and Canterbury joined in the fashion. At the very end, a deep apse was constructed while to the south, a hexagonal stair tower was erected. It is thought that a matching tower lies outside the church to the north, beneath the western walkway of the cloisters.' It is reported in *Current Archaeology* that 'At the same time the arcade walls were strengthened, presumably to take the weight of a substantial arch, and a square tower/porticus was added on the south-east corner. The terminal ends of the apse were constructed of substantial blocks of re-used Roman masonry, up to 1.2 metres across, presumably robbed from a monumental building in the Roman city. Layers of marquise stone chippings in the construction levels also suggest that decorative elements of the Anglo-Saxon cathedral were reused Roman material. This final phase is similar to Ottonian Romanesque churches of mid-tenth to early-11th century date, and may have been built by the Archbishops Lyfing (1013–20) or Aethelnoth (1020–38). Parallels are known at Mainz, Hildersheim, Gernrode and Trier (to name but a few) where the type has a western apse flanked by stair towers, although usually associated with a large central tower. No central tower is indicated in the plan of the westwerk of Canterbury Cathedral'. Having evaluated the archaeological evidence, difficulties remain in assimilating the results to what is known of the history of Canterbury Cathedral from documentary sources.

RECESSED PLATFORMS

Careful fieldwork and excavation have resulted in a reassessment of the many recessed platforms found in western Scotland and especially in the Cowal peninsula in Argyll. Traditionally these platforms, which are cut into the hillside, have been associated with the charcoal burners who fed the developing ironworks of 18th- and 19th-century Scotland. However, the assumption that because the recessed platforms were used by charcoal burners they had

been constructed by them, was challenged by the Cowal Archaeological and Historical Society, which set about a careful investigation of the phenomenon. A starting point was the fact that many of these platforms were above the tree-line and well away from the areas serving the ironworks. The fieldwork and excavation by the Society is summarized by Betty Rennie in *Current Archaeology* (number 138, 1994). Having carried out an extensive field survey and classified various types, ten platforms were excavated totally or in part. 'Each of the ten platforms showed evidence that it had been built to support a round timber-framed structure. Nine of them had a central ring of large postholes which may have been roof-support sockets and at least one ring of perimeter postholes suggesting a timber-framed wall. The tenth platform had perimeter postholes, a central ring of extremely hard "pads" which suggested the "stances" for roof posts. Five of them had been reused as charcoal burners' hearths – the postholes were sealed, and the charcoal was overlying the roof-support sockets. However, of the other five, three had secondary floors which sealed the postholes – one indeed had been used as an area for roasting bog-iron preliminary to smelting it – but the other two had not been reused except that one had very recently been used as the site for burning – probably in this century.' A particular problem was experienced in trying to date all of these sites. 'Unfortunately there were no finds – pottery was not made or used in the west of Scotland from the Iron Age to the Middle Ages – and thus radio-carbon dating is the obvious solution. However this was difficult because so many of the sites had been reused by the charcoal burners, whose charcoal would have contaminated any earlier carbon.'

However, as reported in *Current Archaeology*, 'one of the few sites that could be dated was Ardentraive, which lies above the Kyles of Bute. A carbon date was obtained from it as it had not been reused as a charcoal hearth. Here there was an oval house with a porch which had been rebuilt twice and was finally burnt. Charcoal from a posthole gave a radio-carbon date of 1038 +/− 80 ad which calibrates to between AD 1020 and 1220. There was a similar date from a platform at Barmore wood on the island of Bute. It calibrated to the same dates of between AD 1020 and 1220. A date from another platform at Dunloskin calibrated to between AD 1219 and 1373. 'Taking other evidence into account the conclusion reached was that 'The overall range therefore seems to be in the early medieval period, though beginning in the early Christian period, viz. the first millenium and the early second millenium AD. This shows evidence of the round house tradition lingering on to a date when most of the rest of the country had long adopted rectangular building traditions. The final verdict must be that we have found settlements of people who were living in the west of Scotland in the early Christian/Dark Age/early medieval period. We now know of 92 groups of structures which represent very approximately about 2,000 platforms. Many of these have been found fortuitously and so it follows that there are probably many more sites still to discover.'

## ROMAN MAYFAIR

Most people are aware that the Romans developed the area which is now covered by the City of London, as evidenced by the substantial archaeological discoveries. However, fewer will know of a theory which postulates that the earliest Roman settlement was in the Mayfair area, near the present-day site of Marble Arch. Although this theory has been proposed from time to time over the last 40 years, it has recently been restated in some detail by Bill Sole in an article entitled 'Metropolis in Mayfair?' published in *London Archaeologist* (1993). A complex argument may be reduced to the difference between what happened in London in AD 43 when the Roman Army invaded and developments in AD 50 or thereabouts when Londinium was established. It is postulated that the London of AD 43 and the years immediately following was centred on Mayfair until the need for a deep-water port forced the removal to the newly-established site of Londinium in the years after AD 50, but not before a network of roads had been established at the former location. As Bill Sole puts it 'Marble Arch sits at the junction of three undoubtedly Roman roads – Edgware Road, Bayswater Road and Oxford Street. Edgware Road, the most obvious, leads to Verulamium and Chester; Bayswater Road leads to Brentford, Staines and Bath; Oxford Street is a trifle dubious but leads via High Holborn to Newgate and Londinium and via Old Street to Old Ford on the River Lea. High Holborn and Newgate would not have been built before Londinium was occupied c.AD 50, therefore Oxford Street and Old Street can be said to precede High Holborn ... so the original Roman route to Camulodunum commenced with Oxford Street, Theobalds Road, Old Street, Roman Road, Old Ford (or Stratford – the Ford on the Straight) and Romford Road, thence via Romford and Chelmsford. Thus three main invasion routes radiated from Marble Arch corner. Three main bodies of the Roman Army marched out from the Hyde Park area to bring the province under Roman jurisdiction.' Sole argues for the crucial importance of Park Street in Mayfair:

'Park Street is ancient, and can be considered as the remnant of the via principalis of the HQ fort. Assuming this fort is comparable in size to the later Cripplegate fort its perimeter roads coincide approximately with modern Green Street, North Audley Street, Upper Grosvenor Street and Park Lane. To the junction of the three major roads at Marble Arch from the presumed north gate of the Park Street fort is a distance of a few hundred yards.'

The reason why the Roman occupation of the Mayfair area did not develop was because of the need for better access to the sea. In Bill Sole's words: 'Shipping services would have been essential to the military unit for the provision of equipments and armaments; shipping services for import and export, especially as trade expanded in the hinterland, would bring prosperity and influence to the commercial quarter. Shipping facilities would have been severely handicapped by lack of deep water; that fact dictated the speedy removal of the metropolis to Londinium with its superior port availability. At once, all ports in Gaul and Germany were accessible to the importers and exporters of the relocated metropolis.' Given the uncontested fact of the development of Londinium on the site now occupied by the City of London, Sole argues that 'Londinium acquired its own road system primarily by adapting the Mayfair road system to its own needs, with later additions of main highways emanating from its own centre ... Two highways, obviously Roman, emanate directly from Londinium – Stane Street via London Bridge to Chichester, and Ermine Street via Bishopsgate and Tottenham to Godmanchester on the Lincoln highway. Archaeological dating of these two roads is not at present conclusive enough to provide dating for Londinium. Conversely the dating of Londinium implies that both roads were built later than AD 50'.

It will be very difficult to prove the Sole hypothesis except by further archaeological means, especially in the West End of London where there has been much less excavation than in the City. Until any evidence is found, Bill Sole's thesis, and the ideas of those who preceded him, provide a theoretical explanation of why there are two different centres for the known Roman road system in London.

---

## ROMAN NUMERALS

| | | | | | | | | |
|---|---|---|---|---|---|---|---|---|
| 1 | I | 11 | XI | 30 | XXX | 400 | CD |
| 2 | II | 12 | XII | 40 | XL | 500 | D |
| 3 | III | 13 | XIII | 50 | L | 600 | DC |
| 4 | IV | 14 | XIV | 60 | LX | 700 | DCC |
| 5 | V | 15 | XV | 70 | LXX | 800 | DCCC |
| 6 | VI | 16 | XVI | 80 | LXXX | 900 | CM |
| 7 | VII | 17 | XVII | 90 | XC | 1000 | M |
| 8 | VIII | 18 | XVIII | 100 | C | 1500 | MD |
| 9 | IX | 19 | XIX | 200 | CC | 1900 | MCM |
| 10 | X | 20 | XX | 300 | CCC | 2000 | MM |

*Examples*

| | |
|---|---|
| 43 XLIII | 988 CMLXXXVIII |
| 66 LXVI | 996 CMXCVI |
| 98 XCVIII | 1674 MDCLXXIV |
| 339 CCCXXXIX | 1962 MCMLXII |
| 619 DCXIX | 1995 MCMXCV |

A bar placed over a numeral has the effect of multiplying the number by 1,000, e.g.

| | | | |
|---|---|---|---|
| 6,000 | $\overline{\text{VI}}$ | 160,000 | $\overline{\text{CLX}}$ |
| 16,000 | $\overline{\text{XVI}}$ | 666,000 | $\overline{\text{DCLXVI}}$ |

# Architecture

## NEW OPERA HOUSE
### Glyndebourne, Sussex

*Architect:* Michael Hopkins & Partners

Founded in 1934, Glyndebourne Opera succeeded by virtue of a mix of international standards of music and drama and English idiosyncracy that has raised the concept of opera in a country house setting to cult status. A major part of the attraction of Glyndebourne was the intimacy of the original auditorium, which seated only 830. In 1988 Sir George Christie, the chairman, decided that it was essential to commission a new opera house with an increased audience capacity capable of satisfying the demand for tickets.

The most important requirement of the brief was to maintain the much prized characteristics of Glyndebourne for the opera-goers within the context of a brand new opera house. Hopkins was appointed in February 1989 after an architectural competition among nine selected leading practices. His scheme involved the demolition of the old theatre and rebuilding the opera house on its old site but in a different orientation. This meant that there could be no opera season in 1993 and added great stringency to the programming and analysis of the construction process, which had to be completed in the 16-month period between the end of August 1992 and December 1993 to provide sufficient commissioning time prior to the opening night of the 1994 season.

The primary planning strategy involved turning the new building through 180° from the orientation of the old theatre, so as to allow the audience to enter the opera house on the side closest to the house and gardens. This reinforces the relationship between the musical experience and the enjoyment of the surrounding countryside and gardens, and permits the considerable bulk of the fly tower and backstage areas to be sited further away from the house and partly concealed within the rising contours of the land. Thus the audience can spill out easily from the foyer areas on to the lawns and terraces for the traditional interval picnic, and at the rear access is improved for servicing deliveries to the backstage loading bay.

The plan of the new building is based on the combination of simple bold shapes to give a clear and disciplined framework. The auditorium is circular on plan but with the seating developed into the horseshoe format of the traditional 18th-century theatre. This links with the square fly tower and semi-circular backstage area to form a large race-track plan form, emphasized by the accommodation wrapped around the perimeter on all sides. The choice of materials and methods of construction reflect the context, the requirements for acoustic isolation and the architect's stylistic preoccupations. The requirements for a high-

mass envelope to shield the auditorium from external noise and permit a good acoustic performance suggested the use of brick for the walls, but in keeping with his principles the architect has opted not for modern brick cladding, but for traditional solid load-bearing brickwork.

The bricks are handmade and fired in a traditional kiln, giving the building variety of colour and texture, and match the salmon-coloured walls of the adjoining manor house. They are bedded in traditional thin joints using a lime mortar, thus avoiding the requirement for horizontal and vertical expansion joints. In plan the building has two skins of load-bearing brick. The external skin is in the form of a series of tapering load-bearing brick piers supporting flat gauged brick arches which span the intermediate bays. Around the auditorium half of the plan, the piers are freestanding and define open ambulatories which permit entry to the auditorium from each side and give views out over the complex and beyond to the countryside. Around the backstage half, the bays are infilled to provide accommodation for the offices and support facilities used by the technical and administrative staff.

The internal skin around the auditorium is a drum of load-bearing brickwork built in similar fashion, and forms a further acoustic barrier, but the loads from the auditorium, galleries and roof are taken by an *in-situ* concrete frame. Seen externally, the circular brick form of the auditorium rises clear through the overall building volume and is capped with its own conical lead-clad roof, separately defined from the lower-level lean-to roof over the perimeter walkways and offices. The four-square bulk of the fly tower rises from the centre, clad also in lead panels, its steel frame structure (necessary to save construction time) and deep roof-trusses exposed outside the cladding to reduce the apparent height and volume of the tower.

If the massive brickwork walls have engendered a return to traditional techniques, then the opportunity to create 'temporary' shelter from the elements without the need for mass has produced a totally contemporary approach. Where the curving facade of brick piers addresses the old buildings at the main entry point, the open area between the two is roofed with a tensile fabric canopy supported on steel trusses and tension rods, each bay rising to a porthole-like opening at the apex. The foyer space thus defined is confined between two minimalist glass screens but is otherwise open to the air and the tented canopy is a perfect expression of the open-air informality and rural ambience of the site.

The seating plan of the auditorium, with its gently-sloping bank of stalls and three horseshoe-shaped balconies, is traditional for opera houses. Despite accommodating an increased audience of 1,200 it retains the feeling of intimacy of the old theatre, but offers improved sightlines. In fact the distance from the rear of the new auditorium to the proscenium is some two metres less than in the old one. However, while the layout may be traditional, the interior decor is not and eschews the plush richness typical of many opera houses. The dominant material of the interior is wood, mainly reclaimed 100-year-old pitch pine, which is used for the balcony fronts, panels and seating. This gives the auditorium richness and warmth but with an overriding simplicity that ties in with the traditional Glyndebourne mix of the formal and the informal.

Relief from the timber surfaces is provided by the sparkling silver-grey surfaces of the pre-cast concrete ceiling panels forming the central dome and its aerofoil-shape supporting columns as well as the balcony floor soffits. The pre-cast elements are manufactured to particularly fine tolerances and have been acid-etched to remove the surface cement and reveal the Leemoor sand which is rich in mica. The mica provides 'sparkle' when light is bounced off the surface of the panels from the mixture of concealed and exposed light sources.

The prime function of the building being the presentation of opera, the acoustic performance is crucial to its success. In the new building the acoustic designers aimed at a slightly longer reverberation time, 1.4 seconds compared to 0.8, to improve on the perceived 'dryness' of the acoustic of the earlier theatre. Extensive computer and physical modelling was used to predict reverberation times and estimate the ideal auditorium volume. With Glyndebourne's core repertoire in mind, the key requirement was to balance the opposing factors of clarity and reverberance to achieve the optimum sound quality. Very careful modelling and slotting of timber and concrete surfaces was developed to fine-tune the acoustic performance, e.g. the curved timber balcony panels are acoustically-shaped, being more bulbous towards the centre of the space and flattening out at either side to control reflected sounds.

Early tests indicated that the final acoustic performance was very close to computer predictions, and the acoustics were highly praised when the new opera house opened with a performance of Mozart's *Marriage of Figaro*, 60 years to the day after the opening of its predecessor with the same opera. The building too drew praise, for the architect has contrived to encapsulate the many contradictions and eccentricities that characterize the Glyndebourne tradition while retaining a rigorous approach to all aspects of the design, each element pared down to its essentials and with no superfluous detail. It is a good working building of first-class craftsmanship that should age well.

## HOUSING ASSOCIATION HOSTEL EXTENSION
Castle Lane, Victoria, London

*Architect:* CGHP Architects

This small residential project is an extension to an existing hostel for the Look Ahead Housing Association, which provides homes for single people with special needs. Squeezed into a narrow rectangular site to the rear of the hostel, the extension provides 20 self-catering units for people with physical disabilities and psychiatric problems. It is arranged in a two-storey terrace with balcony access to the upper level.

Though the site constraints were onerous and contributed substantially to the costs of development, the proposals had to fall within the normal funding criteria of the Housing Corporation. The site was a backyard between the existing hostel and a high boundary wall only 19 metres away, immediately adjacent to a secondary school, overlooked by other residential buildings, and with no vehicular access for construction activities. It was therefore necessary to devise a single-aspect scheme, facing northwards towards the hostel, with its back to the wall in order to maintain appropriate daylight angles to the existing rooms in the hostel. Extensive landscaping at ground level together with a roof-garden were incorporated to improve both the amenity for the residents and the view from the surrounding residential buildings.

The 20 units incorporate a range of flat plans that are disposed in pairs and are designed to provide differing levels of shared facilities for two sharers. Each pair of flats shares a front door. Some share bathrooms and kitchens, some only kitchens, and there are two self-contained bed-sits sharing only front door and hall. This mix enables the residents to achieve a level of independence while helping each other as neighbours, encouraging mutual support within varying degrees of privacy.

However the building is far from being 'institutional'. Its external architectural expression is full of undulating curves and spirited detailing. The building façade sets in and out along its whole length, each flat front canted at a shallow angle outward from the central doorways, which are given colour-contrasting brick quoining and a radiused brick arch with central keystone at the upper level. This sets up a rhythm which is picked up by the undulating curves in the balcony and balustrading, and in the glazed canopy at roof level. The line of the balcony is emphasized by alternating black and white pre-cast nosings radiused on the leading edge. These support a robust black painted metal balustrade made of simple vertical balusters between top and bottom rails but given playful form and expression by means of a generous S-curve profile to each one that echoes the undulating curves on plan.

The glazed roof-level canopy undulates in two dimensions, following the balcony curves on plan while also curving upwards and downwards in section, its high points coinciding with the entrances, the low points coming between adjacent flats. The canopy is constructed in panes of translucent clear glass, each with a radiused leading edge like a series of feathers, supported on a series of cantilevered metal brackets and a pierced metal fascia which picks up each glazing bar as it soars up and down over the balcony. The curving lines of the canopy are picked up by the heads of the first-floor windows, further emphasizing the linked pairs of units.

At two points on the façade the metal balustrade swirls forward to embrace two spiral stairs giving access to the roof-garden. Each is surmounted by a smaller glazed canopy of similar construction covering the topmost flight like an elongated umbrella. Each stair continues to ground level, one in spiral form, the other with a straight flight projecting out diagonally into the courtyard space and covered with a further section of glazed canopy roof. The roof-garden itself is generously planted with lawns, shrubs and flowers and makes an enormous contribution to the visual amenity of the surrounding buildings.

The rear wall of the roof-garden is brought forward from the boundary and the section through the building is manipulated to expose the rear of the units on the floors below. This allows daylight to penetrate through continuous strip rooflights into the inner parts of the dwellings, cleverly avoiding many of the lighting problems associated with single-aspect designs.

The use of vibrant colours, such as the balcony nosings and the coloured glass inserts in the doors, coupled with warm Burford yellow brickwork for the main walls, extensive planting and the exuberant forms of stairs, balconies and canopies, provides a visually stimulating appearance that will not only give the residents a very positive sense of 'place' in their home, but provide much enjoyment to those who overlook what was formerly a rather dank backyard. The design received one of the two National Awards given in 1993 by the Housing Design Awards Committee representing the Department of the Environment, the National House Building Council and the RIBA.

## SCHOOL OF ENGINEERING AND MANUFACTURE
De Montfort University, Leicester

*Architects:* Short Ford and Associates

The new School of Engineering and Manufacture at De Montfort University (formerly Leicester Polytechnic) is a key element in the rebuilding programme which the University is carrying out to upgrade the mainly 1960s campus and to create a higher profile in the quest for academic funds and future students.

The new building contains some 10,000 square metres of accommodation and houses a variety of mechanical, electrical and general laboratories, class-rooms and lecture theatres, drawing studios, a computer centre, concourse and administration areas. It cost £8.4 million.

The building is designed on the premise that large buildings, including those whose functions may generate a large amount of heat (such as laboratories), do not need air conditioning and mechanical ventilation systems in order to achieve a satisfactory internal environment. Built largely of brick, it has been designed to be naturally lit and ventilated throughout and this has influenced the building's unconventional appearance, which might best be described as in a free-ranging neo-Gothic style.

To minimize the requirement for artificial lighting and maximize effective daylight, the building has been planned as a collection of narrow, daylit and naturally-ventilated volumes, orientated in accordance with the requirements of their functions. Internal spaces are mainly shallow rather than deep-plan, and orientated to optimize available daylight while controlling solar gain, and are provided with natural means of ventilation, either cross-flow or stack-effect, to remove excess heat and stale air.

A number of strategies have been developed to meet the particular lighting requirements of the different activities in the school. Where possible, spaces are lit from the side and the windows shaded from solar gain. Where good internal distribution of light is required, such as in the two wings of electrical laboratories either side of the entrance, a system of high-level windows is provided, with internal light shelves to bounce light into the middle of the space. In the large double-height space of the general laboratory there is a combination of large side-windows and vertical light shafts that penetrate the floor above; in the single-storey mechanical laboratory a combination of roof lights in the ridge and high-level windows in the gable ends of the pitched roof structure. In the roof-top drawing office and studio areas, where good levels of daylight are required, dramatic north-lights are introduced in the gable ends. The complex multi-level concourse areas are lit from above, with a variety of roof lights allowing shafts of light to penetrate deep into the space.

The building also makes extensive and dramatic use of natural ventilation. A series of eleven tall chimneys rise above the roof-line of the main building and these provide the motive force driving the ventilation system. Fresh air enters the building through open windows and louvres positioned around the building's perimeter and is exhausted from the various spaces by means of roof ventilators and the chimney-stacks. Each chimney connects directly with a shaft which rises the full height of the building and connects to rooms on each floor. The chimneys rise high above the ridge line, partly for architectural effect but also to rise clear of the air turbulence generated by the roof ridges, so that the stack effect induced by pressure differential can operate in stable conditions.

This principle of natural ventilation is applied to all areas of the building, even the lecture theatres, so that no mechanical plant is required either to assist the ventilation or to control summer-time temperatures. The high thermal capacity of the massive and well-insulated building envelope is a necessary adjunct to this strategy, limiting unwanted heat loss and gain. The building envelope is required to perform a number of exacting roles in response to the natural environment. Where a diversity of uses requires a variety of design responses to achieve optimum layout, the result is often, as here, a highly-articulated building form that demands an equally expressive style of architecture to inform and rationalize the structure and detailing of the spaces. This partly explains the buildings unconventional neo-Gothic styling.

The composition is informal and dynamic. The varying spatial components of the building are loosely arranged either side of a central concourse space which rises through four storeys and whose volume is defined by the projecting shapes of the different uses at each level. The effect, though controlled, has a random aspect, as though a large number of smaller buildings, each specifically designed to its own criteria, have been built 'hugger-mugger', with all the odd angles, accidental relationships and impromptu junctions that vernacular buildings often generate.

The main entrance is framed by the two angled wings of the electrical laboratories projecting from the east end, which define a narrow courtyard, and is not a dominant element. It gives access to the concourse, with its forest of steel columns supporting the brickwork walls of the laboratory and theatre spaces overhead.

Though lacking the usual focal point of a main entrance, the exterior of the building has a commanding presence and an appropriate scale and quality. The principal material is a red brick, relieved by string courses, projecting strips and alternate buff colour banding. The pointed lancet windows are emphasized by the red and buff brick striping to the window head arches and quoins. The walls are sometimes expressed as blank planes, the colour of the mortar matching exactly the brickwork to eliminate jointing patterns, and at other times express the brick bonding. The modelling of the exterior produces considerable drama and vitality in the street elevations, most particularly on the north-facing frontage where the volumes of the semi-circular lecture theatres punctuated by the staircase towers are capped by the projecting gable ends of the north-lit drawing studios and the striking T-shaped extract vents surmounting the ridge line. While the pitched roofs are covered with red concrete tiles, the projecting gables and other wall surfaces, such as the projecting wings of teaching rooms on the south elevation, are clad in cedar shingles, which have been given a special fire-retardant treatment. Seen with the strange flared profiles of the roof vents and the tall fluted red-brick chimney-stacks with their four-sided outward-stepping cowls, the whole composition presents an image of fantasy and romanticism far removed from the everyday building forms of most educational establishments.

## CASTLE MALL SHOPPING CENTRE
Norwich

*Architect:* Lambert Scott & Innes

Someone returning recently to Norwich Castle after a number of years might observe that the outlook has been improved considerably by the conversion of an old car-park into terraces, lawns, trees, shrubs and a large conservatory-like structure, unaware that this conceals a new 35,000 square metre shopping centre, with parking for more than 1,000 cars. This has been sensitively threaded into the existing network of the medieval street pattern and jumble of buildings around the base of the castle mound. The scheme is a radical and innovative approach to the organization of vehicular and pedestrian traffic as a way of achieving a viable area of new retail space while respecting the existing fabric of the city centre. It demonstrates the greater benefits to be enjoyed by the community when new life can be breathed into run-down city centre areas, reinforcing the natural focal points for social and commercial activities and exploiting the existing public transport infrastructure.

The key to the scheme was to regard the available site area as ground-space rather than potential airspace, utilizing the level changes around the site to develop several layers of retail space below the existing site levels. The concept of a below-ground-level shopping centre gave rise to a disproportionately large amount of excavation, particularly since some two-thirds of the scheme is cut into the hill-side site of the castle mound and bailey, a scheduled ancient monument. A major archaeological dig and extensive excavation and ground-retaining works were required, involving the removal of over 300,000 cubic metres of spoil and the casting of some 800 contiguous bored piles to create a retaining wall for the huge pit, which reached a depth of 18 metres at the highest point.

Much of the structural design work involved resolving the demands of the sizeable lateral loads from the perimeter ground-retaining supports and taking the substantial vertical loads from the park, with its heavy built-up paving and terraces and, on average, 1.5 metres of topsoil for planting and semi-mature trees. Internally the structural frame combines elements of pre-cast and *in situ* concrete construction bearing on piled pad foundations. Completion of these was not without its difficulties as the engineers encountered a number of 'solution features' in the underlying chalk, areas where the chalk had been dissolved by water percolating down through the ground and which had to be filled by high-pressure grouting techniques.

The retail space is disposed on four levels around a variety of nodal and mall spaces. Much ingenuity has gone into ensuring good visual connections level-to-level and an even distribution of pedestrian flows, to ensure that there are no second-rate areas or dead ends and thereby maximize the retail value. There are two major spaces acting as focal points for the scheme, one a four-storey atrium-type space featuring banks of escalators, wall-climber lifts and a large overhead glazed rooflight, known as St John's Place. The second and larger of the two spaces effectively encompasses the length of mall between the Cattle Market Gate and Castle Meadow Gate entrances, focused on a second atrium space called White Lion Square, but this extends through only two storeys and an open gallery level. The upper mall level is punctuated by large central openings providing views down to the lower mall level, and is a wide and spacious galleria covered by a vaulted roof, lit from one side by a long continuous sloping glazed roof light. Seen from the Castle, this roof light turns out to be the long elegant glazed conservatory construction, reminiscent of the Kew Gardens Palm House, which is visible as the dominant element within the public park which has been created over the roof of the centre. Its 87-metre length is punctuated by a similar circular glazed pavilion giving access from the park terraces direct to the gallery level of the centre.

The individual entrances and new frontages located at points around the site are designed to fit in with their context in terms of scale, form and materials, and to satisfy the conservation area requirements of the planners. External elevations utilize a warm red brick and the occasional use of knapped flint, under tiled and slated roofs. The Farmers Avenue frontage, facing the Castle, shows the effectiveness of the approach; the main terrace apparently comprises at least six separate buildings but only the one at each end is a survival from the previous arrangement. All the rest are new, exhibiting a variety of roof-lines and heights and differing elevational treatments, but simple and familiar in appearance. A series of clear-glazed projecting gable ends on the longest unit give glimpses of the shopping levels within and frame the entry point into the topmost level of the St John's Place atrium. This is the most striking characteristic of the scheme, the way it seems to emerge at all sorts of locations in the immediate area, linking routes and destinations in subtle, unforced and interesting ways, which makes the centre a focal point in the centre of Norwich.

## RESIDENTIAL STAFF TRAINING COLLEGE
Coventry

*Architect:* MacCormac Jamieson Prichard

In 1988 Cable and Wireless decided to relocate their telecommunications training college from Porthcurno, Cornwall to Westwood Heath Business Park on the outskirts of Coventry. The new building is a residential teaching college, and so has to combine residential and social functions with teaching spaces and workshops on the same site. The brief also included the provision of a range of social and sports-based facilities; these have been housed in a separate but linked leisure pavilion. The teaching accommodation ranges from small classrooms for management training to larger workshop areas in which the technical aspects of international communications can be simulated and studied. The residential and social components were required to accommodate up to 300 students, half of them to be able to live on the site for periods ranging from a few days to a couple of years for those reading for a degree.

At an early stage the architects decided to separate the various components into distinct formal elements. The residential accommodation is arranged in a long terrace on the northern side, with groups of study bedrooms arranged around staircases in the Oxford and Cambridge collegiate mode. The terrace is interrupted at the centre by a block containing the kitchen, servery and refectory areas, with offices above. Parallel to this on the south side, but separated by a garden, the teaching spaces are set out in a series of adjacent parallel strips of roughly the same overall length. These two primary elements are joined across the central garden by a large, roofed but open-sided portico. The roof is not continuous, however, as it is sliced in two by a slot running along the central axis of the garden, and which widens out to a pointed oval shape in the centre, clear to the sky. This ocular penetration is the heart of the campus, overlooked on each side by the glazed double-height spaces of the key social areas, the refectory and common-room.

The potentially static arrangement of parallel buildings is given a dramatic thrust at the centre. Here the linked parallel rows of the teaching spaces are sliced apart and a large V-shaped open space has been carved through the stepped and curving planes of the teaching spaces, opening up views of the countryside to the central portico. While the exposed ends of the classrooms follow the line of the diagonal, along each side of the V-shaped cut the roofs of the training wings are stepped in and out, respecting the rhythm and geometry of the structural bays and permitting the resultant freestanding corner columns to become sculptural pointers along the visual line of the cut.

One side of the V is developed as a major diagonal cross-axis running through the central portico, defining one edge of the refectory space and continuing out beyond the north face of the residences into the site beyond, where it becomes a wall in the main car park area, cleverly defining the route back into the building towards the reception area. This strong oblique axis penetrates the entire scheme, being aligned with the main vehicle entry on the south and terminating in the vertical feature of the communications tower on the northern boundary. The meandering drive around the building thus reveals to the visitor all the essential pointers to the spatial organization of the entire complex.

Architecturally the treatment of the two major components in the complex is different and distinctive. The roofs of the teaching blocks provide the most dramatic and memorable image of the building. Each band of classrooms is surmounted by its own profiled roof, in a sinuous double curve like a breaking wave. Each rises to a high point on the north side, generating a clerestorey over the intermediate access corridors which not only admits north light but also enables the deep-plan single-storey building to be naturally ventilated as well. The curve of the roof was specially profiled to ensure that hot air rising from people and equipment collects in the highest zone, where it can be released through openable windows. Cooler replacement air is drawn in through the narrow slit of south-facing windows at the lower eaves level. The curving steel roof beams support an upside-down asphalt roof, insulation outermost, on top of which is a covering of turquoise blue ceramic tiles held in place by a net of stainless steel connectors. The slight variations and richness of colour make the rolling wave metaphor very striking, particularly seen from the southern approach where the western half of the building rises out of an ornamental lake.

The accommodation wing, by contrast, is a three-storey terrace with walls of cream concrete blockwork relieved by thin courses of a contrasting green blockwork. On the south side overlooking the garden the elevation is highly articulated. Projecting bays of bed-sitting rooms clad in a glazed grid of curtain walling overhang the entrances to the communal stairways below, supported at the corners by *in situ* concrete columns. Each column head at first-floor level is developed into a rudimentary capital of the same profile as the concrete edge beams elsewhere, and acts as the springing for three angled steel props supporting intermediate canopies at second-floor level, turning the access walkway below into something of a cloister.

The leisure pavilion is different in form but picks up several of the architectural details of the main building in its elevational handling. It is a symmetrical building in which a sports hall, squash courts, snooker, games and fitness rooms form a U-shape of accommodation set into a hillock around a central swimming pool. It is orientated to frame the view back towards the main building. The pool projects forward, appearing to be cut into the rising contours of the site, creating a large landscaped roof-terrace fronting

the upper-level bar area. The external elevations feature the cream-coloured blockwork in alternating width courses but with bands of polished block, the same needle gunned *in situ* concrete finishes, and hints of the black and white window grid of the residences. The pavilion is centred on the long axis of the central garden, a fact emphasized by the watercourse that links it with the central portico. The gently concave edge of the pool hall plinth is cut away along its length to reveal a shimmering blue waterfall as though the pool is overflowing. The outflow is collected to provide the motive force for the little stream which flows through one of the pairs of aerofoil-shaped copper-clad columns supporting the portico and into a pool under the oval opening in the portico roof.

The building works at many levels, establishing a subtle interrelationship between the various activities on the site, thanks to a basically simple concept, the architect's control of three-dimensional form and the finesse with which natural materials have been handled and juxtaposed.

---

## THE SEVEN WONDERS OF THE WORLD

---

I. THE PYRAMIDS OF EGYPT

The pyramids are found from Gizeh, near Cairo, to a southern limit 60 miles (96 km) distant. The oldest is that of Zoser, at Saqqara, built c.2650 BC. The Great Pyramid of Cheops (built c.2580 BC) covers 13.12 acres (756 × 756 ft (230.4 × 230.4 m) at the base) and was originally 481 ft (146.6 m) in height.

II. THE HANGING GARDENS OF BABYLON

These adjoined Nebuchadnezzar's palace, 60 miles (96 km) south of Baghdad. The terraced gardens, ranging from 75 ft to 300 ft (25–90 m) above ground level, were watered from storage tanks on the highest terrace.

III. THE TOMB OF MAUSOLUS

Built at Halicarnassus, in Asia Minor, by the widowed Queen Artemisia about 350 BC. The memorial originated the term mausoleum.

IV. THE TEMPLE OF ARTEMIS AT EPHESUS

Ionic temple erected about 350 BC in honour of the goddess and burned by the Goths in AD 262.

V. THE COLOSSUS OF RHODES

A bronze statue of Apollo, set up about 280 BC. According to legend it stood at the harbour entrance of the seaport of Rhodes.

VI. THE STATUE OF ZEUS

Located at Olympia in the plain of Elis, and constructed of marble inlaid with ivory and gold by the sculptor Phidias, about 430 BC.

VII. THE PHAROS OF ALEXANDRIA

A marble watch tower and lighthouse on the island of Pharos in the harbour of Alexandria, built c.270 BC.

# Bequests to Charity

The alphabetical list below represents some of the principal charitable bequests from wills published since the last edition. Prior bequests, expenses and inheritance tax have to be deducted from the net figure given below for each estate, so the exact amount left to charity is not certain.

This year's list includes two of the largest charitable bequests ever recorded; Violet Eveson left over £49 million, the bulk of it to charity. The residue is to form the Eveson Charitable Trust, which she stipulated should be used for the support or relief of the physically and mentally handicapped, hospitals and hospices, children in need, the elderly and medical research. Sir Michael Sobell, one of Britain's most generous philanthropists and a pioneer in the electrical goods industry, left over £47 million, most of which was to be added to the charitable trust which he had made in 1977. Other large bequests to charitable trusts included those of Anne Colefax, Roy Wandless, Resi Hulse and Phyllis Cross, who left the residue of her estate to the Gauntlett Trust of the Armourers and Brasiers Company in memory of her husband Christopher. Harold Noakes left the residue of his estate to the Alice Noakes Memorial Charitable Trust, for making donations to animal charities. Evelyn Pratt, the widow of the actor Boris Karloff, left $10,000 to the Actors' Fund of America and the residue of her estate for such charitable purposes as her Trustees selected.

The National Trust figures prominently in the list and was left the residue of the estates of Muriel Hornby, for the maintenance of coastal land from Dartmouth to Mewstone and for 15 miles inland from high tide, and of Arthur Garnett, 'to help them maintain the very best in our heritage for the generations to come'. Canon James Owen left the residue of his estate to the Trust to purchase cliffland, moorland or heathland in Wales to commemorate the Owen family. Thaddeus Mann, a Cambridge professor, left the residue of his estate to Trinity Hall, for exchange of students between that college, western European countries and Poland in particular. Mary Lobel left the residue of her estate between two Oxford colleges and the Historic Towns Trust, on condition that her contribution as founder of the Historic Towns Atlas be acknowledged on the title page of each atlas printed. Elizabeth Clarke, former headmistress of Benenden School, left the residue of her estate to the school, after two life interests, as well as certain effects including a silver sugar bowl given her by Queen Ingrid of Denmark.

Ernest Ellinger left a large number of charitable bequests and stated that most of what he possessed came from compensation from the German government for having been persecuted as a Jew. He felt it was right to pass this on to other refugees and their descendants. Hilda Obott left a third of the residue of her estate to the Officers Association for the relief of those who suffered in the First World War. Anona Lamport, better known as the radio quiz panellist Anona Winn, left the residue of her £167,433 estate (not listed below) for the benefit of policemen, firemen and the armed forces and their relations and dependents, who have suffered since May 1969 or will suffer up to 21 years from her death in the execution of their civil duties, especially in relation to explosive devices.

Gertrude Aboody, of Ellerdale Road, London NW3, £2,616,426 (£1,000 and one 12th of the residue each to the Cancer Research Campaign and RNIB and one 12th of the residue each to Arthritis Care, Age Concern England, Barnardo's, British Heart Foundation, British Red Cross Society, Parkinsons Disease Society, Mencap, National Asthma Campaign, National Society for Epilepsy and SENSE)

Aithna Ingeborg Bertha Andrew, of Exeter, Devon, £1,240,396 (the residue equally between the National Trust and RNLI)

Jean Angus, of Blandford Forum, Dorset, £2,431,654 (the residue equally between the National Trust for Scotland, and the PDSA, Glasgow)

Kitty Violet Apsey, of Maida Vale, London W9, £832,469 (the residue equally between the RNLI and the Cancer Relief Macmillan Fund, but not to fund experiments on animals in any way)

Frank Atkinson, OBE, of Goole, N. Humberside, £604,958 (the residue to the University of Hull, for scientific research)

Kathleen Alice Bailey, of Malvern, Worcs., £1,282,006 (the residue equally between the RNLI, RNIB and RNID)

John Patrick Ernest Grierson Berthoud, of Gloucester Road, London SW7, £4,592,153 (£50,000 to the Motor Neurone Disease Association, and the residue to the Charities Aid Foundation)

James Leslie Blower, of Liphook, Hants, £657,401 (the residue to Help the Aged)

Hugo Blum, of Ellesmere Road, London NW10, £1,253,192 (the residue for such charities in England and Wales as his trustees select)

Avis Mary Eaglesfield Booker, of Paignton, Devon, £592,177 (the residue to the National Trust)

Dorothy Booker, of Bowness-on-Windermere, Cumbria, £2,012,904 (the residue equally between Windermere Motor Boat Racing Club, Friends of the Lake District, Langdale and Ambleside Mountain Rescue Team, Lake District Cheshire Home, Windermere, St John's Hospice, Slyne, Lancaster, RNLI, National Trust, National Equine Defence League, PDSA, RSPCA, British Diabetic Association, and the International Donkey Protection Trust, Sidmouth)

Kathleen Beatrice Bower, of Torquay, Devon, £509,173 (the residue equally between the Guide Dogs for the Blind Association, RNIB, NSPCC, National Trust, Distressed Gentlefolk's Aid Association, RNLI, Torquay Branch, Salvation Army, Torbay Hospital League of Friends, Rowcroft Hospice, Torquay, Cancer Research Campaign, and up to two other charitable institutions as her trustees decide)

Cecil Gordon Browne, of Worthing, W. Sussex, £1,204,297 (the residue equally between the Tarner Homes, Brighton, Copper Cliff Hospice, Brighton, Chichester Cathedral Trust, English-Speaking Union of the Commonwealth, Muscular Dystrophy Group and Barnardo's)

Lt.-Col. Valentine Cambier, of Kenilworth Road, London W5, £609,608 (the residue to the Abbot and Community of Ealing Abbey)

Gladys Carmichael, of Bournemouth, Dorset, £950,053 (£50,000 to the Home of Rest for Horses, Aylesbury, and the residue to the Salvation Army)

Frances Menevia Chadwick, of Ainsworth, Greater Manchester, £569,428 (the residue to the Seedfield Trust, Bury, 'to be used only for preaching the word of the Lord')

Alec Victor Clark, of Kirkham Street, London SE18, £749,913 (his entire estate equally between the RNIB and Salvation Army)

Elizabeth Bleckley Clarke, CVO, of Cranbrook, Kent, £2,935,444 (the residue, after two life interests, to the Benenden School Trust)

Frederick Storey Cockburn, of Sompting, W. Sussex, £725,097 (the residue to the RNLI)

Annie Marie Colefax, of Hungerford, Berks., £7,082,155 (the residue to the Colefax Charitable Trust)

Pauline Cooke, of Surbiton, Surrey, £1,228,929 (three-fifths of the residue to the Cancer Research Campaign and two-fifths of the residue to the British Heart Foundation)

Helen Jean Cope, of Markfield, Leics., £3,228,784 (the residue for such charitable institutions as her trustees think fit)

Maud Craven, of Tiptoe, Hants, £1,028,518 (the residue equally between the NSPCC, Royal Star and Garter Home, Richmond, RAF Benevolent Fund and the Gardeners' Royal Benevolent Society)

Phyllis Josephine Cross, of Princes Gate Mews, London SW7, £1,381,577 (the residue to the Gauntlett Trust of the Armourers and Brasiers Company)

Eunice Denton, of Oldham, Greater Manchester, £1,235,508 (the residue to the Hulme Grammar Schools, Oldham, for assisted places for boys and girls)

Ernest Ellinger, of Higher Compton, Plymouth, Devon, £623,317 (40 per cent of the residue to the Central British Fund for World Jewish Relief, 10 per cent to the National Trust, Plymouth, 5 per cent each to St Luke's Hospice, Plymouth, Arthritis and Rheumatism Council, Barnardo's, Plymouth Age Concern, Salvation Army, Plymouth, Friends of the Hebrew University of Jerusalem, and NSPCC, for their Plymouth and South Devon Child Protection Teams, 4 per cent to the Mental Health Trust, 3 per cent each to the Imperial Cancer Research Fund, and 2 per cent each to the Marie Curie Memorial Foundation, Dame Hannah Rogers School, Ivybridge, British Red Cross Society, Devonshire Branch, and Association of Jewish Refugees)

Fanny Violet Mary Eveson, of Stourton, Staffs., £49,069,977 (£250,000 for surgical equipment and aids for such children's charities in the UK as her trustees select, and the residue to form the Eveson Charitable Trust)

Gwendoline Ruth Forrester, of Gorleston, Norfolk, £690,640 (her entire estate for such charity or charities as her trustees think fit)

Joan Mary Francis, of Stoke Bishop, Bristol, £651,067 (one quarter of the residue to the Salvation Army, half to help children in the London Borough of Camden and half to help the elderly in Bristol, and one-eighth of the residue each to the RNLI, NSPCC, Distressed Gentlefolk's Aid

Association, RNID for work with young children, Bristol Children's Help Society and Cats Protection League)

Raymond Frank Gardner, of Middleton-on-Sea, W. Sussex, £2,477,030 (£500,000 to the Cancer Relief Macmillan Fund)

Arthur Ernest Garnett, of Apperley Bridge, W. Yorks., £1,037,549 (the residue to the National Trust)

Catherine Gaulter, of Thistleton, Lancs., £795,214 (the residue to the Trinity Hospice in the Fylde, Bispham, Blackpool)

William Abercrombie Kidston Glen, of Hurstpierpoint, W. Sussex, £1,659,589 (half the residue to the Macmillan Day Hospice, Brighton, and one quarter of the residue each to the RNID, and King Edward VII's Hospital, London)

Audrey Edith Gray, of Princes Risborough, Bucks., £716,962 (three 17ths of the residue each to the Radiotherapy Fund at Churchill Hospital, Oxford, and Stoke Mandeville Hospital Eye Appeal, two 17ths of the residue each to the Multiple Sclerosis Society, British Kidney Patient Association, and Arthritis and Rheumatism Council, and one 17th of the residue each to the World Wildlife Fund, Imperial Cancer Research Fund, British Heart Foundation, RNLI, and the Iain Rennie Hospice at Home, Pitstone, Bucks.)

Elsie Joyce Green, of Nether Street, London N12, £1,986,293 (the residue equally between the Finchley Meeting of the Society of Friends, National Trust, World Wildlife Fund, RSPB and PDSA)

Isabel Louise Hall, of Southport, Merseyside, £799,800 (the residue equally between the RNLI, RNIB, RSPCA, St John's Ambulance, Royal British Legion, Salvation Army, British Diabetic Association, Arthritis and Rheumatism Council, Leukaemia Research Fund and Imperial Cancer Research Fund)

George Dudley Herbert, of Amesbury, Wilts., £3,655,220 (the residue to the National Trust)

Muriel Stevenson Hornby, of Holland Park, London W11, £1,822,767 (the residue to the National Trust, to maintain coastal land from Dartmouth to Mewstone)

Alice Eliza Mary Hughes, of Westcliff-on-Sea, Essex, £622,961 (the residue equally between the RNLI, Christian Aid, Royal Commonwealth Society for the Blind, Cancer Research Campaign, Arthritis and Rheumatism Council, Leukaemia Research Fund, Multiple Sclerosis Society and the Brain Research Trust of the Institute of Neurology)

Resi Ruth Hulse, of North Hill, London N6, £1,739,460 (half the residue to the Rudi and Resi Hulse Charitable Trust)

Robert Summers Hunter, of Sunderland, Tyne and Wear, £1,177,340 (the residue equally between the RNIB, NSPCC and Guide Dogs for the Blind Association)

Olive Hildegard Hurst, of Rowhook, W. Sussex, £1,217,531 (the residue equally between St Wilfrid's Hospice, Chichester, the Macmillan Fund at King Edward VII Hospital, Midhurst, Royal Star and Garter Home, Richmond, Wildfowl Trust, RSPB, Guide Dogs for the Blind Association, Age Concern, National Trust, Barnardo's, Hospital for Sick Children, Great Ormond Street, London, Leukaemia Research Fund and Childline)

Irene Beatrice Jackson, of Hailsham, East Sussex, £510,096 (the residue to the Worldwide Fund for Nature)

Frank Albert Edward Jeffery, of Bosbury Road, London SE6, £1,018,838 (the residue equally between Lewisham Hospital, London, Brook Hospital, London, Kings College Hospital, London, Maudsley Hospital, London, Multiple Sclerosis Society, Leukaemia Research Fund,

Asthma Research Council, British Heart Foundation, SENSE, Salvation Army, Samaritans, National Association for Mental Health, NSPCC and RNLI)

Ivy Helen Isabel Joseph, of Finchley Road, London NW8, £1,836,942 (the residue for such charities as her executors decide)

Josephine Kehoe, of Aberdare Gardens, London NW6, £833,610 (her entire estate to the British Heart Foundation)

Margaret Atkinson Keitch, of Penrith, Cumbria, £548,306 (half the residue to the RSPB and one quarter of the residue each to the NSPCC and Barnardo's)

Gillian Kimball, of Budleigh Salterton, Devon, £1,483,868 (the residue equally between the RSPCA, Exeter Branch, PDSA, Blue Cross, National Canine Defence League, Brooke Hospital for Animals, National Children's Home, Salvation Army, and the Social Care Unit of St Martin in the Fields, London)

James Lesbirel Kitchin, of Axminster, Devon, £1,390,833 (half the residue to the National Trust, one-fifth of the residue to the Friends of the Elderly and one-tenth of the residue each to the Cancer Relief Macmillan Fund, Salvation Army and RNLI)

Dorothy Tudor Lee, of Elibank Road, London SE9, £531,833 (her entire estate equally between Queens' College, Cambridge, St Paul's Cathedral, London, British and Foreign Bible Society and Methodist Homes for the Aged)

Bertram Bernard Levitus, of Branksome Park, Dorset, £1,614,440 (the residue equally between the Hannah Levy House Trust, Bournemouth, Imperial Cancer Research Fund and the Glasgow Jewish Welfare Board)

Mary Doreen Lobel, of Wardington, Oxon., £514,011 (the residue equally between St Hugh's College, Oxford, Somerville College, Oxford, and the Historic Towns Trust)

Donald Ernest Lockhart, of Berkhamsted, Herts., £747,657 (three-quarters of the residue for such charities as his trustees select, and one quarter of the residue to St Mary's Church, Northchurch, Berkhamsted)

Evelyn Maude Porteous Lord, of Skipton, N. Yorks., £1,317,567 (the residue equally between Holy Trinity Parish Church, Skipton, the Northern Horticultural Society, Harrogate, for Harlow Carr Gardens, the John Charnley Trust, NSPCC, Salvation Army and Giggleswick School)

Prof. Thaddeus Robert Rudolph Mann, CB, FRS, of Cambridge, £522,898 (the residue to Trinity Hall, Cambridge, to promote international relationships)

Robert Geoffrey Mayall, of New Milton, Hants, £581,589 (the residue to the Salvation Army)

Alice Florence Moore, of Barnet, Herts., £530,270 (the residue equally between Battersea Dogs Home and Cancer Relief Macmillan Fund)

Charles Thomas Moore, of Cabourne, Lincs., £2,548,872 (the residue equally between the Salvation Army, Cancer Research Campaign and NSPCC)

Rosemary Newbald, of Bembridge, Isle of Wight, £1,550,224 (one-sixth of the residue each to the Salvation Army and Save the Children Fund)

Magda Newman, of Hersham, Surrey, £707,822 (two-thirds of the residue to the Federation of Women Zionists and one-third of the residue to the National Association for Gifted Children)

Mollie Emily Newman, of Chippenham, Wilts., £1,091,898 (the residue equally between the Donkey Sanctuary, Sidmouth, RSPB, PDSA and RSPCA)

Harold Isaac Noakes, of Great Leighs, Essex, £1,539,950 (£100,000 to the Bishop of Chelmsford for charitable

purposes within his diocese as he thinks fit, and the residue to form the Alice Noakes Memorial Charitable Trust)

Hilda Frances Obott, of Sherbourne, Warks., £1,225,853 (the residue equally between the Royal Horticultural Society, Royal School of Church Music and the Officers Association)

Canon James Owen, of Cambridge, £887,507 (the residue to the National Trust, to purchase cliffland, moorland or heathland in Wales)

Florence Gladys Peak, of Lytham St Annes, Lancs., £2,420,794 (the residue equally between St Mary's Church, Nether Alderley, Cheshire, St Cuthbert's Church, Lytham, St Margaret's Church, St Annes on Sea, the Christie Hospital, Manchester, the YMCA, St Annes on Sea, RUKBA, Barnardo's, John Groom's, Treloar Trust, Salvation Army, Manchester City Mission, Wood Street Mission, Manchester, Not Forgotten Association, Age Concern England, NSPCC, Shelter, Cancer Research Campaign and the Lytham Heritage Group)

Felice Pearson, of Holland Street, London W8, £1,295,722 (the residue equally between the Royal Commonwealth Society for the Blind, Woodland Trust, Abbeyfield Society, Over Forty Association for Women Workers, Help the Aged, Salvation Army, Severn Navigation Restoration Fund, Cancer Relief Macmillan Fund, National Council of the YMCA, Rescue – the British Archaeological Trust, Theatres Trust, Maritime Trust, Redundant Churches Fund, Historic Churches Preservation Trust, Adopt-a-Book Appeal, Architectural Heritage Fund, Chatham Historic Dockyard Trust, Live Music Now, National Art Collections Fund, Royal Opera House Trust, Royal Association in Aid of Deaf People, Disabled Living Foundation, 'the Grace and Compassion Benedictines', King George's Fund for Sailors, Shipwrecked Mariners' Society, British Wireless for the Blind, Yorkshire Derwent Trust, London Association for the Blind, Wood Green Animal Shelter, British Foundation for Age Research, Horticultural Therapy, Children's Society, Children's Country Holidays Fund, National Association for Gifted Children, Pearson's Holiday Fund, National Portrait Gallery Trust Fund, Salisbury Cathedral Spire Appeal, Home Farm Trust, Elizabeth Fitzroy Homes, Greenacre Farm Communities, Hansel Village, Action Water, Harvest Help, Intermediate Technology Development Group, Wings of Friendship, and St Mary Abbot's Church, Kensington (to improve the lighting in St Paul's Chapel)

John David Perry, of College Road, London SE21, £2,018,633 (his entire estate to the Zoological Society of London)

Evelyn Pratt, of Bramshott, Hants, £1,673,712 (the residue for such charitable purposes as her trustees select)

John Geoffrey Drewe Pratt, of West Horsley, Surrey, £2,273,460 (half the residue to the National Trust, for sites of natural beauty or archaeological sites from Roman times or before, and half the residue to the RSPB, for dry land reserves)

Hugh George Gleadow Richardson, of Fowlmere, Cambs., £591,648 (the residue to the Jefferiss Research Wing Trust of St Mary's Hospital, London)

Sadie Rijkeboer, of East Croydon, Surrey, £1,013,899 (the residue equally between the Guide Dogs for the Blind Association, Empire Rheumatism Council, the Chest, Heart and Stroke Association, National Trust, RSPB, Cats Protection League, National Canine Defence League and RNLI)

John Henry Rivett, of Fabian Road, London SW6, £521,696 (the residue to the Marie Curie Memorial Foundation)

Charles Granville Robinson, of Adel, W. Yorks.,
£2,140,263 (the residue equally between the Cancer
Research Campaign, Sue Ryder Foundation, Stoke
Mandeville Hospital and RNLI)

Robert Percival Ross, of Willerby, N. Humberside,
£867,109 (£100,000 for the benefit of Hull Chess Club,
Hull and District Chess Association and any registered
charity promoting chess, and the residue equally between
Hull Boys Club, Salvation Army, Barnardo's and Royal
British Legion Poppy Appeal)

Madeleine Vera Salter, of Windermere Avenue, London
SW19, £703,744 (her entire estate equally between the
Cancer Research Campaign, British Rheumatism and
Arthritis Association, British Heart Foundation and
Royal London Society for the Blind)

Lilian Maud Selway, of Petts Wood, Kent, £523,409 (the
residue to the National Trust)

Catherine Mary Ruth Shirehampton, of Sidmouth, Devon,
£1,751,267 (the residue to the Devon Trust for Nature
Conservation)

Cicely Fay Simpson, of Fincham, Norfolk, £699,602 (the
residue to the Royal College of Surgeons, for cancer
research)

Florence Marion Slater, of Black Notley, Essex, £764,433
(the residue to St Peter and St Paul's Parish Church,
Black Notley)

Agnes Catherine Lampen Smith, of Burcot, Oxon.,
£1,523,328 (the residue to the Parish of St Martin in the
Fields, London, for social welfare work)

Dudley Charles Smith, of Lancing, W. Sussex, £843,327
(the residue to the Imperial Cancer Research Fund)

Minette Henrietta Cairns Smith, of Rye, E. Sussex,
£724,304 ('the remainder of all my cash and investments'
as to five-sixths to the Imperial Cancer Research Fund
and one-sixth to the National Trust, and the residue to
the Cancer Relief Macmillan Fund)

Violet Williamina Harriet Smyth, of Walton on the Hill,
Surrey, £1,027,456 (the residue equally between the
Church Missionary Society, Royal Hospital and Home,
London, Cancer Research Campaign, National Trust for
properties in Hampshire, and the National Trust for
Scotland for properties in Angus)

Sir Michael Sobell, of Englefield Green, Surrey,
£47,291,574 (the residue to the Sobell Foundation)

Emily Stell, of Ilkley, W. Yorks., £1,965,726 (the residue to
the Guide Dogs for the Blind Association)

Hugh MacQuarie Stone, of Sarisbury Green, Hants,
£834,626 (the residue to the RNLI, towards a new
lifeboat for the Harwich station in Essex)

Marie Chambers Stubbs, of Hindhead, Surrey, £836,183
(the residue equally between the RSPCA, the Friends of
the Centre for Spastic Children, London, St Dunstan's,
National Canine Defence League, Wood Green Animal
Shelter and the Guildford Dog Rescue Society)

Gladys Maud Compton Swain, of Brighton, East Sussex,
£670,302 (the residue to the Sussex Eye Hospital,
Brighton)

Natalie Gurney-Taylor, of Redington Road, London NW3,
£604,506 (the residue to the Psychiatry Research Trust)

Constance Mary Thornton, of Uplyme, Devon, £1,053,896
(half the residue for such charitable institutions or objects
in England as her trustees decide)

Yvonne Vilja Townshend, of Chester Close South, London
NW1, £653,064 (£150,000 to the RSPCA, and half the
residue to the Wood Green Animal Shelter)

Clifford Lewis Tucker, of Streatley Place, London NW3,
£803,296 (the residue to St David's University College,
Lampeter, Dyfed)

Phyllis Usher, of Blackpool, Lancs., £517,727 (the residue
equally between the Hawthorne Trust, and the First
Church of Christ Scientist, Blackpool)

Ursula Frances Bowring Vestey, of Hyde Park Gardens,
London W2, £871,935 (the residue equally between the
Winged Fellowship Trust, Friends of the Elderly and
Gentlefolk's Help, SIGN – Campaign for Deaf People,
and the Phyllis Tuckwell Memorial Hospice, Farnham,
Surrey)

Roy Hudson Wandless, of West Parley, Dorset, £6,326,579
(£200,000 and half the residue to the charity known as
the J. V. Trust)

Phoebe Grahame-White, of Brighton, E. Sussex, £1,214,453
(the residue equally between the RSPCA, Royal College
of Veterinary Surgeons, RAF Benevolent Fund, Institute
of Cancer Research and the Home of Rest for Horses)

Kathleen Frances Williams, of Bexhill, E. Sussex, £772,876
(the residue equally between the RNLI and PDSA)

Edith Ethel Williamson, of Chesterton, Cambs., £658,908
(the residue equally between Manchester University and
Cambridge University, both for the study of the history of
biological sciences, Cambridge University Department of
Pathology, Help the Aged, NSPCC, RSPCA, PDSA,
National Trust and Barnardo's)

Mary Roche Woods, of Bexhill, E. Sussex, £1,214,331 (one-
fifth of the residue to the Co-Workers of Mother Teresa
and one-tenth of the residue each to St Mary Magdalen's
RC Church, Bexhill, Parkinson's Disease Society,
RSPCA, PDSA, NSPCC, RNIB, RNID, and the
Benedictine Sisters of Our Lady of Grace and
Compassion at Worth Abbey, Crawley)

Violet Irene Gwendolen Yardley, of Torquay, Devon,
£1,022,128 (three-quarters of the residue to Age Concern
England and one quarter of the residue to the RNLI, for
use in Scotland)

# Broadcasting

## TELEVISION

The long-running, mass-appeal drama series is the motor that drives Britain's main television networks and in 1993–4 the BBC again struggled to keep pace with ITV in this key area of programming. *EastEnders* and *Casualty* excepted, popular drama remained the BBC's Achilles' heel throughout the year. In May 1994 the BBC admitted that it had under-performed in drama over the past ten years. 'ITV drama has not gone down market, as many predicted it would. It has succeeded in catching audiences with expensive quality drama like *Peak Practice* and *Heartbeat*.'

These two programmes achieved audiences of more than 13 million viewers. A new series, *The Knock*, set in the world of the Customs and Excise officer, and *Cadfael*, in which Derek Jacobi played a medieval monk, were two more recent additions to ITV's roster of hit drama series. The network also continued to score with *Sharpe*, featuring Sean Bean as a British officer fighting in the Napoleonic Wars, *Soldier, Soldier*, and a string of detective-based drama including *Anna Lee*, *Taggart* and the critically acclaimed *Prime Suspect*. *Minder*, celebrating its 100th episode, entered its last series. George Cole, who had played Arthur Daley to unanimous approval, said he no longer had the stamina for the part but it was said there were problems with writing fresh scripts. Even so, *Minder* still attracted more than 10 million viewers.

The most talked-about ITV drama of the year was the award-winning *Cracker*, starring Robbie Coltrane as a psychologist assisting the police. *Cracker* generated controversy and was said to be too violent but most critics praised the series for its writing, sense of pace and characterization. ITV had its flops too, notably an eagerly anticipated new series written by *Rumpole*-creator John Mortimer, *Under the Hammer*, set in an auction house and featuring Richard Wilson.

The BBC's attempt to reinvigorate its popular drama was unsuccessful. *Harry*, a BBC 1 series about a hard-drinking Darlington journalist, was the first of several new programmes that failed to live up to the corporation's expectations. Despite being well re-viewed, the series was not a popular success. John Birt, the director-general, later admitted that *Harry*, along with two other new drama series, *Headhunters* and *Grushko*, was a disappointment.

Another high-profile BBC 1 drama, *Scarlet and Black*, serialized from Stendhal's novel, was also a failure. The *Independent*'s television critic likened it to an American mini-series, saying it was 'not so much *Scarlet and Black* as Stendhal's *I'll Take Paris*'. The critics did, however, respond well to *To Play The*

*King*, a four-part sequel to the earlier BBC 1 serial, *House of Cards*, also based on a Michael Dobbs novel. This time the machiavellian Prime Minister Francis Urquhart, facing re-election, clashes with the new king, a leftward-leaning idealist. There was uproar in the press because it was felt the characterization of the monarch bore an uncanny resemblance to Prince Charles and was a slur on his personality.

Another BBC drama, *The Buddha of Suburbia*, adapted by Hanif Kureishi from his own novel, provoked controversy for a different reason. News-papers trailed it as 'the most sexually explicit series ever to be shown on TV'. Scenes involving heterosex-ual and homosexual group sex were criticized by the Broadcasting Standards Council following complaints from viewers, but the serial was a critical success. The BBC's most successful drama of the year was *Middlemarch*, condensed from George Eliot's epic novel into a five-part serial by Andrew Davies, who also wrote the screenplay for *To Play The King*. Observers hailed the £6 million film, praised for its acting and matchless production values, as a return to form in an area – the period literary classic – the BBC had neglected for several years.

There were also kind words for two new BBC dramas set firmly in the late 20th century, *Family*, written by Roddy Doyle, and *Cardiac Arrest*, set in a National Health Service hospital and written by a still-practising junior doctor, John MacUre. Their directness was too much for some people. A Conservative backbencher dismissed *Cardiac Arrest* as 'a piece of anti-Government propaganda, giving a negative view of the NHS'. Reviewers nevertheless welcomed the uncompromising view of contemporary life depicted in *Cardiac Arrest* and *Family*.

### CONCERN OVER QUALITY

Despite such highlights as *Cracker*, *Middlemarch* and *Cardiac Arrest*, there was a widespread feeling that television drama had lost much of its nerve and, in ITV's case, was too reliant on proven formulae. In May 1994 the Independent Television Commission, publishing its first review of the new ITV franchise-holders, complained that 'the predominance of crime-based stories narrowed the range of drama overall'. It mourned the demise of the single play and the one-off film. The ITC was also critical of ITV's general network programme performance, accusing it of being 'cautious and predictable', and adopting a safety first approach. There was little evidence of 'adventure or the surprise of one-off events'. The chairman of the ITV council said the most important judge of ITV's programmes was the viewer and despite a period of severe upheaval, the channel's audience share had remained ahead of its nearest rival, BBC 1.

ITV's Christmas schedule, which had relied heavily on repeats and bought-in feature films, was criticized 'for offering little seasonal material of a quality likely to be attractive to viewers'. The ITC noted an improvement in the quality of regional programmes but two of the new ITV companies, Carlton and the breakfast station GMTV, were singled out for harsh verdicts. Carlton's network programmes 'were, with some exceptions, not distinctive or of noticeable high quality'. GMTV was given a formal warning that unless its service improved, notably in current affairs and children's programming, it could lose its licence. GMTV's news bulletins had initially lacked depth and authority although the situation improved following ITC intervention.

The death in June 1994 of Dennis Potter, the writer who many believed had single-handedly turned television drama into an art form, was seen by some of his peers as symbolizing the demise of the medium as a genuinely creative force. The Directors' Guild expressed its concern over declining standards by publishing a code of practice aimed at improving the quality of television drama. Potter, one of the first to publicly criticize Carlton, had mesmerized viewers when in April 1994 he revealed he was dying of cancer in a lengthy Channel 4 interview with Melvyn Bragg. As a tribute to Potter, Channel 4 and the BBC agreed to collaborate so that his last two television dramas, Karaoke and Cold Lazarus, would be shown on both channels.

SOAP WARS

One sign of increased competition between Britain's television networks was the BBC's decision to show a third episode of EastEnders each week from April 1994. ITV's veteran soap Coronation Street, shown on Mondays, Wednesdays and Fridays, regularly topped the ratings with more than 18 million viewers. The additional episode of EastEnders failed to improve BBC 1's audience share significantly and when, for the first time ever, Coronation Street was shown head-to-head with EastEnders, Coronation Street beat its BBC rival by 5.5 million viewers.

Another ITV soap, Emmerdale, was proving less successful. In an attempt to lift ratings, particularly with younger and more up-market viewers, Phil Redmond, the creator of Grange Hill and Brookside, was employed to give Emmerdale a more contemporary feel. Redmond wrote a Lockerbie-style air disaster into the script, killing off several characters. This and a number of other violent storylines, including armed robbery, abduction and murder, provoked hundreds of complaints from viewers. The ITC censured Emmerdale and its producers, Yorkshire Television, for a shift towards ' a tougher and more violent style' and for being 'insensitive' to the relatives of Lockerbie victims. While audiences for the Emmerdale episodes featuring the air disaster climbed to 18.5 million, overall ratings for the serial still lagged behind Coronation Street and EastEnders.

Another area of concern for the regulators was a tendency for television channels, especially BBC 1 and ITV, to fill their schedules with series based on real-life crime. A BBC 1 documentary, The Underworld, profiling 20th-century British criminals and narrated by Bob Hoskins, was accused of glorifying law-breakers. In June the BBC announced it was introducing new guidelines to avoid the sensational treatment of crime. The BSC also censured the BBC for paying thousands of pounds worth of fees to gangsters for their participation in the series. The BBC said the payments were 'permissible' and the programme was in the public interest. An ITV series, Gangsters, screened at the same time as The Underworld, was also attacked by the BSC for making payments to criminals. Carlton, which commissioned the series, claimed 'the sums involved did not amount to personal gain on a scale which might cause public offence.'

While The Underworld was the BBC's most controversial documentary series of the year, the most celebrated was Thatcher: The Downing Street Years, in which Margaret Thatcher and her Cabinet colleagues gave first-hand accounts of life inside Number Ten. The Observer described the programme as 'riveting from beginning to end'. The BBC also scored with Sir David Attenborough's latest wildlife saga, Life in the Freezer, filmed in the Antarctic, which was watched by more than ten million people. Charles Wheeler's documentary on the D-Day landings was another critical triumph for the BBC.

In the opinion of many, including the ITC, ITV's documentaries were less distinguished. Part of the problem, commentators said, was that there were fewer of them. Such series as Kinnock: The Inside Story were said to be the exception rather than the rule. Some felt that Carlton's Hollywood Women typified ITV's new approach to documentary-making. The ITC accused Hollywood Women of being 'glib and superficial'. First Tuesday, the acclaimed Yorkshire Television series whose 'Windscale, The Nuclear Laundry' had triggered a government inquiry into the nuclear industry to decade earlier, was shown on ITV for the last time in autumn 1993. The new ITV network centre had not recommissioned the series and it was only a decision by Discovery, an American-based satellite channel, to buy the programme that saved First Tuesday from oblivion.

The axing of Viewpoint, another ITV documentary strand, and the anthropological series Disappearing World, was seen as further evidence of a more commercially-minded ITV. The network was praised for its popular history series The Windsors screened in June 1994. Critics, however, thought many viewers had missed a programme they would have enjoyed because it was shown at the relatively late hour of 10.40 p.m. when the series was worthy of a peak-time slot. Another ITV royal documentary, Charles – The Private Man, The Public Role was a subject of much media attention. More than 13 million people watched it. Critics were divided over the programme's merits.

Some reviewers saw Jonathan Dimbleby's interviews with the Prince as part of a public relations campaign instigated by the Prince's supporters. Much of the criticism, however, concerned what was felt to be the protracted nature of the film, which lasted two and a half hours.

## No Laughing Matter

One of the first signs of increased pressure on ITV programmes to deliver instant ratings success or face the consequences, was the axing of Carlton's situation comedy *Brighton Belles* mid-way through its first series in September 1993. Starring Wendy Craig, Jean Boht, Sheila Hancock and Sheila Gish, *Brighton Belles* was seen as an attempt to create a British version of the American hit comedy *The Golden Girls*. The critics were not impressed and when audiences dropped from 7.5 million to seven million within three weeks, the plug was pulled. The general view was that it was the BBC and not ITV that made most of the running in comedy. *Spitting Image*, celebrating its tenth anniversary, was said to have lost its satirical bite. In contrast, *The Day Today*, BBC 2's spoof news series, was hailed as one of the funniest shows of the decade. Its team included the controversial Chris Morris, who was later suspended from his Radio 1 show for broadcasting a hoax phone call to a Conservative MP pretending that Michael Heseltine had died.

The year's great comedy popular success was a series of Morecambe and Wise repeats, *Bring Me Sunshine*, watched regularly by more than ten million viewers on BBC 1 during the summer. Reviewers drew comparisons with today's generation of television comics, pointing out that few of them could attract such big audiences. They concluded that Morecambe and Wise had a warmth lacking in contemporary performers. One of the few current comedies to achieve an audience of more than ten million was the second series of *Absolutely Fabulous*, transferring from BBC 2 to BBC 1. Critics agreed the show had lost none of its appeal.

Overall, the BBC was worried that not enough of its programmes were registering with less well-educated audiences. A survey by the Institute of Practitioners in Advertising, published in September 1993, claimed that 19 of the top 20 television programmes watched by social groups D and E were on ITV. Match Of The Day was the only BBC show included in the list. Worried that it was 'super-serving' middle-class audiences, the BBC launched a number of new shows to address the problem, including the Desmond Lynam-hosted *How Do They Do That?* and *Do The Right Thing*, presented by Terry Wogan. *How Do They Do That?* achieved audiences of more than nine million.

Another programme designed to win over people who did not regard themselves as natural BBC watchers was *Here and Now*, launched in March 1994 as a deliberately populist current affairs show and immediately dubbed 'son of *Nationwide*'. Critics did

not like the show but *Here and Now* was recommissioned for a second series. Meanwhile, commentators noted a resurgence in the quality of BBC television's current affairs flagship *Panorama*, which was 40 years old in November 1993. The so-called Birtian 'mission to explain', with an emphasis on analyses and 'talking-head' journalism had, said reviewers, been abandoned. In its place was a return to more traditional, investigative-style reporting. Programmes on alleged police corruption, 'The Case of India One', and claims of mismanagement at Tottenham Hotspur, 'The Manager', received enthusiastic reviews and audience figures began to improve. However, the most controversial edition of *Panorama* was a programme shown in October 1993, 'Babies on Benefit', claiming that teenagers were deliberately getting pregnant in order to gain council accommodation.

## Future of the BBC

The White Paper on the BBC, published in July 1994, was seen by many commentators as a personal victory for John Birt, the director-general, and his reforms. These were presented as an attempt to create a more efficient, accountable and commercially-minded BBC. MPs on both sides of the House broadly welcomed the White Paper proposals. However, some Conservative MPs wondered why there were no plans to privatize all or part of the BBC's service. Labour's shadow heritage secretary Marjorie Mowlam voiced concern that there was no long-term commitment to linking the licence fee to the rate of inflation.

Outside Parliament, Melvyn Bragg said he was worried that by encouraging the BBC to compete commercially in the international media market place, the Government risked compromising the Corporation's domestic public service role. Bragg said, 'The BBC is being told to ride two horses, the domestic and the international; public service and commercial; should these two race apart then the BBC could be rent asunder'.

In the months leading up to the publication of the White Paper, leading broadcasters had continued to speak out in public about what they saw as the shortcomings of Mr Birt's leadership of the BBC. On being appointed as the new presenter of *Question Time* in December, David Dimbleby told journalists that Mr Birt's regime was 'unhealthy'. In March Johnny Beerling, the former Radio 1 controller said 'I left (the BBC) because in the last two years my life had less and less to do with the creative side and more and more to do with bureaucracy.' In June John Tusa, the former *Newsnight* presenter and ex-head of World Service, criticized Mr Birt's management approach. Delivering the James Cameron Memorial Lecture at London's City University, he said, 'Is the tidy driving out the inspirational? You cannot after all set a quota for inspiration, a performance indicator for genius. But if all the time is spent on measuring the routine, where is the intellectual space for fostering the remarkable?' In July, one of the director-general's most outspoken critics, Mark Tully, the BBC's India correspondent, announced he was leaving the Corporation because he claimed he had been banned from criticizing the BBC in public.

The same month Marmaduke Hussey, the BBC's chairman, said the Corporation would be able to spend an extra £255 million on programmes over the next two years because of efficiency savings. John Birt revealed that the BBC had spent £6 million on consultants in the past eight months alone. He said that the BBC needed to be better managed and that the consultants were necessary to achieve a more efficient organization. He felt, 'Staff will come to understand what the fruits are. What people are bridling against now is change itself'.

## CHANNEL 4

Most commentators agreed that Channel 4 had done well in 1993-4 and in July the ITC praised the station's programmes, saying that 'In many programme areas, high standards of quality, innovation and distinctiveness were achieved.' Critics agreed that one of the channel's most successful programmes was *Rory Bremner . . . Who Else?*, a Saturday night satire show first shown in the autumn and the winner of the BAFTA light entertainment award. Another new entertainment series *Don't Forget Your Toothbrush*, presented by Chris Evans, also attracted excellent reviews despite some adverse pre-transmission publicity suggesting production problems.

Critics also praised a documentary series about life in a Chinese town, *Beyond The Clouds*, made by the acclaimed film-maker Phil Agland. The programme, shown in March 1994, had taken five years to make and was assembled from 55 miles of film. Earlier Channel 4 had been criticized for its decision to screen a number of gay programmes over the Christmas period. The *Daily Express* reported that two bishops and a Conservative minister were furious when it emerged that Quentin Crisp was to deliver an alternative Queen's Christmas Message from Manhattan. *Camp Christmas*, said one critic, was 'an awkward though not unenjoyble affair'. There was further controversy over another item in Channel 4's festive season, *Hookers, Hustlers, Pimps and their Johns*, Beeban Kidron's film about New York's sex industry.

On the drama front, the ITC issued a formal warning to Channel 4 over *Brookside*. It said that scenes transmitted in the early-evening omnibus edition of *Brookside* were unsuitable. The use of a knife in a murder scene was a breach of the programme code. The ITC also criticized *The Word*, often the butt of press attacks for its controversial items. '*The Word*, though popular with 16- to 24-year-olds, was poorly presented and frequently beyond the margins of acceptable taste even very late at night,' the ITC said.

At 11 per cent, Channel 4's average audience share for the year was its highest ever. Channel 4 success was such that in May it launched a campaign to break its final financial links with ITV and end an arrangement that in February 1994 had involved the station giving £38 million to ITV. Michael Grade, Channel 4's chief executive, said that viewers would be better served if this money was spent on the station's programmes. ITV, however, argued that Mr Grade had originally agreed to this arrangement, which provides a financial safety net should Channel 4's share of advertising revenue fall below 14 per cent of total terrestrial television revenue. In 1993-4, the station achieved an 18.2 per cent share of advertising revenue.

## SATELLITE

The financial growth of British Sky Broadcasting continued throughout the year. In July it emerged that BSkyB had made an operating profit of £170 million, an increase of almost 177 per cent on the previous 12 months. However, there was speculation in the press that the rate of satellite dish sales had declined. Sky claimed it had sold 900,000 dishes in the past year; ITV maintained the figure was nearer 400,000. Official figures showed that ratings for Sky One, Sky's main entertainment channel, were decreasing, hit by growing competition from a number of additional satellite channels.

There was, however, no doubt about the business success of BSkyB. In September 1993, the Sky Multichannel package was launched, offering a wider range of services to viewers but ending the practice whereby a number of channels had been available free to anyone with a dish. In January, the television industry was amazed when it was announced that Kelvin MacKenzie, the controversial editor of *Sun*, had been appointed managing director of BSkyB despite a complete lack of broadcasting experience. However, Mr MacKenzie's reign at BSkyB was short-lived and in August he left following a personality clash with Sam Chisholm, BSkyB's chief executive.

On 19 August Sky launched its second sports channel. Four other new channels, Sky Travel, Sky Soap, VH1, a rock channel, and TLC, a learning channel, were due to start in October 1994, when BSkyB will increase its monthly subscription fees by £3 to £22.99.

## RADIO

On 28 March 1994, BBC Radio 5 Live began broadcasting. The news and sports network, which replaced Radio 5, was announced in October 1993. It followed controversy over the BBC's plans to launch an all-news network on Radio 4's long-wave frequency. Thirty thousand listeners had protested about the loss of Radio 4's long-wave transmissions, which would have reduced Radio 4 to an FM-only service. The decision to drop the plan for a 24-hour news service on Radio 4 long-wave and instead kill off Radio 5 to make room for a news and sports station was seen as a compromise. Commentators felt the decision was likely to anger more listeners that it pleased, and there were protests at the closure of Radio 5, especially the loss of children's programmes. Liz Forgan, BBC Radio's managing director, said she regretted the fact that the new network would not broadcast children's programmes but added, 'The children's programmes are very good quality, but the question has to be asked: if the children are not listening, are we providing the right programmes for them?'

It was pointed out that Radio 5 was the only national BBC radio network whose share of the audience was increasing. Critics, however, were less harsh when Radio 5 Live got underway. Writing in the *British Journalism Review*, Gillian Reynolds noted 'It sounds more like local than network radio . . . it is more conversational, younger, less Received Pronunciation . . . Radio 5 Live is not a disaster. It is an unaccustomed mix for BBC listeners, but I think it deserves to be a popular one.'

RADIO 1 RELAUNCHES

The new-look Radio 1, relaunched in October with a number of new presenters including Danny Baker, also provoked controversy. During 1993–4, nine new, young presenters joined the station and a new emphasis was placed on 1990s music of all types, including Afro-Caribbean and Asian music. Although it was generally accepted that changes were necessary, it was felt that the changes to Radio 1 were too extreme and risked alienating traditional listeners. During the year, Radio 1 lost three million listeners, some 15 per cent of its audience. In August 1994 Matthew Bannister, Radio 1's new controller, blamed the loss on increased competition from commercial radio and his attempt to introduce a service that did not simply copy the opposition. 'Any changes in a radio station will upset a part of the audience,' he said. 'The effect of the changes we brought in was to accelerate the losses that were already there. It takes longer for the new audiences to arrive than it does for the old ones to go. But the rate of decline is now slowing.'

Radio 4's continued existence on long wave was hailed by supporters of the Save Radio 4 Long Wave Campaign as a victory for common sense. However, the station did not escape controversy. The introduc-tion of a new afternoon magazine programme *Anderson Country*, presented by Gerry Anderson, was seen as a blatant and misguided attempt to widen Radio 4's appeal beyond its core middle-class, Home Counties audience. Mr Birt said that BBC should reflect the life, activity, culture and events in the whole of the UK, and try to overcome the image of the BBC as 'high brow, stuffy, high-minded and establishment'. Critics and listeners raged against *Anderson Country* because they considered it too unrefined for Radio 4 and claimed it sounded exactly like a local radio show. Liz Forgan said she had never

before in her career as a broadcaster encountered such hostility to a single programme.

The defection of the entire *Gardeners' Question Time* panel to Classic FM, angered by a plan to introduce new, younger panellists, was seen by some critics as further evidence that Radio 4 had lost its way. The death in January of Brian Redhead, the *Today* presenter, was mourned as the end of another Radio 4 institution. More than 6,000 listeners wrote to *Today* to express their grief. Critics praised a unique collaboration between Radio 4 and BBC 2's *Arena*, 'Radio Night', broadcast in December, in which the two networks attempted to hold a conversation with each other. The experiment doubled the size of Radio 4's average audience for a Saturday night.

As competition from the two new national com-mercial stations, Classic FM and Virgin 1215, and the steady growth of new local stations continued to take listeners away from BBC networks, the BBC acknowl-edged that its share of the total radio audience would continue to decline. Overall BBC network radio's audience share declined from 49 to 44 per cent in 1993–4. In the first quarter of 1994 Radio 4 showed a 5 per cent drop in listening. Pundits predicted a further fall in audience levels as the impact of Radio 5 Live became clear. Radio 4 faces further competition from the UK's first speech-based national commercial station, Talk Radio UK, whose licence was awarded in June and which is due on the air in the spring of 1995.

TELEVISION AWARD WINNERS

BAFTA AWARDS 1993

Best Single Drama – *Safe*
Best Drama Series – *Between the Lines*
Best Drama Serial – *Prime Suspect 3*
Best Light Entertainment – *Rory Bremner . . . Who Else?*
Best Comedy – *Drop the Dead Donkey*
Best Actor – Robbie Coltrane, *Cracker*
Best Actress – Helen Mirren, *Prime Suspect 3*
Best Light Entertainment Performance – Richard Wilson, *One Foot in the Grave/One Foot in the Algarve*
Best Factual Series – *The Ark*
Best Arts Programme – 'The Vampire's Life', *Bookmark*
Best Children's Programme – *Old Bear Stories*
Flaherty Documentary – 'The Unforgiving', *True Stories*
Best News and Actuality Coverage – *News at Ten* for its coverage of the storming of the White House in Moscow and the civil war in Georgia
Bafta Fellowship – Michael Grade
Richard Dimbleby Award – Joan Bakewell
Alan Clarke Award – Stephen Frears
Foreign TV Award – *The Oprah Winfrey Show*
Television Award for Originality – *Sarajevo: A Street Under Siege*

# Conservation and Heritage

## THE NATURAL ENVIRONMENT

### BIODIVERSITY

Of the batch of documents published on 25 January 1994 outlining the Government's response to the UN summit held in Rio de Janeiro in 1992, that of greatest interest to British naturalists is *Biodiversity: The UK Action Plan.* The document is in fact not so much a plan as a review of current activities and existing policies relating to conservation, research and education in Britain and British-administered territories overseas. These include measures under the EC Agri-Environment Regulation to manage moorland, a scheme to create or improve a range of wildlife habitats over a 20-year period; and an organic aid scheme to encourage more farmers to convert to organic methods of production. There are also measures relating to the EC Habitats Directive (*see* below) on the sustainable use of vulnerable marine areas and improved protection of certain threatened terrestrial habitats. The report even reviews English Nature's proposals to identify 'prime biodiversity areas' and states a commitment to develop conservation strategies for them. In other respects the document commits the Government to very little, though it promises that more detailed objectives and a timetable to fulfil them will be announced in 1995. The conservation world's almost unanimous reaction to the document was summed up by Jonathon Porritt, who called it 'bioderisory'.

The voluntary conservation sector published its own document, *Biodiversity Challenge: An Agenda for Conservation in the UK,* which contained much crisper proposals for action. This document sets specific objectives, detailing 530 species and 16 vulnerable habitats (not including marine ones) in need of improved protection. It also sets precise targets by which relative success or failure can be judged.

Granted that both documents are essentially platforms for public debate, both are equally significant. *Biodiversity Challenge,* arguing from a position of knowledge in depth and with a clear-sighted view of what needs to be achieved, is timely and necessary. The significance of the Government's 'action plan' and its partner documents is that the buzz-words 'biodiversity' and 'sustainability' have reached the political agenda. What flows from this in terms of policy and regulation remains to be seen.

### HABITATS DIRECTIVE

In October 1993 the Government published its belated response to the 1992 EC directive on the conservation of natural habitats and wild fauna and flora, known as the Habitats Directive. The directive introduces the new designation Special Areas of Conservation (SACs). These are intended to preserve or restore certain kinds of scarce habitat, such as lowland heath and peat bogs, and some 50 rare species, which are regarded as having special value in the European Community as a whole. They also include marine habitats for the first time. The SACs will link up with the existing EC Special Protection Areas (SPAs) for wild birds to form 'a coherent European network of protected sites' both on land and sea. This network will be called Natura 2000.

The Government's paper sets out how it intends to implement the directive. Instead of the primary legislation hoped for by conservationists, the Government is proposing to rely on a modest strengthening of existing safeguards, notably Sites of Special Scientific Interest (SSSIs) and National Nature Reserves, and the use of by-laws. It is believed that the Department of the Environment is under pressure from the Treasury and the Department of Transport to keep changes to the minimum necessary. The draft Regulations were approved by Parliament in July 1994 and will come into force in 1995.

The listing of the proposed SACs is the responsibility of the Government's conservation agencies in England, Wales, Scotland and Northern Ireland. Friends of the Earth has published its own list of 112 sites which it considers should qualify for SAC status. They include places like Asham Wood in the Mendips, Carmel Woods in Dyfed and Ballynahone Bog in Ulster which are threatened by development and other sites which are threatened by the Government's road-building proposals. This might involve the Government in costly compensation, something it has so far refused to contemplate.

### NEW BIRD ATLAS

A new atlas of breeding birds in Britain and Ireland was published in 1993. Undertaken on behalf of the British Trust for Ornithology (BTO) and Irish Wildbird Conservancy, it is the most thorough and objective bird census ever undertaken. The last such survey was undertaken twenty years ago, and comparison with the new one allows the identification of changes and trends during the intervening period. The atlas, which is based on more than one million individual records between 1988 and 1991, is a tribute to the healthy state of British and Irish bird-watching (an expertise that is exported all over the world).

The extent of the change surprised many ornithologists. The period has seen the virtual extinction of two species (the wryneck and the red-backed shrike), the decline of many more, and a compensating increase in others, most remarkably birds of prey like the peregrine and the marsh harrier. The period also saw the spread of the siskin through conifer plantations all over the country, and the northward advance of the blackcap, perhaps linked to its growing tendency to over-winter here.

The most alarming trend revealed by the survey is the decline of a whole community of seed-eating birds on farmland, most notably the turtle-dove, the skylark, the linnet, the corn bunting, the bullfinch and the tree sparrow. The same trend has been noted and quantified by the BTO's Common Bird Census. All of these birds feed not on the crop, but on the seeds of weeds and on their dependent insects. Improved efficiency in farming has taken its toll of 'unwanted' weeds and the final blow has been autumn sowing, which leaves no stubble for the birds to forage in. The new atlas is compelling evidence that, despite the surplus of most crops, modern farming methods continue to undermine the status of even widespread and adaptable birds.

TREES IN TOWNS

The Department of the Environment has published the first national survey of trees in English towns. Its findings reveal that while four out of five town trees grow in gardens and on other private land, the majority of large trees of significant visual impact are in the public domain, especially along streets. The survey also shows that the large street trees of the Victorian era – lime, plane, horse chestnut and others – are being replaced by smaller flowering trees like rowan, whitebeam and cherry, which will never have the same visual effect. Increasingly, fast-growing evergreen shrubs like Leylandia are being planted. Already the latter make up nearly one quarter of all urban trees overall, and in residential areas the proportion rises to more than a third. Few of the local authorities consulted had any idea how many trees were in their care. Although the majority had at least one specialist tree officer, the officer's efforts tend to be directed at supervising tree preservation orders and minimizing the effects of development. There was little evidence of thought-out policies for future urban treescapes.

The greatest threat to street trees is in the laying of cables by cable television companies. The Cable Television Association has been licensed to construct a network of cables beneath the pavements of every city and of all large towns. The trenches, cut by power tools, can easily slice through tree roots, and it is feared that many street trees will sicken and die as a result. No environmental impact assessment has been carried out, and there is no condition in the licences that compels the cable companies to protect trees. The Department of Trade and Industry, which is responsible for licensing, belatedly issued guidelines in autumn 1994 asking the companies to avoid the immediate vicinity of street trees. However the impression given is that the DTI is relying on the problem going unnoticed.

NEW NATIVE TREE DISCOVERED

The possibility of a species of tree lurking unremarked in the British landscape might seem small, but in 1993 the Botanical Society of the British Isles confirmed the presence of a new, apparently native, tree. This is the service tree, *Sorbus domestica*, which has leaves similar to those of rowan but with fruits more like wild pear. Small numbers of gnarled specimens have been found in two places on the limestone coast of the Gower peninsular in Glamorgan. Previously this species, which is widespread on the continent, was known only from a single tree of unknown origin in the Wyre Forest (Hereford and Worcester) where it was known as the 'Whitty Pear'. The newly-discovered service trees are in an area much visited by botanists, and were simply overlooked. Ring counts from the lower branches indicate an age in excess of 400 years. It is quite likely that the species is more widespread and that it will be found in other places now that botanists are aware of it.

KITES AND CORNCRAKES

In certain parts of England and Scotland, the sight of red kites soaring in circles above wooded hillsides is becoming a regular part of the country scene, as it already is in mid-Wales. The programme to introduce red kites from Sweden and Spain to England and Scotland, where they have been extinct for most of the 20th century, began in 1990 in a co-operative effort between the RSPB and the then Nature Conservancy Council. Some of the young kites have fallen victim to agricultural poisons, but on the whole the project shows every appearance of success. In 1994, some 28 pairs reared 50 young in England and Scotland, double the 1993 total. Many people are now seeing this glorious bird in the wild for the first time, and sightings have been widely reported in the press. The native population in Wales had its best season this century in 1993, with 101 breeding pairs; however, because of the cold wet spring only half that number succeeded in raising young.

The fortunes of the once-familiar corncrake continue to decline. A joint report from the RSPB and Irish Wildbird Conservancy published in 1993 reveals that numbers have fallen from 1,494 calling males in 1988 to just 643 in 1993. The greatest decline was in Ireland (including Northern Ireland) where only 174 singing males were heard in 1993, compared with 917 five years earlier. The main causes of the decline seem to be the loss of suitable meadowland and earlier grass cutting, through improved drainage and the use of fertilizers. Despite the availability of EC conservation funds, attempts to halt the decline by paying farmers to use corncrake-friendly methods seem to have failed. The decline of the corncrake in Britain is mirrored in most parts of its world range, and so the outlook for this bird is bleak.

PEATLAND HANDOVER

Fisons, the owner of the largest lowland peat bogs in England, have formally handed over some 3,240 ha of their estate to English Nature. Under the arrangement, English Nature will carry out conservation work to restore damaged habitat and raise the water-level. In return, it will allow Fisons' successor, Levington Horticulture Ltd, to extract peat virtually to exhaustion from the remainder. Eventually much of the restored area is likely to be made a nature reserve, managed by either English Nature or by one of the voluntary conservation bodies.

The newly-acquired areas are parts of Glasson Moss and Wedholme Flow in Cumbria, Thorne Moors and Hatfield Moor in South Yorkshire and Humberside, and Shapwick Heath in Somerset. Shapwick Heath will form part of the 'Avalon Marshes' project in which a large area of former peat cuttings will be encouraged to revert to a wild wetland, to attract wildfowl, reed birds, otters and other wildlife.

Another peat bog saved from peat extraction is Black Snib in Cumbria. A four-year campaign to save the site came to a successful conclusion in January 1994 when the developer's proposal was rejected after a public inquiry. The inspector's report confirmed that nature conservation had been among his main reasons for recommending refusal.

The Peatlands Consortium, the group of conservation charities most concerned with bog preservation, would prefer peat extraction to cease altogether. This would require government intervention and, probably, compensation for those areas with existing planning permission. The use of horticultural alternatives to peat is spreading, and a recent survey by the RSPB indicates that most county councils now use alternatives in publicly-owned parks and gardens.

## THE CAIRNGORMS

The RSPB and the John Muir Trust lost their bid to purchase the Glenfeshie estate, which includes nearly half of the (mainly privately-owned) Cairngorms national nature reserve in the eastern Highlands. The estate was purchased instead by a private company, Will Woodlands, on behalf of a little-known English charity, the Will Charitable Trust. Conservation is a stated aim of the Trust, though none of the trustees are prominent naturalists. It is believed that the non-availability of funds from the National Heritage Memorial Fund to support the RSPB/Muir Trust's bid was in line with the Scottish Office's policy of not taking on commitments that involve public funds and which might antagonize private landowners in the area. This is the second time in the past three years that an opportunity has been missed to acquire parts of this incomparable mountain wilderness for nature conservation. The first was the Scottish Office's refusal to match the £5 million bid from a consortium of conservation bodies to purchase the Mar Lodge estate, which has now been withdrawn from sale.

In the meantime, a working party set up by the Secretary of State for Scotland and chaired by Magnus Magnusson has published its report on the future of the Cairngorms. The working party continues to place its faith in the 'voluntary principle' which, in the view of many, has failed to prevent over-grazing,

the die-back of heather and pine, and the bulldozing of hill tracks. The report's proposals will be presented for public consultation before the Secretary of State decides whether to endorse them.

## MORE ROADS

Roadworks continue to be in the news and to excite organized protest. The case of Twyford Down, now bisected by the four-lane Winchester bypass, has changed the nature of public protest to road development, and similar *causes célèbres* can be expected in the near future. A report published by the Wildlife Trusts of south-east England catalogues a large number of interesting places threatened by roadworks. Ancient woods head the list, with plans to construct or upgrade roads through 101 of them, including 13 'protected' as Sites of Special Scientific Interest. Other places under threat include species-rich grassland, heaths and wetlands. The report also highlights the poor quality of environmental assessments undertaken for road schemes and the piecemeal way in which the whole matter is being tackled.

Among the 'black spots' where conservation and transport are likely to clash again are Canford Heath in Dorset, only recently saved from a housing development at the behest of the President of the Board of Trade, Michael Heseltine; the Newbury bypass, which threatens numerous places rich in wildlife and historical associations, including Snelsmore Common; and a string of five wetland SSSIs on the Gwent Levels near Newport. The last mentioned is one of the most interesting grazing marshes in Britain, but conservationists face an expensive battle to oppose a £500 million motorway and further commercial development in its wake.

---

## THE BUILT ENVIRONMENT

Most government expenditure on architectural conservation in England is channelled through English Heritage, which celebrated its tenth anniversary in 1993.

English Heritage's annual report for 1992-3, published in September 1993, showed a rise of 13.8 per cent to £33 million in the level of grants to owners of listed buildings to assist in repairs. Of this, £13.4 million was spent on secular buildings and monuments, £3 million on cathedrals, and £9.2 million on churches. Conservation Area schemes received £7.4 million and the same sum went on 301 archaeological projects. Among the secular grants, £188,000 went to the purchaser of Barlaston Hall, Staffs., marking the final and successful climax to the campaign by SAVE Britain's Heritage to conserve this outstanding building by Sir Robert Taylor after years of dereliction. It has now become a private house. English Heritage also funded some local authority conservation officer posts, and a grant of £50,000 went to the Cambridgeshire Brick and Tile Company to help restart production of handmade buff Gault bricks and tiles.

## SEEKING ALTERNATIVES

The continued exploration of 'alternative site management' for some English Heritage's 400 'properties in care' moved forward very tentatively in the year under review. There was only one further agreement: with the Dartmoor National Park Authority for the management of three archaeological sites. However, expressions of interest in the administration of 84 properties were received, and negotiations were entered into with 48 local authorities or other bodies.

Early in 1994 the Government announced that its grant to English Heritage for 1994-5 would increase by 4 per cent to £120.7 million. English Heritage itself is confident of a 7 per cent increase in the income it generates from admissions, special events, sales of souvenirs, catering and membership. It is expected that expenditure in 1994-5 will be £61.3 million on conservation grants, advice and statutory work, £33.4 million on preserving and opening English Heritage's own properties, £19.6 million on education, development and promotion, and the remaining £6.4 million on corporate services.

The conservation budget will include £400,000 for the Architectural Heritage Fund (which offers loans to Building Preservation Trusts) and £1 million offered back to the Department of National Heritage as a 'sweetener' to encourage the commencement of long-delayed repairs on the Albert Memorial in London. It is also anticipated that £700,000 will need to be spent, out of a total grant offer of £1 million, on The Crescent at Buxton, Derbys. The Crescent was built between 1779 and 1789 by Carr of York for the fifth Duke of Devonshire as a leisure complex and lodgings for a new spa intended to rival that of Bath. The local authority, High Peak, acquired the building in 1993 with the help of £180,000 from the National Heritage Memorial Fund, after a draft compulsory purchase order had been served by the Secretary of State for National Heritage.

Among the recipients of grant aid in 1994-5 will be 43 cathedrals, which will receive a total of £4,202,000. The two largest grants will be £500,000 for Salisbury Cathedral and £1.5 million over three years for the Roman Catholic Cathedral in Liverpool, designed in the 1960s by Sir Frederick Gibberd. These new grants mean that of the 61 cathedrals in England (both Anglican and Roman Catholic) 54 will have received grant aid totalling £15 million since the launch of the scheme in 1991.

Regarding properties which it administers directly, English Heritage has said that it expects to clear the £56 million backlog of repairs identified in October 1992 by the end of the decade. Two of its properties opening for the first time in 1994 were Camber Castle in Sussex, one of the finest of the forts built by Henry VIII to defend the south coast, and Lulworth Castle in Dorset, the Jacobean hunting lodge converted into a country house in the 18th century and gutted by fire in 1929.

## WALES

The 1992-3 annual report of the Historic Buildings Council for Wales reported a rise in funds for grants to historic buildings of 12 per cent when compared with 1991-2. One of the biggest grants was £500,000, awarded to a scheme of comprehensive repair and restoration for the extraordinary Transporter Bridge at Newport, Gwent. It was built between 1902 and 1906 and is believed to be one of only five such structures in the world. Other recipients included the Shell Grotto in Pontypool Park and the tapestries at Powis Castle, Welshpool.

Wales was also the setting for unusually determined direct government action. The Welsh Office decided to compulsorily acquire the ruins of St Quinten's Castle, and prepared evidence to that effect for a public inquiry that was cancelled at the last moment. At almost the same time the Welsh Office confirmed a compulsory purchase order on Sker House, Porthcawl, a noble composition of the 16th century which has been vacant since 1977.

The Government response to the 1993 report of the House of Commons Welsh affairs committee on the preservation of historic buildings and ancient monuments in the principality has been mainly positive. The Welsh Office has committed its agency, Cadw, to speeding up the resurvey of the statutory lists of protected buildings, including extensive use of the private sector. New momentum will be added to the drive to establish a Redundant Churches Fund for Wales modelled on the Friends of Friendless Churches. The only element of the response not arising out of the findings of the committee was the announcement of the long-term intention to delegate more decisions on listed building consent applications to Welsh planning authorities.

## SCOTLAND

The 1993-4 annual report of Historic Scotland was published in July 1994 and showed a total of £11.2 million disbursed in grants for the repair of listed buildings in Scotland, an increase of 7.5 per cent on 1992-3, with £200,000 paid out towards the conservation of 19 scheduled sites. In 1993-4 310 monuments were newly scheduled, bringing the total of scheduled monuments in Scotland to nearly 6,000.

The conservation programme continued on the 330 properties administered by Historic Scotland on behalf of the Secretary of State. A new vesting for maintenance was promised to Kinnaird Head Lighthouse, Fraserburgh, which will form the focus of the National Lighthouse Museum.

## LISTED BUILDINGS

At the end of 1993 the number of listed buildings in England was 443,470, a larger total than in any other country in Europe. There were only 314 applications to demolish listed buildings in their entirety in

England and Wales in 1993 (compared with 281 in 1992, 465 in 1991 and 455 in 1990), which suggests that most listings are accepted without demur. The reduction compared with earlier years is indicative too of the dampening effect of the recession on development activity, although the same lack of resources may also be impeding programmes of repair and maintenance.

The most important threats in the course of the year included that to demolish four listed buildings of 1620, 1635, 1729 and 1860 respectively, to allow the expansion of Manchester Airport. Also under threat were Holy Trinity Church, Scarborough, designed by Ewan Christian in 1870; Bryn Farm at Halghton, Clwyd, a Grade II* timber-framed 17th-century house; and Christ Church, Waterloo, in Liverpool, built in 1890 by Paley & Austin, which was the subject of a non-statutory public inquiry. However, the proposal for a further arm of the inner ring at Norwich was rejected after an inquiry, and Swansea City Council announced a scheme to save the city's Old Guildhall so that it might house the National Centre for Literature planned as part of the Arts 2000 Year of Literature project in 1995.

ECCLESIASTICAL EXEMPTION

From 1 October 1994 the exemption from listed building consent and conservation area consent legislation previously enjoyed by buildings of all religious denominations was abolished in respect of both interiors and exteriors except for five denominations – the Anglican Church in England and Wales, the Roman Catholic Church, the Methodist Church, the United Reformed Church, and those chapels affiliated to the Baptist Corporation (about half of Baptist places of worship). These five denominations had agreed to introduce internal decision-making processes independent of the congregation concerned, involving consultation with the local planning authority, English Heritage and the National Amenity Societies. The operation of these codes of practice will be reviewed in 1996. There is as yet no agreed timetable for reviewing ecclesiastical exemption in Scotland and Northern Ireland.

In April 1994 the Redundant Churches Fund was rechristened the Churches Conservation Trust. Founded in 1968-9, the Trust now owns 300 disused Anglican churches too important to be demolished or converted. Recent vestings have included the substantial medieval churches of St Mary's in Shrewsbury and St Lawrence's in Norwich, and St Nicholas's Chapel, Kings Lynn. The non-Anglican equivalent to the Churches Conservation Trust is the Historic Chapels Trust, which acquired its first properties in 1994, including the Grade I listed Unitarian Church at Todmorden, W. Yorks.

There was much debate in 1994 on the findings of the Templeman Commission on the future of the churches of the City of London. At present the City has the highest concentration of Grade I churches in the country, a total of 36, most of them designed by

Sir Christopher Wren. Templeman proposed that 24 be closed as active places of worship and demoted to 'reserve' status. The likeliest outcome is the establishment of a trust to administer the 24 churches. In July 1994 the Bishop of London implicitly rejected one of Templeman's recommendations in deciding not to demolish the remains of the medieval church of St Ethelburga's, which was blown up by an IRA bomb in April 1993, but instead to launch a competition for a scheme to retain the remains amid a mixed commercial and ecclesiastical development.

CONSERVATION AREAS

In July 1993 the Department of National Heritage and the Department of the Environment issued a discussion paper in response to pressure to increase controls over damaging alterations within conservation areas, of which there are over 7,000 in England alone. Its tone was clearly against major change, but in March 1994 the Government announced its commitment to tightening up control, principally by allowing local authorities greater autonomy in removing permitted development rights within the areas. A further discussion paper on the technicalities is expected.

The 1993 Royal Institute of Chartered Surveyors Conservation Awards highlighted some projects which had previously escaped national publicity. The National Building Conservation Award went to the repair of Ruthin Library, Clwyd, which was built in the late 18th century as the County Hall and Records Office. The Craftsmanship and Building Conservation Award was won by the reconstruction of the Great Kitchen Chimney at Hampton Court Palace. Commendations in the newly introduced Urban Renewal Award went to the humanizing of the 1960s shopping development known as the Crowngate Development in Worcester, and the repair of one side of the late 18th-century Seymour Terrace in Liverpool, which had long been derelict.

NATIONAL MONUMENTS RECORD

The National Monuments Record, the country's principal archive on historic buildings, moved from London in April 1994 to new headquarters in Swindon. For the first time all sections of the archive are under one roof. There will be a centralized enquiry point for all sections of the National Monuments Record Centre and a specially designed reference library and search room, the former containing over 32,000 books on English architecture and archaeology. A search room is to be maintained in central London for the consultation of material relating to Greater London, and there will be access from the London search room to Swindon via computer, fax and telephone. The principal sections of the Royal Commission on the Historical Monuments of England, the parent body of the National Monuments Record, also relocated to Swindon in April 1994.

# Dance

The year 1993-4 saw radical changes in the contemporary dance scene, with the demise of London Contemporary Dance Theatre as a full-scale company and a change of emphasis for Rambert Dance Company, which plans to relaunch itself as a larger group concentrating more on works bridging the divide between classical ballet and modern dance. After several years of struggling to find a director and an artistic identity, London Contemporary Dance Theatre presented ambitious plans for expansion to the Arts Council in the autumn of 1993; the plans were rejected. Rambert Dance Company had also announced plans for expansion, and when the Arts Council approved these plans and refused to fund LCDT as a large-scale repertory company, LCDT was forced to disband. It will be replaced in the autumn of 1994 by a group of nine dancers and two musicians under the directorship of Richard Alston. Whether Rambert can single-handedly protect and expand the repertoire of large-scale contemporary dance works as well as broadening its repertoire into more classical works remains to be seen. In recent years contemporary dance choreographers have tended to work on a smaller scale with their own groups of dancers and to some extent the new arrangements are merely an acknowledgement of the creative status quo; but the proliferation of small contemporary dance groups performing to small audiences may lead to the art form being marginalized. That would be a sad legacy for LCDT, which was formed in 1967 by Robin Howard and, through the company itself and through the London School of Contemporary Dance, has produced a steady stream of excellent dancers and choreographers and introduced the works of many important American and European choreographers into the British repertoire. LCDT went out on a high note, winning the Olivier award for outstanding achievement in dance for their season at Sadler's Wells Theatre in November–December 1993.

Rambert Dance Company had a transitional season before its relaunch in the autumn of 1994 under the directorship of Christopher Bruce. The company has already demonstrated its new artistic direction with the world première of a work by Bruce in May 1994 and the introduction of one of his most successful existing works, *Land*, into the repertoire. Martha Clarke's theatrical dance-mime work *The Garden of Earthly Delights*, inspired by Bosch's painting of the same title, was also a major departure from the company's recent style and was performed in a programme with a revival of Bruce's 1984 work *Sergeant Early's Dream*. Bruce's plans for Rambert involve a commitment to producing a wide range of new works as well as maintaining works both from the recent past and from Rambert's illustrious history.

In the field of classical ballet, the good news was the reopening of London City Ballet in the autumn of 1993. The company was forced to close down in summer 1993 because of lack of funding but by the autumn sufficient sponsorship had been raised to put the company back on the road with a new production of *Coppélia*. However, there seems little hope of the company obtaining revenue funding from the Arts Council of England as the Council's grant-in-aid from the Government is being cut by £3.2 million to £186 million in 1994-5.

Another result of the grant cut is that the Council's grant to the Royal Opera House will be frozen in 1994-5. This does not bode well for the Royal Ballet; in 1993-4 the company was forced to cut its number of performances from 118 to 96, while the higher-earning (but also higher-spending) Royal Opera was allocated 160 performances. The Royal Opera mounted seven new full-length productions; the Royal Ballet, apart from *The Sleeping Beauty* (performed only in the USA), had four new one-act works at the Opera House and two on a short small-scale regional tour. At the beginning of the season the Royal Ballet's director, Anthony Dowell, said 'I am just grateful we are still in business'. This negative attitude showed in the repertoire for the season, which included the much-criticized production of *Don Quixote* and excellent but over-used works such as *A Month in the Country*, *The Dream* and *Romeo and Juliet*. The latter work, however, did give ballet a rare burst of publicity when a London teacher refused to take her class to a schools performance on the grounds that the work was 'blatantly heterosexual'; a rather unusual criticism to be levelled against ballet. Ashley Page's stylish and exciting new work, *Fearful Symmetries*, was a highlight of the season and could appeal to a wide audience. The 'Dance Bites' tour, on which a group of dancers presented a programme of mainly new works at three regional theatres, was a partially successful venture but appeared to presuppose either that regional audiences are more receptive to new work than the London audience or that they can be used as a sounding-board before risking a new work in London. The new *Sleeping Beauty*, a lavishly-designed production, will be seen in London in the autumn of 1994.

The company's dancers performed admirably during the season in what must have been difficult circumstances. The Royal Ballet management continues to operate an unofficial star system within the company, which could be very destructive in the long term, but a number of younger dancers, particularly Sarah Wildor, Michael Nunn and Gillian Revie, showed the depth of talent which lies at Anthony Dowell's disposal. The Royal Ballet's founder, Dame Ninette de Valois, won the Evening Standard award for her outstanding contribution to ballet.

Birmingham Royal Ballet continued to win praise for the quality of both its programmes and its dancing. The season opened with a new full-length production of *Sylvia* choreographed by David Bintley. The last production of this ballet in Britain was choreographed by Frederick Ashton in 1952; it is based on Greek mythology, and although the Delibes score is universally admired, choreographers have been deterred by the twists and turns of the scenario. Bintley chose to portray a vaguely surreal world in which an Edwardian Eros reads a newspaper in a woodland glade and the barbaric Orion sports a dinner jacket while seducing the nymph Sylvia. It is an amusing, idiosyncratic work, with a traditional happy ending; love is restored to the world when the goddess Diana gives her blessing to the union of Sylvia and Amynta. *Fall River Legend*, which was created in 1948 by Agnes de Mille and entered the company's repertoire during the season, provided a major contrast. It is based on the story of Lizzie Borden of Fall River, Massachusetts, who was tried in 1892 for the axe murder of her father and step-mother; although she was acquitted, she was popularly held to have committed the crime. The work is a sympathetic and dramatic portrayal of the claustro-phobic world which led to the terrible act of violence, but de Mille cannot allow Lizzie Borden to walk away from her deed and the ballet ends with a terrified Lizzie staring at the gallows. The role of Lizzie was taken by BRB's senior ballerina and superb dance-actress, Marion Tait. The company also won an Olivier award for the best new dance production in 1993, for the previous season's revival of *Choreatium*.

CHANGE OF STYLE

English National Ballet had an unusually high-profile season. Derek Deane, who took over the directorship in March 1993, was not afraid to criticize the standards of the company he was inheriting and quickly replaced 14 dancers. In the summer of 1994 Deane publicly criticized the standard of teaching at British ballet schools. He emphasized the high technical standards now expected and seems to favour a more athletic style than is normally associated with British dancers. At its best ENB could provide an interesting stylistic alternative to the Royal Ballet companies, provided that athleticism is not gained at the expense of artistry. Nevertheless, Deane's methods began to bear fruit with ENB's corps de ballet, who have shown a clear improvement. Several interesting guest artists were recruited, and the company's senior principal Thomas Edur won the 1993 Evening Standard award for outstanding performance. The season opened with Ronald Hynd's new production of *The Sleeping Beauty*, which was commissioned before Deane's appointment. ENB also acquired a valuable new work, Balanchine's *Square Dance*. In general the repertoire for the season was safe rather than exciting, but Deane's presence has obviously lifted the company and he has interesting plans for 1994-5.

Scottish Ballet continued to build an interesting and varied repertoire, and mounted Andre Prokov-sky's full-length *Anna Karenina* for the first time in September 1993; the role of Anna was created for the company's director, Galina Samsova, in Australia in 1979. An even more ambitious project was the company's first production of *The Sleeping Beauty*, which opened in Glasgow in March 1994. It was a traditional production in choreographic terms but had arresting, somewhat controversial designs by Patrick Kinmonth, and stylish costumes by Jasper Conran. Reservations were expressed about the standard of dancing below principal level, but the work is a valuable addition to the repertoire and will provide challenging opportunities for the company's dancers at all levels.

Northern Ballet Theatre also mounted a big new production, but not, thankfully, of *The Sleeping Beauty*. The company's director Christopher Gable directed and choreographed a new version of *Cinderella* to an original score by Philip Feeney. The ballet was based on the Brothers Grimm story rather than on the more traditional Perrault fairy-tale and continued the recent NBT tradition of mild contro-versy. It emphasized the darkness and brutality of the story, with hints of an incestuous relationship between Cinderella and her father, and a step-sister so desperate to wear the slipper that she has her toes cut off. The company also celebrated its 25th birthday in 1994, and is planning a ballet based on the Brontë family.

The most publicized contemporary dance venture during the season was in fact led by a celebrated classical dancer, Irek Mukhamedov. Spurred on, perhaps, by the paucity of interesting opportunities for him in the Royal Ballet, he joined with Arc Dance Company to mount a production of *Othello*. It was choreographed by Kim Brandstrup, and Mukhame-dov had no apparent difficulty in adjusting to the new style. It was an interesting and enjoyable work but whether the collaboration has a long-term future remains to be seen.

CONTEMPORARY DANCE

Elsewhere in the field of contemporary dance, Michael Clark presented his first work since *MMM* in 1992. *MMM* involved a highly individual rendering of Stravinsky's *Rite of Spring*; the second half of the new work, *O*, was set to the same composer's *Apollo*. *O* contained deliberate echoes of Balanchine's 1928 *Apollo*; it was less controversial than Clark's earlier pieces and was, on the whole, rapturously received. Shobana Jeyasingh won the 1993 Prudential Award for the Arts, worth £100,000. She works with the ancient southern Indian dance-form of Bharatha Natyam, stripped of its mimetic elements and used in a thoroughly modern and compelling way. Her work *Romance . . . with footnotes* was shown at the Queen Elizabeth Hall, London, in March 1994. John Ashford, the director of The Place, won the £30,000 Digital Premier Award for an outstanding contribution to dance in 1993. The Place once again mounted three ambitious seasons: Resolution, in which unknown choreographers were given a platform; Spring Loaded, a 12-week season during which about 40 groups performed; and The Turning World, which presented 17 European groups including Anna Teresa de Keersmaeker and her company Rosas. Dance Umbrella 1993 presented its usual wide range of contemporary groups, including Batsheva Dance Company from Israel on its first visit to Britain since 1987.

Lea Anderson celebrated the tenth anniversary of the Cholmondeleys by creating a new work, all heavy metal, motorbikes and leather jackets, called *Metalcholia*. Siobhan Davies's new work, *The Glass Blew In*, was set to a highly-praised score by Gavin Bryars and combined Davies's usual fluid style with effective lighting by Peter Mumford. DV8 Physical Theatre performed a new work by Lloyd Newson entitled *MSM*; it was set in a public lavatory and explored the culture of cottaging. It was both funny and moving, although it did not reach the creative heights of his last work, *Strange Fish*. Jonathan Burrows also produced a new work, *Our*. His style is developing in an increasingly interesting and unconventional way, and his dancers are always of the highest quality. On a lighter note, Matthew Bourne's *Highland Fling* for Adventures in Motion Pictures updated *La Sylphide* to a council flat in Glasgow.

The mixed-race Cape Ballet from South Africa ended years of isolation when it presented three programmes at Sadler's Wells Theatre in the summer of 1994. It was the company's first-ever visit outside Africa, although some distinguished South African dancers have made their careers in the UK. The company's current artistic director, Veronica Paeper, is also a prolific choreographer. Two of her full-length works were shown in London; while showing no evidence of an individual choreographic talent, they were intelligent and well-crafted. The popular Twyla Tharp company from the USA performed a rare and enthusiastically-received season at the Riverside Studios in March 1994. The Bolshoi Ballet was due to perform in the open air at various stately home venues in the summer of 1994 but the tour was cancelled after inadequate ticket sales. Participants in the 1994 Edinburgh Festival included the Mark Morris Dance Group, Miami City Ballet, Merce Cunningham and the Lucinda Childs Dance Company.

## PRODUCTIONS

ROYAL BALLET
Founded 1931
Royal Opera House, Covent Garden, London WC2E 9DD

World premières:
*Fanfare* (Matthew Hart), 23 October 1993. A one-act ballet. Music, Brian Elias; design, Yolanda Sonnabend. Cast,

Zoltán Solymosi, Belinda Hatley, Errol Pickford, Michael Nunn, Sarah Wildor, Fiona Brockway
*If This is Still a Problem* (William Tuckett), 23 October 1993. A one-act ballet. Music, Ravel; design, Andy Klunder. Cast led by Lesley Collier, Jonathan Cope and William Trevitt
*Desirable Hostilities* (William Tuckett), 7 February 1994. A one-act ballet premièred at the Haymarket Theatre, Leicester. Music, Bach; design, William Tuckett. Dancers, Leire Ortueta, Adam Cooper, Angela Bescos and Gary Avis
*Caught Dance* (Matthew Hart), 7 February 1994. A pas de deux premièred at the Haymarket Theatre, Leicester. Music, Witold Lutoslawski; design, Yolanda Sonnabend. Dancers, Leanne Benjamin and José Manuel Carreño
*Renard* (Ashley Page), 7 February 1994. A one-act ballet premièred at the Haymarket Theatre, Leicester. Music, Stravinsky; design, Bruce McLean. Cast led by Peter Abegglen, William Trevitt, Adam Cooper and Stuart Cassidy
*The Sleeping Beauty* (Petipa, prod. Anthony Dowell), 6 April 1994. Premièred at the John F. Kennedy Center for the Performing Arts, Washington DC, USA. Music, Tchaikovsky; design, Maria Bjørnson. Cast led by Darcey Bussell, Zoltán Solymosi, Fiona Chadwick and Stephen Wicks
*Fearful Symmetries* (Ashley Page), 18 June 1994. A one-act ballet. Music, John Adams; design, Antony McDonald. Cast led by Jonathan Cope/Irek Mukhamedov, Dana Fouras, Deborah Bull and Sarah Wildor/Ann De Vos

Company première:
*Herman Schmerman* (William Forsythe, 1992), 23 October 1993. Music, Thom Willems; design, William Forsythe and Gianni Versace. Cast, Deborah Bull, Benazir Hussein, Nicola Tranah, Tetsuya Kumakawa, Michael Nunn, Sylvie Guillem, Adam Cooper

Full-length ballets from the repertoire: *Romeo and Juliet* (MacMillan, 1965), *The Nutcracker* (Ivanov, prod. Wright, 1984), *Mayerling* (MacMillan, 1978), *Don Quixote* (Petipa, prod. Baryshnikov, 1978)

One-act ballets from the repertoire: *Different Drummer* (MacMillan, 1984, revised 1991), *Ballet Imperial* (Balanchine, 1941), *Tales of Beatrix Potter* (Ashton, 1971, adapted for the stage by Anthony Dowell, 1992), *The Dream* (Ashton, 1964), *Tombeaux* (Bintley, 1993), *A Month in the Country* (Ashton, 1976), *Danses Concertantes* (MacMillan, 1955), *Winter Dreams* (MacMillan, 1991).

In addition to performances at the Royal Opera House, the company undertook two tours to the USA. In the spring of 1994 (6 April–8 May) it performed in Washington DC, West Palm Beach, Austin, Houston and Orange County. The repertoire comprised the world première of the new production of *The Sleeping Beauty*, *Mayerling*, *The Dream*, *Tales of Beatrix Potter*, *A Month in the Country*, *Tombeaux*, *The Judas Tree* (MacMillan, 1992), *Tchaikovsky Pas de Deux* (Balanchine, 1960), *Meditation from 'Thaïs'* (Ashton, 1971) and *Herman Schmerman*. In July 1994 the company gave a two-week season at the Metropolitan Opera House, New York. The repertoire was *The Sleeping Beauty*, *Mayerling*, *A Month in the Country*, *The Judas Tree* and *Tombeaux*.

A group of 24 Royal Ballet dancers performed in Leicester, Cambridge and Blackpool in February 1994 on a tour entitled Dance Bites. The group performed the world premières of *Renard*, *Desirable Hostilities* and *Caught Dance*, as well as *Monotones II* (Ashton, 1965) and *Herman Schmerman*.

BIRMINGHAM ROYAL BALLET
Founded 1946 as Sadler's Wells Royal Ballet
Birmingham Hippodrome, Thorp Street, Birmingham
B5 4AU

World première:
*Sylvia* (David Bintley), 26 October 1993. A full-length
ballet. Music, Delibes; design, Sue Blane. Cast led by
Miyako Yoshida, Kevin O'Hare, Joseph Cipolla, Michael
O'Hare and Karen Waldie

Company premières:
*Serenade* (Balanchine, 1934), 22 February 1994. Music,
Tchaikovsky; costumes, after Karinska. Cast led by Andrea
Tredinnick, Monica Zamora, Joseph Cipolla, Kevin O'Hare
and Miyako Yoshida
*Fall River Legend* (de Mille, 1948), 31 March 1994. Music,
Morton Gould; set, Oliver Smith; costumes, Miles White.
Cast led by Marion Tait and Joseph Cipolla

Full-length ballets from the repertoire: *The Sleeping Beauty*
(Petipa, prod. Wright, 1984), *The Nutcracker* (Ivanov, prod.
Wright, additional choreography by Vincent Redmon,
1990), *La Fille mal gardée* (Ashton, 1960), *Swan Lake*
(Petipa/Ivanov, prod. Wright and Samsova, 1981)
One-act ballets from the repertoire: *Street* (Hart, 1993),
*The Dream* (Ashton, 1964), *Elite Syncopations* (MacMillan,
1974), *Job* (de Valois, 1931), *Brahms Handel Variations*
(Bintley, 1990, using Brahms's original piano variations
instead of the Rubbra orchestration and with new designs
by Jasper Conran), *Grand Pas* from *Paquita* (Petipa, 1881),
*Theme and Variations* (Balanchine, 1947), *Prodigal Son*
(Balanchine, 1929), *Symphony in Three Movements*
(Balanchine, 1972).
    In addition to four seasons at the Birmingham
Hippodrome, the company toured to Plymouth, Norwich,
Liverpool, Sunderland, Northampton, Southampton (two
seasons), Eastbourne, Bradford, Plymouth, Manchester and
Bristol. The programme of *Serenade*, *Job* and *The Green
Table* given at the Birmingham Hippodrome in February
1994 was the company's contribution to the Towards the
Millennium festival, which celebrated the choreography and
music of the 1930s. The company also performed at the
Royal Opera House, London, with a repertoire of *Sylvia*,
*Serenade*, *Fall River Legend* and *Elite Syncopations*.
    A special performance of *Job* was given at Coventry
Cathedral on 11 November 1993 to celebrate the 950th
anniversary of the founding of the original cathedral. The
company performed *La Fille mal gardée* for one week in
Turin, Italy, in January 1994.

ENGLISH NATIONAL BALLET
Founded 1950 as London Festival Ballet
Markova House, 39 Jay Mews, London SW7 2ES

World premières:
*The Sleeping Beauty* (Petipa, prod. Ronald Hynd), 21
October 1993. Music, Tchaikovsky; design, Peter Docherty.
Cast led by Agnes Oaks, Thomas Edur, Kevin Richmond
and Evelyne Desutter
*X. N. Tricities* (Mauro Bigonzetti), 25 April 1994. A one-
act ballet. Score, Giuseppe Cali; design, Kristopher Millar
and Lois Swandale. Cast led by Yat Sen Chang, Emma
Greenhalgh and Christian Duncan

Company premières:
*Impromptu* (Deane, 1982), 25 April 1994. Music, Schubert;
costumes, Anthony Dowell. Cast, Agnes Oaks and Thomas
Edur
*Square Dance* (Balanchine, 1957, revised 1976), 3 May
1994. Music, Vivaldi and Corelli; costumes, Jane Russell.
Cast led by Giuseppe Picone and Ambra Vallo

Full-length ballets from the repertoire: *The Nutcracker*
(Ivanov, prod. Stevenson, 1972), *Coppélia* (Petipa and
Cecchetti, prod. Hynd, 1985), *Swan Lake* (Petipa/Ivanov,
prod. Struchkova 1993 after Gorsky/Messerer, 1937)
One-act ballets from the repertoire: *La Bayadère* Act III
(Petipa, prod. Makarova, 1980), *Etudes* (Lander, 1948),
*Grand Pas* from *Paquita* (Petipa, staged by Deane), *Dances
from Napoli* (Bournonville, staged by Dinna Bjørn), *Grand
Pas Classique* from *Raymonda* Act III (Petipa, prod.
Franklin, 1993), *Savoy Suite* (Sleep, 1993).
    The full company toured to Southampton (two seasons),
Manchester (three seasons), Liverpool, Bristol, Leeds,
Nottingham, Cardiff and Edinburgh. It also gave two
seasons at the Royal Festival Hall, London, and one at the
London Coliseum. In April–May 1994 the company split
into two groups and went on two mid-scale tours. One had
piano accompaniment and a repertoire of *Grand Pas* from
*Paquita*, *Impromptu*, *Dances from Napoli* and the world
première of *X. N. Tricities*. The other toured with an
orchestra and performed *Grand Pas Classique* from
*Raymonda* Act III, *Savoy Suite* and *Square Dance*. The mid-
scale tours visited Swindon, Newtown, Cambridge, High
Wycombe, Barrow-in-Furness, Crawley, Dartford,
Tunbridge Wells, Darlington, Preston, Basingstoke and
Snape.

RAMBERT DANCE COMPANY
Founded 1926
94 Chiswick High Road, London W4 ISH

World premières:
*Spirit* (Mark Baldwin), 13 October 1993. Music, Poulenc;
design, Natasha Kornilof
*Crossing* (Christopher Bruce), 31 May 1994. Music,
Górecki; design, Marian Bruce
*Banter Banter* (Mark Baldwin), 3 June 1994. Music,
Stravinsky; design, Barney Wan

Company premières:
*Land* (Bruce, 1985), 13 October 1993. Music, Arne
Nordheim; design, Walter Nobbe
*The Garden of Earthly Delights* (Martha Clarke, 1984).
Music, Richard Peaslee; design, Jane Greenwood

Works from the repertoire: *Winnsboro Cotton Mill Blues*
(Davies, 1992), *Gone* (Baldwin, 1992), *Strong Language*
(Alston, 1987), *Embarque* (Davies, 1988), *Sergeant Early's
Dream* (Bruce, 1984).
    The company gave performances in Manchester,
Leicester, Chichester, Oxford, Exeter, Ashton-under-Lyne,
Swindon and Mold. It toured to Brazil in September–
October 1993, performing in Rio de Janeiro, Brasilia,
Salvador and São Paulo. The repertoire was *Winnsboro
Cotton Mill Blues*, *Gone* and *Strong Language*.

LONDON CONTEMPORARY DANCE THEATRE
Founded 1967
The Place, Duke's Road, London WCIH 9AB

World premières:
*Fall Like Rain* (Darshan Singh Bhuller), 29 September
1993. Music, John Martyn; costumes, Claire Sherliker
*Waiting* (Christopher Bruce), 6 October 1993. Music,
Errollyn Wallen; design, Marian Bruce
*The Perilous Night* (Richard Alston), 6 October 1993.
Music, John Cage. A solo danced by Darshan Singh Bhuller
*The Previous Evening* (Amanda Miller), 2 December
1993. Music, Fred Frith; design, Seth Tillet and Amanda
Miller

Company première:
*Sand Skin* (Angelin Preljocaj, 1991), 23 November 1993.
Music, Goran Vejvoda; design, Caroline Antenski

Works from the repertoire: *Rooster* (Bruce, 1991), *Shoes* (Aletta Collins, 1993), *Cell* (Cohan, 1969).

The company toured to High Wycombe, Nottingham, Warwick, Plymouth, Woking, Blackpool, London (two seasons at Sadler's Wells Theatre), Newcastle upon Tyne, Oxford, Northampton, Sheffield, Leicester and Canterbury, where it gave its last performance on 25 June 1994. The company also toured to Tilburg, Holland, in September 1993, performing *Rooster* at the opening ceremony of the newly-built Schouwburg, and to Austria (Linz), Germany (Munich) and France (Chateauvallon) in March 1994, performing *Sand Skin*, *Rooster* and *My Father's Vertigo* (Miller, 1992).

The company held a gala at Sadler's Wells on 17 April 1994 in memory of their founder, Robin Howard. The programme included part of Richard Alston's new work later entitled *Sad Eyes*, *Cell*, *Stabat Mater* (Cohan, 1975, danced by former members of the company) and *Harmonica Breakdown* (Dudley, 1938). Dancers from the company also performed at the Aldeburgh festival in June 1994, giving three new pieces by Richard Alston (*Sad Eyes*, *Three Movements from Petrushka*, and *Rumours*, *Visions*) in a Britten/Stravinsky programme. The company's season at Sadler's Wells Theatre, London, in June 1994 was as part of The Turning World festival of contemporary dance; the programme was entitled In Good Company. The repertoire was *Rikud* (Dror and Ben Gal, 1991) and *My Father's Vertigo*; *St Nick* (Amanda Miller, 1989), and *Two Room Apartment* (Dror and Ben Gal, 1987, shortened version 1988) were given on the same programme.

THE SCOTTISH BALLET
Founded 1956
261 West Princes Street, Glasgow G4 9EE

World première:
*The Sleeping Beauty* (Petipa, prod. Galina Samsova), 10 March 1994. Music, Tchaikovsky; design, Patrick Kinmonth and Jasper Conran. Cast led by Daria Klimentova, Vlasislav Bubnov, Noriko Ohara and Anne Christie

Company premières:
*Bruch Violin Concerto No. 1* (Clark Tippet, 1987), 1 September 1993. Music, Bruch; design, Dain Marcus. Cast, Robert Hampton, Daria Klimentova, Vladislav Bubnov, Anne Christie, Roddie Patrizio, Linda Packer, Rupert Jowett and Nicci Theis

*Anna Karenina* (André Prokovsky, 1979), 8 September 1993. Music, Tchaikovsky, reworked by Guy Woolfenden; design, Peter Farmer. Cast led by Noriko Ohara and Robert Hampton

Full-length ballet from the repertoire: *Peter Pan* (Lustig, 1989).

One-act ballets from the repertoire: *Othello* (Darrell, 1971), *Troy Game* (North, 1974).

The main company performed in Glasgow (four seasons), Edinburgh (two seasons), Aberdeen (three seasons), Liverpool, Hull (two seasons), Sheffield, Inverness (two seasons), Oxford and Newcastle upon Tyne. It also gave a gala performance of *Scotch Symphony* (Balanchine, 1952), *Forgotten Land* (Kylian, 1981) and *Bruch Violin Concerto* at the Edinburgh Festival Theatre in June 1994.

The company staged a small-scale tour to Glenrothes and Broughty Ferry in December 1993, performing *Vespri* (Prokovsky, 1973), *Pas de Quatre* (Perrot, 1845, reconstructed by Dolin, 1941), *Belong* (Vesak, 1972), *Walpurgisnacht* (Samsova, 1993) and *Shoals of Herring* (Maldoom, 1983); and a medium-scale tour to Stirling and Kirkcaldy in June 1994, performing *Scotch Symphony*, *Overgrown Path* (Kylian, 1980), *Belong* and the pas de six from *Raymonda* (Petipa, 1898).

# Masters of the Queen's (King's) Music

'Master of the King's Music' was the title given to the official who presided over the court band during the reign of Charles I. The first Master was appointed in 1626. Today the Master is expected to organize the music for state occasions and to write new music for them, although there are no fixed duties. The post is held for life and the Master receives an annual honorarium of £100.

Nicholas Lanier (1588–1666), appointed 1626
Louis Grabu (?–1674), appointed 1666
Nicholas Staggins (1650–1700), appointed 1674
John Eccles (1668–1735), appointed 1700
Maurice Greene (1695–1755), appointed 1735
William Boyce (1710–79), appointed 1755

John Stanley (1713–86), appointed 1779
Sir William Parsons (1746–1817), appointed 1786
William Shield (1748–1829), appointed 1817
Christian Kramer (?–1834), appointed 1829
François (Franz) Cramer (1772–1848), appointed 1834
George Anderson (?–1870), appointed 1848
Sir William Cusins (1833–93), appointed 1870
Sir Walter Parratt (1841–1924), appointed 1893
Sir Edward Elgar (1857–1934), appointed 1924
Sir Henry Walford Davies (1869–1941), appointed 1934
Sir Arnold Bax (1883–1953), appointed 1941
Sir Arthur Bliss (1891–1975), appointed 1953
Malcolm Williamson (1931–), appointed 1975

# Film

The year was dominated by the achievements of Steven Spielberg. The failure of his long-awaited *Hook* had tarnished Spielberg's reputation; it was self-indulgent, over-produced and sentimental. *Jurassic Park* extinguished all doubts about his magic touch. Already one of the most successful films ever made by the summer of 1993, *Jurassic Park* easily beat the competition from Arnold Schwarzennegger in the expensive post-modern comedy *The Last Action Hero* and went on to become the biggest grossing film of all time (about $1 billion to date). It also opened up previously untapped markets in India and the Far East.

*Jurassic Park* is the story of a modern-day dinosaur nature reserve in which the creatures have been cloned from strands of DNA. It is a straightforward, unsophisticated suspense yarn, and, as critics pointed out, Spielberg and his collaborators were not greatly concerned with characterization or narrative logic. However, the film's success is instructive. By virtue of animatronic special effects, *Jurassic Park* shows dinosaurs apparently living and breathing. At a time when there is much talk about how new inter-active computer technology will supersede films – just as films superseded vaudeville as popular entertainment – Spielberg shows how the cinema might use such technology to its own advantage. He takes us back to the origins of the species, and also to the genesis of cinema itself as a spectacle. Like the eponymous reserve, this film is itself a theme park, providing an emotional rollercoaster ride. There is even an element of self-parody, when Spielberg shows baseball hats and tee-shirts on sale in the park's shop, identical to the marketing tie-ins available in cinemas across the world.

In this respect *Jurassic Park* is the culmination of a process initiated by George Lucas, Spielberg's sometime partner, with *Star Wars*. That film's phenomenal success ushered in a new era of blockbuster 'event' films which required high investment and high returns, and which inevitably raised the stakes for the Hollywood studios. These films inadvertently inspired a more cautious, conservative regime dominated by market research, a handful of powerful stars, and supposedly sure-fire success formulae; sequels, spin-offs, etc.

## GENERAL DISAGREEMENT

It was this brand of cultural commerce which French film-makers decried as colonialism at the acrimonious climax of the latest round of GATT talks. The point at issue here was the American insistence on free trade and the dismantling of quotas designed to safeguard and subsidize European film-making. The debate pitted Spielberg and Martin Scorsese on the one hand against Pedro Almodovar, David Puttnam, Bertrand Tavernier and Stephen Frears on the other.

Claude Berri, whose adaptation of Zola's *Germinal* became a *cause célèbre* for the French, was moved to announce 'I am not about to be buggered by the US industry. We should not allow them to deal with us the way they dealt with the redskins'. In the event the US negotiators gave way, and film and television were exempted from the trade talks.

Notwithstanding the Europeans' brave words, film-making on the continent is stagnating. Production is down everywhere, and in the former Eastern bloc countries government subsidies have dried up and studio facilities have been abandoned. In Germany, only Bernd Eichinger's Neue Constantin production company has anything like an international reputation, and that is based on English-language adaptations such as *The Cement Garden* (a prize-winner at the 1993 Berlin Film Festival) and *The House of the Spirits*. Bille August's version of Isabel Allende's Chilean romance was a huge hit in Germany, but despite stars like Jeremy Irons, Meryl Streep, Winona Ryder, Antonio Banderas and Glenn Close, it was elsewhere deemed a tedious misjudgement, with incongruous casting and a dreary script.

Of Germany's notable directors, Werner Herzog continues to plough his own maverick course, most recently with a documentary about the after-effects of the Gulf war. Wim Wenders appears to be going through some sort of crisis. After the failure of his four-hour science fiction film *Until the End of the World*, Wenders returned to familiar ground with *Faraway So Close*, a sequel to his 1987 masterpiece *Wings of Desire*. The film is a metaphysical caper about an angel who hangs up his wings to live on earth in reunited Berlin. He finds himself embroiled in a plot about arms smuggling with ramifications reaching back into Germany's Nazi past. The film is certainly ambitious, but it is also whimsical and pretentious and has little sense of structure or control. In spite of featuring Willem Dafoe, Nastassja Kinski, Bruno Ganz, Lou Reed, Peter Falk and Mikhail Gorbachev (in a cameo as himself), it was a box-office flop.

The situation is almost as bad in Italy and Spain, where mediocrity prevails. Spain's Bigas Luna joined Pedro Almodavar as a reliable purveyor of sexy kitsch, but the hackneyed shock value of the former's *Jamon Jamon* and *Golden Balls* and the latter's *Kika* seemed like much ado about nothing. The Italian director Gianni Amelio won the Felix award for best European film for the second time for his *Stolen Children*. Other reputable Italian directors, such as Pupi Avati, Maurizio Nichetti, Giuseppe Tornatore, Marco Bellocchio, Ettore Scola and Ermanno Olmi, seem for the most part to be intimidated by the air of corruption and crisis in Italy, which was chillingly captured in Ricky Tognazzi's police thriller *La Scorta*. An exception to the rule is Nanni Moretti, whose

*Dear Diary* was a hilarious and poignant memoir of a year in the life of the film-maker, driving around Rome on his Vespa, popping pills and bemoaning the lack of decent films. The death of Federico Fellini also cast a heavy pall over the Italian film world, but perhaps the promised return of Bernardo Bertolucci (after his insubstantial *Little Buddha* with Keanu Reeves) will rekindle some of the old fire.

Even in France, which is still the most successful European film producer, there is a similar lack of self-belief. Production is down, and the proportion of French films screened theatrically is also down. While government subsidies ensure a certain amount of activity, current film-makers do not measure up to their illustrious forebears. The new directors who emerged in the 1980s (Annaud, Beneix, Besson, Carax) have not sustained their promise with any consistency. Middle-brow talents like Diane Kurys (whose *Apres L'Amour* featured strong performances from Isabelle Huppert and Hippolyte Girardot), Claude Berri (whose *Germinal* was a self-conscious piece with Gerard Depardieu an unlikely starving miner and Miou Miou his mud-streaked wife) and Claude Sautet (who directed the classy chamber work *Coeur en Hiver*) have instead come to the fore. As for the survivors of the *nouvelle vague*, Eric Rohmer continues to make elegant philosophical conversation pieces at regular intervals, though his latest failed to earn a British release; Jacques Rivette scored a modest hit with his interminable Alan Ayckborn adaptation *Smoking/No Smoking*; and the erratic Claude Chabrol was back on form with the intense psychological study *L'Enfer*, based on a screenplay from the 1940s by Henri-Georges Clouzot.

DOUBLE TAKE

One trend that looks set to continue is Hollywood's fondness for remaking French films. Coline Serreau's gentle comedy *Trois Hommes et un Couffin* became *Three Men and a Baby*, and her *Romuald et Juliette* is also being remade by Disney but has yet to reach the screen. Hollywood will almost certainly remake her third film too, although *La Crise* is a much tougher piece, a mid-life crisis comedy about a man who loses his wife and his job on the same day. Nora Ephron is currently remaking *Le Père Noel est une Ordure* with Steve Martin, David Puttnam's production *The War of the Buttons* is based on a French children's film, and James Cameron's blockbuster *True Lies* recycles Claude Zidi's spy comedy *La Totale*. The next remake will inevitably be *Les Visiteurs*, a boisterous farce about two medieval knights who arrive dazed and confused in modern-day France. Easily the biggest grossing French film of the year, *Les Visiteurs* was the only foreign-language production to appear in *Variety*'s top 30 box-office hits of the year – this based almost entirely on its performance in Europe.

By common consent, the best French film of the year was actually made by a Pole, Krzysztof Kieslowski. *Three Colours Blue* was an affecting film about grief; Juliette Binoche loses her husband and child in a car accident and tries to come to terms with the loss and the freedom. This was the first in Kieslowski's *Three Colours* trilogy, loosely inspired by the colours of the *Tricolor* (representing freedom, equality and fraternity), and it shared the best film prize at the Venice Film Festival with Robert Altman's *Short Cuts*. *Three Colours White*, the second piece of the trilogy, was at first sight a much slighter work, an oblique black comedy about a Pole who returns home to make his fortune with the single-minded desire of getting back his French ex-wife. It is a sour, dour satire on post-Communist Poland, a country where everything and everybody has a price. Although it was generally less successful than its predecessor, it was awarded the Golden Bear at the Berlin Film Festival.

The jurors at the Cannes Film Festival, led by Clint Eastwood and Catherine Deneuve, were less receptive than most critics to the trilogy's bitter-sweet endpiece, *Three Colours Red*. A magisterial film about the relationship between a retired judge (Jean Louis Trintignant) and a beautiful model (Irene Jacob), the work brought Kieslowski's agnostic, spiritual concerns to a suitably metaphysical climax. Some judged it a masterpiece, for others it was mannered and unpersuasive. Even so, Kieslowski is undoubtedly pre-eminent among European film directors and it is to be hoped that he does not keep to his announced intention of retiring from film-making.

LOOKING EAST

Hollywood controversially awarded *Belle Epoque* the Oscar for best foreign language film of the year. Fernando Trueba's sunny sex comedy coaxes a certain amount of life out of a disreputable genre and traditional gender roles, but it never entirely outgrows them. Better contenders were the French/Vietnamese *The Scent of Green Papaya*, a delicate, sensuous portrait of domestic Vietnam in the 1950s, made with sensitivity and restraint by first-time director Tran-Anh Hung, and Chen Kaige's *Farewell My Concubine*, a searing melodrama spanning the years of Mao's cultural revolution in China, with an outstanding central performance by China's most famous actress, Gong Li. The film was a world-wide hit and underlined the great strides made by Chinese film-makers over the last decade. The so-called Fifth Generation have made great advances not only in political temerity but also in scope and power. However, the film also suggested that the movement may be on the wane. There is a self-conscious quality about it, and an apparent striving for rhetorical effect; one suspects it was made with half an eye on Hollywood. In contrast, Tian Zhuangzhuang's *The Blue Kite* covered much the same territory with grace and no bombast. It proved less palatable both with the authorities in China, who instigated new measures to curb rebellious film-makers, and with non-Chinese audiences. Elsewhere in the East, the most exciting film-maker to emerge was Takeshi Kitano. A comedian, commentator and cult personality in his native Japan (where he is better known as 'Beat' Takeshi), Kitano made his first film *Violent Cop*, in 1989. Western critics and distributors began to notice him when his bizarre, elegiac yakuza comedy *Sonatine* was shown at Cannes in 1993. *Violent Cop* was more conventional than *Sonatine*, but it showed a charismatic director heading in a new, interesting direction, and his subsequent *Boiling Point* went further, dispensing with a score and highlighting a series of deadpan visual and dramatic non-sequiturs.

In Britain, 1993-4 was the brightest year for some time. However, there have been no significant structural changes, government-backed or otherwise, and therefore the current growth may not be sustained. The New Producers' Alliance launched an initiative known as IMPACT, which lobbied for legislation offering tax incentives to film and video distributors and exhibitors to invest in local production. Distributors and exhibitors were predictably unimpressed with the plan and there was no sign that the Government would respond. The European Parliament is, however, preparing a green paper along broadly similar lines to the IMPACT proposals.

### WEDDED BLISS

Nevertheless, there was no shortage of good films from Britain this year. They were led by the outstandingly successful comedy *Four Weddings and a Funeral*, starring Hugh Grant and Andie MacDowell and directed by Mike Newell. The film was written by Richard Curtis and produced by Working Title for Polygram. It was a cleverly structured and beautifully acted film which benefited from lack of competition at the box-office to take more than $40 million in the USA (the biggest British success since *A Fish Called Wanda*), and it grossed over $100 million world-wide.

No other film could quite match this on a commercial scale, but Kenneth Branagh continued to impress with *Much Ado About Nothing*, featuring an all-star cast including Emma Thompson, Denzel Washington, Michael Keaton and Keanu Reeves. Merchant-Ivory's characteristically self-effacing adaptation *The Remains of the Day* (for which Anthony Hopkins and Emma Thompson were nominated for Oscars) and Richard Attenborough's poignant romance *Shadowlands* (which won an Oscar nomination for Debra Winger) were also very successful.

These films fall into the literary heritage market cornered by Britain in the last ten years. In contrast, others presented raw, angry portraits of contemporary hardship. Mike Leigh's *Naked* was a frightening, hilarious cinematic diatribe with a sensational performance from David Thewlis. Andrew Birkin's *The Cement Garden* was a studiedly bitter look at childhood regression, and Ken Loach continued a remarkably fruitful period with his humane, intense portrait of working-class desperation, *Raining Stones*. Derek Jarman finally succumbed to the AIDS virus he had been living with for many years, but not before completing the haunting, contemplative *Blue*. Peter

Greenaway received a critical and commercial savaging for his cold, ceremonious parable *The Baby of Macon*, but a new avant-garde hero emerged in Patrick Keiller, whose film-essay *London* was warmly received.

The most significant development in the British film world was the emergence of a new breed of young film-makers, dubbed 'The Brit Pack' or 'The Multiplex Generation'. These young directors share a desire to meld British subject-matter with Hollywood entertainment values. They include Danny Cannon, whose output has ranged from *Young Americans* to the new $50 million production *Judge Dredd*, starring Sylvester Stallone; Paul Anderson, whose *Shopping*, much hyped, was a spectacular failure; and Danny Boyle, whose *Shallow Grave* was praised at Cannes.

Faced with a low level of domestic investment in the UK film industry, many young film-makers have followed the example of American counterparts such as Hal Hartley and Spike Lee by making low budget (or no-budget) independent films, with the participants only being paid when and if the film moves into profit. The most successful of these films to date has been Vadim Jean and Gary Sinyor's 1993 production *Leon the Pig Farmer*. Vadim Jean's second film, *Beyond Bedlam*, switched from comedy to horror-thriller, but it proved an incoherent mess and died a quick death at the box-office. Its star, Elizabeth Hurley, subsequently found greater fame as the girlfriend of Hugh Grant.

### VIDEO CENSORSHIP

*Beyond Bedlam* was one of the victims of a stringent new line on the censorship of videos. The Liberal Democrat MP David Alton tabled a bill to the effect that all videos should be cut and classified with a view to the psychological damage they might cause to children. The spur for the Alton bill was the murder of two-year-old James Bulger by two schoolboys in February 1993. The trial judge suggested that violent videos may have influenced the murderers, and the film *Child's Play 3* was singled out for particular criticism. This was despite the fact that the police investigators said that there was no evidence to support the judge's statement, and indeed that there was no proof that the boys had even seen the film in question. Alton commissioned a report from child psychologists to support his view that violent films have a causal relationship with juvenile crime. This was seized on by the press, who largely ignored the results of a study into the viewing habits of juvenile offenders commissioned by the British Board of Film Classification (BBFC); this showed that young offenders watch no more violent videos than the general public, and in fact often come from deprived backgrounds with limited access to television and videos.

Faced with the possibility of the bill being passed, the Home Secretary (Michael Howard) put forward a last-minute amendment reportedly brokered by his then shadow, Tony Blair. While this was presented as a compromise, it met almost all of the bill's objectives except the reclassification of existing videos. It brought in heavy penalties for those who rent inappropriate films to under-age customers, and called on BBFC examiners to 'have regard to' preventing children from seeing videos which may cause 'psychological harm' or which present an 'inappropriate model for children'. The BBFC must also examine 'behaviour or activity likely to stimulate or encourage . . . criminal, violent or horrific behaviour, illegal drugs, and human sexual activity'. For the moment, the new legislation applies only to video. However, the video trade is now such an integral part of film funding that the legislation will inevitably have a knock-back effect on British film-making. The BBFC seems to have been caught out by these developments. Amid much confusion, *Beyond Bedlam* was initially classified for video, but that classification was then withdrawn before finally being confirmed. Meanwhile *The Texas Chainsaw Massacre*, *The Exorcist*, *Bad Lieutenant* and *Reservoir Dogs* are all still denied video classification.

BACK IN THE USA

Quentin Tarantino, the writer-director of *Reservoir Dogs*, has firmly established himself as the brightest American talent of the 1990s and the successor to Martin Scorsese and the so-called 'movie brats'. Tarantino and his colleagues Roger Avery and Lawrence Bender have even been dubbed the 'video brats', since they learned about films from videos or from working in video stores. Tony Scott brought Tarantino's first script to the screen, starring Christian Slater and Patricia Arquette, with memorable cameos from Dennis Hopper and Christopher Walken. *True Romance* was a slick, knowing but immature thriller steeped in pop culture references and designer brutalism. Oliver Stone followed his overblown Vietnam epic *Heaven and Earth* with a satire on the American media's obsession with violence, *Natural Born Killers*, using another Tarantino script as a starting-point. Most impressively, there was Tarantino's own second film, *Pulp Fiction*, a work of dazzling formal invention and wonderful sardonic bite. It caused problems with censors around the world, but was awarded the Palme d'Or at the Cannes Film Festival.

Violence was generally considered *passé* in 1994. This was largely because of the failure of *The Last Action Hero*, but may also have been influenced by the Clinton administration's concern with crime and the media and by the controversy stirred up by Michael Medved's highly publicized book *Hollywood vs America*. The year 1993 was dubbed Hollywood's 'Year of the Woman', a concept much mocked by the few women who work there. In the Academy Awards the best actress and best supporting actress Oscars were both won by the stars of *The Piano*, a French-produced film written and directed by New Zealander Jane Campion. *The Piano* is a sweeping Gothic

romance which was generally rapturously received. There were a handful of good roles for women – for example, Angela Bassett in *What's Love Got To Do With It*, Rosie Perez in *Fearless* and Susan Sarandon in *The Client* – but a handful scarcely represents sexual equality.

ADVANCING AGE

Nevertheless, there were encouraging signs that serious, adult-orientated films were finding an audience. There was Martin Scorsese's immaculate Edith Wharton adaptation, *The Age of Innocence*, a moving tale of love stifled by social convention in late 19th-century New York, sublimely acted by Daniel Day Lewis, Michelle Pfeiffer and Winona Ryder. Day Lewis played, and earned an Oscar nomination for, a very different role, as Gerry Conlon, the Irishman wrongly convicted of terrorism in Jim Sheridan's powerful but controversial *In the Name of the Father*.

There was Peter Weir's artful treatise *Fearless*, in which Jeff Bridges survives a plane crash and learns to confront death; Ivan Reitman's benign political comedy *Dave*, with Kevin Kline; Fred Schepisi's adaptation of John Guare's *Six Degrees of Separation*; and Clint Eastwood's *A Perfect World*, an over-long but memorable film about an escaped convict (an unusually animated Kevin Costner) and the young boy he takes captive. Hollywood finally supported an AIDS film, Jonathan Demme's courtroom drama *Philadelphia*, for which Tom Hanks won an Oscar as a lawyer who sues his former employers for wrongful dismissal with the help of a homophobic prosecutor (Denzel Washington).

This was formulaic film-making at its best, simple and effective. Even more straightforward commercial films – Harrison Ford in *The Fugitive*, Robin Williams in *Mrs Doubtfire*, and three John Grisham thriller adaptations, *The Firm*, *The Pelican Brief* and *The Client* – aspired to some measure of sophistication. There was also a revival of Westerns, after the success of *Unforgiven* and *Dances with Wolves*. This is probably a short-term phenomenon, since many were disappointments either critically or at the box-office – *Tombstone* was an example of the former, *Geronimo* and the under-rated *Wyatt Earp* of the latter, and *Bad Girls* fell into both categories.

The best American films of the year were the most ambitious. Robert Altman's *Short Cuts* was an audacious, panoramic glimpse at the lives of a dozen couples in the suburbs of Los Angeles. Adapted from short stories by Raymond Carver, *Short Cuts* serves as a reminder of how safe and predictable films have become since Altman's prime in the early 1970s. Not all the strands of the film are entirely successful, but those that are take us to the heart of the emotional malaise Altman finds so prevalent in modern relationships.

SCHINDLER'S LIST

The other outstanding American film came from a familiar but still unpredictable source. Steven Spielberg's *Schindler's List* addressed the difficult subject of the Holocaust. Based on Thomas Keneally's book about the German industrialist Oskar Schindler whose factory became a safe-haven for his Jewish employees, *Schindler's List* is an enthralling account of an enigmatic man (an entrepreneur, and an egoist in Liam Neeson's portrayal) inspired to acts of extraordinary courage by the most heinous circumstances. Contrasted with him, we see Ralph Fiennes' psychopathic Nazi, Amon Goeth, compelled by those same circumstances to xenophobia and genocide. What makes this psychological duel so impressive is Spielberg's grasp of the ethical conundrum; that out of ambiguity, ambivalance and random incidence, moral absolutes take form. *Schindler's List* also serves as a penetrating, overwhelming recreation of the Holocaust. Filmed in monochrome, often with a hand-held camera, and lasting nearly three and a half hours, the film is an unforgettably vivid portrait of the 'progress' of the Holocaust from the first bureaucratic designations in census books to the gas chambers at Auschwitz.

Spielberg surpassed himself here – and one senses that he knew it. After the world-wide success of *Schindler's List*, which won seven Oscars including best film and best director, Spielberg took a year's sabbatical to consider his next step. In the meantime he produced the synthetic, witless blockbuster *The Flintstones*, one of many films based on old television series. Other examples were *Maverick* and *The Beverly Hillbillies*, and many more are being developed. Indeed there was a strong sense of *déjà vu* in the summer of 1994, as Spielberg's *Flintstone* dinosaurs vied with Schwarzenegger's action-packed *True Lies*. As it turned out, both were less successful than Robert Zemeckis' sentimental fantasy *Forrest Gump* and Disney's animated *The Lion King*. Escapism proved much in demand, and that Hollywood is always happy to provide.

---

## FILM AWARD WINNERS

---

ACADEMY AWARDS 1993

Best Picture – *Schindler's List*
Best Director – Steven Spielberg, *Schindler's List*
Best Actor – Tom Hanks, *Philadelphia*
Best Actress – Holly Hunter, *The Piano*
Best Supporting Actor – Tommy Lee Jones, *The Fugitive*
Best Supporting Actress – Anna Paquin, *The Piano*
Best Original Screenplay – Jane Campion, *The Piano*
Best Adapted Screenplay – Steven Zaillian, *Schindler's List*
Best Foreign Language Film – *Belle Epoque*, Spain
Best Original Score – John Williams, *Schindler's List*
Best Original Song – Bruce Springsteen, 'Streets of Philadelphia', *Philadelphia*
Best Cinematography – Janusz Kaminski, *Schindler's List*
Best Art Direction – Allan Starski, Ewa Braun, *Schindler's List*
Best Costume Design – Gabriella Pescucci, *The Age of Innocence*
Best Film Editing – Michael Kahn, *Schindler's List*

Best Sound – Gary Summers, Gary Rydstrom, Shawn Murphy, Ron Judkins, *Jurassic Park*
Best Sound Effects Editing – Gary Rydstrom, Richard Hymns, *Jurassic Park*
Best Visual Effects – Dennis Muren, Stan Winston, Phil Tippett, Michael Lantieri, *Jurassic Park*
Best Make-up – Greg Cannom, Ve Neill, Yolanda Toussieng, *Mrs Doubtfire*
Best Animated Short – Nicholas Park, *The Wrong Trousers*
Best Short Documentary – Margaret Lazarus, Renner Wunderlich, *Defending Our Lives*
Best Documentary Feature – Susan Raymond, Alan Raymond, *I Am A Promise: The Children of Stanton Elementary School*
Best Live Action Short – Pepe Danquart, *Black Rider*
Honorary Awards – Deborah Kerr, Paul Newman

BAFTA AWARDS 1994

Best Film – *Schindler's List*
Best Director – Steven Spielberg, *Schindler's List*
Best Actor – Anthony Hopkins, *The Remains of the Day*
Best Actress – Holly Hunter, *The Piano*
Best Supporting Actor – Ralph Fiennes, *Schindler's List*
Best Supporting Actress – Miriam Margolyes, *The Age of Innocence*
Alex Korda Award (British film of the year) – *Shadowlands*
Most Popular Film – *Jurassic Park*

CANNES FESTIVAL 1994

Palme d'Or – *Pulp Fiction*, Quentin Tarantino
Best Director – Nanni Moretti, *Dear Diary*
Best Actor – Ge You, *To Live*
Best Actress – Virna Lisi, *La Reine Margot*
Grand Jury Prize (shared) – *To Live*, Zhang Yimou; *Burnt by the Sun*, Nikita Mikhalkov
Jury Prize – *La Reine Margot*, Patrice Chereau

BERLIN FESTIVAL 1994

Golden Bear – *In the Name of the Father*
Best Director – Krzysztof Kieslowski, *Three Colours Blue*
Best Actor – Tom Hanks, *Philadelphia*
Best Actress – Crissy Rock, *Ladybird, Ladybird*

VENICE FESTIVAL 1993

Golden Lion (shared) – *Short Cuts; Three Colours Blue*
Special Jury Prize – *Bad Boy Buddy*
Best Director – not awarded
Best Actor – Fabrizio Bentivoglio, *Un'Anima Divisa in Due*
Best Actress – Juliette Binoche, *Three Colours Blue*

# Literature

The first volume of Baroness Thatcher's memoirs, *The Downing Street Years*, was published by HarperCollins in October 1993, preceded by much media attention and controversy. The advance for two volumes paid to the former prime minister was reported to be £3.5 million, and was negotiated by an American agent, Marvin Josephson, a choice of middleman that some criticized as unpatriotic.

Serial rights were sold to the *Sunday Times*, for a rumoured £500,000. The former police chief John Stalker was hired to supervise security for the book, and the editor of the *Sunday Times*, Andrew Neil, kept his pre-publication copy in a briefcase handcuffed to his wrist. Nevertheless the *Daily Mirror* got hold of some of the material, and in a spoiler that coincided with the Conservative Party Conference, quoted Lady Thatcher's opinion that her successor John Major was 'small-minded, politically naive and an intellectual lightweight'. HarperCollins and the *Sunday Times* sought an injunction against a breach of copyright. To the consternation of the book trade, anxious to protect the sale of serial rights, the Appeal Court and two High Court judgments said that the *Mirror*'s publication of this material was 'in the public interest'. In May 1994, however, in a separate case, Associated Newspapers paid £200,000 damages plus £330,000 to cover legal costs to the *Sunday Times* after accepting that articles published in the *Mail on Sunday* to coincide with serialization were in breach of copyrights and confidence.

Moments of comparative light relief in *The Downing Street Years* included the assertions that John Major tended to be 'defeated by platitudes', that Nigel Lawson's 'folly' had 'cost us dear' and that Geoffrey Howe's resignation speech was an act of 'bile and treachery'. These leavened what critics generally found an otherwise plodding and detailed self-justification in which the ghost writing was too evident, but which was nevertheless a huge best-seller, apparently exhausting the print run of some 250,000 copies.

## BOOKER DISPUTES

The announcement of the 1993 Booker Prize shortlist in September caused a furore for its exclusion of Vikram Seth's vast and critically feted novel *A Suitable Boy* (Orion), which had been compared to Tolstoy and Dickens. Anthony Cheetham of Orion (which had paid a £250,000 advance for the book) was quoted in the *Guardian* describing the judges as 'a bunch of wankers'. James Wood of the same newspaper was also scathing about the judges and their choices, saying it would be a long time before the Booker recovered from this 'deep wound'; as it turned out, he became a Booker judge himself in 1994. Lord Gowrie, chairman of the 1993 panel, argued that *A Suitable Boy* (at some 1,400 pages the

longest novel published in English since Richardson's *Clarissa*) was inadequately edited. But it won the £10,000 W. H. Smith Award in March 1994 and was very popular with readers; it had sold 120,000 copies in hardback at £20 each by Christmas 1993.

The book that won the Booker Prize in 1993 sold even better – better in fact than any Booker winner in the award's history. Roddy Doyle's *Paddy Clarke Ha Ha Ha*, a ten-year-old boy's narrative about the breakdown of his parents' marriage, had already sold 75,000 copies before it won the Booker in October. It sold a further 135,000 by Christmas, and went on selling, reaching over 320,000 copies in hardback and paperback by September 1994. In February 1994 the British Book Awards named Roddy Doyle author of the year.

The 1994 Booker judging also generated controversy. James Wood attracted some adverse comment of his own about his apparent failure to declare his interest in one of the novels submitted, which was by his wife Clare Messud. Again, some of the most critically admired books of the year were excluded from the shortlist, among them Margaret Atwood's *The Robber Bride* and Candia McWilliam's *Debatable Land*. One inclusion, however, Alan Hollinghurst's poetic and erotic book *The Folding Star* was among the most lauded novels of 1993-4, and so instantly became the bookmakers' favourite to win. Another inclusion attracted wide media comment because it had originally been rejected for publication throughout the UK, despite high praise from publishers' readers. The author of *Knowledge of Angels*, Jill Paton Walsh, eventually decided to publish under the imprint she ran with her husband, Green Bay Books, in association with Colt Books of Cambridge. After the shortlist was announced, she denounced the 'culture of anxiety' that had unsettled Britain's leading fiction houses.

In 1993 Booker celebrated the prize's 25 years of existence by announcing a Booker of Bookers chosen from all the past winners by W. L. Webb (who chaired the first Booker panel in 1969), David Holloway (chair in 1970) and Malcolm Bradbury (1981). It was won by Salman Rushdie for *Midnight's Children*, on the grounds that it had 'changed the novel, removed it from its Eurocentric obsessions and given it a special magic', with the late William Golding's *Rites of Passage* a close second. Waterstone's bookshop then announced its own 'alternative Booker' promotion, of books (chosen by its staff) that should have won but never did, such as Martin Amis's *Money* and Jeanette Winterson's *Oranges Are Not the Only Fruit*. This notion was followed up in July 1994 by Everyman Paperbacks, who initiated an annual 'Booker Prize' for the best book of 100 years ago, to be announced at the Cheltenham Literary Festival after a public discussion among the judges.

The Booker of Bookers accolade was a bright spot in another troubled year for Salman Rushdie. In October his Norwegian publisher was shot in Oslo, and the price on his own head was increased to $2 million. He was, however, received by the US President Bill Clinton (George Bush had refused to meet him). A collection of essays by 100 Arab and Muslim writers and intellectuals upholding his right to freedom of expression was published in France. A new paperback of *The Satanic Verses* was issued in Britain in May 1994 and his first collection of short stories, *East, West* comes out from Cape in October 1994.

The death of Anthony Burgess in December 1993 prompted a poll of authors and critics by the *Sunday Times* in March 1994 to establish who was currently held to be the greatest writer now working in English. The consensus that emerged was that Saul Bellow deserved the title, closely followed by John Updike, with Muriel Spark a contender. Readers' responses were more insistent upon Iris Murdoch, although her latest novel *The Green Knight* was generally given short shrift in September 1993 by critics; a representative comment was that there was 'perhaps for the first time, something forlorn about Murdoch's performance' (Galen Stawson in the *Independent on Sunday*).

Jeanette Winterson, in the *Sunday Times* poll, added to her own notoriety by nominating herself as the greatest living writer: 'No one working in the English language now comes close to my exuberance, my passion, my fidelity to words.' This remark had been preceded in 1991 by her choosing her own novel in the *Telegraph*'s books of the year feature with the comment: 'My own *Written on the Body* is this year's most profound and profoundly misunderstood book', and her nomination the following year of the *Penguin Book of Lesbian Short Stories*, edited by her partner Margaret Reynolds. With this history, it is perhaps no surprise that her new novel *Art and Lies*, published in June, was riding for a critical fall. It was variously accused of 'straining for special effects' and 'fancying itself stupid, literally' (Julie Burchill in the *Spectator*) and containing 'the standard bundle of modernist prejudices and snobberies' (Peter Kemp in the *Sunday Times*).

Winterson's response to such judgements has in the past been unusual for an author. By her own admission, she is not one to accept disparagement easily: 'If people say something about me which is wrong, or appalling, I simply go round to see them. I find it's very effective. I don't like these middle-class manners whereby people can say what they want and there's never any comeback'. When this remark was made, Winterson had already called intimidatingly upon one literary agent and well-known purveyor of gossip late one night, as the papers recorded. It was not her last gesture of this kind: her subsequent doorstepping of a journalist and deputy literary editor whose printed words provoked her also prompted a flurry of media comment.

TRUTH V. TACT

In his lifetime Graham Greene might have laid a claim to being the 'greatest living writer'. This was the year when biographers locked horns over his reputation. Norman Sherry, the official biographer, produced the second volume of his massive *A Life of Graham Greene*, having spent industrious years following in Greene's footsteps. This volume brings Greene's life up to the 1950s and although it contained revelations about, for instance, his extra-marital affairs, was largely a sympathetic portrait. By contrast, *Graham Greene: The Man Within* by Michael Shelden (previously the biographer of George Orwell) was much more damning. Shelden accused Greene of being an alcoholic, a liar, a closet homosexual and an active member of the Secret Service all his life. A third point of view came from Greene's confessor and friend of 27 years, Father Leopoldo Duran. His low-key memoir, *Graham Greene: Friend and Brother*, painted an uncritical (and rather intangible) portrait of a man who was modest, generous and open.

Among other biographies of controversial figures, Humphrey Burton's generally well-received *Leonard Bernstein* revelled in the dark private life of the adulated classical conductor, and Jeremy Treglown's *Roald Dahl* confronted Dahl's reputation for anti-Semitism, bullying and self-publicizing. Burton and Treglown attracted praise, not entirely unmixed, for their books; Bernstein and Dahl came off rather worse.

However, reviewing *Roald Dahl* in the *Sunday Times*, Humphrey Carpenter wrote of him: 'He is outrageous, but he is truthful; and children's literature regularly needs an injection of the outrageously true, as an antidote to the worthy stuff that most adults want to foist on kids.' This remark might be a defence of two award-winning children's books that caused a stir this year. When Babette Cole's bestselling *Mummy Laid an Egg*, a humorous but precise explanation of the facts of life, was submitted for the Smarties Prize in the 0-5 years category, the judges dealt with anxiety about its subject matter by reallocating it to 6-8 years, in contradiction of the author's and the publisher's definition. The Carnegie Prize winner, Robert Swindells' *Stone Cold*, which concerns a serial killer who preys on the homeless, sparked debate about subjects that are suitable for youngsters. Although generally the media was condemnatory about its selection, Sarah Dunnant, who chaired the Carnegie judges, argued in favour of literature for children that helped them to come to terms with terrible truths, while at least one reviewer found the book humane and not at all sensationalizing.

The children's author of the year was undoubtedly Anne Fine, and not only in the estimation of the British Book Awards. Her book *Flour Babies*, the story of an unconventional school project that teaches boys about the responsibilities of parenthood and also a good deal about themselves, won both the Carnegie Medal and the Whitbread children's novel prize.

Furthermore, the Hollywood film of Fine's *Madame Doubtfire* (renamed *Mrs Doubtfire*), starring Robin Williams as an estranged husband impersonating a middle-aged woman in order to become his children's nanny, was a phenomenal box office success. This year made Fine's fortune and reputation.

Reputations were also made, or at least helped along, by a promotion of young poets sponsored by the Poetry Society and the Arts Council, in conjunction with several poetry publishers and backed (some later said rather meanly in terms of air time) by Radio 1. The New Generation Poets were chosen by a panel of six judges chaired by Melvyn Bragg, who put forward 20 collections by poets who were under 40 or who had published their first collection in the last five years. One of these, Carol Ann Duffy, went on to win the £10,000 Forward Poetry Prize for her collection *Mean Time*.

Arguably a landmark in poetry publishing was Craig Raine's *History: The Home Movie*, published in September 1994. It was a semi-autobiographical novel written in verse, submitted for the Booker Prize, and widely praised in the literary pages (although it was cuttingly spoofed in *Private Eye*). Meanwhile Raine's fellow poet and fellow Oxonian James Fenton had defeated the competition from U. A. (Ursula) Fanthorpe and Les Murray to become Oxford Professor of Poetry. This was the second time Fenton had been nominated for the post; on the previous occasion the successful candidate was Peter Levi.

There were some hitherto unknown or little-known writers for whom this last year was something of an *annus mirabilis*. Having stepped into the limelight when her novel *Theory of War* won the Whitbread prize, Joan Brady published her autobiography, *Prologue: An Unconventional Life*. It chronicled her career as a dancer with the New York City Ballet and her unconventional marriage. Two first novelists who were not included in *Granta's* maligned Best of Young British promotion of summer 1993 received notable praise and prizes: Tim Pears for his *In the Place of Fallen Leaves* and Rachel Cusk for *Saving Agnes*, winner of the Whitbread first novel category.

FINE FORTUNES

It was also a good year for making a fortune by writing a first novel. There were four notable instances. Allan Folsom's *The Day After Tomorrow* was the most expensive first novel in history; Little, Brown and Warner paid $2 million, with a further $500,000 on sales of 400,000 copies. The book, the story of an ordinary doctor's pursuit of the Nazi who killed his father, earned some $4.5 million in rights income, not including $1 million from a film rights deal, and was published in May 1994. Folsom had been writing for 30 years, mostly unproduced, for television and film. Also published in May was Carol O'Connell's *Mallory's Oracle*, which was submitted unsolicited to Hutchinson. It earned world rights of over £1 million, selling in nine countries.

The 32-year-old former City trader Michael Ridpath's 'white-collar thriller' *Free to Trade* came out of a literary agent's 'slush pile' of unsolicited manuscripts before five publishers fought over it, each offering 'a substantial six figures' each for this and a subsequent novel. The two-book deal, worth some £750,000, was finally clinched by Heinemann and Mandarin, with publication of *Free to Trade* due in spring 1995. Linda Davies, an Oxford graduate who had been a merchant banker for seven years, earned over $1 million in rights for her first novel *Nest of Vipers* by the time Orion published the book in June 1994. MGM bought the film rights. Davies was pitched by her publisher as 'the female John Grisham'.

John Grisham himself made news by topping the hardback and paperback bestseller lists simultaneously in June 1994 with *The Chamber* and *The Client* respectively. Grisham has become the world's most popular writer, with 30 million books in print, and 40 million books sold in the USA alone since 1991; *The Firm* sold over 1 million in Britain. The sale of film rights in *The Chamber* set an industry record, going to Universal Pictures for $3.7 million before a word of the book was written.

The paperback sensation of the year was Jung Chang's account of three generations of the women of her own Chinese family, *Wild Swans*, which was outsold in 1993 only by Michael Crichton's film-boosted *Jurassic Park*. In terms of turnover, though, *Wild Swans* exceeded all rivals; by Christmas 1993 it had generated sales worth £7.5 million. It was also the first non-fiction paperback to sell over a million copies in one year since *You Can Do the Cube* in 1981. By September 1994 it had spent 55 weeks on the paperback bestseller lists, and at the British Book Awards it was designated the book of the year. Critics had enthused in Britain; in America, though, critical reception was cool.

A novel about which British critics were icy, but which was a huge bestseller in the USA, also made it to the top of the paperback lists in Britain. Robert James Waller's *The Bridges of Madison County*, which reviewers found mawkish, pretentious and clichéd in its characterization, told the story of a married woman who rediscovered passion through a brief affair with a rugged photographer. Mocked and spoofed though it was, it seems that readers generally were moved. Its success followed its republication with its original title after a misguided decision to call it *Love in Black and White*, under which name it made hardly any impact. The same author published a second book, *Slow Waltz in Cedar Bend*, which was even more scathingly received.

In February Viking published the diary of a young girl who had been living in Sarajevo until her evacuation to Paris with her parents at Christmas 1993. *Zlata's Diary*, written by Zlata Filipovic at the age of ten, became the number one bestseller in France, and followed suit on its subsequent appearance in Britain. There was, however, some controversy over whether the text had been tampered with. Detractors found variations between earlier and later editions that suggested the intervention of adults who wished to make political points for an international audience.

Bestsellers of last year that sustained their momentum into this included the hostage books – Terry Waite's *Taken on Trust*, John McCarthy and Jill Morrell's *Some Other Rainbow* and Brian Keenan's *An Evil Cradling*. Alan Clark's readable and rakish *Diaries* topped the 1993 books of the year poll and continued to sell, with an extra fillip in June 1994 when the tabloids came up with new revelations about Clark's love life. He was signed up by Weidenfeld for a rumoured £400,000 to write another volume for publication in 1995. Delia Smith had three books that sold and sold throughout the year despite their seasonal titles: *Delia Smith's Summer Collection, Delia Smith's Christmas* and her *Complete Cookery Course*, reaching, by the end of August 1994, a total of 61, 48 and 84 weeks in the bestseller lists respectively. Joanna Trollope achieved three books in the top 15 paperback sellers of 1993: *The Men and the Girls, The Rector's Wife* and *The Choir*.

The surprise bestseller of Christmas 1993, Andy McNab's story of an SAS unit operating in Iraq during the Gulf War, *Bravo Two Zero* stayed in the hardback bestseller lists well into 1994. The record-breaking *A Brief History of Time* by Stephen Hawking made occasional reappearances in the lists, bringing it up to an astonishing 184 weeks in the top ten.

### CLASSIC APPEAL

One remarkable development was the presence on the bestseller lists of literary classics. George Eliot's *Middlemarch*, and Edith Wharton's *The Age of Innocence* in February were suddenly outselling Catherine Cookson and Danielle Steele, thanks to the BBC's popular and critically well-received television adaptation of *Middlemarch* and Martin Scorsese's film of *The Age of Innocence* starring Daniel Day Lewis. Films also had the power to bring Thomas Keneally's *Schindler's List* (originally titled *Schindler's Ark*) and Kazuo Ishiguro's *The Remains of the Day* back on to the bestseller lists.

The enduring appeal of literary classics was evidenced also by the publication of sequels to well-known works. *Mrs de Winter*, Susan Hill's sequel to Daphne du Maurier's *Rebecca*, vindicated its advance of some £650,000 by being a bestseller, although its critical reception was lukewarm. This was also the case with William Horwood's *The Willows in Winter*, a sequel to Kenneth Grahame's *The Wind in the Willows*, and *Pemberley*, Emma Tennant's sequel to *Pride and Prejudice*. Julia Barrett's *Presumption*, a subsequently published rival sequel to *Pride and Prejudice*, received warmer reviews than Tennant's. Sequels to *The Forsyte Saga* (Suleika Dawson's *The Forsytes*) and *Doctor Zhivago* (Alexander Mollin's *Lara's Child*) were also published during the year, and sequels have been commissioned to *Lady*

*Chatterley's Lover* (Elaine Feinstein's *Lady Chatterley's Daughter*), Anthony Hope's *The Prisoner of Zenda* (John Spurling's *After Zenda*), Frances Hodgson Burnett's *The Secret Garden* (Susan Moody's *Misselthwaite*), and Mary Shelley's *Frankenstein* (Hilary Bailey's *Frankenstein's Bride*). Joseph Heller's 'sequel' to his own modern classic *Catch 22*, is due for publication in October 1994. *Closing Time* brings the characters in *Catch 22* up to the present day.

The trend for signing up celebrities to write novels, or at least to give their names to novels that were written by someone else, also showed no sign of abating. The most blatant example of celebrity endorsement was supermodel Naomi Campbell's *Swan* (written 'with' Carly McIntyre, a.k.a. editor Caroline Upcher). Tennis champion Martina Navratilova (*The Total Zone* written with Liz Nickles) and actress Jill Gascoigne (*Addicted*) also embarked on new careers in fiction. There were reports of the Duchess of York's attempt to cajole American publishers into paying large sums for novels with her name on the cover. She was said to have declined an offer of a $400,000 advance for a series of two or three mystery novels on the grounds that it was not enough money.

Among the more remarkable deals of the year was Reed International's eight-book deal with Peter Ackroyd effectively putting him on a salary until 2004, with one-40th of the total sum payable every quarter. During these ten years he is required to produce four novels and four books of non-fiction. In July there was trouble over an advance paid to Joan Collins by Random House, with rumours of claims and counter-claims by author and publisher. One report had it that the publisher had asked for a $1 million advance to be returned because the book that was submitted was not good enough.

The horrific discoveries at a house in Gloucester that led to the arrest of the builder Frederick West and his wife for multiple murders gave rise during the year to a literary industry of their own. Brian Masters, Gordon Burn and Emma Gilbey were all commissioned to write books about these events, but it was the attempt by Frederick West's solicitor Howard Ogden (who was dismissed by West) to sell his story for £1 million that caused outrage. The novelist Susan Hill resigned after a 35-year association from her literary agency Curtis Brown because it was acting for Ogden. She called the agency's action 'repugnant and grossly unethical', finding it especially insensitive to the relatives of the murdered women. There were also murmurs of disapprobation about the publication and promotion in January of Great Train Robber Ronnie Biggs' autobiography *Odd Man Out*. There were those who considered that the fate of the train driver injured in the robbery made the venture especially distasteful.

Legal disputes included one over David Leavitt's novel *While England Sleeps*; the poet Stephen Spender claimed that Leavitt had 'stolen' an episode from Spender's autobiography *World Within World* for the basis of his novel. Leavitt defended the use of the germ of an idea, but in November his publisher gave the High Court an undertaking that it would not sell the book (already published) until after a full hearing. Proceedings were not for plagiarism but for infringement of copyright, and ultimately the publisher agreed to pulp existing copies and republish with appropriate minor revisions by the author. A writ was issued in August 1994 against the journalist Julie Burchill by Johnny Logan, who claimed that she had plagiarized large sections of his unofficial history of the pop group The Smiths, *The Severed Alliance*, for an article on its lead singer, Morrissey, which was published in the *Sunday Times*.

In April the Health Education Authority's *Your Pocket Guide to Sex*, a guide for teenagers by Nick Fisher, was denounced by the Health Minister Dr Brian Mawhinney as 'smutty and inappropriate'. The HEA asked booksellers to return copies to the wholesalers, but many commentators argued that its style and content were suited to its intended audience and Fourth Estate took over publication.

Publication went ahead of the diaries of Sir Nicholas Henderson, Britain's ambassador to Washington during the Falklands War, despite pressure on the author not to contravene the 'Radcliffe' rules which advise a 15-year silence over ministerial and Foreign Office proceedings. The Cabinet Secretary, Sir Robin Butler, had expressed reservations about publication five years previously, which Sir Nicholas had heeded, but now, according to his publisher, he thought: 'Everyone else – including Mrs Thatcher – has talked about these events; why shouldn't I?' The diaries, entitled *Mandarin*, were critically praised for the elegance of their writing.

A contrast to Margaret Thatcher's memoirs were those of the incumbent Prime Minister's elder brother, Terry Major-Ball, entitled *Major Major*, which were published in summer 1994. They were also widely reviewed, and in general critics enjoyed the often unintentional humour of this ordinary chap's hymn to ordinariness.

Finally, there were two political moves during the year that have implications for readers and publishers alike. Everyone had cause to celebrate in November 1993 when the Chancellor announced that there would be no extension of VAT to books and newspapers. A petition with one million signatures had been delivered in 35 boxes to Downing Street the previous month urging the Chancellor to that decision. Less auspicious for the book trade was the Office of Fair Trading's decision in August 1994 to refer the Net Book Agreement (by which book prices are fixed by the publisher) to the Restrictive Practices Court. Some commentators see this as the writing on the wall for the NBA. Even before this decision, one leading publishing group, Reed International, was allowing some of its books to be sold for less than the published price. In the light of the OFT's referral, others, even those more committed to the NBA, may follow suit.

## LITERARY PRIZE WINNERS

Nobel Prize 1993 – Toni Morrison (USA)
David Cohen British Literature Prize 1993 (biennial) – V. S. Naipul
Commonwealth Writers Prize 1993 – *Such a Long Journey*, Rohinton Mistry (Canada)
Prix Goncourt 1993 – *Texaco*, Patrick Chamoiseau (Martinique)
Booker Prize 1993 – *Paddy Clarke Ha Ha Ha*, Roddy Doyle
    1994 shortlist: *How Late It Was, How Late*, James Kelman; *Reef*, Romesh Gunesekera; *Beside the Ocean of Time*, George Mackay Brown; *The Folding Star*, Alan Hollinghurst; *Knowledge of Angels*, Jill Paton Walsh; *Paradise*, Abdulrazak Gurnah
Whitbread Prize 1993:
    Novel, and overall winner – *Theory of War*, Joan Brady
    First novel – *Saving Agnes*, Rachel Cusk
    Biography – *Philip Larkin: A Writer's Life*, Andrew Motion
    Poetry – *Mean Time*, Carol Ann Duffy
    Children's novel – *Flour Babies*, Anne Fine
David Higham Prize 1993 – *Love Your Enemies*, Nicola Barker
Sunday Express Prize 1993 – *The Blue Afternoon*, William Boyd
Forward Prize 1993 (poetry) – *Mean Time*, Carol Ann Duffy
    First collection – *Nil Nil*, Don Paterson
Catherine Cookson Prize 1993 – *The Sea is My Companion*, Valerie Wood
William Hill Sports Book of the Year 1993 – *Endless Winter*, Stephen Jones
Smarties Prize 1993 (children's books) – *War Game*, Michael Foreman
    Age 0–5 – *Hue Boy*, Rita Phillips Mitchell and Caroline Binch
    Age 6–8 – *War Game*, Michael Foreman
    Age 9–11 – *Listen to the Dark*, Maeve Henry
NCR Award 1994 (non-fiction) – *Edward Heath: A Biography*, John Campbell
Somerset Maugham Prize 1994 – Jackie Kay, A. L. Kennedy, Philip Marsden
Betty Trask Prize 1994 – *Divorcing Jack*, Colin Bateman (£12,000); *Season of the Rainbirds*, Nadeem Aslam (£10,000)
McKitterick Prize 1994 – *Zennor in Darkness*, Helen Dunmore
W. H. Smith Prize 1994 – *A Suitable Boy*, Vikram Seth
Mail on Sunday/John Llewellyn Rhys Prize 1994 – *On Foot to the Golden Horn*, Jason Goodwin
James Tait Black Prize 1994:
    Fiction – *Crossing the River*, Caryl Phillips
    Biography – *Dr Johnson and Mr Savage*, Richard Holmes
Encore Prize 1994 (second novel) – *Afternoon Raag*, Amit Chaudhuri
Cholmondeley Award 1994 (poets) – Ruth Fairlight, Gwen Harwood, Elizabeth Jennings, John Mole
Crime Writers Association Diamond Dagger 1994 – Michael Gilbert
Romantic Novel of the Year 1994 – *Consider the Lily*, Elizabeth Buchan
Carnegie Prize 1994 (children's) – *Stone Cold*, Robert Swindells
Kate Greenaway 1994 (children's illustrated) – Alan Lee, *Black Ships Before Troy* by Rosemary Sutcliff

# Opera

Despite almost universal gloom among opera companies over their financial state – the Department of National Heritage has announced a cut of 1.69 per cent in its grant to the Arts Council, a cut in real terms of nearly 5.3 per cent – the artistic standards of many companies continued to rise. One company unaffected by cuts in Arts Council funding is Glyndebourne Festival Opera, which receives no government subsidy. On 28 May 1994, sixty years to the day since the opening of John Christie's Sussex opera house with Le nozze di Figaro, the new theatre at Glyndebourne was inaugurated with the same opera. Preparatory work had begun on the site at the end of July 1991, the old opera house was demolished in August 1992 and construction was completed, on schedule and within budget, on 31 December 1993.

The new theatre has 1,200 seats, 370 more than the old theatre, and provides standing room for 42 (at £10) and 16 places for wheelchairs. However, it has not lost its intimacy, owing to the horse-shoe shape of the auditorium, which has walls of natural brick with reclaimed pitch pine panels. The acoustics are very kind to the voice and glorious for the orchestra, as the London Philharmonic demonstrated in a revival of Peter Grimes in which the Sea Interludes had a particular vividness and clarity.

The opening Figaro was attended by Roy Henderson, the Scottish baritone who sang Count Almaviva at the opening performance in 1934, and was conducted by Bernard Haitink. It was followed by a new production of Eugene Onegin, staged by Graham Vick, the recently-appointed director of productions, and conducted by Andrew Davis, the Festival's music director. For the revival of The Rake's Progress, with David Hockney's superb, Hogarth-inspired designs, the artist had enlarged his sets to fit the new proscenium arch (which is three metres wider than the old one) and received a personal ovation at curtain-call. A new staging of Don Giovanni, directed by Deborah Warner, was greeted with booing on the first night (only the second time this has ever happened at Glyndebourne), but at later performances the production, the singers, the Orchestra of the Enlightenment and the conductor, Simon Rattle, were all applauded to the echo. The new theatre's first season was universally declared to have been a great success.

Irene Eisinger, a veteran of the pre-war seasons at Glyndebourne, died on 8 April 1994 at the age of 90. The soprano made her début as Despina in Così fan tutte on 29 May 1934, the second night of the first season, and also sang Papagena in Die Zauberflöte, Blonde in Die Entführung aus dem Serail and both Barbarina and Susanna in Le nozze di Figaro. She became a favourite with Glyndebourne audiences, who were enchanted by her personality as well as her singing. In 1940 she played Polly Peachum in The Beggar's Opera at the Theatre Royal, Haymarket and in 1949 sang Despina once more at the Edinburgh Festival.

## ROYAL RETRENCHMENT

The Royal Opera, which generates over 73 per cent of its income through box-office takings and sponsorship (while the Paris Bastille generates 34 per cent, La Scala, Milan, 26 per cent, and the Berlin State Opera only 13 per cent), this year faced a shortfall of £500,000 in calculated revenue from the box-office despite a generally successful season. The company had also made stringent economies, including the disbandment of the Garden Venture. Although its latest production, Thérèse Raquin by Michael Finnissey, a one-act adaptation of Zola's novel, was not a success, the Garden Venture premièred 21 operas and benefited the careers of over 100 young composers, writers, directors, designers and singers during its five-year existence.

The first new production of the season at Covent Garden was Die Meistersinger von Nürnberg; it won universal praise and received the 1993 Evening Standard Award for Outstanding Production – an award embracing the whole ensemble of cast, chorus, orchestra, director and designer. The other successful new productions included Massenet's Chérubin and Janáček's Katya Kabanova, both performed at Covent Garden for the first time. Less popular were Giordano's Fedora, in a production from La Scala, and Rossini's Mosè in Egitto, from the Teatro Communale, Bologna, despite the presence of Mirella Freni and José Carreras in the former, and of Ruggero Raimondi in the latter. After an absence of ten years, Aida returned to the Royal Opera House in a new staging by Elijah Moshinsky, conducted by the company's Verdi specialist, Edward Downes. The production was greeted with reservations, although the musical performance was praised.

A revival of L'Italiana in Algeri marked the last appearance in a Rossini opera by the great coloratura-mezzo Marilyn Horne after a career lasting nearly 40 years. Another successful revival was that of Harrison Birtwistle's Gawain; the tableaux at the end of the first act, The Turning of the Seasons, had been rewritten and the opera scored an even greater triumph than in 1991, despite (or perhaps because of) a minor demonstration against the composer by a group hostile to contemporary music, the Hecklers, when he took a curtain-call.

English National Opera has been determined not to allow financial difficulties to impinge too greatly on artistic decisions. A 'renewal of the core repertory' began with a new production of La Bohème. This was followed by Lohengrin, conducted by Mark Elder, the former music director of ENO, and resourcefully produced by Tim Albery using all the space of the vast Coliseum stage. Jonathan Miller, returning to the company for the first time for several years, offered an equally effective staging of *Der Rosenkavalier*. Judith Weir's third opera, *Blond Eckbert*, was commissioned by ENO and adapted by the composer from a story by the German Romantic writer Ludwig Tieck. The world première was conducted by Sian Edwards, ENO's music director. Although the work itself, economically composed for four singers, a dog, some puppets and a small, off-stage and pre-recorded chorus, was generally praised, Tom Hopkins' production did not please all the critics.

A new production of *Jenufa*, directed by Lucy Bailey, gave soprano Josephine Barstow, once a fine Jenufa, another magnificent role as the Kostelnička. Possibly the most enjoyable event of ENO's season was the revival of Tim Albery's clever staging of *Peter Grimes*, with a beautifully sung and immensely powerful dramatic performance of the title role by Philip Langridge.

John Blatchley, one of the people responsible for the transformation of Sadler's Wells Opera into English National Opera, died on 1 July 1994 at the age of 72. Originally an actor, he was appointed assistant to Glen Byam Shaw, the director of productions at Sadler's Wells, in 1962. During the next two decades he directed more than 20 operas for the company, ranging from Mozart's *Marriage of Figaro* and *Don Giovanni* to Smetana's *Dalibor* and Janáček's *Makropoulos Case* and *Katya Kabanova*. Together with Byam Shaw, he staged *The Mastersingers of Nuremberg* in 1968 and it was the huge success of this production that encouraged the company to move the following year to the London Coliseum, where the two directors staged their even more popular space-age *Ring* cycle, and later *Tristan and Isolde*.

NORTHERN HIGHLIGHTS

Opera North celebrated its fifteenth anniversary with a particularly interesting programme. It opened the season with *Baa-Baa Black Sheep*, Michael Berkeley's Kipling-based opera. On its actual birthday, 15 November, the company mounted a delightful production of Mozart's youthful masterpiece, *Il rè pastore*. This was followed by Britten's *Gloriana*, an opera about Elizabeth I written in honour of Elizabeth II's coronation and now celebrating its own 40th birthday. It was impressively staged by Phyllida Lloyd, with Josephine Barstow a majestic Gloriana, and it was also given two highly praised performances at Covent Garden. The Opera North season in Leeds ended with another new work, Benedict Mason's football opera, *Playing Away*. It was produced by David Pountney and had been successfully premièred by the company in Munich; it proved equally popular at home. Howard Benton's text concerns a Faustian pact between the Great Referee (the devil) and Terry Bond, star player of United, the British champions beaten in the European Cup Final by Germany. Opera North's performances of *Gloriana* were

dedicated to the memory of Joan Cross, the soprano who created the title role in the opera and who died on 12 December 1993 at the age of 93. During an illustrious career, spent mainly at Sadler's Wells and Covent Garden, Joan Cross created four other roles in Britten's operas: Ellen Orford in *Peter Grimes*, the Female Chorus in *The Rape of Lucretia*, Lady Billows in *Albert Herring* and Mrs Grose in *The Turn of the Screw*. The co-founder of the National School of Opera, she retired from performing in 1955 to devote herself to teaching.

Richard Armstrong made his début as Scottish Opera's music director conducting Verdi's *I due Foscari*. He also conducted new productions of *Katya Kabanova*, *Peter Grimes* (a controversial staging by Joachim Herz) and *Tristan und Isolde*. *Grimes* and *Tristan* were both toured to Lisbon, and the Wagner opera was performed at the official opening of the Edinburgh Festival Theatre. The superb sound made by the Scottish Opera Orchestra in the new auditorium (the old Moss Empire, once a bingo hall) demonstrated its magnificent acoustics.

On a smaller scale, Scottish Opera presented *The Turn of the Screw* at Glasgow Tramway, a space perfectly suited to the ghostly nature of Britten's chamber opera. Scottish Opera Go Round toured Gluck's *Orpheus and Eurydice* in autumn 1993 to town, village and school halls in 15 places in Scotland; during March 1994, the same production, with orchestra, was toured to ten medium-scale venues in Scotland and northern England.

Welsh National Opera also ensured that smaller towns were adequately provided with opera. As part of 'the Cinderella Project', Rossini's *Cenerentola* was toured to 29 medium-scale theatres in Wales and England. Other events in the project were performances by schoolchildren of Peter Maxwell Davies' pantomime opera *Cinderella*; a community musical, *The Splott Cinderella*, by Tim Riley and John Lovat, in the Splott district of Cardiff; and, as the project's chief attraction, Massenet's *Cendrillon*, which was magically staged by Robert Carsen and also formed part of the company's main tour.

Other new productions by WNO included Handel's *Ariodante* and Mozart's *La finta giardiniera*, both of which were very popular, and there were admirable revivals of Peter Stein's award-winning production of *Pelléas et Mélisande* and of *Der Rosenkavalier*. This successful season was the culmination of Matthew Epstein's directorship; he left the company at the end of August 1994 and has been succeeded by Anthony Freud.

OPERA HOUSES

Country-house opera continues to rise in popularity. After five seasons, Garsington has emerged as the most successful of recent additions to the genre. This year there were performances of Rossini's *Il barbiere di Siviglia*, Haydn's *L'incontro improviso* and Strauss's *Capriccio*. Another rising star is Broomhill, on the outskirts of Tunbridge Wells. The original small house was rebuilt and enlarged in the early 19th century and a beautiful little theatre was added at the turn of the century. In 1994 Britten's *A Midsummer Night's Dream* alternated with Shakespeare's play. The opera was directed by Stephen Langridge, while the baritone Benjamin Luxon played Bottom – in the play.

The Edinburgh International Festival has finally acquired a theatre in which large-scale opera can be adequately presented. The festival director, Brian McMaster, was therefore able to present Scottish Opera's new *Fidelio* and Australian Opera's spectacular production of *A Midsummer Night's Dream* at the 1994 Festival. Opera North commemorated the centenary of the death of Emmanuel Chabrier with two of the French composer's delightful comic operas, *L'Etoile* and *Le Roi malgré lui*, at the King's Theatre. The latter opera, whose charming score has always been hampered by an extremely complicated libretto, was receiving its British première in a new version by Jeremy Sams and Michael Wilcox entitled *The Reluctant King*. Jeremy Sams also produced, making his début as an opera director.

Smaller British festivals, unable to afford new productions of their own, have had to make do with borrowed productions. Brighton offered Crystal Clear Opera in *Tosca*, Travelling Opera in *The Magic Flute* and Pimlico Opera in *Cavalleria rusticana* and *Pagliacci*. The Pimlico double bill also turned up at the Buxton Festival, with Opera North's *Il rè pastore*.

Opera Factory, a company of uncompromising standards, opened the season with the world première of Iannis Xenakis' *The Bacchae*. This was not so much an opera as Euripides' tragedy with incidental music, of which only the chorus parts were sung. It did not find favour with South Bank audiences and was a financial disaster. The new production of *The Rake's Progress* was a great deal more successful in box-office terms. It was staged by David Freeman with savage realism and the costumes were stunningly original. Conducting his own orchestra, the Première Ensemble, Mark Wigglesworth treated Stravinsky's score with equal robustness. This production certainly achieved Opera Factory's declared aim of 'divesting opera of its grand and élitist image and re-establishing it as a genuinely popular art form.'

## PRODUCTIONS

In the summaries of company activities shown below, the dates in brackets indicate the year that the current production entered the company's repertory.

ROYAL OPERA
Estab. 1946
Royal Opera House, Covent Garden, London WC2E 9DD

Productions from the repertory: *Madama Butterfly* (1950), *L'Italiana in Algeri* (1988), *Mitridate, rè di Ponto* (1991), *Eugene Onegin* (1993), *Tosca* (1964), *Carmen* (1991), *Elektra* (1990), *Rigoletto* (1988), *Un ballo in maschera* (1975),

*Gawain* (1991), *Le nozze di Figaro* (1987), *Manon* (1987), *La fanciulla del West* (1977).

New productions:
*Die Meistersinger von Nürnberg* (Wagner), 8 October 1993. Conductor, Bernard Haitink; director, Graham Vick; designer, Richard Hudson. Gösta Winbergh (Walther von Stolzing), Nancy Gustafson (Eva), Anne Howells (Magdalene), Deon van der Walt (David), Gwynne Howell (Pogner), Thomas Allen (Beckmesser), John Tomlinson (Hans Sachs), Roderick Earle (Kothner)

*Die Zauberflöte* (Mozart), 15 November 1993. Conductor, Andrew Parrott; director, Martin Duncan; designer, Ken Lee. Kurt Streit (Tamino), Peter Coleman-Wright (Papageno), Sumi Jo (Queen of Night), Robin Leggate (Monostatos), Amanda Roocroft (Pamina), Gordon Hawkins (Speaker), Robert Lloyd (Sarastro)

*Chérubin* (Massenet), 14 February 1994. Conductor, Mario Bernardi; director, Tim Albery; designer, Antony McDonald. Robert Lloyd (Philosopher), Jerry Hadley (Duke), Peter Savidge (Baron), Angela Gheorghiu (Nina), Susan Graham (Chérubin), Jane Leslie-Mackenzie (Countess), Fiona Kimm (Baroness), Maria Bayo (L'Ensoleillad)

*Katya Kabanova* (Janáček), 4 March 1994. Conductor, Bernard Haitink; director, Trevor Nunn; designer, Maria Björnson. Christopher Ventris (Kudrjaš), Gwynne Howell (Dikoj), Keith Olsen (Boris), Eva Randova (Kabanicha), Kim Begley (Tichon), Elena Prokina (Katya), Monica Groop (Varvara)

*Fedora* (Giordano), 9 May 1994. Conductor, Edward Downes; director, Lamberto Puggelli; designer, Luisa Spinatelli. Mirella Freni (Fedora), Roderick Earl (Gretch), Jonathan Summers (De Siriex), Michael Druiett (Cirillo), Judith Howarth (Olga), José Carreras (Loris)

*Mosè in Egitto* (Rossini), 23 May 1994. Conductor, Paolo Olmi; director and designer, Hugo de Ana. Bruce Ford (Osiride), Simone Alaimo (Pharaoh), Ann Murray (Amaltea), Ruggero Raimondi (Moses), Justin Lavender (Aaron), Philip Doghan (Mambre), Anna Caterina Antonacci (Elcia), Patricia Bardon (Amenosi)

*Aida* (Verdi), 16 June 1994. Conductor, Edward Downes; director, Elijah Moshinsky; designer, Michael Yeargan. Cheryl Studer (Aida), Luciana d'Intino (Amneris), Dennis O'Neill (Radames), Alexandru Agache (Amonasro), Robert Lloyd (Ramfis), Mark Beesley (King of Egypt)

ENGLISH NATIONAL OPERA
Estab. 1931
London Coliseum, St Martin's Lane, London WC2N 4ES

Productions from the repertory: *Simon Boccanegra* (1987), *Street Scene* (1989), *The Rape of Lucretia* (1984), *The Barber of Seville* (1987), *Figaro's Wedding* (1991), *Die Fledermaus* (1991), *Xerxes* (1985), *Falstaff* (1989), *The Pearl Fishers* (1987), *Peter Grimes* (1991).

New productions:
*La Bohème* (Puccini), 15 September 1993. Conductor, Sian Edwards; director, Steven Pimlott; designers, Tobias Hoheisel (sets), Ingeborg Bernerth (costumes). Roberta Alexander (Mimi), John Hudson (Rodolfo), Jason Howard (Marcello), Cheryl Barker (Musetta), Christopher Booth-Jones (Schaunard), Andrew Slater (Colline), Donald Adams (Benoit/Alcindoro).

*Lohengrin* (Wagner), 20 November 1993. Conductor, Mark Elder; director, Tim Albery; designers, Hildegard Bechtler (sets), Nicky Gillibrand (costumes). John Keyes (Lohengrin), Linda McLeod (Elsa), Malcolm Donnelly (Telramund), Linda Finnie (Ortrud), Michael Druiett (Henry the Fowler), Christopher Booth-Jones (Herald)

*The Two Widows* (Smetana), 20 December 1993. Conductor, Adam Fischer; director, David Pountney; designer, Mark Thompson. Marie McLaughlin (Karolina), Anne-Marie Owens (Anezka), David Rendall (Ladislav), Donald Adams (Mumial), Sally Harrison (Lidka), Mark Le Brocq (Tonik)

*Der Rosenkavalier* (R. Strauss), 2 February 1994. Conductor, Yakov Kreizberg; director, Jonathan Miller; designers, Peter J. Davidson (sets), Sue Blane (costumes). Sally Burgess (Octavian), Anne Evans (The Marschallin), John Tomlinson (Baron Ochs), Rosemary Joshua (Sophie), Christopher Booth-Jones (Faninal)

*Eugene Onegin* (Tchaikovsky), 31 March 1994. Conductor, Alexander Polianichko; director, Julia Hollander; designers, Fotini Dimou (sets), Tahra Kharibian (costumes). Peter Coleman-Wright (Onegin), Cathryn Pope (Tatyana), Bonaventura Bottone (Lensky), Ethna Robinson (Olga), Patricia Payne (Filippyevna), Richard Van Allan (Prince Gremin)

World première of *Blond Eckbert* (Judith Weir), 20 April 1994. Conductor, Sian Edwards; director, Tim Hopkins; designer, Nigel Lowery. Nicholas Folwell (Eckbert), Anne-Marie Owens (Bertha), Christopher Ventris (Walther/Hugo/Old Woman), Nerys Jones (Bird)

*Così fan tutte* (Mozart), 5 May 1994. Conductor, Nicholas Kok; director, Nicolette Molnar; designer, Jacqueline Gunn. Vivian Tierney (Fiordiligi), Susan Bickley (Dorabella), Neill Archer (Ferrando), Christopher Booth-Jones (Guglielmo), Sally Harrison (Despina), Richard Van Allan (Don Alfonso)

*Jenůfa* (Janáček), 8 June 1994. Conductor, Sian Edwards; producer, Lucy Bailey; designer, Simon Vincenzi. Susan Bullock (Jenufa), Josephine Barstow (Kostelnička), Kim Begley (Laca), David Maxwell Anderson (Steva), Shelagh Squires (Grandmother Burya), Nicholas Folwell (Mayor)

OPERA NORTH
Estab. 1978
Grand Theatre, 46 Briggate, Leeds LS1 6NU

Productions from the repertory: *Baa-Baa Black Sheep* (1993), *The Love for Three Oranges* (1988), *La Bohème* (1993), *Tamburlaine (1985)*, *La traviata* (1985), *L'Etoile* (1991).

New productions:

*Il rè pastore* (Mozart), 15 November 1993. Conductor, Paul Daniel; director, David McVicar; designers, Frank Higgins (sets), David McVicar (costumes). Joan Rodgers (Aminta), Mary Hegarty (Elisa), Patricia Bardon (Tamiri), Martyn Hill (Alessandro), Philip Salmon (Agenore)

*Gloriana* (Britten), 18 December 1993. Conductor, Paul Daniel; director, Phyllida Lloyd; designer, Anthony Ward. Josephine Barstow (Queen Elizabeth I), Susan Chilcott (Lady Penelope Rich), Yvonne Burnett (Countess of Essex), Thomas Randle (Earl of Essex), Paul Nilon (Spirit of the Masque), Karl Morgan Daymond (Mountjoy), Eric Roberts (Cecil), Clive Bayley (Sir Walter Raleigh), David Gwynne (Ballad Singer)

*La rondine* (Puccini), 14 April 1994. Conductor, David Lloyd-Jones; director, Francesca Zambello; designer, Bruno Schwengl. Helen Field (Magda), Anna-Maria Panzarella (Lisette), Tito Beltran (Ruggiero), Peter Bronder (Rambaldo)

*The Magic Flute* (Mozart), 30 April 1994. Conductor, Andrew Parrott; director, Annabel Arden; designer, Rae Smith. Eileen Hulse (Queen of Night), Linda Kitchen (Pamina), Susan Bisatt (Papagena), William Burden (Tamino), Paul Wade (Monostatos), William Dazeley (Papageno), Jonathan Best (Speaker), John Rath (Sarastro)

World première of *Playing Away* (Benedict Mason), 19 May 1994, at Munich. British première, 31 May 1994.

Conductor, Paul Daniel; director, David Pountney; designer, Huntley Muir. Pamela Helen Stephen (Cynthia), Rebecca Caine (LA Lola), Philip Sheffield (Terry Bond), Richard Suart (Stan Stock), Clive Bayley (The Great Referee), Adrian Clarke (Jack Spot), Julie Unwin (Mr Y)

British première of *Le Roi malgré lui* (Chabrier), 1 September 1994 at the Edinburgh Festival. Conductor, Paul Daniel; director, Jeremy Sams; designer, Lez Brotherston. Rosa Mannion (Minka), Juliet Booth (Alexina), Justin Lavender (Comte de Nangis), Jamie MacDougall (Basile), Russell Smythe (Henri de Valois), Geoffrey Dolton (Duc de Fritelli), Nicholas Folwell (Count Laski)

Performances of the repertory were given at the Grand Theatre, Leeds and on tour in Sunderland, Manchester, Nottingham, London (Royal Opera House), Norwich, Hull, Munich, Rotterdam, York and at the Edinburgh Festival.

SCOTTISH OPERA
Estab. 1962
39 Elmbank Crescent, Glasgow G2 4PT

Productions from the repertory: *I due Foscari* (1993), *Tosca* (1980), *Salome* (1990), *The Magic Flute* (1992).

New productions:

*Katya Kabanova* (Janáček), 14 October 1993. Conductor, Richard Armstrong; director, Mark Brickman; designer, David Aylwin. Helen Field (Katya), Elizabeth McCormack (Varvara), Elizabeth Vaughan (Kabanicha), Iain Paton (Kudrjas), Richard Brunner (Boris), Anthony Roden (Tikhon), David Gwynne (Dikoy)

*L'elisir d'amore* (Donizetti), 1 February 1994. Conductor, Marco Guidarini; director, Giles Havergal; designer, Russell Craig. Cheryl Barker (Adina), Lisa Milne (Giannetta), Paul Charles Clarke (Nemorino), Simon Keenlyside (Belcore), Claude Corbeil (Dulcamara)

*The Turn of the Screw* (Britten), 15 February 1994, at Glasgow Tramway. Conductor, Timothy Lole; director, David Leveaux; designer, Vicki Mortimer. Anne Williams-King (Governess), Paula Bishop (Flora), Louise Kennedy-Richardson (Miss Jessel), Menai Davies (Mrs Grose), Philip Salmon (Prologue/Peter Quint), Colin McLean (Miles)

*Peter Grimes* (Britten), 12 April 1994. Conductor, Richard Armstrong; director, Joachim Herz; designers, Reinhard Zimmermann (sets), Eleonore Kleiber (costumes). Rita Cullis (Ellen Orford), Patricia Boyden (Auntie), Catherine Wyn-Rogers (Mrs Sedley), Anthony Rolfe-Johnson (Peter Grimes), Anthony Roden (Bob Boles), Russell Smythe (Balstrode), Richard Halton (Ned Keene), Paul Napier-Burrows (Swallow), David Gwynne (Hobson)

*Tristan und Isolde* (Wagner), 6 May 1994. Conductor, Richard Armstrong; director and designer, Yannis Kokkos. Anne Evans (Isolde), Kathryn Harries (Brangaene), Jeffrey Lawton (Tristan), James Johnson (Kerwenal), Kenneth Cox (King Mark)

*Fidelio* (Beethoven), 25 August 1994. Conductor, Richard Armstrong; director, Tim Albery; designer, Stewart Laing. Elizabeth Whitehouse (Leonore), Ai-Lan Zhu (Marzelline), Michael Pabst (Florestan), Richard Coxon (Jaquino), Matthew Best (Don Pizarro), Carsten Stabell (Don Fernando), Stafford Dean (Rocco)

Performances of the repertory were given at the Theatre Royal, Glasgow, and on tour in Edinburgh, Newcastle, Aberdeen, Lisbon and Inverness.

WELSH NATIONAL OPERA
Estab. 1946
John Street, Cardiff CF1 4SP

Productions from the repertory: *Falstaff* (1988), *Eugene Onegin* (1993), *Pelléas et Mélisande* (1992), *Tosca* (1992), *Der Rosenkavalier* (1990).

New productions:
*Lucia di Lammermoor* (Donizetti), 17 September 1993. Conductor, Julian Smith; director, Rennie Wright; designers, Peter J. Davison, (sets), Jon Morrell (costumes). Janice Watson (Lucia), Martin Thompson (Edgardo), Mark Luther (Arturo), Philip Daggett (Normanno), David Barrell (Enrico), Michael Druiett (Raimondo)
    *Cendrillon* (Massenet), 20 November 1993. Conductor, Patrick Fournillier; director, Robert Carsen; designer, Michael Levine. Rebecca Evans (Cendrillon), Lillian Watson (Fairy Godmother), Pamela Helen Stephen (Prince Charming), Paula Bradbury (Noémie), Valerie Seymour (Dorothee), Felicity Palmer (Mme de la Haltière), Donald Maxwell (Pandolfe)
    *Turandot* (Puccini), 12 February 1994. Conductor, Carlo Rizzi; director, Christopher Alden; designer, Paul Steinberg. Mary Jane Johnson (Turandot), Patricia Racette (Liù), Edmund Barham (Calaf), Ieuan Davies (Emperor Altoum), Mark Cartwright (Pang), Anthony Mee (Pong), David Barrell (Ping), Anthony Stuart Lloyd (Timur)
    *Ariodante* (Handel), 24 February 1994. Conductor, Marc Minkowski; director, David Alden; designer, Ian MacNeil. Alwyn Mellor (Ginevra), Susannah Walters (Dalinda), Della Jones (Ariodante), Felicity Palmer (Polinesso), Gregory Cross (Lurcanio), Umberto Chiummo (King)
    *La finta giardiniera* (Mozart), 13 June 1994. Conductor, Ivor Bolton; director, Tim Albery; designer, Tom Cairns. Joan Rodgers (Sandrina), Janice Watson (Arminda), Cyndie Sieden (Serpetta), Ann Taylor-Morley (Ramiro), Paul Groves (Belfiore), Ryland Davies (The Podestà), Neal Davies (Nardo)
    Performances of the repertory were given at the New Theatre, Cardiff, and on tour in Edinburgh, Plymouth, Southampton, Liverpool, Swansea, Birmingham, Oxford, Bristol and Paris.

GLYNDEBOURNE FESTIVAL OPERA
Estab. 1934
Glyndebourne, Lewes, East Sussex BN8 5UU

The Festival ran from 28 May to 25 August 1994. *The Rake's Progress* (1975) and *Peter Grimes* (1992) were revived.

New productions:
*Le nozze di Figaro* (Mozart), 28 May 1994. Conductor, Bernard Haitink; director, Stephen Medcalf; designer, John Gunter. Alison Hagley (Susanna), Renée Fleming (The Countess), Susan Gritton (Barbarina), Wendy Hillhouse (Marcellina), Marie-Ange Todorovitch (Cherubino), Robert Tear (Don Basilio), Gerald Finley (Figaro), Andreas Schmidt (The Count), Manfred Rohr (Don Bartolo)
    *Eugene Onegin* (Tchaikovsky), 2 June 1994. Conductor, Andrew Davis; director, Graham Vick; designer, Richard Hudson. Elena Prokina (Tatyana), Louise Winter (Olga), Yvonne Minton (Larina), Ludmilla Filatova (Filippyevna), Martin Thompson (Lensky), John Fryatt (M. Triquet), Wojciech Drabowicz (Onegin), Frode Olsen (Prince Gremin)
    *Don Giovanni* (Mozart), 10 July 1994. Conductor, Simon Rattle; director, Deborah Warner; designers, Hildegard Bechtler (sets), Sue Blane (costumes). Hillevi Martinpelto (Donna Anna), Amanda Roocroft (Donna Elvira), Juliane Banse (Zerlina), John Mark Ainsley (Don Ottavio), Gilles Cachemaille (Don Giovanni), Sanford Sylvan (Leporello), Roberto Scaltriti (Masetto), Gudjon Oskarsson (Commemdatore)

GLYNDEBOURNE TOURING OPERA performed the world première of *The Second Mrs Kong* , (Harrison Birtwistle), *Eugene Onegin* and *Il barbiere di Siviglia* at Glyndebourne,

Oxford, Norwich, Woking and Manchester from October to December 1994.

ENGLISH TOURING OPERA
Estab. 1980 as Opera 80

*L'elisir d'amore* and *Così fan tutte* were toured to Bath, Halifax, York, Buxton, Canterbury, Weston-super-Mare, Crewe, Coventry, Warwick, Dartford and High Wycombe from October to December 1993.
    *La Bohème* and *L'elisir d'amore* were toured to London (Sadler's Wells), Swindon, Poole, Brighton, Yeovil, Exeter, Reading, Basildon, Crawley, Lincoln, Cambridge, Southsea, Preston, Ulverston and Carlisle from February to May 1994.

OPERA FACTORY
Estab. 1982
South Bank Centre, London SE1

New productions:
World première of *The Bacchae*, Euripides' tragedy with music for chorus by Iannis Xenakis, 1 September 1993. Conductor, Nicholas Kok; director, David Freeman; designer, David Roger
    *The Rake's Progress* (Stravinsky), 22 April 1994. Conductor, Mark Wigglesworth; director, David Freeman; designer, David Roger. Mary Plazas (Anne), Susannah Self (Baba), Annabelle Cheetham (Mother Goose), Mark Tucker (Tom), Howard Milner (Sellem), Geoffrey Dolton (Shadow), Tom MacDonnell (Trulove)

OPERA NORTHERN IRELAND
Estab. 1985
181A Stranmillis Road, Belfast BT9 5DU

There was no autumn season in the Grand Opera House, Belfast, as the theatre was undergoing repair after bomb damage.
    *La Tragédie de Carmen* (Bizet, adapted by Peter Brook and Marius Constant) was performed in the Klondyke Building, Belfast, on 21 September 1993. Conductor, Kenneth Montgomery; director, Ion Caramitru; designer, Maria Miu. Ruby Philogene (Carmen), Melanie Armitstead (Micaela), James Anderson (Don José), Kimm Julian (Escamillo)
    *The Barber of Seville* (Rossini), 26 February 1994, in the restored Grand Opera House. Conductor, Stephen Barlow; director, Stephen Lawless; designers, Christopher Rasche (sets), Jackie Galloway (costumes). Kate McCarney (Rosina), Pauline Tinsley (Berta), William Burden (Almaviva), Geoffrey Dolton (Figaro), Jonathan Veira (Doctor Bartolo), Roger Bryson (Don Basilio)

# Parliament

The House of Lords returned from the summer recess on 11 October and the House of Commons on 18 October.

On 19 October the Secretary of State for Wales (John Redwood) announced that the Government would be accepting all 43 recommendations of the Caines report into the irregularities in the conduct of the Welsh Development Agency in its internal affairs. On 20 October the Minister for Energy (Tim Eggar) brought the Commons up-to-date on developments in the coal industry, including the announcement in the recess that the Government intended that British Coal's mining assets should be offered for sale in five regional packages; he pointed out that despite the subsidies on offer no significant new market for coal had been found since the January review. In the Lords, the Government was defeated on an amendment to the Railways Bill moved by Lord Peyton of Yeovil (C.) protecting the pension rights of former railway workers. On 21 October the Secretary of State for Health (Virginia Bottomley) made a statement on the reorganization of regional health authorities, which are to be replaced by eight regional offices accountable to the NHS Executive in April 1994 and April 1996. Labour's health spokesperson (David Blunkett) condemned the proposal as 'nepotism and bureaucracy gone rampant'.

During the third reading debate on the Railways Bill in the Lords on 27 October the Minister of State at the Department of Transport (the Earl of Caithness) announced that the Government intended to accept the spirit of Lord Peyton's amendment allowing British Rail (BR) to bid for franchises, which had been passed before the recess, but would impose certain restrictions on BR's ability to bid. On 28 October the Home Secretary (Michael Howard) detailed the Government's response to the Sheehy report on police pay and conditions of service, accepting some but not all of the recommendations. The Shadow Home Secretary (Tony Blair) complained that the statement had not been clear and 'while confusion remains, the undermining of police morale . . . will continue and the fight against crime will be impaired'. In the Commons on 29 October the motion to allow the ordination of women priests was passed by 195 votes to 19.

On 1 November the Prime Minister (John Major) reported back on the outcome of the European Council special meeting in Brussels on 29 October. He also reported on his separate meeting with the Irish Taoiseach (Albert Reynolds) agreeing to work together to reach a settlement in Northern Ireland. The Commons debate on the consideration of Lords' amendments to the Railways Bill led to a row when the Leader of the House (Tony Newton) moved a closure motion and tabled a timetable (guillotine) motion on discussion, claiming that the Opposition

had been deliberately filibustering. Labour's deputy leader (Margaret Beckett) accused the Government of trying to curtail discussion on the 500 or so amendments passed in the Lords. On 2 November the timetable motion was passed and the Government overturned defeats in the Lords on allowing BR to bid openly for any franchise, replacing this with its own amendment allowing BR to bid but only under certain circumstances and at the discretion of the Franchise Director. It also overturned a defeat on pensions. On 3 November during the Lords consideration of Commons amendments to the Railways Bill, the Lords accepted the reasons for overturning their amendment on pensions but disagreed with the reasons for rejecting their amendments on allowing BR to bid for franchises freely and rejected the Commons compromise amendment concerning the role of the Franchise Director. There then followed a debate on whether to adjourn until the next day or to wait for the Commons to consider their rejection of these reasons, and eventually the Lords did adjourn at half-past eleven without the Commons having sent the issue back again. In the Commons business was altered to allow them to discuss the Bill at once and after an ill-tempered debate, during which several of the divisions were interrupted, the Commons overturned the amendment on allowing BR to bid freely by 301 votes to 260 and insisted on their compromise amendment by 301 votes to 258, but this all happened too late to send it back to the Lords that day. On 4 November the Lords finally agreed to accept the Commons amendments.

On 2 November the Lords approved the Priests (Ordination of Women) Measure, rejecting an amendment declining to do so by 135 votes to 25. On 3 November MPs approved, by 279 votes to 38, their own 3.9 per cent pay increase. On 4 November the Secretary of State for the Environment (John Gummer) made a statement on the restructuring of economic aid to the regions in England, designed to give local people more influence over spending; five government departments will pool their separate regional aid programmes in areas such as housing development, education, sport and business development into a single budget worth £1,400 million and new integrated offices would be set up to administer the scheme. Labour's environment spokesperson (Jack Straw) welcomed any improved relationship between central and local government but asked the Government 'to back their rhetoric by giving the necessary resources and powers to councils'.

## QUEEN'S SPEECH 1993

The 1992–3 parliamentary session ended on 5 November and The Queen opened the 1993–4 session of Parliament on 18 November. The speech

outlined 13 bills reflecting a 'back to basics' approach to law and order, education and the economy, and continued the policies of privatization, openness and the reform of local government through:
- new law and order measures to help cut crime and to improve the administration of justice (Criminal Justice Bill and Police and Magistrates' Court Bill)
- improving the quality of teacher-training as part of the drive to raise standards in education (Education Bill)
- measures to improve the competitiveness of the British economy through deregulation (Deregulation and Contracting Out Bill)
- a bill to provide for the privatization of British Coal (Coal Industry Bill)
- a bill to put the Secret Intelligence Service and GCHQ on a statutory basis (Intelligence Services Bill)
- bills to reform the structure of local government in Wales and of local government and water supply in Scotland (Local Government (Wales) Bill and Local Government etc. (Scotland) Bill)

The programme also provided for bills:
- to reform the law on Sunday trading (Sunday Trading Bill)
- to provide for changes to the European Community's system of own resources (European Communities Act (Amendment) Bill)
- to provide for raising the main rate of National Insurance contributions paid by employees (Social Security (Contributions) Bill)
- to prepare for an Environmental Protection Agency (England and Wales) and a Scottish Environmental Agency (Environment Agencies Paving Bill)
- to improve and simplify the law on trade marks (Trade Marks Bill)

John Major called it 'a realistic programme that will meet the concerns of the country. It addresses practical problems in a practical way and is light years away from the policies of the Opposition'. The Leader of the Opposition (John Smith) felt it was 'irrelevant to the real aspirations and needs of our people. It is so removed from those aspirations that, instead of going "back to basics", the Government should go back to the drawing board' and that 'the abject failure to tackle the real problems that affect our nation is reflected all too clearly in the legislative programme that has been laid before us'. The Liberal Democrat leader (Paddy Ashdown) said, 'It is a programme the lightness of which portrays the Government's bankruptcy of ideas and complacency about the state of the country, which they have created . . . It looks as though it has been constructed to save the Prime Minister by June rather than save and improve the country by the end of the century.' After the usual six days of debate, a Labour amendment on the economic content was defeated by 317 votes to 276 and a Liberal Democrat amendment calling for further changes was defeated by 324 votes to 24; the speech itself was approved without division.

On 29 November Sir Patrick Mayhew made a statement on the revelations in the media concerning contact between the IRA leadership and the Government over the years. He confirmed that there had been a secret channel of communication between the two but he denied that any negotiations on peace had taken place and said that such a channel could only function if its secrecy was respected on both sides. During the exchanges the Democratic Unionist MP Ian Paisley accused Sir Patrick of lying and refused to withdraw the remark. As a result the Speaker (Betty Boothroyd) named him and Mr Paisley was suspended.

SUNDAY TRADING BILL

The Sunday Trading Bill contained three options: total deregulation, the Keep Sunday Special (KSS) option restricting opening, and the Shopping Hours Reform Council (SHRC) option to allow big stores to be open for a period of six hours on Sundays. It received its second reading in the Commons on 29 November; this was a debate on the principle rather than on the options themselves, which were the subject of a free vote later. The options were debated in a Committee of the Whole House on 8 December, when Sir Peter Emery (C.) introduced but then withdrew an amendment to allow for total deregulation but in the afternoons only. In the free vote the total deregulation option was defeated by 404 votes to 174, the KSS option was defeated by 304 votes to 286 and the SHRC compromise passed by 333 votes to 258. The second day of Committee of the Whole House was on 9 February when amendments dealing with the rights of shopworkers were discussed. The Government announced that workers would be allowed the right to either opt-in or opt-out of Sunday working without fear of dismissal. The bill received its third reading on 23 February. The bill had an unopposed second reading in the Lords on 8 March. A debate on the options on a free vote was held on 29 March when the total deregulation option was defeated by 303 votes to 46, the KSS option was defeated by 206 votes to 151 and the SHRC compromise was therefore kept as the option in the bill. In committee on 14 April an amendment moved by Lord Hacking (C.) exempting garden centres from the provisions was passed. At report stage on 5 May amendments were passed exempting exhibition stands and farm shops, and amendments relating to the structure of dwellings and defining a shopworker. A Government amendment to ensure that Sunday working was undertaken on a voluntary basis was also passed. The Commons accepted the Lords amendments on 21 June, except the exemption for garden centres and DIY shops, which was overturned.

THE BUDGET

On 30 November the Chancellor (Kenneth Clarke) presented his first Budget, the first in the autumn and the first unified financial statement (budget and autumn statement). The main points were:

Fiscal outlook
- PSBR to be brought back towards balance over the medium term and the public sector to borrow no more than is required to finance its net capital spending
- expenditure for 1994-5 to be £3,800 million lower than forecast, for 1995-6 £2,100 million lower and for 1996-7 £4,400 million lower. Aim to reduce total spending from 45 per cent of GDP in 1993-4 to 41 per cent in 1998-9
- fiscal tightening to be achieved by higher taxes. Taxes as a percentage of GDP to rise from 36.5 per cent in 1993-4 to 39.75 per cent in 1996-7 and 40.75 per cent in 1998-9
- public borrowing to fall from £50,000 million in 1993-4 to £38,000 million in 1994-5 (5.5 per cent of GDP), £6,800 million less than March 1993 forecast. PSBR to fall to 0.25 per cent of GDP by 1998-9. Full-funding rule suspended, allowing Chancellor to sell £7,000 million fewer gilts in 1994-5 than otherwise needed to fund PSBR

Taxation
- personal allowance frozen, 20p lower band of income tax to be extended to £3,000
- married couple's allowance rate of relief to be cut to 15 per cent in April 1995
- rate of mortgage relief to be cut to 15 per cent
- from October 1995 an airport departure tax to be levied of £5 per passenger for flights in UK and EU and £10 to other destinations, and an insurance premium tax of 3 per cent
- duty on tobacco to rise by 7.3 per cent immediately and by 3 per cent a year in real terms in future budgets. Wine up 2p per bottle from 1 January 1994. Vehicle excise duty up £5 from 1 December 1993. Petrol and diesel up by 3p per litre and plans for 5 per cent increases in future
- corporation tax profits limit for small companies raised by 20 per cent. Prompt payment measures to be introduced
- employers' National Insurance contributions to fall to 10.2 per cent, and contributions of employees earning less than £200 a week to be cut by 1 per cent
- simpler regime for personal tax. Immediate rise in VAT registration threshold to £45,000. Audit requirement for companies with a turnover of less than £90,000 scrapped
- increase in capital gains tax relief for entrepreneurs selling business on retirement to first £250,000 of gain and half-exemption on next £75,000
- pensioners to receive 50p a week (70p for couples) to compensate for VAT on fuel bills, on top of normal uprating, in April 1994 and April 1995. Cold weather payments up 25 per cent to £7. All pensioners to qualify for energy efficiency grants

Spending
- public sector pay bill to be frozen at this year's level until 1996-7. Pay increases to be financed by greater efficiency
- new single benefit (job seeker's allowance) to replace unemployment benefit and income support from April 1996, to be means tested after six months
- new childcare allowance of £28 a week from autumn 1994 for those on family credit
- employers not to be reimbursed for statutory sick pay from April 1994, except for companies with NI bills of less than £20,000 a year, who will be reimbursed after four weeks
- new incapacity benefit to replace invalidity benefit from April 1995
- state pension age for women to rise to 65, phased in over ten years
- total standard local authority spending rises to be limited to 2.3 per cent in 1994-5
- Housing Corporation's capital programme cut. Control total for housing to be cut by £900 million in real terms over next three years
- reduced plans for roads programmes to allow some extra resources for British Rail and London Underground investment programmes. Overall spending for next year to be £290 million lower than March estimate. Control total to be reduced by £1,300 million in real terms over next three years
- spending on education to rise by £670 million next year (6.8 per cent). Main rate of student grants to be cut by 10 per cent. New control total to increase by £500 million over next three years
- savings on previous defence plans of £250 million in 1994-5 and £500 million in 1995-6. New control total to be reduced by £2,700 million in real terms by 1996-7
- NHS spending to rise by 1.5 per cent in real terms in 1994-5 with a commitment to containing pay and drugs bills. Control total for 1994-5 of £31,700 million
- new apprenticeship scheme to be introduced. Control total for 1994-5 of £3,800 million
- reordering of Home Office priorities to allow for more prison places and victim support. Control total to be £6,260 million in 1994-5

Forecast
- inflation to rise from annual rate of 3 per cent currently to 3.25 per cent in last quarter of 1994-5, before falling to the lower half of the 0-4 per cent target range
- only slow growth in the economy. GDP set to rise 1.5 per cent this year (up from 1.25 per cent forecast in March). Growth expected to rise to 2.25 per cent next year

Kenneth Clarke said 'my Budget puts Britain firmly on course for a sustained period of rising prosperity and falling unemployment, based on low inflation and healthy public finances. This is a no-nonsense

Budget which deals directly and firmly with the main challenges facing the country today. Above all, it is a Budget of a responsible Government which is determined to bring lasting recovery to Britain.' John Smith accused the Government of mounting 'a continued and vicious attack on the welfare state' to pay for public spending cuts and described it as a Budget 'designed to make the British people pay the price of Conservative economic mismanagement . . . a Budget which was a blatant betrayal of election promises, a Budget which continues to pile taxes on the British people and to reduce the services available to them.' The Liberal Democrat Treasury spokesperson (Alan Beith) said 'the Budget will do nothing to aid recovery. It will hold recovery back, through lack of investment and through the huge pile of new taxes and tax increases that it imposes. Ordinary people will be taxed to the hilt, with none of the investment in education or improvement in public services that might have provided some justification for fair and well-chosen tax increases.' After five days of debate the Budget resolutions were approved by 326 votes to 291, after a row during Prime Minister's questions over why there was to be no specific vote on the question of VAT.

In the Lords on 1 December the Government defeated a motion of no confidence moved by the leader of the Labour peers (Lord Richard), by 282 votes to 95. On 2 December John Gummer made a statement on the local authority finance settlement for England for 1994-5, totalling £42,660 million, an increase of 2.3 per cent. Jack Straw claimed that this was in fact a 1.2 per cent cut in cash terms and would lead to many council tax bills increasing by 7 per cent in the coming year.

EDUCATION BILL

The Government bill to create a new Teacher Training Agency and reform the organization of student unions received an unopposed second reading in the Lords on 7 December. In committee on 14 March the Government's plans to allow schools to run their own teacher-training courses received a major setback when an amendment moved by Lord Judd (Lab.) to ensure that schools would only be able to run teacher-training courses in partnership with and having been credited by higher education institutions, was passed by 123 votes to 121. In committee on 22 March the Government faced another reverse when it withdrew its original clause relating to the public funding of student unions and replaced it with a new clause covering requirements to be observed by student unions receiving funding. During the second reading debate in the Commons on 3 May the Education Secretary (John Patten) said he would seek to reverse in committee the defeat in the Lords that would stop schools providing teacher-training schemes. The bill received its third reading on 7 July and royal assent on 21 July.

During 9 December the Opposition announced that it was withdrawing until further notice from the

established pairing arrangements in protest at the Government's attitude to debating important financial bills in the following week only under a guillotine. This caused problems with the progress of business until 28 April, when the Opposition announced that they were ending their campaign of non co-operation and reinstating pairing arrangements.

The Government bill to put the intelligence services on a statutory basis received an unopposed second reading in the Lords on 9 December. With only minor amendments, it completed its third reading on 14 February. An Opposition motion to have the committee stage of the bill discussed on the floor of the Commons was defeated on 22 February and the bill was given an unopposed second reading. The third reading was passed on 27 April and the bill received royal assent on 26 May.

On 13 December John Major reported on the outcome of the European Council meeting in Brussels on 9-11 December. On 14 December the guillotine motion for the Statutory Sick Pay and Social Security (Contributions) Bills was passed by 307 votes to 266 but due to the breakdown of co-operation in the 'usual channels' which this had caused, the evening was dominated by a lengthy series of votes on uncontentious matters which would usually be nodded through, and culminated in the usual pre-recess all-night sitting on a series of backbench debates being curtailed with a cry of 'I spy strangers' when only two MPs voted and so the business under consideration was suspended.

On 14 December in the Lords the bill to reform the structure of local government in Wales through the abolition of existing county and district councils and their replacement by a single tier of unitary authorities was given an unopposed second reading. In committee on 10 February the Government suffered a defeat when an amendment moved by Lord Swansea (C.) to keep the name Powys instead of replacing it with Mid-Wales was passed. In the Commons the bill was given a second reading on 15 March. A motion was passed on 16 March to allow non-Welsh MPs to sit on the committee considering the bill. The third reading was passed on 16 June and the bill received royal assent on 5 July.

On 15 December John Major outlined the details of the joint declaration on Northern Ireland that he had issued with Albert Reynolds, calling it their 'personal priority both to seek a permanent end to the violence and to establish the basis for a comprehensive and lasting political settlement'. John Smith welcomed the declaration 'with enthusiasm'. John Gummer reported the decision to give the go-ahead for authorization for British Nuclear Fuels to begin the commissioning of THORP and that no public inquiry would be held.

After the row over the guillotine, the Statutory Sick Pay Bill to implement the budget proposal on statutory sick pay was given a second reading on 15 December. All other stages were taken at the same time and it received a procedural third reading. In the Lords a Government amendment was added to the bill on third reading on 8 February to allow compensation for employers during periods when they are faced with an exceptionally high level of sickness. The bill received royal assent on 10 February. The Social Security (Contributions) Bill to increase employees' National Insurance contributions, which was the other bill responsible for the row over the guillotine, was given a second reading on 16 December. All other stages were taken at the same time. The bill was not amended in the Lords and received royal assent on 10 February.

CRIMINAL JUSTICE AND PUBLIC ORDER BILL

Returning from the Christmas recess one day later than the Lords on 11 January, the Commons gave a second reading to the Criminal Justice and Public Order Bill, including measures to curb the right to silence, to curb abuses of bail, to give new powers over DNA testing, to introduce a new sentence of secure training orders for persistent young offenders, and providing new powers to deal with mass trespass and the problems of obscenity and pornography. On 21 February there was a Committee of the Whole House to deal with specific new clauses, on a free vote. A new clause introduced by John Greenway (C.) calling for the death penalty for the murder of a police officer was rejected by 383 votes to 186. On the lowering of the age of consent for homosexuals, a new clause introduced by Edwina Currie (C.) to reduce the age to 16 was defeated by 307 votes to 280 but an amendment introduced by Sir Anthony Durant (C.) to reduce the age to 18 was passed by 427 votes to 162. In the remaining stages debate on 12 April an amendment promoted by David Alton (LD) and supported by over 250 MPs of all parties concerning children and so-called video nasties was withdrawn after Michael Howard promised to table a new Government clause to place a duty on the British Board of Film Classification to take account of both the psychological impact of videos on children and the possibility that they would show inappropriate role models and activities. Penalties would also be increased for those who rented inappropriate films to under-age customers. The bill was given a third reading on 13 April. After an unopposed second reading in the Lords on 25 April, the bill progressed through committee; on 16 May an amendment moved by Baroness Faithfull (C.) to delete clause 1 concerning the setting-up of secure training units for children between the ages of 12 and 14 was defeated by 38 votes; on 23 May an amendment moved by Viscount Runciman (Ind.) to delete the clause abolishing the right to silence was defeated by 58 votes; on 14 June the Lords agreed the new clauses on penalties for the sale and distribution of video recordings; on 16 June the Government was defeated when an amendment moved by Lord Ackner (Ind.) to reinstate the old Criminal Injuries Compensation Scheme was passed by 131 votes to 113; on 20 June in the vote on lowering the age of consent for homosexuals the Lords rejected

the age of 16 by 245 votes to 71 and agreed with the Commons on the age of 18 by 176 votes to 113. On report on 5 July the Government was twice defeated on amendments to clause 1 moved by Lord Carr of Hadley (C.): the first, designed to give courts extra powers to help in sentencing young offenders, was passed by 170 votes to 139 and the second, designed to leave the decision on such matters to the court rather than officials, by 147 votes to 128. On 11 July the Government was defeated again when an amendment moved by Lord Stanley of Alderley (C.) designed to prevent genuine gypsies from being moved on from one legal site to another was passed. An amendment from Lord Ponsonby of Shulbrede (Lab.) to make it a crime, with a maximum sentence of life imprisonment, for a man to rape another man was accepted by the Government. On 12 July a new clause introduced by Lord Brightman (C.) concerning the offence of selling confidential financial information was approved against the wishes of the Government, which preferred its own amendment. The bill had its third reading in the Lords on 19 July.

The Non-Domestic Rating Bill to provide continuing help to businesses by phasing in changes in rates bills following the 1990 revaluation and to make it easier for such arrangements to be introduced if necessary following the 1995 revaluation, was given a second reading on 12 January. Plans to complete all its stages in one day were thwarted by an Opposition filibuster and a guillotine motion was introduced so the third reading was delayed by a day. No amendments were passed in the Lords and the bill received royal assent on 24 February.

On 17 January the Local Government etc. (Scotland) Bill, to introduce a single tier of authorities and to reform the water authorities in Scotland, was given a second reading in the Commons. The committee considering the bill sat for 39 sessions and its first session was disrupted by the leader of the Scottish National Party (Alex Salmond) so that the chairman of the committee (Michael Martin) had to return to the Commons on 1 February to propose a motion to give him powers to force Mr Salmond to withdraw; this was passed by 491 votes to 10. The bill was given a third reading on 24 May. After an unopposed second reading in the Lords on 9 June, it completed its committee stage on 21 July.

On 18 January the Coal Industry Bill, to allow for the privatization of the coal industry, was given a second reading in the Commons. The third reading was passed on 23 March. After an unopposed second reading in the Lords on 11 April, the Government was defeated on third reading on 21 June when an amendment moved by Lord Northbourne (Ind.) to clause 12 on restructuring schemes in relation to property was passed by 127 votes to 121, and an amendment moved by Lord Stanley of Alderley to schedule 8 on amendments of the Opencast Coal Act 1958 was passed by 83 votes to 72. The Government also accepted an amendment from Baroness Lockwood (Lab.) to clause 22 on designated mining museums. When the bill was returned to the Commons on 28 June the Government overturned these three Lords amendments, replacing them with similar ones of its own. The bill received royal assent on 5 July.

### POLICE AND MAGISTRATES' COURTS BILL

In the Lords on 18 January the Police and Magistrates' Courts Bill to reform the structure of the police service in England and Wales and to strengthen and modernize the administration of magistrates' courts received an unopposed second reading. This was despite the fact that 22 of the first 23 speakers in the debate spoke against the measure, including Viscount Whitelaw, a former Conservative Home Secretary. On the first day of committee (15 February) Earl Ferrers announced that in return for the Opposition not pressing its amendments on the composition of police authorities, the Government would discuss the issue with interested parties and consider modifying its own proposals on report. He also published an amendment increasing the number of members of police authorities whilst maintaining a 50/50 split between those elected and those appointed, with no more than one-third being independent appointments. The Government was defeated in committee on 21 February when an amendment moved by an adviser to the Police Federation, Lord Bethell (C.), to allow a police officer charged with a disciplinary offence the right to legal representation was passed by 107 votes to 100. As promised the Government withdrew clauses 39 and 45 on police authorities. On 1 March Earl Ferrers announced that the Government would be withdrawing its plans to deprive local councillors of their overall majority on police authorities in England and Wales and they would be allowed a majority of one seat on the new authorities. There would also be a complex new procedure of selection. The Government was defeated on third reading on 24 March when an amendment moved by Baroness Hilton of Eggardon (Lab.) rejecting the proposal to reduce the number of grades in the police force was passed by 133 votes to 107. On second reading in the Commons on 26 April, which was passed by 263 votes to 129, Michael Howard confirmed that he would seek to reverse in committee amendments passed in the Lords on police discipline but that he did accept the amendments on police authorities. The bill had its third reading on 5 July and received royal assent on 21 July.

The Social Security (Incapacity for Work) Bill to introduce a new incapacity benefit to replace sickness benefit and invalidity benefit from April 1995, with new, more objective tests for incapacity was given a second reading in the Commons on 24 January and had its third reading on 8 March. After an unopposed second reading in the Lords on 21 March, the Government was defeated on report on 10 May when an amendment moved by Lord Swinfen (C.) rejecting the Government's plans to delay by 24 weeks the payment of extra incapacity benefits for dependent

children was passed. The Government also accepted an amendment moved by Lord Carter (Lab.) on the disability working allowance, and was defeated on third reading on 19 May when an amendment from Lord Swinfen to restore benefit entitlement to the long-term rate at 196 days for people receiving disability living allowance higher rate care component was passed. In the Commons on 21 June all these amendments were agreed and the bill received royal assent on 5 July.

The Finance Bill to enact the provisions of the Budget was given a second reading in the Commons on 25 January, after an Opposition amendment refusing a second reading unless the VAT provisions of the Finance Act 1993 were repealed was defeated by 17 votes. In Committee of the Whole House on 31 January and 1 February, progress was so slow, with only one clause (air passenger duty) being approved on the first day, that the Government introduced a guillotine motion allowing only 16 days for discussion in committee, which was passed by 315 votes to 284. During the remaining stages debate on 19 and 20 April, the Government added new clauses covering PAYE for expatriates and amendments to the clauses covering insurance premium tax, and the bill was given a third reading by 305 votes to 260. An attempt to delay discussion of the bill in the Lords by a week due to the short notice given for the debate was withdrawn and after a day of debate in the Lords on 29 April, when the arguments over the amount of notice continued, the bill received royal assent on 3 May.

On 2 February there was a series of votes on Statutory Instruments on double taxation relief which had already been debated and would normally have been nodded through; this reflected the withdrawal of co-operation in the 'usual channels'. On 7 February the Minister of State at the Foreign and Commonwealth Office (Alistair Goodlad) responded to a private notice question from Labour's Foreign Affairs spokesperson (Dr Jack Cunningham) on the murder of nearly 70 civilians in a market place in Sarajevo by a mortar attack. Discussions had been held with NATO allies and a meeting of EU foreign ministers was currently discussing a suitable response.

The Deregulation and Contracting Out Bill to remove excessive regulation of business was given a second reading in the Commons on 8 February, after a Liberal Democrat amendment expressing concern at the watering-down of parliamentary accountability had been defeated by 37 votes. During the remaining stages debate on 10 May the chairman of the All-Party Racing and Bloodstock Group (James Paice) introduced a new clause to allow for betting on Sundays (and thus make Sunday racing a reality), which was passed on a free vote by 290 votes to 189. Sir Michael Neubert (C.) moved an amendment on the approval of certain markets, opposing the bill's original proposals to abolish medieval restrictions on markets, which caused the Government to announce that it would be rethinking this part of the bill and would bring forward new proposals in the Lords. The bill was given a third reading on 25 May. After an unopposed second reading in the Lords on 6 June, the new clauses on Sunday betting were approved in committee on 29 June. The Government was defeated in committee on 6 July when an amendment moved by the Labour Transport spokesperson (Lord Clinton-Davis), requiring adverse environmental effects to be taken into consideration in the granting of various licences, was approved by 89 votes to 51. The committee stage was completed on 21 July.

On 10 February the Foreign Secretary (Douglas Hurd) reported on NATO's decision to give the Bosnian Serb gunmen surrounding Sarajevo a ten-day ultimatum to withdraw or face air strikes. Dr Jack Cunningham hoped that the Serbs would heed the warning but 'if they do not, we should not flinch from the decision to use [air power]'.

On 16 February Tim Sainsbury responded to a private notice question from Labour's Trade and Industry spokesperson (Robin Cook) on the decision of the European Commission to impose fines of more than 100 million ECUs on 16 steel companies from six Community and three Scandinavian countries, which for British Steel meant a fine of £24 million, saying that it was entirely a matter for the Commission and the company. Robin Cook said 'the survival of the British steel industry is not something else that the Government can add to the long list of things for which they will take no responsibility'. On 25 February Alistair Goodlad made a statement on the recently-announced decision by the Malaysian Government to ban new contracts with British companies bidding for Government business in Malaysia, following what they saw as unfair reporting by the British press of affairs relating to Malaysia; Mr Goodlad expressed the hope that relations would be restored as soon as possible.

On 1 March Douglas Hurd made a statement on the shooting-down of four Serbian planes in Bosnia by NATO aircraft, and the concerted international effort being made to extend the progress in Bosnia and make the humanitarian effort more effective. On 9 March the draft Prevention of Terrorism (Temporary Provisions) Act 1989 (Continuance) Order 1994, the annual order extending the emergency powers in Northern Ireland, was approved by 328 votes to 242. A motion to approve the setting up of a Northern Ireland select committee was passed by 324 votes to 221, but an Opposition amendment to limit its powers was rejected by 58 votes. On 10 March the Defence Secretary (Malcolm Rifkind) announced that a further 900 British troops would be sent to Bosnia. On 11 March the Civil Rights (Disabled Persons) Bill, a Private Member's Bill sponsored by Roger Berry (Lab.) to secure a statutory right to protection against discrimination was given an unopposed second reading although the Minister for the Disabled (Nicholas Scott), while endorsing the sentiment of the bill, expressed some reservations

and wished to wait for the committee for further discussion.

On 14 March the President of the Board of Trade (Michael Heseltine), in response to a recent judgment of the Court of Appeal which had instructed receivers to wind-up businesses within two weeks, said that the Government would introduce legislation to allow receivers as long as necessary to save a bankrupt company, rather than winding it up so quickly. The Insolvency (No 2) Bill completed all its Commons' stages on 21 March. It was not amended in the Lords and received royal assent on 24 March. Following a statement by Douglas Hurd on the issue on 28 March, John Major made a statement the next day on proposals to adjust qualified majority voting (QMV) when more countries join the European Union. Although expressing regret that the compromise agreement had not gone far enough, he explained that the British Government had not accepted an unqualified extension of the blocking majority to 27. The European Council would be under a legal obligation to seek agreement on the basis of a minority of at least 23 votes and 'a reasonable amount of time' would have to be allowed to sort out any differences; there was no time limit for the fulfilment of this obligation. The binding nature of this obligation was clearly understood by the UK's European partners. John Smith treated the statement with derision and claimed it was a complete climb-down by the Government. One Conservative back-bencher (Tony Marlow) called upon the Prime Minister to resign.

Returning from the Easter recess on 12 April, Douglas Hurd made a statement in response to a private notice question from Dr Jack Cunningham about the situation in the UN safe haven of Gorazde, explaining that the request for air strikes called by the UN leader on the ground in support of UN observers had not been referred to individual countries for approval as approval in principle had already been given under agreed UN and NATO procedures. During the week beginning 18 April there were repeated arguments in the Commons over the suitability of the celebrations planned to commemorate the 50th anniversary of D-Day, originally raised by Peter Mandelson (Lab.) during questions to the National Heritage Secretary (Peter Brooke). On 18 April Malcolm Rifkind reported on events in Gorazde, including the death of a British soldier there and one in Sarajevo, and the shooting-down of a RN Sea Harrier.

CIVIL RIGHTS ROW

On 29 April a motion by Sir John Hannam (C.) calling for sufficient time to be allowed for the completion of the progress of the Civil Rights (Disabled Persons) Bill, which had not been amended in committee and had all-party support, was passed despite the opposition of the Government but this did not have the authority to force the extra time for debate. On 6 May the Civil Rights (Disabled Persons)

Bill returned to the Commons for its remaining stages. There was a major row when Opposition MPs accused the Government of having drafted many of the numerous amendments that had been tabled at this late stage by Conservative backbenchers, in particular Lady Olga Maitland, and which caused the bill to run out of time and to be talked out. Both Nicholas Scott and the MPs concerned denied that the Department of Social Security had drafted the amendments. However, on 10 May Nicholas Scott made a personal statement to the Commons regretting that the explanation he had given during the debate about his department's role in helping to draft backbench amendments had been misleading and apologizing if he had given the wrong impression; whilst his department had not actually drafted the backbench amendments, the Parliamentary Counsel's Office had. This did little to defuse the row and even when the Speaker ruled on 11 May that she would be taking no further action in the case since the Minister had apologized, many Opposition backbenchers were unhappy as they felt this gave *carte blanche* to ministers to lie to the Commons. Following the death of John Smith on 12 May, business in both Houses was cancelled for the day as a mark of respect and they met only briefly to allow tributes to be paid.

On 19 May Michael Heseltine announced the Government's intention to publish a Green Paper on the future of the Post Office; he announced that there would be no change to Post Office Counters and that The Queen had agreed that Royal Mail would be permitted to use a depiction of her head on postage stamps and to be registered as Royal Mail PLC even if it were privatized. Robin Cook wondered why the Government could not accept that 'the best place for the Post Office is in the public sector . . . If they cannot accept that, I warn them that we shall lead a national campaign to demand that the Post Office stays where it belongs – owned by the public, in the public sector and providing a service to the public.'

Because of the simmering row over the Civil Rights (Disabled Persons) Bill, business on 20 May was continually disrupted, with discussion on four Private Members' Bills being curtailed by various procedural devices. On 24 May in the Lords, Lord Ashley of Stoke (Lab.) introduced the Civil Rights (Disabled Persons) (No. 2) Bill, with exactly the same provisions as the bill caught up in the Commons, so that if that bill ever progressed in the Commons, the measure would already have begun its progress in the Lords. In the Commons the Speaker made a statement rebuking Lady Olga Maitland (C.) for misleading the House during the debate on the Civil Rights (Disabled Persons) Bill on 9 May, saying that her conduct fell below the standards the House was entitled to expect from its members; Lady Olga apologized unreservedly. On 17 June an attempt by Dennis Skinner (Lab.) to disrupt business by calling 'I spy strangers' in the hope of forcing further debate on the Civil Rights (Disabled Persons) Bill was defeated when

sufficient MPs were available to vote the motion down.

On 27 June John Major reported back on the outcome of the European Council meeting in Corfu on 24-25 June. On the issue of the next President of the Commission, he had used the UK veto against the candidacy of the Belgian Prime Minister Jean Luc Dehaene not because of any personal criticism, but because the UK did not consider him a suitable candidate and were concerned by the way his candidacy had been handled by the French and the Germans. The acting Labour leader Margaret Beckett, whilst welcoming the positive achievements of the summit, felt that the weekend's events 'show not that he is a Prime Minister who is strong but that he is weak, a prisoner of his Euro-sceptics, and that yet again it is the people of this country who will pay the price for his failure'.

On 12 July the Speaker announced that she would allow a motion on parliamentary privilege to be debated the next day, concerning an article in the *Sunday Times* on 10 July alleging that two Conservative MPs, Graham Riddick and David Treddinick, had accepted money for tabling parliamentary questions. The debate agreed to refer the matter to the Committee of Privileges to investigate the whole affair. In a debate on members' interests on 13 July there was a row over the incomplete disclosure of the details of Lloyd's membership by certain MPs, but a motion to approve proposals concerning registration was approved. On 15 July Nicholas Scott published a consultation document he had promised on measures to tackle discrimination against disabled people in five key areas affecting their lives.

On 18 July the Minister for Housing (Sir George Young) made a statement on the Government's proposals for reform of the homelessness legislation in England and Wales, tightening the rules by which the homeless could apply for local authority housing; in particular, social groups such as single mothers would no longer be given priority treatment. People would have to be 'unintentionally homeless'. Labour's housing spokesperson (John Battle) called it 'an unworthy, mean-spirited statement . . . [it] represents an attack on the basic rights to housing provision that not even Mrs Thatcher was prepared to contemplate . . . The policies will only add to human misery and make the crisis worse.' During the debate to approve the membership of the Committee of Privileges to consider the 'money for questions' affair on 20 July, various Labour backbenchers objected to the inclusion of MPs who had declared outside interests. One Labour MP, Chris Mullin, moved an amendment to remove Sir Marcus Fox (C.) from the committee but this was defeated by 115 votes. The membership of the committee was approved by 151 votes to 23.

After the Government reshuffle on 20 July, the House of Commons rose for the summer recess on 21 July and the House of Lords on 26 July.

# PUBLIC ACTS OF PARLIAMENT

This list is of those Public Acts which received the royal assent after August 1993. The date stated after each Act is the date on which it came into operation; c. indicates the chapter number of each Act

*Welsh Language Act 1993*, c. 38, 21 December 1993, except ss. 30, 31 and 352 on a day or days to be appointed
Brings in provisions to enable use to be made of the Welsh language on an equal footing with English, particularly in the conduct of public business and administration of justice in Wales; and establishes the Welsh Language Board to promote and facilitate the use of the Welsh language

*National Lottery Act 1993*, c. 39, day or days to be appointed
Enables lotteries to be authorized and promoted as part of a National Lottery, regulates their running and controls the distribution of the net proceeds of such schemes

*Noise and Statutory Nuisance Act 1993*, c. 40, various dates, some to be appointed
Makes provision for the effecting of greater control over noise and statutory nuisance; makes noise in the streets a statutory nuisance; makes provisions with regard to the operation of loudspeakers and burglar alarms; enables local authorities to charge expenses incurred in abating or preventing the recurrence of a statutory nuisance

*European Parliamentary Elections Act 1993*, c. 41, various dates
Increases the UK representatives to the European Parliament to 87

*Cardiff Bay Barrage Act 1993*, c. 42, 5 November 1993
Provides for the construction of a barrage across the mouth of Cardiff Bay and authorizes the undertaking of related works and the acquisition and use of land for such purposes; and for connected purposes, including compensation for property damage resulting from the alteration of ground water levels

*Railways Act 1993*, c. 43, various dates, some to be appointed
Provides for the appointment and functions of a Rail Regulator and a Director of Passenger Rail Franchising and makes new provisions with respect to the provision of railway services and the person by whom they are to be provided; and for purposes connected with the railways, inland waterways, tramways and transport police

*Crofters (Scotland) Act 1993*, c. 44, various dates
Consolidates certain enactments relating to crofting, giving effect to the recommendations of the Scottish Law Commission

*Scottish Land Court Act 1993*, c. 45, 5 January 1994
Consolidates various enactments relating to the constitution and proceedings of the Scottish Land Court

*Health Service Commissioners Act 1993*, c. 46, 5 February 1994
Consolidates various enactments relating to the Health Service Commissioners for England, Wales and Scotland, giving effect to the recommendations of the Law Commission and the Scottish Law Commission

*Probation Service Act 1993*, c. 47, 5 February 1994
Consolidates various enactments relating to the probation service and its functions, giving effect to recommendations of the Law Commission

*Pension Schemes Act 1993*, c. 48, day or days to be appointed
Consolidates various enactments relating to pension schemes, giving effect to recommendations of the Law Commission and the Scottish Law Commission

*Pension Schemes (Northern Ireland) Act 1993*, c. 49, day or days to be appointed
Consolidates for Northern Ireland various enactments relating to pension schemes with corrections and minor amendments

*Statute Law (Repeals) Act 1993*, c. 50, various dates, one to be appointed
Provides for the repeals of various enactments which are no longer of practical utility, giving effect to the recommendations of the Law Commission and the Scottish Law Commission

*European Economic Area Act 1993*, c. 51, 5 November 1993
Makes provision in relation to the EEA as established under the 1992 Oporto agreement (2 May 1992) as amended by the 1993 Brussels protocol (17 March 1993)

*Consolidated Fund (No. 3) Act 1993*, c. 52, 17 December 1993
Applies certain sums out of the Consolidated Fund to the service of the years ending 31 March 1994 and 1995

*Social Security (Contributions) Act 1994*, c. 1, 10 February 1994
Increases primary class 1 national insurance contributions; amends the provisions relating to

national health service allocation of those contributions, and clarifies what reliefs should be considered when assessing class 4 contributions

*Statutory Sick Pay Act 1994*, c. 2, various dates
Removes the right of employers, other than small employers, to recover sums paid by them by way of statutory sick pay; gives wider powers to the Secretary of State as to the recovery of those sums

*Non-Domestic Rating Act 1994*, c. 3, 24 February 1994
Makes provision for limiting the increase in non-domestic rates for 1994

*Consolidated Fund Act 1994*, c. 4, 24 March 1994
Applies certain sums out of the Consolidated Fund to the service of the years ending 31 March 1993 and 1994

*New Towns (Amendment) Act 1994*, c. 5, 24 March 1994
Amends Schedule 9 of the 1981 Act in relation to the delegation of powers

*Mental Health (Amendment) Act 1994*, c. 6, 14 April 1994
Amends the definition of managers in section 145(1) of the 1983 Act

*Insolvency Act 1994*, c. 7, 24 March 1994
Makes various amendments to the 1986 Act in relation to contracts of employment adopted by administrators, administrative receivers and certain other receivers

*Transport Police (Jurisdiction) Act 1994*, c. 8, 1 April 1994
Makes various amendments with respect to the jurisdiction of the transport police

*Finance Act 1994*, c. 9, 3 May 1994
Grants certain duties, alters others and amends the law relating to the National Debt and the Public Revenue; e.g. extends the jurisdiction of (and changes the name of) the VAT tribunal to embrace excise appeals; introduces the legislation necessary for current year basis of assessment for Schedule D (traders and professionals) taxpayers and for self-assessment

*Race Relations (Remedies) Act 1994*, c. 10, 3 July 1994
Amends the 1976 Act by removing the limit in s. 56(2) on the amount of compensation which may be awarded and provides for interest to be awarded

*Road Traffic Regulation (Special Events) Act 1994*, c. 11, 3 May 1994
Provides for the amendment of the 1984 Act in order to allow the restriction or regulation of traffic on roads in connection with sporting or social events held on roads

*Insolvency (No. 2) Act 1994*, c. 12, 26 July 1994
Amends the law relating to company insolvency and winding-up and personal insolvency and

bankruptcy so far as it concerns the adjustment of certain transactions relating to acquisitions made in good faith and for value

*Intelligence Services Act 1994*, c. 13, day or days to be appointed
Makes various provisions about the secret intelligence services and GCHQ, including the establishment of a commissioner and a tribunal for the investigation of complaints and the establishment of an Intelligence and Security Committee to oversee the services and GCHQ

*Parliamentary Commissioner Act 1994*, c. 14, 5 September 1994
Extends the jurisdiction of the Commissioner in terms of its investigative powers to include actions taken in exercise of administrative functions by the administrative staff of certain tribunals, such as child support and social security appeal tribunals

*Antarctic Act 1994*, c. 15, day or days to be appointed
Makes provision for giving effect to the Protocol on Environmental Protection to the Antarctic Treaty (Madrid, 4 October 1991); makes provisions consequential on the Convention on the Conservation of Antarctic Marine Living Resources (Canberra, 20 May 1980). The Act restricts entering and remaining in the Antarctic and provides for the protection of minerals, flora, fauna and special areas

*State Hospitals (Scotland) Act 1994*, c. 16, day to be appointed
Amends the National Health (Scotland) Act 1978 and the Mental Health (Scotland) Act 1984 in relation to the provision, control and management of state hospitals in Scotland

*Chiropractors Act 1994*, c. 17, various dates, one to be appointed
Establishes the General Chiropractic Council and provides for the regulation of the chiropractic profession generally, including registration, and monitoring of professional conduct and education; amends the Osteopaths Act 1993

*Social Security (Incapacity for Work) Act 1994*, c. 18, various dates, some to be appointed
Replaces sickness benefit and invalidity benefit with incapacity benefit; and for connected purposes

*Local Government (Wales) Act 1994*, c. 19, various dates, some to be appointed
Makes various provisions relating to the structure and function of local government in Wales; designates new local government areas and facilitates new electoral arrangements; and for connected purposes

*Sunday Trading Act 1994*, c. 20, various dates, one to be appointed
Provides for the reform of the law relating to Sunday trading, amending previous restrictions on that activity; provides for the protection of shop workers

*Coal Industry Act 1994*, c. 21, various dates, some to be appointed
Provides for the establishment of the Coal Authority and the restructuring of the coal industry; makes arrangements for the transfer of the property rights and liabilities of the British Coal Corporation and its subsidiaries to other bodies and for the dissolution of the Corporation; makes appropriate amendments to the Opencast Coal Act 1958 and the Coal Mining Subsidence Act 1991; and for connected purposes

*Vehicle Excise and Registration Act 1994*, c. 22, 1 September 1994
Consolidates the enactments relating to vehicle excise duty and vehicle registration

*Value Added Tax Act 1994*, c. 23, 1 September 1994
Consolidates the enactments relating to VAT, including those relating to VAT tribunals

*Appropriation Act 1994*, c. 24, 24 July 1994
Applies a sum out of the Consolidated Fund to the service of the year ending 31 March 1995; appropriates the supplies granted in this session of Parliament; repeals certain Consolidated Fund and Appropriation Acts

*Land Drainage Act 1994*, c. 25, 21 September 1994
Amends the 1991 Act in relation to the functions of internal drainage boards and local authorities

*Trade Marks Act 1994*, c. 26, day or days to be appointed
Makes new provision for registered trade marks, implementing Directive 89/104/EEC of 21 December 1988 to approximate the laws of the member states regulating trade marks; makes provision in connection with Ref. (EC) 40/94 of 20 December 1993 on the EC trade mark; gives effect to the Madrid Protocol relating to the International Registration of Marks of 27 June 1989 and to certain provisions of the Paris Convention for the Protection of Industrial Property of 20 March 1883; and for connected purposes

*Inshore Fishing (Scotland) Act 1994*, c. 27, day to be appointed
Amends the 1984 Act to make provision for the control of fishing in Scottish inshore waters by vehicles or equipment

*Merchant Shipping (Salvage and Pollution) Act 1994*, c. 28, day or days to be appointed
Makes further provision in relation to marine salvage and marine pollution and the discharge of functions of the Secretary of State in connection therewith; and for connected purposes

*Police and Magistrates' Courts Act 1994*, c. 29, various dates, some to be appointed
Makes provision about police areas, police forces and police authorities; makes provision for England and Wales about magistrates' courts committees, justices' clerks and administrative and financial arrangements for magistrates' courts; and for connected purposes

*Education Act 1994*, c. 30, day or days to be appointed
Makes provision about teacher training, e.g. setting up and funding the Teacher Training Agency, and related matters and with respect to the conduct of students' unions; and for connected purposes

*Firearms (Amendment) Act 1994*, c. 31, 21 September 1994
Creates a new offence of possessing a firearm or imitation firearm with intent to cause fear of violence; applies certain provisions of the 1968 Act to imitation firearms; and for connected purposes

## WHITE PAPERS, REPORTS, ETC.

*Adoption - The Future* was presented to Parliament by the Secretary of State for Health (Virginia Bottomley) on 3 November 1993. Its main recommendations included:
- the wishes of the child to be given greater weight; children aged 12 or over to agree before an adoption order is made
- ethnic origin and culture to be considered only as part of an overall judgment
- married couples to continue to be favoured over single people as adoptive parents
- the present age limit for prospective parents to be raised to include people in their forties
- children to have greater access to information about their natural parents, if the natural parents agree

- more independent members to sit on adoption panels
- step-parent adoption to be simplified
- local authorities to have a statutory duty to process the applications of parents seeking to adopt a child from overseas; new legal protections against abuses of overseas adoption to be introduced; bringing a child to Britain for adoption without authorization to become a criminal offence

*Equality in State Pension Age* was presented to Parliament by the Secretary of State for Social Security (Peter Lilley) on 1 December 1993. It proposed:
- the pension age for women to be raised from 60 to 65 by the year 2020

- the new pension age to be phased in from 2010 and to apply to all women born on or after 6 March 1955
- Family Credit and Disability Working Allowance to be treated as earnings for the purpose of calculating state pension entitlements
- Home Responsibilities Protection, which reduces the required contributory period to qualify for the basic state pension to 20 years for those who stop working for significant periods to look after children or elderly or disabled relatives, to be extended to cover the State Earnings Related Pension Scheme
- the treatment of married couple's pension entitlements to be equalized to allow older spouses of either sex to be able on reaching 65 to claim an increase in pension for a dependent spouse below pensionable age
- the limit for deferral of the pension age to be abolished and the enhancement for each deferred year to be increased from 7.5 per cent to 10 per cent from 2010

*Compensating Victims of Violent Crime: Changes to the Criminal Injuries Compensation Scheme* was presented to Parliament by the Home Secretary (Michael Howard) on 15 December 1993. The proposals, which would speed up payment of awards but in many cases lead to lower payments, included:
- the Criminal Injuries Compensation Board to be replaced by a new Criminal Injuries Compensation Authority
- payments to be made according to a 25-point fixed scale of particular injuries, ranging from £1,000 for moderate shock, a broken nose or a chipped tooth, to £250,000 for severe brain damage or total paralysis
- pain, suffering, medical expenses and loss of earnings no longer to be taken into account
- the time allowed for making a compensation application to be cut from three years to one year

On 25 January 1994 the Government published four documents outlining its plans in response to the main agreements of the United Nations Conference on Environment and Development (the 'Earth Summit') held in Rio de Janeiro in 1992.

*Sustainable Development - The UK Strategy* was published in response to Agenda 21 of the Rio summit, which stated that a comprehensive programme of action is needed throughout the world to achieve a more sustainable pattern of development for the next century. The document looks at the current state of the UK environment and discusses what action should be taken by central and local government, business and industry, voluntary bodies and individuals. The document states that government policies will be aimed at developing instruments which make markets work for the environment and channel development down sustainable paths while reducing unnecessary and over-detailed regulation, although regulation will continue to play an important

role in protecting the environment. The Government also commits itself to establishing Environment Agencies for England and Wales and for Scotland. Commitments include: to integrate environmental considerations into EC agricultural and fisheries policies; to promote environmentally-friendly farming, the conservation of wildlife and habitats, and the protection and restoration of threatened landscapes; to reduce pollution from agricultural inputs and waste; to achieve greater energy efficiency; to improve the environmental performance of transport; to establish good environmental practice by business; to raise consumer awareness; to apply the 'polluter pays' principle.

*Biodiversity - The UK Action Plan* was published in response to the Rio summit's Biodiversity Convention on the protection of the diversity of species and habitats in the world. The document confirms that the Government intends to ratify the Convention given satisfactory progress towards securing safeguards regarding its financial provisions. It reviews the current level of biodiversity and existing conservation programmes in the UK. It commits the Government to conserve and where possible enhance the overall populations and natural ranges of native, internationally-important and threatened species, habitats and ecosystems in the UK; the quality and range of wildlife habitats and ecosystems; species, habitats and ecosystems which are characteristic of local areas; and the biodiversity of natural and semi-natural habitats. Specific commitments include implementing by 2004 the EC Habitats and Species Directive.

*Climate Change - The UK Programme* was published in response to the Rio summit's Climate Change Convention, which established a framework for action to reduce the risks of global warming by limiting the emission of so-called 'greenhouse gases'. It required developed countries to take measures to reduce emissions of greenhouse gases to 1990 levels by the year 2000, and to provide assistance to developing countries. The Convention came into force on 21 March 1994.

For carbon dioxide, the programme is designed to achieve savings equivalent to 10 million tonnes of carbon (6 per cent) against projected emissions in 2000, which should ensure a return to 1990 levels. The programme envisages a 10 per cent reduction in methane emissions and a 75 per cent reduction in nitrous oxide emissions by 2000, and substantial reductions in other less significant greenhouse gases. The overall reduction in emissions, taking account of the relative importance of each gas, should be about 5 per cent. The programme also looks beyond 2000 and considers some of the longer-term options for action.

*Sustainable Forestry - The UK Programme* was published in response to the Rio summit's statement of principles for the management, conservation and sustainable development of all the world's forests. The document states that the Government is also committed to implementing the guidelines for the sustainable management of European forests and for the conservation of their biodiversity adopted at the Ministerial Conference on the Protection of European Forests held in Helsinki in 1993. In the document the Government commits itself to developing a set of national guidelines for the sustainable management of the UK's woodlands and forests. Other policies include: to expand the forest cover of the UK and encourage the regeneration of woodland; to encourage landowners to plant hedgerow trees; to implement plans for restoring Sherwood Forest and creating a new forest in the Midlands; to assist developing countries by supporting bilateral projects and by implementing trade-related incentives to sustainable forest management.

On 4 March 1994 the Government published an interim response to the recommendations of the Royal Commission on Criminal Justice, which were published in July 1993 (*see* Whitaker's Almanack 1994). The response noted that 308 of the Commission's 352 recommendations were intended primarily for consideration by the Government. It said that 128 of these 308 recommendations had been accepted and implemented or were in the course of being implemented, including those relating to the abolition of committal proceedings and the continuous video recording of custody suites in police stations. Fifteen recommendations had been rejected, including the recommendation that no change should be made to the position regarding the accused's right to silence. Another 165 recommendations were the subject of detailed consultations, and a consultation paper about the setting up of the independent Criminal Cases Review Authority would be published soon. The document also stated that although the Royal Commission's ambit was confined to England and Wales, the implications of the Commission's recommendations for Scotland and Northern Ireland would be considered by the relevant Secretaries of State.

The results of a review conducted by the Government into the management of protective security within government departments and agencies were announced by the Prime Minister (John Major) on 23 March 1994. They included the following proposals:

- existing security measures should be examined closely to ensure that they are appropriate
- commercially-available security equipment should be more widely used
- personal vetting enquiries should be streamlined, particularly in routine cases
- a revised system of security classification for documents should be implemented

The revised system of security classification for documents came into force on 4 April 1994. It replaced a system comprising four general levels of classification relating to national security and a complex range of privacy markings with a single system encompassing all information and other assets

held by government. The levels in the new system retain the same labels as the old system (Top Secret, Secret, Confidential, Restricted), but they are more closely defined.

*A Code of Practice on Access to Government Information* was launched by the Chancellor of the Duchy of Lancaster (William Waldegrave) on 29 March 1994 and came into force on 4 April 1994. The code applies to government departments and other bodies within the jurisdiction of the Parliamentary Commissioner for Administration (the Ombudsman). The code commits government departments and public bodies to the following:

- to publish the facts and analyses behind policy proposals
- to make available explanatory material on departments' dealings with the public
- to give reasons for administrative decisions to those affected, except in areas where well-established convention or legal authority limits the disclosure
- to publish full information about how public services are run and what complaints procedures are available
- to release, in response to specific requests, information relating to their policies, actions and decisions

Certain types of information are exempt from the commitments to provide information, including defence, security and international relations; law enforcement and legal proceedings; immigration and nationality; privacy of an individual; a third party's commercial confidences.

The third annual White Paper reporting progress on the 1990 White Paper *This Common Inheritance* was presented to Parliament by the Secretary of State for the Environment (John Gummer) on 24 May 1994. It reviewed progress on more than 500 environmental commitments from previous years and made more than 100 further proposals, some of which had been included in the Rio summit response documents. Other proposals included:

- to establish a single regeneration budget to take over urban regeneration programmes from five government departments from April 1994
- to develop an integrated national air quality monitoring system
- to research the practicability of using economic instruments to reduce the use of pesticides
- to introduce a 30-second restriction on car alarms

*Competitiveness: Helping Business to Win* was presented to Parliament by the President of the Board of Trade (Michael Heseltine) on 24 May 1994. Its main proposals included:

- a new general diploma at GCSE level in England and Wales
- the extension of the modern apprenticeship scheme to 18- and 19-year-olds
- new vocational qualifications for 14- to 16-year-olds

- consultation on the possible introduction of credits worth up to £2,000 for school leavers to buy training
- the extension of the business links scheme
- a regional competition to reward the best ideas for the use of European Union structural funds
- the establishment of a network of regional supply offices in England to help companies identify new business opportunities
- improved information for potential inward investors
- measures to encourage prompt payment of bills
- the simplification of court procedures for debt recovery
- the privatization of the National Air Traffic Services
- a competition for privately-financed trains to operate on London Underground's Northern Line
- the removal or simplification of many health and safety regulations
- a jobseeker's allowance to replace current unemployment benefits in 1996

In May 1994 a consultation document, *Competition and Choice in the Gas Market*, was published jointly by the Department of Trade and Industry and the Office of Gas Supply. Its main proposals included:
- the British Gas tariff formula to continue until at least 1997 and the standing charge to remain at 1986 levels in real terms until at least 1997
- more cost-reflective pricing in both transportation and supply to be introduced
- the transportation and storage division of British Gas to continue to run the pipeline transportation and distribution network under Ofgas regulation, and to remain responsible for providing the emergency service
- new suppliers to be authorized by licence and to be obliged to keep the same procedures as British Gas for debt, disconnection and services to the elderly and disabled

*Security, Equality, Choice: The Future for Pensions* was presented to Parliament by the Social Security Secretary (Peter Lilley) on 23 June 1994. It included 185 of the 218 measures recommended by the Goode Report, which was published in September 1993 after a review of the laws governing pension funds was ordered by the Government in the light of the Maxwell pension fund scandal in 1991. The main recommendations included:
- a statutory regulator to be appointed in place of the Occupational Pensions Board, with powers to investigate schemes with difficulties, impose sanctions and require improvements
- a compensation scheme to be established, financed by a levy on pension funds and administered by the Pensions Ombudsman
- a minimum solvency requirement to apply to all defined-benefit schemes
- pension fund members to be given the right to appoint one-third of the trustees of the scheme

- actuaries, auditors and fund managers to become responsible to the fund's trustees rather than to the employer
- inflation-indexing for all occupational pensions to be at 5 per cent or the RPI, whichever is lower, and to apply to the whole pension
- men and women to receive the same pensions from 2020
- schemes to be subject to a test of overall quality rather than the guaranteed minimum pension being linked to SERPS
- the freedom to delay until the age of 75 the conversion of personal pension schemes into annuities

*The Future of the BBC: Serving the Nation; Competing World-Wide* was presented to Parliament by the Secretary of State for National Heritage (Peter Brooke) on 6 July 1994. It set out the Government's plans for the structure and operation of the BBC under a new royal charter and agreement, to operate for ten years from 1 January 1997. The main proposals included:
- the BBC to continue to be the main public service broadcaster in the UK, and this to remain its primary role
- the BBC to continue to make programmes as well as broadcast them
- the UK services to be financed from the licence fee until at least 2001
- World Service Radio to continue, financed by grant-in-aid from the Foreign Office
- the BBC to expand its commercial activities, ensuring that they are not cross-subsidized from the licence fee
- options including privatization to be explored for injecting private finance into the BBC's transmission services, e.g. digital broadcasting services
- the Broadcasting Standards Council and the Broadcasting Complaints Commission to merge

*The Civil Service: Continuity and Change* was presented to Parliament by the Minister for Public Service and Science (William Waldegrave) on 13 July 1994. It said that the number of civil servants was expected to fall from its present level of 530,000 to significantly below 500,000 by 1998. Its main proposals included:
- a new 3,500-strong Senior Civil Service to be created with individual contracts and salary structures more attractive to private sector applicants
- greater movement between Whitehall and the private sector to be encouraged at all levels
- each government department to review senior management structures with a view to cutting out some layers
- each department to control its own employees' pay and conditions, within tight budget controls

# The Queen's Awards

The Queen's Award for Export Achievement and The Queen's Award for Technological Achievement were instituted by royal warrant in 1976. The two separate awards took the place of The Queen's Award to Industry, which had been instituted in 1965. In 1992 the scheme was extended with the launch of a third award, The Queen's Award for Environmental Achievement.

The export and technological awards are designed to recognize and encourage outstanding achievements in exporting goods or services from the United Kingdom and in advancing process or product technology. The purpose of the environmental award is to recognize and encourage product and process development which has major benefits for the environment and which is commercially successful.

The awards differ from a personal royal honour in that they are given to a unit as a whole, management and employees working as a team. They may be applied for by any organization within the United Kingdom, the Channel Islands or the Isle of Man producing goods or services which meet the criteria for the awards. Eligibility is not influenced in any way by the particular activities of the unit applying, its location, or size. Units or agencies of central and local government with industrial functions, as well as research associations, educational institutions and bodies of a similar character, are also eligible, provided that they can show they have contributed to industrial efficiency.

Each award is formally conferred by a grant of appointment and is symbolized by a representation of its emblem cast in stainless steel and encapsulated in a transparent acrylic block.

Awards are held for five years and holders are entitled to fly the appropriate award flag and to display the emblem on the packaging of goods produced in this country, on the goods themselves, on the unit's stationery, in advertising and on certain articles used by employees. Units may also display the emblem of any previous current awards during the five years.

Awards are announced on 21 April (the birthday of The Queen) and published formally in a special supplement to the London Gazette.

## AWARDS OFFICE

All enquiries about the scheme and requests for application forms (completed forms must be returned by 31 October) should be made to: The Secretary, The Queen's Awards Office, Bridge Place, 88–89 Eccleston Square, London SWIV IPT. Tel: 0171-222 2277.

## EXPORT ACHIEVEMENT

The criterion upon which recommendations for an award for export achievement are based is a substantial and sustained increase in export earnings to a level which is outstanding for the products or services concerned and for the size of the applicant unit's operations. Account will be taken of any special market factors described in the application. Applicants for the award will be expected to explain the basis of the achievement (e.g. improved marketing organization or new initiative to cater for export markets) and this will be taken into consideration. Export earnings considered will include receipts by the applicant unit in this country from the export of goods produced in this country, and for the provision of services to non-residents. Account will be taken of the overseas expenses incurred other than marketing expenses. Income from profits (after overseas tax) remitted to this country from the applicant unit's direct investments in its overseas branches, subsidiaries or associates in the same general line of business will be taken into account, but not receipts from profits on other overseas investments or by interest on overseas loans or credits.

In 1994, The Queen's Award for Export Achievement was conferred on the following concerns:

ABS Electronics Ltd, Bangor, Co. Down
Abbott Laboratories Ltd, Queenborough, Kent
Alan Group Ltd, Horsham, West Sussex
Alifabs Ltd, Woking, Surrey
Allied Distillers Ltd, Dumbarton
Anderson Group Ltd, Motherwell, Lanarkshire
Applied Implant Technology Inc., Horsham, West Sussex
Audio Processing Technology Ltd, Belfast
J. Barbour and Sons Ltd, South Shields, Tyne and Wear
Beardow & Adams (Adhesives) Ltd, Milton Keynes, Bucks
Beautimatic International Ltd, London Colney, Herts
Bechtel Ltd, London w6
Biwater Pipes (a division of Biwater Industries Ltd), Chesterfield, Derbyshire
Bonas Machine Company Ltd, Gateshead, Tyne and Wear
Brewing Products (UK) Ltd, Kirkliston, West Lothian
Bridon Wire (a division of Bridon PLC), Carr Hill, Doncaster
John Brown Engineering Ltd, Clydebank, Dunbartonshire
Burton's Gold Medal Biscuits Ltd, Edinburgh
CRP Marine Ltd, Skelmersdale, Lancs
Cable and Wireless PLC, London wcI
Camtex Fabrics Ltd, Workington, Cumbria
Centurion Furniture PLC, Preston, Lancs
Cherry Valley Farms Ltd, Rothwell, Lincs
Ciba Pigments (a division of Ciba-Geigy PLC), Paisley, Renfrewshire
The Cobb Breeding Company Ltd, Chelmsford, Essex
Constance Carroll Holdings Ltd, Skelmersdale, Lancs
Corin Medical Ltd, Cirencester, Glos
Coulter Electronics Ltd, Luton, Beds
Crossbows Optical Ltd, Craigavon, Co. Armagh
Crowson Fabrics Ltd, Uckfield, East Sussex
Cruachan Ltd, Glasgow
Curdworth International Machine Tools Ltd, Sutton Coldfield
Davy McKee (Sheffield) Ltd Ashlow Guides Division, t/a Davy Int. Ashlow Guides Division, Sheffield

Thomas De La Rue and Company Ltd Security Print (UK), Dunstable, Beds

Deritend Precision Castings Ltd, Droitwich Spa, Worcester

Dunbar & Cook Machine Tools Ltd, Aston, Birmingham

EMI Records UK (EMIR), London W1

Edme Ltd, Manningtree, Essex

Elite Optics Ltd, Llantrisant, Mid Glamorgan

Environmental Resources Ltd, t/a Environmental Resources Management, London W1

The Esmee Fairbairn Research Centre, Riccarton, Edinburgh

Fibre Techniques Ltd, Holywell, Clwyd

Fine Fragrances and Cosmetics Ltd, Hampton, Middx

Finesse Ltd, London W1

FormFlo Ltd, Cheltenham, Glos

GEC ALSTHOM T&D Protection & Control Ltd, Stafford

Gamebore Cartridge Company Ltd, Hull

Genzyme Ltd, Haverhill, Suffolk

Graff Diamonds Ltd, London W1

Private Patients Unit, Great Ormond Street Hospital for Children NHS Trust, London WC1

Guilford Europe Ltd Automotive Business Unit, Somercotes, Derbyshire

Halib Foods International Ltd, Belfast

Frederick Harrington (Nottingham) Ltd, Nottingham

Helena Laboratories (UK) Ltd, Gateshead, Tyne and Wear

Hilti Industries (GB) Ltd, West Bromwich, West Midlands

HIT Entertainment PLC, London W1

Honda Motor Europe Ltd, Reading, Berks

Horton Kirby Paper Mills Ltd, Dartford, Kent

Ilmor Engineering Ltd, Brixworth, Northants

Imperial College of Science, Technology and Medicine, London SW7

Insignia Solutions Ltd, High Wycombe, Bucks

International Banking Information Systems Ltd, London WC2

International Mining Consultants Ltd, Sutton-in-Ashfield, Notts

International Oil Insurers, London EC3

Inveresk Research International Ltd, Tranent, East Lothian

Ives Valves – a division of Alexander Controls Ltd, Birmingham

JCB Hydrapower Ltd, Rugeley, Staffs

Johnson & Higgins Holdings Ltd, London EC3

James Johnston and Company of Elgin Ltd, t/a Johnstons of Elgin, Elgin, Morayshire

KS Process Engineering Ltd, t/a Britannia Soap Machinery Company, Newton Abbot, Devon

Kenwood Appliances PLC, Havant, Hants

LPH Pitman Ltd, London EC3

Lasalle Engineering Ltd Products Division, Inverurie, Aberdeenshire

Loch Fyne Oysters Ltd, Cairndow, Argyll

Lombard Risk Systems Ltd, London EC4

MJS Scientific Ltd, Portchester, Hants

Macphie Exports Ltd (a division of Macphie of Glenberrie Ltd), Stonehaven, Kincardineshire

Madge Networks Ltd, Chalfont St Giles, Bucks

Marathon Belting Ltd, Rochdale, Lancs

Matra Marconi Space UK Ltd, Portsmouth, Hants

McCormick (UK) PLC Food Service Division, Paisley, Renfrewshire

McKey Food Services Ltd, Milton Keynes, Bucks

Memco Ltd, Maidenhead, Berks

Mondbury Ltd, London E1

Munradtech Industrial Generators Ltd, Loughborough, Leics

Nestlé UK Ltd, Croydon, Surrey

Newport Components Ltd, Milton Keynes, Bucks

Nissan Motor Manufacturing (UK) Ltd, Sunderland, Tyne and Wear

Norbrook Laboratories Ltd, Newry, Co. Down

Norfrost Ltd, Castletown, Caithness

Novocastra Laboratories Ltd, Newcastle upon Tyne

Ove Arup Partnership, London W1

PBT International Ltd, Chilcompton, Bath

PFE International Ltd, Loughton, Essex

Parker Plant Ltd, Leicester

Philips Telecom – Private Mobile Radio Paging Business, Cambridge

Photain Controls PLC, Arundel, West Sussex

Portex Ltd, Hythe, Kent

Premier Hazard Systems (UK) Ltd, Yeadon, Leeds

Queen Mary and Westfield College, University of London, London E1

RS Components Ltd, Corby, Northants

RTA Wine Rack Company Ltd, Fakenham, Norfolk

RWS Group PLC, Gerrard Cross, Bucks

Rencol Tolerance Rings (a division of Lilleshall Plastics and Engineering Ltd), Horfield, Bristol

Rosin Engineering Company Ltd, Stourbridge, West Midlands

SCA Nutrition Ltd, Thirsk, North Yorkshire

Scientific Software Intercomp (UK) Ltd, Egham, Surrey

Semefab (Scotland) Ltd, Glenrothes, Fife

Serco Europe Division of Serco International, Southall, Middx

SmithKline Beecham Pharmaceuticals International (a division of SmithKline Beecham PLC), Brentford, Middx

Snap-Drape Europe Ltd, Leominster, Herefordshire

Snell & Wilcox Ltd, Petersfield, Hants

Softel Ltd, Reading, Berks

Sperrin Metal Products Ltd, Draperstown, Co. Londonderry

Stannah Stairlifts Ltd, Andover, Hants

Stirling Cooke Insurance Brokers Ltd, London EC3

Tony Stone Associates Ltd, t/a Tony Stone Images, London NW1

Sunrise Medical Ltd, Brierley Hill, West Midlands

Sunseeker International (Boats) Ltd, Poole, Dorset

Joseph Sykes Brothers Ltd, Lindley, Huddersfield

Taylor & Francis Ltd, London WC1

Technic Group PLC, Burton-on-Trent, Staffs

Tensator Ltd, Milton Keynes, Bucks

Andy Thornton Agricultural Antiques Ltd, Elland, West Yorkshire

Trans Euro PLC, London NW10

Travco, London N1

Tritech International Ltd, Kingswells, Aberdeen

United Distillers PLC, Edinburgh

Unived Technologies Ltd University of Edinburgh, Edinburgh

The University of Buckingham, Buckingham

W. Vinten Ltd, Bury St Edmunds, Suffolk

WBB Devon Clays Ltd, Newton Abbot, Devon

Wade Furniture Ltd, Leeds

Watkiss Automation Ltd, Sandy, Beds

Willett International Ltd, Corby, Northants

Williams Grand Prix Engineering Ltd, Didcot, Oxon

F. G. Wilson (Engineering) Ltd, Larne, Co. Antrim

Zeneca Pharmaceuticals, Macclesfield, Cheshire

Zeus Aluminium Products Ltd, Dudley, West Midlands

## TECHNOLOGICAL ACHIEVEMENT

The criterion upon which recommendations for an award for technological achievement are based is a significant advance, leading to increased efficiency, in the application of technology to a production or development process in British industry or the production for sale of goods which incorporate new and advanced technological qualities.

In 1994 The Queen's Award for Technological Achievement was conferred on the following concerns:

APV Baker Ltd – Liquid Foods Division, Crawley, West Sussex – *Ohmic heating for the production of high-quality ambient-stable food products*

Autotype International Ltd, Wantage, Oxon – *a process for the manufacture of hard coated polyesters for electronic/user interface*

British Aerospace Airbus Ltd, Bristol – *common wing for the Airbus A330/A340 aircraft*

Access Networks Division of BT Laboratories, Ipswich – *'blown fibre' optical fibre cable installation technique*

Chubb Research Ltd, Wolverhampton – *polymer composites as protection materials for high security products*

ConvaTec Ltd, Deeside, Clwyd – *granuflex hydrocolloid moist-wound dressings*

Aircraft Systems Sector, Defence Research Agency, Farnborough, Hants – *Lynx helicopter advanced composite main rotor blade*

Dunn Systems Ltd, Ashby de la Zouch, Leics – *high-speed pack-handling system for food and drinks industry*

EA Technology Ltd, Capenhurst, Chester – *Ohmic heating for the production of high-quality ambient-stable food products*

Extrusion Systems Ltd, Bradford, West Yorkshire – *a process to produce polypropylene yarn suitable for industrial/technical application*

Gooch and Housego Ltd, Ilminster, Somerset – *acousto-optic modulators*

Husky Computers Ltd, Coventry – *Husky FS/2 Rugged Handheld Computer*

IBM United Kingdom Ltd, Havant Division, Havant, Hants – *IBM 0681 high performance disk drive*

Backhoe Loader Division, J C Bamford Excavators Ltd, Rocester, Staffs – *JCB 4CX Servoplus Backhoe Loader*

Kemira Polymers (a division of Kemira Coatings Ltd), Stockport, Cheshire – *polymer composites as protection materials for high security products*

PSION PLC, London NW8 – *pocket computers*

Sonardyne Ltd, Fleet, Hants – *seismic integrated positioning system for sub-sea surveying (SIPS)*

Westland Helicopters Ltd, Yeovil, Somerset – *Lynx helicopter advanced composite main rotor blade*

Combined Power Systems Ltd, Eccles, Greater Manchester – *computer-controlled combined heat and power generators*

Dorman Diesels Ltd, Stafford – *low emission gas engines*

Multicore Solders Ltd, Hemel Hempstead, Herts – *'No Clean' soldering materials*

Seabait Ltd, Ashington, Northumberland – *cultured ragworms for fishing bait*

Shaw, Son & Greenhalgh Ltd, Huddersfield, West Yorkshire – *isolation valves for hazardous chemicals*

Vickers Electronics Ltd, Altrincham, Cheshire – *synchronous burner controls*

## ENVIRONMENTAL ACHIEVEMENT

The criterion upon which recommendations for an award for environmental achievement are based is a significant advance in the application by British industry of the development of products, technology or processes which offer major benefits in environmental terms compared to existing products, technology or processes. An award is only granted for products, technology or processes which have achieved commercial success.

In 1994, The Queen's Award for Environmental Achievement was conferred on the following concerns:

Alida Recycling Ltd, Heanor, Derbyshire – *polythene waste recycling*

Bridgewater Paper Company Ltd, Ellesmere Port, Cheshire – *newsprint from recycled fibre*

# Science and Discovery

## COMET SHOEMAKER-LEVY 9

On 25 March 1993 Jim Scotti of the University of Arizona's Spacewatch Telescope at Kitt Peak was asked to photograph a comet of unusual appearance not far from the planet Jupiter. The charge-coupled device (CCD), a light-sensitive silicon chip used as a light detector in telescopes, showed a number of small comets strung out like a pearl necklace. From positional data, Brian Marsden of the Minor Planet Center in Cambridge, Massachusetts, computed that the object was not in a normal near-parabolic orbit round the Sun, as is usual with comets, but was orbiting around Jupiter in a very elongated ellipse. Further computations by Donald Yeomans and Paul Chadas revealed that comet Shoemaker-Levy 9 (named after the discoverers Caroline and Eugene Shoemaker and David Levy) had been travelling round Jupiter since 1970, but on 8 July 1992 it had passed only 21,000 km from the planet and had been torn apart by the planet's strong gravitational field into about 21 smaller objects. It was these objects that were seen by Scotti. Further calculation showed that these fragments would approach Jupiter again in July 1994 and this time would crash on to the planet at a speed of about 60 km per second.

Such impacts would produce the largest collisions ever predicted and witnessed within the Solar System and an international effort was organized to monitor the event. For observers situated on the Earth, the impacts took place on the side of Jupiter pointing away from the Earth but due to the rapid rotational rate of Jupiter (just under ten hours), the impact points appeared on the limb of the planet within about half an hour and became easily visible within about one and a half hours. The Hubble Space Telescope, the *Galileo* spacecraft and satellites specializing in X-ray, ultraviolet, infrared and radio emissions followed Jupiter during the critical times, and instruments at many large observatories throughout the world monitored the events. All the major nuclei of the fragmented comet were given an identification letter and the behaviour of each nuclei was successfully monitored by the tracking instruments.

Only a few preliminary results have been announced but sufficient to show that the event was far more spectacular than expected. Visually, each impact produced a dark spot which could be seen even with small instruments. In some cases the dark spots were of a size that would dwarf the Earth. What has been surprising is the length of time these spots have survived. They were still evident after a month, although reduced in size. On the evening of 18 July, two of the larger fragments impacted shortly before sunset in the UK but no flashes were seen. A short time afterwards, two very large spots were seen on the disc of the planet, looking just as though Jupiter had two black eyes. On the evening of 19 July, sites H, E, A, C and K appeared as a row of spots extending across the planet. Although visually they appeared as black spots, they were recorded as brilliant white ones at infrared wavelengths just after impact. At radio wavelengths, emission from the planet produced a big surprise. At low frequencies astronomers failed to pick up an expected increase in signal but at higher frequencies, where the intensity of the radiation was expected to drop, there was a dramatic increase in the radio signal.

## BEYOND NEPTUNE

It used to be thought that the planet Pluto and some long-period comets were the only bodies belonging to the Solar System beyond the orbit of Neptune. However, during the last two years 13 objects have been located orbiting the region beyond Neptune. David Jewitt and Jane Luu of the University of Hawaii found the first at the end of 1992 and since then they have discovered a further nine. All the objects discovered to date appear to have a size between 100 and 200 km in diameter. There are three research establishments looking for trans-Neptunian objects and they have only covered about 2 square degrees of sky so far. If the present rate of discovery continues, it implies that there are about 35,000 such objects. This is a very high figure, between 100 and 1,000 times the number of comparable-sized objects in the minor planet belt lying between the orbits of Mars and Jupiter.

Jewitt believes that there may be between one million and 10,000 million objects of the size of Halley's Comet, about 10 km across, and that they may be just the inner edge of a huge disc of objects. This disc has been called the Kuiper belt and it might be the source of long-period comets. The objects discovered so far fall into two groups: some orbit between 32 and 26 AU (astronomical units, i.e. the average distance of the Earth from the Sun), a range of distances comparable to those covered by Pluto; the other group orbits at distances between 42 and 46 AUs. This division into two groups may not be realistic and could be altered when their composition and accurate orbits have been determined.

## FUTURE OF THE SUN

The Sun was formed some 4,500 million years ago, shining with only 70 per cent of its present brilliance. Julianna Sackman and Kathleen Kraemer of Caltech and Arnold Boothroyd of the University of Toronto have calculated new evolutionary models for the Sun and have predicted that it will continue to brighten for the next 1,100 million years, when it will be 10 per cent brighter than it is at present. It will become more than twice its current brightness in 6,500 million years, at which time the helium in its core will start to burn. Over the next 1,300 million years the Sun will expand slowly, turning into a red giant, with a diameter some 170 times its present value, and engulfing the planet Mercury. It will then shrink slightly but after another 110 million years it will start to swell again, and its surface will reach the Earth's present orbit. By this time it will be about 5,200 times brighter than it is today. After this the Sun will gently eject its outer layers, leaving a tiny white dwarf.

The investigators have also considered the effect of the loss of mass of the Sun during its lifetime. By the time it has engulfed Mercury the Sun will have only 72.5 per cent of its present mass and by the time of its expansion to the Earth's orbit, only 59 per cent of its current mass will remain. The weakening of the Sun's gravitational force will cause the orbit of Venus to drift out to 1.22 AU (the Earth's current distance from the Sun is 1 AU), and the radius of the Earth's orbit will increase to about 1.7 AU, approximately the current distance of Mars from the Sun. Even at this distance the Earth will be heated to about 1600 K, a temperature at which rocks will have melted. As the Sun shrinks to a white dwarf, it will lose sufficient mass for Venus and Earth to recede 1.34 and 1.85 times their present distances. At this stage both planets will have frozen and will orbit the Sun for ever.

## ICE ON MERCURY

Mercury is just over a third of the distance of the Earth from the Sun and its surface is exceptionally hot, yet there is evidence that ice exists in the polar regions. The planet's rotational period and its highly eccentric orbit produce a complex pattern of day and night over the planet's surface. But because the planet spins on an axis at right angles to the plane of its orbit round the Sun, the polar regions are always at the edge of the sunlit side of the planet. Consequently these areas receive little solar energy, and possibly none at all at the bottom of craters. Theoretical studies carried out in the United States have shown that shadowed crater floors could be as cold as −213°C (60 K). This is well below the temperature of −161°C (112 K) required to retain water ice for billions of years.

Work carried out in 1991 revealed that the polar regions produced very strong radar signals, similar to those elsewhere in the Solar System where the reflections have come from ice-covered surfaces. John Harmon, of the National Astronomy and Ionosphere Center in Aricebo, Puerto Rico, carried out a further radar survey and the results showed that the areas which showed the strong reflections matched closely the positions of polar craters recorded by *Mariner 10* which flew past the planet in 1974. Working with Martin Slade of the Jet Propulsion Laboratory in Pasadena, the scientists have now analysed more radar data from Earth-based sites. It is possible for Earth-based radar to penetrate the polar craters better than the spacecraft because the orbits of Mercury and the Earth are tilted at an angle of 7° to each other. Results of this work have shown a close correlation between the reflections and the crater floors. Although the data did not prove that the reflections come from ice, there is a very strong case for claiming that ice exists there.

## THE KECK TELESCOPE

The Keck telescope has a segmented mirror 10 metres in diameter; a composite of small mirrors, it is made up of 36 hexagonal segments. It is situated on Mauna Kea, Hawaii, about 4,000 metres above sea-level. Mauna Kea is a vent bulging out of Mauna Loa, a giant volcano which forms the whole of the Hawaiian island of Big Island. The Keck, together with eight other telescopes, can observe the universe over a wide range of wavelengths covering short-wave radio, visual and infrared. The reason for the location of so many telescopes at the summit of Mauna Kea is that it is so high and cold that most of the atmosphere's water vapour has been frozen out. Water vapour absorbs infrared and short-wavelength radio waves, so a telescope at the summit can handle wavelengths not possible at lower altitudes. In addition, the turbulent trade winds are forced to pass either side of the volcano, leaving the summit in a pocket of very stable air. An extra benefit is that Hawaii is far removed from any continent so the air is relatively free from dust.

One of the first results from the Keck, published in 1994, involved its Near Infrared Camera, which revealed a gravitational lens system called MG1131+ 0456. Here a massive galaxy acts as a gravitational lens, bending and focussing light from a more distant quasar to form a double image of the quasar. Whereas a double image was plainly visible at a wavelength of 2.2 microns, nothing was recorded except the intervening galaxy. It is probable that the galaxy contains a lot of dust which blocks out radiation at 1.3 microns. An early success was the separation of the most luminous object known, FSC10214+4724, some 10,000 million light years away, into a cluster of several objects. The clump could be a galaxy feeding voracious quasars at its centre.

Another important discovery is the irregular distribution of galaxies. In the infrared, it was found that the number of galaxies levelled off with distance but in the blue part of the spectrum, the number of galaxies rose with distance. Theories will have to be modified considerably to cope with this. One of the main purposes of the telescope is to provide data which will give a more accurate value for the Hubble constant, which is a measure of the rate of recession of the galaxies.

Close to the Keck telescope a second instrument is under construction. The linking of Keck 1 and Keck 2 will form an interferometer, which will have sufficient resolving power to see planets around other stars.

### Local Galaxy Torn Apart

The two dominant galaxies in the Local Group (the cluster of galaxies to which our galaxy belongs) are the Andromeda galaxy (M31) and our own Milky Way, both of which are spiral galaxies. In addition to the two Magellanic Clouds, there are known to be eight dwarf spheroidal galaxies. The last of these was recently identified by Rodrigo Ibata, Mike Irwin and Gerry Gilmore of the Institute of Astronomy in Cambridge when they were observing stars in the central 'bulge' of the Milky Way using the UK Schmidt telescope in Australia. Out of approximately a million stars whose spectra were examined, there were about 100 which stood out as peculiar. These stars were much younger than the stars of the bulge and were classed as carbon stars, a type virtually absent from the stars of the bulge. When their velocities were measured it was found that the spread in their velocities was much smaller than that of the bulge stars. This shows that the stars are unconnected with the bulge and consequently not members of the Milky Way galaxy.

The brightness of the stars was fairly constant and the investigators concluded that they were part of a dwarf galaxy orbiting beyond the bulge, about 50,000 light years from the centre of our galaxy. This dwarf galaxy, in the constellation of Sagittarius, is the nearest of the dwarf spheroidal galaxies. The galaxy is thought to consist of a few million young stars which are about a few million years old. It is thought that they were formed in a burst of star formation caused by a tidal interaction with the Milky Way. Because of its nearness to the Milky Way, the galaxy is being ripped apart by the Milky Way's gravitational field. A normal dwarf spheroidal galaxy has a diameter of about 1,000 light years but in this case the stars have been scattered over a diameter of ten times this value.

### Magnetic Storms

Magnetic storms are often associated with auroral displays, disrupted radio communications and failures in the electrical power grid system. For decades scientists believed that solar flares were responsible for magnetic storms, but it is now realized that the cause is coronal mass ejections.

Scientists at the Los Alamos National Laboratory and the National Center for Atmospheric Research at the Mauna Loa Observatory at Hawaii, and using the results from the Japanese *Yohkoh* satellite, have shown that in a coronal mass ejection billions of tons of gas are thrown out by the Sun, travelling at up to 2,000 km per second. This gas joins up with the normally slower-moving plasma of energetic particles known as the solar wind, generating a shock-wave ahead of the solar wind. The arrival of this shock-wave and later the gas itself generates a magnetic storm.

Large coronal mass ejections are sometimes followed by flares but the two are distinctly different phenomena. Flares are spectacular events but the coronal mass ejections originate higher in the Sun's atmosphere and are harder to observe because they are relatively faint. These ejections are generated by changes in the Sun's magnetic field. At peak times in the Sun's 11-year activity cycle, it is estimated that the Earth intercepts about 70 coronal mass ejections a year but at minimum sunspot activity there could be less than ten. Studies made during the last maximum period found that 36 out of the 37 largest geomagnetic storms were linked with shock-waves generated by coronal mass ejections.

### Meteorites from Mars

Among the meteorites collected from the Allan Hills region of Antarctica is a group of meteorites which have come from Mars. There are three types, shergottites, nakhlites and chassignites, collectively referred to as SNCs. It is believed they were ejected from Mars millions of years ago.

In 1984 a 1.9 kg meteorite was collected from the Allan Hills area and classed as a diogenite, a class of meteorites dominated by large crystals of a simple magnesium-rich silicate, the large size of the crystals being due to the meteorite cooling very slowly from the magma. The meteorite was thought to be a fragment from the asteroid 4 Vesta. However, in 1993 David Mittlefehldt of Lockheed Engineering and Sciences identified trace elements in this particular meteorite, known as ALH84001, which do not exist in diogenites. He claimed that its composition was more like that of the SNCs but that there were important differences. ALH84001 was therefore classed as a new rock type. Of importance are the traces of carbonates wedged between the silicate crystals; Mittlefehldt believes that they were formed at a high temperature as the rock cooled. The discovery of the carbonates could help to explain the formation and evolution of the carbon dioxide-dominated Martian atmosphere.

### Moon Crater Chains

Certain of the chains of craters on the Moon have been cited as evidence by those who favour the theory of a volcanic origin for the majority of the craters on the lunar surface, as opposed to the more popular impact theories. Many of the chains consist of so-called secondary craters formed by ejected material from larger impacts. However, some of these chains do not point towards a larger crater, and some individual craters within a chain, ranging from 1 km to 3 km in diameter, are better defined than secondary craters. One chain, the Davy chain, consists of 23 craters. Recently an impact origin has become a strong candidate due to observations of the comet Shoemaker-Levy 9's impact on the planet Jupiter in July 1994. Jay Melosh of the University of Arizona has identified crater chains on Jupiter's moon Callisto and he believes that these were formed by fragments of comets caused to disintegrate by Jupiter's gravitational field.

Working with Ewen Whitaker, Melosh has concluded that the Davy chain was formed by cometary impact, the same conclusion as Robert Richman and Charles Wood of the University of North Dakota. They all believe that the chain was formed when a comet with a diameter of about 1 km broke into fragments a few hundred metres across. The Arizonan team also believe that a chain of 24 craters in the vicinity of the crater Abulfeda was caused by the impact of a shattered comet. These craters, of diameters ranging from 5 km to 13 km, are not aligned with any large crater.

There is still controversy as to the rate at which comets impact the Earth or Moon. Because of the far weaker gravitational field of the Earth-Moon system compared with that of Jupiter, the number of observable crater chains is much lower. Melosh claims that one comet approaches the Earth every 10,000 years, a figure much higher than that estimated by Eugene Shoemaker of the US Geological Survey.

NEAR-EARTH ASTEROIDS

Since 1991 three asteroids have been recorded passing the Earth at distances considerably less than the Earth-Moon distance. On 18 January 1991 the asteroid 1991 BA passed within 170,000 km, and on 20 May 1993 the object 1993 KA2 came even closer, at a distance of only 150,000 km. A third object, 1994 ES1, was detected on 13 March 1994 by David Rabinowitz and James Scott, using the 0.9 metre Spacewatch telescope at Kitt Peak, Arizona. It was a 20th magnitude object in the constellation of Virgo, at a distance of 2.2 million km. The next night they found that it had brightened by a factor of 18, indicating that it was approaching the Earth quite rapidly. Brian Marsden of the Minor Planet Center calculated that it would pass the Earth at a distance of 160,000 km om 15 March. Attempts were made to observe the 10 metre-diameter object from observatories throughout the world but these were not successful.

Objects travelling in only slightly different orbits could have hit the Earth, producing widespread devastation. Such objects may not be as rare as was once thought. An object thought to be about 7 metres in diameter and weighing about 400 metric tons entered the atmosphere over the Pacific Ocean on 1 February 1994 at 22.38 Universal Time. The bolide, with a magnitude of −23 (nearly that of the Sun), crossed the sky travelling from the south-east to the north-west as seen by fishermen near to the island of Kusaie. It is estimated that it exploded at a height of about 20 km. Infrared and visible light sensors on six different satellites were activated by the object and from this data a position of 164.1°E. 2.7°N. was calculated. The signals were analysed at the Sandia and Los Alamos Laboratories. Analysis of the observations have shown that the object had the kinetic energy of a nuclear bomb but fortunately it exploded in the upper atmosphere. Eye witnesses say that a smoke trail remained visible for an hour.

SATELLITE OF A MINOR PLANET

Over the last decade there have been several claims for the discovery of binary asteroids i.e. two minor planets in orbit round each other, the pair moving as a single unit in orbit round the Sun. There have also been suggestions of a minor planet having its own satellite, the implication being that the second body was much smaller than the asteroid itself. Proof has now been obtained of the existence of such a system.

Instruments on board the spacecraft *Galileo* as it passed through the minor planet belt on its way to Jupiter have sent back photographs and spectrographic maps showing that the asteroid 243 Ida has an accompanying satellite. This is the first confirmed natural satellite to an asteroid. Ida herself is quite small, only 56 km long, but the satellite has a diameter of about 1 km. It is orbiting Ida at a distance of about 100 km from the planet. The surfaces of both Ida and the satellite appear to be heavily cratered.

*Galileo* recorded the data in August 1993 when it was about 500 million km from the Earth. The photos showing Ida and its moon have only recently been received on Earth because of difficulties with the spacecraft's antenae, which necessitated the slow transmission of data.

At present it is not known how Ida acquired the satellite. It could be a fragment of the same parent from which Ida was formed or it could be the result of a more recent impact with Ida. The team responsible for collecting the data from *Galileo* are confident that more detailed pictures will be sent back in the near future, which may solve this problem.

AMINO ACIDS IN SPACE

Some 20 years ago Fred Hoyle and Chandra Wickramasinghe put forward the theory that, in addition to simple atoms and molecules, space contains complex molecules. This idea was widely dismissed, as was their idea that primitive life may have originated in space and subsequently reached the Earth. This theory was advanced to explain the speed at which life appeared on the Earth, just a few hundred million years after the Earth's crust solidified. The majority of the theories for the origin of life on the Earth are based on the assumption that chemical reactions on the Earth produced increasingly complex molecules, eventually reaching the complexity associated with living molecules. A team of scientists from the University of Illinois, led by Lewis Snyder, have detected spectral lines characteristic of large molecules, including glycine, the simplest amino acid, in a star-forming cloud about one light year across in the constellation of Sagittarius. This discovery is important because amino acids link up to produce proteins.

There have been claims in the last few years for the discovery of more than 100 molecules in space, some of these containing up to 13 atoms, more complex than the 10-atom glycine molecule. Claims for even larger molecules have been made but the discoveries have not been confirmed. The discovery of glycine in space is of fundamental importance because it is an amino acid. Snyder said its discovery shows that the chemistry of prebiotic early Earth is the common chemistry of the galaxy. Wickrama-singhe is reported to have expressed no surprise at the discovery and claims that it will be only a matter of time before other amino acids, together with nucleotide bases, are found in space. These bases are the components of the nucleic acids that make up genetic material. There is already circumstantial evidence for their existence in space. For over half a century astronomers have recorded about a hundred features in the visible and infrared spectra from space. Although large molecules produce such features, as yet they have not been identified.

BUCKMINSTERFULLERENE FINDS

Since the initial discovery of the spherical 60-atom carbon molecule known as buckminsterfullerene in 1985, the molecules have been found in unexpected locations. One place where there is strong evidence of their existence is the tenuous material in the space between stars. For 60 years, astronomers have puzzled over the causes of the diffuse interstellar bands (DIBs), a set of absorption bands seen in the spectra of stars observed through dusty regions of the Galaxy. Due to advances in astronomical instrumentation, the number of DIBs identified has now reached 200. The features are caused by electronic transitions not by free atoms but by large molecules containing six to ten atoms. Recent work has shown that in some cases there is a great similarity to that produced in the laboratory by the buckminsterfuller-ene positive ion $C_{60}^+$. Although the identification is not yet confirmed, the idea of the molecule existing in free space presents exciting prospects.

There is no doubt, however, that the molecule has been found in samples from the clay layer which marks the end of the Cretaceous period 65 million years ago, the time of the impact which formed the huge crater on the Yucatan peninsula, Mexico, and the time of the mass extinction of the dinosaurs. Dieter Heymann of Rice University in Houston found the compound at two sites in New Zealand which are rich in soot thought to originate from global forest fires produced by the Yucatan event. Naturally-occurring buckminsterfullerene have been identified at only two other sites, carbon-rich rocks from Russia known as shungites whose origins are unknown but which are known to have an age of 500 million years. The other is in a sample of fulgurite, formed when lightning strikes and melts a rock. As far as the New Zealand site is concerned, no evidence was found for the existence of the buckminsterfullerene in either the Cretaceous limestone below the clay nor in the Tertiary shales lying above it. Heymann is not sure whether the molecules were formed from the burning of the wood or of fossil fuel such as crude oil released at the time of the impact. In view of this, it is possible that the source was the impacting asteroid.

THE EARTH'S CORE

Little is known about the structure of the Earth's core because of the difficulty of collecting precise data. It is known that the outer part of the core must be liquid because it does not transmit S-waves, the transverse or shear type of earthquake waves, and it is now recognized that an inner section extending about 1,200 km from the centre of the Earth is solid. This inner core is not a uniform sphere of iron, a fact revealed by the time taken for seismic waves to travel through the core and by recent studies of the Earth's natural vibration frequencies.

About ten years ago geophysicists discovered that the time taken by seismic waves to travel through the core in a direction parallel to the Earth's spin axis was two to four seconds faster than if they travelled at right angles to the spin axis, i.e. parallel to the equator. Other researchers recorded that the natural vibration frequencies of the Earth are split. Instead of being a single frequency, they consist of a doublet of two closely-spaced frequencies. A theory was put forward at the time that the core was shaped like a rugby ball but little was done to correlate this with the seismic data.

Jeroen Tromp of Harvard University has now put forward a theory which combines these two fields of study. He claims that the core is anisotropic, i.e. its properties vary with direction. To explain fully the observations, he says that the shape of the inner core would be very unrealistic. However, he proposes that the inner core behaves like a giant asymmetric crystal, aligned with the Earth's axis so that the seismic waves travel faster in that direction. His theory fits well with the suggestion that the inner core is made of a high pressure phase of iron in which the atoms are packed closely in hexagons. This eta-phase of iron has cylindrical symmetry and the idea is in agreement with the results obtained. What causes this is still a mystery.

FLASHES IN UPPER ATMOSPHERE

Electrical flashes in the upper atmosphere have been recorded since 1886. These have taken the form of short-lived phenomena seen above storm clouds but their existence was not taken seriously by many atmospheric researchers until 1989, when a flash was recorded on a video tape by a team from the University of Minnesota. All doubt about their existence was removed by evidence from video cameras on board a NASA aircraft flying at an altitude of 12 km along a row of thunder clouds over Kansas, Iowa and Nebraska between 2200 hours and midnight on 8 July 1994. The scientists responsible, Davis Sentman and Eugene Wescott of the University of Alaska Statewide System, Fairbanks, reported that during the two-hour flight, the low-light-level camera recorded flashes 50 km upwards and 10 km across. They were unable to measure the wavelength of the light emitted so at present the origin and nature of the flashes are unknown. The intensity of the flashes was comparable with the light produced by aurorae but Sentman commented that their short duration means that even at night they can only just be seen. The brightness of the flashes seems to increase with altitude. The large number of flashes recorded indicates that they are not as rare as was thought. There are several possible explanations for the phenomena; they might be caused by lightning-like discharges, or particles in the upper atmosphere might be fluorescing as a result of absorbing ultraviolet light or low energy X-rays from lightning flashes in the clouds at a lower level. Lack of precise data means that further research is needed before the cause is known.

## CHICXULUB CRATER

Research has been carried out recently on the geology of the area around the village of Chicxulub on the Yucatan Peninsula in Mexico, where there exists the remains of a multi-ringed feature buried under sediment. The feature has been identified as the remains of a large impact which occurred some 65 million years ago, triggering off a global biological catastrophe often linked with the extinction of the dinosaurs.

From data obtained from local gravity and magnetic field measurements, it was estimated that the diameter of the feature's third and outermost ring was about 180 km. Results of the work carried out in the autumn of 1993 and a re-analysis of earlier work indicate that there is a fourth ring with a diameter of 300 km. A team of American and Mexican geologists, headed by Virgil Sharpton of the Lunar and Planetary Institute, have come to the conclusion that the 180 km circle marks not the outer ring but the limit of excavation and deformation that took place at the time of the impact. It is thought that the crater produced was unstable and that it subsequently collapsed to form a crater nearly twice as large. The investigators have calculated that to produce a crater of the larger diameter would have required at least five times as much energy as was needed for the 180 km crater, about the equivalent of 10 trillion tons of TNT. They are of the opinion that the Earth has not experienced another impact of this magnitude since the development of multicellular life some thousand million years ago.

Not all impact specialists agree with the findings and some think that the 180 km diameter is the correct value. But other evidence has provided support for the new value. A ring of large sink-holes called cenotes found in the area and centred on the crater has a diameter of 165 km and this is thought to mark the limit of the underlying crater's stable interior floor rather than the jumbled outer ring, giving a diameter of about 240 km.

## THE FIRST FLOWERS

It was generally accepted that the first flowering plants appeared on the Earth about 130 million years ago, at the beginning of the Cretaceous period, and that the first great phase of diversification took place

about 30 million years later. This theory has recently been exploded by evidence of flowering plants, or angiosperms, in Triassic period sediments, which are 220 million years old.

Bruce Cornet of Lamont Doherty Earth Observatory, New York, recently discovered a single small leaf and two flowers of *Pannaulika triassica* in late Triassic shales in North Carolina. Although the fossilized plant is well-preserved, the single critical leaf is not complete. Cornet says that the vein pattern in the leaf fragment is clear and the fragment's asymmetry indicates that it has the typical three-lobed appearance of early angiosperms. Not all scientists have accepted the new evidence because although it is strikingly angiosperm in appearance, it is also similar to certain ferns. In spite of this, evidence is mounting for the earlier date. A group of workers who have used cladistic analysis, in which similar plants are grouped together, to examine the evolutionary relationships of the angiosperms and their link with an extinct group of Triassic plants, have found that the evolving plant lineage that led to the flowering plants must have diverged by late Triassic times. This is supported by the so-called molecular clocks in the DNA of living plants. Cornet has believed in a Triassic origin for a long time, basing his belief on evidence gained from a group of fossil pollens. He has found these particular pollens in Triassic sediments and it is generally accepted that they are very similar to the pollen of angiosperms. Unfortunately the parent plant is not known.

Although Cornet's work is accepted by many workers, they are troubled by the lack of fossil evidence from sediments covering the critical 100 million years in the Jurassic period. Cornet suggests that the unknown Jurassic flowering plants evolved in tropical upland regions where they initially stayed.

## THE EARLIEST VERTEBRATES

Until recently it was generally accepted that the earliest vertebrates existed about 475 million years ago but this has been challenged by new evidence resulting from research carried out by Mark Purnell and colleagues at the University of Leicester.

The previously accepted date was based on a study of heterostracen 'fish' but the new evidence, from fossilized soft tissue taken from an extinct group of eel-like creatures called conodonts, suggests that the date for the emergence of vertebrates should be pushed back by at least 40 million years. Purnell found the most complete conodont fossil to date and used it to reconstruct the anatomy of this microscopic creature. The study has revealed several vertebrate characteristics. In addition to blocks of muscles and complex eyes, the team identified a hardened column which they claim to be the precursor of a backbone. The conodonts were known to live in the sea 520 million years ago. Work carried out at the University of Birmingham has shown the presence of dentine in the hard toothlike material of the conodont's mouth. Dentine is another feature attributed to vertebrates.

If these new discoveries are accepted it is likely that conodonts will be classified as vertebrates. In addition to the earlier date for the emergence of vertebrates, the evidence suggests that vertebrate skeletons evolved not from the protective scales of fish but from teeth.

TRILOBITE FOSSIL

An amateur fossil collector, Ced Conolly, discovered a 475 million-year-old fossil trilobite in marine sedimentary rock near Haverfordwest in Dyfed, Wales. The extraordinary feature about this fossil was that some of its soft tissue was still preserved. Conolly recognized that the find was unusual because he thought he could see the impression of a jointed antenna projecting from the head shield of the trilobite. He sent photographs to the National Museum of Wales where Bob Owens, a palaeontologist at the Museum and a specialist in trilobites, recognized the importance of the find. He examined the specimen and found that although the specimen was distorted, the explanation given by Conolly was correct. He forwarded the specimen to Harry Whittington of the University of Cambridge, an expert on the soft tissue of trilobites. The features spotted by Conolly are normally difficult to interpret because the Ordovician rocks in which the trilobite was found underwent strong deformation during the Caledonian phases of mountain-building. None of the original skeleton remained, all that survived being a mould of the shell in the rocks. This is quite a common feature but in this case the mould was exceptionally good and permitted a detailed study of the soft parts of the animal.

The study has revealed a second antenna. Also, part of the mud-filled gut was found and in the central axial region transverse bars were found at the junctions between the body segments forming the abdomen. It is thought the bars are the remains of tendons to which the muscles were attached. This is the first occasion that these features have been found, although their existence had been predicted.

Trilobite fossils are often found with their bodies curled up, no doubt a method of protecting themselves from predators, but the way the animal curled up has been open to speculation. Whittington suggests that this new evidence supports the argument that longitudinal muscles were attached to a series of transverse bars, providing a mechanism for curling and uncurling.

TYRANNOSAURUS REX

Until 25 years ago it was generally accepted that dinosaurs were cold-blooded creatures but John Ostrom of Yale University upset the establishment by claiming that the small predator dinosaur Deinoychus was warm-blooded. Since then there has been considerable evidence to suggest that dinosaurs in general were warm-blooded but the matter has remained controversial. Strong evidence for the warm-blooded school of thought has now come from the work of two American scientists. Reece Barrick and William Showers of North Carolina State University analysed the ratio of oxygen isotopes in the bones of a Tyrannosaurus rex skeleton. They measured the ratio of oxygen-16 and oxygen-18 from 54 locations on the skeleton. From this data they were able to calculate which parts of the body were warmest. The technique depends on the principle that the cooler the bone when it was formed, the higher the ratio of oxygen-18 to oxygen-16. The technique cannot provide information on the exact temperature because the water the animal drank also affects the ratio.

The examination revealed that the ratio was virtually constant, implying that the animal was evenly heated. The T. rex had less than 4°C body temperature variation overall. Its feet were a little cooler and the base of the tail was a little warmer than the tip. This variation is commonly found in large birds and mammals. Cold-blooded creatures such as lizards have a much larger variation in temperature between their extremities and their bodies. Objections to these findings centre on the possibility that the make-up of T. rex was different from that of the skeleton but Showers claims that the skeleton was particularly well-preserved and that this possibility can safely be ignored. The above results are, of course, based on the assumption that the physiology of the dinosaur and that of modern warm-blooded creatures is the same. This cannot be checked when there are no living analogues to make the comparison.

EARLY MAN IN MALAWI

Most of the evidence for Homo habilis, the earliest-known representative of the chain which led to modern man, has been found in East Africa. The specimens from Olduvai Gorge in Tanzania, where the species was discovered, and from Koobi Fora on the eastern shores of Lake Turkana in Kenya, have ages between 1.9 and 1.6 million years. The discovery of a fragment of a skull near Lake Baringo in Kenya in 1967 created much interest and an examination carried out in 1992 gave an age of 2.4 million years. The only other sites where H. habilis has been found occur in southern Africa. Attention, however, was drawn to a site in Malawi because at Mwimbi in the mid 1980s palaeontologists found simple pebble tools of the Oldowan type, some 3 million to 1.6 million years old and thought to have been made by H. habilis. At Uraha, on the north-west shore of Lake Malawi and only a few kilometres north of Mwimbi, a fossil jawbone belonging to H. habilis was found by a team of scientists from Germany, the USA and Malawi. Its age is thought to be about 2.4 million years.

Such an early date for the start of the Homo lineage had been suspected because Oldowan tools with an age of 2.5 million years have been found in Ethiopia. To fit all these results into a systematic pattern has been difficult. Friedeman Schrenk of the Hessisches Landesmuseum in Darmstadt thinks that there was possibly a migration route through the East African rift valley from the Afar region of Ethiopia to southern Malawi. He suggests that early *Homo* evolved from a smaller-brained australopithecine in East Africa about 2.5 million years ago and that the marked drop in world temperatures at the time could have triggered off a new species; when the climate improved, the larger-brained homonids moved south. However, Schrenk and colleagues have labelled the Uraha specimen *H. rudolfensis* and they are of the opinion that there is too much variation among the early specimens for them all to belong to one species.

## DATING THE PAST

One of the major problems experienced by archaeologists is sorting data given by various techniques used to date the past. For example, a date given by stratigraphical evidence may conflict strongly with that derived by radio-carbon techniques. Recent developments in computer techniques by Caitlin Buck and colleagues at the University of Nottingham have enabled a statistical technique first developed in the 18th century to be used to clarify the discrepancies.

A theorem published in 1763 by an English clergyman, Thomas Bayes, permitted a rigorous mathematical analysis of independent data. The theorem is based on the idea that if the outcome of one event is known, it has an effect on the probability of another event occurring. For example, if in a particular month there is one chance in ten that there will be a clear sky in the evening and also one chance in fifty that it will be raining heavily, if it was clear on a particular night the chances of it raining on the following night is modified. Until recently it was not possible to use Bayes's theorem on the archaeological problem because of the difficulty in presenting the date in a form for statistical analysis. The data were too complicated to allow the necessary integrations to be carried out. However, computer-based simulation techniques called Markov Chain Monte Carlo methods have provided a method of solving the integrations indirectly.

These new techniques have been used by Buck and colleagues on data obtained from copper workings at St Veit-Klinglberg, Austria, an early Bronze Age settlement excavated in the 1980s. Many pieces of copper and pottery were found, the pottery being made from clay mixed with slag. The archaeologists had great difficulty in relating the finds to the stratigraphy of the area. Radio-carbon dating of the artifacts gave dates ranging from 3,400 to 3,900 years ago. By using Bayesian analysis, it was possible to narrow the dates for the deposition of individual objects from about 400 years to 200 years. The results show that smelted copper was stored at the site about 3,500 years ago, although there was no evidence that smelting actually took place there.

## ORIGINS OF DOMESTIC CATTLE

Science is full of examples of well-established facts being overturned by subsequent investigations. In the biological field DNA studies have caused many upsets; one such case is the doubt raised about the belief that the domestication of cattle spread from a single centre in the Near East. Work carried out by Daniel Bradley and colleagues at Trinity College, Dublin, compared DNA from cattle on three continents and has shown this belief to be impossible.

It was thought that wild oxen were first domesticated in south-east Turkey some ten to eight thousand years ago. The domesticated animals then moved eastwards towards India and south-west into Africa in the course of waves of migration and invasion. During this time farmers bred a humped-back variety which was able to survive better in dry climates. Analysis of mitochondrial DNA (mtDNA), a form of DNA passed down only in the maternal line, has provided contrary evidence.

The investigators compared the mtDNA of cattle from six European, four African and three Indian breeds. They expected to find two distinct types of mtDNA, one from the humped (zebu) cattle and another from the non-humped (taurine) variety. They found, however, that there was a geographical distinction between animals from India and those from Europe and Africa. To complicate matters, the African breeds included both zebu and taurine cattle. The differences between the two groups were so large that it would have taken some 200,000 years for the mutations to accumulate and it is impossible for them to have come from a common ancestor 10,000 years ago.

The obvious conclusion is that two distinct domestications occurred from different races of ox. The investigators believe that domestication in Turkey led to the taurine variety and that a separate domestication at about the same time, possibly in the Indus Valley, led to the zebu cattle. In Africa there appears to be no difference in the mtDNA in both zebu and taurine cattle.

## ELIMINATING LOCUST PLAGUES

From time immemorial Africa has been plagued with locusts and the cost has been heavy both in financial terms and in human suffering. Between 1985 and 1989, over $400 million has been spent in attempts to control locusts. Recent work has indicated that locust swarms may be a thing of the past. The success of the new approach depends on a fungus instead of chemical pesticides. Apart from being much cheaper, it is also less damaging to the environment. In the past over 11 million litres of the organophosphorus insecticide Fenitrothion have been spread repeatedly over very large areas with only limited success.

Chris Prior and colleagues at the International Institute of Biological Control (IIBC) at Siwood Park, Berkshire, have developed an anti-locust fungus *Metarhizium flavoviride* which grows only on insects and is pathogenic to locusts. A spore of the fungus lands on an insect and germinates, sending a tube up to 20 micrometres long and only 1–2 micrometres thick into the cuticle. The tip of the tube swells and by a combination of enzymatic digestion and brute force the fungus penetrates through the cuticle into the inside of the insect. Here it breaks into small fragments which disperse through the insect's circulatory system. The system becomes clogged up with the fungus and the insect dies.

Although the fungus is present in the environment, mainly in the soil and dead insects, locusts have developed a way of avoiding it. However, the IIBC has developed a spray which it is difficult for them to avoid. Field trials in Benin, Niger and Mauritania have been very successful. Here the fungus was formulated as a suspension in an oil-based liquid which could be sprayed using existing equipment. When the technology has been perfected it may be possible to develop similar techniques for controlling other pests.

FLATWORM MENACE IN SCOTLAND

The spread of the flatworm *Artioposthia triangulata* throughout much of Scotland could have serious implications for agriculture if it is allowed to multiply uncontrolled. It is thought that it was introduced into the botanical gardens in Edinburgh from New Zealand in about 1965 and since then has spread throughout the country. The flatworm eats the common earthworm, which plays a major part in the aeration of the soil and the provision of nutrients in the soil. The loss of earthworms threatens soil fertility.

B. Boag and colleagues of the Scottish Crop Research Institute in Dundee carried out a systematic survey between July 1991 and February 1993 to provide data on the distribution of the flatworm. They identified the worm in 348 domestic gardens in central Scotland, with a higher concentration around Edinburgh, but it was also identified in the Orkneys and some of the inner islands. It was not found in the Shetlands or the Outer Hebrides. A study centred on botanical gardens, nurseries and garden centres revealed its presence in just over a quarter of these establishments. Its presence on farmland was much lower; this is put down to the fact that there is little mixing of soils between gardens and agricultural lands. However, it is considered to be only a matter of time before agricultural land is seriously affected. Where crops are rotated regularly, farmers tend to use fertilizers and do not depend heavily on earthworms as a source of soil nutrients. They will be less affected by the loss of the earthworm but those who have more permanent pastureland could face serious problems in years to come.

RAT PROBLEM OVERCOME

Throughout the world there are numerous cases of islands and habitats becoming infested by rats that have escaped from visiting ships. In some cases the rats have virtually wiped out the existing fauna and caused considerable damage to the flora. The problem has reached an intolerable level on some of the islands just off South Island, New Zealand. Rowland Taylor and Bruce Thomas of the New Zealand Department of Scientific and Industrial Research have developed techniques which may eliminate the problem, on isolated islands at least.

Having achieved success on a small island, the researchers targeted Breaksea Island, which has an area of 170 hectares. Over a period of more than 150 years, rats had seriously depleted the local invertebrates, lizards and birds, and had gnawed and damaged many trees. Tracks were cut 60 metres apart following the contours of the island, and from the three main ridges down to all the beaches. At 743 points bait containing the anticoagulant rat poison Brodifacoum was put down daily for 22 days, placed inside tubes to protect the island's birds.

On the first night 80 per cent of the bait was taken and most of it on the following three nights. After 21 days there were only two visits to the bait and after a month there was no evidence of rats existing on island. Although the bait was left for a year, together with apples, the rat's favourite food, no rat was recorded. Records over the following four years showed no rat activity at all. During this period the researchers identified a previously absent lizard and noticed that rare nesting South Island robins were unharmed. It is planned to introduce two endangered species of weevil and the South Island saddleback, a forest bird now extinct on the mainland.

PROGRESS IN SUPERCONDUCTORS

For many years scientists have carried out research on compounds which when cooled lose all resistance to the passage of an electric current. The compound is then said to be superconducting. The two main criteria for producing this condition are temperature and pressure. The temperature below which the material is superconducting is called the critical temperature ($T_c$) and the main aim of the research is to find compounds with a $T_c$ as high as possible at a pressure as close to normal as possible. In the summer of 1993, a mercury compound broke the temperature record by going superconducting at 150 K ($-123°C$). To achieve this the compound had to be subjected to a pressure equivalent to 100 times that experienced at the bottom of the deepest ocean. At normal pressure the critical temperature was 135 K.

A team led by Paul Chu of the University of Texas at Houston carried out experiments on a complex molecule containing mercury, barium, calcium and copper, or Hg-1223 for short, and found that by subjecting the compound to a pressure of 150 kbar, a value of 150 K could be reached. Chu has calculated that $T_c$ increases by about .02 K for each additional atmospheric pressure. This indicates that if H-1223 were exposed to a pressure of 7.5 million atmospheres, it would be superconducting at room temperatures. Other research has indicated that modifying the chemical composition has the same effect as reducing the applied pressure. The pressure has the effect of squeezing the atoms closer together so if smaller atoms are used, i.e. replacing barium by strontium, it may be possible to increase the $T_c$ without having to apply such huge pressures.

# Theatre

As in the past, money was a major concern throughout the year. Royal Insurance announced that it would not renew its three-year £2.1 million sponsorship of the Royal Shakespeare Company. The relationship had been a good one but Royal Insurance felt it had no choice after a difficult financial year. Adrian Noble, artistic director of the RSC, said, 'Without their support, six years of large-scale national touring with top-quality RSC productions would not have happened; 700,000 people would not have seen the work of the RSC on their doorsteps and countless others would not have been able to see the work of the RSC in a top-price seat for a quarter of its normal price'. With the help of the Prince of Wales, the RSC's president and a self-professed groupie, who held a party for potential sponsors at Buckingham Palace, a new sponsor was found and in January 1994 the RSC announced a sponsorship deal with Allied-Lyons of £3.3 million over a three-year period.

The Camelot Group overcame strong competition, particularly from Richard Branson, and won the licence to run the new National Lottery due to start in November 1994. The group confidently predicted that there would be more money for charity (£1.54 billion on a turnover of £5.5 billion) including the arts, than the Government itself had hoped. Money for the arts is intended for capital projects, not to supplement revenue. It will provide an opportunity to repair rundown arts buildings and to create new ones, although there are fears that there will be insufficient money to run events within them. Equally there are fears that the lottery will be used as an excuse to cut government funding of the Arts Councils.

Concern continued to be expressed about the state of the West End and the continuing dominance of the musical. Soaring prices have meant that it now costs approximately £250,000 to mount a new play. *Oleanna, Marvin's Room* and *Dead Funny* all transferred into the West End but few new plays were launched there. In July 1994 the producers Frank and Woji Gero announced the formation of the West End Producers Alliance with 16 of London's small independent producers. The purpose is to spread the financial risk, encourage new investors (many of the old investors have been hit by losses at Lloyds), and stage work that is, according to the Geros 'new, innovative and daring'. *900 Oneonta* opened at the Old Vic in July with everybody participating for less than their usual fee, including theatre owner David Mirvish. As a result it was possible to keep seat prices down to £7.50 for previews, with a price range of £7.50 to £14.50 during the run.

The Arts Council lifted its threat of closing ten regional theatres but the reduction of £3.2 million in its grant-in-aid for 1994 meant that nearly all theatres received a grant no higher than last year and that

money for new work and projects was cut by £2 million causing concern that young people would find it increasingly difficult to get started. Lord Gowrie, succeeding Lord Palumbo as Arts Council chairman, expressed his concern that many potential drama students were finding it impossible to obtain grants from their local authorities.

In October 1993, The Lyric Hammersmith launched a campaign to raise £350,000 to keep the theatre open and allow Neil Bartlett to take over as artistic director. The money was raised with the help of £150,000 from the Foundation for Sport and the Arts. Other changes in artistic directorship saw Stephen Daldry taking sole control of the Royal Court. His predecessor Max Stafford-Clark left to start his own touring company, Out of Joint, which opened in a joint production with the Haymarket Leicester of *The Queen and I*, an adaptation of Sue Townsend's novel, and Jim Cartwright's *Road*. Pip Broughton left Nottingham Playhouse after some exciting work concluding with *Pygmalion* with Josie Lawrence as Eliza. Kenny Ireland took over at the Royal Lyceum Edinburgh and opened his season with *The Recruiting Officer*. William Burdett Coutts took over the running of the Riverside Studios, introducing some of the skills he acquired running the Assembly Rooms during the Edinburgh Festival to London. Tim Supple and Julia Bardsley took over the Young Vic. After a troubled beginning, in which productions by both directors were critically panned and proved unpopular with audiences, Bardsley departed, leaving Supple to take sole control.

## MUSICALS

It was a quiet year for new musicals after the succession of high-profile flops the year before. The show that attracted the most publicity was the one that did not go on. Evan Steadman, who once worked for the discredited tycoon Robert Maxwell, wrote a musical about Maxwell's life based on the songs and lyrics of Gilbert and Sullivan. An injunction days before the first preview in February brought the musical to a halt and Steadman lost about £500,000 on the venture. The National Theatre's production of Rodgers and Hammerstein's musical *Carousel* transferred to the Shaftesbury Theatre in September 1993 where it ran until May but was not quite able to find an audience large enough to sustain its enormous running costs. Nicholas Hytner's full-blooded production and Bob Crowley's Shaker-inspired New England designs both won Tony awards when the production was restaged with an American cast on Broadway. *Forever Plaid*, a nostalgic tribute to the clean-cut harmony groups of the 1950s opened at the Apollo in September 1993. Despite worldwide success (over 20 productions have played round the world), this American show looked too small on the Apollo stage, won bad publicity for its high seat prices and quickly closed.

A similar fate met Tim Luscombe's musical play *Eurovision*, a parody of the Eurovision song contest that won *nul points* in the West End after being a cult success at the Drill Hall. It was one of a number of shows this year with a gay theme (parallel love affairs between James Dreyfus' Eurovision buff and a promiscuous air steward and between the ghosts of Emperor Hadrian and the young Antinous) but the task of sending up the song contest, already a send-up of itself in most people's eyes, proved impossible. Far better-received and also hovering between musical and play was *Night after Night*, a joint production between the Royal Court and Gloria, first opening at the Traverse during the 1993 Edinburgh Festival. It was a musical about musicals, and particularly about the homosexual performers and backstage staff who contributed to the boy-meets-girl happy endings in the 1950s shows while their own stories remained untold. Neil Bartlett played his own father who, while waiting outside the theatre in 1958 for his mother to celebrate the news of her pregnancy, is swept into the gay underworld of ushers, barmen and chorus boys climaxing in a pastiche of 1950s numbers. Beverly Klein, the only woman in the show, evoked the spirit of Ethel Merman and Carol Channing.

Sam Mendes transformed the Donmar Warehouse into a sleazy nightclub for his revival of *Cabaret*. The audience sat at tables and were allowed to take drink into the threatre. Alan Cumming, following his success as a punkish, youthful Hamlet in the same theatre, played the Emcee, first satirizing Nazism, then apologizing for it (the first half closed with him exposing his buttocks with a swastika drawn on in lipstick), and finally becoming its victim, forced to wear a pink triangle. Jane Horrocks' waiflike vocally-underpowered Sally with a cutglass accent, was more controversial although much admired for the way in which she transformed the title song from an anthem of survival to one of anger.

*Hot Shoe Shuffle*, at the Queens, was the first full-scale Australian musical ever to open in the West End. The subject-matter was not Australian, but rather a tribute to the American tap-dancer, especially black dancers like the Nicholas Brothers and Bill 'Bojangles' Robinson. For many people bad jokes, over-familiar music, a feeble plot and an appalling sound system obscured the cast's athletic dancing skills, but most were dazzled by the speed of Dein Perry's footwork. The show did well to run for six months but was not able to fulfil the original intention of training an English cast to replace the Australians.

Sir Andrew Lloyd Webber demonstrated his financial and critical clout when he closed the London production of *Sunset Boulevard* for three weeks to introduce changes made for the Los Angeles production. Betty Buckley and John Barrowman took over from Patti LuPone and Kevin Anderson. One new song was introduced, John Napier's designs were less influenced by David Hockney and more by the black and white Billy Wilder film on which the show is based, and Trevor Nunn's production was swifter and sharper. Controversy continued to dog the show; Patti LuPone made her anger known after she was dropped in favour of Glenn Close for the Broadway production. And Faye Dunaway, who was supposed to replace Glenn Close in the Los Angeles production, was dropped three days before the show was due to reopen and threatened to sue Lloyd Webber, claiming that she was hired not as a genuine contract but as a 'stalking horse' to 'test the financial viability' of the show.

A number of critics shamefacedly admitted to enjoying Barry Manilow's *Copacabana* at the Prince of Wales, while others dismissed it as an out-of-season panto. Although he wrote the music, co-wrote the book and did the orchestrations, Manilow himself did not perform, disappointing his fans, who were out in full force. Instead the leading roles were taken by Gary Wilmot and Nicola Dawn. Lavish costumes, soupy music and spectacular visuals provided light relief and the show has survived the criticism. It overshadowed the return of *Fiddler on the Roof* to the West End with Topol repeating his performance as the milkman Tevye, one he has given more than 1,400 times. Although the subject matter of ethnic cleansing was all too topical, that made it all the more frustrating that the production, a replica of the original directed by Hal Prince in 1964, was desperately in need of fresh ideas. Jerry Bock and Sheldon Harnick, who wrote *Fiddler on the Roof*, were also, together with Joe Masteroff, responsible for turning Miklos Laszlo's play *Parfumerie* into *She Loves Me*. First seen in America in 1963, the show flopped in London in 1964, but was revived in July 1994 at the Savoy directed by the American Scott Ellis with John Gordon-Sinclair and Ruthie Henshall in the leads. Its exuberant tunes, human scale and unusual combination of romance (without being saccharine) and wit has, so far, delighted audiences.

REVIVALS

Fears continued to be expressed for the West End, which apart from the productions of Sir Peter Hall, seems incapable of generating new productions of plays on its own but instead leans heavily on transfers from the subsidized sector and the regions. Peter Hall, in collaboration with producer Bill Kenwright, presented three productions in the West End, and a *Hamlet* with Stephen Dinsdale is promised for autumn 1994; in addition his uninspired RSC production of *All's Well That Ends Well* transferred from Stratford to London. *She Stoops to Conquer* failed to rouse much enthusiasm except for Donald Sinden's performance as Mr Hardcastle, veering between apoplectic rage and perplexity. David Essex played an ageing Tony Lumpkin. Pam Gems' *Piaf*, at the Piccadilly, looked less substantial than when the RSC first presented it 15 years ago but provided a star vehicle for Elaine Paige's performance in the title role. Paige delivered the songs with extraordinary accuracy and power, so much so that she diverted attention away from the inadequacy of Gems' trawl through Piaf's life. But when Paige became ill and was no longer able to play the production quickly closed. Feydeau's *Le Dindon* translated by Hall himself and Nicki Frei into *An Absolute Turkey*, opened the same month at the Globe. Gerald Scarfe provided the art nouveau designs and Griff Rhys Jones and Felicity Kendal headed a cast that threw itself into the intricacies of a plot in which lust, typically, is the motivating factor. Again Hall, struggling to do high-class work under commercial pressure, could not quite live up to expectations.

The most controversial and unusual revival in the West End was Deborah Warner's production of Samuel Beckett's 20-minute *Footfalls* (seats £4). Playing twice nightly to packed audiences for just one week at the Garrick, this became a *cause célèbre*, with a row between the Beckett estate and Warner threatening to bring the production to a halt after the first performance. The estate objected to a transposition of lines and changes in the stage directions. Warner, a rigorous and talented director, restored the lines to their rightful owners and the performances were allowed to continue at the Garrick but permission was refused for the production to tour Europe (even to the Bobigny centre in France which had financed the production) or for it to be filmed. Michael Billington, the *Guardian* critic, agreed with the estate's criticisms, describing the production as 'a bit like seeing someone doodling on a Rembrandt'. Undoubtedly some of the rhythmic power of the piece was jarred by using two locations, the stage and the front of the dress circle, to suggest that the whole of the dimly-lit theatre (in which seats were tipped over, areas roped off and lights covered in dust sheets) was a metaphor for the oppression under which May struggled to survive; other changes, especially in Fiona Shaw's appearance as May, made absolute sense, particularly in the light of the building in which the production was playing. The prospect of future productions being unable to seek their own solutions to the problems that Beckett poses is dismaying.

Diana Rigg came into the West End with her award-winning performance as Medea in the Almeida Theatre's production before taking it to Broadway. Helen Mirren scored a personal triumph in Turgenev's *A Month in the Country* at the Albery. It proved an unexpected box-office hit, most people going to see Mirren as Natalya Petrovna, the middle-aged woman who falls in love with her son's student tutor. Mirren managed to encompass both the anguish and absurdity of Petrovna, painfully observed by John Hurt's doting Rakitin.

The RSC brought its entire 1993 Stratford season to London headed by Robert Stephens' deeply moving performance as Lear in Adrian Noble's production. Sadly, Stephens became ill and had to withdraw from the play before the end of the run. David Thacker's production of *The Merchant of*

*Venice*, coinciding with one by the West Yorkshire Playhouse, provoked Arnold Wesker to describe it as a 'deeply unpleasant play' provoking anti-Semitism at a time when there is already a resurgence of anti-Semitism in eastern Europe. Thacker's production was, however, deeply sympathetic to Shylock, played by David Calder as a modern-day broker with a laptop computer on one side of his desk and a Bible on the other. Ian Judge's Edwardian production of *Love's Labours Lost* looked just as pretty but more superficial than it had in Stratford, while Simon Russell Beale won praise for his blonde Ariel, dressed in a Chairman Mao suit and full of hostility for Alec McCowan's Prospero, in Sam Mendes' production of *The Tempest*. Terry Hands' production of *Tamburlaine* expanded from the Swan onto the Barbican stage with African-inspired dance choreographed by Welcome Msomi.

Productions opening in London at the Barbican included a revival of Tom Stoppard's *Travesties*, tightened up by Stoppard with Antony Sher as Henry Carr, the minor diplomat who happened to be present in Zurich at the same time as Joyce, Lenin and Tristan Tzara. This later transferred to the Savoy. Noble came a cropper with a production of *Macbeth* unsuitably cast with Derek Jacobi in the lead and Cheryl Campbell as Lady Macbeth. Tim Albery's truncated version of Schiller's *Wallenstein* was much-praised for its clarity, proved easily able to fill the Pit, and provoked renewed calls from some critics for the staging of more European classics in the UK.

At Stratford, the season opened with Iain Glen's engaging, troubled performance as the King in Mathew Warchus' otherwise muddled *Henry V*. Toby Stephens, son of Robert Stephens and Maggie Smith, had a personal triumph as an arrogant, boyish Coriolanus in the RSC Swan, and John Barton's small-scale *Peer Gynt* with Alex Jennings eclipsed the much flashier Japanese production which visited the RSC the previous autumn. Ian Judge's funny if superficial *Twelfth Night* was dominated by Desmond Barritt's outrageous Malvolio. Soaring over all these productions, however, was Noble's production of *A Midsummer Night's Dream*, both highly original and surreally beautiful with superb leads from Alex Jennings and Stella Gonet as Theseus/Oberon and Hypolyta/Titania.

The Royal National Theatre celebrated the end of 1993 by winning a third of the Olivier awards. It scored a considerable triumph with Stephen Daldry's production of Sophie Treadwell's 1928 feminist play *Machinal* based on a real-life trial in which a young stenographer, wooed by her boss and trapped in a loveless marriage, was executed for killing her husband in order to be with her lover. Treadwell's desire to create an expressionistic indictment of the mechanical age was thrillingly realized in Ian McNeil's designs, which exploited every potential of the Lyttelton theatre. A huge, oppressive iron platform was suspended above the action, and tilted, rose and covered the whole stage. In the final scene the entire floor of the Lyttelton stage was lifted to expose the theatre's nether regions where a naked Fiona Shaw as the Young Woman was executed. A visual spectacle, played without an interval, this was an event and the kind of theatre that attracted attention throughout the year. The production was showered with awards and added to Daldry's already high-flying reputation; but, perhaps because of the bleakness of the piece, audiences did not quite reach the figures necessary for the production to be extended.

Disappointingly, Sean Mathias' production of Cocteau's *Les Parents Terribles*, wittily translated by Jeremy Sams, suffered a similar fate. A crack cast, including Sheila Gish, Frances de la Tour and Alan Howard and newcomers Jude Law and Lynsey Baxter, brilliantly performed this Gallic black farce with an incestuous theme, which moves into tragedy in its final moments. It was an impressively designed production, with Stephen Brimson Lewis providing a stark contrast between the sleazy chaos of the possessive mother's boudoir and the antiseptic order of the girlfriend whose flat was dominated by a towering spiral staircase (not always easy for the actors to negotiate).

After a disastrous production of Charles McArthur's political farce *Johnny on a Spot*, Richard Eyre, director of the National Theatre, recovered his form with Tennessee Williams's *Sweet Bird of Youth*. By introducing scenes that did not appear in the Broadway production Eyre heightened the impact of the Southern racism against which the action takes place. Claire Higgins gave one of the performances of the year as the washed-up screen goddess checked into a Louisiana hotel suite under a false name with her gigolo Chance Wayne, played by Robert Knepper.

Stephen Daldry began his regime at the Royal Court not with a piece of new writing, but a tribute to the Court's historic past, Arnold Wesker's *The Kitchen*, first produced in 1959. In the most expensive production ever put on at the Royal Court, Daldry pulled off another coup, creating a gleaming stainless steel kitchen where the stalls usually are and seating the audience in the circle and on the stage. A cast of 28 chopped, stirred, fried, cleaned and cooked, reaching at times a manic level of activity; only the food was missing. The production was an event, although some doubts were raised as to the quality of Wesker's play. With so many seats lost to the action, demand far outweighed availability and there was talk of transferring the production to the long-dark Roundhouse, but the fact that some of the cast were students and paid below-Equity rates added to the political difficulties of taking the production elsewhere.

NEW PLAYS

Harold Pinter chose to present his first full-length play (only just, at 80 minutes) for 15 years at the Almeida where recent revivals of *Betrayal* and *No*

*Man's Land* have been much acclaimed. The opening of *Moonlight* was a major event for the small Islington theatre, with a cast that included Ian Holm (absent from the stage for 12 years) and Anna Massey. The play turns back from the human rights concerns of his recent plays to more personal pieces like *The Homecoming*. The strength of the piece lies in the relationship between Andy, raging against his encroaching death, and his wife (Anna Massey) apparently disdainful until she tries to persuade their sons to come to the deathbed. False memories, betrayal, fear of the unknowingness of death are partly what the play is about, although few people felt confident enough to state its theme with any certainty, particularly since it is hard to know the role of the daughter floating in a void above the rest of the action, who may or may not be dead. Critical opinion varied from the ecstatic to the dismissive but the overwhelming sense was that this play contained some writing as powerful as anything Pinter has ever produced but was not a match for his early plays.

The second part of Tony Kushner's *Angels in America* at the National was also eagerly awaited. *Perestroika* opened in tandem with a newly-cast revival of the first part *Millennium Approaches* shortly after the opening of both parts on Broadway. *Millennium* finished with an angel dangling over the bed of Prior, a man dying of Aids in New York murmuring 'Very Steven Spielberg'. It was always going to be a hard act to follow and so it proved; *Perestroika* is more repetitive and rambling than its predecessor and concludes with an improbably optimistic ending. It is dominated once more by the real-life character of Roy Cohn, the homophobic homosexual who died of Aids. Whether it is possible to forgive such a man is one of the play's major themes, alongside a damning portrait of Reagan's America.

David Hare concluded his trilogy about the state of the nation at the National Theatre. *Racing Demon* and *Murmuring Judges* were revived to run alongside the newcomer *Absence of War*. *Racing Demon*, a study of how liberalism copes with the rise of fundamentalism, remains the best play, perhaps because it was written before Hare conceived of a grand trilogy. *Murmuring Judges*, a study of the inadequacies of the legal system, is the most flawed, in thrall to its research as Hare himself now admits. *Absence of War* hovers somewhere between, a study of how the Labour Party is losing its ideals in the face of the marketing men. John Thaw played George Jones, an honest, rambling leader who was inevitably compared to Neil Kinnock. There were as many political commentators as critics in the audience on the first night and there was a tendency to judge the play according to how accurately it depicted the state of the current Labour Party rather than as a work of the imagination drawing on some current themes. Hare wrote a book to accompany the play which caused even more of a stir, casting doubt on Neil Kinnock's judgment in allowing a writer to sit in on confidential meetings. It may be some time before the play can be judged as a piece of theatre, although there is one undeniably powerful scene in which Jones attempts to recover his power of oratory only to falter and lose his way. As a trilogy, however, it was generally agreed that it was just what the National Theatre should be putting on and nobody could fault the expertise or artistry with which it was presented.

Terry Johnson had two new plays produced in quick succession, an unusual state of affairs. *Hysteria*, at the Royal Court, was an ambitious combination of farce and melodrama loosely based on an episode towards the end of Freud's life when he was visited by Salvador Dali. It had a surrealist set by Mark Thompson to match. This failed to transfer but *Dead Funny*, an examination of the British sense of humour with a cast headed by Zoe Wanamaker as a witty 40-year-old polytechnic lecturer struggling to get pregnant, opened first at Hampstead and, despite shocking some audiences, transferred to the Vaudeville.

*Me and Mamie O'Rourke* was a rare case of a new play opening immediately in the West End for a short run. The Strand Theatre was always full, but more because of the presence of Dawn French and Jennifer Saunders in the cast than the quality of the play. Nicol Williamson returned to the West End to present his own show about Jack Barrymore, the alcoholic American actor, and displayed some of Barrymore's own temperament when he cut short the second night's performance saying that he did not feel he could give enough of his best to carry on. Michael Palin's *Weekend* was damned as being no better than a TV sitcom, offering no incentive to leave the home. This was despite the best efforts of Richard Wilson, who appeared to be recreating his cantankerous television character Victor Meldrew onstage although Palin's play was written many years before David Renwick's comedy hit the small screen. Kevin Elyot's *My Night with Reg*, a humane comedy, was the first play to transfer directly from the Theatre Upstairs to the West End.

New work of a different sort included Théâtre de Complicité's extraordinary adaptation of a story by John Berger. Called *The Three Lives of Lucie Cabrol*, it opened Manchester's year as the City of Drama and later came to the Riverside Studios in London. The tale of a peasant woman living at the turn of the century in Haute Savoie and struggling to survive solitude, disappointment and poverty won the hearts of almost everybody who saw it. Lilo Baur was exceptional as the gnarled, wizened Lucie Cabrol while the rest of the talented company played everything else, including blueberry bushes and chickens as well as her parents and childhood friends. The Tricycle Theatre scored a huge hit with Richard Norton Taylor's adaptation of the Scott 'arms to Iraq' inquiry, *Half the Picture*, with additional material by John McGrath. The list of characters included John Major, Michael Heseltine, Margaret Thatcher and Alan Clark, and the production caused such a stir that the theatre scored the considerable coup of being invited to play in the House of Commons.

FOREIGN VISITORS

Peter Brook returned to London after more than a decade away with *The Man Who . . .*, described as 'a theatrical research inspired by the work by Oliver Sachs'. His international company, usually based in Paris, toured Newcastle, Glasgow and Nottingham before coming to London. Audiences expecting an epic follow-up to *The Mahabharata* were disappointed but others found this concentrated, humane inquiry into the workings of the mind an absorbing experience.

Robert Lepage, the talented French Canadian, made two visits to this country with his company Théâtre Repère. *Coriolan*, performed in Quebecois, was presented at the Nottingham Playhouse. At the Edinburgh Festival he opened the first two of a seven-part work *The Seven Streams of the River Ota*. Set in Hiroshima and, like most of Lepage's work, visually very exciting, it covers some of the major post-war obsessions.

Yukio Ninagawa directed an international cast in *Peer Gynt* at the Barbican, Unusually, Peer Gynt, young and old, was played by just one actor, an exciting new talent, Michael Sheen. Extraordinary effects recalling the interior of a television set and video games were considered to confuse rather than enhance Ibsen's play. Lev Dodin's Maly Theatre of St Petersburg toured the country with a repertory of five productions including *The Cherry Orchard, Stars in the Morning Sky, Gaudeamus, Brothers and Sisters* and *The Devils*. The company lived up to its description by Peter Brook as 'the finest theatre ensemble in the world'. Peter Zadek's determinedly unromantic Berliner Ensemble production of *Antony and Cleopatra* and Peter Stein's seven-hour Russian version of *The Oresteia* were the highlights of the 1994 Edinburgh Festival.

Finally, the 90th birthday of Sir John Gielgud produced numerous tributes but the most lasting is the naming of a theatre on Shaftesbury Avenue in London after the actor. The Globe is to be renamed the Gielgud in autumn 1994 to coincide with the opening of *Hamlet*, a role in which Gielgud had great success. The change of name also means that the only Globe Theatre in London will in future be the 16th-century recreation in Southwark which was the brainchild of the director Sam Wanamaker, who died this year.

---

## PRODUCTIONS
August 1993 to August 1994

---

LONDON PRODUCTIONS

ADELPHI, WC2 *Sunset Boulevard*, since July 1993

ALBERY, WC2 (22 March 1994) *A Month in the Country* (Turgenev) with Helen Mirren, John Hurt, Polly Adams,

Joseph Fiennes, Anna Livia Ryan, Gawn Grainger, John Standing, Trevor Ray; director, Bill Bryden. (25 July) *Lady Windermere's Fan*, transferred from Birmingham Repertory Theatre

ALDWYCH, WC2 (21 August 1993) *An Inspector Calls* (NT production) with Kenneth Cranham, Julian Glover, Judy Parfitt, Sylvestra le Touzel; director, Stephen Daldry

ALMEIDA, NI (2 September 1993) *Moonlight* (Pinter) with Ian Holm, Anna Massey, Claire Skinner, Michael Sheen, Douglas Hodge, Jill Johnson, Edward de Souza; director, David Leveux. (November) *The LA Plays* (Han Ong) with François Chau, Tony Guilfoyle, Okon Jones, Michelle Newell, David Elliot, Stefan Bednarczyk, Henry Ian Cusick, Richard Cordery, Ramon Tikaram; director, Matthew Lloyd. (2 December) *The School for Wives* (Molière) with Ian McDiarmid, Emma Fielding, Damian Lewis; director, Jonathan Kent. (11 February 1994) *The Life of Galileo* (Brecht) with Richard Griffiths, Michael Gough, Alfred Burke, Edward de Souza, Cara Kelly, Colin Tierney, Timothy Watson; director, Jonathan Kent. (7 April) *Butterfly Kiss* (Phyllis Nagy) with Elizabeth Berridge, Mary MacLeod, Susan Brown, Andrew Woodall, Debora Weston, Larry Lamb, Oliver Cotton, Sandra Dickinson; director, Steven Pimlott. (17 May) *The Bed Before Yesterday* (Ben Travers) with Brenda Blethyn, Charles Kay; director, Peter Wood

AMBASSADORS, WC2 (10 October 1993) *Vita and Virginia* (Eileen Atkins) with Eileen Atkins, Penelope Wilton; director, Patrick Garland. (25 January 1994) *April In Paris* (John Godber) with Gary Olsen, Maria Friedman; director, John Godber. (29 June) *The Cryptogram* (Mamet) with Lindsay Duncan, Eddie Izzard; director, Gregory Mosher

APOLLO, WI (16 September 1993) *Forever Plaid* (Stuart Ross) with Stan Chandler, David Engel, Larry Raben, Guy Stroman; director and choreographer, Stuart Ross. (3 May 1994) *Rough Justice* (Terence Frisby) with Martin Shaw, Diana Quick; director, Robin Herford

APOLLO VICTORIA, SWI. *Starlight Express*, since 1984

ARTS, WC2 (January 1994) *Anorak of Fire* (Stephen Dinsdale) with James Holmes. (May) *Leader!* (Furst and Leigh) with M. Simon Leigh, Steve Furst, Paul Putner

BARBICAN, EC2 (9 September 1993) *Travesties* (Stoppard) with Anthony Sher, David Westhead, Geoffrey Hutchinson, Lloyd Hutchinson, Amanda Harris, Rebecca Saire, Trevor Martin, Darlene Johnson; director, Adrian Noble. (23 September) *Two Gentlemen of Verona*, revival of 1991 production. (13 October) *Tamburlaine* (Marlowe) with Anthony Sher; director, Terry Hands. (16 December) *Macbeth*, with Derek Jacobi, Cheryl Campbell; director, Adrian Noble. (4 April 1994) *The Merchant of Venice*, with David Calder, Penny Downie; transferred from Stratford. (28 April) *Love's Labour's Lost*, transferred from Stratford. (26 May) *King Lear*, with Robert Stephens; transferred from Stratford. (7 July) *The Tempest*, with Alec McCowan; transferred from Stratford

THE PIT (August 1993) *The Odyssey* (Homer, adapt. Derek Walcott) with Ron Cook, Amanda Harris, Stephen Casey, Geoffrey Freshwater, Rudolph Walker. (15 September) *Wallenstein* (Schiller) with Barbara Jefford, Toby Stephens, Philip Voss, Paul Webster, Olivia Williams; director, Tim Albery. (6 October) *All's Well That Ends Well*, with Barbara Jefford, Sophie Thompson, Toby Stephens; transferred from Stratford. (8 December) *Wildest Dreams* (Ayckbourn) with Brenda Blethyn, Barry McCarthy, Peter Laird; director, Alan Ayckbourn. (12 January 1994) *Unfinished Business* (Michael Hastings) with Geoffrey Bayldon, Toby Stephens, Philip Voss, Gemma Jones, Jasper Britton, Ian

Taylor, Angela Vale, Monica Dolan; director, Steven Pimlott. (31 March) *Ghosts* (Ibsen) with Jane Lapotaire, John Carlisle, Simon Russell Beale; transferred from The Other Place, Stratford. (27 April) *Elgar's Rondo*, transferred from the Swan, Stratford. (25 May) *Murder in the Cathedral* (Eliot) with Michael Feast; transferred from the Swan, Stratford. (6 July) *The Country Wife* (Wycherley) with Debra Gillett, Jeremy Northam, Robin Soans; transferred from the Swan, Stratford

BUSH, WI2 (September 1993) *Beautiful Thing* (Jonathan Harvey) with Mark Letheren, Sophie Stanton, Patricia Kerrigan, Jonny Lee Miller, Philip Glenister; director, Hettie Macdonald. (6 October) *Keyboard Skills* (Lesley Bruce); director, Geraldine McEwan. (November) *The Clearing* (Helen Edmundson) with Adrian Rawlins, Susan Lynch, Stephen Boxer; director, Lynne Parker. (18 January 1994) *The Cut* (Mike Cullen) with Billy Riddoch; director, Martin McCardie. (February) *Bad Company* (Simon Bent) with Kemal Sylvester, Stuart Laing, Paul Wyett, Nicola Sanderson, Nicolas Tennant, Suzanne Hitchmough, Gary Sefton, Mark Petrie; director, Paul Miller. (March) *Democracy* (John Murrell) with Hugh Ross, Stanley Townsend. (6 May) *Darwin's Flood* (Snoo Wilson) with John Kane, Rosemary McHale, Paul Bentall, Alex Kingston, Barbara Barnes. (22 June) *Rage* (Richard Zajdlic) with Sue Johnston, Nicky Henson, Sasha Hails, Ian Curtis, Kevin Dignam, Helen Baxendale; director, Mike Bradwell. (August) *In the Heart of America* (Naomi Wallace) with Sasha Hails, Zubin Varla, Toshie Ogura, Robert Glenister; director, Dominic Dromgoole

CAMBRIDGE, WC2 (9 March 1994) *Sinderella*, with Jim Davidson, Charlie Drake

COCKPIT, NW8 (5 October 1993) *Ripped* (Karen Hope) with Victoria Harwood, Lindsey Wilson, David Sibley, Sidney Cole; director, Jessica Dromgoole. (8 February 1994) *Bitter 'n' Twisted*. (1 March) *Paddywack* (Daniel Magee). (16 May) *Peripheral Violence* (Robin Lindsay Wilson) with Ronnie McCann, Rab Christie, Susan Webster, Capbell Morrison, Stuart McGugan; director, Mark Ravenhill

COMEDY, SWI (15 September 1993) *Marvin's Room*, transferred from the Hampstead Theatre. (2 November) *Moonlight*, transferred from the Almeida. (11 January 1994) *September Tide*, with Susannah York, Michael Praed; transferred from the King's Head. (19 July) *The Miracle Worker* (William Gibson) with Jenny Seagrove, Catherine Holman; director, Richard Olivier

CRITERION, WI (11 October 1993) *Looking Through A Glass Onion* (John Waters) with John Waters. (18 May 1994) *Jack - A Night on the Town with John Barrymore* (Nicol Williamson, Leslie Megahey) with Nicol Williamson; director, Leslie Megahey. (18 July) *Juggle and Hyde*, with the Flying Karamazov Brothers

DOMINION, WCI. *Grease*, since July 1993

DONMAR WAREHOUSE, WC2 (16 September 1993) *The Life of Stuff* (Simon Donald) with Forbes Masson, Sandy McDade, Stuart McQuarrie; director, Matthew Warchus. (10 November) *Hamlet* (Shakespeare) with Alan Cumming, Eleanor Bron, Pip Donaghy, Hilary Lyon, Trevor Baxter; director, Stephen Unwin. (2 December) *Cabaret* (Masteroff, Ebb and Kander) with Jane Horrocks, Alan Cumming; director, Sam Mendes. (29 March 1994) *Beautiful Thing*, Bush Theatre production. (26 May) *Glengarry Glen Ross* (Mamet) with James Bolam, Ron Cook; director, Sam Mendes

DRURY LANE THEATRE ROYAL, WC2. *Miss Saigon*, since 1989

DUCHESS, WC2. *Don't Dress for Dinner*, since 1992

DUKE OF YORK'S, WC2 (15 September 1993) *Oleanna*, transferred from the Royal Court. (29 June 1994) *The Rocky Horror Show* (Richard O'Brien) with Jonathon Morris, Nicholas Parsons, Sophie Lawrence, Paul Collis, Patricia Quinn

FORTUNE, WC2. *The Woman in Black*, since 1989

GARRICK, WC2 (8 November 1993) *One Man*, with Steven Berkoff. (14 March 1994) *Footfalls* (Beckett) with Fiona Shaw, Susan Engel; director, Deborah Warner. (6 July) *The Canterbury Tales*, with Brian Glover, Adrian Neil, Nicholas Lumley, David Bailie; directors, Michael Bogdanovitch, Robin Davies

GATE, W11 (September 1993) *Bohemian Lights* (del Valle-Inclán) with Tony Rohr, Ray Callaghan; director, Laurence Boswell. (November) *The Madman of the Balconies* (Mario Vargas Llosa) with Peter Eyre. (December) *The Great Highway* (Strindberg, trans. Kenneth McLeish) with Sylvester Morand, David Sibley; director, David Farr. (January 1994) *Fatzer Material* (Brecht); director, Marc von Henning. (February) *The New Mendoza* (Lenz); director, David Fielding. (14 March 1994) *The Cheating Hearts* (Marivaux, trans. Ranjit Bolt) with John Baxter, Anna Healy, Marcello Magni, Sara Mair-Thomas; director, Laurence Boswell. (May) *Jeppe of the Hill* (Ludwig Holberg) with Jonathan Coyne; director, Ben Crocker. (July) *Jordan* (Anna Reynolds) with Moira Buffini; director, Fiona Buffini

GLOBE, W1 (27 December 1993) *An Absolute Turkey* (Feydeau, trans. Nicki Frei, Peter Hall) with Felicity Kendal, Geoffrey Hutchings, Griff Rhys Jones, Nicholas Le Prevost; director, Peter Hall. (24 August 1994) *The Winslow Boy* (Rattigan) with Peter Barkworth, Simon Williams, Eve Matheson, Nyree Dawn Porter; director, Wyn Jones

GREENWICH, SE10 (2 September 1993) *Amphibious Spangulatos* (Paul Doust), National Youth Theatre production. (11 November) *Doctor Faustus* (Marlowe) with Jonathan Cullen, Hugh Ross; director, Philip Franks. (14 December) *Mr and Mrs Nobody* (Keith Waterhouse) with Patricia Routledge, Clive Swift; director, Matthew Francis. (3 March 1994) *The Old Ladies* (Rodney Ackland) with Faith Brook, Miriam Karlin, Doreen Mantle; directors, Annie Castledine, Sean O'Connor. (9 May) *Falling Over England* (Julian Mitchell) with James Laurensen, Charlotte Cornwell; director, Matthew Francis. (June) *The Browning Version* (Rattigan) with Clive Merrison, Diana Hardcastle; director, Philip Franks. (9 August) *The Sisters Rosensweig* (Wendy Wasserstein) with Janet Suzman, Maureen Lipman, Lynda Bellingham; director, Michael Blakemore

HAMPSTEAD, NW3 (8 September 1993) *A Going Concern* (Stephen Jeffreys) with Henry Stamper, David Killick, David Horovitch, Reece Dinsdale, James Clyde, Adam Godley, Shaun Prendergast, Samantha Holland; director, Matthew Lloyd. (2 February 1994) *Dead Funny* (Terry Johnson) with Zoe Wanamaker, David Haig, Niall Buggy. (12 April) *Ghost from a Perfect Place* (Philip Ridley) with Bridget Turner, John Wood, Trevyn McDowell, Rachel Power, Katie Tyrell; director, Matthew Lloyd. (25 May) *The Lodger*, Royal Exchange Theatre, Manchester, production. (30 June) *A Collier's Friday Night* (D. H. Lawrence) with Edward Peel, Barbara Jefford, Dominic Rowan; director, John Dove

HAYMARKET THEATRE ROYAL, SW1 (13 December 1993) *Two Gentlemen of Verona*, transferred from the Barbican. (23 May 1994) *Arcadia*, with Roger Allam, Joanne Pearce; transferred from the National Theatre

HER MAJESTY'S, SW1. *The Phantom of the Opera*, since 1986

KING'S HEAD, N1 (20 July 1993) *September Tide* (Daphne du Maurier) with Susannah York, Brendan Coyle; director, Mark Rayment. (October) *Parallel Vision* (Stephanie Crawford) with Janie Dee, Diana Kent, Ellie Beavan, Katey Crawford Kastin, Christina Greatrex, Rob Dixon, John Cornwell; director, Dan Crawford. (10 December) *You Can't Take It With You* (Kaufman and Hart) with Janie Dee, Sally George, Frank Middlemass, Bridget Turner, Paul Venables; director, Martin Connor. (3 March) *Elsewhere* (Neal Bell); director, Tracy Thorne. *Invade My Privacy* (Howard Samuels) with Belinda Cryer, Lucy Dixon, Michelle Fine, Tina Jones, Howard Samuels; director, Linda Marlowe

LILIAN BAYLIS, EC1 (October 1993) *The Grubb Street Opera* (Fielding; music adapted by Jonathan Goldstein) with Neil Salvage, Graham Christopher, Susan Dury, Richard Pocock, Jacqueline Charlesworth, Andrew Hesker, Adrian Johnson, Sarah Hayhurst, Vicky Ogden; director, Ben Crocker; choreographer, Imogen Claire. (26 October) *Diary of a New York Queen* (William Barber) with Harold Finlay; director, Lucille O'Flanagan. (2 November) *Battieman Blues* (Oscar Watson) with Idris Elba, Andre Douglas; director, Oscar Watson. (March 1994) *The Eagle Has Two Heads* (Cocteau) with Lisa Harrow, Stash Kirkbridge; director, Susannah York

LONDON PALLADIUM, WC1. *Joseph and the Amazing Technicolour Dreamcoat*, since 1991. (28 June 1994) *Fiddler on the Roof*, with Topol

LYRIC, W1. *Five Guys Named Moe*, since 1990

LYRIC, W6 (August 1993) *Gormenghast* (John Constable; music, John Eacott) with Peter Bailie, Gavin Marshall, Paul Hamilton, Peter Holdway, Di Sherlock, Sarah Cameron, Sally O'Donnell; director, David Glass; choreographer, Sally Owen. (2 September) *In the Summer House* (Jane Bowles) with Rosemary Harris, Dana Ivey, Sophie Thursfield, Robin Weaver; director, Derek Goldby. (November) *Exact Change* (David Epstein) with Kevin McNally, Mick McShane, Steven O'Shea; director, Aaron Mullen. (May 1994) *Uncle Silas* (Le Fanu) with Anne Marie Duff, Terence Wilton; director, Mike Alfreds. (June) *Measure for Measure* (Shakespeare) with Stephen Boxer, Adam Kotz, Anastasia Hille; director, Declan Donnellan (Cheek by Jowl production). (July) *The Lady From the Sea*, joint production with the West Yorkshire Playhouse, Leeds

LYRIC STUDIO (18 August 1993) *The Cenci* (Shelley) with Craig Pender, Louise Bangay, Ninka Scott, Jason Morell, Corin Mellinger; director, Sydnee Blake. (12 October) *Flight* (Bulgakov); director, David Graham-Young. (13 December) *Playhouse Creatures* (April de Angelis). (January 1994) *Breaking the Bank* (Eleanor Zeal). (11 April) *900 Oneonta* (David Beaird) with Leland Brooke, Linda Marlowe, Douglas Hensall, Jon Cryer, Eileen Page; director, David Beaird. (27 April) *The Truman Capote Talkshow* (Bob Kingdom) with Bob Kingdom; director, Kevin Knight

NATIONAL THEATRE, SE1, COTTESLOE (20 November 1993) *Perestroika* (Tony Kushner) with Daniel Craig, Nancy Crane, Stephen Dillane, Susan Engel, Clare Holman, Jason Isaacs, Joseph Myell, David Schofield, Harry Towb; director, Declan Donnellan. *Millennium Approaches* (Kushner), revival of 1992 production then titled *Angels in America*. (3 December) *Mother Courage and Her Children* (Brecht) with Ellie Haddington; director, Anthony Clark. (20 January 1994) *Skriker* (Caryl Churchill) with Kathryn Hunter, Sandy McDade, Jacqueline Defferary; director, Les Waters; music, Judith Weir; choreographer, Ian Spink. (8 March) *Wicked, Yaar!* (Garry Lyons) with Ravi Aujla, Bhasker; director, John Turner. (4 May) *The Man Who . . .*

(Oliver Sachs, adapt. Peter Brook) with David Bennent, Satigui Kouyate, Bruce Myers, Yoshi Oida, Mahmoud Tabrizi-Zadeh; director, Peter Brook. (26 May) *Rutherford and Son* (Githa Sowbery) with Bob Peck, Brid Brennan, Sean Chapman, Wayne Foskett, Tom Mannion, Phoebe Nicholls; director, Katie Mitchell. (21 July) *Le Cid* (Corneille, trans. Ranjit Bolt) with Duncan Bell, Susan Lynch; director, Jonathan Kent

LYTTELTON (15 October 1993) *Machinal* (Sophie Treadwell) with Fiona Shaw, John Woodvine, June Watson, Ciaran Hinds; director, Stephen Daldry. (16 December) *Sweeney Todd*, transferred from the Cottesloe. (11 March 1994) *The Birthday Party* (Pinter) with Anton Lesser, Bob Peck, Dora Bryan, Nicholas Woodeson; director, Sam Mendes. (15 April) *Les Parents Terribles* (Cocteau, trans. Jeremy Sams) with Alan Howard, Frances de la Tour, Sheila Gish, Jude Law, Lynsey Baxter; director, Sean Mathias. (10 June) *Sweet Bird of Youth* (Tennessee Williams) with Robert Knepper, Clare Higgins, Richard Pasco; director, Richard Eyre. (29 July) *Broken Glass* (Arthur Miller) with Henry Goodman, Margot Leicester, Julia Swift; director, David Thacker

OLIVIER (2 September 1993) *Racing Demon*, revival of 1990 production. (9 September) *Murmuring Judges*, revival of 1991 production. (2 October) *Absence of War* (David Hare) with John Thaw, Clare Higgins, Barbara Leigh-Hunt, Michael Bryant, Richard Pasco, Robin Bailey, Oliver Ford Davies; director, Richard Eyre. (1 December) *The Wind in the Willows*, revival of 1990 production. (25 March 1994) *Johnny on a Spot* (Charles MacArthur) with Mark Strong, Janie Dee, James Grout, Diane Langton, Nathan Osgood, Howard Ward, Michael Bryant; director, Richard Eyre. (13 May) *Pericles* (Shakespeare) with Douglas Hodge, Henry Goodman, Susan Lynch, Kathryn Hunter; director, Phyllida Lloyd. (1 July) *The Seagull* (Chekhov) with Judi Dench, Bill Nighy, Anna Calder-Marshall, Helen McCrory, Edward Petherbridge, Norman Rodway; director, John Caird

NEW END, NW3 (February 1994) *A Doll's House* (Ibsen) with Rachel Joyce, Simon Chandler; director, Sue Lefton. (April) *Red* (Anna Reynolds) with Carrie Thomas, Leonora Roger-Wright; director, Fiona Buffini

NEW LONDON, WC2. *Cats*, since 1981

OLD VIC, SE1 (14 September 1993) *Hair* (book, James Rado, Gerome Ragni; music, Galt MacDermott) with John Barrowman, Paul J. Medford, Paul Hipp, Sinitta, Pepsi Lawrie Demacque, Felice Arena, Andree Bernard, Rebecca Vere, Katharine Mehrling; director, Michael Bogdanov; choreographer, Anthony van Laast. (28 December) *A Christmas Carol*, adapted and performed by Patrick Stewart. (18 July) *900 Oneonta*, transferred from the Lyric Studio

OPEN AIR, Regent's Park, NW1 (27 May 1994) *A Midsummer Night's Dream* (Shakespeare) with Paul Freeman, Estelle Kohler, Jenna Russell, Rebecca Egan, Robert Lang, Cameron Blakely; director, Deborah Paige. (13 June) *Hamlet* (Shakespeare) with Damien Lewis; director, Tim Pigott-Smith. (26 July) *The Card* (Drewe and Hatch) with Peter Duncan, Hayley Mills, John Turner, Jessica Martin, Jane Lowe, Jenna Russell

PALACE, WC2. *Les Misérables*, since 1985

PHOENIX, WC2. *Blood Brothers*, since 1991

PICCADILLY, W1 (8 December 1993) *Piaf* (Pam Gems) with Elaine Paige; director, Peter Hall

PLAYERS (14 April 1994) *The Boyfriend* (Sandy Wilson) with Gemma Page, James Davies, Keith John Rutland; director, Maria Charles; choreographer, Geoffrey Webb

PLAYHOUSE, WC2 (1 December 1993) *Jane Eyre* (Brontë, adapt. Fay Weldon) with Alexandra Mathie, Tim Pigott-Smith; director, Helena Kaut-Howson

PRINCE EDWARD, W1. *Crazy For You*, since March 1993

PRINCE OF WALES, W1 (20 December 1993) *Aspects of Love* (Lloyd Webber), revival. (23 June 1994) *Copacabana* (Barry Manilow) with Gary Wilmot, Nicola Dawn

QUEENS, W1 (25 October 1993) *She Stoops To Conquer* (Goldsmith) with Donald Sinden, Miriam Margolyes, David Essex, Emily Morgan, Victoria Hasted, Tom Beard, Peter Gordon, Kate Buckley, Leon Sinden; director, Peter Hall. (16 March 1994) *Hot Shoe Shuffle* (Larry Buttrose, Kathryn Riding) with David Atkins, Dein Perry, Kevin Coyne, Christopher Horsey, Sheldon Perry, Dale Pengelly, Adam Garcia, Rhonda Burchmore, Jack Webster; director, David Atkins; choreographers, David Atkins, Dein Perry

ROYAL COURT, SW1 (27 August 1993) *Hysteria* (Terry Johnson) with Henry Goodman, Tim Potter; director, Phyllida Lloyd. (24 November) *Night After Night* (Neil Bartlett, Nicolas Bloomfield); director, Neil Bartlett. (6 January 1994) *The Cavalcaders* (Billy Roche), Abbey Theatre, Dublin, production. (17 February) *The Kitchen* (Wesker) with Christopher Fulford, Lorraine Ashbourne, Annette Badland, Bambos Karayanis, Teddy Kempner, Stefan Marling, Ric Morgan, Tony Rohr, Christopher Simon, Sandra Voe; director, Stephen Daldry. (8 April) *Hated Nightfall* (Howard Barker) with Ian McDiarmid, Nicholas Jones, Anna Patrick, Rebecca Charles, Paul Gonshaw, Nicola Walker, Jane Wood, Philip Barnes, James Clyde, Keith Osborn, Claire Rushbrook, Raymond Sawyer; director, Howard Barker. (7 June) *The Queen and I*, transferred from the Leicester Haymarket. (10 June) *Road*, transferred from the Leicester Haymarket

THEATRE UPSTAIRS (8 September) *Land of the Living* (David Spencer) with Lorraine Ashbourne, Sue Devaney, Sarah Doherty, Michelle Hardwick; director, Sue Dunderdale. (20 October) *Live Like Pigs* (John Arden) with Kathryn Hunter, Helen Blatch, Trevor Cooper, Jude Law, Ruth Lass, Lizzie McPhee, Paula Jacobs, John Salthouse; director, Katie Mitchell. (18 November) *Hammett's Apprentice* (Kevin Hood) with Ewan Hooper, Gina McKee; director, James MacDonald. (February 1994) *The Madness of Esme and Shaz* (Sarah Daniels) with Marlene Sidaway, Tanya Ronder; director, Jessica Dromgoole. (7 April) *My Night With Reg* (Kevin Elyot) with Anthony Calf, David Bamber, Joe Duttine, John Sessions, Roger Frost, Kenneth Macdonald. (10 June) *Thyestes* (Seneca) with Ewan Stewart; director, James Macdonald

SADLER'S WELLS, EC1 (14 October 1993) *Pickwick*, Chichester Festival Theatre production

ST MARTINS, WC2. *The Mousetrap* (1952), since 1974

SAVOY, WC2 (3 November 1993) *Relative Values*, Cheltenham Festival Theatre production. (24 March 1994) *Travesties*, transferred from the Barbican. (12 July) *She Loves Me* (book, Joe Masteroff; lyrics, Sheldon Harnick; music, Jerry Brock) with Ruthie Henshall, John Gordon-Sinclair; staging, Rob Marshall, Scott Ellis

SHAFTESBURY, WC2 (10 September 1993) *Carousel*, transferred from the National Theatre

STRAND, WC2 (6 September 1993) *A Slice of Saturday Night* (the Heather Brothers) with Dennis Waterman, Sonia, Danny McCall; director, Lea Heather. (3 December) *Me and Mamie O'Rourke* (Mary Agnes Donoghue) with Jennifer Saunders, Dawn French, Sean Chapman, Benedict Blythe; director, Robert Allan Ackerman. (3 May 1994) *The Weekend* (Michael Palin) with Richard Wilson, Angela

Thorne, Marcia Warren, Michael Medwin, Jonathan Coy; director, Robin Lefevre. (21 July) *St Joan* (Shaw) with Imogen Stubbs; director, Gale Edwards

THEATRE ROYAL, E15 (October 1993) *It's a Great Big Shame* (Mike Leigh) with Paul Trusser, Wendy Nottingham, Michelle Austin, Clint Dyer; director, Mike Leigh. (5 February 1994) *Curse of the Werewolf* (Ken Hill) with Robin Nedwell, Toni Palmer, Steven Pacey. (8 April) *Crusade* (Paul Sirett). (12 May) *Party Girls* (Debbie Plentie) with Sharon D. Clarke; director, Indhu Rubasingham

TRICYCLE, NW6 (27 August 1993) *Three Hotels* (Jon Robin Baitz) with Peter Egan, Lindsay Duncan. (30 September) *The Piano Lesson* (August Wilson) with Guy Gregory, Lennie James, Danny John-Jules, Marion Joseph, Tanya Moodie, Eddie Nestor, Cecilia Noble, Cyril Nri; director, Paulette Randall. (9 December) *Playboy of the West Indies* (Synge, adapt. Mustapha Matura). (3 February 1994) *The Government Inspector* (Gogol) with Dan Gordon, Sylvester McCoy, Eileen Pollock, Mark Lambert, Niamh Linehan; director, Pam Brighton. (March) *One Hell of a Do*, with Jon Kenny, Pat Shortt. (June) *Half the Picture* (Richard Norton-Taylor) with Michael Stroud, Jan Chappell, Sylvia Sims; director, John McGrath

VAUDEVILLE, WC2 (10 November 1993) *Eurovision* (Tim Luscombe) with Anita Dobson, James Dreyfus, Charles Edwards; director, Tim Luscombe; choreographer, Richard Sampson. (6 December) *Jamais Vu* (Ken Campbell) with Ken Campbell; directed, Colin Watkeys. (6 April 1994) *Dead Funny*, transferred from the Hampstead Theatre

VICTORIA PALACE, SW1. *Buddy*, since 1989

WHITEHALL, SW1 (20 July 1994) *Patsy Cline*, with Sandy Kelly, George Hamilton IV

WYNDHAM'S, WC2 (18 August 1993) *Lysistrata* (Aristophanes) with Geraldine James; director, Peter Hall. (13 October) *Medea*, with Diana Rigg; an Almeida Theatre/ Liverpool Playhouse production. (11 April 1994) *Rope*, Chichester Festival Theatre production. (21 June) *Home* (David Storey) with Paul Eddington, Richard Briers, Brenda Bruce; director, David Leveaux. (30 August) *Shirley Valentine* (Willy Russell) with Anita Dobson

OUTSIDE LONDON

BIRMINGHAM: REPERTORY (22 October 1993) *Old Times* (Pinter) with Tim Pigott-Smith, Estelle Kohler, Carol Royle; director, Bill Alexander. (3 December) *Blithe Spirit* (Coward) with Eve Matheson, Patsy Byrne; director, Robin Midgley. (December) *The Snowman* (Raymond Briggs) with Perry Douglin, Oliver Ashford/Justyn Towler; director, Bill Alexander. (11 February) *The Atheist's Tragedy* (Tourneur) with Gerard Murphy, Katharine Rogers, Michael Cadman, James Simmons; director, Anthony Clark. (11 March 1994) *Awake and Sing!* (Clifford Odets) with June Alexander; director, Bill Alexander. (15 April) *Lady Windermere's Fan* (Wilde) with Francesca Annis, Amanda Elwes, Rupert Frazer; director, Philip Prowse. (June) *The Playboy of the Western World* (Synge) with J. D. Kelleher, Niamh Linehan; director, Anthony Clark. (July) *Once On This Island* (Ahrens and Flaherty) with Lorna Brown; producers, Gwenda Hughes, David Toguri

BRISTOL: OLD VIC (3 November 1993) *Under Milk Wood* (Dylan Thomas). (February 1994) *The Duchess of Malfi* (Webster) with Sally Dexter, Ewan Stewart, Peter Woodward, Andrew Jarvis; director, Andrew Hay. (March) *The Hairy Ape* (O'Neill) with John Sharian, Helen Fitzgerald; director, Andy Hay. (June) *Stone Free* (Jim Cartwright)

CHICHESTER: FESTIVAL (29 April 1994) *The Rivals* (Sheridan) with James Simmons, Abigail Cruttenden, Patricia Routledge, Timothy West, Emily Raymond, Adam Godley, Richard O'Callaghan; director, Richard Cottrell. (18 May) *Pygmalion* (Shaw) with Fiona Fullerton, Peter Bowles; director, Patrick Garland. (29 June) *The School Mistress* (Pinero) with Patricia Routledge, Guy Henry; director, Matthew Francis. (20 July) *Let's Do It* (Ray and Vosburgh) with David Kernan, Liz Robertson, Robin Ray

MINERVA (13 September 1993) *Elvira '40* (Brigitte Jacques, trans. David Edney) with Keith Baxter, Debra Beaumont; director, Patrick Garland. (2 June 1994) *A Doll's House* (Ibsen) with Sharon Maughan, Peter McEnery; director, Annie Castledine. (7 July) *Dangerous Corner* (Priestley) with Gayle Hunnicutt, Peter McEnery, Christopher Timothy. (11 August) *Three Sisters* (Chekhov) with Greg Hicks, Julia St John, John Warnaby

GLASGOW: CITIZENS (10 September 1993) *The Soldiers* (Jakob Lenz); director, Philip Prowse. (8 October 1993) *Romeo and Juliet* (Shakespeare) with Robert Beck, Shirley Henderson; director, Giles Havergal. (18 November) *Don Juan* (Goldoni) with Andre Wilde, Graham McTavish, Andrea Hurt; director, Robert David MacDonald. (February) *The Second Mrs Tanqueray* (Pinero) with Julie Legrand; director, Philip Prowse. (April 1994) *In Quest of Conscience* (Robert David MacDonald) with Roberta Taylor, Robert David MacDonald, Joanna Tope, Henry Ian Cusick; director, Robert David MacDonald

LEEDS: WEST YORKSHIRE PLAYHOUSE (September 1993) *A Servant of Two Masters* (Goldoni) with Toby Jones, Toby Sedgwick, Tamsin Heatley; director, Phelim McDermott. (23 October) *Brighton Rock* (Graham Greene, adapt. David Horlock) with John Higgins, Catherine Cusack; director, Vicky Featherstone. (7 February 1994) *Death of a Salesman* (Miller) with Ken Stott; director, Matthew Warchus. (28 February) *Postcards from Rome* (Adam Pernak) with Sue Devaney, Beth Goddard, John Gillett, Robin Bowerman, Ann Firbank; director, Janine Wunsche. (14 March) *The Merchant of Venice* (Shakespeare) with Gary Waldhorn, Nichola McAuliffe, Richard Lintern, Michael Cashman; director, Jude Kelly. (16 April) *The Hunchback of Notre Dame* (Victor Hugo, adapt. Phelim McDermott, Julian Crouch) with Niall Ashdown, Susannah Elliott, Martin Gent, Malcolm Ridley, Rory Tapsell, Kate Wilton; director, Phelim McDermott. (30 April) *Forty Years On* (Allan Bennett) with Benjamin Whitrow, David Firth, Harry Burton, Madge Hindle, Susan Porrett, Simon Egerton, Gresby Nash, Mark Denham; director, Jeremy Sams. (June) *The Lady From The Sea* (Ibsen) with Josette Simon, Pip Donaghy; director, Lindsay Posner; joint production with the Lyric Hammersmith

LEICESTER: HAYMARKET (16 September 1993) *The Destiny of Me* (Larry Kramer) with Simon Callow, James Kennedy; director, Simon Callow. (14 October) *Pacific Overtures* (Sondheim) with Russell Dixon; director, Paul Kerryson. (19 November) *Carousel* (Rodgers and Hammerstein); director, Paul Kerryson. (9 December) *Thirst* (Gavin Robertson) with James McKecknie, Gavin Robertson, Simon Williamson, Victoria Worsley. (8 February 1994) *Faust Parts 1 and 2* (Goethe, adapt. Robert David MacDonald); director, Michael Bogdanov. (February) *Macbeth* (Shakespeare) with Rory Edwards, Kathryn Hunter; director, Julia Bardsley. (23 March) *The Queen and I* (Sue Townsend) and *Road* (Jim Cartwright) with Pam Ferris, Toby Salaman, Pearce Quigley; director, Max Stafford-Clark; joint productions with Royal Court Theatre

LIVERPOOL: PLAYHOUSE (21 September 1993) *Misery*, with Nula Conwell, Ray Lonnen. (23 June 1994) *Imagine*, revival of 1992 production

MANCHESTER: ROYAL EXCHANGE (9 September 1993) *Richard II* (Shakespeare) with Linus Roache, Ewan Hooper, Susan Lynch, James Maxwell; director, James Macdonald. (14 October) *Hedda Gabler* (Ibsen) with Geraldine James, Hilton MacRae, Dave Hill; director, Joseph Blatchley. (18 November) *Smoke* (Rod Woodens); director, Braham Murray. (16 December) *The Importance of Being Earnest* (Wilde) with Sam West, Avril Elgar, Marcia Warren, Zara Turner, John Branwell, Neil Dudgeon; director, James Maxwell. (February 1994) *The Lodger* (Simon Burke) with Julia Ford, Philip Jackson, Matthew Marsh, Mark Womack; director, Richard Wilson. (March) *Venice Preserved* (Otway) with Jonathan Cullen, George Anton, David Ryall, Helen McCrory; director, Gregory Hersov. (April) *What the Butler Saw* (Orton) with David Horovitch, Kate Winslet, Deborah Norton, Neil Stuke, Trevor Baxter, Billy Hartman; director, Robert Delamere. (18 May) *The Count of Monte Cristo* (Dumas, adapt. James Maxwell, Jonathan Hackett) with David Threlfall; director, Braham Murray

MOLD: THEATR CLWYD (3 September 1993) *India Song* (Marguerite Duras) with Lilo Baur, Robert Pickavance, Nick Reding; directors, Annabel Arden, Annie Castledine. (4 December) *Great Expectations* (Dickens). (May) *HRH* (Snoo Wilson) with Maria Aitken, David Yelland; director, Giles Havergal

NOTTINGHAM: PLAYHOUSE (10 September 1993) *The Party's Over* (Alan Bleasdale); director, Hettie MacDonald. (22 October) *Crimes of Passion* (Philip Whitchurch); director, Pip Broughton. (23 November) *Coriolan* (Shakespeare); director, Robert Lepage. (31 January 1994) *Neville's Island* (Tim Firth) with Tony Slattery, Jeff Rawle. (28 February) *Of Mice and Men* (Steinbeck) with Joe McGann. (28 March) *Pygmalion* (Shaw) with Josie Lawrence, Christopher Timothy; director, Pip Broughton. (10 June) *Rumpelstiltskin* (Mike Kenny), director, Jennie Darnell

PLYMOUTH: THEATRE ROYAL (16 September 1993) *The Master Forger* (Hugh Janes) with Roy Marsden, Jackie Smith Wood; director, Roger Redfarn. (April 1994) *Angry Old Men* (David Renwick) with Nigel Planer, Nerys Hughes, Sara Crowe, Christopher Ryan; director, Roger Redfarn

SCARBOROUGH: STEPHEN JOSEPH (27 January 1994) *Communicating Doors* (Ayckbourn) with Adie Allen, Liz Crowther, Richard Durden, John Hudson, Nick Stringer, Sara Markland; director, Alan Ayckbourn; music, John Pattison. (22 December) *The End of the Food Chain* (Tim Firth) with Stephen Tompkinson, Mark Benton, Michelle Butterly; director, Connal Orton. (25 April 1994) *Haunting Julia* (Ayckbourn) with Ian Hogg, Damien Goodwin, Adrian McLoughlin

SHEFFIELD: CRUCIBLE (30 September 1993) *Hamlet* (Shakespeare) with Robert Glenister, Susan Tracy, Ian Hogg, Katy Brittain; director, Michael Rudman. (4 November 1993) *Mansfield Park*. (9 December) *Oliver!*

SOUTHAMPTON: NUFFIELD (16 September 1993) *Same Time, Next Year* (Bernard Slade), with Christopher Blake, Gemma Craven. (1 November) *The Taming of the Shrew*. (11 November) *I'm No Angel* (Ayshe Raif). (21 March 1994) *Dr Faustus* (Marlowe) with Alex Hardy, Christopher Godwin; director, Patrick Sandford. (27 July) *Sweet Lorraine*

STRATFORD: MEMORIAL (21 October 1993) *Love's Labour's Lost* (Shakespeare) with Owen Teale, Jeremy Northam, Jenny Quayle, Abigail McKern, Paul Greenwood, Daniel Massey, Christopher Luscombe, John Normington; director, Ian Judge. (15 March 1994) *Macbeth* (Shakespeare) with Derek Jacobi, Cheryl Campbell; director, Adrian Noble. (2 May 1994) *Henry V* (Shakespeare) with Iain Glen; director, Matthew Warchus. (19 May) *Twelfth Night* (Shakespeare) with Emma Fielding, Clive Wood, Haydn Gwynne, Desmond Barrit, Tony Britton, Joanna McCallum; director, Ian Judge. (28 July) *A Midsummer Night's Dream* (Shakespeare) with Stella Gonet, Alex Jennings, Barry Lynch, Desmond Barrit, Emma Fielding, Haydn Gwynne, Toby Stephens, Kevin Doyle; director, Adrian Noble

SWAN (October 1993) *Elgar's Rondo* (David Pownall) with Alec McCowen, Sheila Ballantine, John Carlisle, Ian Hughes; director, Di Trevis. (27 April 1994) *Peer Gynt* with Alex Jennings, Haydn Gwynne; director, John Barton. (18 May) *Coriolanus* (Shakespeare) with Toby Stephens, Caroline Blakiston, Philip Voss, Barry Lynch; director, David Thacker. (27 July) *The Wives' Excuse* (Thomas Southerne) with Olivia Williams, Robert Bowman, Anthony Cochrane, Lesley Manville, Clive Wood; director, Max Stafford-Clark

THE OTHER PLACE (October 1993) *Moby Dick* (Melville, adapt, Rod Wooden) with David Calder, Christopher Hunter, Ray Fearon, David Birrell, Christopher Colquhoun, Lloyd Notice; director, Gerry Mulgrew. (26 May 1994) *After Easter* (Anne Devlin) with Stella Gonet, Doreen Hepburn, Ann Hasson, Katherine Roger, Sean O'Callaghan; director, Michael Attenborough. (27 July) *Henry VI* (Shakespeare) with Jonathan Firth, Lloyd Owen, John Keegan, Tom Smith, Ruth Mitchell; director, Katie Mitchell

WATFORD: PALACE (3 September 1993) *Dogg's Hamlet* and *The Real Inspector Hound* (Stoppard) with Trevor Bannister, James Quinn, Diana Bishop, Terrence Longdon, Patricia Quinn; director, Roger Smith. (8 October) *Duet for One* (Kempinski) with Eve Matheson; director, Lou Stein. (21 January 1994) *A Handful of Dust* (Waugh) with Mark Aiken, Marty Cruickshank, Tim Dutton, Annabelle Apsion, Jason Watkins; director, Mike Alfreds. (25 February) *Private Lives* (Coward) with Patrick Ryecart, Caroline Langrishe; director, Lou Stein. (2 April) *The Return of A. J. Raffles* (Graham Greene) with Brian Protheroe. (5 May) *Desire Under the Elms* (O'Neill) with Sally Dexter, Corey Johnson, James Booth; director, Lou Stein

---

## OLIVIER AWARDS 1994

Best Actor – Mark Rylance, *Much Ado About Nothing*
Best Actress – Fiona Shaw, *Machinal*
Best Actor in a Musical – Alun Armstrong, *Sweeney Todd*
Best Actress in a Musical – Julia McKenzie, *Sweeney Todd*
Best Director (Play) – Stephen Daldry, *Machinal*
Best Director (Musical) – Declan Donnellan, *Sweeney Todd*
Best Revival – *Machinal*
Best Comedy Performance – Griff Rhys Jones, *An Absolute Turkey*
Best Musical Revival – *Sweeney Todd*
Best Entertainment – *A Christmas Carol*
The Times Award – Peter Brook
The Special Award – Sam Wanamaker
Best Play – *Arcadia*
Best Musical – *City of Angels*
Best Comedy – *Hysteria*
Best Supporting Actor – Joseph Mydell, *Perestroika*
Best Supporting Actress – Helen Burns, *The Last Yankee*
Best Supporting Performance in a Musical – Sara Kestelman, *Cabaret*

# Weather

JULY 1993

Rainfall totals were generally above average everywhere for the fourth successive month. From the 2nd to the 7th rain and drizzle fell, mainly over Scotland. A gust of 70.7 kt (89 mph) was recorded at Kirkwall (Orkney) on the 4th. The 8th was wet, with heavy rain at times over western Scotland and the Midlands. On the 9th rain was heavy in many areas in England and Wales and some snow lay in the Scottish Highlands. On the 13th heavy rain spread north-east across England, Wales and Northern Ireland, with 39.1 mm (1.54 in) falling at Davidstow Moor (Devon). Rain and drizzle continued in many areas on the 14th, when 35.8 mm (1.41 in) of rain fell at Burrington (Devon). A ten-year-old girl was struck by lightning in South Croydon (Surrey) but survived. Rain became heavy with thunder in many areas on the 15th, when 63 mm (2.48 in) fell at Louth (Lincs.). On the 16th thunderstorms occurred in Oxfordshire, the Midlands, East Anglia, north-east England and southern Scotland. Floods occurred in Nottinghamshire, with some roads wrecked by burst sewers in Stapleford. Many buildings were flooded in Lincolnshire and the vaults of Lincoln Cathedral were damaged. Heavy rain fell in Northern Ireland and over much of England and Wales on the 18th and over northern England on the 19th. On the 18th 50.3 mm (1.98 in) of rain fell at Davidstow Moor (Devon). Further outbreaks of rain, drizzle or showers continued every day, but the next general heavy rain occurred on the 26th over mainly western areas of England and Wales. The 27th was wet generally, while the 28th brought further heavy rain to England and Wales. On the 29th drizzly rain fell almost everywhere, with 44 mm (1.73 in) falling at Inchmarlo (Grampian).

Monthly mean temperatures were mostly below normal and it was the first month of the year to be cooler than normal over England and Wales. London had its coolest July day on record on the 9th. The highest temperature recorded during the month was 29.7°C (85.5°F) at East Bergholt (Suffolk) on the 4th and the lowest was −1.6°C (29.1°F) at Aros (Strathclyde) on the 19th.

Sunshine totals were mostly below normal except in eastern Scotland. The highst daily total was 15.7 hours at Scilly on the 5th and the highest monthly total was 226.6 hours at Gorey Castle (CI).

## AUGUST 1993

Rainfall totals were generally below normal everywhere, although it was very wet during the first half of the month. The month started with rain and drizzle in the north spreading southwards over most areas. Heavy rain fell over many parts of England and Wales on the 4th and over northern England and

southern Scotland on the 5th. On the 4th 62 mm (2.44 in) of rain fell at Carlton-in-Cleveland (Co. Durham) and 68.2 mm (2.69 in) fell at Osmotherly Filters (N. Yorks.). Rain continued to affect mostly northern and western areas and heavy rain fell over northern England on the 9th. The 11th was a wet day almost everywhere and winds were strong in central areas. On the 12th heavy rain over southern England was followed by thunderstorms in north-west England, the Midlands and East Anglia. Lightning struck the radio mast at Droitwich (Worcs.) and lightning also cut power supplies in Stafford (Staffs.). On the 14th thunderstorms developed over south-east England, becoming widespread over East Anglia on the 15th. A tornado occurred on the 15th at Buckfastleigh (Devon) and 56 mm (2.2 in) of rain fell at Hunstanton (Norfolk) in 40 minutes. On the 16th heavy rain fell in north Yorkshire. Rain continued over Scotland on the 17th and 18th and moved southwards on the 19th. On the 21st rain spread over much of England and Wales and continued on the 22nd, when 74.6 mm (2.93 in) fell at L'Ancresse (CI). Showers or periods of rain continued somewhere in Scotland every day for the rest of the month.

Monthly mean temperatures were below normal everywhere. The highest temperature recorded during the month was 27.2°C (80.96°F) at Torquay (Devon) on the 20th and the lowest was −1.4°C (29.48°F) at Tyndrum (Central) on the 26th.

Sunshine totals were above normal generally except in north and east Scotland where it was the dullest summer (June to August) since 1881. The highest daily total was 14.5 hours at Tiree (Western Isles) on the 5th and the highest monthly total was 271.9 hours at St Helier (CI).

## SEPTEMBER 1993

Rainfall totals were generally above normal, but below normal in north-west Scotland. Rain spread north on the 7th with thunderstorms in the south. Heavy rain fell in northern England on the 8th with thunder in the south. Part of Warwickshire were flooded and a water-main burst on the A2 in London. On the 9th showers were widespread with thunder in Yorkshire. Heavy rain fell in Northern Ireland, with 76 mm (2.99 in) at Carmoney (Co. Londonderry), and gales affected Devon and Cornwall. Rain and showers continued on the 10th and on the 11th in Scotland. Heavy rain fell over most of England on the 12th with gales round coasts in the south and south-west and 114.3 mm (4.5 in) of rain fell at Swincombe (Devon) and 104.5 mm (4.12 in) at Fernworthy (Devon). A man was killed when his car was blown off the road at Wimborne (Dorset). Many roads were blocked by fallen trees and dozens of boats wrecked on the Dorset coast. Very heavy rain fell over northern England on the 13th with thunder in the Midlands and East Anglia. Heavy rain fell in southern England later in the day with gales in the Channel and south-west England. At Gouthwaite Reservoir (N. Yorks.) 79.3 mm (3.12 in) of rain fell. In Falmouth (Cornwall) two shops were badly damaged when two yachts sailed through their windows. In Leigh (Essex) four houses were struck by lightning and several roads flooded. The 14th brought heavy rain to northern England. The 15th was wet over England with thunder in Cornwall. Heavy rain fell in East Anglia, the Midlands and Wales on the 16th and in Northern Ireland on the 18th. On the 16th 76.3 mm (3.0 in) of rain fell at Douglas (IOM). The 19th brought rain to many areas, particularly Scotland, and on the 20th heavy rain fell over much of England. Thunderstorms occurred over the Pennines and the Peak District on the 21st and over north-west and south-east areas on the 22nd. Floods were 0.92 m (3 ft) deep in Battersea and Stockwell (London) and train services were halted as signals were struck by lightning; 46 mm (1.81 in) of rain fell in Putney (London) in three hours. The 23rd and 24th were foggy in many areas. Heavy rain fell in East Anglia on the 26th and over eastern and central England on the 27th. Rain fell in the south on the 28th and over most of England and Wales on the 29th and 30th.

Monthly mean temperatures were below normal everywhere. The highest temperature recorded was 27.2°C (80.96°F) at Great Malvern (Worcs.) on the 1st and the lowest was − 4.8°C (23.36°F) at Carnwath (Strathclyde) on the 28th.

Sunshine totals were above normal over most of Scotland but otherwise below normal. The highest daily total was 12.7 hours at Teignmouth (Devon), Torquay (Devon) and Scilly on the 1st and the highest monthly total was 185.7 hours at Bude (Cornwall).

## OCTOBER 1993

Rainfall totals were above average in most eastern and southern areas but much of Northern Ireland had less than half the normal amount. On the 1st heavy rain fell in eastern Scotland and southern England with thunderstorms in East Anglia and southern England. Flooding occurred around Barnstaple (Devon) and 67.5 mm (2.66 in) of rain fell at Gatwick (Surrey). Severe floods occurred in London, Kent and Surrey. Rain continued on the 2nd, heavy at times, with thunder in the south. Rain fell almost everywhere on the 3rd and in Scotland on the 4th. Rain or showers, often heavy, fell almost everywhere on the 5th and 6th. Thunderstorms occurred over much of England on the 6th. There were gales in northern Scotland, and 77.0 mm (3.03 in) of rain fell at Lentran (Highland). Heavy rain fell over Scotland on the 7th and thunderstorms occurred over southern England on the 8th. Flooding occurred in Scotland, Northumberland and Gloucestershire. Lightning felled the church steeple at Eastleigh (Hants.). Heavy rain fell in northern areas on the 9th and in the far north and the south-west on the 10th. On the 11th

heavy rain with thunder in places affected much of England, Wales and northern Scotland; 87.8 mm (3.46 in) of rain fell at Theberton (Suffolk) and flooding occurred in many parts of the south-east. A whirlwind caused considerable damage in Northborough (Cambs.). The 12th was very wet over England and Wales with showers in Scotland and thunder in East Anglia. Flooding increased. Trains were halted between Exeter and Barnstaple (Devon), and Wedmore and Coklake (Somerset) had 1 m (3 ft) of floodwater. Debenham, Earl Stonham and Framlingham (Suffolk) were cut off and 100 roads were flooded in Norfolk. Parts of Kent were flooded, floods were up to 2 m (6 ft) deep in Lincolnshire, and 96.4 mm (3.80 in) of rain fell at Aldeburgh (Suffolk), 83.2 mm (3.28 in) at Bagstaple (Surrey) and 73.6 mm (2.89 in) at Leverton (Lincs.). On the 13th heavy rain fell over England and Wales, with 141 roads closed and Windsor (Berks.) flooded. The next spell of rain, apart from showers, was over Scotland on the 19th, spreading south on the 20th. Rain fell again in northern Scotland on the 22nd–23rd.

Monthly mean temperatures were below normal everywhere. The highest temperature recorded was 19.2°C (66.54°F) at St James's Park (London) on the 11th and the lowest was − 9.9°C (14.18°F) at Carnwath (Strathclyde) on the 17th.

Sunshine totals were above normal except in northern Scotland. The highest daily total was 10.2 hours at Margate (Kent) on the 18th and the highest monthly total was 160.6 hours at Penzance (Cornwall).

## NOVEMBER 1993

Rainfall totals were below normal, particularly over Scotland and Northern Ireland. Rain fell over the southern half of England and Wales on the 2nd and spread northwards on the 3rd. On the 4th and 5th fog occurred in many places. Rain or drizzle fell almost everywhere on the 7th. The 9th was a wet day everywhere with gales in the north; 61.8 mm (2.43 in) of rain fell at Nantmor (Gwynedd) and a fishery factory ship ran aground in the Shetlands. Rain or drizzle fell over England and Wales on the 10th. On the 12th heavy rain fell in western Scotland, Wales and south-west England, while the 13th brought heavy rain to most of England and Wales which continued in eastern areas on the 15th. Gales occurred over England and Wales on the 14th and a woman was killed by a falling tree near Newmarket (Suffolk). Many roads were closed by falling trees and floods, and a gust of 71 kt (81.8 mph) was recorded in Humberside. A 23 m (75 ft) gap was torn out of the pier at Cromer (Norfolk) by a rig platform which broke from its moorings three miles away. Heavy rain fell in Northern Ireland on the 15th and 16th. On the 20th showers fell, mostly in eastern areas, with snow at times. Snow showers fell mainly in the east on the 21st and 22nd, taking heavy toll of vehicles as drivers ignored the conditions. This was the first November snow to lie in the south since 1969. Freezing fog affected much of England and Wales on the 23rd with snow falling in the south-west. Six people were injured in a 22-vehicle pile-up in fog on the M4 in Wiltshire. Snow fell in Wales and northern England on the 24th and freezing fog occurred in the Midlands. Widespread fog affected East Anglia and the south-east on the 26th. The M4 in Berkshire and the M40 in Buckinghamshire were closed and there was traffic chaos on the M25 in Essex. Fog caused havoc on roads in Merseyside and Cheshire and flights were disrupted at Stansted and Heathrow. The 29th was a very wet day in most areas with gales in the west.

Monthly mean temperatures were generally below normal and in many places it was the coldest November since 1985. This was the fifth successive month with below average temperatures. The highest temperature recorded was 18.0°C (64.4°F) at Jubilee Corner (Kent) on the 4th and the lowest was −14.8°C (5.36°F) at Braemer (Grampian) on the 24th.

Sunshine totals were above normal in the north-west but below normal in the Midlands and north-east England. The highest daily total was 8.3 hours at Eastbourne (E. Sussex) on the 11th and Southsea (Dorset) on the 12th. The highest monthly total was 98.7 hours at Folkestone (Kent).

## DECEMBER 1993

Rainfall totals were above normal everywhere and it was the wettest December since 1979. A total of 634 mm (24.96 in) of rain fell at Moel Cynnedd (Powys) during the month. The month started with strong winds in many areas and on the 3rd most places, particularly in the west, had rain, heavy at times. Most areas had rain or drizzle on the 4th. The 6th brought heavy rain to Northern Ireland, southern Scotland and most of England and Wales except the south-east, with gales in the south-west. Rain was heavy in southern and south-west England on the 7th and the 8th was wet everywhere, with snow in Scotland. Gales were widespread over England and Wales on the 8th and a gust of 84 kt (97 mph) was recorded at Camborne (Cornwall). Overturned lorries and uprooted trees closed many roads throughout the country and Scotland and Northern Ireland were affected by flooding. At least 14 people were killed and many buildings damaged. A tanker was sunk near Plymouth (Devon). Gales continued on the 9th and hundreds of homes were flooded in Wales. On the 10th gales affected western areas and rain or showers fell almost everywhere with sleet, hail and thunder in central areas. On the 11th gales again affected western areas and rain, sleet or hail fell in many places. The 12th was wet, with snow in central and northern areas and gales on western coasts. Heavy snow closed roads in Wales, northern England and Scotland and floods occurred in southern Wales. Rain fell in most areas on the 13th and the 14th was very wet with snow in central and northern areas. The River Wye burst its banks and in Cumbria roads were blocked by snow. Heavy rain fell in northern

England on the 15th and over England and Wales on the 18th, with gales sweeping western areas; 103.4 mm (4.07 in) of rain fell at Llyn Fawr (Powys). Gales and flooding affected many areas on the 19th. The 20th was a wet day over central and southern areas with snow over northern Wales and central England. The railway near Exeter (Devon) was closed by floods. Snow showers with thunder occurred in the north on the 21st. The 22nd and 23rd were wet days with gales in the west, and on the 24th and 25th Shrewsbury (Shropshire) was flooded. Heavy rain fell in the south-west on the 27th and heavy snow fell in many areas on the 28th. Heavy rain fell in the south on the 30th. Several people were killed as a result of the weather in the last few days of the month. There were floods in many parts of the south on the 31st; a 2.3 m (7 ft) wall of water swept through Polperro (Cornwall).

Monthly mean temperatures were above normal in southern and central areas but below normal in the north. The highest temperature recorded was 15.5°C (59.9°F) at Colwyn Bay (Clwyd) on the 18th and at Norwich and Hemsby (Norfolk) on the 19th, and the lowest was −15.8°C (3.56°F) at Altnahara (Highland) on the 26th.

Sunshine totals were generally near or below normal. The highest daily total was 7.2 hours at Manston (Kent) on the 5th and Littlehampton (W. Sussex) on the 11th. The highest monthly total was 68.5 hours at Shanklin (IOW).

## THE YEAR 1993

Rainfall over England, Wales and Northern Ireland was generally above normal and it was the wettest year since 1981. In Scotland rainfall was above normal in Grampian, Fife, Central and Lothian but close to normal elsewhere. Over England and Wales it was the coolest year since 1987, with temperatures only just above normal. Sunshine was below normal everywhere and over Northern Ireland it was the dullest year on record. January was one of the stormiest on record, particularly over Scotland. There were hundreds of accidents and severe flooding affected many areas. The tanker *Braer* broke up and sank in Quendale Bay (Shetland). A gust of 147 kt (169.28 mph) was recorded at Cairngorm (Highland) on the 21st. February was the driest in England, Wales and Northern Ireland since 1986. Further gales caused much damage, particularly in East Anglia. In Northern Ireland it was the dullest February on record. February and March together were the driest over England and Wales since 1929. Gales late in March caused damage and flooding in north-west Scotland. April was a generally wet month. Houses were struck by lightning in Cheddar (Somerset) and there were floods and road accidents in many areas. Over England and Wales it was the dullest April since 1978. May was very wet over central England. Snow made roads hazardous in Scotland, while flooding was severe in northern England early in the month. A violent tornado caused havoc in

Powys in the middle of the month and severe thunderstorms caused flooding in southern counties at the end of the month. June was very wet except in central and southern Scotland. Severe floods occurred in Cornwall, northern Wales (where 40 caravans were washed away at Cardigan and 400 people evacuated at Llandudno), Leicestershire, Yorkshire (with water 7 ft deep in Sheffield), Bedfordshire, Cambridgeshire, Suffolk, Sussex and Cornwall (the North Cornwall show was closed for the first time ever). Armagh (N. Ireland) had its dullest June for 110 years. July was also a wet month, with flooding in Nottinghamshire and Lincolnshire. It was the first month of the year to be colder than normal over England and Wales, and London had its coldest July day on record on the 9th. August was mainly dry but heavy rain did occur, causing flooding in Hunstanton (Norfolk). Lightning damaged the radio mast at Droitwich (Worcs.) and cut off power supplies in Stafford (Staffs.). September was wetter than normal except in north-west Scotland. There were frequent thunderstorms leading to floods in several areas and considerable lightning damage. Gales on the 12th caused much damage in the south-west. October was wet in eastern and southern areas and severe flooding occurred in many places. November was drier but still had spells of severe weather with gales, heavy rain, thick fog and snow. December was the wettest since 1979, with severe flooding and gales in many places.

JANUARY 1994

Rainfall totals were above normal everywhere. The total for December and January was more than the average for the whole winter. Heavy rain fell in most areas from the 1st to the 3rd. Floods occurred in Northern Ireland, with many homes flooded and three men drowned in a capsized boat on the river Bann. Parts of southern England were flooded and water 1 m (3 ft) deep swept through Chichester (W. Sussex). Rain, often heavy and with snow and sleet at times, continued from the 4th to the 6th; 26 cm (10 in) of snow lay at Crowthorne (Berks.) and 16 cm (6 in) lay at Hitchin (Herts.). Snow and floods caused havoc throughout the country and many serious accidents occurred. Several houses collapsed near Haywards Heath (W. Sussex) as rain caused subsidence. Heavy rain fell on the 8th and 9th. On the 11th soldiers and firemen battled to prevent further flood damage to Chichester. Surrey had its worst floods since 1887 as heavy rain fell in England and Wales. Landslips were very severe on the Isle of Wight. The 12th was a wet day with gales in many places which continued on the 13th. Heavy rain fell in southern England on the 15th and snow or sleet fell almost everywhere on the 16th. Heavy rain fell on the 18th with gales in the west. Rain or drizzle fell in many areas until the 21st and heavy rain fell in mainly western areas on the 22nd, with gales and thunder in northern Scotland. Gales continued on the 23rd when gusts of 95 kt (109.4 mph) and 104 kt (119.8 mph)

were recorded at Lerwick and Sumburgh (Shetland) respectively. Rain fell over much of England and Wales. The 25th was wet and windy with gusts over 60 kt (69.1 mph) in many places. A tree fell on a house in Purley (Berks.). Gales were severe on the 27th with frequent showers and thunderstorms. Two lorries were blown over on the M8 bridge over the Clyde and the roof was blown off a building in Glasgow. In Kent a lorry with a 26-ton load of fish was overturned on the M2 near Faversham. Gales continued on the 28th and in Scotland on the 29th–30th when a gust of 118 kt (136 mph) was recorded at Cairngorm (Highland).

Monthly mean temperatures were above normal almost everywhere except northern Scotland. The highest temperature recorded was 13.7°C (56.66°F) at Torquay (Devon) on the 24th and Elmstone (Kent) on the 25th. The lowest was −9.7°C (14.54°F) at Keith (Grampian) and Lairg (Highland) on the 1st.

Sunshine totals were mostly above normal except in north-west Scotland. The highest daily total was 8.3 hours at Hastings (E. Sussex) on the 28th and the highest monthly total was 89.59 hours at Torquay (Devon).

FEBRUARY 1994

Rainfall totals were above normal except in north-west Scotland. It was the wettest February in Northern Ireland since 1990. Heavy rain fell almost everywhere on the 1st. The 3rd was a wet day in the south, with heavy snow in the north and gales in places. A gust of 74 kt (85 mph) was recorded at Llanbedr (Powys) and flooding occurred in the West Country. In West Yorkshire 13 cm (5 in) of snow fell in four hours and Pennine roads were blocked. Rain affected many areas on the 6th. The 8th was wet and windy generally and the 10th was wet in the west. Rain fell in the south and west on the 11th. Widespread frost occurred on the 13th with snow in the south and south-east. Snow fell in many areas on the 14th and was heaviest in the south. Drifting snow in south Wales caused chaos and accidents on many roads. Snow and ice also caused serious accidents in the south, particularly around London. Two people were killed and many injured. The 15th brought snow to most areas and two more people were killed in accidents. Rail services were disrupted and many roads almost impassable. Fog affected much of England and Wales on the 16th and 17th. Rain fell in western areas on the 18th and in the south-west on the 19th. There was snow in many areas on the 20th and 21st and many accidents occurred. In Newcastle upon Tyne lightning struck a tree and a gas main, and an old people's home had to be evacuated. In Cleveland 30 cm (12 in) of snow fell and 13 cm (5 in) fell in Norfolk. There was snow in Northern Ireland, Wales and England on the 22nd, turning to rain in the south and south-west. Snow fell mostly in central areas, with rain in the south, on the 23rd. Many roads were blocked in the Midlands, Lancashire and the Lake District. Rain and snow occurred in most areas on the 25th and

26th and over northern areas on the 27th and 28th. Many roads in Scotland became impassable.

Monthly mean temperatures were mostly below normal and it was the coldest February since 1991. The highest temperature recorded was 14.5°C (58.1°F) at Lacock (Wilts.) on the 27th and the lowest was −16.1°C (3.02°F) at Braemar (Grampian) on the 17th.

Sunshine totals were mostly near or below normal except in the far north of Scotland. The highest daily total was 9.2 hours at Marham (Norfolk) on the 21st and the highest monthly total was 98.28 hours at Cape Wrath (Highland).

## MARCH 1994

Rainfall totals were above normal everywhere and it was the wettest March on record in Scotland. On the 1st 30 cm (12 in) of snow lay at Aviemore (Highland). Rain affected most areas on the 3rd and northern areas on the 4th. Heavy rain fell in northern Scotland on the 6th and in western areas on the 7th and 8th. Rain occurred over most of England and Wales on the 9th and snow fell in Scotland. Gales and rain occurred in the north and west on the 10th and rain fell in western areas on the 11th. The 12th was a wet and windy day everywhere and gales occurred in many areas on the 13th. A gust of 82 kt (94.4 mph) was recorded at Benbecula (Western Isles). A man was killed and five others injured when scaffolding collapsed at Sellafield (Cumbria). The roof was blown off a church in Nottingham. On the 14th a gust of 60 kt (69.1 mph) was recorded at Leeming (N. Yorks.). A man was blown into the canal and drowned at Bassingfield (Notts.), the roof was blown off a school at Redditch (Worcs.) and the end of a house was blown out in York. A gust of 126 kt (145.1 mph) was recorded at Cairngorm (Highland). Rain or showers fell in most areas on the 15th. Gales occurred in the west on the 16th, showers fell in many areas and there were thunderstorms in Leeds, Manchester, Birmingham and London. Rain fell in the south on the 17th and everywhere except northern Scotland on the 18th. Heavy rain fell in the south-west on the 20th–21st and in Scotland and Northern Ireland on the 21st. There was rain in most places on the 22nd. Gales occurred in many places on the 23rd and rain or drizzle fell everywhere. Rain or showers fell on the 24th and 25th with thunder in the north. On the 27th and 28th rain fell in most areas with gales in the west. The 30th and 31st were very wet with gales. Gusts of 65 kt (74.9 mph) at Aberporth (Dyfed) on the 30th, 107 kt (123.2 mph) at Fort William (Highland) and 74 kt (85.2 mph) at Torquay (Devon) on the 31st were recorded. The roof was torn off an inn and a car blown 15 ft into the air at Lulworth Cove (Dorset).

Monthly mean temperatures were above normal except in northern Scotland. The highest temperature recorded was 19.3°C (66.74°F) at Elmstone (Kent) on the 30th and the lowest was −11.2°C (11.84°F) at Dalwhinnie (Highland) on the 21st.

Sunshine totals were generally around normal but above normal in eastern Scotland. The highest daily total was 11.8 hours at Morecambe (Lancs.) on the 29th and the highest monthly total was 165.54 hours at Durris (Grampian).

## APRIL 1994

Rainfall totals were above normal everywhere for the fifth successive month. Heavy rain fell in places on the 1st and gales were widespread in coastal areas with ferry services disrupted at several ports. Flooding occurred in Wales and a gust of 87 kt (100 mph) was recorded at Cardiff (S. Glam.). The 3rd was wet everywhere with strong winds; 54.4 mm (2.15 in) of rain fell at Davidstow Moor (Cornwall). Heavy snow showers fell in many areas on the 4th and ten people were killed in accidents. Many newborn lambs perished in the severe weather. The 7th was wet except over Scotland. The 8th was very wet and heavy snow fell in several areas on the 9th, when 29 cm (11.4 in) lay at Aviemore (Highland). Many roads were closed and accidents occurred throughout the country. On the 10th 50 mm (2 in) of snow fell in southern counties. Freezing fog in eastern areas on the 11th caused a 30-vehicle pile-up on the M6 at Sandbach (Cheshire) which led to further accidents, leaving 120 damaged vehicles on one mile of motorway. The 12th was wet and gales affected eastern areas on the 13th. Rain fell in Scotland on the 18th and across central areas on the 19th; more rain and snow fell on the 21st. Rain fell mainly in the west on the 22nd with snow in northern Scotland. Rain fell in many areas on the 23rd and there were many thunderstorms; rain fell again in many areas on the 25th and in the south and Scotland on the 26th and 27th. On the 26th 54.6 mm (2.2 in) of rain fell at Tulloch Bridge (Highland) and a gust of 92 kt (106 mph) was recorded at Cairngorm (Highland).

Monthly mean temperatures were mostly near or above normal except in western Scotland. The highest temperature recorded was 25.3°C (77.5°F) at Rodney Stoke (Somerset) on the 30th and the lowest was −6.0°C (21.2°F) at Balmoral (Grampian) on the 8th.

Sunshine totals were near or above normal except in western and central Scotland. The highest daily total was 13.9 hours at Bastreet (Cornwall) on the 18th and the highest monthly total was 210 hours at Cleethorpes (Humberside).

## MAY 1994

Rainfall totals were near or above average over England and Wales but below average in Scotland and Northern Ireland. The south-east of England had 77 mm (3 in) of rain in the first 24 days (twice the average for the month). Rain fell in the west on the 3rd and thunderstorms or showers occurred in many areas on the 4th. There was general rain on the 5th and rain fell over England and Wales on the 6th and 7th. Thunderstorms occurred in East Anglia on the 7th and 8th. Rain fell over Northern Ireland on the 10th and in the south-west of England on the 12th.

There was rain in southern areas on the 14th when 32.1 mm (1.26 in) fell at Hadley (Worcs.). Northern England and the Midlands had rain on the 15th and thunderstorms occurred in southern areas on the 16th and 17th, with 37.7 mm (1.49 in) of rain falling at Guernsey on the 16th. There was snow over northern Scotland on the 18th, 19th and 20th and rain fell over England and Wales on the 20th, 21st and 22nd. There was rain in southern England, East Anglia and Wales on the 24th and 25th and over southern England on the 26th.

Monthly mean temperatures were below normal everywhere. The highest temperature recorded during the month was 25.2°C (77.4°F) at Inverailort (Highland) on the 13th and the lowest was −5.6°C (21.9°F) at Dalwhinnie (Highland) on the 20th.

Sunshine totals were above normal in Scotland but below normal in other areas. The highest daily total was 15.8 hours at Stornoway (Western Isles) on the 19th and the highest monthly total was 294 hours, also at Stornoway. This was the highest monthly total ever recorded at Stornoway for any month of the year.

JUNE 1994

Rainfall totals were generally below normal except in western parts of Northern Ireland and the extreme west and north of Scotland. It was the dullest June since 1976 over England and Wales. There were a few scattered thunderstorms from the 1st to the 3rd, mainly in central and eastern areas. Thunderstorms occurred in eastern areas on the 8th. Rain fell in the north from the 15th to the 18th, in the west on the 20th and more generally on the 21st. Gusts of 84 kt (96.7 mph) on the 18th and 80 kt (92.1 mph) on the 22nd were recorded at Cairngorm (Highland). On the 24th thunderstorms, often severe, were widespread over England, Wales and Northern Ireland. A house in Reading was badly damaged by lightning and flooding occurred widely in the area. A house in Ventnor (IOW) was badly damaged by lightning and electricity pylons were struck in Cornwall. Flooding occurred in Kent, Surrey, Sussex and Hampshire, where houses were also badly damaged by lightning. A girl was killed and five other children injured by lightning at Brownhills (W. Midlands). Lightning demolished a chimney in Angle (Pembrokeshire) and an electricity transformer, cutting off power in western Wales. Power was also cut off in large areas of Northern Ireland. On the 24th 49 mm (1.94 in) of rain fell at East Malling (Kent). Thunderstorms occurred in eastern England on the 25th and there was rain in the west and Scotland on the 26th. Thunderstorms were again widespread on the 29th.

Monthly mean temperatures were above normal in parts of southern and eastern England but below normal in western areas, especially north-west England, Northern Ireland and western Scotland. The highest temperature recorded during the month was 31.8°C (89.2°F) at East Bergholt (Suffolk) on the 13th

and the lowest was −0.5°C (31.1°F) at Aberfoyle (Central) on the 6th and 13th.

Sunshine totals were generally above normal but below normal in western areas and the extreme north. The highest daily total was 16.9 hours at Fair Isle (Shetland) on the 16th and the highest monthly total was 305.7 hours at Gorey Castle (Jersey).

*Source:* data provided by The Met Office

## BUCHAN'S WEATHER PERIODS

Dr Alexander Buchan, FRS, secretary of the Scottish Meteorological Society, published in 1867 a paper in the journal of the Society entitled *Interruptions in the regular rise and fall of temperature in the course of the year.* In this paper Buchan claimed the existence of tendencies for short spells of relatively cold and warm weather to occur at certain times of the year. His claims were based on his examination of the mean daily temperature as recorded at stations in Scotland over long periods.

Buchan gave six cold periods and three warm periods:

| Cold periods | Warm periods |
|---|---|
| 7–14 February | 12–15 July |
| 11–14 April | 12–15 August |
| 9–14 May | 3–14 December |
| 29 June–4 July | |
| 6–11 August | |
| 6–13 November | |

Since Buchan's time, these smaller fluctuations of weather superimposed on the normal seasonal changes have been examined from the aspect of tendencies to stormy or anticyclonic spells over the British Isles and have been referred to as 'singularities'. Stormy periods are relatively warm in winter and cool in summer.

The following tendencies have been given:

| | |
|---|---|
| 5–17 January | *stormy* |
| 18–24 January | *anticyclonic* |
| 24 January–1 February | *stormy* |
| 8–16 February | *anticyclonic* |
| 21–25 February | *cold* |
| 26 February–9 March | *stormy* |
| 12–19 March | *anticyclonic* |
| 24–31 March | *stormy* |
| 10–15 April | *stormy* |
| 23–26 April | *unsettled* |
| 1–21 June | *summer monsoon* |
| 10–24 July | *warm* |
| 20–30 August | *stormy* |
| 1–17 September | *anticyclonic* |
| 17–24 September | *stormy* |
| 24 September–4 October | *anticyclonic* |
| 5–12 October | *stormy* |
| 16–20 October | *anticyclonic* |
| 24 October–13 November | *stormy* |
| 15–21 November | *anticyclonic* |
| 24 November–14 December | *stormy* |
| 18–24 December | *anticyclonic* |
| 25 December–1 January | *stormy* |

## AVERAGE AND GENERAL VALUES 1992–4 (MAY)

| | Rainfall (mm) | | | | Temperature (°C) | | | | Bright Sunshine (hrs per day) | | | |
|---|---|---|---|---|---|---|---|---|---|---|---|---|
| | Average 1961–90 | 1992 | 1993 | 1994 | Average 1961–90 | 1992 | 1993 | 1994 | Average 1961–90 | 1992 | 1993 | 1994 |
| **ENGLAND AND WALES** | | | | | | | | | | | | |
| January | 77 | 48 | 113 | 123 | 3.8 | 4.2 | 5.9 | 5.2 | 1.6 | 1.7 | 1.2 | 2.1 |
| February | 55 | 47 | 16 | 82 | 3.8 | 5.9 | 4.8 | 3.3 | 2.3 | 2.3 | 1.8 | 2.3 |
| March | 63 | 85 | 26 | 93 | 5.6 | 7.6 | 6.5 | 7.5 | 3.5 | 2.5 | 3.7 | 3.7 |
| April | 53 | 73 | 94 | 76 | 7.7 | 8.9 | 9.3 | 8.1 | 4.9 | 4.2 | 4.1 | 5.8 |
| May | 56 | 49 | 90 | 61 | 10.9 | 13.5 | 11.4 | 10.6 | 6.2 | 8.2 | 5.7 | 5.1 |
| June | 58 | 38 | 66 | – | 13.9 | 15.8 | 14.7 | – | 6.4 | 7.2 | 6.6 | – |
| July | 56 | 83 | 83 | – | 15.7 | 16.6 | 15.1 | – | 6.0 | 5.3 | 5.6 | – |
| August | 68 | 130 | 55 | – | 15.6 | 15.9 | 14.5 | – | 5.7 | 5.3 | 6.5 | – |
| September | 70 | 92 | 113 | – | 13.6 | 13.8 | 12.5 | – | 4.5 | 3.9 | 3.5 | – |
| October | 77 | 84 | 89 | – | 10.7 | 8.3 | 8.6 | – | 3.2 | 3.1 | 3.6 | – |
| November | 81 | 138 | 74 | – | 6.6 | 7.9 | 4.9 | – | 2.2 | 1.9 | 1.9 | – |
| December | 82 | 83 | 167 | – | 4.7 | 4.2 | 5.4 | – | 1.5 | 1.4 | 1.4 | – |
| YEAR | 796 | 950 | 986 | – | 9.4 | 10.2 | 9.5 | – | 4.0 | 3.9 | 3.8 | – |
| **SCOTLAND** | | | | | | | | | | | | |
| January | 117 | 139 | 306 | 216 | 3.1 | 4.7 | 4.2 | 3.4 | 1.3 | 1.4 | 0.9 | 1.1 |
| February | 78 | 167 | 67 | 99 | 3.1 | 5.5 | 5.6 | 2.3 | 2.3 | 1.9 | 1.3 | 2.2 |
| March | 94 | 208 | 120 | 249 | 4.6 | 6.2 | 5.4 | 4.8 | 3.2 | 2.3 | 3.3 | 3.1 |
| April | 60 | 119 | 116 | 134 | 6.5 | 7.4 | 7.5 | 6.4 | 4.8 | 3.2 | 3.6 | 4.5 |
| May | 67 | 81 | 111 | 30 | 9.3 | 11.7 | 9.2 | 8.7 | 5.6 | 7.4 | 4.5 | 7.5 |
| June | 67 | 39 | 72 | – | 12.1 | 14.3 | 12.3 | – | 5.6 | 6.1 | 3.9 | – |
| July | 74 | 91 | 113 | – | 13.6 | 14.0 | 12.7 | – | 4.9 | 4.0 | 3.7 | – |
| August | 92 | 221 | 74 | – | 13.5 | 13.3 | 12.4 | – | 4.6 | 4.6 | 4.0 | – |
| September | 111 | 177 | 76 | – | 11.5 | 11.7 | 10.9 | – | 3.5 | 3.2 | 3.8 | – |
| October | 120 | 123 | 118 | – | 9.1 | 6.9 | 7.0 | – | 2.6 | 2.4 | 2.6 | – |
| November | 118 | 212 | 76 | – | 5.3 | 6.0 | 4.3 | – | 1.7 | 1.5 | 2.1 | – |
| December | 116 | 159 | 232 | – | 3.9 | 3.7 | 2.8 | – | 1.0 | 0.9 | 0.9 | – |
| YEAR | 1114 | 1736 | 1481 | – | 7.9 | 8.8 | 7.9 | – | 3.4 | 3.2 | 2.9 | – |

## WEATHER RECORDS

### WORLD RECORDS

| | |
|---|---|
| Maximum air temperature | 57.8°C/136°F |
| San Louis, Mexico, 11 August 1933 | |
| Minimum air temperature | – 89.2°C/– 128.56°F |
| Vostok, Antarctica, 21 July 1983 | |
| Greatest rainfall in one day | 1870 mm/73.62 in |
| Cilaos, Isle de Réunion, 16 March 1952 | |
| Greatest rainfall in one calendar month | 9300 mm/366.14 in |
| Cherrapunji, Assam, July 1861 | |
| Greatest annual rainfall total | 22,990 mm/905.12 in |
| Cherrapunji, 1861 | |
| Highest gust of wind | 201 knots/231 mph |
| Mt Washington Observatory, USA, 12 April 1934 | |

### UNITED KINGDOM RECORDS

| | |
|---|---|
| Maximum air temperature | 37.1°C/98.8°F |
| Cheltenham, Glos., 3 August 1990 | |
| Minimum air temperature | – 27.2°C/– 17°F |
| Braemar, Grampian, 11 February 1895 and 10 January 1982 | |
| Greatest rainfall in one day | 280 mm/11 in |
| Martinstown, Dorset, 18 July 1955 | |
| Greatest annual rainfall total | 6528 mm/257 in |
| Sprinkling Tarn, Cumbria, 1954 | |
| Highest gust of wind | 150 knots/173 mph |
| Cairngorm, Highland, 20 March 1986 | |
| Highest low-level gust* | 123 knots/141.7 mph |
| Fraserburgh, Grampian, 13 February 1989 | |
| Highest mean hourly speed | 92 knots/106 mph |
| Great Dun Fell, Cumbria, December 1974 | |
| Highest low-level mean hourly speed* | 72 knots/83 mph |
| Shoreham-by-Sea, Sussex, 16 October 1987 | |

* below 200 m/656 ft

## WIND FORCE MEASURES

The *Beaufort Scale* of wind force has been accepted internationally and is used in communicating weather conditions. Devised originally by Admiral Sir Francis Beaufort in 1805, it now consists of the numbers 0–17, each representing a certain strength or velocity of wind at 10 m (33 ft) above ground in the open.

| Scale no. | Wind Force | mph | knots |
|---|---|---|---|
| 0 | Calm | 1 | 1 |
| 1 | Light air | 1–3 | 1–3 |
| 2 | Slight breeze | 4–7 | 4–6 |
| 3 | Gentle breeze | 8–12 | 7–10 |
| 4 | Moderate breeze | 13–18 | 11–16 |
| 5 | Fresh breeze | 19–24 | 17–21 |
| 6 | Strong breeze | 25–31 | 22–27 |
| 7 | High wind | 32–38 | 28–33 |
| 8 | Gale | 39–46 | 34–40 |
| 9 | Strong gale | 47–54 | 41–47 |
| 10 | Whole gale | 55–63 | 48–55 |
| 11 | Storm | 64–72 | 56–63 |
| 12 | Hurricane | 73–82 | 64–71 |
| 13 | – | 83–92 | 72–80 |
| 14 | – | 93–103 | 81–89 |
| 15 | – | 104–114 | 90–99 |
| 16 | – | 115–125 | 100–108 |
| 17 | – | 126–136 | 109–118 |

TEMPERATURE, RAINFALL AND SUNSHINE
At selected climatological reporting stations, July 1993–June 1994 and calendar year 1993

| | Ht | July 1993 | | | August 1993 | | | September 1993 | | | October 1993 | | |
|---|---|---|---|---|---|---|---|---|---|---|---|---|---|
| | m | °C | Rain mm | Sun hrs | °C | Rain mm | Sun hrs | °C | Rain mm | Sun hrs | °C | Rain mm | Sun hrs |
| Abbotsinch (Glasgow) | 5 | 13.5 | 56 | 4.5 | 13.4 | 57 | 5.6 | 11.7 | 64 | 4.2 | 6.9 | 59 | 3.5 |
| Aberporth | 134 | 14.1 | 74 | 6.2 | 13.7 | 48 | 6.0 | 12.5 | 67 | 4.5 | 8.6 | 46 | 4.4 |
| Aldergrove | 68 | 14.1 | 71 | 3.1 | 13.5 | 62 | 4.9 | 11.8 | 109 | 3.5 | 7.5 | 32 | 3.0 |
| Aspatria | 61 | 14.1 | 64 | 4.4 | 13.3 | 63 | 5.8 | 11.3 | 57 | 4.2 | 6.9 | 57 | 3.7 |
| Auchincruive | 48 | 13.4 | 67 | 2.9 | 12.8 | 67 | 5.3 | 11.5 | 54 | 3.9 | 7.1 | 55 | 3.6 |
| Bala | 163 | 13.2 | 84 | 3.9 | 12.5 | 91 | 4.4 | 10.7 | 76 | 3.4 | 6.4 | 48 | 2.9 |
| Boulmer | 23 | 13.9 | 51 | 6.2 | 13.5 | 51 | 5.6 | 11.3 | 56 | 3.5 | 8.2 | 85 | 3.1 |
| Bradford | 134 | 14.7 | 59 | 4.8 | 13.9 | 69 | 4.5 | 11.8 | 162 | 2.7 | 7.4 | 51 | 2.6 |
| Braemar | 339 | 11.6 | 49 | 4.6 | 11.2 | 45 | 3.9 | 8.7 | 107 | 4.0 | 4.5 | 173 | 2.3 |
| Bristol | 42 | 16.4 | 72 | 6.6 | 16.1 | 27 | 7.1 | 13.7 | 103 | 4.0 | 9.5 | 121 | 4.0 |
| Bude | 15 | 15.1 | 139 | 5.6 | 14.7 | 31 | 7.1 | 12.6 | 94 | 6.2 | 8.9 | 75 | 4.8 |
| Buxton | 307 | 13.3 | 123 | 4.8 | 12.5 | 80 | 4.7 | 10.7 | 133 | 2.8 | 6.1 | 48 | 3.3 |
| Cambridge | 24 | 16.0 | 54 | 5.5 | 15.5 | 37 | 6.3 | 13.1 | 67 | 3.2 | 9.1 | 89 | 3.5 |
| Cheltenham | 65 | 15.7 | 78 | 5.7 | 14.7 | 28 | – | 12.9 | 78 | – | 8.8 | 77 | – |
| Clacton-on-Sea | 16 | 16.5 | 48 | 6.2 | 15.9 | 29 | 6.7 | 13.7 | 102 | 4.0 | 10.1 | 91 | 4.0 |
| Cleethorpes | 23 | 15.7 | 59 | 6.2 | 14.8 | 38 | 6.5 | 12.9 | 125 | 3.4 | 9.2 | 75 | 3.6 |
| Dumfries | 49 | 13.5 | 60 | 3.7 | 13.1 | 43 | 4.4 | 11.3 | 53 | 2.8 | 7.3 | 47 | 3.0 |
| Dundee | 45 | 14.4 | 74 | 5.2 | 13.6 | 49 | 5.2 | 11.4 | 43 | 4.2 | 7.7 | 117 | 4.0 |
| Durham | 102 | 14.4 | 42 | 5.3 | 13.9 | 89 | 5.2 | 11.5 | 118 | 2.9 | 7.6 | 74 | 2.9 |
| Dyce (Aberdeen) | 65 | 13.4 | 121 | 4.7 | 12.9 | 61 | 4.5 | 10.9 | 62 | 3.3 | 7.3 | 113 | 2.9 |
| East Malling | 33 | 16.4 | 46 | 5.9 | 15.9 | 42 | 7.4 | 13.0 | 91 | 3.3 | 9.9 | 107 | 3.3 |
| Edinburgh | 26 | 14.3 | 57 | 5.7 | 13.9 | 34 | 5.1 | 11.5 | 50 | 4.1 | 7.3 | 104 | 3.6 |
| Elmdon (Birmingham) | 98 | 15.6 | 63 | 6.4 | 14.4 | 29 | 5.9 | 12.1 | 73 | 2.7 | 7.7 | 74 | 3.6 |
| Hastings | 45 | 15.5 | 67 | 6.3 | 16.1 | 34 | 7.8 | 13.9 | 104 | 4.3 | 10.4 | 126 | 3.4 |
| Heathrow (London) | 25 | 17.1 | 35 | 5.6 | 16.7 | 24 | 7.1 | 13.7 | 96 | 3.5 | 10.0 | 123 | 3.8 |
| Hurn (Bournemouth) | 10 | 15.9 | 57 | 6.1 | 15.0 | 36 | 7.5 | 12.5 | 153 | 4.3 | 9.0 | 163 | 3.8 |
| Inverness | 4 | 13.8 | 39 | 3.4 | 13.6 | 27 | 3.7 | 11.6 | 26 | 3.8 | – | 140 | 1.9 |
| Isle of Portland | 53 | 15.5 | 53 | 6.6 | 15.7 | 36 | 7.9 | 14.1 | 102 | 5.4 | 10.5 | 81 | – |
| Leeming | 32 | 15.1 | 48 | 4.7 | 14.3 | 87 | 4.8 | 12.1 | 70 | 3.0 | 7.9 | 75 | 2.9 |
| Lerwick | 82 | 10.3 | 51 | 2.8 | 10.7 | 53 | 2.9 | 9.7 | 38 | 3.8 | 6.9 | 100 | 1.5 |
| Long Sutton | 145 | 15.7 | 50 | 5.1 | 15.1 | 35 | 6.4 | 12.5 | 103 | 2.8 | 8.7 | 129 | 3.0 |
| Lowestoft | 25 | 16.3 | 63 | 5.6 | 15.8 | 60 | 6.8 | 13.8 | 137 | 3.8 | 10.4 | 143 | 4.1 |
| Manston | 44 | 16.5 | 53 | 6.3 | 16.4 | 33 | 7.3 | 13.7 | 106 | 4.2 | 10.3 | 121 | 3.5 |
| Morecambe | 7 | 15.0 | 79 | 4.2 | 14.5 | 81 | 6.1 | 12.8 | 61 | 3.7 | 8.5 | 36 | 3.9 |
| Oxford | 63 | 16.5 | 51 | 6.1 | 15.8 | 27 | 7.7 | 13.2 | 96 | 3.6 | 8.9 | 112 | 3.9 |
| Penzance | 19 | 15.8 | 126 | 6.2 | – | 34 | – | 14.1 | 211 | 5.8 | 10.3 | 121 | 5.2 |
| Plymouth | 27 | 15.6 | 106 | 5.9 | 15.3 | 33 | 6.9 | 13.4 | 182 | 5.7 | 9.7 | 99 | 4.9 |
| Presteigne | 175 | 14.6 | 66 | 6.6 | 13.3 | 41 | 5.6 | 10.9 | 101 | 3.2 | 6.9 | 60 | 3.1 |
| Rhoose | 65 | 15.2 | 99 | 6.8 | 14.7 | 44 | 7.0 | 12.8 | 90 | 5.1 | 8.8 | 65 | 4.6 |
| Ringway (Manchester) | 75 | 14.7 | 103 | 4.3 | 13.9 | 79 | 4.7 | 12.5 | 55 | 3.1 | 8.2 | 53 | 3.1 |
| Ronaldsway | 16 | 14.1 | 76 | 5.1 | 13.8 | 53 | 6.6 | 12.5 | 127 | 3.7 | 8.7 | 68 | 3.6 |
| Rustington | 3 | 15.8 | 55 | 5.5 | 15.1 | 28 | 8.0 | 13.3 | 147 | 4.2 | 10.1 | 106 | 4.2 |
| St Mawgan | 103 | 14.9 | 136 | 5.6 | 14.9 | 30 | 7.2 | 13.1 | 160 | 5.5 | 9.1 | 113 | 5.1 |
| Shawbury | 72 | 14.7 | 57 | 6.1 | 13.7 | 52 | 5.5 | 11.7 | 78 | 2.6 | 7.5 | 67 | 3.1 |
| Sheffield | 131 | 15.3 | 85 | 6.4 | 14.3 | 30 | 5.9 | – | 121 | 2.8 | 8.1 | 63 | 2.4 |
| Skegness | 5 | 15.6 | 49 | 5.8 | 14.8 | 62 | 5.4 | 13.3 | 120 | 3.7 | 9.7 | 79 | 3.7 |
| Stornoway | 15 | 11.9 | 81 | 2.3 | 12.0 | 45 | 2.8 | 11.1 | 38 | 3.8 | 7.9 | 79 | 1.7 |
| Tenby | 5 | 14.9 | 98 | 6.3 | 13.7 | 43 | 5.5 | 12.5 | 71 | 4.7 | 9.1 | 57 | 4.9 |
| Terrington St Clement | 2 | 15.4 | 100 | 6.1 | 15.1 | 55 | 6.8 | 13.2 | 79 | 3.2 | 9.3 | 86 | 3.3 |
| Tiree | 9 | 12.3 | 87 | 4.1 | 12.5 | 65 | 4.9 | 11.9 | 63 | 5.4 | 8.5 | 45 | 3.5 |
| Torquay | 8 | 16.5 | 64 | 6.8 | 16.1 | 30 | 8.1 | 14.1 | 153 | 5.5 | 10.5 | 93 | 4.5 |
| Valley | 10 | 14.7 | 46 | 5.0 | 14.4 | 44 | 6.6 | 12.9 | 82 | 4.2 | 8.9 | 32 | 3.8 |
| Ventnor | 135 | 15.3 | 81 | 5.1 | 15.9 | 32 | 8.0 | 14.3 | 110 | 5.0 | 10.3 | 116 | 4.1 |
| Waddington | 68 | 15.2 | 54 | 6.5 | 14.7 | 46 | 5.3 | 12.3 | 102 | 2.8 | 8.3 | 76 | 3.6 |
| Watnall (Nottingham) | 117 | 15.1 | 84 | 6.2 | 14.5 | 61 | 6.1 | 12.3 | 133 | 2.5 | 8.1 | 89 | 3.2 |
| Whitby | 41 | 15.3 | 43 | 5.9 | 14.1 | 138 | 4.8 | 12.4 | 76 | 3.3 | 8.5 | 35 | 2.8 |

Ht        height (in metres) of station above mean sea level
°C        mean air temperature
Rain      total monthly rainfall
Sun       mean daily bright sunshine (hours)
*Source:* data provided by the Met Office

| | November 1993 | | | December 1993 | | | The Year 1993 | | | January 1994 | | | February 1994 | | |
|---|---|---|---|---|---|---|---|---|---|---|---|---|---|---|---|
| | °C | Rain mm | Sun hrs | °C | Rain mm | Sun hrs | °C | Rain mm | Sun hrs | °C | Rain mm | Sun hrs | °C | Rain mm | Sun hrs |
| Abbotsinch (Glasgow) | 3.8 | 82 | 1.9 | 3.1 | 183 | 1.1 | 8.5 | 1081 | 3.3 | 3.9 | 168 | 1.2 | 2.5 | 71 | 1.9 |
| Aberporth | 5.6 | 113 | 2.4 | 6.3 | 143 | 0.9 | 9.4 | 988 | 4.0 | 5.9 | 107 | 1.9 | 4.1 | 87 | 2.2 |
| Aldergrove | 5.6 | 55 | 2.3 | 4.0 | 124 | 1.1 | 8.9 | 941 | 3.0 | 4.0 | 113 | 1.6 | 3.1 | 107 | 1.6 |
| Aspatria | 3.9 | 73 | 2.6 | 3.9 | 191 | 0.9 | 8.5 | 941 | 3.6 | 4.1 | 110 | 1.3 | 2.3 | 57 | 2.9 |
| Auchincruive | 4.6 | 77 | 2.4 | 3.9 | 187 | 0.9 | 8.5 | 934 | 3.1 | 4.4 | 130 | 1.2 | 2.7 | – | 2.7 |
| Bala | 3.9 | 64 | 2.0 | 4.9 | 361 | 0.5 | 8.3 | 1281 | 3.0 | 4.5 | 209 | 1.1 | 2.6 | 116 | 1.8 |
| Boulmer | 4.5 | 66 | 2.0 | 4.0 | 84 | 2.0 | 8.4 | 677 | 3.9 | 4.1 | 90 | 2.5 | 2.7 | 69 | 2.3 |
| Bradford | 3.7 | 44 | 0.9 | 4.3 | 184 | 0.6 | – | 951 | 2.8 | 4.2 | 131 | 1.0 | 1.9 | 83 | 1.3 |
| Braemar | 1.3 | 45 | 1.1 | 0.3 | 84 | 0.8 | 6.3 | – | 2.9 | 1.5 | 124 | 0.7 | −0.3 | 113 | 0.7 |
| Bristol | 6.3 | 50 | 2.1 | 6.9 | 171 | 1.7 | – | – | – | 6.7 | 127 | 2.4 | 5.1 | 73 | 2.6 |
| Bude | 6.8 | 73 | 2.9 | 7.7 | 188 | 1.0 | – | – | – | 7.4 | 132 | 2.1 | 5.7 | 117 | 2.8 |
| Buxton | 2.8 | 86 | 1.2 | 3.3 | 270 | 0.7 | 7.6 | 1189 | 3.2 | 3.5 | 185 | 1.5 | 1.1 | 104 | 1.4 |
| Cambridge | 5.0 | 53 | 2.0 | 5.5 | 78 | 1.4 | 10.0 | 673 | 3.7 | 5.3 | 71 | 2.1 | 3.5 | 34 | 3.0 |
| Cheltenham | 5.1 | 45 | – | 6.3 | 133 | – | 9.9 | 829 | – | 5.5 | 135 | – | 3.7 | 72 | – |
| Clacton-on-Sea | 6.0 | 56 | 2.5 | 5.6 | 78 | 1.3 | 10.1 | 602 | 4.3 | 5.2 | 68 | 2.4 | 3.7 | 38 | 2.7 |
| Cleethorpes | 5.5 | 95 | 1.5 | 5.3 | 69 | 1.9 | – | – | – | 4.9 | 77 | 2.5 | 3.2 | 43 | 2.9 |
| *Dumfries | 3.9 | 68 | 2.0 | 3.5 | 223 | 0.6 | 8.3 | 1078 | 2.8 | 2.4 | 227 | 1.2 | 0.7 | 114 | 1.8 |
| Dundee | 3.9 | 58 | 1.8 | 3.1 | 75 | 1.7 | – | 830 | 3.6 | 3.5 | – | – | 2.5 | – | 2.0 |
| Durham | 3.3 | 65 | 1.1 | 3.7 | 78 | 2.2 | 8.5 | 751 | 3.4 | 3.7 | 71 | 2.3 | 1.7 | 53 | 2.0 |
| Dyce (Aberdeen) | 4.0 | 72 | 1.9 | 2.3 | 110 | 1.2 | 7.9 | 946 | 3.3 | 3.5 | 124 | 1.9 | 2.2 | 146 | 1.2 |
| East Malling | 5.1 | 44 | 2.5 | 6.4 | 96 | 1.6 | 10.3 | 655 | 4.2 | 6.0 | 88 | 2.3 | 3.8 | 35 | 2.3 |
| Edinburgh | 4.1 | 39 | 1.9 | 3.5 | 98 | 1.4 | 8.6 | 782 | 3.4 | 3.9 | – | 1.7 | 2.7 | – | 2.1 |
| Elmdon (Birmingham) | 4.3 | 72 | 1.6 | 5.1 | 101 | 2.0 | 9.3 | 719 | 3.7 | 5.1 | 72 | 2.6 | 2.8 | 59 | 2.2 |
| Hastings | 6.1 | 56 | 2.9 | 6.7 | 140 | 1.8 | 10.2 | 781 | 4.6 | 6.5 | 95 | 2.3 | 4.6 | 35 | 2.2 |
| Heathrow (London) | 5.6 | 29 | 2.4 | 6.4 | 74 | 1.7 | 10.8 | 613 | 4.1 | 6.1 | 80 | 2.4 | 4.5 | 43 | 2.6 |
| Hurn (Bournemouth) | 4.9 | 77 | 2.6 | 6.3 | 179 | 2.1 | 9.9 | 1038 | 4.4 | 5.8 | 130 | 2.4 | 4.1 | 113 | 2.4 |
| Inverness | 4.2 | 16 | 2.2 | 2.1 | 100 | 1.0 | – | 720 | 2.7 | 3.9 | 95 | 0.8 | 2.9 | – | 3.2 |
| Isle of Portland | 7.3 | 66 | 2.3 | 7.7 | 141 | 1.8 | – | – | – | 7.5 | 112 | 2.5 | 6.1 | 120 | 2.5 |
| Leeming | 3.8 | 40 | 1.1 | 4.5 | 66 | 1.9 | 9.0 | 688 | 3.3 | 4.5 | 81 | 2.1 | 1.9 | 54 | 1.8 |
| Lerwick | 5.7 | 64 | 1.2 | 2.6 | 180 | 0.6 | 6.7 | 1121 | 2.5 | 2.7 | 242 | 0.5 | 2.5 | 75 | 1.9 |
| Long Sutton | 5.1 | 47 | 2.3 | – | 124 | 1.7 | – | – | – | 5.0 | 103 | 2.0 | 3.1 | 79 | 2.4 |
| Lowestoft | 6.1 | 177 | 1.9 | 5.4 | 88 | 1.1 | – | 782 | 3.7 | 5.0 | 70 | 1.9 | 3.3 | 23 | 2.7 |
| Manston | 5.4 | 41 | 2.9 | 5.8 | 86 | 1.2 | 10.2 | 628 | 4.5 | 5.5 | 55 | 2.2 | 3.9 | 31 | 2.8 |
| Morecambe | 4.9 | 70 | 2.6 | 4.9 | 206 | 0.7 | 9.6 | 974 | 3.6 | 5.1 | 129 | 1.3 | 3.4 | 45 | 2.1 |
| Oxford | 5.3 | 51 | 2.5 | 6.0 | 98 | 1.8 | 10.2 | 723 | 4.2 | 5.9 | 82 | 2.8 | 4.0 | 62 | 2.8 |
| Penzance | 8.9 | 117 | 2.5 | 8.5 | 246 | 1.7 | – | 1416 | – | 8.1 | 177 | 2.2 | 7.3 | 182 | 2.7 |
| Plymouth | 7.3 | 117 | 3.0 | 7.5 | 225 | 1.8 | 10.6 | 1247 | 4.4 | 7.3 | 161 | 2.5 | 6.1 | 161 | 2.7 |
| Presteigne | 3.7 | 78 | 1.6 | 4.7 | 193 | 1.7 | – | – | – | 4.5 | 127 | 2.6 | 2.1 | 97 | 1.7 |
| Rhoose | 5.7 | 89 | 2.2 | 6.5 | 188 | 1.6 | 9.8 | 933 | 4.3 | 5.9 | 147 | 2.7 | 4.2 | 104 | 2.6 |
| Ringway (Manchester) | 4.3 | 41 | 1.8 | 4.7 | 164 | 1.2 | 9.3 | 786 | 3.4 | 4.7 | 91 | 1.7 | 3.1 | 40 | 1.9 |
| Ronaldsway | 6.9 | 95 | 2.0 | 6.1 | 134 | 1.6 | – | – | – | 6.1 | 98 | 2.0 | 4.3 | 100 | 1.7 |
| Rustington | 5.7 | 68 | 2.9 | 6.5 | 181 | 2.0 | – | – | – | 6.3 | 132 | 2.5 | 4.3 | 61 | 2.7 |
| St Mawgan | 7.3 | 83 | 2.5 | 7.7 | 190 | 1.2 | 10.3 | 1229 | 4.4 | 7.2 | 138 | 2.3 | 5.9 | 164 | 2.5 |
| Shawbury | 3.7 | 58 | 1.6 | 4.7 | 122 | 1.6 | 8.9 | 725 | 3.5 | 4.7 | 63 | 2.2 | 2.7 | 55 | 1.9 |
| Sheffield | 4.2 | 57 | 0.9 | 4.7 | 171 | 0.9 | – | 914 | 3.5 | 4.3 | 124 | 1.4 | 2.1 | 76 | 1.2 |
| Skegness | 5.7 | 87 | 1.9 | – | 78 | 1.6 | – | 724 | 3.9 | – | 95 | 2.4 | 3.3 | 42 | 3.2 |
| Stornoway | 6.4 | 63 | 2.1 | 3.7 | 179 | 0.7 | 8.1 | 1119 | 2.8 | 4.3 | 154 | 0.9 | 4.1 | 57 | 3.1 |
| Tenby | 6.9 | 126 | 1.8 | 7.1 | 201 | – | 10.0 | 1099 | – | 6.5 | 158 | 2.1 | 5.1 | 137 | 1.8 |
| Terrington St Clement | 5.1 | 76 | 1.8 | 5.3 | 71 | 1.6 | – | – | – | 4.9 | 84 | 2.3 | 2.9 | 48 | 3.1 |
| Tiree | 7.2 | 96 | 1.8 | 5.1 | 209 | 1.1 | 8.9 | 1275 | 3.5 | 5.1 | 180 | 1.0 | 4.2 | 71 | 1.4 |
| Torquay | 7.3 | 90 | 2.6 | 7.4 | 202 | 2.0 | 11.2 | 1094 | 4.7 | 7.3 | 122 | 2.9 | 6.1 | 157 | 2.9 |
| Valley | 6.5 | 84 | 2.7 | 6.7 | 109 | 1.2 | 9.9 | 803 | 3.9 | 6.3 | 74 | 1.9 | 4.4 | 86 | 2.8 |
| Ventnor | 7.1 | 53 | 3.1 | 7.0 | 168 | 2.2 | 10.7 | 866 | – | 6.9 | 146 | 2.4 | 5.5 | 72 | 2.8 |
| Waddington | 4.6 | 61 | 1.3 | 4.9 | 75 | 1.8 | 9.3 | 655 | 3.7 | 4.7 | 70 | 2.3 | 2.3 | 46 | 2.9 |
| Watnall (Nottingham) | 4.3 | 73 | 1.5 | 4.7 | 121 | 1.7 | 9.2 | 836 | 3.6 | 4.7 | 95 | 2.2 | 2.6 | 48 | 2.2 |
| Whitby | 4.9 | 75 | 1.7 | 4.8 | 76 | 1.7 | – | – | – | 4.7 | 97 | 2.4 | 2.9 | 61 | 2.5 |

*From Jan. 1994 Dumfries is replaced by Eskdalemuir (Ht 242 m)

TEMPERATURE, RAINFALL AND SUNSHINE *contd.*

| | March 1994 °C | Rain mm | Sun hrs | April 1994 °C | Rain mm | Sun hrs | May 1994 °C | Rain mm | Sun hrs | June 1994 °C | Rain mm | Sun hrs |
|---|---|---|---|---|---|---|---|---|---|---|---|---|
| Abbotsinch (Glasgow) | 5.7 | 180 | 2.9 | 7.1 | 82 | 4.7 | 9.9 | 11 | 6.5 | 12.4 | 77 | 4.9 |
| Aberporth | 7.4 | 115 | 3.4 | 7.4 | 74 | 5.7 | 10.5 | 41 | 6.0 | 12.9 | 28 | 6.1 |
| Aldergrove | 6.1 | 83 | 3.0 | 7.3 | 63 | 6.0 | 9.8 | 29 | 5.0 | 12.6 | 47 | 3.7 |
| Aspatria | 6.1 | 126 | 2.9 | 7.1 | 89 | 5.6 | 9.7 | 19 | 6.5 | 12.7 | 77 | 5.1 |
| Auchincruive | 5.9 | 126 | 2.2 | 6.9 | 74 | 4.2 | 9.7 | 8 | 6.2 | 12.3 | 55 | 3.9 |
| Bala | 6.5 | 204 | 2.5 | 6.8 | 99 | 5.1 | 9.3 | 42 | 4.5 | 12.1 | 51 | 5.0 |
| Boulmer | 6.6 | 20 | 5.1 | 7.2 | 41 | 6.0 | 8.7 | 9 | 6.5 | 13.2 | 45 | 8.6 |
| Bradford | 6.7 | 84 | 3.6 | 8.3 | 69 | 5.3 | 9.7 | 41 | 3.9 | 13.9 | 21 | 5.7 |
| Braemar | 2.9 | 149 | 3.5 | 5.0 | 93 | 4.1 | 6.8 | 12 | 6.5 | – | – | – |
| Bristol | 8.7 | 91 | – | 9.1 | 67 | 5.6 | 12.0 | 82 | 4.3 | 15.3 | 22 | 8.0 |
| Bude | 8.5 | 88 | 2.8 | 8.4 | 61 | 6.0 | 11.1 | 63 | 6.0 | 13.5 | 23 | 7.4 |
| Buxton | 5.3 | 181 | 2.9 | 6.4 | 119 | 5.4 | 8.6 | 31 | 4.7 | 12.5 | 104 | 5.3 |
| Cambridge | 7.9 | 36 | 4.3 | 8.3 | 67 | 5.5 | 11.2 | 44 | 4.4 | 15.3 | 20 | 7.3 |
| Cheltenham | 8.5 | 70 | – | 9.1 | 83 | – | 12.3 | 77 | – | 15.9 | 31 | – |
| Clacton-on-Sea | 8.0 | 38 | 3.8 | 8.1 | 56 | 5.5 | 11.0 | 46 | 5.0 | 15.1 | 31 | 7.6 |
| Cleethorpes | 7.9 | 44 | 4.7 | 8.9 | 41 | 7.0 | – | – | – | – | – | 0.0 |
| Dundee | 5.9 | 42 | 4.8 | 7.3 | 49 | – | 9.5 | 16 | – | 13.9 | – | – |
| Durham | 6.5 | 32 | 4.6 | 7.2 | 38 | 5.7 | 9.0 | 46 | 5.1 | 13.3 | 22 | 6.9 |
| Dyce (Aberdeen) | 5.5 | 27 | 5.3 | 6.9 | 62 | 5.4 | 8.7 | 14 | 7.5 | 13.4 | 28 | 7.4 |
| East Malling | 8.5 | 37 | 4.2 | 8.7 | 73 | 5.6 | 11.3 | 67 | 5.0 | 15.4 | 58 | – |
| Edinburgh | 6.1 | 81 | 4.1 | 7.3 | 52 | 4.8 | 9.7 | 13 | 6.9 | 13.5 | 36 | 6.7 |
| Elmdon (Birmingham) | 7.7 | 73 | 4.0 | 8.0 | 58 | 5.4 | 10.3 | 50 | 4.7 | 14.7 | 23 | 7.9 |
| Eskdalemuir | 4.1 | 262 | 2.3 | 5.1 | 129 | 3.9 | 7.9 | 44 | 5.7 | 11.2 | 107 | 4.5 |
| Hastings | 8.2 | 55 | 4.1 | 8.4 | 90 | 6.1 | 11.3 | 83 | 6.2 | 14.7 | 50 | 8.9 |
| Heathrow (London) | 8.7 | 40 | 4.1 | 9.2 | 53 | 5.8 | 12.1 | 81 | 5.1 | 16.3 | 17 | 8.8 |
| Hurn (Bournemouth) | 8.1 | 66 | 3.6 | 8.2 | 54 | 6.3 | 11.1 | 82 | 5.3 | 14.5 | 19 | 8.9 |
| Inverness | 5.5 | 137 | 2.9 | 7.4 | 79 | 4.1 | 10.3 | – | 7.5 | 13.5 | – | 5.4 |
| Isle of Portland | 8.5 | 64 | 3.2 | 8.5 | 37 | 6.0 | 10.9 | 123 | 5.6 | – | 15 | 9.0 |
| Leeming | 7.3 | 27 | 4.2 | 8.3 | 32 | 5.3 | 9.9 | 27 | 5.3 | 14.5 | 19 | 7.5 |
| Lerwick | 3.1 | 206 | 3.3 | 5.3 | 89 | 5.1 | 6.9 | 34 | 8.1 | 9.2 | 100 | 4.6 |
| Long Sutton | 7.6 | 63 | 3.5 | 7.5 | 66 | 5.8 | 10.5 | 90 | 4.7 | 14.3 | 34 | 7.3 |
| Lowestoft | 7.9 | 45 | 4.3 | 8.6 | 41 | 5.6 | 11.1 | 49 | 5.0 | 15.1 | 28 | 6.3 |
| Manston | 8.0 | 32 | 4.7 | 8.5 | 45 | 5.7 | 11.5 | 69 | 6.1 | 15.2 | 27 | 8.8 |
| Morecambe | 6.6 | 123 | 2.9 | 8.1 | 106 | 5.5 | 11.2 | 35 | 5.6 | 13.7 | 51 | 4.9 |
| Oxford | 8.5 | 42 | 4.1 | 8.7 | 52 | 5.9 | 11.5 | 85 | 5.2 | 15.8 | 13 | 8.5 |
| Penzance | 9.3 | 97 | 2.7 | 9.3 | 74 | – | 11.7 | 81 | – | 14.3 | 28 | – |
| Plymouth | 8.5 | 91 | – | 8.5 | 73 | 6.1 | 11.3 | 99 | 5.8 | 13.9 | 29 | 8.8 |
| Presteigne | 7.0 | 91 | 4.2 | 7.5 | 55 | 5.8 | 9.7 | 69 | 7.3 | 13.5 | 19 | 6.5 |
| Rhoose | 7.9 | 148 | 4.1 | 8.3 | 90 | 6.2 | 11.1 | 93 | 4.9 | 13.5 | 32 | 7.4 |
| Ringway (Manchester) | 7.1 | 99 | 3.1 | 8.1 | 69 | 5.9 | 10.7 | 26 | 5.2 | 14.1 | 39 | 5.1 |
| Ronaldsway | 7.1 | 66 | 3.2 | 7.3 | 67 | 6.0 | 10.1 | 25 | 6.2 | 12.3 | 30 | 4.6 |
| Rustington | 8.1 | 58 | 4.0 | 8.1 | 72 | 6.5 | 11.3 | 78 | 6.1 | 14.3 | 29 | 9.5 |
| St Mawgan | 8.3 | 103 | 2.5 | 8.2 | 80 | 6.4 | 11.0 | 83 | 6.0 | 13.5 | 26 | 8.1 |
| Shawbury | 7.5 | 55 | 3.6 | 7.7 | 48 | 6.3 | 10.3 | 43 | 4.8 | 13.9 | 20 | 6.5 |
| Sheffield | 7.4 | 78 | 4.5 | 8.5 | 55 | 5.8 | 10.3 | 66 | 4.5 | 14.9 | 15 | 6.6 |
| Skegness | 7.7 | 52 | 4.1 | 8.7 | 41 | 5.9 | 10.5 | 37 | 5.4 | 14.9 | 23 | 7.9 |
| Stornoway | 4.5 | 165 | 3.2 | 6.3 | 104 | 4.2 | 8.4 | 36 | 9.5 | 10.9 | 112 | 4.5 |
| Tenby | 7.9 | 123 | 3.4 | 7.9 | 85 | 5.9 | 10.6 | 56 | 5.0 | 12.9 | 48 | 6.4 |
| Terrington St Clement | 7.7 | 59 | 4.0 | 8.6 | 46 | 5.8 | 11.3 | 33 | 5.1 | 14.9 | 18 | 4.8 |
| Tiree | 5.9 | 143 | 3.0 | 7.1 | 107 | 5.5 | 9.8 | 41 | 8.7 | 11.3 | 112 | 4.0 |
| Torquay | 9.3 | 75 | 3.5 | 9.0 | 40 | 6.3 | 11.5 | 125 | 5.3 | 17.5 | 18 | 9.6 |
| Valley | 7.4 | 113 | 3.6 | 7.9 | 95 | 6.0 | 11.0 | 35 | 6.3 | 13.3 | 23 | 5.3 |
| Ventnor | 8.3 | 50 | 3.8 | 8.5 | 63 | 6.8 | 11.6 | 95 | 5.7 | 14.3 | 33 | 9.5 |
| Waddington | 7.4 | 42 | 3.9 | 8.3 | 36 | 6.2 | 10.1 | 45 | 4.8 | 15.1 | 7 | 7.2 |
| Watnall (Nottingham) | 7.2 | 60 | 3.7 | 8.1 | 42 | 6.1 | 10.1 | 52 | 4.6 | 14.5 | 22 | 6.9 |
| Whitby | 7.3 | 36 | 4.7 | 8.2 | 32 | 5.8 | 9.1 | 23 | 5.2 | 14.3 | 18 | 7.4 |

## METEOROLOGICAL OBSERVATIONS London (Heathrow)

Temperature maxima and minima cover the 24-hour period 9–9 h; mean wind speed is 10 metres above the ground; rainfall is for the 24 hours starting at 9 h on the day of entry; sunshine is for the 24 hours

0–24 h; averages are for the period 1961–90
Source: data provided by the Met Office

### JULY 1993

| | Temperature Max. °C | Min. °C | Wind knots | Rain mm | Sun hrs |
|---|---|---|---|---|---|
| Day 1 | 23.9 | 12.8 | 6.1 | 0.0 | 12.5 |
| 2 | 26.1 | 14.3 | 4.1 | 0.0 | 8.8 |
| 3 | 27.6 | 14.5 | 5.4 | 0.0 | 10.6 |
| 4 | 28.1 | 15.3 | 4.7 | 0.0 | 11.1 |
| 5 | 19.5 | 14.2 | 8.2 | 0.0 | 8.2 |
| 6 | 24.1 | 14.2 | 8.2 | 0.0 | 8.2 |
| 7 | 23.0 | 10.0 | 4.9 | 0.0 | 13.0 |
| 8 | 23.0 | 13.4 | 7.5 | Trace | 5.5 |
| 9 | 18.5 | 15.2 | 8.0 | 8.8 | 1.0 |
| 10 | 17.3 | 6.7 | 6.1 | 3.6 | 7.5 |
| 11 | 18.0 | 7.2 | 3.9 | Trace | 8.2 |
| 12 | 18.7 | 7.1 | 4.3 | 0.0 | 6.0 |
| 13 | 18.5 | 8.5 | 6.0 | 6.6 | 0.3 |
| 14 | 23.4 | 13.6 | 7.4 | 1.9 | 2.7 |
| 15 | 22.2 | 14.4 | 6.4 | 5.0 | 0.9 |
| 16 | 22.2 | 15.4 | 7.3 | 0.3 | 1.3 |
| 17 | 22.4 | 13.4 | 7.4 | 0.4 | 8.0 |
| 18 | 20.5 | 10.9 | 5.6 | 1.7 | 4.9 |
| 19 | 21.2 | 12.3 | 4.3 | Trace | 6.5 |
| 20 | 19.2 | 13.5 | 5.3 | 0.1 | 1.4 |
| 21 | 18.1 | 13.0 | 4.8 | 0.0 | 0.3 |
| 22 | 22.7 | 11.5 | 4.1 | 0.0 | 8.9 |
| 23 | 25.2 | 15.2 | 7.3 | 0.9 | 3.6 |
| 24 | 19.1 | 16.0 | 7.0 | 0.5 | 0.4 |
| 25 | 20.4 | 10.1 | 8.7 | 0.2 | 8.8 |
| 26 | 19.1 | 10.8 | 8.9 | 1.4 | 1.0 |
| 27 | 20.3 | 14.3 | 9.3 | 2.5 | 0.6 |
| 28 | 24.4 | 15.2 | 8.1 | Trace | 6.6 |
| 29 | 20.3 | 17.2 | 9.5 | 0.3 | 0.2 |
| 30 | 21.6 | 14.1 | 4.5 | 0.6 | 5.3 |
| 31 | 20.8 | 10.9 | 7.5 | Trace | 6.6 |
| Total | – | – | – | 35.0 | 174.6 |
| Mean | 21.6 | 12.7 | 6.5 | 1.2 | 5.7 |
| Temp. °F | 70.9 | 54.9 | – | – | – |
| Average | 22.5 | 13.1 | 7.4 | 46.0 | 198.5 |

### AUGUST 1993

| | Temperature Max. °C | Min. °C | Wind knots | Rain mm | Sun hrs |
|---|---|---|---|---|---|
| Day 1 | 22.3 | 10.2 | 5.3 | 0.0 | 7.7 |
| 2 | 22.3 | 13.5 | 9.1 | 0.1 | 6.1 |
| 3 | 22.2 | 13.3 | 7.7 | 0.0 | 7.7 |
| 4 | 20.4 | 13.0 | 6.0 | 0.8 | 2.1 |
| 5 | 21.8 | 14.1 | 8.2 | 0.0 | 9.8 |
| 6 | 22.2 | 14.1 | 8.2 | 0.0 | 5.1 |
| 7 | 24.2 | 13.5 | 5.2 | 0.0 | 10.9 |
| 8 | 21.7 | 15.0 | 5.0 | Trace | 5.6 |
| 9 | 23.2 | 14.5 | 8.5 | 0.6 | 1.9 |
| 10 | 19.4 | 13.6 | 7.0 | Trace | 7.7 |
| 11 | 21.1 | 11.0 | 9.4 | 14.5 | 1.1 |
| 12 | 21.0 | 13.5 | 8.9 | 0.0 | 8.8 |
| 13 | 21.2 | 8.2 | 4.2 | 0.0 | 12.2 |
| 14 | 25.9 | 11.5 | 4.1 | 0.0 | 9.8 |
| 15 | 23.1 | 15.3 | 5.3 | Trace | 4.6 |
| 16 | 22.4 | 14.1 | 4.0 | 0.0 | 7.9 |
| 17 | 23.1 | 11.2 | 5.7 | 0.0 | 10.6 |
| 18 | 23.8 | 12.0 | 1.8 | 0.0 | 9.7 |
| 19 | 26.3 | 12.2 | 4.5 | Trace | 6.0 |
| 20 | 25.5 | 14.9 | 6.3 | 0.0 | 6.3 |
| 21 | 23.9 | 13.1 | 3.1 | 7.5 | 6.2 |
| 22 | 17.2 | 12.2 | 7.5 | 0.2 | 2.1 |
| 23 | 17.4 | 10.1 | 5.3 | 0.0 | 8.3 |
| 24 | 18.2 | 9.4 | 5.0 | 0.0 | 10.4 |
| 25 | 18.8 | 6.2 | 3.9 | 0.1 | 4.9 |
| 26 | 18.3 | 8.4 | 5.9 | 0.0 | 3.9 |
| 27 | 18.4 | 8.5 | 6.3 | 0.0 | 9.2 |
| 28 | 20.5 | 8.0 | 2.4 | 0.0 | 9.9 |
| 29 | 22.7 | 7.5 | 2.7 | Trace | 10.0 |
| 30 | 24.1 | 14.2 | 5.0 | 0.0 | 6.6 |
| 31 | 18.3 | 10.0 | 3.3 | 0.0 | 6.3 |
| Total | – | – | – | 23.8 | 219.4 |
| Mean | 21.7 | 11.7 | 5.6 | 0.8 | 7.1 |
| Temp. °F | 71.1 | 53.1 | – | – | – |
| Average | 22.1 | 12.8 | 7.2 | 51.0 | 186.7 |

### SEPTEMBER 1993

| | Temperature Max. °C | Min. °C | Wind knots | Rain mm | Sun hrs |
|---|---|---|---|---|---|
| Day 1 | 24.5 | 11.5 | 2.5 | 0.0 | 8.9 |
| 2 | 20.4 | 12.6 | 3.8 | 0.0 | 4.1 |
| 3 | 19.3 | 12.7 | 4.6 | Trace | 1.5 |
| 4 | 16.6 | 8.2 | 5.2 | 0.0 | 7.7 |
| 5 | 18.0 | 8.4 | 3.1 | 0.0 | 5.5 |
| 6 | 19.2 | 9.2 | 6.1 | 0.0 | 4.1 |
| 7 | 23.4 | 11.9 | 9.3 | 11.4 | 5.8 |
| 8 | 21.4 | 13.7 | 9.5 | 3.5 | 2.8 |
| 9 | 20.7 | 15.2 | 11.3 | 2.7 | 6.0 |
| 10 | 17.2 | 13.8 | 6.7 | 0.3 | 1.2 |
| 11 | 18.1 | 8.2 | 2.1 | Trace | 3.5 |
| 12 | 16.3 | 7.8 | 9.4 | 23.1 | 0.3 |
| 13 | 17.7 | 11.2 | 11.1 | 10.2 | 3.8 |
| 14 | 15.1 | 11.1 | 7.7 | 0.1 | 0.8 |
| 15 | 16.6 | 8.1 | 3.0 | 4.4 | 3.9 |
| 16 | 14.8 | 10.6 | 5.7 | 0.9 | 0.5 |
| 17 | 16.3 | 10.4 | 2.4 | 0.0 | 4.2 |
| 18 | 17.9 | 5.9 | 5.7 | 0.0 | 8.7 |
| 19 | 21.0 | 6.9 | 6.2 | Trace | 10.3 |
| 20 | 16.6 | 12.7 | 4.5 | 7.7 | 0.0 |
| 21 | 19.6 | 12.6 | 6.9 | 0.2 | 7.5 |
| 22 | 18.8 | 11.2 | 1.7 | Trace | 0.7 |
| 23 | 16.6 | 8.6 | 2.3 | 0.0 | 4.6 |
| 24 | 17.4 | 7.5 | 0.9 | 0.1 | 4.2 |
| 25 | 13.7 | 9.9 | 2.5 | 0.4 | 0.0 |
| 26 | 14.3 | 4.5 | 4.6 | 1.3 | 0.5 |
| 27 | 10.0 | 8.0 | 5.7 | 6.2 | 0.0 |
| 28 | 12.5 | 8.3 | 4.0 | 1.2 | 0.0 |
| 29 | 14.8 | 6.7 | 7.3 | 5.0 | 0.1 |
| 30 | 15.0 | 5.7 | 7.9 | 17.6 | 3.3 |
| 31 | | | | | |
| Total | – | – | – | 96.3 | 104.5 |
| Mean | 17.5 | 9.8 | 5.5 | 3.3 | 3.5 |
| Temp. °F | 63.5 | 49.6 | – | – | – |
| Average | 19.3 | 10.8 | 7.1 | 51.0 | 144.7 |

### OCTOBER 1993

| | Temperature Max. °C | Min. °C | Wind knots | Rain mm | Sun hrs |
|---|---|---|---|---|---|
| Day 1 | 13.9 | 6.8 | 7.3 | 24.7 | 0.3 |
| 2 | 14.3 | 10.0 | 4.1 | 3.5 | 1.4 |
| 3 | 17.2 | 7.6 | 4.4 | 1.6 | 6.5 |
| 4 | 16.5 | 10.1 | 6.4 | 1.1 | 5.9 |
| 5 | 16.6 | 10.2 | 8.2 | 1.7 | 4.8 |
| 6 | 15.8 | 10.0 | 8.5 | 9.2 | 3.4 |
| 7 | 14.9 | 9.8 | 6.2 | 4.2 | 6.4 |
| 8 | 16.8 | 8.1 | 6.5 | 1.7 | 1.9 |
| 9 | 14.5 | 9.8 | 6.1 | 1.0 | 4.1 |
| 10 | 15.7 | 9.2 | 3.6 | 8.3 | 4.4 |
| 11 | 18.0 | 11.4 | 6.0 | 6.0 | 4.4 |
| 12 | 16.9 | 11.2 | 3.4 | 59.4 | 2.5 |
| 13 | 14.7 | 11.5 | 7.4 | 0.5 | 0.1 |
| 14 | 11.1 | 7.7 | 9.3 | Trace | 4.5 |
| 15 | 11.1 | 1.4 | 2.5 | Trace | 8.4 |
| 16 | 9.1 | −0.4 | 2.8 | 0.0 | 9.7 |
| 17 | 11.4 | 0.5 | 5.7 | Trace | 6.8 |
| 18 | 12.9 | 3.5 | 5.8 | 0.0 | 9.7 |
| 19 | 10.8 | 1.3 | 2.7 | Trace | 9.0 |
| 20 | 11.1 | 0.5 | 3.0 | Trace | 4.2 |
| 21 | 9.7 | 2.9 | 8.1 | Trace | 4.8 |
| 22 | 11.0 | 5.0 | 7.9 | Trace | 6.4 |
| 23 | 11.0 | 6.2 | 8.9 | Trace | 1.0 |
| 24 | 10.4 | 7.4 | 8.0 | Trace | 0.3 |
| 25 | 11.1 | 6.6 | 6.8 | Trace | 1.0 |
| 26 | 12.0 | 7.5 | 5.8 | Trace | 0.0 |
| 27 | 11.4 | 8.9 | 7.3 | 0.1 | 0.2 |
| 28 | 11.8 | 8.6 | 8.3 | Trace | 0.8 |
| 29 | 12.3 | 7.9 | 6.0 | 0.0 | 4.1 |
| 30 | 10.0 | 7.1 | 6.4 | 0.0 | 0.0 |
| 31 | 9.5 | 8.0 | 6.4 | 0.0 | 0.0 |
| Total | – | – | – | 123.0 | 117.0 |
| Mean | 13.1 | 7.0 | 6.2 | 4.0 | 3.8 |
| Temp. °F | 55.6 | 44.6 | – | – | – |
| Average | 15.4 | 8.0 | 7.2 | 58.0 | 107.2 |

## NOVEMBER 1993

| Day | Temperature Max. °C | Min. °C | Wind knots | Rain mm | Sun hrs |
|---|---|---|---|---|---|
| 1 | 8.1 | 7.4 | 4.7 | 0.0 | 0.0 |
| 2 | 10.4 | 5.9 | 7.1 | Trace | 0.0 |
| 3 | 14.4 | 5.6 | 5.4 | Trace | 0.5 |
| 4 | 15.9 | 10.0 | 1.5 | 0.1 | 0.1 |
| 5 | 16.7 | 10.9 | 4.7 | 0.0 | 3.0 |
| 6 | 11.0 | 7.8 | 7.5 | Trace | 0.4 |
| 7 | 11.3 | 7.9 | 3.8 | Trace | 0.0 |
| 8 | 10.1 | 7.4 | 1.8 | 0.1 | 0.0 |
| 9 | 11.5 | 2.6 | 4.5 | 7.6 | 0.0 |
| 10 | 12.3 | 5.2 | 7.9 | 0.4 | 0.3 |
| 11 | 10.7 | 2.2 | 4.1 | Trace | 5.7 |
| 12 | 11.6 | 1.9 | 4.0 | 7.4 | 8.0 |
| 13 | 13.1 | 5.3 | 8.9 | 6.1 | 0.0 |
| 14 | 8.7 | 5.8 | 14.8 | 0.1 | 1.6 |
| 15 | 10.5 | 2.0 | 3.0 | 0.0 | 6.5 |
| 16 | 8.0 | −0.4 | 3.0 | 0.0 | 0.5 |
| 17 | 6.6 | 0.6 | 8.5 | 0.0 | 7.4 |
| 18 | 5.6 | −0.5 | 7.5 | 0.0 | 6.4 |
| 19 | 6.3 | −1.4 | 4.7 | 0.0 | 7.7 |
| 20 | 5.7 | −1.7 | 4.0 | 0.3 | 3.3 |
| 21 | 2.0 | −0.9 | 4.2 | 0.1 | 1.4 |
| 22 | 1.9 | −5.8 | 1.1 | Trace | 0.9 |
| 23 | 1.9 | −3.5 | 0.7 | Trace | 2.7 |
| 24 | 5.8 | −2.9 | 7.1 | Trace | 0.0 |
| 25 | 11.5 | 0.7 | 3.3 | Trace | 3.4 |
| 26 | 5.7 | 1.8 | 1.5 | 0.0 | 0.0 |
| 27 | 8.1 | 2.2 | 5.5 | 0.0 | 6.0 |
| 28 | 1.7 | −0.5 | 11.5 | 0.0 | 1.5 |
| 29 | 7.5 | −2.7 | 12.6 | 6.7 | 3.1 |
| 30 | 9.7 | −0.5 | 5.0 | 0.6 | 0.9 |
| 31 | | | | | |
| Total | – | – | – | 29.5 | 71.3 |
| Mean | 8.9 | 2.5 | 5.5 | 1.0 | 2.4 |
| Temp. °F | 48.0 | 36.5 | – | – | – |
| Average | 10.4 | 4.1 | 8.0 | 55.0 | 68.1 |

## DECEMBER 1993

| Day | Temperature Max. °C | Min. °C | Wind knots | Rain mm | Sun hrs |
|---|---|---|---|---|---|
| 1 | 11.5 | 4.9 | 5.7 | 0.1 | 2.6 |
| 2 | 12.4 | 4.5 | 9.5 | Trace | 0.0 |
| 3 | 12.8 | 10.0 | 11.7 | 0.6 | 0.0 |
| 4 | 12.2 | 9.9 | 10.6 | 0.6 | 2.0 |
| 5 | 9.2 | 2.4 | 5.3 | Trace | 2.0 |
| 6 | 10.2 | 5.5 | 7.5 | 4.3 | 0.2 |
| 7 | 8.5 | 6.5 | 9.7 | 4.8 | 3.4 |
| 8 | 12.7 | 2.4 | 15.0 | 2.8 | 0.0 |
| 9 | 9.9 | 6.5 | 14.2 | 1.0 | 2.8 |
| 10 | 8.5 | 5.0 | 8.7 | 0.0 | 2.5 |
| 11 | 7.5 | 2.9 | 9.9 | 0.1 | 6.3 |
| 12 | 12.0 | 1.5 | 7.5 | 10.6 | 0.0 |
| 13 | 10.4 | 4.3 | 11.3 | 0.2 | 1.4 |
| 14 | 6.4 | 0.4 | 8.5 | 5.6 | 4.7 |
| 15 | 7.4 | 0.4 | 10.4 | 0.1 | 4.1 |
| 16 | 8.7 | 3.9 | 11.8 | 0.9 | 5.6 |
| 17 | 11.1 | 4.0 | 5.3 | 0.1 | 0.0 |
| 18 | 13.9 | 5.5 | 12.4 | 7.6 | 0.0 |
| 19 | 14.4 | 10.3 | 13.3 | 6.5 | 0.0 |
| 20 | 7.9 | 3.7 | 5.2 | 4.0 | 0.0 |
| 21 | 6.8 | 2.0 | 8.0 | 0.1 | 3.0 |
| 22 | 8.6 | 2.0 | 11.6 | 4.7 | 1.8 |
| 23 | 7.2 | 1.5 | 6.7 | 1.8 | 0.0 |
| 24 | 4.8 | 1.8 | 9.3 | Trace | 0.1 |
| 25 | 4.1 | 0.1 | 2.4 | 0.1 | 0.4 |
| 26 | 3.0 | −0.1 | 3.1 | Trace | 2.4 |
| 27 | 4.6 | −1.3 | 1.7 | 2.6 | 4.7 |
| 28 | 9.4 | −0.3 | 4.8 | 2.2 | 0.0 |
| 29 | 11.7 | 1.9 | 7.5 | 2.8 | 0.7 |
| 30 | 8.8 | 5.5 | 6.4 | 9.6 | 0.0 |
| 31 | 7.5 | 4.6 | 5.9 | Trace | 1.7 |
| Total | – | – | – | 73.8 | 52.4 |
| Mean | 9.2 | 3.7 | 8.5 | 2.4 | 1.7 |
| Temp. °F | 48.6 | 38.7 | – | – | – |
| Average | 8.0 | 2.3 | 8.1 | 57.0 | 46.2 |

## JANUARY 1994

| Day | Temperature Max. °C | Min. °C | Wind knots | Rain mm | Sun hrs |
|---|---|---|---|---|---|
| 1 | 9.1 | −1.7 | 4.3 | 6.1 | 5.8 |
| 2 | 10.0 | 0.5 | 8.5 | Trace | 4.4 |
| 3 | 8.7 | 3.5 | 7.6 | 2.9 | 0.8 |
| 4 | 9.0 | 4.3 | 5.2 | 7.2 | 0.0 |
| 5 | 9.0 | 1.9 | 8.2 | 6.5 | 1.0 |
| 6 | 5.0 | 2.4 | 3.3 | 16.4 | 0.0 |
| 7 | 5.0 | −1.0 | 2.0 | 0.0 | 4.0 |
| 8 | 8.4 | −2.6 | 3.5 | 1.9 | 1.2 |
| 9 | 9.8 | −1.3 | 9.0 | 15.3 | 0.0 |
| 10 | 9.5 | 6.5 | 4.4 | Trace | 0.0 |
| 11 | 10.4 | 4.7 | 6.4 | 3.0 | 2.9 |
| 12 | 13.0 | 6.4 | 12.3 | 2.0 | 0.0 |
| 13 | 11.9 | 7.3 | 13.5 | 2.8 | 5.6 |
| 14 | 9.2 | 5.4 | 9.2 | 1.3 | 5.5 |
| 15 | 7.5 | 2.3 | 4.9 | 2.0 | 0.0 |
| 16 | 5.3 | 2.0 | 6.1 | Trace | 4.9 |
| 17 | 4.5 | 0.5 | 4.3 | Trace | 1.1 |
| 18 | 8.4 | −2.5 | 8.5 | 2.7 | 0.1 |
| 19 | 7.5 | 3.5 | 3.1 | 0.0 | 4.5 |
| 20 | 9.4 | −1.4 | 2.9 | Trace | 1.9 |
| 21 | 10.2 | 4.1 | 4.9 | Trace | 1.3 |
| 22 | 12.0 | 6.3 | 4.5 | 1.4 | 1.3 |
| 23 | 11.8 | 6.7 | 8.3 | 1.2 | 3.0 |
| 24 | 11.8 | 2.9 | 2.7 | 1.2 | 0.0 |
| 25 | 12.7 | 4.3 | 11.9 | 2.3 | 4.2 |
| 26 | 11.1 | 5.0 | 12.9 | 0.1 | 4.1 |
| 27 | 11.2 | 6.2 | 15.4 | 3.2 | 0.8 |
| 28 | 7.9 | 3.9 | 8.5 | 0.3 | 8.0 |
| 29 | 11.4 | 1.1 | 8.4 | 0.2 | 0.0 |
| 30 | 9.9 | 5.5 | 7.8 | 0.0 | 6.6 |
| 31 | 8.7 | 0.3 | 3.6 | Trace | 0.4 |
| Total | – | – | – | 80.0 | 73.4 |
| Mean | 9.4 | 2.9 | 7.0 | 2.6 | 2.4 |
| Temp. °F | 48.9 | 37.2 | – | – | – |
| Average | 7.1 | 1.4 | 8.5 | 52.0 | 51.7 |

## FEBRUARY 1994

| Day | Temperature Max. °C | Min. °C | Wind knots | Rain mm | Sun hrs |
|---|---|---|---|---|---|
| 1 | 9.8 | 3.2 | 11.5 | 3.2 | 0.0 |
| 2 | 7.1 | −0.5 | 4.1 | 5.5 | 3.0 |
| 3 | 11.5 | 1.4 | 14.0 | 6.1 | 0.5 |
| 4 | 9.7 | 4.5 | 7.6 | 0.0 | 1.4 |
| 5 | 11.0 | 1.6 | 2.3 | Trace | 7.7 |
| 6 | 10.0 | 1.4 | 5.6 | 4.9 | 3.4 |
| 7 | 9.2 | 3.6 | 3.0 | Trace | 7.2 |
| 8 | 9.6 | −1.0 | 3.9 | 0.8 | 5.2 |
| 9 | 9.5 | 1.5 | 3.6 | 0.0 | 5.4 |
| 10 | 8.9 | −0.3 | 2.0 | 3.8 | 6.6 |
| 11 | 6.7 | 2.6 | 7.5 | 2.1 | 0.0 |
| 12 | 7.8 | −0.9 | 8.0 | Trace | 8.9 |
| 13 | 3.3 | 1.0 | 9.4 | 0.8 | 0.7 |
| 14 | 0.5 | −4.1 | 15.3 | 1.6 | 1.3 |
| 15 | 6.4 | 0.1 | 6.9 | 0.1 | 0.0 |
| 16 | 8.1 | 0.0 | 2.0 | 0.0 | 0.2 |
| 17 | 6.6 | 2.9 | 2.7 | 0.0 | 0.0 |
| 18 | 7.5 | 3.6 | 7.6 | 0.0 | 0.0 |
| 19 | 6.4 | 0.1 | 4.6 | 0.0 | 6.1 |
| 20 | 3.2 | 1.1 | 9.2 | Trace | 3.5 |
| 21 | 3.4 | −2.0 | 2.6 | 0.2 | 8.9 |
| 22 | 2.7 | −2.2 | 4.9 | 9.3 | 0.0 |
| 23 | 4.8 | 0.0 | 7.9 | 2.1 | 0.0 |
| 24 | 4.2 | 2.2 | 5.8 | Trace | 0.0 |
| 25 | 9.7 | 2.0 | 6.5 | 1.7 | 0.0 |
| 26 | 12.1 | 2.6 | 6.0 | Trace | 0.0 |
| 27 | 12.9 | 7.5 | 7.9 | 0.2 | 1.6 |
| 28 | 11.8 | 7.0 | 3.9 | 0.2 | 0.4 |
| 29 | | | | | |
| 30 | | | | | |
| 31 | | | | | |
| Total | – | – | – | 42.6 | 72.0 |
| Mean | 7.7 | 1.2 | 6.3 | 1.6 | 2.6 |
| Temp. °F | 45.9 | 34.2 | – | – | – |
| Average | 7.5 | 1.5 | 8.8 | 35.0 | 67.3 |

## MARCH 1994

| Day | Temperature Max. °C | Min. °C | Wind knots | Rain mm | Sun hrs |
|---|---|---|---|---|---|
| 1 | 9.1 | 5.2 | 4.0 | 1.9 | 0.1 |
| 2 | 12.5 | 4.5 | 6.5 | 0.0 | 8.2 |
| 3 | 12.0 | 3.2 | 7.7 | 0.6 | 4.0 |
| 4 | 11.3 | 2.9 | 7.3 | 0.1 | 1.4 |
| 5 | 14.6 | 5.8 | 8.7 | Trace | 2.5 |
| 6 | 10.8 | 3.2 | 7.7 | Trace | 0.2 |
| 7 | 13.8 | 6.8 | 8.4 | 2.1 | 0.1 |
| 8 | 13.0 | 10.0 | 8.7 | Trace | 0.1 |
| 9 | 11.9 | 9.6 | 6.3 | 0.6 | 0.0 |
| 10 | 12.4 | 2.4 | 4.0 | 0.0 | 10.0 |
| 11 | 9.7 | 1.1 | 5.3 | Trace | 6.7 |
| 12 | 11.0 | 2.7 | 9.8 | 0.4 | 3.5 |
| 13 | 13.5 | 4.7 | 11.3 | 0.0 | 4.4 |
| 14 | 15.4 | 6.5 | 11.8 | 2.2 | 6.4 |
| 15 | 13.1 | 9.6 | 9.1 | 0.9 | 3.2 |
| 16 | 10.1 | 3.3 | 10.5 | 1.2 | 5.4 |
| 17 | 10.1 | 1.5 | 8.3 | 1.4 | 8.0 |
| 18 | 11.4 | 3.1 | 7.4 | 5.5 | 0.0 |
| 19 | 10.6 | 4.4 | 5.8 | 0.0 | 8.4 |
| 20 | 10.0 | −0.8 | 2.6 | 0.1 | 8.5 |
| 21 | 10.9 | 3.9 | 4.2 | 1.0 | 7.3 |
| 22 | 12.5 | 5.0 | 8.5 | 4.6 | 0.0 |
| 23 | 14.9 | 8.0 | 13.0 | 0.7 | 0.1 |
| 24 | 13.7 | 7.0 | 9.0 | 0.1 | 8.6 |
| 25 | 13.2 | 9.7 | 10.2 | 1.2 | 0.4 |
| 26 | 11.0 | 2.8 | 3.5 | 0.0 | 10.8 |
| 27 | 11.1 | 1.7 | 7.9 | 0.1 | 3.4 |
| 28 | 12.8 | 6.1 | 10.0 | Trace | 0.1 |
| 29 | 16.2 | 9.7 | 9.0 | Trace | 8.3 |
| 30 | 17.5 | 8.7 | 10.3 | 5.5 | 1.1 |
| 31 | 11.7 | 6.0 | 15.6 | 9.8 | 4.3 |
| Total | – | – | – | 40.0 | 126.4 |
| Mean | 12.4 | 5.2 | 8.2 | 1.3 | 4.1 |
| Temp. °F | 54.3 | 41.4 | – | – | – |
| Average | 10.3 | 2.7 | 8.9 | 47.0 | 110.1 |

## APRIL 1994

| Day | Temperature Max. °C | Min. °C | Wind knots | Rain mm | Sun hrs |
|---|---|---|---|---|---|
| 1 | 11.4 | 6.9 | 18.5 | 0.1 | 2.3 |
| 2 | 9.3 | 2.3 | 9.0 | 0.6 | 6.7 |
| 3 | 11.0 | −0.7 | 9.4 | 9.6 | 3.3 |
| 4 | 11.0 | 4.9 | 12.8 | 0.6 | 6.9 |
| 5 | 11.2 | 2.9 | 11.0 | 0.1 | 6.5 |
| 6 | 12.0 | 2.1 | 5.5 | 1.1 | 10.4 |
| 7 | 10.9 | 5.0 | 7.2 | 1.5 | 4.2 |
| 8 | 10.9 | 3.5 | 10.8 | 12.5 | 4.5 |
| 9 | 8.9 | 1.5 | 7.5 | 3.9 | 6.6 |
| 10 | 10.4 | 1.6 | 12.7 | 1.3 | 9.8 |
| 11 | 14.4 | 2.7 | 4.9 | 0.0 | 9.1 |
| 12 | 12.8 | 1.8 | 4.5 | 5.6 | 0.2 |
| 13 | 10.9 | 4.4 | 10.6 | Trace | 6.6 |
| 14 | 8.5 | 3.3 | 10.6 | 2.8 | 3.7 |
| 15 | 8.3 | 3.3 | 12.4 | 3.3 | 0.3 |
| 16 | 12.5 | 5.1 | 11.6 | Trace | 6.4 |
| 17 | 10.2 | 3.2 | 12.5 | Trace | 3.9 |
| 18 | 9.4 | 3.4 | 6.3 | 0.0 | 2.3 |
| 19 | 13.6 | 3.6 | 4.1 | 0.0 | 2.2 |
| 20 | 10.5 | 7.0 | 4.6 | 0.0 | 0.0 |
| 21 | 14.2 | 4.0 | 6.5 | 1.2 | 7.6 |
| 22 | 16.4 | 6.1 | 8.5 | 5.0 | 10.5 |
| 23 | 17.1 | 10.3 | 9.2 | 3.1 | 6.3 |
| 24 | 16.2 | 8.1 | 8.5 | 0.0 | 10.1 |
| 25 | 14.5 | 3.6 | 10.4 | Trace | 7.6 |
| 26 | 19.1 | 9.5 | 9.0 | 0.5 | 10.7 |
| 27 | 19.1 | 10.7 | 8.8 | Trace | 1.0 |
| 28 | 20.4 | 12.3 | 7.3 | 0.0 | 5.8 |
| 29 | 23.1 | 8.9 | 5.7 | 0.0 | 7.2 |
| 30 | 20.0 | 12.2 | 6.1 | 0.0 | 12.3 |
| 31 | | | | | |
| Total | – | – | – | 52.8 | 175.0 |
| Mean | 13.3 | 5.2 | 8.9 | 1.8 | 5.9 |
| Temp. °F | 55.9 | 41.4 | – | – | – |
| Average | 13.1 | 4.7 | 8.5 | 45.0 | 146.9 |

## MAY 1994*

| Day | Temperature Max. °C | Min. °C | Wind knots | Rain mm | Sun hrs |
|---|---|---|---|---|---|
| 1 | 17.4 | 7.2 | – | 0.0 | 12.7 |
| 2 | 17.5 | 6.5 | – | 0.0 | 11.2 |
| 3 | 19.8 | 6.9 | – | 1.4 | 11.1 |
| 4 | 14.6 | 9.1 | – | 2.8 | 4.7 |
| 5 | 13.2 | 6.3 | – | 4.1 | 0.2 |
| 6 | 15.9 | 9.4 | – | 0.2 | 0.8 |
| 7 | 14.0 | 10.9 | – | 6.0 | 0.0 |
| 8 | 16.5 | 6.5 | – | 0.2 | 9.3 |
| 9 | 17.3 | 6.4 | – | Trace | 7.2 |
| 10 | 18.4 | 6.9 | – | 0.0 | 8.2 |
| 11 | 18.3 | 9.9 | – | 4.5 | 9.4 |
| 12 | 17.8 | 11.3 | – | 2.8 | 4.0 |
| 13 | 19.7 | 9.9 | – | 0.0 | 9.5 |
| 14 | 20.1 | 11.5 | – | 11.4 | 2.4 |
| 15 | 20.1 | 9.8 | – | 0.0 | 11.2 |
| 16 | 14.0 | 10.6 | – | 12.0 | 0.0 |
| 17 | 9.4 | 6.6 | – | 1.9 | 0.0 |
| 18 | 14.5 | 6.7 | – | 0.0 | 4.8 |
| 19 | 13.9 | 4.5 | – | 0.1 | 4.8 |
| 20 | 15.7 | 7.7 | – | 5.6 | 2.1 |
| 21 | 13.7 | 10.2 | – | 17.4 | 0.0 |
| 22 | 16.9 | 10.7 | – | 0.3 | 1.6 |
| 23 | 16.1 | 10.5 | – | 0.2 | 0.9 |
| 24 | 13.6 | 10.6 | – | 0.8 | 0.0 |
| 25 | 14.5 | 9.7 | – | 7.8 | 0.1 |
| 26 | 12.9 | 10.3 | – | 1.7 | 0.0 |
| 27 | 12.6 | 6.4 | – | 0.0 | 4.4 |
| 28 | 12.4 | 7.4 | – | Trace | 0.9 |
| 29 | 16.8 | 3.6 | – | 0.0 | 8.6 |
| 30 | 18.0 | 5.0 | – | 0.0 | 13.3 |
| 31 | 21.3 | 6.5 | – | 0.0 | 14.9 |
| Total | – | – | – | 80.9 | 158.3 |
| Mean | 16.1 | 8.3 | – | 2.7 | 5.2 |
| Temp. °F | 61.0 | 46.9 | – | – | – |
| Average | 17.0 | 8.0 | 8.1 | 51.0 | 193.7 |

## JUNE 1994*

| Day | Temperature Max. °C | Min. °C | Wind knots | Rain mm | Sun hrs |
|---|---|---|---|---|---|
| 1 | 25.3 | 7.6 | – | 0.0 | 12.4 |
| 2 | 19.1 | 11.7 | – | 0.2 | 4.0 |
| 3 | 17.8 | 11.5 | – | 1.6 | 6.6 |
| 4 | 12.8 | 8.8 | – | 6.7 | 0.0 |
| 5 | 17.1 | 5.5 | – | 0.1 | 11.1 |
| 6 | 21.5 | 11.1 | – | Trace | 7.0 |
| 7 | 21.3 | 12.6 | – | 1.3 | 4.1 |
| 8 | 17.0 | 12.1 | – | 0.2 | 6.3 |
| 9 | 15.8 | 5.7 | – | 0.2 | 0.1 |
| 10 | 17.0 | 10.5 | – | 0.0 | 6.1 |
| 11 | 19.4 | 7.3 | – | 0.0 | 10.2 |
| 12 | 20.4 | 7.8 | – | 0.0 | 9.4 |
| 13 | 23.3 | 10.6 | – | 0.0 | 13.9 |
| 14 | 24.5 | 12.3 | – | 0.0 | 14.7 |
| 15 | 23.6 | 8.2 | – | 0.0 | 15.3 |
| 16 | 23.6 | 12.0 | – | 0.0 | 14.8 |
| 17 | 25.7 | 11.2 | – | 0.0 | 9.7 |
| 18 | 23.0 | 12.1 | – | 0.0 | 9.1 |
| 19 | 21.4 | 12.5 | – | 0.0 | 5.5 |
| 20 | 18.9 | 13.2 | – | 0.9 | 0.0 |
| 21 | 18.2 | 13.4 | – | 0.1 | 0.0 |
| 22 | 22.0 | 15.2 | – | 0.0 | 14.1 |
| 23 | 24.1 | 9.8 | – | Trace | 15.1 |
| 24 | 29.3 | 14.5 | – | 5.7 | 11.4 |
| 25 | 22.1 | 15.5 | – | Trace | 3.5 |
| 26 | 21.2 | 12.0 | – | 0.0 | 6.2 |
| 27 | 25.7 | 13.1 | – | 0.0 | 10.0 |
| 28 | 28.2 | 13.2 | – | Trace | 15.5 |
| 29 | 21.9 | 15.4 | – | 0.0 | 14.8 |
| 30 | 24.2 | 10.2 | – | 0.0 | 12.1 |
| 31 | | | | | |
| Total | – | – | – | 17.0 | 265.0 |
| Mean | 21.6 | 11.3 | – | 0.6 | 8.9 |
| Temp. °F | 70.9 | 52.3 | – | – | – |
| Average | 20.4 | 11.0 | 7.6 | 50.0 | 198.5 |

*Wind values for May and June were not available at the time of going to press

# Sports Results

## ALPINE SKIING

### WORLD CUP 1993-4

MEN
*Downhill:* Marc Girardelli (Luxembourg), 556 pts
*Slalom:* Alberto Tomba (Italy), 540 pts
*Giant Slalom:* Christian Mayer (Austria), 496 pts
*Super Giant Slalom:* Jan Einer Thorsen (Norway), 280 pts
*Overall:* Kjetil-Andre Aamodt (Norway), 1,392 pts

WOMEN
*Downhill:* Katja Seizinger (Germany), 482 pts
*Slalom:* Vreni Schneider (Switzerland), 860 pts
*Giant Slalom:* Anita Wachter (Austria), 635 pts
*Super Giant Slalom:* Katja Seizinger (Germany), 416 pts
*Overall:* Vreni Schneider (Switzerland), 1,656 pts
*Nations Cup:* Austria, 8,792 pts

## AMERICAN FOOTBALL

*XXVIII American Superbowl 1994* (Atlanta, Georgia, 30 January): Dallas Cowboys beat Buffalo Bills 30–13

## ANGLING

NATIONAL COARSE CHAMPIONSHIPS 1993
*Division:* 1
*Venue:* Leeds and Liverpool Canal; *no. of teams:* 84
*Individual winner:* S. Canty (Goole AA), 5.020 kg
*Team winners:* Liverpool and District, 803 pts

*Division:* 2
*Venue:* River Nene; *no. of teams:* 85
*Individual winner:* M. Parsons (Pro-Rod Bedford MG), 16.350 kg
*Team winners:* Scunthorpe and District, 768 pts

*Division:* 3
*Venue:* 16 and 40 Foot Drains; *no. of teams:* 85
*Individual winner:* G. Whalley (Wigan and District), 26.670 kg
*Team winners:* Chelmsford AA, 832 pts

*Division:* 4
*Venue:* Tidal Trent; *no. of teams:* 79
*Individual winner:* P. Grainger (Bottesford DAA), 20.080 kg
*Team winners:* Langroyd AC, 767 pts

*Division:* 5
*Venue:* River Trent; *no. of teams:* 75
*Individual winner:* R. Bartram (Uppingham and District AS), 5.000 kg
*Team winners:* Team Imex, 700 pts

*Division:* 6
*Venue:* River Witham; *no. of teams:* 27

*Individual winner:* P. Revis (Allerton Bywater), 14.090 kg
*Team winners:* Trev's of Wilmslow, 181 pts

WORLD CHAMPIONSHIPS 1994
Holme Pierrepont, Nottingham, September
*Individual:* Robert Nudd (England), 1,440 kg, 2 pts
*Team:* England, 92 pts

## ASSOCIATION FOOTBALL

### LEAGUE COMPETITIONS 1993-4

ENGLAND AND WALES
*Premiership*
  1. Manchester United, 92 pts
  2. Blackburn Rovers, 84 pts
  *Relegated:* Sheffield United, 42 pts; Oldham Athletic, 40 pts; Swindon Town, 30 pts

*Division 1*
  1. Crystal Palace, 90 pts
  2. Nottingham Forest, 83 pts
  *Third promotion place:* Leicester City
  *Relegated:* Birmingham City, 51 pts; Oxford United, 49 pts; Peterborough United, 37 pts

*Division 2*
  1. Reading, 89 pts
  2. Port Vale, 88 pts
  *Third promotion place:* Burnley
  *Relegated:* Fulham, 52 pts; Exeter City, 45 pts; Hartlepool United, 36 pts; Barnet, 28 pts

*Division 3*
  1. Shrewsbury Town, 79 pts
  2. Chester City, 74 pts
  3. Crewe Alexandra, 73 pts
  *Fourth promotion place:* Wycombe Wanderers
  *No Relegation*

*GM Vauxhall Conference*
  *Champions:* Kidderminster Harriers, 75 pts (not promoted because the necessary improvements to their ground to comply with the Taylor Report had not been made by 31 December 1993)
  *Relegated:* Merthyr Tydfil, 49 pts; Slough Town, 47 pts; Witton Albion, 4 pts

*League of Wales:* Bangor City, 83 pts
*Women's National Premier League:* Doncaster Belles

\*SCOTLAND
*Premier Division*
  1. Rangers, 58 pts
  2. Aberdeen, 55 pts
  *Relegated:* St Johnstone, 40 pts; Raith Rovers, 31 pts; Dundee, 29 pts

*Division 1*
  1. Falkirk, 66 pts
  *Relegated:* Dumbarton, 36 pts; Stirling Albion, 35 pts; Clydebank, 32 pts; Morton, 29 pts, Brechin City, 19 pts

*Division 2*
1. Stranraer, 56 pts
*Relegated:* Alloa, 41 pts; Forfar Athletic, 39 pts; East
Stirling, 37 pts; Montrose, 36 pts; Queens Park,
34 pts; Arbroath, 33 pts; Albion Rovers, 24 pts;
Cowdenbeath, 20 pts

*An extra division is being created in the Scottish league
from the 1994–5 season

NORTHERN IRELAND
*Irish League Championship:* Linfield, 70 pts

## CUP COMPETITIONS

ENGLAND
*FA Cup final 1994* (Wembley, 14 May): Manchester United
beat Chelsea 4–0
*Coca Cola (League) Cup final 1994:* Aston Villa beat
Manchester United 3–1
*Autoglass Trophy final 1994:* Huddersfield Town 1, Swansea
City 1 a.e.t. Swansea City won 3–1 on penalties
*Anglo-Italian Cup final 1994:* Brescia beat Notts County 1–0
*FA Vase final 1994:* Diss Town beat Taunton Town 2–1
a.e.t.
*FA Trophy final 1994:* Woking beat Runcorn 2–1
*Arthur Dunn Cup final 1994:* Old Chigwellians 2, Old
Salopians 2 a.e.t. Replay: Old Chigwellians beat Old
Salopians 5–1
*Women's FA Cup final 1994:* Doncaster Belles beat
Knowsley United 1–0
*Charity Shield 1994:* Manchester United beat Blackburn
Rovers 2–0

WALES
*Welsh FA Cup final 1994:* Barry Town beat Cardiff City 2–1
*Welsh League Cup final 1994:* Afan Lido beat Bangor 1–0

SCOTLAND
*Scottish FA Cup final 1994* (Hampden Park, 21 May):
Dundee United beat Rangers 1–0
*Skol (League) Cup final 1993:* Rangers beat Hibernian 2–1
*B & Q Cup final 1993:* Falkirk beat St Mirren 3–0

NORTHERN IRELAND
*Irish Cup final 1994:* Linfield beat Bangor 2–0

EUROPE
*European Cup final 1994* (Athens): AC Milan beat
Barcelona 4–0
*European Cup-Winners' Cup final 1994* (Copenhagen):
Arsenal beat Parma 1–0
*UEFA Cup final 1994:* Inter Milan beat Salzburg 2–0 on
agg.

## INTERNATIONALS

WORLD CUP QUALIFYING MATCHES 1993

| 13 Oct | Rotterdam | Holland 2, England 0 |
| | Rome | Italy 3, Scotland 1 |
| | Cardiff | Wales 2, Cyprus 0 |
| | Copenhagen | Denmark 1, N. Ireland 0 |
| 17 Nov | Bologna | San Marino 1, England 7 |
| | Valletta | Malta 1, Scotland 0 |
| | Cardiff | Wales 1, Romania 2 |
| | Belfast | N. Ireland 1, Rep. of Ireland 1 |

EUROPEAN CHAMPIONSHIPS QUALIFYING MATCHES
1994

| 20 April | Belfast | N. Ireland 4, Liechtenstein 1 |
| 7 Sept | Helsinki | Finland 0, Scotland 2 |
| | Cardiff | Wales 2, Albania 0 |
| | Belfast | N. Ireland 1, Portugal 2 |

FRIENDLIES 1994

| 9 March | Wembley | England 1, Denmark 0 |
| | Cardiff | Wales 1, Norway 3 |
| 23 March | Glasgow | Scotland 0, Holland 1 |
| | Belfast | N. Ireland 2, Romania 0 |
| 20 April | Vienna | Austria 1, Scotland 2 |
| | Wrexham | Wales 0, Sweden 2 |
| 17 May | Wembley | England 5, Greece 0 |
| 22 May | Wembley | England 0, Norway 0 |
| 23 May | Tallinn | Estonia 1, Wales 2 |
| 27 May | Utrecht | Holland 3, Scotland 1 |
| 4 June | Boston | Colombia 2, N. Ireland 0 |
| 11 June | Miami | Mexico 3, N. Ireland 0 |
| 7 Sept | Wembley | England 2, USA 0 |

WORLD CUP FINALS 1994
USA, 17 June–17 July

FIRST ROUND
*Group A:* Romania, 6 pts; Switzerland, 4 pts; USA, 4 pts;
Colombia, 3 pts
*Group B:* Brazil, 7 pts; Sweden, 5 pts; Russia, 3 pts;
Cameroon, 1 pt
*Group C:* Germany, 7 pts; Spain, 5 pts; S. Korea, 2 pts;
Bolivia, 1 pt
*Group D:* Argentina, 6 pts; Nigeria, 3 pts; Bulgaria, 3 pts;
Greece, 0 pts
*Group E:* Mexico, 4 pts; Rep. of Ireland, 4 pts; Italy, 4 pts;
Norway, 4 pts
*Group F:* Holland, 6 pts; Saudi Arabia, 6 pts; Belgium,
6 pts; Morocco, 0 pts

SECOND ROUND
Germany beat Belgium 3–2; Spain beat Switzerland 3–0;
Romania beat Argentina 3–2; Sweden beat Saudi Arabia
3–1; Brazil beat USA 1–0; Holland beat Rep. of Ireland
2–0; Italy beat Nigeria 2–1 a.e.t.; Mexico 1, Bulgaria 1
(Bulgaria won 3–1 on penalties)

QUARTER-FINALS
Brazil beat Holland 3–2; Italy beat Spain 2–1; Bulgaria beat
Germany 2–1; Romania 2, Sweden 2 (Sweden won 5–4 on
penalties)

SEMI-FINALS
Italy beat Bulgaria 2–1; Brazil beat Sweden 1–0

THIRD PLACE PLAY-OFF
Sweden beat Bulgaria 4–0

FINAL
Pasadena, California, 17 July
Brazil 0, Italy 0 (Brazil won 3–2 on penalties)

## ATHLETICS

WORLD MARATHON CUP
San Sebastian, Spain, 31 October 1993

MEN
*Individual:* Richard Nerurkar (GB), 2 hr. 10 min. 03 sec.
*Team:* Ethiopia, 6 hr. 31 min. 17 sec.

WOMEN
Individual: Wang Junxia (China), 2 hr. 28 min. 16 sec.
Team: China, 7 hr. 27 min. 43 sec.

## AAA INDOOR CHAMPIONSHIPS
Birmingham, 18–19 February 1994

MEN

| | min. | sec. |
|---|---|---|
| 60 metres: Michael Rosswess (Birchfield) | | 6.56 |
| 200 metres: Philip Goedluck (Belgrave) | | 21.16 |
| 400 metres: Du'aine Ladejo (Belgrave) | | 46.54 |
| 800 metres: Tom McKean (Motherwell) | 1 | 48.46 |
| 1,500 metres: Atoi Boru (Kenya) | 3 | 42.25 |
| 3,000 metres: Matthew Barnes (Enfield) | 7 | 56.08 |
| 60 metres hurdles: Hughie Teape (Enfield) | | 7.73 |

| | metres |
|---|---|
| High jump: Brendan Reilly (Corby) | 2.28 |
| Pole vault: Peter Widen (Sweden) | 5.45 |
| Long jump: Mattias Sunneborn (Sweden) | 7.50 |
| Triple jump: Francis Agyepong (Shaftesbury-Barnet) | 16.55 |
| Shot: Paul Edwards (Belgrave) | 18.95 |

WOMEN

| | min. | sec. |
|---|---|---|
| 60 metres: Beverley Kinch (Hounslow) | | 7.35 |
| 200 metres: Maria Staafgard (Sweden) | | 23.78 |
| 400 metres: Tracy Goddard (Basingstoke) | | 54.05 |
| 800 metres: Kirsty Wade (Blaydon) | 2 | 05.60 |
| 1,500 metres: Lynn Gibson (Oxford City) | 4 | 17.01 |
| 3,000 metres: Erika Konig (Austria) | 9 | 25.58 |
| 60 metres hurdles: Samantha Farquharson (Cardiff) | | 8.19 |

| | metres |
|---|---|
| High jump: Hanne Havgland (Norway) | 1.94 |
| Pole vault: Kate Staples (Essex Ladies) | 3.46 |
| Long jump: Denise Lewis (Birchfield) | 6.07 |
| Triple jump: Rachel Kirby (Hounslow) | 13.21 |
| Shot: Maggie Lynes (Croydon) | 15.82 |

## EUROPEAN INDOOR CHAMPIONSHIPS
Paris, 11–13 March 1994

MEN

| | min. | sec. |
|---|---|---|
| 60 metres: Colin Jackson (GB) | | 6.49 |
| 200 metres: Daniel Sangouma (France) | | 20.68 |
| 400 metres: Du'aine Ladejo (GB) | | 46.53 |
| 800 metres: Andrei Loginov (Russia) | 1 | 46.38 |
| 1,500 metres: David Strang (GB) | 3 | 44.57 |
| 3,000 metres: Kim Bauermeister (Germany) | 7 | 52.34 |
| 60 metres hurdles: Colin Jackson (GB) | | 7.41 |
| 5,000 metres walk: Mikhail Shchennikov (Russia) | 18 | 34.32 |

| | metres |
|---|---|
| High jump: Dalton Grant (GB) | 2.37 |
| Pole vault: Pyotr Bochkaryov (Russia) | 5.90 |
| Long jump: Dietmar Haaf (Germany) | 8.15 |
| Triple jump: Leonid Voloshin (Russia) | 17.44 |
| Shot: Aleksandr Bagach (Ukraine) | 20.66 |
| Heptathlon: Christian Plaziat (France) | 6,268 pts |

WOMEN

| | min. | sec. |
|---|---|---|
| 60 metres: Nelli Cooman (Holland) | | 7.17 |
| 200 metres: Galina Malchugina (Russia) | | 22.41 |
| 400 metres: Svetlana Goncharenko (Russia) | | 51.62 |
| 800 metres: Natalya Dukhnova (Belarus) | 2 | 00.42 |
| 1,500 metres: Yekaterina Podkopayeva (Russia) | 4 | 06.46 |

| | | |
|---|---|---|
| 3,000 metres: Fernanda Ribeiro (Portugal) | 8 | 50.47 |
| 60 metres hurdles: Yordanka Donkova (Bulgaria) | | 7.85 |
| 3,000 metres walk: Annarita Sidoti (Italy) | 11 | 54.32 |

| | metres |
|---|---|
| High jump: Stefka Kostadinova (Bulgaria) | 1.98 |
| Long jump: Heike Drechsler (Germany) | 7.06 |
| Triple jump: Inna Lasovskaya (Russia) | 14.88 |
| Shot: Astrid Kumbernuss (Germany) | 19.44 |
| Pentathlon: Larisa Turchinskaya (Russia) | 4,801 pts |

## MEN'S NATIONAL CROSS-COUNTRY CHAMPIONSHIPS
South Shields, 12 March 1994

Individual: David Lewis (Rossendale), 42 min. 35 sec.
Team: Blackheath, 171 pts

## WOMEN'S NATIONAL CROSS-COUNTRY CHAMPIONSHIPS
Blackburn, 13 March 1994

Individual: Paula Radcliffe (Bedford & County), 20 min. 51 sec.
Team: Parkside, 34 pts

## IAAF WORLD CROSS-COUNTRY CHAMPIONSHIPS
Budapest, 26 March 1994

MEN (12,060 metres)
Individual: William Sigei (Kenya), 34 min. 29 sec.
Team: Kenya, 34 pts

WOMEN (6,220 metres)
Individual: Helen Chepngeno (Kenya), 20 min. 45 sec.
Team: Portugal, 55 pts

## LONDON MARATHON
17 April 1994

Men: Dionicio Ceron (Mexico), 2 hr. 08 min. 53 sec.
Women: Katrin Dörre (Germany), 2 hr. 32 min. 34 sec.

## AAA CHAMPIONSHIPS
Sheffield, 11–12 June 1994

MEN

| | min. | sec. |
|---|---|---|
| 100 metres: Linford Christie (TVH) | | 9.91 |
| 200 metres: Solomon Wariso (Haringey) | | 20.67 |
| 400 metres: Roger Black (Team Solent) | | 44.94 |
| 800 metres: Craig Winrow (Wigan) | 1 | 48.45 |
| 1,500 metres: Kevin McKay (Sale) | 3 | 40.59 |
| 5,000 metres: Dermot Donnelly (Annadale) | 13 | 52.63 |
| 10,000 metres: Rob Denmark (Basildon) | 28 | 03.34 |
| 3,000 metres steeplechase: Justin Chaston (Belgrave) | 8 | 28.28 |
| 110 metres hurdles: Andrew Tulloch (Wolverhampton) | | 13.70 |
| 400 metres hurdles: Peter Crampton (Spenborough) | | 49.82 |

| | metres |
|---|---|
| High jump: Brendan Reilly (Loughborough) | 2.24 |
| Pole vault: Andrew Ashurst (Sale) | 5.30 |
| Long jump: Barrington Williams (Cannock) | 7.77 |
| Triple jump: Jon Edwards (Gateshead) | 17.39 |
| Shot: Paul Edwards (Belgrave) | 18.32 |
| Discus: Kevin Brown (Birchfield) | 58.60 |
| Hammer: Peter Vivian (TVH) | 70.80 |
| Javelin: Mick Hill (Leeds) | 84.60 |

WOMEN

| | min. | sec. |
|---|---|---|
| 100 *metres:* Katharine Merry (Birchfield) | | 11.27 |
| 200 *metres:* Katharine Merry (Birchfield) | | 22.85 |
| 400 *metres:* Melanie Neef (City of Glasgow) | | 52.56 |
| 800 *metres:* Diane Modahl (Sale) | 2 | 01.35 |
| 1,500 *metres:* Kelly Holmes (Middlesex Ladies) | 4 | 01.41 |
| 3,000 *metres:* Sonia McGeorge (Brighton) | 9 | 03.80 |
| 10,000 *metres:* Zahara Hyde (Woking) | 33 | 23.25 |
| 100 *metres hurdles:* Clova Court (Birchfield) | | 13.06 |
| 400 *metres hurdles:* Gowry Retchakan (Thurrock) | | 57.08 |

| | metres |
|---|---|
| *High jump:* Julia Bennett (Epsom) | 1.86 |
| *Pole vault:* Katy Staples (Essex Ladies) | 3.65 |
| *Long jump:* Yinka Idowu (Essex Ladies) | 6.58 |
| *Triple jump:* Michelle Griffith (Windsor) | 14.08 |
| *Shot:* Judy Oakes (Croydon) | 18.38 |
| *Discus:* Jackie McKernan (Lisburn) | 56.94 |
| *Hammer:* Lorraine Shaw (Gloucester) | 59.58 |
| *Javelin:* Shelley Holroyd (Sale) | 57.08 |

Horsham, 18–19 June 1994

*Decathlon:* Barry Thomas (Sheffield) 7,458 pts
*Heptathlon:* Vikki Schofield (Rotherham) 5,587 pts
*10,000 metres track walk:* Darrell Stone (Steyning) 43 min. 09.28 sec.
*5,000 metres track walk:* Verity Larby (Aldershot) 23 min. 22.52 sec.

EUROPEAN CUP (BRUNO ZAULI TROPHY)
Birmingham, 25–26 June 1994

MEN

| | min. | sec. |
|---|---|---|
| 100 *metres:* Linford Christie (GB) | | 10.21 |
| 200 *metres:* Linford Christie (GB) | | 20.67 |
| 400 *metres:* Roger Black (GB) | | 45.08 |
| 800 *metres:* Nico Motchebon (Germany) | 1 | 48.10 |
| 1,500 *metres:* Andrei Bulkovsky (Ukraine) | 3 | 49.33 |
| 5,000 *metres:* Dieter Baumann (Germany) | 13 | 48.95 |
| 10,000 *metres:* Francesco Panetta (Italy) | 28 | 38.45 |
| 3,000 *metres steeplechase:* Alessandro Lambruschini (Italy) | 8 | 24.98 |
| 110 *metres hurdles:* Florian Schwarthoff (Germany) | | 13.35 |
| 400 *metres hurdles:* Sven Nylander (Sweden) | | 49.36 |
| 4 × 100 *metres relay:* Great Britain | | 38.72 |
| 4 × 400 *metres relay:* Great Britain | 3 | 02.50 |

| | metres |
|---|---|
| *High jump:* Hendryk Beyer (Germany) | 2.25 |
| *Pole vault:* Jean Galfione (France) | 5.70 |
| *Long jump:* Stanislav Tarasenko (Russia) | 8.02 |
| *Triple jump:* Denis Kapustin (Russia) | 17.30 |
| *Shot:* Paolo dal Soglio (Italy) | 19.69 |
| *Discus:* Dimitri Shevchenko (Russia) | 64.74 |
| *Hammer:* Vasili Sidorenko (Russia) | 78.76 |
| *Javelin:* Andrei Moruyev (Russia) | 87.34 |

*Team points:* Germany 121, GB 106½, Russia 101, Ukraine 87, Italy 84, Sweden 81½, France 80, Romania 56

WOMEN

| | min. | sec. |
|---|---|---|
| 100 *metres:* Zhanna Tarnapolskaya (Ukraine) | | 11.26 |
| 200 *metres:* Silke Knoll (Germany) | | 23.04 |
| 400 *metres:* Svetlana Goncharenko (Russia) | | 52.08 |
| 800 *metres:* Diane Modahl (GB) | 2 | 02.81 |
| 1,500 *metres:* Lyubov Kremlyova (Russia) | 4 | 05.97 |
| 3,000 *metres:* Ludmila Borisova (Russia) | 8 | 52.21 |

| | | |
|---|---|---|
| 10,000 *metres:* Kathrin Wessel (Germany) | 32 | 26.85 |
| 100 *metres hurdles:* Jacqui Agyepong (GB) | | 13.00 |
| 400 *metres hurdles:* Sally Gunnell (GB) | | 54.62 |
| 4 × 100 *metres relay:* Ukraine | | 43.38 |
| 4 × 400 *metres relay:* Great Britain | 3 | 27.33 |

| | metres |
|---|---|
| *High jump:* Tatyana Shevchik (Belarus) | 1.94 |
| *Long jump:* Heike Drechsler (Germany) | 6.99 |
| *Triple jump:* Helga Radtke (Germany) | 13.90 |
| *Shot:* Astrid Kumbernuss (Germany) | 19.63 |
| *Discus:* Ilke Wyludda (Germany) | 68.36 |
| *Javelin:* Natalya Shikolenko (Belarus) | 69.00 |

*Team points:* Germany 98, GB 97, Russia 95, Ukraine 86, Belarus 64, France 60, Romania 60, Spain 50

GREAT BRITAIN v. USA
Gateshead, 20 July 1994

MEN

| | min. | sec. |
|---|---|---|
| 100 *metres:* Kevin Braunskill (USA) | | 10.43 |
| 200 *metres:* John Regis (GB) | | 20.44 |
| 400 *metres:* Calvin Davis (USA) | | 45.34 |
| 800 *metres:* Craig Winrow (GB) | 1 | 47.17 |
| 1,500 *metres:* Kevin McKay (GB) | 3 | 45.70 |
| 5,000 *metres:* Ronnie Harris (USA) | 14 | 02.18 |
| 3,000 *metres steeplechase:* Mark Rowland (GB) | 8 | 41.45 |
| 110 *metres hurdles:* Robert Reading (USA) | | 13.36 |
| 400 *metres hurdles:* Octavius Terry (USA) | | 49.73 |
| 4 × 100 *metres relay:* Great Britain | | 38.91 |
| 4 × 400 *metres relay:* USA | 3 | 01.38 |

| | metres |
|---|---|
| *High jump:* Tony Barton (USA) | 2.28 |
| *Pole vault:* Rory Tarpenning (USA) | 5.80 |
| *Long jump:* Reggie Jones (USA) | 8.15 |
| *Triple jump:* Jonathan Edwards (GB) | 16.80 |
| *Shot:* Gregg Tafralis (USA) | 20.89 |
| *Discus:* Mike Gravelle (USA) | 63.68 |
| *Hammer:* Lance Deal (USA) | 78.28 |
| *Javelin:* Steve Backley (GB) | 84.68 |

*Team points:* USA 206, Great Britain 180

WOMEN

| | min. | sec. |
|---|---|---|
| 100 *metres:* Cheryl Taplin (USA) | | 11.66 |
| 200 *metres:* Flirtisha Harris (USA) | | 23.44 |
| 400 *metres:* Sally Gunnell (GB) | | 51.04 |
| 800 *metres:* Nekita Beasley (USA) | 2 | 02.80 |
| 1,500 *metres:* Yvonne Murray (GB) | 4 | 04.19 |
| 3,000 *metres:* Sonia McGeorge (GB) | 9 | 02.97 |
| 100 *metres hurdles:* Jacqui Agyepong (GB) | | 13.34 |
| 400 *metres hurdles:* Tonja Buford (USA) | | 56.01 |
| 4 × 100 *metres relay:* USA | | 43.35 |
| 4 × 400 *metres relay:* USA | 3 | 26.99 |

| | metres |
|---|---|
| *High jump:* Debbie Marti (GB) | 1.88 |
| *Long jump:* Cynthea Rhodes (USA) | 6.68 |
| *Triple jump:* Ashia Hansen (GB) | 14.00 |
| *Shot:* Judy Oakes (GB) | 18.63 |
| *Discus:* Lacy Barnes (USA) | 56.94 |
| *Javelin:* Donna Mayhew (USA) | 61.50 |

*Team points:* USA 168, Great Britain 152

EUROPEAN CHAMPIONSHIPS
Helsinki, 7–14 August 1994

MEN

| | hr. | min. | sec. |
|---|---|---|---|
| 100 *metres:* Linford Christie (GB) | | | 10.14 |

*200 metres:* Geir Moen (Norway) 20.30
*400 metres:* Du'aine Ladejo (GB) 45.09
*800 metres:* Andrea Benvenuti (Italy) 1 46.12
*1,500 metres:* Fermin Cacho (Spain) 3 35.27
*5,000 metres:* Dieter Baumann (Germany) 13 36.93
*10,000 metres:* Adel Anton (Spain) 28 06.03
*Marathon:* Martin Fiz (Spain) 2 10 31
*3,000 metres steeplechase:* Alessandro 8 22.40
Lambruschini (Italy)
*20 kilometres walk:* Mikhail Shchennikov 1 18 45
(Russia)
*50 kilometres walk:* Valeri Spitsyn (Russia) 3 41 07
*110 metres hurdles:* Colin Jackson (GB) 13.08
*400 metres hurdles:* Oleg Tverdoklev 48.06
(Ukraine)
*4 × 100 metres relay:* France 38.57
*4 × 400 metres relay:* Great Britain 2 59.13
metres
*High jump:* Steinar Hoen (Norway) 2.35
*Pole vault:* Radion Gataullin (Russia) 6.00
*Long jump:* Ivailo Mladenov (Bulgaria) 8.09
*Triple jump:* Denis Kapustin (Russia) 17.62
*Shot:* Aleksandr Klimenko (Ukraine) 20.78
*Discus:* Vladimir Dubrovchik (Belarus) 64.78
*Hammer:* Vasili Sidorenko (Russia) 81.10
*Javelin:* Steve Backley (GB) 85.20
*Decathlon:* Alain Blondel (France) 8,453 pts

WOMEN

| | hr. | min. | sec. |
|---|---|---|---|
| *100 metres:* Irina Privalova (Russia) | | | 11.02 |
| *200 metres:* Irina Privalova (Russia) | | | 22.32 |
| *400 metres:* Maria-José Pérec (France) | | | 50.33 |
| *800 metres:* Lyubov Gurina (Russia) | | 1 | 58.55 |
| *1,500 metres:* Ludmila Rogachova (Russia) | | 4 | 18.93 |
| *3,000 metres:* Sonia O'Sullivan (Rep. of Ireland) | | 8 | 31.84 |
| *10,000 metres:* Fernanda Ribeiro (Portugal) | | 31 | 08.75 |
| *Marathon:* Manuela Machado (Portugal) | 2 | 29 | 54 |
| *10 kilometres walk:* Sari Essayeh (Finland) | | 42 | 37 |
| *100 metres hurdles:* Svetla Dimitrova (Bulgaria) | | | 12.72 |
| *400 metres hurdles:* Sally Gunnell (GB) | | | 53.33 |
| *4 × 100 metres relay:* Germany | | | 42.90 |
| *4 × 400 metres relay:* France | | 3 | 22.34 |

metres
*High jump:* Britta Bilac (Slovenia) 2.00
*Long jump:* Heike Drechsler (Germany) 7.14
*Triple jump:* Anna Biryukova (Russia) 14.89
*Shot:* Viktoria Pavlysh (Ukraine) 19.61
*Discus:* Ilke Wyludda (Germany) 68.72
*Javelin:* Trina Hattestad (Norway) 68.00
*Heptathlon:* Sabine Braun (Germany) 6,419 pts

## GRAND PRIX 1994 FINAL RESULTS

MEN

*100 metres:* Dennis Mitchell (USA)
*400 metres:* Derek Mills (USA)
*1,500 metres:* Noureddine Morceli (Algeria)
*5,000 metres:* Khalid Skah (Morocco)
*400 metres hurdles:* Samuel Matete (Zambia)
*High jump:* Javier Sotomayor (Cuba)
*Triple jump:* Mike Conley (USA)
*Shot:* Randy Barnes (USA)
*Hammer:* Andrei Abduvalyev (Tajikistan)
*Overall winner:* Noureddine Morceli (Algeria)

WOMEN

*100 metres:* Merlene Ottey (Jamaica)
*400 metres:* Marie-José Pérec (France)
*1,500 metres:* Angela Chalmers (Canada)
*5,000 metres:* Sonia O'Sullivan (Rep. of Ireland)
*100 metres hurdles:* Svetla Dimitrova (Bulgaria)
*Long jump:* Jackie Joyner-Kersee (USA)
*Discus:* Ilke Wyludda (Germany)
*Javelin:* Natalya Shikolenko (Belarus)
*Overall winner:* Jackie Joyner-Kersee (USA)

## WORLD CUP
Crystal Palace, 9–11 September 1994

MEN

| | | min. | sec. |
|---|---|---|---|
| *100 metres:* Linford Christie (GB) | | | 10.21 |
| *200 metres:* John Regis (GB) | | | 20.45 |
| *400 metres:* Antonio Pettigrew (USA) | | | 45.26 |
| *800 metres:* Mark Everett (USA) | | 1 | 46.02 |
| *1,500 metres:* Noureddine Morceli (Africa) | | 3 | 34.70 |
| *5,000 metres:* Brahim Lahlafi (Africa) | | 13 | 27.96 |
| *10,000 metres:* Khalid Skah (Africa) | | 27 | 38.74 |
| *3,000 metres steeplechase:* Moses Kiptanui (Africa) | | 8 | 28.28 |
| *110 metres hurdles:* Tony Jarrett (GB) | | | 13.23 |
| *400 metres hurdles:* Samuel Matete (Africa) | | | 48.77 |
| *4 × 100 metres relay:* Great Britain | | | 38.46 |
| *4 × 400 metres relay:* Great Britain | | 3 | 01.34 |

metres
*High jump:* Javier Sotomayor (Americas) 2.40
*Pole vault:* Okkert Brits (Africa) 5.90
*Long jump:* Fred Salle (GB) 8.10
*Triple jump:* Yoelvis Quesada (Americas) 17.61
*Shot:* C. J. Hunter (USA) 19.92
*Discus:* Vladimir Dubrovchik (Europe) 64.54
*Hammer:* Andrei Abduvalyev (Asia) 81.72
*Javelin:* Steve Backley (GB) 85.02
*Team points:* Africa 116, Great Britain 111, Americas 95, Europe 91, Germany 85½, USA 78, Asia 75, Oceania 62½

WOMEN

| | | min. | sec. |
|---|---|---|---|
| *100 metres:* Irina Privalova (Europe) | | | 11.32 |
| *200 metres:* Merlene Ottey (Americas) | | | 22.23 |
| *400 metres:* Irina Privalova (Europe) | | | 50.62 |
| *800 metres:* Maria Mutola (Africa) | | 1 | 58.27 |
| *1,500 metres:* Hassiba Boulmerka (Africa) | | 4 | 01.05 |
| *3,000 metres:* Yvonne Murray (GB) | | 8 | 56.81 |
| *10,000 metres:* Elana Meyer (Africa) | | 30 | 52.51 |
| *100 metres hurdles:* Aliuska Lopez (Americas) | | | 12.91 |
| *400 metres hurdles:* Sally Gunnell (GB) | | | 54.80 |
| *4 × 100 metres relay:* Africa | | | 42.92 |
| *4 × 400 metres relay:* Great Britain | | 3 | 27.36 |

metres
*High jump:* Britta Bilac (Europe) 1.91
*Long jump:* Inessa Kravets (Europe) 7.00
*Triple jump:* Ana Biryuhova (Europe) 14.46
*Shot:* Zhihong Huang (Asia) 19.45
*Discus:* Ilke Wyludda (Germany) 65.30
*Javelin:* Trine Hattestad (Europe) 66.48
*Team points:* Europe 111, Americas 98, Germany 79, Africa 78, Great Britain 73, Asia 67, Oceania 57, USA 48

## BADMINTON

*Thomas Cup final 1994* (Men's World Team Championship): Indonesia beat Malaysia 3–0

*Uber Cup final 1994* (Women's World Team Championship): Indonesia beat China 3–2

ENGLISH NATIONAL CHAMPIONSHIPS 1994

*Men's Singles:* Darren Hall beat Peter Knowles 15–3, 15–13

*Women's Singles:* Suzanne Louis-Lane beat Fiona Smith 11–4, 11–1

*Men's Doubles:* Simon Archer and Chris Hunt beat Nick Ponting and Julian Robertson 15–8, 18–17

*Women's Doubles:* Gillian Gowers and Joanne Wright beat Julie Bradbury and Gillian Clark 15–7, ret.

*Mixed Doubles:* Joanne Wright and Nick Ponting beat Gillian Clark and Chris Hunt 15–9, 15–5

SCOTTISH NATIONAL CHAMPIONSHIPS 1994

*Men's Singles:* Bruce Flockhart beat Jim Mailer 15–6, 15–3

*Women's Singles:* Elinor Allen beat Anne Gibson 12–10, 11–8

*Men's Doubles:* Russell Hogg and Kenneth Middlemiss beat Alastair Gatt and Gordon Haldane 15–9, 11–15, 15–12

*Women's Doubles:* Elinor Allen and Jennifer Allen beat Jillian Haldane and Aileen Travers 15–4, 15–4

*Mixed Doubles:* Elinor Allen and Kenneth Middlemiss beat Jillian Haldane and Gordon Haldane 15–8, 15–5

WELSH NATIONAL CHAMPIONSHIPS 1994

*Men's Singles:* John Leung beat Geraint Lewis 15–5, 15–12

*Women's Singles:* Kelly Morgan beat Rachel Phipps 11–5, 11–7

*Men's Doubles:* David Tonks and Andrew Spencer beat Lyndon Williams and Andrew Carlotti 11–15, 15–6, 15–6

*Women's Doubles:* Kelly Morgan and Rachel Phipps beat Sarah Williams and Rachele Edwards 15–5, 15–9

*Mixed Doubles:* Sarah Williams and Andrew Burke beat Rachel Phipps and David Tonks 15–11, 10–15, 15–8

ALL-ENGLAND CHAMPIONSHIPS 1994

*Men's Singles:* Heryanto Arbi (Indonesia) beat Ardy Wiranata (Indonesia) 15–12, 17–14

*Women's Singles:* Susi Susanti (Indonesia) beat Ye Zhaoying (China) 11–5, 11–9

*Men's Doubles:* Rudy Gunawan and Bambang Suprianto (Indonesia) beat Rexy Mainaky and Ricky Subagya (Indonesia) 15–12, 15–12

*Women's Doubles:* Chung So-Young and Gil Young-Ah (S. Korea) beat Jang Hye-Ock and Shim Eun-Jung (S. Korea) 7–15, 15–8, 15–4

*Mixed Doubles:* Joanne Wright and Nick Ponting (England) beat Gillian Clark and Nick Hunt (England) 15–10, 15–11

## BASKETBALL

MEN

*World Championship final 1994:* USA beat Russia 137–91

*Championship play-off final 1994:* Worthing Bears beat Guildford Kings 71–65

*League Trophy final 1994:* Thames Valley Tigers beat Manchester Giants 79–73

*National Cup final 1994:* Worthing Bears beat Thames Valley Tigers 92–83

*National League Championship 1994:* Thames Valley Tigers

WOMEN

*World Championship final 1994:* Brazil beat China 96–87

*Championship play-off final 1994:* Thames Valley Ladies beat Sheffield Hatters 60–56

*National Cup final 1994:* Sheffield Hatters beat Northampton 76'ers 81–70

*National League Championship 1994:* Sheffield Hatters

## BILLIARDS

*World Professional Championship 1993:* Geet Sethi (India) beat Mike Russell (England) 2,139–1,140

*World Amateur Champion:* Manoj Kothari (India)

*UK Professional Championship 1994:* Mike Russell (England) beat Peter Gilchrist (England) 1,072–330

## BOWLS (MEN)

WORLD INDOOR CHAMPIONSHIPS 1994
Preston, March

*Singles:* Andy Thomson (England) beat Richard Corsie (Scotland) 7–2, 7–0, 6–7, 7–6

*Pairs:* Cameron Curtis and Ian Schuback (Australia) beat Gary Smith and Andy Thomson (England) 7–1, 7–6, 5–7, 7–0

NATIONAL CHAMPIONSHIPS 1994
Worthing, August–September

*Singles:* Brett Morley (GPT, Nottingham) beat Paul Wilkinson (Long Eaton Town) 21–14

*Pairs:* Keith Wood and Mike Bennett (Ponteland) beat Alan Theobald and Davie Webb (Gateshead) 26–6

*Triples:* Torquay beat Reading 15–12

*Fours:* Cheltenham beat Atherley 21–13

NATIONAL INDOOR CHAMPIONSHIPS 1994
Melton Mowbray, April

*Singles:* Mervyn King (Pinewood Park) beat Paul Bennett (Bodmin) 21–12

*Pairs:* Gary Smith and Brian Vickers (Cyphers) beat Mike Newman and Robert Newman (Whiteknights, Reading) 23–22

*Triples:* Blackpool Borough beat Cyphers 27–4

*Fours:* Cyphers beat Paddington 19–16

BRITISH ISLES CHAMPIONSHIPS 1994
Ayr, July

*Singles:* Colin Best (Ireland) beat George Whitelaw (Scotland) 21–20

*Pairs:* Peter Howells and Gareth Jones (Wales) beat Robert Grant and Andrew Grant (Scotland) 25–9

*Triples:* Ireland beat Wales 16–15

*Fours:* Scotland beat England 23–21

BRITISH ISLES INDOOR CHAMPIONSHIPS 1994
Rushcliffe, March

*Singles:* Jeremy Henry (Ireland) beat Russell Morgan (England) 21–18

*Pairs:* Steven Rees and John Price (Wales) beat Ian Bell and Graham Robertson (Scotland) 21–12

*Triples:* Scotland beat England 17–13

*Fours:* England beat Ireland 20–15

*Home International Championships 1994* (Ayr): England
*Home International Indoor Championship 1994* (Nottingham): Scotland

*Middleton Cup final 1994* (Inter-County Outdoor Championship): Cumbria beat Middlesex 102–98
*Liberty Trophy final 1994* (Inter-County Indoor Championship): Somerset beat Kent 125–99

---

## BOWLS (WOMEN)

---

WORLD INDOOR CHAMPIONSHIPS 1994
Cumbernauld, April

*Singles:* Jan Woodley (Scotland) beat Mary Price (England) 5–7, 7–1, 7–5, 5–7, 7–5

NATIONAL CHAMPIONSHIPS 1994
Royal Leamington Spa, July–August

*Singles (four woods):* Ingrid Betke (Thaxted, Essex) beat Pat Kirk (Wealdstone) 21–12
*Singles (two woods):* Brenda Whitehead (Norfolk) beat Gill Fitzgerald (Kettering Lodge) 16–9
*Pairs:* Joan Carpenter and Rhona Darling (Milton Park, Portsmouth) beat Mabel Hodge and Jan Stern (Northolt) 18–15
*Triples:* Egham beat Penryn 17–8
*Fours:* Peterborough and District beat Carlton Conway, Nottinghamshire 25–8

NATIONAL INDOOR CHAMPIONSHIPS 1994
Darlington, March

*Singles:* Mary Price (Desborough) beat Diana Hunt (Swinton) 21–18
*Pairs:* Joan Hills and Janet Tester (Dartford Stone Lodge) beat Joan Beardsley and Jean Baker (South Forest) 18–17
*Triples:* Barwell beat Taunton 21–14
*Fours:* Swinton beat Crystal Palace 21–20

BRITISH ISLES CHAMPIONSHIPS 1994
Llandrindod Wells, June

*Singles:* Dorothy Prior (England) beat Margaret Rosser (Wales) 25–9
*Pairs:* Jenny Davies and Betty Morgan (Wales) beat Irene Minnis and Freda Elliot (Ireland) 30–19
*Triples:* England beat Wales 16–13
*Fours:* Ireland beat Scotland 23–17

BRITISH ISLES INDOOR CHAMPIONSHIPS 1994
Blackpool, March

*Singles:* Julie Davies (Wales) beat Jan Woodley (Scotland) 21–18
*Pairs:* Anne Erridge and Mary Price (England) beat Julie Forrest and Joyce Foster (Scotland) 25–15
*Triples:* Scotland beat Wales 21–19
*Fours:* Scotland beat Ireland 17–14

*Home International Championship 1994* (Llandridnod Wells): England
*Home International Indoor Championship 1994* (Blackpool): Scotland
*Inter-County Championship final 1994:* Middlesex beat Yorkshire 122–106

---

## BOXING

---

## PROFESSIONAL BOXING
as at 22 August 1994

WORLD BOXING COUNCIL (WBC) CHAMPIONS

*Heavy:* Lennox Lewis (GB)
*Cruiser:* Anaclet Wamba (France)

*Light-heavy:* Mike McCallum (Jamaica)
*Super-middle:* Nigel Benn (GB)
*Middle:* Gerald McClellan (USA)
*Super-welter:* Terry Norris (USA)
*Welter:* Pernell Whitaker (USA)
*Super-light:* Julio Cesar Chavez (Mexico)
*Light:* Miguel Gonzalez (Mexico)
*Super-feather:* James Leija (USA)
*Feather:* Kevin Kelley (USA)
*Super-bantam:* Tracy Patterson (USA)
*Bantam:* Yasuei Yakushiji (Japan)
*Super-fly:* Hiroshi Kawashima (Japan)
*Fly:* Yuri Arbachakov (Russia)
*Light-fly:* Humberto Gonzalez (Mexico)
*Straw:* Ricardo Lopez (Mexico)

WORLD BOXING ASSOCIATION (WBA) CHAMPIONS

*Heavy:* Michael Moorer (USA)
*Cruiser:* Orlin Norris (USA)
*Light-heavy:* Virgil Hill (USA)
*Super-middle:* Steve Little (USA)
*Middle:* John Jackson (USA)
*Super-welter:* Julio Cesar Vasquez (Argentina)
*Welter:* Ike Quartey (Ghana)
*Super-light:* Juan Coggi (Argentina)
*Light:* Olzubek Nazarov (Russia)
*Super-feather:* Genaro Hernandez (USA)
*Feather:* Eloy Rojas (Venezuela)
*Super-bantam:* Wilfredo Vazquez (Puerto Rico)
*Bantam:* John Michael Johnson (USA)
*Super-fly:* Katsuya Onizuka (Japan)
*Fly:* Saen Sor Ploenchit (Thailand)
*Light-fly:* Leo Gamez (Venezuela)
*Straw:* Chana Porpaoin (Thailand)

INTERNATIONAL BOXING FEDERATION (IBF) CHAMPIONS

*Heavy:* Michael Moorer (USA)
*Cruiser:* Alfred Cole (USA)
*Light-heavy:* Henry Maske (Germany)
*Super-middle:* James Toney (USA)
*Middle:* Roy Jones (USA)
*Super-welter:* Gianfranco Rosi (Italy)
*Welter:* Felix Trinidad (Puerto Rico)
*Super-light:* Jake Rodriguez (Puerto Rico)
*Light:* Rafael Ruelas (USA)
*Super-feather:* John Molina (Puerto Rico)
*Feather:* Tom Johnson (USA)
*Super-bantam:* Vuyani Bungu (S. Africa)
*Bantam:* Orlando Canizales (USA)
*Super-fly:* Julio Borboa (Mexico)
*Fly:* Pichit Sibranchpagan (Thailand)
*Light-fly:* Humberto Gonzalez (Mexico)
*Straw:* Ratanapol Sovorapin (Thailand)

BRITISH CHAMPIONS

*Heavy:* vacant
*Cruiser:* Carl Thompson
*Light-heavy:* Maurice Coore
*Super-middle:* Cornelius Carr
*Middle:* Neville Brown
*Light-middle:* Robert McCracken
*Welter:* Del Bryan
*Light-welter:* Ross Hale
*Light:* Billy Schwer
*Super-feather:* Floyd Havard
*Feather:* Billy Hardy
*Super-bantam:* Richie Wenton

*Bantam:* Drew Docherty
*Fly:* Francis Ampofo

EUROPEAN CHAMPIONS
*Heavy:* Henry Akinwande (GB)
*Cruiser:* Carl Thompson (GB)
*Light-heavy:* Fabrice Tiozzo (France)
*Super-middle:* Frederic Sellier (France)
*Middle:* Agostino Cardamone (Italy)
*Light-middle:* Javier Castillejos (Spain)
*Welter:* Gary Jacobs (Scotland)
*Light-welter:* Khalid Rahilou (France)
*Light:* Racheed Lawal (Denmark)
*Super-feather:* Jacobin Yoma (France)
*Feather:* Stefano Zoff (Italy)
*Bantam:* Naseem Hamed (GB)
*Fly:* Luigi Camputaro (Italy)

COMMONWEALTH CHAMPIONS
*Heavy:* Henry Akinwande (GB)
*Cruiser:* Franco Wanyama (Uganda)
*Light-heavy:* vacant
*Super-middle:* Henry Wharton (GB)
*Middle:* Richie Woodhall (GB)
*Light-middle:* vacant
*Welter:* Andrew Murray (Guyana)
*Light-welter:* Ross Hale (GB)
*Light:* Billy Schwer (GB)
*Super-feather:* Tony Pep (Canada)
*Feather:* Billy Hardy (GB)
*Bantam:* Johnny Armour (GB)
*Fly:* Darren Fifield (GB)

## AMATEUR BOXING

AMATEUR BOXING ASSOCIATION (ABA)
CHAMPIONSHIP WINNERS 1994
*Super-heavy* (91 + kg): Danny Watts
*Heavy* (91 kg): Steve Burford
*Light-heavy* (81 kg): Kelly Oliver
*Middle* (75 kg): David Starie
*Light-middle* (71 kg): Wayne Alexander
*Welter* (67 kg): Kevin Short
*Light-welter* (63.5 kg): Alan Temple
*Light* (60 kg): Andrew Green
*Feather* (57 kg): Dean Pithie
*Bantam* (54 kg): Spencer Oliver
*Fly* (51 kg): Danny Costello
*Light-fly* (48 kg): Gary Jones

## CHESS

*PCA World Championship 1993:* Garry Kasparov (Russia)
beat Nigel Short (GB) 12½–7½
*FIDE World Championship 1993:* Anatoly Karpov (Russia)
beat Jan Timman (Netherlands) 12½–8½
*Women's World Championship 1993:* Xie Jun (China) beat
Nana Ioseliani (Georgia) 8½–2½
*World Team Championship 1993:* USA
*British Championship 1994:* William Watson
*Women's British Championship 1994:* Kathy Forbes

## CRICKET

### TEST SERIES

WEST INDIES V. ENGLAND
*First Test* (Kingston, Jamaica, 19–24 February 1994): West
Indies won by 8 wickets. England 234 and 267; West
Indies 407 and 95–2
*Second Test* (Georgetown, Guyana, 17–22 March 1994):
West Indies won by an innings and 44 runs. England 322
and 190; West Indies 556
*Third Test* (Port of Spain, Trinidad, 25–30 March 1994):
West Indies won by 147 runs. West Indies 252 and 269;
England 328 and 46
*Fourth Test* (Bridgetown, Barbados, 8–13 April 1994):
England won by 208 runs. England 355 and 394–7 dec.;
West Indies 304 and 237
*Fifth Test* (St John's, Antigua, 16–21 April 1994): Match
drawn. West Indies 593–5 dec.; England 593

ENGLAND V. NEW ZEALAND
*First Test* (Trent Bridge, 2–6 June 1994): England won by
an innings and 90 runs. New Zealand 251 and 226;
England 567–8 dec.
*Second Test* (Lord's, 16–20 June 1994): Match drawn. New
Zealand 476 and 211–5 dec.; England 281 and 254–8
*Third Test* (Old Trafford, 30 June–5 July 1994): Match
drawn. England 382; New Zealand 151 and 308–7

ENGLAND V. SOUTH AFRICA
*First Test* (Lord's, 21–24 July 1994): South Africa won by
356 runs. South Africa 357 and 278–8 dec.; England 180
and 99
*Second Test* (Headingley, 4–8 August 1994): Match drawn.
England 477–9 dec. and 267–5 dec.; South Africa 447
and 116–3
*Third Test* (The Oval, 18–21 August 1994): England won by
8 wickets. South Africa 332 and 175; England 304 and
205–2

AUSTRALIA V. NEW ZEALAND (November–December
1993): Australia won 2–0; one match drawn
PAKISTAN V. ZIMBABWE (December 1993): Pakistan won
2–0; one match drawn
SRI LANKA V. WEST INDIES (December 1993): one
match, drawn
AUSTRALIA V. SOUTH AFRICA (December 1993–
February 1994): Australia 1, South Africa 1; one match
drawn
INDIA V. SRI LANKA (January–February 1994): India won
3–0
NEW ZEALAND V. PAKISTAN (February 1994): Pakistan
won 2–1
SOUTH AFRICA V. AUSTRALIA (March 1994): South Africa
1, Australia 1; one match drawn
NEW ZEALAND V. INDIA (March 1994): one match, drawn
SRI LANKA V. PAKISTAN (August 1994): Pakistan won
2–0

### ONE-DAY INTERNATIONALS

WEST INDIES V. ENGLAND
*Bridgetown* (16 February 1994): England won by 61 runs.
England 202–5; West Indies 141
*Sabina Park* (26 February 1994): West Indies won on a
faster scoring rate. England 253–8; West Indies 240–7
(match interrupted by rain)

*St Vincent* (2 March 1994): West Indies won by 165 runs. West Indies 313–6; England 148–9
*Port of Spain* (5 March 1994): West Indies won on a faster scoring rate. West Indies 265–7; England 193–9 (match interrupted by rain)
*Port of Spain* (6 March 1994): England won on a faster scoring rate. West Indies 250–9; England 201–5 (match interrupted by rain)

### ENGLAND V. NEW ZEALAND

*Edgbaston* (19 May 1994): England won by 42 runs. England 224–8; New Zealand 182
*Lord's* (21–22 May 1994): abandoned due to rain without any play

### ENGLAND V. SOUTH AFRICA

*Edgbaston* (25 August 1994): England won by 6 wickets. South Africa 215–7; England 219–4
*Old Trafford* (27–28 August 1994): England won by 4 wickets. South Africa 181–9; England 182–6

## INTERNATIONAL CUPS

*World Series Cup final 1994:* Australia beat South Africa 2–1
*Sharjah Trophy final 1993:* West Indies beat Pakistan by 6 wickets. Pakistan 284–4; West Indies 285–4
*ICC Trophy final 1994:* United Arab Emirates beat Kenya by 2 wickets. Kenya 281–6; UAE 282–8

### WEST INDIES v. ENGLAND 1994 (Test Averages)

#### WEST INDIES BATTING

|  | I | NO | R | HS | Av. |
|---|---|---|---|---|---|
| B. C. Lara | 8 | 0 | 798 | 375 | 99.75 |
| J. C. Adams | 7 | 1 | 374 | 137 | 62.33 |
| S. Chanderpaul | 6 | 1 | 288 | 77 | 57.60 |
| K. L. T. Arthurton | 7 | 0 | 273 | 126 | 39.00 |
| D. L. Haynes | 7 | 1 | 217 | 63 | 36.16 |
| R. B. Richardson | 7 | 1 | 163 | 63 | 27.16 |
| W. K. M. Benjamin | 6 | 0 | 138 | 44 | 23.00 |
| P. V. Simmons | 4 | 1 | 50 | 22* | 16.66 |
| J. R. Murray | 6 | 1 | 80 | 34 | 16.00 |
| C. E. L. Ambrose | 6 | 0 | 91 | 44 | 15.16 |
| K. C. G. Benjamin | 6 | 2 | 58 | 43* | 14.50 |
| C. A. Walsh | 6 | 2 | 42 | 18* | 10.50 |

Played in one match: S. C. Williams, 3, 21*
*Not out

#### WEST INDIES BOWLING

|  | O | M | R | W | Av. |
|---|---|---|---|---|---|
| C. E. L. Ambrose | 224.2 | 59 | 519 | 26 | 19.96 |
| K. C. G. Benjamin | 181.5 | 38 | 566 | 22 | 25.72 |
| C. A. Walsh | 227.2 | 44 | 646 | 19 | 34.00 |
| W. K. M. Benjamin | 190.2 | 48 | 498 | 12 | 41.50 |
| J. C. Adams | 49.5 | 8 | 173 | 4 | 43.25 |
| S. Chanderpaul | 65 | 10 | 209 | 1 | 209.00 |

Also bowled: P. V. Simmons, 3–1–4–0; K. L. T. Arthurton, 5–1–9–0

#### ENGLAND BATTING

|  | I | NO | R | HS | Av. |
|---|---|---|---|---|---|
| M. A. Atherton | 9 | 0 | 510 | 144 | 56.66 |
| A. J. Stewart | 9 | 0 | 477 | 143 | 53.00 |
| R. A. Smith | 9 | 0 | 320 | 175 | 35.55 |
| G. A. Hick | 9 | 0 | 316 | 96 | 35.11 |
| G. P. Thorpe | 9 | 0 | 239 | 86 | 26.55 |
| R. C. Russell | 9 | 1 | 195 | 62 | 24.37 |
| C. C. Lewis | 9 | 1 | 170 | 75* | 21.25 |
| I. D. K. Salisbury | 4 | 0 | 63 | 36 | 15.75 |

| A. R. Caddick | 6 | 1 | 69 | 29* | 13.80 |
| M. R. Ramprakash | 7 | 0 | 73 | 23 | 10.42 |
| A. R. C. Fraser | 6 | 3 | 11 | 8* | 3.66 |
| A. P. Igglesden | 4 | 2 | 4 | 3* | 2.00 |
| P. C. R. Tufnell | 2 | 1 | 0 | 0* | 0.00 |

Played in one match: M. P. Maynard, 35, 0; D. E. Malcolm, 18, 6
*Not out

#### ENGLAND BOWLING

|  | O | M | R | W | Av. |
|---|---|---|---|---|---|
| A. R. C. Fraser | 168.5 | 39 | 443 | 16 | 27.68 |
| A. R. Caddick | 170.2 | 30 | 545 | 18 | 30.27 |
| I. D. K. Salisbury | 68 | 9 | 276 | 7 | 39.42 |
| C. C. Lewis | 168.3 | 18 | 553 | 14 | 39.50 |
| D. E. Malcolm | 28 | 4 | 132 | 3 | 44.00 |
| A. P. Igglesden | 55.3 | 8 | 183 | 3 | 61.00 |
| P. C. R. Tufnell | 113 | 36 | 291 | 4 | 72.75 |
| G. A. Hick | 77 | 14 | 198 | 2 | 99.00 |

Also bowled: G. P. Thorpe, 2–1–1–0; A. J. Stewart, 3.2–0–13–0; M. R. Ramprakash, 20–3–48–0

### ENGLAND v. NEW ZEALAND 1994 (Test Averages)

#### ENGLAND BATTING

|  | I | NO | R | HS | Av. |
|---|---|---|---|---|---|
| M. A. Atherton | 4 | 0 | 273 | 111 | 68.25 |
| S. J. Rhodes | 4 | 2 | 117 | 49 | 58.50 |
| G. A. Gooch | 4 | 0 | 223 | 210 | 55.75 |
| A. J. Stewart | 4 | 0 | 196 | 119 | 49.00 |
| P. A. J. DeFreitas | 4 | 1 | 134 | 69 | 44.66 |
| G. A. Hick | 4 | 0 | 133 | 58 | 33.25 |
| C. White | 4 | 0 | 121 | 51 | 30.25 |
| R. A. Smith | 4 | 0 | 120 | 78 | 30.00 |
| P. M. Such | 2 | 1 | 9 | 5* | 9.00 |
| A. R. C. Fraser | 4 | 0 | 30 | 10 | 7.50 |

Played in one match: D. Gough, 65; J. P. Taylor, 0, 0*; D. E. Malcolm, did not bat
*Not out

#### ENGLAND BOWLING

|  | O | M | R | W | Av. |
|---|---|---|---|---|---|
| G. A. Hick | 18 | 8 | 21 | 1 | 21.00 |
| P. A. J. DeFreitas | 143.3 | 24 | 451 | 21 | 21.47 |
| D. Gough | 47.5 | 7 | 152 | 6 | 25.33 |
| C. White | 62.1 | 15 | 197 | 6 | 32.83 |
| J. P. Taylor | 26 | 6 | 82 | 2 | 41.00 |
| D. E. Malcolm | 27.4 | 7 | 84 | 2 | 42.00 |
| A. R. C. Fraser | 126 | 37 | 296 | 7 | 42.28 |
| P. M. Such | 123 | 36 | 264 | 6 | 44.00 |

Also bowled: G. A. Gooch, 7–1–26–0

#### NEW ZEALAND BATTING

|  | I | NO | R | HS | Av. |
|---|---|---|---|---|---|
| M. D. Crowe | 6 | 0 | 380 | 142 | 63.33 |
| A. C. Parore | 6 | 1 | 213 | 71 | 42.60 |
| B. A. Young | 6 | 0 | 195 | 94 | 32.50 |
| S. A. Thomson | 6 | 1 | 157 | 69 | 31.40 |
| D. J. Nash | 5 | 2 | 94 | 56 | 31.33 |
| S. P. Fleming | 6 | 0 | 170 | 54 | 28.33 |
| M. N. Hart | 5 | 1 | 99 | 36 | 24.75 |
| K. R. Rutherford | 6 | 0 | 96 | 37 | 16.00 |
| C. Pringle | 2 | 0 | 14 | 14 | 7.00 |
| M. B. Owens | 2 | 1 | 6 | 4 | 6.00 |

Played in one match: B. R. Hartland, 6, 22; M. J. Greatbatch, 0, 21; B. A. Pocock, 10, 2; G. R. Larsen, 8, 2; H. T. Davis, 0*, 0*
*Not out

NEW ZEALAND BOWLING

| | O | M | R | W | Av. |
|---|---|---|---|---|---|
| D. J. Nash | 129 | 28 | 429 | 17 | 25.23 |
| M. B. Owens | 51 | 15 | 168 | 5 | 33.60 |
| G. R. Larsen | 44.4 | 11 | 116 | 2 | 58.00 |
| C. Pringle | 78 | 22 | 201 | 3 | 67.00 |
| M. N. Hart | 147.3 | 60 | 278 | 4 | 69.50 |
| S. A. Thomson | 79 | 19 | 163 | 2 | 81.50 |
| H. T. Davis | 21 | 0 | 93 | 1 | 93.00 |

## ENGLAND v. SOUTH AFRICA 1994
(Test Averages)

ENGLAND BATTING

| | I | NO | R | HS | Av. |
|---|---|---|---|---|---|
| G. P. Thorpe | 4 | 1 | 239 | 79 | 79.66 |
| G. A. Hick | 6 | 1 | 304 | 110 | 60.80 |
| A. J. Stewart | 5 | 1 | 226 | 89 | 56.50 |
| S. J. Rhodes | 4 | 2 | 105 | 65* | 52.50 |
| D. Gough | 4 | 2 | 81 | 42* | 40.50 |
| M. A. Atherton | 6 | 0 | 207 | 99 | 34.50 |
| G. A. Gooch | 6 | 0 | 139 | 33 | 23.16 |
| P. A. J. DeFreitas | 4 | 0 | 73 | 37 | 18.25 |
| J. P. Crawley | 5 | 0 | 59 | 38 | 11.80 |
| A. R. C. Fraser | 3 | 0 | 10 | 6 | 3.33 |

Played in one match: I. D. K. Salisbury, 6*, 0; C. White, 10, 0; D. E. Malcolm, 4; J. E. Benjamin, 0; P. C. R. Tufnell, did not bat
*Not out

ENGLAND BOWLING

| | O | M | R | W | Av. |
|---|---|---|---|---|---|
| D. E. Malcolm | 41.3 | 7 | 138 | 10 | 13.80 |
| J. E. Benjamin | 28 | 3 | 80 | 4 | 20.00 |
| P. C. R. Tufnell | 55 | 21 | 112 | 4 | 28.00 |
| C. White | 16 | 2 | 61 | 2 | 30.50 |
| A. R. C. Fraser | 85.5 | 19 | 245 | 7 | 35.00 |
| D. Gough | 122.3 | 21 | 414 | 11 | 37.63 |
| P. A. J. DeFreitas | 113.3 | 25 | 358 | 9 | 39.77 |
| G. A. Hick | 48 | 23 | 98 | 2 | 49.00 |
| I. D. K. Salisbury | 44 | 6 | 121 | 1 | 121.00 |

Also bowled: G. A. Gooch, 3-0-9-0

SOUTH AFRICA BATTING

| | I | NO | R | HS | Av. |
|---|---|---|---|---|---|
| B. M. McMillan | 5 | 1 | 264 | 93 | 66.00 |
| K. C. Wessels | 6 | 0 | 238 | 105 | 39.66 |
| P. N. Kirsten | 6 | 1 | 179 | 104 | 35.80 |
| J. N. Rhodes | 5 | 1 | 128 | 46 | 32.00 |
| C. R. Matthews | 5 | 1 | 128 | 62* | 32.00 |
| G. Kirsten | 6 | 0 | 190 | 72 | 31.66 |
| D. J. Richardson | 5 | 0 | 138 | 58 | 27.60 |
| A. A. Donald | 4 | 2 | 46 | 27 | 23.00 |
| W. J. Cronje | 6 | 1 | 90 | 38 | 18.00 |
| P. S. de Villiers | 4 | 1 | 35 | 14 | 11.66 |
| A. C. Hudson | 4 | 0 | 30 | 12 | 7.50 |

Played in one match: D. J. Cullinan, 7, 94
*Not out

SOUTH AFRICA BOWLING

| | O | M | R | W | Av. |
|---|---|---|---|---|---|
| B. M. McMillan | 81.2 | 16 | 267 | 9 | 29.66 |
| P. S. de Villiers | 123.3 | 27 | 388 | 12 | 32.33 |
| A. A. Donald | 89.3 | 15 | 410 | 12 | 34.16 |
| C. R. Matthews | 125.3 | 35 | 340 | 8 | 42.50 |

Also bowled: G. Kirsten, 2-1-10-0; W. J. Cronje, 37-9-94-0

## COUNTY CHAMPIONSHIP TABLE 1994

| Order for 1993 in brackets | P | W | L | D | Bt | Bl | Pts |
|---|---|---|---|---|---|---|---|
| Warwickshire (16) | 17 | 11 | 1 | 5 | 41 | 55 | 272 |
| Leicestershire (9) | 17 | 8 | 7 | 2 | 42 | 60 | 230 |
| Nottinghamshire (7) | 17 | 8 | 5 | 4 | 39 | 51 | 218 |
| Middlesex (1) | 17 | 7 | 3 | 7 | 43 | 57 | 212 |
| Northamptonshire (4) | 17 | 8 | 4 | 5 | 28 | 53 | 209 |
| Essex (11) | 17 | 7 | 5 | 5 | 32 | 63 | 207 |
| Surrey (6) | 17 | 7 | 7 | 3 | 32 | 57 | 201 |
| Sussex (10) | 17 | 7 | 5 | 5 | 28 | 60 | 200 |
| Kent (8) | 17 | 6 | 7 | 4 | 44 | 58 | 198 |
| †Lancashire (13) | 17 | 8 | 6 | 3 | 32 | 59 | 194 |
| Somerset (5) | 17 | 7 | 7 | 3 | 32 | 47 | 191 |
| *Gloucestershire (17) | 17 | 5 | 8 | 4 | 28 | 56 | 172 |
| Yorkshire (12) | 17 | 4 | 6 | 7 | 38 | 57 | 159 |
| *Hampshire (13) | 17 | 4 | 7 | 6 | 32 | 55 | 159 |
| Worcestershire (2) | 17 | 4 | 6 | 7 | 42 | 52 | 158 |
| Durham (18) | 17 | 4 | 10 | 3 | 32 | 57 | 153 |
| Derbyshire (15) | 17 | 4 | 9 | 4 | 25 | 54 | 143 |
| Glamorgan (3) | 17 | 2 | 8 | 7 | 29 | 50 | 111 |

*Includes 8pts for batting last in a tied match
†Lancashire had 25 points deducted for starting a match with a damp pitch in July 1994

## FIRST CLASS BATTING AVERAGES 1994

| | I | NO | R | HS | Av. |
|---|---|---|---|---|---|
| J. D. Carr | 27 | 10 | 1,542 | 261* | 90.70 |
| B. C. Lara | 25 | 2 | 2,066 | 501* | 89.82 |
| M. W. Gatting | 27 | 3 | 1,671 | 225 | 69.62 |
| G. A. Gooch | 29 | 2 | 1,747 | 236 | 64.70 |
| C. C. Lewis | 19 | 4 | 881 | 220* | 58.73 |
| B. M. McMillan | 11 | 3 | 467 | 132 | 58.37 |
| M. D. Moxon | 30 | 4 | 1,458 | 274* | 56.07 |
| S. J. Rhodes | 27 | 11 | 896 | 100* | 56.00 |
| G. A. Hick | 29 | 1 | 1,538 | 215 | 54.92 |
| C. L. Hooper | 29 | 0 | 1,579 | 183 | 54.44 |
| R. G. Twose | 31 | 5 | 1,411 | 277* | 54.26 |
| G. P. Thorpe | 25 | 4 | 1,136 | 190 | 54.09 |
| M. R. Ramprakash | 26 | 2 | 1,271 | 135 | 52.95 |
| A. N. Hayhurst | 30 | 6 | 1,250 | 121 | 52.08 |
| D. J. Bicknell | 30 | 4 | 1,354 | 235* | 52.07 |
| C. J. Hollins | 10 | 2 | 415 | 131 | 51.87 |
| P. A. Cottey | 33 | 6 | 1,393 | 191 | 51.59 |
| A. J. Moles | 20 | 3 | 863 | 203* | 50.76 |
| J. P. Crawley | 34 | 3 | 1,570 | 281* | 50.64 |
| N. H. Fairbrother | 22 | 2 | 1,002 | 204 | 50.10 |

*Not out

## FIRST CLASS BOWLING AVERAGES 1994

| | O | M | R | W | Av. |
|---|---|---|---|---|---|
| C. E. L. Ambrose | 540 | 159 | 1,113 | 77 | 14.45 |
| C. A. Walsh | 506.1 | 119 | 1,535 | 89 | 17.24 |
| M. J. McCague | 341.1 | 67 | 1,084 | 57 | 19.01 |
| I. D. Austin | 251.5 | 72 | 662 | 33 | 20.06 |
| F. D. Stephenson | 480.5 | 108 | 1,345 | 67 | 20.07 |
| J. E. Benjamin | 591.2 | 130 | 1,658 | 80 | 20.72 |
| T. A. Munton | 699.4 | 181 | 1,748 | 81 | 21.58 |
| M. M. Patel | 811.2 | 202 | 2,058 | 90 | 22.86 |
| C. White | 235.2 | 53 | 761 | 33 | 23.06 |
| S. R. Lampitt | 512.4 | 127 | 1,484 | 64 | 23.18 |
| A. R. Caddick | 373.1 | 73 | 1,186 | 51 | 23.25 |
| C. C. Lewis | 345.2 | 69 | 1,082 | 46 | 23.52 |
| G. R. Larsen | 226.4 | 73 | 494 | 21 | 23.52 |
| M. C. Ilott | 497.5 | 115 | 1,391 | 59 | 23.57 |
| Wasim Akram | 213.2 | 44 | 646 | 27 | 23.92 |

| P. S. de Villiers | 277.3 | 59 | 922 | 38 | 24.26 |
| W. K. M. Benjamin | 281 | 97 | 585 | 24 | 24.37 |
| E. S. H. Giddins | 450.4 | 89 | 1,463 | 60 | 24.38 |
| C. A. Connor | 574.4 | 131 | 1,764 | 72 | 24.50 |
| D. Gough | 479.2 | 100 | 1,526 | 62 | 24.61 |

*Source for averages and county championship table:* TCCB Official Cricket Statistics

## OTHER RESULTS 1994

*Benson and Hedges Cup final:* Warwickshire beat Worcestershire by 6 wickets. Worcestershire 170–9; Warwickshire 172–4
*NatWest Trophy final:* Worcestershire beat Warwickshire by 8 wickets. Warwickshire 223–9; Worcestershire 227–2
*Sunday League Champions:* Warwickshire
*MCC Trophy* (Minor Counties knockout final): Devon beat Lincolnshire by 18 runs. Devon 281–5; Lincolnshire 263
*Minor Counties' Championship final:* Match drawn. Devon 150–4 dec.; Cambridgeshire 153–6 dec. and 165–4 dec. Devon won 3–2 on bonus points
*National Club Championship final:* Chorley beat Ealing by 5 wickets. Ealing 235–9; Chorley 236–5
*National Village Championship final:* Elvaston beat Werrington by 55 runs. Elvaston 227–5; Werrington 172–9
*Varsity Match:* Match drawn. Oxford 453–9 dec.; Cambridge 253 and 243–8

## CYCLING

*World Cup series overall winner 1993:* Maurizio Fondriest (Italy), 287 pts
· *Tour of Spain 1994:* Tony Rominger (Switzerland)
*Tour of Italy 1994:* Eugeni Berzin (Russia)
*Tour de France 1994:* Miguel Indurain (Spain)
*Tour of Britain 1994:* Maurizio Fondriest (Italy)
*World Professional Road Race Championship 1994:* Luc Leblanc (France)
*World Amateur Road Race Championship 1994:* Alex Pedersen (Sweden)
*World Cyclo-Cross Championship 1994:* Paul Herijgers (Belgium)
*World (Inaugural) Cyclo-Cross Cup 1994:* Paul Herijgers (Belgium)
*British Professional Road Race Championship 1994:* Brian Smith
*British Amateur Road Race Championship 1994:* Robert Harris
*British Open Cyclo-Cross Championship 1994:* Roger Hammond
*Women's World Road Race Championship 1994:* Monica Valvik (Norway)
*Women's National Road Race Championship 1994:* Maxine Johnson
*Women's (Inaugural) British Open Cyclo-Cross Championship 1994:* Caroline Alexander

## EQUESTRIANISM

### SHOW JUMPING
*World Cup final 1994:* Jos Lansink on Bollvorm's Libero (Netherlands)

*World Championship 1994:*
*Individual:* Franke Sloothaak on San Patrignano Weihaiwej (Germany)
*Team:* Germany
*British Jumping Derby 1994* (Hickstead): Capt. John Ledingham on Kilbaha (Ireland)

### THREE-DAY EVENTING
*World Championship 1994:*
*Individual:* Vaughn Jefferis on Bounce (New Zealand)
*Team:* Great Britain
*Badminton Horse Trials 1994:* Mark Todd on Horton Point (New Zealand)
*British Open Horse Trials 1994:* Karen Dixon on Too Smart (GB)
*Burghley Horse Trials 1994:* William Fox-Pitt on Chaka (GB)

## ETON FIVES

*NatWest County Championship 1994:* Middlesex
*Amateur Championship (Kinnaird Cup) 1994:* Robin Mason and Andrew Mole beat Edward Wass and James Halstead 3–2
*Holmwoods Schools' Championship 1994:* Highgate
*Barber Cup final 1994:* Old Cholmeleians beat Old Salopians 3–0
*League Championship (Douglas Keeble Cup) 1994:* Old Cholmeleians

## FENCING (MEN)

### WORLD CHAMPIONSHIPS 1994
*Foil:* Rolando Tuckers (Cuba)
*Epée:* Pavel Kolobkov (Russia)
*Sabre:* Felix Becker (Germany)
*Team Foil:* Italy
*Team Epée:* France
*Team Sabre:* Russia

### BRITISH CHAMPIONSHIPS 1994
*Foil:* Lauren Harper (Salle Boston)
*Epée:* John Llewellyn (Reading)
*Sabre:* Nick Fletcher (Salle Frohlich)
*Team Foil:* Sussex House
*Team Epée:* Reading
*Team Sabre:* Salle Frohlich A
*Challenge Martini International Epée 1994:* Mariusz Strzalka (Germany)
*Eden Cup 1993:* Lorenzo Taddei (Italy)
*Corble Cup 1994:* Kirkham Zavieh (GB)

## FENCING (WOMEN)

### WORLD CHAMPIONSHIPS 1994
*Foil:* Reka Szabo-Lazer (Romania)
*Epée:* Laura Chiesa (Italy)
*Team Foil:* Romania
*Team Epée:* Spain

### BRITISH CHAMPIONSHIPS 1994
*Foil:* Fiona McIntosh (Salle Paul)
*Epée:* Carol Greenway (LTFC)

*Sabre:* Sue Benny (South-West Region)
*Team Foil:* Salle Paul
*Team Epée:* Polytechnic

*Ipswich Cup 1994:* Giongyi Szalay (Hungary)

---

GOLF (MEN)

---

THE MAJOR CHAMPIONSHIPS 1994

*US Masters* (Augusta, Georgia, 7–10 April): José Maria Olazábal (Spain), 279
*US Open* (Oakmont, Pennsylvania, 16–20 June): Ernie Els (South Africa), 279*
*The Open* (Turnberry, 14–17 July): Nick Price (Zimbabwe), 268
*US PGA Championship* (Tulsa, 11–14 August): Nick Price (Zimbabwe), 269

PGA EUROPEAN TOUR 1993

*German Masters* (Stuttgart): Steven Richardson (GB), 271
*Belgian Open* (Knokke-le-Zoute): Darren Clarke (GB), 270
*World Matchplay Championship* (Wentworth): Corey Pavin (USA) beat Nick Faldo (GB) by 1 hole
*Madrid Open:* Des Smyth (Ireland), 272
*Volvo Masters* (Valderrama): Colin Montgomerie (GB), 274
*European Tour Order of Merit 1993:* 1. Colin Montgomerie (GB); 2. Nick Faldo (GB); 3. Ian Woosnam (GB)

PGA EUROPEAN TOUR 1994

*Madeira Island Open:* Mats Lanner (Sweden), 206
*Moroccan Open:* Anders Forsbrand (Sweden), 276
*Dubai Desert Classic:* Ernie Els (S. Africa), 268
*Johnnie Walker Classic* (Phuket, Thailand): Greg Norman (Australia), 277
*Tenerife Open:* David Gilford (GB), 278
*Extremadura Open* (Badajoz, Spain): Paul Eales (GB), 281
*Turespana Masters* (Jerez, Spain): Carl Mason (GB), 278
*Mediterranean Open* (Torrevieja, Spain): José Maria Olazábal (Spain), 276*
*Balearic Open* (Son Vida, Majorca): Barry Lane (GB), 269
*Portuguese Open* (Sintra): Phillip Price (GB), 278
*Lyon Open:* Stephen Ames (Trinidad and Tobago), 282
*Catalonia Open* (Girona): José Coceres (Argentina), 275
*Cannes Open:* Ian Woosnam (GB), 271
*International Open* (St Mellion): Severiano Ballesteros (Spain), 281
*Spanish Open* (Madrid): Colin Montgomerie (GB), 277
*Italian Open* (Rome): Eduardo Romero (Argentina), 272
*PGA Championship* (Wentworth): José Maria Olazábal (Spain), 271
*Belgian Open* (Knokke-le-Zoute): Nick Faldo (GB), 279*
*Honda Open* (Hamburg): Robert Allenby (Australia), 276*
*Jersey Open* (La Moye): Paul Curry (GB), 266
*French Open* (Paris): Mark Roe (GB), 274
*Irish Open* (Thomastown, Co. Kilkenny): Bernhard Langer (Germany), 275
*Scottish Open* (Gleneagles): Carl Mason (GB), 265
*Dutch Open* (Hilversum): Miguel Jimenez (Spain), 270
*Scandinavian Masters* (Drottningholm): Vijay Singh (Fiji), 268
*International Open* (St Eurach, Munich): Mark McNulty (Zimbabwe), 274
*Austrian Open* (Haugschlag): Mark Davis (GB), 270
*English Open* (Forest of Arden): Colin Montgomerie (GB), 274

---

*After a play-off

*German Open* (Dusseldorf): Colin Montgomerie (GB), 269
*European Masters* (Crans-sur-Sierre, Switzerland): Eduardo Romero (Argentina), 266
*European Open* (East Sussex National): David Gilford (GB), 275
*British Masters* (Woburn): Ian Woosnam (GB), 271
*Lancôme Trophy* (Paris): Vijay Singh (Fiji), 263
*German Masters* (Berlin): Seve Ballesteros (Spain), 270*

*World Championship 1993* (Tryall, Jamaica): Larry Mize (USA), 266
*World Cup 1993* (Orlando, Florida): Bernhard Langer (Germany), 272

TEAM EVENTS

*Alfred Dunhill Cup 1993* (St Andrews, 14–17 October): USA beat England 2-1
*World Cup 1993* (Orlando, Florida): USA, 556

AMATEUR CHAMPIONSHIPS 1994

*British Amateur Championship* (Nairn): Lee James (Broadstone)
*Brabazon Trophy* (English Open Strokeplay) (Little Aston): Gary Harris (Broome Manor), 280
*Welsh Open Strokeplay* (St Pierre): Nicholas Van Hootegen (Belgium), 290
*Scottish Open Strokeplay* (Letham Grange): David Downie (Ladybank), 288
*English Amateur Championship* (Moortown): Mark Foster (Worksop)
*Welsh Amateur Championship* (Royal Portcawl): Craig Evans (Brynmawr)
*Scottish Amateur Championship* (Renfrew): Hugh McKibbin (Troon Welbeck)
*Lytham Trophy* (Royal Lytham and St Anne's): Warren Bennett (Ruislip), 285
*Berkshire Trophy* (The Berkshire): James Knight (Sandford Springs) and Andrew Marshall (Dereham), 274
*International Match* (Nimes, France): England beat France 17-7
*Home International Championship* (Ashburnham): England
*European Amateur Championship* (Aura, Finland): Stephen Gallacher (Scotland), 278
*President's Putter* (Rye): Steve Seman
*Halford Hewitt Trophy* (for public schools' old boys) (Royal Cinque Ports, Deal): Tonbridge beat Stowe 3–2
*Varsity Match* (Rye): Oxford beat Cambridge 13–2
*European Amateur Team Championship 1993:* Wales

---

GOLF (WOMEN)

---

*US Women's Open 1994* (Indianwood, Michigan, 21–24 July): Patty Sheehan (USA), 277
*Women's World Championship 1993* (Naples): Dottie Mochrie (USA), 283

WPG EUROPEAN TOUR 1993

*French Open* (St Maxime): Marie-Laure de Lorenzi (France), 220
*European Tour Order of Merit 1993:* 1. Karen Lunn (Australia); 2. Laura Davies (England); 3. Annika Sorenstam (Sweden)

WPG EUROPEAN TOUR 1994

*Ford Classic* (Woburn): Catrin Nilsmark (Sweden), 284
*Costa Azul Open* (Lisbon): Sandrine Mendiburu (France), 140

*Evian Masters:* Helen Alfredsson (Sweden), 287
*OVB Open* (Zell-am-See, Austria): Florence Descampe (Belgium), 277
*European Masters* (Bercuit, Belgium): Helen Wadsworth (GB), 278
*Hennessy Cup* (Refrath, Cologne): Liselotte Neumann (Sweden), 277
*Irish Open* (St Margaret's, Dublin): Laura Davies (England), 282
*Scottish Open* (Dalmahoy): Laura Davies (England), 278
*British Open* (Woburn): Liselotte Neumann (Sweden), 280
*Trygg-Hansa Open* (Haninge, Sweden): Liselotte Neumann (Sweden), 274
*English Open* (Tytherington): Patricia Meunier (France), 288
*Dutch Open* (Nijmegen): Liz Weima (Holland), 214
*Italian Open* (Lignano): Corinne Dibnah (Australia), 277*
*Spanish Open* (La Manga): Marie-Laure de Lorenzi (France), 282*

TEAM EVENT

*Curtis Cup 1994* (Chattanooga, Tennessee): Great Britain and Ireland 9, USA 9. Great Britain and Ireland retained the Cup

AMATEUR CHAMPIONSHIPS 1994

*British Open Championship* (Newport): Emma Duggleby (Malton and Norton)
*English Amateur Championship* (The Berkshire): Julie Hall (Felixstowe Ferry)
*Welsh Amateur Championship* (Royal Porthcawl): Vicki Thomas (Pennard)
*Scottish Amateur Championship* (Gullane): Catriona Matthew (North Berwick)
*British Strokeplay Championship* (Woodhall Spa): Kirsty Speak (Clitheroe), 297
*English Strokeplay Championship* (Ferndown, Bournemouth): Fiona Brown (Heswall), 289
*Welsh Strokeplay Championship* (Newport): Alison Rose, 217
*Home International Championship* (Huddersfield): England
*Espirito Santo Trophy* (world amateur team championship): USA, 569 pts
*European Amateur Team Championship 1993* (The Hague): England

*After a play-off

---

GREYHOUND RACING

*Grand Prix 1993* (Walthamstow): Redwood Girl
*St Leger 1993* (Wembley): Galleydown Boy
*Television Trophy 1994* (Sunderland): Jubilee Rebecca
*Grand National 1994* (Hall Green): Randy Savage
*Derby 1994* (Wimbledon): Moral Standards
*Scurry Gold Cup 1994* (Catford): Rabatino
*The Masters 1994* (Reading): Druids Elprado
*The Regency 1994* (Brighton): Decoy Cougar
*Gold Collar 1994* (Catford): Pearl's Girl
*Cesarewitch 1994* (Manchester): Sandollar Louis

---

GYMNASTICS (MEN)

---

WORLD CHAMPIONSHIPS 1994

*World Champion:* Ivan Ivankov (Belarus)

*World Individual Apparatus Champions:*
  *Floor:* Vitaly Scherbo (Belarus)
  *Pommel Horse:* Marius Urzica (Romania)
  *Rings:* Yuri Chechi (Italy)
  *Vault:* Vitaly Scherbo (Belarus)
  *Parallel Bars:* Huang Liping (China)
  *High Bar:* Vitaly Scherbo (Belarus)

BRITISH CHAMPIONSHIPS 1993

*British Champion:* Marvin Campbell (Central Manchester)
*British Individual Apparatus Champions:*
  *Floor:* Paul Bowler (Central Manchester)
  *Pommel Horse:* = Marvin Campbell (Central Manchester), Lee Ricketts (N. Staffs.), Robert Barber (N. Staffs.)
  *Rings:* Paul Bowler (Central Manchester)
  *Vault:* Paul Bowler (Central Manchester)
  *Parallel Bars:* Paul Bowler (Central Manchester)
  *High Bar:* = Paul Bowler (Central Manchester), Craig Heap (Central Manchester)
*British Team Champions (Adam Shield) 1994:* City of Liverpool

---

GYMNASTICS (WOMEN)

---

WORLD CHAMPIONSHIPS 1994

*World Champion:* Shannon Miller (USA)
*World Individual Apparatus Champions:*
  *Floor:* Dina Kochetkova (Russia)
  *Beam:* Shannon Miller (USA)
  *Vault:* Gina Gogean (Romania)
  *Assymetric Bars:* Luo Li (China)

*World Rhythmics Champion 1993:* Maria Petrova (Bulgaria)

BRITISH CHAMPIONSHIPS 1993

*British Champion:* Jackie Brady (Eltham)
*British Individual Apparatus Champions:*
  *Beam:* Jackie Brady (Eltham)
  *Floor:* Jackie Brady (Eltham)
  *Vault:* Jackie Brady (Eltham)
  *Assymetric Bars:* Jackie Brady (Eltham)
*British Open Club Team Champions 1994:* Heathrow-Hoechst
*British Rhythmics Champion 1993:* Debbie Southwick
*British Rhythmics Champion 1994:* Debbie Southwick

---

HOCKEY (MEN)

---

*National League Champions:* Havant
*Hockey Association Cup final 1994:* Teddington beat Old Loughtonians 1–0
*National Indoor Club Championship final 1994:* St Albans 2, East Grinstead 2. St Albans won 6–5 on penalties
*County Championship final 1994:* Staffordshire beat Surrey 3–1
*Champions Trophy final 1994:* Pakistan 2, Germany 2. Pakistan won 7–6 on penalties
*European Club Championship final 1994:* Uhlenhorst (Germany) beat Bloemendaal (Netherlands) 2–0
*European Indoor Club Championship final 1994:* Rot-Weiss Cologne (Germany) beat Valdeluz (Spain) 13–3
*European Cup Winners' Cup final 1994:* HGC (Netherlands) 3, Atletico Terrassa (Spain) 3. Atletico Terrassa won 5–4 on penalties

*European Indoor Nations Cup final 1994:* Germany beat
  England 9–2
*Varsity Match 1994:* Oxford beat Cambridge 5–0

## HOCKEY (WOMEN)

*National League:* Leicester
*AEWHA Cup final 1994:* Slough 1, Hightown 1. Slough
  won 4–2 on penalties
*National Indoor Club Championship final 1994:* Hightown 5,
  Slough 5. Slough won 3–2 on penalties
*County Championship final 1994:* Yorkshire beat Kent 2–0
*World Cup final 1994:* Australia beat Argentina 2–0
*European Club Championship final 1994:* HGC
  (Netherlands) 0, Russelsheim (Germany) 0. HGC won
  4–3 on penalties
*European Indoor Club Championship final 1994:*
  Russelsheim (Germany) beat Berlin (Germany) 6–5
*European Cup Winners' Cup final 1994:* Bayer Leverkusen
  (Germany) 0, SKIF Moscow (Russia) 0. Bayer
  Leverkusen won 3–1 on penalties

## HORSERACING

### WINNING OWNERS 1993

| Sheikh Mohammed | £1,703,958 |
|---|---|
| Khalid Abdulla | 1,218,433 |
| Hamdan Al-Maktoum | 644,986 |
| Maktoum Al-Maktoum | 638,111 |
| Robert Sangster | 411,286 |
| Jackie Smith | 275,271 |
| Daniel Wildenstein | 273,980 |
| Roldvale Ltd | 262,446 |
| Jeff Smith | 227,700 |
| Peter Savill | 221,772 |

### WINNING TRAINERS 1993

| Henry Cecil | £1,248,318 |
|---|---|
| Richard Hannon | 1,229,046 |
| Michael Stoute | 1,071,842 |
| John Gosden | 1,018,364 |
| John Dunlop | 700,736 |
| Jack Berry | 540,011 |
| Geoff Wragg | 428,417 |
| Peter Chapple-Hyam | 407,059 |
| Clive Brittain | 396,693 |
| Ian Balding | 383,636 |

### LEADING BREEDERS 1993

| | Value |
|---|---|
| Juddmonte Farms | £994,854 |
| Meon Valley Stud | 566,561 |
| Baronrath Stud | 279,381 |
| Dayton | 273,980 |
| Gainsborough Stud Management | 272,312 |
| Gainsborough Farm | 254,311 |
| Sheikh Mohammed | 232,860 |
| Swettenham Stud | 228,722 |
| Lord Howard de Walden | 219,292 |
| Roncon and Swettenham Stud | 200,270 |

### WINNING SIRES 1993

| | Horses | Races won | Total value |
|---|---|---|---|
| Sadler's Wells (1981) by Northern Dancer | 20 | 32 | £994,304 |
| Dancing Brave (1983) by Lyphard | 14 | 30 | £630,631 |
| Last Tycoon (1983) by Try My Best | 8 | 10 | £474,852 |
| Primo Dominie (1982) by Dominion | 25 | 45 | £317,670 |
| Bob Back (1981) by Roberto | 4 | 8 | £299,174 |
| Caerleon (1980) by Nijinsky | 21 | 29 | £297,856 |
| Efisio (1982) by Formidable | 22 | 45 | £277,852 |
| Risk Me (1984) by Sharpo | 15 | 30 | £272,559 |
| Fairy King (1982) by Northern Dancer | 14 | 22 | £272,072 |
| Green Desert (1983) by Danzig | 32 | 51 | £262,844 |

### WINNING FLAT JOCKEYS 1993

| | 1st | 2nd | 3rd | Unpl. | Total mts |
|---|---|---|---|---|---|
| Pat Eddery | 169 | 131 | 83 | 430 | 813 |
| Kevin Darley | 136 | 128 | 105 | 430 | 799 |
| Frankie Dettori | 135 | 114 | 114 | 482 | 845 |
| Willie Carson | 115 | 93 | 120 | 509 | 837 |
| George Duffield | 114 | 91 | 98 | 450 | 753 |
| Michael Roberts | 114 | 96 | 109 | 396 | 715 |
| John Reid | 108 | 108 | 70 | 478 | 764 |
| Richard Quinn | 107 | 106 | 89 | 511 | 813 |
| John Carroll | 92 | 74 | 74 | 379 | 619 |
| Walter Swinburn | 92 | 77 | 77 | 319 | 565 |

### WINNING NATIONAL HUNT JOCKEYS 1993–4

| | 1st | 2nd | 3rd | Unpl. | Total mts |
|---|---|---|---|---|---|
| Richard Dunwoody | 198 | 144 | 117 | 431 | 890 |
| Adrian Maguire | 194 | 175 | 112 | 435 | 916 |
| Jamie Osborne | 105 | 75 | 54 | 262 | 496 |
| Norman Williamson | 104 | 103 | 65 | 309 | 581 |
| Peter Niven | 89 | 70 | 45 | 205 | 409 |
| Mick Fitzgerald | 67 | 53 | 73 | 361 | 554 |
| Graham McCourt | 65 | 58 | 49 | 225 | 397 |
| Declan Murphy | 58 | 52 | 51 | 211 | 372 |
| David Bridgwater | 58 | 40 | 41 | 260 | 399 |
| Lorcan Wyer | 48 | 36 | 42 | 139 | 265 |

The above statistics are the copyright of *The Sporting Life*

### RESULTS

#### CESAREWITCH
(1839) Newmarket, 2 miles and about 2 f

| 1990 | Trainglot (3y), (7st 12lb), W. Carson |
|---|---|
| 1991 | Go South (7y), (7st 11lb), N. Carlisle |
| 1992 | Vintage Crop (5y), (9st 6lb), W. Swinburn |
| 1993 | Aahsaylad (7y), (8st 12lb), J. Williams |

#### CHAMPION STAKES
(1877) Newmarket, 1 mile, 2 f

| 1990 | In the Grove (3y), (8st 9lb), S. Cauthen |
|---|---|
| 1991 | Tel Quel (3y), (8st 12lb), A. Fabre |
| 1992 | Rodrigo de Triano (3y), (8st 12lb), L. Piggott |
| 1993 | Hatoof (4y), (9st), W. Swinburn |

#### *HENNESSY GOLD CUP
(1957) Newbury, 3 miles and about 2½ f

| 1990 | Arctic Call (7y), (11st), J. Osborne |
|---|---|
| 1991 | Chatham (7y), (10st 6lb), P. Scudamore |
| 1992 | Sibton Abbey (7y), (10st), A. Maguire |
| 1993 | Cogent (9y), (10st 8lb), D. Fortt |

*National Hunt

## THE CLASSICS

### ONE THOUSAND GUINEAS

(1814) Rowley Mile, Newmarket, for three-year-old fillies

| Year | Winner | Betting | Owner | Jockey | Trainer | No. of Runners |
|------|--------|---------|-------|--------|---------|----------------|
| 1991 | Shadayid | 4–6 | H. Al-Maktoum | W. Carson | J. Dunlop | 14 |
| 1992 | Hatoof | 5–1 | M. Al-Maktoum | W. Swinburn | C. Head | 14 |
| 1993 | Sayyedati | 4–1 | Mohamed Obaida | W. Swinburn | C. Brittain | 12 |
| 1994 | Las Meninas | 12–1 | R. Sangster | J. Reid | T. Stack | 15 |

### TWO THOUSAND GUINEAS

(1809) Rowley Mile, Newmarket, for three year olds

| Year | Winner | Betting | Owner | Jockey | Trainer | No. of Runners |
|------|--------|---------|-------|--------|---------|----------------|
| 1991 | Mystiko | 13–2 | Lady Beaverbrook | M. Roberts | C. Brittain | 14 |
| 1992 | Rodrigo de Triano | 6–1 | R. Sangster | L. Piggott | P. Chapple-Hyam | 16 |
| 1993 | Zafonic | 5–6 | K. Abdulla | P. Eddery | A. Fabre | 14 |
| 1994 | Mister Baileys | 16–1 | P. Venner | J. Weaver | M. Johnston | 23 |

Record time: 1 minute 35.84 seconds, 1990

### THE DERBY

(1780) Epsom, 1 mile and about 4 f, for three year olds

The first winner was Sir Charles Bunbury's Diomed in 1780. The owners with the record number of winners are Lord Egremont, who won in 1782, 1804, 1805, 1807, 1826 (also won five Oaks); and the late Aga Khan, who won in 1930, 1935, 1936, 1948, 1952 (also won two Oaks). Other winning owners are: Duke of Grafton (1802, 1809, 1810, 1815); Mr J. Bowes (1835, 1843, 1852, 1853); Sir J. Hawley (1851, 1858, 1859, 1868); the 1st Duke of Westminster (1880, 1882, 1886, 1899); and Sir Victor Sassoon (1953, 1957, 1958, 1960).

Record times are: 2 min. 33.80 sec. by Mahmoud in 1936; 2 min. 33.84 sec. by Kahyasi in 1988; 2 min. 33.9 sec. by Reference Point in 1987.

The Derby was run at Newmarket from 1915–18 and from 1940–5.

| Year | Winner | Betting | Owner | Jockey | Trainer | No. of Runners |
|------|--------|---------|-------|--------|---------|----------------|
| 1991 | Generous | 9–1 | Prince Fahd Salman | A. Munro | P. Cole | 13 |
| 1992 | Dr Devious | 8–1 | S. Craig | J. Reid | P. Chapple-Hyam | 18 |
| 1993 | Commander In Chief | 15–2 | K. Abdulla | M. Kinane | H. Cecil | 16 |
| 1994 | Erhaab | 7–2 | H. Al-Maktoum | W. Carson | J. Dunlop | 25 |

### THE OAKS

(1779) Epsom, 1 mile and about 4 f, for three year old fillies

| Year | Winner | Betting | Owner | Jockey | Trainer | No. of Runners |
|------|--------|---------|-------|--------|---------|----------------|
| 1991 | Jet Ski Lady | 50–1 | J. Dunlop | C. Roche | J. Bolger | 9 |
| 1992 | User Friendly | 5–1 | W. Gredley | G. Duffield | C. Brittain | 7 |
| 1993 | Intrepidity | 5–1 | Sheikh Mohammed | M. Roberts | A. Fabre | 14 |
| 1994 | Balanchine | 6–1 | M. Al-Maktoum | F. Dettori | H. Ibrahim | 10 |

### ST LEGER

(1776) Doncaster, 1 mile and about 6 f, for three year olds

| Year | Winner | Betting | Owner | Jockey | Trainer | No. of Runners |
|------|--------|---------|-------|--------|---------|----------------|
| 1991 | Toulon | 5–2 | K. Abdulla | P. Eddery | A. Fabre | 10 |
| 1992 | User Friendly | 7–4 | W. Gredley | G. Duffield | C. Brittain | 8 |
| 1993 | Bob's Return | 3–1 | Mrs J. Smith | P. Robinson | M. Tompkins | 9 |
| 1994 | Moonax | 40–1 | Sheikh Mohammed | P. Eddery | B. Hills | 8 |

*KING GEORGE VI CHASE
(1937) Kempton, about 3 miles

| | | |
|---|---|---|
| 1990 | Desert Orchid (11y), (11st 10lb), R. Dunwoody |
| 1991 | The Fellow (6y), (11st 10lb), A. Kondrat |
| 1992 | The Fellow (7y), (11st 10lb), A. Kondrat |
| 1993 | Barton Bank (7y), (11st 10lb), A. Maguire |

*CHAMPION HURDLE
(1927) Cheltenham, 2 miles and about ½ f

| | |
|---|---|
| 1991 | Morley Street (7y), (12st), J. Frost |
| 1992 | Royal Gait (9y), (12st), G. McCourt |
| 1993 | Granville Again (7y), (12st), P. Scudamore |
| 1994 | Flakey Dove (8y), (11st 9lb), M. Dwyer |

*QUEEN MOTHER CHAMPION CHASE
(1959) Cheltenham, about 2 miles

| | |
|---|---|
| 1991 | Katabatic (8y), (12st), S. McNeill |
| 1992 | Remittance Man (8y), (12st), J. Osborne |
| 1993 | Deep Sensation (8y), (12st), D. Murphy |
| 1994 | Viking Flagship (7y), (12st), A. Maguire |

*CHELTENHAM GOLD CUP
(1924) 3 miles and about 2½ f

| | |
|---|---|
| 1991 | Garrison Savannah (8y), (12st), M. Pitman |
| 1992 | Cool Ground (10y), (12st), A. Maguire |
| 1993 | Jodami (8y), (12st), M. Dwyer |
| 1994 | The Fellow (9y), (12st), A. Kondrat |

LINCOLN HANDICAP
(1965) Doncaster, 1 mile

| | |
|---|---|
| 1991 | Amenable (6y), (8st 1lb), A. Greaves |
| 1992 | High Low (4y), (8st), J. Quinn |
| 1993 | High Premium (5y), (8st 8lb), K. Fallon |
| 1994 | Our Rita (5y), (8st 5lb), D. Holland |

*GRAND NATIONAL
(1837) Liverpool, 4 miles and about 4 f

| | |
|---|---|
| 1991 | Seagram (11y), (10st 6lb), N. Hawke |
| 1992 | Party Politics (8y), (10st 7lb), C. Llewellyn |
| 1993 | Race declared void. Esha Ness (J. White) first past post |
| 1994 | Miinnehoma (11y), (10st 8lb), R. Dunwoody |

Record times: 8 minutes 47.8 seconds by Mr Frisk in 1990;
9 minutes 1.9 seconds by Red Rum in 1973

*WHITBREAD GOLD CUP
(1957) Sandown, 3 miles and about 5 f

| | |
|---|---|
| †1991 | Docklands Express (9y), (10st 13lb), A. Tory |
| 1992 | Topsham Bay (9y), (10st), H. Davies |
| 1993 | Topsham Bay (10y), (10st), R. Dunwoody |
| 1994 | Ushers Island (8y), (10st), C. Swan |

† Cahervillahow finished first but after an objection and a
stewards' inquiry was placed second

JOCKEY CLUB STAKES
(1894) Newmarket, 1½ miles

| | |
|---|---|
| 1991 | Rock Hopper (4y), (8st 7lb), P. Eddery |
| 1992 | Sapience (6y), (8st 12lb), R Cochrane |
| 1993 | Zinaad (4y), (8st 9lb), W. Swinburn |
| 1994 | Silver Wisp (5y), (8st 9lb), M. Hills |

KENTUCKY DERBY
(1875) Louisville, Kentucky, 1¼ miles

| | |
|---|---|
| 1991 | Strike the Gold, C. Antley |
| 1992 | Lil E Tee, P. Day |
| 1993 | Sea Hero, J. Bailey |
| 1994 | Go for Gin, C. McCarron |

*National Hunt

PRIX DU JOCKEY CLUB
(1836) Chantilly, 1½ miles

| | |
|---|---|
| 1991 | Suave Dancer (9st 2lb), C. Asmussen |
| 1992 | Polytain (9st 2lb), L. Dettori |
| 1993 | Hernando (9st 2lb), C. Asmussen |
| 1994 | Celtic Arms (9st 2lb), G. Mossé |

ASCOT GOLD CUP
(1807) Ascot, 2 miles and about 4 f

| | |
|---|---|
| 1991 | Indian Queen (6y), (8st 13lb), W. Swinburn |
| 1992 | Drum Taps (6y), (9st 2lb), L. Dettori |
| 1993 | Drum Taps (7y), (9st 2lb), L. Dettori |
| 1994 | Arcadian Heights (6y), (9st 2lb), M. Hills |

IRISH SWEEPS DERBY
(1866) Curragh, 1½ miles, for three year olds

| | |
|---|---|
| 1991 | Generous (9st), A. Munro |
| 1992 | St Jovite (9st), C. Roche |
| 1993 | Commander In Chief (9st), P. Eddery |
| 1994 | Balanchine (8st 11lb), F. Dettori |

ECLIPSE STAKES
(1886) Sandown, 1 mile and about 2 f

| | |
|---|---|
| 1991 | Environment Friend (3y), (8st 10lb), G. Duffield |
| 1992 | Kooyonga (4y), (9st 4lb), W. O'Connor |
| 1993 | Opera House (5y), (9st 7lb), M. Kinane |
| 1994 | Ezzoud (5y), (9st 7lb), W. Swinburn |

KING GEORGE VI AND QUEEN ELIZABETH DIAMOND
STAKES
(1952) Ascot, 1 mile and about 4 f

| | |
|---|---|
| 1991 | Generous (3y), (8st 9lb), A. Munro |
| 1992 | St Jovite (3y), (8st 9lb), S. Craine |
| 1993 | Opera House (5y), (9st 7lb), M. Stoute |
| 1994 | King's Theatre (3y), (8st 9lb), M. Kinane |

GOODWOOD CUP
(1812) Goodwood, about 2 miles

| | |
|---|---|
| 1991 | Further Flight (5y), (9st), M. Hills |
| 1992 | Further Flight (6y), (9st 5lb), M. Hills |
| 1993 | Sonus (4y), (9st 3lb), P. Eddery |
| 1994 | Tioman Island (4y), (9st 5lb), T. Quinn |

CAMBRIDGESHIRE HANDICAP
(1839) Newmarket, 1 mile

| | |
|---|---|
| 1991 | Mellottie (6y), (9st 1lb), J. Lowe |
| 1992 | Rambo's Hall (7y), (9st 3lb), D. McKeown |
| 1993 | Penny Drops (4y), (7st 13lb), D. Harrison |
| 1994 | Halling (3y), (8st 8lb), L. Dettori |

PRIX DE L'ARC DE TRIOMPHE
(1920) Longchamp, 1½ miles

| | |
|---|---|
| 1991 | Suave Dancer (3y), (8st 11lb), C. Asmussen |
| 1992 | Subotica (4y), (9st 4lb), T. Jarnet |
| 1993 | Urban Sea (4y), (9st 1lb), E. Saint-Martin |
| 1994 | Carnegie (3y), (8st 11lb), T. Jarnet |

---

## ICE HOCKEY

*World Championship final 1994:* Canada 1, Finland 1.
   Canada won 3–2 on penalties
*British Championship final 1994:* Cardiff Devils beat
   Sheffield Steelers 12–1
*League Championship:*
   *Premier Division:* Cardiff Devils
   *First Division:* Milton Keynes Kings
*Stanley Cup final 1994:* New York Rangers beat Vancouver
   Kanucks 4–3 (best of 7 final)

*Women's World Championship final 1994:* Canada beat USA 6–3

---

## ICE SKATING

---

BRITISH CHAMPIONSHIPS 1993
Basingstoke, December

*Men:* Steven Cousins
*Women:* Stephanie Main
*Pairs:* Dana Mednick and Jason Briggs
*Ice Dance* (Sheffield, January 1994): Jayne Torvill and Christopher Dean

EUROPEAN CHAMPIONSHIPS 1994
Copenhagen, January

*Men:* Viktor Petrenko (Ukraine)
*Women:* Surya Bonaly (France)
*Pairs:* Katya Gordeeva and Sergei Grinkov (Russia)
*Ice Dance:* Jayne Torvill and Christopher Dean (GB)

WORLD CHAMPIONSHIPS 1994
Chiba, Japan, March

*Men:* Elvis Stojko (Canada)
*Women:* Yuka Sato (Japan)
*Pairs:* Evgenia Shiskova and Vadim Naumov (Russia)
*Ice Dance:* Oksana Gritschuk and Evgeny Platov (Russia)

---

## JUDO

---

WORLD CHAMPIONSHIPS 1993
Ontario, Canada, September–October

MEN

*Heavyweight* (over 95 kg): David Douillet (France)
*Light-heavyweight* (95 kg): Antal Kovacs (Hungary)
*Middleweight* (86 kg): Yoshio Nakamura (Japan)
*Light-middleweight* (78 kg): Ki-Young Chun (S. Korea)
*Lightweight* (71 kg): Hoon Chung (S. Korea)
*Featherweight* (65 kg): Yukimasa Nakamura (Japan)
*Bantamweight* (60 kg): Ryuki Sonoda (Japan)
*Openweight:* Rafael Kubacki (Poland)

WOMEN

*Heavyweight* (over 72 kg): Johanna Hagn (Germany)
*Light-heavyweight* (72 kg): Chun-Hui Leng (China)
*Middleweight* (66 kg): Min-Sun Cho (S. Korea)
*Light-middleweight* (61 kg): Gella van de Cayeve (Belgium)
*Lightweight* (56 kg): Nicola Fairbrother (GB)
*Featherweight* (52 kg): Rodriguez Verdecia (Cuba)
*Bantamweight* (48 kg): Ryoko Tamura (Japan)
*Openweight:* Beata Maksymow (Poland)

BRITISH NATIONAL CHAMPIONSHIPS 1993
Crystal Palace, December

MEN

*Heavyweight* (over 95 kg): William Etherington
*Light-heavyweight* (95 kg): Lloyd Alexander
*Middleweight* (86 kg): Fitzroy Davis
*Light-middleweight* (78 kg): William Cusack
*Lightweight* (71 kg): Danny Kingston
*Featherweight* (65 kg): Simon Moss
*Bantamweight* (60 kg): Jamie Johnson

WOMEN

*Heavyweight* (over 72 kg): Michelle Rogers
*Light-heavyweight* (72 kg): Kate Howey

*Middleweight* (66 kg): Chloe Cowen
*Light-middleweight* (61 kg): Kirstie Weir
*Lightweight* (56 kg): Cheryl Peel
*Featherweight* (52 kg): Debbie Allan
*Bantamweight* (48 kg): Joyce Heron

---

## LAWN TENNIS

---

MAJOR CHAMPIONSHIPS 1994

AUSTRALIAN OPEN CHAMPIONSHIPS (Melbourne)

*Men's Singles:* Pete Sampras (USA) beat Todd Martin (USA) 7–6, 6–4, 6–4
*Women's Singles:* Steffi Graf (Germany) beat Arantxa Sánchez Vicario (Spain) 6–0, 6–2
*Men's Doubles:* Jacco Eltingh and Paul Haarhuis (Netherlands) beat Byron Black (Zimbabwe) and Jonathan Stark (USA) 6–7, 6–3, 6–4, 6–3
*Women's Doubles:* Gigi Fernandez (USA) and Natalia Zvereva (Belarus) beat Patsy Fendick and Meredith McGrath (USA) 6–3, 4–6, 6–4
*Mixed Doubles:* Larisa Neiland (Latvia) and Andrei Olkhovsky (Russia) beat Natalya Medvedeva (Ukraine) and Paul Haarhuis (Netherlands) 6–1, Haarhuis ret.

FRENCH OPEN CHAMPIONSHIPS (Paris)

*Men's Singles:* Sergi Bruguera (Spain) beat Alberto Berasategui (Spain) 6–3, 7–5, 2–6, 6–1
*Women's Singles:* Arantxa Sánchez Vicario (Spain) beat Mary Pierce (France) 6–4, 6–4
*Men's Doubles:* Byron Black (Zimbabwe) and Jonathan Stark (USA) beat Jan Apell and Jonas Bjorkman (Sweden) 6–4, 7–6
*Women's Doubles:* Gigi Fernandez (USA) and Natalya Zvereva (Belarus) beat Lindsay Davenport and Lisa Raymond (USA) 6–2, 6–2
*Mixed Doubles:* Kristie Boogert and Menno Oosting (Netherlands) beat Larissa Neiland (Latvia) and Andrei Olhovskiy (Russia) 7–5, 3–6, 7–5

ALL ENGLAND CHAMPIONSHIPS (Wimbledon)

*Men's Singles:* Pete Sampras (USA) beat Goran Ivanisevic (Croatia) 7–6, 7–6, 6–0
*Women's Singles:* Conchita Martinez (Spain) beat Martina Navratilova (USA) 6–4, 3–6, 6–3
*Men's Doubles:* Todd Woodbridge and Mark Woodforde (Australia) beat Grant Connell (Canada) and Patrick Galbraith (USA) 7–6, 6–3, 6–1
*Women's Doubles:* Gigi Fernandez (USA) and Natalya Zvereva (Belarus) beat Jana Novotna (Czech Republic) and Arantxa Sánchez Vicario (Spain) 6–4, 6–1
*Mixed Doubles:* Helena Sukova (Czech Republic) and Todd Woodbridge (Australia) beat Lori McNeil and T. J. Middleton (USA) 3–6, 7–5, 6–3

US OPEN CHAMPIONSHIPS (New York)

*Men's Singles:* Andre Agassi (USA) beat Michael Stich (Germany) 6–1, 7–6, 7–5
*Women's Singles:* Arantxa Sánchez Vicario (Spain) beat Steffi Graf (Germany) 1–6, 7–6, 6–4
*Men's Doubles:* Jacco Eltingh and Paul Haarhuis (Netherlands) beat Todd Woodbridge and Mark Woodforde (Australia) 6–3, 7–6
*Women's Doubles:* Arantxa Sánchez Vicario (Spain) and Jana Novotna (Czech Republic) beat Katerina Maleeva (Bulgaria) and Robin White (USA) 6–3, 6–3

*Mixed Doubles:* Elna Reinach (S. Africa) and Patrick Galbraith (USA) beat Jana Novotna (Czech Republic) and Todd Woodbridge (Australia) 6–2, 6–4

*The Grand Slam Cup 1993:* Petr Korda (Czech Republic) beat Michael Stich (Germany) 2–6, 6–4, 7–6, 2–6, 11–9

## TEAM CHAMPIONSHIPS

*Davis Cup final 1993:* Germany beat Australia 4–1
*Federation Cup final 1994:* Spain beat USA 3–0
*LTA County Cup 1994:*
 *Men:* Devon
 *Women:* Essex

## NATIONAL CHAMPIONSHIPS 1993

*Men's Singles:* Jeremy Bates beat Chris Bailey 6–3, 6–3
*Women's Singles:* Clare Wood beat Karen Cross 7–5, 6–0
*Men's Doubles:* Jeremy Bates and Mark Petchey beat Andrew Foster and Miles Maclagan 7–5, 6–7, 13–11
*Women's Doubles:* Shirley-Ann Siddall and Mandy Wainwright beat Jo Durie and Clare Wood 6–3, 0–6, 6–3

*San Marino* (Imola): Michael Schumacher (Germany), Benetton Ford
*Monaco:* Michael Schumacher (Germany), Benetton Ford
*Spanish* (Barcelona): Damon Hill (GB), Williams Renault
*Canadian* (Montreal): Michael Schumacher (Germany), Benetton Ford
*French* (Magny-Cours): Michael Schumacher (Germany), Benetton Ford
*British* (Silverstone): Damon Hill (GB), Williams Renault
*German* (Hockenheim): Gerhard Berger (Austria), Ferrari
*Hungarian* (Budapest): Michael Schumacher (Germany), Benetton Ford
*Belgian* (Spa-Francorchamps): Damon Hill (GB), Williams Renault
*Italian* (Monza): Damon Hill (GB), Williams Renault
*Portuguese* (Estoril): Damon Hill (GB), Williams Renault

*Indianapolis 500 1994:* Al Unser jun. (USA), Penske Mercedes
*Le Mans 24-Hour Race 1994:* Hurley Haywood (USA), Yannick Dalmas (France) and Mauro Baldi (Italy), Porsche

## MOTOR CYCLING

### 500 CC GRAND PRIX 1994
*Australian* (Sydney): John Kocinski (USA), Cagiva
*Malaysian* (Kuala Lumpur): Michael Doohan (Australia), Honda
*Japanese* (Suzuka): Kevin Schwantz (USA), Suzuki
*Spanish* (Jerez): Michael Doohan (Australia), Honda
*Austrian* (Salzburg): Michael Doohan (Australia), Honda
*German* (Hockenheim): Michael Doohan (Australia), Honda
*Dutch* (Assen): Michael Doohan (Australia), Honda
*Italian* (Mugello): Michael Doohan (Australia), Honda
*French* (Le Mans): Michael Doohan (Australia), Honda
*British* (Donington Park): Kevin Schwantz (USA), Suzuki
*Czech Republic* (Brno): Michael Doohan (Australia), Honda
*US* (Laguna Seca): Luca Cadalora (Italy), Yamaha
*Argentinian* (Buenos Aires): Michael Doohan (Australia), Honda

*Senior Manx Grand Prix:* Brian Venables (Honda)
*Senior TT, Isle of Man:* Steve Hislop (Honda)
*Junior TT, Isle of Man:* Joey Dunlop (Honda)

## MOTOR RACING

### FORMULA ONE GRAND PRIX 1993
*Japanese* (Suzuka): Ayrton Senna (Brazil), McLaren Ford
*Australian* (Adelaide): Ayrton Senna (Brazil), McLaren Ford
*Drivers' World Championship 1993:* 1. Alain Prost (France), Williams Renault, 99 pts; 2. Ayrton Senna (Brazil), McLaren Ford, 73 pts; 3. Damon Hill (GB), Williams Renault, 69 pts
*Constructors' World Championship 1993:* 1. Williams Renault, 168 pts; 2. McLaren Ford, 84 pts; 3. Benetton Ford, 72 pts

### FORMULA ONE GRAND PRIX 1994
*Brazilian* (Sao Paulo): Michael Schumacher (Germany), Benetton Ford
*Pacific* (Aida, Japan): Michael Schumacher (Germany), Benetton Ford

## MOTOR RALLYING

### 1993
*San Remo Rally:* Franco Cunico (Italy), Ford Escort
*Catalonia Rally:* François Delecour (France), Ford Escort
*RAC Rally:* Juha Kankkunen (Finland), Toyota Celica
*Drivers' World Championship 1993:* Juha Kankkunen (Finland), Toyota Celica, 135 pts
*Manufacturers' World Championship 1993:* Toyota, 157 pts
*Hong Kong-Beijing Rally:* Ari Vatanen (Finland), Subaru

### 1994
*Monte Carlo Rally:* François Delecour (France), Ford Escort
*Rally of Portugal:* Juha Kankkunen (Finland), Toyota Celica
*Safari Rally:* Ian Duncan (Kenya), Toyota
*Corsican Rally:* Didier Auriol (France), Toyota Celica
*Acropolis Rally:* Carlos Sainz (Spain), Subaru Impreza
*Argentine Rally:* Didier Auriol (France), Toyota Celica
*New Zealand Rally:* Colin McRae (GB), Subaru Impreza
*1,000 Lakes Rally:* Tommi Makinen (Finland), Ford Escort
*Australian Rally:* Colin McRae (GB), Subaru Impreza
*Paris-Dakar-Paris Rally:* Pierre Lartigue (France), Citroën

## NETBALL

### TEST MATCHES 1993

|  |  |  |
|---|---|---|
| 27 Oct | Birmingham | England 40, Trinidad and Tobago 35 |
| 30 Oct | Sheffield | England 40, Trinidad and Tobago 36 |
| 3 Nov | Gateshead | England 50, Trinidad and Tobago 37 |
| 6 Nov | Wembley | England 48, Trinidad and Tobago 36 |
| 10 Nov | Belfast | N. Ireland 51, Trinidad and Tobago 64 |

### INTERNATIONALS 1994

|  |  |  |
|---|---|---|
| 15 Jan | Dublin | Rep. of Ireland 20, Wales 55 |
| 5 Feb | Aberdeen | Scotland 21, England 50 |
| | Cardiff | Wales 58, N. Ireland 15 |
| 19 Feb | Hyndburn | England 60, N. Ireland 34 |
| | East Kilbride | Scotland 65, Rep. of Ireland 15 |
| 19 Mar | Guildford | England 78, Rep. of Ireland 22 |
| | Cardiff | Wales 69, Scotland 32 |

| | | |
|---|---|---|
| 22 Mar | Cardiff | Wales 33, Rep. of Ireland 7 |
| | | Wales 28, Scotland 15 |
| | | Rep. of Ireland 7, Scotland 32 |
| 26 Mar | Portsmouth | England 48, Wales 34 |
| | Belfast | N. Ireland 57, Rep. of Ireland 30 |
| 15 Apr | Belfast | N. Ireland 55, Scotland 37 |

*English Counties League Champions:* Essex Metropolitan
*Inter-County Championship final 1994:* Essex Metropolitan beat Surrey 16–10
*National Clubs League Champions:* New Cambell (Essex Metropolitan)
*National Clubs' Championship final 1994:* Oakwood beat Leeds Athletic 44–37

## POLO

*Prince of Wales's Trophy final 1994:* Cowdray beat Maple Leafs 10–9
*Queen's Cup final 1994:* Black Bears beat Ellerston White 12–11
*Warwickshire Cup final 1994:* Black Bears beat Ellerston White 11–10 a.e.t.
*Gold Cup final 1994* (British Open): Ellerston Black beat Pegasus 13–11
*Coronation Cup final 1994:* England beat South Africa 11–1
*Prince Philip Trophy 1994:* Ellerston Black beat Palmera 12–8
*Varsity Match 1993:* Oxford beat Cambridge 10–2
*Varsity Match 1994:* Cambridge beat Oxford 2–1

## RACKETS

*World Singles Champion:* James Male
*World Doubles Championship 1993:* Shannon Hazell and Neil Smith beat James Male and John Prenn 166–160 in two-leg challenge
*Professional Singles Championship final 1994:* Peter Brake beat Norwood Cripps 3–0
*British Open Singles Championship final 1994:* Neil Smith beat Rupert Owen-Browne 4–3
*British Open Doubles Championship final 1994:* Willie Boone and Tim Cockroft beat Rupert Owen-Browne and John Prenn 4–1
*Amateur Singles Championship final 1993:* Willie Boone beat John Prenn 3–1
*Amateur Doubles Championship final 1994:* Willie Boone and Tim Cockroft beat Rupert Owen-Browne and John Prenn 4–2
*National League final 1994:* Manchester beat Old Etonians 4–2
*Noel Bruce Cup final 1993:* Eton I (Willie Boone and Mark Hue Williams) beat Marlborough I (Alister Robinson and Guy Barker) 4–2
*Public Schools' Singles Championship final 1993:* Richard Carter (Rugby) beat Edward Behn (Radley) 3–0
*Public Schools' Doubles Championship final 1994:* Rugby beat Haileybury 4–2
*Varsity Match 1994:* Cambridge beat Oxford 2–1

## REAL TENNIS

*World Singles Championship 1994:* Robert Fahey (Australia) beat Wayne Davies (Australia) 9–5

*Professional Singles Championship final 1994:* Lachie Deuchar (Australia) beat Mark Devine (GB) 3–0
*Professional Doubles Championship final 1994:* Lachie Deuchar and Robert Fahey (Australia) beat Chris Bray and Mike Gooding (GB) 3–1
*British Open Singles Championship final 1993:* Julian Snow (GB) beat Robert Fahey (Australia) (Fahey retired injured at 1–0)
*British Open Doubles Championship final 1993:* Mike Gooding and Chris Bray beat Julian Snow and Nick Wood 3–0
*Amateur Singles Championship final 1994:* Julian Snow beat Nigel Pendrigh 3–0
*Amateur Doubles Championship final 1994:* James Acheson-Gray and Nigel Pendrigh beat Mike McMurrugh and Julian Snow 3–2
*Henry Leaf Cup final 1994:* Radley beat Charterhouse I 2–0
*Varsity Match 1994:* Oxford beat Cambridge 6–0
*Women's British Open Singles Championship final 1994:* Alex Garside beat Sally Jones 2–0
*Women's British Open Doubles Championship final 1994:* Fiona Deuchar and Mandy Happell (Australia) won on a walk-over against Sally Jones and Alex Garside (GB)

## ROAD WALKING

MEN'S NATIONAL 50 KM WALK
Horsham, 16 October 1993
*Individual:* Les Morton (Sheffield), 4 hr. 3 min. 55 sec.
*Team:* Leicester, 25 pts

WOMEN'S NATIONAL 20 KM WALK
Horsham, 16 October 1993
*Individual:* Elaine Callanin (Solihull), 1 hr. 45 min. 11 sec.
*Team:* Sheffield, 15 pts

MEN'S BRITISH 20 KM WALK
Stoneleigh, 19 March 1994
*Individual:* Darrell Stone (Steyning), 1 hr. 27 min. 24 sec.
*Team:* Steyning, 38 pts

WOMEN'S NATIONAL 10 KM WALK
Stoneleigh, 19 March 1994
*Individual:* Lisa Langford (Wolverhampton), 47 min. 7 sec.
*Team:* Manx, 24 pts

MEN'S BRITISH 30 KM WALK
Horsham, 16 April 1994
*Individual:* Chris Maddocks (Plymouth), 2 hr. 22 min. 45 sec.
*Team:* Leicester, 22 pts

MEN'S NATIONAL 20 KM WALK
Birmingham, 21 May 1994
*Individual:* Chris Cheeseman (Surrey), 1 hr. 29 min. 11 sec.
*Team:* Leicester, 38 pts

WOMEN'S NATIONAL 5 KM WALK
Birmingham, 21 May 1994
*Individual:* Melanie Wright (Nuneaton), 24 min. 27 sec.
*Team:* Dudley & Stourbridge, 20 pts

MEN'S NATIONAL 10 MILES WALK
Victoria Park, 9 July 1994
*Individual:* Chris Cheeseman (Surrey), 1 hr. 13 min. 17 sec.
*Team:* Leicester, 44 pts

MEN'S NATIONAL 50 KM WALK
Chesterfield, 3 September 1994
*Individual:* Les Morton (Sheffield), 4 hr. 32 min. 25 sec.
*Team:* Sheffield, 23 pts

# ROWING

## WORLD CHAMPIONSHIPS 1994
Indianapolis, USA, September
### MEN

*Coxed pairs:* Croatia
*Coxless pairs:* Great Britain
*Coxed fours:* Romania
*Coxless fours:* Italy
*Single sculls:* Andre Wilms (Germany)
*Double sculls:* Norway
*Quad sculls:* Italy
*Eights:* USA

### WOMEN

*Coxless pairs:* France
*Coxless fours:* Holland
*Single sculls:* Trine Hansen (Denmark)
*Double sculls:* New Zealand
*Quad sculls:* Germany
*Eights:* Germany

## NATIONAL CHAMPIONSHIPS 1994
Nottingham, July
### MEN

*Coxed pairs:* Thames Tradesmen
*Coxless pairs:* Cambridge
*Coxed fours:* London
*Coxless fours:* Thames
*Single sculls:* Duncan Nicoll (Upper Thames)
*Double sculls:* Molesey
*Quad sculls:* Tideway Scullers
*Eights:* London

### WOMEN

*Coxless pairs:* Edinburgh University
*Coxed fours:* Bedford
*Coxless fours:* Thames Tradesmen/University of London
*Single sculls:* Sue Appelboon (Mortlake)
*Double sculls:* Tideway Scullers/Henley
*Quad sculls:* Grosvenor/Royal Chester/Nottingham and
   Union/Tideway Scullers
*Eights:* Cambridge University/Capitol/Marlow/
   Nottinghamshire County/Thames/Thames Tradesmen/
   University of Bristol

## THE 140th UNIVERSITY BOAT RACE
Putney–Mortlake, 4 miles 1 f, 180 yd, 26 March 1994
Cambridge beat Oxford by 6½ lengths; 18 min., 9 sec.
Cambridge have won 71 times, Oxford 68 and there has
been one dead heat. The record time is 16 min., 45 sec.,
rowed by Oxford in 1984

WOMEN'S BOAT RACE 1994 (Henley): Cambridge beat
Oxford by 1 length (6 min. 11 sec.)

## HENLEY ROYAL REGATTA 1994

*Grand Challenge Cup:* Charles River/San Diego (USA) beat
   Compiegne/Encouragement (France) easily
*Ladies' Challenge Plate:* College BC (USA) beat London/
   Nottinghamshire County by ⅔ length
*Thames Challenge Cup:* Brown University (USA) beat Goldie
   by 1½ lengths
*Temple Challenge Cup:* Imperial College London A beat
   Trinity College Dublin by 1¾ lengths

*Princess Elizabeth Challenge Cup:* St Paul's School, Concord
   (USA) beat Atlantic City High School (USA) by 1¾
   lengths
*Stewards' Challenge Cup:* Boulogne/Lyon (France) beat
   London by 1½ lengths
*Prince Philip Challenge Cup:* Nottinghamshire County beat
   Leander by ⅔ length
*Queen Mother Challenge Cup:* 'Treviris'/Bollberg (Germany)
   beat London A easily
*Fawley Challenge Cup:* Windsorian/Maidenhead beat
   Bedford School by ¾ length
*Visitors' Challenge Cup:* Imperial College London beat
   University of London easily
*Wyfold Challenge Cup:* Nottinghamshire County A beat Lea
   by ½ length
*Britannia Challenge Cup:* Belfast beat University of London
   A by 1 length
*Silver Goblets and Nickalls' Challenge Cup:* Steve Redgrave
   and Matthew Pinsent (Leander) beat Jaak van Driessche
   and Luc Goiris (Belgium) by 1¾ lengths
*Double Sculls Challenge Cup:* Gabor Mitring and Zsolt Dani
   (Hungary) beat Peter Uhrig and Chistian Handle
   (Germany) by 2½ lengths
*Diamond Challenge Sculls:* Xeno Muller (Switzerland) beat
   Martin Hansen (Denmark) by 1¾ lengths
*Women's Single Sculls:* Marnie McBean (Canada) beat
   Kathrin Boron (Germany) easily

## OTHER ROWING EVENTS

*Oxford Torpids 1994:* **Men,** Oriel; *Women,* Somerville
*Cambridge Lents 1994:* **Men,** Downing; *Women,* Emmanuel
*Oxford Summer Eights 1994:* **Men,** Oriel; *Women,* Osler
   House
*Cambridge Mays 1994:* **Men,** Trinity Hall; *Women,* Jesus
*Head of the River 1994:* **Men,** Munster I (Germany); *Women,*
   Thames A
*Doggett's Coat and Badge 1994*: Christian Bullas
   (Gravesend)
*Wingfield Sculls 1994:* Peter Haining (Auriol Kensington)

# RUGBY FIVES

*National Singles Championship final 1993:* Wayne Enstone
   beat Neil Roberts 15–7, 15–6
*National Doubles Championship final 1994:* Wayne Enstone
   and Neil Roberts beat Ian Fuller and David Hebden
   15–8, 15–0
*Scottish Open Singles Championship final 1994:* Wayne
   Enstone beat Neil Roberts 11–8, 11–6
*Women's National Singles Championship final 1993:* Cherry
   Wood beat Mary Love 15–1, 15–1
*National Schools' Singles Championships final 1994:* James
   Edington (Sedbergh) beat Brian Elphick (Bradfield)
   11–4, 6–11, 11–3
*National Schools' Doubles Championships final 1994:* Nick
   McIver and Nick Hyde (Sherborne) beat Tom
   Barraclough and James Edington (Sedbergh) 11–3, 11–1
*Varsity Match 1994:* Oxford beat Cambridge 257–176

# RUGBY LEAGUE

*World Sevens final 1993* (Sydney): Manly-Warringah beat St
   George 44–12

*World Club Challenge 1994* (Brisbane): Wigan beat
Brisbane Broncos 20–14

INTERNATIONAL MATCHES
1993
3 Oct    Swansea    Wales 19, New Zealand 24

1994
4 March    Cardiff    Wales 13, France 12

TEST MATCHES
1993
16 Oct    Wembley    Great Britain 17, New Zealand 0
30 Oct    Wigan    Great Britain 29, New Zealand 12
6 Nov    Headingley    Great Britain 29, New Zealand 10
1994
20 March    Carcassonne    France 4, Great Britain 12

DOMESTIC COMPETITIONS
*Challenge Cup final 1994* (Wembley, 30 April): Wigan beat
Leeds 26–16
*Premiership Trophy final 1994* (Old Trafford, 22 May):
Wigan beat Castleford 24–20
*Regal Trophy final 1994* (Headingley, 22 January):
Castleford beat Wigan 33–2
*Second Division Premiership final 1994:* Workington Town
beat London Crusaders 30–22
*Stones Bitter Championship 1994:* Wigan, 46 pts
*Division 2 Championship 1994:* Workington Town, 46 pts
*Varsity Match 1994:* Oxford 22, Cambridge 22

AMATEUR RUGBY LEAGUE
*County Championship:* Yorkshire
*National Inter-League Shield Competitions:*
    *Open Age:* York
*National Cup Competitions:*
    *Open Age:* Saddleworth
    *Under 18:* Leigh Miners
    *Under 16:* Rose Bridge
*National League Premier Division Champions:* Woolston
*National League Challenge Cup:* Heworth

RUGBY UNION

INTERNATIONAL MATCHES
1993
16 Oct    Cardiff    Wales 55, Japan 5
10 Nov    Cardiff    Wales 24, Canada 26
14 Nov    Dublin    Ireland 25, Romania 3
20 Nov    Murrayfield    Scotland 15, New Zealand 51
27 Nov    Twickenham    England 15, New Zealand 9

1994
15 Jan    Cardiff    Wales 29, Scotland 6
         Paris    France 35, Ireland 15
5 Feb    Murrayfield    Scotland 14, England 15
         Dublin    Ireland 15, Wales 17
19 Feb    Twickenham    England 12, Ireland 13
         Cardiff    Wales 24, France 15
5 Mar    Paris    France 14, England 18
         Dublin    Ireland 6, Scotland 6
19 Mar    Twickenham    England 15, Wales 8
         Murrayfield    Scotland 12, France 20
17 May    Lisbon    Portugal 11, Wales 102
21 May    Madrid    Spain 0, Wales 54

4 June    Pretoria    South Africa 15, England 32
         Buenos Aires    Argentina 16, Scotland 15
5 June    Brisbane    Australia 33, Ireland 13
11 June    Cape Town    South Africa 27, England 9
         Buenos Aires    Argentina 19, Scotland 17
         Markham    Canada 19, Wales 33
         Sydney    Australia 32, Ireland 18
18 June    Suva    Fiji 8, Wales 23
22 June    Nukualofa    Tonga 9, Wales 18
26 June    Apia    Western Samoa 34, Wales 9

FIVE NATIONS' CHAMPIONSHIP 1994

|  | P | W | D | L | Pts F | A | Total |
|---|---|---|---|---|---|---|---|
| Wales | 4 | 3 | 0 | 1 | 78 | 51 | 6 |
| England | 4 | 3 | 0 | 1 | 60 | 49 | 6 |
| France | 4 | 2 | 0 | 2 | 84 | 69 | 4 |
| Ireland | 4 | 1 | 1 | 2 | 49 | 70 | 3 |
| Scotland | 4 | 0 | 1 | 3 | 38 | 70 | 1 |

DOMESTIC COMPETITIONS
*English League: Division 1,* Bath, 34 pts; *Division 2,* Sale,
    28 pts; *Division 3,* Coventry, 28 pts; *Division 4,* Clifton,
    34 pts; *Division 5,* Reading, 21 pts (*south*); Rotherham,
    21 pts (*north*)
*County Championship final 1994:* Yorkshire beat Durham
    26–3
*Pilkington Cup final 1994* (Twickenham, 7 May): Bath beat
    Leicester 21–9
*Scottish League: Division 1,* Melrose, 24 pts; *Division 2,*
    Glasgow High/Kelvinside, 26 pts; *Division 3,*
    Gordonians, 21 pts; *Division 4,* Trinity Academicals,
    22 pts; *Division 5,* Duns, 20 pts; *Division 6,* Allan Glen's,
    24 pts; *Division 7,* Annan, 24 pts
*Scottish Cup final 1994:* Boroughmuir beat Dundee 48–18
*Welsh League: Division 1,* Swansea, 40 pts; *Division 2,*
    Treorchy, 41 pts; *Division 3,* Abercynon, 42 pts;
    *Division 4,* Builth Wells, 38 pts
*Welsh Challenge Cup final 1994:* Cardiff beat Llanelli 15–8
*Irish League: Division 1,* Garryowen, 16 pts; *Division 2,*
    Instonians, 16 pts; *Division 3,* UCD, 22 pts; *Division 4,*
    Monkstown, 18 pts
*Ulster Cup final 1994:* Dungannon beat Instonians 14–10
*Hospitals' Cup final 1994:* St Mary's beat Charing Cross/
    Westminster 19–18
*Services Championship 1994:* Army beat Royal Navy 18–6;
    RAF beat Royal Navy 22–12; RAF beat Army 28–22
*Varsity Match 1993:* Oxford beat Cambridge 20–8
*Middlesex Sevens final 1994:* Bath beat Orrell 19–12
*Women's World Cup final 1994:* England beat USA 38–23

SHOOTING

125TH NATIONAL RIFLE ASSOCIATION IMPERIAL
MEETING
Bisley, July 1994
*Queen's Prize:* Martin Millar, 291.34 pts
*Grand Aggregate:* Andrew Luckman, 595.80 pts
*Prince of Wales Prize:* Nick Brasier, 75.13 pts
*St George's Vase:* Stuart Collings, 150.21 pts
*Allcomers Aggregate:* Andrew Luckman, 321.45 pts
*National Trophy:* England, 2,050.259 pts
*Kolapore Cup:* Great Britain, 1,285.169 pts
*Chancellor's Trophy:* Cambridge University, 1,156.131 pts
*Musketeers Cup:* Birmingham University, 591.79 pts
*Vizianagram Trophy:* House of Lords, 677.27 pts

*County Long-Range Championship:* Suffolk, 443.56 pts
*Mackinnon Challenge Cup:* Scotland, 1,146.115 pts
*The Ashburton:* Epsom, 525.44 pts
*The Elcho:* England, 1,720.171 pts
*The Albert:* Stuart Collings, 214.24 pts
*Hopton Challenge Cup:* Stuart Collings, 986.118 pts

CLAY PIGEON SHOOTING 1994

*World Down-the-Line Championship:* Terry Humphreys, 896/900
*World Sporting Championship:* Mick Howells, 75/80
*International Cup (Down-the-Line):* England, 7,355/7,500
*British Open Down-the-Line Championship:* Joe O'Kane, 100/300
*Mackintosh Trophy:* Australia, 7,403/7,500
*British Open Skeet Championship:* Allan Coy, 100*
*British Open Sporting Championship:* George Digweed, 97*
*Coronation Cup:* John Timmins, 384*
*after a shoot-off

---

SNOOKER

---

1993
*Dubai Classic:* Stephen Hendry (Scotland) beat Steve Davis (England) 9–3
*Skoda Grand Prix:* Peter Ebdon (England) beat Ken Doherty (Ireland) 9–6
*UK Professional Championship:* Ronnie O'Sullivan (England) beat Stephen Hendry (Scotland) 10–6
*European Open:* Stephen Hendry (Scotland) beat Ronnie O'Sullivan (England) 9–5
*Benson and Hedges Championship:* Steve Davis (England) beat Alan McManus (Scotland) 9–8
*World Amateur Championship:* Chuchat Triratanapradit (Thailand) beat Papruet Chaitanasakun (Thailand) 11–6

1994
*Welsh Open:* Steve Davis (England) beat Alan McManus (Scotland) 9–6
*Benson and Hedges Masters:* Alan McManus (Scotland) beat Stephen Hendry (Scotland) 9–8
*International Open:* John Parrott (England) beat James Wattana (Thailand) 9–5
*Thailand Open:* James Wattana (Thailand) beat Steve Davis (England) 9–7
*Irish Masters:* Steve Davis (England) beat Alan McManus (Scotland) 9–8
*British Open:* Ronnie O'Sullivan (England) beat James Wattana (Thailand) 9–4
*World Professional Championship:* Stephen Hendry (Scotland) beat Jimmy White (England) 18–17
*European League:* Stephen Hendry (Scotland) beat John Parrott (England) 10–7
*Regal Masters:* Ken Doherty (Ireland) beat Stephen Hendry (Scotland) 9–7

*Women's British Open Championship 1993:* Allison Fisher beat Karen Corr 4–1
*Women's World Championship 1994:* Allison Fisher beat Stacey Hillyard 7–3
*Women's National Championship 1994:* Karen Corr beat Allison Fisher 4–0
*Women's UK Championship 1994:* Karen Corr beat Stacey Hillyard 4–3

---

SPEEDWAY

---

*World Individual Championship 1994:* Tony Rickardsson (Sweden)
*World Team Cup 1994:* Sweden, 23 pts
*World Championship, British final 1994:* Andy Smith (Coventry)
*British League Riders' Championship 1993:* Per Jonsson (Reading)
*British League Championship 1993:* Belle Vue Aces
*British League Knock-Out Cup final 1993:* Bradford beat Arena Essex 111–105 on agg.
*British Champion 1994:* Andy Smith (Coventry)

---

SQUASH RACKETS

---

MEN
*World Open Championship final 1993:* Jansher Khan (Pakistan) beat Jahangir Khan (Pakistan) 3–1
*World Open Championship final 1994:* Jansher Khan (Pakistan) beat Peter Marshall (England) 3–1
*World Team Championship final 1993:* Pakistan beat Australia 3–0
*European Team Championship final 1994:* England beat Germany 4–0
*European Club Championship final 1994:* OSC Ingolstadt (Germany) beat St Cloud (France) 3–2
*British Open Championship final 1994:* Jansher Khan (Pakistan) beat Brett Martin (Australia) 3–1
*National Championship final 1994:* Peter Marshall beat Peter Nicol 3–0

WOMEN
*World Open Championship final 1993:* Michelle Martin (Australia) beat Liz Irving (Australia) 3–0
*European Team Championship final 1994:* England beat Germany 3–0
*European Club Championship final 1994:* Richmond Town (England) beat Paderborn (Germany) 3–0
*British Open Championship final 1994:* Michelle Martin (Australia) beat Liz Irving (Australia) 3–0
*National Championship final 1994:* Suzanne Horner beat Sue Wright 3–0

---

SWIMMING

---

WORLD CHAMPIONSHIPS 1994
Rome, September

MEN
*50 metres freestyle:* Alexander Popov (Russia)
*100 metres freestyle:* Alexander Popov (Russia)
*200 metres freestyle:* Anti Casvio (Finland)
*400 metres freestyle:* Kieren Perkins (Australia)
*1,500 metres freestyle:* Kieren Perkins (Australia)
*100 metres backstroke:* Martin Lopez-Zubero (Spain)
*200 metres backstroke:* Vladimir Selkov (Russia)
*100 metres breaststroke:* Norbert Rosza (Hungary)
*200 metres breaststroke:* Norbert Rosza (Hungary)
*100 metres butterfly:* Rafal Szukala (Poland)

*200 metres butterfly:* Denis Pankratov (Russia)
*200 metres medley:* Jani Sievinen (Finland)
*400 metres medley:* Tom Dolan (USA)
*4 × 100 metres freestyle relay:* USA
*4 × 200 metres freestyle relay:* Sweden
*4 × 100 metres medley relay:* USA

WOMEN

*50 metres freestyle:* Le Jingyi (China)
*100 metres freestyle:* Le Jingyi (China)
*200 metres freestyle:* Franziska van Almsick (Germany)
*400 metres freestyle:* Yang Ai Hua (China)
*800 metres freestyle:* Janet Evans (USA)
*100 metres backstroke:* He Cihong (China)
*200 metres backstroke:* He Cihong (China)
*100 metres breaststroke:* Samantha Riley (Australia)
*200 metres breaststroke:* Samantha Riley (Australia)
*100 metres butterfly:* Liu Limin (China)
*200 metres butterfly:* Liu Limin (China)
*200 metres medley:* Lu Bin (China)
*400 metres medley:* Dai Guohong (China)
*4 × 100 metres freestyle relay:* China
*4 × 200 metres freestyle relay:* China
*4 × 100 metres medley relay:* China

NATIONAL CHAMPIONSHIPS 1994
Crystal Palace, July

MEN

*50 metres freestyle:* Michael Fibbens (Barnet Copthall)
*100 metres freestyle:* Nicholas Shackell (Millfield)
*200 metres freestyle:* James Salter (City of Birmingham)
*400 metres freestyle:* Steven Mellor (Satellite)
*1,500 metres freestyle:* Ian Wilson (City of Leeds)
*50 metres backstroke:* Martin Harris (Waltham Forest)
*100 metres backstroke:* Martin Harris (Waltham Forest)
*200 metres backstroke:* Adam Ruckwood (City of Birmingham)
*50 metres breaststroke:* Gavin Bretell (City of Birmingham)
*100 metres breaststroke:* James Parrack (City of Leeds)
*200 metres breaststroke:* Alex Clapper (City of Coventry)
*50 metres butterfly:* Mike Fibbens (Barnet Copthall)
*100 metres butterfly:* Janko Gojkovic (City of Sheffield)
*200 metres butterfly:* James Hickman (Stockport Metro)
*200 metres medley:* David Warren (City of Leeds)
*400 metres medley:* David Warren (City of Leeds)
*4 × 100 metres freestyle relay:* City of Sheffield
*4 × 100 metres medley relay:* City of Leeds
*4 × 200 metres freestyle relay:* City of Leeds

WOMEN

*50 metres freestyle:* Susan Rolph (City of Newcastle)
*100 metres freestyle:* Susan Rolph (City of Newcastle)
*200 metres freestyle:* Karen Pickering (Ipswich)
*400 metres freestyle:* Sarah Hardcastle (Bracknell)
*800 metres freestyle:* Susan Colling (Derwentside)
*50 metres backstroke:* Kathy Osher (Barnet Copthall)
*100 metres backstroke:* Emma Tattan (Portsmouth Northsea)
*200 metres backstroke:* Kathy Osher (Barnet Copthall)
*50 metres breaststroke:* Lorraine Coombes (Ealing)
*100 metres breaststroke:* Marie Hardiman (City of Birmingham)
*200 metres breaststroke:* Marie Hardiman (City of Birmingham)
*50 metres butterfly:* Susan Rolph (City of Newcastle)
*100 metres butterfly:* Samantha Greenep (Ferndown Otters)
*200 metres butterfly:* Helen Slatter (Warrington Warriors)
*200 metres medley:* Susan Rolph (City of Newcastle)

*400 metres medley:* Helen Slatter (Warrington Warriors)
*4 × 100 metres freestyle relay:* Portsmouth Northsea
*4 × 100 metres medley relay:* Portsmouth Northsea
*4 × 200 metres freestyle relay:* Portsmouth Northsea

## TABLE TENNIS

EUROPEAN CHAMPIONSHIPS 1994
Birmingham, April
*Men's Singles:* Jean-Michel Saive (Belgium) beat Jan-Ove Waldner (Sweden) 3–1
*Women's Singles:* Marie Svensson (Sweden) beat Gerdie Keen (Netherlands) 3–0
*Men's Doubles:* Calin Creanga (Greece) and Zoran Kalinic (Ind. Federation) beat Jean-Michel Saive (Belgium) and Zoran Primorac (Croatia) 2–0
*Women's Doubles:* Csilla Batorfy and Krisztina Toth (Hungary) beat Elena Timina and Irina Palina (Russia) 2–0
*Mixed Doubles:* Csilla Batorfy (Hungary) and Zoran Primorac (Croatia) beat Otilia Badescu (Romania) and Calin Creanga (Greece) 2–0
*Men's team event:* France beat Sweden 4–3
*Women's team event:* Russia beat Germany 4–1
*European Nations Cup final 1994:* Sweden beat France 3–2
*Women's European Nations Cup final 1994:* Germany beat Hungary 3–2

ENGLISH NATIONAL CHAMPIONSHIPS 1994
*Men's Singles:* Xinhua Chen beat Alan Cooke 3–1
*Women's Singles:* Lisa Lomas beat Andrea Holt 3–1
*Men's Doubles:* Skylet Andrew and Nicky Mason beat John Holland and Alan Cooke 2–0
*Women's Doubles:* Lisa Lomas and Fiona Mommessin beat Kate Goodall and Andrea Holt 2–1
*Mixed Doubles:* Fiona Mommessin and Skylet Andrew beat Sally Marling and Alex Perry 2–0

## VOLLEYBALL

MEN

*World League final 1994:* Italy beat Cuba 3–0
*National League Championship 1994:* Mizuno Malory Lewisham
*National Cup final 1994:* Mizuno Malory Lewisham beat Tooting Aquila 3–0

WOMEN

*World Grand Prix 1994:* Brazil
*National League Championship 1994:* Woolwich Brixton
*National Cup final 1994:* Britannia Music City beat Sale 3–1

## YACHTING

WHITBREAD ROUND-THE-WORLD RACE
*Started from the Solent, 25 September 1993*
*Maxi class:* New Zealand Endeavour (New Zealand) in 120 days, 5 hours and 9 minutes
*Whitbread 60 class:* Yamaha (New Zealand) in 120 days, 14 hours and 55 minutes

# Winter Olympic Games 1994

*Lillehammer, Norway, 12–27 February 1994*

ALPINE SKIING (MEN)
*Downhill:* Tommy Moe (USA)
*Slalom:* Thomas Stanggassinger (Austria)
*Giant Slalom:* Markus Wasmeier (Germany)
*Super Giant Slalom:* Markus Wasmeier (Germany)
*Alpine Combined:* Lasse Kjus (Norway)

ALPINE SKIING (WOMEN)
*Downhill:* Katya Seizinger (Germany)
*Slalom:* Vreni Schneider (Switzerland)
*Giant Slalom:* Deborah Compagnoni (Italy)
*Super Giant Slalom:* Diann Roffe (USA)
*Alpine Combined:* Pernilla Wiberg (Sweden)

NORDIC SKIING (MEN)
*10 kilometre classical:* Bjorn Dahlie (Norway)
*15 kilometre pursuit:* Bjorn Dahlie (Norway)
*30 kilometre freestyle:* Thomas Alsgaard (Norway)
*50 kilometre classical:* Vladimir Smirnov (Kazakhstan)
*4 × 10 kilometre relay:* Italy

NORDIC SKIING (WOMEN)
*5 kilometre classical:* Lyubov Yegorova (Russia)
*10 kilometre pursuit:* Lyubov Yegorova (Russia)
*15 kilometre freestyle:* Manuela di Centa (Italy)
*30 kilometre classical:* Manuela di Centa (Italy)
*4 × 5 kilometre relay:* Russia

BIATHLON (MEN)
*10 kilometre:* Sergei Chepikov (Russia)
*20 kilometre:* Sergei Tarasov (Russia)
*4 × 7.5 kilometre relay:* Germany

BIATHLON (WOMEN)
*7.5 kilometre:* Myriam Bedard (Canada)
*15 kilometre:* Myriam Bedard (Canada)
*4 × 7.5 kilometre relay:* Russia

FREESTYLE SKIING (MEN)
*Moguls:* Jean-Luc Brassard (Canada)
*Aerials:* Andreas Schonbachler (Switzerland)

FREESTYLE SKIING (WOMEN)
*Moguls:* Stine Lise Hattestad (Norway)
*Aerials:* Lina Cherjasova (Uzbekistan)

NORDIC COMBINED
*Individual:* Fred Borre Lundberg (Norway)
*Team:* Japan

SKI-JUMPING
*90 metre:* Espen Bredesen (Norway)
*120 metre:* Jens Weissflog (Germany)
*120 metre team:* Germany

LUGE (MEN)
*Single:* Georg Hackl (Germany)
*Doubles:* Italy (Kurt Brugger and Wilfried Huber)

LUGE (WOMEN)
*Single:* Gerda Weisensteiner (Italy)

BOBSLEDDING
*2-man:* Switzerland I (Gustav Weder and Donat Acklin)
*4-man:* Germany II

ICE HOCKEY
*Winners:* Sweden

FIGURE SKATING
*Men:* Alexei Urmanov (Russia)
*Women:* Oksana Baiul (Ukraine)
*Pairs:* Ekaterina Gordiyeva and Sergei Grinkov (Russia)
*Ice Dance:* Oksana Gritschuk and Yevgeny Platov (Russia)

SPEED SKATING (MEN)
*500 metres:* Aleksandr Golubyev (Russia)
*1,000 metres:* Dan Jansen (USA)
*1,500 metres:* Johann-Olav Koss (Norway)
*5,000 metres:* Johann-Olav Koss (Norway)
*10,000 metres:* Johann-Olav Koss (Norway)

SPEED SKATING (WOMEN)
*500 metres:* Bonnie Blair (USA)
*1,000 metres:* Bonnie Blair (USA)
*1,500 metres:* Emese Hunyady (Austria)
*3,000 metres:* Svetlana Bazhanova (Russia)
*5,000 metres:* Claudia Pechstein (Germany)

SHORT TRACK SPEED SKATING (MEN)
*500 metres:* Chae Ji-Hoon (Korea)
*1,000 metres:* Kim Ki-Hoon (Korea)
*5,000 metre relay:* Italy

SHORT TRACK SPEED SKATING (WOMEN)
*500 metres:* Cathy Turner (USA)
*1,000 metres:* Chun Lee-Kyung (Korea)
*3,000 metre relay:* Korea

## MEDAL TABLE

|  | Gold | Silver | Bronze | Total |
|---|---|---|---|---|
| Russia | 11 | 8 | 4 | 23 |
| Norway | 10 | 11 | 5 | 26 |
| Germany | 9 | 7 | 8 | 24 |
| Italy | 7 | 5 | 8 | 20 |
| USA | 6 | 5 | 2 | 13 |
| Korea (South) | 4 | 1 | 1 | 6 |
| Canada | 3 | 6 | 4 | 13 |
| Switzerland | 3 | 4 | 2 | 9 |
| Austria | 2 | 3 | 4 | 9 |
| Sweden | 2 | 1 | 0 | 3 |
| Japan | 1 | 2 | 2 | 5 |
| Kazakhstan | 1 | 2 | 0 | 3 |
| Ukraine | 1 | 0 | 1 | 2 |
| Uzbekistan | 1 | 0 | 0 | 1 |
| Belarus | 0 | 2 | 0 | 2 |
| Finland | 0 | 1 | 5 | 6 |
| France | 0 | 1 | 4 | 5 |
| Netherlands | 0 | 1 | 3 | 4 |
| China | 0 | 1 | 2 | 3 |
| Slovenia | 0 | 0 | 3 | 3 |
| Great Britain | 0 | 0 | 2 | 2 |
| Australia | 0 | 0 | 1 | 1 |
|  | 61 | 61 | 61 | 183 |

# Commonwealth Games 1994

*Victoria, Canada, 18–28 August 1994*

ATHLETICS (MEN)

| | hr. | min. | sec. |
|---|---|---|---|
| 100 *metres:* Linford Christie (England) | | | 9.91 |
| 200 *metres:* Frankie Fredericks (Namibia) | | | 19.97 |
| 400 *metres:* Charles Gitonga (Kenya) | | | 45.00 |
| 800 *metres:* Patrick Kinchellah (Kenya) | | 1 | 45.18 |
| 1,500 *metres:* Reuben Chesang (Kenya) | | 3 | 36.70 |
| 5,000 *metres:* Rob Denmark (England) | | 13 | 23.00 |
| 10,000 *metres:* Lameck Aguta (Kenya) | | 28 | 38.22 |
| *Marathon:* Steve Moneghetti (Australia) | 2 | 11 | 49 |
| 3 *km steeplechase:* Johnstone Kipkoech (Kenya) | | 8 | 14.72 |
| 110 *metres hurdles:* Colin Jackson (Wales) | | | 13.08 |
| 400 *metres hurdles:* Samuel Matete (Zambia) | | | 48.67 |
| 4 × 100 *metres relay:* Canada | | | 38.39 |
| 4 × 400 *metres relay:* England | | 3 | 02.14 |
| 30 *km walk:* Nick A'Hern (Australia) | 2 | 07 | 53 |
| 800 *metres wheelchair:* Jeff Adams (Canada) | | 1 | 44.94 |
| *Marathon wheelchair:* Paul Wiggins (Australia) | 1 | 37 | 33 |

| | metres |
|---|---|
| *High jump:* Tim Forsyth (Australia) | 2.32 |
| *Pole vault:* Neil Winter (Wales) | 5.40 |
| *Long jump:* Obinna Eregbu (Nigeria) | 8.05 |
| *Triple jump:* Julian Golley (England) | 17.03 |
| *Shot:* Matt Simson (England) | 19.49 |
| *Discus:* Werner Reiterer (Australia) | 62.76 |
| *Hammer:* Sean Carlin (Australia) | 73.48 |
| *Javelin:* Steve Backley (England) | 82.74 |
| *Decathlon:* Mike Smith (Canada) | 8,326 pts |

ATHLETICS (WOMEN)

| | hr. | min. | sec. |
|---|---|---|---|
| 100 *metres:* Mary Onyali (Nigeria) | | | 11.06 |
| 200 *metres:* Cathy Freeman (Australia) | | | 22.25 |
| 400 *metres:* Cathy Freeman (Australia) | | | 50.38 |
| 800 *metres:* Inez Turner (Trinidad & Tobago) | | 2 | 01.74 |
| 1,500 *metres:* Kelly Holmes (England) | | 4 | 08.86 |
| 3,000 *metres:* Angela Chalmers (Canada) | | 8 | 32.17 |
| 10,000 *metres:* Yvonne Murray (Scotland) | | 31 | 56.97 |
| *Marathon:* Carole Rouillard (Canada) | 2 | 30 | 41 |
| 100 *metres hurdles:* Michelle Freeman (Jamaica) | | | 13.12 |
| 400 *metres hurdles:* Sally Gunnell (England) | | | 54.51 |
| 4 × 100 *metres relay:* Nigeria | | | 42.99 |
| 4 × 400 *metres relay:* England | | 3 | 27.06 |
| 10 *km walk:* Kerry Saxby-Junna (Australia) | | 44 | 25 |

| | metres |
|---|---|
| *High jump:* Alison Inverarity (Australia) | 1.94 |
| *Long jump:* Nicole Boegman (Australia) | 6.82 |
| *Shot:* Judy Oakes (England) | 18.16 |
| *Discus:* Daniela Costian (Australia) | 63.72 |
| *Javelin:* Louise McPaul (Australia) | 63.76 |
| *Heptathlon:* Denise Lewis (England) | 6,325 pts |

BADMINTON

*Men's Singles:* Rashid Sidek (Malaysia)
*Men's Doubles:* Soon Kit Cheah and Beng Kiang Soo (Malaysia)

*Women's Singles:* Lisa Campbell (Australia)
*Women's Doubles:* Jo Muggeridge and Joanne Wright (England)
*Mixed Doubles:* Gillian Clark and Chris Hunt (England)
*Team:* England

BOWLS

*Men's Singles:* Richard Corsie (Scotland)
*Men's Pairs:* Australia
*Men's Fours:* South Africa
*Visually Impaired:* Robert Brand (Scotland)
*Woman's Singles:* Margaret Johnston (N. Ireland)
*Women's Pairs:* Scotland
*Women's Fours:* South Africa
*Visually Impaired:* Katie Portas (New Zealand)

BOXING

*Light-flyweight* (48 kg): Haman Ramadhani (Kenya)
*Flyweight* (51 kg): Paul Shepherd (Scotland)
*Bantamweight* (54 kg): Robert Peden (Australia)
*Featherweight* (57 kg): Casey Patton (Canada)
*Lightweight* (60 kg): Mike Strange (Canada)
*Light-welterweight* (63.5 kg): Peter Richardson (England)
*Welterweight* (67 kg): Neil Sinclair (N. Ireland)
*Light-middleweight* (71 kg): James Webb (N. Ireland)
*Middleweight* (75 kg): Rowan Donaldson (Canada)
*Light-heavyweight* (81 kg): Dale Brown (Canada)
*Heavyweight* (91 kg): Omaar Ahmed (Kenya)
*Super-heavyweight* (91 kg +): Duncan Dokiwari (Nigeria)

CYCLING (MEN)

| | hr. | min. | sec. |
|---|---|---|---|
| *Sprint:* Gary Neiwand (Australia) | | | |
| 1,000 *metres Time Trial:* Shane Kelly (Australia) | | 1 | 05.386 |
| 4,000 *metres Individual Pursuit:* Bradley McGee (Australia) | | 4 | 31.371 |
| 4,000 *metres Team Pursuit:* Australia | | 4 | 10.485 |
| 10 *miles:* Stuart O'Grady (Australia) | | 18 | 50.543 |
| *Team Time Trial:* Australia | 1 | 53 | 19.13 |
| *Individual Road Race:* Mark Rendell (New Zealand) | 4 | 46 | 08 |
| 40 *km points race:* Brett Aitken (Australia) | | | |

CYCLING (WOMEN)

| | hr. | min. | sec. |
|---|---|---|---|
| *Sprint:* Tanya Dubnicoff (Canada) | | | |
| 3,000 *metres Individual Pursuit:* Kathryn Watt (Australia) | | 3 | 48.522 |
| *Team Time Trial:* Australia | 1 | 04 | 03.20 |
| *Individual Road Race:* Kathryn Watt (Australia) | 2 | 48 | 04 |
| 25 *km points race:* Yvonne McGregor (England) | | | |

DIVING (MEN)

1 *metre springboard:* Jason Napper (Canada)
3 *metre springboard:* Michael Murphy (Australia)
10 *metre highboard:* Michael Murphy (Australia)

DIVING (WOMEN)

1 *metre springboard:* Annie Pelletier (Canada)
3 *metre springboard:* Annie Pelletier (Canada)
10 *metre platform:* Anne Montminy (Canada)

GYMNASTICS (MEN)
*Team:* Canada
*Individual:* Neil Thomas (England)
*Floor:* Neil Thomas (England)
*Pommel:* Brennon Dowrick (Australia)
*Vault:* Bret Hudson (Australia)
*Rings:* Lee McDermott (England)
*Parallel Bars:* Peter Hogan (Australia)
*Horizontal Bars:* Alain Nolet (Canada)

GYMNASTICS (WOMEN)
*Team:* England
*Individual:* Stella Umeh (Canada)
*Floor:* Annika Reeder (England)
*Vault:* Stella Umeh (Canada)
*Beam:* Salli Wills (Australia)
*Asymmetrical Bars:* Rebecca Stoyel (Australia)

RHYTHMIC GYMNASTICS
*Team:* Canada
*Individual:* Kasumi Takahashi (Australia)

SHOOTING (MEN)
*Free Pistol:* Michael Gault (England)
*Free Pistol, pairs:* Australia
*Centre-Fire Pistol:* Jaspal Rana (India)
*Centre-Fire Pistol, pairs:* India
*Rapid Fire Pistol:* Michael Jay (Wales)
*Rapid Fire Pistol, pairs;* Australia
*Air Pistol:* Jean-Pierre Huot (Canada)
*Air Pistol, pairs:* Australia
*Small-Bore Prone:* Stephen Petterson (New Zealand)
*Small-Bore Prone, pairs:* New Zealand
*Small-Bore Three Positions:* Michel Dion (Canada)
*Small-Bore Three Positions, pairs:* Canada
*Air Rifle:* Christopher Hector (England)
*Air Rifle, pairs:* Canada
*Running Target:* Bryan Wilson (Australia)
*Running Target, pairs:* Canada

SHOOTING (WOMEN)
*Sport Pistol:* Christine Trefry (Australia)
*Sport Pistol, pairs:* Australia
*Air Pistol:* Helen Smith (Canada)
*Air Pistol, pairs:* Australia
*Small-Bore Prone:* Shirley McIntosh (Scotland)
*Small-Bore Prone, pairs:* Australia
*Small-Bore Three Positions:* Sharon Bowes (Canada)
*Small-Bore Three Positions, pairs:* Canada
*Air Rifle:* Fani Theofanous (Cyprus)
*Air Rifle, pairs:* Sri Lanka

SHOOTING (OPEN)
*Fullbore:* David Calvert (N. Ireland)
*Fullbore, pairs:* Australia
*Trap:* Mansher Singh (India)
*Trap, pairs:* N. Ireland
*Skeet:* Ian Hale (Australia)
*Skeet, pairs:* Cyprus

SWIMMING (MEN)

| | min. | sec. |
|---|---|---|
| 50 *metres freestyle:* Mark Foster (England) | | 23.12 |
| 100 *metres freestyle:* Stephen Clarke (Canada) | | 50.21 |
| 200 *metres freestyle:* Kieren Perkins (Australia) | 1 | 49.31 |
| 400 *metres freestyle:* Kieren Perkins (Australia) | 3 | 45.77 |
| 1,500 *metres freestyle:* Kieren Perkins (Australia) | 14 | 41.66 |
| 4 × 100 *metres freestyle relay:* Australia | 3 | 20.89 |
| 4 × 200 *metres freestyle relay:* Australia | 7 | 20.80 |
| 100 *metres backstroke:* Martin Harris (England) | | 55.77 |
| 200 *metres backstroke:* Adam Ruckwood (England) | 2 | 00.79 |
| 100 *metres breaststroke:* Philip Rogers (Australia) | 1 | 02.62 |
| 200 *metres breaststroke:* Nicholas Gillingham (England) | 2 | 12.54 |
| 100 *metres butterfly:* Scott Miller (Australia) | | 54.39 |
| 200 *metres butterfly:* Danyon Loader (New Zealand) | 1 | 59.54 |
| 200 *metres individual medley:* Matthew Dunn (Australia) | 2 | 02.28 |
| 400 *metres individual medley:* Matthew Dunn (Australia) | 4 | 17.01 |
| 4 × 100 *metres medley relay:* Australia | 3 | 40.41 |
| *Disabled* 100 *metres freestyle:* Andrew Haley (Canada) | | |

SWIMMING (WOMEN)

| | min. | sec. |
|---|---|---|
| 50 *metres freestyle:* Karen van Wirdum (Australia) | | 25.90 |
| 100 *metres freestyle:* Karen Pickering (England) | | 56.20 |
| 200 *metres freestyle:* Susan O'Neill (Australia) | 2 | 00.86 |
| 400 *metres freestyle:* Hayley Lewis (Australia) | 4 | 12.56 |
| 800 *metres freestyle:* Hayley Lewis (Australia) | 8 | 30.18 |
| 4 × 100 *metres freestyle relay:* England | 3 | 46.23 |
| 4 × 200 *metres freestyle relay:* Australia | 8 | 08.06 |
| 100 *metres backstroke:* Nicole Stevenson (Australia) | 1 | 02.68 |
| 200 *metres backstroke:* Nicole Stevenson (Australia) | 2 | 12.73 |
| 100 *metres breaststroke:* Samantha Riley (Australia) | 1 | 08.02 |
| 200 *metres breaststroke:* Samantha Riley (Australia) | 2 | 25.53 |
| 100 *metres butterfly:* Petria Thomas (Australia) | 1 | 00.21 |
| 200 *metres butterfly:* Susan O'Neill (Australia) | 2 | 09.96 |
| 200 *metres individual medley:* Ellinora Overton (Australia) | 2 | 15.59 |
| 400 *metres individual medley:* Ellinora Overton (Australia) | 4 | 44.01 |
| 4 × 100 *metres medley relay:* Australia | 4 | 07.89 |
| *Disabled* 100 *metres freestyle:* Melissa Carlton (Australia) | | |

SYNCHRONISED SWIMMING
*Singles:* Lisa Alexander (Canada)
*Pairs:* Canada

WEIGHTLIFTING
54 kg: Badathala Adisekhar (India)
59 kg: Marcus Stephen (Nauru)
64 kg: Sevdalkin Marinov (Australia)
70 kg: Moji Oluwu (Nigeria)
76 kg: David Morgan (Wales)
83 kg: Kiril Kounev (Australia)

91 kg: Harvey Goodman (Australia)
99 kg: Andrew Callard (England)
108 kg: Nicu Vlad (Australia)
+ 108 kg: Stefan Botev (Australia)

WRESTLING
48 kg: Jacob Isaac (Nigeria)
52 kg: Selwyn Tam (Canada)
57 kg: Robert Dawson (Canada)
62 kg: Marty Calder (Canada)
68 kg: Chris Wilson (Canada)
74 kg: David Hohl (Canada)
82 kg: Justin Abdou (Canada)
90 kg: Scott Bianco (Canada)
100 kg: Greg Edgelow (Canada)
+ 100 kg: Andrew Borodow (Canada)

## MEDAL TABLE

| | Gold | Silver | Bronze | Total |
|---|---|---|---|---|
| Australia | 87 | 52 | 43 | 182 |
| Canada | 40 | 42 | 46 | 128 |
| England | 31 | 45 | 49 | 125 |
| New Zealand | 5 | 16 | 20 | 41 |
| Nigeria | 11 | 13 | 13 | 37 |
| India | 6 | 11 | 7 | 24 |
| Scotland | 6 | 3 | 11 | 20 |
| Kenya | 7 | 4 | 8 | 19 |
| Wales | 5 | 8 | 6 | 19 |
| South Africa | 2 | 4 | 5 | 11 |
| N. Ireland | 5 | 2 | 3 | 10 |
| Jamaica | 2 | 4 | 2 | 8 |
| Malaysia | 2 | 3 | 2 | 7 |
| Zimbabwe | 0 | 3 | 3 | 6 |
| Cyprus | 2 | 1 | 2 | 5 |
| Zambia | 1 | 1 | 2 | 4 |
| Hong Kong | 0 | 0 | 4 | 4 |
| Nauru | 3 | 0 | 0 | 3 |
| Sri Lanka | 1 | 2 | 0 | 3 |
| Pakistan | 0 | 0 | 3 | 3 |
| Namibia | 1 | 0 | 1 | 2 |
| Trinidad and Tobago | 0 | 0 | 2 | 2 |
| Uganda | 0 | 0 | 2 | 2 |
| Papua New Guinea | 0 | 1 | 0 | 1 |
| Western Samoa | 0 | 1 | 0 | 1 |
| Bermuda | 0 | 0 | 1 | 1 |
| Botswana | 0 | 0 | 1 | 1 |
| Ghana | 0 | 0 | 1 | 1 |
| Guernsey | 0 | 0 | 1 | 1 |
| Norfolk Island | 0 | 0 | 1 | 1 |
| Seychelles | 0 | 0 | 1 | 1 |
| Tanzania | 0 | 0 | 1 | 1 |
| Tonga | 0 | 0 | 1 | 1 |
| | 217 | 216 | 242 | 675 |

## THE COMMONWEALTH GAMES

The Games were originally called the British Empire
Games. From 1954 to 1966 the Games were known as the
British Empire and Commonwealth Games, and from 1970
to 1974 as the British Commonwealth Games. Since 1978
the Games have been called the Commonwealth Games.

BRITISH EMPIRE GAMES

| I | Hamilton, Canada | 1930 |
|---|---|---|
| II | London, England | 1934 |
| III | Sydney, Australia | 1938 |
| IV | Auckland, New Zealand | 1950 |

BRITISH EMPIRE AND COMMONWEALTH GAMES

| V | Vancouver, Canada | 1954 |
|---|---|---|
| VI | Cardiff, Wales | 1958 |
| VII | Perth, Australia | 1962 |
| VIII | Kingston, Jamaica | 1966 |

BRITISH COMMONWEALTH GAMES

| IX | Edinburgh, Scotland | 1970 |
|---|---|---|
| X | Christchurch, New Zealand | 1974 |

COMMONWEALTH GAMES

| XI | Edmonton, Canada | 1978 |
|---|---|---|
| XII | Brisbane, Australia | 1982 |
| XIII | Edinburgh, Scotland | 1986 |
| XIV | Auckland, New Zealand | 1990 |
| XV | Victoria, Canada | 1994 |
| XVI | Kuala Lumpur, Malaysia | 1998 |

# Sports Records

## ATHLETICS WORLD RECORDS
### AS AT 3 SEPTEMBER 1994

All the world records given below have been accepted by the International Amateur Athletic Federation except those marked with an asterisk* which are awaiting homologation. Fully automatic timing to 1/100th second is mandatory up to and including 400 metres. For distances up to and including 10,000 metres, records will be accepted to 1/100th second if timed automatically, and to 1/10th if hand timing is used.

## MEN'S EVENTS

| TRACK EVENTS | hr. | min. | sec. |
|---|---|---|---|
| 100 metres | | | 9.85 |
| Leroy Burrell, USA, 1994 | | | |
| 200 metres | | | 19.72 |
| Pietro Mennea, Italy, 1979 | | | |
| 400 metres | | | 43.29 |
| Harry Reynolds, USA, 1988 | | | |
| 800 metres | | 1 | 41.73 |
| Sebastian Coe, GB, 1981 | | | |
| 1,000 metres | | 2 | 12.18 |
| Sebastian Coe, GB, 1981 | | | |
| 1,500 metres | | 3 | 28.86 |
| Noureddine Morceli, Algeria, 1993 | | | |
| 1 mile | | 3 | 44.39 |
| Noureddine Morceli, Algeria, 1993 | | | |
| 2,000 metres | | 4 | 50.81 |
| Saïd Aouita, Morocco, 1987 | | | |
| 3,000 metres | | 7 | 25.11 |
| Noureddine Morceli, Algeria, 1994 | | | |
| 5,000 metres | | 12 | 56.96 |
| Haile Gebresilasie, Ethiopa, 1994 | | | |
| 10,000 metres | | 26 | 52.23 |
| William Sigei, Kenya, 1994 | | | |
| 20,000 metres | | 56 | 55.6 |
| Arturo Barrios, Mexico, 1991 | | | |
| 21,101 metres (13 miles 196 yards 1 foot) | 1 | 00 | 00.0 |
| Arturo Barrios, Mexico, 1991 | | | |
| 25,000 metres | 1 | 13 | 55.8 |
| Toshihiko Seko, Japan, 1981 | | | |
| 30,000 metres | 1 | 29 | 18.8 |
| Toshihiko Seko, Japan, 1981 | | | |
| 110 metres hurdles (3 ft 6 in) | | | 12.91 |
| Colin Jackson, GB, 1993 | | | |
| 400 metres hurdles (3 ft 0 in) | | | 46.78 |
| Kevin Young, USA, 1992 | | | |
| 3,000 metres steeplechase | | 8 | 02.08 |
| Moses Kiptanui, Kenya, 1992 | | | |

| RELAYS | | min. | sec. |
|---|---|---|---|
| 4 × 100 metres | | | 37.40 |
| USA, 1992, 1993 | | | |
| 4 × 200 metres | | 1 | 19.11 |
| Santa Monica TC, 1992 | | | |
| 4 × 400 metres | | 2 | 54.29 |
| USA, 1993 | | | |
| 4 × 800 metres | | 7 | 03.89 |
| GB, 1982 | | | |
| 4 × 1,500 metres | | 14 | 38.8 |
| Federal Republic of Germany, 1977 | | | |

| FIELD EVENTS | metres | ft | in |
|---|---|---|---|
| High jump | 2.45 | 8 | 0½ |
| Javier Sotomayor, Cuba, 1993 | | | |
| Pole vault | 6.14 | 20 | 1¾ |
| Sergei Bubka, Ukraine, 1994 | | | |
| Long jump | 8.95 | 29 | 4½ |
| Mike Powell, USA, 1991 | | | |
| Triple jump | 17.97 | 58 | 11½ |
| Willie Banks, USA, 1985 | | | |
| Shot | 23.12 | 75 | 10¼ |
| Randy Barnes, USA, 1990 | | | |
| Discus | 74.08 | 243 | 0 |
| Jürgen Schult, GDR, 1986 | | | |
| Hammer | 86.74 | 284 | 7 |
| Yuriy Sedykh, USSR, 1986 | | | |
| Javelin | 95.66 | 313 | 10 |
| Jan Zelezny, Czech Rep., 1993 | | | |
| Decathlon† | | | 8,891 pts |
| Dan O'Brien, USA, 1992 | | | |

† Ten events comprising 100 m, long jump, shot, high jump, 400 m, 110 m hurdles, discus, pole vault, javelin, 1500 m

| WALKING (TRACK) | hr. | min. | sec. |
|---|---|---|---|
| 20,000 metres | 1 | 18 | 35.2 |
| Stefan Johansson, Sweden, 1992 | | | |
| 29,572 metres (18 miles 660 yards) | 2 | 00 | 00.0 |
| Maurizio Damilano, Italy, 1992 | | | |
| 30,000 metres | 2 | 01 | 44.1 |
| Maurizio Damilano, Italy, 1992 | | | |
| 50,000 metres | 3 | 41 | 38.4 |
| Raul Gonzalez, Mexico, 1979 | | | |

## WOMEN'S EVENTS

| TRACK EVENTS | min. | sec. |
|---|---|---|
| 100 metres | | 10.49 |
| Florence Griffith-Joyner, USA, 1988 | | |
| 200 metres | | 21.34 |
| Florence Griffith-Joyner, USA, 1988 | | |
| 400 metres | | 47.60 |
| Marita Koch, GDR, 1985 | | |
| 800 metres | 1 | 53.28 |
| Jarmila Kratochvilova, Czechoslovakia, 1983 | | |
| 1,500 metres | 3 | 50.46 |
| Qu Yunxia, China, 1993 | | |
| 1 mile | 4 | 15.61 |
| Paula Ivan, Romania, 1989 | | |
| 3,000 metres | 8 | 06.11 |
| Wang Junxia, China, 1993 | | |
| 5,000 metres | 14 | 37.33 |
| Ingrid Kristiansen, Norway, 1986 | | |
| 10,000 metres | 29 | 31.78 |
| Wang Junxia, China, 1993 | | |
| 100 metres hurdles (2 ft 9 in) | | 12.21 |
| Yordanka Donkova, Bulgaria, 1988 | | |
| 400 metres hurdles (2 ft 6 in) | | 52.74 |
| Sally Gunnell, GB, 1993 | | |

| RELAYS | min. | sec. |
|---|---|---|
| 4 × 100 metres | | 41.37 |
| GDR, 1985 | | |

| | | | |
|---|---|---|---|
| 4 × 200 metres | 1 | 28.15 | |
| GDR, 1980 | | | |
| 4 × 400 metres | 3 | 15.17 | |
| USSR, 1988 | | | |
| 4 × 800 metres | 7 | 50.17 | |
| USSR, 1984 | | | |

| FIELD EVENTS | metres | ft | in |
|---|---|---|---|
| High jump | 2.09 | 6 | 10¼ |
| Stefka Kostadinova, Bulgaria, 1987 | | | |
| Long jump | 7.52 | 24 | 8¼ |
| Galina Chistiakova, USSR, 1988 | | | |
| Triple jump | 15.09 | 49 | 6¼ |
| Ana Biryukova, Russia, 1993 | | | |
| Shot | 22.63 | 74 | 3 |
| Natalya Lisovskaya, USSR, 1987 | | | |
| Discus | 76.80 | 252 | 0 |
| Gabriele Reinsch, GDR, 1988 | | | |
| Javelin | 80.00 | 262 | 5 |
| Petra Felke, GDR, 1988 | | | |
| Heptathlon† | | | 7,291 pts |
| Jackie Joyner-Kersee, USA, 1988 | | | |

†Seven events comprising 100 m hurdles, shot, high jump, 200 m, long jump, javelin, 800 m

## ATHLETICS NATIONAL (UK) RECORDS
AS AT 3 SEPTEMBER 1994

Records set anywhere by athletes eligible to represent Great Britain and Northern Ireland

## MEN

| TRACK EVENTS | hr. | min. | sec. |
|---|---|---|---|
| 100 metres | | | 9.87 |
| Linford Christie, 1993 | | | |
| 200 metres | | | 19.87 |
| John Regis, 1994 | | | |
| 400 metres | | | 44.47 |
| David Grindley, 1992 | | | |
| 800 metres | | 1 | 41.73 |
| Sebastian Coe, 1981 | | | |
| 1,000 metres | | 2 | 12.18 |
| Sebastian Coe, 1981 | | | |
| 1,500 metres | | 3 | 29.67 |
| Sebastian Coe, 1985 | | | |
| 1 mile | | 3 | 46.32 |
| Steve Cram, 1985 | | | |
| 2,000 metres | | 4 | 51.39 |
| Steve Cram, 1985 | | | |
| 3,000 metres | | 7 | 32.79 |
| David Moorcroft, 1982 | | | |
| 5,000 metres | | 13 | 00.41 |
| David Moorcroft, 1982 | | | |
| 10,000 metres | | 27 | 23.06 |
| Eamonn Martin, 1988 | | | |
| 20,000 metres | | 57 | 28.7 |
| Carl Thackery, 1990 | | | |
| 20,855 metres | 1 | | |
| Carl Thackery, 1990 | | | |
| 25,000 metres | 1 | 15 | 22.6 |
| Ron Hill, 1965 | | | |
| 30,000 metres | 1 | 31 | 30.4 |
| Jim Alder, 1970 | | | |
| 3,000 metres steeplechase | | 8 | 07.96 |
| Mark Rowland, 1988 | | | |

| | |
|---|---|
| 110 metres hurdles | 12.91 |
| Colin Jackson, 1993 | |
| 400 metres hurdles | 47.82 |
| Kriss Akabusi, 1992 | |

| RELAYS | | min. | sec. |
|---|---|---|---|
| 4 × 100 metres | | | 37.77 |
| GB team, 1993 | | | |
| 4 × 200 metres | | 1 | 21.29 |
| GB team, 1989 | | | |
| 4 × 400 metres | | 2 | 57.53 |
| GB team, 1991 | | | |
| 4 × 800 metres | | 7 | 03.89 |
| GB team, 1982 | | | |

| FIELD EVENTS | metres | ft | in |
|---|---|---|---|
| High jump | 2.37 | 7 | 9¼ |
| Steve Smith, 1992, 1993 | | | |
| Pole vault | 5.65 | 18 | 6¼ |
| Keith Stock, 1981 | | | |
| Long jump | 8.23 | 27 | 0 |
| Lynn Davies, 1968 | | | |
| Triple jump | 17.57 | 57 | 7¾ |
| Keith Connor, 1982 | | | |
| Shot | 21.68 | 71 | 1½ |
| Geoff Capes, 1980 | | | |
| Discus | 64.32 | 211 | 0 |
| William Tancred, 1974 | | | |
| Hammer | 77.54 | 254 | 5 |
| Martin Girvan, 1984 | | | |
| Javelin | 91.46 | 300 | 1 |
| Steve Backley, 1992 | | | |
| Decathlon | | | 8,847 points |
| Daley Thompson, 1984 | | | |

| WALKING (TRACK) | hr. | min. | sec. |
|---|---|---|---|
| 20,000 metres | 1 | 23 | 26.5 |
| Ian McCombie, 1990 | | | |
| 30,000 metres | 2 | 19 | 18 |
| Christopher Maddocks, 1984 | | | |
| 50,000 metres | 4 | 05 | 44.6 |
| Paul Blagg, 1990 | | | |
| 2 hours | 26,037 metres (16 miles 315 yards) | | |
| Ron Wallwork, 1971 | | | |

## WOMEN

| TRACK EVENTS | min. | sec. |
|---|---|---|
| 100 metres | | 11.10 |
| Kathy Cook, 1981 | | |
| 200 metres | | 22.10 |
| Kathy Cook, 1984 | | |
| 400 metres | | 49.43 |
| Kathy Cook, 1984 | | |
| 800 metres | 1 | 57.42 |
| Kirsty Wade, 1985 | | |
| 1,500 metres | 3 | 59.96 |
| Zola Budd, 1985 | | |
| 1 mile | 4 | 17.57 |
| Zola Budd, 1985 | | |
| 3,000 metres | 8 | 28.83 |
| Zola Budd, 1985 | | |
| 5,000 metres | 14 | 48.07 |
| Zola Budd, 1985 | | |
| 10,000 metres | 30 | 57.07 |
| Liz McColgan, 1991 | | |
| 100 metres hurdles | | 12.82 |
| Sally Gunnell, 1988 | | |

| | min. | sec. |
|---|---|---|
| 400 metres hurdles | | 52.74 |
| Sally Gunnell, 1993 | | |

RELAYS

| | min. | sec. |
|---|---|---|
| 4 × 100 metres | | 42.43 |
| GB team, 1980 | | |
| 4 × 200 metres | 1 | 31.57 |
| GB team, 1977 | | |
| 4 × 400 metres | 3 | 22.01 |
| GB team, 1991 | | |
| 4 × 800 metres | 8 | 23.8 |
| GB team, 1971 | | |

FIELD EVENTS

| | metres | ft | in |
|---|---|---|---|
| High jump | 1.95 | 6 | 4¾ |
| Diana Elliott, 1982 | | | |
| Long jump | 6.90 | 22 | 7¾ |
| Beverley Kinch, 1983 | | | |
| Triple jump | 14.08 | 46 | 2½ |
| Michelle Griffith, 1994 | | | |
| Shot | 19.36 | 63 | 6¼ |
| Judy Oakes, 1988 | | | |
| Discus | 67.48 | 221 | 5 |
| Margaret Ritchie, 1981 | | | |
| Javelin | 77.44 | 254 | 1 |
| Fatima Whitbread, 1986 | | | |
| Heptathlon | 6,623 points | | |
| Judy Simpson, 1986 | | | |

## SWIMMING WORLD RECORDS
AS AT 31 AUGUST 1994

MEN

| | min. | sec. |
|---|---|---|
| 50 metres freestyle | | 21.81 |
| Tom Jager, USA | | |
| 100 metres freestyle | | 48.21 |
| Alexander Popov, Russia | | |
| 200 metres freestyle | 1 | 46.69 |
| Giorgio Lamberti, Italy | | |
| 400 metres freestyle | 3 | 45.00 |
| Evgueni Sadovyi, CIS | | |
| 800 metres freestyle | 7 | 46.00 |
| Kieren Perkins, Australia | | |
| 1,500 metres freestyle | 14 | 41.66 |
| Kieren Perkins, Australia | | |
| 100 metres breaststroke | 1 | 00.95 |
| Karoly Guttler, Hungary | | |
| 200 metres breaststroke | 2 | 10.16 |
| Mike Barrowman, USA | | |
| 100 metres butterfly | | 52.84 |
| Pablo Morales, USA | | |
| 200 metres butterfly | 1 | 55.69 |
| Melvin Stewart, USA | | |
| 100 metres backstroke | | 53.86 |
| Jeff Rouse, USA | | |
| 200 metres backstroke | 1 | 56.57 |
| Martin Lopez-Zubero, Spain | | |
| 200 metres medley | 1 | 59.36 |
| Tamás Darnyi, Hungary | | |
| 400 metres medley | 4 | 12.36 |
| Tamás Darnyi, Hungary | | |
| 4 × 100 metres freestyle relay | 3 | 16.53 |
| USA | | |
| 4 × 200 metres freestyle relay | 7 | 11.95 |
| CIS | | |
| 4 × 100 metres medley relay | 3 | 36.93 |
| USA | | |

WOMEN

| | min. | sec. |
|---|---|---|
| 50 metres freestyle | | 24.79 |
| Yang Wenyi, China | | |
| 100 metres freestyle | | 54.48 |
| Jenny Thompson, USA | | |
| 200 metres freestyle | 1 | 57.55 |
| Heike Friedrich, GDR | | |
| 400 metres freestyle | 4 | 03.85 |
| Janet Evans, USA | | |
| 800 metres freestyle | 8 | 16.22 |
| Janet Evans, USA | | |
| 1,500 metres freestyle | 15 | 52.10 |
| Janet Evans, USA | | |
| 100 metres breaststroke | 1 | 07.91 |
| Silke Hörner, GDR | | |
| 200 metres breaststroke | 2 | 24.76 |
| Rebecca Brown, Australia | | |
| 100 metres butterfly | | 57.93 |
| Mary Meagher, USA | | |
| 200 metres butterfly | 2 | 05.96 |
| Mary Meagher, USA | | |
| 100 metres backstroke | 1 | 00.31 |
| Krisztina Egerszegi, Hungary | | |
| 200 metres backstroke | 2 | 06.62 |
| Krisztina Egerszegi, Hungary | | |
| 200 metres medley | 2 | 11.65 |
| Li Lin, China | | |
| 400 metres medley | 4 | 36.10 |
| Petra Schneider, GDR | | |
| 4 × 100 metres freestyle relay | 3 | 39.46 |
| USA | | |
| 4 × 200 metres freestyle relay | 7 | 55.47 |
| GDR | | |
| 4 × 100 metres medley relay | 4 | 02.54 |
| USA | | |

# Weights and Measures

## SI UNITS

The Système International d'Unités (SI) is an international and coherent system of units devised to meet all known needs for measurement in science and technology. The system was adopted by the eleventh Conférence Générale des Poids et Mesures (CGPM) in 1960. A comprehensive description of the system is given in *SI The International System of Units*, HMSO. The British Standards describing the essential features of the International System of Units are *Specifications for SI units and recommendations for the use of their multiples and certain other units* (BS 5555:1993) and *Conversion Factors and Tables* (BS 350, Part 1:1974).

The system consists of seven base units and the derived units formed as products or quotients of various powers of the base units. Together the base units and the derived units make up the coherent system of units. In the UK the SI base units, and almost all important derived units, are realized at the National Physical Laboratory and disseminated through the National Measurement System.

### BASE UNITS

Metre (m) = unit of length
Kilogram (kg) = unit of mass
Second (s) = unit of time
Ampere (A) = unit of electric current
Kelvin (K) = unit of thermodynamic temperature
Mole (mol) = unit of amount of substance
Candela (cd) = unit of luminous intensity

### DERIVED UNITS

For some of the derived SI units, special names and symbols exist; those approved by the CGPM are as follows:

Hertz (Hz) = unit of frequency
Newton (N) = unit of force
Pascal (Pa) = unit of pressure, stress
Joule (J) = unit of energy, work, quantity of heat
Watt (W) = unit of power, radiant flux
Coulomb (C) = unit of electric charge, quantity of electricity
Volt (V) = unit of electric potential, potential difference, electromotive force
Farad (F) = unit of electric capacitance
Ohm ($\Omega$) = unit of electric resistance
Siemens (S) = unit of electric conductance
Weber (Wb) = unit of magnetic flux
Tesla (T) = unit of magnetic flux density
Henry (H) = unit of inductance
Degree Celsius (°C) = unit of Celsius temperature
Lumen (lm) = unit of luminous flux
Lux (lx) = unit of illuminance
Becquerel (Bq) = unit of activity (of a radionuclide)
Gray (Gy) = unit of absorbed dose, specific energy imparted, kerma, absorbed dose index
Sievert (Sv) = unit of dose equivalent, dose equivalent index

### SUPPLEMENTARY UNITS

The derived units include, as a special case, the supplementary units which may be treated as dimensionless within the SI.

Radian (rad) = unit of plane angle
Steradian (sr) = unit of solid angle

Other derived units are expressed in terms of base units and/or supplementary units. Some of the more commonly-used derived units are the following:

Unit of area = square metre ($m^2$)
Unit of volume = cubic metre ($m^3$)
Unit of velocity = metre per second ($m\ s^{-1}$)
Unit of acceleration = metre per second squared ($m\ s^{-2}$)
Unit of density = kilogram per cubic metre ($kg\ m^{-3}$)
Unit of momentum = kilogram metre per second ($kg\ m\ s^{-1}$)
Unit of magnetic field strength = ampere per metre ($A\ m^{-1}$)
Unit of surface tension = newton per metre ($N\ m^{-1}$)
Unit of dynamic viscosity = pascal second (Pa s)
Unit of heat capacity = joule per kelvin ($J\ K^{-1}$)
Unit of specific heat capacity = joule per kilogram kelvin ($J\ kg^{-1}\ K^{-1}$)
Unit of heat flux density, irradiance = watt per square metre ($W\ m^{-2}$)
Unit of thermal conductivity = watt per metre kelvin ($W\ m^{-1}\ K^{-1}$)
Unit of electric field strength = volt per metre ($V\ m^{-1}$)
Unit of luminance = candela per square metre ($cd\ m^{-2}$)

### SI PREFIXES

Decimal multiples and submultiples of the SI units are indicated by SI prefixes. These are as follows:

| multiples | submultiples |
|---|---|
| yotta (Y) × $10^{24}$ | deci (d) × $10^{-1}$ |
| zetta (Z) × $10^{21}$ | centi (c) × $10^{-2}$ |
| exa (E) × $10^{18}$ | milli (m) × $10^{-3}$ |
| peta (P) × $10^{15}$ | micro ($\mu$) × $10^{-6}$ |
| tera (T) × $10^{12}$ | nano (n) × $10^{-9}$ |
| giga (G) × $10^9$ | pico (p) × $10^{-12}$ |
| mega (M) × $10^6$ | femto (f) × $10^{-15}$ |
| kilo (k) × $10^3$ | atto (a) × $10^{-18}$ |
| hecto (h) × $10^2$ | zepto (z) × $10^{-21}$ |
| deca (da) × $10$ | yocto (y) × $10^{-24}$ |

## UK UNITS

The legal units for the United Kingdom are enacted in the Weights and Measures Act 1985. The Act is due to be amended to take account of the provisions of Council Directive 80/181/EEC as amended by 89/617/EEC on units of measurement, the general effect of which will be to phase out many imperial units. However, at the time of going to press the amending legislation had not been introduced in Parliament.

The United Kingdom primary standards are the yard or the metre as the unit of measurement of length, and the pound or the kilogram as the unit of measurement of mass. Other units of measurement are defined by reference to the primary standards.

Responsibility for the maintenance of the primary standards and for the determination or redetermination of their value rests with the President of the Board of Trade.

The definition of the UK primary standards is as follows:

Yard = 0.9144 metre
Metre is the length of the path travelled by light in vacuum during a time interval of 1/299 792 458 of a second.

Pound = 0.453 592 37 kilogram

Kilogram is equal to the mass of the international prototype of the kilogram

The following list shows the definitions of measures set out in Schedule 1 of the Weights and Measures Act 1985.

## MEASUREMENT OF LENGTH

*Imperial Units*

Mile = 1760 yards

Yard (yd) = 0.9144 metre

Foot (ft) = 1/3 yard

Inch (in) = 1/36 yard

*Metric Units*

Kilometre (km) = 1000 metres

Metre (m) is the length of the path travelled by light in vacuum during a time interval of 1/299 792 458 of a second

Decimetre (dm) = 1/10 metre

Centimetre (cm) = 1/100 metre

Millimetre (mm) = 1/1000 metre

## MEASUREMENT OF AREA

*Imperial Units*

Acre = 4840 square yards

Square yard = a superficial area equal to that of a square each side of which measures one yard

Square foot = 1/9 square yard

*Metric Units*

Hectare (ha) = 100 ares

Decare = 10 ares

Are (a) = 100 square metres

Square metre = a superficial area equal to that of a square each side of which measures one metre

Square decimetre = 1/100 square metre

Square centimetre = 1/100 square decimetre

Square millimetre = 1/100 square centimetre

## MEASUREMENT OF VOLUME

*Metric Units*

Cubic metre (m³) = a volume equal to that of a cube each edge of which measures one metre

Cubic decimetre = 1/1000 cubic metre

Cubic centimetre (cc) = 1/1000 cubic decimetre

Hectolitre = 100 litres

Litre = a cubic decimetre

Decilitre = 1/10 litre

Centilitre = 1/100 litre

Millilitre = 1/1000 litre

## MEASUREMENT OF CAPACITY

*Imperial Units*

Gallon = 4.546 09 cubic decimetres

Quart = 1/4 gallon

Pint (pt) = 1/2 quart

Gill = 1/4 pint

Fluid ounce (fl oz) = 1/20 pint

*Metric Units*

Hectolitre (hl) = 100 litres

Litre (l or L) = a cubic decimetre

Decilitre (dl) = 1/10 litre

Centilitre (cl) = 1/100 litre

Millilitre (ml) = 1/1000 litre

## MEASUREMENT OF MASS OR WEIGHT

*Imperial Units*

Pound (lb) = 0.453 592 37 kilogram

Ounce (oz) = 1/16 pound

*Ounce troy = 12/175 pound

*Metric Units*

Tonne, metric tonne (t) = 1000 kilograms

Kilogram (kg) is the unit of mass; it is equal to the mass of the international prototype of the kilogram

Hectogram (hg) = 1/10 kilogram

Gram (g) = 1/1000 kilogram

†Carat (metric) = 1/5 gram

Milligram (mg) = 1/1000 gram

*Used only for transactions in gold, silver or other precious metals, and articles made therefrom

†Used only for transactions in precious stones or pearls

## OBSOLESCENT UNITS OF MEASUREMENT

Certain units of measurement may no longer be used for trade although the measure may still be used, e.g. it is legal to sell a 112 lb quantity of a commodity but it must be referred to in invoices, etc., as 112 lb, not as 1 cwt. These units are defined as follows:

*Measurement of Length*

Furlong = 220 yards

Chain = 22 yards

*Measurement of Area*

Square mile = 640 acres

Rood = 1210 square yards

Square inch = 1/144 square foot

*Measurement of Volume*

Cubic yard = a volume equal to that of a cube each edge of which measures one yard

Cubic foot = 1/27 cubic yard

Cubic inch = 1/1728 cubic foot

*Measurement of Capacity*

Bushel = 8 gallons

Peck = 2 gallons

Fluid drachm = 1/8 fluid ounce

Minim (min) = 1/60 fluid drachm

*Measurement of Mass or Weight*

Ton = 2240 pounds

Hundredweight (cwt) = 112 pounds

Cental = 100 pounds

Quarter = 28 pounds

Stone = 14 pounds

Dram (dr) = 1/16 ounce

Grain (gr) = 1/7000 pound

Pennyweight (dwt) = 24 grains

Ounce apothecaries = 480 grains

Drachm (ʒ1) = 1/8 ounce apothecaries

Scruple(ϴ1) = 1/3 drachm

Metric tonne = 1000 kilograms

Quintal (q) = 100 kilograms

## MEASUREMENT OF ELECTRICITY

Units of measurement of electricity are defined by the Weights and Measures Act 1985, as follows:

Ampere (A) = that constant current which, if maintained in two straight parallel conductors of infinite length, of negligible circular cross-section and placed 1 metre apart in vacuum, would produce between these conductors a force equal to $2 \times 10^{-7}$ newton per metre of length

Ohm (Ω) = the electric resistance between two points of a conductor when a constant potential difference of 1 volt, applied between the two points, produces in the

conductor a current of 1 ampere, the conductor not being
the seat of any electromotive force
Volt (V) = the difference of electric potential between two
points of a conducting wire carrying a constant current of
1 ampere when the power dissipated between these
points is equal to 1 watt
Watt (W) = the power which in one second gives rise to
energy of 1 joule
Kilowatt (kW) = 1000 watts
Megawatt (MW) = one million watts

## WATER AND LIQUOR MEASURES

1 cubic foot = 62.32 lb
1 gallon = 10 lb
1 cubic cm = 1 gram
1000 cubic cm = 1 litre; 1 kilogram
1 cubic metre = 1000 litres; 1000 kg; 1 tonne
An inch of rain on the surface of an acre (43560 sq. ft) =
3630 cubic ft = 100.992 tons
*Cisterns:* A cistern 4 × 2½ feet and 3 feet deep will hold
brimful 186.963 gallons, weighing 1869.63 lb in addition
to its own weight

### WATER FOR SHIPS

Kilderkin = 18 gallons
Barrel = 36 gallons
Puncheon = 72 gallons
Butt = 110 gallons
Tun = 210 gallons

## WINE MEASURES

Under the Weights and Measures (Intoxicating Liquor)
Order 1988, as amended by the Weights and Measures
(Various Foods) (Amendment) Order 1990, still wines may
be pre-packed only in the following quantities: 10, 25, 37.5,
50 and 75 cl; 1, 1.5, 2, 3, 4, 5, 6, 8, 9 and 10 litres. In addition,
the 18.7 cl size is permitted for consumption on board
aircraft, ships and trains or for sale duty-free, and all
quantities up to and including 25 cl are allowed when for
consumption on the premises of the seller.
   The Intoxicating Liquor Order also provides that sparkling
wines (including champagne) may be pre-packed only in the
following quantities: 12.5, 20, 37.5 and 75 cl; 1.5, 3, 4.5, 6
and 9 litres. However, all quantities are allowed when for
consumption on board aircraft, ships and trains or for sale
duty free.
   Spirits and liqueurs may be pre-packed only in the
following quantities: 2, 3, 4, 5, 7.1, 10, 20, 35, 50 and 70 cl;
1, 1.5, 2, 2.5, 3 and 4.5 litres. In addition, 1.125, 5 and 10
litres are permitted for non-retail sales and all quantities are
allowed when for consumption on board aircraft, ships and
trains or for sale duty free.

### BOTTLES OF WINE

Traditional equivalents in standard champagne bottles:
Magnum = 2 bottles
Jeroboam = 4 bottles
Rehoboam = 6 bottles
Methuselah = 8 bottles
Salmanazar = 12 bottles
Balthazar = 16 bottles
Nebuchadnezzar = 20 bottles

A quarter of a bottle is known as a *nip*.
An eighth of a bottle is known as a *baby*.

## ANGULAR AND CIRCULAR MEASURES

60 seconds (″) = 1 minute (′)
60 minutes = 1 degree (°)
90 degrees = 1 right angle or quadrant
Diameter of circle × 3.141 6 = circumference
Diameter squared × 0.7854 = area of circle
Diameter squared × 3.141 6 = surface of sphere
Diameter cubed × 0.523 = solidity of sphere
One degree of circumference × 57.3 = radius*
Diameter of cylinder × 3.141 6; product by length or height,
gives the surface
Diameter squared × 0.7854; product by length or height,
gives solid content

*Or, one radian (the angle subtended at the centre of a
circle by an arc of the circumference equal in length to the
radius) = 57.3 degrees

## MILLION, BILLION, ETC.

*Value in the United Kingdom*

| | | |
|---|---|---|
| Million | thousand × thousand | $10^6$ |
| Billion | million × million | $10^{12}$ |
| Trillion | million × billion | $10^{18}$ |
| Quadrillion | million × trillion | $10^{24}$ |

*Value in USA*

| | | |
|---|---|---|
| Million | thousand × thousand | $10^6$ |
| Billion | thousand × million | $10^9$ |
| Trillion | million × million | $10^{12}$ |
| Quadrillion | million × billion US | $10^{15}$ |

The American usage of billion (i.e. $10^9$) is increasingly
common, and is now universally used by statisticians

## NAUTICAL MEASURES

### DISTANCE

Distance at sea is measured in nautical miles. The British
standard nautical mile was 6080 feet (the length of a minute
of an arc of a great circle of the earth, rounded off to a mean
value to allow for the length varying at different latitudes).
This measure has been obsolete since 1970 when the
international nautical mile of 1852 metres was adopted by
the Hydrographic Department of the Ministry of Defence as
a result of a recommendation by the International Hydrographic Bureau.
   The cable (600 feet or 100 fathoms) was a measure
approximately one-tenth of a nautical mile. Such distances
are now expressed in decimal parts of a sea mile or in metres.
   Soundings at sea were recorded in fathoms (6 feet). Depths
are now expressed in metres on Admiralty charts.

### SPEED

Speed is measured in nautical miles per hour, called knots. A
ship moving at the rate of 30 nautical miles per hour is said
to be doing 30 knots.

| knots | m.p.h. | knots | m.p.h. |
|---|---|---|---|
| 1 | 1.1515 | 9 | 10.3636 |
| 2 | 2.3030 | 10 | 11.5151 |
| 3 | 3.4545 | 15 | 17.2727 |
| 4 | 4.6060 | 20 | 23.0303 |
| 5 | 5.7575 | 25 | 28.7878 |
| 6 | 6.9090 | 30 | 34.5454 |
| 7 | 8.0606 | 35 | 40.3030 |
| 8 | 9.2121 | 40 | 46.0606 |

## TONNAGE

The tonnage of a vessel is measured in tons of 100 cubic feet.
Gross tonnage = the total volume of all the enclosed spaces
  of a vessel
Net tonnage = gross tonnage less deductions for crew space,
  engine room, water ballast and other spaces not used for
  passengers or cargo

## DISTANCE OF THE HORIZON

The limit of distance to which one can see varies with the
height of the spectator. The greatest distance at which an
object on the surface of the sea, or of a level plain, can be
seen by a person whose eyes are at a height of five feet from
the same level is nearly three miles. At a height of 20 feet
the range is increased to nearly six miles, and an approximate
rule for finding the range of vision for small heights is to
increase the square root of the number of feet that the eye is
above the level surface by a third of itself. The result is the
distance of the horizon in miles, but is slightly in excess of
that in the table below, which is computed by a more precise
formula. The table may be used conversely to show the
distance of an object of given height that is just visible from
a point on the surface of the earth or sea. Refraction is taken
into account both in the approximate rule and in the table.

| Height in feet | range in miles |
|---|---|
| 5 | 2.9 |
| 20 | 5.9 |
| 50 | 9.3 |
| 100 | 13.2 |
| 500 | 29.5 |
| 1,000 | 41.6 |
| 2,000 | 58.9 |
| 3,000 | 72.1 |
| 4,000 | 83.3 |
| 5,000 | 93.1 |
| 20,000 | 186.2 |

## TEMPERATURE SCALES

The SI (International System) unit of temperature is the
Kelvin, which is defined as the fraction 1/273.16 of the
temperature of the triple point of water (i.e. where ice, water
and water vapour are in equilibrium). The zero of the Kelvin
scale is the absolute zero of temperature. The freezing point
of water is 273.15 K and the boiling point (as adopted in the
International Temperature Scale of 1990) is 373.124 K.
  The Celsius scale (formerly centigrade) is defined by
subtracting 273.15 from the Kelvin temperature. The
Fahrenheit scale is related to the Celsius scale by the
relationships:

temperature $°F$ = (temperature $°C$ × 1.8) + 32
temperature $°C$ = (temperature $°F$ − 32) ÷ 1.8

It follows from these definitions that the freezing point of
water is 0°C and 32°F. The boiling point is 99.974°C and
211.953°F.
  The normal temperature of the human body is 36.9°C or
98.4°F.

*Conversion between scales*

| °C | °F | °C | °F | °C | °F |
|---|---|---|---|---|---|
| 100 | 212 | 60 | 140 | 20 | 68 |
| 99 | 210.2 | 59 | 138.2 | 19 | 66.2 |
| 98 | 208.4 | 58 | 136.4 | 18 | 64.4 |
| 97 | 206.6 | 57 | 134.6 | 17 | 62.6 |
| 96 | 204.8 | 56 | 132.8 | 16 | 60.8 |
| 95 | 203 | 55 | 131 | 15 | 59 |
| 94 | 201.2 | 54 | 129.2 | 14 | 57.2 |
| 93 | 199.4 | 53 | 127.4 | 13 | 55.4 |
| 92 | 197.6 | 52 | 125.6 | 12 | 53.6 |
| 91 | 195.8 | 51 | 123.8 | 11 | 51.8 |
| 90 | 194 | 50 | 122 | 10 | 50 |
| 89 | 192.2 | 49 | 120.2 | 9 | 48.2 |
| 88 | 190.4 | 48 | 118.4 | 8 | 46.4 |
| 87 | 188.6 | 47 | 116.6 | 7 | 44.6 |
| 86 | 186.8 | 46 | 114.8 | 6 | 42.8 |
| 85 | 185 | 45 | 113 | 5 | 41 |
| 84 | 183.2 | 44 | 111.2 | 4 | 39.2 |
| 83 | 181.4 | 43 | 109.4 | 3 | 37.4 |
| 82 | 179.6 | 42 | 107.6 | 2 | 35.6 |
| 81 | 177.8 | 41 | 105.8 | 1 | 33.8 |
| 80 | 176 | 40 | 104 | zero | 32 |
| 79 | 174.2 | 39 | 102.2 | − 1 | 30.2 |
| 78 | 172.4 | 38 | 100.4 | − 2 | 28.4 |
| 77 | 170.6 | 37 | 98.6 | − 3 | 26.6 |
| 76 | 168.8 | 36 | 96.8 | − 4 | 24.8 |
| 75 | 167 | 35 | 95 | − 5 | 23 |
| 74 | 165.2 | 34 | 93.2 | − 6 | 21.2 |
| 73 | 163.4 | 33 | 91.4 | − 7 | 19.4 |
| 72 | 161.6 | 32 | 89.6 | − 8 | 17.6 |
| 71 | 159.8 | 31 | 87.8 | − 9 | 15.8 |
| 70 | 158 | 30 | 86 | − 10 | 14 |
| 69 | 156.2 | 29 | 84.2 | − 11 | 12.2 |
| 68 | 154.4 | 28 | 82.4 | − 12 | 10.4 |
| 67 | 152.6 | 27 | 80.6 | − 13 | 8.6 |
| 66 | 150.8 | 26 | 78.8 | − 14 | 6.8 |
| 65 | 149 | 25 | 77 | − 15 | 5 |
| 64 | 147.2 | 24 | 75.2 | − 16 | 3.2 |
| 63 | 145.4 | 23 | 73.4 | − 17 | 1.4 |
| 62 | 143.6 | 22 | 71.6 | − 18 | 0.4 |
| 61 | 141.8 | 21 | 69.8 | − 19 | − 2.2 |

## PAPER MEASURES

*Printing Paper*
516 sheets = 1 ream
2 reams    = 1 bundle
5 bundles  = 1 bale

*Writing Paper*
480 sheets = 1 ream
20 quires = 1 ream
24 sheets = 1 quire

BROWN PAPERS

| | inches | | inches |
|---|---|---|---|
| Casing | 46 × 36 | Imperial Cap | 29 × 22 |
| Double Imperial | 45 × 29 | Haven Cap | 26 × 21 |
| Elephant | 34 × 24 | Bag Cap | 24 × 19½ |
| Double Four | | Kent Cap | 21 × 18 |
| Pound | 31 × 21 | | |

### Printing Papers

| | inches | | inches |
|---|---|---|---|
| Foolscap | 17 × 13½ | Double Large Post | 33 × 21 |
| Double Foolscap | 27 × 17 | Demy | 22½ × 17½ |
| Quad Foolscap | 34 × 27 | Double Demy | 35 × 22½ |
| Crown | 20 × 15 | Quad Demy | 45 × 35 |
| Double Crown | 30 × 20 | Music Demy | 20 × 15½ |
| Quad Crown | 40 × 30 | Medium | 23 × 18 |
| Double Quad Crown | 60 × 40 | Royal | 25 × 20 |
| Post | 19¼ × 15½ | Super Royal | 27½ × 20½ |
| Double Post | 31½ × 19½ | Elephant | 28 × 23 |
| | | Imperial | 30 × 22 |

### Writing and Drawing Papers

| | inches | | inches |
|---|---|---|---|
| Emperor | 72 × 48 | Copy or Draft | 20 × 16 |
| Antiquarian | 53 × 31 | Demy | 20 × 15½ |
| Double Elephant | 40 × 27 | Post | 19 × 15¼ |
| Grand Eagle | 42 × 28¾ | Pinched Post | 18½ × 14¾ |
| Atlas | 34 × 26 | Foolscap | 17 × 13½ |
| Colombier | 34½ × 23½ | Double Foolscap | 26½ × 16½ |
| Imperial | 30 × 22 | Double Post | 30½ × 19 |
| Elephant | 28 × 23 | Double Large Post | 33 × 21 |
| Cartridge | 26 × 21 | Double Demy | 31 × 20 |
| Super Royal | 27 × 19 | Brief | 16½ × 13¼ |
| Royal | 24 × 19 | Pott | 15 × 12½ |
| Medium | 22 × 17½ | | |
| Large Post | 21 × 16½ | | |

## INTERNATIONAL PAPER SIZES

The basis of the international series of paper sizes is a rectangle having an area of one square metre, the sides of which are in the proportion of $1:\sqrt{2}$. The proportions $1:\sqrt{2}$ have a geometrical relationship, the side and diagonal of any square being in this proportion. The effect of this arrangement is that if the area of the sheet of paper is doubled or halved, the shorter side and the longer side of the new sheet are still in the same proportion $1:\sqrt{2}$. This feature is useful where photographic enlargement or reduction is used, as the proportions remain the same.

Description of the A series is by capital A followed by a figure. The basic size has the description A0 and the higher the figure following the letter, the greater is the number of sub-divisions and therefore the smaller the sheet. Half A0 is A1 and half A1 is A2. Where larger dimensions are required the A is preceded by a figure. Thus 2A means twice the size A0; 4A is four times the size of A0.

### Subsidiary Series

A series of B sizes has been devised for use when sizes intermediate between any two adjacent sizes of the A series are needed. In addition there is a series of C sizes which is used much less. A is for magazines and books, B for posters, wall charts and other large items, C for envelopes particularly where it is necessary for an envelope (in C series) to fit into another envelope. The size recommended for business correspondence is A4.

Long sizes (DL) are obtainable by dividing any appropriate sizes from the two series above into three, four or eight equal parts parallel with the shorter side in such a manner that the proportion of $1:\sqrt{2}$ is not maintained, the ratio between the longer and the shorter sides being greater than $\sqrt{2}:1$. In practice long sizes should be produced from the A series only.

It is an essential feature of these series that the dimensions are of the trimmed or finished size.

### A Series

| | mm | | mm |
|---|---|---|---|
| A0 | 841 × 1189 | A6 | 105 × 148 |
| A1 | 594 × 841 | A7 | 74 × 105 |
| A2 | 420 × 594 | A8 | 52 × 74 |
| A3 | 297 × 420 | A9 | 37 × 52 |
| A4 | 210 × 297 | A10 | 26 × 37 |
| A5 | 148 × 210 | | |

### B Series

| | mm | | mm |
|---|---|---|---|
| B0 | 1000 × 1414 | B6 | 125 × 176 |
| B1 | 707 × 1000 | B7 | 88 × 125 |
| B2 | 500 × 707 | B8 | 62 × 88 |
| B3 | 353 × 500 | B9 | 44 × 62 |
| B4 | 250 × 353 | B10 | 31 × 44 |
| B5 | 176 × 250 | | |

| C Series | | DL | |
|---|---|---|---|
| | mm | | mm |
| C4 | 324 × 229 | DL | 110 × 220 |
| C5 | 229 × 162 | | |
| C6 | 114 × 162 | | |

## BOUND BOOKS

The book sizes most commonly used are listed below. Approximate centimetre equivalents are also shown. International sizes are converted to their nearest imperial size, e.g. A4 = D4; A5 = D8.

| | | inches | cm |
|---|---|---|---|
| Crown 32mo | C32 | 2½ × 3¾ | 6 × 9 |
| Crown 16mo | C16 | 3¾ × 5 | 9 × 13 |
| Foolscap 8vo | F8 | 4¼ × 6¾ | 11 × 17 |
| Demy 16mo | D16 | 4⅜ × 5⅝ | 11 × 14 |
| Crown 8vo | C8 | 5 × 7½ | 13 × 19 |
| Demy 8vo | D8 | 5⅝ × 8¾ | 14 × 22 |
| Medium 8vo | M8 | 5¾ × 9 | 15 × 23 |
| Royal 8vo | R8 | 6¼ × 10 | 16 × 25 |
| Super Royal 8vo | suR8 | 6¾ × 10 | 17 × 25 |
| Foolscap 4to | F4 | 6¾ × 8½ | 17 × 22 |
| Crown 4to | C4 | 7½ × 10 | 19 × 25 |
| Imperial 8vo | Imp8 | 7½ × 11 | 19 × 28 |
| Demy 4to | D4 | 8¾ × 11¼ | 22 × 29 |
| Royal 4to | R4 | 10 × 12½ | 25 × 31 |
| Super Royal 4to | suR4 | 10 × 13½ | 25 × 34 |
| Crown Folio | Cfol | 10 × 15 | 25 × 38 |
| Imperial Folio | Impfol | 11 × 15 | 28 × 38 |

Folio = a sheet folded in half
Quarto (4to) = a sheet folded into four
Octavo (8vo) = a sheet folded into eight
Books are usually bound up in sheets of 16 or 32 pages.
Octavo books are generally printed 64 pages at a time, 32 pages on each side of a sheet of quad.

## CONVERSION TABLES FOR WEIGHTS AND MEASURES
Bold figures equal units of either of the columns beside them; thus: 1 cm = 0.394 inches and 1 inch = 2.540 cm

| LENGTH | | | AREA | | | VOLUME | | | WEIGHT (MASS) | | |
|---|---|---|---|---|---|---|---|---|---|---|---|
| *Centimetres* | | *Inches* | *Square cm* | | *Square in* | *Cubic cm* | | *Cubic in* | *Kilograms* | | *Pounds* |
| 2.540 | 1 | 0.394 | 6.452 | 1 | 0.155 | 16.387 | 1 | 0.061 | 0.454 | 1 | 2.205 |
| 5.080 | 2 | 0.787 | 12.903 | 2 | 0.310 | 32.774 | 2 | 0.122 | 0.907 | 2 | 4.409 |
| 7.620 | 3 | 1.181 | 19.355 | 3 | 0.465 | 49.161 | 3 | 0.183 | 1.361 | 3 | 6.614 |
| 10.160 | 4 | 1.575 | 25.806 | 4 | 0.620 | 65.548 | 4 | 0.244 | 1.814 | 4 | 8.819 |
| 12.700 | 5 | 1.969 | 32.258 | 5 | 0.775 | 81.936 | 5 | 0.305 | 2.268 | 5 | 11.023 |
| 15.240 | 6 | 2.362 | 38.710 | 6 | 0.930 | 98.323 | 6 | 0.366 | 2.722 | 6 | 13.228 |
| 17.780 | 7 | 2.756 | 45.161 | 7 | 1.085 | 114.710 | 7 | 0.427 | 3.175 | 7 | 15.432 |
| 20.320 | 8 | 3.150 | 51.613 | 8 | 1.240 | 131.097 | 8 | 0.488 | 3.629 | 8 | 17.637 |
| 22.860 | 9 | 3.543 | 58.064 | 9 | 1.395 | 147.484 | 9 | 0.549 | 4.082 | 9 | 19.842 |
| 25.400 | 10 | 3.937 | 64.516 | 10 | 1.550 | 163.871 | 10 | 0.610 | 4.536 | 10 | 22.046 |
| 50.800 | 20 | 7.874 | 129.032 | 20 | 3.100 | 327.742 | 20 | 1.220 | 9.072 | 20 | 44.092 |
| 76.200 | 30 | 11.811 | 193.548 | 30 | 4.650 | 491.613 | 30 | 1.831 | 13.608 | 30 | 66.139 |
| 101.600 | 40 | 15.748 | 258.064 | 40 | 6.200 | 655.484 | 40 | 2.441 | 18.144 | 40 | 88.185 |
| 127.000 | 50 | 19.685 | 322.580 | 50 | 7.750 | 819.355 | 50 | 3.051 | 22.680 | 50 | 110.231 |
| 152.400 | 60 | 23.622 | 387.096 | 60 | 9.300 | 983.226 | 60 | 3.661 | 27.216 | 60 | 132.277 |
| 177.800 | 70 | 27.559 | 451.612 | 70 | 10.850 | 1147.097 | 70 | 4.272 | 31.752 | 70 | 154.324 |
| 203.200 | 80 | 31.496 | 516.128 | 80 | 12.400 | 1310.968 | 80 | 4.882 | 36.287 | 80 | 176.370 |
| 228.600 | 90 | 35.433 | 580.644 | 90 | 13.950 | 1474.839 | 90 | 5.492 | 40.823 | 90 | 198.416 |
| 254.000 | 100 | 39.370 | 645.160 | 100 | 15.500 | 1638.710 | 100 | 6.102 | 45.359 | 100 | 220.464 |

| *Metres* | | *Yards* | *Square m* | | *Square yd* | *Cubic m* | | *Cubic yd* | *Metric tonnes* | | *Tons (UK)* |
|---|---|---|---|---|---|---|---|---|---|---|---|
| 0.914 | 1 | 1.094 | 0.836 | 1 | 1.196 | 0.765 | 1 | 1.308 | 1.016 | 1 | 0.984 |
| 1.829 | 2 | 2.187 | 1.672 | 2 | 2.392 | 1.529 | 2 | 2.616 | 2.032 | 2 | 1.968 |
| 2.743 | 3 | 3.281 | 2.508 | 3 | 3.588 | 2.294 | 3 | 3.924 | 3.048 | 3 | 2.953 |
| 3.658 | 4 | 4.374 | 3.345 | 4 | 4.784 | 3.058 | 4 | 5.232 | 4.064 | 4 | 3.937 |
| 4.572 | 5 | 5.468 | 4.181 | 5 | 5.980 | 3.823 | 5 | 6.540 | 5.080 | 5 | 4.921 |
| 5.486 | 6 | 6.562 | 5.017 | 6 | 7.176 | 4.587 | 6 | 7.848 | 6.096 | 6 | 5.905 |
| 6.401 | 7 | 7.655 | 5.853 | 7 | 8.372 | 5.352 | 7 | 9.156 | 7.112 | 7 | 6.889 |
| 7.315 | 8 | 8.749 | 6.689 | 8 | 9.568 | 6.116 | 8 | 10.464 | 8.128 | 8 | 7.874 |
| 8.230 | 9 | 9.843 | 7.525 | 9 | 10.764 | 6.881 | 9 | 11.772 | 9.144 | 9 | 8.858 |
| 9.144 | 10 | 10.936 | 8.361 | 10 | 11.960 | 7.646 | 10 | 13.080 | 10.161 | 10 | 9.842 |
| 18.288 | 20 | 21.872 | 16.723 | 20 | 23.920 | 15.291 | 20 | 26.159 | 20.321 | 20 | 19.684 |
| 27.432 | 30 | 32.808 | 25.084 | 30 | 35.880 | 22.937 | 30 | 39.239 | 30.481 | 30 | 29.526 |
| 36.576 | 40 | 43.745 | 33.445 | 40 | 47.840 | 30.582 | 40 | 52.318 | 40.642 | 40 | 39.368 |
| 45.720 | 50 | 54.681 | 41.806 | 50 | 59.799 | 38.228 | 50 | 65.398 | 50.802 | 50 | 49.210 |
| 54.864 | 60 | 65.617 | 50.168 | 60 | 71.759 | 45.873 | 60 | 78.477 | 60.963 | 60 | 59.052 |
| 64.008 | 70 | 76.553 | 58.529 | 70 | 83.719 | 53.519 | 70 | 91.557 | 71.123 | 70 | 68.894 |
| 73.152 | 80 | 87.489 | 66.890 | 80 | 95.679 | 61.164 | 80 | 104.636 | 81.284 | 80 | 78.737 |
| 82.296 | 90 | 98.425 | 75.251 | 90 | 107.639 | 68.810 | 90 | 117.716 | 91.444 | 90 | 88.579 |
| 91.440 | 100 | 109.361 | 83.613 | 100 | 119.599 | 76.455 | 100 | 130.795 | 101.605 | 100 | 98.421 |

| *Kilometres* | | *Miles* | *Hectares* | | *Acres* | *Litres* | | *Gallons* | *Metric tonnes* | | *Tons (US)* |
|---|---|---|---|---|---|---|---|---|---|---|---|
| 1.609 | 1 | 0.621 | 0.405 | 1 | 2.471 | 4.546 | 1 | 0.220 | 0.907 | 1 | 1.102 |
| 3.219 | 2 | 1.243 | 0.809 | 2 | 4.942 | 9.092 | 2 | 0.440 | 1.814 | 2 | 2.205 |
| 4.828 | 3 | 1.864 | 1.214 | 3 | 7.413 | 13.638 | 3 | 0.660 | 2.722 | 3 | 3.305 |
| 6.437 | 4 | 2.485 | 1.619 | 4 | 9.844 | 18.184 | 4 | 0.880 | 3.629 | 4 | 4.409 |
| 8.047 | 5 | 3.107 | 2.023 | 5 | 12.355 | 22.730 | 5 | 1.100 | 4.536 | 5 | 5.521 |
| 9.656 | 6 | 3.728 | 2.428 | 6 | 14.826 | 27.276 | 6 | 1.320 | 5.443 | 6 | 6.614 |
| 11.265 | 7 | 4.350 | 2.833 | 7 | 17.297 | 31.822 | 7 | 1.540 | 6.350 | 7 | 7.716 |
| 12.875 | 8 | 4.971 | 3.327 | 8 | 19.769 | 36.368 | 8 | 1.760 | 7.257 | 8 | 8.818 |
| 14.484 | 9 | 5.592 | 3.642 | 9 | 22.240 | 40.914 | 9 | 1.980 | 8.165 | 9 | 9.921 |
| 16.093 | 10 | 6.214 | 4.047 | 10 | 24.711 | 45.460 | 10 | 2.200 | 9.072 | 10 | 11.023 |
| 32.187 | 20 | 12.427 | 8.094 | 20 | 49.421 | 90.919 | 20 | 4.400 | 18.144 | 20 | 22.046 |
| 48.280 | 30 | 18.641 | 12.140 | 30 | 74.132 | 136.379 | 30 | 6.599 | 27.216 | 30 | 33.069 |
| 64.374 | 40 | 24.855 | 16.187 | 40 | 98.842 | 181.839 | 40 | 8.799 | 36.287 | 40 | 44.092 |
| 80.467 | 50 | 31.069 | 20.234 | 50 | 123.555 | 227.298 | 50 | 10.999 | 45.359 | 50 | 55.116 |
| 96.561 | 60 | 37.282 | 24.281 | 60 | 148.263 | 272.758 | 60 | 13.199 | 54.431 | 60 | 66.139 |
| 112.654 | 70 | 43.496 | 28.328 | 70 | 172.974 | 318.217 | 70 | 15.398 | 63.503 | 70 | 77.162 |
| 128.748 | 80 | 49.710 | 32.375 | 80 | 197.684 | 363.677 | 80 | 17.598 | 72.575 | 80 | 88.185 |
| 144.841 | 90 | 55.923 | 36.422 | 90 | 222.395 | 409.137 | 90 | 19.798 | 81.647 | 90 | 99.208 |
| 160.934 | 100 | 62.137 | 40.469 | 100 | 247.105 | 454.596 | 100 | 21.998 | 90.719 | 100 | 110.231 |

# Abbreviations

A        Associate of
AA       Alcoholics Anonymous
         Anti-Aircraft
         Automobile Association
AAA      Amateur Athletic Association
AB       Able-bodied seaman
ABA      Amateur Boxing Association
abbr(ev) abbreviation
ABM      Anti-ballistic missile
abr      abridged
ac       alternating current
a/c      account
AC       Aircraftman
         (*Ante Christum*) Before Christ
         Companion, Order of Australia
ACAS     Advisory, Conciliation and
         Arbitration Service
ACT      Australian Capital Territory
AD       (*Anno Domini*) In the year of our
         Lord
ADC      Aide-de-Camp
ADC (P)  Personal ADC to The Queen
adj      adjective
Adj      Adjutant
ad lib   (*ad libitum*) at pleasure
Adm      Admiral
         Admission
adv      adverb
         advocate
AE       Air Efficiency Award
AEA      Atomic Energy Authority
AEEU     Amalgamated Engineering and
         Electrical Union
AEM      Air Efficiency Medal
AERE     Atomic Energy Research
         Establishment
AFC      Air Force Cross
         Association Football Club
AFM      Air Force Medal
AFRC     Agricultural and Food Research
         Council
AFV      Armoured fighting vehicle
AG       Adjutant-General
         Attorney-General
AGM      air-to-ground missile
         annual general meeting
AH       (*Anno Hegirae*) In the year of
         the Hegira
AIDS     Acquired immune deficiency
         syndrome
alt      altitude
am       (*ante meridiem*) before noon
AM       (*Anno mundi*) In the year of the
         world
         amplitude modulation
amp      ampere
         amplifier
ANC      African National Congress
anon     anonymous
ANZAC    Australian and New Zealand
         Army Corps
AO       Air Officer
         Officer, Order of Australia
AOC      Air Officer Commanding
AONB     Area of Outstanding Natural
         Beauty
AS       Anglo-Saxon
ASA      Advertising Standards Authority
         Amateur Swimming Association
asap     as soon as possible
ASB      Alternative Service Book
ASEAN    Association of South East Asian
         Nations

ASH      Action on Smoking and Health
ASLEF    Associated Society of
         Locomotive Engineers and
         Firemen
ASLIB    Association for Information
         Management
ASW      anti-submarine warfare
ATC      Air Training Corps
AUC      (*ab urbe condita*) In the year
         from the foundation of Rome
         (*anno urbis conditae*) In the year
         of the founding of the city
AUT      Association of University
         Teachers
AV       Audio-visual
         Authorized Version (*of Bible*)
AVR      Army Volunteer Reserve
AWOL     Absent without leave

b        born
         bowled
BA       Bachelor of Arts
BAA      British Airports Authority
         British Astronomical
         Association
BAF      British Athletics Federation
BAFTA    British Academy of Film and
         Television Arts
BAOR     British Army of the Rhine
Bart     Baronet
BAS      Bachelor in Agricultural Science
         British Antarctic Survey
BB       Boys' Brigade
BBC      British Broadcasting
         Corporation
BBSRC    Biotechnology and Biological
         Sciences Research Council
BC       Before Christ
         British Columbia
BCCI     Bank of Credit and Commerce
         International
B Ch (D) Bachelor of (Dental) Surgery
BCL      Bachelor of Civil Law
B Com    Bachelor of Commerce
BD       Bachelor of Divinity
BDA      British Dental Association
BDS      Bachelor of Dental Surgery
B Ed     Bachelor of Education
BEM      British Empire Medal
B Eng    Bachelor of Engineering
BFI      British Film Institute
BFPO     British Forces Post Office
B Litt   Bachelor of Letters *or* of
         Literature
BM       Bachelor of Medicine
         British Museum
BMA      British Medical Association
B Mus    Bachelor of Music
BOTB     British Overseas Trade Board
Bp       Bishop
B Pharm  Bachelor of Pharmacy
B Phil   Bachelor of Philosophy
Br       Britain
         British
BR       British Rail
BRCS     British Red Cross Society
Brig     Brigadier
Brit     Britain
         British
BSc      Bachelor of Science
BSC      British Steel Corporation
BSI      British Standards Institution

BST      British Summer Time
Bt       Baronet
BTEC     Business and Technology
         Education Council
B Th     Bachelor of Theology
Btu      British thermal unit
BVM      (*Beata Virgo Maria*) Blessed
         Virgin Mary
BVMS     Bachelor of Veterinary
         Medicine and Surgery
BWB      British Waterways Board

c        (*circa*) about
C        Celsius
         Centigrade
         Conservative
CA       Chartered Accountant
         (*Scotland*)
CAA      Civil Aviation Authority
CAB      Citizens' Advice Bureau
Cantab   (of) Cambridge
Cantuar: of Canterbury (*Archbishop*)
CAP      Common Agricultural Policy
Capt     Captain
Caricom  Caribbean Community and
         Common Market
Carliol: of Carlisle (*Bishop*)
CB       Companion, Order of the Bath
CBE      Commander, Order of the
         British Empire
CBI      Confederation of British
         Industry
CC       Chamber of Commerce
         Companion, Order of Canada
         City Council
         County Council
         County Court
CCC      County Cricket Club
CCF      Combined Cadet Force
C Chem   Chartered Chemist
CD       Civil Defence
         compact disc
         Corps Diplomatique
Cdr      Commander
Cdre     Commodore
CDS      Chief of the Defence Staff
CE       Christian Era
         Civil Engineer
C Eng    Chartered Engineer
Cento    Central Treaty Organization
Cestr:   of Chester (*Bishop*)
CET      Central European Time
         Common External Tariff
cf       (*confer*) compare
CF       Chaplain to the Forces
CFC      Chlorofluorocarbon
CGM      Conspicuous Gallantry Medal
CGS      Centimetre-gramme-second
         (*system*)
         Chief of General Staff
CH       Companion of Honour
ChB/M    Bachelor/Master of Surgery
CI       Channel Islands
         The Imperial Order of the
         Crown of India
CIA      Central Intelligence Agency
Cicestr: of Chichester (*Bishop*)
CID      Criminal Investigation
         Department
CIE      Companion, Order of the Indian
         Empire
cif      cost, insurance and freight

| | | | | | |
|---|---|---|---|---|---|
| C-in-C | Commander-in-Chief | DNB | *Dictionary of National* | FA | Football Association |
| CIPFA | Chartered Institute of Public | | *Biography* | FANY | First Aid Nursing Yeomanry |
| | Finance and Accountancy | DNH | Department of National | FAO | Food and Agriculture |
| C Lit | Companion of Literature | | Heritage | | Organization (*UN*) |
| CLJ | Commander, Order of St | do | (*ditto*) the same | FBA | Fellow, British Academy |
| | Lazarus of Jerusalem | DoE | Department of the Environment | FBAA | Fellow, British Association of |
| CM | (*Chirurgiae Magister*) Master of | DOS | Disk operating system | | Accountants and Auditors |
| | Surgery | | (*computer*) | FBI | Federal Bureau of Investigation |
| CMG | Companion, Order of St | DP | Data processing | FBIM | Fellow, British Institute of |
| | Michael and St George | D Ph *or* | | | Management |
| CND | Campaign for Nuclear | D Phil | Doctor of Philosophy | FBS | Fellow, Botanical Society |
| | Disarmament | DPP | Director of Public Prosecutions | FC | Football Club |
| c/o | care of | Dr | Doctor | FCA | Fellow, Institute of Chartered |
| CO | Commanding Officer | D Sc | Doctor of Science | | Accountants in England and |
| | conscientious objector | DSC | Distinguished Service Cross | | Wales |
| COD | Cash on delivery | DSM | Distinguished Service Medal | FCCA | Fellow, Chartered Association |
| C of E | Church of England | DSO | Companion, Distinguished | | of Certified Accountants |
| COHSE | Confederation of Health Service | | Service Order | FCGI | Fellow, City and Guilds of |
| | Employees | DSS | Department of Social Security | | London Institute |
| COI | Central Office of Information | DTI | Department of Trade and | FCIA | Fellow, Corporation of |
| Col | Colonel | | Industry | | Insurance Agents |
| Con | Conservative | DTP | Desk-top publishing | FCIArb | Fellow, Chartered Institute of |
| Cpl | Corporal | Dunelm: | of Durham (*Bishop*) | | Arbitrators |
| CPM | Colonial Police Medal | DV | (*Deo volente*) God willing | FCIB | Fellow, Chartered Institute of |
| CPRE | Council for the Protection of | | | | Bankers |
| | Rural England | | | | Fellow, Corporation of |
| CPS | Crown Prosecution Service | E | East | | Insurance Brokers |
| CPVE | Certificate of Pre-Vocational | Ebor: | of York (*Archbishop*) | FCIBSE | Fellow, Chartered Institution of |
| | Education | EBRD | European Bank for | | Building Services Engineers |
| CRE | Commission for Racial Equality | | Reconstruction and | FCII | Fellow, Chartered Insurance |
| CSA | Child Support Agency | | Development | | Institute |
| CSCE | Conference on Security and Co- | EC | European Community | FCIS | Fellow, Institute of Chartered |
| | operation in Europe | ECG | Electrocardiogram | | Secretaries and Administrators |
| CSE | Certificate of Secondary | ECGD | Export Credits Guarantee | FCIT | Fellow, Chartered Institute of |
| | Education | | Department | | Transport |
| CSI | Companion, Order of the Star of | ECSC | European Coal and Steel | FCMA | Fellow, Chartered Institute of |
| | India | | Community | | Management Accountants |
| CVO | Commander, Royal Victorian | ECU | European Currency Unit | FCO | Foreign and Commonwealth |
| | Order | ED | Efficiency Decoration | | Office |
| | | EEC | European Economic | FCP | Fellow, College of Preceptors |
| | | | Community | FD | (*Fidei Defensor*) Defender of the |
| d | (*denarius*) penny | EEG | Electroencephalogram | | Faith |
| DBE | Dame Commander, Order of | EFA | European Fighter Aircraft | fec | (*fecit*) made this |
| | the British Empire | EFTA | European Free Trade | FEng | Fellow, Royal Academy of |
| dc | direct current | | Association | | Engineering |
| DC | District Council | eg | (*exempli gratia*) for the sake of | ff | (*fecerunt*) made this (*pl*) |
| | District of Columbia | | example | ff | (*fortissimo*) very loud |
| DCB | Dame Commander, Order of | EMS | European Monetary System | FFA | Fellow, Faculty of Actuaries |
| | the Bath | ENEA | European Nuclear Energy | | (*Scotland*) |
| D Ch | (*Doctor Chirurgiae*) Doctor of | | Agency | | Fellow, Institute of Financial |
| | Surgery | EPSRC | Engineering and Physical | | Accountants |
| DCL | Doctor of Civil Law | | Sciences Research Council | FFAS | Fellow, Faculty of Architects |
| DCM | Distinguished Conduct Medal | ER | (*Elizabetha Regina*) Queen | | and Surveyors |
| DCMG | Dame Commander, Order of St | | Elizabeth | FFPHM | Fellow, Faculty of Public Health |
| | Michael and St George | ERD | Emergency Reserve Decoration | | Medicine |
| DCVO | Dame Commander, Royal | ERM | Exchange Rate Mechanism | FGS | Fellow, Geological Society |
| | Victorian Order | ERNIE | Electronic random number | FHS | Fellow, Heraldry Society |
| DD | Doctor of Divinity | | indicator equipment | FHSM | Fellow, Institute of Health |
| DDS | Doctor of Dental Surgery | ESA | European Space Agency | | Service Management |
| DDT | dichlorodiphenyl- | ESP | Extra-sensory perception | FIA | Fellow, Institute of Actuaries |
| | trichloroethane | ESRC | Economic and Social Research | FIBiol | Fellow, Institute of Biology |
| del | (*delineavit*) he/she drew it | | Council | FICE | Fellow, Institution of Civil |
| DFC | Distinguished Flying Cross | ETA | *Euzkadi ta Askatasuna* (Basque | | Engineers |
| DFE | Department for Education | | separatist organization) | FICS | Fellow, Institution of Chartered |
| DFM | Distinguished Flying Medal | et al | (*et alibi*) and elsewhere | | Shipbrokers |
| DG | (*Dei gratia*) By the grace of God | | (*et alii*) and others | FIEE | Fellow, Institution of Electrical |
| | Director-General | etc | (*et cetera*) and the other things/ | | Engineers |
| DH | Department of Health | | and so forth | FIERE | Fellow, Institution of Electronic |
| DHA | District Health Authority | et seq | (*et sequentia*) and the following | | and Radio Engineers |
| Dip Ed | Diploma in Education | EU | European Union | FIFA | International Association |
| Dip H E | Diploma in Higher Education | Euratom | European Atomic Energy | | Football Federation |
| Dip Tech | Diploma in Technology | | Commission | FIM | Fellow, Institute of Metals |
| DJ | Disc jockey | Exon: | of Exeter (*Bishop*) | FIMM | Fellow, Institution of Mining |
| DL | Deputy Lieutenant | | | | and Metallurgy |
| D Litt | Doctor of Letters *or* of | | | FInstF | Fellow, Institute of Fuel |
| | Literature | *f* | (*forte*) loud | FInstP | Fellow, Institute of Physics |
| D Mus | Doctor of Music | F | Fahrenheit | FIQS | Fellow, Institute of Quantity |
| DNA | deoxyribonucleic acid | | Fellow of | | Surveyors |

| | | | | | |
|---|---|---|---|---|---|
| FIS | Fellow, Institute of Statisticians | FRS | Fellow, Royal Society | HMC | Headmasters' Conference |
| FJI | Fellow, Institute of Journalists | FRSA | Fellow, Royal Society of Arts | HMI | Her/His Majesty's Inspector |
| fl | (*floruit*) flourished | FRSC | Fellow, Royal Society of | HML | Her/His Majesty's Lieutenant |
| FLA | Fellow, Library Association | | Chemistry | HMS | Her/His Majesty's Ship |
| FLS | Fellow, Linnean Society | FRSE | Fellow, Royal Society of | HMSO | Her/His Majesty's Stationery |
| FM | Field Marshal | | Edinburgh | | Office |
| | frequency modulation | FRSL | Fellow, Royal Society of | HNC | Higher National Certificate |
| fo | folio | | Literature | HND | Higher National Diploma |
| FO | Flying Officer | FRTPI | Fellow, Royal Town Planning | HOLMES | Home Office Large Major |
| fob | free on board | | Institute | | Enquiry System |
| FPA | Family Planning Association | FSA | Fellow, Society of Antiquaries | Hon | Honorary |
| FPhS | Fellow, Philosophical Society | FSS | Fellow, Statistical Society | | Honourable |
| FRAD | Fellow, Royal Academy of | FSVA | Fellow, Incorporated Society of | hp | horse power |
| | Dancing | | Valuers and Auctioneers | HP | Hire purchase |
| FRAeS | Fellow, Royal Aeronautical | FT | *Financial Times* | HQ | Headquarters |
| | Society | FTI | Fellow, Textile Institute | HRH | Her/His Royal Highness |
| FRAI | Fellow, Royal Anthropological | FTII | Fellow, Institute of Taxation | HSE | Health and Safety Executive |
| | Institute | FZS | Fellow, Zoological Society | | (*hic sepultus est*) here lies buried |
| FRAM | Fellow, Royal Academy of | | | HSH | Her/His Serene Highness |
| | Music | | | HTR | High temperature reactor |
| FRAS | Fellow, Royal Astronomical | GATT | General Agreement on Tariffs | HWM | High water mark |
| | Society | | and Trade | | |
| FRBS | Fellow, Royal Botanic Society | GBE | Dame/Knight Grand Cross, | | |
| | Fellow, Royal Society of British | | Order of the British Empire | I | Island |
| | Sculptors | GC | George Cross | IAAS | Incorporated Association of |
| FRCA | Fellow, Royal College of | GCB | Dame/Knight Grand Cross, | | Architects and Surveyors |
| | Anaesthetists | | Order of the Bath | IAEA | International Atomic Energy |
| FRCGP | Fellow, Royal College of | GCE | General Certificate of Education | | Agency |
| | General Practitioners | GCHQ | Government Communications | IATA | International Air Transport |
| FRCM | Fellow, Royal College of Music | | Headquarters | | Association |
| FRCO | Fellow, Royal College of | GCIE | Knight Grand Commander, | ibid | (*ibidem*) in the same place |
| | Organists | | Order of the Indian Empire | IBRD | International Bank for |
| FRCOG | Fellow, Royal College of | GCLJ | Knight Grand Cross, Order of | | Reconstruction and |
| | Obstetricians and | | St Lazarus of Jerusalem | | Development |
| | Gynaecologists | GCMG | Dame/Knight Grand Cross, | ICAO | International Civil Aviation |
| FRCP | Fellow, Royal College of | | Order of St Michael and St | | Organization |
| | Physicians, London | | George | ICBM | Inter-continental ballistic missile |
| FRCPath | Fellow, Royal College of | GCSE | General Certificate of Secondary | ICFTU | International Confederation of |
| | Pathologists | | Education | | Free Trade Unions |
| FRCPE(d) | Fellow, Royal College of | GCSI | Knight Grand Commander, | ICJ | International Court of Justice |
| | Physicians, Edinburgh | | Order of the Star of India | ICRC | International Committee of the |
| FRCPI | Fellow, Royal College of | GCVO | Dame/Knight Grand Cross, | | Red Cross |
| | Physicians, Ireland | | Royal Victorian Order | id | (*idem*) the same |
| FRCPsych | Fellow, Royal College of | GDP | Gross domestic product | IDA | International Development |
| | Psychiatrists | Gen | General | | Association |
| FRCR | Fellow, Royal College of | GHQ | General Headquarters | IDD | International direct dialling |
| | Radiologists | GM | George Medal | ie | (*id est*) that is |
| FRCS | Fellow, Royal College of | GMB | General, Municipal, | IEA | International Energy Agency |
| | Surgeons of England | | Boilermakers and Allied Trades | IFAD | International Fund for |
| FRCSE(d) | Fellow, Royal College of | | Union | | Agricultural Development |
| | Surgeons of Edinburgh | GMT | Greenwich Mean Time | IFC | International Finance |
| FRCSGlas | Fellow, Royal College of | GNP | Gross national product | | Corporation |
| | Physicians and Surgeons of | GOC | General Officer Commanding | IHS | (*Iesus Hominum Salvator*) Jesus |
| | Glasgow | GP | General Practitioner | | the Saviour of Mankind |
| FRCSI | Fellow, Royal College of | Gp Capt | Group Captain | ILO | International Labour Office/ |
| | Surgeons in Ireland | GSA | Girls' Schools Association | | Organization |
| FRCVS | Fellow, Royal College of | GSO | General Staff Officer | ILR | Independent local radio |
| | Veterinary Surgeons | | | IMF | International Monetary Fund |
| FREconS | Fellow, Royal Economic Society | | | IMO | International Maritime |
| FRGS | Fellow, Royal Geographical | HAC | Honourable Artillery Company | | Organization |
| | Society | HB | His Beatitude | Inc | Incorporated |
| FRHistS | Fellow, Royal Historical Society | HBM | Her/His Britannic Majesty('s) | incog | (*incognito*) unknown, |
| FRHS | Fellow, Royal Horticultural | HCF | Highest common factor | | unrecognized |
| | Society | | Honorary Chaplain to the | INF | International Nuclear Force |
| FRIBA | Fellow, Royal Institute of | | Forces | INLA | Irish National Liberation Army |
| | British Architects | HE | Her/His Excellency | in loc | (*in loco*) in its place |
| FRICS | Fellow, Royal Institution of | | His Eminence | Inmarsat | International Maritime Satellite |
| | Chartered Surveyors | HGV | Heavy Goods Vehicle | | Organization |
| FRMetS | Fellow, Royal Meteorological | HH | Her/His Highness | INRI | (*Iesus Nazarenus Rex Iudaeorum*) |
| | Society | | Her/His Honour | | Jesus of Nazareth, King of the |
| FRMS | Fellow, Royal Microscopical | | His Holiness | | Jews |
| | Society | HIM | Her/His Imperial Majesty | inst | (*instant*) current month |
| FRNS | Fellow, Royal Numismatic | HIV | Human immunodeficiency virus | Intelsat | International |
| | Society | HJS | (*hic jacet sepultus*) here lies | | Telecommunications Satellite |
| FRPharmS | Fellow, Royal Pharmaceutical | | buried | | Organization |
| | Society | HM | Her/His Majesty('s) | Interpol | International Criminal Police |
| FRPS | Fellow, Royal Photographic | HMAS | Her/His Majesty's Australian | | Commission |
| | Society | | Ship | | |

| | | | | | |
|---|---|---|---|---|---|
| IOC | International Olympic Committee | Lit Hum | (*Literae Humaniores*) Faculty of classics and philosophy, Oxford | mph | miles per hour |
| IOM | Isle of Man | Litt D | Doctor of Letters | MR | Master of the Rolls |
| IOU | I owe you | LJ | Lord Justice | MRC | Medical Research Council |
| IOW | Isle of Wight | LLB | Bachelor of Laws | MS | Master of Surgery |
| IPLO | Irish People's Liberation Organization | LLD | Doctor of Laws | | Manuscript (*pl* MSS) Multiple Sclerosis |
| IQ | Intelligence quotient | LLM | Master of Laws | MSc | Master of Science |
| IRA | Irish Republican Army | LM | Licentiate in Midwifery | MSF | Manufacturing, Science and Finance Union |
| IRC | International Red Cross | LMSSA | Licentiate in Medicine and Surgery, Society of Apothecaries | MTh | Master of Theology |
| Is | Islands | loc cit | (*loco citato*) in the place cited | Mus B/D | Bachelor/Doctor of Music |
| ISBN | International Standard Book Number | log | logarithm | MV | Merchant Vessel Motor Vessel |
| ISO | Imperial Service Order | Londin: | of London (*Bishop*) | MVO | Member, Royal Victorian Order |
| ITC | Independent Television Commission | Long | Longitude | MW | medium wave |
| | | LS | (*loco sigilli*) place of the seal | | |
| ITU | International Telecommunication Union | LSA | Licentiate of Society of Apothecaries | N | North |
| | | Lsd | (*Librae, solidi, denarii*) £, shillings and pence | n/a | not applicable |
| ITV | Independent Television | LSE | London School of Economics and Political Science | NAAFI | Navy, Army and Air Force Institutes |
| | | Lt | Lieutenant | NALGO | National and Local Government Officers' Association |
| JP | Justice of the Peace | LTA | Lawn Tennis Association | | |
| | | Ltd | Limited (liability) | NASA | National Aeronautics and Space Administration |
| | | LTh *or* | | | |
| K | Köchel numeration (*of Mozart's works*) | L Theol | Licentiate in Theology | NAS/UWT | National Association of Schoolmasters/Union of Women Teachers |
| | | LVO | Lieutenant, Royal Victorian Order | | |
| KANU | Kenyan African National Union | LWM | Low water mark | NATO | North Atlantic Treaty Organization |
| KBE | Knight Commander, Order of the British Empire | | | NB | New Brunswick (*nota bene*) note well |
| KCB | Knight Commander, Order of the Bath | M | Member of Monsieur | NCC | Nature Conservancy Council |
| KCIE | Knight Commander, Order of the Indian Empire | MA | Master of Arts | NCIS | National Criminal Intelligence Service |
| KCLJ | Knight Commander, Order of St Lazarus of Jerusalem | MAFF | Ministry of Agriculture, Fisheries and Food | NCO | Non-commissioned officer |
| | | Maj | Major | NDPB | Non-departmental public body |
| KCMG | Knight Commander, Order of St Michael and St George | max | maximum | NEB | New English Bible |
| | | MB/D | Bachelor/Doctor of Medicine | nem con | (*nemine contradicente*) no one contradicting |
| KCSI | Knight Commander, Order of the Star of India | MBA | Master of Business Administration | | |
| KCVO | Knight Commander, Royal Victorian Order | MBE | Member, Order of the British Empire | NERC | Natural Environment Research Council |
| KG | Knight of the Garter | MC | Master of Ceremonies Military Cross | nes | not elsewhere specified |
| KGB | (*Komitet Gosudarstvennoi Besopasnosti*) Committee of State Security (USSR) | MCC | Marylebone Cricket Club. | NFT | National Film Theatre |
| | | MCh(D) | Master of (Dental) Surgery | NFU | National Farmers' Union |
| KKK | Ku Klux Klan | MD | Managing Director Doctor of Medicine | NHS | National Health Service |
| KLJ | Knight, Order of St Lazarus of Jerusalem | | | NI | National Insurance Northern Ireland |
| ko | knock out (*boxing*) | MDS | Master of Dental Surgery | NIV | New International Version (*of Bible*) |
| KP | Knight, Order of St Patrick | ME | Middle English | | |
| KStJ | Knight, Order of St John of Jerusalem | | Myalgic Encephalomyelitis | No | (*numero*) number |
| | | MEC | Member of Executive Council | non seq | (*non sequitur*) it does not follow |
| Kt | Knight | MEd | Master of Education | Norvic: | of Norwich (*Bishop*) |
| KT | Knight of the Thistle | mega | one million times | NP | Notary Public |
| kV | Kilovolt | MEP | Member of the European Parliament | NRA | National Rifle Association National Rivers Authority |
| kW | Kilowatt | | | | |
| kWh | Kilowatt hour | MFH | Master of Foxhounds | NS | New Style (*calendar*) Nova Scotia |
| | | Mgr | Monsignor | | |
| | | MI | Military Intelligence | NSPCC | National Society for the Prevention of Cruelty to Children |
| L | Liberal | micro | one-millionth part | | |
| Lab | Labour | milli | one-thousandth part | | |
| Lat | Latitude | min | minimum | NSW | New South Wales |
| lbw | leg before wicket | MIRAS | Mortgage Interest Relief at Source | NT | National Theatre National Trust New Testament |
| lc | lower case (*printing*) | | | | |
| LCJ | Lord Chief Justice | MLA | Member of Legislative Assembly | NUCPS | National Union of Civil and Public Servants |
| LCM | Least/lowest common multiple | | | | |
| LD | Liberal Democrat | MLC | Member of Legislative Council | NUJ | National Union of Journalists |
| LDS | Licentiate in Dental Surgery | Mlle | Mademoiselle | NUM | National Union of Mineworkers |
| LEA | Local Education Authority | MLR | Minimum lending rate | NUPE | National Union of Public Employees |
| LHD | (*Literarum Humaniorum Doctor*) Doctor of Humane Letters/Literature | MM | Military Medal | | |
| | | Mme | Madame | NUS | National Union of Students |
| | | MN | Merchant Navy | NUT | National Union of Teachers |
| Lib | Liberal | MO | Medical Officer/Orderly | NVQ | National Vocational Qualification |
| Lic | (*Licenciado*) lawyer (*Spanish*) | MoD | Ministry of Defence | | |
| Lic Med | Licentiate in Medicine | MoT | Ministry of Transport | NWT | Northwest Territory |
| Lit | Literary | MP | Member of Parliament Military Police | NY | New York |

| | |
|---|---|
| NZ | New Zealand |
| OAPEC | Organization of Arab Petroleum Exporting Countries |
| OAS | Organization of American States |
| OAU | Organization of African Unity |
| Ob *or* obit | died |
| OBE | Officer, Order of the British Empire |
| OC | Officer Commanding |
| ODA | Overseas Development Administration |
| OE | Old English |
| | omissions excepted |
| OECD | Organization for Economic Co-operation and Development |
| OED | *Oxford English Dictionary* |
| Offer | Office of Electricity Regulation |
| Ofgas | Office of Gas Supply |
| OFM | Order of Friars Minor (*Franciscans*) |
| Ofsted | Office for Standards in Education |
| OFT | Office of Fair Trading |
| Oftel | Office of Telecommunications |
| Ofwat | Office of Water Services |
| OHMS | On Her/His Majesty's Service |
| OM | Order of Merit |
| OND | Ordinary National Diploma |
| op | (*opus*) work |
| OP | Opposite prompt side (*of theatre*) |
| | Order of Preachers (*Dominicans*) |
| | out of print (*books*) |
| op cit | (*opere citato*) in the work cited |
| OPCS | Office of Population Censuses and Surveys |
| OPEC | Organization of Petroleum Exporting Countries |
| OPRAF | Office of Passenger Rail Franchising |
| OPSS | Office of Public Service and Science |
| ORR | Office of the Rail Regulator |
| OS | Old Style (*calendar*) |
| | Ordnance Survey |
| OSA | Order of St Augustine |
| OSB | Order of St Benedict |
| OST | Office of Science and Technology |
| O St J | Officer, Order of St John of Jerusalem |
| OT | Old Testament |
| OTC | Officers' Training Corps |
| Oxon | (of) Oxford |
| | Oxfordshire |
| p | page |
| *p* | (*piano*) softly |
| PA | Personal Assistant |
| | Press Association |
| PAYE | Pay as You Earn |
| pc | (*per centum*) in the hundred |
| PC | personal computer |
| | Police Constable |
| | Privy Counsellor |
| PCC | Press Complaints Commission |
| PDSA | People's Dispensary for Sick Animals |
| PE | Physical Education |
| Petriburg: | of Peterborough (*Bishop*) |
| PGA | Professional Golfers Association |
| PhD | Doctor of Philosophy |
| pinx(it) | he/she painted it |
| pl | plural |

| | |
|---|---|
| PLA | Port of London Authority |
| PLC | Public Limited Company |
| PLO | Palestine Liberation Organization |
| pm | (*post meridiem*) after noon |
| PM | Prime Minister |
| PMRAFNS | Princess Mary's Royal Air Force Nursing Service |
| PO | Petty Officer |
| | Pilot Officer |
| | Post Office |
| | postal order |
| POW | Prisoner of War |
| pp | pages |
| | (*per procurationem*) by proxy |
| PPARC | Particle Physics and Astronomy Research Council |
| PPS | Parliamentary Private Secretary |
| PR | Proportional representation |
| | Public relations |
| PRA | President of the Royal Academy |
| Pro tem | (*pro tempore*) for the time being |
| Prox | (*proximo*) next month |
| PRS | President of the Royal Society |
| PRSE | President of the Royal Society of Edinburgh |
| Ps | Psalm |
| PS | (*postscriptum*) postscript |
| PSBR | Public sector borrowing requirement |
| psc | passed Staff College |
| PSV | Public Service Vehicle |
| Pte | Private |
| PTO | Please turn over |
| QARANC | Queen Alexandra's Royal Army Nursing Corps |
| QARNNS | Queen Alexandra's Royal Naval Nursing Service |
| QB | Queen's Bench |
| QBD | Queen's Bench Division |
| QC | Queen's Counsel |
| QED | (*quod erat demonstrandum*) which was to be proved |
| QGM | Queen's Gallantry Medal |
| QHC | Queen's Honorary Chaplain |
| QHDS | Queen's Honorary Dental Surgeon |
| QHNS | Queen's Honorary Nursing Sister |
| QHP | Queen's Honorary Physician |
| QHS | Queen's Honorary Surgeon |
| QMG | Quartermaster General |
| QPM | Queen's Police Medal |
| QS | Quarter Sessions |
| QSO | Quasi-stellar object (quasar) |
| | Queen's Service Order |
| quango | quasi-autonomous non-governmental organization |
| qv | (*quod vide*) which see |
| R | (*Regina*) Queen |
| | (*Rex*) King |
| RA | Royal Academy/Academician |
| | Royal Artillery |
| RAC | Royal Armoured Corps |
| | Royal Automobile Club |
| RADA | Royal Academy of Dramatic Art |
| RADC | Royal Army Dental Corps |
| RAE | Royal Aerospace Establishment |
| RAEC | Royal Army Educational Corps |
| RAeS | Royal Aeronautical Society |
| RAF | Royal Air Force |
| RAM | Random-access memory (*computer*) |
| | Royal Academy of Music |

| | |
|---|---|
| RAMC | Royal Army Medical Corps |
| RAN | Royal Australian Navy |
| RAOC | Royal Army Ordnance Corps |
| RAPC | Royal Army Pay Corps |
| RAVC | Royal Army Veterinary Corps |
| RBA | Royal Society of British Artists |
| RBG | Royal Botanic Garden |
| RBS | Royal Society of British Sculptors |
| RC | Red Cross |
| | Roman Catholic |
| RCM | Royal College of Music |
| RCN | Royal Canadian Navy |
| RCT | Royal Corps of Transport |
| RD | Refer to drawer (*banking*) |
| | Royal Naval and Royal Marine Forces Reserve Decoration |
| | Rural Dean |
| RDI | Royal Designer for Industry |
| RE | Religious Education |
| | Royal Engineers |
| REME | Royal Electrical and Mechanical Engineers |
| Rep | Representative |
| | Republican |
| Rev(d) | Reverend |
| RFU | Rugby Football Union |
| RGN | Registered General Nurse |
| RGS | Royal Geographical Society |
| RHA | Regional Health Authority |
| RHS | Royal Horticultural Society |
| | Royal Humane Society |
| RI | Rhode Island |
| | Royal Institute of Painters in Watercolours |
| | Royal Institution |
| RIBA | Royal Institute of British Architects |
| RIP | (*Requiescat in pace*) May he/she rest in peace |
| RIR | Royal Irish Regiment |
| RL | Rugby League |
| RM | Registered Midwife |
| | Royal Marines |
| RMA | Royal Military Academy |
| RMN | Registered Mental Nurse |
| RMT | National Union of Rail, Maritime and Transport Workers |
| RN | Royal Navy |
| RNIB | Royal National Institute for the Blind |
| RNID | Royal National Institute for the Deaf |
| RNLI | Royal National Lifeboat Institution |
| RNR | Royal Naval Reserve |
| RNVR | Royal Naval Volunteer Reserve |
| RNXS | Royal Naval Auxiliary Service |
| RNZN | Royal New Zealand Navy |
| Ro | (*Recto*) on the right-hand page |
| ROC | Royal Observer Corps |
| Roffen: | of Rochester (*Bishop*) |
| ROI | Royal Institute of Oil Painters |
| ROM | Read-only memory (*computer*) |
| RoSPA | Royal Society for the Prevention of Accidents |
| RP | Royal Society of Portrait Painters |
| rpm | revolutions per minute |
| RRC | Lady of Royal Red Cross |
| RSA | Republic of South Africa |
| | Royal Scottish Academician |
| | Royal Society of Arts |
| RSC | Royal Shakespeare Company |
| RSCN | Registered Sick Children's Nurse |
| RSE | Royal Society of Edinburgh |

| | |
|---|---|
| RSM | Regimental Sergeant Major |
| RSPB | Royal Society for the Protection of Birds |
| RSPCA | Royal Society for the Prevention of Cruelty to Animals |
| RSV | Revised Standard Version (*of Bible*) |
| RSVP | (*Répondez, s'il vous plaît*) Please reply |
| RSW | Royal Scottish Society of Painters in Watercolours |
| RTPI | Royal Town Planning Institute |
| RU | Rugby Union |
| RUC | Royal Ulster Constabulary |
| RV | Revised Version (*of Bible*) |
| RVM | Royal Victorian Medal |
| RWS | Royal Water Colour Society |
| RYS | Royal Yacht Squadron |
| | |
| s | second |
| | (*solidus*) shilling |
| S | South |
| SA | Salvation Army |
| | South Africa |
| | South America |
| | South Australia |
| SAE | stamped addressed envelope |
| Salop | Shropshire |
| Sarum: | of Salisbury (*Bishop*) |
| SAS | Special Air Service Regiment |
| SBS | Special Boat Squadron |
| SBN | Standard Book Number |
| ScD | Doctor of Science |
| SCM | State Certified Midwife |
| SDLP | Social Democratic and Labour Party |
| SDP | Social Democratic Party |
| SEAQ | Stock Exchange Automated Quotations system |
| SEN | State Enrolled Nurse |
| SERC | Science and Engineering Research Council |
| SERPS | State Earnings Related Pension Scheme |
| SFO | Serious Fraud Office |
| SHMIS | Society of Headmasters and Headmistresses of Independent Schools |
| SI | (*Système International d'Unités*) International System of Units |
| | Statutory Instrument |
| sic | So written |
| Sig | Signature |
| | Signor |
| SJ | Society of Jesus (*Jesuits*) |
| SLD | Social and Liberal Democrats |
| SMP | Statutory Maternity Pay |
| SNP | Scottish National Party |
| SOE | Special Operations Executive |
| SOS | Save Our Souls (*distress signal*) |
| sp | (*sine prole*) without issue |
| spgr | specific gravity |
| SPQR | (*Senatus Populusque Romanus*) The Senate and People of Rome |
| SRN | State Registered Nurse |
| SRO | Self Regulating Organizations |
| SS | Saints |
| | *Schutzstaffel* (Nazi paramilitary organization) |
| | Steamship |
| SSC | Solicitor before Supreme Court (*Scotland*) |
| SSF | Society of St Francis |
| SSP | Statutory Sick Pay |
| SSSI | Site of special scientific interest |

| | |
|---|---|
| STD | (*Sacrae Theologiae Doctor*) Doctor of Sacred Theology |
| | Subscriber trunk dialling |
| stet | let it stand (*printing*) |
| stp | Standard temperature and pressure |
| STP | (*Sacrae Theologiae Professor*) Professor of Sacred Theology |
| Sub Lt | Sub-Lieutenant |
| SVQ | Scottish Vocational Qualification |
| | |
| TA | Territorial Army |
| TB | Tuberculosis |
| TCCB | Test and County Cricket Board |
| TCD | Trinity College, Dublin |
| TD | Territorial Efficiency Decoration |
| temp | temperature |
| | temporary employee |
| TES | *Times Educational Supplement* |
| TGWU | Transport and General Workers' Union |
| THES | *Times Higher Education Supplement* |
| TLS | *Times Literary Supplement* |
| TNT | trinitrotoluene (*explosive*) |
| trs | transpose (*printing*) |
| TRH | Their Royal Highnesses |
| TT | Teetotal |
| | Tourist Trophy (*motorcycle races*) |
| | Tuberculin tested |
| TUC | Trades Union Congress |
| TVEI | Technical and Vocational Education Initiative |
| | |
| U | Unionist |
| UAE | United Arab Emirates |
| uc | upper case (*printing*) |
| UCAS | Universities and Colleges Admissions Service |
| UCATT | Union of Construction, Allied Trades and Technicians |
| UDA | Ulster Defence Association |
| UDI | Unilateral Declaration of Independence |
| UDM | Union of Democratic Mineworkers |
| UDR | Ulster Defence Regiment |
| UEFA | Union of European Football Associations |
| UFF | Ulster Freedom Fighters |
| UFO | Unidentified flying object |
| UHF | ultra-high frequency |
| UK | United Kingdom |
| UKAEA | UK Atomic Energy Authority |
| UN | United Nations |
| UNESCO | United Nations Educational, Scientific and Cultural Organization |
| UNHCR | United Nations High Commissioner for Refugees |
| UNICEF | United Nations Children's Fund |
| UNIDO | United Nations Industrial Development Organization |
| Unita | National Union for the Total Independence of Angola |
| UPU | Universal Postal Union |
| URC | United Reformed Church |
| US(A) | United States (of America) |
| USDAW | Union of Shop, Distributive and Allied Workers |
| USM | Unlisted Securities Market |
| USSR | Union of Soviet Socialist Republics |

| | |
|---|---|
| UTC | Co-ordinated Universal Time system |
| UVF | Ulster Volunteer Force |
| | |
| v | (*versus*) against |
| VA | Vicar Apostolic |
| | Victoria and Albert Order |
| VAD | Voluntary Aid Detachment |
| VAT | Value added tax |
| VC | Victoria Cross |
| VD | Venereal disease |
| | Volunteer Officers' Decoration |
| VDU | Visual display unit |
| Ven | Venerable |
| VHF | very high frequency |
| VIP | Very important person |
| Vo | (*Verso*) on the left-hand page |
| VRD | Royal Naval Volunteer Reserve Officers' Decoration |
| VSO | Voluntary Service Overseas |
| VTOL | Vertical take-off and landing (*aircraft*) |
| | |
| W | West |
| WCC | World Council of Churches |
| WEA | Workers' Educational Association |
| WEU | Western European Union |
| WFTU | World Federation of Trade Unions |
| WHO | World Health Organization |
| WI | West Indies |
| | Women's Institute |
| Winton: | of Winchester (*Bishop*) |
| WIPO | World Intellectual Property Organization |
| WMO | World Meteorological Organization |
| WO | Warrant Officer |
| WRAC | Women's Royal Army Corps |
| WRAF | Women's Royal Air Force |
| WRNS | Women's Royal Naval Service |
| WRVS | Women's Royal Voluntary Service |
| WS | Writer to the Signet |
| | |
| YMCA | Young Men's Christian Association |
| YWCA | Young Women's Christian Association |
| | |
| ZANU | Zimbabwe African National Union |
| | |
| Ψ = seaport | |

# Index